1997

68TH EDITION

INTERNATIONAL MOTION PICTURE ALMANAC

Editor
JAMES D. MOSER

Managing Editor
TRACY STEVENS

British Editor
WILLIAM PAY

Canadian Editor
PATRICIA THOMPSON

QUIGLEY PUBLISHING COMPANY, INC.
159 WEST 53RD STREET • NEW YORK, NY 10019

(212) 247-3100

1997 68th Edition
INTERNATIONAL MOTION PICTURE ALMANAC

ISSN: 0074-7084
ISBN: 0-900610-57-3

Contents copyrighted © 1997 by
Quigley Publishing Company, Inc., 159 West 53rd Sreet,
New York, NY 10019. Publications of general circulation may
reproduce material in this volume if proper credit is given to
Motion Picture Almanac; reproduction by all other means,
print or electronic, without written permission
is expressly forbidden.

PRINTED IN THE UNITED STATES OF AMERICA

TABLE OF CONTENTS

ALPHABETICAL INDEX OF SUBJECTS

Company listings for the following sections are not included in this Index: Distributors of 16 mm Films, Buying and Booking Services, The Industry in Great Britain, Canada, and The World Market. For these listings, please find the company in alphabetical order within the relevant section.

A

QUIGLEY'S ENTERTAINMENT
INDUSTRY REFERENCE ON CD-ROM

NEW FOR 1997. INCORPORATING THE MOTION PICTURE ALMANAC AND THE TELEVISION & VIDEO ALMANAC.

For decades, thousands of professionals, librarians and students worldwide have depended on Quigley Publishing's International Motion Picture Almanac and Television & Video Almanac for accurate, timely and accessible information on the ever-changing entertainment industry. And for decades, the only way to get that information was to buy the Almanacs.

That's all about to change. For the first time ever, Quigley Publishing is making the information that makes the Almanacs the most respected entertainment references in the world available in an easy-to-use CD-ROM format.

Quigley's 1997 Entertainment Industry Reference CD-ROM provides the information contained in both the Motion Picture Almanac and the Television & Video Almanac, the data that you've relied on the Almanacs to provide ... all on one CD-ROM. And, as a bonus, we are including thousands of career profiles of industry pioneers from our book, First Century of Film.

Thousands of career profiles. Thousands of product listings. Thousands of corporate listings with key contacts, addresses, branch offices, phone and fax numbers and e-mail addresses. Circuit and independent theatres, television stations, cable carriers and satellite broadcasters. International corporations. And much, much more not available anywhere else.

There's never been a product available like this. In a field where accurate and accessible information is more vital every day, you owe it to yourself to get the best electronic reference available. Order your copy of Quigley's 1997 Entertainment Industry Reference on CD-ROM today!

1997 QUIGLEY'S ENTERTAINMENT INDUSTRY REFERENCE ON CD-ROM

TO ORDER CALL TOLL FREE: (800) 231-8239

MOTION PICTURE YEAR IN REVIEW

The Fall and early Winter of 1995 were particularly strong seasons for the movie industry, with top money-making films such as Disney's digitally animated "Toy Story", MGM/UA's new James Bond franchise entry "Goldeneye", "Get Shorty", the critically acclaimed "Leaving Las Vegas", Warner Brother's "Ace Ventura: When Nature Calls" sequel featuring comedian Jim Carrey, New Line's thriller "Seven", Columbia TriStar's "Jumanji", Buena Vista's sleepers "Dangerous Minds" and "Mr. Holland's Opus". Many of these held over through the first months of 1996.

The late Winter and early Spring season of 1996 showed a notable increase over the previous year, with successful films such as MGM/UA's remake of the French gay-themed farce "La Cage aux Folles", "The Birdcage". Action films were also extremely strong, most notably Warner Bros.' "Executive Decision", New Line's "Rumble in the Bronx", and 20th Century Fox's "Broken Arrow" (both of which, interestingly enough, are by Hong Kong emigrés Jackie Chan and John Woo, respectively).

The Summer season (which seems to start a week earlier every year) started off with especially strong showings by Warner's meteorological thriller "Twister" and Paramount's remake of the classic television series "Mission Impossible". However, 20th Century Fox's "Independence Day" became the top summer film in America, beating both films in the race for the first summer movie to hit $200 million. The science fiction blockbuster, by "Stargate" director Roland Emmerich, featuring nearly 50 minutes of computer generated imagery— CGI (as compared to the ground-breaking "Jurassic Park", which reportedly had only 3 minutes of CGI) is well on the way to becoming one of the top-grossing films of all time with over $450 million in reported world-wide box office receipts 12 weeks into its release. Action adventure hits also included Buena Vista's "The Rock" and the summer's Arnold Schwarzenegger vehicle "Eraser". Other notable entries included Buena Vista's "Phenomenon", Warner's "A Time to Kill", based on the John Grisham novel, Fox's "Courage Under Fire" and Eddy Murphy's remake of "The Nutty Professor" from Paramount. Disney's "The Hunchback of Notre Dame" cartoon musical performed well at the box office, but fell short of the box-office milestones set by Disney animated features of the recent past. Although Columbia's "The Cable Guy", a dark comedy featuring Jim Carrey, passed the $50 million mark, it was a disappointment for the studio, and the first Carrey-starring film not to break the $100 million domestic box office mark. Overall, the Summer of 1996 started off 3% better than the previous year, although admissions actually declined one half of one percent.

Until July. In late July, perhaps due to the broadcast of the 1996 Summer Olympics in Atlanta, perhaps due to mild weather across the country, admissions dropped precipitously, showing only a 5% increase in ticket sales over the previous year. August attendance figures continued this downward trend, showing a drop of 13% compared to 1995 figures. Films released in the late summer and early fall included New Line's "The Island of Doctor Moreau" (a third remake of the H. G. Wells novel), Miramax/ Dimension's "The Crow: City of Angels", John Carpenter's "Escape from L.A." (Paramount), Sony's "Matilda", MGM/UA's "Kingpin", Paramount's "A Very Brady Sequel", Buena Vista's "Jack", Warner's Kevin Costner golf movie "Tin Cup", and Paramount's "First Wives Club", a surprise hit.

One of the more intriguing recent developments in the motion picture industry is the growing dominance of foreign receipts over the domestic box-office. It is now estimated that foreign grosses can average 60% of a films total receipts, up from the estimated 50% previously accepted. "Waterworld", lambasted by the American press for its gigantic budget and performing less than spectacularly at the domestic box-office, earned two-thirds of its total gross overseas and ended up making money for MCA/Universal after all. In fact, many films may be considered to be under-performers in the U.S., but do quite well overseas.

In a climate where opening weekend grosses are routinely reported by the non-trade press and are incorporated immediately into advertising and marketing, and prevailing wisdom relies on the first week's performance of any given film as an indicator of the film's overall performance, the pressure is on for films to show large numbers the first week out, particularly in the case of summer movies. Paramount was criticized for including Thursday figures in its reporting of the opening Memorial Day weekend grosses for "Mission Impossible" and "Independence Day" distributor 20th Century Fox vowed not to include a similar July 1st "preview" of its summer hit, scheduled to "officially" open July 4th.

It was obviously a political campaign year again. Hollywood came under fire for depictions of violence when a scene from the film "Money Train" was blamed by politicians and presidential hopefuls for inciting a copycat New York City subway token booth arson attack (the scene in the movie was based on a real-life incident). At its annual meeting, the Southern Baptist Convention voted to organize a boycott against the Walt Disney company, based on Disney's corporate policy of extending benefits to unmarried domestic partners of employees (including gays), and Disney's distribution of the Miramax film "Priest", which was criticized by Christian groups for its unflattering portrayal of the Catholic clergy. Disney also came under attack from the Assemblies of God, which criticized Disney's venture Hyperion Press for publishing gay-themed books. "Independence Day" (a film in which most of the planet's population was killed) was singled out for praise of its "American values" by presidential hopeful Bob Dole, who at the same time criticized the Demi Moore vehicle "Striptease", and later the films "Pulp Fiction" and "Trainspotting" for glorifying drug abuse (Jack Valenti, president of the MPAA, rightfully criticized Dole, who admitted he hadn't seen either of the latter films, and pointed out that that both "Pulp Fiction" and "Trainspotting" actually contained strong anti-drug messages.

Frank Biondi Jr. was removed from the presidency at Viacom, Inc. and chairman Sumner Redstone replaced him. Biondi was immediately hired by Edgar Bronfman Jr. to head MCA. Barry London, vice chairman an president of the Paramount Motion Picture group departed to pursue production. In early September, Mark Canton was removed as chairman of Columbia Pictures, followed by the resignation on October 2nd of Sony president Alan J. Levine. This followed the replacement of Marc Platt, president of Tri-Star, with former HBO president Robert Cooper. On October 9th, Levine was replaced by John Calley, formerly president of United Artists, who was named president and CEO. Jeff Sagansky, vice president at the Sony Corp., was named co-president, and Masayuki Nozoe became executive vice president and liaison to the Sony home office in Japan.

MGM was purchased (again) by financier Kirk Kerkorian and a consortium of investors, including Australian Kerry Packer, in late July, for a reported $1.3 billion. Kerkorian had earlier settled $125 million worth of debt to Credit Lyonnais assumed by Giancarlo Parretti in his 1990 purchase of the studio.

In late July, the FTC finally approved Time-Warner's bid to acquire Turner Broadcasting and shareholder approval of the merger was given October 10, 1996. The fate of Turner-owned Castle Rock (which has long been rumored to be for sale) was up in the air. Turner chairman Ted Turner personally pushed Time Warner to keep the the profitable New Line Cinema and critically acclaimed Fine Line Cinema company and maintain their separate identity. (For more on the Time Warner—Turner merger see the International Television & Video Almanac.)

Studio bookkeeping, long under intense scrutiny, came under more fire when Winston Grooms, author of "Forrest Gump", and net-profit participant in the film of the same name, disclosed that the Academy Award winning feature had allegedly not broken even and had actually lost money to date, according to Paramount Pictures, and that no profits had been earned. Dreamworks SKG and other studios have designed new accounting practices to counteract the problems inherent in the contract models and to insure that net-profit participants would share in the success of films.

Several of the major studios are reacting to a perceived glut of new releases and the rapidly rising costs of producing, advertising and marketing films. Rupert Murdoch of the News Corporation, which in turn owns 20th Century Fox urged movie executives to cut film production. In June, Disney announced plans to cut its annual output of live-action films by almost one half, and said that it would emphasize the production of what has been the studio's forte, the family film.

Independent films are once again being looked at as an alternative to expensive features, and independent and foreign directors and screenwriters are again being actively courted by the major studios. Italian-made and Miramax-distributed "Il Postino" (The Postman) won a surprise Academy Award nomination for Best Picture, and in its second year of theatrical release has grossed nearly $80 million worldwide. The Scottish film "Trainspotting", a bleak comedy about hero-in addicts, garnered much critical acclaim and showed decent returns at the box office. German director Roland Emmerich, Hong Kong action director John Woo, New Zealand's Peter Jackson and Dutch cinematographer turned director Jan de Bont are among the most successful of this new batch of emigrés.

Eastman Kodak introduced a new silver halide-based color negative film line, named "Vision", which promises increased brightness, decreased graininess and a color consistency which should allow filmmakers to purchase stock as needed, rather than having to purchase all stock in advance in order to insure color and consistency.

In a "Wired" magazine article director James Cameron predicted that within the next decade all films would be scanned into a computer and digitally enhanced or corrected. Although Mr. Cameron may seemingly be going out on a limb, the successes of Disney's all digital animated feature "Toy Story" and the science-fiction extravaganza "Independence Day" prove that CGI is now a mature and sophisticated segment of the filmmaking industry. The big special effects movies are consistently popular with audiences around the world, and almost every big-budget film utilizes some form of CGI processing and/or enhancement (for a listing of the top American special effects and animation houses, see the Services section). In fact, due to the increased sophistication of 3-D animation and rendering technology, more and more small specialized special effects houses have been opening in recent years (causing one wag to call such endeavors "Basement-wood".)

EXHIBITION YEAR IN REVIEW

Carmike Theatres became the largest theatre circuit in the U.S., with 2,478 screens. Carmike has had an ambitious expansion plan over the past several years, not only buying up smaller regional circuits, but building new theatres as well. Other circuits were on a building spree in 1996, building bigger multiplexes, most in the 10-14 screen range, but with AMC building an enormous 30-screen multiplex in Ontario, California, and New York City's first 25-screen multiplex in the Times Square Urban renewal district (plans for this new theatre involve the moving the facade and interior of the landmark Empire Theatre, a former burlesque house, 70 feet down 42nd Street, one of the busiest streets in America). Other circuits are building a limited number of sites with 20-24 screens. Sony's Magic Johnston Theatres are embarked on a program to build theatres in inner cities around the country, areas in which many of the extant theatres have been closed down and who's populations have been underserved in the recent past.

American-based exhibitors continued to move into overseas markets, with United Artists announcing a joint venture with Transeuropa Exhibidora to build new theatres in Argentina, and working with a Malaysian investor to build a ten-screen multiplex in Kuala Lumpur. Both Cinemark and National Amusements continued their expansion into the South American market.

The advantage of multiplexes with higher screen counts is that exhibitors can carry more movies in current release and keep them running longer. A related concern, however, is that without blockbuster films to bring audiences to these multiplexes, screens will operate at far less than the capacity planned.

Independent and regional exhibition companies also continued to grow in 1995 and 1996. One of New York's premier independent houses, the six-screen Angelika Film Center, was sold to City Cinemas in mid-1996. The Angelika has long been one of the top-grossing independent theatres in the country and a pioneer in screening foreign films, independent productions and major revivals of classic films.

According to NATO/MPAA figures ticket prices rose in 1995 to an average of $4.35, up approximately 4% from the 1994 average of $4.17. The domestic box-office gross was up 1.8% to $5.43 billion. As if to balance this, admissions were down approximately 2% to 1.25 billion (see chart following). Several New York theatres increased their admission prices to $8.50.

The number of major releases has proved a mixed blessing to exhibitors. The first quarter of 1996 was a record-setter, with carry-overs from the 1995 holiday season consisting of such hits as "Toy Story", "Seven", "Jumanji" and "Goldeneye", and new releases like "The Birdcage", "Rumble in the Bronx", and "Broken Arrow" pushing theatre receipts over the $1 billion mark. But as the summer season moved in, the number of wide releases (2000 or more prints) was so high that many booking schedules were being severely shortened, with spring films being pushed aside to make room for summer blockbusters like "Twister", "Mission Impossible", "Independence Day", "The Rock", "Eraser", "Phenomenon", "A Time to Kill", "The Nutty Professor" and "The Hunchback of Notre Dame". The advantage to longer booking windows is that, according to most exhibition contracts, exhibitors make more money the longer a film plays in theatres, with most of the studio's share being generated in the first weeks of the movie's run.

NATO's annual ShoWest convention was transformed into a media event this spring, with the convention open to the public for the first time and the awards ceremony broadcast on TNT.

The actual technology used in exhibiting films has dramatically improved over the past decade, and films now look and sound better than ever before. Many features are now being distributed on a polyester base rather than the traditional tri-acetate celluloid. The more durable polyester means that films last longer and look better longer in theatres. There are three major digital sound formats in exhibition, Dolby Digital Sound (installed at 1929 screens in the U.S. and Canada), Sony Dynamic Digital Sound (1502 screens) and Digital Theatre Sound (3305). All films also carry a traditional analog soundtrack. Many theatres carry equipment to decode all three formats. Speaker and amplifier manufacturers have developed new sound equipment to show these new digital soundtracks to their best effect. In addition, professional exhibition standards are being maintained by companies like Lucasfilms' THX Theatre Alignment, which help theatres maintain projection illumination, ambient lighting and sound standards. All of these factors combine to emphasize a new commitment by exhibitors to enhancing the movie-going experience.

In addition, the development of new exhibition technologies such as Imax, Imax 3D, Showscan and several "ride-film" formats have created a whole new exhibition industry. In fact, some of the Imax films show the highest per screen admissions in the industry.

A joint venture between Todd-AO and UA theatres has created the Compact Distribution Print, a print with 2.5 sprocket perforations per frame, rather than the standard 4, and with a length 37.5% shorter than conventional prints, meaning that a 140-minute film could be shipped and shown on a single reel. It is estimated that studios could save million of dollars on prints annually using the CDP. Alternatively, the frame per second count could be pushed up to the far superior 30 fps (as compared to the current 24 fps standard) without lengthening the prints. However, it requires that exhibitors retrofit projection equipment at no little expense, having to replace not only the sprocket spools, but also the lens.

— JIM MOSER

MOTION PICTURE STATISTICS

ADMISSIONS

	Gross ($ millions)	Admissions (millions)	per week (millions)
1946	$1,692.0	4,067.3	78.2
1947	1,594.0	3,664.4	70.5
1948	1,506.0	3,422.7	65.8
1949	1,448.0	3,168.5	60.9
1950	1,379.0	3,017.5	58.0
1951	1,332.0	2,840.1	54.6
1952	1,325.0	2,777.7	53.4
1953	1,339.0	2,630.6	50.6
1954	1,251.0	2,270.4	43.7
1955	1,204.0	2,072.3	39.9
1956	1,125.0	1,893.9	36.4
1957	1,078.0	1,727.6	33.2
1958	1,010.0	1,553.8	29.9
1959	1,006.0	1,488.2	28.6
1960	984.4	1,304.5	25.1
1961	945.5	1,224.7	23.6
1962	874.9	1,080.1	20.8
1963	925.0	1,093.4	21.0
1964	947.6	1,024.4	19.7
1965	1,041.8	1,031.5	19.8
1966	1,067.1	975.4	18.8
1967	1,110.0	926.5	17.8
1968	1,282.0	978.6	18.8
1969	1,294.0	911.9	17.5
1970	1,429.2	920.6	17.7
1971	1,349.5	820.3	15.8
1972	1,583.1	934.1	18.0
1973	1,523.5	864.6	16.6
1974	1,908.5	1,010.7	19.4
1975	2,114.8	1,032.8	19.9
1976	2,036.4	957.1	18.4
1977	2,372.3	1,063.2	20.4
1978	2,643.4	1,128.2	21.7
1979	2,821.3	1,120.9	21.6
1980	2,748.5	1,021.5	19.6
1981	2,965.6	1,067.0	20.5
1982	3,452.7	1,175.4	22.6
1983	3,766.0	1,196.9	23.0
1984	4,030.6	1,199.1	23.1
1985	3,749.4	1,056.1	20.3
1986	3,778.0	1,017.2	19.6
1987	4,252.9	1,088.5	20.9
1988	4,458.4	1,084.8	20.9
1989	5,033.4	1,262.8	24.3
1990	5,021.8	1,188.6	22.9
1991	4,803.2	1,140.6	21.9
1992	4,871.0	1,173.2	22.6
1993	5,154.2	1,244.0	23.9
1994	5,396.2	1,291.7	24.8
1995	5,493.5	1,262.6	24.3

Source: MPAA

ADMISSION PRICES

Admission prices increased slightly in 1995, averaging $4.351 for the year, up from $4.178 in 1994, a 4.1%. Since 1985, admission prices have risen by 22.6%, from $3.55. In New York City the top price is now $8.50.

ATTENDANCE

Total theatre admissions at U.S. theatres in 1995 were 1,262.6 million. The figure is down 2.3% from 1994's figures of 1291.7 million admissions, but over all up a respectable 19.6% from a decade ago, when admissions stood at 1,056.1 million.

ADMISSION DEMOGRAPHICS

All of the following charts are based upon a telephone survey conducted by the Motion Picture Association of America, Inc. that included a national probability sample of 2,000 adults age 18 and over and 250 teenagers, ages 12 to 17.

ADMISSION PERCENTAGE BY AGE GROUP

Age	1995 %	1994 %	1993 %	% of Population
12-15	.9	10	.9	.7
16-20	.16	.17	.17	.8
21-24	.11	.11	.10	.7
25-29	.12	.10	.13	.9
30-39	.20	.8	.19	.17
40-49	.16	.6	.15	.21
50-59	.7	.8	.7	.11
60 +	.10	.12	.11	.20

ALL ATTENDANCE

Age	1995 %	1994 %	1993 %	% of Population
12-17	14	14	15	10
18 +	88	88	86	90

PERCENT OF TOTAL YEARLY ADMISSIONS

Age	1995 %	1994 %	1993 %	% of Population
12-29 years	.48	.45	.49	.31
12-39 years	.68	.63	.68	.52
16-39	.59	.53	.59	.45
40 and over	.33	.36	.33	.48

FREQUENCY OF ATTENDANCE

	Total Public Age 12 & Over			Adult Public Age 18 & Over			Teenagers Age 12 to17		
	1995 %	1994 %	1993 %	1995 %	1994 %	1993 %	1995 %	1994 %	1993 %
Frequent (at least once a month)	31	.30	.26	29	.29	.24	43	.43	.40
Occasional (once in 2 to 6 months)	34	.35	.36	33	.33	.34	48	.45	.48
Infrequent (less than once in 6 months)	9	.11	.11	10	.11	.12	5	.7	.7
Never	26	.25	.27	28	.27	.30	4	.5	.4
Not reported	1	.1	.1	1	.1	*	1	*	.2

* Less than 0.5%

TOTAL MOVIEGOING PUBLIC FREQUENCY
(Based on Moviegoers only)

	1995 %	1994 %	1993 %
Frequent	.41	.39	.36
Occasional	.46	.46	.49
Infrequent	.13	.14	.15

Moviegoing Adults

	1995 %	1994 %	1993 %
Frequent	.40	.40	.34
Occasional	.46	.45	.49
Infrequent	.13	.15	.17

TOTAL MOVIEGOING PUBLIC FREQUENCY
(continued)

MOVIEGOING TEENAGERS

	1995 %	1994 %	1993 %
Frequent	.46	.45	.42
Occasional	.49	.47	.51
Infrequent	.5	7	.7

ADULTS

	Married				Single		
	1995 %	1994 %	1993 %		1995 %	1994 %	1993 %
Frequent	.23	.22	.19		35	.36	.32
Occasional	.33	.35	.34		32	.31	.34
Infrequent	.11	.12	.13		8	.10	.9
Never	.32	.31	.33		24	.23	.24

ADULTS WITH CHILDREN UNDER 18

	1995 %	1994 %	1993 %
Frequent	.27	.25	.27
Occasional	.39	.40	.30
Infrequent	.11	.13	.13
Never	.32	.18	.20

ADULTS WITHOUT CHILDREN

	1995 %	1994 %	1993 %
Frequent	.30	.28	.23
Occasional	.38	.28	.31
Infrequent	9	.10	.10
Never	.32	.33	.36

EDUCATION

	Less Than High School			At Least Some High School			Some College		
	1995 %	1994 %	1993 %	1995 %	1994 %	1993 %	1995 %	1994 %	1993 %
Frequent	.14	.12	.12	24	.23	.19	34	.34	.30
Occasional	.20	.25	.24	30	.34	.33	36	.35	.37
Infrequent	.10	.10	.10	11	.10	.12	10	.12	.11
Never	.55	.52	.54	34	.32	.35	20	.19	.21

SEX (AGE 12 AND OVER)

	Male				Female		
	1995 %	1994 %	1993 %		1995 %	1994 %	1993 %
Frequent	.31	.31%	.28%		30	.27%	.24%
Occasional	.35	.37	.36		33	.33	.35
Infrequent	9	.11	.9		10	.11	.13
Never	.25	.21	.26		27	.29	.28

AGE 18 AND OVER

	Male				Female		
	1995	1994	1993		1995	1994	1993
Frequent	.30%	.30	.26%		27	.25%	.23%
Occasional	.33	.36	.35		32	.33	.35
Infrequent	9	.10	9		11	.11	.14
Never	.27	.23	.26		30	.30	.30

Attendance Demographics Source: MPAA

EXHIBITION

There were a total of 27,805 screens (including drive-ins) in the U.S. at the end of 1995, an increase of 4.6 percent from the 26,586 in 1994. The number of indoor screens was once again on the rise: up 4.9 percent in 1995 to 26,958, as compared to 25,701 in 1994. Drive-in screens fell to 847.

Source: MPAA

THE 15 TOP U.S. THEATRE CIRCUITS

The top 15 circuits account for 16,636 screens out of the reported 27,805 U.S. screens, or almost 60% of all screens.

	Number of Theatres	Total Screens
Carmike Cinemas	566	2469
United Artists	414	2380
American Multi-Cinema, Inc.	240	1950
Cinemark	169	1444
Regal Cinemas	156	1282
General Cinemas	193	1179
Sony Theatres	143	949
Cineplex Odeon	189	869
National Amusements	95	858
Act III Theatres	128	710
Hoyts Cinemas	93	638
Cobb Theatres	70	593
Century Theatres	65	475
Edwards Theatres	76	436
Kerasotes Theatres	95	404

Source: Annual exhibition survey conducted by Quigley Publishing Co., Aug. 1996.

PRODUCTION

NUMBER OF FILMS

Total theatrical releases by all companies in 1995 were 419 including 37 reissues. There were 212 new films released by MPAA members and 22 reissues for a total of 234. All other distributors' releases numbered 170 new films and 15 reissues for a total of 185. Of the 631 films produced in 1995, only the aforementioned 419 were released theatrically.

Source: MPAA

TOP-GROSSING FEATURES

A total of 36 pictures released by MPAA members took in film rentals of $20 million or more in 1995, compared to 33 in 1994, and 28 in 1993. 75 films took in more than $10 million in 1995.

Source: MPAA

PRODUCTION COSTS

The production cost of a feature film averaged $36,369,800 in 1995, a 6.1% increase over the 1994. figure and 21.6% above com-parative 1993 figures. Overall, production costs have risen almost 117 % in the past decade, when the average production cost of a feature film was $16,779,200.

Source: MPAA

PRINTS AND ADVERTISING COSTS OF NEW FEATURES

Total U.S. marketing costs (prints and advertising) increased by 10.4% in 1995 to $17,737,00 from $16,060,000 in 1994. In 1985 the combined marketing costs were $6,454,000. The figure has risen by almost 175% in the past decade. Advertising costs alone averaged $15,383,000 in 1995, up nearly 11% from 1994, and over 193% in the past decade. Advertising dollars in 1995 aver-aged, by media, 19.5% newspaper advertising, 23% network television advertising, 24.4% spot television advertising, 4.6% com-bing attractions trailers and 28.4% in all other advertising costs (including World Wide Web sites, radio advertising and other pro-motional vehicles). Print costs in 1995 were up 7.5% to 2.35 million and up 94% over the past decade. It may be useful to note that screen counts over the past decade have risen 31.5%.

Source: MPAA

EMPLOYMENT

The average number of full and part-time employees the industry was 590,300 in 199 compared to 506,100 in 1994, with 314,400 employed in the production and services sector of the industry (up 32% over 1994), 160,100 in the distribution and video indus-try (a nominal increase—less than 1%) and 115,800 in the exhibition industry (a 5.3% increase over 1994).

Source: MPAA

INDUSTRY FILM RATING SYSTEM:

In 1995, ratings were as follows: 25 rated "G" (3.6%); 99 "PG" (14.2%); 111 "PG-13" (15.9%); 458 "R" (65.7%); 4 "NC-17" (0.6%). This compares with 1994 as follows: 26 "G"; 113 "PG"; 99 "PG-13"; 393 "R"; and 4 "NC-17".
Since the ratings began in 1968 the totals through 1995 for each category are as follows: 1,057 rated "G" (or 8.2%); 3,475 "PG" (27%); 1062 "PG-13" (8.3%); 6,845 "R" (53.3%); and 409 "X" or "NC-17" (3.2%)."

Source: MPAA

QP Top Ten Money-Makers Poll

QP Top Ten Money-Making Stars

In the 1996 annual poll of circuit exhibitors and independent theater owners in the United States conducted by Quigley Publishing, these stars were voted the top ten money-makers of 1995:

Tom Hanks 1
Jim Carrey 2
Brad Pitt 3
Harrison Ford 4
Robin Williams 5
Sandra Bullock 6
Mel Gibson 7
Demi Moore 8
John Travolta 9
Kevin Costner & Michael Douglas 10

The runners up: (12) Bruce Willis, (13) Val Kilmer, (14) Michelle Pfeiffer, (15) Julia Roberts, (16) Morgan Freeman, (17) Pierce Brosnan (18) Anthony Hopkins, (19) Robert De Niro, (20) a tie between Steven Seagal, Winona Ryder & Meg Ryan, (23) Steve Martin, (24) Tommy Lee Jones, (25) Denzel Washington

QP Stars of Tomorrow

Major and independent exhibitors were asked to name those stars they thought would be top money-makers within the next 5-10 years. The overwhelming choices were:

Alicia Silverstone 1
Christina Ricci 2

QP Money-Making Stars of 1933-1994

1994: (1) Tom Hanks; (2) Jim Carrey (3) Arnold Schwarzenegger; (4) Tom Cruise; (5) Harrison Ford; (6) Tim Allen; (7) Mel Gibson; (8) Jodie Foster; (9) Michael Douglas; (10) Tommy Lee Jones.

1993: (1) Clint Eastwood; (2) Tom Cruise; (3) Robin Williams; (4) Kevin Costner; (5) Harrison Ford; (6) Julia Roberts; (7) Tom Hanks; (8) Mel Gibson; (9) Whoopi Goldberg; (10) Sylvester Stallone.

1992: (1) Tom Cruise; (2) Mel Gibson; (3) Kevin Costner; (4) Jack Nicholson; (5) Macaulay Culkin; (6) Whoopi Goldberg; (7) Michael Douglas; (8) Clint Eastwood; (9) Steven Seagal; (10) Robin Williams.

1991: (1) Kevin Costner; (2) Arnold Schwarzenegger; (3) Robin Williams; (4) Julia Roberts; (5) Macaulay Culkin; (6) Jodie Foster; (7) Billy Crystal; (8) Dustin Hoffman; (9) Robert De Niro; (10) Mel Gibson.

1990: (1) Arnold Schwarzenegger; (2) Julia Roberts; (3) Bruce Willis; (4) Tom Cruise; (5) Mel Gibson; (6) Kevin Costner; (7) Patrick Swayze; (8) Sean Connery; (9) Harrison Ford; (10) Richard Gere.

1989: (1) Jack Nicholson; (2) Tom Cruise; (3) Robin Williams; (4) Michael Douglas; (5) Tom Hanks; (6) Michael J. Fox; (7) Eddie Murphy; (8) Mel Gibson; (9) Sean Connery; (10) Kathleen Turner.

1988: (1) Tom Cruise; (2) Eddie Murphy; (3) Tom Hanks; (4) Arnold Schwarzenegger; (5) Paul Hogan; (6) Danny De Vito; (7) Bette Midler; (8) Robin Williams; (9) Tom Selleck; (10) Dustin Hoffman.

1987: (1) Eddie Murphy; (2) Michael Douglas; (3) Michael J. Fox; (4) Arnold Schwarzenegger; (5) Paul Hogan; (6) Tom Cruise; (7) Glenn Close; (8) Sylvester Stallone; (9) Cher; (10) Mel Gibson.

1986: (1) Tom Cruise; (2) Eddie Murphy; (3) Paul Hogan; (4) Rodney Dangerfield; (5) Bette Midler; (6) Sylvester Stallone; (7) Clint Eastwood; (8) Whoopi Goldberg; (9) Kathleen Turner; (10) Paul Newman.

1985: (1) Sylvester Stallone; (2) Eddie Murphy; (3) Clint Eastwood; (4) Michael J. Fox; (5) Chevy Chase; (6) Arnold Schwarzenegger; (7) Chuck Norris; (8) Harrison Ford; (9) Michael Douglas; (10) Meryl Streep.

1984: (1) Clint Eastwood; (2) Bill Murray; (3) Harrison Ford; (4)Eddie Murphy; (5) Sally Field; (6) Burt Reynolds; (7) Robert Redford; (8) Prince; (9) Dan Aykroyd; (10) Meryl Streep.

1983: (1) Clint Eastwood; (2) Eddie Murphy; (3) Sylvester Stallone; (4) Burt Reynolds; (5) John Travolta; (6) Dustin Hoffman; (7)Harrison Ford; (8) Richard Gere; (9) Chevy Chase; (10) Tom Cruise.

1982: (1) Burt Reynolds; (2) Clint Eastwood; (3) Sylvester Stallone; (4) Dudley Moore; (5) Richard Pryor; (6) Dolly Parton; (7) Jane Fonda; (8) Richard Gere; (9) Paul Newman; (10) Harrison Ford.

1981: (1) Burt Reynolds; (2) Clint Eastwood; (3) Dudley Moore; (4)Dolly Parton; (5) Jane Fonda; (6) Harrison Ford; (7) Alan Alda; (8) Bo Derek; (9) Goldie Hawn; (10) Bill Murray.

1980: (1) Burt Reynolds; (2) Robert Redford; (3) Clint Eastwood; (4) Jane Fonda; (5) Dustin Hoffman; (6) John Travolta; (7) Sally Field; (8) Sissy Spacek; (9) Barbra Streisand; (10) Steve Martin.

1979: (1) Burt Reynolds; (2) Clint Eastwood; (3) Jane Fonda; (4) Woody Allen; (5) Barbra Streisand; (6) Sylvester Stallone; (7) John Travolta; (8) Jill Clayburgh; (9) Roger Moore; (10) Mel Brooks.

1978: (1) Burt Reynolds; (2) John Travolta; (3) Richard Dreyfuss; (4) Warren Beatty; (5) Clint Eastwood; (6) Woody Allen; (7) Diane Keaton; (8) Jane Fonda; (9) Peter Sellers; (10) Barbra Streisand.

1977: (1) Sylvester Stallone; (2) Barbra Streisand; (3) Clint Eastwood; (4) Burt Reynolds; (5) Robert Redford; (6) Woody Allen; (7) Mel Brooks; (8) Al Pacino; (9) Diane Keaton; (10) Robert De Niro.

1976: (1) Robert Redford; (2) Jack Nicholson; (3) Dustin Hoffman; (4) Clint Eastwood; (5) Mel Brooks; (6) Burt Reynolds; (7) Al Pacino; (8) Tatum O'Neal; (9) Woody Allen; (10) Charles Bronson.

1975: (1) Robert Redford; (2) Barbra Streisand; (3) Al Pacino; (4)Charles Bronson; (5) Paul Newman; (6) Clint Eastwood; (7) Burt Reynolds; (8) Woody Allen; (9) Steve McQueen; (10) Gene Hackman.

1974: (1) Robert Redford; (2) Clint Eastwood; (3) Paul Newman; (4) Barbra Streisand; (5) Steve McQueen; (6) Burt Reynolds; (7) Charles Bronson; (8) Jack Nicholson; (9) Al Pacino; (10) John Wayne.

1973: (1) Clint Eastwood; (2) Ryan O'Neal; (3) Steve McQueen; (4) Burt Reynolds; (5) Robert Redford; (6) Barbra Streisand; (7) Paul Newman; (8) Charles Bronson; (9) John Wayne; (10) Marlon Brando.

1972: (1) Clint Eastwood; (2) George C. Scott; (3) Gene Hackman; (4) John Wayne; (5) Barbra Streisand; (6) Marlon Brando; (7) Paul Newman; (8) Steve McQueen; (9) Dustin Hoffman; (10) Goldie Hawn.

1971: (1) John Wayne; (2) Clint Eastwood; (3) Paul Newman; (4) Steve McQueen; (5) George C. Scott; (6) Dustin Hoffman; (7) Walter Matthau; (8) Ali MacGraw; (9) Sean Connery; (10) Lee Marvin.

1970: (1) Paul Newman; (2) Clint Eastwood; (3) Steve McQueen; (4) John Wayne; (5) Elliott Gould; (6) Dustin Hoffman; (7) Lee Marvin; (8) Jack Lemmon; (9) Barbra Streisand; (10) Walter Matthau.

1969: (1) Paul Newman; (2) John Wayne; (3) Steve McQueen; (4) Dustin Hoffman; (5) Clint Eastwood; (6) Sidney Poitier; (7) Lee Marvin; (8) Jack Lemmon; (9) Katharine Hepburn; (10) Barbra Streisand.

1968: (1) Sidney Poitier; (2) Paul Newman; (3) Julie Andrews; (4) John Wayne; (5) Clint Eastwood; (6) Dean Martin; (7) Steve McQueen; (8) Jack Lemmon; (9) Lee Marvin; (10) Elizabeth Taylor.

1967: (1) Julie Andrews; (2) Lee Marvin; (3) Paul Newman; (4) Dean Martin; (5) Sean Connery; (6) Elizabeth Taylor; (7) Sidney Poitier; (8) John Wayne; (9) Richard Burton; (10) Steve McQueen.

1966: (1) Julie Andrews; (2) Sean Connery; (3) Elizabeth Taylor; (4) Jack Lemmon; (5) Richard Burton; (6) Cary Grant; (7) John Wayne; (8) Doris Day; (9) Paul Newman; (10) Elvis Presley.

1965: (1) Sean Connery; (2) John Wayne; (3) Doris Day; (4) Julie Andrews; (5) Jack Lemmon; (6) Elvis Presley; (7) Cary Grant; (8) James Stewart; (9) Elizabeth Taylor; (10) Richard Burton.

1964: (1) Doris Day; (2) Jack Lemmon; (3) Rock Hudson; (4) John Wayne; (5) Cary Grant; (6) Elvis Presley; (7) Shirley MacLaine; (8) Ann-Margret; (9) Paul Newman; (10) Jerry Lewis.

1963: (1) Doris Day; (2) John Wayne; (3) Rock Hudson; (4) Jack Lemmon; (5) Cary Grant; (6) Elizabeth Taylor; (7) Elvis Presley; (8) Sandra Dee; (9) Paul Newman; (10) Jerry Lewis.

1962: (1) Doris Day; (2) Rock Hudson; (3) Cary Grant; (4) John Wayne; (5) Elvis Presley; (6) Elizabeth Taylor; (7) Jerry Lewis; (8)Frank Sinatra; (9) Sandra Dee; (10) Burt Lancaster.

1961: (1) Elizabeth Taylor; (2) Rock Hudson; (3) Doris Day; (4) John Wayne; (5) Cary Grant; (6) Sandra Dee; (7) Jerry Lewis; (8)William Holden; (9) Tony Curtis; (10) Elvis Presley.

1960: (1) Doris Day; (2) Rock Hudson; (3) Cary Grant; (4) Elizabeth Taylor; (5) Debbie Reynolds; (6) Tony Curtis; (7) Sandra Dee; (8) Frank Sinatra; (9) Jack Lemmon; (10) John Wayne.

1959: (1) Rock Hudson; (2) Cary Grant; (3) James Stewart; (4) Doris Day; (5) Debbie Reynolds; (6) Glenn Ford; (7) Frank Sinatra; (8) John Wayne; (9) Jerry Lewis; (10) Susan Hayward.

1958: (1) Glenn Ford; (2) Elizabeth Taylor; (3) Jerry Lewis; (4) Marlon Brando; (5) Rock Hudson; (6) William Holden; (7) Brigitte Bardot; (8) Yul Brynner; (9) James Stewart; (10) Frank Sinatra.

1957: (1) Rock Hudson; (2) John Wayne; (3) Pat Boone; (4) Elvis Presley; (5) Frank Sinatra; (6) Gary Cooper; (7) William Holden; (8) James Stewart; (9) Jerry Lewis; (10) Yul Brynner.

1956: (1) William Holden; (2) John Wayne; (3) James Stewart; (4) Burt Lancaster; (5) Glenn Ford; (6) Dean Martin & Jerry Lewis; (7) Gary Cooper; (8) Marilyn Monroe; (9) Kim Novak; (10) Frank Sinatra.

1955: (1) James Stewart; (2) Grace Kelly; (3) John Wayne; (4) William Holden; (5) Gary Cooper; (6) Marlon Brando; (7) Dean Martin & Jerry Lewis; (8) Humphrey Bogart; (9) June Allyson; (10) Clark Gable.

1954: (1) John Wayne; (2) Martin & Lewis; (3) Gary Cooper; (4) James Stewart; (5) Marilyn Monroe; (6) Alan Ladd; (7) William Holden; (8) Bing Crosby; (9) Jane Wyman; (10) Marlon Brando.

1953: (1) Gary Cooper; (2) Martin & Lewis; (3) John Wayne; (4) Alan Ladd; (5) Bing Crosby; (6) Marilyn Monroe; (7) James Stewart; (8) Bob Hope; (9) Susan Hayward; (10) Randolph Scott.

1952: (1) Martin & Lewis; (2) Gary Cooper; (3) John Wayne ; (4) Bing Crosby; (5) Bob Hope; (6) James Stewart; (7) Doris Day; (8) Gregory Peck; (9) Susan Hayward; (10) Randolph Scott.

1951: (1) John Wayne; (2) Martin & Lewis; (3) Betty Grable; (4) Abbott & Costello; (5) Bing Crosby; (6) Bob Hope; (7) Randolph Scott; (8) Gary Cooper; (9) Doris Day; (10) Spencer Tracy.

1950: (1) John Wayne; (2) Bob Hope; (3) Bing Crosby; (4) Betty Grable; (5) James Stewart; (6) Abbott & Costello; (7) Clifton Webb; (8) Esther Williams; (9) Spencer Tracy; (10) Randolph Scott.

1949: (1) Bob Hope; (2) Bing Crosby; (3) Abbott & Costello; (4) John Wayne; (5) Gary Cooper; (6) Cary Grant; (7) Betty Grable; (8) Esther Williams; (9) Humphrey Bogart; (10) Clark Gable.

1948: (1) Bing Crosby; (2) Betty Grable; (3) Abbott & Costello; (4) Gary Cooper; (5) Bob Hope; (6) Humphrey Bogart; (7) Clark Gable; (8) Cary Grant; (9) Spencer Tracy; (10) Ingrid Bergman.

1947: (1) Bing Crosby; (2) Betty Grable; (3) Ingrid Bergman; (4) Gary Cooper; (5) Humphrey Bogart; (6) Bob Hope; (7) Clark Gable; (8) Gregory Peck; (9) Claudette Colbert; (10) Alan Ladd.

1946: (1) Bing Crosby; (2) Ingrid Bergman; (3) Van Johnson; (4) Gary Cooper; (5) Bob Hope; (6) Humphrey Bogart; (7) Greer Garson; (8) Margaret O'Brien; (9) Betty Grable; (10) Roy Rogers.

1945: (1) Bing Crosby; (2) Van Johnson; (3) Greer Garson; (4) Betty Grable; (5) Spencer Tracy; (6) Humphrey Bogart, Gary Cooper; (7) Bob Hope; (8) Judy Garland; (9) Margaret O'Brien; (10) Roy Rogers.

1944: (1) Bing Crosby; (2) Gary Cooper; (3) Bob Hope; (4) Betty Grable; (5) Spencer Tracy; (6) Greer Garson; (7) Humphrey Bogart; (8) Abbott & Costello; (9) Cary Grant; (10) Bette Davis.

1943: (1) Betty Grable; (2) Bob Hope; (3) Abbott & Costello; (4) Bing Crosby; (5) Gary Cooper; (6) Greer Garson; (7) Humphrey Bogart; (8) James Cagney; (9) Mickey Rooney; (10) Clark Gable.

1942: (1) Abbott & Costello; (2) Clark Gable; (3) Gary Cooper; (4) Mickey Rooney; (5) Bob Hope; (6) James Cagney; (7) Gene Autry; (8) Betty Grable; (9) Greer Garson; (10) Spencer Tracy.

1941: (1) Mickey Rooney; (2) Clark Gable; (3) Abbott & Costello; (4) Bob Hope; (5) Spencer Tracy; (6) Gene Autry; (7) Gary Cooper; (8) Bette Davis; (9) James Cagney; (10) Spencer Tracy.

1940: (1) Mickey Rooney; (2) Spencer Tracy; (3) Clark Gable; (4) Gene Autry; (5) Tyrone Power; (6) James Cagney; (7) Bing Crosby; (8) Wallace Beery; (9) Bette Davis; (10) Judy Garland.

1939: (1) Mickey Rooney; (2) Tyrone Power; (3) Spencer Tracy; (4) Clark Gable; (5) Shirley Temple; (6) Bette Davis; (7) Alice Faye; (8) Errol Flynn; (9) James Cagney; (10) Sonja Henie.

1938: (1) Shirley Temple; (2) Clark Gable; (3) Sonja Henie; (4) Mickey Rooney; (5) Spencer Tracy; (6) Robert Taylor; (7) Myrna Loy; (8) Jane Withers; (9) Alice Faye; (10) Tyrone Power.

1937: (1) Shirley Temple; (2) Clark Gable; (3) Robert Taylor; (4) Bing Crosby; (5) William Powell; (6) Jane Withers; (7) Fred Astaire and Ginger Rogers; (8) Sonja Henie; (9) Gary Cooper; (10)Myrna Loy.

1936: (1) Shirley Temple; (2) Clark Gable; (3) Fred Astaire and Ginger Rogers; (4) Robert Taylor; (5) Joe E. Brown; (6) Dick Powell; (7) Joan Crawford; (8) Claudette Colbert; (9) Jeanette MacDonald; (10) Gary Cooper.

1935: (1) Shirley Temple; (2) Will Rogers; (3) Clark Gable; (4) Fred Astaire and Ginger Rogers; (5) Joan Crawford; (6) Claudette Colbert; (7) Dick Powell; (8) Wallace Beery; (9) Joe E. Brown; (10) James Cagney.

1934: (1) Will Rogers; (2) Clark Gable; (3) Janet Gaynor; (4) Wallace Beery; (5) Mae West; (6) Joan Crawford; (7) Bing Crosby; (8) Shirley Temple; (9) Marie Dressler; (10) Norma Shearer.

1933: (1) Marie Dressler; (2) Will Rogers; (3) Janet Gaynor; (4)Eddie Cantor; (5) Wallace Beery; (6) Jean Harlow; (7) Clark Gable; (8) Mae West; (9) Norma Shearer; (10) Joan Crawford.

1932: (1) Marie Dressler; (2) Janet Gaynor; (3) Joan Crawford; (4) Charles Farrell; (5) Greta Garbo; (6) Norma Shearer; (7) Wallace Beery; (8) Clark Gable; (9) Will Rogers; (10) Joe E. Brown.

NATIONAL & INTERNATIONAL AWARDS

ACADEMY AWARD WINNERS
1995

The Academy Awards of 1995 were presented in Los Angeles on March 25, 1996 by the Academy of Motion Pictures Arts and Sciences. The list of winners follows.

PICTURE
Braveheart, An Icon Productions/Ladd Company Production.
ACTOR
Nicolas Cage, Leaving Las Vegas.
ACTRESS
Susan Sarandon, Dead Man Walking.
SUPPORTING ACTOR
Kevin Spacey, The Usual Suspects.
SUPPORTING ACTRESS
Mira Sorvino, Mighty Aphrodite.
DIRECTOR
Mel Gibson, Braveheart.
FOREIGN LANGUAGE FILM
Antonia's Line, A Bergen Theatre-Film-Television Prod., (Dutch).
ORIGINAL SCREENPLAY
Christopher McQuarrie, The Usual Suspects.
ADAPTED SCREENPLAY
Emma Thompson, Sense and Sensibility.
CINEMATOGRAPHER
John Toll, Braveheart.
ART DIRECTION
Eugenio Zanetti, Restoration.
COSTUME DESIGN
James Acheson, Restoration.
FILM EDITING
Mike Hill, Dan Hanley, Apollo 13.
ORIGINAL SCORE
Luis Bacalov, Il Postino (The Postman).
ORIGINAL SONG
"Colors of the Wind," from Pocahontas; Music by Alan Menken, Lyric by Steven Schwartz.
SHORT SUBJECT—ANIMATED
A Close Shave, An Aardman Animations Production; Nick Park.
SHORT SUBJECT—LIVE ACTION
Lierberman In Love, A Chanticleer Films Production; Christine Lahti and Jana Sue Memel.
SOUND
Rick Dior, Steve Pederswon, Scott Millan and David MacMillan, Apollo 13.
SOUND EFFECTS EDITING
Lon Bender, Per Hallberg, Braveheart.
MAKEUP
Peter Frampton, Paul Pattison, Lois Burwell, Braveheart.
VISUAL EFFECTS
Scott E. Anderson, Charles Gibson, Neal Scanlan, John Cox, Babe.
DOCUMENTARY—FEATURE
Anne Frank Remebered, A Jon Blair Film Company Limited Production; Jon Blair, producer.
DOCUMENTARY—SHORT SUBJECT
One Survivor Remembers, A Home Box Office and The United States Holocaust Memorial Museum Production. Kathy Antholis, producer.
HONORARY ACADEMY AWARDS
Kirk Douglas, for 50 years as a creative and moral force in the motion picture community.
Chuck Jones, for the creation of classic cartoons and cartoon characters whose animated lives have brought joy to our real ones for more than half a century.
John Lasseter, for the development and inspired application of techniques that have made possible the first feature-length computer animated film.
SPECIAL AWARDS
Gordon E. Sawyer Award (Academy Statuette); **Donald C. Rogers**.

ACADEMY AWARD WINNERS
1990-1994

Productions, players, directors and craftspersons named for superior merit by the Academy of Motion Picture Arts and Sciences, from 1990 to 1994. For a complete list of winners from the inception of the awards, please see Vols. 1995 and earlier.

1994

PICTURE
Forrest Gump, Steve Tisch/Wendy Finerman Production, Paramount.
ACTOR
Tom Hanks, Forrest Gump.
ACTRESS
Jessica Lange, Blue Sky.
SUPPORTING ACTOR
Martin Landau, Ed Wood.
SUPPORTING ACTRESS
Dianne Wiest, Bullets Over Broadway.
DIRECTOR
Robert Zemeckis, Forrest Gump.
FOREIGN LANGUAGE FILM
Burnt By the Sun, Camera One/Studio Trite; Sony Pictures Classics (Russia).
ORIGINAL SCREENPLAY
Quentin Tarantino, Pulp Fiction.
ADAPTED SCREENPLAY
Eric Roth, Forrest Gump.
CINEMATOGRAPHER
John Toll, Legends of the Fall.
ART DIRECTION
Ken Adam (art direction), Carolyn Scott (set direction), The Madness of King George.
COSTUME DESIGN
Lizzy Gardiner, Tim Chappel, The Adventures of Priscilla, Queen of the Desert.
FILM EDITING
Arthur Schmidt, Forrest Gump.
ORIGINAL SCORE
Hans Zimmer, The Lion King.
ORIGINAL SONG
"Can You Feel the Love Tonight," from the Lion King, Music by Elton John, Lyric by Tim Rice.
SHORT SUBJECT—ANIMATED
Bob's Birthday, Snowden Fine Animation for Channel Four/National Film Board of Canada; Alison Snowden, David Fine, producers.
SHORT SUBJECT—LIVE ACTION
Franz Kafka's It's A Wonderful Life, Conundrum Films, Peter Capaldi, Ruth Kennley-Letts, producers. Trevor, Rajski/Stone, Peggy Rajski, Randy Stone, producers.
SOUND
Gregg Landaker, Steve Maslow, Bob Reemer, David R.B. MacMillan, Speed.
SOUND EFFECTS EDITING
Stephen Hunter Flick, Speed.
MAKEUP
Rick Baker, Ve Neill, Yolanda Toussieng, Ed Wood.
VISUAL EFFECTS
Ken Ralston, George Murphy, Stephen Rosenbaum, Allen Hall, Forrest Gump.
DOCUMENTARY—FEATURE
Maya Lin: A Strong Clear Vision, American Film Foundation/Sanders & Mock; Freida Lee Mock, Terry Sanders, producers.
DOCUMENTARY—SHORT SUBJECT
A Time For Justice, Guggenheim Prods. for the Southern Poverty Law Center; Charles Guggenheim, producer.
HONORARY ACADEMY AWARD
Michelangelo Antonioni, for lifetime achievement.
JEAN HERSHOLT HUMANITARIAN AWARD
Quincy Jones.

IRVING R. THALBERG MEMORIAL AWARD
Clint Eastwood.
SPECIAL AWARDS
Gordon E. Sawyer Award (Academy Statuette)—**Petro Vlahos, Paul Vlahos**, for concept and development of the Ultimatte Electronic Blue Screen Compositing Process. Eastman Kodak, for development of the EXR Color Intermediate Film 5244.

1993

PICTURE
Schindlers List, Universal Pictures/Amblin Entertainment.
ACTOR
Tom Hanks, Philadelphia.
ACTRESS
Holly Hunter, The Piano.
SUPPORTING ACTOR
Tommy Lee Jones, The Fugitive.
SUPPORTING ACTRESS
Anna Paquin, The Piano.
DIRECTOR
Steven Spielberg, Schindlers List.
FOREIGN LANGUAGE FILM
Belle Epoque, Fernando Trueba P.C. (Madrid)/Lola Films (Barcelona)/Animatografo (Lisbon)/French Production (Paris); Sony Pictures Classics (Spain).
ORIGINAL SCREENPLAY
Jane Campion, The Piano.
ADAPTED SCREENPLAY
Steven Zaillian, Schindlers List.
CINEMATOGRAPHER
Janusz Kaminski, Schindlers List.
ART DIRECTION
Allan Starski (art direction), **Ewa Braun** (set decoration); Schindlers List.
COSTUME DESIGN
Gabriella Pescucci, The Age of Innocence
FILM EDITING
Michael Kahn, Schindlers List.
ORIGINAL SCORE
John Williams, Schindlers List.
ORIGINAL SONG
Streets of Philadelphia, from Philadelphia. Music and lyric by Bruce Springsteen.
SHORT SUBJECT—ANIMATED
The Wrong Trousers, Aardman Animations Ltd.; Nicholas Park, producer.
SHORT SUBJECT—LIVE-ACTION
Black Rider (Schwarzfahrer), Trans-Film GmbH; Pepe Danquart, producer.
SOUND
Gary Summers, Gary Rydstrom, Shawn Murphy, Ron Judkins, Jurassic Park.
SOUND EFFECTS EDITING
Gary Rydstrom, Richard Hymns, Jurassic Park.
VISUAL EFFECTS
Dennis Muren, Stan Winston, Phil Tippett, Michael Lantieri, Jurassic Park.
DOCUMENTARY—FEATURE
I Am a Promise: The Children of Stanton Elementary School, Verite Films; Susan Raymond and Alan Raymond, producers.
DOCUMENTARY—SHORT SUBJECT
Defending Our Lives, Cambridge Documentary Films; Margaret Lazarus and Renner Wunderlich, producers.
MAKEUP
Greg Cannom, Ve Neill, Yolanda Toussieng, Mrs. Doubtfire.
HONORARY ACADEMY AWARD
Deborah Kerr, for career achievement.
JEAN HERSHOLT HUMANITARIAN AWARD
Paul Newman, for his humanitarian efforts.
SPECIAL AWARDS
Gordon E. Sawyer Award (Academy Statuette); **Petro Vlahos**, whose technical contributions have brought credit to the motion picture industry.

1992

PICTURE
Unforgiven, Warner Bros. Production, WB, Clint Eastwood, producer.
ACTOR
Al Pacino, Scent of a Woman, Universal Pictures production, Universal.

ACTRESS
Emma Thompson, Howards End, Merchant Ivory production, Sony Pictures Classics.
SUPPORTING ACTOR
Gene Hackman, Unforgiven.
SUPPORTING ACTRESS
Marisa Tomei, My Cousin Vinny, 20th Century Fox production, 20th Century Fox.
DIRECTOR
Clint Eastwood, Unforgiven.
FOREIGN LANGUAGE FILM
Indochine, Paradis Films/La Gaenaerale d'Images/BAC Films/Orly Films/Dine Cinq production, Sony Pictures Classics (France).
ORIGINAL SCREENPLAY
Neil Jordan, The Crying Game, Palace Pictures production, Miramax.
ADAPTED SCREENPLAY
Ruth Prawer Jhabvala, Howards End.
CINEMATOGRAPHER
Philippe Rousselot, A River Runs Through It, Columbia Pictures production, Columbia; Robert Redford, Patrick Markey, producers.
ART DIRECTION
Luciana Arrighi (art direction), **Ian Whittaker** (set decoration), Howards End.
COSTUME DESIGN
Elko Ishioka, Bram Stoker's Dracula, Columbia Pictures production, Columbia; Francis Ford Coppola, Fred Fuchs, Charles Mulvehill, producers.
FILM EDITING
Joel Cox, Unforgiven.
ORIGINAL SCORE
Alan Menken, Aladdin, Walt Disney Pictures production, Buena Vista.
ORIGINAL SONG
"Whole New World," from Aladdin. Music by Alan Menken, lyric by Tim Rice.
SHORT SUBJECT—ANIMATED
Mona Lisa Descending a Staircase, Joan C. Gratz production; Gratz, producer.
SHORT SUBJECT—LIVE ACTION
Omnibus, Lazennec tout court/Le CRRAV production; Sam Karmann, producer.
SOUND
Chris Jenkins, Doug Hemphill, Mark Smith, Simon Kaye, The Last of the Mohicans, 20th Century Fox production, 20th Century Fox.
SOUND EFFECTS EDITING
Tom C. McCarthy, David E. Stone, Bram Stoker's Dracula.
VISUAL EFFECTS
Ken Ralston, Doug Chiang, Doug Smythe, Tom Woodruff, Death Becomes Her, Universal Pictures production, Universal.
DOCUMENTARY—FEATURE
The Panama Deception, Empowerment Project production; Barbara Trent, David Kasper, producers.
DOCUMENTARY—SHORT SUBJECT
Educating Peter, State of the Art Inc. production; Thomas C. Goodwin, Gerardine Wurzburg, producers.
MAKEUP
Greg Cannom, Michele Burke, Matthew W. Mungle, Bram Stoker's Dracula.
HONORARY ACADEMY AWARD
Federico Fellini, "in recognition of his cinematic accomplishments that have thrilled and entertained worldwide audiences."
JEAN HERSHOLT HUMANITARIAN AWARD
Audrey Hepburn, for her UNICEF work;. Elizabeth Taylor for her support of AIDS research.
SPECIAL AWARDS
Gordon E. Sawyer Award (Academy Statuette); **Erich Kaestner**, "whose technical contributions have brought credit to the motion picture industry."

1991

PICTURE
The Silence of the Lambs, Strong Heart/Demme Production, Orion; Edward Saxon, Kenneth Utt and Ron Bozman, producers.
ACTOR
Anthony Hopkins, The Silence of the Lambs.
ACTRESS
Jodie Foster, The Silence of the Lambs.
SUPPORTING ACTOR
Jack Palance, City Slickers, Castle Rock Entertainment in association with Nelson Entertainment presentation of a Face production, Columbia.

SUPPORTING ACTRESS
Mercedes Ruehl, The Fisher King, Hill/Obst production, Tri-Star.
DIRECTOR
Jonathan Demme, The Silence of the Lambs.
FOREIGN LANGUAGE FILM
Mediterraneo, Pentafilm S.p.A./ A.M.A. Film S.r.l. production (Italy), Miramax.
ORIGINAL SCREENPLAY
Callie Khouri, Thelma & Louise, Percy Main production, MGM.
ADAPTED SCREENPLAY
Ted Tally, The Silence of the Lambs.
CINEMATOGRAPHER
Robert Richardson, JFK.
ART DIRECTION
Dennis Gassner (art direction), Nancy Haigh, (set decoration), Bugsy, TriStar Pictures production, TriStar.
COSTUME DESIGN
Albert Wolsky, Bugsy.
FILM EDITING
Joe Hutshing, Pietro Scalia, JFK.
ORIGINAL SCORE
Alan Menken, Beauty and the Beast, Walt Disney Pictures production, Buena Vista.
ORIGINAL SONG
Beauty and the Beast, from Beauty and the Beast. Music by Alan Menken, lyric by Howard Ashman.
SHORT SUBJECT—ANIMATED
Manipulation, Tandem Films production; Daniel Greaves, producer.
SHORT SUBJECTS—LIVE ACTION
Session Man, Chanticleer Films production; Daniel Greaves, producer.
SOUND
Tom Johnson, Gary Rydstrom, Gary Summers, Lee Orloff, Terminator 2: Judgment Day. Mario Kassar presentation of a Pacific Western production in association with Lightstorm Entertainment, TriStar (from Carolco).
SOUND EFFECTS EDITING
Gary Rydstrom, Gloria S. Borders, Terminator 2: Judgment Day.
VISUAL EFFECTS
Dennis Muren, Stan Winston, Gene Warren Jr., Robert Skotak, Terminator 2: Judgment Day.
DOCUMENTARY—FEATURE
In the Shadow of the Stars, Light-Saraf Films production; Allie Light, Irving Saraf, producers.
DOCUMENTARY—SHORT SUBJECT
Deadly Deception: General Electric, Nuclear Weapons and Our Environment, Women's Educational Media Inc. production; Debra Chasnoff, producer.
MAKEUP
Stan Sinston, Jeff Dawn, Terminator 2: Judgment Day.
HONORARY OSCAR
Satyajit Ray.
SPECIAL AWARDS
Gordon E. Sawyer Award (Academy statuette); Ray Harryhausen.

1990

PICTURE
Dances With Wolves, Tig production, Orion, Jim Wilson, Kevin Costner, producers.
ACTOR
Jeremy Irons, Reversal of Fortune, Reversal Films production; Warner Bros.
ACTRESS
Kathy Bates, Misery, Castle Rock Entertainment production, Columbia.
SUPPORTING ACTOR
Joe Pesci, Goodfellas, Warner Bros. production, Warner Bros.
SUPPORTING ACTRESS
Whoopi Goldberg, Ghost, Howard W. Koch production, Paramount.
DIRECTOR
Kevin Costner, Dances With Wolves.
FOREIGN LANGUAGE FILM
Journey of Hope, a Catpics/ Condor Features production (Switzerland).
ORIGINAL SCREENPLAY
Bruce Joel Rubin, Ghost.
ADAPTED SCREENPLAY
Michael Blake, Dances With Wolves.

CINEMATOGRAPHER
Dean Semier, Dances With Wolves.
ART DIRECTION
Richard Sylbert (art direction), Rick Simpson (set decoration), Dick Tracy. Touchstone Pictures production, Buena Vista.
COSTUME DESIGN
Franca Squaricapino, Cyrano de Bergerac, Hachette Premiere production, Orion Classics (France).
FILM EDITING
Neil Travis, Dances With Wolves.
ORIGINAL SCORE
John Barry, Dances With Wolves.
ORIGINAL SONG
Sooner Or Later (I Always Get My Man), from Dick Tracy. Music and lyric by Stephen Sondheim.
SHORT SUBJECTS—ANIMATED
Creature Comforts, Aardman Animations Ltd. production, Nick Park, producer.
SHORT SUBJECTS—LIVE ACTION
The Lunch Date, Adam Davidson production, Adam Davidson, producer.
SOUND
Russell Williams II, Jeffrey Perkins, Bill W. Benton, Greg Watkins, Dances With Wolves.
SOUND EFFECTS EDITING
Cecelia Hall, George Watters II, The Hunt For Red October, Mace Neufeld/Jerry Sherlock production, Paramount.
VISUAL EFFECTS
Eric Brevig, Rob Bottin, Tim McGovern, Alex Funke, Total Recall, Special Achievement Award.
DOCUMENTARY—FEATURE
American Dream, Cabin Creek production, Barbara Kopple, Arthur Cohn, producers.
DOCUMENTARY—SHORT SUBJECT
Days Of Waiting, Mouchette Films production, Steven Okazaki, producer.
MAKEUP
John Caglione Jr., Doug Drexler, Dick Tracy.
HONORARY OSCARS
Sophia Loren and Myrna Loy.
SPECIAL AWARDS
Gordon E. Sawyer Award (Academy statuette); Stefan Kudelski.

CHICAGO FILM CRITICS AWARDS

BEST PICTURE
Apollo 13.
BEST ACTOR
Nicolas Cage, Leaving Las Vegas.
BEST ACTRESS
Elisabeth Shue, Leaving Las Vegas.
BEST SUPPORTING ACTOR
Kevin Spacey, The Usual Suspects.
BEST SUPPORTING ACTRESS
Joan Allen, Nixon.
BEST DIRECTOR
Oliver Stone, Nixon.
BEST SCREENPLAY
Christopher McQuarrie, The Usual Suspects.
BEST CINEMATOGRAPHY
Darius Khondji, Seven.
BEST MUSICAL SCORE
Randy Newman, Toy Story.
MOST PROMISING NEW ACTOR
Greg Kinnear, Sabrina.
MOST PROMISING NEW ACTRESS
Minnie Driver, Circle of Friends.
SPECIAL "COMMITTMENT TO CHICAGO" AWARD
Gary Sinise.

LOS ANGELES FILM CRITICS AWARDS

BEST PICTURE
Leaving Las Vegas.
BEST DIRECTOR
Mike Figgis, Leaving Las Vegas.
BEST ACTOR
Nicolas Cage, Leaving Las Vegas.

BEST ACTRESS
Elisabeth Shue, Leaving Las Vegas.
BEST SUPPORTING ACTOR
Don Cheadle, Devil in a Blue Dress.
BEST SUPPORTING ACTRESS
Joan Allen, Nixon.
BEST SCREENPLAY
Emma Thompson, Sense and Sensibility.
BEST CINEMATOGRAPHY
La Yue, Shanghai Triad.
BEST PRODUCTION DESIGN
Bo Welch, A Little Princess.
BEST MUSICAL SCORE
Patrick Doyle, A Little Princess.
BEST FOREIGN FILM
Wild Reeds, Andre Techine.
CAREER ACHIEVEMENT
Andre de Toth.
BEST DOCUMENTARY
Crumb.
BEST ANIMATION
Toy Story.
DOUGLAS EDWARDS AWARD FOR INDEPENDENT/EXPER-IMENTAL FILM & VIDEO
Mark Rappaport, From the Journals of Jean Seberg.

NATIONAL SOCIETY OF FILM CRITICS AWARDS

BEST PICTURE
Babe.
BEST DIRECTOR
Mike Figgis, Leaving Las Vegas.
BEST ACTOR
Nicolas Cage, Leaving Las Vegas.
BEST ACTRESS
Elisabeth Shue, Leaving Las Vegas.
BEST SUPPORTING ACTOR
Don Cheadle, Devil in a Blue Dress.
BEST SUPPORTING ACTOR
Joan Allen, Nixon.
BEST FOREIGN FILM
Wild Reeds, Andre Techine.
BEST DOCUMENTARY
Crumb, Terry Zwigoff.
BEST SCREENPLAY
Amy Heckerling, Clueless.
BEST CINEMATOGRAPHY
Tak Fujimoto, Devil in a Blue Dress.
SPECIAL ARCHIVAL AWARD
I Am Cuba, Mikhail Kalatozov, (1964).
BEST EXPERIMENTAL FILM
Latcho Drom, Tony Gatlif

AMERICAN FILM INSTITUTE LIFE ACHIEVEMENT AWARD

1996 RECIPIENT
Clint Eastwood.
PAST RECIPIENTS

BRITISH ACADEMY OF FILM AND TELEVISION ARTS (BAFTA) AWARDS

BEST FILM
Sense and Sensibility, Lindsay Doran, Ang Lee.
THE DAVID LEAN AWARD FOR BEST ACHEIVEMENT IN DIRECTING
Michael Radford, Il Postino.
BEST ORIGINAL SCREENPLAY
Christopher McQuarrie, The Usual Suspetcs.
BEST ADAPTED SCREENPLAY
John Hodge, Trainspotting.
BEST ACTRESS
Emma Thompson, Sense and Sensibility.
BEST ACTOR
Nigel Hawthorne, The Madness of King George.
BEST SUPPORTING ACTRESS
Kate Winslet, Sense and Sensibility.
BEST SUPPORTING ACTOR
Tim Roth, Rob Roy.
BEST FILM NOT IN THE ENGLISH LANGUAGE
Il Postino, Mario Cecchi Gori, Vittorio Cecchi Gori, Gaetano Daniele, Michael Radford.
THE ANTHONY ASQUITH AWARD FOR ACHIEVEMENT IN FILM MUSIC
Luis Bacalov, Il Postino.
BEST CINEMATOGRAPHY
John Toll, Braveheart.
BEST PRODUCTION DESIGN
Michael Corenblith, Apollo 13.
BEST COSTUME DESIGN
Charles Knode, Braveheart.
BEST EDITING
John Ottman, The Usual Suspects.
BEST SOUND
Per Hallberg, Lon Bender, Brain Simmons, Andy Nelson, Scott Millan, Anna Behlmer, Braveheart.
BEST SPECIAL EFFECTS
Robert Legato, Michael Kanfer, Matt Sweeney, Leslie Ekker, Apollo 13.
BEST HAIR/MAKE-UP
Lisa Westcott, The Madness of King George.
THE ALEXANDER KORDA AWARD FOR THE OUTSTAND-ING BRITISH FILM OF THE YEAR
The Madness of King George.
THE MICHAEL BALCON AWARD FOR OUTSTANDING BRITISH CONTRIBUTION TO CINEMA
Mike Leigh.
THE FELLOWSHIP
John Schlesinger.
THE CRAFT FELLOWSHIP
Jeanne Moreau.
THE LLOYD'S BANK PEOPLE'S VOTE FOR FAVOURITE FILM
Braveheart.

1996 CANNES FILM FESTIVAL AWARDS

PALME D'OR
Secrets and Lies, Mike Leigh, (France-U.K.)
GRAND JURY PRIZE
Breaking the Waves, Lars Von Trier, (Denmark).
BEST ACTRESS
Brenda Blethyn, Secrets and Lies.
BEST ACTOR (TIE)
Daniel Auteuil, Pascal Duqenne, La huitième Jour.
BEST DIRECTOR
Joel & Ethan Coen, Fargo.
BEST SCREENPLAY
Un héros très Discret.
SPECIAL JURY PRIZE
Crash, David Cronenberg (Canada).
CAMERA D'OR (BEST FIRST FILM)
Love Serenade, Shirley Barrett, (Australia).
TECHNICAL PRIZE
Microcosmos, le peuple de l'herbe, Claude Nurisdany, Marie Perennou (France).

Golden Globe Awards— Motion Pictures

BEST PICTURE—DRAMA
Sense and Sensibility, Columbia (Sony).
BEST ACTOR—DRAMA
Nicolas Cage, Leaving Las Vegas.
BEST ACTRESS—DRAMA
Sharon Stone, Casino.
BEST PICTURE—COMEDY OR MUSICAL
Babe, A Kennedy-Miller Production.
BEST ACTOR—COMEDY OR MUSICAL
John Travolta, Get Shorty.
BEST ACTRESS—COMEDY OR MUSICAL
Nicole Kidman, To Die For.
BEST FOREIGN LANGUAGE FILM
Les Miserables, Les Films 13/TFI Films Prod. with Canal+; Warner Bros. (France).
BEST SUPPORTING ACTOR
Brad Pitt, Twelve Monkeys.
BEST SUPPORTING ACTRESS
Mira Sorvino, Mighty Aphrodite.
BEST DIRECTOR
Mel Gibson, Braveheart.
BEST SCREENPLAY
Emma Thompson, Sense and Sensibility.
BEST ORIGINAL SCORE
Maurice Jarre, A Walk in the Clouds.
BEST ORIGINAL SONG
"Colors of the Wind," Pocahontas, Music by Alan Menken; Lyric by Steven Schwartz.
CECIL B. DEMILLE AWARD
Sean Connery

Independent Spirit Awards

Awarded by the Independent Feature Project West in recognition of the contributions of independent filmmakers.

BEST PICTURE
Leaving Las Vegas, Producers: Lila Cazes, Annie Stewart.
BEST FIRST FEATURE
The Brothers McMullen, Producers: Edward Burns, Dick Fisher.
BEST DIRECTOR
Mike Figgis, Leaving Las Vegas.

BEST ACTOR
Sean Penn, Dead Man Walking.
BEST ACTRESS
Elisabeth Shue, Leaving Las Vegas.
BEST SUPPORTING ACTOR
Benicio Del Toro, The Usual Suspects.
BEST SUPPORTING ACTRESS
Mare Winningham, Georgia.
BEST SCREENPLAY
Christopher McQuarrie, The Usual Suspects.
BEST FIRST SCREENPLAY
Paul Auster, Smoke.
BEST CINEMATOGRAPHY
Newton Thomas Sigel, The Usual Suspects.
BEST FOREIGN FILM
Before the Rain, Milcho Manchevski (Macedonia).
SOMEONE TO WATCH
Christopher Munch, Color of a Bright and Leaping Day.
SPECIAL DISTINCTION AWARD
Sam Fuller, Pickup on South Street, I Shot Jesse James, The Baron of Arizona, Hell and High Water, Forty Gins, The Steel Helmet, Fixed Bayonets, Park Row.

Directors Guild of America Awards

FILM DIRECTOR'S AWARD
Ron Howard, Apollo 13.
D.W. GRIFFITH LIFETIME ACHIEVEMENT AWARD
Woody Allen.

Screen Actors Guild Awards

BEST ACTOR
Nicolas Cage, Leaving Las Vegas.
BEST ACTRESS
Susan Sarandon, Dead Man Walking.
BEST SUPPORTING ACTOR
Ed Harris, Apollo 13.
BEST SUPPORTING ACTRESS
Kate Winslet, Sense and Sensibility.
CAST OF A THEATRICAL MOTION PICTURE
Tom Hanks, Ed Harris, Bill Paxton, Kevin Bacon, Kathleen Quinlan, Gary Sinise, (Apollo 13).

TOP GROSSING FILMS 1990-96

The ten top grossing films per year from 1990-1995 worldwide, as selected by Quigley Publishing. Some films may have been held over from the previous year. The 1996 listing reflects box office rentals from January 1–September 30, 1996.

1996

Independence Day (Fox) 1
Twister (WB) 2
Mission: Impossible (Par) 3
The Rock (BV) 4
Eraser (WB) 5
The Hunchback of Notre Dame (BV) 6
The Birdcage (MGM) 7
The Nutty Professor (Par) 8
Phenomenon (BV) 9
A Time to Kill (WB) 10

1995

Batman Forever 1
Apollo 13 2
Toy Story 3
Pocahontas 4
Ace Ventura: When Nature Calls 5
Casper 6
Die Hard With A Vengeance 7
Goldeneye 8
Crimson Tide 9
Waterworld 10

1994

The Lion King (BV) 1
Forrest Gump (Par) 2
True Lies (Fox) 3
The Santa Clause (BV) 4
The Flintstones (Univ) 5
Dumb and Dumber (New Line) 6
The Mask (New Line) 7
Speed (Univ) 8
Clear and Present Danger (Par) 9
The Client (WB) 10

1993

Jurassic Park (Univ) 1
Mrs. Doubtfire (Fox) 2
The Fugitive (WB) 3
The Firm (Par) 4

Sleepless In Seattle (TriStar) 5
Indecent Proposal (Par) 6
Maverick (WB) 7
The Pelican Brief (WB) 8
In the Line of Fire (Col) 9
Schindler's List (Univ) 10

1992

Aladdin (BV) 1
Batman Returns (WB) 2
Lethal Weapon 3 (WB) 3
A Few Good Men (Col) 4
Sister Act (BV) 5
The Bodyguard (WB) 6
Wayne's World (Par) 7
A Leaugue of Their Own (Col) 8
Basic Instinct (TriStar) 9
Bram Stoker's Dracula (Col) 10

1991

Terminator 2 (TriStar) 1
Home Alone 2: Lost In New York 2
Robin Hood: Prince of Thieves 3
Beauty and the Beast (BV) 4
Hook (TriStar) 5
City Slickers (Col) 6
The Silence of the Lambs (Orion) 7
The Addams Family (Par) 8
Sleeping With the Enemy (Fox) 9
The Naked Gun 2^1/2: The Smell of Fear (Par) 10

1990

Home Alone (Fox) 1
Ghost (Par) 2
Pretty Woman 3
Dances With Wolves (Orion) 4
Teenage Mutant Ninja Turtles (New Line) 5
Die Hard 2 (Fox) 6
Total Recall (TriStar) 7
Dick Tracy (BV) 8
The Hunt for Red October (Par) 9
Back to the Future, Part III (Univ) 10

INTERNATIONAL FESTIVALS & MARKETS

Listed by month. The address and telephone number of Festival Organizers have been provided for your convenience.

JANUARY

Annual Kidfilm Festival, U.S.A. Film Festival
2917 Swiss Ave., Dallas, TX 75205
(214) 821-6300. FAX: (214) 821-6364

Palm Springs International Film Festival
P.O. Box 2930, Palm Springs, CA 92263
(619) 322-2930. FAX: (619) 322-4087

Filmfestival Max Ophuls Prize
Mainzerstrasse 8, 6600 Saarbrucken, Germany
(49-681) 329452. FAX: (49-681) 9051943

Brussels International Film Festival
30 Chausee de Louvain, B-1030 Brussels, Belgium
(2) 2181055. FAX: (2) 2186627

FIPA (Festival International de Programmes Audiovisuel)
Faubourg St. Honore, 75008 Paris, France
(33-1) 45 61 01 66. FAX: (33-1) 40 74 07 96

Fajr International Film Festival
Farhang Cinema, Dr. Shariati Avenue, Gholhak, Tehran 19139
Iran. (21) 2052088. FAX: (21) 267082

Solothurner Filmtage
P.O. Box 1030, CH-4502 Solothurn, Switzerland
(0) 65 233161. FAX: (0) 65 236410

Clermont-Ferrand Short Film Festival
26 rue des Jacobins, 63000 Clermont-Ferrand, France
73 91 65 73. FAX: 73 92 11 93

Rotterdam International Film Festival
P.O. Box 21696, 3001 AR Rotterdam, Netherlands
(10) 411 8080. FAX: (10) 413 5132

Tromso International Film Festival
Georgernes Verft 3, 5011 Bergen, Norway
(55) 322 590. FAX: (55) 323 740

International Film Festival of India
Ministry of Information & Broadcasting, Government of India,
Lok Nayak Bhavan, Khan Market, New Delhi 110003
(11) 461 5963. FAX: (11) 469 4920

CineAsia
Cinema Expo International, 244 W. 49th Street, New York,
NY 10019 (212) 246-6460. FAX: (212) 265-6428

NATPE
2425 Olympic Blvd., Suite 550E, Santa Monica, CA 90404
(310) 453-4440. FAX: (310) 453-5258

Sundance Film Festival
P.O. Box 16450, Salt Lake City, UT 84116 (801) 328-3455.
FAX: (801) 575 5174

FEBRUARY

MILIA
MIDEM Organisation, 179 ave. Victor Hugo, 75016 Paris,
France. (1) 44 34 44 44. FAX: (3301) 44 34 44 00

Berlin International Film Festival
Budapesterstrasse 50, 10787 Berlin, Germany
(49-30) 254 890. FAX: (49-30) 2548 9249

Fantasporto (Opporto International Film Festival)
Rua da Constituicao 311, 4200 Potro, Portugal
(2) 550 8990. FAX: (2) 550 8210

Gothenburg Film Festival
Box 7079, 40232 Gothenburg, Sweden
(31) 410 546. FAX: (31) 410 063

Miami Film Festival
444 Brickell Avenue, Miami, FL 33131
(305) 377-3456. FAX: (305) 577-9768

Hungaria Film Week
Magyar Filmunio, Varoslglieti Sasor 38, 1068 Budapest, Hungary
(1) 269 7760. FAX: (1) 268 0070

Monte Carlo Television Festival & Market
Boulevard Louis II, 98000 Monaco
104 060. FAX: 507 014

American Film Market
Ms. Brady Caine, AMFA, 120850 Wilshire Blvd., 9th fl., Los
Angeles, CA 90024. (310) 446-1000. FAX: (310) 446-1600

Brussels Cartoon & Animated Film Festival, Folioscope
rue de la Rhetorique 19, B-1060 Brussels, Belgium
(2) 534 4125. FAX: (2) 534 2279

Portland International Film Festival
Northwest Film Center, 1219 S.W. Park Ave., Portland, OR
97205. (503) 221-1156. FAX: (503) 226-4842

Aspen Shortfest
P.O. Box 8910, Aspen, CO 81611
(910) 925-6882. FAX: (910) 925-1967

MARCH

NATO ShoWest
116 North Robertson, Suite F, Los Angeles, CA 90048
(310) 654-7724. FAX: (310) 657 4758

Santa Barbara International Film Festival
1216 State St., Santa Barbara, CA 93101
(805) 963-0023. FAX: (805) 962-2524

Fribourg Film Festival
rue de Locarno 8, 1700 Fribourg, Switzerland
(37) 222 232. FAX: (37) 227 950

Dublin Film Festival
1 Suffolk Street, Dublin 2, Ireland
(1) 679 2937. FAX: (1) 679 2939

Tampere International Short Film Festival
Box 305, 33101 Tampere, Finland
(31) 213 0034. FAX: (31) 223 0121

Brussels International Festival of Fantasy, Thriller & Science Fiction Films
111 avenue de la Reine, 1210 Brussels, Belgium
(2) 201 1713. FAX: (2) 201 1469

Bergamo Film Meeting
Via Pascoli 3, 24121 Bergamo, Italy
(35) 234011. FAX: (35) 233129

International Women's Film Festival
Maison des Arts, Place Salvador Allende, 94000 Creteil,
France. (1) 49 80 39 98. FAX: (1) 43 99 04 10

Local Heroes International Screen Festival
10022-103 St., Edmonton, Alberta T5J 0X2, Canada
(403) 421-4084. FAX: (403) 425-8090

New Directors/New Films
The Film Society of Lincoln Center, 70 Lincoln Center Plaza,
New York, NY 10023. (212) 875-5610. FAX: (212) 875-5636

San Francisco Asian American International Film Festival
346 Ninth St., San Francisco, CA 94103
(415) 863-0814. FAX: (415) 863-7428

London Lesbian & Gay Film Festival
National Film Theatre, South Bank, Waterloo, London SE1
8XT, England. (171) 815 1323. FAX: (171) 633 0786

Cartagena Film Festival
P.O. Box 1834, Cartagena, Colombia
(5753) 600 966. FAX: (5753) 600 970

APRIL

MIP – TV
MIDEM Organisation, 179 avenue Victor Hugo, 75016 Paris,
France. (33 1) 44 34 44 44. FAX: (33 1) 44 34 44 00

Los Angeles International Animation Celebration
28024 Dorothy Dr., Agoura Hills, CA 91301
(818) 991-2884. FAX: (818) 991-3773

Istanbul International Film Festival
Istiklal Caddest 146, Luvr Apt. Beyoglu, 80070 Istanbul,
Turkey. (212) 293 31 33. FAX: (212) 249 77 71

Hong Kong International Film Festival
Festivals Office, Level 7, Administration Bldg., Hong Kong
Cultural Centre, 10 Salisbury Rd., Tsimshatsui, Kowloon,
Hong Kong. 734 2903. FAX: 366 5206

Singapore International Film Festival
169 Kim Seng Road, Singapore 0923
738 7567. FAX: 738 7578

Black Filmworks
Black Filmmakers Hall of Fame, P.O. Box 28055, Oakland,
CA 94606. (510) 465-0804. FAX: (510) 839-9858

USA Film Festival
2917 Swiss Ave., Dallas, TX 75204
(214) 821 6300. FAX: (214) 821 6364

Chicago Latino Film Festival
600 South Michigan Ave., Chicago, IL 60605
(312) 431-1330. FAX: (312) 360-0629

Worldfest – Houston
P.O. Box 56566, Houston, TX 77256
(713) 965-9955. FAX: (713) 965-9960

Rivertown: Minneapolis/
St. Paul International Film Festival
425 Ontario St. S.E., Minneapolis, MN 55414
(612) 627-4432. FAX: (612) 627-4111

Cape Town International Film Festival
c/o University of Cape Town, Private Bag, Rondebosch 7700,
Cape Town, South Africa. (21) 238 257. FAX: (21) 242 355

International Cinema Week
Via S. Giacomo alla Pignano. 6, 37121 Verona, Italy
(45) 800 6778. FAX: (45) 590 624

International Short Film Festival Oberhausen
Christian-Steger Strasse 10, 46042 Oberhausen, Germany
(208) 807 008. FAX: (45) 590 624

International Electronic Cinema Festival
P.O. Box 1451, 1820 Montreux, Switzerland
(21) 963 3220. FAX: (21) 963 8851

Baltimore Film Festival
10 Art Museum Drive, Baltimore, MD 21218
(410) 889-1993. FAX: (410) 889-2567

Cleveland International Film Festival
The Cleveland Film Society, 1621 Euclid Ave., Cleveland, OH
44115. (216) 623-0400. FAX: (216) 623-0101

San Francisco International Film Festival
1521 Eddy Street, San Francisco, CA 94115
(415) 929-5000. FAX: (415) 921-5032

Cognac International Film Festival of the Thriller
c/o Promo 2000, 36 rue Perriet, 92200 Neuilly-sur-Seine,
France. 46 40 55 00. FAX: 46 40 55 39

Academic Film Olomuc
Krizkiveskeho 8, 771 47 Olomuc, Czech Republic
(68) 5508 277. FAX: (68) 26 476

Festival of French Cinema
Tel Aviv Cinematheque, 2 Sprintzak St., Tel Aviv, Israel

Lille International Festival of Short & Documentary Films
24-34 rue Washington, 75008 Paris, France

MAY

Cannes Film Festival
99 Boulevard Malesherbes, 75008 Paris, France
(33 1) 45 61 66 00. FAX: (33 1) 45 61 97 60

Philadelphia Festival of World Cinema
Int'l House of Philadelphia, 3701 Chestnut St., Philadelphia,
PA 19104. (215) 895-6593. FAX: (215) 895-6562

Brighton Festival
21-22 Old Steine, Brighton, BN1 1EL, England
(12 73) 713 875. FAX: (12 73) 622 453

Independent Film Days
Filmburo Augsburg, Schroeckstrasse 6, 86152 Augsburg,
Germany. (821) 153 077. FAX: (821) 155 518

Seattle International Film Festival
801 East Pine Street, Seattle, WA 98122
(206) 324-9996. FAX: (206) 324-9998

Ethnogenre Film Festival
184 Dorchester Rd., Rochester, NY 14610
(716) 288-2152. FAX: (716) 288-2156

Prix Danube
Mylneska Dolina, 845 45 Bratislava, Slovakia
(7) 727 448. FAX: (7) 729 440

International Short Film Festival – Kracow
c/o Apollo Film, ul. Pychowicka 7, 30-364 Kracow, Poland
(12) 672 340. FAX: (12) 671 552

Golden Prague International TV Festival
Czechoslovak TV, Kaveci Hory 140 70, Prague 4, Czech
Republic. (2) 6121 2882. FAX: (2) 6121 2891

The Human Rights Watch International Film Festival
485 Fifth Ave., New York, NY 10017
(212) 972-8400. (212) 972-0905

New England Film & Video Festival
Boston Film/Video Foundation, 1126 Boylston St., Boston,
MA 02215. (617) 536-1540. FAX: (617) 536-3576

JUNE

Cinema Expo International
244 West 49th Street, New York, NY 10019
(212) 246-6460. FAX: (212) 265-6428

Sydney Film Festival
Paul Byrnes, P.O. Box 950, Glebe, NSW 2037, Australia
(2) 660 3844. fax: (2) 692 8793

Austrian Film Days
Austrian Film Office, Columbusgasse 2, 1100 Vienna, Austria
(1) 604 0126. FAX: (1) 602 0795

Florida Film Festival
Enzian Theater, 1300 S. Orlando Ave., Maitland, FL 32789
(407) 629-1088. FAX: (407) 629-6870

Melbourne International Film Festival
P.O. Box 2206, Fitzroy Mail Centre, Victoria 3065, Australia
(3) 9417 2011. FAX: (3) 9417 3804

The Montreal International Festival of New
Cinema & Video
3726 Blvd. St. Laurent, Montreal, Quebec H2X 2V8, Canada
(514) 843-4725. FAX: (514) 843-4631

Bellaria Film Festival
Viale Paolo Guidi 108, 47041 Bellaria Igea Marina (RN), Italy
(541) 347 186. FAX: (541) 347 186

Vue Sur Les Docs
3 Square Stalingrad, 13001 Marseille, France
91 84 40 17. FAX: 91 84 38 34

San Francisco Lesbian & Gay Film
Festival and Market
Frameline, 346 Ninth St., San Francisco, CA 94103
(415) 703-8658. FAX: (415) 861-1404

Banff Television Festival
P.O. Box 219, Suite 9000, Banff, Alberta TOL OCO, Canada
(403) 678-9260. FAX: (403) 678-9269

International Advertising Film Festival
c/o 2nd floor, Woolverstone House, 61-62 Berners St., London
W1P 3AE, England. (171) 636 6122. FAX: (171) 636 6086

Munich Film Festival
Kaiserstrasse 39, 80801 Munich, Germany
(89) 381 9040. FAX: (89) 381 90427

London Jewish Film Festival
South Bank, Waterloo, London SE1 8XT, England
(171) 815 1322. FAX: (171) 633 0786

Mystfest (International Mystery Film Festival)
Centro Cultural Polivalente, Piazza Della Repubblica 34, 47033
Catolica (FO), Italy. (541) 967 802. FAX: (541) 967 803.

Donostia Screenings
c/o Euroaim, 210 avenue Winston Churchill, B-1180 Brussels,
Belgium. (2) 346 1500. FAX: (2) 346 3842

La Rochelle International Film Festival
16 rue Saint Sabin, 75011 Paris, France
(1) 48 06 16 66. FAX: (1) 48 06 15 40

Newark Black Film Festival
The Newark Museum Assn., 49 Washington St., P.O. Box 540,
Newark, NJ 07101. (201) 596-6637. FAX: (201) 642-0459

AFI Los Angeles International Film Festival
2021 N. Western Ave., Los Angeles, CA 90027
(213) 856-7707. FAX: (213) 462-4049

Dylan Dog Horror Films
Via M. Buonarotti 38, 20145 Milan, Italy
(2) 4800 2877. FAX: (2) 4801 1937

French American Film Workshop
10 Montee de la Tour, Villeneuve Les Avignon, France
90 25 93 23. FAX: 90 25 93 24

Marketskaya
c/o Seineva Organisation, 10 rue de la Boetie, 75008 Paris, France. (1) 53 76 16 28. FAX: (1) 45 61 94 27

Midnight Sun Film Festival
Malminkatu 36 B 102, Helsinki, Finland
(0) 685 2242. FAX: (0) 694 5560

Pesaro Film Festival
Via Villefranca 20, 00185 Rome, Italy
(6) 445 6643. FAX: (6) 491 163

Festival of Festivals
10 Kamennoostrovsky Ave., St. Petersburg 197101, Russia
(812) 238 5811. FAX: (812) 232 8881

Troia International Film Festival
Troia, 2902 Setubal Codex, Portugal
(65) 441 21. FAX: (65) 441 23

Norwegian Short Film Festival
Storengveien 8B, N-1342 Jar, Norway
(67) 122 013. FAX: (67) 124 865

JULY

Philafilm
IAMPTP, 215 South Broad St., Philadelphia, PA 19107
(215) 977-2831. FAX: (215) 546-8055

19th Asian American International Film Festival
Asian Cinevision, 32 E. Broadway, New York, NY 10002
(212) 925-8685. FAX: (212) 925-8157

Vevey International Comedy Film Festival
Buureau du Festival du Film de Comedie, La Greneyye, Grand Place 29, CH-1800 Vevey, Switzerland.
(21) 922 2027. FAX: (21) 922 2024

Auckland International Film Festival
P.O. Box 9544, Wellington, New Zealand
(4) 385 0162. FAX: (4) 801 7304

Cambridge Film Festival
Cambridge Arts Cinema, 8 Market Passage, Cambridge CB2 2PF, England. (1223) 352 001. FAX: (1223) 462 555

Durban International Film Festival
U. of Natal, King George V Ave., Durban 4001, South Africa.
(31) 811 3978. FAX: (31) 261 7107

International Film Festival of Gijon
Paseo de Begona 24, Entreselvo, 33205 Gijon, Spain
(85) 343 735. FAX: (85) 354 152

Jerusalem Film Festival
P.O. Box 8561, Jerusalem, Israel
(2) 724 131. FAX: (2) 733 076

Karlovy Vary Film Festival
Ministry of Culture, Valdace, Valdstejnsska 12, 11811 Prague 1, Czech Republic. (2) 513 2473. FAX: (2) 530 542

Short & Documentary Film Festival
Farhang Cinema, Dr. Shariati Ave., Gholbak, Tehran 19139, Iran. 265 086. FAX: 678 155

Taormina International Film Festival
Via Pirandello 31, 98039 Taormina, Italy
(942) 211 42. FAX: (942) 233 48

Hometown Video Festival
Buske Group, 30001 J Street, Sacramento, CA 95816
(916) 441-6277. FAX: (916) 441-7670

Wellington Film Festival
P.O. Box 9544, Te Aro, Wellington, New Zealand
(4) 385 0162. FAX: (4) 801 7304

Wine Country Film Festival
12000 Henro Rd., P.O. Box 303, Glen Ellen, CA 95442
(707) 996-2536. FAX: (707) 996-6964

AUGUST

Montreal World Film Festival
Serge Losique, 1432 de Bleury St., Montreal, Quebec, Canada H3A 2J1. (514) 848-3883. FAX: (514) 848-3886

Odense International Film Festival
Vindegade 18, DK-5000 Odense C, Denmark
(45) 6613 1372. FAX: (45) 6591 4318

Giffoni International Film Festival
Piazza Umberto 1, 84095 Giffoni Valle Piana (Salerno), Italy
(89) 868 544. FAX: (89) 866 111

Locarno International Film Festival
Via della Posta 6, Cassella Postale, 6600 Locarno, Switzerland
(93) 310 232. FAX: (93) 317 465

Gramado Cinema Festival
Avenida des Hortensias 2029, Cap. 9567, 1000 Gramado, R.G. Sul, Brazil. (54) 286 2335. FAX: (54) 286 2397

Drambuie Edinburgh Film Festival
88 Lothian Road, Edinburgh EH3 9BZ, Scotland
(131) 228 4051. FAX: (131) 228 5501

Espoo Cine Film Festival
P.O. Box 95, 02101 Espoo, Finland
(0) 466 599. FAX: (0) 466 458

International Animation Festival in Japan-Hiroshima
4-17 Kalo-machi, Naka-ku, Hirshima 730, Japan
(82) 245 0245. FAX: (82) 245 1246

Norwegian International Film Festival
P.O. Box 145, 5501 Haugesund, Norway
(52) 734 430. FAX: (52) 734 420

Brisbane International Film Festival
Level 3, Hoyts Regent Bldg., 167 Queen St. Mall, Brisbane, Queensland 4000, Australia
(7) 3 220 0333. FAX: (7) 3 220 0400.

Alexandria Film Festival
9 Oraby Street, Cairo, Eqypt
578 0042. FAX: 768 727

Weekly Mail/Guardian Film Festival
P.O. Box 2601245, Excom 2023, South Africa
(11) 331 1712. FAX: (11) 331 3339

SEPTEMBER

Toronto International Film Festival
2 Carlton, Toronto, Ontario M5B 1J3, Canada
(416) 967-7371. FAX: (416) 967-9477

Venice Film Festival (Biennale)
Mostra Internazionale d'Arte Cinematografica, La Biennale, San Marco, Ca'Giustinian, 30124 Venice, Italy
(41) 521 8860. FAX: (41) 520 0569. Telex: 410685 BLE-VE-1

San Sebastian International Film Festival
Plaza de Okendo s/n, Donostioa-San Sebastian 20080, Spain
(43) 481 212. FAX: (43) 481 212

Festival International de Cinema Figueira da Foz
Partado dos Correios 50407, 1709 Lisbon Codex, Portugal
(1) 346 9556. FAX: (1) 342 0890

Banco Nacional International Film Festival
Rua Voluntarios de Patria 97, Botafogo, Rio de Janeiro 22270, Brazil. (21) 286 8505. FAX: (21) 286 4029

Telluride Film Festival
Box B-1156, 53 South Main St., Suite 212, Hanover, NH 03755. (603) 643-1255. FAX: (603) 643-5938

Deauville Festival of American Films
c/o Promo, 36 rue Perriet, 92200 Neuilly-sur-Seine, France
(1) 46 40 55 00. FAX: (1) 46 40 55 39

Santa Fe de Bogota Festival
Calle 26 No. 4-92, Apartedo Aereo 23398, Santa Fe de Bogota, Colombia. (1) 282 5196. FAX: (1) 342 2872

International Children's Film Festival
Deutsches Filmmuseum, Schaumainkai 41, 60596 Frankfurt-am-Main, Germany. (69) 2123 3369. FAX: (69) 2123 7881

Boston Film Festival
333 Victory Rd., Quincy, MA 02171
(617) 471-1778. FAX: (617) 479-0778

Prix Italia
c/o RAI, Viale Mazzini 14, 00195 Rome, Italy
(6) 3751 4996. FAX: (6) 3613 3401

Copenhagen Film Festival
Bulowsvej 50A, DK-1870 Frederiksberg C, Copenhagen, Denmark. (45) 3537 2507. FAX: (45) 3135 5758

Independent Feature Film Market
104 West 29th St., New York, NY 10011
(212) 465-8200. FAX: (212) 465-8525

International Film Forum "Arsenals"
Marstalulela 14, P.O. Box 626, LV-1047 Riga, Latvia
(2) 221 620. FAX: (2) 882 0445

Haifa International Film Festival
142 Hanassi Ave., Haifa 34633, Israel
(4) 386 246. FAX: (4) 384 327

Netherlands Film Festival
Hoogt 4, 3512 GW Utrecht, Netherlands
(30) 2 322 684. FAX: (30) 2 313 200

Magdeburg International Film Festival
Coquistrasse 18A, D-39104 Magdeburg, Germany
(391) 401 0875. FAX: (391) 48668

America Film Festival
Museumstrasse 31, A-6020 Innsbruck, Austria
(512) 580 723. FAX: (512) 581 762

British Short Film Festival
Room 313, BBC Threshold House, 65-69 Shepherds Bush
Green, London W12 7RJ, England
(181) 743 8000. FAX: (181) 740 8540

Helsinki Film Festival – Love and Anarchy
Unioninkatu 10 A 27, SF-00130 Helsinki, Finland
(0) 629 528. FAX: (0) 631 450

Europacinema Festival
Via Giulia 66, 00186 Rome, Italy
(6) 686 7581. FAX: (6) 688 05417

Atlantic Film Festival
1541 Barrington St., Suite 326, Halifax, Nova Scotia, Canada
(902) 422-3456. FAX: (902) 422-4006

Aspen Filmfest
P.O. Box 8910, Aspen, Colorado
(303) 925-6882. FAX: (303) 925-1967

Ottawa International Animation Festival
2 Daly Ave., Ottaa, Ontario K1N 6E2, Canada
(613) 232-6727. FAX: (613) 232-6315

Hamburg Film Festival
Friedensallee 7, 22765 Hamburg, Germany
(40) 3982 6210. FAX: (40) 3982 6211

Feminale – International Women's Film Festival
Luxemburgerstrasse 72, D-50674 Cologne, Germany
(221) 416 066. FAX: (221) 417 568

Festival International du Film Francophone
175 rue des Brasseurs, 5000 Namur, Belgium
(81) 241 236. FAX: (81) 241 164

Cairo International Children's Film Festival
17 Kasr El Nil St., Cairo, Eqypt
3923 562. FAX: 3938 979

Tokyo International Film Festival
4th Floor, Landic Ginza Bldg. II, 1-6-5 Ginza, Chuo-Ku,
Tokyo 104, Japan. (3) 3563 6305. FAX: (3) 3563 6310

Vancouver International Film Festival
Ste. 410-1008 Homer St., Vancouver B.C. V6B 2X1, Canada
(604) 685 0260. FAX: (604) 688 8221

OCTOBER

ShowEast
NATO ShowEast, 244 W. 49th Street, Suite 200, New York,
NY 10019. (212) 246-6460. FAX: (212) 265-6428

New York Film Festival
Film Society of Lincoln Center, 70 Lincoln Center Plaza, New
York, NY 10023. (212) 875-5610. FAX: (212) 875-5636

MIPCOM
MIDEM Organisation, 179 avenue Victor Hugo, 75016 Paris,
France. (3301) 44 34 44 44. FAX: (3301) 44 34 44 00

MIFED
Mrs. Elena Lloyd, E.A. Fiera Internazionale di Milano, Largo
Dommodossola 1, 20145 Milano, Italy.
(39-2) 48012 912 x 2920. FAX: (39-2) 49977 020

Shots In The Dark
Broadway, 14 Broad Street, Nottingham, NG1 3 AL, England
(115) 952 6600. FAX: (115) 952 6622

Cork Film Festival
Festival Office, Hatfield House, Tobin St., Cork, Ireland
(21) 271 711. FAX: (21) 275 945

Israel Film Festival
IsraFest Foundation, 6404 Wilshire Blvd., Suite 1151, Los
Angeles CA 90048. (213) 966-4166. FAX: (213) 658-6346

Mill Valley Film Festival
38 Miller Ave., Mill Valley CA 94941
(415) 383-5256. FAX: (415) 383-8606

Warsaw Film Festival
P.O. Box 816, 00-950 Warsaw 1, Poland
Tel/FAX: (2) 635 7591

Flanders International Film Festival
Kortrijksesteenweg 1104, B-9051 Ghent, Belgium
(9) 221 8946. FAX: (9) 221 9074

Sitges Fantasy Film Festival
Calle Rossello 257, 3E, 08008 Barcelona, Spain
(3) 415 3938. FAX: (3) 237 6521

Pordenone Silent Film Festival
c/o La Cineteca del Friuli, Via Osoppo 26, 33013 (UD) Italy
(432) 980 458. FAX: (432) 970 542

Nyon – Visions du Reel
Case Postale 2320, CH-1260, Nyon Switzerland
(22) 3 616 060. FAX: (22) 3 617 071

Independent Film Days
Filmburo Augsburg, Schroeckstrasse 6, 86152 Augsburg,
Germany. (821) 153 079. FAX: (821) 349 5218

Margaret Mead Film Festival
American Museum of Natural History, 79th St. & Central Park
West, New York, NY 10024
(212) 769-5305. FAX: (212) 769-5329

Denver International Film Festival
999 18th Street, Denver, CO 80202
(303) 298-8223. FAX: (303) 298-0209

Leeds International Film Festival
19 Wellington Street, Leeds LS1 4DG, England
(113) 247 8389. FAX: (113) 247 8397

Valencia Film Festival
Plaza del Arzobispo, 2 Bajo, 46003 Valencia, Spain
(96) 392 1506. FAX: (96) 391 5156

Birmingham International Film and Television Festival
c/o Central Independent TV, Central House, Broad Street,
Birmingham B1 2JP, England.
(121) 634 4213. FAX: (121) 634 4392

Viennale (Vienna International Film Festival)
Stiftgasse 6, A-1070 Vienna, Austria
(1) 526 5947. FAX: (1) 934 172

International Filmfestival Mannheim – Heidelberg
Collini Center, Galerie, D-68161 Mannheim, Germany
(621) 102 943. FAX: (621) 291 564

Sportel
6040 Boulevard East, Ste. 27C, West New York, NJ 07093.
(201) 869-4022. FAX: (201) 869-4335

Geneva Film Festival
Case Postale 561, CH-1211 Geneva 11, Switzerland
(22) 321 5466. FAX: (22) 321 9862

Hamptons International Film Festival
3 Newtown Mews, East Hampton, NY 11937
(516) 324-4600

Uppsala International Short Film Festival
Box 1746, S-75147, Uppsala, Sweden
(18) 120 025. FAX: (18) 121 350

Norwich Festival of Women Filmmakers
Cinema City, St. Andrews St., Norwich NR2 4AD, England
(16 3) 622 047

Chicago International Film Festival
415 N. Dearborn, Chicago, IL 60610
(312) 644-3400. FAX: (312) 644-0784

Los Angeles International Film Festival
AFI Festivals, 2021 N. Western Ave., Los Angeles, CA 90027
(213) 856-7707. FAX: (213) 462-4049

Montpellier Festival of Mediterranean Cinema
6 rue Vieille-Aguillerie, 34000 Montpellier, France
67 66 36 36. FAX: 67 66 36 37

Sao Paulo International Film Festival
Al. Lorena 937, CJ 303, 01424-001 Sao Paulo, Brazil
(11) 883 5137. Fax: (11) 853 7936

Valladolid International Film Festival
P.O. Box 646, 47080 Valladoli, Spain
(83) 305 700. FAX: (83) 309 835

International Hofer Filmtage
c/o Heinz Badewitz, Lothstrasse 28, 80335 Munich, Germany
(89) 129 7422. FAX: (89) 123 6868

San Juan Cinemafest
P.O. Box 4543, San Juan, Puerto Rico 00902
(809) 721-6125. FAX: (809) 723-6412

Yamagata International Documentary Film Festival
Kitagawa Building, 4th floor, 6-42 Kagurazaka Shinjuku-ku,
Tokyo 162, Japan. (3) 3266 9704. FAX: (3) 3266 9700

NOVEMBER

London Film Festival
London Film Festival, South Bank, London SE1 8XT, England
(717) 815 1322. FAX: (171) 633 0786

Annual SPAA Conference
Southern Cross Hotel, 131 Exhibition St., Melbourne 3001,
Australia. (2) 262 2277. FAX: (2) 262 2323

Film Art Festival
Cankarjec Dom, Presernova 10, 61000 Ljubljana, Slovenia
(61) 125 8121. FAX: (61) 212 492

Fort Lauderdale International Film Festival
2633 East Sunrise Blvd., Fort Lauderdale, FL 33304-3205
Heartland Film Festival
613 N. East Street, Indianapolis, IN 46202
(317) 464-9405. FAX: (317) 635-4201
Nordic Film Days Lubeck
D-23539 Lubeck, Germany
(451) 122 4105. FAX: (451) 122 7197
Northwest Film & Video Festival
Northwest Film Center, 1219 S.W. Park Ave., Portland, OR
97205. (503) 221-1156. FAX: (503) 226-4842
Amiens International Film Festival
36 rue de Noyon, 8000 Amiens, France
22 91 01 44. FAX: 22 92 53 04
British Film Festival
8 Passage Digard, 50100 Cherbourg, France
33 93 38 94. FAX: 33 01 20 78
Hawaii International Film Festival
700 Bishop St., Suite 400, Honolulu, HI 96813
(808) 528-3456. FAX: (808) 528-1410
Children's Film Festival
Filmburo Augsberg, Schroekstr. 6, 86152 Augsberg, Germany
(821) 153 079. FAX: (821) 349 5218
Duisberg Film Week
Am Konig-Heinrich-Platz, D-47049, Guisberg, Germany
(203) 283 4187. FAX: (203) 283 4130
Cinequest (The San Jose Film Festival)
P.O. Box 720040, San Jose, CA 95172
(408) 995-6305. FAX: (408) 277-3862
Sarasota French Film Festival
5555 North Tamiami Trail, Sarasota, FL 34243
(813) 351-9010. FAX: (813) 351-5796
Worldfest – Charleston
P.O. Box 838, Charleston, SC 29401
(713) 965-9955. FAX: (713) 965-9960
New York Exposition of Short Film & Video
New York Expo, 532 La Guardia Place, Box 330, New York,
NY. (212) 505-7742
Puerto Rico International Film Festival
70 Mayaguez St., Ste. B-1 Hato Rey, Puerto Rico 00918
(809) 764-7044. FAX: (809) 763-4997
International Thessaloniki Film Festival
36 Sina Street, GR 10672 Athens, Greece
(1) 361 0418. FAX: (1) 362 1023
Stockholm International Film Festival
P.O. Box 7673, 10395 Stockholm, Sweden
(8) 200 950
Welsh International Film Festival
Unit 8C, Cefn Llan, Aberystwyth, Dyfed SY23 3AH, Wales
(1970) 617 995. FAX: (1970) 617 942
Festival Sinatron Indonesia
Sekretariat Pantap, Kedoya Center, Jl. Perjuangan-Block II
No. 1, Kebon Jeruk, Jakarta 11063, Indonesia
(21) 533 0467. FAX: (21) 533 0467
Junior Dublin Film Festival
Irish Film Centre, 6 Eustace St., Dublin 2, Ireland
(1) 677 7095. FAX: (1) 677 8755
Oulu International Children's Film Festival
Torikatu 8, 90100 Oulu, Finland
(81) 314 1735. FAX: (81) 314 1730

Tyneside European Film Festival
Tyneside Cinema, 10 Pilgrim St., Newcastle-upon-Tyne NE1
6QG, England. (191) 232 8289. FAX: (191) 221 0535
Festival Internazionale Cinema Giovani
Via Monte di Pieta 1, 10120 Torino, Italy
(11) 562 3309. FAX: (11) 562 9796
Raindance Film Showcase & Market
81 Berwick St., London W1V 3PF, England
(171) 437 3991. FAX: (171) 439 2243
Holland Animation Film Festival
Hoogt 4, 3512 GW Utrecht, The Netherlands
(30) 312 216. FAX: (30) 312 940
International Animated Film Festival
Rua 62, No. 251 4501 Espinho Codex, Portugal
(2) 721 611. FAX: (2) 726 015
Festival dei Popoli
Via Castellani 8, 50122 Firenze, Italy
(55) 294 353. FAX: (55) 213 698
Festival International
du Film Juif et Israelien de Montpellier
500 Boulevard d'Antigone, 34000 Montpellier, France
67 15 08 72. FAX: 67 15 08 72
Cairo International Film Festival
17 Kasr El Nir Street, Cairo, Egypt
(3) 392 3962. FAX: (2) 392 3562
The Americas Film Festival
19th & Constitution Ave., NW, Washington DC 20006
(202) 458-6379. FAX: (202) 458-3122
Festival des 3 Continents
19 Passage Pmmeraye, BP-3306, 44033 Nantes Cedex 01,
France. 40 69 74 14. FAX: 40 73 55 22
Taipei Golden Horse Film Festival
Room 7F, No. 45 Chilin Rd., Taipei 104, Taiwan
(2) 567 5861. FAX: (2) 531 8966

DECEMBER

MIP Asia Screenings & Conferences
Reed Midem Organisation, 179 Victor Hugo, 75116 Paris,
France. (1) 44 34 44 44. FAX: (1) 44 34 44 00
Rencontres du Cinema Italien D'Annecy
Banlieu Scene Nationale, 1 rue Jean Jaures-BP 294, 74007
Annecy Cedex, France. 50 33 44 00. FAX: 50 51 82 09
Noir In Festival
Via dei Coronari 44, 00186 Rome, Italy
(6) 683 3844. FAX: (6) 686 7902
International Documentary Filmfestival
Amsterdam (IFDA)
Kleine Gartmenplantsoen 10, 1017 RR Amsterdam, The
Netherlands. (20) 627 3329. FAX: (20) 638 5388
Festival of International Cinema Students
FFICS Secretariat, c/o Tokyo Agency Inc., 4-8-18 Akasaka,
Minato-ku, Tokyo 107, Japan
(3) 3475 3855. FAX: (3) 5411 0382
Essen International Festival of Films
for Children
Baumstrasse 24, D-45128 Essen, Germany
(201) 794 951. FAX: (201) 794 952

From the publisher of the *International Motion Picture Almanac* and the *International Television & Video Almanac.*

FIRST CENTURY OF FILM.

Who Was Who in the American Motion Picture Industry, 1894-1994

edited and with an introduction by Martin S. Quigley

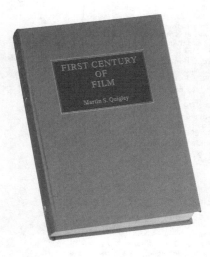

"A BEAUTIFUL PIECE OF BOOK-MAKING... AN ESSENTIAL REFERENCE WORK FOR ANY LIBRARY."

Nicholas B. Scheetz, Manuscripts Librarian, Georgetown University, Washington, DC

- From the world premiere of the Kinetoscope on April 14, 1894 to 1994.
- Over 1300 biographies representing Who Was Who in the American film industry.
- Over 140 photos of the most influential women and men in the motion picture business, from Abbott and Costello to Adolph Zukor.
- A concise chronological review of the century.

ISBN 0-900610-54-9, Hardcover, 7" x 10", 348 pp.

FIRST CENTURY OF FILM $49.50 + 6.00 S&H = $55.50

TO ORDER CALL TOLL-FREE 1-800-231-8239

QUIGLEY PUBLISHING COMPANY
159 West 53rd Street • New York, NY 10019
(212) 247-3100 • Fax (212) 489-0871

WHO'S WHO

IN THE ENTERTAINMENT WORLD

A

AARON, PAUL
Director, Producer, Writer. *B'way*: Salvation, Paris Is Out, '70 Girls '70, Love Me Love My Children.
PICTURES: A Different Story, A Force of One, Deadly Force, Maxie.
TELEVISION: *Movies*: The Miracle Worker, Thin Ice, Maid in America, When She Says No, Save the Dog!, In Love and War, Laurel Avenue (creator, writer, exec. prod.), Under One Roof (creator, writer), Grand Avenue (exec. prod.).

AARON, ROY H.
Arbitrator, Mediator, Entertainment Industry Consultant. b. Los Angeles, CA, April 8, 1929. e. UC Berkeley, BA; USC, LLB. Attorney in L.A. law firm of Pacht, Ross, Warne, Bernhard & Sears (1957-78). Joined Plitt Companies in 1978 as sr. v.p. & gen. counsel. In 1980 was named pres. & chief operating officer of Plitt Theatres, Inc. and related Plitt companies. 1985-93, pres. & CEO of Showscan Corp. 1993, business consultant, pres. of Plitt Entertainment Group Inc., chairman of Pacific Leisure Entertainment Group, L.L.C.

ABARBANEL, SAM X.
Producer, Writer, Publicist. b. Jersey City, NJ, March 27, 1914. e. Cornell U., U. of Illinois, B.S. 1935. Newspaperman in Chicago before joining NY exploitation dept. of Republic, then to studio as asst. publicity director. WWII in Europe with 103rd Div. After war became independent publicist and producer. Formed own co. in Spain, 1966. A founder of the Publicists Guild in Hollywood.
PICTURES: Argyle Secrets (co-prod.), Prehistoric Women (co-s.p., co-prod.), Golden Mistress (exec. prod.), Gunfighters of Casa Grande (assoc. prod.), Son of Gunfighter (assoc. prod.), Narco Men (prod.), Last Day of War (prod., co-s.p.), Summertime Killers (co-s.p).

ABEND, SHELDON
Executive. b. New York, NY, June 13, 1929. Maritime Labor-Rel. Negotiator, 1954-56; chmn., Maritime Union, 1954-56; head, exec. dir. Authors' Research Co. (est. 1957) representing estates of deceased authors. Independent literary negotiator, CC films, A.A.P., RKO General Inc., David O. Selznick, 7 Arts, Warner Bros., 1959-65; pres. American Play Co. Inc., Century Play Co. Inc., 1961-present. Est. Million Dollar Movie Play Library, 1962; pres. Amer. Literary Consultants est. 1965; exec. v.p. Chantec Enterprises Inc. 1969-72. Marketing literary consultant for Damon Runyon Estate. Copyright analyst and literary rights negotiator, United Artists Corp. Founder and chmn., Guild for Author's Heirs, 1970-72. Literary negotiator and prod. consultant for Robert Fryer, 1972. Founder, Copyright Royalty Co. for Authors' Heirs, 1974. Copyright consultant, Films, Inc. 1975; literary agent for Bway. play, Chicago, 1975. Owner of 53 classic RKO motion pictures for the non-theatrical markets, distributed by Films, Inc. Revived publishing of Damon Runyon stories in quality paperback. Published Cornell Woolrich mystery stories-all prod. by Alfred Hitchcock for TV & motion pictures, 1976. 1978, assoc. prod. of film, Why Would I Lie?; Originator of Million Dollar Movie Book Theatre and Million Dollar Movie Sound Track Co., 1980; assoc. prod. of B'way revival, Shanghai Gesture, 1981. Publ. 5 Cornell Woolrich books owned by S. Abend, 1982-83; Co-authored book, The Guardians; 1985, Romance of the Forties by Damon Runyon, 1986; 1985, founder and pres. American Concerts, Inc. and American Theatre Collections, Inc. Published Into the Night by Cornell Woolrich. Packaged m.p. Bloodhounds of Broadway 1988; co-author s.p. Ultimate Demand; 1990, stage adapt. of Bloodhounds of Broadway, Madam La Gimp. Exec. prod. adaptation of Cornell Woolrich stories for TV and movies. In 1990, won landmark copyright case before U.S. Supreme Court protecting Woolrich estate, also affecting other deceased authors, songwriters and their copywright renewals of their work. 1992, acquired Damon Runyon copywrights. 1993 Guys & Dolls handbook published by Viking.

ABRAHAM, F. MURRAY
Actor. b. Pittsburgh, PA, Oct. 24, 1939. r.n. Fahrid Murray Abraham. Attended U. of Texas, 1959-61; trained for stage at Herbert Berghof Studios with Uta Hagen. First NY acting job was as Macy's Santa Claus. Stage debut in Los Angeles in The Wonderful Ice Cream Suit, 1965. New York debut in The Fantasticks, 1966. Full professor of theatre at CUNY Brooklyn College. Honorary Doctorate, Ryder College.
THEATER: Antigone (NYSF, 1982), Uncle Vanya (Obie, LaMamma, etc.), The Golem (NYSF), Madwoman of Chaillot, Othello, Cyrano, A Life in the Theatre, Sexual Perversity in Chicago, Duck Variations, The David Show, Adaptation/Next, Don't Drink the Water, And Miss Reardon Drinks a Little, Where Has Tommy Flowers Gone?, A Christmas Carol, The Seagull, Landscape of the Body, 6 Rms Riv Vu, Survival of St. Joan, Scuba Duba, Teibele & Her Demon, The Ritz, Legend, Bad Habits, Frankie & Johnnie in the Claire De Lune, Twelfth Night, Macbeth, A Midsummer's Night Dream, Waiting for Godot, King Lear, Angels in America: Millenium Aproaches/Perestroika, Little Murders, A Month in the Country; also 5 Children's musicals, Theatreworks.
PICTURES: They Might Be Giants (debut, 1971), Serpico, The Prisoner of 2nd Avenue, The Sunshine Boys, All the President's Men, The Ritz, Madman, The Big Fix, Scarface, Amadeus (Academy Award, 1984), The Name of the Rose, Slipstream, The Favorite, Russicum (The Third Solution), The Betrothed, An Innocent Man, Beyond the Stars, Eye of the Widow, The Bonfire of the Vanities, Cadence, Mobsters, National Lampoon's Loaded Weapon 1, By the Sword, Last Action Hero, Sweet Killing, The Final Card, Surviving the Game, Nostradamus, Jamila, Quiet Flows the Dawn, Money, Dillinger and Capone, Mighty Aphrodite.
TELEVISION: *Series*: Love of Life, How to Survive a Marriage. *Movies*: Sex and the Married Woman, A Season of Giants, Journey to the Center of the Earth. *Guest*: Kojak, All in the Family. *Mini-Series*: Marco Polo, Dream West. *Special*: Largo Desolato.

ABRAHAMS, JIM
Producer, Writer, Director. b. Milwaukee, WI, May 10, 1944. e. U. of Wisconsin. Former private investigator. 1971, with friends David and Jerry Zucker, opened the Kentucky Fried Theatre in Madison, WI, a multimedia show specializing in live improvisational skits mixed with videotaped and film routines and sketches, with the threesome writing and appearing in most. Opened new theatre in Los Angeles in 1972 and developed large following. Co-wrote, co-dir., and co-exec. produced TV series Police Squad!
PICTURES: The Kentucky Fried Movie (co-s.p. with Zuckers), Airplaine! (co-dir., co-exec. prod., co-s.p. with Zuckers), Top Secret! (co-dir., co-s.p., with Zuckers), Ruthless People (co-dir. with Zuckers), Big Business (dir.), The Naked Gun (exec. prod., co-s.p.), Cry-Baby (co-exec. prod.), Welcome Home Roxy Carmichael (co-exec. prod.), The Naked Gun 2-1/2 (co-exec. prod.), Hot Shots! (dir., co-s.p.), Hot Shots Part Deux!. (dir., co-s.p.), Naked Gun 33 1/3: The Final Insult (co-exec. prod.).

ABRAHAMS, MORT
Producer. b. New York, NY. Dir. programming, prod., NTA, 1958-60; exec. prod. Cooga Mooga Prod. Inc., 1960-61. Producer: Target, The Corruptors 1961, Route 66, 1962-63; writer TV shows, 1963-64; prod., Kraft Suspense Theatre, 1965; prod., Man from U.N.C.L.E., 1965-66; exec. v.p., APJAC Prod. 1966. 1969, v.p. in chg. of prod., Rastar Prods.: 1971-74 exec. prod. American Film Theatre & v.p. Ely Landau Organization in charge of West Coast prod. Member of Faculty and producer-in-residence, Center for Advanced Film and TV Studies of A.F.I. Vice-pres. Alph Productions, 1993-present.
PICTURES: *Assoc. Prod.*: Doctor Doolitte, Planet of the Apes, Goodbye Mr. Chips. *Exec. Prod.*: Luther, Homecoming, The Man in the Glass Booth, The Greek Tycoon, Hopscotch, The Chosen

(exec. in chg. prod.), Beatlemania (exec. in chg. prod.), The Deadly Game, Arch of Triumph, The Holcroft Covenant, Seven Hours to Judgment (prod.).

ACKERMAN, BETTYE
Actress. b. Cottageville, SC, Feb. 28, 1928. e. Columbia U., 1948-52. Taught dancing 1950-54.
THEATER: No Count Boy, 1954; Tartuffe, Sophocles' Antigone and Oedipus at Colonus, The Merchant of Venice.
PICTURES: Face of Fire, Rascal, Ted & Venus.
TELEVISION: Series: Ben Casey. Guest: Alcoa Premiere, Alfred Hitchcock Presents, Perry Mason, Breaking Point, Hope-Chrysler Theatre, Bonanza, FBI Story, Mannix, Ironside, Medical Center, Columbo, Sixth Sense, Heat of Anger, Return to Peyton Place, The Rookies, Barnaby Jones, Police Story, Gunsmoke, Harry O, Streets of San Francisco, S.W.A.T., Petrocelli, Wonder Woman, Police Woman, Chips, 240-Robert, The Waltons, Dynasty, Falcon Crest, Me and Mom, Trapper John M.D. Movies: Companions in Nightmare, A Day for Thanks on Walton's Mountain, Confessions of a Married Man.

ACKLAND, JOSS
Actor. b. London, England, Feb. 29, 1928. e. Central Sch. of Speech Training & Dramatic Art. Spent time in Central Africa as a tea planter. Over 400 TV appearances. Autobiography: I Must Be in There Somewhere.
THEATER: The Old Vic (3 yrs.), Mermaid Theatre (artistic dir., 3 yrs.); Hotel in Amsterdam, Jorrocks Come as You Are, The Collaborators, A Streetcar Named Desire, The Madras House, Captain Brassbound's Conversion, Never the Sinner, Henry IV Parts I & II, Peter Pan (dramatic & musical versions), A Little Night Music, Evita, The Visit, etc.
PICTURES: Seven Days to Noon, Crescendo, Trecolonne in Cronaca, The House That Dripped Blood, The Happiness Cage, Villain, England Made Me, The Black Windmill, S.P.Y.S, The Little Prince, Royal Flash, Operation Daybreak, Who Is Killing the Great Chefs of Europe, Saint Jack, The Apple, Rough Cut, Lady Jane, A Zed and Two Noughts, The Sicilian, White Mischief, To Kill a Priest, It Couldn't Happen Here, Lethal Weapon 2, The Hunt for Red October, Object of Beauty, Bill and Ted's Bogus Journey, The Palermo Connection, The Mighty Ducks, Nowhere to Run, Mother's Boys, The Princess and the Goblin (voice), Miracle on 34th Street, Giorgino, Mad Dogs and Englishmen, A Kid in the Court of King Arthur, Occhio Pinocchio, Daisies in December, To the Ends of Time, Mighty Ducks 3, Surviving Picasso, Deadly Voyage, Firelight.
TELEVISION: Movies/Specials: Queenie, Shadowlands, The Man Who Lived at the Ritz, A Quiet Conspiracy, Jekyll and Hyde, First and Last, A Murder of Quality, A Woman Named Jackie, Ashenden, Voices in the Garden, Queenie, The Bible, Citizen X.

ADAM, KEN
Art Director, Prod. Designer. b. Berlin, Germany, Feb. 5, 1921. e. St. Pauls Sch., London; London U., student of architecture. 6 years war service as RAF pilot. Ent. m.p. ind. as draughtsman 1947 (This Was a Woman).
PICTURES: Art Director: The Devil's Pass, Soho Incident, Around the World in 80 Days. Production Designer: Spin a Dark Web, Night of the Demon, Gideon's Day, The Angry Hills, Beyond This Place, The Rough and the Smooth, In the Nick, Let's Get Married, Trials of Oscar Wilde, Dr. No, Sodom and Gomorrah, In the Cool of the Day, Dr. Strangelove, Goldfinger, Woman of Straw, Thunderball, The Ipcress File, Funeral in Berlin, You Only Live Twice, Chitty Chitty Bang Bang, Goodbye Mr. Chips, The Owl and the Pussycat, Diamonds Are Forever, Sleuth, The Last of Sheila, Barry Lyndon (Academy Award, 1975), Madam Kitty, The Seven Percent Solution, The Spy Who Loved Me, Moonraker, Pennies From Heaven (visual consult., assoc. prod.), King David, Agnes of God, Crimes of the Heart, The Deceivers, Dead-Bang, The Freshman, The Doctor, Company Business, Undercover Blues, Addams Family Values, The Madness of King George (Academy Award, 1994), Boys on the Side, Bogus.

ADAMS, BROOKE
Actress. b. New York, NY, Feb. 8, 1949. e. H.S. of Performing Arts; Inst. of American Ballet; Lee Strasberg. Made professional debut at age of six in Finian's Rainbow. Worked steadily in summer stock and TV until age 18. After hiatus resumed acting career.
THEATER: Split, Key Exchange, Linda Hur, The Heidi Chronicles, Lost in Yonkers. Helps run small summer theater upstate NY.
PICTURES: The Lords of Flatbush, Shock Waves (Death Corps), Days of Heaven, Invasion of the Body Snatchers, Cuba, A Man a Woman and a Bank, Tell Me a Riddle, Utilities, The Dead Zone, Almost You, Key Exchange, The Stuff, Man on Fire, The Unborn, Gas Food Lodging, The Baby Sitter's Club.
TELEVISION: Movies: F. Scott Fitzgerald and the Last of the Belles, The Daughters of Joshua Cabe Return, James Dean, Who is the Black Dahlia?, Murder on Flight 502, Nero Wolfe (pilot), Lace, Haunted, Special People, Lace II, The Lion of Africa, Bridesmaids, Sometimes They Come Back, The Last Hit.

Specials: Paul Reiser: Out on a Whim. Series: O.K. Crackerby. Pilot: A Girl's Life. Guest: Kojack, Family, Police Woman, Moonlighting.

ADAMS, CATLIN
Actress, Director. r.n. Barab. b. Los Angeles, CA, October 11, 1950. Began career as actress then studied directing at American Film Institute. Directorial debut: Wanted: The Perfect Guy. Also directed Little Shiny Shoes (short, written and prod. with Melanie Mayron), Stolen: One Husband (TV).
THEATER: Safe House, Scandalous Memories, Dream of a Blacklisted Actor, The Candy Store, Ruby Ruby Sam Sam, Bermuda Avenue Triangle (dir.).
PICTURES: Actress: The Jerk, The Jazz Singer. Director: Sticky Fingers (also co-s.p., co-prod.).
TELEVISION: Specials: How to Survive the 70's and Maybe Even Bump into a Little Happiness, She Loves Me She Loves Me Not. Series: Square Pegs. Movies: Panic in Echo Park, Freaky Friday. Guest: thirtysomething.

ADAMS, DON
Actor. b. New York, NY, April 13, 1926. Won Arthur Godfrey talent contest. Was nightclub impressionist before starting in TV.
PICTURES: The Nude Bomb, Jimmy the Kid, Back to the Beach.
TELEVISION: Series: Perry Como's Kraft Music Hall, The Bill Dana Show, Tennessee Tuxedo (voice), Get Smart (3 Emmy Awards, 2 Clio Awards), The Partners, Don Adams' Screen Test, Three Times Daley, Inspector Gadget (voice), Check It Out!, Get Smart (1995). Movies: The Love Boat, Get Smart Again!

ADAMS, EDIE
Actress, Singer. b. Kingston, PA, April 16, 1927. r.n. Edith Elizabeth Enke. e. Julliard Sch. of Music, Columbia Sch. of Drama.
THEATER: NY: Wonderful Town, Lil Abner (Tony Award), Mame.
PICTURES: The Apartment, Lover Come Back, Call Me Bwana, It's a Mad Mad Mad Mad World, Under the Yum Yum Tree, Love With the Proper Stranger, The Best Man, Made in Paris, The Oscar, The Honey Pot, Up in Smoke, The Happy Hooker Goes Hollywood, Boxoffice.
TELEVISION: Series: Ernie in Kovacsland, The Ernie Kovacs Show (1952-53), The Ernie Kovacs Show (1956), The Chevy Show, Take a Good Look (panelist), Here's Edie, The Edie Adams Show. Movies: Evil Roy Slade, Return of Joe Forrester, Superdome, Fast Friends, Make Me an Offer, A Cry for Love, Ernie Kovacs' Between the Laughter. Guest: Miss U.S. Television, Three to Get Ready, Kovacs on the Corner, Kovacs Unlimited, Jack Paar, Ed Sullivan Show, Perry Como Show, Pat Boone Show, G.E. Theatre, Colgate Comedy House, Dinah Shore Show, Palace, Bob Hope Show. Specials: Cinderella, Tales of the City.

ADAMS, GERALD DRAYSON
Writer. b. Winnipeg, Manitoba, 1904. e. Oxford U. Export exec. 1925-30; literary agt. 1931-45. Member: Screen Writers' Guild.
PICTURES: Magnificent Rogue, Plunderers, Gallant Legion, Big Steal, Dead Reckoning, Battle of Apache Pass, Son of Ali Baba, Flaming Feather, Flame of Araby, Lady from Texas, Steel Town, Untamed, Frontier, Duel at Silver Creek, Princess of the Nile, Three Young Texans, Gambler from Natchez, Wings of the Hawk, Between Midnight and Dawn, Taza Son of Cochise, Gambler from Natchez, Chief Crazy Horse, Golden Horde, Prince Who Was a Thief, Sea Hornet, Three Bad Sisters, Duel on the Mississippi, Black Sleep, War Drums, Gun Brothers, Affair in Reno, Frontier Rangers, Gold Glory & Custer, Kissin' Cousins, Harum Scarum.
TELEVISION: Series: Maverick, G.E. Theatre, Northwest Passage, Broken Arrow, Cheyenne, 77 Sunset Strip.

ADAMS, JULIE
Actress. r.n. Betty May Adams. b. Waterloo, IA, Oct. 17, 1926. e. jr. coll., Little Rock, AK. Coll. dramatics; m.p. debut in Red Hot and Blue (as Betty Adams); Star of Tomorrow, 1953.
PICTURES: Red Hot and Blue (debut, 1949), The Dalton Gang, Crooked River, Hostile Country, West of the Brazos, Colorado Ranger, Fast on the Draw, Marshal of Heldorado. As Julie Adams: Hollywood Story, Finders Keepers, Bend of the River, Bright Victory, Treasure of Lost Canyon, Horizons West, Lawless Breed, Mississippi Gambler, Man From the Alamo, The Stand of Apache River, Wings of the Hawk, The Creature From the Black Lagoon, Francis Joins the WACS, The Looters, One Desire, The Private War of Major Benson, Six Bridges to Cross, Away All Boats, Four Girls in Town, Slim Carter, Slaughter on 10th Avenue, Tarawa Beachhead, Gunfight at Dodge City, Raymie, Underwater City, Tickle Me, Valley of Mystery, The Last Movie, McQ, Psychic Killer, The Wild McCullochs, Killer Inside Me, Goodbye Franklin High, The Fifth Floor, Black Roses.
TELEVISION: Series: Yancy Derringer, General Hospital, The Jimmy Stewart Show, Code Red, Capitol. Movies: The Trackers, Go Ask Alice, Code Red, Backtrack, The Conviction of Kitty Dodds. Guest: Murder She Wrote.

ADAMS, MASON
Actor. b. NY, NY, Feb. 26, 1919. e. U. Wisconsin. B.A., 1940; M.A., 1941. Trained for stage at Neighborhood Playhouse.

Began on radio in 1946, spending nearly two decades in starring role of Pepper Young's Family. B'way debut: Get Away Old Man (1943).
THEATER: Career Angel, Public Relations, Violet, Shadow of My Enemy, Inquest, The Sign in Sidney Brustein's Window, Tall Story, The Trial of the Catonsville Nine, Foxfire, Checking Out, Danger Memory, The Day Room, The Rose Quartet.
PICTURES: God Told Me To, Raggedy Ann and Andy (voice), Northstar, The Final Conflict, F/X, Toy Soldiers, Son-in-Law, Houseguest.
TELEVISION: *Series*: Lou Grant, Morningstar/Eveningstar, Knight and Dave. *Movies*: The Deadliest Season, And Baby Makes Six, The Shining Season, Flamingo Road, The Revenge of the Stepford Wives, The Kid with the Broken Halo, Adam, Passions, Solomon Northrup's Odyssey, The Night They Saved Christmas, Who is Julia?, Under Siege, Rage of Angels: The Story Continues, Perry Mason, Jonathan: The Boy Nobody Wanted, Buying a Landslide, Assault at West Point, Not of This Earth.

ADAMS, MAUD
Actress. r.n. Maud Wikstrum. b. Lulea, Sweden, Feb. 12, 1945. Formerly a model. Film debut as model in The Boys in the Band.
PICTURES: The Boys in the Band, The Christian Licorice Store, U-Turn, Mahoney's Estate, The Man With the Golden Gun, Rollerball, Killer Force, The Merciless Man, Tattoo, Octopussy, Target Eagle, Jane and the Lost City, The Women's Club, A Man of Passion, The Favorite, Soda Cracker.
TELEVISION: *Movies*: Big Bob Johnson and His Fantastic Speed Circus, The Hostage Tower, Playing for Time, Nairobi Affair, The Case of the Wicked Wives. *Series*: Chicago Story, Emerald Point, N.A.S.

ADAMS, TONY
Producer. b. Dublin, Ireland, Feb. 15, 1953. Began career as asst. to dir. John Boorman and was associated with Burt Reynolds prior to joining Blake Edwards as a prod., 1971. Then president, Blake Edwards Entertainment; Pres. & CEO, The Blake Edwards Company, 1988.
PICTURES: *Assoc. Prod.*: Return of the Pink Panther, The Pink Panther Strikes Again. *Exec. Prod.*: Revenge of the Pink Panther. *Prod.*: ``10'', S.O.B., Victor/Victoria, Trail of the Pink Panther, Curse of the Pink Panther, The Man Who Loved Women, Micki & Maude, That's Life, A Fine Mess, Blind Date, Sunset, Skin Deep, Switch, Son of the Pink Panther.
TELEVISION: Julie Andrews (series and specials), Justin Case, Peter Gunn, Julie.

ADDISON, JOHN
Composer. b. West Chobham, Surrey, England, March 16, 1920. e. Wellington and Royal Coll. of Music. Entered m.p. ind. in 1948. Professor, Royal Coll. of Music, 1948-53. Member of bd. of governors of AMPAS 1980-89.
THEATER: The Amazons, Popkiss, The Entertainer, The Chairs, Luther, Midsummer Night's Dream, The Broken Heart, The Workhouse Donkey, Hamlet, Semi-Detached, The Seagull, Saint Joan of the Stockyards, Listen to the Mockingbird, Cranks (revue), Antony & Cleopatra, I Claudius, Twelfth Night, Bloomsbury, Antony and Cleopatra (LA Theatre Centre). *Ballets*: Carte Blanche (at Sadlers Wells and Edinburgh Fest.), Cat's Cradle (Marquis de Cuevas, Paris, Monte Carlo).
PICTURES: Seven Days to Noon, The Man Between, The Maggie, Make Me An Offer, Private's Progress, Reach for the Sky, Lucky Jim, I Was Monty's Double, Carlton Brown of the F. O., The Entertainer, School for Scoundrels, A Taste of Honey, The Loneliness of the Long Distance Runner, Tom Jones (Academy. Award, Grammy Award, 1963), Guns at Batasi, Girl With Green Eyes, The Loved One, Torn Curtain, A Fine Madness, I Was Happy Here, The Honey Pot, Smashing Time, The Charge of the Light Brigade, Start the Revolution Without Me, Country Dance (Brotherly Love), Mr. Forbush and the Penguins, Sleuth, Luther, Dead Cert, Ride a Wild Pony, Seven-Per-Cent Solution, Swashbuckler, Joseph Andrews, A Bridge Too Far (Brit. Acad. Anthony Asquith Award), The Pilot, High Point, Strange Invaders, Grace Quigley, Code Name: Emerald, To Die For.
TELEVISION: Sambo and the Snow Mountains, Detective, Hamlet, The Search for Ulysses, Way of the World, Back of Beyond, Black Beauty, The Bastard, Deadly Price of Paradise, Love's Savage Fury, Like Normal People, The French Atlantic Affair, Mistress of Paradise, Eleanor First Lady of The World, Charles and Diana: A Royal Love Story, Mail Order Bride, Thirteen at Dinner, Dead Man's Folly, Mr. Boogedy, Something in Common, Firefighter, Amazing Stories, Bride of Boogedy, Strange Voices. *Mini-series*: Centennial, Pearl, Ellis Island, Beryl Markham: A Shadow on the Sun, Phantom of the Opera. *Series*: Nero Wolfe, Murder She Wrote (Emmy Award).

ADELMAN, GARY
Executive. b. Los Angeles, CA, March 16, 1944. e. California State U., Long Beach State Coll. 1969, asst. dir. on feature, The Masterpiece; assoc. prod. on The Candy Snatchers. Produced first feature film, The Severed Arm, 1974. Assisted Winston

Hock in development of 3-D process, 1975. 1976-93, pres. & COO of Monarch Prods. Post-prod. consultant for Jerry Gross Organization. 1983, founder and partial owner of New Image Releasing, Inc., new prod. & dist. co. Had post of secty./treas. 1987, named v.p., chg. prod., All-American Group. 1990, assoc. prod. on Nobody's Perfect.

ADELMAN, JOSEPH A.
Executive. b. Winnipeg, Manitoba, Can., Dec. 27, 1933. e. NYU, B.A., 1954; Harvard Law Sch., J.D., 1957, graduated cum laude. Attorney, United Artists Corp., New York, 1958; named west coast counsel, Hollywood, 1964; named exec. asst. to the v.p. in charge of prod. 1968; named v.p., west coast business and legal affairs, 1972; appointed executive v.p., Association of Motion Pictures and Television Producers, 1977; appointed v.p. in chg. of business affairs, Paramount Pictures Corp., 1979; co-founder and exec. v.p. Kidpix, Inc. since 1984; founder and CEO of Kidpix Theaters Corp. since 1985; appointed senior v.p. for business/legal affairs, Color Systems Technology, Inc. 1986; named pres. of CST Entertainment, 1987. Appointed managing dir., Broadway Video Entertainment, 1990. CEO, Intl. Entertainment Enterprises 1991. Admitted to NY, California and U.S. Supreme Court bars; member, Phi Beta Kappa; Alumni Achievement Award, NYU, 1982; American Bar Association; Los Angeles Copyright Society; Academy of Motion Picture Arts and Sciences; bd. of dirs., AMPTP, 1969-1979; National Assn. of Television Programming Executives.; bd. of trustees, Theatre Authority, 1970-79.

ADELSON, GARY
Producer. b. 1954. e. UCLA (B.A.). Son of Merv Adelson. Joined Lorimar Prods. 1970 as prod. asst. on TV movie Helter Skelter. In 1989, formed Adelson/Baumgarten Prods. with Craig Baumgarten.
PICTURES: The Last Starfighter, The Boy Who Could Fly, In The Mood, Tap, Hard to Kill, Hook, Universal Soldier, Nowhere to Run, Blank Check, It Could Happen to You, Jade.
TELEVISION: Helter Skelter (prod. asst.), Sybil (assoc. prod.), Eight Is Enough (prod.), The Blue Knight (prod.). *Exec. prod.*: Too Good To Be True, Our Family Business, Cass Malloy, John Steinbeck's The Winter of Our Discontent, Lace, Detective in the House, Lace II, Studio 5B (series), Glitz.

ADELSON, MERV
Producer. b. Los Angeles, CA, Oct. 23, 1929. e. UCLA. Pres., Markettown Builders Emporium, Las Vegas 1953-63; managing partner Paradise Dev. 1958-; pres. Realty Holdings 1962-; Bd. chmn., Lorimar Inc. 1969-86; chmn. bd. dirs. & CEO, Lorimar Telepictures 1986-.
PICTURES: Twilight's Last Gleaming, The Choirboys, Who Is Killing the Great Chefs of Europe?, Avalanche Express, The Big Red One.
TELEVISION: *Series*: The Waltons, Eight Is Enough, Dallas, Kaz, The Waverly Wonders, Knots Landing. *Movies/Mini-Dir.*: Sybil, A Man Called Intrepid, The Blue Knight, Helter-Skelter.

ADJANI, ISABELLE
Actress. b. Germany, June 27, 1955.
PICTURES: Faustine and the Beautiful Summer, The Slap, The Story of Adele H. (Acad. Award nom.), The Tenant, Barocco, Violette and Francois, The Driver, Nosferatu—The Vampire, The Bronte Sisters, Clara et les Chics Types, Possession, Quartet, Next Year If All Goes Well, One Deadly Summer, Antonieta, Deadly Circuit, Subway, Ishtar, Camille Claudel (also co-prod.; Acad. Award nom.), Toxic Affair, Queen Margot, Diabolique.

ADLER, ALLEN
Executive Producer. b. New York, NY, 1946. e. Princeton U., B.A.; Harvard Business Sch., M.B.A. Started with Standard & Poor's Inter-Capital; then joined Alan Hirschfield at American Diversified Enterprises; next to Columbia Pictures 1973 as corporate officer. 1979, named sr. v.p., Columbia. 1981, teamed with Daniel Melnick in IndieProd Co.
PICTURE: Making Love.

ADLON, PERCY
Director, Writer, Producer. b. Munich, Germany, June 1, 1935. e. Munich Univ. m. Eleonore Adlon, with whom he has worked on several film projects. Created more than forty tv documentaries.
PICTURES: Celeste, The Last Five Days (dir. only), The Swing, Sugarbaby, Bagdad Cafe, Rosalie Goes Shopping, Salmonberries, Younger and Younger.
TELEVISION: The Guardian and His Poet (Adolf Grimme Award).

AGAR, JOHN
Actor. b. Chicago, IL, Jan. 31, 1921. In service WWII.
PICTURES: Fort Apache (debut, 1948), Adventure in Baltimore, I Married a Communist, Sands of Iwo Jima, She Wore a Yellow Ribbon, Breakthrough, Woman on Pier 13, Magic Carpet, Along the Great Divide, Woman of the North Country, Man of Conflict, Bait, Rocket Man, Shield for Murder, Golden Mistress, Revenge of the Creature, Hold Back Tomorrow, Tarantula, Star in the

3

Dust, The Lonesome Trail, The Mole People, Flesh and the Spur, Daughter of Dr. Jekyll, Cavalry Command, The Brain from Planet Arous, Attack of the Puppet People, Ride a Violent Mile, Joe Butterfly, Jet Attack, Frontier Gun, Invisible Invaders, Raymie, Hand of Death, Lisette, Journey to the 7th Planet, Of Love and Desire, The Young and the Brave, Law of the Lawless, Stage to Thunder Rock, Young Fury, Waco, Johnny Reno, Curse of the Swamp Creature, Zontar: The Thing from Venus, Women of the Prehistoric Planet, St. Valentine's Day Massacre, Big Jake, Chisum, King Kong, Perfect Bride, Miracle Mile, Nightbreed, Fear, Invasion of Privacy, Body Bags, Pandora Directive (CD-ROM).

AGOGLIA, JOHN J.
Executive. Worked for 14 years for CBS Entertainment in New York, becoming v.p. business affairs. Joined NBC in 1979 as v.p., program and talent negotiations. 1980, named sr. v.p. business affairs; 1984, exec. v.p. NBC Prods.; 1986, exec. v.p., business affairs NBC-TV Network; 1987, in charge of foreign marketing relating to NBC Productions products. Appointed pres. of NBC Enterprises, 1990. Named pres. of NBC Prods., May 1993.

AGUTTER, JENNY
Actress. b. Taunton, Devonshire, England, Dec. 20, 1952. e. Elmhurst Ballet Sch. Received Variety Club of Great Britain Most Promising Artiste Award, 1971.
THEATER: School for Scandal, Rooted, Arms and the Man, The Ride Across Lake Constance, The Tempest, Spring Awakening, Hedda, Betrayal. Member, Royal Shakespeare Co.-King Lear, Arden of Taversham, The Body. Breaking the Silence, Shrew (Los Angeles), Love's Labour's Lost, Mothers and Daughters.
PICTURES: East of Sudan (debut, 1964), Ballerina (tv in U.S.), Gates of Paradise, Star!, I Start Counting, Walkabout, The Railway Children, Logan's Run, The Eagle Has Landed, Equus (BAFTA Award, 1977), Dominique, China 9 Liberty 37, The Riddle of the Sands, Sweet William, The Survivor, Amy, An American Werewolf in London, Secret Places, Dark Tower, King of the Wind, Dark Man, Child's Play 2, Freddie as F.R.O. 7 (voice), Blue Juice.
TELEVISION: The Great Mr. Dickens, The Wild Duck, The Cherry Orchard, The Snow Goose (Emmy Award, 1972), As Many as Are Here Present, A War of Children, The Man in the Iron Mask, A House in Regent Place, There's Love and Dove, Kiss Me and Die, A Legacy, The Waiting Room, Six Million Dollar Man, School Play, The Mayflower, Voyage of the Pilgrims, Beulah Land, Love's Labour's Lost, This Office Life, Magnum, The Two Ronnies, Silas Marner, The Twilight Zone, Murder She Wrote, No a Penny More Not a Penny Less, Dear John, The Equalizer, The Outsiders, Breaking the Code, Boon, Love Hurts, Heartbeat, The Buccaneers, September.

AIELLO, DANNY
Actor. b. New York, NY, June 20, 1936.
THEATER: Lampost Reunion (Theatre World Award), Wheelbarrow Closers, Gemini (Obie Award), Knockout, The Floating Light Bulb, Hurlyburly (LA Drama Critics Award), The House of Blue Leaves.
PICTURES: Bang the Drum Slowly (debut, 1973), The Godfather Part II, The Front, Fingers, Blood Brothers, Defiance, Hide in Plain Sight, Fort Apache the Bronx, Chu Chu and the Philly Flash, Deathmask, Once Upon a Time in America, Old Enough, The Purple Rose of Cairo, Key Exchange, The Protector, The Stuff, Radio Days, The Pick-Up Artist, Man on Fire, Moonstruck, The January Man, Crack in the Mirror, Do the Right Thing (LA, Chicago & Boston Film Critics Awards; Acad. Award nom.), Russicum (The Third Solution), Harlem Nights, Jacob's Ladder, Once Around, Hudson Hawk, The Closer, 29th Street, Ruby, Mistress, The Cemetery Club, The Pickle, Me and the Kid, The Professional, Ready to Wear (Pret-a-Porter), City Hall, Power of Attorney, He Ain't Heavy, Two Much, 2 Days in the Valley, Mojave Moon.
TELEVISION: Movies: The Last Tenant, Lovey: A Circle of Children Part 2, A Question of Honor, Blood Feud, Lady Blue, Daddy, Alone in the Neon Jungle, The Preppie Murder. Series: Lady Blue. Special: Family of Strangers (Emmy Award), Lieberman in Love.

AIMEE, ANOUK
Actress. r.n. Franccoise Soyra Dreyfus. b. Paris, France, April 27, 1932. Studied dancing at Marseilles Opera, acting at Bauer-Therond dramatic school, Paris. Started in films as teenager billed as Anouk.
PICTURES: La Maison Sous la Mer (debut, 1946), La Fleur de l'age, Les Amants De Verone, The Golden Salamander, Noche de Tormenta, Le Rideau Cramoisi, The Man Who Watched the Trains Go By (Paris Express), Contraband Spain, Forever My Heart, Les Mauvaises Rencontres, Ich Suche Dich, Nina, Stresemann, Pot Bouille, Montparnasse 19, Tous Peuvent Me Tuer, Le Tete Contre Les Murs, The Journey, Les Dragueurs, La Dolce Vita, Le Farceur, Lola, L'Imprevu, Quai Notre-Dame, Il Giudizio Universale, Sodom and Gomorrah, Les Grand Chemins, 8 1/2, Il Terrorista, Il Successo, Liola, Le Voci Bianche,

La Fuga, La Stagione del Nostro Amore, A Man and a Woman (Acad. Award nom.), Lo Sacandalo, Il Morbidonne, Un Soir Un Train, The Model Shop, Justine, The Appointment, Si C'Etait d Refaire, Mon Premier Amour, Salto nel Vuoto (Leap Into the Void), Tragedy of a Ridiculous Man, What Makes David Run?, Le General de l'Armee Morte, Success is the Best Revenge, Viva la Vie, A Man and A Woman: 20 Years Later, Arrivederci e Grazie, La Table Tournante, The House of the Lord, Dr. Bethune, Rabbit Face, Ready to Wear (Pret-a-Porter).

ALBECK, ANDY
Executive. b. U.S.S.R., Sept. 25, 1921. Industry career began in 1939 with Columbia Pictures Intl. Corp. 1947, Central Motion Picture Exchange. 1949, Eagle Lion Classics, Inc. Joined UA in 1951 in intl. dept., functioning in the area of operations. After filling a number of key posts, named asst. treas. in 1970. In 1972 became v.p. of UA and its subsidiary, UA Broadcasting, Inc. 1973, appt. pres. of UA Broadcasting and in 1976 named sr. v.p. operations. Named UA Corp. pres. & chief exec. officer in 1978. Retired, 1981.

ALBERGHETTI, ANNA MARIA
Singer, Actress. b. Pesaro, Italy, May 15, 1936. d. Daniele Alberghetti, cellist. Concert debut in 1948 in Pesaro, then toured Italy, Scandinavia, Spain; Am. debut Carnegie Hall, 1950, sang with NY Philharmonic Society, Phila. Symphony, on television. B'way stage debut: Carnival, 1962 (Tony Award).
PICTURES: The Medium (debut, 1951), Here Comes the Groom, The Stars Are Singing, The Last Command, Duel at Apache Wells, Ten Thousand Bedrooms, Cinderfella.
TELEVISION: Guest: Toast of the Town, Cavalcade of Stars, Arthur Murray Show, Bob Hope, Eddie Fisher, Red Skelton, Dinah Shore, Desilu Playhouse, G.E. Theatre, Chevy Show, Dupont Show, Voice of Firestone, Colgate Hour, Climax, Loretta Young, Ford Jubilee, Perry Como.

ALBERT, EDDIE
Actor. r.n. Eddie Albert Heimberger. b. Rock Island, IL, April 22, 1908. e. U. of Minnesota. Son is actor Edward Albert. Performer on Radio NBC.
THEATER: B'way: Brother Rat, Say Darling, The Music Man, Room Service, The Boys from Syracuse, Seven Year Itch, Our Town, No Hard Feelings, Reuben Reuben, Miss Liberty, You Can't Take It With You.
PICTURES: Brother Rat (debut, 1938), On Your Toes, Four Wives, Brother Rat and a Baby, Angel from Texas, My Love Came Back, Dispatch from Reuter's, Four Mothers, The Wagons Roll at Night, Out of the Fog, Thieves Fall Out, The Great Mr. Nobody, Treat 'em Rough, Eagle Squadron, Ladies' Day, Lady Bodyguard, Bombadier, Strange Voyage, Rendezvous With Annie, Perfect Marriage, Smash-Up, Time Out of Mind, Hit Parade of 1947, Dude Goes West, You Gotta Stay Happy, Fuller Brush Girl, You're in the Navy Now, Meet Me After the Show, Carrie, Actors and Sin, Roman Holiday (Acad. Award nom.), Girl Rush, I'll Cry Tomorrow, Oklahoma!, Attack, Teahouse of the August Moon, The Sun Also Rises, The Joker is Wild, Orders to Kill, Gun Runners, The Roots of Heaven, Beloved Infidel, The Young Doctors, Two Little Bears, Madison Avenue, Who's Got the Action?, The Longest Day, Captain Newman M.D., Miracle of the White Stallions, The Party's Over, Seven Women, The Heartbreak Kid (Acad. Award nom.), McQ, The Take, The Longest Yard, Escape to Witch Mountain, The Devil's Rain, Hustle, Whiffs, Birch Interval, Moving Violations, Yesterday, The Concorde -- Airport 79, Foolin' Around, How to Beat the High Cost of Living, Take This Job and Shove It, Yes Giorgio, Dreamscape, The Act, Stitches, Head Office, The Big Picture, Brenda Starr.
TELEVISION: Series: Leave It To Larry, Nothing But the Best, Saturday Night Revue, Green Acres, Switch!, Falcon Crest, General Hospital. Movies & Specials: The Yeagers, Benjamin Franklin, The Borrowers, Killer Bees, Nutcracker, Anything Goes, Crash, The Word, Evening in Byzantium, Pirates Key, Living in Paradise, Oklahoma Dolls, The Plan, Peter and Paul, Goliath Awaits, Concord, Beyond Witch Mountain, Rooster, Demon Murder Case, Coalfire, In Like Flynn, Dress Gray, Mercy or Murder?, War and Remembrance, Return to Green Acres, The Girl from Mars, The Barefoot Executive. Guest: The Fall Guy, Love Boat, Highway to Heaven, Falcon Crest, Murder She Wrote, thirtysomething, Ray Bradbury Theatre, Twilight Zone, Time Trax, Golden Palace, Dr. Quinn–Medicine Woman.

ALBERT, EDWARD
Actor. b. Los Angeles, CA, Feb. 20, 1951. e. UCLA. Son of actor Eddie Albert and late actress Margo. Was prod. asst. on Patton in Spain. Has appeared with father on radio and TV shows. Is photographer and has exhibited work in L.A.
THEATER: Room Service, Our Town, The Glass Menagerie, Hamlet.
PICTURES: The Fool Killer (debut, 1965), Wild Country, Butterflies Are Free, Forty Carats, Midway, The Domino Principle, Purple Taxi, The Greek Tycoon, When Time Ran Out, The Squeeze, Galaxy of Terror, Butterfly, The House Where Evil Dwells, A Time to Die, Ellie, Getting Even (Hostage: Dallas),

Distortions, Terminal Entry, The Rescue, Mind Games, Fist Fighter, Shoot Fighter, Fight to the Death, Broken Trust, The Ice Runner, Demon Keeper, Guarding Tess.
TELEVISION: *Series*: The Yellow Rose, Falcon Crest. Host: Viva, Different Point of View, On Call. *Guest*: Beauty and the Beast, Houston Knights, Murder She Wrote, Police Story, Hitchhiker, The Love Boat, The Rookies. *Movies*: Killer Bees, Death Cruise, The Millionaire, Silent Victory: The Kitty O'Neil Story, Black Beauty, Blood Feud, The Girl from Mars, Sight Unseen, Body Language. *Mini-Series*: The Last Convertible. *Specials:* Daddy Can't Read, Orson Welles' Great Mysteries (BBC).

ALBRIGHT, LOLA
Actress. b. Akron, OH, July 20, 1925. e. Studied piano 12 years. Switchboard operator and stenographer NBC; stenographer with WHAM and bit player; photographers' model. Screen debut in The Pirate, 1948.
PICTURES: The Pirate (debut, 1947), Easter Parade, Julia Misbehaves, The Girl From Jones Beach, Tulsa, Champion, Bodyhold, Beauty on Parade, The Good Humor Man, When You're Smiling, Sierra Passage, The Killer That Stalked New York, Arctic Flight, The Silver Whip, The Treasure of Ruby Hills, The Magnificent Matador, The Tender Trap, The Monolith Monsters, Pawnee, Oregon Passage, Seven Guns to Mesa, A Cold Wind in August, Kid Galahad, Joy House (The Love Cage), Lord Love a Duck, The Way West, Where Were You When the Lights Went Out?, The Impossible Years, The Money Jungle.
TELEVISION: *Series*: Peter Gunn, Peyton Place. *Guest*: Switch, The Eddie Capra Mysteries, Quincy, Airwolf. *Movies*: Helicopter Spies, How I Spent My Summer Vacation, Delta County USA, Terraces.

ALCAINE, JOSE LUIS
Cinematographer. b. Tangier, Algeria, Dec. 26, 1938. e. Spanish Cinema Sch., Madrid. After graduation joined Madrid's Studio Moros doing commercials.
PICTURES: El Puente, El Sur, Taseo, Rustlers' Rhapsody, Bluebeard Bluebeard, Women on the Verge of a Nervous Breakdown, The Mad Monkey, Tie Me Up Tie Me Down, Ay Carmela, Lovers.

ALDA, ALAN
Actor, Writer, Director r.n. Alphonso D'Abruzzo b. New York, NY, Jan. 28, 1936. e. Fordham U., 1956. Son of actor Robert Alda. Studied at Cleveland Playhouse on Ford Foundation Grant; performed with Second City, then on TV in That Was The Week That Was. For work as director, writer and actor on M*A*S*H won 5 Emmys, 2 Writers Guild Awards, 3 Directors Guild Awards, 6 Golden Globes, 7 People's Choice Awards, Humanitas Award (for Writing).
THEATER: *B'way*: Only in America, The Owl and The Pussycat, Purlie Victorious, Fair Game For Lovers (Theatre World Award), The Apple Tree (Tony nom.), Jake's Women (Tony Award nom.). *London*: Our Town.
PICTURES: Gone Are The Days (debut, 1963), Paper Lion, The Extraordinary Seaman, Jenny, The Moonshine War, The Mephisto Waltz, To Kill a Clown, Same Time Next Year, California Suite, The Seduction of Joe Tynan (also s.p.), The Four Seasons (also dir., s.p.), Sweet Liberty (also dir., s.p.), A New Life (also dir., s.p.), Crimes and Misdemeanors (D.W. Griffith Award, NY Film Critics Award), Betsy's Wedding (also dir., s.p.), Whispers in the Dark, Manhattan Murder Mystery, Canadian Bacon, Flirting With Disaster, Everyone Says I Love You.
TELEVISION: *Series*: That Was the Week That Was, M*A*S*H (11 years), Scientific American Frontiers (PBS, host). *Movies*: The Glass House, Playmates, Isn't It Shocking?, Kill Me If You Can (Emmy nom.), And the Band Played On, Jake's Women, White Mile. *Specials*: Free to Be You and Me, 6 Rms Riv Vu (also dir.), Life's Big Questions (host). *Series creator*: We'll Get By, The Four Seasons. *Guest*: Phil Silvers Show, The Nurses, Route 66, Trials of O'Brien, Coronet Blue, Carol Burnet Show. *Pilots*: Where's Everett, Higher and Higher.

ALDREDGE, THEONI V.
Costume Designer. b. Salonika, Greece, Aug. 22, 1932. m. actor Tom Aldredge. e. American School, Athens; Goodman Theatre School, Chicago, 1949-52.
THEATER: *B'way*: Sweet Bird of Youth, That Championship Season, Sticks and Bones, Two Gentlemen of Verona, A Chorus Line, Annie (Tony Award), Ballroom, Much Ado About Nothing, Barnum (Tony Award), Dream Girls, Woman of the Year, Onward Victoria, La Cage aux Folles (Tony Award), 42nd Street, Merlin, Private Lives, The Corn is Green, The Rink, Blithe Spirit, Chess, Gypsy, Oh Kay!, The Secret Garden, High Rollers.
PICTURES: You're a Big Boy Now, No Way to Treat a Lady, Uptight, Last Summer, I Never Sang for My Father, Promise at Dawn, The Great Gatsby (Acad. Award, 1974), Network, Semi-Tough, The Cheap Detective, The Fury, Eyes of Laura Mars (Sci Fi. Acad. Honor), The Champ, The Rose, Can't Stop the Music, Circle of Two, Loving Couples, A Change of Seasons, Middle Age Crazy, Rich and Famous, Annie, Monsignor, Ghostbusters, Moonstruck, We're No Angels, Stanley & Iris, Other People's Money, Addams Family Values.

ALEANDRO, NORMA
Actress. b. Buenos Aires, Argentina, Dec. 6, 1936. Sister is actress Maria Vaner. As child, performed in parents, in theater troupe. In Argentina performed in every theatrical genre and epoch. Was also director. Has written published short stories (1986) and poems and screenplay for Argentinian film, Los Heloderos. Was in exile in Uruguay (18 months) and Spain 1976-82 because of the military junta in Argentina. Before exile had made 12 films; after return in 1982 starred in theatre and 7 films.
THEATER: U.S.: About Love and Other Stories (one-woman show, toured South America, then at La Mama and later off-B'way at Public Theater 1986); The Senorita of Tacna (written for her by Mario Vargas-Llosa, 1987).
PICTURES: The Official Story (Cannes Film Fest. Award, 1986), Gaby: A True Story (Acad. Award nom.), Cousins, Vital Signs, The Tombs.
TELEVISION: *Movies*: Dark Holiday, One Man's War.

ALEXANDER, JANE
Actress. b. Boston, MA, Oct. 28, 1939. r.n. Jane Quigley. m. director Edwin Sherin. Mother of actor Jace Alexander. e. Sarah Lawrence Coll., U. of Edinburgh. Stage career includes appearances on B'way; at Arena Stage, Washington D.C.; Kennedy Center, D.C.; Music Center, L.A.; and Shakespeare Festival at Stamford, Conn. Appointed chairwoman of the National Endowment for the Arts, 1993.
THEATER: *NY*: The Great White Hope (Tony & Theatre World Awards, 1969), 6 Rms Riv Vu, Find Your Way Home, Hamlet, The Heiress, First Monday in October, Goodbye Fidel, Losing Time, Monday After the Miracle, Old Times, Night of the Iguana, Approaching Zanzibar, Shadowlands, The Visit, The Sisters Rosensweig.
PICTURES: The Great White Hope (debut, 1970), A Gunfight, The New Centurions, All the President's Men, The Betsy, Kramer vs. Kramer, Brubaker, Night Crossing, Testament, City Heat, Square Dance, Sweet Country, Glory.
TELEVISION: *Movies*: Welcome Home Johnny Bristol, Miracle on 34th St., This is the West That Was, Death Be Not Proud, Eleanor and Franklin, Eleanor and Franklin: The White House Years, A Circle of Children, Lovey: A Circle of Children Part II, A Question of Love, Playing for Time (Emmy Award), In the Custody of Strangers, When She Says No, Calamity Jane, Malice in Wonderland, Blood & Orchids, In Love and War, Open Admissions, A Friendship in Vienna, Daughter of the Streets, Stay the Night. *Specials*: Mountain View, A Marriage: Georgia O'Keeffe and Alfred Stieglitz. *Pilot*: New Year.

ALEXANDER, JASON
Actor. r.n. Jay Scott Greenspan. b. Newark, NJ, Sept. 23, 1959. e. Boston Univ.
THEATER: *NY*: Merrily We Roll Along, Forbidden Broadway, The Rink, Personals, Stop the World, Light Up the Sky, Broadway Bound, Jerome Robbins' Broadway (Tony, Drama Desk & Outer Critics' Circle Awards, 1989), Accomplice. *Regional*: Give 'em Hell Harry.
PICTURES: The Burning (debut, 1981), Brighton Beach Memoirs, The Mosquito Coast, Pretty Woman, White Palace, Jacob's Ladder, I Don't Buy Kisses Anymore, Coneheads, The Paper, North, Blankman, For Better or Worse (also dir.), The Last Supper, Dunston Checks In, The Hunchback of Notre Dame (voice).
TELEVISION: *Series*: E/R, Everything's Relative, Seinfeld, Duckman (voice). *Movies*: Senior Trip, Rockabye, Favorite Son, Bye Bye Birdie. *Guest*: Newhart, Dream On. *Special*: Sexual Healing.

ALEXANDER, RALPH
Executive. Began career with Universal Pictures in sales, 1949; various sls. jobs with 20th Century Fox and Lorimar. 1981-82, v.p., theatrical foreign sls., Filmway Pictures; 1982-84, v.p., sls, for Latin America & Southeast Asia, Embassy Pictures Intl. 1984, exec. v.p., multi-media foreign sls. for Robert Meyers Intl. Nov., 1985, joined Dino De Laurentiis Corp. as intl. sls. dir. in chg. all foreign sls. theatrical and ancillary rights except tv. 1986, promoted to v.p., intl. sls., DEG; pres. marketing and sales, Kings Road Intl.; 1989; joined Scotti Bros. Pictures as pres. intl. sales and marketing, 1989.

ALGAR, JAMES
Producer, Writer, Director. b. Modesto, CA, June 11, 1912. e. Stanford U., B.A., M.A. journalism. Entire career since 1934 with Walt Disney Prods. Wrote and co-produced Great Moments with Mr. Lincoln; New York World's Fair; Circarama, America the Beautiful, Circle Vision 1958 Brussels World's Fair, Disneyland, Hall of Presidents, Disney World, Florida. Shares in nine Oscars.
PICTURES: *Animator*: Snow White. *Director*: Fantasia, Bambi, Adventures of Ichabod & Mr. Toad, White Wilderness, Jungle Cat, Ten Who Dared, The Legend of Lobo, The Incredible Journey, The Gnome-Mobile, Rascal. *Documentaries*: True-Life Adventures: Seal Island, The Living Desert, Vanishing Prairie, The African Lion, Secrets of Life.

TELEVISION: *Producer:* Run Light Buck Run, The Not So Lonely Lighthouse Keeper, One Day on Beetle Rock, Wild Heart, Along the Oregon Trail, The Best Doggoned Dog in the World, One Day at Teton Marsh, Solomon the Sea Turtle, Manado the Wolverine, Wild Geese Calling, Two Against the Arctic, Bayou Bay, Secrets of the Pond, Boy Who Talked to Badgers, Big Sky Man.

ALIN, MORRIS
Editor, Writer, Publicist, Lyricist. e. City Coll. of New York. Came into m.p. industry as auditor of Hunchback of Notre Dame roadshow oper., 1924; asst. sls. prom. mgr. Universal, 1926-27; slsmn., Universal, 1927; assoc. editor. The Distributor, MGM publication, 1927; editor, 1928-33; writer, publicist, MGM Studio, 1933-34; writer, publicist, Hollywood, New York, 1935-38; rejoined Universal, 1938, editor, Progress (Univ. publication); twice winner of International Competition on Industrial Journalism; senior publicist and Progress editor, Universal, 1961-67; editor Enterprise Press, 1968; member, executive Enterprise Press 1973; American Guild of Authors and Composers, American Society of Composers, Authors and Publishers, National Academy of Popular Music, and Motion Picture Pioneers.

ALLAND, WILLIAM
Producer. b. Delmar, DE, March 4, 1916. e. Baltimore. Acted in semi-professional groups; with Orson Welles' Mercury Theatre as actor, stage mgr.; asst. prod. Mercury Theatre radio series. Served in U.S. Air Force, WWII; then radio writer; prod., Universal, 1952; Paramount, 1960; Allied Artists, 1963.
PICTURES: *Actor.* Citizen Kane (also dialogue dir.), Macbeth. *Producer.* The Raiders, Flesh and Fury, Stand At Apache River, It Came From Outer Space, The Lawless Breed, Creature From The Black Lagoon, Johnny Dark, This Island Earth, Dawn At Socorro, Four Guns To The Border, Chief Crazy Horse, Revenge Of The Creature, Tarantula, The Creature Walks Among Us, The Mole People, Gun for a Coward, Land Unknown, Deadly Mantis, The Lady Takes a Flyer, As Young As We Are, The Party Crashers, Colossus of New York, Raw Wind in Eden, The Space Children, Look In Any Window (also dir.), The Lively Set, Treasure of the Lost Canyon, The Rare Breed, The Black Castle, Battle Over Citizen Kane.

ALLEN, COREY
Director, Actor. r.n. Alan Cohen. b. Cleveland, OH, June 29, 1934. e. UCLA, 1951-54; UCLA law sch. 1954-55. Actor turned dir. starred in Oscar-winning UCLA student film, appeared in 20 plays at Players Ring, Players Gallery and other L.A. theaters. TV: Perry Mason, Alfred Hitchcock Presents. With partner John Herman Shaner, prod. Freeway Circuit Theatre. Led Actors Workshop with actor Guy Stockwell for 10 years.
PICTURES: *Actor.* Rebel Without a Cause, Key Witness, Sweet Bird of Youth, Private Property, Party Girl, The Chapman Report. *Director.* The Erotic Adventures of Pinocchio, Thunder and Lightning, Avalanche.
TELEVISION: *Series Director.* This is the Life, Mannix, High Chaparral, Dr. Kildare, Streets of San Francisco (DGA nom.), Ironside, Barnaby Jones, Police Woman, Rockford Files, Quincy, Dallas, Lou Grant, McClain's Law, Family Novak, T.J. Hooker, Paper Chase: The Second Year, Hill Street Blues (Emmy), Road Home, Deep Space Nine. *Pilots:* Man Undercover, Capitol, Simon and Simon, Whiz Kids, Murder She Wrote, Code Name: Foxfire, Star Trek: The Next Generation. Unsub. *Movies:* See the Man Run, Cry Rape!, Yesterday's Child, Stone (pilot), Man in the Santa Claus Suit, The Return of Frank Cannon, Code Name: Foxfire (pilot), Brass, Destination America, Beverly Hills Cowgirl Blues, The Last Fling, Ann Jillian Story, Stalking Back.

ALLEN, DAYTON
Performer. b. New York, NY, Sept. 24, 1919. e. Mt. Vernon H.S. Motion picture road shows, 1936-40; disc jockey, WINS, N.Y., 1940-41; writer, vaudeville comedy bits, 1941-45; then radio comic, puppeteer and voices; TV since 1948; film commercials; shows include voices on Terrytoons, Deputy Dawg, Heckle & Jeckle, Lancelot Link: Secret Chimp, Lariat Sam, Oaky Doky, Bonny Maid Varieties, Howdy Doody (voices of Mr. Bluster, Flubadub, The Inspector & many others), Jack Barry's Winky Dink, The Steve Allen Show. 130 Dayton Allen 5 minute shows (synd.). Acted in film The Cotton Club.

ALLEN, DEBBIE
Actress, Choreographer. b. Houston, TX, Jan. 16, 1950. Sister is actress Phylicia Rashad. e. Howard U.
THEATER: Ti-Jean and His Brothers (debut, 1972), Purlie, Raisin, Ain't Misbehavin', West Side Story (revival), Sweet Charity (revival, Tony Award, 1986), Carrie (choreographer).
PICTURES: The Fish That Saved Pittsburgh (1979), Fame, Ragtime, Jo Jo Dancer Your Life is Calling, Blank Check.
TELEVISION: *Series:* The Jim Stafford Show, 3 Girls 3, Fame (series; 3 Emmys as choreographer, 1 nom. as actress), A Different World (prod., dir), In the House. *Mini-Series:* Roots-The Next Generation. *Movies:* The Greatest Thing That Almost Happened, Ebony, Ivory and Jade, Women of San Quentin,

Celebrity, Polly-Comin' Home (dir.), Stompin' at the Savoy (also dir.). *Specials:* Ben Vereen-His Roots, Loretta Lynn in Big Apple Country, Texaco Star Theater—Opening Night, The Kids from Fame, John Schneider's Christmas Holiday, A Tribute to Martin Luther King Jr.—A Celebration of Life, Motown Returns to the Apollo, The Debbie Allen Special (also dir., chor.), Sinbad Live (Afros and Bell Bottoms), Academy Awards (choreographer: 1991-96).

ALLEN, DEDE
Film Editor. r.n. Dorothea Carothers Allen b. Cleveland, OH, 1924. Once a messenger at Columbia Pictures, moved to editing dept., then to commercials and features.
PICTURES: Odds Against Tomorrow (1959), The Hustler, America America, Bonnie and Clyde, Rachel Rachel, Alice's Restaurant, Little Big Man, Slaughterhouse 5, Serpico, Night Moves, Dog Day Afternoon, The Missouri Breaks, Slap Shot, The Wiz, Reds (also exec. prod.), Harry and Son, Mike's Murder, The Breakfast Club, Off Beat, The Milagro Beanfield War (co-ed.), Let It Ride (co-ed.), Henry and June. The Addams Family.

ALLEN, JAY PRESSON
Writer, Producer. r.n. Jacqueline Presson. b. Fort Worth, TX, March 3, 1922. m. prod. Lewis M. Allen.
THEATER: *Writer.*The First Wife, The Prime of Miss Jean Brodie, Forty Carats, Tru (also dir.), The Big Love (also dir.).
PICTURES: *Writer:* Marnie, The Prime of Miss Jean Brodie, Cabaret, Travels with My Aunt, Funny Lady, Just Tell Me What You Want (also prod.), It's My Turn (exec. prod. only), Prince of the City (also exec. prod.), Deathtrap (also exec. prod.).
TELEVISION: *Series:* Family (creator), Hot House (also exec. prod.).

ALLEN, IOAN
Executive. b. Stafford, England, Oct. 25, 1938. e. Rossall School and Dartmouth Naval College, England. Artist management and record production, 1964-1969. Responsible for origination and development of the Dolby Stereo film program. Past Fellow of Society of Morion Picture & Television Engineers, Audio Engineering Society and the British Kinematographic Sound & Television Society. President, International Theatre Equipment Association. U.S. correspondent on the International Standards Organization cinematographic subcommittee. Adjunct professor at USC School of Cinema-Television. Vice president of Dolby Laboratories. Recipient of Scientific & Technical Awards–Academy of Motion Picture Arts & Sciences, 1979 and 1987. Received an Oscar in 1989 for work in Dolby Laboratories film program. 1985 recipient of Samuel L. Warner Award for contribution to motion picture sound.

ALLEN, JOAN
Actress. b. Rochelle, IL, Aug. 20, 1956. Founding member of Steppenwolf Theatre Co., in Chicago where she performed in over 20 shows.
THEATER: *Chicago includes:* A Lesson from Aloes, Three Sisters, The Miss Firecracker Contest, Cloud 9, Balm in Gilead, Fifth of July, Reckless, Earthly Possessions. *Off B'way:* The Marriage of Bette and Boo, And a Nightingale Sang (Clarence Derwent, Drama Desk, Outer Critics' Circle and Theatre World Awards). *B'way debut:* Burn This (1987, Tony Award), The Heidi Chronicles.
PICTURES: Compromising Positions (debut, 1985), Manhunter, Peggy Sue Got Married, Tucker: The Man and His Dream, In Country, Ethan Frome, Searching for Bobby Fischer, Josh and S.A.M., Mad Love, Nixon, The Crucible, The Ice Storm.
TELEVISION: *Special:* All My Sons. *Mini-Series:* Evergreen. Movie: Without Warning: The James Brady Story.

ALLEN, KAREN
Actress. b. Carrollton, IL, Oct. 5, 1951. e. George Washington U., U. of Maryland. Auditioned for theatrical company in Washington, DC and won a role in Saint, touring with it for 7 months. Spent several years with Washington Theatre Laboratory Co. Moved to NY, acting in student films at NYU and studying acting with Lee Strasberg at Theatre Institute.
THEATER: *NY:* Monday After the Miracle (B'way debut, 1982; Theatre World Award), Extremities, The Miracle Worker, The Country Girl. *Williamstown (MA) Theatre:* Tennessee Williams--A Celebration, The Glass Menagerie.
PICTURES: National Lampoon's Animal House (debut, 1978), Manhattan, The Wanderers, Cruising, A Small Circle of Friends, Raiders of the Lost Ark, Shoot the Moon, Split Image, Until September, Starman, Terminus, The Glass Menagerie, Backfire, Scrooged, Animal Behavior, Secret Places of the Heart, Sweet Talker, Exile, Malcolm X, The Sandlot, Ghost in the Machine.
TELEVISION: *Movies:* Lovey: A Circle of Children Part II, Secret Weapon, Challenger, Voyage, Down Home. *Guest:* Alfred Hitcock Presents (1986). *Mini-Series:* East of Eden.

ALLEN, LEWIS M.
Producer. b. Berryville, VA, June 27, 1922. e. Univ. of VA. m. writer-producer Jay Presson Allen.

PICTURES: The Connection, The Balcony, Lord of the Flies, Fahrenheit 451, The Queen (exec. prod.), Fortune and Men's Eyes, Never Cry Wolf, 1918 (exec. prod.), Valentine's Day (exec. prod.), Swimming to Cambodia, O.C. & Stiggs (exec. prod.), End of the Line (co-prod.), Miss Firecracker (exec. prod.).

ALLEN, MEL
TV commentator b. Birmingham, AL, Feb. 14, 1913. e. U. of Alabama, A.B. 1932; U. Alabama Law Sch., LL.B. 1936. Started as sportscaster in Birmingham, while in law school; speech instructor in U. Ala. 1935-37; to N.Y. 1937, as staff announcer CBS to 1943; served in U.S. Army WWII in infantry until the war ended, then before discharge was transferred to work on NBC Army Hour; sportscasting throughout U.S., joined N.Y. Yankees, 1946, concurrently narrating many shorts incl. How to Make a Yankee, appearing on radio & video and in Babe Ruth Story; sports commentator Fox Movietonews; voted best sportscaster in Motion Picture Daily-Fame radio. TV polls; Monitor, NBC; NCAA TV College Football, NBC; World Series (1938-64), CBS-NBC; Rose Bowl (1951-62), NBC; Sports Broadcasters Hall Of Fame.

ALLEN, NANCY
Actress. b. New York, NY, June 24, 1950. e. H.S. Performing Arts, N.Y.
PICTURES: The Last Detail (debut, 1973), Carrie, I Wanna Hold Your Hand, 1941, Home Movies, Dressed to Kill, Blow Out, Strange Invaders, The Buddy System, The Philadelphia Experiment, The Last Victim (Forced Entry), Not for Publication, Terror in the Aisles, Sweet Revenge, Robocop, Poltergeist III, Limit Up, Robocop 2, Robocop 3.
TELEVISION: Movies: The Gladiator, Memories of Murder, Acting on Impulse, The Man Who Wouldn't Die.

ALLEN, REX
Actor. b. Wilcox, AZ, Dec. 31, 1922. e. Wilcox H.S., 1939. Vaudeville & radio actor; WLS, Chicago, 5 yrs.; was rodeo star appearing in shows through U.S.
PICTURES: Arizona Cowboy, Hills of Oklahoma, Under Mexicali Stars, Thunder in God's Country, Rodeo King & the Senorita, I Dream of Jeannie, Last Musketeer, South Pacific Trail, Old Overland Trail, Down Laredo Way, Phantom Stallion, For the Love of Mike, Tomboy and the Champ. Narrator: The Legend of Lobo, The Incredible Journey, Charlotte's Web.
TELEVISION: Guest: Perry Como Special. Voice only: commercials, Wonderful World of Color. Series: Frontier Doctor, Five Star Jubilee.

ALLEN, STEVE
Performer. b. New York, NY, Dec 26, 1921. m. actress Jayne Meadows. Attended Arizona St. Univ. U.S. Army 1942; radio shows, Los Angeles; TV, N.Y., 1950. On NY stage in The Mikado. Composer or lyricist of numerous songs including This Could Be the Start of Something Big, Pretend You Don't See Her, South Rampart St. Parade, Picnic, Houseboat, On the Beach, Sleeping Beauty, Bell Book and Candle, Gravy Waltz, Impossible; score for B'way musical Sophie, and TV musicals: The Bachelor, and Alice in Wonderland.
AUTHOR: Fourteen For Tonight, Steve Allen's Bop Fables, The Funny Men, Wry On the Rocks, The Girls on the Tenth Floor, The Question Man, Mark It and Strike It, Not All of Your Laughter, Not All of Your Tears, Bigger Than a Breadbox, A Flash of Swallows, The Wake, Princess Snip-Snip and the Puppykittens, Curses, Schmock-Schmock!, Meeting of Minds, Ripoff, Meeting of Minds-Second Series, Rip-off, Explaining China, The Funny People, Talk Show Murders, Beloved Son: Story of the Jesus Cults, More Funny People, How To Make a Speech and How To Be Funny, Murder on the Glitter Box, The Passionate Non-smoker's Bill of Rights, Dumbth and 81 Ways to Make Americans Smarter, Murder in Manhattan, Steve Allen on the Bible, Religion and Morality, The Public Hating, Murder in Vegas, Hi-Ho Steverino!: My Adventures in the Wonderful Wacky World of TV, The Murder Game, More Steve Allen on the Bible, Religion & Morality Book II, Make 'em Laugh, Reflections, Murder on the Atlantic, The Man Who Turned Back the Clock and Other Short Stories.
PICTURES: Down Memory Lane (debut, 1949), I'll Get By, The Benny Goodman Story, The Big Circus, College Confidential, Don't Worry We'll Think of a Title, Warning Shot, Where Were You When the Lights Went Out?, The Comic, The Sunshine Boys, Heart Beat, Amazon Women on the Moon, Great Balls of Fire!, The Player, Casino.
TELEVISION: Series: The Steve Allen Show (1950-52), Songs for Sale, Talent Patrol, What's My Line, Steve Allen Show, Tonight, Steve Allen Show (1956-61), (1962-64) (1964-67), I've Got a Secret, Steve Allen Comedy Hour (1967), Steve Allen Show (1967-69), I've Got a Secret (1972-73) Steve Allen's Laugh Back, Meeting of Minds, Steve Allen Comedy Hour (1980-81), Life's Most Embarrassing Moments. Movies: Now You See It Now You Don't, Stone, The Gossip Columnist. Mini-Series: Rich Man Poor Man.

ALLEN, TIM
Actor. r.n. Timothy Allen Dick. b. Denver, CO, June 13, 1953. e. W. Michigan Univ., Univ. of Detroit (studied acting). Worked as creative dir. for adv. agency before becoming stand up comedian. Made stand up tv debut on Showtime Comedy Club All-Stars, 1988. Author: Don't Stand Close to a Naked Man (1994).
PICTURES: Comedy's Dirtiest Dozen, The Santa Clause, Toy Story (voice), Jungle2Jungle.
TELEVISION: Series: Home Improvement. Specials: Tim Allen: Men Are Pigs (also writer), Tim Allen Rewrites America (also exec. prod., writer).

ALLEN, WILLIAM
Executive. e. USC Cinema/TV Sch., Pepperdine Univ. 1979, exec. trainee in CBS Entertainment division, eventually serving as assoc. program exec. in the Comedy Series Programming Dept., mngr./dir. of the CBS Comedy Program Developemnt Dept. 1986- 87, joined MTM as sr. v.p., Comedy Programming; 1987-88, sr. v.p. creative affairs; 1989-91, exec. v.p. MTM Television. 1992, named President of MTM Television.

ALLEN, WOODY
Actor, Director, Writer. r.n. Allan Stewart Konigsberg. b. New York, NY, Dec. 1, 1935. e. NYU, 1953; City Coll. NY, 1953. Began writing comedy at age 17, contributing to various magazines (Playboy, New Yorker) and top TV comedy shows incl. Sid Caesar (1957), Art Carney (1958-59), Herb Shriner (1953). Appeared in nightclubs starting in 1961 as stand-up comic; later performed as a jazz musician at Michael's Pub, NY. Special Award, Berlin Film Fest., 1975.
AUTHOR: Getting Even, Without Feathers, Side Effects.
THEATER: Author: Play It Again Sam (also actor), Don't Drink The Water, The Floating Lightbulb, Central Park West (from Death Defying Acts).
PICTURES: Actor-Screenplay: What's New Pussycat?, What's Up Tiger Lily? (also dubbed and compiled footage; assoc. prod.), Casino Royale (actor only). Director/Screenplay/Actor: Take the Money and Run, Bananas, Play It Again Sam (actor, s.p. only), Everything You Always Wanted to Know About Sex* But Were Afraid to Ask, Sleeper, Love and Death, The Front (actor only), Annie Hall (Academy Awards for Best Director and Original Screenplay, 1977), Interiors (dir., s.p. only), Manhattan, Stardust Memories, A Midsummer Night's Sex Comedy, Zelig, Broadway Danny Rose, The Purple Rose of Cairo (dir., s.p. only), Hannah and Her Sisters (Academy Award for Best Original Screenplay, 1986), Radio Days (dir., s.p.), narrator only,) September (dir., s.p. only), King Lear (actor only), Another Woman (dir., s.p. only), New York Stories (Oedipus Wrecks segment), Crimes and Misdemeanors, Alice (dir., s.p. only), Scenes From a Mall (actor only), Shadows and Fog, Husbands and Wives, Manhattan Murder Mystery, Bullets Over Broadway (dir., s.p. only), Mighty Aphrodite, Everyone Says I Love You (dir. & actor).
TELEVISION: Movies: Don't Drink the Water (also dir., writer), The Sunshine Boys. Specials: The Best on Record, Gene Kelly in New York New York, The Woody Allen Special (also writer, co-dir.), Woody Allen Looks at 1967 (Kraft Music Hall; also writer), Plimpton: Did You Hear the One About ...? Guest: Hullabaloo, Andy Williams, Hippodrome.

ALLEY, KIRSTIE
Actress. b. Wichita, KS, Jan. 12, 1955. m. actor Parker Stevenson. e. KS State U., U. of Kansas. On L.A. stage in Cat on a Hot Tin Roof.
PICTURES: Star Trek II: The Wrath of Khan (debut, 1982), Blind Date, Champions, Runaway, Summer School, Shoot to Kill, Loverboy, Look Who's Talking, Madhouse, Sibling Rivalry, Look Who's Talking Too, Look Who's Talking Now, Village of the Damned, It Takes Two.
TELEVISION: Series: Masquerade, Cheers (Emmy Award, 1991), Untitled. Movies: Sins of the Past, A Bunny's Tale, Stark: Mirror Image, Prince of Bel Air, Infidelity, David's Mother (Emmy Award, 1994). Mini-Series: North and South, North and South Book II. Guest: The Love Boat, The Hitchhiker.

ALLYSON, JUNE
Actress. r.n. Ella Geisman. b. Westchester, NY, Oct. 7, 1917. Started as chorus girl. Voted one of ten top money-making stars in Motion Picture Herald-Fame poll, 1955.
THEATER: B'way: Sing Out the News, Panama Hattie, Best Foot Forward, 40 Carats. Tour: No No Nanette.
PICTURES: Best Foot Foward (debut, 1943), Girl Crazy, Thousands Cheer, Meet the People, Two Girls and a Sailor, Music for Millions, Her Highness and the Bellboy, The Sailor Takes a Wife, Two Sisters From Boston, Till the Clouds Roll By, Secret Heart, High Barbaree, Good News, The Bride Goes Wild, The Three Musketeers, Words and Music, Little Women, The Stratton Story, Meet the People, Reformer and the Redhead, Right Cross, Too Young to Kiss, Girl in White, Battle Circus, Remains to be Seen, Executive Suite, Glenn Miller Story, Woman's World, Strategic Air Command, The Shrike, McConnell Story, Opposite Sex, You Can't Run Away From It, Interlude, My Man Godfrey, Stranger in My Arms, They Only Kill Their Masters, Blackout, That's Entertainment III.
TELEVISION: Series: DuPont Show With June Allyson. Guest: Murder She Wrote, Misfits of Science. Movies: See the Man Run, Letters from Three Lovers, Curse of the Black Widow, Vega$, Three on a Date, The Kid With the Broken Halo. Special: 20th Century Follies.

ALMODOVAR, PEDRO
Director, Writer. b. La Mancha, Spain, Sep. 25, 1951. Grew up in Calzada de Calatrava. At 17 moved to Madrid where worked 10 years for telephone co. while writing comic strips and articles for underground newspapers and working as actor with independent theater co., Los Goliardos. Upon the end of Francoist repression in 1975, made Super-8 experimental films starring friends. Wrote fiction, sang with rock band and created character of porn star, Patty Diphusa, whose fictionalized confessions he published in the magazine La Luna.
PICTURES: Pepi Lucy Bom and Other Girls on the Heap (debut, 1980), Labyrinth of Passion, Dark Habits, What Have I Done to Deserve This?, Matador, Law of Desire, Women on the Verge of a Nervous Breakdown, Tie Me Up! Tie Me Down!, High Heels, Kika.

ALMOND, PAUL
Producer, Director, Writer. b. Montreal, Canada, April 26, 1931. e. McGill U., Balliol Coll., Oxford U. 1954-66 produced and directed over a hundred television dramas in Toronto, London, N.Y., and Hollywood.
PICTURES: Backfire, Isabel, Act of the Heart, Journey, Final Assignment, Ups and Downs, Captive Hearts, The Dance Goes On.

ALONSO, MARIA CONCHITA
Actress, Singer. b. Cuba, 1957. Family moved to Venezuela when she was five. 1971, named Miss Teenager of the World. 1975, Miss Venezuela. 6th runner up, Miss World. Appeared in four feature films and 10 soap operas before coming to U.S. Recorded several albums as singer: 5 gold albums, 1 platinum, 3 Grammy noms.
THEATER: B'way: Kiss of the Spider Woman.
PICTURES: Fear City, Moscow on the Hudson, Touch and Go, A Fine Mess, Extreme Prejudice, The Running Man, Colors, Vampire's Kiss, Predator 2, McBain, The House of the Spirits, Roosters, Caught.
TELEVISION: An American Cousin (RAI mini-series). Specials: Viva Miami!, The Night of the Super Sounds (host). Guest: One of the Boys. Movies: Teamster Boss: The Jackie Presser Story, MacShayne: The Final Roll of the Dice, Texas.

ALONZO, JOHN A
Cinematographer, Director. b. Dallas, TX, 1934.
PICTURES: Bloody Mama, Vanishing Point, Harold and Maude, Get to Know Your Rabbit, Lady Sings the Blues, Sounder, Pete-n-Tillie, Hit, The Naked Ape, Conrack, Chinatown, Farewell My Lovely, The Fortune, I Will ... I Will ... For Now, Once Is Not Enough, The Bad News Bears, Black Sunday, Beyond Reason, Close Encounters of the Third Kind (addtl. photog.), Which Way Is Up?, Casey's Shadow, FM (dir. only), The Cheap Detective, Norma Rae, Tom Horn, Back Roads, Zorro the Gay Blade, Blue Thunder, Cross Creek, Scarface, Out of Control, Terror in the Aisles, Runaway, Jo Jo Dancer Your Life Is Calling, Nothing in Common, 50 Years of Action, Real Men, Overboard, Physical Evidence, Steel Magnolias, Internal Affairs, The Guardian, Navy Seals, Housesitter, Cool World, The Meteor Man, Clifford.
TELEVISION: Champions: A Love Story, Belle Star (also dir.), Blinded By the Light (also dir.), The Kid From Nowhere (also dir.), Roots: The Gift, Knights of the City.

ALTERMAN, JOSEPH GEORGE
Executive. b. New Haven, CT., Dec. 17, 1919. e. Wesleyan U., B.A., 1942; Inst. for Organization Management, Yale U. 1957-59. Exec. assist., SoundScriber Corp., 1945-48; district mgr., Industrial Luncheon Service, 1948-55; asst. secretary and admin. Secretary, Theatre Owners of America, 1955; Exec. dir. and vice pres., Natl. Assn. of Theatre Owners, 1966; Exec. v.p. COMPO., 1970. Retired 1988 from NATO. Consultant m.p. industry, conventions and meetings. Chmn. bd. governors, Institute for Learning in Retirement, Albertus Magnus College.

ALTMAN, ROBERT
Director, Writer, Producer. b. Kansas City, MO, Feb. 20, 1925. e. U. of Missouri. Early film writer credits: Bodyguard (co-story), Corn's-a-Poppin (co-s.p.). Made industrial films and documentaries for the Calvin Company in Kansas City, before dir. first indept. feature in 1957. Received D.W. Griffith Lifetime Achievement Award from Directors Guild of America, 1994.
THEATER: NY: Two By South, Come Back to the Five and Dime Jimmy Dean Jimmy Dean. Operas: The Rake's Progress, McTeague.
PICTURES: Director: The Delinquents (also s.p., prod.), The James Dean Story (also co-prod., edit.), Countdown, That Cold Day in the Park, M*A*S*H (Cannes Film Fest. Golden Palm Award, 1970; Acad. Award nom.), Brewster McCloud, McCabe & Mrs. Miller (also co-s.p.), Images (also s.p.), The Long Goodbye, Thieves Like Us (also co-s.p.), California Split (also co-prod.), Nashville (also prod.; NY Film Critics, Natl. Society of Film Critics & Natl. Board of Review Awards for Best Director & Picture, 1975; Acad. Award noms. for dir. & picture), Buffalo Bill and the Indians: Or Sitting Bull's History Lesson (also co-s.p., prod.), Three Women (also s.p., prod.), A Wedding (also co-s.p.,

prod., co-story), Quintet (also co-s.p., prod., co-story), A Perfect Couple (also co-s.p., prod.), Health (also co-s.p., prod.), Popeye, Come Back to the Five and Dime Jimmy Dean Jimmy Dean, Streamers (also co-prod.), Secret Honor (also prod.), Fool for Love, Beyond Therapy (also co-s.p.), O.C. and Stiggs (also co-prod.), Aria (dir. Les Boreades sequence; also s.p.), Vincent & Theo, The Player (BAFTA & Cannes Film Fest. Awards for Best Director, 1991; Acad. Award nom.), Short Cuts (also co-s.p.; Acad. Award nom. for dir.), Ready to Wear/Pret-a-Porter (also co-s.p.). Producer: The Late Show, Welcome to L.A., Remember My Name, Rich Kids, Mrs. Parker and the Vicious Circle, Kansas City.
TELEVISION: Series (dir., writer, &/or prod. episodes): The Roaring Twenties, The Millionaire, Bonanza, Bus Stop, Combat, Kraft Mystery Theatre (Nightmare in Chicago: Once Upon a Savage Night), The Gallant Men (pilot).Specials: Two by South (also prod.), The Laundromat, The Dumb Waiter (also prod.), Tanner '88 (also co-exec. prod.; Emmy Award for dir. episode The Boiler Room, 1989), The Room, The Real McTeague, Black and Blue. Movie: The Caine Mutiny Court-Martial (also co-prod.).

ALVARADO, TRINI
Actress. b. New York, NY, 1967. e. Fordham U. m. actor Robert McNeill. Began performing at age 7 as flamenco dancer with her parents' troupe. Prof. acting debut at 9 in stage musical Becca.
THEATER: Runaways, Yours Anne, Maggie Magalita, I Love You I Love You Not, Reds, The Magic Show, Godspell.
PICTURES: Rich Kids (debut, 1989), Times Square, Mrs. Soffel, Sweet Lorraine, Satisfaction, The Chair, Stella, American Blue Note, The Babe, American Friends, Little Women, Frighteners.
TELEVISION: Movies: Dreams Don't Die, Prisoner Without a Name, Nitti. Specials: Private Contentment, Unicorn Tales, A Movie Star's Daughter, Stagestruck, Sensibility and Sense. Guest: Kay O'Brien, Kate and Allie.

ALVIN, JOHN
Actor. r.n. John Alvin Hoffstadt; b. Chicago, IL, Oct. 24, 1917. e. Pasadena Playhouse, CA. Attended Morgan Park Military Acad. On radio Chicago & Detroit; on N.Y. stage Leaning on Letty, Life of the Party. Screen debut 1944 in Destination Tokyo. Under contract four years to Warner Bros., featured in 25 films.
PICTURES: Destination Tokyo, Objective Burma, San Antonio, The Beast With Five Fingers, Night and Day, Cheyenne, Missing Women, Two Guys from Texas, Bold Frontiersman, Train to Alcatraz, Shanghai Chest, Carrie, April In Paris, Roughly Speaking, The Very Thought of You, Shadow of a Woman, Three Strangers, Romance on the High Seas, Torpedo Alley, Irma La Douce, Marnie, Inside Daisy Clover, The Legend of Lylah Clare, They Shoot Horses Don't They?, They Call Me Mr. Tibbs, Somewhere in Time, Beethoven's 2nd, Milk Money.
TELEVISION: Meet Millie, Burns and Allen, Death Valley Days, Asphalt Jungle, Climax, Dragnet, Jack Benny Show, My Three Sons, The Texan, Adventures in Paradise, Rawhide, Rifleman, Omnibus, Wells Fargo, Alfred Hitchcock, Mannix, I Spy, Legend of Lizzie Borden, All in the Family, McDuff, Lineup, My Favorite Husband, Family Affair, Get Smart, The Incredible Hulk, The Lucy Show, Ironside, Nightstalker, MASH, Lou Grant Show, Hart to Hart, Yellow Rose, Dennis the Menace (2 Hour Pilot), Murder She Wrote, Monster Squad, House of Evil, Aftermash, General Hospital, Starsky & Hutch, Policewoman, Amazing Stories, Capitol, Passions, The Quest, Visions/KCET, Rachel Sweet Rachel, Swallows Came Back, Return to Green Acres, Moving Target, From Out of the Night, The Walkers, The Bold and the Beautiful.

AMATEAU, ROD
Director. b. New York, NY, Dec. 20, 1923. U.S. Army, 1941; 20th Century-Fox; 2nd unit dir.
PICTURES: The Statue, Where Does It Hurt?, The Wilby Conspiracy, Drive-In, Lovelines, Garbage Pail Kids (also s.p., prod.), Sunset (story only).
TELEVISION: Series: Schlitz Playhouse of Stars, Four Star Playhouse, General Electric Theatre, Private Secretary, Dennis Day Show, Lassie, Ray Milland Show, Bob Cummings Show, Burns & Allen Show (also prod.), Dobie Gillis. Movies: Uncommon Valor, High School U.S.A., Swimsuit (prod.).

AMES, LOUIS B.
Executive. b. St. Louis, MO, Aug. 9, 1918. e. Washington U., St. Louis. m. Jetti Ames. Began as music consultant and staff director of musical programs for NBC; music dir. 1948, WPIX; 1951 appt. program mgr., WPIX; assoc. prod., Today, NBC TV, 1954; feature editor Home, 1957; Adm.-prod. NBC Opera, 1958; dir. cultural prog. N.Y. World's Fair, 1960-63; dir. RCA Pavillion, N.Y. World's Fair, 1963-65; 1966 dir., Nighttime, TV; 1969, dir. of programming N.W. Ayer & Sons, Inc. 1973 Mgr. Station Services, Television Information Office. NYC.

AMIEL, JON
Director. b. London, Eng., 1948. e. Cambridge. Was in charge of the Oxford & Cambridge Shakespeare Co., then literary mngr. for Hampstead Theatre Club where he started directing. Became story edit. for BBC, then director.

PICTURES: Silent Twins, Queen of Hearts, Tune in Tomorrow, Sommersby, Copycat.
TELEVISION: A Sudden Wrench, Gates of Gold, Busted, Tandoori Nights (series), The Singing Detective (mini-series).

AMIN, MARK
Executive. Chairman & Acting CEO, TriMark Pictures.

AMIS, SUZY
Actress. b. Oklahoma City, OK, Jan. 5, 1962. e. Heritage Hall, Oklahoma City. At 16 was introduced on the Merv Griffin Show by Eileen Ford whose modeling agency she worked for, as "The Face of the Eighties." After modeling and living in Europe, made film debut in Fandango (1985). Off-B'way debut: Fresh Horses (Theatre World Award).
PICTURES: Fandango, The Big Town, Plain Clothes, Rocket Gibralter, Twister, Where the Heart Is, Rich in Love, Watch It, The Ballad of Little Jo, Two Small Bodies, Blown Away, The Usual Suspects, Nadja.

AMOS, JOHN
Actor. b. Newark, NJ, Dec. 27, 1941. e. East Orange H.S., Colorado State U, Long Beach City Col. Inducted as honorary Master Chief Petty Officer in U.S. Navy 1993. Worked as professional football player, social worker (heading the Vera Institute of Justice in NY), and advertising copywriter before writing television comedy material (for the Leslie Uggams Show) and performing as stand-up comedian in Greenwich Village. Has dir. theatre with Bahamian Rep. Co. Artistic dir.: John Harms Theatre, Englewood, NJ.
THEATER: L.A.: Norman Is That You? and Master Harold...And the Boys, Split Second, The Emperor Jones. B'way: Tough to Get Him. NYSF: Twelfth Night. Off-B'way: The Past is the Past. Regional: Fences, Halley's Comet (also writer).
PICTURES: Vanishing Point (debut, 1971), Sweet Sweetback's Baadasssss Song, The World's Greatest Athlete, Let's Do It Again, Touched By Love, The Beastmaster, Dance of the Dwarfs, American Flyers, Coming to America, Lock Up, Die Hard 2, Ricochet, Two Evil Eyes (The Black Cat), Mac, Night Trap (Mardi Gras for the Devil).
TELEVISION: Series: Mary Tyler Moore, The Funny Side, Maude, Good Times, Hunter, South by Southwest, 704 Hauser. Mini-Series: Roots. Movies: The President's Plane is Missing, Future Cop, Cops and Robin, Willa, Alcatraz-The Whole Shocking Story, Bonanza-the Next Generation. Pilots: Clippers, 704 Hauser Street; many guest appearances incl. Bill Cosby Show, Love American Style, Sanford and Son, The Love Boat, Cosby Show. Special: Without a Pass.

AMSTERDAM, MOREY
Actor, Producer, Writer, Composer, Musician. b. Chicago, IL, Dec. 14, 1914. e. U. of California, Berkeley. Boy soprano. Radio KPO. Night club performer, Chicago, 1929; comedian, singer, musician. Rube Wolf Orchestra; comedian, Optimistic Doughnuts Program, 1930; writer, performer with, Al Pearce Gang, 1932; writer, MGM, 1937; co-writer, m.p. Columbia, Universal; writer, performer, USO Shows, 1942-43; Owner, the Playgoers Club; v.p. International Pictures. Songs: Rum and Coca Cola, Why Oh Why Did I Ever Leave Wyoming, Yak A Puk, etc.
PICTURES: It Came From Outer Space, Machine Gun Kelly, Murder Inc., Gay Purr-ee (voice), Beach Party, Muscle Beach Party, Don't Worry ... We'll Think of a Title, The Horse in the Gray Flannel Suit, Won Ton Ton the Dog Who Saved Hollywood.
TELEVISION: Series: Stop Me If You've Heard This One, Morey Amsterdam Show, Broadway Open House, Battle of the Ages, Who Said That?, Keep Talking, Dick Van Dyke Show. Can You Top This? (also exec. prod.). Movies: Sooner or Later, Side By Side.

ANDERSON, GERRY
Hon. F.B.K.S., Producer, Director, Writer. b. London, England, 1929. Entered industry in 1946. Chmn./man. dir. Gerry Anderson Productions, Ltd. Over 320 pictures produced for TV worldwide. 1981 Co-founded Anderson Burr Pictures. 1982 prod. Terrahawks in association with London Weekend Television; second series, Terrahawks, 1984; Space Police pilot for series in assoc. with TVS, 1985-6; Dick Spanner stop motion series for Channel Four 1987. Entered commercials as a dir.: numerous commercials incl. Royal Bank of Scotland, Children's World, Domestos, Shout, Scotch Tape, etc. 1992 Anglo Russian Cartoon Series Astro Force and lecture tour An Evening with Garry Anderson.
PICTURES: Thunderbirds Are Go, Thunderbird 6, Journey to the Far Side of the Sun.
TELEVISION: Series: The Adventures of Twizzle, Torchy, The Battery Boy, Four Feather Falls, Supercar, Fireball XL5, Stingray, Thunderbirds, Captain Scarlet, Joe 90, The Secret Service, The Protectors, UFO, Space 1999, Terrahawks, Dick Spanner, Space Precinct.

ANDERSON, HARRY
Actor. b. Newport, RI, Oct. 14, 1952. m. actress-magician Leslie Pollack. Performed magic show prior to plays at Oregon

Shakespeare Festival. Also opening act for Kenny Rogers, Debbie Reynolds and Roger Miller in Las Vegas. Owner of magic shop in Ashland OR. Received Stage Magician of Year Award, National Acad. of Magician Arts and Sciences.
PICTURE: The Escape Artist.
TELEVISION: Series: Night Court (Emmy nom.), Our Time, Dave's World. Movies: Spies, Lies and Naked Thighs; The Absent-Minded Professor, Stephen King's It. Guest: Cheers, The Tonight Show, David Letterman, Saturday Night Live, Wil Shriner. Specials: Comic Relief, Harry Anderson's Sideshow (also exec. prod., writer), Comic Relief II, The Best of Gleason, Magic with the Stars, Nell Carter: Never Too Old to Dream, Hello Sucker.

ANDERSON, J. WAYNE
Executive. b. Clifton Forge, VA, Feb. 19, 1947. e. USA Signal School (1965-67); USN Service Schools (1967). USMC, 1965-69; opened and operated 1st military 35mm m.p. theatre, DaNang, Vietnam, 1967-69; R/C Theatres, dist. mgr., 1971-75; v.p., 1976-83; pres./COO, 1983-present; bd. of dirs., Maryland Permanent Bank & Trust co., 1988-present, chairman, 1992-present. Member of NATO, bd. of dirs., 1987-present, technical advancement committee, 1981-present; chmn., 1991-present; Inter-Society for the Enhancement of Theatrical Presenation, 1986-present; Huntsman bd. of dirs., 1979-83; pres., 1982-83; NRA, 1970-life; Will Rogers Inst., 1988-present; Presidential Task Force, 1990-life.

ANDERSON, KEVIN
Actor. b. Illinois, Jan. 13, 1960. e. Goodman School. Member of Chicago's Steppenwolf Theatre where he starred in Orphans. Moved with the play when it transferred to New York (1985) and later starred in the London production, as well as the film version.
THEATER: NY: Orphans (Theatre World Award), Moonchildren, Brilliant Tracers, Orpheus Descending. London: Sunset Boulevard.
PICTURES: Risky Business (debut, 1983), Pink Nights, A Walk on the Moon, Orphans, Miles From Home, In Country, Sleeping With the Enemy, Liebestraum, Hoffa, The Night We Never Met, Rising Sun.
TELEVISION: Movies: Orpheus Descending, The Wrong Man. Special: Hale the Hero.

ANDERSON, LONI
Actress. b. St. Paul, MN, Aug. 5, 1946. e. U. of Minnesota. Taught school before acting.
PICTURES: Stroker Ace, The Lonely Guy (cameo), All Dogs Go to Heaven (voice), Munchie.
TELEVISION: Series: WKRP in Cincinnati, Partners in Crime, Easy Street, Nurses. Specials: Christmas in Opryland, Shaun Cassidy Special, Bob Hope specials, etc. Movies: The Magnificent Magnet of Mesa, Three on a Date, The Jayne Mansfield Story, Sizzle, Country Gold, My Mother's Secret Life, A Letter to Three Wives, Stranded, Necessity, A Whisper Kills, Too Good to Be True, Sorry Wrong Number, Coins in the Fountain, White Hot: The Mysterious Murder of Thelma Todd, The Price She Paid, Gambler V: Playing for Keeps.

ANDERSON, MELISSA SUE
Actress. b. Berkeley, CA, Sept. 26, 1962. Took up acting at suggestion of a dancing teacher. Did series of commercials; guest role in episode of Brady Bunch; episode of Shaft. Gained fame as Mary Ingalls on Little House on the Prairie series (Emmy nom.).
PICTURES: Happy Birthday to Me, Chattanooga Choo Choo, Dead Men Don't Die.
TELEVISION: Series: Little House on the Prairie. Movies: Little House on the Prairie (pilot), The Loneliest Runner, James at 15 (pilot), Survival of Dana, Midnight Offerings, Advice to the Lovelorn, An Innocent Love, First Affair, Dark Mansions. Special: Which Mother is Mine? (Emmy Award, 1980).

ANDERSON, MICHAEL
Director. b. London, England, Jan. 30, 1920. e. France, Germany. Ent. m.p. industry as actor, 1936. Son is actor Michael Anderson Jr.
PICTURES: Private Angelo (debut, 1949; co-dir. with Peter Ustinov), Waterfront, Hell Is Sold Out, Night Was Our Friend, Will Any Gentleman?, The Dam Busters, 1984, Around the World in 80 Days, Yangtse Incident (Battle Hell), Chase a Crooked Shadow, Shake Hands With the Devil (also prod.), The Wreck of the Mary Deare, All the Fine Young Cannibals, The Naked Edge, Flight From Ashiya, Wild and Wonderful, Operation Crossbow, The Quiller Memorandum, The Shoes of the Fisherman, Pope Joan, Doc Savage: The Man of Bronze, Conduct Unbecoming, Logan's Run, Orca, Dominique (Avenging Spirit), Murder By Phone, Second Time Lucky, Separate Vacations, Jeweller's Shop, Millenium.
TELEVISION: Mini-Series: The Martian Chronicles, Sword of Gideon, Young Catherine. Movies: Regina Vs. Nelles, The Sea Wolf, Harry Oakes, Rugged Gold, Captain's Courageous, 20,000 Leagues Under the Sea.

9

ANDERSON, MICHAEL, JR.
Actor. b. London, England, Aug. 6, 1943. Father is director Michael Anderson. Ent. films as child actor, 1954.
PICTURES: The Moonraker, Tiger Bay, The Sundowners, In Search of the Castaways, Play It Cool, Reach For Glory, Greatest Story Ever Told, Dear Heart, Major Dundee, The Glory Guys, The Sons of Katie Elder, The Last Movie, Logan's Run.
TELEVISION: *Series*: The Monroes. *Mini-Series*: Washington Behind Closed Doors, The Martian Chronicles. *Movies*: The House That Would Not Die, In Search of America, The Family Rico, The Daughters of Joshua Cabe, Coffee Tea or Me? Shootout in a One-Dog Town, Kiss Me Kill Me, The Million Dollar Face, Making of a Male Model, Love Leads the Way.

ANDERSON, RICHARD
Actor. b. Long Branch, NJ, Aug. 8, 1926. e. University H.S., W. Los Angeles. Served in U.S. Army, WWII. Began acting career in summer theatre in Santa Barbara and Laguna Playhouse where spotted by MGM executives who signed him to six yr. contract. Appeared in 26 films for MGM before leaving studio. Spokesperson for Kiplinger Washington Letter since 1985.
PICTURES: 12 O'Clock High, The People Against O'Hara, Scaramouche, The Story of Three Loves, Escape from Fort Bravo, Forbidden Planet, The Search for Bridey Murphy, Paths of Glory, The Long Hot Summer, Curse of the Faceless Man, Compulsion, A Gathering of Eagles, Johnny Cool, Seven Days in May, Seconds, The Ride to Hangman's Tree, Tora! Tora! Tora!, Macho Callahan, Doctors' Wives, Play It As It Lays, The Honkers, The Player, The Glass Shield, An American in Saigon.
TELEVISION: *Series*: Mama Rosa, Bus Stop, The Lieutenant, Perry Mason, Dan August, The Six Million Dollar Man, The Bionic Woman (Emmy nom.), Dynasty, Cover-Up. *Guest*: Ironside, The Big Valley, Mannix, My Friend Tony, The Mod Squad, Land of the Giants, The FBI, Gunsmoke. *Movies*: Along Came a Spider, Kane & Abel, The Return of the Six Million Dollar Man and the Bionic Woman, Pearl, Perry Mason Returns, Hoover vs. the Kennedys, Emminent Domain, Danger High, Stranger on My Land, The Bionic Showdown: The Six Million Dollar Man & The Bionic Woman (also co-prod.), Return of the Six Million Dollar Man and the Bionic Woman III, Kung Fu Revisted, Bionic Breakdown: The Six Million Dollar Man & The Bionic Woman (exec. prod.), Bionic Ever After? (also co-exec. prod.), In A Lake Of The Forest.

ANDERSON, RICHARD DEAN
Actor. b. Minneapolis, MN, Jan. 23, 1950. Planned to become professional hockey player. Became a street mime and jester. Performed with his own rock band, Ricky Dean and Dante.
PICTURES: Young Doctors in Love, Odd Jobs.
TELEVISION: *Series*: General Hospital (1976-81), Seven Brides for Seven Brothers, Emerald Point N.A.S., MacGyver, Legend. *Movies*: Ordinary Heroes, In the Eyes of a Stranger, Through the Eyes of a Killer, MacGyver: Lost Treasure of Atlantis (also co-exec. prod.), MacGyver: Trail to Doomsday, Beyond Betrayal, Past the Bleachers.

ANDERSON, SYLVIA.
Producer, Writer (Pinewood Studios). b. London, England. e. London U. Entered m.p. ind. 1960. First pub. novel, Love and Hisses. UK rep for Home Box Office of America.
TELEVISION: series created include: Thunderbirds, U.F.O., Space 1999.

ANDERSON, WILLIAM H.
Producer. b. Utah, October 12, 1911. e. Compton Coll. Firestone Rubber Co.; Universal Credit Co. Producer & Member of Bd. of Dirs. at Walt Disney Prods.
PICTURES: Old Yeller, Swiss Family Robinson, The Happiest Millionaire, The Computer Wore Tennis Shoes, The Barefoot Executive, $1,000,000 Duck, Superdad, The Strongest Man in the World, The Apple Dumpling Gang, Treasure of Matecumbe, The Shaggy D.A.
TELEVISION: *Series*: Zorro, Pop Warner Football. *Wonderful World of Disney Movies*: Zorro, Texas John Slaughter, Daniel Boone, The Swamp Fox, Johnny Shiloh, Mooncussers, Bristle Face, The Scarecrow of Romney Marsh, The Legend of Young Dick Turpin, Willie and the Yank, A Boy Called Nuthin', The Young Loner, The Wacky Zoo of Morgan City, The Mystery of Dracula's Castle, The Bull from the Sky (co-prod.), Great Sleeping Bear Sled Dog Race (co-prod.).

ANDERSSON, BIBI
Actress. b. Stockholm, Sweden, Nov. 11, 1935. e. Royal Dramatic Theatre School (Kungliga Dramatiska Teatern).
PICTURES: Dum-Bom (debut, 1953), Sir Arne's Treasure, Smiles of a Summer Night, The Seventh Seal, Wild Strawberries, The Magician, Brink of Life, The Face, The Devil's Eye, Square of Violence, Pleasure Garden, The Swedish Mistress, Not to Mention These Women, My Sister My Love, Persona, Duel at Diablo, A Question of Rape, Black Palm Trees, The Girls, Story of a Woman, The Passion of Anna, The Kremlin Letter, The Touch, Scenes From a Marriage, It Is Raining on Santiago, Blondy (Vortex), The Hounds of Spring, I Never

Promised You a Rose Garden, An Enemy of the People, Quintet, The Concorde: Airport '79, Prosperous Times, The Marmalade Revolution, Black Crows, Exposed, The Hill on the Other Side of the Moon, Babette's Feast, Manika, Fordringsagare.
TELEVISION: Wallenberg—A Hero's Story.

ANDRESS, URSULA
Actress. b. Bern, Switzerland, Mar. 19, 1936. To Rome as teen where she landed roles in Italian Films.
PICTURES: Sins of Casanova (debut, 1954), An American in Rome, The Tempest Has Gone, La Catena dell'Odio, Anyone Can Play, Dr. No, Four for Texas, Fun in Acapulco, Nightmare in the Sun, She, The Tenth Victim, What's New Pussycat?, Up to His Ears, Once Before I Die, The Blue Max, Casino Royale, The Southern Star, Perfect Friday, Red Sun, Africa Express, Scaramouche, The Sensuous Nurse, Slave of the Cannibal God, Tigers in Lipstick, The Fifth Musketeer, Primitive Desires, Four Tigers in Lipstick, Clash of the Titans, Reporters, Mexico in Flames, Class Meeting.
TELEVISION: *Mini-Series*: Peter the Great. *Series*: Falcon Crest. *Movies*: Man Against the Mob.

ANDREWS, ANTHONY
Actor. b. London, England, Dec. 1, 1948. e. Royal Masonic Sch., Herts. Regional stage debut, 1967.
PICTURES: Take Me High/Hot Property (debut, 1973), Operation Daybreak, Under the Volcano, The Holcroft Covenant, The Second Victory, The Lighthorsemen, Hanna's War, Lost in Siberia, Haunted (also co-prod.).
TELEVISION: A Beast With Two Backs, Romeo and Juliet, A War of Children, QB VII, Upstairs Downstairs, Danger UXB, Brideshead Revisited, Ivanhoe, The Scarlet Pimpernel, Sparkling Cyanide, A.D., Bluegrass, Suspicion, The Woman He Loved, Columbo Goes to the Guillotine, Daniel Steel's Jewels.

ANDREWS, JULIE
Actress, Singer. r.n. Julia Wells. b. Walton-on-Thames, England. Oct 1, 1935. m. dir./writer Blake Edwards. debut, Eng. Starlight Roof Revue London Hippodrome, 1948.
AUTHOR: Mandy, Last of the Really Great Whangdoodles (1973).
THEATER: *NY*: The Boy Friend, My Fair Lady, Camelot, Putting It Together, Victor/Victoria.
PICTURES: Mary Poppins (debut, 1964; Academy Award), The Americanization of Emily, The Sound of Music (Acad. Award nom.), Hawaii, Torn Curtain, Thoroughly Modern Millie, Star!, Darling Lili, The Tamarind Seed, ``10'', S.O.B, Victor/Victoria (Acad. Award nom.), The Man Who Loved Women, That's Life, Duet for One, A Fine Romance.
TELEVISION: *Specials*: High Tor, Julie and Carol at Carnegie Hall, The Julie Andrews Show, An Evening with Julie Andrews and Harry Belafonte, The World of Walt Disney, Julie and Carol at Lincoln Center, Julie on Sesame Street, Julie Andrews' Christmas Special, Julie and Dick in Covent Garden, Julie Andrews and Jackie Gleason Together, Julie Andrews: My Favorite Things, Julie Andrews:The Sound of Christmas, Julie and Carol: Together Again. *Series*: The Julie Andrews Hour (1972-73), Julie. *Movie*: Our Sons.

ANGERS, AVRIL
Actress, Comedienne, Singer. b. Liverpool, England, April 18. Stage debut at age of 14; screen debut in 1947 in Lucky Mascot (The Brass Monkey).
THEATER: The Mating Game, Cockie, Murder at the Vicarage, Little Me, Norman, Is That You?, Blithe Spirit, Oklahoma!, Gigi, The Killing of Sister George, Cards on the Table, When We Are Married, Cinderella, Easy Virtue, Post Mortem, Crazy for You.
PICTURES: Miss Pilgrim's Progress, Don't Blame the Stork, Women Without Men, Green Man, Devils of Darkness, Be My Guest, Three Bites of the Apple, The Family Way, Two a Penny, The Best House in London, Staircase, There's a Girl in My Soup, Forbush and the Penguins, Gollocks, Confessions of a Driving Instructor, Dangerous Davies.
TELEVISION: How Do You View, Friends and Neighbors, Dear Dotty, Holiday Town, Charlie Fainsbarn Show, Arthur Askey Show, All Aboard, The Gold Hunter, Bob Monkhouse Show, Before The Fringe, Hudd, Coronation Street, Dick Emery Show, Dad's Army, Bright Boffins, The More We Are Together, The Millionairess, Liver Birds, Looks Familiar, No Appointment Necessary, The Songwriters, All Creatures Great and Small, Coronation Concert, Minder, Smuggler, Just Liz, Give Us a Clue, Are You Being Served, Trelawney of the Wells, Cat's Eye, C.A.B., Rude Health, Victoria Wood Playhouse, Common As Muck.

ANHALT, EDWARD
Writer. b. New York, NY. Mar. 28, 1914. e. Columbia U.
PICTURES: Bulldog Drummond Strikes Back, Panic in the Streets (Academy Award for Best Original Story, 1950), Red Mountain, The Member of the Wedding (also prod.), The Sniper, My Six Convicts, Eight Iron Men, Not as a Stranger, The Pride and the Passion, The Young Lions, In Love and War, The Restless Years, The Sins of Rachel Cade, The Young Savages, Girls Girls Girls, A Girl Named Tamiko, Wives and Lovers,

10

Becket (Academy Award for Best Adapted Screenplay, 1964), The Satan Bug, Boeing-Boeing, Hour of the Gun, In Enemy Country, The Boston Strangler, The Madwoman of Chaillot, Jeremiah Johnson, The Man in the Glass Booth, Luther, Escape to Athena, Green Ice, The Holcroft Covenant.
TELEVISION: Peter the Great, QB VII, Contract on Cherry Street, Day That Christ Died, The Neon Empire, The Take, Alexander the Great, The Life and Times of Santa Claus, The Apostles.

ANNAUD, JEAN-JACQUES
Writer, Director. b. Draveil, France, Oct. 1, 1943. Began career as film director in French army, making educational pictures. Also directed 500 commercials. Received 1989 cinema prize from French Acad. for career's work. Directed IMAX film Wings of Courage.
PICTURES: *Director*: Black and White in Color (also s.p., winner of Best Foreign Language Film Oscar, 1978), Coup de Tete (Hothead), Quest for Fire (Cesar Award for best dir., 1982), The Name of the Rose, The Bear (also co-s.p.: Cesar Award for best dir., 1989), The Lover.

ANN-MARGRET
Actress, Singer, Dancer. r.n. Ann-Margret Olsson. b. Valsjobyn, Sweden, April 28, 1941. m. Roger Smith, actor, dir., prod. e. New Trier H.S., Winnetka, IL; Northwestern U. Radio shows, toured with band; worked with George Burns in Las Vegas. TV debut, Jack Benny Show, 1961.
PICTURES: Pocketful of Miracles (debut, 1961), State Fair, Bye Bye Birdie, Viva Las Vegas, Kitten With a Whip, The Pleasure Seekers, Bus Riley's Back in Town, Once A Thief, The Cincinnati Kid, Made in Paris, Stagecoach, The Swinger, Murderer's Row, The Prophet, The Tiger and the Pussycat, Rebus, Criminal Affair, RPM, C. C. & Company, Carnal Knowledge (Acad. Award nom.), The Outside Man, The Train Robbers, Tommy (Acad. Award nom.), The Last Remake of Beau Geste, The Twist, Joseph Andrews, The Cheap Detective, Magic, The Villain, Middle Age Crazy, I Ought To Be in Pictures, Lookin' to Get Out, The Return of the Soldier, Twice in a Lifetime, 52 Pick-up, A Tiger's Tail, A New Life, Newsies, Grumpy Old Men, Grumpier Old Men.
TELEVISION: *Specials*: The Ann-Margret Show, From Hollywood With Love, Dames at Sea, When You're Smiling, Ann-Margret Smith, Ann-Margret Olsson, Memories of Elvis, Rhinestone Cowgirl, Hollywood Movie Girls. *Movies*: Who Will Love My Children?, A Streetcar Named Desire, The Two Mrs. Grenvilles, Our Sons, Nobody's Children, Following Her Heart. *Mini-Series*: Queen, Scarlett, Seduced By Madness: The Diane Borchardt Story.

ANSARA, MICHAEL
Actor. b. Lowell, MA, April 15, 1922. e. Pasadena Playhouse. Served in U.S. Army; then summer stock, little theatre, road shows.
PICTURES: Soldiers Three, Only the Valiant, The Robe, Julius Caesar, Sign of the Pagan, Bengal Brigade, New Orleans Uncensored, Diane, Lone Ranger, Sol Madrid, Daring Game, Dear Dead Delilah, The Bears and I, Mohammad Messenger of God, The Manitou, Gas, Access Code, Knights of the City. Lethal (KGB: The Secret War).
TELEVISION: *Series*: Broken Arrow, Law of the Plainsman, Buck Rogers in the 25th Century. *Mini-Series*: Centennial. *Guest*: The Westerner, Lost in Space, Simon and Simon, Gavilan, George Burns Comedy Week, Hunter, Hardcastle and McCormick. *Movies*: How I Spent My Summer Vacation, Powderkeg, A Call to Danger, Ordeal, Shootout in a One-Dog Town, Barbary Coast, The Fantastic World of D.C. Collins.

ANSPACH, SUSAN
Actress. b. New York, NY, Nov. 23, 1945. e. Catholic U., Washington, DC. After school returned to N.Y. and in 3 years had performed in 11 B'way and off-B'way prods. Moved to Los Angeles and entered films.
PICTURES: The Landlord (debut, 1970), Five Easy Pieces, Play It Again Sam, Blume in Love, The Big Fix, Running, The Devil and Max Devlin, Gas, Montenegro, Misunderstood, Blue Monkey, Into the Fire, Blood Red, Back to Back.
TELEVISION: *Movies*: I Want to Keep My Baby, The Secret Life of John Chapman, Rosetti & Ryan, Mad Bull, The Last Giraffe, Portrait of an Escort, The First Time, Deadly Encounter, Cagney & Lacey: The Return. *Mini-Series*: Space. *Series*: The Yellow Rose, The Slap Maxwell Story.

ANSPAUGH, DAVID
Director, Producer. b. Decatur, IN, Sept. 24, 1946. e. Indiana U., 1965-70; U. of Southern CA, 1974-76. School teacher, Aspen, CO 1970-74.
PICTURES: *Director*: Hoosiers (debut, 1986), Fresh Horses, Rudy, Moonlight and Valentino.
TELEVISION: *Series*: Hill St. Blues (assoc. prod. 1980-81; prod.-dir. 1981-82; prod.-dir. 1983-84, dir. 1985; DGA Award: 1983, 2 Emmy Awards for producing: 1982, 1983), St. Elsewhere (dir.), Miami Vice (dir.). *Movies*: Deadly Care, In the Company of Darkness.

ANTHONY, LYSETTE
Actress. b. London, England, 1963. Stage work incl. Bristol Old Vic, 1988-90.
PICTURES: Krull, The Emperor's New Clothes, Without a Clue, 29 Days in February, Switch, Husbands and Wives, The Pleasure Principle, Look Who's Talking Now, The Advocate, Dr. Jekyll and Ms. Hyde, Dead Cool, Dracula: Dead and Loving It.
TELEVISION: *Series*: Lovejoy (BBC), Three Up Two Down (BBC), Campion, Dark Shadows. *Movies/Specials*: Ivanhoe, Oliver Twist, Dombey and Son, Jemima Shore, Night Train to Murder, The Bretts, Princess Daisy, The Lady and the Highwayman (Dangerous Love), Jack the Ripper, A Ghost in Monte Carlo, Sweet Danger.

ANTHONY, MICHELE
Executive. e. George Washington U.; USC, J.D. Currently exec. v.p., Sony Music Entertainment. Bd. member of the Rock and Roll Halle of Fame, Tock the Vote, Sloan Kettering Cancer Center.

ANTHONY, TONY
Actor, Producer, Writer. b. Clarksburg, WV, Oct. 16, 1939. e. Carnegie Mellon.
PICTURES: Force of Impulse, Pity Me Not, The Wounds of Hunger, A Stranger in Town, The Stranger Returns, A Stranger in Japan, Come Together, Blindman, Pete Pearl and the Pole, Let's Talk About Men, Get Mean, Treasure of the Four Crowns, Comin' at Ya, For Better or For Worse.

ANTON, SUSAN
Actress. b. Oak Glen, CA, Oct. 12, 1950. Concert & night club singer. Country album & single Killin' Time went top 10 on Country charts, received Gold Record in Japan. On B'way in Hurlyburly (debut, 1985), The Will Rogers Follies. Off-B'way in X-mas a Go-Go. 1992, hon. chmn. of Amer. Cancer Soc., Calif. Special Olympics, & hon. capt. U.S. Woman's Olympic Volleyball Team.
PICTURES: Goldengirl, Spring Fever, Cannonball Run II, Options (cameo), Making Mr. Right, Lena's Holiday.
TELEVISION: *Series*: Stop Susan Williams (Cliff Hangers), Presenting Susan Anton. *Movie*: The Great American Beauty Contest. *Guest*: Quantum Leap, Blossom, Murder She Wrote, Night Court, The Famous Teddy Z, Circus of the Stars.

ANTONIO, LOU
Actor, Writer, Producer, Director. b. Oklahoma City, OK, Jan. 23. e. U. of OK. Two Emmy Nominations for TV Movies.
THEATER: *Actor*: The Buffalo Skinner (Theatre World Award), The Girls of Summer, The Good Soup, The Garden of Sweets, Andorra, The Lady of the Camellias, The Ballad of the Sad Cafe, Ready When You Are, C.B. *Dir.*: Private Lives (w Taylor/Burton).
PICTURES: *Actor*: The Strange One, Splendor in the Grass, America America, Hawaii, Cool Hand Luke, The Phynx. *Also*: Mission Batangas (s.p.), Micki and Maude (exec. prod.).
TELEVISION: *Actor*: *Guest*: Picket Fences, Chicago Hope. *Series*: Snoop Sisters, Dog and Cat, Making It, Piece of Blue Sky, The Power and the Glory, Danny Thomas Hour, Partners in Crime, Sole Survivor, Where the Ladies Go, Star Trek. *Director*: *Mini-Series*: Rich Man, Poor Man (co-dir.), Breaking Up Is Hard to Do, The Star Maker. *Movies*: Lanigan's Rabbi, Someone I Touched, Something for Joey, The Girl in the Empty Grave, The Critical List, Silent Victory-The Kitty O'Neil Story, A Real American Hero, The Contender, We're Fighting Back, Something So Right, A Good Sport, Threesome, Rearview Mirror, Face to Face, The Outside Woman (also prod.), Dark Holiday (also exec. prod.), Between Friends, Mayflower Madam, One Terrific Guy, Pals, 13 at Dinner, This Gun for Hire, Lies Before Kisses, The Last Prostitute, The Rape of Dr. Willis, A Taste for Killing, Nightmare in the Daylight.

ANTONIONI, MICHELANGELO
Director, Writer. b. Ferrara, Italy, Sept. 29, 1913. e. Bologna U. Film critic on local newspaper, then script writer and asst. director. First films as director were short documentaries including: Gente del Po (1943-47), N.U., L'Amorosa Menzogna, Superstizione, Sette canne un vestito, followed by latter works La Villa dei Mostri, La Funivia del Faloria, Kumbha Mela, Roma, Noto, Mandorli, Vulcano, Stromboli, Carnevale. Received honorary Academy Award, 1995.
PICTURES: *Dir.-Writer*: Story of a Love Affair (feature debut as dir., 1950), The Vanquished, Lady Without Camelias (Camille Without Camelias), Love in the City (segment: When Love Fails), The Girl Friends, The Outcry, L'Avventura, The Night, Eclipse, The Red Desert, I Tre Volti/Three Faces of a Woman (dir. only; segment: Prefazione), Blow-Up (Acad. Award nom. for dir.), Zabriskie Point, Chung Kuo (documentary), The Passenger, The Oberwald Mystery, Identification of a Woman, The Crew, Beyond the Clouds (co-dir., co-s.p., with Wim Wenders).

ANTONOWSKY, MARVIN
Executive. b. New York, NY, Jan. 31, 1929. e. City Coll. of New York, B.A., M.B.A. Joined Kenyon and Eckhart in 1957 for which was media research dir.; named marketing v.p. With Norman, Craig, & Kummel as v.p., mktg. services. 1965, became v.p. in

11

chg. of media research and spot buying at J. Walter Thompson. In 1969 joined ABC-TV as v.p. in chg. research. Left to become v.p. in chg. of programming at NBC-TV. 1976, sr. v.p., Universal-TV. 1979, joined Columbia Pictures as pres., mktg. & research. Rejoined MCA/Universal Pictures as pres, mktg., Nov. 1983. Formed Marvin Antonowsky & Assoc. marketing consultancy firm, 1989. Rejoined Columbia Pictures in 1990 as exec. v.p. and asst. to chmn. 1993, joined Price Entertainment as exec. v.p.

ANWAR, GABRIELLE
Actress. b. Laleham, England, 1970.
PICTURES: Manifesto (debut, 1989), If Looks Could Kill, Wild Hearts Can't Be Broken, Scent of a Woman, For Love or Money, The Three Musketeers, Body Snatchers, Things to Do in Denver When You're Dead, Innocent Lies, The Grave.
TELEVISION: *Movies:* First Born, In Pursuit of Honor. *Specials:* The Storyteller, Summer's Lease, Dead-End for Delia (Fallen Angels).

APFEL, EDWIN R.
Writer, Executive. b. New York, NY, Jan. 2, 1934. e. Franklin and Marshall Coll., B.A., 1955. Mktg. exec.: Metro-Goldwyn-Mayer, Verve Records, Embassy Pictures. Freelance copywriter. 1990, writer, Edward R. Murrow: This Reporter, Amer. Masters (PBS). 1992, council member, WGA East.

APPLEGATE, CHRISTINA
Actress. b. Hollywood, CA, Nov. 25, 1972.
PICTURES: Jaws of Satan (debut, 1980), Streets, Don't Tell Mom the Babysitter's Dead, Across the Moon, Wild Bill, Nowhere.
TELEVISION: *Series:* Washingtoon, Heart of the City, Married... With Children. *Movies:* Grace Kelly, Dance 'til Dawn. *Guest:* Quincy M.E., Charles in Charge, The New Leave It to Beaver, Amazing Stories, 21 Jump Street.

APTED, MICHAEL
Director, Producer. b. Aylesbury, Eng., Feb. 10, 1941. e. Cambridge. Broke into show business at Granada TV in England in early 1960's as trainee, researcher and finally director. By 1965 was producer-director for local programs and current affairs; then staff drama dir. for TV series, plays and serials. In late 1960's left Granada to freelance.
PICTURES: 14 Up, Triple Echo, Stardust, 21 Up, The Squeeze, Agatha, Coal Miner's Daughter, Continental Divide, Gorky Park, P'Tang Yang, Kipperbang, Firstborn, Bring on the Night, 28 Up, Critical Condition, Gorillas in the Mist, Class Action, 35 Up, Thunderheart, Incident at Oglala, Bram Stoker's Dracula (exec. prod. only), Blink, Nell, Moving the Mountain, Extreme Measures.
TELEVISION: *Director:* Another Sunday and Sweet F.A., Follyfoot, Joy The Style of the Countess, The Reporters, Buggins' Ermine, Jackpoint, Kisses at 50, High Kampf, Poor Girl, Wednesday Love, The Collection, The Long Way Home (doc.), Stronger Than the Sun, My Life and Times, Crossroads, New York News (pilot). *Exec. Producer:* Criminal Justice, Age 7 in America, Intruders, Strapped.

ARAU, ALFONSO
Director, Actor. b. Mexico. e. Univ. of Mexico. Studied drama there and with Saki Sano in Mexico; UCLA film school; studied pantomime in Paris.
PICTURES: *Actor:* The Wild Bunch, El Topo, Used Cars, Romancing the Stone, Three Amigos, Walker, Posse. *Director:* The Barefoot Eagle, Clazonian Inspector, Mojado Power (Wetback Power), Chido One, Like Water for Chocolate (Mexico's Ariel Award), A Walk in the Clouds.
TELEVISION: *Series:* El Show de Arau.

ARCAND, DENYS
Director. b. Deschambault, Quebec, Canada, June 25, 1941. e. U. of Montreal, 1963. While still history student, co-prod. Seul ou avec D'Autres (1962). Joined National Film Board of Canada, where began making documentary shorts (Champlain, Les Montrealistes and La Route de l'ouest) forming a trilogy dealing with colonial Quebec. In 1970 socio-political doc. about Quebec textile workers, On Est au Coton, generated controversy resulting in the NFB banning film until 1976.
PICTURES: On Est au Coton (doc.), Un Maudite Galette (1st fiction feature, 1971). *Dir.-Writer:* Quebec: Duplessis & Apres... (doc.), Rejeanne Padovani, Gina, Le Crime d'Ovide Plouffe, The Decline of the American Empire, Night Zoo (actor only), Jesus of Montreal (Cannes Film Fest. jury prize, 1989), Leolo (actor only), Love and Human Remains.
TELEVISION: Duplessis (s.p., 1977 series), Empire Inc. (series, dir.).

ARCHER, ANNE
Actress. b. Los Angeles, CA. Daughter of actress Marjorie Lord and actor John Archer. Married Terry Jastrow, TV network sports producer-director and pres. Jack Nicklaus Prods.
THEATER: A Coupla White Chicks Sitting Around Talking (off-B'way, 1981), Les Liaisons Dangereuses (Williamstown Fest., 1988).

PICTURES: The Honkers (debut, 1972), Cancel My Reservation, The All-American Boy, Trackdown, Lifeguard, Paradise Alley, Good Guys Wear Black, Hero at Large, Raise the Titanic, Green Ice, Waltz Across Texas (also co-story), The Naked Face, Too Scared to Scream, The Check Is in the Mail, Fatal Attraction (Acad. Award nom.), Love at Large, Narrow Margin, Eminent Domain, Patriot Games, Body of Evidence, Family Prayers, Short Cuts, Clear and Present Danger, There Goes My Baby (narrator), Mojave Moon.
TELEVISION: *Series:* Bob and Carol and Ted and Alice, The Family Tree, Falcon Crest. *Movies:* The Blue Knight, The Mark of Zorro, The Log of the Black Pearl, A Matter of Wife...and Death, The Dark Side of Innocence, Harold Robbins' The Pirate, The Sky's No Limit, A Different Affair, A Leap of Faith, The Last of His Tribe, Nails, Jane's House, Because Mommy Works (also co-prod.), The Man in the Attic. *Mini-Series:* Seventh Avenue. *Special:* Leslie's Folly.

ARCHERD, ARMY
Columnist, TV commentator. r.n. Armand Archerd. b. New York, NY, Jan. 13, 1922. m. actress Selma Archerd. e. UCLA, grad. '41, U.S. Naval Academy Post Graduate Sch., 1943. Started as usher at Criterion Theatre, N.Y., while in high school. After grad. UCLA, worked at Paramount studios before entering Navy. Joined AP Hollywood bureau 1945, Herald-Express, Daily Variety as columnist, 1953. M.C. Hollywood premieres, Emmys and Academy Awards. President, founder Hollywood Press Club. Awards from Masquers, L.A. Press Club, Hollywood Foreign Press Club, and Newsman of the Year award from Publicists Guild, 1970; Movie Game. TV series: People's Choice, co-host. 1987 received Hollywood Women's Press Club Man of the Year Award.

ARDANT, FANNY
Actress. b. Monte Carlo, 1949. Majored in political science in college. Served a 5-year apprenticeship in the French theater acting in Polyeucte, Esther, The Mayor of Santiago, Electra and Tete d'Or. TV debut in Les Dames de la Cote.
PICTURES: Les Chiens (debut, 1979), Les uns et les Autres, The Woman Next Door, The Ins and Outs, Life Is a Novel, Confidentially Yours, Benevenuta, Desire, Swann in Love, Love Unto Death, Les Enrages, L'Ete Prochain, Family Business, Affabulazione, Melo, The Family, La Paltoquet, Three Sisters, Australia, Pleure pas My Love, Adventure of Catherine C., Afraid of the Dark, Rien Que des Mensonges, La Femme du Deserteur, Amok, Colonel Chabert, Beyond the Clouds, Ridicule.

ARGENTO, DARIO
Director, Writer. b. Rome, Italy, 1940. Son of prod. Salvatore Argento.
PICTURES: Today It's Me...Tomorrow It's You (co-s.p.), Cemetery Without Crosses (co-s.p.), Once Upon a Time in the West (co-s.p.), Commandos (co-s.p.), Zero Probability (co-s.p.), The Five Man Army (co-s.p.), One Night at Dinner (co-s.p.), Sex Revolution (s.p.), Legion of the Damned (co-s.p.), Seasons of Love (co-s.p.), Bird With the Crystal Plumage (dir., s.p.), Cat O'Nine Tails (dir., s.p., story), Four Flies on Grey Velvet (dir., s.p.), Five Days in Milan (dir., co-s.p.), Deep Red (dir., s.p.), Suspiria (dir., co-s.p., music), Dawn of the Dead (co-prod., music), Inferno (dir., s.p., story), Tenebrae (Unsane; dir., s.p., story), Creepers (dir., prod., s.p.), Demons (prod., co-s.p.), Demons 2: The Nightmare is Back (s.p., prod.), Opera (Terror at the Opera; dir., s.p.), The Church (prod., s.p., story), Two Evil Eyes (episode: The Black Cat; dir., prod., s.p.), Devil's Daughter (prod., s.p.), Innocent Blood (actor), Trauma (dir., prod., co-s.p.).
TELEVISION: *Series:* Door Into Darkness (It.).

ARKIN, ADAM
Actor. b. Brooklyn, NY, Aug. 19, 1956. Father is actor Alan Arkin. Made acting debut in short film prod. by father, People Soup.
THEATER: I Hate Hamlet (Theatre World Award), Four Dogs and a Bone.
PICTURES: Made for Each Other, Baby Blue Marine, Improper Channels (s.p.), Under the Rainbow, Chu Chu and the Philly Flash, Full Moon High, The Doctor.
TELEVISION: *Series:* Busting Loose, Teachers Only, Tough Cookies, A Year in the Life, Northern Exposure, Chicago Hope. *Mini-Series:* Pearl. *Specials:* Mark Twain's America: Tom Edison, The Fourth Wise Man. *Movies:* It Couldn't Happen to a Nicer Guy, All Together Now, In the Line of Duty: Hunt for Justice.

ARKIN, ALAN
Actor, Director. b. New York, NY, March 26, 1934. e. Los Angeles City Col., Los Angeles State Col., Bennington (VT) Col. m. actress-author Barbara Dana. Father of actor Adam Arkin. Was member of folk singing group The Tarriers; then one of the original members of Chicago's Second City improvisational group. Directed short films T.G.I.F., People Soup (Acad. Award nom.). Author: Tony's Hard Work Day, The Lemming Condition, Halfway Through the Door, The Clearing, Some Fine Grandpa.

THEATER: *Off-B'way:* Second City, Man Out Loud, From the Second City. *B'way:* Enter Laughing (Tony & Theatre World Awards, 1963), Luv. *Director:* Eh?, Little Murders, White House Murder Case (Obie Award), Joan of Lorraine, Rubbers and Yanks Three, The Sunshine Boys, The Sorrows of Stephen, Room Service.
PICTURES: Calypso Heat Wave (debut, 1957), The Russians Are Coming The Russians Are Coming (Golden Globe Award, Acad. Award nom.), Woman Times Seven, Wait Until Dark, Inspector Clouseau, The Heart Is a Lonely Hunter (NY Film Critics Award, Acad. Award nom.), Popi, The Monitors, Catch-22, Little Murders (also dir.), Deadhead Miles, Last of the Red Hot Lovers, Freebie and the Bean, Rafferty and the Gold Dust Twins, Hearts of the West (NY Film Critics Award), The 7 Per Cent Solution, Fire Sale (also dir.), The In-Laws (also exec. prod.), The Magician of Lublin, Simon, Improper Channels, Chu Chu and the Philly Flash, Full Moon High, The Last Unicorn (voice), The Return of Captain Invincible, Joshua Then and Now, Bad Medicine, Big Trouble, Coupe de Ville, Edward Scissorhands, Havana, The Rocketeer, Glengarry Glen Ross, Indian Summer, So I Married an Axe Murderer, North, The Jerky Boys, Steal Big Steal Little, Mother Night.
TELEVISION: *Series:* Harry. *Movies:* The Defection of Simas Kurdirka, The Other Side of Hell, A Deadly Business, Escape from Sobibor, Cooperstown, Taking the Heat, Doomsday Gun. *Specials:* The Love Song of Barney Kempinski, The Fourth Wise Man, A Matter of Principle, Fay (pilot; dir.), Twigs (dir.), The Emperor's New Clothes (Faerie Tale Theatre), The Visit (Trying Times; dir.), The Boss (Trying Times; dir.), Necessary Parties (also co-writer, co-prod.). *Guest:* East Side/West Side, St. Elsewhere.

ARKOFF, SAMUEL Z.
Producer, Executive. b. Fort Dodge, IA, June 12, 1918. e. U. of Colorado, U. of Iowa, Loyola U. Law Sch. Chairman & president of the Samuel Z. Arkoff Company (formed 1980) and Arkoff Int'l Pictures (formed 1981). Served in USAF as cryptographer WWII. Co-founder American Releasing, 1954, and American International Pictures, 1955. Pres. and chmn. of bd. AIP until 1979. 1963, named with partner James H. Nicholson Producers of the Year by Allied States Assoc. of MP Theatre Owners; 1964, Master Showmen of the Decade by the Theatre Owners of America; 1971, he and Nicholson named Pioneers of the Year by the Foundation of the MP Pioneers, Inc. Since appointment in 1973, has served as intl. v.p. of Variety Clubs Intl. V.p., Permanent Charities Committee. Member of the bd. of Trustees of Loyola Marymount U., L.A., in 1979.
PICTURES: *Exec. Producer or Producer:* Reform School Girl, Motorcycle Gang, Machine Gun Kelly, The Bonnie Parker Story, The Fall of the House of Usher, The Pit and the Pendulum, Tales of Terror, Master of The World, Premature Burial, Panic in the Year Zero, The Raven, Beach Party, Haunted Palace, Comedy of Terrors, Bikini Beach, Masque of the Red Death, Muscle Beach Party, Pajama Party Tomb of Ligeia, Wild Angels, Devil's Angels, The Trip, Three in the Attic, Wild in the Streets, The Oblong Box, Scream and Scream Again, Murders in the Rue Morgue, Cry of the Banshee, Bloody Mama, Wuthering Heights, The Abominable Dr. Phibes, Frogs, Blacula, Dillinger, Heavy Traffic, Hennessy, Cooley High, Food of the Gods, Futureworld, The Great Scout and Cathouse Thursday, The Land That Time Forgot, The People That Time Forgot, At the Earth's Core, Island of Dr. Moreau, Our Winning Season, The Amityville Horror, C.H.O.M.P.S., Dressed to Kill, How to Beat the High Cost of Living, The Final Terror, Up the Creek.

ARKUSH, ALLAN
Director. b. Jersey City, NJ, Apr. 30, 1948. e. Franklin & Marshall, NYU. Film Sch. With New World Pictures as film, music and trailer editor 1974-9. Co-directed Hollywood Boulevard and Death Sport and was 2nd unit dir. of Grand Theft Auto before directing on own. Dir. rock videos with Bette Midler and Mick Jagger, Elvis Costello, Christine McVie.
PICTURES: Hollywood Boulevard (co-dir., co-edit.), Deathsport (co-dir.), Rock 'n' Roll High School (also story), Heartbeeps, Get Crazy, Caddyshack II, Shake Rattle and Rock.
TELEVISION: *Series:* Fame, St. Elsewhere, L.A. Law, Moonlighting (Emmy nom.), Shannon's Deal (spv. prod.), Tattinger's, Twilight Zone, Mann & Machine, I'll Fly Away, Middle Ages, Johnny Bago, Central Park West (co-exec. prod.). *Pilots:* The Bronx Zoo, Capital News (prod.), Parenthood (co-exec. prod.), Body of Evidence, Moon Over Miami (exec. prod.). *Movies:* XXX & OOOs (co-exec. prod.), Young at Heart, Desert Breeze (co-exec. prod.).

ARLEDGE, ROONE
Executive. b. Forest Hills, NY, July 8, 1931. e. Columbia U. Entered industry with Dumont Network in 1952; joined U.S. Army, 1953, serving at Aberdeen Proving Ground in Maryland, where produced and directed radio programs. Joined NBC in 1954 where held various production positions. In 1960 went to ABC TV; 1964, named v.p. in chg. of ABC Sports. Created ABC's Wide World of Sports in April, 1961. Named pres. of ABC News in 1968; pres. of ABC News and Sports, 1977. Holds four George Foster Peabody Awards for sports reporting; 19 Emmy awards.

ARLING, ARTHUR E.
Cinematographer. b. Missouri, Sept. 2, 1906. e. N.Y. Inst. of Photography. Entered m.p. Fox studio 1927 as asst. cameraman, 2nd cameraman 1931; operative cameraman on Gone With the Wind which won the Academy Award for technicolor photography 1939. Lt. Comdr. U.S.N.R., WWII. Member: Amer. Soc. of Cinematographers.
PICTURES: The Yearling (Academy Award, 1946), Homestretch, Captain from Castile, Mother Was a Freshman, You're My Everything, Wabash Avenue, My Blue Heaven, Call Me Mister, Belles on Their Toes, The Glass Slipper, Three for the Show, Love Me or Leave Me, I'll Cry Tomorrow, Ransom, Great American Pastime, Tammy & the Bachelor, Pay the Devil, Story of Ruth, Pillow Talk, Lover Come Back, Notorious Landlady, Boys Night Out, My Six Loves, Ski Party, Once Before I Die.

ARMSTRONG, BESS
Actress. b. Baltimore, MD, Dec. 11, 1953. m. producer John Fiedler. e. Brown U.
PICTURES: The House of God (debut, 1979), The Four Seasons, Jekyll and Hyde—Together Again, High Road to China, Jaws 3-D, Nothing in Common, Second Sight, Mother Mother, The Skateboard Kid.
TELEVISION: *Series:* On Our Own, All is Forgiven, Married People, My So-Called Life. *Movies:* Getting Married, How to Pick Up Girls, Walking Through the Fire, 11th Victim, This Girl for Hire, Lace, Take Me Home Again, She Stood Alone: The Tailhook Scandal, Stolen Innocence. *Special:* Barefoot in the Park.

ARMSTRONG, GILLIAN
Director. b. Melbourne, Australia, Dec. 18, 1950. e. Swinburne Coll. Among 1st class in dirs. course at National Aust. Film & TV School, Sydney. Worked as art dir. on a number of films. Dir. numerous shorts (One Hundred a Day, The Singer and the Dancer) and documentaries (A Busy Kind of Bloke, Bingo Bridesmaids and Braces) before turning to features.
PICTURES: My Brilliant Career (Australian Film Inst. Award), Starstruck, Mrs. Soffel, Hard to Handle, High Tide, Fires Within, The Last Days of Chez Nous, Little Women.

ARMSTRONG, GORDON
Executive. b. East Orange, NJ, Nov. 26, 1937. e. Arizona State U., graduate studies at NYU. Joined 20th Century-Fox in 1970 as nat. pub. dir. In 1975 was appointed dir. of adv.-pub.-promo. for Dino De Laurentiis Corp. In 1978, became vice pres., worldwide marketing for the company; 1980, named v.p., adv.-pub.-prom., Universal Pictures; 1984, named exec. v.p., mktg. MCA Recreation. 1991, pres. mktg., Morgan Creek Prods. Pres., Entertainment Marketing Group, 1993. V.P., sales and mktg., ATTICA Cybernetics 1995. V.P., sales and mktg., Doubleclick Network 1996.

ARNALL, ELLIS GIBBS
Lawyer, executive. b. Newnan, GA, March 20, 1907. e. Mercer U., U. of the South, A.B. 1928, D.C.L. 1947; U. of Georgia LL.B. 1931; Atlanta Law Sch., LL.D. 1941; Piedmont Coll., LL.D 1943; Bryant Coll., LL.D. 1948. Georgia state rep. from Coweta County, 1936-38; asst. Attorney-General (GA) 1938-42; Attorney-General (GA) 1942-43; Governor of GA 1943-47; pres. Dixie Life Insurance Co.; pres., Columbus Natl Life Insurance Co.; sr. mem. law firm Arnall Golden & Gregory; pres. Georgia State Jr. Chamber of Commerce 1939. Author: The Shore Dimly Seen (1946), What The People Want (1948). Member U.S. Natl. Com. on UNESCO; member U.S. delegation to 4th annual conference UNESCO, Paris, 1949; SIMPP (pres. 1948, 1952); pres. Indep. Film Prod. Export Corp., 1953; bd. of dir., exec. com., U.S. Nat'l Comm. for UNESCO, 1964-65; AMPAS.

ARNAZ, JR., DESI
Actor, Singer. b. Los Angeles, CA, Jan. 19, 1953. e. Beverly Hills H.S. Son of Lucille Ball and Desi Arnaz. Sister is actress Lucie Arnaz. Gained fame as rock singer and musician with the Dino, Desi and Billy group. Video: A Day at the Zoo. Regional theatre includes Sunday in New York, Grease, Promises Promises, Alone Together, I Love My Wife, Is There Life After High School?, Love Letters, The Boys Next Door.
PICTURES: Red Sky at Morning (debut, 1971), Marco, Billy Two Hats, Joyride, A Wedding, House of the Long Shadows, The Mambo Kings.
TELEVISION: *Series:* Here's Lucy, Automan. *Movies:* Mr. & Mrs. Bo Jo Jones, Voyage of the Yes, She Lives, Having Babies, Flight to Holocaust, Black Market Baby, To Kill a Cop, The Courage and the Passion, How to Pick Up Girls, Crisis in Mid-Air, Gridlock, Advice to the Lovelorn, The Night the Bridge Fell Down. *Guest:* The Love Boat, Fantasy Island, Paul Reiser: Out on a Whim, Matlock.

ARNAZ, LUCIE
Actress. b. Los Angeles, CA, July 17, 1951. Daughter of Lucille Ball and Desi Arnaz. m. actor Laurence Luckinbill. Brother is actor Desi Arnaz Jr. B'way: They're Playing Our Song (Theatre World Award), Lost in Yonkers. National touring companies:

Whose Life is It Anyway?, Educating Rita, My One and Only, Social Security. Nightclubs: Lucie Arnaz-Latin Roots, Irving Berlin in Concert-In Sicily.
PICTURES: Billy Jack Goes to Washington, The Jazz Singer, Second Thoughts.
TELEVISION: Series: Here's Lucy, The Lucy Arnaz Show, Sons and Daughters. Pilot: One More Try. Movies: Who is the Black Dahlia, The Mating Season, The Washington Mistress, Who Gets the Friends? Special: Lucy & Desi: A Home Movie (host, co-exec. prod., co-dir.).

ARNESS, JAMES
Actor. r.n. James Aurness. b. Minneapolis, MN, May 26, 1923. e. Beloit Coll. Brother of actor Peter Graves. Served in U.S. Army; worked in advertising, real estate. Started in films in late 1940's appearing under his real name.
PICTURES: The Farmer's Daughter (debut 1947), Rose Are Red, The Man From Texas, Battleground, Sierra, Two Lost Worlds, Wyoming Mail, Wagon Master, Double Crossbones, Stars in My Crown (1st billing as James Arness), Cavalry Scout, Belle le Grand, Iron Man, The People Against O'Hara, The Girl in White, The Thing, Carbine Williams, Hellgate, Big Jim McLain, Horizons West, Lone Hand, Ride the Man Down, Island in the Sky, Veils of Bagdad, Hondo, Her Twelve Men, Them!, Many Rivers to Cross, Flame of the Islands, The Sea Chase, The First Travelling Saleslady, Gun the Man Down, Alias Jesse James (cameo).
TELEVISION: Series: Gunsmoke (20 years), How the West Was Won, McClain's Law. Movies: The Macahans, The Alamo: 13 Days to Glory, Gunsmoke: Return to Dodge, Red River, Gunsmoke: The Last Apache, Gunsmoke: To the Last Man, Gunsmoke: The Long Ride (also exec. prod.). Mini-Series: How the West Was Won.

ARNOLD, EDDY
Singer. b. Henderson, TN, May 15, 1918. Radio performer, Nashville, TN; recording star since 1946; records include That's How Much I Love You, Anytime, Bouquet of Roses (on the Country Music charts longer than any record in the history of country music), Make the World Go Away. Holds the record for most Country Records on the charts. Elected to Country Music Hall of Fame (1966); Entertainer of the Year (1967), Pioneer Award from Acad. of Country Music (1984), President's Award from Songwriter's Guild (1987).
TELEVISION: Series: Eddy Arnold Show (1952-3), Eddy Arnold Time, Eddy Arnold Show (1956), The Kraft Music Hall (1967-71). Hosted Music from the Land, Tonight Show, more than 20 specials.

ARNOW, TED J.
Executive. b. Brooklyn, NY. e. St. Johns U., Washington and Lee U. Served as dir. of recreation for 262nd General Hospital in Panama. Veteran of over 50 yrs. in amusement industry. Was v.p. for adv., pub., & promo. for Loew's Theatres. Member: Motion Picture Pioneers, Variety Clubs, Will Rogers Hospital; former pres. of AMPA (Assoc. M.P. Advertisers). Retired.

ARQUETTE, PATRICIA
Actress. b. Chicago, IL, Apr. 8, 1968. m. actor Nicolas Cage. Sister of actress Rosanna Arquette and actors Richmond, Alexis and David Arquette. Prof. debut in children's version of Story Theatre. Studied acting with Milton Katselis.
PICTURES: A Nightmare on Elm Street 3: Dream Warriors (debut, 1987), Pretty Smart, Time Out, Far North, Prayer of the Rollerboys, The Indian Runner, Ethan Frome, Trouble Bound, Inside Monkey Zetterland, True Romance, Holy Matrimony, Ed Wood, Beyond Rangoon, Infinity, Flirting With Disaster, The Secret Agent, Nightwatch.
TELEVISION: Movies: Daddy, Dillinger, Wildflower, Betrayed by Love. Special: The Girl With the Crazy Brother. Guest: The Edge (Indian Poker), thirtysomething, Tales From the Crypt.

ARQUETTE, ROSANNA
Actress. b. New York, NY, Aug. 10, 1959. Granddaughter of humorist Cliff Arquette (Charlie Weaver). Daughter of actor-producer Lewis Arquette. Sister of actress Patricia Arquette and actors Richmond, Alexis and David Arquette. Prof. debut in children's version of Story Theatre. Studied acting in San Francisco. Role in LA play led to bit parts on tv then regular role as Shirley Jones' teenage daughter on series Shirley (1979).
PICTURES: More American Graffiti (debut, 1979), Gorp, S.O.B., Baby It's You, Off the Wall, The Aviator, Desperately Seeking Susan, Silverado, After Hours, 8 Million Ways To Die, Nobody's Fool, Amazon Women on the Moon, The Big Blue, New York Stories (Life Lessons), Flight of the Intruder, Wendy Cracked a Walnut, The Linguini Incident, Fathers and Sons, Nowhere to Run, Pulp Fiction, Search and Destroy, Gone Fishin, Crash.
TELEVISION: Series: Shirley. Movies: Having Babies II, The Dark Secret of Harvest Home, Zuma Beach, The Ordeal of Patty Hearst, A Long Way Home, The Wall, The Executioner's Song, Johnny Belinda, One Cooks the Other Doesn't, The Parade, Survival Guide, Promised a Miracle, Sweet Revenge,

Separation, Son of the Morning Star, Black Rainbow, In the Deep Woods, The Wrong Man, Nowhere to Hide. Specials: Mom and Dad Can't Hear Me, A Family Tree (Trying Times).

ARTHUR, BEATRICE
Actress. r.n. Bernice Frankel. b. New York, NY, May 13, 1926. Franklin Inst. of Sciences & Art. Studied with Erwin Piscator at New School for Social Research; first stage role as Lysistrata; professional stage debut in Dog Beneath the Skin, 1947.
THEATER: Gas, Yerma, No Exit, Six Characters in Search of an Author, The Taming of the Shrew, (1948) The Owl and the Pussycat, The Threepenny Opera (1953 revival), The ShoeString Revue, What's the Rush?, Nature's Way, Ulysses in Nighttown, Gay Divorcee, Fiddler on the Roof, Mame (Tony Award, 1966), The Floating Light Bulb, Night of the 100 Stars.
PICTURES: That Kind of Woman, Lovers and Other Strangers, Mame, History of the World Part I.
TELEVISION: Debut: Once Upon a Time (1951), Numerous guest appearances. Series: Caesar's Hour, Maude (Emmy Award, 1977), Amanda's, Golden Girls (Emmy Award, 1988). Specials: All Star Gala at Ford's Theater (host), Jay Leno's Family Comedy Hour. Movie: My First Love.

ARTHUR, KAREN
Director. b. Omaha, NB, Aug. 24, 1941. 1950-68: ballet dancer, choreographer and musical comedy singer, dancer and actress. 1968-75: actress, film, TV and theatre. 1970-95, film, tv director.
PICTURES: Actress: A Guide for the Married Man, Winning. Director: Legacy (1975, Int'l Film Critics & Josef Von Sternberg Awards, 1975), The Mafu Cage, Lady Beware.
TELEVISION: Movies: Charleston, Victims for Victims: The Theresa Saldana Story (Christopher Award), A Bunny's Tale, The Rape of Richard Beck, Evil in Clear River (Christopher Award), Cracked Up, Bridge to Silence, Fall from Grace, Bump in the Night, Shadow of a Doubt, The Secret, The Disappearance of Christina, Against Their Will: Women in Prison. Mini-Series: Love and Betrayal: The Mia Farrow Story, Crossings, Return to Eden, The Jacksons: An American Dream, Dead by Sunset. Pilots: Tin Man, Blue Bayou. Episodes: Rich Man Poor Man Book II, Emerald Point, Boone, Two Marriages, Hart to Hart, Remington Steele, Cagney & Lacey (Emmy Award, 1985).

ARTZ, BOB
Theatre executive. b. Spokane, WA, Aug 21, 1946. e., B.T.A. Pasadena Playhouse College of Theatre Arts. Began in 1968 as doorman; then asst. mgr. to mgr. with National General Theatre Corporation. Joined Plitt Theatres in 1978 as dist. mgr. and ad/pub. director, West Coast. Joined General Cinema Theatres in 1986 as reg. marketing dir.; Western region. Became dir., film marketing in 1993. National dir., Entertainment Marketing & Operations in 1996. Member of Variety Club; Life Member: Pasadena Playhouse Alumni & Assoc.

ASH, RENE
Producer. b. Brussels, Belgium, March 14, 1939; e. U. of Omaha. Member of the Publicists Guild since 1968; Eastern v.p. of Pub Guild 1973-1981; Author of The Film Editor in Motion Pictures & Television. Employed with I.A.T.S.E. 1968-1979, prior to which was assoc. editor, Greater Amusements; various articles published in foreign film magazines; editor-in-chief, Backstage 1979-80; pres., Cinereal Pictures, 1984-85; co-pres., Eagle Films Corp., 1985-94; pres. Rea Film Prods.

ASHER, JANE
Actress. b. London, England, April 5, 1946.
PICTURES: Mandy (Crash of Silence; debut, 1952), Third Party Risk, Dance Little Lady, Adventure in the Hopfields, The Quatermass Experiment (The Creeping Unknown), Charley Moon, Greengage Summer (Loss of Innocence), The Girl in the Headlines (The Model Murder Case), The Masque of the Red Death, Alfie, The Winter's Tale, Deep End, The Buttercup Chain, Henry VIII and His Six Wives (from the BBC series the Six Wives of Henry VIII), Runners, Success is the Best Revenge, Dream Child, Paris By Night, Closing Numbers.
TELEVISION: Movies/Specials: Brideshead Revisited, Voyage 'Round My Father, East Lynne, The Mistress, Wish Me Luck, Tonight at 8:30, The Volunteer.

ASHLEY, ELIZABETH
Actress. b. Ocala, FL, Aug. 30, 1939. e. Studied ballet LA State U., 1957-58; grad. Neighborhood Playhouse, 1961. Author: Postcards From the Road.
THEATER: Take Her She's Mine (1962 Tony & Theatre World Awards), The Highest Tree, Barefoot in the Park, Ring 'Round the Bathtub, The Skin of Our Teeth, Legend, Cat on a Hot Tin Roof (B'way revival), Caesar and Cleopatra, Agnes of God, The Milk Train Doesn't Stop Here Anymore, When She Danced.
PICTURES: The Carpetbaggers (debut, 1964), Ship of Fools, The Third Day, The Marriage of a Young Stockbroker, Paperback Hero, Golden Needles, Rancho DeLuxe, 92 in the Shade, The Great Scout and Cathouse Thursday, Coma, Windows, Paternity, Split Image, Dragnet, Vampire's Kiss, Dangerous Curves, Lost Memories.

TELEVISION: *Series*: Evening Shade. *Movies*: Harpy, The Face of Fear, When Michael Calls, Second Chance, The Heist, Your Money or Your Wife, The Magician, One of My Wives is Missing, The War Between the Tates, A Fire in the Sky, Svengali, He's Fired She's Hired, Stagecoach, Warm Hearts Cold Feet, The Two Mrs. Grenvilles, Blue Bayou, Reason for Living: The Jill Ireland Story, Love and Curses... and All That Jazz, In the Best Interest of the Children. *Pilot*: Tom and Joann. *Guest*: Miami Vice, Hunter, Murder She Wrote, B.L. Stryker.

ASHLEY, JOHN
Actor, Producer. r.n. John Atchley. b. Kansas City, MO, Dec. 25, 1934. e. Oklahoma State U., B.A., 1956. Career started in Tulsa Little Theatre, 1956.
PICTURES: Dragstrip Girl (debut, 1957), Motorcycle Gang, Suicide Battalion, Beach Party, How to Stuff a Wild Bikini.
TELEVISION: *Series*: Straightaway. *Guest*: Men of Annapolis, Sheriff of Cochise, Frontier Doctor, Matinee Theatre, Jefferson Drum. *Movie*: Something is Out There (co-exec. prod.). *Series Prod*: The A-Team, Werewolf, Hardball, Raven, Walker: Texas Ranger.

ASHTON, JOHN
Actor. b. Springfield, MA, Feb. 22, 1948. e. USC (BA in theatre).
THEATER: The Last Meeting of the Knights of the White Magnolia (L.A. Drama Critics Circle Award), True West (Drama-Logue Award), A Flea in Her Ear (L.A. Drama Critics Circle Award).
PICTURES: Oh God!, Breaking Away, Borderline, Honky Tonk Freeway, Adventures of Buckaroo Banzai, Beverly Hills Cop, The Last Resort, King Kong Lives, Some Kind of Wonderful, Beverly Hills Cop II, She's Having a Baby, Midnight Run, I Want to Go Home, Curly Sue, Little Big League, Trapped in Paradise, The Shooter.
TELEVISION: *Series*: Dallas, Breaking Away, Hardball. *Guest*: M*A*S*H*, Police Squad!, The Twilight Zone. *Movies*: Elvis and the Beauty Queen, A Death in California, The Deliberate Stranger, I Know My First Name is Steven, Dirty Work, Stephen King's The Tommyknockers. *Mini-Series*: The Rhinemann Exchange, Love Lies and Murder.

ASNER, EDWARD
Actor. b. Kansas City, MO, Nov. 15, 1929. e. U. of Chicago, where affiliated with campus acting group. Served two years with U.S. Army in France. Returned to Chicago to join Playwright's Theatre Club. Moved to N.Y. NY Shakespeare Festival (1960) and American Shakespeare Festival (1961). In 1961 moved to Hollywood to become active in films and TV. National pres. Screen Actors Guild (1981-85), Prod. TV & feature projects through his company, Quince. Winner of numerous humanitarian awards.
THEATER: *B'way debut*: Face of a Hero, Born Yesterday (1989). *Off-B'way*: Ivanov, Threepenny Opera, Legend of Lovers, The Tempest, Venice Preserved.
PICTURES: Kid Gallahad (debut, 1962), The Slender Thread, The Satan Bug, The Venetian Affair, El Dorado, Gunn, Change of Habit, Halls of Anger, They Call Me Mister Tibbs, The Todd Killings, Skin Game, Gus, Fort Apache-The Bronx, O'Hara's Wife, Daniel, Pinocchio and the Emperor of the Night (voice), Moon Over Parador (cameo), JFK, Happily Ever After (voice), Cat's Don't Dance (voice).
TELEVISION: *Series*: Slattery's People, The Mary Tyler Moore Show (3 Emmy Awards: 1971, 1972, 1975), Lou Grant (2 Emmy Awards: 1978, 1980), Off the Rack, The Bronx Zoo, The Trials of Rosie O'Neill, Fish Police (voice), Hearts Afire, Thunder Alley. *Movies*: The Doomsday Flight, Daughter of the Mind, The House on Greenapple Road, The Old Man Who Cried Wolf, The Last Child, They Call It Murder, Haunts of the Very Rich, The Police Story, The Girl Most Likely To..., The Imposter, Death Scream, Hey I'm Alive, Life and Assassination of the Kingfish, The Gathering, The Family Man, A Small Killing, Anatomy of an Illness, Vital Signs, Kate's Secret, The Christmas Star, A Friendship in Vienna, Not a Penny More Not a Penny Less, Good Cops Bad Cops, Switched at Birth, Silent Motive, Yes Virginia There Is a Santa Claus, Cruel Doubt, Gypsy, Heads. *Mini-Series*: Rich Man Poor Man (Emmy Award, 1976), Roots (Emmy Award, 1977), Tender Is the Night.

ASPEL, MICHAEL
Radio/TV Presenter. b. London, England, Jan. 12, 1933. Entered industry 1954. Early career: BBC Radio as actor/presenter. BBC TV as announcer/newsreader. Presentations incl: Miss World, Crackerjack, Give Us A Clue, Ask Aspel, Family Favourites, Child's Play, ITV Telethon 1988, 1990 & 1992, Aspel and Company, This Is Your Life; BAFTA Awards, Strange ... But True? Awarded OBE in 1993.

ASSANTE, ARMAND
Actor. b. New York, NY, Oct. 4, 1949. e. American Acad. of Dramatic Arts. Appeared with regional theatre groups incl. Arena Stage (D.C.), Long Wharf (New Haven), and Actor's Theatre of Louisville.

THEATER: *B'way*: Boccaccio, Comedians, Romeo and Juliet, Kingdoms. *Off-B'way*: Why I Went Crazy, Rubbers, The Beauty Part, Lake of the Woods, Yankees 3 Detroit 0.
PICTURES: Paradise Alley, Prophecy, Little Darlings, Private Benjamin, Love and Money, I the Jury, Unfaithfully Yours, Belizaire the Cajun, The Penitent, Animal Behavior, Q & A, Eternity, The Marrying Man, The Mambo Kings, 1492: Conquest of Paradise, Hoffa, Fatal Instinct, Trial by Jury, Judge Dredd, Striptease.
TELEVISION: *Movies*: Human Feelings, Lady of the House, The Pirate, Sophia Loren-Her Own Story, Rage of Angels, Why Me?, A Deadly Business, Stranger in My Bed, Hands of a Stranger, Jack the Ripper, Passion and Paradise, Fever, Blind Justice, Kidnapped, Gotti. *Mini-Series*: Napoleon and Josephine: A Love Story, Evergreen. *Series*: The Doctors (1975).

ASSEYEV, TAMARA
Producer. e. Marymont College; UCLA (MA, theatre arts). Began career as asst. to Roger Corman, working on 8 films with him. In 1967 started to produce films independently. Then co-produced films with Alex Rose, starting with Drive-In. In 1966 at 24, became youngest member of Producers Guild of Amer. Member: Costume Council, LA City Museum; founding member LA Museum of Contemporary Art.
PICTURES: The Wild Racers, Paddy, The Arousers, TheHistory of Atlantic Records, Co-produced with Ms. Rose:Drive-In, I Wanna Hold Your Hand, Big Wednesday, Norma Rae.
TELEVISION: *Movies (exec. prod.)*: Penalty Phase, After the Promise, A Shadow on the Sun (also actress), The Secret Life of Kathy McCormick, The Hijacking of the Achille Lauro, Murder By Moonlight.

ASTIN, JOHN
Actor. b. Baltimore, MD, March 30, 1930. e. Washington and Jefferson Coll., Washington Drama Sch., Johns Hopkins U., grad. B.A., U. of Minnesota Graduate School. Father of actors Sean and Mackenzie Astin. First prof. job., Off-B'way, Threepenny Opera; B'way debut, Major Barbara; dir., co-prod., A Sleep of Prisoners, Phoenix Theatre; during 1955-59, did voices in cartoons, commercials. Prod. & dir. short subject Prelude.
THEATER: The Cave Dwellers, Ulysses in Nighttown, Tall Story, Lend Me a Tenor, H.M.S. Pinafore.
PICTURES: The Pusher (debut, 1958), West Side Story, That Touch of Mink, Move Over Darling, The Wheeler Dealers, The Spirit is Willing, Candy, Viva Max!, Bunny O'Hare, Get to Know Your Rabbit, Every Little Crook and Nanny, The Brothers O'Toole, Freaky Friday, National Lampoon's European Vacation, Body Slam, Teen Wolf Too, Return of the Killer Tomatoes, Night Life, Gremlins 2, Killer Tomatoes Eat France, Stepmonster, The Silence of the Hams, Frighteners, Harrison Bergeron.
TELEVISION: *Series*: I'm Dickens... He's Fenster, The Addams Family, The Pruitts of Southampton, Operation Petticoat, Mary, The Addams Family (voice for animated series), The Adventures of Brisco County Jr. *Guest*: Batman, The Flying Nun, Bonanza, Odd Couple, Night Gallery, Partridge Family, Police Woman, Love Boat, Night Court. Specials: Harry Anderson's Sideshow, Halloween With the Addams Family. *Movies*: Two on a Bench, Evil Roy Slade, Skyway to Death, Only with Married Men, The Dream Makers, Operation Petticoat (also dir.), Rossetti and Ryan: Men Who Love Women (dir. only), Huck and the King of Hearts. *Pilots*: Phillip and Barbara, Ethel Is an Elephant.

ASTIN, SEAN
Actor. b. Santa Monica, Feb. 25, 1971. parents are actors John Astin and Patty Duke. Brother is actor Mackenzie Astin. First acting job at 7 opposite mother in Afterschool Special Please Don't Hit Me Mom. Directed short films On My Honor, Kangaroo Court (Acad. Award nom.).
THEATER: Lone Star (L.A.).
PICTURES: The Goonies (debut, 1985), White Water Summer, Like Father Like Son, Staying Together, The War of the Roses, Memphis Belle, The Willies, Toy Soldiers, Encino Man, Where the Day Takes You, Rudy, Safe Passage, The Low Life.
TELEVISION: *Movies*: The Rules of Marriage, The Brat Patrol. *Pilot*: Just Our Luck.

ATHERTON, WILLIAM
Actor. b. New Haven, CT, June 30, 1947. While in high school became youngest member of Long Wharf Theatre Co. Given scholarship to Pasadena Playhouse; then switched to Carnegie Tech Sch. of Drama in 1965. In college years toured with USO prods in Europe and in stock and industrial shows. Came to NY where first prof. job was in nat'l co. of Little Murders.
THEATER: The House of Blue Leaves, The Basic Training of Pavlo Hummel, The Sign in Sidney Brustein's Window, Suggs (Theatre World Award, Outer Circle Critics Award, Drama Desk Award), Rich and Famous, Passing Game, Happy New Year, The American Clock, Three Acts of Recognition, The Caine Mutiny Court-Martial, Child's Play, Loco Motives.
PICTURES: The New Centurions (debut, 1972), Class of '44, The Sugarland Express, The Day of the Locust, The Hindenburg, Looking for Mr. Goodbar, Ghostbusters, Real Genius, No Mercy, Frank and Jesse, Die Hard, Die Hard 2, Grim Prairie Tales, Oscar, The Pelican Brief, Bio-Dome.

TELEVISION: *Mini-Series*: Centennial. *Movies*: Tomorrow's Child, Malibu, Intrigue, Buried Alive, Diagnosis of Murder, Chrome Soldiers, Robin Cook's Virus, Broken Trust. *Guest*: The Equalizer, Twilight Zone, Murder She Wrote, Tales From the Crypt, *Special*: The House of Mirth.

ATKINS, CHRISTOPHER
Actor. b. Rye, NY, Feb. 21, 1961. e. Dennison U., Ohio. Early modeling jobs before being hired for theatrical film debut in The Blue Lagoon (1980).
PICTURES: The Blue Lagoon, The Pirate Movie, A Night in Heaven, Beaks, Mortuary Academy, Listen to Me, Shakma, King's Ransom, Dracula Rising, Die Watching, Exchange Lifeguards, A Bullet Down Under, Trigger Fast, It's My Party.
TELEVISION: *Movies*: Child Bride of Short Creek, Secret Weapons, Fatal Charm. *Series*: Dallas. *Guest*: The Black Stallion. *Also*: The Black Rose, Miami Killer, The Floating Outfit, Deadman's Island, Angel Flight Down.

ATKINSON, ROWAN
Actor, Writer. b. England, Jan. 6, 1955. e. Newcastle U., Oxford.
THEATER: Rowan Atkinson in Revue (also writer), Not in Front of an Audience, The Nerd, Rowan Atkinson at the Atkinson (also writer; NY), Mime Gala, The Sneeze.
PICTURES: The Secret Policeman's Ball (also co-s.p.), The Secret Policeman's Other Ball, Never Say Never Again, The Tall Guy, The Witches, Hot Shots Part Deux, Four Weddings and a Funeral, The Lion King (voice).
TELEVISION: *Series*: Not the Nine O'Clock News (also writer; BAFTA Award for acting), Blackadder. *Specials*: Just for Laughs II, Live from London, Blackadder II, Blackadder the Third, Blackadder Goes Forth, Blackadder IV, Blackadder's Christmas Carol, The Appointments of Dennis Jennings, Mr. Bean (also writer), Mr. Bean Rides Again, The Thin Blue Line.

ATTENBOROUGH, DAVID
Broadcaster. b. London, England, May 8, 1926; e. Wyggeston Sch., Leicester; Clare Coll., Cambridge. Early career, editor in educational publishing house, ent. BBC-TC Sept. 1952. Prod. Zoo Quest series, Travellers Tales, Adventure and other prog., travel, Eastward with Attenborough, The Tribal Eye, Life on Earth, The Living Planet, The First Eden, The Trials of Life. Controller BBC-2, 1965-68; Dir. of Prog. BBC-TV, 1969-72.

ATTENBOROUGH, BARON RICHARD (SAMUEL)
1993, Life Peer of Richmond Upon Thames; Kt 1976; CBE 1967. Actor, Producer, Director. b. Cambridge, England, Aug. 29, 1923. m. 1945 Sheila Beryl Grant Sim. e. Wyggeston Grammar Sch., Leicester. Leverhulme Scholarship to Royal Acad. of Dramatic Art, 1941 (Bancroft Medal). First stage appearance in Ah Wilderness (Palmers Green, 1941). West End debut in Awake and Sing (1942), then The Little Foxes, Brighton Rock. Joined RAF, 1943; seconded to RAF Film Unit, and appeared in training film Journey Together, 1945; demobilized, 1946. Returned to stage, 1949, in The Way Back (Home of the Brave), To Dorothy a Son, Sweet Madness, The Mousetrap (original cast: 1952-54), Double Image, The Rape of the Belt. 1959 formed Beaver Films with Bryan Forbes; 1960 formed Allied Film Makers.
PICTURES: *Actor*: In Which We Serve (debut, 1942), Schweik's New Adventures, The Hundred Pound Window, Journey Together, A Matter of Life and Death (Stairway to Heaven), School for Secrets (Secret Flight), The Man Within (The Smugglers), Dancing With Crime, Brighton Rock (Young Scarface), London Belongs to Me (Dulcimer Street), The Guinea Pig, The Lost People, Boys in Brown, Morning Departure (Operation Disaster), Hell Is Sold Out, The Magic Box, Gift Horse (Glory at Sea), Father's Doing Fine, Eight O'Clock Walk, The Ship That Died of Shame, Private's Progress, The Baby and the Battleship, Brothers in Law, The Scamp, Dunkirk, The Man Upstairs, Sea of Sand (Desert Patrol), Danger Within (Breakout), I'm All Right Jack, Jet Storm, SOS Pacific, The Angry Silence (also co-prod.), The League of Gentlemen, Only Two Can Play, All Night Long, The Dock Brief (Trial & Error), The Great Escape, Seance on a Wet Afternoon (also prod.; San Sebastian Film Fest. & Brit. Acad. Awards for Best Actor), The Third Secret, Guns at Batasi (Brit. Acad. Award), The Flight of the Phoenix, The Sand Pebbles (Golden Globe Award), Dr. Dolittle (Golden Globe Award), The Bliss of Mrs Blossom, Only When I Larf, The Magic Christian, David Copperfield (TV in U.S.), The Last Grenade, A Severed Head, Loot, 10 Rillington Place, Ten Little Indians (And Then There Were None), Rosebud, Brannigan, Conduct Unbecoming, The Chess Players, The Human Factor, Jurassic Park, Miracle on 34th Street. *Producer*: Whistle Down the Wind, The L-Shaped Room. *Director*: Oh! What a Lovely War (also prod.; 16 Intl. Awards incl. Golden Globe and BAFTA UN Award), Young Winston (Golden Globe), A Bridge Too Far (Evening News Best Drama Award, 1977), Magic, Gandhi (also prod.; 8 Oscars, 5 BAFTA Awards, 5 Golden Globes, DGA Award, 1982), A Chorus Line, Cry Freedom (also prod.; Berlinale Kamera, 1987; BFI Award for Tech. Achievement), Chaplin (also prod.), Shadowlands (also prod.; BAFTA Award for Best British Film of 1993), In Love and War.

AUBERJONOIS, RENE
Actor. b. New York, NY, June 1, 1940. e. attended Carnegie Mellon U.
THEATER: *Includes*: Dark of the Moon, Beyond the Fringe, Tartuffe, King Lear, Fire, Julius Caesar, Charley's Aunt, Coco (Tony Award, 1970), Tricks, The Ruling Class, Twelfth Night, The Good Doctor (Tony nom.), Break a Leg, The New York Idea, Every Good Boy Deserves Favor; Richard III, The Misanthrope, Flea in Her Ear, Big River (Tony nom.), Metamorphosis, City of Angels (Tony nom.).
PICTURES: Lilith (debut, 1964), Petulia, M*A*S*H*, Brewster McCloud, McCabe and Mrs. Miller, Pete 'n Tillie, Images, Hindenberg, The Big Bus, King Kong, Eyes of Laura Mars, Where the Buffalo Roam, The Last Unicorn (voice), 3:15, Walker, Police Academy 5: Assignment Miami Beach, My Best Friend is a Vampire, The Little Mermaid (voice), The Feud, Star Trek VI: The Undiscovered Country (unbilled), The Player, Little Nemo (voice), The Ballad of Little Jo.
TELEVISION: *Series*: Benson (Emmy nom.), Star Trek: Deep Space Nine. *Movies*: The Birdmen, Shirts/Skins, Panache, Dark Secret of Harvest Home, Wild Wild West Revisited, More Wild Wild West, Smoky Mountain Christmas, The Christmas Star, Gore Vidal's Billy the Kid, Longarm, A Connecticut Yankee in King Arthur's Court, Absolute Strangers, Ned Blessing: The True Story of My Life, Wild Card. *Mini-Series*: The Rhineman Exchange. *Specials*: Faerie Tale Theatre (The Frog Prince, Sleeping Beauty), King Lear, Legend of Sleepy Hollow (Emmy nom.), Fort Necessity, Incident at Vichy, The Booth, The Cask of Amontillado, Ashenden (BBC), The Lost Language of Cranes (BBC). *Episode Director*: Marble Head Manor, Star Trek: Deep Space Nine.

AUDRAN, STEPHANE
Actress. b. Versailles, France, Nov. 8, 1938. Former wife of French star Jean-Louis Trintignant and director Claude Chabrol.
PICTURES: Les Cousins (debut under direction of Chabrol 1959), Les Bonnes Femmes, Bluebeard, The Third Lover, Six in Paris, The Champagne Murders, Les Biches, La Femme Infidele, The Beast Must Die, The Lady in the Car, Le Boucher, Without Apparent Motive, Dead Pigeon on Beethoven Street, La Rupture, Just Before Nightfall, The Discreet Charm of the Bourgeoisie, Blood Wedding, The Devil's Advocate, Le Cri de Couer, Vincent Francois Paul and the Others, The Black Bird (U.S. film debut), Ten Little Indians, The Silver Bears, Eagle's Wing, The Big Red One, Coup de Torchon (Clean Slate), La Cage ux Folles III: The Wedding, Cop au Vin, Babette's Feast, Seasons of Pleasure, Faceless, Body-To-Body, Sons, Manika: The Girl Who Lived Twice, Quiet Days in Clichy, Mass in C Minor, Betty, Poulet au Vinaigre, Au Petit Marguery.
TELEVISION: Mistral's Daughter, The Blood of Others, The Sun Also Rises, Poor Little Rich Girl: The Barbara Hutton Story, Champagne Charlie.

AUERBACH, NORBERT T.
Executive. b. Vienna, 1923. Educated in U.S. and served with U.S. Army Intelligence in Europe during WWII. Joined m.p. business in 1946 after grad. UCLA. (business admin.). First asst. dir. at Service Studios in CA. Moved to N.Y. to join domestic sales dept. of Film Classics. Joined Columbia Pictures in foreign dept. In 1950 assigned to Paris office, where remained for over decade, except for 18 mos. in Portugal as mgr. Returned to Paris in 1953 and filled number of exec. sls. positions for Columbia, ultimately rising to continental mgr. 1961, left Columbia to produce films in France. Resumed career in dist. as continental mgr. at Paris office of United Artists. 1966 returned to prod. to make The Thief of Paris. 1967, joined Seven Arts Prods. heading theatrical and TV sls. operations in Paris. When Seven Arts acquired Warner Bros., he became continental sls. mgr. for Warners in Paris. 1968, set up European prod. and dist. org. for CBS Cinema Center Films, operating from London. 1972, moved to L.A. as v.p., foreign mgr. for CCF. Returned to London in 1973 to be consultant in prod. and dist. Rejoined UA in 1977 as sls. mgr. for Europe and the Middle East. Named sr. v.p. & foreign mgr. in 1978. Named pres. & COO, Jan. 1981; pres., CEO, Feb. 1981. Co-pres., United Int'l Pictures, London, until 1982. In 1983, formed packaging and financing co., Eliktra, Inc. 1982, acting pres. and chief exec. officer of Almi Distribution Corp. Now Almi consultant, Exec. v.p. American Screen Co.

AUGUST, BILLE
Director. b. Denmark, 1948. e. trained in advertising photography, Danish Film School, grad. 1971, cinematography. As cinematographer shot: Miesta ei voi raiskata (Men Can't Be Raped), Karleken, The Grass is Singing. Became dir. 1978 with short Kim G. and dramas for Danish TV.
PICTURES: Honning Maane/In My Life (also sp.), Zappa (also s.p.), Twist and Shout (also s.p.), Pelle the Conquerer (also s.p.), The Best Intentions (Cannes Film Festival Palm d'Or Award, 1992), The House of the Spirits.

AUMONT, JEAN-PIERRE
Actor. b. Paris, France, Jan. 5, 1911. e. Conservatoire of Drama. Roles French stage and films. In 1943 enlisted in Free French Army. Film debut, Jean de la Lune, 1932.

THEATER: *U.S.:* Tovarich, Incident at Vichy, Hostile Witness, Carnival, Camino Real, Murderous Angels, Gigi, A Talent for Murder.
PICTURES: Hotel du Nord, Assignment in Brittany, The Cross of Lorraine, Heartbeat, Song of Scheherazade, Siren of Atlantis, Affairs of a Rogue, Wicked City, Lili, Life Begins Tomorrow, Gay Adventure, Charge of the Lancers, Hilda Crane, The Seventh Sin, John Paul Jones, The Enemy General, The Devil at 4 O'Clock, Carnival of Crime, Five Miles to Midnight, Cauldron of Blood, Castle Keep, Day for Night, Turn the Other Cheek, The Happy Hooker, Mahogany, Catherine & Co., Entire Days Among the Trees, Cat and Mouse, Blackout, Two Solitudes, Something Short of Paradise, Nana, Sweet Country, The Free Frenchman, Senso, A Star for Two, Becoming Colette, Giorgino, Jefferson in Paris.
TELEVISION: Sins, Windmills of the Gods, A Tale of Two Cities, Young Indiana Jones.

AURELIUS, GEORGE M.
Executive. b. Grasston, MN, Sept. 16, 1911. e. U. of Minnesota. Ent. m.p. ind. 1927 as usher Finkelstein & Ruben, St. Paul; asst. mgr. 1929-30; to Warner Theatres, New York 1931; mgr. Moss' B'way; Minnesota Amusement Co. 1932-41; city mgr. Publix-Rickards-Nace. Paramount-Nace Theatres, Tucson, Ariz. 1941-46; v.p. ABC Theatres. of Arizona, Inc. 1949-67; pres. ABC North Central Theatres, Inc. 1967-72; v.p., ABC Intermountain Theatres, Inc., v.p. ABC Theatres of California, Inc. 1972-1974; Mgmt. Consulting and ShoWest Convention & Trade Show since 1975, named exec. dir., 1979. Retired 1985.

AUSTIN, RAY
Baron Devere-Austin of Delvin, Lord of Bradwell. Producer, Director, Writer. b. London, England, Dec. 5, 1932. Has written, produced and directed many TV series, specials and movies. Lecturer, film & tv techniques, etc., 1978-93. Lecturer U. of VA.
PICTURES: Virgin Witches, House of the Living Dead, Fun & Games (One Woman And A 1,000 Men).
TELEVISION: *Director of Series:* Avengers, The Champions, Department S, Randall & Hopkirk, Ugliest Girl in Town, Journey into the Unknown, Magnum P.I., Simon and Simon, House Calls, Kings Crossing, Fall Guy, Lime Street (pilot), Spencer for Hire, Haven Help Us, JAG. *Writer:* Department S (also prod.). *Producer /Director:* The Perfumed Garden. *Director:* It's the Only Way to Go, Fun and Games, Space 1999, New Avengers, Hawaii Five-O, Sword of Justice, Webb, Barnaby Jones, Hardy Boys, Wonder Woman, Salvage, B.J. and the Bear, Hart to Hart, The Yeagers, Man Called Sloane, From Here to Eternity, Bad Cats, Westworld, Tales of the Gold Monkey (2-hr. pilot), The Return of the Man from U.N.C.L.E. *Director/Writer:* Randall & Hopkirk, Black Beauty, Zany Adventures of Robin Hood, The Master, Hart to Hart (series), V, Air Wolf, Lime Street (pilot and episodes), Spenser for Hire (several episodes), Magnum P.I. (season premiere 2-hr. episode); Return of the Six Million Dollar Man (pilot); Our House (episodes), Dirty Dozen, Alfred Hitchcock Presents, A Fine Romance, Zorro, Boys of Twilight, Crossroads, Highlander, High Tide, Heaven Help Us.

AUTANT-LARA, CLAUDE
Director. Began career as scenic designer for French films in early 1920s; then asst. dir. to Rene Clair. First solo venture experimental film, 1923; in Hollywood, 1930-32. dir. Parlor, Bedroom and Bath, Incomplete Athlete.
PICTURES: Devil in the Flesh, Seven Deadly Sins (segment), Red Inn, Oh Amelia, Game of Love, Ciboulette, Red and the Black.

AUTEUIL, DANIEL
Actor. b. Algeria, Jan. 24, 1950. Parents were lyric opera singers in roving troupe. Lived in Avignon. Performed in Amer. prod. in Paris of Godspell. Then did musical comedy for 2 years. Provided voice of baby for French print of U.S. film Look Who's Talking.
PICTURES: L'Aggression/Sombres Vacanes, Attention Les Yeaux, La Nuit de Saint-Germain des Pres, Monsieuer Papa, L'Amour Viole (Rape of Love), Les Heroes n'ont pas Froid aux Oreilles, A Nous Deux, Bete Mais Discipline, Les Sous-Doues, La Banquiere, Clara et les Chic Types, Men Prefer Fat Girls, Pour 100 Briques t'as Plus Rien Maintentant, Que les Gros Salaires Levent le Doigt!!!, L'Indic, P'tit Con, The Beast, L'Arbalete, Palace, L'Amour en Douce, Jean de Florette, Manon of the Spring, Romuald and Juliette (Mama There's a Man in Your Bed), A Few Days With Me, My Life is Hell, L'Elegant Criminel, Un Coeur en Hiver (A Heart in Winter), Ma Saison Preferee (My Favorite Season), The Separation, According to Pereira, The Eighth Day (Best actor, Cannes 1996).

AUTRY, GENE
Actor. b. Tioga, TX, Sept. 29, 1907. Railroad telegrapher at Sapulpa, OK, 1925; became radio singer and recording artist (Columbia Records) 1928; screen debut 1934 at Mascot Pictures (later became Republic) as screen's first singing cowboy. Starred in 89 feature films and 91 half hour TV films. The Gene Autry Show, 1950-55. Formed Flying A Productions, pro-

duced Annie Oakley, The Range Rider, Buffalo Bill, Jr. and Adventures of Champion TV series. Wrote or co-wrote over two hundred songs, recorded 635 records, has 12 Gold Records, and 6 platinum records, including all-time best seller, Rudolph the Red-Nosed Reindeer. Voted top money making Western star 1937-42, and in top Western stars 1936, 1946-54; first Western star to be in top ten money makers from 1939-42. Served in U.S.A.A.F. as flight officer, 1942-45; on USO tour overseas 3 mos.; immediately thereafter resumed radio career with former sponsor, the Wm. Wrigley Co., formed Gene Autry Productions, Inc., star of Madison Square Garden Rodeo first in 1940; composed & recorded song Here Comes Santa Claus; Be Honest With Me (Acad. Award nom.); owner KSCA FM radio station, California Angels baseball team and chairman of the board of Gene Autry Western Heritage Museum. The only entertainer with five stars on the Hollywood Walk of Fame for radio, recordings, movies, tv and live performances, theatrical and rodeo. Hosted Melody Ranch Theatre on the Nashville Network, 1988-89. TV Specials incl. Biography, 1994; Gene Autry: Melody of the West, 1995.
PICTURES: In Old Santa Fe (debut, 1934), Tumbling Tumbleweeds, The Singing Vagabond, The Big Show, Oh Susannah, The Old Corral, Boots and Saddles, Manhattan Merry-Go-Round, Gold Mine in the Sky, Rhythm of the Saddle, Mexicali Rose, In Old Monterey, South of the Border, Rancho Grande, Melody Ranch, Back in the Saddle, Sierra Sue, Stardust on the Sage, Sioux City Sue, Saddle Pals, Robin Hood of Texas, The Last Round-Up, The Cowboy and the Indians, Cow Town, Mule Train, The Blazing Sun, Valley of Fire, Apache Country, Barbed Wire, Wagon Team, Saginaw Trail, Last of the Pony Riders, Alias Jesse James (cameo), many others.

AVALON, FRANKIE
Singer, Actor. r.n. Francis Thomas Avalone. b. Philadelphia, PA, Sept 18, 1940. e. South Philadelphia H.S. Trumpet prodigy age 9 yrs. Recording contract, Chancellor Records, Inc., 1957; Gold Record: Venus 1959; Gold Album: Swingin' on a Rainbow, 1959.
PICTURES: Jamboree (debut, 1957), Guns of the Timberland, The Alamo, Alakazam the Great (voice), Voyage to the Bottom of the Sea, Sail a Crooked Ship, Panic in the Year Zero, Beach Party, The Castilian, Drums of Africa, Operation Bikini, Bikini Beach, Pajama Party, Muscle Beach Party, How to Stuff a Wild Bikini, Beach Blanket Bingo, Ski Party, I'll Take Sweden, Sgt. Deadhead, Dr. Goldfoot and the Bikini Machine, Fireball 500, The Million Eyes of Su-Muru, Skidoo, Horror House, The Take, Grease, Back to the Beach, Troop Beverly Hills.
TELEVISION: *Series:* Easy Does It... Starring Frankie Avalon. *Guest:* Ed Sullivan, Perry Como, Pat Boone, Arthur Murray, Dick Clark Shows, Milton Berle, Golden Circle Spectacular, Dinah Shore Show, Steve Allen Show, The Patty Duke Show, Hullabaloo, Happy Days.

AVEDON, DOE
Actress, b. Old Westbury, NY, 1928. Bookkeeper, then actress.
THEATER: Young and the Fair, My Name Is Aquilon.
PICTURES: The High and the Mighty, Deep in My Heart, The Boss.
TELEVISION: *Series:* Big Town.

AVILDSEN, JOHN G.
Director, Cinematographer, Editor. b. Chicago, IL, Dec. 21, 1935. m. actress Tracy Brooks Swope. e. NYU. After service in Army made film with friend, Greenwich Village Story, then joined ad agency to write, direct, photograph & edit industrial films. Entered m.p. industry as ass't cameraman on Below the Hill, followed with prod. mgr. job on Italian film made in U.S. Then made first theatrical short, Smiles. Asst. dir: Black Like Me; prod. mgr.: Mickey One, Una Moglie Americana; 2nd unit dir.: Hurry Sundown. Produced, photographed & edited a short, Light, Sound, Diffuse. Returned to industry to make industrial films for ad agencies before resuming theatrical career.
PICTURES: Turn on to Love (debut feature, dir., photo.), Out of It (assoc. prod., dir. of photog.). *Director:* Sweet Dreams (aka Okay, Bill; also photo., edit.), Guess What We Learned in School Today? (also photo., edit.), Joe (also photo.), Cry Uncle (also photo., edit.), The Stoolie (also photo.), Save the Tiger, W. W. and the Dixie Dancekings, Foreplay (also edit., photo.), Rocky (Academy Award, 1976), Slow Dancing in the Big City (also prod., edit.), The Formula, Neighbors (also supv. edit.), Traveling Hopefully (documentary; Acad. Award nom.), A Night in Heaven (also edit., cinematographer), The Karate Kid (also edit.), The Karate Kid: Part II (also edit.), Happy New Year, For Keeps, Lean On Me (also edit.), The Karate Kid Part III (also co-edit.), Rocky V (also co-edit.), The Power of One (also edit.), Steal This Video (documentary), 8 Seconds, Save The Everglades (documentary).
TELEVISION: From No House to Options House (2 On the Town, Emmy Award).

AVNET, JON
Producer, Director. b. Brooklyn, NY, Nov. 17, 1949. e. U. of PA, Sarah Lawrence Coll. Began career as director of off-B'way prods. Produced and directed low-budget film, Confusion's

Circle, which brought a directing fellowship at American Film Institute. Joined Weintraub/Heller Prods. as assoc. prod., where met Steve Tisch, with whom formed Tisch/Avnet Prods. Formed Avnet/Kerner Co., 1986.
PICTURES: Checkered Flag or Crash (assoc. prod.), Outlaw Blues (assoc. prod.), *Producer:* Coast to Coast, Risky Business, Deal of the Century (exec. prod.), Less Than Zero, Men Don't Leave, Funny About Love, Fried Green Tomatoes (also dir., co-s.p.), The Mighty Ducks, The Three Musketeers (co-exec. prod.), When a Man Loves a Woman, The War (also dir.), Miami Rhapsody (co-exec. prod.), Up Close and Personal (also dir.).
TELEVISION: *Producer:* No Other Love, Homeward Bound, Prime Suspect, Something So Right, Silence of the Heart, Calendar Girl Murders, Call to Glory (pilot and series), The Burning Bed, In Love and War (also exec. prod.), Between Two Women (also dir., co-s.p.). *Exec. Prod.:* Side By Side, My First Love, Breaking Point, O Do You Know the Muffin Man?, Heatwave, Backfield in Motion, The Nightman, The Switch, For Their Own Good.

AXEL, GABRIEL
Director. b. Denmark, 1918. e. France, then studied acting at Danish National Conservatory. Returned to France where joined the Paris theater co. of Louis Jouvet as stagehand. Worked as actor in Copenhagen boulevard theater where made directing debut. Went on to dir. Danish TV, mostly classic plays.
PICTURES: Golden Mountains (debut, 1957), Crazy Paradise, The Red Mantle, Danish Blue, Babette's Feast (also s.p.; Academy Award for Best Foreign-Language Feature, 1988), Christian (also s.p.).

AXELMAN, ARTHUR
Executive. b. Philadelphia, PA, Dec. 10, 1944. e. Florida Atlantic U., B.A., 1969. Entered NY offices of William Morris Agency, June 1972; transferred to Bev. Hills offices, 1976, as literary agent. Founded company's original TV Movie dept., 1977. Appointed v.p. in 1980, sr. v.p. in 1991. Among clients represented while overseeing network sales, negotiation, packaging, development, etc. of some 100 TV movies have been EMI TV, Bob Banner, Edward S. Feldman, Lee Grant, Thom Mount, Edward Anhalt, Zev Braun, Marvin Worth, Gilbert Cates, Jerry London, Jeremy Kagan, Dick Berg, Patty Duke, Finnegan-Pinchuk Prods.

AXELROD, GEORGE
Writer, Producer, Director. b. New York, NY, June 9, 1922. Stage mgr., actor, summer stock, 1940-41; radio writer, 1941-52. *Novels:* Beggar's Choice, Blackmailer; co-writer, nightclub musical: All About Love, 1951. *Memoirs:* Where Am I Now When I Need Me?
THEATER: *B'way:* The Seven Year Itch, Will Success Spoil Rock Hunter?, Visit to a Small Planet, Once More with Feeling, Goodbye Charlie (also dir.).
PICTURES: *Writer:* Phffft, The Seven Year Itch, Bus Stop, Breakfast at Tiffany's, The Manchurian Candidate (also co-prod.), Paris When It Sizzles (also co-prod.), How to Murder Your Wife, Lord Love a Duck (also dir., prod.), The Secret Life of an American Wife (also dir., prod.), The Lady Vanishes, The Holcroft Covenant, The Fourth Protocol.

AXELROD, JONATHAN
Writer, Producer. b. New York, NY, July 9, 1950. Stepson of writer George Axelrod. Started as on-set "gofer" before writing screenplays. 1978-80, v.p. primetime drama dev., ABC Entertainment; 1980-82, v.p. exec. dir. in chg. dev. ABC Ent.; 1983-85 exec. v.p., Columbia Pictures TV; 1985-87, pres. New World Pictures; 1987-, co-owner, Camden Artists; 1989, exec. v.p. Ventura Entertainment Group. 1990-93, pres. & CEO Producers Entertainment Group. Exec. Prod. of Hollywood Detective series. 1993-, exec. prod. of Dave's World.

AYKROYD, DAN
Actor, Writer. b. Ottawa, Canada, July 1, 1952. m. actress Donna Dixon. Member of Toronto Co. of Second City Theater. Worked as mgr. of Club 505, after-hours Toronto nightclub 1970-73. Performed and recorded (Briefcase Full of Blues, Made in America) with John Belushi as the Blues Brothers. Co-owner, Hard Rock Cafe.
PICTURES: Love at First Sight (debut, 1977; also co-s.p.), Mr. Mike's Mondo Video, 1941, The Blues Brothers (also co-s.p.), Neighbors, It Came From Hollywood, Doctor Detroit, Trading Places, Twilight Zone—The Movie, Indiana Jones and the Temple of Doom (cameo), Ghostbusters (also co-s.p.), Nothing Lasts Forever, Into the Night, Spies Like Us (also co-s.p.), One More Saturday Night (exec. prod. only), Dragnet (also co-s.p.), The Couch Trip, The Great Outdoors, Caddyshack II, My Stepmother Is an Alien, Ghostbusters II (also co-s.p.), Driving Miss Daisy (Acad. Award nom.), Loose Cannons, Nothing But Trouble (also dir., s.p.), Masters of Menace, My Girl, This Is My Life, Sneakers, Chaplin, Coneheads (also co-s.p.), My Girl 2, North, Exit to Eden, Tommy Boy, Casper (cameo), Canadian Bacon (cameo), Getting Away With Murder, Sgt. Bilko, Celtic Pride, My Fellow Americans.

TELEVISION: Coming Up Rosie (Canada), Saturday Night Live 1975-79 (writer and performer; Emmy Award for writing: 1977). Steve Martin's Best Show Ever (performer, writer). Guest: Tales from the Crypt (Yellow).

AYRES, GERALD
Producer, Writer. e. Yale U. where had four plays produced. Became B'way play doctor and then joined Columbia Pictures as freelance reader. Named story editor; exec. asst. to v.p. Mike Frankovich; then v.p. in chg. creative affairs in Hollywood. Left in 1970 to become independent. Formed Acrobat Films.
PICTURES: *Producer:* Cisco Pike, The Last Detail, Foxes (also s.p.), Rich and Famous (s.p. only; WGA Award, 1981).
TELEVISION: *Movies (writer):* Stormy Weathers (co-writer), Crazy in Love (ACE Award nom.), Liz: The Elizabeth Taylor Story.

AYRES, LEW
Actor. b. Minneapolis, MN, Dec. 28, 1908. Toured Mexico with own orchestra; then with Henry Halstead's Orchestra. Served as medical corpsman & asst. chaplain WWII.
PICTURES: The Sophmore (debut, 1929), The Kiss, All Quiet on the Western Front, Common Clay, East is West, Doorway to Hell, Up for Murder, Many a Slip, Spirit of Notre Dame, Heaven on Earth, Impatient Maiden, Night World, Okay America, State Fair, Don't Bet on Love, My Weakness, Cross Country Cruise, Let's Be Ritzy, She Learned About Sailors, Servants' Entrance, Lottery Lover, Silk Hat Kid, Leathernecks Have Landed, Panic on the Air, Shakedown, Lady Be Careful, Murder With Pictures, The Crime Nobody Saw, Last Train from Madrid, Hold 'Em Navy, King of the Newsboys, Scandal Street, Holiday, Rich Man Poor Girl, Young Dr. Kildare (and subsequent film series), Spring Madness, Ice Follies of 1939, Broadway Serenade, These Glamour Girls, The Golden Fleecing, Maisie Was a Lady, Fingers at the Window, Dark Mirror, Unfaithful, Johnny Belinda (Acad. Award nom.), The Capture, New Mexico, No Escape, Donovan's Brain, Altars to the East (also dir., prod., narrator), Advise and Consent, The Carpetbaggers, The Biscuit Eater, The Man, Battle for the Planet of the Apes, End of the World, Damien-Omen II, Battlestar Galactica.
TELEVISION: *Series:* Frontier Justice (host), Lime Street. *Movies:* Hawaii Five-O (pilot), Marcus Welby M.D. (pilot), Earth II, She Waits, The Stranger, The Questor Tapes, Heatwave, Francis Gary Powers, Suddenly Love, Salem's Lot, Letters from Frank, Reunion, Of Mice and Men, Under Siege, Hart to Hart: Crimes of the Hart.

AZARIA, HANK
Actor. b. Forest Hills, NY. e. Tufts Univ.
PICTURES: Pretty Woman, Cool Blue, Quiz Show, Birdcage.
TELEVISION: *Series:* The Simpsons (voice), Herman's Head, If Not for You. *Guest:* Fresh Prince of Bel-Air, Growing Pains, Mad About You.

AZNAVOUR, CHARLES
Singer, Songwriter, Actor. b. Paris, France, May 22, 1924. r.n. Shahnour Varenagh Aznavourian. Studied dance and drama as a child and was performing at the age of 10. Encouraged by Edith Piaf, became one of France's leading performers by the mid-1950s and an international concert star by the 1970s. Has also composed music for film.
PICTURES: Adieu Cherie (1947), C'est arrive a 36 Chandelles, Les Dragueurs, Shoot the Piano Player, Le testament d'Orphee, Le Passage du Rhin, Un taxi pour Tobrouk, Horace 62, Tempo di Roma, Les Quatres Verites, Le Rat'd Amerique, Pourquoi Paris?, Paris in August, Candy, The Games, The Adventurers, The Blockhouse, Ten Little Indians, The Twist, Sky Riders, Ciao Les Mecs, The Tin Drum, The Magic Mountain, Hatter's Ghosts, What Makes David Run?, Edith and Marcel, Long Live Life!, Mangeclous, Friend to Friend, Il Maestro, Double Game.

B

BABENCO, HECTOR
Director. b. Buenos Aires, Argentina, Feb. 7, 1946. Early years spent in Mar del Plata. Left home at 17 and traveled throughout European capitals for 8 years working as a writer, house-painter, salesman, and, in Rome, as an extra at Cinecitta. Moved to Sao Paulo, Brazil where he made several short documentaries, before turning to features in 1975.
PICTURES: Rei Da Noite (King of the Night; debut, 1975), Lucio Flavio—Passageiro da Agonia, Pixote (also co-s.p.), Kiss of the Spider Woman, Ironweed, Besame Mucho (prod. only), At Play in the Fields of the Lord (also co-s.p.).

BACALL, LAUREN
Actress. r.n. Betty Joan. b. New York, NY, Sept. 16, 1924. e. American Acad. Dram. Arts. Was m. Jason Robards, late Humphrey Bogart. *Autobiographies:* By Myself (1979), Now (1994).
THEATER: *B'way:* Cactus Flower, Goodbye Charlie, Applause (Tony Award), Woman of the Year. London/Australia: Sweet Bird of Youth.

PICTURES: To Have and Have Not (debut, 1944), Two Guys From Milwaukee (cameo), Confidential Agent, The Big Sleep, Dark Passage, Key Largo, Young Man With a Horn, Bright Leaf, How to Marry a Millionaire, Woman's World, Cobweb, Blood Alley, Written on the Wind, Designing Woman, Gift of Love, Flame Over India, Shock Treatment, Sex and the Single Girl, Harper, Murder on the Orient Express, The Shootist, Health, The Fan, Appointment With Death, Mr. North, Innocent Victim, Misery, A Star for Two, All I Want for Christmas, Ready to Wear (Pret-a-Porter), The Mirror Has Two Faces.
TELEVISION: *Specials*: The Girls in Their Dresses, Blithe Spirit, The Petrified Forest, Applause, Bacall on Bogart, A Foreign Field (BBC). *Movies*: Perfect Gentlemen, Dinner at Eight, A Little Piece of Sunshine (BBC), The Portrait, From the Mixed Up Files of Mrs. Basil E. Frankweiler.

BACH, CATHERINE
Actress. b. Warren, Ohio, March 1, 1954.
PICTURES: The Midnight Man, Thunderbolt and Lightfoot, Hustle, Cannonball Run II, Tunnels (Criminal Act), Music City Blues, Driving Force, Street Justice.
TELEVISION: *Series*: The Dukes of Hazzard (1979-85), The Dukes (cartoon, voice), African Skies. Guest on many specials. *Movies*: Matt Helm, Strange New World, Murder in Peyton Place, White Water Rebels.

BACHARACH, BURT
Composer, Conductor, Arranger. b. Kansas City, MO, May 12, 1928. e. McGraw U., Mannes Sch. of Music, Music Acad. of the West. Studied with composers Darius Milhaud, Henry Cowell, and Bohuslav Martinu. Has conducted for Marlene Dietrich, Vic Damone. As a performer albums include: Burt Bacharach; Futures, Man! His Songs. Book: The Bacharach-David Song Book (1978).
THEATER: Promises Promises (Tony Award, 1969).
PICTURES: Lizzie, The Sad Sack, The Blob, Country Music Holiday, Love in a Goldfish Bowl, Wives and Lovers, Who's Been Sleeping in My Bed?, Send Me No Flowers, A House Is Not a Home, What's New Pussycat?, Alfie, Made in Paris, After the Fox, Promise Her Anything, Casino Royale, The April Fools, Butch Cassidy and the Sundance Kid (*2 Academy Awards*: Best Original Score & Best Song: Raindrops Keep Fallin' on My Head; 1969), Something Big, Lost Horizon, Arthur (Academy Award for Best Song: Arthur's Theme; 1981), Night Shift, Best Defense, Tough Guys, Baby Boom, Arthur 2 on the Rocks.
TELEVISION: *Special*: Singer Presents Burt Bacharach (Emmy Award for Best Variety Special, 1971).

BACK, LEON B.
Exhibitor. b. Philadelphia, PA, Oct. 23, 1912. e. Johns Hopkins U., B.E., 1932; U. of Baltimore, LL.B., 1933. Entered m.p. ind. as mgr. for Rome Theatres, Inc., Baltimore, Md., 1934; booker, ass't buyer, 1936; ass't to gen. mgr. 1939; U.S. Navy 1944-46; v.p., gen. mgr., Rome Theatres, 1946; Allied MPTO of Md. 1952-55; nat'l dir. Allied States, 1952-55; nat'l secy. 1954; Pres. NATO of Maryland 1969-80; Pres. USO Council, Greater Baltimore 1969-75; Chairman, board of trustees, Employees Benefit Trust for Health & Welfare Council of Central Maryland, 1970-79.

BACON, KEVIN
Actor. b. Philadelphia, PA, July 8, 1958. m. actress Kyra Sedgwick. Studied at Manning St. Actor's Theatre. Apprentice at Circle-in-the-Square in N.Y. B'way debut in Slab Boys with Sean Penn. Narrated short film A Little Vicious.
THEATER: *B'way*: Slab Boys. *Off-B'way*: Getting Out (debut), Album, Forty Deuce (Obie Award), Poor Little Lambs, Flux, Men Without Dates, The Author's Voice, Loot, Road, Spike Heels.
PICTURES: National Lampoon's Animal House (debut, 1978), Starting Over, Hero at Large, Friday the 13th, Only When I Laugh, Forty Deuce, Diner, Footloose, Enormous Changes at the Last Minute, Quicksilver, White Water Summer (Rites of Summer), End of the Line, Planes Trains and Automobiles, She's Having a Baby, Criminal Law, The Big Picture, Tremors, Flatliners, Queens Logic, He Said/She Said, Pyrates, JFK, A Few Good Men, The Air Up There, The River Wild, Murder in the First, Apollo 13, Balto (voice), Sleepers.
TELEVISION: *Movies*: The Gift, The Demon Murder Case, The Tender Age (The Little Sister), Lemon Sky, Losing Chase (dir. only). *Series*: Search for Tomorrow, The Guiding Light. *Special*: Mr. Roberts.

BADHAM, JOHN
Director. b. Luton, Eng., Aug. 25, 1939. Raised in Alabama. e. Yale U., B.A.; Yale Drama School, M.F.A. Sister is actress Mary Badham. Landed first job at Universal Studio mailroom; later was Universal tour guide, a casting dir. and assoc. prod. to William Sackheim. Twice nominated for Emmy Awards for TV movies. Recipient of George Pal Award.
PICTURES: The Bingo Long Traveling All-Stars and Motor Kings (debut 1976), Saturday Night Fever, Dracula (Best Horror Film award, Science Fiction/Fantasy Academy), Whose Life Is It Anyway? (San Rafael Grand Prize), Blue Thunder, War Games (Best Directing award, Science Fiction/Fantasy Academy),

American Flyers, Short Circuit, Stakeout (also exec. prod.), Disorganized Crime (exec. prod. only), Bird on a Wire, The Hard Way, Point of No Return, Another Stakeout (also exec. prod.), Drop Zone (also exec. prod.), Nick of Time (also prod.).
TELEVISION: *Movies*: Night Gallery (assoc. prod. only), Neon Ceiling (assoc. prod. only), The Impatient Heart, Isn't It Shocking?, The Law, The Gun, Reflections of Murder, The Godchild, The Keegans, Relentless: Mind of a Killer (co-exec. prod. only). *Series episodes*: The Senator (also assoc. prod.), Kung Fu, Night Gallery, Streets of San Francisco, The Doctors, Owen Marshall - Counsellor at Law, Sunshine, Nichols, Sarge, The Sixth Sense, Cannon.

BAILEY, JOHN
Cinematographer. b. Moberly, MO, August 10, 1942. m. film editor Carol Littleton. e. U. of Santa Clara, Loyola U., U.S.C., U. of Vienna. Lecturer, American Film Institute, 1982, 1984, 1994.
PICTURES: Premonition, End of August, Legacy, The Mafu Cage (visual consult.), Boulevard Nights, Winter Kills (add. photog.), American Gigolo, Ordinary People, Honky Tonk Freeway, Continental Divide, Cat People, That Championship Season, Without a Trace, The Big Chill, Racing With the Moon, The Pope of Greenwich Village, Mishima, Silverado, Crossroads, Brighton Beach Memoirs, Light of Day, Swimming to Cambodia, Tough Guys Don't Dance (visual consult.), Vibes, The Accidental Tourist, My Blue Heaven, The Search for Signs of Intelligent Life in the Universe (also dir.), A Brief History of Time, Groundhog Day, In the Line of Fire, China Moon (dir. only), Nobody's Fool, Mariette in Ecstasy (dir. only).
TELEVISION: Battered City in Fear.

BAILEY, ROBIN
Actor. b. Hucknall (Nottingham), Eng., Oct. 5, 1919. e. Henry Mellish School, Nottingham.
THEATER: Barrets of Wimpole Street, Theatre Royal, Nottingham, 1938.
PICTURES: School for Secrets (1946), Private Angelo, Portrait of Clare, His Excellency, Gift Horse, Folly to Be Wise, Single Handed, Sailor of the King, The Young Lovers, For Better, For Worse, Catch Us If You Can, The Whisperers, Spy with a Cold Nose, You Only Live Twice, The Eliminator, Blind Terror, Down by the Riverside, Nightmare Rally, The Four Feathers, Jane and the Lost City.
TELEVISION: Olive Latimer's Husband, Seven Deadly Sins, The Power Game, Public Eye, Person to Person, Troubleshooters, Armchair Theatre, Split Level, The Newcomers, Discharge of Trooper Lusby, Brett, Owen M.D., Solidarity, General Hospital, Murder Must Advertise, Vienna 1900, Justice, The Pallisers, The Couch, Way of the World, Upstairs, Downstairs, Walk with Destiny, North and South, A Legacy, The Velvet Glove, Crown Court, Took and Co., The Good Companions, Cupid's Darts, Sorry, I'm a Stranger Here Myself, Call My Bluff, Jane, Potter, Tales from a Long Room, Sharing Time, Bleak House, Charters and Caldicott, Looks Familiar, On Stage, Rumpole of the Bailey, I Didn't Know You Cared, Number 27, Tinniswood's North Country, Tales From Hollywood, Bed, Dalziel and Pascoe.

BAIO, SCOTT
Actor. b. New York, NY, Sept. 22, 1961. Started career at 9 doing commercials and voice-overs.
PICTURES: Bugsy Malone, Skatetown USA, Foxes, Zapped!, I Love New York.
TELEVISION: *Series*: Blansky's Beauties, Happy Days, Who's Watching the Kids?, We're Movin' (host), Joanie Loves Chachi, Charles in Charge, Baby Talk, Diagnosis Murder. *Specials*: Luke Was There, Muggsy, Stoned, How to Be a Perfect Person, The Truth About Alex. *Guest*: Hotel, The Fall Guy, Full House. *Movies*: The Boy Who Drank Too Much, Senior Trip, Alice in Wonderland.

BAKER, BLANCHE
Actress. r.n. Blanche Garfein. b. New York, NY, Dec. 20, 1956. Daughter of actress Carroll Baker and dir. Jack Garfein. e. Wellesley, Coll., studied acting with Uta Hagen. Acting debut, White Marriage, Yale Repertory Co. (1978), Regional Theater. B'way debut in Lolita (1981).
PICTURES: The Seduction of Joe Tynan (debut, 1979), French Postcards, Sixteen Candles, Raw Deal, Cold Feet, The Handmaid's Tale, Livin' Large, Bum Rap, Dead Funny.
TELEVISION: *Mini-Series*: Holocaust (Emmy Award, 1978). *Movies*: Mary and Joseph, The Day the Bubble Burst, The Awakening of Candra, Nobody's Child. *Special*: Romeo & Juliet.

BAKER, CARROLL
Actress. b. Johnstown, PA, May 28, 1931. e. schools there and St. Petersburg (FL) Junior Coll. Career started as dancer in nightclubs. Actors' Studio N.Y. *Stage debut*: Escapade. Then, All Summer Long. *Autobiography*: Baby Doll.
PICTURES: Easy to Love (debut, 1953), Giant, Baby Doll, The Big Country, But Not for Me, The Miracle, Bridge to the Sun, Something Wild, How the West Was Won, The Carpetbaggers, Station Six Sahara, Cheyenne Autumn, The Greatest Story Ever Told, Sylvia, Mister Moses, Harlow, Jack of Diamonds, The

Sweet Body of Deborah, Paranoia, A Quiet Place to Kill, Captain Apache, The Harem, Honeymoon, My Father's Wife, Bloodbath (The Sky Is Falling), Andy Warhol's Bad, The World is Full of Married Men, Watcher in the Woods, Star 80, The Secret Diary of Sigmund Freud, Native Son, Ironweed, Red Monarch, Kindergarten Cop, Blonde Fist, Cybereden.
TELEVISION: *Specials*: Rain, On Fire, Sharing Time, Coward's: What Mad Pursuit. *Guest*: Tales from the Crypt. *Movies*: Hitler's SS: Portrait in Evil, On Fire, Judgment Day: The John List Story, Men Don't Tell, A Kiss to Die For.

BAKER, DIANE
Actress. b. Hollywood, CA, Feb. 25, 1938. e. USC.
PICTURES: The Diary of Anne Frank (debut, 1959), The Best of Everything, Journey to the Center of the Earth, Tess of the Storm Country, The Wizard of Baghdad, Hemingway's Adventures of a Young Man, 300 Spartans, Nine Hours to Rama, Stolen Hours, The Prize, Straight Jacket, Marnie, Mirage, Sands of Beersheba, The Horse in the Grey Flannel Suit, Krakatoa — East of Java, Baker's Hawk, The Pilot, The Silence of the Lambs, The Closer, The Joy Luck Club, Twenty Bucks, Imaginary Crimes, The Net, The Cable Guy.
TELEVISION: *Series*: Here We Go Again. *Movies*: Dangerous Days of Kiowa Jones, Trial Run, The D.A.: Murder One, The Old Man Who Cried Wolf, Do You Take This Stranger?, Sarge: The Badge or the Cross, Congratulations It's a Boy!, A Little Game, Killer By Night, Police Story (pilot), A Tree Grows in Brooklyn, The Dream Makers, The Last Survivors, Fugitive Family, The Haunted, Perry Mason: The Case of the Heartbroken Bride. *Mini-Series*: The Blue and the Gray.

BAKER, DYLAN
Actor. b. Syracuse, NY. e. Southern Methodist Univ. (BFA), Yale Sch. of Drama (MFA).
PICTURES: Ishtar (debut, 1987), Planes Trains and Automobiles, The Wizard of Loneliness, The Long Walk Home, Delirious, Passed Away, Love Potion No. 9, Life With Mikey, Radioland Murders, Disclosure, The Stars Fell on Henrietta.
TELEVISION: *Series*: Murder One. *Movies*: The Murder of Mary Phagan, Love Honor and Obey: The Last Mafia Marriage. *Mini-Series*: Return to Lonesome Dove. *Guest*: Spenser: For Hire, Miami Vice, Law and Order.
THEATER: *B'way*: Eastern Standard (Theatre World Award), La Bete (Tony nom.). *Off-B'way*: Not About Heroes (Obie Award).

BAKER, GEORGE
Actor, Writer. b. Varna, Bulgaria, April 1, 1931. e. Lancing College, Sussex. Stage debut Deal Repertory Theatre, 1946.
AUTHOR: The Fatal Spring, Imaginary Friends, Going for Broke, The Marches of Wales, The Hopkins, Just a Hunch, Sister, Dear Sister, From Doom With Death, Mouse in the Corner, The Strawberry Tree, Talking About Mira Beau, Dead on Time, The Last Silence.
PICTURES: The Intruder (debut, 1953), The Dam Busters, The Ship That Died of Shame, Woman for Joe, The Extra Day, The Feminine Touch, A Hill in Korea (Hell in Korea), No Time for Tears, These Dangerous Years (Dangerous Youth), The Moonraker, Tread Softly Stranger, Lancelot and Guinevere (Sword of Lancelot), Curse of the Fly, Mister Ten Per Cent, Goodbye Mr. Chips, Justine, The Executioners, On Her Majesty's Secret Service, A Warm December, The Fire Fighters, The Spy Who Loved Me, Thirty-Nine Steps, A Nightingale Sang in Berkeley Square, Hopscotch, North Sea Hijack (ffolkes), For Queen and Country.
TELEVISION: Fan Show, Ron Raudell's programme 1956, Guinea Pig, Death of a Salesman, The Last Troubadour, The Square Ring, Nick of the River, Mary Stuart, Probation Officers, Far Away Music, It Happened Like This, Boule de Suif, Maigret, Zero One, Rupert Henzau, Miss Memory, Any Other Business, The Navigators, Common Ground, Alice, The Queen and Jackson, The Big Man Coughed and Died, Up and Down, Call My Bluff, The Baron, St. Patrick, Love Life, Seven Deadly Virtues, The Prisoner, The Sex Games, Z Cars, Paul Temple, Candida, Fenn Street, Man Outside, The Persuaders, Main Chance, Ministry of Fear, Bowler, Voyage in the Dark, Dial M for Murder, Zodiac, The Survivors, I, Claudius, Print Out, Goodbye, Darling, Chinese Detective, Triangle, Minder, Hart to Hart, Goodbye Mr. Chips, Woman of Substance, The Bird Fancier, Robin of Sherwood, Time after Time, If Tomorrow Comes, Coast to Coast, Dead Head, The Canterville Ghost, Room at the Bottom, Ruth Rendell Mysteries (From Doon With Death; adap.), Journey's End, No Job for a Lady, Little Lord Fauntleroy.

BAKER, JOE DON
Actor. b. Groesbeck, TX, Feb. 12, 1936. e. North Texas State Coll., B.B.A., 1958. Began career on N.Y. stage, in Marathon 33 and Blues for Mr. Charlie. L.A. stage in The Caine Mutiny Court Martial.
PICTURES: Cool Hand Luke (debut, 1967), Guns of the Magnificent Seven, Adam at Six A.M., Wild Rovers, Welcome Home Soldier Boys, Junior Bonner, Walking Tall, Charley Varrick, The Outfit, Golden Needles, Mitchell, Framed, Checkered Flag or Crash, Speedtrap, The Pack, Wacko, Joysticks, The Natural,

Fletch, Getting Even (Hostage Dallas), The Living Daylights, The Killing Time, Leonard Part 6, Criminal Law, The Children, Cape Fear, The Distinguished Gentleman, Reality Bites, Panther, The Underneath, Congo, The Grass Harp, Goldeneye.
TELEVISION: *Movies*: Mongo's Back in Town, That Certain Summer, To Kill a Cop, Power, The Abduction of Kari Swenson, Edge of Darkness (BBC mini-series), Defrosting the Fridge (BBC), Citizen Cohn, Complex of Fear. *Series*: Eischeid. *Guest*: In the Heat of the Night.

BAKER, KATHY
Actress. B. Midland, TX, June 8, 1950. Raised in Albuquerque, NM. e. UC/Berkeley. Stage debut in San Francisco premiere of Fool for Love, won Obie and Theatre World Awards for New York debut in same. Also appeared in Desire Under the Elms, Aunt Dan and Lemon.
PICTURES: The Right Stuff (debut, 1983), Street Smart (Natl. Society of Film Critics Award), Permanent Record, A Killing Affair, Clean and Sober, Jacknife, Dad, Mr. Frost, Edward Scissorhands, Article 99, Jennifer Eight, Mad Dog and Glory, To Gillian on her 37th Birthday.
TELEVISION: *Series*: Picket Fences (2 Emmy Awards: 1993, 1995). Movies: Nobody's Child, The Image, One Special Victory, Lush Life. *Guest*: Amazing Stories.

BAKER, RICK
Makeup Artist, Performer. b. Binghamton, NY, Dec. 8, 1950. Started as assist. to makeup artist Dick Smith before creating his own designs in 1972. Frequent film appearances in makeup, usually as gorillas. Worked on Michael Jackson's video Thriller.
PICTURES: *Actor*: The Thing With Two Heads, King Kong, The Kentucky Fried Movie, The Incredible Shrinking Woman, Into the Night. *Makeup Design*: Shlock, Zebra Force, It's Alive, The Incredible Melting Man, Star Wars (2nd unit), It Lives Again, The Howling (consultant), Funhouse, An American Werewolf in London (Academy Award, 1981), Videodrome, Greystoke: The Legend of Tarzan Lord of the Apes (also costume design; Acad. Award nom.), Ratboy, Harry and the Hendersons (Academy Award, 1987), Coming to America (Acad. Award nom.), Gorillas in the Mist (also assoc. prod.), Missing Link, Wolf, Ed Wood (Academy Award, 1994), Batman Forever (also designed monster bat), The Nutty Professor. Other: Tanya's Island (beast design), Starman (transformation scenes), Cocoon (consultant), My Science Project (Tyrannosaurus Rex sequences consultant), Max My Love (chimpanzee consultant), Gremlins 2: The New Batch (co-prod., f/x supervisor), Baby's Day Out (baby f/x), Just Cause (special bodies), Little Panda (panda suits).
TELEVISION: *Makeup Design*: *Series*: Werewolf, Beauty and the Beast, Harry and the Hendersons. *Movies*: The Autobiography of Miss Jane Pittman (Emmy Award), An American Christmas Carol, Something Is Out There.

BAKER, ROY
Producer, Director. b. London. e. Lycaee Corneille, Rouen; City of London School. Ass't dir. with Gainsborough 1934-40; served in Army 1940-46.
PICTURES: Operation Disaster, Don't Bother to Knock, Inferno, One That Got Away, A Night to Remember, The Singer Not the Song, Flame in the Streets, Quartermass and the Pit, The Anniversary, Vampire Lovers, Dr. Jekyll and Mr. Hyde, Asylum (Paris Grand Prize), Seven Golden Vampires.
TELEVISION: The Human Jungle, The Saint, Gideon's Way, The Baron, The Avengers, The Champions, Department S., The Persuaders, Danger UXB, Minder.

BAKER, DR. WILLIAM F.
Executive. b. 1944. e. Case Western Reserve U., B.A., M.A., Ph.D. Began broadcasting career in Cleveland while still a student. Joined Scripps-Howard Broadcasting, 1971. Joined Group W as v.p. and general mgr., WJZ-TV, 1978; served as pres. and CEO, Group W Productions; pres. of Group W. Television; 1979; chmn., Group W Satellite Communications, 1981; 1983, carried Explorers Club flag to top of world, becoming one of few in history to visit both North and South Poles; April 1987, appointed pres. and CEO, WNET/Thirteen, N.Y. PBS station.

BAKER, WILLIAM M.
Executive. b. Newark, NJ, Dec. 26, 1939. e. University of Virginia 1961. Joined FBI in 1965. From 1987 to 1989, took a haitus from the FBI to serve as dir. of Public Affairs for the CIA. Retired from position as asst. dir., Criminal Investigative Division of FBI in 1991. Currently pres. and CEO Motion Picture Assoc. and exec. v.p., Motion Picture Assoc. of America.

BAKSHI, RALPH
Animator, Writer, Director. b. Haifa, Israel, Oct. 29, 1938. Began career at Terrytoons at age 18 as cell painter and animator, then creative dir. 1966, headed Paramount Cartoons. Pres., Bakshi Prods.
PICTURES: *Director*: Fritz the Cat (also s.p.), Heavy Traffic (also s.p.), Coonskin (also s.p.), Wizards (also s.p., prod.), The Lord of the Rings, American Pop (also co-prod.), Hey Good Lookin' (also s.p., prod.), Fire and Ice (also co-prod.), Cool World.

TELEVISION: Mighty Mouse: The New Adventures (creator), This Ain't Bebop (Amer. Playhouse, dir., s.p.), The Cool and the Crazy (dir., writer).

BAKULA, SCOTT
Actor. b. St. Louis, MO, Oct. 9, 1955. e. Kansas Univ.
THEATER: NY: Marilyn: An American Fable, Three Guys Naked from the Waist Down, Romance/Romance (Tony nom.). LA: Nite Club Confidential.
PICTURES: Sibling Rivalry, Necessary Roughness, Color of Night, A Passion to Kill, My Family/Mi Familia, Lord of Illusions.
TELEVISION: Series: Gung Ho, Eisenhower & Lutz, Quantum Leap (Emmy noms., Golden Globe Award), Murphy Brown, Mr. & Mrs. Smith. Movies: The Last Fling, An Eye for an Eye, In the Shadow of a Killer, Mercy Mission: The Rescue of Flight 771, Nowhere to Hide, The Invaders.

BALABAN, BOB
Actor, Director. b. Chicago, IL, Aug. 16, 1945. Began studying with Second City troupe while still in high school. Attended Colgate U. and NYU while appearing on Broadway in Plaza Suite.
THEATER: You're a Good Man Charlie Brown, The Inspector General, Who Wants to Be the Lone Ranger?, The Basic Training of Pavlo Hummel, The Children, The White House Murder Case, Some of My Best Friends, The Three Sisters, The Boys Next Door, Speed-the-Plow, Some Americans Abroad.
PICTURES: Actor: Midnight Cowboy (debut, 1969), Me Natalie, The Strawberry Statement, Catch-22, Making It, Bank Shot, Report to the Commissioner, Close Encounters of the Third Kind, Girlfriends, Altered States, Prince of the City, Absence of Malice, Whose Life Is It Anyway?, 2010, In Our Hands (doc.), End of the Line, Dead-Bang, Alice, Little Man Tate, Bob Roberts, For Love or Money, Greedy, Pie in the Sky. Director: Parents, My Boyfriend's Back, The Last Good Time (also co-s.p.).
TELEVISION: Movies: Marriage: Year One, The Face of Fear, Unnatural Pursuits, The Late Shift. Series: Miami Vice, Late Shift, Seinfeld. Director: Tales From the Darkside, Amazing Stories, Penn & Teller's Invisible Thread.

BALDWIN, ADAM
Actor. b. Chicago, IL, Feb. 27, 1962. While in high school in Winnetka, was chosen by director Tony Bill for role in My Bodyguard.
THEATER: Album (Chicago).
PICTURES: My Bodyguard (debut, 1980), Ordinary People, D.C. Cab, Reckless, Hadley's Rebellion, Bad Guys, 3:15, Full Metal Jacket, The Chocolate War, Cohen and Tate, Next of Kin, Predator 2, Guilty By Suspicion, Radio Flyer, Where the Day Takes You, Deadbolt, Bitter Harvest, Eight Hundred Leagues Down the Amazon, Wyatt Earp, Independence Day.
TELEVISION: Movies: Off Sides, Poison Ivy, Welcome Home Bobby, Murder in High Places, Cruel Doubt, Cold Sweat, Sawbones. Special: The Last Shot.

BALDWIN, ALEC
Actor. r.n. Alexander Rae Baldwin III. b. Massapequa, NY, April 3, 1958. m. actress Kim Basinger. e. George Washington U., NYU. Brother of actors Stephen, William and Daniel Baldwin. Trained at Lee Strasberg Theatre Inst. and with Mira Rostova, Elaine Aiken. Started career in daytime TV on serial The Doctors. Member, The Creative Coalition.
THEATER: A Midsummer Night's Dream, The Wager, Summertree, A Life in the Theatre (Hartman), Study in Scarlet (Williamstown). NY: Loot (B'way debut; Theatre World Award, 1986), Serious Money, Prelude to a Kiss, A Streetcar Named Desire.
PICTURES: Forever Lulu (debut, 1987), She's Having a Baby, Beetlejuice, Married to the Mob, Working Girl, Talk Radio, Great Balls of Fire!, The Hunt for Red October, Miami Blues, Alice, The Marrying Man, Prelude to a Kiss, Glengarry Glen Ross, Malice, The Getaway, The Shadow, Heaven's Prisoners (also exec. prod.), The Juror, Loosking For Richard, Ghost of Mississippi.
TELEVISION: Series: The Doctors (1980-2), Cutter to Houston, Knots Landing. Movies: Sweet Revenge, Love on the Run, Dress Gray, The Alamo: 13 Days to Glory. Guest: Hotel, Saturday Night Live.

BALDWIN, DANIEL
Actor. b. Long Island, NY, 1961. e. Nassau Comm. Col., Ball St. Univ. Brother of actors Alec, William and Stephen Baldwin.
PICTURES: Born on the Fourth of July, Harley Davidson and the Marlboro Man, Knight Moves, Car 54 Where Are You?, Lone Justice, Mullholland Drive.
TELEVISION: Series: Sydney, Homicide: Life on the Street. Movies: Too Good to Be True, L.A. Takedown, The Heroes of Desert Storm, Ned Blessing: The True Story of My Life, Attack of the 50 Foot Woman. Special: Curse of the Corn People. Guest: Family Ties, Charles in Charge, The Larry Sanders Show.

BALDWIN, STEPHEN
Actor. b. Long Island, NY, 1966. Brother of actors Alec, William and Daniel Baldwin. Stage debut in Off-B'way prod. Out of America.
PICTURES: The Beast, Born on the Fourth of July, Last Exit to Brooklyn, Crossing the Bridge, Bitter Harvest, Posse, New Eden, 8 Seconds, Threesome, A Simple Twist of Fate, Mrs. Parker and the Vicious Circle, Fall Time, The Usual Suspects, Under the Hula Moon, Bio-Dome, Fled.
TELEVISION: Series: The Young Riders. Movies: Jury Duty: The Comedy, Dead Weekend. Specials: The Lawrenceville Stories, In a New Light: Sex Unplugged (co-host). Guest: Family Ties, Kate and Allie, China Beach.

BALDWIN, WILLIAM
Actor. b. Massapequa, NY, Feb. 21, 1963. e. SUNY/Binghamton. Degree in political science; worked in Washington on staff of rep. Thomas J. Downey. Brother of actors Alec, Stephen and Daniel Baldwin. With Ford Model agency, appearing in tv ads while studying acting. Member, The Creative Coalition.
PICTURES: Born on the Fourth of July (debut, 1989), Internal Affairs, Flatliners, Backdraft, Three of Hearts, Sliver, A Pyromaniac's Love Story, Fair Game, Curdled.
TELEVISION: Movie: The Preppie Murder.

BALE, CHRISTIAN
Actor. b. Pembrokeshire, Wales, Jan. 30, 1974. Acting debut at age 9 in U.S. Pac-Man commercial. London stage debut following year in The Nerd.
PICTURES: Empire of the Sun, Land of Faraway, Henry V, Newsies, Swing Kids, Prince of Jutland, Little Women, Pocahontas (voice), The Secret Agent, Portrait of a Lady.
TELEVISION: Specials/Movies: Heart of the Country (BBC), Anastasia: The Mystery of Anna (U.S.), Treasure Island (released theatrically in U.K.), A Murder of Quality.

BALLARD, CARROLL
Director. b. Los Angeles, Oct. 14, 1937. e. UCLA. Prod. of 1967 film Harvest. Camera operator on Star Wars.
PICTURES: The Black Stallion (debut, 1979), Never Cry Wolf, Nutcracker: The Motion Picture, Wind.

BALLARD, KAYE
Actress. b. Cleveland, OH, Nov. 20, 1926. r.n. Catherine Gloria Balotta. Began career as impressionist-singer-actress, toured vaudeville. 17 recordings incl. The Fanny Brice Story, Peanuts, Oklahoma (w/ Nelson Eddy), Unsung Sondheim, Then & Again. Appeared in short film Walking to Waldheim.
THEATER: Three to Make Ready, Carnival, Molly, The Pirates of Penzance, Hey Ma It's Me, Working 42nd Street at Last, Chicago, Touch & Go (London), Nymph Errant (concert version), Hello Dolly, She Stoops to Conquer, Funny Girl, High Spirits, Crazy Words Crazy Times: The Cole Porter-Irving Berlin Revue, Beloved Enemies.
PICTURES: The Girl Most Likely, A House is Not a Home, Which Way to the Front?, The Ritz, Freaky Friday, Falling in Love Again, Pandemonium, Tiger Warsaw, Modern Love, Eternity, The Missing Elephant (Due South).
TELEVISION: Series: Henry Morgan's Great Talent Hunt, The Perry Como Show, The Mothers-in-Law, The Doris Day Show, The Steve Allen Comedy Hour, What a Dummy. Movies: The Dream Merchants, Alice in Wonderland. Guest appearances incl. over 100 spots on The Tonight Show. Pilot: Makin' Out.

BALLHAUS, MICHAEL
Cinematographer. b. Berlin, Germany, August 5, 1935.
PICTURES: Deine Zartlichkeiten, Two of Us, Whity, Beware of a Holy Whore, Tschetan, The Indian Boy, The Bitter Tears of Petra von Kant, Fox and his Friends, Mother Kusters Goes to Heaven, Summer Guests, Satan's Brew, I Only Want You To Love Me, Adolf and Marlene, Chinese Roulette, Bolweiser (The Stationmaster's Wife), Willie and the Chinese Cat, Women in New York, Despair, The Marriage of Maria Braun, Germany in Autumn, German Spring, The Uprising, Big and Little, Malou, Looping, Baby It's You, Friends and Husbands, Dear Mr. Wonderful, Magic Mountain, Edith's Diary, Aus der Familie der Panzereschen, The Autograph, Heartbreakers, Old Enough, Reckless, After Hours, Under the Cherry Moon, The Color of Money, The Glass Menagerie, Broadcast News, The House on Carroll Street, The Last Temptation of Christ, Working Girl, Dirty Rotten Scoundrels, The Fabulous Baker Boys, GoodFellas, Postcards from the Edge, Guilty by Suspicion, What About Bob?, The Mambo Kings, Bram Stoker's Dracula, The Age of Innocence, Quiz Show, Outbreak, Sleepers.

BALSAM, MARTIN
Actor. b. New York, NY, Nov. 4, 1919. e. New School for Social Research. Daughter is actress Talia Balsam. NY stage debut Ghost for Sale, 1941.
THEATER: Lamp at Midnight, The Wanhope Building, High Tor, A Sound of Hunting, Macbeth, Sundown Beach, The Closing Door, You Know I Can't Hear You When the Water's Running (Tony Award, 1968), Cold Storage (Obie Award).
PICTURES: On the Waterfront (debut, 1954), Twelve Angry Men, Time Limit, Marjorie Morningstar, Al Capone, Middle of the Night, Psycho, Ada, Breakfast at Tiffany's, Cape Fear,

Everybody Go Home!, The Conquered City, Who's Been Sleeping in My Bed?, The Carpetbaggers, Youngblood Hawke, Seven Days in May, Harlow, The Bedford Incident, A Thousand Clowns (Academy Award for Best Supporting Actor, 1965), After the Fox, Hombre, Me Natalie, The Good Guys and the Bad Guys, Trilogy, Catch-22, Tora! Tora! Tora!, Little Big Man, The Anderson Tapes, Confessions of a Police Captain, The Man, The Stone Killer, Summer Wishes Winter Dreams, The Taking of Pelham One Two Three, Murder on the Orient Express, Mitchell, Season for Assassins, All The President's Men, Two-Minute Warning, The Sentinel, Silver Bears, Cuba, There Goes the Bride, Cry Onion, The Salamander, The Goodbye People, Innocent Prey, St. Elmo's Fire, Death Wish III, The Delta Force, Whatever It Takes, Private Investigations, Two Evil Eyes (The Black Cat), Cape Fear (1991), The Silence of the Hams.
TELEVISION: Series: Archie Bunker's Place. Guest: Actors Studio Theatre, US Steel Hour, Mr. Peepers, Alfred Hitchcock Presents, Arrest and Trial. Movies: Hunters Are For Killing, The Old Man Who Cried Wolf, Night of Terror, A Brand New Life, Six Million Dollar Man, Trapped Beneath the Sea, Miles to Go Before I Sleep, Death Among Friends, The Lindbergh Kidnapping Case, Raid on Entebbe, Contract on Cherry Street, The Storyteller, Siege, Rainbow, The Millionaire, The Seeding of Sarah Burns, House on Garibaldi Street, Aunt Mary, Love Tapes, People vs. Jean Harris, Little Gloria, Happy at Last, I Want to Live, Murder in Space, Kids Like These. Mini-Series: Space, Queenie. Specials: Cold Storage, Grown Ups.
(d. February 13, 1996)

BANCROFT, ANNE
Actress. r.n. Anna Maria Italiano. b. New York, NY, Sept. 17, 1931. m. director-comedian Mel Brooks. e. American Acad. of Dramatic Arts. Acting debut on TV, Studio One as Anne Marno in Torrents of Spring.
THEATER: Two For the Seesaw (Tony Award, Theatre World Award: 1958), The Miracle Worker (Tony Award, 1960), Mother Courage, The Devils, A Cry of Players, Golda, Duet For One, Mystery of the Rose Bouquet, The Little Foxes.
PICTURES: Don't Bother to Knock (debut, 1952), Tonight We Sing, Treasure of the Golden Condor, The Kid from Left Field, Gorilla at Large, Demetrius and the Gladiators, The Raid, New York Confidential, Life in the Balance, The Naked Street, The Last Frontier, Walk the Proud Land, Nightfall, The Restless Breed, The Girl in Black Stockings, The Miracle Worker (Academy Award for Best Actress, 1962), The Pumpkin Eater, The Slender Thread, Seven Women, The Graduate, Young Winston, The Prisoner of Second Avenue, The Hindenburg, Lipstick, Silent Movie, The Turning Point, Fatso (also dir., s.p.), The Elephant Man, To Be or Not to Be, Garbo Talks, Agnes of God, 'night Mother, 84 Charing Cross Road, Torch Song Trilogy, Bert Rigby You're a Fool, Honeymoon in Vegas, Love Potion No. 9, Point of No Return, Malice, Mr. Jones, How to Make an American Quilt, Home for the Holidays, Dracula–Dead & Loving It, The Sunchaser.
TELEVISION: Mini-Series: Jesus of Nazareth, Marco Polo, Specials: I'm Getting Married, Annie and the Hoods, Annie: The Women in the Life of a Man (also dir.; Emmy Award for Best Variety Special, 1970), Mrs. Cage, The Mother. Movies: Broadway Bound, Oldest Living Confederate Widow Tells All, The Mother, Homecoming.

BAND, ALBERT
Producer, Director. b. Paris, France, May 7, 1924. e. Lyceum Louis le Grand, won French-English Literature Prize 1938; entered film industry as cutter Pathe Lab.; prod. ass't to John Huston at MGM; first screen credit adaptation Red Badge of Courage novel; first direction, The Young Guns; formed Maxim Productions, Inc., Sept. 1956; prod. Recently formed Albert Band Intl. Prods., Inc.
PICTURES: The Young Guns, I Bury the Living, Face of Fire, The Avenger, Grand Canyon Massacre, The Tramplers, The Hellbenders (prod. only), A Minute to Pray a Second to Die, Little Cigars, Dracula's Dog, She Came to the Valley, Metalstorm: The Destruction of Jared-Syn, Swordkill, Buy and Cell (exec. prod. only), Troll, Terrorvision, Ghoulies II, Robotjox.

BAND, CHARLES
Producer-Director. b. Los Angeles, CA, Dec. 27, 1951. e. Overseas Sch. of Rome. Son of Albert Band. Formed Media Home Ent., 1978; formed Empire Ent., 1983; formed Full Moon Ent., 1988; formed Moonbeam Productions, 1993.
PICTURES: Prod.: Mansion of the Doomed, Cinderella, End of the World, Laserblast, Fairytales, Swordkill, Dungeonmaster, Eliminators. Dir.-Prod.: Crash, Parasite, Metalstorm, Trancers, Pulsepounders, Meridian (Kiss of the Beast), Crash & Burn, Trancers II, Dr. Mordrid. Exec. Prod.: Tourist Trap, Day Time Ended, Ghoulies, Re-Animator, Zone Troopers, Troll, Terrorvision, Crawlspace, Dolls, From Beyond, The Caller, Spellcaster, Cellar Dweller, Ghoulies II, Enemy Territory, Deadly Weapon, Robot Jox, Prison, Buy & Cell, Ghost Town, Catacombs, Arena, Puppet Master, Shadowzone, Puppet Master II, The Pit and the Pendulum, Subpecies, Puppet Master III, Arcade, Dollman, Netherworld, Bad Channels, Trancers III,

Shrunken Heads, Oblivion, Dr. Mordrid, Robot Wards, Subspecies II, Mandroid, Invisible, Prehysteria, Remote, Dragonworld, Beanstalk, Pet Shop, Prehysteria II.

BANDERAS, ANTONIO
Actor. b. Malaga, Spain, Aug. 10, 1960. e. School of Dramatic Art, Malaga. Moved to Madrid in 1981 where he made his stage debut in Los Tarantos. Other theatre incl. The City and the Dogs, Daughter of the Air, The Tragedy of Edward II of England.
PICTURES: Labyrinth of Passion (debut, 1982), Pesantas Positzas, Y Del Seguro... Libranos Senor!, Pestanas Positzas, El Senor Galindez, El Caso Almeria, Los Zancos, Casa Cerrado, La Corte de Faraon, Requiem por un Campesino Espanol, 27 Horas, Puzzle, Matador, Asi Como Habian Sido, Law of Desire, The Pleasure of Killing, Baton Rouge, Bajarse Al Moro, Women on the Verge of a Nervous Breakdown, Si Te Dicen Que Cai, Tie Me Up! Tie Me Down!, Contra el Viento, La Blanca Paloma, Truth or Dare, The Mambo Kings, Philadelphia, Dispara, Of Love and Shadows, The House of the Spirits, Interview With the Vampire, Miami Rhapsody, Desperado, Four Rooms, Never Talk to Strangers, Two Much, Assassins, Evita.
TELEVISION: La llave de Hierro, Fragmentos de Interior, La Mujer de Tu Vida.

BANDY, MARY LEA
Director, Dept. of Film, Museum of Modern Art. b. Evanston, IL, June 16, 1943. e. Stanford U., B.A., 1965. Asst. editor, Harry Abrams and Museum of Modern Art. Director (1980-93), Chief Curator (1993-), Dept. of Film, Museum of Modern Art Editor of MOMA film publications incl.: Rediscovering French Film (1983). Member: Advisory Board, AFI's National Center for Preservation of Film and Video; Film Advisory Comm., American Federation of Arts; Advisory Comm. on Film, Japan Society; Advisory Comm. NY State Motion Picture and Television Advisory Board. Co-president, National Alliance of Media Arts Center, 1986-87, 1987-88. Bd. mem.: Intl. Film Seminars, MacDowell Colony, Natl. Film Preservation Board, Library of Congress, Advisory Board, Film Foundation, Board of Directors, Third World Newsreel.

BANJERJEE, VICTOR
Actor. b. Calcutta, India, Oct. 15, 1946. Was instrumental in forming the first Screen Extras Union in India, presently founding secretary. Won international recognition for A Passage to India. Stage: Pirates of Penzance, An August Requiem (director, 1981), Desert Song, Godspell.
PICTURES: The Chess Players (debut), Hullabaloo, Madhurban, Tanaya, Pratidan, Prarthana, Dui Prithri, Kalyug, Arohan, Jaipur Junction (German), A Passage to India, Foreign Body, The Home and the World, Hard to Be a God, Bitter Moon, World Within World Without.
TELEVISION: Movie: Dadah Is Death.

BANNEN, IAN
Actor. b. Airdrie, Scotland, June 29, 1928. Early career Shakespeare Memorial Theatre (now RSC), Stratford-on-Avon.
THEATER: A View From the Bridge, The Iceman Cometh, Long Days Journey Into Night, Sergeant Musgrave's Dance. Royal Shakespeare Thea. Co. 1961-62: Toys in the Attic, Hamlet, As You Like It (with Vanessa Redgrave), Romeo and Juliet, Othello, The Blood Knot, Devil's Disciple, The Iceman Cometh, Hedda Gabler, Translations (Drama Critics Award, 1981); Riverside Mermaid Theatres, 1983; Moon for the Misbegotten (London, Boston, Broadway), All My Sons.
PICTURES: Private's Progress (debut, 1956), The Third Key (The Long Arm), Battle Hell (Yangtse Incident), Miracle in Soho, The Birthday Present, Behind the Mask, A Tale of Two Cities, She Didn't Say No, The French Mistress, Carlton-Browne of the F.O. (Man in Cocked Hat), On Friday at 11, A French Mistress, The Risk (Suspect), Macbeth, Station Six Sahara, Psyche 59, Mister Moses, Rotten to the Core, The Hill, The Flight of the Phoenix (Acad. Award nom.), Penelope, Sailor From Gibraltar, Lock Up Your Daughters!, Too Late the Hero, The Deserter, Fright, Doomwatch, The Offence (BAFTA nom.), The Macintosh Man, The Driver's Seat, The Voyage, Bite the Bullet, From Beyond the Grave, Sweeney!, Inglorious Bastards, Ring of Darkness, The Watcher in the Woods, Eye of the Needle, Night Crossing, Gandhi, The Prodigal, Gorky Park, Defense of the Realm, Lamb, Hope and Glory (BAFTA nom.), The Courier, The Match, Ghost Dad, Crossing the Line (The Big Man), George's Island, The Gamble, Damage, A Pin for the Butterfly, Braveheart, Dead Sea Reels.
TELEVISION: Johnny Belinda, Jane Eyre, Jesus of Nazareth, Tinker Tailor Soldier Spy, Dr. Jekyll and Mr. Hyde, Fifteen Streets, Murder in Eden, Ashenden, Uncle Vanya, The Sound and the Silence, The Treaty, Doctor Finlay, The Politician's Wife, Original Sin.

BANNER, BOB
Producer, Director. b. Ennis, TX, Aug. 15, 1921. e. Southern Methodist U., B.A., 1939-43; Northwestern U., M.A., 1946-48. U.S. Naval Reserve 1943-46; faculty, Northwestern U., 1948-50; staff dir., NBC-TV in Chicago, 1949-50. Pres., Bob Banner Assocs. Visiting Prof.: Southern Methodist U.

TELEVISION: Garroway at Large (dir.), Fred Waring Show (prod., dir.), Omnibus (dir.), Nothing But the Best (prod. dir.), Dave Garroway Show (prod. dir), Dinah Shore Show, Garry Moore Show (exec. prod.), Candid Camera TV Show (exec. prod.), Carnegie Hall Salutes Jack Benny (exec. prod.), Julie & Carol at Carnegie Hall, Carol & Co., Jimmy Dean Show, Calamity Jane, Once Upon a Mattress, The Entertainers, Kraft Summer Music Hall, Carol & Co., Ice Follies, Carol Burnett Show, Peggy Fleming at Madison Square Garden, John Davidson at Notre Dame, Here's Peggy Fleming, Peggy Fleming at Sun Valley, The American West of John Ford, Love! Love! Love!—Hallmark Hall of Fame, To Europe with Love, Peggy Fleming Visits the Soviet Union, Perry Como's Lake Tahoe Holiday, Perry Como's Christmas In Mexico, Perry Como's Hawaiian Holiday, Perry Como's Spring In New Orleans, Don Ho Show, Perry Como Las Vegas Style, Perry Como's Christmas in Austria, All-Star Anything Goes, Peggy Fleming and Holiday on Ice at Madison Square Garden, Julie Andrews, One Step Into Spring, Leapin' Lizards, It's Liberace, Perry Como's Easter By The Sea, Ford Motor Company's 75th Anniversary; Gift of Music, specials starring Bob Hope, Julie Andrews, Andy Williams, Los Angeles Music Center 25th Anniversay. Movies: Mongo's Back in Town, The Last Survivors, Journey From Darkness, My Sweet Charlie, Bud and Lou, Yes Virginia There is a Santa Claus, Crash Landing, With Murder in Mind, The Sea Wolf, Angel Flight Down. Series: Almost Anything Goes, Solid Gold, Star Search, It's Showtime at the Apollo, Uptown Comedy Club.

BAR, JACQUES JEAN LOUIS
Executive, Producer, Exhibitor. b. Chateauroux, France, Sept. 12, 1921. e. Lycaees Lakanal and Saint Louis, France. Formed Citae-Films S.A., 1947; CIPRA in assoc. with MGM, 1961; S.C.B.; Bourges, 8 cinemas; S.C.M., Le Mans, 9 cinemas. Hollywood films: Bridge to the Sun, Once A Thief, Guns for San Sebastian. Prod. 57 films in France, Spain, Italy, Switzerland, Japan and Brazil 1948-89.
PICTURES: Where the Hot Wind Blows, Bridge to the Sun, Rififi in Tokyo, A Very Private Affair, Swordsmen of Siena, Monkey in Winter, The Turfist, Any Number Can Win, The Day and the Hour, Joy House, Guns for San Sebastian, Last Known Address, The Homecoming, Dancing Machine, The Candidate, Once a Thief, My Father the Hero.

BARANSKI, CHRISTINE
Actress. b. Buffalo, NY, May 2, 1952. e. Juilliard Sch. of Music & Dramatic Arts.
THEATER: NY: Private Lives, One Crack Out, Says I Says He, Shadow of a Gunman, Hide and Seek (B'way debhut, 1980), Company, Coming Attractions, Operation Midnight Climax, A Midsummer Night's Dream (Obie Award, 1982), Sally and Marsha, The Real Thing (Tony Award, 1984), Hurlyburly, It's Only a Play, The House of Blue Leaves, Rumors (Tony Award, 1989), Elliot Loves, Nick and Nora, Lips Together Teeth Apart, The Loman Family Picnic.
PICTURES: Soup for One (debut, 1982), Lovesick, Crackers, Nine 1/2 Weeks, Legal Eagles, The Pick-Up Artist, Reversal of Fortune, The Night We Never Met, Life With Mikey, Addams Family Values, New Jersey Drive, Jeffrey, Birdcage.
TELEVISION: Series: Cybill (Emmy Award, 1995). Movie: Playing for Time. Special: The Addams Chronicles.

BARBEAU, ADRIENNE
Actress. b. Sacramento, CA, June 11, 1947. e. Foothill Col.
THEATER: B'way: Fiddler on the Roof, Grease (Tony nom., Theatre World Award). L.A.: Women Behind Bars, Strange Snow, Pump Boys & Dinettes, Drop Dead. Canadian Premiere: Lost in Yonkers. Regional: Love Letters, Best Little Whorehouse in Texas.
PICTURES: The Fog, Cannonball Run, Escape From New York, Swamp Thing, Creepshow, The Next One, Back to School, Open House, Two Evil Eyes, Cannibal Women & the Avocado Jungle of Death, Father Hood.
TELEVISION: Series: Maude, Batman (voice). Movies: The Great Houdinis, Having Babies, Red Alert, Return to Fantasy Island, Crash, Someone's Watching Me!, The Darker Side of Terror, The Top of the Hill, Valentine Magic on Love Island, Tourist, Charlie and the Great Balloon Chase, Seduced, Bridge Across Time, Blood River, Double Crossed, The Burden of Proof, The Parsley Garden, Jailbreakers, Bram Stoker's Burial of the Rats. Guest: Quincy, 8 Is Enough, Tony Orlando and Dawn, The David Frost Special, Bobby Vinton Show, FBI, Head of the Class, Love Boat, Hotel, Twlight Zone, Murder She Wrote, Dream On, Daddy Dearest, The Carlin Show, Babylon 5.

BARBER, FRANCES
Actress. b. Wolverhampton, Eng., May 13, 1957. e. Bangor U.; grad. studies in theatre, Cardiff U. Stage experience with fringe theaters including improvisational troupe Hull Truck Theatre Company, Glasgow Citizens and Tricycle Theatre (Killburn) before joining Royal Shakespeare Co. (Camille, Hamlet).
PICTURES: The Missionary (debut, 1982), A Zed and Two Noughts, White City, Castaway, Prick Up Your Ears, Sammy and Rosie Get Laid, We Think the World of You, The Grasscutter, Chamber ga part (Separate Bedrooms), Young Soul Rebels, Secret Friends.

TELEVISION: Clem, Jackie's Story, Home Sweet Home, Flame to the Phoenix, Reilly, Ace of Spies, Those Glory, Glory Days; Hard Feelings, Behaving Badly, The Nightmare Years.

BARBERA, JOSEPH R.
Executive. b. New York, NY, Mar. 24, 1911. e. NYU, American Institute of Banking. After schooling joined Irving Trust Co. in N.Y.; started submitting cartoon drawings to leading magazines selling one to Collier's. Joined Van Buren Assocs. as sketch artist, later going to work in animation dept. of MGM Studios. At MGM met William Hanna, who became his lifelong business associate. Made first animated short together in 1937, starting the famous Tom & Jerry series which they produced for 20 years. Left MGM in 1957 to form Hanna-Barbera Productions to make cartoons for TV. Hanna-Barbera became a subsidiary of Taft Ent. Co. in 1968 with both men operating the studio under long-term agreements with Taft. Taft and the studio were sold to Great American Broadcasting, 1988. Hanna-Barbera Prods. acquired by Turner Bdcstg. System, 1991. Barbera is co-founder, chmn. Team received Governor's Award from the Academy of Television Arts & Sciences, 1988.
PICTURES: Hey There It's Yogi Bear, A Man Called Flintstone, Charlotte's Web, C.H.O.M.P.S., Heidi's Song, Jetsons: The Movie, The Flintstones (exec. prod. of live action film; also cameo appearance).
TELEVISION: Series: The Huckleberry Hound Show (Emmy Award), Quick Draw McGraw, Yogi Bear, The Flintstones, The Jetsons, Top Cat, Jonny Quest, Scooby-Doo, Smurfs. Specials/Movies: The Gathering (Emmy Award), I Yabba Dabba Do!, Hollyrock-a-Bye Baby.

BARBOUR, ALAN G.
Writer, Editor, Publisher. b. Oakland, CA, July 25, 1933. e. Rutgers U. m. Catherine Jean Callovini, actress, Teacher, AADA, American Mime Theatre. U.S. Army, worked as computer programmer. Formed Screen Facts Press in 1963, Screen Facts Magazine. Compiled, edited: The Serials of Republic, The Serials of Columbia, Great Serial Ads, The B Western, Serial Showcase, Hit the Saddle, The Wonderful World of B-Films, Days of Thrills and Adventure, Serial Quarterly, Serial Pictorial, Karloff—A Pictorial History, Errol Flynn—A Pictorial Biography, A Pictorial History of the Serial, A Thousand and One Delights, Cliffhanger, The Old-Time Radio Quiz Book. Direct Mktg. Div., RCA Records. Mgr., A & R, RCA, BMGVideo Club.

BARBOUR, MALCOLM
Executive. b. London, England, May 3, 1934. e. Radley Coll., Oxford, England, A.B., Columbia Coll. At NBC was press info. asst., 1958-59; asst. magazine ed., 1959-62; assoc. mag. ed., 1962-64; sr. mag. ed., 1964-65; mgr. of magazine pub., National Broadcasting Co., 1965-67; pub. mgr., Buena Vista, 1967-68; Eastern story ed., Walt Disney Prod., 1968-69; dir. of adv. & pub. relations, Buena Vista, 1969. Partner, Producers Creative Services, 1976-79. President, The International Picture Show, 1980-81 (Tim Conway comedies The Billion Dollar Hobo and They Went That-A-Way & That-A-Way; Slayer. Distributor: Soldier of Orange, The Magic of Lassie, The Visitor, etc.). President, Barbour/Langley Productions, 1982-present. Producer, Geraldo Rivera specials: American Vice, Innocence Lost, Sons of Scarface, Murder: Live from Death Row, Satan Worship. Producer, Jack Anderson specials. Writer-Producer, Cocaine Blues. Co-screenplay, P.O.W. The Escape. Exec. producer: Cops, Code 3, Inside the KGB, Cop Files, Deadly Sins (also writer).

BARDOT, BRIGITTE
Actress. b. Paris, France, Sept. 28, 1934. e. Paris Conservatory. Studied ballet, before becoming model. Studied acting with Rene Simon. On stage in L'Invitation au Chateau. Awarded French Legion of Honor, 1985. Active in the movement to preserve endangered animals. Created the Brigitte Bardot Foundation for animal protection, April 1986.
PICTURES: Le Trou Normand (debut, 1952), Nanina la Fille san Voiles, Les Dents Longues, Act of Love, Le Portrait de Son Pere, Royal Affairs in Versailles, Tradita, Le Fils de Caroline Cherie, Helen of Troy, Futures Vedettes, Les Grandes Maneuvres, Doctor at Sea, La Lumiere d'En Face (The Light Across the Street), Cette Sacre Gamine (Mam'zelle Pigalle), Mi Figlio Nerone, En Effeuillant la Marguerite (Please Mr. Balzac), The Bride is Much Too Beautiful, And God Created Woman, Une Parisienne, The Night Heaven Fell, En Cas de Malheur, Le Femme et le Pantin, Babette Goes to War, Come Dance With Me, La Verite (The Truth), La Bride sur le Cou, Les Amours Celebres, A Very Private Affair, Love on a Pillow, Contempt, A Ravishing Idiot, Dear Brigitte, Viva Maria, Masculine-Feminine, Two Weeks in September, Spirits of the Dead (Histories Extraordinaires), Shalako, Les Femmes, L'Ours et la Poupee, Les Novices, Boulevard du Rhum (Rum Runner), Les Petroleuses (The Legend of Frenchie King), Ms. Don Juan, L'Historie Tres Bonne et Tres Joyeuse de Colinot Troussechemise.

BARE, RICHARD L.
Producer, Director. b. Turlock, CA, Aug. 12, 1925. Started as dir. for Warners. SDG Best Dir. TV award, 1959. *Author*: The Film Director (Macmillan, 1971). Pres., United National Film Corp.
PICTURES: *Dir.*: Smart Girls Don't Talk, Flaxy Martin, This Side of the Law, House Across The Street, This Rebel Breed, Girl on the Run, Return of Frontiersman. *Dir.-Prod.-Writer*: Wicked Wicked, Story of Chang & Eng, City of Shame, Sudden Target, Purple Moon.
TELEVISION: 77 Sunset Strip, Maverick, So This is Hollywood, The Islanders, Dangerous Robin, This Rebel Breed, Twilight Zone, Bus Stop, Adventures in Paradise, The Virginian, Kraft Theatre, Run For Your Life, Green Acres, Farraday and Son, Westwind.

BAREN, HARVEY M.
Executive. b. New York, NY, Nov. 25, 1931. e. State U. of New York. Served in U.S. Army, 1952-54; United Artists Corp., 1954-59 (contract dept., print dept., booker—NY branch); asst. to general sls. mgr., Magna Pictures Corp., 1959-61; road show mgr., national sales coordinator, 20th Century-Fox, 1961-71; asst. general sales manager, Allied Artists Pictures, 1971-79; v.p., gen. sls. mgr., Nat'l. Screen Service, 1978-79; v.p., gen. sls. mgr., Cannon Pictures, 1979-80. 1980, pres. of Summit Feature Distributors; 1983, exec. V.P., dir., MGM/UA Classics; 1986, joined New Century/Vista as v.p., sls. admin. 1991, pres. Sea Movies Inc.

BARENHOLTZ, BEN
Executive. b. Kovel, Poland, Oct. 5, 1935. *Asst. theatre manager*: RKO Bushwick, Brooklyn, 1959-60. Manager: Village Theatre (Fillmore East), N.Y., 1966-68. *Owner-operator*: Elgin Cinema, 1968-75, originated Midnight Movie concept with El Topo. *President-owner*: Libra Film Corp., 1972-84. 1984-1992, v.p. & partner: Circle Releasing (which launched and distributed The Family Game, Therese, Blood Simple and prod. Raising Arizona). Pres. Barenholtz Prods. Inc.
PICTURES: *Exec. Prod.*: Miller's Crossing, Barton Fink, Cheat, White Man's Burden (Bleeding Hearts), Georgia.

BARISH, KEITH
Producer. b. Los Angeles, CA. Background in finance. Founded Keith Barish Prods. in 1979. 1984-88 in partnership with Taft Broadcasting Co., Entertainment Div. Founder and chmn. of Planet Hollywood. Appeared in film Last Action Hero.
PICTURES: *Exec. prod.*: Endless Love, Sophie's Choice (prod.), Kiss Me Goodbye, Misunderstood, Nine 1/2 Weeks, Big Trouble in Little China, Light of Day (prod.), The Running Man, The Monster Squad, Ironweed (prod.), The Serpent and the Rainbow, Her Alibi, Firebirds, The Fugitive.
TELEVISION: *Movie*: A Streetcar Named Desire (exec. prod.).

BARKER, BOB
TV host. b. Darrington, WA, Dec. 12. e. Springfield Central H.S., Drury Coll. News writer, announcer, disc jockey KTTS until 1949. News editor, staff announcer, Station WWPG. Pres. Bob Barker Prod., Inc. 1966 started as M.C. for both Miss USA Pageant and Miss Universe Pageant. 1970, first time as M.C. of both Rose Bowl Parade and Pillsbury Bakeoff. Series (emcee or host): The End of the Rainbow, Truth or Consequences (daytime: 1956-65; nighttime synd: 1966-74), Lucky Pair (prod.), That's My Line (1980-1), The Price Is Right (exec. prod. & m.c.; 1972-; received several Emmy Awards as host). *Narrator*: 500 Festival Parade, Indianapolis 1969-81.

BARKER, CLIVE
Writer, Producer, Director. b. Liverpool, England, Oct. 5, 1952. e. Liverpool Univ. Moved to London at twenty-one, forming theatre company. Began writing short stories which were subsequently published as Books of Blood (Vols. 1-3 & Vols. 4-6). *Novels*: Damnation Game, Weaveworld, The Great and Secret Show, Imajica, The Thief of Always, Everville, Sacrament. Also painter with exhibitions in NY, California. *Books*: Clive Barker: Illustrator, The Art of Clive Barker, Incarnations. *Plays*: History of the Devil, Colossus, Frankenstein In Love
PICTURES: Rawhead Rex (from his story), Transmutations (from his story), Hellraiser (dir., s.p.; from his novella The Hellbound Heart), Hellbound: Hellraiser II (co-exec. prod.; from his story), Nightbreed (dir., s.p.; from his novel Cabal), Sleepwalkers (actor), Hellraiser III: Hell on Earth (exec. prod.; from his story), Candyman (exec. prod.; from his story The Forbidden), Candyman: Farewell to the Flesh (exec. prod.; from his story), Lord of Illusions (dir., s.p., co-prod.; from his story The Last Illusion).

BARKER, MICHAEL W.
Executive. b. Nuremberg, Germany, Jan. 9, 1954. e. U. of Texas at Austin, B.S. in International Communications, 1976. Joined Films Inc. 1979-80, then United Artists 1980-83, first as non-theatrical sales manager, then as national sales manager of UA Classics. Co-founder and v.p., Sales & Marketing for Orion Classics, a div. of Orion, 1983-1992. Co-founder and co-pres., Sony Pictures Classics, 1992-present. Member, board of directors of BAFTA New York and Independent Features Project.

BARKETT, STEVE
Actor, Director, Producer, Film Editor, Writer. b. Oklahoma City, OK, Jan. 1, 1950. Exhibited and scored over 52 feature length classic silent films 1966-1968 as dir. of two film series at the Okla. Art Ctr. and Science and Arts Fdn.; prior to coming to LA in 1970. Toured in stage prod. 1971-72: Pajama Tops, Winnie the Pooh. Exec. in several non-theatrical releasing cos., incl. Independent Film Associates and Thunderbird Films. From 1968 to 1974 was active in film preservation and restoration work on early silent and sound films. 1978 founded The Hollywood Book and Poster Company. Est. The Nautilus Film Co., 1978. Founded and operated Capt. Nemo's Video (1985-87). Co-wrote and performed 42 episodes of Capt. Nemo's Video Review for radio (1987).
PICTURES: *Actor*: The Egyptians are Coming, Corpse Grinders, Dillinger, Night Caller, Cruise Missile, Beverly Hills Vampire, Wizard of the Demon Sword, Bikini Drive-In, Cyber Zone, Hard Bounty, Masseuse, Star Hunter. *Prod./Dir./S.P./Edit.*: Collecting, Empire of the Dark, Angels of Death. *Editor only*: Hurricane Express. *Spcl. Fx. only*: Warlords, Sorceress. *Actor/Dir./ S.P./Prod./Edit.*: The Movie People, Cassavetes, The Aftermath, Angels of Death, Empire of the Dark. *Actor/FX*: Dark Universe, Dinosaur Island, Attack of the 60's Centerfold, Invisible Mom.

BARKIN, ELLEN
Actress. b. Bronx, NY, Apr. 16, 1954. e. Hunter Coll.; Actors Studio.
THEATER: Irish Coffee (debut, Ensemble Studio Theatre), Shout Across the River, Killings Across the Last, Tobacco Road, Extremities, Eden Court.
PICTURES: Diner (debut, 1982), Tender Mercies, Daniel, Eddie and the Cruisers, Harry and Son, The Adventures of Buckaroo Banzai Across the Eighth Dimension, Enormous Changes at the Last Minute, Terminal Choice, Desert Bloom, Down by Law, The Big Easy, Siesta, Made in Heaven (unbilled), Sea of Love, Johnny Handsome, Switch, Man Trouble, Mac, This Boy's Life, Into the West, Bad Company, Wild Bill, Mad Dog time.
TELEVISION: *Series*: Search for Tomorrow. *Movies*: Kent State, We're Fighting Back, Parole, Terrible Joe Moran, Act of Vengeance, Clinton and Nadine. *Special*: Faerie Tale Theatre (The Princess Who Never Laughed).

BARLOW, PHIL
Executive. President, Buena Vista Pictures Distribution.

BARNHOLTZ, BARRY
Executive. b. St. Louis, MO, Oct. 12, 1945. e. California State U., Northridge; USC; UCLA; W.L.A.U. (studied law). Concert promotions in So. Calif. 1963-71; with Medallion TV as v.p. in chg. sls.; Barnholtz Organization, representing independent prod. cos. for feature films for cable. Founder, sr. v.p. of Vidmark Inc., and Trimark Films.

BARON, STANLEY N.
Executive. President, Society of Motion Picture and Television Engineers.

BARR, ANTHONY
Producer, Director, Actor. r.n. Morris Yaffe. b. St. Louis, MO, March 14, 1921. e. Washington U., B.S. 1942. Actor, asst. stage mgr., 1944-46; stage mgr., Katherine Dunham Dancers, 1946-47; teacher, actor, dir. in chg. Film Actors' Workshop, Professional Theatre Workshop, Hollywood; v.p. current prime time series, ABC-TV; v.p., current dramatic program production, CBS-TV; v.p., CBS Entertainment Prods.
THEATER: *Actor*: Jacobowsky and the Colonel, Winters' Tale, Embezzled Heaven.
PICTURES: *Actor*: People Against O'Hara, Border Incident, The Hollywood Story, The Mozart Story. *Co-prod.*: Dime with a Halo.
TELEVISION: *Director*: Art Linkletter's Houseparty, About Faces. *Assoc. dir.*: Climax, Shower of Stars. *Prod.*: Climax, Summer Studio One. *Assoc. prod.*: Climax, Playhouse 90, Pursuit, G.E. Theatre, The Law and Mr. Jones, Four-Star.
AUTHOR: Acting for the Camera, 1982.

BARRAULT, MARIE-CHRISTINE
Actress. b. Paris, France, March 21, 1944. m. director Roger Vadim.
PICTURES: My Night at Maud's, Le Distrait (The Daydreamer), Lancelot of the Lake, The Aspern Papers, Les Intrus, La Famille Grossfeld, Chloe in the Afternoon, John Glueckstadt, Cousin Cousine (Acad. Award nom.), By the Tennis Courts, Perceval, The Medusa Touch, Tout est a nous, Femme Entre Chien et Loup, Ma Cherie, Stardust Memories, Table for Five, Josephs Tochter, A Love in Germany, Les Mots Pour le Dire, Swann in Love, Grand Piano, Prisonnieres, Un Etae de orages, Savage State, Necessary Love.

BARRETT, RONA
News Correspondent b. New York, NY, Oct. 8, 1936. e. NYU (communications major). Created the column, Rona Barrett's Young Hollywood, which led to featured column in 1960 in Motion Picture Magazine and a nationally syndicated column

distributed to 125 newspapers by the North American Newspaper Alliance. Turned to TV; initial appearances on ABC Owned Stations in 5 cities, providing two-minute reports for local newscasts. Resulted in Dateline Hollywood a network morning prog., co-hosted by Joanna Barnes. In 1969 created first daily syndicated TV news segment for Metromedia. 1975, became arts and entertainment editor for ABC's Good Morning America. 1980, joined NBC News. Publ. and exec. editor, newsletter, The Rona Barrett Report. 1985, pres., Rona Barrett Enterprises, Inc., sr. corresp., Entertainment Tonight; Mutual Radio Network. 1988: creator of original novels for television, for NBC prods. Appeared in films Sextette, An Almost Perfect Affair.

BARRIE, BARBARA
Actress. b. Chicago, IL, May 23, 1931. e. U. of TX, B.F.A., 1953. Trained for stage at Herbert Berghof Studio. NY stage debut, The Wooden Dish (1955). *Author:* Lone Star (1990), Adam Zigzag (1994).
THEATER: The Crucible, The Beaux Stratagem, The Taming of the Shrew, Conversations in the Dark, All's Well That Ends Well, Happily Never After, Horseman Pass By, Company, The Selling of the President, The Prisoner of Second Avenue, The Killdeer, California Suite, Big and Little, Isn't It Romantic, Torch Song Trilogy, Fugue, After Play.
PICTURES: Giant (debut, 1956), The Caretakers, One Potato Two Potato (best actress, Cannes Film Fest, 1964), The Bell Jar, Breaking Away (Acad. Award nom.), Private Benjamin, Real Men, End of the Line, The Passage.
TELEVISION: *Series:* Love of Life, Diana, Barney Miller, Breaking Away, Tucker's Witch, Reggie, Double Trouble, Love of Life, Big City Story. *Guest appearances:* Ben Casey, The Fugitive, Dr. Kildare, Alfred Hitchcock Presents, The Defenders, Mary Tyler Moore Show, Lou Grant, Trapper John, M.D., Babes, Kojak, Island Son, thirtysomething. *Movies:* Tell Me My Name, Summer of My German Soldier, To Race the Wind, The Children Nobody Wanted, Not Just Another Affair, Two of a Kind, The Execution, Vital Signs, Winnie, My First Love, Guess Who's Coming for Christmas?, The Odd Couple: Together Again, My Breast. *Specials:* To Be Young Gifted and Black, Barefoot in the Park, What's Alan Watching?, Lovejoy: The Lost Colony, My Summer As a Girl. *Mini-Series:* 79 Park Avenue, Backstairs at the White House, Roots: The Next Generation, Scarlett.

BARRON, ARTHUR RAY
Executive. b. Mt. Lake, MN, July 12, 1934. e. San Diego State U. 1956-60, B.S. Accounting. Certified public acc't, Calif., 1960. Coopers & Lybrand, 1960-63; Desilu Productions, Inc., 1963-67; v.p. finance and admin., Paramount TV, 1967-70; v.p. finance, Paramount Pictures Corp., 1970; sr. v.p. finance and admin., 1971; exec. v.p., finance & admin., 1974; exec. v.p. 1980; exec. v.p., Gulf & Western Industries, entertainment & communications group, 1983; promoted to pres., 1984-88. Chmn, Time Warner Enterprises, 1990.

BARRY, GENE
Actor. r.n. Eugene Klass. b. New York, NY, June 14, 1919. e. New Utrecht H.S., Brooklyn.
BROADWAY: Rosalinda, Catherine Was Great, Happy Is Larry, Bless You All, The Would-Be Gentleman, La Cage aux Folles (Tony nom.).
PICTURES: Atomic City (debut, 1952), The Girls of Pleasure Island, The War of the Worlds, Those Redheads from Seattle, Alaska Seas, Red Garters, Naked Alibi, Soldier of Fortune, The Purple Mask, The Houston Story, Back From Eternity, China Gate, The 27th Day, Forty Guns, Thunder Road, Hong Kong Confidential, Maroc 7, Subterfuge, The Second Coming of Suzanne, Guyana: Cult of the Damned.
TELEVISION: *Series:* Our Miss Brooks, Bat Masterson, Burke's Law (1963-66), The Name of the Game, Burke's Law (1994-95). *Movies:* Prescription Murder, Istanbul Express, Do You Take This Stranger?, The Devil and Miss Sarah, Ransom for Alice!, A Cry for Love, The Girl the Gold Watch and Dynamite, Adventures of Nellie Bly, Turn Back the Clock. *Mini-Series:* Aspen.

BARRY, JOHN
Composer, Arranger, Conductor. r.n. John Barry Prendergast. b. York, England, 1933. Started as rock 'n' roll trumpeter. Artist and prod., CBS Records.
PICTURES: Beat Girl, Never Let Go, The L-Shaped Room, The Amorous Mr. Prawn, From Russia With Love, Seance on a Wet Afternoon, Zulu, Goldfinger, The Ipcress File, The Knack, King Rat, Mister Moses, Thunderball, The Chase, Born Free (2 Academy Awards: Best Music Scoring and Best Song: title song, 1966), The Wrong Box, The Quiller Memorandum, The Whisperers, Deadfall, You Only Live Twice, Petulia, The Lion in Winter (Academy Award, 1968), Midnight Cowboy, The Appointment, On Her Majesty's Secret Service, Monte Walsh, The Last Valley, They Might Be Giants, Murphy's War, Walkabout, Diamonds Are Forever, Mary Queen of Scots, Alice's Adventures in Wonderland, The Public Eye (Follow Me), A Doll's House, The Tamarind Seed, The Dove, The Man With the Golden Gun, The Day of the Locust, Robin and Marian, King Kong, The Deep, The Betsy, Hanover Street, Moonraker, The

Black Hole, Starcrash, Game of Death, Raise the Titanic, Somewhere in Time, Inside Moves, Touched By Love, Body Heat, The Legend of the Lone Ranger, Frances, Hammett, High Road to China, Octopussy, The Golden Seal, Mike's Murder, Until September, The Cotton Club, A View to a Kill, Jagged Edge, Out of Africa (Academy Award, 1985), Howard the Duck, Peggy Sue Got Married, The Living Daylights, Hearts of Fire, Masquerade, A Killing Affair, Dances With Wolves (Academy Award, 1990), Chaplin, Indecent Proposal, Deception, My Life, The Specialist.
TELEVISION: Elizabeth Taylor in London, Sophia Loren in Rome.

BARRYMORE, DREW
Actress. b. Los Angeles, CA, Feb. 22, 1975. Father is actor John Barrymore, Jr. (John Drew Barrymore). At 11 months appeared in first commercial. *Author:* Little Girl Lost (1990).
PICTURES: Altered States (debut, 1980), E.T.: The Extra Terrestrial, Firestarter, Irreconcilable Differences, Cat's Eye, See You in the Morning, Far From Home, No Place to Hide, Waxwork II, Poison Ivy, Motorama, Doppelganger, Wayne's World 2, Bad Girls, Inside the Goldmine, Boys on the Side, Mad Love, Batman Forever, Everyone Says I Love You, Scream.
TELEVISION: *Series:* 2000 Malibu Road. *Movies:* Bogie, Suddenly Love, Babes in Toyland, Conspiracy of Love, The Sketch Artist, Guncrazy (also released theatrically), The Amy Fisher Story. *Specials:* Disneyland's 30th Anniversary, Night of 100 Stars II, Con Sawyer and Hucklemary Finn, 15 & Getting Straight.

BARRYMORE, JOHN DREW
Actor. b. Beverly Hills, CA, June 4, 1932. r.n. John Blythe Barrymore Jr. e. St. John's Military Acad., various public and private schools. Son of actors John Barrymore and Delores Costello. Daughter is actress Drew Barrymore. Started acting at age 18 under the name John Barrymore Jr.
PICTURES: Sundowners (debut, 1950), High Lonesome, Quebec, The Big Night, Thunderbirds, While the City Sleeps, Shadow on the Window, Never Love a Stranger, High School Confidential, Night of the Quarter Moon, The Cossacks, The Night They Killed Rasputin, The Pharaoh's Woman, The Trojan Horse, The Centurion, Invasion 1700, War of the Zombies.

BART, PETER
Executive. b. Martha's Vineyard, MA, July 24, 1932. e. Swarthmore Coll. and The London School of Economics. Eight years as corrp. for New York Times and wrote for such magazines as Harper's, The Atlantic, Saturday Review, etc. Joined Paramount Pictures in 1965. Named exec. ass't. to Robert Evans, exec. in charge of world-wide prod. Appointed v.p. prod. Resigned 1973 to develop and produce own films for Paramount. Appointed pres. Lorimar Films, 1978. Resigned, 1979, to be indept. prod. 1983, joined MGM as sr. v.p., prod., m.p. div. Resigned, 1985, to be indep. prod. Editor, Variety. *Novels:* Thy Kingdom Come (1983), Destinies (1979), Fade Out. PICTURES: *Producer:* Islands in the Stream, Fun with Dick and Jane, Revenge of the Nerds (exec. prod.), Youngblood, Revenge of the Nerds II.

BARTEL, PAUL
Director, Writer, Actor. b. New York, NY, Aug. 6, 1938. e. UCLA, B.A. At 13 spent summer working at UPA Cartoons. Later at UCLA won acting and playwriting awards and prod. animated and doc. films. Awarded Fulbright schl. to study film dir. at Centro Sperimentale di Cinematografia in Rome where dir. short Progetti (presented Venice Fest., 1962). Then at Army Pictorial Center, L.I. City. Asst. dir. military training films and writer-dir. monthly news doc. series, Horizontos for U.S. Information Agency. Directed short film The Naughty Nurse. Appeared in 1984 short film Frankenweenie.
PICTURES: *Actor:* Hi Mom!, Private Parts (also dir. debut), Big Bad Mama (2nd unit dir. only), Death Race 2000 (dir. only), Cannonball (also dir., co-s.p.), Eat My Dust!, Hollywood Boulevard, Grand Theft Auto, Mr. Billion, Piranha, Rock 'n' Roll High School, Heart Like a Wheel, Eating Raoul (also dir., s.p.), Trick or Treats, White Dog, Get Crazy, Not for Publication (also dir., s.p.), Lust in the Dust (dir. only), Into the Night, Sesame Street Presents Follow That Bird, Chopping Mall, Killer Party, The Longshot (dir. only), Munchies, Amazon Women on the Moon, Mortuary Academy, Out of the Dark (also exec. prod.), Scenes From the Class Struggle in Beverly Hills (also dir., s.p.), Pucker Up and Bark Like a Dog, Far Out Man, Gremlins 2: The New Batch, The Pope Must Die, Liquid Dreams, Desire and Hell at Sunset Motel, Posse, Grief, The Jerky Boys, The Usual Suspects, Red Ribbon Blues.
TELEVISION: *Actor:* Alfred Hitchcock Presents, Fame, L.A. Law, Acting on Impulse (movie), A Bucket of Blood (movie). *Director:* Amazing Stories (The Secret Cinema, Gershwin's Truck; also writer, actor), The Hustler of Muscle Beach.

BARTKOWIAK, ANDRZEJ
Cinematographer. b. Lodz, Poland, 1950. Attended Polish Film School. Moved to US in 1972, gaining experience in TV commercials and low-budget features. Protege of Sidney Lumet, for whom did several Pictures.

PICTURES: Deadly Hero, Prince of the City, Deathtrap, The Verdict, Daniel, Terms of Endearment, Garbo Talks, Prizzi's Honor, The Morning After, Power, Nuts, Twins, Q&A, Hard Promises, A Stranger Among Us, Falling Down, Guilty As Sin, Speed, A Good Man in Africa, Losing Isaiah, Species, Jade.

BARTY, BILLY
Actor. b. Millsboro, PA, Oct. 25, 1924. e. LA City Col., LA State U. Began performing at age 3 appearing as Mickey Rooney's little brother in the Mickey McGuire shorts. Founded Little People of America, 1957; Billy Barty Foundation, 1975.
PICTURES: Golddiggers of 1933, Footlight Parade, Roman Scandals, Gift of Gab, A Midsummer Night's Dream, Nothing Sacred, The Clown, The Undead, Billy Rose's Jumbo, Roustabout, Harum Scarum, Pufnstuf, The Day of the Locust, The Amazing Dobermans, W.C. Fields and Me, Foul Play, Firepower, Hardly Working, Under the Rainbow, Night Patrol, Legend, Tough Guys, Body Slam, Rumplestiltskin, Willow, Lobster Man From Mars, UHF, The Rescuers Down Under (voice), Life Stinks.
TELEVISION: Series: Ford Festival, The Spike Jones Show, Circus Boy, Club Oasis, Ace Crawford—Private Eye. Movies: Punch and Jody, Twin Detectives.

BARUCH, RALPH M.
Executive. b. Frankfurt, Germany, Aug. 5, 1923. e. The Sorbonne. m. Jean Ursell de Mountford. Administrative aide, SESAC, Inc. 1944-48; account exec., DuMont Television Network, 1950-54; account exec., CBS Films, 1954; account supervisor, 1957; dir. int'l sales, 1959; CBS Group President 1961-70; pres. and CEO Viacom International, 1971-1983, chairman from 1983-1987 and is currently a consultant to Viacom International. Trustee of Lenox Hill Hospital. Chairman Emeritus of the National Academy of Cable Programming and recipient of the Academy's first Governor's Award. Past-president of the International Radio & Television Society and was honored by an IRTS gold medal award. Founder and fellow of the International Council of the National Academy of Television Arts & Sciences. Recipient of an Emmy Award. Former dir., Executive Committee of the National Cable Television Assoc. Co-founder of C-Span. Recipient of the Vanguard Award, three NCTA President's Awards and NCTA Chairman of the Year Award. Chairman of the USIA's Television Communications Board of Advisors under Pres. Reagan. Elected to the Broadcasting/Cable Hall of Fame in 1992. Appointed to New York City Cultural Affairs Advisory Comm. Member of New York Yacht Club.

BARWOOD, HAL
Writer, Producer, Director. e. U. of Southern California Sch. of Cinema. Has written scripts in collaboration with Matthew Robbins, Barwood branching out into producing with Corvette Summer in 1978 and directing with Warning Sign in 1985.
PICTURES: Screenplays (all with Robbins): The Sugarland Express, The Bingo Long Traveling All-Stars and Motor Kings, MacArthur, Corvette Summer (also prod.), Dragonslayer (also prod.), Warning Sign (also dir.).

BARYSHNIKOV, MIKHAIL
Dancer, Actor. b. Riga, Latvia, Jan. 27, 1948. Joined Kirov Ballet, Leningrad, 1969-74; defected to U.S. With American Ballet Theatre 1974-78; New York City Ballet Company 1978-79; named director of the American Ballet Theatre. B'way stage debut, Metamorphosis (1989).
PICTURES: The Turning Point (debut, 1977; Acad. Award nom.), That's Dancing!, White Nights (also co-choreog.), Dancers (also choreog.), Company Business, The Cabinet of Dr. Ramirez.
TELEVISION: Baryshnikov at the White House (Emmy Award, 1979), Bob Hope on the Road to China, Baryshnikov on Broadway (Emmy Award, 1980), AFI Salute to Fred Astaire, Baryshnikov in Hollywood, AFI Salute to Gene Kelly, David Gordon's Made in USA, All Star Gala at Ford's Theater, Dance in America: Baryshnikov Dances Balanchine (Emmy Award, 1989).

BASCH, BUDDY
Print Media Syndicater, Publicist, Producer. b. South Orange, NJ, June 28, 1922. e. Columbia U. Began career as youngest radio editor in U.S. at 15; since written for national mags, syndicates, wire services, and newspapers. Edit. & pub. Top Hit Club News for 7 yrs. Joined Donahue and Coe 1940 on m.p. accounts, U.S. Army in Europe 1942-45. 1945-67: own publicity and promotion office, working on m.p. company accounts and stars such as Burl Ives, Dinah Shore, Tony Martin, Danny Kaye, Peter Lorre, Tony Bennett, Gloria De Haven, McGuire Sisters, Rhonda Fleming, Sammy Davis, Jr., Anna Maria Alberghetti, Polly Bergen, Meyer Davis, The Beatles, Glenn Miller and Tommy Dorsey Orchestras. Produced many shows for radio, TV and stage in New York, Newark, Chicago, Hartford. Asst. to publisher, The Brooklyn Eagle 1962. 1966 formed Buddy Basch Feature Syndicate, covering assignments on show business, travel, health, medicine, food, human interest and general subjects for N.Y. Daily News, A.P., Grit Magazine, Travel/Holiday,

Frontier Magazine, Kaleidoscope, True, United Features, Gannett Westchester-Rockland Newspapers, Bergen (NJ) Record, Argosy, N.A.N.A., Womens' News Service, Today Magazine, Christian Science Monitor, New York Post, Inflight Magazine, Deseret News, California Canadian, Diversion. Provided Associated Press with worldwide exclusives on a number of national and intl. events. Member: Friars Club since 1959. Organized & appointed permanent chairman, VIP Reception and Security for Friars luncheons and dinners since 1970. Served as Chairman of Elections (6 times). Member of Admission Comm. and House Committee. Contributing ed. Friars Epistle.

BASINGER, KIM
Actress. b. Athens, GA, Dec. 8, 1953. m. actor Alec Baldwin. e. Neighborhood Playhouse. Began career as Ford model in New York.
PICTURES: Hard Country (debut, 1981), Mother Lode, Never Say Never Again, The Man Who Loved Women, The Natural, Fool for Love, 9-1/2 Weeks, No Mercy, Blind Date, Nadine, My Stepmother is an Alien, Batman, The Marrying Man, Final Analysis, Cool World, The Real McCoy, Wayne's World 2, The Getaway.
TELEVISION: Series: Dog and Cat, From Here to Eternity. Mini-Series: From Here to Eternity. Movies: Dog and Cat (pilot), The Ghost of Flight 401, Katie: Portrait of a Centerfold, Killjoy. Guest: Charlie's Angels.

BASS, RONALD
Writer. b. Los Angeles, CA. e. Yale, Harvard Law School. Entered industry as entertainment lawyer, while writing novels: The Perfect Thief, Lime's Crisis, The Emerald Illusion.
PICTURES: Code Name: Emerald, Black Widow, Gardens of Stone, Rain Man (Academy Award, 1988), Sleeping With the Enemy, The Joy Luck Club, When a Man Loves a Woman, Dangerous Minds, Waiting to Exhale.
TELEVISION: Series: Dangerous Minds, Moloney.

BASS, SAUL
Director, Producer. b. New York, NY, May 8, 1920. e. Arts Students League. Pres., Saul Bass/Herb Yager & Assoc. Directed short films, m.p. titles/prologues/epilogues, TV commercials. Directorial feature debut in 1974 with Phase IV.
PICTURES: Shorts: The Searching Eye, From Here to There, Why Man Creates (Academy Award, 1968), Notes on the Popular Arts (Acad. Award nom.), The Solar Film (Acad. Award nom.), Bass on Titles, Quest. Feature sequences: Grand Prix, Psycho. Full Features: Carmen Jones, The Big Knife, The Seven Year Itch, The Man With The Golden Arm, Johnny Concho, Saint Joan, Around the World in 80 Days, The Pride and the Passion, Bonjour Tristesse, Cowboy, Vertigo, The Big Country, Anatomy of a Murder, Psycho, Ocean's Eleven, Spartacus, Exodus, West Side Story, Advise and Consent, Walk on the Wild Side, It's a Mad Mad Mad Mad World, Bunny Lake Is Missing, That's Entertainment Part 2, The Human Factor, Broadcast News, Big, The War of the Roses, Goodfellas, Cape Fear, Mr. Saturday Night, The Age of Innocence.
(d. April 25, 1996)

BASSETT, ANGELA
Actress. b. New York, NY, Aug. 16, 1958. Moved to St. Petersburg, FL, at 5 yrs. old. e. Yale.
THEATER: B'way: Ma Rainey's Black Bottom, Joe Turner's Come and Gone. Off-B'way: Colored People's Time, Antigone, Black Girl, Henry IV Part 1. Regional: Beef No Chicken.
PICTURES: F/X (debut, 1986), Kindergarten Cop, Boyz N the Hood, City of Hope, Critters 4, Innocent Blood, Malcolm X, Passion Fish, What's Love Got to Do With It (Acad. Award nom.; Golden Globe Award), Strange Days, Waiting to Exhale, Vampire in Brooklyn.
TELEVISION: Movies: Line of Fire: The Morris Dees Story, The Jacksons: An American Dream. Guest: Cosby Show, 227, thirtysomething, Tour of Duty, Equal Justice.

BATEMAN, JASON
Actor. b. Rye, NY, Jan. 14, 1969. Brother of actress Justine Bateman. Son of prod.-theatrical mgr. Kent Bateman. Started career in commercials until cast in Little House on the Prairie at 12 (1981).
PICTURES: Teen Wolf Too, Necessary Roughness, Breaking the Rules.
TELEVISION: Series: Little House on the Prairie, Silver Spoons, It's Your Move, Valerie (Valerie's Family, The Hogan Family), Simon, Chicago Sons. Movies: The Fantastic World of D.C. Collins, The Thanksgiving Promise, Can You Feel Me Dancing, The Bates Motel, Moving Target, A Taste for Killing, Confessions: Two Faces of Evil, This Can't Be Love, Hart to Hart: Secrets of the Hart. Mini-Series: Robert Kennedy and His Times. Specials: Just a Little More Love, Candid Camera: Eat! Eat! Eat!

BATEMAN, JUSTINE
Actress. b. Rye, NY, Feb. 19, 1966. Brother is actor Jason Bateman. Father, prod.-theatrical mgr. Kent Bateman.

THEATER: Lulu, Self-Storage, The Crucible, Love Letters, Carnal Knowledge, Speed-the-Plow.
PICTURES: Satisfaction, The Closer, Primary Motive, Deadbolt, The Night We Never Met, God's Lonely Man, Kiss & Tell.
TELEVISION: Series: Family Ties, Men Behaving Badly. Guest: Tales from the Dark Side, One to Grow On, It's Your Move, Glitter. Movies: Right to Kill?, Family Ties Vacation, Can You Feel Me Dancing?, The Fatal Image, In the Eyes of a Stranger, The Hunter, Terror in the Night, Another Woman, A Bucket of Blood. Specials: First the Egg, Whatta Year... 1986, Fame Fortune and Romance, Candid Camera: Eat! Eat! Eat!, Merry Christmas Baby, A Century of Women.

BATES, ALAN
Actor. b. Allestree, Derbyshire, England, Feb. 17, 1934. e. Herbert Strutt Grammar Sch.; after natl. service with the RAF studied at RADA with Albert Finney, Peter O'Toole and Tom Courtenay. Professional stage debut 1955 with the Midland Theatre Co. in You and Your Wife.
THEATER: London stage: The Mulberry Tree, Look Back in Anger (also NY, Moscow), Long Day's Journey Into Night, Poor Richard, Richard III, Hamlet, Butley (also NY; Tony Award, 1973), The Taming of the Shrew, Life Class, Otherwise Engaged, The Seagull, Stage Struck, A Patriot for Me, One for the Road, Victoria Station, Dance of Death, Yonadab, Melon, Much Ado About Nothing, Ivanov, Stages, The Showman, Simply Disconnected, Fortune's Fool.
PICTURES: The Entertainer (debut, 1960), Whistle Down the Wind, A Kind of Loving, The Caretaker (The Guest), The Running Man, Nothing But the Best, Zorba the Greek, Georgy Girl, King of Hearts, Far From the Madding Crowd, The Fixer (Acad. Award nom.), Women in Love, Three Sisters, The Go-Between, A Day in the Death of Joe Egg, Impossible Object (Story of a Love Story), Butley, In Celebration, Royal Flash, An Unmarried Woman, The Shout, The Rose, Nijinsky, Quartet, The Return of the Soldier, Britannia Hospital, The Wicked Lady, Duet for One, A Prayer for the Dying, We Think the World of You, Mr. Frost, Hamlet, Force Majeure, Dr. M (Club Extinction), Shuttlecock, Secret Friends, Silent Tongue, Losing Track, The Grotesque.
TELEVISION: The Thug, A Memory of Two Mondays, The Jukebox, The Square Ring, The Wind and the Rain, Look Back in Anger, Three on a Gasring, Duel for Love, A Hero for Our Time, Plaintiff & Defendant, Two Sundays, The Collection, The Mayor of Casterbridge, The Trespasser, Very Like a Whale, Voyage Round My Father, An Englishman Abroad, Separate Tables, Dr. Fischer of Geneva, One for the Road, Pack of Lies, 102 Boulevard Haussmann, Unnatural Pursuits, Hard Times, Oliver's Travels, Hard Times.

BATES, KATHY
Actress. b. Memphis, TN, June 28, 1948. e. S. Methodist U. Regional theatre incl. D.C. and Actor's Theatre in Louisville.
THEATER: Vanities (Off-B'way debut, 1976), Semmelweiss, Crimes of the Heart, The Art of Dining, Goodbye Fidel (B'way debut, 1980), Chocolate Cake and Final Placement, Fifth of July, Come Back to the 5 & Dime Jimmy Dean Jimmy Dean, 'night Mother (Tony nom.), Outer Critics Circle Award), Two Masters: The Rain of Terror, Curse of the Starving Class, Frankie and Johnny in the Clair de Lune (Obie, L.A. Drama Critics Award), The Road to Mecca.
PICTURES: Taking Off (debut, 1971), Straight Time, Come Back to the 5 & Dime Jimmy Dean Jimmy Dean, Two of a Kind, Summer Heat, My Best Friend is a Vampire, Arthur 2 on the Rocks, Signs of Life, High Stakes (Melanie Rose), Men Don't Leave, Dick Tracy, White Palace, Misery (Academy Award, Golden Globe & Chicago Film Critics Awards, 1990), At Play in the Fields of the Lord, Fried Green Tomatoes, Shadows and Fog, The Road to Mecca, Prelude to a Kiss, Used People, A Home of Our Own, North, Dolores Claiborne, Angus, Diabolique, The War at Home.
TELEVISION: Movies: Johnny Bull, No Place Like Home, Roe vs. Wade, Hostages, Curse of the Starving Class, The Late Shift. Mini-Series: Murder Ordained, The Stand. Guest: The Love Boat, St. Elsewhere, Cagney and Lacey, L.A. Law, China Beach. Special: Talking With (also dir.).

BATTY, PETER
Producer, Director, Writer. b. Sunderland, England, June 18, 1931. e. Bede Grammar Sch. and Queen's Coll., Oxford. Feature-writer both sides Atlantic 1954-58. Joined BBC TV 1958 dir. short films. Edited Tonight programme 1963-4. Exec. prod. ATV 1964-68. Awarded Grand Prix for doc. at 1965 Venice and Leipzig festivals. Official entries 1970 and 1971 San Francisco and Melbourne festivals. Nominated Intl. Emmy, 1986. Own company since 1968 prod. TV specials, series, commercials.
TELEVISION: The Quiet Revolution, The Big Freeze, The Katanga Affair, Sons of the Navvy Man, The Fall and Rise of the House of Krupp, The Road to Suez, The Suez Affair, Battle for the Desert, Vietnam Fly-In, The Plutocrats, The Aristocrats, Battle for Cassino, Battle for the Bulge, Birth of the Bomb, Search for the Super, Operation Barbarossa, Farouk: Last of the Pharaohs, Superspy, Spy Extraordinary, Sunderland's Pride and

Passion, A Rothschild and His Red Gold, The World of Television, The Story of Wine, The Rise and Rise of Laura Ashley, The Gospel According to Saint Michael, Battle for Warsaw, Battle for Dien Bien Phu, Nuclear Nightmares. A Turn Up in A Million, Il Poverello, Swindle!, The Algerian War, Fonteyn and Nureyev: The Perfect Partnership, The Divided Union, A Time for Remembrance, Swastika Over British Soil. Contributed 6 episodes to Emmy-winning World at War series.

BAUER, STEVEN
Actor. b. Havana, Cuba, Dec. 2, 1956. r.n. Steve Echevarria. Moved with family to Miami at age 3. e. Miami Dade Jr. Coll. where studied acting. Breakthrough came with selection for role in Que Pasa U.S.A.? for Public TV. Signed by Columbia TV and moved to California.
PICTURES: Scarface, Thief of Hearts, Running Scared, The Beast, Wildfire, Gleaming the Cube, Bloody Murder!, Raising Cain, Woman of Desire, Improper Conduct, Stranger by Night, Wild Side.
TELEVISION: Series: Wiseguy. Guest: The Rockford Files, From Here to Eternity, One Day at a Time, Hill Street Blues. Movies: Doctors' Private Lives, She's in the Army Now, Nichols and Dymes, An Innocent Love, Sword of Gideon, Sweet Poison, False Arrest, Drive Like Lightning. Mini-Series: Drug Wars: The Camarena Story.

BAUM, MARTIN
Executive. b. New York, NY, March 2, 1924. Pres., ABC Pictures; previously partner Baum & Newborn Theatrical Agency; head of West Coast office General Artists Corp., head of m.p. dept., Ashley Famous Agency; pres., Martin Baum Agency; sr. exec. v.p. Creative Management Assoc.; pres., Optimus Productions, Inc., producing Bring Me the Head of Alfredo Garcia, The Wilby Conspiracy, The Killer Elite. Partner with Michael Ovitz, Ron Meyer, Rowland Perkins, Bill Haber in Creative Artists Agency, Inc.

BAUMGARTEN, CRAIG
Executive. b. Aug. 27, 1949. Partner in independent prod. co., New America Cinema. Joined Paramount. Pictures as prod. exec.; named v.p., prod. In 1980 went to Keith Barish Prods., of which was pres. three years. In 1983 appt. exec. v.p. & exec. asst. to the pres. & CEO, Columbia Pictures. Resigned 1985; joined Lorimar Motion Pictures as pres. Joined 20th Century Fox m.p. div. as exec. v.p. of production Oct. 1987. Resigned. 1989 formed Adelson/Baumgarten Prods. with Gary Adelson. Co-Producer: Hard to Kill, Hook, Universal Soldier, Nowhere to Run, Blank Check, It Could Happen to You, Jade, The Shooter, Esmeralda. 1994, formed Baumgarten/Prophet Entertainment Inc.

BAXTER, BILLY
Executive. b. New York, NY, Feb. 8, 1926. e. Holy Cross, 1948. Mgr., Ambassador Brokerage Group, Albany, 1957-58; Bill Doll & Co., 1959-63; organ., prod., radio show, Earl Wilson Celebrity Column, 1962; prod. Broadway show, Mandingo, with Franchot Tone, 1962; dir. of promotion, spec. events, Rumrill Ad Agency, 1963-64; dir. of promotion, exploitation, Landau Co., 1964-65; dir. of adv. and pub., Rizzoli Co., 1965-66. Consultant on special events to the Philip Morris Corp. and American Express.
PICTURES: Coprod.: Love and Anarchy, Daughters-Daughters, Outrageous, One Man, Dawn of the Dead. Prod.: Diary of the Cannes Film Festival with Rex Reed, 1980. Prod.-dir. documentaries: Artists of the Old West, Remington & Russell, Buffalo Bill Cody (1988).

BAXTER, KEITH
Actor. b. Monmouthshire, Wales, April 29, 1933. e. Wales, entered Royal Acad. of Dramatic Art in 1951. 1952-55 in national service; returned to RADA. Did years of repertory work in Dublin, Croydon, Chichester, London's West End, and New York. Biggest stage hit in Sleuth, both London and N.Y. Later in Corpse (London, NY).
PICTURES: The Barretts of Wimpole Street, Peeping Tom, Chimes at Midnight, With Love in Mind, Ash Wednesday, Berlin Blues.
TELEVISION: For Tea on Sunday, Hold My Hand Soldier, Saint Joan.

BAXTER, MEREDITH
Actress. b. Los Angeles, CA, June 21, 1947. e. Interlochen Arts Academy. On stage in Guys and Dolls, Butterflies Are Free, Vanities, Country Wife, Talley's Folly, Love Letters, Diaries of Adam & Eve.
PICTURES: Ben, Stand Up and Be Counted, Bittersweet Love, All the President's Men, Jezebel's Kiss.
TELEVISION: Series: The Interns, Bridget Loves Bernie, Family, Family Ties, The Faculty. Movies: Cat Creature, The Stranger Who Looks Like Me, Target Risk, The Imposter, The Night That Panicked America, Little Women, The Family Man, Beulah Land, Two Lives of Carol Letner, Take Your Best Shot, The Rape of Richard Beck, Kate's Secret, The Long Journey Home (also co-exec. prod.), Winnie: My Life in the Institution, She Knows Too

Much, The Kissing Place, Burning Bridges, Bump in the Night, A Mother's Justice, A Woman Scorned: The Betty Broderick Story, Her Final Fury: Betty Broderick—The Last Chapter, Darkness Before Dawn (also co-exec. prod.), For the Love of Aaron, One More Mountain, My Breast (also co-exec. prod.), Betrayed: A Story of Three Women (also co-exec. prod.). Specials: The Diaries of Adam and Eve, Vanities, Other Mothers (Afterschool Special).

BAXTER, STANLEY
Actor. b. Glasgow, Scotland, May, 1926. e. Hillhead H.S., Glasgow. Principal comedian in Howard & Wyndham pantomimes. Summer revues. Televised regularly on BBC-TV, and also frequent broadcaster. M.P. debut 1955 in Geordie.
THEATER: The Amorous Prawn, On the Brighter Side, Chase Me Comrade (Australia), Cinderella, What the Butler Saw, Phil The Fluter, Mother Goose Pantomime seasons 1970-74. Jack & The Beanstalk, Cinderella, Mother Goose, Aladdin, Cinderella.
PICTURES: Geordie (debut, 1955), Very Important Person, Crooks Anonymous, The Fast Lady, Father Came Too, Joey Boy.
TELEVISION: Baxter on (series) 1964; The Confidence Course, The World of Stanley Baxter, Stanley Baxter Show, Time for Baxter, The Stanley Baxter Big Picture Show, The Stanley Baxter Moving Picture Show, Part III, Stanley Baxter's Christmas Box, Bing Crosby's Merrie Olde Christmas, Stanley Baxter's Greatest Hits, Baxter on Television, Stanley Baxter Series, The Stanley Baxter Hour, Children's Royal, Stanley Baxter's Christmas Hamper, Stanley Baxter's Picture Annual, 1986; Mr. Majeika (series, 1988-89), Fitby, Stanley Baxter Is Back.

BEACHAM, STEPHANIE
Actress. b. Casablanca, Morocco, Feb. 28, 1947. e. RADA. On London stage in The Basement, On Approval, London Cuckolds, etc.
PICTURES: The Games, Tam Lin, The Nightcomers, Dracula A.D., And Now the Screaming Stars, House of Whipcord, Schizo, The Confessional, Horror Planet (Inseminoid), The Wolves of Willoughby Chase, Troop Beverly Hills.
TELEVISION: Series: Tenko (PBS), The Colbys, Dynasty, Sister Kate, seaQuest DSV. Movies/Specials: Napoleon & Josephine: A Love Story, Lucky/Chances, Secrets, To Be the Best, Foreign Affairs, Marked Personal, Jane Eyre, A Sentimental Education.

BEAL, JOHN
Actor. r.n. James Alexander Bliedung. b. Joplin, MO, Aug. 13, 1909. e. Wharton Sch., U. of PA. Author-Illustrator: Actor Drawing. Served in USAAF, WWII.
THEATER: B'way: Another Language, She Loves Me Not, Voice of the Turtle, Teahouse of the August Moon, The Crucible, A Little Hotel on the Side, The Master Builder, The Seagull, Three Men on a Horse. Off B'way: Long Day's Journey into Night, Our Town.
PICTURES: Another Language (debut, 1933), Hat Coat and Glove, The Little Minister, Les Miserables, Laddie, Break of Hearts, M'Liss, We Who Are About to Die, The Man Who Found Himself, Border Cafe, Danger Patrol, Double Wedding, Madame X, Beg Borrow or Steal, Port of Seven Seas, I Am the Law, The Arkansas Traveler, The Cat and the Canary, The Great Commandment, Ellery Queen and the Perfect Crime, Doctors Don't Tell, Atlantic Convoy, One Thrilling Night, Edge of Darkness, Let's Have Fun, Key Witness, So Dear to My Heart, Alimony, Song of Surrender, Chicago Deadline, Messenger of Peace, My Six Convicts, Remains to Be Seen, The Country Parson, The Vampire, That Night, The Sound and the Fury, Ten Who Dared, The House That Cried Murder, Amityville 3-D, The Firm.
TELEVISION: Movies: The Legend of Lizzie Borden, Eleanor and Franklin: The White House Years, Jennifer: A Woman's Story. Specials: The Necklace, Hit the Deck, The Easter Angel.

BEALS, JENNIFER
Actress. b. Chicago, IL, Dec. 19, 1963. Started as fashion model before making film debut in small role in My Bodyguard, 1980.
PICTURES: My Bodyguard, Flashdance, The Bride, Split Decisions, Vampire's Kiss, Layover, Rider in the Dark, The Lizard's Tale, Sons, Jackal's Run, A Reasonable Doubt, Dr. M, Blood and Concrete, In the Soup, Day of Atonement, Caro Diario, Mrs. Parker and the Vicious Circle, Arabian Knight (voice), Devil in a Blue Dress, Four Rooms.
TELEVISION: Series: 2000 Malibu Road. Specials: The Picture of Dorian Grey, Cinderella (Faerie Tale Theatre). Movies: Terror Strikes the Class Reunion, Indecency, Night Owl.

BEAN, ORSON
Actor. b. Burlington, VT, July 22, 1928. r.n. Dallas Burrows. Performed in nightclubs as comic and on Broadway (Never Too Late, Will Success Spoil Rock Hunter?, Subways Are for Sleeping, Roar of the Grease Paint, the Smell of the Crowd, Ilya Darling.) Author: Me and the Orgone. Founder, administrator, dir. 15th St. School, NY.
PICTURES: How to Be Very Very Popular (debut, 1955), Anatomy of a Murder, Lola, Forty Deuce, Innerspace, Instant Karma.

TELEVISION: Series: The Blue Angel (host), I've Got a Secret (panelist), Keep Talking, To Tell the Truth (panelist), Mary Hartman Mary Hartman, One Life to Live, Dr. Quinn: Medicine Woman. Special: Arsenic and Old Lace.

BEAN, SEAN
Actor. b. Sheffield, Yorkshire, England, Apr. 17, 1958.
THEATER: Romeo and Juliet, Fair Maid of the West, Midsummer Night's Dream, Who Knew Mackenzie and Gone, Deathwatch, Last Days of Mankind.
PICTURES: Winter Flight, Caravaggio, Stormy Monday, War Requeim, The Field, Patriot Games. Shopping, Black Beauty, Goldeneye, When Saturday Comes.
TELEVISION: Troubles, Small Zones, 15 Street, My Kingdom for a Horse, Winter Flight, Samson & Delilah, The True Bride, Prince, Tell Me That You Love Me, Clarissa, Scarlett, Jacob.

BEART, EMMANUELLE
Actress. b. Gassin, France, Aug. 14, 1965. Moved to Montreal at age 15. Returned to France and enrolled in drama school.
THEATER: La Repetition ou l'Amour Puni, La Double Inconstance.
PICTURES: Premiers Desirs, L'Enfant Trouve, L'Amour en Douce, Manon of the Spring, Date With an Angel, A Gauche en Sortant de L'Ascenseur, Les Enfants du Desordre, Capitaine Fracasse, La Belle Noiseuse, J'Embrasse Pas, Un Coeur en Hiver (A Heart in Winter), Ruptures, Divertimento, L'Enfer (Hell), Une Femme Francaise, Nelly & Mr. Arnaud, Mission Impossible.
TELEVISION: Zacharius, Raison Perdue.

BEATTY, NED
Actor. b. Lexington, KY, July 6, 1937. Worked at Barter Theatre in Virginia appearing in over 70 plays 1957-66 and with Arena Stage, Washington D.C. 1963-71. Broadway debut: The Great White Hope.
PICTURES: Deliverance (debut, 1972), The Life and Times of Judge Roy Bean, The Thief Who Came to Dinner, The Last American Hero, White Lightning, Nashville, W.W. and the Dixie Dance Kings, All the President's Men, The Big Bus, Network, Mikey and Nicky, Silver Streak, Exorcist II: The Heretic, Gray Lady Down, The Great Georgia Bank Hoax, Superman, Alambistal, Promises in the Dark, 1941, Wise Blood, American Success Company, Hopscotch, The Incredible Shrinking Woman, Superman II, The Toy, Touched, Stroker Ace, Back to School, The Big Easy, The Fourth Protocol, The Trouble With Spies, Switching Channels, Rolling Vengeance, The Unholy, Midnight Crossing, After the Rain, Purple People Eater, Physical Evidence, Time Trackers, Big Bad John, Chattahoochee, A Cry in the Wild, Repossessed, Blind Vision, Going Under, Hear My Song, Prelude to a Kiss, Ed and His Dead Mother, Rudy, Black Water, Radioland Murders, Just Cause.
TELEVISION: Series: Szysznyk, The Boys, Homicide: Life on the Street. Special: Our Town (1977). Movies: Footsteps, Marcus-Nelson Murders, Dying Room Only, The Execution of Private Slovik, Attack on Terror: The FBI vs. the Ku Klux Klan, The Deadly Tower, Tail Gunner Joe, Lucan, A Question of Love, Friendly Fire, Guyana Tragedy: The Story of Jim Jones, All God's Children, The Violation of Sarah McDavid, Splendor in the Grass, Pray TV, A Woman Called Golda, Kentucky Woman, Hostage Flight, Go Toward the Light, Spy, Last Train Home, Back to Hannibal, The Tragedy of Flight 103: The Inside Story, Trial: The Price of Passion, T Bone N Weasel. Guest: Murder She Wrote, M*A*S*H, Rockford Files, Alfred Hitchcock, B.L. Stryker, Roseanne. Mini-Series: Celebrity, The Last Days of Pompeii, Robert Kennedy and His Times.

BEATTY, WARREN
Actor., Producer, Director, Writer. r.n. Henry Warren Beaty. b. Richmond, VA, March 30, 1937. Sister is actress Shirley MacLaine. m. actress Annette Bening. e. Northwestern U. Studied with Stella Adler. Small roles on television; on stage in Compulsion (winter stock, North Jersey Playhouse); Broadway debut: A Loss of Roses (Theatre World Award).
PICTURES: Splendor in the Grass (debut, 1961), The Roman Spring of Mrs. Stone, All Fall Down, Lilith, Mickey One, Promise Her Anything, Kaleidoscope, Bonnie and Clyde (also prod.), The Only Game in Town, McCabe and Mrs. Miller, $ (Dollars), The Parallax View, Shampoo (also prod., co-s.p.), The Fortune, Heaven Can Wait (also prod., co-dir., co-s.p.), Reds (also prod., dir., co-s.p.; Academy Award for Best Director 1981), Ishtar (also prod.), Dick Tracy (also prod., dir.), Bugsy (also co-prod.), Love Affair (also prod, co-s.p.).
TELEVISION: Series: The Many Loves of Dobie Gillis (1959-60). Guest: Kraft Television Theatre, Studio One, Suspicion, Alcoa Presents, One Step Beyond, Wagon Train.

BECK, ALEXANDER J.
Executive. b. Ung. Brod, Czechoslovakia, Nov. 5, 1926. e. Charles U., Prague, NYU. Owns 500 features and westerns for foreign distribution and library of 1400 shorts. Importer and exporter; Pres., chairman of bd. Alexander Beck Films, 1955; formed Albex Films and A.B. Enterprises, 1959; formed & pres., Beckman Film Corp., 1960; formed Alexander Beck

Productions, 1964. In 1969 formed Screencom Int'l Corp., 1986, formed Beck Int'l Corp., 1987; formed Challenger Pictures Corp., 1988.

BECK, JACKSON
Actor-announcer-narrator. b. New York, NY. TV and radio commercials, children's records, comm. industrial films; Narrator.

BECK, MICHAEL
Actor. b. Memphis, TN, Feb. 4, 1949. e. Millsaps Coll. on football scholarship (quarterback). Became active in college theatre. In 1971 attended Central Sch. of Speech and Drama, London; studied 3 years, following which toured England with repertory companies for 2 years. Returned to U.S.; cast as lead in independent film, Madman (shot in Israel in 1977).
PICTURES: Madman, The Warriors, Xanadu, Megaforce, War Lords of the 21st Century, The Golden Seal, Triumphs of a Man Called Horse.
TELEVISION: Mini-Series: Holocaust, Celebrity. Movies: Mayflower: the Pilgrim's Adventure, Alcatraz: The Whole Shocking Story, Fly Away Home, The Last Ninja, Rearview Mirror, Chiller, Blackout, Only One Survived, The Reckoning, Houston: Legend of Texas, Deadly Game, Deadly Aim, Stranger at My Door, Fade to Black. Series: Houston Knights.

BECKER, HAROLD
Director. Dir. documentaries, Eugene Atget, Interview with Bruce Gordon, Blind Gary Davis, Signet, Ivanhoe Donaldson.
PICTURES: The Ragman's Daughter (debut, 1972), The Onion Field, The Black Marble, Taps, Vision Quest, The Boost, Sea of Love, Malice (also co-prod.), City Hall (also co-prod.).

BEDELIA, BONNIE
Actress. b. New York, NY, March 25, 1946. e. Hunter Coll.
THEATER: Enter Laughing, The Playroom, My Sweet Charlie (Theatre World Award).
PICTURES: The Gypsy Moths (debut, 1969), They Shoot Horses Don't They?, Lovers and Other Strangers, The Strange Vengeance of Rosalie, The Big Fix, Heart Like a Wheel, Death of an Angel, Violets Are Blue, The Boy Who Could Fly, The Stranger, Die Hard, The Prince of Pennsylvania, Fat Man and Little Boy, Die Hard 2, Presumed Innocent, Needful Things.
TELEVISION: Series: Love of Life (1961-7), The New Land. Movies: Then Came Bronson, Sandcastles, A Time for Love, Hawkins on Murder (Death and the Maiden), Message to My Daughter, Heatwave!, A Question of Love, Walking Through the Fire, Salem's Lot, Tourist, Fighting Back, Million Dollar Infield, Memorial Day, Alex: The Life of a Child, The Lady from Yesterday, Somebody Has to Shoot the Picture, Switched at Birth, A Mother's Right: The Elizabeth Morgan Story, The Fire Next Time, Judicial Consent, Legacy of Sin: The William Coit Story. Special: The Gift. Guest: Fallen Angels (The Quiet Room).

BEGLEY, ED, JR.
Actor. b. Los Angeles, CA, Sept. 16, 1949. Son of late actor Ed Begley. Debut in a guest appearance on My Three Sons at 17.
THEATER: NY: The Cryptogram.
PICTURES: The Computer Wore Tennis Shoes (debut, 1970), Now You See Him Now You Don't, Showdown, Superdad, Cockfighter, Stay Hungry, Citizens Band (Handle With Care), Blue Collar, The One and Only, Goin' South, Hardcore, Battlestar Gallactica, The In-Laws, The Concorde: Airport '79, Private Lessons, Cat People, Eating Raoul, Get Crazy, This Is Spinal Tap, Streets of Fire, Protocol, Transylvania 6-5000, Amazon Women on the Moon, The Accidental Tourist, Scenes From the Class Struggle in Beverly Hills, She-Devil, Meet the Applegates, Dark Horse, Greedy, Even Cowgirls Get the Blues, Renaissance Man, The Pagemaster, Batman Forever.
TELEVISION: Series: Roll Out, St. Elsewhere (1982-88), Parenthood, Winnetka Road. Guest: Room 222, Love American Style, Happy Days, Columbo, M*A*S*H, Barnaby Jones, Doris Day Show, Mary Hartman Mary Hartman, Faerie Tale Theatre. Movies: Family Flight, Amateur Night at the Dixie Bar and Grill, Elvis, Hot Rod, A Shining Season, Rascals and Robbers - The Secret Adventures of Tom Sawyer and Huck Finn, Tales of the Apple Dumpling Gang, Voyagers, Not Just Another Affair, Still the Beaver, An Uncommon Love, Insight/The Clearing House, Roman Holiday, Spies Lies & Naked Thighs, Not a Penny More Not a Penny Less, In the Best Inerest of the Child, The Big One: The Great Los Angeles Earthquake, Chance of a Lifetime, The Story Lady, In the Line of Duty: Siege at Marion, Exclusive, Running Mates. Cooperstown, World War II: When Lions Roared, Columbo: Undercover, Incident at Deception Ridge, The Shaggy Dog. Specials: Mastergate, Partners.

BELAFONTE, HARRY
Actor, Singer, Producer. b. New York, NY, March 1, 1927. Trained for stage at the Actors Studio, New Sch. for Social Research and American Negro Theatre. Professional debut, Royal Roost nightclub, N.Y., Village Vanguard, 1950. Broadway debut: John Murray Anderson's Almanac, 1953. Recording, concert artist. Emmy Award for Tonight With Harry Belafonte 1961.

THEATER: Juno and the Paycock, John Murray Anderson's Almanac. (Tony Award, 1953), Three for Tonight, A Night With Belafonte, To Be Young Gifted and Black (prod.), Asinamali (co-prod.).
PICTURES: Bright Road (debut, 1953), Carmen Jones, Island in the Sun, Odds Against Tomorrow, The World the Flesh and the Devil, The Angel Levine, Buck and the Preacher, Uptown Saturday Night (also prod.), Beat Street (prod. only), The Player, Ready to Wear (Pret-a-Porter), White Man's Burden, Kansas City.
TELEVISION: Series: Sugar Hill Times. Movie: Grambling's White Tiger. Many variety specials.

BELAFONTE, SHARI
Actress. b. New York, NY, Sept. 22, 1954. Daughter of actor-singer Harry Belafonte. e. Carnegie-Mellon U., BFA, 1976. Worked as publicist's asst. at Hanna Barbera Prods. before becoming successful model (appearing on more than 200 magazine covers and in numerous TV commercials).
PICTURES: If You Could See What I Hear, Time Walker, Murder One Murder Two, The Player.
TELEVISION: Series: Hotel. Pilot: Velvet. Guest: Hart to Hart, Code Red, Trapper John M.D., Different Strokes, The Love Boat, Matt Houston. Movies: The Night the City Screamed, The Midnight Hour, Kate's Secret, Perry Mason: The Case of the All-Star Assassin, French Silk. Host: Big Hex of Little Lulu, AM Los Angeles, Living the Dream: a Tribute to Dr. Martin Luther King, Jr.

BELFER, HAL B.
Executive Producer, Director, Choreographer. b. Los Angeles, CA, Feb. 16. e. USC; U. of CA (writing). Head of choreography depts. at both 20th Century-Fox and Universal Studios. Dir. of entertainment, in Las Vegas, Riviera and Flamingo Hotels. Prod., musical shows for Mexico City, Aruba, Puerto Rico, Montreal, Las Vegas. Dir., TV commercials and industrials. H.R. Pufnstuf TV series. Producer-director-choreographer: Premore, Inc. Develop TV specials and sitcom, tape and film. Exec. prod., Once Upon a Tour and Dora's World, Rose on Broadway, Secret Sleuth, Inn by the Side of the Road, Imagine That! Special staging Tony The Pony Series and prod., segment of What a Way to Run a Railroad; TV specials. Talent development programs, Universal Studios, 20th Century-Fox. Personal management and show packager; 1982, exec. prod., Enchanted Inn (TV Special), Cameo Music Hall I, Stage mgr.: Promises, Promises, A Chorus Line (Sahara Hotel, Las Vegas). Created Hal Belfer Associates Talent and Production Consultant.

BEL GEDDES, BARBARA
Actress. r.n. Barbara Geddes Lewis. b. New York, NY, Oct 31, 1922. Father was Norman Bel Geddes, scenic designer. B'way debut in Out of the Frying Pan; toured USO camps in Junior Miss, 1941; voted Star of Tomorrow, 1949. Author-illustrator children's books: I Like to Be Me (1963), So Do I (1972). Also designer of greeting cards for George Caspari Co.
THEATER: Out of the Frying Pan, Deep Are the Roots, Burning Bright, The Moon Is Blue, Living Room, Cat on a Hot Tin Roof, The Sleeping Prince, Silent Night Holy Night, Mary Mary, Everything in the Garden, Finishing Touches.
PICTURES: The Long Night (debut, 1947), I Remember Mama (Acad Award nom.), Blood on the Moon, Caught, Panic in the Streets, Fourteen Hours, Vertigo, The Five Pennies, Five Branded Women, By Love Possessed, Summertree, The Todd Killings.
TELEVISION: Live TV in 1950s: Robert Montgomery Presents (The Philadelphia Story), Schlitz Playhouse of the Stars; several Alfred Hitchcock Presents episodes (incl. Lamb to the Slaughter), Our Town. Series: Dallas (Emmy Award, 1980).

BELL, TOM
Actor. b. Liverpool, England, 1932. Early career in repertory and on West End stage. First TV appearance in Promenade.
PICTURES: The Concrete Jungle (The Criminal; debut, 1960), Echo of Barbara, Payroll, The Kitchen, H.M.S. Defiant (Damn the Defiant!), A Prize of Arms, The L-Shaped Room, Ballad in Blue (Blues for Lovers), He Who Rides a Tiger, Sands of Beersheba, In Enemy Country, The Long Day's Dying, Lock Up Your Daughters, All the Right Noises, The Violent Enemy, Quest for Love, Straight on Till Morning, Royal Flash, The Sailor's Return, Stronger Than the Sun, The Innocent, Wish You Were Here, Resurrected, The Magic Toy Shop, The Krays, Let Him Have It, Feast of July.
TELEVISION: No Trams to Lime Street, Love on the Dole, A Night Out, The Seekers, Long Distance Blue, Summer Lightning, Hard Travelling, White Knight, The Virginian, The Rainbow, Prime Suspect, The Cinder Path.

BELLAMY, EARL
Producer, Director. b. Minneapolis, MN, March 11, 1917. e. Los Angeles City Coll. President, The Bellamy Productions Co.
PICTURES: Seminole Uprising (debut, 1955), Blackjack Ketchum: Desperado, Toughest Gun in Tombstone, Stagecoach to Dancers' Rock (also prod.), Fluffy, Gunpoint, Munster Go Home!, Incident at Phantom Hill, Three Guns for Texas,

29

Backtack, Sidecar Racers, Seven Alone, Part 2: Walking Tall, Against a Crooked Sky, Sidewinder 1, Speedtrap, Magnum Thrust.
TELEVISION: Bachelor Father, Wells Fargo, Lone Ranger, Alcoa Premiere, Arrest and Trial, The Virginian, The Crusaders, Schlitz Playhouse, Rawhide, The Donna Reed Show, Andy Griffith Show, Wagon Train, Laramie, Laredo, I Spy, Mod Squad, Medical Center.

BELLFORT, JOSEPH
b. New York, NY, Sept. 20, 1912. e. NYU, Brooklyn Law Sch. Joined RKO Service Corp., Feb., 1930; trans. to RKO Radio Pictures, legal dept., 1942; joined RKO Fgn. dept., 1944; handled Far Eastern division, 1946; then asst. to European gen. mgr.; gen. European mgr., 1949-1958; gen. sales mgr. National Screen Service, 1959; home office supv., Europe & Near East, 20th Century-Fox, 1963; home office intl. mgr., 20th Century-Fox, 1966; asst. v.p. & foreign mgr. 20th Cent.-Fox, 1967; v.p. 20th Century-Fox, Intl. Corp. & Inter-America, Inc. 1968; named sr. v.p., 1975. Resigned from Fox, 1977, to become v.p., Motion Picture Export Assn. of America in New York. Retired 1983.

BELLOCCHIO, MARCO
Director, Writer. b. Piacenza, Italy, Nov. 9, 1939. e. Academy of Cinematografia, Rome (studying acting, then film directing); Slade School of Fine Arts, London 1959-63.
PICTURES: Fist in His Pocket (debut, 1965), China Is Near, Amore e Rabbia (segment: Discutiamo Discutiamo), Nel Nome del Padre (In the Name of the Father), Slap the Monster on the Front Page (also co-s.p.), Madmen to Be Released, Triumphal March, Il Gabbiano (The Seagull), The Film Machine, Leap Into the Void, The Eyes and the Mouth, Henry IV, Devil in the Flesh, The Sabba's Vision, The Conviction, The Butterfly's Dream.

BELMONDO, JEAN-PAUL
Actor. b. Neuilly-sur-Seine, France, April 9, 1933. e. private drama school of Raymond Girard, and the Conservatoire d'Art Dramatique. Formed a theater group with Annie Girardot and Guy Bedos.
THEATER: Jean Marais' production of Caesar and Cleopatra, Treasure Party, Oscar, Kean, Cyrano de Bergerac, Tailleur pour Dames.
PICTURES: A Pied a Cheval et En Voiture (By Foot Horse and Car), Look Pretty and Shut Up, Drole de Dimanche, Les Tricheurs, Les Copains du Dimanche, Charlotte et Son Jules, A Double Tour, Breathless, Classe Tous Risques, Moderato Cantabile, La Francaise et l'Amour, Les Distractions, Mademoiselle Ange, La Novice, Two Women, La Viaccia, Une Femme Est une Femme, Leon Morin, Pretre, Les Amours Celebres, Un Singe en Hiver, Le Doulos, L'Aine des Ferchaux, La Mer A Boire, Banana Peel, That Man From Rio, Cent Mille Dollars au Soleil, Echappement Libre, La Chasse a l'Homme, Dieu a Choisi Paris, Weekend a Zuydcocte, Par Un Beau Matin d'Ete, Up to His Ears, Is Paris Burning?, Casino Royale, The Thief of Paris, Pierrot le Fou, The Brain, Love Is a Funny Thing, Mississippi Mermaid, Borsalino, A Man I Like, The Burglars, Tender Scoundrel, Inheritor, Stavisky, Fear Over the City, L'Animal, The Professional, Ace of Aces, The Vultures, Happy Easter, Hold Up, Le Solitaire, Itinerary of a Spoiled Child (also prod.), L'Inconnu dans la Maison, Les Miserables, Desire.

BELSON, JERRY
Producer, Director, Writer. With Garry Marshall, writer of The Dick Van Dyke Show, prod. of The Odd Couple. Co-authoring the Broadway play The Roast (1980).
PICTURES: How Sweet It Is (prod., s.p.), The Grasshopper (s.p., prod.), Smile (s.p.), Fun With Dick and Jane (s.p.), Smokey and the Bandit II (s.p.), Student Bodies (exec. prod.), The End (s.p.), Jekyll and Hyde Together Again (dir.), Surrender (dir., s.p.), For Keeps (prod.), Always (co-s.p.).
TELEVISION: Series: The Dick Van Dyke Show, The Odd Couple, The Tracey Ullmann Show (co-creator, co-exec. prod.; Emmy Awards). Special: Billy Crystal: Midnight Train to Moscow (co-writer; Emmy Award).

BELUSHI, JAMES
Actor. b. Chicago, IL, June 15, 1954. e. DuPage Coll., Southern Illinois U. Brother was late actor John Belushi. Began at Chicago's Second City Theatre.
THEATER: Sexual Perversity in Chicago, The Pirates of Penzance, True West, Conversations With My Father, Baal.
PICTURES: Thief (debut, 1981), Trading Places, The Man with One Red Shoe, Salvador, About Last Night, Jumpin' Jack Flash, Little Shop of Horrors, Number One With a Bullet (co-s.p. only), The Principal, Real Men, Red Heat, Who's Harry Crumb? (cameo), K-9, Homer and Eddie, Wedding Band (cameo), Taking Care of Business, Mr. Destiny, The Palermo Connection, Only the Lonely, Masters of Menace (cameo), Curly Sue, Once Upon a Crime, Diary of a Hitman (cameo), Traces of Red, Last Action Hero (cameo), The Pebble and the Penguin (voice), Destiny Turns on the Radio, Separate Lives, Canadian Bacon (cameo), Race the Sun, Jingle All the Way.

TELEVISION: Series: Who's Watching the Kids?, Working Stiffs, Saturday Night Live. Specials: The Joseph Jefferson Awards, The Best Legs in the 8th Grade, Cinemax's Comedy Experiment's Birthday Boy (also prod., writer). Mini-Series: Wild Palms. Movies: Royce, Parallel Lives, Sahara.

BELZER, RICHARD
Actor, Comedian. b. Bridgeport, CT, Aug. 4, 1944.
PICTURES: The Groove Tube (debut, 1974), Fame, Author Author, Night Shift, Scarface, America, Flicks, The Wrong Guys, Freeway, Fletch Lives, The Big Picture, The Bonfire of the Vanities, Off and Running, Mad Dog and Glory, Girl 6, Get on the Bus.
TELEVISION: Series: The Late Show (host), Homicide: Life on the Street. Specials: On Location: Richard Belzer in Concert (also writer), Belzer on Broadway (also writer, exec. prod.). Movies: Not of This Earth, Prince for a Day.

BENBEN, BRIAN
Actor. b. Winchester, VA, June 18. Raised in Marlboro, NY. m. actress Madeleine Stowe. In regional and alternative theatre before making B'way debut in Slab Boys.
TELEVISION: Series: The Gangster Chronicles, Kay O'Brien, Dream On (Cable ACE Award, 1992). Special: Conspiracy: The Trial of the Chicago 8.
PICTURES: Clean and Sober (debut, 1988), Dangerous Obsession (Mortal Sins), I Come in Peace, Radioland Murders.

BENDICK, ROBERT
Indep. documentary prod., dir. b. New York, NY, Feb. 8, 1917. e. NYU, White School Photography. U.S. Air Force, W.W.II. Documentary and still cameraman before joining CBS Television as cameraman and dir., 1940; rejoined CBS Television as dir. special events, 1946; promoted dir. news & special events; acting program dir. 1947; res. Oct. '51. Collab with Jeanne Bendick on Making the Movies, Electronics for Young People, Television Works Like This, Filming Works Like This, 1971; Prod. Peabody Award-winning U.N. show The U.N. in Action; v.p., Cinerama Prod., co-prod. This Is Cinerama; co-dir., Cinerama Holiday; prod. Dave Garroway Show Today, prod., Wide Wide World 1955-56, NBC prod. dir. C.V. Whitney Pict., June, 1956; Merian C. Cooper Ent., 1957; prod. NBC, 1958. Prod.; Garroway Today Show, Bob Hope 25 Yrs. of Life Show, 1961; Bell Telephone Threshold Science Series, Groucho Marx, Merrily We Roll Along, US Steel Opening New York World's Fair, 1964. Prod. First Look Series 1965 (Ohio St. Award); prod. & dir. American Sportsman, ABC; prod., pilot, Great American Dream Machine (NET) (Emmy Award, 1971 and 1972); 1975, Co-exec. prod., Dick Cavett—Feeling Good. pres. Bendick Assoc. Inc.,; prod. of education audio-visual systems, Bd. of Governors, N.Y. Academy of TV Arts and Sciences. 1976, co-author with Jeanne Bendick, TV Reporting. Consultant, Warner Qube Cable Co., 1978, produced/directed, Fight for Food (PBS). Program consultant to Times-Mirror Cable Co., L.A. Produced segment ABC 20/20. Member awards committee, National TV Acad. Arts & Science. Co-author with Jeanne Bendick of Eureka It's Television (1993). Inducted into Natl. TV Academy Arts & Science, NY chapter, Silver Circle, 1994.

BENEDICT, DIRK
Actor. r.n. Dirk Niewoehner. b. Helena, MT, March 1, 1945. e. Whitman Coll., Walla Walla, WA. Enrolled in John Fernald Academy of Dramatic Arts, Rochester, MI, after which had season with Seattle Repertory Theatre; also in summer stock at Ann Arbor, MI. Broadway debut, 1970, Abelard and Heloise. Author: Confessions of a Kamikaze Cowboy, And Then We Went Fishing. Film debut, Georgia, Georgia, 1972.
PICTURES: Sssssss, W, Battlestar Galactica, Scavenger Hunt, Ruckus, Underground Aces, Body Slam, Blue Tornado, Shadow Force, Cahoots, Tales From the Crypt Presents Demon Knight, Alaska, The Feminine Touch.
TELEVISION: Guest: Love Boat, Murder She Wrote, Hawaii Five-O. Series: Chopper One, Battlestar Galactica, The A Team, Movies: Journey from Darkness, The Georgia Peaches, Scruples, Trenchcoat in Paradise.

BENEDICT, PAUL
Actor, Director. b. Silver City, NM, Sept. 17, 1938. Acted with the Theatre Company of Boston, Arena Stage, D.C.; Trinity Rep., Providence; Playhouse in the Park, Cincinnati; Center Stage, Baltimore; A.R.T., Cambridge.
THEATER: NY: Little Murders, The White House Murder Case, Bad Habits, It's Only a Play, Richard III, The Play's the Thing. LA: The Unvarnished Truth, It's Only a Play. Director: Frankie & Johnnie in the Clair de Lune, Bad Habits, The Kathy and Mo Show, Beyond Therapy, Geniuses, Any Given Day.
PICTURES: They Might Be Giants (debut, 1971), Taking Off, Up the Sandbox, Jeremiah Johnson, The Front Page, The Goodbye Girl, This Is Spinal Tap, Arthur 2 on the Rocks, Cocktail, The Chair, The Freshman, Sibling Rivalry, The Addams Family.
TELEVISION: Series: Sesame Street (1969-74), The Jeffersons, Mama Malone. Movies: Hustling, Baby Cakes, Attack of the 50 Ft. Woman. Mini-Series: The Blue and the Gray. Guest: Kojak, Maude, All in the Family, Harry-O.

BENING, ANNETTE
Actress. b. Topeka, KS, May 29, 1958. Raised in San Diego. e. San Francisco St. Univ. Acted with San Francisco's American Conservatory Theatre. m. actor Warren Beatty.
THEATER: Coastal Disturbances (Tony Award nom., Theatre World & Clarence Derwent Awards), Spoils of War.
PICTURES: The Great Outdoors (debut, 1988), Valmont, Postcards from the Edge, The Grifters (Natl. Society of Film Critics Award, Acad. Award nom., 1990), Guilty by Suspicion, Regarding Henry, Bugsy, Love Affair, The American President, Richard III, Mars Attacks.
TELEVISION: *Guest*: Miami Vice, Wiseguy. *Pilot*: It Had to Be You. *Movies*: Manhunt for Claude Dallas, Hostage.

BENJAMIN, RICHARD
Actor, Director. b. New York, NY, May 22, 1939. m. actress Paula Prentiss. e. Northwestern U.
THEATER: Central Park productions of The Taming of the Shrew, As You Like It; toured in Tchin Tchin, A Thousand Clowns, Barefoot in the Park, The Odd Couple. Broadway debut in Star Spangled Girl (Theatre World Award, 1966), also in The Little Black Book, The Norman Conquests. Directed London productions of Barefoot in the Park.
PICTURES: *Actor*: Goodbye Columbus, Catch-22, Diary of a Mad Housewife, The Marriage of a Young Stockbroker, The Steagle, Portnoy's Complaint, The Last of Sheila, Westworld, The Sunshine Boys (Golden Globe Award), House Calls, Love at First Bite, Scavenger Hunt, The Last Married Couple in America, Witches' Brew, How to Beat the High Cost of Living, First Family, Saturday the 14th. *Director*: My Favorite Year, Racing with the Moon, City Heat, The Money Pit, Little Nikita, My Stepmother Is an Alien, Downtown, Mermaids, Made in America, Milk Money, Mrs. Winterbourne.
TELEVISION: *Series*: He and She (with Paula Prentiss, 1967), Quark. *Special*: Arthur Miller's Fame. *Movies*: No Room to Run (Australia), Packin' It In.

BENNETT, ALAN
Author, Actor. b. Leeds, England, May 9, 1934. e. Oxford U. With Jonathan Miller, Dudley Moore and Peter Cook co-authored and starred in satirical revue Beyond the Fringe in London (1961) and on B'way (special Tony Award, 1963).
THEATER: Forty Years On (actor, author), Getting On, Habeas Corpus (also actor), The Old Country, Enjoy, Kafka's Dick, Single Spies (also dir.), The Madness of George III.
PICTURES: *Actor*: Pleasure at Her Majesty's, The Secret Policeman's Other Ball, Long Shot, Dream Child (voice), Little Dorrit. *Writer*: A Private Function, Prick Up Your Ears, The Madness of King George, The Wind in the Willows (voice).
TELEVISION: Famous Gossips, On the Margin (also actor), An Evening With, A Day Out, Sunset Across the Bay, A Little Outing, A Visit from Miss Prothero, Me—I'm Afraid of Virginia Wood, Doris and Doreen, The Old Crowd, Afternoon Off, All Day on the Sands, The Insurance Man, Talking Heads (6 TV monologues), One Fine Day, Our Winnie, A Woman of No Importance, Rolling Home, Marks, An Englishman Abroad, Intensive Care (also actor), 102 Boulevard Haussmann, Poetry in Motion.

BENNETT, BRUCE
Actor. r.n. Herman Brix. b. Tacoma, WA, May 19, 1909. e. U. of Washington.
PICTURES: My Son Is Guilty, Lone Wolf Keeps a Date, Atlantic Convoy, Sabotage, Underground Agent, The More the Merrier, Sahara, Mildred Pierce, The Man I Love, A Stolen Life, Nora Prentiss, Cheyenne, Dark Passage, Treasure of the Sierra Madre, Smart Girls Don't Talk, Task Force, The Second Face, The Great Missouri Raid, Angels in the Outfield, Sudden Fear, Dream Wife, Dragonfly Squadron, Robber's Roost, Big Tipoff, Hidden Guns, Bottom of the Bottle, Strategic Air Command, Danger Signal, Silver River, Younger Brothers, Without Honor, Mystery Street, The Last Outpost, Three Violent People, The Outsider, Deadhead Miles, The Clones.

BENNETT, HARVE
Producer. r.n. Harve Fischman. b. Chicago, IL, Aug. 17, 1930. e. UCLA. Quiz Kids radio show, 5 yrs.; newspaper columnist, drama critic; freelance writer; Assoc. prod., CBS-TV; freelance TV writer; prod. of special events. CBS-TV; Television film commercials; program exec., ABC, vice pres.; programs west coast, ABC-TV.
PICTURES: Star Trek II: The Wrath of Khan (exec. prod., co-story), Star Trek IV: The Voyage Home (prod., co-s.p.), Star Trek V: The Final Frontier (prod., co-story).
TELEVISION: Pres., Bennett-Katleman. Productions at Columbia Studios. *Series*: Mod Squad (prod., writer), The Young Rebels (creator-writer), Six Million Dollar Man (exec. prod.), Bionic Woman (exec. prod.), American Girls (exec. prod.). From Here to Eternity, Salvage 1, Time Trax (exec. prod.). *Mini-Series*: Rich Man Poor Man. *Movies*: A Woman Named Golda (exec. prod.; Emmy Award), The Jesse Owens Story (exec. prod.), Crash Landing: The Rescue of Flight 232 (writer).

BENNETT, HYWEL
Actor, Director. b. Garnant, South Wales, Apr. 8, 1944. Early career National Youth Theatre where he played many leading Shakespearean roles followed by extensive work in British theatre. 1971-81: directed numerous stage productions.
PICTURES: The Family Way (debut, 1967), Drop Dead My Love, Twisted Nerve, The Virgin Soldiers, The Buttercup Chain, Loot, Percy, Endless Night, Alice in Wonderland, Murder Elite, War Zone.
TELEVISION: Where The Buffalo Roam, Malice Aforethought, Tinker Tailor Soldier Spy, series, Artemis 81, Myself A Mandarin, Frankie and Johnnie, Check Point Chiswick, Twilight Zone, The Idiot, The Traveller, Death of a Teddy Bear, Three's One, Pennies From Heaven, Shelley (series), The Critic, The Consultant, Absent Friends, The Secret Agent, A Mind to Kill, Virtual Murder, The Other Side of Paradise.

BENSON, HUGH
Producer. Exec. Prod., Screen Gems; exec. prod., MGM Television. On staff Col.-TV, pilots and long form.
PICTURES: Nightmare Honeymoon (prod.), Logan's Run (assoc. prod.), Billy Jack Goes to Washington (prod.).
TELEVISION: *Producer*: Contract On Cherry St., Child Stealers, Goldie and the Boxer, A Fire in the Sky, Shadow Riders, Confessions of a Lady Cop, The Dream Merchants, Goldie and the Boxer Go to Hollywood, Goliath Awaits, The Blue and the Gray, Hart to Hart, Master of Ballantrae, Anna Karenina, The Other Lover, I Dream of Jeannie 15 Yrs. Later, Miracle of the Heart: A Boy's Town Story, Crazy Like a Fox, In the Heat of the Night (pilot and series), Daughter of the Streets, Back to Hannibal: Tom and Huck Return, Danielle Steele's Fine Things, Danielle Steele's Changes, Shadow of a Stranger, Diana: Her True Story, Danielle Steele's Message From 'Nam, A Season of Hope, Liz: The Elizabeth Taylor Story.

BENSON, ROBBY
Actor, Writer, Director. r.n. Robert Segal. b. Dallas, TX, Jan. 21, 1956. m. actress Karla DeVito. Father is Jerry Segal, novelist and screenwriter, mother is Ann Benson, veteran of Dallas stage and nat'l summer stock and nat'l spokesperson for Merrill Lynch. Appeared in commercials and summer stock at age 5. B'way debut at age 12 in Zelda. Dir. debut 1989, White Hot (a.k.a. Crack in the Mirror). Composed music for Diana Ross, Karla DeVito and soundtrack of film The Breakfast Club.
THEATER: *NY*: Zelda, The Rothschilds, Dude, The Pirates of Penzance. *Regional*: Oliver!, Evita, The King and I, King of Hearts, Do Black Patent Leather Shoes Really Reflect Up?
PICTURES: Jory (debut, 1973), Jeremy, Lucky Lady, Ode to Billy Joe, One on One (also co-s.p. with father), The End, Ice Castles, Walk Proud (also co-s.p. & co-composer with father), Die Laughing (also prod., co-s.p., co-composer), Tribute, National Lampoon Goes to the Movies, The Chosen, Running Brave, Harry and Son, City Limits, Rent-a-Cop, White Hot (also dir.), Modern Love (also dir., s.p., composed songs), Beauty and the Beast (voice), Betrayal of the Dove (s.p. only), At Home with the Webbers, Deadly Exposure.
TELEVISION: *Movies*: Death Be Not Proud, The Death of Richie, Remember When, Virginia Hill Story, All the Kind Strangers, Two of a Kind, California Girls, Invasion of Privacy, Homewrecker, Precious Victims. *Specials*: Our Town, The Last of Mrs. Lincoln. *Series*: Search for Tomorrow, Tough Cookies. *Guest*: One Day at a Time, Alfred Hitchcock Presents (1985). *Episode Director*: True Confessions (3 episodes), Thunder Alley, Evening Shade, Good Advice, Muddling Through, Monty, Dream On, Friends, Family Album. *Pilot Director*: Bringing Up Jack, George Wendt Show, Game Night.

BENTON, ROBERT
Writer, Director. b. Waxahachie, TX, 1932. e. U. of Texas, B.A. Was art director and later consulting ed. at Esquire Magazine where he met David Newman, a writer-editor, and formed writing partnership. Together wrote a monthly column for Mademoiselle (10 years). Benton made directorial debut with Bad Company, 1972.
THEATER: It's a Bird... It's a Plane... It's Superman (libretto), Oh! Calcutta (one sketch).
PICTURES: Co-writer (with Newman): Bonnie and Clyde, There Was a Crooked Man, What's Up, Doc?. Co-writer: Superman (with Mario Puzo and Tom Mankiewicz). Director/Writer: Bad Company, The Late Show, Kramer vs. Kramer (Academy Awards for Best Director and Adapted Screenplay, 1979), Still of the Night, Places in the Heart (Academy Award for Best Original Screenplay, 1984), Nadine, The House on Carroll Street (co-exec. prod. only), Billy Bathgate (dir. only), Nobody's Fool.

BERENGER, TOM
Actor. b. Chicago, IL, May 31, 1950. e. U. of Missouri (drama). Studied acting at H.B. Studios. Acted in regional theatres and off-off-Broadway. Plays include Death Story, The Country Girl, National Anthems, The Rose Tattoo, Electra, Streetcar Named Desire, End as a Man (Circle Rep.).
PICTURES: The Sentinel (debut, 1977), Looking for Mr. Goodbar, In Praise of Older Women, Butch and Sundance: The

Early Days, The Dogs of War, Beyond the Door, The Big Chill, Eddie and the Cruisers, Fear City, Rustler's Rhapsody, Platoon (Acad. Award nom.), Someone to Watch Over Me, Shoot to Kill, Betrayed, Last Rites, Major League, Born on the Fourth of July, Love at Large, The Field, Shattered, At Play in the Fields of the Lord, Sniper, Sliver, Gettysburg, Major League 2, Chasers, Last of the Dogmen, The Substitute.
TELEVISION: *Series*: One Life to Live (1975-76). *Movies*: Johnny We Hardly Knew Ye, The Avenging Angel, Body Language. *Mini-Series*: Flesh and Blood, If Tomorrow Comes. *Special*: Dear America: Letters Home From Vietnam (reader).

BERENSON, MARISA
Actress. b. New York, NY, Feb. 15, 1947. Granddaughter of haute couture fashion designer Schiaparelli. Great niece of art critic and historian Bernard Berenson. Former model.
PICTURES: Death in Venice (debut, 1971), Cabaret, Barry Lyndon, Casanova & Co., Killer Fish, S.O.B., The Secret Diary of Sigmund Freud, La Tete Dans Le Sac, L'Arbalete, Desire, Quel Treno da Vienna, Il Giardino Dei Cigliegi, Winds of the South, White Hunter Black Heart, Night of the Cyclone, The Cherry Orchard, Flagrant Desire.
TELEVISION: *Movies*: Tourist, Playing for Time, Notorious. *Mini-Series*: Sins, Hemingway. Also: Lo Scialo, Blue Blood, Have a Nice Night, L'Enfant Des Loups, Oceano, Hollywood Detective, Bel Ami, Murder She Wrote (guest).

BERESFORD, BRUCE
Director, Writer. b. Sydney, Australia, Aug. 16, 1940. e. U. of Sydney, B.A. 1962. Worked as teacher in London, 1961. Film editor, East Nigerian Film Unit, 1966; sect. and head of prod., British Film Inst. Production Board, 1966-71.
PICTURES: *Director*: The Adventures of Barry McKenzie (also co-s.p.), Barry McKenzie Holds His Own (also prod., co-s.p.), Don's Party, The Getting of Wisdom, Money Movers, Breaker Morant (also s.p.), The Club, Puberty Blues, Tender Mercies, King David, The Fringe Dwellers (also s.p.), Crimes of the Heart, Aria (sequence), Her Alibi, Driving Miss Daisy, Mister Johnson (also co-s.p.), Black Robe, Rich in Love, A Good Man in Africa, Silent Fall, The Last Dance.
TELEVISION: *Movie*: Curse of the Starving Class (writer, exec. prod.)

BERG, DICK
Writer, Producer. b. New York, NY. e. Lehigh U. 1942; Harvard Business Sch. 1943. Prior to 1960 writer for TV shows Playhouse 90 Studio One, Robert Montgomery Presents, Kraft Television Playhouse. 1961-69 prod., writer for Universal Studios; exec. prod. The Chrysler Theatre, Alcoa Premiere, Checkmate. Created and wrote Staccato (series). 1971-85: prod., writer of over 50 TV movies via his Stonehenge Prods. TV films won 15 Emmies, 23 nominations. Twice elected pres. National Acad. of Television Arts and Sciences.
PICTURES: *Prod*: Counterpoint, House of Cards, Banning Shoot (also s.p.), Fresh Horses.
TELEVISION: Prod. and/or writer: *Mini-Series*: A Rumor of War, The Martian Chronicles, The Word, Space, Wallenberg: A Hero's Story. *Movies*: Rape and Marriage: The Rideout Case, An Invasion of Privacy, Thief, Footsteps, Firehouse, American Geisha, Class of '63, Louis Armstrong, Chicago Style, Everybody's Baby: The Rescue of Jessica McClure (exec. prod.)

BERG, JEFF
Executive. b. Los Angeles, CA, May 26, 1947. e. U of California, Berkeley, B.A., 1969. V.P., head lit. div., Creative Mgt. Associates, Los Angeles, 1969-75; v.p., m.p. dept., International Creative Associates, 1975-80; pres., 1980-. Dir., Joseph Intl. Industries. Named chmn. ICM.

BERG, PETER
Actor. b. New York, NY, 1964. e. Malcalester Col., St. Paul, MN.
PICTURES: Miracle Mile, Heart of Dixie, Race for Glory, Shocker, Genuine Risk, Crooked Hearts, Late for Dinner, A Midnight Clear, Aspen Extreme, Fire in the Sky, Girl 6, The Great White Hype.
TELEVISION: *Series*: Chicago Hope. *Movies*: Rise and Walk: The Dennis Byrd Story, The Last Seduction (also released theatrically).

BERGEN, CANDICE
Actress. b. Beverly Hills, CA, May 9, 1946. m. late dir. Louis Malle. Father was late ventriloquist Edgar Bergen. e. U. of PA. Modeled during college; freelance photo-journalist. Autobiography: Knock Wood (1984). B'way debut in Hurlyburly.
PICTURES: The Group (debut, 1966), The Sand Pebbles, The Day the Fish Came Out, Live for Life, The Magus, The Adventurers, Getting Straight, Soldier Blue, Carnal Knowledge, The Hunting Party, T. R. Baskin, 11 Harrowhouse, The Wind and the Lion, Bite the Bullet, The Domino Principle, A Night Full of Rain, Oliver's Story, Starting Over (Acad. Award nom.), Rich and Famous, Gandhi, Stick.
TELEVISION: *Series*: Murphy Brown (5 Emmy Awards: 1989, 1990, 1992, 1994, 1995). *Mini-Series*: Hollywood Wives. *Movies*:

Arthur the King, Murder: By Reason of Insanity, Mayflower Madam. *Specials*: Woody Allen Special, Moving Day (Trying Times).

BERGEN, POLLY
Singer, Actress. r.n. Nellie Burgin b. Knoxville, TN, July 14, 1930. e. Compton Jr. Coll., CA. Prof. debut radio at 14; in light opera, summer stock; sang with orchestra and appeared in night clubs; Columbia recording star; on B'way stage, John Murray Anderson's Almanac, Champagne Complex, First Impressions. Bd. chmn. Polly Bergen Co.; chmn. Culinary Co., Inc.; co-chmn. Natl. Business Council for Equal Rights Amendment; Humanitarian Award: Asthmatic Research Inst. & Hosp., 1971; Outstanding Mother's Award, 1984.
PICTURES: At War With the Army (debut, 1950), That's My Boy, Warpath, The Stooge, Half a Hero, Cry of the Hunted, Arena, Fast Company, Escape from Fort Bravo, Belle Sommers, Cape Fear, The Caretakers, Move Over Darling, Kisses for My President, A Guide for the Married Man, Making Mr. Right, Mother Mother, Cry-Baby, Dr. Jekyll and Ms. Hyde.
TELEVISION: *Series*: Pepsi-Cola Playhouse (host 1954-55), To Tell the Truth (panelist), The Polly Bergen Show, Baby Talk. *Guest*: G.E. Theatre, Schlitz Playhouse, Playhouse 90, Studio One, Perry Como, Ed Sullivan Show, Bob Hope Show, Bell Telephone, Wonderful World of Entertainment, Dinah Shore Show, Dean Martin Show, Andy Williams Show, Red Skelton Show, Mike Douglas Show. *Special*: The Helen Morgan Story (Emmy Award, 1958). *Movies*: Death Cruise, Murder on Flight 502, Telethon, How to Pick Up Girls, The Million Dollar Face, Born Beautiful, Velvet, Addicted to His Love, She Was Marked For Murder, The Haunting of Sarah Hardy, My Brother's Wife, Lightning Field, Lady Against the Odds, Perry Mason: The Case of the Skin-Deep Scandal, Leave of Absence (also story, co-exec. prod.). *Mini-Series*: 79 Park Avenue, The Winds of War, War and Remembrance.

BERGER, HELMUT
Actor. r.n. Helmut Steinberger. b. Salzburg, Austria, May 29, 1943. e. Feldkirk College and U. of Perugia. First film, small role in Luchino Visconti's The Witches (Le Streghe) in 1966.
PICTURES: The Young Tigers, The Damned, Do You Know What Stalin Did To Women?, The Garden of the Finzi-Continis, Dorian Gray, A Butterfly with Bloody Wings, The Greedy Ones, The Strange Love Affair, Ludwig, Ash Wednesday, Conversation Piece, The Romantic Englishwoman, Orders to Kill, Madam Kitty, Merry-Go-Round, Code Name: Emerald, The Glass Heaven, Faceless, The Betrothed, The Godfather Part III.

BERGER, RICHARD L.
Executive. b. Tarrytown, NY, Oct. 25, 1939. e. Cornell U., UCLA 1963, B.S. In 1964 joined acct. dept., 20th Century-Fox; promoted to exec. position in Fox-TV. Was dir. of programming, then v.p. of programs. Appt. asst. v.p. prod. 20th-Fox. Left in 1975 to join CBS-TV as v.p. dramatic development. Returned to 20th-Fox in 1977 as v.p., domestic prod., 20th Century-Fox Pictures. Joined Disney as pres. Walt Disney Pictures; resigned 1984. Named sr. v.p., United Artists Corp., promoted to pres. MGM/UA Film Group, 1988.

BERGER, SENTA
Actress. b. Vienna, Austria, May 13, 1941. Studied ballet, then acting at VIenna's Reinhardt Seminar. Debuted in German films as teen.
PICTURES: Die Lindenwirtin vom Donanstrand (debut, 1957), The Journey, Katia, The Good Soldier Schweik, The Secret Ways, Sherlock Holmes and the Deadly Necklace, The Testament of Dr. Mabuse, The Victors, Major Dundee, The Glory Guys, Cast a Giant Shadow, Bang! Bang! You're Dead, The Poppy Is Also a Flower, The Quiller Memorandum, To Commit a Murder, The Treasure of San Gennaro, The Ambushers, Diabolically Yours, If It's Tuesday This Must Be Belgium, De Sade, When Women Had Tails, Percy, The Scarlet Letter, Merry-Go-Round, White Mafia, The Swiss Conspiracy, Cross of Iron, Nest of Nipers, The Two Lives of Mattia Pascal, The Flying Devils, Swiss Cheese.

BERGERAC, JACQUES
Actor. b. Biarritz, France, May 26, 1927. Career includes Five Minutes With Jacques Bergerac on radio; in the theatre, on tour in Once More with Feeling; on most major network TV shows.
PICTURES: Twist of Fate, The Time is Now, Strange Intruder, Come Away With Me, Les Girls, Gigi, Man and His Past, Thunder in the Sun, Hypnotic Eye, A Sunday in Summer, Fear No More, Achilles, A Global Affair, Taffy and the Jungle Hunter, The Emergency Operation, Lady Chaplin, The Last Party, One Plus One.

BERGIN, PATRICK
Actor. b. Ireland, 1954.
PICTURES: Those Glory Glory Days, Taffin, The Courier, Mountains of the Moon, Sleeping With the Enemy, Love Crimes, Highway to Hell, Patriot Games, Map of the Human Heart, Double Cross.

TELEVISION: *Movies:* Act of Betrayal, Robin Hood, They, Frankenstein. *Specials:* Morphine and Dolly Mixtures (BBC), The Real Carlotte. *Guest:* Twilight Zone: Lost Classics.

BERGMAN, ALAN
Songwriter. b. Brooklyn, NY. e. U. of North Carolina, UCLA. m. Marilyn Bergman with whom he collaborates.
THEATER: Ballroom, Something More, The Lady and the Clarinet.
PICTURES: Lyrics for: Harlow, Harper, In the Heat of the Night, Fitzwilly, The Thomas Crown Affair (Academy Award for Best Song: The Windmills of Your Mind, 1968), John and Mary, The Happy Ending, Gaily Gaily, The Magic Garden of Stanley Sweetheart, Move, Pieces of Dreams, Wuthering Heights, Doctor's Wives, Sometimes a Great Notion, Pete 'n' Tillie, The Life and Times of Judge Roy Bean, Breezy, 40 Carats, The Way We Were (Academy Award for title song, 1973), Summer Wishes Winter Dreams, Harry and Walter Go to New York, Ode to Billy Joe, A Star Is Born, Same Time Next Year, The Promise, And Justice for All, A Change of Seasons, Back Roads, Author Author, Yes Giorgio, Best Friends, Tootsie, Never Say Never Again, Yentl (Academy Award for song score, 1983), The Man Who Loved Women, Micki and Maude, The January Man, Major League, Shirley Valentine, Welcome Home, Switch, For the Boys.
TELEVISION: Queen of the Stardust Ballroom (Emmy Award), Hollow Image, Sybil (Emmy Award); and themes for Bracken's World, Maude, The Sandy Duncan Show, Good Times, Alice, The Dumplings, Nancy Walker Show, The Powers That Be, Brooklyn Bridge, etc.

BERGMAN, ANDREW
Writer, Director, Producer. b. Queens, NY, 1945. e. Harpur Coll., magna cum laude; U. of Wisconsin, Ph.D, history, 1970. Worked as publicist at United Artists. Author: We're in the Money, a study of Depression-era films, and the mysteries: The Big Kiss-Off of 1944, Hollywood and Levine, Sleepless Nights. Also wrote Broadway comedy, Social Security.
PICTURES: *Writer:* Blazing Saddles, The In Laws, So Fine (also dir.) Oh God You Devil, Fletch, The Freshman (also dir.), Soapdish, Honeymoon in Vegas (also dir.), It Could Happen to You (dir. only), The Scout, Striptease (also dir.). *Exec. Prod.:* Chances Are, Undercover Blues, Little Big League.

BERGMAN, INGMAR
Writer, Director. b. Uppsala, Sweden, July 14, 1918. e. Stockholm U. Directed university play prods.; wrote & dir. Death of Punch, 1940; first theatrical success, dir., Macbeth, 1940; writer-director, Svensk Film-industri, 1942-present; first s.p, Frenzy, 1943; first directorial assignment, Crisis, 1945; chief prod., Civic Malmo, 1956-60. Directed Swedish prod. Hamlet for stage at Brooklyn Acad. of Music, 1988.
PICTURES: *Writer only:* Torment, Woman Without a Face, Eva, The Last Couple Out, Pleasure Garden, Best Intentions, Sunday's Children. *Dir.-Writer:* Crisis It Rains on Our Love, A Ship to India, Night is My Future (dir. only), Port of Call, The Devil's Wanton, Three Strange Loves, To Joy, This Can't Happen Here (dir. only), Summer Interlude (Illicit Interlude), Secrets of Women, Summer With Monika, The Naked Night (Sawdust and Tinsel), A Lesson in Love, Dreams (Journey Into Autumn), Smiles of a Summer Night, The Seventh Seal, Wild Strawberries, Brink of Life, The Magician, The Virgin Spring (dir. only), The Devil's Eye, Through a Glass Darkly, Winter Light, The Silence, All These Women, Persona, Stimulantia (episode), Hour of the Wolf, Shame, The Ritual, The Passion of Anna, The Touch, Cries and Whispers, Scenes from a Marriage, The Magic Flute, Face to Face, The Serpent's Egg, Autumn Sonata, From the Life of the Marionettes, Fanny and Alexander, After the Rehearsal.
U.S. TELEVISION: The Lie.

BERGMAN, MARILYN
Songwriter. b. Brooklyn, NY. e. NYU. m. Alan Bergman with whom she collaborates. Became pres. of ASCAP, 1994.
THEATER: Ballroom, Something More, The Lady and the Clarinet.
PICTURES: Lyrics for: Harlow, Harper, In the Heat of the Night, Fitzwilly, The Thomas Crown Affair (Academy Award for Best Song: The Windmills of Your Mind, 1968), John and Mary, The Happy Ending, Gaily Gaily, The Magic Garden of Stanley Sweetheart, Move, Pieces of Dreams, Wuthering Heights, Doctor's Wives, Sometimes a Great Notion, Pete 'n' Tillie, The Life and Times of Judge Roy Bean, Breezy, 40 Carats, The Way We Were (Academy Award for title song, 1973), Summer Wishes Winter Dreams, Harry and Walter Go to New York, Ode to Billy Joe, A Star Is Born, Same Time Next Year, The Promise, And Justice for All, A Change of Seasons, Back Roads, Author Author, Yes Giorgio, Best Friends, Tootsie, Never Say Never Again, Yentl (Academy Award for song score, 1983), The Man Who Loved Women, Micki and Maude, The January Man, Major League, Shirley Valentine, Welcome Home, Switch, For the Boys.
TELEVISION: Queen of the Stardust Ballroom (Emmy Award), Hollow Image, Sybil (Emmy Award); and themes for Bracken's World, Maude, The Sandy Duncan Show, Good Times, Alice, The Dumplings, Nancy Walker Show, The Powers That Be, Brooklyn Bridge, etc.

BERKOFF, STEVEN
Actor, Director, Writer. b. London, Eng., Aug. 3, 1937. e. studied drama in London and Paris. Founder of London Theatre Group. Author of plays, East, West, Greek Decadence, Sink the Belgrano, Kvetch (London, NY). Staged, adapted and toured with: Kafka's In the Penal Colony, The Trial and Metamorphosis; Agamemnon, The Fall of the House of Usher. Starred in Hamlet and Macbeth. NY theater: Director: Kvetch (also writer, actor), Coriolanus, Metamorphosis (starring Baryshnikov). Also dir. Roman Polanski in Metamorphosis in Paris.
PICTURES: *Actor:* Nicholas and Alexandra, A Clockwork Orange, Barry Lyndon, The Passenger, Outland, McVicar, Octopussy, Beverly Hills Cop, Rambo: First Blood II, Revolution, Underworld, Absolute Beginners, Under the Cherry Moon, The Krays, Decadence (also dir., s.p.), Fair Game.
TELEVISION: Beloved Family, Knife Edge, War and Remembrance, A Season of Giants, Intruders.

BERLE, MILTON
Actor. r.n. Milton Berlinger. b. New York, NY, July 12, 1908. e. Professional Children's Sch., N.Y. Early appearances as child actor incl. film Tillie's Punctured Romance. In vaudeville; on N.Y. stage (Ziegfeld Follies 1936, Life Begins at 8:40, etc.): nightclubs; concurrently on radio & screen. Author: Out of My Trunk (1945), Earthquake (1959), Milton Berle: An Autobiography (1974).
PICTURES: New Faces of 1937, Radio City Revels, Tall Dark and Handsome, Sun Valley Serenade, Rise and Shine, A Gentleman at Heart, Whispering Ghosts, Over My Dead Body, Margin for Error, Always Leave Them Laughing, Let's Make Love, The Bellboy (cameo), It's a Mad Mad Mad Mad World, The Loved One, The Oscar, Don't Worry We'll Think of a Title, The Happening, Who's Minding the Mint?, Where Angels Go... Trouble Follows, For Singles Only, Can Hieronymus Merkin Ever Forget Mercy Humppe and Find True Happiness?, Lepke, Won Ton Ton the Dog Who Saved Hollywood, The Muppet Movie, Cracking Up, Broadway Danny Rose, Driving Me Crazy, Storybook.
TELEVISION: *Series:* Texaco Star Theatre, Kraft Music Hall TV Show, Jackpot Bowling, Milton Berle Show. *Guest:* Doyle Against the House, Dick Powell Show, Chrysler TV special, Lucy Show, F Troop, Batman, Love Boat, many others. *Movies:* Seven in Darkness, Evil Roy Slade, Legend of Valentino, Side By Side.

BERLINGER, WARREN
Actor, b. Brooklyn, NY, Aug. 31, 1937. e. Columbia U.
THEATER: Annie Get Your Gun, The Happy Time, Bernardine, Take A Giant Step, Anniversary Waltz, Roomful of Roses, Blue Denim (Theatre World Award), Come Blow Your Horn, How To Succeed in Business Without Really Trying, (London) Who's Happy Now?, California Suite (1977-78 tour).
PICTURES: Teenage Rebel, Three Brave Men, Blue Denim, Because They're Young, Platinum High School, The Wackiest Ship in the Army, All Hands on Deck, Billie, Spinout, Thunder Alley, Lepke, The Four Deuces, I Will I Will... for Now, Harry and Walter Go to New York, The Shaggy D.A., The Magician of Lublin, The Cannonball Run, The World According to Garp, Going Bananas, Outlaw Force, Ten Little Indians, Hero, Crime and Punishment, Feminine Touch, That Thing You Do!.
TELEVISION: *Series:* Secret Storm (serial), The Joey Bishop Show, The Funny Side, A Touch of Grace, Operation Petticoat, Small & Frye, Shades of L.A. *Guest:* Alcoa, Goodyear, Armstrong, Matinee Theatre, The London Palladium, Kilroy, Bracken's World, Columbo, Friends. *Movies:* The Girl Most Likely To..., The Red Badge of Courage, Ellery Queen, Wanted: The Sundance Woman, Sex and the Single Parent, The Other Woman, Trial By Jury, Death Hits the Jackspot.

BERMAN, BRUCE
Executive. President of Worldwide Production, Warner Bros. Pictures.

BERMAN, PANDRO S.
Producer. b. Pittsburgh, PA, March 28, 1905. Son of late Harry M. Berman, gen. mgr. Universal, FBO. Asst. dir. film ed., FBO; film & title ed. Columbia Studios; chief film ed. RKO, later asst. to William Le Baron & David Selznick; became prod. 1931 (RKO). A Champion of Champions Producer in Fame ratings. Joined MGM 1940.
PICTURES: What Price Hollywood?, Symphony of Six Million, Morning Glory, The Gay Divorcee, Of Human Bondage, Roberta, Alice Adams, The Informer, Quality Street, Top Hat, Follow the Fleet, Winterset, Stage Door, Vivacious Lady, Carefree, Room Service, Gunga Din, Bachelor Mother, The Hunchback of Notre Dame, Ziegfeld Girl, Honky Tonk, Rio Rita, The Seventh Cross, National Velvet, Dragon Seed, The Picture of Dorian Grey, Marriage Is a Private Affair, Undercurrent, Sea of Grass, The Three Musketeers, Madame Bovary, Father of the Bride, Father's Little Dividend, The Prisoner of Zenda, Ivanhoe,

All the Brothers Were Valiant, Knights of the Round Table, The Long Long Trailer, Blackboard Jungle, Bhowani Junction, Tea and Sympathy, Something of Value, The Brothers Karamazov, The Reluctant Debutante, Butterfield 8, Sweet Bird of Youth, The Prize, A Patch of Blue, Justine, Move.

BERMAN, STEVEN H.
Executive. b. Middletown, OH, March 22, 1952. e. Ohio U., B.F.A. in playwriting, 1974; USC, Annenberg Sch. of Communication studied management, 1977. Special research projects Paramount and ABC TV, 1977. Account exec., Gardner Advertising, 1978. Development exec., CBS Television, 1979-82. Dir. of comedy dev., CBS Television, 1982-84. Five years at CBS in series development, comedy and drama. Vice pres., dramatic dev., Columbia Pictures TV, 1984-85. Sr. v.p., Creative Affairs, Columbia Pictures TV, 1985-87. Exec. v.p., Columbia TV, div. of Columbia Entertainment TV, 1987-90. Indept. prod., Columbia Pictures TV, 1990-present.

BERNARD, MARVIN A.
Executive. b. New York, NY, Oct. 1, 1934. e. NYU. Lab technician to v.p. in charge of sales, Rapid Film Technique, Inc., 1949-63; developed technological advances in film rejuvenation and preservation, responsible for public underwriting; 1964-69; real estate sales & investments in Bahamas, then with Tishman Realty (commercial leasing div.); est. B-I-G Capital Properties; v.p. and operating head of International Filmtreat 1970-1973; authored Film Damaged Control Chart, a critical analysis of film care and repair, 1971; founded Filmlife Inc. with latest chemical/mechanical and technical advancement in field of film rejuvenation and preservation. 1973-75 bd. chmn. and chief executive officer of Filmlife Inc., motion picture film rejuvenation, storage and distribution company. Feb. 1975 elected president in addition to remaining bd. chairman. 1979 consultant to National Archives of U.S. on m.p. preservation. 1981 dev. m.p. rejuvenation and preservation for 8mm and S8mm. 1986 introduced this technology to private home movie use before and after transfer to videotape. 1987, active mem. of awards comm. for tech. achievements, National Acad. TV Arts & Sciences. Recognition as leading authority and m.p. conservator from Intl. Communications Industries Assn. (ICIA), 1988. 1989, Filmlife became 1st national film to video transfer lab in U.S.; elected to Princeton Film Preservation Group. Established Film/Video Hospital, repairing broken tapes & videocassettes, Aug. 1990.

BERNARD, TOM
Executive. Co-President, Sony Pictures Classics.

BERNHARD, HARVEY
Producer. b. Seattle, WA, March 5, 1924. e. Stanford U. In real estate in Seattle, 1947-50; started live lounge entertainment at the Last Frontier Hotel, Las Vegas, 1950. Partner with Sandy Howard, 1958-60; v.p. in chg. prod., David L. Wolper Prods., dividing time between TV and feature films, 1961-68; with MPC, v.p., chg. prod., 1968-70. Now pres. of Harvey Bernhard Ent., Inc.
PICTURES: The Mack (1973), The Omen, Damien—Omen II, The Final Conflict, The Beast Within, Ladyhawke (exec. prod.), The Goonies (prod.), The Lost Boys.

BERNHARD, SANDRA
Actress, Comedian, Singer. b. Flint, MI, June 6, 1955. Moved to Scottsdale, AZ at 10. Began career in Los Angeles 1974 as stand-up comedian while supporting herself as manicurist in Beverly Hills. Has written articles for Vanity Fair, Interview, Spin, recorded and written lyrics for album I'm Your Woman (1985) and starred in one-woman off-B'way show Without You I'm Nothing (1988). Published collection of essays, short stories and memoirs, Confessions of a Pretty Lady (1988). Frequent guest on Late Night with David Letterman and Robin Byrd Show.
PICTURES: Cheech and Chong's Nice Dreams (debut, 1981), The King of Comedy, Sesame Street Presents: Follow That Bird, The Whoopee Boys, Track 29, Heavy Petting, Without You I'm Nothing, Hudson Hawk, Inside Monkey Zetterland, Dallas Doll.
TELEVISION: *Series*: The Richard Pryor Show, Roseanne. *Movie*: Freaky Friday.

BERNSEN, CORBIN
Actor. b. North Hollywood, CA, Sept. 7, 1954. m. actress Amanda Pays. Son of actress Jeanne Cooper. e. UCLA, B.A. theater arts; M.F.A playwriting. Teaching asst. at UCLA while working on playwriting degree. 1981 studied acting in NY while supporting self as carpenter and model (Winston cigarettes). Built own theater in loft. Formed theatre co. Theatre of the Night.
PICTURES: Three the Hard Way (debut, 1974), Eat My Dust!, King Kong, S.O.B., Hello Again, Bert Rigby You're a Fool, Major League, Disorganized Crime, Shattered, Frozen Assets, The Killing Box, Savage Land, Major League 2, Trigger Fast, A Brilliant Disguise, The New Age, Radioland Murders, Tales From the Hood, The Great White Hype, The Dentist, Menno's Mind, Circuit Breaker.

TELEVISION: *Series*: Ryan's Hope, L.A. Law, A Whole New Ballgame. *Movies*: Breaking Point, Line of Fire: The Morris Dees Story, Dead on the Money, Grass Roots, Love Can Be Murder, Beyond Suspicion, I Know My Son is Alive, Where Are My Children?, Voice From Within, Dangerous Intentions, In the Heat of the Night: By Duty Bound, Bloodhounds. *Guest*: Anything But Love, Roc, The Larry Sanders Show, Love and War, The Nanny, Night Watch, Seinfeld, Dear John.

BERNSEN, HARRY
Producer, Executive. b. Chicago, IL, June 14, 1935. Served in US Marine Corp., 1953-55. Had own agency, Continental Management, 1956-70. Became producer, 1970.
THEATER: Prod.: Beyond the Rainbow, The Boys in Autumn.
PICTURES: Fool's Parade (assoc. prod.), Something Big (assoc. prod.), Three the Hard Way (prod.), Take a Hard Ride (prod.), Fatal Inheritance (prod.).
TELEVISION: Movie: The Awakening Land (exec. prod.). ABC After School Specials, 1982-88 (exec. prod.).

BERNSTEIN, ARMYAN
Director, Writer, Producer.
PICTURES: Thank God It's Friday (s.p.), One From the Heart (co-s.p.), Windy City (dir. s.p.), Cross My Heart (dir., co-s.p.), Satisfaction (co-exec. prod.), The Commitments (co-exec. prod.), A Midnight Clear (co-exec. prod.), The Baby-sitters Club (co-exec. prod.).

BERNSTEIN, BOB
Executive. Began public relations career 1952 at DuMont TV Network, followed by 2 yrs. as press agent for Liberace. With Billboard Magazine as review editor 3 yrs. Joined Westinghouse Bdg. Co. as p.r. director 1959. In 1963 named p.r. director for Triangle Publications, serving in various capacities to 1971. Joined Viacom Intl. as director of information services. In 1975 formed own co., March Five Inc., p.r. and promotion firm.

BERNSTEIN, ELMER
Composer, Conductor. b. New York, NY, April 4, 1922. Scholarship, Juilliard. e. Walden Sch., NYU., U.S. Army Air Force radio unit. After war 3 yrs. recitals, musical shows, United Nations radio dept; pres., Young Musicians Found.; 1st v.p. Academy of Motion Picture Arts & Sciences; co-chmn. music branch. Music dir. Valley Symphony. Recording artist, United Artists. More than 90 major films. Pres. of Composers & Lyricists Guild of America.
THEATER: How Now Dow Jones?
PICTURES: Never Wave at a WAC, Sudden Fear, Robot Monster, Cat Women of the Moon, It's a Dog's Life, Man With the Golden Arm, Storm Fear, The View From Pompey's Head, The Ten Commandments, Fear Strikes Out, Desire Under the Elms, Drango, The Naked Eye, Sweet Smell of Success, The Tin Star, Anna Lucasta, The Buccaneer, God's Little Acre, Kings Go Forth, Some Came Running, The Miracle, The Story on Page One, From the Terrace, The Magnificent Seven, The Rat Race, By Love Possessed, The Commancheros, Summer and Smoke, The Young Doctors, Birdman of Alcatraz, Walk on the Wild Side, A Girl Named Tamiko, To Kill a Mockingbird, The Great Escape, The Caretakers, Hud, Kings of the Sun, Rampage, Love With the Proper Stranger, The Carpetbaggers, Four Days in November, The World of Henry Orient, The Hallelujah Trail, The Reward, Seven Women, Cast a Giant Shadow, Hawaii, Thoroughly Modern Millie (Academy Award, 1967), I Love You Alice B. Toklas, The Scalphunters, True Grit, The Gypsy Moths, Midas Run, Where's Jack?, Cannon for Cordoba, The Liberation of L.B. Jones, A Walk in the Spring Rain, Doctor's Wives, See No Evil, Big Jake, The Magnificent Seven Ride, Cahill U.S. Marshall, McQ., Gold, The Trial of Billy Jack, Report to the Commissioner, From Noon Till Three, The Incredible Sarah, The Shootist, Slap Shot, National Lampoon's Animal House, Bloodbrothers, Meatballs, The Great Santini, Saturn 3, The Blues Brothers, Airplane!, Zulu Dawn, Going Ape, Stripes, An American Werewolf in London, Honky Tonk Freeway, The Chosen, Five Days One Summer, Airplane II: The Sequel, Spacehunter, Trading Places, Class, Bolero, Ghostbusters, The Black Cauldron, Spies Like Us, Legal Eagles, Three Amigos, Amazing Grace and Chuck, Leonard Part 6, Da, Funny Farm, The Good Mother, Slipstream, My Left Foot, The Grifters, The Field, Oscar, A Rage in Harlem, Rambling Rose, Cape Fear (adapt.), The Babe, The Cemetery Club, Mad Dog and Glory, Lost in Yonkers, The Age of Innocence, The Good Son, I Love Trouble, Roommates, Canadian Bacon, Devil in a Blue Dress.
TELEVISION: *Specials*: Hollywood: The Golden Years, The Race for Space: Parts I & II, D-Day, The Making of the President—1960 (Emmy Award), Hollywood and the Stars, Voyage of the Brigantine Yankee, Crucifiction of Jesus, NBC Best Sellers Theme (1976). *Series*: Julia, Owen Marshall, Ellery Queen, Serpico, The Chisholms. *Movies*: Gulag, Guyana Tragedy.

BERNSTEIN, FRED
Executive. Was sr. v.p. of business affairs and pres. of worldwide prod. for Columbia Pictures in 1980's before serving as sr. v.p. of MCA Inc.'s Motion Picture Group, 1987-94. Named pres. of Coumbia TriStar Motion Pictures, 1994.

BERNSTEIN, JACK B.
Executive. b. New York, NY, May 6, 1937. e. City U. of New York, B.A., sociology. U.S. Army-Europe, 1956-58; research bacteriologist, 1959-61. Entered industry in 1962 with S.I.B. Prods., Paramount, as v.p. gen. mgr.; 1964-66, v.p. gen. mgr. C.P.I. Prods, 1966-73 prod. mgr. asst. dir., free lance. 1973-1982, assoc. prod. exec. prod. at several studios. 1983-86, v.p. worldwide prod., Walt Disney Pictures; 1987, sr. v.p., worldwide prod., United Artists Pictures; 1988-90, sr. v.p. worldwide prod., MGM Pictures. Member: DGA, Friars, Academy of MP Arts & Sciences; Academy of TV Arts & Sciences, AFI.
PICTURES: Asst. dir.: Hearts of the West. Prod. mngr.: Silver Streak. Assoc. Prod.: The Other Side of Midnight, The Fury, Butch and Sundance: The Early Days, Six Pack, Unfaithfully Yours. Exec. Prod.: North Dallas Forty, Monsignor, The Beast Within. Co-Prod.: The Mambo Kings, Under Siege.

BERNSTEIN, JAY
Producer, Personal manager. b. Oklahoma City, OK, June 7, 1937. e. Pomona Coll. 1963-76, pres. of Jay Bernstein Public Relations, representing over 600 clients. Formed Jay Bernstein Enterprises, acting as personal manager for Farrah Fawcett, Suzanne Somers, Kristy McNichol, Susan Hayward, Donald Sutherland, Bruce Boxleitner, Robert Conrad, Susan Saint James, Robert Blake, William Shatner, Linda Evans, Cicely Tyson, etc. Past pres., Bernstein Thompson Entertainment Complex, entertainment and personal mgt. firm.
PICTURES: Exec. prod.: Sunburn, Nothing Personal.
TELEVISION: Exec. prod. Movies: The Return of Mike Hammer, Mickey Spillane's Margin for Murder; Wild, Wild, West, Revisited; More Wild, Wild West. Murder Me Murder You, More Than Murder, The Return of Mike Hammer, Murder Takes All, The Diamond Trap, Final Notice, Double Jeopardy. Series: Bring 'Em Back Alive, Mike Hammer, Houston Knights.

BERNSTEIN, WALTER
Director, Writer. b. New York, NY. Aug. 20, 1919. e. Dartmouth. Wrote for New Yorker Magazine; in W.W.II was roving correspondent for Yank Magazine. Returned to New Yorker after war. Wrote TV scripts; published book Keep Your Head Down (collection of articles).
PICTURES: Writer: Kiss the Blood Off My Hands (co-s.p.), That Kind of Woman, Heller in Pink Tights, A Breath of Scandal (co-s.p.), Paris Blues, The Magnificent Seven (uncredited), Fail Safe, The Money Trap, The Train, The Molly Maguires, The Front, Semi-Tough, The Betsy (co-s.p.), An Almost Perfect Affair, Yanks, Little Miss Marker (dir. debut), The House on Carroll Street.

BERNSTEIN, WILLIAM
Executive. b. New York, NY, Aug. 30, 1933. e. New York U., B.A. 1954; Yale U., L.L.B. 1959. Joined United Artists as an attorney in 1959. 1967-72, v.p., business affairs. Promoted to senior v.p., 1972. Executive v.p., Orion Pictures, 1978-91. Pres. and CEO Orion Pictures, 1991-92. Exec. v.p., Paramount Pictures 1992-present. Member, A.B.A., A.M.P.A.S.

BERRI, CLAUDE
Director, Actor, Producer. b. Paris, July 1, 1934. r.n. Claude Langmann. Started as actor, playing roles in French films and on stage in the 1950s. Began dir. career with short film Jeanine, followed by Le Poulet (The Chicken; also prod.) Academy Award for best live action short subject, 1965). 1963, created Renn Productions. 1973, became partner in AMLF distribution co.
PICTURES: Director: The Two of Us (feature debut, 1967), Marry Me Marry Me (also s.p., actor), Le Pistonne (The Man with Connections), Le Cinema de Papa (Cinema of My Father; also prod.), Le Sex Shop (also s.p.), Male of the Century (also s.p., actor), The First Time (also s.p.), Tess (prod.), Inspecteur la Bavure (prod.), Je Vous Aime (prod., s.p.), In a Wild Moment, Je Vous Aime (I Love You), Le Maitre d' Ecole (The Schoolmaster; also prod., s.p.), A Quarter to Two Before Jesus Christ (prod.), L'Africain (prod.), L'Homme Blesse (prod.), Tchao Pantin (also prod., s.p.), Jean la Florette, Manon of the Spring, The Bear (exec. prod.), Valmont (exec. prod.), Uranus (also s.p.), Germinal (also prod., co-s.p.).

BERRIDGE, ELIZABETH
Actress. b. New Rochelle, NY, May 2, 1962. Studied acting at Lee Strasberg Inst., Warren Robertson Theatre Workshop.
THEATER: NY: The Vampires, The Incredibly Famous Willy Rivers, Outside Waco, Ground Zero Club, Cruise Control, Sorrows and Sons, Crackwalker, Coyote Ugly, Briar Patch. Regional: Tuesday's Child, Hedda Gabler, Lulu, Venus and Thumbtacks.
PICTURES: Natural Enemies, The Funhouse, Amadeus, Smooth Talk, Five Corners, When the Party's Over.
TELEVISION: Series: One of the Boys, The Powers That Be, The John Larroquette Show. Movies: Silence of the Heart, Home Fires Burning, Montana.

BERRY, HALLE
Actress. b. Cleveland, OH, 1968. Named Miss Teen Ohio, Miss Teen All-American, runner up to Miss U.S.A.

PICTURES: Jungle Fever, Strictly Business, The Last Boy Scout, Boomerang, Father Hood, The Program, The Flintstones, Losing Isaiah, Race the Sun, Girl 6, Executive Decision, Rich Man's Wife.
TELEVISION: Movie: Solomon and Sheba. Mini-Series: Queen.

BERRY, JOHN
Director. b. New York, NY, 1917. Directed films in Hollywood mid and late '40s; went abroad during McCarthy era in U.S. where worked in French film industry. Later went to London to do stage work, acting as well as directing. Returned to U.S. to do stage work; returned to Hollywood to do TV.
PICTURES: Cross My Heart, From This Day Forward, Miss Susie Slagle's, Casbah, Tension, He Ran All the Way, CCa Va Barder, The Great Lover, Je Suis un Sentimental, Tamango, On Que Mambo, Claudine, Maya, The Bad News Bears Go to Japan, Thieves, Il y a maldonne, 'Round Midnight (actor only), A Man in Love (actor only), La Voyage a Paimpol (also prod.), Captive in the Land (also prod.).
TELEVISION: One Drink at a Time, Farewell Party, Mr. Broadway, Sister Sister (also prod.), Angel on My Shoulder, Honeyboy, Legitimate Defense.

BERRY, KEN
Actor. b. Moline, IL, Nov. 3, 1933.
PICTURES: Two for the Seesaw, Hello Down There, Herbie Rides Again, The Cat from Outer Space.
TELEVISION: Movies: Wake Me When the War Is Over, The Reluctant Heroes, Every Man Needs One, Letters from Three Lovers, Love Boat II. Series: The Ann Sothern Show, Bob Newhart Show (1962), F Troop, Mayberry RFD, Ken Berry Wow Show, Mama's Family. Guest: Dick Van Dyke Show, Hazel, Lucy Show, Carol Burnett, Sonny & Cher, etc.

BERTINELLI, VALERIE
Actress. b. Wilmington, DE, April 23, 1960. m. musician Eddie Van Halen. Dramatic training at Tami Lynn Academy of Artists in California. Made early TV appearances in the series, Apple's Way, in commercials, and in public service announcements. Started own prod. company to acquire properties for self.
PICTURE: Number One with a Bullet.
TELEVISION: Movies: Young Love First Love, The Promise of Love, The Princess and the Cabbie, I Was a Mail Order Bride, The Seduction of Gina, Shattered Vows, Silent Witness, Rockabye, Pancho Barnes, In a Child's Name, What She Doesn't Know, Murder of Innocence. Specials: The Secret of Charles Dickens, The Magic of David Copperfield. Series: One Day at a Time, Sydney, Cafe Americain. Mini-Series: I'll Take Manhattan.

BERTOLUCCI, BERNARDO
Director, Writer. b. Parma, Italy, May 16, 1940. e. Rome U. Son of Attilio Bertolucci, poet and film critic. At age 20 worked as asst. dir. to Pier Paolo Pasolini on latter's first film, Accatone: in 1962 made debut film, The Grim Reaper, from script by Pasolini. 1962 published poetry book: In Cerca del Mistero. 1965-66: directed and wrote 3-part TV documentary: La vie del Petrolio for Ital. Oil co. in Iran. Collaborated on s.p. Ballata de un Milliardo, Sergio Leone's Once Upon a Time in the West, L'inchiesta. Produced films Sconcerto Rock, Io con te non ci sto piu, Lost and Found.
PICTURES: Director-Writer: The Grim Reaper, Before the Revolution, Love and Rage (episode: Agony), Partner, The Spider's Strategem, The Conformist, Last Tango in Paris, 1900, Luna, Tragedy of a Ridiculous Man, The Last Emperor (Academy Awards for Best Director & Screenplay, 1987), The Sheltering Sky, Little Buddha, Stealing Beauty.

BESCH, BIBI
Actress. b. Vienna, Austria, Feb. 1, 1942. Mother was actress Gusti Huber. Daughter is actress Samantha Mathis. Raised in Westchester County, NY. Appeared on soap daytime dramas as Secret Storm, Love is a Many-Splendored Thing, and Somerset.
THEATER: NY Stage: Fame, The Chinese Prime Minister, Here Lies Jeremy Troy, Once for the Asking.
PICTURES: The Pack, Hardcore, The Promise, Meteor, The Beast Within, Star Trek II: The Wrath of Khan, The Lonely Lady, Date With an Angel, Kill Me Again, Tremors, Steel Magnolias, Betsy's Wedding, My Family/Mi Familia, California Myth, Lonely Hearts, Distance, Black Harvest.
TELEVISION: Series: Secrets of Midland Heights, The Hamptons, The Jeff Foxworthy Show. Movies: Victory at Entebbe, Peter Lundy and the Medicine Hat Stallion, Betrayal, Transplant, The Plutonium Incident, The Sophisticated Gents, Death of a Centerfold: The Dorothy Stratten Story, Secrets of a Mother and Daughter, The Day After, Lady Blue, Crazy From the Heart, Doing Time on Maple Drive, Abandoned and Deceived, Wounded Heart, Rattled, White Dwarf, A.C.E.S., Orleans, Home Video. Mini-Series: Backstairs at the White House. Special: The Last Shot.
(d. September 7, 1996)

BESSON, LUC
Director, Writer, Producer. b. Paris, France, March 18, 1959.
PICTURES: Le Dernier Combat (dir., prod., s.p.), Le Grand
Carnaval (2nd unit dir.), Subway (dir., prod., s.p.), Kamikaze
(prod., s.p.), Taxi Boy (tech. advis.), The Big Blue (dir., s.p.,
lyrics, camera op.), La Femme Nikita (dir., s.p., song), The
Professional (dir., prod., s.p.).

BEST, BARBARA
Publicist. b. San Diego, CA, Dec. 2, 1921. e. U. of Southern
California, AB, 1943. Pub., 20th Century-Fox, 1943-49; reporter,
San Diego Journal, 1950 Stanley Kramer Co. 1950-53; own
agency, Barbara Best & Associates, 1953-66; 1966 exec. v.p.
Jay Bernstein Public rel.; Freeman and Best, 1967-74; Barbara
Best Inc. publ. rel. 1975-85; Barbara Best Personal
Management, current.

BEST, JAMES
Actor. b. Corydon, IN, July 26, 1926. Magazine model; on stage;
in European roadshow cast of My Sister Eileen; served as M.P.
with USAAF, WWII.
PICTURES: One Way Street (debut, 1950), Commanche
Territory, Winchester 73, Peggy, Kansas Raiders, Air Cadet,
Cimarron Kid, Target Unknown, Apache Drums, Ma & Pa Kettle
at the Fair, Steel Town, Francis Goes to West Point, Battle at
Apache Pass, Flat Top, About Face, The Beast from 20000
Fathoms, Seminole, The President's Lady, City of Bad Men,
Column South, Riders to the Stars, The Raid, The Caine Mutiny,
Return from the Sea, They Rode West, Seven Angry Men, The
Eternal Sea, A Man Called Peter, Forbidden Planet, Calling
Homicide, When Gangland Strikes, Come Next Spring, Gaby,
The Rack, Man on the Prowl, Hot Summer Night, Last of the
Badmen, Verboten!, The Naked and the Dead, The Left Handed
Gun, Cole Younger - Gunfighter, The Killer Shrews, Ride
Lonesome, Cast a Long Shadow, The Mountain Road, Shock
Corridor, Black Gold, The Quick Gun, Black Spurs,
Shenandoah, Three on a Couch, First to Fight, Firecreek, The
Brain Machine, Sounder, Ode to Billy Joe, Gator (also assoc.
prod.), Nickelodeon, Rolling Thunder, The End (also assoc.
prod.), Hooper.
TELEVISION: Series: Dukes of Hazzard. Movies: Run Simon
Run, Savages, The Runaway Barge, The Savage Bees. Guest:
Alfred Hitchcock Presents, Twilight Zone, The Andy Griffith
Show, Hawkins, Enos, In the Heat of the Night, etc. Mini-Series:
Centennial.

BETHUNE, ZINA
Actress, Dancer, Singer. b. New York, NY, Feb. 17, 1950. B'way:
Most Happy Fella, Grand Hotel. National tours: Sweet Charity,
Carnival, Oklahoma!, Damn Yankees, Member of the Wedding,
The Owl and The Pussycat, Nutcracker. New York City Ballet
(Balanchine), Zina Bethune & Company Dance Theatre,
Bethune Theatredanse. Special performance at the White
House and Kennedy Center.
PICTURES: Sunrise At Campobello, Who's That Knocking at My
Door, The Boost.
TELEVISION: Series: The Guiding Light, The Nurses, Love of
Life. Guest: Lancer, Cains Hundred, Naked City, Route 66, Little
Women, Santa Barbara, Judy Garland Show, Jackie Gleason
Show, Gunsmoke, Dr. Kildare, Emergency, Planet of The Apes,
Police Story, Chips, Hardy Boys, Dirty Dancing. Movies:
Nutcracker: Money Madness Murder (also choreographer),
Party of Five. Specials: The Gymnast (An ABC Afterschool
Special), Heart Dancing, From the Heart.

BETTGER, LYLE
Actor b. Philadelphia, PA, Feb. 13, 1915. e. Haverford School,
Philadelphia, American Acad. of Dramatic Art, N.Y. m. Mary
Rolfe, actress. Started in summer stock; in road cos. of Brother
Rat, Man Who Came to Dinner.
THEATER: John Loves Mary, Love Life, Eve of St. Mark, The
Male Animal, Sailor Beware, The Moon is Down.
PICTURES: No Man of Her Own, Love Life, First Legion,
Greatest Show on Earth, The Denver & Rio Grande,
Vanquished, Forbidden, The Great Sioux Uprising, All I Desire,
Drums Across the River, Destry, Carnival Story, Sea Chase,
Showdown at Abilene, Gunfight at OK Corral, Town Tamer,
Johnny Reno, Nevada Smith, Return of The Gunfighter,
Impasse, The Hawaiians, The Seven Minutes.
TELEVISION: Court of Last Resort, Grand Jury, Hawaii 5-0,
Police Story, Bonanza, Combat, Gunsmoke, etc.

BEVILLE, HUGH M., JR.
Executive; b. April 18, 1908. e. Syracuse U., NYU (MBA). To
NBC 1930 statistician, chief statistician; Research mgr., dir.,
research; U.S. Army 1942-46; dir. of research and planning
for NBC, v.p., planning and research, 1956; v.p., planning,
1964; consultant, 1968; professor Business Admin.,
Southampton Coll., 1968. Exec. dir., Broadcast Rating
Council, 1971-82, author-consultant, contributing editor,
TV/Radio Age, 1982-85. Author, Audience Ratings; Radio,
Television, Cable, 1985, Elected member, Research Hall of
Fame, 1986.

BEY, TURHAN
Actor. b. Vienna, Austria, March 30, 1922. Came to U.S. in
1930's studying acting at Ben Bard's School of Dramatic Arts,
Pasadena Playhouse.
PICTURES: Footsteps in the Dark (debut, 1941), Burma
Convoy, Raiders of the Desert, Shadows on the Stairs, The Gay
Falcon, Junior G-Men of the Air (serial), The Falcon Takes Over,
A Yank on the Burma Road, Bombay Clipper, Drums of the
Congo, Destination Unknown, Arabian Nights, The Unseen
Enemy, The Mummy's Tomb, Danger in the Pacific, Adventures
of Smilin' Jack (serial), White Savage, The Mad Ghoul,
Background to Danger, Follow the Boys, The Climax, Dragon
Seed, Bowery to Broadway, Ali Baba and the 40 Thieves, Frisco
Sal, Sudan, Night in Paradise, Out of the Blue, The Amazing Mr.
X, Adventures of Casanova, Parole Inc., Song of India,
Prisoners of the Casbah, Stolen Identity (prod. only), Healer,
Possessed by the Night.
TELEVISION: Guest: Seaquest, Murder She Wrote, Babylon 5

BEYMER, RICHARD
Actor. r.n. George Richard Beymer, Jr., b. Avoca, IA, Feb. 21,
1939. e. N. Hollywood H.S., Actors Studio. Performer, KTLA,
Sandy Dreams, Fantastic Studios, Inc., 1949, Playhouse 90.
PICTURES: Indiscretion of an American Wife (debut, 1953), So
Big, Johnny Tremain, The Diary of Anne Frank, High Time, West
Side Story, Bachelor Flat, Five Finger Exercise, Hemingway's
Adventures of a Young Man, The Longest Day, The Stripper,
Grass (Scream Free!), Cross Country, Silent Night Deadly Night
3: Better Watch Out, My Girl 2.
TELEVISION: Series: Paper Dolls, Twin Peaks. Movies:
Generation, With a Vengeance. Guest: The Virginian, Walt
Disney (Boston Tea Party), Dr. Kildare, Man from U.N.C.L.E.,
Moonlighting, Murder She Wrote, The Bronx Zoo.

BIALIK, MAYIM
Actress. b. Dec. 12, 1976.
PICTURES: Pumpkinhead (debut, 1988), Beaches.
TELEVISION: Series: Blossom. Movies: Blossom in Paris, Don't
Drink the Water. Specials: Earth Day Special, Sea World Mother
Earth Celebration (host), Surviving a Break-Up, The Kingdom
Chums: Original Top Ten (voice), I Hate the Way I Look, For Our
Children: The Concert (host). Pilot: Molly. Guest: Webster, Facts
of Life, MacGyver, Empty Nest, The John Larroquette Show.

BICK, JERRY
Producer. b. New York, NY, April 26, 1923. e. Columbia U.,
Sorbonne. Taught English at U. of Georgia, before entering film
industry in pub. dept. of MGM, N.Y. Opened own literary agency
in Hollywood after stint with MCA. Began career as producer in
London; debut film, Michael Kohlhaas, 1969. 1986-89, exec. v.p.
worldwide prod., Heritage Entertainment.
PICTURES: The Long Goodbye, Thieves Like Us, Russian
Roulette, Farewell My Lovely (exec. prod.), The Big Sleep,
Against All Odds (exec. prod.), Swing Shift.

BIEHN, MICHAEL
Actor. b. Anniston, AL, July 31, 1956. Raised in Lincoln, NB, and
Lake Havisu, AZ. At 18 years moved to Los Angeles and stud-
ied acting with Vincent Chase. First professional job in 1977 in
TV pilot for Logan's Run.
PICTURES: Grease (debut, 1978), Coach, Hog Wild, The Fan,
The Lords of Discipline, The Terminator, Aliens, The Seventh
Sign, Rampage, In a Shallow Grave, The Abyss, Navy Seals,
Time Bomb, K2, DeadFall, Tombstone, Deep Red, Jade.
TELEVISION: Series: The Runaways. Guest: Logan's Run, Hill
Street Blues, Police Story, Family. Movies: Zuma Beach, A Fire
in the Sky, China Rose, Deadly Intentions, A Taste for Killing,
Strapped. Pilots: James at 15, The Paradise Connection.

BIGELOW, KATHRYN
Director, Writer. b. 1951. e. SF Art Inst., Columbia. Studied to
be painter before turning to film with short Set-Up, 1978. Was
script supervisor on Union City; appeared in film Born in Flames.
PICTURES: The Loveless (feature debut as co-dir. with Monty
Montgomery, 1981; also co-s.p.), Near Dark (also co-s.p.), Blue
Steel (also co-s.p.), Point Break, Strange Days.
TELEVISION: Mini-Series: Wild Palms (co-dir.).

BIKEL, THEODORE
Actor. b. Vienna, Austria, May 2, 1924. Moved to Palestine
(Israel) as teen where he made stage debut in Tevye the
Milkman. Studied acting at Royal Academy of Dramatic Arts in
London. London stage debut in 1948. Autobiography: Theo
(1995).
THEATER: Tonight in Samarkland, The Lark, The Rope
Dancers, The Sound of Music, Cafe Crown, Fiddler on the
Roof.
PICTURES: The African Queen, Melba, Desperate Moment, The
Divided Heart, The Little Kidnappers, The Vintage, The Pride
and the Passion, The Enemy Below, Fraulein, The Defiant Ones
(Acad. Award nom.), I Want to Live, The Angry Hills, The Blue
Angel, A Dog of Flanders, My Fair Lady, Sands of the Kalahari,
The Russians Are Coming the Russians Are Coming, Sweet

November, My Side of the Mountain, Darker Than Amber, 200 Motels, The Little Ark, Prince Jack, Dark Tower, See You in the Morning.
TELEVISION: The Eternal Light, Look Up and Live, Who Has Seen the Wind?, The Diary of Anne Frank, Killer by Night, Murder on Flight 502, Victory at Entebbe, Testimony of Two Men, Loose Change.

BILBY, KENNETH W.
Executive. b. Salt Lake City, UT, Oct. 7, 1918. e. Columbia U., U. of Arizona, B.A. With N.Y. Herald-Tribune, 47-50; author, New Star in the Near East, 1950; pub. rel. rep. to RCA Victor, Camden, NJ, 1950-54; exec. v.p. National Broadcasting Co., N.Y., 1954-60; v.p. public affairs, RCA, 1960-62, exec. v.p., 1962-75; exec. v.p. corporate affairs, 1976-present.

BILL, TONY
Director, Producer, Actor. b. San Diego, CA, Aug. 23, 1940. e. Notre Dame U. Founded Bill/Phillips Prods. with Julia and Michael Phillips, 1971-73; Tony Bill Prods. 1973-92; Barnstorm Films, 1993-; Acad. of M.P. Arts & Sciences, bd. of govs., bd of trustees, chmn. prods. branch.
PICTURES: Director: My Bodyguard (debut, 1980), Six Weeks, Five Corners (also co-prod.), Crazy People, Untamed Heart (also co-prod.), A Home of Our Own. Prod.: Hearts of the West (exec. prod.), Harry and Walter Go to New York, Boulevard Nights (exec. prod.), Going in Style, Little Dragons (also actor). Co-producer: Deadhead Miles, Steelyard Blues, The Sting (Academy Award for Best Picture, 1973), Taxi Driver. Actor: Come Blow Your Horn (debut, 1963), Soldier in the Rain, Marriage on the Rocks, None But the Brave, You're a Big Boy Now, Ice Station Zebra, Never a Dull Moment, Castle Keep, Flap, Shampoo, Heartbeat, Pee-wee's Big Adventure, Less Than Zero.
TELEVISION: Director: Dirty Dancing (pilot), Love Thy Neighbor, Next Door (movie), One Christmas (movie). Actor: Special: Lee Oswald - Assassin (BBC). Series: What Really Happened to the Class of '65? Movies: Haunts of the Very Rich, Having Babies II, The Initiation of Sarah, With This Ring, Are You in the House Alone?, Portrait of an Escort, Freedom, Washington Mistress, Running Out, The Killing Mind. Guest: Alfred Hitchcock Presents (Night Caller, 1985). Mini-Series: Washington Behind Closed Doors.

BILLS, ELMER E.
Executive. b. Salisbury, MO, July 12, 1936. e. University of Missouri, B.S. Partner B & B Theatres, Inc.

BILSON, BRUCE
Director. b. Brooklyn, NY, May 19, 1928. e. UCLA, BA, Theater Arts, 1950. m. Renne Jarrett. Father was prod. George Bilson, son is prod.-dir. Danny Bilson, daughter is prod. Julie Ahlberg. Asst. film ed. 1951-55; USAF photo unit 1952-53; asst. dir. 1955-65 including Andy Griffith Show, Route 66. Assoc. prod. The Baileys of Balboa. Dir. since 1965 of more than 380 TV shows. Emmy Award, Get Smart, DGA nom. The Odd Couple.
PICTURES: The North Avenue Irregulars, Chattanooga Choo Choo.
TELEVISION: Series: The Sentinel, Touched by an Angel, Viper, The Flash, Dinosaurs, Barney Miller, Get Smart (Emmy Award, 1968), Hogan's Heroes, House Calls, Alice, Private Benjamin, Life With Lucy, Spenser: For Hire, Hotel, Dallas, Hawaii Five-O, Dynasty, The Fall Guy, Nightingales. Movies/pilots: The Odd Couple, The Dallas Cowboys Cheerleaders, BJ and the Bear, The Misadventures of Sheriff Lobo, Half Nelson, Finder of Lost Loves, The Girl Who Came Gift Wrapped, The Ghosts of Buxley Hall, The New Gidget, Barefoot in the Park, The Bad News Bears, Harper Valley PTA.

BINDER, STEVE
Producer, Director, Writer. b. Los Angeles, CA, Dec. 12. e. Univ. of Southern California. 1960-61 announcer in Austria and Germany with AFN, Europe. Prof. of Cinema, Univ. Southern CA. Mem.: DGA, Producers Guild of America, Writers Guild of America, NARAS, ATAS.
PICTURES: Director: The T.A.M.I. Show, Give 'Em Hell Harry!, Melissa.
TELEVISION: Prod./Dir.: Steve Allen Show (1963-65, 1973), Elvis Presley Comeback Special, Barry Manilow Special (also writer, Emmy Award, 1977), Diana Ross '81 (also writer), Ringling Bros & Barnum Bailey Circus (also writer), Pee-wee's Playhouse, Big Fun on Swing Street, Barry Manilow, Pee-wee's Playhouse Christmas Special (prod.), A Tribute to Sam Kinison. Dir.: Diana Ross Sings Jazzy Blues, Diana Ross—World Tour, Diana Ross in Central Park (Cable Ace Award), Diana, The International Special Olimpics, 6th Anniversary of the Grand Ole Opry, The First Annual ESPY Awards. Exec. Prod/Dir.: Disney's Greatest Hits on Ice, John Denver's Montana X-Mas Skies, One Night With You. Exec. Prod.: Pee-wee's Playhouse.

BIONDI, JR. FRANK J.
Executive. b. Jan. 9, 1945. e. Princeton U.; Harvard U., MBA (1968). Various investment banking positions 1968-74; asst.

treas. Children's TV Workshop 1974-78; v.p. programming HBO 1978-82; pres. HBO 1983, then chmn. & chief exec. off. 1984 joined Coca-Cola Co. as exec. v.p., entertainment business arm. Resigned 1987 to join Viacom International as pres. and CEO. Pres, MCA, 1996.

BIRCH, THORA
Actress. b. California. Began acting at age 4. First appeared in commericals.
PICTURES: Paradise, All I Want for Christmas, Patriot Games, Hocus Pocus, Monkey Trouble, Clear and Present Danger, Now and Then, Alaska.
TELEVISION: Series: Parenthood, Day by Day. Guest: Amen, Doogie Howser M.D.

BIRKIN, JANE
Actress. b. London, England, Dec. 14, 1946. Daughter is actress Charlotte Gainsbourg. Sister of director-writer Andrew Birkin. Was subject of Agnes Vardas' 1988 documentary Jane B. par Agnes V.
PICTURES: Blow-Up, Kaleidoscope, Wonderwall, Les Chemins de Katmandou, La Piscine, Cannabis, Romance of a Horse Thief, Trop jolies pour etre honnetes, Dark Places, Projection Privee, La Moutarde me monte au nex, Le Mouton Enrage, 7 Morts sur Ordonnance, Catherine et Cie, La Course a l'echalote, Je T'Aime Moi Non Plus, Seriex comme let plaisir, Le Diable au Coeur, L'Animal, Death on the Nile, Au bout du bout du banc, Melancolie Baby, La Miel, La Fille Prodigue, Evil Under the Sun, L'Ami de Vincent, Circulez u'a rien a voir, Love on the Ground, le Garde du Corps, The Pirate, Beethoven's Nephew, Dust, Leave All Fair, la Femme de ma vie, Comedie!, Kung Fu Master (also story), Soigne ta droite, Daddy Nostalgia, Between the Devil and the Deep Blue Sea.

BIRNBAUM, ROGER
Producer, Executive. b. Teaneck, NJ. e. Univ. of Denver. Was v.p. of both A&M Records and Arista records before becoming m.p. producer. Headed Guber/Peters Company, then named pres. of worldwide prod., United Artists; pres. of worldwide prod. and exec. v.p. of 20th Century Fox. Left Fox in 1993 to become co-founder of Caravan Pictures.
PICTURES: Producer/Exec. Producer: The Sure Thing, Young Sherlock Homes, Who's That Girl, The Three Musketeers, Angie, Angels in the Outfield, A Low Down Dirty Shame, Houseguest, Tall Tale, While You Were Sleeping, Dead Presidents, Powder, Celtic Pride.

BIRNEY, DAVID
Actor. b. Washington, DC, April 23, 1940. e. Dartmouth Coll., B.A., UCLA, M.A. Phd. Southern Utah St. (hon.). Following grad. sch. and the Army spent 2 yrs. in regional theatre, Amer. Shakespeare Festival, Hartford Stage Co., Barter Theatre, to N.Y. where appeared in Lincoln Center prod. of Summertree (Theatre World Award). Appeared for two yrs. on TV daytime series, Love Is a Many Splendored Thing, doing other stage roles in same period. Theatre panelist, Natl. Endowment for the Arts; Board Member, Hopkins Center, Dartmouth College; Board of Foundation for Biomedical Research.
THEATER: NY debut NY Shakespeare Fest (Comedy of Errors); 3 seasons Lincoln Center Rep. Many NY and regional credits incl: Amadeus, Benefactors, Man and Superman, Macbeth, Hamlet, Richard II, III, Romeo & Juliet, Much Ado About Nothing, King John, Titus Andronicus, Major Barbara, Biko Inquest, Playboy of the Western World, The Miser, Antigone, My Fair Lady, Camelot, Love Letters, Present Laughter.
PICTURES: Caravan to Vaccares, Trial by Combat, Oh God Book II, Prettykill, Nightfall.
TELEVISION: Series: Bridget Loves Bernie, Serpico, St. Elsewhere, Glitter, Live Shot, Beyond 2000 (host), Raising Kids (host), Great American TV Poll (host). Mini-Series: Night of the Fox, Seal Morning, Adam's Chronicles, Testimony of Two Men, Master of the Game, Valley of the Dolls, The Bible. Movies: Murder or Mercy, Bronk, Serpico: The Deadly Game, Someone's Watching Me!, High Midnight, Only With Married Men, OHMS, Mom The Wolfman & Me, The Five of Me, The Long Journey Home (also exec. prod.), Love and Betrayal, Always Remember I Love You, Touch and Die, Keeping Secrets. Specials: Missing: Have You Seen This Person? Drop Everything and Read, 15 and Getting Straight, Mark Twain's The Diaries of Adam and Eve (co-prod.). Guest appearances in series & anthology shows.

BISSET, JACQUELINE
Actress. b. Weybridge, England, September 13, 1944. e. French Lyceae, London. After photographic modeling made film debut in The Knack, 1965.
PICTURES: The Knack... and How to Get It (debut, 1965), Cul de Sac, Two For The Road, Casino Royale, The Cape Town Affair, The Sweet Ride, The Detective, Bullitt, The First Time, Secret World, Airport, The Grasshopper, The Mephisto Waltz, Believe in Me, Stand Up and Be Counted, The Life & Times of Judge Roy Bean, The Thief Who Came to Dinner, Day for Night, Le Manifique, Murder on the Orient Express, End of the Game,

The Spiral Staircase, St. Ives, Sunday Woman, The Deep, The Greek Tycoon, Secrets, Who Is Killing the Great Chefs of Europe?, Together? (I Love You I Love You Not), When Time Ran Out, Rich and Famous, Inchon, Class, Under the Volcano, High Season, Scenes From the Class Struggle in Beverly Hills, La Maison de Jade, Wild Orchid, The Maid, A Judgment in Stone.
TELEVISION: Movies: Forbidden, Anna Karenina, Choices, Leave of Absence. Mini-Series: Napoleon and Josephine: A Love Story.

BLACK, ALEXANDER F.
Publicist. b. New Rochelle, NY, Dec. 27, 1918. e. Brown U., BA, 1940. Joined Universal 1941. U.S. Navy 1942-45, Lt. Sr. Grade. Rejoined Universal 1946 serving in various capacities in Foreign Department, becoming director of foreign publicity for Universal International Films, Inc. in 1967; 1974, named exec. in chg. intl. promotion for MCA-TV.

BLACK, KAREN
Actress. b. Park Ridge, IL, July 1, 1942. r.n. Karen Ziegler. e. Northwestern U. Left school for NY to join the Hecscher House, appearing in several Shakespearean plays. In 1965 starred in Playroom, which ran only 1 month but won her NY Drama Critic nom. as best actress.
THEATER: Happily Never After, Keep It in the Family, Come Back to the Five and Dime Jimmy Dean Jimmy Dean.
PICTURES: You're a Big Boy Now (debut, 1966), Hard Contact, Easy Rider, Five Easy Pieces (Acad. Award nom.), Drive He Said, A Gunfight, Born To Win, Cisco Pike, Portnoy's Complaint, The Pyx, Little Laura and Big John, Rhinoceros, The Outfit, The Great Gatsby, Airport 1975, Law and Disorder, Day of the Locust, Nashville, Family Plot, Crime and Passion, Burnt Offerings, Capricorn One, Killer Fish, In Praise of Older Women, The Squeeze, The Last Word, Chanel Solitaire, Come Back to the Five and Dime Jimmy Dean Jimmy Dean, Killing Heat (The Grass is Singing), Can She Bake a Cherry Pie?, Martin's Day, Bad Manners (Growing Pains), Cut and Run (Amazon: Savage Adventure), Invaders from Mars, Flight of the Spruce Goose, It's Alive III, Hostage, Eternal Evil, The Invisible Kid, Out of the Dark, Homer and Eddie, Night Angel, Miss Right, Dixie Lanes, Sister City, Zapped Again, Twisted Justice, Over Exposure, The Children, Mirror Mirror, Haunting Fear, Quiet Fire, Children of the Night, Hotel Oklahoma, Killer's Edge, Club Fed, Evil Spirits, Moon Over Miami, The Legend of the Rollerblade 7, Hitz (Judgment), FInald Judgment (Mrs. Sorrel), Caged Fear, Bound & Gagged: A Love Story, The Player, Rubin & Ed, The Trust, The Double O Kid, Sister Island, Plan 10 From Outer Space, The Wacky Adventures of Dr. Boris & Mrs. Duluth, Odyssey, Every Minute Is Goodbye, A Thousand Stars, Children of the Corn III: The Fever, Crime Time.
TELEVISION: Movies: Trilogy of Terror, The Strange Possession of Mrs. Oliver, Mr. Horn, Power, Where the Ladies Go, Because He's My Friend, Full Circle Again (Canadian TV). Guest: In the Heat of the Night.

BLACK, NOEL
Director. b. Chicago, IL, June 30, 1937. e. UCLA, B.A., 1959; M.A. 1964. Made short film Skaterdater.
PICTURES: Pretty Poison (debut, 1968), Cover Me Babe, Jennifer on My Mind, Mirrors, A Man a Woman and a Bank, Private School, Mischief (s.p., exec. prod.).
TELEVISION: Trilogy, The American Boy, The World Beyond, I'm a Fool, The Golden Honeymoon, The Electric Grandmother, The Doctors Wilde, Meet the Munceys, Eyes of the Panther, The Hollow Boy. Movies: Mulligan's Stew, The Other Victim, Prime Suspect, Happy Endings, Quarterback Princess, Deadly Intentions, Promises to Keep, A Time to Triumph, My Two Loves, Conspiracy of Love, The Town Bully. Mini-series: Deadly Intentions.

BLACK, STANLEY
Composer, conductor, musical director. OBE. b. London, Eng. Resident conductor, BBC, 1944-52. Musical director 105 feature films and Pathe Newsreel music: Music dir. Associated British Film Studios 1958-64. Guest conductor, Royal Philharmonic Orchestra and London Symphony. Orchestra; many overseas conducting engagements including (1977) Boston Pops and Winnipeg Symphony. Associated conductor Osaka Philharmonic Orchestra. Exclusive recording contract with Decca Record Co. since 1944.
PICTURES: Crossplot, The Long the Short and The Tall, Rattle of a Simple Man, The Young Ones, Hell Is a City, Top Secret, Valentino.

BLACKMAN, HONOR
Actress. b. London, England, 1926. Stage debut. The Gleam 1946.
PICTURES: Fame Is the Spur (debut, 1947), Quartet, Daughter of Darkness, A Boy A Girl and a Bike, Diamond City, Conspirator, So Long at the Fair, Set a Murderer, Green Grow the Rushes, Come Die My Love, Rainbow Jacket, Outsiders, Delavine Affair, Three Musketeers, Breakaway, Homecoming, Suspended Alibi, Dangerous Drugs, A Night to Remember, The

Square Peg, A Matter of Who, Present Laughter, The Recount, Serena, Jason & the Golden Fleece, Goldfinger, The Secret of My Success, Moment to Moment, Life at the Top, A Twist of Sand, Shalako, Struggle for Rome, Twinky (Lola), The Last Grenade, The Virgin and the Gypsy, Fright, Something Big, Out Damned Spot, Summer, Cat and the Canary.
TELEVISION: African Patrol, The Witness, Four Just Men, Probation Officer series, Top Secret, Ghost Squad, Invisible Man, The Saint, The Avengers series, Voice of the Heart, The Upper Hand (series).

BLADES, RUBEN
Actor, Composer, Singer, Writer. b. Panama City, Panama, July 16, 1948. e. U. of Panama (law and political science, 1974), Harvard U., L.L.M., 1985. Has recorded more than 14 albums, winning 2 Grammy Awards (1986, 1988). With his band Seis del Solar has toured U.S., Central America and Europe. President of Panama's Papa Egoro political party.
PICTURES: Actor: The Last Fight (debut, 1982), Crossover Dreams (also co-s.p.), Critical Condition, The Milagro Beanfield War, Fatal Beauty, Homeboy, Disorganized Crime, The Lemon Sisters, Mo' Better Blues, The Two Jakes, Predator 2, Homeboy, The Super, Life With Mikey, A Million to Juan, Color of Night. Music: Oliver & Company, Caminos Verdes (Venezuela), Q&A, Scorpion Spring.
TELEVISION: Guest: Sesame Street. Movies: Dead Man Out (ACE Award), One Man's War, The Josephine Baker Story (Emmy nom.), Crazy from the Heart (Emmy nom.), The Heart of the Deal, Miracle on I-880.

BLAIN, GERARD
Actor, Director. b. Paris, Oct. 23, 1930. Began his professional career in 1943 as an extra in Marcel Carne's The Children of Paradise. Appeared on stage in Marcel Pagnol's Topaze (1944). Military service in a parachute regiment. In 1955 Julien Duvivier gave him his first major role in Voici le Temps des Assassins (Murder a la Carte). By 1969 had appeared in more than 30 stage and film roles before becoming a director and co-author.
PICTURES: Les Mistons (1957), Le Beau Serge, Les Cousins. In Italy: The Hunchback of Rome, L'Ora di Roma, I Defini, Run with the Devil, Young Husbands. In Germany: The American Friend, L'Enfant de l'Hiver. As director and author or co-author: Les Amis, Le Pelican (also actor), Un Enfant dans la Foule, Un Second Souffle, Le Rebelle, Portrait sur Michel Tournier, Pierre et Djemila.

BLAIR, JANET
Actress. b. Blair, PA, April 23, 1921. r.n. Martha Janet Lafferty. With Hal Kemp's Orchestra; toured in South Pacific, 1950-52.
PICTURES: Three Girls About Town (debut, 1941), Blondie Goes to College, Two Yanks in Trinidad, Broadway, My Sister Eileen, Something to Shout About, Once Upon a Time, Tonight and Every Night, Tars and Spars, Gdallant Journey, The Fabulous Dorseys, I Love Trouble, The Black Arrow, Fuller Brush Man, Public Pigeon No. 1, Boys Night Out, Burn Witch Burn, The One and Only Genuine Original Family Band, Won Ton Ton the Dog Who Saved Hollywood.
TELEVISION: Series: Leave It to the Girls (panelist), Caesar's Hour, The Chevy Show, The Smith Family. Special: Arabian Nights, Tom Sawyer. Guest: Bell Telephone Hour, Ed Sullivan, Murder She Wrote, etc.

BLAIR, LINDA
Actress. b. St. Louis, MO, Jan. 22, 1959. Model and actress on TV commercials before going into films.
PICTURES: The Sporting Club (debut, 1971), The Exorcist, Airport '75, Exorcist II: The Heretic, Roller Boogie, Wild Horse Hank, Hell Night, Ruckus, Chained Heat, Savage Streets, Savage Island, Red Heat, Night Patrol, Night Force, Silent Assassins, Grotesque, Witchery, The Chilling, Bad Blood, Moving Target, Up Your Alley, Repossessed, Aunt Millie's Will, Zapped Again, Dead Sleep, Double Blast, Temptress.
TELEVISION: Movies: Born Innocent, Sarah T._Portrait of a Teenage Alcoholic, Sweet Hostage, Victory at Entebbe, Stranger in Our House, Calendar Girl Cop Killer? The Bambi Bembenek Story, Perry Mason: The Case of the Heartbroken Bride. Guest: Fantasy Island, Murder She Wrote.

BLAIR, STEWART
Executive. b. Scotland. e. Univ. of Glasgow. Was v.p. of Chase Manhattan Bank N.A. in NY, before joining Tele-Communications Inc. in 1981. Served as vice-chmn. & CEO of United Artists Entertainment Company. 1992, appointed chmn. of CEO of United Artists Theatre Circuit Inc. Bd. member of Foundation of Motion Picture Pioneers, exec. v.p. of Will Rogers Memorial Fund.

BLAKE, JEFFREY
Executive. President, Sony Pictures Releasing.

BLAKE, ROBERT
Actor. b. Nutley, NJ, Sept. 18, 1933. r.n. Michael Gubitosi. Started as a child actor in Our Gang comedies as Mickey

Gubitosi, also appeared as Little Beaver in Red Ryder series. Later was Hollywood stunt man in Rumble on the Docks and The Tijuana Story. First adult acting job was at the Gallery Theater in Hatful of Rain.
PICTURES: I Love You Again (debut, 1940, as Bobby Blake), Andy Hardy's Double Life, China Girl, Mokey, Salute to the Marines, Slightly Dangerous, The Big Noise, Lost Angel, Red Ryder series (as Little Beaver), Meet the People, Dakota, The Horn Blows at Midnight, Pillow to Post, The Woman in the Window, A Guy Could Change, Home on the Range, Humoresque, In Old Sacramento, Out California Way, The Last Round-Up, Treasure of the Sierra Madre, The Black Rose, Blackout (also co-prod.), Apache War Smoke, Treasure of the Golden Condor, Veils of Bagdad, The Rack, Screaming Eagles, Three Violent People, Beast of Budapest, Revolt in the Big House, Pork Chop Hill, The Purple Gang, Town Without Pity, PT 109, The Greatest Story Ever Told, The Connection, This Property Is Condemned, In Cold Blood, Tell Them Willie Boy is Here, Ripped-Off, Corky, Electra Glide in Blue, Busting, Coast to Coast, Second-Hand Hearts, Money Train.
TELEVISION: Series: The Richard Boone Show, Barretta (Emmy Award, 1975), Hell Town (also exec. prod.). Movies: The Big Black Pill (also creator & exec. prod.), The Monkey Mission (also creator & exec. prod.), Of Mice and Men (also exec. prod.), Blood Feud, Murder 1--Dancer 3 (also exec. prod.), Heart of a Champion: The Ray Mancini Story, Judgment Day: The John List Story. Guest: One Step Beyond, Have Gun Will Travel, Bat Masterson.

BLAKELY, SUSAN
Actress. b. Frankfurt, Germany, Sept. 7, 1950, where father was stationed in Army. Studied at U. of Texas. m. prod., media consultant Steve Jaffe. Became top magazine and TV commercial model in N.Y.
PICTURES: Savages (debut, 1972), The Way We Were, The Lords of Flatbush, The Towering Inferno, Report to the Commissioner, Shampoo, Capone, Dreamer, The Concorde—Airport '79, Over the Top, Dream a Little Dream, My Mom's a Werewolf, Russian Holiday.
TELEVISION: Series: Falcon Crest, The George Carlin Show. Mini-Series: Rich Man Poor Man. Movies: Secrets, Make Me an Offer, A Cry For Love, The Bunker, The Oklahoma City Dolls, Will There Really Be A Morning?, The Ted Kennedy Jr. Story, Blood & Orchids, April Morning, Fatal Confession: A Father Dowling Mystery, Broken Angel, Hiroshima Maiden, Ladykillers, Sight Unseen, The Incident, End Run, Dead Reckoning, Murder Times Seven, And the Sea Will Tell, Sight Unseen, Blackmail, Wildflower, Against Her Will: An Incident in Baltimore, Intruders, No Child of Mine, Honor Thy Father and Mother: The True Story of the Menendez Murders. Special: Torn Between Two Fathers. Guest: Step by Step. Pilot: Dad's a Dog.

BLAKLEY, RONEE
Actress, Singer. b. Stanley, ID, 1946. Wrote and performed songs for 1972 film Welcome Home Soldier Boys.
PICTURES: Nashville (debut, 1975; Acad. Award nom.), The Private Files of J. Edgar Hoover, The Driver, Renaldo and Clara, Good Luck Miss Wyckoff (Secret Yearnings/The Sin), The Baltimore Bullet, A Nightmare on Elm Street, Return to Salem's Lot, Student Confidential, Someone to Love.

BLANC, MICHEL
Actor. b. France, 1952.
PICTURES: Que la Fete Commence, The Tenant, Les Bronzes, The Adolescent, Les Bronzes font du Ski, Le Cheval d'Orgueil, Walk in the Shadow, Les Fugitives, Evening Dress, Menage, I Hate Actors!, Story of Women, Monsieur Hire, Chambre a Part, Strike It Rich, Uranus, Merci la Vie, Prospero's Books, The Favor the Watch and the Very Big Fish, Ready to Wear (Pret-a-Porter), Grosse Fatigue (also dir., s.p.), The Grand Dukes, The Monster.

BLANCO, RICHARD M.
Executive, b. Brooklyn, NY. e. electrical engineering, Wentworth Institute. J.C., 1925-27; bus. admin., U. of CA, 1939-40; U.S. Govt. Coll., 1942. Superv. Technicolor Corp., 1931-56; organ. and operator Consumer Products, Kodachrome film process., Technicolor, 1956-62; dir. of MP Govt. and theatre sales, NY & DC, 1963-65; gen. mgr. of Technicolor Florida photo optns. at Kennedy Space Center.; prod. doc. & educ. films for NASA, 1965; v.p. of tv div., Technicolor Corp. of America; 1967 elected corporate v.p. Technicolor, Inc.; 1971 pres., Technicolor Graphic Services, Inc.; 1974, elected chmn. of bd. of Technicolor Graphic Services; 1977, elected to bd. of dirs. of Technicolor Inc.

BLANK, MYRON
Circuit executive. b. Des Moines, IA, Aug. 30, 1911. e. U. of Michigan. Son of A. H. Blank, circuit operator. On leaving coll. joined father in operating Tri-States and Central States circuits. On leave 1943-46 in U.S. Navy, officer in charge visual educ. Now pres. Central States Theatre Corp.; pres. TOA, 1955; chmn. bd. TOA Inc. 1956-57; exec. chmn. of NATO. Pres. of Greater Des Moines Comm. Built Anne Blank Child Guidance Center-Raymond Blank Hospital for Children. Endowed chair for gifted and talented children at Univ. of Iowa; permanent scholarship at Watzman Inst., Israel. Sturdevant Award from NATO, Humanitarian Award from Variety Club in 1980. Partial scholarship for 80 students annually for 3-week seminar at Univ. of Iowa.

BLATT, DANIEL
Producer. e. Philips Andover Acad., Duke U., Northwestern U Sch. of Law.Independent producer since 1976; prior posts: resident counsel, ABC Pictures; exec. v.p. Palomar Pictures.
PICTURES: I Never Promised You a Rose Garden, Winter Kills, The American Success Company, The Howling, Independence Day, Cujo, Restless, The Boost.
TELEVISION: Movies: Circle of Children, Zuma Beach, The Children Nobody Wanted, Sadat, V—The Final Battle, Badge of the Assassin, Raid on Entebbe, Sacred Vows, A Winner Never Quits, Sworn to Silence, Common Ground. Series: V, Against the Law.

BLATTY, WILLIAM PETER
Writer, Director, Producer. b. New York, NY, Jan. 7, 1928. e. George Washington U., Seattle U. Worked as editor for U.S. Information Bureau, publicity dir. for USC and Loyola U. before becoming novelist and screenwriter. Novels include John Goldfarb Please Come Home (filmed), Twinkle Twinkle Killer Kane, The Exorcist, Legion (filmed as Exorcist III).
PICTURES: The Man From the Diner's Club, A Shot in the Dark, Promise Her Anything, What Did You Do in the War Daddy?, Gunn, The Great Bank Robbery, Darling Lili, The Exorcist (also prod.; Academy Award for Best Adapted Screenplay, 1973), The Ninth Configuration (a.k.a. Twinkle Twinkle Killer Kane; also dir., prod.), The Exorcist III (also dir.).

BLAU, MARTIN
Executive. b. New York, NY, June 6, 1924. e. Ohio U., 1948. Employed on newspapers in OH, TX, WV. Pub. dept., Columbia Pictures, 1951; asst. pub. mgr. 1959; pub. mgr., Columbia Int'l, 1961; admin. asst. to v.p. of adv. & pub. Columbia Pictures, 1966. Dir. adv. and publicity, Columbia Pictures Int'l, 1970; v.p., 1971; sr. v.p., 1985. Retired, 1988.

BLAY, ANDRE
Executive. In 1979, sold Magnetic Video to 20th Century Fox, named pres., CEO, 20th Century Fox Home Video; 1981, formed The Blay Corporation; 1982, joined with Norman Lear and Jerry Perenchio, founders of Embassy Communications, as chairman and CEO of Embassy Home Entertainment; 1986, when Embassy sold to Nelson Group, left to form Palisades Entertainment Group with Elliott Kastner.
PICTURES: Exec. Prod.: Prince of Darkness, They Live, Homeboy, The Blob, A Chorus of Disapproval.

BLECKNER, JEFF
Director, Producer. b. Brooklyn, NY, Aug. 12, 1943. e. Amherst College, BA., 1965; Yale Sch. of Drama, MFA 1968. Taught drama at Yale, also participated in the theater co. 1965-68. 1968-75 theater dir. NY Shakespeare Fest. Public Theatre (2 Drama Desk Awards, Tony nom. for Sticks and Bones); Basic Training of Pavlo Hummel (Obie Award, 1971), The Unseen Hand (Obie Award). Began TV career directing The Guiding Light, 1975.
TELEVISION: Hill Street Blues (Emmy Award, DGA Award, 1983), Concealed Enemies (Emmy Award, 1984), Daddy, I'm Their Momma Now (Emmy nom.), Do You Remember Love (Christopher, Humanitas, Peabody Awards, Emmy nom.), Fresno, Terrorist on Trial, Brotherly Love, My Father My Son, Favorite Son, Mancuso F.B.I. (exec. prod.), Lifestories (exec. prod.), Last Wish, In Sickness and In Health, The Round Table (pilot), 7th Avenue (pilot), Serving In Silence (Emmy nom.), A Father For Charlie. Mini-series: In The Best of Families, Beast.

BLEES, ROBERT
Writer, Producer. b. Lathrop, MO, June 9, 1925. e. Dartmouth, Phi Beta Kappa. Writer/photographer, Time and Life Magazines. Fiction: Cosmopolitan, etc. Exec. boards of Writers Guild, Producers Guild. Executive consultant, QM Prods.; BBC (England). Trustee, Motion Picture & TV Fund. Expert witness, copyright and literary litigation, U.S. Federal Court, California Superior Court.
PICTURES: Magnificent Obsession, Autumn Leaves, The Glass Web.
TELEVISION: Producer: Combat!, Bonanza, Bus Stop, Kraft Theater. Writer also: Alfred Hitchcock, Cannon, Barnaby Jones, Harry O, Columbo. Co-creator: The New Gidget.

BLEIER, EDWARD
Executive. b. New York, NY, October 16, 1929. e. Syracuse U., 1951, C.U.N.Y., grad. courses. Reporter/sportscaster: Syracuse and NY newspapers/stations: 1947-50. Prog. service mgr., DuMont Television Network, 1951; v.p., radio-television-film, Tex McCrary, Inc. 1958. American Broadcasting Company, 1952\-57; 1959-68 v.p. in chg. pub. relations (marketing, advertising, publicity), & planning, broadcast div.; v.p. in chg. of daytime sales & programming; v.p./gen. sales mgr., ABC-TV Network. U.S. Army

Psy. War School; Ex-chmn., TV Committee, NASL; Trustee, NATAS; founder-director & vice-chmn., International TV Council (NATAS); past-pres., IRTS; trustee, Keystone Center for Scientific & Environmental Policy, Council on Foreign Relations; ATAS; AMPAS; guest lecturer at universities. Chmn., Steering comm., Aspen B'dcaster's Conference. 1969-present: Warner Bros. Inc.: Pres, pay-TV, cable & network features.

BLIER, BERTRAND
Director. b. Paris, France, 1939. Son of late actor Bernard Blier. Served as asst. dir. to Georges Lautner, John Berry, Christian-Jaque, Denys de la Paatelliere and Jean Delannoy for two years before dir. debut.
PICTURES: Hitler Connais Pas (debut, 1963), Breakdown, C'Est une Valse (s.p. only), Going Places, Femme Fatales (Calmos), Get Out Your Handkerchiefs (Academy Award for Best Foreign-Language Film, 1978), Buffet Froid, Beau-pere, My Best Friend's Girl, Notre Historie, Menage, Too Beautiful for You.

BLOCK, WILLARD
Executive. b. New York, NY, March 18, 1930.; e. Columbia Coll., Columbia U. Law Sch., 1952. Counter-Intelligence Corps., U.S. Army, 1952-54; account exec., Plus Marketing, Inc. 1954-55; joined sales staff, NBC Television Network, 1955-57; sales staff, CBS Enterprises, Inc., 1957; intl. sales mgr, 1960; dir., intl. sales, 1965; v.p., 1967; v.p., Viacom Enterprises, 1971; pres., 1972; v.p MCA-TV, 1973; v.p., gen. mgr., Taft, H-B International, Inc.; pres. Willard Block, Ltd.; 1979, named pres., Viacom Enterprises; 1982-89, pres. Viacom Worldwide Ltd. Currently consultant to Sumitomo Corp., TCI, Starsight Telecast; member bd. dirs. Starsight Telecast.

BLOODWORTH-THOMASON, LINDA
Producer, Writer. b. Poplar Bluff, MO, 1947. With husband Harry Thomason co-owner of Mozark Productions.
TELEVISION: Series; M*A*S*H (writer), Rhoda (writer), Flithy Rich (prod.), Lime Street (co-exec. prod., creator), Designing Women (co-exec. prod., creator, writer), Evening Shade (co-exec. prod., creator, writer), Women of the House. Pilots: Dribble (prod.), Over and Out (writer), London and Davis in New York (prod.)

BLOOM, CLAIRE
Actress. r.n. Claire Blume. b. London, England, Feb. 15, 1931. To U.S. in 1940 during London evacuation. Returned to England in 1943. e. Guildhall School of Music & Drama, Central Sch. Stage debut with Oxford Rep 1946 in It Depends What You Mean. Other Stage work: The White Devil (London debut), The Lady's Not for Burning, Ring Round the Moon, A Streetcar Named Desire; at Stratford-on-Avon, Old Vic seasons, etc. B'way: Rashomon, A Doll's House, Hedda Gabler, Vivat Vivat Regina. Author: Limelight and After: The Education of an Actress (1982).
PICTURES: The Blind Goddess (debut, 1948), Limelight, Innocents in Paris, The Man Between, Richard III, Alexander the Great, The Brothers Karamazov, The Buccaneer, Look Back in Anger, The Royal Game (Schachnovelle/ Brainwashed), The Wonderful World of the Brothers Grimm, The Chapman Report, The Haunting, 80000 Suspects, High Infidelity, Il Maestro di Vigevano, The Outrage, The Spy Who Came in From the Cold, Charly, The Illustrated Man, Three Into Two Won't Go, A Severed Head, Red Sky at Morning, A Doll's House, Islands in the Stream, Clash of the Titans, Deja Vu, Sammy and Rosie Get Laid, Crimes and Misdemeanors, The Princess and the Goblin (voice), Mighty Aphrodite, Daylight.
TELEVISION: Specials/Movies (US/UK): Cyrano de Bergerac, Caesar and Cleopatra, Misalliance, Anna Karenina, Wuthering Heights, Ivanov, Wessex Tales, An Imaginative Woman, A Legacy, In Praise of Love, The Orestaia, Henry VIII, Backstairs at the White House, Brideshead Revisited, Hamlet, Cymbeline, King John, Ann and Debbie, The Going Up of David Lev, Ellis Island, Separate Tables, Florence Nightingale, The Ghost Writer, Time and the Conways, Shadowlands, Liberty, Promises to Keep, The Belle of Amherst, Hold the Dream, Anastasia, Queenie, Intimate Contact, Beryl Markham: A Shadow on the Sun, Oedipus the King, The Lady and the Highwayman, The Camomile Lawn, The Mirror Crack'd From Side to Side, It's Nothing Personal, Barbara Taylor Bradford's Remember.

BLOOM, MARCIE
Executive. Co-President, Sony Pictures Classics.

BLOOM, VERNA
Actress. b. Lynn, MA, Aug. 7, 1938. e. Boston U. Studied drama at Uta Hagen-Herbert Berghof School. Performed with small theatre groups all over country; then started repertory theatre in Denver. Appeared on Broadway in Marat/Sade (played Charlotte Corday), Brighton Beach Memoirs.
PICTURES: Medium Cool (debut, 1969), The Hired Hand, High Plains Drifter, Badge 373, National Lampoon's Animal House, Honkytonk Man, After Hours, The Journey of Natty Gann, The Last Temptation of Christ.

TELEVISION: Movies: Where Have All the People Gone?, Sarah T.: Portrait of a Teenage Alcoholic, The Blue Knight, Contract on Cherry Street, Playing for Time, Rivkin--Bounty Hunter, Gibbsville.

BLOUNT, LISA
Actress. b. Fayetteville, AK, July 1, 1957. e. Univ. of AK. Auditioned for role as extra in film September 30, 1955 and was chosen as the female lead.
PICTURES: September 30, 1955, Dead and Buried, An Officer and a Gentleman, Cease Fire, What Waits Below, Radioactive Dreams, Prince of Darkness, Nightflyers, South of Reno,Out Cold, Great Balls of Fire, Blind Fury, Femme Fatale, Cut and Run, Stalked.
TELEVISION: Series: Sons and Daughters. Pilot: Off Duty. Movies: Murder Me Murder You, Stormin' Home, The Annihilator, Unholy Matrimony, In Sickness and in Health, An American Story, Murder Between Friends, Judicial Consent. Guest: Moonlighting, Magnum P.I., Starman, Murder She Wrote, Hitchhiker, Picket Fences.

BLUM, HARRY N.
Executive. b. Cleveland, OH, Oct. 3, 1932. e. U. of Michigan, B.B.A., LL.B. Toy & hobby industry executive, gen. mngr. Lionel division of General Mills, management consultant, and venture capital and money manager before entering industry. Now heads The Blum Group, entertainment financing, packaging, production and worldwide distrib.
PICTURES: Executive Action (assoc. prod.), The Land That Time Forgot (assoc. prod.), At the Earth's Core (exec. prod.), Drive-In (assoc. prod.), Diamonds (exec. prod.), The Bluebird (assoc. prod.), Obsession (prod.), Skateboard (prod.), The Magician of Lublin (exec. prod.), Duran Duran—Arena (exec. prod.), Young Lady Chatterly II (exec. prod.), Eminent Domain (exec. prod.).

BLUM, MARK
Actor. b. Newark, NJ, May 14, 1950. Studied drama at U. of Minnesota and U. of Pennsylvania. Also studied acting with Andre Gregory, Aaron Frankel and Daniel Seltzer. Extensive Off-B'way work after debut in The Cherry Orchard (1976).
THEATER: NY: Green Julia, Say Goodnight Gracie, Table Settings, Key Exchange, Loving Reno, Messiah, It's Only a Play, Little Footsteps, Cave of Life, Gus & Al (Obie Award), Lost in Yonkers (Broadway). Regional: Brothers (New Brunswick, NJ), Close Ties (Long Wharf), The Cherry Orchard (Long Wharf), Iago in Othello (Dallas). Mark Taper Forum: American Clock, Wild Oats, Moby Dick Rehearsed and An American Comedy.
PICTURES: Desperately Seeking Susan, Just Between Friends, Crocodile Dundee, Blind Date, The Presidio, Worth Winning.
TELEVISION: Series: Sweet Surrender, Capitol News. Pilot: Critical Condition. Guest: Miami Vice, St. Elsewhere, Roseanne. Movies: Condition: Critical, Indictment: The McMartin Trial.

BLUMOFE, ROBERT F.
Producer. b. New York, NY, Sept. 23, 1909. e. Columbia Coll., AB, Columbia U. Sch. of Law, JD. v.p., West Coast oper., U.A., 1953-66; indept. prod., pres. RFB Enterprises, Inc; American Film Institute, director, AFI—West, 1977-81. Now indep. prod.

BLUTH, DON
Animator, Director, Producer, Writer. b. El Paso, TX, Sept. 13, 1938.e. Brigham Young U. Animator with Walt Disney Studios 1956 and 1971-79; animator with Filmation 1967; Co-founder and director with Gary Goldman and John Pomery, Don Bluth Productions, 1979-85; animator, Sullivan Studios, 1986. Joined Fox Animation as dir./prod., 1995.
PICTURES: Animation director. Robin Hood, The Rescuers, Pete's Dragon, Xanadu. Director/Co-Producer: The Secret of NIMH (also co-s.p.), An American Tail, The Land Before Time, All Dogs Go to Heaven (also co-story), Rock-a-Doodle, Hans Christian Andersen's Thumbelina (also s.p.), A Troll in Central Park, The Pebble and the Penguin (presenter).
TELEVISION: Banjo the Woodpile Cat (prod., dir., story, music and lyrics).

BLYTH, ANN
Actress. b. Mt. Kisco, NY, Aug. 16, 1928. e. New Wayburn's Dramatic Sch. On radio in childhood; with San Carlos Opera Co. 3 years; Broadway debut in Watch on the Rhine.
PICTURES: Chip Off the Old Block (debut, 1944), The Merry Monahans, Babes on Swing Street, Bowery to Broadway, Mildred Pierce (Acad. Award nom.), Swell Guy, Brute Force, Killer McCoy, A Woman's Vengeance, Another Part of the Forest, Mr. Peabody and the Mermaid, Red Canyon, Once More My Darling, Free for All, Top o' the Morning, Our Very Own, The Great Caruso, Katie Did It, Thunder on the Hill, I'll Never Forget You, Golden Horde, One Minute to Zero, The World in His Arms, Sally and Saint Anne, All the Brothers Were Valiant, Rose Marie, The Student Prince, King's Thief, Kismet, Slander, The Buster Keaton Story, The Helen Morgan Story.
TELEVISION: Guest: Lux Video Theatre (A Place in the Sun).

BOCHCO, STEVEN
Producer, Writer. b. New York, NY, Dec. 16, 1943. m. actress Barbara Bosson. e. Carnegie Tech, MFA. Won MCA fellowship in college, joined U-TV as apprentice. His shows typically feature several interwoven plots and characters, deal with social issues, and shift from comedy to drama within an episode. Awards incl. Humanitas, NAACP Image, Writers Guild, George Foster Peabody, & Edgar Allen Poe Awards.
PICTURES: Co-Writer: The Counterfeit Killer, Silent Running.
TELEVISION: Writer and story ed.: Name of the Game, Columbo, McMillan and Wife; Delvecchio (writer-prod.), Paris (exec. prod.), Richie Brockelman (co-creator), Turnabout (writer), Invisible Man (writer), Vampire (writer), Hill St. Blues (creator, prod., writer; Emmys 1981, 1982, 1983, 1984), Every Stray Dog and Kid (exec. prod.), Bay City Blues (exec. prod., writer, creator), L.A. Law (Emmy Awards: 1987, 1989), Hooperman, Cop Rock, NYPD Blue (Emmy Award, 1995), Byrds of Paradise, Murder One, Public Morals.

BOCHNER, HART
Actor, Director. b. Toronto, Ontario, Oct. 3, 1956. Son of actor Lloyd Bochner. e. U. of. San Diego. Wrote, prod., dir. short film The Buzz (1992) starring Jon Lovitz. Directed film PCU (1994).
PICTURES: Islands in the Stream (debut, 1977), Breaking Away, Terror Train, Rich and Famous, The Wild Life, Supergirl, Making Mr. Right, Die Hard, Apartment Zero, Mr. Destiny, Mad at the Moon, Batman: Mask of the Phantasm (voice), The Innocent, High School High (dir.).
TELEVISION: Movies: Haywire, Having It All, Fellow Traveller, Complex of Fear. Mini-Series: East of Eden, The Sun Also Rises, War and Remembrance, And the Sea Will Tell, Children of the Dust. Special: Teach 109.

BOCHNER, LLOYD
Actor. b. Toronto, Canada, July 29, 1924. Father of actor Hart Bochner.
PICTURES: Drums of Africa, The Night Walker, Sylvia, Tony Rome, Point Blank, The Detective, The Horse in the Gray Flannel Suit, Tiger by the Tail, Ulzana's Raid, The Man in the Glass Booth, The Lonely Lady, Millenium, The Naked Gun 2 1/2, Morning Glory, It Seemed Like A G ood Idea At The Time, Hot Touch, The Crystal Cage, Berlin Lady, Landslide, Lolita's Affair, The Dozier Case, Fine Gold.
TELEVISION: Series: One Man's Family, Hong Kong, The Richard Boone Show, Dynasty. Movies: Scalplock, Stranger on the Run, Crowhaven Farm, They Call It Murder, Satan's School for Girls, Richie Brockelman: Missing 24 Hours, Terraces, Immigrants, A Fire in the Sky, The Best Place to Be, The Golden Gate Murders, Mary and Joseph: A Story of Faith, Mazes & Monsters, Blood Sport, Race For the Bomb, Double Agent, Eagle One, Our Man Flint. Guest: Fantasy Island, Masquerade, The A-Team, Hotel, Crazy Like a Fox, Greatest Heroes of the Bible, Murder She Wrote, Designing Women, Hart To Hart, Who's The Boss, Golden Girls, The Love Boat, etc..

BODE, RALF
Cinematographer. b. Berlin, Germany. Attended Yale where was actor with drama school and acquired degree in directing. Received on-job training teaching combat photography and making films for Army at Ft. Monmouth. First professional job in films was gaffer on Harry, followed by long association with director John G. Avildsen, for whom served as gaffer and lighting designer on Guess What We Learned in School Today, Joe, and Cry Uncle. Later dir. of photography for Avildsen on Inaugural Ball and as East Coast dir. phot. for Rocky.
PICTURES: Saturday Night Fever, Slow Dancing in the Big City, Rich Kids, Coal Miner's Daughter, Dressed to Kill, Raggedy Man, A Little Sex, Gorky Park, First Born, Bring on the Night, Violets Are Blue, Critical Condition, The Big Town, The Accused, Distant Thunder, Cousins, Uncle Buck, One Good Cop, Love Field, Made in America, George Balanchine's The Nutcracker, Bad Girls, Safe Passage, Don Juan DeMarco.
TELEVISION: PBS Theatre in America, working as lighting designer and dir. of photo. Also many TV commercials. Movie: Gypsy.

BOETTICHER, BUDD
Director, Writer, Producer. r.n. Oscar Boetticher, Jr. b. Chicago, IL, July 29, 1916. e. Culver Military Acad., Ohio State U. bullfighter Novillero; then technical dir., Blood and Sand, 1941; asst. dir., Hal Roach studios and Columbia 1941-44; became feature director at Columbia in 1944; dir. Eagle Lion, 1946; dir., Universal, independ. prod., 1954. Autobiography: When in Disgrace.
PICTURES: As Oscar Boetticher: Behind Locked Doors, Assigned to Danger, Black Midnight, Killer Shark, Wolf Hunters. As Budd Boetticher: The Bullfighter and the Lady (also costory), The Sword of D'Artagnan, The Cimarron Kid, Bronco Busters, Red Ball Express, Horizons West, City Beneath the Sea, Seminole, The Man from the Alamo, Wings of the Hawk, East of Sumatra, The Magnificent Matador (also story), The Killer Is Loose, Seven Men From Now, Decision at Sundown, The Tall T, Buchanan Rides Alone, Ride Lonesome (also prod.),

Westbound, The Rise and Fall of Legs Diamond, Comanche Station (also prod.), Arruza (also prod., co-s.p.), A Time For Dying (also s.p.), My Kingdom For a... (also s.p.).

BOGARDE, SIR DIRK
Actor. b. Hampstead, London, March 28, 1921. r.n. Derek Van Den Bogaerde. e. Allen Glens Coll., Glasgow & University Coll., London. Knighted, Feb. 1992. Started theatrical career with Amersham Repertory Co., then London stage; in Army in WWII. Commandeur des arts et des Lettres, France, 1990. Hon. Doc. Lit.: St. Andrews Univ., Sussex Univ. Top ten British star: 1953-54, 1956-64; number one British money-making star 1955, 1957, 1958, 1959; Variety Club Award—Best Performance 1961-64.
THEATER: U.K.: Power With Glory (1947), Point of Departure, The Shaughraun, The Vortex, Summertime, Jezebel.
PICTURES: Come on George (debut as extra, 1939), Dancing With Crime, Esther Waters, Quartet, Once a Jolly Swagman, Dear Mr. Prohack, Boys in Brown, The Blue Lamp, So Long at the Fair, Blackmailed, Woman in Question, Hunted (Stranger in Between), Penny Princess, The Gentle Gunman, Appointment in London, Desperate Moment, They Who Dare, The Sleeping Tiger, Doctor in the House, For Better or Worse, The Sea Shall Not Have Them, Simba, Doctor at Sea, Cast a Dark Shadow, Spanish Gardener, Ill Met by Moonlight (Night Ambush), Doctor at Large, Campbell's Kingdom, A Tale of Two Cities, The Wind Cannot Read, The Doctor's Dilemma, Libel, The Angel Wore Red, Song Without End, The Singer Not the Song, Victim, H.M.S. Defiant (Damn the Defiant), We Joined the Navy (cameo), The Password Is Courage, I Could Go on Singing, The Mind Benders, The Servant (BFA Award, 1964), Hot Enough for June (Agent 8 3/4), Doctor in Distress, The High Bright Sun (McGuire Go Home), King and Country, Darling (BFA Award, 1965), Modesty Blaise, Accident, Our Mother's House, Sebastian, The Fixer, Justine, Oh! What a Lovely War, The Damned, Death in Venice, The Serpent (Night Flight From Moscow), The Night Porter, Permission to Kill, Providence, A Bridge Too Far, Despair, Daddy Nostalgia.
TELEVISION: The Little Moon of Alban, Blithe Spirit, Upon This Rock, The Patricia Neal Story, May We Borrow Your Husband?, The Vision.
AUTHOR: A Postillion Struck by Lightning (1977), Snakes and Ladders (1978), An Orderly Man (1983), Backcloth, A Particular Friendship, Great Meadow, A Short Walk From Harrods. Novels: A Gentle Occupation, Voices in the Garden, West of Sunset, Jericho, A Period of Adjustment, Cleared For Take Off (autobiography).

BOGART, PAUL
Director. b. New York, NY, Nov. 13, 1919. Puppeteer-actor with Berkeley Marionettes 1946-48; TV stage mgr., assoc. dir. NBC 1950-52; won numerous Christopher Awards; recipient homage from French Festival Internationale Programmes Audiovisuelle, Cannes '91.
PICTURES: Marlowe (debut, 1969), Halls of Anger, Skin Game, Cancel My Reservation, Class of '44 (also prod.), Mr. Ricco, Oh God! You Devil, Torch Song Trilogy.
TELEVISION: U.S. Steel Hour, Kraft Theatre, Armstrong Circle Theatre, Goodyear Playhouse, The Defenders (Emmy Award, 1965), All in the Family (Emmy Award, 1978), The Golden Girls (Emmy Award, 1986). Specials: Ages of Man, Mark Twain Tonight, The Final War of Ollie Winter, Dear Friends (Emmy Award, 1968). Secrets, Shadow Game (Emmy Award, 1970), The House Without a Christmas Tree, Look Homeward Angel, The Country Girl, Double Solitaire, The War Widow, The Thanksgiving Treasure; The Adams Chronicles, Natica Jackson. Movies: In Search of America, Tell Me Where It Hurts, Winner Take All, Nutcracker: Money, Madness and Murder, Broadway Bound, The Gift of Love, The Heidi Chronicles.

BOGDANOVICH, PETER
Director, Producer, Writer, Actor. b. Kingston, NY, July 30, 1939. e. Collegiate Sch., Stella Adler Theatre Sch., N.Y. 1954\-58. Stage debut, Amer. Shakespeare Festival, Stratford, CT, followed by N.Y. Shakespeare Festival, 1958. Off-Bway: dir./prod.: The Big Knife, Camino Real, Ten Little Indians, Rocket to the Moon, Once in a Lifetime. Film critic and feature writer, Esquire, New York Times, Village Voice, Cahiers du Cinema, Los Angeles Times,New York Magazine, Vogue, Variety, etc. 1961–. Owner: The Holly Moon Company Inc. (L.A.), 1992-present.
PICTURES: Voyage to the Planet of the Prehistoric Women (dir., s.p., narrator; billed as Derek Thomas), The Wild Angels (2nd unit dir., co-s.p., actor). Director: Targets (also co-s.p., actor), The Last Picture Show (also co-s.p; N.Y. Film Critics' Award, best s.p., British Academy Award, best s.p. 1971), Directed by John Ford (also s.p., interviewer), What's Up Doc? (also prod., co-s.p.; Writer's Guild of America Award, best s.p., 1972), Paper Moon (also prod.; Silver Shell, Mar del Plata, Spain 1973), Daisy Miller (also prod.; Best Director, Brussels Festival, 1974), At Long Last Love (also prod., s.p.), Nickelodeon (also co-s.p.), Saint Jack (also co-s.p., actor; Pasinetti Award, Critics Prize, Venice Festival, 1979), Opening Night (actor only), They All Laughed (also co-s.p.), Mask,

Illegally Yours (also prod.), Texasville (also co-prod., s.p.), Noises Off (also co-exec. prod.), The Thing Called Love. TELEVISION: *Special*: The Great Professional: Howard Hawks (co-dir., writer, interviewer; BBC). *Series*: CBS This Morning (weekly commentary; 1987-89). *Guest*: Northern Exposure (actor).
AUHTOR: The Cinema of Orson Welles (1961), The Cinema of Howard Hawks (1962), The Cinema of Alfred Hitchcock, (1963), John Ford (1968; enlarged 1978), Fritz Lang in America, (1969), Allan Dwan—The Last Pioneer (1971), Pieces of Time (1973, enlarged 1985), The Killing of the Unicorn: Dorothy Stratten: 1960-1980 (1984), This Is Orson Welles (1992). Also edit., intro. writer to annual Year and a Day Engagement Calendar (1991-).

BOGOSIAN, ERIC
Actor, Writer. b. Woburn, MA, Apr. 24, 1953. e. studied 2 years at U. of Chicago, then Oberlin, theater degree, 1976. In high school, acted in plays with Fred Zollo (now prod.) and Nick Paleologus (now MA congressman). Moved to NY and worked briefly as gofer at Chelsea Westside Theater. Then joined down-town performance space, the Kitchen, first acting in others pieces, then creating his own incl. character Ricky Paul, a stand-up comedian in punk clubs. Theater pieces include: The New World, Men Inside, Voices of America, FunHouse, Drinking in America (Drama Desk and Obie Awards), Talk Radio, Sex Drugs Rock & Roll, Pounding Nails in the Floor With My Forehead (Obie Award), SubUrbia (author only). Book: Notes From Underground.
PICTURES: Special Effects, Talk Radio (also s.p.; Silver Bear Award 1988 Berlin Film Fest.), Sex Drugs Rock & Roll (also s.p.), Naked in New York, Dolores Claiborne, Under Siege 2: Dark Territory, Arabian Knight (voice).
TELEVISION: *Guest*: Miami Vice, Twilight Zone, Law & Order, The Larry Sanders Show. *Movies*: The Caine Mutiny Court Martial, Last Flight Out, Witch Hunt. *Special*: Drinking in America.

BOLAM, JAMES
Actor. b. Sunderland, England. Ent. ind. 1960.
PICTURES: The Kitchen, A Kind of Loving, Loneliness of the Long Distance Runner, HMS Defiant, Murder Most Foul, In Celebration.
TELEVISION: Likely Lads, When The Boat Comes In, Only When I Laugh, The Beiderbecke Affair, Father Matthews Daughter, Room at the Bottom, Andy Capp, The Beiderbecke Tapes, The Beiderbecke Connection, Second Thoughts.

BOLOGNA, JOSEPH
Actor, Writer. b. Brooklyn, NY., Dec. 30, 1938. e. Brown U. m. actress-writer Renee Taylor. Service in Marine Corps and on dis-charge joined ad agency, becoming director-producer of TV commercials. Collaborated with wife on short film, 2, shown at 1966 N.Y. Film Festival. Together they wrote Lovers and Other Strangers, Broadway play, in which both also acted. Wrote s.p. for film version. Both wrote and starred in Made for Each Other, and created and wrote TV series, Calucci's Dept.
PICTURES: Lovers and Other Strangers (co.-s.p. only), Made for Each Other (also co.-s.p.), Cops and Robbers, Mixed Company, The Big Bus , Chapter Two, My Favorite Year, Blame It on Rio , The Woman in Red, Transylvania 6-5000, It Had to Be You (also co-dir., co-s.p.), Coupe de Ville, Jersey Girl, Alligator II: The Mutation, Love Is All There Is.
TELEVISION: *Series*: Calucci's Dept. (creator, co-writer only), Rags to Riches, Top of the Heap. *Movies*: Honor Thy Father, Woman of the Year (also co-writer), Torn Between Two Lovers, One Cooks The Other Doesn't, Copacabana, A Time To Triumph, Prime Target, Thanksgiving Day, Citizen Cohn, The Danger of Love: The Carolyn Warmus Story, Revenge of the Nerds IV: Nerds in Love. *Special*: Acts of Love and Other Comedies (Emmy Award, 1974). *Mini-Series*: Sins.

BONANNO, LOUIE
Actor. b. Somerville, MA, Dec. 17, 1961. e. Bentley Coll., Waltham, MA, BS-economics, finance; AS accountancy, 1983. Moved to NY, 1983 to study at Amer. Acad. of Dramatic Arts. Toured U.S. 1985-86 as Dangermouse for MTV/Nickelodeon. In L.A. appeared as stand-up comedian. Stage debut in The Head.
PICTURES: Sex Appeal (debut, 1986), Wimps, Student Affairs, Cool as Ice, Auntie Lee's Meat Pies.
TELEVISION: Eisenhower & Lutz (series), 227, Tour of Duty, TV 101, Santa Barbara, New York Story.

BOND, DEREK
Actor, Scriptwriter. b. Glasgow Scotland, Jan. 26, 1920. e. Haberdasher' Askes Sch., London. Stage debut in As Husbands Go, 1937; served in Grenadier Guards H.M. Forces 1939-46, awarded Military Cross; author of Unscheduled Stop, Two Young Samaritans, Ask Father Christmas, Packdrill, Double Strung, Order to Kill, The Riverdale Dam, Sentence Deferred, The Mavroletty Fund. Many TV appearances. Pres., British Actors Equity, 1984-86. Author: Steady Old Man.
PICTURES: The Captive Heart (debut, 1946), Nicholas Nickleby, Joanna Godden, Uncle Silas, Scott of the Antarctic, Marry Me,

Poets Pub, Weaker Sex, Broken Journey, Christopher Columbus, Tony Draws a Horse, Quiet Woman, Hour of Thirteen, Distant Trumpet, Love's a Luxury, Trouble in Store, Svengali, High Terrace, Stormy Crossing, Rogues Yarn, Gideon's Day, The Hand, Saturday Night Out, Wonderful Life, Press For Time, When Eight Bells Toll, Intimate Reflections, Vanishing Army.

BONET, LISA
Actress. b. Los Angeles, CA, Nov. 16, 1967. First gained recog-nition on The Cosby Show as Denise Huxtable at the age of 15.
PICTURES: Angel Heart, Dead Connection, Bank Robber, New Eden.
TELEVISION: *Series*: The Cosby Show, A Different World. *Guest*: Tales From the Dark Side. *Special*: Don't Touch.

BONET, NAI
Actress, Producer. Worked in entertainment field since age of 13, including opera, films, TV, stage, night clubs and records.
PICTURES: *Actress*: The Soul Hustlers, The Seventh Veil, Fairy Tales, The Soul of Nigger Charlie, The Spy with the Cold Nose, John Goldfarb Please Come Home, etc. Wrote and starred in Nocturna and Hoodlums.
TELEVISION: Johnny Carson Show, Merv Griffin Show, Joe Franklin Show, Beverly Hillbillies, Tom Snyder Show.

BONHAM-CARTER, HELENA
Actress. b. London, England, May 26, 1966. Great granddaugh-ter of Liberal Prime Minister Lord Asquith. e. Westminster. Appeared on BBC in A Pattern of Roses; seen by director Trevor Nunn who cast her in Lady Jane, 1986, theatrical film debut. On London stage in Trelawny of the Wells.
PICTURES: Lady Jane, A Room with a View, Maurice (cameo), Francesco, La Mascheral (The Mask), Getting It Right, Hamlet, Where Angles Fear to Tread, Howards End, Mary Shelley's Frankenstein, Mighty Aphrodite.
TELEVISION: *Guest*: Miami Vice. *Movies*: A Hazard of Hearts (U.S.), The Vision, Beatrix Potter, Fatal Deception: Mrs. Lee Harvey Oswald, Dancing Queen.

BONO, SONNY
Singer, Actor, Director, Writer. b. Detroit, MI, Feb. 16, 1935. r.n. Salvatore Bono. Started writing songs at age 16; entered record business with Specialty Records as apprentice prod. Became ass't. to Phil Spector, rock music prod. and did background singing. Recorded albums with former wife Cher, made two fea-ture films and formed nightclub act with her. CBS comedy-vari-ety series began as summer show in 1971 and made regular later that year. Elected Mayor, Palm Springs, CA 1988. Published autobiography in 1991. Elected to Congress, 1995.
PICTURES: Wild on the Beach (debut, 1965), Good Times (also wrote songs), Chastity (prod., s.p. only), Escape to Athena, Airplane II: The Sequel, Troll, Hairspray, Under the Boardwalk.
TELEVISION: *Series*: The Sonny & Cher Comedy Hour, The Sonny Comedy Revue. *Movies*: Murder on Flight 502, Murder in Music City, Top of the Hill. *Guest*: Shindig, Hullabaloo, Man from U.N.C.L.E., Love American Style, Murder She Wrote, Parker Lewis Can't Lose.

BOOKMAN, ROBERT
Executive. b. Los Angeles, CA, Jan. 29, 1947. e. U. of California, Yale Law Sch. Motion picture literary agent. IFA 1972-74, ICM 1974-79. 1979-84, ABC Motion Pictures v.p., worldwide produc-tion; 1984-6, Columbia Pictures, exec. v.p., world-wide prod. 1986, Creative Artists Agency, Inc., as motion picture literary and directors' agent.

BOONE, PAT
Singer, Actor. b. Jacksonville, FL, June 1, 1934. e. David Lipscomb Coll., North Texas State Coll., grad. magna cum laude, Columbia U. Winner of Ted Mack's Amateur Hour TV show; joined Arthur Godfrey TV show, 1955. Most promising new male star, Motion Picture Daily-Fame Poll 1957. One of top ten moneymaking stars, M.P. Herald-Fame Poll, 1957. Daughter is singer Debbie Boone. Author: Twixt Twelve and Twenty, Between You & Me and the Gatepost, The Real Christmas, others.
RECORDINGS: Ain't That a Shame, I Almost Lost My Mind, Friendly Persuasion, Love Letters in the Sand, April Love, Tutti Frutti, many others.
PICTURES: Bernardine (debut, 1957), April Love, Mardi Gras, Journey to the Center of the Earth, All Hands on Deck, State Fair, The Main Attraction, The Yellow Canary, The Horror of It All, Never Put It in Writing, Goodbye Charlie, The Greatest Story Ever Told, The Perils of Pauline, The Cross and the Switchblade, Roger and Me.
TELEVISION: *Series*: Arthur Godfrey and His Friends, The Pat Boone-Chevy Showroom (1957-60), The Pat Boone Show (1966-8). *Movie*: The Pigeon.

BOORMAN, JOHN
Director, Producer, Writer. b. London, Eng., Jan. 18, 1933. Wrote film criticism at age of 17 for British publications incl. Manchester Guardian; founder TV Mag. Day By Day; served in National Service in Army; Broadcaster and BBC radio film critic

1950-54; film editor Independent Television News; prod. documentaries for Southern Television; joined BBC, headed BBC Documentary Film Unit 1960-64, indep. doc. about D.W. Griffith; chmn. Natl. Film Studios of Ireland 1975-85; governor Brit. Film Inst. 1985-.
PICTURES: *Director*: Catch Us If You Can (Having a Wild Weekend; debut, 1965), Point Blank, Hell in the Pacific, Leo the Last (also co-s.p.), Deliverance (also prod.; 2 Acad. Award noms.), Zardoz (also prod., s.p.), Exorcist II: The Heretic (also co-prod.), Excalibur (also exec. prod., co-s.p.), Danny Boy (exec. prod. only), The Emerald Forest (also prod.), Hope and Glory (also prod., s.p., actor; 3 Acad. Award noms., Nat'l Film Critics Awards for dir., s.p.; L.A. Film Critics Awards for picture, s.p., dir.; U.K. Critics Awards for picture), Where the Heart Is (also prod., co-s.p.), I Dreamt I Woke Up (also s.p., actor), Two Nudes Bathing (also s.p., prod.), Beyond Rangoon (also co-prod.).
TELEVISION: *Series*: Citizen '63 (dir.), The Newcomers (dir.).

BOOTH, MARGARET
Film editor. b. Los Angeles, CA, 1898. Awarded honorary Oscar, 1977.
PICTURES: Why Men Leave Home, Husbands and Lovers, Bridge of San Luis Rey, New Moon, Susan Lenox, Strange Interlude, Smilin' Through, Romeo and Juliet, Barretts of Wimpole Street, Mutiny on the Bounty, Camille, etc. Supervising editor on Owl and the Pussycat, The Way We Were, Funny Lady, Murder by Death, The Goodbye Girl, California Suite, The Cheap Detective (also assoc. prod.), Chapter Two (also assoc. prod.), The Toy (assoc. prod. only), Annie, The Slugger's Wife (exec. prod. only).

BOOTHE, POWERS
Actor. b. Snyder, TX, 1949. e. Southern Methodist U. On Broadway in Lone Star.
PICTURES: The Goodbye Girl, Cruising, Southern Comfort, A Breed Apart, Red Dawn, The Emerald Forest, Extreme Prejudice, Stalingrad, Rapid Fire, Tombstone, Blue Sky, Sudden Death, Nixon.
TELEVISION: *Series*: Skag, Philip Marlowe. *Movies*: Skag, Plutonium Incident, Guyana Tragedy--The Story of Jim Jones (Emmy Award, 1980), A Cry for Love, Into the Homeland, Family of Spies, By Dawn's Early Light, Wild Card, Marked for Murder, Web of Deception.

BORGE, VICTOR
Comedian, Pianist. b. Copenhagen, Denmark, Jan. 3, 1909. Child prodigy at age 8. Awarded scholarship to study in Berlin and Vienna. Later became humorous concert artist. Wrote and starred in musical plays and films in Denmark. Fled Nazis in 1940, came to America. Appeared on Bing Crosby radio show, concert and nightclub tours, tv variety shows. One-man Broadway shows: Comedy in Music, 1953, 1965, 1977, 1989. Guest conductor with major symphonies around the world. Recent recording, The Two Sides of Victor Borge. Author: My Favorite Intermissions and My Favorite Comedies in Music. Awarded Medal of Honor by Statue of Liberty Centennial Comm. Knighted by 5 Scandinavian countries, honored by U.S. Congress and U.N. Created Thanks to Scandinavia Scholarship Fund, Dana College, Univ. of Conn., SUNY--Purchase Scholarships. Recent video: Onstage with Victor Borge.

BORGNINE, ERNEST
Actor. b. Hamden, CT, Jan. 24, 1917. e. Randall Sch. of Dramatic Art, Hartford, CT. Joined Barter Theatre in Virginia. Served in U.S. Navy; then little theatre work, stock companies; on Broadway in Harvey, Mrs. McThing; many TV appearances. Honors: 33rd Degree of the Masonic Order, Order of the Grand Cross, from same. Named honorary Mayor of Universal City Studios.
PICTURES: China Corsair (debut, 1951), The Mob, Whistle at Eaton Falls, From Here to Eternity, The Stranger Wore a Gun, Demetrius & the Gladiators, Johnny Guitar, Bounty Hunter, Vera Cruz, Bad Day at Black Rock, Marty (Academy Award for Best Actor, 1955), Run for Cover, Violent Saturday, Last Command, Square Jungle, Catered Affair, Jubal, Best Things in Life are Free, Three Brave Men, The Vikings, Badlanders, Torpedo Run, Rabbit Trap, Season of Passion, Man on a String, Pay or Die, Go Naked in the World, Barabbas, McHale's Navy, Flight of the Phoenix, The Oscar, Chuka, The Dirty Dozen, Ice Station Zebra, Legend of Lylah Clare, The Split, The Wild Bunch, The Adventurers, Suppose They Gave a War and Nobody Came?, A Bullet for Sandoval, Bunny O'Hare, Willard, Rain for a Dusty Summer, Hannie Caulder, The Revengers, Ripped Off, The Poseidon Adventure, Emperor of the North Pole, The Neptune Factor, Manhunt, Law and Disorder, Sunday in the Country, The Devil's Rain, Hustle, Shoot, Love By Appointment, The Greatest, Crossed Swords, Convoy, Strike Force, Diary of Madam X, The Black Hole, The Double McGuffin, The Ravagers, When Time Ran Out, High Risk, Super Fuzz, Escape from New York, Deadly Blessing, Young Warriors, Codename: Wild Geese, Skeleton Coast, Spike of Bensonhurst, The Opponent, Any Man's Death, Laser Mission, Turnaround, Captain Henkel, Real Men Don't Eat Gummy Bears, Moving Target, The Last Match, Mistress, All Dogs Go to Heaven 2 (voice).

TELEVISION: *Series*: McHale's Navy, Air Wolf, The Single Guy. *Movies*: Sam Hill: Who Killed the Mysterious Mr. Foster?, The Trackers, Twice in a Lifetime, Future Cop, Jesus of Nazareth, Fire!, The Ghost of Flight 401, Cops and Robin, All Quiet on the Western Front, Blood Feud, Carpool, Love Leads the Way, Last Days of Pompeii, The Dirty Dozen: The Next Mission, Alice in Wonderland, The Dirty Dozen: The Deadly Mission, Treasure Island (Ital. TV), The Dirty Dozen: The Fatal Mission, Jake Spanner-Private Eye, Appearances, The Burning Shore, Mountain of Diamonds (Ital TV). *Guest*: Philco Playhouse, General Electric Theater, Wagon Train, Laramie, Zane Grey Theater, Alcoa Premiere, The Love Boat, Little House on the Prairie, Murder She Wrote, Home Improvement. *Specials*: Billy the Kid, Legend in Granite: The Vince Lombardi Story.

BORIS, ROBERT
Writer, Director. b. NY, NY, Oct. 12, 1945. Screenwriter before also turning to direction with Oxford Blues, 1984.
PICTURES: *Writer*: Electra Glide in Blue, Some Kind of Hero, Doctor Detroit, Oxford Blues (also dir.), Steele Justice (dir.), Buy and Cell (dir.).
TELEVISION: Birds of Prey, Blood Feud, Deadly Encounter, Izzy and Moe, Frank and Jesse (also dir.).

BORODINSKY, SAMUEL
Executive. b. Brooklyn, NY, Oct. 25, 1941. e. Industrial Sch. of Arts & Photography. Expert in film care and rejuvenation. Now exec. v.p., Filmtreat International Corp. Previously with Modern Film Corp. (technician) and Comprehensive Filmtreat, Inc. & International Filmtreat (service manager).

BOSCO, PHILIP
Actor. b. Jersey City, NJ, Sept. 26, 1930. e. Catholic U., Washington, DC, BA. drama, 1957. Studied for stage with James Marr, Josephine Callan and Leo Brady. Consummate stage actor (in over 100 plays, 61 in NY) whose career spans the classics (with NY Shakespeare Fest. and American Shakespeare Fest, CT.), 20 plays with Arena Stage 1957-60, to modern classics as a resident actor with Lincoln Center Rep. Co. in the 1960s, winning Tony and Drama Desk Awards for the farce Lend Me a Tenor, 1988. Recipient: Clarence Derwent Award for General Excellence, Outer Critics Circle Award & Obie for Lifetime Achievement.
THEATER: Auntie Mame (B'way debut, City Center revival, 1958), Measure for Measure, The Rape of the Belt (Tony nom.), Donnybrook, Richard III, The Alchemist, The East Wind, The Ticket of Leave Man, Galileo, Saint Joan, Tiger at the Gates, Cyrano de Bergerac, Be Happy for Me, King Lear, The Miser, The Time of Your Life, Camino Real, Operation Sidewinder, Amphitryon, In the Matter of J. Robert Oppenheimer, The Good Woman of Setzuan, The Playboy of the Western World, An Enemy of the People, Antigone, Mary Stuart, The Crucible, Enemies, Mrs. Warren's Profession, Henry V, The Threepenny Opera, Streamers, Stages, The Biko Inquest, Whose Life Is It Anyway? A Month in the Country, Don Juan in Hell, Inadmissible Evidence, Ah! Wilderness, Man and Superman, Major Barbara, The Caine Mutiny Court Martial, Heartbreak House (Tony nom.), Come Back Little Sheba, Loves of Anatol, Be Happy for Me, Master Class, You Never Can Tell, A Man for All Seasons, Devil's Disciple, Lend Me a Tenor (Tony Award, 1989), The Miser, Breaking Legs, An Inspector Calls, The Heiress, Moon Over Buffalo.
PICTURES: Requiem for a Heavyweight, A Lovely Way to Die, Trading Places, The Pope of Greenwich Village, Walls of Glass, Heaven Help Us, Flanagan, The Money Pit, Children of a Lesser God, Suspect, Three Men and a Baby, Another Woman, Working Girl, The Luckiest Man in the World, Dream Team, Blue Steel, Quick Change, True Colors, FX2, Shadows and Fog, Straight Talk, Angie, Milk Money, Nobody's Fool, Safe Passage, It Takes Two.
TELEVISION: *Series*: TriBeCa. *Specials*: Prisoner of Zenda, An Enemy of the People, A Nice Place to Visit, Read Between the Lines (Emmy Award). *Guest*: Nurses, Trials of O'Brien, Law and Order, Spenser: For Hire, The Equalizer, Against the Law, Janek. *Movies*: Echoes in the Darkness, Second Effort, Internal Affairs, Murder in Black and White, The Return of Eliot Ness, Against the Wall, The Forget-Me-Not Murders, Attica: Line of Fire, Janek: A Silent Betrayal, Young at Heart.

BOSLEY, TOM
Actor. b. Chicago, IL, Oct. 1, 1927. e. DePaul U. Had roles on radio in Chicago and in stock productions before moving to New York. Appeared off-Broadway and on road before signed to play lead in Fiorello! for George Abbott on Broadway. First actor to win Tony, Drama Critics, ANTA and Newspaper Guild awards in one season for that role.
PICTURES: Love with the Proper Stranger, The World of Henry Orient, Divorce American Style, Yours Mine and Ours, The Secret War of Harry Frigg, To Find a Man, Mixed Company, Gus, O'Hara's Wife, Million Dollar Mystery, Wicked Stepmother.
TELEVISION: *Specials*: Alice in Wonderland (1953), Arsenic and Old Lace, The Drunkard, Profiles in Courage. *Guest*: Focus, Naked City, The Right Man, The Nurses, Route 66, The Perry

Como Show. *Series*: That Was the Week That Was, The Debbie Reynolds Show, The Dean Martin Show, Sandy Duncan Show, Wait Til Your Father Gets Home (voice), Happy Days, That's Hollywood (narrator), Murder She Wrote, Father Dowling Mysteries. *Movies*: Marcus Welby M.D.: A Matter of Humanities (pilot), Night Gallery, A Step Out of Line, Vanished, Congratulations It's a Boy!, Mr. & Mrs. Bo Jo Jones, Streets of San Francisco (pilot), No Place to Run, Miracle on 34th Street, The Girl Who Came Gift Wrapped, Death Cruise, Who Is the Black Dahlia?, Last Survivors, The Night That Panicked America, Love Boat, Testimony of 2 Men, Black Market Baby, With This Ring, The Bastard, The Triangle Factory Fire Scandal, The Castaways on Gilligan's Island, The Rebels, Return of the Mod Squad, For the Love of It, Jesse Owens Story, Fatal Confession: A Father Dowling Mystery, The Love Boat: A Valentine Voyage.

BOSTWICK, BARRY
Actor. b. San Mateo, CA, Feb. 24, 1945. e. USIU Sch. of Performing Arts, San Diego, BFA in acting; NYU Grad. Sch. of the Arts. Made prof. stage debut while in coll. working with Walter Pidgeon in Take Her She's Mine, Joined APA Phoenix Rep. Co. making his B'way debut in Cock-A-Doodle Dandy.
THEATER: Salvation, House of Leather, Soon, The Screens, Colette, Grease (created role of Danny Zuko, 1972), They Knew What They Wanted, The Robber Bridegroom (Tony Award, 1977), She Loves Me, L'Historie du Soldat, Nick and Nora.
PICTURES: The Rocky Horror Picture Show, Movie Movie, Megaforce, Eight Hundred Leagues Down the Amazon, Weekend at Bernie's 2, Spy Hard.
TELEVISION: *Series*: Foul Play, Dads. *Movies*: The Chadwick Family, The Quinns, Murder By Natural Causes, Once Upon a Family, Moviola — The Silent Lovers, Red Flag: The Ultimate Game, Summer Girl, An Uncommon Love, Deceptions, Betrayed by Innocence, Body of Evidence, Addicted to His Love, Parent Trap III, Till We Meet Again, Challenger, Captive, Between Love and Hate, Praying Mantis, Danielle Steel's Once in a Lifetime, The Return of Hunter, The Secretary. *Mini-Series*: Scruples, George Washington, I'll Take Manhattan, War and Remembrance. *Specials*: A Woman of Substance, You Can't Take It With You, Working.

BOSUSTOW, NICK
Producer. b. Los Angeles, CA, March 28, 1940. e. Menlo Coll., CA, administration. MCA, intl. sales, 1963. Pres., Stephen Bosustow Productions, 1967; pres., ASIFA-West; Academy Award '70 best short, Is It Always Right to Be Right?; 1973 Acad. Award nom., The Legend of John Henry. TV specials: The Incredible Book Escape, Misunderstood Monsters, A Tale of Four Wishes, Wrong Way Kid (Emmy, 1984); The Hayley Mills Story Book (series). 1973, pres., Bosustow Entertainment, Inc.

BOSWALL, JEFFERY
Producer, Director, Writer. b. Brighton, Eng., 1931. e. Taunton House School, Montpelier Coll., Brighton. Started career as an ornithologist for the Royal Society for the Protection of Birds. Joined BBC in 1958 as radio producer, moving to TV 1964 making films in diverse locations (Ethiopia and Antarctica). Contributed to 50 films as wildlife cameraman. Co-founder of British Library of Wildlife Sounds. 1987: returned to RSPB. Head of Film and Video Unit, 1987. 1992, sr. lecturer in Biological Film & Video, Derby Univ. Chairmanship BKSTS Intl Wildlife Filmmakers' Symposium.
AUTHOR: Birds for All Seasons. Ed. Look and Private Lives. Contrib.: Times, Countryman, the Field, Wildlife and Countryside, BBC Wildlife, Scientific Film, Journal of the Society of Film and TV Arts, Image Technology. Has written for scientific journals and writes annual update for Encyclopaedia Britannica on ornithology.
TELEVISION: 18 films in the Private Lives series of which 4 (about the Kingfisher, Cuckoo, Starling and Jackass Penguin) won intl awards. Animal Olympians, Birds For All Seasons, Where the Parrots Speak Mandarin, Wildlife Safari to Ethiopia.

BOTTOMS, JOSEPH
Actor. b. Santa Barbara, CA, April 22, 1954. Brother of Sam and Timothy Bottoms. Did plays in jr. high school in Santa Barbara and then with community theatre.
PICTURES: The Dove (debut, 1974), Crime and Passion, The Black Hole, Cloud Dancer, King of the Mountain, Blind Date, Open House, Born to Race, Inner Sanctum.
TELEVISION: *Movies*: Trouble Comes to Town, Unwed Father, Stalk the Wild Child, The Intruder Within, Side By Side: The True Story of the Osmond Family, I Married Wyatt Earp, The Sins of Dorian Gray, Time Bomb, Braker, Island Sons, Cop Killer, Gunsmoke: To the Last Man, Treacherous Crossing, Liar's Edge. *Mini-Series*: Holocaust, Celebrity. *Special*: Winesburg Ohio. *Guest*: Owen Marshall, Murder She Wrote.

BOTTOMS, SAM
Actor. b. Santa Barbara, CA, Oct. 17, 1955. Brother of Timothy, Joseph and Ben Bottoms. Co-prod. documentary Picture This. Appeared in documentary Hearts of Darkness.

PICTURES: The Last Picture Show (debut, 1971), Class of '44, Zandy's Bride, The Outlaw Josey Wales, Apocalypse Now, Bronco Billy, Hunter's Blood, Gardens of Stone, After School, Ragin' Cajun, Dolly Dearest, In 'n Out, North of Chiang Mai, Prime Risk, The Trust, Sugar Hill.
TELEVISION: *Series*: Santa Barbara. *Movies*: Savages, Cage Without a Key, Desperate Lives, Island Sons. *Mini-Series*: East of Eden. *Guest*: Greatest Heroes of the Bible, Murder She Wrote, Doc Elliot, Eddie Capra, Lucas Tanner.

BOTTOMS, TIMOTHY
Actor. b. Santa Barbara, CA, Aug. 30, 1951. Brother of actors Joseph and Sam Bottoms. Early interest in acting; was member of S.B. Madrigal Society, touring Europe in 1967. Sang and danced in West Side Story local prod. With brother Sam co-prod. documentary Picture This about making of the Last Picture Show and Texasville.
PICTURES: Johnny Got His Gun (debut, 1971), The Last Picture Show, Love and Pain and the Whole Damn Thing, The Paper Chase, The White Dawn, The Crazy World of Julius Vrooder, Operation Daybreak, A Small Town in Texas, Rollercoaster, The Other Side of the Mountain: Part 2, Hurricane, The High Country, Tin Man, The Census Taker, Hambone and Hillie, In the Shadow of Kilimanjaro, The Sea Serpent, The Fantasist, Invaders from Mars, The Drifter, Mio in the Land of Faraway, Return to the River Kwai, A Case of Law, Texasville, Istanbul, I'll Met By Moonlight, Top Dog.
TELEVISION: *Special*: Look Homeward Angel. *Mini-Series*: The Money Changers, East of Eden. *Movies*: The Story of David, The Gift of Love, A Shining Season, Escape, Perry Mason: The Case of the Notorious Nun. Island Sons. *Series*: Land of the Lost.

BOULTING, ROY
Producer, Director, Writer. b. Bray, Buckinghamshire, England, Nov. 21, 1913. Twin brother of collaborator, producer/director John Boulting (d. 1985). e. McGill U., Montreal. Capt., Brit. Army, WWII. Dir. Charter Film, Charter Film Prod. Ltd. London; dir. British Lion Films, Ltd., 1958. 1977, co-author with Leo Marks of play, Favourites, Danny Travis, 1978.
PICTURES: *Producer*: Trunk Crime (feature debut, 1939), Inquest, Pastor Hall, Thunder Rock, Fame Is the Spur, The Guinea Pig, Singlehanded (Sailor of the King), High Treason, Josephine and Men, Run for the Sun, Brothers in Law, Happy Is the Bride, Carlton-Browne of the F.O. (Man in a Cocked Hat), A French Mistress, The Family Way, Twisted Nerve, There's a Girl in My Soup, Soft Beds and Hard Battles (Undercovers Hero), The Number. *Director*: Journey Together, Brighton Rock (Young Scarface), Seven Days to Noon, The Magic Box, Crest of the Wave (Seagulls Over Sorrento; co-dir., co-prod.), Private's Progress (also co-s.p.), Lucky Jim, I'm All Right Jack (also co-s.p.), The Suspect (The Risk; co-dir., co-prod.), Heaven's Above (also co-.sp.), Rotten to the Core.
TELEVISION: Agatha Christie's The Moving Finger (BBC).

BOUQUET, CAROLE
Actress. b. Neuilly-sur-Seine, France, Aug. 18, 1957. e. Sorbonne, Paris, Paris Conservatoire. Also model for Chanel No. 5 perfume.
PICTURES: That Obscure Object of Desire (debut, 1977), Buffet Froid, Il Cappotto di Astrakan, For Your Eyes Only, Bingo Bongo, Mystere, Nemo, Le Bon Roi Dagobert, Rive Droite Rive Gauche, Special Police, Double Messieurs, Le Mal d'aimer, Jenatsch, Bunker Palace Hotel, New York Stories, Too Beautiful for You, Grosse Fatigue, A Business Affair.

BOUTSIKARIS, DENNIS
Actor. b. Newark, NJ, Dec. 21, 1952. e. Hampshire Col.
THEATER: *Off-B'way*: Another Language (debut, 1975), Funeral March for a One Man Band, All's Well That Ends Well, Nest of the Wood Grouse, Cheapside, Rum and Coke, The Boys Next Door, Sight Unseen. *B'way*: Filomena, Bent, Amadeus.
PICTURES: The Exterminator, Batteries Not Included, Crocodile Dundee II, The Dream Team, Talent for the Game, The Boy Who Cried Bitch, Boys on the Side.
TELEVISION: *Series*: Nurse, Stat, The Jackie Thomas Show, Misery Loves Company. *Movies*: Victim of Love: The Shannon Mohr Story, Love and Betrayal: The Mia Farrow Story.

BOWIE, DAVID
Singer, Actor. b. Brixton, South London, England, Jan. 8, 1947. r.n. David Robert Jones. m. model-actress Iman. Broadway debut: The Elephant Man (1980).
PICTURES: The Virgin Soldiers (debut, 1969), Ziggy Stardust and the Spiders from Mars (1973; U.S. release 1983), The Man Who Fell to Earth, Just a Gigolo, Radio On, Christiane F. Cat People (performed song), The Hunger, Yellowbeard (cameo), Merry Christmas Mr. Lawrence, Into the Night, Absolute Beginners (also songs), Labyrinth (also songs), When the Wind Blows (songs), The Last Temptation of Christ, Imagine—John Lennon, The Linguini Incident, Twin Peaks: Fire Walk With Me, Basquiat.
TELEVISION: *Specials*: Christmas With Bing Crosby, The Midnight Special, Glass Spider Tour.

BOWSER, EILEEN
Curator, Film Archivist, Historian. b. Ohio, Jan. 18, 1928. e. Marietta Coll., B.A., 1950; U. of North Carolina, M.A., history of art, 1953. Joined Dept. of Film, Museum of Modern Art, 1954. Curator, Dept. of Film (1976-1993). Organized major exhib. of the films of D.W. Griffith, Carl-Theodor Dreyer, Art of the Twenties, recent acquisitions and touring shows. On exec. comm. of Federation Internationale des Archives du Film 1969-91, v.p. FIAF 1977-85; pres. FIAF Documentation Commission 1972-81. Film Archives Advisory Comm. since 1971. Assoc. of Univ. Seminars on Cinema and Interdisciplinary Interpretation. Publications: The Transformation of Cinema: 1907-15, Vol II, History of the American Film Series, The Movies, David Wark Griffith, Biograph Bulletins 1908-1912. A Handbook for Film Archives. Has written numerous articles on film history.

BOX, BETTY, OBE
Producer. b. Beckenham, Kent, England, 1920. Assisted Sydney Box in prod. 200 propaganda films in W.W.II. Assoc. prod. Upturned Glass.
PICTURES: Dear Murderer, When the Bough Breaks, Miranda, Blind Goddess, Huggett Family series. It's Not Cricket, Marry Me, Don't Ever Leave Me, So Long At the Fair, The Clouded Yellow, Appointment With Venus (Island Rescue). Venetian Bird (The Assassin), A Day to Remember, Doctor in the House, Mad About Men, Doctor at Sea, The Iron Petticoat, Checkpoint, Doctor at Large, Campbell's Kingdom, A Tale of Two Cities, The Wind Cannot Read, The 39 Steps, Upstairs and Downstairs, Conspiracy of Hearts, Doctor in Love, No Love for Johnnie, No, My Darling Daughter, A Pair of Briefs, The Wild and the Willing, Doctor in Distress, Hot Enough for June (Agent 8 3/4), The High Bright Sun (McGuire Go Home), Doctor in Clover, Deadlier Than the Male, Nobody Runs Forever (The High Commissioner), Some Girls Do, Doctor in Trouble, Percy, The Love Ban, Percy's Progress (It's Not the Size That Counts).

BOXLEITNER, BRUCE
Actor. b. Elgin, IL, May 12, 1950. m. actress Melissa Gilbert. After high school enrolled in Chicago's Goodman Theatre, staging productions and working with lighting and set design in addition to acting.
PICTURES: Six-Pack Annie, The Baltimore Bullet, Tron, The Crystal Eye, Breakaway, Diplomatic Immunity, Kuffs, The Babe.
TELEVISION: Series: How the West Was Won, Bring 'Em Back Alive, Scarecrow and Mrs. King, Babylon 5. Movies: The Chadwick Family, A Cry for Help, The Macahans, Kiss Me—Kill Me, Murder at the World Series, Happily Ever After, Wild Times, Kenny Rogers as The Gambler, Fly Away Home, Bare Essence, I Married Wyatt Earp, Kenny Rogers as The Gambler: The Adventure Continues, Passion Flower, Angel in Green, Kenny Rogers as the Gambler: The Legend Continues, Red River, The Town Bully, From the Dead of Night, The Road Raiders, Till We Meet Again, Murderous Vision, The Secret, Perfect Family, Double Jeopardy (also co-exec. prod.), House of Secrets, Gambler V: Playing for Keeps, Danielle Steel's Zoya. Mini-Series: How the West Was Won, East of Eden, The Last Convertible. Special: Wyatt Earp: Return to Tombstone.

BOYER, PHIL
TV Executive. b. Portland, OR, Dec. 13, 1940. e. Sacramento State U. Began broadcasting career as 12-year-old in Portland, establishing nation's first youth radio facility—a 5-watt facility in the basement of his home. At 16 began working at KPDQ, Portland; two years later joined KPTV, Portland, as announcer. In 1960 joined KEZI-TV, Eugene, OR, heading prod. and prog. depts. In 1965 named staff prod.-dir. for KCRA, TV, Sacramento, CA, becoming prod. mgr. in 1967 and prog. mgr. in 1969. In 1972 joined KNBC-TV, Los Angeles, as prog. dir. In 1974 named v.p., programming, of ABC Owned TV Stations; 1977, v.p.-gen. mgr., WLS-TV, Chicago; 1979, v.p.-gen. mgr. of WABC-TV, NY, 1981; v.p., gen mgr., ABC-owned TV station div.; 1984, joined ABC Video Enterprises as v.p. intl. dev.; 1986 named sr. v.p., intl and prog. dev., CC/ABC Video Ent.

BOYETT, ROBERT LEE
Producer. e. Duke U., B.A.; Col. U., M.A., marketing. Began career in media and mkt. research at Grey Advertising, Inc. Was program development consultant for PBS. In 1973 joined ABC as dir. of prime time series TV, East Coast. In 1975 named ABC TV v.p. & asst. to v.p. programs for West Coast. In 1977 joined Paramount Pictures in newly created position of v.p., exec. asst. to pres. & chief operating officer. 1979, joined Miller-Milkis-Boyett Productions to produce for Paramount Television.
TELEVISION: Exec. prod.: Laverne and Shirley, Happy Days, Bosom Buddies, Mork and Mindy, Valerie, Perfect Strangers.

BOYLE, BARBARA D.
Executive. b. New York, NY, Aug. 11, 1935. e. U. of California, Berkeley, B.A., 1957; UCLA, J.D., 1960. Named to bar: California, 1961; New York, 1964; Supreme Court, 1964. Atty. in busn. affairs dept. & corp. asst. secty., American Intl. Pictures, Los Angeles, 1965-67; partner in entertainment law firm, Cohen & Boyle, L.A., 1967-74; exec. v.p. & gen. counsel, COO, New

World Pictures, L.A., 1974-82. Sr. v.p. worldwide prod., Orion Pictures, L.A., 1982-86; exec. v.p., prod., RKO Pictures, L.A., 1986-87. President, Sovereign Pictures, L.A., 1988-92; Boyle-Taylor Prods., 1993 to present. Co-chmn. 1979-80, Entertainment Law Symposium Advisory Committee, UCLA Law Sch. Member, AMPAS, Women in Film (pres., 1977-78, mem. of bd., chairperson 1981-84), Women Entertainment Lawyers Assn., California Bar Assn., N.Y. State Bar Assn., Beverly Hills Bar Assn., Hollywood Women's Political Committee, American Film Institute. Bd. mem.: Women Director's Workshop, Independent Feature Project/West, Los Angeles Women's Campaign Fund. Founding mem. UCLA Sch. of Law's Entertainment Advisory Council (& co-chairperson 1979 & 80).

BOYLE, LARA FLYNN
Actress. b. Davenport, IA, Mar. 24, 1970. e. Chicago Academy for the Visual and Performing Arts. First studied acting at the Piven Theatre. Professional debut at age 15 in tv mini-series Amerika.
PICTURES: Poltergeist III (debut, 1988), How I Got Into College, Dead Poets Society, May Wine, The Rookie, The Dark Backward, Mobsters, Wayne's World, Where the Day Takes You, The Temp, Eye of the Storm, Equinox, Red Rock West, Threesome, Baby's Day Out, The Road to Wellville, Farmer & Chase, Cafe Society, The Big Squeeze.
TELEVISION: Series: Twin Peaks. Mini-Series: Amerika. Movies: Terror on Highway 91, Gang of Four, The Preppie Murder, The Hidden Room, Past Tense, Jacob.

BOYLE, PETER
Actor. b. Philadelphia, PA, Oct. 18, 1933. e. LaSalle Coll. Was monk in Christian Bros. order before leaving in early 60s to come to N.Y. Acted in off-Broadway shows and joined The Second City in Chicago. Also did TV commercials.
THEATER: NY: Shadow of Heroes, Paul Sills' Story Theatre, The Roast, True West, Snow Orchid.
PICTURES: The Virgin President (debut, 1968), The Monitors, Medium Cool, Joe, Diary of a Mad Housewife, T.R. Baskin, The Candidate, Steelyard Blues, Slither, The Friends of Eddie Coyle, Kid Blue, Ghost in the Noonday Sun, Crazy Joe, Young Frankenstein, Taxi Driver, Swashbuckler, F.I.S.T., The Brink's Job, Hardcore, Beyond the Poseidon Adventure, Where the Buffalo Roam, In God We Trust, Outland, Hammett, Yellowbeard, Johnny Dangerously, Turk 182, Surrender, Walker, The In Crowd, Red Heat, The Dream Team, Speed Zone, Funny, Men of Respect, Solar Crisis, Kickboxer 2, Honeymoon in Vegas, Nervous Ticks, Malcolm X, The Shadow, The Santa Clause, Bulletproof Heart, Born to Be Wild, While You Were Sleeping.
TELEVISION: Series: Comedy Tonight, Joe Bash. Mini-Series: From Here to Eternity. Movies: The Man Who Could Talk to Kids, Tail Gunner Joe, Echoes in the Darkness, Disaster at Silo 7, Guts and Glory: The Rise and Fall of Oliver North, Challenger, In the Line of Duty: Street War, Taking the Heat, Royce. Specials: 27 Wagons Full of Cotton, Conspiracy: The Trial of the Chicago Eight. Guest: Cagney & Lacey, Midnight Caller, X-Files (Emmy Award, 1996). Pilot: Philly Heat.

BRABOURNE, LORD JOHN
Producer. b. London, England, Nov. 9, 1924.
PICTURES: Harry Black and the Tiger, Sink the Bismarck, H.M.S. Defiant (Damn the Defiant!), Othello, The Mikado, Up the Junction, Romeo and Juliet, Dance of Death, Peter Rabbit and Tales of Beatrix Potter, Murder on the Orient Express, Death on the Nile, Stories from a Flying Trunk, The Mirror Crack'd, Evil Under the Sun, A Passage to India, Little Dorrit.

BRACCO, LORRAINE
Actress. b. Brooklyn, NY, 1955. m. actor Edward James Olmos. At 16 began modelling for Wilhelmina Agency appearing in Mademoiselle, Seventeen, Teen magazine. Moved to Paris where modelling career continued and led to TV commercials. After making her film debut in Duo sur Canape became a disc jockey on Radio Luxembourg, Paris. 1983 produced a TV special on fashion and music. In Lincoln Center workshop performance of David Rabe's Goose and Tom Tom, 1986.
PICTURES: Cormorra, The Pick-up Artist, Someone to Watch Over Me, Sing, The Dream Team, On a Moonlight Night, Good Fellas (Acad. Award nom.), Talent for the Game, Switch, Medicine Man, Radio Flyer, Traces of Red, Being Human, The Basketball Diaries, Hackers.
TELEVISION: Movies: Scam, Getting Gotti.

BRACKEN, EDDIE
Actor. b. New York, NY, Feb. 7, 1920. e. Prof. Children's Sch. for Actors, N.Y. m. Connie Nickerson, actress. Vaudeville & night club singer: stage debut in Lottery, 1930.
THEATER: Lady Refuses, Iron Men, So Proudly We Hail, Brother Rat, What A Life, Too Many Girls, Seven Year Itch, Shinbone Alley, Teahouse of the August Moon, You Know I Can't Hear You When The Water's Running, The Odd Couple, Never Too Late, Sunshine Boys, Hotline to Heaven, Hello Dolly, Damn Yankees, Sugar Babies, Show Boat, The Wizard of Oz.

PICTURES: Too Many Girls (debut, 1940), Life With Henry, Reaching for the Sun, Caught in the Draft, The Fleet's In, Sweater Girl, Star Spangled Rhythm, Happy Go Lucky, Young and Willing, The Miracle of Morgan's Creek, Hail the Conquering Hero, Rainbow Island, Bring on the Girls, Duffy's Tavern, Hold That Blonde, Out of This World, Ladies' Man, Fun on a Weekend, The Girl From Jones Beach, Summer Stock, Two Tickets to Broadway, About Face, We're Not Married, Slight Case of Larceny, Wild Wild World (narrator), Shinbone Alley (voice), National Lampoon's Vacation, Preston Sturges: The Rise and Fall of an American Dreamer, Oscar, Home Alone 2: Lost in New York, Rookie of the Year, Baby's Day Out.
TELEVISION: Series: I've Got a Secret (panelist), Make the Connection (panelist), Masquerade Party (host, 1957).Guest: Goodyear Playhouse, Studio One, Climax, Murder She Wrote, Blacke's Magic, Amazing Stories, Tales of the Dark Side, Golden Girls, Wise Guy, Empty Nest, Monsters. Movies: The American Clock, Assault at West Point.

BRADEN, WILLIAM
Executive, Producer. b. Alberta, Canada, June 2, 1939. e. U.S., Vancouver, B.C. and abroad. Began career as stuntman in Hollywood, and has worked in all aspects of industry Worked for Elliott Kastner as prod. exec. and with Jeffrey Bloom, of Feature Films, Inc., as prod. and v.p. in chg. of prod. Also with Dunatai Corp., as head of film and TV prod. With Completion Bond Co. one yr. as prod. exec., Australia then with Filmaker Completion as pres. 4 years. Now indep. prod.
PICTURES: Pyramid (assoc. prod., prod. supv.), Russian Roulette (prod. exec.), 92 in the Shade (prod. exec.), Breakheart Pass (prod. exec.), Dogpound Shuffle (asst. dir.), Dublin Murders (supvr. re-edit), He Wants Her Back (prod.), Goldengirl (prod. exec.), Running Scared (prod.), Death Valley (asst. dir.), The Seduction (prod. exec.), Slapstick of Another Kind (prod. exec.).
TELEVISION: Requiem for a Planet (series, prod./creator). Specials: Nothing Great is Easy (exec. prod.), King of the Channel (exec. prod.), I Believe (prod.), If My People... (prod.), America: Life in the Family (dir./prod.). Also various Movies of the Week for networks and many industrial and doc. films.

BRADFORD, JESSE
Actor. b. 1980. Made first appearance as infant in Q-tip commercial.
PICTURES: Falling in Love (debut, 1984), Prancer, Presmued Innocent, My Blue Heaven, The Boy Who Cried Bitch, King of the Hill, Far From Home: The Adventures of Yello Dog, Hackers.
TELEVISION: Movie: The Boys. Special: Classified Love. Guest: Tribeca.

BRADLEY, ED
Newscaster. b. Philadelphia, Pa., June 22, 1941. e. Cheyney State Coll, B.S. Worked way up through the ranks as local radio reporter in Philadelphia 1963-67 and NY 1967-71. Joined CBS News as stringer in Paris bureau, 1971; then Saigon bureau. Named CBS news correspondent, 1973. Became CBS News White House corr. and anchor of CBS Sunday Night News, 1976-81; principal corr. and anchor, CBS Reports, 1978-81; co-editor and reporter 60 Minutes since 1980. Recipient: Alfred I. duPont-Columbia University and Overseas Press Club Awards, George Foster Peabody and Ohio State Awards, George Polk Award.
TELEVISION: Special reports: What's Happened to Cambodia, The Boat People, The Boston Goes to China, Blacks in America—With All Deliberate Speed, Return of the CIA, Miami... The Trial That Sparked the Riot (Emmy Award), The Saudis, Too Little Too Late (Emmy Award), Murder—Teenage Style (Emmy Award, 1981), In the Belly of the Beast (Emmy Award, 1982), Lena (Emmy Award, 1982).

BRAEDEN, ERIC
Actor. b. Kiel, Germany, Apr. 3, r.n. Hans Gudegast. Awarded Federal Medal of Honor by pres. of Germany for promoting positive, realistic image of Germans in America.
PICTURES: Morituri, Dayton's Devils, 100 Rifles, Colossus: The Forbin Project, Escape from the Planet of the Apes, Lady Ice, The Adulteress, The Ultimate Thrill, Herbie Goes to Monte Carlo, The Ambulance.
TELEVISION: Series: The Rat Patrol, The Young and the Restless (People's Choice Award, Soap Opera Award, 2 Emmy noms.). Movies: Honeymoon With a Stranger, The Mask of Sheba, The Judge and Jake Wyler, Death Race, Death Scream, The New Original Wonder Woman (pilot), Code Name: Diamond Head, Happily Ever After, The Power Within, The Aliens Are Coming, Lucky, The Case of the Wicked Wives.

BRAGA, SONIA
Actress. b. Maringa, Parana, Brazil, 1950. Began acting at 14 on live children's program on Brazilian TV, Gardin Encantado. Stage debut at 17 in Moliere's Jorge Dandin, then in Hair! Starred in many Brazilian soap operas including Gabriella, as well as a prod. of Sesame Street in Sao Paulo.
PICTURES: The Main Road, A Moreninha, Captain Bandeira Vs. Dr. Moura Brasil, Mestica, The Indomitable Slave, The Couple,

Dona Flor and Her Two Husbands, Gabriella, I Love You, A Lady in the Bus, Kiss of the Spider Woman, The Milagro Beanfield War, Moon Over Parador, The Rookie, Roosters.
TELEVISION: Movies: The Man Who Broke 1000 Chains, The Last Prostitute, The Burning Season. Guest: The Cosby Show, Tales From the Crypt.

BRANAGH, KENNETH
Actor, Director, Producer, Author. b. Belfast, Northern Ireland, Dec. 10, 1960. m. actress Emma Thompson. Moved to Reading, England at 9. e. RADA. Went from drama school into West End hit Another Country, followed by Gamblers, The Madness, Francis. Royal Shakespeare Co.: Love Labors Lost, Hamlet, Henry V. Left Royal Shakespeare Company to form his own Renaissance Theater Co. with actor David Parfitt for which he wrote a play Public Enemy (also produced Off-B'way), wrote-directed Tell Me Honestly, directed Twelfth Night, produced-directed-starred in Romeo & Juliet, and played Hamlet, Benedick and Touchstone in a sold-out nationwide tour and London season. L.A.: King Lear, A Midsummer Night's Dream. Author: Beginning (1990). Received BAFTA's Michael Balcon Award for Outstanding Contribution to Cinema (1993). Made Oscar nominated short film Swan Song.
PICTURES: High Season (debut, 1987), A Month in the Country, Henry V (also dir., adapt.; BAFTA & Natl. Board of Review Awards for Best Director, 1989), Dead Again (also dir.), Peter's Friends (also dir., prod.), Swing Kids, Much Ado About Nothing (also dir., adapt.), Mary Shelley's Frankenstein (also dir., co-prod.), In the Bleak Mid-Winter (dir., s.p. only), Anne Frank Remembered (narrator), Othello, Hamlet (also dir, prod..).
TELEVISION: The Boy in the Bush (series), The Billy Plays, Maybury, To the Lighthouse, Coming Through, Ghosts, The Lady's Not For Burning, Fortunes of War (mini-series) Thompson (series), Strange Interlude, Look Back in Anger.

BRANDAUER, KLAUS MARIA
Actor. b., Altaussee, Austria, June 22, 1944. m. film and TV dir.-screenwriter Karin Mueller. e. Acad. of Music and Dramatic Arts, Stuttgart, W. Germany. Was established in the German and Austrian theater before film debut.
PICTURES: The Salzburg Connection (debut, 1972), Mephisto (Cannes Film Fest. Award, 1981). Never Say Never Again, Colonel Redl, Out of Africa, The Lightship, Streets of Gold, Burning Secret, Hanussen, Hitlerjunge Salomon, Das Spinnennetz (The Spider's Web) The French Revolution, The Russia House, White Fang, The Resurrected, Seven Minutes (also dir.), Becoming Colette, Felidae (voice).
TELEVISION: Quo Vadis?

BRANDIS, JONATHAN
Actor. b. Danbury, CT, April 13, 1976. Started as print model at age 4; followed by several tv commercials.
PICTURES: Fatal Attraction, Stepfather 2, Never Ending Story II: The Next Chapter, Ladybugs, Sidekicks.
TELEVISION: Series: seaQuest DSV. Movies: Poor Little Rich Girl, Stephen King's IT, Good King Wenceslas.

BRANDO, MARLON
Actor. b. Omaha, NB, April 3, 1924. Sister is actress Jocelyn Brando. e. Shattuck Military Acad., Faribault, MN. Studied acting at New School's Dramatic Workshop, NY, with Stella Adler; played stock in Sayville, Long Island. Broadway debut: I Remember Mama, followed by Truckline Cafe, Candida, A Flag Is Born, A Streetcar Named Desire. Voted one of top ten Money-Making Stars, M.P. Herald-Fame poll, 1954-55. Autobiography: Brando: Songs My Mother Taught Me (1994).
PICTURES: The Men (debut, 1950), A Streetcar Named Desire, Viva Zapata!, Julius Caesar, The Wild One, On the Waterfront (Academy Award, 1954), Desiree, Guys and Dolls, The Teahouse of the August Moon, Sayonara, The Young Lions, The Fugitive Kind, One-Eyed Jacks (also dir.), Mutiny on the Bounty, The Ugly American, Bedtime Story, The Saboteur—Code Name: Morituri, The Chase, The Appaloosa, A Countess From Hong Kong, Reflections in a Golden Eye, Candy, The Night of the Following Day, Burn!, The Nightcomers, The Godfather (Academy Award, 1972), Last Tango in Paris, The Missouri Breaks, Superman, Apocalypse Now, The Formula, A Dry White Season, The Freshman, Christopher Columbus: The Discovery, Don Juan DeMarco, Divine Rapture, The Island of Dr. Moreau.
TELEVISION: Mini-Series: Roots: The Next Generations (Emmy Award, 1979).

BRANDON, MICHAEL
Actor. b. Brooklyn, NY. e. AADA. Appeared on B'way in Does Tiger Wear a Necktie?
PICTURES: Lovers and Other Strangers, Jennifer on My Mind, Four Flies on Grey Velvet, Heavy Traffic (voice), FM, Promises in the Dark, A Change of Seasons, Rich and Famous.
TELEVISION: Series: Emerald Point, Dempsey & Makepeace, Home Fires. Movies: The Impatient Heart, The Strangers in 7A, The Third Girl From the Left, Hitchhike!, The Red Badge of Courage, Queen of the Stardust Ballroom, Cage Without a Key, James Dean, Scott Free, Red Alert, The Comedy Company, A

Vacation in Hell, A Perfect Match, Between Two Brothers, The Seduction of Gina, Deadly Messages, Rock 'n' Roll Mom, Dynasty: The Reunion, Not in My Family, Moment of Truth: Murder or Memory?

BRANDT, RICHARD PAUL
Executive. b. New York, NY, Dec. 6, 1927. e. Yale U., BS, Phi Beta Kappa. Chmn. Trans Lux Corp.; chmn., Brandt Theatres; dir., Presidential Realty Corp.; chmn. emeritus & trustee, American Film Institute; trustee, American Theatre Wing; member, Tony Awards Management Comm.; vice-chmn. & trustee, College of Santa Fe.

BRAUNSTEIN, GEORGE GREGORY
Producer. b. New York, NY, May 23, 1947. e. Culver Military Acad., U. of California, B.A., biology, chemistry, 1970. U. W.L.A. Law School, J.D. 1987. Father is Jacques Braunstein (Screen Televideo Prods. At War with the Army, Vegas Lions, etc.).
PICTURES: Train Ride to Hollywood, Fade to Black, Surf II, And God Created Woman, Out Cold, Don't Tell Her It's Me.

BRAVERMAN, CHARLES
Producer, Director. b. Los Angeles, CA, March 3, 1944. e. Los Angeles City Coll., U. of Southern California, B.A. m. Kendall Carly Browne, actress. Child actor, 1950-57. Two time Emmy winner.
PICTURES: Dillinger, Soylent Green, Same Time Next Year (all montages, titles), Can't Stop the Music (titles), Hit and Run (prod./dir.).
TELEVISION: An American Time Capsule, The Smothers Brothers Racing Team Special, How to Stay Alive, David Hartman... Birth and Babies, Breathe a Sigh of Relief, The Television Newsman, Getting Married, The Making of a Live TV Show, Televisionland, Nixon: Checkers to Watergate, Braverman's Condensed Cream of Beatles, Two Cops, Peanuts to the Presidency: The Jimmy Carter Campaign, The Making of Beatlemania, Willie Nelson Plays Lake Tahoe, Tony Bennett Sings, What's Up, America?, The Big Laff Off, Englebert at the MGM Grand, Oscar's First 50 Years, Frankie Valli Show, The Sixties, Showtime Looks at 1981, Roadshow, Kenny Rogers' America, St. Elsewhere, DTV (Disney Channel), Crazy Like a Fox, Dreams, The Richard Lewis Special, Prince of Bel Air, Brotherhood of Justice, The Wizard; Heart of the City, Rags to Riches, The New Mike Hammer, Sledge Hammer!, Gabriel's Fire, Life Goes On, Beverly Hills 90210, FBI: Untold Stories, Final Shot: The Hank Gathers Story, Melrose Place, Northern Exposure (DGA nom.), Haunted Lives II.

BRECHER, IRVING
Writer, Director. b. New York, NY, Jan. 17, 1914. e. Roosevelt H.S. in Yonkers. Yonkers Herald reporter; network programs writer for Milton Berle, Willie Howard, Al Jolson, etc., m.p. writer since 1937.
PICTURES: At the Circus, Go West, Du Barry Was a Lady, Shadow of the Thin Man, Best Foot Forward, Meet Me in St. Louis, Summer Holiday, Yolanda and the Thief, Life of Riley (also dir.), Somebody Loves Me (also dir.), Cry for Happy, Sail a Crooked Ship (also dir.), Bye Bye Birdie.
TELEVISION: The People's Choice, The Life of Riley.

BREGMAN, MARTIN
Producer, Writer. b. New York, NY, May 18, 1931. m. actress Cornelia Sharpe. e. Indiana U., NYU. Began career as business and personal mgr. to Barbra Streisand, Faye Dunaway, Candice Bergen, Al Pacino, etc. Chairman NY Advisory Council for Motion Pictures, Radio and TV (co-founder, 1974).
PICTURES: Producer: Serpico, Dog Day Afternoon, The Next Man, The Seduction of Joe Tynan, Simon, The Four Seasons, Eddie Macon's Run, Venom, Scarface, Sweet Liberty, Real Men, A New Life, Sea of Love, Nesting, Betsy's Wedding, Whispers in the Dark, The Real McCoy, Carlito's Way, The Shadow, Gold Diggers: The Secret of Bear Mountain, Matilda.
TELEVISION: Prod.: S*H*E (movie), The Four Seasons (series).

BRENNAN, EILEEN
Actress. b. Los Angeles, CA, Sept. 3, 1935. e. Georgetown U., American Acad. of Dramatic Arts, N.Y. Daughter of silent film actress Jean Manahan. Big break came with lead in off-Broadway musical, Little Mary Sunshine (Obie & Theatre World Awards, 1960).
THEATER: The Miracle Worker (tour), Hello Dolly! (Broadway), and revivals of The King and I, Guys and Dolls, Camelot, Bells Are Ringing; also An Evening with Eileen Brennan, A Couple of White Chicks Sitting Around Talking.
PICTURES: Divorce American Style (debut, 1967), The Last Picture Show (BAFTA nom.), Scarecrow, The Sting, Daisy Miller, At Long Last Love, Hustle, Murder by Death, FM, The Cheap Detective, The Last of the Cowboys (The Great Smokey Roadblock), Private Benjamin (Acad. Award nom.), Pandemonium, The Funny Farm, Clue, Sticky Fingers, Rented Lips, The New Adventures of Pippi Longstocking, It Had to Be You, Stella, Texasville, White Palace, Joey Takes a Cab, I Don't Buy Kisses Anymore, Reckless.

TELEVISION: Series: Rowan & Martin's Laugh-In, All My Children, 13 Queens Boulevard, A New Kind of Family, Private Benjamin (Emmy Award, 1981), Off the Rack. Specials: Working, In Search of Dr. Seuss. Movies: Playmates, My Father's House, The Night That Panicked America, The Death of Richie, When She Was Bad..., My Old Man, When the Circus Came to Town, Incident at Crestridge, Going to the Chapel, Deadly Intentions... Again?, Taking Back My Life: The Nancy Ziegenmeyer Story, Poisoned by Love: The Kern County Murders, Precious Victims, My Name Is Kate, Take Me Home Again, Freaky Friday, Trail of Tears. Mini-Series: The Blue Knight, Black Beauty. Guest: Taxi, Magnum P.I., Newhart, All in the Family, Murder She Wrote.

BREST, MARTIN
Director. b. Bronx, NY, Aug. 8, 1951. e. NYU Sch. of Film. m. producer Lisa Weinstein. Made award-winning short subject, Hot Dogs for Gauguin (featuring Danny DeVito). Accepted into fellowship program at American Film Institute, making first feature, Hot Tomorrows (dir., prod., s.p.), as AFI project. Appeared in Fast Times at Ridgemont High, Spies Like Us. Produced film Josh and S.A.M.
PICTURES: Going in Style (also s.p.), Beverly Hills Cop, Midnight Run (also prod.), Scent of a Woman (also prod.).

BRIALY, JEAN-CLAUDE
Actor. b. Aumale, Algeria, March 30, 1933. e. Strasbourg U. (philosophy) also attended drama classes at Strasbourg Conservatoire. Made several short films with Jacques Rivette and Jean-Luc Godard.
PICTURES: Paris Does Strange Things, Elevator to the Gallows, Les Cousins, Three Faces of Sin, A Woman Is a Woman, Seven Capitol Sins, The Devil and Ten Commandments, Two Are Guilty, Nutty Naughty Chateau, Carless Love, Male Hunt, Circle of Love, King of Hearts, The Oldest Profession, Shock Troops, The Bride Wore Black, Claire's Knee, A Murder is a Murder, The Phantom of Liberty, Catherine et Cie, The Accuser, L'Annee Sainte, Robert and Robert, Eglantine, Les Violets Clos, L'oiseau Rare, Un Amour De Pluie, Bobo Jacco, L'oeil Du Maitre, La Banquiere, La Nuit de Varennes, Cap Canaille, Le Demon Dan L'Isle, Edith and Marcel, Sarah, Stella, The Crime, Papy Fait de la Resistance, Pinot, Simple Flic, Comedie dété.

BRICKMAN, MARSHALL
Writer, Director. b. Rio de Janeiro, Brazil, Aug. 25, 1941. e. U. of Wisconsin. Banjoist, singer, writer with folk groups The Tarriers and The Journeymen before starting to write for TV. Appeared in films Funny and That's Adequate.
PICTURES: Co-writer (with Woody Allen): Sleeper, Annie Hall (Academy Award, 1977), Manhattan, Manhattan Murder Mystery. Director-Writer: Simon (dir. debut, 1980), Lovesick, The Manhattan Project (also prod.). Co-Writer: For the Boys, Intersection.
TELEVISION: Writer: Candid Camera 1966, The Tonight Show 1966-70. Specials: Johnny Carson's Repertory Co. in an Evening of Comedy (1969), Woody Allen Special, Woody Allen Looks at 1967. Prod.: Dick Cavett Show (1970-72, Emmy Award).

BRICKMAN, PAUL
Writer, Director. b. Chicago, IL. e. Claremont Men's Coll. Worked as camera asst., then story analyst at Paramount, Columbia, and Universal.
PICTURES: Handle With Care (Citizen's Band; assoc. prod., s.p.), The Bad News Bears in Breaking Training (s.p.), Risky Business, (dir., s.p.), Deal of the Century (s.p., co-exec. prod.), That's Adequate (interviewee), Men Don't Leave (dir., co-s.p.).

BRICUSSE, LESLIE
Composer, Writer. b. London, England, Jan. 29, 1931. e. Cambridge Univ.
THEATER: Book, music and lyrics (with Anthony Newley): Stop the World—I Want to Get Off, The Roar of the Greasepaint--The Smell of the Crowd, The Good Old Bad Old Days, The Travelling Music Show. Also: Pickwick (lyrics), Over the Rainbow (lyrics), Sherlock Holmes (book, songs), Jekyll and Hyde (book, lyrics).
PICTURES: Wrote songs for: Goldfinger, Penelope, In Like Flint, Gunn, A Guide for the Married Man, Doctor Dolittle (also s.p.; Academy Award for best song: Talk to the Animals, 1967), Sweet November, Goodbye Mr. Chips, Scrooge (also s.p., exec. prod.), Willy Wonka and the Chocolate Factory, Revenge of the Pink Panther, Superman, The Sea Wolves, Sunday Lovers (s.p. only for An Englishman's Home segment), Victor/Victoria (Academy Award, 1982), Santa Claus, That's Life, Home Alone, Hook, Tom & Jerry: The Movie.
TELEVISION: Series Theme Songs: Hart to Hart, I'm a Big Girl Now. Specials: Peter Pan, Babes in Toyland.

BRIDGES, ALAN
Director. b. England, Sept. 28, 1927. Started dir. for the BBC before moving into feature films.

PICTURES: An Act of Murder (debut, 1965), Invasion, Shelley, The Hireling, Out of Season, Summer Rain, The Return of the Soldier, The Shooting Party, Displaced Persons, Apt Pupil, Secret Places of the Heart, Fire Princess.
TELEVISION: The Father, Dial M For Murder, The Intrigue, The Ballade of Peckham Rye, The Initiation, Alarm Call: Z Cars, The Fontenay Murders, The Brothers Karamazov, The Idiot, Days to Come, Les Miserables, Born Victim, The Wild Duck, The Lie, Brief Encounter, Forget Me Not Lane, Double Echo, Saturday, Sunday Monday, Crown Matrimonial.

BRIDGES, BEAU
Actor. r.n. Lloyd Vernet Bridges III. b. Hollywood, CA, Dec. 9, 1941. e. UCLA, U. of Hawaii. Father is actor Lloyd Bridges, brother is actor Jeff Bridges.
PICTURES: Force of Evil (debut, 1948), No Minor Vices, The Red Pony, Zamba, The Explosive Generation, Village of the Giants, The Incident, For Love of Ivy, Gaily Gaily, The Landlord, Adam's Woman, The Christian Licorice Store, Hammersmith Is Out, Child's Play, Your Three Minutes Are Up, Lovin' Molly, The Other Side of the Mountain, Dragonfly (One Summer Love), Swashbuckler, Two-Minute Warning, Greased Lightning, Norma Rae, The Fifth Musketeer, The Runner Stumbles, Silver Dream Racer, Honky Tonk Freeway, Night Crossing, Love Child, Heart Like a Wheel, The Hotel New Hampshire, The Killing Time, The Wild Pair (also dir.), Seven Hours to Judgement (also dir.), The Iron Triangle, Signs of Life, The Fabulous Baker Boys, The Wizard, Daddy's Dyin'...Who's Got the Will?, Married to It, Sidekicks.
TELEVISION: Series: Ensign O'Toole, United States, Harts of the West. Guest: Sea Hunt, Ben Casey, Dr. Kildare, Mr. Novak, Combat, Eleventh Hour, Cimarron Strip, Amazing Stories, The Outer Limits. Movies: The Man Without a Country, The Stranger Who Looks Like Me, Medical Story, The Four Feathers, Shimmering Light, The President's Mistress, The Child Stealer, The Kid from Nowhere (also dir.), Dangerous Company, Witness for the Prosecution, The Red-Light Sting, Alice in Wonderland, Outrage!, Fighting Choice, The Thanksgiving Promise (also dir., co-prod.), Everybody's Baby: The Rescue of Jessica McClure, Just Another Secret, Women & Men: Stories of Seduction (The Man in the Brooks Brothers Shirt), Guess Who's Coming for Christmas?, Without Warning: The James Brady Story (Emmy Award, 1992), Wildflower, Elvis and the Colonel, The Man With 3 Wives, The Positively True Adventures of the Alleged Texas Cheerleader-Murdering Mom (Emmy Award, 1993), Secret Sins of the Fathers (also dir.), Kissinger and Nixon, Losing Chase.

BRIDGES, JEFF
Actor. b. Los Angeles, CA, Dec. 4, 1949. Appeared as infant in 1950 film The Company She Keeps. Made acting debut at eight in the TV series Sea Hunt starring his father, Lloyd Bridges. Studied acting at Herbert Berghof Studio, NY. Mil. service in Coast Guard reserves. Brother is actor-director Beau Bridges. Composed and performed song for film John and Mary. Named Male Star of the Year (1990) by NATO.
PICTURES: Halls of Anger (debut, 1970), The Yin and Yang of Mr. Go, The Last Picture Show (Acad. Award nom.), Fat City, Bad Company, The Iceman Cometh, The Last American Hero, Lolly-Madonna XXX, Thunderbolt and Lightfoot (Acad. Award nom.), Hearts of the West, Rancho Deluxe, Stay Hungry, King Kong, Somebody Killed Her Husband, The American Success Company, Winter Kills, Heaven's Gate, Cutter's Way (Cutter and Bone), Tron, The Last Unicorn (voice only), Kiss Me Goodbye, Against All Odds, Starman (Acad. Award nom.), Jagged Edge, 8 Million Ways to Die, The Morning After, Nadine, Tucker: The Man and His Dream, See You in the Morning, Cold Feet, The Fabulous Baker Boys, Texasville, The Fisher King, The Vanishing, American Heart (also co-prod.), Fearless, Blown Away, Wild Bill, White Squall, The Mirror Has Two Faces.
TELEVISION: Movies: Silent Night, Lonely Night; In Search of America, The Thanksgiving Promise (cameo). Special: Faerie Tale Theatre (Rapunzel). Guest: Lloyd Bridges Show, The FBI, Most Deadly Game.

BRIDGES, LLOYD
Actor. b. San Leandro, CA, January 15, 1913. e. UCLA. Went into stock from college dramatics. Formed off-B'way theater, the Playroom Club. With wife taught drama at private sch. in Darien, CT when signed stock contract with Columbia. B'way stage: Dead Pigeon, Oh Men! Oh Women!, Heart Song, Cactus Flower, Man of La Mancha.
PICTURES: They Dare Not Love, Honolulu Lu, The Lone Wolf Takes a Chance, Cadets on Parade, Son of Davy Crockett, I Was a Prisoner of Devil's Island, Here Comes Mr. Jordan, The Medico of Painted Sprgins, Our Wife, Two Latins From Manhattan, Harmon of Michigan, Three Girls About Town, The Royal Mounted Patrol, Harvard Here I Come, You Belong to Me, The Wife Takes a Flyer, Underground Agent, North of the Rockies, West of Tombstone, Blondie Goes to College, Sing for Your Supper, Shut My Big Mouht, Canal Zone, Stand By All Networks, Tramp Tramp Tramp, Alias Boston Blackie, Hello Annapolis, Sweetheart of the Fleet, Meet the Stewarts, Flight

Lieutenant, Riders of the Northland, Atlantic Convoy, The Talk of the Town, Spirit of Stanford, A Man's World, Pardon My Gun, Commandos Strike at Dawn, Sahara, The Heat's On, Hail to the Rangers, The Crime Doctor's Strangest Case, Destroyer, Two-Man Submarine, Louisiana Hayride, Once Upon a Time, She's a Soldier Too, The Master Race, Saddle Leather Law, A Walk in the Sun, Strange Confession, Secret Agent X-9 (serial), Miss Susie Slage's, Abilene Town, Canyon Passage, Ramrod, The Trouble With Women, Unconquered, Secret Service Investigator, Sixteen Fathoms Deep, Moonrise, Red Canyon, Hideout, Home of the Brave, Calamity Jane and Sam Bass, Trapped, Rocketship XM, Try and Get Me (The Sound of Fury), The White Tower, Colt .45, Little Big Horn, Three Steps North, The Whistle at Eaton Falls, Last of the Comanches, High Noon, Plymouth Adventure, The Tall Texan, The Kid From Left Field, City of Bad Men, The Limping Man, Pride of the Blue Grass, Apache Woman, Wichita, The Deadly Game (Third Party Risk), Wetbacks, The Rainmaker, Ride Out for Revenge, The Goddess, Around the World Under the Sea, Attack on the Iron Coast, The Daring Game, The Happy Ending, To Find a Man, Running Wild, Deliver Us From Evil, The Fifth Musketeer, Bear Island, Airplane!, Airplane II: The Sequel, Weekend Warriors, The Wild Pair, Tucker: The Man and His Dream, Cousins, Winter People, Joe Versus the Volcano, Hot Shots!, Honey I Blew Up the Kid, Hot Shots Part Deux!, Blown Away.
TELEVISION: Series: Police Story, Sea Hunt, The Lloyd Bridges Show, The Loner, San Francisco International Airport, Joe Forrester, Paper Dolls, Capitol News, Harts of the West. Movies: Tragedy in a Temporary Town, The Fortress, The People Next Door, Paper Dolls, Silent Night, Lonley Night, The Thanksgiving Promise, She Was Marked For Murder, Cross of Fire, Leona Helmsley: The Queen of Mean, In the Nick of Time, Devlin, Secret Sins of the Father, The Other Woman. Mini-series: Roots, Disaster on the Coastliner, East of Eden, Movieola, The Blue and the Gray, George Washington, Dress Gray, North & South Book II. Special: Cinderella... Frozen in Time, Nothing Lasts Forever. Guest: Bigelow Theatre, Kraft Suspense Theatre, Robt. Montgomery Present, CBS Playhouse, Alcoa Hour, Philco Playhouse, U.S. Steel Hour, Climax Playhouse 90

BRIGHT, RICHARD
Actor. b. Brooklyn, NY, June 11. e. trained for stage with Frank Corsaro, John Lehne and Paul Mann.
THEATER: The Balcony (1959), The Beard, The Salvation of St. Joan, Gogol, The Basic Training of Pavlo Hummel, Richard III, Kid Twist, Short Eyes as well as regional theater.
PICTURES: Odds Against Tomorrow, Lion's Love, Panic in Needle Park, The Getaway, Pat Garrett and Billy the Kid, The Godfather, The Godfather II, Rancho Deluxe, Marathon Man, Citizens Band, Looking For Mr. Goodbar, On the Yard, Hair, The Idolmaker, Vigilante, Two of a Kind, Once Upon a Time in America, Crackers, Crimewave, Cut and Run, Brighton Beach Memoirs, 52-Pick-up, Time Out, Red Head, The Godfather III.
TELEVISION: Series: Lamp Unto My Feet, Armstrong Circle Theater, The Verdict Is Yours, Kraft Television Theatre, Studio One, Cagney and Lacey, Beacon Hill, Hill Street Blues, From These Roots. Movies: A Death of Innocence, The Connection, The Gun, Cops and Robin, Sizzle, There Must Be A Pony, Penalty Phase. Mini-series: From Here to Eternity, Skag.

BRIGHT, RICHARD S.
Executive. b. New Rochelle, NY, Feb. 28, 1936. e. Hotchkiss Sch., 1953-54; Wharton Sch. of Finance, U. of Pennsylvania, 1954-58. With U.S. Army Finance Corp., 1959-60. Was corporate exec. prior to founding Persky-Bright Organization in 1973, private investment group to finance films. Now bd. chmn, Persky-Bright Productions, Inc.
THEATER: A History of the American Film, Album (Off-B'way, co-prod.).
PICTURES: Last Detail, Golden Voyage of Sinbad, For Pete's Sake, California Split, The Man Who Would Be King, Funny Lady, The Front, and Equus. Financing/production services for: Hard Times, Taxi Driver, Missouri Breaks, Bound for Glory, Sinbad and the Eye of the Tiger, Hair, Body Heat, Still of the Night. Executive Producer: Tribute.
TELEVISION: The President's Mistress (co-producer).

BRILLSTEIN, BERNIE
Producer, Talent Manager. b. New York, NY. 1931. e. NYU, B.S. advertising. Manager whose clients have incl. Lorne Michaels, John Belushi, Jim Henson and the Muppets. Chairman and chief exec. officer, Lorimar Film Entertainment. Founder, chmn., pres., The Brillstein Company. Co-partner of Brillstein-Grey Entertainment and Brillstein-Grey Communications.
PICTURES: Exec. Prod.: The Blues Brothers, Up the Academy, Continental Divide, Neighbors, Doctor Detroit, Ghostbusters, Spies Like Us, Summer Rental, Armed and Dangerous, Dragnet, Ghostbusters II.
TELEVISION: Exec. prod.: Burns and Schreiber Comedy Hour, Buckshot, Open All Night, Show Business, Sitcom, Buffalo Bill, Jump, The Faculty, The Real Ghostbusters (exec. consultant), It's Garry Shandling's Show, The Days and Nights of Molly Dodd, The "Slap" Maxwell Show, The Boys (pilot), The

Wickedest Witch, Normal Life, The Larry Sanders Show, Newsradio, Def Comedy Jam—Prime Time, Hightower 411, Just Shoot Me.

BRIMLEY, WILFORD
Actor. b. Salt Lake City, UT, Sept. 27, 1934. Formerly a blacksmith, ranch hand and racehorse trainer; began in films as an extra and stuntman. Also acted as A. Wilford Brimley. Original member of L.A. Actors Theatre.
PICTURES: True Grit, Lawman, The China Syndrome, The Electric Horseman, Brubaker, Borderline, Absence of Malice, Death Valley, The Thing, Tender Mercies, Tough Enough, High Road to China, 10 to Midnight, Hotel New Hampshire, Harry and Son, The Stone Boy, The Natural, Country, Cocoon, Remo Williams: The Adventure Begins, American Justice, End of the Line, Cocoon: The Return, Eternity, The Firm, Hard Target, Last of the Dogmen.
TELEVISION: *Movies*: The Oregon Trail, The Wild Wild West Revisited, Amber Waves, Roughnecks, Rodeo Girl, The Big Black Pill, Ewoks: The Battle for Endor, Murder in Space, Thompson's Last Run, Act of Vengeance, Gore Vidal's Billy the Kid, Blood River, Tom Clancy's Op Center. *Series*: Our House, Boys of Twilight. *Guest*: The Waltons.

BRINKLEY, DAVID
TV news correspondent. b. Wilmington, NC, July 10, 1920. e. U. of North Carolina, Vanderbilt U. Started writing for hometown newspaper. Joined United Press before entering Army, WWII. After discharge in 1943, joined NBC News in Washington as White House corr. Co-chmn. for many years with late Chet Huntley on NBC Nightly News. Then began David Brinkley's Journal. Moved to ABC to host This Week with David Brinkley.

BRISKIN, MORT
Producer, Writer. b. Oak Park, IL, 1919. e. U. of Southern California; attended Harvard and Northwestern law schools, being admitted to the bar at 20. Practiced law before entering m.p. industry in management with such stars as Mickey Rooney. Turned to production and also wrote screenplays for 16 of his 29 films. Created nine TV series and was prod. or exec. prod. of some 1,350 TV segments of which he wrote more than 300.
PICTURES: The River, The Magic Face, No Time for Flowers, The Second Woman, Quicksand, The Big Wheel, The Jackie Robinson Story, Ben, Willard, Walking Tall, Framed.
TELEVISION: Sheriff of Cochise, U.S. Marshal, The Texan, Grand Jury, The Walter Winchell File, Official Detective, Whirlybirds.

BRITTANY, MORGAN
Actress. r.n. Suzanne Cupito. b. Hollywood, CA, Dec. 5, 1951.
PICTURES: Gypsy, The Birds, Marnie, Yours Mine and Ours, Gable and Lombard, Sundown: The Vampire in Retreat, The Prodigal, Last Action Hero, The Saint.
TELEVISION: *Series*: Dallas, Glitter, Melrose Place. *Guest*: B. L. Stryker. *Movies*: Amazing Howard Hughes, Delta County U.S.A., The Initiation of Sarah, Samurai, Stunt Seven, Death on the Freeway, The Dream Merchants, Moviola: The Scarlett O'Hara War, The Wild Women of Chastity Gulch, LBJ: The Early Years, Perry Mason: The Case of the Scandalous Scoundrel, National Lampoon's Favorite Deadly Sins.

BRITTON, TONY
Actor. b. Birmingham, England, 1924. e. Thornbury Grammar Sch., Glos. Early career as clerk and in repertory; TV debut, 1952, The Six Proud Walkers (serial); m.p. debut, 1955, Loser Takes All.
THEATER: The Guv'nor, Romeo and Juliet, The Scarlet Pimpernel, The Other Man, The Dashing White Sergeant, Importance of Being Earnest, An Ideal Husband, School for Scandal, A Dream of Treason, That Lady, The Private Lives of Edward Whiteley, Affairs of State, The Night of The Ball, Gigi, The Seagull, Henry IV Part 1, Kill Two Birds, Cactus Flower, A Woman of No Importance, The Boston Story, Lady Frederick, My Fair Lady, Move Over Mrs. Markham, No No Nanette, Dame of Sark, The Chairman, Murder Among Friends, The Seven Year Itch, St. Joan, The Tempest, King Lear, A Man for All Seasons.
PICTURES: Birthday Present, Behind the Mask, Operation Amsterdam, The Heart of a Man, The Rough and the Smooth, The Risk, The Horsemasters, Stork Talk, The Break, There's a Girl in My Soup, Forbush and The Penguins, Sunday Bloody Sunday, Night Watch, The Day of the Jackal.
TELEVISION: The Man Who Understood Women, Ooh La La, Call My Bluff, The Nearly Man, Friends and Brothers. Series: Melissa, Father Dear Father, Robins Nest, Don't Wait Up.

BROADBENT, JIM
Actor. b. England. Member of the National Theatre and the Royal Shakespeare Company. Wrote and starred in short film A Sense of History (Clermont-Ferrand Intl. Film Fest. Award).
THEATER: The Recruiting Officer, A Winter's Tale, The Government Inspector, A Flea in Her Ear, Goose Pimples.
PICTURES: The Shout (debut, 1978), The Passage, Breaking Glass, The Dogs of War, Time Bandits, Brazil, The Good Father,

Superman IV: The Quest for Peace, Life Is Sweet, Enchanted April, The Crying Game, Widow's Peak, The Wedding Gift, Princess Caraboo, Bullets Over Broadway, Rough Magic, The Secret Agent, Richard III.
TELEVISION: Not the Nine O'Clock News, Gone to Seed, Sense of History (also writer), Murder Most Horrid, Gone to the Dogs, Only Fools and Horses, The Victoria Wood Show, Silas Marner, Blackladder, Birth of a Nation.

BROADHEAD, PAUL E.
Executive. e. Univ. of MS. Founder of Paul Broadhead & Assocs. real estate development. 1984, sold his interests in that company. Became chmn. of bd. of Theatre Properties, Cinemark USA.

BROADNAX, DAVID
Actor, Producer, Writer. b. Columbus, GA, Dec. 16.
PICTURES: *Actor*: The Landlord, Come Back Charleston Blue, Sharpies (also prod., co-s.p.), Zombie Island Massacre (also prod., story).
TELEVISION: As the World Turns, Another World, Edge of Night, Love Is a Many Splendored Thing, Search for Tomorrow, Saturday Night Live.

BROCCOLI, ALBERT "CUBBY"
Producer. b. New York, NY, April 5, 1909. e. City Coll. of New York. Agriculturist in early years; entered m.p. ind. as asst. director, 20th Century-Fox, 1938. Worked with theatrical agent Charles Feldman 1948-51; prod., Warwick Films 1951-60; prod, Eon Prods., Ltd. since 1961. Thalberg Award, 1982.
PICTURES: Red Beret (Paratrooper), Hell Below Zero, Black Knight, Prize of Gold, Cockleshell Heroes, Safari, Zarak, April in Portugal, Pickup Alley, Fire Down Below, Arrivederci Roma, Interpol, How to Murder a Rich Uncle, Odongo, High Flight, No Time to Die, The Man Inside, Idle on Parade, Adamson of Africa, Bandit of Zhobe, Jazz Boat, Killers of Killimanjaro, In the Nick, Let's Get Married, The Trials of Oscar Wilde, Johnny Nobody, Carolina, Dr. No, Call Me Bwana, From Russia with Love, Goldfinger, Thunderball, You Only Live Twice, Chitty Chitty Bang Bang, On Her Majesty's Secret Service, Diamonds Are Forever, Live and Let Die, The Man with the Golden Gun, The Spy Who Loved Me, Moonraker, For Your Eyes Only, Octopussy, A View to a Kill, The Living Daylights, Licence to Kill, Goldeneye.
(d. June 27, 1996)

BROCKMAN, MICHAEL
Executive. b. Brooklyn, NY, Nov. 19, 1938. e. Ithaca Coll. Became v.p., daytime programming, ABC Entertainment, 1974; later v.p., tape prod. operations and admin. Left to become v.p., daytime programs, NBC Entertainment, 1977-1980. Became v.p. programs, Lorimar Prods. 1980-82; v.p. daytime and children's prog. CBS Entertainment, 1982-89. 1986, title changed to v.p. daytime, children's and late night. Became pres. ABC daytime, children's & late night entertainment 1989-90. Joined Mark Goodson Prods. as v.p. 1991. Became sr. v.p. in 1993. Pres., M. Brockman Broadcast, 1995.

BRODERICK, MATTHEW
Actor. b. New York, NY, Mar. 21, 1962. Son of late actor James Broderick and writer-dir./artist Patricia Broderick. Acted in a workshop prod. of Horton Foote's Valentine's Day with his father (1979).
THEATER: *NY*: Torch Song Trilogy, Brighton Beach Memoirs (Tony & Theatre World Awards, 1983), Biloxi Blues, The Widow Claire, How to Succeed in Business Without Really Trying (Tony Award, 1995).
PICTURES: Max Dugan Returns (debut, 1983), WarGames, Ladyhawke, 1918, On Valentine's Day, Ferris Bueller's Day Off, Project X, Biloxi Blues, Torch Song Trilogy, Glory, Family Business, The Freshman, Out on a Limb, The Night We Never Met, The Lion King (voice), The Road to Wellville, Mrs. Parker and the Vicious Circle, Arabian Knight (voice), Infinity (also dir., co-prod.), The Cable Guy, Infinity (also dir.).
TELEVISION: *Specials*: Master Harold... and the Boys, Cinderella (Faerie Tale Theatre), The Year of the Generals (voice), A Simple Melody. *Movie*: A Life in the Theatre. *Guest*: Lou Grant.

BRODNEY, OSCAR
Writer. b. Boston, MA, 1906. e. Boston U., LL.B., 1927; Harvard, LL.M., 1928. Atty., MA Bar, 1928-35.
PICTURES: She Wrote the Book, If You Knew Susie, Are You With It?, For the Love of Mary, Mexican Hayride, Arctic Manhunt, Yes Sir, That's My Baby, Double Crossbones, Gal Who Took the West, South Sea Sinner, Comanche Territory, Harvey, Frenchie, Francis Goes to the Races, Little Egypt, Francis Covers the Big Town, Willie and Joe Back at the Front, Scarlet Angel, Francis Goes to West Point, Walking My Baby Back Home, Sign of the Pagan, Black Shield of Falworth, Captain Lightfoot, The Spoilers, Purple Mask, Lady Godiva, Day of Fury, Star in the Dust, Tammy and the Bachelor, When Hell Broke Loose, Bobbikins (also prod.), Tammy Tell Me True, The Right Approach, All Hands on Deck, Tammy and the Doctor, The Brass Bottle, I'd Rather Be Rich.

BRODSKY, JACK
Producer. b. Brooklyn, NY, July 3, 1932. e. George Washington H.S. Writer for N.Y. Times. Joined 20th-Fox publicity in N.Y. in 1956. Left in 1961 to head national ad-pub for Filmways. Joined Rastar Productions to work on Funny Girl; later named v.p. in charge of prod. In 1976 named v.p. in chg. film prod. prom., Rogers & Cowan; 1978, Columbia Pictures v.p. of adv., pub., promo.; 1979, named exec. v.p. of Michael Douglas' Big Stick Productions; 1983; joined 20th-Fox as exec. v.p., worldwide adv., pub., exploit. Resigned 1985 to resume career as producer.
PICTURES: Little Murders, Everything You Always Wanted To Know About Sex But Were Afraid to Ask (exec. prod.), Summer Wishes Winter Dreams, The Jewel of the Nile, Dancers (co-exec. prod., actor), King Ralph, Scenes From a Mall (actor), Rookie of the Year (co-exec. prod.).
AUTHOR: The Cleopatra Papers, with Nat Weiss.

BROKAW, CARY
Executive, Producer. b. Los Angeles, CA, June 21, 1951. e. Univ. of CA/Berkeley, UCLA Grad. Sch. Worked at several positions at 20th Century Fox before serving as exec. v.p. for Cineplex Odeon Corp. 1983 became co-chmn., pres. of Island Alive; 1985, became co-chmn., pres. & CEO of Island Pictures. Formed Avenue Entertainment Pictures in 1987, becoming chmn. & CEO.
PICTURES: Executive Producer: Trouble in Mind, Down by Law, Nobody's Fool, Slamdance, Pascali's Island, Signs of Life, Cold Feet, Drugstore Cowboy, After Dark My Sweet, The Object of Beauty, Sex Drugs Rock & Roll, The Player, American Heart. Producer: Short Cuts, Restoration, Voices From a Locked Room.
TELEVISION: Movies: In the Eyes of a Stranger, Amelia Earhart: The Final Flight, See Jane Run, Stranger in Town.

BROKAW, NORMAN R.
Executive. b. New York, NY, April 21, 1927. Joined William Morris Agency as trainee in 1943; junior agent, 1948; sr. agent, company exec. in m.p. and TV, 1951; 1974, v.p., William Morris Agency, World Wide all areas. 1981, named exec. v.p. & mem. of bd., William Morris Agency, worldwide; 1986, named co-chmn. of bd., WMA, worldwide. 1989, named pres. & CEO, William Morris Inc. worldwide. 1991, named Chmn. of Board of CEO. Member Acad. of TV Arts & Sciences, AMPAS. Member bd. of dir. of Cedars-Sinai Medical Center, Los Angeles; pres., The Betty Ford Cancer Center. Clients include former President and Mrs. Gerald R. Ford, Bill Cosby, Gen. Alexander Haig, Priscilla Presley, Andy Griffith, Dr. C. Everett Koop, Marcia Clark, Christopher Darden.

BROKAW, TOM
TV Host, Anchorman. b. Yankton, S.D., Feb. 6, 1940. e. U. of South Dakota. Newscaster, weatherman, staff announcer KTIV, Sioux City, IA, 1960-62. Joined KMTV, NBC affiliate in Omaha, in 1962; 1965, joined WSB-TV, Atlanta. Worked in L.A. bureau of NBC News, anchored local news shows for KNBC, NBC station (1966-73). In 1973 named NBC News' White House correspondent; was anchor of NBC Saturday Night News. Named host of Today show in August, 1976. In 1982 co-anchor, NBC Nightly News. Co-anchor 1993 series NBC newsmagazine, Now With Tom Brokaw & Katie Couric. Special: Conversation with Mikhail S. Gorbachev.

BROLIN, JAMES
Actor, Director. b. Los Angeles, CA, July 18, 1940. r.n. James Bruderlin. e. UCLA. Son is actor Josh Brolin. Debut in Bus Stop (TV series); named most promising actor of 1970 by Fame and Photoplay magazines. Winner, Emmy and Golden Globe Awards. Also nominated for 3 additional Emmys and 2 Golden Globes.
PICTURES: Take Her She's Mine (debut, 1963), John Goldfarb Please Come Home, Goodbye Charlie, Dear Brigitte, Von Ryan's Express, Morituri, Fantastic Voyage, Way ... Way Out, The Cape Town Affair, Our Man Flint, The Boston Strangler, Skyjacked, Westworld, Gable and Lombard, The Car, Capricorn One, The Amityville Horror, Night of the Juggler, High Risk, Pee-wee's Big Adventure, Bad Jim, Super High Score, Ted & Venus, Gas Food Lodging, Cheatin' Hearts (also exec. prod.), Back Stab.
TELEVISION: Series: Marcus Welby M.D. (Emmy Award, 1970), Hotel, Angel Falls, Extreme. Movies: Marcus Welby M.D. (A Matter of Humanities), Short Walk to Daylight, Class of '63, Trapped, Steel Cowboys, The Ambush Murders, Mae West, White Water Rebels, Cowboy, Beverly Hills Cowgirl Blues, Hold the Dream, Intimate Encounters, Voice of the Heart, Finish Line, Nightmare on the 13th Floor, And the Sea Will Tell, Deep Dark Secrets, The Sands of Time, Visions of Murder, Gunsmoke: The Long Ride, The Calling, Parallel Lives, A Perry Mason Mystery: The Case of the Grimacing Governor, Terminal Virus. Special: City Boy (PBS). Director: Hotel (12 episodes), The Young Riders.

BROMHEAD, DAVID M.
Executive. b. Teaneck, NJ, Jan. 7, 1960. e. Leighton Park Sch., Reading, England, 1973-78. Overseas sls. exec., Rank Film Dist., 1980; joined New World Pictures, 1984, dir. intl. dist.; named dir., TV dist., 1986.

BRON, ELEANOR
Actress, Writer. b. Stanmore, Middlesex, Eng., 1938. Started career in Establishment Club, London, and on American tour. Leading lady on British TV show Not So Much a Programme—More a Way of Life. Author of Double Take, The Pillowbook of Eleanor Bron, Life and Other Punchers.
THEATER: The Doctor's Dilemma, Howards End, The Prime of Miss Jean Brodie, Hedda Gabler, The Duchess of Malfi, The Madwoman of Chaillot.
PICTURES: Help!, Alfie, Two for the Road, Bedazzled, The Turtle Diary, Thank You All Very Much, Women in Love, The Millstone, Little Dorrit, Black Beauty, A Little Princess.
TELEVISION: Movies: The Day Christ Died, The Attic: The Hiding of Anne Frank, Intrigue, Changing Step, The Blue Boy. Series: Where Was Spring? (also co-wrote), After That This. Guest: Rumpole of the Bailey, Yes Minister, Absolutely Fabulous.

BRONDFIELD, JEROME
Writer. b. Cleveland, OH, Dec. 9, 1913. e. Ohio State U., 1936. Reporter, ed. on Columbus Dispatch, Associated Press, story ed., script head, RKO Pathe, Oct., 1944; writer, dir. & supvr. of many doc. shorts incl. This Is America series; TV writer; short story writer; collab. s.p., Below the Sahara; s.p. Louisiana Territory; doc. film writer; Author, Woody Hayes, The 100-Yard War, Knute Rockne, The Man and the Legend. Sr. editor, Scholastic, Inc.

BRONFMAN, EDGAR, JR.
Executive. Joined Seagram 1982 as asst. to officeof the pres.; served as mng. dir. of Seagram Europe until he was appointed pres. of The House of Seagram, 1984-88; became pres. & COO in 1989. June 1994 named pres. & CEO of The Seagram Company Ltd. Upon acquisition of MCA Inc. was named acting chairman, 1995.

BRONSON, CHARLES
Actor. b. Ehrenfeld, PA, Nov. 3, 1921. r.n. Charles Buchinsky. Worked as a coal miner. Served in Air Force (1943-46) as tail gunner on B29s in Pacific. Studied acting at Pasadena Playhouse. Started in films billed under real name. Guest in numerous TV shows in addition to those below.
PICTURES: You're in the Navy Now (debut, 1951), The People Against O'Hara, The Mob, Red Skies of Montana, My Six Convicts, The Marrying Kind, Pat and Mike, Diplomatic Courier, Bloodhounds of Broadway, House of Wax, The Clown, Miss Sadie Thompson, Crime Wave, Tennessee Champ, Riding Shotgun, Apache, Drum Beat (lst billing as Charles Bronson), Vera Cruz, Big House U.S.A., Target Zero, Jubal, Run of the Arrow, Machine Gun Kelly, Gang War, Showdown at Boot Hill, When Hell Broke Loose, Ten North Frederick, Never So Few, The Magnificent Seven, Master of the World, A Thunder of Drums, X-15, Kid Galahad, The Great Escape, Four for Texas, The Sandpiper, The Battle of the Bulge, This Property Is Condemned, The Dirty Dozen, Villa Rides, Guns for San Sebastian, Farewell Friend, Once Upon a Time in the West, Rider on the Rain, You Can't Win Em All, The Family, Cold Sweat, Twinky (Lola), Someone Behind the Door, Red Sun, Chato's Land, The Mechanic, The Valachi Papers, The Stone Killer, Chino, Mr. Majestyk, Death Wish, Breakout, Hard Times, Breakheart Pass, From Noon Till Three, St. Ives, The White Buffalo, Telefon, Love and Bullets, Caboblanco, Borderline, Death Hunt, Death Wish II, Ten to Midnight, The Evil That Men Do, Death Wish 3, Murphy's Law, Assassination, Death Wish 4: The Crackdown, Messenger of Death, Kinjite: Forbidden Subjects, The Indian Runner, Death Wish V: The Face of Death.
TELEVISION: Series: Man With a Camera, Empire, Travels of Jamie McPheeters. Guest: Philco Playhouse (Adventure in Java), Medic, A Bell for Adano, Gunsmoke, Have Gun Will Travel, Meet McGraw, The FBI, The Fugitive, The Virginian. Movies: Raid on Entebbe, Act of Vengeance, Yes Virginia There Is a Santa Claus, The Sea Wolf, Donato and Daughter, A Family of Cops.

BROOK, PETER
Director. b. London, England, March 21, 1925. e. Magdalen Coll., Oxford. To London 1943 to dir. his first play, Doctor Faustus; other stage incl. Man and Superman, Marat/Sade, A Midsummer Night's Dream, etc.
PICTURES: The Beggar's Opera (debut, 1953), Moderato Cantabile (also co-s.p.), Lord of the Flies (also s.p., edit), The Persecution and Assassination of Jean-Paul Marat as Performed by the Inmates of the Asylum of Charenton Under the Direction of the Marquis de Sade, Tell Me Lies (also prod.), King Lear (also s.p.), Meetings With Remarkable Men (also s.p.), The Tragedy of Carmen, Swann in Love (s.p. only), The Mahabharata.

BROOKS, ALBERT
Director, Writer, Actor. r.n. Albert Einstein. b. Los Angeles, CA, July 22, 1947. e. Carnegie Tech. Son of late comedian Harry Einstein (Parkyakarkus). Brother is performer Bob Einstein. Sports writer KMPC, L.A. 1962-63. Recordings: Comedy Minus One, A Star is Bought (Grammy nom.).

PICTURES: *Actor.* Taxi Driver, Real Life (also dir., co-s.p.), Private Benjamin, Modern Romance (also dir., co-s.p.), Twilight Zone—The Movie, Terms of Endearment (voice), Unfaithfully Yours, Lost in America (also dir., co-s.p.), Broadcast News (Acad. Award nom.), Defending Your Life (also dir., s.p.), I'll Do Anything, The Scout (also co-s.p.), Mother (also dir.).
TELEVISION: *Series:* Dean Martin Presents the Golddiggers, Saturday Night Live (prod., dir. short films 1975-76), Hot Wheels (voices), The Associates (wrote theme song). *Specials:* Milton Berle's Mad Mad Mad World of Comedy, General Electric's All-Star Anniversary. *Guest:* Love American Style, The Odd Couple, Ed Sullivan Show, Tonight Show, others.

BROOKS, JAMES L.
Director, Producer, Writer. b. North Bergen, NJ, May 9, 1940. e. NYU. Copyboy for CBS News, N.Y.; promoted to newswriter. 1965 moved to L.A. to work for David Wolper's documentary prod. co. In 1969 conceived idea for series, Room 222; formed partnership with fellow writer Allan Burns. Together they created Mary Tyler Moore Show in 1970. 1977, established prod. co. on Paramount lot with other writers, producing and creating the series, The Associates and Taxi. Formed Gracie Films. Directed play Brooklyn Laundry, in L.A.
PICTURES: Real Life (actor), Starting Over (s.p., co-prod.), Modern Romance (actor), Terms of Endearment (dir., prod., s.p.; Academy Awards for Best Picture, Director and Screenplay, 1983), Broadcast News (dir., prod., s.p.), Big (co-prod.), Say Anything (exec. prod), The War of the Roses (co-prod.), I'll Do Anything (dir., prod., s.p.).
TELEVISION: *Movie:* Thursday's Game (writer, prod., 1971). Series: The Mary Tyler Moore Show (co-creator, writer, exec. prod.; 2 Emmy Awards for writing: 1971, 1977; 3 Emmy Awards as exec. prod.: 1975, 1976, 1977), Rhoda (writer, prod.), The New Lorenzo Music Show (writer), Lou Grant (co-exec. prod.). Series (co-creator, and/or exec. prod.): Taxi (3 Emmy Awards as exec. prod.: 1979, 1980, 1981), Cindy, The Associates, Cheers, Tracey Ullman Show (Emmy Award as exec. prod., 1989), The Simpsons (2 Emmy Awards as exec. prod.: 1990, 1991), Sibs, Phenom, The Critics.

BROOKS, JOSEPH
Producer, Director, Writer, Composer, Conductor. Well-known for composing music for TV commercials before turning to producing, directing, writing and scoring theatrical feature, You Light Up My Life, in 1977. Winner of 21 Clio Awards (advertising industry), Grammy, Golden Globe, People's Choice, Amer. Music Awards; created music for 100 commercials. Has also composed for theatrical films. Winner of Cannes Film Festival Advertising Award.
PICTURES: *Scores:* The Garden of the Finzi-Continis, Marjoe, Jeremy, The Lords of Flatbush. *Prod.-Dir.-Writer-Composer:* You Light Up My Life (Academy Award for Best Song: title song, 1977), If Ever I See You Again (also actor).

BROOKS, MEL
Writer, Director, Actor. b. Brooklyn, NY, June 28, 1926. r.n. Melvin Kaminsky. m. actress Anne Bancroft. e. VA Military Inst. 1944. U.S. Army combat engineer 1944-46. As child, did impressions and was amateur drummer and pianist. First appearance as actor in play Separate Rooms in Red Bank, NJ. Was also social dir. of Grossinger's Resort in the Catskills. Became writer for Sid Caesar on TV's Broadway Review and Your Show of Shows. Teamed with Carl Reiner on comedy record albums: The 2000 Year Old Man, The 2000 and 13 Year Old Man. Founded Brooksfilms Ltd., 1981. Won Academy Award for Best Short Subject (animated): The Critic (writer, s.p., narrator). Co-writer of Shinbone Alley.
THEATER: *Writer.* New Faces of 1952 (sketches), Shinbone Alley (book), All-American (book).
PICTURES: New Faces (co-s.p.), The Producers (dir., s.p.; Academy Award for Best Original Screenplay, 1968), The Twelve Chairs (dir., s.p., actor), Blazing Saddles (dir., s.p., actor), Young Frankenstein (dir., co-s.p.; Acad. Award nom. for s.p.), Silent Movie (dir., co-s.p., actor), Frances (exec.-prod.), High Anxiety (dir., prod., co-s.p., actor), The Muppet Movie (actor), History of the World Part 1 (dir., prod., s.p., actor, lyrics), To Be or Not To Be (exec-prod., actor), Spaceballs (dir., prod., co-s.p., actor), My Favorite YEar (exec.-prod.), Look Who's Talking Too (voice), Life Stinks (dir., prod., co-s.p., actor), Robin Hood: Men in Tights (dir., prod., co-s.p., actor), The Silence of the Hams (actor), The Little Rascals (actor), They Fly II (exec.-prod.), Dracula: Dead and Loving It (dir., prod., co-s.p., actor). *Exec. Prod.:* The Elephant Man, The Doctor and the Devils, The Fly, 84 Charing Cross Road, Solarbabies, The Vagrant.
TELEVISION: *Special:* The Sid Caesar-Imogene Coca-Carl Reiner-Howard Morris Special (co-writer; Emmy Award, 1967). *Series:* Get Smart (co-creator, co-writer), When Things Were Rotten (co-creator, co- writer, prod.), The Nutt House (prod., co-writer).

BROSNAN, PIERCE
Actor. b. Navan, County Meath, Ireland, May 16, 1953. Left County Meath, Ireland for London at 11. Worked as commercial

illustrator, then joined experimental theater workshop and studied at the Drama Center. On London stage (Wait Until Dark, The Red Devil Battery Sign, Filumenia, etc.)
PICTURES: The Mirror Crack'd (debut, 1980), The Long Good Friday, Nomads, The Fourth Protocol, Taffin, The Deceivers, Mister Johnson, The Lawnmower Man, Entangled, Mrs. Doubtfire, Love Affair, Goldeneye, Mars Attacks, The Mirror Has Two Faces.
TELEVISION: *Series:* Remington Steele, Frame-Up (NBC Friday Night Mystery). *Movies/Specials:* Murphy's Stroke, The Manions of America, Nancy Astor, Noble House, Around the World in 80 Days, The Heist, Murder 101, Victim of Love, Live Wire, Death Train (Detonator), The Broken Chain, Don't Talk to Strangers, Alistair MacLean's Night Watch.

BROUGH, WALTER
Producer, Writer. b. Phila. PA, Dec. 19, 1935. e. La Salle U. (B.A.), USC (M.A.). Began career with Stage Society Theatre, LA. Currently CEO, Orb Enterprises, Inc.
PICTURES: Gabriella, A New Life, No Place to Hide, Run Wild Run Free, The Desperadoes, Funeral for an Assassin (also prod.), On a Dead Man's Chest (also prod.), Jed and Sonny (also prod.).
TELEVISION: Doctor Kildare, The Fugitive, Branded, Name of the Game, Mannix, Mission Impossible, The Magician, Man From Atlantis, Police Story, Wildside, Heart of the City (also prod.), Thunder Guys (pilot), Spencer for Hire (also co-prod.), Law & Harry McGraw, New Mission Impossible (also co-prod.), Over My Dead Body, Hunter, Tequila & Bonetti, Sirens.

BROUGHTON, BRUCE
Composer. b. Los Angeles, CA , March 8, 1945. e. U. of Southern California, B.M., 1967. Music supvr., CBS-TV, 1967-77. Since then has been freelance composer for TV and films. Member of Academy of TV Arts & Sciences Society of Composers & Lyricists (past pres.), AMPAS (governor). Nominated 15 times for Emmy. Nominated for Grammy for Young Sherlock Holmes.
PICTURES: The Prodigal, The Ice Pirates, Silverado (Acad. Award nom.), Young Sherlock Holmes, Sweet Liberty, The Boy Who Could Fly, Square Dance, Harry and the Hendersons, Monster Squad, Big Shots, Cross My Heart, The Rescue, The Presidio, Last Rites, Moonwalker, Jacknife, Betsy's Wedding, Narrow Margin, The Rescuers Down Under, All I Want for Christmas, Honey I Blew Up the Kid, Stay Tuned, Homeward Bound: The Incredible Journey, So I Married an Axe Murderer, For Love or Money, Tombstone, Holy Matrimony, Baby's Day Out, Miracle on 34th Street.
TELEVISION: *Series:* Hawaii Five-0, Gunsmoke, Quincy, How the West Was Won, Logan's Run, The Oregon Trail, Buck Rogers (Emmy Award), Dallas (Emmy Award), Dinosaurs (theme), Capitol Critters (theme), Tiny Ton Adventures (Emmy Award). *Movies:* The Paradise Connection, Desperate Voyage, The Return of Frank Cannon, Desperate Lives, Killjoy, One Shoe Makes It Murder, The Master of Ballantrae, MADD, The Candy Lightner Story, Cowboy, A Thanksgiving Promise, The Old Man and the Sea, O Pioneers! (Emmy Award). *Mini-Series:* The Blue and the Gray, The First Olympics—Athens: 1896 (Emmy Award), George Washington II, Tiny Toon Adventures.

BROUMAS, JOHN G.
Executive. b. Youngstown, OH, Oct. 12, 1917. e. Youngstown. Usher, Altoona Publix Theatres, 1933, usher to asst. mgr., Warner Thea. 1934-39; mgr. Grand 1939-40; mgr. Orpheum 1940-41. WWII active, Officer Chemical Corps, commanding officer 453rd Chem. Battalion (Reserve); Life member Reserve Officers Assoc.; Gen. mgr. Pitts & Roth Theatres 1946-54; pres., Broumas Theatres; v.p. NATO, 1969; bd. of dir. of NATO of VA, MD, D.C.; pres., Broumas Theatre Service 1954-82; bd. chmn., Showcase Theatres 1965-82; past pres. & bd. chmn. Maryland Theatre Owners; v.p. & bd. of dir., Virginia Theatre Owners; bd. of dir. NATO of D.C.; pres. B.C. Theatres; Past dir. and mem. Motion Picture Pioneers; Advisory Council: Will Rogers Memorial Hospital; Washington, D.C. Variety Club, Tent No. 11, bd. of gov. 1959, 1st asst. chief. barker, 1964 & 71, chief barker 1965-66, 1972, and 1978-79, and bd. chmn., 1980; lecturer, Georgetown Univ., 1972-; Life Patron, Variety Clubs Int'l, 1978 Life Liner, Variety Clubs Intl.; member: Screen Actors Guild. 1994.

BROWN, BLAIR
Actress. b. Washington, DC, 1948. e. National Theatre Sch. of Canada.
THEATER: *NY:* The Threepenny Opera (NY Shakespeare Fest). Comedy of Errors, The Secret Rapture, Arcadia. Acted with Old Globe, San Diego; Stratford, Ont. Shakespeare Fest.; Guthrie Theatre MN; Arena Stage, Wash.; Long Wharf, New Haven; Shaw Festival.
PICTURES: The Paper Chase, The Choirboys, One-Trick Pony, Altered States, Continental Divide, A Flash of Green, Stealing Home, Strapless, Passed Away.
TELEVISION: *Series:* The Days and Nights of Molly Dodd, Talk It Over (discussion). *Mini-series:* Captains and the Kings, James Michener's Space, Arthur Hailey's Wheels, Kennedy. *Movies:*

The 3,000 Mile Chase, The Quinns, And I Alone Survived, The Child Stealer, The Bad Seed, Hands of a Stranger, Eleanor and Franklin: The White House Years, Extreme Close-Up, Those Secrets, Majority Rule, Rio Shannon (pilot), The Day My Parents Ran Away, Moment of Truth: To Walk Again, The Gift of Love. *Specials*: School for Scandal, The Skin of Your Teeth, Lethal Innocence.

BROWN, BRYAN
Actor. b. Sydney, Australia, June 23, 1947. m. actress Rachel Ward. Began acting professionally in Sydney. Worked in repertory theatres in England with the National Theatre of Great Britain. Returned to Australia to work in films while continuing stage work with Theatre Australia.
PICTURES: Love Letters From Teralba Road (debut, 1977), The Irishman, Weekend of Shadows, Newsfront, Third Person Plural, Money Movers, Palm Beach, Cathy's Child, The Odd Angry Shot, Breaker Morant, Blood Money, Stir, Winter of Our Dreams, Far East, Give My Regards to Broad Street, Parker (Bones), The Empty Beach, F/X, Tai-Pan, Rebel, The Good Wife, Cocktail, Gorillas in the Mist, Shall We Dance, FX2 (also co-exec. prod.), Sweet Talker (also co-wrote story), Prisoners of the Sun, Blame It on the Bellboy.
TELEVISION: *Mini-Series*: Against the Wind, A Town Like Alice, The Thorn Birds. Movies: The Shiralee (Aust.), Dead in the Water, Devlin, The Last Hit.

BROWN, CLANCY
Actor. b. Ohio. e. Northwestern Univ.
PICTURES: Bad Boys (debut, 1983), The Adventures of Buckaroo Banzai, The Bride, Highlander, Extreme Prejudice, Shoot to Kill, Season of Fear, Blue Steel, Waiting for the Light, Ambition, Past Midnight, Pet Sematary II, Thunder Alley, The Shawshank Redemption, Dead Man Walking, Donor Unknown, Female Perversions.
TELEVISION: *Series*: Earth 2. *Movies*: Johnny Ryan, Love Lies & Murder, Cast a Deadly Spell, Desperate Rescue: The Cathy Mahone Story, Bloodlines, Last Light.

BROWN, DAVID
Executive, Producer. b. New York, NY, July 28, 1916. m. writer-editor Helen Gurley Brown. e. Stanford U., A.B., 1936; Columbia U. Sch. of Journalism, M.S., 1937. Apprentice reporter, copy-editing, San Francisco News & Wall Street Journal; 1936; night ed. asst. drama critic, Fairchild Publications, N.Y., 1937-39; edit. dir. Milk Research Council, N.Y., 1939-40; assoc. ed., Street & Smith Publ., N.Y., 1940-43; assoc. ed., exec. ed., then ed.-in-chief, Liberty Mag., N.Y., 1943-49; edit. dir., nat'l education campaign, Amer. Medical Assn., 1949; assoc. ed., mng. ed., Cosmopolitan Mag., N.Y., 1949-52; contrib. stories & articles to many nat'l mags.; man. ed., story dept., 20th-Fox, L.A., Jan., 1952; story ed. & head of scenario dept., 1953-56; appt'd. member of exec. staff of Darryl F. Zanuck, 1956; mem. of exec. staff, 20th-Fox studios, and exec. studio story editor, 1956-60; Prod. 20th-Fox Studios, Sept. 1960-62; Editorial v.p. New American Library of World Literature, Inc., 1963-64; exec. story opers., 20th Century-Fox, 1964-67; vp. dir. of story operations, 1967; exec. v.p., creative optns. and mem. bd. of dir., 1969-71. Exec. v.p., mem. bd. of directors Warner Bros., 1971-72; partner and director, The Zanuck/Brown Co., 1972-88. Pres., Manhattan Project Ltd., 1988-; mem., bd. of trustees, American Film Institute, 1972-80. Recipient with Richard D. Zanuck of the Mo. Pic. Acad. of Arts & Sciences' Irving G. Thalberg Memorial Award. Books: Brown's Guide to Growing Gray, Delacorte, Let Me Entertain You, Morrow, The Rest of Your Life is the Best of Your Life, Barricade.
PICTURES: Sssssss, The Sting (Academy Award for Best Picture, 1973), The Sugarland Express, The Black Windmill, Willie Dynamite, The Girl from Petrovka, The Eiger Sanction, Jaws, MacArthur, Jaws 2, The Island, Neighbors, The Verdict, Cocoon, Target, Cocoon: The Return, Driving Miss Daisy (exec. prod.), The Player, A Few Good Men, The Cemetery Club, Watch It, Canadian Bacon.

BROWN, GEORG STANFORD
Actor, Director. b. Havana, Cuba, June 24, 1943. Acted on stage with the New York Shakespeare Fest. in the 1960s. Gained fame as one of the rookie cops in the 1970s TV series, The Rookies, before turning to TV directing.
THEATER: All's Well That Ends Well, Measure for Measure, Macbeth, Murderous Angels, Hamlet, Detective Story.
PICTURES: The Comedians, Dayton's Devils, Bullitt, Colossus: The Forbin Project, The Man, Black Jack (Wild in the Sky), Stir Crazy, House Party 2.
TELEVISION: *Series*: The Rookies. *Movies*: The Young Lawyers, Ritual of Evil, The Rookies (pilot), Dawn: Portrait of a Teenage Runaway, The Night the City Screamed, The Kid With the Broken Halo, In Defense of Kids, The Jesse Owens Story, Murder Without Motive. *Dir. of movies*: Grambling's White Tiger, Kids Like These, Alone in the Neon Jungle, Stuck With Each Other, Father & Son: Dangerous Relations. *Dir. of episodes*: Charlie's Angels, Starsky and Hutch, Dynasty, Hill Street Blues, Great American Hero, Cagney & Lacey (Emmy Award, 1986).

BROWN, HIMAN
M.P. Producer, Director, b. New York, NY, July 21, 1910. e. City Coll. of New York, St. Lawrence U. Radio & TV package prod. since 1927 include: Inner Sanctum, Thin Man, Bulldog Drummond, Dick Tracy, Terry and the Pirates, Joyce Jordan MD, Grand Central Station, CBS Radio Mystery Theatre, pres. Production Center, Inc.
PICTURES: That Night, Violators, The Stars Salute, The Price of Silence, The Road Ahead.

BROWN, JIM
Actor. b. St. Simons Island, GA, Feb. 17, 1936. e. Manhasset H.S., Syracuse U. For nine years played football with Cleveland Browns; in 1964 won Hickock Belt as Professional Athlete of the year. Founder, Black Economic Union.
PICTURES: Rio Conchos (debut, 1964), The Dirty Dozen, Ice Station Zebra, The Split, Riot, Dark Of The Sun, 100 Rifles, Kenner, El Condor, The Phynx, ... tick ... tick ..., The Grasshopper, Slaughter, Black Gunn, I Escaped from Devil's Island, The Slams, Slaughter's Big Rip-Off, Three the Hard Way, Take a Hard Ride, Adios Amigo, Mean Johnny Barrows, Kid Vengeance, Fingers, One Down Two to Go (also exec. prod.), Richard Pryor: Here and Now (exec. prod. only), Pacific Inferno (also exec. prod.), Abducted, The Running Man, I'm Gonna Git You Sucka, L.A. Heat, Crack House, Twisted Justice, The Divine Enforcer, Original Gangstas, Mars Attacks.
TELEVISION: *Movie*: Lady Blue.

BROWN, WILLIAM
Executive. b. Ayr, Scotland, June 24, 1929. e. Ayr Acad., U. of Edinburgh, where graduated Bachelor of Commerce, 1950. Served to Lt., Royal Artillery, 1950-52. Sales mgr. for Scotland Television Ltd. in London, 1958-61, sales dir. 1961-63. Deputy mng. dir. of Scottish Television Ltd. at Glasgow 1963-66, mng. dir. 1966-90. Deputy chmn. 1974-91. Chmn. from 1991. Chmn. Scottish Amicable Life Assurance Society Ltd., 1989-94. Dir., Radio Clyde (now Scottish Radio Holdings) 1973-. Chmn., Scottish Arts Council, 1992-. Dir.: ITN, 1972-77, 1987-90; Channel 4 Co Ltd. 1980-84; Scottish Opera Theatre Royal Ltd. 1974-90. Chmn.: Council, Indept. TV Cos. Assn. 1978-80. C.B.E., 1971. Ted Willis Award 1982. Gold Medal, Royal TV Society 1984. Hon. Doctorates: Edinburgh U. (1990), Strathclyde U. (1992).

BROWNE, ROSCOE LEE
Actor, Director, Writer. b. Woodbury, NJ, May 2, 1925. e. Lincoln U., PA; postgraduate studies in comparative literature and French at Middlebury Coll., VT, Columbia U., N.Y. Taught French and lit. at Lincoln U. until 1952. National sales rep. for Schenley Import Corp. 1946-56; United States' intl. track star and a member of ten A.A.U. teams. Twice American champion in the 1000-yard indoor competition, twice all-American and, in 1951 in Paris, ran the fastest 800 meters in the world for that year. Professional acting debut, 1956, in Julius Caesar at the NY Shakespeare Fest.; published poet and short story writer. Trustee: Millay Colony Arts, NY; Los Angeles Free Public Theatre.
THEATER: *NY*: The Ballad of the Sad Cafe, The Cool World, General Seeger, Tiger Tiger Burning Bright!, The Old Glory, A Hand Is on the Gate (dir., actor), My One and Only. Off-Broadway: The Connection, The Blacks, Aria da Capo, Benito Cereno (Obie Award), Joe Turner's Come and Gone (L.A., S.F., Pittsburgh), Two Trains Running.
PICTURES: The Connection (debut, 1961), Black Like Me, The Comedians, Uptight, Topaz, The Liberation of L. B. Jones, Cisco Pike, The Cowboys, The World's Greatest Athlete, Superfly T.N.T., The Ra Expeditions (narrator), Uptown Saturday Night, Logan's Run, Twilight's Last Gleaming, Nothing Personal, Legal Eagles, Jumpin' Jack Flash, Oliver & Company (voice), Moon 44, The Mambo Kings, Naked in New York, Brother Minister: The Assassination of Malcolm X (narrator), Babe (voice), The Pompatus of Love, Last Summer in the Hamptons.
TELEVISION: *Series*: McCoy, Miss Winslow and Son, Soap, Falcon Crest. *Movies*: The Big Ripoff, Dr. Scorpion, Lady in a Corner, Columbo: Rest in Peace Mrs. Columbo, Meeting of Minds (Peabody Award), A Connecticut Yankee in King Arthur's Court (Peabody Award). *Guest*: All in the Family, Maude, Barney Miller, Soap, Head of the Class, The Cosby Show (Emmy Award, 1986), Falcon Crest. *Mini-Series*: King, Space.

BROWNING, KIRK
TV Director. b. New York, NY, March 28, 1921. e. Brooks School, Andover, MA, Avon Old Farms, Avon, CT., and Cornell U. 1940. Reporter for News-Tribune in Waco, TX; with American Field Service, 1942-45; United States' intl. copywriter for Franklin Spier, 1945-48; became floor mgr. NBC-TV 1949; app't asst. dir. NBC-TV Opera Theatre in 1951 directing NBC Opera Theatre, TV Recital Hall, and Toscanini Simulcasts.
TELEVISION: Trial of Mary Lincoln, Jascha Heifetz Special, Harry and Lena, NBC Opera Theatre, Producers Showcase, Evening with Toscanini, Bell Telephone, The Flood, Beauty and the Beast, Lizzie Borden, World of Carl Sandburg, La Gioconda (Emmy Award, 1980), Big Blonde, Working, Ian McKellan Acting Shakespeare, Fifth of July, Alice in Wonderland, Live From the Met—Centennial.

BROWNLOW, KEVIN
Film Historian, Writer, Director, Film Editor. b. Crowborough, Eng., June 2, 1938. e. University College Sch. Asst. ed./editor, World Wide Pictures, London, 1955-61; film editor, Samaritan Films, 1961-65; film editor, Woodfall Films, 1965-68. Director, Thames Television 1975-90. Dir., Photoplay Productions 1990-present.
PICTURES: It Happened Here (dir. with Andrew Mollo) 1964, Charge of the Light Brigade (editor), Winstanley (with Andrew Mollo), Napoleon (restoration of 1927 film, re-released 1980).
TELEVISION: Charm of Dynamite (dir., ed.), All with David Gill: Hollywood (dir., writer), Unknown Chaplin (dir., prod.; Emmy Award), Buster Keaton: A Hard Act to Follow (prod.; 2 Emmy Awards), Harold Lloyc—The Third Genius, D.W. Griffith: Father of Film, Cinema Europe–The Other Hollywood.
AUTHOR: How It Happened Here (1968), The Parade's Gone By... (1968), Adventures with D.W. Griffith (editor, 1973), The War the West and the Wilderness (1979), Hollywood: The Pioneers (1980), Napoleon: Abel Gance's Classic Film (1983), Behind the Mask of Innocence (1990), David Lean–A Biography (1996).

BRUBAKER, JAMES D.
Producer. b. Hollywood, CA, March 30, 1937. e. Eagle Rock H.S. Transportation coordinator for 15 years before becoming unit prod. mgr., 1978-84. Then assoc. prod., exec. prod. & prod.
PICTURES: Assoc. Prod.: True Confessions, Rocky III, Rhinestone. Unit Proc. Mgr.: New York New York, Comes a Horseman, Uncle Joe Shannon, Rocky II, Raging Bull, True Confessions (also assoc. prod.), Rocky III (also assoc. prod.), Staying Alive, Rhinestone (also assoc. prod.), K-9, Problem Child, Mr. Baseball. Exec. Prod.: The Right Stuff, Beer, Rocky IV, Cobra, Over the Top, Problem Child (also prod. mgr.), Brain Donors (also prod. mgr.), A Walk in the Clouds.
TELEVISION: Movie: Running Mates (prod.)

BRUCE, BRENDA
Actress. b. Manchester, England, 1922. e. privately. London stage debut: 1066 and All That.
THEATER: Gently Does It (1953), This Year Next Year, Happy Days, Woman in a Dressing Gown, Victor Eh!, Merry Wives of Windsor, The Revenger's Tragedy, Little Murders, Winter's Tale, Pericles, Twelfth Night, Hamlet.
PICTURES: Millions Like Us (debut, 1944), Night Boat to Dublin, I See a Dark Stranger (The Adventuress), They Came to a City, Carnival, Piccadilly Incident, While the Sun Shines, When the Bough Breaks, My Brother's Keeper, Don't Ever Leave Me, The Final Test, Law and Disorder, Behind the Mask, Peeping Tom, Nightmare, The Uncle, That'll Be the Day.
TELEVISION: Mary Britton series, Nearer to Heaven, Wrong Side of the Park, The Lodger, The Monkey and the Mohawk, Love Story, A Piece of Resistance, Give the Clown His Supper, Knock on Any Door, The Browning Version, Death of a Teddy Bear, Softly, Softly, The Girl, Happy, Family at War, Budgie.

BRUCKHEIMER, BONNIE
Producer. b. Brooklyn, NY. Started in advertising and public relations eventually working for treasurer of Columbia Pictures. Later worked as asst. to Arthur Penn and Ross Hunter. Became partner with Bette Midler in All Girl Productions, 1985.
PICTURES: Big Business (assoc. prod.), Beaches, Stella, For the Boys, Hocus Pocus, Man of the House.
TELEVISION: Movie: Gypsy (exec. prod.).

BRUCKHEIMER, JERRY
Producer. b. Detroit, MI. e. U. of Arizona. Was art dir./prod. of TV commercials before becoming producer of films. 1983, formed Don Simpson/Jerry Bruckheimer Prods. with the late Don Simpson and entered into deal with Paramount Pictures to produce; company moved onto to Walt Disney in early 1990's.
PICTURES: Assoc. Prod.: The Culpepper Cattle Company, Rafferty and the Gold Dust Twins. Producer: Farewell My Lovely, March or Die, Defiance, American Gigolo, Thief, Cat People (exec. prod.), Young Doctors in Love, Flashdance, Thief of Hearts, Beverly Hills Cop, Top Gun, Beverly Hills Cop II, Days of Thunder, The Ref, Bad Boys, Crimson Tide, Dangerous Minds, The Rock.
TELEVISION: Exec Prod: Dangerous Minds (series).

BRYAN, DORA
Actress. b. Southport, Lancashire, Eng., Feb. 7, 1924. e. Council Sch. Stage debut 1935.
PICTURES: The Fallen Idol (debut, 1949), No Room at the Inn, Once Upon a Dream, Blue Lamp, Cure for Love, Now Barabas, The Ringer, Women of Twilight, The Quiet Woman, The Intruder, You Know What Sailors Are, Mad About Men, See How They Run, Cockleshell Heroes, Child in the House, Green Man, Carry on Sergeant, Operation Bullshine, Desert Mice, The Night We Got the Bird, A Taste of Honey, Two a Penny, Apartment Zero.
TELEVISION: Virtual Murder, Casualty, Presenting Frank Subbs, Heartbeat.

BUCHHOLZ, HORST
Actor. b. Berlin, Germany, Dec. 4, 1933. e. high school. In radio and stage plays. Started in films dubbing foreign movies. Work with Berlin's Schiller Theatre result in film debut in French film.
PICTURES: Marianne (debut, 1955), Emil and the Detectives, Himmel Ohne Sterne (Sky Without Stars), Regine, Teenage Wolfpack, The King in Shadow, The Confessions of Felix Krull, The Legend of Robinson Crusoe, Mompti, Endstation Liebe, Nasser Asphalt, Resurrection, Das Totenschiff, Tiger Bay (English-language debut, 1959), The Magnificent Seven, Fanny, One Two Three, Nine Hours to Rama, The Empty Canvas, Andorra, Marco the Magnificent, That Man in Istanbul, Johnny Banco, Cervantes (The Young Rebel), L'Astragale, How When and With Whom, La Sauveur, La Columba non deve Volare, The Great Waltz, The Catamount Killing, Women in Hospital, The Amazing Captain Nemo, From Hell to Victory, Avalanche Express, Aphrodite, Sahara, Fear of Falling, Code Name: Emerald, And the Violins Stopped Playing, Escape From Paradise, Aces: Iron Eagle III, Far Away So Close.
TELEVISION: Movies: The Savage Bees, Raid on Entebbe, Return to Fantasy Island, Berlin Tunnel 21, Family Affairs, The Lion of Granada, Come Back to Kampen. Mini-Series: The French Atlantic Affair.

BUCKLEY, BETTY
Actress. b. Fort Worth, TX, July 3, 1947. e. Texas Christian U., BA. Studied acting with Stella Adler. NY Stage debut: 1776 (1969); London debut: Promises Promises. Appeared in interactive short film Race for Your Life.
THEATER: Johnny Pott, What's a Nice Country Like You Doing in a State Like This?, Pippin, I'm Getting My Act Together and Taking It on the Road, Cats (Tony Award, 1983), Juno's Swans, The Mystery of Edwin Drood, Song and Dance, Carrie, The Fourth Wall, The Perfectionist, Sunset Boulevard (London/B'way; Olivier Award nom.).
PICTURES: Carrie (debut, 1976), Tender Mercies, Wild Thing, Frantic, Another Woman, Rain Without Thunder, Wyatt Earp.
TELEVISION: Series: Eight is Enough. Movies: The Ordeal of Bill Carney, Roses Are for the Rich, The Three Wishes of Billy Grier, Babycakes, Bonnie & Clyde: The True Story (Emmy nom.), Betrayal of Trust. Specials: Bobby and Sarah, Salute to Lady Liberty, Taking a Stand (Afterschool Special; Emmy nom.), Stephen Sondheim Carnegie Hall Gala. Mini-Series: Evergreen. Guest: L.A. Law, Tribeca.

BUCKLEY, DONALD
Executive. b. New York, NY, June 28, 1955. e. C.W. Post Coll, NY, Sch. of Visual Arts. Ad. mgr., United Artists Theatres, 1975-78; acct. exec., Grey Advertising, 1978-80. Joined Warner Bros. in 1980 as NY adv. mgr.; 1986, promoted to east. dir. of adv./promo. for WB; 1988, named eastern dir. of adv. and publicity. 1991, promoted to v.p., East Coast Adv. & Publicity. 1996, promoted to v.p., Advertising & Publicity/v.p. Warner Bros. On-Line.

BUJOLD, GENEVIEVE
Actress. b. Montreal, Canada, July 1, 1942. e. Montreal Conservatory of Drama. Worked in a Montreal cinema as an usher; American TV debut: St. Joan.
THEATER: The Barber of Seville, A Midsummer Night's Dream, A House...A Day.
PICTURES: La Guerre est Finie, La Fleur de L'Age, Entre La Mer et L'eau Douce, King of Hearts, The Thief of Paris, Isabel, Anne of the Thousand Days, Act of the Heart, The Trojan Women, The Journey, Kamouraska, Earthquake, Swashbuckler, Obsession, Alex and the Gypsy, Another Man Another Chance, Coma, Murder by Decree, Final Assignment, The Last Flight of Noah's Ark, Monsignor, Tightrope, Choose Me, Trouble in Mind, The Moderns, Dead Ringers, False Identity, Secret Places of the Heart, A Paper Wedding, An Ambush of Ghosts, Mon Amie Max.
TELEVISION: Specials: Saint Joan, Antony and Cleopatra. Movies: Mistress of Paradise, Red Earth White Earth.

BULLOCK, SANDRA
Actress. b. Arlington, VA, 1964. Raised in Germany; studied piano in Europe. e. East Carolina Univ., drama major. First prof. acting job in NY in Off-B'way prod. No Time Flat.
PICTURES: Who Shot Patakango?, Love Potion No. 9, When the Party's Over, The Vanishing, The Thing Called Love, Demolition Man, Speed, Me and the Mob, While You Were Sleeping, The Net, Two If by Sea, A Time to Kill, In Love and War.
TELEVISION: Series: Working Girl. Movies: The Preppie Murder, Bionic Showdown: The Six Million Dollar Man and the Bionic Woman, Jackie Collins' Lucky/Chances.

BURGHOFF, GARY
Actor. b. Bristol, CT, May 24, 1943. Winner of Student Hallmark Award while in high school, 1961. Also wildlife artist, with work exhibited in many U.S. galleries.
THEATER: NY: You're a Good Man Charlie Brown, The Nerd. Other: Finian's Rainbow, Bells Are Ringing, Sound of Music, The Boy Friend, Romanoff and Juliet, Whose Life Is It Anyway?

PICTURES: M*A*S*H*, B.S. I Love You, Small Kill (also co-dir.).
TELEVISION: *Series*: The Don Knotts Show, M*A*S*H (Emmy Award, 1977). *Guest*: Good Guys, Name of the Game, Love American Style, Fernwood 2-Night, Sweepstakes, Love Boat, Fantasy Island. *Movies*: The Man in the Santa Claus Suit, Casino. *Special*: Twigs.

BURKE, ALFRED
Actor. b. London, England, 1918.
PICTURES: Touch and Go, The Man Upstairs, The Angry Silence, Moment of Danger, The Man Inside, No Time To Die, Children of the Damned, The Nanny, One Day in the Life of Ivan Denisovitch, Law and Disorder, Yangtse Incident, Interpol, Bitter Victory.
TELEVISION: The Crucible, Mock Auction, Parole, No Gun, No Guilt, The Big Knife, Parnell, The Strong Are Lonely, Home of the Brave, The Birthday Party, The Watching Eye, Public Eye (series).

BURKE, DELTA
Actress. b. Orlando, FL, July 30, 1956. e. LAMDA. m. actor Gerald McRaney. Competed in Miss America contest as Miss Florida, prior to studying acting in England.
TELEVISION: *Series*: The Chisholms, Filthy Rich, 1st & Ten, Designing Women, Delta (also co-exec. prod.), Women of the House (also exec. prod.). *Movies*: Charleston, A Last Cry for Help, Mickey Spillane's Mike Hammer: Murder Me Murder You, A Bunny's Tale, Where the Hell's That Gold?!!? Love and Curses... And All That Jazz (also co-exec. prod.), Day-o.

BURNETT, CAROL
Actress, Singer. b. San Antonio, TX, April 26, 1933. Daughter is actress Carrie Hamilton. e. Hollywood H.S., UCLA. Introduced comedy song, I Made a Fool of Myself Over John Foster Dulles, 1957; regular performer Garry Moore TV show, 1959-62. Recipient outstanding commedienne award Am. Guild Variety Artists, 5 times; TV Guide award for outstanding female performer 1961, 62, 63; Peabody Award, 1963; 5 Golden Globe awards for outstanding comedienne of year; Woman of Year award Acad. TV Arts and Scis. Voted one of the world's 20 most admired women in 1977 Gallup Poll. First Annual National Television Critics Award for Outstanding Performance, 1977. Best Actress Award at San Sebastian Film Fest. for film A Wedding, 1978. Inducted Acad. of Television Arts and Sciences Hall of Fame, 1985. *Author*: Once Upon a Time (1986).
THEATER: *NY*: Once Upon a Mattress (debut, 1959; Theatre World Award), Fade Out-Fade In, Moon Over Buffalo. *Regional*: Calamity Jane, Plaza Suite, I Do I Do, Same Time Next Year.
PICTURES: Who's Been Sleeping in My Bed? (debut, 1963), Pete 'n' Tillie, The Front Page, A Wedding, H.E.A.L.T.H., The Four Seasons, Chu Chu and the Philly Flash, Annie, Noises Off.
TELEVISION: *Series*: Stanley, Pantomime Quiz, The Garry Moore Show (Emmy Award, 1962), The Entertainers, The Carol Burnett Show (1967-78; in syndication as Carol Burnett & Friends), Carol Burnett & Company, Carol & Company, The Carol Burnett Show (1991). *Specials*: Julie & Carol at Carnegie Hall, Carol and Company (Emmy Award for previous 2 specials, 1963), An Evening with Carol Burnett, Calamity Jane, Once Upon a Mattress, Carol + 2, Julie & Carol at Lincoln Center, 6 Rms Riv Vu, Twigs, Sills & Burnett at the Met, Dolly & Carol in Nashville, All-Star Party for Carol Burnett, Burnett Discovers Domingo, The Laundromat, Carol Carl Whoopi & Robin, Julie & Carol—Together Again, The Carol Burnett Show: A Reunion (also co-exec. prod.), Men Movies & Carol. *Movies*: The Grass Is Always Greener Over the Septic Tank, Friendly Fire, The Tenth Month, Life of the Party: The Story of Beatrice, Between Friends, Hostage, Seasons of the Heart. *Mini-Series*: Fresno. *Guest*: Twilight Zone, The Jack Benny Program, Get Smart, The Lucy Show, Fame, Magnum P.I.

BURNETT, CHARLES
Director, Writer, Cinematographer. b. Vicksburg, MI, 1944. e. LA Community Col., UCLA.
PICTURES: *Director*: Killer of Sheep (also prod., s.p., photog., edit.), My Brother's Wedding (also prod., s.p., photog.), To Sleep With Anger (also s.p.), The Glass Shield (also s.p.). Cinematographer: Bless Their Little Hearts (also s.p.), Guest of Hotel Astoria.

BURNS, GEORGE
Actor. r.n. Nathan Birnbaum. b. New York, NY, Jan. 20, 1896. In vaudeville as singer in children's quartet, later as roller skater, then comedian; formed team Burns & (Gracie) Allen, 1925, marrying Gracie in 1926. Team performed many years on Keith and Orpheum vaudeville circuits, then on screen in Paramount short subjects, on radio in England; in 1930 began long career on American radio. Feature picture debut 1932 in The Big Broadcast. Books: I Love Her—That's Why, Living It Up: Or They Still Love Me in Altoona!, How to Live to Be 100—or More!: The Ultimate Diet, Sex and Exercise Book, Dr. Burns' Prescription for Happiness, Dear George: Advice and Answers from America's Leading Expert on Everything from A to Z, Gracie, Wisdom of the 90s.

PICTURES: The Big Broadcast (debut, 1932), International House, College Humor, Six of a Kind, We're Not Dressing, Many Happy Returns, Love in Bloom, Here Comes Cookie, Big Broadcast of 1936, Big Broadcast of 1937, College Swing, College Holiday, A Damsel in Distress, College Swing, Honolulu, The Solid Gold Cadillac (narrator), The Sunshine Boys (Academy Award for Best Supporting Actor, 1975), Oh God!, Sgt. Pepper's Lonely Hearts Club Band, Movie Movie, Just You and Me Kid, Oh God! Book II, Oh God! You Devil, 18 Again, Radioland Murders.
TELEVISION: *Series*: The George Burns & Gracie Allen Show (1950-58), The George Burns Show, Wendy and Me, George Burns Comedy Week. *Specials*: Grandpa Will You Run With Me?, Disney's Magic in the Magic Kingdom (host), A Conversation With... George Burns (Emmy Award, 1990); and numerous others.
(d. March 1, 1996)

BURNS, KEN
Producer, Director, Cinematographer, Writer. b. July 29, 1953. e. Hampshire Col. Producer and director of the following documentaries: Brooklyn Bridge (also photog., edit.; Acad. Award nom.), The Shakers: Hands to Work Hearts to God (also co-writer), The Statue of Liberty (also photog.; Acad. Award nom.), Huey Long (also co-writer), Thomas Hart Benton (also photog.), The Congress, The Civil War (also photog., co-writer; numerous awards incl. Peabody and Emmy), Lindbergh (co-prod. only), Empire of the Air: The Men Who Made Radio (also photog., music dir.), Baseball (co- writer, prod., dir.). Co-author: Shakers: Hands to Work Hearts to God: The History and Visions of the United States's Second Appearance from 1774 to Present, The Civil War: An Illustrated History, Baseball: An Illustrated History. Appeared in film Gettysburg.

BURNS, RALPH
Musical Conductor, Composer. b. Newton, MA, June 29, 1922.
PICTURES: Lenny, Cabaret (Academy Award, 1972), Lucky Lady, New York New York, Movie Movie, All That Jazz (Academy Award, 1979), Urban Cowboy, Annie, My Favorite Year, Jinxed, Kiss Me Goodbye, Star 80, National Lampoon's Vacation, Perfect, Bert Rigby You're a Fool.
TELEVISION: *Specials*: Baryshnikov on Broadway, Liza and Goldie Special. *Movies*: Ernie Kovacs—Between the Laughter, After the Promise, Sweet Bird of Youth.

BURRILL, TIMOTHY
Producer, Executive. b. North Wales, June 8, 1931. e. Eton Coll., Sorbonne U., Paris. Grenadier Guards 2 yrs, then London Shipping Co. Ent. m.p. ind. as resident prod. mgr. Samaritan Films working on shorts, commercials, documentaries, 1954. Ass't. dir.: The Criminal, The Valiant Years (TV series), On The Fiddle, Reach for Glory, War Lover. Prod. mgr: The Cracksman, Night Must Fall, Lord Jim, Yellow Rolls Royce, The Heroes of Telemark, Resident prod. with World Film Services. 1970 prod. two films on pop music for Anglo-EMI. 1972 first prod. administrator National Film School in U.K. 1974 Post prod. administrator The Three Musketeers. Prod. TV Special The Canterville Ghost; assoc. prod, That Lucky Touch; UK Administrator, The Prince and the Pauper; North American Prod. controller, Superman; 1974-1983 council member of BAFTA; mng. dir., Allied Stars (Breaking Glass, Chariots of Fire); 1979-80 V. chmn. Film BAFTA; 1980-83 chmn. BAFTA; 1981-92, Gov. National Film School, executive BFTPA mem. Cinematograph Films Council. 1982-88 Gov Royal National Theatre; 1987-93, chmn., Film Asset Developments, Formed Burrill Prods, 1979-; chmn. First Film Foundation. Exec. member PACT, 1991. Vice-chmn. (film) PACT, 1993.
PICTURES: *Prod.*: Privilege, Oedipus the King, A Severed Head, Three Sisters, Macbeth (assoc. prod.), Alpha Beta, Tess (co-prod.), Pirates of Penzance (co-prod.), Supergirl, The Fourth Protocol, To Kill a Priest (co-prod.), Return of the Musketeers (tv in U.S.), Valmont, The Rainbow Thief, The Lover, Bitter Moon, Sweet Killing.

BURROWS, JAMES
Director, Producer. b. Los Angeles, CA, Dec. 30, 1940. e. Oberlin, B.A.; Yale, M.F.A. Son of late Abe Burrows, composer, writer, director. Directed off-B'way.
PICTURE: Partners.
TELEVISION: *Series* (director): Mary Tyler Moore, Bob Newhart, Laverne and Shirley, Rhoda, Phyllis, Tony Randall Show, Betty White Show, Fay, Taxi (2 Emmy Awards: 1980, 1981), Lou Grant, Cheers (also prod.; 4 Emmy Awards as producer: 1983, 1984, 1989, 1991; 2 Emmy Awards as director: 1983, 1991), Dear John, Night Court, All is Forgiven (also exec. prod.), The Fanelli Boys, Frasier (Emmy Award, 1994), Friends, NewsRadio, Men Behaving Badly, Chicago Sons. *Movie*: More Than Friends.

BURROWS, ROBERTA
Executive. e. Brandeis U; Academia, Florence, Italy. Career includes freelance writing for natl. magazines: GQ, Italian Bazaar, US, Family Circle, and post as dir. of pub. for Howard Stein Enterprises and with Rogers & Cowan and Billings

Associates. Joined Warner Bros. as sr. publicist 1979; named dir. east coast publicity, 1986. Resigned 1989 to dev. novelty products. Proj. co-ordinator at Orion Pictures in NY for The Silence of the Lambs, Little Man Tate, Married to It, Bill & Ted's Bogus Journey. Columnist, Max publication.

BURSTYN, ELLEN
Actress. b. Detroit, MI, Dec. 7, 1932. r.n. Edna Rae Gilhooley. Majored in art; was fashion model in Texas at 18. Moved to Montreal as dancer; then N.Y. to do TV commercials (under the name of Ellen McRae), appearing for a year on the Jackie Gleason show (1956-57). In 1957 turned to dramatics and won lead in B'way show, Fair Game. Then went to Hollywood to do TV and films. Returned to N.Y. to study acting with Lee Strasberg; worked in TV serial, The Doctors. Co-artistic dir. of Actor's Studio. 1982-88. Pres. Actors Equity Assn. 1982-85. On 2 panels of Natl. Endowment of the Arts and Theatre Advisory Council (NY).
THEATER: NY: Same Time Next Year (Tony Award, 1975), 84 Charing Cross Road, Shirley Valentine, Shimada. L.A.: Love Letters. Regional: The Trip to Bountiful.
PICTURES: As Ellen McRae: For Those Who Think Young (debut, 1964), Goodbye Charlie, Pit Stop. As Ellen Burstyn: Tropic of Cancer, Alex in Wonderland, The Last Picture Show, The King of Marvin Gardens, The Exorcist, Harry and Tonto, Alice Doesn't Live Here Anymore (Academy Award, 1974), Providence, A Dream of Passion, Same Time Next Year, Resurrection, Silence of the North, The Ambassador, In Our Hands, Twice in a Lifetime, Hanna's War, Dying Young, The Color of Evening, The Cemetery Club, When a Man Loves a Woman, Roommates, The Baby-sitters Club, How to Make an American Quilt, The Spitfire Grill.
TELEVISION: Movies: Thursday's Game, The People Vs. Jean Harris, Surviving, Act of Vengeance, Into Thin Air, Something in Common, Pack of Lies, When You Remember Me, Mrs. Lambert Remembers Love, Taking Back My Life: The Nancy Ziegenmeyer Story, Grand Isle, Shattered Trust: The Shari Karney Story, Getting Out, Getting Gotti, Trick of the Eye, My Brother's Keeper, Follow the River. Special: Dear America: Letters Home From Vietnam (reader). Series: The Doctors, The Ellen Burstyn Show. Guest: Cheyenne, Dr. Kildare, 77 Sunset Strip, Perry Mason, The Iron Horse.

BURTON, KATE
Actress. b. Geneva, Switzerland, Sept. 10, 1957. e. Brown Univ. (B.A.), Yale Drama Sch. Daughter of late Richard Burton. m. stage manager Michael Ritchie. Worked at Yale Repertory Theatre, Hartford, Stage Co., the Hartman, Huntington Theatre, Williamstown, Berkshire Theatre festivals, The O'Neil Playwright's Conference, Pray Street Theatre.
THEATER: Present Laughter (debut, 1982; Theatre World Award), Alice in Wonderland, Winners, The Accrington Pals, Doonesbury, The Playboy of the Western World, Wild Honey, Measure For Measure, Some Americans Abroad (Drama Desk nom.), Jake's Women, London Suite, Company.
PICTURES: Big Trouble in Little China (debut, 1986), Life With Mikey, August, First Wives Club.
TELEVISION: Mini-Series: Ellis Island, Evergreen. Movies: Alice in Wonderland, Uncle Tom's Cabin, Love Matters, Mistrial, Notes For My Daughter. Series: Home Fires, Monty.

BURTON, LEVAR
Actor. b. Landstuhl, W. Germany, Feb. 16, 1957. e. U. of Southern California. Signed to play role of Kunta Kinte in TV mini-series, Roots, while still in school. Has hosted Public TV children's shows, Rebop, and Reading Rainbow.
PICTURES: Looking for Mr. Goodbar, The Hunter, The Supernaturals, Star Trek: Generations, Star Trek: Forst Contact.
TELEVISION: Mini-Series: Roots. Special: Almos' a Man. Movies: Billy: Portrait of a Street Kid, Battered, One in a Million: The Ron Leflore Story, Dummy, Guyana Tragedy: The Story of Jim Jones, The Acorn People, Grambling's White Tiger, Emergency Room, The Jesse Owens Story, A Special Friendship, Roots: The Gift, Firestorm: 72 Hours in Oakland, Parallel Lives. Series: Star Trek: The Next Generation, Reading Rainbow (PBS; host, co-exec. prod.).

BURTON, TIM
Director, Producer. b. Burbank, CA, Aug. 25, 1958. Cartoonist since grade school in suburban Burbank. Won Disney fellowship to study animation at California Institute of the Arts. At 20 went to Burbank to work as apprentice animator on Disney lot, working on such features as The Fox and the Hound, The Black Cauldron. Made Vincent, 6-minute stop-motion animation short on his own which was released commercially in 1982 and won several film fest. awards. Also made Frankenweenie, 29 minute live-action film. Appeared in film Singles. Wrote and illustrated children's book based on The Nightmare Before Christmas.
PICTURES: Director: Pee-wee's Big Adventure, Beetlejuice, Batman, Edward Scissorhands (also co-story), Batman Returns (also co-prod.), Ed Wood (also co-prod.), Mars Attacks (also prod.). Co-Prod.: The Nightmare Before Christmas (also story), Cabin Boy, James and the Giant Peach, Mars Attacks.

TELEVISION: Episode Director: Aladdin (Faerie Tale Theatre), Alfred Hitchcock Presents, Amazing Stories (Family Dog). Exec. Prod. for animated series: Beetlejuice, Family Dog.

BUSBY, Ann
Executive. Senior v.p., MCA Motion Picture Group.

BUSCEMI, STEVE
Actor. b. Brooklyn, NY, 1957. Started as standup comedian in New York City, also wrote and acted in numerous one-act plays in collaboration with Mark Boone Jr. Acted in many plays by John Jesurun and worked briefly with the Wooster Group; worked as fireman. Studied acting at Lee Strasberg Inst. in NY.
PICTURES: The Way It Is/Eurydice in the Avenue, No Picnic, Parting Glances, Sleepwalk, Heart, Kiss Daddy Good Night, Call Me, Force of Circumstance, Vibes, Heart of Midnight, Bloodhounds of Broadway, Borders, New York Stories (Life Lessons), Slaves of New York, Mystery Train, Tales from the Dark Side, Miller's Crossing, King of New York, Zandalee, Barton Fink, Billy Bathgate, Crisscross, In the Soup, Reservoir Dogs, Trusting Beatrice, Rising Sun, Twenty Bucks, Ed and His Dead Mother, The Hudsucker Proxy, Floundering, Airheads, Me and the Mob, Pulp Fiction, Billy Madison, Desperado, Somebody to Love, The Search for One-Eye Jimmy, Living in Oblivion, Things to Do in Denver When You're Dead, Pistolero, Fargo, Kansas City, Trees Lounge.
TELEVISION: Mini-Series: Lonesome Dove. Movie: The Last Outlaw. Guest: Miami Vice, The Equalizer, L.A. Law, Mad About You, Homicide: Life on the Streets.

BUSCH, H. DONALD
Exhibitor. b. Philadelphia, PA, Sept. 21, 1935. e. U. of Pennsylvania, physics, math, 1956; law school, 1959. 1960 to 1987 practiced law, anti-trust & entertainment. 1984, pres., Budco Theatres, Inc. 1975-87, pres., Busch, Grafman & Von Dreusche, P.C. 1987, pres. & CEO, AMC Philadelphia, Inc. Member: NATO chmn. (1990-91), chmn. emeritus, 1992; Showeast, gen. chmn., 1990-1. Will Rogers Memorial Fund (dir.). 1988, pres. of NATO, Pennsylvania. 1995, dir. Motion Picture Pioneers, Inc.

BUSEY, GARY
Actor, Musician. b. Goose Creek, TX, June 29, 1944. e. Coffeyville Jr. Coll. A.B., 1963; attended Kansas State Coll, OK State U. Played drums with the Rubber Band 1963-70. Also drummer with Leon Russell, Willie Nelson (as Teddy Jack Eddy).
PICTURES: Angels Hard as They Come (debut, 1971), Didn't You Hear?, Little Big Man, The Magnificent Seven Ride, The Last American Hero, Lolly Madonna XXX, Hex, Thunderbolt and Lightfoot, The Gumball Rally, A Star Is Born, Straight Time, Big Wednesday, The Buddy Holly Story (Natl. Society of Film Critics Award; Acad. Award nom., 1978), Foolin' Around, Carny, Barbarosa, D.C. Cab, The Bear, Insignificance, Stephen King's Silver Bullet, Let's Get Harry, Eye of the Tiger, Lethal Weapon, Bulletproof, Act of Piracy, Predator 2, My Heroes Have Always Been Cowboys, Hider in the House, Point Break, The Player, Under Siege, South Beach, The Firm, Rookie of the Year, Surviving the Game, Chasers, Breaking Point, Drop Zone, Man With a Gun, Black Sheep, Carried Away.
TELEVISION: Series: The Texas Wheelers. Guest: High Chaparral (debut, 1970), Gunsmoke, Saturday Night Live, The Hitchhiker (ACE Award). Movies: Bloodsport, The Execution of Private Slovik, The Law, Wild Texas Wind, Chrome Soldiers. Mini-Series: A Dangerous Life, The Neon Empire.

BUSFIELD, TIMOTHY
Actor. b. Lansing, MI, June 12, 1957. e. East Tennessee State U; Actor's Theatre of Louisville (as apprentice and resident). Founded Fantasy Theatre in Sacramento, 1986, a professional acting co., which performs in Northern CA schools, providing workshops on playwriting for children and sponsors annual Young Playwrights contest.
THEATER: Richard II, Young Playwrights Festival (Circle Rep.), A Tale Told, Getting Out (European tour), Green Mountain Guilds Children Theatre, Mass Appeal, The Tempest, A Few Good Men (B'way). Founded & co-prod. The "B" Theatre, 1992, prods. Mass Appeal, Hidden in This Picture.
PICTURES: Stripes, Revenge of the Nerds, Revenge of the Nerds II, Field of Dreams, Sneakers, The Skateboard Kid, Striking Distance, Little Big League, Quiz Show.
TELEVISION: Series: Reggie, Trapper John M.D., thirtysomething (Emmy Award, 1991; also dir. 3 episodes), Byrds of Paradise, Champs. Guest: Family Ties, Matlock, Paper Chase, Love American Style, After M.A.S.H, Hotel. Movies: Strays, Calendar Girl-Cop-Killer?: The Bambi Bembenek Story, Murder Between Friends, In the Shadow of Evil, In the Line of Duty: Kidnapped.

BUTTONS, RED
Actor. r.n. Aaron Chwatt. b. New York, NY, Feb. 5, 1919. Attended Evander Child H.S. in the Bronx. Singer at the age of 13; comic, Minsky's. Served in U.S. Army, during WWII; in Army stage prod. and film version of Winged Victory. Received Golden

Globe Award noms. for Harlow and They Shoot Horses Don't They?; Best Comedian Award for The Red Buttons Show. Performed in most major Variety nightclubs shows.
PICTURES: Winged Victory (1944, debut), 13 Rue Madeleine, Footlight Varieties of 1951, Sayonara (Academy Award fo Best Supporting Actor, 1957; also Golden Globe Award), Imitation General, The Big Circus, One Two Three, The Longest Day, Gay Purr-ee (voice), Five Weeks in a Balloon, Hatari!, A Ticklish Affair, Your Cheatin' Heart, Harlow, Up From the Beach, Stagecoach, They Shoot Horses Don't They?, Who Killed Mary What's 'er Name?, The Poseidon Adventure, Gable and Lombard, Viva Knievel!, Pete's Dragon, Movie Movie, C.H.O.M.P.S., When Time Ran Out..., 18 Again!, The Ambulance, It Could Happen to You.
TELEVISION: Series: The Red Buttons Show (1952-55), The Double Life of Henry Phyfe, Knots Landing. Movies: Breakout, The New Original Wonder Woman, Louis Armstrong: Chicago Style, Telethon, Vega$, The Users, Power, The Dream Merchants, Leave 'Em Laughing, Reunion at Fairborough, Alice in Wonderland, Hansel & Gretel.
oot Boy With Cheek, Hold It, The Admiral Had a Wife, Winged Victory, Tender Trap, Play It Again Sam, The Teahouse of the August Moon, Red Buttons on Broadway, Finian's Rainbow.

BUZZI, RUTH
Actress. b. Westerly, RI, July 24, 1939. e. Pasadena Playhouse Col. of Theatre Arts. On Country Music charts with You Oughta Hear the Song. Has received 5 Emmy nominations; Golden Globe winner, AGVA Variety Artist of the Year, 1977, Rhode Island Hall of Fame, Presidential commendation for outstanding artist in the field of entertainment, 1980, NAACP Image Award.
THEATER: Sweet Charity (Broadway), 4 off-Broadway shows incl. A Man's A Man, Little Mary Sunshine, Cinderella, Wally's Cafe, 18 musical revues and Las Vegas club act.
PICTURES: Record City, Freaky Friday, The Apple Dumpling Gang Rides Again, The North Avenue Irregulars, The Villian, Surf Two, Skatetown USA, Chu Chu and the Philly Flash, The Being, The Bad Guys, Dixie Lanes, Up Your Alley, Diggin' Up Business, My Mom's a Werewolf, It's Your Life Michael Angelo, The Trouble Makers (orig. title: The Fight Before Christmas).
TELEVISION: Series: Rowan & Martin's Laugh-In, The Steve Allen Comedy Hour, Donny & Marie, The Lost Saucer, Betsy Lee's Ghost Town Jamboree, Carol Burnett's The Entertainers, Days of Our Lives, Sesame Street; semi-regular on 12 other series including Flip, Tony Orlando & Dawn, That Girl, Glen Campbell's Goodtime Hour, Leslie Uggums Show, The Dean Martin Variety Hour; guest on many TV series and specials including Medical Center, Adam 12, Trapper John M.D., Love Boat, They Came from Outer Space, Major Dad, Alice, Here's Lucy, Saved by the Bell, etc. Movie: In Name Only. Many cartoon voice-over series and over 150 on-camera commercials.

BYGRAVES, MAX
Comedian, Actor. b. London, England, October 16, 1922. e. St. Joseph's R.C. School, Rotherhithe. After RAF service, touring revues and London stage. TV debut in 1953, with own show. Autobiography: I Wanna Tell You A Story, 1976. Novel: The Milkman's on His Way, 1977. Received O.B.E., New Year's Honours 1983.
PICTURES: Skimpy in the Navy (debut, 1949), Bless 'em All, Nitwits on Parade, Tom Brown's Schooldays, Charley Moon, A Cry from the Streets, Bobbikins, Spare the Rod, The Alf Garnett Saga.
TELEVISION: Roamin' Holiday (series).

BYRD, CARUTH C.
Production Executive. b. Dallas, TX, March 25, 1941. e. Trinity U, San Antonio. Multi-millionaire businessman, chmn. of Caruth C. Byrd Enterprises, Inc., who entered entertainment industry forming Communications Network Inc. in 1972. Was principal investor in film Santee (1972) and in 1973 formed Caruth C. Byrd Prods. to make theatrical features. 1983, chmn., Lone Star Pictures. 1987, formed Caruth C. Byrd Television. Formed Caruth C. Byrd Entertainment Inc. May, 1989. Concerts incl. Tom Jones, Natalie Cole, B.J. Thomas, Tammy Wynette, Seals & Croft, Eddie Rabbit, Helen Reddy, Jim Stafford, Tanya Tucker and many more.
PICTURES: Murph the Surf, The Monkeys of Bandapur (both exec. prod.), Santee, Sudden Death, Hollywood High II, Lone Star Country, Trick or Treats.
TELEVISION: Fishing Fever, Kids Are People Too, Tribute to Mom and Dad, Back to School, Texas 150: A Celebration Special.

BYRNE, DAVID
Actor, Singer, Director. b. Dumbarton, Scotland, May 14, 1952. Moved to Baltimore at 7. e. Rhode Island Sch. of Design studying photography, performance and video, and Maryland Inst. Coll. of Art 1971-72. Prod. and dir. music videos. Awarded MTV's Video Vanguard Award, 1985. Best known as the lead singer and chief songwriter of Talking Heads. Composed and performed original score for choreographer Twyla Tharp's The Catherine Wheel (B'way). Wrote music for Robert Wilson's The Knee Plays.

PICTURES: Stop Making Sense (conceived and stars in concert film), True Stories (director, s.p., narrator), The Last Emperor (music, Academy Award, 1987), Married to the Mob (music), Heavy Petting, Between the Teeth (also co-dir.). Also contributed music to such films as Times Square, The Animals' Film, King of Comedy, America is Waiting, Revenge of the Nerds, Down and Out in Beverly Hills, Dead End Kids, Cross My Heart.
TELEVISION: A Family Tree (Trying Times), Alive From Off-Center (also composed theme), Survival Guides; Rolling Stone Magazine's 20 Years of Rock and Roll.

BYRNE, GABRIEL
Actor. b. Dublin, Ireland, 1950. e. University Coll., Ireland. Worked as archaeologist, then taught Spanish at girls' school. Participated in amateur theater before acting with Ireland's Focus Theatre, an experimental rep. co. and joining Dublin's Abbey Theatre Co. Cast in long-running TV series the Riordans. Also worked with National Theater in London. Author: Pictures in My Head (1994).
PICTURES: On a Paving Stone Mounted, The Outsider, Excalibur, Hanna K, The Keep, Defence of the Realm, Gothic, Lionheart, Siesta, Hello Again, Julia and Julia, A Soldier's Tale, The Courier, Miller's Crossing, Shipwrecked, Dark Obsession (Diamond Skulls), Cool World, Point of No Return, Into the West (also assoc. prod.), A Dangerous Woman, In the Name of the Father (co-prod. only), Prince of Jutland, A Simple Twist of Fate, Trial by Jury, Little Women, The Usual Suspects, Frankie Starlight, Dead Man, Last of the High Kings (also co-s.p.)Mad Dog Time.
TELEVISION: Series: The Riordan's, Branken. Movies/ Specials: Wagner, The Search for Alexander the Great, Treatment, Joyce, Mussolini, Christopher Columbus, Lark in the Clear Air (also dir., writer), Buffalo Girls.

BYRNES, EDD
Actor. b. New York, NY, July 30, 1933. e. Harren H.S. Prof. debut, Joe E. Brown's Circus Show; appeared on stage in Tea and Sympathy, Picnic, Golden Boy, Bus Stop, Ready When You Are C.B., Storm in Summer.
PICTURES: Reform School Girl, Darby's Rangers, Up Periscope, Marjorie Morningstar, Yellowstone Kelly, Girl on the Run, The Secret Invasion, Wicked Wicked, Grease, Stardust, Go Kill and Come Back, Payment in Blood, Troop Beverly Hills.
TELEVISION: Series: 77 Sunset Strip, Sweepstake$. Has appeared in over 300 TV shows incl.: Matinee Theatre, Crossroads, Jim Bowie, Wire Service, Navy Log, Oh Susanna!, Throb, Rags to Riches, Murder She Wrote. Movies: The Silent Gun, Mobile Two, Telethon, Vega$, Twirl.

BYRON, KATHLEEN
Actress. b. London, England, Jan. 11, 1922. e. London U., Old Vic. co. student, 1942. Screen debut in Young Mr. Pitt, 1943.
PICTURES: Silver Fleet, Black Narcissus, Matter of Life and Death, Small Back Room, Madness of the Heart, Reluctant Widow, Prelude to Fame, Scarlet Thread, Tom Brown's Schooldays, Four Days, Hell Is Sold Out, I'll Never Forget You, Gambler and the Lady, Young Bess, Night of the Silvery Moon, Profile, Secret Venture, Hand in Hand, Night of the Eagle, Hammerhead, Wolfshead, Private Road, Twins of Evil, Craze, Abdication, One of Our Dinosaurs Is Missing, The Elephant Man, From a Far Country, Emma.
TELEVISION: The Lonely World of Harry Braintree, All My Own Work, Emergency Ward 10, Probation Officer, Design for Murder, Sergeant Cork, Oxbridge 2000, The Navigators, The Worker, Hereward the Wake, Breaking Point, Vendetta, Play To Win, Who Is Sylvia, Portrait of a Lady, Callan, You're Wrecking My Marriage, Take Three Girls, The Confession of Mariona Evans, Paul Temple, The Worker, The Moonstone, The Challengers, The Golden Bowl, The Edwardians, The New Life, Menace, The Rivals of Sherlock Holmes, The Brontes, On Call, Edward VII, Sutherland's Law, Crown Court, Anne of Avonlea, Heidi, Notorious Woman, General Hospital, North & South, Angelo, Within these Walls, Jubilee, Z Cars, Tales from the Supernatural, Secret Army, An Englishman's Castle, The Professionals, Forty Weeks, Emmerdale Farm, Blake Seven, The Minders, Together, Hedda Gabler, Nancy Astor, God Speed Co-operation, Take Three Women, Reilly, Memoirs of Sherlock Holmes, Moon And Son, The Bill, Casualty, Portrait of a Marriage, Gentlemen & Players.

BYRUM, JOHN
Writer, Director. b. Winnetka, IL, March 14, 1947. e. New York U. Film School. First job as gofer on industrial films and cutting dailies for underground filmmakers. Went to England where wrote 1st s.p., Comeback. From 1970-73, was in NY writing and re-writing scripts for low-budget films.
PICTURES: Writer: Mahogany, Inserts (also dir.) Harry and Walter Go to New York, Heart Beat (also dir), Sphinx, Scandalous, The Razor's Edge (also dir.), The Whoopee Boys (also dir.), The War at Home (also dir.).
TELEVISION: Movie: Murder in High Places (dir., writer). Series: Alfred Hitchcock Presents (1985), Middle Ages (creator, writer, exec. prod.), South of Sunset (creator, writer, exec. prod.), Winnetka Road (creator, writer, exec. prod.).

C

CAAN, JAMES
Actor. b. Bronx, NY, March 26, 1940. e. Hofstra U. Studied with Sanford Meisner at the Neighborhood Playhouse. Appeared off-B'way in La Ronde, 1961. Also on B'way in Mandingo, Blood Sweat and Stanley Poole.
PICTURES: Irma La Douce (debut, 1963), Lady in a Cage, The Glory Guys, Red Line 7000, El Dorado, Games, Countdown, Journey to Shiloh, Submarine X-1, The Rain People, Rabbit Run, T.R. Baskin, The Godfather (Acad. Award nom.), Slither, Cinderella Liberty, The Gambler, Freebie and the Bean, The Godfather Part II, Funny Lady, Rollerball, The Killer Elite, Harry and Walter Go To New York, Silent Movie, A Bridge Too Far, Another Man Another Chance, Comes a Horseman, Chapter Two, Hide in Plain Sight (also dir.), Thief, Bolero, Kiss Me Goodbye, Gardens of Stone, Alien Nation, Dick Tracy, Misery, The Dark Backward, For the Boys, Honeymoon in Vegas, The Program, Flesh & Bone, A Boy Called Hate, Things to Do in Denver When You're Dead, Bottle Rocket, Eraser, Bulletproof.
TELEVISION: Much series guest work (Naked City, Route 66, Wagon Train, Ben Casey, Alfred Hitchcock Presents, etc.) 1962-69. Movie: Brian's Song (Emmy nom.).

CACOYANNIS, MICHAEL
Producer, Director, Writer. b. Cyprus, June 11, 1922. Studied law in London, admitted to bar at age 21. Became a producer of BBC's wartime Greek programs while attending dramatic school. After acting on the stage in England, left in 1952 for Greece, where he made his first film, Windfall in Athens, with his own script. While directing Greek classical plays, he continued making films.
PICTURES: Director/Writer: Windfall in Athens (Sunday Awakening; debut, 1954), Stella, Girl in Black, A Matter of Dignity (The Final Lie), Our Last Spring (Eroica), The Wastrel, Electra, Zorba the Greek, The Day the Fish Came Out, The Trojan Women, Attila '74, Iphigenia, Sweet Country, Up Down and Sideways.

CAESAR, IRVING
Author, Composer, Publisher. b. New York, NY, July 4, 1895. e. City Coll. of New York. Abroad with Henry Ford on Peace Ship, WWI; songwriter since then, songs with George Gershwin, Sigmund Romberg, Vincent Youmans, Rudolph Friml and others; songwriter for stage, screen and radio, including Swanee, Tea for Two, Sometimes I'm Happy, I Want to Be Happy, Lady Play Your Mandolin, Songs of Safety, Songs of Friendship, Songs of Health and Pledge of Allegiance to the Flag.

CAESAR, SID
Actor. b. Yonkers, NY, Sept. 8, 1922. Studied saxophone at Juilliard School; then appeared in service revue Tars and Spars. Cast by prod. Max Liebman in B'way revue Make Mine Manhattan in 1948. Voted best comedian in M.P. Daily's TV poll, 1951, 1952. Best Comedy Team (with Imogene Coca) in 1953. Received Sylvania Award, 1958. Formed Shelbrick Corp. TV. 1959. Appeared in B'way musical Little Me (1962), Off-B'way & B'way revue Sid Caesar & Company (1989). Author: Where Have I Been? (autobiography, 1982).
PICTURES: Tars and Spars (debut, 1945), The Guilt of Janet Ames, It's a Mad Mad Mad Mad World, The Spirit Is Willing, The Busy Body, A Guide for the Married Man, Airport 1975, Silent Movie, Fire Sale, Grease, The Cheap Detective, The Fiendish Plot of Dr. Fu Manchu, History of the World Part 1, Grease 2, Over the Brooklyn Bridge, Cannonball Run II, Stoogemania, The Emperor's New Clothes.
TELEVISION: Series: Admiral Broadway Revue, Your Show of Shows (Emmy Award for Best Actor, 1952), Caesar's Hour (Emmy Award for Best Comedian, 1956), Sid Caesar Invites You (1958), As Caesar Sees It, The Sid Caesar Show. Movies: Flight to Holocaust, Curse of the Black Widow, The Munsters' Revenge, Found Money, Love Is Never Silent, Alice in Wonderland, Freedom Fighter, Side By Side, The Great Mom Swap. Guest: U.S. Steel Hour, G.E. Theatre, The Ed Sullivan Show, Carol Burnett Show, Lucy Show, That's Life, Love American Style, When Things Were Rotten, The Love Boat, Amazing Stories, others. Specials: Tiptoe Through TV, Variety—World of Show Biz, Sid Caesar and Edie Adams Together, The Sid Caesar Imogene Coca Carl Reiner Howard Morris Special, Christmas Snow.

CAGE, NICOLAS
Actor. b. Long Beach, CA, Jan. 7, 1964. r.n. Nicholas Coppola. Nephew of dir. Francis Ford Coppola. Joined San Francisco's American Conservatory Theatre at age 15. While attending Beverly Hills High School won role on tv pilot Best of Times.
PICTURES: Fast Times at Ridgemont High (debut, 1982; billed as Nicholas Coppola), Valley Girl, Rumble Fish, Racing with the Moon, The Cotton Club, Birdy, The Boy in Blue, Peggy Sue Got Married, Raising Arizona, Moonstruck, Vampire's Kiss, Fire Birds, Wild at Heart, Tempo di Mecidere (Time to Kill), Zandalee, Honeymoon in Vegas, Amos & Andrew, DeadFall, Red Rock

West, Guarding Tess, It Could Happen to You, Trapped in Paradise, Kiss of Death, Leaving Las Vegas (Academy Award, Chicago Film Critics Award, Nat'l Society of Film Critics Award; Golden Globe Award), The Rock.

CAINE, MICHAEL
Actor. r.n. Maurice Micklewhite. b. London, England, March 14, 1933. Asst. stage mgr. Westminster Rep. (Sussex, UK 1953); Lowestoft Rep. 1953-55. London stage: The Room, The Dumbwaiter, Next Time I'll Sing For You (1963). Author: Michael Caine's Moving Picture Show or: Not Many People Know This Is the Movies, Acting on Film, What's It All About? (autobiography, 1993). Awarded C.B.E., 1992. Video: Michael Caine—Acting on Film.
PICTURES: A Hill in Korea (debut, 1956; aka Hell in Korea), How to Murder A Rich Uncle, The Key, Two-Headed Spy, Blind Spot, Breakout (Danger Within), Foxhole in Cairo, Bulldog Breed, The Day the Earth Caught Fire, Solo for Sparrow, Zulu, The Ipcress File, Alfie (Acad. Award nom.), The Wrong Box, Gambit, Funeral in Berlin, Hurry Sundown, Woman Times Seven, Billion Dollar Brain, Deadfall, The Magus, Play Dirty, The Italian Job, The Battle of Britain, Too Late the Hero, The Last Valley, Get Carter, Kidnapped, Zee and Company (X,Y & Zee), Pulp, Sleuth (Acad. Award nom.), The Black Windmill, The Destructors (The Marseille Contract), The Wilby Conspiracy, Peeper, The Romantic Englishwoman, The Man Who Would Be King, Harry and Walter Go to New York, The Eagle Has Landed, A Bridge Too Far, The Silver Bears, The Swarm, California Suite, Ashanti, Beyond the Poseidon Adventure, The Island, Dressed to Kill, The Hand, Victory, Deathtrap, Educating Rita (Acad. Award nom.), Beyond the Limit, Blame It on Rio, The Jigsaw Man, The Holcroft Covenant, Hannah and Her Sisters (Academy Award for Best Supporting Actor, 1986), Water, Sweet Liberty, Mona Lisa, Half Moon Street, Jaws—The Revenge, The Whistle Blower, The Fourth Protocol (also exec. prod.), Surrender, Without a Clue, Dirty Rotten Scoundrels, A Shock to the System, Mr. Destiny, Bullseye!, Noises Off, The Muppet Christmas Carol, On Deadly Ground.
TELEVISION: Series: Rickles (1975). In more than 100 British teleplays 1957-63 incl. The Compartment, The Playmates, Hobson's Choice, Funny Noises with Their Mouths, The Way with Reggie, Luck of the Draw, Hamlet, The Other Man. Movies: Jack the Ripper, Jekyll and Hyde, Blue Ice, World War II: When Lions Roared.

CALHOUN, RORY
Actor. r.n. Francis Timothy McCown. b. Los Angeles, CA, Aug. 8, 1922. e. Santa Cruz H.S. Worked as logger, miner, cowpuncher, firefighter before becoming actor.
PICTURES: (as Frank McCown): Something for the Boys (debut, 1944), The Bullfighters, Sunday Dinner for a Soldier, Nob Hill, The Great John L, Where Do We Go From Here?; (as Rory Calhoun): The Red House, Adventure Island, That Hagen Girl, Miraculous Journey, Massacre River, Sand, Return of the Frontiersman, A Ticket to Tomahawk, County Fair, Rogue River, I'd Climb the Highest Mountain, Meet Me After the Show, With a Song in My Heart, Way of a Gaucho, The Silver Whip, Powder River, How to Marry a Millionaire, Yellow Tomahawk, River of No Return, A Bullet Is Waiting, Dawn at Socorro, Four Guns to the Border, The Looters, Ain't Misbehavin', Treasure of Pancho Villa, The Spoilers, Red Sundown, Raw Edge, Flight to Hong Kong, Utah Blaine, Hired Gun, The Domino Kid, The Big Caper, Ride Out for Revenge, Apache Territory, The Saga of Hemp Brown, Thunder in Carolina (Hard Drivin'), The Colossus of Rhodes, Marco Polo, Treasure of Monte Cristo (The Secret of Monte Cristo), Gun Hawk, The Young and the Brave, A Face in the Rain (also co-exec. prod.), Black Spurs, Young Fury, Operation Delilah, Finger on the Trigger, Our Man in Baghdad, The Emerald of Artatama, Apache Uprising, Dayton's Devils, Operation Cross Eagles, Night of the Lepus, Blood Black and White, Won Ton Ton the Dog Who Saved Hollywood, Mule Feathers, Kino the Padre on Horseback, Love and the Midnight Auto Supply, Just Not the Same Without You, Bitter Heritage, The Main Event, Motel Hell, Angel, Rollerblade Warriors, Avenging Angel, Hell Comes to Frogtown, Bad Jim, Fists of Steel, Pure Country.
TELEVISION: Series: U.S. Camera, The Texan, Capitol. Mini-Series: The Blue and the Gray, The Rebels. Movies: Flight to Holocaust, Flatbed Annie and Sweetie Pie: Lady Truckers. Guest: The Road Ahead, Day Is Done, Bet the Wild Queen, Zane Grey Theater, Killer Instinct, Land's End (pilot), Champion, Hart to Hart, Police Woman, Movin' On, Alias Smith & Jones.

CALLAN, MICHAEL
Actor, Singer, Dancer. b. Philadelphia, PA, Nov. 22, 1935. Singer, dancer, Philadelphia nightclubs; to New York in musicals including The Boy Friend and West Side Story; dancer at Copacabana nightclub; in short-run plays, Las Vegas: That Certain Girl, Love Letters.
PICTURES: They Came to Cordura (debut, 1958) The Flying Fontaines, Because They're Young, Pepe, Mysterious Island, Gidget Goes Hawaiian, 13 West Street, Bon Voyage, The Interns, The Victors, The New Interns, Cat Ballou, You Must Be Joking!, The Magnificent Seven Ride!, Frasier the Sensuous

Lion, Lepke, The Photographer, The Cat and The Canary, Record City, Double Exposure (also prod.), Chained Heat, Freeway, Leprechaun III.
TELEVISION: *Series*: Occasional Wife, Superboy. *Guest*: Murder She Wrote, Superboy, etc. *Movies*: In Name Only, Donner Pass: The Road to Survival, Last of the Great Survivors. *Mini-Series*: Blind Ambition, Scruples.

CALLEY, JOHN
Executive. b. New Jersey, 1930. Was dir. of nighttime programming and dir. of programming sales at NBC, 1951-57; prod. exec. & TV prod., Henry Jaffe Enterprises, 1957; in charge of radio & tv for Ted Bates Adv. Agency, 1958; 1960-69, Filmways Inc., exec. v.p. & prod.; 1970, exec. v.p. in chg. of worldwide prod., Warner Bros.; pres. of Warner Bros. 1975-80. Retired from industry for 13 yrs. 1993 appointed pres. of United Artists.

CALLOW, SIMON
Actor, Writer, Director. b. London, June 15, 1949. e. Queens, U. of Belfast, The Drama Centre. Originated role of Mozart in London premiere of Amadeus and Burgess/Chubb in Single Spies. Author: Being an Actor, Acting in Restoration Comedy, Charles Laughton: A Difficult Actor, Shooting the Actor, Orson Welles: The Road to Zanadu.
THEATER: *London*: Plumber's Progress, The Doctor's Dilemma, Soul of the White Ant, Blood Sports, The Resistible Rise of Arturo Ui, Amadeus, Restoration, The Beastly Beatitudes of Balthazar B, Titus Andronicus (Bristol Old Vic), Faust. Shakespeare's Sonnets. Director: Loving Reno, The Infernal Machine (also translator), Jacques and His Master (also trans.; *L.A.*), Single Spies, Shades, My Fair Lady (Natl. tour), Shirley Valentine (*London, NY*), Carmen Jones.
PICTURES: Amadeus, A Room With a View, The Good Father, Maurice, Manifesto, Postcards From the Edge, Mr. and Mrs. Bridge, The Ballad of the Sad Cafe (dir. only), Howards End (unbilled), Four Weddings and a Funeral, Street Fighter, Jefferson in Paris, Ace Ventura: When Nature Calls, James and the Giant Peach.
TELEVISION: Man of Destiny, La Ronde, All the World's a Stage, Wings of Song, The Dybbuk, Instant Enlightenment, Chance of a Lifetime (series), David Copperfield, Honour, Profit and Pleasure, Old Flames, Revolutionary Witness: Palloy.

CALVET, CORINNE
Actress. r.n. Corinne Dibos. b. Paris, France, April 30, 1925. e. U. of Paris School of Fine Arts, Comedie Francaise. On French stage and radio; screen debut in French films, then to U.S. in 1949. Author: Has Corinne Been a Good Little Girl?, The Kirlian Aura.
PICTURES: La Part de L'Ombre (debut, 1946), Nous ne Sommes pas Maries, Petrus, La Chateau de la Derniere Chance, Rope of Sand (U.S. debut), When Willie Comes Marching Home, My Friend Irma Goes West, Quebec, On the Riviera, Peking Express, Sailor Beware, Thunder in the East, What Price Glory?, Powder River, Flight to Tangier, The Far Country, So This Is Paris, The Adventures of Casanova (Sins of Casanova), The Girls of San Frediano, Four Women in the NIhgt, Bonnes a Tuer (One Step to Eternity), Napoleon, Plunderers of Painted Flats, Bluebeard's Ten Honeymoons, Hemingway's Adventures of a Young Man, Apache Uprising, Pound, Too Hot to Handle, Dr. Heckle and Mr. Hype, The Sword and the Sorcerer, Side Roads.
TELEVISION: *Movies*: The Phantom of Hollywood, She's Dressed to Kill, The French Atlantic Affair.

CAMERON, JAMES
Director, Writer. b. Kapuskasing, Ontario, Canada, Aug. 16, 1954. e. Fullerton Junior Col. (physics). 1990, formed Lightstorm Entertainment.
PICTURES: Piranha II—The Spawning (dir.), The Terminator (dir., s.p.), Rambo: First Blood Part II (co-s.p.), Aliens (dir., s.p.), The Abyss (dir., s.p.), Terminator 2: Judgment Day (dir., co-s.p., prod.), Point Break (exec. prod.), True Lies (dir., co-s.p., prod.), Strange Days (co-prod., co-s.p., story).

CAMERON, JOANNA
Actress, Director. r.n. Patricia Cameron. b. Aspen, CO, Sept. 20, 1951. e. U. of California, Sorbonne, Pasadena Playhouse, 1968. Guinness Record: Most network programmed TV commercials. TV Director: Various commercials, CBS Preview Special, closed circuit program host U.S.N., all TV equipped ships–actress and dir. Documentaries: Razor Sharp (prod., dir.), El Camino Real (dir., prod.).
PICTURES: How To Commit Marriage (debut), B.S. I Love You, Pretty Maids All in a Row.
TELEVISION: *Movies*: The Great American Beauty Contest, Night Games, It Couldn't Happen to a Nicer Guy, High Risk, Swan Song. *Series*: Isis. *Guest*: The Survivors, Love American Style, Daniel Boone, Mission Impossible, The Partners, Search, Medical Center, Name of the Game, The Bold Ones, Marcus Welby, Petrocelli, Columbo, Switch, MacMillan, Spiderman. *Specials*: Bob Hope Special, Bob Hope 25th NBC Anniversary Special; numerous commercials.

CAMERON, KIRK
Actor. b. Canoga Park, CA, Oct. 12, 1970. m. actress Chelsea Noble. Sister is actress Candace Cameron. Started doing TV commercials at age 9.
PICTURES: The Best of Times, Like Father, Like Son, Listen to Me.
TELEVISION: *Series*: Two Marriages, Growning Pains, Kirk. *Movies*: Goliath Awaits, Starflight: The Plane That Couldn't Land, A Little Piece of Heaven, Star Struck, The Computer Wore Tennis Shoes. *Specials*: The Woman Who Willed a Miracle, Andrea's Story. Ice Capades with Kirk Cameron.

CAMP, COLLEEN
Actress. b. San Francisco, CA, 1953. Spent 2 years as a bird trainer at Busch Gardens before being noticed by an agent and cast on TV. TV debut on The Dean Martin Show. Assoc. prod. on Martha Coolidge's film The City Girl. Sang several songs in They All Laughed and made Billboard charts with song One Day Since Yesterday.
PICTURES: Battle for the Planet of the Apes (debut, 1973), Swinging Cheerleaders, Death Game (The Seducers), Funny Lady, Smile, The Gumball Rally, Cats in a Cage, Game of Death, Apocalypse Now, Cloud Dancer, They All Laughed, The Seduction, Valley Girl, Smokey and the Bandit III, Rosebud Beach Hotel, The Joy of Sex, Police Academy II, Doin' Time, D.A.R.Y.L., Clue, Walk Like a Man, Illegally Yours, Track 29, Wicked Stepmother, My Blue Heaven, Wayne's World, The Vagrant, Un-Becoming Age, Sliver, Last Action Hero, Greedy, Naked in New York, Die Hard With a Vengeance, The Baby-sitter's Club.
TELEVISION: *Movies*: Amelia Earhart, Lady of the House, Sisterhood, Addicted to His Love, Backfield in Motion, For Their Own Good. *Mini-Series*: Rich Man Poor Man Book II. *Series*: Dallas. *Guest*: Happy Days, Dukes of Hazzard, WKRP in Cincinnati, Magnum PI, Murder She Wrote, Tales from the Crypt. *Guest*: George Burns Comedy Week. *Special*: Going Home Again.

CAMP, JOE
Producer, Director, Writer. b. St. Louis, MO, Apr. 20, 1939. e. U. of Mississippi, B.B.A. Acct. exec. McCann-Erickson Advt., Houston 1961-62; owner Joe Camp Real Estate 1962-64; acct. exec. Norsworthy-Mercer, Dallas 1964-69; dir. TV commercials; founder and pres. Mulberry Square Prods, 1971-present. Author: Underdog.
PICTURES: *Dir./Prod./Writer*: Benji, Hawmps, For the Love of Benji, The Double McGuffin, Oh Heavenly Dog, Benji the Hunted.
TELEVISION: *Specials*: The Phenomenon of Benji (dir., writer, prod.), Benji's Very Own Christmas Story (dir., prod., writer), Benji at Work (prod., writer), Benji at Marineland (dir., writer), Benji Zax and the Alien Prince (dir.).

CAMPANELLA, TOM
Executive. b. Houston, TX, 1944. e. City U. of NY. Joined Paramount Pictures 1968 as asst. business mgr.; later worked for corporate div. and Motion Picture Group. Named exec. dir., nat'l adv. 1979, made v.p., nat'l adv. 1982, appt. sr. v.p., adv., for M.P. Group. of Paramount, 1984. Appointed exec. v.p., adv. & promo., 1990.

CAMPBELL, BRUCE
Actor, Producer. b. Birmingham, MI, 1958.
PICTURES: The Evil Dead (debut, 1983; also exec. prod.), Crimewave (also co-prod.), Evil Dead 2 (also co-prod.), Maniac Cop, Moontrap, Darkman, Maniac Cop 2, Sundown: The Vampire in Retreat, Mindwarp, Lunatics: A Love Story (also prod.), Waxwork II: Lost in Time, Army of Darkness (also co-prod.), The Hudsucker Proxy, Congo.
TELEVISION: *Series:* The Adventures of Brisco County Jr.

CAMPBELL, GLEN
Actor, Singer. b. Delight, AK, April 22, 1936. After forming local band became studio guitarist in Hollywood on records for such performers as Frank Sinatra and Elvis Presley. Won two Grammy awards for record By the Time I Get to Phoenix, 1967. Appeared frequently on Shindig on TV.
PICTURES: The Cool Ones, True Grit, Norwood, Any Which Way You Can, Rock a Doodle (voice).
TELEVISION: *Series*: The Smothers Brothers Comedy Hour, The Glen Campbell Goodtime Hour, The Glen Campbell Music Show; many specials. *Movie*: Strange Homecoming.

CAMPBELL, MICHAEL L.
Executive. b. Knoxville, TN, Jan. 22, 1954. Worked for White Stores, Inc. in a management position until 1982. Founded first theatre venture, Premiere Cinemas in 1982. Premiere grew to 150 screens and was sold to Cinemark in 1989. Founded Regal Cinemas in 1989. President and CEO Regal Cinmeas, Inc which has more than 1200 screens. Named Coopers & Lybrand regional entreprenuer of the year, 1993. Dir. NATO and serves on NATO executive committee.

CAMPBELL, WILLIAM
Actor. b. Newark, NJ, Oct. 30, 1926. e. Feagin Sch. of Drama. Appeared in summer stock; B'way before film debut.
PICTURES: The Breaking Point (debut, 1950), Breakthrough, Inside the Walls of Folsom Prison, Operation Pacific, The People Against O'Hara, Holiday for Sinners, Battle Circus, Small Town Girl, Code Two, The Big Leaguer, Escape from Fort Bravo, The High and the Mighty, The Fast and the Furious, Man Without a Star, Cell 2455— Death Row, Battle Cry, Running Wild, Man in the Vault, Backlash, Love Me Tender, Walk the Proud Land, Eighteen and Anxious, The Naked and the Dead, Money Women and Guns, The Sheriff of Fractured Jaw, Natchez Train, Night of Evil, The Young Racers, The Secret Invasion, Dementia 13, Hush Hush Sweet Charlotte, Blood Bath, Track of the Vampire, Pretty Maids All in a Row, Black Gunn, Dirty Mary Crazy Larry.
TELEVISION: Series: Cannonball, Dynasty, Crime Story. Pilot: The Heat: When You Lie Down With Dogs. Movie: Return of the Six Million Dollar Man and the Bionic Woman.

CAMPION, JANE
Director, Writer. b. Wellington, New Zealand, 1955. e. Victoria Univ. of Wellington (BA, anthropology, 1975), Sydney Coll. of Arts (BA, painting, 1979). Attendend Australian Sch. of Film & TV in early 1980's, where she debuted as dir. & writer with short film Peel (1982; Palme d'Or at Cannes Film Fest., 1986). Other short films: A Girl's Own Story, Passionless Moments, After Hours, Two Friends.
PICTURES: Director-Writer: Sweetie (feature debut, 1989; Australian Film Awards for Best Director & Film; LA Film Critics New Generation Award, American Indept. Spirit Award), An Angel at My Table (Venice Film Fest. Silver Lion Award, Indept. Spirit Award), The Piano (Academy Award, WGA, LA Film Critics, NY Film Critics, & Natl. Society of Film Critics Awards for best screenplay; LA Film Critics & NY Film Critics Awards for best director; Cannes Film Fest. Award for best film), The Portrait of a Lady.

CANBY, VINCENT
Journalist, Critic. b. Chicago, IL, July 27, 1924. e. Dartmouth Coll. Navy officer during WWII. Worked on newspapers in Paris and Chicago. Joined Quigley Publications in 1951 in editorial posts on Motion Picture Herald. Reporter for Weekly Variety 1959-1965. Joined New York Times film news staff, 1965; named film critic, 1969. Author: Living Quarters (1975); End of the War (play, 1978); Unnatural Scenery (1979); After All (play, 1981); The Old Flag (1984).

CANNELL, STEPHEN J.
Writer, Producer. b. Los Angeles, CA, Feb. 5, 1942. e. U. of Oregon, B.A., 1964. After coll. worked at father's decorating firm for 4 years while writing scripts in evening. Sold 1st script for Adam 12, 1966. Asked to serve as head writer at Universal Studios. Chief exec. officer, Stephen J. Cannell Prods. TV prod. co. he formed 1979. Also formed The Cannell Studios, parent co. 1986. Natl. chmn., Orton Dyslexia Society. Received Mystery Writers award 1975; 4 Writers Guild Awards. Acted in films: Identity Crisis, Posse.
TELEVISION: The Rockford Files (creator, writer, prod.; Emmy Award), The Jordan Chance, The Duke, Stone, 10 Speed and Brownshoe, Nightside, Midnight Offerings, The Greatest American Hero, The Quest, Them. Prod.: The A-Team, Hardcastle and McCormick, The Rousters, Riptide, Brothers-in-Law, Creator/Prod.: Baa Baa Black Sheep, Richie Brockelman, Hunter, Wise Guy, 21 Jump Street, J.J. Starbuck, Sonny Spoon, Sirens (co-exec. prod.), Unsub (exec. prod., writer, pilot); Booker (exec. prod.), Top of the Hill (exec. prod.), Scene of the Crime (exec.-prod., creator), The Commish, The Hat Squad, Traps, Greyhounds (exec. prod., writer), Hawkeye, Marker (exec. prod., creator), Renegade (exec. prod., creator), U.S. Customs Classified (exec. prod., host).

CANNON, DYAN
Actress. r.n. Samille Diane Friesen. b. Tacoma, WA, Jan. 4, 1937. e. U. of Washington. Studied with Sanford Meisner. Modelled before becoming actress. Directed, produced and wrote short film Number One (Acad. Award nom.).
THEATER: B'way: The Fun Couple, Ninety-Day Mistress. Tour: How to Succeed in Business Without Really Trying.
PICTURES: The Rise and Fall of Legs Diamond (debut, 1960), This Rebel Breed, Bob & Carol & Ted & Alice (Acad. Award nom.), Doctors' Wives, The Anderson Tapes, The Love Machine, The Burglars, Such Good Friends, Shamus, The Last of Sheila, Child Under a Leaf, Heaven Can Wait (Acad. Award nom.), Revenge of the Pink Panther, Honeysuckle Rose, Coast To Coast, Deathtrap, Author Author, Caddyshack II, The End of Innocence (also dir., prod., s.p.), The Pickle.
TELEVISION: Mini-Series: Master of the Game. Movies: The Virginia Hill Story, Lady of the House, Having It All, Arthur the King, Jenny's War, Rock 'n' Roll Mom, Jailbirds, Christmas in Connecticut, Based on an Untrue Story, A Perry Mason Mystery: The Case of the Jealous Jokester. Guest: Playhouse 90.

CANNON, WILLIAM
Writer, Producer, Director. b. Toledo, OH, Feb. 11, 1937. e. Columbia Coll., B.A., 1959; M.B.A., 1962. Dir. Off-B'way, Death of a Salesman, Pirates of Penzance, 1960. Wrote, prod., dir., Square Root of Zero, Locarno and San Francisco Film Festivals, 1963-65; Distrib., Doran Enterprises, Ltd.; writer Knots Landing, Heaven on Earth, Author, Novel, The Veteran, 1974; Publisher, Highlife and Movie Digest, 1978; The Good Guys, 1987. Co-inventor: Cardz (TM), 1988.
PICTURES: Writer: Skidoo, Brewster McCloud, Hex.

CANOVA, DIANA
Actress. b. West Palm Beach, FL, June 1, 1952. Daughter of actress Judy Canova and musician Filberto Rivero. NY theater: They're Playing Our Song (1981). People's Choice award, favorite female performer, 1981.
THEATER: B'way revival of Company.
PICTURE: The First Nudie Musical.
TELEVISION: Series: Dinah and Her New Best Friends, Soap, I'm a Big Girl Now, Foot in the Door, Throb, Home Free. Guest: Ozzie's Girls (debut), Happy Days, Love Boat, Fantasy Island, Hotel, Chico and the Man, Barney Miller, Murder She Wrote. Movies: The Love Boat II, With This Ring, Death of Ocean View Park, Night Partners.

CANTON, ARTHUR H.
Motion Picture Producer. b. New York, NY. e. NYU, Columbia U. Capt. USAF. Pres., Canton-Weiner Films, indep. foreign films importers, 1947; Van Gogh (Academy Award for best 2-reel short subject, 1949); MGM Pictures, eastern div. publicity mgr., executive liaison, advertising-publicity, Independent Productions; public relations executive, v.p.; pres., Blowitz, Thomas & Canton Inc., 1964; pres., Arthur H. Canton Co. Inc.; prod. exec., Warner Bros., 1968-70; advertising-publicity v.p., Columbia Pictures, 1971; exec. v.p. of advertising and publicity, Billy Jack Productions, 1974-76. Co-founder of Blowitz & Canton Co. Inc., 1976, chmn of bd. Now pres. of Arthur H. Canton Co. Member Academy of Motion Picture Arts and Sciences.

CANTON, MARK
Executive. b. New York, NY, June 19, 1949. e. UCLA, 1978. v.p., m.p. dev., MGM; 1979, exec. v.p., JP Organization; 1980, v.p. prod., Warner Bros.; named sr. v.p., 1983 and pres. worldwide theatrical prod. div., 1985; v.p. worldwide m.p. production, 1989; appointed chmn. of Columbia Pictures, 1991. Promoted to chmn. of Columbia TriStar Motion Pictures, 1994. Resigned, 1996.

CAPRA, FRANK, JR.
Executive. Son of famed director Frank Capra. Served in various creative capacities on TV series (Zane Grey Theatre, Gunsmoke, The Rifleman, etc.). Associate producer on theatrical films (Planet of the Apes, Play It Again Sam, Marooned, etc.). Joined Avco Embassy Pictures, 1981, as v.p., worldwide production. In July, 1981, became pres. of A-E. Resigned May, 1982 to become indep. producer. Now with Pinehurst Industry Studios, NC.
PICTURES: Producer: Born Again, The Black Marble, An Eye for an Eye, Vice Squad, Firestarter, Marie. Exec. prod.: Death Before Dishonor.

CAPSHAW, KATE
Actress. b. Ft. Worth, TX, 1953. r.n. Kathleen Sue Nail. e. U. of Missouri. m. director Steven Spielberg. Taught school before moving to New York to try acting.
PICTURES: A Little Sex (debut, 1982), Indiana Jones and the Temple of Doom, Best Defense, Dreamscape, Windy City, Power, SpaceCamp, Black Rain, Love at Large, My Heroes Have Always Been Cowboys, Love Affair, Just Cause, Duke of Groove (short), How to Make an American Quilt.
TELEVISION: Series: The Edge of Night, Black Tie Affair. Movies: Missing Children: A Mother's Story, The Quick and the Dead, Her Secret Life, Internal Affairs, Next Door.

CARA, IRENE
Singer, Actress. b. New York, NY, March 18, 1959. Off-B'way shows include The Me Nobody Knows, Lotta. On B'way in Maggie Flynn, Ain't Misbehavin', Via Galactica. Received Academy Award for co-writing theme song from Flashdance, 1983.
PICTURES: Aaron Loves Angela, Sparkle, Fame, D.C. Cab, City Heat, Certain Fury, Killing 'em Softly, Paradiso, Busted Up, Maximum Security, Happily Ever After (voice).
TELEVISION: Series: Love of Life, The Electric Company. Mini-Series: Roots—The Next Generation. Movies: Guyana Tragedy, Sister Sister, For Us the Living. Special: Tribute to Martin Luther King, Jr.

CARDIFF, JACK
Cinematographer, Director. b. Yarmouth, Eng., Sept. 18, 1914. Early career as child actor, before becoming cinematographer, then dir. in 1958.

PICTURES: *Cinematographer*. A Matter of Life and Death (Stairway to Heaven), Black Narcissus (Academy Award, 1947), The Red Shoes, Scott of the Antarctic, Black Rose, Under Capricorn, Pandora and the Flying Dutchman, The African Queen, The Magic Box, The Master of Ballantrae, The Barefoot Contessa, The Brave One, War and Peace, Legend of the Lost, The Prince and the Showgirl, The Vikings, The Journey, Fanny, Scalawag, Crossed Swords (The Prince and the Pauper), Death on the Nile, Avalanche Express, The Fifth Musketeer, A Man a Woman and a Bank, The Awakening, The Dogs of War, Ghost Story, The Wicked Lady, Scandalous, Conan the Destroyer, Cat's Eye, Rambo: First Blood II, Blue Velvet, Tai-Pan, Million Dollar Mystery. *Director*: Intent to Kill (debut, 1958), Beyond This Place, Scent of Mystery, Sons and Lovers, My Geisha, The Lion, The Long Ships, Young Cassidy (co-dir.), The Liquidator, Dark of the Sun, Girl on a Motorcycle, Penny Gold, The Mutations, Ride a Wild Pony.
TELEVISION: *As cinematographer*. The Far Pavillions, The Last Days of Pompeii.

CARDINALE, CLAUDIA
Actress. b. Tunis, No. Africa, April 15, 1939. Raised in Italy. Studied acting at Centro Sperimentale film school in Rome. Debuted 1956 in short French film Anneaux d'Or.
PICTURES: Goha (feature debut, 1957), Big Deal on Madonna Street, The Facts of Murder, Upstairs and Downstairs, The Battle of Austerlitz, Il Bell' Antonio, Rocco and His Brothers, Senilita, Girl With a Suitcase, The Love Makers, Cartouche, The Leopard, 8 1/2, Bebo's Girl, The Pink Panther, Circus World, Time of Indifference, The Magnificent Cuckold, Sandra, Blindfold, Lost Command, The Professionals, Don't Make Waves, Mafia, The Queens, Day of the Owl, The Hell With Heroes, Once Upon a Time in the West, A Fine Pair, The Butterfly Affair, The Red Tent, The Legend of Frenchy King, Conversation Piece, Escape to Athena, The Salamander, Careless, Immortal Bachelor, History, The French Revolution, Hiver '54, L'abbe Pierre, Mother, 588 Rue Paradis, Women Only Have One Thing on Their Minds...
TELEVISION: Princess Daisy, Jesus of Nazareth.

CAREY, HARRY JR.
Actor. b. Saugus, CA, May 16, 1921. e. Newhall, CA, public school, Black Fox Military Acad., Hollywood. m. Marilyn Fix. Appeared in Railroads on Parade at 1939-40 NY World's Fair. Summer stock, Skowhegan, ME., with father; page boy, NBC, New York; U.S. Navy 1941-46.
PICTURES: Rolling Home (debut, 1946), Pursued, Red River, Three Godfathers, She Wore a Yellow Ribbon, Wagonmaster, Rio Grande, Copper Canyon, Warpath, Wild Blue Yonder, Monkey Business, San Antone, Island in the Sky, Gentlemen Prefer Blondes, Beneath the 12-Mile Reef, Silver Lode, The Outcast, Long Gray Line, Mister Roberts, House of Bamboo, The Great Locomotive Chase, The Searchers, The River's Edge, Rio Bravo, The Great Imposter, Two Rode Together, Alvarez Kelly, Bandolero, The Undefeated, Dirty Dingus Magee, Big Jake, Something Big, One More Train To Rob, Cahill: U.S. Marshal, Take a Hard Ride, Nickelodeon, The Long Riders, Endangered Species, Mask, Crossroads, The Whales of August, Cherry 2000, Illegally Yours, Breaking In, Bad Jim, Back to the Future Part III, The Exorcist III, Tombstone.
TELEVISION: *Movies*: Black Beauty, The Shadow Riders, Wild Times, Once Upon a Texas Train. *Guest*: Gunsmoke, Rifleman, Laramie, Wagon Train, Have Gun Will Travel, John Ford's America, Legends of the American West. Disney *Series*: Spin & Marty. *Special*: Wyatt Earp: Return to Tombstone.

CARIOU, LEN
Actor. b. St. Boniface, Manitoba, Canada, Sept. 30, 1939. e. St. Paul's Col.
THEATER: *NY stage*: House of Atreus, Henry V, Applause (Theatre World Award), Night Watch, A Sorrow Beyond Dreams, Up from Paradise, A Little Night Music, Cold Storage, Sweeney Todd—The Demon Barber of Fleet Street (Tony Award), Master Class, Dance a Little Closer, Teddy & Alice, Measure for Measure, Mountain, The Speed of Darkness, Papa.
PICTURES: A Little Night Music, One Man, The Four Seasons, There Were Times Dear, Lady in White, Never Talk to Strangers.
TELEVISION: *Movies*: Who'll Save Our Children?, Madame X, Surviving, Miracle on Interstate 880, Class of '61, The Sea Wolf, Witness to the Execution, Love on the Run, The Man in the Attic. *Specials*: The Master Builder, Juno and the Paycock, Kurt Vonnegut's Monkey House (All the King's Men).

CARLIN, GEORGE
Actor, Comedian. b. New York, NY, May 12, 1937. Stand-up comedian and recording artist; received 1972 Grammy Award for Best Comedy Album: FM & AM. Has released 15 comedy albums between 1960-90. Has guested on many TV shows including Talent Scouts, On B'way Tonight, Merv Griffin Show, Saturday Night Live. *Author*: Sometimes a Little Brain Damage Can Help (1984).
PICTURES: With Six You Get Eggroll, Car Wash, Americathon (narrator), Outrageous Fortune, Bill & Ted's Excellent Adventure, Bill and Ted's Bogus Journey, The Prince of Tides.

TELEVISION: *Series*: Kraft Summer Music Hall, That Girl, Away We Go, Tony Orlando and Dawn, Shining Time Station, The George Carlin Show. *Movies*: Justin Case, Working Trash. Appeared in 8 HBO comedy specials.

CARLINO, LEWIS JOHN
Writer, Director. b. New York, NY, Jan. 1, 1932. e. U. of Southern California. Early interest in theatre, specializing in writing 1-act plays. Winner of Obie award (off-B'way play). Won Rockefeller Grant for Theatre, the Int'l. Playwriting Competition from British Drama League, Huntington Hartford Fellowship.
THEATER: Cages, Telemachus Clay, The Exercise, Double Talk, Objective Case, Used Car for Sale, Junk Yard.
PICTURES: *Writer*. Seconds, The Brotherhood, The Fox (co-s.p.), A Reflection of Fear, The Mechanic (also prod.), Crazy Joe, The Sailor Who Fell From Grace With the Sea (also dir.), I Never Promised You a Rose Garden (co-s.p.), The Great Santini (also dir.), Resurrection, Class (dir. only), Haunted Summer.
TELEVISION: Honor Thy Father, In Search of America, Where Have All the People Gone?

CARLTON, RICHARD
Executive. b. New York, NY, Feb. 9, 1919. e. Columbia U., Pace Inst. Columbia Pictures 1935-41; U.S. Army 1941-45; National Screen Serv. 1945-51; Sterling Television 1951-54; U.M. & M. TV Corp. 1955; v.p. in charge of sales, Trans-Lux Television Corp., 1956; exec. v.p., Television Affiliates Corp., 1961; exec. v.p. Trans-Lux Television Corp.; v.p. Entertainment Div. Trans-Lux Corp., 1966. Pres., Schnur Appel, TV, Inc. 1970; Deputy Director, American Film Institute, 1973. Pres., Carlton Communications Corporation, 1982; exec. dir., International Council, National Academy of Television Arts and Sciences, 1983-93. Became writer/consultant, 1994.

CARMEN, JULIE
Actress. b. New York, NY, Apr. 4, 1954. Studied acting at Neighborhood Playhouse. On NY stage in The Creation of the Universe, Cold Storage, Zoot Suit. Also acted with INTAR and the New Conservatory Theater. Recipient of 1992 National Council of La Raza Pioneer Award.
PICTURES: Night of the Juggler, Gloria, Man on the Wall, Comeback, Blue City, The Penitent, The Milagro Beanfield War, Fright Night 2, Kiss Me a Killer, Paint It Black, Cold Heaven, In the Mouth of Madness.
TELEVISION: *Series*: Condo, Falcon Crest. *Movies*: Can You Hear the Laughter?: The Story of Freddie Prinze, Three Hundred Miles for Stephanie, She's in the Army Now, Fire on the Mountain, Neon Empire, Manhunt: Search for the Night Stalker, Billy the Kid, Drug Wars: The Cocaine Cartel, Finding the Way Home, Curacao.

CARMICHAEL, IAN
Actor. b. Hull, England, June 18, 1920. e. Scarborough Coll., Bromsgrove Sch. Stage debut: R.U.R. 1939. B'way debut: Boeing-Boeing (1965). One of the top ten British money making stars Motion Picture Herald Fame Poll 1957, 1958.
PICTURES: Bond Street (debut, 1948), Trottie True (Gay Lady), Mr. Prohack, Time Gentlemen Please, Ghost Ship!, Miss Robin Hood, Meet Mr. Lucifer, Betrayed, The Colditz Story, Storm Over the Nile, Simon and Laura, Private's Progress, The Big Money, Brothers in Law, Lucky Jim, Happy Is the Bride, Left Right and Center, I'm All Right Jack, School for Scoundrels, Light Up the Sky, Double Bunk, The Amorous Prawn, Hide and Seek, Heavens Above, The Case of the 44's, Smashing Time, The Magnificent Seven Deadly Sins, From Beyond the Grave, The Lady Vanishes, Dark Obsession (Diamond Skulls).
TELEVISION: New Faces, Twice Upon a Time, Passing Show, Tell Her The Truth, Lady Luck, Give My Regards to Leicester Square, Jill Darling, Don't Look Now, Regency Room, Globe Revue, Off the Record, Here and Now, The Girl at the Next Table, Gilt and Gingerbread, The Importance of Being Earnest, Simon and Laura, 90 Years On, The World of Wooster (series), The Last of the Big Spenders, The Coward Revue, Odd Man In, Bachelor Father (series), Lord Peter Wimsey (series), Alma Mater, Comedy Tonight, Song by Song, Country Calendar, Down at the Hydro, Obituaries, Strathblair, The Great Kandinsky. *Guest*: Under The Hammer, Bramwell.

CARNEY, ART
Actor. b. Mt. Vernon, NY, Nov. 4, 1918. Started as band singer with the Horace Heidt Orchestra. On many radio shows before and after war. Served in U.S. Army, 1944-45. Regular on Morey Amsterdam's radio show which eventually moved to television.
THEATER: The Rope Dancers. B'way: Take Her She's Mine, The Odd Couple, Lovers, The Prisoner of Second Avenue.
PICTURES: Pot o' Gold (debut, 1941), The Yellow Rolls Royce, A Guide for the Married Man, Harry and Tonto (Academy Award for Best Actor, 1974), W. W. and the Dixie Dancekings, Won Ton Ton the Dog Who Saved Hollywood, The Late Show, Scott Joplin, House Calls, Movie Movie, Ravagers, Sunburn, Going in Style, Defiance, Roadie, Steel, St. Helens, Take This Job and Shove It, Better Late Than Never, Firestarter, The Naked Face, The Muppets Take Manhattan, Night Friend, Last Action Hero.

TELEVISION: *Series*: The Morey Amsterdam Show, Cavalcade of Stars, Henry Morgan's Great Talent Hunt, The Jackie Gleason Show (1951-55; 2 Emmy Awards: 1953, 1954), The Honeymooners (Emmy Award, 1955), The Jackie Gleason Show (1956-57), The Jackie Gleason Show (1966-70; 2 Emmy Awards: 1967, 1968), Lanigan's Rabbi. *Guest*: Studio One, Kraft Theatre, Playhouse 90, Alfred Hitchcock Presents (Safety for the Witness), Sid Caesar Show, Twilight Zone (Night of the Meek), Bob Hope Chrysler Theater (Timothy Heist), Danny Kaye Show, Men From Shiloh, Batman, Carol Burnett Show, Jonathan, Winters Show, Faerie Tale Theatre (The Emperor's New Clothes). *Specials*: Peter and the Wolf, Harvey, Our Town, Charley's Aunt, Art Carney Meets the Sorcerer's Apprentice, Very Important People, Jane Powell Special: Young at Heart, Man in the Dog Suit, The Great Santa Claus Switch. *Movies*: The Snoop Sisters, Death Scream, Katherine, Letters From Frank, Terrible Joe Moran (Emmy Award, 1984), The Night They Saved Christmas, A Doctor's Story, Izzy and Moe, Blue Yonder, Where Pigeons Go to Die.

CARNEY, FRED
Producer, Director. b. Brooklyn, NY, June 10, 1914. e. Mt. Vernon H.S., 1932. Actor on B'way & summer stock; prod. mgr. for radio show, Truth or Consequences; asst. to prod.-dir of Kraft TV Theatre, 3 yrs.; dir., Kraft, Pond's Show; creator-prod., Medical Horizons; dir., Lux Video Theatre. Prod. commercials at Cunningham & Walsh. Assoc. Prod. Everybody's Talking for ABC-TV. Ass't. exec. dir., Hollywood Chpt., Nat'l Acad. TV; Assoc. prod. 40th Acad. Award show, ABC-TV Arts & Sciences.

CARON, GLENN GORDON
Writer, Director, Producer. Started as tv writer for James L. Brooks, Steve Gordon. Prod. of tv series Breaking Away. Formed prod. co., Picturemaker Productions, 1985.
PICTURES: *Director*: Clean and Sober (debut, 1988), Wilder Napalm, Love Affair.
TELEVISION: *Series*: Moonlighting (creator, prod., writer).

CARON, LESLIE
Actress, Dancer. b. Paris, France, July 1, 1931. e. Convent of Assumption, Paris; Nat'l Conservatory of Dance, Paris 1947-50; joined Roland Petit's Ballet des Champs Elysees where she was spotted by Gene Kelly who chose her as his co-star in An American in Paris. Also with Ballet de Paris.
THEATER: Orvet, Ondine, Gigi (London), 13 Rue de l'Amour, The Rehearsal, Women's Games, On Your Toes, One For the Tango.
PICTURES: An American in Paris (debut, 1951), The Man With a Cloak, Glory Alley, The Story of Three Loves, Lili (Acad. Award nom.; BFA Award), The Glass Slipper, Daddy Long Legs, Gaby, Gigi, The Doctor's Dilemma, The Man Who Understood Women, The Subterraneans, Austerlitz, Fanny, Guns of Darkness, Three Fables of Love, The L-Shaped Room (Acad. Award nom.; BFA Award), Father Goose, A Very Special Favor, Promise Her Anything, Is Paris Burning?, Head of the Family, The Beginners, Madron, Chandler, Purple Night, Valentino, The Man Who Loved Women, Golden Girl, Contract, Imperative, The Unapproachable, Dangerous Moves, Warriors and Prisoners, Courage Mountain, Damage, Funny Bones, Let It Be Me.
TELEVISION: *Mini-Series*: QB VIII, Master of the Game. *Guest*: Love Boat, Tales of the Unexpected, Carola, Falcon Crest. *Movie*: The Man Who Lived at the Ritz. *Special*: The Sealed Train.

CARPENTER, CARLETON
Actor. b. Bennington, VT, July 10, 1926 e. Bennington H.S., Northwestern U. (summer scholarship). Began career with magic act, clubs, camps, hospitals in New Eng.; then toured with carnival; first N.Y. stage appearance in Bright Boy. Appeared in nightclubs, radio; as magazine model. TV debut, Campus Hoopla show. Screen debut Lost Boundaries (also wrote book for film, I Wouldn't Mind). Member: SAG, AFTRA, AEA, ASCAP, Dramatists Guild, Mystery Writers of Amer. (ex.-treas., bd. mem.).
THEATER: *NY*: Career Angel, Three To Make Ready, The Magic Touch, The Big People, Out of Dust, John Murray Anderson's Almanac, Hotel Paradiso, Box of Watercolors, A Stage Affair, Greatest Fairy Story Ever Told, Something for the Boys, Boys in the Band, Dylan, Hello Dolly!, Light Up the Sky, Murder at Rutherford House, Rocky Road, Apollo of Bellac, Sweet Adaline, Geo. White's Scandals, Life on the L.I.E. Miss Stanwyck is Still in Hiding, Good Ole Fashioned Revue, What is Turning Gilda So Grey?, Crazy for You, Many Thousands Gone.
PICTURES: Lost Boundries (debut, 1949), Summer Stock, Father of the Bride, Three Little Words, Two Weeks With Love, The Whistle at Eaton Falls, Fearless Fagan, Sky Full of Moon, Vengeance Valley, Up Periscope, Take the High Ground, Some of My Best Friends Are..., The Prowler, Simon, Byline, Cauliflower Cupids, The Bar, Carnegie Hall.
TELEVISION: Over 6,000 shows (live & filmed) since 1945.

CARPENTER, JOHN
Director, Writer, Composer. b. Carthage, NY, Jan. 16, 1948. e. U. of Southern California. At U.S.C. became involved in film

short, Resurrection of Bronco Billy, which won Oscar as best live-action short of 1970. Also at U.S.C. began directing what ultimately became Dark Star, science fiction film that launched his career.
PICTURES: *Director*: Dark Star (also co-s.p., music), Assault on Precinct 13 (also s.p., music), Halloween (also s.p., music), The Fog (also co-s.p., music), Escape from New York (also co-s.p., music), The Thing, Christine (also music), Starman, Big Trouble in Little China (also music), Prince of Darkness (also music, and s.p. as Martin Quatermass), They Live (also music, and s.p. as Frank Armitage), Memoirs of an Invisible Man, In the Mouth of Madness (also co-music), Village of the Damned (also s.p., co-music). *Other*: Eyes of Laura Mars (co-sp., co-story), Halloween II (co- s.p., co-prod., co-music), Halloween III: Season of the Witch (co-prod., co-music), The Philadelphia Experiment (co-exec. prod.), Black Moon Rising (co-s.p., story), The Silence of the Hams (actor).
TELEVISION: *Movies* (director): Elvis, Someone Is Watching Me (also writer), John Carpenter Presents Body Bags (also co-exec. prod., actor). Movies (writer): Zuma Beach, El Diablo, Blood River.

CARPENTER, ROBERT L.
Executive. b. Memphis, TN, March 20, 1927. Joined Universal Pictures in 1949 as booker in Memphis exchange; promoted to salesman, 1952, then branch mgr., 1958; 1963 named Los Angeles branch mgr. 1971, moved to New York to become asst. to gen. sales mgr. Named gen. sls. mgr. 1972, replacing Henry H. Martin when latter became pres. of Universal. Left in 1982 to become consultant and producer's rep. 1984, joined Cannon Releasing Corp. as east. div. mgr. Left in 1989 to become consultant and producers rep.

CARR, MARTIN
Producer, Director, Writer. b. New York, NY, Jan. 20, 1932. e. Williams Coll.
AWARDS: Winner of 5 Emmys; 3 Peabody awards; 2 Du-Pont Col. Journalism awards; Robert F. Kennedy award; Sidney Hillman award; Writers Guild Award.
TELEVISION: PBS Smithsonian World (exec. prod.). For CBS prod., wrote and dir. CBS Reports: Hunger in America, The Search for Ulysses, Gauguin in Tahiti, Five Faces of Tokyo, Dublin Through Different Eyes. For NBC prod., wrote and dir. NBC White Paper: Migrant, NBC White Paper: This Child Is Rated X. Also directed drama, dance, music, opera specials and daytime serial for CBS-TV. ABC Close-Up. The Culture Thieves. PRS Global Paper: Waging Peace, ABC News 20/20; NBC, The Human Animal.

CARRADINE, DAVID
Actor. b. Hollywood, CA, Dec. 8, 1936. e. San Francisco State U. Son of late actor John Carradine. Brother of actors Keith and Robert Carradine. Began career in local repertory; first TV on Armstrong Circle Theatre and East Side, West Side; later TV includes Shane series and Kung Fu; N.Y. stage in The Deputy, Royal Hunt of the Sun (Theatre World Award).
PICTURES: Taggart, Bus Riley's Back in Town, Too Many Thieves, The Violent Ones, Heaven With a Gun, Young Billy Young, The Good Guys and the Bad Guys, The McMasters, Macho Callahan, Boxcar Bertha, Two Gypsies, You and Me (also dir.), A Country Mile (also prod.), Mean Streets, The Long Goodbye, Death Race 2000, Cannonball, Bound for Glory, Thunder and Lightning, The Serpent's Egg, Gray Lady Down, Deathsport, Circle of Iron, Fast Charlie: The Moonbeam Rider, The Long Riders, Cloud Dancer, Americana (also dir., prod.), Q, Trick or Treats, Safari 3000, Lone Wolf McQuade, Warrior and the Sorceress, On the Line, P.O.W. The Escape, Armed Response, The Misfit Brigade, Open Fire, Animal Protector, Warlords, Crime Zone, Night Children, Wizards of the Lost Kingdom 2, Sundown: The Vampire in Retreat, Crime of Crimes, Nowhere to Run, Tropical Snow, Future Force, Think Big, Bird on a Wire, Sonny Boy, Project Eliminator, Evil Toons, Dune Warriors, Kill Zone, Try This One on For Size, Animal Instincts, Capital Punishment, First Force, Roadside Prophets, Double Trouble, Distant Justice, Waxworks II, Midnight Fear, Night Rhythms, Southern Frontier, Crazy Joe, Hollywood Dream.
TELEVISION: *Movies*: Maybe I'll Come Home in the Spring, Kung Fu (1972 pilot), Mr. Horn, Johnny Belinda, Gaugin the Savage, High Noon Part II, Jealousy, The Bad Seed, Kung Fu: The Movie, Oceans of Fire, Six Against the Rock, The Cover Girl & the Cop, I Saw What You Did, Brotherhood of the Gun, The Gambler Returns: Luck of the Draw, The Eagel and the Horse. *Mini-series*: North & South Books I & II. Series: Shane, Kung Fu, Kung Fu: The Legend Continues. *Guest*: Darkroom, Amazing Stories.

CARRADINE, KEITH
Actor. b. San Mateo, CA, Aug. 8, 1949. e. Colorado State U. Daughter is actress Martha Plimpton. Son of late actor John Carradine, brother of David and Robert Carradine. First break in rock opera Hair. Theater: Wake Up It's Time to Go to Bed, Foxfire, The Will Rogers Follies.

PICTURES: A Gunfight (debut, 1971), McCabe and Mrs. Miller, Hex, Emperor of the North Pole, Thieves Like Us, Antoine et Sebastien, Run Joe Run, Idaho Transfer, Nashville (also composed songs; Academy Award for best song: I'm Easy, 1975), You and Me, Lumiere, Welcome to L.A. (also composed songs), The Duellists, Pretty Baby, Sgt. Pepper's Lonely Heart Club Band (cameo), Old Boyfriends, An Almost Perfect Affair, The Long Riders, Southern Comfort, Choose Me, Maria's Lovers (also composed song), Trouble in Mind, The Inquiry (The Investigation), Backfire, The Moderns, Street of No Return, Cold Feet, Daddy's Dyin'...Who's Got the Will?, The Ballad of the Sad Cafe, Crisscross, The Bachelor, Andre, Mrs. Parker and the Vicious Circle, The Tie That Binds, Wild Bill.
TELEVISION: Movies: Man on a String, Kung Fu, The Godchild, A Rumor of War, Scorned and Swindled, A Winner Never Quits, Murder Ordained, Eye on the Sparrow, Blackout, Stones for Ibarra, My Father My Son, The Revenge of Al Capone, Judgment, Payoff, In the Best of Families: Marriage Pride & Madness, Is There Life Out There?, Trial by Fire Mini-Series: Chiefs. Guest: Bonanza, Love American Style.

CARRADINE, ROBERT
Actor. b. Hollywood, CA, March 24, 1954. Son of late actor John Carradine; brother of Keith and David Carradine.
PICTURES: The Cowboys (debut, 1972), Mean Streets, Aloha Bobby and Rose, Jackson County Jail, The Pom Pom Girls, Cannonball, Massacre at Central High, Joyride, Orca, Blackout, Coming Home, The Long Riders, The Big Red One, Heartaches, Tag: The Assassination Game, Wavelength, Revenge of the Nerds, Just the Way You Are, Number One With a Bullet, Revenge of the Nerds II: Nerds in Paradise, Buy and Cell, All's Fair, Rude Awakening, The Player, Bird of Prey, Escape From L.A.
TELEVISION: Series: The Cowboys. Movies: Footsteps, Rolling Man, Go Ask Alice, The Hatfields and the McCoys, The Survival of Dana, The Sun Also Rises, Monte Carlo, The Liberators, I Saw What You Did, The Incident, Clarence, Doublecrossed, Revenge of the Nerds III: The Next Generation, Body Bags, The Disappearance of Christina, Revenge of the Nerds IV: Nerds in Love (also co-prod.), A Part of the Family. Guest: Alfred Hitchcock Presents (1985), The Hitchhiker, Twilight Zone (1986). Specials: Disney's Totally Minnie, As Is.

CARRERA, BARBARA
Actress. b. Nicaragua, Dec. 31, 1951. Fashion model before film career; had bit in film Puzzle of a Downfall Child.
PICTURES: The Master Gunfighter, Embryo, The Island of Dr. Moreau, When Time Ran Out, Condorman, I the Jury, Lone Wolf McQuade, Never Say Never Again, Wild Geese II, The Underachievers, Love at Stake, Wicked Stepmother, Loverboy, Spanish Rose, Night of the Archer, Tryst, Oh No Not Her (Love Is All There Is), Moscow Connection, Ghost Ships of the Kalahari, Love Is All There Is.
TELEVISION: Mini-Series: Centennial, Masada, Emma: Queen of the South Seas. Series: Dallas. Movies: Sins of the Past, Murder in Paradise, Lakota Moon, The Rockford Files.

CARRERE, TIA
Actress. r.n. Althea Janairo. b. Honolulu, HI, 1967. Was prof. model before turning to acting. Received NATO/ShoWest award for Female Star of 1994.
PICTURES: Zombie Nightmare (debut, 1987), Aloha Summer, Fatal Mission, Instant Karma, Showdown in Little Tokyo, Harley Davidson and the Marlboro Man, Wayne's World, Rising Sun, Wayne's World 2, True Lies, Jury Duty, My Generation, The Immortals.
TELEVISION: Series: General Hospital. Mini-Series: James Clavell's Noble House. Movies: The Road Raiders, Fine Gold. Guest: The A-Team, MacGyver, Tales From the Crypt.

CARREY, JIM
Actor. b. Newmarket, Ontario, Canada, Jan. 17, 1962. Began performing act at Toronto comedy clubs while teenager. Moved to LA at 19, performing at the Comedy Store.
PICTURES: Finders Keepers (debut, 1984), Once Bitten, Peggy Sue Got Married, The Dead Pool, Earth Girls Are Easy, Pink Cadillac, High Strung, Ace Ventura: Pet Detective (also co-s.p.), The Mask, Dumb and Dumber, Batman Forever, Ace Ventura: When Nature Calls, The Cable Guy.
TELEVISION: Series: The Duck Factory, In Living Color. Movies: Mickey Spillane's Mike Hammer—Murder Takes All, Doin' Time on Maple Drive. Special: Jim Carrey's Unnatural Act. Canadian TV: Introducing Janet, Copper Mountain: A Club Med Experience.

CARROLL, DIAHANN
Actress, Singer. b. New York, NY, July 17, 1935. r.n. Carol Diahann Johnson. m. singer Vic Damone. Started singing as teen, winning 1st place on tv's Chance of a Lifetime talent show resulting in engagement at Latin Quarter nightclub in New York. Autobiography: Diahann! (1986).
THEATER: B'way: House of Flowers, No Strings (Tony Award, 1962), Agnes of God.

PICTURES: Carmen Jones (debut, 1954), Porgy and Bess, Goodbye Again, Paris Blues, Hurry Sundown, The Split, Claudine (Acad. Award nom.), The Five Heartbeats.
TELEVISION: Series: Julia, The Diahann Carroll Show, Dynasty. Movies: Death Scream, I Know Why the Caged Bird Sings, Sister Sister, From the Dead of Night, Murder in Black and White, A Perry Mason Mystery: The Case of the Lethal Lifestyle. Mini-Series: Roots: The Next Generations; many specials; guest appearances incl. The Naked City, Andy Williams, Judy Garland, Dean Martin Shows.

CARROLL, GORDON
Producer. b. Baltimore, MD, Feb. 2, 1928. e. Princeton U. Advtg. exec., Foote, Cone & Belding, 1954-58; Ent. industry, Seven Arts Prods., 1958-61; v.p., prod., Jalem Prods., 1966-1969; independent producer to present.
PICTURES: How to Murder Your Wife, Luv, Cool Hand Luke, The April Fools, Pat Garrett and Billy the Kid, Alien, Blue Thunder, The Best of Times, Aliens, Red Heat, Alien 3.

CARROLL, PAT
Actress. b. Shreveport, LA, May 5, 1927. e. Immaculate Heart Coll., L.A., Catholic U., Washington, DC. Joined U.S. Army in capacity of Civilian Actress Technician. Night club entertainer in N.Y., 1950.
THEATER: Catch a Star (debut, 1955), Gertrude Stein Gertrude Stein (Drama Desk, Outer Critics Circle, Grammy Awards), Dancing in the End Zone, The Show Off. Shakespeare Theatre at the Folger: Romeo and Juliet (Helen Hayes Award), The Merry Wives of Windsors (as Falstaff; Helen Hayes Award), Mother Courage (Helen Hayes Award), H.M.S. Pinafore, Volpone.
PICTURES: With Six You Get Eggroll, The Brothers O'Toole, The Last Resort, The Little Mermaid (voice).
TELEVISION: Series: Red Buttons Show, Saturday Night Revue, Caesar's Hour (Emmy Award, 1957), Masquerade Party (panelist), Keep Talking, You're in the Picture (panelist), Danny Thomas Show, Getting Together, Busting Loose, The Ted Knight Show, She's the Sheriff. Specials: Cinderella, Gertrude Stein. Guest: Carol Burnett, Danny Kaye, Red Skelton, many others. Movie: Second Chance.

CARSEY, MARCY
Producer. b. Weymouth, MA, Nov. 21, 1944. e. Univ. NH. Was actress in tv commercials, tour guide at Rockefeller Center. Served as exec. story editor, Tomorrow Ent., 1971-74; sr. v.p. for prime time series, ABC-TV, 1978-71; founded Carsey Prods., 1981; owner, Carsey-Werner Co., 1982-.
TELEVISION: Series (exec. prod.): Oh Madeline, The Cosby Show, A Different World, Roseanne, Chicken Soup, Grand, Davis Rules, Frannie's Turn, You Bet Your Life (synd.), Grace Under Fire, Cybill, Cosby (1996-), Men Behaving Badly, Townies. Pilots: Callahan, I Do I Don't. Special: Carol Carl Whoopi and Robin. Movie: Single Bars Single Women.

CARSON, JEANNIE
Actress. b. Yorkshire, England, 1928. Became Amer. Citizen, 1966. Founded Hyde Park Festival Theatre with husband William "Biff" McGuire, 1979. Has taught a musical drama class at U. of WA. Awards: TV Radio Mirror, 1st Recipient of the Variety Club Theatre Award in England.
THEATER: U.K.: Ace of Clubs, Love From Judy, Starlight Roof, Casino Reviews, Aladdin. U.S.: The Sound of Music, Blood Red Roses, Finian's Rainbow (revival). Tours: Camelot, 110 in the Shade, Cactus Flower. Also extensive work with the Seattle Repertory Theatre as actress, and dir. with Seattle Bathhouse Theatre.
PICTURES: A Date with a Dream (debut, 1948), Love in Pawn, As Long as They're Happy, An Alligator Named Daisy, Mad Little Island (Rockets Galore), Seven Keys.
TELEVISION: Best Foot Forward, Little Women, Berkeley Square, The Rivals, Frank Sinatra Show, Heidi, What Every Woman Knows, Jimmy Durante Show, Pat Boone Show, A Kiss for Cinderella. Series: Hey Jeannie, Jeannie Carson Show.

CARSON, JOHNNY
Host, Comedian. b. Corning, IA, Oct. 23, 1925. e. U. of Nebraska, B.A. 1949. U.S. Navy service during WWII; announcer with station KFAB, Lincoln, Neb.; WOW radio-TV, Omaha, 1948; announcer, KNXT-TV, Los Angeles, 1950; then hosted own program, Carson's Cellar (1951-53); latter resulted in job as writer for Red Skelton Show. 1958 guest hosting for Jack Paar on The Tonight Show led to his becoming regular host 4 years later. President, Carson Productions. Recipient: ATAS Governor's Award, 1980. Author: Happiness Is a Dry Martini (1965).
PICTURES: Movies: Looking for Love, Cancel My Reservation.
TELEVISION: Series: Earn Your Vacation (emcee; 1954), The Johnny Carson Show (daytime, 1955; later moved to nighttime, 1955-56), Who Do You Trust? (1957-62), The Tonight Show Starring Johnny Carson (1962-92). Guest: Playhouse 90, U.S. Steel Hour, Get Smart, Here's Lucy, etc. Pilot: Johnny Come Lately.

CARTER, DIXIE
Actress. b. McLemoresville, TN, May 25, 1939. m. actor Hal Holbrook. e. U. of Tennessee, Knoxville, Rhodes Coll.; Memphis, Memphis State U. Off-B'way debut, A Winter's Tale with NY Shakespeare Fest (1963). London debut, Buried Inside Extra (1983). Lincoln Center musicals: The King & I, Carousel, The Merry Widow. Video: Dixie Carter's Unworkout.
THEATER: Pal Joey (1976 revival), Jesse and the Bandit Queen (Theatre World Award), Fathers and Sons, Taken in Marriage, A Coupla White Chicks Sitting Around Talking, Buried Inside Extra, Sextet, Pal Joey.
PICTURE: Going Berserk.
TELEVISION: Series: The Edge of Night, On Our Own, Out of the Blue, Filthy Rich, Diff'rent Strokes, Designing Women. Movies: OHMS, The Killing of Randy Webster, Dazzle, Gambler V: Playing for Keeps, A Perry Mason Mystery: The Case of the Lethal Lifestyle.

CARTER, JACK
Actor. r.n. Jack Chakrin. b. New York, NY, June 24, 1923. e. New Utrecht H.S., Brooklyn Coll., Feagin Sch. of Dramatic Arts. Worked as comm. artist for adv. agencies. Debut B'way in Call Me Mister, 1947; starred in TV Jack Carter Show, NBC Sat. Nite Revue. Hosted first televised Tony Awards. Seen on most major variety, dram. programs, incl. Ed Sullivan Show. Emmy nom. 1962 for Dr. Kildare seg. Played most major nightclubs. On B'way in Top Banana, Mr. Wonderful, Dir. several Lucy Shows. TV incl. specials, HA Comedy Special, Top Banana, Girl Who Couldn't Lose.
PICTURES: The Horizontal Lieutenant, Viva Las Vegas, The Extraordinary Seaman, The Resurrection of Zachary Wheeler, Red Nights, Hustle, The Amazing Dobermans, Alligator, The Octagon, History of the World Part 1, Heartbeeps (voice), The Arena, Deadly Embrace, In the Heat of Passion, Social Suicide, The Opposite Sex, W.A.R., Natl. Lampoon's Last Resort.
TELEVISION: Series: American Minstrels of 1949, Cavalcade of Stars, The Jack Carter Show. Movies: The Lonely Profession, The Family Rico, The Sex Symbol, The Great Houdinis, The Last Hurrah, Human Feelings, Rainbow, The Gossip Columnist, The Hustler of Muscle Beach, For the Love of It. Guest: Blossom, Empty Nest, Nurses, Murder She Wrote, Time Trax, Burke's Law, New Adventures of Superman.

CARTER, LYNDA
Actress. b. Phoenix, AZ, July 24. r.n. Lynda Jean Cordoba. e. Arcadia H.S. Wrote songs and sang professionally in Ariz. from age of 15; later toured 4 yrs. with rock 'n roll band. Won beauty contests in Ariz. and became Miss World-USA 1973. Dramatic training with Milton Katselas, Greta Seacat, and Sandra Seacat.
PICTURE: Lightning in a Bottle.
TELEVISION: Series: Wonder Woman, Hawkeye. Specials: The New Original Wonder Woman Specials; 5 variety specials, Hawkeye. Movies: The New Original Wonder Woman, A Matter of Wife... and Death, Baby Brokers, Last Song, Hotline, Rita Hayworth: The Love Goddess, Stillwatch (also exec. prod.), Mickey Spillane's Mike Hammer, Murder Takes All, Danielle Steel's Daddy, Posing: Inspired By 3 Real Stories, She Woke Up Pregnant, A Secret Between Friends.

CARTER, NELL
Actress. b. Birmingham, AL. Sept. 13, 1948.
THEATER: Hair, Dude, Don't Bother Me I Can't Cope, Jesus Christ Superstar, Ain't Misbehavin' (Tony & Theatre World Awards, 1978), Ain't Misbehaving (1988 revival), Hello Dolly! (L.A.).
PICTURES: Hair, Quartet, Back Roads, Modern Problems, Bebe's Kids (voice), The Grass Harp.
TELEVISION: Series: Lobo, Gimme a Break, You Take the Kids, Hangin' with Mr. Cooper. Specials: Baryshnikov on Broadway, The Big Show, An NBC Family Christmas, Ain't Misbehavin' (Emmy Award), Christmas in Washington, Nell Carter, Never Too Old To Dream, Morton's By the Bay (pilot). Movies: Cindy, Maid for Each Other, Final Shot: The Hank Gathers Story.

CARTLIDGE, WILLIAM
Director, Producer. b. England, June 16, 1942. e. Highgate Sch. Ent. m.p. ind. 1959. Early career in stills dept., Elstree Studio. Later worked as an asst. dir. on The Young Ones, Summer Holiday, The Punch & Judy Man, The Naked Edge. As 1st asst. dir. on such pictures as Born Free, Alfie, You Only Live Twice, The Adventurers, Young Winston, The Spy Who Loved Me, Moonraker. Prod.: Educating Rita, Not Quite Paradise, Consuming Passions, Dealers, The Playboys. Producer of Haunted, Incognito.

CARTWRIGHT, VERONICA
Actress. b. Bristol, Eng., 1949. m. writer-dir. Richard Compton. Sister is actress Angela Cartwright. Began career as child actress. Stage: The Hands of Its Enemies (Mark Taper Forum, LA 1984), The Triplet Connection (off-B'way).
PICTURES: In Love and War (debut, 1958), The Children's Hour, The Birds, Spencer's Mountain, One Man's Way, Inserts,

Goin' South, Invasion of the Body Snatchers, Alien, Nightmares, The Right Stuff, My Man Adam, Flight of the Navigator, Wisdom, The Witches of Eastwick, Valentino Returns, False Identity, Man Trouble, Candyman: Farewell to the Flesh.
TELEVISION: Series: Daniel Boone. Guest: Leave It to Beaver, Twilight Zone. Mini-series: Robert Kennedy and His Times. Movies: Guyana Tragedy—The Story of Jim Jones, The Big Black Pill, Prime Suspect, Intimate Encounters, Desperate for Love, A Son's Promise, Hitler's Daughter, Dead in the Water, It's Nothing Personal, My Brother's Keeper. Specials: Who Has Seen the Wind?, Bernice Bobs Her Hair, Tell Me Not the Mournful Numbers (Emmy Award), Joe Dancer, Abby My Love, On Hope.

CARUSO, DAVID
Actor. b. Queens, NY, Jan. 7, 1956.
PICTURES: Without Warning (debut, 1980), An Officer and a Gentleman, First Blood, Thief of Hearts, Blue City, China Girl, Twins, King of New York, Hudson Hawk, Mad Dog and Glory, Kiss of Death, Jade.
TELEVISION: Series: N.Y.P.D. Blue. Movies: Crazy Times, The First Olmypics—Athens 1896, Into the Homeland, Rainbow Drive, Mission of the Shark, Judgment Day: The John List Story. Guest: Crime Story, Hill Street Blues.

CARVER, STEVE
Director. b. Brooklyn, NY, April 5, 1945. e. U. of Buffalo; Washington U., MFA. Directing, writing fellow, Film Inst. Center for Advanced Studies, 1970. (Writer, dir. films Patent and the Tell-Tale Heart). Teacher of filmmaking art and photo. Florissant Valley Col., MO 1966-68. News photographer, UPI. Instructor, film and photography, Metropolitan Ed. Council in the Arts; St. Louis Mayor's Council on the Arts, Give a Damn (dir., prod.); asst. dir. Johnny Got His Gun; writer, editor with New World Pictures. Member: Sierra Club, Natl. Rifle Assn.
PICTURES: Arena, Big Bad Mama, Capone, Drum, Fast Charlie, The Moonbeam Rider, Steel, An Eye for an Eye, Lone Wolf McQuade (also prod.), Oceans of Fire, Jocks (also co-s.p.), Bulletproof (also co-s.p.), River of Death, Crazy Joe, The Wolves.

CARVEY, DANA
Actor. b. Missoula, MT, Apr. 2, 1955. e. San Francisco State Coll. Won San Francisco Stand-Up Comedy Competition which led to work as stand-up comedian in local S.F., then L.A. comedy clubs. TV debut as Mickey Rooney's grandson on series, One of the Boys, 1982. Received American Comedy Award (1990, 1991) as TV's Funniest Supporting Male Performer.
PICTURES: Halloween II, Racing With the Moon, This is Spinal Tap, Tough Guys, Moving, Opportunity Knocks, Wayne's World, Wayne's World 2, Clean Slate, The Road to Wellville, Trapped in Paradise.
TELEVISION: Series: One of the Boys, Blue Thunder, Saturday Night Live (Emmy Award, 1993). Specials: Superman's 50th Anniversary (host), Salute to Improvisation, Wayne & Garth's Saturday Night Live Music a Go-Go. Guest: The Larry Sanders Show. Pilots: Alone at Last, Whacked Out.

CASEY, BERNIE
Actor. b. Wyco, WV, June 8, 1939. e. Bowling Green U. Played pro-football with San Francisco 49ers and L.A. Rams.
PICTURES: Guns of the Magnificent Seven (debut, 1969), Tick...Tick...Tick, Boxcar Bertha, Black Gunn, Hit Man, Cleopatra Jones, Maurie, Cornbread Earl and Me, The Man Who Fell to Earth, Dr. Black/Mr. Hyde, Brothers, Sharky's Machine, Never Say Never Again, Revenge of the Nerds, Spies Like Us, Steele Justice, Rent-a-Cop, I'm Gonna Git You Sucka, Backfire, Bill and Ted's Excellent Adventure, Another 48 HRS, Under Siege, The Cemetery Club, Street Knight, The Glass Shield.
TELEVISION: Series: Harris and Company, Bay City Blues. Movies: Brian's Song, Gargoyles, Panic on the 5:22, Mary Jane Harper Cried Last Night, It Happened at Lake Wood Manor, Ring of Passion, Love is Not Enough, Sophisticated Gents, Hear No Evil, The Fantastic World of D.C. Collins. Mini-Series: Roots—The Next Generations, The Martian Chronicles.

CASS, PEGGY
Actress. b. Boston, MA, May 21, 1924. On B'way in Burlesque, Bernardine, Auntie Mame (Tony & Theatre World Awards, 1957), A Thurber Carnival, Don't Drink the Water, Front Page, Plaza Suite, Last of the Red Hot Lovers, Once a Catholic, 42nd Street, The Octette Bridge Club.
PICTURES: The Marrying Kind (debut, 1952), Auntie Mame (Acad. Award nom.), Gidget Goes Hawaiian, The Age of Consent, If It's Tuesday This Must Be Belgium, Paddy.
TELEVISION: Series: The Jack Paar Show, Keep Talking, The Hathaways, To Tell the Truth, The Doctors (1978-79), Women in Prison. Movie: Danielle Steel's Zoya. Guest: Garry Moore Show, Barbara Stanwyck Show, Tales from the Darkside, Major Dad.

CASSEL, ALVIN I.
Executive. b. New York , NY, July 26. e. U. of Michigan, B.A., 1938. Capt. in U.S. Army European Theatre, 1941-45. Surveyed Central Africa for MGM, 1946-50, then assumed duties as asst.

mgr. for MGM South Africa. Continued with MGM in West Indies, 1950-51 and Philippines, 1951-57. In 1957 joined Universal as mgr./supvr. for Southeast Asia; back to MGM in 1963 as supvr. S.E. Asia; 1967, with CBS Films as Far East supvr. In 1972, established Cassel Films to secure theatrical films for foreign distributors, principally in Far East. 1979, consultant for Toho-Towa co. of Japan and other Far East distributors.

CASSEL, JEAN-PIERRE
Actor. b. Paris, France, Oct. 27, 1932. Began as dancer, attracting attention of Gene Kelly at Left Bank nightspot, resulting in film debut. Also appeared in plays before becoming established as leading French screen star.
PICTURES: The Happy Road (debut, 1956), A Pied a Cheval et en Voiture, Le Desorde et la Nuit, Love Is My Profession, The Love Game, The Joker, Candide, The Five-Day Lover, Seven Capital Sins, La Gamberge, The Elusive Corporal, Arsene Lupin contre Arsene Lupin, Cyrano and D'Artagnan, The Male Companion, High Infidelity, La Ronde, Those Magnificent Men in Their Flying Machines, Is Paris Burning?, The Killing Game, The Bear and the Doll, Oh! What a Lovely War, The Army of the Shadows, The Rupture, The Boat on the Grass, Baxter!, The Discreet Charm of the Bourgeoisie, The Three Musketeers, Le Mouton Enrage, Murder on the Orient Express, Who Is Killing the Great Chefs of Europe?, Chouans! Grandeson, From Hell to Victory, La Ville des Silence, The Green Jacket, Ehrengard, The Trout, Vive la Sociale! Tranches de Vie, Mangeclous, The Return of the Musketeers, Mr. Frost, Vincent & Theo, The Favor the Watch and the Very Big Fish, Between Heaven and Earth, Petain, Blue Helmet, L'Enfer, Ready to Wear (Pret-a-Porter), La Ceremonie (A Judgment in Stone).
TELEVISION: Casanova (U.S.), The Burning Shore, Notorious, Warburg, Young Indiana Jones Chronicles, From Earth and Blood, Elissa Rhais.

CASSEL, SEYMOUR
Actor. b. Detroit, MI, Jan. 22, 1937. As a boy travelled with a troupe of burlesque performers including his mother. After high school appeared in summer stock in Michigan. Studied acting at American Theatre Wing and Actor's Studio. After joining a workshop taught by John Cassavetes, began a long creative association with the director-actor. B'way: The World of Suzy Wong, The Disenchanted.
PICTURES: Murder Inc., Shadows, Too Late Blues, Juke Box Racket, The Killers, The Sweet Ride, Coogan's Bluff, Faces (Acad. Award nom.), The Revolutionary, Minnie and Moskowitz, Black Oak Conspiracy, Death Game (The Seducers), The Killing of a Chinese Bookie, The Last Tycoon, Scott Joplin, Opening Night, Valentino, Convoy, California Dreaming, Ravagers, Sunburn, The Mountain Men, King of the Mountain, I'm Almost Not Crazy...John Cassavetes—The Man and His Work (doc.), Love Streams, Eye of the Tiger, Survival Game, Tin Men, Johnny Be Good, Plain Clothes, Colors, Track 29, Wicked Stepmother, Dick Tracy, White Fang, Cold Dog Soup, Mobsters, Diary of a Hitman, Honeymoon in Vegas, In the Soup, Trouble Bound, Indecent Proposal, Boiling Point, Chain of Desire, Chasers, There Goes My Baby, When Pigs Fly, Hand Gun, It Could Happen to You, Tollbooth, Dark Side of Genius, Imaginary Crimes, Things I Never Told You, Dead Presidents, The Last Home Run, Dream for an Insomniac, Four Rooms, Cameleone.
TELEVISION: Movies: The Hanged Man, Angel on My Shoulder, Blood Feud, I Want to Live, Beverly Hills Madame, Sweet Bird of Youth, My Shadow, Dead in the Water, Face of a Stranger. Pilot: Rose City. Special: Partners. Series: Good Company.

CASSIDY, DAVID
Actor, Singer. b. New York, NY, April 12, 1950. Son of late actor Jack Cassidy; brother of Shaun and Patrick. Composed and performed theme song for The John Larroquette Show.
THEATER: B'way: The Fig Leaves Are Falling (debut, 1968), Joseph and the Amazing Technicolor Dreamcoat, Blood Brothers. Regional: Little Johnny Jones, Tribute. London: Time.
PICTURES: Instant Karma, The Spirit of '76.
TELEVISION: Series: The Partridge Family, David Cassidy-Man Undercover. Movie: The Night the City Screamed. Guest: The Mod Squad, Bonanza, Adam-12, Ironside, Marcus Welby M.D., Police Story (Emmy nom.), The Love Boat, Alfred Hitchcock Presents, The Flash.

CASSIDY, JOANNA
Actress. b. Camden, NJ, Aug. 2, 1944. e. Syracuse U.
PICTURES: Bullitt (debut, 1968), Fools, The Laughing Policeman, The Outfit, Bank Shot, The Stepford Wives, Stay Hungry, The Late Show, Stunts, The Glove, Our Winning Season, Night Games, Blade Runner, Under Fire, Club Paradise, The Fourth Protocol, Who Framed Roger Rabbit, 1969, The Package, Where the Heart Is, Don't Tell Mom the Babysitter's Dead, All-American Murder, May Wine, Vampire in Brooklyn, Chain Reaction.
TELEVISION: Series: Shields and Yarnell, The Roller Girls, 240-Robert, Family Tree, Buffalo Bill, Code Name: Foxfire, Hotel

Malibu. Movies: She's Dressed to Kill, Reunion, Invitation to Hell, The Children of Times Square, Pleasures, A Father's Revenge, Nightmare at Bitter Creek, Wheels of Terror, Grass Roots, Taking Back My Life, Live! From Death Row, Perfect Family, Barbarians at the Gate, Stephen King's The Tommyknockers, The Rockford Files: I Still Love L.A, Sleep Baby Sleep. Mini-Series: Hollywood Wives. Special: Roger Rabbit and the Secrets of Toontown (host), Other Mothers (Afterschool Special). Pilot: Second Stage. Guest: Taxi, Love Boat, Hart to Hart, Charlie's Angels, Lou Grant.

CASSIDY, PATRICK
Actor. b. Los Angeles, CA, Jan. 4, 1961. Son of late actor Jack Cassidy and actress-singer Shirley Jones.
THEATER: NY: The Pirates of Penzance, Leader of the Pack, Assassins. Regional: Conrack.
PICTURES: Off the Wall, Just the Way You Are, Fever Pitch, Nickel Mountain, Love at Stake, Longtime Companion, I'll Do Anything.
TELEVISION: Series: Bay City Blues, Dirty Dancing. Movies: Angel Dusted, Midnight Offerings, Choices of the Heart, Christmas Eve, Dress Gray, Something in Comon, Follow Your Heart, Three on a Match, How the West Was Fun. Mini-Series: Napoleon and Josephine: A Love Story. Pilot: The Six of Us.

CASTLE, NICK
Writer, Director. b. Los Angeles, CA, Sept. 21, 1947. e. Santa Monica Coll., U. of Southern California film sch. Son of late film and TV choreographer Nick Castle Sr. Appeared as child in films Anything Goes, Artists and Models. Worked with John Carpenter and other USC students on Acad. Award-winning short, The Resurrection of Bronco Billy.
PICTURES: Skatedown USA (co-s.p.), Tag: The Assassination Game (Kiss Me Kill Me; dir., s.p.), Escape from New York (co-s.p.), The Last Starfighter (dir.), The Boy Who Could Fly (dir.), Tap (dir., s.p.), Hook (co-story), Dennis the Menace (dir.), Major Payne (dir.), Mr. Wrong (dir.).

CATES, GILBERT
Director, Producer. r.n. Gilbert Katz. b. New York, NY, June 6, 1934. e. Syracuse U. Brother is dir.-prod. Joseph Cates. Began TV career as guide at NBC studios in N.Y., working way up to prod. and dir. of game shows (Camouflage, Haggis Baggis, Mother's Day, etc.). Created Hootenanny and packaged and directed many TV specials. Pres. Directors Guild of America 1983-87. Awarded DGA's Robert B. Aldrich award 1989. Dir. short film The Painting.
PICTURES: Rings Around the World (debut, 1966), I Never Sang for My Father (also prod.), Summer Wishes Winter Dreams, One Summer Love (Dragonfly; also prod.), The Promise, The Last Married Couple in America, Oh God!—Book II (also prod.), Backfire.
TELEVISION: Specials: International Showtime (1963-65 exec. prod.-dir.), Electric Showcase Specials (dir.-prod.) Academy Awards (prod.; Emmy Award, 1991), After the Fall (prod., dir.). Movies: To All My Friends on Shore (dir., prod.), The Affair (dir.), Johnny, We Hardly Knew Ye (prod., dir.), The Kid from Nowhere (prod.), Country Gold (dir.), Hobson's Choice (dir.), Burning Rage (dir., prod.), Consenting Adult (dir.), Fatal Judgement, My First Love (dir), Do You Know the Muffin Man (dir.), Call Me Anna (dir., prod.), Absolute Strangers (dir., exec. prod.), In My Daughter's Name (co-exec. prod.), Confessions: Two Faces of Evil.
THEATER: Director: Tricks of the Trade, Voices, The Price (Long Wharf Theatre). Producer: Solitaire/Double Solitaire, The Chinese and Mr. Fish, I Never Sang for My Father, You Know I Can't Hear You When the Water's Running.

CATES, JOSEPH
Producer, Director. r.n. Joseph Katz. b. 1924. e. NYU. Brother is dir. Gilbert Cates. Father of actress Phoebe Cates. One of first producers and dirs. of live TV with Look Upon a Star, 1947. Prod., Jackie Gleason Cavalcade of Stars, game shows, ($64,000 Question, $64,000 Challenge, Stop the Music, Haggis Baggis), NBC Spectaculars (1955-60), High Button Shoes, The Bachelor, Accent on Love, Gene Kelly, Ethel Merman, Victor Borge, Yves Montand shows.
THEATER: Prod. on B'way: What Makes Sammy Run?, Joe Egg, Spoon River Anthology, Gantry, Her First Roman.
PICTURES: Director: Who Killed Teddy Bear, The Fat Spy, Girl of the Night.
TELEVISION: Series: International Showtime (Don Ameche Circuses). Prod.-dir. of spectaculars and special programs, 1955-88: Johnny Cash, David Copperfield, Steve Martin; Anne Bancroft: The Woman in the Life of Man (Emmy Award as exec. prod., 1970), Jack Lemmon and Fred Astaire: S'Wonderful S'Marvelous S'Gershwin (Emmy Award as exec. prod., 1972), Annual Ford Theater Salutes to the President, Country Music Awards Show, Miss Teen Age America, Junior Miss pageants, Tony Awards 1992, International Emmies, The Ford Theatre Salute to the President, The 1993 Monte Carlo Circus Festival. Movies: Prod.: The Quick and the Dead, The Last Days of Frank and Jessie James, The Cradle Will Fall, Special People.

CATES, PHOEBE
Actress. b. New York, NY, July 16, 1962. e. Juilliard. Father is prod-dir. Joseph Cates. m. actor Kevin Kline. Dance prodigy and fashion model before launching acting career. NY stage debut The Nest of the Wood Grouse (1984).
PICTURES: Paradise (debut, 1982), Fast Times at Ridgemont High, Private School, Gremlins, Date With an Angel, Bright Lights Big City, Shag, Heart of Dixie, I Love You to Death (unbilled), Gremlins 2: The New Batch, Drop Dead Fred, Bodies Rest and Motion, My Life's in Turnaround, Princess Caraboo.
TELEVISION: Movies: Baby Sister, Lace, Lace II. Special: Largo Desolato.

CATON-JONES, MICHAEL
Director. b. Broxburn, Scotland, 1958.
PICTURES: Scandal (debut, 1989), Memphis Belle, Doc Hollywood (also cameo), This Boy's Life, Rob Roy (also exec. prod.).

CATTRALL, KIM
Actress. b. Liverpool, Eng., Aug. 21, 1956. e. American Acad. of Dramatic Arts, N.Y. Started stage career in Canada's Off-B'way in Vancouver and Toronto; later performed in L.A. in A View from the Bridge, Agnes of God, Three Sisters, etc. On B'way in Wild Honey. Chicago Goodman Theatre in the Misanthrope. Regional: Miss Julie (Princeton).
PICTURES: Rosebud (debut 1975), The Other Side of the Mountain Part II, Tribute, Ticket to Heaven, Porky's, Police Academy, Turk 182, City Limits, Hold-Up, Big Trouble in Little China, Mannequin, Masquerade, Midnight Crossing, Palais Royale, Honeymoon Academy, The Return of the Musketeers, Brown Bread Sandwiches, Bonfire of the Vanities, Star Trek VI: The Undiscovered Country, Split Second, Double Vision, Breaking Point, Unforgettable, Live Nude Girls, Where Truth Lies.
TELEVISION: Series: Angel Falls. Movies: Good Against Evil, The Bastard, The Night Rider, The Rebels, The Gossip Columnist, Sins of the Past, Miracle in the Wilderness, Running Delilah, Tom Clancy's Op Center, Above Suspicion, The Heidi Chronicles, Two Golden Balls. Mini-Series: Scruples, Wild Palms.

CAULFIELD, MAXWELL
Actor. b. Glasgow, Scotland, Nov. 23, 1959. m. actress Juliet Mills. First worked as a dancer at a London nightclub. After coming to NY in 1978, ran the concession stand at the Truck and Warehouse Theatre. Won a Theatre World Award for Class Enemy.
THEATER: Entertaining Mr. Sloane, Salonika, Journey's End, Sleuth, The Elephant Man, An Inspector Calls, Sweet Bird of Youth, The Woman In Black.
PICTURES: Grease 2, Electric Dreams, The Boys Next Door, The Supernaturals, Sundown: The Vampire in Retreat, Mind Games, Alien Intruder, Midnight Witness, Ipi/Tombi, In a Moment of Passion, Calendar Girl, Gettysburg, Inevitable Grace, Empire Records, Prey of the Jaguar.
TELEVISION: Series: The Colbys. Movies: The Parade, Till We Meet Again, Blue Bayou, The Rockford Files.

CAVANAUGH, ANDREW
Executive. Held positions with Norton Simon, Inc. and Equitable Life Insurance Co. before joining Paramount Pictures in 1984 as v.p., human resources. 1985, appt. sr. v.p., administration, mng. personnel depts. on both coasts. Also oversees corp. admin. function for Paramount.

CAVANI, LILIANA
Director. b. near Modena, in Emilia, Italy, Jan. 12, 1937. e. U. of Bologna, diploma in classic literature, 1960; Ph.D. in linguistics. In 1960 took courses at Centro Sperimentale di Cinematografia in Rome where made short films Incontro Notturno and L'Evento. 1961 winner of RAI sponsored contest and started working for the new second Italian TV channel, 1962-66 directing progs. of serious political and social nature incl. History of 3rd Reich, Women in the Resistance, Age of Stalin, Philippe Petain–Trial at Vichy (Golden Lion Venice Fest.), Jesus My Brother, Day of Peace, Francis of Assisi. Has also directed operas Wozzeck, Iphigenia in Tauris and Medea on stage; also dir. opera liriche: Cardillac, Jenufa, Traviata, Vestale, Cena Delle Beffe, Iphigenia in Tauride, Medea.
PICTURES: Galileo, I Cannibali, Francesco d'Assissi, L'Ospite, Milarepa, Night Porter, Beyond Good and Evil, The Skin, Oltre la Porta, The Berlin Affair, Francesco, Sans Pouvoir le Dire.

CAVETT, DICK
Actor, Writer. b. Kearny, NE, Nov. 19, 1936. e. Yale U. Acted in TV dramas and Army training films. Was writer for Jack Paar and his successors on the Tonight Show. Also wrote comedy for Merv Griffin, Jerry Lewis, Johnny Carson. In 1967 began performing own comedy material in night clubs. On TV starred in specials Where It's At (ABC Stage 67) and What's In.
THEATER: B'way: Otherwise Engaged, Into the Woods.

PICTURES: Annie Hall, Power Play, Health, Simon, A Nightmare on Elm Street 3, Beetlejuice, Moon Over Parador, After School, Funny, Year of the Gun, Forrest Gump.
TELEVISION: Series: This Morning (ABC daytime talk show, 1968), The Dick Cavett Show (ABC primetime talk show, summer 1969), The Dick Cavett Show (ABC late night talk show, 1969-72: Emmy Award, 1972), ABC Late Night (talk show, 1973-74; Emmy Award, 1974), The Dick Cavett Show (CBS primetime variety; 1975), Dick Cavett Show (talk show: PBS, 1977-82; USA, 1985-86; CBS, 1986), The Edge of Night (1983), The Dick Cavett Show (CNBC talk show: 1989). Author: Cavett (with Christopher Porter) 1974.

CAZENOVE, CHRISTOPHER
Actor. b. Winchester, Eng., Dec. 17, 1945. m. Angharad Rees. e. Eton, Oxford U., trained at Bristol Old Vic Theatre School. West End theater includes Hamlet (1969), The Lionel Touch, My Darling Daisy, The Winslow Boy, Joking Apart, In Praise of Rattigan, The Life and Poetry of T.S. Eliot, The Sound of Music. B'way debut: Goodbye Fidel (1980).
PICTURES: There's a Girl in My Soup, Royal Flash, East of Elephant Rock, The Girl in Blue Velvet, Zulu Dawn, Eye of the Needle, From a Far Country, Heat and Dust, Until September, Mata Hari, The Fantastist, Hold My Hand I'm Dying, Three Men and a Little Lady, Aces: Iron Eagle III, The Proprietor.
TELEVISION: Series: The Regiment, The Duchess of Duke Street, Dynasty, A Fine Romance, Tales From the Crypt. Specials/Movies: The Rivals of Sherlock Holmes (1971), Affairs of the Heart, Jennie: Lady Randolph Churchill, The Darkwater Hall Mystery, Ladykillers—A Smile Is Sometimes Worth a Million, The Red Signal, Lou Grant, The Letter, Jenny's War, Lace 2, Kane and Abel, Windmills of the Gods, Shades of Love, Souvenir, The Lady and the Highwayman, Tears in the Rain, Ticket to Ride (A Fine Romance), To Be the Best.

CELENTINO, LUCIANO
Producer, Director, Writer. b. Naples, Italy, 1940. e. Rome, Paris, London. Ent. ind. 1959. Wrote, prod., dir. many plays incl: Infamita di Questa Terra, Black Destiny, Honour, Stranger's Heart, Youth's Sin, Wanda Lontano Amore. Stage musicals such as Songs...Dots...And Fantasies, Night Club's Appointment, Filumena, Serenada, Mamma. Since 1964, film critic of Il Meridionale Italiano. From 1962, co-writer and first asst. director to Luigi Capuano and Vittorio De Sica. In 1972, formed own company, Anglo-Fortunato Films. Co-wrote, prod., dir. Blood Money. Dir. Bandito (in Italy). Wrote and dir. Toujours, Parole, Jackpot; 1988: Panache (dir.), 1989: Was There a Way Out? (prod., wrote, dir.), Hobo.

CELLAN-JONES, JAMES
Director. b. Swansea, Wales, July 13, 1931. e. St. John's Coll., Cambridge. Best known for his adaptations of classic novels for the BBC and PBS (shown on Masterpiece Theatre). Won Nymphe d'Or at Monaco Festival.
PICTURE: The Nelson Affair, Chou Chou, Une Vie de Debussy.
TELEVISION: The Scarlet and the Black, The Forsyte Saga, Portrait of a Lady, The Way We Live Now, Solo, The Roads to Freedom, Eyeless In Gaza, The Golden Bowl, Jennie (DGA series award), Caesar and Cleopatra, The Adams Chronicles, The Day Christ Died, The Ambassadors, Unity Mitford, Oxbridge Blues (also prod.), Sleeps Six (also prod.), The Comedy of Errors, Fortunes of War, You Never Can Tell, Arms and the Man, A Little Piece of Sunshine, A Perfect Hero (also prod.), The Gravy Train Goes East, Maigret, Harnessing Peacocks, Brighton Belles.

CHABROL, CLAUDE
Director. b. Paris, France, June 24, 1930. Worked as newsman for Fox, then writer for Cahiers du Cinema. A founding director of the French New Wave.
PICTURES: Le Beau Serge, The Cousins, A Double Tour, Les Bonnes Femmes, Les Godelureaux, The Third Lover, Seven Capital Sins, Ophelia, Landru, Le Tigre Aime la Chair Fraiche, Marie-Chantal Contre le Docteur Kah, Le Tigre Se Parfume a la Dunamite, Paris vu par... Chabrol, La Ligne de Demarcation, The Champagne Murders, The Route to Corinth, Les Biches, Le Femme Infidele, This Man Must Die, Le Boucher, La Rapture, Ten Days' Wonder, Just Before Nightfall, Dr. Popaul, Les Noces Rouges, Nada, The Blood of Others, The Horse of Pride, Alouette je te plumera, Poulet au Vinaigre, Inspector Lavardin, Masques, Le Cri du Hibou, Story of Women, Clichy Days (Quiet Days in Clichy), The Lark (actor only), Doctor M (Club Extinction), Madame Bovary, Betty, L'Enfer (Hell; also s.p.), Through the Eyes of Vichy, A Judgment in Stone (also co-s.p.).

CHAKERES, MICHAEL H.
Executive b. Ohio. e. Wittenberg U, 1935. Pres. and chmn. of bd. of Chakeres Theatres of Ohio and Kentucky. U.S. Army AF 1942-45. Bd. of Dir.: National NATO, NATO of Ohio, Will Rogers Hospital, Motion Picture Pioneers, Society National Bank, Wittenberg U., Springfield Foundation, Variety Club of Palm Beach, Tent No. 65. Member: Masonic Temple, Scottish Rite, I.O.O.F., AHEPA, Leadership 100, ARCHON-Order of St. Andrew, Rotary Club, City of Hope, University Club.

CHAKIRIS, GEORGE
Actor. b. Norwood, OH, Sept. 16, 1933. Entered m.p. industry as chorus dancer.
PICTURES: Song of Love (debut, 1947), The Great Caruso, The 5000 Fingers of Dr. T, Give a Girl a Break, Gentlemen Prefer Blondes, There's No Business Like Show Business, White Christmas, Brigadoon, The Girl Rush, Meet Me in Las Vegas, Under Fire (1st acting role), West Side Story (Academy Award for Best Supporting Actor, 1961), Two and Two Make Six, Diamond Head, Bebo's Girl, Kings of the Sun, Flight From Ashiya, 633 Squadron, McGuire Go Home! (The High Bright Sun), Is Paris Burning?, The Young Girls of Rochefort, The Big Cube, The Day the Hot Line Got Hot, Why Not Stay for Breakfast?, Jekyll and Hyde... Together Again, Pale Blood.
TELEVISION: Series: Dallas (1985-86). Guest: Fantasy Island, CHiPs, Matt Houston, Scarecrow and Mrs. King, Hell Town, Murder She Wrote. Movie: Return to Fantasy Island. Specials: You're the Top, Highways of Melody, Kismet, Notorious Woman (PBS).

CHAMBERLAIN, RICHARD
Actor. r.n. George Richard Chamberlain. b. Los Angeles, CA, March 31, 1935. Studied voice, LA Conservatory of Music 1958; acting with Jeff Corey. Founding mem. City of Angels, LA Theater Company. Became TV star in Dr. Kildare series, 1961-66. Founded prod. co. Cham Enterprises. Had hit record Three Stars Will Shine Tonight (them from Dr. Kildare) in 1962.
THEATER: Breakfast at Tiffany's, Night of the Iguana, Fathers & Sons, Blithe Spirit.
PICTURES: The Secret of the Purple Reef (debut, 1960), A Thunder of Drums, Twilight of Honor, Joy in the Morning, Petulia, The Madwoman of Chaillot, Julius Caesar, The Music Lovers, Lady Caroline Lamb, The Three Musketeers, The Towering Inferno, The Four Musketeers, The Slipper and the Rose, The Swarm, The Last Wave, Murder by Phone (Bells), King Solomon's Mines, Alan Quartermain and the Lost City of Gold, The Return of the Musketeers (tv in U.S.), Bird of Prey.
TELEVISION: Specials: Hamlet, Portrait of a Lady, The Woman I Love, The Lady's Not for Burning. Movies: F. Scott Fitzgerald and the Last of the Belles, The Count of Monte Cristo, The Man in the Iron Mask, Cook and Perry: The Race to the Pole, Wallenberg: A Hero's Story, Casanova, Aftermath: A Test of Love, The Night of the Hunter, Ordeal in the Arctic. Mini-Series: Centennial, Shogun, The Thorn Birds, Dream West, The Bourne Identity. Series: Dr. Kildare, Island Son (also co-exec. prod.) Host: The Astronomers. Guest: Gunsmoke, Thriller, The Deputy, Alfred Hitchcock Presents.

CHAMBERS, EVERETT
Producer, Writer, Director. b. Montrose, CA; Aug. 19, 1926. e. New School For Social Research, Dramatic Workshop, N.Y. Entered industry as actor; worked with Fred Coe as casting dir. and dir., NBC, 1952-57; Author: Producing TV Movies.
PICTURES: Actor. Too Late Blues. Writer: Tess of the Storm Country, Run Across the River, The Kiss (short; dir.: Acad. Award nom.), The Lollipop Cover (also prod., dir.; Chicago Film Fest.), Private Duty Nurses, A Girl to Kill For.
TELEVISION: Producer: Series: Johnny Staccato (also writer), Target the Corrupters, The Dick Powell Theatre, The Lloyd Bridges Show (also writer), Peyton Place, Columbo, Future Cop, Timeslip (exec. prod., writer; 1985 Christopher & A.W.R.T. Awards), Lucan (also writer), Airwolf, Partners in Crime, Rin Tin Tin K-9 Cop (also creative consultant). Movies: Beverly Hills Madam, A Matter of Sex (exec. prod.), Will There Really Be a Morning?, Berlin Tunnel 21 (sprv. prod.), Night Slaves (also writer), Moon of the Wolf, Trouble Comes to Town, The Great American Beauty Contest, Can Ellen Be Saved? (also writer), Jigsaw John, Street Killing, Nero Wolfe, Twin Detectives (also writer), The Girl Most Likely to..., Sacrifice the Queen, Paris Conspiracy, Family Secret, Incident in a Small Town (spv. prod.). Co-writer: The Perfect Town for Murder, Last Chance (pilot).

CHAMPION, JOHN C.
Director, Producer, Writer. b. Denver, CO, Oct. 13, 1923. e. Stanford U., Wittenberg Coll. p. Lee R. Champion, Supreme Court judge. Entered m.p. in Fiesta; did some radio work; in stock at MGM briefly; co-pilot Western Air Lines, Inc., 1943; served in U.S. Army Air Force, air transport command pilot 1943-45; public relations officer AAF; writer & prod. for Allied Artists; v.p. prod. Commander Films Corp.: press. Champion Pictures, Inc.; prod., MGM, Warner, Paramount, Universal, Member: SAG, SWG, SIMPP, SPG; TV Academy. Writer, Mirisch-U.A.; prod. TV Laramie series; created McHales Navy; author, novel, The Hawks of Noon, 1965; National Cowboy, Hall of Fame Award, 1976.
PICTURES: Panhandle, Stampede, Hellgate, Dragonfly Squadron, Shotgun, Zero Hour, The Texican, Attack on the Iron Coast, Submarine X-1, The Last Escape, Brother of the Wind, Mustang Country (dir-prod-writer).

CHAMPION, MARGE
Dancer, Actress, Choreographer. b. Los Angeles, CA, Sept. 2, 1921. r.n. Marjorie Celeste Belcher. e. Los Angeles public schools. Father was Ernest Belcher, ballet master. Was model for Snow White for Disney's animated feature. Debuted in films as Marjorie Bell. Made debut with former husband Gower Champion as dancing team; team was signed by MGM; voted Star of Tomorrow, 1952.
THEATER: Blossom Time, Student Prince (LA Civic Opera), Dark of the Moon. Beggar's Holiday (NY), 3 for Tonight (NY), nvitation to a March (tour). Director: Stepping Out, Lute Song (Berkshire Theatre Fest, 1989), She Loves Me, No No Nanette.
PICTURES: Honor of the West (debut, 1939), The Story of Vernon and Irene Castle, Sorority House, Mr. Music, Show Boat, Lovely to Look At, Everything I Have Is Yours, Give a Girl a Break, Three for the Show, Jupiter's Darling, The Swimmer, The Party, The Cockeyed Cowboys of Calico County. Choreographer only: The Day of the Locust, Whose Life Is It Anyway?.
TELEVISION: Series: Admiral Broadway Revue, Marge and Gower Champion Show. Guest: GE Theatre, Chevy Show, Bell Telephone Hour, Ed Sullivan, Shower of Stars, Fame. Movie: Queen of the Stardust Ballroom (choreographer; Emmy Award, 1975).

CHAN, JACKIE
Actor, Director, Writer. r.n. Chan Kwong-Sang. b. Hong Kong, Apr. 7, 1955. Trained in acrobatics, mime and martial arts at Peking Opera Sch. Was child actor in several films; later became stuntman before being launched as action star by prod.-dir. Lo Wei.
PICTURES: Little Tiger From Canton, New Fist of Fury, Shaolin Wooden Men, To Kill With Intrigue, Snake in the Eagle's Shadow, Snake & Crane Arts of Shaolin, Magnificent Bodyguards, Drunken Master (Drunk Monkey in the Tiger's Eyes), Spiritual Kung Fu, The Fearless Hyena, Dragon Fist, The Young Master (also dir., co-s.p.), Half a Loaf of Kung Fu, The Big Brawl, The Cannonball Run, Dragon Lord (also dir., co-s.p.), Winners and Sinners, The Fearless Hyena Part 2, Cannonball Run II, Project A (also co-dir., co-s.p.), Wheels on Meals, My Lucky Stars, The Protector, Twinkle Twinkle Lucky Stars, Heart of the Dragon (First Mission), Police Story (also dir., co-s.p.), Armour of God (also dir., co-s.p.), Project A Part 2 (also dir., co-s.p.), Dragons Forever, Police Story II (also dir., co-s.p.), Mr. Canton and Lady Rose (Miracle; also dir., co-s.p.), Armour of God II: Operation Condor (also dir., co-s.p.), Island of Fire, Twin Dragons, Police Story III: Super Cop (also dir., co-s.p.), City Hunter, Crime Story, Project S, Drunken Master II, Rumble in the Bronx.

CHANCELLOR, JOHN
TV Anchorman, News Reporter. b. Chicago, IL, 1927. e. U. of Illinois. After military service joined Chicago Sun-Times (1948) and after two years moved to NBC News as Midwest corr. In 1948, assigned to Vienna bureau. Subsequently reported from London; was chief of Moscow bureau before appt. as host of Today program for one year (1961). Left NBC 1965-67 to become dir. of Voice of America. In recent yrs. anchorman for special coverage of moon landings, political conventions, inaugurations etc. Anchorman, NBC Nightly News, 1970-82. Now sr. commentator, NBC News, delivering news commentaries on NBC Nightly News.

CHANNING, CAROL
Actress. b. Seattle, WA, Jan. 31, 1921. e. Bennington Coll.
THEATER: B'way: Gentlemen Prefer Blondes, Lend an Ear (Theatre World Award), Hello Dolly! (Tony Award, 1964), Show Girl, Lorelei. Tour: Legends.
PICTURES: Paid in Full (debut, 1950), The First Traveling Saleslady, Thoroughly Modern Millie (Acad. Award nom.), Skidoo, Shinbone Alley (voice), Sgt. Pepper's Lonely Hearts Club Band (cameo), Happily Ever After (voice), Hans Christian Andersen's Thumbelina (voice), Edie & Pen.
TELEVISION: Specials: Svengali and the Blonde, Three Men on a Horse, Crescendo, The Carol Channing Special; many guest appearances incl. Omnibus, George Burns Show, Lucy Show, Carol Burnett Show, The Love Boat.

CHANNING, STOCKARD
Actress. r.n. Susan Stockard. b. New York, NY, Feb. 13, 1944. e. Radcliffe Coll., B.A., 1965. With Theater Co. of Boston, experimental drama company, 1967.
THEATER: Two Gentlemen of Verona, No Hard Feelings, Vanities (Mark Taper Forum, LA), They're Playing Our Song, The Lady and the Clarinet, Golden Age, The Rink, Joe Egg (Tony Award, 1985), Love Letters, Woman in Mind, House of Blue Leaves, Six Degrees of Separation, Four Baboons Adoring the Sun.
PICTURES: The Hospital (debut, 1971), Up the Sandbox, The Fortune, The Big Bus, Sweet Revenge, Grease, The Cheap Detective, The Fish That Saved Pittsburgh, Safari 3000, Without a Trace, Heartburn, The Men's Club, A Time of Destiny, Staying Together, Meet the Applegates, Married to It, Six Degrees of Separation (Acad. Award nom.), Bitter Moon, Smoke, To Wong Foo—Thanks for Everything—Julie Newmar, Up Close and Personal, Moll Flanders, Edie and Pen.

TELEVISION: *Series*: Stockard Channing in Just Friends, The Stockard Channing Show. *Movies*: The Girl Most Likely To..., Lucan, Silent Victory: The Kitty O'Neil Story, Not My Kid, The Room Upstairs, Echoes in the Darkness, The Perfect Witness, David's Mother. *Guest*: Medical Center, Trying Times (The Sad Professor). *Special*: Tidy Endings.

CHAPIN, DOUG
Producer. Began career as actor; then switched to film production, making debut with When a Stranger Calls, 1979.
PICTURES: Pandemonium, American Dreamer, What's Love Got to Do With It,.
TELEVISION: *Movies*: Belle Starr, Missing Pieces, Second Sight.

CHAPLIN, CHARLES S.
Executive. b. Toronto, Ont., Canada, June 24, 1911. Studied law. Entered m.p. ind. in 1930 as office boy with United Artists; then office mgr. booker, St. John, N.B., 1933; br. mgr. 1935; to Montreal in same capacity, 1941; 1945-62, Canadian gen. mgr.; v.p. Canadian sls. mgr., 7 Arts Prod., 1962; CEO, v.p., dir. TV sls., Europe-Africa, Middle East-Socialist countries, 1968-70; v.p., WB-7 Arts, 1970-72; exec. v.p. intl. film dist., NTA (Canada) Ltd., Toronto Intl. Film Studios, 1972-80; pres., Charles Chaplin Enterprises, specializing in theatrical and TV sls. and prod. Pres.: B'nai Brith, Toronto Bd. of Trade, various charitable org., many trade assns., past pres. Canadian M.P. Dist. Assn., Chmn. m.p. section Com. Chest, chmn. publ. rel. comm. & past-chmn., M.P. Industry Council; Natl. Board Council Christians & Jews, etc. Representing many indept. producers in Europe, Canada, Far East, South America, etc.

CHAPLIN, GERALDINE
Actress. b. Santa Monica, CA, July 3, 1944. e. Royal Ballet School, London. Father was actor-director Charles Chaplin. Starred in over 20 European productions, including seven with Spanish filmmaker, Carlos Saura. On NY stage in The Little Foxes.
PICTURES: Limelight (debut, 1952), Par un Beau Matin d'Ete, Doctor Zhivago, Andremo in Citta, A Countess from Hong Kong, Stranger in the House (Cop-Out), I Killed Rasputin, Peppermint Frappe, Stres es Tres Tres, Honeycomb, Garden of Delights, The Hawaiians, Sur un Arbre Perche, Z.P.G. (Zero Population Growth), Innocent Bystanders, La Casa sin Fronteras, Ana and the Wolves, The Three Musketeers, Le Marriage a la Mode, The Four Musketeers, Summer of Silence, Nashville, Elisa My Love, Noroit, Buffalo Bill and the Indians or Sitting Bull's History Lesson, Welcome to L.A., Cria, In Memorium, Une Page d'Amour, Roseland, Remember My Name, Los Ojos Vendados, The Masked Bride, L'Adoption, A Wedding, The Mirror Crack'd, Le Voyage en Douce, Bolero, Life Is a Bed of Roses, Love on the Ground, The Moderns, White Mischief, Mama Turns 100, The Return of the Musketeers (tv in U.S.), I Want to Go Home, The Children, Buster's Bedroom, Chaplin, The Age of Innocence, Words Upon the Window Pane, Home for the Holidays, Jane Eyre.
TELEVISION: *Specials*: The Corsican Brothers, My Cousin Rachel, The House of Mirth, A Foreign Field. *Mini-Series*: The World. *Movie*: Duel of Hearts.

CHAPLIN, SAUL
Musical Director, Producer. b. Brooklyn, NY, Feb. 19, 1912. e. NYU, 1929-34. Wrote vaudeville material, 1933-36; songwriter Vitaphone Corp.; other, 1934-40; Columbia, 1940-48; MGM, from 1948; songs include: Bei Mir Bist Du Schoen, Shoe Shine Boy, Anniversary Song.
PICTURES: *Scoring/Musical Director/Arranger*. Argentine Nights, Crazy House, Countess of Monte Cristo, An American in Paris (Academy Award, 1951), Lovely to Look At, Give a Girl a Break, Kiss Me Kate, Seven Brides for Seven Brothers (Academy Award, 1954), Jupiter's Darling, Interrupted Melody, High Society, Les Girls (assoc. prod.), Merry Andrew (assoc. prod.), Can-Can (assoc. prod.), West Side Story (Academy Award, 1961), The Sound of Music (assoc. prod.), Star! (prod.), Man of La Mancha (assoc. prod.), That's Entertainment II (co-prod.).

CHAPMAN, MICHAEL
Cinematographer, Director. b. New York, NY, Nov. 21, 1935. m. writer-dir. Amy Jones. Early career in N.Y. area working on documentaries before becoming camera operator for cinematographer Gordon Willis on The Godfather, Klute, End of the Road, The Landlord. Also camera operator on Jaws.
PICTURES: *Cinematographer*. The Last Detail, White Dawn, Taxi Driver, The Front, The Next Man, Fingers, The Last Waltz, Invasion of the Body Snatchers, Hardcore, The Wanderers, Raging Bull, Dead Men Don't Wear Plaid, Personal Best, The Man With Two Brains, Shoot to Kill, Scrooged, Ghostbusters II, Quick Change, Kindergarten Cop, Whispers in the Dark, Rising Sun, The Fugitive. *Director:* All the Right Moves, The Clan of the Cave Bear.
TELEVISION: Death Be Not Proud, King, Gotham. *Dir.*: The Annihilator (pilot).

CHARBONNEAU, PATRICIA
Actress. Stage appearances with Actors Theatre of Louisville, KY. Also in NY in My Sister in This House.
PICTURES: Desert Hearts, Manhunter, Stalking Danger, Call Me, Shakedown, Brain Dead, Captive, The Owl, K2.
TELEVISION: *Series*: Crime Story. *Pilots:* C.A.T. Squad, Dakota's Way. *Guest:* Spenser: For Hire, The Equalizer, Wiseguy, UNSUB, Matlock. *Movies:* Disaster at Silo 7, Desperado: Badlands Justice.

CHARISSE, CYD
Dancer, Actress. r.n. Tula Ellice Finklea. b. Amarillo, TX, March 8, 1921. e. Hollywood Prof. Sch. m. Tony Martin, singer. Toured U.S. & Europe with Ballet Russe starting at age 13. Began in films as bit player using the name Lily Norwood. Signed contract with MGM in 1946. Named Star of Tomorrow 1948. B'way debut 1991 in Grand Hotel.
PICTURES: Something to Shout About (debut, 1943; billed as Lily Norwood), Mission to Moscow; Ziegfeld Follies (1st film billed as Cyd Charisse), The Harvey Girls, Three Wise Fools, Till the Clouds Roll By, Fiesta, Unfinished Dance, On an Island with You, Words and Music, Kissing Bandit, Tension, East Side West Side, Mark of the Renegade, Wild North, Singin' in the Rain, Sombrero, The Band Wagon, Brigadoon, Deep in My Heart, It's Always Fair Weather, Meet Me in Las Vegas, Silk Stockings, Twilight for the Gods, Party Girl, Five Golden Hours, Black Tights, Two Weeks in Another Town, The Silencers, Maroc 7, Won Ton Ton the Dog Who Saved Hollywood, Warlords of Atlantis, That's Entertainment III.
TELEVISION: *Movies*: Portrait of an Escort, Swimsuit, Cinderalla Summer; many specials.

CHARLES, MARIA
Actress. b. London, England, Sept. 22, 1929. Trained at RADA. London stage debut 1946 in Pick Up Girl.
THEATER: *London*: Women of Twilight, The Boy Friend, Divorce Me Darling!, Enter A Free Man, They Don't Grow on Trees, Winnie the Pooh, Jack the Ripper, The Matchmaker, Measure for Measure, Annie (1979-80), Fiddler on the Roof, Steaming, Peer Gynt, The Lower Depths, When We Are Married, Follies, Party Piece, School for Scandal, Driving Miss Daisy, Hay Fever, Blithe Spirit. *Dir.*: Owl and the Pussycat. *Dir./prod.*: The Boy Friend, 40, Starting Here Starting Now.
PICTURES: Folly To Be Wise, The Deadly Affair, Eye of the Devil, Great Expectations, The Return of the Pink Panther, Cuba, Victor/Victoria, Savage Hearts, The Fool.
TELEVISION: The Likes of 'Er, The Moon and the Yellow River, Down Our Street, Easter Passion, Nicholas Nickleby, The Voice of the Turtle, The Fourth Wall, The Good Old Days, Turn Out the Lights, Angel Pavement, The Ugliest Girl in Town, Other Peoples Houses, Rogues Gallery, The Prince and the Pauper, Crown Court, Bar Mitzvah Boy, Secret Army, Agony, Never the Twain, La Ronde, Shine of Harvey Moon, Sheppey, La Ronde, Brideshead Revisited, A Perfect Spy, Casualty, The Fallout Guy, Lovejoy, Anna, Agony Again.

CHARTOFF, ROBERT
Producer. b. New York, NY., Aug. 26, 1933. e. Union College, A.B.; Columbia U., LL.B. Met Irwin Winkler through mutual client at William Morris Agency (N.M.) and established Chartoff-Winkler Prods. Currently pres., Chartoff Prods., Inc.
PICTURES: Double Trouble, Point Blank, The Split, They Shoot Horses Don't They?, The Strawberry Statement, Leo the Last, Believe in Me, The Gang That Couldn't Shoot Straight, The New Centurions, Up the Sandbox, The Mechanic, Thumb Tripping, Busting, The Gambler, S*P*Y*S, Breakout, Nickelodeon, Rocky, New York New York, Valentino, Comes a Horseman, Uncle Joe Shannon, Rocky II, Raging Bull, True Confessions, Rocky III, The Right Stuff, Rocky IV, Beer, Rocky V, Straight Talk.

CHASE, BRANDON
Producer, Director. President MPA Feature Films, Inc.; newscaster-news director NBC-TV 1952-57. Executive director Mardi Gras Productions, Inc. and member of Board of Directors. Now pres., Group I Films, Ltd., and V.I. Prods., Ltd.
PICTURES: The Dead One, The Sinner and the Slave Girl, Bourbon Street Shadows, Verdict Homicide, Face of Fire, Food for the Morgue, Mission To Hell, The Wanton, Harlow, Girl In Trouble, Threesome, Wild Cargo, Alice in Wonderland, The Models, The Four of Us, Against All Odds, The Giant Spider Invasion, House of 1000 Pleasures, The Rogue, Eyes of Dr. Chaney, Alligator, Crash!, Take All of Me, The Psychic, UFOs Are Real, The Actresses, The Sword and the Sorcerer.
TELEVISION: Wild Cargo (series prod.-dir.); This Strange and Wondrous World (prod.-dir.), Linda Evans: Secrets to Stay Young Forever.

CHASE, CHEVY
Actor. r.n. Cornelius Crane Chase. b. New York, NY, Oct. 8, 1943. e. Bard Coll.; B.A. Studied audio research at CCS Institute. Worked as writer for Mad Magazine 1969. Teamed with Kenny Shapiro and Lane Sarasohn while still in school to collaborate on material for underground TV, which ultimately

became off-off-Broadway show and later movie called Groove Tube. Co-wrote and starred in Saturday Night Live on TV, winning 2 Emmys as continuing single performance by a supporting actor and as writer for show. Wrote Paul Simon Special (Emmy Award, 1977).
PICTURES: The Groove Tube (debut, 1974), Tunnelvision, Foul Play, Caddyshack, Oh Heavenly Dog, Seems Like Old Times, Under the Rainbow, Modern Problems, National Lampoon's Vacation, Deal of the Century, Fletch, National Lampoon's European Vacation, Sesame Street Presents Follow That Bird (cameo), Spies Like Us, Three Amigos!, The Couch Trip (cameo), Funny Farm, Caddyshack II, Fletch Lives, National Lampoon's Christmas Vacation, L.A. Story (cameo), Nothing But Trouble, Memoirs of an Invisible Man, Hero (unbilled), Last Action Hero (cameo), Cops and Robbersons, Man of the House.
TELEVISION: Series: Saturday Night Live, The Chevy Chase Show.

CHASE, STANLEY
Producer. b. Brooklyn, NY, May 3. e. NYU, B.A.; Columbia U, postgraduate. m. actress/artist Dorothy Rice. Began career as assoc. prod. of TV show Star Time; story dept., CBS-TV; then produced plays Off-B'way and on B'way, winner Tony and Obie awards for The Threepenny Opera. Joined ABC-TV as dir. in chg. programming; prod., Universal Pictures & TV; exec. consultant, Metromedia Producers Org.; prod. & exec. Alan Landsburg Productions. Formed Stanley Chase Productions, Inc. in 1975, which heads as pres.
THEATER: B'way Producer: The Potting Shed, The Cave Dwellers, A Moon for the Misbegotten, European Tour: Free and Easy. Off-B'way: The Threepenny Opera.
PICTURES: The Hell with Heroes, Colossus: The Forbin Project, Welcome to Blood City, High-Ballin', Fish Hawk, The Guardian, Mack the Knife.
TELEVISION: Inside Danny Baker (pilot), Al Capp special (prod., writer), Happily Ever After (pilot; prod., writer), Bob Hope Presents the Chrysler Theatre series, Jigsaw (pilot), Fear on Trial (Emmy nom.), Courage of Kavik: The Wolf Dog (exec. prod.), An American Christmas Carol, Grace Kelly.

CHASMAN, DAVID
Executive. b. New York, NY, Sept. 28, 1925. e. Sch. of Industrial Art, 1940-43; Academie De La Grande-Chaumiere, 1949-50. Monroe Greenthal Co., Inc. 1950-53; Grey Advertising Agency, Inc., 1953-60. Freelance consultant to industry 1950-60; worked on pictures for UA, 20th-Fox, Columbia, Samuel Goldwyn, City Film; Adv. mgr. United Artists, 1960; exec. dir. adv., United Artists, 1962; exec. production, United Artists, London, 1964; v.p. in prod. United Artists, 1969; v.p. of west coast operations, U.A. 1970; sr. v.p. in charge of prod., U.A. 1972; president, Convivium Productions Inc., 1974. Joined Columbia 1977, named exec. v.p. worldwide theatrical prod. 1979. Joined MGM 1980; named exec. v.p.-worldwide theatrical prod.
PICTURES: Exec. prod.: Brighton Beach Memoirs, The Secret of My Success.

CHAUDHRI, AMIN QAMAR
Director, Producer, Cinematographer, Editor. b. Punjab, India, April 18, 1942. e. Hampstead Polytechnic, London, City U. of New York. Pres., Filmart Enterprises Ltd. & Filmart Int'l Ltd., Pres./CEO, Continental Film Group Ltd. Pres./CEO, Continental Entertainment Group, Ltd., Heron Int'l Pictures, Ltd.
PICTURES: Director: Kashish, Khajuraho, Eternal, Urvasi, Konarak, The Land of Buddha. Producer: Night Visitors, Diary of a Hit Man. Producer/Director: Once Again, An Unremarkable Life, Tiger Warsaw, The Last Day of School, Gunga Din, Golden Chute, Wings of Grey, Call It Sleep. Cinematography: Right On, Sweet Vengeance, The Hopefuls, The Wicked One Slow, Who Says I Can't Ride a Rainbow, Black Rodeo, Medium Is the Message, Death of a Dunbar Girl, Kashish, The Last Day of School.
TELEVISION: Reflections of India (prod.-dir.), Wild Wild East (camera), Nehru (edit.), Medium is the Message (photog.), America... Amerika (prod., dir.).

CHAYKIN, MAURY
Actor. b. Brooklyn, NY, July 27, 1949. e. Univ. of Buffalo. Formed theatre co. Swamp Fox; later acted with Buffalo rep. co., Public Theatre in NY. Moved to Toronto in 1980.
PICTURES: The Kidnapping of the President, Death Hunt, Soup for One, Of Unknown Origin, Harry and Son, Highpoint, Mrs. Soffel, Turk 182!, Meatballs III, The Bedroom Window, Wild Thing, Stars and Bars, Caribe, Iron Eagle II, Twins, Millenium, Breaking In, Where the Heart Is, Mr. Destiny, Dances With Wolves, George's Island, My Cousin Vinny, Leaving Normal, The Adjuster, Hero, Sommersby, Money for Nothing, Josh and S.A.M., Beethoven's 2nd, Camilla, Whale Music (Genie Award), Unstrung Heroes, Devil in a Blue Dress, Cutthroat Island.
TELEVISION: Special: Canada's Sweetheart: The Saga of Hal Banks (Nellie Award)

CHELSOM, PETER
Director, Writer. b. Blackpool, England. Studied acting at London's Central School of Drama. Acted with Royal

Shakespeare Co., Royal Natl. Theatre, Royal Court Theatre. Dir. at Central School of Drama, taught acting at Actors Ints. and at Cornell Univ. Wrote and directed short film Treacle for Channel 4/British Screen. Director of many commercials for television in London and U.S.
PICTURES: Hear My Song (dir., story, co-s.p.), Funny Bones (dir., co-prod., co-s.p.).

CHEN, JOAN
Actress. r.n. Chen Chong. b. Shanghai, China, 1961. Studied acting with actress Zhang Rei Fang at Shanghai Film Studio. Debuted as teenager in Chinese films. Moved to U.S. in 1981.
PICTURES: Little Flower, Awakening, Dim Sum: A Little Bit of Heart, Tai-Pain, The Last Emperor, The Blood of Heroes, Turtle Beach, When Sleeping Dogs Lie, Night Stalker, Heaven and Earth, Golden Gate, On Deadly Ground, Temptation of a Monk, The Hunted, Red Rose/White Rose, Judge Dredd, Wild Side, Precious Find.
TELEVISION: Series: Twin Peaks. Movie: Shadow of a Stranger. Guest: Miami Vice.

CHER
Singer, Actress. r.n. Cherilyn Sarkisian. b. El Centro, CA, May 20, 1946. Began singing as backup singer for Crystals and Ronettes then with former husband Sonny Bono in 1965; first hit record I Got You Babe, sold 3 million copies. Made two films and then debuted nightclub musical-comedy act in 1969. CBS comedy-variety series started as summer show in 1971; became regular series the following December. NY stage debut: Come Back to the Five and Dime Jimmy Dean Jimmy Dean (1982).
PICTURES: Wild on the Beach (debut, 1965), Good Times, Chastity, Come Back to the Five and Dime Jimmy Dean Jimmy Dean, Silkwood, Mask, The Witches of Eastwick, Suspect, Moonstruck (Academy Award for Best Actress, 1987), Mermaids, The Player, Ready to Wear (Pret- a-Porter), Faithful.
TELEVISION: Series: Sonny & Cher Comedy Hour (1971-74), Cher, The Sonny and Cher Show (1976-77). Specials: Cher, Cher... Special, Cher and Other Fantasies, Cher: A Celebration at Caesar's Palace, Cher at the Mirage. Movie: If These Walls Could Speak. Guest: Shindig, Hullabaloo, Hollywood Palace, The Man from U.N.C.L.E., Laugh-In, Glen Campbell, Love American Style.

CHERMAK, CY
Producer, Writer. b. Bayonne, NJ, Sept. 20, 1929. e. Brooklyn Coll., Ithaca Coll.
TELEVISION: Writer, prod., exec. prod.: Ironside, The Virginian, The New Doctors, Amy Prentiss, Kolchak: The Night Stalker, Barbary Coast, CHiPS. Movie: Murder at the World Series (prod., s.p.).

CHERNIN, PETER
Executive. Chairman, Fox, Inc. Formerly pres., Fox Broadcasting.

CHERTOK, JACK
Producer. b. Atlanta, GA, July 13, 1906. Began career as script clerk, MGM; later asst. cameraman, asst. dir., head of music dept., short subjects prod. (including Crime Does Not Pay, Robert Benchley, Pete Smith series). Feature prod. MGM 1939-42 (The Penalty, Joe Smith, American, Kid Glove Killer, The Omaha Trail, Eyes in the Night, etc.). In 1942, apptd. Hollywood prod. chief, Co-Ord. Inter-Amer. Affairs, serving concurrently with regular studio work. Left MGM in 1942 and prod. for Warner Bros. to late 1944; Produced The Corn is Green and Northern Pursuit for Warner Bros. Pres. Jack Chertok TV, Inc.
TELEVISION: Prod.: My Favorite Martian, Lone Ranger, Sky King, Cavalcade, Private Secretary, My Living Doll, Western Marshal, The Lawless Years.

CHETWYND, LIONEL
Executive, Writer, Director. b. London, England, 1940. m. actress Gloria Carlin. Emigrated to Canada, 1948. e. Sir George Williams U., Montreal, BA, economics; BCL-McGill U., Montreal. Graduate Work-Law, Trinity Coll. Oxford. Admitted to bar, Province of Quebec, 1968. C.B.C., TV-Public Affairs and Talks, 1961-1965. CTV network 1965-67. Controller commercial TV and film rights, Expo '67. Freelance writer and consultant 1961-68. Asst. mng. dir. Columbia Pictures (U.K.) Ltd. London 1968-72. Asst. mng. dir. Columbia-Warner UK, 1971. Story and book for musical Maybe That's Your Problem, 1971-1973. Then Bleeding Great Orchids (staged London, and Off-B'way). Also wrote The American 1776, official U.S. Bi-centennial film and We the People/200 Constitutional Foundation. Former mem. of NYU grad. film sch. faculty, lecturer on screenwriting at Frederick Douglass Ctr. Harlem. Mem of Canadian Bar Assc. Served on bd. of gov., Commission on Battered Children, and the Little League.
PICTURES: The Apprenticeship of Duddy Kravitz (s.p.; Acad. Award nom.), Morning Comes (dir., s.p.), Two Solitudes (prod., dir., s.p., Grand Award Salonika), Quintet (s.p.), The Hanoi Hilton (dir., s.p.), Redline, (dir., s.p.).

TELEVISION: Johnny We Hardly Knew Ye (prod., s.p.; George Washington Honor Medal, Freedom Fdn.), It Happened One Christmas (s.p.), Goldenrod (prod., s.p.), A Whale for the Killing (s.p.), Miracle on Ice (s.p.; Christopher Award), Escape From Iran: The Canadian Caper (s.p.), Sadat (s.p.; NAACP Image Award), Children in the Crossfire (s.p.), To Heal a Nation (writer, exec. prod.), Evil in Clear River (exec. prod.; Christopher Award), So Proudly We Hail (exec. prod., dir., s.p.), The Godfather Wars (s.p.), Heroes of Desert Storm, Reverse Angle (PBS; exec. prod., writer), Doom's Day Gun, The Bible... Jacob, The Bible... Joseph.

CHINICH, MICHAEL
Producer. b. New York, NY. e. Boston U. Began career as casting agent in N.Y.; moved to L.A. to join MCA-Universal Pictures as executive in casting. Named head of feature film casting; then prod. v.p.
PICTURES: *Casting dir.*: Dog Day Afternoon, Coal Miner's Daughter, Animal House, Melvin and Howard, The Blues Brothers, Mask, Midnight Run, Twins, Ghostbusters II, Kindergarten Cop, Dave, Junior. *Exec. Prod.*: Pretty in Pink, Ferris Bueller's Day Off, Some Kind of Wonderful, Planes Trains and Automobiles (co-exec. prod.), Commandments.

CHOMSKY, MARVIN J.
Director, Producer. b. Bronx, NY, May 23, 1929. e. Syracuse U., B.S.; Stanford U., M.A. Started in theatre business at early age as art dir. with such TV credits as U.S. Steel Hour, Playhouse 90, Studio One, etc. Later worked with Herbert Brodkin who advanced him to assoc. prod. with such TV shows as The Doctors and The Nurses. Brought to Hollywood in 1965 as assoc. prod. for Talent Associates, producing series of TV pilots. Art dir.: The Bubble.
PICTURES: Evel Knievel, Murph the Surf, Mackintosh and T.J., Good Luck Miss Wycoff, Tank.
TELEVISION: *Series*: The Wild Wild West, Gunsmoke, Star Trek, Then Came Bronson. *Movies*: Assault on the Wayne, Mongo's Back in Town, Family Flight, Fireball Forward, Female Artillery, The Magician, The F.B.I. Story: The F.B.I. Vs. Alvin Karpas, Mrs. Sundance, Attack on Terror: The F.B.I. Vs. the Ku Klux Klan, Kate McShane, Brink's: The Great Robbery, Law and Order, A Matter of Wife and Death, Victory at Entebbe, Little Ladies of the Night, Roots (co-dir.), Danger in Paradise, Holocaust (Emmy Award, 1978), Hollow Image, King Crab, Attica (Emmy Award, 1980), Inside the Third Reich (Emmy Award, 1982), My Body My Child, The Nairobi Affair, I Was a Mail Order Bride, Robert Kennedy and His Times, Evita Peron (also prod.), Peter the Great (also prod.; Emmy Award as prod., 1986), The Deliberate Stranger (also prod.), Anastasia: The Mystery of Anna (also prod.), Billionaire Boys Club (also spv. prod.), Angel in Green, I'll Be Home for Christmas (also prod.), Brotherhood of the Rose (also prod.), Telling Secrets, Strauss Dynasty (also prod.), Hurricane Andrew (also prod.), Catherine the Great (also prod.).

CHONG, RAE DAWN
Actress. b. Vancouver, Canada, 1962. Father is director-comedian Tommy Chong. Debut at 12 in The Whiz Kid of Riverton (TV). B'way debut 1991 in Oh Kay!
PICTURES: Stony Island (debut, 1978), Quest for Fire, Beat Street, The Corsican Brothers, Choose Me, Fear City, City Limits, American Flyers, Commando, The Color Purple, Soul Man, The Squeeze, The Principal, Walking After Midnight, Tales From the Darkside, Far Out Man, The Borrower, Amazon, Chaindance, Time Runner, When the Party's Over, In Exile, Boulevard, Boca, Hideaway, The Break.
TELEVISION: *Movies*: The Top of the Hill, Badge of the Assassin, Curiosity Kills, Prison Stories: Women on the Inside, Father & Son: Dangerous Relations.

CHONG, TOMMY
Actor, Writer, Director. b. Edmonton, Alta., Canada, May 24, 1938. Daughter is actress Rae Dawn Chong. Was guitar player with various Canadian rhythm and blues combinations, before teaming with Richard (Cheech) Marin in improvisational group. Has made comedy recordings.
PICTURES: Up in Smoke, Cheech and Chong's Next Movie (also dir., co-s.p.), Cheech and Chong's Nice Dreams (also dir., co-s.p.), Things Are Tough All Over, It Came from Hollywood, Still Smokin', Yellowbeard, The Corsican Brothers (also dir., s.p.), After Hours, Tripwire (cameo), Far Out Man (also dir., s.p.), The Spirit of 76, FernGully (voice), National Lampoon's Senior Trip.
TELEVISION: Trial and Error (co-exec. prod.).

CHOOLUCK, LEON
Producer, Director. b. New York, NY, March 19, 1920. e. City Coll. of New York, 1938. Production, distribution, editing Consolidated Film Industries Ft. Lee 1936-40; staff sgt., Army Pictorial Service as news photographer 1941-45; prod. for Regal Films (Fox) Clover Prods. (Col.), Hugo Haas Prods. and Orbit Pro. (Col), 1957-58; dir. Highway Patrol, 1958. Prod. mgr., Captain Sinbad, prod. sprv. Encyclopedia Britannica Films, in Spain, 1964; prod. supv., U.S. Pictures, Battle of the Bulge; v.p.

Fouad Said Cinemobile Systems, 1969-70; ABC Pictures 1970-71 (Grissom Gang, Kotch). 1983-present, consultant, intl. film services.
PICTURES: Hell on Devil's Island, Plunder Road, Murder by Contract, City of Fear (prod.), The Fearmakers, Day of the Outlaw, Bramble Bush, Rise and Fall of Legs Diamond (assoc. prod.), Studs Lonigan, Three Blondes in His Life (dir.), El Cid, Midas Run (assoc. prod.), Payday; Three the Hard Way, Take a Hard Ride, Apocalypse Now, Loving Couples, Square Dance. Wonders of China for Disney Circlevision Epcot (supv.).
TELEVISION: Prod. supv.: 1/4 hr. Fireside Theatre, Stoney Burke, The Outer Limits (assoc. prod.), I Spy (assoc. prod.), Lock Up (dir.). *Specials*: Strange Homecoming, James Mitchener's Dynasty, Judge Horton and the Scottsboro Boys, Pearl, A Rumor of War, Murder in Texas, Love Boat, Dynasty, Breakdown (Alfred Hitchcock), On Wings of Eagles.

CHOW, RAYMOND
O.B.E. Producer. b. Hong Kong, 1927. e. St. John's U., Shanghai. Worked for Hong Kong Standard; then joined the Hong Kong office of the U.S. Information Service. In 1959 joined Shaw Brothers as head of publicity, became head of production before leaving in 1970 to start Golden Harvest to produce Chinese-language films in Hong Kong. Kung-fu films featuring Bruce Lee put Harvest into int'l market. Started English-language films in 1977, beginning with The Amsterdam Kill and The Boys in Company C. Named Showman of the Year 1984 by NATO. Awarded O.B.E. in 1988.
PICTURES: Armour of God, The Big Boss (and subsequent Bruce Lee films), The Cannonball Run (and Part II), High Road to China, Lassiter, Miracles, Mr. Boo (a.k.a. The Private Eyes; and many subsequent Michael Hui films), Painted Faces, Police Story (and Part II), Project A (and Part II), Rouge, Teenage Mutant Ninja Turtles (and Part II), The Reincarnation of Golden Lotus.

CHRISTIANSEN, ROBERT W.
Producer. b. Porterville, CA. e. Bakersfield Coll. Spent 3 years in Marine Corps. Worked on Hollywood Reporter in circulation and advertising. Joined Cinema Center Films; prod. asst. on Monte Walsh and Hail Hero. Co-produced first feature in 1970, Adam at Six A.M., with Rick Rosenberg, with whom co-produced all credits listed.
PICTURES: Adam at Six A.M., Hide in Plain Sight.
TELEVISION: *Features*: Suddenly Single, The Glass House, Gargoyles, A Brand New Life, The Man Who Could Talk to Kids, The Autobiography of Miss Jane Pittman, I Love You...Goodbye, Queen of the Stardust Ballroom, Born Innocent, A Death in Canaan, Strangers, Robert Kennedy and His Times, Kids Don't Tell, As Summers Die, Gore Vidal's Lincoln, Red Earth, White Earth, The Heist, A House of Secrets and Lies, The Last Hit, Heart of Darkness, Tad, Kingfish: A Story of Huey P. Long, Redwood Curtain.

CHRISTIE, JULIE
Actress. b. Chukua, Assam, India, April 14, 1941. Father had tea plantation in India. e. in Britian, at 16 studied art in France, then attended Central Sch. of Music & Drama in London. 3 yrs. with Frinton-on-Sea Rep., before TV debut in A for Andromeda. Birmingham Rep.; Royal Shakespeare Co.; East European and American tour. NY stage: Uncle Vanya. London stage: Old Times.
PICTURES: Crooks Anonymous (debut, 1962), Fast Lady, Billy Liar, Young Cassidy, Darling (Academy Award & BFA Award, 1965), Dr. Zhivago, Farenheit 451, Far From the Madding Crowd, Petulia, In Search of Gregory, The Go-Between, McCabe and Mrs. Miller, Don't Look Now, Shampoo, Nashville (cameo), Demon Seed, Heaven Can Wait, Memoirs of a Survivor, The Return of the Soldier, Heat and Dust, Golddiggers, Power, Miss Mary, La Memoire tatouree (Secret Obsession), Fools of Fortune, Dragonheart, Hamlet.
TELEVISION: Debut: A is for Andromeda (UK series, 1962), Sins of the Fathers (Italian TV), Separate Tables, Dadah Is Death (Amer. TV debut, 1988), The Railway Station Man.

CHRISTOPHER, DENNIS
Actor. b. Philadelphia, PA, Dec. 2, 1955. e. Temple U. NY stage debut, the Yeshiva Boy (1974). Other NY theater: Dr. Needle and the Infectious Laughter Epidemic, The Little Foxes, Brothers, Exmass, A Pound on Demand, Advice from a Caterpillar. Regional theater incl. Balm in Gilead, American Buffalo. Appeared in 1991 short The Disco Years.
PICTURES: Blood and Lace, Didn't You Hear?, The Young Graduates, Fellini's Roma, Salome, 3 Women, September 30, 1955, A Wedding, California Dreaming, The Last Word, Breaking Away, Fade to Black, Chariots of Fire, Don't Cry It's Only Thunder, Alien Predator, Flight of the Spruce Goose, Jake Speed, Friends, A Sinful Life, Circuitry Man, Dead Women in Lingerie, Doppelganger, Circuitry Man II: Plughead Rewired.
TELEVISION: *Movies*: The Oregon Trail, Stephen King's IT, False Arrest, Willing to Kill: The Texas Cheerleader Story, Curacao, Deadly Invasion: The Killer Bee Nightmare. *Specials*: Bernice Bobs Her Hair, Jack and the Beanstalk (Faerie Tale

Theatre), Cristabel. *Guest*: Trapper John M.D., Tales of the Unexpected, Stingray, Cagney & Lacey, Moonlighting, Hooperman, The Equalizer, Matlock, Murder She Wrote, Monsters, Civil Wars, Dark Justice, The Watcher, The Cosby Mysteries.

CHRISTOPHER, JORDAN
Actor, Musician. b. Youngstown, OH. Oct. 23, 1941. e. Kent State U. Led rock 'n' roll group, The Wild Ones. B'way debut, Black Comedy, 1967.
PICTURES: Return of the Seven, The Fat Spy, The Tree, Angel Angel Down We Go, Pigeons, Brainstorm, Star 80, That's Life!
TELEVISION: *Series*: Secrets of Midland Heights.

CHUNG, CONNIE
TV News Anchor. r.n. Constance Yu-Hwa Chung. m. anchor Maury Povich. b. Washington, D.C., Aug. 20, 1946. e. U. of Maryland, B.S. Entered field 1969 as copy person, writer then on-camera reporter for WTTG-TV, Washington; 1971, named Washington corr., CBS News; 1976, anchor KNXT, Los Angeles; 1983, anchor, NBC News at Sunrise; anchor, NBC Saturday Nightly News and news specials; 1989 moved to CBS as anchor, Sunday Night Evening News; anchor and reporter, Saturday Night with Connie Chung (later Face ot Face With Connie Chung), 1989-90. Received Emmy Award for Shot in Hollywood (1987), Interview With Marlon Brando (1989); 2 additional Emmy Awards: 1986, 1990. Became co-anchor, with Dan Rather, of CBS Evening News, 1993-95. Prime time series: Eye to Eye With Connie Chung, 1993. Many other awards incl. Peabody, 2 LA Emmy Awards, Golden Mike, Women in Business Award, etc.

CILENTO, DIANE
Actress. b. Queensland, Australia, April 2, 1934. e. Toowoomba. Went to New York and finished schooling and then American Acad. of Dramatic Art. First theatre job at 16; toured U.S. with Barter Co.; returned to London and joined Royal Acad. of Dramatic Art; several small parts and later repertory at Manchester's Library Theatre.
THEATER: *London stage*: Tiger at the Gates (also NY: Theatre World Award), The Third Secret, The Bonne Soup, Heartbreak House. NY: The Big Knife, Orpheus, Altona, Castle in Sweden, Naked, Marys, I've Seen You Cut Lemons.
PICTURES: Wings of Danger (Dead on Course; debut, 1952), Moulin Rouge, Meet Mr. Lucifer, All Halloween, The Angel Who Pawned Her Harp, The Passing Stranger, Passage Home, The Woman for Joe, The Admirable Crichton (Paradise Lagoon), The Truth About Women, Jet Storm, Stop Me Before I Kill! (The Full Treatment), I Thank a Fool, The Naked Edge, Tom Jones (Acad. Award nom.), Rattle of a Simple Man, The Third Secret, The Agony and the Ecstacy, Hombre, Negatives, Z.P.G. (Zero Population Growth), Hitler: The Last Ten Days, The Wicker Man, The Tiger Lily, The Boy Who Had Everything, Duet for Four.
TELEVISION: La Belle France (series), Court Martial, Blackmail, Dial M for Murder, Rogues Gallery, Rain, Lysistrata, The Kiss of Blood, For the Term of His Natural Life.

CIMINO, MICHAEL
Writer, Director. b. New York, NY, 1943. e. Yale U. BFA, MFA. Was tv commecial director before becoming screen writer.
PICTURES: Silent Running (co-s.p.), Magnum Force (co-s.p.). Director: Thunderbolt and Lightfoot (also s.p.), The Deer Hunter (also co-wrote story, co-prod.; Academy Awards for Best Picture & Director, 1978.), Heaven's Gate (also s.p.), Year of the Dragon (also co-s.p.), The Sicilian (also co-prod.), Desperate Hours (also co-prod.), The Sunchasers (also co-s.p., co-prod.).

CIPES, ARIANNE ULMER
Executive. b. New York, NY, July 25, 1937. e. Royal Acad. of Dramatic Art, London, U. of London. Daughter of film director Edgar G. Ulmer. Actress, then production and dubbing, Paris; CDC, Rome; Titra, New York; 1975-77, v.p., Best International Films (international film distributor), Los Angeles; 1977 co-founder and sr. v.p./sales & services of Producers Sales Organization, 1981, named exec. v.p., American Film Marketing Assn. 1982, founded AUC Films, consulting and intl. and domestic sales-producers rep.

CIPES, JAY H.
Executive. b. Mt. Vernon, NY, Dec. 14, 1928. e. Cornell U. 1960-66, independent producer-packager-distributor European features for U.S. TV sales; 1967, producer, 20th Century-Fox TV; 1970, producer, Four Star TV; 1971, marketing exec. Technicolor, Inc.; 1973, v.p., marketing, Technicolor, Inc.; 1979 sr. v.p., director worldwide marketing, Technicolor, Inc. Professional Film Division. 1992, indept. consultant to prod. & post-prod. facilities.

CLARK, BOB
Director, Writer, Producer. b. New Orleans, LA, Aug. 5, 1939. e. Hillsdale Coll.
PICTURES: *Director*: The She Man, The Emperor's New Clothes, Children Shouldn't Play with Dead Things (credited as Benjamin Clark), Deathdream (Dead of Night), Deranged (prod.

only), Black Christmas (Silent Night Evil Night), Breaking Point, Murder by Decree, Tribute, Porky's (also s.p., prod.), Porky's II—The Next Day (also s.p., prod.), A Christmas Story (also s.p., prod.), Rhinestone, Turk 182, From the Hip (also co-s.p.), Loose Cannons (also co-s.p.), It Runs in the Family (also co-s.p.).
TELEVISION: *Movies*: The American Clock, Derby. *Series episode*: Amazing Stories (Remote Control Man).

CLARK, CANDY
Actress. b. Norman, OK, June 20. Was successful model in N.Y. before landing role in Fat City, 1972. Off-B'way debut 1981: A Couple of White Chicks Sitting Around Talking; followed by It's Raining on Hope Street. Appeared in short Blind Curve.
PICTURES: Fat City (debut, 1972), American Graffiti (Acad. Award nom.), I Will I Will... For Now, The Man Who Fell To Earth, Citizens Band (Handle With Care), The Big Sleep, When You Comin' Back Red Ryder, More American Graffiti, National Lampoon Goes to the Movies, Q, Blue Thunder, Amityville 3-D, Hambone and Hillie, Cat's Eye, At Close Range, The Blob, Original Intent, Deuce Coupe, Cool as Ice, Buffy the Vampire Slayer, Radioland Murders.
TELEVISION: *Movies*: James Dean, Amateur Night at the Dixie Bar and Grill, Where the Ladies Go, Rodeo Girl, Johnny Belinda, Cocaine and Blue Eyes, The Price She Paid.

CLARK, DANE
Actor. b. New York, NY, Feb. 18, 1915. e. Cornell U., St. John's. In radio series 2 yrs.; on N.Y. stage (Of Mice and Men, Dead End, The Country Girl, Brecht on Brecht, The Number, The Fragile Fox, A Thousand CLowns, Mike Downstairs, etc.). Natl. Co. of Two for the Seesaw.
PICTURES: The Glass Key (debut, 1942), Sunday Punch, Pride of the Yankees, Tennessee Johnson, Action in the North Atlantic, Destination Tokyo, The Very Thought of You, Hollywood Canteen, Pride of the Marines, God Is My Co-Pilot, Her Kind of Man, A Stolen Life, That Way With Women, Deep Valley, Embraceable You, Moonrise, Whiplash, Without Honor, Backfire, Barricade, Never Trust a Gambler, Fort Defiance, Highly Dangerous, Gambler and the Lady, Go Man Go, Blackout, Paid to Kill, Thunder Pass, Port of Hell, Toughest Man Alive, Massacre, The Man is Armed, Outlaw's Son, Blood Song, The Woman Inside, Last Rites.
TELEVISION: *Series*: Wire Service, Bold Venture, Perry Mason (1973-4). *Specials*: No Exit, The Closing Door, The French Atlantic Affair. Guest: Twilight Zone, I Spy, Mod Squad, Cannon, Hawaii 5-O, Murder She Wrote, Police Story, Highway to Heaven, The Rookies, many others. *Movies*: The Face of Fear, The Family Rico, Say Goodbye Maggie Cole, The Return of Joe Forrester, Murder on Flight 502, James Dean, Condominium. *Mini-Series*: Once an Eagle, The French Atlantic Affair.

CLARK, DICK
Performer; Chairman, CEO, dick Clark Prods., Inc. b. Mt. Vernon, NY, Nov. 30, 1929. e. Syracuse U. graduated 1951, summer announcer WRUN, Utica 1949, staff announcer WOLF, Syracuse 1950. After grad. 1951, took regular job with WOLF. Rejoined WRUN, Utica, then joined WKTV, Utica. Announcer WFIL Philadelphia 1952. *Author*: Your Happiest Years, 1959; Rock, Roll & Remember, 1976; To Goof or Not to Goof, 1963; Dick Clark's Easygoing Guide to Good Grooming, 1986; The History of American Bandstand, 1986. Formed dick clark productions 1956, TV and motion picture production with in-person concert division, cable TV programing dept.Host of two weekly synd. radio programs: Countdown American and Rock Roll & Remember. Founder and principal owner of Unistar Communications Group. Took company public in January, 1987 (NASDAQ: DCPI), serves as chmn. & CEO.
PICTURES: *Actor*: Because They're Young (debut, 1960), The Young Doctors, Killers Three. *Producer*: Psychout, The Savage Seven, Remo Williams: The Adventure Begins.
TELEVISION: *Host*: American Bandstand (also exec. prod.; Emmy Award as exec. prod., 1983), The Dick Clark Beechnut Show, Dick Clark's World of Talent, Record Years, Years of Rock. $25,000 Pyramid (3 Emmy Awards as host: 1979, 1985, 1986), $100,000 Pyramid, The Challengers. *Producer*: Where The Action Is, Swinging Country, Happening, Get It Together, Shebang, Record Years, Years of Rock. *Executive Producer*: American Music Awards, Academy of Country Music Awards, Dick Clark's New Year's Rockin' Eve, ACE Awards, Daytime Emmy Awards, Golden Globe Awards, Soap Opera Awards, Superstars and Their Moms, Caught in the Act (pilot). *Series*: TV's Bloopers & Practical Jokes, Puttin' on the Hits, Puttin' on the Kids, Dick Clark's Nitetime, Inside America, In Person From the Palace, Getting in Touch, Live! Dick Clark Presents! *Movies*: Elvis, Man in the Santa Claus Suit, Murder in Texas, Reaching for the Stars, The Demon Murder Case, The Woman Who Willed a Miracle (Emmy Award, 1983), Birth of the Beatles, Copacabana, Promised a Miracle, The Town Bully, Liberace, Backtrack, Death Dreams, Elvis and the Colonel, Secret Sins of the Father. Specials: Live Aid—An All-Star Concert for African Relief, Farm Aid III, Super Bloopers & New Practical Jokes, American Bandstand's 33 1/3 Celebration,

America Picks the No. 1 Songs, You Are the Jury, Thanks for Caring, Supermodel of the World, Freedom Festival '89, What About Me I'm Only Three, 1992 USA Music Challenge.

CLARK, DUNCAN C.
Executive. b. July, 1952, Sutton, Surrey, England. Entered industry in 1972. Appointed dir. of publicity and adv., CIC, Jan. 1979, taking up similar post in 1981 for United Artists. On formation of U.I.P. in 1982, appt. dir., pub. and adv., & deputy mng. dir., 1983. 1987 appt. v.p. adv. & pub., Columbia Pictures Intl (NY). In 1987, sr. v.p. intl marketing for Columbia (Burbank); appt. sr. v.p., Columbia Tri-Star Film Distribs., Inc., (NY). Relocated to corp. headquarters in Culver City, 1991. Appointed exec. v.p. Worldwide Marketing, Aug. 1994.

CLARK, GREYDON
Producer, Director, Writer. b. Niles, MI, Feb. 7, 1943. e. Western Michigan U., B.A., theatre arts, 1963. Heads own company, World Amusement Corp., Sherman Oaks, CA.
PICTURES: Writer: Satan's Sadists, Psychic Killer. Dir.-writer: Mothers Fathers and Lovers, Bad Bunch. Prod.-writer-dir.: Satan's Cheerleaders, Hi-Riders, Angel's Brigade, Without Warning, Joysticks (prod., dir. only), Uninvited (dir. only), Skinheads.

CLARK, HILARY J.
Executive. e. U. of Southern California, B.A., 1976. Began industry career 1978 as ad-pub admin. in co-op adv. dept., Buena Vista Dist. Co. Promoted to mgr. of natl. field pub & promo., 1980. Acted as unit publicist on numerous films (Explorers, Sylvester, Swing Shift, Twilight Zone, Crossroads, etc.) before returning to BV 1986 as natl. pub. dir. for Walt Disney Pictures. Became exec. dir. of Natl. Publicity for Disney and Touchstone Pictures, 1988; v.p. Intl. Publicity for Buena Vista Intl., 1990.

CLARK, MATT
Actor, Director. b. Washington, DC, Nov. 25, 1936.
THEATER: NY: A Portrait of the Artist as a Young Man, The Subject Was Roses, The Trial of the Catonsville Nine; Regional: One Flew Over the Cuckoo's Nest, Tonight We Improvise.
PICTURES: Black Like Me (debut, 1964), In the Heat of the Night, Will Penny, The Bridge at Remagen, Macho Callahan, Homer (co-s.p. only), Monte Walsh, The Beguiled, The Grissom Gang, The Cowboys, The Culpepper Cattle Company, The Great Northfield Minnesota Raid, Jeremiah Johnson, The Life and Times of Judge Roy Bean, Emperor of the North Pole, The Laughing Policeman, Pat Garrett and Billy the Kid, White Lightning, The Terminal Man, Hearts of the West, Outlaw Blues, Kid Vengeance, The Driver, Dreamer, Brubaker, An Eye for an Eye, Legend of the Lone Ranger, Ruckus, Some Kind of Hero, Honkytonk Man, Love Letters, The Adventures of Buckaroo Banzai, Country, Tuff Turf, Return to Oz, Let's Get Harry, Da (dir. only), The Horror Show, Back to the Future Part III, Cadence, Class Action, Frozen Assets, Fortunes of War, The Harvest, Candyman: Farewell to the Flesh.
TELEVISION: Series: Dog and Cat, The Jeff Foxworthy Show. Mini-Series: The Winds of War, War and Remembrance. Movies: The Execution of Private Slovik, The Great Ice Rip-Off, Melvin Purvis: G-Man, This is the West That Was, The Kansas City Massacre, Dog and Cat (pilot), Lacy and the Mississippi Queen, The Last Ride of the Dalton Gang, The Children Nobody Wanted, In the Custody of Strangers, Love Mary, Out of the Darkness, The Quick and the Dead, The Gambler III: The Legend Continues, Terror on Highway 91, Blind Witness, Deceptions, Dead Before Dawn, Barbarians at the Gate. Specials: Shadow of Fear, Andrea's Story. Pilots: The Big Easy, Highway Honeys, Traveling Man. Guest: Hardcastle and McCormick, Midnight Caller, Bodies of Evidence. Director: Midnight Caller, My Dissident Mom (Schoolbreak Special).

CLARK, PETULA
Actress, Singer. b. Ewell, Surrey, England, Nov. 15, 1932. On British stage in The Sound of Music, Candida, Someone Like You (also composer, co-writer). B'way debut in Blood Brothers (1993). Starred in own BBC TV series 1967-8. Winner of two Grammy Awards, 1964 (Best Rock and Roll Recording: Downtown), 1965 (Best Contemporary R & R Vocal Performance Female: I Know a Place).
PICTURES: Medal for the General (debut, 1944), Strawberry Roan, Murder in Reverse, I Know Where I'm Going, London Town (My Heart Goes Crazy), Vice Versa, Easy Money, Here Come the Huggets, Vote for Hugget, Don't Ever Leave Me, The Huggets Abroad, The Romantic Age (Naughty Arlette), Dance Hall, White Corridors, Madame Louise, The Card (The Promoter), Made In Heaven, The Gay Dog, The Runaway Bus, The Happiness of Three Women, Track the Man Down, That Woman Opposite (City After Midnight), Six-Five Special, A Couteaux Tires (Daggers Drawn), Questi Pazzi Pazzi Italiani, The Big T.N.T. Show, Finian's Rainbow, Goodbye Mr. Chips, Never Never Land.

CLARK, SUSAN
Actress. r.n. Nora Golding. b. Sarnid, Ontario, Canada, March 8, 1943. Trained at Royal Acad. of Dramatic Art, London and Stella Adler Academy.
PICTURES: Banning (debut, 1967), Coogan's Bluff, Madigan, Tell Them Willie Boy Is Here, Colossus: The Forbin Project, Skullduggery, Skin Game, Valdez Is Coming, Showdown, The Midnight Man, Airport 1975, Night Moves, The Apple Dumpling Gang, The North Avenue Irregulars, Murder by Decree, City on Fire, Promises in the Dark, Double Negative, Nobody's Perfekt, Porky's.
TELEVISION: Series: Webster. Movies: Something for a Lonely Man, The Challengers, The Astronaut, Trapped, Babe (Emmy Award, 1976), McNaughton's Daughter, Amelia Earhart, Jimmy B. and Andre (also co-prod.), The Choice, Maid in America (also co-prod.), Snowbound: The Jim and Jennifer Stolpa Story, Tonya and Nancy: The Inside Story, Butterbox Babies. Specials: Hedda Gabler, Double Solitaire.

CLAYBURGH, JILL
Actress. b. New York, NY, April 30, 1944. m. playwright David Rabe. e. Sarah Lawrence Coll. 1966. Former member of Charles Playhouse, Boston.
THEATER: The Nest (off-B'way), The Rothschilds, Jumpers, Pippin, In the Boom Boom Room, Design For Living.
PICTURES: The Wedding Party (debut, 1969), The Telephone Book, Portnoy's Complaint, The Thief Who Came to Dinner, Terminal Man, Gable and Lombard, Silver Streak, Semi-Tough, An Unmarried Woman (Acad. Award nom.), Luna, Starting Over (Acad. Award nom.), It's My Turn, First Monday in October, I'm Dancing as Fast as I Can, Hannah K, Where Are The Children?, Shy People, Beyond the Ocean, Whispers in the Dark, Rich in Love, Day of Atonement, Naked in New York.
TELEVISION: Series: Search For Tomorrow. Movies: The Snoop Sisters (Female Instinct), Miles To Go, Hustling, The Art of Crime, Griffin and Phoenix, Who Gets the Friends?, Fear Stalk, Unspeakable Acts, Reason for Living: The Jill Ireland Story, Trial: The Price of Passion, Firestorm: 72 Hours in Oakland, Honor Thy Father and Mother: The True Story of the Menedez Murders, For the Love of Nancy, The Face on the Milk Carton. Guest: Medical Center, Rockford Files, Saturday Night Live.

CLEESE, JOHN
Actor, Writer. b. Weston-Super-Mare, England, Oct. 27, 1939. e. Clifton Coll., Cambridge U. Began acting with Cambridge University Footlights revue. With classmate Graham Chapman wrote for British TV. Co-creator of Monty Python's Flying Circus. Co-author (with psychiatrist Robin Skynner): Families and How to Survive Them (1983), Life and How to Survive It (1995).
PICTURES: Interlude (debut, 1968), The Bliss of Mrs. Blossom, The Best House in London, The Rise and Rise of Michael Rimmer (also co-s.p.), The Magic Christian (also co-s.p.), The Statue, And Now for Something Completely Different (also co-s.p.), Monty Python and the Holy Grail (also co-s.p.), The Life of Brian (also co-s.p.), The Great Muppet Caper, Time Bandits, The Secret Policeman's Other Ball, Monty Python Live at the Hollywood Bowl (also co-s.p.), Monty Python's The Meaning of Life (also co-s.p.), Yellowbeard, Privates on Parade, Silverado, Clockwise, A Fish Called Wanda (also co-s.p., exec. prod., BAFTA Award, Writer's Guild of America nom., Oscar nom.), The Big Picture (cameo), Erik the Viking, An American Tail: Fievel Goes West (voice), Splitting Heirs, Mary Shelley's Frankenstein, The Swan Princess (voice), Rudyard Kipling's The Jungle Book.
TELEVISION: Special: Taming of the Shrew. Series: The Frost Report, At Last the 1948 Show, Monty Python's Flying Circus, Fawlty Towers. Guest: Cheers (Emmy Award, 1987).

CLEMENS, BRIAN
Writer, Producer, Director. b. Croydon, England. Early career in advertising then wrote BBC TV play. Later TV filmed series as writer, script editor and features. Script editor Danger Man; Won Edgar Allen Poe Award for Best TV Thriller of 1962 (Scene of the Crime for U.S. Steel Hour). Various plays for Armchair Theatre; ATV Drama 70; Love Story. Winner two Edgar Allan Poe Awards, Cinema Fantastique Award for best s.p.
PICTURES: The Tell-Tale Heart, Station Six-Sahara, The Peking Medallion, And Soon The Darkness, The Major, When The Wind Blows, See No Evil, Dr. Jekyll and Sister Hyde, Golden Voyage of Sinbad, Watcher in the Woods, Stiff, Highlander 2, Justine (France), Bugs (UK).
TELEVISION: Wrote and prod.: The Avengers (2 Emmy noms.), The New Avengers, The Professionals, Escapade (U.S.), Perry Mason, Loose Cannon, Fther Dowling..

CLENNON, DAVID
Actor. b. Waukegan, IL. e. Univ. of Notre Dame, Yale Drama School.
THEATER: NY: Unseen Hand, Forensic and the Navigators, As You Like It, Little Eyolf, Medal of Honor Rag, The Cherry Orchard. Regional: Blood Knot, Loot, Marat/Sade, Beyond Therapy, others.
PICTURES: The Paper Chase, Bound for Glory, The Greatest, Coming Home, Gray Lady Down, Go Tell the Spartans, On the

Yard, Being There, Hide in Plain Sight, Missing, The Escape Artist, The Thing, Ladies and Gentlemen the Fabulous Stains, The Right Stuff, Hannah K., Star 80, Falling in Love, Sweet Dreams, Legal Eagles, He's My Girl, The Couch Trip, Betrayed, Downtown, Man Trouble, Light Sleeper, Matinee, Two Crimes.
TELEVISION: *Series:* Rafferty, Park Place, thirtysomething, Almost Perfect. *Movies:* The Migrants, Crime Club, Helter Skelter, Gideon's Trumpet, Marriage is Alive and Well, Reward, Special Bulletin, Best Kept Secrets, Blood and Orchids, Conspiracy: The Trial of the Chicago 8, Nurses on the Line: The Crash of Flight 7, Black Widow Murders, Original Sins, Tecumseh: The Last Warrior. *Guest:* Alfred Hitchcock Presents, Murder She Wrote, Barney Miller, Dream On (Emmy Award, 1993). *Special:* The Seagull.

CLIFFORD, GRAEME
Director. b. England. Worked as film editor on such films as Don't Look Now, The Rocky Horror Picture Show, The Man Who Fell to Earth, F.I.S.T., The Postman Always Rings Twice, before turning to directing.
PICTURES: Frances, Burke & Wills, Gleaming the Cube, Deception, Past Tense.
TELEVISION: The New Avengers, Barnaby Jones, Faerie Tale Theatre, The Turn of the Screw, Twin Peaks, Crossroads.

CLOONEY, GEORGE
Actor. b. Augusta, KY, 1962. Father is tv newscaster-host Nick Clooney. Aunt is singer Rosemary Clooney. e. Northern KY Univ.
PICTURES: Return of the Killer Tomatoes, Red Surf, Unbecoming Age, From Dusk Till Dawn, Batman and Robin.
TELEVISION: *Series:* E/R, The Facts of Life, Roseanne, Sunset Beat, Baby Talk, Sisters, ER.

CLOONEY, ROSEMARY
Singer, Actress. b. Maysville, KY, May 23, 1928. Was singer with sister Betty on radio and with Tony Pastor's band. Won first place on Arthur Godfrey's Talent Scouts in early 1950's. Had first million selling record in 1951 with Come on-a My House. Son is actor Miguel Ferrer. *Autobiography:* This for Remembrance (1977).
PICTURES: The Stars Are Singing (debut, 1953), Here Come the Girls, Red Garters, White Christmas, Deep in My Heart, Radioland Murders.
TELEVISION: *Series:* Songs for Sale, The Johnny Johnston Show, The Rosemary Clooney Show (1956-57), The Lux Show Starring Rosemary Clooney (1957-58). *Movie:* Sister Margaret and the Saturday Night Ladies. *Guest:* Ed Sullivan, Steve Allen, Perry Como's Kraft Music Hall, Red Skelton, Dick Powell Show, Bing Crosby, Hardcastle and McCormick, ER.

CLOSE, GLENN
Actress. b. Greenwich, CT, Mar. 19, 1947. e. Coll. of William and Mary. Began performing with a repertory group Fingernails, then toured country with folk-singing group Up With People. Professional debut at Phoenix Theatre, New York. Also accomplished musical performer (lyric soprano).
THEATER: *NY:* Love for Love, Rules of the Game, Member of the Wedding, Rex, Uncommon Women and Others, The Crucifer of Blood, Wine Untouched, The Winter Dancers, Barnum, Singular Life of Albert Nobbs (Obie Award), The Real Thing (Tony Award, 1984), Childhood, Joan of Arc at the Stake, Benefactors, Death and the Maiden (Tony Award, 1992), Sunset Boulevard (Tony Award, 1995). *Regional:* King Lear, Uncle Vanya, The Rose Tattoo, A Streetcar Named Desire, Brooklyn Laundry, Sunset Boulevard.
PICTURES: The World According to Garp (debut, 1982), The Big Chill, The Natural, The Stone Boy, Greystoke: The Legend of Tarzan Lord of the Apes (dubbed voice), Jagged Edge, Maxie, Fatal Attraction, Light Years (voice), Dangerous Liaisons, Immediate Family, Reversal of Fortune, Hamlet, Meeting Venus, Hook (cameo), The Paper, The House of the Spirits, Anne Frank Remembered (voice), Mary Reilly, Mars Attacks, 101 Dalmatians.
TELEVISION: *Movies:* Too Far To Go, The Orphan Train, Something About Amelia, Stones for Ibarra, Sarah: Plain and Tall, Skylark (also co-exec. prod.), Serving in Silence: The Margarethe Cammermeyer Story (Emmy Award, 1995; also co-exec. prod.). *Specials:* The Elephant Man, Broken Hearts Broken Homes (host, co-exec. prod.).

COATES, ANNE V.
Film editor, Producer. b. Reigate, Surrey, Eng. e. Bartrum Gables Coll. m. late dir. Douglas Hickox. Worked as nurse at East Grinstead Plastic Surgery Hospital. Recipient of 1995 A.C.E. Career Achievement award.
PICTURES: Pickwick Papers, Grand National Night, Forbidden Cargo, To Paris With Love, The Truth About Women, The Horse's Mouth, Tunes of Glory, Don't Bother to Knock, Lawrence of Arabia (Academy Award, 1962; also ACE nom.), Becket (Acad. Award & ACE noms.), Young Cassidy, Those Magnificent Men in Their Flying Machines (co-ed.), Hotel Paridiso, Great Catherine, The Bofors Guns, The Adventurers, Friends, The Public Eye, The Nelson Affair, 11 Harrowhouse, Murder on the Orient Express (BAFTA nom.), Man Friday, Aces High, The Eagle Has Landed, The Medusa Touch (prod. & sprv. ed.), The Legacy, The Elephant Man (Acad. Award nom., BAFTA nom.), The Bushido Blade, Ragtime (co-ed.), The Pirates of Penzance, Greystoke: The Legend of Tarzan Lord of the Apes, Lady Jane, Raw Deal, Masters of the Universe, Farewell to the King (co-ed.), Listen to Me, I Love You to Death, What About Bob?, Chaplin, In the Line of Fire (Acad. Award nom., A.C.E. nom., BAFTA nom., G.B.F.E. award), Pontiac Moon, Congo, Striptease.

COBE, SANDY
Executive, Producer, Distributor. b. New York, NY, Nov. 30, 1928. e. Tulane U., B.A., fine arts. U.S. Army WWII & Korea, combat photographer; produced 11 features for Artmark Pictures, N.Y. General Studios, exec. v.p., distribution; First Cinema Releasing Corp., pres. Formed Sandy Cobe Productions, Inc., producer, packager, European features for U.S. theatrical & television. 1974 pres., Intercontinental Releasing Corporation, domestic and foreign distribution of theatrical features; 1989, named chmn. of bd. and CEO. Member, dir. of bd., American Film Marketing Assn., Dir. of bd., Scitech Corp. USA, 14 year mem., Academy of Television Arts and Sciences, 32nd degree Mason, Shriner, Variety Club Int'l. Special commendations from: Mayor of Los Angeles, California State Senate, City and County of L.A., California Assembly and Senate, and Governor of CA.
PICTURES: Terror on Tour (prod.), Access Code (exec. prod.), A.R.C.A.D.E. (prod.), Terminal Entry (exec. prod.), Open House (prod.).

COBE, SHARYON REIS
Executive, Producer. b. Honolulu, HI, e. U. of Hawaii, Loyola Marymount U. Dancer Fitzgerald, & Sample, N.Y. United Air Lines, N.Y.; v.p.; story editor, Gotham Publishing N.Y.; v.p., distribution-foreign sales, World Wide Film Distributors, L.A.; pres. and chief operating officer, Intercontinental Releasing Corp., L.A. Member of Variety Clubs Intl., Industry Rltns. Com., Amer. Film Mktg. Assoc., Indpt. Feature Projects West. (tent 25), Women in Film.
PICTURES: Home Sweet Home (prod. mgr.), To All a Good Night (assoc. prod.), Access Code (co-prod.), Terminal Entry (prod.), Open House (exec. in chg. of prod.).

COBLENZ, WALTER
Producer.
PICTURES: The Candidate, All the President's Men, The Onion Field, The Legend of the Lone Ranger, Strange Invaders, Sister Sister, 18 Again!, For Keeps, The Babe.
TELEVISION: *Movie:* Jack Reed: Badge of Honor, House of Secrets, Not Our Son.

COBURN, JAMES
Actor. b. Laurel, NB, Aug. 31, 1928. e. Los Angeles City Coll., where he studied drama. Also studied with Stella Adler in NY for 5 years. Served in U.S. Army. First acting role in coast production of Billy Budd. Later to New York, where he worked on TV commercials, then in live teleplays on Studio One, GE Theatre, Robert Montgomery Presents. Summer stock in Detroit before returning to Hollywood. Commercial: Remington Rand.
PICTURES: Ride Lonesome (debut, 1959), Face of a Fugitive, The Magnificent Seven, Hell Is for Heroes, The Great Escape, Charade, The Americanization of Emily, The Loved One, Major Dundee, A High Wind in Jamaica, Our Man Flint, What Did You Do in the War Daddy?, Dead Heat on a Merry-Go-Round, In Like Flint, Waterhole No. 3, The President's Analyst, Duffy, Candy, Hard Contract, Last of the Mobile Hot-Shots, The Carey Treatment, The Honkers, Duck You Sucker, Pat Garrett and Billy the Kid, The Last of Sheila, Harry in Your Pocket, A Reason to Live—A Reason to Die, The Internecine Project, Bite the Bullet, Hard Times, Sky Riders, The Last Hard Men, Midway, Cross of Iron, California Suite (cameo), The Muppet Movie, Goldengirl, Firepower, The Baltimore Bullet, Loving Couples, Mr. Patman, High Risk, Looker, Martin's Day, Death of a Soldier, Phoenix Fire, Walking After Midnight, Train to Heaven, Young Guns II, Hudson Hawk, The Player, Hugh Hefner: Once Upon a Time (narrator), Deadfall, Sister Act 2: Back in the Habit, Maverick, The Nutty Professor, Eraser.
TELEVISION: *Series:* Klondike, Acapulco, Darkroom (host), Hollywood Stuntmakers (host), Fifth Corner. *Movies:* Draw!, Sins of the Fathers, Malibu, The Dain Curse, Valley of the Dolls, Crash Landing: The Rescue of Flight 232, The Hit List, Greyhounds, The Avenging Angel, Ray Alexander: A Menu for Murder, The Set Up. *Specials:* Pinocchio (Faerie Tale Theater), Mastergate. *Pilot:* Silver Fox.

COCA, IMOGENE
Actress. b. Philadelphia, PA, Nov. 18, 1908. p. the late Joe Coca, orchestra leader, and Sadie Brady, vaudevillian. At 11, debut tap dancer in New York vaudeville; solo dancer B'way musicals; as comedienne, in New Faces of 1934; with former husband, Bob Burton, in Straw Hat Revue in 1939, and others through 1942. New York night clubs, Cafe Society and Le Ruban

Bleu, Palmer House, Chicago; Park Plaza, St. Louis, and at Tamiment resort. Seen on early experimental TV telecasts in 1939.1949 to TV via B'way Revue, co-starring with Sid Caesar. Emmy Award, 1951. Returned to B'way in Musical On the Twentieth Century.
PICTURES: Under the Yum Yum Tree, Promises! Promises!, Rabbit Test, National Lampoon's Vacation, Nothing Lasts Forever, Buy and Cell, Papa Was a Preacher.
TELEVISION: Series: Buzzy Wuzzy (host, 1948), Admiral Broadway Revue (1949), Your Show of Shows (1950-54). Imogene Coca Show (1954-55), Sid Caesar Invites You (1958), Grindl (1963-64), It's About Time (1966-67). Special: Ruggles of Red Gap. Guest: Fireside Theatre, Hollywood Palace, Love American Style, Moonlighting. Movies: Alice in Wonderland, Return of the Beverly Hillbillies.

COCCHI, JOHN
Writer, Critic. b. Brooklyn, NY, June 19, 1939. e. Fort Hamilton H.S., 1957; Brooklyn College, A.A.S., 1961. U.S. Army, 1963-65. Puritan Film Labs, manager, 1967-69. Independent-International Pictures, biographer-researcher, 1969. Boxoffice Magazine, critic, reporter, columnist, 1970-79. Co-author: The American Movies Reference Book (Prentice-Hall). Contributor: Screen Facts, Film Fan Monthly, Films in Review. Actor in: The Diabolical Dr. Ongo, Thick as Thieves, Captain Celluloid vs. the Film Pirates. Worked on dubbing: Dirtymouth, 1970. Author of film books incl. The Westerns: a Movie Quiz Book, Second Feature, Best of the B Films. Now free lance writer, researcher, agent. Recent credits: contributor to books, 500 Best American Films, 500 Best British and Foreign-Language Films. Consultant to Killiam Shows, Prof. Richard Brown, Photofest, Star Magazine; research chief for American Movie Classics channel, 1984-present.

COEN, ETHAN
Producer, Writer. b. St. Louis Park, MN, Sep. 21, 1957. e. Princeton U. Co-wrote s.p. with brother, Joel, XYZ Murders (renamed Crimewave).
PICTURES: Producer/Co-Writer: Blood Simple (also co-edited under pseudonym Roderick James), Raising Arizona, Miller's Crossing, Barton Fink, The Hudsucker Proxy, Fargo (Best director, Cannes 1996).

COEN, GUIDO
Producer, Executive. In 1959 became production exec. Twickenham Studios, 1963 Appt. a dir. there, then producer and executive prod. series pictures for Fortress Films and Kenilworth Films.
PICTURES: One Jump Ahead, Golden Link, The Hornet's Nest, Behind the Headlines, Murder Reported, There's Always a Thursday, Date with Disaster, The End of the Line, The Man Without a Body, Woman Eater, Kill Her Gently, Naked Fury, Operation Cupid, Strictly Confidential, Dangerous Afternoon, Jungle Street, Strongroom, Penthouse, Baby Love, One Brief Summer, Burke and Hare, Au Pair Girls, Intimate Games.

COEN, JOEL
Director, Writer. b. St. Louis Park, MN, Nov. 29, 1954. e. Simon's Rock College, MA; studied film at NYU. m. actress Frances McDormand. Was asst. editor on Fear No Evil and Evil Dead. Co-wrote with brother, Ethan, s.p. for XYZ Murders (renamed Crime Wave.) Cameo role in film Spies Like Us, 1985.
PICTURES: Director/Co-Writer: Blood Simple (also co-editor, under pseudonym Roderick Jaynes), Raising Arizona, Miller's Crossing, Barton Fink (also co-editor, as Roderick Jaynes), The Hudsucker Proxy, Fargo (Best director, Cannes 1996).

COHEN, ELLIS A.
Producer, Writer. b. Baltimore, MD, Sept. 15, 1945. e. Baltimore Jr. Coll., A.A. 1967, Univ. of W. LA, mini-law sch., 1992. 1963, talent coord., Cerebral Palsy Telethon, WBAL-TV, Baltimore; 1964, p.r. asst. Campbell-Ewald Adv. Agency, L.A.; 1966, and retail mgr. 1968-69, talent booking; 1968, journalist & editor 1969-72, pr & adv. Camera Mart, NY; 1972-74 creator & editor-in-chief, TV/New York Magazine.; 1974-76 dir., world-wide pub./adv., William Morris Agency, Prod., NY Emmy Awards Telecast (1973 & 1974), WOR-TV (prod.), chmn., exec. prod. of TV Academy Celebrity drop-in luncheon series; 1972, talent coordinator Bob Hope's Celebrity Flood Relief Telethon. Exec. prod., 1976 Democratic Nat'l Conv. Gala. 1978, Account Exec., Solters & Roskin P.R., L.A.; 1978 director of TV Network Boxing Events, Don King Prod., NY; 1979 ,Prod., Henry Jaffe Ent., Inc., 1980, prod.-writer, CBS Entertainment & pres. Ellis A. Cohen Prods. Since 1983, pres., Hennessey Ent., Ltd. Novel: Avenue of the Stars, (1990). Non-fiction: Dangerous Evidence (1995). Member, WGA, Producers Guild of America, World Affairs Council, Friars Club, Amer. Newspaper Guild, Intl. Press Corp.; Israeli Press Corp., Academy of TV Arts & Sciences, SAG. Comm. Public Interest for NYC; Natl. Writers Union.
TELEVISION: Movies: Aunt Mary (prod., story); First Steps (prod.), Love Mary (prod.). Specials: NY Area Emmy Awards (prod. 1973 and 1974).

COHEN, IRWIN R.
Exhibition Executive. b. Baltimore, MD, Sept. 4, 1924. e. U. of Baltimore, (LLB) 1948, admitted to Maryland and U.S. Bar same year. Active limited practice. R/C Theatres outgrowth of family business started in 1932. One of founders of Key Federal Bank, chairman of board Loan Comm., director and member of exec. comm. Pres. NATO of Virginia 1976-78, chairman 1978-80. Director, member of exec. comm., treasurer, chairman of finance comm. National NATO. Member of Motion Picture Pioneers, Will Rogers Hospital, and various other orgs.

COHEN, LARRY
Director, Producer, Writer. b. New York, NY, July 15, 1946. e. CCNY. Started as writer for TV series incl. Kraft Mystery Theatre, The Defenders, Arrest and Trial. Creator of series Branded, The Invaders, Cool Million, Blue Light, Cop Talk.
PICTURES: Daddy's Gone A-Hunting (co-s.p.), El Condor (s.p.), Bone (Housewife; dir., prod., s.p.), Black Caesar (dir., prod., s.p.), It's Alive (dir., prod., s.p.), Demon (God Told Me To; dir., prod., s.p.), The Private Files of J. Edgar Hoover (dir., prod., s.p.), It Lives Again (dir., prod., s.p.), Success (American Success Company; story), Full Moon High (prod., dir., s.p.), Q (dir., prod., s.p.), I The Jury (s.p.), Perfect Strangers (Blind Alley; dir., prod., s.p.), The Man Who Wasn't There (story), Special Effects (dir., s.p.), Scandalous (story), The Stuff (exec. prod., dir., s.p.), Spies Like Us (actor), It's Alive III: Island of the Alive (exec. prod., dir., s.p.), Return to Salem's Lot (dir., exec. prod., s.p.), Best Seller (s.p.), Deadly Illusion (s.p.), Maniac Cop (prod., s.p.), Wicked Stepmother (dir., exec. prod., s.p.), Maniac Cop II (prod., s.p.), The Ambulance (dir., s.p.), The Apparatus (s.p.), Guilty As Sin (s.p.), Original Gangstas (dir.), Invasion of Privacy (writer).
TELEVISION: Movies: Cool Million (Mask of Marcella; writer), Man on the Outside (writer), Shootout in a One Dog Town (co-writer, story) Desperado: Avalanche at Devil's Ridge (writer), As Good as Dead (dir., writer, prod.), 87th Precinct–Ice (writer). Series: NYPD Blue (writer).

COHEN, PAUL
Executive. b. New York, NY, Apr. 16, 1948. e. Hofstra U.; New School for Social Research; Jungian Inst. NY. Started in industry as exec. prod., distributor, screenwriter, producer for Masada Prods. Served as v.p. of Grand Slam Prods., exec. prod. for Moonbeam Assocs. Head of Analysis Films, 1976-84. Founded Aries Film Releasing, 1989, becoming pres. & CEO.
PICTURES: Caligula, My Brilliant Career, Maniac, Basket Case, The Chosen, Butterfly, The Innocent, Mephisto, The Icicle Thief, My Twentieth Century, Superstar: The Life and Times of Andy Warhol, Overseas, The Story of Boys and Girls, Thank You and Goodnight, Lovers, Bad Lieutenant.

COHEN, ROB
Producer, Director. b. Cornwall-on-the-Hudson, NY, March 12, 1949. e. Harvard U. BA. Formerly exec. v.p. in chg of m.p. and TV for Motown. Started as dir. of m.p. for TV at 20th Century-Fox. Joined Motown at age of 24 to produce films. Headed own production co. 1985, appt. pres., Keith Barish Prods.
PICTURES: Mahogany (prod.), The Bingo Long Traveling All-Stars (prod.), Scott Joplin (prod.), Almost Summer (prod.), Thank God It's Friday (prod.), The Wiz (prod.), A Small Circle of Friends (dir.), Scandalous (co-s.p.), The Razor's Edge (prod.), The Legend of Billie Jean (prod.), Light of Day (co-prod.), The Witches of Eastwick (co-exec. prod.), The Monster Squad (co-exec. prod.), Ironweed (co-exec. prod.), The Running Man (co-exec. prod.), The Serpent and the Rainbow (exec. prod.), Disorganized Crime (exec. prod.), Bird on a Wire (prod.), The Hard Way (prod.), Dragon: The Bruce Lee Story (dir., co-s.p., actor), Dragonheart.
TELEVISION: Miami Vice (dir.), Cuba and Claude (exec. prod.), Vanishing Son (exec. prod.).

COHEN, ROBERT B.
Executive. e. George Washington U., B.A., Southern Texas Sch. of Law. 1980-84. Atty. for Pillsbury Madison's Sutro and for Greenberg, Glusker, Fields, Clamans and Machtiger (L.A.). Was asst. gen. counsel for Columbia Pictures. Joined Paramount 1985 as sr. atty. for M.P. Group. to oversee legal functions for assigned feature films; 1988 named v.p. in charge of legal affairs, Motion Picture Group of Paramount; 1990, named sr. v.p. legal affairs, motion picture group, Paramount.

COHEN, SID
Executive. e. Univ. of RI Col. of Business. Served as western div. mngr. for WB tv distrib. in 1970's. 1979-84, v.p. feature planning & sls. develop. for domestic tv distrib. div. of Paramount Pictures Corp. There he created the first satellite- delivered feature-film package for free over-the-air tv on a regularly scheduled natl. basis. 1985-91, pres. of domestic tv distrib. at King World Prods. Sept. 1991, became pres. of MGM Domestic TV Distrib.

COHN, ROBERT
Producer. b. Avon, NJ, Sept. 6, 1920. e. U. of Michigan, B.A., 1941. p. Jack Cohn. Joined Columbia as asst. dir. In WWII, as

Signal Corps film cutter. Air Corps Training Lab. unit mgr., combat aerial m.p. camera man with 13th A.A.F. Awarded: DFC, Air Medal & 3 clusters, Purple Heart. Assoc. prod. Lone Wolf In London, 1947; prod. Adventures in Silverado, 1948, all Col. Headed Robert Cohn prod. unit at Columbia, pres. International Cinema Guild. Columbia European prod.: exec. Columbia Studios. Hollywood: formed Robert Cohn Prod.
PICTURES: Black Eagle, Rusty Leads the Way, Palomino, Kazan, Killer That Stalked New York, The Barefoot Mailman, Mission Over Korea, The Interns, The New Interns, The Young Americans.

COLBERT, CLAUDETTE
Actress. r.n. Lily Chauchoin. b. Paris, Sept. 13, 1905. e. public schools, Paris, New York; Art Students League, N.Y. On N.Y. stage (debut, Wild Wescotts; followed by Marionette Man, We've Got to Have Money, Cat Came Back, Kiss in a Taxi, Ghost Train, The Barker, Dynamo, etc.). First screen role in For the Love of Mike (silent); voted one of ten top Money Making Stars in Fame Poll, 1935, '36, '47.
PICTURES: The Hole in the Wall (talkie debut, 1929), The Lady Lies, The Big Pond, Young Man of Manhattan, Manslaughter, Honor Among Lovers, The Smiling Lieutenant, Secrets of a Secretary, His Woman, The Wiser Sex, Misleading Lady, The Man From Yesterday, Make Me a Star (cameo), The Phantom President, The Sign of the Cross, Tonight is Ours, I Cover the Waterfront, Three Cornered Moon, The Torch Singer, Four Frightened People, It Happened One Night (Academy Award for Best Actress, 1934), Cleopatra, Imitation of Life, The Gilded Lily, Private Worlds, She Married Her Boss, The Bride Comes Home, Under Two Flags, Maid of Salem, I Met Him in Paris, Tovarich, Bluebeard's Eighth Wife, Zaza, Midnight, It's a Wonderful World, Drums Along the Mohawk, Boom Town, Arise My Love, Skylark, Remember the Day, The Palm Beach Story, No Time for Love, So Proudly We Hail, Practically Yours, Since You Went Away, Guest Wife, Tomorrow Is Forever, Without Reservations, The Secret Heart, The Egg and I, Sleep My Love, Family Honeymoon, Bride for Sale, Three Came Home, The Secret Fury, Thunder on the Hill, Let's Make It Legal, Outpost in Malaya (Planter's Wife), Daughters of Destiny, Si Versailles m'etait Conte, Texas Lady, Parrish.
THEATER: Marriage Go Round, Irregular Verb to Love, The Kingfisher, Aren't We All?
TELEVISION: Movie: The Two Mrs. Grenvilles.
(d. July 30, 1996)

COLBY, RONALD
Producer, Director, Writer. b. New York, NY. e. Hofstra U., NYU. Began career as playwright at Cafe La Mama and Caffe Cino; performed in off-B'way shows; spent year as actor-writer in residence at Pittsburgh Playhouse. Served as dialogue coach and asst. to Francis Coppola; was v.p. of Zoetrope Studios. Directed several documentaries and short films.
PICTURES: The Rain People (prod.), Hammett (prod.), Some Kind of Wonderful (exec. prod.), She's Having a Baby (exec. prod.).
TELEVISION: Margaret Bourke-White (co-prod.)

COLE, GARY
Actor. b. Park Ridge, IL, Sept. 20. e. Illinois State, theater major. Dropped out of coll. after 3 years and moved to Chicago where he tended bar, painted houses and worked with Steppenwolf Theatre group. In 1979 helped to form Remains Theatre, left in 1986 to become ensemble member of Steppenwolf.
PICTURES: Lucas, In the Line of Fire, The Brady Bunch Movie.
TELEVISION: Series: Midnight Caller, American Gothic. Movies: Heart of Steel, Fatal Vision, Vital Signs, Those She Left Behind, The Old Man and the Sea, Son of the Morning Star, The Switch, When Love Kills: The Seduction of John Hearn, A Time to Heal, Fall from Grace. Mini-Series: Echoes in the Darkness.

COLE, GEORGE
Actor. b. London, Eng., Apr. 22, 1925. e. secondary sch. Surrey. Stage debut in White Horse Inn, 1939; m.p. debut in Cottage to Let, 1941.
PICTURES: Henry V, Quartet, My Brother's Keeper, Laughter in Paradise, Scrooge, Lady Godiva Rides Again, Who Goes There (Passionate Sentry), Morning Departure (Operation Disaster), Top Secret (Mr. Potts Goes to Moscow), Happy Family, Will Any Gentleman, Apes of the Rock, The Intruder, Happy Ever After (Tonight's the Night), Our Girl Friday (Adventures of Sadie), Belles of St. Trinian's, Prize of Gold, Where There's a Will, Constant Husband, Quentin Durward, The Weapon, It's a Wonderful Life, Green Man, Bridal Path, Too Many Crooks, Blue Murder at St. Trinians, Don't Panic Chaps, Dr. Syn, One Way Pendulum, Legend of Young Dick Turpin, The Great St. Trinian's Train Robbery, Cleopatra, The Green Shoes, Vampire Lovers, Fright, The Bluebird, Mary Reilly.
TELEVISION: Life of Bliss, A Man of Our Times, Don't Forget To Write, The Good Life, Minder (series), Root Into Europe (series), My Good Friend (series), An Independent Man (series).

COLEMAN, DABNEY
Actor. b. Austin, TX, Jan. 3, 1932. e. VA Military Inst. 1949-51; U. Texas 1951-57; Neighborhood Playhouse School Theater 1958-60.
PICTURES: The Slender Thread (debut, 1965), This Property Is Condemned, The Scalphunters, The Trouble With Girls, Downhill Racer, I Love My Wife, Cinderella Liberty, The Dove, The Towering Inferno, The Other Side of the Mountain, Bite the Bullet, The Black Streetfighter, Midway, Rolling Thunder, Viva Knievel, North Dallas Forty, Nothing Personal, How to Beat the High Cost of Living, Melvin and Howard, Nine to Five, On Golden Pond, Modern Problems, Young Doctors in Love, Tootsie, WarGames, The Muppets Take Manhattan, Cloak and Dagger, The Man with One Red Shoe, Dragnet, Hot to Trot, Where the Heart Is, Short Time, Meet the Applegates, There Goes the Neighborhood, Amos & Andrew, The Beverly Hillbillies, Clifford.
TELEVISION: Movies: Brotherhood of the Bell, Savage, Dying Room Only, The President's Plane is Missing, Bad Ronald, Attack on Terror: The FBI Versus the Ku Klux Klan, Returning Home, Kiss Me Kill Me, Maneaters Are Loose!, More Than Friends, Apple Pie, When She Was Bad, Murrow, Guilty of Innocence, Sworn To Silence (Emmy Award, 1987), Baby M, Maybe Baby, Never Forget, Columbo and the Murder of a Rock Star, Judicial Consent, In the Line of Duty: Kidnapped, Devil's Food. Mini-Series: Fresno. Series: That Girl, Bright Promise, Mary Hartman Mary Hartman, Apple Pie, Forever Fernwood, Buffalo Bill, The Slap Maxwell Story, Drexell's Class, Madman of the People. Special: Plaza Suite, Texan.

COLEMAN, GARY
Actor. b. Zion, IL, Feb. 8, 1968. Gained fame as star of TV's Diff'rent Strokes.
PICTURES: On the Right Track, Jimmy the Kid.
TELEVISION: Series: Diff'rent Strokes. Guest: America 2-Night, Good Times, The Jeffersons, Lucy Moves to NBC, The Big Show, etc. Movies: The Kid from Left Field, Scout's Honor, The Kid With the Broken Halo; The Kid with the 200 I.Q., Fantastic World of D.C. Collins, Playing With Fire.

COLEMAN, NANCY
Actress. b. Everett, WA, Dec. 30, 1912. e. U. of Washington. In radio serials; on NY stage in Susan and God, Liberty Jones, Desperate Hours, 1955; American Theatre Guild Rep. Co. tour of Europe and So. America, 1961.
PICTURES: Dangerously They Live, Kings Row (debut, 1941), The Gay Sisters, Desperate Journey, Edge of Darkness, In Our Time, Devotion, Her Sister's Secret, Violence, Mourning Becomes Electra, That Man from Tangier, Slaves.
TELEVISION: Valiant Lady, Producers Showcase, Kraft Theatre, Philco Theatre, Robert Montgomery Presents, Lux Theatre, Alcoa Hour, Theatre Guild Playhouse, Play of the Week, Silver Theatre, Adams Chronicles.

COLEMAN, THOMAS J.
Executive. b. Connecticut, Apr. 13, 1950. e. Boston U. Pres., Twalzo Music Corp., 1972-73; v.p.; natl. sls. mgr., United Intl. Pictures, 1973-74; founded Atlantic Releasing Corp., 1974; Atlantic Television, Inc., 1981. All Atlantic corps. consolidated into Atlantic Entertainment Group, 1986. Co. has distributed over 100 films and produced 30 features and TV movies. Sold Atlantic, March, 1989. Formed Independent Entertainment Group, named chmn. Feb., 1992 formed Rocket Pictures.
PICTURES: Producer or Exec. Prod.: Valley Girl, Alphabet City, Roadhouse, Night of the Comet, Starchaser, Teen Wolf, Extremities, The Men's Club, Modern Girls, Nutcracker, Teen Wolf Too (exec. prod.), Cop (exec. prod.), Patty Hearst (exec. prod.), 1969 (exec. prod.), Bad Golf Made Easier (exec. prod.), Fluke (exec. prod.), A New York Minute (exec. prod.).

COLER, JOEL H.
Executive. b. Bronx, NY, July 27, 1931. e. Syracuse U., B.A., journalism. Worked as adv. asst. NBC; acct. exec. Grey advertising. Joined 20th Century-Fox 1964 as adv. coordinator Fox Intl.; 1967, named intl. adv./pub. mgr. 1974, named v.p. dir., intl. adv./pub. Nov. 1990, named v.p. publicity/promotions Fox Intl. 1991, v.p. Worldwide Distrib. Services. 1984, memb. L.A. Olympic Org. Com. Left Fox in 1992 to form Joel Coler & Friends intl. mktg. consultants.

COLIN, MARGARET
Actress. b. Brooklyn, NY, 1958. Raised on Long Island. Studied acting at Stella Adler Conservatory, Juilliard, Hofstra U. Left Hofstra to pursue acting career in Manhattan where she was cast in daytime TV series The Edge of Night. NY Theatre incl. work at Ensemble Studio, Geva Theatre and Manhattan Theatre Club (Aristocrats, Sight Unseen).
PICTURES: Pretty in Pink, Something Wild, Like Father Like Son, Three Men and a Baby, True Believer, Martians Go Home, The Butcher's Wife, Amos & Andrew, Terminal Velocity, Independence Day.
TELEVISION: Series: The Edge of Night, As the World Turns, Foley Square, Leg Work, Sibs. Movies: Warm Hearts Cold Feet,

The Return of Sherlock Holmes, The Traveling Man, Good Night Sweet Wife: A Murder in Boston, In the Shadow of Evil. *Guest:* Chicago Hope.

COLLERAN, BILL
Producer, Director. b. Edgerton, WI, Nov. 6, 1922. Story department 20th Century-Fox 1945-46; Director Louis de Rochemont 1946-50; stage mgr. NBC 1951; assoc. dir. The Hit Parade 1952-53; dir. The Hit Parade, various TV specs. 1954-56; dir. Cinerama Windjammer film 1956; tv specs. with Bing Crosby, Frank Sinatra, Debbie Reynolds 1957-60; exec. Prod. Judy Garland Show, Dean Martin Show, 1965-66; dir. Richard Burton's Hamlet film; prod. Popendipity ABC-TV spec. and various other TV specs. and series 1967-77. 1978-83, prod., dir., writer for Hill-Eubanks Group and Little Joey, Inc.; 1984-86, dir. music video for Simba; developing film and TV projects for own production co. 1988, semi-retired.

COLLET, CHRISTOPHER
Actor. b. New York, NY, March 13, 1968. Started acting in commercials as teenager.
THEATER: *NY:* Off-B'way: Coming of Age in SoHo, An Imaginary Life, Unfinished Stories. B'way: Torch Song Trilogy, Spoils of War. Regional: The Lion in Winter, The Old Boy, Pterodactyls.
PICTURES: Sleepaway Camp (debut, 1983), Firstborn, The Manhattan Project, Prayer of the Rollerboys.
TELEVISION: *Movies:* Right to Kill?, Stephen King's The Langoliers. *Specials:* Pigeon Feathers, First Love and Other Sorrows, Welcome Home Jelly Bean. *Guest:* The Equalizer, The Cosby Show.

COLLINS, GARY
Actor. b. Boston, MA, Apr. 30, 1938.
TELEVISION: *Series:* The Wackiest Ship in the Army, The Iron Horse, Sixth Sense, Born Free, Hour Magazine (host), Home. *Movies:* Quarantined, Getting Away from It All, Houston We've Got a Problem, The Night They Took Miss Beautiful, The Kid From Left Field, Jacqueline Susann's Valley of the Dolls, Danielle Steel's Secrets. *Mini-Series:* Roots.
PICTURES: The Pigeon That Took Rome, The Longest Day, Cleopatra, Stranded, Angel in My Pocket, Airport, Killer Fish, Hangar 18.

COLLINS, JOAN
Actress. b. London, Eng., May 23, 1933. e. Francis Holland Sch., London. Sister is writer Jackie Collins. Made stage debut in A Doll's House, Arts Theatre 1946. Author: Past Imperfect (autobiography, 1978), Katy, A Fight For Life, Joan Collins Beauty Book, Prime Time, Love & Desire & Hate, My Secrets, Too Damn Famous. On London, LA and NY stage in Private Lives. Video: Secrets of Fitness and Beauty (also exec. prod.)
PICTURES: I Believe in You (debut, 1951), Lady Godiva Rides Again, Judgment Deferred, Decameron Nights, Cosh Boy, The Square Ring, Turn the Key Softly, Our Girl Friday (Adventures of Sadie), The Good Die Young, Land of the Pharaohs, Virgin Queen, Girl in the Red Velvet Swing, Opposite Sex, Sea Wife, Island in the Sun, Wayward Bus, Stopover Tokyo, The Bravados, Rally Round the Flag Boys, Seven Thieves, Esther and the King, Road to Hong Kong, Warning Shot, Can Hieronymus Merkin Ever Forget Mercy Humppe and Find True Happiness?, If It's Tuesday This Must Be Belgium, Subterfuge, The Executioner, Up in the Cellar, Quest for Love, Inn of the Frightened People, Fear in the Night, Tales from the Crypt, Tales That Witness Madness, Dark Places, Alfie Darling, The Devil Within Her, The Bawdy Adventures of Tom Jones, Empire of the Ants, The Big Sleep, The Stud, Zero to Sixty, The Bitch, Game of Vultures, Sunburn, Homework, Nutcracker, Decadence, In the Bleak Mid-Winter, Decadence, In The Bleak Midwinter.
TELEVISION: *Series:* Dynasty. *Movies:* The Cartier Affair, The Making of a Male Model, Her Life as a Man, Paper Dolls, The Wild Women of Chastity Gulch, Drive Hard Drive Fast, Dynasty: The Reunion. *Specials:* Hansel and Gretel (Faerie Tale Theater), Mama's Back. *Mini-Series:* The Moneychangers, Sins, Monte Carlo (also exec. prod.), Annie.

COLLINS, PAULINE
Actress. b. Exmouth, Devon, Eng., Sept. 3, 1940. m. actor John Alderton (Thomas on Upstairs, Downstairs). e. Central School of Speech and Drama. Stage debut A Gazelle in Park Lane (Windsor, 1962). Best known to US audiences as Sarah in Upstairs, Downstairs.
THEATER: Passion Flower Hotel (London debut, 1965), The Erpingham Camp, The Happy Apple, The Importance of Being Earnest, The Night I Chased the Women with an Eel, Come as You Are, Judies, Engaged, Confusions, Romantic Comedy, Woman in Mind, Shirley Valentine (in London won Olivier Award as best actress, in NY won Tony, Drama Desk and Outer Critics Circle Awards.)
PICTURES: Secrets of a Windmill Girl, Shirley Valentine, City of Joy, My Mother's Courage.

TELEVISION: *Series:* Upstairs Downstairs, Thomas and Sarah, Forever Green, No—Honestly (all with husband), Tales of the Unexpected, Knockback, Tropical Moon Over Dorking.

COLLINS, STEPHEN
Actor. b. Des Moines, IA, Oct. 1, 1947. Appeared off-B'way in several Joseph Papp productions before B'way debut in Moonchildren, followed by No Sex We're British, The Ritz, Loves of Anatol, Censored Scenes from King Kong. Off-B'way: Twelfth Night, The Play's the Thing, Beyond Therapy, One of the Guys, The Old Boy, Putting It Together. Author of play Super Sunday (Williamstown Fest.), and novel Eye Contact (1994).
PICTURES: All the President's Men, Between the Lines, The Promise, Fedora, Star Trek: The Motion Picture, Loving Couples, Brewster's Millions, Jumpin' Jack Flash, Choke Canyon, The Big Picture, Stella, My New Gun.
TELEVISION: *Series:* Tales of the Gold Monkey, Tattinger's (revamped as Nick & Hillary), Working it Out. *Movies:* Brink's: The Great Robbery, The Henderson Monster, Dark Mirror, Threesome, Weekend War, A Woman Scorned: The Betty Broderick Story, The Disappearance of Nora, Barbara Taylor Bradford's Remember, A Family Divided. *Mini-Series:* The Rhinemann Exchange, Hold the Dream, Inside the Third Reich, Chiefs, The Two Mrs. Grenvilles, A Woman Named Jackie, Scarlett.

COLT, MARSHALL
Actor, Writer. b. New Orleans, LA, Oct. 26. e. Tulane U., B.S. Physics; Pepperdine U., M.A. Clinical Psychology; Fielding Inst., PhD. candidate student, Clinical Psychology. Combat tour in Southeast Asia during Vietnam War. Captain, U.S. Naval Reserve. Stage productions: (Hotel Universe, Who's Afraid of Virginia Woolf?, Zoo Story, Killer's Head, etc.).
PICTURES: Bimbo (short), North Dallas Forty, Those Lips, Those Eyes, Jagged Edge, Flowers in the Attic, Illegally Yours, Deceptions.
TELEVISION: *Guest:* Family, Paper Chase, Streets of San Francisco, Barnaby Jones, Murder She Wrote. *Series:* McClain's Law, Lottery! *Movies:* Colorado C-1, Sharon: Portrait of a Mistress, Once an Eagle, To Heal a Nation, Mercy or Murder, Guilty of Innocence.

COLTRANE, ROBBIE
Actor. b. Glasgow, Scotland, 1950. Ent. ind. 1977.
THEATER: San Quentin theatre workshop, Oxford Theatre Group, Citizens Theatre, Traverse Theatre, Borderline Theatre, Hampstead Theatre, Bush Theatre; one man shows: Your Obedient Servant,Mistero Buffo.
PICTURES: Bad Business (dir.); Flash Gordon, Death Watch, Subway Riders, Britannia Hospital, Scrubbers, Ghost Dance, Krull, National Lampoon's European Vacation, Caravaggio, Defence of the Realm, Chinese Boxes, The Supergrass, Mona Lisa, Eat the Rich, Bert Rigby You're a Fool, Wonderland (The Fruit Machine), Let It Ride, Henry V, Slipstream, Nuns on the Run, Perfectly Normal, The Pope Must Die, Triple Bogey on a Par 5 Hole, Oh What a Night, The Adventures of Huck Finn, Goldeneye.
TELEVISION: 1981 Take Two, Seven Deadly Sins, Keep It in the Family, Kick Up The Eighties, The Green Door, The Sheep Stealer, House With Green Shutters, The Lost Tribe, Alfresco, Laugh? I Nearly Paid My Licence Fee, Comic Strip Presents Five Go Mad in Dorset, Beat Generation, Susie, Gino, The Bullshitters, Miner's Strike, Tutti Frutti, Danny the Champion of the World (theatrical release in Europe), Jealousy (also dir., co-writer), Space Sluts From Planet Sex, French and Aunders, The Lenny Henry Show, Robbie Coltrane Special, Mistero Buffo (series), Alive & Kicking, The Secret Ingredients, The Bogie Man, Rednose of Courage, A Tour of the Western Isles, Coltrane in a Cadillac (also co-writer), Cracker (BAFTA & Cable ACE Awards).

COLUMBUS, CHRIS
Director, Writer. b. Spangler, PA, 1959. Grew up in Ohio. Started making short super 8 films in high school, studied screenwriting at New York U. Film Sch., graduated 1980. Sold first s.p., Jocks, while at college. Wrote for and developed TV cartoon series, Galaxy High School.
PICTURES: *Writer:* Reckless, Gremlins, The Goonies, Young Sherlock Holmes, Little Nemo: Adventures in Slumberland (co-s.p.). *Director:* Adventures in Babysitting (debut, 1987), Heartbreak Hotel (also s.p.), Home Alone, Only the Lonely (also s.p.), Home Alone 2: Lost in New York, Mrs. Doubtfire, Nine Months (also co-prod.).
TELEVISION: Amazing Stories, Twilight Zone, Alfred Hitchcock Presents.

COMDEN, BETTY
Writer. b. Brooklyn, NY, May 3, 1919. e. Erasmus Hall, NYU sch. of ed., B.S. Nightclub performer and writer with The Revuers, 1939-44. NY City Mayor's Award Art and Culture, 1978. Named to Songwriters Hall of Fame, 1980. NYU Alumnae Assn.'s Woman of Achievement award, 1987. Kennedy Center Honors for Life Achievement, 1991.

THEATER: With Adolph Green: writer book, sketches & lyrics for B'way shows: On the Town (book, lyrics, actress, 1944), Billion Dollar Baby (bk., Lyrics), Bonanza Bound! (bk., lyrics), Two on the Aisle (sketches and lyrics), Wonderful Town (lyrics; Tony Award, 1953), Peter Pan (lyrics), Bells Are Ringing (bk., lyrics), Say Darling (lyrics), A Party With Comden and Green (bk., lyrics, star; 1959 and 1977); Do Re Mi (lyrics), Subways Are For Sleeping (bk., lyrics), Fade Out-Fade In (bk., lyrics), Leonard Bernstein's Theatre Songs, Hallelujah, Baby (lyrics; Tony Award, 1968), Applause (book; Tony Award, 1970), Lorelei (revision to book), By Bernstein (book and some lyrics), On the Twentieth Century (2 Tony Awards, book and lyrics, 1978); A Doll's Life (bk., lyrics), The Will Rogers Follies (Tony Award, 1991). Actress only: Isn't It Romantic.
PICTURES: Writer with Adolph Green: Good News, Take Me Out to the Ballgame (lyricst), On the Town, Barkleys of Broadway, Singin' in the Rain (also lyrics), The Band Wagon (also lyrics), It's Always Fair Weather (also lyrics), Auntie Mame, Bells Are Ringing (also lyrics), What a Way to Go, The Addams Family (lyrics). Actress only: Greenwich Village, Garbo Talks, Slaves of New York.

COMO, PERRY
Singer. r.n. Pierino Como. b. Canonsburg, PA, May 18, 1912. e. Canonsburg local schools. Barber at 15; joined Carlone Band, then Ted Weems Orchestra, 1936-42; played many night clubs; records for RCA Victor. Voted Best Male vocalist M.P. Daily, TV poll, 1952-56; radio poll, 1954. Best TV performer M.P.D. Fame poll 1957. Recipient of Emmy Awards: Best Male Singer (1954, 1955), Best Emcee (1955), Best Male Personality (1956), Best Actor in a Musical or Variety Show (1956).
PICTURES: Something for the Boys (debut, 1944), Doll Face, If I'm Lucky, Words and Music.
TELEVISION: Series: The Chesterfield Supper Club, The Perry Como Show (1950-61), The Kraft Music Hall (1961-63); numerous annual holiday specials.

COMPTON, JOYCE
Actress. b. Lexington, KY, Jan. 27, 1907. e. Tulsa U. r.n. Olivia Joyce Compton. Screen debut in Ankles Preferred.
PICTURES: The Awful Truth, Spring Madness, Sky Murder, Turnabout, A Southern Yankee, If I Had a Million, Christmas in Connecticut, Artists and Models Abroad, Rustlers of Red Dog, The White Parade, Wild Party, Three Sisters, Sorry Wrong Number, Mighty Joe Young, Grand Canyon, Jet Pilot, The Persuader, Girl in the Woods, many others.

CONAWAY, JEFF
Actor. b. New York, NY, Oct. 5, 1950. Started in show business at the age of 10 when he appeared in B'way production, All the Way Home. Later toured in Critics Choice before turning to fashion modeling. Toured with musical group, 3 1/2, as lead singer and guitarist. Entered theatre arts program at NYU. Film debut at 19 in Jennifer on My Mind.
THEATER: Grease, The News.
PICTURES: Jennifer on My Mind (debut, 1971), The Eagle Has Landed, Pete's Dragon, I Never Promised You a Rose Garden, Grease, The Patriot, Elvira: Mistress of the Dark, Cover Girl, Tale of Two Sisters, The Sleeping Car, A Time to Die, Total Exposure, Almost Pregnant, In a Moment of Passion, Alien Intruder.
TELEVISION: Series: Taxi, Wizards and Warriors, Berrenger's, The Bold and the Beautiful. Guest: From Sea to Shining Sea (1974), Joe Forrester, The Mary Tyler Moore Show, Happy Days, Movin' On, Barnaby Jones, Kojak, Mickey Spillane's Mike Hammer. Movies: Having Babies, Delta County, U.S.A., Breaking Up Is Hard to Do, For the Love of It, Nashville Grab, The Making of a Male Model, Bay Coven, The Dirty Dozen: The Fatal Mission, Ghost Writer, Eye of the Storm.

CONDON, CHRIS J.
Producer, Director, Motion Equipment Designer. b. Chicago, IL, Dec. 7, 1922. e. Davidson Inst., U. of Southern California. U.S. Air Force 1943-46. Founded Century Precision Optics, 1948. Designed Athenar telephoto lenses, Century Super wideangle lenses and Duplikins. Co-founded StereoVision International, Inc. 1969 specializing in films produced in new 3-D process. Member SMPTE. Lecturer and consultant on motion picture optics and 3-D motion picture technology.
PICTURES: The Wild Ride, The Surfer, Girls, Airline, The New Dimensions.

CONN, ROBERT A.
Executive. b. Philadelphia, PA, Jan. 16, 1926. e. Lehigh U. 1944; U. of Pennsylvania, 1948. 1st Lt. Days of Eden Army Security Agency, 1944-46, 1951-52; band & act. dept., MCA, 1952-53; dir. of adv. & prom. Official Films NY 1954; head of Official Films Philadelphia sales office serving PA, Baltimore, Washington, Cleveland and Detroit, 1956. Eastern Reg. Sls. Mgr. Flamingo Films, 1957; acct. exec. Dunnan and Jeffrey, Inc., 1961; v.p., Dunnan and Jeffrey, 1962; pres., adv. mgr.; Suburban Knitwear Co., 1963; exec. v.p. Rogal Travel Service, 1964-68. 1968-78, pres. RAC Travel, Inc., Jenkintown, PA. and

pres. Royal Palm Travel, Inc. Palm Beach, Florida, 1978; Rosenbluth Travel Service, 1979; v.p., natl. retail mktg., E.F. Hutton & Co. (N.Y.), 1983.

CONNELLY, JENNIFER
Actress. b. New York, NY, Dec. 1970. e. Yale, Stamford U.
PICTURES: Once Upon a Time in America (debut, 1983), Creepers, Labyrinth, Seven Minutes in Heaven, Some Girls, The Hot Spot, Career Opportunities, The Rocketeer, Of Love and Shadows (De Amor y de Sombra), Higher Education, Mulholland Drive.
TELEVISION: Movie: The Heart of Justice.

CONNERY, SEAN
Actor. b. Edinburgh, Scotland, Aug. 25, 1930. r.n. Thomas Connery. Worked as a lifeguard and a model before landing role in chorus of London prod. of South Pacific, 1953. Prod. dir., The Bowler and the Bonnet (film doc.), I've Seen You Cut Lemons (London stage). Director of Tantallon Films Ltd. (First production: Something Like the Truth). Recipient of Golden Globe Cecil B. Demille Award, 1996.
PICTURES: No Road Back (debut, 1957), Time Lock, Hell Drivers, Action of the Tiger, Another Time Another Place, Darby O'Gill and the Little People, Tarzan's Greatest Adventure, Frightened City, On the Fiddle (Operation Snafu), The Longest Day, Dr. No, From Russia With Love, Marnie, Woman of Straw, Goldfinger, The Hill, Thunderball, A Fine Madness, You Only Live Twice, Shalako, The Molly Maguires, The Red Tent, The Anderson Tapes, Diamonds Are Forever, The Offence, Zardoz, Murder on the Orient Express, The Terrorists, The Wind and the Lion, The Man Who Would Be King, Robin and Marian, The Next Man, A Bridge Too Far, The Great Train Robbery, Meteor, Cuba, Outland, Time Bandits, Wrong Is Right, Five Days One Summer, Sword of the Valiant, Never Say Never Again, Highlander, The Name of the Rose, The Untouchables (Academy Award, best supporting actor, 1987), The Presidio, Memories of Me (cameo), Indiana Jones and the Last Crusade, Family Business, The Hunt for Red October, The Russia House, Robin Hood: Prince of Thieves (cameo), Highlander 2: The Quickening, Medicine Man (also exec. prod.), Rising Sun (also exec. prod.), A Good Man in Africa, Just Cause (also exec. prod.), First Knight, Dragonheart (voice), The Rock.
TELEVISION: Requiem for a Heavyweight, Anna Christie, Boy with the Meataxe, Women in Love, The Crucible, Riders to the Sea, Colombe, Adventure Story, Anna Karenina, Macbeth (Canadian TV).

CONNICK, HARRY, JR.
Musician, Actor. b. New Orleans, LA, Sept. 11, 1967. Began performing with Bourbon Street jazz combos at age 6. Studied classical piano. Albums: Harry Connick, Twenty, When Harry Met Sally..., Lofty's Roach Souffle, We are in Love (Grammy Award, 1991), Blue Light Red Light, Twenty Five, Eleven, When My Heart Finds Christmas, She. Acting debut in Memphis Belle (1990). B'way debut 1990 in An Evening with Harry Connick Jr.
PICTURES: When Harry Met Sally... (special musical performances and arrangements), Memphis Belle (actor), The Godfather Part III (performed theme song), Little Man Tate (actor), Sleepless in Seattle (performed song), Copycat (actor), Independence Day (actor).
TELEVISION: Specials: Swinging Out With Harry, The Harry Connick Jr. Christmas Special, Swinging Out Live, The New York Big Band Concert. Guest: Cheers.

CONNORS, MIKE
Actor. r.n. Krekor Ohanian. b. Fresno, CA, Aug. 15, 1925. e. UCLA. Film debut in Sudden Fear (1952) as Touch Connors.
PICTURES: Sudden Fear (debut, 1952), Sky Commando, 49th Man, Island in the Sky, Day of Triumph, Five Guns West, The Twinkle in God's Eye, Oklahoma Woman, Swamp Woman, The Day the World Ended, The Ten Commandments, Flesh and Spur, Shake Rattle and Rock, Voodoo Woman, Live Fast Die Young, Suicide Battalion, Panic Button, Seed of Violence, Good Neighbor Sam, Where Love Has Gone, Harlow, Situation Hopeless—But Not Serious, Stagecoach, Kiss the Girls and Make Them Die, Avalanche Express, Nightkill, Too Scared to Scream, Fist Fighter, Friend to Friend.
TELEVISION: Series: Tightrope, Mannix (Golden Globe Award), Today's FBI, Crimes of the Century (host). Movies: High Midnight, Beg Borrow or Steal, The Killer Who Wouldn't Die, Revenge for a Rape, Long Journey Back, The Death of Ocean View Park, Casino, Hart to Hart Returns. Mini-Series: War and Remembrance.

CONRAD, ROBERT
Actor, Director. r.n. Conrad Robert Falk. b. Chicago, IL, March 1, 1935. e. public schools, Northwestern U. Prof. debut; nightclub singer. Formed Robert Conrad Productions, 1966 (later A Shane Productions, then Black Sheep Productions).
PICTURES: Thundering Jets (debut, 1958), Palm Springs Weekend, Young Dillinger, The Bandits (also dir.), Murph the Surf (Live a Little Steal a Lot), The Lady in Red, Wrong Is Right, Moving Violations, Uncommon Courage, Jingle All Way.

TELEVISION: *Series*: Hawaiian Eye, Wild Wild West, The D.A., Assignment Vienna, Baa Baa Black Sheep, The Duke, A Man Called Sloane, High Mountain Rangers, Jesse Hawkes, Search and Rescue. *Guest*: Lawman, Maverick, 77 Sunset Strip. *Mini-Series*: Centennial. *Movies*: Weekend of Terror, The D.A.: Conspiracy to Kill, Five Desperate Women, Adventures of Nick Carter, The Last Day, Smash-Up on Interstate 5, Wild Wild West Revisited, Breaking Up Is Hard To Do, More Wild Wild West, Coach of the Year, Will: G. Gordon Liddy, Confessions of a Married Man, Hard Knox, Two Fathers' Justice, Assassin, Charley Hannah, The Fifth Missile, One Police Plaza, High Mountain Rangers (also dir., co-story), Glory Days (also dir.), Anything to Survive, Mario and the Mob, Sworn to Vengeance, Two Fathers: Justice for the Innocent, Search and Rescue.

CONSTANTINE, MICHAEL
Actor. b. Reading, PA, May 22, 1927.
PICTURES: The Hustler, Hawaii, Skidoo, Justine, If It's Tuesday This Must Be Belgium, Peeper, Voyage of the Damned, The North Avenue Irregulars, Pray for Death, In the Mood, Prancer, My Life, The Juror, Thinner.
TELEVISION: *Series*: Hey Landlord, Room 222 (Emmy Award, 1970), Sirota's Court. *Mini-Series*: 79 Park Avenue, Roots: The Next Generations. *Movies*: Suddenly Single, Deadly Harvest, Say Goodbye Maggie Cole, The Bait, Death Cruise, The Night That Panicked America, Conspiracy of Terror, Wanted: The Sundance Woman, The Pirate, Crisis in Mid-Air, The Love Tapes.

CONTE, JOHN
Actor, Singer. b. Palmer, MA, Sept. 15, 1915. e. Lincoln H.S., Los Angeles. Actor, Pasadena Playhouse; radio anncr., m.c.; Armed Forces, WWII. Pres. KMIR-TV, Channel 36, Desert Empire Television Corp., Palm Springs, NBC Affiliate.
THEATER: On B'way in Windy City, Allegro, Carousel, Arms and the Girl.
PICTURES: Thousands Cheer, Lost in a Harem, Trauma, Man With the Golden Arm, The Carpetbaggers.
TELEVISION: *Series*: Van Camp's Little Show (1950-52), Mantovani. *Specials*: Max Liebman Spectaculars and dramatic shows, host and star of NBC Matinee Theatre, TV Hour of Stars.

CONTI, BILL
Composer. b. Providence, RI, April 13, 1942. Studied piano at age 7, forming first band at age 15. e. Louisiana State U., Juilliard School of Music. Moved to Italy with jazz trio where scored first film, Candidate for a Killing. Was: music supvr. on Blume in Love for Paul Mazursky.
PICTURES: Harry and Tonto, Next Stop Greenwich Village, Rocky, Handle With Care, Slow Dancing in the Big City, An Unmarried Woman, F.I.S.T., The Big Fix, Paradise Alley, Uncle Joe Shannon, Rocky II, A Man a Woman and A Bank, Goldengirl, The Seduction of Joe Tynan, The Formula, Gloria, Private Benjamin, Carbon Copy, Victory, For Your Eyes Only, I The Jury, Rocky III, Neighbors, Split Image, Bad Boys, That Championship Season, Unfaithfully Yours, The Right Stuff (Academy Award, 1983), Mass Appeal, The Karate Kid, The Bear, Big Trouble, Gotcha, Beer, Nomads, F/X, The Karate Kid II, A Prayer for the Dying, Masters of the Universe, Baby Boom, Broadcast News, For Keeps, A Night in the Life of Jimmy Reardon, Betrayed, Cohen and Tate, Big Blue, Lean On Me, The Karate Kid Part III, Lock Up, The Fourth War, Backstreet Dreams, Rocky V, Necessary Roughness, Year of the Gun, A Captive in the Land, The Adventures of Huck Finn, Bound By Honor, By the Sword, Rookie of the Year, 8 Seconds, Bushwhacked, Spy Hard.
TELEVISION: Kill Me If You Can, Stark, North and South, The Pirate, Smashup on Interstate 5, Papa & Me, Napoleon and Josephine, Murderers Among Us: The Simon Wiesenthal Story. *Series themes*: Cagney and Lacy, Dynasty, Falcon Crest, The Colbys, Kenya, Heartbeat, Lifestyles of the Rich and Famous, Emerald Point N.A.S., Dolphin Cove, The Elite, Instant Recall, Inside Edition.

CONTI, TOM
Actor. b. Paisley, Scotland, Nov. 22, 1941. Trained at Royal Scottish Academy of Music, Glasgow. Did repertory work in Scotland before London stage debut appearing with Paul Scofield in Savages, 1973.
THEATER: *London*: Devil's Disciple, Whose Life Is It Anyway?, They're Playing Our Song, Romantic Comedy, Two Into One, Italian Straw Hat, Jeffrey Bernard is Unwell. *Director*: Before the Party, The Housekeeper. NY: Whose Life Is It Anyway? (Tony Award, 1979), Last Licks (dir.), Present Laughter (dir.), Chapter Two.
PICTURES: Galileo (debut, 1975), Eclipse, The Duellists, The Haunting of Julia (Full Circle), Merry Christmas Mr. Lawrence, Reuben Reuben (Acad. Award nom.), American Dreamer, Miracles, Saving Grace, Beyond Therapy, The Gospel According to Vic, That Summer of White Roses, Shirley Valentine, Someone Else's America.
TELEVISION: Mother of Men (1959), The Glittering Prizes, Madame Bovery, Treats, The Norman Conquests, The Wall, Nazi

Hunter, The Quick and the Dead, Roman Holiday, The Dumb Waiter, Faerie Tale Theater (The Princess and the Pea), Fatal Judgement, Blade on the Feather, Voices Within: The Lives of Truddi Chase, The Wright Verdicts (series).

CONVERSE, FRANK
Actor. b. St. Louis, MO, May 22, 1938. e. Carnegie-Mellon. Early training on stage in New York. Active in repertory theatres. Two seasons with Amer. Shakespeare Fest.
THEATER: The Seagull, Death of a Salesman, Night of the Iguana, A Man for All Seasons, The House of Blue Leaves, First One Asleep Whistle, Arturo Ui, The Philadelphia Story (1980 revival), Brothers, A Streetcar Named Desire (1988 revival), Design for Living, The Crucible, Hobson's Choice, The Ride Down Mount Morgan, etc.
PICTURES: Hurry Sundown, Hour of the Gun, The Rowdyman, The Pilot, The Bushido Blade, Spring Fever, Everybody Wins, Primary Motive.
TELEVISION: *Movies*: Dr. Cook's Garden, A Tattered Web, In Tandem, Killer on Board, Cruise Into Terror, Sgt. Matlovich Vs. the U.S. Air Force, Marilyn: The Untold Story, The Miracle of Kathy Miller, Anne of Green Gables—The Sequel, Alone in the Neon Jungle. *Guest*: Mod Squad, Medical Center, Wonderworks, Guests of the Nation. *Series*: Coronet Blue, N.Y.P.D., Movin' On, The Family Tree, Dolphin Cove, One Life to Live.

CONWAY, GARY
Actor. r.n. Gareth Carmody. b. Boston, MA, Feb. 4, 1936. e. U. of California at L.A. As college senior was chosen for title role in Teen-Age Frankenstein. After graduating served in military at Ford Ord, CA. In 1960 began contract with Warner Bros., appearing in films and TV. Has also appeared on stage. Has given several one-man shows as painter and is represented in public and private collections.
PICTURES: I Was a Teenage Frankenstein, Young Guns of Texas, Once Is Not Enough, The Farmer (also prod.), American Ninja (also s.p.), Over The Top, American Ninja III: Blood Hunt (s.p.).
TELEVISION: *Series*: Burke's Law, Land of the Giants. *Movie*: The Judge and Jake Wyler. *Guest*: 77 Sunset Strip, Columbo, Police Story, Love Boat.

CONWAY, KEVIN
Actor. b. New York, NY, May 29, 1942.
THEATER: *Actor*: One Flew Over the Cuckoo's Nest, When You Comin' Back Red Ryder? (Obie & Drama Desk Awards), Of Mice and Men, Moonchildren, Life Class, Saved, The Elephant Man, Other Places, King John (NYSF), Other People's Money (Outer Critics Circle Award; also L.A. prod.), The Man Who Fell in Love with His Wife, Ten Below, On the Waterfront. *Director*: Mecca, Short Eyes (revival), One Act Play Fest (Lincoln Center), The Milk Train Doesn't Stop Here Anymore (revival), The Elephant Man (tour), Other People's Money (Chicago, L.A. & S.F.).
PICTURES: Believe in Me, Portnoy's Complaint, Slaughterhouse Five, Shamus, F.I.S.T., Paradise Alley, The Fun House, Flashpoint, Homeboy, The Sun and the Moon (dir., prod.), Funny Farm, One Good Cop, Rambling Rose, Jennifer Eight, Gettysburg, The Quick and the Dead, Lawnmower Man II.
TELEVISION: *Series*: All My Children. *Movies*: Johnny We Hardly Knew Ye, The Deadliest Season, Rage of Angels, The Lathe of Heaven, Attack on Fear, Something About Amelia, Jesse, When Will I Be Loved?, Breaking the Silence, The Whipping Boy. *Specials*: The Scarlet Letter, The Elephant Man. *Mini-Series*: Streets of Laredo.

CONWAY, TIM
Actor. b. Willoughby, OH, Dec. 15, 1933. e. Bowling Green State U. After 2 yrs. Army service joined KYW-TV in Cleveland as writer-director and occasional performer. Comedienne Rose Marie discovered him and arranged audition for the Steve Allen Show on which he became regular. In 1962 signed for McHale's Navy, series. Also has done night club appearances.
PICTURES: McHale's Navy (debut, 1964), McHale's Navy Joins the Air Force, The World's Greatest Athlete, The Apple Dumpling Gang, Gus, The Shaggy D.A., Billion Dollar Hobo, The Apple Dumpling Gang Rides Again, The Prize Fighter, The Private Eyes (also co-s.p.), Cannonball Run II, The Longshot, Dear God.
TELEVISION: *Series*: The Steve Allen Show, McHale's Navy, Rango, The Tim Conway Show (1970), The Tim Conway Comedy Hour, The Carol Burnett Show (3 Emmy Awards as actor: 1973, 1977, 1978; Emmy Award as writer: 1976), The Tim Conway Show (1980-81), Ace Crawford: Private Eye, Tim Conway's Funny America. *Guest*: Hollywood Palace, and shows starring Garry Moore, Carol Burnett, Red Skelton, Danny Kaye, Dean Martin, Cher, Doris Day, Coach (Emmy Award, 1996). *Movie*: Roll Freddy Roll.

COOGAN, KEITH
Actor. b. Palm Springs, CA, Jan. 13, 1970. e. Santa Monica City Col. Grandson of late actor Jackie Coogan. Formerly acted as Keith Mitchell. Appeared in shorts All Summer in a Day and The Great O'Grady.

PICTURES: The Fox and the Hound (voice), Adventures in Babysitting, Hiding Out, Under the Boardwalk, Cousins, Cheetah, Book of Love, Toy Soldiers, Don't Tell Mom the Babysitter's Dead, Forever, In the Army Now, A Reason to Believe.
TELEVISION: *Series*: The MacKenzies of Paradise Cove, The Waltons, Gun Shy. *Movies*: A Question of Love, Million Dollar Infield, Kid With the Broken Halo, Battered, Memorial Day, Spooner. *Specials*: Wrong Way Kid, The Treasure of Alpheus T. Winterborn, Rascal, Over the Limit, A Town's Revenge. *Guest*: Growing Pains, Silver Spoons, Fame, CHips, The Love Boat, Mork and Mindy, 21 Jump Street, 8 is Enough, Fantasy Island, Just the Ten of Us, Sibs, Tales From the Crypt, others. *Pilots*: Norma Rae, Apple Dumpling Gang, Wonderland Cove.

COOK, FIELDER
Director, Producer. b. Atlanta, GA, Mar. 9, 1923. e. Washington & Lee U., B.A.; U. of Birmingham, Eng., post grad. Served with 7th Amphibious Force, WWII.
PICTURES: Patterns (debut, 1956), Home Is the Hero, A Big Hand for the Little Lady (also prod.), How to Save a Marriage and Ruin Your Life, Prudence and the Pill (co-dir.), Eagle in a Cage, From the Mixed Up Files of Mrs. Basil E. Frankweiler.
TELEVISION: *Movies*: Sam Hill: Who Killed the Mysterious Mr. Foster?, Goodbye Raggedy Ann (also exec. prod.), Homecoming, Miracle on 34th Street, This is the West That Was, Miles to Go Before I Sleep, Judge Horton and the Scottsboro Boys, Beauty and the Beast, A Love Affair: The Eleanor and Lou Gehrig Story, Too Far to Go (also released theatrically), I Know Why the Caged Bird Sings, Gaugin the Savage, Family Reunion, Will There Really Be a Morning?, Why Me?, A Special Friendship. *Mini-Series*: Evergreen. *Specials*: The Hands of Carmac Joyce, Teacher Teacher, The Rivalry, Valley Forge, The Price (Emmy Award), Harvey, Brigadoon (also prod.; 2 Emmy Awards), Seize the Day, Third and Oak: The Pool Hall, A Member of the Wedding. *Pilots*: Ben Casey, The 11th Hour, The Waltons.

COOK, RICHARD
Executive. b. Bakersfield, CA, Aug. 20, 1950. e. USC. Began career 1971 as Disneyland sls. rep.; promoted 1974 to mgr. of sls. Moved to studio in 1977 as mgr., pay TV and non-theatrical releases. 1980, named asst. domestic sls. mgr., for Buena Vista; 1981 promoted to v.p. & asst. gen. sls. mgr.; 1984, promoted to v.p. & gen. sls. mgr., B.V.; 1985, appt. sr. v.p., domestic distribution. 1988: appt. pres. Buena Vista Pictures Distribution. 1994, pres., Worldwide Marketing, Buena Vista Pictures Marketing. 1996 named chmn., Walt Disney Motion Picture Group.

COOKE, ALISTAIR
Journalist, Broadcaster. b. Manchester, Eng., Nov. 20, 1908. e. Jesus Coll., Cambridge U.; Yale U.; Harvard U. Film crit. of BBC 1934-37. London corr. NBC 1936-37. BBC commentator in U.S. since 1937. Commentator on radio show Letters From America, starting in 1945. Chief Amer. corr., Manchester Guardian, 1948-72; English narrator, The March of Time, 1938-39. Became U.S. citizen in 1941. Peabody award winner for International reporting, 1952, 1973-83. Hon. Knighthood, KBE, 1973.
AUTHOR: Douglas Fairbanks, Garbo & The Night Watchmen, A Generation on Trial, One Man's America, Christmas Eve, The Vintage Mencken, etc. America, 1973; Six Men, 1977; Talk About America, 1968; The Americans, 1979; Above London (with Robert Cameron), 1980; Masterpieces, 1981; The Patient Has the Floor, 1986, America Observed, 1988; Fun and Games with Alistair Cooke, 1995.
PICTURES: *Narrator*: Sorrowful Jones, The Three Faces of Eve, Hitler—The Last Ten Days
TELEVISION: *Series*: Omnibus (host; 1952-61), m.c. prod. U.N.'s International Zone (host, prod.; Emmy Award, 1958); Masterpiece Theatre (host; 1971-92). *Special doc.*: America: A Personal History of The United States (writer and narrator; 5 Emmy Awards, 1973; Franklin Medal, Royal Society of Arts, 1973).

COOLIDGE, MARTHA
Director, Writer, Producer. b. New Haven, CT, Aug. 17, 1946. e. Rhode Island Sch. of Design. NYU Inst. of Film and TV grad. sch. m. writer Michael Backes. Dir. short films while in school. Wrote and prod. daily children's tv show Magic Tom in Canada Worked on commercials and political doc. film crews. Prod., dir. and writer of docs. which have won festival awards, including Passing Quietly Through; David: Off and On (American Film Fest.), Old Fashioned Woman (CINE Golden Eagle Award, Blue Ribbon Award, American film festival), Bimbo (short), Magic Tom in Canada. First feature film Not a Pretty Picture (won Blue Ribbon Award, Amer. Film Fest.) Helped start assn. of Indep. Video and Filmmakers, Inc. As an AFI/Academy Intern worked with Robert Wise on his film Audrey Rose, 1976. Wrote orig. story that was filmed as the The Omega Connection. DGA, member of bd. of dirs.; WIF, member bd. of dirs. Acted in film Beverly Hills Cop III.
PICTURES: The City Girl, Valley Girl, Joy of Sex, Real Genius, Plain Clothes, That's Adequate (interviewee), Rambling Rose (IFP Spirit Award, 1991), Lost in Yonkers, Angie, Three Wishes.

TELEVISION: The Twilight Zone, Sledge Hammer (pilot), House and Home (pilot). *Movies*: Trenchcoat in Paradise, Bare Essentials, Crazy in Love.

COONEY, JOAN GANZ
Executive, Producer. b. Phoenix, AZ, Nov. 30, 1929. e. U. of Arizona. After working as a reporter in Phoenix, moved to NY in 1953 where she wrote soap-opera summaries at NBC. Then was publicist for U.S. Steel Hour. Became producer of live weekly political TV show Court of Reason (Emmy Award) and documentaries (Poverty, Anti-Poverty and the Poor) before founding Children's Television Workshop and Sesame Street in 1969. Currently chmn., exec. committe, CTW.

COOPER, BEN
Actor. b. Hartford, CT, Sept. 30, 1930. e. Columbia U. On stage in Life with Father (1942); numerous radio, TV appearances starting from 1945.
PICTURES: Side Street (debut, 1950), Thunderbirds, The Woman They Almost Lynched, A Perilous Journey, Sea of Lost Ships, Flight Nurse, The Outcast, Johnny Guitar, Jubilee Trail, Hell's Outpost, The Eternal Sea, The Last Command, Headline Hunters, The Rose Tattoo, Rebel in Town, A Strange Adventure, Duel at Apache Wells, Outlaw's Son, Chartroose Caboose, The Raiders, Gunfight at Comanche Creek, Arizona Raiders, Waco, The Fastest Gun Alive, Red Tomahawk, One More Train to Rob, Support Your Local Gunfighter.

COOPER, HAL
Director, Performer. b. New York, NY, Feb. 22, 1923. e. U. of Michigan. m. Marta Salcido; child actor in various radio prog. starting in 1932; featured Bob Emery's Rainbow House, Mutual, 1936-46; asst. dir. Dock St. Theatre, Charleston, SC, 1946-48.
TELEVISION: Your School Reporter, TV Baby Sitter, The Magic Cottage (writer, prod.). *Director*: Valiant Lady, Search for Tomorrow, Portia Faces Life, Kitty Foyle (also assoc. prod.), Indictment (also prod.), The Happy Time (also assoc. prod.), For Better or Worse (also prod.), The Clear Horizon, Surprise Package (also assoc. prod.), Dick Van Dyke Show, The Art Linkletter Show (also prod.), The Object Is, Death Valley Days, I Dream of Jeannie, That Girl, I Spy, Hazel, Gidget, Gilligan's Island, NYPD, Mayberry, Courtship of Eddie's Father, My World and Welcome to It, The Brady Bunch, The Odd Couple, Mary Tyler Moore, All in the Family. *Exec. prod./Director*: Maude, Phyl and Mikky, Love, Sidney, Gimme a Break, Empty Nest, Dear John, The Powers That Be.

COOPER, JACKIE
Actor, Director, Producer. b. Los Angeles, CA, Sept. 15, 1922. Began theatrical career at age of 3 as m.p. actor; was member of Our Gang comedies (first short was Boxing Gloves in 1929). First starring role in 1931 in Skippy. Worked at every major studio, always with star billing. At 20 enlisted in Navy. After three-yr. tour of duty went to N.Y. to work in live TV. Appeared in 3 plays on B'way stage and in Mr. Roberts on natl. tour and in London. Directed as well as acted in live and filmed TV. Served as v.p. in chg. of TV prod., for Screen Gems, 1964-69, when resigned to return to acting, directing, producing. 2 Emmy Awards for directing M*A*S*H and The White Shadow. Retired 1989.
PICTURES: Fox Movietone Follies (feature debut, 1929), Sunny Side Up, Skippy (Acad. Award nom.), Young Donovan's Kid, Sooky, The Champ, When a Feller Needs a Friend, Divorce in the Family, Broadway to Hollywood, The Bowery, Lone Cowboy, Treasure Island, Peck's Bad Boy, Dinky, O'Shaughnessy's Boy, Tough Guy, The Devil Is a Sissy, Boy of the Streets, White Banners, Gangster's Boy, That Certain Age, Newsboys' Home, Scouts to the Rescue (serial), Spirit of Culver, Streets of New York, What a Life, Two Bright Boys, The Big Guy, The Return of Frank James, Seventeen, Gallant Sons, Life With Henry, Ziegfeld Girl, Glamour Boy, Her First Beau, Syncopation, Men of Texas, The Navy Comes Through, Where Are Your Children?, Stork Bites Man, Kilroy Was Here, French Leave, Everything's Ducky, The Love Machine, Stand Up and Be Counted (dir. only), Chosen Survivors, Superman, Superman II, Superman III, Superman IV: The Quest for Peace, Surrender.
TELEVISION: *Series*: People's Choice (also directed 71 episodes), Hennesey (also dir. 91 epsiodes), Dean Martin Comedy World (host), Mobile One. *Movies*: Shadow on the Land, Maybe I'll Come Home in the Spring, The Astronaut, The Day the Earth Moved, The Invisible Man, Mobile Two, Operation Petticoat. *Director*: Having Babies III, Rainbow, White Mama, Rodeo Girl, Sex and the Single Parent, The Ladies, Deacon Street Deer, Perfect Gentlemen, Marathon, Leave 'Em Laughing, Rosie (also prod.), Glitter, The Night They Saved Christmas, Izzy and Moe.

COOPER, JEANNE
Actress. r.n. Wilma Jean Cooper. b. Taft, CA, Oct. 25. e. College of the Pacific, Pasadena Playhouse. Son is actor Corbin Bernsen. Recipient: 3 Soap Opera Update MVP Awards, Soap Opera Digest, Pasadena Playhouse Woman of the Year and Hollywood Entertainment Museum Award.

THEATER: The Miracle Worker, Plain and Fancy, Picnic, On the Town, The Big Knife, Tonight at 8:30, Dark Side of the Moon, Plaza Suite.
PICTURES: Man From the Alamo, 13 West Street, The Redhead From Wyoming, Let No Man Write My Epitaph, The Glory Guys, Kansas City Bomber, All-American Boy, Frozen Assets.
TELEVISION: *Series*: Bracken's World, The Young and the Restless (1973-).

COOPER, SHELDON
Executive. e. Indiana U. Joined WGN Television, 1950 holding various positions in prod. including floor mgr., dir., prod.; 1961, named mgr. prod.; 1961 became exec. prod. for station; 1964, named asst. prog. mgr.; 1965, mgr. of dept.; 1966, v.p. prog. dev. with WGN Continental Productions Co.; elected to bd. of dir., Continental Broadcasting Co. and appointed station mgr., WGN TV, April 1974.; 1975, named v.p. and gen. mrg., WGN Continental Broadcasting; 1977, dir., broadcasting; 1979, pres. and gen. mgr., WGN Television; 1982, chief exec. of newly formed Tribune Entertainment Co. and dir. of Tribune Co. Syndicate, Inc., 1982-present. One of founders of Operation Prime Time, consortium of independent stations. Awarded Emmys: 1960 as television's man of the year behind the cameras and 1964 for continuing excellence as writer, prod., executive, WGN TV. Chmn., Assoc. of Independent TV Stations, Inc. (INTV), 1980 and 1981; National v.p., Muscular Dystrophy Assoc.; 1980, on bd. National Assoc. of TV Prog. Executives (NATPE); first v.p., Chicago chap. Acad. of TV Arts and Sciences; v.p., trustee of national chap.

COOPERMAN, ALVIN
Producer. b. Brooklyn, NY. Prod., Untouchables, 1961-63; exec. dir., Shubert Theatre Ent. 1963; v.p., special programs, NBC, 1967-68; exec. v.p., Madison Square Garden Center, 1968-72; pres., Madison Square Garden Center, Inc.; founder , Madison Sq. Garden Prods. and Network; chmn. of the board, Athena Communications Corp.; pres., NY Television Academy, 1987-89.
TELEVISION: *Producer*: Romeo and Juliet (Emmy nom.), Pele's Last Game, The Fourth King, Amahl and the Night Visitors, Live from Studio 8H—A Tribute to Toscanini (Emmy Award), Live from Studio 8H—An Evening with Jerome Robbins and the New York City Ballet (Emmy Award), Live from Studio 8H—Caruso Remembered, Ain't Misbehavin' (Emmy nom., NAACP Image Award), Pope John Paul II, My Two Loves, Safe Passage, Family Album, U.S.A. (26 half hrs.), Witness to Survival (26 half hrs.), Mobs and Mobsters, Follow The River, Susan B. Anthony Slept Here (docu.).

COPPOLA, FRANCIS FORD
Director, Writer, Producer. b. Detroit, MI, April 7, 1939. Raised in NYC. Son of late composer Carmine Coppola. Sister is actress Talia Shire. e. Hofstra U, B.A., 1958; UCLA, 1958-68, M.F.A., cinema. While at UCLA was hired as asst. to Roger Corman as dialogue dir., sound man and assoc. prod. 1969; est. American Zoetrope, (later Zoetrope Studios), a prod. center in San Francisco. Publisher, City (magazine, 1975-6). Appeared in documentary Hearts of Darkness: A Filmmaker's Apocalypse.
PICTURES: Tonight for Sure (dir., prod.), The Playgirls and the Bellboy (co-dir., co-s.p. of addtl. sequences for U.S. version), Premature Burial (asst. dir.), Tower of London (dialog. dir.), Battle Beyond the Sun (adapt.), The Young Races (sound, 2nd unit dir.), The Terror (assoc. prod., 2nd unit dir.), Dementia 13 (dir., s.p.), Is Paris Burning? (co-s.p.), This Property Is Condemned (co-s.p.), You're a Big Boy Now (dir., s.p.), The Wild Races (2nd unit dir.), Reflections in a Golden Eye (s.p.), Finian's Rainbow (dir.), The Rain People (dir., s.p.), Patton (co-s.p.; Academy Award, 1970), THX 1138 (exec. prod.), The Godfather (dir., co-s.p.); Academy Award for Best Screenplay, 1972), American Graffiti (exec. prod.), The Great Gatsby (s.p.), The Conversation (dir., co-prod., s.p.), The Godfather Part II (dir., co-s.p., prod.; Academy Awards for Best Picture, Director & Screenplay, 1974), Apocalypse Now (dir., prod., co-s.p., cameo), The Black Stallion (exec. prod.), Kagemusha (co-exec. prod.), One From the Heart (dir., co-s.p.), Hammett (exec. prod.), The Escape Artist (co-exec. prod.), The Black Stallion Returns (exec. prod.), The Outsiders (dir.), Rumble Fish (dir., exec. prod., co-s.p.), The Cotton Club, (dir., co-s.p.), Mishima (co-exec. prod.), Peggy Sue Got Married (dir.), Gardens of Stone (dir., co-prod.), Tough Guys Don't Dance (co-exec. prod.), Lionheart (exec. prod.), Tucker: The Man and His Dream (dir.), New York Stories (Life Without Zoe; dir., co-s.p.), The Godfather Part III (dir., co-s.p., prod.), Wind (co-exec. prod.), Bram Stoker's Dracula (dir., co-prod.), The Secret Garden (exec. prod.), Mary Shelley's Frankenstein (prod.), Don Juan DeMarco (exec. prod.), My Family/Mi Familia (exec. prod.), Haunted (co-exec. prod.), Jack.
TELEVISION: *Movies*: The People (exec. prod.), White Dwarf (co- prod), Tecumseh: The Last Warrior (co-exec. prod.). *Special*: Rip Van Winkle (Faerie Tale Theatre; dir.). *Series*: The Outsiders (exec. prod.).

CORBIN, BARRY
Actor. b. Dawson County, TX, Oct. 16, 1940. e. Texas Tech. Univ.
PICTURES: Urban Cowboy, Stir Crazy, Any Which Way You Can, Dead and Buried, The Night the Lights Went Out in Georgia, The Best Little Whorehouse in Texas, Six Pack, Honkytonk Man, The Ballad of Gregorio Cortez, WarGames, The Man Who Loved Women, Hard Traveling, What Comes Around, My Science Project, Nothing in Common, Under Cover, Off the Mark, Permanent Record, Critters 2: The Main Course, It Takes Two, Who is Harry Crumb?, Short Time, Ghost Dad, The Hot Spot, Career Opportunities.
TELEVISION: *Series*: Boone, Spies, Northern Exposure, The Big Easy. *Mini-Series*: The Thorn Birds, Lonesome Dove. *Movies*: Rage, This House Possessed, The Killing of Randy Webster, Murder in Texas, Bitter Harvest, A Few Days in Weasel Creek, Fantasies, Prime Suspect, Travis McGee, Flight #90: Disaster on the Potomac, The Jesse Owens Story, Fatal Vision, I Know My First Name is Steven, Last Flight Out, The Chase, Conagher, The Keys, Robin Cook's Virus. *Guest*: Call to Glory, Murder She Wrote, Hill Street Blues, Matlock.

CORD, ALEX
Actor. r.n. Alexander Viespi. b. Floral Park, NY, May 3, 1933. Early career in rodeo; left to become actor. Studied at Shakespeare Academy (Stratford, Conn.) and Actor's Studio (N.Y.). Spent two yrs. in summer stock; in 1961 went on tour with Stratford Shakespeare Co. Author of novel Sandsong. Co-founder of Chuckers for Charity polo team which has raised more than $2 million for various charities. Champion rodeo team roper and cutting horse rider.
PICTURES: Synanon (debut, 1965), Stagecoach, A Minute to Pray A Second to Die, The Brotherhood, Stiletto, The Last Grenade, The Dead Are Alive, Chosen Survivors, Inn of the Damned, Sidewinder One, Grayeagle, Jungle Warriors, Street Asylum.
TELEVISION: *Series*: W.E.B., Cassie & Company, Airwolf. *Movies*: The Scorpio Letters, Hunter's Man; Genesis II, Fire !, Beggerman Thief, Goliath Awaits, The Dirty Dozen: The Fatal Mission.

CORDAY, BARBARA
Executive. b. New York, NY, Oct. 15, 1944. Began career as publicist in N.Y. and L.A. Turned to writing for TV; named v.p., ABC-TV, in chg. of comedy series development. 1982-84, headed own production co. in association with Columbia Pictures TV; June, 1984-87 pres., Columbia Pictures TV; 1988, appointed CBS Entertainment, exec. v.p. primetime programs. Member: Caucus of Writers, Producers & Directors; Hollywood Women's Coalition.
TELEVISION: *Writer*: American Dream (pilot), Cagney and Lacey (also co-creator).

COREY, JEFF
Actor. b. New York, NY, Aug. 10, 1914. e. Feagin Sch. of Dram. Art. On stage in Leslie Howard prod. of Hamlet, 1936; Life and Death of an American, In the Matter of J. Robert Oppenheimer, Hamlet-Mark Taper Forum, King Lear, Love Suicide at Schofield Barracks.
PICTURES: All That Money Can Buy, Syncopation, The Killers, Ramrod, Joan of Arc, Roughshod, Black Shadows, Bagdad, Outriders, The Devil and Daniel Webster, My Friend Flicka, Canyon City, Singing Guns, Seconds, In Cold Blood, Golden Bullet, Boston Strangler, True Grit, Butch Cassidy and The Sundance Kid, Beneath the Planet of the Apes, Getting Straight, Little Big Man, They Call Me Mister Tibbs, Clear and Present Danger, High Flying Lowe, Catlow, Something Evil, Premonition, Shine, Rooster, Oh God!, Butch and Sundance: The Early Days, Up River, Conan the Destroyer, Cognac, Messenger of Death, Bird on a Wire, The Judas Project, Deception, Beethoven's 2nd, Surviving the Game, Color of Night.
TELEVISION: *Guest*: The Untouchables, The Beachcomber, The Balcony, Yellow Canary, Lady in a Cage, Outer Limits, Channing, The Doctors and the Nurses, Perry Mason, Gomer Pyle, Wild Wild West, Run for Your Life, Bonanza, Iron Horse, Judd for Defense, Garrisons Gorillas, Gunsmoke, Hawaii Five O, Star Trek, The Psychiatrist, Night Gallery, Alias Smith and Jones, Sixth Sense, Hawkins, Owen Marshall, Police Story, Bob Newhart Show, Six Million Dollar Man, Doctors Hospital, Starsky and Hutch, Land of the Free, Kojak, McCloud, Captains Courageous, Bionic Woman, Barney Miller, One Day at a Time, The Pirate, Lou Grant, The Powers of Jonathan Starr, Cry for the Strangers, Today's FBI, Knots Landing, Archie Bunker's Place, Faerie Tale Theatre, Night Court, Helltown (series), Morning Star/Evening Star (series), New Love American Style, Starman, The A Team, A Deadly Silence (movie), Roseanne, Wolf, Jake and the Fatman, Rose and the Jackal, To My Daughter, Payoff, Sinatra, The Marshal, Home Court, Picket Fences.

CORMAN, GENE
Producer. r.n. Eugene H. Corman. b. Detroit, MI, Sept. 24, 1927. e. Stanford U. Went to work for MCA as agent 1950-57; left to produce his first feature film, Hot Car Girl. Partner with brother

Roger in Corman Company and New World Distributors. Vice pres. 20th Century Fox Television, 1983-87; exec. v.p. worldwide production, 21st Century Film Corp.
PICTURES: Attack of the Giant Leeches, Not of This Earth, Blood and Steel, Valley of the Redwoods, Secret of the Purple Reef, Beast from Haunted Cave, Cat Burglar, The Intruder, Tobruk, You Can't Win Em All, Cool Breeze, Hit Man, The Slams, Von Richthofen and Brown, I Escaped from Devil's Island, Secret Invasion, Vigilante Force, F.I.S.T. (exec. prod.), The Big Red One, If You Could See What I Hear, Paradise, A Man Called Sarge.
TELEVISION: What's In It For Harry, A Woman Called Golda (Emmy and Christopher Awards as prod.), Mary and Joseph, a Love Story, Blood Ties.

CORMAN, ROGER WILLIAM
Executive, Director, Producer, Writer, Distributor. b. Detroit, MI, April 5, 1921. e. Stanford U. 1947; Oxford U., England 1950. U.S. Navy 1944; 20th Century-Fox, production dept., 1948, story analyst 1948-49; Literary agent, 1951-52; story, s.p., assoc. prod., Highway Dragnet. Formed Roger Corman Prod. and Filmgroup. Prod. over 200 feature films and dir. over 60 of them. Formed production-releasing company, org., New World Pictures, Inc., 1970. Formed prod. co., Concorde, 1984; distribution co., New Horizons, 1985. On TV acted in film Body Bags. *Author:* How I Made a Hundred Movies in Hollywood and Never Lost a Dime.
PICTURES: *Director:* Five Guns West (dir. debut, 1955), Apache Woman, Swamp Women, The Day the World Ended, The Oklahoma Woman, The Gunslinger, It Conquered the World, Not of This Earth, Naked Paradise (Thunder Over Hawaii), Attack of the Crab Monsters, Rock All Night, Teenage Doll, Carnival Rock, Sorority Girl, Saga of the Viking Women and Their Voyage to the Waters of the Great Sea Serpent, The Undead, War of the Satellites, She Gods of Shark Reef, Machine Gun Kelly, Teenage Caveman, I Mobster, A Bucket of Blood, The Wasp Woman, Ski Troop Attack, House of Usher, The Little Shop of Horrors, The Last Woman on Earth, Creature From the Haunted Sea, Atlas, The Pit and the Pendulum, The Intruder, The Premature Burial, Tales of Terror, Tower of London, The Raven, The Terror, X—The Man With the X Ray Eyes, The Haunted Palace, The Young Racers, The Secret Invasion, The Masque of the Red Death, Tomb of Ligeia, The Wild Angels, The St. Valentine's Day Massacre, The Trip, Target: Harry (credited as Henry Neill), Bloody Mama, Gas-s-s-s, Von Richtofen and Brown, Frankenstein Unbound. Producer: Boxcar Bertha, Big Bad Mama, Death Race 2000, Eat My Dust, Capone, Jackson County Jail, Fighting Mad, Thunder & Lightning, Grand Theft Auto, I Never Promised You A Rose Garden, Deathsport, Avalanche, Battle Beyond the Stars, St. Jack, Love Letters, Smokey Bites the Dust, Galaxy of Terror, Slumber Party Massacre Part II, Stripped to Kill, Barbarian Queen, Munchies, Stripped To Kill, Big Bad Mama II, Sweet Revenge (co-exec. prod.), The Drifter (exec. prod.), Daddy's Boys, Singles (exec. prod.), Crime Zone (exec. prod.), Watcher (exec. prod.), The Lawless Land (exec. prod.), Stripped to Kill 2 (exec. prod.), The Terror Within, Lords of the Deep (also actor), Two to Tango, Time Trackers, Heroes Stand Alone, Bloodfist, Silk 2, Edgar Allan Poe's The Masque of Red Death, Hollywood Boulevard II (exec. prod.), Rock and Roll High School Forever (exec. prod.), Bloodfist II (prod.), Haunted Symphony, Midnight Tease, One Night Stand (exec. prod.). *Actor:* The Godfather Part II, Cannonball, The Howling, The State of Things, Swing Shift, The Silence of the Lambs, Philadelphia.
TELEVISION: *Movie Series:* Roger Corman Presents (exec. prod.)

CORNELL, JOHN
Producer, Director, Writer. b. Kalgoorlie, Western Australia, 1941. m. actress Delvene Delancy. Grew up Bunbury. e. studied pharmacy for two years in Perth. Won internship at Western Australian Newspapers at 19, becoming columnist then London editor at 26. As Melbourne prod. of TV show, A Current Affair, discovered bridge rigger Paul Hogan. Put him on show, became his manager and formed JP Productions with him in 1972. Prod. and appeared on The Paul Hogan Show. Formed movie co. with Hogan, Rimfire Films.
PICTURES: Crocodile Dundee (prod., co-s.p.), Crocodile Dundee II (prod., dir., editor), Almost an Angel (dir., prod.).

CORNFELD, STUART
Producer. b. Los Angeles, CA. e. U. of California, Berkeley. Entered America Film Institute's Center for Advanced Film Studies as producing fellow, 1975. Joined Brooksfilm as asst. to Mel Brooks on High Anxiety. Assoc. prod., History of the World Part I.
PICTURES: Fatso, The Elephant Man, (exec. prod.), National Lampoon's European Vacation (co-prod.), Girls Just Want to Have Fun (exec. prod.), The Fly, Moving, The Fly II (exec. prod.), Hider in the House (co-prod.), Kafka, Wilder Napalm.

CORRI, ADRIENNE
Actress. r.n. Adrienne Riccoboni. b. Glasgow, Scotland, Nov. 13, 1933. e. RADA at 13; parts in several stage plays including The Human Touch. Numerous TV appearances.

PICTURES: The Romantic Age (Naughty Arlette; debut, 1949), The River, Quo Vadis, The Little Kidnappers, The Sinners, Devil Girl From Mars, Meet Mr. Callaghan, Lease of Life, Make Me an Offer, Triple Blackmail, The Feminine Touch, Behind the Headlines, The Shield of Faith, Three Men in a Boat, Second Fiddle, The Surgeon's Knife, The Big Chance, Corridors of Blood, The Rough and the Smooth (Portrait of a Sinner), The Tell-Tale Heart, Sword of Freedom, The Hellfire, Dynamite Jack, Sword of Lancelot, A Study in Terror, Bunny Lake Is Missing, Doctor Zhivago, Woman Times Seven, The Viking Queen, Africa—Texas Style!, The File of the Golden Goose, Cry Wolf, Moon Zero Two, Vampire Circus, A Clockwork Orange, Madhouse, Rosebud, Revenge of the Pink Panther, The Human Factor.

CORT, BUD
Actor. r.n. Walter Edward Cox. b. New Rochelle, NY, March 29, 1950. e. NYU School of the Arts. Stage debut in Wise Child, B'way. L.A. theatre includes Forget-Me-Not Lane, August 11 1947, Endgame (Dramalogue Award), Demon Wine, The Seagull. Founding member of L.A. Classical Theatre. Theatrical film debut as extra in Up the Down Staircase 1967. Television debut in The Doctors.
PICTURES: Sweet Charity, M*A*S*H, Gas-s-s-s, The Traveling Executioner, Brewster McCloud, Harold and Maude, Die Laughing, Why Shoot the Teacher?, She Dances Alone, Hysterical, Electric Dreams (voice), Love Letters, The Secret Diary of Sigmund Freud, Maria's Lovers, Invaders from Mars, Love at Stake, The Chocolate War, Out of the Dark, Brain Dead, Going Under, Ted and Venus (also dir., co-s.p.), Girl in the Cadillac, Heat, Theodore Rex.
TELEVISION: *Special:* Bernice Bobs Her Hair. *Guest:* Faerie Tale Theatre (The Nightingale), The Hitchhiker (Made for Each Other), The New Twilight Zone, Midnight Caller. *Movies:* Brave New World, The Bates Motel, And the Band Played On.

CORT, ROBERT W.
Executive. e. U. of Pennsylvania (Phi Beta Kappa). Moved into feature prod. after having worked primarily in marketing/advertising. Joined Columbia Pictures as v.p., 1976; elevated to v.p., adv./pub./promo. Named exec. v.p. of mktg. for 20th-Fox, 1980. Moved into feature prod. as senior v.p., 1981. In 1983 named exec. v.p., prod., 20th-Fox Prods. 1985, joined Interscope Communications as pres.
PICTURES: *Prod.:* Critical Condition, Outrageous Fortune, Revenge of the Nerds II, Three Men and a Baby, The Seventh Sign, Cocktail, Bill & Ted's Excellent Adventure (exec. prod.), Renegades (exec. prod.), Blind Fury (exec. prod.), An Innocent Man, The First Power (exec. prod.), Bird on a Wire, Arachnophobia, Three Man and a Little Lady, Eve of Destruction, Class Action, Bill & Ted's Bogus Journey, Paradise, The Hand That Rocks the Cradle, The Cutting Edge, FernGully, The Gun in Betty Lou's Handbag, Out on a Limb, Jersey Girl, Holy Matrimony, Imaginary Crimes, Operation Dumbo Drop, The Tie That Binds, Mr. Holland's Opus.
TELEVISION: *Movies (co-exec. prod.):* A Mother's Courage (Emmy Award), A Part of the Family, Body Language.

CORTESE, VALENTINA
Actress. b. Milan, Italy, Jan. 1, 1924. Started career at 15 in Orizzonte Dipinto while studying at Rome Acad. of Dramatic Art. Following several appearances in European films brought to Hollywood by 20th Century-Fox, 1949; billed in U.S. films as Valentina Cortesa. Experience on dramatic stage in variety of roles inc. Shakespeare, O'Neill, Shaw.
PICTURES: Orrizonte Dipinto (debut, 1940), Primo Amore, A Yank in Rome, A Bullet for Strefano, Les Miserables, The Glass Mountain (English-language debut, 1950), Black Magic, Malaya, Thieves Highway, Shadow of the Eagle, The House on Telegraph Hill, Secret People, Lulu, Forbidden Women (Angels of Darkness), The Barefoot Contessa, Le Amiche, Magic Fire, Calabuch, Barabbas, The Evil Eye, The Visit, The Possessed, Juliet of the Spirits, Black Sun, The Legend of Lylah Clare, The Secret of Santa Vittoria, First Love, Give Her the Moon, The Assassination of Trotsky, Brother Sun Sister Moon, Day for Night (Acad. Award nom.), Tendre Dracula, Widow's Nest, When Time Ran Out, La Ferdinanda, Blue Tango, The Adventures of Baron Munchausen, The Betrothed, Young Toscanini, Buster's Bedroom.

CORTEZ, STANLEY
Director of Photography. r.n. Stanislaus Krantz. b. New York, NY, Nov. 4, 1908. e. NYU. Brother was late actor Ricardo Cortez. Began working with portrait photographers (Steichen, Pirie MacDonald, Bachrach, etc.), N.Y. Entered film indust. with Paramount; to Hollywood as camera asst. and later 2nd cameraman, various studios; pioneer in use of montage. Served Signal Corps WWII. Received Film Critics of Amer. award for work on Magnificent Ambersons. Under personal contract to David O. Selznick, Orson Welles, Walter Wanger, David Wolper. Contributor, Encyclopedia Britannica.
PICTURES: Four Days Wonder, The Forgotten Women, Alias the Deacon, Love Honor and Oh Baby!, Meet the Wildcat, The

Black Cat, Badlands of Dakota, Bombay Clipper, Eagle Squadron, The Magnificent Ambersons (Acad. Award nom.), Flesh and Fantasy, Since You Went Away (Acad. Award. nom.) Smash Up—The Story of a Woman, Secret Beyond the Door, Man on the Eiffel Tower, The Admiral Was a Lady, Fort Defiance, Abbott & Costello Meet Captain Kidd, Stronghold, Diamond Queen, Neanderthal Man, Shark River, Riders to the Stars, The Night of the Hunter, Man from Del Rio, Three Faces of Eve, Top Secret Affair, The Angry Red Planet, Thunder in the Sun, Dinosaurus, Back Street, Shock Corridor, Nightmare in the Sun, The Naked Kiss, Young Dillinger, Ghost in the Invisible Bikini, Blue, The Bridge at Remagen, Another Man Another Chance, Damien: Omen II (special photog.), When Time Ran Out (special photog.).

CORWIN, BRUCE CONRAD
Exhibitor. b. Los Angeles, CA, June 11, 1940. e. Wesleyan U. Pres., Metropolitan Theatres Corp.; Past pres., Variety Children's Charities Tent 25; Board of Trustees U.C.S.B. Foundation; pres. emeritus, L.A. Children's Museum; chmn., Coro Natl. Board of Governors; Past President of the Foundation of Motion Picture Pioneers.

CORWIN, NORMAN
Writer, Producer, Director. b. Boston, MA, May 3, 1910. Sports ed. Greenfield, Mass. Daily Recorder, 1926-29; radio ed., news commentator, Springfield Republican & Daily News, 1929-36; prog. dir., CBS, 1938. Author of Thirteen by Corwin, More by Corwin, Untitled & Other Plays, Prayer to Overthrow Christmas, Dog in the Sky, Overkill and Megalove, Prayer for the 70's, Holes in a Stained Glass Window, Trivializing America; taught courses at UCLA, USC, San Diego State U. Faculty, U.S.C. Sch. of Journalism, 1980-.; sec., M.P. Academy Foundation, 1985. First v.p., Motion Picture Acad., 1985. Inducted into Radio Hall of Fame, Chicago Museum, 1993. Writer-host Academy Leaders (PBS). Chmn. Doc. Award Com., Motion Picture Acad. 1965-91; elected to bd. of gov., 1980; first v.p., 1988-89; chmn., writers' exec. comm., M.P. Academy; co-chmn. scholarship com., M.P. Academy; mem.: Film Advisory Bd.; bd. of trustees, Advisory Board, Filmex; bd. of dirs., WGA. Books incl. Directors Guild Oral History, Years of the Electric Ear, Norman Corwin's Letters.
THEATER: The Rivalry, The World of Carl Sandburg, The Hyphen, Overkill and Megalove, Cervantes. Together Tonight: Jefferson Hamilton and Burr.
PICTURES: Once Upon a Time, The Blue Veil, The Grand Design, Scandal in Scourie, Lust for Life (Acad. Award nom. best adapt. s.p.), The Story of Ruth.
TELEVISION: Inside the Movie Kingdom, The FDR Series, The Plot to Overthrow Christmas, Norman Corwin Presents, The Court Martial of General Yamashita, Network at 50.

COSBY, BILL
Actor, Comedian. b. Philadelphia, PA, July 12, 1938. e. Temple U., U. of Mass., Ed.D. Served in United States Navy Medical Corps. Started as night club entertainer.
AUTHOR: The Wit and Wisdom of Fat Albert, Bill Cosby's Personal Guide to Power Tennis, Fatherhood, Time Flies.
COMEDY ALBUMS: Bill Cosby Is a Very Funny Fellow... Right! (Grammy Award, 1964), I Started Out As a Child (Grammy Award, 1965), Why Is There Air? (Grammy Award, 1966), Wonderfulness (Grammy Award, 1967), Revenge (Grammy Award, 1967), To Russell My Brother Whom I Slept With (Grammy Award, 1969), Bill Cosby Is Not Himself These Days, Rat Own Rat Own Rat Own, My Father Confused Me... What Must I Do? What Must I Do?, Disco Bill, Bill's Best Friend, Cosby and the Kids, It's True It's True, Bill Cosby - Himself, 200 MPH, Silverthroat, Hooray for the Salvation Army Band, 8:15 12:15, For Adults Only, Bill Cosby Talks to Kids About Drugs, Inside the Mind of Bill Cosby.
RADIO: The Bill Cosby Radio Program.
PICTURES: Hickey and Boggs (debut, 1972), Man and Boy, Uptown Saturday Night, Let's Do It Again, Mother Jugs and Speed, A Piece of the Action, California Suite, The Devil and Max Devlin, Bill Cosby Himself, Leonard Part VI (also co-prod., story), Ghost Dad, The Meteor Man, Jack.
TELEVISION: Series: I Spy (3 Emmy Awards for Best Actor: 1966, 1967, 1968), The Bill Cosby Show (1969-71), The New Bill Cosby Show (1972-73), Fat Albert and the Cosby Kids, Cos, The New Fat Albert Show (Emmy Award, 1981), The Cosby Show (1984-92), A Different World (exec. prod. only), You Bet Your Life, Here and Now (exec. prod. only), The Cosby Mysteries, Cosby (also prod., 1996-). Specials: The Bill Cosby Special, The Second Bill Cosby Special, Fat Albert Easter Special (voice), Cosby Salutes Alvin Ailey. Movies: To All My Friends on Shore (also exec. prod., story, music), Top Secret, The Cosby Mysteries (also co-exec. prod.), I Spy Returns (also co-exec. prod.).

COSMATOS, GEORGE PAN
Director, Producer, Writer. b. Tuscany, Italy, Jan. 4, 1947. e. London U., London Film School. Asst. on such films as Exodus, Zorba the Greek.

PICTURES: Director: Restless (also co-prod., s.p.), Massacre in Rome (also co-s.p.), The Cassandra Crossing (also co-s.p.), Escape to Athena (also co-s.p.), Of Unknown Origin, Rambo: First Blood Part II, Cobra, Leviathan, Tombstone, The Shadow Conspiracy.

COSTA-GAVRAS (CONSTANTIN)
Director, Writer. r.n. Konstaninos Gavras. b. Athens, Greece, Feb. 13, 1933. French citizen. e. Studied at the Sorbonne; Hautes Etudes Cinematographique, (IDHEC). Was leading ballet dancer in Greece before the age of 20. Worked as second, then first assistant to Marcel Ophuls, Rene Clair, Rene Clement and Jacques Demy. Pres. of the Cinematheque Francaise, 1982-87. Appeared as actor in film Madame Rosa.
PICTURES: Director: The Sleeping Car Murders (also s.p.; debut, 1965), Un Homme De Trop/Shock Troops (also s.p.), Z (also co-s.p.; 2 Acad. Award noms.), The Confession, State of Siege (also co- s.p.), Special Section (also co-s.p.), Clair de Femme (also s.p.), Missing (also co-s.p.; Academy Award for Best Adapted Screenplay, 1982; Palm d'Or at Cannes Film Fest.), Hannah K. (also prod.), Family Business (also s.p.), Betrayed, Music Box (Golden Bear, Berlin Festival, 1989), The Little Apocalypse.

COSTNER, KEVIN
Actor. b. Lynwood, CA, Jan. 18, 1955. e. CA. State U, Fullerton majored in marketing. Acted with South Coast Actors' Co-op, community theater gp. while at coll. After grad. took marketing job which lasted 30 days. Early film work in low budget exploitation film, Sizzle Beach, 1974. Then one line as Luther Adler in Frances. Role in The Big Chill was edited from final print. 1989, set up own prod. co. Tig Prods. at Raleigh Studios.
PICTURES: Sizzle Beach U.S.A., Shadows Run Black, Night Shift, Chasing Dreams, Table for Five, Testament, Stacy's Knights, The Gunrunner, Fandango, Silverado, American Flyers, The Untouchables, No Way Out, Bull Durham, Field of Dreams, Revenge (also exec. prod.), Dances With Wolves (also dir., co-prod.; Academy Awards for Best Picture & Director, 1990), Robin Hood: Prince of Thieves, JFK, The Bodyguard (also co-prod.), A Perfect World, Wyatt Earp (also co-prod.), Rapa Nui (co-prod. only), The War, Waterworld (also co-prod.), Tin Cup.
TELEVISION: Special: 500 Nations (co-exec. prod., host)

COUNTER, J. NICHOLAS III
Executive. Pres., Alliance of Motion Picture and Television Producers.

COURIC, KATIE
Newcaster. b. Arlington, VA, Jan. 7, 1957. e. Univ. of VA. Started as desk asst. at ABC News, then assignment editor for CNN, reporter for WTVJ, NBC affiliate in Miami. Moved to NBC's Washington D.C. station WRC. Became natl. correspondent for The Today Show, 1989, then co-host in 1991. Served as co-host of Macy's Thanksgiving Day Parade, 1991-present. Co-host of nighttime series Now With Tom Brokaw & Katie Couric.

COURTENAY, TOM
Actor. b. Hull, England, Feb. 25, 1937 e. University Coll., London, Royal Acad. of Dramatic Art, 1960-61; Old Vic.
THEATER: Billy Liar, Andorra, Hamlet, She Stoops to Conquer, Otherwise Engaged (N.Y. debut), The Dresser, Poison Pen, Uncle Vanya, Moscow Stations, etc.
PICTURES: The Loneliness of the Long Distance Runner (debut, 1962), Private Potter, Billy Liar, King and Country, Operation Crossbow, King Rat, Doctor Zhivago (Acad. Award nom.), The Night of the Generals, The Day the Fish Came Out, A Dandy in Aspic, Otley, One Day in the Life of Ivan Denisovich, Catch Me a Spy, The Dresser (Acad. Award nom.), Happy New Year, Leonard Part VI, Let Him Have It, The Last Butterfly.
TELEVISION: Series: The Lads, Ghosts, Private Potter. Movies/Specials: I Heard the Owl Call My Name, Jesus of Nazareth, Absent Friends, Chekhov in Yalta, Redemption, The Old Curiosity Shop.

COURTLAND, JEROME
Actor, Producer, Director. b. Knoxville, TN, Dec. 27, 1926. Began career in 40s as actor, then turned to directing and producing.
PICTURES: Actor: Kiss and Tell, Man from Colorado, Battleground, The Barefoot Mailman, The Bamboo Prison, Tonka, Black Spurs. Director: Run, Cougar, Run, Diamond on Wheels. Producer: Escape to Witch Mountain, Ride a Wild Pony, Return from Witch Mountain, Pete's Dragon.
TELEVISION: Actor: The Saga of Andy Burnett, Tonka. Director: Hog Wild (also co-prod.), Harness Fever. Knots Landing, Dynasty, Hotel, Love Boat, Fantasy Island.

COUSTEAU, JACQUES-YVES, CAPTAIN
Producer. b. St. Andre de Cubzac, Gironde, June 11, 1910. e. French Naval Acad. Trained as Navy flier, switched to Gunnery office and started diving experiments. 1943 with Emile Gagnan conceived and released Aqua-Lung, first regulated compressed air breathing device for deep sea diving. After WWII org.

Experimental Diving Unit, performed oceanographic research. 1951 perfected first underwater camera equipment for TV. Founded environmental org. The Cousteau Society 1973. Awarded Chevalier de la Legion d Honneur for work in Resistance. Member National Acad. of Sciences. Elected to the Academie Francaise.
PICTURES: 20 short documentaries 1942-56; The Silent World (Academy Award, 1957; Grand Prize Cannes, 1956); The Golden Fish (Academy Award, short subject, 1959), World Without Sun (Academy Award, 1965), Voyage to the Edge of the World.
TELEVISION: Nearly 100 TV films on his series: The World of Jacques-Yves Cousteau, The Undersea World of Jacques Cousteau (2 Emmy Awards, 1972), Oasis in Space, The Cousteau Odyssey series, Cousteau/Amazon, Cousteau: Mississippi (Emmy Award, 1985), Rediscovery of the World series (exec. prod.).

COUTARD, RAOUL
Cinematographer. b. Paris, France, Sept. 16, 1924. Spent 4 years in Vietnam working for French Military Info. Service, later a civilian photographer for Time and Paris-Match. During WWII worked in photo labs. After war returned to France and formed prod. co. making documentaries. Joined Jean-Luc Godard as his cinematographer on Breathless (1960). His use of hand-held camera and natural light established him as a seminal camera-man of the French New Wave, working with Godard, Truffaut and later with Costa Gavras. Director: Hoa Binh (1971).
PICTURES: Breathless, Shoot the Piano Player, Lola, Jules and Jim, The Army Game, My Life to Live, Love at Twenty (segment), Les Carabiniers, Contempt, Alphaville, The Soft Skin, Male Companion, Pierrot le Fou, Made in USA, Weekend, Sailor From Gibraltar, The Bride Wore Black, Z, The Confession, Le Crabe Tambour, Passion, First Name: Carmen, Dangerous Moves, Salt on the Skin, La Garce, Max My Love, Burning Beds, Let Sleeping Cops Lie, Bethune: The Making of a Hero.

COWAN, WARREN J.
Publicist. b. New York, NY, Mar. 13. e. Townsend Harris H.S., UCLA, graduated 1941. Entered public relations, 1941, with Alan Gordon & Associates; three yrs. Air Force; joined Henry C. Rogers office in 1945; became partner, 1949, and changed name to Rogers & Cowan Public Relations; advisor, Rogers & Cowan, Inc., 1960; pres., Rogers & Cowan, Inc., 1964; named bd. chmn., 1983. Retired as Rogers & Cowan chmn. in 1992. 1994, started new P.R. company, Warren Cowan & Assocs. Served as natl. communications chmn. for United Way of America. On advisory bd. of the Natl. Assoc. of Film Commissioners; 2nd Decade Council of American Film Inst. On bd. L.A. County High School for the Arts, Scott Newman Center, Young Musicians Foundation.

COX, ALEX
Director, Writer. b. Liverpool, Eng., Dec. 15, 1954. Studied law at Oxford U. where he dir. and acted in plays for school drama society. Studied film prod. Bristol U. Received Fulbright Scholarship to study at UCLA film school, 1981.
PICTURES: Repo Man (also s.p.), Sid and Nancy (also co-s.p.), Straight to Hell (also co-s.p.), Walker (also co-editor), Highway Patrolman, The Glimmer Man.

COX, BRIAN
Actor. b. Dundee, Scotland, June 1, 1946. e. London Acad. of Music & Dramatic Art. Acted with Royal Lyceum Edinburgh and Birmingham Rep. Theatre; also season with Royal Shakespeare Company. Video: Acting and Tragedy. Author: The Lear Diaries, Salem in Moscow.
THEATER: The Master Builder, King Lear, Richard III, Fashion, Rat in the Skull (Olivier Award; also B'way), Titus Andronicus (Olivier Award), Penny for a Song, Misalliance.
PICTURES: Nicholas and Alexandra, In Celebration, Manhunter, Shoot for the Sun, Hidden Agenda, Prince of Jutland, Iron Will, Rob Roy, Braveheart, Chain Reaction.
TELEVISION: Inspector Morse, Therese Raquin, Pope John Paul II, Florence Nightingale, Beryl Markham: A Shadow on the Sun, Murder by Moonlight, Six Characters in Search of an Author, Picasso, The Negotiator, The Big Battalions, Bach, Bothwell, Churchill's People, Master of Ballantrae, Lost Language of Cranes, The Changeling, Secret Weapon.

COX, COURTENEY
Actress. b. Birmingham, AL, June 15, 1964. Left AL to pursue modelling career in NY. Dir. Brian DePalma selected her to be the young woman who jumps out of audience and dances with Bruce Springsteen in his music video Dancing in the Dark. This break led to featured role in short-lived TV series Misfits of Science (1985-86).
PICTURES: Masters of the Universe, Down Twisted, Cocoon: The Return, Mr. Destiny, Blue Desert, Shaking the Tree, The Opposite Sex, Ace Ventura—Pet Detective, Scream.
TELEVISION: Series: Misfits of Science, Family Ties, The Trouble With Larry, Friends. Movies: I'll Be Home for Christmas, Roxanne: The Prize Pulitzer, Till We Meet Again, Curiosity Kills, Battling for Baby, Topper, Sketch Artist II: Hands That See.

COX, RONNY
Actor. b. Cloudcroft, NM, July 23, 1938. e. Eastern New Mexico Univ.
PICTURES: The Happiness Cage (debut, 1972), Deliverance, Hugo the Hippo (voice), Bound for Glory, The Car, Gray Lady Down, Harper Valley P.T.A., The Onion Field, Taps, The Beast Within, Some Kind of Hero, Courage (Raw Courage), Beverly Hills Cop, Vision Quest, Hollywood Vice Squad, Steele Justice, Beverly Hills Cop II, Robocop, One Man Force, Loose Cannons, Martians Go Home!, Total Recall, Scissors, Captain America, Past Midnight.
TELEVISION: Series: Apple's Way, Spencer, St. Elsewhere, Cop Rock, Sweet Justice. Movies: The Connection, A Case of Rape, Who Is the Black Dahlia?, Having Babies, Corey: For the People, The Girl Called Hatter Fox, Lovey: A Circle of Children Part II, Transplant, When Hell Was in Session, Fugitive Family, Courage of Kavik: The Wolf Dog, The Last Song, Alcatraz—The Whole Shocking Story, Fallen Angel, Two of a Kind, The Jesse Owens Story, The Abduction of Kari Swenson, Baby Girl Scott, In the Line of Duty: The FBI Murders, The Comeback, When We Were Young, With Murder in Mind, Perry Mason: The Case of the Heartbroken Bride, A Part of the Family. Mini-Series: Favorite Son. Specials: Our Town, Chicago 7 Trial.

COYOTE, PETER
Actor. r.n. Peter Cohon. b. New York, NY, 1942. Studied with San Francisco Actors Workshop. Theatre includes The Minstrel Show (dir.), Olive Pits (also co-writer), The Red Snake, True West, The Abduction of Kari Swenson, Baby Girl Scott.
PICTURES: Die Laughing (debut, 1980), Tell Me a Riddle, Southern Comfort, The Pursuit of D.B. Cooper, E.T.: The Extra Terrestrial, Endangered Species, Timerider, Cross Creek, Slayground, Stranger's Kiss, Heartbreakers, The Legend of Billie Jean, Jagged Edge, Outrageous Fortune, A Man in Love, Stacking, Heart of Midnight, The Man Inside, Crooked Hearts, Exposure, Bitter Moon, Kika, That Eye The Sky, Moonlight and Valentino, Unforgettable.
TELEVISION: Movies: Alcatraz: The Whole Shocking Story, The People vs. Jean Harris, Isabel's Choice, Best Kept Secrets, Scorned and Swindled, Time Flyer, Child's Cry, Sworn to Silence, Echoes in the Darkness, Unconquered, A Seduction in Travis County, Living a Lie, Keeper of the City, Breach of Conduct. Buffalo Girls. Special: Abraham Lincoln: A New Birth of Freedom (voice).

CRAIG, MICHAEL
Actor. r.n. Michael Gregson. b. Poona, India, Jan. 27, 1929. At 16 joined Merchant Navy. 1949 returned to England and made stage debut in repertory. M.P. debut as extra, 1949.
PICTURES: Passport to Pimlico (debut, 1949), The Magic Box, The Cruel Sea, Malta Story, The Love Lottery, Passage Home, The Black Tent, Yield to the Night, Eye-Witness, House of Secrets, High Tide At Noon, Sea of Sand, Sapphire, Upstairs and Downstairs, The Angry Silence, Cone of Silence, Doctor In Love, Mysterious Island, Payroll, No My Darling Daughter, A Pair of Briefs, A Life for Ruth, The Iron Maiden, Captive City, Summer Flight, Stolen Flight, Of a Thousand Delights, Life at the Top, Modesty Blaise, Star!, Twinky, The Royal Hunt of the Sun, Brotherly Love (Country Dance), A Town Called Bastard, The Fourth Mrs. Anderson, Vault of Horror, Inn of the Damned, Ride a Wild Pony, The Irishman, Turkey Shoot, Stanley, Appointment With Death.

CRAIN, JEANNE
Actress. b. Barstow, CA, May 25, 1925. Model; crowned Miss Long Beach of 1941: Camera Girl of 1942.
PICTURES: The Gang's All Here (debut, 1943), Home in Indiana, In the Meantime Darling, Winged Victory, State Fair, Leave Her to Heaven, Margie, Centennial Summer, You Were Meant for Me, Apartment for Peggy, Letter to Three Wives, The Fan, Pinky, Cheaper by the Dozen, I'll Get By (cameo), Take Care of My Little Girl, People Will Talk, Model and the Marriage Broker, Belles on Their Toes, O. Henry's Full House, City of Bad Men, Dangerous Crossing, Vicki, Duel in the Jungle, Man Without a Star, The Second Greatest Sex, Gentlemen Marry Brunettes, Fastest Gun Alive, Tattered Dress, The Joker is Wild, Guns of the Timberland, Queen of the Nile, Twenty Plus Two, Madison Avenue, Pontius Pilate, Hot Rods to Hell, Skyjacked, The Night God Screamed.

CRAMER, DOUGLAS S.
Executive. e. Northwestern U., Sorbonne, U. of Cincinnati, B.A.; Columbia U.M.F.A. m. Joyce Haber, columnist. Taught at Carnegie Inst. of Tech., 1954-55; Production asst. Radio City Music Hall 1950-51; MGM Script Dept. 1952; Manag. Dir. Cincinnati Summer Playhouse 1953-54. TV supvr. Procter and Gamble 1956-59; Broadcast supvr. Ogilvy Benson and Mather adv. 1959-62; v.p. program dev. ABC-TV 1962-66; v.p. production dev. 20 Cent.-Fox TV 1966; exec. v.p. in chg. of prod., Paramount TV, 1968-71; exec. v.p. Aaron Spelling Prods. 1976-89; pres. Douglas S. Cramer Co, 1989-.
THEATER: Call of Duty, Love is a Smoke, Whose Baby Are You.
TELEVISION: Exec. prod.: Bridget Loves Bernie, QB VII, Dawn:

Portrait of a Runaway, Danielle Steel's Fine Things, Kaleidoscope, Changes, Message from Nam, Daddy, Palamino, Once in a Lifetime, Trade Winds, Lake Success. Co-exec. prod.: Love Boat (1977-86), Vegas (1978-81), Wonder Woman, Dynasty, Matt Houston, Hotel, Colbys.

CRAVEN, GEMMA
Actress. b. Dublin, Ireland, June 1, 1950. e. Loretto Coll. Studied acting at Bush Davies School. London stage debut, Fiddler on the Roof (1970).
THEATER: London: Audrey, Trelawny, Dandy Dick, They're Playing Our Song, Song and Dance, Loot, A Chorus of Disapproval, Three Men on a Horse, Jacobowsky and the Colonel, The Magistrate, South Pacific, The London Vertigo, Private Lives, Present Laughter.
PICTURES: Kingdom of Gifts, Why Not Stay for Breakfast, The Slipper and the Rose, Wagner, Double X: The Name of the Game, Words Upon the Windowpane, Still Life.
TELEVISION: Pennies From Heaven, Must Wear Tights, She Loves Me, Song by Song by Noel Coward, Song by Song by Alan Jay Lerner, East Lynne, Robin of Sherwood, Treasure Hunt, Gemma Girls and Gershwin, Boon, The Bill, The Marshal.

CRAVEN, WES
Director, Writer. b. Cleveland, OH, Aug. 2, 1939. e. Wheaton Coll., B.A.; Johns Hopkins, M.A. (philosophy). Worked as humanities prof. prior to film.
PICTURES: The Last House on the Left (also s.p., ed.), The Hills Have Eyes (also s.p., ed.), Deadly Blessing, Swamp Thing (also s.p.), A Nightmare on Elm Street (also s.p.), The Hills Have Eyes Part II (also s.p.), Deadly Friend, A Nightmare on Elm Street III: Dream Warriors (co-s.p., co-exec. prod. only), The Serpent and the Rainbow, Shocker (also exec. prod., s.p.), The People Under the Stairs (also s.p., co-exec. prod.), Wes Craven's New Nightmare (also actor, s.p.), Vampire in Brooklyn, The Fear (actor only), Scream.
TELEVISION: Series: Twilight Zone (1985, 7 episodes: Word Play, A Little Peace and Quiet, Shatterday, Chameleon, Dealer's Choice, The Road Less Traveled, Pilgrim Soul). The People Next Door (exec. prod.). Movies: A Stranger in Our House, Invitation to Hell, Chiller, Casebusters, Night Visions (also exec. prod., co-writer), Laurel Canyon (exec. prod. only), Body Bags (actor only).

CRAWFORD, MICHAEL
O.B.E. Actor. b. Salisbury, England, Jan.19, 1942. r.n. Michael Dumbell-Smith. Early career as boy actor in children's films, as a boy soprano in Benjamin Britten's Let's Make an Opera and on radio. Later star of TV's Not So Much a Programme, More a Way of Life. Solo albums: Songs from the Stage and Screen, With Love, Performs Andrew Lloyd Weber, A Touch of Music in the Night. Appeared for MGM Grand in production EFX.
THEATER: Come Blow Your Horn, Traveling Light, The Anniversary, White Lies and Black Comedy (N.Y.), No Sex Please We're British, Billy, Same Time Next Year, Flowers for Algernon, Barnum, The Phantom of the Opera (London: Laurence Olivier Award; New York: Tony, Drama Desk, Drama League & Outer Circle Critics Awards, 1988; also L.A.), The Music of Andrew Lloyd Weber (U.S., Canada, U.K. & Australia).
PICTURES: Soap Box Derby (debut, 1957), Blow Your Own Trumpet, A French Mistress, Two Living One Dead, Two Left Feet, The War Lover, The Knack... and How to Get It, A Funny Thing Happened on the Way to the Forum, The Jokers, How I Won the War, Hello Dolly!, The Games, Hello-Goodbye, Alice's Adventures in Wonderland, Condorman, Once Upon a Forest (voice).
TELEVISION: Still Life, Destiny, Byron, Move After Checkmate, Three Barrelled Shotgun, Home Sweet Honeycomb, Some Mothers Do 'ave 'em, Chalk and Cheese, BBC Play for Today, Private View, Barnum.

CRENNA, RICHARD
Actor. b. Los Angeles, CA, Nov. 30, 1927. e. Belmont H.S., USC.
RADIO: Boy Scout Jamboree, A Date With Judy, The Hardy Family, The Great Gildersleeve, Burns & Allen, Our Miss Brooks.
PICTURES: Red Skies of Montana (debut, 1951), Pride of St. Louis, It Grows on Trees, Our Miss Brooks, Over-Exposed, John Goldfarb Please Come Home, Made in Paris, The Sand Pebbles, Wait Until Dark, Star!, Midas Run, Marooned, The Deserter, Doctors' Wives, Red Sky at Morning, Catlow, A Man Called Noon, Dirty Money (Un Flic), Jonathan Livingston Seagull (voice), Breakheart Pass, The Evil, Wild Horse Hank, Death Ship, Stone Cold Dead, Body Heat, First Blood, Table for Five, The Flamingo Kid, Rambo: First Blood Part II, Summer Rental, Rambo III, Leviathan, Hot Shots! Part Deux, A Pyromaniac's Love Story (unbilled), Jade, Sabrina.
TELEVISION: Series: Our Miss Brooks, The Real McCoys, Slattery's People, All's Fair, It Takes Two, Pros & Cons. Movies: Footsteps, Thief, Passions, A Case of Deadly Force, The Day the Bubble Burst, Centennial, The Rape of Richard Beck (Emmy Award, 1985), Doubletake, The Price of Passion, Police Story: The Freeway Killings, Plaza Suite, Kids Like These, On Wings of

Eagles, Internal Affairs, Blood Brothers: The Case of the Hillside Stranglers, Murder in Black and White, Stuck with Each Other, Montana, Last Flight Out, Murder Times Seven, And the Sea Will Tell, Intruders, Terror on Track 9, A Place to Be Loved, The Forget-Me-Not Murders, Jonathan Stone: Threat of Innocence, Janek: A Silent Betrayal, In the Name of Love: A Texas Tragedy.

CRICHTON, CHARLES
Director. b. Wallasey, Eng., Aug. 6, 1910. e. Oundle & Oxford.
PICTURES: For Those in Peril (debut, 1944), Painted Boats (The Girl on the Canal), Dead of Night (Golfing segment), Hue and Cry, Against the Wind, Another Shore, Train of Events (Orchestra Conductor segment), Dance Hall, The Lavender Hill Mob, Hunted (The Stranger in Between), The Titfield Thunderbolt, The Love Lottery, The Divided Heart, Man in the Sky (Decision Against Time), Floods of Fear (also s.p.), The Battle of the Sexes, The Boy Who Stole a Million (also co-s.p.), The Third Secret, He Who Rides a Tiger, Tomorrow's Island (also s.p.), A Fish Called Wanda (also story; 2 Acad. Award noms.).
TELEVISION: The Wild Duck, Danger Man, The Avengers, Man in a Suitcase, The Strange Report, Shirley's World, Black Beauty, The Protectors, Space 1999, Return of the Saint, Dick Turpin 1 & 2 Series, Smuggler, Video Arts Shorts.

CRICHTON, MICHAEL
Writer, Director. r.n. John Michael Crichton. b. Chicago, IL, Oct. 23, 1942. e. Harvard U. Medical School (M.D.), 1969. Postdoctoral fellow, Salk Inst. for Biological Sciences, La Jolla, 1969-70. Visiting writer, MIT, 1988. Recipient Edgar Award, Mystery Writers Amer.: A Case of Need (1968), The Great Train Robbery (1980). Named medical writer of year, Assn. of Amer. Med. Writers: Five Patients (1970). Received Scientific and Technical Achievement Academy Award, 1995.
AUTHOR: Novels: (as John Lange): Odds On, Scratch One, Easy Go (The Last Tomb), The Venom Business, Zero Cool, Grave Descend, Drug of Choice, Binary. (as Jeffery Hudson): A Case of Need (filmed as The Carey Treatment). (as Michael Douglas, with brother Douglas Crichton): Dealing or the Berkeley-to-Boston Forty-Brick Lost-Bag Blues (filmed). (as Michael Crichton): The Andromeda Strain (filmed), The Terminal Man (filmed), The Great Train Robbery, Eaters of the Dead, Congo, Sphere, Jurassic Park, Rising Son, Disclosure, The Lost World. Non-Fiction (as Michael Crichton): Five Patients, Jasper Johns, Electronic Life, Travels.
PICTURES: Westworld (dir., s.p.), Coma (dir., s.p.), The Great Train Robbery (dir., s.p.), Looker (dir., s.p.), Runaway (dir., s.p.), Physical Evidence (dir.), Jurassic Park (co-s.p.), Rising Sun (co-s.p.), Disclosure (co-prod.), Congo (co-s.p.), Twister (co- s.p., co-prod.).
TELEVISION: Movie: Pursuit (dir.; based on Binary). Series: ER (creator, co-exec. prod.; Emmy Award, 1996). Pilot: ER (Writers Guild Award, 1996).

CRIST, JUDITH
Journalist, Critic. b. New York, NY, May 22, 1922. e. Hunter College, Columbia U. School of Journalism. Joined NY Herald Tribune, serving as reporter, arts editor, assoc. drama critic, film critic. Contributing editor COlumbia magazine. Continued as film critic for NY World Journal Tribune, NBC-TV Today Show, New York Magazine, NY Post, Saturday Review, TV Guide, WWOR-TV. Teaches at Col. Grad. School of Journalism.
AUTHOR: The Private Eye the Cowboy and the Very Naked Girl, Judith Crist's TV Guide to the Movies, Take 22: Moviemakers on Moviemaking.

CRISTALDI, FRANCO
Producer. b. Turin, Italy, Oct. 3, 1924. Owner, prod. Vides Cinematografica; President of Italian Producer's Union.
PICTURES: White Nights, The Strawman, The Challenge, Big Deal On Madonna Street, Kapo, The Dauphins, Salvatore Giuliano, The Assassin, Divorce Italian Style, The Organizer, Bebo's Girl, Seduced and Abandoned, Time of Indifference, Sandra, A Rose for Every-One, China Is Near, A Quiet Couple, The Red Tent, Una New Paradise Cinema.
TELEVISION: Marco Polo.

CROMWELL, JAMES
Actor. b. Los Angeles, CA, Jan. 27. Father was director John Cromwell, mother was actress Kate Johnson. e. Carnegie Mellon Univ.
PICTURES: Murder by Death, The Cheap Detective, The Man With Two Brains, House of God, Tank, Revenge of the Nerds, Oh God You Devil, Explorers, A Fine Mess, Revenge of the Nerds II: Nerds in Paradise, The Rescue, Pink Cadillac, The Runnin' Kind, The Babe, Babe, Eraser, The People vs. Larry Flynt, Star Trek: First Contact.
TELEVISION: Series: All in the Family, Hot L Baltimore, The Nancy Walker Show, The Last Precinct, Easy Street, Mama's Boy. Mini-Series: Once an Eagle. Movies: The Girl in the Empty Grave, Deadly Game, A Christmas Without Snow, The Wall, Spraggue, The Shaggy Dog. Guest: M*A*S*H, Dallas, L.A. Law, Star Trek: The Next Generation, Hill Street Blues.

CRONENBERG, DAVID
Writer, Director. b. Toronto, Ont., May 15, 1943. e. U. of Toronto. In college produced two short movies on 16mm. 1971, to Europe on a Canadian Council grant where in 1975 he shot his first feature, They Came From Within (Shivers).
PICTURES: Director: They Came From Within (Shivers; also s.p.), Rabid (also s.p.), Fast Company, The Brood (also s.p.), Scanners (also s.p.), Videodrome, The Dead Zone, The Fly (also co-s.p., cameo), Dead Ringers (also co-prod., co-s.p.), Naked Lunch (also s.p.), M. Butterfly, Crash. Actor: Into the Night, Nightbreed, Trial by Jury, Henry & Verlin.

CRONKITE, WALTER
Correspondent. b. St. Joseph, MO, Nov. 4, 1916. e. U. of Texas. Reporter and editor Scripps-Howard News Service, TX; radio reporter; U.P. correspondent. WW II corres. British Isles, N. Africa. Foreign Correspondent, France, Belgium, Netherlands, Soviet Union. Joined CBS as Washington news correspondent, 1950; anchorman and mng. editor, CBS Evening News, 1962-81; special correspondent, CBS News, 1981-present. Many TV shows including You Are There, Twentieth Century, Eyewitness to History: CBS Reports: 21st Century, Walter Cronkite's Universe. Past nat'l pres. & mem. bd. Trustees, Acad. TV Arts & Sciences. Mng. editor of CBS Evening News 1963-81; Special corres., Children of Apartheid, Walter Cronkite at Large. 1993, formed prod. company with John Ward, Cronkite Ward & Company, which has produced more than 25 award winning documentary hours for the Discovery Channel, PBS and others. Host/commentator of The Cronkite Reports, on the Discovery Channel which investigates current, global news issues. Other Cronkite Ward & Co. productions: Great Books series for the Learning Channel and Understanding: Science programs for the Discovery Channel. Supplied voice for 1995 B'way revival of How to Succeed in Business Without Really Trying.

CRONYN, HUME
Actor, Writer, Director. b. London, Ont., Canada, July 18, 1911. Was married to late actress Jessica Tandy. e. Ridley Coll., McGill U., Amer. Acad. of Dramatic Art.
THEATER: Actor N.Y. plays: High Tor, Escape This Night, Three Men on a Horse, Boy Meets Girl, Three Sisters, Mr. Big, The Survivors, Now I Lay Me Down to Sleep (dir.), Hilda Crane (dir.), The Fourposter (dir.), Madam Will You Walk, The Honeys, A Day by the Sea, The Man in the Dog Suit, The Egghead (dir.), Triple Play (dir. and toured with wife), Big Fish Little Fish (also in London), The Miser, The Three Sisters, Hamlet, The Physicists, Slow Dance on The Killing Ground (prod.), appeared at the White House, Hear America Speaking, Richard III, The Miser, A Delicate Balance (1966 and tour, 1967), The Miser, Hadrian VII (tour), Caine Mutiny Court Martial, Promenade All, Krapp's Last Tape, Happy Days, Act Without Words, Coward In Two Keys, concert recital Many Faces Of Love, Noel Coward in Two Keys (National tour), Merchant of Venice and A Midsummer Night's Dream (Stratford Festival Theatre) Canada, The Gin Game (with Miss Tandy; Long Wharf Thea., New Haven, B'way, 1977, co-prod. with Mike Nichols; also toured U.S., Toronto, London, U.S.S.R., 1978-79). Foxfire (co-author, actor, at Stratford, Ont., 1980, Minneapolis, 1981 and N.Y., 1982-83); Traveler in the Dark (Amer. Repertory Theatre, Cambridge, MA), Foxfire (Ahmanson, LA 1985-86), The Petition (NY 1986).
PICTURES: Shadow of a Doubt (debut, 1943), Phantom of the Opera, The Cross of Lorraine, Lifeboat, The Seventh Cross (Acad. Award nom.), Main Street After Dark, The Sailor Takes a Wife, A Letter for Evie, The Green Years, The Postman Always Rings Twice, Ziegfeld Follies, The Secret Heart (narrator), The Beginning or the End, Brute Force, Rope (adapt. only), The Bride Goes Wild, Top o' the Morning, Under Capricorn (adapt. only), People Will Talk, Crowded Paradise, Sunrise at Campobello, Cleopatra, Hamlet, Gaily Gaily, The Arrangement, There Was a Crooked Man, Conrack, The Parallax View, Honky Tonk Freeway, Rollover, The World According to Garp, Impulse, Brewster's Millions, Cocoon, Batteries Not Included, Cocoon: The Return, The Pelican Brief, Camilla, Marvin's Room.
TELEVISION: Series: The Marriage. Movies: The Dollmaker (co-writer only), Foxfire (also co-writer), Day One, Age-old Friends, Christmas on Division Street, Broadway Bound (Emmy Award, 1992), To Dance With the White Dog (Emmy Award, 1994).

CROSBY, CATHY LEE
Actress. b. Los Angeles, CA, Dec. 2. e. Grad. of U. of Southern California. Studied with Lee Strasberg. Author of Let The Magic Begin.
THEATER: Downside Risk, Almost Perfect (Off-B'way debut), Jellyroll Shoes, They Shoot Horses, Don't They? (wrote, dir. starred in 1st theatrical adapt. Hollywood Amer. Legion), Zoot Suit—The Real Story (writer, dir., actress, adapt., Beverly Hills).
PICTURES: The Laughing Policeman (debut, 1973), Trackdown, The Dark, Coach, Training Camp (s.p.), San Sebastian (s.p.), Call Me By My Rightful Name, The Player.
TELEVISION: Movies: Wonder Woman, Keefer, Roughnecks, World War III, Intimate Strangers, One Child, North & South III: Heaven and Hell, Untamed Love (also co-exec. prod.). Series: That's Incredible. Specials: A Spectacular Evening in Egypt,

Battle of the Network Stars, Circus of the Stars, Bob Hope Specials, Get High on Yourself, Bob Hope: USO Tour of Lebanon & the Mediterranean.

CROSBY, KATHRYN
Actress. r.n. Olive Kathryn Grandstaff. b. Houston, TX, Nov. 25, 1933. e. U. of Texas, Queen of Angels Sch. of Nursing, Immaculate Heart Col. m. late actor-singer Bing Crosby. Author: Bing and Other Things, My Life With Bing.
THEATER: Mama's Baby Boy, The Enchanted, Sunday in New York, Sabrina Fair, The Guardsman, Guys and Dolls, Same Time Next Year, The Crucible, Cyrano de Bergerac, Tonight at 8:30, The Cocktail Hour, Oh Coward, I Do I Do, The Heiress, The Seagull, many others.
PICTURES: Forever Female, Rear Window, Living It Up, Sabrina, Arrowhead, Casanova's Big Night, Unchained, Cell 2455 Death Row, Tight Spot, Five Against the House, Reprisal, Guns of Fort Petticoat, The Phenix City Story, Wild Party, Mister Cory, Gunman's Walk, The Librarian, Anatomy of a Murder, The Brothers Rico, Operation Mad Ball, The Seventh Voyage of Sinbad, The Big Circus.
TELEVISION: Guest: Bob Hope Chrysler Theatre, Bing Crosby Christmas Specials, Suspense Theatre, Ben Casey, The Kathryn Crosby Show (KPIX-TV, San Francisco). Movie: The Initiation of Sarah.

CROSBY, MARY
Actress. b. Los Angeles, CA, Sept. 14, 1959. e. U Tx. Daughter of performers Kathryn Crosby and the late Bing Crosby. Formerly acted as Mary Frances Crosby. Appeared from an early age in several TV variety specials with her parents.
PICTURES: The Last Plane Out, The Ice Pirates, Tapeheads, Body Chemistry, Corporate Affairs, Eating, The Berlin Conspiracy, Desperate Motive (Distant Cousins).
TELEVISION: Series: Brothers and Sisters, Dallas. Movies: With This Ring, A Guide for the Married Woman, Midnight Lace, Golden Gate, Confessions of a Married Man, Final Jeopardy, Stagecoach. Mini-Series: Pearl, Hollywood Wives, North and South Book II.

CROSS, BEN
Actor. r.n. Bernard Cross. b. London, England, Dec. 16, 1947. e. Royal Acad. of Dramatic Art. Worked as stagehand, prop-master, and master carpenter with Welsh Natl. Opera and as set builder, Wimbledon Theatre.
THEATER: The Importance of Being Earnest (Lancaster, debut, 1972), I Love My Wife, Privates on Parade, Chicago, Lydie Breeze (NY debut, 1982), Caine Mutiny Court Martial.
PICTURES: A Bridge Too Far (debut, 1977), Chariots of Fire, The Unholy, The Goldsmith's Shop, Paperhouse, The House of the Lord, Eye of the Widow, Haunted Symphony, The Ascent, First Knight.
TELEVISION: Movies/Specials: Melancholy Hussar of the German Legion (1973, BBC), The Flame Trees of Thika, The Citadel, The Far Pavilions, Coming Out of the Ice, The Assisi Underground, Arthur Hailey's Strong Medicine, Steal the Sky, Pursuit, Twist of Fate, Nightlife, She Stood Alone, Diamond Fleece, Live Wire, Deep Trouble, Cold Sweat. Series: Dark Shadows (1991).

CROUSE, LINDSAY
Actress. b. New York, NY, May 12, 1948. Daughter of playwright Russel Crouse. e. Radcliffe.
THEATER: Was member of Circle Repertory Co. NY. Hamlet, Twelfth Night, Richard II, Childe Byron, Reunion (Obie Award). NY: Serenading Louie, The Shawl, The Stick Wife, The Homecoming (B'way debut; Theatre World Award). Member of L.A. Theatre Co.: The Tavern, Habeus Corpus.
PICTURES: All the President's Men (debut, 1976), Slap Shot, Between the Lines, Prince of the City, The Verdict, Daniel, Iceman, Places in the Heart, House of Games, Communion, Desperate Hours, Being Human, Bye Bye Love, The Indian in the Cupboard, The Arrival.
TELEVISION: Movies: Eleanor and Franklin, Chantilly Lace, Final Appeal, Out of Darkness, Parallel Lives. Mini-Series: The Kennedys of Massachusetts. Specials: Kennedy's Children, Lemon Sky, Between Mother and Daughter. Pilot: American Nuclear.

CROWE, CAMERON
Writer, Director. b. Palm Springs, CA, July 13, 1957. e. Calif. St. Univ., San Diego. Began career as journalist and editor for Rolling Stone. Adapted his book Fast Times at Ridgemont High into Writers Guild Award nominated screenplay for 1982 film.
PICTURES: American Hot Wax (actor). Writer: Fast Times at Ridgemont High, The Wild Life (also co-prod.), Say Anything (also dir.), Singles (also dir.), Singles (also dir.), Jerry Maguire (also dir.).
TELEVISION: Series: Fast Times (creative consultant).

CROWE, KEN
Executive. b. Sewickley, PA, Sep. 3, 1939. e. San Diego U. CPA, public accounting, Coopers & Lybrand, 1968-77; Mann

Theatres, treas./CFO, 1977-86; Paramount Mann Theatres, sr. v.p./CFO, 1986-88; Cinamerica Theatres, exec. v.p./CFO, 1988-present. Member of Motion Picture Pioneers, AICPA, FEI, Variety Club of So. Calif and Sertoma.

CROWE, RUSSELL
Actor. b. New Zealand, 1964. Raised in Australia. Worked as professional musician while appearing on Australian stage in Bad Boy Johnny and the Profits of Doom, Blood Brothers, Rocky Horror Show.
PICTURES: For the Moment, The Silver Brumby, Hammers Over the Anvil, Prisoners of the Sun, Love in Limbo, For the Moment, Proof (Australian Film Inst. Award), The Efficiency Expert, Romper Stomper (Australian Film Inst. Award), The Quick and the Dead, The Sum of Us, Virtuosity, Rough Magic, No Way Back.

CRUEA, EDMOND D.
Executive. b. Jersey City, NJ, June 3. Joined Grand Natl. Pictures, LA, 1935; Monogram Pictures, 1938-41, LA & Seattle; U.S. Army Signal Corps., 1942-46; Monogram Pictures, Seattle, 1946; branch mgr. & district mgr. Allied Artists, 1950-65 (Seattle, Portland, San Francisco, LA); v.p. & gen. sls. mgr., Allied Artists, 1965-71; dir. distribution, Abkco Films div. of Abkco Industries Inc., 1971-3; pres. Royal Dist. Corp, 1974; joined Film Ventures Intl. 1976 as exec. v.p. succeeding to pres. & COO in 1976. Co-founded New Image Releasing Inc., 1982, as pres. & CEO. 1985, v.p. theatrical, Cinetel Films; 1987 theatrical distrib. consultant, Sony Pictures (NY) and Shining Armour Commun (London). Acquisitions & distrib. consultant to Columbia TriStar Home Video, Triumph Pictures and Healing Arts Documentary Prods.; 1995, chmn. and CEO Global International Films Inc.

CRUISE, TOM
Actor. r.n. Thomas Cruise Mapother IV. b. Syracuse, NY, July 3, 1962. m. actress Nicole Kidman. Acted in high school plays; secured role in dinner theatre version of Godspell. Studied acting at Neighborhood Playhouse, before landing small part in Endless Love. Received American Cinema Award for Distinguished Achievement in Film, 1991.
PICTURES: Endless Love (debut, 1981), Taps, Losin' It, The Outsiders, Risky Business, All the Right Moves, Legend, Top Gun, The Color of Money, Cocktail, Rain Man, Born on the 4th of July (Golden Globe Award, Acad. Award nom.), Days of Thunder (also co-wrote story), Far and Away, A Few Good Men, The Firm, Interview With the Vampire, Mission: Impossible.
TELEVISION: Director: The Frightening Framis (episode of series Fallen Angels).

CRYER, JON
Actor. b. New York, NY, Apr. 16, 1965. Son of actor David Cryer and songwriter-actress Gretchen Cryer. On B'way stage in Brighton Beach Memoirs.
PICTURES: No Small Affair (debut, 1984), Pretty in Pink, Morgan Stewart's Coming Home, O.C. and Stiggs, Superman IV: The Quest for Peace, Hiding Out, Dudes, Penn and Teller Get Killed, Hot Shots!, The Pompatus of Love.
TELEVISION: Series: The Famous Teddy Z, Partners. Special: Kurt Vonnegut's Monkey House. Movie: Heads.

CRYSTAL, BILLY
Actor, Writer, Producer, Director. b. Long Island, NY, Mar. 14, 1947. e. Marshall U., Nassau Commun. Col., NYU (BFA in tv & film direction). Father, Jack, produced jazz concerts; family owned Commodore jazz record label. Worked with Alumni Theatre Group at Nassau Commun. College. Later teamed with two friends (billed as We the People, Comedy Jam, 3's Company) and toured coffee houses and colleges. Became stand-up comedian on own, appearing at Catch a Rising Star, The Comedy Story and on TV. Album: Mahvelous!. Book: Absolutely Mahvelous!
PICTURES: Rabbit Test (debut, 1978), Animalympics (voice), This Is Spinal Tap, Running Scared, The Princess Bride, Throw Mama from the Train, Memories of Me (also co-prod., co-s.p.), When Harry Met Sally..., City Slickers (also exec. prod.), Mr. Saturday Night (also dir., prod., co-s.p.), City Slickers II: The Legend of Curly's Gold (also prod., co-s.p.), Forget Paris (also dir., prod., co-s.p.), Hamlet.
TELEVISION: Series: Soap, The Billy Crystal Comedy Hour (also writer), Saturday Night Live (also writer), Sessions (creator, exec. prod. only). Guest: Saturday Night Live with Howard Cosell, Tonight Show, Dinah, Mike Douglas Show, That Was the Year That Was, All in the Family, Love Boat. Specials include: Battle of the Network Stars, Billy Crystal: A Comic's Line (also writer), A Comedy Salute to Baseball (also writer), On Location: Billy Crystal - Don't Get Me Started (also dir., writer), The Three Little Pigs (Faerie Tale Theatre), The Lost Minutes of Billy Crystal, Midnight Train to Moscow (also exec. prod., co-writer; Emmy Award 1990). Movies: SST—Death Flight, Human Feelings, Breaking Up Is Hard to Do, Enola Gay: The Men the Mission and the Atomic Bomb. Host: Grammy Awards (Emmy Awards for hosting, 1988, 1989), Academy Awards (Emmy Award for hosting, 1991; Emmy Award for co-writing, 1992).

CULBERG, PAUL S.
Executive. b. Chicago, IL, June 14, 1942. Began career in record industry, holding positions with Elektra Records & Wherehouse Record; 1977-80; v.p. sls. mktg., Cream Records.; 1980-82, dir. sls. Paramount Home Video; 1982, v.p. sls. mktg., Media Home Entertainment; 1984-89, pres., New World Video; 1989-present, COO, RCA Columbia/TriStar Home Video.

CULKIN, MACAULAY
Actor. b. New York, NY, Aug. 26, 1980. Acting debut at 4 yrs. old in Bach Babies at NY's Symphony Space. Appeared in several TV commercials. Studied ballet at George Ballanchine's School of American Ballet and danced in NY productions of H.M.S. Pinafore and The Nutcracker. Received Comedy Award and Youth in Film Award for role in Home Alone. Appeared in Michael Jackson video Black and White.
THEATER: NY: Afterschool Special, Mr. Softee, Buster B. and Olivia.
PICTURES: Rocket Gibraltar (debut, 1988), See You in the Morning, Uncle Buck, Jacob's Ladder, Home Alone, Only the Lonely, My Girl, Home Alone 2: Lost in New York, The Good Son, George Balanchine's The Nutcracker, Getting Even With Dad, The Pagemaster, Richie Rich.
TELEVISION: Guest: The Equalizer, Saturday Night Live, Bob Hope Christmas Special.

CULLUM, JOHN
Actor. b. Knoxville, TN, Mar. 2, 1930. e. Univ. of TN. Son is actor John David (J.D.) Cullum.
THEATER: NY: Camelot, On a Clear Day You Can See Forever (Theatre World Award, Tony nom.), Hamlet, Man of La Mancha, 1776, Shenandoah (Tony Award, Drama Desk & Outer Circle Critics Awards, 1975), The Trip Back Down, On the Twentieth Century (Tony Award, 1978), Deathtrap, Private Lives, Doubles, The Boys in Autumn, Aspects of Love, Showboat.
PICTURES: All the Way Home, 1776, The Prodigal, The Act, Marie, Sweet Country.
TELEVISION: Series: Buck James, Northern Exposure. Guest: Quantum Leap (also dir.). Movies: The Man Without a Country, The Day After, Shoot Down, With a Vengeance.

CULP, ROBERT
Actor, Writer, Director. b. Berkeley, CA, Aug. 16, 1930. e. Stockton, College of the Pacific, Washington U., San Francisco State; to N.Y. to study with Herbert Berghof (played Potzo in 1st U.S. prod. of Waiting for Godot. Starred in off-Bwdy prod. He Who Gets Slapped. Best Actor of the Year in an off-Bwdy play; motion picture debut, 1962; P.T. 109; television guest appearances in Rawhide, Wagon Train, Bob Hope Presents the Chrysler Theatre; wrote and acted in Rifleman, Cain's Hundred, The Dick Powell Show.
THEATER: Bway.: The Prescott Proposals, A Clearing in the Woods, Diary of a Scoundrel.
PICTURES: PT 109 (debut, 1963), Sunday in New York, Rhino!, Bob & Carol & Ted & Alice, The Grove, Hannie Caulder, Hickey & Boggs (also dir., uncredited co-s.p.), A Name for Evil, The Castaway Cowboy, Inside Out (Golden Heist), Sky Riders, Breaking Point, The Great Scout and Cathouse Thursday, Goldengirl, National Lampoon Goes to the Movies, Turk 182!, Big Bad Mama II, Silent Night Deadly Night 3: Better Watch Out, Pucker Up and Bark Like a Dog, Timebomb, The Pelican Brief, Panther.
TELEVISION: Series: Trackdown, I Spy (also wrote pilot and 6 shows; Emmy noms. as writer and actor), The Greatest American Hero (also wrote 2 shows). Guest: The Cosby Show. Movies: Sammy The Way Out Seal, The Raiders, The Hanged Man, See the Man Run, A Cold Night's Death, Outrage!, Houston We've Got a Problem, Strange Homecoming, A Cry for Help, Flood, Spectre, Last of the Good Guys, Women in White, Hot Rod, The Dream Merchants, The Night the City Screamed, Killjoy, Thou Shalt Not Kill, Her Life as a Man, The Calendar Girl Murders, Brothers-in-Law, The Blue Lightning, The Gladiator, The Key to Rebecca, Combat High, Voyage of Terror: The Achille Lauro Affair, Columbo Goes to College, I Spy Returns.

CUMMINGS, CONSTANCE
C.B.E. Actress. b. Seattle, WA, May 15, 1910. r.n. Constance Cummings Halverstadt. p. D.V. Halverstadt, attorney, and Kate Cummings, concert soprano; m. Benn Levy, English playwright. Was chorus girl in The Little Show and also appeared in June Moon. B'way debut: Treasure Girl, 1928; London debut: Sour Grapes, 1934. Joined National Theatre Co. 1971.
THEATER: Recent work: A Long Day's Journey into Night (with Laurence Olivier), The Cherry Orchard, Wings (Tony & Obie Awards 1979), The Chalk Garden, Tete a Tete.
PICTURES: The Criminal Code (debut, 1931), The Love Parade, Lover Come Back, Guilty Generation, Traveling Husbands, The Big Timer, Behind the Mask, Movie Crazy, Night After Night, American Madness, The Last Man, Washington Merry-Go-Round, Attorney for the Defense, Heads We Go (The Charming Deceiver), Channel Crossing, Billion Dollar Scandal, Broadway Through a Keyhole, The Mind Reader, Glamour, Looking for Trouble, This Man Is Mine, Remember Last Night?, Seven

Sinners (Doomed Cargo), Strangers on a Honeymoon, Busman's Honeymoon (Haunted Honeymoon), This England, The Foreman Went to France (Somewhere in France), Blithe Spirit, Into the Blue, Three's Company, The Scream, John and Julie, The Intimate Stranger (Finger of Guilt), The Battle of the Sexes, Sammy Going South (A Boy 10 Feet Tall), In the Cool of the Day.
TELEVISION: Touch of the Sun, Clutterbuck, The Last Tycoon, Ruth, Late Summer, Long Day's Journey Into Night, Jane Eyre, Wings, Agatha Christie's Dead Man's Folly.

CUMMINS, PEGGY
Actress. b. Prestatyn, North Wales, Dec. 18, 1925. e. Alexandra Sch., Dublin, Gate Theatre, Dublin. Starred in Let's Pretend on London Stage 1938, followed by Junior Miss, Alice in Wonderland, Peter Pan.
PICTURES: Dr. O'Dowd (debut, 1939), Salute John Citizen, Old Mother Riley—Detective, Welcome Mr. Washington, English Without Tears (Her Man Gilbey), The Late George Apley, Moss Rose, Green Grass of Wyoming, Escape, That Dangerous Age (If This Be Sin), Gun Crazy, My Daughter Joy (Operation X), Who Goes There (Passionate Sentry), Street Corner (Both Sides of the Law), Meet Mr. Lucifer, Always a Bride, The Love Lottery, To Dorothy a Son (Cash on Delivery), The March Hare, Carry on Admiral, Night of the Demon, Hell Drivers, The Captain's Table, Your Money or Your Wife, Dentist in the Chair, In the Doghouse.
TELEVISION: The Human Jungle, Looks Familiar.

CUNNINGHAM, SEAN S.
Producer, Director. b. New York, NY, Dec. 31 1941. e. Franklin & Marshall, B.A.; Stanford U., M.F.A. Worked briefly as actor, moving into stage-managing. Became producer of Mineola Theatre (Long Island, NY) and took several productions to B'way. Formed Sean S. Cunningham Films, Ltd., 1971. Produced commercials, industrial film, documentaries, features.
PICTURES: Together (prod., dir.), Last House on the Left (prod.), The Case of the Full Moon Murders (prod.), Here Come the Tigers (prod., dir.), Kick (prod., dir.), Friday the 13th (prod., dir.), A Stranger Is Watching (prod., dir.), Spring Break (prod., dir.), The New Kids (prod., dir.), House (prod.), House II: The Second Story (prod.), Deepstar Six (prod., dir.), The Horror Show (House III; prod.), House IV (prod.), My Boyfriend's Back (prod.), Jason Goes to Hell: The Final Friday (prod.).

CURRY, TIM
Actor. b. Cheshire, England, Apr. 19, 1946. e. Birmingham U. Albums: Read My Lips, Fearless, Simplicity.
THEATER: Hair, A Midsummer Night's Dream, The Rocky Horror Show, Travesties, Amadeus (Tony nom.), The Pirates of Penzance, Me and My Girl (U.S. tour), The Art of Success, My Favorite Year (Tony nom.).
PICTURES: The Rocky Horror Picture Show (debut, 1975), The Shout, Times Square, Annie, The Ploughman's Lunch, Blue Money, Clue, Legend, Pass the Ammo, The Hunt for Red October, Oscar, FernGully... The Last Rainforest (voice), Passed Away, Home Alone 2: Lost in New York, National Lampoon's Loaded Weapon 1, The Three Musketeers, The Shadow, Lovers' Knot, The Pebble and the Penguin (voice), Congo, The Muppet Treasure Island, Lover's Knot.
TELEVISION: Movies: Oliver Twist, Stephen King's IT. Voice work—series: Peter Pan and the Pirates (Emmy Award, 1991), Captain Planet and the Planeteers, Fish Police. Specials: The Life of Shakespeare, Three Men in a Boat, Rock Follies, City Sugar. Guest: Dinosaurs (voice), Earth 2.

CURTIN, JANE
Actress. b. Cambridge, MA, Sept. 6, 1947. e. Northeastern U. On stage in Proposition, Last of the Red Hot Lovers, Candida. Author, actress off-B'way musical revue Pretzel 1974-75.
PICTURES: Mr. Mike's Mondo Video, How to Beat the High Cost of Living, O.C. and Stiggs, Coneheads.
TELEVISION: Series: Saturday Night Live (1974-79), Kate & Allie (Emmy Awards: 1984, 1985), Working It Out. Movies: What Really Happened to the Class of '65, Divorce Wars—A Love Story, Suspicion, Maybe Baby, Common Ground. Special: Candida.

CURTIS, DAN
Producer, Director. b. Bridgeport, CT, Aug. 12, 1928. e. U. of Bridgeport, Syracuse U., B.A. Was sales exec. for NBC and MCA before forming own company, Dan Curtis Productions, which he now heads. Producer/owner of CBS Golf Classic (1963-73).
PICTURES: Dir.-Prod.: House of Dark Shadows, Night of Dark Shadows, Burnt Offerings (also co-s.p.), Me and the Kid.
TELEVISION: Producer: Series: Dark Shadows (ABC daytime serial, 1966-71), Dark Shadows (prime time series, 1991). Movies: Director: The Night Stalker, Frankenstein, The Picture of Dorian Gray. Producer-Director: The Night Strangler, The Norliss Tapes, Scream of the Wolf, Dracula, Melvin Purvis: G-Man, The Turn of the Screw, The Great Ice-Rip Off, Trilogy of Terror, Kansas City Massacre, Curse of the Black Widow, When Every

Day Was the Fourth of July (also co-story). Director: The Last Ride of the Dalton Gang, The Long Days of Summer, Mrs. R's Daughter, Intruders (also co-exec. prod.). Mini-Series (prod./dir.): The Winds of War, War and Remembrance (also co-writer).

CURTIS, JAMIE LEE
Actress. b. Los Angeles, CA, Nov. 22, 1958. m. actor-director Christopher Guest. Daughter of Janet Leigh and Tony Curtis. e. Choat Rosemary Hall, CT; Univ. of the Pacific. While in school won contract with Universal Studios appearing in small parts in several tv shows.
PICTURES: Halloween (debut, 1978), The Fog, Prom Night, Terror Train, Halloween II, Roadgames, Trading Places, Love Letters, Grandview USA, Perfect, Amazing Grace and Chuck, A Man in Love, Dominick and Eugene, A Fish Called Wanda, Blue Steel, Queens Logic, My Girl, Forever Young, My Girl 2, Mother's Boys, True Lies, House Arrest, Death Fish.
TELEVISION: Special: Tall Tales (Annie Oakley). Series: Operation Petticoat (1977-78), Anything But Love (Golden Globe Award). Movies: Operation Petticoat (pilot), She's in the Army Now, Death of a Centerfold: The Dorothy Stratten Story, Money on the Side, As Summers Die, The Heidi Chronicles. Pilot: Callahan. Guest: Quincy, Nancy Drew Mysteries.

CURTIS, TONY
Actor. r.n. Bernard Schwartz. b. New York, NY, June 3, 1925. Daughter is actress Jamie Lee Curtis. e. Seward Park H.S. In U.S. Navy, amateur dramatics, N.Y., started Empire Players Theatre, Newark, NJ; with Dramatic Workshop, Cherry Lane Theatre, Junior Drama workshop of Walt Whitman School; first prod. work with Stanley Woolf Players; m.p. debut unbilled in Criss-Cross; signed with U-I. Star of Tomorrow, 1953. Author: Tony Curtis: The Autobiography (1993).
PICTURES: Criss Cross (debut, 1948), City Across the River, The Lady Gambles, Johnny Stool Pigeon, Francis, Sierra, I Was a Shoplifter, Winchester 73, Sierra, Kansas Raiders, Prince Who Was a Thief, Flesh and Fury, Son of Ali Baba, No Room for the Groom, Houdini, All American, Forbidden, Beachhead, Johnny Dark, Black Shield of Falworth, 6 Bridges to Cross, So This Is Paris, Purple Mask, Square Jungle, Rawhide Years, Trapeze, Mister Cory, Midnight Story, Sweet Smell of Success, The Vikings, Kings Go Forth, The Defiant Ones (Acad. Award nom.), The Perfect Furlough, Some Like It Hot, Operation Petticoat, Who Was That Lady?, The Rat Race, Spartacus, Pepe (cameo), The Great Impostor, The Outsider, Taras Bulba, 40 Pounds of Trouble, The List of Adrian Messenger, Captain Newman, M.D., Paris When it Sizzles, Wild and Wonderful, Sex and the Single Girl, Goodbye Charlie, The Great Race, Boeing-Boeing, Chamber of Horrors (cameo), Not With My Wife You Don't!, Arrivederci Baby!, Don't Make Waves, On My Way to the Crusades I Met a Girl Who—(The Chastity Belt), The Boston Strangler, Rosemary's Baby (voice), Those Daring Young Men in Their Jaunty Jalopies (Monte Carlo or Bust), Suppose They Gave a War and Nobody Came, You Can't Win 'Em All, Lepke, The Last Tycoon, Casanova & Co., The Manitou, The Bad News Bears Go to Japan, Sextette, Little Miss Marker, The Mirror Crack'd, Brainwaves, King of the City, Insignificance, Club Life, The Last of Philip Banter, Balboa, Midnight, Lobster Man From Mars, The High-Flying Mermaid, Prime Target, Center of the Web, Naked in New York, The Reptile Man, The Immortals, The Celluloid Closet.
TELEVISION: Series: The Persuaders, McCoy, Vega$, Hollywood Babylon (host). Movies: The Third Girl from the Left, The Count of Monte Cristo, Vega$, The Users, Moviola: The Scarlett O'Hara War, Inmates: A Love Story, Harry's Back, The Million Dollar Face, Mafia Princess, Murder in Three Acts, Portrait of a Showgirl, Tarzan in Manhattan, Thanksgiving Day, Christmas in Connecticut, A Perry Mason Mystery: The Case of the Grimacing Governor.

CUSACK, JOAN
Actress. b. Evanston, IL, Oct. 11, 1962. Brother is actor John Cusack. e. U. of Wisconsin, Madison. Studied acting at Piven Theatre Workshop, Evanston, IL. While in coll. joined The Ark, local improvisational comedy group.
THEATER: Road, Brilliant Traces (Theatre World Award for both), Cymbeline, The Celestial Alphabet Event, 'Tis Pity She's a Whore, A Midsummer Night's Dream.
PICTURES: My Bodyguard (debut, 1980), Class, Sixteen Candles, Grandview U.S.A., The Allnighter, Broadcast News, Stars and Bars, Married to the Mob, Working Girl (Acad. Award nom.), Say Anything..., Men Don't Leave, My Blue Heaven, The Cabinet of Dr. Ramirez, Hero, Toys, Addams Family Values, Corrina Corrina, Nine Months, Mr. Wrong.
TELEVISION: Series: Saturday Night Live (1985-86). Special: The Mother.

CUSACK, JOHN
Actor. b. Evanston, IL, June 28, 1966. Sister is actress Joan Cusack. Member of Piven Theatre Workshop in Evanston for 10 years beginning when he was 9 years old. Appeared on several tv commercials as teen. Formed Chicago theatrical company, New Criminals.

PICTURES: Class (debut, 1983), Sixteen Candles, Grandview U.S.A., The Sure Thing, The Journey of Natty Gann, Better Off Dead, Stand By Me, One Crazy Summer, Hot Pursuit, Eight Men Out, Tapeheads, Say Anything..., Fat Man and Little Boy, The Grifters, True Colors, Shadows and Fog, Roadside Prophets, The Player, Bob Roberts, Map of the Human Heart, Money for Nothing, Bullets Over Broadway, The Road to Wellville, Floundering, City Hall.

D

D'ABO, OLIVIA
Actress. b. England. Parents, singer Michael d'Abo, actress Maggie London.
THEATER: *LA:* Scenes From an Execution, It's a Girl.
PICTURES: Conan the Destroyer, Bolero, Bullies, Into the Fire, Beyond the Stars, The Spirit of 76, Point of No Return, Wayne's World 2, Bank Robber, Greedy, Clean Slate, The Last Good Time, The Big Green, Kicking and Screaming.
TELEVISION: *Series:* The Wonder Years, The Single Guy. *Movies:* Not My Kid, Crash Course, Midnight's Child.

DAFOE, WILLEM
Actor. r.n. William Dafoe. b. Appleton, WI, July 22, 1955. Worked with experimental group Theatre X on the road before coming to New York. Built sets and debuted with the Wooster Group at the Performing Garage playing (literally) a chicken heart in Elizabeth Le Compte's Nayatt School. Current member of the Wooster Group, performing with them frequently in U.S. and Europe. For them appeared in independent film The Communists Are Comfortable.
PICTURES: Heaven's Gate (debut, 1980), The Loveless, The Hunger, Streets of Fire, Roadhouse 66, To Live and Die in L.A., Platoon (Acad. Award nom.), Off Limits, The Last Temptation of Christ, Mississippi Burning, Triumph of the Spirit, Born on the Fourth of July, Cry-Baby, Wild at Heart, Flight of the Intruder, White Sands, Light Sleeper, Body of Evidence, Faraway So Close!, Clear and Present Danger, Tom and Viv, The Night and the Moment, The English Patient.

DAHL, ARLENE
Actress, Writer, Designer. b. Minneapolis, MN, Aug. 11, 1928. e. MN Business Coll.; U. of Minnesota, summers 1941-44; Minneapolis. Coll. of Music. m. Marc A. Rosen. Mother of actor Lorenzo Lamas. At age 8, played heroine of children's adventure serials on radio. Internationally syndicated beauty columnist, Chgo. Tribune-N.Y. News Syndicate, 1951-71; Pres. Arlene Dahl Enterprises, 1951-75; Sleepwear Designer, A.N. Saab & Co., 1952-57; Natl. Beauty Advisor, Sears Roebuck & Co., 1970-75; v.p. Kenyon & Eckhart Advg. Co., pres., Women's World Div. Kenyon-Eckhart, 1967-72; Fashion Consultant, O.M.A. 1975-78, Int'l. Director of S.M.E.I., 1973-76, Designer, Vogue Patterns 1978-85. Pres., Dahlia Parfums Inc., 1975-80, pres., Dahlia Prods., 1978-81: pres. Dahlmark Prods. 1981-. Publs: Always Ask a Man, 1965, Your Beautyscope, 1969, Secrets of Hair Care, 1971, Secrets of Skin Care, 1973, Your Beautyscope 1977-78, Beyond Beauty, 1980, Lovescopes, 1983. Honrs. include: 8 Motion Picture Laurel Awards, 1948-63; Hds. of Fame Award, 1971, Woman of the Year, N.Y. Adv. Council, 1969. Mother of the Year, 1979; Coup de Chapeau, Deauville Film Fest 1983. Received star on Hollywood Walk of Fame. Lifetime Achievement Award Filmfest 1994.
THEATER: *B'way:* Mr. Strauss Goes to Boston (debut, 1946), Cyrano de Bergerac, Applause. *Major US tours include:* Questionable Ladies, The King and I, One Touch of Venus, I Married an Angel, Mame, Pal Joey, Bell Book and Candle, The Camel Bell, Life With Father, A Little Night Music, Lilliom, Marriage Go Round, Blithe Spirit, Forty Carats, Dear Liar, Murder Among Friends.
PICTURES: My Wild Irish Rose (debut, 1947), The Bride Goes Wild, A Southern Yankee, Ambush, Reign of Terror (The Black Book), Scene of the Crime, The Outriders, Three Little Words, Watch the Birdie, Inside Straight, No Questions Asked, Caribbean, Jamaica Run, Desert Legion, Here Come the Girls, Sangaree, The Diamond Queen, Wicked as They Come, Fortune is a Woman, Bengal Brigade, Woman's World, Slightly Scarlet, She Played With Fire, Journey to the Center of the Earth, Kisses for My President, Les Ponyettes, DuBle en Liasse, Le Chemin du Katmandu. The Landraiders, A Place to Hide, Night of the Warrior.
TELEVISION: Max Factor Playhouse, Lux Television Theater, Pepsi Cola Playhouse, Opening Night, Arlene Dahl's Beauty Spot, Hostess, Model of the Year Show, Arlene Dahl's Starscope, Arlene Dahl's Lovescopes, One Life to Live (1981-84), Night of One Hundred Stars, Happy Birthday Hollywood, Who Killed Max Thorn?, Love Boat, Love American Style, Fantasy Island, Burke's Law, Renegade.

DAHL, JOHN
Director, Writer. b. Montana. e. Univ. of MT, Montana St. In collaboration with David Warfield made 30 minute rock musical, Here Come the Pugs and indept. feature, The Death Mutants.

PICTURES: Private Investigations (co-s.p.), Kill Me Again (dir., co-s.p.), Red Rock West (dir., co-s.p.), The Last Seduction (dir.), Unforgettable (dir., co-s.p.)

DALE, JIM
Actor. b. Rothwell, Northhamptonshire, England, Aug. 15, 1935. Debut as solo comedian at the Savoy, 1951. Joined National Theatre Co. in 1969 playing in Love's Labour's Lost, The Merchant of Venice, The National Health, The Card. U.S. theater: Mark Taper Forum: Comedians, Scapino. NY Theater: Taming of the Shrew, Scapino, Barnum (Tony and Drama Desk Awards, 1980), Joe Egg (Tony Award nom.), Me and My Girl, Privates on Parade, Travels With My Aunt. Has written songs and music for films: Twinky, Shalako, Joseph Andrews, Georgy Girl (Acad. Award nom.). Many tv appearances. Director: Asprin and Elephants.
PICTURES: Six-Five Special (debut, 1958), Raising the Wind, Nurse on Wheels, The Iron Maiden, Carry on Cabby, Carry on Jack, Carry on Spying, Carry on Cleo, The Big Job, Carry on Cowboy, Carry on Screaming, Don't Lose Your Head, The Winter's Tale, The Plank, Follow That Camel, Carry on Doctor, Lock Up Your Daughters, Carry on Again Doctor, The National Health, Digby—The Biggest Dog in the World, Joseph Andrews, Pete's Dragon, Hot Lead Cold Feet, Unidentified Flying Oddball, Scandalous, Carry on Columbus.
TELEVISION: *Movie:* The American Clock.

DALEY, ROBERT
Producer. e. UCLA. Began career in pictures at Universal International and TV at Desilu.
PICTURES: Play Misty For Me, Dirty Harry (exec. prod.), Joe Kidd, High Plains Drifter, Breezy, Magnum Force, Thunderbolt and Lightfoot, The Eiger Sanction, The Outlaw Josey Wales, The Enforcer, The Gauntlet, Every Which Way But Loose, Escape from Alcatraz (exec. prod.), Any Which Way You Can (exec. prod.), Bronco Billy (exec. prod.), Stick (exec. prod.), Real Genius (exec. prod.).
TELEVISION: The Untouchables, Ben Casey, The FBI, 12 O'Clock High, The Invaders, etc.

DALSIMER, SUSAN
Executive. Editor for E.P. Dutton before joining Lorimar Prods., as v.p. of east coast development. Left to become consultant for original programming at Home Box Office. 1987, named v.p., creative affairs, east coast, for Warner Bros. 1994, v.p., publishing for Miramax Films.

DALTON, TIMOTHY
Actor. b. Colwyn Bay, No. Wales, March 21, 1946. Started acting at Natl. Youth Theatre, then studied at RADA. Prof. stage debut in Richard III and As You Like It at Birmingham Rep.
THEATER: Coriolanus, The Merchant of Venice, Richard III, The Doctor's Dilemma, St. Joan, Macbeth, Henry IV, Henry V, The Samaritan, Black Comedy, White Liars, Lunatic Lover and Poet, Love Letters (1991).
PICTURES: The Lion in Winter (debut, 1968), Cromwell, The Voyeur, Wuthering Heights, Mary Queen of Scots, Permission to Kill, Sextette, Agatha, Flash Gordon, El Hombre Que Supo Amar, Anthony and Cleopatra, Chanel Solitaire, The Doctor and the Devils, The Living Daylights, Brenda Starr, Hawks, Licence to Kill, The King's Whore, The Rocketeer, Naked in New York, Saltwater Moose.
TELEVISION: *Mini-Series:* Centennial, Mistral's Daughter, Sins, Scarlett, Framed. *Movies:* The Master of Ballantrae, Lie Down With Lions, Field of Blood. *Specials:* The Three Princes, Five Finger Exercise, Candida, Daerie Tale Theater: The Emperor's New Clothes (narr.), Nature: In The Company of Wolves (docu.). *Series:* Sat'day While Sunday, Judge Dee, Hooked International, Charlie's Angels: Fallen Angel, Tales From the Crypt: Werewolf Concerto, Survival Factor Series (narr.).

DALTREY, ROGER
Singer, Actor. b. London, England, March 1, 1944. Lead vocalist with The Who.
PICTURES: Woodstock, Tommy, Lisztomania, The Legacy, The Kids Are Alright, McVicar (also prod.), Mack the Knife, The Teddy Bear Habit, Father Jim, If Looks Could Kill, Buddy's Song, Lightning Jack.
TELEVISION: *Movie:* Forgotten Prisoners: The Amnesty Files.

DALY, ANN
Executive. Pres., Domestic Home Video, Buena Vista Home Video.

DALY, JIM
Executive Director, Rank Organisation Plc. b. 1938. Managing director of Film and Television division which includes: Pinewood Studios, Rank Film Laboratories, Odeon Cinemas, Rank Film Distributors, Deluxe Hollywood, Deluxe Toronto, Rank Advertising Films, Rank Theatres, Rank Video Services, Rank Video Services America, Rank Video Services Europe, Film House Company, Rank Brimar, Rank Cintel, Strand Lighting, Rank Taylor Hobson. Appt. exec. dir., Rank Org. 1982.

DALY, JOHN
Executive. b. London, England, July 16, 1937. After working in journalism joined Royal Navy. On leaving Service after three years, trained as underwriter with an Assurance Company. In 1966 became David Hemmings manager and in 1967 formed the Hemdale Company with Hemmings (who later sold interest) Chmn. Hemdale Holdings Ltd.
PICTURES: Images, Sunburn (co-prod., co-s.p.), High Risk, Going Ape, Deadly Force, Carbon Copy, Yellowbeard, The Terminator, The Falcon and the Snowman, Salvador, River's Edge, At Close Range, Hoosiers, Platoon, Best Seller, Shag (exec. prod.), Vampire's Kiss (exec. prod.), Miracle Mile (prod.), Criminal Law (co-exec. prod.), War Party (prod.), The Boost, Out Cold (exec. prod.), Staying Together (exec. prod.).

DALY, ROBERT A.
Executive. b. New York, NY, Dec. 8, 1936. e. Brooklyn Coll., Hunter Coll. Joined CBS-TV in 1955; dir. of program acct.; dir. of research and cost planning; dir. of business affairs. Later named v.p., business affairs, NY; exec. v.p. of network on April, 1976. Named president, CBS Entertainment, Oct. 1977. In Oct. 1979 became responsible for CBS Theatrical Films as well as the TV operation. In 1980, appointed co-chmn. and co-chief exec. officer of Warner Bros. Sole title holder since Jan., 1982.

DALY, TIM
Actor. b. New York, NY, March 1, 1956. m. actress Amy Van Nostrand. Son of late actor James Daly, brother of actress Tyne Daly. e. Bennington Coll., B.A. Acted in summer stock while in college. Moved to NY where had own rock and roll band. Has performed in cabaret at Williamstown Theater Festival.
THEATER: Fables for Friends, Oliver Oliver, Mass Appeal, Bus Stop, Coastal Disturbances (Theatre World Award).
PICTURES: Diner, Just the Way You Are, Made in Heaven, Spellbinder, Love or Money, Year of the Comet, Caroline at Midnight, Dr. Jekyll and Ms. Hyde, Denise Calls Up, The Associate.
TELEVISION: Special: The Rise and Rise of Daniel Rocket. Mini-Series: I'll Take Manhattan, Queen. Series: Ryan's Four, Almost Grown, Wings. Movies: I Married a Centerfold, Mirrors, Red Earth White Earth, In the Line of Duty: Ambush in Waco, Dangerous Heart, Witness to the Execution. Guest: Midnight Caller, Hill Street Blues, Alfred Hitchcock Presents.

DALY, TYNE
Actress. r.n. Ellen Tyne Daly. b. Madison, WI, Feb. 21, 1946. Daughter of late actor James Daly and actress Hope Newell; brother is actor Timothy Daly.
THEATER: The Butter and Egg Man, That Summer That Fall, Skirmishes, The Black Angel, Rimers of Eldritch, Ashes, Three Sisters, Come Back Little Sheba (L.A., 1987), Gypsy (Tony Award, 1990), Queen of the Stardust Ballroom, The Seagull, On the Town, Call Me Madam (in concert).
PICTURES: John and Mary, Angel Unchained, Play It As It Lays, The Adulteress, The Enforcer, Telefon, Speedtrap, Zoot Suit, The Aviator, Movers & Shakers.
TELEVISION: Series: Cagney & Lacey (4 Emmy Awards), Christy (Emmy Award, 1996). Movies: In Search of America, A Howling in the Woods, Heat of Anger, The Man Who Could Talk to Kids, Larry, The Entertainer, Better Late Than Never, Intimate Strangers, The Women's Room, A Matter of Life or Death, Your Place or Mine, Kids Like These, Stuck With Each Other, The Last to Go, Face of a Stranger, Columbo: A Bird in the Hand, Scattered Dreams: The Kathryn Messenger Story, The Forget-Me-Not Murders, Columbo: Undercover, Cagney & Lacey: The Return, Cagney & Lacey: Together Again, Bye Bye Birdie. Guest: Medical Center, Columbo, Ray Bradbury Theatre, Wings.

DAMON, MARK
Executive. b. Chicago, IL, April 22, 1933. e. UCLA, B.A. literature, M.A. business administration. Actor: 1958 under contract to 20th Century Fox, 1960 winner Golden Globe Award-Newcomer of the Year; early career includes The Fall of The House of Usher, The Longest Day; 1961 moved to Italy, stayed 16 years appearing in leading roles in 50 films; 1974 head of foreign dept. for PAC, a leading film distributor in Italy; 1976 returned to the U.S. as exec. prod. of The Choirboys and in charge of its foreign distribution; 1979 founder and pres. of Producers Sales Organization, intl. distribution org. 1987 formed Vision Int'l.; 1993, formed MDP Worlwide, intl. prod. & distrib. co.
PICTURES: The Arena (prod.), Exec. prod. or co-exec. prod.: The Choirboys, The Neverending Story, Das Boot, Nine 1/2 Weeks (prod.), Short Circuit, Flight of the Navigator, Lost Boys, High Spirits, Bat 21 (co-prod.), Wild Orchid (prod.), Wild Orchid II: Two Shades of Blue, The Jungle Book.

DAMONE, VIC
Singer, Actor. r.n. Vito Farinola. b. Brooklyn, NY, June 12, 1928. m. actress-singer Diahann Carroll. e. Lafayette H.S., Brooklyn. Winner Arthur Godfrey talent show, 1947; then night clubs, radio, theatres. U.S. Army, 1951-53.

PICTURES: Rich Young and Pretty (debut, 1951), The Strip, Athena, Deep in My Heart, Hit the Deck, Kismet, Hell to Eternity.
TELEVISION: Series: The Vic Damone Show (1956-57), Lively Ones (1962-63), The Vic Damone Show (1967).

DAMSKI, MEL
Director. b. New York, NY, July 21, 1946. e. Colgate U., AFI. Worked as reporter, journalism professor. USC Cinema instructor.
PICTURES: Yellowbeard, Mischief, Happy Together.
TELEVISION: Series: M*A*S*H, Lou Grant, Dolphin Cove. Movies: Long Journey Back, The Child Stealer, Word of Honor, The Legend of Walks Far Woman, American Dream, For Ladies Only, Making the Grade, An Invasion of Privacy, Badge of the Assassin, A Winner Never Quits, Attack on Fear, Hero in the Family, Murder by the Book, Hope Division, The Three Kings, Everybody's Baby: The Rescue of Jessica McClure, Back to the Streets of San Francisco.

DANA, BILL
Actor, Writer. b. Quincy, MA, Oct. 5, 1924. In night clubs and on TV.
PICTURES: Actor: The Busy Body, The Barefoot Executive, The Nude Bomb (also s.p.).
TELEVISION: Series: The Steve Allen Show (performer, head writer, 1961), The Bill Dana Jose Jimenez Show (star, writer), Spike Jones Show (prod., writer, performer), Milton Berle Show (prod., writer, performer), No Soap Radio, Zorro and Son. Writer: All in the Family. Movies: The Snoop Sisters, Rosetti & Ryan: Men Who Love Women, A Guide for the Married Woman, Murder in Texas. Actor: Facts of Life, Too Close for Comfort, Golden Girls, Hollywood Palace, St. Elsewhere.

DANCE, CHARLES
Actor. b. Worcestershire, Eng., Oct. 10, 1946. e. Plymouth Coll. Art., Leicester Coll. of Art (graphic design degree). After first working as a West End theatre stagehand, made acting debut in 1970 in a touring company of It's a Two-Foot-Six-Inches-above-the Ground World. Worked in provincial repertory theaters. Joined the Royal Shakespeare Company 1975-80: Hamlet, Richard III, As You Like It. Lead in Henry V (1975, N.Y.), Coriolanus (Paris, London, Stratford).
THEATER: revival of Irma La Douce (West End), Turning Over (London's Bush Theatre).
PICTURES: The Spy Who Loved Me (debut, 1977), For Your Eyes Only, Plenty, The Golden Child, Good Morning Babylon, White Mischief, The Hidden City, Pascali's Island, Alien 3, The Valley of Stone, Last Action Hero, China Moon, Century, Kabloonak, Exquisite Tenderness, Shortcut to Paradise, Undertow, Michael Collins, Space Truckers, In the Presence of Mine Enemies.
TELEVISION: Very Like a Whale, The McGuffin, The Jewel in the Crown, Edward VII, The Fatal Spring, Little Eyolf, Frost in May, Nancy Astor, Saigon—The Last Day, Out On a Limb, BBC's The Secret Servant, Rainy Day Woman, Out of the Shadows, First Born, Goldeneye, Phantom of the Opera (mini-series).

D'ANGELO, BEVERLY
Actress. b. Columbus, OH, Nov. 15, 1954. Studied visual arts and was exchange student in Italy before working as cartoonist for Hanna-Barbera Studios in Hollywood. Toured Canada's coffeehouse circuit as singer and appeared with rock band called Elephant. Joined Charlotte Town Festival Company. B'way debut in rock musical, Rockabye Hamlet. Off-B'way: Simpatico (Theatre World Award).
PICTURES: The Sentinel (debut 1977). Annie Hall, First Love, Every Which Way But Loose, Hair, Highpoint, Coal Miner's Daughter, Honky Tonk Freeway, Paternity, National Lampoon's Vacation, Finders Keepers, National Lampoon's European Vacation, Big Trouble, Maid to Order, In the Mood, Aria, Trading Hearts, High Spirits, National Lampoon's Christmas Vacation, Daddy's Dyin', Pacific Heights (unbilled), The Miracle, The Pope Must Die, Man Trouble, Lonely Hearts, Lightning Jack, Eye for an Eye, Edie and Pen, Pterodactyl Woman from Beverly Hills.
TELEVISION: Mini-Series: Captains and the Kings. Movies: A Streetcar Named Desire, Doubletake, Slow Burn, Hands of a Stranger, Trial: The Price of Passion, A Child Lost Forever, The Switch, Judgment Day: The John List Story, Jonathan Stone: Threat of Innocence, Menendez: A Killing in Beverly Hills. Special: Sleeping Beauty (Faerie Tale Theater).

DANES, CLAIRE
Actress. b. New York, NY, April 12, 1979. e. Professional Performing Arts School, NY; Lee Strasberg Studio. Acting career began with off-off-B'way appearances in Happiness, Punk Ballet and Kids on Stage.
PICTURES: Dreams of Love (debut), Thirty (short), The Pesky Suitor (short), Little Women, Romeo and Juliet, To Gillian on Her 37th Birthday, Polish Wedding.

TELEVISION: *Series*: My So Called Life. *Guest*: Law and Order. *Movies*: No Room for Opal, The Coming Out of Heidi Leiter.

DANGERFIELD, RODNEY
Actor, Comedian. r.n. Jacob Cohen. b. Babylon, NY, Nov. 22, 1921. Performer in nightclubs as Jack Roy 1941-51. Worked as businessman 1951-63, before becoming stand-up comedian. Founder Dangerfields' Nightclub, 1969. Regular appearances on Dean Martin Show, 1972-3. Appeared in TV movie Benny and Barney: Las Vegas Undercover.
PICTURES: The Projectionist, Caddyshack, Easy Money (also co-s.p.), Back to School, Moving, Rover Dangerfield (voice, exec. prod., s.p., co-story, co-wrote songs), Ladybugs, Natural Born Killers, Casper (cameo), Meet Wally Sparks (also co-s.p.).

DANIEL, SEAN
Executive. b. Aug. 15, 1951. e. California Inst. of Arts film school. BFA, 1973. Was journalist for Village Voice before starting m.p. career as documentary filmmaker and asst. dir. for New World Pictures. In 1976 joined Universal Pictures as prod. exec.; 1979, named v.p., then pres., production. Resigned March, 1989 to become pres., The Geffen Co., film div., resigned from Geffen, Nov. 1989. 1990, with Jim Jacks started own prod. co. Alphaville, in partnership with Universal Pictures.
PICTURES: Pure Luck, American Me, CB4, Hard Target, Heart and Souls, Tombstone.

DANIELS, JEFF
Actor. b. Athens, Georgia. Feb. 19, 1955. e. Central Michigan U. Apprentice with Circle Repertory Theatre, New York. Established Purple Rose Theatre Co. in Chelsea, Michigan. Playwright: The Kingdom's Coming, The Vast Difference.
THEATER: Brontosaurus, Short-Changed Review, The Farm, Fifth of July, Johnny Got His Gun (Obie Award), Lemon Sky, The Three Sisters, The Golden Age, Redwood Curtain.
PICTURES: Ragtime (debut, 1981), Terms of Endearment, The Purple Rose of Cairo, Marie, Heartburn, Something Wild, Radio Days, The House on Carroll Street, Sweet Hearts Dance, Checking Out, Arachnophobia, Welcome Home Roxy Carmichael, Love Hurts, The Butcher's Wife, There Goes the Neighborhood, Rain Without Thunder, Gettysburg, Speed, Terminal Velocity, Dumb & Dumber, 2 Days in the Valley, Fly Away Home, 101 Dalmations.
TELEVISION: *Movies*: A Rumor of War, Invasion of Privacy, The Caine Mutiny Court Martial, No Place Like Home, Disaster in Time, Teamster Boss: The Jackie Presser Story, Redwood Curtain. *Specials*: Fifth of July, The Visit (Trying Times). *Guest*: Breaking Away (pilot), Hawaii 5-0.

DANIELS, PAUL
TV performer, Magician. b. South Bank, England, Apr. 6, 1938. Early career starring in British and overseas theatres. 1983, Magician Of The Year Award by Hollywood's Academy of Magical Arts. 1985, his BBC TV special awarded Golden Rose of Montreux trophy. Presenter of Every Second Counts and Paul Daniels Magic Show. Devised children's TV series, Wizbit and radio series Dealing With Daniels, Secret Magic and Game Show Wipeout.

DANIELS, WILLIAM
Actor. b. Brooklyn, NY, Mar 31, 1927. m. actress Bonnie Bartlett. e. Northwestern U. Traveled around NY area as part of The Daniels Family song and dance troupe. Appeared with family on experimental TV in 1941. Stage debut in Life with Father. Brought to national attention in A Thousand Clowns in original B'way play and film version.
THEATER: The Zoo Story, On a Clear Day You Can See Forever, 1776, Dear Me, The Sky Is Falling, A Little Night Music.
PICTURES: Ladybug Ladybug, A Thousand Clowns, Two for the Road, The Graduate, The President's Analyst, Marlowe, 1776, The Parallax View, Black Sunday, Oh God!, The One and Only, Sunburn, The Blue Lagoon, All Night Long, Reds, Blind Date, Her Alibi.
TELEVISION: *Series*: Captain Nice, The Nancy Walker Show, Freebie and the Bean, Knight Rider (voice), St. Elsewhere (Emmy Awards, 1985, 1986), Boy Meets World. *Guest*: East Side/West Side, For the People, Toma, The Rockford Files. *Movies*: Rooster, Rehearsal for a Murder, Murdock's Gang, A Case of Rape, Sarah T.—Portrait of a Teenage Alcoholic, One of Our Own, Francis Gary Powers, Killer on Board, The Bastard, Big Bob Johnson and His Fantastic Speed Circus, Sgt. Matlovich Vs. the U.S. Air Force, The Rebels, City in Fear, Damien: The Leper Priest, Million Dollar Face, Drop Out Father, The Little Match Girl, Knight Rider 2000 (voice), Back to the Streets of San Francisco. Mini-series: Blind Ambition, The Adams Chronicles.

DANNER, BLYTHE
Actress. b. Philadelphia, PA, Feb. 3, 1943. e. Bard Coll. m. writer-producer Bruce Paltrow. Daughter is actress Gwyneth Paltrow. Appeared in repertory cos. in U.S. before Lincoln Center (N.Y.) productions of Cyrano de Bergerac, Summertree, and The Miser (Theatre World Award for last).
THEATER: *NY*: Butterflies Are Free (Tony Award, 1971), Major Barbara, Twelfth Night, The Seagull, Ring Around The Moon, Betrayal, Blithe Spirit, A Streetcar Named Desire, Much Ado About Nothing, Sylvia. Williamstown: Picnic.
PICTURES: To Kill a Clown (debut, 1972), 1776, Lovin' Molly, Hearts of the West, Futureworld, The Great Santini, Man Woman and Child, Brighton Beach Memoirs, Another Woman, Mr. and Mrs. Bridge, Alice, The Prince of Tides, Husbands and Wives, To Wong Foo—Thanks for Everything—Julie Newmar, Homage.
TELEVISION: *Movies*: Dr. Cook's Garden, F. Scott Fitzgerald and The Last of the Belles, Sidekicks, A Love Affair: The Eleanor and Lou Gehrig Story, Too Far to Go, Eccentricities of a Nightingale, Are You in the House Alone?, Inside the Third Reich, In Defense of Kids, Helen Keller: The Miracle Continues, Guilty Conscience, Money Power Murder, Judgment, Never Forget, Cruel Doubt, Getting Up and Going Home, Oldest Living Confederate Widow Tells All, Leave of Absence. *Series*: Adam's Rib, Tattingers (revamped as Nick & Hillary). *Specials*: To Confuse the Angel, George M, To Be Young Gifted and Black, The Scarecrow., Kiss Kiss Dahlings.

DANSON, TED
Actor. b. San Diego, CA, Dec. 29, 1947. e. Kent Sch., Stanford U., Carnegie-Mellon U, 1972. m. actress Mary Steenburgen. Studied at Actors Inst. New York stage debut, The Real Inspector Hound, 1972; 1978, mgr. and teacher, Actors Inst., L.A. Television debut, The Doctors. Founded Amer. Oceans Campaign; bd. mem. Futures for Children.
PICTURES: The Onion Field (debut, 1979), Body Heat, Creepshow, Little Treasure, Just Between Friends, A Fine Mess, Three Men and a Baby, Cousins, Dad, Three Men and a Little Lady, Made in America, Getting Even With Dad, Pontiac Moon (also co-exec. prod.), Loch Ness.
TELEVISION: An Affectionate Look at Fatherhood (special). *Series*: Somerset, Cheers (2 Emmy Awards: 1990, 1993), Ink (also co-exec. prod.). *Movies*: The Women's Room, Once Upon a Spy, Our Family Business, Cowboy, Something About Amelia, When the Bough Breaks (also prod.), We Are the Children, Mercy Mission: The Rescue of Flight 771, On Promised Land, Fight For Justice, The Canterville Ghost, Gulliver's Travels. *Guest*: Laverne & Shirley, Magnum P.I., Taxi, Saturday Night Live.

DANTE, JOE
Director. b. Morristown, NJ. Managing editor for Film Bulletin before going to Hollywood to work in advertising, creating campaigns for many films. Became protege of Roger Corman, co-directing Hollywood Boulevard. Edited film Grand Theft Auto; co-wrote story for Rock 'n' Roll High School.
PICTURES: *Director*: Piranha (also co-editor), The Howling (also co-editor), Twilight Zone-The Movie (dir. segment), Gremlins, Explorers, Innerspace, Amazon Women on the Moon (co-dir.), The 'Burbs, Gremlins II (also cameo), Matinee. *Actor*: Cannonball, Slumber Party Massacre, Eating Raoul, Sleepwalkers, Beverly Hills Cop III, The Silence of the Hams.
TELEVISION: Amazing Stories, Eerie Indiana. *Movie*: Runaway Daughters.

D'ANTONI, PHILIP
Producer, Director. b. New York, NY, Feb. 19, 1929. e. Fordham U., business administration. Joined CBS in mailroom, advanced into prod., sales development, prog. analysis, mkt. rsrch. Became indep. radio-TV repr. in 1954 for two years; then joined Mutual Broadcasting as sales manager; later, exec. v.p. Resigned in 1962 to form own prod. co. Made theatrical film debut with Bullitt as producer; directing debut with The Seven Ups. Heads D'Antoni Prods.
PICTURES: *Producer*: Bullitt, The French Connection (Academy Award for Best Picture, 1971). *Prod.-Dir.*: The Seven Ups.
TELEVISION: Movin' On (series) Elizabeth Taylor in London, Sophia Loren in Rome, Melina Mercouri in Greece, Jack Jones Special, This Proud Land. Movies: Mr. Inside/Mr. Outside, The Connection, Strike Force, In Tandem, Rubber Gun Squad, Cabo.

DANZ, FREDRIC A.
Executive. b. Seattle, WA, Feb. 28, 1918. Is chairman of Sterling Recreation Organization Co., Seattle; member, Foundation of M.P. Pioneers; v.p., Variety Club Intl.

DANZA, TONY
Actor. b. Brooklyn, NY, Apr. 21, 1951. e. U. of Dubuque, IA on a wrestling scholarship. After grad. professional boxer before tested for role in TV pilot (Fast Lane Blues) which he won. Back to New York and fighting until called to coast to appear as Tony Banta in Taxi series. On L.A. & NY Stage: Wrong Turn at Lungfish.
PICTURES: Hollywood Knights, Going Ape, Cannonball Run II, She's Out of Control, Mob Justice, Angels in the Outfield, The Jerky Boys (co-exec. prod. only).

TELEVISION: *Series*: Taxi, Who's the Boss, Baby Talk (voice), The Mighty Jungle (voice), George (co-exec. prod. only), Hudson Street (also co-exec. prod.). *Movies*: Murder Can Hurt You!, Doing Life (also exec. prod.), Single Bars Single Women, Freedom Fighter (also co-exec. prod.), The Whereabouts of Jenny (also co-exec. prod.), Dead and Alive (also co-exec. prod.), Deadly Whispers.

D'ARBANVILLE-QUINN, PATTI
Actress. b. New York, NY, 1951. Grew up in Greenwich Village. Landed first job as baby in Ivory Soap commercials. In early teens worked as disc jockey where discovered by Andy Warhol and cast in small role in film Flesh. Moved to Paris at 15 where she became successful model and was featured in book Scavullo on Beauty. Made film debut in Gerard Brach's 1969 film La Maison. Fluent in French, worked in French films until 1973 when moved to Los Angeles. Won Dramalogue Award for John Patrick Shanley's Italian-American Reconciliation (L.A., 1987).
PICTURES: La Maison, La Saigne, The Crazy American Girl, Rancho DeLuxe, Bilitis, Big Wednesday, The Main Event, Time After Time, The Fifth Floor, Hog Wild, Modern Problems, Contract: Kill, The Boys Next Door, Real Genius, Call Me, Fresh Horses, Wired.
TELEVISION: *Movies*: Crossing the Mob, Blind Spot. *Mini-Series*: Once an Eagle, New York Undercover. *Guest*: Crime Story, R.E.L.A.X., Tough Cookies, Charlie's Angels, Barnaby Jones, Miami Vice, Murder She Wrote.

DARBY, KIM
Actress. r.n. Deborah Zerby. b. Hollywood, CA, July 8, 1948. e. Swanson's Ranch Sch., Van Nuys H.S. Studied at the Desilu Workshop in Hollywood. Professional debut on the Mr. Novak TV series; screen debut as extra in Bye Bye Birdie.
PICTURES: Bus Riley's Back in Town, The Restless Ones, True Grit, Generation, Norwood, The Strawberry Statement, The Grissom Gang, The One and Only, Better Off Dead, Teen Wolf Too, Halloween: The Curse of Michael Myers.
TELEVISION: *Movies*: The Karate Killers, Ironside (pilot), The People, Streets of San Francisco (pilot), Don't Be Afraid of the Dark, Story of Pretty Boy Floyd, This Was the West That Was, Flatbed Annie & Sweetiepie: Lady Truckers, Enola Gay, Embassy. *Mini-Series*: Rich Man Poor Man, The Last Convertible. *Guest*: Eleventh Hour, Gunsmoke. *Special*: Flesh and Blood.

DARK, JOHN
Producer. Pres. of J.D.Y.T. Producciones S.L., Coin Film City.
PICTURES: Light Up the Sky, Wind of Change, Loss of Innocence (Greengage Summer), The 7th Dawn, Casino Royale, Half a Sixpence, Bachelor of Arts, There's a Girl in My Soup, From Beyond the Grave, Madhouse, Land That Time Forgot, At the Earth's Core, The People That Time Forgot, Warlords of Atlantis, Arabian Adventure, Slayground, Shirley Valentine, Stepping Out.

DARREN, JAMES
Actor. b. Philadelphia, PA, June 8, 1936. e. Thomas Jefferson h.s., South Philadelphia h.s. Studied acting with Stella Adler, NYC.
PICTURES: Rumble on the Docks (debut, 1956), The Brothers Rico, The Tijuana Story, Operation Mad Ball, Gunman's Walk, Gidget, The Gene Krupa Story, Because They're Young, All the Young Men, Let No Man Write My Epitaph, Guns of Navarone, Gidget Goes Hawaiian, Diamond Head, Gidget Goes to Rome, For Those Who Think Young, The Lively Set, Venus in Furs, The Boss' Son.
TELEVISION: *Series*: The Time Tunnel, T.J. Hooker. *Guest*: Police Story, Hawaii Five-0, Vega$, Baa Baa Blacksheep, One Day at a Time. *Movies*: City Beneath the Sea, Police Story, The Lives of Jenny Dolan, Turnover Smith, Scruples. *Director of episodes*: T.J. Hooker, The A Team, Stingray, Werewolf, Hardball, Hunter, Tequila and Bonetti, Raven, Silk Stalkings, Walker: Texas Ranger.

DARRIEUX, DANIELLE
Actress. b. Bordeaux, France, May 1, 1917. e. Lycee LaTour, Conservatoire de Musique.
THEATER: Coco, The Ambassador (B'way).
PICTURES: Le Bal (debut, 1932), La Crise Est Finis, Mayerling, Tarass Boulba, Port Arthur, Un Mauvais Garcon, Club de Femmes, Abus de Confiance, Mademoiselle ma Mere, The Rage of Paris, Katia, Retour a l'Aube, Battlement de Coeur, Premier Rendezvous, Caprices, Adieu Cherie, Au Petit Bonheur, Bethsabee, Ruy Blas, Jean de la Lune, Occupe-toi d'Amelie, La Ronde, Rich Young and Pretty, Five Fingers, Le Plaisir, La Verite sur Bebe Donge, Adorable Creatures, Le Bon Dieu sans Confession, The Earrings of Madame De, Le Rouge et le Noir, Bonnes a Tuer, Napoleon, Alexander the Great, A Friend of the Family, Loss of Innocence (Greengage Summer), Les Lions sont Laches, Les Bras de lat Nuit, Bluebeard (Landru), Patate, Le Coup de Grace, L'Or du Duc, Le Dimanche de la Vie, The Young Girls of Rochefort, La Maison de Campagne, Scene of the Crime, A Few Days With me.

DARTNALL, GARY
Executive. b. Whitchurch, England, May 9, 1937. e. Kings Col., Taunton. Overseas div., Associate British Pathe. European rep., 1958-60; Middle & Far East rep., Lion Intl. Films; U.S. rep., 1962; pres. Lion Intl. 1963; U.S. rep., Alliance Intl. Films Distributors Ltd., and London Indept. Prods. Ltd.; pres. Alliance Intl. Films Corp. and Dartnall Films Ltd., 1966; mng. dir., Overseas div. Walter Reade Org., 1969; pres. EMI Film Distribs., 1971; vice chmn. EMI TV Programs Inc., 1976; pres. EMI Videograms Inc., 1979; pres. VHO Programs Inc. & VHD Disc Mfg. Co, 1980; chmn. Thorn EMI Cinemas; CEO, Thorn EMI Screen Entertainment Ltd. 1987; acquired Southbrook Intl. TV and formed Palladium Inc., chmn. & CEO.

DASSIN, JULES
Director, Writer, Actor. b. Middletown, CT, Dec. 18, 1911. Was married to late actress Melina Mercouri. Actor on dramatic stage several years; radio writer. Joined MGM, 1940, as dir. short subjects; later dir. features.
PICTURES: *Director*: Nazi Agent, Affairs of Martha, Reunion in France, Young Ideas, The Canterville Ghost, A Letter for Evie, Two Smart People, Brute Force, The Naked City, Thieves' Highway, Night and the City, Rififi (also co-s.p., actor), He Who Must Die (also co-s.p.), Where the Hot Wind Blows (also co-s.p.), Never on Sunday (also actor, prod., s.p.), Phaedra (also prod., co-s.p., actor), Topkapi (also prod.), 10:30 p.m. Summer (also prod., co-s.p.), Survival (also co-prod.), Uptight (also prod., co-s.p.), Promise at Dawn (also actor, prod., s.p.), The Rehearsal, A Dream of Passion (also s.p., prod.), Circle of Two.
PLAYS: Ilya Darling, Medicine Show, Magdalena, Joy to the World, Isle of Children, Two's Company, Heartbreak House, Threepenny Opera, Sweet Bird of Youth, A Month in the Country, Who's Afraid of Virginia Woolf?, The Road to Mecca, Death of a Salesman.

DAVENPORT, NIGEL
Actor. b. Cambridge, England, May 23, 1928. e. Trinity Coll., Oxford. Began acting after stint in British military at 18 years. First 10 years of professional career in theatre. Majority of screen work in British films in 1960s and 70s.
PICTURES: Look Back in Anger (debut, 1959), Desert Mice, Peeping Tom, The Entertainer, Lunch Hour, In the Cool of the Day, Operation Snatch, Return to Sender, Ladies Who Do, The Third Secret, Sands of the Kalahari, A High Wind in Jamaica, Where the Spies Are, Life at the Top, A Man for All Seasons, Sebastian, The Strange Affair, Play Dirty, Sinful Davey, The Virgin Soldiers, The Royal Hunt of the Sun, The Mind of Mr. Soames, The Last Valley, No Blade of Grass, Villain, Mary Queen of Scots, L'Attentat, Living Free, Charley-One-Eye, Phase IV, La Regenta, Stand Up Virgin Soldiers, The Island of Dr. Moreau, Zulu Dawn, The Omega Connection, Nighthawks, Chariots of Fire, Greystoke: The Legend of Tarzan Lord of the Apes, Caravaggio, Without a Clue, The Circus Trap.
TELEVISION: A Christmas Carol, Dracula, The Picture of Dorian Gray, The Ordeal of Dr. Mudd, Masada, The Upper Crust.

DAVIAU, ALLEN
Cinematographer. b. New Orleans, LA, June 14, 1942. Started as still photographer and stage lighting designer. Received Gold Clio Award for Tackle (Levi's 501).
PICTURES: Harry Tracy, E.T.: The Extra-Terrestrial (Acad. Award nom.), Twilight Zone: The Movie (co-photog.), Indiana Jones and the Temple of Doom (Calif. unit), The Falcon and the Snowman, The Color Purple (Acad. Award nom.), Harry and the Hendersons, Empire of the Sun (Acad. Award nom.), BAFTA & ASC Awards), Avalon (Acad. Award nom.), Defending Your Life, Bugsy (Acad. Award nom.; ASC Award), Fearless, Congo.
TELEVISION: *Movies*: Rage, Legs. *Special*: The Boy Who Drank Too Much. *Series*: Amazing Stories (pilot).

DAVID, KEITH
Actor. b. New York, NY, June 4, 1954. e. Juilliard.
THEATER: *NY*: The Pirates of Penzance, A Midsummer Night's Dream, Waiting for Godot, Miss Waters to You, La Boheme, Coriolanus, Titus Andronicus, A Map of the World, The Haggadah, Alec Wilder: Clues to a Life, Boesman & Lena, Jelly's Last Jam, Hedda Gabler, Seven Guitars.
PICTURES: The Thing, Platoon, Hot Pursuit, Braddock: Missing in Action III, Off Limits, Stars and Bars, Bird, They Live, Road House, Always, Men at Work, Marked for Death, Final Analysis, Article 99, Reality Bites, The Puppet Masters, The Quick and the Dead, Clockers, Dead Presidents, Johns, Dead Cold (prod.), Marked Man (prod.), Daddy's Girl (prod.), The Dentist (prod.), The Nurse (prod.), The Stranger In The House (prod.), Voodoo (exec. prod.), Serial Killer (prod./dir.), Flipping.
TELEVISION: *Movies*: Ladykillers, Murder in Black and White, There Are No Children Here. *Mini-Series*: Roots: The Next Generations. *Special*: Hallelujah. *Guest*: The Equalizer, A Man Called Hawk, New York Undercover.

DAVID, PIERRE
Executive, Producer. b. Montreal, Canada, May 17, 1944. e. U. of Montreal. Joined radio sta. CJMS 1966 as pub. rel. & spec. events dir., 1969, while running Mutual Broadcasting Network of Canada's live entertainment div., created new film dist. co. Mutual Films. 1972 added prod. unit and as prod. or exec. prod., prod. and dist. 19 French-lang. Canadian films. With filmmaker Roger Corman est. Mutual Pictures of Canada, Ltd to dist. films in English Canada; 1978 teamed Mutual Films with Victor Solnicki and Claude Heroux to prod. Eng.-lang. m.p. Pioneered 3-picture concept for Canadian m.p. investors. Moved to L.A. 1983 where became pres., Film Packages Intl. where prod. exec. on Platoon. Then joined Larry Thompson Org. as partner involved in dev. and/or prod. of m.p., Jan., 1987, named pres. of bd. and chief exec. officer, Image Org., Inc. intl. dist. co. formed by David and Rene Malo. Also pres. Lance Entertainment, prod. co.
PICTURES: Prod.: The Brood, Hog Wild, Scanners, Dirty Tricks, Gas, The Funny Farm, Visiting Hours, Videodrome, Going Berserk, Of Unknown Origin, Covergirl, Breaking All the Rules, For Those I Loved, Blind-Fear (co-prod.), The Perfect Bride, Hot Pursuit, The Perfect Weapon, Bounty Tracker, Distant Cousins, Deep Cover, Marital Outlaw, Stalked, Open Fire, The Force, The Secretary, Scanner Cop 2, The Wrong Woman. Exec. Prod.: Quiet Cool, Scanners II: The New Order, Desire and Hell at Sunset Motel, Martial Law, Scanners III, Dolly Dearest, Mission of Justice, Deadbolt, Internal Affairs, Twin Sisters, Pin, The Neighbor, The Paperboy. Prod.-Dir.: Scanner Cop.

DAVID, SAUL
Producer. b. Springfield, MA., June 27, 1921. e. Classical H.S., Springfield; Rhode Island Sch. of Design. Started in radio, newspaper work and as editorial director for Bantam Books. Worked for Columbia Pictures, 1960-62; Warner Bros., 1962-63; 20th Century-Fox, 1963-67, Universal, 1968-69; Executive story editor at MGM, 1972. Author: The Industry.
PICTURES: Von Ryan's Express, Our Man Flint, Fantastic Voyage, In Like Flint, Skullduggery, Logan's Run, Ravagers (exec. prod.).
(d. June 7, 1996)

DAVIDOVICH, LOLITA
Actress. b. Ontario, Canada, 1961. Also acted under the name Lolita David.
PICTURES: Class, Adventures in Babysitting, The Big Town, Blaze, The Object of Beauty, JFK, The Inner Circle, Raising Cain, Leap of Faith, Boiling Point, Younger and Younger, Cobb, For Better or Worse, Now and Then, Jungle2Jungle.
TELEVISION: Movies: Two Fathers' Justice, Prison Stories: Women on the Inside (Parole Board), Keep the Change, Indictment: The McMartin Trial.

DAVIDSON, JOHN
Actor, Singer. b. Pittsburgh, PA, Dec. 13, 1941. e. Denison U. In numerous school stage prods. before coming to N.Y. in 1964 to co-star with Bert Lahr in B'way show, Foxy. Signed as regular on The Entertainers with Carol Burnett.
PICTURES: The Happiest Millionaire, The One and Only Genuine Original Family Band, The Concorde—Airport '79, The Squeeze, Edward Scissorhands.
TELEVISION: Special: The Fantasticks. Guest: The FBI, The Interns, Owen Marshall, The Tonight Show, (also frequent guest host). Series: The Entertainers, Kraft Summer Music Hall, The John Davidson Show (1969), The Girl With Something Extra, The John Davidson Show (1976), The John Davidson Talk Show (1980), That's Incredible, New Hollywood Squares, Time Machine (game show), Incredible Sunday, The $100,000 Pyramid. Movies: Coffee Tea or Me?, Shell Game, Roger & Harry: The Mitera Target, Dallas Cowboys Cheerleaders II.

DAVIDSON, MARTIN
Director, Writer. b. New York, NY, Nov. 7, 1939.
PICTURES: The Lords of Flatbush, Almost Summer, Hero at Large, Eddie and the Cruisers, Heart of Dixie (also exec. prod.), Hard Promises.
TELEVISION: Series: Our Family Honor, Call to Glory, Law and Order, My Life and Times, Picket Fences, Chicago Hope. Movies: Long Gone, A Murderous Affair: The Carolyn Warmus Story, Follow the River.

DAVIES, JOHN HOWARD
Producer, Director. b. London, England, March 9, 1939. e. Haileybory, I.S.C. and Grenoble Univ. Former child actor played leading roles in Oliver Twist, The Rocking Horse Winner, Tom Brown's Schooldays.
TELEVISION: Prod./Dir.: Monty Python's Flying Circus, Steptoe and Son, Fawlty Towers, The Good Life, The Goodies, The Other One, No Job for a Lady, Mr. Bean.

DAVIS, ANDREW
Director. b. Chicago, IL. e. Univ. of IL. Former journalist and photographer before landing job as asst. cameraman on 1969 film Medium Cool. Was dir. of photog. on several tv commercials and documentaries.

PICTURES: Lepke (dir. of photog.), Stony Island (dir., prod., co-s.p.), Over the Edge (dir. of photog.), The Final Terror (dir.), Angel (dir. of photog.), Beat Street (co-s.p.). Director: Code of Silence, Above the Law (also co-prod., co-story), The Package, Under Siege, The Fugitive, Steal Big Steal Little (also co-prod., co-s.p., co-story), Chain Reaction.

DAVIS, CARL
Composer. b. New York, NY, Oct. 28, 1936. e. Queens Coll., Bard Coll. and New England Coll. of Music. Worked as pianist with Robert Shaw Chorale and wrote music for revue Diversions (1958) and Twists (London). Moved to England 1961 writing incidental music for Joan Littlewood's Theatre Workshop Co., Royal Shakespeare Co. and National Theatre. Other theater music includes Jonathan Miller's Tempest, Forty Years On, and the musical The Vackees. Best known for composing new scores for silent classics (Napoleon, The Crowd, Greed, Intolerance, etc.) for screenings at which he conducts and for Thames TV The Silents series. Concert work: Paul McCartney's Liverpool Oratorio.
PICTURES: The Bofors Gun, Up Pompeii, Rentadick, Man Friday, The Sailor's Return, Birth of the Beatles, The French Lieutenant's Woman, Praying Mantis, The Aerodrome, Champions, Weather in the Streets, George Stevens: A Filmmaker's Journey, King David, The Rainbow, Scandal, Girl in a Swing, Fragments of Isabella, Frankenstein Unbound, Diary of a Madman, Raft of the Medusa, The Voyage.
TELEVISION: That Was the Week That Was, Hollywood, the Pioneers, World at War, Mayor of Casterbridge, Lorna Doone, Unknown Chaplin, Buster Keaton—A Hard Act to Follow, Treasure Island, The Snow Goose, Our Mutual Friend, Naked Civil Servant, Silas Marner, The Accountant, Secret Life of Ian Fleming, Why Lockerbie?, Buried Mirro, A Christmas Carol, Royal Collection, Hotel du Lac, Black Velvet Gown.

DAVIS, COLIN
Executive. Held executive positions in Canada in adv., bdcst., & p.r. with several companies, including Procter & Gamble, Young & Rubicam. Joined MCA TV Canada as v.p. & gen. mgr., 1977. Named dir. intl. sls., 1978. In 1986 appt. pres., MCA TV Int'l.

DAVIS, FRANK I.
Executive. b. Poolesville, MD, Feb. 18, 1919. e. U. of Maryland, A.B., 1941; Harvard Law School, LL.B., 1948. Law firm, Donovan, Leisure, Newton, Lombard and Irvine, 1948-50; v.p., gen. counsel, Vanguard Films, 1951; v.p., gen. counsel, Selznick Releasing Org., 1951-53; pres., The Selznick Company, 1953-55; v.p., Famous Artists Corp., 1956-62; George Stevens Productions Inc., 1962-65; exec. prod., The Greatest Story Ever Told; v.p. in charge of m.p. affairs, Seven Arts, 1966; exec. in chg. talent and exec. asst. to v.p. in chg. prod., MGM, 1967; dir. m.p. business affairs, MGM, 1970; v.p., business affairs, MGM, 1972; sr. v.p., motion picture business affairs, MGM/UA, 1983, exec. v.p., business affairs, MGM Pictures, 1986-88; sr. exec. v.p., business affairs, Pathe Entertainment Inc., 1989-90; sr. exec. v.p. of bus. affairs, MGM, 1990.

DAVIS, GEENA
Actress. r.n. Virginia Elizabeth Davis. b. Wareham, MA, Jan. 21, 1957. e. Boston U. Acted with Mount Washington Repertory Theatre Co., NH. Was NY model before winning role Tootsie, 1982.
PICTURES: Tootsie (debut, 1982), Fletch, Transylvania 6-5000, The Fly, Beetlejuice, The Accidental Tourist (Academy Award, supporting actress, 1988), Earth Girls Are Easy, Quick Change, Thelma & Louise, A League of Their Own, Hero, Angie, Speechless (also prod.), Cutthroat Island, The Long Kiss Goodnight.
TELEVISION: Series: Buffalo Bill (also wrote one episode), Sara. Movie: Secret Weapons. Guest: Family Ties, Riptide, Remington Steele, Saturday Night Live, Trying Times (The Hit List).

DAVIS, GEORGE W.
Art Director, b. Kokomo, IN, Apr. 17, 1914. e. U. of Southern California.
PICTURES: The Ghost and Mrs. Muir, House of Stranger, All About Eve, David and Bathsheba, The Robe (Academy Award, 1953), Love Is a Many-Splendored Thing, Funny Face, The Diary of Anne Frank (Academy Award, 1959), The Time Machine, Butterfield 8, Cimarron, Period of Adjustment, Mutiny on the Bounty, The Wonderful World of the Brothers Grimm, Twilight of Honor, How the West Was Won, The Americanization of Emily, The Unsinkable Molly Brown, A Patch of Blue, Mr. Buddwing, Point Blank, The Shoes of the Fisherman, The Gypsy Moths, Brewster McCloud, Wild Rovers, etc

DAVIS, JOHN
Executive, Producer. e. Bowdoin Col., Harvard Bus. Sch. Served as v.p. at 20th Century Fox before forming Davis Entertainment.

PICTURES: Predator, Three O'Clock High, License to Drive, Little Monsters, The Last of the Finest, Shattered, Storyville, The Firm, The Thing Called Love, Fortress, Gunmen, Grumpy Old Men, Richie Rich, The Hunted, Waterworld, The Grass Harp, Courage Under Fire.
TELEVISION: Movies: Tears and Laughter: The Joan and Melissa Rivers Story, The Last Outlaw, This Can't Be Love.

DAVIS, JUDY
Actress. b. Perth, Australia, 1955. m. actor Colin Friels. Left convent school as teenager to become a singer in a rock band. Studied at West Australia Inst. of Technology and National Inst. of Dramatic Art, Sydney. Worked with theatre companies in Adelaide and Sydney and at Royal Court Theatre, London. Los Angeles stage debut Hapgood.
PICTURES: High Rolling (debut, 1977), My Brilliant Career, Hoodwink, Heatwave, Winter of Our Dreams, The Final Option, A Passage to India (Acad. Award nom.), Kangaroo, High Tide, Georgia, Alice, Impromtu, Barton Fink, Naked Lunch, Where Angels Fear to Tread, Husbands and Wives (Acad. Award nom.), On My Own (Australian Film Inst. Award), The Ref, The New Age.
TELEVISION: Rocket to the Moon, A Woman Called Golda, One Against the Wind, Serving in Silence: The Margarethe Cammermeyer Story (Emmy Award, 1995).

DAVIS, LUTHER.
Writer, Producer. b. New York, NY, Aug. 29, 1921. e. Yale, B.A.
THEATER: Writer: Kiss Them for Me, Kismet (Tony Award), Timbuktu! (also prod.), Grand Hotel (Tony nom.). Co-Prod.: Eden Court, Not About Heroes.
PICTURES: Writer: The Hucksters, B.F.'s Daughter, Black Hand, A Lion Is in the Streets, The Gift of Love, Holiday for Lovers, The Wonders of Aladdin, Lady in a Cage (also prod.), Across 110th Street.
TELEVISION: Writer/Prod.: Kraft Suspense Theatre and many pilots for series (Run for Your Life, Combat, The Silent Force, Eastside, Westside, etc.). Specials: Arsenic and Old Lace (also prod.), The People Trap (prod.). Movies: Daughter of the Mind, The Old Man Who Cried Wolf.

DAVIS, MAC
Singer, Songwriter, Actor. b. Lubbock, TX, Jan 21, 1942. e. Emory U., Georgia State Coll. Employed as ditch digger, service station attendant, laborer, probation officer and record company salesman before gaining fame as entertainer-singer in 1969. Recording artist and composer of many popular songs. On B'way 1992 in The Will Rogers Follies.
PICTURES: North Dallas Forty, Cheaper to Keep Her, The Sting II.
TELEVISION: Series: The Mac Davis Show. Movies: Brothers-In-Law, What Price Victory?, Blackmail.

DAVIS, MARTIN S.
Executive. b. New York, NY, Feb. 5, 1927. U.S. Army, 1943-46; joined Samuel Goldwyn Prod., Inc., 1946; with pub. dept. Allied Artists, 1955; Paramount Pictures, 1958. as dir. sales and marketing then dir. adv., pub. expl. 1960; v.p. in chg. of home office and asst. to pres.; 1963; exec. v.p., 1966; exec. comm. & bd. of dir. Member of Bd., Gulf & Western, 1967, named sr. v.p. 1969; elected Exec. v.p. and mem. exec. comm. Gulf & Western, 1974; elected CEO and chmn. of bd. and chmn. exec. comm. 1983; CEO & managing partner Wellspring Associates, LLC, 1995. Member: bd. trustees, Montefiore Medical Center, Thomas Jefferson Memorial Foundation; Chmn,. NYC Chap, Natl. Multiple Sclerosis Society; bd. of trustees Carnegie Hall. Co-chmn. of Corp. Advisory Committee of the Barbara Bush Foundation for Family Literacy. Board of directors, National Amusements, Inc.

DAVIS, OSSIE
Actor, Writer, Director. b. Cogdell, GA, Dec. 18, 1917. e. Howard U., Washington, DC. m. actress Ruby Dee. Studied acting in N.Y. with Rose McLendon Players, leading to Broadway debut in 1946 in Jeb. For years thereafter was one of best-known black actors on Broadway stage (Anna Lucasta, Jamaica, The Green Pastures, Wisteria Tree, A Raisin in the Sun, I'm Not Rappaport.) Wrote and starred in Purlie Victorious, repeating role for film version. Directed and appeared with Ms. Dee in her musical Take It From the Top. Co-hosted Ossie Davis and Ruby Dee Story Hour on radio (3 years). Published plays: Purlie Victorious, Langston, Escape to Freedom, Curtain Call, Mr. Aldredge, Sir.
PICTURES: Actor: No Way Out, Fourteen Hours, The Joe Louis Story, Gone Are the Days, The Cardinal, Shock Treatment, The Hill, Man Called Adam, The Scalphunters, Sam Whiskey, Slaves, Let's Do It Again, Hot Stuff, House of God, Harry and Son, Avenging Angel, School Daze, Do the Right Thing, Joe Versus the Volcano, Jungle Fever, Gladiator, Malcolm X (voice), Grumpy Old Men, The Client, I'm Not Rappaport, Get on the Bus. Director: Cotton Comes to Harlem (also co-s.p.), Black Girl, Gordon's War, Countdown at Kusini (also actor, prod.).

TELEVISION: Writer: East Side/West Side, The Eleventh Hour. Guest: Name of the Game, Night Gallery, Bonanza, etc. Specials: Martin Luther King: The Dream and the Drum, With Ossie and Ruby (also co-prod.), Today is Ours (writer, dir.). Movies: All God's Children, Don't Look Back, Roots: The Next Generations, King, Teacher Teacher, The Ernest Green Story, Ray Alexander: A Taste for Justice, Ray Alexander: A Menu for Murder, The Android Affair. Series: B.L. Stryker, Evening Shade, John Grisham's The Client. Mini-Series: Queen, Stephen King's The Stand.

DAVIS, PETER
Author, Filmmaker. b. Santa Monica, CA, Jan. 2, 1937. e. Harvard Coll., 1955-57. Parents were screenwriter Frank Davis, and novelist-screenwriter Tess Slesinger. Writer-interviewer, Sextant Prods., FDR Series, 1964-65. Host: The Comers, PBS 1964-65. Author: Hometown (1982), Where Is Nicaragua? (1987), If You Came This Way (1995), articles for Esquire, NY Times Mag., The Nation, NY Woman, TV Guide.
PICTURES: Hearts and Minds (prod., dir.; Academy Award, best documentary, 1975; Prix Sadoul, 1974), Jack (writer/prod.).
TELEVISION: Writer-prod.: Hunger in America (assoc. prod., WGA Award, 1968), The Heritage of Slavery, The Battle of East St. Louis, (Saturday Review Award, 1970; 2 Emmy nom.), The Selling of the Pentagon (WGA, Emmy, Peabody, George Polk, Ohio State, Sat. Review Awards, 1971), 60 Minutes (segment prod.), Middletown (series, prod., Dupont Citation, Emmy noms. 1983), The Best Hotel on Skidrow (ACE Award noms., 1992).

DAVIS, PRESTON A.
Executive. b. Norfolk, VA. Served in US Army. 1976, joined ABC as engineer in Washington DC, later becoming sprv. of Electronic News Gathering; 1979, became tech. mngr. of ENG; 1983, named tech. mngr. then manager of ENG for southeast region, Atlanta; 1986, promoted to gen. mngr. ENG Operations, New York; 1988, named v.p. TV Operations, Broadcast Operations & Engineering, East Coast; 1993, named pres. of Broadcast Operations and Engineering for ABC Television Network Group.

DAVIS, ROGER H.
Executive. Chairman, Motion Picture and Television Fund.

DAVIS, SAMMI
Actress. b. Kidderminster, Worcestershire, Eng., June 21, 1964. Convent-educated before taking drama course. Performed in stage prods. with local drama society in Midlands, then Birmingham Rep. and Big Brum Theatre Co. Plays include The Home Front, The Apple Club, Nine Days, Databased, Choosey Susie. London stage debut: A Collier's Friday.
PICTURES: Mona Lisa, Lionheart, Hope and Glory, A Prayer for the Dying, Consuming Passions, The Lair of the White Worm, The Rainbow, The Horseplayer, Shadow of China, Four Rooms.
TELEVISION: Auf Wiedersehn Pet, The Day After the Fair, Pack of Lies, Chernobyl: The Final Warning, The Perfect Bride, Indecency, Spring Awakening. Series: Homefront.

DAVISON, BRUCE
Actor. b. Philadelphia, PA, June 28, 1946. e. Pennsylvania State U., NYU. debut, Lincoln Center Repertory prod. of Tiger at the Gates, 1967.
THEATER: NY: King Lear (Lincoln Center), The Elephant Man, Richard III (NY Shakespeare Fest.), The Glass Menagerie, The Cocktail Hour. Regional: Streamers (LA Critics Award), The Caine Mutiny Court-Martial, The Normal Heart, To Kill a Mockingbird, A Life in the Theatre, The Front Page, Downside, Breaking the Silence.
PICTURES: Last Summer (debut, 1969), The Strawberry Statement, Willard, Been Down So Long It Looks Like Up To Me, The Jerusalem File, Ulzana's Raid, Mame, Mother Jugs and Speed, Grand Jury, Short Eyes, Brass Target, French Quarter, High Risk, A Texas Legend, Lies, Crimes of Passion, Spies Like Us, The Ladies Club, The Misfit Brigade, Longtime Companion (NY Film Critics, Natl. Society of Film Critics, & Golden Globe Awards, 1990; Acad. Award nom.), Steel and Lace, Short Cuts, An Ambush of Ghosts, Six Degrees of Separation, Far From Home: The Adventures of Yellow Dog, The Cure, The Baby-sitters Club, Homage, Grace of My Heart, The Crucible.
TELEVISION: Movies: Owen Marshall: Counsellor at Law (A Pattern of Morality), The Affair, The Last Survivors, Deadman's Curve, Summer of My German Soldier, Mind Over Murder, The Gathering, Tomorrow's Child, Ghost Dancing, Poor Little Rich Girl: The Barbara Hutton Story, Lady in a Corner, Stolen: One Husband, Live! From Death Row, Desperate Choices: To Save My Child, A Mother's Revenge, Someone Else's Child, Down Out and Dangerous. Specials: Taming of the Shrew, The Lathe of Heaven, The Wave. Guest: Medical Center, Marcus Welby, Love American Style, Police

Story, Lou Grant, Murder She Wrote, Alfred Hitchcok Presents (1985), Amazing Stories. *Series*: Hunter, Harry and the Hendersons.

DAVISON, DALE
Executive. b. North Hollywood, CA, March 21, 1955. e. U.C.L.A., B.A., 1978. Entered the motion picture industry in 1973 working for Pacific Theatres. Employed with Great Western Theatres 1974-77 as manager, dir. of concessions, and asst. vice pres. Partner with Great Western Theatres, 1978-1984. Founder and CEO, CinemaCal Enterprises, Inc., 1985-present.

DAVISON, JON
Producer. b. Haddonfield, NJ, July 21, 1949. e. NYU Film School. 1972, joined New World Pictures as natl. dir. of publ./adv.; 1972, named in charge of prod.; 1980, became indep. prod.
PICTURES: Hollywood Boulevard, Grand Theft Auto, Piranha, Airplane!, White Dog, Twilight Zone—The Movie (episode), Top Secret! Robocop, Robocop 2, Trapped in Paradise.

DAWBER, PAM
Actress, Singer. b. Detroit, MI, Oct. 18, 1954. m. actor Mark Harmon. e. Farmington H.S., Oakland Community Coll. Worked as model and did commercials. First professional performance as singer in Sweet Adeleine at Goodspeed Opera House, East Haddam, CT.
THEATER: Regional: My Fair Lady, The Pirates of Penzance, The Music Man, She Loves Me, Love Letters.
PICTURES: A Wedding, Stay Tuned.
TELEVISION: *Series*: Mork and Mindy, My Sister Sam. *Movies*: The Girl with the Gold Watch and Everything, Remembrance of Love, Through Naked Eyes, Last of the Great Survivors, This Wife For Hire, Wild Horses, Quiet Victory: The Charlie Wedemeyer Story, Do You Know the Muffin Man, The Face of Fear, The Man With 3 Wives, Web of Deception, Trail of Tears. *Specials*: Kennedy Center Honors, Salute to Andy Gibb, Night of the 100 Stars, 3rd Annual TV Guide Special.

DAY, DORIS
Singer, Actress. r.n. Doris Kappelhoff. b. Cincinnati,c OH, Apr. 3, 1924. e. dancing, singing. Toured as dancer; radio and band singer; screen debut in Romance on the High Seas, 1948. Voted one of Top Ten Money-Making Stars in Motion Picture Herald-Fame poll, 1951-52. Best female vocalist. M. P. Daily radio poll, 1952.
PICTURES: Romance on the High Seas (debut, 1948), My Dream is Yours, It's a Great Feeling, Young Man With a Horn, Tea for Two, Storm Warning, West Point Story, Lullaby of Broadway, On Moonlight Bay, I'll See You in My Dreams, Starlift, The Winning Team, April in Paris, By the Light of the Silvery Moon, Calamity Jane, Lucky Me, Young at Heart, Love Me or Leave Me, The Man Who Knew Too Much, Julie, The Pajama Game, Teacher's Pet, Tunnel of Love, It Happened to Jane, Pillow Talk (Acad. Award nom.), Please Don't Eat the Daisies, Midnight Lace, Lover Come Back, That Touch of Mink, Bill Rose's Jumbo, The Thrill of It All, Move Over Darling, Send Me No Flowers, Do Not Disturb, Glass Bottom Boat, Caprice, The Ballad of Josie, Where Were You When the Lights Went Out?, With Six You Get Eggroll.
TELEVISION: *Series*: The Doris Day Show (1968-73), Doris Day's Best Friends (educational cable show; 1985-86).

DAY, LARAINE
Actress. r.n. Laraine Johnson. b. Roosevelt, UT, Oct. 13, 1920. e. Long Beach Polytechnic H.S., Paramount Studio School. In school dramatics; with Players Guild, Long Beach, Calif.; toured in church prod. Conflict; Professionally on stage in Lost Horizon, The Women, Time of the Cuckoo, Angel Street.
PICTURES: Stella Dallas (debut, 1937 as Laraine Johnson), Scandal Street, Border G-Men, Young Dr. Kildare (and subsequent series), And One Was Beautiful, My Son My Son, Foreign Correspondent, The Trial of Mary Dugan, The Bad Man, Unholy Partners, Fingers at the Window, Journey for Margaret, Mr. Lucky, The Story of Dr. Wassell, Bride by Mistake, Those Endearing Young Charms, Keep Your Powder Dry, The Locket, Tycoon, My Dear Secretary, I Married a Communist (Woman on Pier 13), Without Honor, The High and the Mighty, Toy Tiger, Three for Jamie Dawn, The Third Voice.
TELEVISION: Appearances include Climax, Playhouse 90, Alfred Hitchcock, Wagon Train, Let Freedom Ring, Name of the Game, FBI, Sixth Sense, Medical Center, Murder on Flight 504 (movie), Fantasy Island, Love Boat, Lou Grant, Airwolf, Hotel, Murder She Wrote.

DAY, ROBERT
Director. b. England, Sept. 11, 1922. Started as cinematographer before turning to direction.
PICTURES: *Director*: The Green Man (debut, 1956), Stranger's Meeting, Grip of the Strangler (The Haunted Strangler), First Man Into Space, Bobbikins, Two-Way Stretch, Tarzan the Magnificent (also co-s.p.), The Rebel (Call Me

Genius), Corridors of Blood, Operation Snatch, Tarzan's Three Challenges (also co-s.p.), She, Tarzan and the Valley of Gold, Tarzan and the Great River, Tarzan and the Jungle Boy (prod. only), The Man with Bogart's Face.
TELEVISION: *Pilots include*: Banion, Kodiak, Dan August, Sunshine, Switch, Logan's Run, Kingston, Dallas, Matlock. Movies include: Ritual of Evil, The House of Greenapple Road, In Broad Daylight, Having Babies, The Grass Is Always Greener Over the Septic Tank, Peter and Paul, Running Out, Scruples, Cook and Peary—The Race to the Pole, Hollywood Wives, The Lady from Yesterday, Diary of a Perfect Murder, Celebration, Higher Ground, Walking Through the Fire.

DAY-LEWIS, DANIEL
Actor. b. London, England, Apr. 29, 1957. Son of late C. Day-Lewis, poet laureate of Eng., and actress Jill Balcon. Grandson of late Sir Malcolm Balcon who prod. Hitchcock's Brit. films. e. Bristol Old Vic. Theatre School. First professional job at 12 as ruffian scratching cars with broken bottle in film, Sunday Bloody Sunday. Then acted with Bristol Old Vic and Royal Shakespeare Co. Appeared in West End in, among others, Dracula, Another Country, Romeo and Juliet, A Midsummer Night's Dream, Hamlet (Natl Theater, 1989).
PICTURES: Gandhi, The Bounty, A Room With a View, My Beautiful Laundrette, The Unbearable Lightness of Being, Stars and Bars, Nanou, Eversmile New Jersey, My Left Foot (Academy Award, 1989; also BAFTA, NY Film Critics, L.A. Film Critics, Natl. Society of Film Critics Awards), The Last of the Mohicans, The Age of Innocence, In the Name of the Father, The Crucible.
TELEVISION: *BBC Movies/Specials*: A Frost in May, How Many Miles to Babylon?, My Brother Jonathan, The Insurance Man, History of Hamlet (host).

DEAKINS, ROGER
Cinematographer. b. Devon, England, May 24, 1949. Accepted into National Film School in 1972. Working as professional filmmaker from 1975 directing and photographing documentary films including Around the World With Ridgeway, Zimbabwe, Eritrea—Behind the Lines, When the World Changed, Worlds Apart S.E. Nuba, Worlds Apart Rajgonds. Photographed first feature, Another Time Another Place in 1982.
PICTURES: 1984, The Innocent, Sid & Nancy, Shadey, Defense of the Realm, White Mischief, Personal Services, Stormy Monday, Pascali's Island, The Kitchen Toto, Mountains of the Moon, Air America, The Long Walk Home, Barton Fink, Homicide, Thunderheart, Passion Fish, The Secret Garden, The Hudsucker Proxy, The Shawshank Redemption (Acad. Award nom.; ASC Award), Fargo, Courage Under Fire.

DEAN, EDDIE
Actor. r.n. Edgar Dean Glosup. b. Posey, TX, July 9, 1907. 1930-33 in radio throughout middle west; 1934 National Barn Dance, Station WLS; 1935 on CBS & NBC with same program. Featured male singer on TV KTLA Western Varieties 1944-55. Came to Hollywood in 1936; since then has starred in many westerns. Featured performer in western series for PRC in 1945. Voted one of the ten best money making Western Stars in Motion Picture Herald-Fame Poll 1936-47; recording artists, personal appearances, rodeos, fairs, etc.; 1966 v.p. Academy of Country & Western Music; 1967-68 on Bd. of Dir. of Academy of Western Music, Calif. Winner, Pioneer Award of Academy of Country Music, 1978. In 1983 named ACM v.p.; also v.p. in 1985. Recorded video cassette 1986, A Tribute to Eddie Dean. Received two gold records in 1995 for co-writing of "Hillbilly Heaven."

DEAN, JIMMY
Performer. b. Plainview, TX, Aug. 10, 1928. Joined armed forces, 1946-49; first appeared in various clubs in Wash., 1949; then appeared on Town and Country Jamboree; toured Caribbean and Europe with his troupe; appeared in Las Vegas. TNN/Music City News Country Music Awards, Songwriter of the Year Awards.
SONGS: *Composer*: Big Bad John, Little Black Book, I.O.U., To a Sleeping Beauty, PT-109, Dear Ivan.
PICTURES: Diamonds Are Forever, Big Bad John.
TELEVISION: *Series*: The Jimmy Dean Show (1957; 1963-66), Daniel Boone, J.J. Starbuck. *Specials*: Sunday Night at the Palladium (London), Celebrities Offstage. *Movies*: The Ballad of Andy Crocker, Rolling Man, The City.

DEAN, MORTON
Television Newsman. b. Fall River, MA, Aug. 22, 1935. e. Emerson Coll. News dir., N.Y. Herald Tribune Net, 1957; corr. WBZ, 1960, corr. WCBS-TV, 1964; anchor, WCBW-TV News, 1967; corr., CBS News, 1967; anchor, CBS Sunday Night News, 1975; anchor, Sunday edition CBS Evening News, 1976; co-anchor, Independent Network News, 1985.

DEARDEN, JAMES
Writer, Director, b. London, Eng. Sept. 14, 1949. Son of late British director Basil Dearden. e. New Coll., Oxford U. Entered

film industry in 1967 as production runner. After editing commercials and documentaries, and working as asst. dir., wrote, prod. and dir. first short film, The Contraption (Silver Bear Award, 1978 Berlin Film Fest.). 1978, began dir. commercials and made short, Panic (Cert. of Merit, 1980 Chicago Film Fest.). 1979, made 45-min film Diversion, which became basis for Fatal Attraction (Gold Plaque, best short drama, 1980 Chicago Film Fest.).
PICTURES: Fatal Attraction (s.p.), Pascali's Island (dir., s.p.), A Kiss Before Dying (dir., s.p.).
TELEVISION: The Cold Room (dir., writer, Special Jury Prize, dir., 1985 Fest. Intl. d'Avoriaz du Film Fantastique).

De BONT, JAN
Cinematographer, Director. b. Holland, Oct. 22, 1943.Trained at Amsterdam Film Acad. Recipient of Kodak Camera Award and Rembrandt Award.
PICTURES: Cinematographer: Turkish Delight, Cathy Tippel, Max Havelaar, Soldier of Orange, Private Lessons (U.S. debut, 1981), Roar, I'm Dancing as Fast as I Can, Cujo, All the Right Moves, Bad Manners, The Fourth Man, Mischief, The Jewel of the Nile, Flesh + Blood, The Clan of the Cave Bear, Ruthless People, Who's That Girl, Leonard Part 6, Die Hard, Bert Rigby You're a Fool, Black Rain, The Hunt for Red October, Flatliners, Shining Through, Basic Instinct, Lethal Weapon 3. Director: Speed (debut, 1994), Twister.
TELEVISION (Photography): Movie: The Ray Mancini Story. Episode: Tales From the Crypt (Split Personality).

De BROCA, PHILIPPE
Director, Writer. b. Paris, France, Mar. 15, 1933. e. Paris Technical School of Photography and Cinematography.
PICTURES: Director/Writer: Les Jeux de l'Amour (The Love Game), The Joker, The Five Day Lovers, Seven Capitol Sins (dir. segment only), Cartouche (also actor), Les Veinards (segment), That Man From Rio, Male Companion (Un Monsieur de Compagnie), Les Tribulations d'un Chinois en Chine (Up to His Ears), King of Hearts (also prod.), Devil by the Tail, Give Her the Moon, Chere Louise, Le Magnifique, Dear Inspector (also s.p.), The Skirt Chaser, Someone's Stolen the Thigh of Jupiter, The African, Louisiana (TV in U.S.), The Gypsy, Chouans! (dir., co-s.p.), Scheherazade.

De CAMP, ROSEMARY
Actress. b. Prescott AZ, Nov. 14, 1913.
PICTURES: Cheers for Miss Bishop (debut, 1941), Hold Back the Dawn, Jungle Book, Yankee Doodle Dandy, Eyes in the Night, THe Commandos Strike at Dawn, Smith of Minnesota, Without Men, This is the Army, The Merry Monahans, Bowery to Broadway, Blood on the Sun, Practically Yours, Rhapsody in Blue, Pride of the Marines, Danger Signal, Too Young to Know, From This Day Forward, Nora Prentiss, Night Unto Night, The Life of Riley, Look for the Silver Lining, Story of Seabiscuit, The Big Hangover, Night Into Morning, On Moonlight Bay, Scandal Sheet, Treasure of Lost Canyon, By the Light of the Silvery Moon, Main Street to Broadway, So This Is Love, Many Rivers to Cross, Strategic Air Command, 13 Ghosts, Saturday the 14th.
TELEVISION: Series: The Life of Reilly (with Jackie Gleason), The Bob Cummings Show, That Girl. Guest: Death Valley Days, Partridge Family, Love American Style, Police Story, Rockford Files, Days of Our Lives, Misadventures of Sheriff Lobo, Love Boat, B.J. & the Bear. Mini-Series: Blind Ambition. Movie: The Time Machine.

De CAPRIO, AL
Producer, Director. e. Brooklyn Tech., NYU. Started as radio engineer, cameraman, tech. dir., prod. & dir. CBS; dir. series episodes of Sgt. Bilko, Car 54 Where Are You?, Musical specials for ABC, CBS, NBC; v.p. exec. prod. dir., MPO Videotronics, Pres. World Wide Videotape; retired.

De CARLO, YVONNE
Actress. b. Vancouver, B.C., Sept. 1, 1922. e. June Roper School of Dance, Britsh Columbia; Fanchon & Marco, Hollywood. Specialty dancing at Florentine Gardens, Earl Carroll's; m.p. debut in This Gun for Hire, 1942. One-woman club act and 7-person club act. Autobiography, Yvonne (1987).
THEATER: B'way: Follies.
PICTURES: This Gun for Hire (debut, 1942), Harvard Here I Come, Youth on Parade, Road to Morocco, Let's Face It, The Crystal Ball, Salute for Three, For Whom the Bell Tolls, True to Life, So Proudly We Hail, The Deerslayer, Practically Yours, Salome Where She Danced, Frontier Gal, Brute Force, Song of Scheherazade, Slave Girl, Black Bart, Casbah, River Lady, Criss Cross, Gal Who Took the West, Calamity Jane and Sam Bass, Buccaneer's Girl, The Desert Hawk, Tomahawk, Hotel Sahara, Silver City, Scarlet Angel, San Francisco Story, Hurricane Smith, Sombrero, Sea Devils, Fort Algiers, Captain's Paradise, Border River, Passion, Tonight's the Night, Shotgun, Magic Fire, Flame of the Islands, Ten Commandments, Raw Edge, Death of a Scoundrel, Band of Angels, Timbuktu, McLintock!, A Global Affair, Law of the Lawless, Munster Go Home, Hostile Guns, The Power, Arizona Bushwhackers, The Seven Minutes, Play

Dead, It Seemed Like a Good Idea at the Time, Won Ton Ton the Dog Who Saved Hollywood, Blazing Stewardesses, Satan's Cheerleaders, Nocturna, Silent Scream, Guyana Cult of the Damned, The Man With Bogart's Face, Liar's Moon, American Gothic, Cellar Dweller, Mirror Mirror, Oscar, The Naked Truth.
TELEVISION: Series: The Munsters. Movies: The Girl on the Late Late Show, The Mark of Zorro, The Munsters' Revenge, A Masterpiece of Murder. Guest: Bonanza, Man From U.N.C.L.E., Murder She Wrote, Hollywood Sign (special), Johnny Carson, Merv Griffin, Steve Allen, David Frost, Perry Como, Tales from the Crypt, Dream On.

De CORDOVA, FREDERICK
Director. b. New York, NY, Oct. 27, 1910. e. Northwestern U., B.S. 1931. Gen. stage dir. Shubert enterprises, N.Y., 1938-41; same for Alfred Bloomingdale Prods., N.Y., and prod. Louisville (Ky.) Amphitheatre 1942-43. Dir., program planning, Screen Gems, 1944. Author: Johnny Came Lately, 1988.
PICTURES: Dialogue Director: San Antonio, Janie, Between Two Worlds. Director: Too Young to Know (debut, 1945), Her Kind of Man, That Way with Women, Love and Learn, Always Together, Wallflower, For the Love of Mary, The Countess of Monte Cristo, Illegal Entry, The Gal Who Took the West, Buccaneer's Girl, Peggy, The Desert Hawk, Bedtime for Bonzo, Katie Did It, Little Egypt, Finders Keepers, Here Come the Nelsons, Yankee Buccaneer, Bonzo Goes to College, Column South, I'll Take Sweden, Frankie and Johnny.
TELEVISION: Series (prod., dir.): The Burns and Allen Show, December Bride, Mr. Adams and Eve, George Gobel Show, The Jack Benny Program, The Smothers Bros. Show, My Three Sons (dir.), Tonight Show (prod.; 6 Emmy Awards).

DeCUIR, JR., JOHN F.
Art Director, Production Designer. b. Burbank, CA, Aug. 4, 1941. e. U. of Southern California, bachelor of architecture, 1965. Son of John F. De Cuir, Sr. 1966-68, U.S. Coast Guard (holds commission with rank of Lt. Commander, USCGR). 1968-72, project designer, Walt Disney World, Walt Disney Prods. 1972-74, dir. of design, Six Flags Corp. 1974-9, project designer, EPCOT, Walt Disney Prods. 1980-86, pres., John F. De Cuir, Jr. Design Consultants, Inc.; 1987-pres., Cinematix Inc.
PICTURES: Illustrator: Cleopatra, The Honey Pot. Design Concepts: The Agony and the Ecstasy. Art Director: Raise the Titanic, Ghosbusters. Special Effects Consultant: Dead Men Don't Wear Plaid, Monsignor. Producer: Jazz Club, The Baltimore Clipper, The Building Puzzle. Prod. Designer: Fright Night, Top Gun, Apt Pupil, Elvira Mistress of the Dark, Turner & Hooch, True Identity, Sleepwalkers, Sister Act 2: Back in the Habit.
TELEVISION: Art Director: Frank Sinatra Special—Old Blue Eyes Is Back, Annual Academy Awards Presentation 1971, Double Agent. Production Design: Double Switch, Earth * Star Voyager.

DEE, RUBY
Actress. b. Cleveland, OH, Oct. 27, 1924. r.n. Ruby Ann Wallace. e. Hunter Coll. m. actor-dir.-writer Ossie Davis. Worked as apprentice at Amer. Negro Theatre, 1941-44, studied at Actor's Workshop. Stage appearances include Jeb, Anna Lucasta, The World of Sholom Aleichem, A Raisin in the Sun, Purlie Victorious, Wedding Band, Boseman and Lena, Hamlet, Checkmates.
PICTURES: No Way Out, The Jackie Robinson Story, The Tall Target, Go Man Go!, Edge of the City, St. Louis Blues, Take a Giant Step, Virgin Island, A Raisin in the Sun, Gone Are the Days, The Balcony, The Incident, Up Tight, Buck and the Preacher, Black Girl, Countdown at Kusini, Cat People, Do the Right Thing, Love at Large, Jungle Fever, Cop and a Half, Just Cause.
TELEVISION: Movies: Deadlock, The Sheriff, It's Good to Be Alive, I Know Why the Caged Bird Sings, All God's Children, The Atlanta Child Murders, Go Tell it on the Mountain, Windmills of the Gods, The Court-Martial of Jackie Robinson, Decoration Day (Emmy Award, 1991), The Ernest Green Story. Specials: Actor's Choice, Seven Times Monday, Go Down Moses, Twin-Bit Gardens, Wedding Band, To Be Young Gifted and Black, Long Day's Journey into Night, Edgar Allan Poe: Terror of the Soul (narrator). Mini-Series: Roots: The Next Generation, Gore Vidal's Lincoln, The Stand. Series: Peyton Place, With Ossie and Ruby, Middle Ages.

DEE, SANDRA
Actress. r.n. Alexandra Zuck. b. Bayonne, NJ, April 23, 1942. Modeled, Harry Conover and Huntington Hartford Agencies, N.Y., 1954-56; signed long term exclusive contract, U-I, 1957.
PICTURES: Until They Sail (debut, 1957), The Reluctant Debutante, The Restless Years, Stranger in My Arms, Imitation of Life, Gidget, The Wild and the Innocent, A Summer Place, The Snow Queen (voice), Portrait in Black, Romanoff and Juliet, Come September, Tammy Tell Me True, If a Man Answers, Tammy and the Doctor, Take Her She's

Mine, I'd Rather Be Rich, That Funny Feeling, A Man Could Get Killed, Doctor You've Got to Be Kidding!, Rosie, The Dunwich Horror.
TELEVISION: *Movies*: The Daughters of Joshua Cabe, Houston We've Got a Problem, The Manhunter, Fantasy Island (pilot). *Guest*: Steve Allen Show, Night Gallery, Love American Style, Police Woman.

DEELEY, MICHAEL
Producer. b. London, Eng. August 6, 1932. Ent. m.p. ind. 1951 and TV, 1967, as alt. dir. Harlech Television Ltd. Film editor, 1951-58. MCA-TV 1958-61, later with Woodfall as prod. and assoc. prod. Assoc. prod. The Knack, The White Bus, Ride of the Valkyrie. Great Western Investments Ltd.; 1972; Great Western Festivals Ltd.; 1973, mng. dir. British Lion Films Ltd. 1975, purchased BLF, Ltd. Appt. Jnt. man. dir. EMI Films Ltd., 1977; pres., EMI Films, 1978, Member Film Industry Interim Action Committee, 1977-82; Deputy Chairman, British Screen Advisory Council, 1985. Appt. Chief Executive Officer, Consolidated Television Production & Distribution Inc., 1984.
PICTURES: *Prod.*: One Way Pendulum, Robbery, The Italian Job, Long Days Dying (exec. prod.), Where's Jack, Sleep Is Lovely, Murphy's War, The Great Western Express, Conduct Unbecoming, The Man Who Fell to Earth, Convoy, The Deer Hunter (Academy Award for Best Picture, 1978), Blade Runner.
TELEVISION: *Movie:* A Gathering of Old Men (exec. prod.).

DE FINA, BARBARA
Producer. Started as prod. asst. before working at various jobs for such filmmakers as Woody Allen and Sidney Lumet. Became assoc. prod. of development for King/Hitzig Prods., working on Happy Birthday Gemini, Cattle Annie and Little Britches. Was unit mgr./assoc. prod. on Prince of the City. First worked with Martin Scorsese on The King of Comedy as unit mgr. Produced music video Bad.
PICTURES: *Producer*: The Color of Money, The Last Temptation of Christ, New York Stories (segment: Life Lessons), GoodFellas (exec. prod.), The Grifters (exec. prod.), Cape Fear, Mad Dog and Glory, The Age of Innocence, Casino.

De HAVILLAND, OLIVIA
Actress b. Tokyo, Japan, July 1, 1916. e. California schools and Notre Dame Convent, Belmont. Acting debut, Max Reinhardt's stage prod., a Midsummer Night's Dream; going to Warner Bros. for film debut in m.p. version, 1935. Recipient: The Snake Pit (NY Film Critics & Look Awards), The Heiress (NY Film Critics, Women's Natl. Press Club & Look Awards). Autobiography: Every Frenchman Has One (1962).
THEATER: A Midsummer Night's Dream (debut, Hollywood Bowl). B'way: Romeo and Juliet (1951), A Gift of Time. U.S. Tour: Candida (1951-52).
PICTURES: A Midsummer Night's Dream (debut, 1935), Alibi Ike, The Irish in Us, Captain Blood, Anthony Adverse, The Charge of the Light Brigade, Call It a Day, It's Love I'm After, The Great Garrick, Gold is Where You Find It, The Adventures of Robin Hood, Four's a Crowd, Hard to Get, Wings of the Navy, Dodge City, The Private Lives of Elizabeth and Essex, Gone With the Wind, Raffles, My Love Came Back, Santa Fe Trail, Strawberry Blonde, Hold Back the Dawn, They Died With Their Boots On, The Male Animal, In This Our Life, Princess O'Rourke, Thank Your Lucky Stars, Government Girl, The Well Groomed Bride, To Each His Own (Academy Award, 1946), Devotion, Dark Mirror, The Snake Pit, The Heiress (Academy Award, 1949), My Cousin Rachel, That Lady, Not as a Stranger, Ambassador's Daughter, Proud Rebel, Libel, Light in the Piazza, Lady in a Cage, Hush ... Hush Sweet Charlotte, The Adventurers, Pope Joan, Airport '77, The Swarm, The Fifth Musketeer.
TELEVISION: *Special*: Noon Wine (Stage 67). *Movies & Mini-series*: The Screaming Woman, Roots: The Next Generations, Murder is Easy, Charles & Diana: A Royal Romance, North & South Book II, Anastasia, The Woman He Loved.

DELANY, DANA
Actress. b. New York, NY, Mar. 13, 1956. e. Phillips Acad., Wesleyan U.
THEATER: B'way: Translations, A Life. Off-B'way: Blood Woman.
PICTURES: Almost You, Where the River Runs Black, Masquerade, Moon Over Parador, Patty Hearst, Housesitter, Light Sleeper, Batman: Mask of the Phantasm (voice), Tombstone, Exit to Eden, Live Nude Girls.
TELEVISION: *Series*: Love of Life, As the World Turns, Sweet Surrender, China Beach (2 Emmy Awards: 1989, 1992). *Guest*: Moonlighting, Magnum P.I. *Movies*: A Promise to Keep, Donato and Daughter, The Enemy Within, Choices of the Heart: The Margaret Sanger Story. *Mini-Series*: Wild Palms. *Specials*: Texan, Fallen Angels (Good Housekeeping).

De LAURENTIIS, DINO
Producer, Executive. b. Torre Annunziata, Italy, Aug. 8, 1919. Took part in Rome Experimental Film Center; dir., prod. chmn.

of the bd. and CEO, De Laurentiis Entertainment Group Inc.; founded in 1984 the DEG Film Studios in Wilmington, NC. Resigned 1988. Started Dino De Laurentiis Communications, 1990.
PICTURES: L'amore Canta, Il Bandito, La Figlia del Capitano, Riso Amaro, La Lupa, Anna, Ulysses, Mambo, La Strada, Gold of Naples, War and Peace, Nights of Cabiria, The Tempest, Great War, Five Branded Women, Everybody Go Home, Under Ten Flags, The Best of Enemies, The Unfaithfuls, Barabbas, The Bible, Operation Paradise, The Witches, The Stranger, Diabolik, Anzio, Barbarella, Waterloo, The Valachi Papers, The Stone Killer, Serpico, Death Wish, Mandingo, Three Days of the Condor, Drum, Face to Face, Buffalo Bill and the Indians, King Kong, The Shootist, Orca, White Buffalo, The Serpent's Egg, King of the Gypsies, The Brink's Job, Hurricane, Flash Gordon, Halloween II, Ragtime, Conan the Barbarian, Fighting Back, Amityville II: The Possession, Halloween III: Season of the Witch, The Dead Zone, Amityville 3-D, Firestarter, The Bounty, Conan the Destroyer, Stephen King's Cat's Eye, Red Sonja, Year of the Dragon, Marie, Stephen King's Silver Bullet, Raw Deal, Maximum Overdrive, Tai-Pan, Blue Velvet, The Bedroom Window, Crimes of the Heart, King Kong Lives, Million Dollar Mystery, Weeds, Desperate Hours, Kuffs, Once Upon a Crime, Body of Evidence, Army of Darkness, Unforgettable, Assassins, Dragonheart.
TELEVISION: *Movie*: Solomon and Sheba.

De LAURENTIIS, RAFFAELLA
Producer. Daughter of Dino De Laurentiis. Began career as prod. asst. on father's film Hurricane. Independent producer.
PICTURES: Beyond the Reef, Conan the Barbarian, Conan the Destroyer, Dune, Tai-Pan, Prancer, Dragon: The Bruce Lee Story, Trading Mom, Dragonheart, Backdraft (exec. prod.), Daylight (exec. prod.).
TELEVISION: *Series*: Vanishing Son.

De La VARRE, ANDRE, JR.
Producer, Director. b. Vienna, Austria, Oct. 26, 1934. Prod. Grand Tour travelogues; producer of promotion films for KLM, Swissair, tourist offices, recent productions: Bicentennial films for state of Virginia, city of Charleston, NY state; winner, Atlanta Film Festival, Sunset Travel Film Festival; Burton Holmes Travelogue subjects; Corporate Incentive Videos, V-P-R Educational Films; producer, director, lecturer, narrator.

DEL BELSO, RICHARD
Marketing Executive. b. Albany, NY, Aug. 9, 1939. e. Fordham U, 1961, NYU, 1965. Began career in adv./research dept. at Benton & Bowles Advertising, NY. Served as research dept. group head for Kenyon and Eckhart; group head for Grudin/Appell/Haley Research Co. (now known as A/H/F/ Marketing Research, Inc.). Two years as assoc. dir. of mktg., research for Grey Advertising (N.Y.). Joined MCA/Universal in 1976 as assoc. dir., mktg. research. In 1980 named v.p. & dir. of mktg. research for Warner Bros; became worldwide v.p. of mktg. research, 1984; named sr. v.p. worldwide theatrical film market research, 1990.

De LELLIS, BOB
Executive. President, Fox Video.

De LINE, DONALD
Executive. President, Touchstone Pictures.

DELON, ALAIN
Actor. b. Sceaux, France, Nov. 8, 1935. Discovered by Yves Allegret. Served in French Navy as a Marine. Worked as cafe waiter, heavy-load carrier.
PICTURES: When a Woman Gets Involved (debut, 1957), Be Beautiful and Keep Quiet, 3 Murderesses, Christine, Le Chemin Des Ecoliers, Plein Soleil (Purple Noon), Quelle Joie de Vivre!, Rocco and His Brothers, Famous Loves, Eclipse, The Leopard, The Devil and the 10 Commandments, Any Number Can Win, The Black Tulip, The Felines (Joy House), L'Insoumis (also prod., co-s.p.), The Yellow Rolls Royce, Once a Thief, Lost Command, Is Paris Burning?, Texas Across the River, The Adventurers, Spirits of the Dead, Samaurai, Diabolically Yours, Girl on a Motorcycle, Goodbye Friend, The Swimming Pool, Jeff (also prod.), The Sicilian Clan, Borsalino, The Red Circle, Madly (also prod.), Doucement Les Basses, Red Sun, The Widow Cuderc, Assassination of Trotsky, Dirty Money, The Teacher, Scorpio, Shock Treatment, The Burning Barn, Big Guns, Two Men in the City, La Race des Seigneurs, Les Seins de Glace, Borsalino & Company (also prod.), Zorro, Police Story, The Gypsy, Mr. Klein (also prod.), Like a Boomerang (also prod., s.p.), The Gang (also exec. prod.), Armaggedon, L'Homme Presse, Mort d'un Pourri (also prod.), Attention Les Enfants Regardent, The Concorde - Airport 79, The Doctor, Teheran 43, Three Men to Destroy (also prod.), For a Cop's Honor (also dir, s.p., prod.), The Shock (also s.p.), The Cache (also prod., dir., s.p.), Swann in Love, Our Story, Military Police (also exec. prod., s.p.), The Passage (also

prod.), Let Sleeping Cops Lie (also prod., co-s.p.), New Wave, Dancing Machine, The Return of Casanova, Un Crime... L'Ours en Peluche.

DELPY, JULIE
Actress. b. Paris, France, 1970. Made acting debut as teenager for dir. Jean-Luc Godard.
PICTURES: Detective (debut, 1985) Bad Blood, King Lear, Beatrice, The Dark Night, Europa Europa, Voyager, The Three Musketeers, White, Killing Zoe, Younger and Younger, Before Sunrise.

DEL ROSSI, PAUL R.
Executive. b. Winchester, MA, Oct. 19, 1942. e. Harvard Coll, 1964; Harvard Business Sch., 1967. Sr. v.p., The Boston Co., 1977-1980; sr. consultant, Arthur D. Little, Inc.; presently pres. & CEO, General Cinema Theatres.

DeLUCA, MICHAEL
Executive, Writer. b. Brooklyn, Aug., 1965. Left NYU to take intern job at New Line Cinema; became story editor before becoming production exec. in 1989. 1993 named pres. of production of New Line.
PICTURES: Writer: Freddy's Dead: The Final Nightmare, In the Mouth of Madness, Judge Dredd (story).

De LUISE, DOM
Comedian, Actor. b. Brooklyn, NY, Aug. 1, 1933. e. Tufts Coll. m. actress Carol Arthur. Sons: Peter, Michael, David. Spent two seasons with Cleveland Playhouse. Launched TV career on The Garry Moore Show with character, Dominick the Great, a bumbling magician.
THEATER: Little Mary Sunshine, Another Evening With Harry Stoones, All in Love, Half-Past Wednesday, Too Much Johnson, The Student Gypsy, Last of the Red Hot Lovers, Here's Love, Little Shop of Horrors, Die Fledermus (NY Met. Opera: 2 seasons), Peter and the Wolf.
PICTURES: Fail Safe (debut, 1964), Diary of a Bachelor, The Glass Bottom Boat, The Busy Body, What's So Bad About Feeling Good?, Norwood, The Twelve Chairs, Who Is Harry Kellerman...?, Every Little Crook and Nanny, Blazing Saddles, The Adventure of Sherlock Holmes' Smarter Brother, Silent Movie, The World's Greatest Lover, The End, The Cheap Detective, Sextette, The Muppet Movie, Hot Stuff (also dir.), The Last Married Couple in America, Fatso, Wholly Moses, Smokey and the Bandit II, History of the World Part I, The Cannonball Run, The Best Little Whorehouse in Texas, The Secret of NIMH (voice), Cannonball Run II, Johnny Dangerously, Haunted Honeymoon, An American Tail (voice), Spaceballs (voice), A Taxi Driver in New York, Going Bananas, Oliver & Company (voice), All Dogs Go To Heaven (voice), Loose Cannons, Driving Me Crazy, Fievel Goes West (voice), Munchie (voice), The Skateboard Kid (voice), Happily Ever After (voice), Robin Hood: Men in Tights, The Silence of the Hams, A Troll in Central Park (voice), All Dogs Go to Heaven 2 (voice).
TELEVISION: Series: The Entertainers, The Dean Martin Summer Show, Dom DeLuise Show, The Barrum-Bump Show, The Glenn Campbell Goodtime Hour, The Dean Martin Show, Lotsa Luck, Dom DeLuise Show (synd.), The New Candid Camera, Fievel's American Tails (voice). Movies: Evil Roy Slade, Only With Married Men, Happy (also exec. prod.), Don't Drink the Water, The Tin Soldier. Guest: The Munsters, Please Don't Eat the Daises, Ghost and Mrs. Muir, Medical Center, Amazing Stories, Easy Street, B.L. Stryker.

del VALLE, JOHN
Publicist. b. San Francisco, CA, Mar. 23, 1904. e. U. of California. Adv., edit. staff various newspapers including asst. drama ed. S.F. Call-Bulletin, L.A. Mirror; adv.-publicity dir. San Francisco Fox Theatre 1933-36; publicist, Paramount Studio, 1936-42; dir. pub., adv. Arnold Prod. 1946; Chaplin Studios, 1947; Nat Holt Prod., 1948-52; Editor, TV Family mag., N.Y., 1952-53; adv. pub. dir. Century Films, 1954; pub. rel. Academy M.P. Arts & Sciences, 1965; publicist, various U.A. indep. film prod., 1955-56; unit publicist, Paramount, 1956; TC-F 1957-62, Para., 1962-63; Universal 1964-65; Mirisch Corp.-UA Filming, Hawaii, 1965; pub. rel. and editor, Atomics Int'l div. North American Rockwell, 1966-71; present, freelance writer. NY Times Op. Ed. (1985), Gourmet Mag. (1989), others.

DEMME, JONATHAN
Director, Writer, Producer. b. Rockville Centre, NY, Feb. 22, 1944. e. U. of Florida. First job in industry as usher; was film critic for college paper, The Florida Alligator and the Coral Gable Times. Did publicity work for United Artists, Avco Embassy; sold films for Pathe Contemporary Films; wrote for trade paper, Film Daily, 1966-68. Moved to England in 1969; musical co-ordinator on Irving Allen's EyeWitness in 1970. In 1972 co-prod and co-wrote first film, Angels Hard As They Come. Appeared in film Into the Night.
PICTURES: Hot Box (prod., co-s.p.), Black Mama White Mama (story). Director: Caged Heat (also s.p.), Crazy Mama (also s.p.), Fighting Mad (also s.p.), Citizen's Band (Handle

With Care), Last Embrace, Melvin and Howard, Swing Shift, Stop Making Sense, Something Wild (also co-prod.), Swimming to Cambodia, Married to the Mob, Miami Blues (prod. only), The Silence of the Lambs (Academy Award, 1991), Cousin Bobby, Philadelphia (also co-prod.), Devil in a Blue Dress (exec. prod. only).
TELEVISION: Specials: Who Am I This Time?, Accumation With Talking plus Water Motor, Survival Guides, A Family Tree (Trying Times series, PBS), Haiti: Dreams of Democracy. Movie: Women & Men 2 (A Domestic Dilemma; prod. only).
VIDEO: UB40, Chrissie Hynde, Sun City Video of Artists United Against Apartheid, Suzanne Vega's Solitude Standing.

DE MORNAY, REBECCA
Actress. b. Santa Rosa, CA, Aug. 29, 1962. Spent childhood in Europe, graduating from high school in Austria. Returned to America, enrolling at Lee Strasberg's Los Angeles Institute; apprenticed at Zoetrope Studios.
THEATER: Born Yesterday (Pasadena Playhouse), Marat/Sade (Williamstown Fest.).
PICTURES: Risky Business, Testament, The Slugger's Wife, Runaway Train, The Trip to Bountiful, Beauty and the Beast, And God Created Woman, Feds, Dealers, Backdraft, The Hand That Rocks the Cradle, Guilty as Sin, The Three Musketeers, Never Talk to Strangers.
TELEVISION: Movies: The Murders in the Rue Morgue, By Dawn's Early Light, An Inconvenient Woman, Blindside, Getting Out.

DEMPSEY, PATRICK
Actor. b. Lewiston, ME, Jan. 13, 1966. e. St. Dominic Regional h.s. in Lewiston where he became State downhill skiing champion. Juggling, magic and puppetry led to performances before Elks clubs and community orgs. Cast by Maine Acting Co. in On Golden Pond. In 1983 acted in Torch Song Trilogy in San Francisco and toured in Brighton Beach Memoirs. NY Theatre debut, 1991 in The Subject Was Roses.
PICTURES: Heaven Help Us (debut, 1985), Meatballs III, Can't Buy Me Love, In the Mood, In a Shallow Grave, Some Girls, Loverboy, Coupe de Ville, Happy Together, Run, Mobsters, For Better and For Worse (R.S.V.P.), Face the Music, Bank Robber, With Honors, Outbreak.
TELEVISION: Movies: A Fighting Choice, JFK: Reckless Youth, Bloodknot. Series: Fast Times at Ridgemont High. Special: Merry Christmas Baby.

De MUNN, JEFFREY
Actor. b. Buffalo, NY, Apr. 25, 1947. e. Union Col. Studied acting at Old Vic Theatre in Bristol, Eng.
THEATER: NY: Comedians, A Prayer for My Daughter, Modigliani, Augusta, Hands of Its Enemy, Chekhov Sketchbook, A Midsummer Night's Dream, Total Abandon, Country Girl, Bent, K-2, Sleight of Hand, Spoils of War, One Shoe Off, Hedda Gabler.
PICTURES: You Better Watch Out (Christmas Evil), The First Deadly Sin, Resurrection, Ragtime, I'm Dancing as Fast as I Can, Frances, Windy City, Enormous Changes at the Last Minute, Warning Sign, The Hitcher, The Blob, Betrayed, Blaze, Newsies, Eyes of an Angel, The Shawshank Redemption, Safe Passage, Killer, Phenomenon.
TELEVISION: Movies: The Last Tenant, Sanctuary of Fear, King Crab, Word of Honor, I Married Wyatt Earp, The Face of Rage, Sessions, When She Says No, Windmills of the Gods, Lincoln, Doubletake, A Time to Live, Who Is Julia?, Young Harry Houdini, Price of Justice, Switch, Elysian Fields, The Haunted, Treacherous Crossing, Jonathan: The Boy Nobody Wanted, Barbarians at the Gate, Crash: The Fate of Flight 1502, Settle the Score, Under the Influence, Betrayal of Trust, Citizen X, Down Came a Blackbird, Hiroshima, Almost Golden: The Jessica Savitch Story. Specials: Mourning Becomes Electra, Peacemaker (Triple Play II), Sensiblity and Sense, The Joy That Kills, Teacher, Pigeon Feathers, Many Mansions, Wild Jackasses, Ebbie.

DENCH, DAME JUDI
Actress. b. York, England, Dec. 9, 1934. Studied for stage at Central Sch. of Speech and Drama. Theatre debut Old Vic, 1957. Created a Dame in 1988 Honours List. Recent Theatre: Cymbeline, Juno and the Paycock, A Kind of Alaska, The Cherry Orchard, The Plough and the Stars, Importance of Being Earnest, Pack of Lies, Mr. and Mrs. Nobody, Antony and Cleopatra, The Sea, Coriolanus, The Gift of the Gorgon, The Seagull. Director: Much Ado About Nothing, Look Back in Anger, Boys from Syracuse, Romeo and Juliet, Absolute Hell, A Little Night Music.
PICTURES: The Third Secret (debut, 1964), He Who Rides a Tiger, A Study in Terror, Four in the Morning, A Midsummer Night's Dream (RSC Prod.), Luther, Dead Cert, Wetherby, A Room With a View, 84 Charing Cross Road, A Handful of Dust, Henry V, Jack and Sarah, Goldeneye.
TELEVISION: Major Barbara, Pink String and Sealing Wax, Talking to a Stranger, The Funambulists, Age of Kings, Jackanory, Hilda Lessways, Luther, Neighbours, Parade's

End, Marching Song, On Approval, Days to Come, Emilie, The Comedy of Errors (RSC Prod.), Macbeth (RSC Prod.), Langrishe Go Down, On Giant's Shoulders, Love in a Cold Climate, Village Wooing, A Fine Romance (series), The Cherry Orchard, Going Gently, Saigon—Year of the Cat, Ghosts, Behaving Badly, Torch, Can You Hear Me Thinking?, Absolute Hell, As Time Goes By (series).

DENEAU, SIDNEY, G.
Sales executive. Head film buyer Fabian Theatres; U.S. Army 1942-46; gen. mgr. Schine Theatres 1947; v.p., gen. sales mgr., Selznick Releasing Orgn., 1949; 1956; v.p. asst. gen. sls. mgr., Para. Film Dist., 1958; exec. v.p., Rugoff Theatres, 1964. Resigned, September, 1969 to engage in own theatre consultant business.

DENEUVE, CATHERINE
Actress. r.n. Catherine Dorleac. b. Paris, France, Oct. 22, 1943. Sister was the late Francoise Dorleac. Made screen debut as teen using adopting mother's maiden name.
PICTURES: Les Collegiennes (debut, 1956), Wild Roots of Love, L'homme a Femmes, The Doors Slam, La Parisiennes (segment: Sophie), Vice and Virtue, Satan Leads the Dance, Vacances Portugaises, Les Plus Belles Escroqueries du Monde, The Umbrellas of Cherbourg (Cannes Film Fest. Award, 1964), Male Hunt (La Chasse a l'Homme), Male Companion, La Costanza della Ragione, Repulsion, Le Chant du Monde, La Vie de Chateau (A Matter of Resistance), Who Wants to Sleep?, Les Creatures, The Young Girls of Rochefort, Belle de Jour (Venice Film Fest. Award, 1967), Benjamin, Manon 70, Mayerling, La Chamade (Heartbeat), The April Fools, Mississippi Mermaid, Don't Be Blue, Tristana, Donkey Skin, Henri Langolis, Liza, It Only Happens to Others, Dirty Money, Melampo, The Slightly Pregnant Man, Touche Pas a la Femme Blanche, La Grande Bourgeoise, Zig-Zag, La Femme aux Bottes Rouges, Hustle, Lovers Like Us, Act of Agression, The Beach Hut, Second Chance, March or Die, Ecoute voir, L'Argent des Autres, When I Was a Kid I Didn't Dare, Anima Persa, An Adventure for Two, Ils Sont Grandes ces Petits, Courage--Let's Run, The Last Metro, Je vous Aime, Choice of Arms, Hotel des Ameriques, Reporters, Daisy Chain, Le Choc, The African, The Hunger, Le Bon Plaisir, Fort Saganne, Love Songs, Let's Hope It's a Girl, Le Mauvaise Herbe, Scene of the Crime, Agent Trouble, A Strange Place to Meet (also prod.), Hotel Panique, The Man Who Loved Zoos, Frequency Murder, Helmut Newton: Frames From the Edge (doc.), The White Queen, Indochine (Acad. Award nom.), Ma Saison Preferee (My Favorite Season), The Chess Game, The Convent.

DENHAM, MAURICE
O.B.E., 1992: Actor. b. Beckenham, Kent, England, Dec. 23, 1909. e. Tonbridge Sch. Started theatrical career with repertory com. 1934. Served in W.W.II. Played in numerous plays, films & radio shows.
PICTURES: Blanche Fury, London Belongs To Me, It's Not Cricket, Traveller's Joy, Landfall, Spider and the Fly, No Highway in the Sky, The Net, Time Bomb, Street Corner (Both Sides of the Law), Million Pound Note (Man With a Million), Eight O'Clock Walk, Purple Plain, Simon and Laura, 23 Paces to Baker Street, Checkpoint, Carrington V.C. (Court Martial), Doctor at Sea, Night of the Demon, Man With a Dog, Barnacle Bill, The Captain's Table, Our Man in Havana, Sink the Bismark, Two-Way Stretch, Greengage Summer, Invasion, Quartette, The Mark, HMS Defiant, The Very Edge, Paranoiac, The Set Up, Penang, The King's Breakfast, Downfall, Hysteria, The Uncle, Operation Crossbow, Legend of Dick Turpin, The Alphabet Murders, The Night Callers, The Nanny, Those Magnificent Men in Their Flying Machines, Heroes of Telemark, After the Fox, The Torture Garden, The Long Duel, The Eliminator, Danger Route, Attack on the Iron Coast, The Best House in London, Negatives, The Midas Run, Some Girls Do, The Touch of Love, The Virgin and the Gypsy, Bloody Sunday, Countess Dracula, Nicholas and Alexandra, The Day of the Jackal, Luther, Shout at the Devil, Julia, The Recluse, From a Far Country, Mr. Love, The Chain, Monsignor Quixote, Murder on the Orient Express, 84 Charing Cross Road.
TELEVISION: Uncle Harry, Day of the Monkey, Miss Mabel, Angel Pavement, The Paraguayan Harp, The Wild Bird, Soldier Soldier, Changing Values, Maigret, The Assassins, Saturday Spectacular, Vanishing Act, A Chance in Life, Virtue, Somerset Maugham, Three of a Kind, Sapper, Pig in the Middle, Their Obedient Servants, Long Past Glory, Devil in The Wind, Any Other Business, The Retired Colourman, Sherlock Holmes (series), Blackmail, Knock on Any Door, Danger Man, Dr. Finley's Casebook, How to Get Rid of Your Husband, Talking to a Stranger, A Slight Ache, From Chekhov with Love, Home Sweet Honeycomb, St. Joan, Julius Caesar, Golden Days, Marshall Petain, The Lotus Eaters, Fall of Eagles, Carnforth Practice. The Unofficial Rose, Omnibus, Balzac, Loves Labour Lost, Angels, Huggy Bear, The Portrait, The Crumbles Murder, A Chink In The Wall, Porridge, For God's Sake, Bosch, Marie Curie, Upchat Line, Secret Army, My Son, My Son, Edward and Mrs. Simpson, Gate of Eden,

Potting Shed, Double Dealer, Minder, Agatha Christie Hour, Chinese Detective, The Old Men at the Zoo, The Hope and the Glory, Luther, Love Song, Mr. Palfrey, The Black Tower, Boon, Rumpole, All Passions Spent, Trial of Klaus Barbie, Miss Marple, Tears in the Rain, Behaving Badly, Seeing in the Dark, Inspector Morse: Fat Chance, La Nonna, Lovejoy, Memento Mori, Sherlock Holmes, The Last Vampire, Peak Pratice, Bed, The Bill, Prisoner In Time, Pie In The Sky.

De NIRO, ROBERT
Actor. b. New York, NY, Aug. 17, 1943. Studied acting with Stella Adler and Lee Strasberg; 1988, formed Tribeca Film Center in NY. Co-Prod. of film Thunderheart.
THEATER: One Night Stand of a Noisy Passenger (Off-B'way), Cuba and His Teddy Bear (Public Theater and B'way; Theatre World Award).
PICTURES: The Wedding Party (debut, 1969), Greetings, Sam's Song (The Swap), Bloody Mama, Hi Mom, Born to Win, Jennifer on My Mind, The Gang That Couldn't Shoot Straight, Bang the Drum Slowly, Mean Streets, The Godfather Part II (Academy Award, best supporting actor, 1974), Taxi Driver, The Last Tycoon, New York New York, 1900, The Deer Hunter, Raging Bull (Academy Award, 1980), True Confessions, The King of Comedy, Once Upon a Time in America, Falling in Love, Brazil, The Mission, Angel Heart, The Untouchables, Midnight Run, Jacknife, We're No Angels, Stanley and Iris, GoodFellas, Awakenings, Guilty by Suspicion, Backdraft, Cape Fear, Mistress (also co-prod.), Night and the City, Mad Dog and Glory, This Boy's Life, A Bronx Tale (also dir., co-prod.), Mary Shelley's Frankenstein, Casino, Heat, Marvin's Room (also exec. prod.), The Fan, Sleepers, Stolen Flower, Copland, Great Expectations.
TELEVISION: Specials: Night of 100 Stars, Dear America: Letters Home From Vietnam (reader).

DENISON, MICHAEL
C.B.E., Actor. b. Doncaster, York, Eng., Nov. 1, 1915. e. Harrow, Magdalen Coll., Oxford and Webber Douglas Sch. m. Dulcie Gray, actress, 1939. Served overseas, Capt. Intelligence Corps, 1940-46. Debuted on stage 1938 in Charlie's Aunt.
THEATER: Ever Since Paradise, Rain on the Just, Queen Elizabeth Slept Here, Fourposter, Dragon's Mouth, Bad Samaritan; Shakespeare Season Stratford-on-Avon; Edinburgh Festival; Meet Me By Moonlight, Let Them Eat Cake, Candida, Heartbreak House, My Fair Lady (Australia), Where Angels Fear to Tread, Hostile Witness, An Ideal Husband (1965, 1992, 1996), On Approval, Happy Family, No. 10, Out of the Question, Trio, The Wild Duck, The Clandestine Marriage, The Dragon Variation, At the End of the Day, The Sack Race, Peter Pan, The Black Mikado, The First Mrs. Fraser, The Earl and the Pussycat, Robert and Elizabeth, The Cabinet Minister, Old Vic Season: Twelfth Night, Lady's Not for Burning, Ivanov, Bedroom Farce, The Kingfisher, Relatively Speaking, Coat of Varnish, Capt. Brassbound's Conversion, School for Scandal, Song at Twilight, See How They Run, The Tempest, Ring Round the Moon, The Apple Cart, Court in the Act, You Never Can Tell, The Chalk Garden, Joy, Dear Charles, Best of Friends, The Importance of Being Earnest, Pygmalion, The Schoolmistress, Two of a Kind.
PICTURES: Tilly of Bloomsbury, (debut, 1939), Hungry Hill, My Brother Jonathan, The Blind Goddess, The Glass Mountain, Landfall, The Franchise Affair, The Magic Box, Angels One Five, The Importance of Being Earnest, Tall Headlines, There Was a Young Lady, Contraband Spain, The Truth About Women, Faces in the Dark, Shadowlands.
TELEVISION: Marco Millions, The Second Man, What's My Line, Milestones, Waiting for Gillan, Olympia, The Sun Divorce, Rain on the Just, East Lynne, Who Goes Home?, Festival Fever, Boyd QC (80 episodes: 1956-63), The Inside Chance, Frankie Howerd Sketch, The Importance of Being Earnest, Dear Octopus, Village Wooing, Compere for Joan Sutherland, Funeral Games, Unexpectedly Vacant, The Twelve Pound Look, The Provincial Lady, Subject: This Is Your Life (1977, and with Dulcie Gray, 1995), Crown Court, Private Schultz, Blood Money, Bedroom Farce, The Critic, Scorpion, Good Behavior, Rumpole, Cold Warrior, Howard's Way.

DENNEHY, BRIAN
Actor. b. Bridgeport, CT, July 9, 1939. e. Columbia U. In Marine Corps five years, including Vietnam. After discharge in 1965 studied with acting coaches in N.Y., while working at part time jobs as a salesman, bartender, truck driver.
THEATER: Streamers, Galileo (Goodman Th.), The Cherry Orchard, Translations.
PICTURES: Looking for Mr. Goodbar, Semi-Tough, F.I.S.T., Foul Play, 10, Butch and Sundance: The Early Days, Little Miss Marker, Split Image, First Blood, Never Cry Wolf, Gorky Park, Finders Keepers, River Rat, Cocoon, Silverado, Twice in a Lifetime, F/X, Legal Eagles, The Check Is in the Mail, Best Seller, The Belly of an Architect, Return to Snowy River Part II, Miles From Home, Cocoon: The Return, The Last of the Finest, Presumed Innocent, FX2, Gladiator, Seven Minutes, Tommy Boy, The Stars Fell on Henrietta, Midnight Movie.

TELEVISION: *Series:* Big Shamus Little Shamus, Star of the Family, Birdland. *Movies:* Johnny We Hardly Knew Ye, It Happened at Lake Wood Manor, Ruby and Oswald, A Death in Canaan, A Real American Hero, Silent Victory: The Kitty O'Neil Story, The Jericho Mile, Dummy, The Seduction of Miss Leona, A Rumor of War, Fly Away Home, Skokie, I Take These Men, Blood Feud, Off Sides, Acceptable Risks, Private Sessions, The Lion of Africa, A Father's Revenge, Day One, Perfect Witness, Pride and Extreme Prejudice, Rising Son, A Killing in a Small Town, In Broad Daylight, The Burden of Proof, To Catch a Killer, Diamond Fleece, Teamster: The Jackie Presser Story, Deadly Matrimony, Foreign Affairs, Murder in the Heartland, Prophet of Evil: The Ervil LeBaron Story, Final Appeal, Jack Reed: Badge of Honor (also co-exec. prod.), Leave of Absence, Jack Reed: Search for Justice (also dir., co-writer). *Mini-Series:* Evergreen. *Guest:* M*A*S*H, Lou Grant, Cagney and Lacey, Hunter, Tall Tales (Annie Oakley). *Special:* Dear America: Letter Home From Vietnam (reader).

DENVER, BOB
Actor. b. New Rochelle, NY, Jan. 9, 1935. e. Loyola U.
PICTURES: A Private's Affair, Take Her She's Mine, For Those Who Think Young, Who's Minding the Mint? The Sweet Ride, Did You Hear the One About the Travelling Saleslady?, Back to the Beach.
TELEVISION: *Series:* The Many Loves of Dobie Gillis, Gilligan's Island, The Good Guys, Dusty's Trail. *Movies:* Rescue from Gilligan's Island, The Castaways on Gilligan's Island, The Harlem Globetrotters on Gilligans Island, The Invisible Woman, High School USA, Bring Me the Head of Dobie Gillis. Also: Far Out Space Nuts, Scamps.

DENVER, JOHN
Singer, Actor. r.n. Henry John Deutschendorf. b. Roswell, NM, Dec. 31, 1943. Records, concerts, nightclubs.
PICTURES: Oh, God!, Fire and Ice (narrator).
TELEVISION: *Specials:* An Evening with John Denver (Emmy Award for Outstanding Special, 1975), Rocky Mountain Christmas, John Denver and the Muppets, Rocky Mountain Holiday, Salute to Lady Liberty, Jacques Costeau--The First 75 Years, Julie Andrews...The Sound of Christmas, John Denver's Christmas in Aspen. *Movies:* The Christmas Gift, Foxfire, Higher Ground (co-exec. prod., co-music, actor).

De PALMA, BRIAN
Director, Writer, Producer. b. Newark, NJ, Sept. 11, 1940. e. Columbia U.,B.A.; Sarah Lawrence, M.A. While in college made series of shorts, including Wotan's Wake, winner of Rosenthal Foundation Award for best film made by American under 25. Also judged most popular film of Midwest Film Festival (1963); later shown at San Francisco Film Festival. Dir.: The Responsive Eye (doc., 1966).
PICTURES: *Director:* Murder a La Mod (also s.p., edit.), Greetings (also co-s.p. ed.), The Wedding Party (also co-s.p., co-prod., ed.), Hi Mom (also co-story, s.p.), Dionysus in '69 (also co-prod., co-photog., co-ed.), Get To Know Your Rabbit, Sisters (also co-s.p.), Phantom of the Paradise (also co-s.p.), Obsession (also co-story), Carrie, The Fury, Home Movies (also s.p., co-prod.), Dressed to Kill (also s.p.), Blow Out (also s.p.), Scarface, Body Double (also prod., s.p.), Wiseguys, The Untouchables, Casualties of War, The Bonfire of the Vanities (also prod.), Raising Cain (also s.p.), Carlito's Way, Mission: Impossible.

DEPARDIEU, GÉRARD
Actor. b. Chateauroux, France, Dec. 27, 1948. Studied acting at Theatre National Populaire in Paris. Made film debut at 16 in short by Roger Leenhardt (Le Beatnik et Le Minet). Acted in feature film by Agnes Varda (uncompleted).
PICTURES: Le Cri du Cormoran le Soir au-dessis des Jonques, Nathalie Granger, A Little Sun in Cold Water, Le Tueur, L'Affaire Dominici, Au Renedez-vous de la mort joyeuse, La Scoumone, Rude Journee our la Reine, Deux Hommes dans la Ville, The Holes, Going Places, Stavisky, Woman of the Granges, Vincent Francois Paul and the Others, The Wonderful Crook, 7 Morts sur ordonnance, Maitresse, Je t'Aime Moi Non Plus, The Last Woman, 1900, Barocco, Rene la Canne, Baxter Vera Baxter, The Truck, Tell Him I Love Him, At Night All Cats Are Gray, Get Out Your Handkerchiefs, The Left-Handed Woman, Bye Bye Monkey, Violanta, Le Sucre, Les Chiens, L'Ingorgo, Buffet Froid, Temporale Rosy, Mon Oncle d'Amerique, Loulou, The Last Metro, Inspector Blunder, I Love You, Choice of Arms, The Woman Next Door, Le Chevre. The Return of Martin Guerre, The Big Brother, Danton, The Moon in the Gutter, Les Comperes (also co-prod.), Fort Saganne, Le Tartuffe (also dir., co-s.p.), Rive Droite Rive Gauche, Police, One Woman or Two, Menage, Ru du depart, Jean De Florette (also co-prod.), Under Satan's Sun (also co-prod.), A Strange Place for an Enounter (also co-prod.), Camille Claudel (also co-prod.), Dreux, Too Beautiful for You (also co-prod.), I Want to Go Home, Cyrano de Bergerac (also co-prod), Green Card, Uranus, Thanks for Life,

Mon Pere ce Heros (My Father the Hero), 1492: Conquest of Paradise, Tous les Matins du Monde (All the Mornings of the World), Helas Pour Moi (Oh Woe is Me), Une Pure Formalite (A Pure Formality), Germinal, My Father the Hero, Colonel Chabert, La Machine, Elisa, Les Anges Gardiens, The Horseman on the Roof, Bogus, Le Garcu, Hamlet.

DEPP, JOHNNY
Actor. b. Owensboro, KY, June 9, 1963. Raised in Miramar, FL. Played lead guitar with band The Kids, with whom he moved to L.A. in 1983. With no prior acting experience made film debut in A Nightmare on Elm Street.
PICTURES: A Nightmare on Elm Street (debut, 1984), Private Resort, Platoon, Cry-Baby, Edward Scissorhands, Freddy's Dead: The Final Nightmare (cameo), Benny & Joon, What's Eating Gilbert Grape, Arizona Dream, Ed Wood, Don Juan DeMarco, Dead Man, Nick of Time, Divine Rapture, Donnie Brasco.
TELEVISION: *Series:* 21 Jump Street. *Movie:* Slow Burn. *Guest:* Lady Blue.

DEREK, BO
Actress. r.n. Mary Cathleen Collins. b. Torrance, CA., Nov. 20, 1956. Discovered by actor-turned-filmmaker John Derek, whom she married.
PICTURES: Orca (debut, 1977), 10, A Change of Seasons, Fantasies (And Once Upon a Time), Tarzan the Ape Man (also prod.), Bolero (also prod.), Ghosts Can't Do It (also prod.), Hot Chocolate, Sognando la California (California Dreaming), Woman of Desire, Tommy Boy.
TELEVISION: *Movie:* Shattered Image.

DEREK, JOHN
Actor, Producer, Director, Cinematographer. b. Hollywood, CA, August 12, 1926. m. actress Bo Derek. Acting debut as bit player 1945 in I'll Be Seeing You, billed as Derek Harris. Made producer debut 1963 with Nightmare in the Sun, directorial debut 1966 with Once Before I Die.
PICTURES: *Actor:* I'll Be Seeing You (debut, 1945), A Double Life, Knock on Any Door, All the King's Men, Rogues of Sherwood Forest, Saturday's Hero, Mask of the Avenger, Scandal Sheet, The Family Secret, Thunderbirds, Mission Over Korea, The Last Posse, Prince of Pirates, Ambush at Tomahawk Gap, Sea of Lost Ships, The Outcast, The Adventures of Hajji Baba, Prince of Players, Run for Cover, An Annapolis Story, The Leather Saint, The Ten Commandments, Omar Khayyam, Fury at Showdown, High Hell, Prisoner of the Volga, Exodus, Nightmare in the Sun (also prod.), Once Before I Die (also dir., prod.), A Boy ... a Girl, Childish Things (also dir.). *Director-Cinematographer:* Fantasies (And Once Upon a Time), Tarzan The Ape Man, Bolero (also s.p.), Ghosts Can't Do It.
TELEVISION: *Series:* Frontier Circus.

DERN, BRUCE
Actor. b. Chicago, IL, June 4, 1936. e. U. of Pennsylvania. Daughter is actress Laura Dern. Studied acting with Gordon Phillips, member, Actor's Studio, 1959 after N.Y. debut in Shadow of a Gunman. Broadway: Sweet Bird of Youth, Orpheus Descending, Strangers. Film Awards: Natl. Society of Film Critics (Drive He Said, 1971), People's Choice (Coming Home, 1978), Genie (Middle Age Crazy, 1980), Silver Bear (That Championship Season, 1982).
PICTURES: Wild River (debut, 1960), Marnie, Hush...Hush Sweet Charlotte, The Wild Angels, The St. Valentine's Day Massacre, Waterhole No. 3, The Trip, The War Wagon, Psych-Out, Rebel Rousers, Hang 'Em High, Will Penny, Number One, Castle Keep, Support Your Local Sheriff, They Shoot Horses Don't They?, Cycle Savages, Bloody Mama, The Incredible Two-Headed Transplant, Drive He Said, Silent Running, Thumb Tripping, The Cowboys, The King of Marvin Gardens, The Laughing Policeman, The Great Gatsby, Smile, Posse, Family Plot, Won Ton Ton the Dog Who Saved Hollywood, The Twist (Folies Bourgeoises), Black Sunday, Coming Home (Acad. Award nom.), The Driver, Middle Age Crazy, Tattoo, Harry Tracy: Desperado, That Championship Season, On the Edge, The Big Town, World Gone Wild, 1969, The 'Burbs, After Dark My Sweet, Diggstown, Wild Bill, Down Periscope, Mulholland Falls, Last Man Standing.
TELEVISION: *Series:* Stoney Burke. *Mini-Series:* Space. *Movies:* Sam Hill: Who Killed the Mysterious Mr. Foster?, Toughlove, Roses Are for the Rich, Uncle Tom's Cabin, Trenchcoat in Paradise, The Court-Martial of Jackie Robinson, Into the Badlands, Carolina Skeletons, It's Nothing Personal, Deadman's Revenge, Amelia Earhart: The Final Flight, A Mother's Prayer. *Guest:* Naked City, Ben Casey, The Virginian, Twelve O'Clock High, The Big Valley, Gunsmoke, The FBI, Land of the Giants, Saturday Night Live, Fallen Angels (Murder Obliquely).

DERN, LAURA
Actress. b. Los Angeles, CA, Feb. 10, 1967. Daughter of actors Diane Ladd and Bruce Dern. At age 5 appeared with

mother on daytime serial The Secret Storm. Was an extra in several of her father's films and her mother's Alice Doesn't Live Here Anymore. Studied acting at RADA appearing on stage in Hamlet, A Midsummer Night's Dream.
THEATER: NY: The Palace of Amateurs. LA: Brooklyn Laundry.
PICTURES: White Lightning (debut, 1973), Alice Doesn't Live Here Anymore, Foxes, Ladies and Gentlemen: The Fabulous Stains, Teachers, Mask, Smooth Talk, Blue Velvet, Haunted Summer, Fat Man and Little Boy, Wild at Heart, Rambling Rose (Acad. Award nom.), Jurassic Park, A Perfect World, Devil Inside, Citizen Ruth.
TELEVISION: Movies: Happy Endings, Three Wishes of Billy Greer, Afterburn (Golden Globe Award), Down Came a Blackbird. Special: The Gift (dir., co-story only). Guest: Fallen Angels (Murder Obliquely).

DE SANTIS, GREGORY JOSEPH
Producer, Writer, Director. b. Los Angeles, CA, July 12, 1955. e. Durham Univ., Canaan Coll. President, Millenium Mulitmedia.
PICTURES: Prod.: The Companion, Car Trouble, Pass the Buck, Die Sister Die!, Diary of a Surfing Film, Firepower, The Forest.
TELEVISION: Prod.: Volleyball: A Sport Come of Age, The Nature Series, Caribou Crossing, California Day, Midnight Son, Lightning, Mysterious River.

DESCHANEL, CALEB
Cinematographer, Director. b. Philadelphia, PA, Sept. 21, 1944. m. actress Mary Jo Deschanel. e. Johns Hopkins U., U. of Southern California Film Sch. Studied at Amer. Film Inst., interned under Gordon Willis then started making commercials, short subjects, docs.
PICTURES: Cinematographer: More American Graffiti, Being There, The Black Stallion, Apocalypse Now (2nd unit photog.), The Right Stuff, Let's Spend the Night Together (co-cinematographer), The Natural, The Slugger's Wife, It Could Happen to You, Flying Wild. Director: The Escape Artist, Crusoe.

De TOTH, ANDRE
Writer, Director, Producer. b. Hungary. Dir.-writer European films, 1931-39; U.S. assoc. Alexander Korda prod., 1940; dir. Columbia, 1943; assoc. David Selznick, 1943; assoc. Hunt Stromberg-UA, 1944-45; staff dir., Enterprise 1946-47; dir., 20th-Fox, 1948-49; collab. story, The Gunfighter; assoc., Sam Spiegel, Horizon Pictures, Columbia, 1962; Harry Saltzman, Lowndes Prod., U.A. 1966-68; National General, 1969-70.
PICTURES: Passport to Suez, None Shall Escape, Pitfall, Slattery's Hurricane, Springfield Rifle, Thunder Over the Plains, House of Wax, The Stranger Wore a Gun, Bounty Hunter, Tanganyika, The Indian Fighter, Monkey on My Back, Two Headed Spy, Day of the Outlaw, Man on a String, Morgan The Pirate, The Mongols, Gold for the Caesars, Billion Dollar Brain (exec. prod. only), Play Dirty (also exec. prod.), El Condor (prod. only), The Dangerous Game.

DEUTCH, HOWARD
Director. b. New York, NY. e. Ohio State U. m. actress Lea Thompson. Son of music publisher Murray Deutch. Spent almost 10 yrs. working in various film media, including music videos and film trailer advertising, before feature directorial debut with Pretty in Pink, 1986.
PICTURES: Pretty in Pink, Some Kind of Wonderful, The Great Outdoors, Article 99, Getting Even With Dad, Grumpier Old Men.
TELEVISION: Tales from the Crypt (2 episodes; ACE Award for Dead Right).

DEUTCHMAN, IRA J.
Executive. b. Cherry Point, NC, Mar. 24, 1953. e. Northwestern U., B.S., majoring in film. Began career with Cinema 5, Ltd. serving, 1975-79, as non-theatrical sls. mgr.; dir. theatrical adv./pub./dir. acquisitions. Joined United Artists Classics, 1981 as dir. of adv./pub. 1982, left to become one of the founding partners in Cinecom Intl. Films, where headed mktg./dist. div. from inception. Resigned, Jan. 1989 to form the Deutchman Company, Inc., a production company and marketing consultancy firm. Founded and served as pres. of Fine Line Features, a division of New Line Cinema, and sr. v.p. of parent corp, 1991-95. Currenly, pres. of Redeemable Features, a New York-based prod. company. Adjunct prof. Columbia U. film dept. On advisory bds. Sundance U.S. Film Festival and the Sundance Institute.
PICTURES: Exec. Prod.: Swimming to Cambodia, Matewan (assoc. prod.), Miles From Home (co-exec. prod.), Scenes from the Class Struggle in Beverly Hills, Straight Out of Brooklyn, Waterland, The Ballad of Little Jo, Mrs. Parker and the Vicious Circle.

DEUTCHMAN, LAWRENCE SCOT
Executive. b. Bronx, NY, Dec. 10, 1960. e. Rutgers U. Wrote, prod. & dir. Mythbusters campaign. 1986-92, various positions: Entertainment Industries Council, Inc.; wrote, prod., co-dir. That's a Wrap campaign. 1986-88, board member, Public Interest Radio & Television Educational Society. 1987-88, wrote, exec. prod., post-prod. sprv., Buckle Up educational & music video (CINE Golden Eagle). 1989: EIC: An Industry in Action (writer, prod., dir.); Campaigns: Natl. Red Ribbon, Office for Substance Abuse Prevention (writer, dir., exec. prod.), Stop the Madness (co-writer, prod.). 1990, developed: Vince & Larry: The Amazing Crash Test Dummies (series, NBC), Drug Proofing Your Kids (tv special); Campaigns: Alcoholism Runs in Families, Texas Prevention Partnership (dir., exec. prod.), They Do as You Do (writer, exec. prod.). 1991: The Inhalant Problem in Texas docum. (co-exec. prod.), Inhalants: The Silent Epidemic award-winning drama (writer, co-exec. prod.), KBVO Fox Kids Club segments (writer, prod., set designer), The Incredible Crash Dummies toy property (co-creator), Ollie Odorfree property (creator). 1992-present: Pres., Dynamic Commun. Intl. Inc.; v.p. prod. & mktg., EIC. 1993: Hollywood Gets M.A.D.D. tv special (co-prod., TBS, TNT, synd.). 1994: Dinorock Time tv series (exec. prod., writer.); 1994-present, s.r., vp. prod. & mktg, EIC.

DEUTSCH, STEPHEN
Producer. b. Los Angeles, CA, June 30, 1946. e. UCLA, B.A.; Loyola Law Sch., 1974. Son of late S. Sylvan Simon. Stepson of Armand Deutsch. Private law practice before joining Rastar 1976 as asst. to Ray Stark; 1977, sr. v.p., Rastar; prod. head for SLM Inc. Film Co. entered independent prod. 1978.
PICTURES: Somewhere in Time, All the Right Moves, Russkies (co-exec. prod.), She's Out of Control, Bill & Ted's Excellent Adventure (exec. prod.), Lucky Stiff, Bill and Ted's Bogus Journey (co-exec. prod.), Body of Evidence (exec. prod.).

DEVANE, WILLIAM
Actor. b. Albany, NY, Sept. 5, 1939. Appeared in some 15 productions with N.Y. Shakespeare Festival, also B'way & off-B'way shows before heading to California for films and TV.
PICTURES: The Pursuit of Happiness (debut, 1970), The 300 Hundred Year Weekend, Lady Liberty, McCabe and Mrs. Miller, Glory Boy (My Old Man's Place), Irish Whiskey Rebellion, Report to the Commissioner, Family Plot, Marathon Man, Bad News Bears in Breaking Training, Rolling Thunder, The Dark, Yanks, Honky Tonk Freeway, Testament, Hadley's Rebellion, Vital Signs.
TELEVISION: Series: From Here to Eternity, Knots Landing, Phenom, The Monroes. Movies: Crime Club, The Bait, Fear on Trial, Red Alert, Black Beauty, Red Flag: The Ultimate Game, The Other Victim, Jane Doe, With Intent to Kill, Timestalker, Murder C.O.D., Nightmare in Columbia County, Obsessed, The President's Child. Prophet of Evil: The Ervil LeBaron Story, Rubdown, For the Love of Nancy, Falling From the Sky!: Flight 174, Robin Cook's Virus, Alistair MacLean's Night Watch. Special: The Missiles of October. Mini-Series: A Woman Named Jackie.

De VITO, DANNY
Actor, Director, Producer. b. Asbury Park, NJ, Nov. 17, 1944. m. actress Rhea Perlman. e. Oratory Prep Sch. Studied at American Acad. of Dramatic Arts. Wilfred Acad. of Hair and Beauty Culture. At 18 worked as hair dresser for 1 yr. at his sister's shop. NY stage in The Man With a Flower in His Mouth (debut, 1969), Down the Morning Line, The Line of Least Existence, The Shrinking Bride, Call Me Charlie, Comedy of Errors, Merry Wives of Windsor (NYSF). Three By Pirandello. Performance in One Flew Over the Cuckoo's Nest led to casting in the film version. Prod. short films: The Sound Sleeper (1973), Minestrone (1975).
PICTURES: Lady Liberty (debut, 1971), Hurry Up or I'll Be 30, Scalawag, One Flew Over the Cuckoo's Nest, Deadly Hero, The Van, The World's Greatest Lover, Goin' South, Going Ape, Terms of Endearment, Romancing the Stone, Johnny Dangerously, The Jewel of the Nile, Head Office, Wiseguys, Ruthless People, My Little Pony (voice), Tin Men, Throw Momma from the Train (also dir.), Twins, The War of the Roses (also dir.), Other People's Money, Batman Returns, Hoffa (also dir., co-prod.), Jack the Bear, Last Action Hero (voice), Look Who's Talking Now (voice), Reality Bites (co-prod. only), Renaissance Man, Pulp Fiction (co-exec. prod. only), Junior, Get Shorty (also co-prod.), Sunset Park (prod.), Matilda (also dir., co-prod.), Mars Attacks.
TELEVISION: Series: Taxi (Emmy & Golden Globe Awards, 1981; also dir. episodes), Mary (dir. only). Movies: Valentine, The Ratings Game (also dir.). Specials: All the Kids Do It (Afterschool Special), A Very Special Christmas Party, Two Daddies? (voice), What a Lovely Way to Spend an Evening (dir.), The Selling of Vince DeAngelo (dir.). Guest: Police Woman, Saturday Night Live, Amazing Stories (also dir.), The Simpsons (voice).

DEVLIN, DEAN
Actor, Writer, Producer. Began career azs an actor, appearing numerous film and television projects, as well as B'way production of There Must Be a Pony. Met Roland Emmerich while acting in Moon 44. Joined Emmerich as a partner at Centropolis Films.
PICTURES: Writer: Universal Soldier. Co-writer/prod.: Stargate, Independence Day.

De WITT, JOYCE
Actress. b. Wheeling, WV, April 23, 1949. e. Ball State U., B.A., theatre; UCLA, MFA in acting. Classically trained, worked in theater since 13 as actress and dir.
TELEVISION: *Series:* Three's Company. *Guest:* Baretta, The Tony Randall Show, Most Wanted, Risko, Finder of Lost Loves. *Movies:* With This Ring, Spring Fling.

DEY, SUSAN
Actress. b. Pekin, IL, Dec. 10, 1952. Signed as magazine teen model at age 15. Made professional TV debut at 17, appearing in The Partridge Family 1970.
PICTURES: Skyjacked (debut, 1972), First Love, Looker, Echo Park, That's Adequate.
TELEVISION: *Series:* The Partridge Family, Loves Me Loves Me Not, Emerald Point N.A.S., L.A. Law, Love and War. *Movies:* Terror on the Beach, Cage Without a Key, Mary Jane Harper Cried Last Night, Little Women, The Comeback Kid, The Gift of Life, Malibu, Sunset Limousine, I Love You Perfect, Bed of Lies, Lies and Lullabies (also co-prod.), Whose Child Is This? The War for Baby Jessica, Beyond Betrayal, Deadly Love.

DE YOUNG, CLIFF
Actor. b. Inglewood, CA, Feb. 12, 1947. e. California State Coll., Illinois State U. On stage in Hair, Sticks and Bones, Two By South, The Three Sisters, The Orphan.
PICTURES: Harry and Tonto, Blue Collar, Shock Treatment, Independence Day, The Hunger, Reckless, Protocol, Secret Admirer, F/X, Flight of the Navigator, Fear, Pulse, Rude Awakening, Glory, Flashback, Crackdown, Dr. Giggles, Carnosaur II, Final Frontier, The Craft, The Substitute.
TELEVISION: *Series:* Sunshine, Robocop. *Special:* Sticks and Bones. *Mini-Series:* Centennial, Master of the Game, Captains and the Kings, King, Robert Kennedy and His Times, Andersonville, Seduced By Madness. *Movies:* Sunshine, The 3000 Mile Chase, The Lindbergh Kidnapping Case, Scared Straight: Another Story, Invasion of Privacy, The Seeding of Sarah Burns, The Night That Panicked America, This Girl for Hire, The Awakening of Candra, Deadly Intentions, Sunshine Christmas, Fun and Games, Where Pigeons Go to Die, Fourth Story, Criminal Behavior, Love Can Be Murder, The Tommyknockers, Precious Victims, Heaven & Hell: North and South Book III, JAG, Element of Truth.

DIAMANT, LINCOLN
Executive, Biographer, Historian. b. New York, NY, Jan. 25, 1923. e. Columbia Coll., A.B. cum laude 1943. Cofounder, Columbia U. radio station. WKCR-FM; served in Wash. as prod., Blue Network (NBC), then in NY as CBS newswriter; 1949 joined World Pub. Co. as adv. and promo. dir.; 1952-69 worked in creative/TV dept. McCann-Erickson, Grey, then Ogilvy & Mather ad agencies (winning 6 Clio Awards). Prod. Lend Us Your Ears (Met. Museum Art broadcast series); founder, pres., Spots Alive, Inc., broadcast adv. consultants, 1969; Author, The Broadcast Communications Dictionary, Anatomy of a Television Commercial, Television's Classic Commercials, biography of Bernard Romans, Chaining the Hudson (Sons of Revolution Book Award), Stamping Our History, Yankee Doodle Days. Contrib., to Effective Advertising, to Messages and Meaning; New Routes to English; columnist Back Stage/Shoot. Member, Broadcast Pioneers, Acad. TV Arts & Sciences; v.p. Broadcast Advertising Producer's Society of America. Adjunct faculty member, Pace U., Hofstra U. Fellow, Royal Society of Arts.

DIAMOND, BERNARD
Theatre Executive. b. Chicago, IL, Jan. 24, 1918. e. U. of Indiana, U. of Minnesota. Except for military service was with Schine Theatre chain from 1940 to 1963, working up from ass't. mng., booker, buyer, dir. of personnel to gen. mgr. Then joined Loews Theatres; last position, exec. v.p. Retired, 1985.

DIAMOND, NEIL
Singer, Songwriter. b. Brooklyn, NY, Jan. 24, 1941. Many concert tours.
PICTURES: Jonathan Livingston Seagull (music), Every Which Way But Loose (music), The Last Waltz (actor), The Jazz Singer (actor, music).
TELEVISION: *Specials:* Neil Diamond... Hello Again, I Never Cared for the Sound of Being Alone, I'm Glad You're Here With Me Tonight, Greatest Hits Live, Neil Diamond's Christmas Special.

DIAZ, CAMERON
Actress. Began career as model for Elite. Feature debut was in The Mask. Received ShoWest 1996 Female Star of Tomorrow Award.
PICTURES: The Mask, Feeling Minnesota, Head Above Water, The Last Supper, She's the One.

DI CAPRIO, LEONARDO
Actor. b. Hollywood, CA, Nov. 11, 1974. Started acting at age 14 in commercials and educational films. Appeared in short film The Foot Shooting Party.

PICTURES: Critters III (debut, 1991), Poison Ivy, This Boy's Life, What's Eating Gilbert Grape (Natl. Board of Review, Chicago Film Critics & LA Film Critics Awards, Acad. Award nom.), The Quick and the Dead, The Basketball Diaries, Total Eclipse, Marvin's Room, Romeo and Juliet.
TELEVISION: *Series:* Growing Pains, Parenthood.

DICKERSON, ERNEST
(A.S.C.): Cinematographer, Director. b. Newark, NJ, 1952. e. Howard U., architecture, NYU, grad. film school. First job, filming surgical procedures for Howard U. medical school. At NYU film school shot classmate Spike Lee's student films Sarah, and Joe's Bed Stuy Barbershop: We Cut Heads. Also shot Nike commercial and several music videos including Bruce Springsteen's Born in the U.S.A., Patti LaBelle's Stir It Up and Miles Davis' Tutu; and Branford Marsalis' Royal Garden Blues directed by Spike Lee. Admitted into Amer. Soc. of Cinematographers in 1989.
PICTURES: *Cinematographer:* The Brother From Another Planet, She's Gotta Have It (also cameo), Krush Groove, School Daze, Raw, Do the Right Thing, Def By Temptation, The Laser Man, Mo' Better Blues, Jungle Fever, Sex Drugs Rock & Roll, Cousin Bobby (co-photog.), Malcolm X. *Director:* Juice (also co-s.p., story), Surviving the Game, Tales Fromt he Crypt Presents Demon Knight.
TELEVISION: Do it Acapella (dir.; PBS).

DICKINSON, ANGIE
Actress. r.n. Angeline Brown. b. Kulm, ND, Sept. 30, 1931. e. Immaculate Heart Coll., Glendale Coll., secretarial course. Beauty contest winner.
PICTURES: Lucky Me (debut in bit part, 1954), Man With the Gun, The Return of Jack Slade, Tennessee's Partner, The Black Whip, Hidden Guns, Tension at Table Rock, Gun the Man Down, Calypso Joe, China Gate, Shoot Out at Medicine Bend, Cry Terror, I Married a Woman, Rio Bravo, The Bramble Bush, Ocean's 11, A Fever in the Blood, The Sins of Rachel Cade, Jessica, Rome Adventure, Captain Newman M.D., The Killers, The Art of Love, Cast a Giant Shadow, The Chase, The Poppy is Also a Flower, The Last Challenge, Point Blank, Sam Whiskey, Some Kind of a Nut, Young Billy Young, Pretty Maids All in a Row, The Resurrection of Zachary Wheeler, The Outside Man, Big Bad Mama, Klondike Fever, Dressed to Kill, Charlie Chan and the Curse of the Dragon Queen, Death Hunt, Big Bad Mama II, Even Cowgirls Get the Blues, The Maddening, Sabrina, The Sun, The Moon and The Stars.
TELEVISION: *Series:* Police Woman, Cassie & Co. *Movies:* The Love War, Thief, See the Man Run, The Norliss Tapes, Pray for the Wildcats, A Sensitive Passionate Man, Overboard, The Suicide's Wife, Dial M for Murder, One Shoe Makes It Murder, Jealousy, A Touch of Scandal, Stillwatch, Police Story: The Freeway Killings, Once Upon a Texas Train, Prime Target, Treacherous Crossing, Danielle Steel's Remembrance. *Mini-Series:* Pearl, Hollywood Wives, Wild Palms.

DICKINSON, WOOD
Executive, Exhibitor. r.n. Glen Wood Dickinson III. b. Fairway, KS, Sept. 14, 1952. e. Texas Christian U (BFA Communications, MA Film). CEO and pres. Dickinson, Inc. and Dickinson Operating Company, commonly known as Dickinson Theatres.

DILLER, BARRY
Executive. b. San Francisco, CA, Feb. 2, 1942. Joined ABC in April, 1966, as asst. to v.p. in chg. programming. In 1968, made exec. asst. to v.p. in chg. programming and dir. of feature films. In 1969, named v.p., feature films and program dev., east coast. In 1971, made v.p., Feature Films and Circle Entertainment, a unit of ABC Entertainment, responsible for selecting, producing and scheduling The Tuesday Movie of the Week, The Wednesday Movie of the Week, and Circle Film original features for airing on ABC-TV, as well as for acquisition and scheduling of theatrical features for telecasting on ABC Sunday Night Movie and ABC Monday Night Movie. In 1973, named v.p. in chg. of prime time TV for ABC Entertainment. In 1974 joined Paramount Pictures as bd. chmn. and chief exec. officer. 1983, named pres. of Gulf & Western Entertainment and Communications Group, while retaining Paramount titles. Resigned from Paramount in 1984 to join 20th Century-Fox as bd. chmn. and chief. exec. officer. Named chmn. & CEO of Fox, Inc. (comprising 20th Fox Film Corp., Fox TV Stations & Fox Bdcstg. Co.), Oct., 1985. Named to bd., News Corp. Ltd., June, 1987. Resigned from Fox in Feb., 1992. Named CEO of QVC Network Inc. TV shopping concern. Resigned QVC in 1995. CEO and bd. chair, Silver King Communications, Inc, Aug. 1995. Bd. chairman, Home Shopping Network, Nov. 1995.

DILLER, PHYLLIS
Comedienne, Actress. b. Lima, OH, July 17, 1917. r.n. Phyllis Ada Driver. e. Sherwood Music Sch., 1935-37; Bluffton Coll., OH, 1938-39. Started as publicist at San Francisco radio sta-

tion before becoming nightclub comic at the age of 37. Recordings: Phyllis Diller Laughs, Are You Ready for Phyllis Diller?, Great Moments of Comedy, Born to Sing. Performed with many U.S. symphonies, 1971-90.
AUTHOR: Phyllis Diller's Housekeeping Hints, Phyllis Diller's Marriage Manual, Phyllis Diller's The Complete Mother, The Joys of Aging and How to Avoid Them.
THEATER: Hello Dolly! (B'way), Everybody Loves Opal, Happy Birthday, The Dark at the Top of the Stairs, Subject to Change, The Wizard of Oz, Nunsense, Cinderella.
PICTURES: Splendor in the Grass (debut, 1961), Boy Did I Get a Wrong Number!, The Fat Spy, Mad Monster Party (voice), Eight on the Lam, Did You Hear the One About the Traveling Saleslady?, The Private Navy of Sgt. O'Farrell, The Adding Machine, The Sunshine Boys (cameo), A Pleasure Doing Business, Pink Motel, Pucker Up and Bark Like a Dog, Dr. Hackenstein, Friend to Friend, The Nutcracker Prince (voice), The Boneyard, Wisecracks, Happily Ever After (voice), The Perfect Man, The Silence of the Hams.
TELEVISION: Series: Showstreet, The Pruitts of Southampton, The Beautiful Phyllis Diller Show. Specials: The Phyllis Diller Special, An Evening With Phyllis Diller, Phyllis Diller's 102nd Birthday Party. Guest: Laugh In, Love American Style, The Muppet Show, The Love Boat, CHiPs, etc.

DILLMAN, BRADFORD
Actor. b. San Francisco, CA, April 14, 1930. m. actress-model Suzy Parker. e. Yale U., 1951. Studied at Actors Studio.
Author: Inside the New York Giants.
THEATER: The Scarecrow (1953), Third Person, Long Day's Journey into Night (premiere; Theatre World Award), The Fun Couple.
PICTURES: A Certain Smile (debut, 1958), In Love and War, Compulsion, Crack in the Mirror, Circle of Deception, Sanctuary, Francis of Assisi, A Rage to Live, The Plainsman, Sergeant Ryker, Helicopter Spies, Jigsaw, The Bridge at Remagen, Suppose They Gave a War and Nobody Came, Brother John, The Mephisto Waltz, Escape from the Planet of the Apes, The Resurrection of Zachary Wheeler, The Iceman Cometh, The Way We Were, Chosen Survivors, 99 and 44/100% Dead, Gold, Bug, Mastermind, The Enforcer, The Lincoln Conspiracy, Amsterdam Kill, The Swarm, Piranha, Love and Bullets, Guyana: Cult of the Damned, Sudden Impact, Treasure of the Amazon, Man Outside, Lords of the Deep, Heroes Stand Alone.
TELEVISION: Series: Court-Martial, King's Crossing, Dynasty. Movies: Fear No Evil, Black Water Gold, Longstreet, Five Desperate Women, Revenge, Eyes of Charles Sand, The Delphi Bureau, Moon of the Wolf, Deliver Us From Evil, Murder or Mercy, Disappearance of Flight 412, Adventures of the Queen, Force Five, Widow, Street Killing, Kingston: The Power Play, The Hostage Heart, Jennifer: A Woman's Story, Before and After, The Memory of Eva Ryker, Tourist, The Legend of Walks Far Woman, Covenant, Heart of Justice.

DILLON, KEVIN
Actor. b. Mamaroneck, NY, Aug. 19, 1965. Younger brother of actor Matt Dillon. Stage work includes Dark at the Top of the Stairs, The Indian Wants the Bronx.
PICTURES: No Big Deal, Heaven Help Us, Platoon, Remote Control, The Rescue, The Blob, War Party, Immediate Family, The Doors, A Midnight Clear, No Escape.
TELEVISION: Movie: When He's Not a Stranger. Special: Dear America: Letters Home from Vietnam (reader). Guest: Tales From the Crypt.

DILLON, MATT
Actor. b. New Rochelle, NY, Feb. 18, 1964. Discovered at age 14 in junior high school by casting dir. who cast him in Over the Edge. Brother is actor Kevin Dillon.
THEATER: NY: The Boys of Winter (B'way debut, 1985).
PICTURES: Over the Edge (debut, 1979), Little Darlings, My Bodyguard, Liar's Moon, Tex, The Outsiders, Rumble Fish, The Flamingo Kid, Target, Rebel, Native Son, The Big Town, Kansas, Bloodhounds of Broadway, Drugstore Cowboy, A Kiss Before Dying, Singles, Mr. Wonderful, The Saint of Fort Washington, Golden Gate, To Die For, Frankie Starlight, Beautiful Girls, Grace of My Heart, Albino Alligator.
TELEVISION: Movie: Women & Men 2: In Love There Are No Rules (Return to Kansas City). Specials: The Great American Fourth of July and Other Disasters, Dear America: Letters Home From Vietnam (reader).

DILLON, MELINDA
Actress. b. Hope, AR, Oct. 13, 1939. e. Chicago Sch. of Drama, Art Inst., Goodman Theatre. Launched career on Broadway in original prod. of Who's Afraid of Virginia Woolf? (Theatre World Award, Tony Award nom., Drama Critics Award).
PICTURES: The April Fools (debut, 1969), Bound for Glory (People's Choice Award), Slap Shot, Close Encounters of the Third Kind (Acad. Award nom.), F.I.S.T., Absence of Malice (Acad. Award nom.), A Christmas Story, Songwriter, Harry

and the Hendersons, Staying Together, Spontaneous Combustion, Capt. America, The Prince of Tides, Sioux City, To Fong Woo—Thanks for Everything Julie Newmar, How to Make an American Quilt, Dorothy Day, The Effects of Magic.
TELEVISION: Series: Paul Sills Story Theatre. Guest: Twilight Zone, The Defenders, Bonanza, East Side West Side, The Paul Sand Show, The Jeffersons, Good Morning America, The Today Show, Dick Cavett Show, Dinah Shore Show, Picket Fences, The Client. Mini-Series: Space. Movies: Critical List, Transplant, Marriage is Alive and Well, The Shadow Box, Fallen Angel, Hellinger's Law, Right of Way, Shattered Spirits, Shattered Innocence, Nightbreaker, Judgment Day: The John List Story, Slow Bleed, State of Emergency, Confessions: Two Faces of Evil, Naomi & Wynonna: Love Can Build a Bridge.

Di PIETRA, ROSEMARY
Executive. Joined Paramount Pictures in 1976, rising through ranks to become director-corporate administration. 1985, promoted to exec. dir.-corporate administration.

DiNOVI, DENISE
Producer. b. Canada. Started as journalist, reporter, film critic in Toronto before entering film industry as unit publicist. 1980, joined Montreal's Film Plan production co. as co-prod., assoc. prod. and exec. in charge of prod. working on such movies as Visiting Hours, Going Berserk, Videodrome. Became exec. v.p. of prod. at New World, then head of Tim Burton Prods., 1989-92.
PICTURES: Heathers, Edward Scissorhands, Meet the Applegates, Batman Returns, The Nightmare Before Christmas, Cabin Boy, Ed Wood, James and the Giant Peach.

DISHY, BOB
Actor. b. Brooklyn, NY. e. Syracuse U.
THEATER: Damn Yankees, From A to Z, Second City, Flora the Red Menace, By Jupiter, Something Different, The Goodbye People, The Good Doctor, The Unknown Soldier at His Wife, The Creation of the World and Other Business, An American Millionaire, Sly Fox, Murder at Howard Johnson's, Grown Ups, Cafe Crown.
PICTURES: The Tiger Makes Out, Lovers and Other Strangers, The Big Bus, I Wonder Who's Killing Her Now?, The Last Married Couple in America, First Family, Author! Author!, Brighton Beach Memoirs, Critical Condition, Stay Tuned, Used People, My Boyfriend's Back, Don Juan DeMarco.
TELEVISION: Series: That Was the Week That Was. Specials: Story Theatre (dir.), The Cafeteria. Guest: The Comedy Zone. Movies: It Couldn't Happen to a Nicer Guy, Thicker Than Blood: The Larry McLinden Story.

DISNEY, ROY E.
Producer, Director. Writer, Cameraman, Film editor. b. Los Angeles, CA, Jan. 10, 1930. e. Pomona Coll., CA. 1951 started as page, NBC-TV. Asst. film editor Dragnet TV series. 1952-78, Walt Disney Prods., Burbank, Calif., various capacities; vice chmn. of the board, The Walt Disney Co.; bd. chmn., Shamrock Holdings, Inc., bd. dir., Walt Disney Co.
PICTURES: Perri, Mysteries of the Deep, Pacific High.
TELEVISION: Walt Disney's Wonderful World of Color, The Hound That Thought He Was A Raccoon, Sancho, The Homing Steer, The Silver Fox and Sam Davenport, Wonders of the Water World, Legend of Two Gypsy Dogs, Adventure in Wildwood Heart, The Postponed Wedding, Zorro series, An Otter in the Family, My Family is a Menagerie, Legend of El Blanco, Pancho, The Fastest Paw in the West, The Owl That Didn't Give A Hoot, Varda the Peregrine Falcon, Cristobalito, The Calypso Colt, Three Without Fear, Hamade and the Pirates, Chango, Guardian of the Mayan Treasure, Nosey the Sweetest Skunk in the World, Mustang!, Call It Courage, Ringo the Refugee Raccoon, Shokee the Everglades Panther, Deacon the High-Noon Dog, Wise One, Whale's Tooth, Track of African Bongo, Dorsey the Mail-Carrying Dog.

DIXON, BARBARA
Executive. b. Pasadena CA. e. USC, grad. degree from Johns Hopkins U. Served as staff member of Senate Judiciary Committee and was dir. of legislation for Sen. Birch Bayh, 1974-79. Left to become dir. of Office of Government & Public Affairs of Natl. Transportation Safety Board. Named v.p., Fratelli Group, p.r. firm in Washington; took leave of absence in 1984 to serve as deputy press secty. to Democratic V.P. candidate, Geraldine Ferraro. In 1985 joined Motion Picture Assn. of America as v.p. for public affairs.

DIXON, DONNA
Actress. b. Alexandria, VA, July 20, 1957. m. actor-writer Dan Aykroyd. e. Studied anthropology and medicine, Mary Washington U. Left to become a model, both on magazine covers and in TV commercials (Vitalis, Max Factor, Gillette).
PICTURES: Dr. Detroit, Twilight Zone--The Movie, Spies Like Us, The Couch Trip, It Had To Be You, Speed Zone, Lucky Stiff, Wayne's World.

TELEVISION: *Series*: Bosom Buddies, Berrenger's. *Movies*: Mickey Spillane's Margin for Murder, No Man's Land, Beverly Hills Madam. *Specials*: Women Who Rate a "10," The Shape of Things, The Rodney Dangerfield Show: I Can't Take it No More.

DIXON, WHEELER WINSTON
Educator, Writer, Filmmaker. b. New Brunswick, NJ, March 12, 1950. e. Rutgers U. In 1960s asst. writer for Time/Life publications; also writer for Interview magazine. 1976, directed TV commercials in NY. One season with TVTV, Los Angeles, as post-prod. suprv. 1978, formed Deliniator Films, Inc., serving as exec. prod./dir. Since 1988 has directed film program at Univ. of Nebraska, where holds rank of tenured full prof. and chair, Film Studies Prog.; received Rockefeller Foundation grant. Author: The `B' Directors, 1985; The Cinematic Vision of F. Scott Fitzgerald, 1986; PRC: A History of Producer's Releasing Corp., 1986; books on Freddie Francis, Terence Fisher, Reginald Le Borg, 1992-93. Prod., dir. with Gwendolyn Audrey-Foster: Women Who Made the Movies (video). Books: The Early Film Criticism of Francois Truffaut, Re-Viewing British Cinema, 1900-92, It Looks at You, 1994. Prod/Dir: What Can I Do?, Squatters. 1992, guest programmer at the British Film Inst./Natl. Film Theatre. 1993, Distinguished Teaching Award. Invited lecturer at Yale, 1995.

DMYTRYK, EDWARD
Director. b. Grand Forks, B.C., Canada, Sept. 4, 1908. Entered employ Paramount 1923, working as messenger after school. Film editor 1930-39. One of the ``Hollywood Ten" who was held in contempt by the House UnAmerican Activities Comm. 1947. The only one to recant. Autobiography: It's a Hell of a Life But Not a Bad Living (1979).
PICTURES: The Hawk (debut, 1935), Television Spy, Emergency Squad, Golden Gloves, Mystery Sea Raider, Her First Romance, The Devil Commands, Under Age, Sweetheart of the Campus, The Blonde From Singapore, Confessions of Boston Blackie, Secrets of the Lone Wolf, Counter-Espionage, Seven Miles From Alcatraz, Hilter's Children, The Falcon Strikes Back, Behind the Rising Sun, Captive Wild Woman Tender Comrade, Murder My Sweet, Back to Bataan, Cornered, Till the End of Time, Crossfire (Acad. Award nom.), So Well Remembered, Obsession (The Hidden Room), Give Us This Day, Mutiny, The Sniper, Eight Iron Men, The Juggler, The Caine Mutiny, Broken Lance, The End of the Affair, The Left Hand of God, Soldier of Fortune, The Mountain (also prod.), Raintree County, The Young Lions, Warlock (also prod.), The Blue Angel, The Reluctant Saint (It.), Walk on the Wild Side, The Carpetbaggers, Where Love Has Gone, Mirage, Alvarez Kelly, Shalako, Anzio, Bluebeard, The Human Factor, He Is My Brother.

DOBSON, KEVIN
Actor. b. New York, NY, Mar. 18, 1943.
PICTURES: Love Story, Bananas, Klute, The Anderson Tapes, The French Connection, Carnal Knowledge, Midway, All Night Long.
TELEVISION: *Series*: Kojak, Shannon, Knots Landing (also dir. 9 episodes). *Movies*: The Immigrants, Transplant, Orphan Train, Hardhat and Legs, Reunion, Mark I Love You, Mickey Splillane's Margin for Murder, Money Power Murder (also prod.), Casey's Gift: For Love of a Child, Sweet Revenge, Fatal Friendship, Dirty Work, House of Secrets and Lies, The Conviction of Kitty Dodds, If Someone Had Known. *Guest*: The Nurses, The Doctors, Greatest Heroes of the Bible.

DOCTOROW, ERIC
Executive. Pres., Home Video Division of Viacom, Inc. Worldwide Video.

DOERFLER, RONALD J.
Executive. e. Fairleigh Dickinson Univ. Became CPA in 1967. 1972, received M.B.A. from Fairleigh Dickinson. Joined Capital Cities 1969 as asst. controller. Became treas. in 1977; v.p. & CFO, 1980. 1983, named sr. v.p.,.then sr. v.p. & CFO.

DOHERTY, SHANNEN
Actress. b. Memphis, TN, April 12, 1971. On stage in The Mound Builders.
PICTURES: Night Shift, The Secret of NIMH (voice), Girls Just Want to Have Fun, Heathers, Freeze Frame, Blindfold, Mall Rats.
TELEVISION: *Series*: Little House on the Prairie, Our House, Beverly Hills 90210. *Movies*: The Other Lover, Obsessed, Jailbreakers, A Burning Passion: The Margaret Mitchell Story. *Mini-Series*: Robert Kennedy and His Times. *Pilot*: His and Hers. *Guest*: 21 Jump Street.

DOLGEN, JONATHAN L.
Executive. b. New York, NY, Apr. 27, 1945. e. Cornell U., NYU Sch. of Law. Began career with Wall Street law firm, Fried, Frank, Harris, Shriver & Jacobson. In 1976 joined Columbia Pictures Industries as asst. gen. counsel and deputy gen.

counsel. 1979, named sr. v.p. in chg. of worldwide business affairs; 1980, named exec. v.p. Joined Columbia m.p. div., 1981; named pres. of Columbia Pay-Cable & Home Entertainment Group. Also pres. Columbia Pictures domestic operations, overseeing Music Group. 1985, joined 20th-Fox in newly created position of sr. exec. v.p. for telecommunications. Became pres. of Sony Motion Picture Group, 1991. Appointed chmn. Viacom Entertainment Group, 1994.

DONAHUE, ELINOR
Actress. b. Tacoma, WA, Apr. 19, 1937.
PICTURES: Mr. Big, Tenth Avenue Angel, Unfinished Dance, Three Daring Daughters, Love is Better Than Ever, Girls Town, Pretty Woman, Freddy's Dead: The Final Nightmare.
TELEVISION: *Series*: Father Knows Best, The Andy Griffith Show, Many Happy Returns, The Odd Couple, Mulligan's Stew, Please Stand By, Days of Our Lives,The New Adventures of Beans Baxter, Get a Life. *Pilot*: The Grady Nutt Show. *Guest*: One Day at a Time, Sweepstakes$, The Golden Girls. *Movies*: In Name Only, Gidget Gets Married, Mulligan's Stew (pilot), Doctors' Private Lives, Condominium, High School U.S.A. *Special*: Father Knows Best Reunion.

DONAHUE, PHIL
Television Host. b. Cleveland, OH, Dec. 21, 1935. e. Notre Dame, BBA. m. actress Marlo Thomas. Worked as check sorter, Albuquerque Natl. Bank, 1957, then as announcer at KYW-TV & AM, Cleveland; news dir. WABJ radio, Adrian, MI; morning newscaster WHIO-TV. Interviews with Jimmy Hoffa and Billy Sol Estes picked up nationally by CBS. Host of Conversation Piece, phone-in talk show. Debuted The Phil Donahue Show, daytime talk show in Dayton, Ohio, 1967. Syndicated 2 years later. Moved to Chicago, 1974. Host, Donahue, now in 165 outlets in U.S. In 1979 a mini-version of show became 3-times-a-week segment on NBC's Today Show. Winner of several Emmys. *Books*: Donahue: My Own Story (1980), The Human Animal (1985).

DONAHUE, TROY
Actor. r.n. Merle Johnson, Jr. b. New York, NY, Jan. 27, 1937. e. Bayport H.S., N.Y. Military Acad. Columbia U., Journalism. Directed, wrote, acted in school plays. Summer stock, Bucks County Playhouse, Sayville Playhouse; contract, Warner Brothers, 1959.
PICTURES: Man Afraid (debut, 1957), The Tarnished Angels, This Happy Feeling, The Voice in the Mirror, Live Fast Die Young, Monster on the Campus, Summer Love, Wild Heritage, The Perfect Furlough, Imitation of Life, A Summer Place, The Crowded Sky, Parrish, Susan Slade, Rome Adventure, Palm Springs Weekend, A Distant Trumpet, My Blood Runs Cold, Blast-Off! (Those Fantastic Flying Fools), Come Spy With Me, Sweet Savior, Cockfighter, Seizure, The Godfather Part II, Tin Man, Grandview U.S.A., Low Blow, Cyclone, Deadly Prey, American Revenge, Dr. Alien (I Was a Teenage Sex Mutant), Sexpot, Hard Rock Nightmare, Bad Blood, John Travis, Solar Survivor, The Chilling, The Housewarming, Deadly Spy Games, Assault of the Party Nerds, Deadly Diamonds, Deadly Embrace, Cry-Baby, Double Trouble.
TELEVISION: *Series*: Hawaiian Eye, Surfside 6. *Guest*: Matt Houston. *Movies*: Split Second to an Epitaph, The Loneliest Profession, Malibu.

DONALDSON, ROGER
Director. b. Ballarat, Australia, Nov. 15, 1945. Emigrated to New Zealand at 19. Established still photography business; then began making documentaries. Directed Winners and Losers, a series of short dramas for NZ-TV.
PICTURES: Sleeping Dogs (also prod.), Smash Palace (also s.p. prod.), The Bounty, Marie, No Way Out, Cocktail, Cadillac Man (also prod.), White Sands, The Getaway, Species.

DONEN, STANLEY
Director, Producer, Choreographer. b. Columbia, SC, April 13, 1924. e. USC. Former dancer, B'way debut 1940 in chorus of Pal Joey starring Gene Kelly. Assisted Kelly as choreog. on stage prod. of Best Foot Forward; hired by MGM to repeat duties in film version. Choreographer or co-choreographer on such films as Cover Girl, Holiday in Mexico, This Time for Keeps, A Date With Judy, Take Me Out to the Ballgame (also co-story credit).
PICTURES: *Director*: On the Town (debut, 1949; co-dir. with Gene Kelly), Royal Wedding, Singin' in the Rain (co-dir., co-choreog. with Gene Kelly), Fearless Fagan, Love Is Better Than Ever, Give a Girl a Break (also co-choreog.), Seven Brides for Seven Brothers, Deep in My Heart (also co-choreog.), It's Always Fair Weather (co-dir., co-choreog. with Gene Kelly), Funny Face, The Pajama Game (co-dir., co-prod. with George Abbott), Kiss Them for Me. *Director-Producer*: Indiscreet, Damn Yankees (co-dir., co-prod. with George Abbott), Once More With Feeling, Surprise Package, The Grass Is Greener, Charade, Arabesque, Two for the Road, Bedazzled, Staircase, The Little Prince, Lucky Lady (dir. only), Movie Movie, Saturn 3, Blame It on Rio.

DONIGER, WALTER
Writer, Director, Producer. b. New York NY. e. Valley Forge Military Academy, Duke U., Harvard U. Graduate Business Sch. Entered m.p. business as writer later writer-prod-dir. Wrote documentaries in Army Air Forces M.P. Unit in W.W.II. WGA award nominee and other awards.
PICTURES: Rope of Sand, Desperate Search, Cease Fire, Safe At Home (dir.), House of Women (dir.), Duffy of San Quentin (dir.), Along the Great Divide, Tokyo Joe, Alaska Seas, Steel Cage (dir.), Steel Jungle (dir.), Hold Back the Night, Guns of Fort Petticoat, Unwed Mother (dir.), Stone Cold (exec. prod.).
TELEVISION: Series: Delvecchio, Mad Bull, Switch, Moving On, Baa Baa Blacksheep, McCloud, The Man and the City, Sarge, Owen Marshall, Peyton Place, Mr. Novak, The Greatest Show on Earth, Travels of Jaimie McPheeters, Outlaws, Hong Kong, Checkmate, Bat Masterson, The Web, Bold Venture, Tombstone Territory, Maverick, Rough Riders, Lockup, Dick Powell, The Survivors, Bracken's World, Bold Ones, Kung Fu, Barnaby Jones, Marcus Welby, Lucas Tanner, etc.

DONNELLY, DONAL
Actor. b. Bradford, Eng. July 6, 1931. Studied for theatre at the Dublin Gate Theatre.
THEATER: NY Theatre: Philadelphia Here I Come (B'way debut, 1966), Joe Egg, Sleuth (NY and U.S. tour), The Elephant Man, The Faith-Healer, The Chalk Garden, My Astonishing Self, Big Maggie, Execution of Justice, Sherlock's Last Case, Ghetto, Dancing at Lughnasa, Translations.
PICTURES: Rising of the Moon (1957), Gideon's Day, Shake Hands With the Devil, Young Cassidy, The Knack, Up Jumped a Swagman, The Mind of Mr. Soames, Waterloo, The Dead, The Godfather Part III, Squanto: A Warrior's Tale, Korea.
TELEVISION: Juno and the Paycock (BBC, 1958), Home Is the Hero, The Venetian Twins, The Plough and the Stars, Playboy of the Western World, Sergeant Musgrave's Dance, Yes-Honestly (series).

DONNELLY, RALPH E.
Executive. b. Lynbrook, NY, Jan. 20, 1932. e. Bellmore, NY public school; W. C. Mepham H.S., 1949. Worked for Variety (publication) as writer, 1950; Long Island Press as daily columnist, 1951; joined Associated Independent Theatres, 1953, as gen. mgr.; later film buyer; in 1973 left to become independent buyer and booker for Creative Films; film buyer and v.p., RKO/Stanley Warner Theatres, 1976-79; pres. & gen. mgr. for Cinema 5 Ltd. circuit, N.Y., 1980-87; 1987-93, exec. v.p. City Cinemas, N.Y. Now chmn. of Cinema Connection.

DONNER, CLIVE
Director. b. London, Eng., Jan 21, 1926. Ent. m.p. ind. 1942. Asst. film ed. Denhem Studios, 1942. Dir. London stage: The Formation Dancers, The Front Room Boys, Kennedy's Children (also NY). Film editor: A Christmas Carol (Scrooge), The Card (The Promoter), Genevieve, Man With a Million (The Million Pound Note), The Purple Plain, I Am a Camera.
PICTURES: The Secret Place (debut, 1957), Heart of a Child, Marriage of Convenience, The Sinister Man, Some People, The Caretaker (The Guest), Nothing But the Best, What's New Pussycat?, Luv, Here We Go Round the Mulberry Bush (also prod.), Alfred the Great, Old Dracula (Vampira), The Nude Bomb, Charlie Chan and the Curse of the Dragon Queen, Stealing Heaven.
TELEVISION: Danger Man, Sir Francis Drake, Mighty and Mystical, British Institutions, Tempo, Spectre, The Thief of Baghdad, Oliver Twist, Rogue Male, The Scarlet Pimpernel, Arthur the King, To Catch a King, Three Hostages, She Fell Among Thieves, A Christmas Carol, Dead Man's Folly, Babes in Toyland, Not a Penny More Not a Penny Less, Coup de Foudre (Love at First Sight), Terror Strikes the Class Reunion (For Better or Worse), Charlemagne.

DONNER, RICHARD
Director. b. New York, NY, 1939. Began career as actor off-B'way. Worked with director Martin Ritt on TV production of Maugham's Of Human Bondage. Moved to California 1958, directing commercials, industrial films and documentaries. First TV drama: Wanted: Dead or Alive.
PICTURES: X-15 (debut, 1961), Salt and Pepper, Twinky (Lola), The Omen, Superman, Inside Moves, The Final Conflict (exec. prod. only), The Toy (also exec. prod.), Ladyhawke (also prod.), The Goonies (also prod.), Lethal Weapon (also prod.), The Lost Boys (exec. prod. only), Scrooged (also prod.), Lethal Weapon 2 (also prod.), Delirious (exec. prod. only), Radio Flyer, Lethal Weapon 3 (also prod.), Free Willy (co-exec. prod. only), Maverick (also prod.), Tales From the Crypt Presents Demon Knight (co-exec. prod. only), Assassins (also prod.).
TELEVISION: Series episodes: Have Gun Will Travel, Perry Mason, Cannon, Get Smart, The Fugitive, Kojak, Bronk, Gilligan's Island, Man From U.N.C.L.E., Wild Wild West, Tales From the Crypt, Two Fisted Tales, Twilight Zone, The Banana Splits, Combat. Movies: Lucas Tanner (pilot), Sarah T.: Portrait

of a Teen-Age Alcoholic, Senior Year, A Shadow in the Streets, Tales From the Crypt (exec. prod.; also dir. episode: Dig That Cat... He's Real Gone).

D'ONOFRIO, VINCENT PHILLIP
Actor. b. Brooklyn, NY, 1960. Studied acting with the American Stanislavsky Theatre in NY, appearing in Of Mice and Men, The Petrified Forest, Sexual Perversity in Chicago, and The Indian Wants the Bronx.
THEATER: B'way: Open Admissions.
PICTURES: The First Turn On! (debut, 1984), Full Metal Jacket, Adventures in Babysitting, Mystic Pizza, Signs of Life, The Blood of Heroes, Crooked Hearts, Dying Young, Fires Within, Naked Tango, JFK, The Player, Desire, Household Saints, Mr. Wonderful, Being Human, Ed Wood, Imaginary Crimes, Stuart Saves His Family, Strange Days, Feeling Minnesota.

DONOHOE, AMANDA
Actress. b. England, 1962. e. Francis Holland Sch. for Girls, Central Sch. of Speech & Drama. Member of Royal Exchange Theatre in Manchester. B'way dbut 1995 in Uncle Vanya.
PICTURES: Foreign Body (debut, 1986), Castaway, The Lair of the White Worm, The Rainbow, Tank Malling, Diamond Skulls (Dark Obsession), Paper Mask, The Madness of King George.
TELEVISION: Series: L.A. Law (Golden Globe Award). Movies: Married to Murder, Shame, It's Nothing Personal (also co-exec. prod.), The Substitute, Shame II: The Secret (also co-exec. prod.). Special: Game Set and Match (Mystery!).

DONOVAN, ARLENE
Producer. b. Kentucky. e. Stratford Coll., VA. Worked in publishing before entering industry as asst. to late dir. Robert Rosen on Cocoa Beach, uncompleted at his death. Worked as story editor, Columbia Pictures. 1969-82, literary head of m.p. dept. for ICM; involved in book publishing as well as stage and screen projects.
PICTURES: Still of the Night, Places in the Heart, Nadine, The House on Carroll Street (co-exec. prod.), Billy Bathgate.

DONOVAN, HENRY B.
Executive, Producer. b. Boston, MA. Entered m.p. ind. for RKO Pathe Studios, property master, special effects dir., unit mgr., asst. dir., prod. mgr.; worked on over 310 pictures; Harry Sherman, Hopalong Cassidy features (for Paramount). 10 yrs., U.S. Army Signal Corps, as head of dept. of California studios prod. training m.p.; pres.: Telemount Pictures, Inc. Prod., dir., writer Cowboy G Men (TV series). Wrote: Corkscrewed (novel), 7 Zane Grey westerns for Paramount.
PICTURES: Hopalong Cassidy Features, Gone with the Wind, Becky Sharp, Our Flag (dir.), Magic Lady (13 one-reel features), others. Cowboy G Men (prod., writer; 39 films).
TELEVISION: programming, financing, distribution. Global Scope; International TV; Dist., Financing, programming; sls. consultant, Intl. TV & motion pictures. Cable TV & distribution & program development, collector of movie memorabilia; DBS TV programming & financing: production software. Worldwide TV consultant. Created Silicon Valley for satellite B.D. Frontier Lawyer: Historical United States of America.

DONOVAN, TATE
Actor. b. New York, NY, 1964. Raised in New Jersey. Studied acting at USC. Worked as still photographer for two Mutual of Omaha documentaries.
THEATER: Ruffian on the Stair, The American Plan, The Rhythm of Torn Stars, Bent. B'way: Picnic.
PICTURES: SpaceCamp, Clean and Sober, Dead Bang, Memphis Belle, Love Potion No. 9, Ethan Frome, Equinox, Holy Matrimony.
TELEVISION: Series: Partners. Movies: Not My Kid, Into Thin Air, A Case of Deadly Force, Nutcracker: Money Madness Murder. HBO Special: Vietnam War Stories.

DOOHAN, JAMES
Actor. b. Vancouver, B.C., Canada, Mar. 3, 1920. WWII capt. in Royal Canadian Artillery. 1946 won scholarship to Neighborhood Playhouse in NY and later taught there. 1953, returned to Canada to live in Toronto, becoming engaged in acting career on radio, TV and in films. Went to Hollywood and chief fame as Chief Engineer Scott in TV series, Star Trek.
PICTURES: The Wheeler Dealers, The Satan Bug, Bus Riley's Back in Town, Pretty Maids All in a Row, Star Trek—The Motion Picture, Star Trek II: The Wrath of Khan, Star Trek III: The Search for Spock, Star Trek IV: The Voyage Home, Star Trek V: The Final Frontier, Star Trek VI: The Undiscovered Country, Double Trouble, National Lampoon's Loaded Weapon 1, Star Trek: Generations.
TELEVISION: Series: Star Trek. Guest: Hazel, Bonanza, The Virginia, Gunsmoke, Peyton Place, The Fugitive, Marcus Welby MD, Ben Casey, Bewitched, Fantasy Island, etc. Movie: Scalplock.

DOOLEY, PAUL
Actor. b. Parkersburg, WV, Feb. 22, 1928. Began career on
NY stage in Threepenny Opera. Later member of Second City.
B'way credits include The Odd Couple, Adaptation/Next, The
White House Murder Case, Hold Me, etc. Co-creator and
writer for The Electric Company on PBS. Owns co. called All
Over Creation.
PICTURES: What's So Bad About Feeling Good? (debut,
1968), The Out-of-Towners, Death Wish, The Gravy Train,
Slap Shot, A Wedding, A Perfect Couple, Breaking Away, Rich
Kids, Popeye, Health (also co-s.p.), Paternity, Endangered
Species, Kiss Me Goodbye, Strange Brew, Going Berserk,
Sixteen Candles, Big Trouble, O.C. and Stiggs, Monster in the
Closet, Last Rites, Flashback, Shakes the Clown, The Player,
My Boyfriend's Back, A Dangerous Woman, The Underneath,
God's Lonely Man.
TELEVISION: Specials: Faerie Tale Theater, The Firm,
Traveler's Rest, Tales of the City. Movies: The Murder of Mary
Phagan, Lip Service, Guts and Glory: The Rise and Fall of
Oliver North, When He's Not a Stranger, The Court Martial of
Jackie Robinson, Guess Who's Coming for Christmas?, White
Hot: The Mysterious Murder of Thelma Todd, Cooperstown,
Mother of the Bride, State of Emergency, The Computer Wore
Tennis Shoes. Series: The Dom DeLuise Show, Coming of
Age. Guest: Dream On, ALF, The Golden Girls, thirtysome-
thing, Mad About You, Evening Shade, Coach, Wonder Years,
The Boys, L.A. Law, The Mommies, Star Trek: Deep Space
Nine, many others.

DORAN, LINDSAY
Executive. b. Los Angeles, CA. e. U. of California at Santa
Cruz. Moved to London where was contributing author to The
Oxford Companion to Film and the World Encyclopedia of
Film. Returned to U.S. to write and produce documentaries
and children's programs for Pennsylvania public affairs station
WPSX-TV. Career in m.p. industry began in story dept. at
Embassy Pictures which she joined in 1979; 1982 promoted to
dir. of development; then v.p., creative affairs. 1985, joined
Paramount Pictures as v.p., production, for M.P. Group. 1987,
promoted to senior v.p., production. 1989, appointed pres.,
Mirage Productions.

DORFF, STEPHEN
Actor. b. July 29, 1973. Started acting at age 9.
PICTURES: The Gate (debut, 1987), The Power of One, An
Ambush of Ghosts, Judgment Night, Rescue Me, BackBeat,
S.F.W., Reckless, Innocent Lies, I Shot Andy Warhol.
TELEVISION: Series: What a Dummy. Movies: I Know My First
Name Is Steven, Always Remember I Love You, Do You Know
the Muffin Man?, A Son's Promise. Guest: Empty Nest,
Roseanne, The Outsiders, Married... With Children, Empty
Nest.

DORTORT, DAVID
Executive Producer. b. New York, NY, Oct. 23, 1916. e. City
Coll. of New York. Served U.S. Army, 1943-46. Novelist and
short story writer, 1943-49. Also TV writer. Now pres. of
Xanadu Prods., Aurora Enterprises, Inc., and Bonanza
Ventures, Inc. & Pres. TV branch, WGA, West, 1954-55; TV-
radio branch, 1955-57; v.p. PGA, 1967; pres. 1968. Chmn.,
Caucus for Producers, Writers and Directors, 1973-75. Pres.,
PGA, 1980-81; campaign dir., Permanent Charities Comm.,
1980-81; chmn., Interguild Council 1980-81. Received
WGA/West noms. for TV work on An Error in Chemistry
(Climax), and The Ox-Bow Incident (20th Century Fox Hour).
Author: novels include Burial of the Fruit, The Post of Honor.
PICTURES: The Lusty Men, Reprisal, The Big Land, Cry in
the Night, Clash by Night, Going Bananas (exec. prod.).
TELEVISION: Creator and exec. prod.: Bonanza, High
Chaparral, The Chisholms, Hunter's Moon, Bonanza: Legends
of the Ponderosa. Producer: The Restless Gun, The Cowboys.
Creator, story and exec. prod.: Bonanza: The Next Generation.

DOUGHERTY, MARION
Executive. e. Penn St. U. Gained fame as casting director.
Casting dir. on series Naked City, Route 66. Formed own co.
in 1965. Acted as co-executive producer on Smile, 1975. In
1977 named v.p. in chg. talent for Paramount Pictures. In 1979
joined Warner Bros. as sr. v.p. in chg. talent to work with production dept. and producers and directors.
CASTING: A Little Romance, Urban Cowboy, Honky Tonk
Freeway, Reds, Firefox, Honkytonk Man, The World According
to Garp, Sudden Impact, The Man With Two Brains, The Killing
Fields, Swing Shift, The Little Drummer Girl, Lethal Weapon
(also 2 & 3), Batman, Batman Returns, Forever Young, Falling
Down.

DOUGLAS, ILLEANA
Actress. Grandfather was actor Melvyn Douglas. Directed
short films The Perfect Woman (Aspen Film Fest. prize, 1994),
Boy Crazy—Girl Crazier.
THEATER: NY: Takes on Women, As Sure as You Live, Black
Eagles.

PICTURES: Hello Again, New York Stories (Life Lessons),
GoodFellas, Guilty By Suspicion, Cape Fear, Alive, Household
Saints, Grief, Quiz Show, Search and Destroy, To Die For,
Grace of My Heart.

DOUGLAS, KIRK
Actor, Producer, Director. r.n. Issur Danielovitch (changed to
Demsky). b. Amsterdam, NY, Dec. 9, 1916. m. Anne Buydens,
pres. of Bryna Prod. Co. Father of Michael, Joel, Peter, Eric. e.
St. Lawrence U, B.A, AADA. Stage debut in New York: Spring
Again. U.S. Navy during W.W.II; resumed stage work. Did
radio soap operas. Signed by Hal B. Wallis for film debut.
Autobiography: The Ragman's Son (1988). Novels: Dance
With the Devil, The Secret, Last Tango in Brooklyn. Recipient
of U.S. Presidential Medal of Freedom, 1981. Career achieve-
ment award, National Board of Review, 1989. Received AFI
Lifetime Achievement Award, 1991.
THEATER: Spring Again, Three Sisters, Kiss and Tell, Trio,
The Wind is Ninetry, Star in the Window, Man Bites Dog, One
Flew Over the Cuckoo's Nest, The Boys of Autumn.
PICTURES: The Strange Love of Martha Ivers (debut, 1946),
Out of the Past, I Walk Alone, Mourning Becomes Electra, The
Walls of Jericho, My Dear Secretary, Letter to Three Wives,
Champion, Young Man with a Horn, The Glass Menagerie,
Ace in the Hole (The Big Carnival), Along the Great Divide,
Detective Story, The Big Trees, The Big Sky, Bad and the
Beautiful, Story of Three Loves, The Juggler, Act of Love,
20,000 Leagues Under the Sea, Ulysses, Man Without a Star,
The Racers, The Indian Fighter (also prod.), Lust for Life, Top
Secret Affair, Gunfight at the OK Corral, Paths of Glory, The
Vikings (also prod.), Last Train from Gun Hill, The Devil's
Disciple, Strangers When We Meet, Spartacus (also prod.),
The Last Sunset, Town Without Pity, Lonely Are the Brave
(also prod.), Two Weeks in Another Town, The Hook, List of
Adrian Messenger (also prod.), For Love or Money, Seven
Days in May (also prod.), In Harm's Way, The Heroes of
Telemark, Cast a Giant Shadow, Is Paris Burning?, The Way
West, The War Wagon, A Lovely Way to Die, The Brotherhood
(also prod.), The Arrangement, There Was a Crooked Man, A
Gunfight, Summertree (prod. only), The Light at the Edge of
the World (also prod.), Catch Me a Spy, Scalawag (also dir.,
prod.), Master Touch, Once is Not Enough, Posse (also dir.,
prod.), The Chosen, The Fury, The Villain, Saturn III, Home
Movies, The Final Countdown, The Man from Snowy River,
Eddie Macon's Run, Tough Guys, Oscar, Welcome to Veraz,
Greedy.
TELEVISION: Movies: Mousey, The Money Changers, Draw!
(HBO), Victory at Entebbe, Remembrance of Love, Amos,
Queenie, Inherit the Wind, The Secret, Take Me Home Again.
Guest: The Lucy Show, Tales From the Crypt (Yellow).
Specials: Legend of Silent Night, Dr. Jekyll & Mr. Hyde.

DOUGLAS, MICHAEL
Actor, Producer. b. New Brunswick, NJ, Sept 25, 1944. p. Kirk
Douglas and Diana Dill. e. Black Fox Military Acad., Choate,
U. of California. Worked as asst. director on Lonely Are the
Brave, Heroes of Telemark, Cast a Giant Shadow; after TV
debut in The Experiment (CBS Playhouse), appeared off-
Broadway in City Scene, Pinkville (Theatre World Award).
Produced 1993 Off-B'way show The Best of Friends.
PICTURES: Hail Hero (debut, 1969), Adam at 6 A.M.,
Summertree, Napoleon and Samantha, One Flew Over the
Cuckoo's Nest (co-prod. only; Academy Award for Best
Picture, 1975), Coma, The China Syndrome (also prod.),
Running (also exec. prod.), It's My Turn, The Star Chamber,
Romancing the Stone (also prod.), Starman (exec. prod. only),
A Chorus Line, The Jewel of the Nile (also prod.), Fatal
Attraction, Wall Street (Academy Award; Natl. Board of Review
Award, 1987), Black Rain, The War of the Roses, Flatliners
(co-exec. prod. only), Shining Through, Radio Flyer (co-exec.
prod. only), Basic Instinct, Falling Down, Made in America (co-
exec. prod. only), Disclosure, The American President, The
Ghost and the Darkness.
TELEVISION: Series: Streets of San Francisco. Guest: The
FBI, Medical Center. Movies: Streets of San Francisco (pilot),
When Michael Calls.

DOUGLAS, MIKE
TV host. r.n. Michael Delaney Dowd, Jr. b. Chicago, IL, Aug.
11, 1925. Started career singing with bands in and around
Chicago. 1950-54 featured singer with Kay Kyser's band. In
1953 became host of WGN-TV's Hi Ladies in Chicago; also
featured on WMAQ-TV, NBC, Chicago, as singer and host.
Moved to Hollywood in late '50s, working as piano bar singer.
In 1961 hired as host for new show on station KYW-TV in
Cleveland, owned by Westinghouse Bdg. Co., featuring
celebrity guests. This became the Mike Douglas Show which
was later nationally syndicated and moved base of operations
to Philadelphia, then Los Angeles. Ran 21 years til Mid-1982.
Books: The Mike Douglas Cookbook (1969), Mike Douglas My
Story (1978), When the Going Gets Tough.
PICTURES: Gator, Nasty Habits, The Incredible Shrinking
Woman.

DOURIF, BRAD
Actor. b. Huntington, WV, Mar. 18, 1950. Studied with Stanford Meisner. Stage actor, three years with Circle Repertory Co., NY (When You Comin' Back Red Ryder?), before films and TV.
PICTURES: Split, One Flew Over the Cuckoo's Nest (Acad. Award nom., Golden Globe & BAFTA Awards, 1975), Group Portrait with Lady, Eyes of Laura Mars, Wise Blood, Heaven's Gate, Ragtime, Dune, Impure Thoughts, Istanbul, Blue Velvet, Fatal Beauty, Child's Play, Mississippi Burning, Medium Rare, The Exorcist: 1990, Spontaneous Combustion, Grim Prairie Tales, Sonny Boy, Graveyard Shift, Child's Play II, Hidden Agenda, Dead Certain, Jungle Fever, The Horseplayer, Body Parts, Child's Play 3, Common Bonds, Scream of Stone, Critters 4, London Kills Me, Diary of the Hurdy Gurdy Man, Murder Blues, Final Judgment, Amos & Andrew, Trauma, Color of Night, Murder in the First.
TELEVISION: Movies: Sgt. Matlovitch vs. the U.S. Air Force, Guyana Tragedy—The Story of Jim Jones, I Desire, Vengeance: The Story of Tony Cimo, Rage of Angels: The Story Continues, Desperado: The Outlaw Wars, Class of '61, Escape From Terror: The Teresa Stamper Story, Escape to Witch Mountain. Mini-Series: Studs Lonigan, Wild Palms. Specials: Mound Builders, The Gardener's Son. Guest: Miami Vice, The Hitchhiker, Spencer for Hire, Tales of the Unexpected, Moonlighting, The Equalizer, Murder She Wrote, Babylon 5, Voyager.

DOWN, LESLEY-ANNE
Actress. b. London, England, March 17, 1954. At age of 10 modeled for TV and film commercials, leading to roles in features. Film debut at 14 in The Smashing Bird I Used to Know (billed as Lesley Down).
THEATER: Great Expectations, Hamlet, etc.
PICTURES: The Smashing Bird I Used to Know (debut, 1969), All the Right Noises, Countess Dracula, Assault, Pope Joan, Scalawag, From Beyond the Grave, Brannigan, The Pink Panther Strikes Again, The Betsy, A Little Night Music, The Great Train Robbery, Hanover Street, Rough Cut, Sphinx, Nomads, Scenes from the Goldmine, Mardi Gras for the Devil, Death Wish V: The Face of Death, Munchie Stikes Back, The Unfaithful.
TELEVISION: Series: Upstairs, Downstairs, Dallas. Movies: Agatha Christie's Murder is Easy, Hunchback of Notre Dame, The One and Only Phyllis Dixey, Arch of Triumph, Indiscreet, Lady Killers, Night Walk. Mini-Series: North and South Books I & II & III, Last Days of Pompeii. Specials: Unity Mitford. Heartbreak House. Pilots: Shivers, 1775.

DOWNEY, ROBERT, JR.
Actor. b. New York, NY, April 4, 1965. Father is indep. filmmaker Robert Downey. Film debut at age 5 in his father's film Pound.
PICTURES: Pound (debut, 1970), Greaser's Palace, Jive, Up the Academy, Baby Its You, Firstborn, Tuff Turf, Weird Science, To Live and Die in L.A., Back to School, America, The Pick-Up Artist, Less Than Zero, Johnny B. Good, Rented Lips, 1969, True Believer, Chances Are, That's Adequate, Air America, Too Much Sun, Soapdish, Chaplin (Acad. Award nom., BAFTA Award), Hail Caesar, Heart and Souls, The Last Party, Short Cuts, Natural Born Killers, Only You, Restoration, Danger Zone, Home for the Holidays, Richard III.
TELEVISION: Series: Saturday Night Live. Mini-Series: Mussolini: The Untold Story. Special: Dear America (reader).

DOWNS, HUGH
Broadcaster. b. Akron, OH, Feb. 14, 1921. e. Bluffton Coll., 1938. Wayne U., 1941. Col. U., N.Y., 1955; Supervisor of Science Programming, NBC's Science Dept. one yr.; science consultant for Westinghouse Labs., Ford Foundation, etc.; chmn. of bd., Raylin Prods., Inc. Today, Chairman, U.S. Committee for UNICEF. Chm. of bd. of governors, National Space Society. Books: Thirty Dirty Lies About Old, Rings Around Tomorrow, School of Stars, Yours Truly Hugh Downs, On Camera: My Ten Thousand Hours on Television, Perspectives, Fifty to Forever.
TELEVISION: Series: Kukla Fran & Ollie (announcer), Home, Sid Caesar (announcer), The Jack Paar Show, Concentration, The Tonight Show (announcer, 1962), Today. Host: 20/20, Over-Easy (Emmy Award, 1981), Live From Lincoln Center.
RADIO: NBC's Monitor, ABC's Perspectives.

DOYLE, KEVIN
Executive. b. Sydney, Australia, June 21, 1933. e. N. Sydney Tech. HS., Aust. Jr. exec., asst. adv. & pub. div., 20th Century-Fox, Aust., 1947-59; adv. & pub. dir., Columbia Pictures Aust., 1960-66; international ad/pub. mgr.; Columbia Pictures Int'l, N.Y. 1966; intl. pub./promo. mgr., 1980; 1987, Columbia Int'l. rep., Coca-Cola promotions/mktg. sub-committee; int'l pub./promo. mgr. Columbia Tri-Star Film Distributors Inc., 1988; int'l pub./promo. dir. Columbia/Tri-Star Film distrib. Inc. 1990. Retired 1992.

DOYLE-MURRAY, BRIAN
Actor, Writer. b. Chicago, IL., Oct. 31. Brother is comedian Bill Murray. Started as member of Chicago's Second City improv. troupe, before joining the Organic Theatre of Chicago and the Boston Shakespeare Co. Appeared Off-B'way in The National Lampoon Show and on radio on weekly National Lampoon Show.
PICTURES: Caddyshack (also co-s.p.), Modern Problems, National Lampoon's Vacation, Sixteen Candles, The Razor's Edge, Legal Eagles, Club Paradise (also co-s.p.), Scrooged, The Experts, How I Got Into College, Ghostbusters II, National Lampoon's Christmas Vacation, Nothing But Trouble, JFK, Wayne's World, Groundhog Day, Cabin Boy, Jury Duty, Multiplicity.
TELEVISION: Series: Saturday Night Live (also writer), Get a Life, Good Sports, Bakersfield P.D. Movies: Babe Ruth, My Brother's Keeper. Special: Texan.

DRAGOTI, STAN
Director. b. New York, NY, Oct. 4, 1932. e. Cooper Union and Sch. of Visual Arts. 1959 hired as sketch at ad agency, promoted to sr. art dir., later TV dept. and art dir. of Young & Rubicam. Studied acting HB Studios. Directed Clio awarding-winning TV commercials (including I Love New York campaign).
PICTURES: Dirty Little Billy (debut, 1972; also co-prod., co-s.p.), Love at First Bite, Mr. Mom, The Man With One Red Shoe, She's Out of Control, Necessary Roughness.

DRAI, VICTOR
Producer. b. Casablanca, Morocco, July 25, 1947. e. Lycee de Port Lyautey, 1957-63. In real estate in Los Angeles 1976-82; clothing designer/mfg. in Paris, France, 1969-76. Began producing features in 1984, The Woman in Red.
PICTURES: The Man with One Red Shoe, The Bride, Weekend at Bernie's, Folks!, Weekend at Bernie's 2.

DRAZEN, LORI
Executive. Began career as asst. to dir. of adv. for Orion Pictures; creative dept. mgr., Kenyon & Eckhardt; gen. mgr., Seiniger Advertising; joined Warner Bros. 1985 as v.p., world-wide adv. & pub. services.

DREYFUSS, RICHARD
Actor. b. Brooklyn, NY, Oct. 29, 1947. e. Beverly Hills H.S.; San Fernando Valley State Coll. 1965-67. Prof. career began at Gallery Theatre (L.A.) in In Mama's House. Co-Exec. Prod. of film Quiz Show.
THEATER: Journey to the Day, Incident at Vichy, People Need People, Enemy Line, Whose Little Boy Are You, But Seriously, Major Barbara, The Time of Your Life, The Hands of Its Enemy (L.A.), The Normal Heart, Death and the Maiden, others.
PICTURES: The Graduate, Valley of the Dolls, The Young Runaways, Hello Down There, Dillinger, American Graffiti, The Second Coming of Suzanne, The Apprenticeship of Duddy Kravitz, Jaws, Inserts, Close Encounters of the Third Kind, The Goodbye Girl (Academy Award, 1977), The Big Fix (also co-prod.) The Competition, Whose Life Is It Anyway?, The Buddy System, Down and Out in Beverly Hills, Stand by Me, Tin Men, Stakeout, Nuts, Moon Over Parador, Let It Ride, Always, Postcards from the Edge, Once Around, Rosencrantz and Guildenstern Are Dead, What About Bob?, Lost in Yonkers, Another Stakeout, Silent Fall, The American President, Mr. Holland's Opus, James and the Giant Peach, Night Falls on Manhattan, Mad Dog Time.
TELEVISION: Series: Karen. Host: American Chronicles. Guest: Love on a Rooftop, Occasional Wife, The Big Valley, Room 222, Judd for the Defense, Mod Squad, The Bold Ones. Special: Funny You Don't Look 200 (host, co-prod., co-writer). Movies: Two for the Money, Victory at Entebbe, Prisoner of Honor (also prod.), The Last Word.

DROMGOOLE, PATRICK
Director, Producer, Executive. b. Iqueque, Chile, Aug. 30, 1930; e. Dulwich Coll., University Coll., Oxford. Joined BBC Radio as dir. 1954, later directing TV plays for BBC and ABC, incl. Armchair Theatre, Frontier, Dracula, Mystery Imagination. Joined HTV as West Country Programme Controller, 1968; dir. award-winning dramas; Thick as Thieves, Machinegunner. Developed Company's drama output and promoted policy of international pre-sales with such dramas as Jamaica Inn, Separate Tables, Catholics, Kidnapped, Robin of Sherwood, Arch of Triumph, Mr. Halpern and Mr. Johnson, Jenny's War, Codename Kyril, Wall of Tyranny, Strange Interlude, The Woman He Loved, Grand Larceny, Maigret. Made Fellow of RTS, 1978; chief exec. HTV Group since 1988. Fellow of RSA, 1989.
THEATER: Director: incl. first plays of Charles Wood, Joe Orton, David Halliwell, Colin Welland; Peter O'Toole in Man and Superman.
PICTURES: Two Vale South, Hidden Face, Dead Man's Chest, Anthony Purdy Esq., Point of Dissent, The Actors, King of the Wind (exec. prod.), Visage du Passe (dir.), Meutres en Douce.

DRU, JOANNE
Actress. r.n. Joanne La Cock. b. Logan, WV, Jan. 31, 1923. Sister of Peter Marshall. John Robert Powers model: on stage as showgirl in Hold on to Your Hats; a Samba Siren at Ritz Carlton & Paramount; with theatrical group under Batami Schneider.

PICTURES: Abie's Irish Rose (debut, 1946), Red River, She Wore a Yellow Ribbon, All the King's Men, Wagonmaster, 711 Ocean Drive, Vengeance Valley, Mr. Belvedere Rings the Bell, My Pal Gus, Return of the Texan, Pride of St. Louis, Thunder Bay, Outlaw Territory, Forbidden, Siege at Red River, Duffy of San Quentin, Southwest Passage, Three Ring Circus, Day of Triumph, Hell on Frisco Bay, The Warriors, Sincerely Yours, Drango, Light in the Forest, Wild and the Innocent, September Storm, Sylvia, Super Fuzz.
TELEVISION: *Series*: Guestward Ho. *Guest*: Ford Theatre, Schlitz Playhouse, Playhouse 90, Climax, Lux Video Theatre, David Niven Show, The Green Hornet, Marcus Welby M.D.
(d. September 10, 1996)

DRURY, JAMES
Actor. b. New York, NY, Apr. 18, 1934. e. New York U. Acting debut at age 8 in biblical play for children at Greenwich Settlement Playhouse. Performed on stage while youngster. Signed by MGM in 1955, working one day in each of seven movies that year, including Blackboard Jungle. Then got two-year contract at 20th-Fox. Gained fame as hero of TV series, The Virginian, which had nine-year run.
PICTURES: Forbidden Planet, Love Me Tender, Bernardine, Toby Tyler, Pollyana, Ten Who Dared, Ride the High Country, The Young Warriors.
TELEVISION: *Series*: The Virginian, Firehouse. *Movies*: Breakout, Alias Smith and Jones, The Devil and Miss Sarah, The Gambler Returns: Luck of the Draw.

DUBAND, WAYNE
Executive. b. Sydney, Australia, Feb. 13, 1947. Joined Warner Bros. 1969 as mgr. trainee in Australia. 1973, transferred to South Africa as mgr. dir.; 1977 gen. mgr. of CIC/Warner Bros. joint venture, also managing the CIC theatre operation there. 1980, named exec. asst. to Myron D. Karlin, pres. WB Intl., in Burbank. 1981, mgr. dir. of Warner/Columbia joint venture in France. 1985, appt. v.p. of sls. for WB Intl. division. 1987, appt. senior v.p. for Warner Bros. Intl. division. 1992, appt. pres. Intl. Theatrical div., WB Intl.

DUBE, JACKSON E.
Executive. b. New York, NY. e. U. of North Carolina. m. Pat Lavelle, actress. USAF 1942-45 Radar-Gunner, AAF, Italy. Writer: Television and Sponsor Magazine 1947-48; reviews of recorded music. 1947-51, Consol Film Inds. Penthouse Prods. Dist.: E. sales mgr. Atlas Tel. Corp. 1951-54; vp & gen. mgr., Craftsman Film Greatest Fights of the Century 1954; vp, Conquest Prods. CBS Net. Docus. 1954-57. TV and radio dir. Cote Fischer & Rogow Adv., 1957-59; exec. vp, Bon Ami Film; dist.: UA Feats. abroad 1959-63; prod's rep. Le Vien Prods.—Finest Hours King's Story; Eastern sales mgr. Desilu, 1964-67; exec. vp, UCC Films; dist. RKO feature Library abroad, 1969-70; pres. JED Rrns. Corp. Dist. London Films, Rank chidren's features, 1967-88. Consultant: New Century Ent., Windsor Pdns., Rurner Program Services, 1985-88. Agent for Weiss Global, Medallion TV Enterprises, Turner International, Morin International, 1988-92. Agent for Aries S.A. and Sidney Beckerman Prods. Agent for Otto Preminger Films Ltd. JED Productions Corp. owner or partner in remake rights to 125 US feature motion pictures 1992 to present.

DUBS, ARTHUR R.
Executive, Producer, Director, Writer, President and Owner of Pacific International Enterprises. b. Medford, OR, Feb. 26, 1930. e. Southern Oregon State Coll. Founded Pacific International Enterprises, 1969.
PICTURES: *Producer-Director*: American Wilderness, Vanishing Wilderness, Wonder of It All. *Exec. Prod.*: Challenge to Be Free. *Prod.*: Adventures of the Wilderness Family, Wilderness Family Part 2 (also s.p.), Mountain Family Robinson (also s.p.), Across the Great Divide, Sacred Ground, Mystery Mansion, Dream Chasers (also co-dir.). *Co-Prod.*: Windwalker.

DUCHOVNY, DAVID
Actor. b. New York, NY, Aug. 7, 1960. e. Yale. Was teaching asst. at Yale before landing first acting job in beer commercial.
PICTURES: Working Girl (debut, 1988), New Year's Day, Bad Influence, Julia Has Two Lovers, Don't Tell Mom the Babysitter's Dead, The Rapture, Ruby, Venice/Venice, Chaplin, Kalifornia.
TELEVISION: *Series*: Twin Peaks, The X Files.

DUDELHEIM, HANS RUDOLF
Communications Executive. b. Berlin, Germany, June 17, 1927. e. Sch. of Photography Berlin, School of Radio & TV NY. Film editor, ABC, 1951-66. Prod/Dir/Edit.: Cinema Arts Assn. 1966-90; served as pres. Founder, 1961, Cinema Arts Film Soc. Editor of documentaries: Saga of Western Man, Comrade Student, Sublimated Birth (also prod.), Kent State, Sigmund Freud, IBM Motivation Project, The Forgotten Pioneers of Hollywood, Painting With Love. Producer: Sesame Street, 60 Minutes: Ranaissance Community, American Dream Machine, Voyage of the Barba Negra. Presently film and video consultant.

DUDIKOFF, MICHAEL
Actor. b. Torrance, CA, Oct. 8, 1954.
PICTURES: Making Love, I Ought to Be in Pictures, Tron, Bachelor Party, Bloody Birthday, American Ninja, Radioactive Dreams, Avenging Force, American Ninja II: The Confrontation, Platoon Leader, River of Death, American Ninja 4: The Annihilation, Midnight Ride, Human Shield, Rescue Me, Virtual Assassin.
TELEVISION: *Mini-Series*: North and South Book II. *Movie*: The Woman Who Sinned. *Series*: Star of the Family, Cobra. *Pilot*: Sawyer and Finn. *Guest*: Happy Days, Dallas.

DUFFY, JAMES E.
Executive. b. Decatur, IL, April 2, 1926. e. Beloit Coll. Radio announcer, then reporter; joined publicity dept., ABC in 1949; named dir. of adv. & promo., then account exec. for Central division of ABC Radio Network; dir. of sales ABC Radio, 1957; central div. account exec., ABC TV Network, 1955; natl. dir. of Sales, ABC Radio central division, 1960; v.p., ABC Radio Network, 1961; exec. v.p. & natl. dir. of sales, 1962; v.p. in charge of sales, ABC TV Network, 1963; pres., ABC TV Network, 1970-85; pres., communications, 1985-86; v.p. Capital Cities/ABC, Inc.; pres., communications, ABC Network & Bdgst. Divisions.

DUFFY, PATRICK
Actor. b. Townsend, MT, March 17, 1949. e. U. of Washington. Became actor-in-residence in state of Washington, where performed with various statefunded groups. Acted off-B'way Taught mime and movement classes in summer camp in Seattle. Moved to L.A. and began TV acting career.
PICTURE: Vamping (also co-exec prod.).
TELEVISION: *Specials*: The Last of Mrs. Lincoln, Freedom Festival '89 (host). *Movies*: The Stranger Who Looks Like Me, Hurricane, Man From Atlantis, Enola Gay, Cry for the Strangers, Strong Medicine, Alice in Wonderland, Too Good to Be True, Unholy Matrimony, Murder C.O.D, Children of the Bride, Danielle Steel's Daddy, Texas. *Series*: Man from Atlantis, Dallas, Step By Step. *Guest*: Switch, George Burns' Comedy Week.

DUGAN, DENNIS
Actor, Director. b. Wheaton, IL, Sept. 5, 1946. m. actress Joyce Van Patten. Studied acting at Goodman Theatre School.
THEATER: *NY*: A Man's Man, The House of Blue Leaves. *LA*: Once in a Lifetime, Rainbows for Sales, Estonia, The Dining Room, The Kitchen.
PICTURES: Night Call Nurses, The Day of the Locust, Night Moves, Smile, Harry and Walter Go to New York, Norman ... Is That You?, Unidentified Flying Oddball, The Howling, Water, Can't Buy Me Love, She's Having a Baby, The New Adventures of Pippi Longstocking, Parenthood, Problem Child (also dir.), Brain Donors (dir. only), Happy Gilmore (dir. only).
TELEVISION: *Series*: Richie Brockelman: Private Eye, Empire, Shadow Chasers. *Movies*: Death Race, The Girl Most Likely To..., Last of the Good Guys, Country Gold, The Toughest Man in the World, Columbo: Butterfly in Shades of Grey. *Mini-Series*: Rich man Poor Man. *Guest*: Hooperman, Moonlighting, M*A*S*H, The Rockford Files, Scene of the Crime, Making a Living, Hill Street Blues. *Pilots*: Alice, Father O Father, Did You Hear About Josh and Kelly?, Full House, Channel 99. *Director*: Hunter, Sonny Spoon, Wiseguy, Moonlighting, The Shaggy Dog (movie).

DUGGAN, ERVIN S.
Executive. Started as reporter for the Washington Post in early 1960's. As member of President Lydon Johnson's staff helped define government's role in supporting public broadcasting with the Public Broadcasting Act of 1967. Served as special asst. to Senators Lloyd Bentsen and Adlai Stevenson III, Health Education and Welfare Secretary Joseph Califano; and as member of the State Dept. Policy Planning Staff. 1981-90, managed communications and consulting firm. Served 4 years as Commissioner of the Federal Communications Commission. Feb. 1994 joined PBS as pres. and CEO.

DUIGAN, JOHN
Director, Writer. Lived in England and Malaysia before moving to Sydney, Australia. e. Univ. of Melbourne, philosophy, M.A. Taught for several years at Univ. of Melbourne and Latrobe U. before entering films. Directed and wrote experimental short, The Firm Man (1974). Novels: Badge, Players, Room to Move.
PICTURES: *Dir.-Writer*: Trespassers, Mouth to Mouth, Winter of Our Dreams (Australian Writers Guild Award), Far East, The Year My Voice Broke (Australian Acad. Award for best dir., s.p.) Romero (dir. only), Flirting, Wide Sargasso Sea, Sirens (also actor), The Journey of August King.
TELEVISION: *Mini-Series*: Vietnam (co-dir.). *Movie*: Fragments of War: The Story of Damien Parer.

DUKAKIS, OLYMPIA
Actress. b. Lowell, MA, June 20, 1931. m. actor Louis Zorich. e. Boston U., B.A., M.F.A. Founding mem. of The Charles

Playhouse, Boston, establishing summer theatre 1957-60. Taught acting at NYU: 1967-70 as instructor, 1974-83 as master teacher, and at Yale U. 1976. With husband conceived and guided artistic dev. of Whole Theatre of Monclair, NJ, 1977-90; producing artistic dir. Adapted plays for her co. and dir. theater there; also at Williamstown Theatre Fest. and Delaware Summer Fest. Appeared in more than 100 plays on B'way, Off-B'way and in regional and summer theater.
THEATER: Who's Who in Hell, The Aspern Papers, Night of the Iguana, The Breaking Wall, Curse of the Starving Class, Snow Orchid, The Marriage of Bette and Boo (Obie Award), Social Security.
PICTURES: Lilith, Twice a Man, John and Mary, Made for Each Other, Death Wish, Rich Kids, The Wanderers, The Idolmaker, National Lampoon Goes to the Movies, Flanagan, Moonstruck (Academy Award, best supporting actress, 1987), Working Girl, Look Who's Talking, Steel Magnolias, Dad, In the Spirit, Look Who's Talking Too, The Cemetery Club, Over the Hill, Look Who's Talking Now, Naked Gun 33 1/3: The Final Insult (cameo), I Love Trouble, Jeffrey, Mighty Aphrodite, Mr. Holland's Opus.
TELEVISION: Specials: The Rehearsal, Sisters, Last Act is a Solo, A Century of Women. Series: Search for Tomorrow, One of the Boys. Movies: Nicky's World, The Neighborhood, FDR-The Last Year, King of America, Lucky Day, Fire in the Dark, Sinatra, Young at Heart. Mini-Series: Tales of the City.

DUKE, BILL
Actor, Director. b. Poughkeepsie, NY, Feb. 26, 1943. e. Boston Univ., NY Univ. Sch. of the Arts. Recieved AFI Best Young Director Award for short The Hero (Gold Award, Houston Film Festival). Has written poetry, short stories for children. Member bd. of dirs. American Film Institute.
PICTURES: Actor: Car Wash, American Gigolo, Commando, Predator, No Man's Land, Action Jackson, Bird on a Wire, Street of No Return, Menace II Society. Director: A Rage in Harlem, Deep Cover, The Cemetery Club, Sister Act 2: Back in the Habit.
TELEVISION: Actor: Movies: Love is Not Enough, Sgt. Matlovich Vs. the U.S. Air Force. Series: Palmerstown U.S.A. Director: Series: A Man Called Hawk, Cagney & Lacey, Hill Street Blues, Miami Vice, Dallas. Specials: The Killing Floor, A Raisin in the Sun, The Meeting. Movie: Johnnie Mae Gibson.

DUKE, PATTY
Actress. r.n. Anna Marie Duke. b. New York, NY, Dec. 14, 1946. e. Quintano Sch. for Young Professionals. Mother of actors Sean and Mackenzie Astin. Pres., Screen Actors Guild, 1985-88. Author: Surviving Sexual Assault (1983), Call Me Anna (1987).
THEATER: The Miracle Worker (Theatre World Award), Isle of Children.
PICTURES: I'll Cry Tomorrow (debut as extra 1955), The Goddess, Happy Anniversary, The 4-D Man, The Miracle Worker (Academy Award, best supporting actress, 1962), Billie, Valley of the Dolls, Me Natalie, The Swarm, By Design, Something Special, Prelude to a Kiss.
TELEVISION: Series: The Brighter Day, The Patty Duke Show, It Takes Two, Hail to the Chief, Karen's Song, Amazing Grace. Guest: Armstrong Circle Theatre, The SS Andrea Doria, U.S. Steel Hour, All's Fair. Specials: The Prince and the Pauper, Wuthering Heights, Swiss Family Robinson, Meet Me in St. Louis, The Power and the Glory. Movies: My Sweet Charlie (Emmy Award, 1970), Two on a Bench, If Tomorrow Comes, She Waits, Deadly Harvest, Nightmare, Look What's Happened to Rosemary's Baby, Fire!, Rosetti & Ryan: Men Who Love Women, Curse of the Black Widow, Killer on Board, The Storyteller, Having Babies III, A Family Upside Down, Women in White, Hanging by a Thread, Before and After, The Miracle Worker (Emmy Award, 1980), The Women's Room, Mom The Wolfman and Me, The Babysitter, Violation of Sarah McDavid, Something So Right, September Gun, Best Kept Secrets, Fight for Life, Perry Mason: The Case of the Avenging Angel, A Time to Triumph, Fatal Judgment, Everybody's Baby: The Rescue of Jessica McClure, Amityville: The Evil Escapes, Call Me Anna, Always Remember I Love You, Absolute Strangers, Last Wish, Grave Secrets: The Legacy of Hilltop Drive, A Killer Among Friends, Family of Strangers, No Child of Mine, A Matter of Justice, One Woman's Courage, Cries From the Heart. Mini-Series: Captains and the Kings (Emmy Award, 1977), George Washington. Host: Fatal Passions, Angels: The Mysterious Messengers.

DUKES, DAVID
Actor. b. San Francisco, CA, June 6, 1945.
THEATER: B'way: Don Juan, The Great God Brown, Chemin de Fer, The Visit, Holiday, School for Wives, The Play's the Thing, Love for Love, Rules of the Game, Dracula, Travesties, Frankenstein, Bent, Amadeus, M. Butterfly, Love Letters, Someone Who'll Watch Over Me, Broken Glass.
PICTURES: The Strawberry Statement, The Wild Party, A Little Romance, The First Deadly Sin, Only When I Laugh,

Without a Trace, The Men's Club, Catch the Heat, Rawhead Rex, Date With an Angel, Deadly Intent, See You in the Morning, The Handmaid's Tale, Me and the Kid, Fled.
TELEVISION: Series: Beacon Hill, All That Glitters, Sisters, The Mommies. Mini-Series: 79 Park Avenue, Space, George Washington, The Winds of War, War and Remembrance, Kane & Abel. Specials: Strange Interlude, Cat on a Hot Tin Roof. Movies: Go West Yound Girl, A Fire in the Sky, Some Kind of Miracle, The Triangle Factory Fire Scandal, Mayflower—The Pilgrim Adventure, Margaret Sanger— Portrait of a Rebel, Miss All-American Beauty, Sentimental Journey, Turn Back the Clock, Snowkill, Held Hostage: The Sis and Jerry Levin Story, The Josephine Baker Story, Wife Mother Murderer, She Woke Up, Look at It This Way (BBC), Spies. Guest: All in the Family, The Jeffersons, Once Day at a Time, Barney Miller, Hawaii 5-0, Police Story, Police Woman, Cannon, etc.

DULLEA, KEIR
Actor. b. Cleveland, OH, May 30, 1936. e. Rutgers Univ., San Francisco State Coll., Sanford Meisner's Neighborhood Playhouse. Acted as resident juvenile at the Totem Pole Playhouse in PA. NY theatre debut in the revue Sticks and Stones, 1956; appeared in stock co. prods. at the Berkshire Playhouse and Philadelphia's Hedgerow Theatre, 1959; off-Broadway debut in Season of Choice, 1969. Won San Francisco Film Festival Award for performance in film David and Lisa, 1963.
THEATER: Dr. Cook's Garden, Butterflies Are Free, Cat on a Hot Tin Roof, P.S. Your Cat is Dead, The Other Side of Paradise.
PICTURES: The Hoodlum Priest (debut, 1961), David and Lisa, The Thin Red Line, Mail Order Bride, The Naked Hours, Bunny Lake Is Missing, Madame X, The Fox, 2001: A Space Odyssey, De Sade, Pope Joan, Paperback Hero, Il Diavolo nel Cervello, Paul and Michelle, Black Christmas (Silent Night Evil Night), Leopard in the Snow, Welcome to Blood City, The Haunting of Julia (Full Circle), Because He's My Friend, The Next One, Brainwaves, Blind Date, 2010.
TELEVISION: Movies: Black Water Gold, Law and Order, Legend of the Golden Gun, Brave New World, The Hostage Tower, No Place to Hide. Special: Mrs. Miniver.

DUNAWAY, FAYE
Actress. b. Bascom, FL, Jan. 14, 1941. e. Texas, Arkansas, Utah, Germany, U. of Florida. Awarded a Fulbright scholarship in theatre. Boston U. of Fine Applied Arts. With Lincoln Center Rep. Co. for 3 years. NY Stage: A Man for All Seasons, After the Fall, Hogan's Goat (Theatre World Award), The Curse of an Aching Heart.
PICTURES: Hurry Sundown (debut, 1967), The Happening, Bonnie and Clyde, The Thomas Crown Affair, The Extraordinary Seaman, A Place for Lovers, The Arrangement, Puzzle of a Downfall Child, Little Big Man, The Deadly Trap, Doc, Oklahoma Crude, The Three Musketeers, Chinatown, The Towering Inferno, The Four Musketeers, Three Days of the Condor, Network (Academy Award, 1976), Voyage of the Damned, Eyes of Laura Mars, The Champ, The First Deadly Sin, Mommie Dearest, The Wicked Lady, Ordeal by Innocence, Supergirl, Barfly, Midnight Crossing, Burning Secret, The Handmaid's Tale, Wait Until Spring Bandini, The Gamble, On a Moonlit Night, Scorchers, Double Edge, The Temp, Arizona Dream, Don Juan DeMarco, Drunks, Dunston Checks In, Albino Alligator, The Chamber.
TELEVISION: Movies: The Woman I Love, The Disappearance of Aimee, Evita, Peron, 13 at Dinner, Beverly Hills Madam, The Country Girl, Casanova, The Raspberry Ripple, Cold Sassy Tree, Silhouette, Columbo: It's All in the Game (Emmy Award, 1994), A Family Divided. Mini-Series: Ellis Island, Christopher Columbus. Specials: Hogan's Goat, After the Fall, Supergirl: The Making of the Movie (host), Inside the Dream Factory (host). Series: It Had to Be You.

DUNCAN, LINDSAY
Actress. Stage actress with National Theatre, Royal Shakespeare Company.
THEATER: Plenty, The Provok'd Wife, The Prince of Homburg, Top Girls, Progress, The Merry Wives of Windsor, Les Liaisons Dangereuses (RSC, West End, Broadway; Theatre World Award), Cat On A Hot Tin Roof, Hedda Gabler, A Midsummer Night's Dream, Cryptogram.
PICTURES: Loose Connections, Samson & Delilah, Prick Up Your Ears, Manifesto, The Reflecting Skin, Body Parts, City Hall, A Midsummer Night's Dream.
TELEVISION: Reilly, Ace of Spies, Dead Head (serial), Traffik, A Year in Provence, The Rector's Wife, G.B.H., Jake's Progress.

DUNCAN, SANDY
Actress. b. Henderson, TX, Feb. 20, 1946. m. singer-dancer Don Correia. e. Len Morris Coll.
THEATER: The Music Man (NY debut, 1965); The Boyfriend, Ceremony of Innocence (Theatre World Award), Your Own Thing, Canterbury Tales, Peter Pan, Five Six Seven Eight Dance!, My One and Only.

107

PICTURES: $1,000,000 Duck, Star Spangled Girl, The Cat from Outer Space, Rock a Doodle (voice), The Swan Princess (voice).
TELEVISION: *Series*: Funny Face, The Sandy Duncan Show, Valerie's Family (later called The Hogan Family). *Movies*: My Boyfriend's Back, Miracle on Interstate 880. *Mini-Series*: Roots. *Specials*: Pinocchio, Sandy in Disneyland, The Sandy Duncan Special.

DUNING, GEORGE
Composer, Conductor, Arranger. b. Richmond, IN, Feb. 25, 1908. e. Cincinnati Conservatory of Music, U. of Cincinnati. Music dir. Aaron Spelling Prods., 1970-71, Bobby Sherman Show, Movies of the Week. Board of Directors, ASCAP, 1969-83. V.P. ASCAP, 1977-79. Society for Preservation of Film Music Career Achievement Award, 1987; Indiana Composer of the Year, 1993.
PICTURES: Down to Earth, The Guilt of Janet Ames, Johnny O'Clock, To the Ends of the Earth, Jolson Sings Again, The Eddy Duchin Story, From Here to Eternity, Picnic, Pal Joey, Cowboy, The Last Angry Man, The World of Susie Wong, Devil at 4 O'Clock, The Notorious Landlady, Toys in the Attic, Ensign Pulver, Dear Brigitte, Any Wednesday, Terror in the Wax Museum, The Man with Bogart's Face.
TELEVISION: No Time for Sergeants, Wendy and Me, The Farmer's Daughter, Big Valley, The Long Hot Summer, The Second Hundred Years, Star Trek, Mannix, Then Came Bronson.

DUNLAP, RICHARD D.
Producer, Director. b. Pomona, CA, Jan. 30, 1923. e. Yale U., B.A., 1944; M.F.A., 1948. U.S. Navy 1943-46; Instructor, English dept., Yale U., 1947-48; Prod.-dir., Kraft TV Theatre, 3 years; Dir, Assoc. Prod., Omnibus, 3 seasons; Dir., 25 half-hr. Dramatic Film Shows. Frank Sinatra Specials, Prod.-Dir., 11 Academy Award Shows, 4 Emmy Award Shows.

DUNNE, DOMINICK
Producer. Writer. b. Hartford, CT, Oct. 29, 1925. e. Canterbury Sch., 1944; Williams Col., 1949. Son is actor-prod. Griffin Dunne. Began career as stage manager at NBC-TV; then produced shows for CBS Studio One. Later exec. prod. at 20th-Fox TV, v.p. at Four Star. Novels: The Winners, The Two Mrs. Grenvilles, People Like Us, An Inconvenient Woman, A Season in Purgatory, Fatal Charms, The Mansions of Limbo.
PICTURES: The Boys in the Band (exec. prod.), The Panic in Needle Park, Play It as It Lays, Ash Wednesday.

DUNNE, GRIFFIN
Actor, Producer. b. New York, NY, June 8, 1955. Son of prod.-writer Dominick Dunne. foremerly m. actress Carey Lowell. Formed Double Play Prods. with Amy Robinson. Studied at Neighborhood Playhouse and with Uta Hagen. On Stage in Album, Marie and Bruce, Coming Attractions, Hotel Play, Search and Destroy (B'way debut; Theatre World Award).
PICTURES: *Actor*: The Other Side of the Mountain (debut, 1975), Chilly Scenes of Winter (also prod.), The Fan, American Werewolf in London, Cold Feet, Almost You, Johnny Dangerously, After Hours (also co-prod.), Golden Globe nom.), Who's That Girl, Amazon Women on the Moon, Big Blue, Me and Him, Once Around (also co-prod.), My Girl, Straight Talk, Big Girls Don't Cry... They Get Even, The Pickle, Naked in New York, Quiz Show, I Like It Like That, Search and Destroy. *Producer only*: Baby It's You, Running on Empty, White Palace. *Director/Writer*: Duke of Groove (short, Oscar nom.).
TELEVISION: *Movies*: The Wall, Secret Weapon, Love Matters, The Android Affair, Love Matters (Ace nom.). *Specials*: Lip Service, Trying Times: Hunger Chic, Partners. *Pilot*: Graham.

DURNING, CHARLES
Actor. b. Highland Falls, NY, Feb. 28, 1923. e. NYU. Studied acting on the G.I. Bill. Prof. stage debut, 1960. Made several appearances with Joseph Papp's NY Shakespeare Festival.
THEATER: That Championship Season, Knock Knock, Au Pair Man, In the Boom Boom Room, The Happy Time, Indians, Cat on a Hot Tin Roof (Tony Award, 1990), Queen of the Stardust Ballroom, Inherit the Wind.
PICTURES: Harvey Middleman—Fireman (debut, 1965), I Walk the Line, Hi Mom!, The Pursuit of Happiness, Dealing: or the Berkeley-to- Boston Forty-Brick Lost-Bag Blues, Deadhead Miles, Sisters, The Sting, The Front Page, Dog Day Afternoon, The Hindenburg, Breakheart Pass, Harry and Walter Go to New York, Twilight's Last Gleaming, The Choirboys, An Enemy of the People, The Fury, The Greek Tycoon, Tilt, The Muppet Movie, North Dallas Forty, Starting Over, When a Stranger Calls, Die Laughing, The Final Countdown, True Confessions, Sharky's Machine, The Best Little Whorehouse in Texas (Acad. Award nom.), Tootsie, To Be or Not to Be (Acad. Award nom.), Two of a Kind, Hadley's Rebellion, Mass Appeal, Stick, The Man With One Red Shoe, Stand Alone, Big Trouble, Tough Guys, Where the River Runs Black, Solarbabies, Happy New Year, The Rosary Murders, A

Tiger's Tail, Cop, Far North, Cat Chaser, Dick Tracy, V. I. Warshawski, Brenda Starr, Etolie, Fatal Sky, The Music of Chance, The Hudsucker Proxy, I.Q., Home for the Holidays, The Last Supper, The Grass Harp, Spy Hard.
TELEVISION: *Series*: Another World (1972), The Cop and the Kid, Eye to Eye, Evening Shade. *Mini-Series*: Captains and the Kings, Studs Lonigan, The Kennedys of Massachusetts, A Woman of Independent Means. *Specials*: The Rivalry, The Dancing Bear, Working, Mr. Roberts, Side by Side (pilot), P.O.P. (pilot), Eye to Eye, Tales from Hollywood, Normandy (narrator), Texan, Leslie's Folly. *Movies*: The Connection, The Trial of Chaplain Jensen, Queen of the Stardust Ballroom, Switch, Special Olympics, Attica, Perfect Match, Crisis at Central High, The Best Little Girl in the World, Dark Night of the Scarecrow, Death of a Salesman, Kenny Rogers as The Gambler III—The Legend Continues, The Man Who Broke 1000 Chains, Case Closed, Unholy Matrimony, Prime Target, It Nearly Wasn't Christmas, Dinner at Eight, The Return of Eliot Ness, The Story Lady, The Water Engine, Roommates. *Guest*: Madigan, All in the Family, Barnaby Jones, Hawaii Five-O, Amazing Stories.

DURWOOD, EDWARD D.
Executive. e. Univ. of KS, B.S., 1975; M.B.A., 1985. Started with AMC Entertainment in 1976 as asst. film buyer, then head film buyer of Midwest Division. 1983, promoted to v.p. of AMC; 1985, with Real Estate Dept.; 1989, exec. v.p.; 1989 elected pres. & vice-chmn. of AMC.

DURWOOD, RICHARD M.
Executive. b. Kansas City, MO, Aug. 18, 1929. e. Brown U., A.B. Pres. Crown Cinema Corp.
MEMBER: Motion Picture Assn. of Kansas City (pres.), United Motion Pictures Assn. (pres. 1972-73), Young NATO (chmn., 1968-69), Past Chief Barker, Tent No. 8. Past mem., exec. comm., National NATO.

DURWOOD, STANLEY H.
Executive. b. 1920. e. Harvard Coll., B.S. Air Force navigator 3 years. Chmn. of bd. American Multi-Cinema Inc. Member: Harvard Club of Kansas City; Harvard Club of New York. On board of United Missouri Bankshares.

DUSSAULT, NANCY
Actress. b. Pensacola, FL, Jun. 30, 1936. e. Northwestern U.
THEATER: *B'way*: Street Scene, The Mikado, The Cradle Will Rock, Do Re Mi (Theatre World Award), Sound of Music, Carousel, Fiorello, The Gershwin Years, Into the Woods. *L.A. stage*: Next in Line.
PICTURE: The In-Laws.
TELEVISION: *Special*: The Beggars Opera. *Host*: Good Morning America. *Series*: The New Dick Van Dyke Show, Too Close for Comfort (The Ted Knight Show).

DUTTON, CHARLES S.
Actor. b. Baltimore, MD, Jan. 30, 1951. e. Towson St., Yale Sch. of Drama.
THEATER: *Yale Rep*: The Works, Beef No Chicken, Astopovo, Othello. *NY*: Ma Rainey's Black Bottom (Theatre World Award, 1983), Joe Turner's Come and Gone, The Piano Lesson.
PICTURES: No Mercy, Crocodile Dundee II, Jacknife, An Unremarkable Life, Q & A, Mississippi Masala, Alien3, The Distinguished Gentleman, Menace II Society, Rudy, Foreign Student, A Low Down Dirty Shame, Cry the Beloved Country, Nick of Time, The Last Dance, A Time to Kill, Get on the Bus.
TELEVISION: *Series*: Roc. *Guest*: Miami Vice, The Equalizer, Cagney and Lacey. *Movies*: Apology, The Murder of Mary Phagan, Jack Reed: Search for Justice, The Piano Lesson, Zooman. *Special*: Runaway.

DUVALL, ROBERT
Actor. b. San Diego, CA, Jan. 5, 1931. e. Principia College, IL. Studied at the Neighborhood Playhouse, NY.
THEATER: *Off-B'way*: The Days and Nights of Bee Bee Fenstermaker, Call Me By My Rightful Name, A View From the Bridge (Obie Award, 1965). *B'way*: Wait Until Dark, American Buffalo.
PICTURES: To Kill a Mockingbird (debut, 1962), Captain Newman M.D., Nightmare in the Sun, The Chase, Countdown, The Detective, Bullitt, True Grit, The Rain People, M*A*S*H, The Revolutionary, THX-1138, Lawman, The Godfather, Tomorrow, The Great Northfield Minnesota Raid, Joe Kidd, Lady Ice, Badge 373, The Outfit, The Conversation, The Godfather Part II, Breakout, The Killer Elite, The Seven Percent Solution, Network, We're Not the Jet Set (dir., co-prod. only), The Eagle Has Landed, The Greatest, The Betsy, Invasion of the Body Snatchers (cameo), Apocalypse Now, The Great Santini, True Confessions, The Pursuit of D.B. Cooper, Tender Mercies (Academy Award, 1983; also co-prod, songwriter), Angelo My Love (dir., prod., s.p. only), The Stone Boy, The Natural, Belizaire the Cajun (cameo; also creative consultant), The Lightship, Let's Get Harry, Hotel Colonial, Colors, The Handmaid's Tale, A Show of Force, Days of

Thunder, Rambling Rose, Convicts, Newsies, Falling Down, The Plague, Geronimo: An American Legend, Wrestling Ernest Hemingway, The Paper, Something to Talk About, The Stars Fell on Henrietta, The Scarlet Letter, A Family Thing (also co-prod.), Phenomenon.
TELEVISION: *Movies*: Fame Is the Name of the Game, The Terry Fox Story, Stalin. *Mini-Series*: Ike, Lonesome Dove. *Guest*: Great Ghost Tales, The Outer Limits, Naked City, Route 66, The Defenders, Alfred Hitchcock Presents, Twilight Zone, Combat, Wild Wild West, The FBI, Mod Squad.

DUVALL, SHELLEY
Actress, Producer. b. Houston, TX, July 7, 1949. Founded Think Entertainment, TV prod. co. Appeared in 1984 short film Frankenweenie.
PICTURES: Brewster McCloud (debut, 1970), McCabe and Mrs. Miller, Thieves Like Us, Nashville, Buffalo Bill and the Indians, Three Women (Cannes Fest. Award, 1977), Annie Hall, The Shining, Popeye, Time Bandits, Roxanne, Suburban Commando, The Underneath, Portrait of a Lady.
TELEVISION: *Actress*: Bernice Bobs Her Hair, Lily, Twilight Zone, Mother Goose Rock 'n' Rhyme, Faerie Tale Theatre (Rumpelstiltskin, Rapunzel), Tall Tales and Legends (Darlin' Clementine). *Exec. Producer*: Faerie Tale Theatre, Tall Tales and Legends, Nightmare Classics, Dinner at Eight (movie), Mother Goose Rock 'n' Rhyme, Stories from Growing Up, Backfield in Motion (movie), Bedtime Stories, Mrs. Piggle-Wiggle.

DYSART, RICHARD A.
Actor. b. Brighton, MA, Mar. 30, 1929. e. Emerson Coll., B.S., M.S., L.L.D.(honorary). Univ. of Maine, PhD (honorary). Off-B'way in The Quare Fellow, Our Town, Epitaph for George Dillon, Six Characters in Search of an Author, on B'way in A Man for All Seasons, All in Good Time, The Little Foxes, A Place without Doors, That Championship Season, Another Part of the Forest.
PICTURES: Petulia, The Lost Man, The Sporting Club, The Hospital, The Terminal Man, The Crazy World of Julius Vrooder, The Day of the Locust, The Hindenberg, Prophecy, Meteor, Being There, An Enemy of the People, The Thing, The Falcon and the Snowman, Mask, Warning Signs, Pale Rider, Wall Street, Back to the Future Part III.
TELEVISION: *Movies*: The Autobiography of Miss Jane Pittman, Gemini Man, It Happened One Christmas, First You Cry, Bogie, The Ordeal of Dr. Mudd, Churchill and the Generals (BBC), People Vs. Jean Harris, Bitter Harvest, Missing, Last Days of Patton, Children--A Mother's Story, Malice in Wonderland, Day One, Bobby and Marilyn: Her Final Affair, Truman, A Child Is Missing. *Special*: Sandburg's Lincoln, Jay Leno's Family Comedy Hour, Concealed Enemies (PBS), Charlie Smith and the Fritter Tree (PBS), Moving Target. *Mini-Series*: War and Rememberance. *Series*: L.A. Law (Emmy Award, 1992).

DZUNDZA, GEORGE
Actor. b. Rosenheim, Germany, 1945. Spent part of childhood in displaced-persons camps before he was moved to Amsterdam in 1949. Came to NY in 1956 where he attended St. John's U. as speech and theater major.
THEATER: King Lear (NY Shakespeare Fest., debut, 1973), That Championship Season (tour, 1973), Mert and Phil, The Ritz, Legend, A Prayer for My Daughter.
PICTURES: The Happy Hooker, The Deer Hunter, Honky Tonk Freeway, Streamers, Best Defense, No Mercy, No Way Out, The Beast, Impulse, White Hunter Black Heart, The Butcher's Wife, Basic Instinct, Crimson Tide, Dangerous Minds.
TELEVISION: *Series*: Open All Night, Law and Order. *Movies*: The Defection of Simas Kudirka, Salem's Lot, Skokie, A Long Way Home, The Face of Rage, The Last Honor of Kathryn Beck, When She Says No, The Rape of Richard Beck, Brotherly Love, The Execution of Raymond Graham, Something is Out There, The Ryan White Story, Terror on Highway 91, What She Doesn't Know, The Enemy Within. Guest: Starsky and Hutch, The Waltons.

E

EASTWOOD, CLINT
Actor, Producer, Director. b. San Francisco, CA, May 31, 1930; e. Oakland Technical H.S., Los Angeles City Coll. Worked as a lumberjack in Oregon before being drafted into the Army, Special Services 1950-54. Then contract player at Universal Studios. Starred in TV series Rawhide, 1958-65. Formed Malpaso Productions, 1969. Made a Chevalier des Lettres by French gov., 1985. Mayor, Carmel, CA, 1986-88. Best Director for Bird: Hollywood Foreign Press Assoc., Orson Award. Made Commandeur de Ordre des Arts & Lettres by French Government, 1994. Received Irving G. Thalberg Award, 1995. Received American Film Institute Life Achievement Award, 1996.
PICTURES: Revenge of the Creature (debut, 1955), Francis in the Navy, Lady Godiva, Tarantula, Never Say Goodbye, Away

All Boats, The First Traveling Saleslady, Star in the Dust, Escapade in Japan, Ambush at Cimarron Pass, Lafayette Escadrille, A Fistful of Dollars, For a Few Dollars More, The Witches, The Good The Bad and The Ugly, Hang 'Em High, Coogan's Bluff, Where Eagles Dare, Paint Your Wagon, Kelly's Heroes, Two Mules For Sister Sara, Beguiled, Play Misty For Me (also dir.), Dirty Harry, Joe Kidd, Breezy (dir. only), High Plains Drifter (also dir.), Magnum Force, Thunderbolt & Lightfoot, The Eiger Sanction (also dir.), The Outlaw Josey Wales (also dir.), The Enforcer, The Gauntlet (also dir.), Every Which Way But Loose, Escape from Alcatraz, Bronco Billy (also dir.), Any Which Way You Can, Firefox (also dir., prod.), Honky Tonk Man (also dir., prod.), Sudden Impact (also dir., prod.), Tightrope (also prod.), City Heat, Pale Rider (also dir., prod.), Heartbreak Ridge (also dir., prod.), The Dead Pool (also prod.), Bird (dir. only), Thelonius Monk: Straight, No Chaser (exec. prod. only), Pink Cadillac, White Hunter Black Heart (also dir., prod.), The Rookie (also dir., prod.), Unforgiven (also dir., prod.; Acad. Awards for Best Picture & Director; L.A. Film Critics Awards for Best Actor, Director & Picture; Natl. Society of Film Critics Awards for Best Director & Picture; Golden Globe Award for Best Director; DGA Award, 1992), In the Line of Fire, A Perfect World (also dir.), Casper (cameo), The Bridges of Madison County (also dir., prod.), The Stars Fell on Henrietta (co-prod. only), Absolute Power (also dir., prod.).
TELEVISION: *Series*: Rawhide. *Specials*: Fame Fortune and Romance, Happy Birthday Hollywood, Clint Eastwood: The Man From Malpaso, Don't Pave Main Street: Carmel's Heritage. *Dir.*: Amazing Stories (Vanessa in the Garden). *Guest*: Navy Log, Maverick, Mr. Ed, Danny Kaye Show.

EBERSOL, DICK
Executive 1968, started at ABC as Olympic Television researcher; 1974, joined NBC as dir. of weekend late- night programming; named v.p. late night programming; 1977, became v.p. of Comedy Variety and Event Programming; 1981-85, served as exec. prod. of series Saturday Night Live; 1983, formed his own production company, No Sleep Productions, creating Friday Night Videos, Saturday Night's Main Event, Later With Bob Costas; 1989, named pres. of NBC Sports; served as exec. prod. of NBC's coverage of the 1992 Barcelona Summer Olympics.

EBERTS, JOHN DAVID (JAKE)
Producer, Financier. b. Montreal, Canada, July 10, 1941. e. McGill Univ. Harvard. President Goldcrest, founder & CEO 1976-83, 1985-6; 1984 joined Embassy Communications Intl. 1985 founded and chief exec. of Allied Filmmakers. Film Prods. Award of Merit 1986; Evening Standard Special Award 1987. Publication: My Indecision Is Final (1990).
PICTURES: Chariots of Fire, Gandhi, Another Country, Local Hero, The Dresser, Cal, The Emerald Forest, The Name of the Rose, Hope and Glory, Cry Freedom, The Adventures of Baron Munchausen, Driving Miss Daisy, Dances With Wolves, Black Robe, Get Back, City of Joy, A River Runs Through It, Super Mario Bros., No Escape, Arabian Knight.

EBSEN, BUDDY
Actor. r.n. Christian Ebsen, Jr. b. Belleville, IL, April 2, 1908. e. U. of Florida, Rollins Coll. Won first Broadway role as dancer in Ziegfeld's Whoopee in 1928. Sister, Vilma, became dancing partner and they played nightclubs and did road tours. Went to Hollywood and appeared in Broadway Melody of 1936 with Vilma then in many musicals as single. Later became dramatic actor and appeared on TV. Co-wrote title song for film Behave Yourself.
PICTURES: Broadway Melody of 1936 (debut, 1935), Born to Dance, Captain January, Banjo on My Knee, Yellow Jack, Girl of the Golden West, My Lucky Star, Broadway Melody of 1938, Four Girls in White, Parachute Battalion, They Met in Argentina, Sing Your Worries Away, Thunder in God's Country, Night People, Red Garters, Davy Crockett--King of the Wild Frontier, Davy Crockett and the River Pirates, Between Heaven and Hell, Attack!, Breakfast at Tiffany's, The Interns, Mail Order Bride, The One and Only Genuine Original Family Band, The Beverly Hillbillies.
TELEVISION: *Series*: Davy Crockett, Northwest Passage, The Beverly Hillbillies, Barnaby Jones, Matt Houston. *Guest*: Hawaii Five-O, Gunsmoke. *Movies*: Stone Fox, The Daughters of Joshua Cabe, Horror at 37000 Feet, Smash-Up on Interstate 5, The President's Plane is Missing, Leave Yesterday Behind, The Paradise Connection, Fire on the Mountain, The Return of the Beverly Hillbillies, The Bastard, Tom Sawyer, Stone Fox, Working Trash. *Special*: The Legend of the Beverly Hillbillies.
THEATER: Flying Colors, Yokel Boy, The Male Animal, Ziegfeld Follies, Take Her She's Mine, Our Town, The Best Man.

ECKERT, JOHN M.
Producer, Production Executive. b. Chatham, Ontario, Canada, e. Ryerson Polytechnical Inst., 1968-71 (film major). Member: DGA, DGC.

PICTURES: Power Play (assoc. prod.), Running (co-prod.), Middle Age Crazy (co-prod.), Dead Zone (unit prod. mgr.), Cats Eye (exec. in charge of prod.), Silver Bullet (assoc. prod.), Home Is Where the Heart Is (prod.), Millenium (suprv. prod.), Deep Sleep (prod.), Car 54 Where Are You? (s.p., prod.), Legends of the Fall (unit prod. mngr.), The Scarlet Letter (unit prod. mngr.), Flying Wild (assoc. prod.).
TELEVISION: Terry Fox Story (assoc. prod.), Special People (prod., Christopher Award), Danger Bay (series supv. prod., 1985-87), Family Pictures (unit prod. mngr.), Getting Gotti (prod.).

EDEN, BARBARA
Actress. b. Tucson, AZ, Aug. 23, 1934. r.n. Barbara Jean Huffman. e. San Francisco Conservatory of Music. Pres. Mi-Bar Productions. Dir. Security National Bank of Chicago.
PICTURES: Back From Eternity (debut, 1956), The Wayward Girl, A Private's Affair, From the Terrace, Twelve Hours to Kill, Flaming Star, All Hands on Deck, Voyage to the Bottom of the Sea, Five Weeks in a Balloon, Swingin' Along (Double Trouble), The Wonderful World of the Brothers Grimm, The Yellow Canary, The Brass Bottle, The New Interns, Ride the Wild Surf, 7 Faces of Dr. Lao, Quick Let's Get Married, The Amazing Dobermans, Harper Valley PTA, Chattanooga Choo Choo.
TELEVISION: Series: How to Marry a Millionaire, I Dream of Jeannie, Harper Valley P.T.A., A Brand New Life, Dallas. Movies: The Feminist and the Fuzz, A Howling in the Woods, The Woman Hunter, Guess Who's Sleeping in My Bed, The Stranger Within, Let's Switch, How to Break Up a Happy Divorce, Stonestreet: Who Killed the Centerfold Model?, The Girls in the Office, Condominium, Return of the Rebels, I Dream of Jeannie: 15 Years Later, The Stepford Children, The Secret Life of Kathy McCormick (also co-prod.), Your Mother Wears Combat Boots, Opposites Attract, Her Wicked Ways, Hell Hath No Fury, I Still Dream of Jeannie, Visions of Murder, Eyes of Terror, Dean Man's Island (also co-prod.).

EDWARDS, ANTHONY
Actor. b. Santa Barbara, CA, July 19, 1962. Grandfather designed Walt Disney Studios in the 1930s and worked for Cecil B. De Mille as conceptual artist. Joined Santa Barbara YHouth Theatre; acted in 30 plays from age 12 to 17. At 16 worked professionally in TV commercials. 1980 attended Royal Acad. of Dramatic Arts, London, and studied drama at USC. On NY stage 1993 in Ten Below.
PICTURES: Fast Times at Ridgemont High (debut, 1982), Heart Like a Wheel, Revenge of the Nerds, The Sure Thing, Gotcha!, Top Gun, Summer Heat, Revenge of the Nerds II (cameo), Mr. North, Miracle Mile, How I Got Into College, Hawks, Downtown, Delta Heat, Pet Sematary II, The Client.
TELEVISION: Series: It Takes Two, Northern Exposure, ER. Movies: The Killing of Randy Webster, High School U.S.A., Going for the Gold: The Bill Johnson Story, El Diablo, Hometown Boy Makes Good. Specials: Unpublished Letters, Sexual Healing.

EDWARDS, BLAKE
Director, Writer, Producer. r.n. William Blake McEdwards. b. Tulsa, OK, July 26, 1922. m. actress Julie Andrews. e. Beverly Hills H.S. Coast Guard during war. Film acting debut, Ten Gentlemen from West Point (1942).
RADIO: Johnny Dollar, Line-up; writer-creator: Richard Diamond.
PICTURES: Writer only: Panhandle, Stampede, Sound Off, All Ashore, Cruising Down the River, Rainbow Round My Shoulder, Drive a Crooked Road, The Atomic Kid (story), My Sister Eileen, Operation Mad Ball, Notorious Landlady, Soldier in the Rain. Producer only: Waterhole $NO3. Director: Bring Your Smile Along (also s.p.), He Laughed Last (also s.p.), Mister Cory (also s.p.), This Happy Feeling (also s.p.), The Perfect Furlough (also s.p.), Operation Petticoat, High Time, Breakfast at Tiffany's, Experiment in Terror, Days of Wine and Roses, The Pink Panther (also s.p.), A Shot in the Dark (also s.p., prod.), The Great Race (also s.p., prod.), What Did You Do in the War Daddy? (also s.p., prod.), Gunn (also prod.), The Party (also s.p., prod.), Darling Lili (also s.p., prod.), Wild Rovers (also s.p., prod.), The Carey Treatment (also s.p., prod.), The Tamarind Seed (also s.p.), The Return of the Pink Panther (also s.p., prod.), The Pink Panther Strikes Again (also s.p., prod.), Revenge of the Pink Panther (also s.p., prod.), "10" (also co-prod., s.p.), S.O.B. (also co-prod., s.p.), Victor/Victoria (also co-prod., s.p.), Trail of the Pink Panther (also co-prod., co-s.p.), The Curse of the Pink Panther (also co-prod., s.p.), The Man Who Loved Women (also prod., co-s.p.), Micki and Maude, A Fine Mess (also s.p.), That's Life (also co-prod.), Blind Date, Sunset (also s.p.), Skin Deep (also s.p.), Switch (also s.p.), Son of the Pink Panther (also s.p.).
TELEVISION: City Detective (prod., 1953), The Dick Powell Show (dir.). Creator: Dante's Inferno, Mr. Lucky, Justin Case (exec. prod., dir., writer), Peter Gunn (exec. prod., dir., writer), Julie (exec. prod., dir.). Specials: Julie! (prod., dir.), Julie on Sesame St. (exec. prod.), Julie and Dick in Covent Garden (dir.).

EDWARDS, JAMES H.
Executive. President & CEO, Storey Theatres, Inc. b. Cedartown, GA, Aug. 14, 1927. e. Georgia State. U.S. Navy, 1948-50. With Ga. Theatre Co., 1950-1952; Storey Theatres, 1952-present. Formerly pres. & chmn., NATO of GA; formerly pres., Variety Club of Atlanta. Former dir. at large, Nat'l. NATO. Director, numerous theatre cos.

EDWARDS, RALPH
Producer, Emcee. b. Merino, CO, June 13, 1913. e. U. of California, Berkeley. Began career in radio in 1929 as writer-actor-producer-announcer at station KROW, Oakland. Later joined CBS & NBC Radio in New York as announcer. Originated, produced and emceed Truth or Consequences, This Is Your Life and The Ralph Edwards Show for both radio & TV.
PICTURES: Seven Days Leave, Radio Stars on Parade, Bamboo Blonde, Beat the Band, I'll Cry Tomorrow, Manhattan Merry-go-round, Radio Stars of 1937.
TELEVISION: Producer/Creator: It Could Be You, Place the Face, About Faces, Funny Boners, End of the Rainbow, Who in the World, The Woody Woodbury Show. Producer/Host: This Is Your Life (specials for NBC). Producers: Wide Country, Name That Tune, Cross Wits, Knockout. Producer (with partner, Stu Billett): The People's Court, So You Think You Got Troubles?, Family Medical Center, Love Stories, Superior Court, Bzzz.

EGGAR, SAMANTHA
Actress. b. London, Eng., March 5, 1939. e. student Webber-Douglas Dramatic Sch., London; Slade Sch. of Art.
PICTURES: The Wild and the Willing, Dr. Crippen, Doctor in Distress, Psyche '59, The Collector (Acad. Award nom.), Return From the Ashes, Walk Don't Run, Doctor Dolittle, The Molly Maguires, The Lady in the Car With Glasses and a Gun, The Walking Stick, The Grove, The Light at the Edge of the World, The Dead Are Alive, The Seven Percent Solution, The Uncanny, Welcome to Blood City, The Brood, The Exterminator, Demonoid, Why Shoot the Teacher?, Curtains, Hot Touch, Loner, Ragin' Cajun, Dark Horse, Inevitable Grace, The Phantom.
TELEVISION: Series: Anna and the King. Movies: Double Indemnity, All The Kind Strangers, The Killer Who Wouldn't Die, Ziegfeld: the Man and His Women, The Hope Diamond, Love Among Thieves, A Ghost in Monte Carlo. A Case for Murder. Mini-Series: For the Term of His Natural Life, Davy Crockett, Great Escapes: Secrets of Lake Success. Guest: Columbo, Baretta, Love Story, Kojak, McMillan & Wife, Streets of San Francisco, Starsky and Hutch, Hart to Hart, Murder She Wrote, Finder of Lost Loves, George Burns Comedy Week, Lucas Tanner, Hotel, Fantasy Island, Magnum P.I., Stingray, Tales of the Unexpected, Heartbeat, Love Boat, 1st & Ten, Outlaws, Alfred Hitchcock Presents, Matlock, L.A. Law, Star Trek: The Next Generation. Specials: Man of Destiny, Hemingway Play.

EGOYAN, ATOM
Director. b. Cairo, Egypt, 1960. Raised in Victoria, British Columbia, Canada. e. Univ. of Toronto. Made short films, one of which, Open House appeared on tv series Canadian Reflections. Appeared in film Camilla.
PICTURES: Next of Kin (feature debut, 1984), Family Viewing, Speaking Parts, The Adjuster, Calendar, Exotica.
TELEVISION: In This Corner, Looking for Nothing, Gross Misconduct: The Life of Brian Spencer, Twilight Zone, Alfred Hitchcock Presents (The Final Twist).

EICHHORN, LISA
Actress. b. Reading, PA, Feb. 4, 1952. e. Queen's U. Kingston, Canada and Eng. for literature studies at Oxford. Studied at Royal Acad. of Dramatic Art.
THEATER: The Hasty Heart (debut, LA). NY: The Common Pursuit, The Summer Winds, The Speed of Darkness, Down the Road, Any Given Day.
PICTURES: Yanks, The Europeans, Why Would I Lie?, Cutter and Bone, Weather in the Streets, Wild Rose; Opposing Force, Moon 44, Grim Prairie Tales, The Vanishing, King of the Hill, A Modern Affair.
TELEVISION: Series: All My Children (1987). Movies: The Wall, Blind Justice, Devlin. Mini-Series: A Woman Named Jackie.

EIKENBERRY, JILL
Actress. b. New Haven, CT, Jan. 21, 1947. e. Yale U. Drama Sch. m. actor Michael Tucker.
THEATER: B'way: All Over Town, Watch on the Rhine, Onward Victoria, Summer Brave, Moonchildren. Off-B'way: Lemon Sky, Life Under Water, Uncommon Women and Others, Porch, The Primary English Class.
PICTURES: Between the Lines, The End of the World in Our Usual Bed in a Night Full of Rain, An Unmarried Woman, Butch and Sundance: The Early Days, Rich Kids, Hide in Plain Sight, Arthur, The Manhattan Project.

TELEVISION: *Movies*: The Deadliest Season, Orphan Train, Swan Song, Sessions, Kane & Abel, Assault and Matrimony, Family Sins, A Stoning in Fulham Country, My Boyfriend's Back, The Diane Martin Story, The Secret Life of Archie's Wife, An Inconvenient Woman, Living a Lie, A Town Torn Apart, Chantilly Lace, Parallel Lives, Without Consent, Rugged Gold, The Other Woman. *Series*: L.A. Law, The Best of Families (PBS). *Specials*: Uncommon Women & Others, Destined to Live (prod., host), A Family Again, On Hope.

EILBACHER, LISA
Actress. b. Saudi Arabia, May 5. Moved to California at age 7; acted on TV as child.
PICTURES: The War Between Men and Women (debut, 1972), Run for the Roses (Thoroughbred), On the Right Track, An Officer and a Gentleman, Ten to Midnight, Beverly Hills Cop, Deadly Intent, Leviathan, Never Say Die, The Last Samurai.
TELEVISION: *Series*: The Texas Wheelers, The Hardy Boys Mysteries, Ryan's Four, Me and Mom. *Movies*: Bad Ronald, Panache, Spider Man, The Ordeal of Patty Hearst, Love for Rent, To Race the Wind, This House Possessed, Monte Carlo, Deadly Deception, Joshua's Heart, Blind Man's Bluff, Deadly Matrimony, The Return of Hunter. *Mini-Series*: Wheels, The Winds of War. *Guest*: Wagon Train, Laredo, My Three Sons, Gunsmoke, Combat.

EISNER, MICHAEL D.
Executive. b. Mt. Kisco, NY, March 7, 1942. e. Denison U., B.A. Started career with programming dept. of CBS TV network. Joined ABC in 1966 as mgr. talent and specials. Dec., 1968 became dir. of program dev., east coast. 1968, named v.p., daytime programming, ABC-TV. 1975 made v.p., prog. planning and dev. 1976 named sr. v.p., prime time production and dev., ABC Entertainment. 1976, left ABC to join Paramount Pictures as pres. & chief operating officer. 1984, joined The Walt Disney Company as chmn. & CEO.

EKBERG, ANITA
Actress. b. Malmo, Sweden, Sept. 29, 1931. Came to U.S. in 1951 as Miss Universe contestant. Worked as model before becoming actress appearing in small roles in Europe.
PICTURES: Mississippi Gambler, Abbott & Costello Go to Mars, Take Me to Town, The Golden Blade, Blood Alley, Artists and Models, Man in the Vault, War and Peace, Back from Eternity, Hollywood or Bust, Zarak, Pickup Alley, Valerie, Paris Holiday, The Man Inside, Screaming Mimi, Sign of the Gladiator, La Dolce Vita, The Dam on the Yellow River (Last Train to Shanghai), Little Girls and High Finance, Behind Locked Doors, The Last Judgment, The Mongols, Boccaccio '70, Call Me Bwana, 4 for Texas, L'Incastro, Who Wants to Sleep?, The Alphabet Murders, Way Way Out, How I Learned to Love Women, Woman Times Seven, The Glass Sphinx, The Cobra, Malenka the Vampire (Fangs of the Living Dead), If It's Tuesday This Must Be Belgium, The Clowns, Valley of the Widows, Killer Nun, Daisy Chain, Intervista.
TELEVISION: *Movies*: Gold of the Amazon Women, S*H*E.

EKLAND, BRITT
Actress. b. Stockholm, Sweden, Oct. 6, 1942. Was model before debuting in European films.
PICTURES: Short Is the Summer (debut, 1962), Il Commandante, After the Fox, The Double Man, The Bobo, The Night They Raided Minsky's, Stiletto, Cannibals, Machine Gun McCain, Tintomara, Percy, Get Carter, A Time for Loving, Endless Night, Baxter, Asylum, The Wicker Man, Ultimate Thrill, The Man With the Golden Gun, Royal Flash, Casanova & Co., High Velocity, Slavers, King Solomon's Treasure, The Monster Club, Satan's Mistress (Demon Rage), Hellhole, Fraternity Vacation, Marbella, Moon in Scorpio, Scandal, Beverly Hills Vamp, The Children.
TELEVISION: *England*: Carol for Another Christmas, Too Many Thieves, A Cold Peace. *USA*: *Guest*: Trials of O'Brien, McCloud, Six Million Dollar Man. *Movies*: Ring of Passion, The Great Wallendas, The Hostage Tower, Valley of the Dolls 1981, Dead Wrong.

ELAM, JACK
Actor. b. Miami, AZ, Nov. 13, 1916. e. Santa Monica Jr. Coll., Modesto Jr. Coll. Worked in Los Angeles as bookkeeper and theatre mgr.; civilian employee of Navy in W.W.II; Introduction to show business was as bookkeeper for Sam Goldwyn. Later worked as controller for other film producers. Given first acting job by producer George Templeton in 1948; has since appeared in over 100 films.
PICTURES: Wild Weed (debut, 1949), Rawhide, Kansas City Confidential, Rancho Notorious, Ride Vaquero, Appointment in Honduras, The Moonlighter, Vera Cruz, Cattle Queen of Montana, The Far Country, Moonfleet, Kiss Me Deadly, Artists and Models, Gunfight at the OK Corral, Baby Face Nelson, Edge of Eternity, Girl in Lovers Lane, The Last Sunset, The Comancheros, The Rare Breed, The Way West, Firecreek, Never a Dull Moment, Once Upon a Time in the West, Support

Your Local Sheriff, Rio Lobo, Dirty Dingus Magee, Support Your Local Gunfighter, The Wild Country, Hannie Caulder, Last Rebel, Pat Garrett and Billy the Kid, Hawmps, Grayeagle, Hot Lead Cold Feet, The Norsemen, The Villain, The Apple Dumpling Gang Rides Again, The Cannonball Run, Jinxed, Cannonball Run II, The Aurora Encounter, Big Bad John, Suburban Commando.
TELEVISION: *Series*: The Dakotas, Temple Houston, The Texas Wheelers, Struck by Lightning, Detective in the House, Easy Street. *Movies*: The Over-the-Hill Gang, The Daughters of Joshua Cabe, Black Beauty, Once Upon a Texas Train, Where the Hell's That Gold!!!?.

ELEFANTE, TOM
Executive. Began career as usher at Loews Riviera in Coral Gables, FL; progressed through ranks to asst. mgr., mgr. & Florida division mgr. 1972, joined Wometco Theatres as gen. mgr. 1975, returned to Loews Theatres as southeast div. mgr.; 1979, named natl. dir. of concessions, moving to h.o. in New York. 1987, appt. sr. v.p. & gen. mgr., Loews. Served as pres. and chmn. of NATO of Florida. 1990, then pres. of NATO of NY.

ELFAND, MARTIN
Executive. b. Los Angeles, CA, 1937. Was talent agent for ten years with top agencies; joined Artists Entertainment Complex in 1972. First film project as producer: Kansas City Bomber, first venture of AEC, of which he was sr. v.p. In 1977 joined Warner Bros. as production chief.T
PICTURES: *Prod.*: Dog Day Afternoon, It's My Turn, An Officer and a Gentleman, King David, Clara's Heart. *Exec. prod.*: Her Alibi.

ELFMAN, DANNY
Composer. b. Los Angeles, CA, May 29, 1953. Member of rock band Oingo Boingo, recorded songs for such films as The Tempest, Fast Times at Ridgemont High, 16 Candles, Beverly Hills Cop, Weird Science, Texas Chainsaw Massacre 2, Something Wild. Appeared in Hot Tomorrows, Back to School.
PICTURES: Forbidden Zone, Pee-wee's Big Adventure, Back to School, Wisdom, Summer School, Beetlejuice, Midnight Run, Big-Top Pee-wee, Hot to Trot, Scrooged, Batman, Nightbreed, Dick Tracy, Darkman, Edward Scissorhands, Pure Luck, Article 99, Batman Returns, Sommersby, The Nightmare Before Christmas (also vocalist), Black Beauty, Dolores Claiborne, To Die For, Dead Presidents, Mission: Impossible, The Frighteners.
TELEVISION: *Series*: Pee-wee's Playhouse, Sledgehammer, Fast Times, Tales from the Crypt, The Simpsons, The Flash, Beetlejuice, segments of Amazing Stories (Mummy Dearest, Family Dog), Alfred Hitchcock Presents (The Jar).

ELG, TAINA
Actress, Dancer. b. Helsinki, Finland, March 9, 1930. Trained and performed with Natl. Opera of Finland. Attended Sadler's Wells Ballet Sch. Toured with Swedish Dance Theatre, then Marquis de Cuevas Ballet.
THEATER: Look to the Lilies, Where's Charley?, The Utter Glory of Morrissey Hall, Strider, Nine.
PICTURES: The Prodigal (debut, 1955), Diane, Gaby, Les Girls, Watusi, Imitation General, The 39 Steps, The Bacchae, Liebestraum, The Mirror Has Two Faces.
TELEVISION: *Movie*: The Great Wallendas. *Mini-Series*: Blood and Honor: Youth Under Hitler (narrator). *Special*: O! Pioneers.

ELIAS, HAL
Executive. b. Brooklyn, NY, Dec. 23, 1899. Publicity dir., State Theatre, Denver; western exploitation mgr., MGM; adv. dept., pub. dept., MGM, Culver City studios; Head, MGM cartoon studio (Tom and Jerry); UPA Pictures, Inc., vice-pres. studio mgr.: Hollywood Museum; bd. dir., Academy of Motion Picture Arts & Sciences, 35 years; treasurer, AMPAS 1976-1979. Academy Oscar, 1979, for dedicated and distinguished service to AMPAS.

ELIZONDO, HECTOR
Actor. b. New York, NY, Dec. 22, 1936. m. actress Carolee Campbell. Studied with Ballet Arts Co. of Carnegie Hall and Actors Studio. Many stage credits in N.Y. and Boston.
THEATER: The Prisoner of Second Avenue, Dance of Death, Steambath (Obie Award), The Great White Hope, Sly Fox, The Price.
PICTURES: The Fat Black Pussycat, Valdez Is Coming, Born to Win, Pocket Money, Deadhead Miles, Stand Up and Be Counted, The Taking of Pelham One Two Three, Report to the Commissioner, Thieves, Cuba, American Gigolo, The Fan, Young Doctors in Love, The Flamingo Kid, Private Resort, Nothing in Common, Overboard, Beaches, Leviathan, Pretty Woman (Golden Globe nom.), Taking Care of Business, Necessary Roughness, Frankie and Johnny, Final Approach, Samantha, There Goes the Neighborhood, Being Human, Beverly Hills Cop III, Getting Even With Dad, Exit to Eden, Perfect Alibi, Dear God, Turbulence.
TELEVISION: *Series*: Popi (1976), Casablanca, Freebie and

the Bean; A.K.A. Pablo (also dir.), Foley Sq, Down and Out in Bevery Hills, Fish Police (voice), Chicago Hope. *Guest:* The Wendie Barrie Show (1947), The Impatient Heart, Kojack, the Jackie Gleason Show, All in the Family, The Pirates of Dark Water (voice), Tales of the Crypt. *Movies:* The Impatient Heart, Wanted: The Sundance Woman, Honeyboy, Women of San Quentin, Courage, Out of the Darkness, Addicted to His Love, Your Mother Wears Combat Boots, Forgotten Prisoners: The Amnesty Files, Finding the Way Home, Chains of Gold, The Burden of Proof. *Mini-Series:* The Dain Curse. *Specials:* Medal of Honor Rag, Mrs. Cage.

ELKINS, HILLARD
Producer. b. New York, NY, Oct. 18, 1929. e. NYU, B.A., 1951. Exec., William Morris Agy., 1949-51; exec. v.p., Gen. Artists Corp., 1952-53; pres., Hillard Elkins Mgmt., 1953-60; Elkins Prods. Intl. Corp., N.Y., 1960-71; Elkins Prods. Ltd., 1972-; Hillard Elkins Entertainment Corp., 1974; Media Mix Prods., Inc., 1979-82.
MEMBER: Academy of Motion Picture Arts & Sciences, Acad. of TV Arts & Sciences, Dramatists Guild, League of New York Theatres, American Fed. of TV & Radio Artists.
THEATER: Come On Strong, Golden Boy, Oh Calcutta!, The Rothschilds, A Doll's House, An Evening with Richard Nixon, Sizwe Banzi Is Dead, etc.
PICTURES: Alice's Restaurant, A New Leaf, Oh Calcutta!, A Doll's House, Richard Pryor Live in Concert, Sellers on Sellers.
TELEVISION: The Importance of Being Earnest, The Deadly Game, Princess Daisy, The Meeting (exec. prod.), Father & Son: Dangerous Relations.

ELKINS, SAUL
Producer. b. New York, NY, June 22, 1907. e. City Coll. of New York, B.S., 1927. Radio writer, dir., prod. 1930-2; dir., prod. stock co. touring Latin America 1932-34; writer Fox Films, 20th Century-Fox; writer RKO, Columbia 1937-42; writer, dial-dir., dir. Warner Bros. 1943-7; prod. Warner Bros. since 1947.
Member: AMPAS, Screen Writer's Guild. Exec. prod., Comprenetics, Inc. Dir., Pioneer Prods., 1982.
PICTURES: Younger Brothers, One Last Fling, Homicide, House Across the Street, Flaxy Martin, Barricade, Return of the Frontiersmen, This Side of the Law, Colt .45, Sugarfoot, Raton Pass, The Big Punch, Smart Girls Don't Talk, Embraceable You.

ELLIOTT, CHRIS
Actor, Writer. b. New York, NY, May 31, 1960. Father is come-dian Bob Elliott. Was performer in improv. theatres, summer stock; also tour guide at Rockefeller Center. Became writer/performer for David Letterman starting in 1982. *Author:* Daddy's Boy: A Son's Shocking Account of Life With a Famous Father (1989).
PICTURES: Manhunter (debut, 1986), The Abyss, Hyperspace, Groundhog Day, CB4, Cabin Boy (also co-story), Kingpin.
TELEVISION: *Series:* Late Night With David Letterman (also co- writer; 2 Emmy Awards for writing: 1984, 1985), Nick and Hillary, Get a Life (also creator, co-writer, prod.). *Specials:* Late Night With David Letterman Anniversary Specials (also co-writer; 2 Emmy Awards for writing: 1986, 1987), Chris Elliott's FDR: One-Man Show (also writer, prod.).

ELLIOTT, LANG
Producer, Director. b. Los Angeles, CA, Oct. 18, 1949. Began acting in films at an early age, influenced by his uncle, the late actor William Elliott (known as Wild Bill Elliott). Employed by, among others the McGowan Brothers. Turned to film produc-tion; co-founded distribution co., The International Picture Show Co., serving as exec. v.p. in chg. of financing, production & distribution. In 1976 formed TriStar Pictures, Inc. to finance and distribute product. In 1980 sold TriStar to Columbia, HBO and CBS. 1982, formed Lang Elliott Productions, Inc. Co-founded Longshot Enterprises with actor Tim Conway to prod. films and home videos, 1985. Videos include Dorf on Golf (the first made-for-home-video comedy), 'Scuse Me!, Dorf and the First Olympic Games. Formed Performance Pictures, Inc., in 1989, a prod. & distrib. company. Received Academy Award nom. for Soldier of Orange and The Magic of Lassie.
PICTURES: *Prod:* Ride the Hot Wind, Where Time Began, The Farmer, The Billion Dollar Hobo, They Went That-a-Way & That-a-Way, The Prize Fighter. *Prod.-dir.:* The Private Eyes, Cage, Cage II, and over 40 other pictures.
TELEVISION: Experiment in Love (prod.), Boys Will Be Boys (writer).

ELLIOTT, SAM
Actor. b. Sacramento, CA, Aug. 9, 1944. m. actress Katharine Ross. e. U. of Oregon.
PICTURES: Butch Cassidy and the Sundance Kid (debut in bit, 1969), The Games, Frogs, Molly and Lawless John, Lifeguard, The Legacy, Mask, Fatal Beauty, Shakedown, Road House, Prancer, Sibling Rivalry, Rush, Gettysburg, Tombstone.

TELEVISION: *Movies:* The Challenge, Assault on the Wayne, The Blue Knight, I Will Fight No More Forever, The Sacketts, Wild Times, Murder in Texas, Shadow Riders, Travis McGee, A Death in California. The Blue Lightning, Houston: The Legend of Texas, The Quick and the Dead, Conagher (also co-writer, exec. prod.), Fugitive Nights: Danger in the Desert, Buffalo Girls, The Ranger the Cook and a Hole in the Sky. *Series:* Mission: Impossible, The Yellow Rose. *Mini-Series:* Once and Eagle, Aspen (The Innocent and the Damned). *Guest:* Lancer, The FBI, Gunsmoke, Streets of San Francisco, Hawaii 5-0, Police Woman. *Pilot:* Evel Knievel.

ELWES, CARY
Actor. b. London, England, Oct. 26, 1962. e. Harrow. Studied for stage with Julie Bovasso at Sarah Lawrence, Bronxville, NY.
PICTURES: Another Country (debut 1984), Oxford Blues, The Bride, Lady Jane, The Princess Bride, Glory, Days of Thunder, Leather Jackets, Hot Shots!, Bram Stoker's Dracula, The Crush, Robin Hood: Men in Tights, Rudyard Kipling's The Jungle Book, Twister.

EMMERICH, ROLAND
Director, Writer, Exec. Producer. b. Germany. Studied pro-duction design in film school in Munich. First film was student production, The Noah's Ark Principle, which opened the 1984 Berlin Film Festival and was sold to more than 20 countries. Formed Centropolis Film Productions.
PICTURES: *Co-s.p./Dir.:*Making Contact (a.k.a. Joey; dir. only), Ghost Chase, Eye of the Storm (prod. only), Moon 44, Universal Soldier, Stargate, Independence Day.

ENGEL, CHARLES F.
Executive. b. Los Angeles, CA, Aug. 30. e. Michigan State U., UCLA. Son of writer-producer Samuel G. Engel. Pgm. devel., ABC-TV, 1964-68; v.p. Univ.-TV 1972; sr. v.p., 1977; exec. v.p., 1980; pres., MCA Pay-TV Programming, 1981. ACE Award, 1988 for outstanding contribution to cable; v.p. Universal TV, exec. in chg. ABC Mystery Movie, 1989. Sr. v.p. 1992 in chg. Columbo, Murder She Wrote, SeaQuest, The Rockford Files. Founding member board of governors, the National Academy of Cable Programming. Member, Television Academy.
TELEVISION: The Aquarians (exec. prod.), Run a Crooked Mile (exec. prod.), Road Raiders (prod.), ABC Mystery Movie (exec. in chg. of prod.).

ENGELBERG, MORT
Producer. b. Memphis, TN. e. U. of Illinois, U. of Missouri. Taught journalism; worked as reporter for UPI, AP. Worked for US government, including USIA, Peace Corps., Office of Economic Opportunity; President's Task Force on War on Poverty. Left gov. service in 1967 to become film unit publicist, working on three films in Europe: Dirty Dozen, Far From the Madding Crowd, The Comedians. Returned to U.S.; appt. pub. mgr. for United Artists. Sent to Hollywood as asst. to Herb Jaffe, UA head of west coast prod., which post he assumed when Jaffe left. Left to join indep. prod., Ray Stark.
PICTURES: Smokey and the Bandit, Hot Stuff, The Villain, The Hunter, Smokey and the Bandit II, Smokey and the Bandit III, Nobody's Perfekt, The Heavenly Kid, The Big Easy, Maid to Order, Dudes, Three For the Road, Russkies, Pass the Ammo, Trading Hearts, Fright Night Part 2, Rented Lips, Remote Control.

ENGLANDER, MORRIS K.
Executive. b. New York, NY, July 5, 1934. e. Wharton Sch., U. of Pennsylvania. With General Cinema Corp. circuit before joining RKO Century Warner Theatres 1984 as exec. v.p., develp.; later exec.-vice chmn. of circuit. 1986, sr. real estate advisor, American Multi-Cinema. 1988: v.p. real estate Hoyts Cinemas Corp.; 1990 COO of Hoyts; pres. & COO of Hoyts. 1991.

ENGLUND, ROBERT
Actor. b. Glendale, CA, June 6, 1949. e. UCLA, RADA. First significant role was in the Cleveland stage production of Godspell, 1971.
PICTURES: Buster and Billie, Hustle, Stay Hungry, Death Trap (Eaten Alive), The Last of the Cowboys, St. Ives, A Star is Born, Big Wednesday, Bloodbrothers, The Fifth Floor, Dead and Buried, Galaxy of Terror, Don't Cry It's Only Thunder, A Nightmare on Elm Street, A Nightmare on Elm Street Part 2: Freddy's Revenge, Never Too Young to Die, A Nightmare on Elm Street 3: Dream Warriors, A Nightmare on Elm Street 4: The Dream Master, 976-EVIL (dir. only), A Nightmare on Elm Street: The Dream Child, Phantom of the Opera, The Adventures of Ford Fairlane, Danse Macabre, Freddy's Dead: The Final Nightmare, Eugenie, Wes Craven's New Nightmare, The Mangler, The Paper Route, Vampyre Wars, Killer Tongue, Regeneration.
TELEVISION: *Series:* Downtown, V, Freddy's Nightmares, Nightmare Cafe. *Specials and Movies:* Hobson's Choice, Young Joe: The Forgotten Kennedy, The Ordeal of Patty

Hearst, The Courage and the Passion, Mind Over Murder, Thou Shalt Not Kill, The Fighter, Journey's End, Starflight: The Plane That Couldn't Land, I Want to Live, Infidelity, A Perry Mason Mystery: The Case of the Lethal Lifestyle, Robin Cook's Mortal Fear, The Unspoken Truth. *Mini-Series*: V, North and South Book II. *Host*: Horror Hall of Fame.

EPHRON, NORA
Writer, Director. b. New York, NY, May 19, 1941. e. Wellesley Col. Daughter of writers Henry and Phoebe Ephron. m. writer Nicholas Pileggi. *Author*: Heartburn, Crazy Salad, Scribble Scribble. Appeared in films Crimes and Misdemeanors, Husbands and Wives.
PICTURES: *Writer*: Silkwood, Heartburn, When Harry Met Sally... (also assoc. prod.), Cookie (also exec. prod.), My Blue Heaven (also exec. prod.), This is My Life (also dir.), Sleepless in Seattle (also dir.), Mixed Nuts (also dir.), Michael (also dir.).
TELEVISION: *Movie (writer)*: Perfect Gentlemen.

EPSTEIN, JULIUS J
Screenwriter. b. New York, NY, Aug. 22, 1909. e. Pennsylvania State U. Worked as publicist before going to Hollywood where began writing. Had long collaboration with twin brother, Philip G. Epstein. Under contract with Warner Bros. over 17 years.
PICTURES: In Caliente, Broadway Gondolier, Four Daughters, Daughters Courageous, Four Wives, Saturday's Children, No Time for Comedy, The Strawberry Blonde, The Bride Came C.O.D., The Man Who Came to Dinner, The Male Animal, Casablanca (Academy Award, 1943), Arsenic and Old Lace, Mr. Skeffington (also co-prod.), Romanc on the High Seas, My Foolish Heart, Forever Female, The Last Time I Saw Paris, Young at Heart, The Tender Trap, Kiss Them for Me, Take a Giant Step (also prod.), Tall Story, Fanny, Light in the Piazza, Send Me No Flowers, Return From the Ashes, Any Wednesday (also prod.), Pete n' Tillie (also prod.), Jacqueline Susann's Once Is Not Enough, Cross of Iron, House Calls, Reuben Reuben (also co-prod.).

EPSTEIN, MEL
Producer. b. Dayton, OH, Mar. 25, 1910; e. Ohio State U. Adv. & edit. depts. on newspapers; entered m.p. ind. as player in 1931; then asst. dir., unit prod. mgr., second unit & shorts dir.; U.S. Army Signal Corps (1st Lt.); apptd. Paramount prod., 1946. Now retired.
PICTURES: Whispering Smith, Hazard, Copper Canyon, Dear Brat, Branded, The Savage, Alaska Seas, Secret of the Incas.
TELEVISION: Broken Arrow, Men into Space, The Islanders, Asphalt Jungle, Rawhide, Long Hot Summer, The Monroes, Custer, Lancer (pilot), Lancer (unit mngr., series), Medical Center (series).

ERDMAN, RICHARD
Actor, Director. b. Enid, OK, June 1, 1925. e. Hollywood H.S.
PICTURES: *Actor*: Janie, Objective Burma, Time of Your Life, Four Days Leave, The Men, Cry Danger, Jumping Jacks, Happy Time, The Stooge, Stalag 17, The Power and the Prize, Saddle the Wind, Namu The Killer Whale. *Director*: Bleep, The Brothers O'Toole. *Writer-Prod.*: The Hillerman Project.
TELEVISION: Ray Bolger Show, Perry Mason, Police Story, Tab Hunter Show, Alice, Bionic Woman, One Day at a Time, Playhouse of Stars, Twilight Zone, The Lucy Show, Lou Grant, Cheers, Wings. *Movie*: Jesse. *Director*: The Dick Van Dyke Show, Mooch (special). *Writer-Prod.*: More Than a Scarecrow.

ERICSON, JOHN
Actor. b. Detroit, MI, Sept. 25, 1926. e. American Acad. of Dramatic Arts. Appeared in summer stock; then Stalag 17 on Broadway.
PICTURES: Teresa (debut, 1951), Rhapsody, The Student Prince, Green Fire, Bad Day at Black Rock, The Return of Jack Slade, The Cruel Tower, Oregon Passage, Forty Guns, Day of the Bad Man, Pretty Boy Floyd, Under Ten Flags, Slave Queen of Babylon, 7 Faces of Dr. Lao, Operation Atlantis, The Money Jungle, The Destructors, Treasure of Pancho Villa, The Bamboo Saucer (Collision Course), Heads or Tails, Bednobs and Broomsticks, Hustle Squad, Crash, Final Mission, Alien Zone, Project Saucer, Golden Triangle, Queens Are Wild, Hustler Squad, $10,000 Caper.
TELEVISION: *Series*: Honey West. *Movies*: The Bounty Man, Hog Wild, Hunter's Moon, House on the Rue Riviera, Tenafly. *Mini-Series*: Robert Kennedy and His Times, Space. *Specials*: Saturday's Children, Heritage of Anger, The Innocent Sleep. *Guest*: Marcus Welby, Mannix, Streets of San Francisco, Fantasy Island, Bonanza, Medical Center, Route 66, Murder She Wrote, Police Story, General Hospital, Air Wolf, Gunsmoke, Police Woman, The FBI, One Day at a Time, Magnum P.I.

ERMAN, JOHN
Director. b. Chicago, IL, Aug. 3, 1935. e. U. of California. Debut as TV director, Stoney Burke, 1962.
PICTURES: Making It, Ace Eli and Rodger of the Skies, Stella.

TELEVISION: *Movies*: Letters From Three Lovers, Green Eyes, Alexander the Other Side of Dawn, Just Me and You, My Old Man, Moviola (This Year's Blonde; Scarlett O'Hara War; The Silent Lovers), The Letter, Eleanor: First Lady of the World, Who Will Love My Children? (Emmy Award, 1983), Another Woman's Child, A Streetcar Named Desire, Right to Kill?, The Atlanta Child Murders, An Early Frost, The Two Mrs. Grenvilles (also sprv. prod.), When the Time Comes, The Attic: The Hiding of Anne Frank (also prod.), David (also sprv. prod.), The Last Best Year (also sprv. prod.), The Last to Go (also prod.), Our Sons, Carolina Skeletons, Breathing Lessons (also prod.), The Sunshine Boys (also prod.). *Mini-Series*: Roots: The Next Generations (co-dir.), Queen (also co-prod.), Scarlett (also prod.).

ESBIN, JERRY
Executive. b. Brooklyn, NY, 1931. Started in mailroom at Columbia at 17 and worked for co. nearly 25 years. Then joined American Multi Cinema. Joined Paramount Pictures in 1975 as mgr. of branch operations; later named v.p., asst. sls. mgr. In 1980 named v.p., gen. sls. mgr. 1981, as domestic sls. & mktg. 1981, joined United Artists as sr. v.p., mktg. & dist.; 1982, named pres., MGM/UA m.p. dist. & mktg. div; 1983, sr. v.p., domestic dist., Tri-Star Pictures; 1985, promoted to exec. v.p.; 1989, joined Loews Theaters as sr. exec. v.p. and chief oper. officer, also in 1989 named pres. as well as chief operating officer, Loews Theater Management Corp.

ESMOND, CARL
Actor. b. Vienna, Austria, June 14, 1906. e. U. of Vienna. On stage Vienna, Berlin, London (Shakespeare, Shaw, German modern classics). Acted in many European films under the name Willy Eichberger. Originated part of Prince Albert in Victoria Regina (London). On screen in Brit. prod. incl. Blossom Time, Even Song, Invitation to the Waltz. To U.S. in 1938. Guest star on many live and filmed TV shows. US stage incl. The Woman I Love, Four Winds. Appeared in Oscar nom. docum. Resisting Enemy Interrogation.
PICTURES: Dawn Patrol, First Comes Courage, Little Men, Sergeant York, Panama Hattie, Seven Sweethearts, Address Unknown, Margin for Error, Master Race, Ministry of Fear, Experiment Perilous, Story of Dr. Wassell. The Catman of Paris, Smash-up, Story of a Woman, Casablanca, Climax, Slave Girl, Walk a Crooked Mile, The Navy Comes Through, Sundown, Lover Come Back, This Love of Ours, Without Love, Mystery Submarine, The Desert Hawk, The World in His Arms, Thunder in the Sun, From the Earth to the Moon, Brushfire, Kiss of Evil, Agent for H.A.R.M., Morituri.
TELEVISION: My Wicked Wicked Ways. *Guest*: The Man From Uncle, Lassie, The Big Valley, Treasury Agent, etc.

ESPOSITO, GIANCARLO
Actor. b. Copenhagen, Denmark, April 26, 1958. Made B'way debut as child in 1968 musical Maggie Flynn.
THEATER: *B'way*: Maggie Flynn, The Me Nobody Knows, Lost in the Stars, Seesaw, Merrily We Roll Along, Don't Get God Started. *Off-B'way*: Zooman and the Sign (Theatre World Award, Obie Award), Keyboard, Who Loves the Dancer, House of Ramon Iglesias, Do Lord Remember Me, Balm in Gilead, Anchorman, Distant Fires, Trafficking in Broken Hearts.
PICTURES: Running, Taps, Trading Places, The Cotton Club, Desperately Seeking Susan, Maximum Overdrive, Sweet Lorraine, School Daze, Do the Right Thing, Mo'Better Blues, King of New York, Harley Davidson and the Marlboro Man, Night on Earth, Bob Roberts, Malcolm X, Amos & Andrew, Fresh, Smoke, The Usual Suspects, Kla$h, Blue in the Face, Reckless.
TELEVISION: *Series*: Bakersfield P.D. *Movies*: The Gentleman Bandit, Go Tell It on the Mountain, Relentless: Mind of a Killer. *Special*: Roanok. *Guest*: Miami Vice, Spencer: For Hire, Legwork.

ESSEX, DAVID
Actor, Singer, Composer. b. Plaistow, London, Eng. July 23, 1947. e. Shipman Sch., Custom House. Started as a singer-drummer in East London band. 1967: Joined touring Repertory Co. in The Fantasticks, Oh, Kay. 1970: West End debut in Ten Years Hard, 1972: Jesus Christ in Godspell, Che in Evita; Lord Byron in Childe Byron, 1983-84: Fletcher Christian in own musical Mutiny! on album and stage. International recording artist. Variety Club of Great Britain show business personality of 1978. Many gold & silver disc intl. awards. 1989, Royal Variety performance. World concerts since 1974.
PICTURES: Assault, All Coppers Are..., That'll Be the Day, Stardust, Silver Dream Racer (also wrote score), Shogun Mayeda.
TELEVISION: Top of the Pops, Own Specials, The River (also composed music), BBC series. U.S.: Merv Griffin, Johnny Carson, Dinah Shore, American Bandstand, Midnight Special, Grammy Awards, Salute To The Beatles, Don Kirshner's Rock Concert, A.M. America, Phil Everly in Session, Paul Ryan Show.

ESSEX, HARRY J.
Writer. b. New York, NY, Nov. 29, 1915. e. St. John's U., Brooklyn, B.A. With Dept. Welfare. Wrote orig. story, Man Made Monster, for Universal. During W.W.II in U.S. Army Signal Corps; scenarist, training films on combat methods, censorship. Novels: I Put My Right Foot In, Man and Boy, Marina.
THEATER: Something for Nothing, Stronger Than Brass, Neighborhood Affair, One for the Dame, Fatty, Twilight, When the Bough Breaks, Dark Passion, Casa D'Amor, I Remember It Well, Maurice Chevalier.
PICTURES: Boston Blackie and the Law, Dangerous Business, Desperate, Bodyguard, He Walked by Night, Dragnet, Killer That Stalked New York, Wyoming Mail, The Fat Man, Undercover Girl, Las Vegas Story, Models Inc., Kansas City Confidential, The 49th Man, It Came From Outer Space, I the Jury (also dir.), Creature from the Black Lagoon, Southwest Passage, Devil's Canyon, Mad at the World (also dir.), Teen-age Crime Wave, Raw Edge, Lonely Man, The Sons of Katie Elder, Man and Boy, Octoman, The Cremators (also prod., dir.), The Amigos.
TELEVISION: Untouchables, The Racers, Alcoa Hour, Westinghouse, Desilu; story consultant and head writer: Target, The Corruptors, The Dick Powell Show, Bewitched, I Dream of Jeannie, Kraft Suspense Theatre, Hostage Flight.

ESTEVEZ, EMILIO
Actor, Director, Writer. b. New York, NY, May 12, 1962. Father is actor Martin Sheen; brother is actor Charlie Sheen. Made prof. debut at age 20 in tv movie starring his father, In the Custody of Strangers.
PICTURES: Tex (debut, 1982), The Outsiders, Nightmares, Repo Man, The Breakfast Club, St. Elmo's Fire, That Was Then This is Now (also s.p.), Maximum Overdrive, Wisdom (also dir., s.p.), Stakeout, Young Guns. Men at Work (also dir., s.p.), Young Guns II, Freejack, The Mighty Ducks, National Lampoon's Loaded Weapon 1, Another Stakeout, Judgment Night, D2: The Mighty Ducks, The Jerky Boys (co- exec. prod. only), The War at Home, Mighty Ducks 3.
TELEVISION: Movies: In the Custody of Strangers. Nightbreaker.

ESTRADA, ERIK
Actor. r.n. Enrique Estrada. m. actress Peggy Rowe. b. New York, NY, Mar. 16, 1949. Began professional career in Mayor John Lindsay's Cultural Program, performing in public parks. Joined American Musical Dramatic Acad. for training. Feature film debut in The Cross and the Switchblade (1970).
PICTURES: The New Centurions, Airport '75, Midway, Trackdown, Where Is Parsifal?, Lightblast, The Repentant, Hour of the Assassin, The Lost Idol, A Show of Force, Night of the Wilding, Twisted Justice, Caged Fury, Guns, Spirits, Do or Die, The Divine Enforcer, Alien Seed, Night of the Wilding, National Lampoon's Loaded Weapon 1, The Last Riders, Gang Justice.
TELEVISION: Series: CHiPS. Guest: Hawaii Five-0, Six Million Dollar Man, Police Woman, Kojak, Medical Center, Hunter, Alfred Hitchcock Presents (1988), Cybill. Movies: Fire!, Honeyboy, The Dirty Dozen: The Fatal Mission, She Knows Too Much, Earth Angel.

ESZTERHAS, JOE
Writer. Author of novel Charlie Simpson's Apocalypse (nom. National Book Award, 1974), Nark!, and novelization of F.I.S.T.
PICTURES: F.I.S.T., Flashdance, Jagged Edge, Big Shots, Betrayed, Checking Out, Music Box (also co-exec. prod.), Basic Instinct, Nowhere to Run (co-sp., co-exec. prod.), Sliver (also co-exec. prod.), Jade (exec. prod. only), Hearts of Fire.

ETTINGER, EDWIN D.
Publicist. b. New York, NY, 1921. Entered m.p. ind. as office boy, MGM; pub. rel. and publ. for industrial, comm. clients, 1946-52; joined Ettinger Co., pub. rel., 1952; pub. rel. dir., Disneyland Inc., 1955; marketing dir., Disneyland, 1955-65; v.p., M.C.A. Enterprises, Inc., 1965-66; Board chmn. & CEO Recreation Environments, Inc., 1967-70; Board chmn. & CEO Recreations Inc., 1967-70; Pres., Ettinger, Inc., 1975-85; semi-retired in 1985.

ETTLINGER, JOHN A.
Producer, Director, Distributor. b. Chicago, IL, Oct. 14, 1924. e. Peddie Inst., Cheshire Acad. Signal Corps Photog. Center, 1942-45; with Paramount Theatres Corp., 1945-47; dir., KTLA, Paramount TV Prod., Inc., Los Angeles, 1948-50; radio-TV dir., Nat. C. Goldstone Agency, 1950-53; pres. Medallion TV Enterprises, Inc.; TV prod., View the Clue, Greenwich Village, High Road to Danger, Sur Demande, Star Route, Las Vegas Fights, Celebrity Billiards; Pres., KUDO-FM, Las Vegas.

EVANS, BARRY
Actor, Director. b. Guildford, England, 1943. Trained Central School. Repertory: Barrow, Nottingham, Chester, Royal Court, Nat. Theatre, Hampstead Th. Club, Chips with Everything, London and B'way Young Vic. Theatre Clwyd Mold.
PICTURES: The White Bus, Here We Go 'Round the Mulberry Bush, Alfred the Great, Die Screaming, Marriane, The Adventures of a Taxi-Driver, Under the Doctor.
TELEVISION: Redcap, Undermined, The Baron, The Class, Armchair Theatre, Love Story, Doctor in the House, Doctor at Large, Short Story, Crossroads, Mind Your Language, Dick Emery Show.

EVANS, GENE
Actor. b. Holbrook, AZ, July 11, 1924. e. Colton H.S. Started career in summer stock, Penthouse Theatre, Altadena, CA. Screen debut: Under Colorado Skies, 1947.
PICTURES: Crisscross, Larceny, Berlin Express, Assigned to Danger, Mother Was a Freshman, Sugarfoot, Armored Car Robbery, Steel Helmet, I Was an American Spy, Force of Arms, Jet Pilot, Fixed Bayonets, Mutiny, Park Row, Thunderbirds, Donovan's Brain, Golden Blade, Hell and High Water, Long Wait, Cattle Queen of Montana, Wyoming Renegades, Crashout, Helen Morgan Story, Bravados, Sad Sack, The Hangman, Operation Petticoat, Support Your Local Sheriff, War Wagon, Nevada Smith, Young and Wild, Ballad of Cable Hogue, There Was a Crooked Man, Support Your Local Gunfighter, Camper John, Walking Tall, People Toys, Pat Garrett and Billy the Kid, Magic of Lassie, Blame It on the Night.
TELEVISION: Series: My Friend Flicka, Matt Helm, Spencer's Pilots. Movies: Kate Bliss & Ticker Tape Kid, Fire, The Sacketts, Shadow Riders, Travis McGee, The Alamo: 13 Days to Glory, Once Upon a Texas Train, Casino, Concrete Cowboys, Shootout in a One-Dog Town.

EVANS, LINDA
Actress. b. Hartford, CT, Nov. 18, 1942. e. Hollywood H.S., L.A. TV commercials led to contract with MGM.
PICTURES: Twilight of Honor (debut, 1963), Those Calloways, Beach Blanket Bingo, The Klansman, Mitchell, Avalanche Express, Tom Horn.
TELEVISION: Series: The Big Valley, Hunter, Dynasty. Movies: Nakia, Nowhere to Run, Standing Tall, Gambler: The Adventure Continues, Bare Essence, The Last Frontier, I'll Take Romance, Dynasty: The Reunion, The Gambler Returns: Luck of the Draw. Mini-Series: North & South Book II, Dazzle.

EVANS, RAY
Songwriter. b. Salamanca, NY, Feb. 4, 1915. e. Wharton Sch. of U. of Pennsylvania. Musician on cruise ships, radio writer spec. material. Hellzapoppin', Sons o' Fun. Member: exec. bd. Songwriters Guild of America, Dramatists Guild, West Coast advisory bd. ASCAP., bd., Myasthenia Gravis Fdn. CA chap., Songwriters Hall of Fame, Motion Picture Acad. Received star on Hollywood Blvd. Walk of Fame.
SONGS: To Each His Own, Golden Earrings, Buttons and Bows (Academy Award, 1948), Mona Lisa (Academy Award, 1950), Whatever Will Be Will Be (Academy Award, 1956), A Thousand Violins, I'll Always Love You, Dreamsville, Love Song from Houseboat, Tammy, Silver Bells, Dear Heart, Angel, Never Let Me Go, Almost in Your Arms, As I Love You, In the Arms of Love, Wish Me a Rainbow.
PICTURES: The Paleface, Sorrowful Jones, Fancy Pants, My Friend Irma, Aaron Slick From Punkin Crick, Son of the Paleface, My Friend Irma Goes West, The Night of Grizzly, Saddle the Wind, Isn't It Romantic, Capt. Carey U.S.A., Off Limits, Here Come the Girls, Red Garters, Man Who Knew Too Much, Stars Are Singing, Tammy, Houseboat, Blue Angel, A Private's Affair, All Hands on Deck, Dear Heart, The Third Day, What Did You Do in the War Daddy?, This Property Is Condemned.
BROADWAY MUSICALS: Oh Captain! Let It Ride!, Sugar Babies.
TELEVISION THEMES: Bonanza, Mr. Ed, Mr. Lucky, To Rome With Love.

EVANS, ROBERT
Producer. b. New York, NY, June 29, 1930. Son is actor Josh Evans. Radio actor at age 11; went on to appear in more than 300 radio prog. (incl. Let's Pretend, Archie Andrews, The Aldrich Family, Gangbusters) on major networks. Also appeared on early TV. At 20 joined brother, Charles, and Joseph Picone as partner in women's clothing firm of Evan-Picone, Inc., 1952-67. In 1957 signed by Universal to play Irving Thalberg in Man of a Thousand Faces after recommendation by Norma Shearer, Thalberg's widow. Guest columnist NY Journal American, 1958. Independent prod. at 20th Century-Fox. 1966-76, with Paramount Pictures as head of prod., then exec. v.p. worldwide prod. (supervising Barefoot in the Park, Rosemary's Baby, Barbarella, Goodbye Columbus, Love Story, The Godfather I & II, The Great Gatsby, etc.). Resigned to become indep. prod. again; with exclusive contract with Paramount. Autobiography: The Kid Stays in the Picture (1994).
PICTURES: Actor: Man of a Thousand Faces, The Sun Also Rises, The Fiend Who Walked the West, The Best of

Everything. *Producer*: Chinatown, Marathon Man, Black Sunday, Players, Urban Cowboy, Popeye, The Cotton Club, The Two Jakes, Sliver, Jade, The Phantom.
TELEVISION: *Actor*: Elizabeth and Essex (1947), Young Widow Brown, The Right to Happiness. *Prod.*: Get High on Yourself.

EVERETT, CHAD
Actor. r.n. Raymond Lee Cramton. b. South Bend, IN, June 11, 1937. e. Wayne State U., Detroit. Signed by William T. Orr, head of TV prod. for Warner Bros. to 7-year contract. Appeared in many TV series as well as films. Next became contract player at MGM (1963-67). Received star on Hollywood Walk of Fame.
PICTURES: Claudelle Inglish (debut, 1961), The Chapman Report, Rome Adventure, Get Yourself a College Girl, The Singing Nun, Made in Paris, Johnny Tiger, The Last Challenge, Return of the Gunfighter, First to Fight, The Impossible Years, Firechasers, Airplane II: The Sequel, Fever Pitch, Jigsaw, Heroes Stand Alone, Official Denial.
TELEVISION: *Series*: The Dakotas, Medical Center, Hagen, The Rousters, McKenna, Dark Skies (narr. of pilot). *Guest*: Hawaiian Eye, 77 Sunset Strip, Surfside Six, Lawman, Bronco, The Lieutenant, Redigo, Route 66, Ironside, Hotel, Murder She Wrote, Shades of L.A., Cybil. *Movies*: Intruder, The Love Boat, Police Story, Thunderboat Row, Malibu, The French Atlantic Affair, Mistress in Paradise, Journey to the Unknown, In the Glitter Palace. *Mini-Series*: Centennial.

EVERETT, RUPERT
Actor. b. Norfolk, England, 1959. e. Ampleforth Central School for Speech & Drama. Apprenticed with Glasgow's Citizen's Theatre. Originated role of Guy Bennett in Another Country on London stage in 1982 and made feature film debut in screen version in 1984. Author: Are You Working Darling?
PICTURES: Another Country, Real Life, Dance with a Stranger, Duet for One, Chronicle of a Death Foretold, The Right Hand Man, Hearts of Fire, The Gold-Rimmed Glasses, Jigsaw, The Comfort of Strangers, Inside Monkey Zetterland, Ready to Wear (Pret-a-Porter), The Madness of King George, Dunston Checks In, Cemetary Man.
TELEVISION: Arthur the King, The Far Pavilions, Princess Daisy.

EVERSON, WILLIAM K.
Writer. b. Yeovil, Eng., April 8, 1929. Pub. dir., Renown Pictures Corp., Ltd., London, 1944; film critic; m.p. journalist; in armed forces, 1947-49; thea. mgr., pub. & booking consultant, Monseigneur News Theatres, London, 1949; pub. dir., Allied Artists Inc. Corp., 1951; prod., writer Paul Killiam Dorg., 1956. Writer-editor-researcher on TV series Movie Museum and Silents Please, also on TV specials and theatrical features Hollywood the Golden Years, The Valentino Legend, The Love Goddesses and The Great Director. Lecturer, archival consultant, American Film Institute representative. Film History instructor at NYU, The New School and Sch. of Visual Arts, all in NY. Also, Harvard U.
AUTHOR: The Western, The Bad Guys, The American Movie, The Films of Laurel & Hardy, The Art of W. C. Fields, Hal Roach, The Detective in Film, Classics of the Horror Film, Claudette Colbert.
(d. April 14, 1996)

EVIGAN, GREG
Actor. b. South Amboy, NJ, Oct. 14, 1953. Appeared on NY stage in Jesus Christ Superstar and Grease.
PICTURES: Stripped to Kill, DeepStar Six.
TELEVISION: *Series*: A Year at the Top, B.J. and the Bear, Masquerade, My Two Dads, P.S. I Luv U, Tek War. *Movies*: B.J. and the Bear (pilot), Private Sessions, The Lady Forgets, Lies Before Kisses, Tek War, Tek Justice, One of Her Own, Tek Lab, Tek Lords. *Guest*: One Day at a Time, Barnaby Jones, Murder She Wrote, New Mike Hammer, Matlock.

F

FABARES, SHELLEY
Actress. b. Los Angeles, CA, Jan. 19, 1944. r.n. Michele Marie Fabares. m. actor Mike Farrell. Earned gold record for 1962 single Johnny Angel.
PICTURES: Never Say Goodbye, Rock Pretty Baby, Marjorie Morningstar, Summer Love, Ride the Wild Surf, Girl Happy, Hold On!, Spinout, Clambake, A Time to Sing, Hot Pursuit, Love or Money.
TELEVISION: *Series*: Annie Oakley, The Donna Reed Show, The Little People (The Brian Keith Show), The Practice, Mary Hartman Mary Hartman, Highcliffe Manor, One Day at a Time, Coach. *Guest*: Twilight Zone, Mr. Novak, Love American Style, The Rookies, Marcus Welby, Hello Larry. *Movies*: U.M.C., Brian's Song, Two for the Money, Sky Hei$t, Pleasure Cove, Friendships Secrets & Lies, The Great American Traffic Jam (Gridlock), Memorial Day, Class Cruise, Deadly Relations, The Great Mom Swap.

FAHEY, JEFF
Actor. b. Olean, NY, Nov. 29, 1956. Family moved to Buffalo when he was 10 years old. Was member of Joffrey Ballet for 3 years. Appeared on B'way in Brigadoon (1980), tour of Oklahoma!, Paris prod. of West Side Story, and London prod. of Orphans.
PICTURES: Silverado (debut, 1985), Psycho III, Split Decisions, Backfire, Outback, True Blood, Out of Time, Last of the Finest, Impulse, White Hunter Black Heart, Body Parts, Iron Maze, The Lawnmower Man, Wrangler, Woman of Desire, Freefall, Wyatt Earp, Temptation.
TELEVISION: *Series*: One Life to Live, The Marshal. *Movies*: Execution of Raymond Graham, Parker Kane, Curiosity Kills, Iran: Days of Crisis, Sketch Artist, In the Company of Darkness, The Hit List, Blindsided, Quick, Sketch Artist II: Hands That See, Virtual Seduction.

FAIMAN, PETER
Director. b. Australia. Entered entertainment business through TV, involved in production-direction of major variety series in Australia. Assoc. prod.-dir. of over 20 programs for The Paul Hogan Show and two Hogan specials filmed in England (1983). Developed Australia's most popular and longest-running national variety program, The Don Lane Show. Responsible for creative development of the TV Week Logie Awards on the Nine Network. For 4 years headed Special Projects Division of the Nine Network Australia. Resigned to establish own prod. co., Peter Faiman Prods. Pty Ltd. 1984. Made m.p. theatrical film debut as director of Crocodile Dundee, followed by Dutch.

FAIRBANKS, DOUGLAS, JR.
K.B.E., (Hon.) D.S.C., M.A., (Oxon), (Hon.) D.F.I., Westminster (Fulton, MO), (Hon.) LL.D (Denver). **Actor, Producer, Executive**. b. New York, NY, Dec. 9, 1909. e. Pasadena (CA) Polytech. Sch.; Harvard Mil. Acad., Los Angeles; Bovee and Collegiate Sch., N.Y.; was also tutored in Paris, London. Son of late Douglas Fairbanks. Began as screen actor 1923 in Stephen Steps Out; thereafter in more than 80 pictures. On U.S. stage from 1926. Formed own film prod. co. 1935; commissioned Lieut. (j.g.) USNR, 1940; Appt. Presidential envoy to certain South Amer. nations by Pres. Roosevelt. Helped org. British War Relief and was natl. chmn., Committee for CARE. W.A. White Committee to Defend America 1939-41. Promoted through ranks to Capt., USNR, Now retired. Awarded U.S. Silver Star, Combat Legion of Merit with "V" Attachment; Knight Commander of Order of British Empire, 1949. Distinguished Service Cross, Knight of Justice of Order of St. John of Jerusalem; French Legion of Honor, Croix de Guerre with Palm, etc. Chairman, American Relief for Korea. Entered TV film prod., 1952. Autobiographies: The Fairbanks Album (1975; with Richard Schickel), The Salad Days (1988), A Hell of a War (1993). FYI: republished in England, 1995.
THEATER: U.S.: Young Woodley, Saturday's Children, Present Laughter, Out on a Limb, Sleuth, The Pleasure of His Company (also U.K., Ireland, Canada, Australia, Hong Kong), The Winding Journey, Moonlight in Silver, My Fair Lady, The Secretary Bird.
PICTURES: (since sound): The Forward Pass, The Careless Age, The Show of Shows, Party Girl, Loose Ankles, The Little Accident, The Dawn Patrol, Little Caesar, Outward Bound, One Night at Susie's, Chances, I Like Your Nerve, Union Depot, It's Tough to Be Famous, Love is a Racket, Parachute Jumper, Morning Glory, Life of Jimmy Dolan, The Narrow Corner, Captured, Catherine the Great, Success at Any Price, Mimi, The Amateur Gentleman (also prod.), Man of the Moment, Accused, When Thief Meets Thief, The Prisoner of Zenda, Joy of Living, Having Wonderful Time, The Rage of Paris, The Young in Heart, Gunga Din, The Sun Never Sets, Rulers of the Sea, Green Hell, Safari, Angels Over Broadway, The Corsican Brothers, Sinbad the Sailor, That Lady in Ermine, The Exile, The Fighting O'Flynn, State Secret, Mr. Drake's Duck, Another Man's Poison (prod. only), Chase a Crooked Shadow (prod. only), Ghost Story.
TELEVISION: *Series*: Douglas Fairbanks Presents (also prod.). *Guest*: The Rheingold Theatre (also prod.), The Chevy Show, Route 66, Dr. Kildare, The Love Boat, B.L. Stryker. *Special*: The Canterville Ghost (ABC Stage '67). *Movies*: The Crooked Hearts, The Hostage Tower.

FAIRBANKS, JERRY
Executive Producer. b. San Francisco, CA, Nov. 1, 1904. Cameraman, 1924-29; prod., shorts, Universal, 1929-34; prod., Popular Science, Unusual Occupations, Speaking of Animals Series, Para., 1935-49; Winner two Acad. Awards; set up film div., NBC, 1948; formed NBC Newsreel, 1949; devel. Zoomar Lens and Multicam System; formed Jerry Fairbanks Prods., 1950.
PICTURES: The Last Wilderness, Down Liberty Road, With This Ring, Counterattack, Collision Course, Land of the Sea, Brink of Disaster, The Legend of Amaluk, North of the Yukon, Damage Report, The Boundless Seas.
TELEVISION: Public Prosecutor (first film series for TV); other series: Silver Theatre, Front Page Detective, Jackson and Jill, Hollywood Theatre, Crusader Rabbit.

FAIRCHILD, MORGAN
Actress. b. Dallas, TX, Feb. 3, 1950. e. Southern Methodist U.
PICTURES: Bullet for Pretty Boy, The Seduction, Pee-wee's Big Adventure, Red-Headed Stranger, Campus Man, Sleeping Beauty, Midnight Cop, Deadly Illusion, Phantom of the Mall, Body Chemistry 3: Point of Seduction, Freaked, Virgin Hunters, Naked Gun 33 1/3: The Final Insult.
TELEVISION: Series: Search for Tomorrow, Flamingo Road, Paper Dolls, Falcon Crest, Roseanne. Movies: The Initiation of Sarah, Murder in Music City, Concrete Cowboys, The Memory of Eva Ryker, Flamingo Road (pilot), The Dream Merchants, The Girl with the Gold Watch and Dynamite, Honeyboy, The Zany Adventures of Robin Hood, Time Bomb, Street of Dreams, The Haunting of Sarah Harding, How to Murder a Millionare, Menu for Murder, Writer's Block. Perry Mason: The Case of the Skin-Deep Scandal, Based on an Untrue Story. Mini-Series: 79 Park Avenue, North and South Book II.

FAIRCHILD, WILLIAM
Writer, Director. b. Cornwall, England, 1918. e. Royal Naval Coll., Dartmouth. Early career Royal Navy.
AUTHOR: A Matter of Duty, The Swiss Arrangement, Astrology for Dogs, Astrology for Cats, Catsigns (U.S.), The Poppy Factory, No Man's Land (U.S.), Tierra de Nadie (Spain).
THEATER: Sound of Murder, Breaking Point, Poor Horace, The Pay-Off, The Flight of the Bumble B.
PICTURES: Writer: Don Juan (debut, 1956), The Iceman Outcast of the Islands, The Gift Horse, The Net, Newspaper Story, Malta Story, The Seekers, Passage Home, Value For Money, John and Julie (also dir.), The Extra Day (also dir.), The Silent Enemy (also dir.), Star!, Embassy, The Darwin Adventure, Invitation to the Wedding, Bruno Rising, The Promise, Statues in a Garden. Director only: The Horsemasters (tv in U.S.).
TELEVISION: The Man with the Gun, No Man's Land, The Signal, Four Just Men, Some Other Love, Cunningham 5101, The Break, The Zoo Gang, Lady with a Past.

FALK, PETER
Actor. b. New York, NY, Sept. 16, 1927. e. New Sch. for Social Research, B.A., 1951; Syracuse U. M.F.A. Studied with Eva Le Galliene and Sanford Meisner. Worked as efficiency expert for Budget Bureau State of CT.
THEATER: Off-B'way: Don Juan (debut, 1956), The Iceman Cometh, Comic Strip, Purple Dust, Bonds of Interest, The Lady's Not for Burning, Diary of a Scoundrel. On Broadway: Saint Joan, The Passion of Josef D., The Prisoner of Second Avenue.
Regional: Light Up the Sky (L.A.), Glengarry Glen Ross (tour).
PICTURES: Wind Across the Everglades (debut, 1958), The Bloody Brood, Pretty Boy Floyd, The Secret of the Purple Reef, Murder Inc. (Acad. Award nom.), Pocketful of Miracles (Acad. Award nom.), Pressure Point, The Balcony, It's a Mad Mad Mad Mad World, Robin and the 7 Hoods, Italiano Brava Gente (Attack and Retreat), The Great Race, Penelope, Luv, Anzio, Castle Keep, Machine Gun McCann, Operation Snafu, Husbands, A Woman Under the Influence, Murder by Death, Mikey and Nicky, The Cheap Detective, The Brink's Job, Opening Night, The In-Laws, The Great Muppet Caper, All the Marbles, Big Trouble, Happy New Year, The Princess Bride, Wings of Desire, Vibes, Cookie, In the Spirit, Tune in Tomorrow, The Player, Faraway So Close!, Roommates.
TELEVISION: Series: The Trials of O'Brien, Columbo (1971-77; Emmy Awards: 1972, 1975, 1976), Columbo (1989, also co-exec. prod.; Emmy Award, 1990). Guest: Studio One, Kraft Theatre, Alcoa Theatre, N.T.A. Play of the Week, Armstrong Circle Theatre, Omnibus, Robert Montgomery Presents, Brenner, Deadline, Kraft Mystery Theatre, Rendezvous, Sunday Showcase, The Untouchables, Dick Powell Show (The Price of Tomatoes; Emmy Award, 1962), Danny Kaye Show, Edie Adams Show, Bob Hope Chrysler Theatre. Movies: Prescription: Murder, A Step Out of Line, Ransom for a Dead Man, Griffin and Phoenix: A Love Story, Columbo Goes to College, Caution: Murder Can Be Hazardous to Your Health, Columbo and the Murder of a Rock Star, Death Hits the Jackpot, Columbo: No Time to Die, Columbo: A Bird in the Hand (also exec. prod.), Columbo: It's All in the Game (also writer, exec. prod.), Columbo: Butterfly in Shades of Grey (also exec. prod.), Columbo: Undercover, Columbo: Strange Bedfellows (also exec. prod.). Specials: The Sacco-Vanzetti Story, The Million Dollar Incident, Brigadoon, A Hatful of Rain, Clue: Movies Murder and Mystery.

FARBER, BART
Executive. Joined United Artists Corp. in early 1960s when UA acquired ZIV TV Programs. Served as v.p. United Artists Television and United Artists Broadcasting. 1971 named v.p. in charge of legal affairs of the cos. 1978, named sr. v.p.—TV, video and special markets; indep. consultant, TV, Pay TV, home video. 1982, joined Cable Health Network as v.p., legal & business affairs; 1984, v.p., business & legal affairs, Lifetime Network; 1986, independent communications consultant.

FARENTINO, JAMES
b. Brooklyn, NY, Feb. 24, 1938. e. American Acad. of Dramatic Arts.

THEATER: B'way: Death of a Salesman, A Streetcar Named Desire (revival, 1973; Theatre World Award). Off-B'way: The Days and Nights of Bebe Fenstermaker, In the Summerhouse. Regional: One Flew Over the Cuckoo's Nest (Jos. Jefferson, Chas. MacArthur & Chicago Drama Critics League Awards), California Suite, The Best Man, Love Letters.
PICTURES: Psychomania (Violent Midnight), Ensign Pulver, The War Lord, The Pad ... And How to Use It (Golden Globe Award, 1966), The Ride to Hangman's Tree, Banning, Rosie!, Me Natalie, The Story of a Woman, The Final Countdown, Dead and Buried, Her Alibi, Bulletproof.
TELEVISION: Series: The Lawyers (The Bold Ones), Cool Million, Dynasty, Blue Thunder, Mary, Julie. Guest: Naked City, daytime soap operas, Laredo, Route 66, The Alfred Hitchcock Hour, Ben Casey, Twelve O'Clock High. Special: Death of a Salesman, DOS Pasos USA. Mini-Series: Sins, Jesus of Nazareth (Emmy nom.). Movies: Wings of Fire, Sound of Anger, The Whole World is Watching, Vanished, Longest Night, Family Rico, Cool Million, The Elevator, Crossfire, Possessed, Silent Victory: The Kitty O'Neil Story, Son Rise: A Miracle of Love, Evita Peron, That Secret Sunday, Something So Right (Emmy nom.), The Cradle Will Fall, License to Kill, A Summer to Remember, That Secret Sunday, Family Sins, The Red Spider, Who Gets the Friends?, Common Ground, In the Line of Duty: A Cop for the Killing, Miles From Nowhere, When No One Would Listen, Secrets of the Sahara (Italy), One Woman's Courage, Honor Thy Father and Mother: The True Story of the Menendez Murders, Dazzled. Pilot: American Nuclear.

FARGAS, ANTONIO
Actor. b. Bronx, NY, Aug. 14, 1946. Studied acting at Negro Ensemble Co. and Actor's Studio.
THEATER: The Great White Hope, The Glass Menagerie, Mod Hamlet, Romeo and Juliet, The Slave, Toilet, The Amen Corner.
PICTURES: The Cool World (debut, 1964), Putney Swope, Pound, Believe in Me, Shaft, Cisco Pike, Across 110th Street, Cleopatra Jones, Busting, Foxy Brown, Conrack, The Gambler, Cornbread Earl and Me, Next Stop Greenwich Village, Car Wash, Pretty Baby, Up the Academy, Firestarter, Streetwalkin', Night of the Sharks, Shakedown, I'm Gonna Git You Sucka, The Borrower, Howling VI: The Freaks, Whore.
TELEVISION: Series: Starsky and Hutch, All My Children. Movies: Starsky and Hutch (pilot), Huckleberry Finn, Escape, Nurse, The Ambush Murders, A Good Sport, Florida Straits, Maid for Each Other, Percy and Thunder. Guest: Ironside, The Bill Cosby Show, Sanford and Son, Police Story, Kolchak The Night Stalker, Miami Vice, Kojak.

FARGO, JAMES
Director. b. Republic, WA, Aug. 14, 1938. e. U. of Washington, B.A.
PICTURES: The Enforcer, Caravans, Every Which Way But Loose, Forced Vengeance, Born to Race, Voyage of the Rock Aliens, Riding the Edge (also actor).
TELEVISION: Tales of the Gold Monkey, Gus Brown and Midnight Brewster, The Last Electric Knight, Hunter, Snoops, Sky High.

FARINA, DENNIS
Actor. b. Chicago, IL, Feb. 29, 1944. Served 18 years with Chicago police before being introduced to producer-director Michael Mann who cast him in film Thief. Celebrity Chmn. of Natl. Law Enforcement Officers Memorial in Washington, D.C.
THEATER: A Prayer for My Daughter, Streamers, Tracers, Bleacher Bums, Some Men Need Help, The Time of Your Life.
PICTURES: Thief (debut, 1981), Jo Jo Dancer Your Life Is Calling, Manhunter, Midnight Run, Men of Respect, We're Talkin' Serious Money, Mac, Another Stakeout, Striking Distance, Romeo Is Bleeding, Little Big League, Get Shorty, Eddie.
TELEVISION: Series: Crime Story. Mini-Series: Drug Wars: Columbia. Movies: Six Against the Rock, Open Admissions, The Hillside Stranglers, People Like Us, Blind Faith, Cruel Doubt, The Disappearance of Nora, One Woman's Courage, The Corpse Had a Familiar Face, Bonanza: Under Attack, Out of Annie's Past. Guest: Miami Vice, Hunter, Tales from the Crypt. Special: The Killing Floor.

FARLEY, CHRIS
Actor. b. Madison, WI, 1960. e. Marquette Univ. Started with The Ark Improv. Theatre Group; performed comedy at Main Stage at Second City in Chicago where he met producer Lorne Michaels.
PICTURES: Coneheads (debut, 1993), Wayne's World 2, Airheads, Bill Madison (cameo), Tommy Boy, Black Sheep.
TELEVISION: Series: Saturday Night Live.

FARNSWORTH, RICHARD
Actor. b. Los Angeles, CA, Sept. 1, 1920. Active as stuntman for 40 years before turning to acting.
PICTURES: Comes a Horseman, Tom Horn, Resurrection, The Legend of the Lone Ranger, Ruckus, Waltz Across Texas, The Grey Fox, The Natural, Rhinestone, Into the Night, Sylvester, Space Rage, The Two Jakes, Misery, Highway to Hell, The Getaway, Lassie.

TELEVISION: *Series*: Boys of Twilight. *Movies*: Strange New World, A Few Days in Weasel Creek, Travis McGee, Ghost Dancing, Anne of Green Gables, Chase, Wild Horses, Red Earth White Earth, Good Old Boy, The Fire Next Time.

FARR, FELICIA
Actress. b. Westchester, NY, Oct. 4, 1932. e. Pennsylvania State Coll. m. Jack Lemmon. Stage debut: Picnic (Players Ring Theatre).
PICTURES: Timetable, Jubal, Reprisal, The First Texan, The Last Wagon, 3:10 to Yuma, Onionhead, Hell Bent for Leather, Kiss Me Stupid, The Venetian Affair, Kotch, Charley Varrick, That's Life!, The Player.

FARR, JAMIE
Actor. r.n. Jameel Joseph Farah. b. Toledo, OH, July 1, 1934. e. Columbia Coll. Trained for stage at Pasadena Playhouse. PICTURES: Blackboard Jungle (debut, 1955), The Greatest Story Ever Told, Ride Beyond Vengeance, Who's Minding the Mint?, With Six You Get Eggroll, The Gong Show Movie, Cannonball Run, Cannonball Run II, Happy Hour, Scrooged, Speed Zone, Curse II: The Bite.
TELEVISION: *Series*: The Chicago Teddy Bears, M*A*S*H (also dir. episodes), The Gong Show (panelist), The $1.98 Beauty Show (panelist), After M*A*S*H (also dir. episodes). *Guest*: Dear Phoebe, The Red Skelton Show, The Dick Van Dyke Show, The Danny Kaye Show, The Love Boat, The New Love American Style, Murder She Wrote. *Movies*: The Blue Knight, Amateur Night at the Dixie Bar and Grill, Murder Can Hurt You!, Return of the Rebels, For Love or Money, Run Till You Fall.

FARRELL, HENRY
Writer. Author of novels and screenplays
PICTURES: Whatever Happened to Baby Jane? Hush ... Hush Sweet Charlotte, What's the Matter with Helen?
TELEVISION: *Movies*: How Awful About Allan, The House That Would Not Die, The Eyes of Charles Sand.

FARRELL, MIKE
Actor, Producer. b. St. Paul, MN, Feb. 6, 1939. m. actress Shelley Fabares.
PICTURES: Captain Newman M.D., The Americanization of Emily, The Graduate, Targets. *Prod.*: Dominick and Eugene.
TELEVISION: *Series*: Days of Our Lives, The Interns, The Man and the City, M*A*S*H. *Specials*: JFK: One Man Show (PBS), The Best of Natl. Geographic Specials (host/narrator). *Movies*: The Longest Night, She Cried Murder!, The Questor Tapes, Live Again Die Again, McNaughton's Daughter, Battered, Sex and the Single Parent, Letters from Frank, Damien: The Leper Priest, Prime Suspect, Memorial Day, Choices of the Heart, Private Sessions, Vanishing Act, A Deadly Silence, Price of the Bride, The Whereabouts of Jenny, Memorial Day (also prod.), Incident at Dark River (also prod.), Silent Motive (also prod.), Hart to Hart: Old Friends Never Die. *Director*: Run Till You Fall.

FARROW, MIA
Actress. b. Los Angeles, CA, Feb. 9. 1945. r.n. Maria de Lourdes Villiers Farrow. d. of actress Maureen O'Sullivan and late dir. John Farrow. e. Marymount, Los Angeles, Cygnet House, London.
THEATER: The Importance of Being Earnest (debut, Madison Ave. Playhouse, NY, 1963); Royal Shakespeare Co. (Twelfth Night, A Midsummer Night's Dream, Ivanov, Three Sisters, The Seagull, A Doll's House), Mary Rose (London), Romantic Comedy (B'way debut, 1979).
PICTURES: Guns at Batasi (debut, 1964), A Dandy in Aspic, Rosemary's Baby, Secret Ceremony, John and Mary, See No Evil, The Public Eye, Dr. Popaul (High Heels), The Great Gatsby, Full Circle (The Haunting of Julia), Avalanche, A Wedding, Death on the Nile, Hurricane, A Midsummer Night's Sex Comedy, The Last Unicorn (voice), Zelig, Broadway Danny Rose, Supergirl, The Purple Rose of Cairo, Hannah and Her Sisters, Radio Days, September, Another Woman, New York Stories (Oedipus Wrecks), Crimes and Misde-meanors, Alice (Natl. Board of Review Award, 1990), Shadows and Fog, Husbands and Wives, Widow's Peak, Miami Rhapsody, Reckless.
TELEVISION: *Series*: Peyton Place. *Specials*: Johnny Belinda, Peter Pan. *Movie*: Goodbye Raggedy Ann.

FAWCETT, FARRAH
Actress. b. Corpus Christi, TX, Feb. 2, 1947. e. U. of Texas. Picked as one of the ten most beautiful girls while a freshman; went to Hollywood and signed by Screen Gems. Did films, TV shows, and made over 100 TV commercials. Off B'way debut: Extremities (1983).
PICTURES: Love Is a Funny Thing, Myra Breckinridge, Logan's Run, Somebody Killed Her Husband, Sunburn, Saturn 3, Cannonball Run, Extremities, See You in the Morning, Man of the House.
TELEVISION: *Series*: Charlie's Angels, Good Sports. *Guest*: Owen Marshall Counselor at Law, The Six Million Dollar Man, Rockford Files, Harry-O. *Movies*: Three's a Crowd, The Feminist

and the Fuzz, The Great American Beauty Contest, The Girl Who Came Gift-Wrapped, Murder on Flight 502, Murder in Texas, The Burning Bed, Red Light Sting, Between Two Women, Nazi Hunter: The Beate Klarsfeld Story, Poor Little Rich Girl: The Barbara Hutton Story, Margaret Bourke-White, Small Sacrifices, Criminal Behavior, The Substitute Wife, Children of the Dust.

FAY, PATRICK J.
Director, Producer. b. June 7, 1916. e. Carnegie Tech. Dumont TV Network, 10 years. Director of over 100 Army training films; also dir. IBM Industrials.
AUTHOR: Melba, The Toast of Pithole, The Last Family Portrait in Oil, Coal Oil Johnny, French Kate, No Pardon in Heaven, An Ill Wind, Tighten Your G-String, As It Was in the Beginning (Television 50 Yrs. Ago).
PICTURES: Director for RCA, General Electric H.G. Peters Company, Bransby Films. *Screenplays:* Sanctuary, The Burning of New York City, Johnson's Island.
TELEVISION: Bishop Sheen, Broadway to Hollywood, Cavalcade of Stars, Manhattan Spotlight, Life is Worth Living, Front Row Center, Ilona Massey Show, Alec Templeton Show, Maggi McNellis Show, Key to Missing Persons, Kids and Company, Confession (also prod.), The Big Picture.

FAYE, ALICE
Actress, Singer. r.n. Alice Jeanne Leppert. b. New York, NY, May 5, 1912. m. bandleader-actor-singer Phil Harris. Started dancin and singing in choruses as teen; hired by Rudy Vallee as singer for his band which resulted in movie debut at Fox, 1934.
PICTURES: George White's Scandals (debut, 1934), She Learned About Sailors, Now I'll Tell, 365 Nights in Hollywood, George White's 1935 Scandals, Every Night at Eight, Music Is Magic, Poor Little Rich Girl, Sing Baby Sing, King of Burlesque, Stowaway, On the Avenue, Wake Up and Live, You Can't Have Everything, You're a Sweetheart, In Old Chicago, Sally Irene and Mary, Alexander's Ragtime Band, Tail Spin, Hollywood Cavalcade, Barricade, Rose of Washington Square, Lillian Russell, Little Old New York, Tin Pan Alley, That Night in Rio, The Great American Broadcast, Weekend in Havana, Hello Frisco Hello, The Gang's All Here, Four Jills in a Jeep (cameo), Fallen Angel, State Fair, Won Ton Ton the Dog Who Saved Hollywood (cameo), The Magic of Lassie.

FEHR, RUDI
Editor, Executive. b. Berlin, Germany, July 6, 1911. m. Maris Wrixon, actress. Started career with Tobis-Klangfilm, Berlin. Joined Warner Bros. editorial department, 1936. Became pro-ducer, 1952; promoted to executive, 1956; Post Production Exec. Warner Bros.; WB title changed to dir. of editorial & post-prod. operations. Now retired; is consultant to industry.
PICTURES: *Editor*: Invisible Enemies, Honeymoon for Three, Desperate Journey, Watch on the Rhine, The Conspirators, Humoresque, Possessed, Key Largo, The Inspector General, House of Wax, Dial M for Murder, One From the Heart, Prizzi's Honor.

FEINGOLD, BEN
Executive. President, Columbia TriStar Home Video.

FEINSTEIN, ALAN
Actor. b. New York, NY, Sept. 8, 1941.
THEATER: *NY*: Malcolm, Zelda, A View from the Bridge (NY Drama Desk Award), As Is, A Streetcar Named Desire.
PICTURE: Looking for Mr. Goodbar.
TELEVISION: *Series*: Edge of Night, Love Of Life, Search for Tomorrow, Jigsaw John, The Runaways, The Family Tree, Berrenger's. *Movies*: Alexander: The Other Side of Dawn, Visions, The Hunted Lady, The Users, The Two Worlds of Jenny Logan, On Fire. *Mini-Series*: Masada.

FEITSHANS, BUZZ
Executive. b. Los Angeles, CA. e. USC. Started in film business as editor. Worked for 10 years at American-International as supvr. of prod. In 1975 formed A-Team Productions with John Milius. With Carolco Pictures: producer, 1981-6; exec. v.p. for mo. pic. production, member bd. dir. 1986-90. 1990\-, v.p. for Cinergi Prods.; 1994, pres. of Cinergi.
PICTURES: *Producer*: Dillinger, Act of Vengeance, Foxy Brown, Big Wednesday, Hardcore, 1941, Extreme Prejudice (exec. prod.), Conan the Barbarian, First Blood, Uncommon Valor, Rambo II, Red Dawn, Rambo III, Total Recall, Tombstone (exec. prod.), Color of Night.

FELDMAN, COREY
Actor. b. Reseda, CA, July 16, 1971. Has been performing since the age of 3 in over 100 commercials, television (Love Boat, Father Murphy, Foul Play, Mork and Mindy, Eight Is Enough, Alice, Gloria) and films.
PICTURES: Time After Time, The Fox and the Hound (voice), Friday the 13th—The Final Chapter, Gremlins, Friday the 13th—A New Beginning, The Goonies, Stand by Me, Lost Boys, License to Drive, The 'Burbs, Dream a Little Dream, Teenage Mutant Ninja Turtles (voice only), Rock 'n' Roll High School

Forever, Edge of Honor, Meatballs 4, Round Trip to Heaven, Stepmonster, Blown Away, National Lampoon's Loaded Weapon 1, Lipstick Camera, National Lampoon's Last Resort, Maverick, Dream a Little Dream 2, A Dangerous Place, Evil Obsession, Tales From the Crypt: Bordello of Blood.
TELEVISION: *Series*: The Bad News Bears, Madame's Place. *Movies*: Willa, Father Figure, Kid with a Broken Halo, Still the Beaver, Out of the Blue, When the Whistle Blows, I'm a Big Girl Now, Exile. *Specials*: 15 & Getting Straight, How to Eat Like a Child.

FELDMAN, EDWARD S.
Producer. b. New York, NY, Sept. 5, 1929. e. Michigan State U. Trade press contact, newspaper and mag. contact, 20th Century Fox, 1950; dir. info. services, Dover Air Force Base. 1954-56; publ. coordinator, The World of Suzie Wong, 1960; joined Embassy, dir. of publicity, 1969; v.p. in chg., adv. & pub, 7 Arts Prods., 1962; v.p. exec. asst. to head prod. Warner-7 Arts Studio 1967; pres., m.p. dept., Filmways, 1970; Formed Edward S. Feldman Co., 1978.
PICTURES: What's the Matter With Helen? (exec. prod.), Fuzz (exec. prod.), Save the Tiger (exec. prod.), The Other Side of the Mountain (prod.), Two-Minute Warning (prod.), The Other Side of the Mountain Part 2 (prod.), The Last Married Couple in America (co-prod.), Six Pack (co-exec. prod.), The Sender (prod.), Hot Dog ... The Movie! (co-prod.), Witness (prod.), Explorers (co-prod.), The Golden Child (co-prod.), The Hitcher (exec. prod.), Near Dark (exec. prod.), Wired (prod.), Green Card (exec. prod.), The Doctor (exec. prod.), Honey I Blew Up the Kid (prod.), Forever Young (exec. prod.), My Father the Hero (exec. prod.), The Jungle Book (prod.).
TELEVISION: *Exec. Prod.*: Moon of the Wolf, My Father's House, Valentine, 300 Miles for Stephanie, Charles and Diana: A Royal Love Story, 21 Hours at Munich, King, Not in Front of the Children, Obsessed with a Married Woman.

FELDON, BARBARA
Actress. b. Pittsburgh, PA, Mar. 12, 1941. e. Carnegie Tech. Former fashion model, also appeared in many commercials. On NY stage in Past Tense, Cut the Ribbons.
PICTURES: Fitzwilly, Smile, No Deposit No Return.
TELEVISION: *Series*: Get Smart, The Marty Feldman Comedy Machine, The Dean Martin Comedy Hour (host), Special Edition (host), The 80's Woman (synd.; host), Get Smart (1995). *Movies*: Getting Away From It All, Playmates, What Are Best Friends For?, Let's Switch, A Guide for the Married Woman, Sooner or Later, A Vacation in Hell, Before and After, Children of Divorce, Get Smart Again!

FELDSHUH, TOVAH
Actress. b. New York, NY, Dec. 27, 1953. e. Sarah Lawrence Col., Univ. of MN. For humanitarian work received the Israel Peace Medal and the Eleanor Roosevelt Humanitarian Award.
THEATER: *NY*: Cyrano, Straws in the Wind, Three Sisters, Rodgers and Hart, Yentl (Theatre World Award), Sarava, The Mistress of the Inn, Springtime for Henry, She Stoops to Conquer, Lend Me a Tenor, A Fierce Attachment, Sarah and Abraham, Six Wives, Hello Muddah! Hello Fadduh!
PICTURES: White Lies, Nunzio, The Idolmaker, Cheaper to Keep Her, Daniel, Brewster's Millions, The Blue Iguana, A Day in October, Comfortably Numb.
TELEVISION: *Series*: As the World Turns, Mariah. *Movies*: Scream Pretty Peggy, The Amazing Howard Hughes, Terror Out of the Sky, The Triangle Factory Fire Scandal, Beggarman Thief, The Women's Room, Citizen Cohn, Sexual Considerations. *Specials*: Dosvedanya Mean Goodbye, Saying Kaddish. *Mini-Series*: Holocaust. Guest: LA Law, Law and Order, etc.

FELL, NORMAN
Actor. b. Philadelphia, PA, March 24, 1924. e. Temple U. Studied acting with Stella Adler. Member, Actors Studio. Professional debut at Circle-in-the-Square Theatre in N.Y. in Bonds of Interest. Summer Stock; appearances on TV; moved to Hollywood in 1958 to begin theatrical film career.
PICTURES: Pork Chop Hill, Ocean's Eleven, The Rat Race, Inherit the Wind, It's a Mad Mad Mad Mad World, The Graduate, Bullitt, If It's Tuesday This Must Be Belgium, Catch-22, The Stone Killer, Rabbit Test, The End, On the Right Track, Paternity, Stripped to Kill, C.H.U.D.II: Bud the Chud, The Boneyard, For the Boys, Hexed.
TELEVISION: Over 150 live plays from NY and some 200 shows filmed in Hollywood. *Series*: Joe and Mabel, 87th Precinct, Dan August, Needles and Pins, Three's Company, The Ropers, Teachers Only. *Guest*: Matt Houston, Crazy Like a Fox, Simon and Simon, It's Garry Shandling's Show, The Boys (pilot). *Mini-Series*: Rich Man Poor Man, Roots: The Next Generations. *Movies*: The Hanged Man, Three's a Crowd, The Heist, Thursday's Game, Death Stalk, Richie Brockelman, Moviola: This Year's Blonde, For the Love of It, Uncommon Valor, The Jessie Owens Story.

FELLMAN, DANIEL R.
Executive. b. Cleveland, OH, March 14, 1943. e. Rider Coll., B.S., 1964. Paramount Pictures, 1964-69; Loews Theatres,

1969-71; Cinema National Theatres, 1971-76; 1976-78, pres., American Theatre Mgmt. Joined Warner Bros. in 1978, named exec. v.p. Warner Bros. domestic distribution, Jan. 1993. President Variety Club Tent 35, 1977-78. Bd. member, Will Rogers Foundation; Chairman, Foundation of Motion Picture Pioneers.

FELLMAN, NAT D.
Executive. b. New York, NY, Feb. 19, 1910. Started as office boy, Warner Bros. Pictures, 1928; transferred to Warner Bros. Theatres, asst. to chief booker; handled pool, partnership operations; head buyer, booker for Ohio zone, 1941; asst. to chief film buyer in New York, 1943; apptd. chief film buyer, 1952; exec. asst. to v.p. and gen. mgr., Stanley Warner Theatres, 1955; asst. gen. mgr., Stanley Warner Theatres, 1962; acting gen. mgr., Stanley Warner Theatres, July, 1964; Stanley Warner Theatres, v.p. and gen. mgr., 1965; v.p., NGC Theatre Corp. and division mgr. Fox Eastern Theatres, 1968; v.p. National General Corp., and pres., National General Theatres, 1969; 1974, formed Exhibitor Relations Co., operations consultant; sold it and retired in 1982. Served as vice pres., Variety Clubs International and NATO, Chmn., presidents' advisory comm.

FENADY, ANDREW J.
Producer, Writer. b. Toledo, OH, Oct. 4, 1928. e. U. of Toledo, 1946-50. Radio-prod.-actor-writer. *Novels*: The Man With Bogart's Face, The Secret of Sam Marlow, The Claws of the Eagle, The Summer of Jack London, Mulligan, Runaways.
PICTURES: Stakeout on Dope Street, The Young Captives, Ride Beyond Vengeance, Chisum, Terror in the Wax Museum, Arnold, The Man with Bogart's Face.
TELEVISION: *Series*: Confidential File, The Rebel, Branded, Hondo. *Movies*: The Woman Hunter, Voyage of the Yes, The Stranger, The Hanged Man, Black Noon, Sky Heist, Mayday 40,000 Ft., The Hostage Heart, Mask of Alexander, Masterpiece of Murder, Who Is Julia?, Jake Spanner—Private Eye, The Love She Sought, Yes Virginia There Is a Santa Claus, The Sea Wolf.

FENN, SHERILYN
Actress. b. Detroit, MI, Feb. 1, 1965.
PICTURES: The Wild Life (debut, 1984), Just One of the Guys, Out of Control, Thrashin', The Wraith, Zombie High, Two Moon Junction, Crime Zone, True Blood, Meridian: Kiss of the Beast, Wild at Heart, Backstreet Dreams, Ruby, Desire and Hell at Sunset Motel, Diary of a Hit Man, Of Mice and Men, Three of Hearts, Boxing Helena, Fatal Instinct.
TELEVISION: *Series*: Twin Peaks. *Movies*: Silence of the Heart, Dillinger, Spring Awakening, Liz: The Elizabeth Taylor Story. *Guest*: Cheers, 21 Jump Street, Heart of the City. *Specials*: Tales From the Hollywood Hills (A Table at Ciro's), Divided We Stand, A Family Again.

FENNEMAN, GEORGE
M.C., Announcer. b. Peking, China, Nov. 10, 1919. e. San Francisco State U.
PICTURES: The Thing, How to Succeed in Business Without Really Trying.
TELEVISION: *Series*: You Bet Your Life, Surprise Package, Anybody Can Play, Tell It to Groucho, Your Funny Funny Films, Talk About Pictures, On Campus, Donny & Marie (announcer). *Commercials*: Spokesman for Home Savings of America/ Savings of America.

FERRARA, ABEL
Director, Writer. b. Bronx, NY, 1951. Moved to Peekskill, NY, as teenager where he made short films with future writer Nicholas St. John. Traveled to England, worked for the BBC. Returned to U.S. to attended SUNY/Purchase, making short Could This Be Love, which received some theatrical distribution. Has used the pseudonymn Jimmy Laine.
PICTURES: Driller Killer (also actor, s.p. songs), Ms. 45 (also actor), Fear City, China Girl (also songs), Cat Chaser, King of New York, Bad Lieutenant (also co-s.p.), Dangerous Game, Body Snatchers, The Addiction, The Funeral.

FERRARO, JOHN E.
Executive. b. Greenwich, CT, July 20, 1958. e. Emerson College, B.S. in Mass Communications, 1980. Joined Paramount Pictures Corp. 1980. 1983-84, story analyst, Paramount TV. 1984-85 supervisor, Drama Development. 1985-87 manager, Current Programs & Special Projects. 1987-88, dir. Drama Development. 1988, exec. dir., Acquisitions, Paramount Pictures. 1990, v.p., acquisitions & co-productions.

FERRAZZA, CARL J.
Executive. b. Cleveland, OH, Aug. 29, 1920. e. Catholic U. of America, Washington, DC. Started career 1945: as asst. mgr. & mgr. for Loews Theatres. 1952, joined Cincinnati Theatre Co., first as mgr. for Keith's Theatre, Cincinnati, and after prom. dir. for circuit. 1963, field rep. for United Artists, covering midwest. 1968, UA prom. mgr., N.Y. 1975-83, dir. of field activities, MGM/UA; 1984, joined Orion Pictures Distributing Corp. as v.p. promotional and field activities.

FERRELL, CONCHATA
Actress. b. Charleston, WV, Mar. 28, 1943. e. Marshall Univ.
THEATER: *NY*: The Three Sisters, Hot L Baltimore, Battle of Angels, The Sea Horse (Theatre World, Obie & Vernon Rice Drama Desk Awards), Wine Untouched. *LA*: Getting Out, Picnic.
PICTURES: Deadly Hero, Network, Heartland, Where the River Runs Black, For Keeps?, Mystic Pizza, Edward Scissorhands, Family Prayers, True Romance, Samuari Cowboy, Heaven and Earth.
TELEVISION: *Series*: Hot L Baltimore, B.J. and the Bear, McClain's Law, E/R, Peaceable Kingdom, L. A. Law, Hearts Afire. *Movies*: The Girl Called Hatter Fox, A Death in Canaan, Who'll Save My Children?, Before and After, The Seduction of Miss Leona, Reunion, Rape and Marriage: The Rideout Case, Life of the Party: The Story of Beatrice, Emergency Room, Nadia, The Three Wishes of Billy Grier, North Beach and Rawhide, Samaritan: The Mitch Snyder Story, Eye on the Sparrow, Your Mother Wears Combat Boots, Goodbye Miss 4th of July, Opposites Attract, Deadly Intentions... Again?, Backfield in Motion. *Guest*: Good Times, Love Boat, Lou Grant, St. Elsewhere, Frank's Place, Murder She Wrote, Who's the Boss?, Matlock. *Specials*: The Great Gilly Hopkins, Portrait of a White Marriage, Runaway Ralph, Picnic.

FERRER, MEL
Actor, Producer, Director. r.n. Melchoir Ferrer. b. Elberon, NJ, Aug. 25, 1917. e. Princeton U. During coll. and early career spent summers at Cape Cod Playhouse, Dennis, MA; then writer in Mexico, authored juvenile book, Tito's Hats; later ed. Stephen Daye Press, VT. Left publishing upon reaching leading-man status at Dennis; on B'way as dancer in You'll Never Know, Everywhere I Roam, others; also in Kind Lady, Cue For Passion; then to radio, serving apprenticeship in small towns; prod.-dir. for NBC Land of the Free, The Hit Parade, and Hildegarde program. Entered m.p. ind., 1945, when signed by Columbia as dial. dir.: The Girl of the Limberlost; later, returned to Broadway, leading role, Strange Fruit; signed by David Selznick as producer-actor, on loan to John Ford as prod. asst. on The Fugitive; then to RKO for Vendetta.
THEATER: Kind Lady, Cue for Passion, Strange Fruit, Ondine, The Best Man (L.A., 1987).
PICTURES: *Actor*: Lost Boundaries (debut, 1949), Born to Be Bad, The Brave Bulls, Rancho Notorious, Scaramouche, Lili, Saadia, Knights of the Round Table, Oh Rosalinda!, Proibito (Forbidden), War and Peace, Paris Does Strange Things, The Sun Also Rises, The Vintage, Fraulein, The World the Flesh and the Devil, L'Homme a Femmes, The Hands of Orlac, Blood and Roses, Legge di Guerra, Devil and the 10 Commandments, The Longest Day, The Fall of the Roman Empire, Paris When It Sizzles (cameo), Sex and the Single Girl, El Greco (also prod.), El Senor de la Salle, The Black Pirate, The Girl From the Red Cabaret, Brannigan, The Tempter (The Antichrist), Death Trap (Eaten Alive), Hi-Riders, Pyjama Girl, Island of the Fish Men, The Norsemen, Yesterday's Tomorrow, The Visitor, The Fifth Floor, Nightmare City, Lili Marleen, Deadly Game, Screamers, Mad Dog Anderson. *Director*: The Girl of the Limberlost (debut, 1945), The Secret Fury, Vendetta (co-dir.), Green Mansions, Cabriola (Every Day Is a Holiday; also exec. prod., co-s.p.). *Producer*: Wait Until Dark, The Night Visitor, A Time for Loving, Embassy, W.
TELEVISION: *Series*: Behind the Screen, Falcon Crest. *Movies*: One Shoe Makes It Murder, Seduced, Outrages, Dream West, Peter the Great, Christine Cromwell, A Thanksgiving Promise (prod.). *Special*: Mayerling.

FERRER, MIGUEL
Actor. b. Santa Monica, CA, Feb. 7, 1954. m. actress Leilani Sarelle. Son of actor Jose Ferrer and singer Rosemary Clooney. Began performing as a drummer. With actor Bill Mumy created comic book The Comet Man.
PICTURES: Heartbreaker (debut, 1983), Lovelines, Star Trek III: The Search for Spock, Flashpoint, Robocop, Deepstar Six, Valentino Returns, Revenge, The Guardian, Twin Peaks: Fire Walk With Me, Point of No Return, Hot Shots! Part Deux, Another Stakeout, It's All True (narrator), The Harvest, Blank Check.
TELEVISION: *Series*: Twin Peaks, Broken Badges, On the Air. *Guest*: Miami Vice, Hill Street Blues, Cagney & Lacey, Shannon's End. *Pilot*: Badlands 2005. *Mini-Series*: Drug Wars: The Camarena Story, The Stand. *Movies*: Downpayment on Murder, C.A.T. Squad, Guts & Glory: The Rise and Fall of Oliver North, Murder in High Places, In the Shadow of a Killer, Cruel Doubt, Scam, Royce, Incident at Deception Ridge, Jack Reed: Search for Justice, A Promise Kept: The Oksana Baiul Story, The Return of Hunter, In the Line of Duty: Hunt for Justice.

FIEDLER, JOHN
Executive. Launched m.p. career in 1975 working in commercials and industrial and ed. films. Joined Technicolor as sr. exec. in prod. svcs. in mktg. Joined Rastar 1980 as v.p., prod. dev. and asst. to Guy McElwaine, pres. & CEO. Joined Paramount as v.p. in prod.; then to Tri-Star Pictures in same post. Resigned to join Columbia Pictures as exec. v.p., worldwide prod., 1984, then pres. of prod. 1986. 1987, left to become independent prod. 1989 named pres. of prod., Rastar IndieProd.
PICTURES: The Beast, Tune in Tomorrow (prod.).

FIELD, DAVID M.
Executive. b. Kansas City, MO, Apr. 22, 1944. e. Princeton U. Worked as reporter on city desk at Hartford (CT) Courant. In 1968 with NBC News in N.Y. and Washington, DC. Entered film school at U. of Southern California (L.A.) after which joined Columbia Pictures as west coast story editor. In 1973 went to ABC-TV Network as mgr., movies of the week. 1975, moved to 20th-Fox as v.p., creative affairs. Joined United Artists in 1978; named sr. v.p.—west coast production. Left in 1980 to become 20th-Fox exec. v.p. in chg. of worldwide production 1983, resigned to enter independent production deal with 20th-Fox, Consultant, Tri-Star Pictures. Wrote and produced Amazing Grace and Chuck, 1987.

FIELD, SALLY
Actress. b. Pasadena, CA, Nov. 6, 1946. m. prod. Alan Greisman. Daughter of Paramount contract actress Maggie Field Mahoney. Stepdaughter of actor Jock Mahoney. e. Actor's Studio 1973-75. Acting classes at Columbia studios. Picked over 150 finalists to star as lead in TV series, Gidget, 1965.
PICTURES: The Way West (debut, 1967), Stay Hungry, Smokey and the Bandit, Heroes, The End, Hooper, Norma Rae (Academy Award, 1979), Beyond the Poseidon Adventure, Smokey and the Bandit II, Back Roads, Absence of Malice, Kiss Me Goodbye, Places in the Heart (Academy Award, 1984), Murphy's Romance (also exec. prod.), Surrender, Punchline, Steel Magnolias, Not Without My Daughter, Soapdish, Dying Young (co-prod. only), Homeward Bound: The Incredible Journey (voice), Mrs. Doubtfire, Forrest Gump, Eye for an Eye, Homeward Bound II: Lost in San Francisco (voice).
TELEVISION: *Series*: Gidget, The Flying Nun, Alias Smith and Jones, The Girl With Something Extra. *Movies*: Maybe I'll Come Home in the Spring, Marriage Year One, Mongo's Back in Town, Home for the Holidays, Hitched, Bridger, Sybil (Emmy Award, 1977). *Mini-Series*: A Woman of Independent Means (also co-exec. prod.). *Host*: Barbara Stanwyck: Fire and Desire. *Guest*: Hey Landlord, Marcus Welby M.D., Bracken's World. *Special*: All the Way Home.

FIELD, SHIRLEY-ANNE
Actress. b. London, Eng., June 27. Ent. films after repertory experience. Under contract to Ealing-M.G.M. 1958.
THEATER: The Lily White Boys, Kennedy's Children, Wait Until Dark, The Life and Death of Marilyn Monroe, How the Other Half Loves.
PICTURES: It's Never Too Late, The Silken Affair, The Good Companions, Horrors of the Black Museum, Upstairs and Downstairs, Beat Girl, The Entertainer, Man in the Moon, Once More With Feeling, Peeping Tom, Saturday Night and Sunday Morning, These Are the Damned, The War Lover, Kings of the Sun, Alfie, Doctor in Clover, Hell Is Empty, With Love in Mind, House of the Living Dead (Doctor Maniac), My Beautiful Laundrette, Getting It Right, The Rachel Papers, Shag, Hear My Song, At Risk, Carrington.
TELEVISION: *U.S.*: Bramwell, Santa Barbara, Anna Lees, Lady Chatterly.

FIELD, TED
Producer. r.n. Frederick W. Field. e. U. of Chicago, Pomona Coll. Started career as one of owners of Field Enterprises of Chicago; transferred to west coast, concentrating on movies and records. Founded Interscope Communications, diversified co., which develops and produces theatrical films; Interscope Records, 1990.
PICTURES: Revenge of the Nerds, Turk 182, Critical Condition, Outrageous Fortune, Three Men and a Baby, The Seventh Sign, Cocktail, Bill & Ted's Excellent Adventure (exec. prod.), Renegades (exec. prod), Innocent Man, The First Power (exec. prod.), Bird on a Wire, Three Men and a Little Lady, Paradise, The Hand That Rocks the Cradle, The Cutting Edge, FernGully, The Gun in Betty Lou's Handbag, Out on a Limb, Jersey Girl, Holy Matrimony, Imaginary Crimes, Operation Dumbo Drop, The Tie That Binds, Mr. Holland's Opus.
TELEVISION: The Father Clements Story (co-exec. prod.), Everybody's Baby: The Rescue of Jessica McClure (co-exec. prod.), My Boyfriend's Back, A Mother's Courage: The Mary Thomas Story (co-exec. prod.), Crossing the Mob, Murder Ordained, Foreign Affairs (co-exec. prod.), A Part of the Family (co-exec. prod.), Body Language (co-exec. prod.).

FIELDS, ALAN
Executive. Spent five years with Madison Square Garden before joining Paramount Pictures. Career there included various positions: v.p. for pay-TV and Home Video TV. Spent two years at studio lot in L.A. as part of network TV organization. 1981, named bd. director for Paramount Pictures (U.K.) in London, serving as liaison to United Intl. Pictures and Cinema Intl. Corp., serving on operating committees of both. 1985, appt.

v.p., Entertainment & Communications Group of Gulf & Western Industries, Inc., parent co. of Paramount; C.O.O., exec. v.p. Madison Square Garden Corp.

FIELDS, FREDDIE
Executive. b. Ferndale, NY, July 12, 1923. Vice-pres., member of bd. of directors, MCA-TV, MCA Canada Ltd., MCA Corp.; mem., Pres. Club, Wash., D.C.; pres., Freddie Fields Associates Ltd., 1960; Founder pres., chief exec. officer Creative Management Assoc. Ltd. Agency, Chicago, Las Vegas, Miami, Paris, Los Angeles, N.Y., London, Rome, 1961. Was exclusive agent of Henry Fonda, Phil Silvers, Judy Garland, Paul Newman, Peter Sellers, Barbra Streisand, Steve McQueen, Woody Allen, Robert Redford, Ryan O'Neal, Liza Minnelli and others. In 1975 sold interest in CMA (now International Creative Mgt.) but continued as consultant. Produced for Paramount Pictures. 1977: Looking for Mr. Goodbar. American Gigolo, Citizen's Band; Victory. In 1983 named pres. and COO, MGM Film Co. Resigned 1985 to become independent producer for MGM/UA.
PICTURES: Fever Pitch. Poltergeist II, Crimes of the Heart, Millenium, Glory. Exec. Prod. of The Montel Williams Show.

FIENNES, RALPH
Actor. b. Suffolk, England, Dec. 22, 1962. e. Chelsea College of Art & Design, RADA. Stage work with the Royal Shakespeare Co. includes King Lear, Troilus and Cressida, Love's Labour's Lost. B'way debut in Hamlet (Tony & Theatre World Awards, 1995).
PICTURES: Wuthering Heights (tv in U.S.), The Baby of Macon, Schindler's List (Acad. Award nom.; Natl. Society of Film Critics, NY Film Critics & BAFTA Awards), Quiz Show, Strange Days, The English Patient.
TELEVISION: Prime Suspect, A Dangerous Man: Lawrence After Arabia, The Cormorant (theatrical release in U.S.).

FIERSTEIN, HARVEY
Actor, Writer. b. New York, NY, June 6, 1954. e. Pratt Inst.
THEATER: Actor: Andy Warhol's Pork, The Haunted Host, Pouf Positive. Actor-Writer: Torch Song Trilogy (NY & London; Tony Awards for best actor & play; Theatre World Award), Safe Sex. Writer: Spookhouse, La Cage Aux Folles (Tony Award), Legs Diamond.
PICTURES: Garbo Talks, The Times of Harvey Milk (narrator), Torch Song Trilogy (also s.p.), The Harvest, Mrs. Doubtfire, Bullets Over Broadway, Dr. Jekyll & Ms. Hyde, Independence Day.
TELEVISION: Movies: The Demon Murder Case (voice), Apology. Series: Daddy's Girls. Guest: Miami Vice, The Simpsons (voice), Cheers, Murder She Wrote. Specials: Tidy Endings, In the Shadow of Love.

FIGGIS, MIKE
Director, Writer, Musician. b. Kenya, 1949. At age 8 family moved to Newcastle, England. Studied music before performing with band Gas Boad; joined experimental theatre group The People Show in early 70's as musician. Began making indept. films including Redheugh, Slow Fade, Animals of the City. Made 1-hr. film The House for U.K.'s Channel 4.
PICTURES: Director: Stormy Monday (debut, 1988; also s.p., music), Internal Affairs (also music), Liebestraum (also s.p., music), Mr. Jones, Leaving Las Vegas (also s.p., music; IFP Independent Spirit Award, 1996; Nat'l Society of Film Critics Award).

FINCH, JON
Actor. b. London, England, Mar. 2, 1943. Came to acting via backstage activities, working for five years as company manager and director.
PICTURES: The Vampire Lovers (debut, 1970), The Horror of Frankenstein, Sunday Bloody Sunday, L'affaire Martine Desclos, Macbeth, Frenzy, Lady Caroline Lamb, The Final Programme (The Last Days of Man on Earth), Diagnosis: Murder, Une Femme Fidele, The Man With the Green Cross, El Segundo Poder, Battle Flag, El Mister, Death on the Nile, La Sabina, Gary Cooper Which Art in Heaven, Breaking Glass, The Threat, Giro City (And Nothing But the Truth), Plaza Real, Streets of Yesterday, Game of Seduction, The Voice, Beautiful in the Kingdom, Mirror Mirror, Darklands.
TELEVISION: The Martian Chronicles (U.S.), Peter and Paul, The Rainbow, Unexplained Laughter, Dangerous Curves, Maigret, Beautiful Lies, Make or Break, The Oddjob Man (series), Sherlock Homes, Counterstrike (series), Mary Queen of Scots, Riviera, White Men Are Cracking Up, A Love Renewed, Merlin of the Crystal Cave, Richard II, Henry IV, Much Ado About Nothing, South of the Border, Hammer House of Horrors, Ben Hall (series).

FINESHRIBER, WILLIAM H., JR.
Executive. b. Davenport, IA, Nov. 4, 1909. e. Princeton U., B.A., 1931. Pub., CBS, 1931-34; mgr. Carnegie Hall, N.Y., 1934-37; script writer, dir., music comm., dir. of music dept., CBS, 1937-40; dir. of short wave programs, CBS, 1940-43; gen. mgr. CBS program dept. 1943-49; v.p. in charge of programs MBS, 1949-51; exec. v.p. & dir., MBS, 1951-53; v.p. & gen. mgr. of networks, NBC, 1953-54; v.p. in charge of Radio Network, NBC, 1955; v.p. Television Programs of America, 1956; director International operations, Screen Gems, 1957; v.p., Motion Picture Assoc. of America and Motion Picture Export Assoc. of America, 1960; bd. of dir., NARTB: exec. comm., bd. of dir., R.A.B; v.p. Radio Pioneers. Author, Stendhal the Romantic Rationalist.

FINLAY, FRANK
Actor. C.B.E. b. Farnworth, Eng., Aug. 6, 1926. Rep. in Troon, 1951, Halifax and Sunderland, 1952-3, before winning Sir James Knott Scholarship to RADA. e. Studied acting at RADA. Appeared with Guildford Repertory Theatre Co. 1957. London stage debut: The Queen and the Welshman, 1957. Broadway debut, Epitaph for George Dillon, 1958.
THEATER: Work with Royal Court, Chichester Fest., National Theatre includes: Sergeant Musgrave's Dance, Chicken Soup with Barley, Roots, Platonov, Chips with Everything, Saint Joan, Hamlet, Othello, Saturday Sunday Monday, Plunder, Watch It Come Down, Weapons of Happiness, Tribute to a Lady, Filumena (and N.Y.), Amadeus, The Cherry Orchard, Mutiny, Beyond Reasonable Doubt, Black Angel, A Slight Hangover.
PICTURES: The Loneliness of the Long Distance Runner (debut, 1962), The Longest Day, Life for Ruth (Walk in the Shadow), Private Potter, Doctor in Distress, Underworld Informers, The Comedy Man, Agent 8 3/4 (Hot Enough for June), The Wild Affair, A Study in Terror, Othello (Acad. Award nom.), The Sandwich Man, The Jokers, The Deadly Bees, Robbery, I'll Never Forget What's 'is Name, The Shoes of the Fisherman, Inspector Clouseau, Twisted Nerve, The Molly Maguires, Cromwell, The Body (narrator), Assault (The Devil's Garden), Gumshoe, Danny Jones, Sitting Target, Neither the Sea Nor the Sand, Shaft in Africa, The Three Musketeers, The Four Musketeers, The Wild Geese, Murder by Decree, Enigma, The Ploughman's Lunch, The Return of the Soldier, The Key, 1919, Lifeforce, The Return of the Musketeers (tv in U.S.), King of the Wind, Cthulhu Mansion.
TELEVISION: The Adventures of Don Quixote, Casanova, Candide, Julius Caesar, Les Miserables, This Happy Breed, The Lie, The Death of Adolph Hitler, Voltaire, The Merchant of Venice, Bouquet of Barbed Wire, 84 Charing Cross Road, Saturday Sunday Monday, Count Dracula, The Last Campaign, Thief of Bagdad, Betzi, Sakharov, A Christmas Carol, Arch of Triumph, The Burning Shore, In the Secret State, Verdict of Erebus, Mountain of Diamonds, Encounter, Stalin.

FINNEY, ALBERT
Actor. b. Salford, England, May 9, 1936. Studied for stage at Royal Acad. Dramatic Art making his West End debut 1958 in The Party. Appeared at Stratford-Upon-Avon 1959, playing title role in Coriolanus, etc.
THEATER: The Lily White Boys, Billy Liar, Luther (also NY), Much Ado About Nothing, Armstrong's Last Goodnight, Love for Love, Miss Julie, Black Comedy, A Flea in Her Ear, Joe Egg (NY), Alpha Beta, Krapp's Last Tape, Cromwell, Chez Nous, Hamlet, Tamburlaine, Uncle Vanya, Present Laughter. National Theatre, The Country Wife, The Cherry Orchard, Macbeth, The Biko Inquest, Sergeant Musgrave's Dance (also dir.), Orphans, Another Time (also Chicago), Reflected Glory.
PICTURES: The Entertainer (debut, 1960), Saturday Night and Sunday Morning, Tom Jones, The Victors, Night Must Fall (also co-prod.), Two for the Road, Charlie Bubbles (also dir.), The Picasso Summer (tv in U.K.), Scrooge, Gumshoe, Alpha Beta (tv in U.K.), Murder on the Orient Express, The Adventure of Sherlock Holmes' Smarter Brother (cameo), The Duellists, Wolfen, Looker, Loophole, Shoot the Moon, Annie, The Dresser, Under the Volcano, Orphans, Miller's Crossing, The Playboys, Rich in Love, The Browning Version, A Man of No Importance, The Run of the Country.
TELEVISION: The Claverdon Road Job, The Miser, Pope John Paul II, Endless Game, The Image, The Green Man.

FIORENTINO, LINDA
Actress. b. Philadelphia, PA, 1960. e. Rosmont Col. To New York, 1980, studing acting at Circle in the Square Theatre School.
PICTURES: Vision Quest (debut, 1985), Gotcha!, After Hours, The Modrens, Queens Logic, Shout, Chain of Desire, The Last Seduction, Bodily Harm, Jade, Unforgettable, Men in Black.
TELEVISION: Movies: The Neon Empire, Acting on Impulse, The Desperate Trail.

FIRSTENBERG, JEAN
Director. The American Film Institute.

FIRTH, COLIN
Actor. b. Grayshott, Hampshire, Eng., Sept. 10, 1960. Studied acting at the Drama Centre at Chalk Farm. On stage in Doctor's Dilemma, Another Country, Desire Under the Elms.
PICTURES: Another Country, 1919, A Month in the Country, Apartment Zero, Valmont, Wings of Fame, The Pleasure Principle, Femme Fatale, Playmaker, The Advocate, Circle of Friends.

TELEVISION: *Series*: Lost Empires. *Movies*: Camille, Dutch Girls, Tumbledown, Hostages. *Special*: Tales from the Hollywood Hills (Pat Hobby Teamed With Genius).

FIRTH, PETER
Actor. b. Bradford, Yorkshire, Oct. 27, 1953. Appeared in local TV children's show where casting director spotted him and got him role in series, The Flaxton Boys. Moved to London and worked in TV, first in children's show, later on dramas for BBC. Breakthrough role in Equus at National Theatre, 1973 which he repeated in film.
THEATER: Equus (Theatre World Award), Romeo and Juliet, Spring Awakening, Amadeus.
PICTURES: Diamonds on Wheels (debut, 1972; tv in U.S.), Brother Sun Sister Moon, Daniel and Maria, Equus (Acad. Award nom.), Joseph Andrews, Aces High, When You Comin' Back Red Ryder, Tess, Lifeforce, Letter to Brezhnev, Trouble in Paradise, White Elephant, A State of Emergency, Born of Fire, The Tree of Hands, Prisoner of Rio, Burndown, The Hunt for Red October, The Rescuers Down Under (voice), The Perfect Husband, White Angel, Shadowlands, An Awfully Big Adventure.
TELEVISION: *Series*: The Flaxon Boys, Home and Away, Country Matters. *Movies and specials*: Here Comes the Doubledeckers, Castlehaven, The Sullen Sisters, The Simple Life, The Magistrate, The Protectors, Black Beauty, Arthur, Her Majesty's Pleasure, the Picture of Dorian Gray, Lady of the Camillias, The Flip Side of Domenic Hide, Blood Royal, Northanger Abbey, The Way, The Truth: the Video, The Incident, Children Crossing, Prisoner of Honor, Married to Murder, The Laughter of God, Murder in Eden, Brighton Boy.

FISCHER, JOSEPH A.
Executive. Executive v.p., MCA Motion Picture Group.

FISHBURNE, LAURENCE
Actor. b. Augusta, GA, July 30, 1961. Raised in Brooklyn. Landed role on daytime serial One Life to Live at age 11. On NY stage in Short Eyes, Two Trains Running (Tony and Theatre World Awards), Riff Raff (also wrote and directed).
PICTURES: Cornbread Earl and Me (debut, 1975), Fast Break, Apocalypse Now, Willie and Phil, Death Wish II, Rumble Fish, The Cotton Club, The Color Purple, Quicksilver, Band of the Hand, A Nightmare on Elm Street 3: Dream Warriors, Gardens of Stone, School Daze, Red Heat, King of New York, Cadence, Class Action, Boyz N the Hood, Deep Cover, What's Love Got to Do With It (Acad. Award nom.), Searching for Bobby Fischer, Higher Learning, Bad Company, Just Cause, Othello, Fled, Hoodlums.
TELEVISION: *Series*: One Life to Live, Pee-wee's Playhouse. *Guest*: M*A*S*H, Trapper John, M.D., Spenser: For Hire, Tribeca (Emmy Award, 1993). *Movies*: A Rumor of War, I Take These Men, Father Clements Story, Decoration Day, The Tuskegee Airmen.

FISHER, AL
Executive. b. Brooklyn, NY. Entered m.p. industry as office boy, Fox Metropolitan Theatres; U.S. Army Provost Marshal General's Office, 1942-46; Universal Pictures, mgr., Park Avenue Theatre, N.Y. & Copley Plaza Theatre, Boston, 1946; Eagle Lion Film Co., mgr., Red Shoe's Bijou Theatre, N.Y., 1947; Stanley Kramer Prods., exploitation, Cyrano de Bergerac, 1951; press agent, 1951; prod., Bway show, Daphine, 1952; joined United Artists Corporation, 1952, named dir. of exploitation; now freelancing as producer's repr.

FISHER, CARRIE
Actress, Writer. b. Beverly Hills, CA, Oct. 21, 1956. e. London Central Sch. of Speech & Drama. Daughter of actress Debbie Reynolds and singer Eddie Fisher. On Broadway in the chorus of revival of Irene (1972; with mother); later in Censored Scenes from King Kong. *Author*: Postcards From the Edge (1987), Surrender the Pink (1990), Delusions of Grandma (1994).
PICTURES: Shampoo (debut, 1975), Star Wars, Mr. Mike's Mondo Video, The Empire Strikes Back, The Blues Brothers, Under the Rainbow, Return of the Jedi, Garbo Talks, The Man with One Red Shoe, Hannah and Her Sisters, Hollywood Vice Squad, Amazon Women on the Moon, Appointment with Death, The 'Burbs, Loverboy, She's Back, When Harry Met Sally..., The Time Guardian, Postcards From the Edge (s.p. only), Sibling Rivalry, Drop Dead Fred, Soapdish, This Is My Life.
TELEVISION: *Movies*: Leave Yesterday Behind, Liberty, Sunday Drive, Sweet Revenge. *Specials*: Come Back Little Sheba, Classic Creatures: Return of the Jedi, Thumbelina (Faerie Tale Theatre), Paul Reiser: Out on a Whim, Two Daddies? (voice), Trying Times (Hunger Chic), Carrie Fisher: The Hollywood Family (also writer). *Guest*: Laverne and Shirley, George Burns' Comedy Week.

FISHER, EDDIE
Singer. b. Philadelphia, PA, Aug. 10, 1928. Daughter is actress Carrie Fisher. Band, nightclub, hotel singer; discovered by Eddie Cantor, 1949; U.S. Army, 1951-53; many hit records include Wish You Were Here, Lady of Spain; radio & TV shows, NBC.

PICTURES: Bundle of Joy, Butterfield 8, Nothing Lasts Forever.
TELEVISION: *Series*: Coke Time With Eddie Fisher (1953-57), The Eddie Fisher Show (1957-59).

FISHER, FRANCES
Actress. b. Milford-on-Sea, England, May 11. Father was intl. construction supervisor. Raised in Colombia, Canada, France, Brazil, Turkey. Made stage debut in Texas in Summer and Smoke.
THEATER: *NY*: Fool for Love, Desire Under the Elms, Cat on a Hot Tin Roof, The Hitch-Hikers, Orpheus Descending, A Midsummer Night's Dream.
PICTURES: Can She Bake a Cherry Pie? (debut, 1983), Tough Guys Don't Dance, The Principal, Patty Hearst, Bum Rap, Heavy Petting, Pink Cadillac, Lost Angels, Welcome Home Roxy Carmichael, L.A. Story, Unforgiven, Babyfever, The Stars Fell on Henrietta, Waiting for Guffman, Female Perversion.
TELEVISION: *Series*: The Edge of Night (1976-81), The Guiding Light (1985), Strange Luck. *Movies*: Broken Vows, Devlin, Lucy & Desi: Before the Laughter, The Other Mother. *Pilots*: Elysian Fields. *Guest*: The Equalizer, Matlock, Newhart.

FISHER, GEORGE M.C.
Executive. b. Anna, IL. e. Univ. of IL, Brown Univ. Worked in research and devlop. at Bell Labs before joining Motorola in 1976, eventually becoming pres. & CEO in 1988. 1990, elected chmn. & CEO. Named chmn., pres. & CEO of Eastman Kodak Company, Dec. 1993.

FISHER, LUCY
Executive. b. Oct. 2, 1949. e. Harvard U., B.A. Exec. chg. creative affairs, MGM; v.p., creative affairs, 20th Century Fox; prod., Fox. 1980, head of prod., Zoetrope Studios; 1980-82, v.p., sr. prod. exec., Warner Bros.; 1983, sr. v.p. prod., WB. Joined Columbia TriStar in March, 1996 as vice chmn.

FISK, JACK
Director. b. Ipava, IL, Dec. 19, 1934. e. Cooper Union-Pa. Acad. of the Fine Arts. m. actress Sissy Spacek. Began in films as designer; turning to direction with Raggedy Man (1981).
PICTURES: *Director*: Raggedy Man, Violets Are Blue, Daddy's Dyin', ... Who's Got the Will? *Art Director*: Badlands, Phantom of the Paradise, Carrie, Days of Heaven, Heart Beat.

FITZGERALD, GERALDINE
Actress. b. Dublin, Ireland, Nov. 24, 1914. e. Dublin Art Sch. Mother of director Michael Lindsay-Hogg. On stage Gate Theat., Dublin; then in number of Brit. screen prod. including Turn of the Tide, Mill on the Floss. On N.Y. stage in Heartbreak House. Founded Everyman Street Theatre with Brother Jonathan Ringkamp.
THEATER: Sons and Soldiers, Portrait in Black, The Doctor's Dilemma, King Lear, Hide and Seek, A Long Day's Journey Into Night, (1971), Ah, Wilderness, The Shadow Box, A Touch of the Poet, Songs of the Streets (one woman show), Mass Appeal (dir. only), The Lunch Girls (dir.).
PICTURES: Blind Justice (debut, 1934), Open All Night, The Lad, The Aces of Spades, Three Witnesses, Lieutenant Daring RN, Turn of the Tide, Radio Parade of 1935, Bargain Basement (Department Store), Debt of Honor, Cafe Mascot, The Mill on the Floss, Wuthering Heights (U.S. debut, 1939; Acad. Award nom.), Dark Victory, A Child Is Born, 'Til We Meet Again, Flight from Destiny, Shining Victory, The Gay Sisters, Watch on the Rhine, Ladies Courageous, Wilson, The Strange Affair of Uncle Harry, Three Strangers, O.S.S., Nobody Lives Forever, So Evil My Love, The Late Edwina Black (The Obsessed), 10 North Frederick, The Fiercest Heart, The Pawnbroker, Rachel Rachel, The Last American Hero, Harry and Tonto, Cold Sweat, Echoes of a Summer, The Mango Tree, Bye Bye Monkey, Lovespell (Tristan and Isolde), Arthur, Blood Link, Easy Money, Poltergeist II, Arthur 2: On the Rocks.
TELEVISION: *Series*: Our Private World, The Best of Everything. *Movies*: Yesterday's Child, The Quinns, Dixie: Changing Habits, Do You Remember Love?, Circle of Violence, Night of Courage, Bump in the Night. *Mini-Series*: Kennedy. *Specials*: The Moon and Sixpence, Street Songs.

FITZGERALD, TARA
Actress. b. England, 1968. e. London's Drama Centre, 1990.
THEATER: *London*: Our Song. *NY*: Hamlet.
PICTURES: Hear My Song (debut, 1991), Sirens, A Man of No Importance, The Englishman Who Went Up a Hill But Came Down a Mountain.
TELEVISION: The Black Candle, The Camomille Lawn, Anglo-Saxon Attitudes, Six Characters in Search of an Author, Fall From Grace.

FLAGG, FANNIE
Actress, Writer. b. Birmingham, AL, Sept. 21, 1944. e. Univ. of AL. Studied acting at Pittsburgh Playhouse, Town & Gown Theatre. Had her own 50 minute tv show in Birmingham. To NY where she wrote and appeared in revues for Upstairs at the Downstairs Club. *Comedy albums*: Rally 'Round the Flagg, My

Husband Doesn't Know I'm Making This Phone Call. *Author:* Coming Attractions: A Wonderful Novel (Daisy Fay and the Miracle Man), Fried Green Tomatoes at the Whistle Stop Cafe, Fannie Flagg's Original Whistle Stop Cafe Cookbook.
THEATER: *B'way:* Patio Porch, Come Back to the Five and Dime Jimmy Dean Jimmy Dean, The Best Little Whorehouse in Texas. Regional: Private Lives, Gypsy, Mary Mary, Tobacco Road, Old Acquaintance, etc.
PICTURES: Five Easy Pieces (debut, 1970), Some of My Best Friends Are..., Stay Hungry, Grease, Rabbit Test, My Best Friend Is a Vampire, Fried Green Tomatoes (also co-s.p.; Acad. Award nom. for s.p.).
TELEVISION: *Series:* The New Dick Van Dyke Show, Match Game P.M., Liar's Club, Harper Valley P.T.A. *Movies:* The New Original Wonder Woman, Sex and the Married Woman. *Pilots:* Comedy News, Home Cookin'. *Producer:* Morning Show.

FLATTERY, THOMAS L.
Executive-Lawyer b. Detroit, MI, Nov. 14, 1922. e. U.S. Military Acad., West Point, B.S., 1944-47; UCLA, J.D., 1952-55; USC, LL.M. 1955-65. Radioplane Company, staff counsel and asst. contract admin. 1955-7. Gen'l counsel and asst. sec'y, McCulloch Corp., CA, 1957-64; sec. & corp. counsel, Technicolor, Inc., 1964-70; v.p., sec. & gen. counsel, Amcord, Inc. 1970-72; v.p., sec. & gen. counsel, Schick Inc., 1972-75; counsel asst. sec., C.F. Braun & Co., 1975-76; sr. v.p., sec. & gen. counsel PCC Technical Industries, Inc. 1976-86; v.p., gen. counsel & sec., G & H Technology, Inc. 1986.-93. Attorney at law, 1993.

FLAXMAN, JOHN P.
Producer. b. New York, NY, March 3, 1934. e. Dartmouth U., B.A. 1956. 1st Lt. U.S. Army, 1956-58. Ent. m.p. industry in executive training program, Columbia Pictures Corp., 1958-63; exec. story consultant, Profiles in Courage, 1964-65; head of Eastern Literary Dept., Universal Pictures, 1965; writer's agent, William Morris Agency, 1966; partner with Harold Prince in Media Productions, Inc. 1967; founded Flaxman Film Corp., 1975. President-Tricorn Productions 1977; pres. Filmworks Capital Corp., 1979-83; Becker/Flaxman & Associates, 1979-83; pres., Cine Communications, 1983-present. Producer Off-Broadway, Yours, Anne (1985). Co-prod. with NY Shakespeare Fest., The Petrified Prince.
PICTURES: Something for Everyone, Jacob Two-Two Meets the Hooded Fang.
TELEVISION: The Caine Mutiny Court-Martial (prod.).

FLEISCHER, RICHARD
Director. b. Brooklyn, NY, Dec. 8, 1916. e. Brown U., B.A.; Yale U., M.F.A. Son of animator Max Fleischer. Stage dir.; joined RKO Pathe 1942. Dir. and wrote This Is America shorts, prod./dir. Flicker Flashbacks. Author: Just Tell Me When to Cry.
PICTURES: Child of Divorce (debut, 1946), Banjo, Design for Death (also co-prod.; Academy Award for Best Feature-Length Documentary, 1948), So This Is New York, Bodyguard, Follow Me Quietly, Make Mine Laughs, The Clay Pigeon, Trapped, Armored Car Robbery, The Narrow Margin, The Happy Time, Arena, 20000 Leagues Under the Sea, Violent Saturday, Girl in the Red Velvet Swing, Bandido, Between Heaven and Hell, The Vikings, These Thousand Hills, Compulsion, Crack in the Mirror, The Big Gamble, Barabbas, Fantastic Voyage, Doctor Dolittle, The Boston Strangler, Che!, Tora! Tora! Tora!, 10 Rillington Place, The Last Run, See No Evil, The New Centurions, Soylent Green, The Don Is Dead, The Spikes Gang, Mr. Majestyk, Mandingo, The Incredible Sarah, Crossed Swords (The Prince and the Paupre), Ashanti, The Jazz Singer, Tough Enough, Amityville 3-D, Conan the Destroyer, Red Sonja, Million Dollar Mystery, Call From Space (Showcan).

FLEMING, JANET BLAIR
Executive. b. Ottawa, Canada, November 29, 1944. e. Carlton U., Ottawa, Canada, B.A. Secretary to Canada's Federal Minister of Transport 1967-72; 1973-77, asst. to Sandy Howard—business affairs; 1977, co-founder and v.p./sales & admin. of Producers Sales Organization; 1981, named sr. v.p., admin.; 1982, sr. v.p., acquisitions; 1983, exec. v.p., Skouras Pictures; 1985 promoted to pres., intl. div.; 1987-88 mgr. Lift Haven Inn, Sun Valley, ID; 1989-present, owner/partner Premiere Properties (prop. management, Sun Valley, ID).

FLEMING, RHONDA
Actress. r.n. Marilyn Louis. b. Los Angeles, CA, Aug. 10. m. Ted Mann (Mann Theatres). e. Beverly Hills H.S. Member, several charity orgs. Bd. of Dir. trustee of World Opportunities Intl. (Help the Children). Alzheimer Rsch., Childhelp USA, bd. of trustees of the UCLA Foundation, etc. Opened Rhonda Fleming Mann Resource Center for Women with Cancer at UCLA Medical Center, 1994. Many awards incl. Woman of the Year Award from City of Hope 1986 & 1991, and for Operaton Children, etc. Stage incl. The Women (B'way), Kismet (LA), The Boyfriend (tour), one woman concerts.
PICTURES: Spellbound, Abiline Town, Spiral Staircase, Adventure Island, Out of the Past, A Connecticut Yankee in King Arthur's Court, The Great Lover, The Eagle and the Hawk, The Redhead and the Cowboy, The Last Outpost, Cry Danger, Crosswinds, Little Egypt, Hong Kong, Golden Hawk, Tropic Zone, Pony Express, Serpent of the Nile, Inferno, Those Redheads from Seattle, Jivaro, Yankee Pasha, Tennessee's Partner, While the City Sleeps, Killer Is Loose, Slightly Scarlet, Odongo, Queen of Babylon, Gunfight at the OK Corral, Buster Keaton Story, Gun Glory, Bullwhip, Home Before Dark, Alias Jesse James, The Big Circus, The Crowded Sky, The Patsy (cameo), Won Ton Ton The Dog Who Saved Hollywood, The Nude Bomb.
TELEVISION: *Guest:* Wagon Train, Police Woman, Love Boat, McMillian and Wife, Legends of the Screen, Road to Hollywood, Wildest West Show of Stars. *Movies:* The Last Hours Before Morning, Love for Rent, Waiting for the Wind.

FLEMYNG, ROBERT
Actor. b. Liverpool, England, Jan. 3, 1912. e. Halleybury Coll. Stage debut: Rope, 1931.
PICTURES: Head Over Heels (debut, 1937), Bond Street, The Guinea Pig, The Conspirators, The Blue Lamp, Blackmailed, The Magic Box, The Holly and the Ivy, Cast a Dark Shadow, Man Who Never Was, Funny Face, Let's Be Happy, Wisdom's Way, Blind Date, A Touch of Larceny, Radtus (Italian), The King's Breakfast, The Deadly Affair, The Spy with the Cold Nose, The Quiller Memorandum, Deathhead Avenger, Oh! What a Lovely War, Battle of Britain, Cause for Alarm, Young Winston, The Darwin Adventure, Travels with My Aunt, Golden Rendezvous, The Medusa Touch, The Four Feathers, The Thirty-Nine Steps, Paris By Night, Kafka.
TELEVISION: appearances in England, U.S. inc.: Rainy Day, Playhouse 90, Wuthering Heights, Browning Version, After the Party, Boyd Q.C., They Made History, Somerset Maugham Show, Woman in White, The Datchet Diamonds, Probation Officer, Family Solicitor (series), Man of the World, Zero One, Compact (serial), Day by the Sea, The Living Room, Hawks and Doves, Vanity Fair, The Inside Man, The Doctor's Dilemma, The Persuaders, Major Lavender, Public Eye, Florence Nightingale, Edward VIII, Spy Trap, The Venturers' Loyalties, The Avengers, Crown Court, Enemy at the Door, Rebecca, Edward and Mrs. Simpson, The Ladykiller, Professionals, Fame Is the Spur, Crown Court, Spider's Webb, Executive Suite, Small World, Perfect Scoundrels, Short Story.

FLETCHER, LOUISE
Actress. b. Birmingham, AL, July 22, 1934. e. U. of North Carolina, B.A. Came to Hollywood at age 21; studied with Jeff Corey. Worked on TV shows (including Playhouse 90, Maverick). Gave up career to be a mother for 10 yrs.; returned to acting in 1973. Board of Directors: Deafness Research Foundation, 1980-. Honorary Degrees: Doctor of Humane Letters from Gallaudet U. and West Maryland Col. Advisory board: The Caption Center, The Nat'l Institute on Deafness and Other Communication Disorders.
PICTURES: Thieves Like Us, Russian Roulette, One Flew Over the Cuckoo's Nest (Academy Award, 1975), Exorcist II: The Heretic, The Cheap Detective, Natural Enemies, The Magician of Lublin, The Lucky Star, The Lady in Red, Strange Behavior, Mamma Dracula, Brainstorm, Strange Invaders, Firestarter, Once Upon a Time in America, Overnight Sensation, Invaders from Mars, The Boy Who Could Fly, Nobody's Fool, Flowers in the Attic, Two Moon Junction, Best of the Best, Shadow Zone, Blue Steel, Blind Vision, The Player, Georgino, Tollbooth, Return to Two Moon Junction, Virtuosity.
TELEVISION: *Series:* Boys of Twilight. *Movies:* Can Ellen Be Saved?, Thou Shalt Not Commit Adultery, A Summer to Remember, Island, Second Serve, J. Edgar Hoover, The Karen Carpenter Story, Final Notice, Nightmare on the 13th Floor, In a Child's Name, The Fire Next Time, The Haunting of Seacliff Inn, Someone Else's Child. *Guest:* Twilight Zone, Tales from the Crypt, Civil Wars, Deep Space Nine, Dream On, VR5.

FLINN, JOHN C.
Publicist. b. Yonkers, NY, May 4, 1917. e. U. of California. p. late John C. Flinn, pioneer m.p. executive. In pub. dept. David O. Selznick, 1936-39; unit publicist, then head planter, Warner, 1936-46; joined Monogram as asst. to nat'l adv. & pub. head & pub. mgr. 1946; apptd. nat'l dir. of pub. & adv. of Allied Artists Pictures, 1951; appt'd studio dir. adv. & pub., Columbia, 1959; v.p., Jim Mahoney & Assocs. (p.r. firm) 1971. Joined MGM West Coast publ. dept. as publ. coordinator, 1973; rejoined Columbia Pictures in 1974 as studio publ. dir.; 1979, promoted to dir. industry relations. Joined MGM/UA publ. staff, 1988 to work on m.p. academy campaign for Moonstruck. Engaged by Paramount 1988-89 to assist in Acad. Award campaigns. Retired.

FLOREA, JOHN
Producer, Director, Writer. b. Alliance, OH, May 28, 1916. Served as photo journalist with Life magazine, 1940-50; assoc. editor Colliers magazine, 1950-53. Prod.-dir. with David Gerber 1979-84.
PICTURES: A Time to Every Purpose, The Astral Factor, The Invisible Strangler, Hot Child in the City.

TELEVISION: Dir. several episodes: Sea Hunt series, 1957-60; Bonanza, Outlaws, Outpost (pilot), The Virginian, Honey West, Daktari, Gentle Ben, Cowboy in Africa, High Chapparal, Flipper, Destry Rides Again, Not For Hire, Ironside, Highway Patrol, V, Target, Everglades, (also prod.), CHiPS, MacGyver. Prod.-dir. of film Islands of the Lost. With Ivon Tors Films. Nominated as one of the Top 10 directors in America by DGA for 1968 Mission Impossible episode. Dir. several Ironside episodes. Doc: Kammikazi, Attack Hawaiian Hospitality, Million Dollar Question, Marineland, Brink of Disaster. (Valley Freedom Award), Dangerous Report, (for CIA), The Runaways (Emmy Award), Down the Long Hills, Dark Canyon.

FLYNN, JOHN
Director, Writer. b. Chicago IL. e. George Washington U, Stanford, UCLA, B.A. (Eng.). Worked in mailroom at MCA then with p.r. firm. Began career as trainee script supvr. for dir. Robert Wise on West Side Story. Soon working as ass't. dir. on MGM-TV shows. Made dir. debut with The Sergeant, 1969.
PICTURES: The Jerusalem File, The Outfit (also s.p.), Rolling Thunder, Defiance, Touched, Best Seller, Lock Up, Brainscan.
TELEVISION: Marilyn—The Untold Story (dir.).

FOCH, NINA
Actress. b. Leyden, Holland, April 20, 1924. Daughter of Consuelo Flowerton, actress, & Dirk Foch, symphony orch. conductor. Adjunct Prof., USC, 1966-67; 1978-80, Adjunct professor, USC Cinema-TV grad. sch. 1986-; sr. faculty, American Film Inst., 1974-77; bd. of Governors, Hollywood Acad. of Television Arts & Sciences, 1976-77; exec. Comm. Foreign Language Film Award, Acad. of Motion Picture Arts & Sciences, 1970-. Co-chmn., exec. comm. Foreign Language Film Award 1983-.
PICTURES: The Return of the Vampire (debut, 1943), Nine Girls, Cry of the Werewolf, She's a Soldier Too, She's a Sweetheart, Shadows in the Night, I Love a Mystery, Prison Ship, Song to Remember, My Name is Julia Ross, Boston Blackie's Rendezvous, Escape in the Fog, The Guilt of Jane Ames, Johnny O'Clock, The Dark Past, Johnny Allegro, Undercover Man, St. Benny the Dip, An American in Paris, Young Man With Ideas, Scaramouche, Sombrero, Fast Company, Executive Suite (Acad. Award nom.), Four Guns to the Border, The Ten Commandments, Illegal, You're Never Too Young, Three Brave Men, Cash McCall, Spartacus, Such Good Friends, Salty, Mahogany, Jennifer, Rich and Famous, Skin Deep, Sliver, Morning Glory.
TELEVISION: Series: Q.E.D. (panelist), It's News to Me (panelist), Shadow Chasers. Movies: Outback Bound, In the Arms of a Killer, The Sands of Time. Mini-series: War and Remembrance. Special: Tales of the City. Guest star, most major series incl. Studio One, Playhouse 90, US Steel Hour, L.A. Law, Dear John, Hunter; talk shows, specials.

FOGARTY, JACK V.
Executive, Producer, Writer. b. Los Angeles, CA. e. UCLA. Management, MGM, 1960-62; exec. prod. mgr., Cinerama, Inc., 1962-64; assoc. prod., The Best of Cinerama, 1963; est. own p.r. firm, 1965; pres., AstroScope, Inc., 1969-74.
TELEVISION: Writer/prod.: The Rookies, S.W.A.T., Charlie's Angels, Most Wanted, Barnaby Jones, A Man Called Sloane, Trapper John, T.J. Hooker, Crazy Like a Fox, The Equalizer, Jake and the Fatman, Murder She Wrote, Charlie's Angels (story edit.). Exec. Story consultant: Most Wanted, A Man Called Sloane, Sheriff Lobo, T.J. Hooker. Producer: T.J. Hooker, Jessie.

FOLEY, JAMES
Director. b. New York, NY. E. NYU, USC. While at USC directed two short films, Silent Night and November which brought him attention. Directed two Madonna videos: Live to Tell and Papa Don't Preach.
PICTURES: Reckless, At Close Range, Who's That Girl, After Dark My Sweet, Glengarry Glen Ross, A Day to Remember, Fear, Two Bits, The Chamber.

FOLSEY, GEORGE, JR
Producer, Editor. b. Los Angeles, CA, Jan. 17, 1939. Son of late cinematographer George Folsey Sr. e. Pomona Coll., B.A., 1961.
PICTURES: Editor: Glass Houses, Bone, Hammer, Black Caesar, Schlock, Trader Horn, Bucktown, J.D.'s Revenge, Norman... Is That You?, Tracks, The Chicken Chronicles, The Kentucky Fried Movie, National Lampoon's Animal House, Freedom Road, The Great Santini (addt'l editing), The Blues Brothers (also assoc. prod.). Producer: An American Werewolf in London, Twilight Zone—The Movie (assoc. prod.); Trading Places (also prod. & 2nd unit dir.), Into the Night (co-prod.), Spies Like Us (co-prod.), Clue (co-exec. prod.), Three Amigos, Coming to America (co-prod., co-editor), Greed (co-exec. prod.), Grumpier Old Men.
VIDEO: Michael Jackson's Thriller (co-prod., editor).

FONDA, BRIDGET
Actress. b. Los Angeles, CA, Jan. 27, 1964. Daughter of actor Peter Fonda. Grew up in Los Angeles and Montana. e. NYU the-

ater prog. Studied acting at Lee Strasberg Inst., and with Harold Guskin. Starred in grad. student film PPT. Workshop stage performances include Confession and Pastels.
PICTURES: Aria (Tristan and Isolde sequence; debut, 1987), You Can't Hurry Love, Light Years (voice), Scandal, Shag, Strapless, Frankenstein Unbound, The Godfather Part III, Drop Dead Fred (unbilled), Doc Hollywood, Leather Jackets, Out of the Rain, Iron Maze, Single White Female, Singles, Army of Darkness, Point of No Return, Bodies Rest and Motion, Little Buddha, It Could Happen to You, The Road to Wellville, Camilla, Rough Magic, Balto (voice), City Hall.
TELEVISION: Specials: Jacob Have I Loved (Wonderworks), The Edge (The Professional Man). Guest: 21 Jump Street.

FONDA, JANE
Actress. b. New York, NY, Dec. 21, 1937. e. Emma Willard Sch., Troy, NY. Active in dramatics, Vassar. Father was late actor Henry Fonda. Brother is actor Peter Fonda. m. executive Ted Turner. Appeared with father in summer stock production, The Country Girl, Omaha, NB. Studied painting, languages, Paris. Art Students League, N.Y. Appeared in The Male Animal, Dennis, MA. Modeled, appeared on covers, Esquire, Vogue, The Ladies Home Journal, Glamour, and McCall's, 1959. Appeared in documentaries: Introduction to the Enemy, No Nukes.
THEATER: There Was A Little Girl (Theatre World Award), Invitation to a March, The Fun Couple, Strange Interlude.
PICTURES: Tall Story (debut, 1960), Walk on the Wild Side, The Chapman Report, Period of Adjustment, In the Cool of The Day, Sunday in New York, The Love Cage (Joy House), La Ronde (Circle of Love), Cat Ballou, The Chase, La Curee (The Game is Over), Any Wednesday, Hurry Sundown, Barefoot in the Park, Barbarella, Spirits of the Dead, They Shoot Horses Don't They? (Acad. Award nom.), Klute (Academy Award, 1971), F.T.A. (also prod.), Tout va Bien, Steelyard Blues, A Doll's House, The Bluebird, Fun With Dick and Jane, Julia (Acad. Award nom.), Coming Home (Academy Award, 1978), Comes a Horseman, California Suite, The China Syndrome (Acad. Award nom.), The Electric Horseman, Nine To Five, On Golden Pond (Acad. Award nom.), Rollover, Agnes of God, The Morning After (Acad. Award nom.), Leonard Part 6 (cameo), Old Gringo, Stanley and Iris.
TELEVISION: Specials: A String of Beads, Lily—Sold Out, The Helen Reddy Special, I Love Liberty, Tell Them I'm a Mermaid, Fonda on Fonda (host), A Century of Women (narrator). Movie: The Dollmaker (Emmy Award, 1984). Series: 9 to 5 (exec. prod. only).

FONDA, PETER
Actor, Director. b. New York, NY, Feb. 23, 1939. e. studied at U. of Omaha. Son of late actor Henry Fonda. Sister is actress Jane Fonda; daughter is actress Bridget Fonda.
PICTURES: Tammy and the Doctor (debut, 1963), The Victors, Lilith, The Young Lovers, The Wild Angels, The Trip, Spirits of the Dead, Easy Rider (also co-s.p., prod.), Idaho Transfer (dir.), The Last Movie, The Hired Hand (also dir.), Two People, Dirty Mary Crazy Larry, Open Season, Race With the Devil, 92 in the Shade, Killer Force, Fighting Mad, Futureworld, Outlaw Blues, High Ballin!, Wanda Nevada (also dir.), Cannonball Run (cameo), Split Image, Certain Fury, Dance of the Dwarfs, Mercenary Fighters, Jungle Heat, Diajobu My Friend, Peppermint Frieden, Spasm, The Rose Garden, Fatal Mission, Family Spirit, Reckless, South Beach, Bodies Rest & Motion, DeadFall, Molly & Gina, Love and a .45, Nadja.
TELEVISION: Movies: A Reason to Live, The Hostage Tower, A Time of Indifference, Sound, Certain Honorable Men, Montana.

FONER, NAOMI
Writer, Producer. b. New York, NY. e. Barnard Col., Columbia U. m. dir. Stephen Gyllenhaal. Was media dir. of Eugene McCarthy's 1968 political campaign, then prod. asst. & researcher at PBS. 1968 joined Children's Television Workshop on staff of Sesame Street. Later helped develop series The Electric Company, 3-2-1 Contact. Creator and co-prod. of series The Best of Families. Wrote teleplay Blackout for PBS series Visions.
PICTURES: Writer: Violets Are Blue, Running on Empty (Golden Globe Award, Acad. Award nom.; also exec. prod.), A Dangerous Woman (also prod.), Losing Isaiah (also prod.).

FONTAINE, JOAN
Actress. b. Tokyo, Oct. 22, 1917. r.n. Joan de Beauvoir de Havilland. e. American School in Japan. Sister is actress Olivia de Havilland. Started on stage in L.A., Santa Barbara and San Francisco in Kind Lady; then as Joan Fontaine in Call it a Day (L.A.), where she was spotted and signed to contract by prod. Jesse Lasky. Sold contract to RKO. On B'way in Tea and Sympathy (1954). Author: No Bed of Roses (1978) Appeared in The Lion in Winter at Vienna's English Speaking Theatre 1979.
PICTURES: No More Ladies (debut, 1935), Quality Street, You Can't Beat Love, Music for Madame, Maid's Night Out, A Damsel in Distress, Blonde Cheat, The Man Who Found Himself, The Duke of West Point, Sky Giant, Gunga Din, Man of Conquest, The Women, Rebecca (Acad. Award nom.), Suspicion (Academy Award, 1941), This Above All, The Constant Nymph

(Acad. Award nom.), Jane Eyre, Frenchman's Creek, Affairs of Susan, From This Day Forward, Ivy, The Emperor Waltz, Letter From an Unknown Woman, Kiss the Blood Off My Hands, You Gotta Stay Happy, Born to Be Bad, September Affair, Darling How Could You?, Something to Live For, Othello (cameo), Ivanhoe, Decameron Nights, Flight to Tangier, The Bigamist, Casanova's Big Night, Serenade, Beyond a Reasonable Doubt, Island in the Sun, Until They Sail, A Certain Smile, Voyage to the Bottom of the Sea, Tender Is the Night, The Devil's Own.
TELEVISION: Crossings, Dark Mansions, Cannon, The Users, Bare Essence, Good King Wenceslas, etc.

FOOTE, HORTON
Writer. b. Wharton, TX, March 14, 1916. Actor before becoming playwright. Plays include Only the Heart, The Chase, Trip to Bountiful, Traveling Lady, Courtship, 1918, The Widow Claire, Habitation of Dragons, Lily Dale, Valentine's Day, Dividing the Estate, Talking Pictures, The Roads to Home, Night Seasons.
PICTURES: Storm Fear, To Kill a Mockingbird (Academy Award, 1962), Baby the Rain Must Fall, The Chase, Hurry Sundown, Tomorrow, Tender Mercies (Academy Award, 1983), 1918 (also co-prod.), The Trip to Bountiful (also co-prod.), On Valentine's Day, Convicts, Of Mice and Men.
TELEVISION: Only the Heart, Ludie Brooks, The Travelers, The Old Beginning, Trip to Bountiful, Young Lady of Property, Death of the Old Man, Flight, The Night of the Storm, The Roads to Home, Drugstore: Sunday Night, Member of the Family, Traveling Lady, Old Man, Tomorrow, The Shape of the River, The Displaced Person, Barn Burning, The Habitation of Dragons.

FORBES, BRYAN
Actor, Writer, Producer, Director. b. Stratford (London), July 22, 1926. m. actress Nanette Newman. Former head of prod., man. dir., Associated British Prods. (EMI). Stage debut, The Corn Is Green (London), 1942; screen debut, The Small Back Room, 1948. Pres.: National Youth Theatre of Great Britain, 1985–; Pres.: Writers Guild of Great Britain, 1988-91.
AUTHOR: Short stories: Truth Lies Sleeping. Novels: The Distant Laughter, Familiar Strangers (U.S.: Stranger), The Rewrite Man, The Endless Game, A Song at Twilight (U.S.: A Spy at Twlight), The Twisted Playground, Partly Cloudy, Quicksand. Novelizations: The Slipper and the Rose, International Velvet. Non-Fiction: Ned's Girl (bio. of Dame Edith Evans) That Despicable Race (history of the British acting tradition). Autobiographies: Notes for a Life, A Divided Life.
THEATER: Director: Macbeth, Star Quality, Killing Jessica, The Living Room.
PICTURES: Actor: Tired Men, The Small Back Room All Over the Town, Dear Mr. Prohack, Green Grow The Rushes, The Million Pound Note (Man With a Million), An Inspector Calls, The Colditz Story, Passage Home, Appointment in London, Sea Devils, The Extra Day, Quatermass II, It's Great To be Young, Satellite in The Sky, The Baby and The Battleship, Yesterday's Enemy, The Guns of Navarone, A Shot in The Dark, Of Human Bondage, Restless Natives. Writer: The Cockleshell Heroes, The Black Tent, Danger Within, I Was Monty's Double (also actor), The League of Gentlemen (also actor), The Angry Silence (also prod., actor), Man in the Moon, Only Two Can Play, Station Six Sahara, Of Human Bondage (also actor), Hopscotch, Chaplin. Director-Writer: Whistle Down the Wind (dir. only), The L-Shaped Room (also actor), Seance on a Wet Afternoon (also prod.), King Rat, The Wrong Box, The Whisperers, Deadfall, The Madwoman of Chaillot (dir. only), The Raging Moon (Long Ago Tomorrow; also actor), The Stepford Wives (dir., actor), The Slipper and the Rose (also actor), International Velvet (also actor), Sunday Lovers (co-dir. only), Better Late Than Never (Menage a Trois), The Naked Face. Exec. Prod.: Hoffman, Forbush and the Penguins, The Railway Children, Peter Rabbit and the Tales of Beatrix Potter, The Go-Between, And Soon The Darkness, On The Buses, Dulcima.
TELEVISION: Actor: Johnnie Was a Hero, The Breadwinner, French Without Tears, Journey's End, The Gift, The Road, The Heiress, December Flower, First Amongst Equals. Writer/Dir.: I Caught Acting Like The Measles (documentary on the life of Dame Edith Evans) Goodbye Norma Jean and Other Things (documentary on the life of Elton John) Jessie, The Endless Game.

FORD, GLENN
Actor. r.n. Gwylin Ford. b. Quebec, Canada, May 1, 1916. Moved to Southern California as child. On stage with various West Coast theatre cos.; featured in The Children's Hour 1935; Broadway in Broom for a Bride, Soliloquy. Signed contract for film career with Columbia Pictures, 1939. Served in U.S. Marine Corps 1942-45.
PICTURES: Heaven With a Barbed Wire Fence (debut, 1940), My Son Is Guilty, Convicted Women, Men Without Souls, Babies for Sale, Blondie Play Cupid, The Lady in Question, So Ends Our Night, Texas, Go West Young Lady, The Adventures of Martin Eden, Flight Lieutenant, Destroyer, The Desperadoes, A Stolen Life, Gilda, Gallant Journey, Framed, The Mating of Millie, The Return of October, The Loves of Carmen, The Man from Colorado, Mr. Soft Touch, The Undercover Man, Lust for Gold,

The Doctor and the Girl, The White Tower, Convicted, The Flying Missile, The Redhead and the Cowboy, Follow the Sun, The Secret of Convict Lake, Green Glove, Young Man with Ideas, Affair in Trinidad, Time Bomb (Terror on a Train), The Man from the Alamo, Plunder of the Sun, The Big Heat, Appointment in Honduras, Human Desire, The Americano, The Violent Men, Blackboard Jungle, Interrupted Melody, Trial, Ransom, The Fastest Gun Alive, Jubal, The Teahouse of the August Moon, 3:10 to Yuma, Don't Go Near the Water, Cowboy, The Sheepman, Imitation General, Torpedo Run, It Started With a Kiss, The Gazebo, Cimarron, Cry for Happy, Pocketful or Miracles, The Four Horsemen of The Apocalypse, Experiment in Terror, Love Is a Ball, The Courtship of Eddie's Father, Advance to the Rear, Fate Is the Hunter, Dear Heart, The Rounders, The Money Trap, Is Paris Burning?, Rage, A Time for Killing, The Last Challenge, Day of the Evil Gun, Heaven With a Gun, Smith!, Santee, Midway, Superman, The Visitor, Virus, Happy Birthday to Me, Border Shootout, Raw Nerve.
TELEVISION: Series: Cade's County, Friends of Man (narrator), The Family Holvak, When Havoc Struck (narrator). Movies: Brotherhood of the Bell, The Greatest Gift, Punch and Jody, The 3000 Mile Chase, Evening in Byzantium, The Sacketts, Beggarman Thief, The Gift, Final Verdict. Mini-Series: Once an Eagle.

FORD, HARRISON
Actor. b. Chicago, IL, July 13, 1942. e. Ripon Coll. Started acting in summer stock at Williams Bay, WI, in Damn Yankees, Little Mary Sunshine. Moved to L.A. where he acted in John Brown's Body. Signed by Columbia Studios under seven-year contract. Took break from acting to undertake carpentry work which included building Sergio Mendes' recording studio. Returned to acting in American Graffiti.
PICTURES: Dead Heat on a Merry-Go-Round (debut, 1966), Luv, A Time for Killing, Journey to Shiloh, Zabriskie Point, Getting Straight, American Graffiti, The Conversation, Star Wars, Heroes, Force 10 from Navarone, Hanover Street, The Frisco Kid, More American Graffiti (cameo), Apocalypse Now, The Empire Strikes Back, Raiders of the Lost Ark, Blade Runner, Return of the Jedi, Indiana Jones and the Temple of Doom, Witness (Acad. Award nom.), The Mosquito Coast, Frantic, Working Girl, Indiana Jones and the Last Crusade, Presumed Innocent, Regarding Henry, Patriot Games, The Fugitive, Jimmy Hollywood (cameo), Clear and Present Danger, Sabrina, Devil's Own.
TELEVISION: Movies: The Intruders, James A. Michener's Dynasty, The Possessed. Guest: The Virginian, Ironside, The FBI, Love American Style, Gunsmoke, The Young Indiana Jones Chronicles. Special: Trial of Lt. Calley.

FORMAN, SIR DENIS
O.B.E., M.A.: Executive. b. Moffat, Dumfriesshire, Scot., Oct. 13, 1917. e. Loretto Sch., Musselburgh, Pembroke Coll., Cambridge. Served in Argyll & Sutherland Highlanders, W.W.II. Entered film business 1946, production staff Central Office of Information, 1947; Chief Production Officer C.O.I. 1948; appointed dir. of the British Film Inst.; 1949; joined Granada Television Ltd., 1955. Jnt. Mng. Dir., 1965 chmn., British Film Inst., bd. of Gov., 1971-73. Chmn. Granada T.V. 1975-87. Chmn. Novello & Co. 1972. Fellow, British Acad. Film & TV Arts, 1976. Dep. chmn. Granada Group, 1984-90, consultant, 1990-96. Deputy chmn. Royal Opera House, 1983-92.

FORMAN, JEROME A.
Executive. b. Hood River, Oregon, June 20, 1934. e. U Arizona. 1966, became gen. mgr. Forman and United Theatres of the Northwest. 1971, joined Pacific Theatres; 1972, appointed v.p. & gen. mgr.; 1978-87, exec. v.p.; 1987-present, pres. One of the original founders of the ShoWest Convention. Currently chmn. emeritus, NATO of Calif. Presently 1991 chmn. NATO. 1991 elected chmn. bd. of Will Rogers Memorial Fund. Board member of the Foundation of the Motion Picture Pioneers.

FORMAN, MILOS
Director. b. Caslav, Czechoslovakia, Feb. 18, 1932. Trained as writer at Czech Film Sch. and as director at Laterna Magika. Directed short films Audition (Competition), If There Were No Music. Won Int'l. attention with first feature length film Black Peter, 1963. Emigrated to U.S. after collapse of Dubcek govt. in Czechoslovakia, 1969. Appeared as actor in films Heartburn, New Year's Day.
PICTURES: Peter and Pavla/Black Peter (also co-s.p.; Czech Film Critics & Grand Prix Locarno Awards), Loves of a Blonde (also co- s.p.), The Firemen's Ball (also co-s.p.), Taking Off (U.S. debut, 1971), Visions of Eight (Decathalon segment), One Flew Over the Cuckoo's Nest (Academy Award, 1975), Hair, Ragtime, Amadeus (Academy Award, 1984), Valmont, The People vs. Larry Flynt.

FORREST, FREDERIC
Actor. b. Waxahachie, TX, Dec. 23, 1936. e. Texas Christian U., U. of Oklahoma, B.A. Studied with Sanford Meisner and Lee Strasberg. Began career off-off B'way at Caffe Cino in The

Madness of Lady Bright then off-B'way in Futz, Massachusetts Trust and Tom Paine, all with La Mama Troupe under direction of Tom O'Horgan. Moved to Hollywood in 1970.
PICTURES: Futz (debut, 1969), When the Legends Die, The Don Is Dead, The Conversation, The Gravy Train, Permission to Kill, The Missouri Breaks, It Lives Again!, Apocalypse Now, The Rose (Acad. Award nom.), One From the Heart, Hammett, Valley Girl, The Stone Boy, Return, Where Are the Children?, Stacking, Tucker: The Man and His Dream, Valentino Returns, Music Box, The Two Jakes, Cat Chaser, Rain Without Thunder, Falling Down, Trauma, Chasers, One Night Stand.
TELEVISION: Movies: Larry, Promise Him Anything, Ruby and Oswald, Calamity Jane, Right to Kill?, The Deliberate Stranger, Quo Vadis, Little Girl Lost, Saigon: Year of the Cat (U.K.), Best Kept Secrets, Who Will Love My Children? A Shadow on the Sun, Margaret Bourke-White, Citizen Cohn, The Habitation of Dragons, Against the Wall. Mini-Series: Die Kinder.

FORREST, STEVE
Actor. b. Huntsville, TX, Sept. 29, 1925. r.n. William Forrest Andrews. Brother of late actor Dana Andrews. e. UCLA, 1950. Acted at La Jolla Playhouse; appeared on radio, TV; m.p. debut in Crash Dive billed as William Andrews.
PICTURES: Crash Dive (debut, 1942), The Ghost Ship, Geisha Girl, Sealed Cargo, Last of the Comanches, The Bad and the Beautiful (1st billing as Steve Forrest), Dream Wife, Battle Circus, The Clown, The Band Wagon, So Big, Take the High Ground, Phantom of the Rue Morgue, Prisoner of War, Rogue Cop, Bedevilled, The Living Idol, It Happened to Jane, Heller in Pink Tights, Five Branded Women, Flaming Star, The Second Time Around, The Longest Day, The Yellow Canary, Rascal, The Wild Country, The Late Liz, North Dallas Forty, Mommie Dearest, Sahara, Spies Like Us, Amazon Women on the Moon.
TELEVISION: Movies: The Hatfields and the McCoys, Wanted: The Sundance Women, The Last of the Mohicans, Testimony of Two Men, Maneaters are Loose, Hollywood Wives, Gunsmoke: Return to Dodge, Columbo: A Bird in the Hand. Series: The Baron, S.W.A.T., Dallas.

FORSTATER, MARK
Producer. b. Philadelphia, PA, 1943. e. City Coll. of New York, Temple U. In 1967 moved to England; studied at U. of Manchester and London Intl. Film School. First job in industry with Anglia TV on program, Survival. Began producing in 1970 with British Film Institute. Set up Chippenham Films to make documentaries. Moved into features in 1974 with Monty Python and the Holy Grail.
PICTURES: The Odd Job, Marigolds in August, The Grass Is Singing, Xtro, Paint It Black, Wherever She Is, The Wolves of Willoughby Chase, Death of a Schoolboy, Streets of Yesterday, Wherever You Are (exec. prod.). Shorts: The Glitterball, Wish You Were Here, The Silent Touch, Between the Devil and the Deep Blue Sea, Provocateur.
TELEVISION: The Cold Room, Forbidden, Separation, Grushko, Doing Rude Things.

FORSTER, ROBERT
Actor. b. Rochester, NY, July 13, 1941. e. Heidelberg Coll., Alfred U., Rochester U., B.S.
THEATER: Mrs. Dally Has a Lover, A Streetcar Named Desire, The Glass Menagerie, 12 Angry Men, The Sea Horse, One Flew Over the Cuckoo's Nest, The Big Knife.
PICTURES: Reflections in a Golden Eye (debut, 1967), The Stalking Moon, Medium Cool, Justine, Cover Me Babe, Pieces of Dreams, Journey Through Rosebud, The Don is Dead, Stunts, Avalanche, The Black Hole, Lady in Red (unbilled), Crunch, Alligator, Vigilante, Walking the Edge, Hollywood Harry (also prod., dir.), The Delta Force, Committed, Esmeralda Bay, Heat from Another Sun, The Banker, Peacemaker, Diplomatic Immunity, 29th Street, In Between, Badge of Silence, Maniac Cop 3: Badge of Silence, South Beach, Cover Story, Body Chemistry 3: Point of Seduction.
TELEVISION: Series: Banyon, Nakia, Once a Hero. Movies: Banyon, The Death Squad, Nakia, The City, Standing Tall, The Darker Side of Terror, Goliath Awaits, In the Shadow of a Killer, Sex Love and Cold Hard Cash. Pilots: Checkered Flag, Mickie & Frankie.

FORSYTH, BILL
Director. Writer. b. Glasgow, Scotland, July 29, 1946. At 16 joined film co. For next 10 years made industrial films, then documentaries. Joined Glasgow Youth Theater.
PICTURES: Director-Writer: That Sinking Feeling (debut, 1979; also prod.), Gregory's Girl, Local Hero, Comfort and Joy, Housekeeping, Breaking In, Rebecca's Daughters, Being Human.
TELEVISION: Andrina.

FORSYTHE, JOHN
Actor. b. Penn's Grove, NJ, Jan. 29, 1918. r.n. John Freund. Former commentator for Brooklyn Dodgers, prior to becoming actor. Debuted on tv in 1947.
THEATER: Mr. Roberts, All My Sons, Yellow Jack, Teahouse of the August Moon, and others.

PICTURES: Destination Tokyo (debut, 1943), The Captive City, It Happens Every Thursday, The Glass Web, Escape From Fort Bravo, The Trouble With Harry, The Ambassador's Daughter, Everything But the Truth, Kitten With a Whip, Madame X, In Cold Blood, The Happy Ending, Topaze, Goodbye and Amen, And Justice for All, Scrooged.
TELEVISION: Series: Bachelor Father, The John Forsythe Show, To Rome With Love, Charlie's Angels (voice only), Dynasty, The Powers That Be. Movies: See How They Run, Shadow on the Land, Murder Once Removed, The Letters, Lisa—Bright and Dark, Cry Panic, Healers, Terror on the 40th Floor, The Deadly Tower, Amelia Earhart, Tail Gunner Joe, Never Con a Killer, Cruise Into Terror, With This Ring, The Users, A Time for Miracles, Sizzle, The Mysterious Two, On Fire, Opposites Attract, Dynasty: The Reunion. Guest: Studio One, Kraft Theatre, Robert Montgomery Presents.

FORSYTHE, WILLIAM
Actor. b. Brooklyn, NY.
THEATER: A Streetcar Named Desire, A Hatful of Rain, Othello, Julius Caesar, 1776, Hair, Godspell.
PICTURES: King of the Mountain, Smokey Bites the Dust, Once Upon a Time in America, Cloak and Dagger, Savage Dawn, The Lightship, Raising Arizona, Extreme Prejudice, Weeds, Patty Hearst, Dead Bang, Torrents of Spring, Dick Tracy, Career Opportunities, Out for Justice, Stone Cold, Sons, American Me, The Waterdance, The Gun in Betty Lou's Handbag, Relentless 3, Direct Hit, The Immortals, Virtuosity, Things to Do in Denver When You're Dead, The Substitute, Palookaville.
TELEVISION: Series: The Untouchables (1993). Movies: The Miracle of Kathy Miller, The Long Hot Summer, Cruel Doubt, Willing to Kill: The Texas Cheerleader Story, A Kiss to Die For, Gotti. Guest: CHiPs, Fame, Hill Street Blues. Mini-Series: Blind Faith.

FORTE, FABIAN
Singer. Actor. b. Philadelphia, PA, Feb. 6, 1943. e. South Philadelphia H.S. At 14, signed contract with Chancellor Records. Studied with Carlo Menotti. Formerly billed simply as Fabian.
RECORDS: Turn Me Loose, Tiger, I'm a Man, Hound Dog Man, The Fabulous Fabian (gold album).
PICTURES: Hound Dog Man (debut, 1959), High Time, North to Alaska, Love in a Goldfish Bowl, Five Weeks in a Balloon, Mr. Hobbs Takes a Vacation, The Longest Day, Ride the Wild Surf, Dear Brigitte, Ten Little Indians, Fireball 500, Dr. Goldfoot and the Girl Bombs, Thunder Alley, Maryjane, The Wild Racers, The Devil's Eight, A Bullet for Pretty Boy, Lovin' Man, Little Laura and Big John, Disco Fever, Kiss Daddy Goodbye, Get Crazy.
TELEVISION: Movies: Getting Married, Katie: Portrait of a Centerfold, Crisis in Mid-Air. Guest: Bus Stop, Love American Style, Laverne & Shirley, The Love Boat.

FOSSEY, BRIGITTE
Actress. b. Tourcoing, France, Mar. 11, 1947. After debut at the age of 5 in Rene Clement's Forbidden Games (1952) returned to school, studying philosophy and translating. Rediscovered by director Jean-Gabriel Albicocco and cast in Le Grand Meaulnes (1967).
PICTURES: Forbidden Games (debut, 1952), The Happy Road, Le Grand Meaulnes (The Wanderer), Adieu l'Ami, M Comme Mathieu, Raphael ou le DeBauche, Going Places, La Brigade, The Blue Country, Femme Fetales, The Good and the Bad, The Man Who Loved Women, The Swiss Affair, Quintet, Mais ou et donc Orincar, The Triple Death of the Third Character, A Bad Son, The Party, Chanel Solitaire, A Bite of Living, Imperativ, The Party-2, Enigma, Au nom de tous les Meins, Scarlet Fever, A Strange Passion, A Case of Irresponsibility, The Future of Emily, The False Confidences, Cinema Paradiso.

FOSTER, CHRISTINE
Executive. r.n. Mary Christine Foster. b. Los Angeles, CA, March 19, 1943. e. Immaculate Heart Coll, B.A. 1964. UCLA MJ, 1968. Teacher while member of Immaculate Heart Community, 1962-65. Teacher, Pacific U., Tokyo, 1968; dir., research and dev. Metromedia Producers Corp., 1968-71; dir., dev. & prod. services, Wolper Org. 1971-76; mgr., film progs. NBC TV 1976-77; v.p. movies for TV & mini-series, Columbia Pictures TV, 1977-81; v.p. series programs, Columbia TV, 1981; v.p. prog. dev., Group W. Prods. 1981-87; v.p., The Agency, 1988-90; agent, Shapiro-Lichtman Talent Agency, 1990-. Member: exec. comm. Humanitas Awards, 1986-; exec. comm. Catholics in Media, 1993-; Activities Committee, Acad. of TV Arts & Sciences, 1989-91; L.A. Roman Catholic Archdiocesan Communications Comm., 1986-89; Women in Film, bd. of dirs., 1977-78; teacher UCLA Extension, 1987-. Foreign and domestic university and public group lecturer and speaker.

FOSTER, DAVID
Producer. b. New York, NY, Nov. 25, 1929. e. Dorsey H.S., U. of Southern California Sch. of Journalism. U.S. Army, 1952-54; entered public relations field in 1952 with Rogers, Cowan &

Brenner; Jim Mahoney, 1956; Allan, Foster, Ingersoll & Weber, 1958; left field in 1968 to enter independent m.p. production. Partner in Turman-Foster Co.
PICTURES: *Produced* (with Mitchell Brower): McCabe and Mrs. Miller, The Getaway. Produced (with Lawrence Turman): The Nickel Ride (exec. prod.), The Drowning Pool, The Legacy, Tribute (exec. prod.), Caveman, The Thing, Second Thoughts, Mass Appeal, The Mean Season, Short Circuit, Running Scared, Full Moon in Blue Water, Short Circuit II, Gleaming the Cube, The Getaway (1993), The River Wild.
TELEVISION: Jesse (co-exec. prod), Between Two Brothers, Surrogate Mother.

FOSTER, JODIE
Actress. r.n. Alicia Christian Foster. b. Los Angeles, CA, Nov. 19, 1962. e. Yale U. Started acting in commercials including famous Coppertone ad. Acting debut on Mayberry, R.F.D. TV series (1968). Followed with many TV appearances, from series to movies of the week.
PICTURES: Napoleon and Samantha (debut, 1972), Kansas City Bomber, Tom Sawyer, One Little Indian, Alice Doesn't Live Here Anymore, Taxi Driver (Acad. Award nom.), Echoes of a Summer, Bugsy Malone, Freaky Friday, The Little Girl Who Lives Down the Lane, Il Casotto (The Beach Hut), Moi fleur bleue (Stop Calling Me Baby!), Candleshoe, Foxes, Carny, O'Hara's Wife, The Hotel New Hampshire, Mesmerized (also co-prod.), Siesta, Five Corners, Stealing Home, The Accused (Academy Award, 1988), The Silence of the Lambs (Academy Award, 1991), Little Man Tate (also dir.), Shadows and Fog, Sommersby, Maverick, Nell (Acad. Award nom.; also co-prod.), Home for the Holidays (dir., co-prod. only), Hate, Contact.
TELEVISION: *Series*: Bob & Carol & Ted & Alice, Paper Moon. *Guest*: The Courtship of Eddie's Father, Gunsmoke, Julia, Mayberry R.F.D., Ironside, My Three Sons. *Specials*: Alexander, Rookie of the Year, Menace on the Mountain, The Secret Life of T.K. Dearing, The Fisherman's Wife. *Movies*: Smile Jenny--You're Dead, The Blood of Others, Svengali, Backtrack.

FOSTER, JULIA
Actress. b. Lewes, Sussex, England, 1941. First acted with the Brighton Repertory Company, then two years with the Worthing, Harrogate and Richmond companies. 1956, TV debut as Ann Carson in Emergency Ward 10.
THEATER: The Country Wife, What the Butler Saw.
PICTURES: Term of Trial (debut, 1962), The Loneliness of the Long Distance Runner, Two Left Feet, The Small World of Sammy Lee, The System (The Gir Getters), The Bargee, One Way Pendulum, Alfie, Half a Sixpence, All Coppers Are ..., The Great McGonagall.
TELEVISION: A Cosy Little Arrangement, The Planemakers, Love Story, Taxi, Consequences, They Throw It at You, Crime and Punishment, The Image.

FOSTER, MEG
Actress. b. Reading, PA, May 14, 1948. e. N.Y. Neighborhood Playhouse.
PICTURES: Adam at 6 A.M. (debut, 1970), Thumb Tripping, Welcome to Arrow Beach (Tender Flesh), A Different Story, Once in Paris, Carny, Ticket to Heaven, The Osterman Weekend, The Emerald Forest, Masters of the Universe, The Wind, They Live, Leviathan, Relentless, Stepfather 2, Blind Fury, Tripwire, Jezebel's Kiss, Diplomatic Immunity, Dead One: Relentless II, Project Shadowchaser, Immortal Combat.
TELEVISION: *Movies*: The Death of Me Yet, Sunshine, Things In This Season, Promise Him Anything, James Dean, Sunshine Christmas, Guyana Tragedy, Legend of Sleepy Hollow, Desperate Intruder, Best Kept Secrets, Back Stab, To Catch a Killer. *Series*: Sunshine, Cagney & Lacey. *Guest*: Here Come the Brides, Mod Squad, Men at Law, Hawaii Five-O, Murder She Wrote, Miami Vice. *Mini-Series*: Washington: Behind Closed Doors. *Special*: The Scarlet Letter.

FOWKES, RICHARD O.
Executive. b. Yonkers, NY, April 15, 1946. e. NYU, Geo. Washington U. Staff attorney for The Dramatists Guild, 1973-77; joined Paramount as assoc. counsel, 1977-80; moved to UA (NYC) as prod. attorney from 1980-82; returned to Paramount as v.p., legal & bus. affairs., MoPic division (LA) 1983; promoted to sr. v.p., bus. affairs & acquisitions, 1989; promoted to sr. v.p. in charge of bus. affairs, 1994.

FOWLER, HARRY
Actor. b. London, England, Dec. 10, 1926. e. West Central Sch., London. Stage debut, Nothing Up My Sleeve (London) 1950; Screen debut, 1941.
PICTURES: Demi-Paradise, Don't Take It to Heart, Champaigne Charlie, Painted Boats, Hue and Cry, Now Barabbas, The Dark Man, She Shall Have Murder, The Scarlet Thread, High Treason, The Last Page, I Believe in You, Pickwick Papers, Top of the Form, Angels One Five, Conflict of Wings (Fuss Over Feathers), A Day to Remember, Blue Peter, Home and Away, Booby Trap, Town on Trial, Lucky Jim, Birthday Present, Idle on Parade, Don't Panic Chaps, Heart of a Man, Crooks Anonymous, The

Longest Day, Lawrence of Arabia, Flight from Singapore, The Golliwog, Ladies Who Do, Clash By Night, The Nanny, Life at the Top, Start the Revolution Without Me, The Prince and The Pauper, Fanny Hill, Chicago Joe and the Showgirl.
TELEVISION: Stalingrad, I Remember the Battle, Gideon's Way, That's for Me, Our Man at St. Mark's, Dixon of Dock Green, Dr. Finlay's Case Book, I Was There, Cruffs Dog Show, The Londoners, Jackanory, Get This, Movie Quiz, Get This (series), Going a Bundle, Ask a Silly Answer, London Scene, Flockton Flyer, Sun Trap, The Little World of Don Camillo, World's End, Minder, Dead Ernest, Morecambe Wise Show, Gossip, Entertainment Express, Fresh Fields, Supergram, A Roller Next Year, Harry's Kingdom, Body Contact, Davro's Sketch Pad, The Bill, In Sickness and in Health, Casualty, Leaves on the Line, Young Indiana Jones Chronicles, Southside Party, London Tonight.

FOWLEY, DOUGLAS
Actor. b. New York, NY, May 30, 1911. e. St. Francis Xavier's Mil. Acad., N.Y. In stock; operated dramatic sch. N.Y.; on screen in bit parts. From 1934 in regular roles.
PICTURES: Battleground, Just This Once, This Woman Is Dangerous, Singin' in the Rain, Man Behind the Gun, Slight Case of Larceny, Naked Jungle, Casanova's Big Night, Lone Gun, The High and the Mighty, Three Ring Circus, Texas Lady, Broken Star, Girl Rush, Bandido, Nightmare in the Sun, The North Avenue Irregulars, From Noon Till Three, The White Buffalo.
TELEVISION: The Moneychangers, Starsky and Hutch, Sunshine Christmas, Oregon Trail. *Series*: The Life and Legend of Wyatt Earp, Pistols and Petticoats, Gunsmoke.

FOX, EDWARD
Actor. b. London, England, April 13, 1937. Comes from theatrical family; father was agent for leading London actors; brother is actor James Fox.
PICTURES: The Mind Benders (debut, 1962), Morgan!, The Frozen Dead, The Long Duel, The Naked Runner, The Jokers, I'll Never Forget What's 'is Name, The Battle of Britain, Oh! What a Lovely War, Skullduggery, The Go-Between, The Day of The Jackal, A Doll's House, Galileo, The Squeeze, A Bridge Too Far, The Duellists, The Big Sleep, Force 10 from Navarone, The Cat and the Canary, Soldier of Orange, The Mirror Crack'd, Gandhi, Never Say Never Again, The Dresser, The Bounty, Wild Geese II, The Shooting Party, Return From the River Kwai, A Feast at Midnight, A Month by the Lake, Prince Valiant.
TELEVISION: Edward and Mrs. Simpson, A Hazard of Hearts, Anastasia: The Mystery of Anna, Quartermaine's Terms, They Never Slept, Shaka Zulu, Robin Hood, The Crucifer of Blood.

FOX, JAMES
Actor. b. London, England, May 19, 1939. Brother is actor Edward Fox. Ent. films as child actor in 1950 as William Fox. Left acting in 1973 to follow spiritual vocation. Returned to mainsteam films in 1982. B'way debut 1995 in Uncle Vanya.
PICTURES: The Miniver Story, 1950; as William Fox), The Magnet, One Wild Oat, The Lavender Hill Mob, Timbuktu, The Queen's Guards, The Secret Partner, She Always Gets Their Man, What Every Woman Wants, The Loneliness of the Long-Distance Runner; Tamahine (1st film billed as James Fox), The Servant, Those Magnificent Men in Their Flying Machines, King Rat, The Chase, Thoroughly Modern Millie, Arabella, Duffy, Isadora, Performance, No Longer Alone, Runners, Greystoke: The Legend of Tarzan, A Passage to India, Pavlova, Absolute Beginners, The Whistle Blower, Comrades, High Season, The Mighty Quinn, Farewell to the King, The Boys in the Island, The Russia House, Patriot Games, Afraid of the Dark, The Remains of the Day.
TELEVISION: The Door, Espionage, Love Is Old, Love Is New, Nancy Astor, Country, New World, Beryl Markham: A Shadow on the Sun, Sun Child, She's Been Away (BBC; shown theatrically in U.S.), Never Come Back, Slowly Slowly in the Wind, Patricia Highsmith Series, As You Like It, A Question of Attribution, Heart of Darkness, Fall from Grace, Hostage, Doomsday Gun, Headhunters, The Old Curiosity Shop.

FOX, MICHAEL J.
Actor. b. Edmonton, Alberta, Canada, June 9, 1961. r.n. Michael Andrew Fox. m. actress Tracy Pollan. Appeared in Vancouver TV series Leo and Me, and on stage there in The Shadow Box. Moved to Los Angeles at age 18.
PICTURES: Midnight Madness (debut, 1980), The Class of 1984, Back to the Future, Teen Wolf, Light of Day, The Secret of My Success, Bright Lights Big City, Casualties of War, Back to the Future Part II, Back to the Future Part III, The Hard Way, Doc Hollywood, Homeward Bound: The Incredible Journey (voice), Life With Mikey, For Love or Money, Where the Rivers Flow North, Greedy, Coldblooded (also co-prod.), Blue in the Face, The American President, Homeward Bound II: Lost in San Francisco (voice), The Frighteners, Mars Attacks.
TELEVISION: *Series*: Palmerstown U.S.A., Family Ties (3 Emmy Awards), Spin City. *Guest*: Lou Grant, The Love Boat, Night Court, Trapper John M.D., Tales from the Crypt (The Trap; also

dir.). *Specials*: Teachers Only, Time Travel: Fact Fiction and Fantasy, Dear America: Letters Home From Vietnam (reader), James Cagney: Top of the World (host). *Movies*: Letters From Frank, High School USA, Poison Ivy, Family Ties Vacation, Don't Drink the Water. *Director*: Brooklyn Bridge (episode).

FOX, RICHARD
Executive. b. New York, NY, Feb. 24, 1947. Joined Warner Bros. Intl. as mgt. trainee in October 1975, working in Australia and Japan. 1977, named gen. mgr. of Columbia-Warner Dist., New Zealand. Served as gen. mgr. of WB in Tokyo, 1978\-1981. Joined WB in L.A. as exec. asst. to Myron D. Karlin, pres. of WB Intl., 1981; appt. v.p., sls. 1982; 1983, promoted to exec. v.p. of intl. arm; 1985, named pres. of WB Intl., assuming post vacated by Karlin. 1992, promoted to exec. v.p., Intl. Theatrical Enterprises, WB.

FOX, RICHARD A.
Executive. b. Buffalo, NY, Jan 5, 1929. e. U. of Buffalo, 1950. Chmn., Fox Theatres Management Corp. Pres., Nat'l NATO 1984-86; chmn., Nat'l NATO 1986-1988.

FOXWELL, IVAN
Producer, Writer. b. London, Eng., Feb. 22, 1914. Entered m.p. ind. 1933 as technician with British & Dominions Film Corp., subsequently with Paramount British & London Films; Assoc. with Curtis Bernhardt in Paris 1937 becoming producer & collaborating on story, s.p. of Carefour, Le Train pour Venise, De Mayerling Sarajevo, others. WWII with BEF and AEF 1939-46. Returned to British films 1947. Director, Foxwell Film Prods. Ltd. PICTURES: *Producer*: No Room at the Inn (also co-s.p.), Guilt Is My Shadow (also co-s.p.), Twenty-Four Hours of a Woman's Life, The Intruder (also co-s.p.), Manuela, A Touch of Larceny, Tiara Tahiti, The Quiller Memorandum, Decline and Fall (also s.p.). TELEVISION: The Intruder (co-writer), The Colditz Story (prod.).

FOXWORTH, ROBERT
Actor. b. Houston, TX, Nov. 1, 1941. e. Carnegie-Mellon U. Began acting at age 10 at Houston Alley Theatre and stayed with stage part-time while completing formal education. Returned to theatre on full-time basis after graduation. Made TV debut in Sadbird, 1969. THEATER: *NY*: Henry V, Terra Nova, The Crucible (Theatre World Award), Love Letters, Candida. *Regional*: Antony & Cleopatra, Uncle Vanya, Cyrano de Bergerac, Who's Afraid of Virginia Woolf?, Othello, Habeus Corpus, The Seagull, Macbeth. PICTURES: Treasure of Matecumbe (debut, 1976), The Astral Factor, Airport '77, Damien: Omen II, Prophecy, The Black Marble, Beyond the Stars. TELEVISION: *Series*: The Storefront Lawyers, Falcon Crest. *Movies*: The Devil's Daughter, Frankenstein, Mrs. Sundance, The Questor Tapes (pilot), The FBI Story: The FBI Vs. Alvin Karpis, James Dean, It Happened at Lakewood Manor, Death Moon, The Memory of Eva Ryker, Act of Love, Peter and Paul, The Return of the Desperado, Double Standard, Face to Face, The Price of the Bride, With Murder in Mind, For Love and Glory. *Specials*: Hogan's Goat, Another Part of the Forest.

FRAKER, WILLIAM A.
Cinematographer, Director. b. Los Angeles, CA, 1923. e. U. of Southern California Film Sch. Worked as camera operator with Conrad Hall; moved to TV before feature films. Photographed and co-prod. doc. Forbid Them Not. PICTURES: *Cinematographer*: Games, The Fox, The President's Analyst, Fade In, Rosemary's Baby, Bullitt, Paint Your Wagon, Dusty and Sweets McGee, The Day of the Dolphin, Rancho Deluxe, Aloha Bobby and Rose, Lipstick, The Killer Inside Me, Gator, Exorcist II--The Heretic, Looking for Mr. Goodbar, American Hot Wax, Heaven Can Wait, Old Boyfriends, 1941, The Hollywood Knights, Divine Madness, Sharky's Machine, The Best Little Whorehouse in Texas, WarGames, Irreconcilable Differences, Protocol, Fever Pitch, Murphy's Romance, SpaceCamp, Burglar, Baby Boom, Chances Are, An Innocent Man, The Freshman, Memoirs of an Invisible Man, Honeymoon in Vegas, Tombstone (also co-assoc. prod.), Street Fighter, Father of the Bride II. *Director*: Monte Walsh, Reflection of Fear, Legend of the Lone Ranger. TELEVISION: Stony Burke, Outer Limits, Ozzie and Harriet, Daktari, B.L. Stryker: The Dancer's Touch (dir.).

FRANCIOSA, ANTHONY
Actor. b. New York, NY, Oct. 25, 1928. e. Ben Franklin h.s. in NY. Erwin Piscator's Dramatic Workshop (4-year scholarship). First stage part in YWCA play; joined Off-Broadway stage group; stock at Lake Tahoe, CA, Chicago and Boston. THEATER: *B'way*: End as a Man, The Wedding Breakfast, A Hatful of Rain (Theatre World Award, Tony nom.), Rocket to the Moon, Grand Hotel. Tour: Love Letters. PICTURES: A Face in the Crowd (debut, 1957), This Could Be The Night, A Hatful of Rain (Acad. Award nom.), Wild Is The Wind, The Long Hot Summer, The Naked Maja, Career, The Story on Page One, Go Naked in the World, Senilita (Carless), Period of Adjustment, Rio Conchos, The Pleasure Seekers, A

Man Could Get Killed, Assault on a Queen, The Swinger, Fathom, In Enemy Country, The Sweet Ride, A Man Called Gannon, Ghost in the Noonday Sun, Across 110th Street, The Drowning Pool, Firepower, The World is Full of Married Men, Death Wish II, Julie Darling, Ghost in the Noonday Sun, Death Is in Fashion, Tenebrae, Help Me Dream, The Cricket, A Texas Legend, Backstreet Dreams, Death House, Brothers in Arms, Double Threat, City Hall. TELEVISION: *Series*: Valentine's Day, The Name of the Game, Search, Matt Helm, Finder of Lost Loves. *Movies*: Fame is the Name of the Game, Deadly Hunt, Earth II, The Catcher, This is the West That Was, Matt Helm, Curse of the Black Widow, Side Show, Till Death Do Us Part, Ghost Writer. *Mini-Series*: Aspen, Wheels. *Guest*: Kraft Theatre, Philco Playhouse, Danger, Naked City, Arrest & Trial, Playhouse 90, etc.

FRANCIS, ANNE
Actress b. Ossining, NY, Sept. 16, 1932. Child model; radio, TV shows as child & adult; on B'way in Lady in the Dark. PICTURES: Summer Holiday (debut, 1948), So Young So Bad, Whistle at Eaton Falls, Elopement, Lydia Bailey, Dream Boat, A Lion Is in the Streets, Rocket Man, Susan Slept Here, Rogue Cop, Bad Day at Black Rock, Battle Cry, Blackboard Jungle, The Scarlet Coat, Forbidden Planet, The Rack, The Great American Pastime, The Hired Gun, Don't Go Near the Water, Crowded Sky, Girl of the Night, Satan Bug, Brainstorm, Funny Girl, Hook Line and Sinker, More Dead Than Alive, The Love God?, Impasse, Pancho Villa, Survival, Born Again, The High Fashion Murders, The Return, Little Vegas. TELEVISION: *Series*: Honey West, My Three Sons, Dallas, Riptide. *Guest*: Partners in Crime, Crazy Like a Fox, Jake and the Fatman, Twilight Zone, Finder of Lost Loves, Golden Girls, Matlock, Murder She Wrote, Burke's Law. *Movies*: Wild Women, The Intruders, The Forgotten Man, Mongo's Back in Town, Fireball Forward, Haunts of the Very Rich, Cry Panic, FBI Vs. Alvin Karpis, The Last Survivors, A Girl Named Sooner, Banjo Hackett, Little Mo, The Rebels, Beggarman Thief, Detour to Terror, Rona Jaffe's Mazes and Monsters, Poor Little Rich Girl: The Barbara Hutton Story, Laguna Heat, My First Love, Love Can Be Murder, Fortune Hunter.

FRANCIS, ARLENE
Actress. r.n. Arlene Francis Kazanjian; b. Boston, MA, Oct. 20, 1908. e. Convent of Mount St. Vincent Acad., Riverdale, NY, Finch Finishing Sch., Theatre Guild Sch., NY. m. Martin Gabel, late actor. *Author*: That Certain Something (1960); Arlene Francis--A Memoir (1978). THEATER: The Women (1937), Horse Eats Hat (Mercury Theater), Danton's Death, All That Glitters, Doughgirls, The Overtons, Once More With Feeling, Tchin-Tchin, Beekman Place, Mrs. Dally, Dinner at Eight, Kind Sir, Lion in Winter, Pal Joey, Who Killed Santa Claus?, Gigi, Social Security. PICTURES: Murders in the Rue Morgue, Stage Door Canteen, All My Sons, One Two Three, The Thrill of It All, Fedora. TELEVISION: Soldier Parade 1949-55, Blind Date, What's My Line; Home, Arlene Francis Show, Talent Patrol, etc. RADIO: Arlene Francis Show, Emphasis, Monitor, Luncheon at Sardis.

FRANCIS, CONNIE
Singer. r.n. Constance Franconero. b. Newark, NJ, Dec. 12, 1938. Appeared, Star Time when 12 years old; won Arthur Godfrey's Talent Scout Show, 12 years old. Autobiography: Who's Sorry Now (1984). Regular on series The Jimmie Rodgers Show, 1959. Gold Records: Who's Sorry Now, My Happiness. Numerous vocalist awards. PICTURES: Where the Boys Are, Follow the Boys, Looking For Love.

FRANCIS, FREDDIE
Producer, Director, Cinematographer. b. London, 1917. Joined Gaumont British Studios as apprentice to stills photographer; then clapper boy at B.I.P. Studios, Elstree; camera asst. at British Dominion. After W.W.II returned to Shepperton Studios to work for Korda and with Powell and Pressburger as cameraman. PICTURES: *Director*: Two and Two Make Six (A Change of Heart/The Girl Swappers; debut, 1962), Paranoiac, Vengeance, The Evil of Frankenstein, Nightmare, Traitor's Gate, Hysteria, Dr. Terror's House of Horrors, The Skull, The Psychopath, The Deadly Bees, They Came from Beyond Space, Torture Garden, Dracula Has Risen from the Grave, Mumsy Nanny Sonny and Girly, Trog, Tales from the Crypt, The Creeping Flesh, Tales That Witness Madness, Son of Dracula, Craze, The Ghoul, Legend of the Werewolf, The Doctor and the Devils, Dark Tower. *Cinematographer*: Moby Dick (second unit photo., special effects), A Hill in Korea (Hell in Korea), Time Without Pity, Room at the Top, The Battle of the Sexes, Saturday Night and Sunday Morning, Sons and Lovers (Academy Award, 1960), The Innocents, Night Must Fall, The Elephant Man, The French Lieutenant's Woman, Dune, Memed My Hawk, Clara's Heart, Her Alibi, Brenda Starr, Glory (Academy Award, 1989), Man in the Moon, Cape Fear, School Ties, Princess Caraboo. TELEVISION: *Movie*: A Life in the Theatre.

FRANCIS, KEVIN
Producer, Executive. b. London, England, 1949. Produced It's Life, Passport, Troubl with Canada, Persecution, The Ghoul, Legend of the Werewolf, etc. Executive produ. The Masks of Death, Murder Elite, A One-Way Ticket to Hollywood, etc. 1976, prod. Film Technique Educational course for BFI. 1972-94, CEO Tyburn Prods. Ltd. 1994-present, Ar;ington Productions Ltd.

FRANKENHEIMER, JOHN
Director. b. Malba, NY, Feb. 19, 1930. e. Williams Coll. Actor, dir., summer stock; radio-TV actor, dir., Washington, DC; then joined CBS network in 1953. Theater: The Midnight Sun (1959). PICTURES: The Young Stranger (debut, 1957), The Young Savages, Birdman of Alcatraz, All Fall Down, The Manchurian Candidate (also co-prod.), Seven Days in May, The Train, Seconds, Grand Prix, The Fixer, The Extraordinary Seaman, The Gypsy Moths, I Walk the Line, The Horsemen, The Impossible Object (Story of a Love Story), The Iceman Cometh, 99 and 44/100% Dead, French Connection II, Black Sunday, Prophecy, The Challenge, The Holcroft Covenant, 52 Pick-Up, Dead-Bang, The Fourth War, Year of the Gun, The Island of Dr. Moreau.
TELEVISION: Series dir.: I Remember Mama, You Are There, Danger, Climax, Studio One, Playhouse 90, Du Pont Show of the Month, Ford Startime, Sunday Showcase. Specials: The Comedian, For Whom the Bell Tolls, The Days of Wine and Roses, Old Man, The Turn of the Screw, The Browning Version, The Rainmaker. Movies: Against the Wall (Emmy Award, 1994), The Burning Season (Emmy Award, 1995; also co-prod.). Mini-Series: Andersonville (Emmy Award, 1996).

FRANKLIN, BONNIE
Actress. b. Santa Monica, CA, Jan. 6, 1944. e. Smith College & UCLA. On B'way: Applause (Theatre World Award, Tony nom. Outer Critics Circle award), Dames At sea, Your Own Thing. Off-B'way in Frankie and Johnny in the Claire de Lune.
TELEVISION: Series: One Day at a Time. Movies: The Law, A Guide for the Married Woman, Breaking Up Is Hard to Do, Portrait of a Rebel: Margaret Sanger, Your Place or Mine, Sister Margaret and Saturday Night Ladies, Shalom Sesame.

FRANKLIN, MICHAEL HAROLD
Executive. b. Los Angeles, CA, Dec. 25, 1923. e. U. of California, A.B., USC, LL.B. Admitted to CA bar, 1951; pvt. practice in L.A. 1951-52; atty. CBS, 1952-54; atty. Paramount, 1954-58; exec. dir. Writers Guild Am. West, Inc. 1958-78; natl exec. dir., Directors Guild of America 1978-. Mem. Am. Civil Liberties Union, Los Angeles Copyright Soc.

FRANKLIN, PAMELA
Actress. b. Tokyo, Japan, Feb. 4, 1950. Attended Elmshurst Ballet Sch., Camberley, Surrey.
PICTURES: The Innocents (debut, 1961), The Lion, The Third Secret, Flipper's New Adventure, The Nanny, Our Mother's House, The Prime of Miss Jean Brodie, The Night of the Following Day, And Soon the Darkness, Necromancy, Ace Eli and Rodger of the Skies, The Legend of Hell House, The Food of the Gods.
TELEVISION: Movies: The Horse Without a Head (theatrical in U.K.), See How They Run, David Copperfield (theatrical in U.K.), The Letters, Satan's School for Girls, Crossfire, Eleanor and Franklin.

FRANKLIN, RICHARD
Director, Producer, Writer. b. Melbourne, Australia, July 15, 1948. e. USC (Cinema, 1967).
PICTURES: Director: The True Story of Eskimo Nell (also co-prod., co-s.p.), Patrick (also co-prod., co-s.p.), The Blue Lagoon (co-prod. only), Road Games (also prod., co-s.p.), Psycho II, Cloak and Dagger, Into the Night (actor only), Link (also prod.), FX2, Hotel Sorrento (also prod.).
TELEVISION: Pilots: Beauty and the Beast, A Fine Romance. Movie: Running Delilah.

FRANKLIN, ROBERT A.
Executive. b. New York, NY, April 15. e. U. of Miami, B.B.A., 1958; Columbia Pacific U., M.B.A., 1979; Ph.D., 1980 majoring in marketing. Before entering film industry worked with House of Seagram, Canada Dry Corp., J. M. Mathes Adv. 1967, joined 20th Century-Fox as dir. of mkt. planning. Formed RP Marketing Intl. (entertainment consulting firm) in 1976 and World Research Systems (computer software marketer). 1981 joined MPAA; 1983, named v.p., admin. & info. services. 1986, named v.p. worldwide market research. Chmn., MPAA research comm.; member, AMA and ESOMAR.

FRANZ, ARTHUR
Actor. b. Perth Amboy, NJ, Feb. 29, 1920. e. Blue Ridge Coll., MD. U.S. Air Force. Radio, TV shows.
THEATER: A Streetcar Named Desire, Second Threshold.
PICTURES: Jungle Patrol (debut, 1948), Roseanna McCoy, The Red Light, The Doctor and the Girl, Sands of Iwo Jima, Red Stallion in the Rockies, Three Secrets, Tarnished, Abbott and Costello Meet the Invisible Man, Flight to Mars, Submarine Command, Strictly Dishonorable, The Sniper, Rainbow 'Round My Shoulder, The Member of the Wedding, Eight Iron Men, Invaders From Mars, Bad for Each Other, The Eddie Cantor Story, Flight Nurse, The Caine Mutiny, Steel Cage, Battle Taxi, New Orleans Uncensored, Bobby Ware Is Missing, Beyond a Reasonable Doubt, The Wild Party, Running Target, The Devil's Hairpin, Back From the Dead, The Unholy Wife, Hellcats of the Navy, The Young Lions, The Flame Barrier, Monster on the Campus, Atomic Submarine, The Carpetbaggers, Alvarez Kelly, Anzio, The Sweet Ride, The Human Factor, Sister of Death, That Championship Season.
TELEVISION: Movies: Murder or Mercy, Jennifer: A Woman's Story, Bogie.

FRANZ, DENNIS
Actor. b. Chicago, IL, Oct. 28, 1944. Started in Chicago Theatre.
PICTURES: Stony Island, Dressed to kill, Blow Out, Psycho II, Body Double, A Fine Mess, The Package, Die Hard 2, The Player, American Buffalo.
TELEVISION: Series: Chicago Story, Bay City Blues, Hill Street Blues, Beverly Hills Buntz, Nasty Boys, N.Y.P.D. Blue (Emmy Award, 1994, 1996). Movies: Chicago Story (pilot), Deadly Messages, Kiss Shot, Moment of Truth: Caught in the Crossfire (also co-prod.), Texas Justice.

FRASER, BRENDAN
Actor. b. Indianapolis, IN, 1968. Raised in Holland, Switzerland, Canada. e. Actors' Conservatory, Cornish College of the Arts, Seattle. Member of Laughing Horse Summer Theatre in Ellensburg, WA.
THEATER: Waiting for Godot, Arms and the Man, Romeo and Juliet, A Midsummer Night's Dream, Moonchildren, Four Dogs and a Bone.
PICTURES: Dogfight (debut, 1991), Encino Man, School Ties, Twenty Bucks, Younger and Younger, With Honors, Airheads, The Scout, Now and Then, The Passion of Darkly Noon, Mrs. Winterbourne.
TELEVISON: Movie: Guilty Until Proven Innocent. Pilot: My Old School.

FRAZIER, SHEILA E.
Actress, Producer. b. Bronx, NY, Nov. 13. e. Englewood, NJ. Was exec. sect'y. and high-fashion model. Steered to acting career by friend Richard Roundtree. Studied drama with N.Y. Negro Ensemble Co. and New Federal Theatre, N.Y., also with Bob Hickey at H.B. Studios, N.Y. Currently owrking as a TV producer.
PICTURES: Super Fly (debut), Superfly T.N.T., The Super Cops, California Suite, What Does It Take?, Three the Hard Way, The Hitter, I'm Gonna Git You Sucker.
TELEVISION: Movie: Firehouse. Mini-Series: King. Series: The Lazarus Syndrome.

FREARS, STEPHEN
Director. b. Leicester, Eng., June 20, 1941. e. Cambridge, B.A in law. Joined Royal Court Theatre, working with Lindsay Anderson on plays. Later assisted Karel Reisz on Morgan: A Suitable Case for Treatment, Albert Finney on Charlie Bubbles, and Lindsay Anderson on If ... Worked afterwards mostly in TV, directing and producing. First directorial credit was 30-minute film The Burning, 1967.
PICTURES: Gumshoe (dir. debut 1971), Bloody Kids, The Hit, My Beautiful Laundrette, Prick Up Your Ears, Sammy and Rosie Get Laid, Dangerous Liaisons, The Grifters, Hero (GB: Accidental Hero), The Snapper, Mary Reilly, The Van.
TELEVISION: A Day Out (1971), England Their England, Match of the Day, Sunset Across the Bay, Three Men in a Boat, Daft as a Brush, Playthings, Early Struggles, Last Summer, 18 Months to Balcomb Street, A Visit from Miss Protheroe, Abel's Will, Cold Harbour, Song of Experience; series of six Alan Bennett plays; Long Distance Information, Going Gently, Loving Walter, Saigon: Year of the Cat, December Flower.

FREDERICKSON, H. GRAY, JR.
Producer. b. Oklahoma City, OK, July 21, 1937. e. U. of Lausanne, Switzerland, 1958-59; U. of Oklahoma. B.A., 1960. Worked one yr. with Panero, Weidlinger & Salvatori Engineering Co., Rome Italy. In 1979 named v.p. of feature films, Lorimar Films.
PICTURES: Candy, Inspector Sterling, Gospel 70, An Italian in America, The Man Who Wouldn't Die, The Good, the Bad and the Ugly, Intrigue in Suez, How to Learn to Love Women, God's Own Country, Wedding March, An American Wife, Natika, Echo in the Village, Little Fauss and Big Halsey, Making It, The Godfather (assoc. prod.), The Godfather Part II (co-prod; Academy Award for Best Picture, 1974), Hit (exec. prod.), Apocalypse Now (co.-prod.; Acad. Award nom.), One From the Heart, The Outsiders, UHF, The Godfather Part III (co-prod.), Ladybugs (exec. prod.), Bad Girls (story), Heaven's Prisoners.
TELEVISION: Producer. The Return of Mickey Spillane's Mike Hammer, Houston Nights, Staying Afloat.

FREEDMAN, JERROLD
Director, Writer. b. Philadelphia, PA, Oct.29, 1942. e. Univ. of PA. Novel: Against the Wind.
PICTURES: Kansas City Bomber, Borderline, Native Son.
TELEVISION: *Director-Writer*. Blood Sport, Betrayal, Some Kind of Miracle, Legs, This Man Stands Alone. *Director*. The Streets of L.A., The Boy Who Drank Too Much, Victims, The Seduction of Gina, Best Kept Secrets, Seduced, Family Sins, Unholy Matrimony, The Comeback, Night Walk, A Cold Night's Death, The Last Angry Man, Goodnight Sweet Wife: A Murder in Boston, Condition: Critical.

FREEMAN, AL, JR.
Actor. b. San Antonio, TX, March 21, 1934. e. LA City Coll.
THEATER: The Long Dream (1960), Kicks and Co., Tiger Tiger Burning Bright, Trumpets of the Lord, Blues for Mister Charlie, Conversation at Midnight, Look to the Lilies, Are You Now or Have You Ever Been?, The Poison Tree.
PICTURES: Torpedo Run, Black Like Me, Dutchman, Finian's Rainbow, The Detective, Castle Keep, The Lost Man, A Fable (also dir.), Seven Hours to Judgement, Malcolm X.
TELEVISION: *Movies*: My Sweet Charlie, Assault at West Point. *Mini-Series*: Roots: The Next Generations, King. *Series*: Hot L Baltimore, One Life to Live (Emmy Award, 1979).

FREEMAN, JOEL
Producer. b. Newark, NJ, June 12, 1922. e. Upsala Coll. Began career at MGM studios, 1941. Air Force Mot. Pic. Unit 1942-46. Became assist. dir. at RKO, 1946. 1948 returned to MGM as asst. dir.; later assoc. prod. 1956 entered indep. field as prod. Supv. on various features and TV series. 1960 to Warner Bros., assoc. producing Sunrise at Campobello, The Music Man and Act One. After such films as Camelot and Finian's Rainbow, became studio exec. at Warners. Presently senior v.p. prod., New Century Entertainment Corp.
PICTURES: *Producer*. The Heart Is a Lonely Hunter, Shaft, Trouble Man, Love at First Bite, Octagon, The Kindred.

FREEMAN, KATHLEEN
Actress. b. Chicago, IL, Feb. 17, 1919.
PICTURES: Casbah (debut, 1948), The Saxon Charm, The Naked City, Behind Locked Doors, Mr. Belvedere Goes to College, The Reformer and the Redhead, A Life of Her Own, The House by the River, Lonely Hearts Bandits, Appointment With Danger, A Place in the Sun, The Company She Keeps, O. Henry's Full House, Singin' in the Rain, Talk About a Stranger, Love Is Better Than Ever, She's Back on Broadway, The Affairs of Dobie Gillis, Half a Hero, Athena, Artists and Models, The Far Country, The Midnight Story, Kiss Them for Me, Houseboat, The Fly, The Missouri Traveler, The Buccaneer, North to Alaska, The Ladies Man, The Errand Boy, Madison Avenue, The Nutty Professor, The Disorderly Orderly, Mail Order Bride, The Rounders, Marriage on the Rocks, Three on a Couch, Point Blank, Hook Line and Sinker, The Good Guys and the Bad Guys, Myra Breckinridge, The Ballad of Cable Hogue, Which Way to the Front?, Support Your Local Gunfighter, Stand Up and Be Counted, Where Does It Hurt?, Unholy Rollers, Your Three Minutes Are Up, The Strongest Man in the World, The Norsemen, The Blues Brothers, Heartbeeps, The Best of Times, Malibu Bikini Shop, Dragnet, Innerspace, In the Mood, The Willies, Gremlins 2: The New Batch, Joey Takes a Cab, Dutch, FernGully ... The Last Rainforest (voice), Little Nemo: Adventures in Slumberland (voice), Hocus Pocus, Naked Gun 33 1/3: The Final Insult, At First Sight.
TELEVISION: *Series*: Topper, Mayor of the Town, It's About Time, Funny Face, Lotsa Luck. *Movies*: But I Don't Want to Get Married!, Call Her Mom, Hitched, The Daughters of Joshua Cabe Return, The Last Ride of the Dalton Gang.

FREEMAN, MORGAN
Actor. b. Memphis, TN, June 1, 1937. e. LA City Coll. Served in Air Force 1955-59 before studying acting. Worked as dancer at NY's 1964 World's Fair. Broadway debut in Hello Dolly! with Pearl Bailey. Took over lead role in Purlie. Became known nationally when he played Easy Reader on TV's The Electric Company (1971-76).
THEATER: *NY*: Ostrich Feathers, The Nigger Lovers, Hello Dolly!, Scuba Duba, Purlie, Cockfight, The Last Street Play, The Mighty Gents (Drama Desk & Clarence Derwent Awards), Coriolanus (Obie Award), Julius Caesar, Mother Courage, Buck, Driving Miss Daisy (Obie Award), The Gospel at Colonus (Obie Award), The Taming of the Shrew.
PICTURES: Who Says I Can't Ride a Rainbow? (debut, 1972), Brubaker, Eyewitness, Death of a Prophet, Harry and Son, Teachers, Marie, That Was Then...This Is Now, Street Smart (NY & LA Film Critics & Natl. Board of Review Awards; Acad. Award nom., 1987), Clean and Sober, Lean on Me, Johnny Handsome, Glory, Driving Miss Daisy (Natl. Board of Review & Golden Globe Awards; Acad. Award nom., 1989), The Bonfire of the Vanities, Robin Hood: Prince of Thieves, The Power of One, Unforgiven, Bopha (dir. only), The Shawshank Redemption (Acad. Award nom.), Outbreak, Seven, Moll Flanders, Chain Reaction.

TELEVISION: *Movies*: Hollow Image, Attica, The Marva Collins Story, The Atlanta Child Murders, Resting Place, Flight For Life, Roll of Thunder Hear My Cry, Charlie Smith and the Fritter Tree, Clinton and Nadine. *Series*: The Electric Company, Another World (1982-4). *Specials* (narrator): The Civil War, Follow the Drinking Gourd, The Promised Land.

FREEZER, HARLENE
Executive. Pres., New York Women in Film & Television.

FRESCO, ROBERT M.
Writer. b. Burbank, CA, Oct. 18, 1928. e. Los Angeles City Coll. Newspaperman. Los Angeles, 1946-47; U.S. Army, 1948-49; staff writer, Hakim Prod., 1950-51; various screenplays, 1951-56.
PICTURES: Tarantula, They Came to Destroy the Earth, Monolith.
TELEVISION: Scripts for Science Fiction Theatre, Highway Patrol.

FREWER, MATT
Actor. b. Washington, D. C., Jan. 4, 1958. Raised in Victoria, British Columbia. Studied drama at the Bristol Old Vic Theatre, appearing in Romeo and Juliet, Macbeth, Waiting for Godot, Deathtrap.
PICTURES: The Lords of Discipline (debut, 1983), Supergirl, Spies Like Us, Ishtar, The Fourth Protocol, Far From Home, Speed Zone, Honey I Shrunk the Kids, Short Time, The Taking of Beverly Hills, Twenty Bucks, National Lampoon's Senior Trip, Lawnmower Man II.
TELEVISION: *BBC*: Tender is the Night, Robin of Sherwood; U.S. *Series*: Max Headroom, Doctor Doctor, Shaky Ground, The Pink Panther (voice), Outer Limits. *Movie*: The Positively True Adventures of the Alleged Texas Cheerleader-Murdering Mom, The Day My Parents Ran Away, Kissinger and Nixon. *Mini-Series*: The Stand. *Guest*: Miami Vice. Specials: Long Shadows, In Search of Dr. Seuss.

FRICKER, BRENDA
Actress. b. Dublin, Ireland, Feb. 17, 1945. Appeared in short film The Woman Who Married Clark Gable. Theatre work includes appearances with the RSC, Royal Court Theatre, and The National Theatre.
PICTURES: Quatermass Conclusion, Bloody Kids, Our Exploits at West Poley, My Left Foot (Academy Award, best supporting actress, 1989), The Field, Utz, Home Alone 2: Lost in New York, So I Married an Axe Murderer, Angels in the Outfield, A Man of No Importance, Moll Flanders, A Time to Kill.
TELEVISION: *Series*: Casualty. *Specials*: Licking Hitler, The House of Bernarda Alba, The Ballroom Romance. *Mini-Series*: Brides of Christ, The Sound and the Silence, A Woman of Independent Means.

FRIEDBERG, A. ALAN
Executive. b. New York, NY, Apr. 13, 1932. e. Columbia Coll., B.A. 1952, Junior Phi Beta Kappa, Summa Cum Laude; Harvard Law School 1955. Past pres. and chmn. of bd. NATO, currently memb. of exec. committee. V.P. Foundation of Motion Picture Pioneers. 1990, named chmn. Loews Theatre Mgmt. Co. Retired.

FRIEDKIN, JOHN
Executive. b. New York, NY, Dec. 9, 1926. e. Columbia Univ. Entered industry in New York as publicist for Columbia Pictures; spent eight years at Young & Rubicam adv. agency. Formed Sumner & Friedkin with Gabe Sumner as partner; left to join Rogers & Cowan, where named v.p. In 1967 resigned to join 20th-Fox, moving to California in 1972 when home offices were transferred. Appointed Fox v.p. worldwide publ. & promo. In 1979 joined Warner Bros. as v.p., adv. pub. for intl. div; 1988, joined Odyssey Distributors Ltd. as sr. v.p., intl. marketing. 1990, formed indept. marketing firm.

FRIEDKIN, WILLIAM
Director, Writer. b. Chicago, IL, Aug. 29, 1939. m. producer Sherry Lansing. Joined WGN-TV, 1957, worked for National Education TV, did TV documentaries before feature films. Dir. B'way play Duet for One.
PICTURES: *Director*: Good Times (debut, 1967), The Night They Raided Minsky's, The Birthday Party, The Boys in the Band, The French Connection (Academy Award, 1971), The Exorcist, Sorcerer (also prod.), The Brink's Job, Cruising (also s.p.), Deal of the Century, To Live and Die in L.A. (also co-s.p.), Rampage (also s.p.), The Guardian (also co-s.p.), Blue Chips, Jade.
TELEVISION: *Movies*: C.A.T. Squad (also exec. prod.), C.A.T. Squad: Python Wolf, Jailbreakers. *Special*: Barbra Streisand: Putting It Together. *Series*: Tales From the Crypt (On a Dead Man's Chest).

FRIEDMAN, JOSEPH
Executive. b. New York, NY. e. City Coll. of New York, 1940-42, NYU, 1946-47. U.S. Navy 3 yrs. Asst. to nat'l dir. field exploita-

tion, Warner Bros. Pictures, 1946-58; nat'l exploitation mgr., Paramount 1958-60; exec. asst. to dir. of adv., publicity & exploitation, Para., 1961; dir. adv. & pub., Paramount 1964; v.p., Para., 1966; v.p. in charge of mktg., 1968; v.p., adv., and p.r., Avco Embassy, 1969; v.p., p.r. American Film Theatre, 1973; v.p., adv. and p.r., ITC, motion picture div., 1976, pres., Joseph Friedman Mktg. & Adv., Inc., 1977. Exec. dir. New Jersey M.P. & T.V. Commission, 1978; v.p. worldwide adv./pub. /promo., Edie & Ely Landau, Inc., 1980; exec. dir., NJ Motion Picture & Television Commission, 1981.

FRIEDMAN, PAUL
Executive. e. Princeton U. Woodrow Wilson Sch. of Public & Intl. Affairs, Columbia Sch. of Journalism. 1967, joined NBC News as newswriter in NY; 1970-75, served as reporter for WRC-TV in D.C., field prod. for The Huntley-Brinkley Report, sr. prod. for NBC Weekend Nightly News, exec. prod. of News 4 New York, sr. prod. NBC Nightly News; 1976-79, was exec. prod. of Today; 1982, joined ABC News as sr, prod. in London; there became dir. of news coverage for Europe, Africa, Middle East, while as operating the ABC News Bureaus in those areas; 1988-92, exec. prod. of World News Tonight With Peter Jennings; Jan. 1993 named exec. v.p. of ABC News.

FRIEDMAN, ROBERT L.
Executive. b. Bronx, NY, March 1, 1930. e. DeWitt Clinton H.S, Bronx. Started as radio announcer and commentator with Armed Forces Radio Service in Europe and U.S. sr. v.p., distrib. & mktg., United Artists Corp.; pres. domestic distribution, Columbia Pictures. 1984, named pres., AMC Entertainment Int'l Inc. 1992, named pres. of AMC Entertainment - the Motion Picture Group. On Century City bd. of dirs.; chmn. of Entertainment Industry Council. Member: M.P. Associates Foundation, Phila., pres. 2 yrs.; Variety Club (on board) M.P. Pioneers; (on board) area chmn. Distrib., chmn., Will Rogers Hospital Foundation, American Film Inst., Academy of M.P. Arts & Sciences.

FRIEDMAN, SEYMOUR MARK
Director. b. Detroit, MI, Aug. 17, 1917. e. Magdalene Coll., Cambridge, B.S. 1936; St. Mary's Hospital Medical Sch., London. Entered m.p. ind. as asst. film ed. 1937; 2nd asst. dir. 1938; 1st asst. dir. 1939, on budget pictures; entered U.S. Army 1942; returned to ind. 1946; dir. Columbia Pictures 1947. Vice president & executive production for Columbia Pictures Television, division of Columbia Pictures Industries, 1955. Member: Screen Directors Guild.
PICTURES: To the Ends of the Earth, Rusty's Birthday, Prison Warden, Her First Romance, Rookie Fireman, Son of Dr. Jekyll, Loan Shark, Flame of Calcutta, I'll Get You, Saint's Girl Friday, Khyber Patrol, African Manhunt, Secret of Treasure Mountain.

FRIEDMAN, STEPHEN
Producer, Writer. b. March 15, 1937. e. U. of Pennsylvania, Harvard Law School. Worked as lawyer for Columbia Pictures (1960-63) and Ashley-Famous Agency. 1963-67: Paramount Pictures. Formed and heads Kings Road Productions.
PICTURES: Producer: The Last Picture Show, Lovin' Molly (also s.p.), Slap Shot, Bloodbrothers, Fast Break, Hero at Large, Little Darlings, Eye of the Needle, All of Me, Creator, Enemy Mine, Morgan Stewart's Coming Home, The Big Easy, There Goes the Neighborhood.

FRIELS, COLIN
Actor. b. Scotland, e. Australia Natl. Inst. of Dramatic Art. m. actress Judy Davis. First began acting with the State Theatre Co. of So. Australia and the Sydney Theatre Co. Theatre includes Sweet Bird of Youth and Hedda Gabler. TV includes special Stark.
PICTURES: Buddies, Monkey Grip, For the Term of His Natural Life, Kangaroo, Malcolm, High Tide, Ground Zero, Grievous Bodily Harm, Warm Nights on a Slow Moving Train, Darkman, Class Action, Dingo, A Good Man in Africa., Angel Baby, Back of Beyond.

FRIENDLY, FRED W.
Producer, Journalist, Writer, Educator. r.n. Fred Wachenheimer. b. New York, NY, October 30, 1915. e. Cheshire Acad., Nichols Junior Coll. U.S. Army, Information and Education Section 1941-45. Editor and correspondent for China, Burma and India for CBI Roundup 1941-45. President, CBS News 1964-66: Edward R. Murrow Professor of Broadcast Journalism, Columbia U., 1966-present; advisor on TV, Ford Foundation, 1966-; member: Mayor's Task Force on CATV and Telecommunications, NYC, 1968; teacher and director: Television Workshop, Columbia U. Sch. of Journalism. RADIO Producer-writer-narrator: Footprints in the Sand of Time, 1938; co-prod. Hear It Now, 1951. Ten George Foster Peabody Awards; DeWitt Carter Reddick Award, 1980; See It Now (35 major awards incl. Overseas Press Club, Page One Award, New York Newspaper Guild, National Headliners Club Award, 1954); CBS Reports (40 major awards). Honorary L.H.D. degrees: U. of Rhode Island, Grinnell U., Iowa U. Military: Legion of Merit

medal, Soldier's Medal for heroism, 4 Battle Stars.
AUTHOR: See It Now (1955); Due to Circumstances Beyond Our Control (1967); The Good Guys, the Bad Guys and the First Amendment: Free Speech vs. Fairness in Broadcasting (1976), Minnesota Rag: The Dramatic Story of the Landmark Supreme Court Case that Gave New Meaning to Freedom of the Press (1981); The Constitution: That Delicate Balance (1984); The Presidency and the Constitution (1987).

FRIES, CHARLES W.
Executive, Producer. b. Cincinnati, OH. e. Ohio State U., B.S. Exec.-prod., Ziv Television; v.p., prod., Screen Gems; v.p., prod., Columbia Pictures; exec. v.p., prod. and exec. prod., Metromedia Prod. Corp., 1970-74; pres., exec. prod., Alpine Prods. and Charles Fries Prods. 1974-83; chmn. & pres., Fries Entertainment, 1984. Nat'l. treas., TV Academy; pres., Alliance TV Film Producers; exec. comm., MPPA. Chmn., Caucus of Producers, Writers and Directors, board of governors and exec. comm. of Academy of TV Arts and Sciences. Bd. trustees, secretary, Exec. committee & vice-chmn., American Film Institute. V.P. & dir. of the Center Theatre Group.
PICTURES: Prod.: Cat People, Flowers in the Attic, Troop Beverly Hills, Screamers.
TELEVISION: Movies: Toughlove, The Right of the People, Intimate Strangers, Bitter Harvest, A Rumor of War, Blood Vows: The Story of a Mafia Wife, The Alamo: 13 Days to Glory, Intimate Betrayal, Drop Out Mother, Crash Course, Supercarrier, Bridge to Silence, The Case of the Hillside Strangler, Deadly Web. Small Sacrifices, The Martian Chronicles. Specials: It's Howdy Doody Time: A 40 Year Celebration.

FRONTIERE, DOMINIC
Executive, Composer. b. New Haven, CT, June 17, 1931. e. Yale School of Music. Studied composing, arranging and conducting; concert accordionist, World's Champion Accordionist, 1943; An Hour with Dominic Frontiere, WNHC-TV, New Haven, 3 years, 1947; exec. vice-pres., musical dir., Daystar Prods. Composer or arranger over 75 films.
PICTURES: Giant, Gentlemen Prefer Blondes, Let's Make Love, High Noon, Meet Me in Las Vegas, 10,000 Bedrooms, Hit the Deck, Marriage-Go-Round, The Right Approach, One Foot in Hell, Hero's Island, Hang 'Em High, Popi, Barquero, Chisum, A for Alpha, Cancel My Reservation, Hammersmith is Out, Freebie and the Bean, Brannigan, The Gumball Rally, Cleopatra Jones and the Casino of Gold, The Stunt Man, Modern Problems, The Aviator.
TELEVISION: Composer-conductor: The New Breed, Stoney Burke, Bankamericard commercials (Venice Film Fest. Award for best use of original classical music for filmed TV commercials), Outer Limits, Branded, Iron Horse, Rat Patrol, Flying Nun, The Invaders, Name of the Game, That Girl, Twelve O'Clock High, Zig Zag, The Young Rebel, The Immortal, Fugitive, The Love War. Movie: Washington Behind Closed Doors.

FUCHS, LEO L.
Independent producer. b. Vienna, June 14, 1929. Moved to U.S., 1939. e. Vienna and New York. U.S. Army cameraman 1951-53; int'l. mag. photographer until entered motion pictures as producer with Universal in Hollywood in 1961.
PICTURES: Gambit, A Fine Pair, Sunday Lovers, Just the Way You Are.

FUCHS, MICHAEL
Executive. b. New York, NY, March 9, 1946. e. Union Coll., NYU Law School (J.D. degree). Show business lawyer before joining Home Box Office in 1976, developing original and sports programming. Named chmn. and CEO of HBO in 1984. 1982-87, v.p. Time Inc. in NY; 1987-1995, exec. v.p. Time Inc.

FUEST, ROBERT
Director. b. London, 1927. Early career as painter, graphic designer. Ent. TV industry as designer with ABC-TV, 1958. 1962: directing doc., commercials. 1966: Wrote and dir. Just Like a Woman, 1967-68; dir. 7 episodes of The Avengers, 1969: wrote and directed 6 episodes of The Optimists.
PICTURES: And Soon the Darkness, Wuthering Heights, Doctor Phibes, Doctor Phibes Rides Again (also s.p.), The Final Programme (also s.p., design), The Devil's Rain, The Geller Effect (s.p. only), The New Avengers, The Gold Bug, Revenge of the Stepford Wives, The Big Stuffed Dog, Mystery on Fire Island, Aphrodite, Worlds Beyond, Cat's Eyes.

FULLER, SAMUEL
Director, Writer, Producer, Actor. b. Worcester, MA, Aug. 12, 1912. m. actress Christa Lang. Copy boy, N.Y. Journal; reporter, rewrite man, N.Y. Graphic, N.Y Journal, San Diego Sun; journeyman reporter many papers. Writer of many orig. s.p.; in U.S. Army, 16th Inf. 1st U.S. Inf. Div. 1942-45.
AUTHOR: Crown of India, 144 Piccadilly Street, Dead Pigeon on Beethoven Street, The Rifle, The Big Red One, The Dark Page, La Grande Melee (Battle Royal), Pecos Bill and the Soho Kid, Once Upon Samuel Fuller (Stories of America; interview book). PICTURES: Director-Writer: I Shot Jesse James, Baron of

Arizona, The Steel Helmet (also prod.), Fixed Bayonets, Park Row (also prod.), Pickup On South Street, Hell and High Water, House of Bamboo, Run of the Arrow (also prod.), China Gate (also prod.), Forty Guns, Verboten!, The Crimson Kimono (also prod.), Underworld U.S.A. (also prod.), Merrill's Marauders, Shock Corridor (also prod.), The Naked Kiss (also prod.), Dead Pigeon on Beethoven Street, The Big Red One, White Dog (also actor), Thieves After Dark, Street of No Return (also actor, edit.), Tini Kling. Actor: The Last Movie, The American Friend, Scott Joplin, 1941, Hammett, State of Things, Slapstick of Another Kind, Return to Salem's Lot, Helsinki Napoli All Night Long, Sons, Somebody to Love, Tigrero: A Movie That Was Never Made.

FUNT, ALLEN
Producer, Performer. b. New York, NY, Sept. 16, 1914. e. Cornell U. Best known as producer and creator of Candid Camera series which originated on radio in 1947 as Candid Microphone which inspired theatrical film shorts. TV version began in 1948 as Candid Mike, changed in 1949 to Candid Camera which played off and on until 1960 when became regular series on CBS, lasting until 1967. Revived briefly in early '70s and again in mid '80s in new format; then syndicated as The New Candid Camera. Joined in 1988 by son Peter Funt as host and prod. Specials: Candid Camera Christmas Special, Candid Camera: Eat! Eat! Eat!, Candid Camera on Wheels, Candid Camera's Vacation, Candid Camera Getting Physical, Candid Camera Goes to the Doctor, Candid Camera's Sporting Life. Produced and starred in film, What Do You Say to a Naked Lady?, Candid Camera's 50th Anniversary.

FURIE, SIDNEY J.
Director, Writer, Producer. b. Toronto, Canada, Feb. 28, 1933. Ent. TV and films 1954. Canadian features include: Dangerous Age, A Cool Sound from Hell. Also dir. many Hudson Bay TV series. To England 1960. 1961 appt. exec. dir. Galaworldfilm Productions, Ltd.
PICTURES: The Snake Woman, Doctor Blood's Coffin, Wonderful to Be Young, Night of Passion (also prod., s.p.), The Young Ones, The Leather Boys, Wonderful Life, The Ipcress File, The Appaloosa, The Naked Runner, The Lawyer, Little Fauss and Big Halsy, Lady Sings the Blues, Hit!, Sheila Levine Is Dead and Living in New York, Gable and Lombard, The Boys in Company C, The Entity, Purple Hearts (also prod., s.p.), Iron Eagle, Superman IV: The Quest For Peace, Iron Eagle II (also co-s.p.), The Taking of Beverly Hills, Ladybugs, Hollow Point, Iron Eagle IV.

FURLONG, EDWARD
Actor. b. Glendale, CA, Aug. 2, 1977. Discovered by casting agent for Terminator 2, having no previous acting experience. Appeared in Aerosmith video Livin' on the Edge.
PICTURES: Terminator 2: Judgment Day (debut, 1991), Pet Sematary 2, American Heart, A Home of Our Own, Brainscan, Little Odessa, The Grass Harp, Before and After.

FURMAN, ROY L.
Attorney, Executive. b. New York, NY, April 19, 1939. e. Brooklyn Coll., A.B. 1960; Harvard U., L.L.B. 1963. Pres., Furman Selz. Chmn., Film Society of Lincoln Center.

FURST, AUSTIN O.
Executive. e. Lehigh U., B.S. in economics/marketing. Began career in mktg. dept., Proctor and Gamble; 1972, joined Time Inc. as dir., new subscription sales for Time magazine; later joined Time Inc.'s new magazine dev. staff for People magazine; named circulation mgr., People magazine, 1974; 1975 named pres., Time Inc.'s Computer Television Inc., a pay-per-view hotel operation and was responsible for successful turnaround and sale of co.; 1976, v.p., programming, Home Box Office; named exec. v.p. HBO, 1979; appointed pres. and CEO, Time-Life Films, Inc., 1980; 1981 established Vestron after acquiring home video rights to Time/Life Video Library; chmn. and CEO, Vestron, Inc.

G

GABOR, ZSA ZSA
Actress. r.n. Sari Gabor. b. Hungary, Feb. 6, 1918. e. Lausanne, Switzerland. Stage debut in Europe. Author: Zsa Zsa's Complete Guide to Men (1969), How to Get a Man How to Keep a Man and How to Get Rid of a Man (1971), One Lifetime is Not Enough (1991). As accomplished horsewoman has won many prizes in various intl. horse shows. Stage work incl. 40 Carats, Blithe Spirit.
PICTURES: Lovely to Look At, We're Not Married, Moulin Rouge, The Story of Three Loves, Lili, Three Ring Circus, The Most Wanted Man in the World, Death of a Scoundrel, Girl in the Kremlin, The Man Who Wouldn't Talk, Touch of Evil, Queen of Outer Space, Country Music Holiday, For the First Time, Pepe, Boys' Night Out, Picture Mommy Dead, Arrivederci Baby, Jack of Diamonds, Won Ton Ton the Dog

Who Saved Hollywood, Frankenstein's Great Aunt Tillie, A Nightmare on Elm Street 3, The Naked Gun 2 1/2: The Smell of Fear, Happily Ever After (voice).

GAIL, MAX
Actor. b. Grosse Ile, MI, Apr. 5, 1943. e. William Coll. B.A. Economics, Univ. of Mich M.B.A.
THEATER: NY: The Babe, One Flew Over the Cuckoo's Nest (also S.F.). LA: Visions of Kerouac.
PICTURES: The Organization, Dirty Harry, D.C. Cab, Heartbreakers, Pontiac Moon, Mind Lies, Sodbusters, Ox and the Eye, Lords of Tanglewood.
TELEVISION: Series: Barney Miller, Whiz Kids, Normal Life. Mini-Series: Pearl. Movies: The Priest Killer, Like Mom Like Me, Desperate Women, The 11th Victim, The Aliens Are Coming, Fun and Games, Letting Go, The Other Lover, Killer in the Mirror, Intimate Strangers, Can You Feel Me Dancing?, Tonight's the Night, Man Against the Mob, The Outside Woman, Ride With the Wind, Robin Cook's Mortal Fear, Naomi & Winona: Love Can Build a Bridge, Secret Agent (prod.), Wrong Side of the Fence (prod.).

GALE, BOB
Writer, Producer. b. St. Louis, MO, May 25, 1951. e. USC Sch. of Cinema. Joined with friend Robert Zemeckis to write screenplays, starting with episode for TV series, McCloud. Also co-wrote story for The Nightstalker series. Turned to feature films, co-writing with Zemeckis script for I Wanna Hold Your Hand, on which Gale also acted as associate producer. Exec. prod. of CBS animated series Back to the Future. Wrote and directed feature Mr. Payback.
PICTURES: I Wanna Hold Your Hand (co-s.p., co-assoc. prod.), 1941 (co-s.p.), Used Cars (prod., co-s.p.), Back to the Future (co.-prod., s.p.), Back to the Future Part II (prod., co-s.p.), Back to the Future Part III (prod., s.p.), Trespass (co-exec. prod., co-s.p.), Tales From the Crypt: Bordello of Blood (co-s.p.).
TELEVISION: Series: Back to the Future (animated; exec. prod.), Tales From the Crypt (wrote, dir. House of Horror).

GALE, GEORGE
Executive. b. Budapest, Hungary, May 26, 1919. e. Sorbonne U., Paris, France. Feature editor, Budapest Ed., U.S. Army Pictorial Service. Feature and TV editor MGM, Hal Roach, Disney Studios; prod. and prod. exec. Ivan Tors; American National Enterprises, Inc. Producer and director. Supervised the production of over 30 features for tv syndication and numerous theatrical features. Member ACE and Academy of Motion Picture Arts and Sciences. Formed George Gale Productions, Inc. in 1976.

GALLAGHER, PETER
Actor. b. New York, NY, Aug. 19, 1955. e. Tufts Univ.
THEATER: NY: Hair (1977 revival), Grease, A Doll's Life (Theatre World Award), The Corn is Green, The Real Thing (Clarence Derwent Award), Long Day's Journey Into Night (Tony Award nom.; also London), Guys & Dolls. Also: Another Country, Pride & Prejudice (both Long Wharf). PICTURES: The Idolmaker (debut, 1980), Summer Lovers, Dream Child, My Little Girl, High Spirits, Sex Lies and Videotape, Tune in Tomorrow, Late for Dinner, The Cabinet of Dr. Ramirez, The Player, Bob Roberts, Watch It, Malice, Short Cuts, Mother's Boys, The Hudsucker Proxy, Mrs. Parker and the Vicious Circle, While You Were Sleeping, The Underneath, Cafe Society, The Last Dance, To Gillian on Her 37th Birthday.
TELEVISION: Series: Skag. Movies: Skag, Terrible Joe Moran, The Caine Mutiny Court-Martial, The Murder of Mary Phagan, I'll Be Home for Christmas, Love and Lies, An Inconvenient Woman, White Mile. Specials: The Big Knife, Long Day's Journey Into Night, Private Contentment, Guys & Dolls: Off the Record.

GALLIGAN, ZACH
Actor. b. New York, NY, Feb. 14, 1964. e. Columbia U.
PICTURES: Gremlins, Nothing Lasts Forever, Waxwork, Mortal Passions, Rising Storm, Gremlins II, Zandalee, Lost in Time, Round Trip to Heaven, All Tied Up, Waxwork II, Warlock: The Armageddon, Ice, Caroline at Midnight, The First to Go.
TELEVISION: Movies: Jacobo Timerman: Prisoner Without a Name Cell Without a Number, Surviving, Psychic, For Love and Glory. Specials: The Prodigious Hickey, The Return of Hickey, The Beginning of the Firm, A Very Delicate Matter, The Hitchhiker: Toxic Shock. Mini-Series: Crossings. Pilot: Interns in Heat. Guest: Tales From the Crypt (Strung Along), Melrose Place, Extreme.

GAMBON, MICHAEL
Actor. b. Dublin, Ireland, Oct. 19, 1940. Ent. Ind. 1966. Early experience in theatre. 1985-87 Acting at National Theatre and London's West End. 1988: in Harold Pinter's Mountain Language.
PICTURES: Othello, The Beast Must Die, Turtle Diary, Paris By Night, The Rachel Papers, A Dry White Season, The Cook

the Thief His Wife and Her Lover, Mobsters, Toys, Clean Slate, The Browning Version, Squanto: A Warrior's Tale, A Man of No Importance, Bullet to Beijing, The Innocent Sleep, Nothing Personal.
TELEVISION: Uncle Vanya, Ghosts, Oscar Wilde, The Holy Experiment, Absurd Person Singular, The Singing Detective (serial), The Heat of the Day, The Storyteller, Maigret Sets a Trap.

GAMMON, JAMES
Actor. b. Newman, IL, Apr. 20. e. Boone H.S., Orlando, FL. Former television cameraman. First acting role was small part on Gunsmoke. Head of Los Angeles' Met Theatre for 10 years.
THEATER: The Dark at the Top of the Stairs (L.A. Critics Circle Award, best actor), Bus Stop (L.A. Drama Critics award, best director), Curse of the Starving Class (NY, L.A.), A Lie of the Mind (NY, L.A.).
PICTURES: Cool Hand Luke (debut, 1967), Journey to Shiloh, Macho Callahan, A Man Called Horse, Macon County Line, Black Oak Conspiracy, Urban Cowboy, Any Which Way You Can, Smithereens, Vision Quest, Sylvester, Silverado, Silver Bullet, Made in Heaven, Ironweed, The Milagro Beanfield War, Major League, Revenge, Coupe de Ville, I Love You to Death, Leaving Normal, Crisscross, The Painted Desert, Running Cool, Cabin Boy, Vegas Vice, Natural Born Killers, Wild Bill.
TELEVISION: Series: Bagdad Cafe. Guest: Bonanza, The Wild Wild West, Cagney & Lacey, The Equalizer, Crime Story, Midnight Caller. Movies: Kansas City Massacre, Rage, Women of San Quentin, M.A.D.D.: Mothers Against Drunk Drivers, Hell Town, The Long Hot Summer, Roe vs. Wade, Dead Aim, Conagher, Stranger at My Door, Men Don't Tell, Truman. Mini-Series: Lincoln.

GANIS, SIDNEY M.
Executive. b. New York, NY, Jan. 8, 1940. e. Brooklyn Coll. Staff writer, newspaper and wire service contact, 20th Century-Fox 1961-62; radio, TV contact and special projects, Columbia Pictures 1963-64. Joined Seven Arts Prod. 1965 as publicity mgr.; 1967, appt. prod. publicity mgr. Warner-7 Arts, Ass't prod., There Was a Crooked Man, 1969. Studio publicity dir., Cinema Center Films, 1970. Director of Ad-Pub for Mame, Warner Bros., 1973; Director of Advertising, Warner Bros., 1974; named WB v.p., worldwide adv. & pub., 1977; 1979, sr. v.p., Lucasfilm, Ltd.; 1982 Emmy winner, exec. prod., best documentary, The Making of Raiders of the Lost Ark. 1986, joined Paramount Pictures as pres., worldwide mktg; 1986, named pres., Paramount Motion Picture Group. 1988, elected trustee University Art Museum, Berkeley, CA. 1991, appointed exec. v.p., Sony Pictures Ent. Exec. v.p., pres. mktg & distrib., Columbia Pictures, 1992. Elected to bd. of govs. AMPAS, 1992. Vice chmn., Columbia Pictures, 1994. Pres., worldwide mktg., Columbia TriStar.

GANZ, BRUNO
Actor. b. Zurich, Switzerland, March 22, 1941.
THEATER: Member of the Berlin Theater troupe, Schaubuhne. Hamlet (1967), Dans La Jungle Des Villes, Torquato Tasso, La Chevauchee Sur Le Lac de Constance, Peer Gynt.
PICTURES: Der Sanfte Lauf (1967), Sommergaste, The Marquise of O, Lumiere, The Wild Duck, The American Friend, The Lefthanded Woman, The Boys from Brazil, Black and White Like Day and Night, Knife in the Head, Nosferatu the Vampyre, Return of a Good Friend, 5% Risk, An Italian Woman, Polenta, La Provinciale, La Dame Aux Camelias, Der Erfinder, Etwas Wird Sichtbar, Circle of Deceit, Hande Hoch, Logik Der Gerfuhls, War and Peace, In the White City, System Ohne Schatten, Der Pendler, Wings of Desire, Bankomatt, Strapless, The Last Days of Chez Nous, Especially on Sunday, Faraway So Close!
TELEVISION: Father and Son (German TV).

GANZ, LOWELL
Writer, Producer, Director. b. New York, NY, Aug. 31, 1948. e. Queens Col. Worked as staff writer on tv series The Odd Couple. Met writing partner Babaloo Mandel at The Comedy Store in the early 1970s. Was co-creator Laverne & Shirley. First teamed with Mandel on script for 1982 comedy Night Shift.
PICTURES: Writer: Night Shift, Splash (Acad. Award nom.; also actor), Spies Likes Us, Gung Ho, Vibes, Parenthood (also actor), City Slickers, A League of Their Own (also actor), Mr. Saturday Night (also actor), Greedy (also actor), City Slickers II: The Legend of Curly's Gold, Forget Paris, Multiplicity.
TELEVISION: Writer-Exec. Prod (series): The Odd Couple, Happy Days, Busting Loose, The Ted Knight Show, Makin' It, Joanie Loves Chachi, Gung Ho, Knight and Dave, Parenthood. Producer: Laverne & Shirley (also writer).

GANZ, TONY
Producer. b. New York, NY. e. studied film at Harvard U. Produced documentaries for PBS in N.Y. Moved to L.A. 1973

where in charge of dev., Charles Fries Productions. Then joined Ron Howard Productions 1980. Left to form own prod. co. with Deborah Blum.
PICTURES: Gung Ho, Clean and Sober, Vibes.
TELEVISION: Series: American Dream Machine, Maximum Security (exec. prod.). Movies: Bitter Harvest, Into Thin Air.

GARCIA, ANDY
Actor. b. Havana, Cuba, Apr. 12, 1956. r.n. Andres Arturo Garcia Menendez. Family moved to Miami Beach in 1961. e. Florida International U, Miami. Spent several years acting with regional theaters in Florida; also part of improv. group. Music producer of album: Cachao Master Sessions Vol. I (Grammy Award), Chachao Master Sessions Vol II (Grammy nom.).
PICTURES: The Mean Season, 8 Million Ways to Die, The Untouchables, Stand and Deliver, American Roulette, Black Rain, Internal Affairs, A Show of Force, The Godfather Part III (Acad. Award nom.), Dead Again, Hero, Jennifer Eight, Cachao... Como Su Ritmo No Hay Dos (Like His Rhythm There Is No Other; also dir., co-prod.), When a Man Loves a Woman, Steal Big Steal Little, Things to Do in Denver When You're Dead, Night Falls on Manhattan, Death in Granada.
TELEVISION: Movie: Clinton and Nadine.

GARDINER, PETER R.
Executive. b. Santa Monica, CA, Apr. 25, 1949. Independent still photographer and industrial filmmaker before joining Paramount, 1973, in feature post-prod. 1979, joined Warner Bros. as asst. dir., corporate services. 1987, promoted to v.p., opns., WB corporate film-video services. 1993, promoted to v.p. Warner Bros. corp. film & video services.

GARDNER, ARTHUR
Producer. b. Marinette, WI, June 7. e. Marinette h.s. Entered m.p. ind. as actor, in orig. cast All Quiet on the Western Front, 1929. Juvenile leads in: Waterfront, Heart of the North, Assassin of Youth, Religious Racketeer; production, asst. dir. King Bros. 1941, then asst. prod. U.S. Air Force 1st Motion Picture Unit, 1943-45. Formed Levy-Gardner-Laven Prods. with Jules Levy, Arnold Laven, 1951.
PICTURES: (Asst. dir.): Paper Bullets, I Killed That Man, Rubber Racketeers, Klondike Fury, I Escaped From the Gestapo, Suspense; Asst. prod.: Gangster, Dude Goes West, Badmen of Tombstone, Gun Crazy, Mutiny, Southside 1-1000. Prod.: Without Warning, Vice Squad, Down Three Dark Streets, Return of Dracula, The Flame Barrier, The Vampire, The Monster that Challenged the World. Geronimo, The Glory Guys, Clambake, Scalphunters, Sam Whiskey, Underground, McKenzie Break, The Honkers, Hunting Party, Kansas City Bomber, White Lightning, McQ, Brannigan, Gator, Safari 3000.
TELEVISION: The Rifleman, Robert Taylor's Detectives, Law of the Plainsman, The Big Valley.

GARFIELD, ALLEN
Actor. b. Newark, NJ, Nov. 22, 1939. r.n. Allen Goorwitz. e. Upsala Col, Actors Studio. Worked as journalist for Newark Star Ledger and Sydney Morning Herald (Australia) prior to becoming an actor. Has also acted as Allen Goorwitz. Life Member of the Actors Studio, NYC.
PICTURES: Greetings, Putney Swope, Hi Mom!, The Owl and the Pussycat, Bananas, Believe in Me, Roommates, The Organization, Taking Off, Cry Uncle!, You've Got to Walk it Like You Talk It or You'll Lose That Beat, Get to Know Your Rabbit, The Candidate, Top of the Heap, Deadhead Miles, Slither, Busting, The Conversation, The Front Page, Nashville, Gable and Lombard, Mother Jugs & Speed, The Brink's Job, Skateboard, Paco, One-Trick Pony, The Stunt Man, Continental Divide, One from the Heart, The State of Things, The Black Stallion Returns, Get Crazy, Irreconcilable Differences, Teachers, The Cotton Club, Desert Bloom, Beverly Hills Cop II, Rich Boys, Let it Ride, Night Visitor, Dick Tracy, Club Fed, Until the End of the World, Jack and His Friends, Family Prayers, The Patriots, The Glass Shadow, Miracle Beach, Sketches of a Strangler, Destiny Turns on the Radio, Diabolique.
TELEVISION: Movies: Footsteps, The Marcus-Nelson Murders, The Virginia Hill Story, Serpico: The Deadly Game, The Million Dollar Rip-Off, Nowhere to Run, Ring of Passion, Leave 'Em Laughing, Citizen Cohn, Killer in the Mirror, Incident at Vichy, Judgment: The Trial of Julius and Ethel Rosenberg. Guest: Law and Order, Equal Justice, Eddie Dodd, Jack's Place, Taxi, etc.

GARFINKLE, LOUIS
Writer, Director, Producer. b. Seattle, WA, February 11, 1928. e. U. of California, U. of Washington, U. of Southern California (B.A., 1948). Writer KOMO, Seattle 1945; Executive Research, Inc., 1948; writer, educ. doc. screenplays, Emerson Films, EBF 1948-50; s.p. You Can Beat the A-Bomb (RKO), 1950; writer-dir. training films, info. films, Signal Photo, 1950-53; copy, Weinberg Adv., 1953; head of doc. research in TV, U. of California, Berkeley, 1954-55; staff, Sheilah Graham Show,

1955; formed Maxim Prod. Inc. with Albert Band, 1956. Co-creator Collaborator Interactive Computer Software to asst. in writing stories for screen & TV, 1990; formed Collaborator Systems Inc. with Cary Brown and Francis X. Feighan, 1991. Received Best Screenwriting Tool Award from Screen Writers Forum, 1991. Member: AMPAS, WGA West, ATAS, Dramatists Guild, Board of Advisers Filmic Writing Major, USC School of Cinema & TV.
PICTURES: *Screenplay*: The Young Guns (also story), I Bury the Living (also story, co-prod.), Face of Fire (also co-prod.), Hellbenders, A Minute to Pray A Second to Die, The Love Doctors (also story, prod.), Beautiful People, The Models (also story), The Doberman Gang (also story), Little Cigars (also story), The Deer Hunter (story collab.; Acad. Award nom.)
TELEVISION: *Writer*: 712 teleplays for Day in Court, Morning Court, Accused, 1959-66. *Co-writer-creator*: Direct Line (pilot), June Allyson Show, Threat of Evil, Death Valley Days, Crullers At Sundown, Captain Dick Mine, No. 3 Peanut Place (pilot).

GARFUNKEL, ART
Singer, Actor. b. New York, NY, Nov. 5, 1942. e. Columbia Coll. Began singing at age 4. Long partnership with Paul Simon began in grade school at 13 in Queens, NY; first big success in 1965 with hit single, Sound of Silence. Partnership dissolved in 1970. Winner of 4 Grammy Awards.
PICTURES: Catch-22 (debut, 1970), Carnal Knowledge, Bad Timing/A Sensual Obsession, Good to Go, Boxing Helena.

GARLAND, BEVERLY
Actress. b. Santa Cruz, CA, Oct. 17, 1930. r.n. Beverly Fessenden. e. Glendale Coll., 1945-47.
PICTURES: D.O.A., The Glass Web, Miami Story, Bittercreek, Two Guns and a Badge, Killer Leopard, The Rocket Man, Sudden Danger, Desperate Hours, Curucu: Beast of the Amazon, Gunslinger, Swamp Woman, The Steel Jungle, It Conquered the World, Not of This Earth, Naked Paradise, The Joker is Wild, Chicago Confidential, Badlands of Montana, The Saga of Hemp Brown, Alligator People, Stark Fever, Twice Told Tales, Pretty Poison, The Mad Room, Where the Red Fern Grows, Airport 1975, Roller Boogie, It's My Turn, Death Falls, Haunted Symphony.
TELEVISION: *Series*: Mama Rosa, Pantomime Quiz, The Bing Crosby Show, My Three Sons, Scarecrow & Mrs. King, Decoy. *Guest*: Twilight Zone, Dr. Kildare, Medic (Emmy nom.), Magnum P.I., Remington Steele, Lois and Clark. *Movies*: Cutter's Trail, Say Goodbye Maggie Cole, Weekend Nun, Voyage of the Yes, Unwed Father, Healers, Day the Earth Moved, This Girl for Hire, The World's Oldest Living Bridesmaid, Finding the Way Home.

GARNER, JAMES
Actor. r.n. James Baumgarner. b. Norman, OK, April 7, 1928. e. Norman H.S. Joined Merchant Marine, U.S. Army, served in Korean War. Prod. Paul Gregory suggested acting career. Studied drama at N.Y. Berghof School. Toured with road companies; Warner Bros. studio contract followed.
PICTURES: Toward the Unknown (debut, 1956), The Girl He Left Behind, Shoot Out at Medicine Bend, Sayonara, Darby's Rangers, Up Periscope, Alias Jesse James (cameo), Cash McCall, The Children's Hour, Boys' Night Out, The Great Escape, The Thrill of It All, The Wheeler Dealers, Move Over Darling, The Americanization of Emily, 36 Hours, The Art of Love, Mister Buddwing, A Man Could Get Killed, Duel at Diablo, Grand Prix, Hour of the Gun, The Pink Jungle, How Sweet It Is, Support Your Local Sheriff, Marlowe, A Man Called Sledge, Support Your Local Gunfighter, Skin Game, They Only Kill Their Masters, One Little Indian, The Castaway Cowboy, Health, The Fan, Victor/Victoria, Tank, Murphy's Romance (Acad. Award nom.), Sunset, The Distinguished Gentleman, Fire in the Sky, Maverick, My Fellow Americans.
TELEVISION: *Series*: Maverick, Nichols, The Rockford Files, Bret Maverick, Man of the People. *Movies*: The Rockford Files (pilot), The New Maverick (pilot), The Long Summer of George Adams, The Glitter Dome, Heartsounds, Promise (also exec. prod.), Obsessive Love, My Name Is Bill W. (also exec. prod.), Decoration Day, Barbarians at the Gate, The Rockford Files: I Still Love L.A. (also co-exec. prod.), The Rockford Files: A Blessing in Disguise (also co-exec. prod.). *Mini-Series*: Space. *Specials*: Sixty Years of Seduction, Lily for President.

GARR, TERI
Actress. b. Lakewood, OH, Dec. 11, 1949. Began career as dancer, performing S.F. Ballet at 13. Later appeared with L.S. Ballet and in original road show co. of West Side Story. Several film appearances as a dancer incl. Fun in Acapulco, Viva Las Vegas, What a Way to Go, Roustabout, etc. Did commercials; appeared in film Head written by a fellow acting student, Jack Nicholson. Career boosted by appearance on TV as semi-regular on The Sonny and Cher Show.
PICTURES: Maryjane, Head, The Moonshine War, The Conversation, Young Frankenstein, Won Ton Ton the Dog Who Saved Hollywood, Oh God!, Close Encounters of the Third

Kind, Mr. Mike's Mondo Video, The Black Stallion, Witches' Brew, Honky Tonk Freeway, One from the Heart, The Escape Artist, Tootsie (Acad. Award nom.), The Sting II, The Black Stallion Returns, Mr. Mom, Firstborn, Miracles, After Hours, Full Moon in Blue Water, Out Cold, Let It Ride, Short Time, Waiting for the Light, The Player, Mom and Dad Save the World, Dumb & Dumber, Ready to Wear (Pret-a-Porter), Michael.
TELEVISION: *Series regular*: Shindig, The Ken Berry "Wow" Show, (1972), Burns and Schreiber Comedy Hour, Girl With Something Extra, The Sonny and Cher Comedy Hour, The Sonny Comedy Revue, Good and Evil, Good Advice, Women of the House. *Movies*: Law and Order, Doctor Franken, Prime Suspect, Winter of Our Discontent, To Catch a King, Intimate Strangers, Pack of Lies, A Quiet Little Neighborhood A Perfect Little Murder, Stranger in the Family, Deliver Them From Evil: The Taking of Alta View, Fugitive Nights: Danger in the Desert. *Specials*: The Frog Prince (Faerie Tale Theatre), Drive She Said (Trying Times), Paul Reiser: Out on a Whim, Mother Goose Rock 'n' Rhyme, The Whole Shebang, Aliens for Breakfast. *Mini-Series*: Fresno. *Guest*: Tales from the Crypt (The Trap), The Larry Sanders Show.

GARRETT, BETTY
Singer, Actress. b. St. Joseph, MO, May 23, 1919. e. scholarships: Annie Wright Seminary, Tacoma, WA; Neighborhood Playhouse, N.Y. Sang in night clubs, hotels, Broadway shows: Call Me Mister (Donaldson Award, 1946), Spoon River Anthology, A Girl Could Get Lucky, Meet Me in St. Louis (1989). Motion Picture Herald, Star of Tomorrow, 1949. Starred in one woman show, Betty Garrett and Other Songs, beginning in 1974 and touring through 1993 (Bay Area Critics & LA Drama Critics Awards); also in autobiographical show, No Dogs or Actors Allowed (Pasadena Playhouse, 1989), So There! (with Dale Gonyear; Pasadena Playhouse, 1993). Given Life Achievement Award by Los Angeles Drama Critics Circle, 1995.
PICTURES: The Big City (debut, 1948), Words and Music, Take Me Out to the Ball Game, Neptune's Daughter, On the Town, My Sister Eileen, Shadow on the Window.
TELEVISION: *Series*: All in the Family, Laverne and Shirley. *Guest*: Love Boat, Black's Magic, Somerset Gardens, Murder She Wrote, Harts of the West, The Good Life. *Movies*: All the Way Home, Who's Happy Now.

GARSON, GREER
Actress. b. County Down, Northern Ireland, Sept. 29, 1908. e. London U., B.A. cum laude; post grad. studies, Grenoble U. France. After early career in art research and editing for Encyclopaedia Britannica and market research with Lever's Intl. Advertising Service became actress with Birmingham Rep. Co. starring in 13 West End prods. before lured to Hollywood by MGM, 1938. Screen debut 1939 in Goodbye, Mr. Chips. Academy Award best actress, 1942 Mrs. Miniver. Voted one of the ten best Money-Making Stars in Motion Picture Herald-Fame Poll 1942-46 inclusive. Photoplay Mag. Gold Medal 1944-45 and top British Award 1942, 1943, 1944. Numerous other awards incl. L.A. Times Woman of the Year, Woman of the World Award from Intl. Orphans, Inc. 1987 Gov. Award for contrib. to arts NM, 1988 USA Film Fest. Master Screen Artist. Active in civic and benevolent activities. With late husband Col. E.E. (Buddy) Fogelson, awarded Dept. of Interior's citation for environmental preservation efforts. Founded Fogelson Museum NM 1987. Established The Greer Garson Theatre and Fogelson Library Center at the College of Santa Fe; founding donor for Fogelson Forum at Dallas Presbyterian Hospital, Garson Communications Center at Col. of Santa Fe, Fogelson Pavillion in Dallas. Donor for The Greer Garson Theatre at Southern Methodist Univ., Dallas.
THEATER: Stage debut Birmingham (England) Rep. theat. 1932 in Street Scene; London debut 1935 in Golden Arrow (opposite Laurence Olivier); continued London stage to 1938 (Vintage Wine, Mademoiselle, Accent on Youth, Page from a Diary, Old Music, etc.).
PICTURES: Goodbye Mr. Chips (debut, 1939), Remember?, Pride and Prejudice, Blossoms in the Dust, When Ladies Meet, Mrs. Miniver (Academy Award, 1942), Random Harvest, Madame Curie, The Youngest Profession (cameo), Mrs. Parkington, Valley of Decision, Adventure, Desire Me, Julia Misbehaves, That Forsyte Woman, The Miniver Story, The Law and the Lady, Scandal at Scourie, Julius Caesar, Her Twelve Men, Strange Lady in Town, Sunrise at Campobello, Pepe, The Singing Nun, The Happiest Millionaire.
TELEVISION: *Specials*: The Little Foxes, Crown Matrimonial, My Father Gave Me America, The Little Drummer Boy, Holiday Tribute to Radio City, Perry Como's Christmas in New Mexico, A Gift of Music (host), Bicentennial Tribute to Los Angeles. *Movie*: Little Women.
(d. April 6, 1996)

GARY, LORRAINE
Actress. b. New York, NY, Aug. 16, 1937. r.n. Lorraine Gottfried. m. executive Sidney J. Scheinberg. e. Columbia Univ.

PICTURES: Jaws, Car Wash, I Never Promised You a Rose Garden, Jaws 2, Just You and Me Kid, 1941, Jaws-The Revenge.
TELEVISION: *Movies*: The City, The Marcus-Nelson Murders, Partners in Crime, Pray for the Wildcats, Man on the Outside, Lanigan's Rabbi, Crash.

GASSMAN, VITTORIO
Actor. b. Genoa, Italy, Sept. 1, 1922. e. Acad. of Dramatic Art, Rome. Stage actor, 1943; m.p. debut, 1946.
PICTURES: Daniele Cortis, Mysterious Rider, Bitter Rice, Lure of Sila, The Outlaws, Anna, Streets of Sorrow; to U.S., Cry of the Hunted, Sombrero, The Glass Wall, Rhapsody, Girls Marked Danger, Mambo, War and Peace, World's Most Beautiful Woman, Tempest, The Love Specialist, The Great War, Let's Talk About Women, Il Successo, The Tiger, Woman Times Seven, Ghosts-Italian Style, Scent of a Woman, Viva Italia!, A Wedding, Quintet, Immortal Bachelor, The Nude Bomb, Sharky's Machine, Tempest, I Picari, The Family, The Sleazy Uncle, The House of the Lord, The Hateful Dead, To Forget Palermo, Los Alegres Picaro, Scheherzade, The Long Winter, Sleepers.

GATES, WILLIAM H.
Executive. b. 1957. Started computer programming at age 13. 1974, developed BASIC for the first microcomputer, MITS Altair. 1975, with Paul Allen formed Microsoft to develop software for personal computers. Chmn. & CEO of Microsoft Corp. leading provider of worldwide software for personal computers.

GATWARD, JAMES
Executive. b. London, England. Ent. Ind. 1957. Early career as freelance drama prod. dir. in Canada, USA, UK (with ITV & BBC). Prod. dir. various intern. co-productions in UK, Ceylond, Australia, Germany. Currently chief executive and Dep. chmn. TVS Television Ltd., chmn. Telso Communications Ltd., dir. of ITN, Channel Four, Super Channel, Oracle Teletext.

GAVIN, JOHN
Executive, Diplomat, Former Actor. b. Los Angeles, CA, April 8, 1932. m. actress Constance Towers. e. St. John's Military Acad., Villanova Prep at Ojai, Stanford Univ., Naval service: air intelligence officer in Korean War. Broadway stage debut: Seesaw, 1973. 1961-73 public service experience as spec. advisor to Secretary Gen. of OAS, performed gp. task work for Dept. of State and Exec. Office of the President. Pres. Screen Actors Guild, 1971-73. Named U.S. Ambassador to Mexico, 1981-86. Partner in Gavin & Dailey, a venture capital firm; Pres., Gamma Services Corp. (Intl. Consultants); dir., Atlantic Richfield Co., Dresser Industries, Pinkerton, Inc., The Hotchkiss and Wiley Funds, International Wire Group Co. Consultant to Dept. of State and serves pro-bono on several boards.
PICTURES: Behind the High Wall (debut, 1956), Four Girls in Town, Quantez, A Time to Love and a Time to Die, Imitation of Life, Psycho, Midnight Lace, Spartacus, A Breath of Scandal, Romanoff and Juliet, Tammy Tell Me True, Back Street, Thoroughly Modern Millie, The Madwoman of Chaillot, Pussycat Pussycat I Love You.
TELEVISION: *Movies*: Cutler's Trail, The New Adventures of Heidi, Sophia Loren: Her Own Story. *Series*: Destry, Convoy. *Mini-Series*: Doctors' Private Lives.

GAY, JOHN
Writer. b. Whittier, CA, April 1, 1924. e. LA City Coll.
PICTURES: Run Silent, Run Deep, Separate Tables, The Happy Thieves, Four Horsemen, The Courtship of Eddie's Father, The Hallelujah Trail, The Last Safari, The Power, No Way to Treat a Lady, Soldier Blue, Sometimes a Great Notion, Hennessey, A Matter of Time.
TELEVISION: Amazing Howard Hughes, Kill Me If You Can, Captains Courageous, Red Badge of Courage, All My Darling Daughters, Les Miserables, Transplant, A Private Battle, A Tale of Two Cities, The Bunker, Berlin Tunnel 21, Stand By Your Man, Dial "M" For Murder, The Long Summer of George Adams, A Piano for Mrs. Cimino, The Hunchback of Notre Dame, Ivanhoe, Witness for the Prosecution, Samson and Delilah, Fatal Vision, Doubletake, Uncle Tom's Cabin, Outlaw, Six Against the Rock, Around the World in 80 Days, Blind Faith, Cruel Doubt.

GAYNOR, MITZI
Actress. r.n. Francisca Mitzi Von Gerber. b. Chicago, IL, Sept. 4, 1931. e. Powers Professional H.S., Hollywood. Studied ballet since age four; was in L.A. Light Opera prod. Roberta. Stage: Anything Goes (natl. co., 1989).
OPERA: Fortune Teller, Song of Norway, Louisiana Purchase, Naughty Marietta, The Great Waltz.
PICTURES: My Blue Heaven (debut, 1950), Take Care of My Little Girl, Golden Girl, We're Not Married, Bloodhounds of Broadway, The I Don't Care Girl, Down Among the Sheltering Palms, There's No Business Like Show Business, Three

Young Texans, Anything Goes, The Birds and the Bees, The Joker Is Wild, Les Girls, South Pacific, Happy Anniversary, Surprise Package, For Love or Money.
TELEVISION: *Specials*: Mitzi, Mitzi's Second Special, The First Time, A Tribute to the American Housewife, Mitzi and a Hundred Guys, Roarin' in the 20s, Mitzi...Zings Into Spring, What's Hot What's Not.

GAZZARA, BEN
Actor. b. New York, NY, Aug. 28, 1930. e. Studied at CCNY 1947-49. Won scholarship to study with Erwin Piscator; joined Actor's Studio, where students improvised a play, End as a Man, which then was performed on Broadway with him in lead. Screen debut (1957) in film version of that play retitled The Strange One.
THEATER: Jezebel's Husband, End as a Man, Cat on a Hot Tin Roof, A Hatful of Rain, The Night Circus, Epitaph for George Dillon, Two for the Seesaw, Strange Interlude, Traveler Without Luggage, Hughie, Who's Afraid of Virginia Woolf, Dance of Death, Thornhill, Shimada.
PICTURES: The Strange One (debut, 1957), Anatomy of a Murder, The Passionate Thief, The Young Doctors, Convicts Four, Conquered City, A Rage to Live, The Bridge at Remagen, Husbands, The Neptune Factor, Capone, Killing of a Chinese Bookie, Voyage of the Damned, High Velocity, Opening Night, Saint Jack, Bloodline, They All Laughed, Inchon, Tales of Ordinary Madness, Road House, Quicker Than the Eye, Don Bosco, A Lovely Scandal, Girl from Trieste, Il Camorrista, Tattooed Memory, Beyond the Ocean (also dir., s.p.), Forever, Farmer & Chase, The Shadow Conspiracy.
TELEVISION: *Series*: Arrest and Trial, Run for Your Life. *Movies*: When Michael Calls, Maneater, QB VII, The Death of Ritchie, A Question of Honor, An Early Frost, A Letter to Three Wives, Police Story: The Freeway Killings, Downpayment on Murder, People Like Us, Lies Before Kisses, Blindsided, Love Honor & Obey: The Last Mafia Marriage, Parallel Lives, Fatal Vows: The Alexandria O'Hara Story.

GEARY, ANTHONY
Actor. b. Coalville, UT, May 29, 1947. e. U. of Utah.
PICTURES: Blood Sabbath (debut, 1969), Johnny Got His Gun, Private Investigations, Disorderlies, Penitentiary III, You Can't Hurry Love, Pass the Ammo, Dangerous Love, It Takes Two, UHF, Night Life, Crack House, Night of the Warrior, Scorchers.
TELEVISION: *Series*: Bright Promise, General Hospital (1978-83; 1990-). *Guest*: The Young and the Restless, Osmond Family Holiday Special, Sunset Beat, Murder She Wrote, Hotel, All in the Family, Streets of San Francisco. *Movies*: Intimate Agony, Sins of the Past, The Imposter, Kicks, Perry Mason: The Case of the Murdered Madam, Do You Know the Muffin Man?

GEBHARDT, FRED
Producer, Writer, Exhibitor. b. Vienna, Austria, Mar. 16, 1925. e. Schotten Gymnasium, Vienna, UCLA, 1939. Usher Boyd Theatre, Bethlehem, PA; Mgr., Rivoli Thea. L.A.; 1944; 18 yrs. mgr. many theatres. Fox West Coast, then Fine Arts Theatre. Writer, prod.: 12 To the Moon, The Phantom Planet; prod., Assignment Outer Space, Operation M; s.p., All But Glory, The Starmaker, Shed No Blood, Fortress in Heaven, Eternal Woman. Pres., Four Crown Prods., Inc.; recipient of Medal of Americanism, D.A.R., 1963; Honorary Lifetime Member, P.T.A., Young Man of The Year Award, 1956, 24 Showmanship Awards; Mem. Acad. M.P. Arts and Sciences, Ind. M.P. Prod. Assoc.
AUTHOR: Mental Disarmament, All But Glory, Starmaker, Shed No Blood, The Last of the Templars.

GEDRICK, JASON
Actor. b. Chicago, IL, Feb. 7, 1965.
PICTURES: Massive Retaliation (debut, 1984), The Zoo Gang, The Heavenly Kid, Iron Eagle, Stacking, Promised Land, Rooftops, Born on the Fourth of July, Backdraft, Crossing the Bridge.
TELEVISION: *Series*: Class of 96, Murder One.

GEESON, JUDY
Actress. b. Arundel, Sussex, England, Sept. 10, 1948. e. Corona Stage Sch. Began professional career on British TV, 1960.
THEATER: Othello, Titus Andronicus, Two Gentlemen of Verona, Section Nine, An Ideal Husband.
PICTURES: To Sir with Love, Berserk, Here We Go Round the Mulberry Bush, Prudence and the Pill, Hammerhead, Three into Two Won't Go, The Oblong Box, Two Gentlemen Sharing, The Executioner, Nightmare Hotel, 10 Rillington Place, Doomwatch, Fear in the Night, It's Not the Size That Counts, Brannigan, Diagnosis Murder, The Eagle Has Landed, Carry On England, Dominique, Horror Planet, The Plague Dogs (voice).
TELEVISION: Dance of Death, Lady Windermere's Fan, Room with a View, The Skin Game, Star Maidens, Poldark, She, The Coronation, Murder She Wrote, Astronomy (Triple Play II). *Movie*: The Secret Life of Kathy McCormick.

GEFFEN, DAVID
Executive, Producer. b. Brooklyn, NY, Feb. 21, 1943. Began in mailroom of William Morris Agency before becoming agent there and later at Ashley Famous. With Elliott Roberts founded own talent management co. for musicians. Founded Asylum Records, 1970. Pres. then chmn. Elektra-Asylum Records 1973-76. Sold co. to Warner Communications for whom he headed film prod. unit. Vice-chmn. Warner Bros. Pictures, 1975; exec. asst. to chmn., Warner Communications, 1977; Member music faculty Yale U., 1978. Formed Geffen Records 1980 and Geffen Film Co. Producer of Broadway shows Master Harold... and the Boys, Cats, Good, Dreamgirls, Social Security, Chess. 1990, sold record co. to MCA, Inc. With Steven Spielberg and Jeffrey Katzenberg formed Dreamworks entertainment company, 1995.
PICTURES: Personal Best, Risky Business, Lost in America, After Hours, Little Shop of Horrors, Beetlejuice (exec. prod.), Men Don't Leave, Defending Your Life, M. Butterfly, Interview With the Vampire.

GELBART, LARRY
Writer. b. Chicago, IL, Feb. 25, 1928. Began at age 16 writing for Danny Thomas on Fanny Brice Show. Followed by Duffy's Tavern, Bob Hope and Jack Paar radio shows.
THEATER: The Conquering Hero, A Funny Thing Happened on the Way to the Forum (with Burt Shevlove; Tony Award, 1962), Sly Fox, Mastergate, City of Angels (Tony Award, 1990), Power Failure.
PICTURES: The Notorious Landlady, The Thrill of It All, The Wrong Box, Not With My Wife You Don't, The Chastity Belt, A Fine Pair, Oh God!, Movie Movie, Neighbors, Tootsie, Blame It on Rio.
TELEVISION: Series: Caesar's Hour, M*A*S*H (Emmy Award, 1974; also co-prod.), United States. Movie: Barbarians at the Gate (Cable Ace Award, 1993). Special: Mastergate.

GELFAN, GREGORY
Executive. b. Los Angeles, CA, Aug. 7, 1950. Was entertainment atty. with Kaplan, Livingston et. al., and Weissmann, Wolff et. al. before joining Paramount Pictures in 1983 as dir. of business affairs. 1985, named v.p., business affairs, for M.P. Group of Paramount; 1989 promoted to sr. v.p. in chg. of business affairs. 1994, named exec. v.p. in chg. of business & legal affairs, 20th Century Fox.

GELLER, BRIAN L.
Executive. b. New York, NY, Feb. 3, 1948. e. Queens Coll. Entered industry with Columbia Pictures as sls. trainee in 1966, leaving in 1968 to go with American Intl. Pictures as asst. branch mgr. In 1969 joined Cinemation Industries as eastern div. sls. mgr.; 1978, left to become gen. sls. mr. of NMD Film Distributing Co. 1982, named dir. of dist., Mature Pictures Corp. 1983, gen. sls. mgr., Export Pix.; with Cinema Group as east. sls. mgr.; joined Scotti Brothers Pictures as national sales, mgr. Member of Motion Picture Bookers Club of N.Y.; Variety Tent 35, Motion Picture Pioneers.

GENDECE, BRIAN
Producer, Executive. b. St. Louis, MO, Dec. 3, 1956. e. Drury Coll., Springfield, MO. 1981-85, Director of Business Affairs, Weinstein/Skyfield Productions and Skyfield Management. 1986-87, dir. of business affairs, Cannon Films; 1987-89, dir. creative affairs, Cannon Films; 1989 co-pres., Sheer Entertainment; indie first look Epic Prods.; 1991 owner The Gendece Film Co.; 1991-93, prod./dir., 21st Century Film; 1993-96, dir. of mktg., Raleigh Film and Television Studios.
THEATER: Jack Klugman as Lyndon.
PICTURES: Runaway Train, Salsa, Rope Dancin', The Hunters, The American Samurai, Ceremony.
VIDEO: Bad Habits, Shape Up with Arnold, Laura Branigan's Your Love, How to Become a Teenage Ninja, L.A. Raiders' Wild Wild West, The Making of Crime and Punishment.

GEORGE, GEORGE W.
Writer, Producer. b. New York, NY, Feb.8, 1920. e. Williams Coll. U.S. Navy, 1941-44; screen-writer since 1948. President, Jengo Enterprises, dev. theatrical and m.p. projects.
THEATER: Prod.: Dylan, Any Wednesday, Ben Franklin in Paris, The Great Indoors, Happily Never After, Night Watch, Via Galactica, Bedroom Farce, Program for Murder (also co-author).
PICTURES: Writer: Bodyguard, The Nevadan, Woman on Pier 13, Peggy, Mystery Submarine, Red Mountain Experiment, Alcatraz, Fight Town, Smoke Signal, Desert Sands, Uranium Boom, Halliday Brand, Doc, The James Dean Story, The Two Little Bears. Prod.: The James Dean Story, A Matter of Innocence, Twisted Nerve, Hello-Goodbye, Night Watch, Rich Kids, My Dinner With Andre.
TELEVISION: Climax, Screen Gems, Loretta Young Show, The Rifleman, Peter Gunn, The Real McCoys, Adventures in Paradise, Hong Kong, Follow the Sun, Bonanza.

GEORGE, LOUIS
Executive. b. Karavas, Kyrenia, Cyprus, June 7, 1935. e. Kyrenia Business Acad., Cyprus (honored 1951). Emigrated to U.S. in

1952. After brief stint in Foreign Exchange Dept. of City National Bank, New York, served in U.S. Army, 1953-55. Entered industry in 1956 as theatre manager with Loew's Theatres in N.Y. metro area, managing Metropolitan, Triboro, New Rochelle, between 1958-66. 1966 joined MGM as dir. of intl. theatre dept. 1969 promoted to dir. of world-wide non-theatrical sales. 1972-74 served as regional dir. of MGM Far East operations. 1974 left MGM to establish Arista Films, Inc., an indep. prod./dist. co. Pres. & CEO, Arista Films, Inc. Also bd. member, American Film Marketing Assn., chmn. Copywright and Film Security Committee of the Assn.
PICTURES: Slaughterhouse Rock, Buying Time, Violent Zone (exec. prod.), Angels Brigade, Final Justice, Surf II, Crackdown.

GEORGE, SUSAN
Actress, Producer. b. Surrey, England, July 26, 1950. m. actor-prod. Simon MacCorkindale. e. Corona Acad.
PICTURES: Billion Dollar Brain, The Sorcerers, Up the Junction, The Strange Affair, The Looking Glass War, All Neat in Black Stockings, Twinky (Lola), Spring and Port Wine, Eye Witness (Sudden Terror), Die Screaming Marianne, Fright, Straw Dogs, Sonny and Jed, Dirty Mary Crazy Larry, Mandingo, Out of Season, A Small Town in Texas, Tintorera, Tomorrow Never Comes, Enter the Ninja, Venom, The House Where Evil Dwells, Jigsaw Man, Lightning: The White Stallion, Stealing Heaven (exec. prod. only), That Summer of White Roses (also exec. prod.), The House That Mary Bought (also exec. prod.).
TELEVISION: Swallows and Amazons, Adam's Apple, Weaver's Green, Compensation Alice, The Right Attitude, Dracula, Lamb to the Slaughter, Royal Jelly, Masquerade, Czechmate, Hotel, Blacke's Magic, Jack the Ripper, Castle of Adventure, Cluedo, Stay Lucky.

GERALD, HELEN
Actress. b. New York, NY, Aug. 13. e. U. of Southern California, 1948. Stage: Italian Teatro D'Arte, Les Miserables, The Civil Death, Feudalism.
PICTURES: The Gay Cavalier, The Trap, Tarzan and the Leopard Woman, Cigarette Girl, Meet Miss Bobby Socks, G.I. War Brides, Gentleman's Agreement, A Bell for Adano, Tomorrow Is Forever, Janie, Grand Prix, The Sandpiper, Make Mine Mink, Best of Everything.
TELEVISION: Robert Montgomery Presents, Frontiers of Faith, Valiant Lady, Kraft Theatre, Gangbusters, Adventures of The Falcon, Schlitz Playhouse of Stars, This Is the Answer, Man from U.N.C.L.E., Run for Your Life, Perry Mason.

GERARD, GIL
Actor. b. Little Rock, AK, Jan. 23, 1943. e. Arkansas State Teachers Coll. Appeared in over 400 TV commercials. On stage in I Do! I Do!, Music Man, Stalag 17, Applause, etc.
PICTURES: Some of My Best Friends Are (1971), Man on a Swing, Hooch (also co-prod.), Airport '77, Buck Rogers in the 25th Century, Soldier's Fortune.
TELEVISION: Series: The Doctors, Buck Rogers in the 25th Century, Nightingales, Sidekicks, E.A.R.T.H. Force, Code 3 (host). Movies: Ransom for Alice, Killing Stone, Help Wanted: Male, Not Just Another Affair, Hear No Evil, Johnny Blue (pilot), For Love or Money, Stormin' Home, International Airport, Final Notice, The Elite, Last Electric Knight.

GERARD, LILLIAN
Publicist, Writer b. New York, NY, Nov. 25, 1914. e. Baruch CCNY, Columbia U. Publicity, Rialto Theatre, 1936; publicity-adv. Filmarte Theatre, 1938, Gerard Associates, 1938-47; V.P. and managing dir. of Paris Theatre, 1948-62; publicity-adv. dir., Rugoff Theatres, 1962. Film consultant to Times Films, Lopert Films, Landau Co., 1962-65. Adjunct Professor, Film, 1968-70, Columbia U., Sch. of the Arts, Special Projects Co-Ordinator, Museum of Modern Art, 1968-80. Now associated with Philip Gerard in Gerard Associates.

GERARD, PHILIP R.
Executive. b. New York, NY, Aug. 23, 1913. e. City Coll. of New York, B.B.A. 1935; Columbia U.. Publicity dir. Mayer-Burstyn 1936-39; Gerard Associates, 1939-41; in public relations U.S. War Dept. 1942-44; with MGM 1944-48; with Universal Pictures since 1948; Eastern pub. mgr., 1950-59; Eastern ad. and pub. dir., Dec. 1959-68; N.Y. Production Exec., 1968-76. As of Jan. 1, 1977 formed Gerard Associates, film consultants on marketing, production and acquisitions. N.Y.C. Board member of CSS/RSVP (Retired Seniors Volunteer Program); Community Service Society. Member: Visitor's Day Comm., New York Hospital; volunteer at the International Center.

GERBER, DAVID
Executive. b. Brooklyn, NY. e. U. of the Pacific. m. actress Laraine Stephens. Joined Batten, Barton, Durstine and Osborn ad agency in N.Y. as TV supvr. Left to become sr. v.p. of TV at General Artists Corp. 1956, named v.p. in chg. sales at 20th-Fox TV where sold and packaged over 50 prime-time

series and specials. Entered indep. prod. with The Ghost and Mrs. Muir, followed by Nanny and the Professor. 1970 was exec. prod. of The Double Deckers, children's series made in England. 1972 joined Columbia Pictures Television as indep. prod.; 1974 was named exec. v.p. worldwide prod. for CPT. 1976 returned to indep. prod. 1985, joined MGM/UA TV broadcasting group in chg. world-wide prod. 1986 named president, MGM/UA Television. 1988-92, chmn & CEO, MGM/UA Television Prods. group.
TELEVISION: *Exec. prod.*: Cade's County, Police Story (Emmy, best dramatic series), Police Woman, The Lindbergh Kidnapping Case, Joe Forrester, The Quest and Gibbsville, To Kill a Cop, Power, Medical Story, Born Free, Beulah Land, The Night the City Screamed, Follow the North Star, Nothing Lasts Forever.

GERBER, MICHAEL H.
Executive. b. New York, NY, Feb. 6, 1944. e. St. Johns U., B.A., 1969; St. Johns U. School of Law, J.D., 1969. Atty. for Screen Gems, 1969-71; asst. secy. & asst. to gen. counsel, Columbia Pictures Industries, 1971-74; corporate counsel and secretary, Allied Artists Pictures, 1974, v.p. corporate affairs, Allied Artists, 1978; v.p., business affairs, Viacom Intl. 1980-86; 1986-89, sr. v.p.; 1989-93, pres., first run, intl. distrib. & acquisitions, Viacom Enterprises.

GERE, RICHARD
Actor. b. Philadelphia, PA, Aug. 29, 1949. e. U. of Massachusetts. Started acting in college; later joined Provincetown Playhouse and Seattle Repertory Theatre. Composed music for productions of these groups.
THEATER: *B'way*: Grease, Soon, Habeas Corpus, Bent (Theatre World Award), A Midsummer Night's Dream (Lincoln Center). *Off-B'way* in Killer's Head. *London*: Taming of the Shrew (with Young Vic).
PICTURES: Report to the Commissioner (debut, 1975), Baby Blue Marine, Looking for Mr. Goodbar, Days of Heaven, Bloodbrothers, Yanks, American Gigolo, An Officer and a Gentleman, Breathless, Beyond the Limit, The Cotton Club, King David, Power, No Mercy, Miles From Home, Internal Affairs, Pretty Woman, Rhapsody in August, Final Analysis (also co-exec. prod.), Sommersby (also co-exec. prod.), Mr. Jones (also co-exec. prod.), Intersection, First Knight, Primal Fear.
TELEVISION: *Movies*: Strike Force, And the Band Played On. *Guest*: Kojak. *Pilot*: D.H.P.

GERTZ, IRVING
Composer, Musical director. b. Providence, RI, May 19, 1915. e. Providence Coll. of Music, 1934-37. Assoc. with Providence Symph. Orch., comp. choral works for Catholic Choral Soc.; music dept., Columbia, 1939-41; U.S. Army, 1941-46; then comp. arranger, mus. dir. for many ocs. incl. Columbia, Universal International, NBC, 20th Century Fox. Compositions: Leaves of Grass, Serenata for String Quartet, Divertimento for String Orchestra, Tableau for Orchestra.
PICTURES: Bandits of Corsica, Gun Belt, Long Wait, The Fiercest Heart, First Travelling Saleslady, Fluffy, Nobody's Perfect, Marines Let's Go!, It Came from Outer Space, The Man from Bitter Ridge, Posse from Hell, The Creature Walks Among Us, The Incredible Shrinking Man, Hell Bent for Leather, Seven Ways from Sundown, Francis Joins the WACS, Raw Edge, East of Sumatra, A Day of Fury, To Hell and Back, Cult of the Cobra, Plunder Road, Top Gun, Tombstone Express, The Alligator People, Khyber Patrol, The Wizard of Baghdad. Fluffy, Marines, Let's Go!
TELEVISION: *Orig. theme & scores*: America, The Golden Voyage, Across the Seven Seas, The Legend of Jesse James, Daniel Boone, Voyage to the Bottom of the Sea, Peyton Place, Land of the Giants, Lancer, Medical Center, Boutade for Wood-Wind Quartet, Salute to All Nations, A Village Fair, Liberty! Liberte! (for symphony orchestra).

GERTZ, JAMI
Actress. b. Chicago, IL, Oct. 28, 1965. e. NYU. Won a nationwide talent search competition headed by Norman Lear to cast TV comedy series Square Pegs. Following series studied at NYU drama school. Los Angeles theater includes Out of Gas on Lovers' Leap and Come Back Little Sheba. On NY stage in Wrong Turn at Lungfish. Also appeared in the Julian Lennon music video Stick Around.
PICTURES: Endless Love (debut, 1981), On the Right Track, Alphabet City, Sixteen Candles, Mischief, Quicksilver, Crossroads, Solarbabies, The Lost Boys, Less Than Zero, Listen to Me, Renegades, Silence Like Glass, Don't Tell Her It's Me, Sibling Rivalry, Jersey Girls, Twister.
TELEVISION: *Series*: Square Pegs, Dreams, Sibs. *Guest*: Diff'rent Strokes, The Facts of Life. *Movie*: This Can't Be Love.

GETTY, BALTHAZAR
Actor. b. California, Jan. 22, 1975. Spotted by talent agent while at Bel Air Prep School, winning lead role in remake of Lord of the Flies.

PICTURES: Lord of the Flies (debut, 1990), Young Guns II, My Heroes Have Always Been Cowboys, The Pope Must Die, December, Where the Day Takes You, Red Hot, Natural Born Killers, White Squall.
TELEVISION: *Special*: The Turn of the Screw.

GETTY, ESTELLE
Actress. b. New York, NY, July 25, 1923. e. attended New School for Social Research. Trained for stage with Gerald Russak and at Herbert Berghof Studios. Worked as comedienne on Borscht Belt circuit and as actress with Yiddish theatre. Founder Fresh Meadows Community theater. Also worked as acting teacher and coach and secretary. Author, If I Knew What I Know Now... So What? (1988).
THEATER: The Divorce of Judy and Jane (off-B'way debut, 1971), Widows and Children First, Table Settings, Demolition of Hannah Fay, Never Too Old, A Box of Tears, Hidden Corners, I Don't Know Why I'm Screaming, Under the Bridge There's a Lonely Place, Light Up the Sky, Pocketful of Posies, Fits and Starts, Torch Song Trilogy (off-B'way, B'way and tour, Drama Desk nom., 1982, Helen Hayes Award, best supp. performer in a touring show).
PICTURES: The Chosen, Tootsie, Protocol, Mask, Mannequin, Stop Or My Mom Will Shoot.
TELEVISION: *Series*: The Golden Girls (Golden Globe Award, Emmy Award, 1988), The Golden Palace, Empty Nest. *Movies*: No Man's Land, Victims for Victims: The Teresa Saldana Story, Copacabana. *Guest*: Cagney and Lacey, Nurse, Baker's Dozen, One of the Boys, Fantasy Island.

GETZ, JOHN
Actor. e. Univ Iowa, Amer. Conservatory Theatre (SF). Appeared on B'way in They're Playing Our Song, M. Butterfly. LA stage: Money & Friends.
PICTURES: Tattoo, Thief of Hearts, Blood Simple, The Fly, The Fly II, Born on the Fourth of July, Men at Work, Don't Tell Mom the Babysitter's Dead, Curly Sue, A Passion to Kill.
TELEVISION: *Series*: Rafferty, Suzanne Pleshette is Maggie Briggs, MacGruder & Loud, Mariah. *Movies*: Killer Bees, A Woman Called Moses, Kent State, Rivkin: Bounty Hunter, Muggable Mary: Street Cop, Not in Front of the Children, Concrete Beat, The Execution, In My Daughter's Name, Betrayal of Trust, Untamed Love, Awake to Danger. *Mini-Series*: Loose Change.

GHOSTLEY, ALICE
Actress. b. Eve, MO, Aug. 14, 1926. e. Univ. of OK.
THEATER: New Faces of 1952, Sandhog, Trouble in Tahiti, Maybe Tuesday, A Thurber Carnival, The Sign in Sidney Brustein's Window (Tony Award, 1965), Stop Thief Stop, Annie, The Beauty Part, Livin' The Life, Nunsense, Come Blow Your Horn, Bye Bye Birdie, Arsenic and Old Lace, Shangri-La.
PICTURES: New Faces (debut, 1954), To Kill a Mockingbird, My Six Loves, Ace Eli and Rodger of the Skies, Gator, Rabbit Test, Grease, Not for Publication, Viva Ace, The Flim Flam Man, With Six You Get Egg Roll, The GRaduate, Blue Sunshine, Record City.
TELEVISION: *Series*: The Jackie Gleason Show (1962-64), Captain Nice, The Jonathan Winters Show, Bewitched, Mayberry R.F.D., Nichols, The Julie Andrews Hour, Temperatures Rising, Designing Women. *Movie*: Two on a Bench. *Specials*: Cinderella, Twelfth Night, Shangri-La, Everybody's Doin' It. *Guest*: Please Don't Eat the Daisies, Get Smart, Love American Style, Hogan's Heroes, The Odd Couple, What's Happening!, Good Times, Gimme a Break, The Golden Girls, The Client, Cybill, etc.

GIANNINI, GIANCARLO
Actor. b. Spezia, Italy, Aug. 1, 1942. Acquired degree in electronics but immediately after school enrolled at Acad. for Drama in Rome. Cast by Franco Zeffirelli as Romeo at age of 20. Subsequently appeared in a play also directed by Zeffirelli, Two Plus Two No Longer Make Four, written by Lina Wertmuller.
PICTURES: Rita la Zanzara, Arabella, Anzio, Fraulein Doktor, The Secret of Santa Vittoria, Love and Anarchy, The Seduction of Mimi, Swept Away by an Unusual Destiny in the Blue Sea of August, Seven Beauties, How Funny Can Sex Be?, A Night Full of Rain, The Innocent, Buone Notizie (also prod.), Revenge, Travels with Anita, Lili Marleen, Lovers and Liars, La Vita e Bella, Picone Sent Me, Immortal Bachelor, American Dreamer, Fever Pitch, Saving Grace, New York Stories (Life Without Zoe), Il Picari, The Sleazy, Uncle, Snack Bar Budapest, Oh King, Blood Red, Brown Bread Sandwiches, Killing Time, Short Cut, Once Upon a Crime, A Walk in the Clouds.
TELEVISION: Sins, Jacob.

GIANOPULOUS, JIM
Executive. Pres., Fox International Theatrical Distribution, Twentieth Century Fox, Inc.

GIBBS, DAVID
Executive. b. 1944. Ent. motion picture industry 1961, Kodak research, worked as a photographer for Kodak 1963-66.

Lectured at Harrow College of Technology and Kodak Photographic School until 1972. Left Kodak, 1975, after three years as a market specialist to join Filmatic Laboratories. Appt. asst. man. director, 1977, becoming chmn. and man. director, 1988. Member of RTS, SMPTE and IVCA. Past Chmn. BISFA 1988-90. Past president of the British Kinematograph, Sound and Television Society.

GIBBS, MARLA
Actress. b. Chicago, IL, June 14, 1931. e. Cortez Peters Business School, Chicago. Worked as receptionist, switchboard operator, travel consultant (1963-74) before co-starring as Florence Johnston on the Jeffersons (1974-85). Formed Marla Gibbs Enterprises, Los Angeles, 1978. Member of CA State Assembly, 1980. Image Award NAACP, 1979-83.
PICTURES: Black Belt Jones, Sweet Jesus, Preacher Man.
TELEVISION: *Series:* The Jeffersons, Checking In, 227. *Movies:* The Missing One, Tell Me Where It Hurts, Nobody's Child. *Mini-Series:* The Moneychangers. *Special:* You Can't Take It With You.

GIBSON, DEREK
Executive. b. Huyton, England, July 7, 1945. e. Wigan Col. Head of Prod. at Astral Bellevue Pathe, 1979-80; v.p. Sandy Howard Prods.; Pres. Hemdale Film Group., 1982-present.
PICTURES: *Prod./Exec.:* The Terminator, Hoosiers, Salvador, Platoon (Academy Award winner for Best Picture, 1986), River's Edge, Best Seller, Criminal Law.

GIBSON, HENRY
Actor. b. Germantown, PA, Sept. 21, 1935. e. Catholic U. of America. Appeared as child actor with stock companies, 1943-57; B'way debut in My Mother My Father and Me, 1962.
PICTURES: The Nutty Professor, Kiss Me Stupid, The Outlaws Is Coming, Charlotte's Web (voice), The Long Goodbye, Nashville (Nat'l Soc. Film Critics Award, 1975), The Last Remake of Beau Geste, Kentucky Fried Movie, A Perfect Couple, The Blues Brothers, Tulips, Health, The Incredible Shrinking Woman, Monster in the Closet, Brenda Starr, Inner Space, Switching Channels, The 'Burbs, Night Visitor, Gremlins II, Tune in Tomorrow, Tom and Jerry: The Movie (voice), A Sailor's Tattoo, Biodome.
TELEVISION: *Series:* Rowan and Martin's Laugh-In (1968-72). *Movies:* Evil Roy Slade, Every Man Needs One, The New Original Wonder Woman (pilot), Escape from Bogen County, The Night They Took Miss Beautiful, Amateur Night at the Dixie Bar & Grill, For the Love of It, Nashville Grab, Long Gone, Slow Burn, Return to Green Acres, Return to Witch Mountain. *Mini-Series:* Around the World in 80 Days.

GIBSON, MEL
Actor, Director. b. Peekskill, NY, Jan. 3, 1956. Emigrated in 1968 to Australia with family. Attended Nat'l Inst. of Dramatic Art in Sydney; in 2nd yr. was cast in his first film, Summer City. Graduated from NIDA, 1977. Joined South Australian Theatre Co. in 1978, appearing in Oedipus, Henry IV, Cedoona. Other plays include Romeo and Juliet, No Names No Pack Drill, On Our Selection, Waiting for Godot, Death of a Salesman.
PICTURES: Summer City (Coast of Terror; debut, 1977), Mad Max, Tim, Chain Reaction (unbilled), Attack Force Z, Gallipoli, The Road Warrior (Mad Max II), The Year of Living Dangerously, The Bounty, The River, Mrs. Soffel, Mad Max Beyond Thunderdome, Lethal Weapon, Tequila Sunrise, Lethal Weapon 2, Bird on a Wire, Air America, Hamlet, Lethal Weapon 3, Forever Young, The Man Without a Face (also dir.), Maverick, Braveheart (also dir., co-prod.; Academy Award, 1996; Golden Globe, 1996), Casper (cameo), Pocahontas (voice), Ransom.
TELEVISION: *Series:* The Sullivans, The Oracle. *Specials:* The Ultimate Stuntman: A Tribute to Dar Robinson, Australia's Outback: The Vanishing Frontier (host). *Guest host:* Saturday Night Live.

GIELGUD, SIR JOHN
Actor. b. London, England, Apr. 14, 1904. e. Westminster Sch., Lady Benson's Sch. (dram.), London; Royal Acad. of Dramatic Art. Knighted, 1953. Autobiography: Early Stages (1983). Honorary degress: Oxford, London, St. Andrews, Brandeis (U.S.), Assoc. Legion of Honor.
THEATER: Began stage career in Shakespearean roles; on London stage also in the Constant Nymph, The Good Companions, Dear Octopus, The Importance of Being Earnest, Dear Brutus, etc., various Shakespearean seasons, London & N.Y. 1988: The Best of Friends.
PICTURES: Who is the Man? (debut, 1924), The Clue of the New Pin; Insult (sound debut, 1932), The Good Companions, Secret Agent, The Prime Minister, Julius Caesar (1953), Romeo and Juliet, Richard III, Around the World in 80 Days, The Barretts of Wimpole Street, Saint Joan, Hamlet, Becket (Acad. Award nom.), To Die in Madrid (narrator), The Loved One, Chimes at Midnight (Falstaff), Sebastian, Assignment to Kill, The Charge of the Light Brigade, The Shoes of the Fisherman, Oh What a Lovely War, Julius Caesar (1971),

Eagle in a Cage, Lost Horizon, Galileo, 11 Harrowhouse, Gold, Murder on the Orient Express, Aces High, Providence, Portrait of the Artist as a Young Man, Joseph Andrews, Murder by Decree, Caligula, The Human Factor, The Elephant Man, The Formula, Sphinx, Lion of the Desert, Arthur (Academy Award, best supporting actor, 1981), Chariots of Fire, Priest of Love, Gandhi, The Wicked Lady, Invitation to the Wedding, Scandalous, The Shooting Party, Plenty, Time After Time, Whistle Blower, Appointment With Death, Bluebeard Bluebeard, Arthur 2 on the Rocks, Getting It Right, Strike It Rich, Prospero's Books, Shining Through, The Power of One, First Knight, Haunted, Shine, The Leopard Son (narrator), Hamlet.
TELEVISION: *Specials/Movies/Mini-Series:* A Day by the Sea, The Browning Version, The Rehearsal, Great Acting, Ages of Man, Mayfly and th Frog, Cherry Orchard, Ivanov, From Chekhov With Love, St. Joan, Good King Charles' Golden Days, Conversation at Night, Hassan, Deliver Us from Evil, Heartbreak House, Brideshead Revisited, The Canterville Ghost, The Hunchback of Notre Dame, Inside the Third Reich, Marco Polo, The Scarlet and the Black, The Master of Ballantrae, Wagner, The Far Pavillions, Camille, Romance on the Orient Express, Funny You Don't Look 200, Oedipus the King, A Man For All Seasons, War and Remembrance, Summer Lease (Emmy Award, 1991), The Best of Friends, Inspector Alleyn: Hand in Glove, Leave All Fair, Ages of Man, John Gielgud: An Actor's Life, Lovejoy: The Lost Colony, Scarlett.

GILBERT, ARTHUR N.
Producer. b. Detroit, MI, Oct. 17, 1920. Lt., U.S.M.C., 1941-45. e. U. of Chicago, 1946. Special Agent, FBI, 1946-53; world sales dir., Gen. Motors, Cadillac Div., 1953-59; investments in mot. pictures and hotel chains, 1959-64; exec. prod., Mondo Hollywood, 1965; exec. prod. Jeannie-Wife Child, 1966; assoc. prod., The Golden Breed, 1967; commissioned rank of Colonel U.S.M.C., 1968; 1970-80, exec. prod. Jaguar Pictures Corp; Columbia, 1981-86; Indi Pic. Corp. Also account exec. and v.p. Pacific Western Tours. v.p., Great Basion Corp. Bev. Hills 1987-9; v.p., Lawrence 3-D TV 1990-present; v.p Cougar Prods. Co. 1990-91. Producer in development at Jonte Prods. of Paris/London, 1992-94.
PICTURES: The Glory Stompers, Fire Grass, Cycle Savages, Bigfoot, Incredible Transplant, Balance of Evil.

GILBERT, BRUCE
Producer. b. Los Angeles, CA, March 28, 1947. e. U. of California. Pursued film interests at Berkeley's Pacific Film Archive; in summer involved in production in film dept. of San Francisco State U. Founded progressive pre-school in Bay Area. Became story editor in feature film division of Cine-Artists; involved in several projects, including Aloha, Bobby and Rose. Formally partnered with Jane Fonda in IPC Films, Inc., then pres., American Filmworks.
PICTURES: Coming Home (assoc. prod.), The China Syndrome (exec. prod.). *Producer:* Nine to Five, On Golden Pond, Rollover, The Morning After, Man Trouble, Jack the Bear.
TELEVISION: *Series:* Nine to Five (exec. prod.). *Movies:* The Dollmaker (exec. prod.), By Dawn's Early Light (writer, exec. prod.).

GILBERT, LEWIS
Producer, Writer, Director, Former Actor. b. London, England, Mar. 6, 1920. In RAF, W.W.II. Screen debut, 1932; asst. dir. (1930-39) with London Films, Assoc. British, Mayflower, RKO-Radio; from 1939-44 attached U.S. Air Corps Film Unit (asst. dir., Target for Today). In 1944 joined G.B.I. as writer and dir. In 1948, Gainsborough Pictures as writer, dir., 1949; Argyle Prod. 1950; under contract Nettlefold Films, Ltd. as dir.
PICTURES: *Actor:* Under One Roof, I Want to Get Married, Haunting Melody. Director: The Little Ballerina, Marry Me (s.p. only), Once a Sinner, Scarlet Thread, There Is Another Sun, Time Gentlemen Please, Emergency Call, Cosh Boy, Johnny on the Run, Albert R.N., The Good Die Young, The Sea Shall Not Have Them, Reach for the Sky, Cast a Dark Shadow, The Admirable Crichton, Carve Her Name with Pride, A Cry from the Street, Ferry to Hong Kong, Sink the Bismarck, Light Up the Sky, The Greengage Summer, H.M.S. Defiant, The Patriots, Spare the Rod, The Seventh Dawn, Alfie, You Only Live Twice, The Adventurers, Friends (also prod., story), Paul & Michelle (also prod., story), Operation Daybreak, Seven Nights in Japan, The Spy Who Loved Me, Moonraker, Educating Rita (also prod.), Not Quite Paradise, Shirley Valentine (also prod.), Stepping Out (also co-prod.), Haunted (also s.p.).

GILBERT, MELISSA
Actress. b. Los Angeles, CA, May 8, 1964. m. actor Bruce Boxleitner. Made debut at age of 3 in TV commercial. Comes from show business family: father, late comedian Paul Gilbert; mother, former dancer-actress Barbara Crane. Grandfather,

Harry Crane created The Honeymooners. NY Off-B'way debut A Shayna Madel (1987; Outer Critics Circle & Theatre World Awards).
PICTURES: Sylvester (debut, 1985), Ice House.
TELEVISION: *Series*: Little House on the Prairie, Stand By Your Man, Sweet Justice. *Guest*: Gunsmoke, Emergency, Tenafly, The Hanna-Barbera Happy Hour, Love Boat. *Movies*: Christmas Miracle in Caulfield U.S.A., The Miracle Worker, Splendor in the Grass, Choices of the Heart, Choices, Penalty Phase, Family Secrets, Killer Instincts, Without Her Consent, Forbidden Nights, Blood Vows: The Story of a Mafia Wife, Joshua's Heart, Donor, The Lookalike, With a Vengeance, Family of Strangers, With Hostile Intent, Shattered Trust: The Shari Karney Story, House of Secrets, Dying to Remember, Babymaker: The Dr. Cecil Jacobson Story, Against Her Will: The Carrie Buck Story, Cries From the Heart, A Touch of Truth, Danielle Steel's Zoya.

GILER, DAVID
Producer, Writer, Director. b. New York, NY. Son of Bernie Giler, screen and TV writer. Began writing in teens; first work an episode for ABC series, The Gallant Men. Feature film career began as writer on Myra Breckenridge (1970).
PICTURES: *Writer*: The Parallax View, Fun with Dick and Jane, The Blackbird (also dir.), Southern Comfort (also prod.). *Prod.*: Alien, Rustlers' Rhapsody, Let It Ride, Alien³.
TELEVISION: *Writer*: The Kraft Theatre, Burke's Law, The Man from U.N.C.L.E., The Girl from U.N.C.L.E., Tales From the Crypt (exec. prod.).

GILLIAM, TERRY
Writer, Director, Actor, Animator. b. Minneapolis, MN, Nov. 22, 1940. e. Occidental Coll. Freelance writer and illustrator for various magazines and ad agencies before moving to London. Animator for BBC series Do Not Adjust Your Set, We Have Ways of Making You Laugh. Member, Monty Python's Flying Circus (1969-76). Books incl. numerous Monty Python publications. Honorary degrees: DFA Occidental Col. 1987, DFA Royal Col. of Art 1989.
PICTURES: And Now for Something Completely Different (animator, co-s.p., actor), Monty Python and the Holy Grail (co-dir., co-s.p., actor, animator), Jabberwocky (dir., co-s.p.), Life of Brian (actor, co-s.p., animator), The Do It Yourself Animation Film, Time Bandits (prod., dir., co-s.p.), Monty Python Live at the Hollywood Bowl (actor, co-s.p., animator, designer), The Miracle of Flight (animator, s.p.), Monty Python's The Meaning of Life (co-s.p., actor, animator), Spies Like Us (actor), Brazil (co-s.p., dir.), The Adventures of Baron Munchausen (dir., co-s.p.), The Fisher King (dir.), Twelve Monkeys (dir.).
TELEVISION: *Series*: Monty Python's Flying Circus (also animator, dir.), Do Not Adjust Your Set, We Have Ways of Making You Laugh, The Mart Feldman Comedy Machine, The Last Machine (1995).

GILMORE, WILLIAM S.
Producer. b. Los Angeles, CA, March 10, 1934. e. U. of California at Berkeley. Started career in film editing before becoming asst. dir. and prod. mgr. at Universal Studios, where worked on 20 feature films. Headed prod. for Mirisch Co. in Europe; then to Zanuck/Brown Co. as exec. in chg. prod. Sr. v.p./prod. of Filmways Pictures, supervising literary development, prod. and post-prod.
PICTURES: Jaws (prod. exec.), The Last Remake of Beau Geste, Defiance, Deadly Blessing, Tough Enough, Against All Odds, White Nights, Little Shop of Horrors, The Man in the Moon, The Player, A Few Good Men, Watch It, The Sandlot, Curse of the Starving Class.
TELEVISION: Just You and Me, One in a Million--The Ron Leflore Story, The Legend of Walks Far Woman, S.O.S. Titanic, Another Woman's Child, Women and Men, Women and Men 2.

GILROY, FRANK D.
Writer, Director. b. New York, NY, Oct. 13, 1925. e. Dartmouth; postgrad. Yale School of Drama. TV writer: Playhouse 90, US Steel Hour, Omnibus, Kraft Theatre, Lux Video Theater, Studio One. B'way playwright.
AUTHOR: *Plays*: Who'll Save the Plowboy?, The Subject Was Roses (Pulitzer Prize & Tony Award, 1965), The Only Game in Town, Present Tense, The Housekeeper, Last Licks, Any Given Day. *Novels*: Private, Little Ego (with Ruth Gilroy), From Noon to 3. *Book*: I Wake Up Screening!: Everything You Need to Know About Making Independent Films Including a Thousand Reasons Not To (1993).
PICTURES: *Writer*: The Fastest Gun Alive, The Gallant Hours, The Subject Was Roses, The Only Game in Town. *Dir.-Writer*: Desperate Characters (also prod.), From Noon Till Three, Once in Paris, The Gig, The Luckiest Man in the World.
TELEVISION: *Writer-Dir.*: Nero Wolfe, Turning Point of Jim Malloy.

GILULA, STEPHEN
Executive. b. Herrin, IL, Aug. 20, 1950. e. Stanford U. UA Theatre Circuit, film booker for San Francisco area, 1973; Century Cinema Circuit, film buyer, LA, 1974. Co-founder,

Landmark Theatre Corp., 1974; serving as pres., 1982-present. Landmark merged with Samuel Goldwyn Co. in 1991. Chmn. NATO of California/Nevada, 1991-present; also on bd. of dirs. of NATO, 1992-present.

GIMBEL, ROGER
Producer, Executive. b. March 11, 1925. e. Yale. Began tv prod. career as creative chief of RCA Victor TV, then became assoc. prod. of the Tonight Show for NBC; named head of prog. dev. of NBC daytime programming; then prod. of the 90-minute NBC Tonight Specials, including The Jack Paar Show and the Ernie Kovacs Show. Became prod. and co-packager of the Glen Campbell Goodtime Hour for CBS, 1969; v.p. in chg. of prod. for Tomorrow Entertainment, 1971. Formed his own prod. co., Roger Gimbel's Tomorrow Enterprises, Inc., 1975; prod. Minstrel Man. Became U.S. pres. of EMI-TV, 1976. Received special personal Emmy as exec. prod. of War of the Children, 1975. Produced 33 movies for TV under the EMI banner and won 18 Emmys. In 1984, EMI-TV became The Peregrine Producers Group, Inc., of which he was pres. & COO. 1987, spun off Roger Gimbel Prods. as an independent film co; 1988-89, pres./exec. prod., Carolco/Gimbel Productions, Inc. 1989-96, pres. & exec. prod. of Roger Gimbel Prods Inc. in association with Multimedia Motion Pictures Inc.
TELEVISION: *Movies/Specials*: The Autobiography of Miss Jane Pittman, Born Innocent, Birds of Prey, Brand New Life, Gargoyles, Glass House, In This House of Brede, I Heard the Owl Call My Name, I Love You Goodbye, Larry, Miles to Go Before I Sleep, Queen of the Stardust Ballroom, Tell Me Where It Hurts, The Man Who Could Talk to Kids, Things in Their Season, A War of Children (Emmy Award), The Amazing Howard Hughes, Deadman's Curve, Steel Cowboy, Betrayal, The Cracker Factory, Survival of Diana, Can You Hear the Laughter?, S.O.S. Titanic, Walks-Far Woman, Sophia Loren: Her Own Sotory, Manions of America, A Question of Honor, The Killing of Randy Webster, Broken Promise, A Piano for Mrs. Cimino, Deadly Encounter, Aurora, Rockabye, Blackout, Apology, Montana, Shattered Dreams, Chernobyl: The Final Warning, Desperate Rescue: The Cathy Mahone Story, Murder Between Friends, etc.

GINNA, ROBERT EMMETT, JR.
Producer, Writer. b. New York, NY, Dec. 3, 1925. e. U. of Rochester, Harvard U., M.A. In U.S. Navy, WWII. Journalist for Life, Scientific American, Horizon, 1950-55; 1958-61, contributor to many magazines. Staff writer, producer, director NBC-TV, 1955-58; v.p., Sextant, Inc.; dir., Sextant Films Ltd., 1961-64. Founded Windward Productions, Inc., Windward Film Productions, Ltd., 1965. Active in publishing 1974-82; sr. ed. People; ed. in chief, Little Brown; asst. mgr., Life. Resumed pres., Windward Prods, Inc., 1982; publishing consultant.
PICTURES: Young Cassidy (co-prod.), The Last Challenge (co-s.p.), Before Winter Comes (prod.), Brotherly Love (prod.).

GINNANE, ANTHONY I.
Executive, Producer. e. Melbourne U (law), 1976. 1977 formed joint venture with financier William Fayman for Australian film production and distribution. 1981 established company Film and General Holdings Inc. for locating film projects/financing.
PICTURES: *Producer or Exec. Prod*: Sympathy in Summer (debut, 1970; also dir.), Fantasm, Patrick, Snapshot, Thirst, Harlequin, Race for the Yankee Zephyr, Strange Behavior, Turkey Shoot, Prisoners, Second Tim Lucky, Mesmerized, Dark Age, Slate Wyn & Me, Initiation, High Tide, The Lighthorsemen, Time Guardian, Incident at Raven's Gate, The Everlasting Secret Family, The Dreaming, Grievous Bodily Harm, Boundaries of the Heart, Killer Instinct, Savage Justice, Outback, A Case of Honor, Siege of Firebase Gloria, Driving Force, Demonstone, Fatal Sky, No Contest, Screamers, Bonjour Timothy.

GINSBERG, SIDNEY
Executive. b. New York, NY, Oct. 26, 1920. e. City Coll. of New York, 1938. Entered m.p. ind., as asst. mgr., Loew's Theatres; joined Trans-Lux 1943, as theatre mgr.; film booker; helped form Trans-Lux Distributing Corp., 1956; asst. to pres., Trans-Lux Dist. Corp.; asst. vice-pres., Trans-Lux Picture, Distributing and TV Corp., 1961, V.P. Trans-Lux Dist. Corp., 1967, V.P. in charge of worldwide sales, 1969. Haven International Pictures, Inc., Haven Int'l 1970; IFIDA gov., 1970, v.p. sales, Scotia International Films, Inc., 1971; exec. v.p., Scotia American Prods; 1977, pres., Rob-Rich Films Inc.; 1979, exec. v.p., A Major Studio, Inc.; 1980, exec. v.p., The Health and Entertainment Corp. of America; 1982, sr. acct. rep., 3M-Photogard; 1984, pres., Rob-Rich Films.

GINSBURG, LEWIS S.
Distributor, Importer, Prod. b. New York, NY, May 16, 1914. e. City Coll. of New York, 1931-32. Columbia U., 1932-33. Ent. film industry, tabulating dept., United Artists, 1933; sls. contract dept. 1934; asst. to eastern district mgr., 1938; slsmn.,

New Haven exch., 1939. Army, 1943. Ret. to U.S., then formed first buying & booking service in Connecticut, 1945-55; in chg., New England Screen Guild Exchanges, 1955; TV film distr., 1955; Formed & org. International Film Assoc., Vid-EX Film Distr. Corp., 1961. Prod., TV half-hour series; vice-pres. in chg., dist., Desilu Film Dist. C., 1962; organized Carl Releasing Co., 1963; Walter Reade-Sterling Inc., 1964-65; formed L.G. Films Corp.; contract and playdate mgr., 20th Fox, 1965-68. Cinerama Releasing Corp. Adm. Ass't to sales mgr., 1968-69; 20th Cent.-Fox. Nat'l sales coordinator, 1969-present. 1970, 20th Century-Fox, Asst. to the Sales Mgr. 1971, Transnational Pictures Corp., v.p. in chg. of dist., pres., Stellar IV Film Corp., 1972.

GIRARDOT, ANNIE
Actress. b. Paris, France, Oct. 25, 1931. Studied nursing. Studied acting at the Paris Conservatory, made her acting debut with the Comedie Franccaise. Has acted on the French stage and in reviews in the Latin Quarter.
PICTURES: Trezie a Table (debut, 1955), Speaking of Murder, Inspector Maigret, Love and the Frenchwoman, Rocco and His Brothers, Le Rendezvous, Crime Does Not Pay, Vice and Virtue, The Organizer, La Bonne Soupe (Careless Love), Male Companion, The Dirty Game, The Witches, Live for Life, Les Galoises Bleues, Dillinger Is Dead, The Seed of Man, Trois Chambres a Manhattan (Venice Film Fest. Award), The Story of a Woman, Love Is a Funny Thing, Shock!, Where THere's Smoke, Juliette et Juliette, The Slap, It Is Raining in Santiago, No Time for Breakfast (Cesar Award), Dear Inspector, The Skirt Chaser, Traffic Jam, Jupiter's Thigh, Five Days in June, La Vie Continue, Prisonniers, Comedie D'Amour, Girls With Guns, Les Miserables.

GISH, ANNABETH
Actress. b. Albuquerque, NM, Mar. 13, 1971. e. Duke U ('93). Started acting at age 8; appeared in several TV commercials in Iowa.
PICTURES: Desert Bloom, Hiding Out, Mystic Pizza, Shag, Coupe de Ville, Wyatt Earp, The Red Coat, Nixon, The Last Supper, Beautiful Girls.
TELEVISION: Series: Courthouse. Movies: Hero in the Family, When He's Not a Stranger, The Last to Go, Lady Against the Odds, Silent Cries. Mini-Series: Scarlett.

GIVENS, ROBIN
Actress. b. New York, NY, Nov. 27, 1964. e. Sarah Lawrence Col., Harvard Univ. Graduate Sch. of Arts & Sciences. While at college became model, made appearances on daytime dramas The Guiding Light and Loving.
PICTURES: A Rage in Harlem (debut, 1991), Boomerang, Foreign Student, Blankman.
TELEVISION: Series: Head of the Class, Angel Street, Courthouse, Sparks, Sparls and Sparks. Movies: Beverly Hills Madam, The Women of Brewster Place, The Penthouse, Dangerous Intentions.

GLASER, PAUL MICHAEL
Actor, Director. b. Cambridge, MA, March 25, 1943. e. Tulane U., Boston U., M.A. Did five seasons in summer stock before starting career in New York, making stage debut in Rockabye Hamlet in 1968. Appeared in numerous off-B'way plays and got early TV training as regular in daytime series, Love of Life and Love Is a Many Splendored Thing.
PICTURES: Actor: Fiddler on the Roof, Butterflies Are Free, Phobia. Director: Band of the Hand, The Running Man, The Cutting Edge, The Air Up There, Kazaam (also prod., story).
TELEVISION: Series: Starsky and Hutch. Guest: Kojak, Toma, The Streets of San Francisco, The Rockford Files, The Sixth Sense, The Waltons. Movies: Trapped Beneath the Sea, The Great Houdinis, Wail Till You Mother Gets Home!, Princess Daisy, Jealousy, Attack on Fear, Single Bars Single Women, Amazons (dir. only).

GLAZER, WILLIAM
Executive. b. Cambridge, MA. e. State U. of New York, Entered m.p. ind. with Ralph Snider Theatres 1967-69; General Cinema Corp. 1969-71; Loews Theatres 1971-73; Joined Sack Theatres 1973 as Dist. mgr.; 1974 Exec. Asst. to Pres.; 1976 Gen. Mgr.; 1980 V.P. Gen. Mgr.; 1982 Exec. V.P. Member of SMPTE; NATO (Bd of Dir); Theatre Owners of New England Bd of Dir, also pres.; 1982-1985.

GLEASON, LARRY
Executive. b. Boston, MA, Apr. 30, 1938. e. Boston Coll., M.A., 1960. Held various positions, western div., mgr., General Cinema Corp.; 1963-73; gen. mgr., Gulf States Theatres, New Orleans, 1973-74; pres., Mann Theatres, 1974-85; joined DeLaurentiis Entertainment Group as pres., mktg./dist., 1985. Named sr. v.p., Paramount Pictures Corp, theatrical exhibition group, 1989. Named pres. Paramount Pictures Corp. theatrical exhib. group, 1991. Joined MGM/UA as pres. of Worlwide Distrib., 1994. Foundation of Motion Picture Pioneers v.p. Member, Variety Club, Will Rogers Foundation.

GLEN, JOHN
Director. b. Sunbury on Thames, Eng., May 15, 1932. Entered industry in 1947. Second unit dir.: On Her Majesty's Secret Service, The Spy Who Loved Me, Wild Geese, Moonraker (also editor). Editor: The Sea Wolves.
PICTURES: For Your Eyes Only (dir. debut, 1981), Octopussy, A View to a Kill, The Living Daylights, Licence to Kill, Aces: Iron Eagle III, Christopher Columbus: The Discovery.
TELEVISION: Series: Space Precinct (7 episodes).

GLENN, CHARLES OWEN
Executive. b. Binghamton, NY, March 27, 1938. e. Syracuse U., B.A., U. of PA. Capt., U.S. Army, 1961-63. Asst. to dir. of adv., 20th Cent. Fox, 1966-67; asst. adv. mgr., Paramount, 1967-68; acct. spvsr. & exec., MGM record & m.p. div., 1968-69; nat'l adv. mgr., Paramount, 1969-70; nat'l. dir. of adv., Paramount, 1970-71; v.p. adv.-pub.-prom., 1971-73; v.p. marketing, 1974; v.p. prod. mktg., 1975; joined American Intl. Pictures as v.p. in chg. of adv./creative affairs, 1979. 1980, when Filmways took over AIP and it was named their v.p. in chg. worldwide adv./pub./promo.; joined MCA/Universal in 1982 as exec. v.p., adv.-promo.; 1984, appt. Orion Pictures adv.-pub.-promo. exec. v.p.; 1987, appt. Orion mktg. exec. v.p. 1989 recipient Outstanding Performance Award Leukemia Society of Amer. for completing NYC Marathon. 1993, pres. mktg., Bregman/Baer Prods. Featured actor in 1993 film Philadelphia. Member: Exec. comm. public relations branch, Academy of M.P. Arts & Sciences. Holder of NATO mktg. exec. of year (1983) award, Clio Award for U.S. adv. of Platoon; Variety Club, Motion Picture Pioneers, Screen Actors Guild.

GLENN, SCOTT
Actor. b. Pittsburgh, PA, Jan. 26, 1942. e. William & Mary Coll. Worked as U.S. Marine, newspaper reporter before going to New York to study drama at Actors Studio in 1968.
THEATER: Off-B'way: Zoo Story, Fortune in Men's Eyes, Long Day's Jack Street, Journey into Night. B'way: The Impossible Years, Burn This, Dark Picture.
PICTURES: The Baby Maker (debut, 1970), Angels Hard as They Come, Hex, Nashville, Fighting Mad, More American Graffiti, Apocalypse Now, Urban Cowboy, Cattle Annie and Little Britches, Personal Best, The Challenge, The Right Stuff, The Keep, The River, Wild Geese II, Silverado, Verne Miller, Man on Fire, Off Limits, Miss Firecracker, The Hunt for Red October, The Silence of the Lambs, My Heroes Have Always Been Cowboys, Backdraft, The Player, Night of the Running Man, Tall Tale, Reckless, Edie and Pen, Courage Under Fire, Carla's Song, Courage Under Fire, Edue & Pen.
TELEVISION: Movies: Gargoyles, As Summers Die, Intrigue, The Outside Woman, Women & Men 2, Shadowhunter, Slaughter of the Innocents, Past Tense.

GLENNON, JAMES M.
Cinematographer. b. Burbank, CA, Aug. 29, 1942. e. UCLA. m. actress Charmaine Glennon. Focus Awards judge 1985-; bd. or dirs., UCLA Theatre Arts Alumni Assoc. 1985-. ASC - member of American Society of Cinematographers, AMPAS.
PICTURES: Return of the Jedi, El Norte, The Wild Life, Smooth Talk, Flight of the Navigator, Time of Destiny, A Show of Force, December, The Gift.
TELEVISION: Lemon Sky (American Playhouse), Laurel Ave, DEA (pilot), Bakersfield (pilot), Judicial Consent.

GLESS, SHARON
Actress. b. Los Angeles, CA, May 31, 1943. m. producer Barney Rosenzweig. London stage: Misery.
PICTURES: Airport 1975, The Star Chamber.
TELEVISION: Series: Marcus Welby M.D., Faraday and Co., Switch, Turnabout, House Calls, Cagney and Lacey (2 Emmy Awards, Golden Globe Award), The Trials of Rosie O'Neill (Golden Globe Award). Mini-Series: Centennial, The Immigrants, The Last Convertible. Movies: The Longest Night, All My Darling Daughters, My Darling Daughters' Anniversary, Richie Brockelman: Missing 24 Hours, The Flying Misfits, The Islander, Crash, Whisper in the Gloom (Disney), Hardhat and Legs, Moviola: The Scarlett O'Hara War, Revenge of the Stepford Wives, The Miracle of Kathy Miller, Hobson's Choice, The Sky's No Limit, Letting Go, The Outside Woman, Honor Thy Mother, Separated by Murder, Cagney & Lacey: The Return, Cagney & Lacey: Together Again.

GLICK, PHYLLIS
Executive. b. New York, NY. e. Queens Coll. of C.U.N.Y. Began career with Otto-Windsor Associates, as casting director; left to be independent. 1979, joined ABC-TV as mgr. of comedy series development; promoted 1980 to director, involved with all comedy series developed for network. 1985, joined Paramount Pictures as exec. dir., production, for M.P. Group; 1989, co-exec. prod., Living Dolls.

GLOBUS, YORAM
Producer. b. Israel, Came to U.S. 1979. Has co-produced many films with cousin and former partner Menahem Golan.

Sr. exec. v.p., Cannon Group; Pres. and CEO Cannon Entertainment and Cannon Films; 1989 named chmn. and C.E.O Cannon Entertainment and officer of Cannon Group Inc.; then co-pres. Pathe Communications Corp. and chmn. and C.E.O. Pathe Intl. Left MGM/Pathe in 1991.
PICTURES: All as producer or exec. prod. with Menahem Golan: Sallah; Trunk to Cairo; My Margo; What's Good for the Goose; Escape to the Sun; I Love You, Rosa; The House on Chelouch Street; The Four Deuces; Kazablan; Diamonds; God's Gun; Kid Vengeance, Operation Thunderbolt, The Uranium Conspiracy, Savage Weekend, The Magician of Lublin, The Apple, The Happy Hooker Goes to Hollywood, Dr. Heckyl and Mr. Hype, The Godsend, New Year's Evil, Schizoid, Seed of Innocence, Body and Soul, Death Wish II, Enter the Ninja, Hospital Massacre, The Last American Virgin, Championship Season, Treasure of Four Crowns, 10 to Midnight, Nana, I'm Almost Not Crazy..., John Cassavetes: The Man and His Work, The House of Long Shadows, Revenge of the Ninja, Hercules, The Wicked Lady, Sahara, The Ambassador, Bolero, Exterminator 2, The Naked Face, Missing in Action, Hot Resort, Love Streams, Breakin', Grace Quigley, Making the Grade, Ninja III-The Domination, Breakin' 2: Electric Boogaloo, Lifeforce, Over the Brooklyn Bridge, The Delta Force, The Assisi Underground, Hot Chili, The Berlin Affair, Missing in Action 2-The Beginning, Rappin', Thunder Alley, American Ninja, Mata Hari, Death Wish 3, King Solomon's Mines, Runaway Train, Fool for Love, Invasion U.S.A., Maria's Lovers, Murphy's Law, The Naked Cage, P.O.W.: The Escape, The Texas Chainsaw Massacre, Part 2, Invaders from Mars, 52 Pick-Up, Link, Firewalker, Dumb Dicks, The Nutcracker: The Motion Picture, Avenging Force, Hashigaon Hagadol, Journey to the Center of the Earth, Prom Queen, Salome, Otello, Cobra, America 3000, American Ninja 2: The Confrontation, Allan Quartermain and the Lost City of Gold, Assassination, Beauty and the Beast, Down Twisted, Duet for One, The Emperor's New Clothes, The Hanoi Hilton, The Barbarians, Dutch Treat, Masters of the Universe, Number One with a Bullet, Rumpelstiltskin, Street Smart, UnderCover, The Assault, Hansel and Gretel, Going Bananas, Snow White, Sleeping Beauty, Tough Guys Don't Dance, Shy People, Dancers, Red Riding Hood, King Lear, Braddock: Missing in Action III, Too Much, Die Papierene Brucke, Field of Honor, Barfly (exec. prod.), Surrender (exec. prod.), Death Wish 4: The Crackdown (exec. prod.), Gor (exec. prod.), Business as Usual (exec. prod.), Over the Top, Superman IV: The Quest for Peace. Prod.: Delta Force, Operation Crackdown, Manifesto, Stranglehold, Delta Force II, Cyborg, Step By Step. Exec. prod.: The Kitchen Toto, Doin' Time on Planet Earth, Kickboxer, Kinjite, A Man Called Sarge, The Rose Garden, The Secret of the Ice Cave.

GLOVER, CRISPIN
Actor. b. New York, NY, 1964. e. Mirman School. Trained for stage with Dan Mason and Peggy Feury. Stage debut, as Friedrich Von Trapp, The Sound of Music, Los Angeles, 1977. Wrote books, Rat Catching (1987), Oak Mot (1990), Concrete Inspection (1992), What It Is and How It Is Done (1995). Recorded album The Big Problem Does Not Equal the Solution- The Solution Equals Let it Be.
PICTURES: My Tutor, Racing with the Moon, Friday the 13th-The Final Chapter, Teachers, Back to the Future, At Close Range, River's Edge, Twister, Where the Heart Is, Wild at Heart, The Doors, Little Noises, Rubin and Ed, Thirty Door Key, What's Eating Gilbert Grape, Chasers, Even Cowgirls Get the Blues, Crime and Punishment, Dead Man, What Is It? (dir. and wrote), The People vs. Larry Flynt.
TELEVISION: Movie: High School U.S.A. Special: Hotel Room (Blackout).

GLOVER, DANNY
Actor. b. San Francisco, CA, July 22, 1947. e. San Francisco State U. Trained at Black Actors Workshop of American Conservatory Theatre. Appeared in many stage productions (Island, Macbeth, Sizwe Banzi Is Dead, etc.). On N.Y. stage in Suicide in B Flat, The Blood Knot, Master Harold... and the Boys (Theatre World Award).
PICTURES: Escape from Alcatraz (debut, 1979), Chu Chu and the Philly Flash, Out (Deadly Drifter), Iceman, Places in the Heart, Witness, Silverado, The Color Purple, Lethal Weapon, Bat-21, Lethal Weapon 2 To Sleep with Anger (also co-exec. prod.), Predator 2, Flight of the Intruder, A Rage in Harlem, Pure Luck, Grand Canyon, Lethal Weapon 3, Bopha!, The Saint of Fort Washington, Maverick (cameo), Angels in the Outfield, Operation Dumbo Drop.
TELEVISION: Mini-Series: Chiefs, Lonesome Dove, Queen. Movies: Face of Rage, Mandela, Dead Man Out. Series: Storybook Classics (host), Civil War Journal (host). Specials: And the Children Shall Lead, How the Leopard Got Its Spots (narrator), A Place at the Table, A Raisin in the Sun, Override (dir. only), Shelley Duvall's Tall Tales and Legends: John Henry. Guest: Lou Grant, Palmerstown U.S.A., Gimme a Break, Hill Street Blues, Many Mansions.

GLOVER, JOHN
Actor. b. Kingston, NY, Aug. 7, 1944. e. Towson State Coll., Baltimore.
THEATER: On regional theatre circuit; Off-B'way in A Scent of Flowers, Subject to Fits, The House of Blue Leaves, The Selling of the President, Love! Valour! Compassion! (also B'way; Tony Award, 1995). With APA Phoenix Co. in Great God Brown (Drama Desk Award), The Visit, Don Juan, Chermin de Fer, Holiday. Other NY stage: The Importance of Being Earnest, Hamlet, Frankenstein, Whodunnit, Digby. L.A.: The Traveler (L.A. Drama Critics Award), Lips Together Teeth Apart.
PICTURES: Shamus, Annie Hall, Julia, Somebody Killed Her Husband, Last Embrace, Success, Melvin and Howard, The Mountain Men, The Incredible Shrinking Woman, A Little Sex, The Evil That Men Do, A Flash of Green, 52 Pick-Up, White Nights, Something Special, Masquerade, A Killing Affair, Rocket Gibraltar, The Chocolate War, Scrooged, Meet the Hollowheads, Gremlins 2: The New Batch, Robocop 2, Ed and His Dead Mother, Night of the Running Man, In the Mouth of Madness, Schemes, Automatics, Batman and Robin.
TELEVISION: Movies: A Rage of Angels, The Face of Rage, Ernie Kovacs-Between the Laughter, An Early Frost (Emmy nom.), Apology, Moving Target, Hot Paint, Nutcracker: Money Madness and Murder (Emmy nom.), David, The Traveling Man (ACE nom.), Twist of Fate, Breaking Point, El Diablo, What Ever Happened to Baby Jane?, Dead on the Money, Drug Wars: The Cocaine Cartel, Grass Roots, Majority Rule, Assault at West Point. Specials: An Enemy of the People, Paul Reiser: Out on a Whim, Crime and Punishment (Emmy nom.). Mini-Series: Kennedy, George Washington. Series: South Beach. Guest: L.A. Law (Emmy nom.), Frasier (Emmy nom.)

GLYNN, CARLIN
Actress. b. Cleveland, OH, Feb. 19, 1940. m. actor-writer-dir. Peter Masterson. Daughter is actress Mary Stuart Masterson. e. Sophie Newcomb College, 1957-58. Studied acting with Stella Adler, Wynn Handman and Lee Strasberg in NY. Debut, Gigi, Alley Theatre, Houston, TX 1959. NY stage debut Waltz of The Toreadors, 1960. On stage in The Best Little Whorehouse in Texas (Tony, Eleanora Duse & Olivier Awards), Winterplay, Alterations, Pal Joey (Chicago; Jos. Jefferson Award), The Cover of Life, The Young Man From Atlanta (winner, Pulitzer Prize for Drama, 1995). Adjunct professor at Columbia U film sch. Resource advisor at the Sundance Inst.
PICTURES: Three Days of the Condor, Continental Divide, Sixteen Candles, The Trip to Bountiful, Gardens of Stone, Blood Red, Night Game, Convicts.
TELEVISION: Series: Mr. President. Mini-Series: A Woman Named Jackie.

GODARD, JEAN-LUC
Writer, Director. b. Paris, France, Dec. 3, 1930. e. Lycee Buffon, Paris. Journalist, film critic Cahiers du Cinema. Acted in and financed experimental film Quadrille by Jacques Rivette, 1951. 1954: dir. first short, Operation Beton, followed by Une Femme Coquette. 1956, was film editor. 1957: worked in publicity dept. 20th Century Fox.
PICTURES: Director/Writer: Breathless (A Bout de Souffle; feature debut, 1960), Le Petit Soldat, A Woman Is a Woman, My Life to Live, Les Carabiniers, Contempt, Band of Outsiders, The Married Woman, Alphaville, Pierrot le Fou, Masculine-Feminine, Made in USA, Two or Three Things I Know About Her, La Chinoise, Weekend, Sympathy for the Devil, Le Gai Savoir, Tout a Bien (co-dir.), Numero Deux, Every Man For Himself, First Name Carmen, Hail Mary, Aria (Armide segment), King Lear, Keep Up Your Right (also edit, actor), Nouvelle Vogue (New Wave), Helas Pour Moi (Oh Woe is Me). Germany Year, J.L.G. by J.L.G., The Kids Play Russian.

GOLAN, MENAHEM
Producer, Director, Writer. b. Tiberias, Israel, May 31, 1929. e. NYU. Studied theater dir. at Old Vic Theatre London, m.p. prod. at City Coll, NY. Co-founder and prod. with cousin Yoram Globus, Golan-Globus Prods., Israel, then L.A., 1962. Later Noah Films, Israel, 1963, Ameri-Euro Pictures Corp, before buying controlling share in Cannon Films, 1979. Sr. exec. v.p., Cannon Group; chmn. of bd., Cannon Entertainment and Cannon Films. 1988, dir. and sr. exec. v.p Cannon Group, chmn. and head of creative affairs, Cannon Entertainment when it became div. of Giancarlo Parretti's Pathe Communications Corp. Resigned March, 1989 to form 21st Century Film Corp as chmn. and CEO.
PICTURES: Director/co-writer: Kasablan, Diamonds, Entebbe (Operation Thunderbolt), Teyve and His Seven Daughters, What's Good for the Goose? Lepke, The Magician of Lublin, The Godsend, Happy Hooker Goes to Hollywood, Enter the Ninja. Producer-Writer-Director: Mack the Knife, Hanna's War. Producer-Director: The Uranium Conspiracy, Delta Force, Over the Brooklyn Bridge, Over the Top. Producer/Exec. prod.: Sallah, Runaway Train, Sallah, Fool For Love, Maria's Lovers, Cobra, Evil Angels, I Love You Rosa, Body and Soul, also:

Deathwish II, The Last American Virgin, That Championship Season, House of Long Shadows, Revenge of the Ninja, Hercules, The Movie Tales (12 children's fairy tales films), The Wicked Lady, Cobra, Barfly (exec. prod.), Breakin', Missing in Action, Dancers (prod.), Surrender (exec. prod.), Death Wish 4: The Crackdown (exec. prod.), King Lear (prod.), Too Much (prod.), Powaqquatsi (exec. prod.), Mercenary Fighters (prod.), Doin' Time on Planet Earth (prod.), Manifesto (prod.), Kinjite (exec. prod.), Messenger of Death (exec. prod.), Alien From L.A. (prod.), Hero and the Terror (prod.), Haunted Summer (exec. prod.), A Cry in the Dark (exec. prod.), Delta Force-Operation Crackdown (prod.), A Man Called Sarge (exec. prod.), Strangehold: Delta Force II (prod.), Cyborg (prod.), The Rose Garden (exec. prod.), Rope Dancing (exec. prod.), The Phantom of the Opera.

GOLCHAN, FREDERIC
Producer. b. Neuilly sur Seine, France, Nov. 20, 1955. e. UCLA Film School, HEC in Paris, NYU Bus.Sch. Journalist/photographer for various European magazines. Worked for American Express, 1979-80. Started indept. investment banking firm, 1980-84. Started own production co., 1985. Directed Victory of the Deaf.
PICTURES: Flagrant Desire, Quick Change, Intersection, The Associate.
TELEVISION: Freedom Fighter, Home by Midnight, In The Deep Woods.

GOLD, ERNEST
Composer, Conductor. b. Vienna, Austria, July 13, 1921. e. State Acad. for Music and Performing Arts, Austria 1937-38; private study, 1939-49 in U.S. Worked as song writer 1939-42 and taught in private schools, 1942. Composed first score for Columbia Pictures, 1945. Musical dir., Santa Barbara Symphony, 1958-59. Taught at UCLA, 1973 and 1983-90 (adult ed.). Gold record for soundtrack of Exodus, 1968. Received star on Walk of Fame on Hollywood Blvd., 1975. Elected to bd. of govs., AMPAS, 1984.
PICTURES: Smooth as Silk, Wyoming, Witness for the Prosecution, The Pride and the Passion, Too Much Too Soon, On the Beach (Acad. Award nom.), Exodus (Academy Award, 1960), Inherit the Wind, The Last Sunset, Judgment at Nuremberg, Pressure Point, A Child Is Waiting, It's a Mad Mad Mad Mad World (Acad. Award nom.), Ship of Fools, The Secret of Santa Vittoria (Acad. Award nom.), The Wild McCullochs, Cross of Iron, Fun With Dick and Jane, Good Luck Miss Wyckoff, The Runner Stumbles, Tom Horn.
TELEVISION: Small Miracle, Wallenberg: a Hero's Story.

GOLDBERG, FRED
Executive. b. New York, NY, Aug. 26, 1921. e. Pace Col., Sch. of Marketing & Advertising. Expl. Paramount, 1946; asst. expl. mgr. trade contact, syndicate contact, NY newspaper contact promotion mgr., 1946-52; asst. publ. mgr. RKO, 1952; natl. publ. mgr., IFE, 1953; v.p. Norton and Condon, pub., 1953; returned to IFE Sept. 1954 as natl. pub. mgr.; head of NY office, Arthur Jacobs, then Blowitz-Maskel, 1956; exec. asst. to dir. pub., adv. UA Corp., 1958; exec. dir., adv., pub. exploitation, UA Corp., 1961; named v.p., 1962; sr. v.p., 1972; sr. v.p., dir. of mrkt., 1977. Left in 1978 to be consultant with Diener, Hauser & Bates Agency. In 1979 joined Columbia Pics. as sr. v.p. in chg. of adv./pub. Left in 1981 to form new company. Became teacher of M.P. Marketing & Distrib. at Univ. of Miami's Sch. of Communications. Author: Motion Picture Marketing & Distribution.

GOLDBERG, LEONARD
Executive, Producer. b. Brooklyn, NY, Jan. 24, 1934. e. Wharton ch., U. of Pennsylvania. Began career in ABC-TV research dept.; moved to NBC-TV research div.; 1961 joined BBD&Q ad agency in charge of overall bdcst. coordinator. In 1963 rejoined ABC-TV as mgr. of program devel. 1964-66, v.p., Daytime programs. 1966 named VP in chg of network TV programming. Resigned in 1969 to join Screen Gems as VP in chg. of prod. Left for partnership with Aaron Spelling in Spelling/Goldberg Prods.; later produced TV and theatrical films under own banner, Mandy Prods. 1986, named pres., COO, 20th Century Fox. Resigned, 1989. Elected to the board of Spectradyne Inc.
PICTURES: Prod.: All Night Long, WarGames, Space Camp, Sleeping With the Enemy, The Distinguished Gentleman, Aspen Extreme.
TELEVISION: Series: The Rookies, SWAT, Starsky and Hutch, Charlie's Angels, Family, Hart to Hart, T.J. Hooker, Fantasy Island, Paper Dolls, The Cavanaughs, Class of '96. Movies: Brian's Song, Little Ladies of the Night, The Legend of Valentino, The Boy in the Plastic Bubble, Something About Amelia, Alex: The Life of a Child, She Woke Up.

GOLDBERG, WHOOPI
Actress. b. New York, NY, Nov. 13, 1949. r.n. Caryn Johnson. e. Sch. for the Performing Arts. Began performing at age 8 in N.Y. with children's program at Hudson Guild and Helena

Rubenstein Children's Theatre. Moved to San Diego, CA, 1974, and helped found San Diego Rep. Theatre appearing in Mother Courage, Getting Out. Member: Spontaneous Combustion (improv. group). Joined Blake St. Hawkeyes Theatre in Berkeley, partnering with David Schein. Went solo to create The Spook Show, working in San Francisco and later touring U.S. & Europe. 1983 performance caught attention of Mike Nichols which led to B'way show (for which she received a Theatre World Award) based on it and directed by him. Founding member of Comic Relief benefits. Theatrical film debut in The Color Purple (1985; Image Award NAACP, Golden Globe).
THEATER: small roles in B'way prods. of Pippin, Hair, Jesus Christ Superstar. 1988: toured in Living on the Edge of Chaos.
PICTURES: The Color Purple (debut, 1985; Acad. Award nom.), Jumpin' Jack Flash, Burglar, Fatal Beauty, The Telephone, Clara's Heart, Beverly Hills Brats (cameo), Homer and Eddie, Ghost (Academy Award, best supporting actress, 1990), The Long Walk Home, Soapdish, House Party 2 (cameo), The Player, Sister Act, Wisecracks, Sarafina!, The Magic World of Chuck Jones, National Lampoon's Loaded Weapon 1 (cameo), Made in America, Sister Act 2: Back in the Habit, Naked in New York (cameo), The Lion King (voice), The Little Rascals, Corrina Corrina, Star Trek: Generations, Theodore Rex, The Pagemaster (voice), Liberation (narrator), Boys on the Side, Moonlight and Valentino, The Celluloid Closet, Bogus, Eddie, The Associate, Ghosts of Mississippi.
TELEVISION: Series: Star Trek: The Next Generation, Bagdad Cafe, The Whoopi Goldberg Show (synd. talk show). Specials: Whoopi Goldberg Direct From Broadway, Comic Relief, Carol Carl Whoopi and Robin, Scared Straight: 10 Years Later, Funny You Don't Look 200, Comedy Tonight (host), My Past is My Own (Schoolbreak Special), Free to Be... a Family, The Debbie Allen Special, Cool Like That Christmas (voice). Guest: Moonlighting (Emmy nom.), A Different World. Movie: Kiss Shot.

GOLDBLUM, JEFF
Actor. b. Pittsburgh, PA, Oct. 22, 1952. Studied at Sanford Meisner's Neighborhood Playhouse in New York. On B'way in Two Gentleman of Verona, The Moony Shapiro Songbook. Off-B'way: El Grande de Coca Cola, City Sugar, Twelfth Night.
PICTURES: Death Wish (debut, 1974), California Split, Nashville, Next Stop Greenwich Village, St. Ives, Special Delivery, The Sentinel, Annie Hall, Between the Lines, Remember My Name, Thank God It's Friday, Invasion of the Body Snatchers, Threshold, The Big Chill, The Right Stuff, The Adventures of Buckaroo Banzai, Into the Night, Silverado, Transylvania 6-5000, The Fly, Beyond Therapy, Vibes, Earth Girls Are Easy, Twisted Obsession, The Tall Guy, Mr. Frost, The Player, Deep Cover, The Favor the Watch and the Very Big Fish, Fathers and Sons, Jurassic Park, Hideaway, Nine Months, Powder, The Great White Hype, Independence Day, Mad Dog Time.
TELEVISION: Movies: The Legend of Sleepy Hollow, Rehearsal for Murder, Ernie Kovacs: Between the Laughter, The Double Helix (BBC), Framed, Lush Life. Series: Tenspeed and Brownshoe, Future Quest (host). Guest: The Blue Knight, It's Garry Shandling's Show.

GOLDEN, HERBERT L.
b. Philadelphia, PA, Feb. 12, 1914. e. Temple U., 1936, B.S. Reporter, rewrite man. asst. city ed., Philadelphia Record, 1933-38; joined Variety, 1938; on leave of absence, 1942-43, when asst. to John Hay Whitney and Francis Alstock, directors, M.P. Division, Coordinator of Inter-American Affairs (U.S.); in U.S. Navy, 1943-46; then returned to Variety. m.p. ed. Consultant on motion pictures, Good Housekeeping magazine McGraw-Hill Publications, American Yearbook. Ent. Ind. Div. Bankers Trust Co., NY, 1952; named v.p. 1954-56; v.p. & mem. of bd. Associated Artists Corp., 1958; member of board, MPAA, 1959; pres., Lexington Int., Inc. investments, 1962; mem. bd., chmn. exec. com., Perfect Photo Inc., 1962; 1965 sect. & mem. bd. Century Broadcasting Group; chmn. G & G Thea. Corp.; pres. Diversifax Corp., 1966; consult. Pathe Lab, 1967; Mem. bd. Childhood Prod. Inc., Music Makers Group, Inc.; Cinecom Corp. pres., Vere/Swiss Corp., 1977; mem. bd., Coral Reef Publications, Inc., 1977. Returned to Bankers Trust, 1979, to head its Media Group (service to film and TV industries). Retired, 1992.

GOLDEN, JEROME B.
Executive, Attorney. b. New York, NY, Nov. 26, 1917. e. St. Lawrence U., LL.B., 1942. Member legal dept., Paramount Pictures, Inc., 1942-50; United Paramount Theatres, Inc., 1950-53; ABC, Inc., 1953; secy., ABC, 1958-86; v.p., ABC, 1959-86. Consultant.

GOLDEN, PAT
Casting Director, Director. b. Pittsburgh, PA, July 21, 1951. e. U Pittsburgh, Carnegie-Mellon U. Has directed plays for theatre incl. Homeboy at Perry St. Th. in NY. Was in casting dept. of NY Shakespeare Festival Public Th. Served as assoc.

prod. on PBS series The Negro Ensemble Company's 20th Anniversary. Assoc. prod.: Hallelujah (PBS); dir.: House Party 2 documentary, My Secret Place (tv pilot).
PICTURES: Ragtime, Beat Street, Krush Groove, The Killing Fields, Blue Velvet, Platoon (Awarded Casting Society of America Award), Dear America, The Handmaid's Tale, House Party 2 (assoc. prod.), Voyager, Posse.

GOLDENSON, LEONARD H.
Executive. b. Scottsdale, PA, December 7, 1905. e. Harvard Coll., B.A., Harvard Law School, LL.B. Practiced law, NY; counsel in reorg. Paramount theatres in New England, 1933-37; 1937 apptd. asst. to v.p. Paramount in charge theat. operations; became head of theat. operations, 1938; elected pres. Paramount Theat. Service Corp., v.p. Paramount Pictures, 1938; dir. Paramount Pictures, 1942 (also pres. various Paramount theat. subsids) Pres., CEO & dir. United Paramount Theatres, Inc., 1950, and of American Broadcasting-Paramount Theatres, Inc., 1953, result of merger of ABC and United Paramount Theatres, Inc.; chmn. of bd. & CEO of ABC to 1986. Then chmn. of exec. comm. & bd. Capital Cities/ABC, Inc. 1972; mem., International Radio and TV Society, Natl. Acad. of TV Arts & Sciences, Broadcast Pioneers, Motion Picture Pioneers; founder/member of Hollywood Museum; grad. dir. of Advertising Council, Inc.; Trustee Emeritus Museum of TV & Radio; Hon. Chmn. Acad. of TV Arts & Sciences.

GOLDMAN, BO
Writer. b. New York, NY, Sept. 10, 1932. e. Princeton U., B.A., 1953. Wrote lyrics for B'way musical version of Pride and Prejudice entitled First Impressions (1959). Assoc. prod. & script editor for Playhouse 90 1958-60; writer-prod., NET Playhouse 1970-71, Theater in America 1972-74.
PICTURES: One Flew Over the Cuckoo's Nest (co-s.p.; WGA & Academy Awards, 1975), The Rose (co-s.p.), Melvin and Howard (NY Film Critics, WGA & Academy Awards, 1980), Shoot the Moon, Swing Shift (uncredited), Little Nikita (co-s.p.), Dick Tracy (uncredited), Scent of a Woman (Golden Globe Award, Acad. Award nom.), First Knight (co-s.p.), City Hall (co-s.p.).

GOLDMAN, EDMUND
Executive, Producer. b. Shanghai, China, Nov. 12, 1906. e. Shanghai and San Francisco. Entered ind. as asst. mgr., for Universal in Shanghai, 1935-36; named mgr. Columbia Pictures' Philippine office, 1937. 1951 named Far East. supvr. for Columbia, headquartering in Tokyo. 1953-91 indep. m.p. dist., specializing in foreign marketing, representing indep. producers and distributors. Retired, 1991.
PICTURES: Surrender Hell (prod.), The Quick and the Dead (exec. prod.).

GOLDMAN, MICHAEL F.
Executive. b. Manila, Philippines, Sept. 28, 1939. e. UCLA, B.S. in acct., 1962 California C.P.A. certificate issued June, 1972. In 1962 incorporated Manson International, which was sold in 1986. Incorporated Quixote Prods., 1979. Also owner and sole proprietor Taurus Film co. of Hollywood, founded 1964. Co-founder and first chief financial officer of American Film Marketing Association, sponsor of First American Film Market in Los Angeles in 1981; v.p. of AFMA 1982 and 1983, President AFMA 1984 and 1985. Chmn. AFMA, 1992-3. AFMA bd. mbr., 1981-87, 1988-present; Co-founder, Cinema Consultants Group, 1988. Produced feature, Jessi's Girls in 1975. Founded Manson Interactive, 1995. Member A.M.P.A.S. since 1979. Director, Foundation of Motion Picture Pioneers.

GOLDMAN, MITCHELL
Executive. Pres., of Theatrical Distribution, New Line Distribution, Inc.

GOLDMAN, STEVE
Executive. e. Univ. of IL. 1980, joined Paramount as Midwest division mngr., Chicago. Then served in NY as v.p. Eastern regional mngr. 1983, to Hollywood office. 1985, exec. v.p., sls. & mktg. 1989, exec. v.p. 1992, pres. Paramount Domestic Television. 1995, named exec. v.p. of Paramount Television Group.

GOLDMAN, WILLIAM
Writer. b. Chicago, IL, Aug. 12, 1931. e. Oberlin College, B.A., Columbia U., M.A. Novels include The Temple of Gold, Your Turn to Curtsy, My Turn to Bow, Soldier in the Rain (filmed), Boys and Girls Together, The Thing of It Is, No Way to Treat a Lady (filmed), Father's Day, The Princess Bride (filmed), Marathon Man (filmed), Magic (filmed), Tinsel, Control, Heat (filmed), The Silent Gondoliers, The Color of Light, Brothers. Non-fiction: The Season, Adventures in the Screen Trade, Wait Until Next Year (w/Mike Lupica), Hype and Glory.
PICTURES: Harper, Butch Cassidy and the Sundance Kid (Academy Award, 1969), The Hot Rock, The Stepford Wives, The Great Waldo Pepper, All the President's Men (Academy

Award, 1976), Marathon Man (based on his novel), A Bridge Too Far, Magic (based on his novel), Heat (based on his novel), The Princess Bride (based on his novel), Misery, Memoirs of an Invisible Man (co-s.p.), Year of the Comet, Chaplin (co-s.p.), Maverick, The Ghost and the Darkness.

GOLDSMITH, JERRY
Composer. b. Los Angeles, CA, Feb. 10, 1929. e. Los Angeles City Coll. Studied piano with Jacob Gimpel and music composition, harmony, theory with Mario Castelnuovo-Tedesco. With CBS radio first with own show (Romance) and then moved on to others (Suspense). Began scoring for TV, including Climax, Playhouse 90, Studio One, Gunsmoke, etc. Emmy Awards for QB VIII, Masada, Babe, The Red Pony, Star Trek Voyager Theme.
PICTURES: Black Patch (debut, 1957), Lonely Are the Brave, Freud (Acad. Award nom.), The Stripper, The Prize, Seven Days in May, Lilies of the Field, In Harm's Way, Von Ryan's Express, Our Man Flint, A Patch of Blue (Acad. Award nom.), The Blue Max, Seconds, Stagecoach, The Sand Pebbles (Acad. Award nom.), In Like Flint, Planet of the Apes (Acad. Award nom.), The Ballad of Cable Hogue, Tora! Tora! Tora!, Patton (Acad. Award nom.), The Wild Rovers, The Other, Papillon (Acad. Award nom.), The Reincarnation of Peter Proud, Chinatown (Acad. Award nom.), Logan's Run, The Wind and the Lion (Acad. Award nom.), The Omen (Academy Award, 1976), Islands in the Stream, MacArthur, Coma, Damien: Omen II, The Boys From Brazil (Acad. Award nom.), The Great Train Robbery, Alien, Star Trek-The Motion Picture (Acad. Award nom.), The Final Conflict, Outland, Raggedy Man, The Secret of NIMH, Poltergeist (Acad. Award nom.), First Blood, Twilight Zone—The Movie, Psycho II, Under Fire (Acad. Award nom.), Gremlins, Legend (European ver.), Explorers, Rambo: First Blood II, Poltergeist II: The Other Side, Hoosiers (Acad. Award nom.), Extreme Prejudice, Innerspace, Lionheart, Rent-a-Cop, Rambo III, Criminal Law, The 'Burbs, Leviathan, Star Trek V: The Final Frontier, Total Recall, Gremlins 2: The New Batch (also cameo), The Russia House, Not Without My Daughter, Sleeping With the Enemy, Medicine Man, Basic Instinct (Acad. Award nom.), Mom and Dad Save the World, Mr. Baseball, Love Field, Forever Young, Matinee, The Vanishing, Dennis the Menace, Malice, Rudy, Six Degrees of Separation, Angie, Bad Girls, The Shadow, The River Wild, I.Q., Congo, First Knight, Powder, City Hall, 2 Days in the Valley, Executive Decision, Powder, Chain Reaction.

GOLDSMITH, MARTIN M.
Writer. b. New York, NY, Nov. 6, 1913. Bush pilot, playwright, novelist, screenwriter.
AUTHOR: Novels: Double Jeopardy, Detour, Shadows at Noon, Miraculous Fish of Domingo Gonzales. Play: Night Shift.
PICTURES: Detour, Blind Spot, Narrow Margin, Mission Over Korea, Overland Pacific, Hell's Island, Fort Massacre, Bat Masterson, It Happens Every Thursday, Shakedown.
TELEVISION: Playhouse 90, Goodyear Playhouse, Twilight Zone.

GOLDSMITH, MARVIN F.
Executive. b. Brooklyn, NY. e. NY Inst. of Tech. Started as page at CBS, eventually becoming film editor. Was tv group supervisor with Batten Barton Durstine & Osborne. 1973, joined ABC as mgr. nighttime sales proposals; 1976-78, account exec. in sports sales, then v.p. prime time sales proposals, then v.p. Eastern Sales. 1986, promoted to sr. v.p., natl. sls. mngr.; 1989, became sr. v.p. gen. sls. mngr. 1992, promoted to pres., sls. & marketing, ABC Television Network.

GOLDSTEIN, MILTON
Executive. b. New York, NY, Aug. 1, 1926. e. NYU, 1949. In exec. capac., Paramount; foreign sales coord., The Ten Commandments, Psycho; v.p. foreign sales, Samuel Bronston org.; asst. to Pres., Paramount Int'l, special prods., 1964; Foreign sales mgr., 1966; v.p., world wide sales, 1967, Cinerama; Sr. v.p. Cinema Center Films, 1969; pres., Cinema Center Films, 1971; v.p. Theatrical Mktg. & Sales, Metromedia Producers Corp., 1973; in March, 1974, formed Boasberg-Goldstein, Inc., consultants in prod. and dist. of m.p.; 1975, named exec. vice pres., Avco Embassy Pictures; 1978, named exec. v.p. & chief operating officer, Melvin Simon Prods. 1980, named pres.; 1985, pres. Milt Goldstein Enterprises, Inc.; 1990, chairman and ceo, HKM Films. 1991, pres., Introvision movies.

GOLDSTONE, JAMES
Director. b. Los Angeles, CA. June 8, 1931. e. Dartmouth Coll., B.A., Bennington Coll., M.A. Film editor from 1950. Writer, story editor from 1957. Dir. starting from 1958.
PICTURES: Jigsaw (debut, 1968), A Man Called Gannon, Winning, Brother John, Red Sky at Morning, The Gang That Couldn't Shoot Straight, They Only Kill Their Masters, Swashbuckler, Rollercoaster, When Time Ran Out.

142

TELEVISION: Pilots: Star Trek, Ironside, Iron Horse, The Senator, etc. Specials-Movies: A Clear and Present Danger (Emmy nom.), Eric (Virgin Islands Int'l. Film Fest. Gold Medal). Journey from Darkness (Christopher Award). Studs Lonigan (miniseries 1978), Kent State, (Emmy, best dir., special), Things in Their Season, Calamity Jane, The Sun Also Rises, Dreams of Gold, Earthstar Voyager.

GOLDTHWAIT, BOBCAT (BOB)
Comedian, Actor. b. Syracuse, NY, May 1, 1962. Performed with comedy troupe The Generic Comics in early 1980's. Album: Meat Bob.
PICTURES: Police Academy 2: Their First Assignment (debut, 1985), One Crazy Summer, Police Academy 3: Back in Training, Burglar, Police Academy 4: Citizens on Patrol, Hot to Trot, Scrooged, Shakes the Clown (also dir., s.p.), Freaked, Radioland Murders, Destiny Turns on the Radio, Hercules.
TELEVISION: Series: Capitol Critters (voice), Unhappily Ever After (voice). Specials: Bob Goldthwait: Don't Watch This Show, Share the Warmth, Is He Like That All the Time? (also dir., writer), Bob Saget: In the Dream Suite, Comic Relief, Medusa: Dare to Be Truthful. Guest: Tales From the Crypt, Married... With Children, The Larry Sanders Show, E.R., Beavis and Butthead, Comic Relief, The John Laroquette Show.

GOLDWATER, CHARLES
Executive, Exhibitor. b. New Orleans, LA. e. Boston U., B.S. Broadcasting & Film. Began career with Walter Reade Organization as usher in 1971-74, promoted to manager. Sack Theatres/USA Cinemas 1974-88, began as manager, promoted to s.v.p. & general manager. National Amusements, exec. dir. Project Development, 1988-90. Loews/Sony Theatres, sr. v.p. & general manager, 1990-1995. Currently pres. & CEO, Cinamerica/Mann Theatres. NATO bd. of dir. 1987-present. Chmn. CARA/Product Committee, 1991-present. General chmn. Showeast 1992-1995; chmn of the bd. Showeast, 1995-present. Bd. of directors, Motion Picture Pioneers, Will Riogers Organization, Theatre Owners of New England. Past bd. of directors, Variety Clubs of New England & New York.

GOLDWYN, SAMUEL, JR.
Producer, Director. b. Los Angeles, CA, Sept. 7, 1926. e. U. of Virginia. Father of actor Tony Goldwyn. U.S. Army, 1944; following war writer, assoc. prod., J. Arthur Rank Org.; prod. Gathering Storm on London stage; returned to U.S., 1948; assoc. prod., Universal; recalled to Army service, 1951; prod., dir., Army documentary films including Alliance for Peace (Edinburgh Film Festival prize); prod. TV shows, Adventure series for CBS, 1952-53; prod. TV series, The Unexpected, 1954; pres., The Samuel Goldwyn Company, 1955-. Also established Samuel Goldwyn Home Entertainment, and Goldwyn Pavilion Cinemas.
PICTURES: Prod.: Man With the Gun, The Sharkfighters, The Proud Rebel, The Adventures of Huckleberry Finn, The Young Lovers (also dir.), Cotton Comes to Harlem, Come Back Charleston Blue, The Golden Seal, Mystic Pizza (exec. prod.), Stella.
TELEVISION: The Academy Awards, 1987, 1988; April Morning (co-exec. prod.).

GOLDWYN, TONY
Actor. b. Los Angeles, CA, May 20, 1960. e. Brandeis U., London Acad. of Music & Dramatic Art.
THEATER: Digby, The Foreigner, The Real Thing, Pride and Prejudice, The Sum of Us, Spike Heels, Inherit the Wind.
PICTURES: Friday the 13th Part VI: Jason Live (debut, 1986), Gaby-A True Story, Ghost, Kuffs, Traces of Red, The Pelican Brief, Reckless, The Substance of Fire, Nixon, The Substance of Fire.
TELEVISION: Movies: Favorite Son, Dark Holiday, Iran: Days of Crisis, Taking the Heat, Love Matters, Doomsday Gun, The Last Word, The Boys Next Door, Truman. Mini-Series: A Woman of Independent Means. Special: The Last Mile. Guest: L.A. Law, Tales from the Crypt.

GOLINO, VALERIA
Actress. b. Naples, Italy, Oct. 22, 1966. Raised in Athens, Greece. Was model at age 14 before being discovered by dir. Lina Wertmuller for film debut.
PICTURES: A Joke of Destiny (debut, 1983), Blind Date, My Son Infinitely Beloved, Little Fires, Dumb Dicks, Storia d'Amore (Love Story), Last Summer in Tangiers, The Gold-Rimmed Glasses, Three Sisters, Big Top Pee-wee, Rain Man, Torrents of Spring, The King's Whore, Traces of an Amorous Life, Hot Shots!, The Indian Runner, Hot Shots! Part Deux, Clean Slate, Immortal Beloved, Leaving Las Vegas, Four Rooms.

GONZALEZ-GONZALEZ, PEDRO
Actor. r.n. Ramiro Gonzalez-Gonzalez. b. Aguilares, TX, May 24, 1925. Comedian in San Antonio Mexican theatres.
PICTURES: Wings of the Hawk, Ring of Fear, Ricochet

Romance, The High and the Mighty, Strange Lady in Town, Bengazi, I Died a Thousand Times, Bottom of the Bottle, The Sheepman, Gun the Man Down, Rio Bravo, The Young Land, The Adventures of Bullwhip Griffin, The Love Bug, The Love God, Hellfighters, Hook Line and Sinker, Chisum, Support Your Local Gunfighter, Zachariah, Six-Pack Annie, Won Ton Ton the Dog Who Saved Hollywood, Dreamer, Lust in the Dust, Uphill All the Way, Deception.
TELEVISION: Guest: O'Henry Playhouse, Felix the Fourth, Ann Southern Show, No Time for Sergeants, Gunsmoke, Perry Mason, The Monkees, Love American Style, Adam 12, Farmer's Daughter, Danny Kaye Show, National Velvet, Bachelor Father, Bonanza, The Fall Guy, Moonlighting, many others. Movies: Donor, Ghost Writer, Bates Motel (pilot).

GOOD, CHARLES E.
Executive. b. 1922. Joined Buena Vista in 1957 in Chicago office; progressed from salesman to branch mgr. and then district mgr. Later moved to Burbank as domestic sales mgr. in 1975; 1978, named v.p. & general sales mgr.; 1980, appointed pres., BV Distribution Co. Resigned presidency 1984; became BV consultant until retirement, 1987.

GOODALL, CAROLINE
Actress. b. London, England, Nov. 13, 1959. e. Natl Youth Theatre of Great Britain; Bristol Univ. On stage with Royal Court Theatre, Royal Natl. Theatre, Royal Shakespeare Co. Toured Australia in Richard III for RSC, 1986.
PICTURES: Every Time We Say Goodbye (debut, 1986), Hook, The Silver Brumby, The Webbers' 15 Minutes, Cliffhanger, Schindler's List, Disclosure, Hotel Sorrento, White Squall.
TELEVISION: Movies (Australia): Cassidy, Ring of Scorpio, The Great Air Race, Diamond Swords (Fr.). Mini-Series: After the War. Guest: Remington Steele, Tales of the Unexpected, Quantum Leap, The Commish, Rumpole of the Bailey, Poirot: Curse of the Western Star.

GOODING, CUBA, JR.
Actor. b. Bronx, NY, Sept. 2, 1968. Son of rhythm and blues vocalist Cuba Gooding. Raised in California. Prof. debut as dancer backing up Lionel Richie at 1984 Olympic Games. Recipient of NAACP Image Awards for Boyz in the Hood and tv movie Murder Without Motive. Voted by NATO/Showest as Newcomer of the Year, 1992.
PICTURES: Coming to America (debut, 1988), Sing, Boyz in the Hood, Hitz, Gladiator, A Few Good Men, Judgment Night, Lightning Jack, Outbreak, Losing Isaiah, Jerry Maguire.
TELEVISION: Movies: Murder Without Motive: The Edmund Perry Story, Daybreak, The Tuskegee Airmen. Special: No Means No.

GOODMAN, DAVID Z.
Writer. e. Queens Coll., Yale School of Drama.
PICTURES: Lovers and Other Strangers, Straw Dogs, Farewell My Lovely, Logan's Run, Eyes of Laura Mars, Man Woman and Child (co.-s.p.).

GOODMAN, JOHN
Actor. b. Afton, MO, June 20, 1952. e. Southwest Missouri State U. Moved to NY in 1975 where he appeared on stage (incl. A Midsummer Night's Dream) and in commercials. On Broadway in Loose Ends, Big River. L.A. stage in Antony and Cleopatra.
PICTURES: Eddie Macon's Run (1983, debut), The Survivors, Revenge of the Nerds, C.H.U.D., Maria's Lovers, Sweet Dreams, True Stories, Raising Arizona, Burglar, The Big Easy, The Wrong Guys, Punchline, Everybody's All-American, Sea of Love, Always, Stella, Arachnophobia, King Ralph, Barton Fink, Babe, Matinee, Born Yesterday, We're Back! A Dinosaur's Story (voice), The Flintstones, Pie in the Sky, Mother Night.
TELEVISION: Series: Roseanne. Movies: The Face of Rage, Heart of Steel, The Mystery of Moro Castle, Murder Ordained, Kingfish: A Story of Huey P. Long (also co-prod.), A Streetcar Named Desire. Mini-Series: Chiefs. Guest: The Equalizer, Moonlighting.

GOODRICH, ROBERT EMMETT
Executive. b. Grand Rapids, MI, June 27, 1940. e. U. of Michigan, B.A., 1962; J.D., 1964; NYU. LL.M, 1966. Pres. & Secty., Goodrich Quality Theaters, Inc. 1967-present, developed circuit from father's one theater to 154 screens at 19 locations in 9 Mich. cities, 4 Indiana cities, 2 Illinois cities. Owns and operates 6 FM/AM radio stations in Grand Rapids, MI, Muskegon, MI. Member: NATO; Will Rogers Inst. advisory comm; bd.; Mich. Millers Mutual Insurance Co.; State of MI Bar Assn.

GOODWIN, RICHARD
Producer. b. Bombay, India, Sept. 13, 1934. e. Rugby. Entered film world by chance: while waiting to go to Cambridge U. took temporary job as tea boy at studio which led to 20-year-long association with producer Lord Brabourne.

PICTURES: *Prod. Mgr.*: The Sheriff of Fractured Jaw, Carve Her Name with Pride, The Grass Is Greener, Sink the Bismarck, HMS Defiant. *Prod.*: The Tales of Beatrix Potter. *Co-Prod.*: Murder on the Orient Express, Death on the Nile, The Mirror Crack'd, Evil Under the Sun, A Passage to India, Little Dorrit.

GOODWIN, RONALD
Composer, Arranger, Conductor. b. Plymouth, Eng., Feb. 17, 1925. e. Pinner County Grammar Sch. Early career: arranger for BBC dance orchestra; mus. dir., Parlophone Records; orchestra leader for radio, TV and records. Fut. m.p. ind., 1958. Many major film scores. Guest cond. R.P.O., B.S.O., Toronto Symph. Orch. New Zealand Symphony Orch., Sydney Symphony Orch. Royal Scottish Natl. Orch., BBC Scottish Symphony Orch., BBC Welsh Symphony Orch., BBC Radio Orch., BBC Concert Orch., London Philharmonic Orch., Gothenberg Symphony Orch., Norwegian Opera Orch. & Chorus, Halle Orchestra, Singapore Symphony Orch., Australian Pops Orch, Detroit Symphony Orchestra, Danish Radio Orchestra, Odense Symphony Orch., Norrkoping Symphony Orch.
PICTURES: Whirlpool, I'm All Right Jack, The Trials of Oscar Wilde, Johnny Nobody, Village of the Damned, Murder She Said, Follow the Boys, Murder at the Gallop, Children of the Damned, 633 Squadron, Murder Most Foul, Murder Ahoy, Operation Crossbow, The ABC Murders, Of Human Bondage, Those Magnificent Men in Their Flying Machines, The Trap, Mrs. Brown, You've Got a Lovely Daughter; Submarine X-1, Decline and Fall, Where Eagles Dare, Monte Carlo or Bust, Battle of Britain, The Executioner, The Selfish Giant, Frenzy, Diamonds on Wheels, The Little Mermaid, The Happy Prince, One of Our Dinosaurs Is Missing, Escape From the Dark, Born to Run, Beauty and the Beast, Candleshoe, Force Ten from Navarone, Spaceman and King Arthur, Clash of Loyalties, Valhalla.

GORDON, ALEX
Producer. b. London, Eng., Sept. 8, 1922. e. Canford Coll., Dorset, 1939. Writer, m.p. fan magazines, 1939-41; British Army, 1942-45; pub. dir. Renown Pictures Corp., 1946-47; P.R. and pub. rep. for Gene Autry, 1948-53; v.p. and prod. Golden State Productions, 1954-58; prod. Alex Gordon Prods., 1958-66; producer Twentieth Century-Fox Television, 1967-76; film archivist/preservationist, 1976-84; v.p., Gene Autry's Flying A Pictures, 1985.
PICTURES: Lawless Rider, Bride of the Monster, Apache Woman, Day the World Ended, Oklahoma Woman, Girls in Prison, The She-Creature, Runaway Daughters, Shake Rattle and Rock, Flesh and the Spur, Voodoo Woman, Dragstrip Girl, Motorcycle Gang, Jet Attack, Submarine Seahawk, Atomic Submarine, The Underwater City, The Bounty Killer, Requiem for a Gunfighter.
TELEVISION: Movie of the Year, Golden Century, Great Moments in Motion Pictures.

GORDON, BERT I.
Producer, Director, Writer. b. Kenosha, WI, Sept. 24, 1932. e. Univ. of WI. Started on tv as commercial prod.
PICTURES: *Dir./Prod.*: Serpent Island (debut, 1954), King Dinosaur, Beginning of the End, Cyclops (also s.p.), The Amazing Colossal Man (also co-s.p.), Attack of the Puppet People (also story), War of the Colossal Beast, The Spider, Tormented, The Boy and the Pirates, The Magic Sword (also story), Village of the Giants (also story), Picture Mommy Dead, How to Succeed With Sex (dir., s.p.), Necromancy (also s.p.), The Mad Bomber (also s.p.), The Police Connection (also s.p.), The Food of the Gods (also s.p.), Empire of the Ants (also s.p.), The Coming (also s.p.), Satan's Princess, Malediction.

GORDON, BRUCE
Executive. b. Sidney, Australia, Feb. 4, 1929. Began career in Australian entertainment industry 1952 with Tivoli Circuit, live theatre chain; acted as advance man, front-of-house mgr., adv. dir.; promoted to busn. mgr., 1958. Named Tivoli membr. bd. of management, 1960-62. Joined Desilu Studios in 1962, developing Far East territories; promoted 1968 when Paramount acquired Desilu to mng. dir. Para. Far East opns. Named to bd. of TV Corp., 1969, operator of Channel 9 TV stns. & co.'s theatres in Sydney, Melbourne. Dir. on bd. of Academy Investments, operator of Perth theatre chain; responsible for building Perth Entertainment Centre. Named pres., Paramount TV Intl. Services, Ltd., 1974, in New York office. 1981, pres. Intl. Television of Paramount Pictures.

GORDON, CHARLES
Executive, Producer. b. Belzoni, MS. Began career as a talent agent with William Morris Agency. Left to write and develop innovative programming creating and producing 5 pilots and 3 series. Left TV to enter motion picture production in partnership with brother Lawrence Gordon. President and chief operating officer, The Gordon Company.

PICTURES: *Exec. prod.*: Die Hard, Leviathan. *Co-prod.*: Night of the Creeps, The Wrong Guys, Field of Dreams, K-9, Lock Up, The Rocketeer, The Super, Unlawful Entry, Waterworld. TELEVISION: *Writer-creator*. When the Whistle Blows. *Exec. prod.*: The Renegades. *Exec. prod.-creator*. Just Our Luck, Our Family Honor.

GORDON, DON
Actor. b. Los Angeles, CA, Nov. 13, 1926. r.n. Donald Walter Guadagno. Served, U.S. Navy, 1941-45. Studied acting with Michael Chekhov. e. Columbia U. Theatre includes On an Open Roof, Stockade.
PICTURES: Bullitt, The Lollipop Cover (best actor, Chicago Film Fest.), W.U.S.A., The Last Movie, Papillon, The Gambler, Out of the Blue, The Final Conflict, The Beast Within, Lethal Weapon, Skin Deep, The Exorcist III, The Borrower.
TELEVISION: *Series*: The Blue Angels, Lucan, The Contender. *Guest*: The Defenders, Remington Steele, Charlie's Angels, Twilight Zone, Simon & Simon, Outer Limits, MacGyver, etc. *Movies*: Happiness is a Warm Clue, Street Killing, Confessions of a Married Man.

GORDON, KEITH
Actor, Director, Writer. b. Bronx, NY, Feb. 3, 1961.
THEATER: A Traveling Companion, Richard III, Album, Back to Back The Buddy System, Third Street.
PICTURES: *Actor*. Jaws 2 (debut, 1978), All That Jazz, Home Movies, Dressed to Kill, Christine, The Legend of Billie Jean, Static (also co-s.p., co-prod.), Back to School, I Love Trouble. *Director-Writer*. The Chocolate War, A Midnight Clear, Mother Night.
TELEVISION: *Mini-Series*: Studs Lonigan, Wild Palms (co-dir.). *Movies*: Kent State, Single Bars Single Women, Combat High. *Special*: My Palikari (Amer. Playhouse).

GORDON, JEROME
Executive, Exhibitor. b. Newport News, VA, Mar. 1, 1915. Began movie career at age 10 as usher in father's theatre. At age 18, owned and operated two theatres. Spent one year in theater decorating business in Philadelphia. Worked for Fox West Coast circuit in Los Angeles, 1937-40. Returned to VA and developed small theater circuit with brothers. Served as pres. of Virginia NATO for 4 yrs. 1975-, exec. dir., Virginia NATO; 1976-, exec. dir., Maryland & D.C. NATO. Coordinated Mid-Atlantic NATO convention from 1975 until it merged with ShowEast in 1989. Currently exec. dir., Mid-Atlantic NATO. 1978-86, spec. asst. to pres.; NATO; coordinated campaigns to pass Anti-Blind Bidding Laws in individual states. Edited Regional Presidents' NATO Handbook. Member, bd. of dirs., NATO; chmn., NATO Membership Development Committee. Exec. Committee, ShowEast. Recipient of Distinguished Service Award, ShowEast, 1992; B.V. Sturdivant Award, NATO ShowEast, 1992.

GORDON, LAWRENCE
Producer, Executive. b. Belzoni, MS, March 25, 1936. e. Tulane U. (business admin.). Assist. to prod. Aaron Spelling at Four Star Television, 1964. Writer and assoc. prod. on several Spelling shows. 1965, joined ABC-TV as head of west coast talent dev; 1966, TV and motion pictures exec. with Bob Banner Associates; 1968 joined AIP as v.p. in charge of project dev.; 1971 named v.p., Screen Gems (TV div. of Columbia Pictures) where he helped dev. Brian's Song and QB VII. Returned to AIP as v.p. worldwide prod. Formed Lawrence Gordon Prods. at Columbia Pictures; 1984-86, pres. and COO 20th Century Fox. Currently indep. prod. with 20th Century Fox. Producer of B'way musical Smile.
PICTURES: Dillinger (1973), Hard Times, Rolling Thunder, The Driver, The End, Hooper, The Warriors, Xanadu, Paternity, Jekyll and Hyde, Together Again, 48 Hours, Streets of Fire, Brewster's Millions, Lucas, Jumpin' Jack Flash, Predator, The Couch Trip, The Wrong Guys, Die Hard, Leviathan (exec. prod.), K-9, Field of Dreams, Lock Up, Family Business, Another 48 HRS, Die Hard 2, Predator 2, The Rocketeer, Used People.
TELEVISION: (Co-creator and co-exec. prod.) Dog and Cat, Matt Houston, Renegades, Just Our Luck, Our Family Honor.

GORDON, RICHARD
Producer. b. London, Eng., Dec. 31, 1925. e. U. of London, 1943. Served in Brit. Royal Navy, 1944-46; ed. & writer on fan magazines & repr. independent American cos. 1946, with publicity dept. Assoc. Brit. Pathe 1947; org. export-import business for independent, British and American product; formed Gordon Films, Inc., 1949; formed Amalgamated prod., 1956; formed Grenadier Films, Ltd. 1971. 1992, prod. of A Tribute to Orson Welles.
PICTURES: The Counterfeit Plan, The Haunted Strangler, Fiend Without a Face, The Secret Man, First Man into Space, Corridors of Blood, Devil Doll, Curse of Simba, The Projected Man, Naked Evil, Island of Terror, Tales of the Bizarre, Tower of Evil, Horror Hospital, The Cat and the Canary, Inseminoid.

GORDON, STUART
Director, Writer. b. Chicago, IL, Aug. 11, 1947. e. Univ. of WI. Worked at commercial art studio prior to founding Broom Street Theater in Madison, WI. Later founder and prod. dir. of Organic Theater Co. in Madison, then Chicago, 1969-85. Was fight choreographer on 1976 film The Last Affair.
PICTURES: *Director*: Re-Animator (also co-s.p.), From Beyond (also co-s.p.), Dolls, Robot Jox (also wrote story), Honey I Shrunk the Kids (co-story only), The Pit and the Pendulum, Honey I Blew Up the Kid (exec. prod., co-story only), Fortress, Body Snatchers (co-s.p. only), Castle Freak (also co-story), Space Truckers (dir., prod., co-story).
TELEVISION: *Director*: Bleacher Bums (special), Daughter of Darkness (movie).

GORDY, BERRY
Executive. b. Detroit, MI, Nov. 28, 1929. Was working on auto assembly line in Detroit when decided to launch record co., Motown. In 1961 wrote song, Shop Around; recording by Smokey Robinson made it his first million dollar record. Expanded into music publishing, personal mgt., recording studios, film and TV, also backing stage shows. Former bd. chmn., Motown Industries. Chmn. The Gordy Co. Received Business Achievement Award, Interracial Council for Business Opportunity, 1967; Whitney M. Young Jr. Award, L.A. Urban League, 1980; Inducted into Rock and Roll Hall of Fame, 1988. Recipient of NARAS Trustee Award, 1991. Author of To Be Loved (1994). Member BMI, NAACP, A.M.P.A.S., DGI, NARAS.
PICTURES: Lady Sings the Blues (prod.), Bingo Long Traveling All-Stars and Motor Kings (exec. prod.), Mahogany (dir.), Almost Summer, The Last Dragon (exec. prod.).

GORE, MICHAEL
Composer, Producer. b. New York City, New York, March 5, 1951. e. Yale University and studied in Paris with composer Max Deustch. Began writing pop songs for his sister singer Lesley Gore; as a staff songwriter for Screen Gems-Columbia; and as a producer of classical recordings for CBS Records. Prod. for Philips Classics recording of The King and I (with Julie Andrews, Ben Kingsley). Wrote Whitney Houston's hit single All the Man That I Need.
PICTURES: Fame (2 Academy Awards for Best Score and Title Song, 1980), Terms of Endearment, Footloose, Pretty in Pink, Broadcast News, Defending Your Life, The Butcher's Wife, Mr. Wonderful.
TELEVISION: Generations (theme); Fame (theme).

GORING, SIR MARIUS
Actor. b. Newport, Isle of Wight, May 23, 1912. e. Cambridge U., Universities of Frankfurt-on-Main, Munich, Vienna, Paris. Early career with Old Vic; stage debut 1927, Jean Sterling Rackinlay's Children's Matinees. 1940-46 served with H. M. Forces and Foreign Office.
PICTURES: Rembrandt, Dead Men Tell No Tales, Flying 55, Consider Your Verdict, Spy in Black, Pastor Hall, The Case of the Frightened Lady, The Big Blockade, The Night Raider, Lilli Marlene, Stairway to Heaven, Night Boat to Dublin, Take My Life, Red Shoes, Mr. Perrin and Mr. Traill, Odette, Pandora and the Flying Dutchman, Circle of Danger, Highly Dangerous, So Little Time, The Man Who Watched Trains Go By, Rough Shoot, The Barefoot Contessa, Break in the Circle, Quentin Durward, Ill Met by Moonlight, The Moonraker, Family Doctor, Angry Hills, Whirlpool, Treasure of St. Teresa, Monty's Double, Beyond the Curtain, Desert Mice, The Inspector, Girl on a Motorcycle, Subterfuge, Zeppelin.
TELEVISION: Numerous appearances, Sleeping Dog, Man in a Suitcase, Scarlet Pimpernel, The Expert.

GOROG, LASZLO
Writer. b. Hungary, Sept. 30, 1903. e. U. of Sciences, Budapest. Playwright, short story writer, asst. editor, Budapest, 1928-39.
PICTURES: Tales of Manhattan, The Affairs of Susan, She Wouldn't Say Yes, The Land Unknown, Mole People.
TELEVISION: 4 Star, Dupont, The Roaring Twenties, 77 Sunset Strip, Maverick, etc.

GORSHIN, FRANK
Actor. b. Pittsburgh, PA, Apr. 5, 1933. Also nightclub comic and impresionist. On B'way stage in Jimmy.
PICTURES: Hot Rod Girl, Dragstrip Girl, Invasion of the Saucer Men, Portland Exposse, Warlock, Bells Are Ringing, Studs Lonigan, Where the Boys Are, The Great Impostor, Ring of Fire, The George Raft Story, Sail a Crooked Ship, That Darn Cat, Ride Beyond Vengeance, Batman, Skidoo, Record City, Underground Aces, The Uppercrust, Hot Resort, Uphill All the Way, Hollywood Vice Squad, Midnight, Beverly Hills Bodysnatchers, Hail Caesar, The Meteor Man, Twelve Monkeys.
TELEVISION: *Series*: ABC Comedy Hour (The Kopycats), The Edge of Night. *Movies*: Sky Heist, Death on the Freeway, Goliath Awaits, A Masterpiece of Murder. *Guest*: Hennessey,

The Detectives, Have Gun Will Travel, The Defenders, Naked City, The Munsters, Batman, Police Woman, SWAT, The Fall Guy, Murder She Wrote, etc.

GORTNER, MARJOE
Actor, Producer. b. Long Beach, CA, Jan. 14, 1944. Was child evangelist, whose career as such was basis for Oscar-winning documentary film, Marjoe. Acted in films and TV; turned producer in 1978 for When You Comin' Back Red Ryder?
PICTURES: Earthquake, Bobbie Joe and the Outlaw, The Food of the Gods, Viva Knievel, Sidewinder One, Acapulco Gold, Starcrash, When You Comin' Back Red Ryder?, Mausoleum, Jungle Warriors, Hellhole, American Ninja III: Blood Hunt, Wild Bill.
TELEVISION: *Movies*: The Marcus-Nelson Murders, Pray for the Wildcats, The Gun and the Pulpit, Mayday at 40000 Feet. *Guest*: Police Story, Barnaby Jones, The A-Team. *Series*: Falcon Crest.

GOSSETT, LOUIS, JR.
Actor. b. Brooklyn, NY, May 27, 1936. e. NYU, B.S. Also nightclub singer during 1960s.
THEATER: Take a Giant Step (debut, 1953), The Desk Set, Lost in the Stars, A Raisin in the Sun, Golden Boy, The Blacks, Blood Knot, The Zulu and the Zayda, My Sweet Charlie, Carry Me Back to Morningside Heights, Murderous Angels (L.A. Drama Critics Award).
PICTURES: A Raisin in the Sun (debut, 1961), The Bushbaby, The Landlord, Skin Game, Travels With My Aunt, The Laughing Policeman, The White Dawn, The River Niger, J.D.'s Revenge, The Deep, The Choirboys, An Officer and a Gentleman (Academy Award, best supporting actor, 1982), Jaws 3-D, Finders Keepers, Enemy Mine, Iron Eagle, Firewalker, The Principal, Iron Eagle II, Toy Soldiers, The Punisher, Aces: Iron Eagle III, Diggstown, Monolith, Flashfire, Blue Chips (unbilled), A Good Man in Africa, Iron Eagle IV, Inside.
TELEVISION: *Series*: The Young Rebels, The Lazarus Syndrome, The Powers of Matthew Star, Gideon Oliver. *Movies*: Companions in Nightmare, It's Good to Be Alive, Sidekicks, Delancey Street, The Crisis Within, Don't Look Back, Little Ladies of the Night, To Kill a Cop, The Critical List, This Man Stands Alone, Sadat, The Guardian, A Gathering of Old Men, The Father Clements Story, Roots: The Gift, El Diablo, Sudie and Simpson, The Josephine Baker Story, Carolina Skeletons, Father & Son: Dangerous Relations (also co-exec. prod.), Ray Alexander: A Taste for Justice, A Father for Charlie (also co-exec. prod.), Curse of the Starving Class, Zooman, Ray Alexander: A Menu for Murder. *Mini-Series*: Roots (Emmy Award, 1977), Backstairs at the White House. Return to Lonesome Dove. *Specials*: Welcome Home, A Triple Play: Sam Found Out, Zora Is My Name, The Century Collection Presents Ben Vereen: His Roots. *Guest*: The Mod Squad, Bill Cosby Show, Partridge Family, The Rookies, Love American Style, Police Story, Rockford Files, many others.

GOTTESMAN, STUART
Executive. b. New York, NY, June 11, 1949. Started career in mailroom of Warner Bros., 1972; later named promo. asst. to southwestern regional fieldman; promoted to that post which held for 10 years. 1987, named WB dir. field activities; 1990, appointed v.p. WB national field operations.

GOTTLIEB, CARL
Writer, Director, Actor. b. New York, NY, March 18. e. Syracuse U., B.S., 1960. Directed short film The Absent-Minded Waiter.
PICTURES: *Actor*: Maryjane, M*A*S*H, Up the Sandbox, Cannonball, The Sting II, Johnny Dangerously, The Committee, Into the Night, Clueless. *Director*: Caveman (also co-s.p.), Amazon Women on the Moon (co-dir.). *Co-Writer*: Jaws (also actor), Which Way Is Up?, Jaws II, The Jerk (also actor), Doctor Detroit, Jaws 3-D.
TELEVISION: *Writer*: Smothers Bros. Comedy Hour (Emmy Award, 1969), The Odd Couple, Flip Wilson, Bob Newhart Show, The Super, Crisis at Sun Valley, The Deadly Triangle. *Director*: Paul Reiser: Out on a Whim, Partners In Life, Campus Cops. *Director-Co-creator*: Leo & Liz in Beverly Hills. *Co-creator*: George Burns' Comedy Week.

GOTTLIEB, MEYER
Executive. Pres. & COO, The Samuel Goldwyn Company.

GOUGH, MICHAEL
Actor. b. Malaya, Nov. 23, 1917. e. Rose Hill Sch., in Kent, England, and at Durham School. Studied at Old Vic School in London; first stage appearance in 1936 at Old Vic Theatre. N.Y. stage debut 1937 in Love of Women. London debut in 1938 in The Zeal of Thy House. Won 1979 Tony Award for Bedroom Farce.
PICTURES: Blanche Fury (debut, 1947), Anna Karenina, Saraband for Dead Lovers, The Small Back Room, The Man in the White Suit, Rob Roy, The Sword and the Rose, Richard III,

Reach for the Sky, Horror of Dracula (Dracula), Horrors of the Black Museum, The Horse's Mouth, Konga, Candidate for Murder, I Like Money (Mr. Topaze), The Phantom of the Opera, Black Zoo, Dr. Terror's House of Horrors, The Skull, Berserk, They Came From Beyond Space, A Walk With Love and Death, Women in Love, Trog, Julius Caesar, The Go-Between, Savage Messiah, Legend of Hell House, Horror Hospital (Computer Killers), Galileo, The Boys from Brazil, Venom, The Dresser, Top Secret!, Oxford Blues, Out of Africa, Caravaggio, Memed My Hawk, The Fourth Protocol, The Serpent and the Rainbow, Batman, Strapless, Let Him Have It, Blackeyes, Batman Returns, Little Nemo (voice), The Age of Innocence, Wittgenstein, Uncovered, Batman Forever.
TELEVISION: The Search for the Nile, Six Wives of Henry VIII, QB VII, Shoulder to Shoulder, The Citadel, Smiley's People, Brideshead Revisited, Mistral's Daughter, Lace II, Inside the Third Reich, To the Lighthouse, Suez, Vincent the Dutchman, Heart Attack Hotel, After the War, The Shell Seekers, Children of the North, Dr. Who, Sleepers.

GOULD, ELLIOTT
Actor. r.n. Elliott Goldstein. b. Brooklyn, NY, August 29, 1938. e. Professional Children's Sch., NY 1955. Vaudeville: appeared at Palace Theater, 1950. Broadway debut in Rumple (1957). Son is actor Jason Gould.
THEATER: Say Darling, Irma La Douce, I Can Get It for You Wholesale, On the Town (London), Fantasticks (tour), Drat the Cat, Little Murders, Luv (tour), Hit the Deck (Jones Beach), Rumors, Breakfast With Les & Bess.
PICTURES: Quick Let's Get Married (debut, 1965), The Night They Raided Minsky's, Bob & Carol & Ted & Alice (Acad. Award nom.), M*A*S*H, Getting Straight, Move, I Love My Wife, Little Murders (also prod.), The Touch, The Long Goodbye, Busting, S*P*Y*S!, California Split, Who?, Nashville (cameo), Whiffs, I Will I Will... For Now, Harry and Walter Go to New York, Mean Johnny Barrows, A Bridge Too Far, Capricorn One, Matilda, The Silent Partner, Escape to Athena, The Muppet Movie, The Last Flight of Noah's Ark, The Lady Vanishes, Falling in Love Again, The Devil and Max Devlin, Dirty Tricks, The Naked Face, Over the Brooklyn Bridge, The Muppets Take Manhattan, Inside Out, My First 40 Years, Lethal Obsession (Der Joker), The Telephone, The Big Picture, Dangerous Love, Night Visitor, The Wounded King, The Lemon Sisters, Judgment, Dead Men Don't Die, Bugsy, Strawanser, The Player, Exchange Lifeguards, Wet and Wild Summer, Naked Gun 33 1/3: The Final Insult (cameo), White Man's Burden, The Glass Shield, Kicking and Screaming, A Boy Called Hate, Johns.
TELEVISION: Specials: Once Upon A Mattress, Come Blow Your Horn, Jack and the Beanstalk (Faerie Tale Theater), Paul Reiser: Out on a Whim, Prime Time, Out to Lunch, Casey at the Bat (Tall Tales & Legends). Guest: Twilight Zone, Electric Company, Saturday Night Live, George Burns Comedy Week, Ray Bradbury Theatre, The Hitchhiker, Friends. Movies: The Rules of Marriage, Vanishing Act, Conspiracy: The Trial of Chicago 8, Stolen: One Husband, Somebody's Daughter, Bloodlines: Murder in the Family. Series: E/R, Together We Stand, Sessions (HBO).

GOULD, HAROLD
Actor. b. Schenectady, NY, Dec. 10, 1923. e. SUNY, Albany, B.A. Cornell U., MA., Ph.D. Instructor of theatre and speech, 1953-56, Randolph Macon's Woman's Col., Lynchburg, VA. Asst. prof. drama and speech, 1956-60, Univ. of Calif., Riverside. Acted with Ashland, OR Shakespeare Fest. in 1958 and Mark Taper Forum (The Miser, Once in a Lifetime). Won Obie Award for Off-B'way debut in The Increased Difficulty of Concentration, 1968. ACE Award for Ray Bradbury Theatre. L.A. Drama Critics Award, 1994.
THEATER: The House of Blue Leaves, Fools, Grown Ups, Artist Descending a Staircase, I Never Sang for My Father, Freud (one man show), Love Letters, Incommunicado, King Lear (Utah Shakespearean Fest.), Mixed Emotions, Old Business, The Tempest (Utah Shakespearean Fest.), Substance of Five (San Diego Olde Globe).
PICTURES: Two for the Seesaw, The Couch, Harper, Inside Daisy Clover, Marnie, An American Dream, The Arrangement, The Lawyer, Mrs. Pollifax: Spy, Where Does It Hurt?, The Sting, The Front Page, Love and Death, The Big Bus, Silent Movie, The One and Only, Seems Like Old Times, Playing for Keeps, Romero, Flesh Suitcase, Killer.
TELEVISION: Series: Rhoda (Emmy nom.), Park Place, Foot in the Door, Under One Roof, Singer and Sons, Golden Girls, Feather and Father Gang. Movies: To Catch a Star, Moviola (Emmy nom.), Washington Behind Closed Doors, Aunt Mary, Better Late Than Never, King Crab, Have I Got a Christmas for You, Man in the Santa Claus Suit, I Never Sang For My Father, Get Smart Again!, Mrs. Delafield Wants to Marry (Emmy nom.), Love Bug II, Fox Hope. Special: The Sunset Gang. Guest: Police Story (Emmy nom.), Tales from the Hollywood Hills: The Closed Set, Ray Bradbury Theater (Emmy nom.).

GOULET, ROBERT
Singer, Actor. b. Lawrence, MA., Nov. 26, 1933. e. Edmonton; scholarship, Royal Conservatory of Music. Sang in choirs, appeared with numerous orchestras; disk jockey, CKUA, Edmonton; pub. rel., Rogo & Rove,Inc.
THEATER: NY: Camelot (as Lancelot; Theatre World Award), The Happy Time (Tony Award, 1968), Camelot (as King Arthur; 1993 revival). Regional: numerous tours including I Do I Do, Carousel, On a Clear Day You Can See Forever, Kiss Me Kate, South Pacific, The Fantasticks, Camelot (as King Arthur).
PICTURES: Gay Purr-ee (voice), Honeymoon Hotel, I'd Rather Be Rich, I Deal in Danger, Atlantic City, Beetlejuice, Scrooged, The Naked Gun 2 1/2: The Smell of Fear, Mr. Wrong.
TELEVISION: Series: Robert Goulet Show, Blue Light. Guest: The Ed Sullivan Show, Garry Moore, The Enchanted Nutcracker, Omnibus, The Broadway of Lerner and Loewe, Rainbow of Stars, Judy Garland Show, Bob Hope Show, The Bell Telephone Hour, Granada-TV special (U.K.), Jack Benny, Dean Martin, Andy Williams, Jack Paar, Red Skelton, Hollywood Palace, Patty Duke Show, The Big Valley, Mission : Impossible, Police Woman, Cannon, Murder She Wrote, Mr. Belvedere, Fantasy Island, Matt Houston, Glitter, WKRP in Cincinnati. Pilot: Make My Day. Specials: Brigadoon, Carousel, Kiss Me Kate. Movie: Based on an Untrue Story.

GOWDY, CURT
Sportscaster. b. Green River, WY, July 31, 1919. Basketball star at U. of Wyoming. All-Conference member; graduated U. of Wyoming. 1942. Officer in U.S. Air Force WWII, then became sportscaster. Voted Sportscaster of the Year, 1967, Nat'l Assn. of Sportswriters Broadcasters. Best Sportscaster, Fame, 1967. Did play-by-play telecasts for 16 World Series, 7 Super Bowls, 12 Rose Bowls, 8 Orange Bowls, 18 NCAA Final 4 college basketball championships. In 1970 was the first individual from the field of sports to receive the George Foster Peabody Award. Hosted the American Sportsman outdoor TV show on ABC for 20 years. (Received 8 Emmy Awards). Inducted into the Sportscasters Hall of Fame in 1981, the Fishing Hall of Fame in 1982, and the Baseball Hall of Fame in 1984, Pro Football Hall of Fame in 1992.

GRADE, LORD LEW
Executive. r.n. Louis Winogradsky. b. Tokmak, Russia, Dec. 25, 1906. Brother of Lord Bernard Delfont. Came to Eng. 1912. Was first a music hall dancer until 1934 when he became an agent with Joe Collins, founding Collins and Grade Co. Joint managing dir. Lew & Leslie Grade Ltd. theatrical agency until 1955; Chmn. & mng. dir., ITC Entertainment Ltd. 1958-82; chmn. & chief exec., Associated Communications Corp. Ltd., 1973-82; pres. ATV Network Ltd., 1977-82; chmn., Stoll Moss Theatres Ltd., 1969-82; chmn. & chief exec., Embassy Communications International Ltd., 1982-85; chmn. & chief exec., The Grade Co. 1985-; Dir. Euro Disney S.C.A. Paris 1988, v.p. British Olympic Assn. Fellow BAFTA, 1979, KCSS 1979. Chairman for Life Active–I.T.C., 1995. Consultant to Polygram Entertainment Group. Autobiography: Still Dancing (1988).
NY THEATER: Prod.: Merrily We Roll Along, Starlight Express, Sly Fox.

GRADE, MICHAEL
Executive. b. London, England, March 8, 1943. e. Stowe. Entered industry 1966. Early career as newspaper columnist, became an executive at London Weekend Television then Embassy Television in Hollywood. Joined BBC Television, 1983 as controller of BBC 1 and director of Programmes (TV), 1986. Joined Channel 4 as chief executive, 1988.

GRAFF, RICHARD B.
Executive. b. Milwaukee, WI, Nov. 9, 1924. e. U. of Illinois. Served U.S. Air Force; Universal Pictures 1946 to 1964 in Chicago, Detroit, Chicago and NY home office as asst. to genl. sales mgr.; 1964 joined National General in Los Angeles. 1967 became v.p. and general sales mgr. of National General Pictures, formed and operated company. 1968, exec. v.p. in charge of world-wide sales and marketing. 1968 made v.p. of parent company; v.p. general sales mgr. AIP in 1971; 1975, pres. Cine Artists Pictures; 1977, pres. Richard Graff Company Inc; 1983, pres. of domestic distribution, MGM/UA. 1987, pres., worldwide distribution, Weintraub Entertainment Group. 1990, pres. The Richard Graff Company, Inc.

GRAFF, TODD
Actor, Writer. b. New York, NY, Oct. 22, 1959. e. SUNY/Purchase.
THEATER: NY: Baby (Tony nom., Theatre World Award), Birds of Paradise. Author: The Grandma Plays, Sheila Levine.
PICTURES: Actor: Sweet Lorraine (also composed songs), Five Corners, Dominick & Eugene, The Abyss, An Innocent Man, Opportunity Knocks, City of Hope. Writer: Used People, The Vanishing (also co-prod.), Fly by Night (also actor), Angie (also co-prod., cameo).
TELEVISION: Special: Vietnam War Story.

GRANET, BERT
Producer, Writer. b. New York, NY, July 10, 1910. e. Yale U. Sch. of Fine Arts (47 workshop). From 1936 author s.p. orig. & adapt. numerous pictures. Exec. prod.: Universal, 1967-69, CBS, Desilu Studios.
PICTURES: Quick Money, The Affairs of Annabel, Mr. Doodle Kicks Off, Laddie, A Girl a Guy and a Gob, My Favorite Wife, Bride by Mistake, Sing Your Way Home, Those Endearing Young Charms, The Locket, Do You Love Me?, The Marrying Kind, Berlin Express, The Torch, Scarface Mob.
TELEVISION: Desilu (1957-61), Twilight Zone (pilot), The Untouchables (pilot), Scarface Mob; Loretta Young Show (1955-56), Walter Winchell File 1956-57, Lucille Ball-Desi Arnaz Show 1957-60, Westinghouse Desilu Playhouse, The Great Adventure.

GRAMMER, KELSEY
Actor. b. St. Thomas, Virgin Islands, Feb. 20, 1955. e. Juilliard. Acting debut on tv in Another World. On B'way in Sunday in the Park With George. Supplied voice for Disney/Mickey Mouse short Runaway Brain.
PICTURE: Down Periscope.
TELEVISION: Series: Cheers, Frasier (2 Emmy Awards, 1994, 1995; Golden Globe, 1996), Fired Up (exec. prod.). Guest: Simpsons (voice). Movies: Dance 'Til Dawn, Beyond Suspicion, The Innocent.

GRANGER, FARLEY
Actor. b. San Jose, CA, July 1, 1925. e. Hollywood. U.S. Armed Forces 1944-46. Joined Eva Le Gallienne's National Rep. Co. in 1960s (The Sea Gull, The Crucible, Ring Round the Moon).
PICTURES: The North Star (debut, 1943), The Purple Heart, Rope, Enchantment, The Live By Night, Roseanna McCoy, Side Street, Our Very Own, Edge of Doom, Strangers on a Train, Behave Yourself, I Want You, O. Henry's Full House, Hans Christian Andersen, Story of Three Loves, Small Town Girl, Senso, Naked Street, Girl in the Red Velvet Swing, Rogue's Gallery, Something Creeping in the Dark, They Call Me Trinity, Replica of a Crime, Amuk, The Slasher, The Redhead with the Translucent Skin, Kill Me My Love, Planet Venus, Night Flight From Moscow, Man Called Neon, Arnold, Savage Lady, The Co-ed Murders, Deathmask, The Prowler, The Imagemaker.
TELEVISION: Series: One Life to Live (1976-7), As the World Turns (1986-8). Movies: The Challengers, The Lives of Jenny Dolan, Widow, Black Beauty. Guest: Playhouse of Stars, U.S. Steel Hour, Producer's Showcase, Climax, Ford Theatre, Playhouse 90, 20th Century Fox Hour, Robert Montgomery Presents, Arthur Murray Dance Party, Wagon Train, Masquerade Party, Kojak, 6 Million Dollar Man, Ellery Queen.

GRANATH, HERBERT A.
Executive. e. Fordham U. Started with ABC TV in sales, marketing and production. 1979, became v.p. of Capital Cities/ABC Video Enterprises Inc.; 1982-93, served as pres. of same; Oct. 1993, named pres. ABC Cable and International Broadcast Group, sr. v.p. Capital Cities/ABC Inc.

GRANT, DAVID MARSHALL
Actor. b. New Haven, CT, June 21, 1955. e. Yale School of Drama.
THEATER: NY: Sganarelle, Table Settings, The Tempest, Bent, The Survivor, Making Movies, Angels in America: Millenium Approaches/Perestroika. Regional: Bent (also dir.), Once in a Lifetime, Lake Boat, Free and Clear, True West, The Wager, Rat in the Skull, Snakebit (author).
PICTURES: French Postcards (debut, 1979), Happy Birthday Gemini, The End of August, American Flyers, The Big Town, Bat 21, Air America, Strictly Business, Forever Young.
TELEVISION: Series: thirtysomething. Movies: Kent State, Legs, Sessions, Dallas: The Early Years, What She Doesn't Know, Citizen Cohn, Through the Eyes of a Killer. Special: A Doonesbury Special (voice). Pilot: Graham. Host: The Legend of Billy the Kid.

GRANT, HUGH
Actor. b. London, Eng., Sept. 9, 1960. e. New Coll., Oxford U. Acted with OUDS before landing role in Oxford Film Foundation's Privileged. Acted at Nottingham Playhouse and formed revue group, The Jockeys of Norfolk.
PICTURES: Privileged (debut, 1982), Maurice, White Mischief, The Lair of the White Worm, The Dawning, Remando al Viento (Rowing With the Wind), Bengali Night, Impromptu, Crossing the Line, The Remains of the Day, Night Train to Venice, Sirens, Four Weddings and a Funeral (BAFTA & Golden Globe Awards), Bitter Moon, The Englishman Who Went Up a Hill But Came Down a Mountain, Nine Months, An Awfully Big Adventure, Restoration, Sense and Sensibility, Extreme Measures (also prod.).
TELEVISION: Mini-Series: The Last Place on Earth. Series: The Demon Lover, Ladies in Charge. Movies/Specials: The

Detective, Handel: Honour, Profit and Pleasure, Jenny's War, The Lady and the Highwayman, Champagne Charlie, 'Til We Meet Again, Our Sons (U.S.), The Changeling.

GRANT, LEE
Actress. r.n. Lyova Rosenthal. b. New York, NY, Oct. 31, 1931. m. producer Joseph Feury. Daughter is actress Dinah Manoff. At 4 was member of Metropolitan Opera Company; played princess in L'Orocolo. Member of the American Ballet at 11. e. Juilliard Sch. of Music, studied voice, violin and dance. At 18 with road co. Oklahoma as understudy. Acting debut: Joy to the World.
THEATER: acted in a series of one-acters at ANTA with Henry Fonda. Detective Story (Critics Circle Award, 1949), Lo and Behold, A Hole in the Head, Wedding Breakfast; road co. Two for the Seesaw, The Captains and the Kings; toured with Electra, Silk Stockings, St. Joan, Arms and the Man, The Maids (Obie Award), Prisoner of Second Avenue.
PICTURES: Detective Story (debut, 1951; Acad. Award nom.), Storm Fear, Middle of the Night, Affair of the Skin, The Balcony, Terror in the City, Divorce American Style, In the Heat of the Night, Valley of the Dolls, Buona Sera Mrs. Campbell, The Big Bounce, Marooned, The Landlord (Acad. Award nom.), There Was a Crooked Man, Plaza Suite, Portnoy's Complaint, The Internecine Project, Shampoo (Academy Award, best supporting actress, 1975), Voyage of the Damned (Acad. Award nom.), Airport '77, Damien: Omen II, The Swarm, The Mafu Cage, When You Comin' Back Red Ryder, Little Miss Marker, Charlie Chan and the Curse of the Dragon Queen, Visiting Hours, Teachers, The Big Town, Defending Your Life, Under Heat. Dir.: Tell Me a Riddle, Willmar Eight, Staying Together.
TELEVISION: Series: Search for Tomorrow (1953-4), Peyton Place (Emmy Award, 1965), Fay. Guest: Studio One, The Kraft Theatre, Slattery's People, The Fugitive, Ben Casey, The Nurses, The Defenders, East Side/West Side, One Day at a Time, Bob Hope Show (Emmy nom.). Movies: Night Slaves, The Love Song of Bernard Kempenski, BBC's The Respectful Prostitute, The Neon Ceiling (Emmy Award, 1971), Ransom for a Dead Man, Lt. Schuster's Wife, Partners in Crime, What Are Best Friends For?, Perilous Voyage, The Spell, Million Dollar Face, For Ladies Only, Thou Shalt Not Kill, Bare Essence, Will There Really Be A Morning?, The Hijacking of the Achille Lauro, She Said No, Something to Live For: The Alison Gertz Story, In My Daughter's Name, Citizen Cohn. Mini-Series: Backstairs at the White House, Mussolini--The Untold Story. Special: Plaza Suite. Director: Nobody's Child, Shape of Things, When Women Kill, A Matter of Sex, Down and Out in America, No Place Like Home, Following Her Heart.

GRANT, RICHARD E.
Actor. b. Mbabane, Swaziland, May 5, 1957. e. Cape Town U., South Africa (combined English and drama course). Co-founded multi-racial Troupe Theatre Company with fellow former students and members of Athol Fugard and Yvonne Bryceland's Space Theatre, acting in and directing contemporary and classic plays. Moved to London 1982 where performed in fringe and rep. theater. Nominated most promising newcomer in Plays and Players, 1985, for Tramway Road.
PICTURES: Withnail and I, Hidden City, How to Get Ahead in Advertising, Killing Dad, Mountains of the Moon, Henry and June, Warlock, L.A. Story, Hudson Hawk, The Player, Bram Stoker's Dracula, Franz Kafka's It's A Wonderful Life (short), The Age of Innocence, Ready to Wear (Pret-a-Porter), Jack and Sarah, Twelfth Night.
TELEVISION: Series: Sweet Sixteen. Movies/Specials: Honest Decent and True, Lizzie's Pictures, Codename Kyril, Thieves in the Night (also released theatrically), Here Is the News, Suddenly Last Summer, Hard Times, Bed.

GRASGREEN, MARTIN
Executive. b. New York, NY, July 1, 1925. Entered m.p. ind. 1944, Columbia Pictures in contract dept. Promoted to travelling auditor 1947. Appt. office mgr. Omaha branch 1948; salesman Omaha, 1950. To Indianapolis, 1952, as city salesman; transferred to Cleveland as sales mgr., 1953. Left Columbia in 1960 to become 20th-Fox branch mgr. in Cleveland. Transferred to Philadelphia in 1965 as branch mgr.; transferred to NY in 1967 as Eastern dist. mgr. Resigned in 1970 to form Paragon Pictures, prod.-dist. co. 1975, formed Lanira Corp., representing producers for U.S. sales and dist. of films in U.S. Retired 1980.

GRASSHOFF, ALEX
Director. b. Boston, MA, Dec. 10, 1930. e. USC. 3 Acad. Award nominations for feature documentaries; Really Big Family; Journey to the Outer Limits; Young Americans (Acad. Award, 1968).
PICTURES: A Billion For Boris, J.D. and the Salt Flat Kid, The Last Dinosaur, The Jailbreakers.
TELEVISION: Series: The Rockford Files, Toma, Chips, Night Stalker, Barbary Coast, Movin' On. Specials: The Wave (Emmy Award), Future Shock (1973 Cannes Film Fest. Awards), Frank Sinatra, Family and Friends.

GRASSO, MARY ANN

Executive. b. Rome, NY, Nov. 3, 1952. e. U. of Calif., Riverside, B.A. art history, 1973; U. of Oregon, Eugene, Master of Library Science, 1974. Dir., Warner Research Collection, 1975-85; mgr., CBS-TV, docu-drama, 1985-88; Instructor 1980-88 UCLA Extension, American Film Institute. exec. dir. National Association of Theater Owners, 1988-present. Member: Acad. Motion Picture Arts & Sciences, Friends of the Motion Picture Pioneers, American Society of Association Executives , Phi Beta Kappa. Woman of Achievement, BPOA Awarded 1984. TV credits: The Scarlet O'Hara Wars, This Year's Blonde, The Silent Lovers, A Bunnies Tale, Embassy.

GRAVES, PETER

Actor. r.n. Peter Aurness. b. Minneapolis, MN, March 18, 1926. e. U. of Minnesota. Brother of actor James Arness. Played with bands, radio announcer, while at school; U.S. Air Force 2 yrs.; summer stock appearances.
PICTURES: Rogue River (debut, 1950), Fort Defiance, Red Planet Mars, Stalag 17, East of Sumatra, Beneath the 12-Mile Reef, Killers From Space, The Raid, Black Tuesday, Wichita, Long Gray Line, Night of the Hunter, Naked Street, Fort Yuma, Court Martial of Billy Mitchell, It Conquered the World, The Beginning of the End, Death in Small Doses, Poor White Trash (Bayou), Wolf Larsen, A Rage to Live, Texas Across the River, Valley of Mystery, The Ballad of Josie, Sergeant Ryker, The Five Man Army, Sidecar Racers, Parts: The Clonus Horror, Survival Run, Airplane!, Savannah Smiles, Airplane II: The Sequel, Number One With a Bullet, Addams Family Values.
TELEVISION: Series: Fury, Whiplash, Court-Martial, Mission Impossible, New Mission: Impossible. Movies: A Call to Danger, The President's Plane is Missing, Scream of the Wolf, The Underground Man, Where Have All the People Gone?, Dead Man on the Run, SST-Death Flight, The Rebels, Death on the Freeway, The Memory of Eva Ryker, 300 Miles for Stephanie, If It's Tuesday It Still Must Be Belgium. Mini-Series: Winds of War, War and Remembrance. Host/narrator: Discover! The World of Science, Biography.

GRAVES, RUPERT

Actor. b. Weston-Super-Mare, England, June 30, 1963. Before film debut worked as a clown with the Delta travelling circus in England.
THEATER: The Killing of Mr. Toad, 'Tis Pity She's a Whore, St. Ursula's in Danger, Sufficient Carbohydrates, Amadeus, Torch Song Trilogy, Candida, Pitchfork Disney, History of Tom Jones, A Madhouse in Goa, A Midsummer Night's Dream, Design for Living.
PICTURES: A Room with a View, Maurice, A Handful of Dust, The Children, Where Angels Fear to Tread, Damage, The Madness of King George, The Innocent Sleep, Different for Girls.
TELEVISION: Vice Versa, All for Love, A Life of Puccini, Fortunes of War, The Plot to Kill Hitler, The Sheltering Desert, Union Matters, Starting Out, Royal Celebration, Good and Bad at Games, Inspector Morse, Doomsday Gun.

GRAY, COLEEN

Actress. r.n. Doris Jensen. b. Staplehurst, NB, Oct. 23, 1922. e. Hamline U., B.A. summa cum laude, 1943, Actor's Lab. m. Fritz Zeiser. Member: Nat'l Collegiate Players, Kappa Phi, a capella choir, little theatres, 1943-44.
PICTURES: State Fair (debut, 1945), Kiss of Death, Nightmare Alley, Fury at Furnace Creek, Red River, Sleeping City, Riding High, Father Is a Bachelor, Apache Drums, Lucky Nick Cain, Models Inc., Kansas City Confidential, Sabre Jet, Arrow in the Dust, The Fake, The Vanquished, Las Vegas Shakedown, Twinkle in God's Eye, Tennessee's Partner, The Killing, Wild Dakotas, Death of a Scoundrel, Frontier Gambler, Black Whip, Star in the Dust, The Vampire, Hell's Five Hours, Copper Sky, Johnny Rocco, The Leech Woman, The Phantom Planet, Town Tamer, P.J., The Late Liz, Cry from the Mountain.
TELEVISION: Series: Window on Main Street, Days of Our Lives, (1966-67), Bright Promise (1968-72). Guest: Family Affair, Ironside, Bonanza, Judd for the Defense, Name of the Game, The FBI, The Bold Ones, World Premiere, Mannix, Sixth Sense, McCloud, Tales from the Dark Side. Movies: Ellery Queen: Don't Look Behind You, The Best Place to Be.

GRAY, DULCIE

C.B.E., F.L.S., F.R.S.A. Actress b. Malaya, Nov. 20, 1919. e. Webber Douglas Sch. Stage debut 1939, Aberdeen, Hay Fever, Author: Love Affair (play), 18 detective novels, book of short stories. 8 radio plays; co-author with husband Michael Denison, An Actor and His World; Butterflies on My Mind, The Glanville Women, Anna Starr; Mirror Image, Looking Forward Looking Back.
THEATER: Over 50 West End plays including Little Foxes, Brighton Rock, Dear Ruth, Rain on the Just, Candida, An Ideal Husband (1965, 1962, 1996 London & NY), Where Angels Fear to Tread, Heartbreak House, On Approval, Happy Family, No. 10, Out of the Question, Village Wooing, Wild

Duck, At The End of the Day, The Pay Off, A Murder Has Been Announced, Bedroom Farce, A Coat of Varnish, School for Scandal, The Living Room, Tartuffe, Cavell, Pygmalion, The School Mistress (Chicester), Two of a Kind.
PICTURES: Two Thousand Women, A Man About the House, Mine Own Executioner, My Brother Jonathan, The Glass Mountain, They Were Sisters Wanted for Murder, The Franchise Affair, Angels One Five, There Was a Young Lady, A Man Could Get Killed, The Trail of the Pink Panther, The Curse of the Pink Panther, The Black Crow.
TELEVISION: Milestones, The Will, Crime Passionel, Art and Opportunity, Fish in the Family, The Governess, What the Public Wants, Lesson in Love, The Happy McBaines, Winter Cruise, The Letter, Tribute to Maugham, Virtue, Beautiful Forever, East Lynne, Unexpectedly Vacant, The Importance of Being Earnest, This Is Your Life (1977; and with Michael Denison, 1995), Crown Court, Making Faces, Read All About It, The Voysey Inheritance, Life After Death, The Pink Pearl, Britain in the Thirties, Rumpole (The Old Boy Net.), Cold Warrior, Hook, Line and Sinker, Howard's Way (series; 6 yrs.), Three Up, Two Down, The Time and the Place.

GRAY, LINDA

Actress. b. Santa Monica, CA, Sept. 12, 1940.
PICTURES: Under the Yum Yum Tree, Palm Springs Weekend, Dogs, Fun With Dick and Jane, Oscar.
TELEVISION: Series: Dallas, Model Inc. Guest: Touched By an Angel. Movies: The Big Ripoff, Murder in Peyton Place, The Grass is Always Greener Over the Septic Tank, Two Worlds of Jennie Logan, Haywire, The Wild and the Fire, Not in Front of the Children, The Entertainers, Highway Heartbreaker, Moment of Truth: Why My Daughter?, Bonanza: The Return, To My Daughter with Love, Accidental Meeting, Moment of Truth: Broken Pledges.

GRAY, SPALDING

Performance artist, Actor, Writer. b. Barrington, RI, June 5, 1941. Began career as actor in 1965 at Alley Theater, Housten, then off-B'way in Tom Paine at LaMama Co. In 1969 joined the Wooster Group, experimental performance group. Has written and performed autobiographical monologues (Three Places in Rhode Island, Sex and Death to the Age 14, Swimming to Cambodia, Monster in a Box, Gray's Anatomy) throughout U.S, Europe and Australia. Taught theater workshops for adults and children and is recipient of Guggenheim fellowship. Artist in resident Mark Taper Forum, 1986-87. B'way debut: Our Town (1988).
PICTURES: Actor: Almost You, The Killing Fields, Hard Choices, True Stories, Swimming to Cambodia (also s.p.), Stars and Bars, Clara's Heart, Beaches, Heavy Petting, Straight Talk, Monster in a Box (also s.p.), The Pickle, King of the Hill, Twenty Bucks, The Paper, Bad Company, Beyond Rangoon, Drunks, Diabolique.
TELEVISION: Special: Terrors of Pleasure (HBO). Movies: The Image, To Save a Child, Zelda.

GRAY, THOMAS K.

Executive, producer. b. New York City, N. Y., July 1, 1945. e. U. of Arizona, B.A., post grad work at American Graduate School of Int'l Management, Phoenix. Began career as management trainee with United Atists film exchange in Spain, 1970, and year later became managing director, UA, Chile. Also managing director for UA, New Zealand, 1972; Columbia, 1973; South and East Africa, 1974. Joined Cinema Int'l Corp., London, as exec. assist. to co-chairman, 1974, and moved up to managing director of CIC/Warner, South Africa, 1976. Returned to UA as vice pres. Far East, Latin America, Africa and Australia, 1977. Joined Golden Communications Overseas Ltd., London, as vice pres. foreign sales, 1980. With Golden Harvest Films, Inc. since 1984 as sr. vice. pres., production. Executive in charge of prod. for Golden Harvest features: Flying, The Protector, China O'Brien, China O'Brien II, A Show of Force, Teenage Mutant Ninja Turtles, Best of Martial Arts (prod.), Teenage Mutant Ninja Turtles II: Secret of the Ooze (prod.), Teenage Mutant Ninja Turtles III. 1992, pres. and CEO of Rim Film Distribution Inc.

GRAYSON, KATHRYN

Actress, Singer. r.n. Zelma Hedrick. b. Winston-Salem, NC, Feb. 9, 1923. e. St. Louis schools.
THEATER: Camelot, Rosalinda, Merry Widow, Kiss Me Kate, Showboat.
PICTURES: Andy Hardy's Private Secretary (debut, 1941), The Vanishing Virginian, Rio Rita, Seven Sweethearts, Thousands Cheer; Anchors Aweigh, Ziegfeld Follies, Two Sisters from Boston, Till the Clouds Roll By, It Happened in Brooklyn, The Kissing Bandit, That Midnight Kiss, The Toast of New Orleans, Grounds for Marriage, Show Boat, Lovely to Look At, The Desert Song, So This Is Love, Kiss Me Kate, The Vagabond King.
TELEVISION: Guest: GE Theatre (Emmy nom.), Playhouse 90, Lux Playhouse, Murder She Wrote. Special: Die Fliedermaus.

GRAZER, BRIAN
Producer. b. Los Angeles, CA, July 12, 1951. e. U. of
Southern California. Started as legal intern at Warner Bros.;
later script reader (for Brut/Faberge) & talent agent. Joined
Edgar J. Scherick-Daniel Blatt Co.; then with Ron Howard as
partner in Imagine Films Entertainment. Received
NATO/ShoWest Producer of the Year Award, 1992.
PICTURES: Night Shift, Splash (also co-story), Real Genius,
Spies Like Us, Armed and Dangerous (also co-story), Like
Father Like Son, Vibes, The 'Burbs, Parenthood, Cry-Baby
(co-exec. prod.), Kindergarten Cop, The Doors (co-exec.
prod.), Closet Land (co-exec. prod.), Backdraft (exec. prod.),
My Girl, Far and Away, Housesitter, Boomerang, CB4 (co-
exec. prod.), Cop and a Half, For Love or Money, My Girl 2,
Greedy, The Paper, The Cowboy Way, Apollo 13, Fear, Sgt.
Bilko, The Nutty Professor.
TELEVISION: *Movies*: Zuma Beach, Thou Shalt Not Commit
Adultery, Splash Too. Series (executive prod.): Shadow
Chasers, Take Five, Ohara, Parenthood. *Special*: Poison
(prod.)

GREEN, ADOLPH
Writer, Actor. b. New York, NY, Dec. 2, 1915. m. actress-
singer Phyllis Newman. Began career in the cabaret act The
Revuers with partner Betty Comden and Judy Holliday (1944).
THEATER: Wrote book, sketches and/or lyrics for many
Broadway shows including: On the Town (also actor), Billion
Dollar Baby, Bonanza Bound! (also actor), Two on the Aisle,
Wonderful Town (Tony Award for lyrics, 1953), Peter Pan
(Mary Martin), Say Darling, Bells Are Ringing, A Party with
Comden and Green (1959 & 1977), Do Re Mi, Subways Are
For Sleeping, Fade Out Fade In, Halleuljah Baby (Tony
Awards for lyrics & best musical, 1968), Applause (Tony
Award for book, 1970), Lorelei: Or Gentlemen Still Prefer
Blondes (new lyrics), By Bernstein (book), On the Twentieth
Century (Tony Awards for book & lyrics, 1978), A Doll's Life,
The Will Rogers Follies (Tony Award for lyrics, 1991).
PICTURES: *Writer* (with Betty Comden): Good News, On the
Town, The Barkleys of Broadway, Take Me Out to the Ball
Game (co-lyrics), Singin' in the Rain, The Band Wagon, It's
Always Fair Weather, Auntie Mame, What a Way to Go. *Actor*:
Greenwich Village, Simon, My Favorite Year, Lily in Love,
Garbo Talks, I Want to Go Home.

GREEN, GUY
Director. b. Somerset, Eng. Nov. 5, 1913. Joined Film
Advertising Co. as projectionist & camera asst. 1933; camera
asst., Elstree Studios (BIP) 1935; started as camera operator
on films including One of Our Aircraft Is Missing, In Which We
Serve, This Happy Breed. 1944: Director of Photography; Dir
of Allied Film Makers Ltd.
PICTURES: *Dir. of Photography*: The Way Ahead, Great
Expectations (Academy Award, 1947), Oliver Twist, Captain
Horatio Hornblower, I Am a Camera. *Director*: River Boat
(debut, 1954), Portrait of Alison, Tears for Simon, House of
Secrets, The Snorkel, Desert Patrol (Sea of Sand), The Angry
Silence, The Mark, Light in the Piazza, Diamond Head, A
Patch of Blue (also co-exec. prod., s.p.), Pretty Polly (A Matter
of Innocence), The Magus, A Walk in the Spring Rain (also co-
exec. prod.), Luther, Once Is Not Enough, The Devil's
Advocate.
TELEVISION: (U.S.) Incredible Journey of Dr. Meg Laurel;
Isabel's Choice; Jennifer: A Woman's Story; Arthur Hailey's
Strong Medicine, Jimmy B. and Andre, Inmates.

GREEN, JACK N.
Cinematographer. b. San Francisco. Started as camera oper-
ator for Bruce Surtees.
PICTURES: *Camera operator*: Fighting Mad, Firefox, Honky
Tonk Man, Risky Business, Sudden Impact, Tightrope, Beverly
Hills Cop, City Heat, Pale Rider, Ratboy. *Cinematographer*:
Heartbreak Ridge, Like Father Like Son, The Dead Pool, Bird,
Pink Cadillac, Race for Glory, White Hunter Black Heart, The
Rookie, Deceived, Unforgiven, Rookie of the Year, A Perfect
World, Bad Company, The Bridges of Madison County, The
Net, The Amazing Panda Adventure, Twister.

GREEN, JOSEPH
Executive, Producer, Director. b. Baltimore, MD, Jan. 28,
1938. e. U. of Maryland, B.A. Since 1970 has headed own distribution co. Joseph Green Pictures and released its library of
150 features to theatres, TV and cable.
PICTURES: The Brain that Wouldn't Die (dir., s.p.), The Perils
of P.K. (assoc. prod., dir.), Psychedelic Generation (prod., dir.,
s.p.).

GREEN, MALCOLM C.
Theatre Executive. b. Boston, MA, Mar. 1, 1925. e. Harvard
Coll. Began career as asst. mgr., Translux Theatre, Boston &
Revere Theatre, Revere, MA. Treas., Interstate Theatres,
1959-64. Film Buyer, Interstate, 1959-72. Formed Theatre
Management Services in 1972 with H. Rifkin and P. Lowe and
Cinema Centers Corp. with Rifkin and Lowe families in 1973.

Treas., Cinema Center, & pres., Theatre Mgmt. Services.
Cinema Center grew to 116 theatres in 6 Northeast states,
sold to Hoyts Cinemas Corp., 1986. Sr. v.p., Hoyts Cinemas
Corp. 1986-89. Pres., Theatre Owners of New England, 1964-
65; chmn bd., 1965-69; treas., 1970-84. Pres., NATO, 1986-
88, Chmn Bd, 1988-90. Dir., Natl. Assoc. Theatre Owners.
Chmn., NATO of New York State. Director, Vision Foundation.
Dir., The Lyric Stage, Boston 1990-94; dir. & v.p., New
Hampshire Music Festival, 1988-1996.

GREENAWAY, PETER
Director, Writer. b. Newport, Wales, Apr. 5, 1942. Trained as
a painter, first exhibition was at Lord's Gallery in 1964. Started
making short films and documentaries in 1966, including: A
Walk Through H, The Falls, Act of God, Vertical Features
Remake. Directorial feature debut in 1982. Author of numer-
ous books including, 100 Objects to Represent the World, The
Physical Self, Les Bruits des Nuages.
PICTURES: The Draughtsman's Contract, A Zed and Two
Noughts, The Belly of an Architect, Drowning By Numbers,
The Cook The Thief His Wife and Her Lover, Prospero's
Books, The Baby of Macon, The Pillow Book.
TELEVISION: Death in the Seine, series of 9 Cantos from
Dante's Inferno in collaboration with painter Tom Phillips, MIs
for Man Music Mozart, Darwin.

GREENE, CLARENCE
Producer, Writer. b. New York, NY, 1918. e. St. John's U.,
L.L.B. Author of play Need a Lawyer. Formed Greene-Rouse
prods. with Russell Rouse; Acad. Oscar co-orig. story Pillow
Talk. Acad. award nom. co-orig. s.p. The Well. Two Writers
Guild nominations. Writers Guild award outstanding teleplay,
One Day in the Life of Ivan Denisovitch. Co-prod., writer TV
series Tightrope.
PICTURES: *Prod., collab. s.p.*: The Town Went Wild, D.O.A.,
The Well, The Thief, Wicked Woman, New York Confidential, A
House Is Not a Home, The Oscar. *Prod.*: Unidentified Flying
Objects, The Gun Runners, Fastest Gun Alive, Thunder in the
Sun, The Caper of the Golden Bulls, D.O.A. (story, 1988).

GREENE, DAVID
Director, Writer. b. Manchester, Eng., Feb. 22, 1921. Early
career as actor. To U.S. with Shakespeare company early
1950's; remained to direct TV in Canada, New York and
Hollywood.
PICTURES: The Shuttered Room, Sebastian, The Strange
Affair, I Start Counting, Godspell, Gray Lady Down, Hard
Country (prod., dir.).
TELEVISION: The Defenders. *Movies*: The People Next Door,
Mdame Sin, Count of Monte Cristo, Friendly Fire, The Trial of
Lee Harvey Oswald, A Vacation in Hell, The Choice, World
War III, Rehearsal For Murder, Take Your Best Shot, Ghost
Dancing, Prototype, Sweet Revenge, The Guardian, Fatal
Vision (Emmy nom.), Guilty Conscience, This Child Is Mine,
Vanishing Act, Miles to Go, Circle of Violence, The Betty Ford
Story, After the Promise; Inherit the Wind, Liberace: Behind
the Music, Red Earth, White Earth; The Penthouse (dir., exec.
prod.), Small Sacrifices (Peabody Award), Honor Thy Mother.

GREENE, ELLEN
Actress, Singer. b. Brooklyn, NY, Feb. 22. e. Ryder Coll. After
coll. joined musical road show. Appeared in cabaret act at The
Brothers & the Sisters Club and Reno Sweeney's, NY. Off-
B'way debut, Rachel Lily Rosenbloom. B'way in the The Little
Prince and The Aviator. With NY Shakespeare Fest. in the
Boom Boom Room, The Sorrows of Steven, The Threepenny
Opera (Tony nom.). Film debut Next Stop, Greenwich Village
(1976). Off B'way co-starred in musical Little Shop of Horrors
1982, repeated role in film. Also Off-B'way in Weird Romance.
L.A. stage: David's Mother.
PICTURES: Next Stop Greenwich Village (debut, 1976), I'm
Dancing as Fast as I Can, Little Shop of Horrors, Me and Him,
Talk Radio, Pump Up the Volume, Stepping Out, Rock a
Doodle (voice), Fathers and Sons, Naked Gun 33 1/3: The
Final Insult, Wagons East!, The Professional.
TELEVISION: *Special*: Rock Follies. *Movie*: Glory Glory. *Mini-
Series*: Seventh Avenue. Pilot: Road Show.

GREENE, GRAHAM
Actor. b. Six Nations Reserve, Ontario, Canada. Member of
the Oneida tribe. First show business job as audio technician
for several rock bands. Began acting in theater in England.
THEATER: Diary of a Crazy Boy, Coming Through Slaughter,
Crackwalker, Jessica, Dry Lips Oughta Move to Kapuskasing.
PICTURES: Running Brave, Revolution, Powwow Highway,
Dances With Wolves (Acad. Award nom.), Thunderheart,
Clearcut, Savage Land, Rain Without Thunder, Benefit of the
Doubt, Maverick, North, Camilla, Die Hard With a Vengeance.
TELEVISION: *U.S.*: *Series*: Northern Exposure. *Movies*:
Unnatural Causes, The Last of His Tribe, Cooperstown, Huck
and the King of Hearts, Rugged Gold. *Guest*: Adderly, *L.A.
Law*. Canada: *Series*: 9B, Spirit Bay. Movies: Murder Sees the
Light, The Great Detective, Street Legal.

GREENFIELD, LEO

Executive, b. New York, NY, April 26, 1916. e. St. John's U, Coll. of Arts & Sciences. v.p., gen. sales mgr. Buena Vista, 1962; Columbia road show sales mgr. 1966; v.p.-gen. sales mgr., Cinerama Rel. Corp. 1966; pres.-gen. sales mgr., Warners, 1969; sr. v.p. worldwide distribution, MGM 1975; v.p. distribution & marketing, Marble Arch Productions, 1978; exec. v.p. Associated Film Distribution, 1979; pres., distribution, F/M, 1986; pres., dist., Kings Road Entertainment, 1987; pres., Greenlee Assoc., 1988.

GREENHUT, ROBERT

Producer. b. New York, NY. e. Univ. of Miami. Began career as prod. asst. on Arthur Hiller's The Tiger Makes Out, 1967. Worked as prod. manager and asst. director on such films as Pretty Poison, The Night They Raided Minsky's, Where's Poppa?, The Owl and the Pussycat, Husbands, Born to Win, Panic in Needle Park, The Last of the Red Hot Lovers. Received Crystal Apple from city of NY and Eastman Kodak Award for lifetime achievement.
PICTURES: Huckleberry Finn (assoc. prod.), Lenny (assoc. prod.), Dog Day Afternoon (assoc. prod.), The Front (assoc. prod.), Annie Hall (exec. prod.), Interiors (exec. prod.), Hair (assoc. prod.), Manhattan (prod.), Stardust Memories (prod.), Arthur (prod.), A Midsummer Night's Sex Comedy (prod.), The King of Comedy (exec. prod.), Zelig (prod.), Broadway Danny Rose (prod.), The Purple Rose of Cairo (prod.), Hannah and Her Sisters (prod.), Heartburn (prod.), Radio Days (prod.), September (prod.), Big (exec. prod.), Another Woman (prod.), Working Girl (exec. prod.), New York Stories (prod.), Crimes and Misdemeanors (prod.), Quick Change (prod.), Postcards From the Edge (co-exec. prod.), Alice (prod.), Regarding Henry (exec. prod.), Shadows and Fog (prod.), A League of Their Own (prod.), Husbands and Wives (prod.), Manhattan Murder Mystery (prod.), Renaissance Man (prod.), Wolf (co-exec. prod.), Bullets Over Broadway (prod.), Mighty Aphrodite (prod.), Everyone Says I Love You (prod.), The Preacher's Wife (prod.).
TELEVISION: *Movie*: Don't Drink the Water.

GREENWALD, ROBERT

Director, Producer, Teacher. b. New York, NY, Aug. 28, 1948. e. Antioch Coll., New School for Social Research. Teaches film and theatre at NYU, New Lincoln, New School. Formed Robert Greenwald Prods.
THEATER: A Sense of Humor, I Have a Dream, Me and Bessie.
PICTURES: *Director*: Xanadu, Sweet Hearts Dance (also exec. prod.), Hear No Evil.
TELEVISION: *Prod.*: The Desperate Miles, 21 Hours at Munich, Delta Country USA, Escape From Bogen County, Getting Married, Portrait of a Stripper, The Texas Rangers, The First Time. *Exec. prod.*: My Brother's Wife, Hiroshima, Zelda, The Portrait, Daddy, Scattered Dreams, Murder in New Hampshire, Death in Small Doses. *Director*: Sharon: Portrait of a Mistress, In the Custody of Strangers, The Burning Bed, Katie: Portrait of a Centerfold, Flatbed Annie and Sweetpie: Lady Truckers, Shattered Spirits (also exec. prod.), Forgotten Prisoners, A Woman of Independent Means (also co-exec. prod.).

GREENWOOD, BRUCE

Actor. b. Noranda, Quebec, Canada, Aug. 14, 1956. e. Univ. of British Columbia, London Sch. of Speech and Learning, AADA. Worked in Canadian theater and as lead singer/guitarist with blues/rock band in Vancouver before arriving in LA in 1983.
PICTURES: Bear Island (debut, 1980), First Blood, Malibu Bikini Shop, Another Chance, Wild Orchid, Passenger 57, Exotica, Paint Cans, Dream Man.
TELEVISION: *Series*: Legmen, St. Elsewhere, Knots Landing, Hardball, Nowhere Man. *Movies*: Peyton Place: The Next Generation, Destination: America, In the Line of Duty: The FBI Murders, Perry Mason: The Case of the All-Star Assassin, Spy, Summer Dreams: The Story of the Beach Boys, The Great Pretender, Rio Diablo, Adrift, The Heart of a Child, Bitter Vengeance, Treacherous Beauties, The Companion, Servants of Twilight, Little Kindappers, Twist of Fate, Woman on the Run: The Lawrencia Bembenek Story, Jazzle, The Judds: Love Can Build a Bridge. *Guest*: Hitchhiker, Jake and the Fatman, Road to Avonlea.

GREER, JANE

Actress. b. Washington, DC, Sept. 9, 1924. r.n. Bettyjane Greer. Orchestra singer; photograph as WAC on Life Magazine cover won screen debut in Pan-Americana (as Bettejane Greer).
PICTURES: Pan American (debut, 1945), Two O'Clock Courage, George White's Scandals; Dick Tracy (1st film as Jane Greer), Falcon's Alibi, Bamboo Blonde, Sunset Pass, Sinbad the Sailor, They Won't Believe Me, Out of the Past, Station West, Big Steal, You're in the Navy Now, The Company She Keeps, You For Me, The Prisoner of Zenda, Desperate

Search, The Clown, Down Among the Sheltering Palms, Run for the Sun, Man of a Thousand Faces, Where Love Has Gone, Billie, The Outfit, Against All Odds, Just Between Friends, Immediate Family.
TELEVISION: *Movie*: Louis L'Amour's The Shadow Riders. *Guest*: Murder She Wrote, Twin Peaks.

GREGORY, JOHN R.

Executive, Producer, Writer. b. Brooklyn, NY, Nov. 19, 1918. e. Grover Cleveland H.S., 1935, New Inst. of M.P. & Telev., 1952; Sls., adv. dept. Fotoshop, Inc., N.Y., 1938-42; Spec. Serv., Photo. instructor, chief projectionist, supv., war dept. theatres, U.S. Army, 1942-46; sls. mgr., J. L. Galef & Son, N.Y.; 1948-49, gen. mgr., Camera Corner Co.; 1949-58, pres.; City Film Center, Inc., 1957; exec. v.p., Talent Guild of New York, 1958; pres., Teleview Prods., Inc., 1961; executive producer, City Film Productions, 1970. Executive post-production supervisor, Jerry Liotta Films, 1977. Author of many articles in nat'l publications dealing with m.p. practices and techniques; tech. editor, Better Movie-Making magazine, 1962; editor, pub., National Directory of Movie-Making Information, 1963; assoc. ed., Photographic Product News, 1964; contrib. editor, U.S. Camera. M.P. columnist, contributing ed. Travel and Camera magazine, 1969; Advisory panelist, Photo-methods (N.Y.), 1975. Consultant, Photographic Guidance Council, 1957, assoc. Society of M.P. & Television-Engineers, 1952.

GREIST, KIM

Actress. b. Stamford, CT, May 12, 1958. e. New Sch. for Social Research.
THEATER: Second Prize: Two Months in Leningrad, Twelfth Night (NY Shakespeare Fest.).
PICTURES: C.H.U.D. (debut, 1984), Brazil, Manhunter, Throw Momma from the Train, Punchline, Why Me?, Homeward Bound: The Incredible Journey, Houseguest, Homeward Bound II: Lost in San Francisco.
TELEVISION: *Guest*: Miami Vice, Tales From the Darkside, Chicago Hope (recurring). *Movies*: Payoff, Duplicates, Roswell.

GREY, JENNIFER

Actress. b. New York, NY, Mar. 26, 1960. Father is actor Joel Grey. Appeared as dancer in Dr. Pepper commercial before making NY stage debut in Off-B'way play Album. B'way in The Twilight of the Golds.
PICTURES: Reckless (debut, 1984), Red Dawn, The Cotton Club, American Flyers, Ferris Bueller's Day Off, Dirty Dancing, Bloodhounds of Broadway, Stroke of Midnight (If the Shoe Fits), Wind.
TELEVISION: *Movies*: Murder in Mississippi, Criminal Justice, Eyes of a Witness, A Case for Murder.

GREY, JOEL

Actor, Singer, Dancer. b. Cleveland, OH, April 11, 1932. r.n. Joel Katz. Father was performer Mickey Katz; daughter is actress Jennifer Grey. e. Alexander Hamilton H.S., L.A. Acting debut at 9 years in On Borrowed Time at Cleveland Playhouse. Extensive nightclub appearances before returning to theatre and TV.
THEATER: *NY*: Come Blow Your Horn, Stop the World—I Want to Get Off, Half a Sixpence, Harry: Noon and Night, Littlest Revue, Cabaret (Tony Award, 1967), George M!, Goodtime Charley, The Grand Tour, Cabaret (1987, B'way revival). *Regional*: Herringbone.
PICTURES: About Face (debut, 1952), Calypso Heat Wave, Come September, Cabaret (Academy Award, best supporting actor, 1972), Man on a Swing, Buffalo Bill and the Indians or Sitting Bull's History Lesson, The Seven Percent Solution, Remo Williams: The Adventure Begins..., Kafka, The Player, The Music of Chance, The Fantasticks.
TELEVISION: *Specials*: Jack and the Beanstalk, George M! *Guest*: Maverick, December Bride, Ironside, Night Gallery, The Burt Bacharach Show, The Tom Jones Show, The Englebert Humperdinck Show, The Carol Burnett Show, The Julie Andrews Hour, Dallas, Brooklyn Bridge. *Movies*: Man on a String, Queenie.

GREY, VIRGINIA

Actress. b. Los Angeles, CA, March 22, 1917. Screen career started 1927 with Uncle Tom's Cabin.
PICTURES: Misbehaving Ladies, Secrets, Dames, The Firebird, The Great Ziegfeld, Rosalie, Test Pilot, The Hardys Ride High, Hullaballoo, Blonde Inspiration, The Big Store, Grand Central Murder, Idaho, Strangers in the Night, Blonde Ranson, Unconquered, Who Killed Doc Robbin, The Bullfighter and the Lady, Highway 301, Slaughter Trail, Desert Pursuit, Perilous Journey, Forty-Niners, Target Earth, Eternal Sea, Last Command, Rose Tattoo, All That Heaven Allows, Crime of Passion, Jeanne Eagles, The Restless Years, No Name on the Bullet, Portrait in Black, Tammy Tell Me True, Back Street, Bachelor In Paradise, Black Zoo, The Naked Kiss, Love Has Many Faces, Madame X, Rosie, Airport.

GRIECO, RICHARD
Actor. b. Watertown, NY, 1966. Started with Elite Modeling Agency. Studied acting at Warren Robertson Theatre Workshop appearing in prods. of Orphans, Golden Boy. As musician released album Waiting for the Sky to Fall.
PICTURES: Born to Ride, If Looks Could Kill, Mobsters, Tomcat: Dangerous Desires, Bolt.
TELEVISION: Series: One Life to Live, 21 Jump Street, Booker, Marker. Movies: Sin and Redemption, A Vow to Kill

GRIEM, HELMUT
Actor. b. Hamburg, Germany, 1940. e. Hamburg U.
PICTURES: The Girl From Hong Kong, The Damned, The Mackenzie Break, Cabaret, Ludwig, Children of Rage, Desert of the Tartars, Voyage of the Damned, Germany in Autumn, The Glass Cell, Sgt. Steiner (Breakthrough), Berlin Alexanderplatz, Malou, La Passante, The Second Victory.
TELEVISION: Mini-Series: Peter the Great.

GRIER, DAVID ALAN
Actor. b. Detroit, MI, June 30, 1955. e. Univ. of MI, Yale. Acted with Yale Rep.
THEATER: NY: A Soldier's Play, The First (Theatre World Award), Richard III, Dreamgirls, The Merry Wives of Windsor.
PICTURES: Streamers (debut, 1983), A Soldier's Story, Beer, From the Hip, Amazon Women on the Moon, Off Limits, I'm Gonna Git You Sucka, Me and Him, Loose Cannons, Almost an Angel, The Player, Boomerang, In the Army Now, Blankman, Tales From the Hood, Jumanji.
TELEVISION: Series: All Is Forgiven, In Living Color, The Preston Episodes (also co-exec. prod.).

GRIER, PAM
Actress. b. Winston-Salem, NC, 1949.
PICTURES: The Big Doll House, Big Bird Cage, Black Mama White Mama, Cool Breeze, Hit Man, Women in Cages, Coffy, Scream Blacula Scream, Twilight People, The Arena, Foxy Brown, Bucktown, Friday Foster, Sheba Baby, Drum, Greased Lightning, Fort Apache The Bronx, Tough Enough, Something Wicked This Way Comes, The Vindicator, On the Edge, Stand Alone, The Allnighter, Above the Law, The Package, Class of 1999, Bill & Ted's Bogus Journey, Posse, Original Gangstas, Mars Attacks.
TELEVISION: Mini-Series: Roots: The Next Generations. Movie: A Mother's Right: The Elizabeth Morgan Story. Guest: Miami Vice, Crime Story, Pacific Station, Frank's Place, The Cosby Show, Night Court, In Living Color, Sinbad Show, Fresh Prince of Bel Air.

GRIFFIN, MERV
Executive, Singer, Emcee. b. San Mateo, CA, July 6, 1925. e. U. of San Francisco. Host of The Merv Griffin Show, KFRC-Radio, 1945-48; vocalist, Freddy Martin's orch., 1948-52; recorded hit song I've Got a Lovely Bunch of Coconuts; contract Warner Bros., 1952-54; Prod. Finian's Rainbow, City Center, NY, 1955. Chairman, Merv Griffin Prods.
PICTURES: By the Light of the Silvery Moon, So This Is Love, Boy From Oklahoma, Phantom of the Rue Morgue, Hello Down There, Two Minute Warning, The Seduction of Joe Tynan, The Man With Two Brains, The Lonely Guy, Slapstick of Another Kind.
TELEVISION: Series: The Freddy Martin Show (vocalist), Summer Holiday, Morning Show, The Robert Q. Lewis Show, Keep Talking (emcee), Play Your Hunch (emcee), Saturday Prom, The Merv Griffin Show (1962-63), Talent Scouts, Word for Word, The Merv Griffin Show (1965-86; Emmy Award for writing, 2 Emmy Awards for hosting), Secrets Women Never Share (exec. prod., host, 1987). Creator: Jeopardy, Wheel of Fortune.

GRIFFIN, ANDY
Actor. b. Mount Airy, NC, June 1, 1926. e. U. of North Carolina. Began career as standup comedian, monologist, recording artist (What It Was Was Football, 1954). TV acting debut in U.S. Steel Hour production of No Time for Sergeants, which he later played on Broadway and film.
THEATER: B'way: No Time for Sergeants (Theatre World Award), Destry Rides Again.
PICTURES: A Face in the Crowd (debut, 1957), No Time for Sergeants, Onionhead, The Second Time Around, Angel in My Pocket, Hearts of the West, Rustler's Rhapsody, Spy Hard.
TELEVISION: Series: The Andy Griffith Show, The Headmaster, The New Andy Griffith Show, Salvage One, Matlock. Movies: Strangers in 7A, Go Ask Alice, Pray for the Wildcats, Winter Kill, Savages, Street Killing, Girl in the Empty Grave, Deadly Games, Salvage, Murder in Texas, For Lovers Only, Murder in Coweta County, The Demon Murder Case, Fatal Vision, Crime of Innocence, Diary of a Perfect Murder, Return to Mayberry, Under the Influence, Matlock: The Vacation (also co-exec. prod.), The Gift of Love, Gramps. Mini-Series: Washington Behind Closed Doors, Centennial, From Here to Eternity, Roots: The Next Generations.

GRIFFITH, MELANIE
Actress. b. New York, NY, Aug. 9, 1957. m. Anotnio Banderas. Mother is actress Tippi Hedren. Moved to Los Angeles at 4. e. Catholic academies until Hollywood Prof. Sch., 1974. Did some modeling before being cast in Night Moves at 16. Studied acting with Stella Adler, Harry Mastrogeorge and Sandra Seacat.
PICTURES: The Harrad Experiment (debut, 1973), Smile, Night Moves, The Drowning Pool, One on One, Joyride, Underground Aces, Roar, Fear City, Body Double, Something Wild, Cherry 2000, The Milagro Beanfield War, Stormy Monday, Working Girl (Acad. Award nom.), In the Spirit, Pacific Heights, The Bonfire of the Vanities, Paradise, Shining Through, A Stranger Among Us, Born Yesterday, Milk Money, Nobody's Fool, Now and Then, Two Much, Mulholland Falls, Lolita.
TELEVISION: Series: Carter Country. Mini-Series: Once an Eagle. Movies: Daddy I Don't Like This, Steel Cowboy, The Star Maker, She's in the Army Now, Golden Gate, Women & Men: Stories of Seduction (Hills Like White Elephants), Buffalo Girls. Guest: Vega$, Miami Vice, Alfred Hitchcock Presents.

GRILLO, BASIL F.
Executive. b. Angel's Camp, CA, Oct. 8, 1910. e. U. of California, Berkeley, A.B. Certified public accountant, exec. v.p., dir., Bing Crosby Ent., Inc., 1948-57; bus. mgr., Bing Crosby, 1945; co-organizer, dir., 3rd pres., & treas., Alliance of T.V. Film Producers, 1950-54; exec. prod., BCE, Inc., shows incl. Fireside Thea., Rebound, Royal Playhouse, The Chimps; dir., KCOP, Inc., 1957-60; dir KFOX, Inc., 1958-62; pres., dir., Bing Crosby Prods., 1955-72; dir., Seven Leagues Ent., Inc., 1958; dir. Electrovision Prods., 1970, CEO, Bing Crosby Enterprises.

GRIMALDI, ALBERTO
Producer. b. Naples, Italy, Mar. 28, 1925. Studied law, serving as counsel to Italian film companies, before turning to production with Italian westerns starring Clint Eastwood and Lee Van Cleef. Is owner of P.E.A. (Produzioni Europee Associate, s.r.l.).
PICTURES: For a Few Dollars More, The Good the Bad and the Ugly, The Big Gundown, Three Steps in Delirium, A Quiet Place in the Country, The Mercenary, Satyricon, Burn!, The Decameron, Man of the East, The Canterbury Tales, Last Tango in Paris, Bawdy Tales, Arabian Nights, Salo or the 100 Days of Sodom, Burnt Offerings, Fellini's Casanova, 1900, Illustrious Corpses, Lovers and Liars, Hurricane Rosy, Ginger and Fred.

GRIMES, GARY
Actor. b. San Francisco, CA, June 2, 1955. Family moved to L.A. when he was nine. Made film debut at 15 in Summer of '42, 1971. Voted Star of Tomorrow in QP poll, 1971.
PICTURES: Summer of '42, The Culpepper Cattle Company, Cahill: U.S. Marshal, Class of '44, The Spikes Gang, Gus.
TELEVISION: Mini-Series: Once an Eagle.

GRIMES, TAMMY
Actress. b. Boston, MA, Jan. 30, 1934. Daughter is actress Amanda Plummer. e. Stephens Coll, The Neighborhood Playhouse. Recipient: Woman of Achievment Award (ADL), Mother of the Year Award, Mayor's Outstanding Contribution to the Arts Award (NYC). Member: bd. dirs. & v.p. of the Upper East-Side Historic Preservation District (NYC).
THEATER: Look After Lulu (Theatre World Award, 1959), Clerambard, The Littlest Revue, Stratford (Ont.) Shakespeare Fest., Bus Stop, The Cradle Will Rock, The Unsinkable Molly Brown (Tony Award, 1961), Rattle of a Simple Man, High Spirits, Private Lives (Tony Award, 1970), Trick, California Suite, 42nd Street, Tartuffe, A Month in the Country, The Guardsman, The Millionairess, Imaginary Invalid, The Importance of Being Earnest, Mademoiselle Columbe, Blythe Spirit, Waltz of the Toreadors, Molly, Taming of the Shrew, Orpheus Descending, Tammy Grimes: A Concert in Words and Music, A Little Night Music, Pygmalion.
PICTURES: Three Bites of the Apple (debut, 1967), Play It as It Lays, Somebody Killed Her Husband, The Runner Stumbles, Can't Stop the Music, The Last Unicorn (voice), The Stuff, No Big Deal, America, Mr. North, Slaves of New York, A Modern Affair.
TELEVISION: Specials: Omnibus, Hollywood Sings, Hour of Great Mysteries, Four Poster. Guest: St. Elsewhere, The Young Riders. Series: The Tammy Grimes Show. Movies: The Other Man, The Horror at 37,000 Feet, The Borrowers, You Can't Go Home Again, An Invasion of Privacy.

GRISSMER, JOHN
Executive, Producer, Director. b. Houston, TX, Aug. 28, 1933. e. Xavier U., B.S., 1955; Catholic U., M.F.A., dramatic writing, 1959. Taught drama courses, directed student productions at U. of CT & American U., Washington, DC. Produced and co-wrote House That Cried Murder, 1973; co-produced,

wrote and directed Scalpel; directed Nightmare at Shadow Woods. Partner in P.J. Productions Co. & North Salem Prods., Inc. Guest Director, Xavier Univ. Theatre.

GRIZZARD, GEORGE
Actor. b. Roanoke Rapids, NC, April 1, 1928. e. U. of North Carolina, B.A., 1949. Has been member of Arena Stage, Washington, D.C., APA repertory company and Tyrone Guthrie resident company in Minneapolis.
THEATER: The Desperate Hours. (B'way debut, 1955), The Happiest Millionaire (Theatre World Award), The Disenchanted, Face of a Hero, Big Fish, Little Fish, Who's Afraid of Virginia Woolf?, The Glass Menagerie, You Know I Can't Hear You When the Water's Running, The Gingham Dog, Inquest, The Country Girl, The Creation of the World and Other Business, Crown Matrimonial, The Royal Family, California Suite, Man and Superman, Another Antigone, Show Boat, A Delicate Balance (Tony Award, 1996).
PICTURES: From the Terrace, Advise and Consent, Warning Shot, Happy Birthday Wanda June, Comes a Horseman, Firepower, Seems Like Old Times, Wrong Is Right, Bachelor Party.
TELEVISION: Movies: Travis Logan D.A., Indict & Convict, The Stranger Within, Attack on Terror: The FBI vs. the Ku Klux Klan, The Lives of Jenny Dolan, The Night Rider, Attica, Not In Front of the Children, The Deliberate Stranger, Underseige, That Secret Sunday, International Airport, Embassy, The Shady Hill Kidnapping, Oldest Living Graduate (Emmy Award, 1980), Perry Mason: The Case of the Scandalous Scoundrel, David, Caroline?, Iran: Days of Crisis, Not in My Family, Triumph Over Disaster: The Hurricane Andrew Story. Special: Enemy of the People. Mini-Series: The Adams Chronicles, Robert Kennedy and His Times, Queen, Scarlett.

GRODIN, CHARLES
Actor, Director, Writer. b. Pittsburgh, PA, April 21, 1935. e. U. of Miami. After time with Pittsburgh Playhouse studied acting with Uta Hagen and Lee Strasberg; began directing career in New York 1965 as asst. to Gene Saks. Has appeared in some 75 plays all over the country. Has also written scripts, produced plays. Books: It Would Be So Nice If You Weren't Here, How I Get Through Life, We're Ready for You Mr. Grodin.
THEATER: Tchin-Tchin (B'way debut, 1962), Absence of a Cello, Same Time Next Year, It's a Glorious Day... And All That (dir., co-author), Lovers and Other Strangers (dir.), Thieves (prod., dir.), Unexpected Guests (prod., dir.), Price of Fame (also author), One of the All-Time Greats (author).
PICTURES: Sex and the College Girl (debut, 1964), Rosemary's Baby, Catch-22, The Heartbreak Kid, 11 Harrowhouse (also adapt.), King Kong, Thieves, Heaven Can Wait, Real Life, Sunburn, It's My Turn, Seems Like Old Times, The Incredible Shrinking Woman, The Great Muppet Caper, The Lonely Guy, The Woman in Red, Movers and Shakers (also s.p., co-prod.), Last Resort, Ishtar, The Couch Trip, You Can't Hurry Love, Midnight Run, Taking Care of Business, Beethoven, Dave, So I Married an Axe Murderer, Heart and Souls, Beethoven's 2nd, Clifford, It Runs in the Family (My Summer Story).
TELEVISION: Specials (writer): Candid Camera (also dir.), The Simon & Garfunkel Special, Paul Simon Special (also dir.; Emmy Award for writing, 1978). Specials (dir.): Acts of Love and Other Comedies, Paradise (also prod.). Actor: Guest: The Defenders, My Mother the Car, The FBI, Guns of Will Sonnett, The Big Valley. Specials: Grown Ups, Love Sex and Marriage (also writer), Charley's Aunt. Movies: Just Me and You, The Grass Is Always Greener over the Septic Tank. Mini-Series: Fresno. Series: Charles Grodin (talk).

GROSBARD, ULU
Director. b. Antwerp, Belgium. Jan. 9, 1929. e. U. of Chicago, B.A. 1950, M.A. 1952. Trained at Yale Sch. of Drama 1952-53. Asst. dir. to Eliza Kazan on Splendor in the Grass, 1961; asst. dir.: West Side Story, The Hustler, The Miracle Worker. Unit mgr.: The Pawnbroker.
THEATER: The Days and Nights of Beebee Fenstermaker, The Subject Was Roses, A View From the Bridge, The Investigation, That Summer—That Fall, The Price, American Buffalo, The Woods, The Wake of Jamie Foster, The Tenth Man.
PICTURES: The Subject Was Roses (debut, 1968), Who Is Harry Kellerman and Why Is He Saying Those Terrible Things About Me? (also co-prod.), Straight Time, True Confessions, Falling in Love, Georgia (also co-prod.).

GROSS, KENNETH H.
Executive. b. Columbus, OH, Feb. 12, 1949. e. New School for Social Research, U. of London. Conducted film seminars at New School and active in several indep. film projects. Published film criticism in various journals and magazines. Joined ABC Ent. 1971. Named supvr. of feature films for ABC-TV. Appt. mgr. of feature films, 1974. Promoted 1975 to program exec., ABC Ent. Prime Time/West Coast. Promoted to

exec. prod., movies for TV, ABC Ent. 1976 in L.A.; 1978, with literary agency F.C.A. as partner in L.A.; 1979 prod. for Lorimar; then with Intl. Creative Mgt; 1982, formed own literary talent agency, The Literary Group; 1985, merged agency with Robinson-Weintraub & Assoc. to become Robinson-Weintraub-Gross & Assoc. 1993, founding partner of Paradigm, a talent and literary agency.

GROSS, MARY
Actress. b. Chicago, IL, March 25, 1953. Brother is actor Michael Gross. e. Loyola U. Is also student of the harp. In 1980 discovered by John Belushi who saw her perform as resident member of Chicago's Second City comedy troupe, where she won Chicago's Joseph Jefferson Award as best actress for the revue, Well, I'm Off to the Thirty Years War. First came to national attention as regular on Saturday Night Live, 1981-85.
PICTURES: Club Paradise, The Couch Trip, Casual Sex?, Big Business, Feds, Troop Beverly Hills, The Santa Clause.
TELEVISION: Series: Saturday Night Live, The People Next Door. Specials: Comic Relief I, The Second City 25th Anniversary Reunion.

GROSS, MICHAEL
Actor. b. Chicago, IL, June 21, 1947. m. casting dir. Elza Bergeron. Sister is actress Mary Gross. e. U. Illinois, B.A., Yale School of Drama, M.F.A.
THEATER: NY Shakespeare Fest. (Sganarelle, An Evening of Moliere Farces, Othello). Off-B'way: Endgame, No End of Blame (Obie Award), Put Them All Together, Geniuses, Territorial Rites. B'way: Bent, The Philadelphia Story. L.A. stage: Hedda Gabler, The Real Thing, Love Letters, Money & Friends.
PICTURES: Just Tell Me What You Want, Big Business, Tremors, Midnight Murders, Cool as Ice, Alan & Naomi, Tremors II: Aftershocks.
TELEVISION: Series: Family Ties. Movies: A Girl Named Sooner, FDR: The Last Year, Dream House, The Neighborhood, Little Gloria Happy at Last, Cook and Peary-The Race to the Pole, Summer Fantasy, Family Ties Vacation, A Letter to Three Wives, Right to Die, In the Line of Duty: The FBI Murders, A Connecticut Yankee in King Arthur's Court, Vestige of Honor, In the Line of Duty: Manhunt in the Dakotas, With a Vengeance, Snowbound: The Jim and Jennifer Stolpa Story, In the Line of Duty: The Price of Vengeance, Avalanche, Awake to Danger, Deceived by Trust.

GROSSBART, JACK
Producer. b. Newark, NJ, Apr. 18, 1948. e. Rutgers Univ. Was agent , 1975-80, then personal manager, Litke-Grossbart Mgmt., 1980-87. Became tv prod., Jack Grossbart Prods., 1987.
TELEVISION: Movies (exec. prod./prod.): Shattered Vows, The Seduction of Gina, Rockabye, Killer in the Mirror, Something in Common, Dangerous Affection, Echoes in the Darkness, She Was Marked for Murder, The Preppie Murder, Joshua's Heart, Lies Before Kisses, Honor Bright, Last Wish, Something to Live For: The Alison Gertz Story, A Jury of One, Comrades of Summer, The Woman Who Loved Elvis, One of Her Own, Leave of Absence. Series (exec. prod.): Sydney, Cafe Americain.

GROSSBERG, JACK
Producer, Executive. b. Brooklyn, NY, June 5, 1927. Member: AMPAS.
PICTURES: Requiem for a Heavyweight, Pretty Poison, The Producers, Don't Drink the Water, Take the Money and Run, Bananas, Everything You Always Wanted To Know About Sex, Sleeper, A Delicate Balance, Luther, Rhinoceros, Leadbelly, King Kong, The Betsy, Fast Break, A Stranger is Watching, Brainstorm, Strange Brew, Touch and Go, The Experts, Little Monsters.

GROSSMAN, ERNIE
Executive. b. New York, NY, Sept. 19, 1924. Still dept., press-book edit., asst. field mgr., Warner Bros., 1940-58; Studio publicist, 1958-60; exploitation, promo. mgr. field dept., 1960-64; nat'l mgr., pub., exploit., promo.; 1964-67 exec. co-ord. advt., pub. & promo., Warner-7 Arts, 1967; WB nat'l supv. ad.-pub., 1970. exec. assist. to Richard Lederer, 1971-72; 1973 nat'l dir. of Pub. & Promotion, Warner Bros. Inc.; 1977, natl. dir. of adv.-pub.; 1980-85, natl. dir. promo. 1987, named southwest special events dir. Retired, 1994.

GRUEN, ROBERT
Executive. b. New York, NY, Apr. 2, 1913. e. Carnegie Mellon U., B.A. Stage designer, 1934-35; designer, 20th-Fox, 1936; prod. exec., National Screen Service Corp., 1936; head, Robert Gruen Associates, ind. design org., 1940; nat. pres. Industrial Designers Inst., 1954-55; dir. and v.p., National Screen Service Corp. since 1951; senior v.p. 1975-78; dir., NSS Corp., Continental Lithograph and NSS, Ltd., 1978-85. Retired 1985.

GRUENBERG, ANDY
Executive. b. Minneapolis, MN, March 10, 1950. e. University of Wisconsin. Held various sales positions with 20th Century Fox and Warner Bros. from 1976 to 1984. Joined Columbia Pictures as general sales mgr. Lorimar Pictures s.v.p. and general sales mgr. 1985-89. Hemdale Prods. pres. of distribution, 1989-91. Joined MGM/UA in 1991, currently exec. v.p. of distribution.

GRUENBERG, LEONARD S.
Executive. b. Minneapolis, MN, Sept. 10, 1913, e. U. of Minnesota. Began as salesman Republic Pictures, Minneapolis, 1935; with RKO in same capacity, 1936; promoted to city sales mgr., St. Louis, 1937, then branch mgr., Salt Lake City, 1941; later that year apptd. Rocky Mt. Dist. Mgr. (hqts., Denver, CO); 1946 Metropolitan, div. mgr., v.p. NTA, v.p. Cinemiracle Prods.; Pres., Chmn. of bd., Sigma III Corp. 1962. Chmn. of bd., Filmways, 1967. Chmn. of bd. Gamma III Dist. Co. & Chmn of bd. and Pres. Great Owl Corp., 1976. Member Variety Club, Sigma Alpha Mu Fraternity; Lieut. Civil Air Patrol, Lieut. Comdr., U.S.N.R.

GRUSIN, DAVID
Composer, Conductor, Performer. b. Littleton, CO, June 26, 1934. Directed music for the Andy Williams Show on TV for 7 yrs in the 1960s, where met Norman Lear and Bud Yorkin, producers of the series, who signed him to score their first feature film, Divorce, American Style (1967).
PICTURES: Waterhole No. 3, The Graduate, Candy, The Heart Is a Lonely Hunter, Winning, Where Were You When the Lights Went Out?, Generation, A Man Called Gannon, Tell Them Willie Boy Is Here, Adam at 6 A.M., Halls of Anger, The Gang That Couldn't Shoot Straight, The Pursuit of Happiness, Shoot Out, Fuzz, The Great Northfield Minnesota Raid, The Friends of Eddie Coyle, The Midnight Ride, W.W. and the Dixie Dancekings, The Yakuza, Three Days of the Condor, Murder By Death, The Front, Fire Sale, Mr. Billion, Bobby Deerfield, The Goodbye Girl, Heaven Can Wait, And Justice for All, The Champ, The Electric Horseman, My Bodyguard, Absence of Malice, On Golden Pond, Reds, Author! Author!, Tootsie, Scandalous, Racing with the Moon, The Pope of Greenwich Village, The Little Drummer Girl, Falling in Love, Goonies, The Milagro Beanfield War (Acad. Award, 1988), Clara's Heart, Tequila Sunrise, A Dry White Season, Havana, The Bonfire of the Vanities, For the Boys, The Firm, Mulhalland Falls.
TELEVISION: Movies: Deadly Dream, Prescription: Murder, Scorpio Letters, Eric, The Family Rico, The Death Squad; themes to many series.

GUBER, PETER
Producer. b. 1942. e. Syracuse U., B.A.; U. at Florence (Italy), S.S.P.; Sch. of Law, J.D., L.L.M. Recruited by Columbia Pictures as exec. asst. in 1968 while at NYU. Graduate Sch. of Business Adm. With Col. seven yrs. in key prod. exec. capacities, serving last three as studio chief. Formed own company, Peter Guber's Filmworks, which in 1976 was merged with his Casablanca Records to become Casablanca Record and Filmworks where he was co-owner & chmn. bd. 1980 formed Polygram Pictures later bringing in Jon Peters as partner. 1983 sold Polygram and formed Guber-Peters. 1988 merged co. with Burt Sugarman's Barris Industries to form Guber-Peters-Barris Entertainment Co. Co-chmn. & man. dir. 1989 took full control of co. with Sugarman's exit and addition of Australia's Frank Lowy as new partner. 1989 became CEO of Columbia Pictures Ent.; 1992 became chairman and CEo of Sony Pictures Ent. Awards: Producer of Year, NATO, 1979; NYU Albert Gallatin Fellowship; Syracuse U Ardent Award. Visiting prof., & chmn. producer's dept., UCLA Sch. of Theatre Arts. Member of NY, CA and Wash. DC Bars. Books: Inside the Deep, Above the Title.
PICTURES: The Deep (first under own banner), Midnight Express. Co-Prod. with Jon Peters: An American Werewolf in London, Missing, Flashdance (exec. prod.), D.C. Cab (exec. prod.), Endless Love, Vision Quest (exec. prod.), The Legend of Billie Jean, Head Office, Clan of the Cave Bear, Six Weeks (exec. prod.), The Pursuit of D.B. Cooper (exec. prod.), Clue (exec. prod.), The Color Purple (exec. prod.), The Witches of Eastwick (prod.), Innerspace (exec. prod.), Who's That Girl (exec. prod.), Gorillas in the Mist (exec. prod.), Caddyshack II, Rain Man (exec. prod), Batman (prod.), Johnny Handsome, Tango and Cash (prod.), Batman Returns, This Boy's Life (exec. prod.), With Honors (exec. prod.).
TELEVISION: Mysteries of the Sea (doc. Emmy Award). Exec. prod.: Television and the Presidency, Double Platinum, Dreams (series). Movies: Stand By Your Man, The Toughest Man in the World (exec. prod.), Bay Coven, Oceanquest, Brotherhood of Justice, Nightmare at Bitter Creek, Finish Line.

GUEST, CHRISTOPHER
Actor, Writer, Composer. b. New York, NY, Feb. 5, 1948. m. actress Jamie Lee Curtis. Brother is actor Nicholas Guest. Wrote the musical score and acted in National Lampoon's Lemmings off-B'way. On B'way in Room Service, Moonchildren.

PICTURES: The Hospital (debut, 1971), The Hot Rock, Death Wish, The Fortune, Girlfriends, The Last Word, The Long Riders, Heartbeeps, This Is Spinal Tap (also co-s.p.), Little Shop of Horrors, Beyond Therapy, The Princess Bride, Sticky Fingers, The Big Picture (dir. co-s.p., story), A Few Good Men, Waiting for Guffman (also dir.).
TELEVISION: Series: Saturday Night Live (1984-5). Movies: It Happened One Christmas, Haywire, Million Dollar Infield, A Piano for Mrs. Cimino, Attack of the 50 Ft. Woman (dir.). Specials: The TV Show, The Chevy Chase Special (also writer), The Billion Dollar Bubble, Lily Tomlin (also writer, Emmy Award, 1976), A Nice Place to Visit (writer only), Spinal Tap Reunion (also co-writer). Mini-Series: Blind Ambition.

GUEST, LANCE
Actor. b. Saratoga, CA, July 21, 1960. e. UCLA.
PICTURES: Halloween II, I Ought To Be in Pictures, The Last Starfighter, Jaws-The Revenge, The Wizard of Loneliness.
TELEVISION: Series: Lou Grant, Knots Landing. Guest: St. Elsewhere. Movies: Confessions of a Married Man. Specials: One Too Many, My Father My Rival, The Roommate. Mini-Series: Favorite Son.

GUEST, VAL
Writer, Director, Producer. b. London, England, 1911. e. England and America. Journalist with Hollywood Reporter, Zit's Los Angeles Examiner and Walter Winchell. Debuted as dir. & writer of 1942 short film The Nose Has It.
PICTURES: Director/Writer: Miss London Ltd. (feature debut, 1943), Murder at the Windmill, Miss Pilgrim's Progress, The Body Said No, Mr. Drake's Duck, Happy Go Lovely, Another Man's Poison, Penny Princess, The Runaway Bus, Life With the Lyons, Dance Little Lady, Men of Sherwood Forest, Lyons in Paris, Break in the Circle, It's A Great Life, The Quatermass Experiment (The Creeping Unknown), They Can't Hang Me, The Weapon, It's a Wonderful World, Quatermass II (Enemy From Space), The Abominable Snowman, Carry on Admiral, The Camp on Blood Island, Up the Creek, Further Up the Creek, Yesterday's Enemy, Expresso Bongo (also prod.), Life Is a Circus, Hell Is a City, Full Treatment (Stop Me Before I Kill; also prod.), The Day the Earth Caught Fire (also prod.), Jigsaw (also prod.), 80,000 Suspects (also prod.), The Beauty Jungle (Contest Girl; also co-prod.), Where the Spies Are (also co-prod.), Casino Royale (co-dir.), Assignment K, When Dinosaurs Ruled the Earth, Tomorrow, The Persuaders, Au Pair Girls, Confessions of a Window Cleaner, Killer Force (Diamond Mercenaries; dir. only), The Boys in Blue.
TELEVISION: Space 1999, The Persuaders, The Adventurer, The Shillingbury Blowers, The Band Played On, Sherlock Holmes & Dr. Watson, Shillingbury Tales, Dangerous Davies, The Last Detective, In Possession, Mark of the Devil, Child's Play, Scent of Fear.

GUILLAUME, ROBERT
Actor. b. St. Louis, MO, Nov. 30, 1937. e. St. Louis U., Washington U. Scholarship for musical fest. in Aspen, CO. Then apprenticed with Karamu Theatre where performed in operas and musicals. B'way plays and musicals include Fly Blackbird, Kwamina, Guys and Dolls, Purlie, Jacques Brel is Alive and Well and Living in Paris, Cyrano. In L.A. in Phantom of the Opera.
PICTURES: Super Fly T.N.T. (debut, 1973), Seems Like Old Times, Prince Jack, They Still Call Me Bruce, Wanted Dead or Alive, Lean On Me, Death Warrant, The Meteor Man, The Lion King (voice), First Kid.
TELEVISION: Series: Soap (Emmy Award, 1979), Benson (Emmy Award, 1985), The Robert Guillaume Show, Saturdays, Pacific Station, Fish Police (voice), Happily Ever After... Fairytales for Every Child. Guest: Dinah, Mel and Susan Together, Rich Little's Washington Follies, Jim Nabors, All in the Family, Sanford and Son, The Jeffersons, Marcus Welby, M.D., Carol & Company, Sister Kate, A Different World. Mini-Series: North and South. Movies: The Kid From Left Field, The Kid with the Broken Halo, You Must Remember This, The Kid with the 100 I.Q. (also exec. prod.), Perry Mason: The Case of the Scandalous Scoundrel, The Penthouse, Fire and Rain, Greyhounds, Children of the Dust. Specials: Purlie, 'S Wonderful 'S Marvellous 'S Gershwin, John Grin's Christmas, Martin Luther King: A Look Back A Look Forward, Living the Dream: A Tribute to Dr. Martin Luther King Jr. (host), The Debbie Allen Special, Carol & Company, Sister Kate, Story of a People (host), Mastergate, Cosmic Slop. Pilot: Driving Miss Daisy.

GUILLERMIN, JOHN
Director, Producer, Writer. b. London, England, Nov. 11, 1925. e. City of London Sch., Cambridge U. RAF pilot prior to entering film industry.
PICTURES: Director: Torment (debut, 1949; also co-prod., s.p.), Smart Alec, Two on the Tiles, Four Days, Song of Paris, Miss Robin Hood, Operation Diplomat (also co-s.p.), Adventure in the Hopfields, The Crowded Day, Dust and Gold, Thunderstorm, Town on Trial, The Whole Truth, I Was Monty's

Double, Tarzan's Greatest Adventure (also co-s.p.), The Day They Robbed the Bank of England, Never Let Go (also co-story), Waltz of the Torreadors, Tarzan Goes to India (also co-s.p.), Guns at Batasi, Rapture, The Blue Max. P.J. (U.S. debut, 1968), House of Cards, The Bridge of Remagen, El Condor, Skyjacked, Shaft in Africa, The Towering Inferno, King Kong, Death on the Nile, Mr. Patman, Sheena, King Kong Lives, The Favorite.
TELEVISION: *Movie*: The Tracker.

GUINNESS, SIR ALEC
Actor. r.n. Alec Guinness. b. London, Eng., April 2, 1914. e. Pembroke Lodge, Southbourne & Roborough Sch., Eastbourne. Studied acting at Fay Compton Studio of Dramatic Art. Created C.B.E. 1955; Knighted 1959. C.H., 1994. Honorary degrees in literature: Oxford, 1977; Canterbury, 1991. Stage debut: London, 1934. First film appearance was extra in 1934 in Evensong. Special Academy Award, 1980, for services to film. *Autobiography*: Blessings in Disguise (1985). Also author of Blessings in Disguise, and My Name Escapes Me.
THEATER: Libel! (walk-on debut, 1934), Queer Cargo, Hamlet (1934), Noah, Romeo & Juliet (1935), The Seagull, Love's Labour's Lost, As You Like It, The Witch of Edmonton, Hamlet (1937), Twelfth Night (1937), Henry V, Richard III, School for Scandal, The Three Sisters, The Merchant of Venice (1937), The Doctor's Dilemma, Trelawny of the Wells, Hamlet (1938), Henry V, The Rivals, The Ascent of F.6, Romeo and Juliet (1939), Great Expectations (also adapt.), Cousin Muriel, The Tempest, Thunder Rock, Flare Path (B'way), Heart of Oak, The Brothers Karamazov, Vicious Circle, King Lear, An Inspector Calls, Cyrano de Bergerac, The Alchemist, Richard II, Saint Joan, The Government Inspector, Coriolanus, Twelfth Night (1948; also dir.), The Human Touch, The Cocktail Party (Edinburgh; B'way), Hamlet (1951; also dir.), Under the Sycamore Tree, All's Well That Ends Well, Richard III, The Prisoner, Hotel Paradiso, Ross, Exit the King, Dylan (B'way; Tony Award, 1964), Time Out of Mind, Voyage Round My Father, Habeas Corpus, A Family and a Fortune, Yahoo (also author), The Old Country, The Merchant of Venice (1984), A Walk in the Woods.
PICTURES: Great Expectations (debut, 1946), Oliver Twist, Kind Hearts and Coronets, A Run for Your Money, Last Holiday, The Mudlark, The Lavender Hill Mob (Acad. Award nom.), The Man in the White Suit, The Card (The Promoter), Malta Story, The Captain's Paradise, Father Brown (The Detective), To Paris With Love, The Prisoner, The Ladykillers, The Swan, The Bridge on the River Kwai (Academy Award, 1957), Barnacle Bill (All at Sea), The Horse's Mouth (also s.p.; Acad. Award nom. for s.p.), The Scapegoat (also co-prod.), Our Man in Havana, Tunes of Glory, A Majority of One, H.M.S. Defiant (Damn the Defiant!), Lawrence of Arabia, The Fall of the Roman Empire, Situation Hopeless But Not Serious, Doctor Zhivago, Hotel Paradiso, The Quiller Memorandum, The Comedians, Cromwell, Scrooge, Brother Sun Sister Moon, Hitler: The Last Ten Days, Murder by Death, Star Wars (Acad. Award nom.), The Empire Strikes Back, Raise the Titanic!, Lovesick, Return of the Jedi, A Passage to India, A Handful of Dust, Little Dorrit (Acad. Award nom.), Kafka.
TELEVISION: *Movies/Specials/Mini-Series*: The Wicked Scheme of Jebel Deeks, Twelfth Night, Conversation at Night, Solo, Little Gidding, The Gift of Friendship, Caesar and Cleopatra, Little Lord Fauntleroy, Tinker Tailor Soldier Spy (mini-series; BAFTA Award), Smiley's People (mini-series; BAFTA Award), Edwin, Monsignor Quixote, Tales From Hollywood, A Foreign Field, Eskimo Day.

GULAGER, CLU
Actor. b. Holdenville, OK, Nov. 16, 1928. Father, John Gulager, cowboy entertainer. e. Baylor U. Starred at school in original play, A Different Drummer, where spotted by prod. of TV's Omnibus; invited to New York to recreate role on TV.
PICTURES: The Killers, Winning, The Last Picture Show, Company of Killers, McQ, The Other Side of Midnight, A Force of One, Touched by Love, The Initiation, Lies, Into the Night, Prime Risk, The Return of the Living Dead, Hunter's Blood, The Hidden, Tapeheads, Uninvited, I'm Gonna Git You Sucka, Teen Vamp, My Heroes Have Always Been Cowboys, The Killing Device.
TELEVISION: *Series*: The Tall Man, The Virginian, The Survivors, San Francisco International Airport, MacKenzies of Paradise Cove. *Movies*: San Francisco International, Glass House, Footsteps, Smile Jenny You're Dead, Houston We've Got a Problem, Hit Lady, Killer Who Wouldn't Die, Charlie Cobb: Nice Night for a Hanging, Ski Lift to Death, Sticking Together, A Question of Love, Willa, This Man Stands Alone, Kenny Rogers as The Gambler, Skyward, Living Proof: The Hank Williams Jr. Story, Bridge Across Time. *Mini-Series*: Once an Eagle, Black Beauty, King, North and South II, Space.

GUMBEL, BRYANT
Announcer, News Show Host. b. New Orleans, LA, Sept. 29, 1948. e. Bates Coll. Started as writer for Black Sports

Magazine, NY, 1971; sportscaster, then sports dir., KNBC, Los Angeles. Sports host NBC Sports NY 1975-82. Now host on Today Show, New York (Emmy Awards, 1976, 1977).
TELEVISION: Super Bowl games, '88 Olympics, Games People Play, The R.A.C.E.

GUMPERT, JON
Executive. e. Cornell U. Law Sch. Sr. v.p., business affairs, MGM/UA Entertainment; pres., World Film Services, Inc., indep. prod. co. in N.Y. 1985, named v.p., business affairs, Warner Bros; 1986 sr. v.p. Vista Films. Named sr. v.p. legal bus. affairs, Universal Pictures 1990. Named exec. v.p., legal business affairs, Universal Pictures, 1994.

GUNSBERG, SHELDON
Executive. b. Jersey City, NJ, Aug. 10, 1920. e. St. Peters Coll., New Jersey State Normal, NYU. With Night of Stars, Madison Sq. Garden, 1942; for. pub., 20th-Fox 1942; United Artists, 1945-47; Universal, roadshows. Rank product, asst. adv., pub. dir., 1947-54; v. pres., Walter Reade Theatres; exec. v.p. & dir., Walter Reade Org. 1962; Made chief operating officer, 1971; president, and Chief Executive Officer, 1973; chmn. & CEO, 1984. Member: Film Society of Lincoln Center: bd. of dirs. (1955-present), chmn., bldg. committee, Walter Reade Theatre (1986-92), exec. v.p. (1987-90).

GUNTON, BOB
Actor. b. Santa Monica, CA, Nov. 15, 1945. e. UCal. Served in army during Vietnam War. Prof. acting debut at Cumberland County Playhouse in Tennesse U.S.A.
THEATER: *Off-B'way*: Who Am I? (debut, 1971), How I Got That Story (Obie Award), Tip Toes, The Death of Von Richthofen. *B'way*: Happy End (debut, 1977), Working, Evita (Drama Desk Award; Tony nom.), Passion, King of Hearts, Big River, Rozsa, Sweeney Todd (Drama Desk Award; Tony nom.).
PICTURES: Rollerover (debut, 1981), Static, Matewan, The Pick-Up Artist, Cookie, Born on the Fourth of July, Glory, JFK, Patriot Games, The Public Eye, Jennifer Eight, Demolition Man, The Shawshank Redemption, Dolores Claiborne, Ace Ventura: When Nature Calls, Broken Arrow.
TELEVISION: *Series*: Comedy Zone, Hot House, Courthouse. *Movies*: Lois Gibbs and the Love Canal, A Woman Named Jackie, Finnegan Begin Again, Ned Blessing, Dead Ahead: The Exxon Valdez Disaster, Murder in the Heartland, Sinatra. *Mini-Series*: Wild Palms.

GURIAN, PAUL R.
Executive, Producer. b. New Haven, CT, Oct.18, 1946. e. Lake Forest Coll., U. of Vienna, NYU. Started producing films in 1971 with Cats and Dogs, a dramatic short which won prizes at Chicago Int. Film Fest and Edinburgh Fest. In 1977 formed Gurian Entertainment Corp., to acquire film properties for production.
PICTURES: Cutter and Bone, Peggy Sue Got Married, The Seventh Sign (exec. prod.).
TELEVISION: The Garden Party (PBS program), Profile Ricardo Alegria (short), Bernice Bobs Her Hair (shown at 1977 N.Y. Film Festival)

GUTTENBERG, STEVE
Actor. b. Brooklyn, NY, Aug. 24, 1958. e. Sch. of Performing Arts, N.Y. Off-B'way in The Lion in Winter; studied under John Houseman at Juilliard; classes with Lee Strasberg and Uta Hagen. Moved to West Coast in 1976; landed first TV role in movie, Something for Joey. B'way debut 1991 in Prelude to a Kiss.
PICTURES: Rollercoaster, The Chicken Chronicles, The Boys from Brazil, Players, Can't Stop the Music, Diner, The Man Who Wasn't There, Police Academy, Police Academy 2: Their First Assignment, Cocoon, Bad Medicine, Police Academy 3: Back in Training, Short Circuit, The Bedroom Window, Police Academy 4: Citizens on Patrol (also prod. assoc.), Amazon Women on the Moon, Surrender, Three Men and a Baby, High Spirits, Cocoon: The Return, Don't Tell Her It's Me, Three Men and a Little Lady, The Big Green, Home for the Holidays, It Takes Two.
TELEVISION: *Guest*: Police Story, Doc. *Series*: Billy, No Soap Radio. *Movies*: Something for Joey, To Race the Wind, Miracle on Ice, The Day After. *Specials*: Gangs (co-prod.), Pecos Bill: King of the Cowboys.

GYLLENHAAL, STEPHEN
Director. b. Pennsylvania. e. Trinity Col, CT. Started career in NYC making industrial films. Directed short film Exit 10.m.. writer-producer Naomi Foner.
PICTURES: Waterland, A Dangerous Woman, Losing Isaiah.
TELEVISION: *Movies*: The Abduction of Kari Swenson, Promised a Miracle, Leap of Faith, Family of Spies, A Killing in a Small Town, Paris Trout.

H

HAAS, LUKAS
Actor. b. West Hollywood, CA, Apr. 16, 1976. Kindergarten school principal told casting dir. about him which resulted in film debut in Testament. NY theater debut in Mike Nichols' Lincoln Center production of Waiting for Godot (1988). Appeared in AFI film The Doctor.

PICTURES: Testament (debut, 1983), Witness, Solarbabies, Lady in White, The Wizard of Loneliness, See You in the Morning, Music Box, Rambling Rose, Convicts, Alan and Naomi, Leap of Faith, Warrior Spirit, Boys, Johns, Palookaville, Mars Attacks!, Everyone Says I Love You.
TELEVISION: Movies: Love Thy Neighbor, Shattered Spirits, The Ryan White Story, The Perfect Tribute. Guest: Amazing Stories (Ghost Train), Twilight Zone, The Young Indiana Jones Chronicles. Pilot: Brothers-in-Law. Specials: A Place at the Table, My Dissident Mom, Peacemaker (Triple Play II).

HACK, SHELLEY
Actress. b. Greenwich, CT, July 6, 1952. e. Smith Coll. and U. of Sydney, Australia. Made modeling debut at 14 on cover of Glamour Magazine. Gained fame as Revlon's Charlie Girl on TV commercials.
PICTURES: Annie Hall, If Ever I See You Again, Time After Time, The King of Comedy, Troll, The Stepfather, Blind Fear, Me Myself and I, The Finishing Touch.
TELEVISION: Series: Charlie's Angels, Cutter to Houston, Jack and Mike. Movies: Death on the Freeway, Trackdown: Finding the Goodbar Killer, Found Money, Single Bars Single Women, Bridesmaids, Casualty of War, Taking Back My Life: The Nancy Ziegenmeyer Story, Not in My Family, The Case of the Wicked Wives, Falling From the Sky: Flight 174, Freefall, Frequent Flyer.

HACKER, CHARLES R.
Executive. b. Milwaukee, WI, Oct. 8, 1920. e. U. of Wisconsin. Thea. mgr., Fox Wisc. Amuse. Corp., 1940; served in U.S.A.F., 1943-45; rejoined Fox Wisconsin Amusement Corp.; joined Standard Theatres Management Corp. 1947, on special assignments; apptd. district mgr. of Milwaukee & Waukesha theatres 1948; joined Radio City Music Hall Corp. as administrative asst. July, 1948; mgr. of oper., 1952; asst. to the pres., Feb. 1957; v.p.; Radio City Music Hall Corp., 1964; appointed executive vice president and chief operating officer, February 1, 1973. Pres., Landmark Pictures, May, 1979. Treas. Will Rogers Memorial Fund, 1978-95. Award: Quigley Silver Grand Award for Showmanship, 1947. Member: U.S. Small Business Admin. Region 1, Hartford Advisory Council 1983-93.

HACKETT, BUDDY
Actor. r.n. Leonard Hacker. b. Brooklyn, NY, Aug. 31, 1924. Prof. debut, borscht circuit.
THEATER: B'way: Call Me Mister, Lunatics and Lovers, I Had a Ball.
PICTURES: Walking My Baby Back Home (debut, 1953), Fireman Save My Child, God's Little Acre, Everything's Ducky, All Hands on Deck, The Music Man, The Wonderful World of the Brothers Grimm, It's a Mad Mad Mad Mad World, Muscle Beach Party, The Golden Head, The Good Guys and the Bad Guys (cameo), The Love Bug, Loose Shoes, Hey Babe!, Scrooged, The Little Mermaid (voice).
TELEVISION: Series: School House, Stanley, Jackie Gleason Show, Jack Paar Show, You Bet Your Life (1980), Fish Police (voice). Movie: Bud and Lou. Specials: Entertainment 55, Variety, The Mama Cass TV Program, Plimpton: Did You Hear the One About...?, Jack Frost (voice), Circus of the Stars, Buddy Hackett—Live and Uncensored.

HACKFORD, TAYLOR
Director, Producer. b. Santa Barbara, CA, Dec. 31, 1944. e. USC, B.A. (international relations). Was Peace Corps volunteer in Bolivia 1968-69. Began career with KCET in Los Angeles 1970-77. As prod.-dir. won Oscar for short, Teenage Father, 1978. Theatrical film debut as director with The Idolmaker (1980).
PICTURES: Director: The Idolmaker, An Officer and a Gentleman. Dir./Prod.: Against All Odds, White Nights, Chuck Berry: Hail! Hail! Rock 'n' Roll (dir. only), Everyone's All-American, Bound By Honor/Blood In Blood Out, Dolores Claiborne. Prod.: La Bamba. Exec. Prod.: Rooftops, The Long Walk Home, Sweet Talker, Queens Logic, Defenseless, Mortal Thoughts.

HACKMAN, GENE
Actor. b. San Bernardino, CA, Jan. 30, 1930. First major broadway role in Any Wednesday. Other stage productions include: Poor Richard, Children from Their Games, A Rainy Day in Newark, The Natural Look, Death and the Maiden. Formed own production co., Chelly Ltd.
PICTURES: Mad Dog Coll (debut, 1961), Lilith, Hawaii, A Covenant With Death, Bonnie and Clyde (Acad. Award nom.), First to Fight, Banning, The Split, Riot, The Gypsy Moths, Downhill Racer, Marooned, I Never Sang for My Father (Acad. Award nom.), Doctors' Wives, The Hunting Party, The French Connection (Academy Award, 1971), Cisco Pike, Prime Cut, The Poseidon Adventure, Scarecrow, The Conversation, Zandy's Bride, Young Frankenstein, Night Moves, Bite the Bullet, French Connection II, Lucky Lady, The Domino Principle, A Bridge Too Far, March or Die, Superman, All Night Long, Superman II, Reds, Eureka, Under Fire, Uncommon Valor, Misunderstood, Target, Twice in a Lifetime, Power, Hoosiers, Superman IV, No Way Out, Another Woman, Bat-21, Split Decisions, Full Moon in

Blue Water, Mississippi Burning (Acad. Award nom.), The Package, Loose Cannons, Postcards From the Edge, Narrow Margin, Class Action, Company Business, Unforgiven (Academy Award, Natl. Soc. of Film Critics, NY Film Critics, BAFTA, LA Film Critics & Golden Globe Awards, best supporting actor, 1992), The Firm, Geronimo: An American Legend, The Quick and the Dead, Crimson Tide, Get Shorty, Birdcage, Extreme Measures, The Chamber.
TELEVISION: Guest: U.S. Steel Hour, The Defenders, Trials of O'Brien, Hawk, CBS Playhouse's My Father My Mother, The F.B.I., The Invaders, The Iron Horse. Movie: Shadow on the Land.

HADLOCK, CHANNING M.
Marketing. TV Executive. b. Mason City, IA. e. Duke U., U. of North Carolina. Newspaperman, Durham, NC Herald, war corr., Yank; NBC, Hollywood; television prod.-writer, Cunning-ham & Walsh Adv.; v.p. account supr. Chirug & Cairns Adv.; v.p. Marketing Innovations; dir. mktg. Paramount Pictures; mktg. svcs, Ogilvy & Mather; mktg, Time Life Books.

HAGERTY, JULIE
Actress. b. Cincinnati, OH, June 15, 1955. Studied drama for six years before leaving for NY where studied with William Hickey. Made acting debut in her brother Michael's theatre group in Greenwich Village called the Production Company.
THEATER: The Front Page (Lincoln Center), The House of Blue Leaves (Theatre World Award, 1986), Wild Life, Born Yesterday (Phil. Drama Guild), The Years, Three Men on a Horse, Wifey, A Cheever Evening.
PICTURES: Airplane! (debut, 1980), A Midsummer Night's Sex Comedy, Airplane II: The Sequel, Lost in America, Goodbye New York, Bad Medicine, Beyond Therapy, Aria, Bloodhounds of Broadway, Rude Awakening, Reversal of Fortune, What About Bob?, Noises Off, The Wife.
TELEVISION: Series: Princesses. Specials: The Visit (Trying Times). House of Blue Leaves, Necessary Parties. Movie: The Day the Women Got Even.

HAGGAR, PAUL JOHN
Executive. b. Brooklyn, NY, Aug. 5, 1928. e. LA h.s. Veteran of over 40 yrs. with Paramount Pictures, working way up from studio mail room to become apprentice editor in 1953; promoted to asst. editor 1955; music editor, 1957. 1968, named head of post-prod. for all films and TV made by Paramount. 1985, named sr. v.p., post-prod. for the Motion Picture Group.

HAGGARD, PIERS
Director. b. London, 1939. e. U. of Edinburgh. Son of actor Stephen Haggard; great grandnephew of author Rider Haggard. Began career in theatre in 1960 as asst. to artistic dir. at London's Royal Court. Named director of Glasgow Citizens' Theatre, 1962. 1963-65 worked with the National Theatre, where co-directed Hobson's Choice and The Dutch Courtesan. Has directed many prize winning TV commercials.
PICTURES: Wedding Night (debut, 1969; also co-s.p.), Blood on Satan's Claw (Satan's Skin), The Fiendish Plot of Dr. Fu Manchu, Venom, A Summer Story.
TELEVISION: Series: Pennies from Heaven, Quatermass, Return to Treasure Island, Centrepoint, Space Precinct. Specials/Movies: A Triple Play: Sam Found Out (Liza Minnelli special), The Fulfillment of Mary Gray, Back Home, Quatermass Conclusion, Chester Cycle of Mystery Plays, Mrs. Reinhardt, Knockback, Visitors, Heartstones, I'll Take Romance, Four Eyes and Six-Guns, Eskimo Day, Heartstones.

HAGMAN, LARRY
Actor. b. Fort Worth, TX, Sept. 21, 1931. e. Bard Coll. Son of late actress Mary Martin. First stage experience with Margo Jones Theatre in the Round in Dallas. Appeared in N.Y. in Taming of the Shrew; one year with London production of South Pacific. 1952-56 was in London with US Air Force where produced and directed show for servicemen. Returned to N.Y. for plays on and off B'way: God and Kate Murphy (Theatre World Award), The Nervous Set, The Warm Peninsula, The Beauty Part.
PICTURES: Ensign Pulver, Fail Safe, In Harm's Way, The Group, The Cavern, Up in the Cellar, Son of Blob (aka: Beware! The Blob; also dir.), Harry and Tonto, Stardust, Mother Jugs and Speed, The Big Bus, The Eagle Has Landed, Checkered Flag or Crash, Superman, S.O.B., Nixon.
TELEVISION: Series: The Edge of Night, I Dream of Jeannie, The Good Life, Here We Go Again, Dallas. Movies: Three's a Crowd, Vanished, A Howling in the Woods, Getting Away from It All, No Place to Run, The Alpha Caper, Blood Sport, What Are Best Friends For?, Sidekicks, Hurricane, Sarah T.-Portrait of a Teenage Alcoholic, The Big Rip-Off, Return of the World's Greatest Detective, Intimate Strangers, The President's Mistress, Last of the Good Guys, Deadly Encounter, Staying Afloat, In the Heat of the Night: Who Was Geli Bendl? (dir. only), Dallas: Who Killed Jr?. Special: Applause.

HAHN, HELENE
Executive. b. New York, NY. e. Loyola U. Sch. of Law. Instructor of entertainment law at Loyola. Attorney for ABC before joining

Paramount in 1977 in studio legal dept. 1979, moved to business affairs; promoted to dir. 1980, v.p., 1981; sr. v.p., 1983. Left in 1985 to join Walt Disney Pictures as sr. v.p., business & legal affairs for m.p. division. 1987, promoted to exec. v.p., Walt Disney Studios.

HAID, CHARLES
Actor, Director, Producer. b. San Francisco, CA, June 2, 1943. e. Carnegie Tech. Appeared on NY stage in Elizabeth the First. Co-produced Godspell. Prod. & dir. short film The Last Supper.
PICTURES: *Actor*: The Choirboys, Who'll Stop the Rain, Oliver's Story, House of God, Altered States, Square Dance (co-exec. prod. only), Cop, The Rescue, Nightbreed, Storyville. *Director*: Iron Will.
TELEVISION: *Series*: Kate McShane, Delvecchio, Hill Street Blues, Cop Rock (prod. only). *Movies*: The Execution of Private Slovik, Remember When, Things in Their Season, Kate McShane (pilot), Foster and Laurie, A Death in Canaan, The Bastard, Death Moon, Twirl, Divorce Wars, Children in the Crossfire (also co-prod.), Code of Vengeance, Six Against the Rock, Weekend War, The Great Escape II: The Untold Story, A Deadly Silence, Fire and Rain, Man Against the Mob: The Chinatown Murders, In the Line of Duty: A Cop for the Killing (also co-prod.), In the Line of Duty: Siege at Marion (dir. only), The Nightman (dir., prod. only), Cooperstown (also dir.), For Their Own Good, The Fire Next Time, Broken Trust.

HAIM, COREY
Actor. b. Toronto, Canada, Dec. 23, 1972. Performed in TV commercials at 10; signed as regular on children's show, The Edison Twins.
PICTURES: Firstborn (debut, 1984), Secret Admirer, Silver Bullet, Murphy's Romance, Lucas, The Lost Boys, License to Drive, Watchers, Dream a Little Dream, Fast Getaway, Prayer of the Roller Boys, The Dream Machine, Oh What a Night, Blown Away, The Double-O Kid, National Lampoon's Last Resort, Fast Getaway 2, Tales From the Crypt: Bordello of Blood.
TELEVISION: *Movies*: A Time to Live, Just One of the Girls. *Series*: Roomies.

HAINES, RANDA
Director. b. Los Angeles, CA, Feb. 20, 1945. Raised in NYC. Studied acting with Lee Strasberg. e. School of Visual Arts. 1975 accepted into AFI's Directing Workshop for Women. Dir. & co-wrote short film August/September, which led to work as writer for series Family. Appeared in documentary Calling the Shots.
PICTURES: Children of a Lesser God, The Doctor, Wrestling Ernest Hemingway, A Family Thing (co-prod. only).
TELEVISION: *Series*: Family (writer), Hill Street Blues (dir. of 4 episodes), Alfred Hitchcock Presents (Bang You're Dead), Tales from the Crypt (Judy You're Not Yourself Today). *Movie*: Something about Amelia. *Specials*: Under This Sky, The Jilting of Granny Weatherall, Just Pals.

HALE, BARBARA
Actress. b. DeKalb, IL, April 18, 1922. Was married to late actor Bill Williams. Son is actor William Katt. e. Chicago Acad. of Fine Arts. Beauty contest winner, Little Theatre actress. Screen debut, 1943.
PICTURES: Gildersleeve's Bad Day, The Seventh Victim, Higher and Higher, Belle of the Yukon, The Falcon Out West, Falcon in Hollywood, Heavenly Days, West of the Pecos, First Yank in Tokyo, Lady Luck, A Likely Story, Boy with Green Hair, The Clay Pigeon, Window, Jolson Sings Again, And Baby Makes Three, Emergency Wedding, Jackpot, Lorna Doone, First Time, Last of the Comanches, Seminole, Lone Hand, A Lion Is in the Streets, Unchained, Far Horizons, Houston Story, 7th Cavalry, Oklahoman, Slim Carter, Desert Hell, Buckskin, Airport, Soul Soldier, Giant Spider Invasion, Big Wednesday.
TELEVISION: *Series*: Perry Mason (Emmy Award, 1959). *Movies*: Perry Mason Returns (1985) and 29 other Perry Mason's incl. The Case of the... Murdered Madam, Avenging Ace, Lady in the Lake, Scandalous Scoundrel, Lethal Lesson, Poisoned Pen, Fatal Fashion, Reckless Romeo.

HALEY, JR., JACK
Executive, Director. b. Los Angeles, CA, Oct.25, 1933. e. Loyola U. Son of late actor Jack Haley. 1959-67 Wolper Prods., 1967-73. sr. v.p. at Wolper before joining MGM. Named dir. of creative affairs. Left in 1974, to join 20th Century-Fox as pres. of TV div. and v.p., TV for 20th-Fox Film Corp. Winner of 2 Peabody Awards, best prod. at Int'l. TV Festival at Monte Carlo and 3 Silver Lion Awards at Venice Film Festival. Won Emmy for best dir. in music or variety shows for Movin' On with Nancy. Directed Academy Awards Show in 1970; prod. it in 1974 and 1979. Left Fox 1976 to be indep. prod.
PICTURES: *Director*: Norwood, The Love Machine, That's Entertainment (also prod, s.p.), Better Late Than Never (prod. only), That's Dancing (also co-prod., s.p.).
TELEVISION: The Incredible World of James Bond, The Legend of Marilyn Monroe, The Supremes, The Hidden World, Movin' with Nancy (Emmy Award, dir., 1968), With Love Sophia, Monte Carlo, Life Goes to War: Hollywood and the Homefront; Heroes

of Rock n' Roll (exec. prod.), 51st Academy Awards (Emmy Award, 1979), Hollywood, the Golden Years (with David Wolper), Ripley's Believe It or Not, The Night They Saved Christmas, Cary Grant: A Celebration (exec. prod.).

HALL, ANTHONY MICHAEL
Actor. b. Boston, MA, Apr. 14, 1968.
PICTURES: Six Pack (debut, 1982), National Lampoon's Vacation, Sixteen Candles, The Breakfast Club, Weird Science, Out of Bounds, Johnny Be Good, Edward Scissorhands, A Gnome Named Norm, Into the Sun, Hail Caesar (also dir.), Six Degrees of Separation, Me and the Mob.
TELEVISION: *Series*: Saturday Night Live (1985-86). *Mini-Series*: Texas. *Movies*: Rascals and Robbers: The Secret Adventures of Tom Sawyer and Huck Finn, Running Out, A Bucket of Blood. *Guest*: NYPD Blue, Tales from the Crypt, Boys and Girls.

HALL, ARSENIO
Actor, Comedian. b. Cleveland, OH. Feb. 12, 1959. e. Kent State U. Became interested in magic at 7, which later led to own local TV special, The Magic of Christmas. Switched from advertising career to stand-up comedy, 1979. Discovered at Chicago nightclub by singer Nancy Wilson.
PICTURES: Amazon Women on the Moon (debut, 1987), Coming to America, Harlem Nights, Bopha! (exec. prod. only), Blankman.
TELEVISION: *Series*: The 1/2 Hour Comedy Hour (1983, co-host), Thicke of the Night, Motown Revue, The Late Show (1987, host), The Arsenio Hall Show, The Party Machine With Nia Peeples (prod. only).

HALL, CONRAD
Cinematographer. b. Papeete, Tahiti, June 21, 1926. Worked as camera operator with Robert Surtees, Ted McCord, Ernest Haller; moved to TV as director of photography before feature films.
PICTURES: Wild Seed, The Saboteur—Code Name: Morituri, Harper, The Professionals, Rogue's Gallery, Incubus, Divorce American Style, In Cold Blood, Cool Hand Luke, Hell in the Pacific, Butch Cassidy and the Sundance Kid (Academy Award, 1969), Tell Them Willie Boy Is Here, The Happy Ending, Fat City, Electra Glide in Blue, The Day of the Locust, Smile, Marathon Man, Black Widow, Tequila Sunrise, Class Action, Jennifer Eight, Searching for Bobby Fischer, Love Affair.
TELEVISION: *Movie*: It Happened One Christmas, Stoney Burke. *Series*: Outer Limits.

HALL, KURT C.
Executive. b. Burlington, VT. e. Univ. of VT. Served as dir. of financial reporting, dir. of finance, and v.p. & treas. of UA Entertainment before becoming v.p. & treas. of United Artists Theatre Circuit, 1990-91. Named exec. v.p. and CFO of United Artists Theatre Circuit, Inc.

HALL, HUNTZ (HENRY)
Actor. b. Boston, MA, Aug 15, 1920. In 1937 appeared in stage and screen production Dead End.
PICTURES: Dead End (debut, 1937), Crime School, Angels with Dirty Faces, They Made Me a Criminal, Hell's Kitchen, Muggs Rides Again, Live Wires, A Walk in the Sun, Jinx Money, Smuggler's Cove, Fighting Fools, Blues Busters, Bowery Battalion, Ghost Chasers, Crazy Over Horses, Let's Go Navy, Here Come the Marines, Hold That Line, Feudin' Fools, No Holds Barred, Private Eyes, Paris Playboys, Bowery Boys Meet the Monsters, Clipped Wings, Jungle Gents, Bowery to Bagdad, High Society, Spy Chasers, Jail Busters, Dig That Uranium, Up in Smoke, Second Fiddle to a Steel Guitar, Gentle Giant, The Phynx, Herbie Rides Again, The Manchu Eagle Murder Caper Mystery, Won Ton Ton the Dog Who Saved Hollywood, Valentino, Gas Pump Girls, The Escape Artist, Cyclone.
TELEVISION: *Series*: The Chicago Teddy Bears. *Movie*: Escape. *Guest*: Barefoot in the Park, Diff'rent Strokes, Night Heat.

HALL, MONTY; O.C.
Actor. b. Winnipeg, Manitoba, Canada, Aug. 25, 1925. e. U. of Manitoba, B.S. Host of Let's Make a Deal, 1964-86. International chmn., Variety Clubs International.

HALLSTROM, LASSE
Director. b. Stockholm, Sweden, 1946. m. actress Lena Olin. As teenager made 16mm film which was eventually screened on Swedish tv. Began professional career filming and editing inserts for Swedish TV. Directed program Shall We Dance? for Danish TV, followed by TV prod. on The Love Seeker, dir. of program Shall We Got to My or to Your Place or Each Go Home Alone?.
PICTURES: A Love and His Lass (debut, 1974), ABBA: The Movie, Father-to-Be, The Rooster, Happy We, The Children of Bullerby Village, More About the Children of Bullerby Village, My Life as a Dog (also co-s.p.; Acad. Award noms. for dir. & s.p.), Once Around (U.S. debut, 1991), What's Eating Gilbert Grape (also co-exec. prod.), Something to Talk About.

HALMI, ROBERT SR.
Producer. b. Budapest, Hungary, Jan 22, 1924. Originally writer-photographer under contract to Life Magazine.
PICTURES: Created documentaries for U.N. Features include: Hugo the Hippo, Visit to a Chief's Son, The One and Only, Brady's Escape, Cheetah, Mr. and Mrs. Bridge.
TELEVISION: Bold Journey (dir.-cin.), American Sportsman, The Oriental Sportsman, The Flying Doctor, The Outdoorsman, Julius Boros Series, Rexford, Who Needs Elephants, Calloway's Climb, Oberndorf Revisited, True Position, Wilson's Reward, Nurse, Buckley Sails, A Private Battle, My Old Man, Mr. Griffin and Me, When the Circus Came to Town, Best of Friends, Bush Doctor, Peking Encounter, Svengali, China Rose, Cook and Peary-The Race to the Pole, Terrible Joe Moran, Nairobi Affair, The Night They Saved Christmas, Spies, Lies and Naked Thighs, exec. prod.: The Prize Pulitzer, Paradise, Bridesmaids, Face to Face, Margaret Bourke-White, The Incident, Josephine Baker Story, The Secret, An American Story, Call of the Wild, Blind Spot, Incident in a Small Town, Spoils of War, The Yearling, A Promise Kept: The Oksana Baiul Story, A Mother's Gift, Scarlett, Reunion, My Brother's Keeper, White Dwarf, Secrets, Bye Bye Birdie, Kidnapped, Gulliver's Travels (Emmy Award, 1996), Captains Courageous, Dead Man's Walk.

HAMADY, RON
Producer. b. Flint, MI, June 16, 1947. e. U. of California, B.A. 1971. Co-founder of The Crystal Jukebox, record productions, music management and music publishing co. Produced 12 hit albums for Decca Records of England and London Records, U.S. Entered m.p. industry in 1975, producing Train Ride to Hollywood for Taylor-Laughlin dist. Co.
PICTURES: Fade to Black, Surf II, And God Created Woman (1987), Out Cold, Don't Tell Her It's Me.

HAMEL, VERONICA
Actress. b. Philadelphia, PA, Nov. 20, 1943. e. Temple U. Moved to NY and began a modelling career with Eileen Ford Agency. Off B'way debut: The Big Knife. Acted in dinner theater prods. Moved to L.A. 1975.
THEATER: B'way: Rumors. Off B'way: The Big Knife, The Ballad of Boris K.
PICTURES: Cannonball, Beyond the Poseidon Adventure, When Time Ran Out, A New Life, Taking Care of Business.
TELEVISION: Movies: The Gathering, Ski Lift to Death, The Gathering II, The Hustler of Muscle Beach, Valley of the Dolls, Sessions, Twist of Fate, She Said No, Stop at Nothing, Deadly Medicine (also co-exec. prod.), Baby Snatcher (also co-exec. prod.), The Disappearance of Nora, The Conviction of Kitty Dodds, Shadow of Obsession, A Child's Cry for Help, Intensive Care, Secrets, Here Come the Munsters, Blink of an Eye, Brother's Keeper. Mini-Series: 79 Park Avenue, Kane & Abel. Series: Hill Street Blues. Guest: Kojak, Rockford Files, Bob Newhart Show, Switch.

HAMILL, MARK
Actor. b. Oakland, CA, Sept. 25, 1951. While studying acting at LA City Col. made prof. debut in episode of The Bill Cosby Show, 1970. Featured in CD-ROM interactive game Wing Commander III.
THEATER: NY: The Elephant Man (B'way debut), Amadeus (also Natl. tour), Harrigan 'n' Hart, Room Service (off-B'way), The Nerd.
PICTURES: Star Wars (debut, 1977), Wizards (voice), Corvette Summer, The Empire Strikes Back, The Big Red One, The Night the Lights Went Out in Georgia, Britannia Hospital, Return of the Jedi, Slipstream, Midnight Ride, Black Magic Woman, Sleepwalkers (cameo), Time Runner, The Guyver, Batman: Mask of the Phantasm (voice), Village of the Damned.
TELEVISION: Series: General Hospital, The Texas Wheelers, Batman (voice). Movies: Sarah T.-Portrait of a Teenage Alcoholic, Eric, Delancey Street: The Crisis Within, Mallory: Circumstantial Evidence, The City, Earth Angel, Body Bags, Hollyrock-a-Bye Baby (voice). Guest: Room 222, The Partridge Family, Headmaster, Medical Center, Owen Marshall, The FBI, Streets of San Francisco, One Day at a Time, Manhunter, Hooperman, Alfred Hitchcock Presents, Amazing Stories, The Flash, seaQuest DSV. Specials: Get High on Yourself, Night of 100 Stars.

HAMILTON, GEORGE
Actor. b. Memphis, TN, Aug. 12, 1939. e. grammar, Hawthorne, CA; military sch., Gulfport, MS, N.Y. Hackley Prep Sch., FL, Palm Beach H.S. Won best actor award in Florida, high sch. contest.
PICTURES: Crime and Punishment USA (debut, 1959), Home From the Hill, All the Fine Young Cannibals, Where the Boys Are, Angel Baby, By Love Possessed, A Thunder of Drums, Light in the Piazza, Two Weeks in Another Town, Act One, The Victors, Looking for Love, Your Cheatin' Heart, Viva Maria, That Man George, Doctor You've Got to Be Kidding!, Jack of Diamonds, A Time for Killing, The Power, Togetherness, Evel Knievel (also co-p, The Man Who Loved Cat Dancing, Once Is Not Enough, The Happy Hooker Goes to Washington, Love at First Bite (also co-

exec. prod.), Sextette, From Hell to Victory, Zorro the Gay Blade (also co-prod.), The Godfather Part III, Doc Hollywood, Once Upon a Crime.
TELEVISION: Mini-Series: Roots. Movies: Two Fathers' Justice, Monte Carlo, Poker Alice, Caution: Murder Can Be Hazardous to Your Health, The House on Sycamore Street, Two Fathers: Justice for the Innocent, Danielle Steel's Vanished. Series: The Survivors, Paris 7000, Dynasty, Spies, The George and Alana Show (also prod.). Guest: Rin Tin Tin, The Donna Reed Show. Special: The Veil.

HAMILTON, GUY
Director. b. Paris, France, Sept. 24, 1922. Ent. m.p. industry 1939 as apprentice at Victorine Studio, Nice; Royal Navy, 1940-45, in England asst. dir., Fallen Idol, Third Man, Outcast of the Islands, African Queen.
PICTURES: The Ringer, The Intruder, An Inspector Calls, Colditz Story, Manuela, The Devil's Disciple, A Touch of Larceny, The Best of Enemies, The Party's Over, Man in the Middle, Goldfinger, Funeral in Berlin, Battle of Britain, Diamonds Are Forever, Live and Let Die, The Man with the Golden Gun, Force Ten from Navarone, The Mirror Crack'd, Evil Under the Sun, Remo Williams.

HAMILTON, LINDA
Actress. b. Salisbury, MD, Sept. 26, 1956. Appeared on NY stage in Looice and Richard III.
PICTURES: Tag: The Assassination Game, Children of the Corn, The Stone Boy, The Terminator, Black Moon Rising, King Kong Lives!, Mr. Destiny, Terminator 2: Judgment Day, Silent Fall, The Shadow Conspiracy.
TELEVISION: Series: Secrets of Midland Heights, King's Crossing, Beauty and the Beast. Movies: Reunion, Rape and Marriage-The Rideout Case, Country Gold, Secrets of a Mother and Daughter, Secret Weapons, Club Med, Go Toward the Light, A Mother's Prayer. Guest: Hill Street Blues, Murder She Wrote.

HAMLIN, HARRY
Actor. b. Pasadena, CA, Oct. 30, 1951. e. U. of California, Yale U., 1974 in theatre, psychology. Awarded IT&T Fulbright Grant, 1977. Joined American Conservatory Theatre, San Francisco, for two years' study before joining McCarter Theatre, Princeton (Hamlet, Faustus in Hell.) B'way debut Awake and Sing! (1984).
PICTURES: Movie Movie (debut, 1978), King of the Mountain, Clash of the Titans, Making Love, Blue Skies Again, Maxie, Save Me.
TELEVISION: Mini-series: Studs Lonigan, Master of the Game, Space, Favorite Son. Movies: Laguna Heat, Deceptions, Deadly Intentions... Again?, Deliver Them From Evil: The Taking of Alta View, Poisoned By Love: The Kern County Murders, In the Best of Families: Marriage Pride & Madness, Tom Clancy's Op Center, Her Deadly Rival. Series: L.A. Law.

HAMLISCH, MARVIN
Composer. b. New York, NY, June 2, 1944. e. Juilliard. Accompanist and straight man on tour with Groucho Marx 1974-75; debut as concert pianist 1975 with Minn. Orch. Scores of Broadway shows: A Chorus Line (Tony Award); They're Playing Our Song, Smile, The Goodbye Girl. Winner 4 Grammy Awards.
PICTURES: The Swimmer, Take the Money and Run, Bananas, Save the Tiger, Kotch, The Way We Were (2 Acad. Awards for orig. score and title song, 1973), The Sting (Acad. Award for music adapt., 1973), The Spy Who Loved Me, Same Time Next Year, Ice Castles, Chapter Two, Seems Like Old Times, Starting Over, Ordinary People, The Fan, Sophie's Choice, I Ought to Be in Pictures, Romantic Comedy, D.A.R.Y.L., Three Men and a Baby, Little Nikita, The January Man, The Experts, Frankie and Johnny, Open Season.
TELEVISION: Series: Good Morning America (theme), Brooklyn Bridge. Movies: The Entertainer (also prod.), A Streetcar Named Desire, The Two Mrs. Grenvilles, Women & Men: Stories of Seduction, Switched at Birth, Seasons of the Heart.

HAMMOND, PETER
Actor, Writer, Director. b. London, Eng., Nov.15, 1923. e. Harrow Sch. of Art. Stage debut: Landslide, Westminster Theatre. Screen debut: Holiday Camp. Dir./writer, 1959-61, tv plays.
PICTURES: The Huggetts, Helter Skelter, Fools Rush In, The Reluctant Widow, Fly Away Peter, The Adventurers, Operation Disaster, Come Back, Peter, Little Lambs Eat Ivy, Its Never Too Late, The Unknown, Morning Departure, Confession. Dir.: Spring and Port Wine.
TELEVISION: Series: William Tell, Robin Hood, The Buccaneers. Dir.: Avengers, 4 Armchair Theatres, Theatre 625, BBC classic serials Count of Monte Cristo, Three Musketeers, Hereward the Wake, Treasure Island, Lord Raingo, Cold Comfort Farm, The White Rabbit, Out of the Unknown, Follyfoot; Lukes Kingdom, Time to Think, Franklin's Farm, Sea Song, Shades of Greene, Our Mutual Friend, The House that Jack Built, The King of the Castle, The Black Knight, Kilvert's Diary, Turgenev's Liza, Wuthering Heights, Funnyman, Little World of Don Camillo, Rumpole of the Bailey, Bring on the Girls, Hallelujah Mary Plum,

Aubrey Beardsley, The Happy Autumn Fields, The Combination, Tales of the Unexpected, The Glory Hole, The Hard Word, Shades of Darkness-The Maze, The Blue Dress.

HAMNER, EARL
Producer, Writer. b. Schuyler, VA, July 10, 1923. e. U. of Richmond 1940-43, Northwestern U.; U of Cincinnati, Coll. Conservatory of Music, B.F.A., 1958. With WLW, Cincinnati, as radio writer-producer; joined NBC 1949 as writer; (The Georgia Gibbs Show, The Helen O'Connell Show); freelance 1961-71; writer, prod. Lorimar Prods. 1971-86; writer prod. Taft Entertainment 1986-; Pres. Amanda Prods.
PICTURES: Palm Springs Weekend, Spencer's Mountain, The Tamarind Seed, Charlotte's Web (adaptor), Where the Lilies Bloom.
TELEVISION: *Exec. prod.: Series*: The Waltons (creator, co-prod., narrator), Apple's Way (creator), The Young Pioneers (creator), Joshua's World, Falcon Crest, Boone (also creator), Morning Star/Evening Star (also narrator). *Movies*: The Homecoming: A Christmas Story (writer only), You Can't Get There From Here (writer only), A Wedding on Walton's Mountain, Mother's Day on Walton's Mountain, A Day of Thanks on Walton's Mountain (also actor), The Gift of Love--A Christmas Story (also writer).

HAMPSHIRE, SUSAN
O.B.E., 1995. Actress. b. London, Eng., May 12, 1941.
THEATER: Expresso Bongo, Follow That Girl, Fairy Tales of New York, Ginger Man, Past Imperfect, She Stoops to Conquer, On Approval, The Sleeping Prince, A Doll's House, Taming of the Shrew, Peter Pan, Romeo & Jeanette, As You Like It, Miss Julie, The Circle, Arms and the Man, Man and Superman, Tribades, An Audience Called Edward, The Crucifer of Blood, Night and Day, The Revolt, House Guest, Blithe Spirit, Married Love, A Little Night Music, The King and I, Noel & Gertie, Relative Values, Susanna Andler, Black Chiffon.
PICTURES: The Three Lives of Thomasina, Night Must Fall, Wonderful Life, Paris Au Mois d'Aout, The Fighting Prince of Donegal, The Trygon Factor, Monte Carlo or Bust, Rogan, David Copperfield, A Room in Paris, Living Free, Time for Loving, Malpertius, Baffled, Neither the Sea nor the Sand, Roses and Green Peppers, David the King, Bang.
TELEVISION: Andromeda, The Forsyte Saga, Vanity Fair, Katy, The First Churchills: An Ideal Husband, The Lady Is a Liar, The Improbable Mr. Clayville, Dr. Jekyll and Mr. Hyde (musical), The Pallisers, Barchester Chronicles, Leaving, Leaving II, Going to Pot (I, II, and III), Don't Tell Father.

HAMPTON, JAMES
Actor. b. Oklahoma City, OK, July 9, 1936. e. N. Texas St. Univ.
PICTURES: Fade In, Soldier Blue, The Man Who Loved Cat Dancing, The Longest Yard, W.W. & The Dixie Dancekings, Hustle, Hawmps!, The Cat from Outer Space, Mackintosh & T.J., The China Syndrome, Hangar 18, Condorman, Teen Wolf, Teen Wolf Too, Police Academy 5, Pump Up the Volume, The Giant of Thunder Mountain.
TELEVISION: *Series*: F Troop, The Doris Day Show, Love—American Style, Mary, Maggie. *Movies*: Attack on Terror: The FBI Versus the Ku Klux Klan, Force Five, The Amazing Howard Hughes, Three on a Date, Thaddeus Rose and Eddie, Stand By Your Man, Through the Magic Pyramid, World War III, The Burning Bed. *Mini-Series*: Centennial.

HANCOCK, JOHN
Director. b. Kansas City, MO, Feb. 12, 1939. e. Harvard. Was musician and theatre director before turning to films. Dir. play A Man's a Man, NY 1962. Artistic dir. San Francisco Actors Workshop 1965-66, Pittsburgh Playhouse 1966-67. Obie for dir. Midsummer Night's Dream, NY 1968. Nominated for AA for short, Sticky My Fingers, Fleet My Feet.
PICTURES: Let's Scare Jessica to Death, Bang the Drum Slowly, Baby Blue Marine, California Dreaming, Weeds (also co-s.p.), Prancer.
TELEVISION: The Twilight Zone (1986), Hill Street Blues.

HAND, BETHLYN J.
Executive. b. Alton, IL. e. U. of Texas. Entered motion picture industry in 1966 as administrative assistant to president of Motion Picture Association of America, Inc. In 1975 became associate director of advertising administration of MPAA. In 1976 became director of advertising administration; in 1979 became; v.p.-west coast activities, board of directors, Los Angeles. S.P.C.A. 1981, appointed by Governor to Calif. Motion Picture Council 1983, elected vice chmn., California Motion Picture Council. 1990, named sr. v.p. MPAA.

HANDEL, LEO A.
Producer, Director. b. Vienna, Austria, Mar. 7, 1924. e. Univ. of Vienna (Ph.D. economics). Dir. audience research, MGM, 1942-51; organized Meteor Prod., 1951; organized Leo A. Handel Prod., for TV films, 1953; author, Hollywood Looks at Its Audience, also TV plays; pres., Handel Film Corp. Exec. prod. & v.p., Four Crown Prods., Inc. Prod.-writer-dir., feature film, The Case of Patty Smith, 1961; book, A Dog Named Duke, 1965.

TELEVISION: prod. TV series including Everyday Adventures, Magic of the Atom. exec. prod., Phantom Planet, Americana Series. Also produced numerous educational specials and videos.

HANKS, TOM
Actor. b. Concord, CA, July 9, 1956. m. actress Rita Wilson. Traveled around Northern CA. with family before settling in Oakland, CA. e. Chabot Jr. Col., California State U. Began career with Great Lakes Shakespeare Festival, Cleveland (3 seasons) and NY's Riverside Theater (Taming of the Shrew).
PICTURES: He Knows You're Alone (debut, 1980), Splash, Bachelor Party, The Man With One Red Shoe, Volunteers, The Money Pit, Nothing in Common, Every Time We Say Goodbye, Dragnet, Big (Acad. Award nom.), Punchline, The 'Burbs, Turner and Hooch, Joe Versus the Volcano, The Bonfire of the Vanities, Radio Flyer (unbilled), A League of Their Own, Sleepless in Seattle, Philadelphia (Academy Award, 1993; Golden Globe Award), Forrest Gump (Academy Award, 1994; Golden Globe Award), Apollo 13, Toy Story (voice), That Thing You Do! (also dir.).
TELEVISION: *Series*: Bosom Buddies. *Guest*: The Love Boat, Taxi, Happy Days, Family Ties, Saturday Night Live, Tales From the Crypt (None but the Lonely Heart; also dir.), Fallen Angels (I'll Be Waiting; also dir.), The Naked Truth. *Movie*: Rona Jaffe's Mazes and Monsters. *Episode Dir.*: A League of Their Own.

HANNA, WILLIAM
Executive. b. Melrose, NM, July 14, 1910. e. Compton Coll. Studied engineering and journalism. Joined firm in CA as structural engineer; turned to cartooning when Leon Schlessinger's company in Hollywood. In 1937 hired by MGM as director and story man in cartoon dept. There met Joseph R. Barbera and created famous cartoon series Tom & Jerry, continuing to produce it from 1938 to 1957. Left MGM in 1957 to form Hanna-Barbera Productions to make cartoons for TV. Series have included Yogi Bear, Huckleberry Hound, The Flintstones, The Jetsons. Hanna-Barbera became a subsidiary of Taft Broadcasting Co. in 1968 with both men operating studio under long-term agreements with Taft (which became Great American Broadcasting, 1987). Received Governor's Award from Academy of Television Arts & Sciences, 1988.
PICTURES: Hey There It's Yogi Bear, A Man Called Flintstone, Charlotte's Web, C.H.O.M.P.S., Heidi's Song, Once Upon a Forest, The Flintstones (co-exec. prod. of live-action film; also cameo appearance).
TELEVISION: *Series*: The Huckleberry Hound Show (Emmy Award), Quick Draw McGraw, The Flintstones, The Jetsons, Jonny Quest, Top Cat, Scooby-Doo, Smurfs (2 Emmy Awards). *Movies*: I Yabba Dabba Do!, Hollyrock-a-Bye Baby.

HANNAH, DARYL
Actress. b. Chicago, IL, 1960. Niece of cinematographer Haskell Wexler. e. UCLA. Studied ballet with Maria Tallchief. Studied acting with Stella Adler.
PICTURES: The Fury (debut, 1978), The Final Terror, Hard Country, Blade Runner, Summer Lovers, Reckless, Splash, The Pope of Greenwich Village, Clan of the Cave Bear, Legal Eagles, Roxanne, Wall Street, High Spirits, Crimes and Misdemeanors, Steel Magnolias, Crazy People, At Play in the Fields of the Lord, Memoirs of an Invisible Man, Grumpy Old Men, The Little Rascals, The Tie That Binds, Two Much, Grumpier Old Men.
TELEVISION: *Movies*: Paper Dolls, Attack of the 50 Ft. Woman (also co-prod.).

HANNEMANN, WALTER A.
Film editor. b. Atlanta, GA, May 2, 1914. e. USC, 1935. Editorial training, RKO 1936-40; edit. supvr., Universal, 1941-42; consultant 1970-75 national educational media. Bd. of govs., TV Academy (2 terms, 1960 & 1970); bd. of govs., AMPAS. 1983-86; board of dir., Motion Picture Film Editors, 1944-48, 1981-88, past v.p., American Cinema Editors.
PICTURES: Interval, The Revengers, Dream of Kings, Guns of the Magnificent Seven, Krakatoa: East of Java, The Bob Mathias Story, Pay or Die, Al Capone. (Amer. Cinema Editor's Award, 1959), Hell's Five Hours, Armoured Command, Only the Valiant, Time of Your Life, Kiss Tomorrow Goodbye, Blood on the Sun, Guest in the House, Texas Masquerade, Cannon for Cardoba, El Condor, Maurie, Lost in the Stars, Big Mo, Two Minute Warning (Acad. Award nom.) Smokey and the Bandit (Acad. Award nom.), The Other Side of the Mountain-Part II, The Visitor, The Villain, The Nude Bomb, Charlie Chan and the Curse of the Dragon Queen.
TELEVISION: *Series*: Death Valley Days, Reader's Digest, Rosemary Clooney Show, The New Breed, The Fugitive, Twelve O'Clock High, The Invaders, Hawaii Five-O, Streets of San Francisco, Cannon, Barnaby Jones, Caribe. Movies: The Man Who Broke a 1000 Chains, Intimate Strangers, The Abduction of Saint Anne, The Day the Loving Stopped.Han

HANSON, CURTIS
Director, Writer. b. Los Angeles, CA, 1946. Editor of Cinema magazine before becoming screenwriter.

PICTURES: *Writer*: The Silent Partner, White Dog, Never Cry Wolf. *Director*: The Arousers (Sweet Kill), Little Dragons, The Bedroom Window (also s.p.), Bad Influence, The Hand That Rocks the Cradle, The River Wild.
TELEVISION: *Movie*: The Children of Times Square.

HARBACH, WILLIAM O.
Producer. b. Yonkers, NY, Oct. 12, 1919, e. Brown U. Father was lyricst Otto Harbach. Served with U.S. Coast Guard, 1940-45; actor, MGM, 1945-47; broadcast co-ordinator. NBC, 1947-49; stage mgr., 1949-50; dir., NBC, 1950-53
TELEVISION: *Producer*: Tonight, Steve Allen Show, Bing Crosby shows (also dir.), Milton Berle Special, Hollywood Palace, The Julie Andrews Show (Emmy Award, 1973), Shirley MacLaine's Gypsy in My Soul (Emmy Award, 1976), Bob Hope Specials.

HARBERT, TED
Executive. e. Boston Univ. 1976-77, prod. of new dept. at WHDH radio in Boston. Joined ABC, 1977 as feature film coordinator; 1979, named supervisor, feature film and late-night program planning, then assst. to v.p., program planning & scheduling; 1981, became dir. program planning & scheduling; 1984, promoted to v.p. program planning & scheduling; 1987, named v.p. motion pictures and scheduling, ABC Entertainment; 1988, v.p., prime time, ABC Entertainment; 1989, became exec. v.p., Prime Time, ABC Entertainment; 1993, promoted to pres. of ABC Entertainment.

HARDEN, MARCIA GAY
Actress. b. La Jolla, CA, Aug. 14, 1959.
Father was naval captain. Schooled in Athens, Munich, then returned to states attending Univ. of TX, NYU. Stage work in Washington D.C. in Crimes of the Heart, The Miss Firecracker Contest.
THEATER: *Off-B'way*: The Man Who Shot Lincoln (debut, 1989), Those the River Keeps, The Skin of Our Teeth, The Years, Simpatico. *B'way*: Angels in America: Millenium Approaches/Perestroika (Theatre World Award; Tony nom.)
PICTURES: Miller's Crossing (debut, 1990), Late for Dinner, Used People, Crush, Safe Passage, The Spitfire Grill, The First Wives Club, Spy Hard.
TELEVISION: *Mini-Series*: Sinatra. *Movie*: Fever.

HARDISON, KADEEM
Actor. b. Brooklyn, NY, July 24, 1966. Studied acting with Earl Hyman and at H.B.Studios.
PICTURES: Beat Street (debut, 1984), Rappin', School Daze, I'm Gonna Git You Sucka, Def by Temptation, White Men Can't Jump, Gunmen, Renaissance Man, Panther, Vampire in Brooklyn.
TELEVISION: *Series*: A Different World. *Specials*: The Color of Friendship, Amazing Grace, Don't Touch, Go Tell It on the Mountain. *Movie*: Dream Date. *Guest*: The Cosby Show, Spenser for Hire.

HARE, DAVID
Writer, Director. b. St. Leonards, Sussex, England, June 5, 1947. e. Lancing Coll., Jesus Coll., Cambridge. After leaving univ. in 1968 formed Portable Theatre Company, experimental touring group. Hired by Royal Court Theater as literary manager, 1969. 1970, first full-length play, Slag, prod. at Hampstead Theatre Club. Resident dramatist, Royal Court (1970-71), and Nottingham Playhouse (1973). Assoc. dir., National Theatre. West End debut, Knuckle.
THEATER: Slag, The Great Exhibition, Brassneck, Knuckle, Fanshen, Teeth 'n' Smiles, Plenty, A Map of the World, Pravda, The Bay at Nice, Secret Rapture, Racing Demon, Murmuring Judges, Rules of the Game (new version of Pirandello Play), Brecht's The Absence of War, Skylight, Galileo, Mother Courage.
PICTURES: *Writer*: Plenty, Wetherby (also dir.), Paris by Night (also dir.), Strapless (also dir.), Damage.
TELEVISION: *Writer*: Licking Hitler (also dir.), Dreams of Leaving (also dir.), Saigon: Year of the Cat, Knuckle, Heading Home (also dir.).

HAREWOOD, DORIAN
Actor. b. Dayton, OH, Aug. 6, 1950. m. actress Ann McCurry. e. U. of Cincinnati.
THEATER: Jesus Christ Superstar (road co.), Two Gentlemen of Verona, Miss Moffat, Streamers, Over Here, Don't Call Back (Theatre World Award), The Mighty Gents.
PICTURES: Sparkle (debut, 1976), Gray Lady Down, Looker, Tank, Against All Odds, The Falcon and the Snowman, Full Metal Jacket, Pacific Heights, Solar Crisis, The Pagemaster (voice), Sudden Death.
TELEVISION: *Series*: Strike Force, Trauma Center, Glitter, The Trials of Rosie O'Neill, Viper. *Mini-Series*: Roots: The Next Generations, Amerika. *Movies*: Foster and Laurie, Panic in Echo Park, Siege, An American Christmas Carol, High Ice, Beulah Land, The Ambush Murders, I Desire, The Jesse Owens Story, Guilty of Innocence, God Bless the Child, Kiss Shot, Polly, Polly-Comin' Home!, Getting Up and Going Home, Bermuda Grace, Shattered Image. *Pilot*: Half 'n' Half.

HARGREAVES, JOHN
Executive. b. Freckleton, Lancashire, Eng., July 1921. Joined Gainsborough Pictures 1945. Transferred to Denham Studios 1946 and later Pinewood Studios. Joined Allied Film Makers 1960, then Salamander Productions as Bryan Forbes' financial controller and asst. prod. 1965. Joined EMI Film Prods. Ltd. as asst. man. dir. and prod. controller 1969-72. 1983-, U.K. dir. and production executive for Completion Bond Company, Inc. Cal. USA.
PICTURES: Don Quixote (prod.), The Slipper and the Rose (prod. asst.), International Velvet (assoc. prod.), The Awakening (prod. rep.), The Fiendish Plot of Dr. Fu Manchu (post-prod. exec.), Excalibur (prod. rep.), The Year of Living Dangerously, Carrington (financial consultant).

HARKINS, DANIEL E.
Executive, Exhibitor. b. Mesa, AZ, Feb. 6, 1953. e. Arizona State U. Joined Harkins Theatres in 1968. Acquired company in 1975. President and CEO Harkins Amusement Enterprises, Inc. National NATO bd. member. Pres., Arizona Theatre Assoc. V.P., Governor's Film Commission. Recipient of United Motion Picture Assoc. National Showman of the Year award 1976, 1980, 1981. Hollywood Reported Marketing Concept award, 1983. Box Office Showmandizer award, 1976, 1978, and several others.

HARLIN, RENNY
Director. b. Helsinki, Finland, 1958. e. Univ. of Helsinki film school. Formed prod. co. Midnight Sun Pictures. m. actress Geena Davis.
PICTURES: Born American (debut, 1986), Prison, A Nightmare on Elm Street IV: The Dream Master, Die Hard 2, The Adventures of Ford Fairlane, Rambling Rose (prod. only), Cliffhanger, Speechless (co-prod. only), Cutthroat Island (also prod.), The Long Kiss Goodnight.

HARMON, MARK
Actor. b. Burbank, CA, Sept. 2, 1951. Son of actress Elyse Knox and football star Tom Harmon. m. actress Pam Dawber. Brother of actresses Kelly and Kristin Harmon. On stage in Wrestlers, The Wager (both L.A.), Key Exchange (Toronto).
PICTURES: Comes a Horseman, Beyond the Poseidon Adventure, Let's Get Harry, Summer School, The Presidio, Stealing Home, Worth Winning, Till There Was You, Cold Heaven, Wyatt Earp, Magic in the Water, The Last Supper.
TELEVISION: *Series*: Sam, 240-Robert, Flamingo Road, St. Elsewhere, Reasonable Doubts, Charlie Grace. *Movies*: Eleanor and Franklin: The White House Years, Getting Married, Little Mo, Flamingo Road (pilot), The Dream Merchants, Goliath Awaits, Intimate Agony, The Deliberate Stranger, Prince of Bel Air, Sweet Bird of Youth, Dillinger, Fourth Story, Long Road Home, Shadow of a Doubt. *Guest*: Adam-12, Laverne & Shirley, Nancy Drew, Police Story, Moonlighting. *Mini-Series*: Centennial.

HARNELL, STEWART D.
Executive. b. New York, NY, Aug. 18, 1938. e. U. of Miami, UCLA, New School for Social Research. Entertainer with Youth Parade in Coral Gables, FL, 1948-55, performing for handicapped children, Variety Club, etc. as singer, dancer, musician. Had own bands, Teen Aces & Rhythm Rascals, 1950-56; performed on Cactus Jim TV show and Wood & Ivory, 1953-54, WTVJ, Miami. Catskills, Sand Lake, NY, 1954-55. Joined National Screen Service as exec. trainee in 1960 in Chicago; worked as booker & salesman. Transferred to NY home office, 1963; worked in special trailer production. Promoted to gen. sls. mgr., 1964-66; New Orleans branch mgr., 1966-67; Atlanta division mgr., 1967-70. Formed own distribution co., 1970-77 Harnell Independent Productions. Resumed post as gen. sls. mgr. of NSS, New York, 1977-78; In 1986, founded Cinema Concepts. In 1995, founded Silver Screen Signs & Display, Inc. Chief barker of Variety Club of Atlanta, Tent 21, 1972, 1976, 1979, 1988, 1989, 1993, 1994. In 1986 formed Cinema Concepts Communications, film-video animation studio in Atlanta. Motion Picture Pioneers Bd. of Directors (1990-97).

HARPER, JESSICA
Actress. b. Chicago, IL, Oct. 10, 1949. m. prod. exec. Thomas E. Rothman. e. Sarah Lawrence Coll. Understudied on Broadway for Hair for one year. Appeared in summer stock and off-B'way shows (Richard Farina: Long Time Coming Longtime Gone, Doctor Selavy's Magic Theatre.)
PICTURES: Taking Off, Phantom of the Paradise, Love and Death, Inserts, Suspiria, The Evictors, Stardust Memories, Shock Treatment, Pennies from Heaven, My Favorite Year, The Imagemaker, Once Again, The Blue Iguana, Big Man on Campus, Mr. Wonderful, Safe.
TELEVISION: *Series*: Little Women, It's Garry Shandling's Show. *Mini-Series*: Studs Lonigan, Aspen (The Innocent and the Damned), When Dreams Come True. *Special*: The Garden Party. *Guest*: Tales From the Darkside, The Equalizer, Trying Times (Bedtime Story), Wiseguy.

HARPER, TESS
Actress. b. Mammoth Springs, AR, 1952. e. Southwest Missouri State Coll., Springfield. Worked in Houston, then Dallas in children's theater, dinner theater, and commercials.

PICTURES: Tender Mercies (debut, 1983), Amityville 3-D, Silkwood, Flashpoint, Crimes of the Heart (Acad. Award nom.), Ishtar, Far North, Her Alibi, Criminal Law, Daddy's Dyin'... Who's Got the Will?, My Heroes Have Always Been Cowboys, The Man in the Moon, My New Gun.
TELEVISION: Mini-Series: Chiefs, Celebrity. Movies: Kentucky Woman, Starflight: The Plane That Couldn't Land, A Summer to Remember, Promises to Keep, Little Girl Lost, Unconquered, In the Line of Duty: Siege at Marion, Willing to Kill: The Texas Cheerleader Story, Death in Small Doses.

HARPER, VALERIE
Actress. b. Suffern, NY. Aug. 22, 1940. e. Hunter Coll, New Sch. for Social Research. Started as dancer in stage shows at Radio City Music Hall. First professional acting in summer stock in Conn.; actress with Second City Chicago 1964-69; Appeared on B'way. in Lil' Abner, Take Me Along, Wildcat, Subways Are for Sleeping, Something Different, Story Theatre, Metamorphoses. Won 3 Emmys for best performance in supporting role in comedy for portrayal of Rhoda on The Mary Tyler Moore Show and 1 for best leading actress on Rhoda. Off B'way, Death Defying Acts (1995-96).
PICTURES: Rock Rock Rock, Lil Abner, Freebie and the Bean, Chapter Two, The Last Married Couple in America, Blame It on Rio.
TELEVISION: Series: The Mary Tyler Show, Rhoda, Valerie, City, The Office. Movies: Thursday's Game, Night Terror, Fun and Games, The Shadow Box, The Day the Loving Stopped, Farrell for the People (pilot), Don't Go to Sleep, An Invasion of Privacy, Execution, Strange Voices, Drop Out Mother, The People Across the Lake, Stolen: One Husband, A Friend To Die For, The Great Mom Swap.

HARRELSON, WOODY
Actor. b. Midland, TX, July 23, 1961. e. Hanover Col. First professional acting job as understudy for B'way production of Biloxi Blues.
THEATER: NY: The Boys Next Door. LA: 2 on 2 (also wrote & prod.), The Zoo Story (also prod.), Brooklyn Laundry.
PICTURES: Wildcats (debut, 1986), Cool Blue, L.A. Story, Doc Hollywood, Ted and Venus, White Men Can't Jump, Indecent Proposal, I'll Do Anything, The Cowboy Way, Natural Born Killers, Money Train, The Sunchaser, Kingpin, The People vs. Larry Flynt.
TELEVISION: Series: Cheers (Emmy Award, 1989). Movies: Bay Coven, Killer Instinct. Special: Mother Goose Rock 'n' Rhyme.

HARRINGTON, CURTIS
Director, Writer. b. Los Angeles, CA, Sept. 17, 1928. e. U. of Southern California, B.A. Exec. asst. to Jerry Wald, 1955-61 Associate producer at 20th Cent. Fox.
PICTURES: Assoc. Prod.: Mardi Gras (also story), Hound Dog Man, Return to Peyton Place, The Stripper. Director: Night Tide (also s.p.), Queen of Blood (Planet of Blood; also s.p.), Games (also co-story), What's the Matter with Helen?, Who Slew Auntie Roo?, The Killing Kind, Ruby, Mata Hari.
TELEVISION: Series episodes: Hotel, Dynasty, The Colby's, Tales of the Unexpected, Twilight Zone, Baretta, Vega$, Glitter, Logan's Run. Movies: How Awful About Allan, The Cat Creature, Killer Bees, The Dead Don't Die, Devil Dog: The Hound of Hell.

HARRINGTON, PAT
Actor. b. New York, NY, Aug. 13, 1929. e. Fordham U. Served USAF as 1st Lt., 1952-54. Time salesman for NBC, 1954-58.
PICTURES: The Wheeler Dealers, Move Over Darling, Easy Come Easy Go, The President's Analyst, 2000 Years Later, The Candidate.
TELEVISION: Series: The Steve Allen Show, The Danny Thomas Show, The Jack Paar Show, Stump the Stars (host), Mr. Deeds Goes to Town, One Day at a Time (Emmy Award, 1984).

HARRIS, BARBARA
Actress. b. Evanston, IL, July 25, 1935. r.n. Sandra Markowitz. e. Wright Junior Coll., Chicago; Goodman Sch. of the Theatre; U. of Chicago. Joined acting troup, The Compass. Founding member, Second City Players, 1960. Came to NY where first role was in Oh Dad Poor Dad Mama's Hung You in the Closet and I'm Feeling So Sad (Theatre World Award), repeating role in film version.
THEATER: Mother Courage and Her Children, Dynamite Tonight, On a Clear Day You Can See Forever, The Apple Tree (Tony Award, 1967), Mahogany.
PICTURES: A Thousand Clowns (debut, 1965), Oh Dad Poor Dad Mama's Hung You in the Closet and I'm Feeling So Sad, Plaza Suite, Who Is Harry Kellerman and Why Is He Saying Those Terrible Things About Me? (Acad. Award nom.), The War Between Men and Women, The Manchu Eagle Murder Caper Mystery, Mixed Company, Nashville, Family Plot, Freaky Friday, Movie Movie, The North Avenue Irregulars, The Seduction of Joe Tynan, Second Hand Hearts, Peggy Sue Got Married, Nice Girls Don't Explode, Dirty Rotten Scoundrels.
TELEVISION: Guest: Alfred Hitchcock Presents, Naked City, The Defenders.

HARRIS, BURTT
Producer, Actor. Began career as actor; later worked with Elia Kazan as prod. asst. and asst. dir. on America America, Splendor in the Grass, and The Arrangement. Worked as second unit dir. and asst. dir. on many films as well as producer and actor.
PICTURES: Associate Producer: Little Murders, The Wiz, Cruising, Gilda Live. Executive Producer: The Verdict, Just Tell Me What You Want,. See No Evil, Hear No Evil, Family Business. Producer: Prince of the City, Daniel, Deathtrap, Garbo Talks, The Glass Menagerie, Q & A. Co-Producer: D.A.R.Y.L. Actor: Splendor in the Grass, Fail Safe, The Taking of Pelham 1-2-3, The Wanderers, The Verdict, Daniel, Garbo Talks, D.A.R.Y.L., Running on Empty, Hudson Hawk, Undertow, A Stranger Among Us.

HARRIS, ED
Actor. b. Tenafly, NJ, Nov. 28, 1950. m. actress Amy Madigan. Played football 2 years at Columbia U. prior to enrolling in acting classes at OK State U. Summer stock. Grad. CA Institute of the Arts, B.F.A. 1975. Worked in West Coast Theater.
THEATER: NY: Fool For Love (Off-B'way debut; Obie Award), Precious Sons (B'way debut; Theatre World Award), Simpatico, Taking Sides. LA: Scar.
PICTURES: Coma (debut, 1978), Borderline, Knightriders, Dream On, Creepshow, The Right Stuff, Under Fire, Swing Shift, Places in the Heart, Alamo Bay, A Flash of Green, Sweet Dreams, Code Name: Emerald, Walker, To Kill a Priest, Jacknife, The Abyss, State of Grace, Glengarry Glen Ross, The Firm, Needful Things, China Moon, Milk Money, Just Cause, Apollo 13, Eye for an Eye, Nixon, The Rock.
TELEVISION: Movies: The Amazing Howard Hughes, The Seekers, The Aliens Are Coming (Alien Force), The Last Innocent Man, Paris Trout, Running Mates, Riders of the Purple Sage. Mini-Series: The Stand.

HARRIS, JAMES B.
Producer, Director, Writer. b. New York, NY, Aug. 3, 1928. e. Juilliard Sch. U.S. film export, 1947; Realart Pictures, 1948; formed Flamingo Films, 1949; formed Harris-Kubrick Productions, 1954. formed James B. Harris Prods., Inc., 1963.
PICTURES: Producer: The Killing, Paths of Glory, Lolita, The Bedford Incident (also dir.), Some Call It Loving (also dir., s.p.), Telefon, Fast-Walking (also dir., s.p.), Cop (also dir., s.p.), Boiling Point (dir., s.p.).

HARRIS, JULIE
Designer. b. London, England. e. Chelsea Arts Sch. Entered industry in 1945 designing for Gainsborough Studios. First film, Holiday Camp.
PICTURES: Greengage Summer, Naked Edge, The War Lover, Fast Lady, Chalk Garden, Psyche 59, A Hard Day's Night, Darling, Help!, The Wrong Box, Casino Royale, Deadfall, Prudence and the Pill, Decline and Fall, Goodbye Mr. Chips, Sherlock Holmes, Follow Me!, Live and Let Die, Rollerball, Slipper and The Rose, Dracula.
TELEVISION: Laura (with Lee Radziwill), Candleshoe, The Sailor's Return, Lost and Found, The Kingfisher, Arch of Triumph, Sign of Four, Hound of the Baskervilles, A Hazard of Hearts, A Perfect Hero.

HARRIS, JULIE
Actress. b. Grosse Pointe, MI, Dec. 2, 1925. e. Yale Drama Sch.
THEATER: Sundown Beach, Playboy of the Western World, Macbeth, Young and the Fair, Magnolia Alley, Monserrat, Member of the Wedding, I Am a Camera (Tony Award, 1952), Colombe, The Lark (Tony Award, 1956), A Shot in the Dark, Marathon 33, Ready When You Are, C.B., Break a Leg, Skyscraper, Voices, And Miss Reardon Drinks a Little, 40 Carats (Tony Award, 1969), The Last of Mrs. Lincoln (Tony Award, 1973), In Praise of Love, The Belle of Amherst (Tony Award, 1973), Driving Miss Daisy (Natl. co.), Lucifer's Child, Lettice & Lovage (tour), The Fiery Furnace (Off-B'way debut, 1993), The Glass Menagerie.
PICTURES: The Member of the Wedding (debut, 1952; Acad. Award nom.), East of Eden, I Am a Camera, The Truth About Women, The Poacher's Daughter, Requiem for a Heavyweight, The Haunting, Harper, You're a Big Boy Now, Reflections in a Golden Eye, The Split, The People Next Door, The Hiding Place, Voyage of the Damned, The Bell Jar, Nutcracker: The Motion Picture (voice), Gorillas in the Mist, Housesitter, The Dark Half, Carried Away.
TELEVISION: Specials: Little Moon of Alban (Emmy Award, 1959), Johnny Belinda, A Doll's House, Ethan Frome, The Good Fairy, The Lark, He Who Gets Slapped, The Heiress, Victoria Regina (Emmy Award, 1962), Pygmalion, Anastasia, The Holy Terror, The Power and The Glory, The Woman He Loved. Movies: The House on Greenapple Road, How Awful About Alan, Home for the Holidays, The Greatest Gift, The Gift, Too Good To Be True, The Christmas Wife, They've Taken Our Children: The Chowchilla Kidnapping, When Love Kills: The Seduction of John Hearn, One Christmas. Series: Thicker Than Water, The Family Holvak, Knots Landing. Mini-Series: Backstairs at the White House, Scarlett.

HARRIS, MEL
Actress. b. Bethlehem, PA, July 12, 1957. r.n. Mary Ellen Harris. e. Columbia. Career as successful model before turning to acting in 1984. NY theatre debut in Empty Hearts, 1992 (Theatre World Award).
PICTURES: Wanted: Dead or Alive, Cameron's Closet, K-9, Raising Cain, Desperate Motive (Distant Cousins), Suture, The Pagemaster.
TELEVISION: *Series*: thirtysomething, Something So Right. *Guest*: M*A*S*H, Alfred Hitchcock Presents, Rags to Riches, Heart of the City, The Wizard. *Movies*: Seduced, Harry's Hong Kong, Cross of Fire, My Brother's Wife, The Burden of Proof, Grass Roots, Child of Rage, With Hostile Intent, Desperate Journey: The Allison Wilcox Story, Ultimate Betrayal, The Spider and the Fly, The Women of Spring Break, Sharon's Secret.

HARRIS, NEIL PATRICK
Actor. b. Albuquerque, NM, June 15, 1973. While attending week-long theatre camp at New Mexico St. Univ. met writer Mark Medoff who suggested him for co-starring role in Clara's Heart.
THEATER: Luck Pluck and Virtue (Off-B'way debut, 1995).
PICTURES: Clara's Heart (debut, 1988), Purple People Eater, Hairspray.
TELEVISION: *Series*: Doogie Howser M.D., Capitol Critters (voice). *Movies*: Too Good to Be True, Home Fires Burning, Cold Sassy Tree, Stranger in the Family, A Family Torn Apart, Snowbound: The Jim and Jennifer Stolpa Story, Not Our Son, My Antonia, The Man in the Attic, Legacy of Sin: The William Coit Story. *Guest*: B. J. Stryker, Carol & Company, Roseanne, Quantum Leap, Murder She Wrote.

HARRIS, RICHARD
Actor. b. Limerick, Ireland, Oct. 1, 1930. Attended London Acad. of Music and Dramatic Arts. Prod.-dir. Winter Journey 1956. Prof. acting debut in Joan Littlewood's prod. of The Quare Fellow, Royal Stratford, 1956. Recorded hit song MacArthur's Park, 1968. Author of novel Honor Bound (1982) and poetry compilation: I in the Membership of My Days (1973).
THEATER: *London*: A View from the Bridge, Man Beast and Virtue, The Ginger Man. *B'way*: Camelot.
PICTURES: Alive and Kicking (debut, 1958), Shake Hands With the Devil, The Wreck of the Mary Deare, A Terrible Beauty (Night Fighters), The Long The Short and The Tall (Jungle Fighters), The Guns of Navarone, Mutiny on the Bounty, This Sporting Life (Acad. Award nom.), Red Desert, Major Dundee, The Heroes of Telemark, The Bible, Hawaii, Caprice, Camelot, The Molly Maguires, A Man Called Horse, Cromwell, The Hero (Bloomfield; also dir., s.p.), Man in the Wilderness, The Deadly Trackers, 99 and 44/100% Dead, Juggernaut, Echoes of a Summer (also co-exec. prod.), Robin and Marian, Return of a Man Called Horse (also co-exec. prod.), The Cassandra Crossing, Gulliver's Travels, Orca, Golden Rendezvous, The Wild Geese, Ravagers, The Last Word, Game for Vultures, Your Ticket Is No Longer Valid, Highpoint, Tarzan the Ape Man, Martin's Day, Triumphs of a Man Called Horse, Mack the Knife, The Field (Acad. Award nom.), Patriot Games, Unforgiven, Wrestling Ernest Hemingway, Silent Tongue, Savage Hearts, Cry the Beloved Country.
TELEVISION: *Specials*: Ricardo, The Iron Harp, The Snow Goose, Camelot. *Movies*: Maigret, The Return.

HARRIS, ROBERT A.
Archivist, Producer. b. New York, NY, Dec. 27, 1945. e. NYU, Sch. of Commerce and Sch. of Arts, 1968. Worked as exec. trainee with 7 Arts assoc., NY while in school, 1960-68; worked in corp. communications, Pepsico, 1970-71; formed Center for Instructional Resources, SUNY Purchase, 1971-73; organized Images Film Archive, dist. of classic theatrical and non theat. films, 1974; pres., Images Video and Film Archive, 1985; formed Davnor Prods., president 1986-present; formed The Film Preserve, Inc. pres. 1989-. 1975-80: restored Abel Gance films Beethoven, J'Accuse, Lucretia Borgia; 1974-79: worked with Kevin Brownlow to complete restoration of Abel Gance's Napoleon. Partnered with Francis Coppola/Zoetrope Studios to present Napoleon at Radio City Music Hall, 1981 and worldwide tour; 1986-89; reconstruction and restoration of David Lean's Lawrence of Arabia for Columbia Pictures, released 1989; The Grifters (prod.); restoration and reconstruction of Stanley Kubrick's Spartacus for Univ. Pictures, 1991; restoration of George Cukor's My Fair Lady for CBS Video, 1994, restoration in SuperVistaVision 70 of Alfred Hitchcock's Vertigo, 1996.

HARRIS, ROSEMARY
Actress. b. Ashby, Suffolk, Sept. 19, 1930. e. India and England. Early career, nursing; studied Royal Acad. of Dramatic Art, 1951-52.
THEATER: Climate of Eden (NY debut 1952), Seven Year Itch, Confidential Clerk (Paris Festival), and with Bristol Old Vic in The Crucible, Much Ado About Nothing, Merchant of Venice. With Old Vic, 1955-56; U.S. tour, 1956-57; U.S. stage, 1958-63. Chichester Festivals 1962 and 63; Nat'l Theatre 1963-64; You Can't Take It With You, 1965; The Lion in Winter (Tony Award, 1966), 1967, APA Repertory Co., Heartbreak House, The Royal Family, The New York Idea (Obie Award), Pack of Lies, Hay Fever, Lost in Yonkers, An Inspector Calls, A Delicate Balance.
PICTURES: Beau Brummell, The Shiralee, A Flea in Her Ear, The Boys from Brazil, The Ploughman's Lunch, Crossing Delancey, Tom and Viv (Acad. Award nom.), Hamlet.
TELEVISION: *Series*: The Chisholms. *Specials*: Cradle of Willow (debut, 1951), Othello, The Prince and the Pauper, Twelfth Night, Wuthering Heights, Notorious Woman (Emmy Award, 1976), Blithe Spirit, Profiles in Courage, To the Lighthouse, Strange Interlude, Tales From the Hollywood Hills: The Old Reliable. *Mini-Series*: Holocaust (Golden Globe Award), The Chisholms.

HARRIS, TIMOTHY
Writer, Producer. b. Los Angeles, CA, July 21, 1946. e. Charterhouse, 1963-65; Peterhouse Coll., Cambridge, 1966-69, M.A. Honors Degree, Eng. lit. Author of novels, Kronski/McSmash, Kyd For Hire, Goodnight and Goodbye; author of novelizations, Steelyard Blues, Hit, Heatwave, American Gigolo.
PICTURES: Co-writer with Herschel Weingrod: Cheaper to Keep Her, Trading Places (BAFTA nom., orig. s.p.; NAACP Image Awards, best m.p. 1983), Brewster's Millions, My Stepmother is an Alien, Paint It Black, Twins (People's Choice Award, best comedy, 1988), Kindergarten Cop, Pure Luck. Co-Prod.: Falling Down.
TELEVISION: Street of Dreams (based on his novel Goodnight and Goodbye; also exec. prod.).

HARRISON, GEORGE
Singer, Composer, Producer. b. Liverpool, England, Feb. 25, 1943. Former member, The Beatles. Winner of 2 Grammys on own in addition to Beatles' group awards. Founder of Handmade Films.
PICTURES: *Performer*: A Hard Day's Night (debut, 1964), Help!, Yellow Submarine (cameo), Let It Be, The Concert for Bangladesh (also prod.). *Exec. Prod.*: Little Malcolm. *Exec. Prod.* (for Handmade Films): Life of Brian (also cameo), Time Bandits, Monty Python Live at the Hollywood Bowl, The Missionary, Privates on Parade, Scrubbers, Bullshot, A Private Function, Water (also cameo), Mona Lisa, Shanghai Surprise (also songs, cameo), Withnail and I, Five Corners, Bellman and True, The Lonely Passion of Judith Hearne, Track 29, How to Get Ahead in Advertising, Powwow Highway, Checking Out, Cold Dog Soup, Nuns on the Run, The Raggedy Rawney.

HARRISON, GREGORY
Actor, Producer, Director. b. Avalon, Catalina Island, CA, May 31, 1950. Started acting in school plays; then joined Army (1969-71). Studied at Estelle Harman Actors Workshop; later with Lee Strasberg and Stella Adler. Formed Catalina Productions with Franklin Levy, 1981.
THEATER: Child's Play, Carnal Knowledge, Picnic, The Hasty Heart, Love Letters, Festival, Billy Budd, The Subject Was Roses, The Promise, The Music Man, Paper Moon- The Musical.
PICTURES: Jim: the World's Greatest (debut, 1976), Fraternity Row, Razorback, North Shore (also 2nd unit dir.), Voice of a Stranger (also 2nd unit dir.), Cadillac Girls, It's My Party.
TELEVISION: *Series*: Logan's Run, Trapper John M.D. (also dir. 6 episodes), Falcon Crest, The Family Man, True Detectives, New York News. *Guest*: M*A*S*H, Barnaby Jones, Sisters. *Movies* (actor): The Gathering, Enola Gay, Trilogy in Terror, The Best Place To Be, The Women's Room, For Ladies Only (also co-prod.), The Fighter, Seduced (also exec. prod.), Oceans of Fire, Hot Paint, Red River, Dangerous Pursuit, Angel of Death, Bare Essentials, Breaking the Silence, Duplicates, Split Images, Caught in the Act, A Family Torn Apart, Lies of the Heart: The Story of Laurie Kellogg, Robin Cook's Mortal Fear, A Christmas Romance, A Dangerous Affair, Nothing Lasts Forever. *Mini-series*: Centennial, Fresno, 500 Nations (narrator). *Movies* (exec. prod. only): Thursday's Child, Legs, Samson & Delilah, The Tower.

HARROLD, KATHRYN
Actress. b. Tazewell, VA, Aug. 2, 1950. e. Mills Coll. Studied acting at Neighborhood Playhouse in N.Y., also with Uta Hagen. Appeared in Off-Off-B'way. plays for year; then joined experimental theatre group, Section Ten, touring East, performing and teaching at Connecticut Coll. and NYU. Cast in TV daytime serial, The Doctors.
PICTURES: Nightwing (debut, 1979), The Hunter, Modern Romance, The Pursuit of D.B. Cooper, Yes Gorgio, The Sender, Heartbreakers, Into the Night, Raw Deal, Someone to Love, The Companion.
TELEVISION: *Movies*: Son-Rise: A Miracle of Love, Vampire, The Women's Room, Bogie, An Uncommon Love, Women in White, Man Against the Mob, Dead Solid Perfect, Capital News, Rainbow Drive, Deadly Desire, The Companion. *Series*: The Doctors (1976-78), MacGruder and Loud, Bronx Zoo, I'll Fly Away, The Larry Sanders Show.

HARRYHAUSEN, RAY
Special Effects Expert, Producer, Writer. b. Los Angeles, CA, June 29, 1920. e. Los Angeles City Coll. While at coll. made

16mm animated film, Evolution, which got him job as model animator for George Pal's Puppetoons in early '40s. Served in U.S. Signal Corps; then made series of filmed fairy tales with animated puppets for schools and churches. In 1946 worked on Mighty Joe Young as ass't. to Willis O'Brien. Designed and created special visual effects for The Beast from 20,000 Fathoms; then began evolving own model animation system called Dynarama. In 1952 joined forces with prod. Charles H. Schneer, using new process for first time in It Came from Beneath the Sea. Subsequently made many films with Schneer in Dynamation. Received Gordon E. Sawyer Award for Acad. of Motion Picture Arts & Sciences, 1992. Appeared in films Spies Like Us, Beverly Hills Cop III.
PICTURES: Mighty Joe Young, The Beast From 20000 Fathoms, It Came From Beneath the Sea, Earth Vs. the Flying Saucers, Animal World, Twenty Million Miles to Earth, 7th Voyage of Sinbad, The Three Worlds of Gulliver, Mysterious Island, Jason and the Argonauts, First Men in the Moon, One Million Years B.C., The Valley of Gwangi, The Golden Voyage of Sinbad, Sinbad and the Eye of the Tiger (also co-prod.), Clash of the Titans (also co. prod.).

HART, GARRETT S.
Executive. e. Univ. of MA, Amherst; Queens Col/CUNY. 1979, joined Paramount as mngr. then v.p. of research; 1982, became dir. of comedy develp. Served as sr. v.p., research for Lorimar-Telepictures Corp. before joining Universal 1987; 1990, became sr. v.p., current programs. 1993, named pres. of the network tv division of the Paramount Television Group.

HARTLEY, HAL
Director, Writer. b. Long Island, NY, 1959. e. SUNY/Purchase (film). Following graduation made 3 short movies: Kid, The Cartographer's Girlfriend, Dogs. For PBS made the shorts Theory of Achievement, Ambition, Surviving Desire; also NYC 3/94, Opera No. 1. Music videos: The Only Living Boy in New York (Everything But the Girl), From a Motel 6 (Yo La Tengo), Iris.
PICTURES: Director/Writer: The Unbelievable Truth (debut, 1990), Trust, Simple Men, Amateur, Flirt (also actor, editor).

HARTLEY, MARIETTE
Actress. b. New York, NY, June 21, 1940. Student Carnegie Tech. Inst. 1956-57; studied with Eva Le Gallienne. Appeared with Shakespeare Festival, Stratford 1957-60. Co-host Today Show, 1980. Co-host on CBS Morning Show, 1987. Returned to stage in King John (NYSF in Central Park), 1989. Nominated for 6 Emmys for Best Actress. Received 3 Clio Awards, 1979, 1980, and 1981, for acting in commercials. Autobiography: Breaking the Silence.
PICTURES: Ride the High Country (debut, 1962), Drums of Africa, Marnie, Marooned, Barquero, The Return of Count Yorga, Skyjacked, The Magnificent Seven Ride!, Improper Channels, O'Hara's Wife, 1969, Encino Man.
TELEVISION: Series: Peyton Place, The Hero, Good Night Beantown, WIOU. Guest: The Rockford Files, The Incredible Hulk (Emmy Award, 1979), Stone. Movies: Earth II, Sandcastles, Genesis II, Killer Who Wouldn't Die, Last Hurrah, M.A.D.D.: Mothers Against Drunk Drivers, Drop-Out Father, One Terrific Guy, Silence of the Heart, My Two Loves, Murder C.O.D., Diagnosis of Murder, The House on Sycamore Street, Child of Rage, Heaven & Hell: North and South Book III, Falling From the Sky!: Flight 174. Mini-Series: Passion and Paradise. Special: The Halloween That Almost Wasn't.

HARTMAN, LISA
Actress. Houston, TX, June 1, 1956. m. musician Clint Black. Attended NYC's H.S. of Performing Arts prior to becoming a nightclub performer.
PICTURES: Deadly Blessing, Where the Boys Are.
TELEVISION: Series: Tabitha, Knots Landing, High Performance, 2000 Malibu Road. Movies: Murder at the World Series, Valentine Magic on Love Island, Where the Ladies Go, Gridlock, Jacqueline Susann's Valley of the Dolls 1981, Beverly Hills Cowgirl Blues, Full Exposure: The Sex Tapes Scandal, The Operation, The Take, Bare Essentials, Fire: Trapped on the 39th Floor, Not of This World, Red Wind, The Return of Eliot Ness, Without a Kiss Goodbye, Search for Grace, Dazzle, Someone Else's Child, Have You Seen My Son?

HARTMAN, PHIL
Actor. b. Branford, Ontario, Canada, Sept. 24, 1948. Raised in Connecticut and Los Angeles. e. Cal State Northridge (graphic design). Designed album covers before joining improv. comedy group the Groundlings.
PICTURES: Jumpin' Jack Flash, Three Amigos!, Blind Date, Fletch Lives, Quick Change, Coneheads, So I Married an Axe Murderer, Greedy, Houseguest, Sgt. Bilko, Jingle All the Way.
TELEVISION: Series: Six O'Clock Follies, Saturday Night Live, NewsRadio. Pilots: Top Ten, The Natural Snoop.

HARTZ, JIM
TV Newsman, Panelist. b. Tulsa, OK, Feb. 3, 1940. Pre-med student at U. of Tulsa, where worked in spare time as reporter

for radio station KRMG. 1963 left studies for career as newsman and joined KOTV in Tulsa. 1964 moved to NBC News in New York, acting as reporter and anchorman. 1974 became co-host of Today Show, joined Barbara Walters.

HARU, SUMI
Executive. Acting pres., Screen Actors Guild.

HARVEY, ANTHONY
Director, Editor. b. London, Eng., June 3, 1931. Royal Acad. of Dramatic Art. Two yrs. as actor. Ent. m.p. ind. 1949 with Crown Film Unit.
PICTURES: Editor: Private's Progress, Brothers-in-Law, Man in a Cocked Hat (Carlton Brown of the F.O.), I'm Alright Jack, The Angry Silence, The Millionairess, Lolita, The L-Shaped Room, Dr. Strangelove, The Spy Who Came In From the Cold, The Whisperers. Director: Dutchman (debut, 1966), The Lion in Winter, They Might Be Giants, Eagles' Wing, Players, The Abdication, Richard's Things, Grace Quigley.
TELEVISION: Movies: The Disappearance of Aimee, Svengali, The Patricia Neal Story, The Glass Menagerie, This Can't Be Love.

HARWOOD, RONALD
Writer. b. Cape Town, South Africa, 1934. e. Royal Acad. of Dramatic Art.
THEATER: The Dresser, Interpreters, J.J. Farr, Another Time, Reflected Glory, Poison Pen, Taking Sides.
PICTURES: Barber of Stamford Hill, Private Potter, High Wind in Jamaica, Arrivederci Baby, Diamonds for Breakfast, Sudden Terror (Eye Witness), One Day in the Life of Ivan Denisovich, Operation Daybreak (Price of Freedom), The Dresser, The Doctor and the Devils, The Browning Version, Cry the Beloved Country.
TELEVISION: The Barber of Stamford Hill, Private Potter, Take a Fellow Like Me, The Lads, Convalescence, Guests of Honor, The Guests. Adapted several of the Tales of the Unexpected, Mandela, Breakthrough at Rykjavik, Countdown to War, All the World's a Stage (series).

HASSANEIN, RICHARD C.
Executive. b. New York, NY, Aug. 13, 1951; e. Staunton Military Acad., 1966-70; American U., 1970-74. Booker/real estate dept. opns., United Artists Theater Circuit, 1974-77; joined United Film Distribution Co., 1977; 1978-88, pres. of UFD. 1988-91 served as pres., producers' rep., foreign & U.S. sls., of Myriad Enterprises. Joined Todd-AO Glen Glenn Studios in 1991 as v.p. of new bus. ventures. 1991 appointed exec. v.p. of Todd-AO Studios East, NY. 1993, elected to bd. of dirs. of Todd-AO Corp. 1995, appointed v.p. of Todd-AO Studios West, Los Angeles; 1996, pres. and COO of Todd-AO Studios West.

HASSANEIN, SALAH M.
Executive. b. Suez, Egypt, May 31, 1921. e. British Sch., Alexandria, Egypt. Nat'l Bank of Egypt, Cairo, 1939-42. Asst. division mgr. Middle East, 20th-Fox, Cairo, Egypt, 1942-44: U.S. armed forces, 1945-47; usher, asst. mgr., Rivoli Theatre, N.Y., 1947-48. Film buyer, booker, oper. v.p. U.A. Eastern Theas., 1948-59; pres. 1960; exec. v.p. U.A. Communications, Inc. 1960; v.p. United Artists Cable Corp., 1963. Exec. v.p., Todd-AO Corp., 1980. President, Warner Bros. International Theaters, 1988. President, Todd AO Corp., 1994.
PICTURES: Exec. prod.: Knightriders, Creepshow, Hello Again, Love or Money.

HASSELHOFF, DAVID
Actor. b. Baltimore, MD, July 17, 1952.
PICTURES: Starcrash, Witchery, W.B. Blue and the Bean.
TELEVISION: Series: The Young and the Restless, Knight Rider, Baywatch, Baywatch Nights. Movies: Griffin and Phoenix, Semi Tough, The Cartier Affair, Bridge Across Time, Perry Mason: The Case of the Lady in the Lake, Baywatch: Panic at Malibu Pier, Knight Rider 2000, Avalanche.

HASTINGS, DON
Actor. b. Brooklyn, NY, Apr. 1, 1934. e. Professional Children's Sch., Lodge H.S. On B'way in I Remember Mama, Summer and Smoke, etc.; Natl. co. of Life With Father; on various radio shows. Also wrote scripts for tv series The Guiding Light.
TELEVISION: Series: Captain Video, The Edge of Night, As the World Turns (also writer).

HATFIELD, HURD
Actor. b. New York, NY, Dec. 7, 1918. e. Morristown prep, Horace Mann, Riverdale Acad., Bard Col., Chekhov Drama Sch., Devonshire, Eng.
THEATER: Lower Depths, Twelfth Night, Cricket on the Hearth, King Lear, Venus Observed, Camino Real, Love's Labor's Lost, Bullfight, Julius Caesar, The Count of Monte Cristo, Son Juan in Hell, Son of Whistler's Mother, Stuttgart.
PICTURES: Dragon Seed (debut, 1944), The Picture of Dorian Gray, Diary of a Chambermaid, The Beginning or the End?, The Unsuspected, The Checkered Coat, Joan of Arc, Chinatown at

Midnight, Destination Murder, Tarzan and the Slave Girl, The Left-Handed Gun, King of Kings, El Cid, Harlow, Mickey One, The Boston Strangler, Von Richtofen and Brown, King David, Crimes of the Heart, Her Alibi.
TELEVISION: *Movies*: Thief, The Norliss Tapes, You Can't Go Home Again, Lies of the Twins. *Mini-Series*: The Word.

HATFIELD, TED
Executive. b. Wilton Junction, IA, Aug. 26, 1936. e. Hot Springs, AR. U.S. Army-NCO Academy, 1954. 1949-67 ABC Paramount Theatres, advanced from usher to district mgr. 1967-70 MGM asst. exploitation dir.; 1970-83, MGM national advertising coordinator; 1983-87, MGM/UA v.p., field operations. 1987-91, MGM/UA v.p., exhibitor relations. 1991-, Sony Pictures Releasing, v.p., exhib. rltns. Member: Motion Picture Pioneers, Western LA Council, Boy Scout Commissioner, Culver City Chamber of Commerce, past v.p./presidents award, Jaycees, Past State v.p., Advertising Federation, past state pres., Culver City Commissioner.

HAUER, RUTGER
Actor. b. Breukelen, Netherlands, Jan. 23, 1944. Stage actor in Amsterdam for six years.
PICTURES: Repelsteeltje (debut, 1973), Turkish Delight, Pusteblume, The Wilby Conspiracy, Keetje Tippel, Het Jaar van de Kreeft, Max Havelaar, Griechische Feigen, Soldier of Orange, Pastorale 1943, Femme Entre Chien et Loup, Mysteries (also co-prod.), Gripsta en de Gier, Spetters, Nighthawks, Chanel Solitaire, Blade Runner, Eureka, The Osterman Weekend, A Breed Apart, Ladyhawke, Flesh and Blood, The Hitcher, Wanted: Dead or Alive, The Legend of the Holy Drinker, Bloodhounds of Broadway, The Blood of Heroes, Blind Fury, Ocean Point, On a Moonlit Night, Past Midnight, Split Second, Buffy the Vampire Slayer, Arctic Blue, Beyond Forgiveness, Surviving the Game, Nostradamus, The Beans of Egypt Maine, Angel of Death.
TELEVISION: *Movies*: Escape from Sobibor, Inside The Third Reich, Deadlock, Blind Side, Voyage, Amelia Earhart: The Final Flight, Fatherland. *Series*: Floris (Netherlands TV). *Mini-Series*: Maketub: The Law of the Desert (Italy).

HAUG, WILLIAM F.
Executive. Pres. and CEO, Motion Picture and Television Fund.

HAUSER, WINGS
Actor. b. Hollywood, CA, 1947. Nickname derived from playing wing back on h.s. football team. Began studying acting in 1975.
PICTURES: First to Fight, Who'll Stop the Rain, Homework, Vice Squad, Deadly Force, Uncommon Valor (assoc. prod., story only), Mutant (Night Shadows), A Soldier's Story, Jo Jo Dancer Your Life is Calling, 3:15, Tough Guys Don't Dance, Nightmare at Noon, The Wind, Hostage, Dead Man Walking, The Carpenter, The Siege of Firebase Gloria, No Safe Haven (also co-s.p.), L.A. Bounty, Bedroom Eyes II, Beastmaster 2: Through the Portal of Time, Watchers 3.
TELEVISION: *Series*: The Young and the Restless, The Last Precinct, Lightning Force, Command 5, Roseanne. *Movies*: Hear No Evil, Ghost Dancing, The Long Hot Summer, Perry Mason: The Case of the Scandalous Scoundrel, Highway Man.

HAUSMAN, MICHAEL
Producer. Former stockbroker and still photographer. Entered film industry as assoc. prod. and prod. mgr. on The Heartbreak Kid and Taking Off. Worked as head of prod. for Robert Stigwood on Saturday Night Fever.
PICTURES: I Never Promised You a Rose Garden, Alambrista!, Heartland, Rich Kids, One-Trick Pony, Ragtime (exec. prod., 1st asst. dir.), The Ballad of Gregorio Cortez, Silkwood, Amadeus (exec. prod.), Places in the Heart (exec. prod.), Desert Bloom, Flight of the Spruce Goose, No Mercy, House of Games, Things Change, Valmont, State of Grace, Homicide, Nobody's Fool.
TELEVISION: Lip Service (exec. prod.).

HAVERS, NIGEL
Actor. b. London, Eng., Nov. 6, 1949. e. Leicester U., trained for stage at Arts Educational Trust. Father, Sir Michael Havers, was Attorney General of Britain. As child played Billy Owen on British radio series, Mrs. Dale's Diary. Records voice overs and books for the blind.
THEATER: Conduct Unbecoming, Richard II, Man and Superman (RSC), Family Voices, Season's Greetings, The Importance of Being Earnest.
PICTURES: Pope Joan (debut, 1972), Full Circle, Who is Killing the Great Chefs of Europe?, Chariots of Fire, A Passage to India, Burke and Wills, The Whistle Blower, Empire of the Sun, Farewell to the King, Clichy Days.
TELEVISION: *Series*: A Horseman Riding By, Don't Wait Up. *Mini-Series*: The Glittering Prizes, Nicholas Nickleby, Pennies From Heaven, Winston Churchill: The Wilderness Years, Nancy Astor, The Little Princess, Death of the Heart, Naked Under Capricorn, Sleepers. *Movies*: The Charmer, Private War of Lucina Smith, Lie Down With Lions, The Burning Season. *Guest*: Thriller, Star Quality: Noel Coward Stories (Bon Voyage), A Question of Guilt, Aspects of Love, Upstairs Downstairs, Edward VII, Liz: The Elizabeth Taylor Story.

HAVOC, JUNE
Actress. r.n. Hovick. b. Seattle, WA, Nov. 8, 1916. Sister was late Gypsy Rose Lee. Made film bow at 2 yrs. old in Hal Roach/Harold Lloyd productions billed as Baby June. Danced with Anna Pavlova troupe, then entered vaudeville in own act. Later, joined Municipal Opera Company, St. Louis, and appeared in Shubert shows. Musical comedy debut: Forbidden Melody (1936). To Hollywood, 1942. Author: Early Havoc (1959), More Havoc (1980).
THEATER: Pal Joey, Sadie Thompson, Mexican Hayride, Dunnigan's Daughter, Dream Girl, Affairs of State, The Skin of Our Teeth, A Midsummer Night's Dream (Stratford, CT. American Shakespeare Fest., 1958), Tour for U.S. Dept. of St., 1961; wrote Marathon 33. The Ryan Girl, The Infernal Machine, The Beaux Strategem, A Warm Peninsula, Dinner at Eight, Habeas Corpus. An Unexpected Evening with June Havoc (one woman show, London 1985), The Gift (tour), Eleemosynary, The Old Lady's Guide to Survival.
PICTURES: Four Jacks and a Jill (debut, 1941), Powder Town, My Sister Eileen, Sing Your Worries Away, Hi Diddle Diddle, Hello Frisco Hello, No Time for Love, Casanova Burlesque, Timber Queen, Sweet and Low Down, Brewster's Millions, Intrigue, Gentleman's Agreement, When My Baby Smiles at Me, The Iron Curtain, The Story of Molly X, Red Hot and Blue, Chicago Deadline, Mother Didn't Tell Me, Once a Thief, Follow the Sun, Lady Possessed, Three for Jamie Dawn, The Private Files of J. Edgar Hoover, Can't Stop the Music, Return to Salem's Lot.
TELEVISION: Anna Christie, The Bear, Cakes and Ale, Daisy Mayme, The Untouchables, Willy, MacMillan & Wife, The Paper Chase, Murder She Wrote. *Series*: More Havoc (1964-65), Search for Tomorrow, General Hospital.

HAWKE, ETHAN
Actor. b. Austin, TX, Nov. 6, 1970. Attended NYU. Studied acting at McCarter Theatre in Princeton, NJ, the British Theatre Assn., Carnegie Mellon U. Stage debut in St. Joan. Co-founder of Malaparte Theatre Co. in NYC. Dir. & wrote short film Straight to One.
THEATER: *NY*: Casanova (Off-B'way debut, 1991), A Joke, The Seagull (B'way debut, 1992), Sophistry, Hesh, The Great Unwashed.
PICTURES: Explorers (debut, 1985), Dead Poets Society, Dad, White Fang, Mystery Date, A Midnight Clear, Waterland, Alive, Rich in Love, Reality Bites, White Fang 2: Myth of the White Wolf (cameo), Quiz Show (cameo), Floundering, Before Sunrise, Search and Destroy.

HAWN, GOLDIE
Actress, Producer. b. Washington, DC, November 21, 1945. Started as professional dancer (performed in Can-Can at the N.Y. World's Fair, 1964), and made TV debut dancing on an Andy Griffith Special.
PICTURES: The One and Only Genuine Original Family Band (debut, 1968), Cactus Flower (Academy Award, best supporting actress, 1969), There's a Girl in My Soup, $ (Dollars), Butterflies Are Free, The Sugarland Express, The Girl From Petrovka, Shampoo, The Duchess and the Dirtwater Fox, Foul Play, Private Benjamin (Acad. Award nom.; also exec. prod.), Seems Like Old Times, Lovers and Liars (Travels With Anita), Best Friends, Swing Shift, Protocol (also exec. prod.), Wildcats (also exec. prod.), Overboard (also exec. prod.), Bird on a Wire, My Blue Heaven (co-exec. prod. only), Deceived, Crisscross (also co-exec. prod.), Housesitter, Death Becomes Her, Something to Talk About (exec. prod. only), The First Wives Club, Everyone Says I Love You.
TELEVISION: *Series*: Good Morning World, Rowan & Martin's Laugh-In (1968-70). *Specials*: The Goldie Hawn Special, Goldie & Liza Together, Goldie and the Kids: Listen to Us.

HAWTHORNE, NIGEL
Actor. b. Coventry, England, Apr. 5, 1929. Extensive career on stage. Ent. TV ind. 1953. Films, 1957. Won 1991 Tony Award for best actor for Shadowlands; Olivier & Evening Standard Awards for The Madness of George III (Natl. Th.).
PICTURES: Young Winston, The Hiding Place, Watership Down (voice), History of the World Part 1, Plague Dogs (voice), Firefox, Gandhi, The Black Cauldron (voice), The Chain, Turtle Diary, Freddie as F.R.O.7 (voice), Demolition Man, The Madness of King George (Acad. Award nom., BAFTA Award), Richard III, Inside, Twelfth Night.
TELEVISION: Mapp and Lucia, The Knowledge, The Miser, The Critic, Barchester Chronicles, Marie Curie, Edward and Mrs. Simpson, Yes Minister, Yes Prime Minister (series), The Oz Trials, Flea-Bites. The Shawl, Relatively Speaking, Late Flowering Lust.

HAYES, ISAAC
Musician, Actor. b. Covington, TN, Aug. 20, 1942. Was session musician with Stax Records in Memphis, eventually working as composer, producer. Debuted with solo album Presenting Isaac Hayes in 1968.
PICTURES: *Music*: Shaft (Academy Award for best song: Theme from Shaft, 1971), Shaft's Big Score. *Actor*: Wattstax,

Save the Children, Three Tough Guys (also music), Truck Turner (also music), Escape From New York, I'm Gonna Git You Sucka, Guilty as Charged, Posse, Robin Hood: Men in Tights, It Could Happen to You, Flipper.
TELEVISION: *Series theme:* The Men.

HAYES, JOHN MICHAEL
Writer. b. Worcester, MA, May 11, 1919. e. U. of Massachusetts, 1941.
PICTURES: Red Ball Express, Thunder Bay, Torch Song, War Arrow, Rear Window, To Catch a Thief, The Trouble with Harry, It's a Dog's Life, The Man Who Knew Too Much, The Matchmaker, Peyton Place, But Not for Me, Butterfield 8, The Children's Hour, Where Love Has Gone, The Chalk Garden, Judith, Nevada Smith.
TELEVISION: Pancho Barnes.

HAYES, PETER LIND
Actor. b. San Francisco, CA, June 25, 1915. m. Mary Healy. Was radio singer, actor, vaudeville, night clubs. Producer, Grace Hayes Lodge Review: on TV show with Mary Healy.
PICTURES: Million Dollar Legs, All Women Have Secrets, These Glamour Girls, Seventeen, Dancing on a Dime, Playmates, Seven Days Leave, The 5000 Fingers of Dr. T., Once You Kiss a Stranger.

HAYS, ROBERT
Actor. b. Bethesda, MD, July 24, 1947. e. Grossmont Coll., San Diego State U. Left school to join San Diego's Old Globe Theatre five years, appearing in such plays as The Glass Menagerie, The Man in the Glass Booth, Richard III.
PICTURES: Airplane! (debut, 1980), Take This Job and Shove It!, Utilities, Airplane II: The Sequel, Trenchcoat, Touched, Scandalous, Cat's Eye, Honeymoon Academy, Hot Chocolate, Homeward Bound: The Incredible Journey, Fifty Fifty, Raw Justice, Hoemward Bound II: Lost in San Francisco.
TELEVISION: *Series*: Angie, Starman, FM, Cutters. *Movies*: Young Pioneers, Young Pioneers' Christmas, Delta County U.S.A., The Initiation of Sarah, The Girl The Gold Watch and Everything, California Gold Rush, The Fall of the House of Usher, The Day the Bubble Burst, Murder by the Book, Running Against Time, No Dessert Dad 'Til You Mow the Lawn, Deadly Invasion: The Killer Bee Nightmare, Danielle Steel's Vanished. *Mini-Series*: Will Rogers: Champion of the People. *Specials*: Mr. Roberts, Partners. *Guest*: Love Boat, Harry O, Laverne and Shirley.

HAYSBERT, DENNIS
Actor. b. San Mateo, CA, June 2.
THEATER: Wedding Band, Yanks-3 Detroit-0 Top of the Seventh, Diplomacy, Othello, On the Death of, All Over Town, Blood Knot, No Place to Be Somebody, Jimmy Shine, The Time of Your Life, Ten Little Indians.
PICTURES: Major League, Navy SEALS, Mr. Baseball, Love Field, Suture, Major League 2, Amanda, Waiting to Exhale.
TELEVISION: *Series*: Code Red, Off the Rack. *Mini-Series*: Queen. Movies: A Summer to Remember, Grambling's White Tiger, K-9000. *Specials*: The Upper Room, Hallelujah.

HEADLY, GLENNE
Actress. b. New London, CT, March 13, 1957. e. High Sch. of Performing Arts. Studied at HB Studios. In Chicago joined St. Nicholas New Works Ensemble. Won 3 Joseph Jefferson awards for work with Steppenwolf Ensemble in Say Goodnight Gracie, Miss Firecracker Contest, Balm in Gilead, Coyote Ugly, Loose Ends. Directed Canadian Gothic.
THEATER: *NY*: Balm in Gilead, Arms and the Man, Extremities, The Philanthropist (Theatre World Award).
PICTURES: Four Friends (debut, 1981), Dr. Detroit, Fandango, The Purple Rose of Cairo, Eleni, Making Mr. Right, Nadine, Stars and Bars, Dirty Rotten Scoundrels, Paperhouse, Dick Tracy, Mortal Thoughts, Getting Even With Dad, Mr. Holland's Opus, Sgt. Bilko, 2 Days in the Valley.
TELEVISION: *Movies*: Seize the Day, Grand Isle, And the Band Played On. *Mini-Series*: Lonesome Dove (Emmy nom.).

HEALD, ANTHONY
Actor. b. New Rochelle, NY, Aug. 25, 1944. e. Michigan St. Univ.
THEATER: *B'way*: The Wake of Jamey Foster, The Marriage of Figaro, Anything Goes, A Small Family Business, Love! Valour! Compassion! *Off-B'way*: The Glass Menagerie, The Electra Myth, Inadmissible Evidence, Misalliance (Theatre World Award), The Caretaker, The Fox, The Philanthropist, Henry V, The Foreigner, Digby, Principia Scriptoriae, The Lisbon Traviata, Elliot Loves, Lips Together Teeth Apart, Pygmalion, Later Life, Love! Valour! Compassion! *Regional*: Quartermaine's Terms, J.B., Look Back in Anger, The Rose Tattoo, Bonjour la Bonjour, The Matchmaker.
PICTURES: Silkwood (debut, 1983), Teachers, Outrageous Fortune, Happy New Year, Orphans, Postcards From the Edge, The Silence of the Lambs, The Super, Whispers in the Dark, Searching for Bobby Fisher, The Ballad of Little Jo, The Pelican Brief, The Client, Kiss of Death.

TELEVISION: *Movies*: A Case of Deadly Force, Royce. *Mini-Series*: Fresno. Pilot: After Midnight. *Special*: Abby My Love. *Guest*: Hard Copy, Crime Story, Spenser for Hire, Miami Vice, Tales From the Darkside, Against the Law, Law and Order, Class of '96, Cheers, Murder She Wrote, Under Suspicion.

HEARD, JOHN
Actor. b. Washington, D.C., Mar. 7, 1946. e. Catholic U. Career began at Organic Theatre, starring in Chicago & N.Y. productions of Warp. Other stage roles include Streamers, G.R. Point (Theatre World Award), Othello, Split, The Glass Menagerie, Total Abandon, The Last Yankee.
PICTURES: Between the Lines (debut, 1977), First Love, On the Yard, Head Over Heels (Chilly Scenes of Winter), Heart Beat, Cutter and Bone (Cutter's Way), Cat People, Best Revenge, Violated, Heaven Help Us, Lies, C.H.U.D., Too Scared to Scream, After Hours, The Trip to Bountiful, The Telephone, The Milagro Beanfield War, The Seventh Sign, Big, Betrayed, Beaches, The Package, Home Alone, End of Innocence, Awakenings, Rambling Rose, Deceived, Mindwalk, Radio Flyer, Gladiator, Waterland, Home Alone 2: Lost in New York, In the Line of Fire, Me and Veronica, The Pelican Brief, Before and After.
TELEVISION: *Series*: John Grisham's The Client. *Specials*: The Scarlet Letter, Edgar Allan Poe: Terror of the Soul. *Mini-Series*: Tender Is the Night. *Movies*: Will There Really Be a Morning?, Legs, Out on a Limb, Necessity, Cross of Fire, Dead Ahead: The Exxon Valdez Disaster, There Was a Little Boy, Spoils of War, Because Mommy Works.

HECKART, EILEEN
Actress. b. Columbia, OH, Mar. 29, 1919. e. Ohio State U., American Theatre Wing. m. Jack Yankee.Inducted into Theatre Hall of Fame, 1995. Awards: Foreign Press, and Donaldson, Oscar nom. and Film Daily Citation (Bad Seed), TV Sylvania for the Haven, Variety Poll of N.Y. and Drama Critics (Dark at The Top of the Stairs); Emmy (Save Me a Place at Forest Lawn). Also 5 Tony noms., 5 Emmy noms. Honorary Doctorates from: Ohio St. Univ., Sacred Heart, Niagara Univ.
THEATER: Voice of the Turtle, Brighten the Corner, They Knew What They Wanted, Hilda Crane, Picnic (Theatre World & Outer Critics Circle Awards), The Bad Seed, A View From the Bridge, Family Affair, Pal Joey, Invitation to a March, Everybody Loves Opal, The Dark at the Top of the Stairs, And Things That Go Bump in the Night, You Know I Can't Hear You When the Water's Running, Too True to Be Good, Barefoot in the Park, Butterflies Are Free, Veronica's Room, The Effect of Gamma Rays on Man in the Moon Marigolds, Eleemosynary, The Cemetery Club, Love Letters, Driving Miss Daisy.
PICTURES: Miracle in the Rain (debut, 1956), Somebody Up There Likes Me, The Bad Seed, Bus Stop, Hot Spell, Heller in Pink Tights, My Six Loves, Up the Down Staircase, No Way to Treat a Lady, The Tree, Butterflies Are Free (Academy Award, best supporting actress, 1972), Zandy's Bride, The Hiding Place, Burnt Offerings, Heartbreak Ridge.
TELEVISION: *Series*: The Five Mrs. Buchanans. *Guest*: Kraft, Suspense, Philco Playhouse, The Web, Mary Tyler Moore, Annie McGuire, Love and War (Emmy Award, 1994). *Movies*: The Victim, FBI Story: The FBI Versus Alvin Karpis, Sunshine Christmas, Suddenly Love, White Mama, FDR: The Last Year, The Big Black Pill, Games Mother Never Taught You, Seize the Day, Ultimate Betrayal. *Mini-Series*: Backstairs at the Whitehouse.

HECKERLING, AMY
Director. b. New York, NY, May 7, 1954. e. Art & Design H.S., NYU, (film and TV), American Film Institute. Made shorts (Modern Times, High Finance, Getting It Over With), before turning to features.
PICTURES: Fast Times at Ridgemont High, Johnny Dangerously, Into the Night (actor only), National Lampoon's European Vacation, Look Who's Talking, Look Who's Talking Too, Look Who's Talking 3 (co-exec. prod. only), Clueless.
TELEVISION: George Burns Comedy Hour, Fast Times, They Came From Queens. *Series*: Clueless.

HEDAYA, DAN
Actor. b. Brooklyn, NY. e. Tufts Univ. Taught junior high school for seven yrs. before turning to acting. Joined NY Shakespeare Fest. in 1973.
THEATER: *NY*: Last Days of British Honduras, Golden Boy, Museum, The Basic Training of Pavlo Hummel, Conjuring an Event, Survivors, Henry V.
PICTURES: The Passover Plot (debut, 1976), The Seduction of Joe Tynan, Night of the Juggler, True Confessions, I'm Dancing As Fast As I Can, Endangered Species, The Hunger, The Adventures of Buckaroo Banzai, Blood Simple, Reckless, Tightrope, Commando, Wise Guys, Running Scared, Joe Vs. the Volcano, Pacific Heights, Tune in Tomorrow, The Addams Family, Boiling Point, Benny & Joon, Rookie of the Year, For Love or Money, Mr. Wonderful, Maverick, Search and Destroy, Clueless, The Usual Suspects, To Die For, Marvin's Room, Freeway.
TELEVISION: *Series*: The Tortellis, One of the Boys. *Movies*: The Prince of Central Park, Death Penalty, The Dollmaker,

Courage, Slow Burn, A Smoky Mountain Christmas, Betrayal of Trust, Reluctant Agent, The Whereabouts of Jenny. *Guest*: Hill Street Blues, Cheers, L.A. Law. *Pilots*: The Earthlings, The Flamingo Kid, The Rock. *Special*: Just Like Family, Mama's Boy, Veronica Clare.

HEDLUND, DENNIS
Executive. b. Hedley, TX, Sept. 3, 1946. e. U. of Texas, Austin, B.A., business admin., 1968. Captain U.S. Marine Corp, 1966-72. 1970-74, newscaster and disc jockey, KGNC Amarillo, TX; KOMA Oklahoma City, OK; WTIX New Orleans, LA; WFLA Tampa, FL; 1974-77, nat'l sales mgr., Ampex Corp., NY; 1977-80, v.p., Allied Artists Video Corp., NY; 1980-present, founder and president, Kultur International Films Ltd. 1990, created White Star Films to produce original programs for tv. TELEVISION: Roger Miller: King of the Road, Jackie Mason: An Equal Opportunity Offender, Merle Haggard: A Portrait of a Proud Man, History of Talk Radio.

HEDREN, TIPPI
Actress. r.n. Nathalie Hedren. b. Lafayette, MN, Jan. 18, 1935. Daughter is actress Melanie Griffith. Was hired by Alfred Hitchcock for leading role in The Birds after being spotted on a commercial on the Today Show. Author of The Cats of Shambala. Founder and pres. of The Roar Foundation. Bd. memeber, The Wildlife Safari, The Elsa Wild Animal Appeal, The ASPCA, The American Heart Assoc., etc.
PICTURES: The Birds (debut, 1963), Marnie, A Countess From Hong Kong, The Man and the Albatross, Satan's Harvest, Tiger By the Tail, Mr. Kingstreet's War, The Harrad Experiment, Where the Wind Dies, Roar (also prod.), Deadly Spygames, Foxfire Light, In the Cold of the Night, Pacific Heights, Inevitable Grace, Teresa's Tattoo, Mind Lies, The Devil Inside.
TELEVISION: *Series*: The Bold and the Beautiful. *Guest*: Run for Your Life, The Courtship of Eddie's Father, Alfred Hitchcock Presents (1985), Baby Boom, Hart to Hart, In the Heat of the Night, Hotel, Improv (guest host), Tales From the Darkside, Murder She Wrote. *Movies*: Alfred Hitchcock Presents..., Through the Eyes of a Killer, Shadow of a Doubt, Perry Mason: The Case of the Skin-Deep Scandal, The Birds II: Land's End, Treacherous Beauties, Heroes Die Hard, Return to Green Acres, Kraft Suspense Theatre: The Trains of Silence.

HEFFNER, RICHARD D.
Executive. b. New York, NY, Aug. 5, 1925. e. Columbia U. Instrumental in acquisition of Channel 13 (WNET) as New York's educational tv station; served as its first gen. mngr. Previously had produced and moderated Man of the Year, The Open Mind, etc. for commercial and public TV. Served as dir. of public affairs programs for WNBC-TV in NY. Was also dir. of special projects for CBS TV Network and editorial consultant to CBS, Inc. Editorial Board. Was radio newsman for ABC. Exec. editor of From The Editor's Desk on WPIX-TV in NY. Taught history at U. of California at Berkeley, Sarah Lawrence Coll., Columbia U. and New School for Social Research, NY. Served as American specialist in communications for U.S. Dept. of State in Japan, Soviet Union, Germany, Yugoslavia, Israel, etc. Prof. of Communications and Public Policy at Rutgers U. 1974-94, chmn. of classification and rating admin. rating board. 1994-95, sr. fellow, Freedom Forum Media Studies Center at Columbia Univ.

HEFFRON, RICHARD T.
Director. b. Chicago, Oct. 6, 1930.
PICTURES: Fillmore, Newman's Law, Trackdown, Futureworld, Outlaw Blues, I the Jury, The French Revolution.
TELEVISION: The Morning After, Dick Van Dyke Special, I Will Fight No More Forever, Toma (pilot), Rockford Files (pilot), North and South (mini-series). *Movies*: The California Kid, Young Joe Kennedy, A Rumor of War, A Whale for the Killing, The Mystic Warrior, V: The Final Battle, Anatomy of an Illness, Convicted: A Mother's Story, Guilty of Innocence, Samaritan, Napoleon and Josephine: A Love Story, Broken Angel, Pancho Barnes.

HEIDER, FREDERICK
Producer. b. Milwaukee, WI, Apr. 9, 1917. e. Notre Dame U., Goodman Theatre, Chicago. Actor in Globe Theatre, Orson Welles' Mercury Theatre.
TELEVISION & RADIO: Chesterfield Supper Club, Sammy Kaye's So You Want to Lead a Band, Frankie Carle Show, Jo Stafford Show, Paul Whiteman Goodyear Revue, Billy Daniels Show, Martha Wright Show, Earl Wrightson Show, Club Seven, Mindy Carson Show; Ted Mack Family Hour, Dr. I.Q., Miss America Pageant, Bishop Sheen's Life Is Worth Living, Voice of Firestone, Music for a Summer Night. Music for a Spring Night, The Bell Telephone Hour. Publisher, Television Quarterly, National Academy of Television Arts and Sciences. Became columnist, The Desert Sun, Palm Springs, CA.

HEILMAN, CLAUDE
Executive. b. Cologne, Germany, June 27, 1927. Early career in Europe in prod. and distribution. In U.S. joined Fox in Hollywood and NY; incl. mgmt. of Grauman's Chinese and other Fox the-aters. Formed Vintage Prods. Inc., United Film Associates Intlo., Inter Road Shows. Currently pres./chief. exec. GEM Communications and Islandia Enterprises.
PICTURES: This Earth Is Mine, Odyssey of Justice Lee, The Adventure of Gulliver, Desamor, Sound General Quarters, Islandia.

HELGENBERGER, MARG
Actress. b. Nebraska. e. Northwestern U. Came to NY where she landed first professional job as regular on daytime serial Ryan's Hope.
PICTURES: After Midnight (debut, 1989), Always, Crooked Hearts, The Cowboy Way, Species.
TELEVISION: *Series*: Ryan's Hope, Shell Game, China Beach (Emmy Award, 1990). *Movies*: Blind Vengeance, Death Dreams, The Hidden Room, Deadline (pilot), The Tommyknockers, When Love Kills: The Seduction of John Hearn, Where Are My Children?, Red Eagle. *Special*: Fallen Angels. *Guest*: Spenser for Hire, thirtysomething, Tales From the Crypt.

HELLER, FRANKLIN
Producer, Director. b. Dover, NJ, Sept. 15, 1911. e. Carnegie Inst. of Technology, B.A., 1934. Actor, 1934-36; stage mgr., Sam Harris-Max Gordon Prods., 1936-44; exec. prod., USO shows N.Y., 1944-45; prod. & dir., Paramount, 1945-47; dir., summer stock, 1947-48; prod. & dir., CBS TV, 1949-54; exec., prod. and dir. Goodson-Todman Prods., 1954-69; exec. prod. Protocol Prods., 1969-72 Literary Representative 1972. Dirs. Guild of America, Nat'l bd. 1965-77; Treas. 1965-69; Sec. 1970-73; Chr. Publications 1966-76. Retired.
TELEVISION: What's My Line?, Beat the Clock, The Front Page, The Web, Danger, To Tell the Truth, I've Got a Secret.

HELLER, PAUL M.
Producer. b. New York, NY, Sept. 25, 1927. e. Hunter Coll., Drexel Inst. of Technology. President, Intrepid Productions. Studied engineering until entry into U.S. Army as member of security agency, special branch of signal corps. Worked as set designer (Westport, East Hampton, Palm Beach) and in live TV and then on theatrical films. Produced the NY Experience and South Street Venture. Debut as film producer, David and Lisa, 1963. From 1964 to 1969 was president of MPO Pictures Inc. Joined Warner Bros. as prod. exec., 1970. Founded the Community Film Workshop Council for the American Film Institute. In 1972 founded Sequoia Pictures, Inc. with Fred Weintraub. Pres. of Paul Heller Prods. Inc. formed in 1978. Founded the Audrey Skirball-Kenis Theatre. Board of Directors, the British Academy of Film and Television - Los Angeles.
PICTURES: David and Lisa, The Eavesdropper, Secret Ceremony, Enter the Dragon, Truck Turner, Golden Needles, Dirty Knight's Work, Outlaw Blues, The Pack, The Promise, First Monday in October, Withnail and I, My Left Foot (exec. prod.), The Lunatic.
TELEVISION: Pygmalion.

HELLMAN, JEROME
Producer. b. New York, NY, Sept. 4, 1928. e. NYU. Joined ad dept. of New York Times then went to William Morris Agency as apprentice. Made asst. in TV dept. Worked as agent for Jaffe Agency. After hiatus in Europe joined Ashley-Steiner Agency (later IFA) where clients included Franklin Schaffner, Sidney Lumet, George Roy Hill, John Frankenheimer. Functioned as TV prod., including Kaiser Aluminum Hour. Left to form own agency, Ziegler, Hellman and Ross. Switched to feature prod. with The World of Henry Orient in 1964.
PICTURES: The World of Henry Orient, A Fine Madness, Midnight Cowboy (Academy Award for Best Picture, 1969), The Day of the Locust, Coming Home, Promises in the Dark (also dir.), The Mosquito Coast.

HELLMAN, MONTE
Director, Editor. b. New York, NY, 1932. e. Stanford Univ., UCLA. Started by working for Roger Corman's company as director, editor, 2nd Unit director. Replaced deceased directors on the films The Greatest, The Awakening. Dialogue Director: St. Valentine's Day Massacre. Acted in The Christian Licorice Store, Someone to Love.
PICTURES: *Director*: The Beast from Haunted Cave, Back Door to Hell, Flight to Fury, Ride in the Whirlwind (also edit., prod.), The Shooting (also edit., prod.), Two-Lane Blacktop (also edit., prod.), Cockfighter, China 9 Liberty 37 (also prod.), Iguana (also s.p., edit.), Silent Night Deadly Night 3 (also story). *Editor*: The Wild Angels, The Long Ride Home, How to Make It, The Killer Elite. *Second Unit Director*: The Last Woman on Earth, Ski Troop Attack, Creature from the Haunted Sea, The Terror. *Exec. Prod.*: Reservoir Dogs.

HELMOND, KATHERINE
Actress. b. Galveston, TX, July 5, 1934. Initial stage work with Houston Playhouse and Margo Jones Theatre, Dallas. Joined APA Theatre, NY, and Trinity Square Rep. Co., RI, Hartford Stage, CT and Phoenix Rep. NY. In 1950s opened summer stock theatre in the Catskills. Taught acting at American Musical and

Dramatic Acad., Brown U. and Carnegie-Mellon U. 1983, accepted into AFI's Directing Workshop for Women. Directed Bankrupt.
THEATER: The Great God Brown, House of Blue Leaves (Clarence Derwent, NY and LA Drama Critics Awards, 1972), Mixed Emotions.
PICTURES: The Hindenberg, Baby Blue Marine, Family Plot, Time Bandits, Brazil, Shadey, Overboard, Lady in White, Inside Monkey Zetterland.
TELEVISION: Series: Soap, Who's The Boss? (also episode dir), Benson (episode dir. only), Coach. Movies: Dr. Max, Larry, Locusts, The Autobiography of Miss Jane Pittman, The Legend of Lizzie Borden, The Family Nobody Wanted, Cage Without a Key, The First 36 Hours of Dr. Durant, James Dean, Wanted: The Sundance Woman, Little Ladies of the Night, Getting Married, Diary of a Teenage Hitchhiker, Scout's Honor, World War III, For Lovers Only, Rosie: The Rosemary Clooney Story, Meeting of the Minds, When Will I Be Loved?, The Perfect Tribute, Deception: A Mother's Secret, Grass Roots, Liz: The Elizabeth Taylor Story. Special: Christmas Snow.

HEMINGWAY, MARIEL
Actress. b. Ketchum, ID, Nov. 22, 1961. Granddaughter of writer Ernest Hemingway. Sister of actress-model Margaux Hemingway.
PICTURES: Lipstick (debut, 1976), Manhattan (Acad. Award nom.), Personal Best, Star 80, The Mean Season, Creator, Superman IV: The Quest for Peace, Sunset, The Suicide Club (also co-prod.), Delirious, Falling From Grace, Naked Gun 33 1/3: The Final Insult, Bad Moon.
TELEVISION: Series: Civil Wars, Central Park West. Movies: I Want to Keep My Baby, Steal the Sky, Into the Badlands, Desperate Rescue: The Cathy Mahone Story. Mini-Series: Amerika. Guest: Tales From the Crypt.

HEMMINGS, DAVID
Actor, Director. b. Guildford, England, Nov.18, 1941. Early career in opera. Ent. m.p. ind. 1956. Former co-partner in Hemdale Company.
THEATER: Adventures in the Skin Trade, Jeeves.
PICTURES: Five Clues to Fortune, Saint Joan, The Heart Within, In the Wake of a Stranger, No Trees in the Street, Men of Tomorrow, The Wind of Change, The Painted Smile (Murder Can Be Deadly), Some People, Play It Cool, Two Left Feet, West 11, Live It Up (Sing and Swing), The System (The Girl-Getters), Be My Guest, Dateline Diamonds, Eye of the Devil, Blow-Up, Camelot, The Charge of the Light Brigade, Only When I Larf, Barbarella, The Long Day's Dying, The Best House in London, Alfred the Great, The Walking Stick, Fragment of Fear, The Love Machine, Unman Wittering and Zigo, Voices, Juggernaut, Running Scared (dir.only), The 14 (dir. only), Mr. Quilp, Deep Red, Islands in the Stream, The Squeeze, The Disappearance, Blood Relatives, Crossed Swords, Power Play, Murder by Decree, Just a Gigolo (also dir.), Thirst, Beyond Reasonable Doubt, The Survivor (dir. only), Harlequin, Race to the Yankee Zephyr (dir., prod. only), Man Woman and Child, Prisoners (also exec. prod.), Coup D'Grat (also prod.), The Rainbow, Dark Horse (dir. only).
TELEVISION: Auto Stop, The Big Toe, Out of the Unknown, Beverly Hills Cowgirl Blues, Clouds of Glory, Davy Crockett: Rainbow in the Thunder (also dir.). Director only: Hardball, Magnum PI, A-Team, Airwolf, Murder She Wrote, In the Heat of the Night, Quantum Leap, The Turn of the Screw, Tales From the Crypt, Passport to Murder (movie). Guest: Northern Exposure, The Raven, Ned Blessing.

HEMSLEY, SHERMAN
Actor. b. Philadelphia, PA, Feb. 1, 1938.
THEATER: NY: Purlie.
PICTURES: Love at First Bite, Stewardess School, Ghost Fever, Mr. Nanny.
TELEVISION: Series: All in the Family, The Jeffersons, Amen, Dinosaurs (voice), Goode Behavior. Guest: The Rich Little Show, Love Boat, E/R, 227, Family Matters, Lois & Clark, Fresh Prince of Bel Air, Sister Sister.

HENDERSON, FLORENCE
Actress, Singer. b. Dale, IN, Feb. 14, 1934. e. AADA. Made B'way debut while teenager in musical Wish You Were Here.
THEATER: Oklahoma!, The Great Waltz, Fanny, The Sound of Music, The Girl Who Came to Supper, South Pacific. Tour: Annie Get Your Gun.
PICTURES: Song of Norway, Shakes the Clown, Naked Gun 33 1/3: The Final Insult, The Brady Bunch Movie.
TELEVISION: Series: Sing Along, The Jack Paar Show, Oldsmobile Music Theatre, The Brady Bunch, The Brady Bunch Hour, The Brady Brides, Florence Henderson's Home Cooking, The Bradys. Movies: The Love Boat (pilot), The Brady Girls Get Married, A Very Brady Christmas, Fudge-A-Mania. Guest: Car 54 Where Are You?, Garry Moore Show, Ed Sullivan Show, Medical Center, The Love Boat, Fantasy Island, It's Garry Shandling's Show, Police Squad, many others. Specials: Huck Finn, Little Women, An Evening With Richard Rodgers, etc.

HENDERSON, SKITCH
Music Director. r.n. Lyle Cedric Henderson. b. Birmingham, England, Jan. 27, 1918. e. U. of California. Began as pianist in dance bands, then theatre orchestras, films and radio on West Coast. Accompanist to Judy Garland on tour. Served, USAF, WW II. Music director radio, Bing Crosby. Toured with own dance band, 47-49. Music Director for NBC Network, Steve Allen Show, Tonight Show, Today Show, Street Scene (NY Opera). Guest conductor, symphony orchestras including NY Philharmonic, London Philharmonic. Founder and Music Director, NY Pops Orchestra. Music Director, Florida Orchestra Pops, Virginia Symphony Pops, Louisville Orchestra Pops. Grammy Award for RCA album NY Philharmonic with Leontyne Price and William Warfield, highlights from Porgy and Bess. Instrumental works: Skitch's Blues, Minuet on the Rocks, Skitch in Time, Come Thursday, Curacao. Scores: American Fantasy, Act One (film).

HENNER, MARILU
Actress. b. Chicago, IL, Apr. 6, 1952. e. U. of Chicago. Studied singing and dancing, appearing in musicals in Chicago and on Broadway in Over Here and Pal Joey. Autobiography: By All Means Keep on Moving (1994).
PICTURES: Between the Lines (debut, 1977), Blood Brothers, Hammett, The Man Who Loved Women, Cannonball Run II, Johnny Dangerously, Rustler's Rhapsody, Perfect, L.A. Story, Noises Off, Chasers.
TELEVISION: Series: Taxi, Evening Shade, Marilu. Movies: Dream House, Stark, Love with a Perfect Stranger, Ladykillers, Chains of Gold, Abandoned and Deceived (co-exec. prod. only), Fight for Justice.

HENNING, LINDA KAYE
Actress, Singer. b. Toluca Lake, CA, Sept. 16, 1944. Daughter of prod. Paul Henning. e. Cal State Northridge, UCLA. Member of California Artists Radio Theatre.
THEATER: Gypsy, Applause, Damn Yankees, I Do, I Do, Pajama Game, Sugar, Wonderful Town, Fiddler on the Roof, Sound of Music, Vanities, Born Yesterday, Mary, Mary, Bus Stop, etc.
PICTURE: Bye Bye Birdie.
TELEVISION: Series: Petticoat Junction, Sliders. Guest: Beverly Hillbillies, Happy Days, Mork & Mindy, Double Trouble, Barnaby Jones, The New Gidget, Hunter. Pilots: Kudzu, The Circle, Family. Movie: The Return of the Beverly Hillbillies.

HENNING, PAUL
Producer, Writer. b. Independence, MO, Sept. 16, 1911. e. Kansas City Sch. of Law, grad. 1932. Radio singer and disc jockey. Also acted, ran sound effects, sang, wrote scripts. To Chicago 1937-38, to write for Fibber McGee and Molly. To Hollywood as writer for Rudy Vallee, 1939. Wrote scripts for Burns and Allen 10 years, including transition radio to TV.
PICTURES: Writer: Lover Come Back, Bedtime Story, Dirty Rotten Scoundrels.
TELEVISION: Series (creator, writer, producer): The Bob Cummings Show, The Beverly Hillbillies, Petticoat Junction, Green Acres (exec. prod.)

HENRIKSEN, LANCE
Actor. b. New York, NY, May 5, 1943. Appeared on B'way in The Basic Training of Pavo Hummel, Richard III.
PICTURES: It Ain't Easy (debut, 1972), Dog Day Afternoon, The Next Man, Mansion of the Doomed, Close Encounters of the Third Kind, Damien: Omen II, The Visitor, The Dark End of the Street, Prince of the City, Piranha II: The Spawning, Nightmares, The Right Stuff, Savage Dawn, The Terminator, Jagged Edge, Choke Canyon, Aliens, Near Dark, Deadly Intent, Pumpkinhead, Hit List, The Horror Show, Johnny Handsome, Survival Quest, The Last Samurai, Stone Cold, Comrades in Arms, Delta Heat, Alien[3], Jennifer Eight, Excessive Force, The Outfit, Super Mario Bros., Hard Target, Man's Best Friend, No Escape, Color of Night, The Quick and the Dead, Powder.
TELEVISION: Series: Millenium. Guest: Scene of the Crime, Paul Reiser: Out on a Whim, Tales From the Crypt (Cutting Cards). Movies: Return to Earth, Question of Honor, Blood Feud, Reason for Living: The Jill Ireland Story, Wes Craven Presents Mind Ripper.

HENRY, BUCK
Actor, Writer. b. New York, NY, Dec. 9, 1930. r.n. Henry Zuckerman. e. Dartmouth Coll. Acted in Life with Father, (tour, 1948), Fortress of Glass, Bernardine, B'way; 1952-54, U.S. Army; No Time for Sergeants (Nat'l. Co.), The Premise, improvisational theatre, off-B'way.
PICTURES: Actor: The Secret War of Harry Frigg, Is There Sex After Death?, Taking Off, The Man Who Fell to Earth, Old Boyfriends, Gloria, Eating Raoul, Aria, Dark Before Dawn, Rude Awakening, Tune in Tomorrow, Defending Your Life, The Player, The Linguini Incident, Short Cuts, Even Cowgirls Get the Blues, Grumpy Old Men. Writer: Candy, The Owl and the Pussycat, What's Up Doc?, The Day of the Dolphin, Protocol. Actor-Writer: The Troublemaker, The Graduate, Catch-22, To Die For. Actor-Writer-Director: Heaven Can Wait (co-dir.), First Family.

TELEVISION: *Series*: Garry Moore Show (writer), Steve Allen Show (writer, performer), The Bean Show (writer), That Was the Week That Was (writer, performer), Get Smart (co-creator, story editor), Captain Nice (writer, exec. prod.), Alfred Hitchcock Presents (1985, actor, writer), Quark (writer), The New Show (performer, writer), Falcon Crest (actor), Trying Times: Hunger Chic (dir.). *Guest:* Saturday Night Live, Murphy Brown. *Movies:* Keep the Change, Harrison Bergeron. *Special:* Mastergate.

HENRY, JUSTIN
Actor. b. Rye, NY, May 25, 1971. Debut at age 8 in Kramer vs. Kramer, 1979 for which he received an Academy Award nomination.
PICTURES: Kramer vs Kramer, Sixteen Candles, Martin's Day, Sweet Hearts Dance.
TELEVISION: *Movies*: Tiger Town, Andersonville.

HENSON, LISA
Executive. b. 1960. e. Harvard U. Father was performer-puppeteer-director Jim Henson. Joined Warner Bros., 1983, as exec. asst. to head of prod. 1985, named dir. of creative affairs. 1985, promoted to v.p., prod. 1992, became exec. v.p., production. 1993, named pres. of worldwide prod. of Columbia Pictures. 1994, named pres. of Columbia Pictures. Resigned in 1996 to form own production company.

HEPBURN, KATHARINE
Actress. b. Hartford, CT, May 12, 1907. *Author*: The Making of the African Queen (1987), Me: Stories of My Life (1991). Received a record 12 Academy Award nominations for acting.
THEATER: Death Takes a Holiday, The Warrior's Husband, The Lake, The Philadelphia Story, As You Like It, The Millionairess, The Merchant of Venice, The Taming of the Shrew, Measure for Measure, Coco, A Matter of Gravity, West Side Waltz.
PICTURES: A Bill of Divorcement (debut, 1932), Christopher Strong, Morning Glory (Academy Award, 1933), Little Women, Spitfire, The Little Minister, Break of Hearts, Alice Adams, Sylvia Scarlett, Mary of Scotland, A Woman Rebels, Quality Street, Stage Door, Bringing Up Baby, Holiday, The Philadelphia Story, Woman of the Year, Keeper of the Flame, Stage Door Canteen, Dragon Seed, Without Love, Undercurrent, The Sea of Grass, Song of Love, State of the Union, Adam's Rib, The African Queen, Pat and Mike, Summertime, The Iron Petticoat, The Rainmaker, The Desk Set, Suddenly Last Summer, Long Day's Journey Into Night, Guess Who's Coming to Dinner (Academy Award, 1967), The Lion in Winter (Academy Award, 1968), The Madwoman of Chaillot, The Trojan Women, A Delicate Balance, Rooster Cogburn, Olly Olly Oxen Free, On Golden Pond (Academy Award, 1981), Grace Quigley, Love Affair.
TELEVISION: *Movies*: The Glass Menagerie, Love Among the Ruins (Emmy Award, 1975), The Corn Is Green, Mrs. Delafield Wants To Marry, Laura Lansing Slept Here, The Man Upstairs, This Can't Be Love, One Christmas. *Special*: Katharine Hepburn: All About Me (host, co-writer).

HERALD, PETER
Executive. b. Berlin, Germany, Dec. 20, 1930. e. UCLA, B.A. US Gov't. film officer in Europe 8 years. In charge of continental European prod. operation for Walt Disney Prods., 6 years. Supervisory prod. manager, Columbia Pictures, 3 years. Corporate Prod. mgr. Universal 3 years.
PICTURES: *Executive-, Co-, Assoc.-, Line Producer and/or Production Mgr.*: Almost Angels, Magnificent Rebel, Miracle of the White Stallions, Emil and the Detectives, There Was a Crooked Man, Outrageous Fortune, National Lampoon's Class Reunion, Doctor Detroit, D. C. Cab; The Great Waltz, Foul Play, Nightwing. W. W. and the Dixie Dancekings, Mandingo, W. C. Fields and Me, Alex and the Gypsy, Silver Streak, Star Wars, Stick, Married to It, many others.

HEREK, STEPHEN
Director. b. San Antonio, TX, Nov. 10, 1958.
PICTURES: Critters (debut, 1986), Bill & Ted's Excellent Adventure, Don't Tell Mom the Babysitter's Dead, The Mighty Ducks, The Three Musketeers, Mr. Holland's Opus, 101 Dalmatians.

HERMAN, NORMAN
Producer, Director. b. Newark, NJ, Feb. 10, 1924. e. Rutgers U., NYU. Was accountant in California; in 1955 switched to film ind., joining American Int'l Pictures. Headed AIP prod. dept. 4 years, incl. prod., post-prod., labor negotiations, supervising story dept., etc. Pres. of Century Plaza Prods. for 9 yrs. Sr. v.p./staff writer DEG, 1986-9; Pres. No. Carolina Studios, 1989-90.
PICTURES: *Prod. except as noted*: Sierra Stranger, Hot Rod Girl, Hot Rod Rumble, Crime Beneath Seas, Look in any Window (exec. prod. mgr.), Tokyo After Dark (also dir., s.p.), Everybody Loves It (dir.), Mondy Teeno (also dir. co-s.p.), Glory Stompers, Three in the Attic (assoc. prod.), Pretty Boy Floyd, Dunwich Horror, Three in the Cellar, Angel Unchained, Psych-Out, Sadismo (s.p.), Bloody Mama, Bunny O'Hare, Killers Three, Frogs (exec. prod.), Planet of Life (s.p.), Blacula, Dillinger (s.p.), Legend of Hell House, Dirty Mary Crazy Larry, Rolling Thunder, In God We Trust (exec. prod.), Blue Velvet (consultant).

TELEVISION: *Writer*: Robert Taylor Detective, Iron Horse, Invaders, Adam 12, Lancer. *Director-Producer*: Hannibal Cobb, You Are the Judge.

HEROUX, CLAUDE
Producer. b. Montreal, Canada, Jan. 26, 1942. e. U. of Montreal. 1979, prod. v.p., Film Plan Intl., Montreal.
PICTURES: Valerie, L'Initiation, L'Amour Humain, Je t'aime, Echoes of a Summer, Jacques Brel Is Alive and Well and Living in Paris, Breaking Point,Born for Hell, Hog Wild, City of Fire, Dirty Tricks, Gas, Visiting Hours, Videodrome, The Funny Farm, Going Berserk, Of Unknown Origin, Covergirl.
TELEVISION: The Park is Mine, Popeye Doyle.

HERRMANN, EDWARD
Actor. b. Washington, DC, July 21, 1943. Raised in Grosse Pointe, MI. e. Bucknell U. Postgrad. Fulbright scholar, London Acad. Music and Dramatic Art 1968-69. Acted with Dallas Theater Center for 4 years.
THEATER: *NY*: The Basic Training of Pavlo Hummel, Moonchildren, Mrs. Warren's Profession (Tony Award, 1976), Journey's End, The Beach House, The Philadelphia Story, Plenty, Tom and Viv, Julius Caesar, Not About Heroes, Life Sentences. London: A Walk in the Woods. Regional: many prods. with Williamstown Playhouse; Harvey, Twelfth Night, Love Letters, Three Sisters.
PICTURES: Lady Liberty, The Paper Chase, The Day of the Dolphin, The Great Gatsby, The Great Waldo Pepper, The Betsy, Brass Target, Take Down, The North Avenue Irregulars, Harry's War, Reds, Death Valley, A Little Sex, Annie, Mrs. Soffel, The Purple Rose of Cairo, The Man With One Red Shoe, Compromising Positions, The Lost Boys, Overboard, Big Business, Hero (unbilled), Born Yesterday, My Boyfriend's Back, Foreign Student, Richie Rich.
TELEVISION: *Series*: Beacon Hill, Our Century (host). *Guest*: M*A*S*H, St. Elsewhere. *Mini-Series*: Freedom Road. *Movies*: Eleanor and Franklin, Eleanor and Franklin: The White House Years, A Love Affair: The Eleanor and Lou Gehrig Story, Portrait of a Stripper, The Gift of Life, Memorial Day, So Proudly We Hail, Sweet Poison, Fire in the Dark, The Face on the Milk Carton. Specials: Sorrows of Gin, The Private History of The Campaign That Failed, Murrow, Dear Liar, Concealed Enemies, The Return of Hickey, The Beginning of the Firm, Last Act is a Solo, The End of a Sentence, A Foreign Field.

HERSHEY, BARBARA
Actress. r.n. Barbara Herzstein. b. Los Angeles, CA, Feb. 5, 1948. e. Hollywood H.S. m. painter Stephen Douglas. Briefly, in the mid-1970's, acted under the name Barbara Seagull.
PICTURES: With Six You Get Eggroll (debut, 1968), Heaven With a Gun, Last Summer, The Liberation of L.B. Jones, The Baby Maker, The Pursuit of Happiness, Dealing, Boxcar Bertha, Angela (Love Comes Quietly), The Crazy World of Julius Vrooder, Diamonds, You and Me, The Last Hard Men, Dirty Knights' Work, The Stunt Man, Americana, Take This Job and Shove It, The Entity, The Right Stuff, The Natural, Hannah and Her Sisters, Hoosiers, Tin Men, Shy People (Cannes Film Fest. Award, 1987), A World Apart (Cannes Film Fest. Award, 1988), The Last Temptation of Christ, Beaches, Tune in Tomorrow, Defenseless, The Public Eye, Falling Down, Swing Kids, Splitting Heirs, A Dangerous Woman, Last of the Dogmen, Portrait of a Lady, The Pallbearer.
TELEVISION: *Series*: The Monroes, From Here to Eternity. *Guest*: Gidget, The Farmer's Daughter, Run for Your Life, The Invaders, Daniel Boone, CBS Playhouse, Chrysler Theatre, Kung Fu, Alfred Hitchcock Presents (1985). *Movies*: Flood, In the Glitter Palace, Just a Little Inconvenience, Sunshine Christmas, Angel on My Shoulder, My Wicked Wicked Ways... The Legend of Errol Flynn, Passion Flower, A Killing in a Small Town (Emmy & Golden Globe Awards, 1990), Paris Trout, Stay the Night. *Mini-Series*: A Man Called Intrepid, Return to Lonesome Dove. *Special*: Working.

HERSKOVITZ, MARSHALL
Producer, Director, Writer. b. Philadelphia, PA, Feb. 23, 1952. e. Brandeis U., BA, 1973; American Film Inst., MFA. 1975. Worked as freelance writer, dir., and prod. on several TV shows. Received Humanitas Award, 1983 and Writers Guild award, 1984.
PICTURE: Jack the Bear (dir.), Legends of the Fall (co-prod.).
TELEVISION: Family (writer, dir.), White Shadow (writer), Special Bulletin (prod., writer, 2 Emmys for writing and dramatic special), thirtysomething (exec. prod., co-writer, dir; 2 Emmy awards for writing and dramatic series, 1988; Also Humanitas Award and Directors Guild Award, 1988 & 1989, Peabody Award, 1989.), Relativity.

HERTZ, WILLIAM
Executive. b. Wishek, ND, Dec. 5, 1923. Began theatre career in 1939 with Minnesota Amusement in Minneapolis; 1946 joined Fox West Coast Theatres; theatre mgr., booking dept.; 1965 appointed Los Angeles first-run district mgr.; promoted to Pacific

Coast Division Mgr., National General Corp., 1967; v.p. Southern Pacific Div. Mgr., National General Theatres, Inc. 1971. Joined Mann Theatres as dir. of marketing, public relations.

HERZOG, WERNER
Director, Producer, Writer. r.n. Werner Stipetic. b. Sachrang, Germany, September 5, 1942. e. U. of Munich, Duquesne U., Pittsburgh. Wrote first s.p. 1957; 1961 worked nights in steel factory to raise money for films; 1966, worked for U.S. National Aeronautics and Space Admin.
PICTURES: Signs of Life (debut, 1968), Even Dwarfs Started Small, Fata Morgana, The Land of Silence and Darkness, Aguirre—Wrath of God, Every Man for Himself and God Against All (The Mysery of Kaspar Hauser), Heart of Glass, Stroszek, Nosferatu: The Vampyre (also cameo), Woyzeck, Fitzcarraldo, Where the Green Ants Dream, Cobra Verde, It Isn't Easy Being God, Echoes of a Somber Empire.

HESSEMAN, HOWARD
Actor. b. Salem, OR, Feb. 27, 1940. Started with the San Francisco group, The Committee and worked as a disc jockey in San Francisco in the late 1960s.
PICTURES: Petulia, Billy Jack, Steelyard Blues, Shampoo, The Sunshine Boys, Jackson County Jail, The Big Bus, The Other Side of Midnight, Silent Movie, Honky Tonk Freeway, Private Lessons, Loose Shoes, Doctor Detroit, This is Spinal Tap, Police Academy 2: Their First Assignment, Clue, My Chauffeur, Flight of the Navigator, Heat, Amazon Women on the Moon, Rubin and Ed, Little Miss Millions.
TELEVISION: Series: WKRP in Cincinnati, One Day at a Time, Head of the Class. Guest: Mary Hartman Mary Hartman, Fernwood 2night, George Burns Comedy Week. Movies: Hustling, The Blue Knight (pilot), Tail Gunner Joe, The Amazing Howard Hughes, Tarantulas: The Deadly Cargo, The Ghost on Flight 401, The Comedy Company, More Than Friends, Outside Chance, The Great American Traffic Jam, Victims, One Shoe Makes It Murder, Best Kept Secrets, The Diamond Trap, Call Me Anna, Murder in New Hampshire: The Pamela Smart Story, Quiet Killer, Lethal Exposure.

HESSLER, GORDON
Producer, Director. b. Berlin, Germany, 1930. e. Reading U., England. Dir., vice pres., Fordel Films, Inc., 1950-58; dir., St. John's Story (Edinborough Film Festival), March of Medicine Series, Dr. Albert Lasker Award; story edit., Alfred Hitchcock Presents 1960-62; assoc. prod., dir., Alfred Hitchcock Hour, 1962; prod., Alfred Hitchcock Hour; prod., dir., Universal TV 1964-66.
PICTURES: The Woman Who Wouldn't Die, The Last Shot You Hear, The Oblong Box, Scream and Scream Again, Cry of the Banshee, Murders of the Rue Morgue, Sinbad's Golden Voyage, Medusa, Embassy, Puzzle, Pray for Death, Rage of Honour, The Misfit Brigade, The Girl in a Swing (also s.p.), Out on Bail, Mayeda, Journey of Honor.
TELEVISION: Series: Alfred Hitchcock Presents (1960-62), Alfred Hitchcock Hour, Run for Your Life, Convoy, Bob Hope Chrysler Show, ABC Suspense Movies of the Week, ABC Movies of the Week, Lucas Tanner, Night Stalker, Amy Prentiss, Switch, Kung Fu, Sara, Hawaii Five-O, Blue Knight, Wonder Woman, Master, CHiPs, Tales of the Unexpected, Equilizer. Pilots: Tender Warriors.

HESTON, CHARLTON
Actor. b. Evanston, IL, Oct. 4, 1924. e. Northwestern U. Sch. of Speech. Radio, stage, TV experience. Following coll. served 8 yrs. 11th Air Force, Aleutians. After war, dir. and co-starred with wife at Thomas Wolfe Memorial Theatre, Asheville, NC in State of the Union, Glass Menagerie; member, Katharine Cornell's Co., during first year on Broadway; Antony and Cleopatra, other Bway. plays, Leaf and Bough, Cockadoodle Doo; Studio One (TV): Macbeth, Taming of the Shrew, Of Human Bondage, Julius Caesar. Pres. Screen Actors Guild 1966-71; Member, Natl. Council on the Arts, 1967-72; Trustee: Los Angeles Center Theater Group, American Film Inst. 1971, chmn. 1981-; Received Jean Hersholt Humanitarian award, 1978. Autobiographies: The Actor's Life (1978), In the Arena (1995).
RECENT THEATER: A Man for All Seasons, The Caine Mutiny (dir., in China).
PICTURES: Dark City (debut, 1950), The Greatest Show on Earth, The Savage, Ruby Gentry, The President's Lady, Pony Express, Arrowhead, Bad for Each Other, The Naked Jungle, The Secret of the Incas, The Far Horizons, Lucy Gallant, The Private War of Major Benson, The Ten Commandments, Three Violent People, Touch of Evil, The Big Country, The Buccaneer, Ben-Hur (Academy Award, 1959), The Wreck of the Mary Deare, El Cid, The Pigeon That Took Rome, 55 Days at Peking, Major Dundee, The Agony and the Ecstasy, The War Lord, The Greatest Story Ever Told, Khartoum, Counterpoint, Planet of the Apes, Will Penny, Number One, Beneath the Planet of the Apes, Julius Caesar, The Hawaiians, The Omega Man, Antony and Cleopatra (also dir.), Skyjacked, Soylent Green, The Three Musketeers, Airport 1975, Earthquake, The Four Musketeers, The Last Hard Men, Midway, Two Minute Warning, Crossed Swords (The Prince and the Pauper), Gray Lady Down,

Mountain Men, The Awakening, Mother Lode (also dir.), Almost an Angel (cameo), Solar Crisis, Wayne's World 2 (cameo), Tombstone, True Lies, In the Mouth of Madness, Alaska, Hamlet.
TELEVISION: Series: The Colbys. Mini-Series: Chiefs. Movies: The Nairobi Affair, The Proud Men, A Man For All Seasons (also dir.), Original Sin, Treasure Island, The Little Kidnappers, The Crucifer of Blood, Crash Landing: The Rescue of Flight 232, The Avenging Angel, Texas (narrator). Special: Charlton Heston Presents the Bible (also writer).

HEYMAN, JOHN
Producer. b. Germany, 1933. e. Oxford U. Started with Independent British Television creating,. writing and producing entertainment and documentary programs. Had 5 top-ten programs 1955-57. Expanded into personal management, forming International Artsists, representing Elizabeth Taylor, Richard Burton, Richard Harris, Shirley Bassey among others. In 1963, formed World Film Services Ltd. to produce packafe and finance films and World Film Sales Ltd., the first major independent film sales co. Co-financed 250 major studio films 1969-91. In 1973, formed Genesis Project. In 1989 formed Island World and Islet. In 1994, formed World Group of Companies Ltd., parent co. to World Production Ltd.
PICTURES: Privilege, Boom!, Secret Ceremony, Twinky, Bloomfield, The Go-Between (Grand Prix, Cannes 1971), Superstars, Hitler: The Last Ten Days, Black Gunn, Divorce His, Divorce Hers, The Hireling (Grand Prix, Cannes 1973), A Doll's House, Daniel, Beyond the Limit, The Dresser, A Passage to India (co-prod.), Martin's Day, Steaming, D.A.R.Y.L.

HEYWOOD, ANNE
Actress. r.n. Violet Pretty. b. Birmingham, England, Dec. 11, 1931. Family tree dates back to Shakespearean actor Thomas Heywood (1570-1641). e. scholarship London Acad. of Dramatic Art and Music. Joined Highbury Theater Players and Birmingham Rep. Starred as Peter Pan, Shakespeare Memorial Theatre, Stratford on Avon.
PICTURES: Lady Godiva Rides Again (debut, 1951; billed as Violet Pretty), Find the Lady, Checkpoint, Doctor at Large, Dangerous Exile, The Depraved, Violent Playground, Floods of Fear, The Heart of a Man, Upstairs and Downstairs, A Terrible Beauty (The Night Fighters), Carthage in Flames, Petticoat Pirates, Stork Talk, Vengeance (The Brain), The Very Edge, 90 Degrees in the Shade, The Fox, Midas Run, The Chairman, The Nun of Monza, I Want What I Want, Trader Horn, Good Luck Miss Wyckoff, Ring of Darkness, What Waits Below.
TELEVISION: Guest: The Equalizer.

HICKEY, WILLIAM
Actor. b. Brooklyn, NY, 1928.
PICTURES: A Hatful of Rain (debut, 1957), Something Wild, Invitation to a Gunfighter, The Producers, The Boston Strangler, Little Big Man, Happy Birthday Wanda June, 92 in the Shade, Mikey and Nicky, The Sentinel, Nunzio, Prizzi's Honor (Acad. Award nom.), Remo Williams: The Adventure Begins, Flanagan, One Crazy Summer, The Name of the Roses, Bright Lights Big City, Da, Pink Cadillac, Puppet Master, Sea of Love, It Had to Be You, National Lampoon's Christmas Vacation, Tales From the Darkside: The Movie, Any Man's Death, Mob Boss, My Blue Heaven, The Nightmare Before Christmas (voice), The Jerky Boys, Major Payne, Forget Paris.

HICKS, CATHERINE
Actress. b. New York NY, Aug. 6, 1951. e. St. Mary's Notre Dame; Cornell U. (2 year classical acting prog.). On B'way. in Tribute, Present Laughter.
PICTURES: Death Valley, Better Late Than Never, Garbo Talks, The Razor's Edge, Fever Pitch, Peggy Sue Got Married, Star Trek IV: The Voyage Home, Like Father Like Son, Child's Play, She's Out of Control, Cognac, Liebestraum.
TELEVISION: Series: Ryan's Hope (1976-8), The Bad News Bears, Tucker's Witch. Movies: Love for Rent, To Race the Wind, Marilyn- the Untold Story, Valley of the Dolls 1981, Happy Endings, Laguna Heat, Spy, Hi Honey I'm Dead, Redwood Curtain. Pilot: The Circle Game.

HIFT, FRED
Executive. b. Vienna, Nov. 27, 1924. e. Vienna, London, Chicago. Early career reporter Chicago Sun and radio work with CBS News, New York; radio desk of NY Times. 1946 joined Boxoffice magazine; 1947 Quigley Publications; 1950 Variety. 1960 began career as publicist on Exodus. 1961 dir. pub., The Longest Day for Darryl Zanuck. 1962 joined Fox in Paris as ad-pub. dir. for Europe. 1964 became dir. European prod. pub. with headquarters London. Formed own pub., p.r. co., Fred Hift Assoc., 1970. 1979, joined Columbia as dir. of eastern adv.-pub operations in N.Y.; 1980, to United Artists as intl. adv./pub. v.p. Left to establish Fred Hift Assoc., intl. mktg. consultant in New York. 1983, joined Almi Pictures as v.p., mktg. 1985, reactivated F.H.A. 1986, returned to freelance journalism. Currently contributes to a variety of magazines and newspapers and also does reports on radio.
d. July 6,1996

HILL, ARTHUR

Actor. b. Melfort, Saskatchewan, Canada, Aug. 1, 1922. e. U. of British Columbia. Moved to England in 1948, spending ten years in varied stage & screen pursuits
THEATER: *B'way*: The Matchmaker, Home of the Brave, The Male Animal, Look Homeward Angel, All the Way Home, Who's Afraid of Virginia Woolf? (Tony Award, 1963), More Stately Mansions.
PICTURES: Miss Pilgrim's Progress, Scarlet Thread, Mr. Drake's Duck, A Day to Remember, Life With the Lyons, The Crowded Day, The Deep Blue Sea, Raising a Riot, The Young Doctors, The Ugly American, In the Cool of the Day, Moment to Moment, Harper, Petulia, The Chairman, Rabbit Run, The Pursuit of Happiness, The Andromeda Strain, The Killer Elite, Futureworld, A Bridge Too Far, A Little Romance, Butch and Sundance: The Early Days, The Champ, Dirty Tricks, Making Love, The Amateur, Something Wicked This Way Comes (narrator), One Magic Christmas.
TELEVISION: *Series*: Owen Marshall: Counselor-At-Law, Hagen, Glitter. *Movies*: The Other Man, Vanished, Ordeal, Owen Marshall: Counselor at Law (pilot; a.k.a. A Pattern of Morality), Death Be Not Proud, Judge Horton and the Scottsboro Boys, Tell Me My Name, The Ordeal of Dr. Mudd, Revenge of the Stepford Wives, The Return of Frank Cannon, Angel Dusted, Tomorrow's Child, Intimate Agony, Prototype, Love Leads the Way, Murder in Space, Churchill and the Generals, The Guardian, Perry Mason: The Case of the Notorious Nun.

HILL, BERNARD

Actor: b. Manchester, Eng., Dec. 17, 1944. Joined amateur dramatic society in Manchester then studied drama at Manchester Art Coll. Joined Liverpool Everyman rep. co. West End debut as John Lennon in John, Paul, George, Ringo... and Bert. Also in Normal Service, Shortlist, Twelfth Night, Macbeth, Cherry Orchard, Gasping, A View From the Bridge.
PICTURES: Gandhi, The Bounty, The Chain, Restless Natives, No Surrender, Bellman and True, Drowning by Numbers, Shirley Valentine, Mountains of the Moon, Double X: The Name of the Game, Skallagrigg, Madagascar Skin, The Ghost and the Darkness.
TELEVISION: I Claudius, Squaring the Circle, John Lennon: A Journey in the Life, New World, St. Luke's Gospel, Boys from the Blackstuff, Burston Rebellion.

HILL, DEBRA

Producer, Director, Writer. b. Philadelphia, PA. Career on feature films started with work as script supvr., asst. dir. and 2nd unit dir. of 13 pictures. Producer's debut with Halloween, 1980, for which also co-wrote script with director John Carpenter.
PICTURES: Halloween (also co-s.p.), The Fog (and co-s.p.), Escape from New York, Halloween II (and co-s.p.), Halloween III: Season of the Witch, The Dead Zone, Clue, Head Office, Adventures in Babysitting, Big Top Pee-wee, Heartbreak Hotel, Gross Anatomy, The Fisher King.
TELEVISION: Adventures in Babysitting (pilot, exec. prod.), Monsters (dir. episodes), Dream On (dir. episodes). *Movies*: El Diablo, Attack of the 50 Ft. Woman. *Rebel Highway Film Series*: Roadracers, Confessions of a Sorority Girl (also co-writer), Dragstrip Girl, Shake Rattle and Roll, The Cool and the Crazy, Runaway Daughters, Motocycle Gang, Drag Strip Girl, Reform School Girl, Jailbreakers (also co-writer), Girls in Prison.

HILL, GEORGE ROY

Director. b. Minneapolis, MN, Dec. 20, 1921. e. Yale U., Trinity Coll., Dublin. Started as actor, Irish theatres and U.S. Margaret Webster's Shakespeare Repertory Co., also off-B'way. Served as Marine pilot in WWII and Korean War. Wrote TV play, My Brother's Keeper, for Kraft Theatre, later rose to director with show.
THEATER: Look Homeward Angel (B'way debut, 1957), The Gang's All Here, Greenwillow, Period of Adjustment, Moon on a Rainbow Shawl (also prod.), Henry Sweet Henry.
PICTURES: Period of Adjustment (debut, 1962), Toys in the Attic, The World of Henry Orient, Hawaii, Thoroughly Modern Millie, Butch Cassidy and the Sundance Kid, Slaughterhouse Five, The Sting (Academy Award, 1973), The Great Waldo Pepper (also prod., story), Slap Shot, A Little Romance (also co-exec. prod.), The World According to Garp (also co-prod., cameo), The Little Drummer Girl, Funny Farm.
TELEVISION: *Writer-Dir.*: A Night to Remember, The Helen Morgan Story, Judgment at Nuremberg, Child of Our Time.

HILL, TERENCE

Actor, Director. r.n. Mario Girotti. b. Venice, March 29, 1939. Debuted as actor under his real name. First attracted attention as actor in Visconti's The Leopard, 1963. Gained fame in European-made westerns. Formed Paloma Films.
PICTURES: *as Mario Girotti*: Vacanze col Gangster (debut, 1951), Hannibal, Carthage in Flames, Joseph and His Brethren, The Wonders of Aladdin, Magdalena, Seven Seas to Calais, The Leopard, Games of Desire, Arizona Wildcat, Rampage at Apache Wells, Flaming Frontier, Whom the Gods Destroy, Blood River; *as Terence Hill*: God Forgives I Don't, Boot Hill, Ace High, Barbaglia, Anger of the Wind, They Call Me Trinity, The True and the False, Trinity Is Still My Name, Man of the East, Baron Blood, All the Way Boys!, My Name Is Nobody, Crime Busters, Mr. Billion, March or Die, Super Fuzz, Two Super Cops, Don Camillo (also dir.), Renegade Luke (also exec. prod.), Go for It!, Lucky Luke (also dir.), The F(N)ight Before Christmas (also dir.).
TELEVISION: *Series*: Lucky Luke (also dir.)

HILL, WALTER

Director, Writer, Producer. b. Long Beach, CA, Jan. 10, 1942. e. Michigan State U.
PICTURES: Hickey and Boggs (s.p.), The Getaway (1972; s.p.), Thief Who Came to Dinner (s.p.), The Mackintosh Man (s.p.), The Drowning Pool (s.p.), Hard Times (dir., s.p.), The Driver (dir., s.p.), The Warriors (dir., s.p.), Alien (prod.), The Long Riders (dir.), Southern Comfort (dir., s.p.), 48 HRS (dir., s.p.), Streets of Fire (dir., s.p.), Brewster's Millions (dir.), Crossroads (dir.), Blue City (prod., s.p.), Aliens (exec. prod., story), Extreme Prejudice (dir.), Red Heat (dir., s.p., prod.), Johnny Handsome (dir.), Another 48 HRS (dir.), Alien 3 (s.p., prod.), Trespass (dir.), Geronimo: An American Legend (dir., co-prod.), The Getaway (1993; co-s.p.), Tales From the Crypt Presents Demon Knight (co-exec. prod.), Wild Bill (dir., s.p.), Last Man Standing (dir.).
TELEVISION: *Series*: Dog and Cat (creator, writer), Tales From the Crypt (exec. prod.; also dir. & writer of episodes: The Man Who Was Death, Cutting Cards, Deadline: ACE Award).

HILLER, ARTHUR

Director. b. Edmonton, Alberta, Can., Nov. 22, 1923. e. U. of Alberta, U. of Toronto, U. of British Columbia. Worked for Canadian Broadcasting Corp. as dir. of live tv before moving to L.A. Pres. of DGA. 1993, became pres. of AMPAS. Appeared in Beverly Hills Cop III.
PICTURES: The Careless Years (debut, 1957), Miracle of the White Stallions, The Wheeler Dealers, The Americanization of Emily, Promise Her Anything, Penelope, Tobruk, The Tiger Makes Out, Popi, The Out-of-Towners, Love Story, Plaza Suite, The Hospital, Man of La Mancha, The Crazy World of Julius Vrooder (also co-prod.), The Man in the Glass Booth, W. C. Fields and Me, Silver Streak, Nightwing, The In-Laws (also co-prod.), Making Love, Author Author, Romantic Comedy, The Lonely Guy (also prod.), Teachers, Outrageous Fortune, See No Evil Hear No Evil, Taking Care of Business, The Babe, Married to It.
TELEVISION: Matinee Theatre, Playhouse 90, Climax, Alfred Hitchcock Presents, Gunsmoke, Ben Casey, Rte. 66, Naked City, The Dick Powell Show.

HILLER, DAME WENDY

Actress. D.B.E., 1975, O.B.E., 1971, Hon. LLD, Manchester, 1984. b. Bramhall, Cheshire, Eng., Aug. 15, 1912. e. Winceby House Sch., Bexhill. On stage 1930, Manchester Repertory Theatre, England; then on British tour. London debut 1935 in Love On the Dole; to N.Y., same role 1936. m.p. debut in Lancashire Luck, 1937.
THEATER: First Gentleman, Cradle Song, Tess of the D'Urbervilles, Heiress (NY & London), Ann Veronica, Waters of the Moon, Night of the Ball, Old Vic Theatre, Wings of the Dove, Sacred Flame, Battle of Shrivings, Crown Matrimonial, John Gabriel Borkman, Waters of the Moon (revival), Aspern Papers (revival), The Importance of Being Earnest, Driving Miss Daisy.
PICTURES: Lancashire Luck (debut, 1937), Pygmalion, Major Barbara, I Know Where I'm Going, Outcast of the Islands, Single Handed (Sailor of the King), Something of Value, How to Murder a Rich Uncle, Separate Tables (Academy Award, best supporting actress, 1958) Sons and Lovers, Toys in the Attic, A Man For All Seasons, Murder on the Orient Express, Voyage of the Damned, The Cat and the Canary, The Elephant Man, Making Love, The Lonely Passion of Judith Hearne.
TELEVISION: The Curse of King Tut's Tomb, David Copperfield (theatrical in U.K.), Witness for the Prosecution, Anne of Green Gables-The Sequel, Peer Gynt, The Kingfisher, All Passion Spent, A Taste for Death, Ending Up, The Best of Friends, The Countess Alice.

HILLERMAN, JOHN

Actor. b. Denison, TX, Dec. 20, 1932. e. U. of Texas. While in U.S. Air Force joined community theatre group and went to New York after completing military service. Studied at American Theatre Wing, leading to summer stock and off-B'way.
PICTURES: The Last Picture Show, Lawman, The Carey Treatment, What's Up Doc?, Skyjacked, High Plains Drifter, The Outside Man, The Thief Who Came to Dinner, Paper Moon, Blazing Saddles, Chinatown, At Long Last Love, The Nickel Ride, The Day of the Locust, Lucky Lady, Audrey Rose, Sunburn, History of the World Part I, Up the Creek.
TELEVISION: *Series*: Ellery Queen, The Betty White Show, Magnum P.I. (Emmy Award, 1987), The Hogan Family. *Movies*: Sweet Sweet Rachel, The Great Man's Whiskers, The Law, Ellery Queen, The Invasion of Johnson County, Relentless, Kill Me If You Can, A Guide for the Married Woman, Betrayal, Marathon, The Murder That Wouldn't Die, Little Gloria... Happy at Last, Assault and Matrimony, Street of Dreams, Hands of a Murderer. *Mini-Series*: Around the World in 80 Days.

HILLMAN, WILLIAM BRYON
Writer, Director, Producer. b. Chicago, IL, Feb. 3, 1951. e. Oklahoma Military Acad., UCLA. Head of production at Intro-Media Prod.; Fairchild Ent.; Spectro Prod.; Double Eagle Ent. Corp; Excellent Films Inc.; Creative consultant for The Hit 'Em Corp. Presently head of SpectroMedia Ent.
AUTHOR: *Novels:* Silent Changes, The Combination, The Liar, Additives The Perfect Crime, Why Me, The Loner.
PICTURES: *Dir.-Writer:* His Name is Joey (also exec. prod.), Tis the Season (also co-prod.), Strangers (also co-prod.), Back on the Street (also co-prod.), Loner (also co-prod.), Fast & Furious, The Master, Lovelines (s.p. only), Double Exposure (also co-prod.), The Passage, Campus, The Photographer (also prod.), The Man From Clover Grove (also co-prod.), Thetus, The Trail Ride (also co-prod.), Betta Betta (also prod.), Ragin' Cajun (also co-prod.).
TELEVISION: Working Together (pilot writer), Disco-Theque Pilot (dir., writer), Everything Will Be Alright (writer), Money (dir., writer), RIPA (writer).

HINES, GREGORY
Actor, Dancer. b. NY, Feb. 14, 1946. Early career as junior member of family dancing act starting at age 2. Nightclub debut at 5 as Hines Kids with brother Maurice (later renamed Hines Brothers as teenagers) and joined by father as Hines, Hines and Dad. B'way debut at 8 in The Girl in Pink Tights. Continued dancing with brother until 1973. Formed and performed with jazz-rock band, Severance. Solo album, Gregory Hines (1988).
THEATER: The Last Minstral Show (closed out of town). B'way: Eubie (Theatre World Award), Comin' Uptown (Tony nom.), Sophisticated Ladies (Tony nom.), Twelfth Night, Jelly's Last Jam (Tony Award, 1992).
PICTURES: History of the World Part 1 (debut, 1981), Wolfen, Deal of the Century, The Muppets Take Manhattan, The Cotton Club (also choreog.), White Nights, Running Scared, Off Limits, Tap (also choreog.), Eve of Destruction, A Rage in Harlem, Renaissance Man, Waiting to Exhale, Mad Dog Time.
TELEVISION: *Movies:* White Lie, T Bone N Weasel, Dead Air, A Stranger in Town. *Guest:* The Tonight Show, Motown Returns to the Apollo, Saturday Night Live.

HINGLE, PAT
Actor. b. Miami, FL, July 19, 1924. e. U. of Texas, 1949. Studied at Herbert Berghof Studio, American Theatre Wing, Actor's Studio.
THEATER: End as a Man (N.Y. debut, 1953), The Rainmaker, Festival, Cat on a Hot Tin Roof, Girls of Summer, Dark at the Top of the Stairs, J.B., The Deadly Game, Macbeth and Troilus and Cresida (with American Shakespeare Festival, Stratford, CT), Strange Interlude, Blues for Mr. Charlie, A Girl Could Get Lucky, The Glass Menagerie, The Odd Couple, Johnny No-Trump, The Price, Child's Play, The Selling of the President, That Championship Season, The Lady from the Sea, A Life, Thomas Edison: Reflections of a Genius (one man show).
RADIO: Voice of America.
PICTURES: On the Waterfront (debut, 1954), The Strange One, No Down Payment, Splendor in the Grass, All the Way Home, The Ugly American, Invitation to a Gunfighter, Nevada Smith, Sol Madrid, Hang 'em High, Jigsaw, Norwood, Bloody Mama, WUSA, The Carey Treatment, One Little Indian, Running Wild, Nightmare Honeymoon, The Super Cops, The Gauntlet, When You Comin' Back Red Ryder?, Norma Rae, America: Lost and Found (narrator), Sudden Impact, Running Brave, Going Berserk, The Falcon and the Snowman, Brewster's Millions, Maximum Overdrive, Baby Boom, The Land Before Time (voice), Batman, The Grifters, Batman Returns, Lightning Jack, The Quick and the Dead, Batman Forever, Large As Life.
TELEVISION: *Series:* Stone. *Guest:* Gunsmoke, MASH, Blue Skies, Matlock, Twilight Zone, The Untouchables, Trapper John M.D., Murder She Wrote, In the Heat of the Night, Cheers, Wings, American Gothic. *Movies:* The Ballad of Andy Crocker, A Clear and Present Danger, The City, Sweet Sweet Rachel, If Tomorrow Comes, Trouble Comes to Town, The Last Angry Man, The Secret Life of John Chapman, Escape from Bogen County, Sunshine Christmas, Tarantulas, Elvis, Stone (pilot), Disaster at the Coastliner, Wild Times, Of Mice and Men, Washington Mistress, The Fighter, Stranger on My Land, The Town Bully, Everybody's Baby: The Rescue of Jessica McClure, Not of This World, Gunsmoke: To the Last Man, Citizen Cohn, The Habitation of Dragons, Simple Justice, Against Her Will: The Carrie Buck Story, Truman. *Mini-Series:* War and Remembrance, The Kennedy's of Massachusetts.

HINKLE, ROBERT
Actor, Producer, Director. b. Brownfield, TX, July 25, 1930. e. Texas Tech. U. Joined Rodeo Cowboys Association, 1950 and rodeoed professionally until 1953 when began acting career in Outlaw Treasure. Pres. Cinema Pictures, Inc.
PICTURES: *Actor:* Giant, All the Fine Young Cannibals, Hud, The First Texan, Dakota Incident, Gun the Man Down, The Oklahoman, First Traveling Saleslady, No Place to Land, Under Fire, Speed Crazy, The Gunfight at Dodge City, Broken Land, Law in Silver City, *Producer-Director:* Ole Rex, Born Hunter,

Trauma, Something Can Be Done, Mr. Chat, Stuntman, Jumping Frog Jubilee, Mr. Chat-Mexico Safari, Trail Ride, Virginia City Cent., Texas Today, Texas Long Horns, Kentucky Thoroughbred Racing, Country Music, Guns of a Stranger.
TELEVISION: *Prod. & Dir.:* Test Pilot, Dial 111, Juvenile Squad, X13 Vertijet, Cellist Extraordinary, Sunday Challenge, The Drifter, Country Music Tribute, World of Horses, Country Music Videos.

HIRD, DAME THORA
Actress. b. Morecambe, Lancashire, Eng., May28, 1911. e. The Nelson Sch., Morecambe.
PICTURES: (Screen debut, 1940) The Black Sheep of Whitehall; Street Corner, Turn the Key Softly, Personal Affair, The Great Game, Storks Don't Talk, Shop Soiled, For Better or Worse; Love Match, One Good Turn, Quatermass Experiment, Simon and Laura, Lost, Sailor Beware, Home and Away, Good Companions, The Entertainer, A Kind of Loving, Term of Trial, Bitter Harvest, Rattle of a Simple Man, Some Will Some Won't, The Nightcomers, Consuming Passions.
TELEVISION: The Winslow Boy, The Bachelor, What Happens to Love, The Witching Hour, So Many Children, The Queen Came By, Albert Hope, All Things Bright and Beautiful, Say Nothing, Meet the Wife, Who's a Good Boy Then? I AM! Dixon of Dock Green, Romeo and Juliet, The First Lady, Ours Is a Nice House, The Foxtrot, Seasons, She Stoops to Conquer, Villa Maroc, When We Are Married, In Loving Memory, Flesh and Blood, Your Songs of Praise Choice, Hallelujah, Happiness, That's the Main Thing, Intensive Care, In Loving Memory, Praise Be, Last of the Summer Wine, The Fall, Cream Cracker Under the Settee (Talking Heads), Perfect Scoundrels, Wide Eyed and Legless... It's a Girl, Pat & Margaret, Thora on the Broad 'n' Narrow... South Bank Show.

HIRSCH, JUDD
Actor. b. New York, NY, March 15, 1935. e. City Coll. of New York. Studied physics but turned to acting; studied at Amer. Acad. of Dramatic Arts., HB Studios. First acting job in 1962 in Crisis in the Old Sawmill in Estes, Colorado; then to Woodstock Playhouse, before returning to N.Y.C.
THEATER: *NY:* On the Necessity of Being Polygamous, Barefoot in the Park, Scuba Duba, Mystery Play, HotL Baltimore, King of the United States, Prodigal, Knock Knock, Chapter Two, Talley's Folly (Obie Award), I'm Not Rappaport (Tony Award), Conversations With My Father (Tony Award).
PICTURES: Serpico (debut, 1973), King of the Gypsies, Ordinary People (Acad. Award nom.), Without a Trace, The Goodbye People, Teachers, Running on Empty, Independence Day.
TELEVISION: *Series:* Delvecchio, Taxi (2 Emmy Awards: 1981, 1983), Detective in the House, Dear John. *Movies:* The Law, Fear on Trial, Legend of Valentino, The Keegans, Sooner or Later, Marriage is Alive and Well, Brotherly Love, First Steps, The Great Escape II: The Untold Story, She Said No, Betrayal of Trust. *Special:* The Halloween That Almost Wasn't.

HIRSCHFIELD, ALAN J.
Executive. b. Oklahoma City, OK; Oct.10, 1935. e. U. of Oklahoma, B.A.; Harvard Business School, M.B.A. V.P., Allen & Co., 1959-66; Financial v.p. & dir. Warner/7 Arts, 1967-68; v.p. & dir., American Diversified Enterprises, 1969-73; pres. & chief exec. officer, Columbia Pictures Industries, 1973-78; consultant, Warner Communications, 1979, 1980-85, chmn. and chief exec. officer, 20th Century-Fox. Current: Co-CEO Data Broadcasting Corp. Dir., Cantel Inc., Chyron Corp.

HIRSHAN, LEONARD
Theatrical Agent. b. New York, NY, Dec.27, 1927. e. NYU. Joined William Morris Agency as agent trainee, New York, 1951. Agent legit theatre & TV dept. 1952-54. Sr. exec. agent M.P. dept., California office, 1955; sr. v.p., 1983; head of m.p. dept., west coast, 1986; named exec. v.p. and mem. bd. of dir., William Morris Agency, 1989; mem. bd. of dir., Center Theater Group, 1988; bd. governors Cedars-Sinai Hospital in L.A. 1987.

HIRSCHHORN, JOEL
Composer. b. Bronx, NY, Dec. 18, 1937. e. HS for the Performing Arts, Hunter Col.
PICTURES: *Songs* (with collaborator Al Kasha): The Fat Spy, The Cheyenne Social Club, The Poseidon Adventure (Academy Award for best song: The Morning After, 1972), The Towering Inferno (Academy Award for best song: We May Never Love Like This Again, 1974), Freaky Friday, Pete's Dragon, Hot Lead Cold Feet, The North Avenue Irregulars, All Dogs Go to Heaven, Rescue Me
TELEVISION: *Series:* Kids Inc., First and Ten, Getting in Touch, The Challengers. *Specials:* Kingdom Chums, A Precious Moments Christmas, The Magic Paintbrush, Caddie Woodlawn. *Movies:* Trapped Beneath the Sea, Someone I Touch, Charles Dickens' David Copperfield.

HITZIG, RUPERT
Producer, Director. b. New York, NY, Aug. 15, 1942. e. Harvard. At CBS as doc. writer-producer-director; later moved into dramas and comedy. Alan King's partner in King-Hitzig Prods.

PICTURES: *Prod.*: Electra Glide in Blue, Happy Birthday Gemini, Cattle Annie and Little Britches, Wolfen (also 2nd unit dir.), Jaws 3-D, The Last Dragon, The Squeeze. *Dir.*: Night Visitor, Backstreet Dreams, The Legend of O.B. Taggart, Last Lives (dir.).
TELEVISION: Much Ado About Nothing, The Wonderful World of Jonathan Winters, Playboy After Dark, How to Pick Up Girls, Return to Earth, Saturday Night Live, Birds of Prey, Date My Dad, Save Our Streets, annual comedy awards, television series and numerous specials.

HOBERMAN, DAVID
Executive. b. 1953. Started career as prod. exec. with TAT Communications for five years. 1982-85, worked as m.p. agent with Writers and Artists Agency and later at Ziegler Associates and ICM. 1985, named v.p. of prod. for Walt Disney Pictures based at studio. 1987, promoted to sr. v.p., prod. 1988, named president, production. 1989, pres. Touchstone Pictures. 1994, appointed head of all motion pictures produced by Walt Disney. Resigned from Disney, 1995, to form Mandeville Films.

HOCK, MORT
Executive. Blaine-Thompson Agency; A. E. Warner Bros., 1948; David Merrick B'way Prod., 1958; asst. adv. mgr., Paramount Pictures Corp., 1960; adv. mgr., United Artists Corp., 1962; dir. adv., UA Corp., 1964; adv. dir., Paramount, 1965; v.p. adv. & public rltns., Paramount, 1968-71; v.p., marketing, Rastar Prods., 1971; exec. v.p., Charles Schlaifer & Co., 1974; sr. v.p. entertainment div., DDB Needham Worldwide, 1983; exec. v.p. DDB, 1994.

HODGE, PATRICIA
Actress. b. Cleethorpes, Lincolnshire, England, Sept. 29, 1946. Studied at London Acad. of Music and Dramatic Arts.
THEATER: Popkiss, Two Gentlemen of Verona, Pippin, The Mitford Girls, Benefactors, Noel and Gertie, Separate Tables, The Prime of Miss Jean Brodie.
PICTURES: The Elephant Man, Betrayal, Sunset, Thieves in the Night, Diamond's Edge.
TELEVISION: The Naked Civil Servant, Rumpole of the Bailey, Edward and Mrs. Simpson, Holding the Fort, Jemima Shore Investigates, Hay Fever, Hotel Du Lac, The Life and Loves of a She-Devil, Exclusive Yarns, Let's Face the Music of..., Inspector Morse, The Shell Seekers, The Secret Life of Ian Fleming, The Heat of the Day, Rich Tea and Sympathy, The Cloning of Joanna May.

HOFFMAN, DUSTIN
b. Los Angeles, CA, Aug. 8, 1937. m. Lisa Hoffman. e. Los Angeles Conservatory of Music, Santa Monica Coll., Pasadena Playhouse, 1958. Worked as an attendant at a psychiatric institution, a demonstrator in Macy's toy dept., and a waiter. First stage role 1960 in Yes Is for a Very Young Man, at Sarah Lawrence Coll. Acted in summer stock, television and dir. at community theatre. Asst. dir. Off-B'way of A View From the Bridge.
THEATER: *Broadway and Off Broadway*: A Cook for Mr. General (bit part, B'way debut), Harry Noon and Night, Journey of the Fifth Horse (Obie Award), Eh? (Vernon Rice & Theatre World Awards), Jimmy Shine, All Over Town (dir. only), Death of a Salesman (Drama Desk Award), The Merchant of Venice (also London).
PICTURES: The Tiger Makes Out (debut, 1967), Madigan's Millions, The Graduate, Midnight Cowboy, John and Mary, Little Big Man, Who Is Harry Kellerman and Why Is He Saying Those Terrible Things About Me?, Straw Dogs, Alfredo Alfredo, Papillon, Lenny, All the President's Men, Marathon Man, Straight Time, Agatha, Kramer vs. Kramer (Academy Award, 1979), Tootsie, Ishtar, Rain Man (Academy Award, 1988), Family Business, Dick Tracy, Billy Bathgate, Hook, Hero, Outbreak, American Buffalo, Sleepers.
TELEVISION: *Specials*: Journey of the Fifth Horse, The Star Wagons, Free to Be You and Me, Bette Midler: Old Red Hair Is Back, Common Threads: Stories from the Quilt (narrator), The Earth Day Special. *Movies*: The Point (narrator), Death of a Salesman (Emmy Award, 1985). *Guest*: Naked City, The Defenders.

HOFFMAN, JOSEPH
Writer. b. New York, NY, Feb. 20, 1909. e. UCLA. Newspaperman, screen writer, magazine writer. TV prod. Now TV and screen freelance writer.
PICTURES: China Sky, Don't Trust Your Husband, Gung-Ho, And Baby Makes Three, Weekend with Father, Duel at Silver Creek, At Sword's Point, Has Anybody Seen My Gal?, Against All Flags, No Room for the Groom, Lone Hand, Yankee Pasha, Rails into Laramie, Tall Man Riding, Chicago Syndicate, Live a Little, How to Make Love and Like It, Sex and the Single Girl.
TELEVISION: *Producer*: Ford Theatre, Colt 45. *Writer*: Leave It to Beaver, My Three Sons, The Virginian, Love American Style, Bonanza, Patty Duke Show, Family Affair, etc.

HOGAN, HULK
Actor. r.n. Terry Gene Bollea. b. Augusta, GA, Aug. 11, 1953. Former bodyguard then prof. wrestler using names Sterling Golden, Terry Boulder, then finally Hulk Hogan.

PICTURES: Rocky III (debut, 1982), No Holds Barred, Gremlins 2: The New Batch, Suburban Commado, Mr. Nanny, Santa with Muscles.
TELEVISION: *Series*: Hulk Hogan's Rock 'n' Wrestling (voice), Thunder in Paradise (also exec. prod.). *Pilot*: Goldie and the Bears. *Guest*: The A-Team, The Love Boat.

HOGAN, PAUL
Actor, Writer. b. Lightning Ridge, Australia, Oct. 8, 1939. m. actress Linda Kozlowski. Worked as rigger before gaining fame on Australian TV as host of nightly current affairs show (A Current Affair) and The Paul Hogan Show. Shows now syndicated in 26 countries. In U.S. gained attention with commercials for Australian Tourist Commission. 1985, starred in dramatic role on Australian TV in series, Anzacs. Live one-man show, Paul Hogan's America, 1991.
PICTURES: Fatty Finn (debut, 1980), Crocodile Dundee (also co-s.p.), Crocodile Dundee II (also exec. prod., co-s.p.), Almost an Angel (also exec. prod., s.p.), Lightning Jack (also s.p., co-prod.), Flipper.
TELEVISION: Anzacs: The War Down Under.

HOLBROOK, HAL
Actor. b. Cleveland, OH, Feb. 17, 1925. m. actress Dixie Carter. e. Denison U., 1948. Summer stock 1947-53. Gained fame and several awards for performance as Mark Twain on stage in Mark Twain Tonight over a period of years throughout the US and abroad.
THEATER: Mark Twain Tonight (Tony Award, 1966), Do You Know the Milky Way?, Abe Lincoln in Illinois, American Shakespeare Fest., Lincoln Center Repertory (After the Fall, Marco Millions, Incident at Vichy, Tartuffe), The Glass Menagerie, The Apple Tree, I Never Sang For My Father, Man of La Mancha, Does a Tiger Wear a Necktie?, Lake of the Woods, Buried Inside Extra, The Country Girl, King Lear. Regional: Our Town, The Merchant of Venice, Uncle Vanya.
PICTURES: The Group (debut, 1966), Wild in the Streets, The People Next Door, The Great White Hope, They Only Kill Their Masters, Jonathan Livingston Seagull (voice), Magnum Force, The Girl From Petrovka, All the President's Men, Midway, Julia, Rituals (The Creeper), Capricorn One, Natural Enemies, The Fog, The Kidnapping of the President, Creepshow, The Star Chamber, Girls Night Out (The Scaremaker), Wall Street, The Unholy, Fletch Lives, The Firm, Carried Away.
TELEVISION: *Series*: The Bold Ones: The Senator (Emmy Award, 1971), Designing Women, Portrait of America (4 annual ACE Awards, 2 Emmy Awards, 1988, 1989), Evening Shade. *Movies*: Coronet Blue, The Whole World is Watching, A Clear and Present Danger, Travis Logan, Suddenly Single, Goodbye Raggedy Ann, That Certain Summer, Murder by Natural Causes, Legend of the Golden Gun, When Hell Was in Session, Off the Minnesota Strip, The Killing of Randy Webster, Under Siege, Behind Enemy Lines, Dress Gray, The Fortunate Pilgrim, Three Wishes for Billy Grier, Emma, Queen of the South Seas, Day One, Sorry Wrong Number, A Killing in a Small Town, Bonds of Love, A Perry Mason Mystery: The Case of the Lethal Lifestyle, A Perry Mason Mystery: The Case of the Grimacing Governor, A Perry Mason Mystery: The Case of the Jealous Jokester, She Stood Alone: The Tailhook Scandal. *Specials*: Mark Twain Tonight, Pueblo (Emmy Award, 1974), Sandburg's Lincoln (Emmy Award, 1976), Our Town, Plaza Suite, The Glass Menagerie, The Awakening Land, The Oath: 33 Hours in the Life of God, Omnibus. *Mini-Series*: North and South Books I & II, Celebrity, George Washington, Rockport Christmas.

HOLDRIDGE, LEE
Composer. b. Port-au-Prince, Haiti, March 3, 1944. e. Manhattan School of Music. Music arranger for Neil Diamond, 1969-73, with whom he collaborated on the score for Jonathan Livingston Seagull. Wrote score for B'way musical Into the Light (1986). With Alan Raph wrote score for the Joffrey Ballet's Trinity. One-act opera for L.A. Opera commission: Journey to Cordoba.
PICTURES: Jeremy, Jonathan Livingston Seagull, Forever Young Forever Free, Mustang Country, The Other Side of the Mountain—Part 2, The Pack, Moment By Moment, Oliver's Story, French Postcards, Tilt, American Pop, The Beastmaster, Mr. Mom, Micki and Maude, Splash, Sylvester, 16 Days of Glory, Transylvania 6-5000, The Men's Club, Big Business, Old Gringo, Pastime, Freefall.
TELEVISION: *Series*: One Life to Live, Hec Ramsey, Moonlighting, Beauty and the Beast, Bob. *Movies*: East of Eden, Fly Away Home, The Day the Loving Stopped, For Ladies Only, The Sharks, The Story Lady, One Against the Wind, In Love With an Older Woman, Running Out, Thursday's Child, Wizards and Warriors, The Mississippi, Legs, I Want to Live, Letting Go, Fatal Judgment, The Tenth Man, I'll Take Manhattan, Do You Know the Muffin Man?, Incident at Dark River, A Mother's Courage, In the Arms of a Killer, Face of a Stranger, Deadly Matrimony, Killer Rules, One Against the Wind, Call of the Wild, Torch Song, Barcelona '92: 16 Days of Glory, Jack Reed: Badge of Honor, Incident in a Small Town, The Yearling, Heidi, Texas, Tyson, Buffalo Girls, The Tuskegee Airmen, Nothing Lasts Forever.

HOLLAND, AGNIESZKA
Director, Writer. b. Warsaw, Poland, Nov. 28, 1948. e. FAMU, Prague. m. director Laco Adamik. Studied filmmaking in Czechoslovakia. Worked in Poland with director Andrzej Wajda. Moved to Paris in 1981.
PICTURES: Screen Tests (dir., s.p. episode), Provincial Actors (dir., s.p.), Bez Znieczulenia (s.p.), A Woman Alone (dir., co-s.p.), Danton (co-s.p.), Interrogation (actor), A Love in Germany (co-s.p.), Angry Harvest (dir., co-s.p.), Anna (s.p., story), Les Possedes (co-s.p.), La Amiga (co-s.p.), To Kill a Priest (dir., co-s.p.), Korczak (s.p.), Europa Europa (dir., s.p.), Olivier Olivier (dir., s.p.), The Secret Garden (dir.), Total Eclipse (dir.).
TELEVISION: Evening With Abdon, The Children of Sunday, Something for Something, Lorenzaccio, The Trial, Largo Desolato.

HOLLAND, TOM
Director, Writer. b. Highland, NY, July 11, 1945. e. Northwestern U. Started as actor, working at Bucks County Playhouse in PA and HB Studios in NY. Appeared on daytime serials Love of Life, Love is a Many-Splendored Thing. Turned to commercial prod. while attended UCLA law school, then took up screenwriting.
PICTURES: Writer: The Beast Within, The Class of 1984, Pyscho II (also actor), Scream for Help, Cloak and Dagger. Director: Fright Night (also s.p.), Fatal Beauty, Child's Play (also co-s.p.), The Temp, Thinner.
TELEVISION: Movie: The Stranger Within. Series: Tales From the Crypt (dir. 3 episodes: Love Come Hack to Me-also co-writer, Four-Sided Triangle-also co-writer, King of the Road). Mini-Series: Stephen King's The Langoliers (also writer, actor).

HOLLIMAN, EARL
Actor. b. Delhi, LA, Sept. 11, 1928. e. U. of Southern California, Pasadena Playhouse. Pres., Actors and Others for Animals.
THEATER: Camino Real (Mark Taper Forum), A Streetcar Named Desire (Ahmanson).
PICTURES: Scared Stiff, The Girls of Pleasure Island, Destination Gobi, East of Sumatra, Devil's Canyon, Tennessee Champ, The Bridges at Toko-Ri, Broken Lance, The Big Combo, I Died a Thousand Times, Forbidden Planet, Giant, The Burning Hills, The Rainmaker, Gunfight at the OK Corral, Trooper Hook, Don't Go Near the Water, Hot Spell, The Trap, Last Train From Gun Hill, Visit to a Small Planet, Armored Command, Summer and Smoke, The Sons of Katie Elder, A Covenant With Death, The Power, Anzio, The Biscuit Eater, Good Luck Miss Wyckoff, Sharky's Machine.
TELEVISION: Series: Hotel de Paree, Wide Country, Police Woman, P.S. I Luv You, Delta. Pilot: Twilight Zone. Movies: Tribes, Alias Smith and Jones, Cannon, The Desperate Mission, Trapped, Cry Panic, I Love You... Goodbye, Alexander: The Other Side of Down, The Solitary Man, Where the Ladies Go, Country Gold, Gunsmoke: Return to Dodge, American Harvest, P.S. I Luv You (pilot). Mini-Series: The Thorn Birds. Specials: The Dark Side of the Earth, The Return of Ansel Gibbs.

HOLM, CELESTE
Actress. b. New York, NY, Apr. 29, 1919. e. Univ. Sch. for Girls, Chicago, Francis W. Parker, Chicago, Lyceae Victor Durui (Paris), U. of Chicago, UCLA. p. Theodor Holm and Jean Parke Holm. m. actor Wesley Addy.
THEATER: B'way: Gloriana, The Time of Your Life, 8 O'Clock Tuesday, Another Sun, Return of the Vagabond, My Fair Ladies, Papa Is All, All the Comforts of Home, The Damask Cheek, Oklahoma!, Bloomer Girl, She Stoops to Conquer, Affairs of State, Anna Christie, The King and I, Interlock, Third Best Sport, Invitation to a March, Mame, Candida, Habeas Corpus, The Utter Glory of Morrissey Hall, I Hate Hamlet. Off-B'way: A Month in the Country. Theatre-in-Concert for the U.S. State Department in 8 countries May-July 1966. Regional: Janet Flanner's Paris Was Yesterday. Natl. Tour: Mame (Sarah Siddons Award), Hay Fever, Road to Mecca, Cocktail Hour.
PICTURES: Three Little Girls in Blue (debut, 1946), Carnival in Costa Rica, Gentleman's Agreement (Academy Award, best supporting actress, 1947), Road House, The Snake Pit, Chicken Every Sunday, Come to the Stable (Acad. Award nom.), A Letter to Three Wives (voice), Everybody Does It, Champagne for Caesar, All About Eve (Acad. Award nom.), The Tender Trap, High Society, Bachelor Flat, Doctor You've Got To Be Kidding, Tom Sawyer, Bittersweet Love, The Private Files of J. Edgar Hoover, Three Men and a Baby.
TELEVISION: Specials: A Clearing in the Wood, Play of the Week, Cinderella, Nora's Christmas Gift. Mini-Series: Backstairs at the White House (Emmy nom.). Movies: Underground Man, Death Cruise, Love Boat II, Midnight Lace, The Shady Hill Kidnapping, This Girl for Hire, Murder by the Book, Polly, Polly-Comin' Home! Pilot: Road Show. Series: Honestly Celeste, Who Pays, Nancy, Jessie, Falcon Crest, Christine Cromwell, Loving. Guest: Love Boat, Trapper John M.D., Magnum P.I.
RADIO: People at the U.N., Theatre Guild on the Air, Mystery Theatre.

HOLM, IAN
C.B.E. Actor. b. Ilford, Essex, England, Sept. 12, 1931. r.n. Ian Holm Cuthbert. e. RADA. On British stage in Love Affair, Titus Andronicus, Henry IV, Ondine, Becket, The Homecoming (B'way: Tony Award, 1967), Henry V, Richard III, Romeo and Juliet, The Sea, etc.
PICTURES: The Bofors Gun (debut, 1968), A Midsummer Night's Dream, The Fixer, Oh! What a Lovely War, A Severed Head, Nicholas and Alexandra, Mary Queen of Scots, Young Winston, The Homecoming, Juggernaut, Robin and Marian, Shout at the Devil, March or Die, Alien, Chariots of Fire (Acad. Award nom.), Time Bandits, Return of the Soldier, Greystoke: The Legend of Tarzan Lord of the Apes, Dance With a Stranger, Wetherby, Dreamchild, Brazil, Laughterhouse, Another Woman, Henry V, Hamlet, Kafka, Naked Lunch, The Advocate, Mary Shelley's Frankenstein, The Madness of King George, Big Night, Night Falls On Manhattan, The Fifth Element.
TELEVISION: Mini-Series/Movies: Les Miserables, S.O.S. Titanic, Napoleon, We the Accused, All Quiet on the Western Front, Holocaust, Man in the Iron Mask, Jesus of Nazareth, Thief of Bagdad, Game Set and Match, A Season of Giants, The Borrowers. Specials: The Browning Version, Murder By the Book, Uncle Vanya, Tailor of Gloucester, The Lost Boys, The Last Romantics.

HOMEIER, SKIP
Actor. r.n. George Vincent Homeier. b. Chicago, IL, Oct. 5, 1930. e. UCLA. Started in radio, 1936-43; on B'way stage, Tomorrow the World, 1943-44 which led to film debut in adaptation of same (billed as Skippy Homeier).
PICTURES: Tomorrow the World (debut, 1944), Boys' Ranch, Mickey, Arthur Takes Over, The Big Cat, The Gunfighter, Halls of Montezuma, Fixed Bayonets, Sealed Cargo, Sailor Beware, Has Anybody Seem My Gal?, The Last Posse, The Lone Gun, Beachhead, Black Widow, Dawn at Socorro, Ten Wanted Men, The Road to Denver, At Gunpoint, Cry Vengeance, The Burning Hills, Between Heaven and Hell, Dakota Incident, No Road Back, Stranger at My Door, Thunder Over Arizona, The Tall T, Lure of the Swamp, Decision at Durango, Day of the Badman, Journey Into Darkness, The Punderers of Painted Flats, Commanche Station, Showdown, Bullet for a Badman, Stark Fear, The Ghost and Mr. Chicken, Dead Heat on a Merry-Go-Round, Tiger By the Tail, The Greatest.
TELEVISION: Series: Dan Raven, The Interns. Guest: Playhouse 90, Alcoa Hour, Kraft Theatre, Studio 1, Armstrong Circle Theatre, Alfred Hitchcock. Movies: The Challenge, Two for the Money, Voyage of the Yes, Helter Skelter, Overboard, The Wild Wild West Revisited. Mini-Series: Washington: Behind Closed Doors.

HOOKS, KEVIN
Actor, Director. b. Philadelphia, PA, Sept. 19, 1958. Son of actor-director Robert Hooks.
PICTURES: Sounder, Aaron Loves Angela, A Hero Ain't Nothin' But a Sandwich, Take Down, Innerspace, Strictly Business (also dir.), Passenger 57 (dir. only), Fled.
TELEVISION: Series: The White Shadow, He's the Mayor. Movies: Just an Old Sweet Song, The Greatest Thing That Almost Happened, Friendly Fire, Can You Hear the Laughter?-The Story of Freddie Prinze, Roots: The Gift (dir.), Murder Without Motive: The Edmund Perry Story (dir.). Mini-Series: Backstairs at the White House. Special: Home Sweet Homeless (dir.).

HOOKS, ROBERT
Actor, Director, Producer. b. Washington, D.C., April 18, 1937. Father of actor-director Kevin Hooks. Co-founder and exec. dir. Negro Ensemble Co. NY 1968-present. Founder DC Black Theatre, Washington, D.C. 1973-77. Co-star of TV series NYPD, 1967-69.
THEATER: Tiger Tiger Burning Bright (B'way. debut, 1962), Ballad for Bimshire, The Blacks, Dutchman, Henry V, Happy Ending, Day of Absence, Where's Daddy? (Theatre World Award for last two), Hallelujah, Baby?, Kongi's Harvest, A Soldier's Play (Mark Taper Forum, LA). Co-prod.: with Gerald S. Krone: Song of the Lusitanian Bogey, Daddy Goodness, Ceremonies in Dark Old Men, Day of Absence, The Sty of the Blind Pig, The River Niger, The First Breeze of Summer.
PICTURES: Sweet Love Bitter, Hurry Sundown, The Last of the Mobile Hot-Shots, Trouble Man, Aaron Loves Angela, Airport '77, Fast-Walking, Star Trek III: The Search For Spock, Passenger 57, Posse, Fled.
TELEVISION: Series: N.Y.P.D., Supercarrier. Pilots: The Cliff Dweller, Two for the Money, Down Home. Movies: Carter's Army, Vanished, The Cable Car Murder, Crosscurrent, Trapped, Ceremonies in Dark Old Men, Just an Old Sweet Song, The Killer Who Wouldn't Die, The Courage and the Passion, To Kill a Cop, A Woman Called Moses, Hollow Image, Madame X, The Oklahoma City Dolls, The Sophisticated Gents, Cassie and Co., Starflight-The Plane that Couldn't Land, Feel the Heat, Sister Sister, The Execution.

HOOL, LANCE
Producer, Director. b. Mexico City, Mex., May 11, 1948. e. Univ. of the Americas.
PICTURES: Producer: Cabo Blanco, Ten to Midnight, The Evil That Men Do, Missing in Action (also s.p.), Missing in Action 2

(dir.), Steel Dawn (also dir.), Options, Damned River, Pure Luck, The Air Up There, Gunmen, Road Flower, Flipper, McHale's Navy.
TELEVISION: The Tracker, Born To Run, Cover Girl Murders,. Flashfire.

HOOPER, TOBE
Director. b. Austin, Texas, Jan. 25, 1943. e. Univ. of TX. Began film career making documentary and industrial films and commercials in Texas. Was asst. dir. of U. of Texas film program, continuing filmmaking while working with students. First feature film: documentary Peter Paul & Mary, followed by Eggshells. Directed Billy Idol video Dancing With Myself.
PICTURES: The Texas Chainsaw Massacre (also prod., co-s.p.), Eaten Alive (Death Trap), The Funhouse, Poltergeist, Lifeforce, Invaders from Mars, The Texas Chainsaw Massacre Part 2 (also co-prod., co- music), Spontaneous Combustion, Sleepwalkers (actor only), Night Terrors, The Mangler (also co-s.p.).
TELEVISION: Movie: I'm Dangerous Tonight. Mini-Series: Salem's Lot. Series episodes: Amazing Stories, Freddy's Nightmares (No More Mr. Nice Guy-1st episode), Equalizer (No Place Like Home), Tales from the Crypt (Dead Wait). Pilots: Haunted Lives, Body Bags.

HOPE, BOB
Actor. r.n. Leslie Townes Hope. b. Eltham, England, May 29, 1903. To U.S. at age 4; raised in Cleveland, OH. Became American citizen in 1920. Was amateur boxer before appearing in vaudeville as comedian/song and dance man. Debuted on B'way 1933 in Roberta, followed by stage work in Ziegfeld Follies, Red Hot & Blue. Began film career 1934, appearing in 8 short films made in NY, before going to Hollywood for feature debut, 1938, signing contract with Paramount. Starred on radio, 1938-56; made countless trips overseas to entertain U.S. troops during wartime; lent name to Bob Hope Desert Classic golf tournament. Voted one of top ten Money-Making Stars in M.P. Herald-Fame Poll: 1941-47, 1949-53. Recipient: 5 special Academy Awards (1940, 1944, 1952, 1959, 1965); special Emmy Awards: Trustees Award (1959), Governors Award (1984); Kennedy Center Honors (1985); Presidential Medal of Freedom, and many other awards. Author (or-co-author): They Got Me Covered, I Never Left Home, So This Is Peace, Have Tux Will Travel, I Owe Russia $1,200, Five Women I Love: Obit Hope's Vietnam Story, The Last Christmas Show, The Road to Hollywood: My 40-Year Love Affair With the Movies, Confessions of a Hooker: My Lifelong Love Affair With Golf, Don't Shoot It's Only Me.
PICTURES: The Big Broadcast of 1938 (feature debut, 1938), College Swing, Give Me a Sailor, Thanks for the Memory, Never Say Die, Some Like It Hot, The Cat and the Canary, Road to Singapore, The Ghost Breakers, Road to Zanzibar, Caught in the Draft, Louisiana Purchase, My Favorite Blonde, Road to Morocco, Nothing But the Truth, They Got Me Covered, Star Spangled Rhythm, Let's Face It, Road to Utopia, The Princess and the Pirate, Monsieur Beaucaire, My Favorite Brunette, Where There's Life, Road to Rio, The Paleface, Sorrowful Jones, The Great Lover, Fancy Pants, The Lemon Drop Kid, My Favorite Spy, Son of Paleface, Road to Bali, Off Limits, Scared Stiff (cameo), Here Come the Girls, Casanova's Big Night, The Seven Little Foys, That Certain Feeling, The Iron Petticoat, Beau James, Paris Holiday (also prod., story), Alias Jesse James (also prod.), The Five Pennies (cameo), The Facts of Life, Bachelor in Paradise, The Road to Hong Kong, Call Me Bwana, A Global Affair, I'll Take Sweden, The Oscar (cameo), Boy Did I Get a Wrong Number!, Not With My Wife You Don't (cameo), Eight on the Lam, The Private Navy of Sgt. O'Farrell, How to Commit Marriage, Cancel My Reservation (also exec. prod.), The Muppet Movie (cameo), Spies Like Us (cameo).
TELEVISION: Series: Chesterfield Sound Off Time, Colgate Comedy Hour (rotating host), Bob Hope Presents the Chrysler Theatre (Emmy Award as exec. prod. and host, 1966). Movie: A Masterpiece of Murder. Many specials incl. prod. of Roberta, annual variety shows; also was frequent host of annual Academy Award telecast.

HOPE, HARRY
Producer, Director, Writer. b. May 26, 1926. e. UCLA, Etudes Universitaires Internationales, Ph.D. Entered m.p. industry as special effects man, Republic Studios, 1944; associate producer Star Productions; formed Blue Bird Film Co. Has since produced, directed and written 33 feature films, including Like the Gull, 1967, which won creative classical film award as Asian Film Festival. Founded Western International and directed First Leisure Corp. as exec. v.p. until 1972. From then until present, pres. of Harry Hope Production. Among recent film credits: Smokey and the Judge, Sunset Cove, Doomsday Machine, Death Dimension, Thunderfist, Tarzana, The Mad Butcher, Death Blow, Pop's Oasis.

HOPKINS, SIR ANTHONY
C.B.E.: Actor. b. Port Talbot, South Wales, Dec. 31, 1937. Trained at Royal Acad. of Dramatic Art; Welsh Coll. of Music & Drama. Joined National Theatre, gaining fame on stage in England, then TV and films. Appeared in short The White Bus. Recordings: Under Milk Wood (1988), Shostakovich Symphony No. 13 Babi Yar (reciting Yevtushenko's poem, 1994). Dir. An Evening With Dylan Thomas, 1993. Received special award at Montreal Film Festival for Career Excellence, 1992; Evening Standard Film Awards Special Award for Body of Work, 1994; BAFTA Britannia Award for Outstanding Contribution to the International Film and TV Industry, 1995.
THEATER: Julius Caesar (debut, 1964), Juno and the Paycock, A Flea in Her Ear, The Three Sisters, Dance of Death, As You Like It, The Architect and the Emperor of Assyria, A Woman Killed With Kindness, Coriolanus, The Taming of the Shrew, Macbeth, Equus (NY, 1974-75; Outer Critics Circle, NY Drama Desk, US Authors & Celebrities Forum Awards), Equus (LA 1977, also dir.; LA Drama Critics Award), The Tempest, Old Times, The Lonely Road, Pravda (Variety Club Stage Actor Award, 1985; British Theatre Association Best Actor, Laurence Olivier & Observer Awards), King Lear, Antony and Cleopatra, M. Butterfly, August (also dir.).
PICTURES: The Lion in Winter (debut, 1967), The Looking Glass War, Hamlet, When Eight Bells Toll, Young Winston, A Doll's House, The Girl from Petrovka, Juggernaut, Audrey Rose, A Bridge Too Far, International Velvet, Magic, The Elephant Man, A Change of Seasons, The Bounty (Variety Club UK Film Actor Award, 1983), 84 Charing Cross Road (Moscow Film Fest. Award, 1987), The Good Father, The Dawning, A Chorus of Disapproval, Desperate Hours, The Silence of the Lambs (Academy Award, Natl. Board of Review, NY Film Critics, Boston Film Critics & BAFTA Awards, 1991), Freejack, One Man's War, Howards End, The Efficiency Expert (Spotswood), Bram Stoker's Dracula, Chaplin, The Remains of the Day (BAFTA, Variety Club UK Film Actor, LA Film Critics, Japan Critics Awards, 1993), The Trial, Shadowlands (Natl. Board of Review & LA Film Critics Award, 1993), The Road to Wellville, Legends of The Fall, The Innocent, August (also dir.), Nixon, Surviving Picasso.
TELEVISION: A Heritage and Its History, Vanya, Hearts and Flowers, Decision to Burn, War & Peace, Cuculus Canorus, Lloyd George, QB VII, Find Me, A Childhood Friend, Possessions, All Creatures Great and Small, The Arcata Promise, Dark Victory, The Lindbergh Kidnapping Case (Emmy Award, 1976), Victory at Entebbe, Kean, Mayflower: The Pilgrim's Adventure, The Bunker (Emmy Award, 1981), Peter and Paul, Othello, Little Eyolf, The Hunchback of Notre Dame, A Married Man, Corridors of Power, Strangers and Brothers, Arch of Triumph, Mussolini and I / Mussolini: The Rise and Fall of Il Duce (ACE Award), Hollywood Wives, Guilty Conscience, Blunt, The Dawning, Across the Lake, Heartland, The Tenth Man, Great Expectations, One Man's War, To Be the Best, A Few Selected Exits, Big Cats.

HOPKINS, BO
Actor. b. Greenwood, SC, Feb. 2, 1942. Studied with Uta Hagen in N.Y. then with Desilu Playhouse training school in Hollywood. Parts in several prods. for that group won him an agent, an audition with director Sam Peckinpah and his first role in latter's The Wild Bunch.
PICTURES: The Wild Bunch (debut, 1969), Monte Walsh, The Moonshine War, The Culpepper Cattle Co., The Getaway, White Lightning, The Man Who Loved Cat Dancing, American Graffiti, The Nickel Ride, The Day of the Locust, Posse, The Killer Elite, A Small Town in Texas, Tentacles, Midnight Express, More American Graffiti, The Fifth Floor, Sweet Sixteen, Night Shadows, Trapper Country, What Comes Around, War, The Bounty Hunter, The Stalker, Nightmare at Noon, The Tenth Man, Big Bad John, Center of the Web, Inside Monkey Zetterland, The Ballad of Little Jo, Cheyenne Warrior, Radioland Murders, Riders in the Storm, The Feminine Touch.
TELEVISION: Series: Doc Elliott, The Rockford Files, Dynasty. Movies: The Runaway Barge, Kansas City Massacre, Charlie's Angels (pilot), The Invasion of Johnson County, Dawn: Portrait of a Teenage Runaway, Thaddeus Rose and Eddie, Crisis in Sun Valley, Plutonium Incident, A Smoky Mountain Christmas, Beggerman Thief, Down the Long Hills, Last Ride of the Dalton Gang, Casino, Rodeo Girl, Ghost Dancing, Blood Ties. Special: Wyatt Earp: Return to Tombstone.

HOPPER, DENNIS
Actor, Director. b. Dodge City, KS, May 17, 1936. e. San Diego, CA, public schools. Author: Out of the Sixties (1988; book of his photographs).
PICTURES: Rebel Without a Cause, I Died a Thousand Times, Giant, The Steel Jungle, The Story of Mankind, Gunfight at the OK Corral, From Hell to Texas, The Young Land, Key Witness, Night Tide, Tarzan and Jane Regained Sort Of, The Sons of Katie Elder, Queen of Blood, Cool Hand Luke, Glory Stompers, The Trip, Panic in the City, Hang 'Em High, True Grit, Easy Rider (also dir., co-s.p.), The Last Movie (also dir., s.p.), Kid Blue, James Dean-The First American Teenager, Bloodbath (The Sky Is Falling), Mad Dog Morgan, Tracks, The American Friend, Couleur Chair, The Sorcerer's Apprentices, L'Ordre et la Securite du Monde, Resurrection, Apocalypse Now, Out of the Blue (also dir.), King of the Mountain, Renacida, White Star, Human

Highway, Rumble Fish, The Osterman Weekend, My Science Project, The Texas Chainsaw Massacre Part 2, Hoosiers (Acad. Award nom.), Blue Velvet, Black Widow, River's Edge, Straight to Hell, The Pick Up Artist, O.C. and Stiggs, Riders of the Storm, Blood Red, Colors (dir. only), Flashback, Chattachoochee, The Hot Spot (dir. only), Superstar: The Life and Times of Andy Warhol, The Indian Runner, Hearts of Darkness: A Filmmaker's Apocalypse, Midnight Heat, Eye of the Storm, Boiling Point, Super Mario Bros., True Romance, Red Rock West, Chasers (also dir.), Speed, Search and Destroy, Waterworld, Acts of Love, Basquiat, Carried Away.
TELEVISION: Movies: Wild Times, Stark, Paris Trout, Double-crossed, Backtrack (also dir.), Nails, The Heart of Justice, Witch Hunt. Guest: Pursuit, Espionage, Medic, Loretta Young Show.

HORN, ALAN
Executive. b. New York, NY, Feb. 28, 1943. e. Union Coll., Harvard Business Sch. 1971, joined Tandem Prods., 1972; named v.p., business affairs, and of sister co., T.A.T. Communications, 1973; 1977, exec. v.p. & COO; pres., 1978. In 1983 named chmn. Embassy Communications. 1986 joined 20th Century Fox as pres. COO. Left Fox Sept. 1986. Co-founded Castle Rock Entertainment 1987; Chmn. & CEO after being acquired by Turner Broadcasting System Inc. in 1994.

HORNE, LENA
Singer, Actress. b. Brooklyn, NY, June 30, 1917. Radio with Noble Sissle, Charlie Barnet, other bands. Floor shows at Cotton Club, Cafe Society, Little Troc, etc. Started screen career 1942. Appeared in short subjects Harlem Hotshots, Boogie Woogie Dream. Autobiographies: In Person (1950), Lena (1965) Recipient Kennedy Center Honors for Lifetime contribution to the Arts, 1984. Spingarn Award, NAACP, 1983; Paul Robeson Award, Actors Equity Assn., 1985.
THEATER: Blackbirds, Dance With Your Gods, Jamaica, Pal Joey (L.A. Music Center), Lena Horne: The Lady and Her Music (Tony Award).
PICTURES: The Duke Is Tops (debut, 1938), Panama Hattie, Cabin in the Sky, Stormy Weather, I Dood It, Thousands Cheer, Broadway Rhythm, Swing Fever, Two Girls and a Sailor, Ziegfeld Follies, Till the Clouds Roll By, Words and Music, Duchess of Idaho, Meet Me in Las Vegas, Death of a Gunfighter, The Wiz, That's Entertainment III.
TELEVISION: Guest: Music '55, Perry Como Show, Here's to the Ladies, The Flip Wilson Show, Dean Martin Show, Sesame Street, Ed Sullivan Show, Sanford & Sons, Laugh-In, Hollywood Palace, The Cosby Show. Specials: The Lena Horne Show (1959), The Frank Sinatra Timex Show, Lena in Concert, Harry and Lena, The Tony & Lena Show, Lena Horne: The Lady and Her Music.

HORNER, JAMES
Composer. b. Los Angeles, CA. e. Royal Col. of Music: London, USC, UCLA. Received Grammy Awards for the song Somewhere Out There (from the film An American Tail), and for instrumental composition from Glory.
PICTURES: The Lady in Red, Battle Beyond the Stars, Humanoids From the Deep, Deadly Blessing, The Hand, Wolfen, The Pursuit of D.B. Cooper, 48 HRS, Star Trek II: The Wrath of Khan, Something Wicked This Way Comes, Krull, Brainstorm, Testament, Gorky Park, The Dresser, Uncommon Valor, The Stone Boy, Star Trek III: The Search for Spock, Heaven Help Us, Cocoon, Volunteers, Journey of Natty Gann, Commando, Aliens, Where the River Runs Black, The Name of the Rose, An American Tail, P.K. and the Kid, Project X, Batteries Not Included, Willow, Red Heat, Vibes, Cocoon: The Return, The Land Before Time, Field of Dreams, Honey I Shrunk the Kids, Dad, Glory, I Love You to Death, Another 48 HRS., Once Around, My Heroes Have Always Been Cowboys, Class Action, The Rocketeer, An American Tail: Fievel Goes West, Thunderheart, Patriot Games, Unlawful Entry, Sneakers, Swing Kids, A Far Off Place, Jack the Bear, Once Upon a Forest, Searching for Bobby Fischer, The Man Without a Face, Bopha!, The Pelican Brief, Clear and Present Danger, Legends of the Fall, Braveheart, Casper, Apollo 13, Jumanji, Courage Under Fire.

HORSLEY, LEE
Actor. b. Muleshoe, TX, May 15, 1955. e. U. of No. Colorado. On stage in Mack and Mabel, West Side Story, Sound of Music, Oklahoma!, Forty Carats.
PICTURE: The Sword and the Sorcerer, Unlawful Passage.
TELEVISION: Series: Nero Wolfe, Matt Houston, Guns of Paradise, Bodies of Evidence, Hawkeye. Mini-series: Crossings, North and South Book II. Movies: The Wild Women of Chastity Gulch, Infidelity, When Dreams Come True, Thirteen at Dinner, Single Women Married Men, The Face of Fear, Danielle Steel's Palomino, French Silk, The Corpse Had a Familiar Face, Home Song. Documentary: Western Ranching Culture In Crisis, AThe Forest Wars.

HORTON, PETER
Actor. b. Bellevue, WA, Aug. 20. e. Univ. of CA, Santa Barbara. Stage work includes appearances with Lobero Rep. Co. Theatre in Santa Barbara, Butterflies Are Free in L.A.

PICTURES: Serial, Fade to Black, Split Image, Children of the Corn, Where the River Runs Black, Amazon Women on the Moon (also co-dir.), Sideout, Singles, The Cure (dir. only), The Baby-sitters Club, 2 Days in the Valley.
TELEVISION: Series: Seven Brides for Seven Brothers, thirtysomething (also dir., episodes), Class of '96 (consultant, dir., actor). Pilot: Sawyer and Finn. Movies: She's Dressed to Kill, Miracle on Ice, Freedom, Choices of the Heart, Children of the Dark. Special: The Gift. Guest: The White Shadow, St. Elsewhere. Director: The Wonder Years, One Too Many (Afterschool Special).

HORTON, ROBERT
Actor. b. Los Angeles, CA, July 29, 1924. e. U. of Miami, UCLA, Yale. With U.S. Coast Guard; many legit. plays; many radio & TV appearances. Star of Broadway musical 110 in the Shade.
PICTURES: A Walk in the Sun, The Tanks Are Coming, Return of the Texan, Pony Soldier, Apache War Smoke, Bright Road, The Story of Three Loves, Code Two, Arena, Prisoner of War, Men of the Fighting Lady, The Green Slime, The Dangerous Days of Kiowa Jones, The Spy Killer, Foreign Exchange.
TELEVISION: Series: Kings Row, Wagon Train, A Man Called Shenandoah, As the World Turns. Movie: Red River. Guest: Alfred Hitchcock Presents, Suspense, Houston Knights, Murder She Wrote.

HOSKINS, BOB
Actor. b. Bury St. Edmunds, Suffolk, England, Oct. 26, 1942. Porter and steeplejack before becoming actor at 25. Veteran of Royal Shakespeare Co. Appeared with Britain's National Theatre (Man Is Man, King Lear, Guys and Dolls, etc.)
PICTURES: The National Health (debut, 1973), Royal Flash, Inserts, Zulu Dawn, The Long Good Friday, Pink Floyd: The Wall, Beyond the Limit, Lassiter, The Cotton Club, Brazil, Sweet Liberty, Mona Lisa (Acad. Award nom.), A Prayer for the Dying, The Lonely Passion of Judith Hearne, Who Framed Roger Rabbit, The Raggedy Rawney (also dir., co-s.p.), Heart Condition, Mermaids, Shattered, The Inner Circle, The Favor the Watch and the Very Big Fish, Hook, Passed Away, Super Mario Bros., The Rainbow, The Secret Agent, Nixon, Balto (voice), Joseph Conrad's The Secret Agent.
TELEVISION: Villains on the High Road (debut, 1972), New Scotland Yard, On the Move, Rock Follies, In the Looking Glass, Napoleon, Flickers, Pennies from Heaven, Othello, Mussolini, The Dunera Boys, World War II: When Lions Roar, The Changeling.

HOUGH, JOHN
Director. b. London, Eng., Nov. 21, 1941. Worked in British film prod. in various capacities; impressed execs. at EMI-MGM Studios, Elstree, London, so was given chance to direct The Avengers series for TV. Began theatrical films with Sudden Terror for prod. Irving Allen, 1971.
PICTURES: Sudden Terror, The Practice, Twins of Evil, Treasure Island, The Legend of Hell House, Dirty Mary Crazy Larry, Escape to Witch Mountain, Return From Witch Mountain, Brass Target, The Watcher in the Woods, The Incubus, Triumphs of a Man Called Horse, Biggles: Adventures in Time, American Gothic, Howling IV—The Original Nightmare.
TELEVISION: A Hazard of Hearts (also co-prod.), The Lady and the Highwayman (also prod.), A Ghost in Monte Carlo (also prod.), Duel of Hearts (also prod.), Distant Scream, Black Carrion, Check-Mate.

HOWARD, ARLISS
Actor. b. Independence, MO, 1955. e. Columbia Col.
THEATER: American Buffalo, Lie of the Mind.
PICTURES: The Prodigal, Sylvester, Door to Door, The Ladies Club, The Lightship, Full Metal Jacket, Plain Clothes, Tequila Sunrise, Men Don't Leave, For the Boys, Ruby, Crisscross, The Sandlot, Wilder Napalm, Natural Born Killers, To Wong Foo—Thanks for Everything—Julie Newmar.
TELEVISION: Movies: Hands of a Stranger, I Know My First Name is Steven, Somebody Has to Shoot the Picture, Iran: Days of Crisis, Till Death Us Do Part, Those Secrets, The Infiltrator.

HOWARD, CLINT
Actor. b. Burbank, CA, Apr. 20, 1959. Brother is director Ron Howard; father is actor Rance Howard.
PICTURES: Rock 'n' Roll High School, Evil Speak, Night Shift, Spalsh, Cocoon, Gung Ho, The Wraith, End of the Line, Freeway, Parenthood, Tango and Cash, Disturbed, Backdraft, The Rocketeer, Far and Away, Carnosaur, The Ice Cream Man, Forget Paris, Apollo 13.
TELEVISION: Series: The Baileys of Balboa, Gentle Ben, The Cowboys, Gung Ho. Movies: The Red Pony, The Death of Richie, Cotton Candy.

HOWARD, JAMES NEWTON
Composer. Started as keyboard player for Elton John, before composing and producing for such artists as Cher, Diana Ross, Barbra Streisand, Chaka Khan, Randy Newman.

PICTURES: 8 Million Ways to Die, Five Corners, Promised Land, Some Girls, Everybody's All-American, Major League, The Package, Pretty Woman, Coupe de Ville, Flatliners, Three Men and a Little Lady, Dying Young, The Man in the Moon, My Girl, The Prince of Tides, Grand Canyon, Glengarry Glen Ross, Night and the City, Alive, Falling Down, Dave, The Fugitive, The Saint of Fort Washington, Wyatt Earp, Outbreak, Eye for an Eye, Thr Juror, Primal Fear.

HOWARD, KEN
Actor. b. El Centro, CA, March 28, 1944. e. Yale Drama Sch. Left studies to do walk-on in B'way. musical, Promises Promises.
THEATER: Promises Promises, 1776 (Theatre World Award), Child's Play (Tony Award, 1970), Seesaw, 1600 Pennsylvania Avenue, The Norman Conquests, Equus, Rumors, Camping With Henry and Tom.
PICTURES: Tell Me That You Love Me Junie Moon (debut, 1970), Such Good Friends, The Strange Vengeance of Rosalie, 1776, Second Thoughts, Oscar, Clear and Present Danger, The Net.
TELEVISION: Series: Adam's Rib, The Manhunter, The White Shadow, It's Not Easy, The Colbys, Dynasty, Dream Girl U.S.A., What Happened? (host). Guest: Bonanza, Medical Center. Movies: Manhunter, Superdome, Critical List, A Real American Hero, Damien: The Leper Priest, Victims, Rage of Angels, The Trial of George Armstrong Custer, He's Not Your Son, Rage of Angels: The Story Continues, Murder in New Hampshire: The Pamela Smart Story, Memories of Midnight, Hart to Hart Returns, Moment of Truth: To Walk Again, Tom Clancy's Op Center. Specials: Strange Interlude, The Man in the Brown Suit, Mastergate. Mini-Series: The Thorn Birds.

HOWARD, RON
Actor, Director, Producer. b. Duncan, OK, March 1, 1954. e. Univ. of So. Calif. Los Angeles Valley Col. Acting debut as Ronny Howard at age of 2 with parents, Rance and Jean Howard, in The Seven Year Itch at Baltimore's Hilltop Theatre. Two years later traveled to Vienna to appear in first film, The Journey. Brother is actor Clint Howard, also former child actor. Co-Chairman of Imagine Films Entertainment.
PICTURES: Actor: The Journey (debut, 1959), Five Minutes to Live (Door-to-Door Maniac), The Music Man, The Courtship of Eddie's Father, Village of the Giants, The Wild Country, American Graffiti, Happy Mother's Day... Love George (Run Stranger Run), The Spikes Gang, Eat My Dust!, The Shootist, The First Nudie Musical (cameo), Grand Theft Auto (also dir., co-s.p.), More American Graffiti. Director: Grand Theft Auto (dir. debut, 1977; also actor, co-s.p.), Night Shift, Splash, Cocoon, Gung Ho (also exec. prod.), Willow, Parenthood (also co-story), Backdraft, Far and Away (also co-prod., co-story), The Paper, Apollo 13. Exec. Prod.: Leo & Loree, No Man's Land, Vibes, Clean and Sober, Closet Land, Ransom.
TELEVISION: Series: The Andy Griffith Show, The Smith Family, Happy Days, Fonz and the Happy Days Gang (voice for animated series). Guest: Red Skelton Hour, Playhouse 90, Dennis the Menace, Many Loves of Dobie Gillis, Five Fingers, Twilight Zone, Dinah Shore Show, The Fugitive, Dr. Kildare, The Big Valley, I Spy, Danny Kaye Show, Gomer Pyle USMC, The Monroes, Love American Style, Gentle Ben, Gunsmoke; Disney TV films (incl. A Boy Called Nuthin', Smoke). Movies: The Migrants, Locusts, Huckleberry Finn, Act of Love, Bitter Harvest, Fire on the Mountain, Return to Mayberry. Director (Movies): Cotton Candy (also co-writer), Skyward (also co-exec. prod.), Through the Magic Pyramid (also exec. prod.). Co-Exec. Prod. (Movies): When Your Lover Leaves, Into Thin Air, Splash Too. Exec. Prod. (Series): Gung Ho, Parenthood.

HOWARD, SANDY
Producer. b. Aug. 1, 1927. e. Florida So. Coll. Ent. m.p. ind. 1946. PICTURES: Perils of the Deep, One Step to Hell, Jack of Diamonds, Tarzan and the Trappers, A Man Called Horse, Man in the Wilderness, Together Brothers, Neptune Factor, The Devil's Rain, Sky Riders, The Last Castle, Embryo, Magna I-Beyond the Barrier Reef, The Battle, Island of Dr. Moreau, City on Fire, Death Ship (exec. prod.), Avenging Angel, The Boys Next Door, Street Justice (exec. prod.), Nightstick, Dark Tower (exec. prod.), Truk Lagoon (exec. prod.).

HOWELL, C. THOMAS
Actor. b. Los Angeles, CA, Dec. 7, 1966. m. actress Rae Dawn Chong. Former junior rodeo circuit champion.
PICTURES: E.T.: The Extra Terrestrial (debut, 1982), The Outsiders, Tank, Grandview U.S.A., Red Dawn, Secret Admirer, The Hitcher, Soul Man, A Tiger's Tale, Young Toscanini, Side Out, Far Out Man, The Return of the Musketeers, Kid, Nickel and Dime, Breaking the Rules, First Force, That Night, Tattle Tale, Streetwise, To Protect and Serve, Gettysburg, Jail Bate, Teresa's Tattoo, Power Play, Treacherous, Mad Dogs and Englishmen.
TELEVISION: Series: Little People (only 4 yrs. old), Two Marriages. Movies: It Happened One Christmas, Into the Homeland, Curiosity Kills, Acting on Impulse, Dark Reflection. Guest: Nightmare Classics (Eye of the Panther).

HOWELLS, URSULA
Actress. b. Sept. 17, 1922. e. St. Paul's Sch., London. Stage debut, 1939, at Dundee Repertory with Bird in Hand followed by several plays inc. Springtime for Henry in N.Y., 1951; m.p. debut in Flesh and Blood, 1950; TV debut in Case of the Frightened Lady for BBC, 1948.
PICTURES: Lolly Madonna XXX, Catch My Soul, Hardcore, Escape from New York, Vice Squad, Total Exposure, Twist of Fate.
TELEVISION: The Small Back Room, A Woman Comes Home, For Services Rendered, Mine Own Executioner, The Cocktail Party.

HUBLEY, SEASON
Actress. b. New York, NY, Mar. 14, 1951. Studied acting with Herbert Berghoff.
THEATER: LA: Heat, Triplet Collection, Rhythm of Torn Stars.
PICTURES: The Oracle (Horse's Mouth), Track the Man Down, They Can't Hang Me, Keep It Clean, Long Arm (Third Key), Death and The Sky Above, Mumsy Nanny Sonny and Girly, Crossplot.
TELEVISION: Series: Kung Fu, Family, All My Children, Pilots: Lond and Davis in New York, Blues Skies, The City. Movies/Specials: She Lives, The Healers, SST—Death Flight, Loose Change, Elvis, Mrs. R's Daughter, Three Wishes of Billy Grier, Under the Influence, Christmas Eve, Shakedown on Sunset Strip, Unspeakable Acts, Child of the Night, Steel Justice, Key to Rebecca, All I Could See From Where I Stood, Stepfather III, Caribbean Mystery, Black Carrion, Vestige of Honor. Guest: The Partridge Family, The Rookies, Kojak, Twilight Zone, Alfred Hitchcock Presents, Twilight Zone, Hitchhiker.

HUDDLESTON, DAVID
Actor, Producer. b. Vinton, VA, Sept. 17, 1930. e. American Acad. of Dramatic Arts. Son is actor Michael Huddleston.
THEATER: A Man for All Seasons, Front Page, Everybody Loves Opal, Ten Little Indians, Silk Stockings, Fanny, Guys and Dolls, The Music Man, Desert Song, Mame. Broadway: The First, Death of a Salesman.
PICTURES: All the Way Home (debut, 1963), A Lovely Way to Die, Slaves, Norwood, Rio Lobo, Fools, Parade, Bad Company, Blazing Saddles, McQ, The World's Greatest Lover, Capricorn One, Gorp, Smokey and the Bandit II, The Act, Santa Claus, Frantic, Life With Mikey, Cultivating Charlie. Something to Talk About (unbilled).
TELEVISION: Series: Tenafly, Petrocelli, The Kallikaks, Hizzoner. Movies: Sarge, The Badge or the Cross, The Priest Killer, Suddenly Single, The Homecoming, Brian's Song, Tenafly (pilot), Brock's Last Case, Hawkins on Murder, Heatwave, The Gun and the Pulpit, The Oregon Trail, Shark Kill, Sherlock Holmes in New York, Kate Bliss and the Ticker Tape Kid, Oklahoma City Dolls, Family Reunion, Computeruide, M.A.D.D.: Mothers Against Drunk Drivers, Finnegan Begin Again, Family Reunion, Spot Marks the X, The Tracker, Margaret Bourke-White, In a Child's Name. Mini-Series: Once an Eagle.

HUDSON, ERNIE
Actor. b. Benton Harbor, MI, Dec. 17, 1945. e. Wayne St. Univ., Yale Sch. of Drama. Former Actors Ensemble Theater while in Detroit. Professional stage debut in L.A. production of Daddy Goodness.
PICTURES: Leadbelly (debut, 1976), The Main Event, The Jazz Singer, Penitentiary II, Spacehunter: Adventures in the Forbidden Zone, Going Berserk, Ghostbusters, The Joy of Sex, Weeds, Leviathan, Ghostbusters II, The Hand That Rocks the Cradle, Sugar Hill, No Escape, The Crow, The Cowboy Way, Airheads, Speechless, The Basketball Diaries, Congo, The Substitute.
TELEVISION: Series: Highcliffe Manor, The Last Precinct, Broken Badges. Mini-Series: Roots: The Next Generations, Wild Palms. Movies: White Mama, Dirty Dozen: The Fatal Mission, Love on the Run. Guest: Fantasy Island, Little House on the Praire, One Day at a Time, Diff'rent Strokes, St. Elsewhere.

HUDSON, HUGH
Producer, Director. b. England. e. Eton. Began career as head of casting dept. with ad agency in London; left for Paris to work as editor for small film co. Returned to London to form Cammell-Hudson-Brownjohn Film Co., production house., turning out award-winning documentaries (Tortoise and Hare, A is for Apple). 1970, joined Ridley Scott to make TV commercials. 1975, formed Hudson Films to produce.
PICTURES: Director: Chariots of Fire, Greystoke: The Legend of Tarzan Lord of the Apes (also prod.), Revolution, Lost Angels.

HUGH KELLY, DANIEL
Actor. b. Hoboken, NJ, Aug. 10, 1949. Began acting with the National Players touring U.S. in such plays as Henry IV Part 1, Charlie's Aunt, School for Wives.
THEATER: Arena Stage (DC): An Enemy of the People, Once in a Lifetime, Long Day's Journey Into Night. Actors Theatre (Louisville): Much Ado About Nothing, The Best Man, The Taming of the Shrew, The Rainmaker. Off-B'way: Hunchback of

Notre Dame, Miss Margarita's Way, Juno's Swans, Fishing, Short-Changed Revue. *B'way*: Born Yesterday, Cat on a Hot Tin Roof.
PICTURES: Cujo, Nowhere to Hide, Someone to Watch Over Me, The Good Son, Bad Company.
TELEVISION: *Series*: Chicago Story, Hardcastle and McCormick. *Movies*: Nutcracker, Thin Ice, Murder Ink, Night of Courage, Citizen Cohn, Moment of Truth: A Mother's Deception, A Child's Cry for Help, The Tuskegee Airmen.

HUGHES, BARNARD
Actor. b. Bedford Hills, NY, July 16, 1915. Winner of Emmy for role as Judge in Lou Grant series (1978) and Tony Award for Da (1978). Inducted into Theatre Hall of Fame (1993).
PICTURES: Midnight Cowboy, Where's Poppa?, Cold Turkey, The Pursuit of Happiness, The Hospital, Rage, Sisters, Deadhead Miles, Oh God!, First Monday in October, Tron, Best Friends, Maxie, Where Are the Children?, The Lost Boys, Da, Doc Hollywood, Sister Act 2: Back in the Habit, The Fantasticks.
TELEVISION: *Series*: Doc, Mr. Merlin, The Cavanaughs, Blossom. *Movies*: Guilty or Innocent, The Sam Sheppard Murder Case, See How She Runs, The Caryl Chessman Story, Tell Me My Name, Look Homeward, Angel, Father Brown: Detective, Nova, Homeward Bound, The Sky's No Limit, A Caribbean Mystery, Night of Courage, A Hobo's Christmas, Day One, Home Fires Burning, Guts and Glory: The Rise and Fall of Oliver North, The Incident, Miracle Child, Trick of the Eye, Past the Bleachers. *Guest*: Homicide, The Marshal.

HUGHES, JOHN
Writer, Director, Producer. b. Detroit, MI, Feb. 18, 1950. e. Univ. of AZ. Editor of National Lampoon before writing film script of National Lampoon's Class Reunion (1982). Made directorial debut with Sixteen Candles in 1984 which also wrote. In 1985 entered into deal with Paramount Pictures to write, direct and produce films with his own production unit, The John Hughes Co.
PICTURES: *Writer*: National Lampoon's Class Reunion, National Lampoon's Vacation, Mr. Mom, Nate and Hayes, Sixteen Candles (also dir.), The Breakfast Club (also dir., co-prod.), National Lampoon's European Vacation, Weird Science (also dir.), Pretty in Pink (also co-exec. prod.), 101 Dalmations. *Writer/Prod.*: Ferris Bueller's Day Off (also dir.), Some Kind of Wonderful, Planes Trains & Automobiles (also dir.), She's Having a Baby (also dir.), The Great Outdoors (exec. prod., s.p.), Uncle Buck (also dir.), National Lampoon's Christmas Vacation, Home Alone, Career Opportunities (exec. prod., co-s.p.), Only the Lonely (co-prod. only), Dutch, Curly Sue (also dir.), Home Alone 2: Lost in New York, Dennis the Menace, Baby's Day Out, Miracle on 34th Street.

HUGHES, KATHLEEN
Actress. r.n. Betty von Gerkan; b. Hollywood, CA, Nov. 14, 1928. e. Los Angeles City Coll., UCLA. m. Stanley Rubin, producer, mother of 4, Michael played Baby Matthew on Peyton Place. Studied drama; under contract, 20th-Fox, 1948-51; starred in Seven Year Itch 1954, La Jolla Playhouse; signed by UI, 1952. Theatre includes You Can't Take It With You, An Evening With Tennessee Williams, The Bar Off Melrose.
PICTURES: Road House, Mother is a Freshman, Mr. Belvedere Goes to College, Take Care of My Little Girl, It Happens Every Spring, When Willie Comes Marching Home, My Blue Heaven, Mister 880, The Way Out, I'll See You in My Dreams, Thy Neighbor's Wife, For Men Only (The Tall Lie), Sally and Saint Anne, Golden Blade, It Came From Outer Space, Dawn at Socorro, Glass Web, Cult of the Cobra, Three Bad Sisters, Promise Her Anything, The President's Analyst, The Take, Pete and Tillie, Ironweed, The Couch Trip, Revenge.
TELEVISION: *Guest*: Bob Cummings Show, Hitchcock, 77 Sunset Strip, G.E. Theatre, Bachelor Father, Frank Sinatra Show, Ed Wynn Show, Alan Young Show, The Tall Man, Dante, Tightrope, Markham, I Dream of Jeannie, Peyton Place, Gomer Pyle, Kismet, Ghost and Mrs. Muir, Bracken's World, The Survivors, Julia, Here's Lucy, To Rome with Love, The Interns, The Man and the City, Mission Impossible, The Bold Ones, Lucas Tanner, Marcus Welby, Barnaby Jones, Medical Center, M.A.S.H., General Hospital, Quincy, Finder of Lost Loves, The Young and the Restless. *Movies*: Babe, Forbidden Love, The Spell, Portrait of an Escort, Capitol, Mirror, Mirror, And Your Name is Jonah.

HUGHES, KEN
Director, Writer. b. Liverpool, Eng., 1922. Ent. ind. as sound engineer with BBC, 1940; Doc. films, Army training films. Wrote book and lyrics for stage musical Oscar. Member: Assn. Cine Technicians, Writers' Guild of Great Britain.
AUTHOR: High Wray, The Long Echo, An Enemy of the State. Scripts: The Matarese Circle, Tussy is Me, The Queen's Own, RatsHallo Berlin.
PICTURES: *Dir./Writer*: Wide Boy, The House Across the Lake, Black 13 (dir. only), The Brain Machine, Case of the Red Monkey, Confession (The Deadliest Sin), Timeslip (The Atomic Man), Joe Macbeth, Wicked as They Come, The Long Haul,

Jazz Boat, In the Nick, The Trials of Oscar Wilde, The Small World of Sammy Lee, Of Human Bondage (dir. only), Arrivederci Baby (also prod.), Casino Royale (co-dir.), Chitty Chitty Bang Bang, Cromwell, The Internecine Project, Alfie Darling (Oh Alfie!), Sextette (dir. only), Night School.
TELEVISION: Eddie (Emmy Award for writing, 1959), Sammy (Brit. Acad. Award). *Serials*: Solo for Canary, Enemy of the State. *Series*: Lenin 1917 (The Fall of Eagles), The Haunting, The Voice, Oil Strike North, Colditz, Churchill (BBC).
AWARDS: Golden Globe, Emmy, British TV Acad. Award (Script Writer of Year), Avorias Festival Merit Award, British Writer's Guild Award, British Critics Award (best serial).

HUGHES, WENDY
Actress. b. Melbourne, Australia. Studied acting at National Institute of Dramatic Art, Sydney.
PICTURES: Sidecar Racers, High Rolling, Newsfront, My Brilliant Career, Kostas, Touch and Go, Hoodwink, Lonely Hearts, Careful He Might Hear You, My First Wife, An Indecent Obsession, Happy New Year, Warm Nights on a Slow Moving Train, Boundaries of the Heart, Luigi's Ladies (also co-s.p.), Wild Orchid II, Princess Caraboo.
TELEVISION: Amerika, Coralie Landsdowne Says No, Can't Get Started, The Heist, A Woman Named Jackie, Homicide: Life on the Street.

HUIZENGA, HARRY WAYNE
Entrepreneur, Entertainment Executive. b. Evergreen Park, IL, Dec 29, 1939. e. Calvin College, 1957-58. m. Martha Jean Pike, Apr. 17, 1972. Vice chmn., pres., chief operating officer Waste Mgmt. Inc., Oak Brook, IL, 1968-84; prin. Huizenga Holdings, Inc., Ft. Lauderdale, FL, 1984–; chmn., chief exec. officer Blockbuster Entertainment Corp., Ft. Lauderdale, 1987-1995; owner Florida Marlins, Miami, 1992–; co-owner Miami Dolphins, Joe Robbie Stadium. Mem. Florida Victory Com., 1988-89, Team Repub. Nat. com., Washington, 1988-90. Recipient Entrepenuer of Yr. award Wharton Sch. U. Pa., 1989, Excalibur award Bus. Leader of Yr. News/Sun Sentinel, 1990, Silver Medallion Brotherhood award Broward Region Nat. Conf. Christians and Jews, 1990, Laureates award Jr. Achievement Broward and Palm Beach Counties, 1990, Jim Murphy Humanitarian Award The Emerald Soc., 1990, Entrepreneur of Yr. award Disting. Panel Judges Fla., 1990, Man of Yr. Billboard/Time Mag., 1990, Man of Yr. Juvenile Diabetes Found., 1990, Florida Free Enterpriser of Yr. award Fla. Coun. on Econ. Edn., 1990, commendation for youth restricted video State of Fla. Office of Gov., 1989, Hon. Mem. Appreciation award Bond Club Ft. Lauderdale, 1989, honored with endowed teaching chair Broward Community Coll., 1990. Mem. Lauderdale Yacht Club, Tournament Players Club, Coral Ridge Country Club, Fisher Island Club, Ocean Reef Club, Cat Cay Yacht Club, Linville Ridge Country Club. Avocations: golf, collecting antique cars. Office: 200 S. Andrews Ave., Ft. Lauderdale, FL 33301.

HULCE, TOM
Actor. b. White Water, WI, Dec. 6, 1953. e. NC School of the Arts. Understudied and then co-starred in Equus on Broadway. Directorial stage debut Sleep Around Town. Appeared in IMAX film Wings of Courage. Recipient of Emmy Award, 1996.
THEATER: A Memory of Two Mondays, Julius Caesar, Candida, The Sea Gull, The Rise and Rise of Daniel Rocket, Eastern Standard, A Few Good Men (Tony nom.), Hamlet.
PICTURES: September 30, 1955 (debut, 1978), National Lampoon's Animal House, Those Lips Those Eyes, Amadeus (Acad. Award nom.), Echo Park, Slamdance, Dominick and Eugene, Parenthood, Shadowman, The Inner Circle, Fearless, Mary Shelley's Frankenstein, The Hunchback of Notre Dame (voice).
TELEVISION: *Specials*: Emily Emily, The Rise and Rise of Daniel Rocket, Song of Myself, Forget-Me-Not Lane, Tall Tales and Legends (John Henry). *Mini-Series*: The Adams Chronicles. *Movies*: Murder in Mississippi, Black Rainbow.

HUNNICUT, GAYLE
Actress. b. Fort Worth, TX, February 6, 1943. e. UCLA, B.A., with honors, theater arts & English major. Early career, community theatres in Los Angeles.
THEATER: The Ride Across Lake Constance, Twelfth Night, The Tempest, Dog Days, The Admirable Crichton, A Woman of No Importance, Hedda Gabler, Peter Pan, Macbeth, Uncle Vanya, The Philadelphia Story, Miss Firecracker Contest, Exit The King, The Doctor's Dilemma, So Long on Lonely Street, The Big Knife, Edith Wharton at Home, The Little Foxes, Dangerous Corner.
PICTURES: The Wild Angels (debut, 1966), P.J., Eye of the Cat, Marlowe, Fragment of Fear, The Freelance, Voices, Running Scared, Legend of Hell House, Scorpio, L'Homme Sans Visage, The Spiral Staircase, The Sell Out, Strange Shadows in an Empty Room, Once in Paris, One Take Two, Fantomas, Privilege, Sherlock Holmes, Target, Dream Lover, Turnaround, Silence Like Glass.
TELEVISION: *Series*: Dallas (1989-91). *Movies*: The Smugglers, The Million Dollar Face, The Return of the Man From U.N.C.L.E., The First Olympics: Athens 1896. *Specials*: Man and Boy, The

Golden Bowl, The Ambassadors, The Ripening Seed, Fall of Eagles, The Switch, Humboldt's Gift, The Life and Death of Dylan Thomas, Return of the Saint, The Lady Killers, Savage in the Orient, Strong Medicine. *Mini-Series*: A Man Called Intrepid, The Martian Chronicles, Dream West. *Guest*: Taxi.

HUNT, HELEN
Actress. b. Los Angeles, CA, June 15, 1963. Daughter of director Gordon Hunt.
THEATER: Been Taken, Our Town, The Taming of the Shrew, Methusalem.
PICTURES: Rollercoaster, Girls Just Want to Have Fun, Peggy Sue Got Married, Project X, Miles From Home, Trancers, Stealing Home, Next of Kin, The Waterdance, Only You, Bob Roberts, Mr. Saturday Night, Kiss of Death, Twister.
TELEVISION: *Series*: Swiss Family Robinson, Amy Prentiss, The Fitzpatricks, It Takes Two, Mad About You (Emmy Award, 1996). *Movies*: Pioneer Woman, All Together Now, Death Scream, The Spell, Transplant, Angel Dusted, Child Bride of Short Creek, The Miracle of Kathy Miller, Quarterback Princess, Bill: On His Own, Sweet Revenge, Incident at Dark River, Into the Badlands, Murder in New Hampshire: The Pamela Smart Story, In the Company of Darkness. *Specials*: Weekend, Land of Little Rain. *Special*: Sexual Healing. *Guest*: St. Elsewhere, Family, Mary Tyler Moore Show, The Hitchhiker.

HUNT, LINDA
Actress. b. Morriston, NJ, Apr. 2, 1945. e. Interlochen Arts Acad., MI, and Chicago's Goodman Theatre & Sch. of Drama. Narrated documentary Ecological Design: Inventing the Future.
THEATER: *Long Wharf (New Haven)*:Hamlet, The Rose Tattoo, Ah Wilderness. *NY*: Mother Courage, End of the World (Tony nom.), A Metamorphosis in Miniature (Obie Award), Top Girls (Obie Award), Aunt Dan and Lemon, The Cherry Orchard. *Regional*: The Three Sisters.
PICTURES: Popeye (debut, 1980) The Year of Living Dangerously (Academy Award, best supporting actress, 1983), The Bostonians, Dune, Silverado, Eleni, Waiting for the Moon, She-Devil, Kindergarten Cop, If Looks Could Kill, Rain Without Thunder, Twenty Bucks, Younger and Younger, Ready to Wear (Pret-a-Porter), Pocahontas (voice).
TELEVISION: *Series*: Space Rangers. *Movie*: The Room Upstairs. *Specials*: Ah Wilderness, The Room. *Guest*: Fame.

HUNT, MARSHA
Actress. b. Chicago, IL, Oct. 17, 1917.
THEATER: *B'way*: Joy to the World, Devils Disciple, Legend of Sarah, Borned in Texas, Tunnel of Love, The Paisley Convertible.
PICTURES: The Virginia Judge (debut, 1935), College Holiday, Easy to Take, Blossoms in the Dust, Panama Hattie, Joe Smith American, These Glamour Girls, Winter Carnival, Irene, Pride and Prejudice, Flight Command, The Affairs of Martha, Kid Glove Killer, Seven Sweethearts, Cheers for Miss Bishop, Trial of Mary Dugan, Thousands Cheer, The Human Comedy, None Shall Escape, Lost Angel, Cry Havoc, Bride by Mistake, Music for Millions, Valley of Decision, A Letter for Evie, Smash-Up, Carnegie Hall, The Inside Story, Raw Deal, Jigsaw, Take One False Step, Actors and Sin, Happy Time, No Place to Hide, Back from the Dead, Bombers B-52, Blue Denim, The Plunderers, Johnny Got His Gun.
TELEVISION: *Series*: Peck's Bad Girl. *Guest*: Philco, Studio One, Ford Theatre, Show of Shows, G.E. Theatre, Climax, Hitchcock, The Defenders, Twilight Zone, Cains Hundred, Gunsmoke, The Breaking Point, Outer Limits, Profiles in Courage, Ben Casey, Accidental Family, Run For Your Life, My Three Sons, The Outsiders, Name of the Game, Univ.'s 120, Ironside, Marcus Welby, M.D., Police Story, The Young Lawyers, Harry-O, The Mississippi, Hot Pursuit, Shadow Chaser, Matlock, Murder She Wrote, Star Trek: The Next Generation.

HUNT, PETER
Director, Editor. b. London, Eng., March 11, 1928. e. Romford, England and Rome, Italy, London Sch. of Music. Actor English Rep. Entered film as camera asst. documentary, later asst film editor documentary, then asst editor features, London Films.
PICTURES: *Editor*: Hill in Korea, Admirable Crichton, Cry From the Streets, Greengage Summer (Loss of Innocence), Ferry to Hong Kong, H.M.S. Defiant (Damn the Defiant). *Supervising editor/2nd Unit Director*: Dr. No, Call Me Bwana, From Russia With Love, Goldfinger, The Ipcress File, Thunderball, You Only Live Twice. *Assoc. Prod.*: Chitty Chitty Bang Bang. *Director*: On Her Majesty's Secret Service, Gullivers Travels, Gold, Shout at the Devil, Death Hunt, Wild Geese II, Hyper Sapien, Assassination.
TELEVISION: *Director*: *Series*: The Persuaders, Shirley's World, The Pencil, Smart Alec Kill (Philip Marlowe). *Movies*: The Beasts Are in the Streets, Eye of a Witness. *Mini-Series*: Last Days of Pompeii.

HUNT, PETER H.
Director. b. Pasadena, CA, Dec. 16, 1938. e. Hotchkiss, Yale U., Yale Drama Sch. m. actress Barbette Tweed. Director for Williamston Theatre since 1957. Lighting designer on B'way. (1963-69) Awards: Tony, Ace, Peabody (twice), N.Y. Drama Critics, London Drama Critics, Edgar Allan Poe, Christopher.

THEATER: 1776 (London & B'way.), Georgy (B'way.), Scratch (B'way.), Goodtime Charley (B'way.), Give 'Em Hell Harry, Magnificent Yankee (Kennedy Center). *Tours*: Bully, Three Penny Opera, Sherlock Holmes, Bus Stop.
PICTURES: 1776, Give 'Em Hell Harry.
TELEVISION: *Specials*: Adventures of Huckleberry Finn, Life on the Mississippi, A Private History of a Campaign That Failed, A New Start, Mysterious Stranger, Sherlock Holmes (cable), Bus Stop (cable). *Movies*: Flying High, Rendezvous Motel, When She Was Bad, Skeezer, The Parade, Sins of the Past, It Came Upon the Midnight Clear, Charley Hannah, Danielle Steel's Secrets, Sworn to Vengeance. *Pilots*: Adam's Rib, Hello Mother Goodbye, Ivan the Terrible, Quark, Mixed Nuts, Wilder and Wilder, The Main Event, Nuts and Bolts, The Good Witch of Laurel Canyon, Masquerade, Stir Crazy, The Wizard of Elm Street, Travelling Man, My Africa.

HUNT, WILLIE
Executive Producer. b. Van Nuys, CA, Oct. 1, 1941. e. Utah State U., B.A., 1963. m. writer Tim Considine. Started in industry as secretary at Warner Bros., 1965; named exec. secty. to Ted Ashley, WB, 1969; story analyst, WB, 1974; story editor, WB, 1975; named West Coast story editor for WB, 1978; joined MGM in 1979 as v.p., motion picture development. Moved to United Artists as v.p.-prod., 1982. 1983 sr. v.p. of prod. at Rastar Prods.; 1984, indep. prod., Tri-Star; 1986, sr. v.p., Freddie Fields Prods. 1988: Loverboy (co-prod.) 1989, sr. v.p. Considine Prods. 1993, partner, Creative Entertainment Group.

HUNTER, HOLLY
Actress. b. Conyers, GA. March 20, 1958. e. studied acting, Carnegie-Mellon Univ. Appeared Off-B'way in Battery (1981) and Weekend Near Madison. Appeared in 5 Beth Henley plays: The Miss Firecracker Contest (Off-B'way), as a replacement in Crimes of the Heart (B'way) The Wake of Jamey Foster (B'way), Lucky Spot (Williamstown Theater Festival), and Control Freaks (L.A.; also co-prod.). Also: A Lie of the Mind (L.A.).
PICTURES: The Burning (debut, 1981), Swing Shift, Raising Arizona, Broadcast News (NY Film Critics, LA Film Critics and Natl. Board of Review Awards, Acad. Award nom., 1987), End of the Line, Miss Firecracker, Animal Behavior, Always, Once Around, The Firm (Acad. Award nom.), The Piano (Academy Award, Cannes Film Fest., LA Film Critics, NY Film Critics, Natl. Board of Review, Natl. Society of Film Critics & Golden Globe Awards, 1993), Home for the Holidays, Copycat, Crash.
TELEVISION: *Movies*: Svengali, An Uncommon Love, With Intent to Kill, A Gathering of Old Men, Roe vs. Wade (Emmy Award, 1989), Crazy in Love, The Positively True Adventures of the Alleged Texas Cheerleader-Murdering Mom (Emmy Award, 1993). *Guest*: Fame (pilot).

HUNTER, KIM
Actress. r.n. Janet Cole. b. Detroit, MI, Nov. 12, 1922. e. public schools. d. Donald and Grace Mabel (Lind) Cole. Studied acting with Charmine Lantaff Camine, 1938-40, Actors Studio; First stage appearance, 1939; played in stock, 1940-42; Broadway debut in A Streetcar Named Desire, 1947; frequent appearances in summer stock and repertory theater, 1940-; appeared Am. Shakespeare Festival, Stratford, CT, 1961. Autobiography-cookbook: Loose in the Kitchen (1975).
THEATER: *NY*: Darkness at Noon, The Chase, The Children's Hour (revival), The Tender Trap, Write Me a Murder, Weekend, The Penny Wars, The Women, The Cherry Orchard, To Grandmother's House We Go, When We Dead Awaken, Territorial Rites, Man and Superman, A Murder of Crows, Eye of the Beholder, All The Way Home. *Tours*: Two Blind Mice, They Knew What They Wanted, And Miss Reardon Drinks a Little, In Praise of Love, The Gin Game. *Regional*: The Glass Menagerie, The Lion in Winter, The Chalk Garden, Elizabeth the Queen, Semmelweiss, The Belle of Amherst, The Little Foxes, Another Part of the Forest, Ghosts, Death of a Salesman, Cat on a Hot Tin Roof, Life With Father, Sabrina Fair, Faulkner's Bicycle, Antique Pink, The Belle of Amherst, Painting Churches, A Delicate Balance, Jokers, Remembrance, The Gin Game, A Murder of Crows, Watch on the Rhine, Suddenly Last Summer, A Smaller Place, Open Window, The Cocktail Hour, The Belle of Amherst, Love Letters, Do Not Go Gentle.
PICTURES: The Seventh Victim (debut, 1943), Tender Comrade, When Strangers Marry (Betrayed), You Came Along, Stairway to Heaven (A Matter of Life and Death), A Canterbury Tale, A Streetcar Named Desire (Academy Award, best supporting actress, 1951), Anything Can Happen, Deadline: U.S.A., The Young Stranger, Bermuda Affair, Storm Center, Money Women and Guns, Lilith, Planet of the Apes, The Swimmer, Beneath the Planet of the Apes, Escape from the Planet of the Apes, Dark August, The Kindred, Two Evil Eyes.
TELEVISION: Made TV debut on Actors Studio Program, 1948. *Series*: The Edge of Night (1979-80). *Specials*: Requiem for a Heavyweight, The Comedian (both on Playhouse 90); Give Us Barabbas, Stubby Pringle's Christmas, Project: U.F.O., Three Sovereigns for Sarah, Vivien Leigh: Scarlett and Beyond, Martin Luther King: The Dream and the Drum, Hurricane Andrew Project. *Guest*: Love American Style, Columbo, Cannon, Night

177

Gallery, Mission Impossible, Marcus Welby, Hec Ramsey, Griff, Police Story, Ironside, Medical Center, Baretta, Gibbsville, The Oregon Trail, Scene of the Crime, Hunter, Murder She Wrote, Class of '96, Mad About You, L.A. Law. Movies: Dial Hot Line, In Search of America, The Magician (pilot), Unwed Father, Born Innocent, Bad Ronald, Ellery Queen (Too Many Suspects), The Dark Side of Innocence, The Golden Gate Murders, F.D.R.: The Last Year, Skokie, Private Sessions, Drop-Out Mother, Cross of Fire, Bloodlines: Murder in the Family. Mini-Series: Once an Eagle, Backstairs at the White House.

HUNTER, ROSS
Producer. r.n. Martin Fuss. b. Cleveland, OH, May 6, 1926. e. Western Reserve U., M.A. Was school teacher before becoming actor at Columbia Pictures; returned to school teaching; stage prod. & dir.; m.p. dialogue dir.; assoc. prod. Universal-International, 1950-51; prod., U-I, 1951. Moved production Co. from Universal to Columbia, 1971. Moved to Paramount, 1974. Moved to NBC, 1978-82.
PICTURES: As actor: Louisiana Hayride, Ever Since Venus, She's a Sweetheart, Out of the Depths, Submarine Below, Hit the Hay, Eve Knew Her Apples, Bandit of Sherwood Forest, Groom Wore Spurs. As producer: Take Me to Town, All I Desire, Tumbleweed, Taza Son of Cochise, Magnificent Obsession, Naked Alibi, Yellow Mountain, Captain Lightfoot, One Desire, The Spoilers, All That Heaven Allows, There's Always Tomorrow, Battle Hymn, Tammy and the Bachelor, Interlude, My Man Godfrey, The Restless Years, This Happy Feeling, Stranger in My Arms, Imitation of Life, Pillow Talk, Portrait in Black, Midnight Lace, Back Street, Flower Drum Song, Tammy Tell Me True, If a Man Answers, Tammy and the Doctor, The Thrill of It All, The Chalk Garden, I'd Rather Be Rich, The Art of Love, Madame X, The Pad, Thoroughly Modern Millie, Rosie, Airport, Lost Horizon.
TELEVISION: Movies: Lives of Jenny Dolan, The Moneychangers, The Best Place to Be, A Family Upside Down, Suddenly Love.
d. March 10, 1996.

HUNTER, TAB
Actor. r.n. Arthur Gelien. b. New York, NY, July 11, 1931. Served with U.S. Coast Guard. Entered industry in 1948.
PICTURES: The Lawless (debut, 1950), Island of Desire, Gun Belt, Steel Lady, Return to Treasure Island, Track of the Cat, Battle Cry, Sea Chase, The Burning Hills, The Girl He Left Behind, Lafayette Escadrille, Gunman's Walk, Damn Yankees, That Kind of Woman, They Came to Cordura, The Pleasure of His Company, Operation Bikini, The Golden Arrow, Ride the Wild Surf, The Loved One, War Gods of the Deep, Birds Do It, Fickle Finger of Fate, Hostile Guns, The Arousers (Sweet Kill), Life and Times of Judge Roy Bean, Timber Tramp, Won Ton Ton the Dog Who Saved Hollywood, Polyester, Pandemonium, Grease 2, Lust in the Dust (also co-prod.), Cameron's Closet, Grotesque, Out of the Dark, Dark Horse (also story).
TELEVISION: Movies: San Francisco International, Katie: Portrait of a Centerfold. Series: The Tab Hunter Show, Mary Hartman Mary Hartman.

HUNTER, TIM
Director. e. Harvard, AFI.
PICTURES: Over the Edge (co-s.p.). Dir.: Tex (also s.p.), Sylvester, River's Edge, Paint It Black, The Saint of Fort Washington.
TELEVISION: Movie: Lies of the Twins.

HUPPERT, ISABELLE
Actress. b. Paris, France, March 16, 1955. e. Conservatoire National d'Art Dramatique.
PICTURES: Faustine and the Beautiful Summer (Growing Up; debut, 1971), Cesar and Rosalie, Going Places, Rosebud, The Rape of Innocence, The Judge and the Assassin, The Lacemaker, Violette (Cannes Fest. Award, 1977), The Bronte Sisters, Loulou, Heaven's Gate, Coup de Torchon, Every Man for Himself, The True Story of Camille, Wings of the Dove, Deep Water, Entre Nous, The Trout, Cactus, Signed Charlotte, The Bedroom Window, The Possessed, Story of Women (Venice Fest Award, 1988), Milan Noir, Madame Bovary, Revenge of a Woman, Malina, Apres l'Amour (After Love), Amateur, The Separation, A Judgment in Stone.

HURD, GALE ANNE
Producer. b. Los Angeles, CA, Oct. 25, 1955. e. Stanford U., Phi Beta Kappa, 1977. Joined New World Pictures in 1977 as exec. asst. to pres. Roger Corman, then named dir. of advertising and pub. and moved into prod. management capacities on several New World films. Left in 1982 to form own co., Pacific Western Productions. Honored by NATO with special merit award for Aliens. Served as juror, U.S. Film Fest., Utah, 1988 and for 1989 Focus Student Film Awards. Member, Hollywood Women's Political Committee. Board of Trustees, AFI. The Amer. Film Inst. created Gale Anne Hurd production grants for Institute's Directing Workshop for Women. Bd. of dir. The Independent Feature Project/West.

PICTURES: Smokey Bites the Dust (co-prod. with Roger Corman, 1981), The Terminator (Grand Prix, Avoriaz Film Fest., France), Aliens (Hugo Award) Alien Nation (Saturn nom.), The Abyss, Downtown (exec. prod.), Tremors (exec. prod.), Terminator 2 (exec. prod.), The Waterdance, Raising Cain, No Escape, Safe Passage, The Relic, The Ghost and The Darkness.
TELEVISION: Movies: Cast a Deadly Spell, Witch Hunt, Sugartime.

HURLOCK, ROGER W.
Pres. Hurlock Cine-World. b. Cambridge, MD, May 30, 1912. e. Baltimore City Coll. Ent. m.p. ind. as publicist, Hippodrome Theatre, Balt.; asst. mgr., Lessor-operator Imperial and Majestic Theatres, Balt., 1931-35; real estate, bldg., farming, Maryland and Alaska, 1936-58; elected bd. mem., Allied Artists, 1958; asst. to pres., 1961-63; chmn. budget comm., 1963; chmn. policy comm., 1964; c.p. exec. comm. member, 1964; v.p., chf. operating officer 1965; chmn. exec. comm., 1966; pres., 1967. pres., Hurlock Cine-World, 1969.

HURT, JOHN
Actor. b. Shirebrook, Derbyshire, Jan. 22, 1940. e. St. Martin's Sch. for Art, London, RADA.
THEATER: The Dwarfs, Little Malcolm and His Struggle Against the Eunuchs, Man and Superman, Belcher's Luck, Ride a Cock Horse, The Caretaker, Romeo and Juliet, Ruffian on the Streets, The Dumb Waiter, Travesties, The Arrest, The Seagull, The London Vertigo, A Month in the Country.
PICTURES: The Wild and the Willing (debut, 1962), This is My Street, A Man for All Seasons, The Sailor from Gibraltar, Before Winter Comes, Sinful Davey, In Search of Gregory, 10 Rillington Place, Mr. Forbush and the Penguins, The Pied Piper, Little Malcolm, The Ghoul, East of Elephant Rock, Disappearance, Midnight Express (Acad. Award nom.) Watership Down (voice), The Lord of the Rings (voice), The Shout, Alien, The Elephant Man (Acad. Award nom.), Heaven's Gate, History of the World Part I, Night Crossing, Partners, The Plague Dogs (voice), The Osterman Weekend, Champions, The Hit, Success Is the Best Revenge, 1984, The Black Cauldron (voice), Jake Speed, From the Hip, Spaceballs, Aria, Vincent (voice), White Mischief, Little Sweetheart, Scandal, Frankenstein Unbound, The Field, King Ralph, Romeo-Juliet, Resident Alien, I Dreamt I Woke Up, Lapse of Memory, Dark at Noon, Monolith, Hans Christian Andersen's Thumbelina (voice), Even Cowgirls Get the Blues, Crime and Punishment, Great Moments in Aviation, Second Best, Rob Roy, Wild Bill, Two Nudes Bathing, Dead Man.
TELEVISION: Playboy of the Western World, A Tragedy of Two Ambitions, Green Julia, Nijinsky, Shades of Green, Ten from the Twenties, The Peddler, The Naked Civil Servant, I Claudius, Spectre, Crime and Punishment, The Storyteller (series host), Deadline, The Jim Henson Hour, The Investigation: Inside a Terrorist Bombing, Six Characters in Search of an Author.

HURT, MARY BETH
Actress. b. Marshalltown, IA, Sept. 26, 1946. m. writer-director Paul Schrader. e. U. of Iowa, NYU Sch. of Arts. Stage debut in 1973 with N.Y. Shakespeare Fest. (More Than You Deserve, Pericles, The Cherry Orchard).
THEATER: As You Like It (Central Park), 2 seasons with Phoenix Theater, Love For Love, Tralawny of the Wells, Secret Service, Boy Meets Girl, Father's Day, Crimes of the Heart, The Misanthrope, Benefactors, The Nest of the Wood Grouse, The Day Room, Othello, A Delicate Balance.
PICTURES: Interiors (debut, 1978), Head Over Heels (Chilly Scenes of Winter), A Change of Seasons, The World According to Garp, D.A.R.Y.L., Compromising Positions, Parents, Slaves of New York, Defenseless, Light Sleeper, My Boyfriend's Back, The Age of Innocence, Six Degrees of Separation, From the Journals of Jean Seberg.
TELEVISION: Series: Nick and Hillary. Movies: Baby Girl Scott, Shimmer. Specials: The Five-Forty-Eight, Secret Service (NET Theatre). Guest: Kojak.

HURT, WILLIAM
Actor. b. Washington, DC, Mar. 20, 1950. Lived as child in South Pacific when father was dir. of Trust Territories for U.S. State Dept. e. Tufts as theology major, switched to drama in jr. year, Juilliard. Acted with Oregon Shakespearean Fest. Leading actor with New York's Circle Repertory Company (Theatre World Award), since 1976.
THEATER: NY: The Fifth of July, My Life (Obie Award), Ulysses in Traction, The Runner Stumbles, Hamlet, Childe Byron, Beside Herself. NY Shakespeare Festival: Henry V, A Midsummer's Night's Dream, Hurlyburly (off-B'way and B'way). Regional: Good (S.F.), Ivanov (Yale).
PICTURES: Altered States (debut, 1980), Eyewitness, Body Heat, The Big Chill, Gorky Park, Kiss of the Spider Woman (Academy Award, 1985), Children of a Lesser God, Broadcast News, A Time of Destiny, The Accidental Tourist, I Love You to Death, Alice, The Doctor, Until the End of the World, Mr. Wonderful, The Plague, Trial by Jury, Second Best, Smoke, Jane Eyre, Secrets Shared With a Stranger, Michael.
TELEVISION: Specials: Verna: USO Girl, Best of Families, All the Way Home, The Odyssey of John Dos Passos (voice).

HUSSEY, OLIVIA
Actress. b. Buenos Aires, Apr. 17, 1951. Attended Italia Conti Stage School, London. Began acting at age 8.
PICTURES: The Battle of the Villa Fiorita (debut, 1965), Cup Fever, All the Right Noises, Romeo and Juliet, Summertime Killer, Lost Horizon, Black Christmas, Death on the Nile, The Cat and the Canary, Virus, The Man With Bogart's Face, Turkey Shoot, Distortions, The Jeweler's Shop, The Undeclared War, Save Me, Ice Cream Man.
TELEVISION: Movies/Mini-Series: *Jesus of Nazareth, The Pirate, The Ba*startd, Ivanhoe, Last Days of Pompeii, The Corsican Brothers, Psycho IV: The Beginning, Stephen King's IT, Save Me, Quest of the Delta Knights, H-Bomb. *Guest*: Murder She Wrote.

HUSTON, ANJELICA
Actress. b. Santa Monica, CA, July 8, 1951. Father was late writer-dir.-actor, John Huston. Brother is director Danny Huston. Raised in St. Clerans, Ireland. Studied acting at the Loft Studio and with Peggy Furey, Martin Landau. Appeared in 3-D Disney short Captain Eo.
PICTURES: A Walk With Love and Death (debut, 1969), Sinful Davey, Swashbuckler, The Last Tycoon, The Postman Always Rings Twice, Frances, The Ice Pirates, This is Spinal Tap, Prizzi's Honor (Academy Award, best supporting actress, 1985), Good to Go (Short Fuse), Gardens of Stone, The Dead, A Handful of Dust, Mr. North, Crimes and Misdemeanors, Enemies a Love Story (Acad. Award nom.), The Witches, The Grifters (Acad. Award nom.), The Addams Family, The Player, Manhattan Murder Mystery, Addams Family Values, The Perez Family, The Crossing Guard, Bstard Out of Carolina (also prod.).
TELEVISION: Movies: The Cowboy and the Ballerina, Family Pictures, And the Band Played On, Buffalo Girls. Specials: Faerie Tale Theatre, A Rose for Miss Emily. Mini-Series: Lonesome Dove.

HUSTON, DANNY
Director. b. Rome, Italy, May 14, 1962. Youngest son of director-actor John Huston and actress Zoe Sallis. Brother of actress Anjelica and screenwriter Tony Huston. e. Overseas School, Rome; Intl branch of Milfield School in Exeter, London Film School. A constant visitor to his father's sets throughout the world, he began working on his father's films, beginning in Cuernavaca, Mexico as second-unit dir. on Under the Volcano. Directed TV doc. on Peru and on making of Santa Claus: The Movie; and TV features Bigfoot and Mr. Corbett's Ghost.
PICTURES: Mr. North (debut, 1988), Becoming Colette, The Maddening.

HUTTE, ROBERT E.
Exhibitor. b. Escanaba, MI, Oct. 22, 1917. e. Wisc. Inst. of Technology. Mgr. insp. lab. Iowa Ord. Plant 1940-42, Army Artil. 1942, Entered business as exhibitor in Southern Iowa 1943; then theatre owner and manager there. Elected board of directors, Allied Theatre Owners of Iowa, Nebraska & Missouri 1948, 1950, 1952. Democratic candidate Iowa State Auditor 1960; Pres. Insurance Advisors, Des Moines, IA; pres Leisure Homes, Nursing Homes; pres., Leisure Homes of Texas; pres. Wodon & Romar Prods., Austin, TX 1970-75. Real estate broker & pres Leisure Mor, theatres in West TX; elected board of dir. National Independent Theatre Exhibitors 1979; Pres. Southwestern Indep. Theatre Exhibitors Assn. of TX, OK, AR, LA & NM; 1979 elected pres. Natl. Independent Theatre Exhibitors Assn. 1980-present. Lifetime member, Foundation of Motion Picture Pioneers.

HUTTON, BETTY
Actress. r.n. Betty June Thornburg. b. Battle Creek, MI, Feb. 26, 1921. Sister was singer-actress Marion Hutton. Was vocalist for Vincent Lopez orchestra earning nickname the Blonde Bombshell. Debuted on B'way 1940 in Two for the Show, followed by Panama Hattie. Signed by Paramount in 1941. Returned to stage in Fade Out Fade In, Annie.
PICTURES: The Fleet's In (debut, 1942), Star Spangled Rhythm, Happy Go Lucky, Let's Face It, The Miracle of Morgan's Creek, And the Angels Sing, Here Come the Waves, Incendiary Blonde, Duffy's Tavern, The Stork Club, Cross My Heart, The Perils of Pauline, Dream Girl, Red Hot and Blue, Annie Get Your Gun, Let's Dance, Sailor Beware (cameo), The Greatest Show on Earth, Somebody Loves Me, Spring Reunion.
TELEVISION: Series: The Betty Hutton Show (1959-60). Special: Satins and Spurs. Guest: Dinah Shore Chevy Show, Greatest Show on Earth, Burke's Law, Gunsmoke.

HUTTON, BRIAN, G.
Director. b. New York, NY, 1935. Started as bit player in films (incl. Fear Strikes Out, Gunfight at the O.K. Corral) before dir. for tv, then features.
PICTURES: The Wild Seed (debut, 1965), The Pad and How to Use It, Sol Madrid, Where Eagles Dare, Kelly's Heroes, X Y and Zee (Zee & Company), Night Watch, The First Deadly Sin, High Road to China, Hostile Takeover.
TELEVISION: Institute For Revenge.

HUTTON, LAUREN
Actress. r.n. Mary Hutton. b. Charleston, SC, Nov. 17, 1943. e. U. of South Florida, Sophie Newcombe Coll. As model featured on more covers than any other American. Stage debut at LA Public Theatre in Extremities.
PICTURES: Paper Lion (debut, 1968), Pieces of Dreams, Little Fauss and Big Halsy, Rocco Papaleo, The Gambler, Gator, Welcome to L.A., Viva Knievel!, A Wedding, American Gigolo, Paternity, Zorro the Gay Blade, Tout Feu tout Flamme (Hecate), Lassiter, Once Bitten, Flagrant Desire, Malone, Blue Blood, Bulldance (Forbidden Sun), Run For Your Life, Billions, Guilty as Charged, Missing Pieces, My Father the Hero.
TELEVISION: Mini-Series: The Rhinemann Exchange, Sins. Movies: Someone Is Watching Me, Institute for Revenge, Starflight, The Cradle Will Fall, Scandal Sheet, The Return of Mike Hammer, Time Stalker, Monte Carlo, Perfect People, Fear. Series: Paper Dolls, Falcon Crest, Lauren Hutton and... (talk show), Central Park West.

HUTTON, TIMOTHY
Actor. b. Malibu, CA, Aug. 16, 1960. Father was late actor Jim Hutton. Debut in bit part in father's film Never Too Late. Acted in high school plays; toured with father in Harvey during vacation. Directed Cars video Drive (1984).
THEATER: NY: Love Letters (B'way debut, 1989), Prelude to a Kiss, Babylon Gardens.
PICTURES: Never Too Late (debut, 1965), Ordinary People (Academy Award, best supporting actor, 1980; also Golden Globe & LA Film Critics Awards), Taps, Daniel, Iceman, The Falcon and The Snowman, Turk 182, Made in Heaven, A Time of Destiny, Betrayed (cameo), Everybody's All American, Torrents of Spring, Q&A, Strangers, The Temp, The Dark Half, French Kiss, Beautiful Girls, The Substance of Fire.
TELEVISION: Movies: Zuma Beach, Friendly Fire, The Best Place to Be, And Baby Makes Six, Young Love First Love, Father Figure, A Long Way Home, Zelda, The Last Word. Director: Amazing Stories (Grandpa's Ghost).

HUYCK, WILLARD
Writer, Director. e. U. of Southern California. Worked as reader for Larry Gordon, executive at American-International Pictures; named Gordon's asst., working on scene rewrites for AIP films. First screen credit on The Devil's Eight as co-writer with John Milius.
PICTURES: Writer: French Postcards (also dir.), Indiana Jones and the Temple of Doom, Best Defense (also dir.), Howard the Duck (also dir.), Radioland Murders, Mission: Impossible.
TELEVISION: A Father's Homecoming (co-exec. prod., co-s.p.), American River (co-exec. prod., co-s.p.).

HYAMS, JOSEPH
Advertising & Publicity Executive. b. New York, NY, Sept. 21, 1926. e. NYU Ent. industry, 1947. Various publicity posts, 20th Century-Fox, Columbia Pictures, 1947-55; eastern pub. mgr., Figaro Prods., 1955-56; West Coast pub. mgr., Hecht-Hill-Lancaster, 1955-58; pub. adv. dir., Batjac Prods. 1959-60 national adv. & pub. dir., Warner Bros.-7 Arts, 1960. v.p., world-wide pub., Warner Bros., Inc., 1970-87; appointed sr. v.p., special projects, 1987.

HYAMS, PETER
Director, Writer, Cinematographer. b. New York, NY, July 26, 1943. e. Hunter Coll., Syracuse U. Joined CBS news staff N.Y. and made anchor man. Filmed documentary on Vietnam in 1966. Left CBS in 1970 and joined Paramount in Hollywood as writer. Hired by ABC to direct TV features.
PICTURES: Writer: T.R. Baskin (also prod.), Telefon, The Hunter. Exec. Prod.: The Monster Squad. Director: Busting (dir. debut 1974; also s.p.), Our Time (also s.p.), Peeper, Capricorn One (also s.p.), Hanover Street (also s.p.), Outland (also s.p.), The Star Chamber (also s.p.), 2010 (also prod., s.p., photog.), Running Scared (also exec. prod., photog.), The Presidio (also photog.), Narrow Margin (also s.p., photog.), Stay Tuned (also photog.), Timecop (also photog.), Sudden Death (also phtg.).
TELEVISION: Movies (dir., writer): The Rolling Man, Goodnight My Love.

HYDE, TOMMY
Executive. r.n. Thomas L. b. Meridian, MS, June 29, 1916. e. Lakeland H.S., grad., 1935. Worked E.J. Sparks Theatres, 1932-41. Florida State Theatres, 1941-42; Navy, 1942-46. Florida State Theatres, 1946-47; city mgr. (Tallahassee). Talgar Theatres, 1947-58; v.p. and gen. mgr. Kent Theatres, 1958-86; vice-pres. Motion Picture Films, Inc.; pres., NATO of Florida, 1961-62; chmn. bd. 1963-70; 1987-, theatre consultant.

HYER, MARTHA
Actress. b. Fort Worth, TX, Aug. 10, 1924. e. Northwestern U., Pasadena Playhouse.
PICTURES: The Locket (debut, 1946), Thunder Mountain, Born to Kill, Woman on the Beach, The Velvet Touch, Gun Smugglers, The Judge Steps Out, Clay Pigeon, Roughshod, The Rustlers, The Lawless, Outcast of Black Mesa, Salt Lake Raiders, Frisco

Tornado, Geisha Girl, The Kangaroo Kid, The Invisible Mr. Unmei, Wild Stallion, Yukon Gold, Abbott and Costello Go to Mars, So Big, Riders to the Stars, Scarlet Spear, Battle of Rogue River, Lucky Me, Down Three Dark Streets, Sabrina, Cry Vengeance, Wyoming Renegades, Kiss of Fire, Paris Follies of 1956, Francis in the Navy, Red Sundown, Showdown at Abilene, Battle Hymn, Kelly and Me, Mister Cory, The Delicate Delinquent, My Man Godfrey, Paris Holiday, Once Upon a Horse, Houseboat, Some Came Running (Acad. Award nom.), The Big Fisherman, The Best of Everything, Ice Palace, Desire in the Dust, Mistress of the World, The Right Approach, The Last Time I Saw Archie, Girl Named Tamiko, The Man from the Diner's Club, Wives and Lovers, Pyro, The Carpetbaggers, First Men in the Moon, Blood on the Arrow, Bikini Beach, The Sons of Katie Elder, The Chase, Night of the Grizzly, Picture Mommy Dead, War Italian Style, The Happening, Some May Live, Lo Scatenato (Catch as Catch Can), House of 1000 Dolls, Once You Kiss a Stranger, Crossplot, The Tyrant.

HYLER, JOAN
Executive. Pres., Women In Film.

I

IANNUCCI, SALVATORE J.
Executive. b. Brooklyn, NY, Sept. 24, 1927. e. NYU, B.A., 1949; Harvard Law School, J.D., 1952. 2 yrs. legal departments RCA and American Broadcasting Companies, Inc.; 14 yrs. with CBS Television Network: asst. dir. of bus. affairs, dir. of bus. affairs, v.p. of bus. affairs; 2 yrs. v.p. admin. National General Corp.; 2-1/2 yrs. pres. of Capital Records; 4-1/2 yrs. Corp. v.p. and dir. of Entertainment Div. of Playboy Enterprises, Inc.; 4 yrs. partner with Jones, Day Reavis & Pogue in Los Angeles office, handling entertainment legal work; Pres., Filmways Entertainment, and sr. v.p., Filmways, Inc.; exec. v.p., Embassy Communications; COO, Aaron Spelling Prods.; sr. partner Bushkin, Gaines, Gaines & Jonas; pres. and chief operating officer, Brad Marks International; prod. of features, tv movies and infomercials.

IBBETSON, ARTHUR
Cinematographer. b. England, Sept. 8, 1922.
PICTURES: The Horse's Mouth, The Angry Silence, The League of Gentlemen, Tunes of Glory, Whistle Down the Wind, Lisa (The Inspector), Nine Hours to Rama, I Could Go on Singing, The Chalk Garden, A Countess from Hong Kong, Inspector Clouseau, Where Eagles Dare, The Walking Stick, Anne of the Thousand Days (Acad. Award nom.), The Railway Children, Willy Wonka and the Chocolate Factory, A Doll's House, 11 Harrow House, A Little Night Music, The Medusa Touch, The Prisoner of Zenda, Hopscotch, Nothing Personal (co-cin.), The Bounty, Santa Claus: The Movie.
TELEVISION: Frankenstein: the True Story, Little Lord Fauntleroy (Emmy Award), Brief Encounter, Babes in Toyland, Witness for the Prosecution, Master of the Game.

IBERT, LLOYD
Executive. Began career as mgng. editor, Independent Film Journal. 1973, joined Paramount Pictures pub. dept.; named sr. publicist. 1985, appointed dir., natl. pub. for M.P. Group.

ICE CUBE
Actor, Singer. r.n. O'Shea Jackson. b. Los Angeles, 1969. e. Phoenix Inst. of Tech. Debuted as rap performer with group N.W.A. Solor debut 1990 with album Amerikka's Most Wanted.
PICTURES: Boyz N the Hood (debut, 1991), Trespass, Higher Learning, Friday (also co-s.p., co-exec. prod.), The Glass Shield.

ICE-T
Actor, Singer. r.n. Tracy Morrow. b. Newark, NJ. Raised in Los Angeles. Served 4 yrs. as ranger in U.S. army. Made debut as rap performer with 1982 single The Coldest Rap. Received Grammy Award 1990 for Back on the Block.
PICTURES: Breakin' (debut, 1984), Breakin' 2: Electric Boogaloo, New Jack City, Ricochet, Trespass, Who's the Man?, Surviving the Game, Tank Girl, Johnny Mnemonic.
TELEVISION: Guest: New York Undercover.

IDLE, ERIC
Actor, Writer. b. South Shields, Co. Durham, Eng., March 29, 1943. e. Pembroke Coll., Cambridge, 1962-65. Pres. Cambridge's Footlights appearing at Edinburgh Fest. 1963-64. Member Monty Python's Flying Circus appearing on BBC, 1969-74.
THEATER: Oh What a Lovely War, Monty Python Live at the Hollywood Bowl, Monty Python Live, The Mikado (English Natl. Opera, 1986).
BOOKS: Hello Sailor, The Rutland Dirty Weekend Book, Pass the Bulter; as well as co-author of Monty Python books: Monty Python's Big Red Book, The Brand New Monty Python Book, Monty Python and the Holy Grail, The Complete Works of Shakespeare and Monty Python.

PICTURES: And Now for Something Completely Different (also co-s.p.), Monty Python and the Holy Grail (also co-s.p.), Monty Python's Life of Brian (also co-s.p.), Monty Python Live at the Hollywood Bowl (also co-s.p.), Monty Python's The Meaning of Life (also co-s.p.), Yellowbeard, National Lampoon's European Vacation, Transformers (voice), The Adventures of Baron Munchausen, Nuns on the Run, Too Much Sun, Missing Pieces, Mom & Dad Save the World, Splitting Heirs (also s.p., exec. prod.), Casper.
TELEVISION: Isadora (debut, 1965), The Frost Report (writer), Do Not Adjust Your Set, Monty Python's Flying Circus, Rutland Weekend Television (series), All You Need is Cash (The Rutles), Faerie Tale Theater (The Frog Prince; dir., writer ACE Award, 1982; The Pied Piper), Saturday Night Live, The Mikado, Around the World in 80 Days, Nearly Departed (series).

IGER, ROBERT
Executive. b. New York, NY, 1951. e. Ithaca Col. Joined ABC in 1974 as studio supervisor. 1976 moved to ABC Sports. 1985, named v.p. in charge of program plan. & dev. as well as scheduling and rights acquisitions for all ABC Sports properties. 1987, named v.p. program. for ABC Sports and mgr. & dir. for ABC's Wide World of Sports; 1988, appt. exec. v.p., ABC Network Group. 1989 named pres., ABC Entertainment. 1992 became pres. of ABC TV Network Group.; 1993, sr. v.p. CC/ABC Inc., exec. v.p. of Capital Cities/ABC Inc. Sept., 1994, elected pres. & COO.

IMAMURA, SHOHEI
Director, Producer, Writer. b. Tokyo, Japan, Sept. 15, 1926. e. Waseda U. Joined Shochiku Ofuna Studio 1951 asst. dir., transferred Nikkatsu in 1954 as asst. dir., director Stolen Desire 1958 then 4 more films before refusing to work on any film distasteful to him; and wrote play later made into film directed by him in 1968; later turned to documentaries and from 1976 onward as independent; Ballad of Narayama awarded Golden Palm Prize, Cannes Festival, 1983.
PICTURES: Stolen Carnal Desire, Big Brother, Hogs and Warships, Insect Woman, God's Profound Desire, The Pornographers, A Man Vanishes, Human Evaporation, History of Postwar Japan, Vengeance Is Mine, Eijanaika, The Ballad of Nurayama, Zegen, Black Rain.

IMI, TONY
Cinematographer. b. London, March 27, 1937. Ent. ind. 1959.
PICTURES: The Raging Moon, Dulcima, The Slipper and the Rose, International Velvet, Brass Target, Ffolkes, The Sea Wolves, Night Crossing, Nate and Hayes, Not Quite Jerusalem, Enemy Mine, Empire State, American Roulette, Buster, Options, Wired, Fire Birds, Pretty Hattie's Baby, Shopping.
TELEVISION: Queenie, The Return of Sherlock Holmes, Oceans of Fire, The Last Days of Frank and Jesse James, Reunion at Fairborough, A Christmas Carol, Sakharov, Princess Daisy, John Paul II, Little Gloria–Happy at Last, Inside the Third Reich, Dreams Don't Die, For Ladies Only, Nicholas Nickleby, A Tale of Two Cities, Babycakes, Old Man and the Sea, Fourth Story, The Last to Go, Our Sons, Carolina Skeletons, Child of Rage, Queen, Cobb's Law, For the Love of My Child: The Anissa Ayala Story, Blind Angel, Scarlett, The Sunshine Boys, The Turn of the Screw, Dalva, The Abduction, Desperate Justice.

IMMERMAN, WILLIAM J.
Producer, Attorney, Executive. b. New York, NY, Dec. 29, 1937. e. Univ. Wisconsin, BS, 1959; Stanford Law, J.D., 1963. 1963-65, served as deputy district attorney, LA County. 1965-72, assoc. counsel, v.p.-bus. affairs, American Intl. Pictures. 1972-77, v.p., business affairs, sr. v.p. feature film division 20th Century-Fox. 1977-1979, producer at Warner Bros. 1979-82, founder and chmn. of bd. of Cinema Group Inc. 1978-present, pres. Salem Productions. 1988-94, pres. Distribution Expense Co. 1988-present, pres., ImmKirk Financial Corp. 1988-89, spec. consultant to office of pres., Pathe Communications. 1989-90, vice chmn. Cannon Pictures. 1986-90, dir. Heritage Ent., Inc. 1991-present, v.p. The Crime Channel, 1983-93, of counsel to law firm of Barash and Hill. 1993-present, of Counsel to law firm of Kenoff and Machtinger (LA). 1990-present, Regional Adjudicator (Southwest). Member of AFMA Arbitration Panel. Member of AMPAS. Stage Productions: Berlin to Broadway (LA), The Knife Thrower's Assistant (LA, tour), The Wiz (B'way).
PICTURES: Exec. prod.: Highpoint, Southern Comfort, Hysterical, Mind Games, Take this Job and Shove It, Where the Red Ferns Grows Part II, The St. Tammany Miracle. Prod.: Primal Rage, Nightmare Beach (Welcome to Spring Break).

INGALLS, DON
Producer, Writer. b. Humboldt, NE, July 29, 1928. e. George Washington U., 1948. Columnist, Washington Post; producer-writer, ATV England and Australia; writer-prod., Have Gun Will Travel, also prod. for TV: The Travels of Jamie McPheeters,

The Virginian, Honey West, Serpico, Kingston: Confidential. Exec. story consultant The Sixth Sense; prod.: Fantasy Island, T.J. Hooker, Duel at Shiloh, Smile of the Dragon, In Preparation: Watchers on the Mountain, Hearts & Diamonds. PICTURES: Airport—1975, Who's Got the Body? TELEVISION: *Writer*: Gunsmoke, Have Gun Will Travel, The Bold Ones, Marcus Welby M.D., Mod Squad, Star Trek, Honey West, Bonanza, The Sixth Sense, Then Came Bronson, Police Story, World Premier Movie, Shamus, Flood, Capt. America, The Initiation of Sarah, Blood Sport, and others.

INGELS, MARTY
Actor, Former Comedian, Executive. b. Brooklyn, NY, Mar. 9, 1936. m actress-singer Shirley Jones. U.S. Infantry 1954-58. Ent. show business representing Army, Name That Tune. Stage: Sketchbook revue, Las Vegas. Pres., Celebrity Brokerage, packaging celebrity events and endorsements. Active in community affairs and charity funding.
PICTURES: The Ladies Man, Armored Command, The Horizontal Lieutenant, The Busy Body, Wild and Wonderful, A Guide for the Married Man, If It's Tuesday It Must be Belgium, For Singles Only, Instant Karma.
TELEVISION: *Series*: I'm Dickens... He's Fenster, The Phyllis Diller Show. *Guest*: Phil Silvers Show, Steve Allen, Jack Paar, Playboy Penthouse, Bell Telephone Hour, Manhunt, Ann Sothern Show, Peter Loves Mary, The Detectives, Joey Bishop Show, Hennessey, Dick Van Dyke Show, Burke's Law, Hollywood Palace, Family, Murder She Wrote.

INGSTER, BORIS
Writer, Director. b. 1913.
PICTURES: Writer: The Last Days of Pompeii, Dancing Pirate, Thin Ice, Happy Landing, Paris Underground, Something for the Birds, Abdullah's Harem, California, Cloak & Dagger, The Amazing Mrs. Holliday. Director: The Judge Steps Out, Southside 1-1000.
TELEVISION: Wagon Train, The Alaskans, The Roaring 20's, Travels of Jaimie McPheeters, The Man From U.N.C.L.E.

INSDORF, ANNETTE
Film Professor, Critic, Translator, TV Host. b. Paris, France, July 27, 1950. e. 1968-studied voice, Juilliard Sch. of Music and performed as singer; Queens Coll. (summa cum laude), B.A. 1972; Yale U., M.A., 1973; Yale U., Ph.D., 1975. 1973: soloist in Leonard Bernstein's Mass (European premiere in Vienna and BBC/WNET TV). 1975-87: professor of film, Yale U. Author of Francois Truffaut (1979; updated 1989), Indelible Shadows: Film and the Holocaust (1983, updated 1989). Since 1979: frequent contributor to NY Times (Arts and Leisure), Los Angeles Times, San Francisco Chronicle, Elle, and Premiere. Named Chevalier dans l'ordre des arts et lettres by French Ministry of Culture, 1986. Since 1987, dir. of Undergrad. Film Studies, Columbia U., and prof. Graduate Film Div. 1990 named chmn. of Film Div. 1987: exec.-prod. Shoeshine (short film nom. for Oscar). 1989: exec. prod., Abrams' Performance Pieces (named best fiction short, Cannes Fest).

IRONS, JEREMY
Actor. b. Isle of Wight, Sept. 19, 1948. m. actress Sinead Cusack. e. Sherborne Sch., Dorset. Stage career began at Marlowe Theatre, Canterbury, where he was student asst. stage manager. Accepted at Bristol Old Vic Theatre Sch. for two-yr. course; then joined Bristol Old Vic Co. In London played in Godspell, Much Ado About Nothing, The Caretaker, Taming of the Shrew, Wild Oats, Rear Column, An Audience Called Edouard, etc. N.Y. stage debut, The Real Thing (Tony Award, 1984).
PICTURES: Nijinsky (debut, 1980), The French Lieutenant's Woman, Moonlighting, Betrayal, The Wild Duck, Swann in Love, The Mission, Dead Ringers, A Chorus of Disapproval, Danny the Champion of the World (tv in U.S.), Australia, Reversal of Fortune (Academy Award, 1990), Kafka, Waterland, Damage, M. Butterfly, The House of the Spirits, The Lion King (voice), Die Hard With a Vengeance.
TELEVISION: The Pallisers, Notorious Woman, Love for Lydia, Langrishe Go Down, Brideshead Revisited, The Captain's Doll, Autogeddon, Tales From Hollywood, The Dream of a Ridiculous Man.

IRONSIDE, MICHAEL
Actor. b. Toronto, Ontario, Canada, Feb. 12, 1950. e. Ontario Col. of Art.
PICTURES: Scanners, Visiting Hours, Spacehunter: Adventures in the Forbidden Zone, The Falcon and the Snowman, Jo Jo Dancer Your Life Is Calling, Top Gun, Extreme Prejudice, Nowhere to Hide, Hello Mary Lou: Prom Night II, Watchers, Total Recall, McBain, Highlander II: The Quickening, The Vagrant, Fortunes of War, The Killing Man, Free Willy, The Next Karate Kid, Major Payne, The Glass Shield.
TELEVISION: *Series*: V, ER, seaQuest DSV. *Movie*: Probable Cause (also co-exec. prod.).

IRVIN, JOHN
Director. b. Cheshire, England, May 7, 1940. In cutting rooms at Rank Organisation before making first film documentary, Gala Day, on grant from British Film Inst.; made other award-winning documentaries before turning to features.
PICTURES: The Dogs of War (debut, 1981), Ghost Story, Champions, Turtle Diary, Raw Deal, Hamburger Hill, Next of Kin, Eminent Domain, Widow's Peak, A Month by the Lake.
TELEVISION: The Nearly Man, Hard Times, Tinker Tailor Soldier Spy, Robin Hood (foreign theatrical), Crazy Horse.

IRVING, AMY
Actress. b. Palo Alto, CA, Sept. 10, 1953. e. American Conservatory Theatre, London Acad. of Dramatic Art. Daughter of late theatre dir. Jules Irving and actress Priscilla Pointer. m. director Bruno Barreto.
THEATER: *NY*: Amadeus, Heartbreak House, Road to Mecca, Broken Glass. *LA*: The Heidi Chronicles.
PICTURES: Carrie (debut, 1976), The Fury, Voices, Honeysuckle Rose, The Competition, Yentl (Acad. Award nom.), Micki and Maude, Rumpelstiltskin, Who Framed Roger Rabbit (voice), Crossing Delancey, Show of Force, An American Tail: Fievel Goes West (voice), Benefit of the Doubt, Kleptomania, Acts of Love (also co- exec. prod.), I'm Not Rappaport, Carried Away.
TELEVISION: *Movies*: James Dean, James A. Michener's Dynasty, Panache, Anastasia: The Mystery of Anna. Mini-*Series*: Once an Eagle, The Far Pavilions. *Specials*: I'm a Fool, Turn of the Screw, Heartbreak House, Twilight Zone: Rod Serling's Lost Classics: The Theater. *Guest*: The Rookies, Police Woman.

IRWIN, BILL
Actor. b. Santa Monica, CA, April 11, 1950.
THEATER: *B'way*: Accidental Death of an Anarchist, 5-6-7-8 Dance, Largely New York, Fool Moon. *Off-B'way*: The Regard of Flight, The Courtroom, Not Quite New York, Waiting for Godot. Regional: Scapin (also dir., adaptation).
PICTURES: Popeye (debut, 1980), A New Life, Eight Men Out, My Blue Heaven, Scenes From a Mall, Hot Shots, Stepping Out, Silent Tongue.
TELEVISION: *Specials*: The Regard of Flight, Bette Midler— Mondo Beyondo, The Paul Daniels Magic Show (BBC), The Last Mile. *Guest*: Saturday Night Live, Tonight Show, Cosby Show, Northern Exposure.

ISAACS, CHERYL BOONE
Executive. b. Springfield, MA. Entered m.p. industry 1977 as staff publicist for Columbia Pictures. Worked five years after that for Melvin Simon Prods., named v.p. Left to become dir. of adv./pub. for The Ladd Co. 1984, named dir., pub. & promo., West Coast, for Paramount Pictures. Promoted vice pres., publicity, Paramount Pictures in 1986. Promoted to sr. v.p., Worldwide Publicity, Paramount in 1991. Member A.M.P.A.S. Board of Governors since 1988. Promoted to exec. v.p. in 1994.

ISAACS, PHIL
Executive. b. New York, NY, May 20, 1922. e. City Coll. of New York. In U.S. Navy, 1943-46. Joined Paramount Pictures in 1946 as bookers asst., N.Y. exch. Branch mgr. in Washington; then mgr. Rocky Mt. div. In 1966 was Eastern-Southern sls. mgr.; 1967 joined Cinema Center Films as v.p. domestic dist. In 1972 named v.p., marketing, for Tomorrow Entertainment; Joined Avco-Embassy 1975 as v.p., gen. sls. mgr., named exec. v.p., 1977. 1978 joined General Cinema Corp. as v.p 1980 v.p., gen. sls. mgr., Orion Pictures. 1983, formed Phil Isaacs Co; 1988, v.p., general sales mgr., TWE Theatrical; 1989, appointed pres. Became pres. South Gate Entertainment 1989.

ISRAEL, NEAL
Writer, Director, Producer. m. actress Romy Walthall.
PICTURES: Tunnelvision (exec. prod., s.p., actor), Cracking Up (s.p., actor), Americathon (dir., s.p.), Police Academy (s.p.), Bachelor Party (dir., s.p.), Johnny Dangerously (actor), Moving Violations (dir., s.p.), Real Genius (s.p.), It's Alive III (s.p.), Buy and Cell (co-s.p.), Look Who's Talking Too (co-prod., actor), Spurting Blood (exec. prod., s.p.), All I Want for Christmas (co-s.p.), Breaking the Rules (dir.), Surf Ninjas (dir., actor).
TELEVISION: Lola Falana Special (writer), Mac Davis Show, Ringo, Marie (prod.), Twilight Theatre (writer, prod.), Man of the People (co-prod.), The Wonder Years (dir.), Hearts of the West (dir.). Movies: The Cover Girl and the Cop (dir.), Woman With a Past (co-exec. prod.), Combat High (dir.), Taking the Heat (co-prod.), Dream Date (prod.), Bonnie and Clyde: The True Story (co-prod.), A Quiet Little Neighborhood (co-prod.), Foster's Field Trip (dir., writer), Family Reunion: A Relative Nightmare (dir., co-writer, co-prod.).

ITAMI, JUZO
Director, Actor. b. Kyoto, Japan, 1933. m. actress Nobuko Miyamoto. Son of Mansaku Itami, pioneering Japanese film

director. After successful stint as commercial artist, became an actor as well as essayist (Listen, Women, a collection of his work). Directing debut The Funeral (1984).
PICTURES: *Actor:* 55 Days at Peking, Lord Jim, I Am a Cat, The Makioka Sisters, The Family Game. *Director:* The Funeral (5 Japanese Acad. Awards), Tampopo, A Taxing Woman (8 Japanese Acad. Awards), A Taxing Woman's Return (dir., s.p.), Sweet Home (exec. prod. only), Tales of a Golden Geisha, The Gangster's Moll.

IVANEK, ZELJKO
Actor. b. Ljubljana, Yugoslavia, Aug. 15, 1957. Came to U.S. with family in 1960 and returned to homeland before settling in Palo Alto, CA, in 1967. Studied at Yale, majoring in theatre studies; graduated in 1978. Also graduate of London Acad. of Music and Dramatic Arts. Regular member of Williamstown Theatre Festival, appearing in Hay Fever, Charley's Aunt, Front Page. B'way debut in The Survivor.
THEATER: *B'way:* The Survivor, Brighton Beach Memoirs, Loot, Two Shakespearean Actors, The Glass Menagerie. Regional: Master Harold... and the Boys (Yale Rep. premiere prod.), Hamlet (Guthrie), Ivanov (Yale Rep.). *Off B'way:* Cloud 9, A Map of the World, The Cherry Orchard.
PICTURES: Tex, The Sender, The Soldier, Mass Appeal, Rachel River, School Ties.
TELEVISION: *Movies:* The Sun Also Rises, Echoes in the Darkness, Aftermath: A Test of Love, Our Sons, My Brother's Keeper, Truman. *Special:* All My Sons. *Guest:* Homicide: Life on the Street.

IVANY, PETER
Executive. b. Melbourne, Australia, Aug. 23, 1954. e. Monash U. Melbourne, B.A., M.B.A. Victoria Health Commission as strategic planning analyst, 1978-80. Kodak Australia, estimating and planning analyst, 1980-81. Joined Hoyts Corporation Pty Ltd. in 1981 as cinema mgr., then general mgr., Hoyts Video; general mgr., corporate development, 1986-88. Chairman and CEO Hoyts US Holdings, Inc. 1986 then CEO to present.

IVERS, IRVING N.
Executive. b. Montreal, Canada, Feb. 23, 1939. e. Sir George Williams U. Worked for 10 years in radio and TV in variety of executive capacities in station management before entering film business. Joined Columbia Pictures in 1973, serving as director of mktg. and dir. of adv. 1973-77; named Canadian sls. mgr. 1977-78; v.p. of adv./pub. 1978-80. 1980 joined 20th Century-Fox as sr. v.p. of adv./pub./promo.; exec. v.p., worldwide adv., pub., promo. 1980-83; pres., worldwide mkt., MGM/UA/Entertainment Co., 1983-86. 1986 to Warner Bros. as v.p., intl. adv./pub. 1991 to Astral Commun., Toronto as pres. of Astral Films and Astral Video.

IVEY, JUDITH
Actress. b. El Paso, TX, Sept. 4, 1951. m. ind. prod., Tim Braine. e. Illinois State U. Stage debut in The Sea in Chicago, 1974.
THEATER: Bedroom Farce, The Goodbye People, Oh Coward!, Design for Living, Piaf, Romeo and Juliet, Pastorale, Two Small Bodies, Steaming (Tony & Drama Desk Awards), Second Lady (off-B'way work she helped develop), Hurlyburly (Tony & Drama Desk Awards), Precious Sons (Drama Desk nom.), Blithe Spirit, Mrs. Dally Has a Lover, Park Your Car in Harvard Yard (Tony nom.), The Moonshot Tape (Obie Award).
PICTURES: Harry and Son (debut, 1984), The Lonely Guy, The Woman in Red, Compromising Positions, Brighton Beach Memoirs, Hello Again, Sister Sister, Miles from Home, In Country, Everybody Wins, Alice, Love Hurts, There Goes the Neighborhood.
TELEVISION: *Series:* Down Home, Designing Women, The Critic (voice), The Five Mrs. Buchanans. *Movies:* The Shady Hill Kidnapping, Dixie: Changing Habits, We Are the Children, The Long Hot Summer, Jesse and the Bandit Queen, Decoration Day, Her Final Fury: Betty Broderick—The Last Chapter, On Promised Land, Almost Golden: The Jessica Savitch Story. *Special:* Other Mothers (Afterschool Special).

IVORY, JAMES
Director. b. Berkeley, CA, June 7, 1928. e. U. of Oregon, B.F.A., 1951; U. of Southern California, M.A. (cinema) 1956. First film Venice: Theme and Variations (doc. made as M.A. thesis, 1957). Early work: The Sword and the Flute, The Delhi Way. Formed Merchant Ivory Productions with prod. Ismail Merchant and script writer Ruth Prawer Jhabvala. Received D.W. Griffith Lifetime Achievement Award from DGA, 1995.
PICTURES: The Householder, Shakespeare Wallah (also co-s.p.), The Guru (also co-s.p.), Bombay Talkie (also co-s.p.), Savages, The Wild Party, Roseland, The Europeans (also cameo), Quartet, Heat and Dust, The Bostonians, A Room With a View, Maurice (also co-s.p.), Slaves of New York, Mr. and Mrs. Bridge, Howards End, The Remains of the Day, Jefferson in Paris, Surviving Picasso.

TELEVISION: Noon Wine (exec. prod.). Dir: Adventures of a Brown Man in Search of Civilization, Autobiography of a Princess (also released theatrically), Hullabaloo Over George and Bonnie's Pictures, Jane Austen in Manhattan (also released theatrically), The Five Forty Eight.

J

JACKSON, ANNE
Actress. b. Allegheny, PA, Sept. 3, 1926. e. Neighborhood Playhouse, Actors Studio. Married to actor Eli Wallach. Stage debut in The Cherry Orchard, 1944. Autobiography: Early Stages.
THEATER: Major Barbara, Middle of the Night, The Typist and the Tiger, Luv, Waltz of the Toreadors, Twice Around the Park, Summer and Smoke, Nest of the Woodgrouse, Marco Polo Sings a Solo, The Mad Woman of Chaillot, Cafe Crown, Lost in Yonkers, In Persons, The Flowering Peach.
PICTURES: So Young So Bad (debut, 1950), The Journey, Tall Story, The Tiger Makes Out, How to Save a Marriage and Ruin Your Life, The Secret Life of an American Wife, The Angel Levine, Zig Zag, Lovers and Other Strangers, Dirty Dingus Magee, Nasty Habits, The Bell Jar, The Shining, Sam's Son, Funny About Love, Folks!
TELEVISION: *Series:* Everything's Relative. *Special:* 84 Charing Cross Road. *Movies:* The Family Man, A Woman Called Golda, Private Battle, Blinded By the Light, Leave 'em Laughing, Baby M.

JACKSON, BRIAN
Actor, Film & Theatre Producer. b. Bolton, England, 1931. Early career in photography then numerous stage performances incl. Old Vic, Royal Shakespeare. Ent. film/TV industry 1958. Formed Quintus Plays, 1965; formed Brian Jackson Productions 1966; formed Hampden Gurney Studios Ltd. 1970. Co-produced The Others 1967; presented The Button, 1969; co-produced the documentary film Village in Mayfair, 1970; 1971: Formed Brian Jackson Films Ltd.; produced Yesterday, The Red Deer, The Story of Tutankhamen.
THEATER: Mame, Drury Lane, Fallen Angels, In Praise of Love.
PICTURES: Incident in Karandi, Carry On Sergeant, Gorgo, Jack the Ripper, Taste of Fear, Heroes of Telemark, Only the Lonely, The Deadly Females, The Revenge of the Pink Panther, Deceptions, Shadow Chasers.
TELEVISION: Moon Fleet, Private Investigator, Life of Lord Lister, Z Cars, Vendetta, Sherlock Holmes, Mr. Rose, Hardy Heating International, Nearest & Dearest, The Persuaders, The Paradise Makers, The New Avengers, Smugglers Bay, The Tomorrow People, Secret Army, Last Visitor for Hugh Peters, Six Men of Dorset, Commercials: featured as the man from Delmonte for 5 years.

JACKSON, GLENDA
Actress. b. Birkenhead, England, May 9, 1936. Stage debut: Separate Tales (Worthing, Eng. 1957). 1964 joined Peter Brooks' Theatre of Cruelty which led to film debut. Became member of Parliament, 1992.
THEATER: (Eng.): All Kinds of Men, Hammersmith, The Idiot, Alfie. Joined Royal Shakespeare Co in experimental Theatre of Cruelty season. Marat Sade (London, N.Y.), Three Sisters, The Maids, Hedda Gabler, The White Devil, Rose, Strange Interlude (N.Y.), Macbeth (N.Y.), Who's Afraid of Virginia Woolf? (L.A.).
PICTURES: The Persecution and Assassination of Jean-Paul Marat as Performed by the Inmates of the Asylum at Charenton Under the Direction of the Marquis de Sade (debut, 1967), Tell Me Lies, Negatives, Women in Love (Academy Award, 1970), The Music Lovers, Sunday Bloody Sunday, Mary Queen of Scots, The Boy Friend, Triple Echo, The Nelson Affair, A Touch of Class (Academy Award, 1973), The Maids, The Temptress, The Romantic Englishwoman, The Devil is a Woman, Hedda, The Incredible Sarah, Nasty Habits, House Calls, Stevie, The Class of Miss McMichael, Lost and Found, Health, Hopscotch, Giro City, The Return of the Soldier, Turtle Diary, Beyond Therapy, Business as Usual, Salome's Last Dance, The Rainbow, The Visit.
TELEVISION: *Movies:* The Patricia Neal Story, Sakharov. *Mini-Series:* Elizabeth R (2 Emmy Awards, 1972). *Special:* Strange Interlude, A Murder of Quality, The House of Bernarda Alba.

JACKSON, KATE
Actress. b. Birmingham, AL, Oct. 29, 1949. e. U. of Mississippi, Birmingham Southern U. Did summer stock before going to N.Y. to enter American Acad. of Dramatic Arts, appearing in Night Must Fall, The Constant Wife, Little Moon of Alban. Worked as model and became tour guide at NBC. First role on TV in Dark Shadows (series).
PICTURES: Night of Dark Shadows, Limbo, Thunder and Lightning, Dirty Tricks, Making Love, Loverboy.
TELEVISION: *Movies:* Satan's School for Girls, Killer Bees, Death Cruise, Death Scream, Charlie's Angels (pilot), Death at Love House, James at 15 (pilot), Topper, Inmates: A Love

Story, Thin Ice, Listen to Your Heart, The Stranger Within, Quiet Killer, Homewrecker (voice), Adrift, Empty Cradle, Armed and Innocent, Justice in a Small Town. *Series*: Dark Shadows, The Rookies, Charlie's Angels, Scarecrow and Mrs. King, Baby Boom. *Guest*: The Jimmy Stewart Show.

JACKSON, MICHAEL
Singer, Composer. b. Gary, IN, Aug. 29, 1958. Musical recording artist with family group known as Jackson 5: all brothers, Jackie, Jermaine, Tito, Marlon, and Michael. Sister is singer Janet Jackson.
PICTURES: Save the Children, The Wiz, Moonwalker (also exec. prod., story).
TELEVISION: *Series*: The Jacksons (1976-77). *Specials*: Free to Be You and Me, Sandy in Disneyland, Motown on Showtime: Michael Jackson.

JACKSON, MICK
Director. b. Grays, England. e. Bristol Univ. Joined BBC as film editor, following post-grad work in film & tv. Produced and directed many documentaries for the BBC.
PICTURES: Chattahoochee, L.A. Story, The Bodyguard, Clean Slate.
TELEVISION: *Documentaries*: The Ascent of Man, Connections, The Age of Uncertainty. *Movies/Specials*: Threads, The Race for the Double Helix, Yuri Nosenko KGB (HBO), Indictment: The McMartin Trial. *Mini-Series*: A Very British Coup.

JACKSON, PETER
Director. b. New Zealand.
PICTURES: Meet the Feebles, Bad Taste, Dead Alive, Heavenly Creatures, The Frighteners.

JACKSON, SAMUEL L.
Actor. b. 1949. e. Morehouse Col. m. actress LaTanya Richardson. Co-founder, member of the Just Us Theatre Co. in Atlanta.
THEATER: *Negro Ensemble Company*: Home, A Soldier's Story, Sally/Prince, Colored People's Time. *NY Shakespeare Fest*: Mother Courage, Spell No. 7, The Mighty Gents. *Yale Rep*: The Piano Lesson, Two Trains Running. *Seattle Rep*: Fences.
PICTURES: Ragtime (debut, 1981), Eddie Murphy Raw, School Daze, Coming to America, Do the Right Thing, A Shock to the System, Def by Temptation, Betsy's Wedding, Mo' Better Blues, The Exorcist III, GoodFellas, Mob Justice, Jungle Fever (Cannes Film Fest. & NY Film Critics Awards, 1991), Strictly Business, Juice, White Sands, Patriot Games, Johnny Suede, Jumpin at the Boneyard, Fathers and Sons, National Lampoon's Loaded Weapon 1, Amos & Andrew, Menace II Society, Jurassic Park, True Romance, Hail Caesar, Fresh, The New Age, Pulp Fiction (Acad. Award nom.), Losing Isaiah, Kiss of Death, Die Hard With a Vengeance, Fluke (voice), The Great White Hype, A Time to Kill, The Long Kiss Goodnight.
TELEVISION: *Movies*: Assault at West Point: The Court-Martial of Johnson Whittaker, Against the Wall.

JACOBI, DEREK
O.B.E. Actor. b. London, England, Oct. 22, 1938. e. Cambridge. On stage in Pericles, The Hollow Crown, Hobson's Choice, The Suicide, Breaking the Code (London, NY).
PICTURES: Othello (debut, 1965), Interlude, The Three Sisters, The Day of the Jackal, Blue Blood, The Odessa File, The Medusa Touch, The Human Factor, Enigma, The Secret of NIMH (voice), Little Dorrit, Henry V, Dead Again, Hamlet.
TELEVISION: She Stoops to Conquer, Man of Straw, The Pallisers, I, Claudius, Philby, Burgess and MacLean, Hamlet. Movies: Othello, Three Sisters, Interlude, Charlotte, The Man Who Went Up in Smoke, The Hunchback of Notre Dame, Inside the Third Reich, The Secret Garden, The Tenth Man (Emmy Award). *Series*: Minder, Tales of the Unexpected, Mr. Pye, The Leper of St. Giles.

JACOBS, JOHN
Executive. b. New York, NY. e. Syracuse U.'s Newhouse Communications Sch. Full-service agency background, including 13 years with Grey Advertising agency, where handled Warner Bros. & Warner Home Video accts. Supvr. media on RCA, ABC-TV, Murdoch Publishing, Radio City Musical Hall, etc. Named v.p. & group media dir. for Grey. 1986, left to join Warner Bros. as v.p., media; then sr. v.p. worldwide media.

JACOBS, MICHAEL
Producer, Writer. b. New Brunswick, NJ. Studied at Neighborhood Playhouse in NY. Had first play, Cheaters, prod. on B'way when he was only 22 yrs. old, followed by Getting Along Famously.
PICTURE: Quiz Show.
TELEVISION: *Series* (creator/prod.): Charles in Charge, No Soap Radio, Together We Stand, Singer and Songs, My Two Dads (also dir.), Dinosaurs, The Torkelsons (Almost Home), Boy Meets World, Where I Live.

JACOBSEN, JOHN M.
Producer, Executive. b. Oslo, Norway, Dec. 27, 1944. Produced number of feature films incl. Pathfinder (Acad. Award nom.), Shipwrecked, Head Above Water. Pres., Norwegian Film and Video Producers Assn.; Pres. AB Svensk Filmindustri Norwegian Operation.

JACOBY, FRANK DAVID
Director, Producer. b. New York, NY, July 15, 1925. e. Hunter Coll., Brooklyn Coll. m. Doris Storm, actress. 1949-52, NBC network tv dir.; 1952-56, B.B.D.O., Biow Co., tv prod./dir.; 1956-58 Metropolitan Educational TV Assn., dir. of prod.; 1958-65, United Nation, film prod./dir.; 1965 to present, pres., Jacoby/Storm Prods., Inc., Westport, CT—documentary, industrial, educational films and filmstrips. Clients include Xerox Corp., Random House, Publ., Lippincott Co., IBM, Heublein, G.E., and Pitney Bowes. Winner, Sherwood Award, Peabody Award. Member, Director's Guild of America; winner, Int'l TV & Film Festival, National Educational Film Festival, American Film Festival.

JACOBY, JOSEPH
Producer, Director, Writer. b. Brooklyn, NY, Sept. 22, 1942. e. NYU. Sch. of Arts and Sciences, majoring in m.p. As undergraduate worked part-time as prod. asst. on daytime network TV shows and as puppeteer for Bunin Puppets. 1964 joined Bil Baird Marionettes as full-time puppeteer, working also on Baird film commercials. Made feature m.p. debut as prod.-dir of Shame Shame Everybody Knows Her Name, 1968. Contributing essayist, NY Woman Magazine. Founder/Dir.-Prod., Children's Video Theatre starring The Bil Baird Marionettes.
PICTURES: *Dir./Prod./Writer*: Hurry Up or I'll Be 30, The Great Bank Hoax, Davy Jones' Locker.

JACOBY, SCOTT
Actor. b. Chicago, IL, Nov. 19, 1956.
PICTURES: The Little Girl Who Lives Down the Lane, Love and the Midnight Auto Supply, Our Winning Season, Return to Horror High, To Die For, To Die For II.
TELEVISION: *Movies*: No Place to Run, That Certain Summer (Emmy Award, 1973), The Man Who Could Talk to Kids, Bad Ronald, Smash-Up on Interstate 5, No Other Love, The Diary of Anne Frank. *Mini-Series*: 79 Park Avenue. *Series*: One Life to Live (1973-74). *Guest*: Medical Center, Marcus Welby M.D., The Golden Girls.

JAECKEL, RICHARD
Actor. b. Long Beach, NY, Oct. 10, 1926. e. Hollywood H.S., 1943. Worked as delivery boy in mail room, 20th Century-Fox.
PICTURES: Guadalcanal Diary (debut, 1943), Wing and a Prayer, Jungle Patrol, City Across the River, Battleground, Sands of Iwo Jima, The Gunfighter, Sea Hornet, Hoodlum Empire, My Son John, Come Back Little Sheba, The Big Leaguer, Sea of Lost Ships, Shanghai Story, The Violent Men, Apache Ambush, Attack!, 3:10 to Yuma, The Naked and the Dead, Platinum High School, The Gallant Hours, Town Without Pity, The Young and the Brave, Four for Texas, Town Tamer, The Dirty Dozen, The Devil's Brigade, The Green Slime, Chisum, Sometimes a Great Notion (Acad. Award nom.), Ulzana's Raid, Pat Garrett and Billy the Kid, The Outfit, Chosen Survivors, The Drowning Pool, Part 2—Walking Tall, Grizzly, Mako: The Jaws of Death, Day of the Animals, Twilight's Last Gleaming, Delta Fox, Speedtrap, The Dark, Herbie Goes Bananas, ... All the Marbles, Cold River, Airplane II: The Sequel, Killing Machine, Starman, Black Moon Rising, Delta Force II, Ghetto Blasters, Martial Outlaw.
TELEVISION: *Series*: Frontier Circus, Banyon, Firehouse, Salvage One, At Ease, Spenser for Hire, Supercarrier, Baywatch. *Guest*: U.S. Steel Hour, Elgin Hour, Goodyear Playhouse, Kraft, Producer's Showcase. *Special*: The Petrified Forest. *Movies*: The Deadly Dream, Firehouse, The Red Pony, Partners in Crime, Born Innocent, The Last Day Go West Young Girl, Champions: A Love Story, Salvage, The $5.20 an Hour Dream, Reward, The Awakening of Candra, Dirty Dozen: The Next Mission, Baywatch: Panic at Malibu Pier.

JAFFE, LEO
Executive. b. April 23, 1909. e. NYU. Started at Columbia, 1930; v.p., Columbia Pictures, 1954; 1st v.p., treas., bd. memb., 1956; v.p. & treas., 1958; exec. v.p., Columbia, 1962; pres. Columbia, 1968; pres., Columbia Pictures Industries, Inc, 1970; pres. & CEO, Columbia Pictures Industries, Inc.; chmn. of bd. of dirs. to 1978. Currently chmn. emeritus. Industry honors: Motion Picture Pioneer of the Year, 1972; Acad. of Motion Picture Arts and Sciences Jean Hersholt Humanitarian Award, 1979; NATO Award-Knight of Malta. Gloria Swanson Humanitarian Award, 1984. Chairman, President's Motion Picture Council–Motion Pictures & TV under Pres. Reagan. Dean Madden Award from NYU.

JAFFE, STANLEY R.
Producer. b. New York, NY, July, 31, 1940. Graduate of U. of Pennsylvania Wharton Sch. of Finance. Joined Seven Arts

Associates, 1962; named exec. ass't to pres., 1964; later, head of East Coast TV programming. Produced Goodbye, Columbus, in 1968 for Paramount; then joined that company as exec. v.p., 1969. Named pres. of Paramount in 1970; resigned 1971 to form own prod. unit. Joined Columbia as exec. v.p. of global prod. in 1976, but resigned to be independent producer. Named pres. & COO of Paramount Communications in 1991.
PICTURES: Goodbye Columbus, A New Leaf, Bad Company, Man on a Swing, The Bad News Bears, Kramer vs. Kramer (Academy Award for Best Picture, 1979), Taps, Without a Trace (also dir.). Co-prod.(with Sherry Lansing): Racing with the Moon, Firstborn, Fatal Attraction, The Accused, Black Rain, School Ties.

JAFFE, STEVEN-CHARLES
Producer. b. Brooklyn, NY, 1954. e. U. of Southern California, cinema. First professional job as documentary prod. on John Huston's Fat City. Served as prod. asst. on The Wind and the Lion in Spain. Assoc. prod. on Demon Seed (written by brother Robert); served as location mgr. on Who'll Stop the Rain; assoc. prod. on Time After Time. On tv worked as 2nd unit dir. on The Day After.
PICTURES: Those Lips Those Eyes, Motel Hell (also co-s.p.), Scarab (dir.), Flesh + Blood (2nd unit. dir.), Near Dark, Plain Clothes (exec. prod.), The Fly II, Ghost (exec. prod., 2nd unit dir.), Company Business, Star Trek VI: The Undiscovered Country, Strange Days.

JAGGER, MICK
Singer, Composer, Actor. b. Dartford, Kent, England, July 26, 1943. Lead singer with the Rolling Stones.
PICTURES: The Rolling Stones Rock and Roll Circus, Performance, Ned Kelly, Popcorn, Gimme Shelter, Sympathy for the Devil, Ladies and Gentlemen: The Rolling Stones, The London Rock 'n' Roll Show, Let's Spend the Night Together, At the Max, Freejack.
TELEVISION: Special: The Nightingale (Faerie Tale Theatre).

JAGGS, STEVE
Executive. b. London, England, June 29, 1946. Ent. motion picture industry, 1964. Gained experience in the film production and laboratory areas with Colour Film Service and Universal Laboratories. Joined Agfa-Gevaert Ltd., Motion Picture Division, 1976. Appt. sales manager, 1979; divisional manager, 1989. Joined Rank Organisation, 1992. Appoint. mng. dir. of Pinewood Studios, 1993.

JAGLOM, HENRY
Director, Writer, Editor, Actor. b. London, Eng., Jan. 26, 1943. Studied acting, writing and directing with Lee Strasberg and at Actors Studio. Did off-B'way. shows; went to West Coast where guest-starred in TV series (Gidget, The Flying Nun, etc.). Shot documentary film in Israel during Six Day War. Hired as edit consultant for Easy Rider by producer Bert Schneider. Acted in Psych Out, Drive He Said, The Last Movie, Thousand Plane Raid, Lili Aime Moi, The Other Side of the Wind (Orson Welles' unreleased last film). Wrote and dir. first feature, A Safe Place, in 1971. Created The Women's Film Co. (to prod. and distrib. motion pictures by women filmmakers), and Jagfilms Inc., Rainbow Film Company, and Rainbow Releasing. Presented Academy Award winning documentary Hearts and Minds, 1974.
PICTURES: Dir.-Writer-Prod.-Editor. A Safe Place, Tracks, Sitting Ducks (also actor), National Lampoon Goes to the Movies (co-dir. only), Can She Bake a Cherry Pie?, Always (also actor), Someone To Love (also actor), New Year's Day (also actor), Eating, Venice Venice (also actor), Babyfever, Last Summer in the Hamptons (dir., co-s.p., edit., actor).

JALBERT, JOE JAY
Executive. e. U. of Washington. Was ski captain in school and began film career as technical director on Downhill Racer, 1969, also cinematographer and double for Robert Redford, 1970, produced Impressions of Utah, documentary, with Redford. Won Emmy for cinematography on TV's Peggy Fleming Special. In 1970 formed Jalbert Productions, Inc., to make feature films, TV sports, specials, commercials, etc. Co. has produced Winter Sportscast and 9 official films at Innsbruck Winter Olympics (1976), Lake Placid (1980), Sarajevo (1984). Albertville Winter Olympic Games official film, One Light One World.

JAMES, BRION
Actor. b. Beaumont, CA, Feb. 20, 1945. e. Beaumont h.s., San Diego St. U., 1968. On stage in LA, San Diego, NY, as well as performing stand-up comedy at Comedy Store, The Improv.
THEATER: Long Day's Journey Into Night, Picnic, Basic Training Pavlo Hummell, Mother Courage, George Washington Slept Here, West Side Story, Spec, Lady Windermere's Fan.
PICTURES: Harry and Walter Go to New York (debut, 1976), Treasure of Matecumbe, Bound for Glory, Nickelodeon, Blue

Sunshine, Black Sunday, Corvette Summer, Wholly Moses, The Postman Always Rings Twice, Southern Comfort, The Ballad of Gregorio Cortez, Blade Runner, 48 HRS, A Breed Apart, Silverado, Crimewave, Flesh $PL Blood, Enemy Mine, Armed and Dangerous, Steel Dawn, Dead Man Walking, Cherry 2000, Nightmare at Noon, The Wrong Guys, Red Heat, Red Scorpion, The Horror Show, Mom, Time of the Beast, Tango & Cash, Street Asylum, Savage Land, Another 48 HRS, The Player, Nemesis, Ultimate Desires, Brain Smasher—A Love Story, Nature of the Beast, Time Runner, Wishman, Future Shock, Striking Distance, Pterodactyl Women of Beverly Hills, The Soft Kill, Cyberjack, The Dark, Scanner Cop, Dominion, Cabin Boy, The Companion, Art Deco Detective, F.T.W., Radioland Murders, Steel Frontier, From the Edge, Hong Kong '97. Evil Obsession, Malevolence, Precious Find.
TELEVISION: Movies: Flying High, Mrs. Sundance, Kiss Meets the Phantom of the Park, Trouble in High Timber Country, Killing at Hell's Gate, Hear No Evil, Precious Victims, Rio Diablo, Kenny Rogers As The Gambler: The Adventure Continues, Overkill: The Aileen Wuornos Story, Precious Victims, The Companion, Sketch Artist II: Hands That See, Terminal Virus. Guest: Rockford Files, Hunter, The Young Riders, Cagney & Lacey, Quincy, Little House on the Prairie, Dynasty, Amazing Stories, Tales from the Crypt, A Team, etc.

JAMES, CLIFTON
Actor. b. Portland, OR, May 29, 1925. e. U. of Oregon. Studied at Actors Studio. Made numerous appearances on stage and TV, as well as theatrical films.
THEATER: NY: B'way: J.B., All the Way Home, The Shadow Box, American Buffalo. Off-B'way: All the King's Men.
PICTURES: On The Waterfront, The Strange One, The Last Mile, Something Wild, Experiment in Terror, David and Lisa, Black Like Me, The Chase, The Happening, Cool Hand Luke, Will Penny, The Reivers, ...tick...tick...tick..., WUSA, The Biscuit Eater, The New Centurions, Kid Blue, Live and Let Die, The Iceman Cometh, Werewolf of Washington, The Last Detail, Bank Shot, Juggernaut, The Man with the Golden Gun, Rancho DeLuxe, Silver Streak, The Bad News Bears in Breaking Training, Superman II, Where Are the Children?, Whoops Apocalypse, Eight Men Out, The Bonfire of the Vanities.
TELEVISION: Series: City of Angels, Lewis and Clark. Movies: Runaway Barge, Friendly Persuasion, The Deadly Tower, Hart to Hart (pilot), Undercover With the KKK, Guyana Tragedy: The Story of Jim Jones, Carolina Skeletons, The John Vernon Story. Mini-Series: Captains and the Kings, Lone Star.

JAMES, DENNIS
Performer. b. Jersey City, NJ, Aug. 24, 1917. e. St. Peter's Coll., Jersey City. Received Doctorate in 1988. Formerly M.C., actor, sports commentator on radio; award winning sports commentator for wrestling, 25 TV first to credit; currently pres., Dennis James Prod. For 47 years has been host of Cerebral Palsy Telethon, having helped raised over 675 million dollars. 1970-present, Natl. Commercial Spokesman for Physicians Mutual Insurance Company of Omaha. Given star on Hollywood Walk of Fame and Palm Springs Walk of Stars.
THEATER: Impossible YEars, Who Was That Lady?, Murder at the Howard Johnson, Two For the Seasaw.
PICTURES: The One and Only, Rocky III, Mr. Universe, The Method.
TELEVISION: Series: Cash and Carry, Prime Time Boxing, The Original Amateur Hour (1948-60), Chance of a Lifetime (host), Two for the Money, Judge for Yourself, The Name's the Same, High Finance, Haggis Baggis, Your First Impression, People Will Talk, The Price Is Right, PDQ, Your All-American College Show, New Price Is Right, Name That Tune. Actor: Kraft Theatre, Dick Powell Theatre, Tycoon, Batman, 77 Sunset Strip.

JAMES, POLLY
Writer. b. Ancon, Canal Zone. e. Smith Coll. Newspaper work, Panama; with trade mag., N.Y.; screenwriter since 1942.
PICTURES: Mrs. Parkington, The Raiders, Redhead from Wyoming, Quantrill's Raiders.

JAMESON, JERRY
Director. b. Hollywood, CA. Started as editorial asst.; then editor and supv. editor for Danny Thomas Prods. Turned to directing.
PICTURES: Dirt Gang, The Bat People, Brute Core, Airport '77, Raise the Titanic.
TELEVISION: Movies: Heatwave!, The Elevator, Hurricane, Terror on the 40th Floor, The Secret Night Caller, The Deadly Tower, The Lives of Jenny Dolan, The Call of the Wild, The Invasion of Johnson County, Superdome, A Fire in the Sky, High Noon--Part II, The Return of Will Kane, Stand By Your Man, Killing at Hell's Gate, Hotline, Starflight: The Plane That Couldn't Land, Cowboy, This Girl for Hire, Last of the Great Survivors, The Cowboy and the Ballerina, Stormin' Home, One Police Plaza, The Red Spider, Terror on Highway 91, Fire and Rain, Gunsmoke: The Last Ride.

JANKOWSKI, GENE F.
Executive. b. Buffalo, NY, May 21, 1934. e. Canisius Coll., B.S., Michigan State U., M.A. in radio, TV and film. Joined CBS radio network sls, 1961 as acct. exec.; eastern sls. mgr., 1966; moved to CBS-TV as acct. exec. 1969; gen. sls. mgr. WCBS-TV, 1970; dir. sls, 1971; v.p. sls., CBS-TV Stations Divisions, 1973; v.p.; finance & planning, 1974; v.p., controller, CBS Inc. 1976; v.p. adm., 1977; exec. v.p. CBS/Broadcast Group, 1977; pres., CBS/Broadcast Group, 1977; chmn. CBS/Broadcast Group, 1988-89; chmn. Jankowski Communications Systems, Inc. 1989-. Member: pres., Intl. Council of National Acad. of Television Arts & Sciences; chmn. & trustee Amer. Film Institute; trustee, Catholic U. of Amer.; director, Georgetown U.; bd. of gov. American Red Cross; vice chmn., business comm. Metropolitan Museum of Art. Member, Library of Congress Film Preservation Board; adjunct prof. telecommunications, Michigan St. U.AWARDS: Received Distinguished Communications Medal from South Baptist Radio & Television Commission; honorary Doctorate of Humanities, Michigan State U.; Humanitarian Award, National Conference of Christians and Jews, etc.

JARMAN, CLAUDE, JR.
Actor. b. Nashville, TN, Sept. 27, 1934. e. MGM Sch. Received special Oscar for The Yearling. Exec. prod. of concert film Fillmore.
PICTURES: The Yearling (debut, 1946), High Barbaree, The Sun Comes Up, Intruder in the Dust, Roughshod, The Outriders, Inside Straight, Rio Grande, Hangman's Knot, Fair Wind to Java, The Great Locomotive Chase.
TELEVISION: *Mini-Series*: Centennial.

JARMUSCH, JIM
Director, Writer, Composer, Actor. b. Akron, OH, 1953. e. attended Columbia U., went to Paris in senior year. NYU Film Sch., studied with Nicholas Ray and became his teaching asst. Appeared as an actor in Red Italy and Fraulein Berlin. Composed scores for The State of Things and Reverse Angle. Wrote and directed New World using 30 minutes of leftover, unused film from another director. (Won International Critics Prize, Rotterdam Film Festival.) Expanded it into Stranger Than Paradise.
PICTURES: *Dir.-Writer*: Permanent Vacation (dir. debut, 1980; also prod., music, edit.), Stranger Than Paradise (also edit., Golden Leopard, Locarno Film Festival; Camera d'Or best new director, Cannes), Down by Law, Mystery Train, Night on Earth, Dead Man. *Actor*: Straight to Hell, Candy Mountain, Mystery Train, Leningrad Cowboys Go America, In the Soup, Tigrero: A Film That Was Never Made.

JARRE, MAURICE
Composer. b. Lyons, France, Sept. 13, 1924. Studied at Paris Cons. Was orchestra conductor for Jean Louis Barrault's theatre company four years. 1951 joined Jean Vilar's nat'l theatre co., composing for plays. Musical dir., French National Theatre for 12 years before scoring films. Also has written ballets (Masques de Femmes, Facheuse Rencontre, The Murdered Poet, Maldroros, The Hunchback of Notre Dame) and served as cond. with Royal Phil. Orch, London, Japan Phil. Orch, Osaka Symph. Orch., Quebec Symp. Orch, Central Orchestra of People's Republic of China.
PICTURES: La Tete contre les Murs (The Keepers; feature debut, 1959), Eyes Without a Face, Crack in the Mirror, The Big Gamble, Sundays and Cybele, The Longest Day, Lawrence of Arabia (Academy Award, 1962), To Die in Madrid, Behold a Pale Horse, The Train, The Collector, Is Paris Burning?, Weekend at Dunkirk, Doctor Zhivago (Academy Award, 1965), The Professionals, Grand Prix, Gambit, The Night of the Generals, Villa Rides!, Five Card Stud, Barbarella, Isadora, The Extraordinary Seaman, The Damned, Topaz, The Only Game in Town, El Condor, Ryan's Daughter, Plaza Suite, Red Sun, Pope Joan, The Life and Times of Judge Roy Bean, The Effect of Gamma Rays on Man-in-the-Moon Marigolds, The Mackintosh Man, Ash Wednesday, Island at the Top of the World, Mandingo, Posse, The Man Who Would Be King, Shout at the Devil, The Last Tycoon, Crossed Swords, Winter Kills, The Magician of Lublin, Resurrection, The American Success Company, The Black Marble, Taps, Firefox, Young Doctors in Love, Don't Cry It's Only Thunder, The Year of Living Dangerously, Dreamscape, A Passage to India (Academy Award, 1984), Top Secret!, Witness (BAFTA Award, 1985), Mad Max Beyond Thunderdome, Solarbabies, The Mosquito Coast, Tai-Pan, No Way Out, Fatal Attraction, Gaby--A True Story, Julia and Julia, Moon Over Parador, Gorillas in the Mist, Wildfire, Distant Thunder, Chances Are, Dead Poets Society (BAFTA Award, 1989), Prancer, Enemies a Love Story, Ghost, After Dark My Sweet, Jacob's Ladder, Almost an Angel, Only the Lonely, Fires Within, School Ties, Shadow of the Wolf, Mr. Jones, Fearless, A Walk in the Clouds (Golden Globe, 1996).

JARRICO, PAUL
Writer, Producer. b. Los Angeles, CA, Jan. 12, 1915. e. USC, 1936.
PICTURES: *Prod.*: Salt of the Earth. *Writer*: Beauty for the Asking, The Face Behind the Mask, Tom Dick and Harry

(Acad. Award nom.), Thousands Cheer, Song of Russia, The Search, The White Tower, Not Wanted, The Day the Hot Line Got Hot, Messenger of Death.
TELEVISION: Call to Glory, Fortune Dane, Seaway, The Defenders.

JARROTT, CHARLES
Director. b. London, England, June 16, 1927. Joined British Navy; wartime service in Far East. After military service turned to theatre as asst. stage mgr. with Arts Council touring co. 1949 joined Nottingham Repertory Theatre as stage dir. and juvenile acting lead. 1953 joined new co. formed to tour Canada; was leading man and became resident leading actor for Ottawa Theatre. 1955 moved to Toronto and made TV acting debut opposite Katharine Blake whom he later wed. 1957 dir. debut in TV for Canadian Bdcstg. Co. Became CBC resident dir. Moved to London to direct for Armchair Theatre for ABC-TV. Then became freelance dir., doing stage work, films, TV. Received BAFTA Best Director Award, 1962. Golden Globe Awards, 1969, 1987.
THEATER: The Duel, Galileo, The Basement, Tea Party, The Dutchman, etc.
PICTURES: Time to Remember (debut, 1962), Anne of the Thousand Days, Mary Queen of Scots, Lost Horizon, The Dove, The Littlest Horse Thieves, The Other Side of Midnight, The Last Flight of Noah's Ark, Condorman, The Amateur, The Boy in Blue, Morning Glory (co-s.p. only).
TELEVISION: The Hot Potato Boys, Roll On, Bloomin' Death, Girl in a Birdcage, The Picture of Dorian Gray, Rain, The Rose Affair, Roman Gesture, Silent Song, The Male of the Species, The Young Elizabeth, A Case of Libel, Dr. Jekyll and Mr. Hyde. U.S. *Movies/Mini-Series*: A Married Man, Poor Little Rich Girl: The Barbara Hutton Story, The Woman He Loved, Till We Meet Again (mini-series), Night of the Fox (mini-series), Lucy & Desi: Before the Laughter, Changes, Yes Virginia There is a Santa Claus, Stranger in the Mirror, Jackie Collins' Lady Boss, Treacherous Beauties, Trade Winds, A Promise Kept: The Oksana Baiul Story (Emmy Award for dir.), At The Midnight Hour.

JASON, RICK
Actor. b. New York, NY, May 21, 1926. e. American Acad. of Dramatic Arts. B'way debut in Now I Lay Me Down To Sleep (Theatre World Award). Has acted in over 400 TV shows, beginning with Live TV (1945) and over 40 feature films.
PICTURES: Sombrero, Saracen Blade, This Is My Love, Lieutenant Wore Skirts, Wayward Bus, Partners, Illegally Yours.
TELEVISION: *Series*: The Case of the Dangerous Robin, Combat. *Mini-Series*: Around the World in 80 Days. *Movies*: The Monk, Who is the Black Dahlia?, The Best Place to Be.

JAYSTON, MICHAEL
Actor. b. Nottingham, England, Oct. 28, 1935. Member of Old Vic theatre Co. & Bristol Old Vic.
PICTURES: A Midsummer Night's Dream, Cromwell, Nicholas and Alexandra, The Public Eye (Follow Me), Alice's Adventures in Wonderland, The Nelson Affair, Tales That Witness Madness, The Homecoming, Craze, The Internecine Project, Dominique, Zulu Dawn.
TELEVISION: She Fell Among Thieves, Tinker Tailor Soldier Spy.

JEFFREYS, ANNE
Actress. b. Goldsboro, NC, Jan. 26. m. actor Robert Sterling. Named by Theatre Arts Magazine as one of the 10 outstanding beauties of the stage. Trained for operatic career. Sang with NY's Municipal Opera Co. while supplementing income as a Powers model. Appeared as Tess Trueheart in Dick Tracy features.
THEATER: *B'way*: in Street Scene, Kiss Me Kate, Romance, Three Wishes for Jamie, Kismet. Stock: Camelot, King & I, Kismet, Song of Norway, Bells Are Ringing, Marriage Go Round, No Sex Please, We're British, Take Me Along, Carousel, Anniversary Waltz, Do I Hear a Waltz, Ninotchka, Pal Joey, Name of the Game, Destry Rides Again, The Merry Widow, Bitter Sweet, Desert Song, High Button Shoes, Sound of Music.
PICTURES: I Married an Angel, Billy the Kid, Trapped, Joan of Ozark, The Old Homestead, Tarzan's New York Adventure, X Marks the Spot, Yokel Boy, Catterbox, Man from Thunder River, Nevada, Step Lively, Dillinger, Sing Your Way Home, Those Endearing Young Charms, Zombies on Broadway, Dick Tracy Vs. Cueball, Genius at Work, Step By Step, Vacation in Reno, Trail Street, Riffraff, Return of the Bad Men, Boys' Night Out, Panic in the City, Southern Double Cross, Clifford.
TELEVISION: *Series*: Topper, Love That Jill, Bright Promise, Delphi Bureau, General Hospital, Finder of Lost Loves. *Guest*: Falcon Crest, Hotel, Murder She Wrote, L.A. Law, Baywatch. *Movies*: Beggarman Thief, A Message From Holly.

JEFFRIES, LIONEL
Actor, Director. b. Forest Hill, London, England, 1926. e. Queens Elizabeth's Grammar Sch, Wimbone Dorset. Ent. m.p. ind. 1952.
THEATER: Hello, Dolly!, See How They Run, Two Into One, Pygmalion (U.S.), The Wild Duck.

PICTURES: The Black Rider, The Colditz Story, No Smoking, Will Any Gentleman?, Windfall, All for Mary, Bhowani Junction, Eyewitness, Jumping for Joy, Lust for Life, Creeping Unknown (Quatermass Experiment), Baby and the Battleship, Decision Against Time, Doctor at Large, High Terrace, Hour of Decision, Up in the World, Behind the Mask, Blue Murder at St. Trinian's, Dunkirk, Girls at Sea, Law and Disorder, Orders to Kill, Revenge of Frankenstein, Up the Creek, Bobbikins, The Circle (The Vicious Circle), Idol on Parade, Nowhere to Go, The Nun's Story, Jazzboat, Let's Get Married, Trials of Oscar Wilde, Please Turn Over, Tarzan the Magnificent, Two-Way Stretch, Fanny, The Hellions, Life is a Circus, Kill or Cure, Mrs. Gibbons' Boys, Operation Snatch, The Notorious Landlady, The Wrong Arm of the Law, Call Me Bwana, The Crimson Blade, First Men in the Moon, The Long Ships, Murder Ahoy, The Secret of My Success, The Truth About Spring, You Must Be Joking!, Arrivederci Baby!, The Spy With a Cold Nose, Oh Dad Poor Dad, Blast Off! (Rocket to the Moon), Camelot, Chitty Chitty Bang Bang, Sudden Terror, The Railway Children (dir., s.p. only), Lola (Twinky), Who Slew Auntie Roo?, The Amazing Mr. Blunden (dir., s.p. only), Baxter (dir. only), Royal Flash, Wombling Free (voice, also dir., s.p.), The Water Babies (dir. only), The Prisoner of Zenda, Better Late Than Never, A Chorus of Disapproval.
TELEVISION: Father Charlie, Tom Dick and Harriet, Cream in My Coffee, Minder, Danny: the Champion of the World, Jekyll and Hyde, Boon Morse, Ending Up, Look at It This Way, Bed.

JENKINS, DAN
Public Relations Consultant. b. Montclair, NJ, Dec. 5, 1916. e. U. of Virginia. 1938. U.S. Army, 1940-45; major, infantry. P.R. officer, Hq. Eighth Army. Mng. ed., Motion Picture Magazine, 1946-48; editor, Tele-Views Magazine, 1949-50; TV editor, columnist, Hollywood Reporter, 1950-53; Hollywood bureau chief, TV Guide, 1953-63; v.p., exec. dir. TV dept., Rogers, Cowan & Brenner, Inc., 1963-71. Formed Dan Jenkins Public Relations, Inc. 1971. Joined Charles A. Pomerantz Public Relations, Ltd. as v.p., 1975, while retaining own firm. Sr. associate, Porter, Novelli, Assocs., 1981. Mem. bd. trustees, Natl. Academy of TV Arts & Sciences; bd. gov., Hollywood chapter, Natl. Academy of TV Arts & Sciences, 1967-71. Rejoined Rogers & Cowan, 1983, v.p., TV dept. Retired, 1988.

JENKINS, GEORGE
Art Director. b. Baltimore, MD, Nov. 19, 1908. e. U. of Pennsylvania. Hollywood-New York art dir. since 1946; TV pictures for Four Star Playhouse and Revue productions; NBC-TV opera, Carmen; color dir., CBS-TV, 1954; NBC color spec. Annie Get Your Gun, 1957; TV music with Mary Martin, 1959. Professor, Motion Picture Design, UCLA, 1985-88.
THEATER: Mexican Hayride, I Remember Mama, Dark of the Moon, Lost in the Stars, Bell Book and Candle, The Bad Seed, The Happiest Millionaire, Two for the Seesaw, Ice Capades, Song of Norway, Paradise Island, Around the World in 80 Days, Mardi Gras, The Miracle Worker, Critic's Choice, A Thousand Clowns, Jennie, Generation, Wait Until Dark, Only Game in Town, Night Watch, Sly Fox.
PICTURES: The Best Years of Our Lives, The Secret Life of Walter Mitty, A Song Is Born, Rosanna McCoy, The Miracle Worker, Mickey One, Up the Down Staircase, Wait Until Dark, The Subject Was Roses, Klute, 1776, The Paper Chase, The Parallax View, Night Moves, Funny Lady, All the President's Men (Academy Award, 1976), Comes a Horseman, The China Syndrome (Acad. Award nom.), Starting Over, The Postman Always Rings Twice, Rollover, Sophie's Choice, Orphans, See You in the Morning, Presumed Innocent.
TELEVISION: Movie: The Dollmaker.

JENNINGS, PETER
TV News Anchor. b. Toronto, Canada, July 29, 1938. Son of Canadian broadcaster Charles Jennings. e. Carleton U.; Rider Coll. Worked as a bank teller and late night radio host in Canada. Started career as host of Club Thirteen, a Canadian American Bandstand-like dance prog., then as a newsman on CFJR (radio), Ottawa; then with CJOH-TV and CBC. Joined ABC in 1964 as NY corr.; 1965, anchor, Peter Jennings with the News; 1969, overseas assignments for ABC news; 1975, Washington correspondent and anchor for AM America; 1977, chief foreign corr.; 1978, foreign desk anchor, World News Tonight; 1983-, anchor, sr. editor, World News Tonight.

JENS, SALOME
Actress. b. Milwaukee, WI, May 8, 1935. e. Northwestern U. Member Actors Studio.
THEATER: The Disenchanted, Far Country, Night Life, Winter's Tale, Mary Stuart, Antony and Cleopatra, After the Fall, Moon For the Misbegotten, The Balcony.
PICTURES: Angel Baby (debut, 1961), The Fool Killer, Seconds, Me Natalie, Cloud Dancer, Harry's War, Just Between Friends, Coming Out Under Fire (narrator).
TELEVISION: Movies: In the Glitter Palace, Sharon: Portrait of a Mistress, The Golden Moment: An Olympic Love Story, A

Killer in a Family, Playing with Fire, Uncommon Valor. Guest: Mary Hartman, Mary Hartman. Series: Falcon Crest. Mini-Series: From Here to Eternity.

JERGENS, ADELE
Actress. b. Brooklyn, NY, Nov. 26, 1917. Began career in musical shows during summer vacation at 15; won contest, New York's World Fair, as model; appeared on New York stage; night clubs, U.S. and abroad.
PICTURES: A Thousand and One Nights, She Wouldn't Say Yes, The Corpse Came C.O.D., Dwon to Earth, Woman From Tangier, The Fuller Brush Man, The Dark Past, Treasure of Monte Cristo, SLightly French, Edge of Doom, Side Street, Abbott and Costello Meet the Invisible Man, Sugarfoot, Try and Get Me, Show Boat, Somebody Loves Me, Aaron Slick from Punkin' Crick, Overland Pacific, Miami Story, Fireman Save My Child, Big Chase, Strange Lady in Town, The Cobweb, Girls in Prison, The Lonesome Trail, Treasure of Monte Cristo.

JETER, MICHAEL
Actor. b. Lawrenceberg, TN, Aug. 20, 1952.e. Memphis State Univ.
THEATER: Alice, G.R. Point (Theatre World Award), Cloud 9, Greater Tuna, Once in a Lifetime, Zoo Story, Waiting for Godot, Only Kidding, The Boys Next Door, Grand Hotel (Tony Award, 1990).
PICTURES: Hair, Ragtime, Soup for One, Zelig, The Money Pit, Dead-Bang, Tango & Cash, Just Like in the Movies, Miller's Crossing, The Fisher King, Bank Robber, Sister Act 2: Back in the Habit, Drop Zone, Waterworld.
TELEVISION: Series: One Life to Live, Hothouse, Evening Shade (Emmy Award, 1992). Movies: My Old Man, Sentimental Journey, When Love Kills: The Seduction of John Hearn, Gypsy. Mini-Series: From Here to Eternity. Guest: Lou Grant, Designing Women.

JEWISON, NORMAN
Producer, Director. b. Toronto, Canada, July 21, 1926. e. Malvern Collegiate Inst., Toronto, 1940-44; Victoria Coll., U. of Toronto, 1946-50, B.A. Stage and TV actor 1950-52. Director, Canadian Broadcasting Corp 1953-58. Awarded 1988 Acad. of Canadian Cinema and Television Special Achievement Award. Made Companion Order of Canada, 1992.
PICTURES: Director: 40 Pounds of Trouble (debut, 1962), The Thrill of It All, Send Me No Flowers, The Art of Love, The Cincinnati Kid. Director-Producer: The Russians Are Coming the Russians Are Coming (Acad. Award nom. for picture), In the Heat of the Night (dir. only; Acad. Award nom.), The Thomas Crown Affair, Gaily Gaily, Fiddler on the Roof (Acad. Award nom. for dir. & picture), Jesus Christ Superstar (also co-s.p.), Rollerball, F.I.S.T., ... And Justice for All, Best Friends, A Soldier's Story (Acad. Award nom. for picture), Agnes of God, Moonstruck (Acad. Award noms. for dir. & picture), In Country, Other People's Money, Only You, Bogus. Producer: The Landlord, Billy Two Hats, The Dogs of War (exec. prod.), Iceman, The January Man.
TELEVISION: Exec. prod. of 8 episodes of The Judy Garland Show. Prod.-Dir.: Judy Garland specials, The Andy Williams Show. Dir. of Specials: Tonight with Harry Belafonte, The Broadway of Lerner and Loewe.

JHABVALA, RUTH PRAWER
Writer. b. Cologne, Germany, May 7, 1927. Emigrated with her family to England, 1939. e. Hendon County Sch., Queen Mary Coll., London U. (degree in English). m. architect C.S.H. Jhabvala, 1951 and moved to Delhi. Has written most of the screenplays for the films of Ismail Merchant and James Ivory.
AUTHOR: To Whom She Will, Esmond in India, The Nature of Passion, The Householder, Get Ready for Battle, Heat and Dust, In Search of Love and Beauty, Three Continents, Poet and Dancer, Shards of Memory.
PICTURES: The Householder (debut, 1963; based on her novel), Shakespeare Wallah (with Ivory), The Guru (with Ivory), Bombay Talkie (with Ivory), Autobiography of a Princess, Roseland, The Europeans, Jane Austen in Manhattan, Quartet, Heat and Dust (based on her own novel; BAFTA Award), The Bostonians, A Room with a View (Academy Award, 1986), Madame Sousatzka (co.-s.p. with John Schlesinger), Mr. and Mrs. Bridge (NY Film Critics Award), Howards End (Academy Award, 1992), The Remains of the Day, Jefferson in Paris.
TELEVISION: Hullabaloo Over Georgie and Bonnie's Pictures.

JILLIAN, ANN
Actress. b. Cambridge, MA, Jan. 29, 1951. Began career at age 10 in Disney's Babes in Toyland; in film version of Gypsy at age 12. Broadway debut in musical, Sugar Babies, 1979. Formed own company: 9-J Productions, developing TV movies and series.
PICTURES: Babes in Toyland, Gypsy, Mr. Mom, Sammy the Way Out Seal.

TELEVISION: *Series*: Hazel, It's a Living, Jennifer Slept Here, Ann Jillian. *Guest*: Love Boat, Fantasy Island, Twilight Zone, Ben Casey, etc. *Mini-Series*: Ellis Island (Emmy & Golden Globe nom.), Alice in Wonderland, Malibu. *Movies*: Mae West (Emmy & Golden Globe nom.), Death Ride to Osaka, Killer in the Mirror, Convicted: A Mother's Story, Perry Mason: The Case of the Murdered Madam, The Ann Jillian Story (Golden Globe Award; Emmy nom.), Original Sin, This Wife for Hire, Little White Lies, Mario and the Mob, Labor of Love: The Arlette Schweitzer Story, Heart of a Child, The Disappearance of Vonnie, Fast Company, It's Him Or Us, My Son The Match Maker.

JOANOU, PHIL
Director. b. La Canada, CA, Nov. 20, 1961. e. UCLA, USC. Student film The Last Chance Dance won him first professional job directing 2 episodes of tv's Amazing Stories (Santa 85, The Doll).
PICTURES: Three O'Clock High (debut, 1987), U2: Rattle and Hum (also edit., camera operator), State of Grace, Final Analysis, Heaven's Prisoners.
TELEVISION: *Mini-Series*: Wild Palms (co-dir.). *Series*: Fallen Angels (Dead-End for Delia).

JOFFE, CHARLES H.
Executive. b. Brooklyn, NY, July 16, 1929. e. Syracuse U. Joined with Jack Rollins to set up management-production org., clients including Woody Allen, Ted Bessell, Billy Crystal, David Letterman, Tom Poston, Robin Williams.
PICTURES: *Producer*: Don't Drink the Water, Take the Money and Run, Everything You Always Wanted to Know About Sex but Were Afraid To Ask, Love and Death, Annie Hall (Academy Award for Best Picture, 1977), House of God. *Exec. prod.*: Play It Again Sam, Bananas, Sleeper, Manhattan, Interiors, Stardust Memories, Arthur, A Midsummer Nights' Sex Comedy, Zelig, Broadway Danny Rose, The Purple Rose of Cairo, Hannah and Her Sisters, Radio Days, September, Another Woman, New York Stories (Oedipus Wrecks), Crimes and Misdemeanors, Alice, Shadows and Fog, Husbands and Wives, Manhattan Murder Mystery, Bullets Over Broadway.
TELEVISION: Woody Allen specials. Star of the Family, Good Time Harry, Triplecross.

JOFFE, EDWARD
Producer, Director, Writer, Production Consultant. Worked in m.p., theatre, commercial radio and as journalist before ent. TV ind. in Britain as writer/prod with ATV. 1959-61 staff prod. Granada TV. 1962, dir., Traitor's Gate & Traveling Light for Robt Stigwood; prod. dir., numerous series for Grampian TV; 1967, dir. film The Price of a Record—Emmy finalist; 1967-68 films, Columbia's Folk & So Many Partings ITV entries in Golden Harp Fest.; 1968, prod., dir. Tony Hancock Down Under in Australia, prod. dir. Up At The Cross; prod. dir. ind. film, Will Ye No' Come Back Again?; This Is... Tom Jones; prod. dir., The Golden Shot; 1971, senior production lecturer, Thomson TV College; dir., films for U.S. for London Television Service; Evening Standard Commercials for Thames TV. Co. prod. dir.,ind. film Sound Scene, 1972-8, Contract prod. dir. Thames TV various series: Magpie, Today, Opportunity Knocks, The David Nixon Show, Seven Ages of Man, Problems, Finding Out; 1980 production consultant, CBC-TV; 1978-82, prod. dir. series Writers' Workshop, About Books; 1978, film, Places & Things (British Academy Award nom.) film, Who Do You Think You Are? (British Academy Award nom., ITV's Japan Prize entry, Special Jury Award San Francisco Intl. Film Fest.), 1981, Film Images, (British Academy Award nom.; Gold Plaque Chicago Intl. Film Fest.); The Protectors (medal winner Intl. Film & TV Festival, N.Y.). 1982-86: film Rainbow Coloured Disco Dancer. Various Series: Taste of China, Jobs Ltd., Spin-Offs, The Buzz. Doc.: War Games in Italy. 1989-95, devised, prod., dir. Video View for ITV Network; Co-prod. & dir. 2 series Sprockets; Dir. Challenge. Dir. Screen Scene Prods, String of Pearls, PLC, String of Pearls 2 PLC. Companies produced mopics Double X, Little Devils - The Birth, To Catch a Yeti, Big Game, Shepherd on the Rock.

JOFFE, ROLAND
Director, Producer. b. London, Eng., Nov. 17, 1945. e. Lycee Francaise, Carmel Col. Manchester U., England. Worked in British theatre with the Young Vic, the National Theatre and the Old Vic. 1973 became youngest director at National Theatre. 1978, moved into directing TV for Granada TV, then Thames and B.B.C. before feature debut in 1984 with The Killing Fields.
PICTURES: *Director*: The Killing Fields (debut, 1984), The Mission, Fat Man and Little Boy (also co-s.p.), City of Joy (also co-prod.), The Scarlett Letter. *Producer*: Made in Bangkok, Super Mario Bros.
TELEVISION: *Documentaries*: Rope, Ann, No Mama No. Plays: The Spongers, Tis Pity She's a Whore, The Legion Hall Bombing, United Kingdom (also co-wrote). *Series*: Coronation Street, Bill Brand, The Stars Look Down.

JOHNS, GLYNIS
Actress. b. Durban, South Africa, Oct. 5, 1923. e. in England. Daughter of Mervyn Johns, actor, and Alys Steele, pianist. On London stage from 1935 (Buckie's Bears, The Children's Hour, A Kiss for Cinderella, Quiet Week-End; Gertie, N.Y. stage, 1952; Major Barbara, N.Y., 1956-57.) Voted one of top ten British Money-making stars in Motion Picture Herald-Pathe poll, 1951-54.
THEATER: Too Good to Be True (NY), The King's Mare, Come as You Are, The Marquise (tour), A Little Night Music (NY; Tony Award), Cause Celebre, Harold and Maude (Canada, Hay Fever (U.K. tour), The Boy Friend (Toronto), The Circle (NY).
PICTURES: South Riding (debut, 1938), Murder in the Family, Prison Without Bars, On the Night of the Fire, Mr. Brigg's Family, Under Your Hat, The Prime Minister, 49th Parallel, Adventures of Tartu, Half-Way House, Perfect Strangers, This Man Is Mine, Frieda, An Ideal Husband, Miranda, Third Time Lucky, Dear Mr. Prohack, State Secret, Flesh and Blood, No Highway in the Sky, Appointment With Venus (Island Rescue), Encore, The Magic Box, The Card (The Promoter), The Sword and the Rose, Rob Roy the Highland Rogue, Personal Affair, The Weak and the Wicked, The Seekers (Land of Fury), The Beachcomber, Mad About Men, Court Jester, Josephine and Men, Loser Takes All, All Mine to Give, Around the World in 80 Days, Another Time Another Place, Shake Hands with the Devil, The Sundowners, The Spider's Web, The Cabinet of Caligari, The Chapman Report, Papa's Delicate Condition, Mary Poppins, Dear Brigette, Don't Just Stand There, Lock Up Your Daughters, Under Milk Wood, Vault of Horror, Zelly and Me, Nukie, The Ref, While You Were Sleeping.
TELEVISION: *Series*: Glynis, Coming of Age. *Guest*: Dr. Kildare, Roaring Twenties, Naked City, The Defenders, Danny Kaye Show. Also: Noel Coward's Star Quality, Mrs. Amworth, All You Need Is Love, Across a Crowded Room, Little Gloria... Happy at Last, Skagg.

JOHNSON, ARTE
Actor. b. Chicago, IL, Jan. 20, 1934. e. Univ. of IL. To NY in 1950's where he landed role on B'way in Gentlemen Prefer Blondes. Also worked in nightclubs, summer stock, tv commercials. Gained fame on Rowan and Martin's Laugh-In in late 1960's. Much voice work on tv cartoons.
PICTURES: Miracle in the Rain, The Subterraneans, The Third Day, The President's Analyst, Love at First Bite, A Night at the Magic Castle, What Comes Around, Tax Season, Evil Spirits, Munchie, Second Chance, Captiva.
TELEVISION: *Series*: It's Always Jan, Sally, Hennesey, Don't Call Me Charlie, Rowan & Martin's Laugh-In (Emmy Award, 1969), Ben Vereen... Comin' at Ya!, The Gong Show (panelist), Games People Play, Glitter, General Hospital. *Movies*: Twice in a Lifetime, Bud and Lou, If Things Were Different, Detour to Terror, The Love Tapes, Condominium, Making of a Male Model, Alice in Wonderland, Dan Turner--Hollywood Detective.

JOHNSON, BEN
Actor. b. Pawhuska, OK, June 13, 1918. Stunt rider & performer in rodeos, touring country; did stunt work in many films before acting debut.
PICTURES: Three Godfathers, Mighty Joe Young, She Wore a Yellow Ribbon, Wagonmaster, Rio Grande, Wild Stallion, Fort Defiance, Shane, Rebel in Town, War Drums, Slim Carter, Fort Bowie, Ten Who Dared, Tomboy and the Champ, One-Eyed Jacks, Cheyenne Autumn, Major Dundee, The Rare Breed, Will Penny, Hang 'Em High, The Wild Bunch, The Undefeated, Chisum, Something Big, The Last Picture Show (Academy Award, best supporting actor, 1971), Corky, Junior Bonner, The Getaway, Dillinger, The Train Robbers, Kid Blue, The Sugarland Express, Bite the Bullet, Hustle, Breakheart Pass, The Town That Dreaded Sundown, The Greatest, Grayeagle, The Swarm, The Hunter, Terror Train, Soggy Bottom U.S.A., Ruckus, High Country Pursuit, Tex, Champions, Red Dawn, Let's Get Harry, Trespasses, Dark Before Dawn, Cherry 2000, Back to Back, My Heroes Have Always Been Cowboys, Radio Flyer, Angels in the Outfield.
TELEVISION: *Series*: The Monroes. *Movies*: Runaway!, Bloodsport, Dream West, Locusts, The Shadow Riders, Red Pony, The Sacketts, Wild Horses, Wild Times, Stranger on My Land, The Chase, Bonanza: The Return, Bonanza: Under Attack. *Guest*: Alfred Hitchcock Presents (1958), Laramie, Have Gun Will Travel, Bonanza, The Virginian.
(d. April 8, 1996)

JOHNSON, DON
Actor. b. Flatt Creek, MO, Dec. 15, 1949. Worked at ACT (Amer. Conservatory Th.), San Francisco. On stage there in Your Own Thing. In L.A. in Fortune and Men's Eyes. Recording: Heartbeat (1986).
PICTURES: The Magic Garden of Stanley Sweetheart (debut, 1970), Zachariah, The Harrad Experiment, A Boy and His Dog, Return to Macon County, Soggy Bottom USA, Cease Fire, Sweet Hearts Dance, Dead-Bang, The Hot Spot, Harley Davidson and the Marlboro Man, Paradise, Born Yesterday, Guilty as Sin, Tin Cup.

TELEVISION: *Series*: From Here to Eternity, Miami Vice. *Mini-Series*: The Rebels, Beulah Land, The Long Hot Summer. *Movies*: First You Cry, Ski Lift to Death, Katie: Portrait of a Centerfold, Revenge of the Stepford Wives, Amateur Night at the Dixie Bar and Grill, Elvis and the Beauty Queen, The Two Lives of Carol Letner, In Pursuit of Honor. *Special*: Don Johnson's Heartbeat (music video, also exec. prod.). *Guest*: Kung Fu, The Bold Ones, Police Story.

JOHNSON, G. GRIFFITH
Executive. b. New York, NY, Aug. 15, 1912. e. Harvard U., 1934, A.M. 1936, Ph.D. 1938. U.S. Treasury Dept. 1936-39; Dept. of Comm., 1939-40; O.P.A. & predecessor agencies, 1940-46; consulting economist, 1946-47; dir., Econ. Stab. Div., Nat'l. Security Resources Bd., 1948-49; chief econ., U.S. Bur. of Budget, 1949-50; econ. advisor to Econ. Stab. Admin. 1950-52; Exec. v.p. MPEAA, 1965, MPAA, 1971; Asst. Sec'y of State for Economic Affairs, 1962-65; v.p. MPAA, 1953-62. Author of several books & articles.

JOHNSON, J. BOND
Producer, Executive. b. Fort Worth, TX, June 18, 1926. e. Texas Wesleyan Univ., B.S., 1947; Texas Christian U., M.Ed., 1948; Southern Methodist U., B.D., 1952; USC, Ph.D., 1967. Army Air Forces, WWII; public information officer, captain, U.S. Marine Corps, Korean War. Formerly member Marine Corps Reserve, Motion Picture Production Unit, Hollywood. Was Colonel, U.S. Army; now retired. Newspaper reporter, Fort Worth Star-Telegram, 1942-48; pres., West Coast News Service, 1960; pres., exec. prod., Bonjo Prods., Inc., 1960, President, chief executive officer, Cine-Media International, 1975 managing partner, Capra-Johnson Productions, Ltd., 1978.
PICTURES: Sands of Iwo Jima, Retreat Hell, Flying Leathernecks; photographed aerial portions, Jamboree 53, Norfleet, Devil at My Heels, Kingdom of the Spiders, Ordeal at Donner Pass, Place of the Dawn, Lies I Told Myself, Backstretch, Airs Above The Ground, The Jerusalem Concert, The Berkshire Terror, The Seventh Gate.
TELEVISION: *Series*: Creator, story consultant, tech. advisor, Whirlpool. *Exec. producer, creator*: On The Go (TV News-Sports), Coasties, Desert Rangers. *Producer*: Fandango.

JOHNSON, LAMONT
Director, Producer. b. Stockton, CA, Sept. 30, 1922. e. UCLA. 4 time winner of Director's Guild Award for TV work. Directed plays The Egg, Yes Is For a Very Young Man. Dir. two operas, L.A. Philharmonic, 1964; founder, dir., UCLA Professional Theatre Group.
PICTURES: A Covenant With Death (debut, 1967), Kona Coast, The McKenzie Break, A Gunfight, The Groundstar Conspiracy, You'll Like My Mother, The Last American Hero, Visit to a Chief's Son, Lipstick, One on One (also actor), Somebody Killed Her Husband, Cattle Annie and Little Britches, Spacehunter: Adventures in the Forbidden Zone.
TELEVISION: *Series*: The Defenders, Profiles in Courage, Twilight Zone. *Movies/Mini-Series*: Deadlock, My Sweet Charlie, That Certain Summer, The Execution of Pvt. Slovik, Fear on Trial, Off the Minnesota Strip, Crisis at Central High, Escape from Iran, Dangerous Company, Life of the Party: The Story of Beatrice, Ernie Kovacs: Between the Laughter, Wallenberg: A Hero's Story (also co-prod.; Emmy Award, 1985), Unnatural Causes, Gore Vidal's Lincoln (Emmy Award, 1988), The Kennedys of Massachusetts, Voices Within: The Lives of Truddi Chase, Crash Landing: The Rescue of Flight 232, The Broken Chain (also prod.).

JOHNSON, MARK
Producer. b. Washington, DC, Dec. 27, 1945. Moved to Spain at age 7, lived there for eleven years before returning to America. e. Univ. of VA, Univ. of IA. Joined Directors Guild training program receiving first credit on Next Stop Greenwich Village. Worked as prod. asst., then asst. dir. on High Anxiety, Movie Movie, The Brink's Job, and Escape From Alcatraz. Starting with Diner in 1982 served as executive prod. or prod. on all Barry Levinson films. With Levinson formed Baltimore Pictures in 1989.
PICTURES: Diner (exec. prod.). *Producer*: The Natural, Young Sherlock Holmes, Tin Men, Good Morning Vietnam, Rain Man (Academy Award for Best Picture of 1988), Avalon, Kafka (co-exec. prod.), Bugsy (L.A. Film Critics & Golden Globe Awards for Best Picture of 1991), Toys, Sniper, Wilder Napalm, A Perfect World, A Little Princess.

JOHNSON, RICHARD
Actor. b. Upminster, Essex, England, July 30, 1927. Studied at Royal Acad. of Dramatic Art. First stage appearance Opera House, Manchester, then with John Gielgud's repertory season, 1944. Served in Royal Navy 1945-48. Subsequent stage appearances incl. The Madwoman of Chaillot, The Lark. Visited Moscow with Peter Brook's production of Hamlet. Royal Shakespeare Thea.: Stratford, London, 1957-62. Royal Shakespeare Co. 1972-73. National Theatre, 1976-77. Founded United British Artists, 1983.

PICTURES: Captain Horatio Hornblower (debut, 1951), Calling Bulldog Drummond, Scotland Yard Inspector (Lady in the Fog), Saadia, Never So Few, Cairo, The Haunting, 80,000 Suspects, The Pumpkin Eater, The Amorous Adventures of Moll Flanders, Operation Crossbow, Khartoum, The Witch in Love, Deadlier Than the Male, The Rover, Danger Route, A Twist of Sand, Oedipus the King, Lady Hamilton, Some Girls Do, Julius Caesar, The Tyrant, The Beloved, Behind the Door, Hennessy, Night Child, The Cursed Medallion, Aces High, The Last Day of Spring, The Comeback, Zombie, The Monster Club, Screamers, What Waits Below, Lady Jane, Turtle Diary, Foreign Student, Diving In. Producer: Turtle Diary, Castaway, The Lonely Passion of Judith Hearne.
TELEVISION: The Flame is Love, Haywire, The Four Feathers, Portrait of a Rebel: Margaret Sanger, A Man For All Seasons, Voice of the Heart, The Crucifer of Blood, Duel of Hearts. Guest: Wagon Train, Lou Grant, Ironside, Knots Landing, That Girl, MacGyver, Police Story, Route 66, many others. Live TV incl. Lux Video Theatre, Front Row Center, Hallmark Hall of Fame.

JOHNSON, RUSSELL
Actor. b. Ashley, PA, Nov. 10, 1924. e. Girard Coll, Actors Laboratory, L.A. W.W.II, Army Air Corps. Author: Here on Gilligan's Isle (1993).
PICTURES: A Town of the 80's, Stand at Apache Landing, A Distant Trumpet, Ma & Pa Kettle at Waikiki, Rogue Cop, Loan Shark, Seminole, Tumbleweed, Blue Movies, It Came From Outer Space, Many Rivers to Cross, Law and Order, Black Tuesday, This Island Earth, Rock All Night, Attack of the Crab Monsters, The Space Children, For Men Only, The Greatest Story Ever Told, Hitchhike to Hell, MacArthur.
TELEVISION: *Series*: Black Saddle, Gilligan's Island. *Guest*: Studio One, Front Row Center, Playhouse 90, Lux Video Theatre, Mobile One, The Great Adventure Jane Powell Show, Climax, You Are There, Rawhide, Twilight Zone, Gunsmoke, Outer Limits, Cannon, Marcus Welby, That Girl, The FBI, Dallas, Fame, Dynasty, My Two Dads, Bosom Buddies, Buffalo Bill, Vanished, Harry Truman Biography, Truman vs. MacArthur, Knots Landing, Santa Barbara, Roseanne, many others. *Movie*: With a Vengeance.

JOHNSON, VAN
Actor. b. Newport, RI, Aug. 25, 1916. Began in vaudeville; then on N.Y. stage New Faces of 1937, Eight Men of Manhattan, Too Many Girls, Pal Joey. Voted one of the top ten Money Making Stars in Motion Picture Herald-Fame Poll 1945-46. Stage includes The Music Man (London), La Cage aux Folles (NY) and numerous tours.
PICTURES: Too Many Girls (debut, 1940), Murder in the Big House, Somewhere I'll Find You, War Against Mrs. Hadley, Dr. Gillespie's New Assistant, The Human Comedy, Pilot No. 5, Dr. Gillespies's Criminal Case, Guy Named Joe, White Cliffs of Dover, Three Men in White, Two Girls and a Sailor, Thirty Seconds Over Tokyo, Between Two Women, Thrill of Romance, Weekend at the Waldorf, Easy to Wed, No Leave No Love, Till the Clouds Roll By, High Barbaree, Romance of Rosy Ridge, Bride Goes Wild, State of the Union, Command Decision, Mother is a Freshman, In the Good Old Summertime, Scene of the Crime, Battleground, Big Hangover, Duchess of Idaho, Three Guys Named Mike, Grounds for Marriage, Go For Broke, Too Young to Kiss, It's a Big Country, Invitation, When in Rome, Washington Story, Plymouth Adventure, Confidentially Connie, Remains to Be Seen, Easy to Love, Caine Mutiny, Siege at Red River, Men of the Fighting Lady, Brigadoon, Last Time I Saw Paris, End of the Affair, Bottom of the Bottle, Miracle in the Rain, 23 Paces to Baker Street, Slander, Kelly and Me, Action of the Tiger, The Last Blitzkreig, Subway in the Sky, Beyond This Place, Enemy General, Wives and Lovers, Divorce American Style, Yours Mine and Ours, Where Angels Go ... Trouble Follows, Company of Killers, Eagles Over London, The Kidnapping of the President, The Purple Rose of Cairo, Down There in the Jungle, Escape From Paradise, Three Days to a Kill.
TELEVISION: *Special*: Pied Piper of Hamelin. *Mini-Series*: Rich Man Poor Man, Black Beauty. *Movies*: Doomsday Flight, San Francisco International, Call Her Mom, The Girl on the Late Late Show, Superdome. *Guest*: I Love Lucy, G.E. Theatre, Batman, Love American Style, The Love Boat, Murder She Wrote.

JOHNSTON, MARGARET
Actress. b. Sydney, Australia, Aug. 10, 1918. e. Sydney U., Australia; RADA. London stage debut: Murder Without Crime.
THEATER: Ring of Truth, The Masterpiece, Lady Macbeth, Merchant of Venice, Measure for Measure, Othello.
PICTURES: The Prime Minister, The Rake's Progress (The Notorious Gentleman), A Man About the House, Portrait of Clare, The Magic Box, Knave of Hearts, Touch and Go, Burn With Burn (Night of the Eagle), The Nose on My Face, Girl in the Headlines (The Model Murder Case), Life at the Top, The Psychopath, Schizo, Sebastian.

TELEVISION: Always Juliet, Taming of the Shrew, Man with a Load of Mischief, Light of Heart, Autumn Crocus, Androcles and the Lion, Sulky Five, Windmill Near a Frontier, The Shrike, The Out of Towners, Looking for Garrow, The Typewriter, The Glass Menagerie, That's Where the Town's Going, The Vortex.

JOLLEY, STAN
Producer, Director, Production Designer, Art Director. b. New York, NY, May 17, 1926. e. U. of Southern California, col. of architecture. Son of actor I. Stanford Jolley. In Navy in W.W.II. Has acted in capacities listed for many feature films and TV series. One of orig. designers of Disneyland.
PICTURES: *Prod./Prod. Designer*: Knife for the Ladies. *Assoc. Prod./ Prod. Designer*: The Good Guys and the Bad Guys. 2nd Unit Dir.: Superman. *Prod. Designer*: Dutch, The Good Mother, Witness (Acad. Award nom.), Taps, Caddyshack, Cattle Annie and Little Britches, Americathon (also second unit director), The Swarm, Drum, Framed, Dion Brothers, Mixed Company, Walking Tall, Terror in the Wax Museum, Night of the Lepus (also second unit director), War Between Men and Women, Law Man, The Phynx. *Art Director*: Young Billy Young, Ride Beyond Vengeance, Broken Saber, The Restless Ones, Mail Order Bride, Toby Tyler. *Assoc. Prod./Prod. designer & 2nd unit dir.*: Happily Ever After.
TELEVISION: *Movies* (2nd Unit Dir./Prod. Designer): Swiss Family Robinson, Adventures of the Queen, Woman Hunter. *Prod. Designer*: Abduction of Carrie Swenson, Eagle One, No Man's Land, Last of the Great Survivors, Like Normal People, Rescue From Gilligan's Island, Flood, Voyage of the Yes, The Stranger, Punch & Jody, City Beneath the Sea, Women of San Quentin, The Amazing Mr. Hughes. *TV Series*: *Assoc. Prod./Prod. Designer*: Jessie. *Art Director*: Walt Disney Presents, Pete and Gladys, Gunsmoke, Mr. Ed., Branded, Voyage to the Bottom of the Sea, Land of the Giants, O'Hara, Shane, Acapulco, The Racers. *Prod. Designer*: Walking Tall, Today's F.B.I., For Love and Honor, Macgyver, Under Fire, Donald in Mathmagic Land, Crisis in the Wetlands (prod./dir.).

JONAS, TONY
Executive. Pres., Warner Bros. Television.

JONES, AMY HOLDEN
Director, Writer. b. Philadelphia, PA, Sept. 17, 1953. m. cinematographer, Michael Chapman. e. Wellesley Coll., B.A., 1974; film and photography courses, Massachusetts Inst. of Technology. Winner, first place, Washington National Student Film Festival, 1973.
PICTURES: *Editor*: Hollywood Boulevard (debut, 1976), American Boy, Corvette Summer, Second Hand Hearts. *Director*: Slumber Party Massacre, Love Letters (also s.p.), Mystic Pizza (s.p. only), Maid to Order (also co-s.p.), It Had to Be Steve (also co-s.p.), Rich Man's Wife (also s.p.). *Writer*: Beethoven, Indecent Proposal, The Getaway.
TELEVISION: *Pilot* (writer): Jack's Place.

JONES, CHUCK
Producer, Director, Writer, Animator. b. Spokane, WA, Sept. 21, 1912. e. Chouinard Art Inst. Dir., Warner Bros. Animation until 1962 where he created and directed Road Runner & Wile E. Coyote, Pepe le Pew; directed and helped create Bugs Bunny, Porky Pig, Daffy Duck etc. Created Snafu character, U.S. Armed Service. Later headed MGM Animation Dept. Lecturer at many Universities. Establisehd indept. co. Chuck Jones Enterprises. Academy Awards for best animated short subjects: For Scentimental Reasons (1950), The Dot and the Line (1965), best documentary short subject: So Much for So Little (1950). 1989, published Chuck Amuck: The Life and Times of an Animated Cartoonist. 1990, chmn. Chuck Jones Prods.; currently consultant and good-will representative to Warner Bros.
PICTURES: The Phantom Tollbooth, The Bugs Bunny/Road Runner Movie, The Magical World of Chuck Jones; created animated sequences for live-action features Stay Tuned, Mrs. Doubtfire.
TELEVISION: The Bugs Bunny Show (co-prod., writer, dir.). *Dir.*: How the Grinch Stole Christmas, Horton Hears a Who, Pogo. *Producer- Director-Writer*: The Cricket in Times Square, A Very Merry Cricket, Yankee Doodle Cricket, Rikki-Tikki-Tavi, The White Seal, Mowgli's Brothers, The Carnival of the Animals, A Connecticut Rabbit in King Arthur's Court, Raggedy Ann and Andy In The Great Santa Claus Caper, The Pumpkin Who Couldn't Smile, Daffy Duck's Thanks-for-Giving Special, Bugs Bunny's Bustin' Out All Over.

JONES, DAVID
Director, Producer. b. Poole, Eng., Feb. 19, 1934. e. Christ's Coll., Cambridge U., B.A., 1954, M.A., 1957. Immigrated to U.S. in 1979. Artistic controller, then assoc. dir., Royal Shakespeare Co., 1964-75; artistic dir, RSC at Aldwych Theatre 1975-78; artistic dir, Brooklyn Acad. of Music Theatre Co., NY 1979-81; prof. Yale Sch. of Drama, 1981.
THEATER: Sweeney Agonistes (debut, 1961); *U.S.*: Summerfolk, Loves Labour's Lost, Winter's Tale, Barbarians, Jungle of Cities.
PICTURES: Betrayal, Jacknife, The Trial.

TELEVISION: *Prod.*: Monitor 1958-64 (BBC series), Play of the Month, The Beaux' Stratagem, Langrishe Go Down, Ice Age. *Dir.*: Shakespeare series, BBC 1982-83, Devil's Disciple, The Christmas Wife, Sensibility and Sense, Is There Life Out There?

JONES, DEAN
Actor. b. Decatur, AL, Jan. 25, 1931. e. Asbury Coll., Wilmore, KY. Prof. debut as blues singer, New Orleans; U.S. Navy, 1950-54. Author: Under Running Laughter.
PICTURES: Tea and Sympathy (debut, 1956), The Rack, The Opposite Sex, These Wilder Years, The Great American Pastime, Designing Woman, Ten Thousand Bedrooms, Jailhouse Rock, Until They Sail, Imitation General, Torpedo Run, Handle with Care, Night of the Quarter Moon, Never So Few, Under the Yum-Yum Tree, The New Interns, That Darn Cat, Two on a Guillotine, Any Wednesday, The Ugly Dachshund, Monkeys Go Home, Blackbeard's Ghost, The Horse in the Grey Flannel Suit, The Love Bug, $1,000,000 Duck, Snowball Express, Mr. Super Invisible, The Shaggy D.A., Herbie Goes to Monte Carlo, Born Again, Other People's Money, Beethoven, Clear and Present Danger.
TELEVISION: *Series*: Ensign O'Toole, The Chicago Teddy Bears, What's It All About World?, Herbie the Love Bug, Beethoven (animated; voice). *Movies*: Guess Who's Sleeping in My Bed?, When Every Day Was the 4th of July, Long Days of Summer, Fire and Rain, The Great Man's Whiskers, Saved By the Bell: Hawaiian Style, The Computer Wore Tennis Shoes. *Special*: Journey to Mars.
THEATER: There Was a Little Girl, Under the Yum-Yum Tree, Company, Into the Light.

JONES, GEMMA
Actress. b. London, Eng., Dec. 4, 1942. e. Royal Acad. of Dramatic Art.
THEATER: Baal, Alfie, The Cavern, The Pastime of M Robert, Portrait of a Queen, Next of Kin, The Marriage of Figaro, And A Nightingale Sang, reaking the Silence, Howards End, A Midsummer Night's Dream, The Homecoming, Mount Morgan, The Winter's Tale, etc.
PICTURES: The Devils, The Paper House, On the Black Hill, The Devils Feast of July, Sense and Sensibility.
TELEVISION: The Lie, The Way of the World, The Merchant of Venice, The Duchess of Duke Street (series), The Jim Henson Hour, Forget Me Not Lane,Call My Bluff, Dial M For Murder, The Way of the World, Churchill's People, The Cherry Orchard, The Lie, Man In A Sidecar, Shadows of Fear, Crimes of Passion, The Spoils of Poynton, The Duchess of Duke Street, The Importance of Being Earnest, Chelworth, After The Dance, Inspector Morse, The Storyteller, Sevises and Desires, Some Life Some Die, Wycliffe, The Borrowers, Faith.

JONES, GRACE
Singer, Actress. b. Spanishtown, Jamaica, May 19, 1952. e. Syracuse U. Modelled and appeared in several Italian pictures before career as singer.
PICTURES: Conan the Destroyer, A View to a Kill, Vamp, Straight to Hell, Siesta, Boomerang.

JONES, HENRY
Actor. b. Philadelphia, PA, Aug. 1, 1912. e. St. Joseph's Coll. On stage in Hamlet, Henry IV, Time of Your Life, My Sister Eileen, The Solid Gold Cadillac, Bad Seed, Sunrise at Campobello (Tony Award, 1958), Advise and Consent.
PICTURES: This is the Army, Lady Says No, Taxi, The Bad Seed, The Girl He Left Behind, The Girl Can't Help It, Will Success Spoil Rock Hunter?, 3:10 to Yuma, Vertigo, Cash McCall, The Bramble Bush, Angel Baby, Never Too Late, The Champagne Murders, Stay Away Joe, Project X, Support Your Local Sheriff, Rascal, Angel in My Pocket, Butch Cassidy and the Sundance Kid, Rabbit Run, Dirty Dingus Magee, Skin Game, Support Your Local Gunfighter, Napoleon and Samantha, Pete 'n' Tillie, Tom Sawyer, The Outfit, Nine to Five, Deathtrap, Balboa, Caddo Lake, Nowhere to Run, Dick Tracy, Arachnophobia, The Grifters.
TELEVISION: *Series*: Honestly Celeste!, Channing, The Girl With Something Extra, Phyllis, Kate Loves a Mystery, Gun Shy, Code Name: Foxfire, I Married Dora. *Movies*: The Crucible, Something for a Lonely Man, The Movie Murderer, Love Hate Love, Who is the Black Dahlia?, Tail Gunner Joe, CaliforniaGold Rush, The Leftovers, Grass Roots. *Guest*: Lost in Space, We'll Get By, B.J. and the Bear, Falcon Crest.

JONES, JAMES EARL
Actor. b. Arkabutla, MS, Jan. 17, 1931. e. U. of Michigan. Son of actor Robert Earl Jones. Awarded Hon. Doctor of Fine Arts (Yale, Princeton); Medal for Spoken Language (Amer. Acad. and Inst. of Arts and Letter; Hon. Doctor of Humane Letters (Columbia Coll. & U. of Michigan).
THEATER: Moon on a Rainbow Shawl (Theatre World Award), The Cool World, Othello, Paul Robeson, Les Blancs, The Great White Hope (Tony Award, 1969), The Iceman Cometh, Of Mice and Men, A Lesson from Aloes, Master Harold ... and the Boys, Fences (Tony Award, 1986).

PICTURES: Dr. Strangelove, or: How I Learned to Stop Worrying and Love the Bomb (debut, 1964), The Comedians, King: A Filmed Record ... Montgomery to Memphis, End of the Road, The Great White Hope (Acad. Award nom.), Malcolm X (narrator), The Man, Claudine, Deadly Hero, Swashbuckler, The Bingo Long Travelling All-Stars and Motor Kings, The River Niger, The Greatest, Star Wars (voice), Exorcist II: The Heretic, The Last Remake of Beau Geste, A Piece of the Action, The Bushido Blade, The Empire Strikes Back (voice), Conan the Barbarian, Blood Tide (The Red Tide), Return of the Jedi (voice), City Limits, My Little Girl, Soul Man, Allan Quartermain and the Lost City of Gold, Gardens of Stone, Matewan, Pinocchio and the Emperor of the Night (voice), Coming to America, Three Fugitives, Field of Dreams, Best of the Best, The Hunt for Red October, Grim Prairie Tales, The Ambulance, True Identity, Convicts, Patriot Games, Sneakers, Sommersby, The Sandlot, The Meteor Man, Naked Gun 33 1/3: The Final Insult, Clean Slate, The Lion King (voice), Clear and Present Danger, Jefferson in Paris, Judge Dredd (voice), Cry the Beloved Country, Lone Star, A Family Thing.
TELEVISION: Series: As the World Turns, The Guiding Light, Paris, Me and Mom, Gabriel's Fire (Emmy Award, 1991), Pros & Cons, Under One Roof. Movies: The UFO Incident, Jesus of Nazareth, The Greatest Thing That Almost Happened, Guyana Tragedy—The Story of Jim Jones, Golden Moment: An Olympic Love Story, Philby, Burgess and MacLean, The Atlanta Child Murders, The Vegas Strip War, By Dawn's Early Light, Heat Wave (Emmy Award, 1991), Last Flight Out, The Last Elephant, Percy & Thunder, The Vernon Johns Story, Confessions: Two Faces of Evil. Mini-Series: Roots: The Next Generations. Specials: King Lear, Soldier Boy, Mathnet, Bailey's Bridge, Third and Oak: The Pool Hall, Teach 109, Hallelujah. Host: Black Omnibus, Vegetable Soup, Summer Show, Long Ago and Far Away.

JONES, JEFFREY
Actor. b. Buffalo, NY, Sept. 28, 1947. e. Lawrence U., Wisconsin. While pre-med student, performed in 1967 prod. of Hobson's Choice and was invited by Sir Tyrone Guthrie to join Guthrie Theatre in Minneapolis. After short time in South America, studied at London Acad. of Music and Dramatic Arts before joining Stratford Theater in Ontario. 1973-74 worked with Vancouver touring children's theater co. Playhouse Holiday. Moved to N.Y. where performed on stage.
THEATER: The Elephant Man (B'way debut), Trelawney of the Wells, Secret Service, Boy Meets Girl, Cloud Nine, Comedy of Errors, The Tempest, The Death of Von Richtoven, London Suite.
PICTURES: The Revolutionary, The Soldier, Easy Money, Amadeus, Transylvania 6-5000, Ferris Bueller's Day Off, Howard the Duck, The Hanoi Hilton, Beetlejuice, Without a Clue, Who Is Harry Crumb?, Valmont, The Hunt for Red October, Over Her Dead Body, Mom and Dad Save the World, Stay Tuned, Out on a Limb, Heaven and Earth (unbilled), Ed Wood, Houseguest, The Pest.
TELEVISION: Mini-Series: George Washington: The Forging of a Nation, Fresno. Movies: Kenny Rogers as The Gambler III—The Legend Continues, The Avenging Angel. Guest: Amazing Stories, Twilight Zone, Remington Steele. Series: The People Next Door.

JONES, JENNIFER
Actress. r.n. Phyllis Isley. b. Tulsa, OK, Mar. 2, 1919. e. Northwestern U., American Acad. of Dramatic Arts. Daughter of Phil R., Flora Mae (Suber) Isley, exhib. m. industrialist Norton Simon. Son is actor Robert Walker Jr. Toured with parents stock company as child; in summer stock in East; little theat. East & West. Began screen career as Phyllis Isley. Pres., Norton Simon Museum.
PICTURES: Dick Tracy's G-Men (debut, 1939), The New Frontier, The Song of Bernadette (Academy Award, 1943; first film billed as Jennifer Jones), Since You Went Away, Love Letters, Cluny Brown, Duel in the Sun, Portrait of Jennie, We Were Strangers, Madame Bovary, Carrie, Wild Heart (Gone to Earth), Ruby Gentry, Indiscretion of an American Wife (Terminal Station), Beat the Devil, Love Is a Many-Splendored Thing, Good Morning Miss Dove, The Man in the Gray Flannel Suit, The Barretts of Wimpole Street, A Farewell to Arms, Tender Is the Night, The Idol, Angel Angel Down We Go (Cult of the Damned), The Towering Inferno.

JONES, KATHY
Executive. b. Aug. 27, 1949. Began career as acct. exec. for m.p. clients, Stan Levinson assoc., Dallas. Joined Paramount Pictures in 1977 as sr. publicist in field marketing then exec. dir., field mktg. Left to join Time-Life Films as v.p., domestic mktg., for m.p. div. Returned to Paramount 1981 as v.p., domestic pub. & promo. 1984, appt. sr. v.p., domestic pub. & promo. for Motion Picture Group, Paramount. Formed m.p. consultancy with Buffy Shutt, 1987. 1989, appt. exec. v.p., marketing, Columbia Pictures. 1991, appt. exec. v.p. marketing, TriStar Pictures.

JONES, QUINCY
Producer, Composer, Arranger, Recording Artist. b. Chicago, IL, March 14, 1933. e. Seattle U., Berklee Sch. Music, Boston Conservatory. Trumpeter and arranger for Lionel Hampton's orch. 1950-53, played with Dizzy Gillespie, Count Basie and arranged for orchs., singers-Frank Sinatra, Sarah Vaughn, Peggy Lee, Dinah Washington and led own orch. for European tours, and recordings. Prod. recordings for Michael Jackson, Tevin Campbell, Barbra Streisand, Donna Summer. Music dir. and v.p., Mercury Records 1961-64 before scoring films. Prod. & arranged We Are the World recording. Owns own Qwest Records record company. Received Jean Hersholt Humanitarian Award, 1995.
PICTURES: The Pawnbroker, Mirage, The Slender Thread, Made in Paris, Walk Don't Run, Banning, The Deadly Affair, In the Heat of the Night, In Cold Blood (Acad. Award nom.), Enter Laughing, A Dandy in Aspic, For Love of Ivy, The Hell With Heroes, The Split, Up Your Teddy Bear, Jocelyn, McKenna's Gold, The Italian Job, Bob & Carol & Ted & Alice, The Lost Man, Cactus Flower, John and Mary, The Last of the Mobile Hotshots, The Out-of-Towners, They Call Me Mister Tibbs, Brother John, $ (Dollars), The Anderson Tapes, Yao of the Jungle, The Hot Rock, The New Centurions, Come Back Charleston Blue, The Getaway, The Wiz (also cameo), The Color Purple (also co-prod.; Acad. Award nom.), Listen Up.
TELEVISION: Mini-Series: Roots (Emmy, 1977). Special: An American Reunion (exec. prod.). Series: Fresh Prince of Bel Air.

JONES, SAM J.
Actor. b. Chicago, IL, Aug. 12, 1954.
PICTURES: "10," Flash Gordon, My Chauffeur, Silent Assassins, White Fire, One Man Force, Double Trouble, Driving Force, From the Edge, Vegas Vice.
TELEVISION: Series: Code Red, The Highwayman. Movies: The Incredible Journey of Dr. Meg Laurel, Stunts Unlimited, Code Red (pilot), No Man's Land.

JONES, SHIRLEY
Actress. b. Smithton, PA, March 31, 1934. m. actor-prod. Marty Ingels. Mother of actors Shaun and Patrick Cassidy. Former Miss Pittsburgh. Natl. chair, Leukemia Foundation. Book: Shirley & Marty: An Unlikely Love Story (Wm. Morrow, 1990). Received hom. Doctor of Humane Letters degree from Point Park Col. 1991.
THEATER: Appeared with Pittsburgh Civic Light Opera in Lady in the Dark, Call Me Madam. B'way: South Pacific, Me and Juliet, Maggie Flynn.
PICTURES: Oklahoma! (debut, 1955), Carousel, April Love, Never Steal Anything Small, Bobbikins, Elmer Gantry (Academy Award, best supporting actress, 1960), Pepe, Two Rode Together, The Music Man, The Courtship of Eddie's Father, A Ticklish Affair, Dark Purpose, Bedtime Story, Fluffy, The Secret of My Success, The Happy Ending, The Cheyenne Social Club, Beyond the Poseidon Adventure, Tank, There Were Times Dear.
TELEVISION: Movies: Silent Night Lonely Night, But I Don't Want to Get Married, The Girls of Huntington House, The Family Nobody Wanted, Winner Take All, The Lives of Jenny Dolan, Yesterday's Child, Evening in Byzantium, Who'll Save Our Children, A Last Cry For Help, Children of An Lac, Intimates: A Love Story, Widow. Series: The Partridge Family, Shirley, The Slap Maxwell Story. Guest: McMillan, The Love Boat, Hotel, Murder She Wrote, Empty Nest.

JONES, TERRY
Writer, Actor, Director. b. Colwyn Bay, North Wales, Feb. 1, 1942. Worked with various rep. groups before joining BBC script dept. Was member of Monty Python's Flying Circus.
PICTURES: Actor: And Now for Something Completely Different (also co-s.p.), Monty Python and the Holy Grail (also co-dir., co-s.p.), Monty Python's Life of Brian (also dir., co-s.p.), Monty Python's The Meaning of Life (also co-s.p., dir., music), Labyrinth (s.p. only), Personal Services (dir. only), Erik the Viking (also dir., s.p.).
TELEVISION: Late Night Lineup, The Late Show, A Series of Birds, Do Not Adjust Your Set, The Complete and Utter History of Britain, Monty Python's Flying Circus, Secrets, The Crusades (also dir., writer).

JONES, TOMMY LEE
Actor. b. San Saba, TX, Sept. 15, 1946. Worked in oil fields; graduated Harvard, where earned a degree, cum laude, in English. Broadway debut in A Patriot for Me; appeared on stage in Four in a Garden, Ulysses in Nighttown, Fortune and Men's Eyes.
PICTURES: Love Story (debut, 1970), Eliza's Horoscope, Jackson County Jail, Rolling Thunder, The Betsy, Eyes of Laura Mars, Coal Miner's Daughter, Back Roads, Nate and Hayes, The River Rat, Black Moon Rising, The Big Town, Stormy Monday, The Package, Firebirds, JFK (Acad. Award nom.), Under Siege, House of Cards, The Fugitive (Academy Award, best supporting actor, 1993; LA Film Critics & Golden Globe Awards), Heaven and Earth, Blown Away, The Client, Natural Born Killers, Blue Sky, Cobb, Batman Forever.

TELEVISION: *Movies*: Charlie's Angels (pilot), Smash-Up on Interstate 5, The Amazing Howard Hughes, The Executioner's Song (Emmy Award, 1983), Broken Vows, The Park is Mine, Yuri Nosenko: KGB, Gotham, Stranger on My Land, April Morning, The Good Old Boys (also dir., co-writer). *Mini-Series*: Lonesome Dove. *Specials*: The Rainmaker, Cat on a Hot Tin Roof.

JORDAN, GLENN
Director, Producer, b. San Antonio, TX, April 5, 1936. e. Harvard, B.A.; Yale Drama Sch. Directed plays off-B'way. and on tour.
PICTURES: *Director*: Only When I Laugh, The Buddy System, Mass Appeal.
TELEVISION: *Specials*: Hogan's Goat, Paradise Lost, Benjamin Franklin (prod.; Emmy Award), Eccentricities of a Nightingale, The Oath, The Court Martial of Gen. George Armstrong Custer. *Movies*: Frankenstein, The Picture of Dorian Gray, Shell Game, One of My Wives is Missing, Delta County U.S.A., In the Matter of Karen Ann Quinlan, Sunshine Christmas, Les Miserables, Son Rise: A Miracle of Love, The Family Man, The Women's Room (also prod.), The Princess and the Cabbie, Lois Gibbs and the Love Canal, Heartsounds, Dress Grey, Promise (also prod.; 2 Emmy Awards), Something in Common (also prod.), Echoes in the Darkness (also prod.), Jesse (also prod.), Home Fires Burning (also prod.), Challenger (also prod.), Sarah: Plain and Tall (also prod.), Aftermath: A Test of Love (also prod.), The Boys (also prod.), O Pioneers! (also prod.), Barbarians at the Gate (Emmy Award; also co-exec. prod.), To Dance With the White Dog (also prod.), Jane's House (also prod.), My Brother's Keeper (also prod.), A Streetcar Named Desire (also prod.), Jake's Women (also prod.), After Jimmy (also prod.).

JORDAN, NEIL
Director, Writer. b. Sligo, Ireland, Feb. 25, 1950. e. University Coll, Dublin, B.A., 1972. Novels: The Past, Night in Tunisia, Dream of a Beast.
PICTURES: Traveller (s.p.), The Courier (co-exec. prod.). *Dir.-Writer*: Angel, The Company of Wolves, Mona Lisa (LA Film Critics Award for s.p., 1986), High Spirits, We're No Angels (dir. only), The Miracle, The Crying Game (Academy Award, WGA & NY Film Critics Awards for s.p., 1992), Interview With the Vampire, Michael Collins.
TELEVISION: Mr. Solomon Wept (BBC), RTE (Ireland), Seduction, Tree, Miracles and Miss Langan.

JOSEPHSON, BARRY
Executive. Pres., of production, Sony Pictures Entertainment, Inc.

JOSEPHSON, ERLAND
Actor, Director, Writer. b. Stockholm, Sweden, June 15, 1923. Acted in over 100 plays in Sweden. Joined Sweden's Royal Dramatic Theatre in 1956 replacing Ingmar Bergman as head of the theater, 1966-76. Closely associated with Bergman, with whom he staged plays in his late teens. Co-authored s.p. The Pleasure Garden and Now About These Women. Also has pub. poetry, six novels, and scripts for stage, screen and radio. American stage debut: The Cherry Orchard, 1988.
PICTURES: It Rains on Our Love, To Joy, Brink of Life, The Magician, Hour of the Wolf, The Passion of Anna, Cries and Whispers, Scenes from a Marriage, Face to Face, Beyond Good and Evil, I'm Afraid, Autumn Sonata, To Forget Venice, One and One (also dir.), The Marmalade Revolution (also dir., s.p.), Montenegro, Sezona Mira u Parizu, Fanny and Alexander, Bella Donna, Nostalgia, House of the Yellow Carpet, After the Rehearsal, Angela's War, Behind the Shutters, A Case of Irresponsibility, Dirty Story, Amarosa, The Flying Devils, Garibaldi, The General, The Last Mazurka, The Sacrifice, Saving Grace, Unbearable Lightness of Being, Hanussen, Meeting Venus, The Ox, Sofie, Ulysses' Gaze.

JOSEPHSON, MARVIN
Executive. b. Atlantic City, NJ, March 6, 1927. e. Cornell U., B.A., 1949; L.L.B. NYU, 1952. Lawyer at CBS Television 1952-55; founded company which today is ICM Holdings Inc. in 1955. ICM Holdings Inc. is the parent company of Intl. Creative Management Inc. and ICM Artists Ltd.

JOSIAH, JR., WALTER J.
Executive. b. New York, NY, Nov. 9, 1933. e. Fordham U., B.S., 1955: Harvard Law School, LL.B., 1962. U.S. Air Force, 1955-58, First Lt. and Pilot. Associate, Simpson Thacher & Bartlett, 1962-67. Legal staff, Paramount Pictures, 1967-69. Asst. resident counsel, 1969; chief resident counsel, 1970 and v.p. & chief resident counsel, 1971-82. ex.-v.p. & general counsel, Motion Picture Association of America, Inc., 1983-93. Professional Associations: Chmn., Committee 307, Authors Rights, 1981-82, Patent, Trademark & Copyright Law Section of the American Bar Assn.; Association of the Bar of the City of NY (Committee on Copyright and Literary Property, 1976-

79, 1982-85, chmn. 1986-89): Copyright Society of the U.S.A.—Member of the Board of Trustees commencing 1981; v.p., from 1988; pres. beginning 1990; member, Motion Picture Academy of Arts and Sciences; Copyright Office Advisory Committee, 1981-82; National Sculpture Society advisor to the president; Advisory Board, Publication: Communications and the Law; Member, President's Club Executive Committee and Annual Fund Council, Fordham U.

JOURDAN, LOUIS
Actor, r.n. Louis Gendre. b. Marseille, France, June 19, 1921. Stage actor prior to m.p. On B'way in The Immoralist, Tonight in Samarkand, On a Clear Day You Can See Forever (Boston, previews), 13 Rue de l'Amour.
PICTURES: Le Corsaire (debut, 1940), Her First Affair, La Boheme, L'Arlesienne, La Belle, Adventure, Felicie Nanteuil, The Paradine Case, Letter from an Unknown Woman, No Minor Vices, Madame Bovary, Bird of Paradise, Anne of the Indies, The Happy Time, Decameron Nights, Three Coins in the Fountain, The Swan, Julie, The Bride is Much Too Beautiful, Dangerous Exile, Gigi, The Best of Everything, Can-Can, Leviathan, Streets of Montmartre, Story of the Count of Monte Cristo, Mathias Sandorf, The VIPs, Made in Paris, To Commit a Murder, A Flea in Her Ear, Young Rebel (Cervantes), The Silver Bears, Double Deal, Swamp Thing, Octopussy, The Return of Swamp Thing, Counterforce, Year of the Comet.
TELEVISION: *Series*: Paris Precinct, Romance Theatre (host). *Mini-Series*: The French Atlantic Affair, Dracula. *Movies*: Run a Crooked Mile, Fear No Evil, Ritual of Evil, The Great American Beauty Contest, The Count of Monte Cristo, The Man in the Iron Mask, The First Olympics-Athens, Beverly Hills Madam. *Guest*: Ford Theatre, The FBI, Name of the Game, Charlie's Angels.

JOY, ROBERT
Actor. b. Montreal, Canada, Aug. 17, 1951. e. Memorial Univ. of Newfoundland; Rhodes Scholar. Acted in regional and off-Broadway theatre. Off-B'way debut The Diary of Anne Frank (1978). Has composed music for stage, radio and film.
THEATER: NY Shakespeare Fest. (Found a Peanut, Lenny and the Heartbreakers, The Death of von Richtofen), Life and Limb, Fables for Friends, Welcome to the Moon, What I Did Last Summer, Lydie Breeze, Romeo and Juliet (La Jolla Playhouse; Drama-Logue Award), Hay Fever (B'way debut), Big River (premiere), The Nerd, Hyde in Hollywood, The Taming of the Shrew, Shimada, Goodnight Desdemona (Good Morning Juliet), Abe Lincoln in Illinois.
PICTURES: Atlantic City, Ragtime, Ticket to Heaven, Threshold, Terminal Choice, Amityville 3-D, Desperately Seeking Susan, Joshua Then and Now, Adventure of Faustus Bidgood (also co-prod. music), Radio Days, Big Shots, The Suicide Club, She's Back!, Millenium, Longtime Companion, Shadows and Fog, The Dark Half, Death Wish 5: The Face of Death, I'll Do Anything, Henry & Verlin, Waterworld, A Modern Affair, Pharoah's Army, Harriet the Spy.
TELEVISION: *Series*: One Life to Live. *Guest*: The Equalizer, Moonlighting, Law and Order, The Marshal, New York Undercover, Wings. *Specials*: The Prodigious Hickey, The Return of Hickey, The Beginning of the Firm, Hyde in Hollywood. *Movies*: Escape from Iran: The Canadian Caper, Gregory K, Woman on the Run: The Lawrencia Bembenek Story.

JURADO, KATY
Actress. r.n. Maria Christina Jurado Garcia. b. Guadalajara, Mexico, Jan. 16, 1927. Appeared in numerous Mexican films beginning in 1943. Also m.p. columnist for Mexican publications.
PICTURES: No Maturas (debut, 1943), El Museo del Crimen, Rosa del Caribe, The Bullfighter and the Lady (U.S. debut, 1951), High Noon, San Antone, Arrowhead, Broken Lance (Acad. Award nom.), The Sword of Granada, The Racers, Trial, Trapeze, Man from Del Rio, Dragoon Wells Massacre, The Badlanders, One Eyed Jacks, Barabbas, Seduction of the South, Target for Killing, Smoky, A Covenant With Death, Stay Away Joe, Bridge in the Jungle, Pat Garrett and Billy the Kid, Once Upon a Scoundrel, The Children of Sanchez, Reasons of State, Under the Volcano.
TELEVISION: *Movies*: Any Second Now, A Little Game, Evita Peron, Lady Blue. *Series*: A.K.A. Pablo.

K

KAGAN, JEREMY
Director, Writer. b. Mt. Vernon, NY, Dec. 14, 1945. e. Harvard; NYU, MFA; student Amer. Film Inst. 1971. Film animator, 1968; multi-media show designer White House Conf. on Youth and Ed. Previously credited as Jeremy Paul Kagan.
PICTURES: Scott Joplin, Heroes, The Big Fix, The Chosen (Montreal World Film Fest. Prize, 1981), The Sting II, The Journey of Natty Gann (Gold Prize, Moscow Film Fest., 1987), Big Man on Campus, By the Sword.

TELEVISION: *Series*: Columbo, The Bold Ones, Chicago Hope (Emmy Award, 1996). *Movies*: Unwed Father, Judge Dee and the Monastery Murders, Katherine (also writer), Courage, Roswell (also co-prod., co-story). *Specials*: My Dad Lives in a Downtown Hotel, Conspiracy: The Trial of the Chicago 8 (also writer; ACE Award, 1988).

KAHN, MADELINE
Actress, Singer. b. Boston, MA., Sept. 29. e. Hofstra U. Broadway bow in New Faces of '68. Trained as opera singer and appeared in La Boheme, Showboat, Two by Two, Candide. Appeared in short film The Dove.
THEATER: Promenade, Two by Two, In the Boom Boom Room, On the Twentieth Century, Born Yesterday, The Sisters Rosensweig (Tony Award, 1993).
PICTURES: What's Up Doc? (debut, 1972), Paper Moon (Acad. Award nom.), From the Mixed-Up Files of Mrs. Basil E. Frankweiler (The Hideaways), Blazing Saddles (Acad. Award nom.), Young Frankenstein, At Long Last Love, The Adventures of Sherlock Holmes' Smarter Brother, Won Ton Ton the Dog Who Saved Hollywood, High Anxiety, The Cheap Detective, The Muppet Movie, Simon, Happy Birthday Gemini, Wholly Moses, First Family, History of the World—Part 1, Yellowbeard, Slapstick of Another Kind, City Heat, Clue, My Little Pony (voice), An American Tail (voice), Betsy's Wedding, Mixed Nuts, Nixon.
TELEVISION: *Series*: Comedy Tonight, Oh Madeline!, Mr. President, New York News. *Specials*: Harvey, The Perfect Guy (afterschool special), Celebrating Gershwin: The Jazz Age, Irving Berlin Gala, Stephen Sondheim Gala. *Movie*: For Richer For Poorer.

KAHN, MILTON
Publicist. b. Brooklyn, NY, May 3, 1934. e. Syracuse U., Ohio U., B.S.J. 1957. Formed Milton Kahn Associates, Inc. in 1958. Represented: Gregory Peck, Joan Crawford, Steve Allen, Glenn Ford, Lee Grant, Herb Alpert, Roger Corman, Robert Aldrich, Arthur Hiller, Chuck Norris, Bob Cousy, Adam Oates, Michael Landon, Dean Hargrove, Bill Conti, etc. and New World Pictures (1970-83), Avco-Embassy, Vista Films, Roger Corman's Concorde (1983-), Electric Shadow Prods.

KAHN, RICHARD
Executive. b. New Rochelle, NY, Aug. 19, 1929. e. Wharton Sch. of Finance and Commerce, U. of Pennsylvania, B.S., 1951; U.S. Navy, 3 yrs.; joined Buchanan & Co., 1954; ent. m.p. ind. as pressbook writer, Columbia Pictures, 1955; exploitation mgr., 1958; natl. coord. adv. and pub., 1963; natl. dir. of adv., pub. and exploitation, 1968; v.p., 1969; 1974 v.p. in chg. of special marketing projects; 1975 moved to MGM as v.p. in chg. of worldwide advertising, publicity and exploitation; 1978, named sr. v.p. in chg. worldwide mktg. & pres., MGM Intl. 1980, elected bd. of govs., Academy of M.P. Arts & Sciences. 1982, named exec. v.p. of adv., pub., promo. for MGM/UA; 1983, formed the Richard Kahn Co., dist. & mktg. consultancy, 1984-88. Faculty mem. Peter Stark m.p. producing prog., USC Sch. of Cinema & TV. Exec. chmn., Film Inf. Council. 1982-95 elected secretary Acad. of Motion Picture Arts & Sciences; elected v.p. 1983-87; elected pres. 1988.

KALB, MARVIN
TV news reporter. e. City Coll. of NY; Harvard, M.A., 1953, Russian Language Sch., Middlebury Coll. Worked for U.S. State Dept., American Embassy, Moscow; CBS News, 1957; writer, reporter-researcher. Where We Stand: reporter-assignment editor; Moscow Bureau Chief, 1960-63; first diplomatic corresp., Washington Bureau, 1963. Chief diplomatic corresp. CBS News and NBC News, moderator Meet the Press; Teacher and lecturer; first Murr. Joan Shorenstein Barone Center on the Press, Politics and Public Policy at John F. Kennedy Sch. of Govt. of Harvard U., since 1987. Host of PBS series, Candidates '88. Author: Eastern Exposure, Kissinger, Dragon in the Kremlin, Roots of Involvement, The U.S. in Asia 1784-1971, Candidates '88 (with Hendrik Hertzberg).

KALISH, EDDIE
Executive. b. New York, NY, Apr. 27, 1939. Reporter/reviewer, Variety, 1959-64; sr. publicist, Paramount Pictures, 1964-65; adv./pub./promo dir., Ken Greengras Personal Management, 1965-66; pub. dir., Harold Rand & Co., 1966-67; indept. publicist overseas, 1967-75; rejoined Paramount Pictures in 1975 as dir. of intl. mktg.; later named v.p.; 1978, named v.p., worldwide pub. & promo. 1979 appt. sr. v.p., worldwide mktg. 1980 joined United Artists as v.p. domestic mktg.; sr. v.p., adv., pub., promo, for MGM/UA 1981-82; became sr. v.p., worldwide mkt., PSO, 1982-1986. Now pres., Kalish/Davidson Marketing, Inc.

KAMBER, BERNARD M.
Executive. e. U. of Pennsylvania. New England exploitation rep. U.A. 1940; Army service 1941-43; dir. special events dept. U.A., 1943; asst. to Gradwell L. Sears, nat'l distrib. chmn. 6th War Loan Drive; dir. pub. 7th War Loan Drive, 1943-47; dir. pub. & prom. Eagle Lion Classics, 1951; org. Kamber Org.,

pub. rel. rep. for ind. prod. v.p. sales, adv. pub. Ivan Tors Prod. Greene-Rouse Prods. 1953; exec. asst. Hecht-Hill-Lancaster, chg. of N.Y. off., 1957; v.p. Hecht-Hill-Lancaster Companies, 1958; formed Cinex Distr. Corp., 1962; Pres. Cinex and Posfilm, Inc.; 1967, v.p. in chg. sls. Du Art Film Lab. Inc; 1975 joined Technicolor, Inc.

KAMEY, PAUL
b. New York, NY, Aug. 25, 1912. Worked on newspapers including NY Journal American. Ent. m.p. industry 1938; worked for MGM and 20th Century Fox; during war was writer, Office of War information; joined Universal, 1949; eastern pub. mgr., Universal Pictures. 1968. Freelance publicist.

KANE, CAROL
Actress. b. Cleveland, OH, June 18, 1952. e. Professional Children's Sch., NY. Began professional acting career at age 14, touring, then on B'way in The Prime of Miss Jean Brodie.
THEATER: The Tempest, The Effect of Gamma Rays on Man-in-the-Moon Marigolds, Are You Now or Have You Ever Been? Arturo Ui, The Enchanted, The Tempest, Macbeth, Tales of the Vienna Woods, Frankie and Johnny in the Claire de Lune, Control Freaks.
PICTURES: Carnal Knowledge (debut, 1971), Desperate Characters, Wedding in White, The Last Detail, Dog Day Afternoon, Hester Street, Harry and Walter Go to New York, Annie Hall, Valentino, The World's Greatest Lover, The Mafu Cage, The Muppet Movie, When a Stranger Calls, Pandemonium, Norman Loves Rose, Over the Brooklyn Bridge, Racing With the Moon, The Secret Diary of Sigmund Freud, Transylvania 6-5000, Jumpin' Jack Flash, Ishtar, The Princess Bride, Sticky Fingers, License to Drive, Scrooged, Flashback, Joe Vs. the Volcano, My Blue Heaven, The Lemon Sisters, Ted and Venus, In the Soup, Addams Family Values, Even Cowgirls Get the Blues, Big Bully, The Pallbearer, Sunset Park.
TELEVISION: *Series*: Taxi (2 Emmy Awards: 1982, 1983), All Is Forgiven, American Dreamer. *Movies*: An Invasion of Privacy, Burning Rage, Drop Out Mother, Dad the Angel and Me, Freaky Friday. *Specials*: Faerie Tale Theatre, Paul Reiser: Out on a Whim, Tales From the Crypt (Judy, You're Not Yourself Today).

KANE, JOHN
Publicity Manager. b. New York, NY. e. Rutgers, B.A.; NYU, M.A. Publicist, Solters & Roskin, 1976-80. Unit publicist: Fame, Tender Mercies, Prince of the City, 1980-82. 1982-90, Home Box Office, unit publicist, manager. 1991, unit publ. for Ricochet, Arizona Dream.

KANE, STANLEY D.
Judge. b. Minneapolis, MN, Dec. 21, 1907. e. U of MN, B.A. (magna cum laude), 1930;, M.A., 1931; MN Coll. of Law, LL.B., 1940. Instructor, U. of Minnesota, 1930-33. Exec. sec. Allied Theatre Owners of the Northwest, 1933-37; city attorney, 1940-60; exec. v.p. & gen. counsel, North Central Allied Independent Theatre Owners, 1946-63; dist. court judge, then sr. judge, Hennepin County, 1963-90.

KANER, MARK
Executive. Pres. of International Television, Fox, Inc.

KANEW, JEFF
Director.
PICTURES: Black Rodeo (also prod., edit.), Natural Enemies (also s.p., edit.), Eddie Macon's Run (also s.p., edit.), Revenge of the Nerds, Gotcha!, Tough Guys, Troop Beverly Hills, V. I. Warshawski.
TELEVISION: Alfred Hitchcock Presents (1985).

KANIN, FAY
Writer. b. New York, NY, May 9. e. Elmira Coll., U. of Southern California, 1937. m. Michael Kanin, writer. Contrib. fiction to mags., Writers Guild of Amer. pres. screen branch, 1971-73; Acad. Motion Picture Arts & Sciences 1983-88. also bd. mem. of latter. Co-chair, National Center for Film and Video Preservation; Bd. of trustees, Amer. Film Institute; Chair, Natl. Film Preservation Board.
THEATER: Goodbye My Fancy, His and Hers, Rashomon, The High Life, Grind (1985).
PICTURES: My Pal Gus, Rhapsody, The Opposite Sex, Teacher's Pet, Swordsman of Siena, The Right Approach.
TELEVISION: Heat of Anger, Tell Me Where It Hurts (Emmy Award, 1974), Hustling (also co-prod.), Friendly Fire (also co-prod., Emmy Award, San Francisco Film Fest. Award, Peabody Award), Heartsounds (Peabody Award; also co-prod.).

KANIN, GARSON
Director, Writer. b. Rochester, NY, Nov. 24, 1912. e. American Acad. of Dramatic Arts. Was married to actress Ruth Gordon (d: 8/28/85). m. actress Marian Seldes, 1990. Started as musician, actor, appearing in Spring Song, Little Ol' Boy, and others.

Prod. assist. to George Abbott on plays Three Men on a Horse, Brother Rat, Room Service. 1937 joined Samuel Goldwyn's prod. staff; 1938, joined RKO, as prod.-dir. 1942, prod. for U.S. Office of Emergency Management. Joined armed forces, WWII. Documentary director: Fellow Americans, Ring of Steel, Night Shift, Final Glory (co-dir. with Carol Reed; Academy Award, 1945), Salute to France (co-dir. with Jean Renoir). 1989, received Writers Guild Valentine Davies Award with brother Michael. Pres., Authors League of America.
AUTHOR: Remembering Mr. Maugham, Cast of Characters, Tracy and Hepburn, Hollywood, Blow Up a Storm, The Rat Race, A Thousand Summers, One Hell of an Actor, It Takes a Long Time to Become Young, Moviola, Smash, Together Again!, Cordelia.
THEATRE: *Writer/Dir.*: Born Yesterday, The Smile of the World, The Rat Race, The Live Wire, A Gift of Time, Do Re Mi, Come on Strong, Small War on Murray Hill, The Amazing Adele, The Good Soup, Dreyfus in Rehearsal, Happy Ending, Peccadillo. *Dir.*: Hitch Your Wagon, Too Many Heroes, The Rugged Path, Years Ago, How I Wonder, The Leading Lady, The Diary of Anne Frank, Into Thin Air, Hole in the Head, Sunday in New York, Funny Girl, I Was Dancing, A Very Rich Woman, We Have Always Lived in the Castle, Idiot's Delight, Ho! Ho! Ho!.
PICTURES: *Dir.*: A Man to Remember, Next Time I Marry, The Great Man Votes, Bachelor Mother, Tom Dick & Harry, My Favorite Wife, They Knew What They Wanted. *Dir./Writer*: Where It's At, Some Kind of a Nut. *Writer*: From This Day Forward, A Double Life, Adam's Rib, The Marrying Kind, Pat and Mike, It Should Happen To You, The Rat Race.
TELEVISION: *Movie*: Hardhat and Legs (co-writer). *Series*: Mr. Broadway.

KANTER, HAL
Writer, Director, Producer. b. Savannah, GA, Dec. 18, 1918. On B'way contributor to Hellzapoppin. Then began writing radio dramas before mil. service, WW II. Served as combat corresp. Armed Forces Radio; writer, Paramount, 1951-54; dir., RKO, 1956; writer, prod. for Lucille Ball Prods., 1979-80. Savannah Prods., 1982-86. Received Writers Guild Paddy Chayefsky Laurel Award, 1989. Writer (radio): Danny Kaye Show, Amos 'n Andy, Bing Crosby Show, Jack Paar, Beulah. Winner 3 Emmy Awards for writing, 1954, 1991, 1992. Member: bd. of dir., WGAW; bd. of govs. AMPAS; v.p. Writers Guild Foundation.
PICTURES: *Writer*: My Favorite Spy, Off Limits, Road to Bali, Casanova's Big Night, About Mrs. Leslie, Money from Home, Artists and Models, The Rose Tattoo, I Married a Woman (dir. only), Loving You (also dir.), Mardi Gras, Once Upon a Horse (also dir., prod.), Blue Hawaii, Pocketful of Miracles, Bachelor in Paradise, Move Over Darling, Dear Brigitte.
TELEVISION: *Writer*: Ed Wynn Show, George Gobel Show (also creator, prod.), Kraft Music Hall (also dir., prod.; 1958-59), Chrysler Theatre (also prod., dir.; 1966-67), Julia (also dir., prod., creator), Jimmy Stewart Show (also prod., dir., creator), All In The Family (exec. prod.: 1975-76), Chico & The Man (spv. prod., 1976-77), You Can't Take It With You. *Specials (writer)*: AFI Life Achievement Awards for Henry Fonda & Alfred Hitchcock, 26 Annual Academy Awards.

KANTER, JAY
Executive. b. Chicago, IL, Dec. 12, 1926. Entered industry with MCA, Inc., where was v.p. Left after more than 20 yrs. to become indep. prod., then pres. of First Artists Production Co., Ltd. 1975 joined 20th-Fox as v.p. prod.; 1976, named sr. v.p., worldwide prod. Named v.p., The Ladd Co., 1979. Joined MGM/UA Entertainment Co. as pres., worldwide prod., Motion Picture Division, 1984. 1985, named pres., worldwide prod., UA Corp.; then pres., production MGM Pictures Inc.; 1989, named chmn. of prod. of Pathe Entertainment Co. 1991, became COO & chmn. of prod., MGM-Pathe Commun. Co. (MGM Communi-cations, 1992). 1994-95, MGM consultant. March, 1995, independent prod.

KANTOR, IGO
Producer, Film Editor. b. Vienna, Austria, Aug. 18, 1930. e. UCLA, A.A. 1950; B.S., 1952; M.S., 1954. Foreign corres., Portugal magazine, FLAMA, 1949-57; music supvr., Screen Gems, Columbia 1954-63; post-prod. supvr., film ed., features, TV; assoc. prod., 1963-64; prod., exec., International Entertainment Corp., 1965. pres., Synchrofilm, Inc., post-production co. and Duque Films, Inc., production co. 1968-74. 1975-present, produced and edited films. 1982, pres., Laurelwood Prods; 1988, pres. Major Arts Corp.
PICTURES: *Assoc. Producer*: Bye Bye Birdie, Under the Yum Yum Tree, Gidget Goes to Rome, A House Is Not a Home, Pattern for Murder, Willy. Producer: Assault on Agathon (also edit.), FTA, Dixie Dynamite (assoc. prod., edit.), Kingdom of the Spiders (also edit., music spvr.), The Dark (assoc. prod.), Good Luck Miss Wyckoff (prod. spvr.), Hardly Working, Kill and Kill Again, Mutant, Shaker Run, Act of Piracy, They Call Me Bruce Levy.

TELEVISION: From Hawaii with Love (1984), The Grand Tour, It's a Wonderful World (prod.-dir.), Nosotros Golden Eagle Awards (prod.), United We Stand (pre-Olympic special), Legends of the West With Jack Palance, Mom U.S.A., A Desperate Affair, Holiday Classics Cartoons (special).

KAPLAN, GABRIEL
Actor, Comedian. b. Brooklyn, NY, March 31, 1945. After high school worked as bellboy at Lakewood, NJ hotel, spending free time studying comedians doing routines. Put together a comedy act, landing engagements in small clubs and coffee houses all over U.S. Made several appearances on Tonight Show, Merv Griffin Show, Mike Douglas Show, etc. Has played Las Vegas clubs.
PICTURES: Fast Break, Tulips, Nobody's Perfekt.
TELEVISION: *Series*: Welcome Back Kotter, Gabriel Kaplan Presents the Future Stars, Lewis and Clark. *Movie*: Love Boat (pilot).

KAPLAN, JONATHAN
Director, Writer. b. Paris, Nov. 25, 1947. Son of composer Sol Kaplan. e. U. of Chicago, B.A.; NYU, M.F.A. Made short film Stanley Stanley. Member of tech. staff Fillmore East, NY 1969-71. New World Pictures' Roger Corman post-grad. sch. of filmmaking, Hollywood, 1971-73. As actor on B'way in Dark at the Top of the Stairs. Appeared in films: Cannonball, Hollywood Boulevard.
PICTURES: *Director*: Night Call Nurses, Student Teachers, The Slams, Truck Turner, White Line Fever (also co-s.p.), Mr. Billion, Over the Edge, Heart Like a Wheel, Project X, The Accused, Immediate Family, Unlawful Entry, Love Field, Bad Girls.
TELEVISION: *Movies*: The 11th Victim, The Hustler of Muscle Beach, The Gentleman Bandit, Girls of the White Orchid.

KAPOOR, SHASHI
Actor. b. Calcutta, India, Mar. 18, 1938. Son of late Prithviraj Kapoor, Indian film and stage actor. As child worked in Prithvi Theatre and in brother, Raj's films. Toured with father's co. at 18 and joined the Kendals' Shakespeareana Co. in India. Starred in over 200 Indian films as well as several Merchant-Ivory Prods.
PICTURES: Pretty Polly, Siddhartha, The Householder, Bombay Talkie, Shakespeare Wallah, Heat and Dust, USTAV (Festival of Love, also prod.), The New Delhi Times, Sammy and Rosie Get Laid, The Deceivers, Nomads, Ajuba.

KARDISH, LAURENCE
Curator, Dept. of Film, Museum of Modern Art. b. Ottawa, Ontario, Canada, Jan. 5, 1945. e. Carlton U. Ottawa, Canada, 1966, Honors B.A. in philosophy; Columbia U., Sch. of the Arts, 1968, M.F.A. in film, radio, and television. 1965-66: Canadian Film Inst., programmer for National Film Theatre, Ottawa; researched a history of Canadian filmmaking. 1965: founded first film society in Canada to exhibit Amer. avant-garde films (Carleton U. Cine Club); directed summer seminar on film, Carleton U., 1966. 1966-68: New American Cinema Group, Inc., NY, worked for the Film-Makers' Distribution Center. 1968: joined Dept. of Film, MOMA; made curator 1984. Since 1968 involved with Cineprobe prog. Since 1972 participated in selection of films for New Directors/New Films series; dir. exhibitions of surveys of national cinemas (Senegal, Scandinavia, French-speaking Canada) and retrospectives of ind. Amer. filmmakers (includ. Rudolph Burkhardt, Stan Brakhage, Shirley Clarke), The Lubitsch Touch, Columbia Pictures, Warner Bros., MGM, Universal, RKO, and directors. 1980: toured Europe with prog. of indep. Amer. films. Author: Reel Plastic Magic (1972); also essays and monographs. Dir.feature Slow Run (1968). On jury for Channel 13's Indep. Focus series and on Board of Advisors, Collective for Living Cinema, NY. 1982-82: bd. of dirs. of National Alliance of Media Arts Centers; 1987-89: on Jerome Foundation panel. 1986 on Camera d'Or jury, Cannes Film Fest.

KARLIN, FRED
Composer, Conductor. b. Chicago, IL, June 16, 1936. e. Amherst Coll., B.A. Composer and arranger for Benny Goodman. Won Academy Award for Best Song for For All We Know (from Lovers and Other Strangers) and Emmy for original music in The Autobiography of Miss Jane Pittman. 4 Acad. Award noms., 11 Emmy Award noms.; Image Award for score to Minstrel Man. Author: On the Track: A Guide to Contemporary Film Scoring (with Rayburn Wright), Listening to Movies. Creator and instructor of the ASCAP/Fred Karlin Film Scoring Workshop, since 1988.
PICTURES: Up the Down Staircase, Yours Mine and Ours, The Sterile Cuckoo (including music for song, Come Saturday Morning; Acad. Award nom.), The Stalking Moon, Westworld, Futureworld, Lovers and Other Strangers, Leadbelly, Loving Couples.
TELEVISION: The Autobiography of Miss Jane Pittman, The Awakening Land, The Plutonium Incident, Minstrel Man, Sophia Loren—Her Own Story, Green Eyes, Strangers: The

Story of a Mother and Daughter, Calamity Jane, Ike: the War Years, Inside the Third Reich, Hollywood—The Gift of Laughter, Homeward Bound, Dream West, Hostage Flight, A Place to Call Home, Robert Kennedy and His Times, Dadah is Death, Bridge to Silence, The Secret, Film Music Masters: Jerry Goldsmith (prod. and dir.), Film Music Masters: Elmer Bernstein (prod. and dir.).

KARLIN, MYRON D.
Executive. b. Revere, MA, Sept. 21, 1918. e. UCLA. Joined m.p. business in 1946 as gen. mgr. for MGM in Ecuador. Two yrs. later assigned same spot for MGM in Venezuela. 1952-53 was gen. sales mgr. for MGM in Germany, after which managing dir. in Argentina, returning to Germany as mgr. dir. in 1956. Named mgn. dir. for United Artists in Italy. 1960-68 was pres. of Brunswick Int'l., while also serving as advisor to World Health Organization and UNESCO. 1969 was European mgr. for MGM and mgn. dir. in Italy. Joined Warner Bros. Int'l. in 1970 as v.p. of European dist. 1972 appt. v.p. in chg. of int'l. operations for WB; 1977, appt. pres., WB Intl. & exec. v.p., Warner Bros., Inc; 1985, named exec. v.p., intl. affairs, WB, Inc. Now pres. & COO, Motion Picture Export Assn. July, 1994, sr. consultant, Motion Picture assoc.

KARP, ALLEN
Executive. b. Toronto, Ontario, Canada, Sept. 18, 1940. e. Univ. of Toronto, bachelor of law degree, 1964; called to Ontario bar in 1966; masters of business law degree 1975, from Osgoode Hall Law School, York Univ. Served as buiness lawyer and senior legal advisor, becoming dir. of Odeon Theatre Film circuit, 1977. 1986, named sr. exec. v.p. of Cineplex Odeon Corp. 1988, became pres. North American Theatres Division; 1989, pres. & COO; 1990, elected pres. & CEO.

KARRAS, ALEX
Actor. b. Gary, IN, July 15, 1935. e. Univ. of Iowa. As football player with Iowa State U., picked for All Amer. team. Received Outland Trophy, 1957. Former professional football player with Detroit Lions, 1958-62, and 1964-71. Sportswriter, Detroit Free Press, 1972-73. Also worked as prof. wrestler, salesman, steel worker and lecturer. m. actress Susan Clark. With her formed Georgian Bay Prods., 1979. Books: Even Big Guys Cry (with Herb Gluck, 1977), Alex Karras: My Life in Football Television and Movies (1979), Tuesday Night Football (1991).
PICTURES: Paper Lion (as himself; debut, 1968), Blazing Saddles, FM, Win Place or Steal, Jacob Two-Two Meets the Hooded Fang, When Time Ran Out, Nobody's Perfekt, Porky's, Victor/Victoria, Against All Odds.
TELEVISION: *Commentator and host:* Monday Night Football (1974-76). *Mini-Series:* Centennial. *Movies:* Hardcase, The 500-Pound Jerk, Babe, Mulligan's Stew, Mad Bull, Jimmy B. & Andre (also exec. prod.), Alcatraz: The Whole Shocking Story, Word of Honor (also exec. prod.), Maid in America (also exec. prod.), Fudge-a-Mania, Tracy Takes On.... *Series:* Webster (also co-prod.).

KARTOZIAN, WILLIAM F.
Executive. b. San Francisco, CA, July 27, 1938. e. Stanford U., 1960; Harvard Law Sch., 1963. Deputy Attorney General State of CA, 1963-64; assoc. in law firm of Lillick, McHose Wheat Adams & Charles, San Francisco, 1964-65; corp. counsel and dir., Natl. Convenience Stores, Houston, 1965-67; v.p. and corp. counsel, UA Theatre Circuit, 1967-75; owner, Festival Enterprises, Inc., 1970-86; chmn. San Francisco Theatre Employers Assoc., 1973-76; Theatre Assoc. of CA, Inc., dir. 1972-86, v.p. 1974-75, pres. 1975-79, chmn. of bd. 1979-81; member, State of CA Industrial Welfare Comm. Amusement and Recreation Industries Wage Board, 1975-76; Natl Assoc. of Theatre Owners: dir. 1976-86, v.p. 1980-86, president 1988-present. Owner, Regency Enterprises, Inc., 1986-present; chmn. of bd., Lakeside Inn & Casino, Stateline, NV 1985-present. Member: Calif. Film Commission, 1988-present.

KASDAN, LAWRENCE
Writer, Director, Producer. b. West Virginia, Jan. 14, 1949. e. U. of Michigan. Clio award-winning advertising copywriter, Detroit and LA before becoming screen writer. Became director with Body Heat (1981).
PICTURES: The Empire Strikes Back (co-s.p.), Raiders of the Lost Ark (co-s.p.), Continental Divide (s.p.), Body Heat (dir., s.p.), Return of the Jedi (co-s.p.), The Big Chill (dir., co-s.p., co-exec. prod.), Into the Night (actor), Silverado (dir., co-s.p., prod.), Cross My Heart (prod.), The Accidental Tourist (dir., co-prod., co-s.p.), Immediate Family (exec. prod.), I Love You to Death (dir., actor), Grand Canyon (dir., co-prod., co-s.p., actor), Jumpin at the Boneyard (exec. prod.), The Bodyguard (s.p., co-prod.), Wyatt Earp (dir., co-prod., co-s.p.), French Kiss (dir.).

KASLOFF, STEVE
Writer. b. New York, NY, Nov. 13, 1952. e. Pratt Institute, 1974, cum laude. Writer/supvr., Young & Rubicam, 1974-76;

writer/sprv., Ally & Gargano, 1976; writer/supvr., Marsteller Inc., 1976-79; writer/creative supvr., Scali, McCabe, Sloves, 1979-82. hired as youngest v.p., Columbia Pictures, 1982; promoted to sr. v.p., creative dir., Columbia, 1983. Sr. v.p. creative dir., 20th Century Fox, 1992. Member, WGA. Winner of numerous Clio and Key Arts Awards and over 200 others for creative work (trailers, TV commercials, posters, etc.) on such films as Tootsie, Ghostbusters, Total Recall, Home Alone, Dances With Wolves, Terminator 2, Home Alone 2, Last Action Hero, Jurassic Park, Schindler's List, Dumb and Dumber, etc. Has directed stage productions, commercials & special teaser trailers. Screen-writing/Production deal with Columbia Pictures, 1988; 20th Century Fox Films, 1993-present.

KASSAR, MARIO
Executive, Producer. b. Lebanon, Oct. 10, 1951. At age of 18 formed own foreign distribution co. Kassar Films International, specializing in sale, dist. and exhibition of films in Asia and Europe. In 1976 became partners with Andrew Vajna who had own dist. co., forming Carolco. First prod. First Blood, followed by Rambo: First Blood Part II. Became sole chmn. of Carolco in 1989. Formed own production co. in 1996.
PICTURES: *Exec. Prod.:* Angel Heart, Extreme Prejudice, Rambo III, Red Heat, Iron Eagle II, Deep Star Six, Johnny Handsome, Mountains of the Moon, Total Recall, Air America, Jacob's Ladder, L.A. Story, The Doors, Terminator 2: Judgment Day, Rambling Rose, Basic Instinct, Universal Soldier, Light Sleeper, Chaplin, Cliffhanger, Stargate, Showgirls.

KASTNER, ELLIOTT
Producer. b. New York, NY, Jan. 7, 1933. e. U. of Miami, Columbia U. Was agent then v.p. with MCA, before becoming indep. prod., financing and personally producing 65 feature films in 25 yrs. Based in London, NY & LA.
PICTURES: Harper, Kaleidoscope, The Bobo, Sweet November, Sol Madrid, Michael Kohlaas, Laughter in the Dark, Night of the Following Day, Where Eagles Dare, A Severed Head, Tam Lin, The Walking Stick, X Y and Zee (Zee & Company), The Nightcomers, Big Truck and Poor Clare, Face to the Wind, Fear Is the Key, The Long Goodbye, Cops and Robbers, Jeremy, 11 Harrowhouse, Spot, Rancho Deluxe, 92 in the Shade, Farewell My Lovely, Russian Roulette, Breakheart Pass, The Missouri Breaks, Swashbuckler, Equus, A Little Night Music, The Medusa Touch, The Big Sleep, Absolution, Goldengirl, Yesterday's Hero, ffolkes, The First Deadly Sin, Death Valley, Man Woman and Child, Garbo Talks, Oxford Blues, Nomads, Heat, Angel Heart, Jack's Back, The Blob, White of the Eye, Zombie High, Never on Tuesday, Homeboy, A Chorus of Disapproval, The Last Party.
TELEVISION: *Movie:* Frank and Jesse.

KATLEMAN, HARRIS L.
Executive. b. Omaha, NB, Aug. 19, 1928. e. UCLA. Joined MCA in 1949; 1952 transferred to NY as head of TV Packaging Dept. Left to join Goodson-Todman Prods. in 1955, where named v.p., 1956; exec. v.p., 1958; sr. exec. v.p., 1968. Was directly responsible for all programs prod. in L.A., including The Rebel, Branded, The Richard Boone Show, and Don Rickles Show, on which was exec. prod. Joined M-G-M in 1972 as v.p. of MGM-TV; promoted following year to pres., MGM-TV and sr. v.p. of MGM, Inc. Resigned as pres.- MGM-TV, 1977. Formed Bennett/ Katleman Productions under contract to Columbia Pictures. Exec. prod.: From Here to Eternity, Salvage 1; 1980, named bd. chmn. 20th-Fox Television. Appointed pres. & CEO, Twentieth TV, 1982. Oversaw prod. of final years of M*A*S*H, as well as Mr. Belvedere, The Fall Guy, Trapper John M.D., L.A. Law, Hooperman, Anything But Love, Tracey Ullman Show, Alien Nation, The Simpsons, In Living Color. Resigned, 1992. Formed Shadow Hill Prods. under contract to Twentieth TV. Joined Mark Goodson Prods., 1993, as COO.

KATSELAS, MILTON GEORGE
Director, Writer, Teacher, Painter. b. Pittsburgh, PA, Feb. 22, 1933. e. drama dept., Carnegie Inst. of Technology (now Carnegie-Mellon U.). Acting teacher-owner, Beverly Hills Playhouse. Has exhibited paintings in several major solo exhibitions. Awards: 3 time recipient of the L.A. Drama Critics Circle Award, Drama Logue Best Director Award, NAACP and Tony Nominations for Best Director.
THEATER: *B'way:* The Rose Tattoo, Butterflies are Free, Camino Real. *Off-B'way:* Call Me By My Rightful Name, The Zoo Story.
PICTURES: Butterflies Are Free, 40 Carats, Report to the Commissioner, When You Comin' Back Red Ryder?
TELEVISION: *Movies:* The Rules of Marriage, Strangers—The Story of a Mother and Daughter.

KATT, WILLIAM
Actor. b. Los Angeles, CA, Feb. 16, 1955. Son of actors Barbara Hale and Bill Williams. e. Orange Coast Coll. Majored in music, playing piano and guitar. Acted with South Coast

Repertory Theatre, later working in productions at the Ahmanson and Mark Taper Theatres in L.A. Phoenix Rep (N.Y.): Bonjour La Bonjour. Regional: Sarah and Abraham, Days of Wine and Roses.
PICTURES: Carrie (debut, 1976), First Love, Big Wednesday, Butch and Sundance: The Early Days, Baby, Rising Storm, House, White Ghost, Wedding Band, Naked Obsession, Double X: The Name of the Game, House IV: Home Deadly Home, Desperate Motive (Distant Cousins), Tollbooth, The Paperboy, Stranger by Night.
TELEVISION: *Series*: The Greatest American Hero, Top of the Hill, Good Sports. *Movies*: Night Chase, The Daughters of Joshua Cabe, Can Ellen Be Saved?, Perry Mason Returns and several Perry Mason follow-ups (Case of the... Murdered Madam, Avenging Ace, Scandalous Scoundrel, Lady in the Lake, Notorious Nun, Shooting Star, Lost Love, Sinister Spirit), Swim Suit, Problem Child 3: Junior in Love, Piranha. *Specials*: Pippin, The Rainmaker.

KATZ, GLORIA
Producer, Writer. e. UCLA. Film Sch. Joined Universal Pictures as editor, cutting educational films. Later joined forces with Willard Huyck, whom she had met at U.C.L.A. Pair signed by Francis Ford Coppola to write and direct for his newly created company, American Zoetrope.
PICTURES: *Writer*: American Graffiti, Lucky Lady, French Postcards (also prod.), Indiana Jones and the Temple of Doom, Best Defense (also prod.), Howard the Duck (also prod.), Radioland Murders.
TELEVISION: *Co-Producer, Co-Writer*: A Father's Homecoming, Mothers Daughters and Lovers.

KATZ, JAMES C.
Producer, Executive. b. New York, NY, March 17, 1939. e. Ohio St. U. Started in publicity dept. of United Artists, 1963, eventually serving as v.p. of publicity for UA, 1966-68. Publicity co-ord. on film Khartoum, 1964. To London, 1968 as unit publicist for The Charge of the Light Brigade, Joanna. Prod. & dir. for C.I.C. special shorts and documentaries. 1973-78, prod./dir. commercials from own company in London. 1980, pres. Universal Classics Dept.; 1984, v.p. prod, Universal Pictures. With Robert A. Harris worked on restoration of Spartacus, My Fair Lady.
PICTURES: Three Sisters (co-prod.), Lust in the Dust (exec. prod.), Nobody's Fool (prod.), Scenes From the Class Struggle in Beverly Hills (prod.).

KATZ, MARTY
Producer. b. Landsburg, West Germany, Sept. 2, 1947. e. UCLA, U. of Maryland. Served in Vietnam War as U.S. Army first lieut.; awarded Bronze Star as combat pictorial unit director. 1971, dir. of film prod., ABC Circle Films; 1976, exec. v.p., prod., Quinn Martin Prods; 1978-80, producer and consultant, Paramount Pictures' 1981-85, independent producer (Lost in America, Heart Like a Wheel). 1985, joined Walt Disney Prods. as sr. v.p., motion picture & TV prod. Named exec. v.p. motion picture and TV production, 1988-92. 1992-present, prod. Marty Katz Prods./Walt Disney Studios. Producer of Mr. Wrong.

KATZ, NORMAN B.
Executive. b. Scranton, PA, Aug. 23, 1919. e. Columbia U. In U.S. Army 1941-46 as intelligence officer, airborne forces. Entered m.p. industry in 1947 with Discina Films, Paris, France, as prod. asst. Named exec. asst. to head of prod. in 1948. 1950 named v.p. Discina Int'l. Films and in 1952 exec. v.p. 1954 joined Associated Artists Prods. as foreign mgr.; named dir. of foreign operation in 1958. 1959 became dir. of foreign operations for United Artists Associated. 1961 joined 7 Arts Associated Corp. as v.p. in charge of foreign optns.; 1964, named exec. v.p., 7 Arts Prods. Int'l.; 1967, exec. v.p. Warner Bros.-7 Arts 1969 appt. exec. v.p. & CEO WB Intl. & bd. mem. of WB Inc. 1974 named sr. v.p. int'l. div. of American Film Theatre. Pres. of Cinema Arts Assoc. Corp. 1979, exec. v.p. and bd. member, American Communications Industries and pres., CEO of ACI subsidiary, American Cinema; 1983, pres., The Norkat Co., Also, bd. chmn., CEO, American Film Mktg. Assoc., 1985-87; chmn. Amer. Film Export Assn. 1988-92.

KATZENBERG, JEFFREY
Executive. b. 1950. Entered motion picture industry in 1975 as asst. to Paramount Pictures chmn. and CEO Barry Diller in NY. In 1977, became exec. dir. of mktg.; later same year moved to west coast as v.p. of programming for Paramount TV. Promoted to v.p., feature production for Paramount Pictures 1978; 2 years later assumed role of sr. v.p. prod. of m.p. div; 1982, pres. of prod., m.p. and TV, Paramount Pictures. Left to join The Walt Disney Company, 1984; chairman of The Walt Disney Studios, 1984-94. With Steven Spielberg and David Geffen formed Dreamworks entertainment company, 1995.

KAUFMAN, HAL
Creative director, TV Writer, Producer. b. New York, NY, Dec. 16, 1924. e. U. of TX, 1943-44; U. of MI, 1944-47. Started career as petroleum geologist, Western Geophysical Co., 1947-48; TV writer-prod-dir., KDYL-TV, Salt Lake City, 1948-49; prog. dir., WLAV-TV, Grand Rapids, 1949-51; prod. mgr., WOOD-TV, Grand Rapids, 1951-54; TV writer-prod., Leo Burnett Company, Chicago, 1954-56; TV writer-prod., Gordon Best Company, Chicago, 1957-58; with Needham Louis & Brorby Inc.: 1959, sr. writer, TV/Radio creative dept.; 1962, v.p., asst. copy dir.; 1963, dir., tv, radio prod.; 1964, dir., broadcast design, production; assoc. creat. dir., asst. exec. v.p., Needham, Harper & Steers, Inc., 1965; creat. dir. L.A.; 1966; sr. v.p. and mem. bd. of dir., 1966. 1969, creative & marketing consultant in Beverly Hills. 1970, exec. v.p., principle, Kaufman, Lansky Inc., Beverly Hills and San Diego; 1974 editor and publisher Z Magazine; program dir., Z Channel, Theta Cable TV. 1979, sr. v.p./adv. & p.r. & asst. to pres. & bd. chmn., World Airways, Inc. 1982, v.p., creative dir., Admarketing, Inc., Los Angeles. 1985, mktg. & adv. consultant copy dir., Teleflora, Inc.; pres. Hal Kaufman Inc., mktg. & adv. consultant; pres. Brochures on Video, library division, creators and prods. of promotional videos, distribs. religious videos to libraries; pres. Pious Publications, prods. and distribs. of religious videos. Member, Directors Guild of America, SAG, AFTRA. 1974.

KAUFMAN, LEONARD B.
Producer, Writer, Director. b. Newark, NJ, Aug. 31, 1927. e. NYU. In W.W.II served with Army Special Services writing and directing camp shows. Nat'l magazine writer, 1945-48; radio writer, including Errol Flynn Show, 1948-50; radio and TV writer, 1950-52. Headed own public relations firm: Kaufman, Schwartz, and Associates, 1952-64. Joined Ivan Tors Films as writer-prod., 1964. Films Corp. 1958.
PICTURES: Clarence the Cross-eyed Lion, Birds Do It (story)
TELEVISION: Daktari, Ivan Tors' Jambo, O'Hara U.S. Treasury (pilot feature and series). Producer: Hawaii-Five O, The New Sea Hunt, Scruples (mini-series), The Hawaiian (pilot), Writer: Knightrider, Dukes of Hazzard, Hawaii-Five O, Wet Heat (pilot), Hawaiian Heat, Island Sons (movie).

KAUFMAN, LLOYD
Executive. e. Yale Univ., 1969. From 1974-present, pres. of Troma, Inc.
PICTURES: The Girl Who Returned (prod., dir., s.p.), Cry Uncle (prod. mgr.), Joe (prod. asst.), Sugar Cookie (exec. prod., s.p.), Silent Night Bloody Night (assoc. prod.), Battle of Love's Return (dir., prod., s.p., actor), Big Gus What's the Fuss (dir., prod.), Sweet Savior (prod. mgr.), Mother's Day (assoc. prod.), Rocky (pre-prod. spvr.), Slow Dancing in the Big City (prod. spvr.), The Final Countdown (assoc. prod.), Squeeze Play (dir., prod.), Waitress (Co-dir., prod.), Stuck on You (co-dir., co-prod., co-s.p.), The First Turn-On (co-dir., co-prod.), Screamplay (exec. prod.), When Nature Calls (assoc. prod.), The Toxic Avenger (co-dir., co-prod., co-s.p., story), Blood Hook (exec. prod.), Girl School Screams (exec. prod.), Class of Nuke 'Em High (co-dir., co-prod.), Lust for Freedom (exec. prod.), Monster in the Closet (exec. prod.), Troma's War (Co-dir., co-prod., co-s.p., story), Toxic Avenger Part II (co-dir., co-prod., co-s.p., story), Fortress of Amerikkka (prod.), Toxic Avenger III: The Last Temptation of Toxie (co-dir., co-s.p., co-prod.), Class of Nuke 'Em High Part II: Subhumanoid Meltdown (co-dir., co-prod., co-prod., story), Sgt. Kabukiman N.Y.P.D. (co-dir., co-prod., co-s.p.), The Good the Bad and the Subhumanoid (co-s.p., co-prod., co-story).

KAUFMAN, PHILIP
Writer, Director, Producer. b. Chicago, IL, Oct. 23, 1936. e. U. of Chicago, Harvard Law Sch. Was teacher in Italy and Greece before turning to film medium.
PICTURES: *Co-Writer*: The Outlaw Josey Wales, Raiders of the Lost Ark. *Director*: Goldstein (co-dir., co-s.p., co-prod.), Fearless Frank (also s.p., prod.), The Great Northfield Minnesota Raid (also s.p., prod.), The White Dawn, Invasion of the Body Snatchers, The Wanderers (also co-s.p.), The Right Stuff (also s.p.), The Unbearable Lightness of Being (also co-s.p.), Henry & June (also co-s.p.), Rising Sun (also co-s.p.).

KAUFMAN, VICTOR
Executive. b. New York, NY, June 21, 1943. e. Queens Coll.; NYU Sch. of Law, J.D., 1967. Taught criminal law at UCLA before joining Wall St. law firm, Simpson Thacher & Bartlett. Joined Columbia Pictures as asst. general counsel, 1974. Named chief counsel, 1975; then made vice chmn. Columbia Pictures. Later exec. v.p. Columbia Pictures Industries and vice chmn. Columbia Pictures motion picture div. when conceived a new studio as a joint venture between Coca-Cola, Time Inc.'s Home Box Office and CBS, Inc. forming Tri-Star Pictures. Named chmn. and CEO Tri-Star, 1983. When Columbia Pictures and Tri-Star merged in late 1987, became pres. and CEO of new entity, Columbia Pictures Entertainment. In June 1988, dropped title of chmn. of Tri-Star. 1993 became head of Savoy Pictures.

KAUFMANN, CHRISTINE
Actress. b. Lansdorf, Graz, Austria, Jan. 11, 1945. e. school in Munich, Germany. Film debut as a dancer. Salto Mortale at 7 yrs of age.
PICTURES: Rosenrosli (Little Rosie), Schweigende Engel (Silent Angel), Maedchen in Uniform, Winter Vacation, The Last Days of Pompeii, Red Lips, Taras Bulba (U.S debut), Town Without Pity, Murder in the Rue Morgue, Bagdad Cafe, Der Geschichtenerzahler.

KAURISMAKI, AKI
Director, Writer. b. Finland, April 4, 1957. Brother is filmmaker Mika Kaurismaki. First film credit was acting and writing his brother's The Liar in 1980. Directed short subjects: Rocky VI, Thru the Wire, Those Were the Days, These Boots. Served as writer on brother's features: Jackpot 2, The Worthless (also actor), The Clan: The Tale of the Frogs, Rosso.
PICTURES: Director: The Saimaa Gesture (co-dir., with Mika), Crime and Punishment, Calamari Union, Shadows in Paradise, Hamlet Goes Business, Ariel, Leningrad Cowboys Go America, The Match Factory Girl, I Hired a Contract Killer, La Vie de Boheme (The Bohemian Life), Leningrad Cowboys Meet Moses (also s.p., prod., edit.), Take Care of Your Scarf Tatiana (also s.p., prod., edit.).

KAVNER, JULIE
Actress. b. Los Angeles, CA, Sept. 7, 1951. e. San Diego State U. Professional debut as Brenda Morgenstern on TV's Rhoda, 1974.
THEATER: Particular Friendships (Off-B'way), Two for the Seesaw (Jupiter, FLA), It Had to Be You (Canada).
PICTURES: National Lampoon Goes to the Movies, Bad Medicine, Hannah and Her Sisters, Radio Days, Surrender, New York Stories (Oedipus Wrecks), Awakenings, Alice, This Is My Life, Shadows and Fog, I'll Do Anything, Forget Paris.
TELEVISION: Series: Rhoda (Emmy Award, 1978), The Tracey Ullman Show, The Simpsons (voice). Special: The Girl Who Couldn't Lose (Afternoon Playbreak). Movies: Katherine, No Other Love, The Revenge of the Stepford Wives, Don't Drink the Water. Pilot: A Fine Romance. Guest: Lou Grant, Petrocelli, Taxi.

KAYLOR, ROBERT
Director. b. Plains, MT, Aug. 1, 1934. e. Art Center Sch. of Design. Received awards at Cannes, San Francisco and Dallas Film Festivals, Guggenheim Fellow, Amer. Film Inst.
PICTURES: Derby, Carny, Nobody's Perfect.

KAZAN, ELIA
Director. b. Constantinople, Turkey, Sept. 7, 1909. e. Williams Coll., Yale Dramatic Sch. With Group Theatre as apprentice & stage mgr.; on stage, 1934-41; plays include: Waiting for Lefty, Golden Boy, Gentle People, Five-Alarm, Lilliom. Author (novels): The Arrangement, The Assassins, The Understudy, Acts of Love, The Anatolian, A Life (autobiography, 1988), Beyond the Aegean (1994).
THEATER: Director: Skin of Our Teeth, All My Sons, Streetcar Named Desire, Death of a Salesman, Cat on a Hot Tin Roof (co-dir.), One Touch of Venus, Harriet, Jocobowsky and the Colonel, Tea and Sympathy, Dark at the Top of the Stairs, J.B., Sweet Bird of Youth, Lincoln Center Repertory Theatre (co-dir., prod.), After The Fall, But For Whom Charlie.
PICTURES: Actor: City for Conquest, Blues in the Night. Director: A Tree Grows in Brooklyn (debut, 1945), Boomerang!, The Sea of Grass, Gentleman's Agreement (Academy Award, 1947), Pinky, Panic in the Streets, A Streetcar Named Desire, Viva Zapata!, Man on a Tightrope, On the Waterfront (Academy Award, 1954). Producer/Director: East of Eden, Baby Doll, A Face in the Crowd, Wild River, Splendor in the Grass, America America (also s.p.), The Arrangement (also s.p.), The Visitors, The Last Tycoon.

KAZAN, LAINIE
Singer, Actress. b. New York, NY, May 15, 1942. e. Hofstra U.
PICTURES: Dayton's Devils, Lady in Cement, Romance of a Horse Thief, One from the Heart, My Favorite Year, Lust in the Dust, The Delta Force, The Journey of Natty Gann, Harry and the Hendersons, Beaches, Eternity, 29th Street, I Don't Buy Kisses Anymore, The Cemetery Club.
TELEVISION: Series: The Dean Martin Summer Show, Tough Cookies, Karen's Song. Pilot: Family Business, The Lainie Kazan Show. Movies: A Love Affair: The Eleanor and Lou Gehrig Story, A Cry for Love, Sunset Limousine, The Jerk Too, Obsessive Love, Prince for a Day. Guest: Too Close for Comfort, Dick Van Dyke Show, Beverly Hills 90210, Tales From the Crypt, Faerie Tale Theatre (Pinocchio), Hotel, Johnny Carson Show, Dean Martin, Merv Griffin, Joan Rivers, Amazing Stories, Pat Sajak Show, The Famous Teddy Z, Murder She Wrote.

KAZANJIAN, HOWARD G.
Producer. b. Pasadena, CA, July 26, 1943. e. U. of Southern California Film Sch.; DGA Training Program. Exec. Prod.: The Making of Raiders of the Lost Ark.

PICTURES: Asst. Dir.: Camelot, Finian's Rainbow, The Wild Bunch, The Arrangement, The Front Page, The Hindenberg, Family Plot. Assoc. Prod.: Rollercoaster. Producer: More American Graffiti, Raiders of the Lost Ark, Return of the Jedi, Demolition Man.

KAZURINSKY, TIM
Actor, Writer. b. Johnstown, PA, March 3, 1950. Raised in Australia. Worked as copywriter for Chicago ad agency. Took acting class at Second City and quit job to become actor and head writer for Chicago troupe. Co-starred with John Candy in CTV/NBC's series Big City Comedy, 1980. Joined cast of Saturday Night Live as writer-actor 1981-84.
PICTURES: Actor: My Bodyguard, Somewhere in Time, Continental Divide, Neighbors, Police Academy II: Their First Assignment, Police Academy III: Back in Training, About Last Night (also co-s.p.), Police Academy IV: Citizens on Patrol, For Keeps (s.p. only), Road to Ruin (also s.p.), Hot to Trot, Wedding Band, A Billion for Boris, Shakes the Clown, Plump Fiction.
TELEVISION: Movies: This Wife for Hire, Dinner at Eight.

KEACH, STACY
Actor, Director, Producer. b. Savannah, GA, June 2, 1942. Brother is actor James Keach. Began professional acting career in Joseph Papp's 1964 Central Park prod. of Hamlet.
THEATER: Long Day's Journey into Night (Obie Award), Macbird (Drama Desk & Obie Awards), Indians (Drama Desk Award & Tony nom.), Hamlet, Deathtrap, Hughie, Barnum, Cyrano de Bergerac, Peer Gynt, Henry IV Parts I & II, Idiot's Delight, Solitary Confinement, Richard III, The Kentucky Cycle (Helen Hayes Award), Steiglitz Loves O'Keefe.
PICTURES: The Heart Is a Lonely Hunter (debut, 1968), End of the Road, The Traveling Executioner, Brewster McCloud, Doc, The New Centurions, Fat City, Watched!, The Life and Times of Judge Roy Bean, Luther, The Gravy Train, The Killer Inside Me, Conduct Unbecoming, Street People, The Squeeze, The Duellists (narrator), Slave of the Cannibal God, The Great Battle, Gray Lady Down, Up in Smoke, The Ninth Configuration (Twinkle Twinkle Killer Kane), The Long Riders (also exec. prod., co-s.p.), Nice Dreams, Road Games, Butterfly, That Championship Season, Class of 1999, False Identity, Milena, Raw Justice, Batman: Mask of the Phantasm (voice), New Crime City, Escape from L.A., Prey of the Jaguar.
TELEVISION: Series: Caribe, Mickey Spillane's Mike Hammer, Case Closed (host). Movies: All the Kind Strangers, Caribe, The Blue and the Gray, Princess Daisy, Murder Me Murder You, More Than Murder, Wait Until Dark, Mistral's Daughter, Hemingway, Mickey Spillane's Mike Hammer: Murder Takes All, The Forgotten, Mission of the Shark, Revenge on the Highway, Rio Diablo, Body Bags, Against Their Will: Women in Prison, Texas, Amanda & the Alien. Director: Incident at Vichy, Six Characters in Search of an Author.

KEACH, SR., STACY
Executive. b. Chicago, IL, May 29, 1914. Father of actors, Stacy and James. e. Northwestern U., B.S. & M.A. Was instructor in theatre arts at Northwestern and Armstrong Coll. and dir. at Pasadena Playhouse before entering industry. For 4-1/2 yrs. under contract at Universal Pictures; 3 yrs. at RKO; had own prod. on NBC, CBS. In 1946 began producing and directing industrial stage presentations for Union Oil Co. and from then on became full-time prod. of m.p. and stage industrial shows. In 1946 formed Stacy Keach Productions, of which he is pres. In addition to directing, producing and writing occasionally appears as actor in films (Cobb, etc.). Played Clarence Birds Eye on TV commercials as well as other commercials. Voiceovers/ spokesman for many major American Cos. Autobiography: Stacy Keach, Go Home! (1996). Received Man of the Year Award from Pasadena Playhouse Alumni in 1995. Recipient of the Diamond Circle Award from the Pacific Pioneers Broadcasters Assoc., 1996.

KEATON, DIANE
Actress, Director. r.n. Diane Hall. b. Santa Ana, CA, Jan. 5, 1946. e. Santa Ana Coll. Appeared in summer stock and studied at Neighborhood Playhouse in N.Y. Made prof. debut in B'way prod. of Hair (1968); then co-starred with Woody Allen in Play It Again Sam, repeating role for film version. Off-B'way: The Primary English Class. Author: photography books: Reservations (co-ed.), Still Life. Directed 1982 short What Does Dorrie Want?
PICTURES: Lovers and Other Strangers (debut, 1970), The Godfather, Play It Again Sam, Sleeper, The Godfather Part II, Love and Death, I Will I Will... for Now, Harry and Walter Go to New York, Annie Hall (Academy Award, 1977), Looking for Mr. Goodbar, Interiors, Manhattan, Reds, Shoot the Moon, The Little Drummer Girl, Mrs. Soffel, Crimes of the Heart, Radio Days, Heaven (dir. only), Baby Boom, The Good Mother, The Lemon Sisters (also prod.), The Godfather Part III, Father of the Bride, Manhattan Murder Mystery, Look Who's Talking Now (voice), Unstrung Heroes (dir. only), Father of the Bride 2, Marvin's Room, The First Wives Club.

TELEVISION: *Movies*: Running Mates, Amelia Earhart: The Final Flight. *Guest*: Love American Style, The FBI, Mannix. *Director*: The Girl With the Crazy Brother, Twin Peaks, Wildflower (movie).

KEATON, MICHAEL
Actor. r.n. Michael Douglas. b. Coraopolis, PA, Sept. 5, 1951. Speech major, Kent State U, 2 years. Drove cab and ice-cream truck, worked for PBS station in Pittsburgh and appeared in regional theatre prods. while performing in local coffeehouses. Became memb. of improvisational troupe Jerry Vale. Moved to L.A. where honed craft at Comedy Store and Second City Improv. Workshops as stand-up comic.
PICTURES: Night Shift (debut, 1982), Mr. Mom, Johnny Dangerously, Gung Ho, Touch and Go, The Squeeze, Beetlejuice, Clean and Sober, The Dream Team, Batman, Pacific Heights, One Good Cop, Batman Returns, Much Ado About Nothing, My Life, The Paper, Speechless, Multiplicity.
TELEVISION: *Series*: All's Fair, Mary, The Mary Tyler Moore Hour, Working Stiffs, Report to Murphy. *Movie*: Roosevelt and Truman.

KEEL, HOWARD
Actor. r.n. Harold Keel. b. Gillespie, IL, April 13, 1919. e. high school, Fallbrook, CA. Began career following George Walker scholarship award for singing, L.A.; appeared in plays, Pasadena Auditorium, concerts; won awards, Mississippi Valley and Chicago Musical Festivals. Stage debut: Carousel, 1945; followed by London prod. of Oklahoma! which led to contract with MGM.
THEATER: Carousel, Oklahoma!, Saratoga, No Strings, The Ambassador, Man of La Mancha.
PICTURES: The Small Voice (debut, 1948), Annie Get Your Gun, Pagan Love Song, Three Guys Named Mike, Show Boat, Texas Carnival, Callaway Went Thataway, Lovely to Look At, Desperate Search, I Love Melvin (cameo), Ride Vaquero!, Fast Company, Kiss Me Kate, Calamity Jane, Rose Marie, Seven Brides for Seven Brothers, Deep in My Heart, Jupiter's Darling, Kismet, Floods of Fear, The Big Fisherman, Armored Command, The Day of the Triffids, The Man From Button Willow (voice), Waco, Red Tomahawk, The War Wagon, Arizona Bushwhackers, That's Entertainment III.
TELEVISION: *Series*: Dallas. *Movie*: Hart to Hart: Home Is Where the Hart Is. *Guest*: Zane Grey Theatre, Bell Telephone Hour, Tales of Wells Fargo, Death Valley Days, Here's Lucy, Sonny and Cher, The Love Boat, etc. *Specials*: A Toast to Jerome Kern, Roberta, Music of Richard Rodgers.

KEESHAN, BOB
Performer. b. Lynbrook, NY, June 27, 1927. e. Fordham U. As network page boy became assistant to Howdy Doody's Bob Smith and originated role of Clarabelle the Clown; created children's programs Time for Fun, Tinker's Workshop, Mister Mayor, Captain Kangaroo (1955-85).

KEITEL, HARVEY
Actor. b. Brooklyn, NY, May 13, 1939. Served in U.S. Marine Corps. Studied with Frank Corsaro, Lee Strasberg, Stella Adler. Member of the Actors' Studio. Debuted in Martin Scorsese's student film Who's That Knocking at My Door?
THEATER: *NY*: Up to Thursday, Death of a Salesman, Hurlyburly, A Lie of the Mind.
PICTURES: Who's That Knocking at My Door? (debut, 1968), Mean Streets, Alice Doesn't Live Here Anymore, That's the Way of the World, Taxi Driver, Mother Jugs and Speed, Buffalo Bill and the Indians or: Sitting Bull's History Lesson, Welcome to L.A., The Duellists, Fingers, Blue Collar, Eagle's Wing, Deathwatch, Saturn 3, Bad Timing, The Border, Exposed, La Nuit de Varennes, Corrupt, Falling in Love, Knight of the Dragon (Star Knight), Camorra, Off Beat, Wise Guys, The Men's Club, The Investigation (The Inquiry), The Pick-Up Artist, The Last Temptation of Christ, The January Man, The Two Jakes, Mortal Thoughts, Thelma & Louise, Two Evil Eyes (The Black Cat), Bugsy (Acad. Award nom.), Sister Act, Reservoir Dogs (also co-prod.), Bad Lieutenant, Point of No Return, Rising Sun, The Piano, Dangerous Game, The Young Americans, Monkey Trouble, Pulp Fiction, Imaginary Crimes, Somebody to Love, Smoke, Clockers, Blue in the Face, Ulysses' Gaze, From Dusk Till Dawn, Head Above Water, Somebody to Love.
TELEVISION: *Movie*: The Virginia Hill Story. *Special*: This Ain't Bebop (Amer. Playhouse).

KEITH, BRIAN
Actor. r.n. Robert Brian Keith. b. Bayonne, NJ, Nov. 14, 1921. Father was actor Robert Keith. U.S. Marines, 1942-45; worked in stock co., radio shows, comm. films for TV; on B'way in Mr. Roberts, Darkness at Noon.
PICTURES: Arrowhead (debut, 1953), Jivaro, Alaska Seas, Bamboo Prison, Violent Men, Tight Spot, Five Against the House, Nightfall, Storm Center, Run of the Arrow, Chicago Confidential, Hell Canyon Outlaws, Dino, Appointment With a Shadow, Desert Hell, Fort Dobbs, Sierra Baron, Villa!, Violent

Road, The Young Philadelphians, Ten Who Dared, The Deadly Companions, The Parent Trap, Moon Pilot, Savage Sam, The Pleasure Seekers, The Raiders, A Tiger Walks, Those Calloways, The Hallelujah Trail, The Rare Breed, Nevada Smith, The Russians Are Coming the Russians Are Coming, Way Out, Reflections in a Golden Eye, With Six You Get Egg Roll, Krakatoa: East of Java, Gaily Gaily, Suppose They Gave a War and Nobody Came, The McKenzie Break, Scandalous John, Something Big, The Yakuza, The Wind and the Lion, Joe Panther, Nickelodeon, Hooper, Meteor, Mountain Men, Charlie Chan and the Curse of the Dragon Queen, Sharky's Machine, Death Before Dishonor, Young Guns, After the Rain, Welcome Home.
TELEVISION: Numerous dramas on Studio One, Suspense, Philco Playhouse, etc. *Series*: Crusader, The Westerner, Family Affair, The Little People (The Brian Keith Show), Archer, Hardcastle and McCormick, Pursuit of Happiness, Heartland, Walter & Emily. *Mini-Series*: Centennial, The Chisholms, Great Escapes: Secrets of Lake Success. *Movies*: Second Chance, The Quest, The Loneliest Runner, In the Matter of Karen Ann Quinlan, The Seekers, Moviola: The Silent Lovers, World War III, Cry for the Strangers, The Alamo: 13 Days to Glory, Perry Mason: The Case of the Lethal Lesson, Lady in a Corner, The Gambler Returns: Luck of the Draw, The Return of Hunter.

KEITH, DAVID
Actor, Director. b. Knoxville, TN, May 8, 1954. e. U. of Tennessee, B.A., speech and theater. Appearance at Good-speed Opera House in musical led to role in CBS sitcom pilot, Co-Ed Fever.
PICTURES: The Rose (debut, 1979), The Great Santini, Brubaker, Back Roads, Take This Job and Shove It, An Officer and a Gentleman, Independence Day, The Lords of Discipline, Firestarter, The Curse (dir. only), White of the Eye, The Further Adventures of Tennessee Buck (also dir.), Heartbreak Hotel, The Two Jakes, Off and Running, Desperate Motive (Distant Cousins), Caged Fear, Raw Justice, Temptation, Major League 2, Liar's Edge, Till the End of the Night, Born Wild, Gold Diggers: The Secret of Bear Mountain, Deadly Sins, The Indian in the Cupboard, A Family Thing, Invasion of Privacy, Judge & Jury, Red Blooded American Girl.
TELEVISION: *Series*: Co-ed Fever, Flesh 'N' Blood, Strangers, High Incident. *Movies*: Are You in the House Alone?, Friendly Fire, Gulag, Whose Child Is This?: The War for Baby Jessica, XXX's & OOO's (pilot), James Michener's Texas, If Looks Could Kill: From the Files of America's Most Wanted. *Mini-Series*: If Tomorrow Comes, Golden Moment: An Olympic Love Story, Guts and Glory: The Rise and Fall of Oliver North. Guest: Happy Days, Runaways.

KEITH, PENELOPE
O.B.E. Actress. b. Sutton, Surrey, Eng., 1939. London stage debut, The Wars of the Roses (RSC, 1964). Extensive theater work including The Norman Conquests, Donkey's Years, The Apple Cart, Hobson's Choice, Captain Brassbound's Conversion, Hay Fever.
PICTURES: Think Dirty (Every Home Should Have One), Take a Girl Like You, Penny Gold, Priest of Love.
TELEVISION: *Series*: Kate, The Good Life, To the Manor Born, Executive Stress. *Movies-Specials*: Private Lives, The Norman Conquests, Donkey's Years.

KELLER, MARTHE
Actress. b. Basel, Switzerland, 1945. e. Stanislavsky Sch., Munich. Joined a Heidelberg repertory group and Schiller Rep. in Berlin. Started acting in France and attracted attention of U.S. directors after appearing in Claude Lelouch's And Now My Love. Has acted in over 50 plays in French, German, Eng. & Italian.
PICTURES: Funeral in Berlin (debut, 1967), The Devil by the Tail, Give Her the Moon, La Vieille Fille, The Loser, Elle Court (Love in the Suburbs), And Now My Love, Down the Ancient Staircase, Le Guepier, Marathon Man, Black Sunday, Bobby Deerfield, Fedora, The Formula, Les Uns et les Autres, The Amateur, Wagner, Femmes de Personne, Joan Lui, I Come on Monday, Dark Eyes, Rouge Basier, The Artisan, Una Vittoria, Lapse of Memory, Mon Amie Max, According to Pereira.
TELEVISION: The Charterhouse of Parma, The Nightmare Years.

KELLERMAN, SALLY
Actress. b. Long Beach, CA, June 2, 1936. m. Jonathan Krane. e. Hollywood H.S. Studied acting in N.Y. at the Actors Studio and in Hollywood with Jeff Corey. Recorded album Roll With the Feeling. Has done voice-overs for many commercials.
THEATRE: Women Behind Bars, Holiday.
PICTURES: Reform School Girl (debut, 1959), Hands of a Stranger, The Third Day, The Boston Strangler, The April Fools, M*A*S*H (Acad. Award nom.), Brewster McCloud, Last of the Red Hot Lovers, Lost Horizon, Slither, Reflection of Fear, Rafferty and the Gold Dust Twins, The Big Bus,

Welcome to L.A., The Mouse and His Child (voice), Magee and the Lady, A Little Romance, Serial, Head On (Fatal Attraction), Foxes, Loving Couples, Moving Violations, Lethal (KGB: The Secret War), Back to School, That's Life!, Meatballs III, Three For the Road, Someone to Love, You Can't Hurry Love, Paramedics (voice), All's Fair, Limit Up, The Secret of the Ice Cave, The Player, Doppelganger, Happily Ever After (voice), Younger and Younger, Ready to Wear (Pret-a-Porter). TELEVISION: Mini-Series: Centennial. Movies: For Lovers Only, Dempsey, Secret Weapons, September Gun, Drop Dead Gorgeous, Boris and Natasha (also assoc. prod.). Specials: Big Blonde, Verna: USO Girl, Elena, Faerie Tale Theatre, Dr. Paradise. Guest: Mannix, It Takes a Thief, Chrysler Theatre.

KELLEY, DeFOREST
Actor. b. Atlanta, GA, Jan. 20, 1920. e. Decatur Boys' H.S. PICTURES: Fear in the Night (debut, 1947), Variety Girl, Canon City, The Men, House of Bamboo, Taxi, Illegal, The Man in the Gray Flannel Suit, Tension at Table Rock, Gunfight at the O.K. Corral, Raintree County, The Law and Jake Wade, Warlock, Where Love Has Gone, Marriage on the Rocks, Apache Uprising, Night of the Lepus, Star Trek: The Motion Picture, Star Trek II: The Wrath of Khan, Star Trek III: The Search for Spock, Star Trek IV: The Voyage Home, Star Trek V: The Final Frontier, Star Trek VI: The Undiscovered Country. TELEVISION: Series: Star Trek. Guest: Gunsmoke, The Lineup, Matinee Theatre, The Web, Playhouse 90, Bonanza, Bat Masterson, The Deputy, Perry Mason, The Virginian, Room 222.

KELLEY, SHEILA
Actress. b. Philadelphia, PA, 1964.
PICTURES: Wish You Were Here, Some Girls, Breaking In, Staying Together, Mortal Passions, Where the Heart Is, Soapdish, Pure Luck, Singles, Passion Fish, Wild Blade. TELEVISION: Series: L.A. Law, Sisters. Movie: The Secretary.

KELLOGG, PHILIP M.
Executive. b. March 17, 1912, Provo, WA. e. UCLA. Special feature writer for Hearst papers and magazines, 1933-34; MGM story dept., production dept., Irving Thalberg unit, 1934-35; Warner Bros. film editor, 1935-41; Berg-Allenberg Agency, 1941-50; U.S. Naval Reserve officer, 1941-46; William Morris Agency, 1950-present, co-head of m.p. dept., dir. WMA, Ltd., London.

KELLY, FRANK
Executive. Was assoc. prod. of AM Los Angeles, then exec. prod./program dir. for KABC-TV prior to joining Paramount. 1983, named v.p. programming for Paramount domestic tv division; 1985, promoted to sr. v.p. 1989, became exec. v.p. programming. 1995, named pres. of creative affairs for domestic tv division of Paramount Television Group.

KELLY, GENE
Actor, Director, Dancer, Choreographer. b. Pittsburgh, PA, Aug. 23, 1912. e. Pennsylvania State U., U. of Pittsburgh. Bricklayer, concrete mixer, soda clerk, dance instructor before going on B'way stage. Special Academy Award for advancing dance films, 1951. Received American Film Institute Life Achievement Award, 1985; Kennedy Center Honors, 1982.
THEATER: Actor: Leave It to Me, One for the Money, The Time of Your Life, Pal Joey. Choreographer: The Time of Your Life, Best Foot Forward, Billy Rose's Diamond Horsehoe. Director: Flower Drum Song.
PICTURES: For Me and My Gal (debut, 1942), Pilot No. 5, Du Barry Was a Lady, Thousands Cheer, The Cross of Lorraine, Cover Girl (also choreog.), Christmas Holiday, Anchors Aweigh (Acad. Award nom.; also choreog.), Ziegfeld Follies, Living in a Big Way (also choreog.), The Pirate (also co-choreog.), The Three Musketeers, Words and Music, Take Me Out to the Ball Game (also co-choreog.), On the Town (also co-dir., choreog.), Black Hand, Summer Stock, An American in Paris (also choreog.), It's a Big Country, Singin' in the Rain (also co-dir., co-choreog.), The Devil Makes Three, Love Is Better Than Ever (cameo), Brigadoon (also choreog.), Crest of the Wave (Seagulls Over Sorrento), Deep in My Heart, It's Always Fair Weather (also co-dir., choreog.), Invitation to the Dance (also dir., s.p., choreog.), The Happy Road (also dir., prod.), Les Girls, Marjorie Morningstar, The Tunnel of Love (dir. only), Inherit the Wind, Let's Make Love, Gigot (dir. only), What a Way to Go!, A Guide for the Married Man (dir. only), The Young Girls of Rochefort, Hello Dolly! (dir. only), The Cheyenne Social Club (dir., prod. only), 40 Carats, That's Entertainment, That's Entertainment Part 2 (also dir.), Viva Knievel!, Xanadu, That's Dancing, That's Entertainment III.
TELEVISION: Series: Going My Way, The Funny Side. Specials: Salute to Baseball, Dancing Is a Man's Game (Omnibus), The Gene Kelly Pontiac Show, The Gene Kelly Show, The Julie Andrews Show, Gene Kelly in New York New York, Jack and the Beanstalk (also prod., dir.; Emmy Award as prod., 1967), Hollywood Stars of Tomorrow, Gene Kelly's

Wonderful World of Girls, The Changing Scene, Magnavox Presents Frank Sinatra, Dick Cavett's Backlot USA, The Dorothy Hamill Special, America Salutes Richard Rodgers: The Sound of His Music, Cinderella at the Palace, Oscar's Best Actors, The Stars Salute Israel at 30, The Movie Palaces, Christmas at the Movies, others. Mini-Series: North and South, Sins. Guest: Ed Sullivan Show, $64000 Question, Mary Tyler Moore Hour, Password, The Love Boat.
(d. February 2, 1996)

KELLY, MOIRA
Actress. b. 1969. e. Marymount Col. In addition to acting also trained as violinist, operatic soprano.
PICTURES: The Boy Who Cried Bitch (debut, 1991), Billy Bathgate, The Cutting Edge, Twin Peaks: Fire Walk With Me, Chaplin, With Honors, The Lion King (voice), Little Odessa, The Tie That Binds.
TELEVISION: Movies: Love Lies and Murder, Daybreak.

KELSEY, LINDA
Actress. b. Minneapolis, MN, July 28, 1946. e. U. of Minnesota, B.A.
TELEVISION: Series: Lou Grant, Day by Day, Sessions. Movies: The Picture of Dorian Gray, Something for Joey; Eleanor and Franklin: The White House Years, The Last of Mrs. Lincoln, A Perfect Match, Attack on Fear, His Mistress, Nutcracker, Baby Girl Scott, A Place to Be Loved, A Family Torn Apart, If Someone Had Known. Special: Home Sweet Homeless. Mini-Series: Captains and the Kings.

KEMENY, JOHN
Producer. b. Budapest, Hungary. Producer for National Film Board of Canada, 1957-69. Formed International Cinemedia Center, Ltd. in 1969 in Montreal, as partner.
PICTURES: The Apprenticeship of Duddy Kravitz, White Line Fever, Shadow of the Hawk, Ice Castles, Atlantic City, Bay Boy, The Wraith, Quest for Fire (co-prod.), Nowhere to Hide (exec. prod.), Iron Eagle II, Gate II.
TELEVISION: Murderers Among Us: The Simon Wiesenthal Story (co-prod.), Josephine Baker.

KEMP, JEREMY
Actor. b. Chesterfield, England, Feb. 3, 1935. e. Abbottsholme Sch., Central Sch. of Speech and Drama. Service with Gordon Highlanders. Early career on stage incl. Old Vic Theatre Company, 1959-61. Recent theatre: Celebration, Incident at Vichy, Spoiled, The Caretaker. National Theatre, 1979-80.
PICTURES: Cleopatra (debut, 1963), Dr. Terror's House of Horrors, Face of a Stanger, Operation Crossbow (The Great Spy Mission), Cast a Giant Shadow, The Blue Max, Assignment K, Twist of Sand, The Strange Affair, Darling Lili, The Games, Sudden Terror (Eye Witness), Pope Joan, The Bellstone Fox, The Blockhouse, The Seven Percent Solution, East of Elephant Rock, Queen of Diamonds, A Bridge Too Far, The Thoroughbreds (Treasure Seekers), Leopard in the Snow, Caravans, The Prisoner of Zenda, The Return of the Soldier, Top Secret!, When the Whales Came, Angels and Insects.
TELEVISION: Z Cars, The Lovers of Florence, The Last Reunion, Colditz, Brassneck, Rhinemann Exchange, Lisa, Goodbye, Henry VIII, St. Joan, The Winter's Tale, Unity, The Contract, Sadat, King Lear, Sherlock Holmes, George Washington, Peter the Great, The Winds of War, War and Remembrance, Slip-Up (The Great Paper Chase), Cop-out, Summers Lease, Prisoner of Honor, Duel of Hearts, Star Trek: The Next Generation (guest).

KEMPER, VICTOR J.
Cinematographer. b. Newark, NJ, April 14, 1927. e. Seton Hall, B.S./Engineer. Channel 13, Newark 1949-54; Tech. supervisor EUE Screen Gems NY 1954-56; v.p. engineering General TV Network. Pres. VJK Prods.
PICTURES: Husbands, The Magic Garden of Stanley Sweetheart, They Might Be Giants, Who is Harry Kellerman?, The Hospital, The Candidate, Last of the Red Hot Lovers, Shamus, The Friends of Eddie Coyle, Gordon's War, The Hideaways, The Gambler, The Reincarnation of Peter Proud, Dog Day Afternoon, Stay Hungry, The Last Tycoon, Mikey and Nicky, Slapshot, Audrey Rose, Oh God!, The One and Only, Coma, Eyes of Laura Mars, Magic, Night of the Juggler, And Justice for All, The Jerk, The Final Countdown, Xanadu, The Four Seasons, Chu Chu and the Philly Flash, Partner, Author! Author!, National Lampoon's Vacation, Mr. Mom, The Lonely Guy, Cloak and Dagger, Secret Admirer, Pee-wee's Big Adventure, Clue, Bobo, Hot to Trot, Cohen and Tate, See No Evil, Hear No Evil, Crazy People, FX2, Another You, Married to It, Beethoven, Tommy Boy, Eddie.

KENNEDY, BURT
Director, Writer. b. Muskegon, MI, Sept. 3, 1922. e. Ravenna H.S. U.S. Army 1942-46; awarded Silver Star, Bronze Star and Purple Heart with Oak Leaf Cluster. Began as writer of TV and film scripts, and was writer, producer and director of Combat series and many TV and theatrical westerns.

PICTURES: *Writer*: Seven Men From Now, Gun the Man Down, Man in the Vault, the Tall T, Fort Dobbs, Ride Lonesome, Yellostone Kelly, Comanche Station, Six Black Horses, Stary Away Joe, The Littlest Horse Thiefs, White Hunter Black Heart. *Director*: The Canadians (debut, 1961; also s.p.), Mail Order Bride (also s.p.), The Rounders (also s.p.), The Money Trap, Return of the Seven, The War Wagon, Welcome to Hard Times (also s.p.), Support Your Local Sheriff, The Good Guys and the Bad Guys, Young Billy Young (also s.p.), Dirty Dingus Magee, Support Your Local Gunfighter (also exec. prod.), Hannie Caulder (also s.p. as Z.X. Jones), The Deserter, The Train Robbers (also s.p.), The Killer Inside Me, Wolf Lake (also s.p.), The Trouble with Spies (also prod., s.p.), Big Bad John (also s.p.), Suburban Commando.
TELEVISION: *Series*: Combat (prod., writer) The Rounders (also writer), How the West Was Won, The Yellow Rose, Simon & Simon, Magnum P.I. *Mini-Series*: The Rhinemann Exchange. *Movies*: Shoot out in a One-Dog Town, Side kicks (also prod.), All the Kind Strangers, Kate Bliss and the Ticker Tape Kid, The Wild Wild West Revisted, The Concrete Cowboys, More Wild Wild West, The Alamo-Thirteen Days to Glory, Down the Long Hills, Once Upon a Texas Train (also prod., writer), Where the Hell's That Gold?!!? (also prod., writer).

KENNEDY, GEORGE
Actor. b. New York, NY, Feb. 18, 1925. At 2 acted in touring co. of Bringing Up Father. At 7, disc jockey with his own radio show for children. Served in Army during WWII, earning two Bronze Stars and combat and service ribbons. In Army 16 years, became Capt. and Armed Forces Radio and TV officer. 1957, opened first Army Information Office, N.Y. Served as technical advisor to Phil Silvers's Sergeant Bilko TV series. Began acting in 1959 when discharged from Army.
PICTURES: The Little Shepard of Kingdom Come (debut, 1961), Lonely Are the Brave, The Man From the Diner's Club, Charade, Strait- Jacket, Island of the Blue Dolphins, McHale's Navy, Hush... Hush... Sweet Charlotte, Mirage, In Harm's Way, The Sons of Katie Elder, The Flight of the Phoenix, Shenandoah, Hurry Sundown, The Dirty Dozen, Cool Hand Luke (Academy Award, best supporting actor, 1967), The Ballad of Josie, The Pink Jungle, Bandolero!, The Boston Strangler, The Legend of Lylah Claire, Guns of the Magnificent Seven, Gaily Gaily, The Good Guys and the Bad Guys, Airport, ... tick ... tick ... tick ..., Zigzag, Dirty Dingus Magee, Fool's Parade, Lost Horizon, Cahill: U.S. Marshal, Thunderbolt and Lightfoot, Airport 1975, Earthquake, The Human Factor, The Eiger Sanction, Airport '77, Ningen no Shomei (Proof of the Man), Mean Dog Blues, Death on the Nile, Brass Target, The Concorde—Airport '79, Death Ship, The Double McGuffin, Steel, Virus, Just Before Dawn, Modern Romance, A Rare Breed, Search and Destroy, Wacko, The Jupiter Menace, Bolero, Chattanooga Choo Choo, Hit and Run, Savage Dawn, The Delta Force, Radioactive Dreams, Creepshow 2, Born to Race, Demonwarp, Counterforce, Nightmare at Noon, Private Roads, Uninvited, The Terror Within, The Naked Gun: From the Files of Police Squad, Esmeralda Bay, Ministry of Vengeance, Brain Dead, Hangfire, The Naked Gun 2 1/2: The Smell of Fear, Driving Me Crazy, Distant Justice, Naked Gun 33 1/3: The Final Insult.
TELEVISION: *Series*: The Blue Knight, Sarge, Counterattack: Crime in America, Dallas. *Guest*: Sugarfoot, Cheyenne. *Movies*: See How They Run, Sarge: The Badge or the Cross, Priest Killer, A Great American Tragedy, Deliver Us From Evil, A Cry in the Wilderness, The Blue Knight, The Archer: Fugitive from the Empire, Jesse Owens Story, Liberty, International Airport, Kenny Rogers as the Gambler III, The Gunfighters, What Price Victory, Good Cops Bad Cops, Final Shot: The Hank Gathers Story. *Mini-Series*: Backstairs at the White House.

KENNEDY, JOSEPH W.
Executive. a.k.a. Scott Kennedy. b. New York, NY, Feb. 11, 1934. e. La Salle, NYU. Started as office boy at NBC in 1950, before studying acting in NY. Appeared on TV in The Defenders and The Naked City, in film Advise and Consent. Host of Scott Kennedy Luncheon radio show in 1964. Joined United Artists in Boston in 1967 as salesman. UA Chicago sls. mgr. 1969-72; Jacksonville branch mgr. 1972-78; southern div. mgr. 1978-79. 1980 named v.p. & asst. gen. sls. mgr. responsible for UA eastern sls. territories. 1983 joined Tri-Star Pictures as v.p. southern div. mgr. Dallas.

KENNEDY, KATHLEEN
Producer. b. 1954. Raised in Weaverville and Redding in No. Calif. e. San Diego State U. Early TV experience on KCST, San Diego, working as camera operator, video editor, floor director and news production coordinator. Produced talk show, You're On. Left to enter m.p. industry as prod. asst. on Steven Spielberg's 1941. Founding member and pres. of Amblin Entertainment. 1992, with husband and partner Frank Marshall formed the Kennedy/Marshall Company.

PICTURES: Raiders of the Lost Ark (prod. assoc.), Poltergeist (assoc. prod.), E.T.: The Extra-Terrestrial (prod.), Twilight Zone: The Movie (co-assoc. prod.), Indiana Jones and the Temple of Doom (assoc. prod.). *Exec. prod.* (with Frank Marshall): Gremlins, The Goonies, Back to the Future, The Color Purple (prod.), Young Sherlock Holmes (co-prod.), An American Tail, Innerspace, Empire of the Sun, Batteries Not Included, Who Framed Roger Rabbit, The Land Before Time, Indiana Jones and the Last Crusade, (prod. exec.), Dad, Always (prod.), Joe Versus the Volcano, Gremlins II, Hook (co-prod.), Noises Off, Alive, A Far Off Place, Jurassic Park, Milk Money, The Bridges of Madison County, Congo, The Indian in the Cupboard, Twister. *Exec. Prod*: Schindler's List, A Dangerous Woman, The Flintstones, Lost World.
TELEVISION: Amazing Stories (spv. prod.), You're On (prod.), Roger Rabbit & the Secrets of Toontown (exec. prod.).

KENNEY, H. WESLEY
Producer, Director. b. Dayton, OH, Jan. 3, 1926. e. Carnegie Inst. of Tech. Guest Instructor, UCLA; guest lecturer, Televisia: Mexico City.
THEATER: *Dir*: Ten Little Indians (Advent Th., L.A.), The Best Christmas Pageant Ever, Love Letters (WV State Theatre), Shadowlands (Tracey Roberts Theatre).
TELEVISION: *Series*: All in the Family (dir.), The Jefferson (pilot dir.), Days of Our Lives (exec. prod. 1979-81), Ladies Man (dir.), Filthy Rich (dir.), Flo (dir.), The Young and the Restless (exec. prod. 1981-86), General Hospital (exec. prod. 1986-89). Dir. Sopa Break. Infomercials (dir.): Elements of Beauty, Merle Norman Experience,

KENSIT, PATSY
Actress. b. London, England, Mar. 4, 1968. Made film debut at the age of 4 in The Great Gatsby. Later appeared in commercials directed by Tony Scott and Adrian Lyne.
PICTURES: The Great Gatsby (debut, 1974), Alfie Darling, The Blue Bird, Hanover Street, Absolute Beginners, Lethal Weapon 2, A Chorus of Disapproval, Chicago Joe and the Showgirl, Timebomb, Twenty-One, Blue Tornado, Blame It on the Bellboy, Beltenebros, Kleptomania, The Turn of the Screw, Bitter Harvest, Angels and Insects, Grace of My Heart.
TELEVISION: *BBC*: Great Expectations, Silas Marner, Tycoon: The Story of a Woman, Adam Bede. *U.S.*: The Corsican Brothers, Fall from Grace, Love and Betrayal: The Mia Farrow Story.

KENT, JEAN
Actress. r.n. Joan Summerfield. b. London, England, June 29, 1921. e. Marist Coll., Peekham, London. First stage appearance at 3; at age 10 played in parents' act; chorus girl at Windmill Theatre, London, 1935; 2 yrs. repertory before debuting on screen under real name.
PICTURES: The Rocks of Valpre (High Treason; debut, 1934), It's That Man Again (first film as Jean Kent, 1943), Fanny by Gaslight (Man of Evil), Champagne Charlie, 2000 Women, Madonna of the Seven Moons, The Wicked Lady, The Rake's Progress (The Notorious Gentleman), Caravan, The Magic Bow, The Man Within (The Smugglers), Good Time Girl, Bond Street, Sleeping Car to Trieste, Trottie True (Gay Lady), Her Favorite Husband, The Woman in Question, The Browning Version, The Big Frame (The Lost Hours), Before I Wake (Shadow of Fear), The Prince and the Showgirl, Bonjour Tristesse, Grip of the Strangler (The Haunted Strangler), Beyond This Place (Web of Evidence), Please Turn Over, Bluebeard's Ten Honeymoons, Shout at the Devil, The Saving of Aunt Esther.
TELEVISION: A Call on the Widow, The Lovebird, The Morning Star, November Voyage, Love Her to Death, The Lion and the Mouse, The Web, Sir Francis Drake series, Yvette, Emergency Ward 10, County Policy, Coach 7, Smile on the Face of the Tiger, No Hiding Place, Kipling, This Man Craig, The Killers, Vanity Fair, A Night with Mrs. Da Tanka, United serial. The Family of Fred, After Dark, Thicker than Water series, The Young Doctors, Brother and Sister, Up Pompei, Steptoe and Son, Doctor at Large, Family at War, K is for Killing, Night School, Tycoon series, Crossroads (series), Lyttons Diary, Lovejoy (series), Missing Persons, After Henry (series), Shrinks (series).

KENT, JOHN B.
Theatre executive, Attorney. b. Jacksonville, FL, Sept. 5, 1939. e. Yale U., U. of FL, Law Sch., NYU grad. sch. of law (L.L.M. in taxation, 1964). Partner in Kent Ridge & Crawford, P.A.; pres. & dir, Kent Investments, Inc. 1977-; v.p. & gen. counsel, Kent Theatres, Inc. 1970-; dir. & v.p., Kent Enterprises, Inc. 1961-; dir. & v.p. Kent Cinemas Inc. 1993-. Was pres. of Kent Theatres Inc. 1967-70; resigned to devote full time to law practice. NATO dir. 1972 and Presidents' Advisory Cabinet, 1979-; v.p./dir. NATO of FL, 1968-. Member of Rotary Club ofJacksonville, Fla. Bar Ass'n., American Bar Ass'n.

KENYON, CURTIS
Writer. b. New York, NY, March 12, 1914.
PICTURES: Woman Who Dared, Lloyds of London, Wake Up and Live, Love and Hisses, She Knew All the Answers, Twin

Beds, Seven Days' Leave, Thanks for Everything, Bathing Beauty, Fabulous Dorseys, Tulsa, Two Flags West, Mr. Ricco. TELEVISION: Cavalcade of America, Fireside Theatre, Schlitz Playhouse, U.S. Steel Hour, 20th Century-Fox Hour. Series: Hawaii 5-O.

KERASOTES, GEORGE G.
Exhibitor. b. Springfield, IL. e. U. of IL, 1929-33; Lincoln Coll. of Law 1935-37. Past pres. & chmn., Kerasotes Theatres, 1935-85; Pres. & chmn., George Kersotes Corp. & GKC Theatres, Inc., 1984-96.Past pres. Theatre Owners of Illinois. Past pres. & chmn. Kerasotes Theatres, 1935-85. Past pres., Theatre Owners of America, 1959-60. Chmn. of board of TOA 1960-62; chmn. ACE Toll TV com.; bd. mem. NATO; treas., bd. of dirs., memebr, exec. comm., chmn., insurance comm. Director, St. Anthony's Hellenic Church, Hellenic Golf Classic. Director, Will Rogers Hospitals; Director, Pioneers. Robert W. Selig ShoWester of the Year, NATO, Las Vegas, 1992.

KERKORIAN, KIRK
Executive. b. Fresno, CA, June 6, 1917. e. Los Angeles public schools. Served as capt., transport command, RAF, 1942-44. Commercial air line pilot from 1940; founder Los Angeles Air Service (later Trans Intl. Airlines Corp.), 1948; Intl. Leisure Corp., 1968; controlling stockholder, Western Airlines, 1970; chief exec. officer, MGM, Inc., 1973-74; chmn. exec. com., vice-chmn. bd., 1974-1978. Stepped down from exec. positions while retaining financial interest in MGM/UA. Repurchased MGM in the summer of 1996.

KERNER, JORDAN
Producer. e. Stanford U, A.B. Political Science & Communications; U.C. Berkely, J.D.-M.B.A.. Bgean career in entertainment working for CBS affiliate KPIX-TV. Joined law firm of Ball, Hunt, Brown & Baerwitz. Talent & Program Negotiator for CBS. Worked for Universal Pictures & QM Prods., 1978-81. Joined ABC Entertainment as dir., Dramatic Series Develop-ment. Promoted to v.p., 1983. While at ABC, placed Moonlight-ing, MacGyver, Dynasty, Spencer for Hire, Call To Glory. Founded the Avnet/Kerner Co. in 1986 with Jordan Kerner. Currently dir., Allied Communications, Inc. Member, bd. of dirs., The Starbright Foundation, The Chrysalis Foundation. Member, President's Advisory Council for the City of Hope, Sen. Dianne Feinstein's California Cabinet, Planned Parenthood, Earth Communications Office, A.M.P.A.S., A.F.I. Former secy., Academy of Television Arts & Sciences. Founder and former co-chmn., Committee for the Arts of the Beverly Hills Bar Asoc. Founder, COMM/ENT, the Journal of Communications & Entertainment Law.
PICTURES: Less Than Zero, Funny About Love, The Mighty Ducks, Fried Green Tomatoes, The War, The Three Musketeers, When A Man Loves A Woman, D2: The Mighty Ducks, D3: The Mighty Ducks, George of the Jungle, Miami Rhapsody (exec. prod.), Up Close and Personal, Swiss Family Robinson, Dinner For Two at the El Cortez, To Live For, Friday Night Lights, Blaze of Glory, sequel to Fried Green Tomatoes (as yet, untitled), Mula 18.
TELEVISION: The Switch, For Their Own Good, Side By Side, My First Love, Do You Know the Muffin Man, The Nightman, Backfield in Motion, Heat Wave, Breaking Point.

KERNS, JOANNA
Actress. b. San Francisco, CA, Feb. 12, 1953. r.n. Joanna de Varona. Former gymnast, became dancer, appeared on tv commercials. Sister is Olympic swimmer and tv commentator Donna de Varona. NY stage: Ulysses in Nighttown.
PICTURES: Coma, Cross My Heart, Street Justice, An American Summer.
TELEVISION: Series: The Four Seasons, Growing Pains (also wrote one episode). Guest: Three's Company, Magnum P.I., Hill Street Blues, Hunter, etc. Movies: The Million Dollar Rip-Off, Marriage Is Alive and Well, Mother's Day on Walton's Mountain, A Wedding on Walton's Mountain, A Day of Thanks on Walton's Mountain, The Return of Marcus Welby M.D., A Bunny's Tale, The Rape of Richard Beck, Stormin' Home, Mistress, Those She Left Behind, Like Mother Like Daughter, The Preppie Murder, Blind Faith, Captive, The Nightman, Not in My Family, The Man With 3 Wives, Shameful Secrets, No Dessert Dad 'Til You Mow the Lawn, Robin Cook's Mortal Fear, See Jane Run, Whose Daughter Is She?

KERR, DEBORAH
Actress. b. Helensburgh, Scotland, Sept. 30, 1921; e. Phyllis Smale Ballet Sch. On stage 1939 in repertory before Brit. screen career began the following year. Voted Star of Tomorrow by Motion Picture Herald-Fame Poll, 1942. Voted one of top ten British money-making stars in Motion Picture Herald-Fame Poll, 1947. B'way debut in Tea and Sympathy, 1953. Received special Academy Award, 1994.
PICTURES: Major Barbara (debut, 1940), Love on the Dole, Penn of Pennsylvania, Hatter's Castle, The Day Will Dawn (The Avengers), The Life and Death of Colonel Blimp, Perfect Strangers (Vacation From Marriage), I See a Dark Stranger

(The Adventuress), Black Narcissus (Acad. Award nom.), The Hucksters (U.S. debut), If Winter Comes, Edward My Son, Please Believe Me, King Solomon's Mines, Quo Vadis, The Prisoner of Zenda, Thunder in the East, Dream Wife, Julius Caesar, Young Bess, From Here to Eternity (Acad. Award nom.), End of the Affair, The King and I (Acad. Award nom.), The Proud and the Profane, Tea and Sympathy, Heaven Knows Mr. Allison (Acad. Award nom.), An Affair to Remember, Bonjour Tristesse, Separate Tables (Acad. Award nom.), The Journey, Count Your Blessings, Beloved Infidel, The Sundowners (Acad. Award nom.), The Grass Is Greener, The Innocents, The Naked Edge, The Chalk Garden, The Night of the Iguana, Marriage On the Rocks, Casino Royale, Eye of the Devil, Prudence and the Pill, The Gypsy Moths, The Arrangement, The Assam Garden.
TELEVISION: Movies: A Woman of Substance, Reunion at Fairborough, Hold the Dream, Witness for the Prosecution.

KERR, FRASER
Actor. b. Glasgow, Scotland, Feb. 25, 1931. Early career in repertory. Tours of Canada and America. Ent. TV 1956. Series incl. Emergency Ward 10, Dixon of Deck Green, Murder Bag. Many Shakespeare plays. Radio: BBC Drama Rep. Co., 39 Steps, The Ringer, The Bible, What Every Woman Knows, The Ruling Class.
THEATER & TELEVISION: Night Must Fall, Never a Cross Word, The Inside Man, On the Buses, Dr. Finlay's Casebook, Wicked Woman, Madelaine July, Doctor in the House, Counterstrike, Waggoner's Walk, Juno and the Paycock, Aquarius, Ev, Upstairs and Downstairs, Cover to Cover, Janine, Robert the Bruce, Caliph of Bagdad, Watch it, Sailor!, The Fosters, Weekend World, Doctor at Sea, Dads Army, Algernon Blackwood, Waiting for Sheila, Weekend Show, Mind Your Language, Yes, Minister, Dick Emery Show, Bottle Boys, The Hard Man, Brigadoon, Hair of the Dog.
PICTURES: What a Whopper, Carry on Regardless, Way of McEagle, Thomasina, Theatre of Death, Tom, Dick and Harriet, Granny Gets the Point, Nothing but the Night, The Lord of the Rings, Kidnapped, The Derelict, Bloomfield, Ace of Diamonds, Andy Robson, It's a Deal!, Howard's Way, One Step Beyond, The Trawler.
RECORD PRODUCER: Tales of Shakespeare Series, The Casket Letters of Mary Queen of Scots.

KERSHNER, IRVIN
Director. b. Philadelphia, PA, April 29, 1923. e. Tyler Sch. of Fine Arts of Temple U., 1946; Art Center Sch., U. of Southern California. Designer, photography, adv., documentary, architectural; doc. filmmaker, U.S.I.S., Middle East, 1950-52; dir., cameraman, TV doc., Confidential File, 1953-55; dir.-prod.-writer, Ophite Prod. Appeared as actor in film The Last Temptation of Christ.
PICTURES: Stakeout on Dope Street (debut, 1958; also co-s.p.), The Young Captives, The Hoodlum Priest, A Face in the Rain, The Luck of Ginger Coffey, A Fine Madness, The Flim-Flam Man, Loving, Up the Sandbox, S*P*Y*S, The Return of a Man Called Horse, Eyes of Laura Mars, The Empire Strikes Back, Never Say Never Again, Robocop 2.
TELEVISION: Series: The Rebel, Naked City, numerous pilots and other nat'l. shows. Movies: Raid on Entebbe (theatrical in Europe), The Traveling Man. Pilot: seaQuest dsv.

KERWIN, BRIAN
Actor. b. Chicago, IL, Oct. 25, 1949. e. USC.
THEATRE: NY: Emily (Theatre World Award), Lips Together Teeth Apart, Raised in Captivity. LA: Strange Snow (LA Drama Critics Award), Who's Afraid of Virginia Woolf?, A Loss of Roses, Torch Song Trilogy.
PICTURES: Hometown USA (debut, 1979), Nickel Mountain, Murphy's Romance, King Kong Lives, Torch Song Trilogy, S.P.O.O.K.S., Hard Promises, Love Field, Gold Diggers: The Secret of Bear Mountain, Getting Away With Murder, Jack.
TELEVISION: Series: The Young and the Restless (1976-77), The Misadventures of Sheriff Lobo, Angel Falls. Mini-Series: The Chisholms, The Blue and the Gray, Bluegrass. Movies: A Real American Hero, Power, Miss All-American Beauty, Intimate Agony, Wet Gold, The Greatest Thing That Almost Happened, Challenger, Switched at Birth, Against Her Will: An Incident in Baltimore, Abandoned and Deceived, It Came From Outer Space, Sins of Silence. Special: Natica Jackson (Tales of the Hollywood Hills). Guest: St. Elsewhere, The Love Boat, B.J. and the Bear, Roseanne, Murder She Wrote, Simon & Simon, Highway to Heaven.

KEYES, EVELYN
Actress. b. Port Arthur, TX, Nov. 20, 1919. e. high school. Began career as a dancer in night clubs.
AUTHOR: Novel: I Am a Billboard (1971). Autobiographies: Scarlett O'Hara's Younger Sister (1977), I'll Think About That Tomorrow (1991).
PICTURES: Artists and Models (debut, 1937), The Buccaneer, Men With Wings, Artists and Models Abroad, Sons of the Legion, Dangerous to Know, Paris Honeymoon,

Union Pacific, Sudden Money, Gone with the Wind, Slightly Honorable, Before I Hang, Beyond Sacramento, The Lady in Question, The Face Behind the Mask, Here Comes Mr. Jordan, Ladies in Retirement, The Adventures of Martin Eden, Flight Lieutenant, There's Something About a Soldier, Dangerous Blondes, The Desperadoes, Nine Girls, Strange Affair, A Thousand and One Nights, The Jolson Story, Renegades, The Thrill of Brazil, The Mating of Millie, Johnny O'Clock, Enchantment, Mrs. Mike, Mr. Soft Touch, The Killer That Stalked New York, Smuggler's Island, The Iron Man, The Prowler, One Big Affair, Shoot First, 99 River Street, Hell's Half Acre, It Happend in Paris, Top of the World, The Seven Year Itch, Around the World in 80 Days, Across 110th Street, Return to Salem's Lot, Wicked Stepmother.
TELEVISION: Guest: Murder She Wrote.

KEYLOUN, MARK
Actor. b. Dec. 20, 1960. e. Georgetown U. Worked in New York theatre.
PICTURES: Those Lips Those Eyes, Sudden Impact, Forty-Deuce, Mike's Murder.
TELEVISION: Evergreen, War Stories: The Mine.

KIDD, MICHAEL
Choreographer, Dancer, Actor. r.n. Milton Greenwald. b. Brooklyn, NY, Aug. 12, 1919. e. CCNY. Studied dance at School of the American Ballet. Was dancer with Lincoln Kirstein's Ballet Caravan, Eugene Loring's Dance Players, Ballet Theatre. Became stage choreographer starting in 1945.
THEATER: B'way (choreographer): Finian's Rainbow (Tony Award, 1947), Love Life, Arms and the Girl, Guys and Dolls (Tony Award, 1951), Can-Can (Tony Award, 1954), Li'l Abner (Tony Award, 1957; also dir., prod.), Destry Rides Again (Tony Award, 1960; also dir.), Wildcat (also dir., co-prod.), Subways Are for Sleeping (also dir.), Here's Love, Ben Franklin in Paris, Skyscraper, The Rothschilds (also dir.). B'way (dir.): Cyrano, Good News, Pal Joey, The Music Man, The Goodbye Girl.
PICTURES: Choreographer: Where's Charley?, The Band Wagon, Knock on Wood, Seven Brides for Seven Brothers, Guys and Dolls, Merry Andrew (also dir.), Li'l Abner, Star!, Hello Dolly!, Movie Movie (also actor). Actor: It's Always Fair Weather, Smile, Skin Deep.
TELEVISION: Specials (choreographer): Baryshnikov in Hollywood, Academy Awards. Movie (actor): For the Love of It.

KIDDER, MARGOT
Actress. r.n. Margaret Kidder. b. Yellowknife, Canada, Oct. 17, 1948.
PICTURES: The Best Damned Fiddler From Calabogie to Kaladar (debut, 1968), Gaily Gaily, Quackser Fortune Has a Cousin in the Bronx, Sisters, A Quiet Day in Belfast, The Gravy Train, Black Christmas, The Great Waldo Pepper, 92 in the Shade, The Reincarnation of Peter Proud, Superman, Mr. Mike's Mondo Video, The Amityville Horror, Willie and Phil, Superman II, Heartaches, Shoot the Sun Down, Some Kind of Hero, Trenchcoat, Superman III, Little Treasure, GoBots (voice), Superman IV: The Quest for Peace, Miss Right, Mob Story, White Room, Crime and Punishment.
TELEVISION: Series: Nichols, Shell Game. Movies: Suddenly Single, The Bounty Man, Honky Tonk, Louisiana, The Glitter Dome, Picking Up the Pieces, Vanishing Act, Body of Evidence, To Catch a Killer, One Woman's Courage, Bloodknot. Specials: Bus Stop, Pygmalion. Guest: Murder She Wrote. Director: White People, Love 40.

KIDMAN, NICOLE
Actress. b. Hawaii, June 20, 1967. m. actor Tom Cruise. Raised in Australia. Made acting debut at 14 in Australian film Bush Christmas. On Australian stage in Steel Magnolias (Sydney Theatre Critics Award for Best Newcomer).
PICTURES: Bush Christmas (debut, 1982), BMZ Bandits, Windrider, Dead Calm, Emerald City, Days of Thunder, Billy Bathgate, Far and Away, Flirting, Malice, My Life, Batman Forever, To Die For (Golden Globe, 1996), Portrait of a Lady.
TELEVISION: Mini-Series (Australia): Five-Mile Creek, Vietnam, Bangkok Hilton.

KIDRON, BEEBAN
Director. b. London, England. e. National Film School. Made co-dir. debut (with Amanda Richardson) with documentary Carry Greenham Home (Chicago Film Fest. Hugo Award, 1983).
PICTURES: Antonia and Jane, Used People, Great Moments in Aviation, To Wong Foo—Thanks for Everything—Julie Newmar.
TELEVISION: The Global Gamble, Vroom, Oranges Are Not the Only Fruit.

KIEL, RICHARD
Actor. b. Detroit, MI, Sept. 13, 1939. Former nightclub bouncer.
PICTURES: The Phantom Planet (debut, 1961), Eegah!, House of the Damned, The Magic Sword, Roustabout, The Human Duplicators, Las Vegas Hillbillies, A Man Called Dagger, Skidoo, The Longest Yard, Flash and the Firecat, Silver Streak, The Spy Who Loved Me, Force 10 from Navarone, They Went Thataway and Thataway, Moonraker, The Humanoid, So Fine, Hysterical, Cannonball Run II, Pale Rider, Think Big, The Giant of Thunder Mountain (also co-s.p., co-exec. prod.).
TELEVISION: Series: The Barbary Coast, Van Dyke & Company. Movies: Now You See It Now You Don't, The Barbary Coast (pilot).

KIERZEK, TERRY
Executive. b. Chicago, IL, Feb. 15, 1951. e. U. of Il. Joined Paramount Pictures Domestic Distrib., as booker in Chicago, 1974. Promoted to Sales in 1976, Dallas, TX. Named branch mgr., Dallas/OK City, 1978. V.P., Eastern Division in Washington, D.C., 1982-84. V.P., Southern Division, Dallas, TX., 1984-86. V.P., Western Division, Los Angeles, 1986-89. Orion Pictures v.p., Western Division, 1990-92. Joined National Film Service in 1993 as v.p., sales & mktg. Named exec. v.p., 1995. Appointed pres., National Film Service in 1996.

KIESLOWSKI, KRZYSZTOF
Director. b. Warsaw, Poland, June 27, 1941. Studied at Lodz Film School. Autobiography: Kieslowski on Kieslowksi.
PICTURES: Picture, Workers, First Love, Personnel, Biography, Scar, Politics, Hospital, Calm, Seen by the Night Porter, Station, Anator/Camera Buff, Talking Heads, A Short Day's Work, No End, Blind Chance, A Short Film About Killing/Thou Shalt Not Kill, A Short Film About Life, City Life (Seven Days a Week episode), The Double Life of Veronique, Blue, White, Red.
(d. March 13, 1996)

KILEY, RICHARD
Actor. b. Chicago, IL, Mar. 31, 1922. e. Loyola U. Started prof. career on radio in Jack Armstrong, Tom Mix, Ma Perkins, etc.
THEATER: A Streetcar Named Desire (tour), Misalliance, Kismet, Time Limit, Redhead (Tony Award, 1959), No Strings, Man of LaMancha (Tony Award, 1966), Her First Roman, The Incomparable Max, Voices, Absurd Person Singular, All My Sons.
PICTURES: The Mob (debut, 1951), The Sniper, Eight Iron Men, Pick-Up on South Street, Blackboard Jungle, The Phenix City Story, Spanish Affair, Pendulum, The Little Prince, Looking for Mr. Goodbar, Endless Love, Howard the Duck (voice), Jurassic Park (voice), Phenomenon.
TELEVISION: Series: A Year in the Life (Emmy Award, 1988). Mini-Series: The Thorn Birds (Emmy Award, 1983), George Washington, If Tomorrow Comes, A.D. Movies: Night Gallery, Incident in San Francisco, Murder Once Removed, Jigsaw, Friendly Persuasion, The Macahans, Angel on My Shoulder, Golden Gate, Isabel's Choice, Pray TV, The Bad Seed, Do You Remember Love?, My First Love, The Final Days, Gunsmoke: The Last Apache, Separate But Equal, Absolute Strangers, The Cosby Mysteries, A Passion for Justice: The Hazel Brannon Smith Story, Secrets. Specials: Mastergate, 30 Years of National Geographic Specials (narrator). Guest: Picket Fences (Emmy Award, 1994).

KILMER, VAL
Actor. b. Los Angeles, CA, Dec. 31, 1959. e. Hollywood Professional Sch., Juilliard, NY. Appeared in IMAX film Wings of Courage.
THEATRE: NY: Electra and Orestes, How It All Began (also co-writer), Henry IV Part One, Slab Boys (B'way debut), 'Tis Pity She's a Whore. Also: As You Like It (Gutherie MN), Hamlet (Colorado Shakespeare Fest.).
PICTURES: Top Secret! (debut, 1984), Real Genius, Top Gun, Willow, Kill Me Again, The Doors, Thunderheart, True Romance, The Real McCoy, Tombstone, Batman Forever, Heat, The Island of Dr. Moreau, The Ghost and the Darkness, The Saint.
TELEVISION: Movies: Murders in the Rue Morgue, The Man Who Broke 1000 Chains, Gore Vidal's Billy the Kid.

KIMBLEY, DENNIS
Executive. Early career in Kodak Testing Dept. responsible for quality control motion picture films. Joined Marketing Division 1966. Chairman BKSTS FILM 75 and FILM 79 Conference Committee. President BKSTS 1976-78. Governor, London International Film School, 1983. Bd. member, British Board of Film Classification; dir. of Children's Film Unit.

KIMBROUGH, CHARLES
Actor. b. St. Paul, MN, May 23, 1936. e. Indiana U., Yale U.
THEATER: NY: All in Love (debut, 1961), Cop-Out (B'way debut, 1969), Company (Tony nom.), Candide, Love for Love, The Rules of the Game, Secret Service, Mr. Happiness, Same Time Next Year, Drinks Before Dinner, The Dining Room, Sunday in the Park With George, Hay Fever. Several prods. with Milwaukee Rep. Theatre (1966-73).

PICTURES: The Front (debut, 1976), The Seduction of Joe Tynan, Starting Over, It's My Turn, Switching Channels, The Good Mother, The Hunchback of Notre Dame (voice).
TELEVISION: *Series*: Murphy Brown (Emmy nom.). *Movies*: For Ladies Only, A Doctor's Story, Weekend War, Cast the First Stone. *Pilot*: The Recovery Room. *Special*: Sunday in the Park With George.

KING, ALAN
Actor, Producer. r.n. Irwin Alan Kingberg. b. Brooklyn, NY, Dec. 26, 1927. Started as musician, stand-up comedian in Catskills, then nightclubs. Author: Anybody Who Owns His Own Home Deserves It, Help I'm a Prisoner in a Chinese Bakery.
THEATER: The Impossible Years, The Investigation, Dinner at Eight, The Lion in Winter, Something Different.
PICTURES: *Actor*: Hit the Deck (debut, 1955), Miracle in the Rain, The Girl He Left Behind, The Helen Morgan Story, On the Fiddle (Operation Snafu), Bye Bye Braverman, The Anderson Tapes, Just Tell Me What You Want, Prince of the City (cameo), Author! Author!, I the Jury, Lovesick, Cat's Eye, You Talkin' to Me?, Memories of Me (also co-prod.), Enemies a Love Story, The Bonfire of the Vanities, Night and the City, Casino. *Producer*: Happy Birthday Gemini, Cattle Annie and Little Britches (co-prod.), Wolfen (exec. prod.).
TELEVISION: *Guest/Host*: The Tonight Show, Kraft Music Hall. *Prod-star NBC-TV specials*: Comedy is King, On Location: An Evening With Alan King at Carnegie Hall, etc. *Mini-Series*: Seventh Avenue. *Movies*: Return to Earth (co-exec. prod. only), How to Pick Up Girls (also exec. prod.), Pleasure Palace, Dad the Angel and Me, The Infiltrator. *Host*: Alan King: Inside the Comic Mind (Comedy Central).

KING, ANDREA
Actress. r.n. Georgette Barry. b. Paris, France, Feb. 1, 1919. e. Edgewood H.S., Greenwich, CT. m. N.H. Willis, attorney. Started career on NY stage, following high school; in Growing Pains & Fly Away Home, Boy Meets Girl, Angel Street (Boston); Life with Father (Chicago); signed by Warner, 1943. Screen debut as Georgette McKee in The Ramparts We Watch, 1940.
PICTURES: Hotel Berlin, God is My Co-Pilot, The Very Thought of You, The Man I Love, The Beast With Five Fingers, Shadow of a Woman, Roughly Speaking, My Wild Irish Rose, Ride the Pink Horse, Mr. Peabody and the Mermaid, Song of Surrender, Southside 1-10001, I Was a Shoplifter, Dial 1119, The Lemon Drop Kid, Mark of the Renegade, World in His Arms, Red Planet Mars, Darby's Rangers, Band of Angels, Daddy's Gone A-Hunting, The Linguini Incident, The Color of Evening.
TELEVISION: *Movie*: Prescription Murder. *Specials*: Dream Girl, Officer and the Lady, Witness for the Prosecution. *Guest*: Fireside Theatre, Maya.

KING, LARRY
Talk Show Host, Writer. b. Brooklyn, NY, Nov. 19, 1933. Started as disc jockey on various Miami radio stations from 1958-64. Became host of radio talk show, broadcast from Miami before moving to Arlington, VA, in 1978. Show has run since then on Mutual Broadcasting System. Host of CNN tv talk show since 1985, Larry King Live. Starred in tv special Larry King Extra. Columnist for Miami Beach Sun-Reporter, Sporting News, USA Today. Appeared in films Ghostbusters, Eddie and the Cruisers II: Eddie Lives, The Exorcist III.
AUTHOR: Larry King by Larry King, Tell It to the King, Mr. King You're Having a Heart Attack, Tell Me More, How to Talk to Anyone Anytime Anywhere: The Secrets of Good Conversation.

KING, PERRY
Actor. b. Alliance, OH, Apr. 30, 1948. e. Yale. Studied with John Houseman at Juilliard. B'way debut 1990 in A Few Good Men.
PICTURES: Slaughterhouse-Five (debut, 1972), The Possession of Joel Delaney, The Lords of Flatbush, Mandingo, The Wild Party, Lipstick, Andy Warhol's Bad, The Choirboys, A Different Story, Search and Destroy (Striking Back), Class of 1984, Killing Hour (The Clairvoyant), Switch, A Cry in the Night.
TELEVISION: *Series*: The Quest, Riptide, Almost Home, The Trouble With Larry. *Guest*: Medical Center, Hawaii Five-O, Apple's Way, Cannon. *Mini-Series*: Aspen, The Last Convertible, Captain and the Kings. *Movies*: Foster and Laurie, The Cracker Factory, Love's Savage Fury, City in Fear, Inmates: A Love Story, Golden Gate, Helen Keller: The Miracle Continues, Stranded, Perfect People, Shakedown on Sunset Strip, The Man Who Lived at the Ritz, Disaster at Silo 7, The Prize Pulitzer, Danielle Steel's Kaleidoscope, Only One Survived, Something to Live For, Sidney Sheldon's A Stranger in the Mirror, Jericho Fever, Good King Wenceslas, She Led Two Lives. *Pilot*: Half 'n' Half.

KING, PETER
Executive, Barrister-at-law. b. London, England, Mar. 22, 1928. e. Marlborough, Oxford U. (MA, honors). Bd., Shipman

& King Cinemas Ltd., 1956; borough councillor, 1959-61; chmn., London & Home counties branch, CEA, 1962-63; pres., CEA, 1964; mang. dir. Shipman & King Cinemas Ltd., 1959-68; chmn. & mang. dir. Paramount Pictures (U.K.) Ltd. Britain, 1968-70; mang. dir., EMI Cinemas and Leisure Ltd., 1970-74; chmn. & mang. dir. King Publications/pub. Screen Intl., 1974-89; pres., Screen Intl., 1989-90; chmn. & mang. dir., Rex Publications Ltd., 1990-; pub., Majesty, 1990-; pub. Preview.

KING, STEPHEN
Writer. b. Portland, ME, Sept. 21, 1947. e. Univ. of Maine at Orono (B.S.). Best-selling novelist specializing in thrillers many of which have been adapted to film by others. *Movie adaptations*: Carrie, The Shining, The Dead Zone, Christine, Cujo, Children of the Corn, Firestarter, Cat's Eye, Stand By Me (The Body), The Running Man, Pet Sematary, Misery, Apt Pupil, The Lawnmower Man, The Dark Half, Needful Things, The Shawshank Redemption, The Mangler, Dolores Claiborne. *TV adaptations*: Salem's Lot, IT, Sometimes They Come Back, The Tommyknockers, The Langoliers.
PICTURES: Knightriders (actor), Creepshow (s.p., actor), Children of the Corn (s.p.), Silver Bullet (s.p.), Maximum Overdrive (dir., s.p., actor), Creepshow II (actor), Pet Sematary (s.p., actor), Sleepwalkers (s.p., actor).
TELEVISION: *Series*: Golden Years (creator, writer). *Mini-Series*: The Stand (writer, actor), The Langoliers (actor).

KING, ZALMAN
Actor, Director, Writer. b. Trenton, NJ, 1941. r.n. Zalman King Lefkowitz. m. writer Patricia Knop.
PICTURES: *Actor*: The Ski Bum, You've Got to Walk It Like You Talk It or You'll Lose the Beat, Neither by Day Nor Night, Some Call It Loving, Trip with the Teacher, Sammy Somebody, The Passover Plot, Blue Sunshine, Tell Me a Riddle, Galaxy of Terror. *Exec. Prod.*: Roadie (also co-story), Endangered Species, Siesta. *Prod./Writer*: 9 1/2 Weeks. *Director-Writer*: Wildfire, Two Moon Junction, Wild Orchid, Wild Orchid II: Two Shades of Blue, Delta of Venus.
TELEVISION: *Series*: The Young Lawyers, Red Shoe Diaries (exec. prod., creator, dir. episodes). *Guest*: Alfred Hitchcock Presents, Land of the Giants, Gunsmoke, Adam 12, Charlie's Angels, etc. *Movies*: The Dangerous Days of Kiowa Jones, Stranger on the Run, The Young Lawyers (pilot), The Intruders, Smile Jenny You're Dead, Like Normal People, Lake Consequence (co-prod., co-writer).

KINGMAN, DONG
Fine Artist. b. Oakland, CA, Mar. 31, 1911. e. Hong Kong 1916-1920. 1928, mem. motion picture co., Hong Kong branch; 1935; began to exhibit as fine artist in San Francisco; promotional, advertising or main title artwork for following films: World of Suzie Wong, Flower Drum Song, 55 Days of Peking, Circus World, King Rat, The Desperados, The Sand Pebbles, Lost Horizon. 1966-67, created 12 paintings for Universal Studio Tour for posters and promotion; 1968, cover painting for souvenir program for Ringling Bros.,Barnum and Bailey Circus; treasurer for Living Artist Production since 1954; Exec. V.P. 22nd-Century Films, Inc. since 1968, Prod. & dir. short, Hongkong Dong. Also short subject film Dong Kingman, filmed and directed by James Wong Howe. 1993 Chinese-American Arts Council exhibition of all motion picture work. 1996, created official poster for Olympic Games.

KINGSLEY, BEN
Actor. r.n. Krishna Banji. b. Snaiton, Yorkshire, England, Dec. 31, 1943. Started career with Salford Players, amateur co. in Manchester. Turned pro in 1966 and appeared on London stage at a Chichester Festival Theatre. 1967, joined Royal Shakespeare Co., appearing in A Midsummer Night's Dream, Tempest, Measure for Measure, Merry Wives of Windsor, Volpone, Cherry Orchard, Hamlet, Othello, Judgement. On NY stage in Kean. Played Squeers in Nicholas Nickleby in 1980 in London.
PICTURES: Fear Is the Key (debut, 1972), Gandhi (Academy Award, 1982), Betrayal, Turtle Diary, Harem, Maurice, Testimony, Pascali's Island, Without a Clue, Bugsy (Acad. Award nom.), Sneakers, Dave, Searching for Bobby Fisher (Innocent Moves), Schindler's List, Death and the Maiden, Species, Twelfth Night.
TELEVISION: *Movies/Specials*: Silas Marner, Kean, Oxbridge Blues, Camille, Murderers Among Us: The Simon Wiesenthal Story, Joseph, Moses.

KINGSLEY, WALTER
Executive. b New York, NY, Oct. 20, 1923. e. Phillips Acad., Andover; Amherst Coll., B.A., 1947. Charter member Big Brothers of Los Angeles. WCOP, Boston, 1948-50; Ziv Television Programs, Inc., 1950-58; pres., Independent Television Corp. (ITC), 1958-62; member bd. dir Big Brothers of Amer.; pres. Kingsley Co., 1962-66; exec. v.p. Wolper Prods. Metromedia Prods. Corp., 1966-72; faculty, Inter-Racial Council of Business Opportunity, N.Y.; 1972-82, pres.,

Kingsley Company, Commercial Real Estate; 1983-present, special consultant, American Film Inst.; bd. mem.: Big Brothers/Big Sisters of America; Big Brothers of Greater Los Angeles.

KINOY, ERNEST
Writer. Started career in radio writing sci. fic. programs (X Minus One, Dimension X). Wrote for nearly all early dramatic shows, including Studio One, Philco Playhouse, Playhouse 90.
PICTURES: Brother John, Buck and the Preacher, Leadbelly, White Water Summer (co-s.p.).
TELEVISION: The Defenders (Emmy Award, 1964), Naked City, Dr. Kildare, Jacob and Joseph, David the King, Roots I & II, Victory at Entebbe, Skokie, Murrow, The President's Plane is Missing, Stones for Ibarra, Gore Vidal's Lincoln, The Fatal Shore.

KINSKI, NASTASSJA
Actress. r.n. Nastassja Nakszynski. b. Berlin, Germany, Jan. 24, 1960. m. prod and talent agent, Ibrahim Moussa. Daughter of late actor Klaus Kinski.
PICTURE: Falsche Bewegung (The Wrong Move; debut, 1975), To the Devil a Daughter, Passion Flower Hotel, Stay as You Are, Tess, One From the Heart, Cat People, For Your Love Only, Exposed, The Moon in the Gutter, Unfaithfully Yours, The Hotel New Hampshire, Maria's Lovers, Paris Texas, Revolution, Symphony of Love, Harem, Malady of Love, Silent Night, Torrents of Spring, On a Moonlit Night, Magdalene, The Secret, Night Sun, Faraway So Close!, Crackerjack, Terminal Velocity, The Blonde.

KIRBY, BRUNO
Actor. b. New York, NY, Apr. 28, 1949. Also acted as B. Kirby Jr., and Bruce Kirby Jr. Father is actor Bruce Kirby. On B'way 1991 in Lost in Yonkers.
PICTURES: The Harrad Experiment (debut, 1973), Cinderella Liberty, Superdad, The Godfather Part 2, Baby Blue Marine, Between the Lines, Almost Summer, Where the Buffalo Roam, Borderline, Modern Romance, This Is Spinal Tap, Birdy, Flesh + Blood, Tin Men, Good Morning Vietnam, Bert Rigby You're a Fool, When Harry Met Sally ..., We're No Angels, The Freshman, City Slickers, Hoffa (unbilled), Golden Gate, The Basketball Diaries, Donnie Brasco.
TELEVISION: Series: The Super. Movies: All My Darling Daughters, A Summer Without Boys, Some Kind of Miracle, Million Dollar Infield. Specials: Run Don't Walk (Afterschool Special), The Trap, Mastergate. Guest: Room 222, Columbo, Kojak, Emergency, It's Garry Shandling's Show, Tales From the Crypt, The Larry Sanders Show, Fallen Angels (I'll Be Waiting).

KIRK (BUSH), PHYLLIS
Actress. r.n. Phyllis Kirkegaard. b. Syracuse, NY, Sept. 18, 1926. Perfume repr. model, Conover Agcy.; B'way debut in My Name Is Aquilon followed by Point of No Return. Worked as interviewer-host on all three major networks Executive with ICPR and Stone Associates. Joined CBS News in Los Angeles, 1978; 1988 named v.p. media relations Stone/Hallinan Associates.
PICTURES: Our Very Own (debut, 1950), A Life of Her Own, Two Weeks with Love, Mrs. O'Malley and Mr. Malone, Three Guys Named Mike, About Face, The Iron Mistress, Thunder Over the Plains, House of Wax, Crime Wave, River Beat, Canyon Crossroads, Johnny Concho, Back From Eternity, City After Midnight, The Sad Sack.
TELEVISION: Series: The Red Buttons Show, The Thin Man.

KIRKLAND, SALLY
Actress. b. NY, NY, Oct. 31, 1944. e. Actors Studio, studied acting with Uta Hagen and Lee Strasberg. Achieved notoriety in the 1960s for on-stage nudity (Sweet Eros, Futz), for work in experimental off-off B'way theater and as part of Andy Warhol's inner circle. Appeared as featured actress in over 25 films and countless avant-garde shows, before winning acclaim (and Acad. Award nom.) as the star of Anna (1987). 1983 founded Sally Kirkland Acting Workshop, a traveling transcendental meditation, yoga and theatrical seminar. Formed Artists Alliance Prods. with Mark and David Buntzman, 1988.
THEATER: The Love Nest, Futz, Tom Paine, Sweet Eros, Witness, One Night Stand of a Noisy Passenger, The Justice Box, Where Has Tommy Flowers Gone?, In the Boom Boom Room (L.A., Drama-Logue's best actress award, 1981), Largo Desolato.
PICTURES: The Thirteen Most Beautiful Woman (1964), Blue, Futz!, Coming Apart, Going Home, The Young Nurses, The Way We Were, Cinderella Liberty, The Sting, Candy Stripe Nurses, Big Bad Mama, Bite the Bullet, Crazy Mama, Breakheart Pass, A Star is Born, Pipe Dreams, Hometown U.S.A., Private Benjamin, The Incredible Shrinking Woman, Human Highway, Love Letters, Fatal Games, Talking Walls, Anna, Melanie Rose (High Stakes), Crack in the Mirror (White

Hot), Paint It Black, Cold Feet, Best of the Best, Revenge, Bullseye, Two Evil Eyes, JFK, In the Heat of Passion, The Player, Blast 'Em, Primary Motive, Double Threat, Forever, Cheatin' Hearts (also co-exec. prod.).
TELEVISION: Movies: Kansas City Massacre, Death Scream, Stonestreet: Who Killed the Centerfold Model?, Georgia Peaches, Heat Wave, The Haunted. Double Jeopardy, The Woman Who Loved Elvis, Double Deception. Specials: Willow B—Women in Prison, Summer, Largo Desolato. Series: Falcon Crest. Guest: Roseanne.

KIRKWOOD, GENE
Producer. Company: Kanter-Kirkwood Entertainment.
PICTURES: Rocky, New York New York (assoc. prod.), Comes a Horseman, Uncle Joe Shannon, The Idolmaker, A Night in Heaven, Gorky Park, The Keep, The Pope of Greenwich Village, Ironweed, UHF (co-prod.).

KITT, EARTHA
Actress, Singer. b. Columbia, SC, Jan. 26, 1928. Professional career started as dancer in Katherine Dunham group; toured U.S., Mexico & Europe with group, then opened night club in Paris; in Orson Welles stage prod. of Faust (European tour); N.Y. night clubs before B'way debut in New Faces of 1952. Author: Thursday's Child, A Tart Is Not a Sweet, Alone with Me, Confessions of a Sex Kitten.
THEATRE: NY: New Faces of 1952, Shinbone Alley, Mrs. Patterson, The Skin of Our Teeth, The Owl and the Pussycat, Timbuktu.
PICTURES: New Faces (debut, 1954), The Mark of the Hawk (Accused), St. Louis Blues, Anna Lucasta, Saint of Devil's Island, Synanon, Uncle Tom's Cabin, Up the Chastity Belt, Friday Foster, The Last Resort, The Serpent Warriors, The Pink Chiquitas (voice), Master of Dragonard Hill, Erik the Viking, Ernest Scared Stupid, Boomerang, Fatal Instinct.
TELEVISION: Movies: Lt. Schuster's Wife, To Kill a Cop. Guest: Batman (as Catwoman), I Spy, Miami Vice.

KLEES, ROBERT E.
Executive. b. New York, NY, Feb. 21, 1927. e. Duke U., 1947-51. Univ. of CA Graduate Sch. of Mgt., 1973-75. U.S. Navy, 1944-46; Union Carbide Corp., 1951-57; Beckman Instruments Inc., 1957-69; International Biophysics Corp, 1969-73; sr. v.p., mktg., Deluxe Laboratories Inc., div. of 20th Century Fox, 1975-83. Retired member of AMPAS, ACE, AFI, ASC, SMPTE.

KLEIN, ALLEN
Producer. b. New Jersey, Dec. 18, 1931. e. Upsala. Pres. ABKCO Films, a division of ABKCO Music & Records, Inc.
PICTURES: Force of Impulse, Pity Me Not, Charlie is My Darling, Stranger in Town, Sympathy for the Devil, Mrs. Brown You've Got a Lovely Daughter, The Stranger Returns, The Silent Stranger, Come Together, Pearl & The Pole, Let It Be, Gimme Shelter, El Topo, Blind Man, The Concert for Bangladesh, The Holy Mountain, The Greek Tycoon, Personal Best, It Had to Be You, The Rolling Stones Rock and Roll Circus.

KLEIN, HAROLD J.
Executive. b. New York, NY, e. U. of West Virginia, New York Law Sch. Reviewer, sales staff. Showman's Trade Review; booker, Brandt Theatres; booker, later vice-pres., gen. mgr.; JJ Theatres, 1941-59; account exec., exec. v.p., dir. of world-wide sales, ABC Films, Inc., N.Y., Pres., Klein Film Assn.; exec. v.p., Plitt Theatres, Inc. to Nov., 1985; pres., H.J.K. Film Associates, also acting consultant to P.E.G. (Plitt Entertainment Gp.). Retired.

KLEIN, MALCOLM C.
Executive. b. Los Angeles, CA, Nov. 22, 1927. e. UCLA, grad., 1948; U. of Denver. Prod. dir. management, KLAC-TV (KCOP), L.A., 1948-52; acct. exec., KABC-TV, 1952-56; asst. gen. sales mgr., KABC-TV, 1956-59; exec. v.p. gen. mgr., NTA Broadcasting, N.Y., 1959; v.p., gen. mgr., RKO-General-KHJ-TV, 1960; joined National General Corp. 1968, v.p. creative services and marketing. Pres. National General TV Prods., Inc. Pres. NGC Broadcasting Corp.; 1971, pres. Filmways TV Presentations; 1972, pres. Malcolm C. Klein & Assoc. mgmt. & mktg. consultants; 1973 gen'l. exec. Sterling Recreation Org. & Gen'l Mgr. Broadcast Division; pres., American Song Festival 1976; memb. of faculty, UCLA, USC. Exec. v.p., Telease Inc. & American Subscription Television; 1981, sr. v.p., mng. dir., STAR-TV (subscription TV); 1982, sr. v.p., InterAmerican Satellite TV Network. 1983: Pres. Malcolm C. Klein & Assoc., management consultant. exec. dir. programming, Interactive Network. V.p., bus. development, Interactive Network Inc.

KLEIN, ROBERT
Actor, Comedian. b. New York, NY, Feb. 8, 1942. e. Alfred U, Yale Drama School. Was member of Chicago's Second City comedy group. Comedy albums: Child of the '50s (Grammy nom.), Mind Over Matter, New Teeth, Let's Not Make Love.

THEATRE: *NY*: The Apple Tree, Morning Noon and Night, New Faces of 1968, They're Playing Our Song (Tony Award nom.), The Sisters Rosensweig.
PICTURES: The Landlord, The Owl and the Pussycat, Rivals, The Bell Jar, Hooper, Nobody's Perfekt, The Last Unicorn (voice), Tales from the Darkside—The Movie, Radioland Murders, Mixed Nuts, Jeffrey.
TELEVISION: *Series*: Comedy Tonight, Robert Klein Time, TV's Bloopers and Practical Jokes, Sisters. *Movies*: Your Place or Mine, Poison Ivy, This Wife for Hire. *Guest*: The Tonight Show, ABC Comedy Special, George Burns Comedy Week, Twilight Zone, Late Night With David Letterman. Also appeared in HBO comedy specials.

KLEINER, HARRY
Writer, Producer. b. Philadelphia, PA, Sept. 10, 1916. e. Temple U., B.S.; Yale U., M.F.A.
PICTURES: Fallen Angel, The Street With No Name, Red Skies of Mountain, Kangaroo, Miss Sadie Thompson, Salome, Carmen Jones, The Violent Men, The Garment Jungle (also prod.), Cry Tough (also prod.), The Rabbit Trap (prod. only), Ice Palace, Fever in the Blood, Fantastic Voyage, Bullitt, Le Mans, Extreme Prejudice, Red Heat.
TELEVISION: *Writer*: Rosenberg Trial.

KLEISER, RANDAL
Director, Producer. b. Lebanon, PA, July 20, 1946. e. U. of Southern California. For Disney Theme Parks dir. 70mm 3-D film Honey I Shrunk the Audience.
PICTURES: Street People (s.p.). *Director:* Grease, The Blue Lagoon, Summer Lovers (also s.p.), Grandview U.S.A., Flight of the Navigator, North Shore (exec. prod., co-story only), Big Top Pee-Wee, Getting it Right (also co-prod.), White Fang, Return to the Blue Lagoon (exec. prod. only), Honey I Blew Up the Kid, It's My Party.
TELEVISION: *Movies*: All Together Now, Dawn: Portrait of a Teenage Runaway, The Boy in the Plastic Bubble, The Gathering. *Series*: Marcus Welby, M.D., The Rookies, Starsky and Hutch, Family.

KLINE, FRED W.
Publicist. b. Oakland, CA, May 17, 1918. e. U. of California, Berkeley. M.P. pub. rel. since 1934; pres. & owner The Fred Kline Agency; pres. Kline Communications Corp.; Kline Communications Corp.; Fred W. Kline Prod., Inc.; Capitol News Service, Sacramento; L.A. News Bureau; Capitol Radio News Service, Inc.; Advisor, Calif. Film Commission. Member, Regional Filming Task Force Committee, Los Angeles City Council.

KLINE, KEVIN
Actor. b. St. Louis, MO, Oct. 24, 1947. m. actress Phoebe Cates. e. Indiana U. Studied at Juilliard Theater Center (1968-72), and became founding member of John Houseman's The Acting Company, touring in classics, incl. The School for Scandal, She Stoops to Conquer, The Lower Depths, The Way of the World.
THEATER: Understudied Raul Julia in Lincoln Center's The Threepenny Opera; The Three Sisters (B'way debut, 1973), On the Twentieth Century (Tony Award, 1978), Loose Ends, The Pirates of Penzance (Tony Award, 1981), Richard III, Henry V (Central Park), Arms and the Man, Hamlet, Much Ado About Nothing, Hamlet (1990, also dir.), Measure for Measure.
PICTURES: Sophie's Choice (debut, 1982), The Pirates of Penzance, The Big Chill, Silverado, Violets Are Blue, Cry Freedom, A Fish Called Wanda (Academy Award for Best Supporting Actor, 1988), The January Man, I Love You to Death, Soapdish, Grand Canyon, Consenting Adults, Chaplin, Dave, George Balanchine's The Nutcracker (narrator), Princess Caraboo, French Kiss, Fierce Creatures, The Hunchback of Notre Dame (voice), The Ice Storm.
TELEVISION: *Series*: Search For Tomorrow (1976-77). *Specials*: The Time of Your Life, Hamlet (also co-dir.).

KLINGER, TONY
Producer, Director, Writer, Educator. b. London, 1950. Entered m.p. industry, 1966. In addition to continuing work in m.p. industry, currently lecturing on Film & TV at Bournemouth & Poole College of Art & Design Film School.
PICTURES: The Kids are Alright, Extremes, The Butterfly Ball, Mr. J, The Festival Game, Rock of Ages, Promo Man, Rachel's Man, Gold, Shout at the Devil (assoc. prod.), Electric Sound Sandwich, Deep Purple Rises Over Japan, Riding High (co-prod.).
TELEVISION: *Series*: You Can, Starsigns, Make the Grade (exec. prod.), Make Your Mark, Angles on Horseback.

KLUGMAN, JACK
Actor. b. Philadelphia, PA, April 27, 1922. e. Carnegie Tech. Much tv work in 1950's incl. Captain Video, Tom Corbett—Space Cadet, U.S. Steel Hour, Kraft Television Theatre, Playhouse 90.

THEATRE: *B'way*: Saint Joan, Stevedore, Mister Roberts, Gypsy, I'm Not Rappaport, Three Men on a Horse. *Tour/Stock*: The Odd Couple.
PICTURES: Timetable (debut, 1956), Twelve Angry Men, Cry Terror, The Scarface Mob, Days of Wine and Roses, I Could Go on Singing, The Yellow Canary, Act One, Hail Mafia, The Detective, The Split, Goodbye Columbus, Who Says I Can't Ride a Rainbow?, Two Minute Warning.
TELEVISION: *Series*: The Greatest Gift (daytime serial; 1954-55), Harris Against the World, The Odd Couple (2 Emmy Awards: 1971, 1973), Quincy M.E., You Again? *Guest*: The Defenders (Emmy Award, 1964), The Twilight Zone, The FBI, Ben Casey, 90 Bristol Court. *Movies*: Fame Is the Name of the Game, Poor Devil, The Underground Man, One of My Wives Is Missing, The Odd Couple: Together Again, Parallel Lives. *Mini-Series*: Around the World in 80 Days.

KNIGHT, SHIRLEY
Actress. b. Goessell, KS, July 5, 1936. e. Lake Forest Coll., D.F.A., 1978. Won 1976 Tony Award for Kennedy's Children; Joseph Jefferson Award for Landscape of the Body, 1977; New Jersey Drama Critics Awards for A Streetcar Named Desire, 1979.
PICTURES: Five Gates to Hell (debut, 1959), Ice Palace, The Dark at the Top of the Stairs (Acad. Award nom.) The Couch, Sweet Bird of Youth (Acad. Award nom.), House of Women, Flight from Ashiya, The Group, Dutchman (Venice Film Fest. Award), Petulia, The Counterfeit Killer, The Rain People, Juggernaut, Secrets, Beyond the Poseidon Adventure, Endless Love, The Sender, Prisoners, Color of Night, Stuart Saves His Family, Diabolique, Somebody if Waiting, The Man Who Counted.
TELEVISION: *Movies*: The Outsider, Shadow Over Elveron, Friendly Persuasion, Medical Story, Return to Earth, 21 Hours at Munich, The Defection of Simas Kudirka, Champions: A Love Story, Playing for Time (Emmy nom.), Billionaire Boys Club, Bump in the Night, Shadow of a Doubt, To Save a Child, When Love Kills: The Seduction of John Hearn, A Mother's Revenge, Baby Brokers, The Yarn Princess, A Part of the Family, Children of the Dust, Indictment: The McMartin Trial (Emmy Award, 1995; Golden Glove Award, 1996), Ties That Bind, Tim, The Haunting of Patricia Johnson. *Specials*: The Country Girl, The Lie. *Guest*: The Equalizer (Emmy nom.), thirtysomething (Emmy Award), Law and Order (Emmy nom.), NYPD Blue (Emmy Award, 1995), Cybill, Outer Limits Tribute.

KNOTTS, DON
Actor. b. Morgantown, WV, July 21, 1924. e. WV U., U. of AZ. Drafted into U.S. Army where became part of show called Stars and Gripes, teamed with comedian Mickey Shaughnessy. After schooling resumed was offered teaching fellowship but went to New York to try acting instead. Started out in radio show Bobby Benson and the B Bar B's. Appeared on TV, leading to role in No Time for Sergeants on B'way; appeared in film version.
PICTURES: No Time for Sergeants (debut, 1958), Wake Me When It's Over, The Last Time I Saw Archie, It's a Mad Mad Mad Mad World, Move Over Darling, The Incredible Mr. Limpet, The Ghost and Mr. Chicken, The Reluctant Astronaut, The Shakiest Gun in the West, The Love God?, How to Frame a Figg (also co-story), The Apple Dumpling Gang, No Deposit No Return, Gus, Herbie Goes to Monte Carlo, Hot Lead and Cold Feet, The Apple Dumpling Gang Rides Again, The Prize Fighter, Ther Private Eyes, Cannonball Run II, Pinocchio and the Emperor of the Night (voice), Big Bully.
TELEVISION: *Series*: Search for Tomorrow (1953-55), The Steve Allen Show, The Andy Griffith Show (5 Emmy Awards: 1961, 1962, 1963, 1966, 1967), The Don Knotts Show, Three's Company, What a Country, Matlock. *Movies*: I Love a Mystery, Return to Mayberry.

KOCH, HOWARD W.
Producer, Director. b. New York, NY, Apr. 11, 1916. Runner on Wall St. Began film career in Universal's contracts and playdate dept. in NY; asst. cutter, 20th-Fox; asst. dir., 20th-Fox, Eagle Lion, MGM; 2nd unit dir., freelance; In 1953, joined Aubrey Schenck Prod. forming Bel Air Prods., made films for U.A.; 1961-64, prod. Frank Sinatra Enterprises; v.p., chg. prod., Paramount Pictures Corp., 1964-66, Past pres. of the Academy of Motion Picture Arts and Sciences, 1977-79. 1977, elected to the National Board of Directors Guild of America for two year term. 1980 honored by NATO as prod. of year. 1985 Silver Medallion Award of Honor, Motion Picture Television Fund. Produced eight Academy Award shows, 1972-1983. Has had a 24 year relationship with Paramount as exec., prod., and dir. 1990, received Jean Hersholt Humanitarian Award, honored by Amer. Society of Cinematographers. 1991: Frank Capra Award from Directors Guild, Motion Picture Showmanship Award from the Publicists Guild; 1995: David O. Selznick Lifetime Achievement Award from the Producers Guild.
PICTURES: *Executive Producer*: Sergeants 3, The Manchurian Candidate, Come Blow Your Horn, X-15, Robin and the 7 Hoods, None But the Brave, The President's

Analyst, For Those Who Think Young, Dragonslayer. *Producer:* War Paint, Beachhead, Yellow Tomahawk, Desert Sands, Fort Yuma, Frontier Scout, Ghost Town, Broken Star, Crimes Against Joe, Three Bad Sisters, Emergency Hospital, Rebel in Town, The Black Sheep, Pharaoh's Curse, Tomahawk Trail, Revolt at Fort Laramie, War Drums, Voodoo Island, Hellbound, The Dalton Girls, The Odd Couple, On a Clear Day You Can See Forever, Plaza Suite, Star Spangled Girl, Last of the Red Hot Lovers, Jacqueline Susann's Once Is Not Enough, Some Kind of Hero, Airplane II: The Sequel, Collision Course. A Howard W. Koch *Production:* A New Leaf, Airplane!, Ghost. Director: Jungle Heat, Shield for Murder, Big House USA, Fort Bowie, Violent Road, Untamed Youth, Born Reckless, Frankenstein 1970, Andy Hardy Comes Home, The Last Mile, Girl in Black Stockings, Badge 373 (also prod.). TELEVISION: *Director:* Miami Undercover, The Untouchables, Maverick, Cheyenne, Hawaiian Eye. *Mini-Series: Prod.:* The Pirate, Hollywood Wives, Crossings. *Movie:* The Odd Couple: Together Again (prod.). *Specials: Prod.:* Ol' Blue Eyes Is Back, Oscar's Best Actors (also dir.), Oscar's Best Movies (also dir.), Who Loves Ya Baby, On the Road with Bing (also dir.), The Stars Salute the Olympics.

KOCH, HOWARD W., JR.
Producer. b. Los Angeles, CA, Dec. 14, 1945. Was asst. dir. and in industry posts before turning to production. Pres. & chief exec. off., Rastar (Peggy Sue Got Married, The Secret of My Success, Nothing in Common, Violets Are Blue, Amazing Chuck and Grace prod. under presidency); 1987, set up own prod. co. at De Laurentiis Entertainment Group. Oct. 1987: named president of the De Laurentiis Entertainment Group, Resigned April 1988 to produce independently. PICTURES: Heaven Can Wait, The Other Side of Midnight, The Frisco Kid (exec. prod.). *Co-prod./prod.:* The Idolmaker, Gorky Park, Honky Tonk Freeway, The Keep, A Night in Heaven, The Pope of Greenwich Village, Rooftops, The Long Walk Home, Necessary Roughness, Wayne's World, The Temp, Sliver, Wayne's World 2, Losing Isaiah, Virtuosity, Primal Fear.

KOCH, JOANNE
Executive Director, The Film Society of Lincoln Center. b. NY, NY, Oct. 7, 1929. e. Goddard College, B.A. political science, 1950. Dept. of Film, Museum of Modern Art, as circulation asst., film researcher, motion picture stills archivist, 1950. Early 1960s, technical dir., film dept. MOMA, supervised the implementation of MOMA's film preservation program. 1967, asst. to publisher of Grove Press, active in preparation of Grove's case in I Am Curious Yellow censorship trial. Joined film div., Grove, first in distribution then as tech. dir. and prod. coord. 1971 joined Film Society of Lincoln Center as prog. dir. of Movies-in-the-Parks. 1971 made admin. dir. Exec. dir. of N.Y. Film Festival, Film Comment magazine, Film-in-Education, New Directors/New Films, annual Film Society Tribute and Walter Reade Theater at Lincoln Center.

KOENEKAMP, FRED J.
Cinematographer. b. Los Angeles, CA, Nov. 11, 1922. Father was special effects cinematographer Hans F. Koenekamp. Member of American Society of Cinematographers. PICTURES: Doctor You've Got to Be Kidding, Sol Madrid, Stay Away Joe, Live a Little Love a Little, Heaven With a Gun, The Great Bank Robbery, Patton (Acad. Award nom.), Beyond the Valley of the Dolls, Flap, Skin Game, Billy Jack, Happy Birthday Wanda June, Stand Up and Be Counted, Kansas City Bomber, The Magnificent Seven Ride, Rage, Harry in Your Pocket, Papillon, Uptown Saturday Night, The Towering Inferno (Academy Award, 1974), The Wild McCullochs, Doc Savage, Posse, Embryo, Fun With Dick and Jane, The Other Side of Midnight, Islands in the Streams (Acad. Award nom.), The Bad News Bears in Breaking Training, The Dominic Principle, White Line Fever, The Swarm, The Champ, The Amityville Horror, Love and Bullets, When Time Ran Out, The Hunter, First Family, First Monday in October, Carbon Copy, Yes Giorgio, It Came From Hollywood, Two of a Kind, The Adventures of Buckaroo Banzai: Across the 8th Dimension, Stewardess School, Listen to Me, Welcome Home, Flight of the Intruder. TELEVISION: *Movies:* Disaster on the Coastline, Tales of the Gold Monkey, Money on the Side, Return of the Man from U.N.C.L.E., Summer Fantasies, Whiz Kids, Flight 90—Disaster on the Potomac, Obsessive Love, City Killer, Las Vegas Strip War, A Touch of Scandal, Not My Kid, Hard Time on Planet Earth (pilot), Return of the Shaggy Dog, Foreign Exchange, Splash Too, Hard Times, many others. *Series:* The Man From U.N.C.L.E. (Emmy nom.)

KOENIG, WALTER
Actor, Writer. b. Chicago, IL, Sept. 14, 1936. e. Grinnell Coll. (IA), U. of California. Performed in summer stock; after college enrolled at Neighborhood Playhouse, N.Y.; first acting job in TV's Day in Court. *Books:* Chekov's Enterprise, Buck Alice and the Actor Robot. Creator and writer of comic book series Raver.

PICTURES: Strange Lovers, The Deadly Honeymoon, Star Trek—The Motion Picture, Star Trek II: The Wrath of Khan, Star Trek III: The Search for Spock, Star Trek IV: the Voyage Home, Star Trek V: the Final Frontier, Moontrap, Star Trek VI: The Undiscovered Country, Star Trek: Generations. TELEVISION: *Series:* Star Trek. *Guest:* Colombo, Medical Center, Ironside, Mannix, Alfred Hitchcock Presents, Mr. Novak, Ben Casey, The Untouchables, Combat, Babylon V. *Movies:* The Questor Tapes, Goodbye Raggedy Ann. *Writer:* Family, The Class of '65, The Powers of Matthew Starr.

KOHN, HOWARD EDWARD, II
Executive. b. McKeesport, PA, Oct. 25, 1920. e. NYU. National dir. of adv., publicity, roadshow dept., United Artists; indep. prod., Hidden Fear, 1957; pres. Lioni-Warren-Kohn, Inc., 1958; national roadshow dir., Columbia Pictures, Porgy and Bess, 1959; World wide co-ordinator, national co-ordinator adv. & pub. for El Cid, 1961; named world wide co-ordinator adv., pub. all Samuel Bronston Productions, 1962; pres., Starpower Inc., 1968; exec. v.p., Avanti Films, 1970; v.p. Avariac Prods., 1971; pres., Blossom Films, 1973. Elected member of ASCAP, 1975. Pres., Avanti Associates, 1976. Pres. Channel Television Prods., Inc., 1985; pres. Search Television Prods. 1988. Pres. Avanti Music Co. 1991. Exec. v.p., Petard TV and Video Prods.

KOHNER, PANCHO
Producer. b. Los Angeles, CA, Jan. 7, 1939. e. U. of Southern California, U. of Mexico, Sorbonne. PICTURES: The Bridge in the Jungle (also dir., s.p.), The Lie, Victoria (also s.p.), Mr. Sycamore (also dir., s.p.), St. Ives, The White Buffalo, Love and Bullets, Why Would I Lie?, 10 to Midnight, The Evil That Men Do, Murphy's Law, Assassination, Death Wish IV, Messenger of Death, Kinjite.

KOHNER, SUSAN
Actress, b. Los Angeles, CA. Nov. 11, 1936. m. designer & author John Weitz. Sons Paul and Christopher Weitz are screenwriters. Mother, Lupita Tovar, was one of Mexico's leading film actresses. Father was talent rep. Paul Kohner. e. U. of California, 1954-55. Received Golden Globe Awards, 1959 and 1960. Retired from acting in 1964. Co-chair, Juilliard Council, Juilliard Sch. NY. THEATER: Love Me Little, He Who Gets Slapped, A Quiet Place, Rose Tatoo, Bus Stop, St. Joan, Sunday in New York, Take Her She's Mine, Pullman Car, Hiawatha, as well as summer stock. PICTURES: To Hell and Back (debut, 1955), The Last Wagon, Trooper Hook, Dino, Imitation of Life (Acad. Award nom.), The Big Fisherman, The Gene Krupa Story, All the Fine Young Cannibals, By Love Possessed, Freud. TELEVISION: Alcoa Hour, Schlitz Playhouse, Four Star Theatre, Matinee Theatre, Climax, Suspicion, Playhouse 90, Route 66, Dick Powell Theatre.

KONCHALOVSKY, ANDREI
Director, Writer. a.k.a. Mikhalkov Konchalovski. b. Moscow, Soviet Union, Aug. 20, 1937. Great grandfather: painter Sourikov; grandfather: painter Konchalovski; father is a writer; mother poet Natalia Konchalovskaia; brother is director Nikita Mikhalkov. e. as pianist Moscow Conservatoire, 1947-57; State Film Sch. (VGIK) under Mikhail Romm (1964). Dir. debut with 1961 short film The Boy and the Pigeon. Worked as scriptwriter during 1960s especially with Andrei Tarkovsky. 1962: asst. to Tarkovsky on Ivan's Childhood. In 1980, moved to US. In 1991, moved back to Russia. THEATRE/OPERA: The Seagull (Theatre de L'Odeon, Paris), Eugene Onegin (La Scala, Milan), La Pique Dame (La Scala, Milan & Bastille Opera, Pairs). PICTURES: *Writer:* The Steamroller and the Violin, Andrey Rublev, Tashkent City of Bread, The Song of Manshuk, The End of Chieftain. *Director:* The First Teacher (feature debut, 1965), Asya's Happiness, A Nest of Gentlefolk, Uncle Vanya, Romance for Lovers, Siberiade (Cannes Film Fest. Award, 1979), Maria's Lovers, Runaway Train, Duet for One, Shy People (also co-s.p.), Tango and Cash, Homer and Eddie, Ryaba, My Chicken (writer, dir.), The Inner Circle (also co-s.p.). TELEVISION: Split Cherry Terry (short).

KONIGSBERG, FRANK
Executive. b. Kew Gardens, NY, March 10, 1933. e. Yale, Yale Law Sch. Worked as lawyer at CBS for six years; moved to NBC 1960-65 in legal dept. as dir. prog. and talent administration. Left to package TV special for Artists Agency Rep. (later AFA) in Los Angeles; sr. v.p. of West Coast office seven years. Executive producer of many TV series, pilots, variety specials and made-for-TV movies. Formed own Konigsberg Company. Theatrical film debut as prod., Joy of Sex (1984). TELEVISION: *Movies* (all exec. prod.): Pearl, Ellis Island, Bing Crosby: His Life and Legend, Dummy, Before and After, Guyana Tragedy, A Christmas Without Snow, The Pride of Jesse Hallam, Hard Case, Divorce Wars, Coming Out of the

Ice, Onassis: The Richest Man in the World, Where the Hell's That Gold?!!?, Senior Prom, Babycakes. *Series* (exec. prod.): It's Not Easy, Breaking Away, Dorothy.

KOPELSON, ARNOLD
Producer, Financier, Intl. Distributor. b. New York, NY, Feb. 14, 1935. e. New York Law Sch., J.D., 1959; NYU, B.S. 1956. Has executive-produced, produced, packaged, developed or distributed with partner, Anne Kopelson over 100 films. Handled intl. dist. of Twice in a Lifetime, Salvador, Warlock, Triumph of the Spirit and prod. Platoon. Chmn. Arnold Kopelson Prods., Co-chmn. Inter-Ocean Film Sales, Ltd. Named NATO/ShoWest Producer of the Year, 1994.
PICTURES: *Exec. Prod.*: The Legacy, Lost and Found, Night of the Juggler, Dirty Tricks, Final Assignment, Gimme an "F", Fire Birds, Warlock. *Producer*: Foolin' Around, Platoon (Academy Award for Best Picture, 1986), Triumph of the Spirit, Out for Justice, Falling Down, The Fugitive (Acad. Award nom.), Outbreak, Seven, Eraser.
TELEVISION: *Movie*: Past Tense.

KOPPEL, TED
TV News Correspondent, Anchor, Host. b. Lancashire, England, Feb. 8, 1940. To U.S. in 1953; became citizen, 1963. e. Syracuse U, Stanford U. Started as writer and news correspondent for WMCA radio in NYC. Joined ABC News in New York, 1963, serving as correspondent in Vietnam, 1967, 1969-71; Miami Bureau chief, 1968; Hong Kong Bureau chief, 1969-71; diplomatic correspondent, 1971-76, 1977-79. Anchor of NBC Saturday Night News, 1976-77. Host of Nightline, beginning in 1980. Author: The Wit and Wisdom of Adlai Stevenson, In the National Interest.
TELEVISION: *Series*: ABC News (1971-80), ABC Saturday Night News (1975-77); Nightline (1980-), 20/20 (1986). Host/anchor/writer of many ABC news specials.

KORMAN, HARVEY
Actor, Director. b. Chicago, IL, Feb. 15, 1927. e. Wright Junior Coll. Began dramatic studies at Chicago's Goodman Sch. of Drama at the Arts Inst. Acted in small roles in Broadway plays and did TV commercials until break came as comedian for Danny Kaye Show on TV. Staged comedy sketches for Steve Allen variety series in 1967. Became Carol Burnett's leading man on her show 1967-77. Directed two episodes of The New Dick Van Dyke Show.
PICTURES: Living Venus (debut, 1961), Gypsy, Lord Love a Duck, The Last of the Secret Agents?, The Man Called Flintstone (voice), Three Bites of the Apple, Don't Just Stand There, The April Fools, Blazing Saddles, Huckleberry Finn, High Anxiety, Americathon, Herbie Goes Bananas, First Family, History of the World Part I, Trail of the Pink Panther, Curse of the Pink Panther, The Longshot, Munchie, The Flintstones (voice), Radioland Murders, Dracula: Dead and Loving It.
TELEVISION: *Series*: The Danny Kaye Show, The Carol Burnett Show (4 Emmy Awards: 1969, 1971, 1972, 1974), The Tim Conway Show, Mama's Family, Leo and Liz in Beverly Hills, The Nutt House. *Movies*: Three's a Crowd, Suddenly Single, The Love Boat (pilot), Bud and Lou, The Invisible Woman, Carpool, Crash Course, Based on an Untrue Story. *Special*: The Carol Burnett Show: A Reunion (also co-exec. prod.).

KORMAN, LEWIS J.
Executive. b. 1945. Partner, Kaye, Scholer, Fierman, Hays & Handler 1978; founding partner, Gelberg & Abrams where pioneered dev. of public limited partnerships, Delphi Partners, to help finance Columbia Pictures' and Tri-Star Pictures' films. 1986, became consultant to Tri-Star involved in negotiations that led to acquisition of Loews Theatre Corp. that year. Joined Tri-Star, 1987, as sr. exec. v.p. 1988 appt. to additional post of COO and named dir. of Columbia Pictures Entertainment Inc.; 1989 also became chmn, Motion Picture Group. 1990, resigned his positions after Columbia sale to Sony. Co-founder, pres. & COO of Savoy Pictures Ent., Inc., 1992.

KORTY, JOHN
Director, Producer, Writer, Animator. b. Lafayette, IN, June 22, 1936. e. Antioch Coll. B.A. 1959. President, Korty Films. Documentary: Who Are the DeBolts? And Where Did They Get Nineteen Kids? (Academy Award: 1977; Emmy & DGA Awards: 1978-79). Short Films: The Language of Faces (AFSC, 1961), Imogen Cunningham: Photographer (AFI grant, 1970), The Music School. Animation: Breaking the Habit (Oscar nom.), Twice Upon a Time.
PICTURES: Crazy Quilt (1966), Funnyman, Riverrun, Alex and the Gypsy, Oliver's Story, Twice Upon a Time.
TELEVISION: *Movies*: The People, Go Ask Alice, Class of '63, The Autobiography of Miss Jane Pittman (Emmy & DGA Awards, 1974), Farewell to Manzanar (Humanitas, Christopher Awards), Forever, A Christmas Without Snow (also writer, prod.), The Haunting Passion, Second Sight: A

Love Story, The Ewok Adventure, Resting Place, Baby Girl Scott, Eye on the Sparrow, Winnie, Cast the First Stone, A Son's Promise, Line of Fire: The Morris Dees Story, Long Road Home, Deadly Matrimony, They, Getting Out, Redwood Curtain.

KOTCHEFF, TED
Director. r.n. William Theodore Kotcheff. b. Toronto, Canada, Apr. 7, 1931. Ent. TV ind. 1952. After five years with Canadian Broadcasting Corp. joined ABC-TV in London, 1957.
THEATER: *London*: Progress the Park, Play with a Tiger, Luv, Maggie May, The Au Pair Man, Have You Any Dirty Washing, Mother Dear?
PICTURES: Tiara Tahiti (debut, 1963), Life at the Top, Two Gentlemen Sharing, Wake in Fright, Outback, Billy Two Hats, The Apprenticeship of Duddy Kravitz, Fun with Dick and Jane, Who Is Killing the Great Chefs of Europe?, North Dallas Forty (also co-s.p.), First Blood, Split Image (also prod.), Uncommon Valor (also exec. prod.), Joshua Then and Now, The Check is in the Mail (prod. only), Switching Channels, Winter People, Weekend at Bernie's (also actor), Folks!, The Shooter.
TELEVISION: *Specials*: Of Mice and Men, Desperate Hours, The Human Voice.

KOTEAS, ELIAS
Actor. b. Montreal, Quebec, Canada, 1961. e. AADA.
PICTURES: One Magic Christmas, Some Kind of Wonderful, Gardens of Stone, Tucker: The Man and His Dream, Full Moon in Blue Water, Malarek, Blood Red, Friends Lovers and Lunatics, Teenage Mutant Ninja Turtles, Backstreet Dreams, Desperate Hours, Look Who's Talking Too, Almost an Angel, The Adjuster, Teenage Mutant Ninja Turtles III, Chain of Desire, Camilla, Exotica, The Prophecy.

KOTTO, YAPHET
Actor. b. New York, NY, Nov. 15, 1937. Has many stage credits, including starring roles on Broadway in The Great White Hope, The Zulu and the Zayda. Off-B'way: Blood Knot, Black Monday, In White America, A Good Place To Raise a Boy.
PICTURES: The Limit (also prod.), 4 for Texas, Nothing But a Man, 5 Card Stud, Thomas Crown Affair, The Liberation of L. B. Jones, Man and Boy, Across 110th Street, Bone, Live and Let Die, Truck Turner, Report to the Commissioner, Sharks' Treasure, Friday Foster, Drum, Monkey Hustle, Blue Collar, Alien, Brubaker, Fighting Back, Star Chamber, Eye of the Tiger, Warning Sign, Prettykill, The Running Man, Midnight Run, Nightmare of the Devil (also prod., dir.), Terminal Entry, Jigsaw, A Whisper to a Scream, Tripwire, Ministry of Vengeance, Hangfire, Freddy's Dead, Almost Blue, Intent to Kill, The Puppet Masters, Two If By Sea.
TELEVISION: *Series*: Homicide. *Movies*: Night Chase, Raid on Entebbe, Rage, Playing With Fire, The Park Is Mine, Women of San Quentin, Badge of the Assassin, Harem, Desperado, Perry Mason: The Case of the Scandalous Scoundrel, Prime Target, After the Shock, Chrome Soldiers, It's Nothing Personal, Extreme Justice, The American Clock, The Corpse Had a Familiar Face, Deadline for Murder: From the Files of Edna Buchanan. *Guest*: Alfred Hitchcock Presents.

KOVACS, LASZLO
Cinematographer. b. Hungary, May 14, 1933. Came to U.S. 1957; naturalized 1963. e. Acad. Drama and M.P. Arts, Budapest, MA 1956.
PICTURES: Hell's Angels on Wheels, Hell's Bloody Devils, Psych Out, The Savage Seven, Targets, A Man Called Dagger, Single Room Furnished, Easy Rider, That Cold Day in the Park, Getting Straight, Alex in Wonderland, Five Easy Pieces, The Last Movie, Marriage of a Young Stockbroker, The King of Marvin Gardens, Pocket Money, What's Up Doc?, Steelyard Blues, Paper Moon, Slither, A Reflection of Fear, Huckleberry Finn, For Pete's Sake, Freebie and the Bean, Shampoo, At Long Last Love, Baby Blue Marine, Nickelodeon, Close Encounters of the Third Kind (addl. photog. only), Harry and Walter Go to New York, New York New York, F.I.S.T., The Last Waltz, Paradise Alley, Butch and Sundance: The Early Days, The Runner Stumbles, Heart Beat, Inside Moves, The Legend of the Lone Ranger, Frances, The Toy, Crackers, Ghostbusters, Mask, Legal Eagles, Little Nikita, Say Anything, Shattered, Radio Flyer, Life With Mikey, Deception, The Next Karate Kid, The Scout, Free Willy 2: The Adventure Home, Copycat, Multiplicity.

KOZAK, HARLEY JANE
Actress. b. Wilkes-Barre, PA, Jan. 28, 1957. e. NYU's School of the Arts. Member of Nebraska Repertory Theatre.
PICTURES: House on Sorority Row, Clean and Sober, When Harry Met Sally..., Parenthood, Sideout, Arachnophobia, Necessary Roughness, The Taking of Beverly Hills, All I Want for Christmas, The Favor, Magic in the Water.
TELEVISION: *Series*: The Guiding Light, Santa Barbara, Texas, Harts of the West, Bringing Up Jack. *Guest*: L.A. Law, Highway to Heaven. *Movies*: So Proudly We Hail, The Amy Fisher Story, The Android Affair.

KOZLOWSKI, LINDA
Actress. b. 1956. m. actor Paul Hogan. Began professional acting career soon after graduating from Juilliard Sch., N.Y., 1981. Stage debut in How It All Began at the Public Theatre. In regional theatre appeared in Requiem, Translations, Make and Break, as well as on Broadway and on tour with Dustin Hoffman in Death of a Salesman and the TV adaptation.
PICTURES: Crocodile Dundee, Crocodile Dundee II, Pass the Ammo, Helena, Almost an Angel, The Neighbor, Village of the Damned.
TELEVISION: Mini-Series: Favorite Son.

KRABBE, JEROEN
Actor. b. Amsterdam, The Netherlands, Dec. 5, 1944. Trained for stage at De Toneelschool, Acad. of Dramatic Art, Amsterdam, 1965. Also studied at painting at Acad. of Fine Arts, grad. 1981. Founded touring theater co. in the Netherlands and translated plays into Dutch. Also costume designer. As a painter, work has been widely exhibited (one-man show at Francis Kyle Galleries, London). Author: The Economy Cookbook. Dir. debut, new stage adaptation of The Diary of Anne Frank, 1985 in Amsterdam.
PICTURES: Soldier of Orange, A Flight of Rainbirds, Spetters, The Fourth Man, Turtle Diary, Jumpin' Jack Flash, No Mercy, The Living Daylights, Shadow of Victory, A World Apart, Crossing Delancey, Shadowman, Scandal, The Punisher, Melancholia, Till There Was You, Kafka, The Prince of Tides, For a Lost Soldier, The Fugitive, King of the Hill, Immortal Beloved, Farinelli, Blood of a Poet.
TELEVISION: Danton's Death (debut, 1966), William of Orange, World War III. Movies: One for the Dancer, Family of Spies, After the War, Secret Weapon, Robin Hood (theatrical in Europe), Murder East Murder West, Dynasty: The Reunion, Stalin.

KRAMER, LARRY
Writer, Producer. b. Bridgeport, CT, June 25, 1935. e. Yale U., B.A. 1957. Ent. m.p. ind. 1958. Story edit. Columbia Pictures, N.Y. London 1960-65. Asst. to David Picker and Herb Jaffe, UA, 1965. Assoc. prod. and additional dialogue Here We Go Round the Mulberry Bush, 1968. Writ. prod. Women in Love (Acad. Award nom. for s.p., 1970). Lost Horizon, 1973 (s.p.). Novel: Faggots (1978). Theater: The Normal Heart (NY Shakespeare Festival and throughout the world), Just Say No, The Destiny of Me. Cofounder: Gay Men's Health Crisis, Inc. (community AIDS org.). Founder: ACT UP: AIDS Coalition to Unleash Power (AIDS activist and protest org.). Book of Essays: Reports from the Holocaust: The Story of an AIDS Activist (St. Martin's Press, 1995).

KRAMER, SIDNEY
Sales executive. b. New York, NY, Oct. 25, 1911. e. New York Law Sch., LL.B., City Coll. of New York. Gen. sales mgr., RKO Pathe, June 1953; dir. and v.p. Cellofilm Corp. 1941-56; foreign sales mgr., RKO Radio, 1954-59; v.p. Cinemiracle Intl. 1960-61; v.p. T.P.E.A., 1960-61; foreign sls. mgr., Cinerama, Inc., 1962-65; exec. Commonwealth Theatres, Puerto Rico, Inc., 1965-68; exec. v.p. Cobian Jr. Enterprises Inc. 1968; m.p. consultant, exhibition, dist., foreign and Caribbean area, 1968-70; pres. Coqui Int'l Inc.; 1970-80; v.p. of UAPR, Inc., Puerto Rico, U.A. Communications, Inc. 1981-91. Retired.

KRAMER, STANLEY E.
Producer, Director. b. New York, NY, Sept. 29, 1913. e. NYU, B.Sc., 1933. Entered m.p. ind. via backlot jobs; with MGM research dept.; film cutter 3 yrs.; film ed.; m.p. & radio writer; served in U.S Signal Corps, 1st Lt. during WWII. Recipient of Irving G. Thalberg Award, 1961.
PICTURES: Assoc. Prod.: So Ends Our Night, The Moon and Sixpence. Producer: So This Is New York, Champion, Home of the Brave, The Men, Cyrano de Bergerac, Death of a Salesman, High Noon, My Six Convicts, The Sniper, The Four Poster, The Happy Time, Eight Iron Men, The 5000 Fingers of Dr. T, The Wild One, The Juggler, Caine Mutiny, Pressure Point, A Child Is Waiting, Invitation to a Gunfighter. Director-Producer: Not as a Stranger (dir. debut, 1955), The Pride and the Passion, The Defiant Ones, On the Beach, Inherit the Wind, Judgment at Nuremberg, It's a Mad Mad Mad Mad World, Ship of Fools, Guess Who's Coming to Dinner, The Secret of Santa Vittoria, R.P.M., Bless the Beasts and Children, Oklahoma Crude, The Domino Principle, The Runner Stumbles.
TELEVISION: Guess Who's Coming to Dinner? (pilot).

KRANE, JONATHAN
Executive. b. 1952. m. actress Sally Kellerman. e. St. Johns Coll. grad. with honors, 1972; Yale Law Sch., 1976. Joined Blake Edwards Entertainment in 1981, becoming pres. Formed talent management co. Management Company Entertainment Group representing clients such as John Travolta, Sally Kellerman, Kathryn Harrold, Sandra Bernhard, Howie Mandel, Drew Barrymore, others. Began producing vehicles for clients and transformed co. into production, distri-

bution, management and finance co. Chairman and chief exec. officer, Management Company Entertainment Group (MCEG).
PICTURES: Exec. prod./prod.: Boardwalk, Honeymoon, Fly Away Home, The Man Who Loved Women, Micki & Maude, A Fine Mess, That's Life, The Chocolate War, The Experts, Fatal Charm, Boris and Natasha, Look Who's Talking, Chud II: Bud the Chud, Without You I'm Nothing (prod.), Look Who's Talking Too, Convicts, Cold Heaven, Breaking the Rules, Look Who's Talking Now.
TELEVISION: Prod.: Howie Mandel Life at Carnegie Hall, Howie Mandel: The North American Watusi Tour.

KRANTZ, STEVE
Executive. b. New York, NY, May 20, 1923. m. novelist Judith Krantz. e. Columbia U., B.A. Dir. progs., NBC, New York, 1953; dir. prog. dev., Screen Gems, N.Y., 1955; v.p., gen. mgr. Screen Gems, Canada, 1958; dir. int. sls., 1960; formed Steve Krantz Productions, Inc. 1964.
PICTURES: Producer: Fritz the Cat, Heavy Traffic, The Nine Lives of Fritz the Cat, Cooley High, Ruby, Which Way Is Up?, Jennifer. Swap Meet (also writer).
TELEVISION: Series: Steve Allen Show, Kate Smith Show, Hazel, Dennis the Menace, Winston Churchill—The Valiant Years, Marvel Super Heroes, Rocket Robin Hood. Mini-series: Princess Daisy, Sins, Mistral's Daughter, I'll Take Manhattan. Movies: Dadah is Death (exec. prod.), Till We Meet Again, Deadly Medicine, Deadly Matrimony, Torch Song, Jack Reed: Badge of Honor, House of Secrets, Children of the Dark, Dazzle.

KREIMAN, ROBERT T.
Executive. b. Kenosha, WI, Sept. 16, 1924. Served WWII, Capt Army Corps of Engineers-ETO. e. Stanford U.; U. of WI. Dir., sales training, mgr., audio visual sales, Bell & Howell Co., 1949-58; v.p., Argus Cameras, Inc., 1958-61; v.p., gen. mgr., Commercial & Educ. Div., Technicolor 1961-69. v.p. gen. mgr., The Suburban Companies; 1969-71, pres. & CEO, Deluxe General, Inc. pres. & dir. of Movietonews, Inc.; bd. chmn. Keith Cole Photograph, Inc. 1972-78; bd. chmn., pres. & CEO, Pace International Corp., 1969-; past pres. of UCLA. Executive Program Ass'n. Fellow SMPTE, Member M.P. Academy; TV Academy; assoc. mem., American Society of Cinematographers.

KRESS, HAROLD F.
Film Editor, Director. b. Pittsburgh, PA, June 26, 1913. e. UCLA. Film ed., Command Decision, Madame Curie, Mrs. Miniver, The Yearling; crime shorts; 5-reel Army documentary short, Ward Care for Psychotic Patients. Member: Acad. of M.P. Arts and Sciences, Screen Directors Guild, Film Editors Guild.
PICTURES: Director: Painted Hills, No Questions Asked, Apache War Smoke. Editor: Ride Vaquero, Saadia, Rose Marie, Valley of the Kings, The Cobweb, The Prodigal, I'll Cry Tomorrow, The Teahouse of the August Moon, Silk Stockings, Until They Sail, Merry Andrew, Imitation General, The World the Flesh and the Devil, Count Your Blessings, Home from the Hill, How the West Was Won (Academy Award, 1963), The Greatest Story Ever Told, Walk Don't Run, Alvarez Kelly, The Poseidon Adventure, The Iceman Cometh, 99 and 44/100% Dead, The Towering Inferno (Academy Award, 1974).

KREUGER, KURT
Actor. b. St. Moritz, Switzerland, July 23, 1917. e. U. of Lausanne, Polytechnic. London. Came to U.S 1937, partner in travel bureau: acted in Wharf Theat. group. Cape Cod, 1939; Broadway debut in Candle in the Wind with Helen Hayes, 1941.
PICTURES: The Moon Is Down, Edge of Darkness, The Strange Death of Adolph Hitler, Sahara, Mademoiselle Fifi, None Shall Escape, Escape in the Desert, Hotel Berlin, Paris Underground, The Spider, Dark Corner, Unfaithfully Yours, Spy Hunt, Fear, The Enemy Below, Legion of the Doomed, What Did You Do in the War Daddy?, The St. Valentine's Day Massacre.

KRIER, JOHN N.
Executive. b. Rock Island, IL. e. Augustana Coll. Joined A. H. Blank Theatres, Grad. Publix Theatres Manager Training Sch.; 1930: managed theatres in Illinois, Iowa, Nebraska; joined Intermountain Theatres, Salt Lake City, 1937: appointed Purchasing Head, 1946: buyer-booker, 1952: v.p., gen. mgr., 1955: appt. v.p. gen mgr. ABC Theas., Arizona, 1968: appt. v.p. gen'l mgr. director Film Buying ABC Theatres of California & ABC Intermountain Theatres, Feb. 1972. Became consultant ABC Southern Theatres, 1974. Joined Exhibitors Relations Inc. as partner, 1978. Elected pres., 1982. Became owner, 1988.

KRIGE, ALICE
Actress. b. Upington, South Africa. Moved to London at 22 and studied at School of Speech and Drama. Professional

debut on British TV: The Happy Autumn Fields. In London prod. of Forever Yours, Maylou. West End debut, Arms and the Man, 1981. Two seasons with Royal Shakespeare Co. at Stratford and London (The Tempest, King Lear, The Taming of the Shrew, Cyrano de Bergerac, Bond's Lear.), Venice Preserved.
PICTURES: Chariots of Fire (debut, 1981), Ghost Story, King David, Barfly, Haunted Summer, See You in the Morning, S.P.O.O.K.S., Sleepwalkers, Habitat, Institute Benjamenta, Amanda.
TELEVISION: *Movies*: Wallenberg: A Hero's Story, Dream West, A Tale of Two Cities, Second Serve, Baja Oklahoma, Max and Helen, Iran: Days of Crisis, Ladykiller, Judgment Day: The John List Story, Double Deception, Jack Reed: Badge of Honor, Scarlet & Black, Sharpes Honour, Summer, Devil's Advocate, Donor Unknown, Joseph. *Mini-Series*: Ellis Island.

KRISTOFFERSON, KRIS
Actor, Singer. b. Brownsville, TX, June 22, 1936. e. Pomona Coll., Oxford U. (Rhodes Scholar). Joined U.S. Army briefly and taught English literature at West Point. Started writing songs (country music), hits have included Me and Bobby McGee, Why Me, Lord, Sunday Mornin' Comin' Down, etc.
PICTURES: The Last Movie (debut, 1971), Cisco Pike, Pat Garrett and Billy the Kid, Blume in Love, Bring Me the Head of Alfredo Garcia, Alice Doesn't Live Here Anymore, Vigilante Force, The Sailor Who Fell from Grace with the Sea, A Star Is Born, Semi-Tough, Convoy, Heaven's Gate, Rollover, Flashpoint, Songwriter, Trouble in Mind, Big Top Pee-wee, Millennium, Welcome Home, Original Intent, Night of the Cyclone, Sandino, No Place to Hide, Cheatin' Hearts, Lone Star.
TELEVISION: *Movies/Mini-Series*: Freedom Road, The Lost Honor of Kathryn Beck, The Last Days of Frank and Jesse James, Blood and Orchids, Stagecoach, The Tracker, Dead or Alive, Pair of Aces, Another Pair of Aces, Miracle in the Wilderness, Christmas in Connecticut, Troubleshooters: Trapped Beneath the Earth, Big Dreams & Broken Hearts: The Dottie West Story, Tad. *Mini-Series*: Amerika.

KRONICK, WILLIAM
Writer, Director. b. Amsterdam, NY. e. Columbia Coll., A.B. U.S. Navy photography; wrote, dir. featurette, A Bowl of Cherries.
PICTURES: Nights in White Satin (s.p.), Horowitz in Dublin (dir., s.p.), Flash Gordon and King Kong (2nd unit dir.).
TELEVISION: *Documentaries: Wrote, dir., prod.*: The Ultimate Stuntman: a Tribute to Dar Robinson, To the Ends of the Earth, Mysteries of the Great Pyramid; George Plimpton Specials; National Geographic, Ripley's Believe It or Not, The World's Greatest Stunts. *Prod.*: In Search of... Series. *Dir.*: (movie) The 500 Pound Jerk.

KRUEGER, RONALD P.
Executive. b. St. Louis, MO, Oct. 19, 1940. e. Westminister Coll., 1961. Began working in theatres as a teenager. Assumed presidency Wehrenberg Theatres, 1963. Member: NATO, bd. member, regional v.p.; American Film Inst.; advisory bd. mbr., Salvation Army; Motion Picture Pioneers; Demolay Legion of Honor; bd. trustees, Westminster Col. at Fulton, MO; Divan mbr. Moolah Temple Shrine; past Master Tuscan Lodge 360 AF & AM; Scottish Rite 32 KCCH.

KRUGER, HARDY
Actor, Writer. b. Berlin, Germany, April 12, 1928. Ent. m.p. ind. 1943; on stage since 1945. Starred in approx. 25 German films. Has published 8 books, novels, travelogues, etc.
PICTURES: The One That Got Away, Bachelor of Hearts, The Rest Is Silence (German film of Hamlet), Blind Date, Taxi Pour Tobrouk, Sundays and Cybele, Hatari! (U.S. debut, 1963), Le Gros Coup, Les Pianos Mecaniques (The Uninhibited), Le Chant du Monde, Flight of the Phoenix, The Defector, La Grande Sauterelle, Le Franciscain de Bourges, The Nun of Monza, The Secret of Santa Vittoria, The Battle of Neretva, The Red Tent, Night Hair Child, Death of a Stranger, Barry Lyndon, Paper Tiger, Un Solitaire, Potato Fritz, A Bridge Too Far, L'Autopsie d'un Monstre, The Wild Geese, Society Limited, Wrong Is Right, The Inside Man.
TELEVISION: *Mini-Series*: War and Remembrance. Series: Globetrotter (writer, prod; 1986).

KUBRICK, STANLEY
Director, Producer, Writer. b. Bronx, NY, July 26, 1928. e. Taft H.S. Staff photog. Look magazine; dir., edit., cinematog. of short documentaries Day of the Fight, Flying Padre; dir., cinematog. of documentary The Seafarers. Received Luchino Visconti Award in Italy for contribution to the cinema, 1988.
PICTURES: *Director*: Fear and Desire (also prod., co-s.p., photog., edit.), Killer's Kiss (also co-prod., co-s.p., story, photog., edit.), The Killing (also s.p.), Paths of Glory (also co-s.p.), Spartacus, Lolita. *Director-Producer-Writer*: Dr. Strangelove, or: How I Learned to Stop Worrying and Love the Bomb, 2001: A Space Odyssey (also special photog. effects design. & dir.; Academy Award for special effects, 1968), A Clockwork Orange, Barry Lyndon, The Shining, Full Metal Jacket.

KUHN, THOMAS G.
Executive/Executive Producer. e. Northwestern U., B.A.; USC, M.B.A. KNBC-TV sales; NBC business affairs; dir. live night time progs. Warner Bros. TV, v.p. prod.; exec. prod., TV, Alice, The Awakening Land, Torn Between Two Lovers, The Jayne Mansfield Story, Long Way Home. Pres., RCA Video Prods.; pres., Lightyear Ent., 1987. Exec. prod.: Aria, The Return of Swamp Thing, Heaven, The Lemon Sisters, Stories to Remember. With partner Fred Weintraub: The JFK Assassination: The Jim Garrison Tapes, Trouble Bound, Gypsy Eyes, Backstreet Justice, Guinevere, Triplecross, Young Ivanhoe, Young Connecticut Yankee, Undertow, Playboy's Really Naked Truth.

KULIK, SEYMOUR (BUZZ)
Producer, Director. b. New York, NY, 1923. Joined CBS-TV as prod.-dir., 1956; 1964: v.p. chg. West Coast Prods., Bob Banner Associates Inc., 1965; 1967 Prod-Dir. with Paramount Studios.
PICTURES: The Explosive Generation, The Yellow Canary, Warning Shot (also prod.), Villa Rides, Riot, To Find a Man, Shamus, The Hunter.
TELEVISION: *Series*: Lux Video Theatre, Kraft Theatre, You Are There, Climax, Playhouse 90, The Defenders, Dr. Kildare, Twilight Zone, Dick Powell Playhouse, Kentucky Jones (exec. prod.). Movies: Vanished, Owen Marshall—Counsellor at Law (A Pattern of Morality), Brian's Song (DGA Award), Incident on a Dark Street, Pioneer Woman, Remember When, Bad Ronald, Cage Without a Key, Matt Helm, Babe, The Lindbergh Kidnapping Case, Never Con a Killer, Kill Me If You Can, Ziegfeld: The Man and His Women, From Here to Eternity, Rage of Angels, George Washington (also sprv. prod.), Kane and Abel, Her Secret Life, Women of Valor, Too Young the Hero, Around the World in 80 Days, Jackie Collins' Lucky/Chances, Miles From Nowhere.

KURALT, CHARLES
TV News Correspondent, Author. b. Wilmington, NC, Sept. 10, 1934. e. U. of North Carolina. Reporter-columnist for Charlotte News until joining CBS News as writer in 1957. Promoted to news assignment desk in 1958. Became first host of CBS News series, Eyewitness, in 1960. Named CBS News chief Latin American correspondent (based in Rio de Janeiro) in 1961 Appt. CBS News chief west coast correspondent in 1963; transferred to New York, 1964. Has worked on CBS Reports, CBS News Specials, and On the Road series for CBS Evening News (Emmy Award, 1969). Host of CBS News Sunday Morning, 1979-94. Retired from CBS News, May 1994. Author: To the Top of the World (1968), Dateline America (1979), On the Road with Charles Kuralt (1985), A Life on the Road (1990), Charles Kuralt's America (1995).

KUREISHI, HANIF
Writer. b. South London, Eng., Dec. 5, 1956. e. King's Coll. (philosophy). At 18, first play presented at Royal Court Theatre where he ushered before becoming writer in residence. Early in career, wrote pornography as Antonia French. Stage and TV plays include: The Mother Country, Outskirts, Borderline and adaptations (Mother Courage). The Rainbow Sign, With Your Tongue Down My Throat (novella) and short stories have been pub. Anglo-Pakistani writer's first s.p. My Beautiful Laundrette earned Acad. Award nom., 1986 and began creative relationship with dir. Stephen Frears.
PICTURES: My Beautiful Laundrette, Sammy and Rosie Get Laid, London Kills Me (also dir.).

KURI, EMILE
Set Decorator. b. Cuernavaca, Mex., June 11, 1907. e. Chaminade Coll., 1924-27. Career began with 50 Hopalong Cassidy episodes for Harry Sherman. Under contract to Selznick Intl., Liberty Films, and Walt Disney Prods., supv. all film and tv sets, and all decor for both Disneyland and Disney World.
PICTURES: 71 films incl.: The Silver Queen (Acad. Award nom.), I'll Be Seeing You, Spellbound, It's a Wonderful Life, Duel in the Sun, Paradine Case, The Heiress (Academy Award, 1949), Fancy Pants, A Place in the Sun, Carrie (Acad. Award nom.), The War of the Worlds, Shane, The Actress, Executive Suite (Acad. Award nom.), 20,000 Leagues Under the Sea (Academy Award, 1954), Old Yeller, The Absent-Minded Professor (Acad. Award nom.), The Parent Trap, Mary Poppins (Acad. Award nom.), Bedknobs & Broomsticks (Acad. Award nom.).
TELEVISION: 15 seasons of The Wonderful World of Disney (Emmy Award, 1963), The Academy Awards (1960-70).

KURI, JOHN A.
Producer, Writer. b. Los Angeles, CA, Feb. 16, 1945. Son of set decorator and Disneyland co-designer, Emile Kuri. Began

13 yr. employment with Disney at age 16 in construction and maintenance at Disneyland. Progressed through mgmt. in Park Operations. 1969 transferred to Disney Studios in set decorating. 1973 became art director. 1975 at 20th Century Fox as exec. asst. to prod. Irwin Allen. 1976, formed own co., wrote and prod. both television and motion picture projects. 1979 thru 1982 developed and prod. television in partnership with Ron Howard. 1988 thru 1990 as pres. of Sheffield Ent. developed master broadcasting plan for KCMY TV, Sacramento, CA. Published works: Determined to Live: An American Epic, Remember Wes.
PICTURES: Captive Hearts (prod., co-s.p. 2nd unit dir., co-lyrics.) *Set decorator*: Apple Dumpling Gang, Leadbelly, Report to the Commissioner, Castaway Cowboy, Superdad, Mad Mad Movie Makers.
TELEVISION: One More Mountain (prod., writer, 2nd unit dir.; Christopher Award, 1994), Conagher (prod.; Western Heritage Award from Cowboy Hall of Fame), O'Hara (co-creator of series), Airwolf (2nd unit prod., dir.), Skyward (prod., 2nd unit dir.; Golden Halo Award), Skyward Christmas (prod., 2nd unit dir.), Through the Magic Pyramid (assoc. prod., art dir.). Art dir.: The Plutonium Incident, Scared Straight Another Story, Young Love First Love, Marriage is Alive and Well, Little Shots, The Red Pony (and set decorator, Emmy nom., 1973). Set decorator: Michael O'Hara IV, The Mouse Factory (22 episodes).

KUROSAWA, AKIRA
Director, Writer. b. Japan. March 23, 1910. e. Attended Tokyo Acad. of Fine Arts, 1928. Asst. dir. to Kajiro Yamamoto, Photo-Chemical Laboratories (PCL Studios, later renamed Toho Films), 1936-43. Became dir., 1943. Founded Kurosawa Prods., 1960; Dir. Yonki Kai Prods., 1971. Autobiography: Something Like An Autobiography (1982).
PICTURES: *Director/Writer*: Sanshiro Sugata (debut, 1943), The Most Beautiful, The Men Who Tread on the Tiger's Tail, Sanshiro Sugata Part 2, No Regrets for Our Youth, Those Who Make Tomorrow (co- dir.), One Wonderful Sunday, Drunken Angel, The Quiet Duel, Stray Dog, Scandal, Rashomon, The Idiot, Ikiru, The Seven Samurai, I Live in Fear, The Lower Depths (also co-prod.), Throne of Blood (also co-prod.), The Bad Sleep Well (also co-prod.), The Hidden Fortress (also co-prod.), Yojimbo (also exec. prod.), Sanjuro (also exec. prod.), High and Low (also exec. prod.), Red Beard (also exec. prod.), Dodes 'Ka-Den (also co-prod.), Dersu Uzala, Kagemusha (also co-prod.), Ran, Runaway Train (adapt. from orig. s.p. only), Akira Kurosawa's Dreams, Rhapsody in August.

KURTZ, GARY
Producer, Director. b. Los Angeles, CA, July 27, 1940. e. USC Cinema Sch. Began prof. career during college. Has worked as cameraman, soundman, editor, prod. supervisor and asst. dir. on documentaries and features. Worked on many low budget features for Roger Corman including: The Terror, Beach Ball, Track of the Vampire, Planet of Blood, The Shooting, Ride in the Whirlwind. Drafted into Marines. Spent 2 yrs. in photo field as cameraman, editor and still photo.
PICTURES: The Hostage (prod. spvr., ed.), Two-Lane Blacktop (line prod.), Chandler (line prod.), American Graffiti (co.-prod.); Star Wars (prod.), The Empire Strikes Back (prod.), The Dark Crystal (prod., 2nd unit dir.), Return to Oz (exec. prod.), Slipstream (prod.).

KURTZ, SWOOSIE
Actress. b. Omaha, NE, Sept. 6, 1944. e. Studied at U. Southern Calif., London Acad. of Music and Dramatic Art.
THEATER: A History of the American Film (Drama Desk Award), Ah Wilderness (Tony nom.), Who's Afraid of Virginia Woolf? (with Mike Nichols and Elaine May), The Effect of Gamma Rays on Man-in-the-Moon Marigolds, Fifth of July (Tony, Outer Critics Circle & Drama Desk Awards), House of Blue Leaves (Tony and Obie Awards), Uncommon Women and Others (Obie & Drama Desk Awards), Hunting Cockroaches (Drama League nom.), Six Degrees of Separation, Lips Together Teeth Apart.
PICTURES: Slap Shot, First Love, Oliver's Story, The World According to Garp, Against All Odds, Wildcats, True Stories, Vice Versa, Bright Lights Big City, Dangerous Liaisons, Stanley and Iris, A Shock to the System, Reality Bites, Storybook, Citizen Ruth, Emma, Citizen Ruth.
TELEVISION: *Series*: As the World Turns (1971), Mary, Love Sidney (Emmy noms.), Sisters (Emmy & SAG noms). *Movies*: Walking Through the Fire, Marriage Is Alive and Well, Mating Season, A Caribbean Mystery, Guilty Conscience, A Time to Live, Baja Oklahoma (Golden Globe nom.), The Image (Emmy & Cable ACE noms.), Terror on Track 9, The Positively True Adventures of the Alleged Texas Cheerleader-Murdering Mom, And the Band Played On (Emmy & Cable Ace noms.), One Christmas, Betrayed: A Story of Three Women, A Promise to Carolyn. *Specials*: Uncommon Women, Fifth of July, House of Blue Leaves, The Visit (Trying Times). *Guest*: Kojak, Carol & Company (Emmy Award, 1990).

KURYS, DIANE
Director, Writer. b. Lyons, France, Dec. 3, 1948. In 1970 joined Jean-Louis Barrault's theatre group, acted for 8 years on stage, television and film. Adapted and translated staged plays. 1977, wrote screenplay for Dibolo Menthe (Peppermint Soda) which she also directed and co-prod. Film won Prix Louis Deluc, Best Picture. Co-prod. Alexandre Arcady's Coup de Sirocco and Le Grand Pardon.
PICTURES: *Dir./Writer*: Peppermint Soda (also co-prod.), Cocktail Molotov, Entre Nous, A Man in Love, C'est la vie.

KUSTURICA, EMIR
Director. b. Sarajevo, Yugoslavia, 1955. e. FAMU.
PICTURES: Do You Remember Dolly Bell? (debut, 1981; Golden Lion Award at Venice Film Fest.), When Father Was Away on Business (Golden Palme at Cannes Film Fest., 1985), Time of the Gypsies (also co-s.p.), Arizona Dream, Underground (Golden Palme at Cannes Film Fest., 1995).

KWAN, NANCY
Actress. b. Hong Kong, May 19, 1939. Trained as dancer at British Royal Ballet.
PICTURES: The World of Suzie Wong (debut, 1960), Flower Drum Song, The Main Attraction, Tamahine, Fate Is the Hunter, The Wild Affair, Honeymoon Hotel, Arrivederci Baby, Lt. Robin Crusoe USN, The Corrupt Ones, Nobody's Perfect, The Wrecking Crew, The Girl Who Knew Too Much, The McMasters, Girl From Peking, Supercock, The Pacific Connection, Project: Kill, Night Creature, Streets of Hong Kong, Angkor, Walking the Edge, Night Children, Cold Dog Soup, Dragon: The Bruce Lee Story.
TELEVISION: *Movies*: The Last Ninja, Blade in Hong Kong, Miracle Landing.

KWIT, NATHANIEL TROY, JR.
Executive. b. New York, NY, May 29, 1941. e. Cornell U., B.A.; NYU, M.B.A. 1964-68, American Broadcasting Co., Inc., exec. asst. to pres. of ABC Films. 1968-71, National Screen Service Corp., New York branch mgr., asst. genl. sls. mgr. 1971, founder, CEO Audience Marketing, Inc., later acquired by Viacom International as operating subsidiary. 1974 named v.p. marketing services, Warner Bros., Inc. 1979, named v.p. in charge video and special markets division, United Artists Corp.; 1981, named sr. v.p. in chg. UA television, video, special market div. Following acquisition of UA Corp. by MGM in 1981 promoted to pres., dist. & mktg. for MGM/UA Entertainment Co. 1983, pres. & CEO, United Satellite Communications, direct broadcast TV co. 1986, founder, pres. Palladium Entertainment, Inc.

L

LACHMAN, ED
Cinematographer. b. 1948. Son of a Morristown, NJ movie theater owner. e. Ohio U., BFA. Filmed documentaries Ornette: Made in America, Strippers, Huie's Sermon. Assisted Sven Nykvist on King of the Gypsies, Hurricane; Vittorio Storaro on Luna; Robby Muller on The American Friend and They All Laughed. Co-director of photography on Werner Herzog's La Soufriere and Stroszek and Wim Wenders' Lightning Over Water and A Tokyo Story.
PICTURES: Scalpel, Union City, Say Amen Somebody, Little Wars, Split Cherry Tree, Strippers, The Little Sister, Insignificance (American sequences) Desperately Seeking Susan, True Stories, Making Mr. Right, Chuck Berry: Hail Hail Rock 'n' Roll, Less Than Zero, El Dia Que Me Quieras, Mississippi Masala, Light Sleeper, London Kills Me, My New Gun, My Family/Mi Familia.
TELEVISION: Get Your Kicks on Route 66 (dir., cinematography, American Playhouse.), A Gathering of Old Men, Backtrack.

LACK, ANDREW
Executive. b. New York, NY, May 16, 1947. e. Sorbonne, Boston Univ. School of Fine Arts (BFA). Starting in 1976, worked at CBS as prod. for Who's Who, 60 Minutes, CBS Reports. 1981, named sr. prod. of CBS Reports and CBS News correspondent, 1983 became exec. prod. Exec. prod. and creator of Face to Face with Connie Chung, West 57th, Crossroads,, Our Times With Bill Moyers. Exec. prod. of Street Stories, specials The 20th Anniversary of Watergate, Malcolm X. 1993, appointed pres. of NBC News.

LADD, JR., ALAN
Executive. b. Los Angeles, CA, Oct. 22, 1937. Son of late actor Alan Ladd. Motion picture agent, Creative Management Associates, 1963-69. M.p. producer, 1969-73. Joined 20th Century-Fox in 1973 in chg. of creative affairs in feature div. Promoted to v.p., prod., 1974. 1975 named sr. v.p. for world-wide prod.; 1976, promoted to pres. of 20th Century-Fox Pictures. Resigned & formed The Ladd Co., 1979. 1985 appt. pres. & COO, MGM/UA Entertainment Film Corp; appointed

chairman of board, CEO Metro-Goldwyn-Mayer Pictures Inc., 1986; resigned 1988; 1989 named co-chmn. Pathe Communications Corp. and chmn., CEO, Pathe Entertainment. Chmn., & CEO, MGM-Pathe Ent., 1989-92. Chmn & CEO MGM-Pathe Commun. Co., 1991-92. Co-chmn. & Co-CEO, MGM, 1992-93. Founded Ladd Pictures.
PICTURES: *Prod.*: Walking Stick, A Severed Head, Tam Lin, Villian, Zee and Co. *Exec. prod.*: Fear Is the Key, Nightcomers, Vice Versa, The Brady Bunch Movie, Braveheart (Academy Award).

LADD, CHERYL
Actress. r.n. Cheryl Stoppelmoor. b. Huron, S.D., July 12, 1951. Joined professional Music Shop Band while in high school; after graduation toured with group ending up in Los Angeles. Cast as voice of Melody character in animated Josie and the Pussycats. Studied acting with Milton Katselas. Did TV commercials, small parts in TV. Film debut 1972 in Jamaica Reef (aka Evil in the Deep, unreleased).
PICTURES: Purple Hearts, Now and Forever, Millennium, Lisa, Poison Ivy.
TELEVISION: *Series*: The Ken Berry "Wow" Show, Charlie's Angels, One West Waikiki. *Specials*: Ben Vereen... His Roots, General Electric's All-Star Anniversary, John Denver and the Ladies; The Cheryl Ladd Special, Looking Back: Souvenirs, Scenes From a Special. *Guest*: Police Woman, Happy Days, Switch, etc. *Movies*: Satan's School for Girls, When She Was Bad, Grace Kelly Story, Romance on the Orient Express, A Death in California, Crossings, Deadly Care, Bluegrass, Kentucky Woman, Jekyll & Hyde, The Fulfillment of Mary Gray, The Girl Who Came Between Them, Crash: The Mystery of Flight 1501, Danielle Steel's Changes, Locked Up: A Mother's Rage, Dead Before Dawn, Broken Promises: Taking Emily Back, Dancing With Danger.

LADD, DAVID ALAN
Actor, Producer, Motion Picture Executive. b. Los Angeles, CA, Feb. 5, 1947. e. USC. Son of late actor Alan Ladd. On stage in The Glass Menagerie. Exec. v.p. motion picture prod. at Pathe Entertainment and Metro-Goldwyn-Mayer.
PICTURES: *Actor*: The Big Land, The Proud Rebel (Golden Globe Award), The Sad Horse, A Dog of Flanders, Raymie, Misty, R.P.M., Catlow, Deathline (Raw Meat), The Klansman, The Day of the Locust, Wild Geese. Producer: The Serpent and the Rainbow.
TELEVISION: *Guest*: Zane Gray Theatre, Wagon Train, Pursuit, Ben Casey, Gunsmoke, Love American Style (pilot), Kojak, Emergency, Tom Sawyer, Bonanza, Quest, Police Story, Medical Story, etc. *Producer*: When She Was Bad, ABC Variety specials.

LADD, DIANE
Actress. b. Meridian, MS, Nov. 29. r.n. Diane Rose Lanier. Daughter is actress Laura Dern. e. St. Aloysius Acad.; trained for stage at Actors Studio with Frank Corsaro in N.Y. Worked as model and as Copacabana nightclub dancer. At 18 in touring co. of Hatful of Rain. NY debut: Orpheus Descending.
THEATER: Carry Me Back to Morningside Heights, One Night Stands of a Noisy Passenger. The Wall, The Goddess, The Fantastiks, Women Speak, Texas Trilogy; Lu Ann Hampton Laverty, Love Letters.
PICTURES: Wild Angels (debut, 1966), Rebel Rousers, The Reivers, Macho Calahan, WUSA, White Lightning, Chinatown, Alice Doesn't Live Here Anymore (Acad. Award nom.), Embryo, All Night Long, Sweetwater, Something Wicked This Way Comes, Black Widow, Plain Clothes, National Lampoon's Christmas Vacation, Wild at Heart (Acad. Award nom.), A Kiss Before Dying, Rambling Rose (Acad. Award nom.), The Cemetery Club, Forever, Carnosaur, Hold Me Thrill Me Kiss Me, Father Hood.
TELEVISION: *Movies*: The Devil's Daughter, Black Beauty, Thaddeus Rose and Eddie, Willa, Guyana Tragedy, Desperate Lives, Grace Kelly, Crime of Innocence, Bluegrass, Rock Hudson, The Lookalike, Shadow of a Doubt, Hush Little Baby, Mrs. Munck (also dir., writer). *Guest*: Hazel, Gunsmoke, City of Angels, The Love Boat, Dr. Quinn Medicine Woman (pilot). *Series*: The Secret Storm, Alice (Golden Globe Award). *Special*: The Gift.

LAFFERTY, PERRY
Executive. b. Davenport, IA, Oct. 3, 1920. e. Yale U. With CBS-TV as v.p., programs, Hollywood, 1965-76. Sr. v.p., programs and talent, west coast, for NBC Entertainment, 1979-85.
TELEVISION: Maybe Baby (exec. prod.), Murder C.O.D. (exec. prod.), An Early Frost (prod.).

LaGRAVENESE, RICHARD
Writer. b. Brooklyn, NY, 1960.
PICTURES: Rude Awakening, The Fisher King (Acad. Award nom.), The Ref (also prod.), A Little Princess, The Bridges of Madison County, Unstrung Heroes.

LAHTI, CHRISTINE
Actress. b. Birmingham, MI, April 4, 1950. m. dir. Thomas Schlamme. e. U. of Michigan. Trained for stage at Herbert Berghof Studios with Uta Hagen. TV commercials. As a mime, performed with Edinburgh Scotland's Travis Theatre. N.Y. stage debut in The Woods, 1978.
THEATER: The Zinger, Hooter (Playwrights Horizon), Loose Ends, Division St., The Woods (Theatre World Award), Scenes and Revelations, Present Laughter, The Lucky Spot, Summer and Smoke (LA), The Heidi Chronicles, Three Hotels.
PICTURES: ...And Justice For All (debut, 1979), Whose Life Is It Anyway?, Ladies and Gentlemen the Fabulous Stains, Swing Shift (Acad. Award nom.), Just Between Friends, Housekeeping, Stacking, Running on Empty, Miss Firecracker (cameo), Gross Anatomy, Funny About Love, The Doctor, Leaving Normal, Hideaway, Pie in the Sky, A Weekend in the Country, Lieberman In Love (short; Academy Award).
TELEVISION: *Series*: Chicago Hope. *Movies*: Dr. Scorpion, The Last Tenant, The Henderson Monster, The Executioner's Song, Love Lives On, Single Bars Single Women, No Place Like Home, Crazy From the Heart, The Fear Inside, The Good Fight, The Four Diamonds. *Mini-Series*: Amerika.

LAI, FRANCIS
Composer. b. France, April 26, 1932.
PICTURES: A Man and a Woman, I'll Never Forget What's 'is Name, The Bobo, Three Into Two Won't Go, Hello Goodbye, Hannibal Brooks, The Games, Mayerling, House of Cards, Rider on the Rain, Love Story (Academy Award, 1970), Le Petit Matin, Another Man, Another Chance, Wanted: Babysitter, Bilitis, The Good and the Bad, Widow's Nest, Cat and Mouse, The Body of My Enemy, Emmanuelle 2; The Forbidden Room, International Velvet, Oliver's Story, Passion Flower Hotel, Robert and Robert, The Small Timers, By the Blood Brothers, Beyond the Reef, Bolero, A Second Chance, Edith and Marcel, My New Partner, Marie, A Man and a Woman: 20 Years Later, Bernadette, Itinerary of a Spoiled Child., Der Aten (The Spirit), La Belle Histoire.
TELEVISION: The Berlin Affair, The Sex Symbol, Sins.

LAKE, RICKI
Actress. b. New York, NY, Sept. 21, 1968. e. Manhattan's Professional Children's School. Won role in Hairspray while attending Ithaca Col. Theatre in LA: A Girl's Guide to Chaos.
PICTURES: Hairspray (debut, 1988), Working Girl, Cookie, Cry-Baby, Last Exit to Brooklyn, Where the Day Takes You, Inside Monkey Zetterland, Skinner, Cabin Boy, Serial Mom, Mrs. Winterbourne.
TELEVISION: *Series*: China Beach, Ricki Lake (synd. talk show). *Movies*: Babycakes, The Chase, Based on an Untrue Story.

LAMARR, HEDY
Actress. r.n. Hedwig Kiesler. b. Vienna, Austria, Nov. 9, 1915. Started in films as script girl, bit player before gaining fame for role in 1933 Czech film. Ecstasy. To Hollywood, 1938. Autobiography: Ecstasy and Me (1966).
PICTURES: Ecstasy, Algiers (U.S. debut, 1938), Lady of the Tropics, I Take This Woman, Boom Town, Comrade X, Come Live With Me, Ziegfeld Girl, H. M. Pulham Esq., Tortilla Flat, Crossroads, White Cargo, The Heavenly Body, The Conspirators, Experiment Perilous, Her Highness and the Bellboy, The Strange Woman, Dishonored Lady, Let's Live a Little, Samson and Delilah, A Lady Without a Passport, Copper Canyon, My Favorite Spy, Love of 3 Queens, The Story of Mankind, The Female Animal.

LAMAS, LORENZO
Actor. b. Los Angeles, CA, Jan. 20, 1958. e. Santa Monica City Coll. Son of the late actor Fernando Lamas and actress Arlene Dahl. Studied at Tony Barr's Film Actors Workshop (Burbank Studios). Appeared on commercials for Diet Coke, BVD, Coors (Hispanic).
PICTURES: Grease, Tilt, Take Down, Body Rock, Snakeater, Night of the Warrior, Snakeater II, Final Impact, Snakeater III: His Law, Killing Streets, CIA Code Name: Alexa, CIA: Target Alexa, The Swordsman, Bounty Tracker, Final Round, C.I.A.: Target Alexa II, Bad Blood.
TELEVISION: *Series*: California Fever, Secrets of Midland Heights, Falcon Crest, Dancin' to the Hits (host), Renegade. *Guest*: The Love Boat, Switch, Sword of Justice, The Hitchhiker, Dear John. *Movies*: Detour to Terror, CIA: Code Name Alexa.

LAMBERT, CHRISTOPHER (also CHRISTOPHE)
Actor, Producer. b. New York , NY, Mar. 29, 1957; reared in Geneva; parents French. Studied at Paris Conservatoire Drama Academy.
PICTURES: La Bar du Telephone (debut, 1981), Putain d'Historie d'Amour, Legitime Violence, Greystoke: The Legend of Tarzan Lord of the Apes, Love Songs, Subway (Cesar Award), Highlander, I Love You, The Sicilian, Love Dream, To Kill a Priest, Un Plan d'Enfer, Why Me?, Highlander 2: The Quickening, Priceless Beauty, Knight Moves, Fortress, Gunmen, Road Flower, Highlander III: The Sorcerer, The Hunted, Nine Months (exec. prod. only), Mortal Kombat, North Star (also exec. prod.), When Saturday Comes (exec. prod. only).

LAMBERT, MARY
Director. b. Arkansas. e. attended U. of Denver, Rhode Island Sch. of Design where began making short films. Worked in variety of prod. jobs before moving to Los Angeles and directing TV commercials and music videos (includ. Madonna's Material Girl, Like a Virgin, Like a Prayer, others for Sting, Janet Jackson and Mick Jagger).
PICTURES: Siesta, Pet Sematary, Pet Sematary 2.
TELEVISION: *Movie:* Dragstrip Girl.

LAMBERT, VERITY
Producer. b. London, England, Nov. 27. Ent. TV 1961; prod. Dr. Who, Adam Adamant Lives, Detective, Somerset Maugham (all BBC series). Since 1971: (series), Budgie, Between The Wars. 1974: Appt. controller of Drama, Thames Television. 1979: Chief exec. Euston Films. 1983: Director of Production Thorn EMI Films Ltd. Relinquished her position as controller of Drama Thames Television and retained position as chief exec., Euston Films. Became indep. prod. developing projects for film and TV incl. BBC. Founded own company, Cinema Verity Ltd., 1985.
PICTURES: Link, Morons from Outer Space, Restless Natives, Dreamchild, Not for Publication, Clockwise, A Cry in the Dark.
TELEVISION: May to December, The Boys from the Bush, Sleepers, GBH, So Haunt Me, Comics, Coasting, Sam Saturday, Running Late, Class Act, She's Out, Heavy Weather.

LAMOUR, DOROTHY
Actress. r.n. Mary Leta Dorothy LaPorte. b. New Orleans, LA, Dec. 10, 1914. e. Spencer's Business Sch. Miss New Orleans 1931. Sang with bands before being signed to contract by Paramount Pictures. Had two radio shows, Sealtest Variety Hour & Chase and Sanborn Hour. *Autobiography:* My Side of the Road (1980).
PICTURES: The Jungle Princess (debut, 1936), Swing High Swing Low, High Wide and Handsome, Last Train From Madrid, Thrill of a Lifetime, The Hurricane, Big Broadcast of 1938, Her Jungle Love, Tropic Holiday, Spawn of the North, St. Louis Blues, Man About Town, Disputed Passage, Johnny Apollo, Typhoon, Road to Singapore, Moon Over Burma, Chad Hanna, Road to Zanzibar, Caught in the Draft, Aloma of the South Seas, The Fleet's In, Beyond the Blue Horizon, Road to Morocco, Star Spangled Rhythm, They Got Me Covered, Dixie, Riding High, And the Angels Sing, Rainbow Island, A Medal for Benny, Duffy's Tavern, Masquerade in Mexico, Road to Utopia, My Favorite Brunette, Road to Rio, Wild Harvest, Variety Girl, On Our Merry Way, Lulu Belle, The Girl From Manhattan, The Lucky Stiff, Slightly French, Manhandled, Here Comes the Groom (cameo), The Greatest Show on Earth, Road to Bali, The Road to Hong Kong, Donovan's Reef, Pajama Party, The Phynx (cameo), Won Ton Ton the Dog Who Saved Hollywood (cameo), Creepshow 2.
TELEVISION: *Movie:* Death at Love House. *Guest:* Murder She Wrote, I Spy, Marcus Welby, Love Boat, Crazy Like a Fox, Remington Steele, Damon Runyon Theatre, Hart to Hart. *Specials:* Bob Hope Specials, Entertaining the Troops, Remembering Bing, many others.
(d. September 22, 1996)

LANDAU, MARTIN
Actor. b. Brooklyn, NY, June 20, 1930. e. Pratt Inst., Art Students League, Was cartoon and staff artist on NY Daily News; studied at Actors Studio. Daughter is actress Juliet Landau. Recipient: Lifetime Achievement Awards from Houston Film Fest. and Charleston Film Fest.
THEATER: Middle of the Night, Uncle Vanya, Stalag 17, Wedding Breakfast, First Love, The Goat Song.
PICTURES: Pork Chop Hill (debut, 1959), North by Northwest, The Gazebo, Stagecoach to Dancer's Rock, Cleopatra, The Hallelujah Trail, The Greatest Story Ever Told, Decision at Midnight, Alien Attack, Nevada Smith, They Call Me Mister Tibbs, Situation Normal But All Fouled Up, A Town Called Hell, Black Gunn, Strange Shadows in an Empty Room, Meteor, Destination Moonbase Alpha, Without Warning, Trial By Terror, Cosmic Princess, Journey Through the Black Sun, The Last Word, The Return (The Alien's Return), Alone in the Dark, The Being, Access Code, Treasure Island, Run ... If You Can, Death Blow, W.A.R.: Women Against Rape, Sweet Revenge, Cyclone, Real Bullets, Empire State, Delta Fever, Tucker: The Man and His Dream (Acad. Award nom.), Crimes and Misdemeanors (Golden Globe Award, Acad. Award nom.), Paint It Black, Firehead, Tipperary, The Color of Evening, Mistress, Eye of the Stranger, Sliver, Intersection, Time Is Money, Ed Wood (Academy Award, best supporting actor, 1994; also Golden Globe, SAG, American Comedy, NY Film Critics, LA Film Critics, Natl. Society of Film Critics, Boston Film Critics, Chicago Film Critics & Texas Film Critics Awards), City Hall, Pinocchio.
TELEVISION: *Series:* Mission Impossible (1966-69; 3 Emmy noms., Golden Globe Award), Space 1999. *Movies:* Welcome Home Johnny Bristol, Savage, The Death of Ocean View Park,

Harlem Globetrotters on Gilligan's Island, Fall of the House of Usher, Max and Helen (ACE Award nom.), The Neon Empire, By Dawn's Early Light (ACE Award nom.), Something to Live For: The Alison Gertz Story, Legacy of Lies (ACE Award), 12:01, Joseph. Numerous guest appearances.

LANDES, MICHAEL
Executive. b. Bronx, NY, Feb. 4, 1939. e. Fairleigh Dickinson, B.A., 1961; Rutgers, J.D., 1964; NYU, L.L.M., 1965. 17 years of corporate law and financing experience as sr. partner in law firm of Hahn and Hessen. Co-chairman of The ALMI Group formed, 1978. Co-chmn. & CEO of Almi Pictures Inc. formed, 1982. 1986, Almi sold its 97-screen RKO Century Warner Theatre chain to Cineplex Odeon. 1986, purchased Video Shack Inc. assets and formed RKO Warner Video, Inc.; Chmn since inception. 1988, became chairman, Damon Creations, Inc. which merged with Enro Holding Corp. and Enro Shirt Co. into Damon Creations. Sold Damon, 1988. Chmn./CEO, RKO Warner Intl. Ltd. a video franchisor and chmn./CEO of The Lexington Group Ltd., org. 1990. Member: World Presidents Organization (WPO). Chief Executives Organization (CEO); Association for a Better New York; bd. of dirs. Motion Picture Pioneers; Academy of Motion Picture Arts and Sciences; bd. of dirs. Periwinkle Theatre Productions. Produced more than ten pictures throughout his career.

LANDIS, JOHN
Director, Producer, Writer, Actor. b. Chicago, IL, Aug. 3, 1950. Raised in Los Angeles. Started in mailroom at 20th Century-Fox, then worked in Europe as prod. asst. and stunt-man before making first low-budget film, Schlock.
PICTURES: *Director:* Schlock (also actor, writer), The Kentucky Fried Movie (also actor), National Lampoon's Animal House, The Blues Brothers (also co-s.p.), An American Werewolf in London (also s.p., actor), Trading Places, Twilight Zone—The Movie (sequence dir., also s.p., co-prod.), Into the Night (also actor), Spies Like Us, Clue (co-exec. prod., co-story only), Three Amigos!, Amazon Women on the Moon (sequence dir.; also co-exec. prod.), Coming to America, Oscar, Innocent Blood, Beverly Hills Cop III, The Stupids. *Actor:* Battle for the Planet of the Apes, Death Race 2000, 1941, The Muppets Take Manhattan, Spontaneous Combustion, Darkman, Diva Las Vegas, Sleepwalkers, Venice/Venice, The Silence of the Hams.
TELEVISION: *Series:* Dream On (exec. prod., dir., actor), Topper (exec. prod., dir.), Weird Science (exec. prod.), Sliders (exec. prod.), Campus Cops (exec. prod.). *Movie:* Psycho IV (actor), The Stand (actor). *Videos:* Thriller, Black or White (both for Michael Jackson). *Specials:* B.B. King Into the Night, Disneyland's 35th Anniversary Celebration.

LANDRES, PAUL
Director. b. New York, NY, Aug. 21, 1912. e. UCLA. Started as asst. film editor at Universal 1931. Editor 1937 to 1949 of many feature films. Director of feature films and TV since 1949. Under directorial contract to Warner Bros. 1961-62. Director of 22 feature films for theatrical release.
PICTURES: Oregon Passage, A Modern Marriage, Mark of the Vampire, Navy Bound, The Curse of Dracula, Miracle of the Hills, 54 Washington Street, Son of a Gunfighter, etc.
TELEVISION: *Series:* Bonanza, Daktari, The Rifleman, 77 Sunset Strip, Maverick Hawaiian Eye, The Plainsman, Readers Digest, Topper, Wyatt Earp, Blondie.

LANDSBURG, ALAN
Executive, Producer, Writer. b. New York, NY, May 10, 1933. e. NYU. Producer for NBC News Dept., 1951-59; producer-writer, CBS, 1959-60; exec. prod., Wolper Productions/Metromedia Producers Corp., 1961-70; chairman, The Alan Landsburg Company, 1970-present.
PICTURES: Co-exec. prod.: Jaws 3-D, Porky's II: The Next Day.
TELEVISION: *Exec. prod.:* Biography, National Geographic Specials (1965-70): The Undersea World of Jacques Cousteau; In Search of..., That's Incredible. *Movies:* Adam, Fear on Trial, Parent Trap II, Adam: His Song Continues, The George McKenna Story, Long Gone, Strange Voices, Bluegrass, A Place at the Table, Too Young the Hero, A Stoning in Fulham County, High Risk, Destined to Live, Quiet Victory: The Charlie Wedemeyer Story, The Ryan White Story, Unspeakable Acts (co-exec. prod., writer), A Mother's Right: The Elizabeth Morgan Story (writer), The Hunter (writer).

LANE, DIANE
Actress. b. New York, NY, Jan. 2, 1965. Acted in stage classics (Medea, Electra, As You Like It) at La Mama Experimental Theatre Club, NY. Addtl. stage: The Cherry Orchard, Agamemnon, Runaways, Twelfth Night.
PICTURES: A Little Romance (debut, 1979), Touched by Love, National Lampoon Goes to the Movies, Cattle Annie and Little Britches, Six Pack, Ladies and Gentlemen the Fabulous Stains, The Outsiders, Rumble Fish, Streets of Fire, The Cotton Club, The Big Town, Lady Beware, Priceless Beauty, Vital Signs, My New Gun, Chaplin, Knight Moves, Indian Summer, Judge Dredd, Wild Bill, Mad Dog Time, Jack.

TELEVISION: *Movies*: Child Bride of Short Creek, Miss All-American Beauty, Descending Angel, Oldest Living Confederate Widow Tells All. *Special*: Edith Wharton's Summer. *Guest*: Fallen Angels (Murder Obliquely). *Mini-Series*: Lonesome Dove.

LANE, NATHAN
Actor. r.n. Joseph Lane. b. Jersey City, NJ, Feb. 3, 1956. Received 1992 Obie Award for Sustained Excellence in Off-B'way Theatre.
THEATER: *B'way*: Present Laughter (Drama Desk nom.), Merlin, The Wind in the Willows, Some Americans Abroad, On Borrowed Time, Guys & Dolls (Drama Desk & Outer Critics Circle Awards; Tony nom.), Laughter on the 23rd Floor, Love! Valour! Compassion! (Drama Desk, Outer Critics Circle and Obie Awards; also Off-B'way), A Funny Thing Happened On The Way To The Forum (Tony Award). *Off-B'way*: A Midsummer Night's Dream, Measure for Measure, The Merry Wives of Windsor, She Stoops to Conquer, Claptrap, The Common Pursuit (Dramalogue Award), In a Pig's Valise, The Film Society, Uncounted Blessings, Hidden in This Picture, Love, The Lisbon Traviata (also L.A.; Drama Desk, Lucille Lortel, LA Drama Critics Circle & Dramalogue Awards), Bad Habits, Lips Together Teeth Apart (also L.A.).
PICTURES: Ironweed (debut, 1987), Joe Vs. the Volcano, The Lemon Sisters, He Said She Said, Frankie and Johnny, Life With Mikey, Addams Family Values, The Lion King (voice of Timon), Jeffrey (American Comedy Award nom.), The Birdcage.
TELEVISION: *Series*: One of the Boys. *Guest*: The Days and Nights of Molly Dodd, Miami Vice, Frasier (Emmy nom.). *Movie*: Hallmark Hall of Fame's The Boys Next Door. *Specials*: Alice in Wonderland, The Last Mile, Co-host 1995 Tony Awards, 1995 Kennedy Center Honors.

LANG, CHARLES
Cinematographer. b. Bluff, UT, March 27, 1902. e. Lincoln H.S., Los Angeles; U. of Southern California. Entered m.p. ind. with Paramount Film Laboratory, then asst. cameraman; dir. of photography, Paramount, 1929-52; then freelance.
PICTURES: Innocents of Paris, The Devil and the Deep, A Farewell to Arms (Academy Award, 1933), She Done Him Wrong, Death Takes a Holiday, Lives of a Bengal Lancer, Souls at Sea, Tovarich, Spawn of the North, Midnight, Arise My Love, The Shepherd of the Hills, The Uninvited, Blue Skies, The Ghost and Mrs. Muir, A Foreign Affair, Miss Tatlock's Millions, Fancy Pants, September Affair, Ace in the Hole, Sudden Fear, The Big Heat, It Should Happen to You, Sabrina, Phffft!, Queen Bee, The Man from Laramie, The Rainmaker, The Solid Gold Cadillac, Gunfight at the O.K. Corral, A Farewell to Arms (1957), Wild Is the Wind, The Matchmaker, Some Like It Hot, The Magnificent Seven, Strangers When We Meet, The Facts of Life, One-Eyed Jacks, Summer and Smoke, Charade, Father Goose, Inside Daisy Clover, How to Steal a Million, Hotel, The Flim Flam Man, Wait Until Dark, The Stalking Moon, Cactus Flower, Bob & Carol & Ted & Alice, The Love Machine, Doctors' Wives, Butterflies Are Free, 40 Carats.

LANG, JENNINGS
Executive. b. New York, NY, May 28, 1915. e. St. John's U. Law Sch. m. actress-singer Monica Lewis. Went into law practice in 1937 with Seligsburg and Lewis, m.p. law specialists. 1938 to Hollywood as 2nd asst. dir. at Grand National Studios. Opened own office as actor's agent; first client, comedian Hugh Herbert. 1940 joined Jaffe Agency; made partner and v.p. in 1942. Was pres. 1948-50, resigned to join MCA. Worked in all phases of MCA operations; 1952 made v.p. of MCA TV Ltd., and bd. mem. Involved with prod. and sales of TV prods. from inception of Revue (now Universal City Studios) in 1950. Organized Revue's New Projects Dept., creator and exec. in chg. of prog. dev. Involved with creation and sales of such series as Wagon Train, The Robert Cummings Show, Bachelor Father, Wells Fargo, Mike Hammer. Supvr. of Universal's World Premiere films. Made exec. prod. at MCA (Universal) for motion pictures.
PICTURES: *Exec. prod.*: Coogan's Bluff, Winning, Tell Them Willie Boy Is Here, Puzzle of a Downfall Child, The Beguiled, They Might Be Giants, Act of the Heart, Play Misty for Me, Slaughterhouse 5, Joe Kidd, The Great Northfield Minneota Raid, Pete 'n Tillie, High Plains Drifter, Charley Varrick, Breezy, Earthquake, Airport 1975, The Front Page, The Great Waldo Pepper, The Eiger Sanction, The Hindenburg, Airport '77. *Producer*: Swashbuckler, Rollercoaster, House Calls, Nunzio, The Concorde—Airport' 79, Little Miss Marker, The Nude Bomb, The Sting II, Stick.
(d. May 29, 1996)

LANG, OTTO
Producer, Director. b. Tesanj, Austria (now Yugoslavia), Jan. 21, 1908. e. Salzburg, Austria. Four Academy Award nominations for Cinemascope Specials, Twentieth Century-Fox Film Corp.

PICTURES: *Dir.*: Search for Paradise. *Prod.*: Call Northside 777, Five Fingers, White Witch Doctor. *Assoc. prod*: Tora! Tora! Tora!
TELEVISION: Man from U.N.C.L.E., Daktari, Iron Horse, Cheyenne, Dick Powell Show, Zane Gray Theatre, Ann Sothern Show, Rifleman, Bat Masterson, Seahunt, The Deputy, Surfside 6, Hawaiian Eye. Prod. Twentieth Century Fox Hour. *Dir.*: Man and the Challenge, Aquanauts, World of Giants, The Legend of Cortez, Beethoven: Ordeal and Triumph, Saga of Western Man.

LANG, STEPHEN
Actor. b. Queens, NY, July 11, 1952. e. Swarthmore Col. Professional debut 1974 at Washington D.C.'s Folger Theatre.
THEATER: *NY*: Rosencrantz and Guildenstern Are Dead, Henry V, Bloomsday on Broadway, The Shadow of a Gun, Saint Joan, Hamlet, Johnny on the Spot, Death of a Salesman, Barbarians, The Winter's Tale, A Few Good Men, The Speed of Darkness.
PICTURES: Twice in a Lifetime (debut, 1985), Band of the Hand, Manhunter, Project X, Last Exit to Brooklyn, The Hard Way, Another You, Guilty As Sin, Gettysburg, Tombstone, Tall Tale, The Amazing Panda Adventure, The Shadow Conspiracy, An Occasional Hell.
TELEVISION: *Series*: Crime Story. *Movies*: King of America, Death of a Salesman, Stone Pillow, Babe Ruth, Taking Back My Life: The Nancy Ziegenmeyer Story, Darkness Before Dawn, Murder Between Friends, A Season of Hope, The Possession of Michael D., The Phantoms, Strangers *Specials*: Anyone for Tennyson?, The Mother. *Guest*: Tribeca.

LANGE, HOPE
Actress. b. Redding Ridge, CT, Nov. 28, 1936. e. Reed Coll., Portland, OR; Barmore Jr. Coll., N.Y. Parents: John Lange, musician and Minnette Buddecke Lange, actress. Prof. stage debut in The Patriots on Broadway
THEATER: The Hot Corner (understudy), Same Time Next Year, The Supporting Cast.
PICTURES: Bus Stop (debut, 1956), The True Story of Jesse James, Peyton Place (Acad. Award nom.), The Young Lions, In Love and War, The Best of Everything, Wild in the Country, Pocketful of Miracles, Love Is a Ball, Jigsaw, Death Wish, I Am the Cheese, The Prodigal, A Nightmare on Elm Street Part 2, Blue Velvet, Tune in Tomorrow, Clear and Present Danger, Just Cause.
TELEVISION: *Series*: The Ghost and Mrs. Muir (2 Emmy Awards: 1969, 1970), The New Dick Van Dyke Show, Knight and Dave. *Movies*: Crowhaven Farm, That Certain Summer (Emmy nom.), The 500 Pound Jerk, I Love You— Goodbye, Fer-de-Lance, The Secret Night Caller, Love Boat II, Like Normal People, The Day Christ Died, Beulah Land, Pleasure Palace, Private Sessions, Dead Before Dawn, Cooperstown. *Special*: A Family Tree (Trying Times). *Mini-Series*: The Henry Ford Story: Man and the Machine, Message from Nam. *Guest*: Murder She Wrote.

LANGE, JESSICA
Actress. b. Cloquet, MN, Apr. 20, 1949. e. U. of Minnesota. Left to study mime 2 years under Etienne Decroux in Paris. Dancer, Opera Comique, Paris; model with Wilhelmina, NY. Worked in experimental theatre in New York. Broadway debut 1992 in A Streetcar Named Desire (Theatre World Award).
PICTURES: King Kong (debut, 1976), All That Jazz, How to Beat the High Cost of Living, The Postman Always Rings Twice, Frances, Tootsie (Academy Award, best supporting actress, 1982), Country (also co-prod.), Sweet Dreams, Crimes of the Heart, Far North, Everybody's All-American, Music Box, Men Don't Leave, Cape Fear, Night and the City, Blue Sky (Academy Award, 1994), Losing Isaiah, Rob Roy.
TELEVISION: *Special*: Cat on a Hot Tin Roof. *Movies*: O Pioneers!, A Streetcar Named Desire (Golden Globe, 1996).

LANGELLA, FRANK
Actor. b. Bayonne, NJ, Jan. 1, 1938. Studied acting at Syracuse U.; later in regional repertory, summer stock, and On- and Off- B'way. Joined Lincoln Ctr. Rep. Co., 1963.
THEATER: *NY*: The Immoralist (Off-B'way debut, 1963), Benito Cereno, The Old Glory (Obie Award), Good Day (Obie Award), The White Devil (Obie Award), Long Day's Journey Into Night, Yerma, Seascape (B'way debut, 1975; Tony Award), Dracula, A Cry of Players, Cyrano de Bergerac, The Tooth of the Crime, Ring Around the Moon, Amadeus, Passion, Design for Living, Sherlock's Last Case, The Tempest, Booth. *L.A.*: The Devils, Les Liaisons Dangereuses, My Fair Lady, Scenes From an Execution.
PICTURES: Diary of a Mad Housewife (debut, 1970), The Twelve Chairs, The Deadly Trap, The Wrath of God, Dracula, Those Lips Those Eyes, Sphinx, The Men's Club, Masters of the Universe, And God Created Woman, True Identity, 1492: Conquest of Paradise, Body of Evidence, Dave, Brainscan, Junior, Bad Company, Cutthroat Island, Eddie.
TELEVISION: *Specials*: Benito Cereno, The Good Day, The Ambassador, The Sea Gull, The American Woman: Portrait in

Courage, Eccentricities of a Nightingale, Sherlock Holmes, Fortitude (Kurt Vonnegut's Monkey House). *Movies*: The Mark of Zorro, Liberty, Doomsday Gun.

LANGFORD, FRANCES
Singer, Actress. b. Lakeland, FL, April 4, 1913. e. Southern Coll. Stage experience in vaudeville, nightclubs, national radio programs.
PICTURES: Every Night at Eight, Collegiate, Broadway Melody of 1936, Palm Springs, Born to Dance, The Hit Parade, Hollywood Hotel, Dreaming Out Loud, Too Many Girls, The Hit Parade of 1941, All-American Coed, Mississippi Gambler, Yankee Doodle Dandy, Cowboy in Manhattan, This Is the Army, Never a Dull Moment, Career Girl, The Girl Rush, Dixie Jamboree, Radio Stars on Parade, Bamboo Blonde, Make Mine Laughs, People Are Funny, Deputy Marshall, Purple Heart Diary, The Glenn Miller Story.

LANGNER, PHILIP
Producer, b. New York, NY, Aug. 24, 1926. e. Yale U. President of The Theatre Guild and Theatre Guild Films, Inc. Producer the Westport Country Playhouse 1947-53. Joined The Theatre Guild 1954.
THEATER: The Matchmaker, Bells Are Ringing, The Tunnel of Love, Sunrise at Campobello, A Majority of One, The Unsinkable Molly Brown, A Passage to India, Seidman and Son, The Royal Hunt of the Sun, The Homecoming, Absurd Person Singular, Golda.
PICTURES: *Producer*: The Pawnbroker, Slaves, Born to Win. Associate Prod.: Judgment at Nuremberg, A Child Is Waiting.

LANSBURY, ANGELA
Actress. b. London, England, Oct. 16, 1925. Brothers are producers Bruce and Edgar Lansbury. e. South Hampstead Sch. for Girls, England; Acad. of Music, London; Feagin Dramatic Sch., N.Y. Mother was actress Moyna Macgill. To NY 1940 to study drama. Signed to contract by MGM, 1944. Exercise and lifestyle video: Positive Moves, 1988. *Book*: Positive Moves, 1990.
THEATER: *B'way*: Hotel Paradiso (NY debut, 1957), A Taste of Honey, Anyone Can Whistle, Mame (Tony Award, 1966), Dear World (Tony Award, 1969), Prettybelle (closed out of town), All Over, Gypsy (Tony Award, 1975), Hamlet, The King and I, Sweeney Todd: The Demon Barber of Fleet Street (Tony Award, 1979), A Little Family Business, Mame (1983 revival).
PICTURES: Gaslight (debut, 1944; Acad. Award nom.), National Velvet, The Picture of Dorian Gray (Acad. Award nom.), The Harvey Girls, The Hoodlum Saint, The Private Affairs of Bel Ami, Till the Clouds Roll By, If Winter Comes, Tenth Avenue Angel, State of the Union, The Three Musketeers, The Red Danube, Samson and Delilah, Kind Lady, Mutiny, Remains to Be Seen, The Purple Mask, A Lawless Street, The Court Jester, Please Murder Me, The Key Man (A Life at Stake), The Long Hot Summer, The Reluctant Debutante, The Summer of the 17th Doll (Season of Passion), The Dark at the Top of the Stairs, A Breath of Scandal, Blue Hawaii, All Fall Down, The Manchurian Candidate (Acad. Award nom.), In the Cool of the Day, The World of Henry Orient, Dear Heart, The Greatest Story Ever Told, Harlow, The Amorous Adventures of Moll Flanders, Mister Buddwing, Something for Everyone, Bedknobs and Broomsticks, Death on the Nile, The Lady Vanishes, The Mirror Crack'd, The Last Unicorn (voice), The Pirates of Penzance, The Company of Wolves, Beauty and the Beast (voice).
TELEVISION: *Special*: Sweeney Todd. *Movies*: Little Gloria... Happy at Last, The Gift of Love: A Christmas Story, The First Olympics: Athens 1896, A Talent for Murder, Lace, Rage of Angels: The Story Continues, Shootdown, The Shell Seekers, The Love She Sought, Mrs. 'arris Goes to Paris. *Series*: Pantomime Quiz, Murder She Wrote (also exec. prod.). *Guest*: Robert Montgomery Presents, Four Star Playhouse, Studio 57, Playhouse 90.

LANSBURY, BRUCE
Executive. b. London, England, Jan. 12, 1930. Brother of Angela and twin Edgar. e. UCLA. Mother was actress Moyna Macgill. Writer, prod. KABC-TV, Los Angeles, 1957-59; joined CBS-TV, 1959, was ass't. dir., program dev., Hollywood, director for daytime and nighttime programs, and v.p., programs, New York; 1964-66, indep. prod.; Broadway stage; 1966-69 producer, Wild Wild West, CBS series; 1969-72, prod. Mission: Impossible, Paramount Movies of Week; now v.p., creative affairs, Para-mount TV.
TELEVISION: Great Adventure (series; prod.), Wings of the Water (exec. prod.), Murder She Wrote.

LANSBURY, EDGAR
Producer, Director, Designer. b. London, England, Jan. 12, 1930. e. UCLA. Brother of Angela and Bruce Lansbury. Started career as scenic designer and art director. 1955-60, art dir., CBS; 1962-63, exec. art dir. prod. for WNDT-TV, educational sta.; THEATER: *Producer—B'way*: The Subject Was Roses, Promenade, Waiting for Godot, Long Day's Journey

into Night, Gypsy, The Night That Made America Famous, American Buffalo, Amphigorey: The Musical, Any Given Day, etc. Director on stage: Without Apologies, Advice From a Caterpillar, The Country Club.
PICTURES: *Producer*: The Subject Was Roses, Godspell, The Wild Party, Squirm, Blue Sunshine, He Knows You're Alone, The Clairvoyant.
TELEVISION: The Defenders (art. dir.), Summer Girl (exec. prod.), Wings of the Water (exec. prod.), A Stranger Waits.

LANSING, SHERRY
Executive. b. Chicago, IL, July 31, 1944. e. Northwestern U. m. director William Friedkin. Taught math and English in L.A. city high schools, 1966-69. Acted in films (Loving, Rio Lobo) and numerous TV shows. Story editor for Wagner Intl. Prod. Co., 1972-74. Talent Associates, in chg. West Coast development (all projects), 1974-75. Appt. MGM story editor, 1975. In 1977, named MGM v.p. of creative affairs; Nov., 1977, appointed vice pres., production, at Columbia Pictures. January, 1980, appointed pres., Twentieth Century-Fox Productions. Resigned 1982 to form new production co. with Stanley R. Jaffe: Jaffe—Lansing Prods. Appointed chmn. and CEO, Paramount Motion Picture Group, 1992.
PICTURES: Co-prod.: Racing with the Moon, Firstborn, Fatal Attraction, The Accused, Black Rain, School Ties, Indecent Proposal (prod.).
TELEVISION: When the Time Comes (exec. prod.), Mistress.

LaPAGLIA, ANTHONY
Actor. b. Adelaide, Australia, 1959. Former teacher, moved to U.S. in 1984. Made Off-B'way debut in Bouncers, followed by On the Open Road. *B'way*: The Rose Tattoo (Theatre World Award).
PICTURES: Slaves of New York (debut, 1989), Dangerous Obsession (Mortal Sins), Betsy's Wedding, He Said/She Said, One Good Cop, 29th Street, Whispers in the Dark, Innocent Blood, So I Married an Axe Murderer, The Client, The Custodian, Mixed Nuts, Bulletproof Heart, Lucky Break, Empire Records, Nowhere Man, The Funeral, Brilliant Lies.
TELEVISION: *Movies*: Criminal Justice, Keeper of the City, Black Magic, Past Tense, Nitti: The Enforcer. *Series*: Murder One.

LARDNER, RING W., JR.
Writer. b. Chicago, IL, Aug. 19, 1915. p. writer-humorist Ring W. and Ellis A. e. Phillips Andover Acad., Princeton U. Was reporter on New York Daily Mirror. Publ. writer, Selznick International. 1947, member of "Hollywood 10." In collab. with Ian Hunter conceived and wrote under pseudonyms many episodes in 5 TV series while blacklisted. Uncredited writer of such films as A Breath of Scandal, The Cardinal. 1989, received Writers Guild Laurel Award. Author of novels: The Ecstacy of Owen Muir, All For Love, and memoir, The Lardners My Family Remembered. Also collab. on B'way musical Foxy. 1992. WGA Ian McLellan Hunter Memorial Award for Lifetime Achievement.
PICTURES: Woman of the Year (Academy Award, 1942), The Cross of Lorraine, Tomorrow the World, Forever Amber, Forbidden Street, Four Days Leave, Cloak and Dagger, The Cincinnati Kid, M*A*S*H (Academy Award, 1970), Lady Liberty, The Greatest.

LARKIN, JAMES J.
Executive. b. Brooklyn, NY, Nov. 2, 1925. e. Columbia U., 1947-52. U.S. Air Force, 1943-46; BOAC rep. to entertainment ind., 1948-60; pres., Transportation Counselors Inc., 1960-62; pres., Larkin Associates, Inc., 1962-65; exec. Radio N.Y. Worldwide, 1965-68; v.p. Grolier Educational Corp., 1968-69; v.p. Visual Informational Systems, 1969-73; pres., Business TV Services, Inc., 1973; exec. prod., Madhouse Brigade, 1977-79; prod.-writer, All Those Beautiful Girls, 1979-80.

LARROQUETTE, JOHN
Actor. b. New Orleans, LA., Nov. 25, 1947. Disc jockey on FM radio during 1960s and early 70s. Acted on L.A. stage from 1973 (The Crucible, Enter Laughing, Endgame). Prof. debut, TV series Doctor's Hospital, 1976-78. Was narrator for film Texas Chainsaw Massacre.
PICTURES: Altered States, Heart Beat, Green Ice, Stripes, Cat People, Hysterical, Twilight Zone—The Movie, Choose Me, Meatballs Part II, Star Trek III: The Search for Spock, Summer Rental, Blind Date, Second Sight, Madhouse, Tune in Tomorrow, Richie Rich.
TELEVISION: *Series*: Doctor's Hospital, Baa Baa Black Sheep, Night Court (4 Emmy Awards, 1985-88), The John Larroquette Show. *Movies*: Bare Essence, The Last Ninja, Hot Paint, Convicted, One Special Victory (also co-exec. prod.).

LASSALLY, WALTER
Cinematographer. b. Berlin, Germany, Dec. 18, 1926. Entered indust. as clapper-boy at Riverside Studios. During 1950s allied himself with Britain's Free Cinema filmmakers working for Lindsay Anderson, Gavin Lambert, Tony Richardson and Karel Reisz.

PICTURES: A Girl in Black (feature debut, 1956), Beat Girl, A Taste of Honey, Electra, The Loneliness of the Long Distance Runner, Tom Jones, Zorba the Greek (Academy Award, 1964), The Day the Fish Came Out, Joanna, Oedipus the King, The Adding Machine, Three Into Two Won't Go, Something for Everyone, Twinky (Lola), Savages, Happy Mother's Day... Love George, To Kill a Clown, The Wild Party, Pleasantville, The Great Bank Hoax, The Woman Across the Way, Hullabaloo Over George and Bonnie's Pictures, Something Short of Paradise, The Blood of Hussain, Angel of Iron, Memoirs of a Survivor, Too Far to Go, Heat and Dust, Private School, The Bostonians, The Deceivers, Fragments of Isabella, The Perfect Murder, Ballad of the Sad Cafe, The Little Dolphins.
TELEVISION: Mrs. Delafield Wants to Marry, The Man Upstairs.

LASSER, LOUISE
Actress. b. New York, NY, April 11, 1939. e. Brandeis U., New School for Social Research. Appeared on stage before theatrical film debut in 1965 with What's New Pussycat? Won first Clio Award for best actress in a commercial.
THEATER: I Can Get it For You Wholesale, The Third Ear, Henry Sweet Henry, Lime Green/Khaki Blue, The Chinese, Marie & Bruce, A Coupla White Chicks Sitting Around Talking.
PICTURES: What's Up Tiger Lily? (voice), Take the Money and Run, Bananas, Such Good Friends, Everything You Always Wanted to Know About Sex, Slither, Simon, In God We Trust, Stardust Memories, Crimewave, Nightmare at Shadow Woods (Blood Rage), Surrender, Sing, Rude Awakening, Modern Love, Frankenhooker, The Night We Never Met.
TELEVISION: Series: Mary Hartman Mary Hartman, It's a Living. Movies: Coffee Tea or Me?, Isn't It Shocking?, Just Me and You (also writer), For Ladies Only. Guest: Bob Newhart Show, Mary Tyler Moor Show, Taxi, St. Elsewhere, Empty Nest, many others. Special: The Lie.

LASZLO, ANDREW
Cinematographer. b. Papa, Hungary, Jan. 12, 1926. To U.S. in 1947, working as cameraman on tv before turning to feature films.
PICTURES: One Potato Two Potato, You're a Big Boy Now, The Night They Raided Minskys, Popi, The Out of Towners, Lovers and Other Strangers, The Owl and the Pussycat, Jennifer on My Mind, To Find a Man, The Effect of Gamma Rays on Man-in-the-Moon Marigolds, Class of '44, Countdown at Kusini, Thieves, Somebody Killed Her Husband, The Warriors, The Funhouse, Southern Comfort, I the Jury, First Blood, Streets of Fire, Thief of Hearts, Remo Williams: The Adventure Begins, Poltergeist II, Innerspace, Star Trek V: The Final Frontier, Ghost Dad, Newsies.
TELEVISION: Documentaries: High Adventure with Lowell Thomas, The Twentieth Century. Series: The Phil Silvers Show, Joe and Mabel, Mama, Brenner, Naked City, The Nurses, Doctors and Nurses, Coronet Blue. Specials: New York New York, The Beatles at Shea Stadium, Ed Sullivan Specials. Movies and feature pilots: The Happeners, The Cliffdwellers, Daphne, Teacher Teacher, Blue Water Gold, The Man Without a Country, The Unwanted, Spanner's Key, Thin Ice, Love is Forever. Mini-series: Washington Behind Closed Doors, The Dain Curse, Top of the Hill, Shogun, and numerous commericals.

LATSIS, PETER C.
Publicist. b. Chicago, IL, Mar. 9, 1919. e. Wright Jr. Coll., Chicago. Newspaper reporter, Chicago Herald-American, 1942-45; Army, 1943; joined Fox West Coast Theatres, Los Angeles, in theatre operations 1945; adv.-pub. dept. 1946; asst. dir. adv.-pub. 1955; press rep. National Theatres, 1958; press relations dir., National General Corp., 1963; home office special field pub. repr., American International Pictures, 1973; Filmways Pictures, 1980-82; Recipient of Publicists Guild's Robert Yeager Award, 1983. Member, Motion Picture Pioneers. Unit rep., Executive Bd. of Publicists Guild of America, 1993-95.

LATTANZI, MATT
Actor. m. actress-singer Olivia Newton-John.
PICTURES: Xanadu (1980), Rich and Famous, Grease 2, My Tutor, That's Life!, Roxanne, Blueberry Hill, Catch Me If You Can, Diving In.
TELEVISION: Series: Paradise Beach.

LATTUADA, ALBERTO
Director. b. Milan, Italy, 1914. Son of Felice Lattuada, musician, opera composer, and writer of scores of many of son's films. Studied architecture; founded the periodical Cominare. Later founded Italian Film Library of which he still pres. Also, pres., Cinema D'Essay. First screen work as scriptwriter and asst. dir. of two films, 1940.
PICTURES: Mill on the Po, Anna, The Overcoat, La Lupa, Love in the City, White Sister, Flesh Will Surrender, Without Pity, The She Wolf, Tempest, The Unexpected, Mafioso, The Mandrake, Matchless, The Betrayal, The Steppe, Oh Serafina, Stay as You Are.

LAUGHLIN, TOM
Actor, Producer, Director, Writer. b. Minneapolis, MN, 1938. e. U. of Indiana, U. of Minnesota where had athletic scholarships. m. actress Delores Taylor. Travelled around world, studying in Italy with Dr. Maria Montessori. Established, ran a Montessori school in Santa Monica for several yrs. Worked his way to Hollwood, where acted in bit parts until stardom came in Born Losers in 1967. Produced and starred in Billy Jack and The Trial of Billy Jack, also writing b.p. with wife under pseudonym Frank Christina. Heads own prod. co., Billy Jack Enterprises.
PICTURES: Actor: Tea and Sympathy, South Pacific, Gidget, Tall Story, The Slime People. Actor-Dir.-Prod.-Writer: The Proper Time, The Young Sinner, Born Losers, Billy Jack, The Trial of Billy Jack, The Master Gunfighter, Billy Jack Goes to Washington.

LAUNER, DALE
Writer. b. Cleveland, OH. E. Cal State Northridge. Son of actor John S. Launer.
PICTURES: Ruthless People, Blind Date, Dirty Rotten Scoundrels, My Cousin Vinny, Love Potion #9 (also dir.).

LAURENTS, ARTHUR
Writer, Director. b. New York, NY, July 14, 1917. e. Cornell U., B.A., 1937. First Professional writing as radio script writer in 1939. In Army 1941-45. Member of the Council of the Dramatists Guild; Theatre Hall of Fame.
THEATER: Author: Home of the Brave (Sidney Howard Award), Heartsong, The Bird Cage, The Time of the Cuckoo, A Clearing in the Woods, Invitation to a March, West Side Story, Gypsy, Hallelujah, Baby! (Tony Award), Scream, The Enclave, Running Time, Jolson Sings Again, The Radical Mystique. Director: Invitation to a March, I Can Get It for You Wholesale, La Cage aux Folles (Tony Award), Birds of Paradise. Author-Director: Anyone Can Whistle, Do I Hear a Waltz?, The Madwoman of Central Park West, Gypsy (revival), Nick and Nora.
PICTURES: Writer: The Snake Pit, Rope, Caught, Anna Lucasta, Anastasia, Bonjour Tristesse, The Way We Were (from his own novel), The Turning Point (also co-prod.; Golden Globe, Writer's Guild Award).

LAURIA, DAN
Actor. b. Brooklyn, NY, April 12, 1947. e. So Conn. St. Col., Univ. of Conn. Served in U.S. Marine Corps., 1970\-73.
PICTURES: Without a Trace, Stakeout, Another Stakeout, Excessive Force II: Force on Force.
TELEVISION: Series: Love of Life, One Life to Live, Hooperman, The Wonder Years. Movies: Johnny Brass, Johnny Bull, Doing Life, At Mother's Request, Angel in Green, David, Howard Beach: Making the Case for Murder, The Big One: The Great Los Angeles Earthquake, Overexposed, Dead and Alive, From the Files of Joseph Wambaugh: A Jury of One, In the Line of Duty: Ambush in Waco, In the Line of Duty: Hunt for Justice. Guest: Growing Pains, Mike Hammer, Moonlighting, Hill Street Blues. Special: Between Mother and Daughter.

LAURIE, PIPER
Actress. r.n. Rosetta Jacobs. b. Detroit, MI, Jan. 22, 1932. e. Los Angeles H.S. Acted in school plays, signed by U.I. in 1949.
THEATER: The Glass Menagerie (revival), Marco Polo Sings a Solo, The Innocents, Biography, Rosemary, The Alligators, The Last Flapper (tour), The Destiny of Me.
PICTURES: Louisa (debut, 1950), The Milkman, Francis Goes to the Races, The Prince Who Was a Thief, Son of Ali Baba, Has Anybody Seen My Gal, No Room for the Groom, Mississippi Gambler, Golden Blade, Dangerous Mission, Johnny Dark, Dawn at Socorro, Smoke Signal, Ain't Misbehavin', Kelly and Me, Until They Sail, The Hustler (Acad. Award nom.), Carrie (Acad. Award nom.), Ruby, The Boss's Son, Tim, Return to Oz, Children of a Lesser God (Acad. Award nom.), Distortions, Appointment with Death, Tiger Warsaw, Dream a Little Dream, Mother Mother, Other People's Money, Storyville, Rich in Love, Trauma, Wrestling Ernest Hemingway, The Crossing Guard, The Grass Harp.
TELEVISION: Specials: Days of Wine and Roses (Emmy nom.), The Road That Led Afar (Emmy nom.), The Deaf Heart (Emmy nom.), The Secret Life of Margaret Sanger. Movies: In the Matter of Karen Ann Quinlan, Rainbow, Skag, The Bunker (Emmy nom.), Mae West, Love Mary, Toughlove, Promise (Emmy Award, 1987), Go To the Light, Rising Son, Poisoned By Love: The Kern County Murders, Lies and Lullabies, Shadows of Desire, Fighting for My Daughter. Series: Skag, Twin Peaks (Golden Globe Award, Emmy nom.). Mini-Series: The Thorn Birds (Emmy nom.), Tender is the Night. Guest: St. Elsewhere (Emmy nom.)

LAUTER, ED
Actor. b. Long Beach, NY, Oct. 30, 1940.
PICTURES: The New Centurions, Hickey & Boggs, The Last

American Hero, Executive Action, Lolly Madonna XXX, The Longest Yard, French Connection II, Breakheart Pass, Family Plot, King Kong, The Chicken Chronicles, Magic, The Amateur, Death Hunt, Timerider, The Big Score, Eureka, Lassiter, Cujo, Finders Keepers, Death Wish 3, Girls Just Want to Have Fun, Youngblood, 3:15, Raw Deal, Chief Zabu, Revenge of the Nerds II, Gleaming the Cube, Fat Man and Little Boy, Tennessee Waltz, School Ties, Wagons East!, Trial by Jury, Girl in the Cadillac.
TELEVISION: *Series*: B.J. and the Bear. *Movies*: Class of '63, The Migrants, The Godchild, Satan's Triangle, A Shadow in the Streets, Last Hours Before Morning, The Clone Master, The Jericho Mile, Love's Savage Fury, Undercover with the KKK, The Boy Who Drank Too Much, Guyana Tragedy—The Story of Jim Jones, AlcatrazThe Whole Shocking Story, In the Custody of Strangers, Rooster, The Seduction of Gina, Three Wishes of Billy Grier, The Last Days of Patton, The Thanksgiving Promise, Calendar Girl Cop Killer?: The Bambi Bembenek Story, Extreme Justice.

LAVEN, ARNOLD
Director, Producer. b. Chicago, IL, Feb. 23, 1922.
PICTURES: Without Warning (debut, 1952), Vice Squad, Down Three Dark Streets, The Rack, The Monster That Challenged the World, Slaughter on Tenth Ave., Anna Lucasta, Geronimo (also prod.), The Glory Guys (also co-prod.), Clambake (co-prod. only), Rough Night in Jericho, Sam Whiskey (also co-prod.).
TELEVISION: Part creator and director TV pilots: The Rifleman, Robert Taylor's Detectives, The Plainsmen.

LAVIN, LINDA
Actress. b. Portland, ME, Oct. 15, 1937. e. Coll. of William & Mary. First professional job in chorus of Camden County (N.J.) Music Circus. Worked in plays both off and on Broadway before turning to TV, where guest-starred on such series as Family, Rhoda, Phyllis and Harry O.
THEATER: Oh Kay! (Off-B'way debut, 1960), A Family Affair (B'way debut), Revues: Wet Paint (Theatre World Award), The Game Is Up, The Mad Show, member acting co.: Eugene O'Neil Playwright's Unit, 1968; It's a Bird It's a Plane... It's Superman, Something Different, Little Murders (Outer Critics Circle & Sat. Review Awards), Cop Out, The Last of the Red Hot Lovers (Tony nom.), Story Theatre, Dynamite Tonight, Broadway Bound (Tony, Drama Desk, Outer Critics Circle & Helen Hayes Awards), Gypsy, The Sisters Rosensweig, Death Defying Acts.
PICTURES: The Muppets Take Manhattan, See You in the Morning, I Want to Go Home.
TELEVISION: *Series*: Barney Miller, Alice (2 Golden Globe Awards; 2 Emmy noms.), Room for Two (also co-exec. prod.). *Movies*: The Morning After, Like Mom and Me, The $5.20 an Hour Dream, A Matter of Life and Death (also exec. prod. & developed), Another Woman's Child, A Place to Call Home (also exec. prod. & developed), Lena: My Hundred Children.

LAW, JOHN PHILLIP
Actor. b. Hollywood, CA, Sept. 7, 1937. e. Neighborhood Playhouse. B'way debut in Coming on Strong. Appeared at Lincoln Center in After the Fall, Marco Millions, The Changeling, and Tartuffe. Has made more than 50 films in more than 20 countries world wide.
PICTURES: High Infidelity, Three Nights of Love, The Russians Are Coming The Russians Are Coming the Russians Are Coming (U.S. debut), Hurry Sundown, Barbarella, Danger Diabolik, The Sergeant, Death Rides a Horse, Skidoo, Diary of a Telephone Operator, Von Richtofen and Brown, The Hawaiians, Michael Strogoff, The Love Machine, The Last Movie, The Golden Voyage of Sinbad, Stardust, Open Season, Your God My Hell, The Spiral Staircase, Dr. Justice, African Rage, Whisper in the Dark, Portrait of an Assassin, The Crystal Man, Death in November, Ring of Darkness, Tarzan the Ape Man, Night Train to Terror, The Tin Man, Rainy Day Friends (L.A. Bad), No Time to Die, American Commandos (Mr. Salvage), Johann Strauss, The Moon Under the Trees, Moon in Scorpio, Striker (Combat Force), The Overthrow, Mutiny in Space, Thunder Warrior III, A Case of Honor, Blood Delirium, Alienator, L.A. Heat, Gorilla, The Guest, Alaska Stories, Angel Eyes, Shining Blood, Marilyn Behind Bars, Day of the Pig, The Mountain of the Lord, Europa Mission.
TELEVISION: *Series*: The Young and the Restless (1989). *Movie*: The Best Place to Be, A Great Love Story (It.), Experiences (It.), The Fourth Man (Austrian), Little Women of Today (It.). *Guest*: The Love Boat, Murder She Wrote.

LAW, LINDSAY
Producer. e. NYU School of the Arts. Producer of specials for Warner Bros. Television, head of drama for WNET/New York and prod. for Theatre in America before becoming exec. prod. of American Playhouse. Advisory Board of Independent Feature Project/West, Sundance Film Festival.

PICTURES: *Exec. prod.*: On Valentine's Day, Smooth Talk, Native Son, In a Shallow Grave, Stand and Deliver, The Thin Blue Line, El Norte, The Wizard of Loneliness, Signs of Life, Bloodhounds of Broadway, Big Time, Eat a Bowl of Tea, Longtime Companion, Thousand Pieces of Gold, Straight Out of Brooklyn, Daughters of the Dust, Thank You and Goodnight, All the Vermeers in New York, Brother's Keeper, Ethan Frome, The Music of Chance, Golden Gate, I Shot Andy Warhol.
TELEVISION: *Prod.*: The Girls in Their Summer Dresses, The Time of Your Life, You Can't Take It With You, The Good Doctor, The Most Happy Fella, The Eccentricities of a Nightingale, Cyrano de Bergerac (assoc. prod.). *Prod. for American Playhouse*: Working, for Colored Girls Who Have Considered Suicide/When the Rainbow Is Enuf, Private Contentment, *Exec. prod.*: Concealed Enemies (Emmy Award, 1984), Land of Little Rain, Ask Me Again, The Diaries of Adam and Eve, A Walk in the Woods, Fires in the Mirror.

LAWRENCE, BARBARA
Actress. b. Carnegie, OK, Feb. 24, 1930. e. UCLA. Mother Berenice Lawrence. Child model; successful screen try-out, 1944; screen debut in Billy Rose Diamond Horse Shoe (1945).
PICTURES: Margie, Captain from Castile, You Were Meant for Me, Give My Regards to Broadway, Street with No Name, Unfaithfully Yours, Letter to Three Wives, Mother Is a Freshman, Thieves Highway, Two Tickets to Broadway, Here Come the Nelsons, The Star, Arena, Paris Model, Her 12 Men, Oklahoma, Man with the Gun, Joe Dakota, Kronos.

LAWRENCE, JOEY
Actor. b. Montgomery, PA, Apr. 20, 1976. e. USC.
PICTURES: Summer Rental, Oliver and Company (voice), Pulse, Radioland Murders.
TELEVISION: *Series*: Gimme a Break, Blossom, Brotherly Love. *Pilots*: Scamps, Little Shots. *Specials*: Andy Williams and the NBC Kids, Don't Touch, Alvin Goes Back to School, Umbrella Jack, Adventures in Babysitting, Disney's Countdown to Kids' Day, All That, Blossom in Paris, Kids' Choice Awards (host), etc. *Movies*: Chains of Gold, Prince for a Day.

LAWRENCE, MARC
Actor. r.n. Max Goldsmith. b. New York, NY, Feb. 17, 1914. e. City Coll. of New York. On stage in The Tree (Eva La Galliene Rep. Theatre.), Sour Mountain, Waiting for Lefty, Golden Boy, View From the Bridge.
PICTURES: White Woman, Little Big Shot, Dr. Socrates, Road Gang, San Quentin, The Ox Bow Incident, I Am the Law, While New York Sleeps, Dillinger, Flame of Barbary Coast, Club Havana, Don't Fence Me In, The Virginian, Life with Blondie, Yankee Fakir, Captain from Castile, I Walk Alone, Calamity Jane and Sam Bass, The Asphalt Jungle, Hurricane Island, My Favorite Spy, Girls Marked Danger, Helen of Troy, Johnny Cool, Nightmare in the Sun, Savage Pampas, Johnny Tiger, Custer of the West, Nightmare in the Sun (dir. co- prod., co-story only), Krakatoa East of Java, The Kremlin Letter, Fraser: The Sensuous Lion, The Man With the Golden Gun, Marathon Man, A Piece of the Action, Foul Play, Goin' Cocoanuts, Hot Stuff, Night Train to Terror, The Big Easy, Ruby, Newsies, Marilyn I Love You.

LAWRENCE, MARTIN
Actor, Comedian. b. Frankfurt, Germany, 1965. Started as stand-up comic in Washington D.C.
PICTURES: Do the Right Thing (debut, 1989), House Party, Talkin' Dirty After Dark, House Party 2, Boomerang, You So Crazy (also exec. prod.), Bad Boys.
TELEVISION: *Series*: What's Happening Now?, Kid 'n' Play (voice), Russell Simmons' Def Comedy Jam (host, prod. con-sultant), Martin (also co-exec. prod.). *Pilots*: Hammer Slammer & Slade, A Little Bit Strange. *Guest*: Stand Up Spotlight, Yo! MTV Laffs, An Evening at the Improv.

LAWRENCE, STEVE
Actor. b. New York, NY, July 8, 1935. m. singer Eydie Gorme. Singer in nightclubs and on TV.
THEATER: What Makes Sammy Run?, Golden Rainbow.
PICTURES: Stand Up and Be Counted, The Blues Brothers, The Lonely Guy.
TELEVISION: *Specials*: Steve and Eydie Celebrate Irving Berlin (also co-exec. prod.; Emmy Award, 1979), many spe-cials. *Series*: Tonight, The Steve Lawrence-Eydie Gorme Show (1958), The Steve Lawrence Show (1965), Foul-Ups Bleeps and Blunders (host). *Guest*: Police Story, Murder, She Wrote. *Movie*: Alice in Wonderland.

LAWRENCE, VICKI
Actress. b. Inglewood, CA, March 26, 1949. Singer and recording artist appearing with Young Americans (1965-67). Gained fame on The Carol Burnett Show as comedienne (1967-78), winning Emmy Award in 1976. Gold record for The Night the Lights Went Out in Georgia (1972). Author: *Vicki!: The True Life Adventures of Miss Fireball* (Simon & Schuster, 1995).

TELEVISION: *Movies*: Having Babies, Hart to Hart: Old Friends Never Die. *Series*: Carol Burnett Show, Jimmie Rodgers Show, Mama's Family. *Host*: Win Lose or Draw (1987-88), Vicki! (synd. talk show).

LAWSON, SARAH
Actress. b. London, Eng., Aug. 6, 1928. e. Heron's Ghyll Sch., Sussex. Stage debut in Everyman (Edinburgh Festival) 1947.
PICTURES: The Browning Version (debut, 1951), The Night Won't Talk, Street Corner, Street Corner (Both Sides of the Law), Three Steps in the Dark, Meet Mr. Malcolm, You Know What Sailors Are, Blue Peter (Navy Heroes), It's Never Too Late, Links of Justice, Three Crooked Men, The Solitary Child, Night Without Pity, On the Run, The World Ten Times Over, Island of the Burning Doomed, The Devil's Bride (The Devil Rides Out), Battle of Britain, The Stud, The Dawning (prod.).
TELEVISION: Face to Face, River Line, Whole Truth, Lady From the Sea, Mrs. Moonlight, Silver Card, An Ideal Husband, Love and Money, Rendezvous, Invisible Man, Saber Buccaneers, White Hunter, Flying Doctor, On the Night of the Murder, Haven in Sunset, The Odd Man, Zero 1 (series), The Innocent Ceremony, Department S, The Marrying Kind, The Expert, The Persuaders, Trial, Starcast, The Midsummer of Colonel Blossum, Callen, Crime of Passion, Full House, Father Brown, Within These Walls These Walls Series, The Standard, The Purple Twilight, The Professionals, Bergerac, Cuffy, Lovejoy.

LAYBOURNE, GERALDINE
Executive. e. Vassar College, B.A.; U. Penn, M.S. Joined Nickelodeon in 1980. Was vice chmn., MTV Networks; pres., Nickelodeon/Nick at Nite. Bd. member Viacom exec. committee. Left Nickelodeon to join ABC as pres., Disney/ABC Cable Network. Inducted into Broadcast and Cable Hall of Fame, 1996.

LAZARUS, PAUL N.
Executive. b. Brooklyn, NY, March 31, 1913. e. Cornell U., B.A., 1933. In U.S. Army, W.W. II. Entered m.p. ind. 1933 as gen. asst., press book dept., Warner Bros.; pres., AMPA, 1939-40. Joined Buchanan & Co., 1942 as m.p. account exec. To United Artists 1943 as dir. adv. & pub. Named asst. to pres.; 1948; joined Columbia exec. staff, New York, 1950; elected v.p. Columbia, 1954-62; exec. v.p. Samuel Bronston Prods., 1962-64; v.p., chg. Motion Pictures, Subscription Television Inc., 1964; exec. officer and partner, Landau Releasing Organization, 1964-65; exec. v.p., member bd. of dir., Nat'l Screen Serv. Corp., 1965-75; lecturer and consultant, Film Studies Program, U. of CA at Santa Barbara, 1975-. Consultant to Kenya Film Corp., Nairobi, 1983. Director, Santa Barbara Intl. Film Festival, 1986-87. Chief of Staff, Santa Barbara Writers' Conference, 1976-. Vice-chmn. Santa Barbara County Film Council, 1989-92.

LAZARUS, PAUL N. III
Executive. b. New York, NY, May 25, 1938. e. Williams Coll., BA.; Yale Law Sch., L.L.B. Third generation film exec. Began career with Palomar Pictures Int'l. as exec. v.p.; joined ABC Pictures Corp. as v.p. in chg. of creative affairs. Mng. dir., CRM Productions, maker of educational films; v.p. for motion pictures. Marble Arch Productions; 1983, v.p. in chg. of prod., Home Box Office. 1985, Film Commissioner, New Mexico; 1987, Dir. of Film Program, U of Miami.
PICTURES: *Prod.*: Extreme Close-Up, Westworld, Futureworld, Capricorn One, Hanover Street, Barbarosa, Doubles.

LAZENBY, GEORGE
Actor. b. Goulburn, Australia, Sept. 5, 1939. Appeared in Australian and British tv commericals before being chosen to star as James Bond.
PICTURES: On Her Majesty's Secret Service (debut, 1969), Universal Soldier, Who Saw Her Die?, The Dragon Flies, Stoner, The Man From Hong Kong, The Kentucky Fried Movie, Death Dimension, The Falcon's Ultimatum, Saint Jack, L'ultimo Harem, Never Too Young to Die, Hell Hunters, Gettysburg.
TELEVISION: Is Anybody There?, Cover Girls, The Newman Shame, The Return of the Man From U.N.C.L.E.

LEACHMAN, CLORIS
Actress. b. Des Moines, IA, April 30, 1926. e. Northwestern U. Broadway stage, television, motion pictures.
PICTURES: Kiss Me Deadly (debut, 1955), The Rack, The Chapman Report, Butch Cassidy and the Sundance Kid, Lovers and Other Strangers, The People Next Door, W.U.S.A., The Steagle, The Last Picture Show (Academy Award, best supporting actress, 1971), Dillinger, Charlie and the Angel, Happy Mother's Day... Love George, Daisy Miller, Young Frankenstein, Crazy Mama, High Anxiety, The Mouse and His Child (voice), The North Avenue Irregulars, The Muppet Movie, Scavenger Hunt, Foolin' Around, Yesterday, Herbie Goes Bananas, History of the World—Part I, My Little Pony

(voice), Shadow Play, Walk Like a Man, Hansel and Gretel, Prancer, Texasville, Love Hurts, My Boyfriend's Back, The Beverly Hillbillies, A Troll in Central park (voice), Now and Then.
TELEVISION: *Series*: Hold It Please, Charlie Wild: Private Detective, Bob and Ray, Lassie, Mary Tyler Moore Show (Emmy Awards 1974, 1975), Phyllis (Golden Globe Award), The Facts of Life, The Nutt House, Walter & Emily. *Movies*: Silent Night Lonely Night, Suddenly Single, Haunts of the Very Rich, A Brand New Life (Emmy Award, 1973), Crime Club, Dying Room Only, The Migrants, Hitchhike!, Thursday's Game, Death Sentence, Someone I Touched, A Girl Named Sooner, Death Scream, The New Original Wonder Woman, The Love Boat (pilot), It Happened One Christmas, Long Journey Back, Willa, Mrs. R's Daughter, S.O.S. Titanic, The Acorn People, Advice to the Lovelorn, Miss All-American Beauty, Dixie: Changing Habits, Demon Murder Case, Ernie Kovacs: Between the Laughter, Deadly Intentions, Love Is Never Silent, Wedding Bell Blues, Danielle Steel's Fine Things, In Broad Daylight, A Little Piece of Heaven, Fade to Black, Without a Kiss Goodbye, Miracle Child, Double Double Toil and Trouble, Between Love and Honor. *Specials*: Oldest Living Graduate, Of Thee I Sing, Breakfast With Les and Bess, Screen Actors Guild 50th Anniversary Celebration (Emmy Award, 1984). *Guest*: Twilight Zone, Untouchables, Big Valley, That Girl, Marcus Welby, Night Gallery, Cher (Emmy Award, 1975), Love Boat.

LEAR, NORMAN
Producer, Director, Writer. b. New Haven, CT, July 27, 1922. e. Emerson Coll. In public relations 1945-49. Began in TV as co-writer of weekly one-hour variety show, The Ford Star Revue in 1950. Followed as writer for Dean Martin and Jerry Lewis on the Colgate Comedy Hour and for the Martha Raye and George Gobel TV shows. With partner, Bud Yorkin, created and produced such specials as Another Evening with Fred Astaire, Henry Fonda and the Family, An Evening with Carol Channing, and The Many Sides of Don Rickles. In 1965 their company, Tandem Productions, also produced the original Andy Williams Show. Moved into motion pictures in 1963, writing and producing Come Blow Your Horn. Formed Act III Communications, 1987.
PICTURES: Come Blow Your Horn (co-prod., s.p.), Never Too Late (prod.), Divorce-American Style (prod., s.p.), The Night They Raided Minsky's (co-prod., co-s.p.), Start the Revolution Without Me (exec. prod.), Cold Turkey (dir., s.p., prod.), The Princess Bride (exec. prod.), Fried Green Tomatoes (co-exec. prod.).
TELEVISION: *Creator-dir.*: TV Guide Award Show (1962), Henry Fonda and the Family (1963), Andy Williams Specials, Robert Young and the Family. Exec. prod. and creator or developer: All in the Family (3 Emmy Awards), Maude, Good Times, Sanford and Son, The Jeffersons, Mary Hartman Mary Hartman, One Day at a Time, All's Fair, A Year at the Top, All that Glitters, Fernwood 2 Night, The Baxters, Palmerstown, Love Liberty, Heartsounds, Sunday Dinner, The Powers That Be, 704 Hauser.

LEARNED, MICHAEL
Actress. b. Washington, DC, Apr. 9, 1939. Studied ballet and dramatics in school. Many stage credits include Under Milkwood, The Three Sisters, A God Slept Here, The Sisters Rosensweig, etc.; resident performances with Shakespeare festivals in Canada, Stratford, CT, and San Diego, CA. Gained fame on hit TV series, The Waltons, as the mother, Olivia.
PICTURES: Touched by Love, Shanghai Shadows (narrator), Power, Dragon: The Bruce Lee Story.
TELEVISION: *Series*: The Waltons (3 Emmy Awards: 1973, 1974, 1976), Nurse (Emmy Award, 1982), Hothouse, Living Dolls. *Guest*: Gunsmoke, Police Story, St. Elsewhere, Murder She Wrote, Who's the Boss?. *Movies*: Hurricane, It Couldn't Happen to a Nicer Guy, Widow, Little Mo, Nurse (pilot), Off the Minnesota Strip, A Christmas Without Snow, Mother's Day on Walton Mountain, The Parade, A Deadly Business, Mercy or Murder?, Roots: The Gift, Gunsmoke: The Last Apache, Aftermath: A Test of Love, Keeping Secrets, A Walton Thanksgiving Reunion, A Walton Wedding. *Specials*: All My Sons, Picnic.

LEARY, DENIS
Actor. b. 1957. e. Emerson Coll., Boston. Performed with the New Voices Theater Company, Charlestown Working Theater. Debuted one-man stand-up show No Cure for Cancer at Edinburgh Intl. Arts Fest., then later in London, Off-B'way, and cable tv. Appeared in and dir. short film for Showtime, Thy Neighbor's Wife.
PICTURES: Strictly Business (debut), National Lampoon's Loaded Weapon 1, The Sandlot, Who's the Man?, Gunmen, Demolition Man, Judgment Night, The Ref, Operation Dumbo Drop, The Neon Bible, Two If by Sea (also co-s.p.).

LEAUD, JEAN-PIERRE
Actor. b. Paris, France, May 5, 1944. Parents were screen-writer Pierre Leaud and actress Jacqueline Pierreux. At 14

chosen to play Antoine Doinel in Truffaut's The 400 Blows and subsequent autobiographical films love at 20, Stolen Kisses, Bed and Board, Love on the Run. Also closely identified with major films by Jean-Luc Godard.
PICTURES: The 400 Blows, The Testament of Orpheus, Love at Twenty, Masculine-Feminine, Made in USA, Le Depart, La Chinoise, Weekend, Stolen Kisses, Le Gai Savoir, Pigsty, The Oldest Profession, Bed and Board, Two English Girls, Last Tango in Paris, Day for Night, Lola's Lolos, Love on the Run, Rebelote, Detective, Just a Movie, Seen by... 20 Years After, Treasure Island, The Grandeur and Decadence of a Small-Time Filmmaker, With All Hands, Time to Aim, Jane B, par Agnes V.; 36 Fillete, La Femme de Paille (The Straw Woman), The Color of the Wind, Femme de Papier, Bunker Palace Hotel, Treasure Island, I Hired a Contract Killer, Paris at Dawn, The Birth of Love.

LEDER, HERBERT JAY
Writer, Director, Producer. b. New York, NY, Aug. 15, 1922. e. B.A., Ph.D. Play Doctor on Broadway; Director TV dept., Benton and Bowles Adv. chg. all T.V. & Film production, 13 yrs. Sponsored Films: Child Molester, Bank Robber, Shoplifter, Untouchables.
PICTURES: *Writer.* Fiend Without a Face, Pretty Boy Floyd (also dir., co-prod.), Nine Miles to Noon (also dir., co-prod.), Aquarius Mission, Love Keeps No Score of Wrongs, The Frozen Dead (also dir., prod.), It (also dir., prod.), Candyman (also dir.), The Winners, The Way It Is, The Cool Crazies.

LEDERER, RICHARD
Executive. b. New York, NY, Sept. 22, 1916. e. U. of Virginia, B.S., 1938. Freelance writer, 1939-41; U.S. Army. Cryptanalyst, Signal Intell. Serv 1941-45; Adv. copywriter, Columbia Pictures, 1946-50; Adv. copywriter, Warner Bros., 1950-53; copy chief, Warner Bros., 1950-53; copy chief, Warner Bros., 1953-57; Asst. Nat'l Adv. mgr., Warner Bros. studios, 1957-59; Prod., theatrical, TV. Warner Bros. studios, 1959-60; Dir. of adv., publicity, Warner Bros. Pictures, 1960; v.p. Warner Bros. Pictures, 1963. V.P. production, Warner Bros. Studio, 1969-70; indep. prod. to 1971, when returned to WB as adv.-pub., v.p. Independent producer. 1980: Hollywood Knights. Joined Orion Pictures as v.p., adv. Resigned, 1984.

LEE, ANNA
Actress. M.B.E. r.n. Joan Boniface Winnifrith. b. Kent, England, Jan. 2, 1913. e. Central School of Speech Training and Dramatic Art, Royal Albert Hall. With London Repertory Theatre; toured in the Constant Nymph and Jane Eyre. In 1930s known as Britain's Glamour Girl. 1939 came to US to star in My Life With Caroline. Entertained troops with U.S.O. during WWII. 1950 moved to N.Y. to appear in live TV.
PICTURES: Ebb Tide (debut, 1932), Yes Mr. Brown, Say It With Music, Mayfair Girl, King's Cup, Chelsea Life, Mannequin, Faces, The Bermondsey Kid, Lucky Loser, The Camels Are Coming, Rolling in Money, Heat Wave, Passing of the Third Floor Back, First a Girl, The Man Who Changed His Mind, O.H.M.S. (You're in the Army Now), King Solomon's Mines, Non-Stop New York, The Four Just Men (The Secret Four), Return to Yesterday, Young Man's Fancy, Seven Sinners, My Life With Caroline, How Green Was My Valley, Flying Tigers, The Commandos Strike at Dawn, Hangmen Also Die, Flesh and Fantasy, Forever and a Day, Summer Storm, Abroad With Two Yanks, Bedlam, G.I. War Brides, High Conquest, The Ghost and Mrs. Muir, Best Man Wins, Fort Apache, Prison Warden, Wyoming Mail, Boots Malone, Daniel Boone—Trail Blazer, Gideon of Scotland Yard, The Last Hurrah, The Horse Soldiers, Jet Over the Atlantic, This Eath Is Mine, The Big Night, The Crimson Kimono, Jack the Giant Killer, Two Rode Together, The Man Who Shot Liberty Valance, What Ever Happend to Baby Jane?, The Prize, The Unsinkable Molly Brown, For Those Who Think Young, The Sound of Music, Torn Curtain, Seven Women, Picture Mommy Dead, In Like Flint, Star!, Clash.
TELEVISION: Guest on many major television shows from 1950-77. *Series:* General Hospital (1978-present). *Movies:* Eleanor and Franklin, The Night Rider, The Beasts are Loose, Scruples.

LEE, CHRISTOPHER
Actor. b. London, England, May 27, 1922. e. Wellington Coll. Served RAF 1940-46. Ent. m.p. ind. 1947. *Autobiography:* Tall, Dark and Gruesome (1977).
PICTURES: include: Corridor of Mirrors (debut, 1947), One Night With You, A Song for Tomorrow, Scott of the Antarctic, Hamlet, The Gay Lady, Capt. Horatio Hornblower, Valley of the Eagles, The Crimson Pirate, Babes in Bagdad, Moulin Rouge, Innocents of Paris, That Lady, The Warriors, Cockleshell Heroes, Storm Over the Nile, Port Afrique, Private's Progress, Beyond Mombasa, Battle of the River Plate, Night Ambush, She Played With Fire, The Traitors, Curse of Frankenstein, Bitter Victory, Truth About Women, Tale of Two Cities, Dracula, Man Who Could Cheat Death, The Mummy, Too Hot to Handle, Beat Girl, City of the Dead

(Horror Hotel), Two Faces of Dr. Jekyll, The Terror of the Tongs, The Hands of Orlac, Taste of Fear, The Devil's Daffodil, Pirates of Blood River, Devil's Agent, Red Orchid, Valley of Fear, Katharsis, Faust '63, The Virgin of Nuremberg, The Whip and the Body, Carmilla, The Devil Ship Pirates, The Gorgon, The Sign of Satan, The House of Blood, Dr. Terror's House of Horrors, She, The Skull, The Mask of Fu Manchu, Dracula, Prince of Darkness, Rasputin, Theatre of Death, Circus of Fear, The Brides of Fu Manchu, Five Golden Dragons, Vengeance of Fu Manchu, Night of the Big Heat, The Pendulum, The Face of Eve, The Devil Rides Out, The Blood of Fu Manchu, The Crimson Altar, Dracula Has Risen from the Grave, The Oblong Box, De Sade 70, Scream and Scream Again, The Magic Christian, Julius Caesar, One More Time, Count Dracula, Bloody Judge, Taste the Blood of Dracula, The Private Life of Sherlock Holmes, El Umbragolo, Scars of Dracula, The House That Dripped Blood, I Monster, Hannie Caulder, Dracula A.D. 1972, Horror Express, Death Line (Raw Meat), Nothing But the Night (also co-exec. prod.), The Creeping Flesh, The Wicker Man, Poor Devil, Dark Places, Satanic Rites of Dracula, Eulalie Quitte les Champs, The Three Musketeers, Earthbound, The Man with the Golden Gun, The Four Musketeers, Killer Force, Diagnosis—Murder, Whispering Death, The Keeper, To the Devil a Daughter, Dracula and Son, Airport '77, Starship Invasions (Alien Encounters), The End of the World, Return from Witch Mountain, Caravans, The Passage, Arabian Adventure, Jaguar Lives, Circle of Iron (The Silent Flute), 1941, Bear Island, Serial, The Salamander, An Eye for an Eye, Safari 3000, House of Long Shadows, The Return of Captain Invincible, The Rosebud Beach Hotel, Roadtrip, Dark Mission, The Howling II: Your Sister is a Werewolf, Olympus Force, Jocks, Murder Story, Mio In the Land of Faraway, The Girl, The Return of the Musketeers, Honeymoon Academy, The French Revolution, Gremlins 2: The New Batch, Curse III: Blood Sacrifice, The Rainbow Thief, L'Avaro, Jackpot, Double Vision, Shogun Mayeda, Special Class, Journey of Honor, Cybereden, Funny Man, Police Academy: Mission to Moscow, A Feast at Midnight, The Stupids, Sorellina.
TELEVISION: The Disputation, Metier du Seigneur, Movies: Poor Devil, Harold Robbins' The Pirate, Captain America II, Once a Spy, Charles and Diana: A Royal Love Story, Far Pavilions, Shaka Zulu, Goliath Awaits, Massarati and the Brain, Around the World in 80 Days, Treasure Island, Young Indiana Jones, The Care of Time, Sherlock Holmes & the Leading Lady, Sherlock Holmes and the Incident at Victoria Falls, Death Train, The Tomorrow People, Tales of Mystery & Imagination, Moses, Ivanhoe.

LEE, JASON SCOTT
Actor. b. Los Angeles, CA, 1966. Raised in Hawaii. e. Fullerton Col., Organge County, CA.
PICTURES: Born in East L.A. (debut, 1987), Back to the Future II, Map of the Human Heart, Dragon: The Bruce Lee Story, Rapa Nui, Rudyard Kipling's The Jungle Book.
TELEVISION: *Movie:* Vestige of Honor. *Special:* American Eyes.

LEE, JOIE
Actress. b. 1968. e. Sarah Lawrence Col. Brother is director-writer Spike Lee. On NY stage in Mulebone. Appeared in short film Coffee and Cigarettes Part Two. Has also been billed as Joy Lee, Joie Susannah Lee.
PICTURES: She's Gotta Have It (debut, 1986), School Daze, Do the Right Thing, Bail Jumper, Mo' Better Blues, A Kiss Before Dying, Fathers and Sons, Crooklyn (also story, co-s.p., assoc. prod.), Losing Isaiah.

LEE, MICHELE
Actress. b. Los Angeles, CA, June 24, 1942. On Broadway in How to Succeed in Business Without Really Trying, Seesaw.
PICTURES: How to Succeed in Business Without Really Trying, The Love Bug, The Comic.
TELEVISION: *Series:* Knots Landing (also dir. several episodes). *Movies:* Dark Victory, Bud and Lou, Letter to Three Wives, Single Women Married Men (also exec. prod.), The Fatal Image, My Son Johnny, Broadway Bound, When No One Would Listen (also exec. prod.), Big Dreams & Broken Hearts: The Dottie West Story (also exec. prod.).

LEE, PEGGY
Singer, Actress. r.n. Norma Egstrom. b. Jamestown, ND, May 26, 1920. Began career as night club vocalist in Fargo; became radio singer, WDAY, then with bandleader Sev Olsen in Minneapolis, Will Osborne, Benny Goodman. Collaborated with Dave Barbour on such songs as Manana, It's a Good Day, What More Can a Woman Do?, Fever, Johnny Guitar, So What's New. Also leading recording artist. PICTURES: Stage Door Canteen, Mr. Music, The Jazz Singer, Pete Kelly's Blues (Acad. Award nom.), Lady and the Tramp (voices, co- compser).
TELEVISION: *Series:* TV's Top Tunes, Songs for Sale. *Guest:* Jimmy Durante, Dean Martin, Ed Sullivan, many others.

LEE, SPIKE
Director, Producer, Writer, Actor. b. Atlanta, GA, Mar. 20, 1957. r.n. Shelton Jackson Lee. Son of jazz bass musician, composer Bill Lee. Sister is actress Joie Lee. e. Morehouse Coll B.A., Mass Comm., MFA NYU Film Sch. Completed 2 student features and hour-long thesis: Joe's Bed-Stuy Barbershop: We Cut Heads which won student Acad. Award from Acad. M.P. Arts & Sciences. Wrote, prod., dir., co-starred in indep. feature, She's Gotta Have It, budgeted at $175,000. Appeared in films Lonely in America, Hoop Dreams. Author of five books on his films. Director of numerous tv commercials for Nike, Levi's, ESPN and others. Director of over 35 music videos for Michael Jackson, Stevie Wonder, Miles Davis, and others.
PICTURES: Joe's Bed-Stuy Barbershop: We Cut Heads (co-prod., dir., s.p., editor). *Dir.-Prod.-Writer-Actor.* She's Gotta Have It (LA Film Critics Award for best new director, 1986), School Daze, Do the Right Thing (LA Film Critics Awards for best picture & director, 1989), Mo' Better Blues, Jungle Fever, Malcolm X, Crooklyn, Clockers, Girl 6, Get On the Bus. *Executive Producer.* Drop Squad also actor), New Jersey Drive, Tales From the Hood.
TELEVISION: *Guest:* The Debbie Allen's Special, Spike & Co. Do It A Capella.

LEEDS, MARTIN N.
Film-TV Executive. b. New York, NY, Apr. 6, 1916. e. NYU, B.S., 1936; J.D., 1938. Admitted NY Bar, 1938, CA Bar, 1948; dir. ind. rltns. Wabash Appliance Corp., 1943-44; ind. bus. rltns. cons. Davis & Gilbert, 1944-45; dir. ind. rltns. Flying Tiger Lines, 1947; dir. bus. affairs CBS TV div., 1947-53; exec. v.p. Desilu Productions, Inc., 1953-60; v.p. Motion Picture Center Studios, Inc.: memb. Industry comm. War Manpower Comm., 1943; chmn. to form Television Code of Ethics: U.S. Army 1941. Exec. v.p. in chg. of West Coast oper. & member of bd. of dir. Talent Associates—Paramount Ltd., Hollywood, 1962; TV production consultant; exec. v.p., Electronovision Prods. Inc., 1964; TV prod. & MP prod. consultant, 1965; pres., CEO, memb. of bd., Beverly Hills Studios, Inc., 1969; sr. v.p., American Film Theatre, 1973; 1975, motion picture and TV attorney & consultant.

LEEWOOD, JACK
Producer. b. New York, NY. May 20, 1913. e. Upsala Coll., Newark U., NYU. 1926-31 with Gottesman-Stern circuit as usher, asst. and relief mgr.; 1931-43 Stanley-Warner, mgr. of Ritz, Capitol and Hollywood theatres 1943-47. Joined Warner Bros. field forces in Denver-Salt Lake; Seattle-Portland, 1947-48. Dir. pub. & adv. Screen Guild Prod.; 1948-52, Lippert Productions; prod. exec., 1953-56, Allied Artists; 1957-62 prod. 20th Cent. Fox; 1965-68, prod., Universal; 1976-78. Affiliated Theatre S.F. & HTN.; 1978-83. Hamner Prod.
PICTURES: Holiday Rhythm, Gunfire, Hi-Jacked, Roaring City, Danger Zone, Lost Continent, F.B.I. Girl, Pier 23, Train to Tombstone, I Shot Billy the Kid, Bandit Queen, Motor Patrol, Savage Drums, Three Desperate Men, Border Rangers, Western Pacific Agent, Thundering Jets, Lone Texan, Little Savage, Alligator People, 13 Fighting Men, Young Jesse James, Swingin' Along, We'll Bury You, 20,000 Eyes, Thunder Island, The Plainsman.
TELEVISION: Longest 100 Miles, Escape to Mindanao, Dallas Cowboys Cheerleaders, When Hell Was in Session, Fugitive Family, Dallas Cowboys Cheerleaders II, Million Dollar Face, Portrait of a Showgirl, Margin For Murder, Anatomy of an Illness, Malibu.

LEFFERTS, GEORGE
Producer, Writer, Director. b. Paterson, NJ. e. Univ. of MI. Dir., numerous award-winning TV series, films. Exec. prod.-Time-Life films prod./writer, Movie of the Week (NBC) Biog: Who's Who in America, Who's Who in the World. Exec. prod., Bing Crosby Productions, prod., NBC 10 yrs, Independent. Exec. prod. David Wolper prods. 4 Emmy Awards, 2 Golden Globe Awards, 2 New England Journalism Awards, 1 Cine Golden Eagle Award.
THEATER: Hey Everybody.
PICTURES: The Stake, Mean Dog Blues, The Living End, The Boat, The Teenager.
TELEVISION: *Specials:* Teacher Teacher (Emmy Award, 1969), Benjamin Franklin (Emmy Award, 1975), Purex Specials for Women (Emmy Award, Producer's Guild Award; writer, prod. dir.), Our Group (writer), Jean Seberg Story. *Series:* Breaking Point (exec. prod.), The Bill Cosby Show, Studio One, Kraft Theatre, Chrysler Theatre, Sinatra Show, Lights Out, Alcoa, The Bold Ones, One Life to Live (WGA Award), Ryan's Hope (prod.). *Movies:* The Harness, She's Dressed to Kill, The Night They Took Miss Beautiful, Smithsonian Institution Specials (exec. prod.).

LEGRAND, MICHEL JEAN
Composer, Conductor. b. France, Feb. 24, 1932. Son of well-known arranger, composer and pianist, Raymond Legrand. At 11 Michel, a child prodigy, entered Paris Cons. and graduated nine years later with top honors in composition and as solo pianist. In late fifties turned to composing for films and has composed, orchestrated and conducted scores of more than 140 films.
PICTURES: Lola, Eva, Vivre Sa Vie, La Baie des Anges, The Umbrellas of Cherbourg, Banda a Part, Un Femme Mariee, Une Femme est une Femme, The Young Girls of Rochefort, Ice Station Zebra, The Thomas Crown Affair (Academy Award for best song: The Windmills of Your Mind, 1968), Pieces of Dreams, The Happy Ending, Picasso Summer, Wuthering Heights, The Go-Between, Summer of '42 (Academy Award, 1971), Lady Sings the Blues, The Nelson Affair, Breezy, The Three Musketeers, Sheila Levine, Gable and Lombard, Ode to Billy Joe, The Savage, The Other Side of Midnight, The Fabulous Adventures of the Legendary Baron Munchausen, The Roads of the South, The Hunter, The Mountain Men, Atlantic City, Falling in Love Again, Best Friends, A Love in Germany, Never Say Never Again, Yentl (Academy Award, 1983), Hell Train, Micki and Maude, Secret Places, Spirale, Parking, Switching Channels, Three Seats for the 26th Cinq jours en juin (dir. debut, s.p., music), Dingo, The Pickle, Ready to Wear (Pret-a-Porter).
TELEVISION: *Movies:* Brian's Song, The Jesse Owens Story, A Woman Called Golda, As Summers Die, Crossings, Sins, Promises to Keep, Not a Penny More Not a Penny Less, The Burning Shore.

LE GROS, JAMES
Actor. b. Minneapolis, MN, Apr. 27, 1962.
THEATER: The Cherry Orchard, Galileo, Ceremony of Innocence, Table Settings, Curse of the Starving Class, American Buffalo, Bits and Bytes, Becoming Memories, Slab Boys.
PICTURES: Solarbabies, Near Dark, Fatal Beauty, Phantasm II, Drugstore Cowboy, Point Break, Blood & Concrete, The Rapture, Where the Day Takes You, Singles, My New Gun, Bad Girls, Floundering, Mrs. Parker and the Vicious Circle, Destiny Turns on the Radio, Panther, Safe, Living in Oblivion, Infinity, The Low Life, Boys, The Destiny of Marty Fine.
TELEVISION: *Movie:* Gun Crazy.

LEGUIZAMO, JOHN
Actor. b. Bogota, Colombia, July 22, 1964. Moved to Queens, NY at age 5. e. NYU. Appeared in award-winning student film Five Out of Six, while in school. Studied acting with Lee Strasberg and Wynn Handman. Made professional debut on Miami Vice on tv.
THEATER: A Midsummer Night's Dream, La Puta Vida, Parting Gestures, Mambo Mouth (also writer; Obie & Outer Critics Circle Awards), Spic-O-Rama (also writer; Drama Desk & Theatre World Awards).
PICTURES: Casualties of War, Revenge, Die Hard 2, Gentile Alouette, Street Hunter, Out for Justice, Hangin' With the Homeboys, Regarding Henry, Whispers in the Dark, Super Mario Bros., Night Owl, Carlito's Way, A Pyromaniac's Love Story, To Wong Foo—Thanks for Everything—Julie Newmar, Executive Decision, Spawn, Romeo and Juliet, The Pest.
TELEVISION: *Series:* House of Buggin'. *Specials:* Talent Pool Comedy Special (ACE Award), Mambo Mouth (also writer), Spic-O-Rama (also writer; 3 Cable ACE Awards).

LEHMAN, ERNEST
Writer, Producer, Director. b. New York, NY, 1923. e. City Coll. of New York. Began career as free-lance journalist and magazine fiction writer. First pub. books, The Comedian, The Sweet Smell of Success. First hardcover novel, The French Atlantic Affair followed by Farewell Performance, and first non-fiction book, Screening Sickness. Pres., WGAW, 1983-85.1987, 1988, 1990: Acad. Awards show (co-writer). The Ernest Lehman Collection is archived at the Humanities Research Center, Univ. of TX at Austin, and in part at USC Film Library and Margaret Herrick Library. Co-prod. of musical stage adaptation of Sweet Smell of Success. Laurel Award for Screen Achievement, WGAW, 1973. Five Best Screenplay Awards, WGAW.
PICTURES: *Writer:* Executive Suite, Sabrina (co-s.p.; Acad. Award nom.), The King and I, Somebody Up There Likes Me, Sweet Smell of Success (co-s.p.; based on his own novelette), North By Northwest (Acad. Award nom.), From the Terrace, West Side Story (Acad. Award nom.), The Prize, The Sound of Music, Who's Afraid of Virginia Woolf? (also prod.; 2 Acad. Award noms. for picture & s.p.), Hello Dolly! (also prod.; Acad. Award nom. for picture), Portnoy's Complaint (also dir., prod.), Family Plot, Black Sunday (co-s.p.).

LEHMANN, MICHAEL
Director. b. San Francisco. e. UCal, Berkeley, Columbia U. Started in industry supervising video systems used in the Francis Ford Coppola films One From the Heart, Rumble Fish, The Outsiders. Dir. short films for Saturday Night Live incl. Ed's Secret Life. Served as exec. prod. on Ed Wood.
PICTURES: Heathers (debut, 1989), Meet the Applegates, Hudson Hawk, Airheads, The Truth About Cats and Dogs.

LEHRER, JIM
News Anchor. b. Wichita, KS, 1934. e. Victoria Col., Univ. of MO. Served in US Marine Corps. 1959-66, reporter for Dallas Morning News, Dallas Times-Herald; 1968 became Times-Herald's city editor before moving into tv as exec. dir. of public affairs, host and editor of news program on KERA-TV in Dallas. To Washington where he became public affairs coord. for PBS, then corresp. for the Natl. Public Affairs Center for Television. 1973 first teamed with Robert MacNeil to cover Senate Watergate hearings. 1975, served as D.C. corresp. for the Robert MacNeil/Lehrer Report on PBS (showed was re-named The MacNeil/Lehrer Report in 1976). 1983, started The MacNeil/Lehrer NewsHour. 1995, became exec. editor and anchor of new version of series The NewsHour With Jim Lehrer.

LEIBMAN, RON
Actor. b. New York, NY, Oct. 11, 1937. m. actress Jessica Walter. e. Ohio Wesleyan U. Joined Actor's Studio in N.Y.; first professional appearance in summer theatre production of A View from the Bridge.
THEATER: The Premise, Dear Me, The Sky Is Falling, We Bombed in New Haven (Theatre World Award), Cop Out, Room Service, I Oughta Be in Pictures, The Deputy, Bicycle Ride to Nevada, Doubles, Rumors, Angels in America: Millenium Approaches (Tony & Drama Desk Awards).
PICTURES: Where's Poppa (debut, 1970), The Hot Rock, Slaughterhouse Five, Your Three Minutes Are Up, Super Cops, Won Ton Ton the Dog Who Saved Hollywood, Norma Rae, Up the Academy, Zorro the Gay Blade, Romantic Comedy, Phar Lap, Rhinestone, Door to Door, Seven Hours to Judgement, Night Falls on Manhattan.
TELEVISION: Series: Kaz (Emmy Award, 1979), Pacific Station, Central Park West. Movies: The Art of Crime, A Question of Guilt, Rivkin: Bounty Hunter, Many Happy Returns, Christmas Eve, Terrorist on Trial: The United States vs. Salim Ajami.

LEIDER, GERALD J.
Producer, Executive. b. Camden, NJ, May 28, 1931. e. Syracuse U., 1953; Bristol U., Eng., 1954, Fulbright Fellowship in drama. m. Susan Trustman. 1955 joined MCA, Inc., N.Y.; 1956-59 theatre producer in NY, London: Shinbone Alley, Garden District, and Sir John Gielgud's Ages of Man. 1960-61; director of special programs, CBS/TV; 1961-62, dir. of program sales, CBS-TV; 1962-69, v.p., tv optns., Ashley Famous Agency, Inc.; 1969-74, pres. Warner Bros. TV, Burbank; 1975-76, exec. v.p. foreign prod. Warner Bros. Pictures, Rome; 1977-82, indept. prod. under Jerry Leider Prods.; 1982-87, pres., ITC Prods., Inc; named pres. and CEO, ITC Entertainment Group, 1987-present.
PICTURES: Wild Horse Hank, The Jazz Singer, Trenchcoat.
TELEVISION: Movies: And I Alone Survived, Willa, The Hostage Tower, The Scarlet and the Black, Secrets of a Married Man, The Haunting Passion, Letting Go, A Time to Live, The Girl Who Spelled Freedom, Unnatural Causes, Poor Little Rich Girl.

LEIGH, JANET
Actress. r.n. Jeanette Helen Morrison. b. Merced, CA, July 6, 1927. Mother of actresses Jamie Lee Curtis and Kelly Curtis. e. Coll. of Pacific, music. Author: There Really Was a Hollywood (autobiography, 1984), Behind the Scenes of Psycho (1995), House of Destiny (novel; 1995).
THEATER: includes: Murder Among Friends, Love Letters (with Van Johnson).
PICTURES: The Romance of Rosy Ridge (debut, 1947), If Winter Comes, Hills of Home, Words and Music, Act of Violence, Little Women, That Forsyte Woman, Red Danube, Doctor and the Girl, Holiday Affair, Two Tickets to Broadway, Strictly Dishonorable, Angels in the Outfield, It's a Big Country, Just This Once, Scaramouche, Fearless Fagan, Naked Spur, Confidentially Connie, Houdini, Walking My Baby Back Home, Prince Valiant, Living It Up, Black Shield of Falworth, Rogue Cop, My Sister Eileen, Pete Kelly's Blues, Safari, Jet Pilot, Touch of Evil, The Vikings, The Perfect Furlough, Who Was That Lady?, Psycho (Acad. Award nom.), Pepe, The Manchurian Candidate, Bye Bye Birdie, Wives and Lovers, Three on a Couch, Harper, An American Dream, Kid Rodelo, Grand Slam, Hello Down There, One Is a Lonely Number, Night of the Lepus, Boardwalk, The Fog, Other Realms.
TELEVISION: Movies: Honeymoon With a Stranger, House on Green Apple Road, The Monk, Deadly Dream, Mirror Mirror, Telethon, Murder at the World Series. Guest: Matt Houston, Starman, Murder She Wrote. Addtl.: Carriage from Britain, Murder in the First, Dear Deductible, Catch Me If You Can, One for My Baby, My Wives, Jane, The Chairman, Death's Head, This Is Maggie Mulligan, Tales of the Unexpected, On the Road.

LEIGH, JENNIFER JASON
Actress. b. Los Angeles, CA, Feb. 5, 1962. r.n. Jennifer Leigh Morrow. Daughter of late actor Vic Morrow and TV writer

Barbara Turner. At age 14 debuted in Disney tv movie The Young Runaway. Won L.A. Valley Coll. best actress award for stage prod. The Shadow Box (1979).
PICTURES: Eyes of a Stranger (debut, 1981), Wrong Is Right, Fast Times at Ridgemont High, Easy Money, Grandview U.S.A., The Hitcher, Flesh + Blood, The Men's Club, Undercover, Sister Sister, Heart of Midnight, The Big Picture, Miami Blues (NY Film Critics Award, 1990), Last Exit to Brooklyn (NY Film Critics Award, 1990), Backdraft, Crooked Hearts, Rush, Single White Female, Short Cuts, The Hudsucker Proxy, Mrs. Parker and the Vicious Circle (Natl. Society of Film Critics & Chicago Film Critics Awards, 1994), Dolores Claiborne, Georgia (also co-prod.), Kansas City.
TELEVISION: Movies: The Young Runaway, Angel City, The Killing of Randy Webster, The Best Little Girl in the World, The First Time, Girls of the White Orchid, Buried Alive.

LEIGH, MIKE
Director, Writer. b. Salford, England, Feb. 20, 1943. e. RADA, Camberwell Art Sch., Central Sch. of Arts & Crafts, London Film Sch. m. actress Alison Steadman. Directed 1977 TV drama Abigail's Party. 1987 short: The Short and Curlies. Recipient of 1995 BAFTA Award for Outstanding British Contribution to Cinema.
PICTURES: Bleak Moments, Hard Labour, Nuts in May, The Kiss of Death, Who's Who, Grown-Ups, Home Sweet Home, Meantime, Four Days in July, High Hopes, Life Is Sweet, Naked, Secrets & Lies (Palme d'Or, Cannes 1996).

LEIGH, SUZANNA
Actress. b. Reading, England, 1945. Studied at the Arts Educational Sch. and Webber Douglas Sch. 1965-66, under contract to Hal Wallis and Paramount.
PICTURES: Oscar Wilde, Bomb in High Street, Boeing Boeing, Paradise Hawaiian Style, The Deadly Bees, Deadlier Than the Male, The Lost Continent, Subterfuge, Lust for a Vampire (To Love a Vampire), Beware My Brethren, Son of Dracula.
TELEVISION: Series: Three Stars (France), One on an Island (West Indies). Special: The Plastic People. Guest: The Persuaders.

LEITCH, DONOVAN
Actor. Son of folksinger Donovan. Brother of actress Ione Skye. Acted in jr. high sch. musical then had bit part in PBS show K.I.D.S.
PICTURES: And God Created Women (1988), The Blob, The In Crowd, Cutting Class, Glory, Gas Food Lodging, Dark Horse, I Shot Andy Warhol.
TELEVISION: Movie: For the Very First Time. Guest: Life Goes On.

LELAND, DAVID
Director, Writer, Actor. b. Cambridge, Eng., April 20, 1947. Began as actor at Nottingham Playhouse. Then joined newly formed company at Royal Court Theatre, London. Also appeared in films Time Bandits, The Missionary, and his own Personal Services (Peter Sellers Award for Comedy) and on TV in The Jewel in the Crown. As stage director specialized in complete seasons of new works at the Crucible in Sheffield and London venues. Wrote play Psy-Warriors.
PICTURES: Mona Lisa (co-s.p.), Personal Services (s.p.), Wish You Were Here (dir., s.p.; BAFTA Award for s.p.), Checking Out (dir.), The Big Man (dir.; a.k.a. Crossing the Line).
TELEVISION: Wrote Birth of a Nation, Flying Into the Wind, Rhino, Made in Britain, Beloved Enemy, Ligmalion, Psy-Warriors.

LELOUCH, CLAUDE
Director, Writer, Producer, Cinematographer, Editor. b. Paris, France, Oct. 30, 1937. Began m.p. career with short subjects, 1956; French military service, motion picture department, 1957-60; formed Films 13, 1960; publicity Films and Scopitones, 1961-62.
PICTURES: Le Propre de l'Homme (The Right of Man; debut, 1960; also s.p., prod., actor), L'amour avec des Si (Love With Ifs; aalso prod., s.p.), La Femme Spectacle (Night Women; also prod., photog.), Une Fille et des Fusils (To Be a Crook; also co-s.p., prod., edit.), Les Grands Moments (also co-prod.), A Man and A Woman (also co-s.p., story, prod., photog., edit.; Academy Awards for Best Foreign Language Film & Original Screenplay, 1966; also Acad. Award nom. for dir.), Live for Life (also co-s.p., co-photog. , edit.), Farm From Vietnam (segment), 13 Jours en France (Grenoble; co-dir., co-s.p.), Life Love Death (also co-s.p.), Love Is a Funny Thing (also photog., co-s.p.), The Crook (also co- photog., co-s.p.), Smic Smac Smoc (also prod., s.p., photog., actor), Money Money Money (also s.p., prod., photog.), La Bonne Annee (Happy New Year; also prod., s.p., co-photog.), Visions of Eight (segment: The Losers), And Now My Love (also s.p., prod.), Marriage (also co-s.p.), Cat and Mouse (also s.p.), The Good and Bad (also s.p., photog.), Second Chance (also s.p.,

prod.), Another Man Another Chance (also s.p.), Robert and Robert (also s.p.), Adventure for Two, Bolero (also s.p., prod.), Edith and Marcel (also prod., s.p.), Vive la Vie (also prod., s.p., photog.), Partier Revenir (also prod., co-s.p.), A Man and a Woman: 20 Years Later (also prod., co-s.p.), Bandits (also prod., s.p.), Itinerary of a Spoiled Child (also co-prod., s.p.), There Were Days and Moons (also prod., co-s.p.), Les Miserables.
TELEVISION: Moliere (prod. only).

LE MAT, PAUL
Actor. b. Rahway, NJ, Sept. 22, 1945. Studied with Milton Katselas, Herbert Berghof Studio, A.C.T., San Francisco, Mitchel Ryan-Actor's Studio.
PICTURES: American Graffiti (debut, 1973), Aloha Bobby and Rose, Citizens Band (Handle With Care), More American Graffiti, Melvin and Howard, Death Valley, Jimmy the Kid, Strange Invaders, P.K. and the Kid, Rock & Rule (voice), The Hanoi Hilton, Private Investigations, Puppet Master, Easy Wheels, Deuce Coupe, Grave Secrets, Veiled Threats, Wishman, Caroline at Midnight.
TELEVISION: Movies: Firehouse, The Gift of Life, The Night They Saved Christmas, The Burning Bed, Long Time Gone, Secret Witness, On Wings of Eagles, Into the Homeland, In the Line of Duty: Siege at Marion, Woman With a Past, Blind Witness.

LEMBERGER, KENNETH
Executive. Exec. v.p., Sony Pictures Entertainment, Inc.

LEMMON, JACK
Actor. b. Boston, MA. Feb. 8, 1925. r.n. John Uhler Lemmon III. e. Harvard U. m. actress Felicia Farr. Father of actor Chris Lemmon. Stage debut as a child; radio actor on soap operas; stock companies; U.S. Navy, W.W.II; many TV shows. Narrated film Stowaway in the Sky. Appeared in AFI short Wednesday. Albums: A Twist of Lemmon, Jack Lemmon Plays and Sings Music From Some Like It Hot. Recipient: American Film Institute Life Achievement Award (1988), Lincoln Center Tribute (1993).
THEATER: B'way: Room Service (debut, 1953), Face of a Hero, Tribute (also L.A., Denver), Long Day's Journey into Night (also London, Israel, D.C.). Off-B'way: Power of Darkness. L.A.: Idiot's Delight, Juno and the Paycock, A Sense of Humor (also Denver, S.F.). London: Veterans Day.
PICTURES: It Should Happen to You (debut, 1953), Phffft!, Three for the Show, Mister Roberts (Academy Award, best supporting actor, 1955), My Sister Eileen, You Can't Run Away from It, Fire Down Below, Operation Mad Ball, Cowboy, Bell Book and Candle, Some Like It Hot (Acad. Award nom.), It Happened to Jane, The Apartment (Acad. Award nom.), Pepe, The Wackiest Ship in the Army, The Notorious Landlady, Days of Wine and Roses (Acad. Award nom.), Irma La Douce, Under the Yum Yum Tree, Good Neighbor Sam, How to Murder Your Wife, The Great Race, The Fortune Cookie, Luv, The Odd Couple, The April Fools, The Out-of-Towners, Kotch (dir. debut; also cameo), The War Between Men and Women, Avanti!, Save the Tiger (Academy Award, 1973), The Front Page, The Prisoner of Second Avenue, Alex and the Gypsy, Airport '77, The China Syndrome (Cannes Film Fest. Award; Acad. Award nom., 1979), Tribute (Acad. Award nom.), Buddy Buddy, Missing (Cannes Film Fest. Award; Acad. Award nom., 1982), Mass Appeal, Macaroni, That's Life, Dad, JFK, The Player, Glengarry Glen Ross, Short Cuts, Grumpy Old Men, Getting Away With Murder, The Grass Harp, Grumpier Old Men, A Weekend in the Country, Hamlet, My Fellow Americans.
TELEVISION: Series: That Wonderful Guy, Toni Twin Time (host), Ad Libbers, Heaven For Betsy, Alcoa Theatre. Guest on numerous dramatic shows: Studio One, Playhouse 90 (Face of a Hero), Kraft Theatre, The Web, Suspense, etc. Specials: The Day Lincoln Was Shot, 'S Wonderful 'S Marvelous 'S Gershwin, Get Happy, The Entertainer, Long Day's Journey into Night, The Wild West (narrator), A Life in the Theatre. Movies: The Murder of Mary Phagan, For Richer For Poorer.
RADIO: Serials: The Brighter Day, Road of Life.

LENO, JAY
Comedian, Actor. r.n. James Leno. b. New Rochelle, NY, April 28, 1950. e. Emerson College, B.A. speech therapy, 1973. Raised in Andover, MA. Worked as Rolls Royce auto mechanic and deliveryman while seeking work as stand-up comedian. Performed in comedy clubs throughout the U.S. and as opening act for Perry Como, Johnny Mathis, John Denver and Tom Jones. Guest on numerous talk shows and specials.
PICTURES: Fun With Dick and Jane, The Silver Bears, American Hot Wax, Americathon, Collision Course, What's Up Hideous Sun Demon? (voice), Dave, We're Back! (voice), Wayne's World 2, Major League 2, The Flintstones.
TELEVISION: Series: The Marilyn McCoo & Billy Davis Jr. Show, The Tonight Show (guest host: 1987-92; host: 1992-; Emmy Award, 1995). Specials: Jay Leno and the American Dream (also prod.), The Jay Leno Show, Our Planet Tonight, Jay Leno's Family Comedy Hour.

LENZ, KAY
Actress. b. Los Angeles, CA, March 4, 1953.
PICTURES: Breezy (debut, 1973), White Line Fever, The Great Scout and Cathouse Thursday, Moving Violation, Mean Dog Blues, The Passage, Fast-Walking, House, Stripped to Kill, Death Wish IV: The Crackdown, Headhunter, Physical Evidence, Fear, Streets, Falling From Grace.
TELEVISION: Series: Reasonable Doubts. Movies: The Weekend Nun, Lisa, Bright and Dark, A Summer Without Boys, Unwed Father, The Underground Man, The FBI Story: The FBI Versus Alvin Karpis, Journey from Darkness, Rich Man, Poor Man, The Initiation of Sarah, The Seeding of Sarah Burns, Sanctuary of Fear, The Hustler of Muscle Beach, Murder by Night, Heart in Hiding, How the West Will: Traveling Man, Escape, Hitler's Daughter, Against Their Will: Women in Prison, Trapped in Space, Shame II: The Secret. Guest: Midnight Caller (Emmy Award, 1989), Moonlighting, Hill St. Blues, Hotel, Cannon, McGyver, Cagney & Lacey, McCloud, Riptide, many others. Mini-Series: Rich Man Poor Man—Book II.

LEON, SOL
Executive. b. New York, NY, July 2, 1913. e. NYU, City Coll. of New York, Brooklyn Law Sch., B.B.L., master of law. Exec. v.p., William Morris Agency, L.A.

LEONARD, ROBERT SEAN
Actor. b. Westwood, NJ, Feb. 28, 1969. Raised in Ridgewood, NJ. Started acting at age 12 in local summer stock. Joined NY Shakespeare Festival at 15.
THEATER: Off-B'way: Coming of Age in Soho, Sally's Gone—She Left Her Name, The Beach House, When She Danced, Romeo and Juliet, Good Evening, The Great Unwashed. B'way: Brighton Beach Memoirs, Breaking the Code, The Speed of Darkness, Candida (Tony nom.), Philadelphia Here I Come!, Arcadia. Regional: Biloxi Blues (tour), Rocky and Diego, Long Day's Journey Into Night, King Lear, The Double Inconstancy.
PICTURES: The Manhattan Project (debut, 1986), My Best Friend Is a Vampire, Dead Poets Society, Mr. & Mrs. Bridge, Swing Kids, Married to It, Much Ado About Nothing, The Age of Innocence, Safe Passage, Killer: A Journal of Murder, I Love You—I Love You Not.
TELEVISION: Movies: My Two Loves, Bluffing It. Pilot: The Robert Klein Show.

LEONARD, SHELDON
Actor, Producer. r.n. Sheldon Leonard Bershad. b. New York, NY, Feb. 22, 1907. e. Syracuse U., B.A. Theatre mgr., N.Y. stage, 10 yrs.; sec., Directors Guild of America. 3 Emmy awards, Sylvania award, 4 TV Director of the Year nominations by D.G.A, Cinematographers Governors Award, D.G.A. Aldrich Award. Inducted into TV Hall of Fame, 1992.
PICTURES: Another Thin Man, Tall, Dark and Handsome, Private Nurse, Buy Me That Town, Week-End in Havana, Tortilla Flat, Rise and Shine, Street of Chance, Lucky Jordan, Hit the Ice, Uncertain Glory, To Have and Have Not, The Falcon in Hollywood, Why Girls Leave Home, Captain Kidd, Froniter Gal, Somewhere in the Night, Her Kind of Man, It's a Wonderful Life, The Gangster, If You Knew Susie, Sinbad the Sailor, My Dream Is Yours, Take One False Step, Iroquois Trail, Behave Yourself, Here Come the Nelsons, Young Man with Ideas, Stop You're Killing Me, Diamond Queen, Money from Home, Guys and Dolls, Pocketful of Miracles, The Brinks Job.
TELEVISION: Series (actor): The Duke, Make Room for Daddy/The Danny Thomas Show (also dir., prod.; Emmy Awards for dir.: 1956, 1961), Big Eddie. Series (exec. prod.): The Andy Griffith Show, The Dick Van Dyke Show, Gomer Pyler USMC, I Spy, My World and Welcome to It (Emmy Award, 1970). Movies: Top Secret (exec. prod., actor), The Islander (actor), I Spy Returns (co-exec. prod.). Dir.: Damon Runyon, G.E. Theatre, Electric Theatre, Jewelers' Showcase, Jimmy Durante Show.

LERNER, JOSEPH
Producer, Director, Writer. m. Geraldine Lerner. Actor on Broadway; radio actor & dir.; with RKO, Columbia and Republic as dir., dial. dir., writer, 2nd unit dir., test dir.; dir.-writer & head of special productions U.S. Army Signal Corps Photographic Center; writer of commercial and educational films 1946-47; v.p. in chg. of prod. Visual Arts Productions 1947; v.p. in chg. prod. Laurel Films 1949; Girl on the Run, comm. ind. films; dir., prod., writer, many TV commercials, documentaries 1967-73; pres., The Place for Film Making, Inc.; pres., Astracor Associates Ltd.; writer & line prod. for Gold Shield Prods; also lecturer and instructor at NYU, Wm. Patterson Coll., Broward Community Coll. (FL), College at Boca Raton. Member: Eastern Council of the Directors Guild of America.
TELEVISION: Dir./Prod.: Gangbusters, Grand Tour, Three Musketeers, United Nations Case Book. Dir./Writer: C-Man, Guilty Bystander, Mr. Universe, Daek of the Day, The Fight Never Ends, etc. Prod./Writer: Olympic Cavalcade, King of The Olympics, and many other documentaries.

LERNER, MICHAEL
Actor. b. Brooklyn, NY, June 22, 1941. e. Brooklyn Col., Univ. of CA, Berkeley. Prior to acting was professor of dramatic literature at San Francisco St. Col., 1968-69. Studied acting in London on Fullbright Scholarship. Was member of San Francisco's American Conservatory Theatre. On NY stage in Twelfth Night; L.A. stage in The Women of Trachis, Hurlyburly.
PICTURES: Alex in Wonderland (debut, 1970), The Candidate, Busting, Newman's Law, Hangup (Superdude), St. Ives, The Other Side of Midnight, Outlaw Blues, Goldengirl, Borderline, Coast to Coast, The Baltimore Bullet, The Postman Always Rings Twice, National Lampoon's Class Reunion, Threshold, Strange Invaders, Movers and Shakers, Anguish, Vibes, Eight Men Out, Harlem Nights, Any Man's Death, The Closer, Barton Fink (Acad. Award nom.), Newsies, Amos & Andrew, Blank Check, No Escape, Radioland Murders, The Road to Wellville, Girl in the Cadillac, A Pyromaniac's Love Story.
TELEVISION: Series: Courthouse. Movies: Thief, Marriage Year One, What's a Nice Girl Like You...?, Magic Carpet, Firehouse (pilot), Reflections of Murder, The Rockford Files (pilot), The Death of Sammy (The Dream Makers), A Cry for Help, Starsky and Hutch (pilot), Sarah T: Portrait of a Teenage Alcoholic, Dark Victory, F. Scott Fitzgerald in Hollywood (The Screen Test), Scott Free, Killer on Board, A Love Affair: The Eleanor and Lou Gehrig Story, Vega$ (pilot), Ruby & Oswald, Hart to Hart (pilot), Moviola: This Year's Blonde, Gridlock (The Great American Traffic Jam), Blood Feud, Rita Hayworth: Love Goddess, The Execution, This Child is Mine, Betrayal of Trust (That Secret Sunday), Hands of a Stranger, King of Love, Framed, Omen IV: The Awakening, The Comrades of Summer. Special: The Missiles of October. Guest: Amazing Stories, Macgyver. Pilots: Grandpa Max, The Boys, I Gave at the Office.

LESLIE, ALEEN
Writer. b. Pittsburgh, PA, Feb. 5, 1908. e. Ohio State U. Contributor to magazines; columnist Pittsburgh Press; orig. & wrote radio series A Date with Judy 1941-50. B'way play Slightly Married, 1943; wrote, prod. Date with Judy, TV series; author, The Scent of the Roses, The Windfall.
PICTURES: Doctor Takes a Wife, Affectionately Yours, Henry Aldrich Plays Cupid, Stork Pays Off, Henry Aldrich Gets Glamour, It Comes Up Love, Rosie the Riveter, A Date With Judy, Father Was a Fullback, Father Is a Bachelor.

LESLIE, JOAN
Actress. r.n. Joan Brodell. b. Detroit, MI, January 26, 1925. e. St. Benedicts, Detroit; Our Lady of Lourdes, Toronto; St. Mary's Montreal; Immaculate Heart. H.S., L.A. Child performer on stage as part of The Three Brodels. Became model before going to Hollywood in 1936. Voted Star of Tomorrow, 1946. Now on bd. of dir., St. Anne's Maternity Home, Damon Runyon Foundation.
PICTURES: (as Joan Brodel): Camille (debut, 1937), Men with Wings, Nancy Drew—Reporter, Love Affair, Winter Carnival, Two Thoroughbreds, High School, Young as You Feel, Star Dust, Susan and God, Military Academy, Foreign Correspondent, Laddie. (as Joan Leslie): Thieves Fall Out, The Wagons Roll at Night, High Sierra, The Great Mr. Nobody, Sergeant York, The Hard Way, The Male Animal, Yankee Doodle Dandy, The Sky's the Limit, This Is the Army, Thank Your Lucky Stars, Hollywood Canteen, Rhapsody in Blue, Where Do We Go From Here?, Too Young to Know, Janie Gets Married, Cinderella Jones, Two Guys From Milwaukee, Repeat Performance, Northwest Stampede, Born To Be Bad, The Skipper Surprised His Wife, Man in the Saddle, Hellgate, Toughest Man in Arizona, The Woman They Almost Lynched, Flight Nurse, Hell's Outpost, Jubilee Trail, The Revolt of Mamie Stover.
TELEVISION: Guest: Ford Theatre, G.E. Theatre, Queen for a Day, Simon and Simon, Murder, She Wrote. Movies: Charley Hannah, The Keegans, Turn Back the Clock. Various commercials.

LESTER, MARK
Actor. b. Oxford, England, July 11, 1958. Ent. m.p. ind. 1963.
THEATER: The Murder Game, The Prince and the Pauper 1976.
PICTURES: Allez France (The Counterfeit Constable; debut, 1963), Spaceflight IC-1, Fahrenheit 451, Arrividerci Baby!, Our Mother's House, Oliver!, Run Wild Run Free, Sudden Terror (Eye Witness), Melody, Black Beauty, Who Slew Auntie Roo?, Redneck, Scalawag, Jungle Boy, Crossed Swords (The Prince and the Pauper).
TELEVISION: The Boy Who Stole the Elephants, Graduation Trip, Danza Alla Porto Gli Olmi (Italian Entry Berlin '75), Seen Dimly Before Dawn.

LESTER, MARK LESLIE
Director. b. Cleveland, OH, Nov. 26, 1949. e. U. of California, Northridge, B.A.
PICTURES: Steel Arena (debut, 1973; also co-prod., s.p.), Truck Stop Women (also prod., co-s.p.), Bobbie Jo and the

Outlaw (also prod.), Stunts, Roller Boogie, The Funhouse (co-exec. prod. only), The Class of 1984 (also co-exec. prod., co-s.p.), Firestarter, Commando, Armed and Dangerous, Class of 1999 (also prod., story), Showdown in Little Tokyo, Night of the Running Man.
TELEVISION: Gold of the Amazon Women, Extreme Justice.

LESTER, RICHARD
Director. b. Philadelphia, PA, Jan. 19, 1932. e. Univ. of PA. Started as stagehand at tv studio before becoming dir. and music. dir. CBS-TV in Philadelphia, then CBC-TV, Toronto. To England in 1956 where he resumed work as tv dir. TV dir. The Goon Shows. Composed (with Reg. Owen) Sea War Series. Short Film: composer and dir., The Running Jumping and Standing Still Film. Directed sequences for Mondo Teeno/Teenage Rebellion, Superman.
PICTURES: It's Trad Dad (debut, 1962; aka Ring-a-Ding Rhythm; also prod.), The Mouse on the Moon, A Hard Day's Night, The Knack... and How to Get It, Help!, A Funny Thing Happened on the Way to the Forum, How I Won the War (also prod.), Petulia, The Bed-Sitting Room (also co-prod.), The Three Musketeers, Juggernaut, The Four Musketeers, Royal Flash, Robin & Marian (also co-prod.), The Ritz, Butch and Sundance: The Early Days, Cuba, Superman II, Superman III, Finders Keepers (also exec. prod.), The Return of the Musketeers (tv in U.S.), Get Back.

LESTZ, EARL
Executive. Chmn. of the bd., Permanent Charities Committee of the Entertainment Industries.

LETTERMAN, DAVID
Performer, Writer. b. Indianapolis, IN, Apr. 12, 1947. e. Ball State U. Began career as weatherman and talk show host on Indianapolis TV before going to Hollywood. Cameo appearance in film Cabin Boy.
TELEVISION: Series Writer: Good Times, Paul Lynde Comedy Hour. Writer (specials): John Denver Special, Bob Hope Special. Series Performer: The Starland Vocal Band (also writer), Mary (1978), Tonight Show (guest host 1978-82), The David Letterman Show (Daytime Emmy Award for writing, 1981), Late Night with David Letterman (1982-93, on NBC; 4 Emmy Awards for Writing), Late Show With David Letterman (1993-, on CBS). Guest performer: An NBC Family Christmas, The Larry Sanders Show.

LEVIN, GERALD M.
Executive. b. Philadelphia, PA, May 6, 1939. e. Haverford Col., Univ. of PA Law Sch. Attorney, 1963-67. Gen. mgr. & COO of Development Sources Corp., 1969. IBEC rep. in Tehran, Iran, 1971. Joined HBO in 1972 as v.p. of programming, then pres. & CEO, 1973-76; promoted to chmn, 1976. Became v.p. Time Inc., 1975; group v.p., video, 1979; exec. v.p. in 1984; on bd. of dirs., 1983-87. Named vice-chmn, Time Warner, 1989; COO, 1991; pres. & co-CEO of Time Warner, Inc., 1992; chmn. & CEO of Time Warner Inc., 1993.

LEVIN, ROBERT B.
Executive. b. Chicago, IL. e. U. of Illinois. Operated own adv. firm for five years. 1982, named sr. v.p., Needham Harper World Wide Advertising Agency, Chicago. 1985, joined Walt Disney Pictures as sr. v.p., mktg. 1988: Named pres. Buena Vista Pictures marketing.

LEVINE, ALAN J.
Attorney, Executive. b. Los Angeles, CA, Mar. 8, 1947. e. UCLA 1968, J.D. 1971. Partner at Pacht, Ross, Warne, Bernhard & Sears, 1971-78; Shiff, Hirsch & Schreiber, 1978-80; Armstrong, Hirsch & Levine, 1980-89. Named COO of Sony Pictures Entertainment, 1989. Promoted to pres. and CEO. Member CA Bar, L.A. County Bar, A.M.P.A.S., Academy TV Arts & Sciences.

LEVINSON, ART
Producer. Began film career as office boy at Universal Studios where he entered training program and rapidly rose from asst. director to production manager on Harry and Tonto. Assoc. prod.: Breaking Away, Mr. Mom, Teachers.
PICTURES: Assoc. Prod.: Breaking Away, Mr. Mom, Teachers, Stop or My Mom Will Shoot!. Prod.: My Favorite Year, Racing with the Moon, The Money Pit, Mannequin, Little Nikita. Exec. Prod.: My Stepmother Is an Alien, Great Balls of Fire.
TELEVISION: Billionaire Boys Club (assoc. prod.), Curacao (prod.).

LEVINSON, BARRY
Director, Producer, Writer, Actor. b. Baltimore, MD, Apr. 6, 1942. e. American Univ. Wrote and acted in L.A. comedy show leading to work on network tv incl. writing and performing on The Carol Burnett Show. Co-wrote film scripts with Mel Brooks, and then-wife Valerie Curtin. Apppeared as actor in History of the World Part 1, Quiz Show.

PICTURES: *Writer*: Silent Movie (also actor), High Anxiety (also actor), ... And Justice for All (Acad. Award nom.), Inside Moves, Best Friends, Unfaithfully Yours. *Director*: Diner (also s.p.; Acad. Award nom. for s.p.), The Natural, Young Sherlock Holmes, Tin Men (also s.p.), Good Morning Vietnam, Rain Man (also actor; Academy Award for Best Director, 1988), Avalon (also s.p.; WGA Award, Acad. Award nom. for s.p.), Bugsy (Acad. Award nom.), Toys (also co-s.p.), Jimmy Hollywood (also s.p., co-prod.), Disclosure (also co-prod.), Sleepers (also s.p., co-prod.).
TELEVISION: *Series*: The Tim Conway Comedy Hour (writer), The Marty Feldman Comedy Machine (writer), The Carol Burnett Show (writer; Emmy Awards: 1974, 1975), Harry (exec. prod.), Homicide: Life on the Streets (dir., co-exec. prod.; Emmy Award for directing, 1993). *Pilot*: Diner (exec. prod., dir.). *Specials*: Stopwatch 30 Minutes of Investigative Ticking (exec. prod.).

LEVINSON, NORM
Executive. b. New Haven, CT, Mar. 17, 1925. Started theatre business as usher for Loew's Theatres, 1940. U.S. Army, 1943-46. Returned Loew's Theatres managerial positions New Haven and Hartford, CT. MGM press representative, Minneapolis, Jacksonville, Atlanta, Dallas. General Manager, Trans-Texas Theatres, Dallas. President, Academy Theatres, Inc., Dallas. Promoted World Championship Boxing, Dallas and Johannesburg, South Africa. Executive Vice President, Cobb Theatres, Birmingham, Alabama; v.p., world-wide mktg., Artists Releasing Corp., Encino, CA.; head film buyer, Chakeres Theatres, Ohio & Kentucky.

LEVY, BERNARD
Executive. b. Boca Raton, FL. e. Brooklyn Law Sch., L.L.B. Legal staff of Superintendent of Insurance of the state of New York in the rehabilitation and liquidation of guaranteed title and mortgage companies, 1934-36; private practice of law, 1936-46; legal staff, Paramount Pictures, Inc., 1946-50; legal staff, United Paramount Theatres, 1950-51; exec. asst. to Edward L. Hyman, v.p., ABC, Inc., in chg. of theatre administration, north, 1951-62; apptd. exec. liaison officer for southern motion picture theatres, ABC, Inc., 1962-64; exec. liaison officer, m.p. theas., ABC, Inc., 1965-72; v.p., ABC Theatre Division, 1973. Retired, 1976.

LEVY, BUD
Executive. b. Jackson Heights, NY, April 3, 1928. e. NYU. Member: Variety Clubs Int'l., M.P. Pioneers, President's Advisory Board-NATO; director: NATO, TOP, CATO. Elected pres., Trans-Lux Corp., 1980. Pres. Trans Lux Theatres, (a subsidiary of Cinamerica Theatres, later Crown Theatres). Will Rogers Memorial Fund, Chmn., Cara Committee for NATO; chmn. ShowEast; v.p. NATO; dir. Motion Picture Pioneers.

LEVY, DAVID
Executive, Producer, Writer. b. Philadelphia, PA, Jan. 2. e. Wharton Sch., U. of PA, B.S. in Eco., M.B.A., as v.p. & assoc. dir., Young & Rubicam. Inc., 1938-59, acquisitions for clients include: People's Choice, Kate Smith Hour, Wagon Train, Four Star Playhouse, What's My Line, Father Knows Best, Goodyear Playhouse, Life of Riley, Gunsmoke, Arthur Godfrey's Talent Scouts, I Married Joan, The Web, Treasury Men in Action, Person to Person, Maverick, etc. Prod. We the People, Manhattan at Midnight. Writer: Kate Smith radio series, Manhattan at Midnight, Reunion, Robert Montgomery Presents, Grand Central Station, CBS Radio Workshop, Alcoa/Goodyear. With War Finance div. of U.S. Treasury Dept. on detached duty from U.S. Navy, 1944-46. Was v.p. in chg. of network TV progs. & talent, NBC, 1959-61. Acquisitions for network include: Sing-a-Long With Mitch, Peter Pan, Bonanza, Dr. Kildare, Bob Newhart Show, Thriller, Car 54 Where Are You?, Loretta Young Show, Sunday Showcase, Alfred Hitchcock Presents, Dick Powell Show, Saturday Night at the Movies, Hazel, Klondike, Victory at Sea, Joey Bishop Show, Shirley Temple Show, etc. Created: Bat Masterson, The Addams Family, Americans, Outlaws, Pruitts of Southampton, Sarge, Hollywood Screen Test, Face the Music, etc. Developed: Double Life of Henry Phyffe, Name That Tune, You Asked for It, etc. Assigned as writer, training film section, photographic div., Bureau of Aeronautics, U.S. Navy, 1944. Novels: The Chameleons, The Gods of Foxcroft, Network Jungle, Potomac Jungle, as well as numerous TV plays and short stories. Currently creative consultant to Mark Goodson Prods. Pres., Wilshire Prods. Exec. dir., Caucus for Prods., Writers and Dirs.

LEVY, EUGENE
Actor, Writer, Director. b. Hamilton, Canada, Dec. 17, 1946. e. McMaster U. Acted with coll. ensemble theater. Film debut in Ivan Reitman's Cannibal Girls, 1970, before joining Toronto's Second City troupe which eventually led to his work as writer-performer on Second City Television's various programs, 1977-83. *Canadian theater*: Godspell (1971), The Owl and the Pussycat, Love Times Four.

PICTURES: Cannibal Girls, Running, Heavy Metal (voice), National Lampoon's Vacation, Strange Brew, Going Berserk, Splash, Armed and Dangerous, The Canadian Conspiracy, Club Paradise, Speed Zone, Father of the Bride, Once Upon a Crime (also dir.), Stay Tuned, I Love Trouble, Multiplicity.
TELEVISION: *Series*: Second City TV, SCTV Network 90, SCTV Network (Emmy Award as writer, 1983). *Movies*: Partners in Love, Sodbusters (dir., co-writer, co-exec. prod.), Harrison Bergeron.

LEVY, HERMAN M.
Attorney. b. New Haven, CT, Sept. 27, 1904. e. Yale, B.A., 1927, Yale Law Sch., LL.B., 1929; Phi Beta Kappa, was in legal dept. RCA Photophone; newspaper reporter; admitted to Connecticut bar, 1929. 1939 elected exec. secy. of MPTO of Connecticut. 1943 elected gen. counsel MPTOA. Gen. counsel, Theatre Owners of America, 1947-63. Pres., New Haven County Bar Assn., 1964; legislative agent, CT Assn. of Theatre Owners. Retired as legislative agent, 1981. Received Distinguished Service Award from ShowEast '93. *Author*: More Sinned Against, Natl. Bd. of Review Magazine, 1941. Proving the Death of a Non-Resident Alien, Conn. Bar Journal, 1950; Need for a System of Arbitration M.P. Ind., Arbitration Journal, 1950; reprint of Industry Case Digest, 20th Century-Fox vs. Boehm in the Journal (Screen Producers Guild); Book Review of Antitrust in the Motion Picture Industry, by Michael Conant (Univ. of Calif. Law Review).

LEVY, JULES
Producer. b. Los Angeles, CA, Feb. 12, 1923. e. USC. Started in property dept. of WB, 1941; first m.p. unit Army Air Force, Culver City, CA.
PICTURES: The Vampire, Return of Dracula, Vice Squad, Without Warning, Down Three Dark Streets, Geronimo, The Glory Guys, Clambake, The Scalphunters, Sam Whiskey, The McKenzie Break, The Hunting Party, Kansas City Bomber, The Honkers, McQ, Branningan, White Lightning, Gator, Safari 3000.
TELEVISION: *Series*: The Rifleman, Robert Taylor in The Detectives, Law of the Plainsman, The Big Valley.

LEVY, MICHAEL
Executive. b. Brooklyn, NY. e. Brown U. Started in industry in editorial dept. of trade-paper Variety; held posts in New York with ABC Motion Pictures and with Diener/Hauser/Bates Advertising. Worked for Lawrence Gordon Productions as exec. asst. to Gordon and as story editor. Joined 20th Century Fox in January, 1985, as dir. of creative affairs for studio. 1986, named v.p., production, m.p. div., Fox; appointed sr. v.p. production, 20th Century Fox, 1988; named pres., Silver Pictures, 1989.

LEVY, NORMAN
Executive. b. Bronx, NY, Jan. 3, 1935. e. City Coll. of New York. 1957 joined Universal Pictures, holding various sales positions; 1967, went to National General Pictures, ultimately being named v.p. and exec. asst. to pres.; 1974, Columbia Pictures, v.p., gen. sls. mgr. 1975 named Columbia exec. v.p. in chg. of domestic sls.; 1977, exec. v.p., mktg; 1978. pres., Columbia Pictures Domestic Distribution. 1980 joined 20th-Fox as pres. of Entertainment Group; 1981, vice-chmn., 20th Century-Fox Film Corp. Resigned 1985 to become chmn, ceo, New Century/Vista Film Co. 1991, chmn. and CEO, Creative Film Enterprises.

LEWELLEN, A. WAYNE
Executive. b. Dallas, TX, Feb. 16, 1944. e. U. of Texas. Joined Paramount Pictures 1973 as brch. mgr., Dallas-Oklahoma City territory; 1978, v.p. Southern div.; 1984, exec. v.p., gen. sls. mngr.; 1986, pres. domestic distrib.; 1993, pres. M.P. distrib.

LEWIS, ARTHUR
Producer, Director, Writer. b. New York, NY, Sept. 15, 1918. e. USC, Yale U. Began career as writer and assoc. prod. on the Jones Family TV series. Five years in U.S. Army; returned to screenwriting before producing Three Wishes for Jamie on Broadway and producing and directing Guys and Dolls in London's West End. In mid-60s and 70s produced over 25 plays with Bernard Delfont in the West End of London.
PICTURES: *Producer*: Loot, Baxter, The Killer Elite, Brass Target.
TELEVISION: Brenner, The Asphalt Jungle, The Nurses. *Movies*: The Diary of Anne Frank, Splendor in the Grass.

LEWIS, EDWARD
Producer. b. Camden, NJ, Dec. 16, 1922. e. Bucknell U. Began entertainment career as script writer, then co-produced The Admiral Was a Lady and teamed with Marion Parsonnet to bring the Faye Emerson Show to TV. Subsequently prod. first Schlitz Playhouse and China Smith series. Was v.p. of Kirk Douglas' indep. prod. co., where was assoc. prod. and writer-prod. Collaborated with John Frankenheimer on 8 films.

PICTURES: Lizzie (assoc. prod.), The Careless Years (prod., s.p.), Spartacus, The Last Sunset, Lonely Are the Brave, The List of Adrian Messenger, Seconds, Grand Prix, The Fixer (exec. prod.), The Gypsy Moths (exec.), I Walk the Line (exec.), The Horsemen, The Iceman Cometh (exec.), Executive Action, Rhinoceros, Lost in the Stars, Missing (co-prod.), Crackers, The River, Brothers (prod., s.p.).
TELEVISION: Ishi: The Last of His Tribe (exec. prod.), The Thorn Birds (exec. prod.).

LEWIS, GEOFFREY
Actor. b. San Diego, CA, 1935. Father of actress Juliette Lewis, actors Lightfield & Peter Lewis.
PICTURES: Welcome Home Soldier Boys, The Culpepper Cattle Company, Bad Company, High Plains Drifter, Dillinger, Thunderbolt and Lightfoot, Macon County Line, The Great Waldo Pepper, Smile, The Wind and the Lion, Lucky Lady, The Return of a Man Called Horse, Every Which Way But Loose, Tilt, Human Experiments, Tom Horn, Broncho Billy, Heaven's Gate, Any Which Way You Can, Shoot the Sun Down, I the Jury, Ten to Midnight, Night of the Comet, Lust in the Dust, Stitches, Fletch Lives, Out of the Dark, Pink Cadillac, Catch Me If You Can, Disturbed, Double Impact, The Lawnmower Man, Point of No Return, Wishman, The Man Without a Face, Only the Strong, Army of One, Maverick.
TELEVISION: *Series*: Flo, Gun Shy. *Movies*: Moon of the Wolf, Honky Tonk, The Great Ice Rip-Off, Attack on Terror: The FBI Versus the Ku Klux Klan, The New Daughters of Joshua Cabe, The Great Houndinis, The Deadly Triangle, The Hunted Lady, When Every Day Was the Fourth of July, The Jericho Mile, Samurai, Salem's Lot, Belle Starr, The Shadow Riders, Life of the Party: The Story of Beatrice, The Return of the Man From U.N.C.L.E., Travis McGee, September Gun, Stormin' Home, Dallas: The Early Years, Day of Reckoning, Gambler V: Playing for Keeps, When the Dark Man Calls, Kansas. *Guest*: Mannix, Barnaby Jones, Starsky and Hutch, Streets of San Francisco, Police Woman, Little House on the Prairie, Laverne & Shirley, Lou Grant, Magnum P.I., Amazing Stories, Murder She Wrote, Paradise.

LEWIS, HAROLD G.
Executive. b. New York, NY, Sept. 18, 1938. e. Union Coll., 1960, electrical engineer. Joined ATA Trading Corp. in 1960 and has been pres. since 1977. Producer of feature animation. Importer and exporter for theatrical and TV features, documentaries, series, classics. Pres., ATA Trading Corp., and Favorite TV, Inc.

LEWIS, JERRY
Actor, Director, Writer, Producer. r.n. Joseph Levitch. b. Newark, NJ, Mar. 16, 1926. e. Irvington H.S. Parents Danny and Rae Lewis, prof. entertainers. Debut at 5 at a NY Borscht Circuit hotel singing Brother Can You Spare a Dime? 1946 formed comedy-team with Dean Martin at 500 Club, Atlantic City, NJ; then appeared on NBC tv, performed many theatres before being signed by Hal Wallis for m.p. debut. Voted Most Promising Male Star in Television in m.p. Daily's 2nd annual TV poll, 1950. Voted (as team) one of top ten money making stars in m.p. Herald-Fame poll: 1951-56 (including no. 1 position in 1952), voted as solo performer: 1957-59, 1961-64; named best comedy team in m.p. Daily's 16th annual radio poll, 1951-53. 1956 formed Jerry Lewis Prods. Inc., functioning as prod., dir., writer & star. National Chairman & bd. member, Muscular Dystrophy Association. Full professor USC; taught grad. film dir. Book: The Total Filmmaker (1971) based on classroom lectures. *Autobiography*: Jerry Lewis In Person (1982).
THEATER: Hellzapoppin (regional), Damn Yankees (B'way debut, 1995).
PICTURES: My Friend Irma (debut, 1949), My Friend Irma Goes West, At War With the Army, That's My Boy, Sailor Beware, Jumping Jacks, Scared Stiff, The Stooge, Road to Bali (cameo), The Caddy, Money From Home, Living It Up, Three Ring Circus, You're Never Too Young, Artists and Models, Pardners, Hollywood or Bust, The Delicate Delinquent (also prod.), The Sad Sack, Rock-a-Bye Baby, The Geisha Boy (also prod.), Don't Give Up the Ship, Li'l Abner (cameo), Visit to a Small Planet, Cinderfella (also prod.), The Bellboy (also dir., prod., s.p.), The Ladies Man (also dir., prod., co-s.p.), The Errand Boy (also dir., co-s.p.), It's Only Money, The Nutty Professor (also dir., co-s.p.), Who's Minding the Store?, It's a Mad Mad Mad Mad World (cameo), The Patsy (also dir., co-s.p.), The Disorderly Orderly, Boeing-Boeing, The Family Jewels (also dir., prod., co-s.p.), Three on a Couch (also dir., prod.), Way... Way Out, The Big Mouth (also dir., prod., co-s.p.), Don't Raise the Bridge Lower the River, Hook Line and Sinker (also prod.), Which Way to the Front? (also dir., prod.), One More Time (dir. only), The Day the Clown Cried (also dir., co-s.p.), Hardly Working (also dir., co-s.p.), The King of Comedy, Smorgasbord (Cracking Up; also dir., co-s.p.), Slapstick of Another Kind, Cookie, Mr. Saturday Night (cameo), Arizona Dream, Funny Bones.
TELEVISION: *Movie*: Fight for Life. *Series*: Colgate Comedy Hour, The Jerry Lewis Show (1963), The Jerry Lewis Show (1967-69). *Guest*: Wiseguy (5 episodes).

LEWIS, JOSEPH H.
Director. b. New York, NY, Apr. 6, 1907. e. DeWitt Clinton H.S. Camera boy, MGM; then asst. film ed. in chge. film ed., Republic; dir. in chge. 2nd units; debuted as dir. at Universal; served in U.S. Signal Corps., WW II. Dir. musical numbers for The Jolson Story.
PICTURES: Navy Spy (co-dir. with Crane Wilbur; debut, 1937), Courage of the West, Singing Outlaw, The Spy Ring, Border Wolves, The Last Stand, Two-Fisted Rangers, The Return of Wild Bill, That Gang of Mine, The Invisible Ghost, Pride of the Bowery, Arizona Cyclone, Bombs Over Burma, The Silver Bullet, Secrets of a Co-Ed, The Boss of Hangtown Mesa, The Mad Doctor of Market Street, Minstrel Man, The Falcon in San Francisco, My Name is Julia Ross, So Dark the Night, The Swordsman, The Return of October, The Undercover Man, Gun Crazy, A Lady Without Passport, Retreat Hell!, Desperate Search, Cry of the Hunted, The Big Combo, A Lawless Street, The Seventh Cavalry, The Halliday Brand, Terror in a Texas Town.
TELEVISION: *Series*: The Rifleman, The Big Valley.

LEWIS, JULIETTE
Actress. b. California, June 21, 1973. Father is actor Geoffrey Lewis.
PICTURES: My Stepmother Is an Alien (debut, 1988), Meet the Hollowheads, National Lampoon's Christmas Vacation, Crooked Hearts, Cape Fear (Acad. Award nom.), Husbands and Wives, That Night, Kalifornia, What's Eating Gilbert Grape, Romeo Is Bleeding, Natural Born Killers, Mixed Nuts, The Basketball Diaries, Strange Days, From Dusk Till Dawn, The Evening Star.
TELEVISION: *Series*: Homefires, I Married Dora, A Family for Joe. *Movie*: Too Young to Die?

LEWIS, MICHAEL J.
Composer. b. Wales, 1939. First film score 1969, The Mad Woman of Chaillot, won Ivor Novello Award for best film score. 1973: first Broadway musical, Cyrano, Grammy nomination '74, Caesar and Cleopatra (T.V. '76), The Lion the Witch and the Wardrobe (Emmy, 1979).
PICTURES: The Man Who Haunted Himself, Julius Caesar, Upon This Rock, Unman Wittering and Zigo, Running Scared, Baxter, Theatre of Blood, 11 Harrowhouse, 92 in the Shade, Russian Roulette, The Stick-Up, The Medusa Touch, The Legacy, The Passage, The Unseen, ffolkes, Sphinx, Yes Giorgio, The Hound of the Baskervilles, On the Third Day, The Naked Face.

LEWIS, RICHARD
Comedian, Actor. b. Brooklyn, NY, June 29, 1949. e. Ohio St. Univ. (marketing degree). Was copywriter for adv. agency before becoming stand-up comic performing in nightclubs in NYC, Las Vegas, 1971.
PICTURES: The Wrong Guys (debut, 1988), That's Adequate, Once Upon a Crime, Robin Hood: Men in Tights, Wagons East!, Leaving Las Vegas, Drunks.
TELEVISION: *Series*: Harry, Anything But Love. *Specials*: Richard Lewis: I'm in Pain, Richard Lewis: I'm Exhausted, Richard Lewis: I'm Doomed, Living Against the Odds (also writer). *Pilot*: King of the Building.

LIBERMAN, FRANK P.
Publicist. b. New York, NY, May 29, 1917. e. Cheshire Acad., CT, 1934; Lafayette Coll., Easton, PA, B.A. 1938. m. Patricia Harris, casting dir. Worked as copy boy, N.Y. Daily News, 1938-39. Began career as publicist at Warner Bros., home office as messenger, 1939, promoted to pressbooks dept., transferred to Warner's Chicago office as field exploitation man. U.S. Signal Corps, 1941, public relations officer, Army Pictorial Service, on temporary duty with War Dept., Bureau of Public Relations in Pentagon. Discharged as Capt., 1946. Rejoined Warner Bros. on coast 2 years, 1947, est. own public relations office, 1947. Owner, Frank Liberman and Associates, Inc.

LIBERTINI, RICHARD
Actor. b. Cambridge, MA, May 21. Original member of Second City troupe in Chicago. With MacIntyre Dixon appeared as the Stewed Prunes in cabaret performances.
THEATER: Three by Three (1961), Plays for Bleecker Street, The Cat's Pajamas, The Mad Show, Bad Habits. Solo: The White House Murder Case, Don't Drink the Water, Paul Sill's Story Theatre, Ovid's Metamorphoses, The Primary English Class, Neopolitan Ghosts, Love's Labour's Lost, As You Like It.
PICTURES: The Night They Raided Minsky's, Don't Drink the Water, Catch-22, The Out-of-Towners, Lovers and Other Strangers, Lady Liberty, Fire Sale, Days of Heaven, The In-Laws, Popeye, Sharky's Machine, Soup for One, Best Friends, Deal of the Century, Going Berserk, Unfaithfully Yours, All of Me, Fletch, Big Trouble, Betrayed, Fletch Lives, Animal Behavior, Duck Tales: The Movie (voice), Lemon Sisters, Awakenings, The Bonfire of the Vanities, Cultivating Charlie, Nell.

TELEVISION: *Series*: Story Theatre, The Melba Moore-Clifton Davis Show, Soap, Family Man, The Fanelli Boys, Pacific Station. *Guest*: George Burns Comedy Week, Barney Miller, Bob Newhart. *Pilots*: Calling Dr. Storm, M.D., Fair Game. *Movies*: Three on a Date, Extreme Close-Up. *Specials*: Let's Celebrate, The Fourth Wise Man, Fame (Hallmark Hall of Fame), The Trial of Bernhard Goetz, Equal Justice, Murder She Wrote, Law and Order, L.A. Law.

LICCARDI, VINCENT G.
Executive. b. Brooklyn, NY. Started as messenger at Universal Pictures, asst. adv. mgr. on Around the World in 80 Days, asst. to exec. coord. of sales & Adv. on Spartacus; National Dir. of Adv. & Publ., Continental; Nat. Dir. Adv. & Publ., Braintree Prod., adv. pub. mgr. Allied Artists, ad. mgr. Paramount, National Dir. Adv.-Pub., UMC Pictures, Screenwriter, Playboy to Priest, The Rivals, The Rivals-Part II, The Greatest Disaster of All Time, The Lady on the 9:40, All That Heaven Allows, All Mine to Love, Twice Over, Lightly!, Mr. Jim.

LIEBERFARB, WARREN N.
Executive. e. Wharton Sch. of Commerce and Finance, U. of PA, B.S., economics; U. of Michigan. Started career in industry at Paramount Pictures as dir. of mktg. and exec. asst. to Stanley Jaffe, then pres. Later joined 20th-Fox as v.p., special market dist. (cable, pay-TV, non-theatrical). Joined Warner Bros. as v.p., exec. asst. to Ted Ashley, bd. chmn.; later named v.p., intl. adv.-pub. In 1979 joined Lorimar as v.p., of Lorimar Productions, Inc., the parent company, based in New York. Promoted to sr. v.p. 1982, named v.p. mktg., Warner Home Video; named pres., 1984.

LIEBERMAN, HAL
Executive. Pres. of production, Universal Pictures.

LIEBERMAN, ROBERT
Director, Producer. b. Buffalo, NY, July 16, 1947. e. Univ. of Buffalo. m. actress Marilu Henner. Moved to LA, became editor for Desort-Fisher commercial production house, which led to dir. tv ad spots. Formed own commercial company, Harmony Pictures.
PICTURES: Table for Five, All I Want for Christmas, Fire in the Sky.
TELEVISION: *Movies*: Fighting Back: The Story of Rocky Blier, Will: G. Gordon Liddy, To Save a Child (also exec. prod.). *Series*: thirtysomething, Dream Street (pilot), The Young Riders (pilot), Gabriel's Fire (also exec. prod.), Pros and Cons (exec. consultant), Under Suspicion (also exec. prod.), Medicine Ball (also exec. prod.).

LIEBERSON, SANFORD
Producer. b. Los Angeles, CA, 1936. Early career with William Morris Agency. 1961-62, agent in Rome for Grade Org. Returned to LA as Founding Member CMA agency then exec. in charge of European operations. 1979, named pres. of 20th-Fox Productions, which company he joined in 1977 as v.p. European production. Previously an independent producer forming Good Times. With David Putnam formed Visual Programming Systems to produce, acquire and consult in the Home Video area for CBS, Phillips, Time/Life, etc. As v.p. intl. prod. at Fox, spv. intl. release of such films as Star Wars, 1900, Alien, Chariots of Fire, Nine to Five, Quest for Fire. V.P. Intl. prod. for The Ladd Company. Outland, Body Heat, Blade Runner, The Right Stuff, Police Academy, etc. Chief of prod. at Goldcrest Harvest: Dance With a Stranger, Room With a View, Absolute Beginners, etc. Pres. intl. prod. MGM spv. Russia House, Thelma & Louise, Liebestraum, Not Without My Daughter, Criss Cross, etc. Currently head of prod. at the Natl. Film and Television School of Great Britain.
PICTURES: *Producer*: Melody, Pied Piper, Radio Wonderful, James Dean: First American Teenager, Bugsy Malone, Slade in Flame, Final Programme, Stardust, That'll Be the Day, Brother Can You Spare a Dime, Swastika, Double Headed Eagle, All This and World War II, Mahler, Lisztomania, Jabberwocky, Rita Sue and Bob Too, Stars and Bars, The Mighty Quinn.
TELEVISION: *Movie*: Frank & Jessie (exec. prod.).

LIGHT, JUDITH
Actress. b. Trenton, NJ, Feb. 9. e. Carnegie-Mellon Univ. (BFA). Toured with USO in prod. of Guys and Dolls during college. Acted with Milwaukee and Seattle rep. companies. Made B'way debut in 1975 prod. of A Doll's House with Liv Ullmann. Other stage work: A Streetcar Named Desire, As You Like It, Richard III. Landed role of Karen Wolek on daytime serial One Life to Live in 1977.
TELEVISION: *Series*: One Life to Live (2 Emmy Awards), Who's the Boss?, Phenom. *Movies*: Intimate Agony, Dangerous Affection, The Ryan White Story, My Boyfriend's Back, In Defense of a Married Man, Wife Mother Murderer, Men Don't Tell, Betrayal of Trust, Against Their Will: Women in Prison, Lady Killer, A Husband, A Wife and A Lover. *Guest*: St. Elsewhere, Family Ties, Remington Steele.

LIGHTMAN, M. A.
Exhibitor. b. Nashville, TN, Apr. 21, 1915. e. Southwestern U., Vanderbilt U., 1936, B.A. Bd. chmn. Malco Theatres, Inc., Memphis, Tenn.

LINDBLOM, GUNNEL
Actress, Director. b. Gothenburg, Sweden, 1931. Discovered by Ingmar Bergman while studying at drama school of Gothenburg Municipal Theatre, 1950-53; she moved to Malmo, where he was director of the local Municipal Theatre. Under Bergman's direction she played in Easter, Peer Gynt, Faust, etc. between 1954-59. Later appeared in many Bergman films. Since 1968 has been on staff of Stockholm's Royal Dramatic Theatre, assisting Bergman and then beginning to direct on her own. Made film debut as director with Summer Paradise in 1977.
PICTURES: *Actress*: Love, Girl in the Rain, Song of the Scarlet Flower, The Seventh Seal, Wild Strawberries, The Virgin Spring, Winter Light, The Silence, My Love Is a Rose, Rapture, Loving Couples, Hunger, Woman of Darkness, The Girls, The Father, Brother Carl, Scenes From a Marriage, Misfire, Bakom Jalusin. *Director*: Summer Paradise (also co-s.p.), Sally and Freedom, Summer Nights on Planet Earth (also s.p.).

LINDEN, HAL
Actor. b. Bronx, NY, March 20, 1931. e. City Coll. of New York. Began career as saxophone player and singer, playing with bands of Sammy Kaye, Bobby Sherwood, etc. Drafted and performed in revues for Special Services. After discharge enrolled at N.Y.'s American Theatre Wing; appeared on B'way in Bells Are Ringing, replacing Sydney Chaplin.
THEATER: Wildcat, Something More, Subways Are for Sleeping, Ilya Darling, The Apple Tree, The Education of H*Y*M*A*N K*A*P*L*A*N, On a Clear Day You Can See Forever, Three Men on a Horse, The Pajama Game, The Rothschilds (Tony Award, 1971), I'm Not Rappaport, Unfinished Stories, The Sisters Rosensweig.
PICTURES: Bells Are Ringing, When You Comin' Back Red Ryder?, A New Life.
TELEVISION: *Series*: Animals Animals Animals (host), Barney Miller, Blacke's Magic, F.Y.I. (Emmy Awards, 1983, 1984), Jack's Place, The Boys Are Back. *Specials*: I Do! I Do!, The Best of Everything. *Movies*: Mr. Inside/Mr. Outside, The Love Boat (pilot), How to Break Up a Happy Divorce, Father Figure, Starflight: The Plane That Couldn't Land, The Other Woman, My Wicked Wicked Ways: The Legend of Errol Flynn, The O'Connors, Dream Breakers, The Colony.

LINDHEIM, RICHARD D.
Executive. e. Univ. of Redlands, USC. Started as wrtier/prod. for KNBC in LA. 1969, to NBC as administrator of program testing; 1974, v.p., NBC program research; then v.p. current drama progs. NBC. 1979, joined Universal TV as prod.; 1981, appointed to v.p. of current programming, then sr. v.p. series programming; 1987, named exec. v.p., creative affairs. 1992, became exec. v.p. of Paramount Television Group.

LINDO, DELROY
Actor. b. London, England, Nov. 18, 1952. Received NAACP Image Awards for film Malcolm X and play A Raisin in the Sun. THEATER: *B'way*: Joe Turner's Come and Gone (Tony nom.), Master Harold and the Boys. *Off-B'way*: District Line, As You Like It, Romeo and Juliet, Spell #7, The Heliotrope Bouquet. *Regional*: Othello, Mrs. Ever's Boys, Cobb, A Raisin in the Sun, My Mark My Name, Union Boys, Macbeth, Black Branch, Home.
PICTURES: The Blood of Heroes (Salute to the Jugger; debut, 1990), Mountains of the Moon, Perfect Witness, The Hard Way, Bright Angel, Malcolm X, Bound by Honor, Mr. Jones, Behanzin, Crooklyn, Congo, Clockers, Get Shorty, Feeling Minnesota, Broken Arrow, Ransom.
TELEVISION: *Guest*: Going to Extremes, Against the Law, Hawk, Beauty and the Beast.

LINDSAY, ROBERT
Actor. b. Ilkeston, Derbyshire, Eng., Dec. 13, 1949. e. GLadstone Boys School, Ilkeston, Royal Acad. of Dramatic Art. With Manchester's Royal Exchange Theatre Co. (Hamlet, The Cherry Orchard, The Lower Depths). Also in Godspell, The Three Musketeers, Me and My Girl, (London—Olivier Award, NY—Tony, Theatre World & Drama Desk Awards, 1987), Becket (Olivier & Variety Club Awards), Cyrano de Bergerac.
PICTURES: That'll Be the Day (debut, 1974), Bert Rigby You're a Fool, Strike It Rich, Fierce Creatures.
TELEVISION: *Series*: Citizen Smith, Give Us A Break. *Mini-series*: Confessional. *Specials*: King Lear, G.B.H. (BAFTA Award), Genghis Cohn, Jake's Progress.

LINDSAY-HOGG, MICHAEL
Director. b. England, 1940. Mother is actress Geraldine Fitzgerald.
PICTURES: Let It Be, Nasty Habits, The Object of Beauty (also s.p.), Frankie Starlight.
TELEVISION: Brideshead Revisted (co-dir.), Master Harold ... and the Boys, As Is.

LINK, WILLIAM
Writer, Producer. b. Philadelphia, PA, Dec. 15, 1933. e. U. of Pennsylvania, B.S., 1956. With partner, late Richard Levinson, wrote and created numerous TV series and movies, specializing in detective-mystery genre. *Books*: Fineman, Stay Tuned: An Inside Look at the Making of Prime-Time Television, Off Camera. *Stage incl.*: Prescription Murder, Guilty Conscience, Merlin.
PICTURES: The Hindenberg, Rollercoaster.
TELEVISION: *Series writer-creator.* Mannix, Ellery Queen, Tenafly, Columbo (Emmy Award as writer, 1972), Murder She Wrote. *Movies* writer-prod.: That Certain Summer, My Sweet Charlie (Emmy Award as writer, 1970), The Judge and Jake Wyler, Savage (exec. prod., writer), The Execution of Private Slovik, The Gun, A Cry for Help (prod. only), The Storyteller, Murder by Natural Causes, Stone, Crisis at Central High, Rehearsal For Murder (also exec. prod.), Take Your Best Shot, Prototype (also exec. prod.), The Guardian (also exec. prod.), Guilty Conscience (also exec. prod.), Vanishing Act (also exec. prod.), The United States Vs. Salim Ajami, The Boys (also co-exec. prod.).

LINKLATER, RICHARD
Director, Writer, Producer. b. Houston, TX, 1961. Founded Austin Film Society, serving as artistic director. Filmed several super 8 films incl. feature It's Impossible to Learn to Plow by Reading Books.
PICTURES: *Director/Writer:* Slacker (also prod.), Dazed and Confused (also co-prod.), Before Sunrise.

LINKLETTER, ART
Emcee, Producer, Author. b. Moose Jaw, Saskatchewan, Canada, July 17, 1912. Raised in San Diego. e. San Diego State Coll. Radio prg. mgr., San Diego Exposition, 1935; radio pgm. mgr. S.F. World's Fair, 1937-39; freelance radio announcer and m.c. 1939-42; m.c. series People Are Funny starting in 1942. Author: The Secret World of Kids, 1959; Kids Say the Darndest Things, 1957; Linkletter Down Under, 1969; Yes You Can, 1979; Old Age Is Not For Sissies, 1988; Cavalcade of the Golden West; Cavalcade of America. Recorded albums: Howls, Boners & Shockers and We Love You, Call Collect (Grammy Award winner, 1966).
PICTURES: People Are Funny, Champagne for Caesar, The Snow Queen.
TELEVISION: *Series*: Art Linkletter's House Party, Life With Linkletter, People Are Funny (emcee), The Art Linkletter Show (emcee), Hollywood Talent Scouts. *Specials*: Inside Salute to Baseball (exec. prod., host), Art Linkletter's Secret World of Kids (host), Ford Startime, Young Man With A Band. *Movies*: Sane Grey Theatre, G.E. Theatre.

LINN-BAKER, MARK
Actor, Director. b. St. Louis, MO, June 17, 1954. e. Yale Univ., Yale Sch. of Drama (M.F.A., 1979). Founding memb. American Repertory Th. in Cambridge, MA; founding prod./dir. NY Stage & Film Co. in NYC & Poughkeepsie. Co-founder of True Pictures, 1990.
THEATER: *B'way*: Doonesbury, Laughter on the 23rd Floor, A Funny Thing Happened On The Way To The Forum.
PICTURES: Manhattan (bit), The End of August, My Favorite Year, Me and Him (voice only), Noises Off, Me and Veronica (co-prod. only).
TELEVISION: *Series*: Comedy Zone, Perfect Strangers, Hangin' With Mr. Cooper (dir. only). *Movies*: Wedding Bell Blues, Bare Essentials. *Specials*: Doonesbury (voice of Rick), The Ghost Writer (Amer. Playhouse), The Whole Shebang. *Director*: episodes of Family Matters, Family Man, Going Places.

LINSON, ART
Producer, Director. b. Chicago, IL, 1942. e. UCLA; LLD. UCLA, 1967. Was rock music manager with record prod. Lou Adler and ran own record co., Spin Dizzy records before turning to film production. Debuted as director also with Where the Buffalo Roam.
PICTURES: Rafferty and the Gold Dust Twins (co.-prod.), Car Wash, American Hot Wax (also co-s.p.), Where the Buffalo Roam (also dir.), Melvin and Howard, Fast Times at Ridgemont High (co-prod.), The Wild Life (also dir.), The Untouchables (prod.), Scrooged (co-prod.), Casualties of War (prod.), We're No Angels (prod.), Dick Tracy (exec. prod.), Singles, Point of No Return, This Boy's Life (prod.).

LIOTTA, RAY
Actor. b. Newark, NJ, Dec. 18, 1955. e. Univ. of Miami. First prof. job on tv commercial, followed by continuing role on daytime serial, Another World.
PICTURES: The Lonely Lady (debut, 1983), Something Wild, Dominick and Eugene, Field of Dreams, GoodFellas, Article 99, Unlawful Entry, No Escape, Corrina Corrina, Operation Dumbo Drop, Unforgettable, Turbulence.
TELEVISION: *Series*: Another World, Casablanca, Our Family Honor. *Movies*: Harhat and Legs, Crazy Times, Women and Men 2: In Love There Are No Rules (Domestic Dilemma).

LIPPERT, ROBERT L., JR.
Producer, Exhibitor. b. Alameda, CA, Feb. 28, 1928. e. St Mary's Coll., 1946; all conference football 1947. Career began in theatre exhibition. Entered m.p. production in 1951. Film editor of 45 "b" features. Produced 9 pictures for Lippert Features and 20th Century Fox Films. Returned in 1966 to theatre exhibition. Became pres. of Affiliated, Lippert, Transcontinental theatrs (180 theatres nation-wide). Semi-retired as of 1994.

LIPSTONE, HOWARD H.
Executive, Producer. b. Chicago, IL, Apr. 28, 1928. e. UCLA, USC. Ass't to gen. mgr. at KLTA, 1950-55; program dir. at KABC-TV, 1955-65; exec. ass't to pres. at Selmur Prods., ABC subsidiary, 1965-69. Ivan Tors Films & Studios as exec. v.p., 1969-70; pres., Alan Landsburg Prods., 1970-1985; The Landsburg Co., 1985-. Co-exec. prod.: The Outer Space Connection, The Bermuda Triangle, Mysteries, The White Lions, Jaws 3-D.
TELEVISION: *Exec. in charge of prod.*: The Savage Bees, Ruby and Oswald, The Triangle Factory Fire Scandal, Strange Voices, A Place at the Table, Kate & Allie, Gimme a Break, A Stoning in Fulham County, The Ryan White Story, Quiet Victory, Unspeakable Acts, In Defense of a Married Man, Triumph of the Heart, Nightmare in Columbia County, A Mother's Right, The Elizabeth Morgan Story, The diamond Fleece, Terror in the Night, If Someone Had Known.

LIPTON, PEGGY
Actress. b. New York, NY, Aug. 30, 1947. Former model. Co-wrote song L.A. is My Lady (recorded by Frank Sinatra). Recorded album Peggy Lipton.
PICTURES: The Purple People Eater, Kinjite (Forbidden Subjects), Twin Peaks: Fire Walk With Me.
TELEVISION: *Series*: The John Forsythe Show, The Mod Squad (Golden Globe Award, 1971), Twin Peaks, Angel Falls. *Movies*: The Return of the Mod Squad, Addicted to His Love, Fatal Charm, The Spider and the Fly, Deadly Vows.

LISI, VIRNA
Actress. r.n. Virna Pieralisi. b. Ancona, Italy, Nov. 8, 1936.
PICTURES: Desiderio e Sole, Violenza sul Lago, The Doll That Took the Town, Luna Nova, Vendicatta, La Rossa, Caterina Sforza, Il Mondo dei Miracoli, Duel of the Titans, Eva, Don't Tempt the Devil, The Black Tulip, The Shortest Day, How To Murder Your Wife, Casanova 70, The Possessed, A Virgin for a Prince, Kiss the Other Sheik, The Birds the Bees and the Italians, Made in Italy, La Bambole (The Dolls), Not With My Wife You Don't, Assault on a Queen, The 25th Hour, Anyone Can Play, The Girl and the General, Arabella, Better a Widow, The Girl Who Couldn't Say No, The Christmas Tree, The Secret of Santa Vittoria, If It's Tuesday This Must Be Belgium, Roma Bene, The Statue, Bluebeard, The Serpent, Ernesto, I Love N.Y., I Ragazzi di Via Panisperna, Beyond Good and Evil, Merry Christmas Happy New Year, Miss Right, Queen Margot (Cannes Film Fest. Award, 1994).
TELEVISION: *US*: Christopher Columbus.

LITHGOW, JOHN
Actor. b. Rochester, NY, Oct. 19, 1945. Father was prod. of Shakespeare Fests. in midwest. e. Harvard. Fulbright fellowship to study at London Acad. of Music and Dramatic Art. Interned in London with Royal Shakespeare Co. and Royal Court Theatre.
THEATER: *NY*: The Changing Room (Tony & Drama Desk Awards, 1973), My Fat Friend, Trelawney of the Wells, Comedians, Anna Christie, A Memory of Two Mondays, Once in a Lifetime, Spokesong, Bedroom Farce, Salt Lake City Skyline, Division Street (also LA), Kaufman at Large (also dir., writer), Beyond Therapy, Requiem for a Heavyweight (Drama Desk Award), The Front Page, M Butterfly. Regional: The Beggar's Opera, Pygmalion, Of Mice and Men, Troilus and Cressida, The Roar of the Greasepaint, What Price Glory?, The Lady's Not for Burning, Who's Afraid of Virginia Woolf? (LA Drama Critics Circle Award).
PICTURES: Dealing or the Berkeley-to-Boston Forty-Brick Lost-Bag Blues (debut, 1972), Obsession, The Big Fix, Rich Kids, All That Jazz, Blow Out, I'm Dancing as Fast as I Can, The World According to Garp (Acad. Award nom.), Twilight Zone—The Movie, Terms of Endearment (Acad. Award nom.), Footloose, The Adventures of Buckaroo Banzai: Across the Eighth Dimension, 2010, Santa Claus, The Manhattan Project, Mesmerized, Harry and the Hendersons, Distant Thunder, Out Cold, Memphis Belle, Ricochet, At Play in the Fields of the Lord, Raising Cain, Cliffhanger, The Pelican Brief, A Good Man in Africa, Princess Caraboo, Silent Fall, Hollow Point.
TELEVISION: *Series*: Third Rock from the Sun (Emmy Award, 1996). *Guest*: Amazing Stories (Emmy Award, 1987), Saturday Night Live. *Movies*: Mom The Wolfman and Me, Not in Front of the Children, The Day After, The Glitter Dome, Resting Place, Baby Girl Scott, The Traveling Man, The Last Elephant (Ivory Hunters), The Boys, The Wrong Man, Love Cheat and Steal, World War II: When Lions Roared, Redwood

Curtain, The Tuskegee Airmen. *Specials*: The Country Girl (TV debut, 1973), Secret Service, Big Blonde, The Oldest Living Graduate, Goldilocks and the Three Bears (Faerie Tale Theatre).

LITTLE, RICH
Actor. b. Ottawa, Canada, Nov. 26, 1938. Started as radio disc jockey, talk show host in Canada; then impressionist in night clubs.
PICTURES: Dirty Tricks, Happy Hour, Bebe's Kids (voice).
TELEVISION: *Series*: Love on a Rooftop, The John Davidson Show, ABC Comedy Hour (The Kopycats), The Julie Andrews Hour, The Rich Little Show, The New You Asked For It (host). *Specials*: The Rich Little Show, Rich Little's Christmas Carol (also writer), Rich Little's Washington Follies, The Rich Little Specials (HBO), Rich Little's Robin Hood, Come Laugh With Me, Night of 42 Stars, The Christmas Raccoons, Rich Little and Friends in New Orleans, etc.

LITTLEFIELD, WARREN
Executive. b. Montclair, NJ. e. American Univ. in DC, School of Government and Public Admin.; Hobart Col. (psych. degree). 1975-79, Westfall Prods., developing prime-time specials and movies before being promoted to v.p., develop. & prod. 1979, served as WB TV dir., comedy develop. Joined NBC 1979, as mngr. comedy develop. 1981, v.p. current comedy programs at NBC. 1985, sr. v.p. series specials & variety progs., NBC Entertainment; 1987, exec. v.p., Prime-Time progs. NBC Entertainment. 1990, named pres. NBC Entertainment.

LITTMAN, LYNNE
Director, Producer. b. New York, NY, June 26. e. Sarah Lawrence. B.A., 1962; Student the Sorbonne 1960-61. Researcher for CBS News 1965; assoc. prod. Natl. Educational TV 1964-68; dir. NIMH film series on drug abuse UCLA Media Center 1970; prod., dir. documentary films, news and pub. affairs series KCET Community TV, So. Calif. 1971-77; dir. WNET non-fiction film, Once a Daughter 1979; exec. v.p., movies-for-TV, ABC, 1980-81; Received Ford Fdn. Grant 1978 and numerous awards. Acad. Award film tribute to women, 1993.
PICTURES: In the Matter of Kenneth (doc.), Wanted-Operadoras (doc.), Till Death Do Us Part (doc.), Number Our Days (doc. short; Academy Award 1977), Testament (co-prod., dir.), In Her Own Time.

LITTO, GEORGE
Producer. b. Philadelphia, PA. e. Temple U. Joined William Morris Agency in New York and then became indep. literary agent. Opened own office in Hollywood, 1965. Packaged film and TV productions, including M*A*S*H, Hang 'Em High, Hawaii Five-O for TV prior to entering indep. prod.; 1981-82, chmn. bd. & CEO, Filmways; 1983-85 indep. prod. 20th Century Fox.
PICTURES: Thieves Like Us (exec. prod.), Drive-In (exec. prod.), Obsession (prod.), Over the Edge (prod.), Dressed To Kill (prod.). Blow Out (prod.), Kansas (prod.), Night Game (prod.).

LITVINOFF, SI
Producer, Executive. b. New York, NY, April 5. e. Adelphi Coll., A.B.; NYU Sch. of Law, LL.B. Theatrical lawyer, personal and business manager in New York until 1967 when left firm of Barovick, Konecky & Litvinoff to produce plays and films. June, 1987: sr. v.p. for production and dev., Hawkeye Entertainment, Inc.
THEATER: Leonard Bernstein's Theatre Songs, Cry of the Raindrop, Girl of the Golden West, Little Malcolm and His Struggle Against the Eunuchs, I and Albert (London).
PICTURES: The Queen, All the Right Noises, Walkabout, A Clockwork Orange (exec. prod.), Glastonbury Fayre (exec. in chg. prod.), The Man Who Fell to Earth (exec. prod.)
TELEVISION: *Exec. prod.*: 15th Annual Saturn Awards, Doobie Brothers Retrospective, Listen to the Music 1989.

LIVINGSTON, JAY
Composer, Lyricist. b. McDonald, PA, March 28, 1915. e. U. of PA, 1937, UCLA, 1964-65. Army, WWII. Accompanist and arranger for various NBC singers and singing groups 1940-42, NY; author music and special material for Olsen & Johnson, including various editions of Hellzapoppin', and Sons O'Fun: began composing m.p. songs, 1944. Under contract to Paramount, 1945-55; then freelanced. Cameo appearance in Sunset Boulevard. Writer of songs and special material for Bob Hope starting in 1945. Has written songs for over 100 pictures. Elected to Songwriters Hall of Fame, 1975. Received star on Hollywood Blvd. Walk of Fame, 1995.
SONGS INCLUDE: G'bye Now, Stuff Like That There, To Each His Own, Golden Earrings, Silver Bells, Buttons and Bows (Academy Award, 1949), Mona Lisa (Academy Award, 1951), Que Sera Sera/Whatever Will Be Will Be (Academy Award, 1957), Tammy (Acad. Award nom.), Almost In Your Arms

(Acad. Award nom.), Dear Heart, (Acad. Award nom.), Wish Me a Rainbow, In the Arms of Love, Never Let Me Go, As I Love You, All the Time, Maybe September.
THEATER: *B'way*: Oh Captain!, Let It Ride, Sugar Babies (2 songs).
PICTURES: Monsieur Beaucaire, My Favorite Brunette, The Paleface, My Friend Irma, Sorrowful Jones, My Friend Irma Goes West, Streets of Laredo, Isn't It Romantic?, Fancy Pants, Here Comes the Groom, The Lemon-Drop Kid, Son of Paleface, The Stars Are Singing, Here Come the Girls, Somebody Loves Me, Aaron Slick from Punkin' Crick, Red Garters, The Man Who Knew Too Much, Houseboat, Tammy and the Bachelor, Dear Heart, The Night of the Grizzly, This Property Is Condemned, The Oscar, Never Too Late, Harlow, What Did You Do in the War Daddy?, Wait Until Dark.
TELEVISION: Series themes: Bonanza, Mister Ed.

LLOYD, CHRISTOPHER
Actor. b. Stamford, CT, Oct. 22, 1938. Studied at Neighborhood Playhouse, NY.
THEATER: *NY*: Kaspar (Drama Desk & Obie Awards, 1973), Happy End, Red White and Maddox. Regional: The Father, Hot L Baltimore, The Possessed, A Midsummer Night's Dream.
PICTURES: One Flew Over the Cuckoo's Nest (debut, 1975), Goin' South, Butch and Sundance: The Early Days, The Onion Field, The Lady in Red, Schizoid, The Black Marble, The Postman Always Rings Twice, The Legend of the Lone Ranger, National Lampoon Goes to the Movies, Mr. Mom, To Be or Not to Be, Star Trek III: The Search for Spock, The Adventures of Buckaroo Banzai Across the Eighth Dimension, Joy of Sex, Back to the Future, Clue, Legend of the White Horse, Miracles, Walk Like a Man, Who Framed Roger Rabbit, Track 29, Eight Men Out, The Dream Team, Back to the Future Part II, Why Me?, Back to the Future Part III, Duck Tales: The Movie (voice), White Dragon, Suburban Commando, The Addams Family, Dennis the Menace, Twenty Bucks, Addams Family Values, Angels in the Outfield, Camp Nowhere, Radioland Murders, The Pagemaster, Things to Do in Denver When You're Dead, Cadillac Ranch.
TELEVISION: *Series*: Taxi (Emmy Awards: 1982, 1983), Back to the Future (voice for animated series), Deadly Games. *Specials*: Pilgrim Farewell, The Penny Elf, Tales From Hollywood Hills: Pat Hobby—Teamed With Genius, In Search of Dr. Seuss. *Movies*: Lacy and the Mississippi Queen, The Word, Stunt Seven, Money on the Side, September Gun, The Cowboy and the Ballerina, T Bone N Weasel, Dead Ahead: The Exxon Valdez Disaster. *Guest*: Barney Miller, Best of the West, Cheers, Amazing Stories, Avonlea (Emmy Award, 1992).

LLOYD, EMILY
Actress. b. North London, Eng., Sept. 29, 1970. r.n. Emily Lloyd Pack. Father is stage actor Roger Lloyd Pack, mother worked as Harold Pinter's secretary. Father's agent recommended that she audition for screenwriter David Leland's directorial debut Wish You Were Here when she was 15.
PICTURES: Wish You Were Here (Natl. Society of Film Critics & London Evening Standard Awards, 1987; BAFTA nom.), Cookie, In Country, Chicago Joe and the Showgirl, Scorchers, A River Runs Through It, Under the Hula Moon, When Saturday Comes.

LLOYD, EUAN
Producer. b. Rugby, Warwick, England, Dec. 6, 1923. e. Rugby. Entered m.p. ind. in 1939 as theatre manager, then pub. dir.; dir. of Publ. Rank, 1946; joined Associated British-Pathe, Ltd. in same capacity; 1952 asst. to prod., Warwick Film Prod. Ltd. v.p. Highroad Productions, 1962-64. Rep. Europe Goldwyn's Porgy & Bess 1959.
PICTURES: April in Portugal, Heart of Variety, Invitation to Monte Carlo, The Secret Ways, Genghis Khan, Poppy Is Also a Flower, Murderer's Row, Shalako, Catlow, The Man Called Noon, Paper Tiger, The Wild Geese, The Sea Wolves, Who Dares Wins, Wild Geese II, The Final Option.

LLOYD, NORMAN
Actor, Producer, Director. b. Jersey City, NJ, Nov. 8, 1914. e. NYU, 1932. Acted on B'way in: Noah, Liberty Jones, Everywhere I Roam, 1935-44; in various stock companies. Joined Orson Welles and John Houseman in the original company of Mercury Theatre, NY, 1937-38. Prod. asst. on films Arch of Triumph, The Red Pony. Produced film Up Above the World.
THEATER: Village Green, King Lear, The Cocktail Party, The Lady's Not for Burning, Madame Will You Walk, The Golden Apple, Major Barbara, The Will & Bart Show, Quiet City. With La Jolla Playhouse (1948-55).
PICTURES: *Actor*: Saboteur, Spellbound, The Southerner, A Walk in the Sun, A Letter for Evie, The Unseen, Green Years, The Beginning or The End, Limelight, Young Widow, No Minor Vices, The Black Book, Scene of the Crime, Calamity Jane and Sam Bass, Buccaneer's Girl, The Flame and the Arrow,

He Ran All the Way, The Light Touch, Audrey Rose, FM, The Nude Bomb, Jaws of Satan, Dead Poets Society, Journey of Honor (Shogun Mayeda), The Age of Innocence.
TELEVISION: *Assoc. prod./exec. prod.*: The Alfred Hitchcock Show. *Prod.-Dir.*: The Alfred Hitchcock Hour, The Name of the Game, Hollywood Television Theater, Tales of the Unexpected, Omnibus (dir. of The Lincoln Films, 1952). *Actor.* St. Elsewhere (series). *Movies* (prod.-dir.): The Smugglers, Companions in Nightmare, What's a Nice Girl Like You (prod.), The Bravos (prod.), Amityville: The Evil Escapes.

LOACH, KEN
Director, Writer. b. Nuneaton, England, June 17, 1936. e. Oxford (studied law). Served in Royal Air Force; then became actor. Began dir. career on British tv in early 1960's.
PICTURES: Poor Cow (debut, 1968; also co-s.p.), Kes (also co-s.p.), Family Life, Black Jack (also co-s.p.), Looks and Smiles (also co- s.p.), Fatherland (Singing the Blues in Red), Hidden Agenda, Riff- Raff, Raining Stones, Land and Freedom.
TELEVISION: Diary of a Young Man, 3 Clear Sundays, The End of Arthur's Marriage, Up the Junction, Coming Out Party, Cathy Come Home, In Two Minds, The Golden Vision, The Big Flame, In Black and White, After a Lifetime, The Rank and the File, Days of Hope, The Price of Coal, Auditions: The Gamekeeper, A Question of Leadership, Which Side Are You On.

LOBELL, MICHAEL
Producer. b. Brooklyn, NY, May 7, 1941. e. Michigan State U. on athletic baseball scholarship. Worked briefly in garment indust. Entered film industry in 1974 by buying Danish distribution rights to The Apprenticeship of Duddy Kravitz. Formed Lobell/ Bergman Prods. with Andrew Bergman.
PICTURES: Dreamer, Windows, So Fine, The Journey of Natty Gann, Chances Are, The Freshman, White Fang, Honeymoon in Vegas, Undercover Blues, Little Big League, It Could Happen to You, Striptease.

Lo BIANCO, TONY
Actor. b. New York, NY. Oct. 19, 1936. Performed on N.Y. stage as well as in films and TV. Former artistic dir. Triangle Theatre, NY.
THEATER: Yanks 3—Detroit 0—Top of the Seventh (Obie Award), The Office, The Rose Tattoo, A View From the Bridge (Outer Critics Circle Award), The Royal Hunt of the Sun, Hizzoner, Other People's Money (tour).
PICTURES: The Honeymoon Killers (debut, 1970), The French Connection, The Seven Ups, Demon (God Told Me To), F.I.S.T., Bloodbrothers, Separate Ways, City Heat, Too Scared to Scream (dir. only), Mean Frankie and Crazy Tony, La Romana, City of Hope, The Spiders Web, Boiling Point, The Ascent, The Last Home Run (dir. only), The Juror.
TELEVISION: *Series*: Love of Life, Jessie, Palace Guard. *Guest*: Police Story. *Movies/Mini-Series*: Mr. Inside Mr. Outside, The Story of Joseph and Jacob, Magee and the Lady (She'll Be Sweet), Jesus of Nazareth, Hidden Faces, Legend of the Black Hand, Lady Blue, Marco Polo, Welcome Home Bobby, Blood Ties, A Last Cry for Help, Marciano, Another Woman's Child, The Last Tenant, Goldenrod, Shadow in the Streets, Eugene O'Neill's A Glory of Ghosts, Police Story: The Freeway Killings, The Ann Jillian Story, Body of Evidence, Off Duty, True Blue, Perry Mason: The Case of the Poisoned Pen, Malcolm Takes a Shot, In the Shadow of a Killer, Stormy Weathers, Teamster Boss: The Jackie Presser Story, The First Circle, The Maharajah's Daughter, Tyson. *Specials*: Hizzoner (Emmy Award), A Glory of Ghosts. *Director*: Police Story, Kaz, Cliffhangers, When the Whistle Blows, The Duke.

LOCKE, SONDRA
Actress, Director. b. Shelbyville, TN, May 28, 1947.
PICTURES: The Heart Is a Lonely Hunter (debut, 1968; Acad. Award nom.), Cover Me Babe, Willard, A Reflection of Fear, The Second Coming of Suzanne, Death Game (The Seducers), The Outlaw Josey Wales, The Gauntlet, Every Which Way But Loose, Bronco Billy, Any Which Way You Can, Sudden Impact, Ratboy (also dir.), Impulse (dir. only).
TELEVISION: *Movies*: Friendships, Secrets and Lies, Rosie: The Rosemary Clooney Story. *Guest*: Amazing Stories. *Director*: Death in Small Doses (movie).

LOCKHART, JUNE
Actress. b. New York, NY, June 25, 1925. p. actors, Gene and Kathleen Lockhart. B'way debut For Love or Money, 1947.
PICTURES: A Christmas Carol (debut, 1938), All This and Heaven Too, Adam Had Four Sons, Sergeant York, Miss Annie Rooney, Forever and a Day, White Cliffs of Dover, Meet Me in St. Louis, Son of Lassie, Keep Your Powder Dry, Easy to Wed, She-Wolf of London, Bury Me Dead, The Yearling, T-Men, It's a Joke Son, Time Limit, Butterfly, Deadly Games, Strange Invaders, Troll, Rented Lips, The Big Picture, Dead Women in Lingerie, Tis the Season, Sleep With Me.
TELEVISION: *Series*: Who Said That? (panelist), Lassie, Lost in Space, Petticoat Junction, General Hospital. *Movies*: But I

Don't Want to Get Married, The Bait, Who is the Black Dahlia?, Curse of the Black Widow, The Gift of Love, Walking Through the Fire, The Night They Saved Christmas, Perfect People, A Whisper Kills, Danger Island. *Mini-Series*: Loose Change.

LOCKLEAR, HEATHER
Actress. b. Los Angeles, CA, Sept. 25, 1961. e. UCLA. Appeared in commercials while in college.
PICTURES: Firestarter (debut, 1984), The Return of Swamp Thing, The Big Slice, Illusions, Wayne's World 2, The First Wives Club.
TELEVISION: *Series*: Dynasty, T.J. Hooker, Fright Night Videos (host), Going Places, Melrose Place. *Movies*: Return of the Beverly Hillbillies, Twirl, City Killer, Blood Sport, Rich Men Single Women, Jury Duty: The Comedy, Her Wicked Ways, Dynasty: The Reunion, Body Language, Highway Heartbreaker, Fade to Black, Texas Justice. *Specials*: Battle of the Network Stars, Hollywood Starr, TV Guide 40th Anniversary Special (host). *Guest*: Fantasy Island, The Fall Guy, Matt Houston, Hotel, The Love Boat.

LOCKWOOD, GARY
Actor. r.n. John Gary Yusolfsky. b. Van Nuys, CA, Feb. 21, 1937. Began in Hollywood as stuntman.
PICTURES: Tall Story, Splendor in the Grass, Wild in the Country, The Magic Sword, It Happened at the World's Fair, Firecreek, 2001: A Space Odyssey, They Came to Rob Las Vegas, Model Shop, The Body, R.P.M., Stand Up and Be Counted, The Wild Pair, Night of the Scarecrow.
TELEVISION: *Series*: Follow the Sun, The Lieutenant. *Movies*: Earth II, Manhunter, The FBI Story: The FBI Versus Alvin Karpus—Public Enemy, The Ghost of Flight 401, The Incredible Journey of Dr. Meg Laurel, Top of the Hill, The Girl The Gold Watch & Dynamite, Emergency Room.

LOCKWOOD, ROGER
Executive. b. Middletown, CT, June 7, 1936. e. Ohio Wesleyan U. Sports writer for Akron Beacon Journal, 1960-62. On executive staff of Lockwood & Gordon Theatres; exec. v.p. SBC Theatres, 1969-73. 1974 asst. to exec. v.p., General Cinema Corp. 1975 formed Lockwood/Friedman Theatres, buying-booking and exhibition organization. Pres., Theatre Owners of New England, 1971-72; pres., Young NATO 1965-67; bd. of dir. NATO, 1962-1968. Board of dir. Tone, 1968-present; pres., Jimmy Fund, present; 1979-80, Variety Club of New England, pres. Director, Dana-Farber Cancer Institute, 1983-present. 1988, formed Lockwood/McKinnon Company Inc. operating theatres and Taco Bell Restaurants.

LOEKS, BARRIE LAWSON
Executive. b. Pittsburgh, PA. e. Univ. of MI, Univ. of MI Law Sch., 1979. Began career as associate in Grand Rapids, MI, law firm of Warner Norcross & Judd before serving for 7 yrs. as v.p. and gen. counsel of Jack Loeks Theatres; promoted to pres. of Loeks Michigan Theatres & Loeks-Star joint venture, 1988; Nov. 1992 named co-chmn., with husband Jim Loeks, of Sony Theatres, a Sony Retail Entertainment Co.

LOEKS, JIM
Executive. b. Grand Rapids, MI. e. Univ. of MI. Started as gen. mgr. of John Ball Concessions Inc, becoming chmn. of bd. and owner, 1976-91. 1978, elected v.p. of Jack Loeks Theatres Inc.; named pres. of chain in 1983. 1988, became chmn. & co-owner of Loeks Michigan Theatres Inc., also gen. partner & operating agent of Loeks-Star joint venture with Sony Pictures Entertainment. Nov., 1992 named co-chmn., with wife Barrie Lawson Loeks, of Sony Theatres.

LOEKS, JOHN D. Jr.
Executive. b. E. Grand Rapids, MI, Feb 24, 1945. e. Wheaton Coll., B.A. 1967; Wayne State U., J.D. 1970. Began own law practice in 1970 until 1990. President, Showspan Inc., 1982-present. President, Jack Loeks Theatres Inc., 1990-present. Chmn., Ansable Institute of Environmental Studies; 1988-present, bd. member, Intervaristy Christian Fellowship; 1992-present, bd. of dirs., NATO.

LOESCH, MARGARET
Executive. e. U. of S. MS, B.A; grad. work at U. of New Orleans. President, Fox Children's Network.

LOGAN, JEFF
Exhibitor. b. Mitchell, SD, Dec. 29, 1950. e. Dakota Wesleyan U. & U. of SD. Started working in family's Roxy Theatre at 9 yrs. old. Worked as announcer on KORN radio, 1969-70. Announcer, reporter & photgrapher, KUSD-TV, 1970-71. Relief anchor, KXON-TV, 1972-78. Took over management of family theatre. Built co. into present circuit, Logan Luxury Theatres. Member, bd. of trustess, Dakota Wesleyan U., 1990-present; bd. of trustees, Queen of Peace Hospital, 1991-present. V.P., Variety Club of SD, 1994-96. Dir., NATO/North Central, 1980-90. V.P., VSDA of SD, 1989-present.

LOGGIA, ROBERT
Actor. b. New York, NY, Jan. 3, 1930. e. U. of Missouri, B.A. journalism, 1951. Studied with Stella Adler and at The Actors Studio. Broadway debut, The Man with the Golden Arm, 1955. THEATER: Toys in the Attic, The Three Sisters, In the Boom Boom Room, Wedding Band.
PICTURES: Somebody Up There Likes Me (debut, 1956), The Garment Jungle, Cop Hater, The Lost Missile, Cattle King, The Greatest Story Ever Told, Che, First Love, Speed Trap, Revenge of the Pink Panther, The Ninth Configuration (Twinkle Twinkle Killer Kane), S.O.B., An Officer and a Gentleman, Trail of the Pink Panther, Psycho II, Curse of the Pink Panther, Scarface, Prizzi's Honor, Jagged Edge (Acad. Award nom.), Armed and Dangerous, That's Life, Over the Top, Hot Pursuit, The Believers, Gaby: A True Story, Big, Oliver & Company (voice), Relentless, S.P.O.O.K.S. (Code Name: Chaos), Triumph of the Spirit, Opportunity Knocks, The Marrying Man, Necessary Roughness, Gladiator, Innocent Blood, The Last Tattoo, Bad Girls, I Love Trouble, Man With a Gun, Independence Day, Lost Highway.
TELEVISION: Series: T.H.E. Cat, Emerald Point N.A.S., Mancuso FBI, Sunday Dinner. Specials: Miss Julie, The Nine Lives of Elfego Baca, Conspiracy: The Trial of the Chicago 8, Merry Christmas Baby. Movies: Mallory: Circumstantial Evidence, Street Killing, Scott Free, Raid on Entebbe, No Other Love, Casino, A Woman Called Golda, A Touch of Scandal, Streets of Justice, Intrigue, Dream Breakers (The O'Connors), Afterburn, Lifepod, Nurses on the Line: The Crash of Flight 7, White Mile, Jake Lassiter: Justice on the Bayou, Between Love and Honor, Mercy Mission: The Rescue of Flight 771, Right to Remain Silent. Mini-Series: Arthur Hailey's The Moneychangers, Echoes in the Darkness, Favorite Son, Wild Palms.

LOLLOBRIGIDA, GINA
Actress. b. Subiaco, Italy, July 4, 1927. e. Acad. of Fine Arts, Rome. Film debut (Italy) L'aguila nera, 1946. Published several volumes of her photography incl. Italia Mia, The Wonder of Innocence.
PICTURES: Pagliacci, The City Defends Itself, The White Line, Fanfan the Tulip, Times Gone By, Beat the Devil, Crossed Swords, The Great Game, Beauties of the Night, Wayward Wife, Bread Love and Dreams, Bread Love and Jealousy, Young Caruso, World's Most Beautiful Woman, Trapeze, Hunchback of Notre Dame, Solomon and Sheba, Never So Few, The Unfaithfuls, Fast and Sexy, Where the Hot Wind Blows, Go Naked in the World, Come September, Imperial Venus, Woman of Straw, That Splendid November, Hotel Paradiso, Buona Sera Mrs. Campbell, Plucked, The Private Navy of Sgt. O'Farrell, Bad Man's River, King Queen Knave, The Lonely Woman, Bambole.
TELEVISION: Movie: Deceptions. Series: Falcon Crest.

LOMITA, SOLOMON
Executive. b. New York, NY, April 23, 1937. Started industry career with United Artists Corp. as follows: adm., intl. dept., 1962; asst., intl. sales, same year. 1963, asst. intl. print mgr.; 1965, intl. print mgr. 1973 appt. dir. of film services. 1981, v.p., film services. 1985 named v.p., post-prod., Orion Pictures; 1989-92; then sr. v.p. post-prod.

LONDON, BARRY
Executive. Joined Paramount Pictures 1971 in L.A. branch office as booker; later salesman. 1973, sls. mgr., Kansas City-St. Louis; 1974, branch mgr. Transferred to San Francisco, first as branch mgr.; later as district mgr. 1977, eastern div. mgr. in Washington, DC, 1978-81; western div. mgr. 1981, named v.p., gen. sls. mgr. 1983, advanced to sr. v.p., domestic distrib.1984, named pres., domestic div., for Motion Picture Group of Paramount; 1985, named pres., marketing and domestic distrib.; 1988, named pres. worldwide distrib., Motion Picture Group.

LONDON, JASON
Actor. b. San Diego, CA, 1973. Twin brother of actor Jeremy London. Raised in Oklahoma and Texas. Appeared in Aerosmith video Amazing.
PICTURES: The Man in the Moon (debut, 1991), December, Dazed and Confused, Safe Passage, To Wong Foo—Thanks for Everything—Julie Newmar, My Generation.
TELEVISION: Movie: A Matter of Justice. Guest: I'll Fly Away, Tales From the Crypt.

LONDON, JERRY
Director. b. Los Angeles, CA, Jan 21, 1937. Apprentice film editor, Desilu Prods., 1955; film ed., Daniel Boone, 1962; staged plays in local theater workshops; editor, assoc. prod., then dir. Hogan's Heroes. Formed Jerry London Prods., 1984.
PICTURE: Rent-a-Cop (feature debut, 1988).
TELEVISION: Series: Mary Tyler Moore Show, Love American Style, The Bob Newhart Show, Marcus Welby, M.D., Kojak, The Six Million Dollar Man, Police Story, Rockford Files. Mini-series: Wheels, Shogun (DGA, best dir., special award),

Chiefs (also sprv. prod.), Ellis Island (also sprv. prod.), If Tomorrow Comes, A Long Way From Home. Movies: Killdozer, McNaughton's Daughter, Cover Girls, Evening in Byzantium, Women in White, Father Figure, The Chicago Story, The Ordeal of Bill Carney (also prod.), The Gift of Life (also prod.), The Scarlet and the Black, Arthur Hailey's Hotel (also prod.), With Intent to Kill (exec. prod. only), Dark Mansions, Manhunt For Claude Dallas, Harry's Hong Kong, Family Sins (exec. prod. only), Macgruder and Loud (also prod.), Dadah Is Death (also prod.), Kiss Shot (also exec. prod.), The Haunting of Sarah Hardy (also exec. prod.), Vestige of Honor, A Season of Giants, Victim of Love, Grass Roots, Calendar Girl Cop Killer?: The Bambi Bembenek Story (also prod.), A Twist of the Knife, Labor of Love: The Arlette Schweitzer Story, A Mother's Gift.

LONDON, JULIE
Singer, Actress. r.n. Julie Peck. b. Santa Rosa, CA, Sept. 26, 1926. Launched as actress by agent Sue Carol (wife of Alan Ladd) who arranged screen test, followed by contract for 6 films. As singer has appeared in nightclubs and recorded.
PICTURES: Nabonga (Jungle Woman; debut, 1944), On Stage Everybody, Billy Rose's Diamond Horseshoe, Night in Paradise, The Red House, Tap Roots, Task Force, Return of the Frontiersman, The Fat Man, Fighting Chance, The Great Man, The Girl Can't Help It, Crime Against Joe, Drango, Saddle the Wind, Man of the West, Voice in the Mirror, A Question of Adultery, The Wonderful Country, Night of the Quarter Moon, The Third Voice, The George Raft Story.
TELEVISION: Series: Emergency. Guest: Perry Como Show, Steve Allen Show, Ed Sullivan Show. Movie: Emergency (pilot).

LONDON, MILTON H.
Executive. b. Detroit, MI, Jan. 12, 1916. e. U. of Michigan, B.A., 1937. Wayne U. Law Sch., 1938. U.S. Army 1943-46. Invented Ticograph system of positive admissions control for theatres, 1950; pres. Theatre Control Corp., 1950-62; secytreas. Co-op. Theas. of Michigan Inc., 1956-63; exec. comm., Council of M.P. Organizations, 1957-66; dir. M.P. Investors, 1960-67; exec. dir. Allied States Assoc. of M.P. Exhib., 1961-66; exec. dir. National Assoc. of Theatre Owners, 1966-69; pres., NATO of Michigan, 1954-74; Chief Barker, Variety Club of Detroit, Tent No. 5. 1975-76; Life Patron and Lifeliner, Variety Clubs International; trustee, Variety Club Charity for Children; chmn., Variety Club Myoelectric Center; dir., Motion Picture Pioneers; dir., Will Rogers Inst.; trustee, Detroit Inst. for Children; pres., Metropolitan Adv. Co.; Intl. ambassador, Variety Clubs Int'l; Detroit News 1991 Michiganian of the Year.

LONE, JOHN
Actor. b. Hong Kong. Studied at Chin Ciu Academy of the Peking Opera in Hong Kong, Moved to LA where he studied acting at Pasadena's American Acad. of Dramatic Art, becoming member of the East-West Players.
THEATER: F.O.B., The Dance and the Railroad (Obie Awards for both plays), Paper Angels (dir.), Sound and Beauty (also dir.).
PICTURES: Iceman (debut, 1984), Year of the Dragon, The Last Emperor, The Moderns, Echoes of Paradise, Shadow of China, Shanghai 1920, M. Butterfly, The Shadow, The Hunted.
TELEVISION: The Dance and the Railroad, Paper Angels (dir.).

LONG, SHELLEY
Actress. b. Ft. Wayne, IN, Aug. 23, 1949. e. Northwestern U. Was co-host, assoc. prod. of local tv show Sorting It Out.
PICTURES: A Small Circle of Friends (debut, 1980), Caveman, Night Shift, Losin' It, Irreconcilable Differences, The Money Pit, Outrageous Fortune, Hello Again, Troop Beverly Hills, Don't Tell Her It's Me, Frozen Assets, The Brady Bunch Movie, A Very Brady Sequel.
TELEVISION: Series: Cheers (Emmy Award, 1983), Good Advice. Movies: The Cracker Factory, Princess and the Cabbie, Promise of Love, Voices Within: The Lives of Truddi Chase, Fatal Memories, A Message From Holly, The Women of Spring Break, Freaky Friday. Special: Basic Values: Sex Shock & Censorship in the '90's.

LONGSTREET, STEPHEN
Writer, Painter. b. New York, NY, April 18, 1907. e. Rutgers U.; Parsons Coll.; Rand Sch., London, B.A. Humorist, cartoonist (New Yorker, Collier's, etc.) 1930-37; ed. Free World Theatre, radio plays; edit. film critic, Saturday Review of Literature, 1940, U.S. at War, Time 1942-43. On staff UCLA. Elected pres. Los Angeles Art Assoc. 1970. 1973, joined USC as prof. Film and book critic for Readers' Syndicate starting in 1970.
AUTHOR: Decade, Last Man Around the World, Chico Goes to the Wars, Pedlocks, Lion at Morning, Promoters, Sometimes I Wonder (with Hoagy Carmichael), Wind at My Back (with Pat O'Brien), Goodness Had Nothing to Do With It (with Mae West), The Young Men of Paris, The Wilder Shore, War Cries on Horseback, Yoshiwara, Geishas and Courtesans, Canvas

Falcons, Men and Planes of World War I, We All Went to Paris. Chicago 1860-1919 (show business & society), Divorcing (a novel), The General (novel), All Star Cast (Hollywood), The Queen Bees, Our Father's House, Storyville to Harlem, Dictionary of Jazz, Dreams that Swallowed the World: The Movies, Jazz Solos (poems & images), My Three Nobel Prizes, Life With Faulkner/Hemingway/Lewis.
THEATER: High Button Shoes (book, revived in Jerome Robbins' Broadway, 1989).
PICTURES: The Gay Sisters, Golden Touch, Stallion Road, The Jolson Story, Silver River, Helen Morgan Story, The First Traveling Saleslady, Untamed Youth, The Crime, Uncle Harry, Rider on a Dead Horse, The Imposter.
TELEVISION: Casey Jones (series), Clipper Ship (Playhouse 90), Man Called X, The Sea, Press & Clergy, Viewpoint, Boy in the Model T, John Kennedy Young Man From Boston, Blue and the Grey.

LONSDALE, PAMELA
Producer and Executive Producer for Children's drama, Thames TV for 15 years. Now freelance. Prod. short feature film, Exploits at West Poley (for CFTF), Prod.: News at Twelve (Central TV comedy series). Exec. prod. for E.B.U.'s world drama exchange for 2 years. Winner British Acad. Award for Rainbow, 1975.

LORD, JACK
Actor, Writer, Artist, Director, Producer. r.n. John Ryan. b. New York, NY, Dec. 30, 1930. e. NYU. (Chancellor Chase scholarship), B.S., Fine Arts, 1954. Studied at Sanford Meisner's Neighborhood Playhouse and with Lee Strasberg at the Actors Studio. Made film debut 1949 under his real name. Artist, represented in various museums worldwide. Received Fame Award as new male star, 1963. Awards: St. Gauden's Artist Award, G. Washington Honor Medal from Freedom Foundation at Valley Forge, Veterans Admin., Administrator's Award, East-West Center Distinguished Service Award. Author: Jack Lord's Hawaii...A Trip Through the Last Eden, 1971. Pres., Lord and Lady Enterprises, Inc. Appeared in Williamsburg documentary Story of a Patriot.
THEATER: B'way: Traveling Lady (Theatre World Award, 1959), Cat on a Hot Tin Roof.
PICTURES: The Red Menace (debut, 1949), Project X, Cry Murder, The Tattooed Stranger, The Court Martial of Billy Mitchell, Tip on a Dead Jockey, God's Little Acre, Man of the West, The Hangman, True Story of Lynn Stuart, Walk Like a Dragon, Dr. No, Ride to Hangman's Tree, The Counterfeit Killer, The Name of the Game Is Kill.
TELEVISION: Series: Stoney Burke (1962-63), Hawaii Five-O (1968-79; also dir. episodes), creator of Tramp Ship, McAdoo, Yankee Trader, The Hunter TV series. Guest: Man Against Crime (debut), Playhouse 90, Goodyear Playhouse, Studio One, U.S. Steel. Have Gun Will Travel (pilot), Untouchables, Naked City, Rawhide, Bonanza, The Americans, Route 66, Gunsmoke, Stagecoach West, Dr. Kildare, Greatest Show on Earth, Combat, Chrysler Theatre, 12 O'Clock High, The Loner, Laredo, The FBI, The Invaders, The Fugitive, The Virginian, Man from U.N.C.L.E., High Chaparral, Ironside. Movie: Doomsday Flight. Director: Death with Father, How to Steal a Masterpiece, Honor Is an Unmarked Grave, The Bells Toll at Noon, Top of the World, Why Won't Linda Die, Who Says Cops Don't Cry; episodes of Hawaii Five-O. Special: M Station: Hawaii (creator, dir., exec. prod.).

LOREN, SOPHIA
Actress. b. Rome, Italy, Sept. 20, 1934. e. Naples. m. producer Carlo Ponti. Autobiography: Sophia: Living and Loving (with A.E. Hotchner, 1979).
PICTURES: Africa Beneath the Seas, Village of the Bells, Good People's Sunday, Neapolitan Carousel, Day in the District Court, Pilgrim of Love, Aida, Two Nights with Cleopatra, Our Times, Attila, Scourge of God, Gold of Naples, Too Bad She's Bad, Scandal in Sorrento, Miller's Beautiful Wife, Lucky to Be a Woman, Boy on a Dolphin (U.S. debut, 1957), The Pride and the Passion, Legend of the Lost, Desire Under the Elms, The Key, Houseboat, The Black Orchid, That Kind of Woman, Heller in Pink Tights, It Started in Naples, A Breath of Scandal, The Millionairess, Two Women (Academy Award, 1961), El Cid, Boccaccio 70, Madame Sans-Gene, Five Miles to Midnight, The Condemned of Altona, Yesterday Today and Tomorrow, The Fall of the Roman Empire, Marriage Italian Style, Operation Crossbow, Lady L, Judith, Arabesque, A Countess from Hong Kong, More than a Miracle, Ghosts—Italian Style, Sunflower, The Priest's Wife, Lady Liberty, White Sister, Man of La Mancha, The Voyage, The Verdict (Jury of One), The Cassandra Crossing, A Special Day, Angela, Brass Target, Firepower, Blood Feud (Revenge), Ready to Wear (Pret-a-Porter), Grumpier Old Men.
TELEVISION: Movies/Specials: Brief Encounter, Sophia Loren—Her Own Story, Softly Softly, Rivals of Sherlock Holmes, Fantasy Island, Aurora, Courage, Mario Puzo's The Fortunate Pilgrim.

LOUDON, DOROTHY
Actress. b. Boston, MA, Sept. 17, 1933.
THEATER: B'way: Nowhere to Go But Up (Theatre World Award), The Fig Leaves Are Falling, Sweet Potato, Three Men on a Horse, The Women, Annie (Tony Award, 1977), Ballroom, Sweeney Todd, West Side Waltz, Noises Off, Jerry's Girls, Comedy Tonight. Off-B'way: The Matchmaker. Regional: Driving Miss Daisy, Love Letters.
PICTURE: Garbo Talks.
TELEVISION: Series: It's a Business?, Laugh Line, The Garry Moore Show, Dorothy, The Thorns (sang opening song). Specials: Many appearances on the Tony Awards; also Carnegie Hall Salutes Stephen Sondheim.

LOUGHLIN, LORI
Actress. b. Long Island, NY, July 28, 1964. Started modeling at age 7 for catalogues, then tv commercials. First professional acting job at 18 as regular on daytime serial The Edge of Night.
THEATER: Grease.
PICTURES: Amityville 3-D (debut, 1983), The New Kids, Secret Admirer, Back to the Beach, The Night Before.
TELEVISION: Series: The Edge of Night, Full House, Hudson Street. Movies: North Beach and Rawhide, Brotherhood of Justice, A Place to Call Home, Doing Time on Maple Drive, A Stranger in the Mirror, Empty Cradle, One of Her Own, Abandoned and Deceived.

LOUIS-DREYFUS, JULIA
Actress. b. New York, NY, Jan. 13, 1961. e. Northwestern Univ. Member of Second City comedy troupe which resulted in casting on Saturday Night Live.
PICTURES: Troll (debut, 1986), Hannah and Her Sisters, Soul Man, National Lampoon's Christmas Vacation, Jack the Bear, North.
TELEVISION: Series: Saturday Night Live (1982-85), Day by Day, Seinfeld (Emmy Award, 1996). Specials: The Art of Being Nick, Spy Magazine's Hit List (host), Sesame Street's All-Star 25th Birthday.

LOUISE, TINA
Actress. r.n. Tina Blacker. b. New York, NY, Feb. 11. e. Miami U., N.Y. Neighborhood Playhouse, Actors Studio.
THEATER: Two's Company, The Fifth Season, John Murray Anderson's Almanac, Li'l Abner, Fade Out Fade In, Come Back to the 5 and Dime Jimmy Dean Jimmy Dean.
PICTURES: God's Little Acre (debut), The Trap, The Hangman, Day of the Outlaw, The Warrior Empress, Siege of Syracuse, Armored Command, For Those Who Think Young, The Wrecking Crew, The Good Guys and the Bad Guys, How to Commit Marriage, The Happy Ending, The Stepford Wives, Mean Dog Blues, Dogsday, Hellriders, Evils of the Night, O.C. and Stiggs, Dixie Lanes, The Pool, Johnny Suede.
TELEVISION: Series: Jan Murray Time, Gilligan's Island, Dallas, Rituals. Guest: Mannix, Ironside, Kung Fu, Police Story, Kojak, Roseanne. Movies: But I Don't Want to Get Married, A Call to Danger, Death Scream, Look What's Happened to Rosemary's Baby, Nightmare in Badham Country, SST—Death Flight, Friendships Secrets and Lies, The Day the Women Got Even, Advice to the Lovelorn, The Woman Who Cried Murder.

LOVITZ, JON
Actor, Comedian. b. Tarzana, CA, July 21, 1957. e. U. of California at Irvine. Studied acting at Film Actors Workshop. Took classes at the Groundlings, L.A. comedy improvisation studio, 1982. Performed with Groundling's Sunday Company, before joining main company in Chick Hazzard: Olympic Trials. Developed comedy character of pathological liar which he later performed when he became regular member of Saturday Night Live in 1985.
PICTURES: The Last Resort, Ratboy, Jumpin' Jack Flash, Three Amigos, Big, My Stepmother Is an Alien, The Brave Little Toaster (voice), Mr. Destiny, An American Tail: Fievel Goes West (voice), A League of Their Own, Mom and Dad Save the World, National Lampoon's Loaded Weapon 1, Coneheads, City Slickers II: The Legend of Curly's Gold, North, Trapped in Paradise, The Great White Hype, High School High.
TELEVISION: Series: Foley Square, Saturday Night Live (1985-90), The Critic (voice). Special: The Please Watch the Jon Lovitz Special. Guest: The Paper Chase.

LOWE, CHAD
Actor. b. Dayton, OH, Jan. 15, 1968. Brother is actor Rob Lowe. Stage debut in L.A. production of Blue Denim. On NY stage in Grotesque Love Songs.
PICTURES: Oxford Blues (debut, 1984), Apprentice to Murder, True Blood, Nobody's Perfect, Highway to Hell.
TELEVISION: Movies: Silence of the Heart, There Must Be a Pony, April Morning, So Proudly We Hail, An Inconvenient Woman, Captive, Candles in the Dark, Fighting for My Daughter. Series: Spencer, Life Goes On (Emmy Award, 1993). Special: No Means No (Emmy nom.).

LOWE, PHILIP L.
Executive. b. Brookline, MA, Apr. 17, 1917. e. Harvard. Army 1943-46. Checker, Loew's 1937-39; treasurer, Theatre Candy Co., 1941-58; Pres., ITT Sheraton Corp., 1969-70; Principal, Philip L. Lowe and Assoc.

LOWE, PHILIP M.
Executive. b. New Rochelle, NY, May 9, 1944. e. Deerfield Acad., Harvard Coll., cum laude in psychology, 1966; Columbia Business Sch., 1968. Work experience includes major marketing positions at General Foods, Gillette, Gray Advertising, and Estee Lauder Cosmetics before co-founding Cinema Centers Corp. and Theatre Management Services in Boston. Pres. of Lowe Group of Companies (cable television, broadcasting, hotels, real estate and management consulting). Past pres. and chmn. of the bd; National Association of Concessionaires (NAC); past director, National Association of Theater Owners (NATO). Professor of Marketing, Bentley Coll., Waltham, MA.; Contributing Editor; The Movie Business Book, Prentice-Hall, Inc. 1983.

LOWE, ROB
Actor. b. Charlottesville, VA, Mar. 17, 1964. Raised in Dayton, OH. Started acting as child appearing in commercials, local tv spots, summer stock. Family moved to Malibu when he was 12 yrs. old. Job in Coca Cola commercial was followed by role on series A New Kind of Family. Made B'way debut 1992 in A Little Hotel on the Side. Brother is actor Chad Lowe.
PICTURES: The Outsiders (debut, 1983), Class, The Hotel New Hampshire, Oxford Blues, St. Elmo's Fire, Youngblood, About Last Night..., Square Dance, Masquerade, Illegally Yours, Bad Influence, Stroke of Midnight (If the Shoe Fits), The Dark Backward, Wayne's World, The Finest Hour, Tommy Boy, Mulholland Falls.
TELEVISION: Series: A New Kind of Family. Movies: Thursday's Child, Frank and Jesse (also co-prod.), First Degree. Mini-Series: Stephen King's The Stand. Specials: A Matter of Time, Schoolboy Father, Suddenly Last Summer.

LOWRY, DICK
Director. b. Oklahoma City, OK. e. U. of Oklahoma. Commercial photographer before being accepted by AFI. Dir. short film The Drought.
PICTURE: Smokey and the Bandit Part 3.
TELEVISION: Mini-Series: Dream West. Movies: OHMS, Kenny Rogers as the Gambler, The Jayne Mansfield Story, Angel Dusted, Coward of the County, A Few Days in Weasel Creek, Rascals and Robbers: The Secret Adventures of Tom Sawyer and Huck Finn, Missing Children—A Mother's Story, Living Proof: The Hank Williams Jr. Story, Kenny Rogers as the Gambler—The Adventure Continues (also prod.), Off Sides (Pigs Vs. Freaks), Wet Gold, The Toughest Man in the World, Murder with Mirrors, American Harvest, Kenny Rogers as The Gambler III (also co-exec. prod.), Case Closed, In the Line of Duty: The FBI Murders, Unconquered (also prod.), Howard Beach: Making the Case For Murder, Miracle Landing (also prod.), Archie: To Riverdale and Back, In the Line of Duty: A Cop for the Killing (also prod.), In the Line of Duty: Manhunt in the Dakotas (also prod.), A Woman Scorned: The Betty Broderick Story (also co-prod.), In the Line of Duty: Ambush in Waco (also prod.), In the Line of Duty: The Price of Vengeance, One More Mountain, A Horse for Danny, In The Line of Duty: Hunt for Justice (also prod.), Forgotten Sins, Project Alf, In The Line of Duty: Smoke Jumpers (also prod.).

LOWRY, HUNT
Producer. b. Oklahoma City, OK, Aug. 21, 1954. e. Rollins Coll., & Wake Forest. Abandoned plans to study medicine to enter film-making industry; first job for New World Pictures where he met Jon Davison, with whom was later to co-produce. Next made TV commercials as prod. asst. and then producer. Left to go freelance as commercials producer. 1980, appt. assoc. prod. to Davison on Airplane!
PICTURES: Humanoids from the Deep, Get Crazy, Top Secret!, Revenge, Career Opportunities, Only the Lonely, Last of the Mohicans, Striking Distance, My Life, First Knight, A Time to Kill.
TELEVISION: Movies (exec. prod.): Rascals and Robbers: The Secret Adventures of Tom Sawyer and Huckleberry Finn, Baja Oklahoma. Movies (prod.): His Mistress, Surviving, Wild Horses. Mini-Series: Dream West (prod.).

LUBCKE, HARRY R.
Registered Patent Agent. b. Alameda, CA, Aug. 25, 1905. e. U. of California, B.S., 1929. Holds numerous U.S. and foreign patents on television. In 1931: station W6XAO went on air on what is now television Channel No. 2 to become first station of kind in nation. Built Mt. Lee studios 1941 housing then largest TV stage. Pioneered present television standard of 525 line (Aug., 1940). 1942, television programs to promote war bond sale. 1942-46 dir. war research for which certificates of commendation were received from Army & Navy.

LUCAS, GEORGE
Producer, Director, Writer. b. Modesto, CA, May 14, 1944. e. USC, cinema. Made short film called THX-1138 and won National Student Film Festival Grand Prize, 1967. Signed contract with WB. Ass't. to Francis Ford Coppola on The Rain People, during which Lucas made 2-hr. documentary on filming of that feature entitled Filmmaker. Appeared as actor in film Beverly Hills Cop III. Novel: Shadow Moon (1995). Pres., Lucas Films, Industrial Light & Magic.
PICTURES: Director/Writer: THX-1138, American Graffiti, Star Wars. Executive Producer: More American Graffiti, The Empire Strikes Back (also story), Raiders of the Lost Ark (also co-story), Return of the Jedi (also co-s.p., story), Twice Upon a Time, Indiana Jones and the Temple of Doom (also story), Mishima, Labyrinth, Howard the Duck, Willow (also story), Tucker: The Man and His Dream, The Land Before Time, Indiana Jones and the Last Crusade (also co-story), Radioland Murders (also story).
TELEVISION: Exec. Prod.: The Ewok Adventure (movie), Ewoks: The Battle for Endor (movie); The Young Indiana Jones Chronicles (series).

LUCCHESI, GARY
Executive. b. San Francisco, CA, 1955. e. UCLA. Entered industry as a trainee with the William Morris Agency, 1977. Joined Tri-Star, 1983, as vice pres. of production, became sr. vice pres., 1985. Joined Paramount Pictures as exec. vice pres., April 1987; pres. of motion picture production division, 1987-92. Pres. of the Really Useful Film Company, Inc., 1994-present.
PICTURES: Producer: Jennifer Eight, Three Wishes, Virtuosity, Primal Fear.

LUCCI, SUSAN
Actress. b. Scarsdale, NY, Feb. 23, 1948. e. Marymount Col. Was semifinalist in NY State Miss Universe Pageant. First professional job as "color girl" for CBS, sitting for cameras as new lighting system for color tv was developed. Had bit parts in films Me Natalie and Goodbye Columbus. Performed on 1983 album Love in the Afternoon.
PICTURES: Daddy You Kill Me, Young Doctors in Love (cameo).
TELEVISION: Series: All My Children (1970-). Movies: Invitation to Hell, Mafia Princess, Anastasia: The Story of Anna, Haunted By Her Past, Lady Mobster, The Bride in Black, The Woman Who Sinned, Double Edge, Between Love and Hate, French Silk, Seduced and Betrayed.

LUCKINBILL, LAURENCE
Actor. b. Fort Smith, AR, Nov. 21, 1934. m. actress Lucie Arnaz. e. U. of Arkansas, Catholic U. of America.
THEATER: NY: A Man for All Seasons, Arms and the Man, The Boys in the Band, Alpha Beta, The Shadow Box, Poor Murderer, Chapter Two, Past Tense.
PICTURES: The Boys in the Band, Such Good Friends, The Promise, Not for Publication, Cocktail, Messenger of Death, Star Trek V: The Final Frontier.
TELEVISION: Series: The Secret Storm, Where the Heart Is, The Delphi Bureau. Movies: The Delphi Bureau (pilot), Death Sentence, Panic on the 5:22, Winner Take All, The Lindbergh Kidnapping Case, The Mating Season, To Heal a Nation. Mini-Series: Ike. Specials: Lyndon Johnson (one-man show), Voices and Visions (narrator), The 5:48, Lucy & Desi: A Home Movie (co-exec. prod., co-dir., writer).

LUDDY, TOM
Producer. e. U. of California at Berkeley where he operated student film societies and rep. cinemas. Entered industry via Brandon Films. 1972, prog. dir. and curator of Pacific Film Archives. 1979, joined Zoetrope Studios as dir. of special projects where dev. and supervised revival of Gance's Napoleon and Our Hitler—A Film From Germany. Coordinated Koyaanis-qatsi, Every Man For Himself, Passion. A founder, Telluride Film Fest. Served on selection comm., N.Y. and pres. San Francisco Film Fest.
PICTURES: Mishima (co-prod.), Tough Guys Don't Dance (co-exec. prod.), Barfly, King Lear (assoc. prod.), Manifesto (exec. prod.), Powwaqatsi (assoc. prod.), Wait Until Spring Bandini, Wind, The Secret Garden (co-prod.).

LUDWIG, IRVING H.
Executive. b. Nov. 3. Rivoli Theatre, N.Y., mgr., theatre oper., Rugoff and Becker, 1938-39; opened first modern art type theatre, Greenwich Village, 1940. With Walt Disney Prod. in charge of theatre oper. on Fantasia, 1940-41; buyer-booker, Rugoff and Becker, 1942-45; film sales admin., Walt Disney Prod. home office, 1945-53; v.p. and domestic sales mgr., Buena Vista Dist. Co., 1953; pres. sales & mktg., 1959-80. Member of bd. of dirs., Will Rogers Memorial Fund, Foundation of M.P. Pioneers; Motion Picture Club; Academy of M.P. Arts & Sciences.

LUEDTKE, KURT
Writer. b. Grand Rapids, MI, Sept. 29, 1938. e. Brown U., B.A., 1961. Reporter Grand Rapids Press 1961-62. Miami Herald, 1963-65; Detroit Free Press (reporter, asst. photography dir., asst. mgr. ed., asst. exec. ed., exec. ed. 1965-78.).
PICTURES: Absence of Malice, Out of Africa (Academy Award, 1985), Walls.

LUFT, LORNA
Actress, Singer. b. Hollywood, CA, Nov. 21, 1952. Daughter of actress-singer Judy Garland and producer Sid Luft. Has sung in nightclubs. Appeared on 1990 recording of Girl Crazy.
THEATER: NY: Judy Garland at Home at the Palace, Promises Promises, Snoopy, Extremities. Tours: They're Playing Our Song, Grease, Little Shop of Horrors, Jerry Herman's Broadway, The Unsinkable Molly Brown, Guys and Dolls.
PICTURES: I Could Go on Singing (extra, unbilled), Grease 2, Where the Boys Are.
TELEVISION: Series: Trapper John. Movie: Fear Stalk. Guest: Twilight Zone, Hooperman, Murder She Wrote, Tales from the Dark Side, The Cosby Show.

LUKE, PETER
Writer, Director. b. England, Aug. 12, 1919. Autobiography: Sisyphus & Reilly.
THEATER: Hadrian VII, Bloomsbury.
TELEVISION: Writer: Small Fish Are Sweet, Pigs Ear with Flowers, Roll on Bloomin' Death, A Man on Her Back (with William Sansom), Devil a Monk Won't Be, Anach 'Cuan (also dir.), Black Sound—Deep Song (also dir.).

LUMET, SIDNEY
Director. b. Philadelphia, PA, June 25, 1924. e. Professional Children's Sch.; Columbia U. Child actor in plays: Dead End, George Washington Slept Here, My Heart's in the Highlands, and films: The 400 Million, One Third of a Nation. U.S. Armed Forces, WWII, 1942-46; dir. summer stock, 1947-49; taught acting, H.S. of Prof. Arts. Assoc. dir. CBS, 1950, dir. 1951. Appeared in documentary Listen Up: The Lives of Quincy Jones. Author: Making Movies (Alfred A. Knopf, 1995).
PICTURES: 12 Angry Men (debut, 1957), Stage Struck, That Kind of Woman, The Fugitive Kind, A View From the Bridge, Long Day's Journey Into Night, Fail-Safe, The Pawnbroker, The Hill, The Group, The Deadly Affair (also prod.), Bye Bye Braverman (also prod.), The Sea Gull (also prod.), The Appointment, The Last of the Mobile Hotshots (also prod.), King: A Filmed Record ... Montgomery to Memphis (co-dir., prod.), The Anderson Tapes, Child's Play, The Offence, Serpico, Lovin' Molly, Murder on the Orient Express, Dog Day Afternoon (also co-prod.), Network, Equus, The Wiz, Just Tell Me What You Want (also co-prod.), Prince of the City (also co-s.p.), Deathtrap, The Verdict, Daniel (also co-exec. prod.), Garbo Talks, Power, The Morning After, Running on Empty, Family Business, Q & A (also s.p.), A Stranger Among Us, Guilty As Sin, Night Falls On Manhattan (also s.p.).
TELEVISION: Series episodes: Mama, Danger, You Are There, Omnibus, Best of Broadway, Alcoa, Goodyear Playhouse, Kraft Television Theatre (Mooney's Kid Don't Cry, The Last of My Gold Watches, This Property is Condemned), Playhouse 90, Play of the Week (The Dybbuk, Rashomon, The Iceman Cometh—Emmy Award). Specials: The Sacco and Vanzetti Story, John Brown's Raid, Cry Vengeance.

LUNDGREN, DOLPH
Actor. b. Stockholm, Sweden, Nov. 3, 1959. e. Washington State U., won Fulbright to Massachusetts Inst. of Technology, Royal Inst. of Technology, Stockholm, M.S.C. Was doorman at Limelight disco in NY while studying acting. Full Contact Karate champion. Made workout video, Maximum Potential. On stage in Another Octopus.
PICTURES: A View to a Kill, Rocky IV, Masters of the Universe, Red Scorpion, The Punisher, I Come in Peace, Cover-Up, Showdown in Little Tokyo, Universal Soldier, Army of One, Pentathlon, Men of War, Johnny Mnemonic, The Shooter, The Algonquin Goodbye.

LUPONE, PATTI
Actress. b. Northport, NY, Apr. 21, 1949. e. Juilliard.
THEATER: School for Scandal, Three Sisters, The Beggars Opera, The Robber Bridegroom, Meaure for Measure, Edward II, The Water Engine, Working, Evita (Tony Award, 1980), Oliver!, Anything Goes, Les Miserables (London), Sunset Boulevard (London), Master Class.
PICTURES: 1941, Fighting Back, Witness, Wise Guys, Driving Miss Daisy, Family Prayers.
TELEVISION: Series: Life Goes On. Movies: LBJ: The Early Years, The Water Engine.

LYDON, JAMES
Actor. b. Harrington Park, NJ, May 30, 1923; e. St. Johns Mil. Sch. On N.Y. stage in Prologue to Glory, Sing Out the News. For 20th Century Fox tv was assoc. prod. of series Anna and the King, Roll Out. Prod./Writer/Dir. of special The Incredible 20th Century. Dir. for Universal TV: 6 Million Dollar Man, Simon & Simon, Beggarman Thief.
PICTURES: Actor: Back Door to Heaven (debut, 1939), Two Thoroughbreds, Racing Luck, Tom Brown's Schooldays, Little Men, Naval Academy, Bowery Boy, Henry Aldrich for President, Cadets on Parade, The Mad Martindales, Star Spangled Rhythm, Henry Aldrich— Editor, Henry Aldrich Gets Glamour, Henry Aldrich Swings It, Henry Aldrich Haunts a House, Henry Aldrich Plays Cupid, Aerial Gunner, Henry Aldrich—Boy Scout, My Best Gal, The Town Went Wild, Henry Aldrich's Little Secret, When the Lights Go on Again, Out of the Night, Twice Blessed, The Affairs of Geraldine, Life With Father, Cynthia, Sweet Genevieve, The Time of Your Life, Out of the Storm, Joan of Arc, An Old-Fashioned Girl, Bad Boy, Miss Mink of 1949, Tucson, Gasoline Alley, Tarnished, When Willie Comes Marching Home, Destination Big House, Hot Rod, September Affair, The Magnificent Yankee, Island in the Sky, The Desperado, Battle Stations, Chain of Evidence, The Hypnotic Eye, I Passed for White, The Last Time I Saw Archie, Brainstorm, Death of a Gunfighter, Scandalous John, Bonnie's Kids, Vigilante Force. Assoc. Prod.: My Blood Runs Cold, An American Dream, A Covenant With Death, First to Fight, The Cool Ones, Chubasco, Countdown, Assignment to Kill, The Learning Tree.
TELEVISION: Guest: Frontier Circus (also assoc. prod.). Co-ordin. Prod.: Wagon Train, Alfred Hitchcock Hour. Assoc. Prod.: McHale's Navy, 77 Sunset Strip, Mr. Roberts. Series (actor): So This Is Hollywood, The First Hundred Years, Love That Jill. Movies: Ellery Queen, The New Daughters of Joshua Cabe, Peter Lundy and the Medicine Hat Stallion.

LYLES, A. C.
Producer. b. Jacksonville, FL. May 17, 1918. e. Andrew Jackson H.S. Paramount Publix's Florida Theatre, 1928; interviewed Hollywood celebrities, Jacksonville Journal, 1932; mail boy, Paramount Studios, Hollywood, 1937; publicity dept., 1938; hd. of adv., publ. dept., Pine-Thomas unit at Paramount, 1940; assoc. prod., The Mountain. President, A. C. Lyles Productions, Inc. (Paramount Pictures).
PICTURES: Short Cut to Hell, Raymie, The Young and the Brave, Law of the Lawless, Stage to Thunder Rock, Young Fury, Black Spurs, Hostile Guns, Arizona Bushwackers, Town Tamer, Apache Uprising, Johnny Reno, Waco, Red Tomahawk, Fort Utah, Buckskin, Rogue's Gallery, Night of the Lepus, The Last Day, Flight to Holocaust.
TELEVISION: Rawhide (series; assoc. prod.), A Christmas for Boomer, Here's Boomer (series), Dear Mr. President, Conversations With the Presidents.

LYNCH, DAVID
Director, Writer. b. Missoula, MT, Jan. 20, 1946. e. Pennsylvania Acad. of Fine Arts, where received an independent filmmaker grant from America Film Institute. Made 16mm film, The Grandmother. Accepted by Center for Advanced Film Studies in Los Angeles, 1970. Wrote and directed Eraserhead (with partial AFI financing). Acted in films Zelly & Me, Nadja (also exec. prod.).
PICTURES: Director-Writer: Eraserhead (also prod., edit., prod.-design, f/x), The Elephant Man, Dune, Blue Velvet, Wild at Heart, Twin Peaks: Fire Walk With Me (also co-exec. prod., actor), Crumb (presenter).
TELEVISION: Series: Twin Peaks (dir., exec. prod., writer), On the Air (exec. prod., dir., writer). Special: Hotel Room (co-dir., co-exec. prod.).

LYNCH, KELLY
Actress. b. Minneapolis, MN, 1959. Former model.
PICTURES: Osa, Bright Lights Big City, Cocktail, Road House, Warm Summer Rain, Drugstore Cowboy, Desperate Hours, Curly Sue, For Better and For Worse, Three of Hearts, Imaginary Crimes, The Beans of Egypt Maine, Virtuosity, White Man's Burden.
TELEVISION: Guest: Miami Vice, The Equalizer, Spenser for Hire, The Hitcher, The Edge (Black Pudding). Movie: Something in Common. Pilot: San Berdoo.

LYNCH, PAUL M.
Director.
PICTURES: Hard Part Begins, Blood and Guts, Prom Night, Cross Country, Flying, Blindside, Bullies.
TELEVISION: Series: Voyagers, Blacke's Magic, Murder She Wrote, In the Heat of the Night, Tour of Duty, Beauty and the Beast, Twilight Zone (1987), Moonlighting, Star Trek: The Next Generation, Dark Shadows, Tour of Duty, Top Cops, Mike Hammer, Hooperman, Bronx Zoo. Movies: Cameo By Night, Going to the Chapel, She Knows Too Much, Murder by Night, Drop Dead Gorgeous.

LYNCH, RICHARD
Actor. b. Brooklyn, NY, Feb. 12. Made B'way debut in The Devils, both on and off B'way. Also in Live Like Pigs, The Orphan, The Basic Training of Pavlo Hummel, The Lady From the Sea, Arturo-U, Lion in Winter.
PICTURES: Scarecrow (debut, 1973), The Seven Ups, The Delta Fox, The Premonition, Steel, The Formula, The Sword and the Sorcerer, Savage Dawn, Invasion U.S.A., Cut and Run, Night Force, The Barbarians, Little Nikita, Bad Dreams, Melanie Rose (High Stakes), Spirit, Aftershock, Return to Justice, One Man Force, The Forbidden Dance, October 32nd, Alligator II: The Mutation, Double Threat, H.P. Lovecraft's Necromonicon, Scanner Cop, Crime & Punishment.

TELEVISION: *Series*: Battlestar Gallactica, The Phoenix. *Movies*: Starsky and Hutch (pilot), Roger & Harry: The Mitera Target, Good Against Evil, Dog and Cat, Vampire, Alcatraz—The Whole Shocking Story, Sizzle, White Water Rebels, The Last Ninja.

LYNDON, VICTOR
Producer, Writer. b. London. e. St. Paul's. Ent. m.p. ind. 1942 as asst. dir., Gainsborough Pictures. Novel: Bermuda Blue (1984).
PICTURES: *Prod. mgr.*: The African Queen. *Assoc. Prod.*: Dr. Strangelove, Darling, 2001: A Space Odyssey. *Prod.*: Spare The Rod, Station Six—Sahara, The Optimists.

LYNE, ADRIAN
Director. b. Peterborough, England, March 4, 1941. Started as director of commercials.
PICTURES: Foxes, Flashdance, Nine 1/2 Weeks, Fatal Attraction, Jacob's Ladder, Indecent Proposal.

LYNLEY, CAROL
Actress. b. New York, NY, Feb. 13, 1942. Was model as teenager.
PICTURES: The Light in the Forest (debut, 1958), Holiday for Lovers, Blue Denim, Hound-Dog Man, Return to Peyton Place, The Last Sunset, The Stripper, Under the Yum-Yum Tree, The Cardinal, The Pleasure Seekers, Shock Treatment, Harlow, Bunny Lake Is Missing, The Shuttered Room, Danger Route, Once You Kiss a Stranger, The Maltese Bippy, Norwood, Beware the Blob!, The Poseidon Adventure, Cotter, The Four Deuces, The Washington Affair, The Cat and the Canary, The Shape of Things to Come, Vigilante, Dark Tower, Blackout, Howling VI: The Freaks.
TELEVISION: *Series*: The Immortal. *Movies*: Shadow on the Land, The Smugglers, The Immortal, Weekend of Terror, The Cable Car Murder, The Night Stalker, The Elevator, Death Stalk, Willow B, Women in Prison, Flood, Fantasy Island, Having Babies II, Cops and Robin, The Beasts Are on the Streets.

LYNN, ANN
Actress. b. London, England, 1934. Ent. films and TV, 1958.
PICTURES: Johnny You're Wanted (debut, 1955), Moment of Indiscretion, Naked Fury, Piccadilly Third Stop, The Wind of Change, Strip Tease Murder, Strongroom, Flame in the Streets, HMS Defiant (Damn the Defiant), The Party's Over, Doctor in Distress, The Black Torment, The System (The Girl Getters), A Shot in the Dark, The Uncle, Four in the Morning, Separation, I'll Never Forget What's 'is Name, Baby Love, Hitler—The Last Ten Days, Screamtime.
TELEVISION: *Specials/Movies*: After The Show, All Summer Long, Trump Card, Man at the Top, The Expert, Hine, The Intruders, Too Far, King Lear, The Zoo Gang, Morning Tide, Estuary, Who Pays the Ferryman, The Professionals, Zeticula, Westway, The Perfect House, Minder, To the Sound of Guns, Crown Court, Just Good Friends, Starting Out, Paradise Park. *Series*: The Cheaters, The Other Side of the Underneath.

LYNN, JONATHAN
Director, Writer, Actor. b. Bath, England, Apr. 3, 1943. Was artistic dir. of Cambridge Theatre Company, 1976-81; Company Director of Natl. Theatre, 1987. Playwright: Pig of the Month. Books: A Proper Man, The Complete Yes Minister, Mayday. Appeared as actor in Into the Night, Three Men and a Little Lady.
PICTURES: The Internecine Project (s.p.). *Director*: Clue (also s.p.), Nuns on the Run (also s.p.), My Cousin Vinny, The Distinguished Gentleman, Greedy (also actor), Sgt. Bilko.
TELEVISION: Doctor on the Go, My Name is Harry Worth, My Brother's Keeper, Yes Minister, Yes Prime Minister.

LYNTON, MICHAEL
Executive. Pres., Hollywood Pictures.

LYON, FRANCIS D. "PETE"
Director, Editor. b. Bowbells, ND, July 29, 1905. e. Hollywood H.S., UCLA. WWII: writer, prod., dir., OWI; assoc. with training, exploitation and information films. Maj. U.S. Army Signal Corps. Author: Twists of Fate: An Oscar Winner's International Career.
PICTURES: *Editor*: Things to Come (co-edit.), Knight Without Armour, Rembrandt, Intermezzo, Adam Had Four Sons, The Great Profile, Four Sons, Daytime Wife, Body and Soul (Academy Award, 1947), He Ran All the Way. Director: Crazylegs, The Bob Mathias Story (Christopher Award), The Great Locomotive Chase, Cult of the Cobra, The Oklahoman, Gunsight Ridge, Bailout at 43,000, Escort West, Cinerama South Seas Adventure (co-dir.), The Young and the Brave, Destination Inner Space, The Destructors, The Money Jungle, The Girl Who Knew Too Much. *Producer*: Tiger by the Tail.
TELEVISION: *Series*: Laramie, Perry Mason, Zane Grey Theatre, Bus Stop, M. Squad, Wells Fargo, Kraft Suspense Theatre, Death Valley Days, Follow the Sun, etc.

LYON, SUE
Actress. b. Davenport, IA, July 10, 1946. e. Hollywood Prof. Sch.
PICTURES: Lolita (debut, 1962), The Night of the Iguana, Seven Women, Tony Rome, The Flim Flam Man, Evel Knievel, Crash, End of the World, Alligator, Invisible Strangler.
TELEVISION: *Movies*: But I Don't Want to Get Married!, Smash-Up on Interstate 5, Don't Push—I'll Charge When I'm Ready.

LYONS, STUART
Producer. b. Manchester, England, Dec. 27, 1928. e. Manchester U. Ent. m.p. ind. 1955. Asst. dir. TV series 1955-56. Casting dir. Associated British, 1956-60. Freelance cast. dir., 1960-63. Joined 20th Century-Fox Productions as cast. dir., 1963. Appt. director 20th Century-Fox Productions Ltd., 1967, man. dir. 1968. 1971 left Fox on closure Europe prod., to resume indep. prod. London Prod. Rep. for Neue Constantin Film, Munich: Salt on Our Skin, House of the Spirits.
PICTURES: *Casting Director*: Those Magnificent Men in Their Flying Machines, Cleopatra, The Long Ships, Guns at Batasi, High Wind in Jamaica, The Blue Max, many others. Producer: The Slipper and the Rose, Meetings with Remarkable Men, Danses Sacrees, Turnaround. *Prod. Consultant*: Eleni, The Witches, A Dangerous Life, Delta Force II, State of Grace, Captive in the Land (as rep. of Completion Bond Co.). *Prod. Spvr.*: Death Train.

M

MAC ARTHUR, JAMES
Actor. b. Los Angeles, CA, Dec. 8, 1937. e. Harvard. p. actress Helen Hayes, writer Charles MacArthur. Stage debut, summer stock; The Corn Is Green, Life with Father.
PICTURES: The Young Stranger (debut, 1957), The Light in the Forest, Third Man on the Mountain, Kidnapped, Swiss Family Robinson, The Interns, Spencer's Mountain, Cry of Battle, The Truth About Spring, The Battle of the Bulge, The Bedford Incident, Ride Beyond Vengeance, The Love-Ins, Hang 'em High, The Angry Breed.
TELEVISION: *Series*: Hawaii Five-0. *Movies*: Alcatraz—The Whole Shocking Story, The Night the Bridge Fell Down. *Special*: Willie and the Yank (Mosby's Marauders).

MACCHIO, RALPH
Actor. b. Long Island, NY, Nov. 4, 1962. Started in TV commercials at age 16 before winning role in series Eight Is Enough. Broadway debut in Cuba and His Teddy Bear, 1986; Off-B'way in Only Kidding.
PICTURES: Up the Academy (debut, 1980), The Outsiders, The Karate Kid, Teachers, Crossroads, The Karate Kid Part II, Distant Thunder, The Karate Kid Part III, Too Much Sun, My Cousin Vinny, Naked in New York.
TELEVISION: *Series*: Eight Is Enough. *Movies*: Journey to Survival, Dangerous Company, The Three Wishes of Billy Grier, The Last P.O.W.?: The Bobby Garwood Story.

MAC CORKINDALE, SIMON
Actor, Producer, Director, Writer. b. Isle-of-Ely, England, Feb. 2, 1952. m. actress Susan George. On stage in Dark Lady of the Sonnets, Pygmalion, French Without Tears, etc.
PICTURES: *Actor*: Death on the Nile, Quatermass Conclusion, Caboblanco, Robbers of the Sacred Mountain, The Sword and the Sorcerer, Jaws 3-D, The Riddle of the Sands, Sincerely Violet. *Producer*: Stealing Heaven, That Summer of White Roses (also co-s.p.), The House That Mary Bought (also dir., co-s.p.).
TELEVISION: *Specials*: I Claudius, Romeo and Juliet, Quatermass. *Movies*: The Manions of America, Falcon's Gold, Jesus of Nazareth, Twist of Fate, Obsessive Love, No Greater Love, At The Midnight Hour, A Family of Cops. *Mini-Series*: Pursuit, The Way to Dusty Death. *Series*: Manimal, Falcon Crest, Counterstrike.

MAC DOWELL, ANDIE
Actress. b. Gaffney, SC, Apr. 21, 1958. r.n. Rose Anderson MacDowell. Started as model for Elite Agency in NY appearing for L'Ordeal Cosmetics, The Gap, Calvin Klein.
PICTURES: Greystoke: The Legend of Tarzan Lord of the Apes (debut, 1984), St. Elmo's Fire, Sex Lies and Videotape (L.A. Film Critics Award, 1989), Green Card, The Object of Beauty, Hudson Hawk, The Player, Groundhog Day, Short Cuts, Deception, Four Weddings and a Funeral, Bad Girls, Unstrung Heroes, Michael, Multiplicity.
TELEVISION: *Movie*: Women and Men 2: In Love There Are No Rules (Domestic Dilemma). *Mini-Series* (Italy): Sahara's Secret.

MAC GRAW, ALI
Actress. b. Pound Ridge, NY, Apr. 1, 1939. e. Wellesley Coll. Son is actor Josh Evans. Editorial asst. Harper's Bazaar Mag.; asst. to photographer Melvin Sokolsky. Was top fashion model. *Author*: Moving Pictures (autobiography, 1991), Yoga Mind & Body (1995).

PICTURES: A Lovely Way to Die (debut, 1968). Goodbye Columbus, Love Story (Acad. Award nom.), The Getaway, Convoy, Players, Just Tell Me What You Want, Natural Causes. TELEVISION: *Mini-Series*: The Winds of War. *Movies*: China Rose, Survive the Savage Sea, Gunsmoke: The Long Ride. *Series*: Dynasty.

MAC LACHLAN, KYLE
Actor. b. Yakima, WA, Feb. 22, 1959. e. Univ. of WA. Acted in high school and college, then in summer stock. Joined Oregon Shakespeare Festival (Romeo and Juliet, Julius Caesar, Henry V). Cast as lead in Dune by director David Lynch in a nationwide search.
THEATRE: *NY*: Palace of Amateurs (Off-B'way).
PICTURES: Dune (debut, 1984), Blue Velvet, The Hidden, Don't Tell Her It's Me, The Doors, Twin Peaks: Fire Walk With Me, Where the Day Takes You, Rich in Love, The Trial, The Flintstones, Showgirls, Trigger Effect, Mad Dog Time.
TELEVISION: *Series*: Twin Peaks. *Guest*: Tales From the Crypt (Carrion Death). *Movies*: Dream Breakers, Against the Wall, Roswell.

MAC LAINE, SHIRLEY
Actress. b. Richmond, VA, April 24, 1934. r.n. Shirley MacLean Beaty. Brother is actor-prod. Warren Beatty. e. Washington and Lee H.S., Arlington, VA. Started as dancer; on B'way as understudy for Carol Haney in The Pajama Game, which resulted in contract with film prod. Hal Wallis. Producer, writer and co-director of Oscar-nominated film documentary: The Other Half of The Sky: A China Memoir. Returned to stage in Gypsy in My Soul, Shirley MacLaine on Broadway. Videos: Shirley MacLaine's Inner Workout, Relaxing Within.
AUTHOR: Don't Fall off the Mountain, You Can Get There from Here, Out on a Limb, Dancing in the Light, It's All In the Playing, Going Within, Dance While You Can, My Lucky Stars. *Editor*: McGovern: The Man and His Beliefs (1972).
PICTURES: The Trouble With Harry (debut, 1955), Artists and Models, Around the World in 80 Days, Hot Spell, The Matchmaker, The Sheepman, Some Came Running (Acad. Award nom.), Ask Any Girl, Career, Can-Can, The Apartment (Acad. Award nom.), Ocean's Eleven (cameo), All in a Night's Work, Two Loves, My Geisha, The Children's Hour, Two for the Seesaw, Irma La Douce (Acad. Award nom.), What a Way to Go!, John Goldfarb Please Come Home, The Yellow Rolls Royce, Gambit, Woman Times Seven, The Bliss of Mrs. Blossom, Sweet Charity, Two Mules for Sister Sara, Desperate Characters, The Possession of Joel Delaney, The Turning Point (Acad. Award nom.), Being There, Loving Couples, A Change of Seasons, Terms of Endearment (Academy Award, 1983), Cannonball Run II, Madame Sousatzka, Steel Magnolias, Postcards From the Edge, Waiting for the Light, Defending Your Life (cameo), Used People, Wrestling Ernest Hemingway, Guarding Tess, Mrs. Winterbourne, The Celluloid Closet, Evening Star.
TELEVISION: *Series*: Shirley's World. Variety *Specials*: The Other Half of the Sky: A China Memoir (also prod., co-writer), If They Could See Me Now, Where Do We Go From Here?, Shirley MacLaine at the Lido, Every Little Movement (Emmy Award for co-writing, 1980), Illusions, The Shirley MacLaine Show. *Movies*: Out on a Limb (also co-writer), The West Side Waltz.

MACLEOD, GAVIN
Actor. b. Mt. Kisco, NY, Feb. 28, 1931. e. Ithaca Coll.
PICTURES: I Want to Live, Compulsion, Operation Petticoat, McHale's Navy, McHale's Navy Joins the Air Force, The Sand Pebbles, Deathwatch, The Party, Kelly's Heroes.
TELEVISION: *Series*: McHale's Navy, The Mary Tyler Moore Show, The Love Boat. *Movies*: The Intruders, Only with Married Men, Ransom for Alice, Murder Can Hurt You, Student Exchange, The Love Boat: The Valentine Voyage. *Mini-Series*: Scruples. *Specials*: Last Act Is a Solo, If I Die Before I Wake.

MAC NAUGHTON, ROBERT
Actor. b. New York, NY, Dec. 19, 1966. Entered entertainment industry in 1979. Member Circle Rep. Co., N.Y.
THEATER: Critic's Choice, A Thousand Clowns, Camelot, The Diviners, The Adventures of Huckleberry Finn, Henry V, Tobacco Road, Master Harold... and the Boys, Tomorrow's Monday, Talley and Son.
PICTURES: E.T.: The Extra-Terrestrial, I Am the Cheese.
TELEVISION: *Movies*: Angel City, A Place to Call Home. *Specials*: Big Bend Country, The Electric Grandmother, Hear My Cry.

MAC NICOL PETER
Actor. b. Dallas, TX. e. U. of Minnesota.
THEATER: Manhattan Theatre Club: Crimes of the Heart. NY Shakespeare Fest: Found a Peanut, Rum and Coke, Twelfth Night, Richard II, Romeo & Juliet. Regional theatre includes Guthrie, Alaska Rep., Long Wharf, Dallas Theatre Center, Trinity Rep. B'way: Crimes of the Heart (Theatre World Award), The Nerd, Black Comedy/White Liars.

PICTURES: Dragonslayer (debut, 1981), Sophie's Choice, Heat, Ghostbusters II, American Blue Note, Hard Promises, Housesitter, Addams Family Values, Radioland Murders, Dracula: Dead and Loving It.
TELEVISION: *Movies*: Johnny Bull, By Dawn's Early Light, Roswell. *Guest*: Faerie Tale Theatre, Days and Nights of Molly Dodd, Cheers. *Series*: Powers That Be, Chicago Hope.

MACY, WILLIAM H.
Actor. b. Miami, FL, Mar. 13, 1950. e. Goddard Col.
THEATER: *NY*: The Man in 605 (debut, 1980), Twelfth Night, Beaurecrat, A Call From the East, The Dining Room, Speakeasy, Wild Life, Flirtations, Baby With the Bathwater, The Nice and the Nasty, Bodies Rest and Motion, Oh Hell!, Life During Wartime, Mr. Gogol and Mr. Preen, Oleanna, Our Town (B'way).
PICTURES: Without a Trace, The Last Dragon, Radio Days, House of Games, Things Change, Homicide, Shadows and Fog, Benny and Joon, Searching for Bobby Fischer, The Client, Oleanna, Murder in the First, Mr. Holland's Opus, Down Periscope, Fargo, Ghosts of Mississippi.
TELEVISION: *Series*: Chicago Hope. *Movies*: The Murder of Mary Phagan, Texan, A Murderous Affair, The Water Engine, Heart of Justice, A Private Matter. *Guest*: ER, Law and Order.

MADDEN, BILL
Executive. b. New York, NY, March 1, 1915. e. Boston U. Joined Metro-Goldwyn-Mayer as office boy, 1930; student salesman, 1938; asst. Eastern div. sales mgr., 1939; U.S. Navy, 1942-46; Boston sales rep., 1947-53; Philadelphia branch mgr., 1954-59; Midwest div. sales mgr., 1960-68; roadshow sales mgr., 1969; v.p., gen. sales mgr., 1969-74, MGM; corp., v.p. & gen. sls. mgr., MGM, 1974; retired from MGM, 1975; 1976-present, exec. consultant to motion picture industry; lecturer and instructor at UCLA. Member: AMPAS, Motion Picture Associates, American Film Institute. Motion Picture Pioneers.

MADDEN, DAVID
Executive, Producer, Director. b. Chicago, IL, July 25, 1955. e. Harvard U., 1976; UCLA, M.A., 1978. Joined 20th Century-Fox in 1978 as story analyst. Named story editor, 1980; exec. story editor, 1982. Appt. v.p., creative affairs for 20th-Fox Prods., 1983; v.p., prod., 20th Century-Fox Prods; 1984, v.p., production, Paramount Pictures. Joined Interscope Commun., 1987, as prod.
PICTURES: *Producer*: Renegades, Blind Fury (exec. prod.), The First Power, Eve of Destruction, Jersey Girls, The Hand That Rocks the Cradle, Holy Matrimony, Operation Dumbo Drop, The Tie That Binds.
TELEVISION: *Movies*: A Part of the Family (dir., writer), Body Language (co-exec. prod.).

MADIGAN, AMY
Actress. b. Chicago, IL, Sept. 11, 1951. m. actor Ed Harris. For 10 years traveled country performing in bars and clubs with band. Then studied at Lee Strasberg Inst., L.A. NY Stage: The Lucky Spot (Theatre World Award), A Streetcar Named Desire.
PICTURES: Love Child (debut, 1982), Love Letters, Streets of Fire, Places in the Heart, Alamo Bay, Twice in a Lifetime (Acad. Award nom.), Nowhere to Hide, The Prince of Pennsylvania, Field of Dreams, Uncle Buck, The Dark Half, Female Perversions.
TELEVISION: *Special*: The Laundromat. *Movies*: Crazy Times, The Ambush Murders, Victims, Travis McGee, The Day After, Roe vs. Wade, Lucky Day, And Then There Was One, Riders of the Purple Sage.

MADONNA
Singer, Actress. r.n. Madonna Louise Veronica Ciccone. b. Pontiac, MI, Aug. 16, 1958. e. U. of Michigan. Gained fame as rock & recording star before professional acting debut in Desperately Seeking Susan, 1985. NY stage debut: Speed-the-Plow, 1988. Author: Sex (1992).
PICTURES: A Certain Sacrifice (debut, 1983), Vision Quest, Desperately Seeking Susan, Shanghai Surprise, Who's That Girl?, Bloodhounds of Broadway, Dick Tracy, Truth or Dare (also exec. prod.), Shadows and Fog, A League of Their Own, Body of Evidence, Dangerous Game, Blue in the Face, Four Rooms, Girl 6, Evita.

MADSEN, MICHAEL
Actor. b. Chicago, IL, Sept. 25, 1958. Sister is actress Virginia Madsen. Started acting with Chicago's Steppenwolf Theatre appearing in such plays as Of Mice and Men, A Streetcar Named Desire. On B'way in A Streetcar Named Desire (1992).
PICTURES: WarGames (debut, 1983), Racing With the Moon, The Natural, The Killing Time, Shadows in the Storm, Blood Red, Kill Me Again, The End of Innocence, The Doors, Thelma & Louise, Straight Talk, Inside Edge, Reservoir Dogs, Trouble Bound, House in the Hills, Free Willy, Money for Nothing, Fixing the Shadow, The Getaway, Beyond the Law, Dead Connection, Wyatt Earp, Man With a Gun, Species, Free Willy 2: The Adventure Home, Mulholland Falls, Donnie Brasco.
TELEVISION: *Movies*: Our Family Honor, Montana, Baby Snatcher. *Pilot*: Diner.

MADSEN, VIRGINIA
Actress. b. Chicago, IL, Sept. 11, 1963. Mother is Emmy-winning Chicago filmmaker; brother is actor Michael Madsen. Studied with Chicago acting coach Ted Liss. Prof. debut, PBS, A Matter of Principle. Received Avoriaz & Saturn Awards for Best Actress for Candyman.
PICTURES: Class (debut, 1983), Electric Dreams, Dune, Creator, Fire With Fire, Modern Girls, Zombie High, Slam Dance, Mr. North, Hot to Trot, Heart of Dixie, The Hot Spot, Highlander 2: The Quickening, Candyman, Becoming Colette, Caroline at Midnight, Blue Tiger, The Prophecy.
TELEVISION: *Movies*: Mussolini: The Untold Story, The Hearst and Davies Affair, Long Gone, Gotham, Third Degree Burn, Ironclads, Victim of Love, Love Kills, Linda, A Murderous Affair: The Carolyn Warmus Story, Bitter Revenge. *Guest*: The Hitchhiker.

MAGNOLI, ALBERT
Director, Writer, Editor.
PICTURES: Jazz (dir., editor, s.p.), Reckless (edit.), Purple Rain (dir., edit., s.p.), American Anthem (dir. only).
TELEVISION: *Movie*: Born to Run.

MAGNUSON, ANN
Actress, Writer, Performance Artist. b. Charleston, WV, Jan. 4, 1956. e. Denison U. Intern at Ensemble Studio Theatre when she came to NY in 1978. Ran Club 57, an East Village club, 1979. Has performed Off-B'way, in East Village clubs, downtown art spaces, on college campuses since 1980, and at Whitney Museum, Soguestu Hall (Tokyo), Walker Art Ctr. (Minn.), Lincoln Center, Serious Fun Festival, Joseph Papp's Public Theatre. Also performed with band Bongwater. Debut as solo recording artist on Geffen Records with The Luv Show, 1995.
PICTURES: Vortex, The Hunger, Perfect Strangers, Desperately Seeking Susan, Making Mr. Right, A Night in the Life of Jimmy Reardon, Sleepwalk, Mondo New York, Tequila Sunrise, Checking Out, Heavy Petting, Love at Large, Cabin Boy, Clear and Present Danger, Tank Girl, Before and After.
TELEVISION: Night Flight, Made for TV, Alive from Off Center (co-host), Vandemonium, Table at Ciro's (Tales From the Hollywood Hills), The Hidden Room, The Adventures of Pete and Pete. *Series*: Anything But Love, The John Laroquette Show.

MAHARIS, GEORGE
Actor. b. Astoria, NY, Sept. 1, 1928. Studied at The Actors Studio.
PICTURES: Exodus (debut, 1960), Quick Before It Melts, Sylvia, The Satan Bug, A Covenant With Death, The Happening, The Desperadoes, Last Day of the War, The Land Raiders, The Sword and the Sorcerer, Doppelganger.
TELEVISION: *Series*: Search for Tomorrow, Route 66, Most Deadly Game. Guest: Naked City. *Movies*: Escape to Mindanao, The Monk, The Victim, Murder on Flight 502, Look What's Happened to Rosemary's Baby, SST—Death Flight, Return to Fantasy Island, Crash, A Small Rebellion. *Mini-Series*: Rich Man Poor Man. *Special*: A Death of Princes.

MAHONEY, JOHN
Actor. b. Manchester, Eng., June 20, 1940. Mem. of Stratford Children's Theatre from age 10\-13. Moved to U.S. at 19, taught Eng. at Western Illinois U. Then freelance ed. of medical manuscripts; assoc. ed., Quality Review Bulletin. At 35 quit medical book editing to become an actor. Studied acting, Chicago's St. Nicholas Theatre. Prof. debut, The Water Engine, 1977. Joined Steppenwolf Theatre Co., 1979. (The Hothouse, Taking Steps, Death of a Salesman).
THEATER: Orphans (Theatre World Award), The House of Blue Leaves (Tony and Clarence Derwent Awards), The Subject Was Roses.
PICTURES: Mission Hill, Code of Silence, The Manhattan Project, Streets of Gold, Tin Men, Suspect, Moonstruck, Frantic, Betrayed, Eight Men Out, Say Anything, Love Hurts, The Russia House, Barton Fink, Article 99, In the Line of Fire, Striking Distance, Reality Bites, The Hudsucker Proxy, The American President, Primal Fear.
TELEVISION: *Series*: Lady Blue, H.E.L.P., The Human Factor, Frasier. *Movies*: The Killing Floor, Chicago Story, First Steps, Listen to Your Heart, Dance of the Phoenix, First Steps, Trapped in Silence, Favorite Son, The Image, Dinner at Eight, The 10 Million Dollar Getaway, The Secret Passion of Robert Clayton, Unnatural Pursuits. *Special*: The House of Blue Leaves.

MAJORS, LEE
Actor. r.n. Lee Yeary. b. Wyandotte, MI, April 23, 1939. Star athlete in high school; turned down offer from St. Louis Cardinals in final year at Eastern Kentucky State Coll. to pursue acting career. In L.A. got job as playground supervisor for park dept. while studying acting at MGM Studio. Debuted in films 1964 under his real name.
PICTURES: Strait-Jacket (debut, 1964), Will Penny, The Liberation of L. B. Jones, The Norsemen, Killer Fish, Steel, Agency, The Last Chase, Scrooged, Keaton's Cop.

TELEVISION: *Series*: The Big Valley, The Men From Shiloh, Owen Marshall-Counselor at Law, The Six Million Dollar Man, The Fall Guy, Tour of Duty, Raven. *Pilot*: Road Show (also exec. prod.). *Movies*: The Ballad of Andy Crocker, Weekend of Terror, The Gary Francis Powers Story, The Cowboy and the Ballerina, A Rocky Mountain Christmas, The Return of the Six Million Dollar Man and the Bionic Woman, Danger Down Under (exec. prod., actor), The Bionic Showdown: the Six Million Dollar Man and the Bionic Woman, Fire!, Trapped on the 37th Floor, The Cover Girl Murders, Bionic Ever After?

MAKEPEACE, CHRIS
Actor. b. Montreal, Canada, April 22, 1964. e. Jarvis Collegiate Institute. Trained for stage at Second City Workshop.
PICTURES: Meatballs (debut, 1979), My Bodyguard, The Last Chase, The Oasis, The Falcon and the Snowman, Vamp, Captive Hearts, Aloha Summer.
TELEVISION: *Movies*: The Terry Fox Story, The Mysterious Stranger, Mazes and Monsters, The Undergrads. *Series*: Going Great (host, 1982-84), Why On Earth?

MAKO
Actor. r.n. Makoto Iwamatsu. b. Kobe, Japan, Dec. 10, 1933. e. Pratt Inst.
THEATER: *NY*: Pacific Overtures (Tony nom.), Shimada. *Regional*: Rashomon.
PICTURES: The Ugly Dachshund, The Sand Pebbles (Acad. Award nom.), The Private Navy of Sgt. O'Farrell, The Great Bank Robbery, The Hawaiians, The Island at the Top of the World, Prisoners, The Killer Elite, The Big Brawl, The Bushido Blade, Under the Rainbow, An Eye for an Eye, Conan the Barbarian, The House Where Evil Dwells, Testament, Conan the Destroyer, Armed Response, P.O.W. The Escape, Silent Assassins, The Wash, Tucker: The Man and His Dream, An Unremarkable Life, Taking Care of Business, Pacific Heights, The Perfect Weapon, Sidekicks, Robocop 3, Rising Sun, Cultivating Charlie, A Dangerous Place, Highlander III: The Sorcerer.
TELEVISION: *Series*: Hawaiian Heat. *Movies*: The Challenge, If Tomorrow Comes, The Streets of San Francisco (pilot), Judge Dee and the Monastery Murders, Farewell to Manzanar, When Hell Was in Session, The Last Ninja, Girls of the White Orchid. *Guest*: McHale's Navy, Ensign O'Toole, 77 Sunset Strip, I Spy, F Troop, Hawaii Five-O.

MALDEN, KARL
Actor. r.n. Mladen Sekulovich. b. Gary, IN, Mar. 22, 1914. e. Art Inst. of Chicago 1933-36; Goodman Theatre Sch. Elected pres., Acad. of Motion Picture Arts & Sciences, 1989.
THEATER: *B'way*: Golden Boy, Key Largo, Flight to West, Missouri Legend, Uncle Harry, Counterattack, Truckline Cafe, All My Sons, Streetcar Named Desire, Desperate Hours, Desire Under the Elms, The Egghead.
PICTURES: They Knew What They Wanted (debut, 1940), Winged Victory, 13 Rue Madeleine, Boomerang!, Kiss of Death, The Gunfighter, Where the Sidewalk Ends, Halls of Montezuma, A Streetcar Named Desire (Academy Award, best supporting actor, 1951), The Sellout, Diplomatic Courier, Operation Secret, Ruby Gentry, I Confess, Take the High Ground, Phantom of the Rue Morgue, On the Waterfront (Acad. Award nom.), Baby Doll, Bombers B-52, Time Limit (dir. only), Fear Strikes Out, The Hanging Tree, One Eyed Jacks, Pollyanna, The Great Impostor, Parrish, All Fall Down, Birdman of Alcatraz, Gypsy, How the West Was Won, Come Fly With Me, Cheyenne Autumn, Dead Ringer, The Cincinnati Kid, Nevada Smith, Murderer's Row, Hotel, Blue, The Adventures of Bullwhip Griffin, Billion Dollar Brain, Hot Millions, Patton, Cat O'Nine Tails, Wild Rovers, Summertime Killer, Beyond the Poseidon Adventure, Meteor, The Sting II, Twilight Time, Billy Galvin, Nuts.
TELEVISION: *Series*: Streets of San Francisco, Skag. *Movies*: Captains Courageous, Word of Honor, With Intent to Kill, Alice in Wonderland, Fatal Vision (Emmy Award, 1985), My Father My Son, The Hijacking of the Achille Lauro, Call Me Anna, Absolute Strangers, Back to the Streets of San Francisco.

MALIN, AMIR JACOB
Executive. b. Tel-Aviv, Israel, Mar. 22, 1954. e. Brandeis U., 1972-76; Boston U. Sch. of Law, 1976-79. Staff atty., WGBH-TV, Boston, 1979-81; pres. and co-CEO, Cinecom Entertainment Group Inc., 1982-92. Films acquired and distributed include Come Back to the Five and Dime Jimmy Dean Jimmy Dean, Metropolis, The Brother from Another Planet, Stop Making Sense, Coca-Cola Kid, A Room with a View, Swimming to Cambodia, Matewan, A Man in Love, Maurice, Miles From Home. Partner, October Films, Inc. Films acquired and distrib.: Life Is Sweet, Adam's Rib, The Living End, Tous les Matins du Monde (All the Mornings of the World), Ruby in Paradise, A Heart in Winter, Bad Behavior, Kika, Cronos, The Cement Garden, The Last Seduction, Search & Destroy, The Funeral, Breaking the Waves, Girlstown.
PICTURES: *Exec. prod.*: Swimming to Cambodia, Matewan, Miles From Home, Scenes from the Class Struggle in Beverly Hills, The Handmaid's Tale, Tune in Tomorrow.

MALKOVICH, JOHN
Actor, Producer, Director. b. Christopher, IL, Dec. 9, 1953. e. Illinois State U. Founding member Steppenwolf Ensemble in Chicago with group of college friends, 1976. Starred in Say Goodnight Gracie and True West (Obie Award) which then was brought to New York. NY Stage work includes Death of Salesman, Burn This, States of Shock. Director: Balm in Gilead, Arms and the Man, The Caretaker, Libra (also writer).
PICTURES: Places in the Heart (Acad. Award nom.), The Killing Fields, Eleni, Making Mr. Right, The Glass Menagerie, Empire of the Sun, Miles From Home, Dangerous Liaisons, The Accidental Tourist (co-exec. prod. only), The Sheltering Sky, Queens Logic, The Object of Beauty, Shadows and Fog, Of Mice and Men, Jennifer Eight, Alive, In the Line of Fire (Acad. Award nom.), The Convent, Beyond the Clouds, Mary Reilly, Mulholland Falls, Portrait of a Lady.
TELEVISION: Special: Rocket to the Moon. Movies: Word of Honor, American Dream, Death of a Salesman (Emmy Award, 1986), Heart of Darkness.

MALLE, LOUIS
Director, Producer, Writer. b. Thumeries, France, Oct. 30, 1932. m. actress Candice Bergen. e. Sorbonne (Pol. Science). Studied filmmaking at Institut des Hautes Etudes Cinematographiques 1951-53. Started on film industry as assistant to Robert Bresson and cameraman to oceanographer Jacques Cousteau, 1954-55 then corres. for French TV in Algeria, Vietnam and Thailand 1962-64. Became internationally known with Les Amants (The Lovers) in 1958. Has also acted in films (A Very Private Affair, A Very Curious Girl, Milky Way, La Vie de Boheme).
PICTURES: Silent World (co-dir., photog. with J. Y. Cousteau), A Conedmned Man Escapes (prod. asst. to Bresson), Mon Oncle (photog. only). Director: Elevator to the Gallows (also s.p.), The Lovers (also s.p.), Calcutta (doc.; also s.p., photog., actor), Zazie in the Metro (also s.p.), A Very Private Affair (also s.p., actor), Vive Le Tour (doc.; also s.p., photog., actor), The Fire Within (also s.p.), Viva Maria (also prod., s.p.), The Thief of Paris (also prod., s.p.), Spirits of the Dead (co-dir.), Phantom India (doc.; also photog.), Murmur of the Heart (also s.p.; Acad. Award nom. for best s.p.), Humain Trop Humain (doc.; also prod., photog.), Place de la Republique (doc.; also prod., photog.), Lacombe Lucien (also prod., s.p.), Black Moon (also s.p.), Pretty Baby (also prod., story), Atlantic City (Acad. Award nom.), My Dinner With Andre, Crackers, Alamo Bay (also prod.), Au Revoir Les Enfants (Goodbye Children; also s.p., prod.; Golden Lion Award, Venice Film Fest., 1987), May Fools (Milou en Mai; also co-s.p.), Damage (also prod.), Vanya on 42nd Street.
TELEVISION: Documentaries: God's Country, And the Pursuit of Happiness.
(d. November 23, 1995)

MALMUTH, BRUCE
Director, Actor. b. Brooklyn, NY, Feb. 4, 1937. e. City Coll. of New York, Brooklyn Coll. Grad. studies in film, Columbia U. and U. of Southern California. Acted in and dir. college productions. Moved to California and obtained job as page at NBC. In Army assigned to special services as director; reassigned to New York. Upon release began 10-year Clio-winning career as dir. of TV commercials. Debut as director of features with Nighthawks, 1981. Founder, Los Angeles Aspiring Actors and Directors Workshop. Theatre incl.: Two Guys Second Wind (writer, dir., prod.), Thanksgiving Cries (writer, dir.).
PICTURES: Director: Nighthawks, The Man Who Wasn't There, Where Are the Children? (also actor), Hard to Kill, Pentathalon (also actor). Actor: The Karate Kid (also Part II), For Keeps?, Happy New Year, Laine.
TELEVISION: Baseballs or Switchblades? (prod., writer, dir., Emmy Award), A Boy's Dream, Twilight Zone, Beauty and the Beast, Heartbreak Winner.

MALONE, DOROTHY
Actress. b. Chicago, IL, Jan. 30, 1925. e. Southern Methodist U., USC, AADA. Started as RKO starlet, 1943. Stage work incl. Little Me, Practice to Deceive.
PICTURES: The Big Sleep, Night and Day, One Sunday Afternoon, Two Guys From Texas, The Nevadan, The Bushwackers, Jack Slade, The Killer That Stalked New York, Scared Stiff, Torpedo Alley, The Lone Gun, Pushover, Security Risk, Private Hell 36, The Fast and the Furious, Young at Heart, Battle Cry, Sincerely Yours, Artists and Models, At Gunpoint, Five Guns West, Tall Man Riding, Pillars of the Sky, Tension at Table Rock, Written on the Wind (Academy Award, best supporting actress, 1956), Man of a Thousand Faces, Quantez, The Tarnished Angels, Tip on a Dead Jockey, Too Much Toon Soon, Warlock, The Last Voyage, The Last Sunset, Beach Party, Fate is the Hunter (unbilled), Abduction, Golden Rendezvous, Good Luck Miss Wyckoff, Winter Kills, The Day Time Ended, The Being, Basic Instinct, Beverly Hills.
TELEVISION: Series: Peyton Place. Guest: Dick Powell Theatre, Loretta Young Show (twice hosted), Philip Morris Playhouse, Dr. Kildare, Bob Hope Show, Jack Benny Show, The Untouchables, Phyllis Diller Show, Ken Murray's Blackouts, Death Valley Days.

Movies: The Pigeon, Little Ladies of the Night, Murder in Peyton Place, Katie: Portrait of a Centerfold, Condominium, Peyton Place: The Next Generation. Mini-Series: Rich Man Poor Man. Specials: Gertrude Stein Story, The Family That Prays Together.

MALONE, JOHN C.
Executive. b. Milford, CT, Mar. 7, 1941. e. Yale U. Pres. & CEO of Telecommunications Inc., 1973-present. With National Cable Television Association as: dir., 1974-77; treasurer, 1977-78; dir., 1980-94. Dir. of TCI; on bd. of dirs. for Turner Bordacasting, Cable Television Laboratories Inc. BET, Discovery.

MAMET, DAVID
Writer, Director. b. Chicago, IL, Nov. 30, 1947. e. Goddard Coll. Artist-in-residence, Goddard Coll. 1971-73. Artistic dir. St. Nicholas Theatre Co., Chicago, 1973-75. Co-founder Dinglefest Theatre; assoc. artistic dir., Goodman Theatre, Chicago. Appeared as actor in film Black Widow. Novel: The Village (1994).
THEATER: Lakefront, The Woods, American Buffalo, Sexual Perversity in Chicago, Duck Variations, Edmond, A Life in the Theatre, The Water Engine, Prairie du Chien, Glengarry Glen Ross (Pulitzer Prize, Tony Award, 1984), Speed-the-Plow, Sketches of War (benefit for homeless Vietnam Veterans), Oleanna, An Interview (Death Defying Acts), The Cryptogram.
PICTURES: Writer: The Postman Always Rings Twice, The Verdict, The Untouchables, House of Games (also dir.), Things Change (also dir.), We're No Angels, Homicide (also dir.), Hoffa, Vanya on 42nd Street (adaptation), Oleanna (also dir.).
TELEVISION: Lip Service (exec. prod.), Hill Street Blues, A Life in the Theatre, Texan.

MANASSE, GEORGE
Producer. b. Florence, Italy, Jan. 1, 1938. e. U. of North Carolina.
PICTURES: Prod.: Who Killed Mary What's 'er Name?, Squirm, Blue Sunshine, He Knows You're Alone. Prod. Mgr.: Greetings, Joe, Fury on Wheels, Slow Dancing in the Big City, Tribute, Porky's II: The Next Day, Neighbors, Death Wish III, Torch Song Trilogy, Indecent Proposal, Coneheads, Lassie, Die Hard With a Vengeance, Eraser.
TELEVISION: Line Prod.: Series: American Playwright's Theatre (Arts & Ent.) The Saint in Manhattan (pilot), Movie: The Killing Floor, Vengeance: The Story of Tony Cimo. Prod. Mgr.: Series: St. Elsewhere, Annie McGuire. Movies: Sanctuary of Fear, Mr. Griffith and Me, Peking Encounter, When the Circus Came to Town, Murder, Inc. Muggable Mary, Running Out, Dropout Father, He's Hired, She's Fired, Intimate Strangers, Drop Out Mother, Vengeance: The Story of Tony Cimo, The Saint in Manhattan, The Diamond Trap, The Prize Pulitzer (also suprv. prod.), Orpheus Descending (also suprv. prod.), John and Yoko, Marilyn and Me, The Woman Who Sinned.

MANCIA, ADRIENNE
Curator, Dept. of Film, Museum of Modern Art. b. New York, NY. e. U. of Wisconsin. B.A.; Columbia U., M.A. Worked in film distribution industry in New York prior to joining Dept. of Film & Video, Museum of Modern Art, 1964; responsible for film exhibition since 1965. 1977, appointed curator. Restructured Museums' Auditorium Exhibition Prog., creating a balance between classic cinema and contemporary work. Initiated innovative programs such as Cineprobe and New Documentaries (formerly What's Happening?) Served on numerous int'l film juries. Co-founder New Directors/New Films. Chevalier de l'Ordre des Arts et des Lettres (France, 1985). Ufficiale dell Ordine al Merito della Repubblica Italiana, 1988.

MANCUSO, FRANK G.
Executive. b. Buffalo, NY, July 25, 1933. e. State U. of New York. Film buyer and operations supvr. for Basil Enterprises, theatre circuit, 1958-62. Joined Paramount as booker in Buffalo branch, 1962. Named sls. repr. for branch in 1964 and branch mgr. in 1967. 1970 appt. v.p./gen. sls. mgr., Paramount Pictures Canada, Ltd., becoming pres. in 1972. 1976 relocated with Paramount in U.S. as western div. mgr. in LA. 1977, appt. gen. sls. mgr. of NY, office; two months later promoted to v.p. domestic distribution; 1979, named exec. v.p., distrib. & mktg. 1983 made pres. of entire Paramount Motion Picture Group. 1984, appointed chmn. and CEO, Paramount Pictures; resigned 1991. Named Motion Picture Pioneers Man of the Year, 1987. Member of Board: AMPAS, M.P. Assoc. of America, Will Rogers Memorial Fund, Variety Clubs Intl., Sundance Institute, Amer. Film Institute, Museum of Broadcasting, Motion Picture Pioneers. Appointed Chmn. & CEO of MGM, 1993.

MANCUSO, FRANK, JR.
Producer. b. Buffalo, NY, Oct. 9, 1958. Son of Frank G. Mancuso. e. Upsala Coll. Began with industry at age 14, booking short subjects in Canadian theatres. Worked in gross receipts dept. in Paramount corporate offices in New York and later with paralegal div. Initial prod. work as location asst. for Urban Cowboy in Houston, TX. Served as assoc. prod. of Friday the 13th Part II and prod. of Friday the 13th Part III in 3-D.

PICTURES: Off the Wall, The Man Who Wasn't There, April Fool's Day, Friday the 13th, Part IV: The Final Chapter; Friday the 13th—A New Beginning (exec. prod.), Friday the 13th, Part VII (exec. prod.); Back to the Beach; Permanent Record, Internal Affairs, He Said/She Said, Species, Fled.
TELEVISION: Friday the 13th: The Series (exec. prod.).

MANDEL, BABALOO
Writer. r.n. Marc Mandel. b. 1949. Started as comedy writer for Joan Rivers, among others. First teamed with Lowell Ganz on script for 1982 film Night Shift.
PICTURES: Night Shift, Splash (Acad. Award nom.; also actor), Spies Like Us, Gung Ho, Vibes, Parenthood, City Slickers, A League of Their Own, Mr. Saturday Night (also cameo), Greedy, City Slickers II: The Legend of Curly's Gold, Forget Paris, Multiplicity.
TELEVISION: Series co-writer: Laverne and Shirley, Busting Loose, Take Five (also co-creator). Series co-exec. prod.: Gung Ho, Knight and Daye, Parenthood.

MANDEL, LORING
Writer. b. Chicago, IL, May 5, 1928. e. U. of Wisconsin, B.S. 1949. Long career writing scripts for TV, dating back to 1955 when penned Shakedown Cruise. Governor, Natl. Acad. of TV Arts & Sciences 1964-68; Pres. Writers Guild of America East 1975-77; Natl. Chmn. 1977-79.
PICTURES: Countdown, Promises in the Dark, The Little Drummer Girl.
TELEVISION: Do Not Go Gentle Into That Good Night (Emmy, 1967), Breaking Up, Project Immortality (Sylvania Award, 1959), A House His Own, Trial of Chaplain Jensen, The Raider, etc.

MANDEL, ROBERT
Director. e. Columbia Univ.
PICTURES: Night at O'Rears (also prod.), Independence Day, F/X, Touch and Go, Big Shots, School Ties, The Substitute.
TELEVISION: Hard Time on Planet Earth.

MANDELL, ABE
Executive. b. Oct. 4, 1922. e. U. of Cincinnati. Entered broadcasting as actor on Cincinnati radio station prior to W.W.II. Served U.S. Army in Southwest Pacific, 1942-45. Formed indep. motion picture distribution co. in the Far East. Company, which became the largest indep. motion picture dist. in the Far East, also operated and owned motion picture theaters throughout the Phillipines and Indonesia, 1946-56; network-regional sales exec., Ziv Television, 1956-58; dir. foreign operations, Independent Television Corporation, 1958; v.p.-foreign oper., 1960; v.p.-sales and adm., 1961; exec. v.p., 1962; pres. 1965. 1976 corporate name changed from Independent Television Corp. to ITC Entertainment, Inc. President to 1983 of ITC Entertainment; with Robert Mandell heads New Frontier Prods.

MANDOKI, LUIS
Director. b. Mexico City, Mexico. e. San Francisco Art Institute, London Intl. Film School, London College's School of Film. Dir. short film Silent Music which won Intl. Amateur Film Fest. Award at 1976 Cannes Film Fest. Back in Mexico dir. shorts and documentaries for the Instituto Nacional Indignista Concaine, Centro de Produccionde Cortometraje. Won Ariel
PICTURES: Motel (debut, 1982), Gaby--A True Story, White Palace, Born Yesterday, When a Man Loves a Woman.

MANES, FRITZ
Producer. b. Oakland, CA, Apr. 22, 1936. e. U.C., Berkeley, B.A. UCLA, 1956. Armed Service: 1951-54. U.S. Marines, Korea, Purple Heart. TV ad. exec. and stuntman before becoming exec. prod. on films for Clint Eastwood. Has formed own production co., Sundancer Prods. Membership, DGA, SAG.
PICTURES: in various capacities: The Outlaw Josey Wales, The Enforcer. Assoc. prod.: The Gauntlet, Every Which Way But Loose, Escape From Alcatraz, Bronco Billy. Prod.: Any Which Way You Can (also 2nd asst. dir.), Firefox (exec. prod.), Honky Tonk Man (exec. prod.), Tightrope (prod.), Sudden Impact (exec. prod.), City Heat (prod.), Pale Rider (exec. prod.), Ratboy (exec. prod.), Heartbreak Ridge (exec. prod., prod. mgr.), James Dean.

MANKIEWICZ, DON M.
Writer. b. Berlin, Germany, Jan. 20, 1922. p. Herman J. Mankiewicz. e. Columbia, B.A., 1942; Columbia Law Sch. Served in U.S. Army, 1942-46; reporter, New Yorker magazine, 1946-48; author of novels See How They Run, Trial, It Only Hurts a Minute; magazine articles, short stories. President, Producers Guild of America, 1987; on Board of Directors, Writers Guild of America, 1992.
PICTURES: Trial, I Want to Live, (Acad. Award nom.), The Chapman Report, The Black Bird.
TELEVISION: Studio One, On Trial, One Step Beyond, Playhouse 90, Profiles in Courage. Value. story consultant: Hart to Hart, Simon & Simon, Crazy Like a Fox, Adderly. Pilots: Ironside, Marcus Welby M.D., Sarge, Lanigan's Rabbi (collab.), Rosetti and Ryan (collab.).

MANKIEWICZ, TOM
Writer, Director. b. Los Angeles, CA, June 1, 1942. e. Yale U.
PICTURES: Writer: The Sweet Ride (debut), Diamonds Are Forever, Live and Let Die, The Man with the Golden Gun, Mother Jugs and Speed (also prod.), The Cassandra Crossing, The Eagle Has Landed, Ladyhawke. Exec. Prod.: Hot Pursuit. Creative consultant: Superman, Superman II. Director: Dragnet (also s.p.), Delirious.
TELEVISION: Pilot: Hart to Hart (writer, dir.). Movie: Taking the Heat (dir.). Episode: Tales of the Crypt (dir.)

MANKOWITZ, WOLF
Writer, Producer. b. London, Nov. 7, 1924. Was journalist before ent. m.p. industry in 1952.
THEATRE: Expresso Bongo (from his story), Make Me An Offer, Belle, Pickwick, Passion Flower Hotel, Casanova's Last Stand, etc.
PICTURES: Make Me an Offer, A Kid for Two Farthings, The Bespoke Overcoat, Expresso Bongo, The Millionairess, The Long and the Short and the Tall, The Day the Earth Caught Fire, Waltz of the Toreadors, Where the Spies Are, Casino Royale (co-writer), The Assassination Bureau, Bloomfield, Black Beauty, Treasure Island, The Hebrew Lesson, The Hireling, Almonds and Raisins.
TELEVISION: The Killing Stones, A Cure for Tin Ear, The Battersea Miracle, Series: Conflict, Dickens of London.

MANN, ABBY
Writer. b. Philadelphia, PA, 1927. e. NYU. First gained fame on TV writing for Robert Montgomery Theatre, Playhouse 90, Studio One, Alcoa, Goodyear Theatre. Acad. Award for film adaptation of own teleplay Judgment at Nuremberg into theatrical film.
PICTURES: Judgment at Nuremberg, A Child Is Waiting, The Condemned of Altona, Ship of Fools (Academy Award nom.), The Detective, Report to the Commissioner.
TELEVISION: Series: Kojak (creator), Skag, Medical Story. Movies: The Marcus-Nelson Murders (Emmy Award, 1973; also exec. prod.), Medical Story (also exec. prod.), The Atlanta Child Murders, King (Emmy nom.), Murderers Among Us: The Simon Wiesenthal Story (Emmy Award, 1989; co-writer, co-exec. prod.), Teamster Boss: The Jackie Presser Story (also co-exec. prod.), Indictment: The McMartin Trial (also co-exec. prod.; Emmy Award, 1995, Golden Globe Award).

MANN, DELBERT
Director, Producer. b. Lawrence, KS, Jan. 30, 1920. e. Vanderbilt U., Yale U. U.S. Air Force, 1942-45. Stage mgr., summer stock, dir. Columbia, S.C. Town Theatre, 1947-49. Asst. dir. NBC-TV, 1949; dir., NBC-TV, 1949-55. Past pres., Directors Guild of America.
THEATER: A Quiet Place, Speaking of Murder, Zelda, The Glass Menagerie, The Memoirs of Abraham Lincoln; opera: Wuthering Heights (NY City Center).
PICTURES: Marty (Academy Award, 1955), The Bachelor Party, Desire Under the Elms, Separate Tables, Middle of the Night, The Dark at the Top of the Stairs, The Outsider, Lover Come Back, That Touch of Mink, A Gathering of Eagles, Dear Heart, Quick Before It Melts (also prod.), Mister Buddwing (also prod.), Fitzwilly, The Pink Jungle, Kidnapped, Birch Interval, Night Crossing.
TELEVISION: Philco-Goodyear TV Playhouse, Producer's Showcase, Omnibus, Playwrights '56, Playhouse 90, Ford Star Jubilee, Lights Out, Mary Kay and Johnny, The Little Show, Masterpiece Theatre, Ford Startime. Movies/Specials: Heidi, David Copperfield, No Place to Run, She Waits (also prod.), Jane Eyre, The Man Without a Country, A Girl Named Sooner, Francis Gary Powers: The True Story of the U-2 Spy Incident, Tell Me My Name, Breaking Up, Home to Stay, Love's Dark Ride, Thou Shalt Not Commit Adultery, All Quiet on the Western Front, Torn Between Two Lovers, To Find My Son, All the Way Home, The Member of the Wedding, The Gift of Love, Bronte, Love Leads the Way, A Death in California, The Last Days of Patton, The Ted Kennedy, Jr. Story, April Morning (also co-prod.), Ironclads, Against Her Will: An Incident in Baltimore (also prod.), Incident in a Small Town (also prod.), Lily in Winter.

MANN, MICHAEL
Director, Writer, Producer. b. Chicago, IL, Feb. 5, 1943. e. U. of Wisconsin, London Film Sch. Directed shorts, commercials and documentaries in England. Returned to U.S. in 1972. Wrote for prime-time TV (episodes of Starsky and Hutch, Police Story, created Vegas).
PICTURES: Exec. Prod.: Band of the Hand. Director-Writer: Thief (also exec. prod.), The Keep, Manhunter, The Last of the Mohicans (also co-prod.), Heat (also s.p.).
TELEVISION: The Jericho Mile (writer, dir.; DGA Award, Emmy Award for writing, 1980), Miami Vice (exec. prod.), Crime Story (exec. prod.), L.A. Takedown (dir., writer, exec. prod.). Mini-Series: Drug Wars: The Camarena Story (exec. prod.; Emmy Award, 1990), Drug Wars: The Cocaine Cartel (exec. prod.).

MANNING, MICHELLE
Executive. Exec. v.p., Production Division, Viacom, Inc.

MANOFF, DINAH
Actress. b. New York, NY, January 25, 1958. e. CalArts. Daughter of actress-director Lee Grant and late writer Arnold Manoff. Prof. debut in PBS prod., The Great Cherub Knitwear Strike. Guest starred on Welcome Back Kotter.
THEATER: I Ought to Be in Pictures (Tony & Theatre World Awards, 1980), Gifted Children, Leader of the Pack, Alfred and Victoria: A Life (L.A. Theatre Center), Kingdom of Earth (TheatreWest).
PICTURES: Grease (debut, 1978), Ordinary People, I Ought to Be in Pictures, Child's Play, Staying Together, Bloodhounds of Broadway, Welcome Home Roxy Carmichael.
TELEVISION: Series: Soap, Empty Nest. Movies: Raid on Entebee, Night Terror, The Possessed, For Ladies Only, A Matter of Sex, The Seduction of Gina, Flight No. 90: Disaster on the Potomac, Classified Love, Crossing the Mob, Backfire, Babies, Maid for Each Other (also co-exec. prod., co-story). Mini-Series: Celebrity.

MANSON, ARTHUR
Executive. b. Brooklyn, NY, Feb. 21, 1928. e. City Coll. of New York, grad. Inst. Film Technique, 1945. Editor, American Traveler, U.S. Army, 1946. Advance agent, co. mgr., Henry V, U.S., 1948-50; producer's publ. rep., Stanley Kramer Distributing Corp., Samuel Goldwyn Productions, 1951-52, dir. of adv. and publ., MGM Pictures of Canada, Ltd., 1952-53; publ. and adv. rep., Cinerama widescreen process, 1953-58; dir. worldwide ad-pub Cinerama 1958-60; adv. mgr., Columbia Pictures, 1961-62; nat'l dir. of adv., publ., Dino De Laurentiis, 1962-64; exec. asst. to v.p. adv. & pub., 20th Century-Fox, 1964-67; v.p., adv. & pub. Cinerama. Inc., and Cinerama Releasing Corp.; 1967-74; exec. v.p., sales & marketing, BCP, service of Cox Broadcasting Corp., 1974-75; v.p. worldwide marketing Warner Bros., 1976. 1977 formed own company, Cinemax Mkt. & Dist. Corp. and is pres. Chmn., NY events committee, AMPAS.

MANTEGNA, JOE
Actor. b. Chicago, IL, Nov. 13, 1947. e. Morton Jr. Coll., Goodman Sch. of Drama, 1967-69. Member: The Organic Theatre Company, Chicago (The Wonderful Ice Cream Suit, Cops, and 2 European tours with ensemble). Later member of Goodman Theater where he began long creative assoc. with playwright-dir. David Mamet (A Life in the Theatre, The Disappearance of the Jews). In national co. of Hair, Godspell, Lenny. B'way debut: Working. Narrated documentaries Crack U.S.A. and Death on the Job.
THEATER: Bleacher Bums (also conceived and co-author), Leonardo (L.A., co-author), Glengarry Glen Ross (Tony Award), Speed-the-Plow.
PICTURES: Who Stole My Wheels? (Towing), Second Thoughts, Compromising Positions, The Money Pit, Off Beat, Three Amigos, Critical Condition, House of Games, Weeds, Suspect, Things Change (Venice Film Fest. Award, 1988), Wait Until Spring Bandini, Alice, The Godfather Part III, Queens Logic, Homicide, Bugsy, Body of Evidence, Family Prayers, Searching for Bobby Fisher, Baby's Day Out, Airheads, For Better or Worse, Forget Paris, Up Close and Personal, Eye for an Eye, Thinner, Albino Alligator.
TELEVISION: Series: Comedy Zone. Guest: Soap, Bosom Buddies, Archie Bunker's Place, Magnum P.I., Open All Night, Fallen Angels (The Quiet Room). Special: Bleacher Bums (Emmy Award). Movies: Elvis, Comrades of Summer, The Water Engine, State of Emergency, Above Suspicion.

MANULIS, MARTIN
Producer, Director. b. New York, NY, May 30, 1915. e. Columbia Col., B.A. 1935. Lt. USN, 1941-45. Head of prod. John C. Wilson, 1941-49; mgr. dir., Westport Country Playhouse, 1945-50; dir. B'way plays; staff prod. & dir. CBS-TV, 1951-58; head prod. 20th-Fox Television. Now pres., Martin Manulis Prods. Ltd. 1987, artistic dir., Ahmanson Theatre, L.A.
THEATER: B'way/and on tour: Private Lives, Made in Heaven, The Philadelphia Story, Pride's Crossing, Laura, The Men We Marry, The Hasty Heart, The Show Off.
PICTURES: Producer: Days of Wine and Roses, Dear Heart, Luv, Duffy, The Out-of-Towners.
TELEVISION: Suspense, Studio One, Climax, Best of Broadway, Playhouse 90. Mini-Series: Chiefs, Space, The Day Christ Died, Grass Roots.

MARA, ADELE
Actress. r.n. Adelaida Delgado; b. Dearborn, MI, April 28, 1923. m. writer-prod. Roy Huggins. Singer, dancer with Xavier Cugat orchestra.
PICTURES: Navy Blues (feature debut, 1941), Shut My Big Mouth, Blondie Goes to College, Alias Boston Blackie, You Were Never Lovelier, Lucky Legs, Vengeance of the West, Reveille With Beverly, Riders of the Northwest Mounted, The Magnificent Rogue, Passkey to Danger, Traffic in Crime, Exposed, The Trespasser, Blackmail, Campus Honeymoon, Twilight on the Rio Grande, Robin Hood of Texas, Nighttime in Nevada, The Gallant Legion, Sands of Iwo Jima, Wake of the Red Witch, Rock Island Trail, California Passage, The Avengers, The Sea Hornet, Count The Hours, The Black Whip, Back from Eternity, Curse of the Faceless Man, The Big Circus.
TELEVISION: Series: Cool Million. Mini-Series: Wheels.

MARAIS, JEAN
Actor. b. Cherbourg, France, Dec. 11, 1913. e. Coll. St. Germain, Lycee Janson de Sailly, Lycee Condorcet. Painter; photog; stage actor; French Air Army; m.p. debut in Pavillon Brule.
PICTURES: Carmen, Eternal Return, Beauty and the Beast, Ruy Blas, Les Parents Terribles, Secret of Mayerling, Souvenir, Orpheus, Eagle with Two Heads, Inside a Girl's Dormitory, Royal Affairs in Versailles, Paris Does Strange Things, Le Capitan, Le Bossu, La Princesse de Cleves, Le Capitaine Fracasse, Honorable Stanilleu, Agent Secret, Patute, Fantomas, Le Gentleman de Cocody, Stealing Beauty.

MARCHAND, NANCY
Actress. b. Buffalo, NY, June 19, 1928. m. actor-dir. Paul Sparer. e. Carnegie Tech. Stage debut The Late George Apley (1946).
THEATER: The Taming of the Shrew (B'way debut, 1951), The Balcony (Obie Award, 1960), Morning's at Seven (Drama Desk & Outer Critics Circle Awards), Sister Mary Ignatius Explains It All to You, Taken in Marriage, The Plough and the Stars, Awake and Sing, The Cocktail Hour (Obie Award, 1990), The End of the Day, Black Comedy/White Liars. Was an original mem of APA-Phoenix Theater.
PICTURES: The Bachelor Party (debut, 1957), Ladybug Ladybug, Me Natalie, Tell Me That You Love Me Junie Moon, The Hospital, The Bostonians, From the Hip, The Naked Gun: From the Files of Police Squad, Jefferson in Paris, Sabrina.
TELEVISION: Specials: Little Women, Marty, Kiss Kiss Dahlings, many others. Series: Beacon Hill, Adams Chronicles, Love of Life, Search for Tomorrow, Lou Grant (4 Emmy Awards: 1978, 1980, 1981, 1982). Movies: Some Kind of Miracle, Willa, Once Upon a Family, Killjoy, The Golden Moment—An Olympic Love Story, Sparkling Cyanide. Mini-Series: North and South Book II.

MARCOVICCI, ANDREA
Actress, Singer. b. New York, NY, Nov. 18, 1948. e. Bennett Col. Studied acting with Herbert Berghof. Acted on NY stage in The Wedding of Iphigenia, The Ambassadors, Nefertiti, Hamlet, Any Given Day. Frequent performer in night clubs.
PICTURES: The Front (debut, 1976), The Concorde: Airport 1979, The Hand, Spacehunter: Adventures in the Forbidden Zone, Kings and Desperate Men, The Stuff, Someone to Love, White Dragon, Jack the Bear.
TELEVISION: Series: Love Is a Many-Splendored Thing, Berrenger's, Trapper John M.D. Movies: Cry Rape!, Smile Jenny You're Dead, Some Kind of Miracle, A Vacation in Hell, Packin' It In, Sprague, Velvet, The Canterville Ghost, The Water Engine.

MARCUS, MICHAEL E.
Executive. b. Pittsburgh, PA, June 5, 1945. e. Penn State, 1963-67. Moved to LA where he started in industry in mailroom of General Artists Corp. Promoted to agent when co. merged with Creative Management Assocs. 1972 joined Bart/Levy Agency; 1980, became full partner and co-owner of Kohner/Levy/Marcus Agency. 1981, became sr. agent at Creative Artists Agency. 1993, named pres. & COO of MGM Pictures.

MARCUS, MORT
Executive. Pres., Buena Vista Television Production.

MARENSTEIN, HAROLD
Executive. b. New York, NY, Nov. 30, 1916. e. City Coll. of New York, 1937. Shipping, picture checking service, Warner Bros., 1935-45; booking, Loew's Inc., 1945-48; booking, contracts, Selznick Rel. Org., 1948-51; contracts, Paramount, 1951-52; asst. sls. gr., International Rel. Org., 1952; asst. sls. mgr., Janus Films, 1961-64; sls. exec., Rizzoli Films, 1965; 1967, nat'l sales dir., Continental Dist.; gen. sales mgr., Cinemation Industries, 1968; v.p.-sales, dir., Cinemation Industries, 1971; 1976, gen. sls. mgr., General National Films; 1980, gen. sls. mgr., Lima Productions. Now retired.

MARENZI, GARY
Executive. Pres., MGM/UA Communications Group.

MARGOLIN, STUART
Actor, Director, Writer. b. Davenport, IA, Jan. 31, 1940. Wrote play Sad Choices which was produced Off-B'way when he was only 20.
PICTURES: The Gamblers, Kelly's Heroes, Limbo, Death Wish, The Big Bus, Futureworld, Days of Heaven, S.O.B., Class, Running Hot, A Fine Mess, Paramedics (dir. only), Iron Eagle II, Bye Bye Blues, Guilty By Suspicion.
TELEVISION: Series: Occasional Wife, Love American Style, Nichols, The Rockford Files (Emmy Awards, 1979, 1980), Bret Maverick, Mr. Smith. Guest: Hey Landlord, He & She, The

Monkees, M*A*S*H, Gunsmoke, The Mary Tyler Moore Show (also dir.), Rhoda, Magnum P.I., Hill Street Blues. *Movies*: The Intruders, The Ballad of Andy Crocker (writer, associate prod. only), A Summer Without Boys (voice), The Rockford Files (pilot), The California Kid, This is the West That Was, Lanigan's Rabbi, Perilous Voyage, A Killer in the Family, Three of a Kind, To Grandmother's House We Go, How the West Was Fun (dir. only), The Rockford Files: I Still Love L.A, The Rockford Files: A Blessing in Disguise. *Director*: Suddenly Love, A Shining Season, The Long Summer of George Adams, Double Double Toil and Trouble.

MARGULIES, STAN
Producer. b. New York, NY, Dec. 14, 1920. e. De Witt Clinton H.S., NYU, B.S., June, 1940. Army Air Force, May, 1942; p.r., Air Force and the Infantry, wrote service magazines, newspapers including Yank; spec. feature writer & asst. Sunday editor, Salt Lake City Tribune; publicist, RKO Studios, Hollywood, March, 1947; continued publicity work at CBS-Radio, 20th Century-Fox, Walt Disney Productions. Bryna Films, 1955; became vice-pres., 1958; also served exec. prod., TV series, Tales of the Vikings; prod. asst., Spartacus.
PICTURES: 40 Pounds of Trouble, Those Magnificent Men in Their Flying Machines, Don't Just Stand There, The Pink Jungle, If It's Tuesday This Must Be Belgium, I Love My Wife, Willy Wonka and the Chocolate Factory, One Is a Lonely Number, Visions of Eight.
TELEVISION: *Movies*: The 500 Pound Jerk, She Lives, The Morning After, Unwed Father, Men of the Dragon, I Will Fight No More Forever, Roots (Emmy Award, 1977), Roots: The Next Generations (Emmy Award, 1979), Moviola, Agatha Christie's Murder Is Easy, The Thorn Birds, Agatha Christie's A Caribbean Mystery, A Killer in the Family, Sparkling Cyanide, The Mystic Warrior, A Bunny's Tale, Out on a Limb, Broken Angel, Crossing to Freedom, Separate But Equal (Emmy Award, 1991).

MARILL, ALVIN H.
Writer. b. Brockton, MA, Jan. 10, 1934. e. Boston U., 1955. Director music programming, writer/prod., WNAC, Boston 1961-65; dir. music prog., WRFM, NY 1966-67; publicity writer, RCA Records 1967-72; sr. writer/editor, RCA Direct Marketing 1972-80; partner, TLK Direct Marketing 1977-80; mgr., A & R Administration, RCA Direct Marketing 1980-83; exec. editor, CBS TV (1984-88); editor, Carol Publ. Group (1988-94); v.p., Sandal Enterprises (1994-present). Television editor, Films in Review 1973-84. Writer/researcher: The Great Singers (record/tape collections). Jury member: 1983 Locarno Film Fest. Television Movie Hall of Fame.
AUTHOR: Samuel Goldwyn Presents, Robert Mitchum on the Screen, The Films of Anthony Quinn, The Films of Sidney Poitier, Katharine Hepburn: A Pictorial Study, Boris Karloff—A Pictorial Biography, Errol Flynn—A Pictorial Biography, The Complete Films of Edward G. Robinson, More Theatre: Stage to Screen to Television, Movies Made for Television 1964-96, The Films of Tyrone Power; Editor: Moe Howard & The 3 Stooges, The Films of Tommy Lee Jones, The Ultimate John Wayne Trivia Book. Assoc. editor: Leonard Maltin's Movie & Video Guide.

MARIN, CHEECH (RICHARD)
Actor, Writer. b. Los Angeles, CA, July 13, 1946. e. California State U, B.S. Teamed with Tommy Chong in improvisational group, City Works (Vancouver). Comedy recordings include Sleeping Beauty, Cheech and Chong Big Bama, Los Cochinos, The Wedding Album (Grammy Award), Get Out of My Room.
PICTURES: Up in Smoke (also co-s.p.), Cheech and Chong's Next Movie (also co-s.p.), Cheech and Chong's Nice Dreams (also co-s.p.), Things Are Tough All Over (also co-s.p.), It Came from Hollywood, Still Smokin' (also co-s.p.), Yellowbeard, Cheech and Chong's The Corsican Brothers (also co-s.p.), After Hours, Echo Park, Born in East L.A. (also s.p., dir.), Fatal Beauty, Oliver & Company (voice), Troop Beverly Hills (cameo), Ghostbusters II (cameo), Rude Awakening, Far Out Man, The Shrimp on the Barbie, FernGully... The Last Rainforest (voice), A Million to Juan, The Lion King (voice), Desperado, From Dusk Till Dawn, The Great White Hype, Tin Cup.
TELEVISION: *Series*: The Golden Palace, Nash Bridges. *Movie*: The Cisco Kid. *Specials*: Get Out of My Room (also dir., songs), Charlie Barnett—Terms of Enrollment.

MARK, LAURENCE M.
Producer, Executive. b. New York, NY. e. Wesleyan U., B.A.; NYU, M.A. Started career as trainee and publicist for United Artists; also asst. to producer on Lenny, Smile, etc. Joined Paramount Pictures as mktg./prod. liaison dir. and then exec. dir., pub. for m.p. division in NY. Named v.p., prod./mktg. at Paramount Studio; 1980, v.p., west coast mktg.; 1982 promoted to post as v.p., prod. 1984 (projects incl. Trading Places, Terms of Endearment, Falling in Love, Lady Jane); joined 20th Century-Fox as exec. v.p., prod. (projects incl. The Fly, Broadcast News); 1986, established Laurence Mark Productions at Fox; 1989 moved headquarters to Walt Disney Studios.
THEATER: Brooklyn Laundry (L.A.).

PICTURES: Black Widow (exec. prod.), Working Girl (exec. prod.), My Stepmother is an Alien (exec. prod.), Cookie (prod.), Mr. Destiny (exec. prod.), True Colors (prod.), One Good Cop (prod.), The Adventures of Huck Finn (prod.), Gunmen (prod.), Sister Act 2: Back in the Habit (exec. prod.), Cutthroat Island (prod.), Tom & Huck (prod.), Jerry Maguire (prod.), Romy & Michele's High School Reunion (prod.), Tom and Huck.
TELEVISION: Sweet Bird of Youth (exec. prod.).

MARKHAM, MONTE
Actor. b. Manatee, FL, June 21, 1938. e. U. of Georgia. Military service in Coast Guard after which joined resident theatre co. at Stephens College, MO, where he also taught acting. Joined Actor's Workshop Theatre, San Francisco, for three years. Made TV debut in Mission: Impossible episode. June, 1992 formed Perpetual Motion Films with Adam Friedman.
THEATER: *B'way*: Irene (Theatre World Award), Same Time Next Year.
PICTURES: Hour of the Gun, Guns of the Magnificent Seven, One Is a Lonely Number, Midway, Airport '77, Ginger in the Morning, Off the Wall, Jake Speed, Hot Pursuit, Defense Play (also dir.), Neon City (also dir.), At First Sight.
TELEVISION: *Series*: The Second Hundred Years, Mr. Deeds Goes to Town, The New Perry Mason, Dallas, Rituals, Baywatch (also dir. episodes), Melrose Place, Campus Cops. *Movies*: Death Takes a Holiday, The Astronaut, Visions, Hustling, Ellery Queen, Relentless, Drop-Out Father, Hotline, Baywatch: Panic at Malibu Pier. *Host-narrator-prod.-dir.*: Air Combat, Combat at Sea, Master of War, Epic Biographies, The Great Ships.

MARKLE, PETER
Director. b. Danville, PA, Sept. 24, 1946.
PICTURES: The Personals (also s.p., photog.), Hot Dog ... The Movie, Youngblood (also co-story, s.p.), Bat-21, Wagons East!
TELEVISION: *Movies*: Desperate, Nightbreaker, Breaking Point, El Diablo, Through the Eyes of a Killer, Jake Lassiter: Justice on the Bayou, White Dwarf.

MARKOWITZ, ROBERT
Director. b. Irvington, NJ, Feb. 7, 1935. e. Boston Univ. Mostly on TV before theatrical debut with Voices, 1979.
TELEVISION: *Movies*: Children of the Night, Phantom of the Opera, The Deadliest Season, The Storyteller, Kojak: The Belarus File, My Mother's Secret Life, Pray TV, A Long Way Home, Alex: The Life of a Child, Adam: His Song Continues, The Wall, A Cry for Help: The Tracey Thurman Story, Too Young to Die, A Dangerous Life, Decoration Day, Love Lies and Murder, Afterburn, Overexposed, Murder in the Heartland, Because Mommy Works, The Tuskegee Airmen. *Special*: Twilight Zone: Rod Serling's Lost Classics.

MARKS, ALFRED
O.B.E. Actor-Comedian. b. London, 1921. TV, own series, Alfred Marks Time with wife, comedienne Paddie O'Neil.
PICTURES: Desert Mice, There Was a Crooked Man, Weekend with Lulu, The Frightened City, She'll Have to Go, Scream and Scream Again, Our Miss Fred, Valentino, Sleeps Six.
TELEVISION: Blanding's Castle, Hobson's Choice, Paris 1900, The Memorandum.

MARKS, ARTHUR
Producer, Director, Writer, Film Executive. b. Los Angeles, CA, Aug. 2, 1927. At 19 began work at MGM Studios as production messenger. Became asst. dir. in 1950, youngest dir. member of Directors Guild of Amer., 1957. President and board member of Arthur Prod., Inc.
PICTURES: Togetherness (prod., dir., s.p.), Class of '74 (dir., s.p.), Bonnie's Kids (dir., s.p.), Roommates (dir., s.p.), Detroit 9000 (prod., dir.), The Centerfold Girls (prod., dir.), A Woman For All Men (dir.), Wonder Woman (exec. prod.), The Candy Snatchers (exec. prod.), Bucktown (dir.), Friday Foster (prod., dir.), J.D.'s Revenge (prod., dir.), Monkey Hustle (prod., dir.).
Writer: Empress of the China Seas, Gold Stars, Mean Intentions, Hot Times, Starfire, There's A Killer in Philly.
TELEVISION: *Series*: Perry Mason series (1961-66; prod., also dir. of over 100 episodes); writer-dir. of numerous TV shows including: I Spy, Mannix, Starsky & Hutch, Dukes of Hazzard, Young Daniel Boone, My Friend Tony.

MARKS, RICHARD E.
Executive. e. UCLA Sch. of Law. 1978-82, v.p., legal & business affairs for Ziegler/Diskant Literary Agency. Joined Paramount Pictures 1984 as sr. atty. for Network TV Div., as project atty. for Family Ties, Cheers, etc. 1985, named sr. atty. for M.P. Group for The Golden Child, Beverly Hills Cop II, etc.; 1987 joined Weintraub Entertainment Group as v.p. business affairs, m.p. div. 1990, counsel for Disney projects such as The Rocketeer, Beauty and the Beast. 1991, joined Media Home Entertainment as sr. v.p. in charge of all business and legal affairs. 1994, joined the Kushner-Locke Company as sr. v.p., business affairs for feature division.

MARS, KENNETH
Actor. b. Chicago, IL, 1936.
PICTURES: The Producers, Butch Cassidy and the Sundance Kid, Desperate Characters, What's Up Doc?, The Parallax View, Young Frankenstein, Night Moves, The Apple Dumpling Gang Rides Again, Full Moon High, Yellowbeard, Protocol, Prince Jack, Beer, Fletch, Radio Days, For Keeps?, Illegally Yours, Rented Lips, Police Academy 6: City Under Siege, The Little Mermaid (voice), Shadows and Fog, We're Back (voice).
TELEVISION: *Series:* He & She, The Don Knotts Show, Sha Na Na, The Carol Burnett Show (1979). *Guest:* The Facts of Life. *Movies:* Second Chance, Guess Who's Sleeping in My Bed?, Someone I Touched, The New Original Wonder Woman, Before and After, The Rules of Marriage, Get Smart Again.

MARSH, JEAN
Actress, Writer. b. London, Eng., July 1, 1934. NY stage debut in Much Ado About Nothing, 1959. As a child appeared in films: Tales of Hoffman; as principal dancer in Where's Charley. Co-creator, co-author and starred as Rose, in Upstairs, Downstairs.
THEATER: *B'way:* Travesties, The Importance of Being Earnest, Too True to Be Good, My Fat Friend, Whose Life Is It Anyway?, Blithe Spirit.
PICTURES: Cleopatra, Unearthly Stranger, The Limbo Line, Frenzy, Dark Places, The Eagle Has Landed, The Changeling, Return to Oz, Willow.
TELEVISION: Upstairs Downstairs (Emmy Award, 1975), Nine to Five, The Grover Monster, A State Dinner with Queen Elizabeth II, Mad About the Boy: Noel Coward—A Celebration, Habeas Corpus, Uncle Vanya, Twelfth Night, Pygmalion, On the Rocks Theatre, The Corsican Brothers, Master of the Game, Danny, the Champion of the World, Act of Will, A Connecticut Yankee in King Arthur's Court.

MARSHALL, ALAN
Producer. b. London, Eng., Aug. 12, 1938. Co-founder Alan Parker Film Company, 1970. Formerly film editor. Received Michael Balcon Award, British Acad., Outstanding Contribution to Cinema, 1985.
PICTURES: Bugsy Malone, Midnight Express, Fame, Shoot the Moon, Pink Floyd: The Wall, Another Country (Cannes Film Fest. Award, 1984), Birdy (Special Jury Award, Cannes Film Fest., 1985), Angel Heart, Homeboy, Jacob's Ladder, Basic Instinct, Cliffhanger, Showgirls.
TELEVISION: No Hard Feelings, Our Cissy, Footsteps.

MARSHALL, E. G.
Actor. r.n. Everett G. Marshall. b. Owatonna, MN, June 18, 1910. e. Univ. of MN. Acting debut with Oxford Players, 1933.
THEATER: *B'way:* Jason, Jacobowsky and the Colonel, Skin of Our Teeth, Iceman Cometh, Woman Bites Dog, The Survivors, The Gambler, The Crucible, The Little Foxes.
PICTURES: The House on 92nd Street (debut, 1945), 13 Rue Madeleine, Call Northside 77, The Caine Mutiny, Pushover, Bamboo Prison, Broken Lance, The Silver Chalice, The Left Hand of God, The Scarlet Hour, The Mountain, 12 Angry Men, The Bachelor Party, Man on Fire, The Buccaneer, The Journey, Compulsion, Cash McCall, Town Without Pity, The Chase, The Bridge at Remagen, Tora! Tora!, The Pursuit of Happiness, Billy Jack Goes to Washington, Interiors, Superman II, Creepshow, Power, My Chauffeur, La Gran Fiesta, National Lampoon's Christmas Vacation, Two Evil Eyes (The Black Cat), Consenting Adults, Nixon.
TELEVISION: *Series:* The Defenders (2 Emmy Awards: 1962, 1963), The Bold Ones (The New Doctors), Chicago Hope. *Movies:* Collision Course, The Winter of Our Discontent, Under Siege, At Mother's Request, Emma, Queen of the South Seas, The Hijacking of the Achille Lauro, Ironclads, Stephen King's The Tommyknockers, Oldest Living Confederate Widow Tells All.

MARSHALL, FRANK
Producer, Director. b. 1954. Raised in Newport Beach, CA. Worked on first feature film in 1967 while still a student at UCLA. Protege of Peter Bogdanovich, working on his production crew and as asst. on Targets, location manager on The Last Picture Show, What's Up Doc?, assoc. prod. on Paper Moon, Daisy Miller, Nickelodeon, etc. Line producer on Orson Welles' The Other Side of the Wind (unreleased) and Martin Scorsese's The Last Waltz. Worked with Walter Hill on The Driver (assoc. prod.) and The Warriors (exec. prod.). Began collaboration with Steven Spielberg as prod. for Raiders of the Lost Ark. 1992, with wife and partner Kathleen Kennedy formed The Kennedy/Marshall Company.
PICTURES: Raiders of the Lost Ark (prod.), Poltergeist (prod.), E.T.: The Extra-Terrestrial (prod. supvr.). Exec. *Producer:* Twilight Zone—The Movie, Indiana Jones and the Temple of Doom, Fandango, Gremlins, The Goonies, Back to the Future (also 2nd unit dir.), The Color Purple (prod.), Young Sherlock Holmes, An American Tail, Innerspace, The Money Pit (prod.), Empire of the Sun (prod.), Who Framed Roger Rabbit (prod., 2nd unit dir.), The Land Before Time, Indiana

Jones and the Last Crusade, Dad, Back to the Future Part II, Always (prod.), Joe Versus the Volcano, Back to the Future Part III, Gremlins II, Arachnophobia (also dir.), Cape Fear, An American Tail: Fievel Goes West, Hook (co-prod.), Noises Off (prod.), Alive (also dir.), Swing Kids, A Far Off Place, We're Back, Milk Money, Congo (also dir.), The Indian in the Cupboard.
TELEVISION: Amazing Stories (series exec. prod.), Roger Rabbit and the Secrets of Toontown (exec. prod.), Alive: The Miracle of the Andes (exec. prod.).

MARSHALL, GARRY
Producer, Director, Writer, Actor. b. New York, NY, Nov. 13, 1934. r.n. Garry Marscharelli. Sister is director-actress Penny Marshall. e. Northwestern U. Copy boy and reporter for NY Daily News while writing comedy material for Phil Foster, Joey Bishop. Was drummer in his own jazz band and successful stand-up comedian and playwright. Turned Neil Simon's play The Odd Couple into long running TV series (1970). Partner with Jerry Belson many years. *Playwright:* The Roast (with Belson, 1980), Wrong Turn at Lungfish (with Lowell Ganz, 1992; also dir., actor). *Autobiography:* Wake Me When It's Funny (1995).
PICTURES: *Writer-Producer:* How Sweet It Is, The Grasshopper. *Director:* Young Doctors in Love (also exec. prod.), The Flamingo Kid (also co-s.p.), Nothing in Common, Overboard, Beaches, Pretty Woman, Frankie and Johnny (also co-prod.), Exit to Eden. *Actor:* Psych-Out, Lost in America, Jumpin' Jack Flash, Soapdish, A League of Their Own, Hocus Pocus, Dear God.
TELEVISION: *Series Writer:* Jack Paar Show, Joey Bishop Show, Danny Thomas Show, Lucy, Dick Van Dyke Show, I Spy. *Series creator/exec. prod./writer:* Hey Landlord (also dir.), The Odd Couple, The Little People (The Brian Keith Show), Happy Days, Laverne & Shirley, Makin' It (creator only), Angie. *Series exec. prod./writer:* Blansky's Beauties (also dir.), Who's Watching the Kids?, Mork and Mindy (also dir.), Joanie Loves Chachi. *Series exec. prod.:* The New Odd Couple, Nothing in Common. *Series actor:* The Ugliest Girl in Town, A League of Their Own. *Movie:* Evil Roy Slade (co-prod., co-writer). *Special:* The Last Shot (actor).

MARSHALL, PENNY
Actress, Director. b. New York, NY, Oct. 15, 1942. Father: industrial filmmaker and Laverne and Shirley prod., Tony Marscharelli. Brother is producer-director Garry Marshall. Daughter is actress Tracy Reiner. Dropped out of U. of New Mexico to teach dancing. Acted in summer stock and competed on The Original Amateur Hour before going to Hollywood to make TV debut in The Danny Thomas Hour (1967-68).
PICTURES: *Actress:* How Sweet It Is, The Savage Seven, The Grasshopper, 1941, Movers and Shakers, The Hard Way, Hocus Pocus. *Director:* Jumpin' Jack Flash (debut, 1986), Big, Awakenings, A League of Their Own, Renaissance Man, The Preacher's Wife. *Exec. Prod.:* Calendar Girl.
TELEVISION: *Series:* The Bob Newhart Show, The Odd Couple, Friends and Lovers, Laverne and Shirley. *Guest:* Danny Thomas Hour, The Super, Happy Days, Saturday Night Live, Comedy Zone, Chico and the Man. *Movies:* The Feminist and the Fuzz, Evil Roy Slade, The Couple Takes a Wife, The Crooked Hearts, Love Thy Neighbor, Let's Switch, More Than Friends, Challenge of a Lifetime, The Odd Couple: Together Again. *Specials:* Lily for President, The Laverne and Shirley Reunion. *Series Director:* Laverne and Shirley, Working Stiffs, Tracey Ullman Show, A League of Their Own.

MARSHALL, PETER
Actor, TV Show Host. r.n. Pierre La Cock. b. Clarksburg, WV, March 30. Sister is actress Joanne Dru. Began career as NBC page in N.Y. Teamed with the late Tommy Noonan in comedy act for nightclubs, guesting on Ed Sullivan Show and other variety shows. In 1950, made Las Vegas stage debut and since has been headliner there and in Reno and Lake Tahoe. New York stage, in B'way musical Skyscraper. On London stage in H.M.S. Pinafore, Bye Bye Birdie. In La Cage aux Folles (national company and B'way), 42nd St. (Atlantic City), Rumors (natl. co.).
PICTURES: The Rookie, Swingin' Along (Double Trouble), Ensign Pulver, The Cavern, Americathon, Annie.
TELEVISION: *Host:* Two of the Most (local N.Y. show), The Hollywood Squares, NBC Action Playhouse, The Peter Marshall Variety Show, Mrs. America Pageant, Mrs. World; many guest appearances.

MARTEL, GENE
Producer, Director. b. New York, NY, June 19, 1906. e. City Coll. of New York , U. of Alabama, Sorbonne, Paris. Newspaperman, New York and Birmingham, Ala.; dancer, actor, choreographer, director Broadway; prod. dir., many documentaries; films for State Dept., others; dir. for Paramount Pictures. Joined Princess Pictures 1952 to make films in Europe; formed own co., Martel Productions Inc., 1956.
PICTURES: Check-mate, Double-Barrelled Miracle, The Lie, Double Profile, Sergeant and the Spy, Black Forest, Eight Witnesses, Fire One, Phantom Caravan, Doorway to Suspicion, Diplomatic Passport, Immediate Disaster.

MARTIN, ANDREA
Actress. b. Portland, ME, Jan. 15, 1947.
THEATRE: NY: My Favorite Year (Tony Award & Theatre World Award), The Merry Wives of Windsor.
PICTURES: Cannibal Girls, Soup for One, Club Paradise, Rude Awakening, Worth Winning, Too Much Sun, Stepping Out, All I Want for Christmas, Ted and Venus,. Bogus.
TELEVISION: Series: Second City TV, SCTV Network 90 (2 Emmy Awards for writing), The Martin Short Show. Special: In Search of Dr. Seuss. Movie: Harrison Bergeron.

MARTIN, DEAN
Actor, Singer. r.n. Dino Crocetti. b. Steubenville, OH, June 7, 1917. e. Steubenville H.S. Was amateur prizefighter; worked at odd jobs, mill hand, gasoline attendant, prior to singing career. Joined comedian Jerry Lewis at 500 Club, Atlantic City, NJ, as straight man-singer, 1946; as team played many theatres, night clubs until 1956. Voted (with Jerry Lewis) one of the top ten Money-Making Stars in Motion Picture Herald-Fame poll, 1951, 1953-55; number One, 1952; solo: 1967, 1968.
PICTURES: My Friend Irma (debut, 1949), My Friend Irma Goes West, At War With the Army, That's My Boy, Sailor Beware, Jumping Jacks, The Stooge, The Caddy, Road to Bali (cameo), Scared Stiff, Money from Home, Living It Up, Three Ring Circus, You're Never Too Young, Artists and Models, Pardners, Hollywood or Bust, Ten Thousand Bedrooms, The Young Lions, Some Came Running, Rio Bravo, Career, Who Was That Lady?, Bells Are Ringing, Ocean's Eleven, Pepe, All in a Night's Work, Ada, The Road to Hong Kong (cameo), Sergeants 3, Who's Got the Action?, Toys in the Attic, Come Blow Your Horn (cameo), Who's Been Sleeping in My Bed?, Four for Texas, What a Way to Go!, Robin and the Seven Hoods, Kiss Me Stupid!, The Sons of Katie Elder, Marriage on the Rocks, The Silencers, Texas Across the River, Murderers' Row, The Ambushers, Rough Night in Jericho, Bandolero, Five Card Stud, How to Save a Marriage and Ruin Your Life, The Wrecking Crew, Airport, Something Big, Showdown, Mr. Ricco, The Cannonball Run, Cannonball Run II.
TELEVISION: Series: The Colgate Comedy Hour, The Dean Martin Show (1965-74), Half Nelson. Guest: Club Oasis, Danny Thomas Show, Rawhide, Lucy Show, Carol Burnett, Sheriff Lobo, many others.
(d. December 25, 1995)

MARTIN, DEWEY
Actor. b. Katemcy, TX, Dec. 8, 1923. e. U. of Georgia. U.S. Navy, WWII. In stock before film debut in 1949.
PICTURES: Knock on Any Door, Kansas Raiders, The Thing, The Big Sky, Tennessee Champ, Prisoner of War, Men of the Fighting Lady, Land of the Pharaohs, Desperate Hours, The Proud and Profane, 10,000 Bedrooms, Battle Ground, The Longest Day, Savage Sam, Seven Alone.
TELEVISION: G.E. Theatre, U.S. Steel, Playhouse 90, Playwrights 56, Daniel Boone, Doc Holliday, Wheeler and Murdoch, Outer Limits, Twilight Zone.

MARTIN, EDWIN DENNIS
Executive. b. Columbus, GA, Jan. 30, 1920. e. U. of Georgia, B.S., 1940. Past pres., Martin Theatre Cos.; past pres., TOA, International, past pres., Variety. Retired.

MARTIN, GARY
Executive. b. Aug, 14, 1944. V.P. of production, Columbia Pictures, 1984-86; exec. v.p., production, 1986-88. Named pres. of production admin., 1988. Member, AMPAS., D.G.A.

MARTIN, MILLICENT
Actress, Singer. b. Romford, Eng., June 8, 1934. Toured U.S. in The Boy Friend, 1954-57.
THEATER: Expresso Bongo, The Crooked Mile, Our Man Crichton, Tonight at 8:30, The Beggar's Opera, Puss 'n Boots, Aladdin, Peter Pan, The Card, Absurd Person Singular, Aladdin, Side by Side by Sondheim, King of Hearts, Move Over Mrs. Markham, Noises Off, One Into Two, 42nd Street (N.Y. & L.A.), The Cemetery Club, Shirley Valentine, The Boyfriend, Noel, Follies.
TELEVISION: Series: The Picadilly Palace, From a Bird's Eye View, Mainly Millicent, Millie, Dowtown. Also: Harry Moorings, Kiss Me Kate, London Palladium Color Show, Tom Jones, Englebert Humperdinck show, That Was the Week That Was, LA Law, Max Headroom, Newhart, Murphy Brown.
PICTURES: Libel, The Horsemasters (tv in U.S.), The Girl on the Boat, Nothing But the Best, Those Magnificent Men in Their Flying Machines, Alfie, Stop the World I Want To Get Off, Invasion Quartet.

MARTIN, PAMELA SUE
Actress. b. Westport, CT, Jan. 15, 1953. Did modelling and TV commercials before entering films.
PICTURES: To Find a Man, The Poseidon Adventure, Buster and Billie, Our Time, The Lady in Red, Torchlight (also assoc. prod. & s.p.), Flicks, A Cry in the Wild.
TELEVISION: Series: Nancy Drew Mysteries, Hardy Boys Mysteries, Dynasty, The Star Games (host). Movies: The Girls of Huntington House, The Gun and the Pulpit, Human Feelings, Bay Coven.

MARTIN, STEVE
Actor, Writer. b. Waco, TX, Aug. 14, 1945. e. Long Beach Col., UCLA. Raised in Southern California. Worked at Disneyland, teaching himself juggling, magic and the banjo. Became writer for various TV comedy shows, incl. Smothers Brothers Comedy Hour (Emmy Award for writing, 1968-69), Glen Campbell Show, Sonny & Cher. Co-writer for special Van Dyke and Company. Wrote and starred in Acad. Award nominated short The Absent-Minded Waiter. Author: Cruel Shoes (1980). Albums: Let's Get Small (Grammy Award, 1977), A Wild and Crazy Guy (Grammy Award, 1978), Comedy Is Not Pretty, The Steve Martin Brothers. Gold Record for single King Tut.
THEATER: Actor: Waiting for Godot (Off-B'way debut, 1988). Author: Picasso at the Lapin Agile (regional, 1993), WASP (Off-B'way).
PICTURES: Sgt. Pepper's Lonely Hearts Club Band (debut, 1978), The Kids Are Alright, The Muppet Movie, The Jerk (also co-s.p.), Pennies From Heaven, Dead Men Don't Wear Plaid (also co-s.p.), The Man With Two Brains (also co-s.p.), The Lonely Guy, All of Me (NY Film Critics & Natl. Board of Review Awards, 1984), Movers and Shakers, Three Amigos! (also co-s.p., exec. prod.), Little Shop of Horrors, Roxanne (also s.p., exec. prod.; Natl. Society of Film Critics & L.A. Film Critics Awards for actor, WGA Award for adapt. s.p., 1987), Planes Trains & Automobiles, Dirty Rotten Scoundrels, Parenthood, My Blue Heaven, L.A. Story (also s.p., co-exec. prod.), Father of the Bride, Grand Canyon, Housesitter, Leap of Faith, A Simple Twist of Fate (also s.p., exec. prod.), Mixed Nuts, Father of the Bride 2, Sgt. Bilko.
TELEVISION: Series: Andy Williams Presents Ray Stevens, The Ken Berry "WOW" Show, Half the George Kirby Comedy Hour, The Sonny and Cher Comedy Hour, The Smothers Brothers Show (1975), The Johnny Cash Show. Guest: The Tonight Show, Cher, The Carol Burnett Show, Saturday Night Live, The Muppet Show, Steve Allen Comedy Hour. Specials: HBO On Location: Steve Martin, Steve Martin—A Wild and Crazy Guy, Comedy Is Not Pretty, All Commercials: A Steve Martin Special, Steve Martin's Best Show Ever, The Winds of Whoopie, Texas 150--A Celebration, The Smothers Brothers Comedy Hour 20th Reunion, Learned Pigs and Fireproof Women. Producer: Domestic Life (series). Pilot: Leo & Liz in Beverly Hills (writer, creator, co-prod., dir.). Movies: The Jerk Too (exec. prod. only), And the Band Played On.

MARTIN, TONY
Singer, Musician, Actor. b. Oakland, CA, Dec. 25, 1913. r.n. Alvin Morris. e. Oakland H.S., St. Mary's Coll. m. actress-dancer Cyd Charisse. Sang, played saxophone & clarinet in high school band, engaged by nearby theatres for vaudeville; with Five Red Peppers, jazz group at 14 yrs.; two yrs. later with band, Palace Hotel, San Francisco; radio debut Walter Winchell program, 1932; joined Tom Gerund's band, World's Fair Chicago, 1933; played night clubs. First starring radio show, Tune Up Time (singer & emcee); on Burns and Allen program; own show for Texaco, Carnation Contented Hour. Recordings: Begin the Beguine, Intermezzo, The Last Time I Saw Paris, I'll See You in My Dreams, Domino, September Song, For Every Man There's a Woman.
PICTURES: Pigskin Parade (debut, 1936), Banjo on My Knee, Sing Baby Sing, Follow the Fleet, Back to Nature, The Holy Terror, Sing and Be Happy, You Can't Have Everything, Life Begins in College, Ali Baba Goes to Town, Sally Irene and Mary, Kentucky Moonshine, Thanks for Everything, Up the River, Winner Take All, Music in My Heart, Ziegfeld Girl, The Big Store, Till the Clouds Roll By, Casbah, Two Tickets to Broadway, Here Come the Girls, Easy to Love, Deep in My Heart, Hit the Deck, Quincannon—Frontier Scout, Let's Be Happy, Dear Mr. Wonderful.

MASLANSKY, PAUL
Producer. b. New York, NY, Nov. 23, 1933. e. Washington and Lee U., 1954. Moved to Europe performing as jazz musician in Paris, 1959-60. Entered film business with documentary, Letter from Paris. Asst. to prods. Charles Shneer and Irving Allan in England, Italy and Yugoslavia, 1961-62. In charge of physical prod. in Europe for UA, 1965-67.
PICTURES: Castle of the Living Dead, Revenge of the Blood Beast, Sudden Terror (Eye Witness), Raw Meat, Deathline, Sister of Satan, Big Truck, Poor Claire, Deathline, Sugar Hill (also dir.), Race With the Devil, Hard Times, The Blue Bird, Circle of Iron, Damnation Alley (co-prod.), When You Comin' Back Red Ryder (co-prod.), Hot Stuff, The Villain, Scavenger Hunt, The Salamander, Ruckus, Love Child, Police Academy, Police Academy 2: Their First Assignment, Return to Oz, Police Academy 3: Back in Training, Police Academy 4: Citizens on Patrol, Police Academy 5: Assignment Miami Beach, For Better or Worse (exec. prod.), Police Academy 6: City Under Siege, Ski Patrol (exec. prod.), Honeymoon Academy (exec. prod.), The Russia House, Cop and a Half, Police Academy: Mission to Moscow, Fluke.
TELEVISION: Movie: The Gun and the Pulpit. Mini-Series: King.

MASON, JACKIE
Comedian, Actor. b. Sheboygan, WI June 9, 1934. e. City College. Was a rabbi before becoming stand-up comedian. Records include The World According to Me! Has lectureship in his name at Oxford Univ. in England.
THEATER: Enter Solly Gold (1965), A Teaspoon Every Four Hours (Amer. National Theatre & Academy Theatre), Sex-a-Poppin (revue, prod. only), The World According to Me! (one-man show, special Tony Award, 1987), Jackie Mason: Brand New, Politically Incorrect.
PICTURES: Operation Delilah (debut, 1966), The Stoolie (also prod.), The Jerk, History of the World Part I, Caddyshack II.
TELEVISION: Guest: Steve Allen, Ed Sullivan, Jack Paar, Garry Moore, Perry Como and Merv Griffin Shows. Johnny Carson, Arsenio Hall, Evening at the Improv, Late Night with David Letterman. Series: Chicken Soup, Jackie Mason (synd.). Specials: Jack Paar is Alive and Well!, The World According to Me! (ACE Award), Jackie Mason on Broadway (Emmy Award for Writing).

MASON, JOHN DUDLEY
Executive. b. Ashland, KY, Oct 29, 1949. e. Amherst Coll., B.A., cum laude, 1971; Claremont Graduate Sch. and University Center, M.A., 1973; Amos Tuck Sch. of Business Administration, Dartmouth Coll., M.B.A., 1978. Program officer, National Endowment for the Humanities, 1972-76; analyst (1978-79), asst. mgr. (1979-80), mgr. (1980) strategic planning, Consolidated Rail Corp.; Consultant, Frito-Lay, Division, PepsiCo (1980-82); mgr, corporate planning, Dun & Bradstreet Corp. (1982-86); finance director, anti-piracy (1986-90), v.p. finance, anti-piracy (1990-92), Motion Picture Association of America, Inc. Chmn, New Century Artists' Mgmt., 1990-present. Chmn., Finance Comm. and mem., bd. of dir. Association de Gestion Int'l. Collective des Oeuvres Audiovisuelles (AGICOA) 1987-88. Director, Institutio Venezolano de Representacion Cinematografica (INVERECI), Caracas, Venezuela (1988-92). Director: Foundation for the Protection of Film & Video Works (FVWP), Taipei, Taiwan (1987-92). Dir. sec. Korean Federation Against Copyright Theft, 1990-92; Dir., Japan & Intl. M.P. Copyright Assn., Tokyo, 1990-92; Trustee and Treasurer, Design Industries Foundation for AIDS, 1990-1994.

MASON, KENNETH M.
Executive. b. Rochester, NY; Sept. 21, 1917. e. Washington and Jefferson Coll. (BA, 1938); U. of Rochester, graduate work; Dr. of Laws (H), Washington & Jefferson Coll., 1989. Began career with Eastman Kodak Co. in Kodak Park cine processing dept. in 1935; transferred following year to film dev. dept., Kodak Research Lab. Later joined film planning dept., remaining there until entering U.S. Navy in 1943. Returned to Kodak in 1946 as staff engineer in Kodak Office motion picture film dept. 1950 appt. mgr. of Midwest Division, of M.P. Film Dept.; became gen. mgr., Midwest Division, m.p. products sales dept. in 1963; named sls. mgr. of NYC region in 1965; appt. regional sls. mgr., Pacific Southern Region, Hollywood, in 1970; 1974 appt. mgr., product programs and research, Motion Picture and Audiovisual Markets Division, Kodak Office; 1974 named gen. mgr. of that division. Elected asst. v.p. of co., 1974, then v.p., 1978. Retired 1982. Former chmn., Inter-Society Committee for the Enhancement of Theatrical Presentation. Member, Trustee emeritus, Board of Trustees of Washington and Jefferson Coll. (and former chmn); past pres. of Society of Motion Picture & Television Engineers and honorary member; honorary fellow of British Kinematograph Sound & Television Society; mem. of University Film & Video Assn., Motion Picture Academy, American Society of Cinematographers. Board of dir.: Univ. Film & Video Foundation.

MASON, MARSHA
Actress. b. St. Louis. April 3, 1942. e. Webster Coll. Came to N.Y. to continue dramatic studies and embark on theatre career. Member of American Conservatory Theatre, San Francisco.
THEATER: The Deer Park, Cactus Flower, The Indian Wants the Bronx, Happy Birthday Wanda June, Private Lives, You Can't Take It With You, Cyrano de Bergerac, A Doll's House, The Crucible, The Good Doctor, Old Times, The Big Love, Lake No Bottom. Dir.: Juno's Swans.
PICTURES: Hot Rod Hullabaloo (debut, 1966), Blume in Love, Cinderella Liberty (Acad. Award nom.), Audrey Rose, The Goodbye Girl (Acad. Award nom.), The Cheap Detective, Promises in the Dark, Chapter Two (Acad. Award nom.), Only When I Laugh (Acad. Award nom.), Max Dugan Returns, Heartbreak Ridge, Stella, Drop Dead Fred, I Love Trouble, Nick of Time, 2 Days in the Valley.
TELEVISION: Series: Love of Life, Sibs. Specials: Brewsie and Willie, The Good Doctor, Cyrano de Bergerac. Movies: Lois Gibbs and the Love Canal, Surviving, Trapped in Silence, The Image, Dinner at Eight, Broken Trust. Dir.: Little Miss Perfect.

MASON, PAMELA
Actress, Writer. b. Westgate. England. Mar. 10, 1918. Stage debut, 1936, The Luck of the Devil, London; also playwright (in collab. with James Mason: Flying Blind, Made in Heaven),

AUTHOR: This Little Hand, A Lady Possessed, The Blinds Are Down, Ignoramus, Marriage Is the First Step Toward Divorce, The Female Pleasure Hunt. Columnist for Movieline Magazine.
PICTURES: I Met a Murderer, They Were Sisters, The Upturned Glass, Pandora and the Flying Dutchman, Lady Possessed, Everything You Always Wanted to Know About Sex.
TELEVISION: Series (synd): The Pamela Mason Show, The Weaker Sex?.

MASSEN, OSA
Actress. b. Denmark, Copenhagen. Jan. 13, 1916.
PICTURES: Honeymoon in Bali, Honeymoon for Three, A Woman's Face, Accent on Love, You'll Never Get Rich, The Devil Pays Off, Iceland, Jack London, Cry of the Werewolf, Tokyo Rose, Strange Journey, Night Unto Night, Deadline at Dawn, Gentleman Misbehaves, Rocketship XM, Outcasts of the City.

MASSEY, ANNA
Actress. b. Sussex, England, Aug. 11, 1937. Daughter of late actor Raymond Massey. Brother is actor Daniel Massey. On London stage in The Reluctant Debutante (debut, 1958), The Prime of Jean Brodie, Slag, The Importance of Being Earnest, Spoiled, Doctor's Delimma, School for Scandal, With National Theatre, 1989.
PICTURES: Gideon of Scotland Yard, Peeping Tom, Bunny Lake Is Missing, DeSade, The Looking Glass War, David Copperfield (TV in U.S.), Frenzy, A Doll's House, Vault of Horror, A Little Romance, Sweet William, Another Country, The Chain, Five Days One Summer, Foreign Body, Mountains of the Moon, La Couleur du Vent, The Tall Guy, Killing Dad, Impromptu, Haunted.
TELEVISION: Remember the Germans, Wicked Woman, The Corn Is Green, Sakharov, Hotel Du Lac (BAFTA Award), A Hazard of Hearts, Around the World in 80 Days, Tears in the Rain, The Man from the Pru.

MASSEY, DANIEL
Actor. b. London, Eng., Oct. 10, 1933. e. Eaton and King's Colleges, Cambridge U. Father was later actor Raymond Massey. Sister is actress Anna Massey. On B'way in She Loves Me, Gigi. Recent London theatre incl. Follies, The Devil's Disciple.
PICTURES: In Which We Serve (debut, 1942), Girls at Sea, Upstairs and Downstairs, The Queen's Guard, Go to Blazes, The Entertainer, Operation Bullshine (Girls in Arms), The Amorous Adventures of Moll Flanders, The Jokers, Star! (Acad. Award nom.), Fragment of Fear, Mary Queen of Scots, Vault of Horror, The Incredible Sarah, The Devil's Advocate, Warlords of Atlantis, Bad Timing: A Sensual Obsession, The Cat and the Canary, Victory, Scandal, In the Name of the Father.
TELEVISION: Series: The Roads to Freedom. Mini-series: The Golden Bowl. Movies/Specials: Aren't We All (debut, 1958), Love with a Perfect Stranger, Intimate Contact, Inspector Morse, Look of Love, Bye Bye Columbus, Stalin, GBH.

MASTERS, BEN
Actor. b. Corvallis, OR, May 6, 1947. e. Univ. of Oregon.
THEATER: The Cherry Orchard, Waltz of the Toreadors, Plenty, Captain Brassbound's Conversion, The Boys in the Band, Eden Court, What the Butler Saw, The White Whore and the Bit Player, Key Exchange.
PICTURES: Mandingo, All That Jazz, Key Exchange, Dream Lover, Making Mr. Right.
TELEVISION: Series: Heartbeat. Guest: Barnaby Jones, Kojack. Movies: One of Our Own, The Shadow Box, The Neighborhood, Illusions, The Deliberate Stranger, Street of Dreams, Cruel Doubt, Running Mates, A Twist of the Knife, A Time to Heal, Lady Killer. Mini-Series: Loose Change, Celebrity, Noble House.

MASTERSON, MARY STUART
Actress. b. Los Angeles, CA, June 28, 1966. Daughter of writer-director-actor Peter Masterson and actress Carlin Glynn. e. Goddard Col. Made film debut at age 8 in The Stepford Wives (1975), which featured her father. Spent summer at Stage Door Manor in Catskills; two summers at Sundance Inst. Studied acting with Gary Swanson. Member of the Actor's Studio. Off-off B'way debut in Been Taken. Off-B'way debut in Lily Dale followed by The Lucky Spot (Manhattan Theatre Club). Regional: Moonlight and Valentines, Three Sisters.
PICTURES: The Stepford Wives (debut, 1975), Heaven Help Us, At Close Range, My Little Girl, Some Kind of Wonderful, Gardens of Stone, Mr. North, Chances Are, Immediate Family (Natl. Board of Review Award, 1989), Funny About Love, Fried Green Tomatoes, Mad at the Moon, Married to It, Benny & Joon, Bad Girls, Radioland Murders, Heaven's Prisoners, Bed of Roses.
TELEVISION: Movie: Love Lives On. Guest: Amazing Stories (Go to the Head of the Class).

MASTERSON, PETER
Actor, Writer, Director. r.n. Carlos Bee Masterson, Jr. b. Houston, TX, June 1, 1934. m. actress Carlin Glynn. Daughter is actress Mary Stuart Masterson. e. Rice U., Houston, BA. 1957. NY stage debut, Call Me By My Rightful Name, 1961.

THEATER: Marathon '33, Blues for Mr. Charlie, The Trial of Lee Harvey Oswald, The Great White Hope, That Championship Season, The Poison Tree, The Best Little Whorehouse in Texas (co-author, dir.), The Last of the Knucklemen (dir.).
PICTURES: *Actor*: Ambush Bay (debut, 1965), Counterpoint, In the Heat of the Night, Tomorrow, The Exorcist, Man on a Swing, The Stepford Wives, Gardens of Stone. *Writer*: The Best Little Whore House in Texas. *Director*: The Trip to Bountiful, Full Moon in Blue Water, Blood Red, Night Game, Convicts.
TELEVISION: Camera Three, Pueblo; The Quinns; A Question of Guilt.

MASTORAKIS, NICO
Writer, Director, Producer. b. Athens, Greece, 1941. Writer of novels and screenplays, including Fire Below Zero, and Keepers of the Secret (co-author). Pres. Omega Entertainment Ltd. since 1978.
PICTURES: *Writer/dir./prod.*: The Time Traveller, Blind Date, Sky High, The Zero Boys, The Wind, Terminal Exposure, Nightmare at Noon, Glitch, Ninja Academy, Hired to Kill, In the Cool of the Night, At Random. *Prod.*: The Greek Tycoon, Red Tide, Grandmother's House, Darkroom, Bloodstone (prod., co-s.p.).

MASTRANTONIO, MARY ELIZABETH
Actress. b. Oak Park, IL, Nov. 17, 1958. e. U. of Illinois 1976-78 where she trained for opera. m. director Pat O'Connor. Worked as singer & dancer for summer at Opryland Theme Park in Nashville. Came to NY as understudy and vacation replacement as Maria in West Side Story revival.
THEATER: *NY*: Copperfield (1981), Oh Brother, Amadeus, Sunday in the Park With George (Playwright's Horizons), The Human Comedy, Henry V, The Marriage of Figaro, Measure for Measure, The Knife, Twelfth Night.
PICTURES: Scarface (debut, 1983), The Color of Money (Acad. Award nom.), Slamdance, The January Man, The Abyss, Fools of Fortune, Class Action, Robin Hood: Prince of Thieves, White Sands, Consenting Adults, A Day to Remember, Three Wishes, Two Bits.
TELEVISION: *Mini-Series*: Mussolini: The Untold Story. *Special*: Uncle Vanya (BBC).

MASTROIANNI, MARCELLO
Actor. b. Fontana Liri, Italy, Sept. 28, 1924. e. U. of Rome theatrical company. Draftsman in Rome, 1940-43. WWII, drew military maps until captured by Nazis and escaped. Theatrical debut in Rome in Angelica, 1948. Formed indep. prod. co., Master Films, 1966.
THEATER: Death of a Salesman, Streetcar Named Desire, Ciao Rudy.
PICTURES: I Miserabili (debut, 1947), Too Bad She's Bad, A Dog's Life, Three Girls from Rome, The Miller's Beautiful Wife, Fever to Live, The Ladykillers of Rome, Love a La Carte, Days of Love, White Nights, Big Deal on Madonna Street, Where the Hot Wind Blows, The Tailor's Maid, Most Wonderful Moment, Bell Antonio, La Dolce Vita, Divorce Italian Style, Ghosts of Rome, La Notte, A Very Private Affair, The Organizer, 8 1/2, Yesterday Today and Tomorrow, Marriage Italian Style, Casanova '70, The 10th Victim, The Poppy Is Also a Flower, Shoot Loud Louder... I Don't Understand, The Stranger, Ghosts Italian Style (cameo), Kiss the Other Shiek, The Man With the Balloons, A Place for Lovers, Leo the Last, Diamonds for Breakfast, Sunflower, The Pizza Triangle, The Priest's Wife, Fellini's Roma (cameo), It Only Happens to Others, What?, The Grande Bouffe, Massacre in Rome, Down the Ancient Stairs, The Sunday Woman, The Gangster's Doll, The Divine Nymph, A Special Day, Lunatics and Lovers, One Way or Another, Ladies and Gentlemen Good Night, Wifemistress, Bye Bye Monkey, Stay as You Are, Blood Feud, Neapolitan Mystery, City of Women, The Terrace, Ghost of Love, The Skin, Beyond the Door, Gabriella, La Nuit de Varennes, The General of the Dead Army, Piera's Story, Henry IV, The Last Horror Film (cameo), Macaroni, Ginger and Fred, Intervista, Dark Eyes, Miss Arizona, Traffic Jam, The Two Lives of Martia Pascal, Splendor, What Time Is It?, Everybody's Fine, Toward Evening, The Suspended Step of the Stork, A Fine Romance, Used People, The Beekeeper, The Children Thief, 1-2-3 Sun, I Don't Want to Talk About It, Pret-a-Porter (Ready to Wear), A Hundred and One Nights, According to Pereira, Beyond the Clouds, Three Lives and Only One Death.

MASUR, RICHARD
Actor. b. New York, NY, Nov. 20, 1948. Directed Oscar-nominated short, Love Struck, 1987.
THEATRE: *B'way*: The Changing Room.
PICTURES: Whiffs (debut, 1975), Bittersweet Love, Semi-Tough, Who'll Stop the Rain, Hanover Street, Scavenger Hunt, Heaven's Gate, I'm Dancing as Fast as I Can, The Thing, Timerider, Risky Business, Under Fire, Nightmares, The Mean Season, My Science Project, Head Office, Heartburn, The Believers, Walker, Rent-a-Cop, Shoot to Kill, License to Drive, Far from Home, Flashback, Going Under, My Girl, Encino Man, The Man Without a Face, Six Degrees of Separation, My Girl 2, Forget Paris, Multiplicity.

TELEVISION: *Series*: Hot L Baltimore, One Day at a Time, Empire. *Mini-Series*: East of Eden. *Movies*: Having Babies, Betrayal, Mr. Horn, Walking Through the Fire, Fallen Angel, Money on the Side, An Invasion of Privacy, The Demon Murder Case, Adam, John Steinbeck's The Winter of Our Discontent, Flight #90: Disaster on the Potomac, The Burning Bed, Obsessed With a Married Woman, Wild Horses, Embassy, Adam: His Song Continues, Roses Are for the Rich, Cast the First Stone, When the Bough Breaks, Settle the Score, Always Remember I Love You, Stephen King's IT, The Story Lady, And the Band Played On, Search for Grace, My Brother's Keeper, The Face on the Milk Carton, Hiroshima. *Director*: Torn Between Two Fathers (After School Special).

MATHESON, TIM
Actor. b. Los Angeles, CA, Dec. 31, 1947. e. California State U. Debut on TV at age 12 in Window on Main Street. At 19, contract player for Universal. 1985, turned to direction: St. Elsewhere episode and music videos. Set up own production co. at Burbank Studios 1985; acted off-B'way in True West. With partner Daniel Grodnick bought National Lampoon from founder Matty Simons, becoming exec. officer and chmn. 1989; resigned in 1991. Co-prod. film Blind Fury.
PICTURES: Divorce American Style (debut, 1967), Yours Mine and Ours, How to Commit Marriage, Magnum Force, Almost Summer, National Lampoon's Animal House, Dreamer, The Apple Dumpling Gang Rides Again, 1941, House of God, A Little Sex, To Be or Not To Be, Up the Creek, Impulse, Fletch, Speed Zone, Drop Dead Fred, Solar Crisis, Black Sheep.
TELEVISION: *Movies*: Owen Marshall: Counselor-at-Law, Lock Stock and Barrel, Hitched, Remember When, The Last Day, The Runaway Barge, The Quest, Mary White, Listen to Your Heart, Obsessed with a Married Woman, Blind Justice, Warm Hearts Cold Feet, Bay Coven, The Littlest Victims, Little White Lies, Buried Alive, Joshua's Heart, Stephen King's Sometimes They Come Back, The Woman Who Sinned, Quicksand: No Escape, Relentless: Mind of a Killer, Trial & Error, Dying to Love You, A Kiss to Die For, Robin Cook's Harmful Intent, Target of Suspicion, Breach of Conduct (dir., co-exec. prod. only), While Justice Sleeps, Fast Company. *Series*: Window on Main Street, Jonny Quest (voice), The Virginian, Bonanza, The Quest, Tucker's Witch, Just in Time (also co-exec. prod.), Charlie Hoover. *Pilot*: Nikki & Alexander. *Special*: Bus Stop.

MATHIS, SAMANTHA
Actress. b. New York, NY, 1971. Mother is actress Bibi Besch; grandmother was actress Gusti Huber. Began acting as teen landing role in tv pilot Aaron's Way at age 16.
PICTURES: The Bulldance (debut, 1988 in Yugoslav film), Pump Up the Volume, This Is My Life, FernGully ... The Last Rainforest (voice), Super Mario Bros., The Music of Chance, The Thing Called Love, Little Women, Jack and Sarah, How to Make an American Quilt, The American President, Broken Arrow.
TELEVISION: *Series*: Knightwatch. *Movies*: Cold Sassy Tree, To My Daughter, 83 Hours 'Til Dawn.

MATLIN, MARLEE
Actress. b. Morton Grove, IL, Aug. 24, 1965. e. John Hersey H.S., Chicago, public school with special education program for deaf; William Rainey Harper Coll., majoring in criminal justice. Performed at Children's Theatre of the Deaf in Des Plaines at age 8, playing many leading roles. As adult appeared in only one stage show. Theatrical film debut in Children of a Lesser God. Production company, Solo One Productions.
PICTURES: Children of a Lesser God (debut, 1986; Academy Award, Golden Globe), Walker, The Player, The Linguini Incident, Hear No Evil, It's My Party, Snitch.
TELEVISION: *Series*: Reasonable Doubts, The Outer Limits, Picket Fences. *Movies*: Bridge to Silence, Against Her Will: The Carrie Buck Story. *Specials*: Face the Hate, Meaning of Life, Free to Laugh, Creative Spirit, The Big Help, People In Motion (host). *Guest*: Sesame Street, Adventures in Wonderland, Picket Fences (Emmy Award nom.), Seinfeld (Emmy Award nom.).

MATTHAU, CHARLES
Director. b. New York, NY, Dec. 10, 1964. Son of actor Walter Matthau. e. U. of Southern California Film School. While at USC wrote and dir. The Duck Film, a silent comedy short (Golden Seal Award, London Amateur Film Fest. and C.I.N.E. Eagle Award.) Also dir. short, I Was a Teenage Fundraiser. President, The Matthau Company, organized 1989.
PICTURES: Doin' Time on Planet Earth. (nom. Saturn Award, best dir., Acad. of Science Fiction.), The Grass Harp (dir., prod.)
TELEVISION: *Movie*: Mrs. Lambert Remembers Love (dir., prod.; Golden Eagle, Golden Medal & Houston Fest. Grand & Angel Awards).

MATTHAU, WALTER
Actor. b. New York, NY, Oct. 1, 1920. Served in Air Force WWII. Studied journalism at Columbia U. and acting at New Sch. for Social Research's dramatic workshop, 1946, then acted in summer stock.

THEATER: *B'way*: Anne of the Thousand Days (debut, 1948), Will Success Spoil Rock Hunter?, Once More With Feeling, Once There Was a Russian, A Shot in the Dark (Tony Award, 1962), The Odd Couple (Tony Award, 1965). LA: Juno and the Paycock.
PICTURES: The Kentuckian (debut, 1955), The Indian Fighter, Bigger Than Life, A Face in the Crowd, Slaughter on Tenth Avenue, King Creole, The Voice in the Mirror, Ride a Crooked Trial, Onionhead, Strangers When We Meet, The Gangster Story (also dir.), Lonely Are the Brave, Who's Got the Action?, Island of Love, Charade, Ensign Pulver, Fail Safe, Goodbye Charlie, Mirage, The Fortune Cookie (Academy Award, best supporting actor, 1966), A Guide for the Married Man, The Odd Couple, The Secret Life of an American Wife, Candy, Cactus Flower, Hello Dolly!, A New Leaf, Plaza Suite, Kotch (Acad. Award nom.), Pete n' Tillie, Charley Varrick, The Laughing Policeman, Earthquake, The Taking of Pelham One Two Three, The Front Page, The Sunshine Boys (Acad. Award nom.), The Bad News Bears, Casey's Shadow, House Calls, California Suite, Little Miss Marker (also exec. prod.), Hopscotch, First Monday in October, Buddy Buddy, I Ought to Be in Pictures, The Survivors, Movers and Shakers, Pirates, The Couch Trip, Il Piccolo Diavolo (The Little Devil), JFK, Dennis the Menace, Grumpy Old Men, I.Q., The Grass Harp, I'm Not Rappaport, Grumpier Old Men.
TELEVISION: Many appearances 1952-65 on Philco-Goodyear Playhouse, Studio One, Playhouse 90, Kraft Theatre, Awake and Sing, Insight. *Series*: Tallahassee 7000 (1961). *Movies*: The Incident, Mrs. Lambert Remembers Love, Against Her Will: An Incident in Baltimore, Incident in a Small Town. *Special*: The Stingiest Man in Town (voice).

MATURE, VICTOR
Actor. b. Louisville, KY, Jan. 29, 1913. Acted with Pasadena Playhouse before film debut. On B'way in Lady in the Dark; served with U.S. Coast Guard, WWII.
PICTURES: The Housekeeper's Daughter (debut, 1939), One Million B.C., Captain Caution, No No Nanette, I Wake Up Screaming, Shanghai Gesture, Song of the Islands, My Gal Sal, Footlight Serenade, Seven Days Leave, My Darling Clementine, Moss Rose, Kiss of Death, Fury at Furnace Creek, Cry of the City, Red Hot and Blue, Easy Living, Samson and Delilah, Wabash Avenue, I'll Get By (cameo), Stella, Gambling House, Las Vegas Story, Androcles and the Lion, Million Dollar Mermaid, Something for the Birds, Glory Brigade, Affair with a Stranger, The Robe, Veils of Bagdad, Dangerous Mission, Betrayed, Demetrius & the Gladiators, The Egyptian, Chief Crazy Horse, Violent Saturday, Last Frontier, The Sharkfighters, Safari, Zarak, The Long Haul, Pickup Alley, China Doll, Tank Force, The Bandit of Zhobe, Escort West, Big Circus, Timbuktu, Hannibal, The Tartars, After the Fox, Head, Every Little Crook and Nanny, Won Ton Ton the Dog Who Saved Hollywood, Firepower, The Screamer.
TELEVISION: *Movie*: Samson and Delilah.

MAURA, CARMEN
Actress. b. Madrid, Spain, Sept. 15, 1945. e. Madrid's Catholic Inst. Daughter of ophthalmologist; faced family disapproval and custody battle when she became an actress. After working as cabaret entertainer, translator (has degree in French), and occasional voiceover dubber, met aspiring director Pedro Almodovar when they were cast in stage prod. of Sartre's Dirty Hands and starred in several of his films. Hosted weekly Spanish tv talk show Esta Noche.
PICTURES: El Hombre Oculto (debut, 1970), El Love Feroz, The Petition, Paper Tigers, Que Hace una Chica Como tu en un Sitio Como Este?, Pepi Luci Bom ... And Other Girls on the Heap (1980), El Cid Cabreador, Dark Habits, What Have I Done to Deserve This?, Extramuros, Se Infiel y No Mires Con Quien, Matador, Law of Desire, Women on the Verge of a Nervous Breakdown, Baton Rouge, Ay Carmela!, Between Heaven and Earth, The Anonymous Queen, Shadows in a Conflict, Louis the Child King, How to Be Miserable and Enjoy It, The Flowers of My Secret.

MAUREY, NICOLE
Actress. b. France, Dec. 20, 1926. Studied dancing; French films include Blondine, Pamela, Le Cavalier Noir, Journal D'Un Cure De Campagne, Les Compagnes de la Nuit; many television and stage appearances in France; U.S. film debut in Little Boy Lost (1953).
PICTURES: Little Boy Lost, The Secret of the Incas, The Bold and the Brave, The Weapon, The Constant Husband, The Scapegoat, Me and the Colonel, The Jayhawkers, House of the Seven Hawks, High Time, Day of the Triffids, Why Bother to Knock?, The Very Edge.
TELEVISION: U.S. and U.K.: Tomorrow We Will Love, Casablanca, The Billion Franc Mystery, Champion House, I Thought They Died Years Ago.

MAXWELL, LOIS
Actress. r.n. Lois Hooker. b. Canada, 1927. Started in U.S. films in late 1940's before working in Italy then Britain. Has done numerous Canadian films for tv.

PICTURES: That Hagen Girl, The Decision of Christopher Blake, The Big Punch, The Dark Past, Kazan, Domani e troppa Tardi (Tomorrow Is Too Late), La Grande Speranza (The Great Hope), Aida, Passport to Treason, Satellite in the Sky, Time Without Pity, Lolita, Dr. No, Come Fly With Me, The Haunting, From Russia With Love, Goldfinger, Thunderball, Operation Kid Brother, You Only Live Twice, On Her Majesty's Secret Service, Adventure in Rainbow Country, The Adventurers, Diamonds Are Forever, Live and Let Die, The Man With the Golden Gun, The Spy Who Loved Me, Moonraker, Mr. Patman, For Your Eyes Only, Octopussy, A View to a Kill, Martha Ruth and Eddie.

MAXWELL, RONALD F.
Director, Writer, Producer. b. Jan. 5, 1947. e. NYU Coll. of Arts & Sciences; NYU Sch. of the Arts, Inst. of Film & Television Graduate Sch., M.F.A., 1970. Producer-Director for PBS Theater-in-America (1974-78).
PICTURES: *Director*: The Guest, Little Darlings, The Night the Lights Went Out in Georgia, Kidco, Gettysburg (also co-s.p.).
TELEVISION: *Director*: Sea Marks (also prod.), Verna: USO Girl (also prod.), Parent Trap II.

MAY, ELAINE
Actress, Director, Writer. b. Philadelphia, PA, April 21, 1932. Daughter is actress Jeannie Berlin. Father was prod.-dir. Jack Berlin whose travelling theater she acted with from age 6 to 10. Repertory theatre in Chicago, 1954; comedy team with Mike Nichols starting in 1955. Appeared with improvisational theater group, The Compass, Chicago. Co-starred in An Evening with Mike Nichols and Elaine May.
THEATRE: *Playwright*: A Matter of Position, Not Enough Rope, Hot Line, Better Point of Valour, Mr. Gogol & Mr. Preen, Hotline (Death Defying Acts).
PICTURES: Luv (actress), Enter Laughing (actress), A New Leaf (actress, dir., s.p.), Such Good Friends (s.p. as Esther Dale), The Heartbreak Kid (dir.), Mikey and Nicky (dir., s.p.), Heaven Can Wait (co-s.p.), California Suite (actress), Ishtar (dir., s.p.), In the Spirit (actress), The Birdcage (s.p.).
TELEVISION: *Series regular*: Keep Talking (1958-59). *Guest*: Jack Paar, Omnibus, Dinah Shore Show, Perry Como, Laugh Lines.

MAYER, GERALD
Producer, Director. b. Montreal, Canada, 1919. Father was Jerry G. Mayer, mgr. MGM studio. e. Stanford U., journalism; corresp. for San Francisco Examiner; pres. Sigma Delta Chi, prof. journalism soc. Navy lieut., amphibious forces, WWII. Entered m.p. ind. in prod. dept. MGM studios; first dir. assignment Dial 1119 (1950).
PICTURES: Dial 1119, Inside Straight, The Sellout, Holiday for Sinners, Bright Road (Christopher Award for direction), The Marauders, African Drumbeat, The Man Inside (Canadian).
TELEVISION: Canadian Broadcasting Corp. (prod./dir., TV drama), prod. The Swiss Family Robinson (British-Canadian-West German TV series). Director for U.S. TV: One Last Ride (mini-series), Airwolf, Night Heat, Lou Grant, Eight Is Enough, Quincy, Logan's Run, Mannix, Mission Impossible, Police Surgeon, Cimarron Strip, Peyton Place, Judd for the Defense, Bonanza, The Fugitive, Chrysler Thea., Ben Casey, Slattery's People, Profiles in Courage, The Defenders, Gunsmoke, etc.

MAYER, MICHAEL F.
Attorney, Executive. b. White Plains, NY, Sept. 8, 1917. e. Harvard Coll., B.S., 1939; Yale Law Sch., L.L.B., 1942. Armed Forces 1942-46, Air Medal (1945). V.P., Kingsley International Pictures Corp., 1954-62. Exec. dir. and gen. counsel, Independent Film Importers and Distributors of America Inc. (IFIDA), 1959-67. Special Counsel, French Society of Authors, Composers and Publishers, 1961-72; British Performing Rights Society, 1962-67. Author: Foreign Films on American Screens (1966), Divorce and Annulment (1967), What You Should Know About Libel and Slander (1968), Rights of Privacy (1972), The Film Industries (1973, revised ed. pub. in 1978). Teacher of courses on Business Problems in Film, New School (1971-82). Secty. of Film Society of Lincoln Center, Inc. (1972-88).

MAYER, ROGER LAURANCE
Executive. b. New York, NY, Apr. 21, 1926. e. Yale U., B.A. 1948; Yale Law Sch., L.L.B. and J.D. 1951. In 1952 was practicing attorney; joined Columbia Pictures that year as atty. and named general studio exec., 1957. Left in 1961 to join MGM Studio as asst. gen. mgr. With MGM as follows: v.p., operations, 1964; v.p., administration, 1975-84. Also exec. v.p. MGM Laboratories, 1974-83. Named pres., MGM Laboratories and sr. v.p., studio admin.; MGM Entertainment Co. 1983-86; joined Turner Entertainment Co. as pres. and COO, 1986-present. Member of Los Angeles County Bar Assn., Calif. Bar Assn., Los Angeles Copyright Society, bd of dirs., Acad. of Motion Picture Arts & Sciences. Trustee, chmn. Motion Picture & TV Fund, bd. of dirs., Permanent Charities Fund.

MAYO, VIRGINIA
Actress. r.n. Virginia Jones. b. St. Louis, MO, Nov. 30, 1920. e. St. Louis dramatic school. With Billy Rose's Diamond Horseshoe; then N.Y. stage, Banjo Eyes.

PICTURES: Jack London (debut, 1943), Up in Arms, The Princess and the Pirate, Wonder Man, The Kid from Brooklyn, The Best Years of Our Lives, The Secret Life of Walter Mitty, Out of the Blue, A Song Is Born, Smart Girls Don't Talk, The Girl from Jones Beach, Flaxy Martin, Colorado Territory, Always Leave Them Laughing, White Heat, Red Light, Backfire, The Flame and the Arrow, West Point Story, Along the Great Divide, Captain Horatio Hornblower, Painting the Clouds with Sunshine, Starlift, She's Working Her Way Through College, Iron Mistress, She's Back on Broadway, South Sea Woman, Devil's Canyon, King Richard and the Crusaders, The Silver Chalice, Pearl of the South Pacific, Great Day in the Morning, The Proud Ones, Congo Crossing, The Big Land, The Story of Mankind, The Tall Stranger, Fort Dobbs, Westbound, Jet Over the Atlantic, Young Fury, Fort Utah, Castle of Evil, Won Ton Ton the Dog Who Saved Hollywood, French Quarter, Evil Spirits, Seven Days Ashore.

MAYRON, MELANIE
Actress, Director. b. Philadelphia, PA, Oct. 20, 1952. e. American Academy of Dramatic Arts, 1972. Debut Godspell (tour), NY stage debut: The Goodbye People, 1979. Gethsemane Springs, (Mark Taper Forum, 1976), Crossing Delancey, (1986, Jewish Rep. Theatre, 1992). With Catlin Adams, co-prod., co-wrote short, Little Shiny Shoes.
PICTURES: Actress: Harry and Tonto (debut, 1974), Gable and Lombard, Car Wash, The Great Smokey Roadblock, You Light Up My Life, Girl Friends (Locarno Film Fest. Award) Heartbeeps, Missing, The Boss' Wife, Sticky Fingers (also co-s.p., co-prod), Checking Out, My Blue Heaven. Director: The Babysitters Club.
TELEVISION: Series: thirtysomething (Emmy Award, 1989). Movies: Playing For Time, Will There Really Be a Morning?, Hustling, The Best Little Girl in the World, Wallenberg: A Hero's Story, Ordeal in the Arctic, Other Women's Children. Guest: Rhoda. Specials: Lily Tomlin: Sold Out, Cinder Ella: A Modern Fairy Tale, Wanted: The Perfect Guy. Director: Tribeca: Stepping Back (also writer), thirtysomething, Sirens, Moon Over Miami, Winnetka Road, Freaky Friday (movie).

MAYSLES, ALBERT
Director, Cinematographer. b. Boston, MA, Nov. 1926. e. Syracuse (B.A.), Boston U, M.A. Taught psychology there for 3 years. With late brother David (1932-87) pioneer in direct cinema documentary filmmaking, using a hand-held synchronous sound camera, no narration, to capture the drama of daily life, without need to invent stories. Entered filmmaking photographing Primary with D.A. Pennebaker, Richard Leacock and Robert Drew, 1960. Formed Maysles Films, Inc. 1962, making non-fiction feature films, commercials and corp. films.
PICTURES: Showman (1962), Salesman, What's Happening! The Beatles in the U.S.A., Meet Marlon Brando, Gimme Shelter, Christo's Valley Curtain, Grey Gardens, Running Fence, Vladimir Horowitz: The Last Romantic, Ozawa, Islands, Horowitz Plays Mozart, Fellow Passengers, Christo in Paris, Soldiers of Music: Rostropovitch Returns to Russia, Baroque Duet, Umbrellas.
TELEVISION: Vladimir Horowitz: The Last Romantic (Emmy Award, 1987), Soldiers of Music: Rostopovich Returns to Russia (Emmy Award, 1991). Sports Illustrated: The Making of the Swimsuit Issue (co-dir.), Abortion: Desperate Choices.

MAZURSKY, PAUL
Producer, Director, Writer, Actor. b. Brooklyn, NY, April 25, 1930. e. Brooklyn Coll. Started acting in 1951 Off-B'way (Hello Out There, The Seagull, Major Barbara, Death of a Salesman, He Who Gets Slapped), TV and films. Was nightclub comic 1954-1960 and directed plays. Began association with Larry Tucker by producing, directing, writing and performing in Second City, semi-improvisational revue. For four years they wrote the Danny Kaye TV show and created and wrote the Monkees series. First theatrical film I Love You Alice B. Toklas, 1968, which he wrote and exec. produced with Tucker. Exec. prod. of film Taking Care of Business.
PICTURES: Dir.-Writer: Bob and Carol and Ted and Alice, Dir.-Prod.-Writer-Actor: Alex in Wonderland, Blume in Love, Harry and Tonto, Next Stop Greenwich Village (dir., prod., s.p. only), An Unmarried Woman, Willie and Phil, Tempest, Moscow on the Hudson, Down and Out in Beverly Hills, Moon Over Parador, Enemies: a Love Story, Scenes From a Mall, The Pickle, Faithful. Actor: Fear and Desire, Blackboard Jungle, Deathwatch, A Star Is Born, A Man a Woman and a Bank, History of the World Part 1, Into the Night, Punchline, Scenes From the Class Struggle in Beverly Hills, Man Trouble, Carlito's Way, Love Affair, Miami Rhapsody, 2 Days in the Valley.

MAZZELLO, JOSEPH
Actor. b. Rhineback, NY, Sept. 21, 1983. Made acting debut at age 5 in tv movie Unspeakable Acts.
PICTURES: Presumed Innocent (debut, 1990), Radio Flyer, Jurassic Park, Shadowlands, The River Wild, The Cure, Three Wishes.
TELEVISION: Movies: Unspeakable Acts, Desperate Choices: To Save My Child, A Father for Charlie.

McBRIDE, JIM
Director, Writer. b. New York, NY, Sept. 16, 1941. e. NYU. m. costume designer Tracy Tynan. Began in underground film scene in New York. First film: David Holzman's Diary, 1967, which won grand prize at Mannheim and Pesaro Film Festivals, and was named to the Library of Congress' list of important American films designated for preservation in 1991. Appeared as actor in film Last Embrace.
PICTURES: Director: David Holzman's Diary (also prod.), My Girlfriend's Wedding (also actor, s.p.), Glen and Randa (also s.p.), Hot Times (also s.p., actor), Breathless (also co-s.p.), The Big Easy, Great Balls of Fire (also co-s.p.), Uncovered (also co-s.p.).
TELEVISION: Series: The Wonder Years (3 episodes), Twilight Zone (The Once and Future King, 1986). Movies: Blood Ties, The Wrong Man, Field of Blood, Pronto. Special: Fallen Angels (Fearless).

McCALL, JOAN
Writer, Actress. b. Grahn, KY. e. Berea Coll. Staff writer for Days of Our Lives, Another World, As the World Turns, under the pen name Joan Pommer; also Search for Tomorrow, Capitol, Santa Barbara, Divorce Court. Starred on B'way in Barefoot in the Park, The Star Spangled Girl, A Race of Hairy Men, and road companies of Barefoot in the Park, Any Wednesday, Star Spangled Girl, and Don't Drink the Water, Los Angeles co. of Jimmy Shine.
PICTURES: Grizzly, Act of Vengeance, The Devil Times Five. Screenwriter: Predator, Between Two Worlds, Timelapse, Heart Like a Wheel.

McCALLUM, DAVID
Actor. b. Glasgow, Scotland, Sept. 19, 1933. Early career in rep. theatres and dir. plays for Army. Entered industry in 1953.
PICTURES: The Secret Place (debut, 1957), Hell Drivers, Robbery Under Arms, Violent Playground, A Night to Remember, The Long and the Short and the Tall, Carolina, Jungle Street, Billy Budd, Freud, The Great Escape, The Greatest Story Ever Told, To Trap a Spy, The Spy With My Face, Around the World Under the Sea, One Spy Too Many, Three Bites of the Apple, Sol Madrid, Mosquito Squadron, The Kingfisher Caper, Dogs, King Solomon's Treasure, The Watcher in the Woods, Terminal Choice, The Wind, The Haunting of Morella, Hear My Song, Dirty Weekend, Healer.
TELEVISION: Series: The Man From U.N.C.L.E., Colditz (BBC, 1972-74), The Invisible Man, Sapphire and Steel (BBC), Trainer (BBC). Guest: Hitchcock, Murder She Wrote. Movies: Teacher Teacher, Hauser's Memory, Frankenstein: The True Story, Behind Enemy Lines, Freedom Fighters, She Waits, The Man Who Lived at the Ritz, The Return of Sam McCloud, Mother Love (BBC), Shattered Image.

McCAMBRIDGE, MERCEDES
Actress. b. Joliet, IL, March 17, 1918. e. Mundelein Coll., Chicago, B.A. Did some radio work while in college; opposite Orson Welles two seasons, on Ford Theatre, other air shows; New York stage in: Hope for the Best, (1945); Place of Our Own, Twilight Bar, Woman Bites Dog, The Young and Fair, Lost in Yonkers. Starred on own radio show, 1952. Member of National Inst. Alcohol Abuse and Alcoholism, Washington. Autobiography: The Two of Us.
PICTURES: All the King's Men (debut, 1949; Academy Award, best supporting actress), Lightning Strikes Twice, Inside Straight, The Scarf, Johnny Guitar, Giant, A Farewell to Arms, Touch of Evil (unbilled), Suddenly Last Summer, Cimarron, Angel Baby, 99 Women, Like a Crow on a June Bug (Sixteen), The Exorcist (voice), Thieves, The Concorde—Airport '79, Echoes.
TELEVISION: Series: One Man's Family, Wire Service; also numerous guest appearances. Movies: Killer By Night, Two For the Money, The Girls of Huntington House, The President's Plane Is Missing, Who Is the Black Dahlia?, The Sacketts.

McCARTHY, ANDREW
Actor. b. Westfield, NJ, Nov. 29, 1962. Raised in Bernardsville, NJ. e. NYU. While at college won role in film Class. Studied acting at Circle-in-the-Square.
THEATER: B'way: The Boys of Winter. Off B'way: Bodies Rest and Motion, Life Under Water, Neptune's Hips, Mariens Kammer.
PICTURES: Class (debut, 1983), Heaven Help Us, St. Elmo's Fire, Pretty in Pink, Mannequin, Waiting for the Moon, Less Than Zero, Kansas, Fresh Horses, Weekend at Bernie's, Quiet Days in Clichy, Dr. M (Club Extinction), Year of the Gun, Only You, Weekend at Bernie's 2, The Joy Luck Club, Getting In (Student Body), Night of the Running Man, Mrs. Parker & the Vicious Circle, Dream Man, Dead Funny, Mulholland Falls, Things I Never Told You.
TELEVISION: Movie: The Courtyard. Specials: Dear Lola, Common Pursuit. Guest: Amazing Stories (Grandpa's Ghost), Tales From the Crypt (Loved to Death).

McCARTHY, KEVIN
Actor. b. Seattle, WA, Feb. 15, 1914. Sister was late author Mary McCarthy. e. U. of Minnesota. Acted in sch. plays, stock; B'way debut in Abe Lincoln in Illinois. Served in U.S. Army.
THEATER: B'way: Flight to West, Winged Victory, Truckline Cafe, Joan of Lorraine, The Survivors, Death of a Salesman (London), Anna Christie, The Deep Blue Sea, Red Roses For Me, A Warm Body, Something About a Soldier, Love's Labour's Lost, Advise and Consent, The Day The Money Stopped, Two For the Seesaw, Cactus Flower, Alone Together, The Three Sisters, Happy Birthday Wanda June.
PICTURES: Death of a Salesman (debut, 1951; Acad. Award nom.), Drive a Crooked Road, The Gambler From Natchez, Stranger on Horseback, Annapolis Story, Nightmare, Invasion of the Body Snatchers, The Misfits, 40 Pounds of Trouble, A Gathering of Eagles, The Prize, The Best Man, An Affair of the Skin, Mirage, A Big Hand for the Little Lady, Three Sisters, Hotel, The Hell With Heroes, If He Hollers Let Him Go, Revenge in El Paso, Ace High, Kansas City Bomber, Alien Thunder (Dan Candy's Law), Order to Kill, Buffalo Bill and the Indians, Piranha, Invasion of the Body Snatchers (1978, cameo), Hero at Large, Those Lips Those Eyes, The Howling, My Tutor, Twilight Zone— The Movie, Hostage, Innerspace, UHF, Fast Food, Dark Tower, Love or Money, The Sleeping Car, Eve of Destruction, Final Approach, The Distinguished Gentleman, Matinee, Greedy, Just Cause, Steal Big Steal Little.
TELEVISION: Active on TV since 1949. Movies: U.M.C., A Great American Tragedy, Exo-Man, Mary Jane Harper Cried Last Night, Flamingo Road, Portrait of an Escort, Rosie: The Story of Rosemary Clooney, Making of a Male Model, Invitation to Hell, Deadly Intentions, The Midnight Hour, A Masterpiece of Murder, Poor Little Rich Girl: The Barbara Hutton Story, The Long Journey Home, Once Upon a Texas Train, In the Heat of the Night, Channel 99, The Rose and the Jackal, Dead on the Money, Duplicates, The Sister-in-Law. Mini-series: Passion and Paradise. Series: The Colbys, The Survivors, Flamingo Road, Amanda's, Second Start. Guest: Dynasty. Pilot: Second Stage.

McCARTNEY PAUL
Singer, Musician. r.n. James Paul McCartney. b. Liverpool, England, June 18, 1942. Formerly with The Beatles, Wings.
PICTURES: Performer: A Hard Day's Night, (debut, 1964; also songs) Help! (also songs), Yellow Submarine (cameo; also songs), Let It Be (also songs; Academy Award for best original song score, 1970), Rockshow (concert film), Give My Regards to Broad Street (also s.p., songs), Eat the Rich (cameo), Get Back (concert film) Songs for films: Live and Let Die (title song; Acad. Award nom.), Oh Heavenly Dog, Spies Like Us. Scores: The Family Way, Beyond the Limit.
TELEVISION: Specials: James Paul McCartney, Sgt. Pepper: It Was 20 Years Ago Today, Put It There, Paul McCartney Live in the New World, The Beatles Anthology.

McCLANAHAN, RUE
Actress. b. Healdton, OK, Feb. 21. e. U. of Tulsa (B.A. cum laude). Member: Actors Studio, NYC.
THEATER: On B'way in Sticks and Bones, Jimmy Shine, California Suite. Off-B'way: Who's Happy Now? (Obie Award, 1970), After Play. Vienna: Lettice and Lovage. London: Harvey.
PICTURES: Five Minutes to Love, Hollywood After Dark, How to Succeed With Girls, They Might Be Giants, The People Next Door, The Pursuit of Happiness, Modern Love, This World Then The Fireworks, Dear God, Starship Troopers.
TELEVISION: Series: Maude, Mama's Family, The Golden Girls (Emmy Award, 1987), The Golden Palace, Apple Pie, Balckbird Hall. Movies: Having Babies III, Sgt. Matlovich Vs. the U.S. Air Force, Rainbow, Topper, The Great American Traffic Jam, Word of Honor, The Day the Bubble Burst, The Little Match Girl, Liberace, Take My Daughters Please, Let Me Hear You Whisper, To the Heroes, After the Shock, Children of the Bride, To My Daughter, The Dreamer of Oz, Baby of the Bride, Mother of the Bride (also co-exec. prod.), A Burning Passion: The Margaret Mitchell Story, Innocent Victims, A Christmas Love. Specials: The Wickedest Witch, The Man in the Brown Suit, Nunsense 2: The Sequel. Mini-Series: Message From Nam.

McCLORY, SEÁN
Actor. b. Dublin, Ireland, March 8, 1924. e. Jesuit Coll., Nat'l U. at Galway (medical sch.). With Gaelic Theatre, Galway; Abbey Theatre, Dublin. Brought to U.S. in 1946 under contract to RKO Pictures, then Warners, then Batjac (John Wayne's co.). Prod. and dir. numerous plays, member of the Directors Guild of America and author of drama, Moment of Truth; Pax: The Benedictions in China. Editor: The Jester: The Masques Club 50th Anniv. Mng. Editor: A.N.T.A. News (2 yrs). For past 4 years starred in 40 ninety-minute radio dramas for California Artists Radio Theatre and written some 90 min. shows for National Public Radio.
THEATER: Shining Hour, Juno and the Paycock, Anna Christie, Escape to Autumn, King of Friday's Men, Lady's Not for Burning, Billy Budd, Dial M for Murder, The Winslow Boy, Shadow of a Gunman (Dramalogue Award), Saint Joan, The Importance of Being Earnest, many others.

PICTURES: Roughshod, Beyond Glory, The Daughter of Rosie O'Grady, Anne of the Indies, Storm Warning, Lorna Doone, What Price Glory?, The Quiet Man, Rogue's March, Plunder of the Sun, Island in the Sky, Them, Ring of Fear, Man in the Attic, The Long Grey Lane, Diane, I Cover the Underworld, The King's Thief, Moonfleet, Guns of Fort Petticoat, Valley of the Dragons, Cheyenne Autumn, Follow Me Boys, The Gnome-Mobile, Bandolero, Day of the Wolves, Roller Boogie, In Search of Historic Jesus, My Chauffeur, The Dead.
TELEVISION: Series: The Californians (also dir. episodes), Kate McShane, Bring 'Em Back Alive, General Hospital. Mini-Series: The Captains and the Kings, Once an Eagle. Movies: Kate McShane (pilot), The New Daughters of Joshua Cabe, Young Harry Houdini. Guest: Matinee Theatre, Climax, Lost in Space, My Three Sons, Suspense, The Untouchables, Hitchcock, Thriller, Beverly Hillbillies, Bonanza, Gunsmoke, Mannix, Little House on the Prairie, Perry Mason, S.W.A.T., Fish, Columbo, How the West Was Won, Fantasy Island, Battlestar Galactica, Trapper John M.D., Blue Knight, Falcon Crest, Simon and Simon, Murder She Wrote.

McCLUGGAGE, KERRY
Executive. b. 1955. e. USC, Harvard U. 1978, programming asst. at Universal; 1979, dir. of current srs. programming; 1980, became v.p., Universal TV. 1982, sr. v.p. creative affairs. Served as v.p. of production, Universal Pictures and supv. prod. on series Miami Vice. 1987-991, pres. of Universal Television. 1991, joined Paramount as pres. of the Television Group. 1992, named chmn. of the Television Group of Paramount Pictures.

McCLURE, MARC
Actor. b. San Mateo, CA, Mar. 31, 1957.
PICTURES: Freaky Friday, Coming Home, I Wanna Hold Your Hand, Superman, Superman II, Superman III, Supergirl, Back to the Future, Superman IV: The Quest for Peace, Amazon Women on the Moon, Perfect Match, Chances Are, After Midnight, Back to the Future Part III, Grim Prairie Tales, The Vagrant, Apollo 13, Sleepstalker.
TELEVISION: Series: California Fever. Movies: James at 15, Little White Lies. Guest: The Commish.

McCLURG, EDIE
Actress. b. Kansas City, MO, July 23, 1951. e. Syracuse Univ. Newswriter and documentary producer for National Public Radio affiliate, KCUR-FM. Joined the Pitschel Players in LA in 1975; then became member of the Groundlings Improv Comedy Revue.
PICTURES: Carrie (debut, 1976), Cheech and Chong's Next Movie, Oh God Book II, Secret of NIMH (voice), Pandemonium, Cracking Up, Eating Raoul, Mr. Mom, The Corsican Brothers, Ferris Bueller's Day Off, Back to School, The Longshot, Planes Trains and Automobiles, She's Having a Baby, Elvira: Mistress of the Dark, The Little Mermaid (voice), Curly Sue, A River Runs Through It, Stepmonster, Airborne, Natural Born Killers, Under the Hula Moon.
TELEVISION: Series: Tony Orlando and Dawn, The Kallikaks, The Big Show, Harper Valley PTA, No Soap Radio, Madame's Place, Small Wonder, Toegther We Stand, Valerie (The Hogan Family), Drexell's Class, Life with Louie, Martin Mull's White POlitics in America. Specials: Cinderella (Faerie Tale Theatre), The Pee-wee Herman Show, Martin Mull's History of White People in America, Once Upon a Brothers Grimm, The Chevy Chase Show, A Home Run for Love. Guest: WKRP in Cincinnati, The Richard Pryor Show, The Jeffersons, Trapper John M.D., Alice, Diff'rent Strokes, The Incredible Hulk, Madame's Place, Picket Fences. Movies: Bill on His Own, Crash Course, Dance 'til Dawn, Menu for Murder. Voice Characterizations: The Snorks, The 13 Ghosts of Scooby Doo, The New Jetsons, Casper, Problem Child, Bobby's World of Monsters.

McCORMICK, PAT
Writer, Actor. b. July 17, 1934. Served as comedy writer for such performers as Jonathan Winters, Phyllis Diller.
PICTURES: Actor: Buffalo Bill and the Indians, Smokey and the Bandit, A Wedding, Hot Stuff, Scavenger Hunt, Smokey and the Bandit 2, History of the World Part 1, Under the Rainbow (also co-s.p.), Smokey and the Bandit 3, Bombs Away, Rented Lips, Scrooged, Beverly Hills Vamp.
TELEVISION: Series (as writer): Jack Paar Show, Tonight Show, etc. Series (as actor): The Don Rickles Show, The New Bill Cosby Show, Gun Shy. Movies (as actor): Mr. Horn, Rooster, The Jerk Too.

McCOWEN, ALEC
Actor. b. Tunbridge Wells, England, May 26, 1925. e. Royal Acad. of Dramatic Art. On stage in London in Hadrian the Seventh, among others. On B'way in Antony and Cleopatra, After the Rain, The Philanthropist, The Misanthrope, Equus, Someone Who'll Watch Over Me, etc.
PICTURES: The Cruel Sea, The Divided Heart, The Deep Blue Sea, The Good Companions, The Third Key (The Long Arm),

Time Without Pity, Town on Trial, The Doctor's Dilemma, A Night to Remember, The One That Got Away, Silent Enemy, The Loneliness of the Long Distance Runner, In the Cool of the Day, The Devil's Own (The Witches), The Hawaiians, Frenzy, Travels with My Aunt, Stevie, Hanover Street, Never Say Never Again, The Assam Garden, Personal Services, Cry Freedom, Henry V, The Age of Innocence.

McCRANE, PAUL
Actor. b. Philadelphia, PA, Jan. 19, 1961. Stage debut at age 16 in NY Shakespeare Fest. prod. of Landscape of the Body.
THEATER: NY: Dispatches, Runaway, Split, The House of Blue Leaves, The Palace of Amateurs, Hooters, The Hostage, Curse of an Aching Heart
PICTURES: Rocky II (debut, 1979), Fame (also songwriter), The Hotel New Hampshire, Purple Hearts, Robocop, The Blob, The Shawshank Redemption.
TELEVISION: Series: Cop Rock.

McDERMOTT, DYLAN
Actor. b. Connecticut, Oct. 26, 1961. Raised in New York City. e. Fordham U., studied acting at Neighborhood Playhouse with Sanford Meisner.
THEATER: The Seagull, Golden Boy, The Glass Menagerie, Biloxi Blues (B'way), Floating Rhoda and the Glue Man.
PICTURES: Hamburger Hill, The Blue Iguana, Twister, Steel Magnolias, Where Sleeping Dogs Lie, Hardware, In the Line of Fire, The Cowboy Way, Miracle on 34th Street, Destiny Turns on the Radio, Home for the Holidays.
TELEVISION: Movies: The Neon Empire, Into the Badlands, The Fear Inside.

McDONNELL, MARY
Actress. b. Ithaca, NY, 1952.
THEATER: NY: Buried Child, Savage in Limbo, All Night Long, Black Angel, A Weekend Near Madison, Three Ways Home, Still Life, The Heidi Chronicles. Regional: National Anthems, A Doll's House, A Midsummer Night's Dream, The Three Sisters.
PICTURES: Matewan, Tiger Warsaw, Dances With Wolves (Acad. Award nom.), Golden Globe Award), Grand Canyon, Sneakers, Passion Fish (Acad. Award nom.), Blue Chips, Mariette in Ecstasy, Independence Day.
TELEVISION: Series: E/R, High Society. Movies: Money on the Side, Courage, The American Clock. Special: O Pioneers!

McDORMAND, FRANCES
Actress. b. Illinois, 1958. Daughter of a Disciples of Christ preacher, traveled Bible Belt with family settling in PA at 8. e. Yale Drama School. Regional theater include Twelfth Night, Mrs. Warren's Profession, The Three Sisters, All My Sons. Two seasons with O'Neill Playwrights Conference.
THEATER: Awake and Sing, Painting Churches, On the Verge, A Streetcar Named Desire (Tony nom.), The Sisters Rosensweig, The Swan.
PICTURES: Blood Simple, Raising Arizona, Mississippi Burning (Acad. Award nom.), Chattahoochee, Dark Man, Miller's Crossing (unbilled), Hidden Agenda, The Butcher's Wife, Passed Away, Short Cuts, Beyond Rangoon, Fargo, Lone Star, Primal Fear, Palookaville.
TELEVISION: Series: Leg Work. Guest: Twilight Zone, Spenser: For Hire, Hill St. Blues. Movies: Crazy in Love, The Good Old Boys.

McDOWALL, BETTY
Actress. b. Sydney, Australia. e. Mt. Bernard Convent, N. Sydney. Early career radio, stage in Australia; ent. BBC TV, 1952; since in West End plays, many TV and radio plays and films. Radio plays include: Anna Christie, The Little Foxes, Another Part of the Forest, The Archers.
THEATER: Age of Consent, Ghost Train, The Kidders, The Dark Halo, Period of Adjustment, Rule of Three, Signpost to Murder, Hippolytus, The Winslow Boy, Woman in a Dressing Gown, As Long as It's Warm, Caprice—in a Pink Palazzo, Sweet Bird of Youth, There Was an Old Woman, What the Butler Saw, Two Dozen Red Roses, A Boston Story, The Man Most Likely To..., Sleeping Partner.
PICTURES: Timelock, She Didn't Say No, Jack the Ripper, The Shiralee, Jackpot, Dead Lucky, Spare the Rod, Golliwog, Echo of Diana, First Men in the Moon, Ballad in Blue, The Liquidators, Willy Wagtails by Moonlight, The Omen.
TELEVISION: Mid-Level and Glorification of Al Toolum, The Black Judge, Phone Call for Matthew Quade, Thunder on the Snowy, Shadow of Guilt, Traveling Lady, Torment, Biography, Notes for a Love Song, Esther's Altar, The Corridor People, The Braden Beat, The Douglas Fairbanks, Ivanhoe, The Foreign Legion, Fabian of the Yard, Four Just Men, Flying Doctor, No Hiding Place, Z' Cars, Days of Vengeance, Flower of Evil, Outbreak of Murder, Call Me Sam, The Prisoner, Public Eye, The Forgotten Door, All Out for Kangaroo Valley, Barry Humphries Scandals, Castle Haven, Albert and Victoria, Follyfoot, The Man Who Came to Dinner, Anne of Avoniea, Little Lord Fauntleroy, The Bass Player and the Blond (4 plays), The Gingerbread Lady.
Series: Boyd Q.C.

McDOWALL, RODDY
Actor. b. London, England, Sept. 17, 1928. e. St. Joseph's, London. First appeared in British film Murder in the Family at age of 9. In 1940, was signed by 20th Century-Fox. Voted Star of Tomorrow, 1944. Named Screen Actors Guild representative on National Film Preservation Bd., 1989. Published four volumes of his photography: Double Exposure (& II, III, IV).
THEATER: B'way: Misalliance, Escapade, Doctor's Dilemma, No Time for Sergeants, Good as Gold, Compulsion, Handful of Fire, Look After Lulu, The Fighting Cock (Tony Award, 1960), Camelot, The Astrakhan Coat.
PICTURES: Murder in the Family (debut, 1938), I See Ice, John Halifax Gentleman, Convict 99, Scruffy, Yellow Sands, Hey Hey USA, Poison Pen, The Outsider, Dead Man's Shoes, Just Williams, His Brother's Keeper, Saloon Bar, You Will Remember, This England, Man Hunt (U.S. debut, 1941), How Green Was My Valley, Confirm or Deny, Son of Fury, On the Sunny Side, The Pied Piper, My Friend Flicka, Lassie Come Home, White Cliffs of Dover, The Keys of the Kingdom, Thunderhead Son of Flicka, Molly and Me, Holiday in Mexico, Macbeth, Rocky, Kidnapped, Tuna Clipper, Black Midnight, Killer Shark, Everybody's Dancin', Big Timber, Steel Fist, The Subterraneans, Midnight Lace, The Longest Day, Cleopatra, Shock Treatment, The Greatest Story Ever Told, That Darn Cat, The Loved One, The Third Day, Inside Daisy Clover, Lord Love a Duck, The Defector, It, The Adventures of Bullwhip Griffin, The Cool Ones, Planet of the Apes, Five Card Stud, Hello Down There, Midas Run, Angel Angel Down We Go (Cult of the Damned), Pretty Maids All in a Row, Escape from the Planet of the Apes, Bedknobs and Broomsticks, Corky (unbilled), Conquest of the Planet of the Apes, The Devil's Widow (Tam Lin; dir. only), Life and Times of Judge Roy Bean, The Poseidon Adventure, The Legend of Hell House, Arnold, Battle for the Planet of the Apes, Dirty Mary Crazy Larry, Funny Lady, Mean Johnny Barrows, Embryo, Sixth and Main, Rabbit Test, Laserblast, The Cat from Outer Space, Circle of Iron, Scavenger Hunt, The Black Hole (voice), Charlie Chan and the Curse of the Dragon Queen, Evil Under the Sun, Class of 1984, Fright Night, GoBots: Battle of the Rock Lords (voice), Dead of Winter, Overboard (also exec. prod.), Doin' Time on Planet Earth, The Big Picture, Destroyer, Fright Night Part 2, Cutting Class, Shakma, Going Under, The Color of Evening, Double Trouble, The Naked Target, Mirror Mirror 2, Angel 4: Undercover, Last Summer in the Hamptons, The Grass Harp.
TELEVISION: Series: Planet of the Apes, Fantastic Journey, Tales of the Gold Monkey, Bridges to Cross. Specials: Stratford Shakespeare Festival, Heart of Darkness, He's for Me, Not Without Honor (Emmy Award, 1961), The Fatal Mistake, Camilla (Nightmare Classics). Movies: Night Gallery, Terror in the Sky, A Taste of Evil, What's a Nice Girl Like You...?, Miracle on 34th Street, The Elevator, Flood, Thief of Baghdad, The Immigrants, The Martian Chronicles, Hart to Hart (pilot), The Memory of Eva Ryker, Million Dollar Face, Mae West, This Girl for Hire, The Zany Adventures of Robin Hood, Alice in Wonderland, Earth Angel, An Inconvenient Woman, Deadly Game, The Sands of Time, Heads, Hart to Hart: Home Is Where the Hart Is. Mini-Series: The Rhinemann Exchange, Hollywood Wives, Around the World in 80 Days. Guest: Goodyear TV Playhouse, Ponds Theatre, Oldsmobile Music Theatre, Campbell Soundstage, Batman, The Invaders, Love American Style, Carol Burnett Show, George Burns Comedy Week, Love Boat, Matlock, Murder She Wrote, many others.

McDOWELL, MALCOLM
Actor. b. Leeds, England, June 13, 1943. Was spearholder for the Royal Shakespeare Co. in season of 1965-66 when turned to TV and then to films. NY stage: Look Back in Anger (also on video), In Celebration, Another Time. LA stage: Hunting Cockroaches.
PICTURES: Poor Cow (debut, 1967), If..., Figures in a Landscape, The Raging Moon (Long Ago Tomorrow), A Clockwork Orange, O Lucky Man!, Royal Flash, Voyage of the Damned, Aces High, The Passage, Time After Time, Caligula, Cat People, Britannia Hospital, Blue Thunder, Cross Creek, Get Crazy, Sunset, Buy and Cell, The Caller, Class of 1999, Disturbed, In the Eye of the Snake, Moon 44, The Maestro, Schweitzer (The Light in the Jungle), Assassin of the Tsar, The Player, Happily Ever After (voice), Chain of Desire, East Wind, Night Train to Venice, Bopha!, Milk Money, Star Trek: Generations, Tank Girl, Kids of the Round Table, Where Truth Lies.
TELEVISION: Series: Pearl. Guest: Faerie Tale Theatre (Little Red Riding Hood), Tales fromt the Crypt (Reluctant Vampire). Movies: Arthur the King, Gulag, Monte Carlo, Seasons of the Heart, The Man Who Wouldn't Die.

McELWAINE, GUY
Executive. b. Culver City, CA, June 29, 1936. Started career in pub. dept. of MGM, 1955; 1959, joined m.p. div. of Rogers and Cowen; 1964, formed own public relations firm; then joined CMA. Left to become sr. exec. v.p. in chg. worldwide m.p. production, Warner Bros., 1975. 1977 became sr. exec. v.p. in chg. worldwide m.p. activities and pres. of intl. film mktg. at Intl. Creative Management (ICM), formerly CMA. 1981, named pres.

and CEO, Rastar Films. Left in 1982 to become pres., Columbia Pictures; given additional title of CEO, 1983. 1985 named chmn. and on board of Columbia Pictures Industries. Resigned, 1986. Joined Weintraub Entertainment Group as exec. v.p. and chmn., m.p. div. 1987-89; returned to ICM, 1989 as vice chmn.

McEVEETY, BERNARD
Director. Father was pioneer as unit mgr. at New York's Edison Studios; Brothers dir. Vincent and writer Joseph. Began career in 1953 at Paramount where he was asst. dir. for 6 yrs. Dir. debut on TV series, The Rebel.
PICTURES: Ride Beyond Vengeance, Brotherhood of Satan, Napoleon and Samantha, One Little Indian, The Bears and I.
TELEVISION: Numerous episodes on Bonanza, Gunsmoke, Combat and Cimarron Strip (also prod.), Centennial, Roughnecks, The Machans.

McEVEETY, VINCENT
Director. Brother is dir. Bernard McEveety. Joined Hal Roach Studios in 1954 as second asst. dir. Then to Republic for The Last Command. First Disney assignments: Davy Crockett shows and Mickey Mouse Club. Moved to Desilu as first asst. dir. on The Untouchables; made assoc. prod. with option to direct. Did segments of many series, including 34 Gunsmoke episodes.
PICTURES: Firecreek (debut, 1968), $1,000,000 Duck, The Biscuit Eater, Charley and the Angel, Superdad, The Strongest Man in the World, Gus, Treasure of Matecumbe, Herbie Goes to Monte Carlo, The Apple Dumpling Gang Rides Again, Herbie Goes Bananas, Amy.
TELEVISION: Blood Sport, Wonder Woman, High Flying Spy, Ask Max, Gunsmoke: Return to Dodge, Murder She Wrote, Simon and Simon (26 episodes), Columbo: Rest in Peace Mrs. Columbo.

McGAVIN, DARREN
Actor. b. Spokane, WA, May 7, 1922. e. Coll. of the Pacific. Studied acting at Neighborhood Playhouse, Actors Studio. Landed bit roles in films starting in 1945.
THEATER: Death of a Salesman, My Three Angels, The Rainmaker, The Lovers, The King and I, Dinner at Eight (revival), Captain Brassbound's Conversion (LA), The Night Hank Williams Died, Greetings.
PICTURES: A Song to Remember (debut, 1945), Kiss and Tell, Counter-Attack, She Wouldn't Say Yes, Fear, Queen for a Day, Summertime, The Man With the Golden Arm, The Court Martial of Billy Mitchell, Beau James, The Delicate Delinquent, The Case Against Brooklyn, Bullet for a Badman, The Great Sioux Massacre, Ride the High Wind, Mission Mars, Mrs. Polifax—Spy, Happy Mother's Day... Love George (Run Stranger Run; dir. only), No Deposit No Return, Airport '77, Hot Lead and Cold Feet, Zero to Sixty, Hangar 18, Firebird 2015 A.D., A Christmas Story, The Natural, Turk 182, Raw Deal, From the Hip, Dead Heat, Blood and Concrete: A Love Story, Billy Madison.
TELEVISION: Series: Crime Photographer, Mike Hammer, Riverboat, The Outsider, Kolchak: The Night Stalker, Small & Frye. Movies: The Outsider (pilot), The Challenge, The Challengers, Berlin Affair, Tribes, Banyon, The Death of Me Yet, Night Stalker, Something Evil, The Rookies, Say Goodbye Maggie Cole, The Night Strangler, The Six Million Dollar Man (pilot), Brink's: The Great Robbery, Law and Order, The Users, Love for Rent, Waikiki, Return of Marcus Welby M.D., My Wicked Wicked Ways, Inherit the Wind, The Diamond Trap, By Dawn's Early Light, The American Clock, Danielle Steel's A Perfect Stranger, Derby. Specials: Unclaimed Fortunes (host), Clara (ACE Award), Mastergate, Miracles and Ohter Wonders (host), The Secret Discovery of Noah's Ark (host). Mini-Series: Ike, The Martian Chronicles, Around the World in 80 Days. Guest: Goodyear TV Playhouse, Alfred Hitchcock Presents, Route 66, U.S. Steel Hour, The Defenders, Love American Style, The Name of the Game, Owen Marshall, Police Story, The Love Boat, Murphy Brown (Emmy Award, 1990), many others.

McGILLIS, KELLY
Actress. b. Newport Beach, CA, July 9, 1957. Studied acting at Pacific Conservatory of Performing Arts in Santa Maria, CA; Juilliard. While at latter, won role in film Reuben Reuben.
THEATER: D.C. Stage: The Merchant of Venice, Twelfth Night, Measure for Measure, Much Ado About Nothing. NY Stage: Hedda Gabler.
PICTURES: Reuben Reuben (debut, 1983), Witness, Top Gun, Once We Were Dreamers (Promised Land), Made in Heaven, The House on Carroll Street, The Accused, Winter People, Cat Chaser, Before and After Death, The Babe, North.
TELEVISION: Movies: Sweet Revenge, Private Sessions, Grand Isle (also prod.), Bonds of Love, In the Best of Families: Marriage Pride & Madness. Special: Out of Ireland (narrator).

McGINLEY, JOHN C.
Actor. b. New York, NY, Aug. 3, 1959. e. NYU (M.F.A.), 1984.
THEATRE: NY: Danny and the Deep Blue Sea, The Ballad of Soapy Smith, Jesse and the Games, Requiem for a Heavyweight, Love as We Know It, Talk Radio, Florida Crackers, Breast Men.

PICTURES: Sweet Liberty, Platoon, Wall Street, Shakedown, Talk Radio, Lost Angels, Fat Man and Little Boy, Born on the Fourth of July, Point Break, Highlander 2: The Quickening, Article 99, Little Noises, A Midnight Clear, Fathers and Sons, Hear No Evil, Watch It (also co-prod.), Car 54 Where Are You?, On Deadly Ground, Surviving the Game, Suffrin' Bastards (also co-s.p.), Wagons East!, Born to Be Wild, Captive (co-prod. only), Seven, Nixon, Johns, The Rock.
TELEVISION: Movies: Clinton & Nadine, Cruel Doubt, The Last Outlaw, The Return of Hunter. Guest: Frasier.

McGOOHAN, PATRICK
Actor, Director. b. New York, Mar. 19, 1928. Early career in repertory in Britain. London stage 1954 in Serious Charge; 1955, Orson Welles' Moby Dick. On B'way in Pack of Lies (1987).
PICTURES: The Dam Busters (debut, 1954), I Am a Camera, The Dark Avenger (The Warriors), Passage Home, Zarak, High Tide at Noon, Hell Drivers, The Gypsy and the Gentleman, Nor the Moon by Night (Elephant Gun), Two Living One Dead, All Night Long, Life for Ruth (Walk in the Shadow), The Quare Fellow, The Three Lives of Thomasina, Dr. Syn: Alias the Scarecrow (U.S. tv as: The Scarecrow of Romney Marsh), Ice Station Zebra, The Moonshine War, Mary—Queen of Scots, Catch My Soul (dir. only), Un Genio due Campari e un Pollo (The Genius), Porgi d'altra Guancia (Nobody's the Greatest), Silver Streak, Brass Target, Escape From Alcatraz, Scanners, Kings and Desperate Men, Finding Katie, Baby: Secret of the Lost Legend, Braveheart, The Phantom, A Time to Kill.
TELEVISION: Series: Danger Man (also dir. episodes), Secret Agent, The Prisoner (also creator, prod.), Rafferty. Movies/Specials: The Hard Way, Jamaica Inn, Of Pure Blood, The Man in the Iron Mask, Three Sovereigns for Sarah. Guest: Columbo (Emmy Awards: 1975, 1990; also dir. episodes).

McGOVERN, ELIZABETH
Actress. b. Evanston, IL, July 18, 1961. Family moved to Southern California when she was 10. Acted in high school in North Hollywood; performance in prod. of The Skin of Our Teeth won her agency represenation. Studied at American Conservatory Theatre, San Francisco and Juilliard Sch. of Dramatic Art. Open audition for Ordinary People resulted in her film debut. Appeared in IMAX film Wings of Courage.
THEATER: NY: To Be Young Gifted and Black (1981, debut), My Sister in This House (Theatre World, Obie Awards), Painting Churches, The Hitch-Hiker, A Map of the World, Aunt Dan and Lemon (L.A.), Two Gentlemen of Verona, A Midsummer Night's Dream (NY Shakespeare Fest.), Love Letters, Twelfth Night (Boston), Major Barbara (Alaska), Ring Around the Moon (D.C.), Maids of Honor, The Three Sisters, As You Like It.
PICTURES: Ordinary People (debut, 1980), Ragtime (Acad. Award nom.), Lovesick, Racing with the Moon, Once Upon a Time in America, Native Son, The Bedroom Window, She's Having a Baby, Johnny Handsome, The Handmaid's Tale, A Shock to the System, Tune in Tomorrow, King of the Hill, Me and Veronica, The Favor.
TELEVISION: Series: If Not for You. Movies: Women and Men: Stories of Seduction (The Man in the Brooks Brothers Shirt), Broken Trust. Specials: Ashenden, Tales From Hollywood, The Changeling (BBC).

McGRATH, JUDY
Executive. e. Cedar Crest Coll. President, MTV. Began at MTV as on-air promotions writer. Created Unplugged, MTV Books, MTV Online.

McGRATH, THOMAS J.
Producer, Attorney, Writer, Lecturer. b. New York, NY, Oct. 8, 1932. e. Washington Square Coll. of NYU, B.A., 1956; NYU Sch. of Law, LL.B., 1960. Served in Army with U.S. Army, 1953-54. Has practiced law in N.Y. from 1960 to date. Became indep. prod. with Deadly Hero in 1976; Author, Carryover Basis Under The 1976 Tax Reform Act, published in 1977. Cobntributing author, Estate and Gift Tax After ERTA, 1982. Lecturer and writer: American Law Institute 1976-81; Practicing Law Institute, 1976-present. Dir., New York Philharmonic; Oloffson Corp.; East Food Development Corp. Trustee: American Austrian Foundation; Tanzania Wildlife Fund.

McGREGOR, CHARLES
Executive. b. Jersey City, NJ, April 1, 1927. e. NYU. 1958-69, co-founder, pres. and CEO, Banner Films, Inc. (World Wide TV Distribution); 1955-58, salesman and div. mgr., Flamingo Films (domestic TV Dist.); Professional mgr. ABC Music Publishing. 1951-53: Prod. and partner Telco Prods. and GM Productions (prods. of network and local shows). 1969-77: exec. v.p. in chg. of worldwide dist., WB-TV; 1977-89, pres. WB-TV Distribution; 1989, named exec. v.p., corp. projects, WB.

McGUIRE, DOROTHY
Actress. b. Omaha, NE, June 14, 1919. e. Ladywood convent, Indianapolis; Pine Manor, Wellesley, MA. Acting debut as teenager at Omaha Community Playhouse. Following summer

stock and radio work, made B'way debut in 1938 as Martha Scott's understudy in Our Town. Came to Hollywood to repeat stage role in film version of Claudia.
THEATER: Our Town, My Dear Children, Swinging the Dream, Claudia, Legend of Lovers, Winesberg Ohio, Night of the Iguana (1976), Cause Celebre, Another Part of the Forest, I Never Sang for My Father.
PICTURES: Claudia (debut, 1943), A Tree Grows in Brooklyn, The Enchanted Cottage, The Spiral Staircase, Claudia and David, Till the End of Time, Gentleman's Agreement (Acad. Award nom.), Mother Didn't Tell Me, Mister 880, Callaway Went Thataway, I Want You, Invitation, Make Haste to Live, Three Coins in the Fountain, Trial, Friendly Persuasion, Old Yeller, The Remarkable Mr. Pennypacker, This Earth Is Mine, A Summer Place, The Dark at the Top of the Stairs, Swiss Family Robinson, Susan Slade, Summer Magic, The Greatest Story Ever Told, Flight of the Doves, Jonathan Livingston Seagull (voice).
TELEVISION: Series: Little Women. Movies: She Waits, The Runaways, Little Women, The Incredible Journey of Dr. Meg Laurel, Ghost Dancing, Amos, Between the Darkness and the Dawn, Caroline? Mini-Series: Rich Man Poor Man. Specials: The Philadelphia Story, To Each His Own, Another Part of the Forest, I Never Sang for My Father. Guest: The Love Boat, The Young & the Restless, Highway to Heaven, Fantasy Island, St. Elsewhere.

McGURK, CHRIS
Executive. Pres., The Walt Disney Motion Pictures Group.

McHATTIE, STEPHEN
Actor. b. Antigonish, Nova Scotia, Canada, Feb. 3, e. Acadia U. Trained for stage at American Acad. of Dramatic Arts.
THEATER: NY: The American Dream (debut, 1968), Pictures in the Hallway, Twelfth Night, Mourning Becomes Electra, The Iceman Cometh, Alive and Well in Argentina, The Winter Dancers, Casualties, The Three Sisters, The Misanthrope, Heartbreak House, Mensch Meier, Haven, Search and Destroy.
PICTURES: Von Richthofen and Brown (debut, 1970), The People Next Door, The Ultimate Warrior, Moving Violation, Tomorrow Never Comes, Death Valley, Best Revenge, Belizaire the Cajun, Salvation!, Call Me, Sticky Fingers, Caribe, Bloodhounds on Broadway, Erik, The Dark, Geronimo: An American Legend, Beverly Hills Cop III, Art Deco Detective.
TELEVISION: Series: Highcliffe Manor, Mariah, Scene of the Crime. Mini-series: Centennial. Movies: Search for the Gods, James Dean, Look What's Happened to Rosemary's Baby, Mary and Joseph: A Story of Faith, Roughnecks, Terror on Track 9, Jonathan Stone: Threat of Innocence, Deadlocked: Escape From Zone 14, Convict Cowboy.

McKEAN, MICHAEL
Actor, Writer. b. NYC, Oct. 17, 1947. e. NYU. Featured on L.A. radio show, The Credibility Gap.
THEATRE: Accomplice (Theatre World Award).
PICTURES: 1941, Used Cars, Young Doctors in Love, This is Spinal Tap (also co-s.p., co-wrote songs), D.A.R.Y.L., Clue, Jumpin' Jack Flash, Light of Day, Planes Trains and Automobiles, Short Circuit 2, Earth Girls Are Easy, The Big Picture (also co-s.p.), Hider in the House, Flashback, Book of Love, True Identity, Memoirs of an Invisible Man, Man Trouble, Coneheads, Airheads, Radioland Murders, Across the Moon, The Brady Bunch Movie, Edie and Pen, Jack.
TELEVISION: Series: Laverne & Shirley, Grand, Sessions, Saturday Night Live, Dream On. Movies: More Than Friends, Classified Love, Murder in High Places, MacShayne: The Final Roll of the Dice. Specials: Spinal Tap Reunion, The Laverne and Shirley Reunion.

McKELLEN, SIR IAN
Actor. b. Burnley, England, May 25, 1939. e. Cambridge. C.B.E. 1979, Knighted 1991.
THEATRE: London: A Scent of Flowers (debut, 1964), Trelawny of the Wells, A Lily in Little India, The Man of Destiny, Black Comedy, Dr. Faustus, Henceforward, Bent, Uncle Vanya, Hamlet, Macbeth, Romeo & Juliet, Richard III. B'way: The Promise, Amadeus (Tony Award, 1981), Ian McKellen Acting Shakespeare, Wild Honey (also London), Richard III (Brooklyn), A Knight Out. Assoc. Dir. Nat'l Theatre. Prof. of Contemporary Theatre, Oxford Univ., 1991.
PICTURES: Alfred the Great, Thank You All Very Much, A Touch of Love, Priest of Love, The Keep, Plenty, Zina, Scandal, Last Action Hero, The Ballad of Little Jo, Six Degrees of Separation, The Shadow, Jack & Sarah, Restoration, Thin Ice, Richard III (also co-s.p.), Apt Pupil.
TELEVISION: Hamlet, David Copperfield, The Scarlet Pimpernel, Hedda Gabler, Ian McKellen Acting Shakespeare, Every Good Boy Deserves Favor, Loving Walter, Windmills of the Gods, Macbeth, Othello, Countdown to War, And the Band Played On, Mister Shaw's Missing Millions, Tales of the City, Cold Comfort Farm, Rasputin.

McKEON, DOUG
Actor. b. Pompton Plains, NJ, June 10, 1966.
THEATRE: Dandelion Wine, Truckload, Brighton Beach Memoirs, Death of a Buick, The Big Day.

PICTURES: Uncle Joe Shannon, On Golden Pond, Night Crossing, Mischief, Turnaround, Where the Red Fern Grows Part 2, The Empty Mirror.
TELEVISION: Series: Edge of Night, Big Shamus Little Shamus, Little Niagra. Mini-Series: Centennial. Movies: Tell Me My Name, Daddy I Don't Like It Like This, The Comeback Kid, An Innocent Love, Desperate Lives, At Mother's Request, Silent Eye, Heart of a Champion: The Ray Mancini Story, Breaking Home Ties, Without Consent.

McKEON, NANCY
Actress. b. Westbury, NY, Apr. 4, 1966.
PICTURE: Where the Day Takes You.
TELEVISION: Series: Stone, The Facts of Life, Can't Hurry Love. Movies: A Question of Love, The Facts of Life Goes to Paris, High School U.S.A., This Child Is Mine, Poison Ivy, Firefighter (also co-exec. prod.), The Facts of Life Down Under, Strange Voices (also co-exec. prod.), A Cry for Help: The Tracey Thurman Story, A Mother's Gift. Specials: Schoolboy Father, Scruffy (voice), Please Don't Hit Me Mom, Candid Kids (co-host).

McKERN, LEO
Actor. r.n. Reginald McKern. b. Sydney, New South Wales, Australia, Mar. 16, 1920.
THEATER: She Stoops to Conquer, Hamlet, Merry Wives of Windsor, Cat on a Hot Tin Roof, A Man for All Seasons, Boswell for the Defence, Hobson's Choice.
PICTURES: Murder in the Cathedral, All For Mary, X the Unknown, Time Without Pity, A Tale of Two Cities, The Mouse That Roared, Yesterday's Enemy, Scent of Mystery, Jazz Boat, Mr. Topaze (I Like Money), The Day the Earth Caught Fire, Lisa (The Inspector), Doctor in Distress, A Jolly Bad Fellow, King and Country, Agent 8 3/4 (Hot Enough for June), Help!, The Amorous Adventures of Moll Flanders, A Man for All Seasons, Assignment K, Decline and Fall of a Bird Watcher, The Shoes of the Fisherman, Ryan's Daughter, Massacre in Rome, The Adventure of Sherlock Holmes' Smarter Brother, The Omen, Candleshoe, Damien: Omen II, The Last Tasmanian, The Blue Lagoon, The French Lieutenant's Woman, Ladyhawke, The Chain, Traveling North (Australian Film Award), Dave and Dad on Our Selection.
TELEVISION: King Lear, Murder with Mirrors, House on Garibaldi Street, Reilly: Ace of Spies, Rumpole of the Bailey, The Master Builder, The Last Romantics, A Foreign Field, Good King Wenceslas.

McLAGLEN, ANDREW V.
Director. b. London, Eng., July 28, 1920. Son of late actor Victor McLaglen. e. U. of Virginia, 1939-40. Asst. m.p. dir., 1944-54.
PICTURES: Gun the Man Down (debut, 1956), Man in the Vault, The Abductors, Freckles, The Little Shepherd of Kingdom Come, McLintock!, Shenandoah, The Rare Breed, The Way West, Monkeys Go Home!, The Ballad of Josie, The Devil's Brigade, Bandolero, Hellfighters, The Undefeated, Chisum, Fool's Parade (also prod.), Something Big (also prod.), One More Train to Rob, Cahill: U.S. Marshal, Mitchell, The Last Hard Men, The Wild Geese, Breakthrough (Sergeant Steiner), ffolkes (North Sea Hijack), The Sea Wolves, Sahara, Return to the River Kwai, Eye of the Widow.
TELEVISION: Series: Gunsmoke, Have Gun—Will Travel, Perry Mason, Rawhide, The Lineup, The Lieutenant. Movies: Log of the Black Pearl, Stowaway to the Moon, Banjo Hackett: Roamin' Free, Murder at the World Series, Louis L'Amour's The Shadow Riders, Travis McGee, The Dirty Dozen: The Next Mission. Mini-Series: The Blue and the Gray, On Wings of Eagles.

McLERIE, ALLYN ANN
Actress. b. Grand Mere, Quebec, Canada, Dec. 1, 1926. e. Prof. childrens school. m. actor-singer George Gaynes. e. high school, N.Y. Dancer since 15 in many B'way shows.
THEATER: One Touch of Venus, On the Town, Finian's Rainbow, Where's Charley?, Miss Liberty, Time Limit, South Pacific, Night of the Iguana, Julius Caesar, West Side Story, My Fair Lady, The Beast in Me, To Dorothy a Son.
PICTURES: Words and Music (debut 1948), Where's Charley?, Desert Song, Calamity Jane, Phantom of the Rue Morgue, Battle Cry, They Shoot Horses Don't They?, Monte Walsh, The Cowboys, Jeremiah Johnson, The Magnificent Seven Ride, The Way We Were, Cinderella Liberty, All the President's Men.
TELEVISION: Series: Tony Randall Show, Punky Brewster, Days and Nights of Molly Dodd. Mini-Series: The Thorn Birds, Beulah Land. Specials: Oldest Living Graduate, The Entertainer, Return Engagement, Shadow of a Gunman. Guest: WKRP in Cincinnati, Barney Miller, St. Elsewhere, Hart to Hart, Love Boat, Dynasty.

McMAHON, ED
Performer. b. Detroit, MI, March 6, 1923. e. Boston Coll.; Catholic U. of America, B.A., 1949. U.S. Marines, 1942-53. First job on TV was as the clown on Big Top, 1950-51. First joined Johnny Carson as his sidekick on daytime quiz show Who Do You Trust? in 1958.
THEATRE: stock; B'way: Impossible Years.

PICTURES: The Incident, Slaughter's Big Rip-Off, Fun with Dick and Jane, The Last Remake of Beau Geste (cameo), Butterfly, Full Moon High, Love Affair.
TELEVISION: *Series*: Big Top, Who Do You Trust?, The Tonight Show (1962-92), Missing Links (emcee), Snap Judgment (emcee), The Kraft Music Hall (host, 1968), Concentration (emcee), NBC Adventure Theatre (host), Whodunnit? (emcee), Star Search (host), TV's Bloopers and Practical Jokes (host). *Movies*: Star Marker, The Great American Traffic Jam (Gridlock), The Kid From Left Field. *Specials*: Macy's Thanksgiving Day Parade (host), Jerry Lewis Labor Day Telethon (co-host).

McMAHON, JOHN J.
Executive. b. Chicago, IL, 1932. e. Northwestern U. Served with U.S. Army in Korea, beginning career on WGN-TV, Chicago; associated with ZIV-United Artists TV Productions during 1950s; joined ABC in 1958; v.p. & gen. mgr., WXYTZ-TV, Detroit, then KABC-TV, Los Angeles, 1968; v.p., ABC, 1968-72; joined NBC in 1972 as v.p., programs, west coast, NBC-TV; president, Hollywood Radio & Television Society; board member, Permanent Charities Committee. 1980, named pres. of Carson Prods. (Johnny Carson's prod. co.).
TELEVISION: If It's Tuesday It Still Must Be Belgium (exec. prod.), My Father My Son (exec. prod.).

McMARTIN, JOHN
Actor. Warsaw, IN, e. Columbia U. Off-B'way debut: Little Mary Sunshine (1959: Theatre World Award).
THEATER: The Conquering Hero, Blood Sweat and Stanley Poole, Children from Their Games, A Rainy Day in Newark, Pleasures and Palaces (Detroit), Sweet Charity (Tony nom.), Follies, The Great God Brown (Drama Desk Award), Sondheim: A Musical Tribute, Forget-Me-Not-Lane (Mark Taper Forum), The Visit, Chemin de Fer, The Rules of the Game, A Little Family Business, Passion (Mark Taper), Solomon's Child, Julius Caesar, A Little Night Music (Ahmanson), Love for Love, Happy New Year, Don Juan (Drama Desk Award, Tony nom.), Artist Descending a Staircase, Henry IV (Kennedy Ctr.), Custer (Kennedy Ctr.), Money & Friends (L.A.), Show Boat (Tony nom.).
PICTURES: A Thousand Clowns, What's So Bad About Feeling Good?, Sweet Charity, All The President's Men, Thieves, Brubaker, Blow Out, Pennies From Heaven, Dream Lover, Legal Eagles, Native Son, Who's That Girl, A Shock to the System.
TELEVISION: *Series*: Falcon Crest, Beauty and the Beast. *Guest*: Cheers, Mary Tyler Moore Show, Murder She Wrote, Magnum P.I., The Golden Girls, Empty Nest, Law and Order, others. American Playhouse *Specials*: Edith Wharton Story, Rules of the Game, The Greatest Man in the World, Private Contentment, The Fatal Weakness, Concealed Enemies. *Movies*: Ritual of Evil, Fear on Trial, The Defection of Simas Kudirka, The Last Ninja, Murrow, Day One, Roots: The Gift, Separate But Equal, Citizen Cohn.

McNAMARA, WILLIAM
Actor. b. Dallas, TX, 1965. e. Columbia U. Joined Act I theatre group at Williamstown Theatre Festival, 1986; studied acting at Lee Strasberg Institute.
PICTURES: The Beat (debut, 1988), Stealing Home, Dream a Little Dream, Stella, Texasville, Terror at the Opera, Aspen Extreme, Surviving the Game, Chasers, Storybook, Girl in the Cadillac, Copycat.
TELEVISION: *Series*: Island Son. *Specials*: Soldier Boys (Afterschool Special), Secret of the Sahara, The Edge (Indian Poker), It's Only Rock 'n' Roll (Afterschool Special). *Movies*: Wildflower (ACE Award nom.), Doing Time on Maple Drive, Honor Thy Mother, Sworn to Vengeance, Radio Inside, Liz: The Elizabeth Taylor Story. *Pilot*: The Wyatts.

McNAUGHTON, JOHN
Director. b. Chicago, IL, Jan. 13, 1950.
PICTURES: Henry: Portrait of a Serial Killer, The Borrower, Sex Drugs Rock & Roll, Mad Dog and Glory, Normal Life.

McNICHOL, KRISTY
Actress. b. Los Angeles, CA, Sept. 11, 1962. Brother is actor Jimmy McNichol. Made debut at age of 7 performing in commercials. Given regular role in Apple's Way; began appearing on such series as Love American Style and The Bionic Woman. Attracted attention of Spelling-Goldberg Productions, who cast her as Buddy Lawrence in Family series, 1976-80.
PICTURES: The End (debut, 1978), Little Darlings, The Night the Lights Went Out in Georgia, Only When I Laugh, White Dog, The Pirate Movie, Just the Way You Are, Dream Lover, You Can't Hurry Love, Two Moon Junction, The Forgotten One.
TELEVISION: *Series*: Apple's Way, Family (2 Emmy Awards: 1977, 1979), Empty Nest. *Movies*: The Love Boat II, Like Mom Like Me, Summer of My German Soldier, My Old Man, Blinded by the Light, Love Mary, Women of Valor, Children of the Bride, Mother of the Bride (also co-exec. prod.).

McRANEY, GERALD
Actor. b. Collins, MS, Aug. 19, 1948. m. actress Delta Burke. e. U. of Mississippi. Left school to become surveyor in oil fields

after which joined acting company in New Orleans. Studied acting with Jeff Corey; landed guest role on TV series, Night Gallery.
PICTURES: Night of Bloody Horror, Keep Off My Grass, The Neverending Story, American Justice.
TELEVISION: *Series*: Simon & Simon, Major Dad (also exec. prod.), Home of the Brave. *Guest*: The Incredible Hulk, The Rockford Files, The Dukes of Hazzard, Eight Is Enough, How the West Was Won, Hawaii Five-O, Barnaby Jones, Gunsmoke, Designing Women. *Movies*: Roots II, The Jordan Chance, Women in White, Trial of Chaplain Jenson, The Law, The Haunting Passion, A Hobo's Christmas, Where the Hell's That Gold?!!?, The People Across the Lake, Dark of the Moon, Murder By Moonlight, Blind Vengeance, Vestige of Honor, Love and Curses... And All That Jazz (also dir., co-exec. prod.), Fatal Friendship, Scattered Dreams: The Kathryn Messenger Story, Armed and Innocent, Motorcycle Gang, Deadly Vows, Someone She Knows, Not Our Son, Simon & Simon: In Trouble Again, The Stranger Beside Me, Nothing Lasts Forever. *Special*: Fast Forward.

McSHANE, IAN
Actor. b. Blackburn, England, Sept. 29, 1942. e. RADA. Stage work includes The House of Fred Ginger, The Easter Man, The Glass Menagerie (England). *NY*: The Promise. *LA*: Inadmissible Evidence, Betrayal.
PICTURES: The Wild and the Willing (debut, 1962), The Pleasure Girls, Gypsy Girl (Sky West and Crooked), If It's Tuesday This Must Be Belgium, The Battle of Britain, Freelance, Pussycat Pussycat I Love You, The Devil's Widow (Tam-Lin), Villain, Sitting Target, The Left Hand of Gemini, The Last of Sheila, Ransom, Journey Into Fear, The Fifth Musketeer, Yesterday's Hero, Cheaper to Keep Her, Exposed, Torchlight, Ordeal By Innocence, Too Scared to Scream.
TELEVISION: Wuthering Heights, The Pirate, Disraeli, The Letter, Marco Polo, Bare Essence, Grace Kelly, Evergreen, A.D., The Murders in the Rue Morgue, Grand Larceny, War and Remembrance, Chain Letter (pilot), The Great Escape II: the Untold Story, The Young Charlie Chaplin, Lovejoy (also II), Sauce For Goose, Dick Francis Mysteries (Blood Sport), Perry Mason: The Case of the Desperate Deception, Columbo: Rest in Peace Mrs. Columbo.

McTIERNAN, JOHN
Director. b. Albany, NY, Jan. 8, 1951. e. Juilliard (acting), SUNY/Old Westbury (filmmaking). m. prod. Donna Dubrow. First effort was film The Demon's Daughter, unreleased to date. Appeared in film Death of a Soldier.
PICTURES: Nomads (also s.p.), Predator, Die Hard, The Hunt for Red October, Medicine Man, Last Action Hero (also co-prod.), Die Hard With a Vengeance.

MEADOWS, JAYNE
Actress. b. Wu Chang, China, Sept. 27, 1924. m. performer Steve Allen. Sister of deceased actress Audrey Meadows. Parents were Episcopal missionaries. Came to U.S. in early 1930's. Studied acting with Stella Adler, Lee Strasberg, David Craig. Made B'way debut in 1941 in Spring Again.
THEATRE: *NY*: Spring Again, Another Love Story, Kiss Them for Me, The Gazebo, Once in a Lifetime (revival), Many Happy Returns, etc. Regional: Love Letters, Lost in Yonkers, The Fourposter, Cinderella, Tonight at 8:30, Powerful Women in History (1 woman show).
PICTURES: Undercurrent (debut, 1946), Dark Delusion, Lady in the Lake, Song of the Thin Man, Luck of the Irish, Enchantment, David and Bathsheba, The Fat Man, College Confidential, Da Capo (Finland), Norman Is That You?, City Slickers (voice), The Player, City Slickers II: The Legend of Curly's Gold (voice), Casino.
TELEVISION: *Series*: I've Got a Secret, The Steve Allen Show, Art Linkletter Show, Steve Allen Comedy Hour, Medical Center, Steve Allen's Laugh Back, Meeting of Minds, It's Not Easy, High Society. *Movies*: Now You See It Now You Don't, James Dean, Sex and the Married Woman, The Gossip Columnist, Miss All-American Beauty, The Ratings Game, Alice in Wonderland, A Masterpiece of Murder, Parent Trap Hawaiian Honeymoon. *Guest*: Robert Montgomery Presents, The Web, Ann Sothern Show, Love American Style, Here's Lucy, The Paper Chase, Fantasy Island, The Love Boat, St. Elsewhere, Sisters, Murder She Wrote, many others.

MEANEY, COLM
Actor. b. Ireland. Started acting as a teen, appearing at Gate Theatre in Dublin in play, The Hostage. Studied at Abbey Theatre then joined London's 7-84 Theatre Co., Half Moon Theatre Co., Belt and Braces touring co. On NY stage in Breaking the Code. Also acted with Great Lakes Fest. in Cleveland, OH, in Nicholas Nickelby.
PICTURES: The Dead, Dick Tracy, Die Hard 2, Come See the Paradise, The Commitments, The Last of the Mohicans, Under Siege, Far and Away, Into the West, The Snapper (Golden Globe nom.), The Road to Wellville, The Englishman Who Went Up a Hill But Came Down a Mountain, The Van, Last of the High Kings.
TELEVISION: *Series*: Star Trek: The Next Generation, Deep Space Nine. *Mini-Series*: Scarlett.

MEANEY, DONALD V.
Executive. b. Newark, NJ. e. Rutgers U. Sch. of Journalism. Worked as reporter for Plainfield (NJ) Courier-News, Newark Evening News. Became news director of radio station WCTC in New Brunswick, NJ; later for WNJR, Newark. Joined NBC in 1952 as news writer; two years later became nat'l TV news editor. Promoted to mgr., national news, 1960 and mrg., special news programs, 1961. Appt. dir. of news programs 1962 and gen. mgr., NBC News, 1965; v.p., news programming, NBC, 1967; v.p. news, Washington, 1974; mng. dir., affiliate & intl. liaison, 1979; sr. mng. editor, intl. liaison, 1984; retired from NBC, 1985. Now on faculty of American U. Sch. of Communications.

MEARA, ANNE
Actress, Writer. b. Brooklyn, NY Sept. 20, 1929. m. actor-writer Jerry Stiller. Son is actor-director Ben Stiller; daughter is actress Amy Stiller. e. Herbert Berghof Studio, 1953-54. Apprenticed in summer stock on Long Island and Woodstock NY, 1950-53. Acted with NY Shakespeare Fest. 1957 and 1988 (Romeo and Juliet). With husband joined St. Louis improv. theater The Compass, 1959 and Chicago's Medium Rare. They formed comedy act in 1962 appearing (34 times) on The Ed Sullivan Show and making the nightclub and comedy club circuit incl. The Village Gate, The Blue Angel, The Establishment. Formed own prod. company, writing, prod. and recording award-winning radio and TV commercials. With husband co-hosted and wrote video, So You Want to Be an Actor?
THEATER: A Month in the Country, Maedchen in Uniform, Ulysses in Nightown, The House of Blue Leaves, Spookhouse, Bosoms and Neglect, Eastern Standard, Anna Christie (Tony nom.), After-Play (also author).
PICTURES: The Out-of-Towners, Lovers and Other Strangers, Nasty Habits, The Boys From Brazil, Fame, The Perils of P.K., The Longshot, My Little Girl, Awakenings, Highway to Hell, Reality Bites, Heavyweights, Kiss of Death, An Open Window, The Daytrippers.
TELEVISION: Guest on numerous TV game and talk shows and variety shows. Series: The Greatest Gift (1954 soap opera), The Paul Lynde Show, The Corner Bar, Take Five with Stiller and Meara (1977-78; synd.), Kate McShane, Rhoda, Archie Bunker's Place, ALF (also writer), All My Children. Movies: Kate McShane (pilot), The Other Woman. Specials: The Sunset Gang, Avenue Z Afternoon.

MECHANIC, BILL
Executive. b. Detroit, MI. e. Michigan State U., B.A.; U. of Southern California, Ph.D. in film pending. Entered industry 1978 as dir. of programming for SelecTV; promoted to v.p., 1980. Joined Paramount 1982; 1984, to Disney as v.p., pay TV sls. 1985, named sr. v.p., video, of new Walt Disney video div.; 1987, named president, int'l theatrical distribution and worldwide video, Walt Disney. Became pres. 20th Century Fox, 1993.

MEDAK, PETER
Director. b. Budapest, Hungary, Dec. 23, 1940. Appeared in film Beverly Hills Cop III.
THEATRE: Miss Julie. Operas: Salome, La Voix Humaine, Rigoletto.
PICTURES: Negatives, A Day in the Death of Joe Egg, The Ruling Class, Ghost in the Noonday Sun, The Odd Job, The Changeling, Zorro the Gay Blade, The Men's Club, The Krays, Let Him Have It, Romeo Is Bleeding, Pontiac Moon.
TELEVISION: Third Girl from the Left, The Babysitter, The Dark Secret of Black Bayou, Mistress of Paradise, Cry for the Stranger, Faerie Tale Theatre, Twilight Zone, Nabokov, Crime Story, Mount Royal, La Voix Humaine, Tales From the Crypt, Homicide, The Kindred, Falls Road.

MEDAVOY, MIKE
Executive. b. Shanghai, China, Jan. 21, 1941. Lived in China until 1947 when family moved to Chile. Came to U.S. in 1957. e. UCLA, grad. 1963 with honors in history. Started working in mail room at Universal Studios and became a casting director, then went to work for Bill Robinson as an agent trainee. Two years later joined GAC and CMA where he was a v.p. in the motion picture dept. 1971 joined IFA as v.p. in charge of motion picture dept. Represented American and foreign creative talents, incl. Jane Fonda, Donald Sutherland, Michelangelo Antonioni, Jean-Louis Trintignant, Karel Reisz, Steven Spielberg, Robert Aldrich, George Cukor, John Milius, Terry Malick, Raquel Welch, Gene Wilder and Jeanne Moreau. While at IFA was involved in packaging The Sting, Young Frankenstein, Jaws and others, before joining United Artists Corp. in 1974, as sr. v.p. in chg. of West Coast prod. While at UA, was responsible for One Flew Over the Cuckoo's Nest, Annie Hall and Rocky among others. 1978 named exec. v.p., Orion Pictures Co. where he was responsible for Platoon, Amadeus, Dances With Wolves and Silence of the Lambs. (In 1982 Orion team took over Filmways, Inc.) 1990, appointed chairman Tri-Star Pictures, & member Columbia Pictures Board of Directors. Resigned in 1994. Became chmn. and CEO of Phoenix Pictures in 1995. Co-chmn., St. Petersburg Film Festival, 1994. Chmn. of the Jury, Tokyo Film Festival, 1994. Member of Filmex board; board of trustees, UCLA

Foundation; advisory board, College for Intl. Strategic Affairs at UCLA; steering committee of Royce 270, UCLA; visiting committee, Boston Museum of Fine Arts; advisory bd., Tel Aviv U.; bd., Museum of Science & Industry; Co-Chmn.: Olympic Sports Federation, Music Center Unified Fund Campaign; bd. of governors, Sundance Inst.

MEDOFF, MARK
Writer. e. U. of Miami, Stanford U. Honorary doctor of humane letters, Gallaudet Univ. Prof. & dramatist in residence, New Mexico St. Univ. Novel: Dreams of Long Lasting.
THEATER: When You Comin' Back Red Ryder? (Obie Award), Children of a Lesser God (Tony Award), The Wager, Kringle's Window.
PICTURES: Off Beat, Children of a Lesser God, Clara's Heart, City of Joy, Homage (also prod.).
TELEVISION: Movie: Apology.

MEDWIN, MICHAEL
Actor, Writer, Producer. b. London, England, 1923. e. Institut Fischer, Switzerland. Stage debut 1940; m.p. acting debut in Root of All Evil, 1946. Acted with National Theatre 1977-78.
THEATRE: Spring and Port Wine, Joe Egg, Forget-me-not Lane, Chez Nous, Alpha Beta, Another Country, Crystal Clear, Interpreters, Orpheus, Noises Off.
PICTURES: Actor: My Sister and I, Mrs. Christopher, Gay One, Children of Chance, Operation Diamond, Black Memory, Just William's Luck, Ideal Husband, Picadilly Incident, Night Beat, Courtney's of Curzon Street, Call of the Blood, Anna Karenina, William Comes to Town, Woman Hater, Look Before You Love, Forbidden, For Them That Trespass, Queen of Spades, Trottie True, Boys in Brown, Trio, Long Dark Hall, Curtain Up, Street Corner (Both Sides of the Law), I Only Asked, Carry on Nurse, Wind Cannot Read, Heart of a Man, Crooks Anonymous, It's All Happening, Night Must Fall, I've Gotta Horse, 24 Hours To Kill, Scrooge, The Jigsaw Man. Prod.: Charlie Bubbles, If..., Spring and Port Wine, O Lucky Man! Gumshoe, Law and Disorder, Memoirs of a Survivor, Diamond's Edge.
TELEVISION: Granada's Army Game, Shoestring, The Love of Mike, Three Live Wires.

MELCHIOR, IB
Director, Writer. b. Copenhagen, Denmark, Sept. 17, 1917. Son of late singer Lauritz Melchior. e. Coll., Stenhus, Denmark, 1936; U. of Copenhagen, 1937. Actor. stage mgr., English Players, 1937-38; co-dir. 1938; actor in 21 stage prod. in Europe and U.S. on radio; set designer; stage man. dept., Radio City Music Hall, 1941-42; U.S. Military Intelligence, 1942-45; writer, dir., m.p. shorts for TV, 1947-48; TV actor, 1949-50; assoc. dir., CBS-TV, 1950; assoc. prod., G-L Enterprises, 1952-53; dir., Perry Como Show, 1951-54; dir. March of Medicine, 1955-56. Documentary writ. & dir., received Top Award by Nat'l. Comm. for Films for Safety, 1960. Golden Scroll Award, Acad. of Science Fiction, Best Writing, 1976; Hamlet Award, Shakespeare Society of America, excellence in playwriting, Hour of Vengeance, 1982.
AUTHOR: Order of Battle, Sleeper Agent, The Haigerloch Project, The Watchdogs of Abaddon, The Marcus Device, The Tombstone Cipher, Eva, V-3, Code Name: Grand Guignol, Steps & Stairways, Quest, Order of Battle: Hitler's Werewolves, Case by Case.
PICTURES: Writer: When Hell Broke Loose, Live Fast—Die Young, The Angry Red Planet (also dir.), The Case of Patty Smith (assoc. prod.), Reptilicus, Journey to the Seventh Planet, Robinson Crusoe on Mars, The Time Travellers (also dir.), Ambush Bay, Planet of the Vampires, Death Race 2000.

MELEDANDRI, CHRIS
Executive. Pres., Fox Family Films.

MELNICK, DANIEL
Executive. b. New York, NY, April 21, 1934. e. NYU. 1952-54, prod. The Children's Theatre at Circle in the Sq., NY. In 1954 was (youngest) staff prod. for CBS-TV; then exec. prod., East Side West Side and N.Y.P.D. Joined ABC-TV as v.p. in chg. of programming. Partner in Talent Associates. Joined MGM as v.p. in chg. of prod.; in 1974 named sr. v.p. & worldwide head of prod.; 1977 in charge of worldwide production, Columbia Pictures; named pres., 1978. Resigned to form independent production co., IndieProd. Company.
PICTURES: Prod.: Straw Dogs, That's Entertainment (exec. prod.), That's Entertainment Part 2, All That Jazz (exec. prod.), Altered States (exec. prod.), First Family, Making Love, Unfaithfully Yours (exec. prod.), Footloose (exec. prod.), Quicksilver, Roxanne, Punchline, Mountains of the Moon, Total Recall, Air America, L.A. Story.
TELEVISION: Specials: Death of a Salesman (prod.; Emmy Award, 1967), The Ages of Man (prod.; Emmy Award, 1966). Exec. prod.: East Side/West Side, N.Y.P.D., Get Smart, Chain Letter (pilot, exec. prod.). Movie: Get Smart Again! (exec. prod.).

MELNIKER, BENJAMIN
Producer, Attorney. b. Bayonne, NJ. e. Brooklyn Coll., LL.B., Fordham Law Sch. Loew's Theatres usher; private law practice;

employed by Legal Department MGM, v.p. & gen. counsel, 1954-69; exec. v.p., 1968-70; resigned from MGM, 1971; also member MGM bd. of dirs. and mem. MGM exec. com.; adjunct assoc. prof., NY Law Sch., 1976-77; prod. & exec. prod. motion pictures, 1974-86; former m.p. chmn. Anti-Defamation League, B'nai Brith; Mem. Amer., NY State bar assns., Bar Assn. of City NY, AMPAS.
PICTURES: Mitchell, Shoot, Winter Kills, Swamp Thing, Batman (exec. prod.), The Return of the Swamp Thing (prod.), Batman Returns, Batman: Mask of the Phantasm (prod.), Batman Forever (exec. prod.), Batman & Robin (exec. prod.).
TELEVISION: Three Sovereigns for Sarah, Television's Greatest Bits, Where On Earth Is Carmen Sandiego (exec. prod., Emmy Award), Little Orphan Annie's Very Animated Christmas (exec. prod.), Swamp Thing (exec. prod.), Harmful Intent (exec. prod.), Fish Police (exec. prod.), Dinosaucers (exec. prod.).

MELVIN, MURRAY
Actor. b. London, England, 1932. On stage with Theatre Workshop.
PICTURES: The Criminal (debut, 1960), A Taste of Honey, HMS Defiant (Damn the Defiant), Sparrows Can't Sing, The Ceremony, Alfie, Kaleidoscope, Smashing Time, The Fixer, Start the Revolution Without Me, A Day in the Death of Joe Egg, The Devils, The Boy Friend, Ghost in the Noonday Sun, Barry Lyndon, The Bawdy Adventures of Tom Jones, Joseph Andrews, Comrades, Testimony, Little Dorrit, The Krays, Let Him Have It, Princess Caraboo.
TELEVISION: Little World of Don Camillo, The Soldiers Tale, A Christmas Carol, This Office Life, Bulman, William Tell, Stuff of Madness, Sunday Pursuit, The Memorandum, The Stone of Montezuma, Surprises, England My England, The Village.

MENGES, CHRIS
Cinematographer, Director. b. Kington, Eng., Sept. 15, 1940.
PICTURES: Cinematographer. Kes, Gumshoe, The Empire Strikes Back (second unit), Local Hero, Comfort and Joy, The Killing Fields (Acad. Award, 1984), Marie, The Mission (Acad. Award, 1986), Singing the Blues in Red, Shy People, High Season. Director: A World Apart, Crisscross, Second Best.
TELEVISION: World in Action, Opium Warlords, Opium Trail, East 103rd Street, etc.

MENKEN, ALAN
Composer. b. New York, NY, July 22, 1949. Raised in New Rochelle, NY. e. NYU. Began composing and performing at Lehman Engel Musical Theatre Workshop at BMI, where he met future partner, lyricist Howard Ashman. With Ashman made Off-B'way debut in 1979 with score of God Bless You Mr. Rosewater. Wrote music for workshop Battle of the Giants, and music and lyrics for Manhattan Theatre Club Prod. of Real Life Funnies. With Ashman wrote 1982 Off-B'way hit Little Shop of Horrors. Other theatre credits include: The Apprenticeship of Duddy Kravitz, Diamonds, Personals, Let Freedom Sing, Weird Romance, Beauty and the Beast, A Christmas Carol. Grammy Awards: The Little Mermaid (2), Beauty and the Beast (3), Aladdin (4), Pocahontas (1).
PICTURES: Little Shop of Horrors (Acad. Award nom. for song Mean Green Mother From Outer Space), The Little Mermaid (2 Academy Awards: best song, Under the Sea, and music score, 1989), Rocky V (song), Beauty and the Beast (2 Academy Awards: best song, title song, and music score, 1991), Newsies, Aladdin (2 Academy Awards: for song, A Whole New World, and music score, 1992), Home Alone 2: Lost in New York (song), Life With Mikey, Pocahontas (Academy Awards for Best Score & Best Original Song), The Hunchback of Notre Dame.
TELEVISION: Special: Lincoln. Movie: Polly (song).

MERCHANT, ISMAIL
Producer, Director. b. Bombay, India, Dec. 25, 1936. e. St. Xavier's Coll., Bombay; NYU, M.A. business admin. Formed Merchant Ivory Prods., 1961 with James Ivory. First film, The Creation of Women (theatrical short, 1961, nom. for Acad. Award). Published 3 cookbooks: Ismail Merchant's Indian Cuisine, Ismail Merchant's Passionate Meals, Ismail Merchant's Florence; and book Hullabaloo in Old Jeypore: The Making of The Deceivers (1989).
PICTURES: Producer. The Householder, Shakespeare Wallah, The Guru, Bombay Talkie, Savages, Autobiography of a Princess, The Wild Party, Roseland, Hullabaloo Over Georgie and Bonnie's Pictures, The Europeans, Jane Austen in Manhattan, Quartet, Heat and Dust, The Bostonians, A Room With a View, Maurice, My Little Girl (exec. prod.), The Deceivers, Slaves of New York, The Perfect Murder (exec. prod.), Mr. and Mrs. Bridge, Ballad of the Sad Cafe, Howards End (BAFTA Award), The Remains of the Day, In Custody (dir. debut), Jefferson in Paris (also cameo), Feast of July (exec. prod.), The Proprietor.
TELEVISION: Director: Mahatma and the Mad Boy, Courtesans of Bombay.

MEREDITH, BURGESS
Actor. b. Cleveland, OH, Nov. 16, 1907. e. Amherst Coll., M.A. (hon.). m. Kaja Sundsten. Served as Capt. U.S. Army Air Corps, WWII. Stage debut, 1929, Civic Repertory Co., NY. Autobiography: So Far So Good (1994).
THEATER: Little Ol' Boy, She Loves Me Not, The Star Wagon, Winterset, High Tor, The Remarkable Mr. Pennypacker, James Joyce's Women (dir.), etc.
PICTURES: Winterset (debut, 1936), There Goes the Groom, Spring Madness, Idiot's Delight, Of Mice and Men, Castle on the Hudson, Second Chorus, San Francisco Docks, That Uncertain Feeling, Tom Dick and Harry, Street of Chance, The Story of G.I. Joe, Diary of a Chambermaid (also s.p., co-prod.), Magnificent Doll, On Our Merry Way (also prod.), Mine Own Executioner, Jigsaw, The Man on the Eiffel Tower (also dir.), The Gay Adventure, Joe Butterfly, Advise and Consent, The Cardinal, In Harm's Way, A Big Hand for the Little Lady, Madame X, Batman, Crazy Quilt (narrator), Hurry Sundown, Torture Garden, Stay Away Joe, Skidoo, Mackenna's Gold, Hard Contract, The Reivers (narrator), There Was a Crooked Man, Clay Pigeon, Such Good Friends, A Fan's Notes, The Man, Golden Needles, The Day of the Locust (Acad. Award nom.), 92 in the Shade, The Hindenburg, Burnt Offerings, Rocky (Acad. Award nom.), The Sentinel, Golden Rendezvous, The Manitou, Foul Play, Magic, The Great Bank Hoax, Rocky II, Final Assignment, When Time Ran Out, Clash of the Titans, True Confessions, The Last Chase, Rocky III, Twilight Zone: The Movie (narrator), Broken Rainbow (voice), Santa Claus, King Lear, Hot to Trot (voice), Full Moon in Blue Water, State of Grace, Rocky V, Odd Ball Hall, Grumpy Old Men, Camp Nowhere, Across the Moon, Tall Tale, Grumpier Old Men.
TELEVISION: Movies: Lock Stock and Barrel, Getting Away From It All, The Last Hurrah, Johnny We Hardly Knew Ye, Tail Gunner Joe (Emmy Award, 1977), Probe, Outrage!, Wet Gold, Night of the Hunter. Series: Mr. Novak, Batman (frequent guest), Search, Those Amazing Animals (host), Gloria. Specials: Faerie Tale Theatre (Thumbelina), From Sea to Shining Sea, The Wickedest Witch, Mastergate. Guest: G.E. Theatre, Studio One, DuPont Show of the Month, The Twilight Zone, Ben Casey, Wild Wild West, Night Gallery, Love American Style, CHiPs, In the Heat of the Night.

MERRICK, DAVID
Producer. r.n. David Margulois. b. Hong Kong, Nov. 27, 1912. e. Washington U.; St. Louis U. L.L.B.
THEATER: B'way: Fanny, The Matchmaker, Look Back in Anger, The Entertainer, Jamaica, The World of Suzie Wong, La Plume de Ma Tante, Epitaph for George Dillon, Destry Rides Again, Gypsy, Take Me Along, Irma La Douce, A Taste of Honey, Becket (Tony Award, 1961), Do Re Mi, Carnival, Sunday in New York, Ross, Subways Are For Sleeping, I Can Get It for You Wholesale, Stop the World—I Want to Get Off, Tchin Tchin, Oliver!, Luther, 110 in the Shade, Arturo Ui, Hello Dolly! (Tony Award, 1964), Oh What a Lovely War, Pickwick, The Roar of the Greasepaint—The Smell of the Crowd, Inadmissible Evidence, Cactus Flower, Marat/Sade (Tony Award, 1966), Philadelphia Here I Come, Don't Drink the Water, I Do! I Do!, How Now Dow Jones, The Happy Time, Rosencrantz and Guildenstern Are Dead (Tony Award, 1968), 40 Carats, Promises and Promises, Play It Again Sam, Child's Play, Four in a Garden, A Midsummer Night's Dream, Sugar, Out Cry, Mack and Mabel, Travesties, Very Good Eddie, Private Lives, 42nd Street (Tony Award, 1981), Oh Kay!.
PICTURES: Child's Play (debut, 1972), The Great Gatsby, Semi-Tough, Rough Cut.

MERRILL, DINA
Actress. r.n. Nedenia Hutton. b. New York, NY, Dec. 29, 1928. Fashion model, 1944-46. A co-owner and vice-chmn., RKO Pictures, m.p. and TV prod. co.
THEATER: Regional: My Sister Eileen, Major Barbara, Misalliance, Othello, Twelfth Night, Loved, Surprise. Off-B'way: Importance of Being Earnest, Smile of the Cardboard Man, Suddenly Last Summer. B'way: Angel Street, Are You Now or Have You Ever Been?, On Your Toes.
PICTURES: The Desk Set (debut, 1957), A Nice Little Bank That Should Be Robbed, Don't Give Up the Ship, Operation Petticoat, The Sundowners, Butterfield 8, Twenty Plus Two, The Young Savages, The Courtship of Eddie's Father, I'll Take Sweden, Running Wild, The Meal (Deadly Encounter), The Greatest, A Wedding, Just Tell Me What You Want, Twisted, Caddyshack II, True Colors, The Player, Open Season, The Point of Betrayal.
TELEVISION: Debut: Kate Smith Show 1956. Guest: Four Star Theatre, Playwrights '56, Climax!, Playhouse 90, Westinghouse Presents, The Investigators, Checkmate, The Rogues, Bob Hope Presents, To Tell the Truth, The Doctors, The Name of the Game, Hotel, Hawaii Five-O, Murder She Wrote, Something Wilder. Series: Hot Pursuit. Mini-Series: Roots: The Next Generations. Movies: The Sunshine Patriot, Seven in Darkness, The Lonely Profession, Mr. & Mrs. Bo Jo Jones, Family Flight, The Letters, Kingston: The Power Play, The Tenth Month, Repeat Performance, Turn Back the Clock, Fear, Brass Ring, Anne to the Infinite, Not in My Family.

MERSON, MARC
Producer. b. New York, NY, Sept. 9, 1931. e. Swarthmore Coll. Entered Navy in 1953; assigned as publicist to Admiral's Staff of Sixth Fleet Command in the Mediterranean. Upon discharge joined trade paper Show Business as feature editor. Joined CBS-TV as asst. to casting director. Left after 3 yrs. to work for Ely Landau as casting dir., packager and sometime producer of The Play of the Week on TV. Returned to CBS for 3-yr. stint doing specials and live programs. Left to organize Brownstone Productions as indep. prod. Partner with Alan Alda in Helix Productions to package and produce TV shows.
PICTURES: The Heart Is a Lonely Hunter, People Soup (short), Leadbelly, Doc Hollywood (exec. prod.).
TELEVISION: Series: Kaz, We'll Get By, Off the Rack, Jessica Novak, Waverly Wonders, Stage 67, Androcles and the Lion, Dummler and Son (pilot), The David Frost Revue (synd. series), We'll Get By. Movie: Rules of Marriage (spr. prod.).

MESSICK, DON
Actor. b. Buffalo, NY, Sept. 7, 1926. e. Nanticoke H.S., Maryland; Ramsay Street Sch. of Acting, Baltimore; American Theatre Wing, NY. Began performing as ventriloquist at age 13 in rural Maryland. Own radio show at 15 in Salisbury, MD (WBOC) for two years, writing and portraying all the characters in a one-man weekly comedy show. Worked in Hanna-Barbera cartoons since company began in 1957, voicing Ruff in their first series on NBC, 1958. Voices: Boo Boo Bear and Ranger Smith on Yogi Bear Show, Astro on The Jetsons, Scooby Doo and Scrappy Doo on Scooby Doo series, Papa Smurf and Azrael on Smurfs, Droopy on Droopy & Dripple, Dr. Benton Quest on Jonny Quest (all Hanna-Barbera Prods.); Hamton J. Pig on Tiny Toon Adventures (WB). Has done numerous national commercials.

MESTRES, RICARDO A. III
Executive. b. New York, NY, Jan. 23, 1958. e. Harvard U., A.B. 1980. Gained filmmaking experience during summers as prod. asst. on TV features. Joined Paramount Pictures as creative exec. 1981. Promoted to exec. dir. of production in 1982 and to v.p., prod. in 1984. Named v.p. of prod., Walt Disney Pictures, 1985. Promoted to sr. v.p., prod.,1986-88. Named pres. production, Touchstone Pictures, 1988-89. In 1989, became pres., Hollywood Pictures. Resigned, 1994. Co-founder Great Oaks Entertainment with John Hughes, 1995-present. Member, AMPAS.
PICTURES: Prod.: Jack, 101 Dalmatians, Flubber, Reach the Rock.

METCALF, LAURIE
Actress. b. Edwardsville, IL, June 16, 1955. e. Illinois St. Univ. One of the original members of the Steppenwolf Theatre Company. On B'way in My Thing of Love.
THEATRE: Chicago: True West, Fifth of July. NY: Balm in Gilead (Obie & Theatre World Awards). LA: Wrong Turn at Lungfish.
PICTURES: Desperately Seeking Susan (debut, 1985), Making Mr. Right, Candy Mountain, Stars and Bars, Miles From Home, Uncle Buck, Internal Affairs, Pacific Heights, JFK, Mistress, A Dangerous Woman, Blink, Leaving Las Vegas, Dear God.
TELEVISION: Series: Roseanne (3 Emmy Awards: 1992-4). Movie: The Execution of Raymond Graham.

METZLER, JIM
Actor. b. Oneonta, NY, June 23, 1951. e. Dartmouth Coll.
PICTURES: Four Friends, Tex, River's Edge, Hot to Trot, Sundown: The Vampire in Retreat, 976-EVIL, Old Gringo, Circuitry Man, Delusion, One False Move, Waxwork II: Lost in Time, A Weekend with Barbara und Ingrid, Gypsy Eyes, C.I.A. Trackdown, Plughead Rewired: Circuitry Man II, Children of the Corn III: Urban Harvest, Cadillac Ranch, A Gun A Car A Blonde.
TELEVISION: Series: Cutter to Houston, The Best Times. Mini-Series: North and South, North and South Book II, On Wings of Eagles. Movies: Do You Remember Love, Princess Daisy, Christmas Star, The Alamo: 13 Days to Glory, The Little Match Girl, Murder By Night, Crash: The Mystery of Flight 1501, Love Kills, French Silk, The Gulf.

MEYER, BARRY M.
Executive. b. New York, NY, Nov. 28, 1943. With ABC-TV in legal and business affairs depts. before joining Warner Bros. TV in 1971 as dir. of business affairs. 1972, named v.p. of business affairs for Warner TV arm; promoted to exec. v.p. of div. 1978. 1984, named exec. v.p. of Warner Bros., Inc. 1994, named COO.

MEYER, NICHOLAS
Director, Writer. b. New York, NY, Dec. 24, 1945. e. U. of Iowa. Was unit publicist for Love Story, 1969. Story ed. Warner Bros. 1970-71.
AUTHOR: The Love Story Story, The Seven Percent Solution, Target Practice, The West End Horror, Black Orchid, Confession of a Homing Pigeon, The Canary Trainer.

PICTURES: The Seven Percent Solution (s.p.), Time After Time (s.p., dir.), Star Trek II: The Wrath of Khan (dir.), Volunteers (dir.), The Deceivers (dir.), Company Business (dir., s.p.) Star Trek VI: The Undiscovered Country (dir., co-s.p.), Sommersby (co-s.p.).
TELEVISION: Movies: Judge Dee (writer), The Night That Panicked America (writer), The Day After (dir.).

MEYER, RON
Executive. b. 1945. Served in US Marine Corps. 1985, co-founded, with Mike Ovitz, Creative Artists talent agency, eventually serving as pres. 1995, appointed pres. & COO of MCA.

MEYER, RUSS
Producer, Director. b. Oakland, CA, March 21, 1922. In 1942 joined Army Signal Corps, learned m.p. photography and shot combat newsreels. Worked as photographer for Playboy Magazine. Pres., RM Films Intl. Inc. 3 vol. autobiography: A Clean Breast: The Life and Loves of Russ Meyer.
PICTURES: The Immoral Mr. Teas, Eve and the Handyman, Erotica, Wild Gals of the Naked West, Heavenly Bodies, Lorna, Motor Psycho, Fanny Hill, Mudhoney, Mondo Topless, Faster Pussycat Kill Kill, Finders Keepers Lovers Weepers, Goodmorning and Goodbye, Common Law Cabin, Vixen, Cherry Harry & Raquel, Beyond the Valley of the Dolls, The Seven Minutes, Black Snake, Supervixens, Up, Beneath the Valley of the Ultra Vixens, Amazon Women on the Moon (actor).

MEYERS, NANCY
Writer, Producer. b. Philadelphia, PA. e. American U., D.C. Began as story editor for Ray Stark. First teamed with Charles Shyer to write screenplay for Private Benjamin.
PICTURES: Writer/Producer: Private Benjamin (Acad. Award nom., Writers Guild Annual Award), Irreconcilable Differences, Baby Boom, Father of the Bride, I Love Trouble, Father of the Bride II.

MEYERS, ROBERT
Executive. b. Mount Vernon, NY, Oct. 3, 1934. e. NYU. Entered m.p. industry as exec. trainee in domestic div. of Columbia Pictures, 1956; sales and adv. 1956-60; transferred to sales dept. Columbia Pictures Int'l, NY: posts there included supervisor of int'l roadshows and exec. assistant. to continental mgr. Joined National General Pictures as v.p.-foreign sales, 1969. Created JAD Films International Inc. in Feb. 1974 for independent selling and packaging of films around the world. September, 1977, joined Lorimar Productions Inc. as sr. v.p. of Lorimar Distribution Intl. Became pres. in 1978. Joined Filmways Pictures in 1980, named pres. & COO. Pres. of American Film Mktg. Assn.; 1982, formed new co., R.M. Films International. Rejoined Lorimar 1985. as pres., Lorimar Motion Pictures, int'l distribution. 1988-92, pres., Orion Pictures Int'l. 1993-94, pres., Odyssey Entertainment. In 1995, joined Village Roadshow International as pres.

MICHAELS, JOEL B.
Producer. b. Buffalo, NY, Oct. 24, 1938. Studied acting with Stella Adler. Many co-prods. with Garth Drabinsky, Cineplex Corp. Pres. of Cineplex Odeon, 1986-90.
PICTURES: The Peace Killers, Your Three Minutes Are Up (prod. spvr.), Student Teachers (prod. spvr.), The Prisoners (assoc. prod.), Lepke (assoc. prod.), The Four Deuces (asso. prod.), Bittersweet Love, The Silent Partner, The Changeling, Tribute, The Amateur, Losin' It (exec. prod.), The Philadelphia Experiment, Three of Hearts (exec. prod.), Cutthroat Island (co-prod.).

MICHAELS, LORNE
Writer, Producer. b. Toronto, Canada, Nov. 17, 1944. e. U. of Toronto, 1966. CEO, Broadway Video, since 1979. Named Broadcaster of the Year by the International Radio and Television Society, 1992.
THEATER: Gilda Radner Live From New York (prod., dir.).
PICTURES: Producer: Gilda Live (also co-s.p.), Nothing Lasts Forever, Three Amigos (also co-s.p.), Wayne's World, Coneheads, Wayne's World 2, Lassie, Tommy Boy, Stuart Saves His Family, Black Sheep.
TELEVISION: Series: Rowan and Martin's Laugh-In (writer, 1968-69), Saturday Night Live (creator, prod., writer: 1975-80, 4 Emmy Awards; 1985-), The New Show (prod.), The Kids in the Hall (series co-prod.), Late Night With Conan O'Brien (exec. prod.). Specials: Lily Tomlin Specials (writer, prod.: 1972-75, 2 Emmy Awards), Perry Como (writer, prod., 1974), Flip Wilson (writer, prod.), Beach Boys (writer, prod.), The Paul Simon Special (writer, prod., Emmy Award, 1978), The Rutles: All You Need Is Cash (writer, prod.), Steve Martin's Best Show Ever (prod.), Simon and Garfunkel: The Concert in the Park (exec. prod.), The Coneheads (exec. prod.), 1988 Emmy Awards (prod.), Coca-Cola Presents Live: The Hard Rock, On Location: Kids in the Hall (exec. prod.), The Rolling Stones: Steel Wheels Concert (exec. prod.), Paul Simon: Born at the Right Time in Central Park (exec. prod.).

MICHAELS, RICHARD
Director. b. Brooklyn, NY, Feb. 15, 1936. e. Cornell U. Script supervisor 1955-64 and associate producer before starting directing career in 1968 with Bewitched (54 episodes; also assoc. prod.).
PICTURES: How Come Nobody's On Our Side?, Blue Skies Again.
TELEVISION: *Series*: Love American Style, The Odd Couple, Delvecchio, Ellery Queen, Room 222. *Movies*: Once an Eagle (mini-series), Charlie Cobb, Having Babies II, Leave Yesterday Behind, My Husband Is Missing, ... And Your Name Is Jonah (winner, Christopher Award), Once Upon a Family, The Plutonium Incident, Scared Straight, Another Story (Scott Newman Drug Abuse Prevention Award), Homeward Bound (Banff Intl. TV Fest. Special Jury Award & Christopher Award), Berlin Tunnel 21, The Children Nobody Wanted, One Cooks, The Other Doesn't, Jessie (pilot), Silence of the Heart, Heart of a Champion: The Ray Mancini Story, Rockabye, Kay O'Brien (pilot), Leg Work (pilot), Red River (movie), Indiscreet, Love and Betrayal, Her Wicked Ways, Leona Helmsley: The Queen of Mean, Triumph of the Heart: The Ricky Bell Story, Backfield in Motion, Miss America: Behind the Crown, Father and Scout. *Mini-series*: Sadat, I'll Take Manhattan.

MICHEL, WERNER
Executive. e. U. of Berlin, U. of Paris, Ph.D., Sorbonne, 1931. Radio writer, dir., co-author two Broadway revues, 1938, 1940. Broadcast dir., Voice of America, 1942-46. Prod. & dir., CBS, 1946-48; asst. prog. dir., CBS, 1948-50. Prod. Ford TV Theatre, 1950-52 Prod. DuMont TV network, 1952-55. Dir. Electronicam TV-Film Prod., 1955-56. Prod. of Edge of Night, Procter and Gamble, 1956-57. V.P. & dir., TV-radio dept., Reach, McClinton Advertising, Inc., 1957-62. Consultant, TV Programming & Comm'l-Prod., N.W. Ayer & Son Inc. V.P. & dir., TV dept., SSCB Advertising, 1963. Program exec. at ABC-TV Hollywood, 1975. Sr. v.p. of creative affairs, MGM-TV, 1977. Exec. v.p., Wrather Entertainment Intl., 1979. Returned to MGM-TV as sr. v.p., creative affairs, 1980-82. COO, Guber-Peters TV, 1982-84. Sr. v.p., corporate TV dept., Kenyon & Eckhart, & NY, 1984-85. Currently sr. v.p., sr. partner of TV dept., Bozell, Inc. NY.

MICHELL, KEITH
Actor. b. Adelaide, Australia, Dec. 1, 1926. Early career as art teacher, radio actor; toured Australia with Stratford Shakespearean Co. 1952-53; Stratford Memorial Theatre 1954-55, Old Vic Theatre 1956-57. Served as Artistic Director, Chichester Festival Theatre, touring Australia.
THEATER: Irma la Douce, Art of Seduction, The First 400 Years, Robert & Elizabeth, Kain, The King's Mare, Man of La Mancha, Abelard & Heloise, Hamlet, Crucifer of Blood, On the Twentieth Century, Pete McGynty, Captain Beaky Christmas Show, On the Rocks, The Tempest, Amadeus, La Cage aux Folles, Portraits, The Bacarat Scandal, Henry VIII, Aspects of Love, Scrooge, Brazilian Blue, Caesar & Cleopatra.
PICTURES: True as a Turtle, Dangerous Exile, Gypsy and the Gentleman, The Hellfire Club, All Night Long, Seven Seas to Calais, Prudence and the Pill, House of Cards, Henry VIII and his Six Wives, Moments, The Deceivers.
TELEVISION: *U.K.*: Pygmalion, Act of Violence, Mayerling Affair, Wuthering Heights, The Bergonzi Hand, Ring Round The Moon, Spread of the Eagle, The Shifting Heart, Loyalties, Julius Caesar, Antony and Cleopatra, Kain, The Ideal Husband, The Six Wives of Henry VIII (series), Dear Love, Captain Beaky & His Band, Captain Beaky, Volume 2, The Gondoliers, The Pirates of Penzance, Ruddigore. *U.S.*: Story of the Marlboroughs, Jacob and Joseph, Story of David, The Tenth Month, The Day Christ Died, The Miracle, Murder She Wrote. *Australia*: *Series*: My Brother Tom, Captain James Cook.

MIDLER, BETTE
Actress, Singer. b. Honolulu, HI, Dec. 1, 1945. e. U. of Hawaii. Studied acting at Berghof Studios. Appeared on B'way in Fiddler on the Roof, Salvation; also in Tommy with Seattle Opera Co., 1971. Gained fame as singer-comic in nightclubs and cabarets. Has toured extensively with own stage shows: The Divine Miss M, Clams on the Half-Shell, Divine Madness, Art of Bust, Experience the Divine. Grammy Awards: The Divine Miss M, The Rose, Blueberry Pie (from In Harmony), Wind Beneath My Wings. *Author*: A View From a Broad, The Saga of Baby Divine. Special Tony Award, 1973.
PICTURES: Hawaii (debut, 1966), The Rose (Acad. Award nom.; 2 Golden Globe Awards), Divine Madness, Jinxed, Down and Out in Beverly Hills, Ruthless People, Outrageous Fortune, Big Business, Oliver & Company (voice), Beaches (also co-prod.), Stella, Scenes from a Mall, For the Boys (Acad. Award nom., Golden Globe Award; also co-prod.), Hocus Pocus, Get Shorty, First Wives Club.
TELEVISION: *Specials*: The Fabulous Bette Midler Show, Ol' Red Hair is Back (Emmy Award, 1978; also co-writer), Art or Bust (also prod., co-writer), Bette Midler's Mondo Beyondo (also creator, co-writer), Mud Will Be Flung Tonight. Movie: Gypsy. *Guest*: Cher, The Tonight Show (Emmy Award, 1992).
RECORDINGS: The Divine Miss M, Bette Midler, Songs for the New Depression, Live at Last, The Rose, Thighs and Whispers, Divine Madness, No Frills, Mud Will Be Flung Tonight, Beaches, Some People's Lives, For the Boys, Experience the Divine, Bette of Roses.

MIFUNE, TOSHIRO
Actor. b. Tsingtao, China, April 1, 1920. e. Japanese schools. Served five years Japanese army. Joined Toho Studio 1946.
PICTURES: Snow Trail, Drunken Angel, Eagle of Pacific, Seven Samurai, I Live in Fear, Legend of Musashi, Throne of Blood, Riksha Man, Three Treasures, Last Gunfight, I Bombed Pearl Harbor, Rose in Mud, Rashomon, Yojimbo, Animus Trujano, Kiska, Red Beard, High and Low, Judo Saga, Grand Prix, Rebellion, Tunnel to the Sun, The Lost World of Sinbad, Admiral Yamamoto, Hell in the Pacific, Under the Banner of the Samurai, Red Sun, Paper Tiger, Midway, Winter Kills, 1941, The Challenge, Inchon, The Bushido Blade, Princess from the Moon, The Death of a Master, Journey of Honor, Shadow of the Wolf, Picture Bride.
TELEVISION: *US*: Shogun.

MIGDEN, CHESTER L.
Executive. b. New York, NY, May 21, 1921; e. City Coll. of New York, B.A., 1941, Columbia U., J.D., 1947. Member New York Bar. Attorney for National Labor Relations Board 1947-51. Exec of Screen Actors Guild 1952-81. Nat'l exec. dir., 1973-81. Exec. dir., Assn. of Talent Agents, 1982-94.

MIKELL, GEORGE
Actor. b. Lithuania. In Australia 1950-56 acting with Old Vic Co. Ent. films 1955. TV 1957. To England 1957.
THEATER: Five Finger Exercise, Altona, The Millionairess, Love from a Stranger, Portrait of a Queen, Farewell, Judas, Flare Path.
PICTURES: The Guns of Navarone, The Password Is Courage, The Great Escape, Deadline for Diamonds, Where The Spies Are, The Spy Who Came in From the Cold, I Predoni Del Sahara (Italy), Sabina (Israel), The Double Man, Attack on the Iron Coast, Zeppelin, Young Winston, Scorpio, The Tamarind Seed, Sweeney Two, The Sea Wolves, Victory, Emerald, Kommissar Zufall (Germany).
TELEVISION: Counsel at Law, Six Eyes on a Stranger, The Mask of a Clown, Green Grows the Grass, Opportunity Taken, OSS Series, Espinage, The Danger Man, Strange Report, The Survivors, The Adventurer, Colditz, The Hanged Man, Quiller, Martin Hartwell, Flambards, Sweeney, The Secret Army, Sherlock Holmes, When the Boat Comes In, Brack Report, Bergerac, The Brief, Glass Babies (Australia), Hannay, Night of the Fox (mini-series), Secrets (Australia), Stark (Australia).

MILCHAN, ARNON
Producer. b. Israel, Dec. 6, 1944. Began producing and financing films in Israel. Also producer of stage plays including: Ipi Tombi, It's So Nice to be Civilized, and Amadeus in Paris starring Roman Polanski. Appeared in film Can She Bake a Cherry Pie?
PICTURES: Black Joy, The Medusa Touch, Dizengoff 99, The King of Comedy, Once Upon a Time in America (also actor), Brazil, Stripper (exec. prod.), Legend, Man on Fire, Who's Harry Crumb?, The War of the Roses, Big Man on Campus, Pretty Woman, Q & A, Guilty by Suspicion, JFK (exec. prod.), The Mambo Kings, Memoirs of an Invisible Man (exec. prod.), The Power of One, Under Siege, Sommersby, Falling Down (exec. prod.), Made in America, Free Willy (exec. prod.), That Night, Striking Distance, George Balanchine's The Nutcracker (exec. prod.), Six Degrees of Separation, Heaven and Earth, The Client, The New Age, Second Best, Boys on the Side, Copycat (co-prod.), Under Siege 2: Dark Territory, Free Willy 2: The Adventure Home, Heat, Bogus, Tin Cup (exec. prod.), A Time to Kill.
TELEVISION: *Mini-Series*: Masada. *Series*: John Grisham's The Client (exec. prod.)

MILES, CHRISTOPHER
Director. b. London, England, April 19, 1939. e. I.D.H.E.C., 1962. Sister is actress Sarah Miles. Studied film in Paris at the Institut des Hautes Etudes Cinematographiques.
PICTURES: The Six-Sided Triangle, Up Jumped a Swagman, The Virgin and the Gypsy, Time for Loving, The Maids (also co-s.p.), That Lucky Touch, Alternative 3 (also co-s.p.), Priest of Love (also prod.), The Marathon (also co-s.p.), Aphrodisias (also co-s.p.), Some Stones of No Value (also s.p.), Love In The Ancient World (also s.p.).

MILES, SARAH
Actress. b. Ingatestone, Eng., Dec. 31, 1941. e. RADA. Was married to late writer Robert Bolt. Brother is actor Christopher Miles. Appeared in short film Six-Sided Triangle.
THEATER: Dazzling, World War 2 1/2, Kelly's Eye, Vivat! Vivat Regina!
PICTURES: Term of Trial (debut, 1962), The Servant, The Ceremony, Those Magnificent Men in Their Flying Machines, I Was Happy Here (Time Lost and Time Remembered), Blow-Up,

Ryan's Daughter (Acad. Award nom.), Lady Caroline Lamb, The Man Who Loved Cat Dancing, The Hireling, Bride to Be (Pepita Jimenez), The Sailor Who Fell From Grace With the Sea, The Big Sleep, Priest of Love, Venom, Ordeal by Innocence, Steaming, Hope and Glory, White Mischief, The Silent Touch.
TELEVISION: Loving Walter (Walter and June), James Michener's Dynasty, Great Expectations, Harem, Queenie, A Ghost in Monte Carlo, Dandelion Dead, Ring Round the Moon, The Rehearsal.

MILES, SYLVIA
Actress. b. New York, NY, Sept. 9, 1934. Attended Pratt Inst., NYC. e. Washington Irving H.S., Actors Studio, Dramatic Workshop of the New School.
THEATER: Rosebloom, The Iceman Cometh, The Balcony, The Riot Act, Vieux Carre, Before Breakfast, The Night of the Iguana, Tea with Mommy and Jack, Ruthless.
PICTURES: Murder Inc. (debut, 1960), Parrish, Pie in the Sky, Violent Midnight, Terror in the City, Midnight Cowboy (Acad. Award nom.), The Last Movie, Who Killed Mary Whats'ername?, Heat, 92 in the Shade, Farewell My Lovely (Acad. Award nom.), The Great Scout and Cathouse Thursday, The Sentinel, Shalimar (Deadly Thief), Zero to Sixty, The Funhouse, Evil Under the Sun, No Big Deal, Critical Condition, Sleeping Beauty, Wall Street, Crossing Delancey, Spike of Bensonhurst, She-Devil, Denise Calls Up.
TELEVISION: Series: All My Children. Guest: Miami Vice, The Equalizer, Tonight Show, etc.

MILES, VERA
Actress. r.n. Vera Ralston. b. Boise City, OK, Aug. 23, 1929. e. public schools, Pratt and Wichita, KS.
PICTURES: Two Tickets to Broadway (debut, 1951), For Men Only, Rose Bowl Story, Charge at Feather River, So Big, Pride of the Blue Grass, Tarzan's Hidden Jungle, Wichita, The Searchers, 23 Paces to Baker Street, Autumn Leaves, Wrong Man, Beau James, Web of Evidence, FBI Story, Touch of Larceny, Five Branded Women, Psycho, Back Street, The Man Who Shot Liberty Valance, A Tiger Walks, Those Calloways, Follow Me Boys!, The Spirit Is Willing, Gentle Giant, Sergeant Ryker, Kona Coast, It Takes All Kinds, Hellfighters, Mission Batangas, The Wild Country, Molly and Lawless John, One Little Indian, The Castaway Cowboy, Twilight's Last Gleaming, Thoroughbred, Run for the Roses, Brainwaves, Psycho II, The Initiation, Into the Night.
TELEVISION: Movies: The Hanged Man, In Search of America, Cannon (pilot), Owen Marshall: Counselor at Law (pilot), A Howling in the Woods, Jigsaw, A Great American Tragedy, Baffled!, Runaway!, Live Again Die Again, Underground Man, The Strange and Deadly Occurence, NcNaughton's Daughter, Judge Horton and the Scottsboro Boys, Smash-up on Interstate 5, Fire!, And I Alone Survived, Roughnecks, Our Family Business, Rona Jaffe's Mazes and Monsters, Travis McGee, Helen Keller: The Miracle Continues, The Hijacking of the Achille Lauro. Guest: Climax, Pepsi Cola Playhouse, Schlitz Playhouse, Ford Theatre.

MILGRAM, HANK
Theatre Executive. b. Philadelphia, PA, April 20, 1926. e. U. of PA, Wharton Sch. Exec. v.p., Milgram Theatres. Variety Club Board member, past president and chairman of the board of Variety Club of Philadelphia; past Variety Club Intl. v.p.; President's council. Served for 12 yrs. as bd. member, Hahneman Univ. until 1993.

MILIUS, JOHN
Writer, Director. b. St. Louis, MO. April 11, 1944. e. Los Angeles City Coll., U. of Southern California (cinema course). While at latter, won National Student Film Festival Award. Started career as ass't. to Lawrence Gordon at AIP. Began writing screenplays, then became director with Dillinger (1973). Appeared in documentary, Hearts of Darkness.
PICTURES: The Devil's Eight (co-s.p.), Evel Knievel (co-s.p.), The Life and Times of Judge Roy Bean (s.p.), Jeremiah Johnson (co-s.p.), Deadhead Miles (actor), Dillinger (dir. debut, 1973; also s.p.), Magnum Force (co-s.p.), The Wind and the Lion (dir., s.p.), Big Wednesday (dir., co-s.p., actor), Hardcore (exec. prod.), Apocalypse Now (s.p.), 1941 (exec. prod., co-story), Used Cars (co-exec. prod.), Conan the Barbarian (dir., co-s.p.), Uncommon Valor (co-prod.), Red Dawn (dir., co-s.p.), Extreme Prejudice (story), Farewell to the King (dir., s.p.), Flight of the Intruder (dir., co-s.p.), Geronimo: An American Legend (co-s.p., story), Clear and Present Danger (co-s.p.).

MILKIS, EDWARD
Producer. b. Los Angeles, CA, July 16, 1931. e. U. of Southern California. Began career as asst. editor, ABC-TV, 1952; Disney, 1954; MGM, 1957; editor, MGM, 1960-65; assoc. prod., Star Trek, 1966-69; exec. in chg. post-prod., Paramount, 1969-72; formed Miller-Milkis Prods., 1972; Miller-Milkis-Boyett, 1979. Now heads Edward K. Milkis Prods.
PICTURES: Silver Streak, Foul Play, The Best Little Whorehouse in Texas.
TELEVISION: Petrocelli, Bosom Buddies (exec. prod.), Happy Days, Laverne and Shirley, Feel the Heat.

MILLAR, STUART
Producer, Director. b. New York, NY, 1929. e. Stanford U.; Sorbonne, Paris. Ent. industry working for Motion Picture Branch, State Dept., Germany. documentaries, Army Signal Corps, Long Island, Germany; journalist, International News Service, San Francisco; assoc. prod.-dir., The Desperate Hours; assoc. prod.-dir., Friendly Persuasion.
PICTURES: Producer: The Young Stranger, Stage Struck, Birdman of Alcatraz, I Could Go On Singing, The Young Doctors, Stolen Hours, The Best Man, Paper Lion, Little Big Man, When The Legends Die (also dir.), Rooster Cogburn (dir. only), Shoot the Moon (co-exec. prod.).
TELEVISION: Producer: Isabel's Choice, Vital Signs (also dir.), Killer Instinct, Dream Breaker (also dir.), Lady in a Corner.

MILLER, ANN
Actress. r.n. Lucille Ann Collier. b. Houston, TX, Apr. 12, 1923. e. Albert Sidney Johnson H.S., Houston; Lawler Prof. Sch., Hollywood. Studied dance as child; played West Coast vaudeville theatres. Autobiography: Miller's High Life (1974), Tapping Into the Force.
THEATER: George White's Scandals, Mame, Sugar Babies.
PICTURES: Anne of Green Gables (debut, 1934), The Good Fairy, Devil on Horseback, New Faces of 1937, Life of the Party, Stage Door, Radio City Revels, Having Wonderful Time, Room Service, You Can't Take It with You, Tarnished Angel, Too Many Girls, Hit Parade of 1941, Melody Ranch, Time Out for Rhythm, Go West Young Lady, True to the Army, Priorities on Parade, Reveille with Beverly, What's Buzzin' Cousin?, Jam Session, Hey Rookie, Carolina Blues, Eadie Was a Lady, Eve Knew Her Apples, Thrill of Brazil, Easter Parade, The Kissing Bandit, On the Town, Watch the Birdie, Texas Carnival, Two Tickets to Broadway, Lovely To Look At, Small Town Girl, Kiss Me Kate, Deep in My Heart, Hit the Deck, The Opposite Sex, The Great American Pastime, Won Ton Ton the Dog Who Saved Hollywood, That's Entertainment III.
TELEVISION: Specials: Dames at Sea, Disney-MGM Special. Guest: Love American Style, The Love Boat.

MILLER, ARTHUR
Writer. b. New York, NY, Oct. 17, 1915. e. U. of Michigan. Plays include All My Sons, Death of a Salesman (Pulitzer Prize, 1949), The Crucible (Tony Award), A View from the Bridge, After the Fall, Incident at Vichy, The Price, Up From Paradise, Situation Normal, The American Clock, I Can't Remember Anything, Some Kind of Love Story, Clara, Broken Glass. Novel: Focus. Novella: Homely Girl. Autobiography: Timebends (1987).
PICTURES: Film versions of plays: All My Sons, Death of a Salesman, The Crucible, A View From the Bridge. Original s.p.: The Misfits, Everybody Wins, The Crucible.
TELEVISION: Death of a Salesman (Emmy Award, 1967), Fame, After The Fall, Playing for Time (Emmy Award, 1981).

MILLER, BARRY
Actor. b. Los Angeles, CA, Feb. 6, 1958. New York stage debut, My Mother My Father and Me, 1980.
THEATER: Forty Deuce, The Tempest, Biloxi Blues (Tony, Theatre World, Outer Critics Circle and Drama Desk Awards, 1985), Crazy He Calls Me.
PICTURES: Lepke (debut, 1975), Saturday Night Fever, Voices, Fame, The Chosen, The Journey of Natty Gann, Peggy Sue Got Married, The Sicilian, The Last Temptation of Christ, Love at Large, The Pickle, Love Affair.
TELEVISION: Specials: The Roommate, Conspiracy: The Trial of the Chicago Eight. Series: Joe and Sons, Szysznyk, Equal Justice. Guest: The Bill Cosby Show. Movies: Brock's Last Case, Having Babies, The Death of Richie.

MILLER, CHERYL
Actress. b. Sherman Oaks, CA, Feb. 4, 1942. e. UCLA, Los Angeles Conservatory of Music.
PICTURES: Casanova Brown, Marriage is a Private Affair, Unconquered, Cheaper by the Dozen, Fourteen Hours, Mr. 880, Executive Suite, The Next Voice You Hear, The Matchmaker, Blue Denim, North by Northwest, The Parent Trap, The Monkey's Uncle, Clarence the Cross-Eyed Lion, The Initiation, Doctor Death, Mr. too Little.
TELEVISION: Series: Daktari, Bright Promise. Guest: Perry Mason, Bachelor Father, Flipper, Donna Reed, Leave It to Beaver, Farmer's Daughter, Wonderful World of Color, Moutain Man, Dobie Gillis, Bright Promise, Love American Style, Emergency, Cade's County. Movie: Gemini Man.

MILLER, DENNIS
Comedian, Actor. b. Pittsburgh, PA, Nov. 3, 1953. e. Point Park Coll., (journalism degree). Began as stand-up comic in local clubs, then moved to NY appearing at Catch a Rising Star and the Comic Strip. Back in Pittsburgh wrote essays for PM Magazine and hosted Saturday-morning series for teens, Punchline. Recording: The Off-White Album.
PICTURES: Madhouse, Disclosure, The Net, Tales From the Crypt: Bordello of Blood.

TELEVISION: *Series*: Saturday Night Live (1985-91), The Dennis Miller Show (talk), Dennis Miller Live (also writer; Emmy Award for writing, 1996). *Specials* (also exec. prod./writer): Mr. Miller Goes to Washington, Dennis Miller: Black and White, They Shoot HBO Specials Don't They?, MTV Video Awards (host, 1996), Dennis Miller: Citizen Arcane (also exec. prod./writer; Emmy Award, 1996).

MILLER, DENNIS
Executive. Exec. v.p., Sony Pictures Entertainment, Inc.

MILLER, DICK (RICHARD)
Actor, Writer. b. New York, NY, Dec. 25, 1928. e. City Coll. of New York, Columbia U. Grad. NYU. Theater Sch. of Dramatic Arts. Commercial artist, psychologist (Bellevue Mental Hygiene Clinic, Queens General Hosp. Psychiatric dept.) Served in U.S. Navy, WWII. Boxing champ, U.S. Navy. Semi-pro football. Broadway stage, radio disc jockey, The Dick Miller Show, WMCA, WOR-TV. Over 500 live shows. Did first live night talk show with Bobby Sherwood, Midnight Snack, CBS, 1950. Wrote, produced and directed radio and TV shows in NY in early 1950s. Wrote screenplays; T.N.T. Jackson, Which Way to the Front, Four Rode Out and others. Has appeared on many major TV series and was a regular on Fame (3 years) and The Flash.
PICTURES: Has appeared in over 150 features, including: Apache Woman, Oklahoma Woman, It Conquered the World, The Undead, Not of This Earth, The Gunslinger, War of the Satellites, Naked Paradise, Rock All Night, Sorority Girl, Carnival Rock, A Bucket of Blood, Little Shop of Horrors, Atlas, Capture That Capsule, Premature Burial, X—The Man With the X Ray Eyes, The Terror, Beach Ball, Ski Party, Wild Wild Winter, Wild Angels, Hell's Angels on Wheels, The Trip, St. Valentine's Day Masacre, A Time for Killing, The Dirty Dozen, Targets, The Legend of Lilah Clare, Wild Racers, Target Harry, Which Way to the Front (also co-s.p.), Night Call Nurses, The Grissom Gang, Ulzana's Raid, Executive Action, The Slams, Student Nurses, Big Bad Mama, Truck Turner, Capone, T.N.T. Jackson, The Fortune, White Line Fever, Crazy Mama, Moving Violation, Hustle, Cannonball, Vigilante Force, New York New York, Mr. Billion, Hollywood Boulevard, Grand Theft Auto, I Wanna Hold Your Hand, Piranha, Corvette Summer, Rock 'n' Roll High School, Lady in Red, Dr. Heckle and Mr. Hype, The Happy Hooker Goes Hollywood, Used Cars, The Howling, Heartbeeps, White Dog, Get Crazy, Lies, Heart Like a Wheel, All the Right Moves, Twilight Zone: The Movie, National Lampoon Goes to the Movies, Space Raiders, Swing Shift, Gremlins, The Terminator, Explorers, After Hours, Night of the Creeps, Project X, Armed Response, Chopping Mall, Amazon Women on the Moon, Innerspace, Angel III, The 'Burbs, Under the Boardwalk, Far From Home, Mob Boss, Gremlins 2: The New Batch, Unlawful Entry, Amityville 1992: It's About Time, Motorama, Matinee, Batman: Mask of the Phantasm (voice), Mona Must Die, Number One Fan, Tales From the Crypt Presents Demon Knight.

MILLER, (DR.) GEORGE
Director, Producer. b. Chinchilla, Queensland, Australia, 1945. Practiced medicine in Sydney; quit to work on films with Byron Kennedy, who became longtime partner until his death in 1983. Early work: Violence in the Cinema Part One (short: dir. s.p.), Frieze—An Underground Film (doc.: editor only), Devil in Evening Dress (doc.: dir., s.p.). First worldwide success with Mad Max.
PICTURES: Mad Max (dir., s.p.), Chain Reaction (assoc. prod.), The Road Warrior (dir., co-s.p.), Twilight Zone—The Movie (dir. segment), Mad Max Beyond Thunderdome (co-dir., prod., co-s.p.), The Witches of Eastwick (dir.), The Year My Voice Broke (exec. prod.), Dead Calm (exec. prod.), Flirting (exec. prod.), Lorenzo's Oil (dir., co-s.p., co-prod.), Babe (dir.).
TELEVISION: The Dismissal (mini-series; exec. prod., co-writer & dir. of first episode). Prod.: Bodyline, The Cowra Breakout. Exec. Prod.: Vietnam (mini-series), Dirtwater Dynasty, Sports Crazy.

MILLER, GEORGE
Director. b. Australia.
PICTURES: In Search of Anna (asst. dir.), The Man from Snowy River, The Aviator, The Never Ending Story II, Over the Hill, Frozen Assets, Gross Misconduct, Andre.
TELEVISION: Cash and Company, Against the Wind, The Last Outlaw, All the Rivers Run.

MILLER, JAMES R.
Executive. Began m.p. industry career in 1971 in legal dept. of United Artists (N.Y.). Left to go with Paramount Pictures in legal dept.; then moved to Columbia in 1977 as sr. counsel; later assoc. gen. counsel. In 1979, named Warner Bros. v.p., studio business affairs; 1984, v.p. in chg. world-wide business affairs; 1987, sr. v.p.; 1989, exec. v.p. business and acquisition.

MILLER, JP
Writer. b. San Antonio, TX, Dec. 18, 1919. e. Rice U., 1937-41; Yale Drama Sch., 1946-47. U.S. Navy, Lieut., 1941-46; pub. poetry, short stories. Author of novels The Race for Home, Liv, The Skook.

THEATER: Days of Wine and Roses, The People Next Door, Privacy.
PICTURES: The Rabbit Trap, (story, s.p.) Days of Wine and Roses (story, s.p.) The Young Savages (co-author, s.p.) Behold a Pale Horse (s.p.) The People Next Door (story, s.p.).
TELEVISION: Philco TV Playhouse: Hide and Seek, Old Tasslefoot, The Rabbit Trap, The Pardon-me Boy; Playhouse 90, Days of Wine and Roses, CBS Playhouse, The People Next Door (Emmy Award, 1969), The Unwanted, The Lindbergh Kidnapping Case, Helter Skelter, Gauguin the Savage, I Know My First Name is Steven (story, co-s.p.).

MILLER, JASON
Writer, Actor. b. Scranton, PA, April 22, 1939. Entered regional playwriting contest during high school in Scranton, PA and since has moved back and forth between acting and writing. Wrote Nobody Hears a Broken Dream, That Championship Season (NY Drama Critics & Tony Awards, Pulitzer Prize, 1973). Acted on stage in Juno and the Paycock, Long Day's Journey Into Night.
PICTURES: Actor: The Exorcist (Acad. Award nom.), The Nickel Ride, The Ninth Configuration (Twinkle Twinkle Killer Kane), Monsignor, Toy Soldiers, Light of Day, The Exorcist III, Rudy. Director-Writer: That Championship Season.
TELEVISION: Movies: A Home of Our Own, F. Scott Fitzgerald in Hollywood, Vampire, The Henderson Monster, Marilyn: The Untold Story, The Best Little Girl in the World, Deadly Care, A Mother's Courage: The Mary Thomas Story. Mini-Series: The Dain Curse.

MILLER, MAX B.
Executive. b. Los Angeles, Feb. 23, 1937. Father, Max Otto Miller, producer silent features and shorts. Great grandfather was Brigham Young. e. Los Angeles Valley Coll., UCLA, Sherwood Oaks Coll. Writer of articles on cinema for American Cinematographer and other publications. Owns and manages Fotos Intl., entertainment photo agency with offices in 46 countries. Recipient of Golden Globe Award in 1976 for Youthquake, documentary feature. Also director of Films International (prod., Shoot Los Angeles) and pres. of MBM Prod., Inc. Active member of Hollywood Foreign Press Assn. (from 1974-82 bd member; twice chmn.), Independent Feature Project, Acad. of TV Arts & Sciences, L.A. Int'l, Film Exhibition, Soc. of M.P. & TV Engineers, Film Forum, Amer. Cinemateque.

MILLER, PENELOPE ANN
Actress. b. Los Angeles, CA, Jan. 13, 1964. Daughter of actor-filmmaker Mark Miller and journalist-yoga instructor Bea Ammidown. e. studied acting with Herbert Berghof.
THEATER: NY: The People From Work (1984), Biloxi Blues (B'way and LA), Moonchildren, Our Town (Tony nom.), On the Waterfront.
PICTURES: Adventures in Babysitting (1987, debut), Biloxi Blues, Big Top Pee-Wee, Miles From Home, Dead-Bang, Downtown, The Freshman, Awakenings, Kindergarten Cop, Other People's Money, Year of the Comet, The Gun in Betty Lou's Handbag, Chaplin, Carlito's Way, The Shadow, The Relic.
TELEVISION: Series: The Guiding Light, As the World Turns, The Popcorn Kid. Guest: Tales From the Darkside, Miami Vice, St. Elsewhere, Family Ties, The Facts of Life. Specials: Tales From the Hollywood Hills: The Closed Set, Our Town. Movie: Witchhunt.

MILLER, ROBERT ELLIS
Director. b. New York, NY, July 18, 1932. e. Harvard U. Worked on Broadway and TV before feature film debut with Any Wednesday (1966).
PICTURES: Any Wednesday (debut, 1966), Sweet November, The Heart Is a Lonely Hunter, The Buttercup Chain, The Big Truck, The Girl from Petrovka, The Baltimore Bullet, Reuben Reuben, Brenda Starr, Hawks, Bed and Breakfast.
TELEVISION: The Voice of Charlie Pont, The Other Lover, Madame X, Just an Old Sweet Song, Her Life as a Man, Ishi: Last of His Tribe, Intimate Strangers, Killer Rules, Point Man (pilot), A Walton Wedding.

MILLS, DONNA
Actress. b. Chicago, IL, Dec. 11, 1945. e. U. of Illinois. Left school to pursue career in theatre, beginning as dancer with stage companies around Chicago and touring. In NY became regular on soap opera, The Secret Storm. On B'way in Don't Drink the Water.
PICTURES: The Incident (debut, 1968), Play Misty for Me.
TELEVISION: Series: Love Is a Many Splendored Thing, The Good Life, Knots Landing. Guest: Lancer, Dan August. Movies/Mini-Series: Haunts of the Very Rich, Rolling Man, Night of Terror, The Bait, Live Again Die Again, Who is the Black Dahlia?, Beyond the Bermuda Triangle, Look What's Happened to Rosemary's Baby, Smash-Up on Interstate 5, Fire!, Curse of the Black Widow, The Hunted Lady, Superdome, Doctors' Private Lives, Hanging by a Thread, Waikiki, Bare Essence, He's Not Your Son, Woman on the Run, Outback Bound, The Lady Forgets, Intimate Encounters (also exec. prod.), The World's Oldest Living Bridesmaid (also exec. prod.), Runaway Father

(also co-exec. prod.), False Arrest, In My Daughter's Name (also co-exec. prod.), The President's Child, Barbara Taylor Bradford's Remember, My Name Is Kate (also exec. prod.), Dangerous Intentions, Element of Truth (exec. prod.), Stepford Husbands.

MILLS, HAYLEY
Actress. b. London, Eng., April 18, 1946. Father is actor John Mills. Sister is actress Juliet Mills. e. Elmhurst Boarding Sch., Surrey, and Institute Alpine Vidamanette, Switz. Made m.p. debut in Tiger Bay 1959 with father; then signed Disney contract 1960. Received special Academy Award for her role in Pollyanna.
THEATER: The Wild Duck, Peter Pan, Trelawney of the Wells, The Three Sisters, A Touch of Spring, The Importance of Being Earnest, Rebecca, The Summer Party, Hush & Hide, My Fat Friend, Tally's Folly, Dial M for Murder, The Secretary Bird, Toys in the Attic, The Kidnap Game, The King and I (Australian tour), Fallen Angels (U.K., Australia, New Zealand), Dead and Guilty.
PICTURES: Tiger Bay (debut, 1959), Pollyanna, The Parent Trap, Whistle Down the Wind, In Search of the Castaways, Summer Magic, The Chalk Garden, The Moonspinners, That Darn Cat, The Truth About Spring, Sky West and Crooked (Gypsy Girl), The Trouble With Angels, The Family Way, A Matter of Innocence (Pretty Polly), Twisted Nerve, Take a Girl Like You, Mr. Forbush and the Penguins (Cry of the Penguins), Endless Night, Deadly Strangers, Silhouettes, What Changed Charley Farthing, The Kingfisher Caper, Appointment with Death, After Midnight, A Troll in Central Park (voice).
TELEVISION: The Flame Trees of Thika (mini-series), Parent Trap (Parts II, III, IV, V), Amazing Stories, Illusion of Life, Good Morning Miss Bliss (series), Murder She Wrote, Back Home (series), Tales of the Unexpected, Deadly Strangers, Only a Scream Away, Walk of Life.

MILLS, SIR JOHN
Actor, Producer. b. Suffolk, England, February 22, 1908. m. Mary Hayley Bell. Father of actresses Hayley and Juliet Mills. Worked as clerk before becoming actor. One of top ten money-making Brit. stars in Motion Picture Herald-Fame Poll, 1945, 1947, 1949-50, 1954, 1956-58. Knighted, 1977. Recipient special award 1988, British Academy of Film and Television Arts. Autobiography: Up in the Clouds Gentlemen Please (1981).
THEATER: London: Good Companions, Great Expectations, Separate Tables, Goodbye Mr. Chips, Little Lies (also Toronto), The Petition, Pygmalion (NY), An Evening With John Mills.
PICTURES: The Midshipmaid (debut, 1932), Britannia of Billingsgate, The Ghost Camera, The River Wolves, A Political Party, The Lash, Those Were the Days, Blind Justice, Doctor's Orders, Regal Cavalcade, Born for Glory, Car of Dreams, Charing Cross Road, First Offence, Nine Days a Queen, OHMS (You're in the Army Now), The Green Cockatoo (Four Dark Hours), Goodbye Mr. Chipes, Old Bill and Son, Cottage to Let, The Black Sheep of Whitehall, The Big Blockade, The Young Mr. Pitt, In Which We Serve, We Dive at Dawn, This Happy Breed, Waterloo Road, The Way to the Stars, Great Expectations, So Well Remembered, The October Man, Scott of the Antarctic, The History of Mr. Polly, The Rocking Horse Winner (also prod.), Morning Departure (Operation Disaster), Mr. Denning Drives North, The Gentle Gunman, The Long Memory, Hobson's Choice, The End of the Affair, The Colditz Story, Above Us the Waves, Escapade, It's Great to Be Young, War and Peace, Around the World in 80 Days, Baby and the Battleship, Town on Trial, Vicious Circle, I Was Monty's Double, Dunkirk, Ice Cold in Alex, Summer of the 17th Doll (Season of Passion), Tiger Bay, Tunes of Glory, The Singer Not the Song, Swiss Family Robinson, Flame in the Streets, Tiara Tahiti, The Valiant, The Chalk Garden, The Truth About Spring, Operation Crossbow (The Great Spy Mission), King Rat, The Wrong Box, Sky West and Crooked (Gypsy Girl; dir., prod. only), The Family Way, Africa—Texas Style, Chuka, Emma Hamilton, La Morte non ha Sesso (A Black Veil For Lisa), Oh! What a Lovely War, Run Wild Run Free, Ryan's Daughter (Academy Award; best supporting actor, 1970), A Black Veil for Lisa, Adam's Woman, Dulcima, Oklahoma Crude, Young Winston, Lady Caroline Lamb, The Human Factor, Trial By Combat (Dirty Knight's Work), The Devil's Advocate, The Big Sleep, Zulu Dawn, The 39 Steps, Gandhi, Sahara, Who's That Girl, When the Wind Blows (voice), Deadly Advice.
TELEVISION: Masks of Death, Murder with Mirrors, Woman of Substance, Hold the Dream, Edge of the Wind, When the Wind Blows, Around the World in 80 Days, The Lady and the Highwayman, The True Story of Spit MacPhee, A Tale of Two Cities, Ending Up, Frankenstein, The Big Freeze.

MILLS, JULIET
Actress. b. London, England, Nov. 21, 1941. m. actor Maxwell Caulfield. Father is actor John Mills. Sister is actress Hayley Mills. Made stage debut at 14 in Alice Through the Looking Glass. Also toured with Fallen Angels with sister; 1995, The Cherry Orchard, in Canada. Also in 1995, The Molière Comedies and Time of My Life.
PICTURES: So Well Remembered, The History of Mr. Polly, No My Darling Daughter, Twice Round the Daffodils, Nurse on

Wheels, Carry on Jack, The Rare Breed, Oh! What a Lovely War, Avanti!, Beyond the Door, The Man With the Green Cross, Primevals.
TELEVISION: Series: Nanny and the Professor. Movies: Wings of Fire, The Challengers, Letters from Three Lovers, Alexander: The Other Side of Dawn, The Cracker Factory, Barnaby and Me (Australia), Columbo: No Time to Die, A Stranger in the Mirror. Mini-Series: QB VII (Emmy Award, 1975), Once an Eagle. Guest: Hotel, Dynasty, The Love Boat. Special: She Stoops to Conquer.

MILNER, MARTIN
Actor. b. Detroit, MI, Dec. 28, 1931. e. USC. Army 1952-54, directed 20 training films.
PICTURES: Life With Father (debut, 1947), Sands of Iwo Jima, The Halls of Montezuma, Our Very Own, Operation Pacific, I Want You, The Captive City, Battle Zone, Mr. Roberts, Pete Kelly's Blues, On the Threshold of Space, Gunfight at the O.K. Corral, Sweet Smell of Success, Marjorie Morningstar, Too Much Too Soon, Compulsion, 13 Ghosts, Valley of the Dolls.
TELEVISION: Series: The Stu Erwin Show, The Life of Riley, Route 66, Adam-12, Swiss Family Robinson. Movies: Emergency!, Runaway!, Hurricane, Swiss Family Robinson (pilot), Flood, SST—Death Flight, Black Beauty, Little Mo, Crisis in Mid-Air, The Seekers, The Ordeal of Bill Carney. Mini-Series: The Last Convertible.

MIMIEUX, YVETTE
Actress. b. Los Angeles, CA, Jan. 8, 1942. e. Vine Street Sch., Le Conte Jr. H.S., Los Angeles, Los Ninos Heroes de Chapultepec, Mexico City, Hollywood H.S., CA. Appeared with a theatrical group, Theatre Events; Concerts: Persephone, Oakland Orchestra, 1965, N.Y. Philharmonic, Lincoln Center, L.A. Philharmonic, Hollywood Bowl.
THEATER: I Am a Camera (1963), The Owl and the Pussycat.
PICTURES: Platinum High School (debut, 1960), The Time Machine, Where the Boys Are, The Four Horsemen of the Apocalypse, Light in the Piazza, The Wonderful World of the Brothers Grimm, Diamond Head, Toys in the Attic, Joy in the Morning, The Reward, Monkeys Go Home, The Caper of the Golden Bulls, Dark of the Sun, The Picasso Summer, Three in the Attic, The Delta Factor, Skyjacked, The Neptune Factor, Journey Into Fear, Jackson County Jail, The Black Hole, Mystique (Circle of Power), Lady Boss.
TELEVISION: Series: The Most Deadly Game, Berrenger's. Movies: Death Takes A Holiday, Black Noon, Hit Lady (also writer), The Legend of Valentino, Snowbeast, Ransom for Alice, Devil Dog: The Hound of Hell, Outside Chance, Disaster on the Coastliner, Forbidden Love, Night Partners, Obsessive Love (also co-prod., co-writer), Perry Mason: The Case of the Desperate Deception.

MINER, STEVE
Director. b. Chicago, IL, June 18, 1951. e. Dean Junior Col. Began career as prod. asst. on Last House on the Left (1970). Launched a NY-based editorial service, and dir., prod., edited sport, educational and indust. films.
PICTURES: Here Come the Tigers! (co-prod.), Manny's Orphans (co-prod., s.p.), Friday the 13th (assoc. prod.). Director: Friday the 13th Part 2 (also prod.), Friday the 13th Part 3, Soul Man, House, Warlock (also prod.), Wild Hearts Can't Be Broken, Forever Young, My Father the Hero, Big Bully.
TELEVISION: Series: The Wonder Years (sprv. prod., dir., DGA Award for pilot). Pilots: B-Men, Elvis, Laurie Hill, Against the Grain.

MINNELLI, LIZA
Actress, Singer. b. Los Angeles, CA, Mar. 12, 1946. p. actress-singer Judy Garland & dir. Vincente Minnelli. e. attended sch. in CA, Switzerland, and the Sorbonne. Left to tour as lead in The Diary of Anne Frank, The Fantastiks, Carnival and The Pajama Game. In concert with mother, London Palladium 1964. In concert Carnegie Hall, 1979, 1987, 1993. Film debut as child in mother's film In the Good Old Summertime (1949). Recordings incl. Liza with a Z, The Singer, Live at the Winter Garden, Tropical Nights, Live at Carnegie Hall, Liza Minnelli at Carnegie Hall, Results, Live at Radio City Music Hall, The Day After That.
THEATER: Best Foot Forward (off-B'way debut, 1963, Theatre World Award), Flora The Red Menace (Tony Award, 1965), Liza at the Winter Garden (special Tony Award, 1974), Chicago, The Act (Tony Award, 1978), Are You Now or Have You Ever Been?, The Rink (Tony nom.).
PICTURES: In the Good Old Summertime, Journey Back to Oz (voice; 1964, released in U.S. in 1974), Charlie Bubbles, The Sterile Cuckoo (Acad. Award nom.), Tell Me That You Love Me Junie Moon, Cabaret (Academy Award; also British Acad. & Golden Globe Awards, 1972), That's Entertainment!, Lucky Lady, Silent Movie, A Matter of Time, New York New York, Arthur, The Muppets Take Manhattan, That's Dancing!, Rent-a-Cop, Arthur 2 on the Rocks, Stepping Out.
TELEVISION: Specials: Judy and Liza at the London Palladium, The Dangerous Christmas of Red Riding Hood, Liza, Liza with a Z (Emmy Award, 1972). Goldie and Liza Together, Baryshnikov

on Broadway, Liza in London, Faerie Tale Theater (Princess and the Pea), A Triple Play: Sam Found Out, Frank Sammy and Liza: The Ultimate Event, Liza Minnelli Live From Radio City Music Hall. *Movies*: A Time to Live (Golden Globe Award), Parallel Lives, The West Side Waltz.

MIOU-MIOU
Actress r.n. Sylvette Herry. b. Paris, France, Feb. 22, 1950. First job as apprentice in upholstery workshop. In 1968, helped to create Montparnasse cafe-theatre, Cafe de la Gare, with comedian Coluche. Returned to stage in Marguerite Duras' La Musica, 1985.
PICTURES: La Cavale (debut, 1971), Themroc, Quelques Messieurs Trop Tranquilles, Elle Court, Elle Court La Banlieue, Les Granges Brulees, The Mad Adventures of Rabbi Jacob, Going Places, Un Genie Deux Associes une Cloche, D'Amour et D'Eau Fraiche, Victory March, F... comme Fairbanks, On Aura Tout Vu, Jonah Who Will Be 25 in the Year 2000, Dites-lui Que Je l'aime, Les Routes du Sud, Le Grand Embouteillage, Memoirs of a French Whore, Au Revoir...a Lundi, La Femme Flic (Lady Cop), Est-ce Bien Raisonnable?, La Geule du Loup, Josepha, Guy De Maupassant, Coup de Foudre (Entre Nous), Canicule, Le Vol du Sphinx, Blanche et Marie, Menage, The Revolving Doors, La Lectrice, Milou in May, La Totale, Le Bal des Casse-Pieds, Tango, Montparnasse-Pondichery, Germinal.

MIRISCH, DAVID
Executive. b. Gettysburg, PA, July 24, 1935. e. Ripon Coll. United Artists Corp., 1960-63; former exec. with Braverman-Mirisch adv. public rel. firm.

MIRISCH, MARVIN E.
Executive. b. New York, NY, March 19, 1918. e. CCNY, B.A., 1940. Print dept., contract dept., asst. booker, NY exch.; head booker, Grand National Pictures, Inc., 1936-40; officer, gen. mgr. vending concession operation 800 theatres, Midwest, Theatres Candy Co., Inc., Milwaukee, Wisc., 1941-52; exec., corporate officer in chg., indep. producer negotiations, other management functions, Allied Artists Pictures, Inc., 1953-57; chmn. of bd., CEO in chg. of all business affairs, admin. & financing, distr. liaison, The Mirisch Company, Inc., 1957 to present. Member of Board of Governors and former v.p., AMPAS. Member Motion Pictures Pioneers. Past president of AMPAS Foundation.
PICTURES: *Exec. prod.*: Dracula, Romantic Comedy.

MIRISCH, WALTER
Producer. b. New York, NY, Nov. 8, 1921. e. U. of Wisconsin, B.A., 1942; Harvard Grad. Sch. of Business Admin., 1943. In m.p. indust. with Skouras Theatres Corp., 1938-40; Oriental Theatre Corp., 1940-42. 1945 with Monogram/Allied Artists; apptd. exec. prod. Allied Artists, 1951 (spv. such films as The Big Combo, The Phoenix City Story, Invasion of the Body Snatchers, Friendly Persuasion, Love in the Afternoon); established The Mirisch Company, supervising such films as Some Like It Hot, The Horse Soldiers, The Apartment, West Side Story, Irma La Douce, The Great Escape, The Pink Panther, A Shot in the Dark, The Fortune Cookie, The Russians Are Coming the Russians Are Coming, Fiddler on the Roof; 1960-61 Pres. of Screen Prod. Guild; 1962, mem. bd. dir., MPAA; bd. Gvnrs., AMPAS, 1964, 1972; 1967, pres., Center Thea. Group of L.A.; named pres. and exec. head of prod., The Mirisch Corporation, 1969; pres., Permanent Charities Committee 1962-63; pres., AMPAS, 1973-77. Recipient: Irving Thalberg Award 1978, Jean Hersholt Humanitarian Award 1984, Honorary Doctor of Humanities, Univ. of WI 1989, UCLA Medal 1989.
PICTURES: *Producer or Exec. Producer*: Fall Guy, I Wouldn't Be in Your Shoes, Bomba on Panther Island, Bomba the Jungle Boy, Bomba and the Hidden City, County Fair, The Lost Volcano, Cavalry Scout, Elephant Stampede, Flight to Mars, The Lion Hunters, Rodeo, African Treasure, Wild Stallion, The Rose Bowl Story, Flat Top, Bomba and the Jungle Girl, Hiawatha, Safari Drums, The Maze, The Golden Idol, Killer Leopard, The Warriors, Annapolis Story, Lord of the Jungle, Wichita, The First Texan, The Oklahoman, The Tall Stranger, Fort Massacre, Man of the West, Cast a Long Shadow, Gunfight at Dodge City, The Man in the Net, The Magnificent Seven, By Love Possessed, Two for the Seesaw, Toys in the Attic, In the Heat of the Night (Academy Award for Best Picture, 1967), Sinful Davey, Some Kind of a Nut, Halls of Anger, The Hawaiians, They Call Me Mister Tibbs, The Organization, Scorpio, Mr. Majestyk, Midway, Gray Lady Down, Same Time Next Year, The Prisoner of Zenda, Dracula, Romantic Comedy.
TELEVISION: *Movies* (exec. prod.): Desperado, Return of Desperado, Desperado: Avalanche at Devil's Ridge, Desperado: The Outlaw Wars, Desperado: Badlands Justice, Troubleshooters: Trapped Beneath the Earth, Lily In Winter, A Case for Life.

MIRREN, HELEN
Actress. b. London, England, 1946.
THEATER: Troilus and Cressida, 2 Gentlemen of Verona, Hamlet, Miss Julie, Macbeth, Teeth 'n' Smiles, The Seagull, Bed Before Yesterday, Henry VI, Measure for Measure, The Duchess

of Malfi, Faith Healer, Antony and Cleopatra, Roaring Girl, Extremities, Madame Bovary, Two Way Mirror, Sex Please We're Italian!, Woman in Mind (LA), A Month in the Country (also B'way).
PICTURES: A Midsummer's Night Dream (debut, 1968), Age of Consent, Savage Messiah, O Lucky Man!, Hamlet, Caligula, Hussy, The Fiendish Plot of Dr. Fu Manchu, Excalibur, The Long Good Friday, Cal, 2010, White Nights, Heavenly Pursuits, The Mosquito Coast, Pascali's Island, When the Whales Came, The Cook The Thief His Wife and Her Lover, The Comfort of Strangers, Where Angels Fear to Tread, Dr. Bethune, The Gift, The Hawk, Prince of Jutland, The Madness of King George (Acad. Award nom.; Cannes Film Fest. Award), Losing Chase, Some Mother's Son.
TELEVISION: Miss Julie, The Applecart, The Little Minister, The Changeling, Blue Remembered Hills, As You Like It, A Midsummer Night's Dream, Mrs. Reinhart, After the Party, Cymbeline, Coming Through, Cause Celebre, Red King White Knight, Prime Suspect (BAFTA Award), Prime Suspect 2, Prime Suspect 3 (Emmy Award, 1996).

MISCHER, DON
Producer, Director. b. San Antonio, TX, March 5, 1941. e. U. of TX, B.A. 1963, M.A. 1965. Pres., Don Mischer Productions. Founded Don Mischer Productions, 1978. Recipient of 11 Emmy Awards.
TELEVISION: *Producer*: Opening and closing ceremonies of the 1996 Centennial Olympics Games, Michael Jackson's Super Bowl XXVII Halftime Show, The Kennedy Center Honors (Emmy Awards, 1981, 1987, 1994, 1996), Tony Awards (3 yrs; Emmy Awards, 1987, 1989), Carnegie Hall 100th Anniversary, Gregory Hines Tap Dance in America, Opening of EuroDisney, The Muppets Celebrate Jim Henson, AFI Salutes to Billy Wilder and Gene Kelly, Irving Berlin's 100th Birthday (Emmy Award, 1988), Baryshnikov by Tharp, Motown 25: Yesterday Today Forever (Emmy Award, 1983), Motown Returns to the Apollo (Emmy Award, 1985), Grand Reopening of Carnegie Hall specials with Goldie Hawn, Liza Minnelli, Bob Hope, Robin Williams, Pointer Sisters. Also: The Great American Dream Machine, Donohue and Kids: Project Peacock (Emmy Award, 1981), The Presidential Inaugural, 6 Barbara Walters Specials, Ain't Misbehavin', It's Garry Shandling's Show.

MITCHUM, ROBERT
Actor. b. Bridgeport, CT, Aug. 6, 1917. Joined Long Beach Players Guild; appeared in Hopalong Cassidy series with William Boyd; in Westerns 8 yrs.
PICTURES: Hoppy Serves a Writ (debut, 1943), The Leather Burners, Border Patrol, Follow the Band, Colt Comrades, The Human Comedy, We've Never Been Licked, Beyond the Last Frontier, Bar 20, Doughboys in Ireland, Corvette K-225, Aerial Gunner, The Lone Star Trail, False Colors, The Dancing Masters, Riders of the Deadline, Cry Havoc, Gung Ho, Johnny Doesn't Live Here Anymore, When Strangers Marry, The Girl Rush, Thirty Seconds Over Tokyo, Nevada, West of the Pecos, The Story of G.I. Joe (Acad. Award nom.), Undercurrent, Locket, Till the End of Time, Pursued, Desire Me, Crossfire, Out of the Past, Rachel and the Stranger, Blood on the Moon, The Red Pony, The Big Steal, Holiday Affair, Where Danger Lives, My Forbidden Past, His Kind of Woman, The Racket, Macao, One Minute to Zero, The Lusty Men, Angel Face, White Witch Doctor, Second Chance, She Couldn't Say No, River of No Return, Track of the Cat, Night of the Hunter, Not as a Stranger, Man with the Gun, Foreign Intrigue, Bandido, Heaven Knows Mr. Allison, Fire Down Below, The Enemy Below, Thunder Road (also exec. prod., story, wrote song), The Hunters, The Angry Hills, The Wonderful Country (also exec. prod.), Home from the Hill, A Terrible Beauty (Night Fighters), The Grass is Greener, The Sundowners, The Last Time I Saw Archie, Cape Fear (1962), The Longest Day, Two for the Seesaw, The List of Adrian Messenger, Rampage, Man in the Middle, What a Way to Go!, Mr. Moses, The Way West, El Dorado, Villa Rides, Anzio, Five Card Stud, Secret Ceremony, Young Billy Young, The Good Guys and the Bad Guys, Ryan's Daughter, Going Home, The Wrath of God, The Friends of Eddie Coyle, The Yakuza, Farewell My Lovely, Midway, The Last Tycoon, The Amsterdam Kill, The Big Sleep, Breakthrough, Matilda, Nightkill, Agency (Mind Games), That Championship Season, Maria's Lovers, The Ambassador, Mr. North, Scrooged, Midnight Ride, Presumed Dangerous, Cape Fear (1991), Woman of Desire, Tombstone (voice), Dead Man.
TELEVISION: *Series*: A Family for Joe, African Skies. *Mini-Series*: The Winds of War, North and South, War and Remembrance. *Movies*: One Shoe Makes It Murder, A Killer in the Family, The Hearst and Davies Affair, Reunion at Fairborough, Promises to Keep, Thompson's Last Run, Brotherhood of the Rose, Jake Spanner: Private Eye, A Family for Joe (pilot).

MOCIUK, YAR W.
Executive. b. Ukraine, Jan. 26, 1927. e. CCNY; World U.; Peoples U. of Americas, Puerto Rico. Expert in field of m.p. care and repair; holds U.S. patent for method and apparatus for

treating m.p. film. Has also been film producer and director. Founder and pres. of CM Films Service, Inc. until 1973. Now chmn. of bd. and pres. of Filmtreat International Corp. Member: M.P. & TV Engineers; Univ. Film Assn. Pres., Ukrainian Cinema Assn. of America.

MODINE, MATTHEW
Actor. b. Loma Linda, CA, March 22, 1959. Raised in Utah. Studied acting with Stella Adler. Stage work incl. Our Town, Tea and Sympathy, The Brick and the Rose.
PICTURES: Baby It's You (debut, 1983), Private School, Streamers, The Hotel New Hampshire, Mrs. Soffel, Birdy, Vision Quest, Full Metal Jacket, Orphans, Married to the Mob, La Partita (The Gamble), Gross Anatomy, Pacific Heights, Memphis Belle, Wind, Equinox, Short Cuts, The Browning Version, Bye Bye Love, Fluke, Cutthroat Island.
TELEVISION: Movies: And the Band Played On, Jacob. Specials: Amy and the Angel, Eugene O'Neill: Journey Into Greatness. Series: Texas (daytime serial).

MOFFAT, DONALD
Actor. b. Plymouth, England, Dec. 26, 1930. Studied acting Royal Academy of Dramatic Art, 1952-54. London stage debut Macbeth, 1954. With Old Vic before Broadway debut in Under Milkwood, 1957. Worked with APA-Phoenix Theatre Co. and as actor and dir. of numerous B'way and regional productions.
THEATER: The Bald Soprano, Jack, Ivanov, Much Ado About Nothing, The Tumbler, Duel of Angels, A Passage to India, The Affair, The Taming of the Shrew, The Caretaker, Man and Superman, War and Peace, You Can't Take It With You, Right You Are... If You Think You Are, School for Scandal, The Wild Duck, The Cherry Orchard, Cock-a-Doodle Dandy, Hamlet, Chemin de Fer, Father's Day, Forget-Me-Not-Lane, Terra Nova, The Kitchen, Waiting for Godot, Painting Churches, Play Memory, Passion Play, The Iceman Cometh, Uncommon Ground, Love Letters, As You Like It, The Heiress.
PICTURES: Pursuit of the Graf Spee (The Battle of the River Plate; debut, 1957), Rachel Rachel, The Trial of the Catonsville Nine, R.P.M., The Great Northfield Minnesota Raid, Showdown, The Terminal Man, Earthquake, Land of No Return (Snowman), Promises in the Dark, Health, On the Nickel, Popeye, The Thing, The Right Stuff, Alamo Bay, The Best of Times, Monster in the Closet, The Unbearable Lightness of Being, Far North, Music Box, The Bonfire of the Vanities, Class Action, Regarding Henry, Housesitter, Clear and Present Danger, Trapped in Paradise.
TELEVISION: Series: The New Land, Logan's Run. Guest: Camera Three (1958), You Can't Have Everything (U.S. Steel Hour), Murder, She Wrote, Dallas. Specials: Forget-Me-Not Lane, Tartuffe, Waiting for Godot. Movies: Devil and Miss Sarah, Call of the Wild, Eleanor and Franklin: The White House Years, Exo-Man, Mary White, Sergeant Matlovich vs. the U.S. Air Force, The Word, The Gift of Love, Strangers: The Story of a Mother and Daughter, Ebony Ivory and Jade, Mrs. R's Daughter, The Long Days of Summer, Jacqueline Bouvier Kennedy, Who Will Love My Children?, Through Naked Eyes, License to Kill, Cross of Fire, A Son's Promise, Kaleidoscope, The Great Pretender, Babe Ruth, Columbo: No Time to Die, Teamster Boss: The Jackie Presser Story, Majority Rule, Love Cheat and Steal, Is There Life Out There? Mini-Series: Tales of the City.

MOGER, STANLEY H.
Executive. b. Boston, MA, Nov. 13, 1936. e. Colby Coll., Waterville, ME, B.A., 1958. Announcer/TV personality/WVDA and WORL (Boston) 1953-54; WGHM (Skowhegan) 1955-56; WTWO-TV (Bangor) 1955; WMHB (Waterville) 1956-57; WTVL (Waterville) 1957-58; unit pub. dir., Jaguar Prods., 1958-59; US Army reserve, 1958-64, with calls to active duty in 1958-59, 1961-62. Account exec., NBC Films/California National Productions, Chicago 1959-60; asst. sales mgr., Midwest, RCA/NBC Medical Radio System, 1960; acct. exec. Hollingbery Co., Chicago, 1960-63; and NY 1963-66; acct. exec., Storer TV Sales, 1966-69; co-founded SFM, 1969. 1978, named pres., SFM Entertainment which was responsible for the revival of Walt Disney's Mickey Mouse Club, The Adventures of Rin-Tin-Tin; Mobil Showcase Network, SFM Holiday Network. Pres., SFM Entertainment, Exec. Vice Pres., SFM Media Corp. Exec. prod.: Television-Annual, 1978-79: Your New Day with Vidal Sassoon, The Origins Game, Believe You Can and You Can, Walt Disney Presents Sport Goofy (series), The World of Tomorrow, March of Time ... on the March (England), Sports Pros and Cons, Unclaimed Fortunes, Sea World Summer Night Magic, America's Dance Honors, Allen & Rossi's 25th Anniversary Special, Paris '89 Celebration, U.S. Sports Academy Awards, K-Nite Color Radio, Into the Night With Brad Garrett (ABC-TV).

MOKAE, ZAKES
Actor. b. Johannesburg, South Africa, Aug. 5, 1935. e. RADA. Came to US in 1969. Has appeared in many plays written by Athol Fugard incl. Master Harold...and the Boys, Blood Knot.
PICTURES: The Comedians, The Island, Roar, Cry Freedom, The Serpent and the Rainbow, A Dry White Season, Gross Anatomy, Dad, A Rage in Harlem, The Doctor, Body Parts, Dust Devil, Outbreak, Waterworld, Vampire in Brooklyn.

TELEVISION: Special: Master Harold... and the Boys. Movies: One in a Million: The Ron LeFlore Story, Parker Kane, Percy & Thunder, Slaughter of the Innocents, Rise & Walk: The Dennis Byrd Story.

MOLEN, GERALD R.
Producer. Unit prod. mngr. on The Postman Always Rings Twice, Tootsie, Let's Spend the Night Together, A Soldier's Story, The Color Purple. Assoc. prod. on Batteries Not Included. Co-prod. on Rain Man. Joined Amblin Entertainment to oversee prod. of feature film projects.
PICTURES: Exec. Producer: Bright Lights Big City, Days of Thunder, A Far Off Place, The Flintstones, The Little Rascals, Little Giants, Casper, To Wong Foo Thanks for Everything Julie Newmar, Twister. Producer: Hook, Jurassic Park, Schindler's List (Academy Award for Best Picture, 1993).

MOLINA, ALFRED
Actor. b. London, Eng., May 24, 1953. e. Guildhall Sch. of Music and Drama. Began acting with the National Youth Theatre. Worked as stand-up comic for street theatre group. Joined Royal Shakespeare Co., 1977.
THEATER: Frozen Assets, The Steve Biko Inquest, Dingo, Bandits, Taming of the Shrew, Happy End, Serious Money, Speed-the-Plow, Accidental Death of an Anarchist (Plays and Players' Most Promising New Actor Award), The Night of the Iguana, Molly Sweeney (off-B'way).
PICTURES: Raiders of the Lost Ark (debut, 1981), Meantime, Number One, Ladyhawke, Eleni, Water, Letter to Brezhnev, Prick Up Your Ears, Manifesto, Not Without My Daughter, Enchanted April, American Friends, The Trial, When Pigs Fly, Cabin Boy, White Fang 2: Myth of the White Wolf, Maverick, Hideaway, The Perez Family, The Steal, Species, Before and After, Dead Man, Scorpion Spring, Anna Karenina.
TELEVISION: The Losers, Anyone for Dennis, Joni Jones, Cats' Eyes, Blat, Casualty, Virtuoso, Apocolyptic Butterflies, The Accountant, Drowning in the Shallow End, El C.I.D., Ashenden, Hancock, A Polish Practice, Year in Provence, Requiem Apache, Nervous Energy.

MOLL, RICHARD
Actor. b. Pasadena, CA, Jan. 13, 1943.
PICTURES: Caveman, The Sword and the Sorcerer, Metalstorm: The Destruction of Jared-Syn, The Dungeonmaster, House, Wicked Stepmother, Think Big, Driving Me Crazy, National Lampoon's Loaded Weapon 1, Sidekicks, The Flintstones, Storybook, Galaxis, The Glass Cage, The Secret Agent Club, The Perils of Being Walter Wood.
TELEVISION: Series: Night Court. Movies: The Jericho Mile, The Archer: Fugitive from the Empire, Combat High, Dream Date, Class Cruise, Summertime Switch, The Ransom of Red Chief. Specials: Reach for the Sun, The Last Halloween, Words Up! Guest: Remington Steele, Facts of Life, Sledge Hammer, My Two Dads, Highlander, Weird Science, Married...With Children.

MONASH, PAUL
Producer, Writer. b. New York, NY, June 14, 1917. e. U. of WI, Columbia U. Was in U.S. Army Signal Corps and Merchant Marine; newspaper reporter, high school teacher, and civilian employee of U.S. gov't. in Europe. Wrote two novels: How Brave We Live, The Ambassadors. Entered industry writing TV scripts for Playhouse 90, Studio One, Theatre Guild of the Air, Climax, etc. Authored two-part teleplay which launched The Untouchables. 1958 won Emmy award for The Lonely Wizard (Schlitz Playhouse of Stars), dramatization of life of German-born electrical inventor Charles Steinmetz. Made m.p. debut as exec. prod. of Butch Cassidy and the Sundance Kid, 1969.
PICTURES: Exec. Prod.: Butch Cassidy and the Sundance Kid. Producer: Slaughterhouse-Five, The Friends of Eddie Coyle (also s.p.), The Front Page, Carrie, Big Trouble in Little China.
TELEVISION: Series: Peyton Place (exec. prod.). Movies (exec. prod.): The Trial of Chaplain Jensen, The Day the Loving Stopped, Child Bride of Short Creek, Killer Rules (writer), Stalin (writer), Kingfish: A Story of Huey P. Long (writer).

MONICELLI, MARIO
Director. b. Rome, Italy, May 15, 1915. Ent. m.p. industry in pro-duction; later co-authored, collab., comedies.
PICTURES: The Tailor's Maid (also s.p.), Big Deal on Madonna Street (also s.p.), The Great War, The Passionate Thief, Boccaccio '70 (dir. segment; cut for U.S. release), The Organizer (also s.p.), Casanova '70 (also s.p.), Girl With a Pistol, The Queens, Lady Liberty (Mortadella), Romanzo Popolare (also s.p.), My Friends, Caro Michele, Signore e Signori Buonanotte (also s.p.), The New Monsters, Hurricane Rosy, Sono Fotogenico, Lovers and Liars (Travels With Anita; also s.p.), Il Marchese del Grillo (also s.p.), Amici Miei Atto (All My Friends 2; also s.p.), Bertoldo Bertoldino e Cacasenna (also s.p.), The Two Lives of Mattia Pascal (also s.p.), Let's Hope It's a Girl (also s.p.), The Rogues (also co-s.p.), The Obscure Illness (also s.p.), Looking for Paradise.

MONKHOUSE, BOB
Comedian, Writer. b. Beckenham, Kent, England, June 1, 1928. e. Dulwich Coll. Debut 1948 while serving in RAF, own radio comedy series 1949-83 (winters), own TV series, BBC 1952-56, ITV 1956-83, BBC 1983-90, ITV 1990-. Major cabaret attraction. Voted Comedian of the Year, 1987. After-Dinner Speaker of the Year, 1989.
THEATER: The Boys from Syracuse, Come Blow Your Horn; The Gulls, several West End revues.
PICTURES: Carry On Sergeant, Weekend with Lulu, Dentist in the Chair, She'll Have to Go, The Bliss of Mrs. Blossom
TELEVISION: Series: What's My Line?; Who Do You Trust?, Mad Movies, Quick on the Draw, Bob Monkhouse Comedy Hour, The Golden Shot, Celebrity Squares, I'm Bob He's Dickie!, Family Fortunes, Bob Monkhouse Tonight (1983-86), Bob's Full House (1984-90), Bob Says Opportunity Knocks (1987-89), $64,000 Question (1990-ongoing).

MONKS, JOHN, JR.
Writer, Actor, Producer, Director. b. Brooklyn, NY, June 25, 1910. e. Virginia Military Inst., A.B. Actor, stock, B'way, radio, m.p. U.S. Marines, 1942; commissioned Major, 1945. Co-author of Brother Rat. Wrote book A Ribbon and a Star.
PICTURES: Writer: Brother Rat, Brother Rat and a Baby, Strike Up the Band, The House on 92nd Street, 13 Rue Madeleine, Wild Harvest, Dial 1119, The West Point Story, People Against O'Hara, Where's Charley, So This Is Love, Knock on Any Door, No Man Is an Island.
TELEVISION: Climax (The Gioconda Smile, A Box of Chocolates), 20th Century-Fox Hour (Miracle on 34th St.), Gen. Electric Theatre (Emily), CBS Special: High Tor, SWAT. Creator serial: Paradise Bay.

MONTAGNE, EDWARD J.
Producer, Director. b. Brooklyn, NY, May 20, 1912. e. Loyola U., Univ. of Notre Dame. RKO Pathe, 1942; U.S. Army, 1942-46; prod. many cos. after army. Exec. prod. of film-CBS-N.Y. Prod. & head of programming, Wm. Esty Co., 1950; Program consultant, William Esty Co.; v.p. Universal TV prod. & dir.
PICTURES: Tattooed Stranger, The Man with My Face, McHale's Navy, McHale's Navy Joins the Air Force, P.J., The Reluctant Astronaut, Angel in My Pocket.
TELEVISION: Man Against Crime, Cavalier Theatre, The Vaughn Monroe Show, The Hunter, I Spy, McHale's Navy, Phil Silvers Show. TV Movies: Ellery Queen: A Very Missing Person, Short Walk to Daylight, Hurricane, Terror on the 40th Floor, Francis Gary Powers, Million Dollar Ripoff, Crash of Flight 401, High Noon—Part 2.

MONTALBAN, RICARDO
Actor. b. Mexico City, Mex., Nov. 25, 1920. Appeared in Mexican pictures 1941-45. On B'way in Her Cardboard Lover with Tallulah Bankhead. Later in Jamaica, The King and I, Don Juan in Hell. Autobiography: Reflections: A Life in Two Worlds (1980).
PICTURES: Fiesta (U.S. debut, 1947), On an Island with You, The Kissing Bandit, Neptune's Daughter, Battleground, Border Incident, Mystery Street, Right Cross, Two Weeks with Love, Across the Wide Missouri, Mark of the Renegade, My Man and I, Sombrero, Latin Lovers, The Saracen Blade, The Courtesans of Babylon (Queen of Babylon), Sombra Verde, A Life in the Balance, Untouched, The Son of the Sheik, Three for Jamie Dawn, Sayonara, Let No Man Write My Epitaph, The Black Buccaneer, Hemingway's Adventures of a Young Man, The Reluctant Saint, Love Is a Ball, Cheyenne Autumn, The Money Trap, Madame X, The Singing Nun, Sol Madrid, Blue, Sweet Charity, The Deserter, Escape From the Planet of the Apes, Conquest of the Planet of the Apes, The Train Robbers, Joe Panther, Won Ton Ton the Dog Who Saved Hollywood, Star Trek II: The Wrath of Khan, Cannonball Run II, The Naked Gun: From the Files of Police Squad.
TELEVISION: Series: Fantasy Island, The Colbys, Heaven Help Us. Guest: How the West Was Won Part II (Emmy Award, 1978). Movies: The Longest Hundred Miles, The Pigeon, Black Water Gold, The Aquarians, Sarge: The Badge or the Cross, Face of Fear, Desperate Mission, Fireball Foreward, Wonder Woman, The Mark of Zorro, McNaughton's Daughter, Fantasy Island (pilot), Captains Courageous, Return to Fantasy Island.

MONTGOMERY, GEORGE
Actor. r.n. George Montgomery Letz. b. Brady, MT, Aug. 29, 1916. e. U. of MT. Armed Services, WWII. Was champion heavyweight boxer. Debuted in films as extra, stuntman, then bit player billed as George Letz.
PICTURES: Singing Vagabond (debut, 1935), Cisco Kid and the Lady, Star Dust, Young People, Charter Pilot, Jennie, Cowboy and the Blonde, Accent on Love, Riders of the Purple Sage, Last of the Duanes, Cadet Girl, Roxie Hart, Ten Gentlemen from West Point, Orchestra Wives, China Girl, Brasher Doubloon, Three Little Girls in Blue, Lulu Belle, Belle Starr's Daughter, Girl From Manhattan, Sword of Monte Cristo, Texas Rangers, Indian Uprising, Cripple Creek, Pathfinder, Jack McCall Desperado, Fort Ti, Gun Belt, Battle of Rogue River, The Lone Gun, Masterson of Kansas, Seminole Uprising, Robbers' Roost, Too

Many Crooks, Stallion Trail, The Steel Claw, Watusi, Samar, Hallucination Generation, Hostile Guns, Ransom in Blood.
TELEVISION: Series: Cimarron City.

MOODY, RON
Actor. r.n. Ronald Moodnick. b. London, England, Jan. 8, 1924. e. London Sch. of Economics. Novels: The Devil You Don't, Very Very Slightly Imperfect, Off The Cuff, The Amazon Box.
THEATER: London: Intimacy at Eight (debut, 1952), For Adults Only, Candide, Oliver! (also NY revival: Theatre World Award), Joey Joey (Bristol; also writer, composer, lyricist), Peter Pan, Hamlet, The Clandestine Marriage, The Showman (also writer), Sherlock Holmes—The Musical. Author: Saturnalia, Move Along Sideways.
PICTURES: Davy (debut, 1958), Follow a Star, Make Mine Mink, Five Golden Hours, The Mouse on the Moon, A Pair of Briefs, Summer Holiday, Ladies Who Do, Murder Most Foul, San Ferry Ann, The Sandwich Man, Oliver! (Acad. Award nom.), The Twelve Chairs, Flight of the Doves, Dogpound Shuffle, Dominique, Unidentified Flying Oddball, Wrong Is Right, Where Is Parsifal?, A Kid in King Arthur's Court.
TELEVISION: Series: Nobody's Perfect, Tales of the Gold Monkey. Mini-Series: The Word. Movies: David Copperfield (theatrical in U.K.), Dial M for Murder (U.S.), The Caucasian Chalk Circle, Hideaway. Specials: Portrait of Petulia, Bing Crosby's Merrie Olde Christmas, Winter's Tale, Othello, Other Side of London, Baden Powell, Lights Camera Action, Last of the Summer Wine.

MOONJEAN, HANK
Producer, Director. Began as asst. dir. at MGM. Later turned to producing.
PICTURES: Assoc. Prod.: The Great Gatsby, WUSA, The Secret Life of An American Wife, Child's Play, Welcome to Hard Times, The Singing Nun. Exec. Prod.: The Fortune, The End. Producer: Hooper, Smokey and the Bandit II, The Incredible Shrinking Woman, Paternity, Sharky's Machine, Stroker Ace, Stealing Home, Dangerous Liaisons.

MOORE, CONSTANCE
Actress. b. Sioux City, IA, Jan. 18, 1922. Sang on radio: Lockheed program, Jurgen's Show. Screen debut 1938. TV shows, nightclubs. N.Y. Stage: The Boys from Syracuse, By Jupiter, Annie Get Your Gun, Bells Are Ringing, Affairs of State.
PICTURES: Prison Break, A Letter of Introduction, You Can't Cheat an Honest Man, I Wanted Wings, Take a Letter Darling, Show Business, Atlantic City, Delightfully Dangerous, Earl Carroll Vanities, In Old Sacramento, Hit Parade of 1947, Spree.

MOORE, DEMI
Actress. b. Roswell, NM, Nov. 11, 1962. r.n. Demi Guynes. m. actor Bruce Willis. Began modeling at age 16. Off-B'way debut: The Early Girl, 1987 (Theatre World Award).
PICTURES: Choices (debut, 1981), Parasite, Young Doctors in Love, Blame It on Rio, No Small Affair, St. Elmo's Fire, About Last Night, One Crazy Summer, Wisdom, The Seventh Sign, We're No Angels, Ghost, Nothing But Trouble, Mortal Thoughts (also co-prod.), The Butcher's Wife, A Few Good Men, Indecent Proposal, Disclosure, The Scarlett Letter, Now and Then (also co-prod.), The Juror, The Hunchback of Notre Dame, Striptease.
TELEVISION: Series: General Hospital. Guest: Kaz, Vega$, Moonlighting, Tales from the Crypt (Dead Right). Specials: Bedrooms, The New Homeowner's Guide to Happiness. Movies: If These Walls Could Speak.

MOORE, DICKIE
Actor. b. Los Angeles, CA, Sept. 12, 1925. m. actress Jane Powell. Began picture career when only 11 months old, playing John Barrymore as a baby in The Beloved Rogue. Appeared in numerous radio, television and stage prods. in NY and L.A. and over 100 films; appeared in several Our Gang shorts. Co-author and star, RKO short subject, The Boy and the Eagle (Acad. Award nom.). Author: Opportunities in Acting, Twinkle Twinkle Little Star (But Don't Have Sex or Take the Car), 1984. Now public relations executive.
PICTURES: Passion Flower, The Squaw Man, Manhattan Parade, Million Dollar Legs, Blonde Venus, So Big, Gabriel Over the White House, Upper World, Little Men, Peter Ibbetson, So Red the Rose, The Story of Louis Pasteur, The Life of Emile Zola, The Arkansas Traveler, The Under-Pup, The Blue Bird, A Dispatch From Reuters, Sergeant York, Adventures of Martin Eden, Miss Annie Rooney, Heaven Can Wait, The Happy Land, The Eve of St. Mark, Youth Runs Wild, Out of the Past, Killer Shark, 16 Fathoms Deep, Eight Iron Men, The Member of the Wedding.

MOORE, DUDLEY
Actor, Writer, Musician. b. Dagenham, Essex, Eng., April 19, 1935. e. Oxford, graduating in 1958. Toured British Isles with jazz group before joining Peter Cook, Jonathan Miller and Alan Bennett in creating hit revue, Beyond the Fringe, in U.K. and N.Y. Appeared later with Peter Cook on B'way in Good Evening. Composed film scores: Inadmissible Evidence, Staircase.

PICTURES: The Wrong Box (debut, 1966), Bedazzled (also composer), 30 is a Dangerous Age Cynthia (also co-s.p., composer), Monte Carlo or Bust (Those Daring Young Men in Their Jaunty Jalopies), The Bed Sitting Room, Alice's Adventures in Wonderland, The Hound of the Baskervilles, Foul Play, "10", Wholly Moses, Arthur (Acad. Award nom.), Six Weeks, Lovesick, Romantic Comedy, Unfaithfully Yours, Best Defense, Micki and Maude, Santa Claus, Like Father Like Son, Arthur 2 On the Rocks (also exec. prod.), The Adventures of Milo and Otis (narrator), Crazy People, Blame It on the Bellboy, The Pickle, A Weekend in the Country.
TELEVISION: Series: Dudley, Daddy's Girls. Movie: Parallel Lives.

MOORE, ELLIS
Consultant. b. New York, NY, May 12, 1924. e. Washington and Lee U., 1941-43. Newspaperman in AK, TN, 1946-52. Joined NBC 1952; mgr. of bus. pub., 1953; dir. press dept., 1954; dir., press & publicity, 1959; vice-pres., 1961; pub. rel. dept., Standard Oil Co. (N.J.), 1963-66; v.p. press relations, ABC-TV Network, 1966-68; v.p. public relations ABC-TV Network, 1968-70; v.p. public relations, ABC, 1970, v.p. public relations, ABC, Inc., 1972; v.p. corporate relations, ABC, Inc., 1979; v.p., public affairs, ABC, Inc., 1982-85. P.R. consultant, 1985. Retired, 1992.

MOORE, JULIANNE
Actress. b. 1961. e. Boston Univ. Sch. for the Arts.
THEATRE: Off-B'way: Serious Money, Ice Cream/Hot Fudge, The Road to Nirvana, Hamlet, The Father.
PICTURES: Tales From the Darkside (debut, 1990), The Hand That Rocks the Cradle, Body of Evidence, Benny & Joon, The Fugitive, Short Cuts, Vanya on 42nd Street, Roommates, Safe, Nine Months, Assassins, Surviving Picasso.
TELEVISION: Series: As the World Turns (Emmy Award). Movies: I'll Take Manhattan, The Last to Go, Cast a Deadly Spell.

MOORE, KIERON
Actor. r.n. Kieron O'Hanrahan. b. Skibereen, Co. Cork, Eire, 1925. e. St. Mary's Coll., Dublin. Stage debut, 1945 in Desert Rats; appeared in Red Roses For Me. Debuted in films under his real name.
PICTURES: The Voice Within (debut, 1945), A Man About the House (1st billing as Kieron Moore), Anna Karenina, Mine Own Executioner, Saints and Sinners, The Naked Heart, Honeymoon Deferred, Ten Tall Men, David and Bathsheba, Man Trap (Woman in Hiding), Conflict of Wings (Fuss Over Feathers), The Green Scarf, Blue Peter, Satellite in the Sky, The Steel Bayonet, Three Sundays to Live, The Key, The Angry Hills, Darby O'Gill and the Little People, The Day They Robbed the Bank of England, League of Gentlemen, The Siege of Sidney Street, Faces of Evil, Lion of Sparta, I Thank a Fool, Double Twist, The Day of the Triffids, The Thin Red Line, The Main Attraction, Crack in the World, Son of a Gunfighter, Never Love a Savage, Arabesque, Run Like a Thief, Custer of the West. Director: The Progress of Peoples, The Parched Land.

MOORE, MARY TYLER
Actress. b. Brooklyn. NY, Dec. 29, 1936. Began as professional dancer and got first break as teenager in commercials (notably the elf in Hotpoint appliance ads); then small roles in series Bachelor Father, Steve Canyon, and finally as the switchboard oper. in series Richard Diamond Private Detective (though only her legs were seen). Chairman of Bd., MTM Enterprises, Inc, which she founded with then-husband Grant Tinker.
THEATER: B'way: Breakfast at Tiffany's (debut), Whose Life Is It Anyway? (special Tony Award, 1980), Sweet Sue.
PICTURES: X-15 (debut, 1961), Thoroughly Modern Millie, Don't Just Stand There, What's So Bad About Feeling Good?, Change of Habit, Ordinary People (Acad. Award nom.), Six Weeks, Just Between Friends, Flirting With Disaster.
TELEVISION: Series: Richard Diamond—Private Detective, The Dick Van Dyke Show (2 Emmy Awards: 1964, 1966), The Mary Tyler Moore Show (1970-77; 4 Emmy Awards: 1973, 1974 (2), 1976), Mary (1978), The Mary Tyler Moore Hour (1979), Mary (1985-86), Annie McGuire, New York News. Guest: Bachelor Father, Steve Canyon, 77 Sunset Strip, Hawaiian Eye, Love American Style, Rhoda. Movies: Run a Crooked Mile, First You Cry, Heartsounds, Finnegan Begin Again, Gore Vidal's Lincoln, The Last Best Year, Thanksgiving Day, Stolen Babies (Emmy Award, 1993). Specials: Dick Van Dyke and the Other Woman, How to Survive the 70's, How to Raise a Drugfree Child.

MOORE, MICHAEL
Director, Writer. b. Davison, MI, 1954. e. Univ. of MI. Was editor of The Michigan Voice and Mother Jones magazine, commentator on radio show All Things Considered, before gaining fame with first film Roger & Me. Established Center for Alternative Media to support indept. filmmakers.
PICTURES: Dir./Prod./Writer/Actor: Roger & Me (debut, 1989), Canadian Bacon.
TELEVISION: Series: TV Nation (dir., exec. prod., writer, host). Special: Pets and Meat: The Return to Flint.

MOORE, ROGER
Actor. b. London, England, Oct. 14, 1927. e. art school, London; Royal Acad. of Dramatic Art. Had bit parts in British films Vacation From Marriage, Caesar and Cleopatra, Piccadilly Incident, Gay Lady. Appointed Special Ambassador for UNICEF, 1991.
THEATER: Mr. Roberts, I Capture the Castle, Little Hut, others. B'way: A Pin to See the Peepshow.
PICTURES: The Last Time I Saw Paris, Interrupted Melody, The King's Thief, Diane, The Miracle, Gold of the Seven Saints, The Sins of Rachel Cade, Rape of the Sabines, Crossplot, The Man Who Haunted Himself, Live and Let Die, Gold, The Man With the Golden Gun, That Lucky Touch, Street People, Shout at the Devil, The Spy Who Loved Me, The Wild Geese, Escape To Athena, Moonraker, ffolkes (North Sea Hijack), The Sea Wolves, Sunday Lovers, For Your Eyes Only, The Cannonball Run, Octopussy, The Curse of the Pink Panther, The Naked Face, A View to a Kill, The Magic Snowman (voice), Fire Ice and Dynamite, Bed and Breakfast, Bullseye!, The Quest.
TELEVISION: Series: The Alaskans, Maverick, The Saint, The Persuaders. Movies: Sherlock Holmes in New York, The Man Who Wouldn't Die (also co-exec. prod.).

MOORE, TERRY
Actress. r.n. Helen Koford. b. Los Angeles, CA, Jan. 7, 1929. Mother was Luella Bickmore, actress. Photographer's model as a child; acted on radio; with Pasadena Playhouse 1940. Voted Star of Tomorrow: 1958. Author: The Beauty and the Billionaire (1984). Formed Moore/Rivers Productions, 1988 with partner-manager Jerry Rivers. Has also acted as Helen Koford, Judy Ford, and Jan Ford.
PICTURES: Maryland (debut as Helen Koford, 1940), The Howards of Virginia, On the Sunny Side (billed as Judy Ford), A-Haunting We Will Go, My Gal Sal, True to Life, Date With Destiny, Gaslight, Since You Went Away, Son of Lassie, Sweet and Low Down, Shadowed, Summer Holiday, Devil on Wheels, The Return of October (1st billing as Terry Moore), Mighty Joe Young, The Great Ruppert, He's a Cockeyed Wonder, Gambling House, The Barefoot Mailman, Two of a Kind, Sunny Side of the Street, Come Back Little Sheba (Acad. Award nom.), Man on a Tightrope, Beneath the 12-Mile Reef, King of the Khyber Rifles, Daddy Long Legs, Shack Out on 101, Postmark for Danger (Portrait of Alison), Between Heaven and Hell, Peyton Place, Bernardine, A Private's Affair, Cast a Long Shadow, Why Must I Die?, Platinum High School, City of Fear, Black Spurs, Town Tamer, Waco, A Man Called Dagger, Daredevil, Death Dimension (Black Eliminator), Double Exposure, Hellhole, W.A.R., Beverly Hills Brats (also co-prod., co-story).
TELEVISION: Series: Empire. Movies: Quarantined, Smash-Up on Interstate 5, Jake Spanner: Private Eye.

MOORE, THOMAS W.
Executive. e. U. of Missouri. Naval aviator, USNR, 1940-45. Adv. dept., The Star, Meridian, MS; v.p., adv. mgr., Forest Lawn Memorial Park; account exec., CBS-TV Film Sales, Los Angeles; gen. sales mgr., CBS-TV Film Sales, 1956; v.p. in chg. programming & talent, 1958; pres., ABC-TV Network, 1962; chmn. bd., Ticketron, 1968; pres., Tomorrow Entertainment, Inc. 1971; chmn., 1981.

MORALES, ESAI
Actor. b. Brooklyn, NY, 1963. e. NY's High School for the Performing Arts. NY stage debut at age 17 in NY Shakespeare Fest. prod. of The Tempest, 1981.
THEATRE: Short Eyes, Tamer of Horses, El Mermano, Salome.
PICTURES: Forty Deuce (debut, 1982), Bad Boys, L.A. Bad, Rainy Day Friends, La Bamba, The Principal, Bloodhounds of Broadway, Naked Tango, Amazon, Freejack, In the Army Now, Rapa Nui, My Family/Mi Familia, Scorpion Spring.
TELEVISION: Mini-Series: On Wings of Eagles. Movies: The Burning Season, Deadlocked: Escape From Zone 14. Special: The Great Love Experiment. Guest: The Equalizer, Miami Vice.

MORANIS, RICK
Actor, Writer. b. Toronto, Canada, Apr. 18, 1954. Began career as part-time radio engineer while still in high school. Hosted own comedy show on radio then performed in Toronto cabarets and nightclubs and on TV. Joined satirical TV series SCTV during its 3rd season on CBC, for which he won Emmy for writing when broadcast in U.S. Created characters of the McKenzie Brothers with Dave Thomas and won Grammy nom. for McKenzie Brothers album. With Thomas co-wrote, co-directed and starred in film debut Strange Brew, 1983. Supplied voice for cartoon series Rick Moranis in Gravedale High.
PICTURES: Strange Brew (debut, 1983; also co-dir., co-s.p.), Streets of Fire, Ghostbusters, The Wild Life, Brewster's Millions, Head Office, Club Paradise, Little Shop of Horrors, Spaceballs, Ghostbusters II, Honey I Shrunk the Kids, Parenthood, My Blue Heaven, L.A. Story, Honey I Blew Up the Kid, Splitting Heirs, The Flintstones, Little Giants, Big Bully.

MOREAU, JEANNE
Actress. b. Paris, France, Jan. 23, 1928. e. Nat'l Conservatory of Dramatic Art. Stage debut with Comedie Francaise, acting there

until 1952 when she joined the Theatre Nationale Populaire. Directorial debut: La Lumiere (film), 1976. Recipient of 1995 BAFTA Film Craft Fellowship Award.
THEATER: A Month in the Country, La Machine Infernale, Pygmalion, Cat on a Hot Tin Roof.
PICTURES: The She-Wolves, Elevator to the Scaffold, The Lovers, Le Dialogue Des Carmelites, Les Liaisons Dangereuses, Moderato Cantabile, La Notte, Jules and Jim, A Woman Is a Woman, Eva, The Trial, Bay of Angels, The Victors, Le Feu Follet, Diary of a Chambermaid, The Yellow Rolls-Royce, The Train, Mata Hari, Viva Maria, Mademoiselle, Chimes at Midnight, Sailor From Gibraltar, The Bride Wore Black, The Immortal Story, Great Catherine, Monte Walsh, Alex in Wonderland, The Little Theatre of Jean Renoir, Louise, The Last Tycoon, French Provincial, La Lumiere (also dir., s.p.), Mr. Klein, The Adolescent (dir., s.p. only), Plein Sud, Querelle, The Trout, Le Miracule, La Femme Nikita, The Suspended Step of the Stork, La Femme Farde, Until the End of the World, Alberto Express, The Lover (voice), Map of the Human Heart, Anna Karamazova, The Summer House, See You Tomorrow, My Name Is Victor, The Old Lady Who Walks in the Sea, Beyond the Clouds, I Love You I Love You Not, The Proprietor.
TELEVISION: A Foreign Field (BBC).

MORENO, RITA
Actress. r.n. Rosa Dolores Alvario. b. Humacao, Puerto Rico, Dec. 11, 1931. Spanish dancer since childhood; night club entertainer. Has won all 4 major show business awards: Oscar, Tony, 2 Emmys and Grammy (for Best Recording for Children: The Electric Company, 1972).
THEATER: Skydrift (debut, 1945), The Sign in Sidney Brustein's Window, Gantry, Last of the Red Hot Lovers, The National Health (Long Wharf, CT), The Ritz (Tony Award, 1975), Wally's Cafe, The Odd Couple (female version).
PICTURES: So Young So Bad (debut, 1950, as Rosita Moreno), Pagan Love Song, The Toast of New Orleans, Singin' in the Rain, The Ring, Cattle Town, Ma and Pa Kettle on Vacation, Latin Lovers, Fort Vengeance, Jivaro, El Alamein, Yellow Tomahawk, Garden of Evil, Untamed, Seven Cities of Gold, Lieutenant Wore Skirts, The King and I, The Vagabond King, The Deerslayer, This Rebel Breed, Summer and Smoke, West Side Story (Academy Award, best supporting actress, 1961), Cry of Battle, The Night of the Following Day, Marlowe, Popi, Carnal Knowledge, The Ritz, The Boss' Son, Happy Birthday Gemini, The Four Seasons, Life in the Food Chain (Age Isn't Everything), The Italian Movie, Blackout, I Like It Like That, Angus.
TELEVISION: Series: The Electric Company, Nine to Five, B.L. Styker, Top of the Heap, The Cosby Mysteries. Movies: Evita Peron, Anatomy of a Seduction, Portrait of a Showgirl. Guest: The Muppet Show (Emmy Award, 1977), The Rockford Files (Emmy Award, 1978). Special: Tales From the Hollywood Hills: The Golden Land.

MORGAN, ANDRE
Producer. b. Morocco, 1952. e. U. of Kansas. Golden Harvest Films 1972-84, Producer. Exec. v.p., Golden Communications 1976-84. Formed Ruddy-Morgan Organization with Albert S. Ruddy, 1984.
PICTURES: Enter the Dragon, The Amsterdam Kill, The Boys in Company C, Cannonball Run II, High Road to China, Lassiter, Farewell to the King, Speed Zone, Impulse, Ladybugs, Bad Girls, The Scout, Heaven's Prisoners.
TELEVISION: Series: Walker Texas Ranger. Movies: Miracle in the Wilderness, Staying Afloat.

MORGAN, HARRY
Actor. r.n. Harry Bratsburg. b. Detroit, MI, Apr. 10, 1915. e. U. of Chicago. Previously acted as Henry Morgan.
THEATER: Gentle People, My Heart's in the Highlands, Thunder Rock, Night Music, Night Before Christmas.
PICTURES: To the Shores of Tripoli (debut, 1942), The Loves of Edgar Allen Poe, Crash Dive, Orchestra Wives, The Ox-Bow Incident, Happy Land, Wing and a Prayer, A Bell for Adano, Dragonwyck, From This Day Forward, The Gangster, All My Sons, The Big Clock, Moonrise, Yellow Sky, Madame Bovary, The Saxon Charm, Dark City, Appointment with Danger, The Highwayman, When I Grow Up, The Well, The Blue Veil, Bend of the River, Scandal Sheet, My Six Convicts, Boots Malone, High Noon, What Price Glory, Stop You're Killing Me, Arena, Torch Song, Thunder Bay, The Glenn Miller Story, About Mrs. Leslie, Forty-Niners, The Far Country, Not as a Stranger, Backlash, Strategic Air Command, The Teahouse of the August Moon, Inherit the Wind, The Mountain Road, How the West Was Won, John Goldfarb Please Come Home, What Did You Do in the War Daddy?, Frankie and Johnny, The Flim Flam Man, Support Your Local Sheriff, Viva Max!, The Barefoot Executive, Support Your Local Gunfighter, Scandalous John, Snowball Express, Charlie and the Angel, The Apple Dumpling Gang, The Greatest, The Shootist, The Cat From Outer Space, The Apple Dumpling Gang Rides Again, Dragnet.

TELEVISION: Series: December Bride, Pete and Gladys, The Richard Boone Show, Kentucky Jones, Dragnet, The D.A., Hec Ramsey, M*A*S*H (Emmy Award, 1980), After M*A*S*H, Blacke's Magic, You Can't Take It With You. Movies: Dragnet (pilot), But I Don't Want to Get Married!, The Feminist and the Fuzz, Ellery Queen: Don't Look Behind You, Hec Ramsey (pilot), Sidekicks, The Last Day (narrator), Exo-Man, The Magnificent Magnet of Santa Mesa, Maneaters Are Loose!, Murder at the Mardi Gras, The Bastard, Kate Bliss and the Ticker Tape Kid, The Wild Wild West Revisited, Better Late Than Never, Roughnecks, Scout's Honor, More Wild Wild West, Rivkin: Bounty Hunter, Agatha Christie's Sparkling Cyanide, The Incident, Against Her Will: An Incident in Baltimore, Incident in a Small Town. Mini-Series: Backstairs at the White House, Roots: The Next Generations.

MORGAN, MICHELE
Actress. r.n. Simone Roussel. b. Paris, France, Feb. 29, 1920. e. Dieppe, dramatic school, Paris. Won starring role at 17 opposite Charles Boyer in Gribouille (The Lady in Question). Made several pictures abroad; to U.S. 1941. Recent theatre includes Les Monstres Sacres. Autobiography: With Those Eyes (1977).
PICTURES: Gribouille, Port of Sahadows, Joan of Paris (U.S. debut, 1942), The Heart of a Nation, Two Tickets to London, Higher and Higher, Passage to Marseilles, The Chase, La Symphonie Pastorale, The Fallen Idol, Fabiola, Souvenir, The Naked Heart (Maria Chapdelaine), The Moment of Truth, Daughters of Destiny, The Proud and the Beautiful, Napoleon, Grand Maneuver, Marguerite de la Nuit, Marie Antoinette, There's Always a Price Tag, The Mirror Has Two Faces, Maxime, Love on the Riviera, Three Faces of Sin, Crime Does Not Pay, Landru (Bluebeard), Web of Fear, Lost Command, Benjamin, Cat and Mouse, Robert et Robert, A Man and a Woman: 20 Years Later, Everybody's Fine.

MORIARTY, CATHY
Actress. b. Bronx, NY, Nov. 29, 1960. Raised in Yonkers, NY.
PICTURES: Raging Bull (debut, 1980; Acad. Award nom.), Neighbors, White of the Eye, Burndown, Kindergarten Cop, Soapdish, The Mambo Kings, The Gun in Betty Lou's Handbag, Matinee, Another Stakeout, Me and the Kid, Pontiac Moon, Forget Paris, Casper, Foxfire, Opposite Corners.
TELEVISION: Series: Bless This House. Movie: Another Midnight Run. Guest: Tales from the Crypt (ACE Award).

MORIARTY, MICHAEL
Actor. b. Detroit, MI, April 5, 1941. e. Dartmouth. Studied at London Acad. of Music and Dramatic Arts. Appeared with New York Shakespeare Festival, Charles Street Playhouse (Boston), Alley Theatre (Houston) and Tyrone Guthrie Theatre (Minneapolis). B'way debut in The Trial of the Catonsville Nine.
THEATER: Find Your Way Home (Tony & Theatre World Awards, 1974), Richard III, Long Day's Journey Into Night, Henry V, GR Point, Whose Life Is It Anyway (Kennedy Center), The Ballad of Dexter Creed, Uncle Vanya, The Caine Mutiny Court-Martial, My Fair Lady.
PICTURES: Glory Boy (debut, 1971), Hickey and Boggs, Bang the Drum Slowly, The Last Detail, Shoot It Black Shoot It Blue, Report to the Commissioner, Who'll Stop the Rain, Q, Blood Link, Odd Birds, Pale Rider, The Stuff, Troll, The Hanoi Hilton, It's Alive III: Island of the Alive, Return to Salem's Lot, Dark Tower, Full Fathom Five, The Secret of the Ice Cave, Courage Under Fire.
TELEVISION: Series: Law and Order. Movies: A Summer Without Boys, The Glass Menagerie (Emmy Award, 1974), The Deadliest Season, The Winds of Kitty Hawk, Too Far to Go (also distributed theatrically), Windmills of the Gods, Frank Nitti: The Enforcer, Tailspin: Behind the Korean Airline Tragedy, Born Too Soon, Children of the Dust. Mini-Series: Holocaust (Emmy Award, 1978). Guest: The Equalizer.

MORITA, NORIYUKI "PAT"
Actor. b. Isleton, CA, June 28, 1932. Began show business career as comedian in nightclubs for such stars as Ella Fitzgerald, Johnny Mathis, Diana Ross and the Supremes, Glen Campbell, etc. Worked in saloons, coffee houses, and dinner theatres before becoming headliner in Las Vegas showrooms, Playboy Clubs, Carnegie Hall, etc. Guest on most TV talk, variety shows and comics: M*A*S*H, Love Boat, Magnum, P.I. etc.
PICTURES: Thoroughly Modern Millie, Every Little Crook and Nanny, Cancel My Reservation, Where Does It Hurt?, Midway, When Time Ran Out, Full Moon High, Savannah Smiles, Jimmy the Kid, The Karate Kid (Acad. Award nom.), Night Patrol, Slapstick of Another Kind, The Karate Kid Part II, Captive Hearts, Collision Course, The Karate Kid Part III, Do Or Die, Lena's Holiday, Honeymoon in Vegas, Miracle Beach, Even Cowgirls Get the Blues, The Next Karate Kid, American Ninja 5.
TELEVISION: Series: The Queen and I, Sanford and Son, Happy Days, Mr. T and Tina, Blansky's Beauties, Ohara, The Karate Kid (voice for animated series). Movies: Evil Roy Slade, A Very Missing Person, Brock's Last Case, Punch and Jody, Farewell to Manzanar, Human Feelings, For the Love of It, The Vegas Strip Wars, Amos, Babes in Toyland, Hiroshima: Out of the Ashes, Greyhounds, Hart to Hart: Secrets of the Hart.

MORITZ, MILTON I
Executive. b. Pittsburgh, PA, Apr. 27, 1933. e. Woodbury Coll., grad. 1955. Owned, operated theatres in L.A., 1953-55; U.S. Navy 1955-57; American International Pictures asst. gen. sls. mgr., 1957; nat'l. dir. of adv. and publ. 1958; v.p. and bd. mem. of American International Pictures, 1967; pres. of Variety Club of So. Cal, Tent 25, 1975-76; 1975, named sr. v.p.; in 1980, formed own co., The Milton I. Moritz Co., Inc., Inc., mktg. & dist. consultant. 1987-94, joined Pacific Theatres as v.p. in chg. of adv., p.r. & promotions. 1995, reactivated the Milton I. Morvitz Co., Inc.

MORRICONE, ENNIO
Composer, Arranger. b. Rome, Italy, Nov. 10, 1928. Studied with Goffredo Petrissi at the Acad. of Santa Cecilia in Rome. Began career composing chamber music and symphonies as well as music for radio, TV and theater. Wrote for popular performers including Gianni Morandi. Early film scores for light comedies. Gained recognition for assoc. with Italian westerns of Sergio Leone (under name of Dan Davio).
PICTURES: Il Federal (1961, debut), A Fistful of Dollars, The Good the Bad and the Ugly, El Greco, Fists in the Pocket, Battle of Algiers, Matcheless, Theorem, Once Upon a Time in the West, Investigation of a Citizen, Fraulein Doktor, Burn, The Bird with the Crystal Plumage, Cat O'Nine Tails, The Red Tent, Four Flies in Grey Velvet, The Decameron, The Black Belly of the Tarantula, Bluebeard, The Serpent, Blood in the Streets, Eye of the Cat, The Human Factor, Murder on the Bridge, Sunday Woman, The Inheritance, Partner, Orca, Exorcist II: The Heretic, 1900, Days of Heaven, La Cage aux Folles, Bloodline, Stay as You Are, The Humanoid, The Meadow, A Time to Die, Travels With Anita (Lovers and Liars), When You Comin' Back Red Ryder?, Almost Human, La Cage aux Folles II, The Island, Tragedy of a Ridiculous Man, Windows, Butterfly, So Fine, White Dog, Copkiller, Nana, The Thing, Treasure of the Four Crowns, Sahara, Once Upon a Time in America, Thieves After Dark, The Cage, La Cage aux Folles III, The Forester's Sons, The Red Sonja, Repentier, The Mission, The Venetian Woman, The Untouchables, Quartiere (Neighborhood), Rampage, Frantic, A Time of Destiny, Casualties of War, Cinema Paradiso, State of Grace, Hamlet, Bugsy, City of Joy, The Bachelor, In the Line of Fire, Wolf, Love Affair, Disclosure.
TELEVISION: U.S.: Marco Polo, Moses—The Lawgiver, Scarlet and the Black, C.A.T. Squad, The Endless Game, Octopus 4, Abraham.

MORRIS, ERROL
Director, Writer. b. Hewlett, NY, 1948. e. Univ. of WI, Univ. of CA/Berkeley.
PICTURES: Gates of Heaven, Vernon Florida, The Thin Blue Line, A Brief History of Time, The Dark Wind.

MORRIS, GARRETT
Actor. b. New Orleans, LA, Feb. 1, 1937. e. Dillard Univ., Julliard Sch. of Music, Manhattan Sch. of Music. Was singer and arranger for Harry Belafonte Folk Singers and B'way actor before achieving fame as original cast member of Saturday Night Live.
THEATER: Porgy and Bess, I'm Solomon, Show Boat, Hallelujah Baby!, The Basic Training of Pavlo Hummel, Finian's Rainbow, The Great White Hope, Ain't Supposed to Die a Natural Death, The Unvarnished Truth.
PICTURES: Where's Poppa? (debut, 1970), The Anderson Tapes, Cooley High, Car Wash, How to Beat the High Cost of Living, The Census Taker, The Stuff, Critical Condition, The Underachievers, Dance to Win, Motorama.
TELEVISION: Series: Roll Out, Saturday Night Live (1975-80), It's Your Move, Hunter, Martin, Cleghorne! Movies: The Invisible Woman, Maid for Each Other, Black Scorpion. Guest: Scarecrow and Mrs. King, Love Boat, Married With Children, Murder She Wrote, The Jeffersons.

MORRIS, HOWARD
Actor, Director, Writer. b. New York, NY, Sept. 4, 1919. e. NYU. U.S. Army, 4 yrs.
THEATER: Hamlet, Call Me Mister, John Loves Mary, Gentlemen Prefer Blondes, Finian's Rainbow.
PICTURES: Director: Who's Minding the Mint?, With Six You Get Egg Roll, Don't Drink the Water, Goin' Cocoanuts. Actor: Boys' Night Out, 40 Pounds of Trouble, The Nutty Professor, Fluffy, Way... Way Out, High Anxiety, History of the World Part 1, Splash, Transylvania Twist, Life Stinks.
TELEVISION: Series: Your Show of Shows (also writer), Caesar's Hour. Movies: The Munster's Revenge, Portrait of a Showgirl, Return to Mayberry. Voices: Jetsons, Flintstones, Mr. Magoo. Producer: The Corner Bar. Director: Dick Van Dyke Show, Get Smart, Andy Griffith Show (also frequent guest); also many commericals.

MORRIS, JOHN
Composer, Conductor, Arranger. b. Elizabeth, NJ, Oct. 18, 1926. e. student Juilliard Sch. Music 1946-48, U. of Washington. 1947, New Sch. Social Research 1946-49. Member: ASCAP, Acad. of M.P. Arts & Sciences, American Federation of Musicians.

THEATER: Composer. B'way: My Mother My Father and Me, A Doll's House, Camino Real, A Time For Singing (musical), Take One Step, Young Andy Jackson, 15 Shakespeare plays for NY Shakespeare Fest. & Amer. Shakespeare Fest, Stratford CT. Musical supervisor, conductor, dance music arranger: Mack and Mabel, Much Ado About Nothing, Bells Are Ringing, Bye Bye Birdie and 23 other B'way musicals. Off-B'way: Hair.
PICTURES: The Producers, The Twelve Chairs, Blazing Saddles (Acad. Award nom.), Bank Shot, Young Frankenstein, The Adventure of Sherlock Holmes' Smarter Brother, Silent Movie, The Last Remake of Beau Geste, The World's Greatest Lover, High Anxiety, The In-Laws, In God We Trust, The Elephant Man (Acad. Award nom.), History of the World Part 1, Table for Five, Yellowbeard, To Be or Not to Be, The Woman in Red, Johnny Dangerously, The Doctor and the Devils, Clue, Haunted Honeymoon, Dirty Dancing, Spaceballs, Ironweed, The Wash, Second Sight, Stella, Life Stinks.
TELEVISION: Composer. Fresno, Katherine Anne Porter, Ghost Dancing, The Firm, The Mating Season, Splendor in the Grass, The Electric Grandmother, The Scarlet Letter, Georgia O'Keeffe, The Adams Chronicles, The Franken Project, The Tap Dance Kid (Emmy Award, 1986), Make Believe Marriage, The Desperate Hours, The Skirts of Happy Chance, Infancy and Childhood, The Fig Tree, The Little Match Girl, Favorite Son, The Last Best Year, The Last to Go, The Sunset Gang, Our Sons, When Lions Roared, Scarlett. Themes: ABC After School Special, Making Things Grow, The French Chef, Coach. Musical sprv., conductor, arranger Specials: Anne Bancroft Special (Emmy Award), S'Wonderful S'Marvelous S'Gershwin (Emmy Award), Hallmark Christmas specials.
RECORDINGS: Wildcat, All-American, Bells Are Ringing, First Impressions, Bye Bye Birdie, Kwamina, Baker Street, Rodgers and Hart, George Gershwin Vols. 1 & 2, Jerome Kern, Lyrics of Ira Gershwin, Cole Porter, others.

MORRIS, OSWALD
Cinematographer. b. London, Eng., Nov. 22, 1915. Left school at 16 to work for two years as camera dept. helper at studios. Was lensman for cameraman Ronald Neame who gave Morris first job as cameraman; in 1949, when Neame directed The Golden Salamander, he made Morris dir. of photography.
PICTURES: The Golden Salamander, The Card, The Man Who Never Was, Moulin Rouge, Beat the Devil, Moby Dick, Heaven Knows Mr. Allison, A Farewell to Arms, The Roots of Heaven, The Key, The Guns of Navarone, Lolita, Term of Trial, Of Human Bondage, The Pumpkin Eater (BFA Award, 1964), Mister Moses, The Hill (BFA Award, 1965), The Spy Who Came in from the Cold, Life at the Top, Stop the World- -I Want to Get Off, The Taming of the Shrew, Reflections in a Golden Eye, Oliver!, Gooodbye Mr. Chips, Scrooge, Fiddler on the Roof (Academy Award, 1971), Sleuth, Lady Caroline Lamb, The Mackintosh Man, The Odessa File, The Man Who Would Be King, The Seven Per Cent Solution, Equus, The Wiz, Just Tell Me What You Want, The Great Muppet Caper, The Dark Crystal.
TELEVISION: Dracula (1974).

MORRISSEY, PAUL
Writer, Director, Photographer. b. New York, NY, 1938. e. Fordham U. 2nd lt. in Army. A writer, cameraman and director in independent film prod. prior to becoming Andy Warhol's mgr. in all areas except painting. Discovered and managed The Velvet Underground and Nico. Founded Intrreview magazine. Story, casting, dir. & photog. for Warhol's Chelsea Girls, Four Stars, Bike Boy, I A Man, Lonesome Cowboys, Blue Movie, and San Diego Surf.
PICTURES: writer/photog./edit.: Flesh, Trash, Heat, L'Amour, Women in Revolt. writer/dir.: Andy Warhol's Frankenstein, Andy Warhol's Dracula, The Hound of the Baskervilles, Forty Deuce, Mixed Blood, Beethoven's Nephew, Spike of Bensonhurst.

MORROW, ROB
Actor. b. New Rochelle, NY, Sept. 21, 1962.
THEATRE: NY: The Substance of Fire, Aven'U Boys, The Chosen, Scandal (workshop), Soulful Scream of a Chosen Son, The Boys of Winter, Slam, Third Secret.
PICTURES: Private Resort, Quiz Show, The Last Dance, Mother.
TELEVISION: Series: Tattinger's, Northern Exposure. Guest: Spenser: For Hire, Everything's Relative, Fame.

MORSE, DAVID
Actor. b. Beverly, MA, Oct. 11, 1953.
THEATRE: B'way: On the Waterfront.
PICTURES: Inside Moves, Desperate Hours, The Indian Runner, The Good Son, The Getaway, The Crossing Guard, Twelve Monkeys, The Rock.
TELEVISION: Series: St. Elsewhere, Big Wave Dave's. Movies: Shattered Vows, When Dreams Come True, Prototype, Downpayment on Murder, Six Against the Rock, Winnie, Brotherhood of the Rose, Cross of Fire, A Cry in the Wild: The Taking of Peggy Ann, Dead Ahead: The Exxon Valdez Disaster, Miracle on Interstate 880, Tecumseh: The Last Warrior. Mini-Series: Stephen King's The Langoliers. Guest: Nurse. Special: A Place at the Table.

MORSE, ROBERT
Actor. b. Newton, MA, May 18, 1931. Served U.S. Navy. Studied with American Theatre Wing, New York. Following radio work, appeared on B'way stage in The Matchmaker, 1956.
THEATER: B'way: The Matchmaker, Say Darling (Theatre World Award), Take Me Along, How to Succeed in Business Without Really Trying (Tony Award, 1962), Sugar, So Long 174th Street, Tru (Tony Award, 1990).
PICTURES: The Proud and the Profane (debut, 1956), The Matchmaker, The Cardinal, Honeymoon Hotel, Quick Before It Melts, The Loved One, Oh Dad Poor Dad Mama's Hung You in the Closet and I'm Feeling So Sad, How to Succeed in Business Without Really Trying, A Guide for the Married Man, Where Were You When the Lights Went Out?, The Boatniks, Hunk, The Emperor's New Clothes.
TELEVISION: Series: The Secret Storm (1954), That's Life. Specials: The Stingiest Man in Town (voice), Kennedy Center Tonight—Broadway to Washington, Tru (Emmy Award, 1993). Movie: The Calendar Girl Murders. Mini-Series: Wild Palms. Guest: Masquerade, Alfred Hitchcock Presents, Naked City, Love American Style, Twilight Zone, Murder She Wrote.

MORTON, ARTHUR
Composer, Arranger. b. Duluth, MN, Aug. 8, 1908. e. U. of MN, 1929.
PICTURES: Night Life of the Gods, Princess O'Hara, Riding on Air, Fit for a King, Turnabout, Walking Hills, The Nevadan, Rogues of Sherwood Forest, Father is a Bachelor, Never Trust a Gambler, Harlem Globetrotters, Big Heat, Pushover, He Laughed Last. Orchesrtal Arrangements: Laura, From Here to Eternity, Jolson Story, Salome, Born Yesterday, The Long Gray Line, Man from Laramine, My Sister Eileen, Picnic, Strangers When We Meet, That Touch of Mink, Diamond Head, Toys in the Attic, Von Ryan's Express, In Harm's Way, What a Way to Go, The New Interns, Our Man Flint, Planet of the Apes, Patton, Tora Tora Tora, Papillon, Chinatown, Logan's Run, The Omen, MacArthur, The Boys from Brazil, Magic, Superman, Alien, Star Trek: The Motion Picture, Poltergeist, First Blood, Gremlins, Rambo: First Blood Part II, Hoosiers, The 'Burbs, Star Trek V: The Final Frontier, Total Recall, Medicine Man, Gladiator, Mr. Baseball, Forever Young, The Vanishing, Rudy, Angie, The Shadow, The River Wild, many others.
TELEVISION: Black Saddle, Laramie, Bus Stop, Follow the Sun, My Three Sons, Peyton Place, Medical Center, Daniel Boone, Lancers, National Geographic, Say Goodbye, How to Stay Alive, Hooray For Hollywood, The Waltons, Apple's Way, Masada, Medical Story.

MORTON, JOE
Actor. b. New York, NY, Oct. 18, 1947. e. Hofstra U.
THEATRE: NY: Hair, Raisin (Theatre World Award), Oh Brother, Honky Tonk Nights, A Midsummer Night's Dream, King John, Cheapside, Electra, A Winter's Tale, Oedipus Rex, Julius Caesar, The Tempest. Director: Heliotrope Bouquet.
PICTURES: ...And Justice for All, The Brother From Another Planet, Trouble in Mind, Zelly and Me, The Good Mother, Tap, Terminator 2: Judgment Day, City of Hope, Of Mice and Men, Forever Young, The Inkwell, Speed, The Walking Dead, Lone Star, Executive Decision.
TELEVISION: Series: Grady, Equal Justice, Tribeca (also dir.), Under One Roof, New York News. Movies: The Challenger, Terrorist on Trial: The United States vs. Salim Ajami, Howard Beach: Making a Case for Murder, Death Penalty, Legacy of Lies, In the Shadow of Evil. Special: The File of Jill Hatch. Guest: A Different World, Hawk, Homicide: Life on the Street.

MOSES, CHARLES ALEXANDER
Executive, Writer, Producer. b. Chicago, IL, March 1, 1923. e. Aeronautical U., Northwestern U., Englewood Eve. Jr. Coll., Antioch U. Field adv-promo exec., United Artists, unit publicist for over 30 films; exec., Screen Gems; European adv-publ. suprv., Paris, United Artists; adv-pub dir., Bel Air Prod., v.p. adv-pub dir., Associates & Aldrich Co.; adv-pub dir., Sinatra Enterprises; assoc. studio publ. dir., Universal Studios; adv-pub rep., Universal Studios from Paris for Europe; exec-in-chg NY domestic & foreign adv-publ. dept., Universal; adv-pub superv., Orion Pictures Co. Started own firm, Charles A. Moses Co., adv-marketing-pub. rel., acc'ts included United Artists, Columbia Picts., 20th Century-Fox, UA-TV, Cinemation Industries, Hemdale Leisure Corp., American Internat'l Picts., Filmways, etc. Orig. story: Frankenstein 1970. Prod.: Radio Free Europe, Munich, Goldblatt radio, TV shows (WGN); Writer-prod-dir., documentaries: Carson Prod., Mason City. Past pres., The Publicists Guild of America (IATSE, Local 818).

MOSK, RICHARD M.
Executive. b. Los Angeles, CA, May 18, 1939. e. Stanford U, Harvard Law School. Admitted to California Bar, 1964. Principal in firm of Sanders Barnet Goldman Simons & Mosk, a prof. corp. Named chmn. of the movie industry's voluntary rating system, the Classification & Rating Administration, June 1994.

MOSLEY, ROGER E.
Actor. b. Los Angeles, CA. Planned career in broadcasting but turned to acting, first appearing in small roles on TV in: Night Gallery, Baretta, Kojak, Cannon, Switch.
PICTURES: The New Centurions (debut, 1972), Hit Man, Terminal Island, Stay Hungry, Leadbelly, The Greatest, Semi-Tough, Steel, Heart Condition, Unlawful Entry.
TELEVISION: Series: Magnum P.I., You Take the Kids. Guest: Baretta, Kojak, Cannon, Switch. Movies: Cruise Into Terror, I Know Why the Caged Bird Sings, The Jericho Mile, Attica. Mini-Series: Roots: The Next Generations.

MOSS, FRANK L.
Writer, Producer. b. New York, NY, Aug. 25, 1913. e. Duke U., Columbia U. Reporter, drama & film critic, N.Y. U.S. Army Air Force, 1942-46. Instructor, UCLA, 1985-86 on advanced screenplay writing. 1987-88, private tutoring on screenplay and TV writing. For military made 22 Air Force training films, 17 documentaries. Author: The Hack.
THEATER: Author: Glamour Girl, Call To Arms (collab), So Goes the Nation (collab), Some People's Children, American Pastoral, City on a Hill.
PICTURES: To Have and Have Not, The Unvanquished, Whiphand, Sangaree, Papago Wells, The Half Breed, Sweetheart of Sigma Chi.
TELEVISION: Writer: Telephone Hour, Four Star Playhouse, Winston Churchill's Valiant Years, Route 66, Wagon Train, Laramie, Wild Wild West, The Texan, G.E. Theater, Wire Service, U.S. Marshall, M-Squad, Stoney Burke, Tales of the Texas Rangers, T.V. Reader's Digest, Sheriff of Cochise, Whirlybirds, Line-Up, Wyatt Earp, Rin Tin Tin, Walter Winchell File, Daniel Boone, Man Who Never Was, Felony Squad, Richard Diamond, Lassie, Like the Rich People, Hired Mother, Shenandoah, Counterspy, White Hunter, Hondo, Northwest Mounted Police, Casey Jones, Cowboy in Africa. Pilots: Outer Limits, Grand Jury, The Texam, Bush Pilot, Lafitte, Cortez. Prod./Story Ed.: Screen Televideo, Sovereign Prod., Wire Service, T.V. Reader's Digest, Wyatt Earp.

MOSS, IRWIN
Executive. e. Syracuse U., Harvard Law Sch. Member NY State Bar. Began industry career as director of package negotiations for CBS-TV; 1970-80, exec. v.p. & natl. head of business affairs for I.C.M.; 1978-80, sr. v.p., NBC Entertainment; 1980, pres., Marble Arch TV. 1982, joined Paramount Pictures as sr. v.p. for motion picture div. 1984, exec. v.p., L. Taffner Ltd.

MOSTEL, JOSH
Actor, Director. b. New York, NY, Dec. 21, 1946. Father was late actor Zero Mostel. m. producer Peggy Rajski. e. Brandeis U., B.A. 1970. Part of The Proposition, a Boston improvisational comedy group. Stage debut, The Homecoming (Provincetown Playhouse, MA).
THEATER: Actor: Unlikely Heroes, The Proposition, An American Millionaire, A Texas Trilogy, Gemini, Men in the Kitchen, The Dog Play, The Boys Next Door, A Perfect Diamond, Threepenny Opera, My Favorite Year, The Flowering Peach. Director: Ferocious Kisses, Love As We Know It, Misconceptions, Red Diaper Baby.
PICTURES: Going Home (debut, 1971), The King of Marvin Gardens, Jesus Christ Superstar, Harry and Tonto, Deadly Hero, Fighting Back, Sophie's Choice, Star 80, Almost You, The Brother from Another Planet, Windy City, Compromising Positions, The Money Pit, Stoogemania, Radio Days, Matewan, Wall Street, Heavy Petting, Animal Behavior, City Slickers, Naked Tango, Little Man Tate, City of Hope, Searching for Bobby Fischer, The Chase, City Slickers II: The Legend of Curly's Gold, Billy Madison, The Basketball Diaries, The Maddening.
TELEVISION: Series: Delta House, At Ease, Murphy's Law. Mini-Series: Seventh Avenue. Special: The Boy Who Loved Trolls (PBS). Co-writer: Media Probes: The Language Show.

MOUND, FRED
Executive. b. St. Louis, MO, April 10, 1932. e. St. Louis U., Quincy Coll. 1946-52, assoc. with father, Charles Mound, at Park Theatre in Valley Park, Mo.; 1952-53, Universal Pictures (St. Louis); 1953, booker, UA, St. Louis; 1955 promoted to salesman in Kansas City; 1957, salesman, St. Louis; 1962, Indianapolis branch mgr. 1967 named UA regional mgr., Dallas and in 1970 became S.W. div. mgr.; 1976-77, asst. gen. sls. mgr. for Southern, N.W. and S.W. div. operating out of Dallas. 1977 appt. v.p., asst. gen. sls. mgr. of UA; 1978, appt. v.p. gen sls. mgr. for AFD Pictures in Los Angeles; 1981, v.p. asst. gen. sls. mgr. for Universal; 1984, sr. v.p., gen. sls. mgr., Universal Pictures Distribution; named exec. v.p. 1988. Foundation of Motion Picture Pioneers v.p., 1989. Appointed pres. Universal distrib., 1990.

MOUNT, THOM
Executive. b. Durham, NC, May 26, 1948. e. Bard Coll.; CA Institute of the Arts, MFA. Started career with Roger Corman and as asst. to prod., Danny Selznick at MGM. Moved to Universal under prod. exec. Ned Tanen. At 26, named pres. and

head of prod. at Universal. During 8-year tenure, was responsible for dev. and prod. of more than 140 films (including Smokey and the Bandit, Animal House, others).
THEATER: Open Admissions (co-prod.), Death and the Maiden.
PICTURES: Pirates (exec. prod.), My Man Adam, Can't Buy Me Love, Frantic, Bull Durham (co-prod.), Stealing Home, Tequila Sunrise, Roger Corman's Frankenstein Unbound, The Indian Runner (exec. prod.), Death and the Maiden.
TELEVISION: Son of the Morning Star, Open Admissions.

MOYERS, BILL
TV Correspondent. b. Hugo, OK, June 5, 1934. e. U. of Texas; Southwestern Baptist Theological Sem. Aide to Lyndon B. Johnson; assoc. dir., Peace Corps, 1961-2, and deputy dir., 1963. Spec. asst. to Pres. Johnson, 1963-65 and press secty., 1965-67. Editor and chief corr., CBS Reports. Bill Moyers Journal on PBS. Established Public Affairs TV, Inc., 1986.

MUDD, ROGER
Newscaster. b. Washington, DC, Feb. 9, 1928. e. Washington & Lee U., U. of North Carolina. Reporter for Richmond News-Leader, 1953; news. dir., WRNL, 1954; WTOP, Washington, 1956; joined CBS News 1961 as Congressional correspondent (2 Emmy Awards). 1977, Natl. Aff. corr.; 1978, corr., CBS Reports; 1980-87: NBC News as chief Washington corr., chief political corr., co-anchor; 1987 joined The MacNeil/Lehrer News Hour as special correspondent; essayist, and chief congressional correspondent. 1992 became contributing correspondent.

MUELLER-STAHL, ARMIN
Actor. b. Tilsit, East Prussia, Dec. 17, 1930. Moved to West Germany in 1980. e. Berlin Conservatory. Studied violin before turning to acting. Author: Verordneter Sonntag (Lost Sunday), Drehtage.
PICTURES: Naked Among the Wolves, The Third, Jacob the Liar, The Flight, Lite Trap, Lola, Wings of Night, Veronika Voss, A Cop's Sunday, A Love in Germany, Thousand Eyes, Trauma, Colonel Redl, L'Homme blesse, God Doesn't Believe in Us Anymore, Angry Harvest, The Blind Director, Following the Fuhrer, Momo, The Jungle Mission, Lethal Obsession, Midnight Cop, Music Box, Das Spinnenetz, Just for Kicks, Avalon, Bronstein's Children, Kafka, The Power of One, Night on Earth, Utz, The House of the Spirits, Holy Matrimony, The Last Good Time, A Pyromaniac's Love Story, Taxandria, Shine, Theodore Rex.
TELEVISION: Mini-Series: Amerika.

MUHL, EDWARD E.
Executive, Producer. b. Richmond, IN, Feb. 17, 1907. Gen. mgr., Universal 1948-53; v.p.; studio in charge of prod. 1953-68. Consultant, Alcor Prods., Ft. Smith, AR, 1985-90. Co-author, consultant, s.p., Soldier: Other Side of Glory, 1991-92.

MUIR, E. ROGER
Producer. b. Canada, Dec. 16, 1918. e. U. of Minnesota. Partner Minn. Advertising Services Co.; Photographer, Great Northern Railway; motion picture producer Army Signal corps; NBC TV producer, Howdy Doody; exec. producer, Concentration. Now pres. Nicholson-Muir Prods, TV program packager, U.S. Spin-Off, Pay Cards, Canada Pay Cards, Headline Hunters, Definition, Celebrity Dominoes; co-creator Newlywed Game, exec. prod. I Am Joe's Heart, I Am Joe's Lung, I Am Joe's Spine, I Am Joe's Stomach, The New Howdy Doody Show, Supermates, Second Honeymoon, Groaner, Generation Jury, Shopping Game, Guess What, I Am Joe's Kidney, I Am Joe's Liver, It's Howdy Doody Time: A 40 Year Celebration. Retired 1993.

MULDAUR, DIANA
Actress. b. New York, NY, Aug. 19, 1943. e. Sweet Briar Coll. Began on New York stage then turned to films and TV, appearing on numerous major network shows.
PICTURES: The Swimmer (debut, 1968), Number One, The Lawyer, One More Train to Rob, The Other, McQ, Chosen Survivors, Beyond Reason.
TELEVISION: Series: The Secret Storm, The Survivors, McCloud, Born Free, The Tony Randall Show, Hizzoner, Fitz and Bones, A Year in the Life, L.A. Law, Star Trek: The Next Generation. Movies: McCloud: Who Killed Miss U.S.A.?, Call to Danger, Ordeal, Planet Earth, Charlie's Angels (pilot), Pine Canyon is Burning, Deadly Triangle, Black Beauty, To Kill a Cop, Maneaters Are Loose!, The Word, The Miracle Worker, The Return of Frank Cannon, Terror at Alcatraz, The Return of Sam McCloud.

MULGREW, KATE
Actress. b. Dubuque, IA, April 29, 1955. e. NYU. Stage work includes stints with American Shakespeare Festival, NY Shakespeare Festival, Seattle Rep. Theatre, Mark Taper Forum (LA). B'way: Black Comedy.
PICTURES: Lovespell, A Stranger Is Watching, Remo Williams: The Adventure Begins, Throw Momma from the Train, Camp Nowhere.

TELEVISION: Series: Ryan's Hope (1975-77), Kate Columbo (Kate Loves a Mystery), Heartbeat, Man of the People, Star Trek: Voyager. Movies: The Word, Jennifer: A Woman's Story, A Time for Miracles, The Manions of America, Roses Are for the Rich, Roots: The Gift, Danielle Steel's Daddy, Fatal Friendship, For Love and Glory.

MULHERN, MATT
Actor. b. Philadelphia, PA, July 21, 1960. e. Rutgers Univ.
THEATRE: NY: Biloxi Blues, Wasted, The Night Hank Williams Died.
PICTURES: One Crazy Summer, Extreme Prejudice, Biloxi Blues, Junior.
TELEVISION: Series: Major Dad. Movie: Gunsmoke: To the Last Man, Terror in the Night, A Burning Passion: The Margaret Mitchell Story.

MULHOLLAND, ROBERT E.
Executive. b. 1933. e. Northwestern U. Joined NBC News as newswriter in Chicago in 1962. 1964 made midwestern field producer for Huntley-Brinkley Report. 1964 moved to London as European producer for NBC News; 1965, named Washington producer of Huntley-Brinkley Report. Transferred to L.A. in 1967 to be director of news, west coast. Named exec. prod. of NBC Nightly News. 1973 appt. v.p., NBC News; 1974 exec. v.p. of NBC News. 1977 appt. pres. of NBC Television Network; also elected to board of directors; 1981, pres. & CEO. Resigned, 1984. Dir. Television Info. Office, NYC 1985-87. Prof. Northwestern U. 1988-.

MULL, MARTIN
Actor. b. Chicago, IL, Aug. 18, 1943. e. Rhode Island Sch. of Design. Started as humorist, making recordings for Warner Bros., Capricorn, ABC Records, etc.
PICTURES: FM (debut, 1978), My Bodyguard, Serial, Take This Job and Shove It, Flicks, Mr. Mom, Bad Manners, Clue, O.C. and Stiggs, Home Is Where the Hart Is, Rented Lips (also s.p., exec. prod.), Cutting Class, Ski Patrol, Far Out Man, Think Big, Ted and Venus, The Player, Miracle Beach, Mrs. Doubtfire, Mr. Write, Edie and Pen.
TELEVISION: Series: Mary Hartman Mary Hartman, Fernwood 2-Night, America 2-Night, Domestic Life, His and Hers, Roseanne, The Jackie Thomas Show, Family Dog (voice). Specials: The History of White People in America (also prod.), Candid Camera Christmas Special (1987), Portrait of a White Marriage, The Whole Shebang. Movies: Sunset Limousine, California Girls, The Day My Parents Ran Away, How the West Was Fun.

MULLER, ROBBY
Cinematographer. b. Netherlands, April 4, 1940. e. Dutch Film Acad. Asst. cameraman in Holland before moving to Germany where he shot 9 films for Wim Wenders.
PICTURES: Kings of the Road, Alice in the Cities, Wrong Move, The American Friend, Saint Jack, Honeysuckle Rose, They All Laughed, Body Rock, Repo Man, Paris Texas, To Live and Die in L.A., THe Longshot, Down By Law, Tricheurs, The Believers, Barfly, Il Piccolo Diavolo (The Little Devil), Mystery Train, Korczak, Until the End of the World, Mad Dog and Glory.

MULLIGAN, RICHARD
Actor. b. New York, NY Nov. 13, 1932.
THEATER: Nobody Loves an Albatross, All the Way Home, Never Too Late, Mating Dance, Hogan's Goat, Thieves, etc.
PICTURES: Love With the Proper Stranger (debut, 1963), One Potato Two Potato, The Group, The undefeated, Little Big Man, Irish Whiskey Rebellion, From the Mixed-Up Files of Mrs. Basil E. Frankweiler, The Big Bus, Scavenger Hunt, S.O.B., Trail of the Pink Panther, Meatballs Part II, Teachers, Micki and Maude, Doin' Time, The Heavenly Kid, A Fine Mess, Quicksilver, Oliver & Company (voice).
TELEVISION: Movies: Having Babies III, Malibu, Jealousy, Poler Alice, Gore Vidal's Lincoln, Guess Who's Coming for Christmas? Series: The Hero, Diana, Soap (Emmy Award, 1980), Reggie, Empty Nest (Emmy Award, 1989)

MULLIGAN, ROBERT
Director. b. Bronx, NY. Aug. 23, 1925. e. Fordham U. Served in Navy during WWII. After working as copyboy for NY Times joined CBS in mailroom. Eventually became TV director before moving into features.
PICTURES: Fear Strikes Out (debut, 1957), The Rat Race, The Great Imposter, Come September, The Spiral Road, To Kill a Mockingbird, Love With the Proper Stranger, Baby the Rain Must Fall, Inside Daisy Clover, Up the Down Staircase, The Stalking Moon, The Pursuit of Happiness, Summer of '42, The Other, The Nickel Ride, Bloodbrothers, Same Time Next Year, Kiss Me Goodbye, Clara's Heart, The Man in the Moon.
TELEVISION: The Moon and the Sixpence (Emmy Award, 1960), Billy Budd, Ah Wilderness, A Tale of Two Cities, The Bridge of San Luis Rey, Playhouse 90, Philco-Goodyear, Suspense, Studio One, Hallmark Hall of Fame.

MULRONEY, DERMOT
Actor. b. Alexandria, VA, Oct. 31, 1963. e. Northwestern Univ.
PICTURES: Sunset, Young Guns, Survival Quest, Staying Together, Longtime Companion, Career Opportunities, Bright Angel, Where the Day Takes You, Samantha, Point of No Return, The Thing Called Love, Silent Tongue, Bad Girls, Angels in the Outfield, There Goes My Baby, Living in Oblivion, Copycat, How to Make an American Quilt, Kansas City, Trigger Effect.
TELEVISION: Movies: Sin of Innocence, Daddy, Unconquered, Long Gone, The Heart of Justice, Family Pictures, The Last Outlaw. Special: Toma: The Drug Knot.

MUMY, BILL
Actor. r.n. Charles William Mumy Jr. b. El Centro, CA, Feb. 1, 1954. Began acting as Billy Mumy at age 6. Played with band America in 1970's, also with bands Bill Mumy & The Igloos, and The Jenerators. Has made 8 albums with Barnes & Barnes. With actor Miguel Ferrer, wrote comic books Comet Man and Trip to the Acid Dog. Has also written stories for Star Trek, The Hulk, and Spiderman comic books, and Lost in Space comic published by Innovation. Wrote music for Disney's Adventures in Wonderland series (Emmy nom.)
PICTURES: Tammy Tell Me True, Palm Springs Weekend, A Ticklish Affair, A Child is Waiting, Dear Brigitte, Rascal, Bless the Beasts and Children, Papillon, Twilight Zone—The Movie, Hard to Hold, Captain America, Double Trouble.
TELEVISION: Series: Lost in Space, Sunshine. Movies: Sunshine, The Rockford Files (pilot), Sunshine Christmas. Guest: The Twilight Zone, Alfred Hitchcock Presents, Bewitched, The Virginian, I Dream of Jeannie, The Adventures of Ozzie and Harriet, Ben Casey, The Red Skelton Show, Lancer, Here Come the Brides, Riverboat, Have Gun Will Travel, Matlock, Me and Mom, The Flash, Superboy, Babylon 5. Pilots: The Two of Us, Archie, Space Family Robinson. Host: Inside Space (SciFi Channel).

MURDOCH, RUPERT
Executive. b. Australia, March 11, 1931. Son of Sir Keith Murdoch, head of The Melbourne Herald and leading figure in Australian journalism. e. Oxford U., England. Spent two years on Fleet St. before returning home to take over family paper, The Adelaide News. Acquired more Australian papers and in 1969, expanded to Britain, buying The News of the World. Moved to U.S. in 1973, buying San Antonio Express and News. Conglomerate in 1985 included New York Post, New York Magazine, The Star, The Times of London, The Boston Herald, The Chicago Sun-Times along with TV stations, book publishing companies, airline, oil and gas companies, etc. 1985, made deal to buy 20th Century-Fox Film Corp. from owner Martin Davis. Sold the NY Post, 1988 to conform with FCC regulations. Purchased Triangle Publications 1988 (including TV Guide).

MURPHY, BEN
Actor. b. Jonesboro, AR, March 6, 1942. e. U. of Illinois. Degree in drama from Pasadena Playhouse. Acted in campus productions and toured in summer stock. Film debut with small role in The Graduate, 1967.
PICTURES: Yours Mine and Ours, The Thousand Plane Raid, Sidecar Racers, Time Walker.
TELEVISION: Series: The Name of the Game, Alias Smith and Jones, Griff, Gemini Man, The Chisholms, Lottery!, Berrenger's, The Dirty Dozen. Movies: The Letters, Wild Bill Hickock, Bridger, Heat Wave, Runaway, This Is the West That Was, Gemini Man, Hospital Fire, The Cradle Will Fall, Stark: Mirror Image. Mini-Series: The Winds of War.

MURPHY, EDDIE
Actor. b. Brooklyn, NY, Apr. 3, 1961. e. Roosevelt High Sch. Wrote and performed own comedy routines at youth centers and local bars at age 15. Worked on comedy club circuit; at 19 joined TV's Saturday Night Live as writer and performer. Recordings: Eddie Murphy, Eddie Murphy: Comedian, How Could It Be?, Love's Alright. Voted Top-Money Making Star of 1988 on Quigley Poll, NATO/ShoWest Star of the Decade, for 1980's.
PICTURES: 48 HRS. (debut, 1982), Trading Places, Best Defense, Beverly Hills Cop, The Golden Child, Beverly Hills Cop II, Eddie Murphy Raw (also s.p.; exec. prod.), Coming to America (also story), Harlem Nights (also dir., s.p, exec. prod.), Another 48 HRS., Boomerang (also story), The Distinguished Gentleman, Beverly Hills Cop III, Vampire in Brooklyn (also co-prod.), The Nutty Professor (also co-exec. prod.).
TELEVISION: Series: Saturday Night Live (1981-84). Pilots (exec. prod.): What's Alan Watching? (also cameo), Coming to America. Movie (exec. prod.): The Kid Who Loved Christmas.

MURPHY, LAWRENCE P.
Executive. Exec. v.p. of strategic planning & development, The Walt Disney Company.

MURPHY, MICHAEL
Actor. b. Los Angeles, CA, May 5, 1938. e. U. of Arizona. m. actress Wendy Crewson. Taught English and Drama in L.A. city school system, 1962-64. N.Y. stage debut as director of Rat's Nest, 1978.

PICTURES: Double Trouble (debut, 1967), Countdown, The Legend of Lylah Clare, The Arrangement, That Cold Day in the Park, M*A*S*H, Count Yorga: Vampire, Brewster McCloud, McCabe and Mrs. Miller, What's Up Doc?, The Thief Who Came to Dinner, Phase IV, Nashville, The Front, An Unmarried Woman, The Great Bank Hoax, The Class of Miss MacMichael, Manhattan, The Year of Living Dangerously, Strange Behavior, Cloak and Dagger, Salvador, Mesmerized, Shocker, Folks!, Batman Returns, Clean Slate, Bad Company, Kansas City.
TELEVISION: Series: Two Marriages, Hard Copy. Guest: Saints and Sinners, Ben Casey, Dr. Kildare, Bonanza, Combat. Movies: The Autobiography of Miss Jane Pittman, The Caine Mutiny Court-Martial, Tailspin: Behind the Korean Airlines Tragedy. Specials: John Cheever's Oh Youth and Beauty, Tanner '88.

MURPHY, THOMAS S.
Executive. e. Cornell Univ (B.S.M.E.), Harvard U. Grad. Sch. of Bus. Admin. (M.B.A.). Joined Capital Cities at its inception in 1954. Named a dir. in 1957, then pres. in 1964. Chmn. & CEO of Capital Cities, 1966-90. Company named Capital Cities/ABC Inc. in 1986 after acquistion of American Broadcasting Companies Inc. 1990-94, chmn. of bd. Resumed position of chmn. & CEO in Feb., 1994.

MURRAY, BARBARA
Actress. b. London, England, Sept. 27, 1929. Stage debut in Variety, 1946.
PICTURES: Badger's Green (debut, 1948), Passport to Pimlico, Don't Ever Leave Me, Boys in Brown, Poets Pub, Tony Draws a Horse, Dark Man, Frightened Man, Mystery Junction, Another Man's Poison, Hot Ice, Street Corner (Both Sides of the Law), Meet Mr. Lucifer, Doctor at Large, Campbell's Kingdom, A Cry from the Streets, Girls in Arms, A Dandy in Aspic, Tales From the Crypt.
TELEVISION: Series: The Power Game, The Bretts.

MURRAY, BILL
Actor. b. Wilmette, IL, Sept. 21, 1950. e. attended Regis Coll. Was pre-med student; left to join brother, Brian Doyle-Murray, in Second City the Chicago improvisational troupe. Appeared with brother on radio in National Lampoon Radio Hour, and in off-B'way revue, National Lampoon Show. Also on radio provided voice of Johnny Storm the Human Torch on Marvel Comics' Fantastic Four. Hired by ABC for Saturday Night Live with Howard Cosell; then by NBC for Saturday Night Live, 1977.
PICTURES: Jungle Burger (debut, 1975), Meatballs, Mr. Mike's Mondo Video, Where the Buffalo Roam, Loose Shoes (Coming Attractions), Caddyshack, Stripes, Tootsie, Ghostbusters, The Razor's Edge (also co-s.p.), Nothing Lasts Forever, Little Shop of Horrors, Scrooged, Ghostbusters II, Quick Change (also co-dir., co-prod.), What About Bob?, Groundhog Day, Mad Dog and Glory, Ed Wood, Space Jam, Larger Than Life, Kingpin.
TELEVISION: Series: Saturday Night Live (1977-80; also writer; Emmy Award for writing 1977). Pilot: The TV TV Show. Movie: All You Need Is Cash. Specials: It's Not Easy Being Me—The Rodney Dangerfield Show, Steve Martin's Best Show Ever, Second City—25 Years in Revue.

MURRAY, DON
Actor, Director, Writer. b. Hollywood, CA, July 31, 1929. e. AADA. Mother was a Ziegfeld Girl, father was dance dir. for Fox Studio.
THEATER: B'way: Insect Comedy, The Rose Tattoo, The Skin of Our Teeth, The Hot Corner, Smith (musical), The Norman Conquests, Same Time Next Year. National tours: California Suite, Chicago.
PICTURES: Bus Stop (debut, 1956; Acad. Award nom.), The Bachelor Party, A Hatful of Rain, From Hell to Texas, These Thousand Hills, Shake Hands With the Devil, One Foot in Hell, The Hoodlum Priest (also co-prod., co-s.p. as Don Deer), Advise and Consent, Escape From East Berlin, One Man's Way, Baby the Rain Must Fall, Kid Rodelo, The Plainsman, Sweet Love Bitter, The Viking Queen, Childish Things (Confession of Tom Harris; also prod., co-s.p.), The Cross and the Switchblade (dir., co-s.p. only), Happy Birthday Wanda June, Conquest of the Planet of the Apes, Cotter, Call Me by My Rightful Name (also prod., co-s.p.), Deadly Hero, Damien (dir., s.p. only), Endless Love, I Am the Cheese, Radioactive Dreams, Peggy Sue Got Married, Scorpion, Made in Heaven, Ghosts Can't Do It.
TELEVISION: Series: Made in America (panelist), The Outcasts, Knots Landing, Brand New Life, Sons and Daughters. Movies: The Borgia Stick, Daughter of the Mind, The Intruders, The Girl on the Late Late Show, The Sex Symbol, A Girl Named Sooner, Rainbow, Crisis in Mid-Air, If Things Were Different, The Boy Who Drank to Much, Fugitive Family, Return of the Rebels, Thursday's Child, Quarterback Princess, License to Kill, A Touch of Scandal, Something in Common, Stillwatch, The Stepford Children, Mistress, Brand New Life. Specials: For I Have Loved Strangers (also writer), Hasty Heart, Billy Budd, Winterset, Alas Babylon, Justin Morgan Had a Horse, My Dad Isn't Crazy Is He?, Montana Crossroads (Emmy nom.)

MURRAY, JAN
Comedian, Actor. b. Bronx, NY, Oct. 4, 1917. Started as comedian, nightclub performer, continuing on radio, tv.
THEATER: A Funny Thing Happened on the Way to the Forum, Guys and Dolls, Silk Stockings, Bye Bye Birdie, A Thousand Clowns, Come Blow Your Horn, The Odd Couple, Make a Million, Don't Drink the Water, Critic's Choice, You Know I Can't Hear You When the Water Is Running.
PICTURES: Who Killed Teddy Bear? (debut, 1965), Tarzan and the Great River, The Busy Body, A Man Called Dagger, Which Way to the Front?, History of the World Part I, Fear City.
TELEVISION: Series (emcee/host): Songs for Sale, Go Lucky, Sing It Again, Blind Date, Dollar a Second (also creator, prod.), Jan Murray Time, Treasure Hunt (also creator, prod.), Charge Account (also creator, prod.), Chain Letter. Guest: Zane Grey Theatre, Dr., Kildare, Burke's Law, The Lucy Show, Love American Style, Mannix, Ellery Queen, Hardcastle and McCormick. Movies: Roll Freddy Roll, Banjo Hackett: Roamin' Free, The Dream Merchants.

MUSANTE, TONY
Actor. b. Bridgeport, CT, June 30. e. Oberlin Coll. B.A. Directed local theatre, then appeared off-Broadway, in regional theater, and on Dupont Show of the Month (Ride With Terror).
THEATER: B'way: The Lady From Dubuque, P.S. Your Cat Is Dead, 27 Wagons Full of Cotton, Memory of Two Mondays. Off-B'way: Grand Magic, Cassatt, A Gun Play, Benito Cereno, L'Histoire du Soldat, Match-Play, The Zoo Story, The Pinter Plays (The Collection), Kiss Mama, The Balcony, Snow Orchid, The Flip Side, Frankie and Johnny in the Claire de Lune. Regional: The Big Knife, A Streetcar Named Desire, The Taming of the Shrew, Widows, The Archbishop's Ceiling, Dancing in the Endzone, Two Brothers, Souvenir, APA Shakespeare Rep., Wait Until Dark, Anthony Rose, Mount Allegro, Double Play, Falling Man, Breaking Legs, Love Letters, others. Regional: The Sisters, Italian Funerals and Other Festive Occasions.
PICTURES: Once a Thief, The Incident, The Detective, The Mercenary, The Bird with the Crystal Plumage, The Grissom Gang, The Last Run, Anonymous Venetian, Collector's Item, The Repenter, The Pisciotta Case, Goodbye and Amen, Break Up, Nocturne, The Pope of Greenwich Village, One Night at Dinner, Appointment in Trieste, Devil's Hill.
TELEVISION: Series: Toma. Guest: Chrysler Theatre, Alfred Hitchcock Hour, N.Y.P.D., The Fugitive, Trials of O'Brien, Police Story, Medical Story, Thomas Gottschallk's Late Night TV. Movies: Rearview Mirror, The Court Martial of Lt. William Calley, Desperate Miles, The Quality of Mercy, Nowhere to Hide, My Husband is Missing, The Story of Esther, High Ice, Last Waltz on a Tightrope, Weekend (Amer. Playhouse), Nutcracker: Money Madness & Murder, Breaking Up Is Hard To Do, The Baron.

MYERS, JULIAN F.
Public Relations Executive. b. Detroit, MI, Feb. 22, 1918. e. Wayne U., 1935-37, USC, 1937-39. Distribution, Loew's Detroit, 1941-42; asst. story editor, idea man, Columbia, 1942-46; publicist, 20th Century-Fox, 1948-62; public relations, Julian F. Myers, Inc., 1962; pres., Myers Studios, Inc., 1966; pres., New Horizons Broadcasting Corp., 1968-69; sr. publicist American Intl. Pictures, 1970-80. Pres., Hollywood Press Club; former member Variety Club; Academy of Motion Pictures Arts & Sciences; Board of Governors Film Industry Workshops, Inc. 1977, 1979, western v.p., Publicists Guild; Recipient of Publicists Guild's Robert Yeager Award. First male member Hollywood Women's Press Club. Co-founder HANDS (Hollywood Answering Needs of Disaster Survivors). Member, M.P. Pioneers. Winner, 1980 Publicists Guild Les Mason Award. Instructor in publicity, UCLA, 1979-present, and at Loyola Marymount U, 1991-present. Filmways Pictures, pub. dept. 1980-81. Exec. v.p., worldwide m.p. and TV pub./mktg., Hanson & Schwam Public Relations 1981-91. Author of Myersystem and Myerscope guides. Member: USC Cinema & TV Alumni Assn., West Coast P.R. Will Rogers Inst., Acad. TV Arts Sciences; p.r. co-ord. committee Academy of Motion Picture Arts & Sciences. Bd. of Dirs., Show Biz Expo. Publicist, Prods. Guild of America. Pres. Julian Myers Public Relations, nominated MoPic Showmanship of the Year, Publicists Guild of America, 1993.

MYERS, PETER S.
Executive. b. Toronto, Ont., Canada, May 13, 1923. e. U. of Toronto. Toronto branch mgr., 20th Century-Fox, 1948; mng. dir., Canada, 1951; gen. sales mgr. in charge of domestic distrib., US & Canada, 1968; sr. v.p., 20th-Fox Ent.; pres., 20th-Fox Classics, 1983; pres., Hemdale Releasing Corp., 1986; pres. & CEO, Four Seasons Entertainment, 1989.

MYERS, STANLEY
Composer. b. London, England, 1939.
PICTURES: Kaleidoscope (debut, 1966), Ulysses, No Way to Treat a Lady, Michael Kohlhaas, Otley, Two Gentlemen Sharing, Take a Girl Like You, Tropic of Cancer, The Walking Stick, Long Ago Tomorrow, A Severed Head, Tam Lin, King Queen Knave, Sitting Target, Summer Lightning, X Y & Zee, The Blockhouse, The Apprenticeship of Duddy Kravitz, Caravan to Vaccares,

Little Malcolm, The Wilby Conspiracy, Coup de Grace, The Greek Tycoon, The Deer Hunter, The Class of Miss MacMichael, A Portrait of the Artist as a Young Man, The Secret Policeman's Other Ball, Yesterday's Hero, Watcher in the Woods, Absolution, The Incubus, Lady Chatterly's Lover, Eureka, Moonlighting, Blind Date, Beyond the Limit, The Next One, Success is the Best Revenge, The Chain, Dreamchild, Insignificance, The Lightship, The Wind, Castaway, My Beautiful Laundrette, Prick Up Your Ears, Wish You Were Here, The Second Victory, Taffin, Track 29, Stars and Bars, Trading Hearts, Sammy and Rosie Get Laid, Scenes From the Class Struggle in Beverly Hills, Torrents of Spring.
TELEVISION: Series (U.K.): Widows (parts 1 & 2), Nancy Astor, Diana. Series (U.S.): The Martian Chronicles, Florence Nightingale. Movies: Strong Medicine, Smart Money, Baja Oklahoma, Monte Carlo.

MYERSON, BERNARD
Executive. b. New York, NY, March 25, 1918. Entered m.p. ind. with Fabian Theatres, 1938-63; last position as exec. v.p.; joined Loew's Theatres as v.p., 1963; exec. v.p. and board member, Loew's Corp.; pres. Loew's Theatres, 1971. Chmn. & pres., Loews Theatre Management Corp., 1985, presently retired. Member of Executive Committee Greater N.Y. Chapter, National Foundation of March of Dimes; Honorary chmn., bd. mem., & former pres., Will Rogers Memorial Fund; exec. comm., bd., National Assn. Theatre Owners; bd. member & former pres., Motion Picture Pioneers; treas. Variety Intl.; member bd. of dirs., Burke Rehabilitation Center; member, N.Y.S. Governor's Council on M.P. & T.V. Development; vice-chmn., adv. bd. of Tisch Sch. of Arts, NYU.

N

NABORS, JIM
Actor. b. Sylacauga, AL, June 12, 1932. Discovered performing in an L.A. nightclub in early 1960's by Andy Griffith, who asked him to appear on his series. Developed a second career as a singer. Between 1966-72 had 12 albums on best selling charts.
PICTURES: The Best Little Whorehouse in Texas, Stroker Ace, Cannonball Run II.
TELEVISION: Series: The Andy Griffith Show, Gomer Pyle USMC, The Jim Nabors Hour, The Lost Saucer, The Jim Nabors Show (synd. talk show). Movie: Return to Mayberry.

NADER, GEORGE
Actor. b. Pasadena, CA, Oct. 19, 1921. e. Occidental Coll., B.A.; Pasadena Playhouse, B.T.A. Served in U.S. Navy. Wrote novel: Chrome (Putnam).
PICTURES: Monsoon (debut, 1953), Memory of Love, Robot Monster, Rustlers on Horseback, Overland Telegraph, Carnival Story, Miss Robin Crusoe, Sins of Jezebel, Phone Call from a Stranger, Four Guns to the Border, Six Bridges to Cross, Lady Godiva, The Second Greatest Sex, Away All Boats, Appointment With a Shadow, Congo Crossing, The Unguarded Moment, Four Girls in Town, Man Afraid, The Female Animal, Flood Tide, Joe Butterfly, Nowhere to Go, The Secret Mark of D'Artagnan, The Great Space Adventure, Zigzag, The Human Duplicators, House of a Thousand Dolls, The Million Eyes of Sumuru, Alarm on 83rd Street, Murder at Midnight, Count-Down for Manhattan, Dynamite in Green Silk, The Check and an Icy Smile, Murder Club from Brooklyn, Death in Red Jaguar, End Station of the Damned, Beyond Atlantis.
TELEVISION: Series: Ellery Queen, Man and the Challenge, Shannon. Guest: Letter to Loretta, Fireside Theatre, Chevron Theatre, Alfred Hitchcock, Andy Griffith Show, etc. Movie: Nakia.

NAIFY, MARSHALL
Executive. Chairman, Todd-AO/Glenn Studios.

NAIFY, ROBERT
Executive. b. Sacramento, CA. e. Attended Stanford U. Worked for United California Theatres starting in 1946 in various capacities including: theatre manager, purchasing agent, film buyer, general manager and president. 1963 became exec. v.p. United Artists Communications; 1971 became pres. & CEO until 1987. Currently president, Todd-AO Corporation.

NAIR, MIRA
Director, Producer. b. Bhubaneswar, India, 1957. e. Irish Catholic Missionary School in India, Delhi U., Harvard U. A course in documentary filmmaking at Harvard led to directing 4 non-fiction films including India Cabaret (1985) and Children of Desired Sex.
PICTURES: Director-Producer: Salaam Bombay! (Cannes Film Fest. Camera d'Or/Prix du Publique; Acad. Award nom.), Mississippi Masala (also s.p.), The Perez Family.

NALLE, BILLY
Theatre Concert Organist, Composer. b. Fort Myers, FL, Apr. 24, 1921. Postgrad, Juilliard Sch. Over 5,000 major tele-

casts from NY; now artist emeritus, Wichita Theatre Organization, Inc. RCA, Telarc, Reader's Digest & WTO Records Artist. Now residing in Fort Myers, FL.

NAMATH, JOE
Actor. b. Beaver Falls, PA, May 31, 1943. e. U. of Alabama. Former professional football star.
PICTURES: Norwood (debut, 1970), C.C. & Company (Chrome Hearts), The Last Rebel, Avalanche Express, Chattanooga Choo Choo, Going Under.
TELEVISION: *Series*: The Waverly Wonders. *Host*: Monday Night Football (1985). *Movie*: Marriage Is Alive and Well. *Guest*: Here's Lucy, The Brady Bunch, The Love Boat, Kate and Allie.

NARDINO, GARY
Executive. b. Garfield, NJ, Aug. 26, 1935. e. Seton Hall U. Awarded honorary degree of Doctor of Laws. Entered industry in 1959 as agent, representing Lorimar Prods. and Talent Associates, among others. Named sr. v.p. of ICM's New York TV dept; then v.p. of William Morris Agency, heading N.Y. TV dept. Pres. of Paramount TV Production Division, 1977-83. Pres. of Gary Nardino Prods., Inc., formed 1983, to dev. and produce theatrical features and TV programming; 1988-90, chmn. & CEO, Orion Television Entertainment.
PICTURES: Star Trek III: The Search for Spock (exec. prod.), Fire with Fire (prod.).
TELEVISION: *Exec. prod.*: Brothers, At Your Service, Joanna.

NARIZZANO, SILVIO
Producer, Director. b. Montreal, Canada, Feb. 8, 1927. e. U. of Bishop's, Lennoxville, Quebec, B.A. Was active as actor-director in Canadian theatre before going to England for TV and theatrical film work.
PICTURES: *Director*: Under Ten Flags (co-dir.), Die! Die! My Darling! (Fanatic), Georgy Girl, Blue, Loot, Redneck (also prod.), The Sky Is Falling, Why Shoot the Teacher?, The Class of Miss MacMichael, Choices, Double Play. *Producer*: Negatives, Fadeout.
TELEVISION: Come Back Little Sheba, Staying On, Young Shoulders, Miss Marple (series).

NASH, N. RICHARD
Writer. b. Philadelphia, PA, June 8, 1913.
AUTHOR: Cry Macho, East Wind, Rain, The Last Magic, Aphrodite's Cave, Radiance, Behold the Man, The Wildwood.
THEATER: *B'way*: Second Best Bed, The Young and Fair, See the Jaguar, The Rainmaker, Girls of Summer, Handful of Fire, Wildcat, 110 in the Shade, Fire, The Happy Time, Echoes, Wildfire, The Torch, Magic, The Bluebird of Happiness, The Loss of D-Natural, Breaking the Tie, Come As You Are, Everybody Smile, Life Anonymous, The Green Clown.
PICTURES: Nora Prentiss, Welcome Stranger, The Vicious Years, The Rainmaker, Dear Wife, Porgy and Bess, Sainted Sisters, Dragonfly.
TELEVISION: Many TV plays for Television Playhouse, U.S. Steel, General Electric.

NAUGHTON, DAVID
Actor, Singer. b. Hartford, CT, Feb. 13, 1951. Brother is actor James Naughton. e. U. of Pennsylvania, B.A. Studied at London Acad. of Music and Dramatic Arts. Numerous TV commercials, including music for Dr. Pepper. On B'way in Hamlet, Da, Poor Little Lambs.
PICTURES: Midnight Madness (debut, 1980), An American Werewolf in London, Separate Ways, Hot Dog... The Movie, Not for Publication, The Boy in Blue, Separate Vacations, Kidnapped, Quite By Chance, Beanstalk, The Sleeping Car, Overexposed, Wild Cactus, Desert Steel, Ice Cream Man, Midnight Madness, The Boy In Blue.
TELEVISION: *Series*: Making It, At Ease, My Sister Sam, Temporary Insanity, The Belles of Bleeker St., Those Two. *Movies*: I Desire, Getting Physical, Goddess of Love. *Guest*: Twilight Zone, Murder She Wrote.

NAUGHTON, JAMES
Actor. b. Middletown, CT, Dec. 6, 1945. Father of actor Greg Naughton. e. Brown U., A.B., 1967; Yale U., M.F.A., drama, 1970.
THEATER: *NY*: I Love My Wife (B'way debut, 1977), Long Day's Journey Into Night (Theatre World, Drama Desk and New York Critics Circle Awards), 1971), Whose Life Is It Anyway?, Losing Time, Drinks Before Dinner, City of Angels (Tony & Drama Desk Awards, 1990), Four Baboons Adoring the Sun. Regional: Who's Afraid of Virginia Woolf? (Long Wharf), The Glass Menagerie (Long Wharf), Hamlet (Long Wharf), Julius Caesar (Amer. Shakespeare Festival), 8 seasons at Williamstown Theatre Festival.
PICTURES: The Paper Chase (debut, 1973), Second Wind, A Stranger is Watching, Cat's Eye, The Glass Menagerie, The Good Mother, First Kid.
TELEVISION: *Special*: Look Homeward Angel (1972). *Series*: Faraday and Company, Planet of the Apes, Making the Grade, Trauma Center, Raising Miranda, The Cosby Mysteries. *Movies*: F. Scott Fitzgerald and the Last of the Belles, The Last

36 Hours of Dr. Durant, The Bunker, My Body My Child, Parole, The Last of the Great Survivors, Between Darkness and the Dawn, Sin of Innocence, Traveling Man, Antigone, The Cosby Mysteries (pilot), The Birds II: Land's End, Cagney & Lacey: The Return, Cagney & Lacey: Together Again, Raising Caines.

NEAL, PATRICIA
Actress. b. Packard, KY, Jan. 20, 1926. e. Northwestern U. Worker as doctor's asst., cashier, hostess, model, jewelry store clerk prior to prof. career as actress. In summer stock before B'way debut in The Voice of the Turtle, 1946. Autobiography: As I Am (with Richard DeNeut, 1988).
THEATER: *NY*: The Voice of the Turtle, Another Part of the Forest (Tony, Donaldson & Drama Critic Awards), The Children's Hour, Roomful of Roses, The Miracle Worker. *England*: Suddenly Last Summer.
PICTURES: John Loves Mary (debut 1949), The Fountainhead, It's a Great Feeling, The Hasty Heart, Bright Leaf, Three Secrets, The Breaking Point, Raton Pass, Operation Pacific, The Day the Earth Stood Still, Weekend With Father, Diplomatic Courier, Washington Story, Something for the Birds, Stranger From Venus (Immediate Disaster), Your Woman, A Face in the Crowd, Breakfast at Tiffany's, Hud (Academy Award, BFA Award, 1963), Psyche '59, In Harm's Way (BFA Award, 1965), The Subject Was Roses (Acad. Award nom.), The Night Digger, Baxter, Happy Mother's Day Love George (Run Stranger Run), "B" Must Die, The Passage, Ghost Story, An Unremarkable Life.
TELEVISION: *Movies*: The Homecoming, Things in Their Season, Eric, Tail Gunner Joe, A Love Affair: The Eleanor and Lou Gehrig Story, The Bastard, All Quiet on the Western Front, Shattered Vows, Love Leads the Way, Caroline?, A Mother's Right: The Elizabeth Morgan Story, Heidi. *Guest*: Little House on the Prairie, Murder She Wrote. *BBC*: Days & Nights of Beebee Finstermaker, The Country Girl, Clash By Night, The Royal Family.

NEAME, RONALD
Cinematographer, Producer, Director. b. Hendon, Eng. April 23, 1911. e. U. Coll. Sch., London. p. Elwin Neame, London photog., & Ivy Close, m.p. actress. Entered m.p. ind. 1928; asst. cameraman on first full-length Brit. sound film, Blackmail, dir. by Alfred Hitchcock, 1929; became chief cameraman & lighting expert, 1934; in 1945 joint assoc. prod., Noel Coward Prods.
PICTURES: *Cinematographer*: Girls Will Be Boys (co-cine.), Happy (co-cine.), Elizabeth of England, Honours Easy (co-cine.), Invitation to the Waltz (co-cine.), Joy Ride, Music Hath Charms, The Crimes of Stephen Hawke, The Improper Dutchess, A Star Fell From Heaven, Against the Tide, Brief Ecstasy, Feather Your Nest, Keep Fit, Weekend Millionaire, Gaunt Stranger, The Phantom Strikes, The Crime of Peter Frame, Dangerous Secrets, I See Ice (co-cine.), Penny Paradise, Who Goes Next? Cheers Boys Cheer, Sweeney Todd: The Demon Barber of Fleet Street, Let's Be Famous, Trouble Brewing, The Ware Case, It's In the Air (co-cine.), Let George Do It, Return to Yesterday, Saloon Bar, Four Just Men, Major Barbara, A Yank in the R.A.F. (Brit. flying sequence), One of Our Aircraft is Missing, In Which We Serve, This Happy Breed, Blithe Spirit, Brief Encounter, Great Expectations (also co-s.p.), Oliver Twist (also co-s.p.), A Young Man's Fancy, Passionate Friends. *Director*: Take My Life, Golden Salamander (also co-s.p.), The Card (The Promoter; also prod.), Man With a Million (The Million Pound Note), The Man Who Never Was, The Seventh Sin, Windom's Way, The Horse's Mouth, Tunes of Glory, Escape from Zahrain, I Could Go on Singing, The Chalk Garden, Mister Moses, Gambit, A Man Could Get Killed (co-dir.), Prudence and the Pill (co-dir.), The Prime of Miss Jean Brodie, Scrooge, The Poseidon Adventure, The Odessa File, Meteor, Hopscotch, First Monday in October, Foreign Body, The Magic Balloon.

NEEDHAM, HAL
Director, Writer. b. Memphis, TN, March 6, 1931. e. Student public schools. Served with Paratroopers, U.S. Army 1951-54. Founder Stunts Unlimited, Los Angeles, 1970; stuntman Stunts Unlimited, 1956-65; dir. and stunt coordinator second unit, 1965-75. Chmn. of bd., Camera Platforms International, Inc. 1985. Owner Budweiser Rocket Car (fastest car in the world). Member Screen Actors Guild, AFTRA, Writers Guild of America, Directors Guild of America.
PICTURES: *Dir.*: Smokey and the Bandit (debut, 1977; also co-story), Hooper, The Villain, Smokey and the Bandit II, The Cannonball Run, Megaforce (also co-s.p.), Stroker Ace (also co-s.p.), Cannonball Run II (also co-s.p.), RAD, Body Slam.
TELEVISION: *Series*: Hal Needham's Wild World of Stunts (synd. series; also writer, star). *Movie*: Death Car on the Freeway. *Pilot*: Stunts Unlimited (pilot). *Episode*: B.L. Stryker.

NEESON, LIAM
Actor. b. Ballymena, Northern Ireland, June 7, 1952. m. actress Natasha Richardson. Former amateur boxer. Was driving

a fork lift truck for a brewery when he joined the Lyric Player's Theatre in Belfast. Made prof. debut in The Risen (1976) and stayed with rep. co. 2 years. Moved to Dublin as freelance actor before joining the Abbey Theatre.
THEATER: The Informer (Dublin Theatre Fest.), Translations (National Theatre, London). NY theatre debut 1992 in Anna Christie (Theatre World Award).
PICTURES: Excalibur (debut, 1981), Krull, The Bounty, Lamb, The Innocent, The Mission, Duet For One, A Prayer for the Dying, Suspect, Satisfaction, The Dead Pool, The Good Mother, High Spirits, Next of Kin, Dark Man, Crossing the Line (The Big Man), Shining Through, Under Suspicion, Husbands and Wives, Leap of Faith, Ethan Frome, Deception, Schindler's List (Acad. Award nom.), Nell, Rob Roy, Before and After, Michael Collins.
TELEVISION: Merlin and the Sword, Across the Water (BBC), Ellis Island, A Woman of Substance, Sweet As You Are.

NEILL, SAM
Actor. b. Northern Ireland, Sept. 14, 1947. Raised in New Zealand. e. U. of Canterbury. In repertory before joining N.Z. National Film Unit, acting and directing documentaries and shorts. 1992, awarded the O.B.E. for his services to acting. Co-directed, co-wrote and appeared in New Zealand documentary Cinema of Unease: A Personal Journey by Sam Neill.
PICTURES: Sleeping Dogs (debut, 1977), The Journalist, My Brilliant Career, Just Out of Reach, Attack Force Z, The Final Conflict, Possession, Enigma, Le Sang des Autres, Robbery Under Arms, Plenty, For Love Alone, The Good Wife, A Cry in the Dark (Australian Film Inst. Award), Dead Calm, The French Revolution, The Hunt for Red October, Until the End of the World, Hostage, Memoirs of an Invisible Man, Death in Brunswick, Jurassic Park, The Piano, Sirens, Rudyard Kipling's The Jungle Book, In the Mouth of Madness, Country Life, Restoration, Victory.
TELEVISION: The Sullivans, Young Ramsay, Lucinda Brayford, The Country Girls. Mini-Series: Kane and Abel, Reilly Ace of Spies, Amerika. Movies: From a Far Country: Pope John Paul II, Ivanhoe, The Blood of Others, Arthur Hailey's Strong Medicine, Leap of Faith, Fever, One Against the Wind, The Sinking of the Rainbow Warrior, Family Pictures.

NELLIGAN, KATE
Actress. b. London, Ontario, Canada, March 16, 1951.
THEATER: Barefoot in the Park, A Streetcar Named Desire, Playboy of the Western World, Private Lives, Plenty, Serious Money, Spoils of War, Bad Habits.
PICTURES: The Romantic Englishwoman (debut, 1975), Dracula, Mr. Patman, Eye of the Needle, Without a Trace, The Mystery of Henry Moore, Eleni, Frankie and Johnny (BAFTA Award), The Prince of Tides (Acad. Award nom.), Shadows and Fog, Fatal Instinct, Wolf, Margaret's Museum, How to Make an American Quilt, Up Close and Personal.
TELEVISION: Movies/Specials: The Onedin Line, The Lady of the Camelias, Therese Raquin, Count of Monte Cristo, Victims, Kojak: The Price of Justice, Love and Hate: The Story of Colin and Joann Thatcher, Three Hotels, Terror Strikes the Class Reunion, Diamond Fleece, Liar Liar, Shattered Trust: The Shari Karney Story, Spoils of War, Million Dollar Babies.

NELSON, BARRY
Actor. r.n. Robert Neilson. b. Oakland, CA, Apr. 16, 1920. e. U. of California. London stage in No Time for Sergeants, 1957.
THEATER: B'way: Light Up the Sky, The Rat Race, The Moon Is Blue, Mary Mary, Cactus Flower, Everything in the Garden, Seascape, The Norman Conquests, The Act, 42nd Street.
PICTURES: Shadow of the Thin Man, Johnny Eager, Dr. Kildare's Victory, Rio Rita, Eyes in the Night, Bataan, The Human Comedy, A Guy Named Joe, Winged Victory, The Beginning or the End, Undercover Maisie, The Man With My Face, The First Traveling Saleslady, Mary Mary, Airport, Pete 'n' Tillie, The Shining, Island Claws.
TELEVISION: Series: The Hunter, My Favorite Husband. Mini-Series: Washington: Behind Closed Doors. Movies: The Borgia Stick, Seven in Darkness, Climb an Angry Mountain. Guest: Suspense, Alfred Hitchcock Presents, Longstreet, Taxi, Magnum P.I., Murder She Wrote.

NELSON, CRAIG T.
Actor. b. Spokane, WA, April 4, 1946. Began career as writer/performer on Lohman and Barkley Show in Los Angeles. Teamed with Barry Levinson as a comedy writer. Wrote for Tim Conway Show, Alan King TV special; guest appearances on talk shows and Mary Tyler Moore Show. Produced series of 52 half-hour films on American artists, American Still. Returned to L.A. in 1978 and acting career.
PICTURES: And Justice for All (debut, 1979), Where the Buffalo Roam, Private Benjamin, Stir Crazy, The Formula, Poltergeist, Man Woman and Child, All the Right Moves, The Osterman Weekend, Silkwood, The Killing Fields, Poltergeist II, Red Riding Hood, Action Jackson, Rachel River, Me and Him, Troop Beverly Hills, Turner & Hooch, I'm Not Rappaport, Ghosts of Mississippi.

TELEVISION: Series: Call to Glory, Coach (Emmy Award, 1992).Guest: Wonder Woman, Charlie's Angels, How the West Was Won. Movies: Diary of a Teenage Hitchhiker, Rage, Promise of Love, Inmates: A Love Story, Chicago Story, Paper Dolls, Alex: The Life of a Child, The Ted Kennedy Jr. Story, Murderers Among Us, The Simon Wiesenthal Story, Extreme Close-Up, The Josephine Baker Story, The Switch, The Fire Next Time, Ride With the Wind (also co-writer), Probable Cause, Take Me Home Again. Mini-Series: Drug Wars: The Camarena Story.

NELSON, DAVID
Actor. b. New York, NY, Oct. 24, 1936. e. Hollywood H.S., U. of Southern California. Son of Ozzie Nelson and Harriet Hilliard Nelson; brother of late Rick Nelson.
PICTURES: Here Comes the Nelsons, Peyton Place, The Remarkable Mr. Pennypacker, Day of the Outlaw, The Big Circus, "30," The Big Show, No Drums No Bugles, Cry-Baby.
Director: A Rare Breed, The Last Plane Out.
TELEVISION: Series: The Adventures of Ozzie and Harriet (also dir. episodes). Movies: Smash-Up on Interstate 5, High School U.S.A. Guest: Hondo, The Love Boat. Dir.: Easy To Be Free (special), OK Crackerby (series).

NELSON, GENE
Dancer, Actor, Director, Choreographer. r.n. Gene Berg. b. Seattle, WA, March 24, 1920. e. Santa Monica, CA, H.S. Began dancing and ice skating in school; joined Sonja Henie Hollywood Ice Revue, featured in It Happens on Ice in NY; served in WWII. Joined Hollywood group prod. stage musical, Lend an Ear; to Warner for Daughter of Rosie O'Grady (1950). Prof. of Theatre Arts at San Francisco State U. School of Creative Arts, 1989-90.
THEATER: B'way: Actor. Lend an Ear, Follies, The Music Music, Good News. Director: Follies, Elephant Man, Oklahoma!, Stepping Out.
PICTURES: Actor: This Is the Army (debut, 1943), I Wonder Who's Kissing Her Now, Gentleman's Agreement, Apartment For Peggy, The Daughter of Rosie O'Grady, Tea for Two, Starlift, The West Point Story, Lullaby of Broadway, Painting the Clouds With Sunshine, She's Back on Broadway, Three Sailors and a Girl, Crime Wave, So This Is Paris, Oklahoma!, The Way Out (Dial 999), The Atomic Man (Timeslip), 20,000 Eyes, The Purple Hills, Thunder Island, S.O.B. Director: The Hand of Death, Hootenany Hoot, Your Cheatin' Heart, Kissin' Cousins, Harum Scarum, The Cool Ones (also s.p.).
TELEVISION: Series Director: Mod Squad, I Dream of Jeannie, FBI, 12 O'Clock High, Hawaii Five-O, Farmer's Daughter, Donna Reed Show, Burke's Law, Felony Squad, Laredo, The Rifleman, The Wackiest Ship, Iron Horse, FBI, The Rookies, Quincy, Operation Petticoat. Movies (Director): Wake Me When the War is Over (also co-prod.), The Letters. Movies (Actor): Family Flight, A Brand New Life.

NELSON, JUDD
Actor. b. Portland, ME, Nov. 28, 1959. e. Haverford/Bryn Mawr Coll. Studied acting at Stella Adler Conservatory. NY theatre includes Carnal Knowledge.
PICTURES: Making the Grade (debut, 1984), Fandango, The Breakfast Club, St. Elmo's Fire, Blue City, Transformers (voice), From the Hip, Relentless, Far Out Man, New Jack City, The Dark Backward, Primary Motive, Entangled, Conflict of Interest, Caroline at Midnight, Hail Caesar, Every Breath (also s.p.), Flinch, Circumstances Unknown, Blackwater Trail.
TELEVISION: Series: Suddenly Susan. Guest: Moonlighting. Movies: Billionaire Boys Club, Hiroshima: Out of the Ashes, Conflict of Interest, Blindfold: Acts of Obsession.

NELSON, LORI
Actress. r.n. Dixie Kay Nelson. b. Santa Fe, NM, Aug. 15, 1933. e. Canoga Park H.S. Started as child actress, photographer's model before film debut in 1952.
THEATER: The Pleasure of His Company, Who Was That Lady I Saw You With, Affairs of Mildred Wilde, Sweet Bird of Youth, Picnic, 'Night Mother.
PICTURES: Ma and Pa Kettle at the Fair (debut, 1952), Bend of the River, Francis Goes to West Point, All I Desire, All-American, Walking My Baby Back Home, Tumbleweed, Underwater, Destry, Revenge of the Creature, I Died a Thousand Times, Sincerely Yours, Mohawk, Day the World Ended, Pardners, Hot Rod Girl, Ma and Pa Kettle at Waikiki, Gambling Man, Untamed Youth.
TELEVISION: Series: How to Marry a Millionaire. Guest: Wagon Train, Laramie, Family Affair, The Texan, Wanted Dead or Alive, Sam Spade, G.E. Theatre, Riverboat, Sugarfoot, The Young and the Restless, Climax, The Millionaire, Wells Fargo, etc. Special: The Pied Piper of Hamelin.

NELSON, TRACY
Actress, Singer, Dancer. b. Santa Monica, CA, Oct., 1963. e. Bard Coll. Daughter of late singer-actor Rick Nelson. Sister of singers Matthew & Gunnar Nelson. Studied acting in England.
THEATER: Grease (Nat'l touring co. & B'way).

PICTURES: Yours Mine and Outs (debut, 1968), Maria's Lovers, Down and Out in Beverly Hills, Chapters.
TELEVISION: *Series*: Square Pegs, Glitter, Father Dowling Mysteries, A League of Their Own, Melrose Place, The Man from Snowy River. *Movies*: Katie's Secret, Tonight's the Night, If It's Tuesday It Still Must Be Belgium, Fatal Confessions, For Hope, In the Shadow of Evil, Pleasures, Highway Heartbreaker, Ray Alexander: Murder in Mind, Ray Alexander: A Taste for Justice, No Child of Mine. *Guest*: The Adventures of Ozzie and Harriet, Hotel, Family Ties, The Love Boat.

NELSON, WILLIE
Composer, Singer, Actor. b. Abbott, TX, April 30, 1933. Worked as salesman, announcer, host of country music shows on local Texas stations; bass player with Ray Price's band. Started writing songs in the 60's; performing in the 70's.
PICTURES: The Electric Horseman (debut, 1979), Honeysuckle Rose, Thief, Barbarosa, Hell's Angels Forever, Songwriter, Red-Headed Stranger (also prod.), Walking After Midnight.
TELEVISION: *Movies*: The Last Days of Frank and Jesse James, Stagecoach, Coming Out of the Ice, Baja Oklahoma, Once Upon a Texas Train, Where the Hell's That Gold?!!?, Pair of Aces, Another Pair of Aces, Wild Texas Wind, Big Dreams & Broken Hearts: The Dottie West Story. *Special*: Willie Nelson—Texas Style (also prod.).

NEMEC, CORIN
Actor. r.n. Joseph Charles Nemec IV. b. Little Rock, AR, Nov. 5, 1971. Began acting in commercials at age 13.
PICTURES: Tucker: The Man and His Dream, Solar Crisis, Drop Zone, Operation Dumbo Drop.
TELEVISION: *Series*: Parker Lewis Can't Lose. *Movies*: I Know My First Name is Steven (Emmy nom.), For the Very First Time, My Son Johnny, The Lifeforce Experiment. *Mini-Series*: The Stand. *Pilot*: What's Alan Watching? *Guest*: Webster, Sidekicks.

NERO, FRANCO
Actor. r.n. Franceso Sparanero. b. Parma, Italy, Nov. 23, 1942. e. Univ. La Bocconi, Milan.
PICTURES: Celestina (Made at Your Service; debut, 1964), The Deadly Diaphanoids, I Knew Her Well, Wild Wild Planet, The Third Eyes, The Bible, The Tramplers, Django, The Avenger (Texas Addio), Hired Killer, The Brute and the Beast, Mafia, Camelot, L'uomo l'Orgoglio la Vendetta, Island of Crime, The Mercenary, The Day of the Owl, A Quiet Place in the Country, The Battle of Neretva, Detective Belli, Sardinia: Ramsom, Companeros, Tristana, The Virgin and the Gypsy, Drop Out!, Confessions of a Police Commissioner, Killer From Yuma, Redneck, The Monk, The Vacation, Pope Joan, Deaf Smith and Johnny Ears, The Fifth Day of Peace, The Aquarian, High Crime, Blood Brothers (I Guappi), Cry Onion, The Anonymous Avenger, Challenge to White Fang, Death Drive, Violent Breed, Submission, The Last Days of Mussolini, Force Ten From Navarone, The Man With Bogart's Face, The Visitor, Shark Hunter, Blue-Eyed Bandit, Danzig Roses, Day of the Cobra, The Falcon, The Salamander, Sahara Cross, Enter the Ninja, Mexico in Flames, Querelle, Wagner, Sweet Country, The Girl, Garibaldi the General, Race to Danger, Marathon, Django Strikes Again, Top Line, Silent Night, Young Toscanini, The Betrothed, The Magistrate, Heart of Victory, The Repenter, The Forester's Sons, Die Hard 2, Brothers and Sisters, Crimson Down, Oro, Deep Blue, The Lucona Affair, Babylon Complot, A Breath of Life, Jonathan of the Bears, Conflict of Interest, The Dragon's Ring, Talk of Angels, The Innocent Sleep, The King and Me.
TELEVISION: *Mini-series*: The Last Days of Pompeii. *Movies*: The Legend of Valentino, 21 Hours at Munich, The Pirate, Young Catherine.

NESMITH, MICHAEL
Musician, Producer. b. Houston, TX, Dec. 30, 1942. Original member of The Monkees, later became producer of videos and films. Chmn. & CEO Pacific Arts Publishing video company. Won Grammy award for music video Elephant Parts. Exec. prod. & performer in video Dr. Duck's Super Secret All-Purpose Sauce.
PICTURES: *Actor*: Head, Burglar (cameo). *Exec. Prod.*: Timerider (also co-s.p.), Repo Man, Square Dance, Tapeheads.
TELEVISION: *Series*: The Monkees, Michael Nesmith in Television Parts (also prod.). *Special*: 33-1/3 Revolutions Per Monkee.

NETTER, DOUGLAS
Executive, Producer. b. Seattle, WA. 1955-57, gen. mgr. Todd A.O.; 1958-60, Sam Goldwyn Productions; 1961-67, formed own co. representing producers; 1968-69, Jalem Productions; 1969-75, exec. v.p. MGM. Films: Mr. Ricco (prod.), The Wild Geese (co-prod.).
TELEVISION: Louis L'Amour's The Sacketts (prod.), The Buffalo Soldiers (exec. prod.), Wild Times (prod.),

Roughnecks (exec. prod.), Cherokee Trail (exec. prod.), Five Mile Creek (exec. prod.; Australian based TV series for Disney Channel), Captain Power and the Soldiers of the Future (exec. prod.), Stealth F22 (exec. prod.), Babylon 5 (exec. prod.).

NETTLETON, LOIS
Actress. b. Oak Park, IL, 1931. e. Studied at Goodman Theatre, Chicago and Actors Studio. Replaced Kim Hunter in Darkness at Noon on B'way. Emmy Award: Performer Best Daytime Drama Spec., The American Woman: Portraits in Courage (1977). Also Emmy: Religious Program, Insight (1983).
THEATER: Cat on a Hot Tin Roof, Silent Night, Lonely Night, God and Kate Murphy, The Wayward Stork, The Rainmaker, A Streetcar Named Desire.
PICTURES: A Face in the Crowd (debut, 1957), Period of Adjustment, Come Fly with Me, Mail Order Bride, Valley of Mystery, Bamboo Saucer, The Good Guys and the Bad Guys, Dirty Dingus Magee, The Sidelong Glances of a Pigeon Kicker, The Honkers, The Man in the Glass Booth, Echoes of a Summer, Deadly Blessing, Butterfly, Soggy Bottom U.S.A., The Best Little Whorehouse in Texas.
TELEVISION: *Series*: Accidental Family, You Can't Take It With You. *Guest*: Medical Center, Barnaby Jones, Alfred Hitchcock, All That Glitters, In the Heat of the Night. *Movies*: Any Second Now, Weekend of Terror, The Forgotten Man, Terror in the Sky, Women in Chains, Fear on Trial, Tourist, Brass, Manhunt for Claude Dallas. *Mini-Series*: Washington: Behind Closed Doors, Centennial. *Specials*: Rendezvous, Meet Me in St. Louis, Traveler's Rest.

NEUFELD, MACE
Producer. b. New York, NY, July 13, 1928. e. Yale Col. Started as professional photographer, before becoming prod. asst. at Dumont Television Network. Wrote musical material for performers incl. Sammy Davis Jr., Dorothy Loudon, Ritz Brothers, etc., and theme for Heckle and Jeckle animated series. In 1951, formed independent TV prod. and personal mgmt. co. For TV produced programs for Dick Van Dyke, Elaine May and Mike Nichols. Formed independent production co. with Nichols and Buck Henry. In 1980, created Neufeld-Davis Prods. with Marvin Davis. Formed Neufeld/Rehme Prods. with Robert G. Rehme in 1989. On B'way, prod. Flying Karamazov Brothers show. Voted Producer of the Year by NATO/ShoWest, 1992.
PICTURES: The Omen, Damien: Omen II, The Frisco Kid, The Funhouse, The Aviator, Transylvania 6-5000, No Way Out, The Hunt for Red October, Flight of the Intruder, Necessary Roughness, Patriot Games, Gettysburg, Beverly Hills Cop III, Clear and Present Danger.
TELEVISION: *Movies/Miniseries*: East of Eden, Angel on My Shoulder, American Dream, Cagney and Lacey (pilot), A Death in California. *Specials*: The Magic Planet, The Flying Karamazov Brothers.

NEUWIRTH, BEBE
Actress. b. Newark, NJ, Dec. 31. e. Juilliard. Started as chorus dancer.
THEATER: *NY*: Little Me, Dancin', Upstairs at O'Neal, The Road to Hollywood, Sweet Charity (Tony Award, 1986), Showing Off, Damn Yankees. *Tour*: A Chorus Line. *Regional*: Just So, Kicks (also choreog.), Chicago. *London*: Kiss of the Spider Woman.
PICTURES: Say Anything... (debut, 1989), Green Card, Bugsy, Paint Job, Malice, Jumanji, All Dogs Go to Heaven (voice), The Associate.
TELEVISION: *Series*: Cheers (2 Emmy Awards). *Movies*: Without Her Consent, Unspeakable Acts. *Mini-Series*: Wild Palms. *Guest*: Frasier.

NEWELL, MIKE
Director. b. St. Albans, England, 1942. e. Cambridge U. Took directorial training course at Granada Television.
PICTURES: The Awakening (debut, 1980), Bad Blood, Dance With a Stranger, The Good Father, Amazing Grace and Chuck, Common Ground, Enchanted April, Into the West, Four Weddings and a Funeral, An Awfully Big Adventure, Donnie Brasco.
TELEVISION: Baa Baa Black Sheep, Silver Wedding, Jill and Jack, Ready When You Are Mr. McGill, Lost Your Tongue, Mr. & Mrs. Bureaucrat, Just Your Luck, The Man in the Iron Mask, The Gift of Friendship, Destiny, Tales Out of School, Birth of a Nation, Blood Feud.

NEWHART, BOB
Actor, Comedian. b. Chicago, IL, Sept. 5, 1929. e. Loyola U. In Army 2 yrs., then law school; left to become copywriter and accountant. Acted with theatrical stock co. in Oak Park; hired for TV man-in-street show in Chicago. Recorded hit comedy album for Warner Bros., The Button-Down Mind of Bob Newhart (Grammy Award, 1960), followed by two more successful albums. Did series of nightclub engagements and then acquired own TV variety series in 1961. Grand Marshall: Tournament of Roses Parde, 1991. Inducted into TV Hall of Fame, 1993.

PICTURES: Hell Is for Heroes (debut, 1962), Hot Millions, Catch-22, On a Clear Day You Can See Forever, Cold Turkey, The Rescuers (voice), Little Miss Marker, First Family, The Rescuers Down Under (voice).
TELEVISION: *Series*: The Bob Newhart Show (1961-62, variety), The Entertainers, The Bob Newhart Show (1972-78, sitcom), Newhart, Bob. *Movies*: Thursday's Game, Marathon, The Entertainers.

NEWLAND, JOHN
Actor, Director. b. Cincinnati, OH, Nov. 23, 1917. Began as a singer-dancer in vaudeville and on B'way; many TV appearances, especially as host of One Step Beyond. Actor, dir., Robert Montgomery Show, My Lover, My Son. Turned to full-time dir. and prod. in the 1960's.
PICTURES: Bulldog Drummond, That Night, The Violators, The Spy With My Face, Hush-a-Bye Murder, Purgatory.
TELEVISION: *Series*: One Man's Family, Robert Montgomery Presents, Alcoa Presents: One Step Beyond (host), The Next Step Beyond (host, prod.). *Guest*: Philco TV Playhouse, Eye Witness, Schlitz Playhouse of Stars, Loretta Young Show, Thriller. *Director*: Star Trek, Route 66, Dr. Kildare, Man from U.N.C.L.E.

NEWLEY, ANTHONY
Actor, Writer, Composer, Singer. b. Hackney, Eng., Sept. 24, 1931. Recipient of Male Singer of the Year Award, Las Vegas, 1972; Elected to Songwriters Hall of Fame, 1989. Gold records for composing Goldfinger, Candy Man, What Kind of Fool Am I?
THEATER: *West End stage*: Cranks (also dir., writer), Stop The World—I Want to Get Off (also composer with Leslie Bricusse, dir., writer; also NY), The Roar of the Greasepaint—The Smell of the Crowd (also composer with Bricusse, writer, dir.; also NY), The Good Old Bad Old Days (also composer with Bricusse, writer, dir.), Royalty Follies (also dir., writer), The World's Not Entirely to Blame, It's a Funny Old World We Live In. *Regional*: Chaplin, Once Upon a Song. *British tour*: Scrooge (1992-95).
PICTURES: Adventures of Dusty Bates (debut, 1946), Little Ballerina, The Guinea Pig, Vice Versa, Oliver Twist, Vote for Huggett, Don't Ever Leave Me, A Boy a Girl and a Bike, Golden Salamander, Madeleine, Highly Dangerous, Those People Next Door, Top of the Form, The Weak and the Wicked, Up to His Neck, Blue Peter, The Cockleshell Heroes, Battle of the River Plate, Above Us the Waves, Port Afrique, The Last Man to Hang, Fire Down Below, How to Murder a Rich Uncle, Good Companions, X the Unknown, High Flight, No Time to Die (Tank Force), The Man Inside, The Bandit of Zhobe, The Lady Is a Square, Idle on Parade, Killers of Kilimanjaro, Let's Get Married, Jazz Boat, In the Nick, The Small World of Sammy Lee, Play It Cool, Stop the World I Want to Get Off (songs only), Doctor Dolittle, Sweet November, Can Hieronymus Merkin Ever Forget Mercy Humppe and Find True Happiness? (also dir., s.p., songs), Willie Wonka and the Chocolate Factory (songs only), Summertree (dir. only), Mr. Quilp (also music), It Seemed Like a Good Idea at the Time, The Garbage Pail Kids Movie.
TELEVISION: *Specials*: Sunday Night Palladium, Saturday Spectaculars, Anthony Newley Special (London). *Guest*: The Johnny Darling Show, Hollywood Squares, Merv Griffin Show, The Tonight Show, Limited Partners, Fame, Magnum P.I., Alfred Hitchcock Theatre, Murder She Wrote, Simon & Simon. *Movies*: Malibu, Alice in Wonderland, Blade in Hong Kong, Stagecoach, Coins in a Fountain, Polly Comin' Home, Boris and Natasha, Anna Lee: Dupe. *Series* (BBC): Sammy, The Strange World of Gurney Slade, The Anthony Newley Show (1972).

NEWMAN, ALFRED S.
Executive. b. Brooklyn, NY, Nov. 16. e. NYU. Public relations work for Equitable Life Insurance, Trans World Airlines prior to joining Columbia Pictures in 1968 as writer in publicity dept.; named New York publicity mgr.; 1970; national publicity mgr., 1972; joined MGM as East adv.-pub. dir., 1972; named director of adv., pub. and promotion, 1974; named v.p., worldwide adv., pub., promo., 1978; v.p., pub.-promo., MGM/UA, 1981. With 20th Century-Fox as v.p. adv.-pub.-promo. for TV & corporate, 1984-85; joined Rogers & Cowan as sr. v.p. & head of corporate entertainment, 1985; named exec. v.p., 1987; Oct. 1988 named pres. and CEO. Sterling Entertainment Co. and exec. v.p. worldwide marketing of parent co. MCEG; formed Newman & Associates, 1989; joined Hill and Knowl Entertainment as founding mng. dir., 1990. Re-opened Newman and Assocs., 1991.

NEWMAN, BARRY
Actor. b. Boston, MA, Nov. 7, 1938. e. Brandeis U.
PICTURES: Pretty Boy Floyd (debut, 1960), The Moving Finger, The Lawyer, Vanishing Point, The Salzburg Connection, Fear is the Key, City on Fire, Amy.
TELEVISION: *Series*: Petrocelli, Nightingales. *Movies*: Night Games, Sex and the Married Woman, King Crab, Fantasies, Having It All, Second Sight: A Love Story, Fatal Vision, My Two Loves, The Mirror Crack'd (BBC).

NEWMAN, DAVID
Composer. b. Los Angeles, CA, Mar. 11, 1954. e. USC (masters degree). Son of late composer Alfred Newman. Cousin of composer Randy Newman. Music director at Robert Redford's Sundance Institute.
PICTURES: Critters, Vendetta, The Kindred, My Demon Lover, Malone, Dragnet, Throw Momma from the Train, Pass the Ammo, Bill & Ted's Excellent Adventure, Disorganized Crime, The Brave Little Toaster, Heathers, Little Monsters, Gross Anatomy, The War of the Roses, Madhouse, Fire Birds, The Freshman, DuckTales: The Movie, Mr. Destiny, Meet the Applegates, The Marrying Man, Talent for the Game, Don't Tell Mom the Babysitter's Dead, Bill & Ted's Bogus Journey, Rover Dangerfield, Paradise, Other People's Money, The Runestone, The Mighty Ducks, Hoffa, The Sandlot, Coneheads, The Air Up There, My Father the Hero, The Flintstones, The Cowboy Way, Tommy Boy, Operation Dumbo Drop, The Phantom, Mathilda, The Nutty Professor.

NEWMAN, DAVID
Writer. b. New York, NY, Feb. 4, 1937. e. U. of Michigan, M.S., 1959. Was writer-editor at Esquire Magazine where he met Robert Benton, an art director, and formed writing partnership. All early credits co-written with Benton; later ones with Leslie Newman and others.
THEATER: It's a Bird... It's a Plane... It's Superman (libretto), Oh! Calcutta (one sketch).
PICTURES: Bonnie and Clyde, There Was a Crooked Man, What's Up Doc?, Bad Company, Superman, Superman II, Jinxed, Still of the Night (co-story), Superman III, Sheena, Santa Claus, Moonwalker.

NEWMAN, EDWIN
News Correspondent. b. New York, NY, Jan. 25, 1919. Joined NBC News in 1952, based in N.Y. since 1961. Reports news on NBC-TV and often assigned to anchor instant specials. Has been substitute host on Today, appeared on Meet the Press and has reported NBC News documentaries. Series host: Edwin Newman Reporting, The Nation's Future, What's Happening to America, Comment, Speaking Freely, Television (PBS series).

NEWMAN, JOSEPH M.
Producer, Director, Writer. b. Logan, UT, Aug. 7, 1909. Started as office boy MGM, 1925; jobs in production dept. to 1931; asst. to George Hill, Ernst Lubitsch, etc., 1931-37; asstd. in organization of MGM British studios 1937; dir. short subjects 1938; dir. Crime Does Not Pay series 1938-42; Major in U.S. Army Signal Corps 1942-46; dir. 32 Army Pictorial Service Pictures. TV work includes Alfred Hitchcock Presents, Twilight Zone. Member of AMPAS, SDG Masons.
PICTURES: Northwest Rangers, Abandoned, Jungle Patrol, Great Dan Pitch, 711 Ocean Drive, Lucky Nick Cain, The Guy Who Came Back, Love Nest, Red Skies of Montana, Outcasts of Poker Flat, Pony Soldier, Dangerous Crossing, Human Jungle, Kiss of Fire, This Island Earth, Flight to Hong Kong, Fort Massacre, The Big Circus, Tarzan the Ape Man, King of the Roaring Twenties, Twenty Plus Two, The George Raft Story, Thunder of Drums.

NEWMAN, LARAINE
Actress. b. Los Angeles, CA, Mar. 2, 1952. Founding member of comedy troupe the Groundlings.
THEATER: *B'way*: Fifth of July.
PICTURES: Tunnelvision (debut, 1976), American Hot Wax, Wholly Moses!, Stardust Memories (unbilled), Perfect, Sesame Street Presents Follow That Bird (voice), Invaders from Mars, Problem Child 2, Witchboard II, Coneheads, The Flintstones.
TELEVISION: *Series*: Manhattan Transfer, Saturday Night Live. *Guest*: George Burns Comedy Week, St. Elsewhere, Laverne & Shirley, Alfred Hitchcock Presents, Amazing Stories, Faerie Tale Theatre (The Little Mermaid), Twilight Zone, Dream On, Likely Suspects. *Specials*: Steve Martin's Best Show Ever, The Lily Tomlin Special, Bob Ray Jane Laraine & Gilda. *Movies*: Her Life as a Man, This Wife for Hire.

NEWMAN, NANETTE
Actress, Writer. b. Northampton, Eng., 1936. m. prod.-dir.-writer Bryan Forbes. Ent. films in 1946 and TV in 1951.
AUTHOR: God Bless Love, That Dog, Reflections, The Root Children, Amy Rainbow, Pigalev, Archie, Christmas Cookbook, Summer Cookbook, Small Beginnings, Bad Baby, Entertaining with Nanette Newman and Her Daughters, Charlie the Noisy Caterpillar, Sharing, The Pig Who Never Was, ABC, 123, Cooking for Friends, Spider the Horrible Cat, There's a Bear in the Bath, Karmic Mothers (Teleplay), There's a Bear in the Classroom, The Importance of Being Ernest the Earwig, Take 3 Cooks.
PICTURES: The Personal Affair, The League of Gentlemen, The Rebel, Twice Around the Daffodils, The L-Shaped Room, The Wrong Arm of the Law, Of Human Bondage, Seance on a Wet Afternoon, The Wrong Box, The Whisperers, Deadfall,

The Madwoman of Chaillot, Captain Nemo and the Underwater City, The Raging Moon (Long Ago Tomorrow), The Stepford Wives, It's a 2'2" Above the Ground World (The Love Ban), Man at the Top, International Velvet, The Endless Game. TELEVISION: The Glorious Days, The Wedding Veil, Broken Honeymoon, At Home, Trial by Candlelight, Diary of Samuel Pepys, Faces in the Dark, Balzac (BBC), Fun Food Factory, TV series, Stay with Me Till Morning, Let There Be Love (series), West Country Tales, Jessie, Late Expectations (series).

NEWMAN, PAUL
Actor, Director, Producer. b. Cleveland, OH, Jan. 26, 1925. m. actress Joanne Woodward. e. Kenyon Coll., Yale Sch. of Drama, The Actors Studio. Formed First Artists Prod. Co., Ltd. 1969 with Sidney Poitier, Steve McQueen and Barbra Streisand. Appeared in documentaries: King: A Filmed Record... Memphis to Montgomery, Hello Actors Studio. Recipient of special Academy Award, 1986; Jean Hersholt Humanitarian Award, 1994.
THEATER: B'way: Picnic, The Desperate Hours, Sweet Bird of Youth, Baby Want a Kiss.
PICTURES: The Silver Chalice (debut, 1954), The Rack, Somebody Up There Likes Me, The Helen Morgan Story, Until They Sail, The Long Hot Summer, The Left-Handed Gun, Cat on a Hot Tin Roof, Rally 'Round the Flag Boys!, The Young Philadelphians, From the Terrace, Exodus, The Hustler, Paris Blues, Sweet Bird of Youth, Hemingway's Adventures of a Young Man, Hud, A New Kind of Love, The Prize, What a Way to Go!, The Outrage, Harper, Lady L, Torn Curtain, Hombre, Cool Hand Luke, The Secret War of Harry Frigg, Rachel Rachel (dir. prod. only), Winning, Butch Cassidy and the Sundance Kid, WUSA (also prod.), Sometimes a Great Notion (also dir.), Pocket Money, The Life and Times of Judge Roy Bean, The Effect of Gamma Rays on Man-in-the-Moon Marigolds (dir., prod. only), The Mackintosh Man, The Sting, The Towering Inferno, The Drowning Pool, Buffalo Bill and the Indians or Sitting Bull's History Lesson, Silent Movie, Slap Shot, Quintet, When Time Ran Out..., Fort Apache the Bronx, Absence of Malice, The Verdict, Harry and Son (also dir., co-s.p., co-prod.), The Color of Money (Academy Award, 1986), The Glass Menagerie (dir. only), Fat Man & Little Boy, Blaze, Mr. and Mrs. Bridge, The Hudsucker Proxy, Nobody's Fool.
TELEVISION: Guest (on 1950's anthology series): The Web (Bell of Damon, One for the Road), Goodyear TV Playhouse (Guilty is the Stranger), Danger (Knife in the Dark), Appointment With Adventure (Five in Judgment), Philco TV Playhouse (Death of Billy the Kid), Producers Showcase (Our Town), Kaiser Aluminum Hour (The Army Game, Rag Jungle), U.S. Steel Hour (Bang the Drum Slowly), Playhouse 90 (The 80-Yard Run). Movie (dir. only): The Shadow Box.

NEWMAN, RANDY
Composer, Singer. b. Los Angeles, CA, Nov. 28, 1943. Nephew of musicians Lionel and Alfred Newman. Studied music at UCLA. Debut album: Randy Newman Creates Something New Under the Sun. Songs include Short People, I Think It's Gonna Rain Today, I Love L.A. Was music director on film Performance. Began writing songs and scores for films in 1971 with The Pursuit of Happiness. Composed opera, Faust.
PICTURES: Pursuit of Happiness, Cold Turkey, Ragtime, The Natural, Three Amigos (also co-wrote s.p.), Parenthood, Avalon, Awakenings, The Paper, Maverick, James and the Giant Peach, The Quest.

NEWMAN, SYDNEY
Producer, Writer. O. C., F.R.S.A., F.R.T.S. for Canadian Film Development Corp. b. Toronto, Canada, Apr. 1, 1917. Studied painting, drawing, commercial art at Central Tech. Sch. To Hollywood in 1938. Joined National Film Board of Canada under John Grierson. Prod. over 300 shorts. Later became exec. prod. all Canadian government cinema films, 1947-52; Canadian Broadcasting Corp., 1952, as dir. outside broadcasts, features and documentaries. Later became drama sup. and prod. General Motors Theatre. Joined ABC-TV in England, 1958 as sup. of drama and prod. of Armchair Theatre: Head of Drama Group, TV, BBC, 1963. Commissioned and prod. first TV plays by Arthur Hailey, Harold Pinter, Mordecai Richler, Alun Owen, Angus Wilson, Peter Luke. Devised, created Dr. Who (1962) and The Avengers (1959). Fellow of Society of Film & TV Arts, 1968; Fellow of Royal Television Society, 1990. Prod. Associated British Pictures. SFTA award 1968; Zeta award, Writers Guild, Gt. Btn., 1970. 1970, special advisor, ch. dir., Broadcast Programmes branch, Canadian Radio & TV Commission, Ottawa. 1970, appt. Canadian Govt. Film Commissioner and chmn., National Film Board of Canada; Trustee, National Arts Centre, Ottawa; bd. mem., Canadian Broadcasting Corporation, Canadian Film Development Corp. Recognition Award from S.M.P.T.E. (USA), Canadian Picture Pioneers Special Award. Special Advisor on Film to the Secretary of State for Canada, 1975-77; pres., Sydney Newman

Enterprises. 1981, made officer of the Order of Canada. Left Canadian Film Develop. Corp. 1983. At present Creative Consultant to film & tv producers.

NEWMAR, JULIE
Actress. r.n. Julie Newmeyer. b. Hollywood, CA, Aug. 16, 1933. e. UCLA. Studied acting with Lee Strasberg at the Actor's Studio. Holds patent for special panty hose design. Appeared in George Michael video Too Funky.
THEATER: NY: Silk Stockings, Li'l Abner, The Marriage-Go-Round (Tony Award, 1959). Other: In the Boom Boom Room (L.A.), Damn Yankees, Irma La Douce, Guys and Dolls, Dames at Sea, Stop the World, The Women.
PICTURES: Just for You (debut, 1952), Seven Brides for Seven Brothers, The Rookie, Li'l Abner, The Marriage-Go-Round, For Love or Money, McKenna's Gold, The Maltese Bippy, Hysterical, Streetwalkin', Body Beat, Nudity Required, Ghosts Can't Do It, Oblivion, To Wong Foo—Thanks for Everything—Julie Newmar.
TELEVISION: Series: My Living Doll, Batman (frequent guest; as Catwoman). Movies: McCloud: Who Killed Miss U.S.A.?, The Feminist and the Fuzz, A Very Missing Person, Terraces. Guest: Omnibus, Route 66, Jonathan Winters Show, Beverly Hillbillies, The Monkees, Love American Style, Love Boat, Half Nelson, Fantasy Island, Hart to Hart, Buck Rogers.

NEWTON-JOHN, OLIVIA
Actress, Singer. b. Cambridge, Eng. Sept. 26, 1948. m. actor Matt Lattanzi. Brought up in Melbourne, Australia, where won first talent contest at 15, winning trip to England. Stayed there 2 yrs. performing as part of duo with Australian girl singer Pat Carroll (Farrar) in cabarets and on TV. Started recording; several hit records. Became a regular guest on TV series, It's Cliff Richard. Gained world-wide prominence as singer, winning several Grammys and other music awards. 1983 opened Koala Blue, U.S. Clothing Stores featuring Australian style clothes and goods.
PICTURES: Tomorrow (debut, 1970), Grease, Xanadu, Two of a Kind.
TELEVISION: Specials: Olivia Newton-John: Let's Get Physical, Standing Room Only: Olivia Newton-John, Olivia Newton-John in Australia, Christmas in Washington. Movies: A Mom for Christmas, A Christmas Romance.

NEY, RICHARD
Actor, Writer, Producer, Financier. b. New York, NY, Nov. 12, 1917. e. Columbia U., B.A., 1940. Acted in RCA TV demonstration, New York World's Fair; on stage in Life with Father. Was Naval Officer in WWII. Financial advisor consultant, Richard Ney and Associates; financial advisor, lecturer; author, The Wall Street Jungle, The Wall Street Gang, Making it in the Market.
PICTURES: Mrs. Miniver, The War Against Mrs. Hadley, The Late George Apley, Ivy, Joan of Arc, The Fan, Secret of St. Ives, Lovable Cheat, Babes in Bagdad, Miss Italia, Sergeant and The Spy, Midnight Lace, The Premature Burial.

NGOR, HAING S.
Actor. b. Cambodia, 1947. Started as doctor in Cambodia, serving as medical officer in the Cambodian Army. Escaped to Thailand following four years in captivity under the Khmer Rouge, then immigrated to U.S. in 1980, resuming career as doctor before being picked for debut role in The Killing Fields. Subject of documentaries: A Man Without a Country, Beyond the Killing Field. Autobiography: A Cambodia Odyssey (1987).
PICTURES: The Killing Fields (debut, 1984; Academy Award, best supporting actor; also BAFTA & Golden Globe Awards), Iron Triangle, Vietnam Texas, Ambition, My Life, Heaven and Earth, Fortunes of War.
TELEVISION: Movies: In Love and War, Last Flight Out. Series: Vanishing Son. Guest: Hotel, China Beach, Miami Vice, Highway to Heaven. Special: Vietnam War Story (The Last Outpost), The Doctors Wilde.
(d. March 3, 1996)

NICHOLAS, DENISE
Actress, Writer. b. Detroit, MI, July 12, 1945. e. Univ. of MI., USC. Short story published in Essence Magazine.
THEATER: Productions with The Free Southern Theatre, The Negro Ensemble Company, Cross Roads Theatre Co., New Federal Theatre incl. Daddy Goodness, Ceremonies in Dark Old Men, Dame Lorraine, Summer of the 17th Doll, Poetry Show, Their Eyes Were Watching God. Author: Buses (prod. at Crossroads theatre, New Brunswick, NJ).
PICTURES: Blacula, The Soul of Nigger Charley, Mr. Ricco, Let's Do It Again, A Piece of the Action, Capricorn One, Marvin and Tige, Ghost Dad.
TELEVISION: Series: Room 222, Baby I'm Back, In the Heat of the Night (also wrote 6 episodes). Movies: Five Desperate Women, The Sophisticated Gents, On Thin Ice, Mother's Day, Ring of Passion, Return to the Valley of the Dolls, In the Heat of the Night: By Duty Bound. Guest: NYPD, The FBI, Night Gallery, Love American Style, Police Story, The Love Boat, The Paper Chase, Magnum P.I., Benson, The Cosby Show, A Different World, many others.

NICHOLS, MIKE
Director, Producer, Performer. r.n. Michael Igor Peschkowsky. b. Berlin, Germany, Nov. 6, 1931. m. news correspondent Diane Sawyer. e. U. of Chicago. Member of Compass Players; later teamed with Elaine May in night clubs.
THEATER: *Director:* Barefoot in the Park (Tony Award), The Knack, Luv (Tony Award), The Odd Couple, The Apple Tree, The Little Foxes, Plaza Suite (Tony Award), Uncle Vanya, The Prisoner of 2nd Avenue (Tony Award), Streamers, Comedians, The Gin Game, Drinks Before Dinner, Annie (prod. only; Tony Award), The Real Thing (2 Tony Awards), Hurlyburly, Social Security, Waiting for Godot, Elliot Loves, Death and the Maiden.
PICTURES: *Director:* Who's Afraid of Virginia Woolf? (debut, 1966), The Graduate (Academy Award, 1967), Catch-22, Carnal Knowledge, The Day of the Dolphin, The Fortune, Gilda Live, Silkwood (also co-prod.), The Longshot (exec. prod. only), Heartburn, Biloxi Blues, Working Girl, Postcards From the Edge, Regarding Henry, The Remains of the Day (co-prod. only), Wolf, The Birdcage.
TELEVISION: *Specials:* B'way, An Evening with Mike Nichols and Elaine May. *Exec. prod.:* Family, The Thorns.

NICHOLS, NICHELLE
Actress. b. Robbins, IL, 1936. Started singing and dancing with Duke Ellington and his band at age 16. Was appointee to the bd. of dirs. of the National Space Institute in the 1970's; recruited women and minority astronauts for Space Shuttle Program. Received NASA's distinguished Public Service Award. Member of the bd. of govs. of the National Space Society. One of the original founders of KWANZA Foundation. Awarded star on Hollywood Walk of Fame (1992). *Autobiography:* Beyond (1994). Novels: Saturn's Child (1995), Saturna's Quest (1996).
THEATER: Horowitz and Mrs. Washington, Reflections (one woman show). Nominated for Sarah Siddons Award for performances in Kicks and Company, The Blacks.
PICTURES: Porgy and Bess, Mr. Buddwing, Made in Paris, Truck Turner, Star Trek: The Motion Picture, Star Trek II: The Wrath of Khan, Star Trek III: The Search for Spock, Star Trek IV: The Voyage Home, The Supernaturals, Star Trek V: The Final Frontier, Star Trek VI: The Undiscovered Country.
TELEVISION: *Series:* Star Trek. *Guest:* The Lieutenant, Tarzan. *Special:* Antony and Cleopatra.

NICHOLSON, JACK
Actor, Producer, Director, Writer. b. Neptune, NJ, April 22, 1937. Began career in cartoon department of MGM. Made acting debut in Hollywood stage production of Tea and Sympathy. Made directing debut with Drive, He Said (1971). Has received 10 Academy Award nominations for acting. Recipient of American Film Institute's Life Achievement Award, 1994.
PICTURES: Cry Baby Killer (debut, 1958), Too Soon to Love, Little Shop of Horrors, Studs Lonigan, The Wild Ride, The Broken Land, The Raven, The Terror, Thunder Island (co-s.p. only), Back Door to Hell, Flight to Fury (also s.p.), Ensign Pulver, Ride in the Whirlwind (also co-prod., s.p.), The Shooting (also co-prod.), The St. Valentine's Day Massacre, Rebel Rousers, Hell's Angels on Wheels, The Trip (s.p. only), Head (also co-prod., co-s.p.), Psych-Out, Easy Rider, On a Clear Day You Can See Forever, Five Easy Pieces, Carnal Knowledge, Drive He Said (dir., co-prod., co-s.p. only), A Safe Place, The King of Marvin Gardens, The Last Detail, Chinatown, Tommy, The Passenger, The Fortune, One Flew Over the Cuckoo's Nest (Academy Award, 1975), The Missouri Breaks, The Last Tycoon, Goin' South (also dir.), The Shining, The Postman Always Rings Twice, Reds, The Border, Terms of Endearment (Academy Award, best supporting actor, 1983), Prizzi's Honor, Heartburn, The Witches of Eastwick, Broadcast News, Ironweed, Batman, The Two Jakes (also dir.), Man Trouble, A Few Good Men, Hoffa, Wolf, The Crossing Guard, Mars Attacks!, The Evening Star.
TELEVISION: *Guest:* Tales of Wells Fargo, Cheyenne, Hawaiian Eye, Dr. Kildare, Andy Griffith Show, Guns of Will Sonnett.

NICHOLSON, WILLIAM
Writer. b. England, 1948. e. Cambridge U. Was graduate trainee at BBC, becoming prod./dir./writer of over 40 documentaries.
THEATER: Shadowlands, Map of the Heart.
PICTURES: Sarafina!, Shadowlands (Acad. Award nom.), Nell, First Knight.
TELEVISION: *Exec. Prod.:* Everyman, Global Report, Lovelaw. *Writer:* Martin Luther, New World, Life Story, The Vision, Sweet as You Are, The March.

NICKSAY, DAVID
Executive, Producer. e. Mass., Hampshire Coll. Entered industry through Directors Guild of America's training program, apprenticing on Rich Man Poor Man and rising to second asst. dir. on Oh, God. Producer of many TV projects and theatrical films with Edgar Scherick prod. co. In 1986, joined Paramount Pictures as v.p., prod., for M.P. Group. Assoc. prod., prod. mgr.: I'm Dancing as Fast as I Can. Became sr. v.p., prod. Paramount, M.P. Group, 1987; resigned 1989 to become pres. and head of prod. at Morgan Creek Prods. Mem. of bd.
PICTURES: *Prod.:* Mrs. Soffel, Lucas, Up Close and Personal. *Sprv. prod.:* Big Top Pee-Wee, Summer School, Coming to America, The Untouchables, Scrooged, Star Trek V: The Final Frontier, Major League, Were No Angels, Harlem Nights, The Two Jakes, White Sands, Stay Tuned.
TELEVISION: Call to Glory (pilot), Little Gloria Happy at Last.

NICOL, ALEX
Actor, Director. b. Ossining, NY, Jan. 20, 1919. e. Fagin Sch. of Dramatic Arts, Actor's Studio. U.S. Cavalry.
THEATER: Forward the Heart, Sundown Beach, Hamlet, Richard II, South Pacific, Mr. Roberts, Cat on a Hot Tin Roof.
PICTURES: The Sleeping City, Tomahawk, Target Unknown, Air Cadet, Raging Tide, Meet Danny Wilson, Red Ball Express, Because of You, Redhead From Wyoming, Lone Hand, Law and Order, Champ for a Day, Black Glove, Heat Wave, About Mrs. Leslie, Dawn at Socorro, Strategic Air Command, Man from Laramie, Great Day in the Morning, The Gilded Cage, Sincerely Yours, Five Branded Women, Via Margutta, Under 10 Flags, Gunfighters at Casa Grande, The Screaming Skull (dir.), Then There Were Three (dir.), The Brutal Land, Bloody Mama, Homer, Point of Terror (dir.), The Night God Screamed, A-P-E.

NIELSEN, LESLIE
Actor. b. Regina, Sask., Canada, Feb. 11, 1926. e. Victoria H.S., Edmonton. Disc jockey, announcer for Canadian radio station; studied at Lorne Greene's Acad. of Radio Arts, Toronto and at Neighborhood Playhouse; N.Y. radio actor summer stock. Toured country in one-man show, Darrow, 1979. *Author:* The Naked Truth (1993), Leslie Nielsen's Stupid Little Golf Book (1995).
PICTURES: Ransom (debut, 1956), Forbidden Planet, The Vagabond King, The Opposite Sex, Hot Summer Night, Tammy and the Bachelor, The Sheepman, Night Train To Paris, Harlow, Dark Intruder, Beau Geste, The Plainsman, Gunfight in Abilene, The Reluctant Astronaut, Rosie!, Counterpoint, Dayton's Devils, How to Commit Marriage, Change of Mind, Four Rode Out, The Resurrection of Zachary Wheeler, The Poseidon Adventure, And Millions Will Die, Day of the Animals, Viva Knievel!, The Amsterdam Kill, City on Fire, Airplane!, Prom Night, The Creature Wasn't Nice, Wrong Is Right, Creepshow, The Patriot, Soul Man, Nightstick, Nuts, Home Is Where the Hart Is, The Naked Gun: From the Files of Police Squad!, Dangerous Curves, Repossessed, The Naked Gun 2 1/2: The Smell of Fear, All I Want for Christmas, Surf Ninjas, Naked Gun 33 1/3: The Final Insult, Dracula: Dead and Loving It, Spy Hard (also co-exec. prod.).
TELEVISION: *Series:* The New Breed, Peyton Place, The Protectors, Bracken's World, The Explorers (host), Police Squad, Shaping Up. *Guest:* Studio One, Kraft, Philco Playhouse, Robert Montgomery Presents, Pulitzer Prize Playhouse, Suspense, Danger, Justice, Man Behind the Badge, Ben Casey, Walt Disney (Swamp Fox), Wild Wild West, The Virginian, The Loner. *Special:* Death of a Salesman. *Movies:* See How They Run, Shadow Over Elveron, Hawaii Five-O (pilot), Companions in Nightmare, Trial Run, Deadlock, Night Slaves, The Aquarians, Hauser's Memory, Incident in San Francisco, They Call It Murder, Snatched, The Letters, The Return of Charlie Chan (Happiness Is a Warm Clue), Can Ellen Be Saved?, Brink's: The Great Robbery, Little Mo, Institute for Revenge, OHMS, The Night the Bridge Fell Down, Cave-In!, Reckless Disregard, Blade in Hong Kong, Fatal Confession: A Father Dowling Mystery, Chance of a Lifetime. *Mini-Series:* Backstairs at the White House.

NIMOY, LEONARD
Actor, Director. b. Boston, MA, Mar. 26, 1931. e. Boston Col. Joined Pasadena Playhouse. Along with active career in films, TV and stage, has been writer and photographer. Author of three books on photography and poetry, as well as autobiography, I Am Not Spock. Has also been speaker on college lecture circuit. Created comic book Primortals.
THEATER: Full Circle, Equus, Sherlock Holmes, Vincent (also dir., writer; one-man show), Love Letters.
PICTURES: Queen for a Day, Rhubarb, Francis Goes to West Point, Them!, Satan's Satellite (edited from serial Zombies of the Stratosphere), The Brain Eaters, The Balcony, Catlow, Invasion of the Body Snatchers, Star Trek—The Motion Picture, Star Trek II: The Wrath of Khan, Star Trek III: The Search for Spock (also dir.), Transformers: The Movie (voice), Star Trek IV: The Voyage Home (also dir., co-story), Three Men and a Baby (dir. only), The Good Mother (dir. only), Star Trek V: The Final Frontier, Funny About Love (dir. only), Star Trek VI: The Undiscovered Country (also exec. prod., co-story), Holy Matrimony (dir. only), The Pagemaster (voice).
TELEVISION: *Series:* Star Trek, Mission: Impossible, In Search Of... (host), Outer Limits. *Movies:* Assault on the Wayne, Baffled, The Alpha Caper, The Missing Are Deadly,

The Sun Also Rises, A Woman Called Golda, Never Forget (also co-prod.), Bonanza: Under Attack. *Mini-Series:* Marco Polo. *Guest:* Bonanza, Twilight Zone, Perry Mason, Laramie, Wagon Train, Man From U.N.C.L.E., The Virginian, Get Smart, Night Gallery, Columbo, T.J. Hooker, Star Trek: The Next Generation. *Special:* Seapower: A Global Journey (narrator). *Episode Dir.:* Deadly Games.

NIVEN, DAVID, JR.
Executive. b. London, England, Dec. 15, 1942. e. Univ. of Grenoble; London Sch. of Economics. Joined William Morris Agency in Beverly Hills in 1963. Transferred same yr. to New York; over next five yrs. worked for agency's European offices in Rome, Madrid and London. 1968-72, Columbia Pictures' U.K. office as v.p. of production; 1972-76, mng. dir. and v.p. of Paramount Pictures in U.K. 1976 became indep. prod. West Coast corresp. & interviewer for Inside Edition. Appeared as actor in films Lisa, Cool Surface, and on tv series, America's Most Wanted. 1993, became chmn. of R.A.D.D. (Recording-Artists Against Drunk Driving)
PICTURES: *Producer.* The Eagle Has Landed, Escape to Athena, Monsignor, Better Late Than Never, Kidco, That's Dancing!, Pyscho Cop II, Girl With the Hungry Eyes, Cool Surface (also actor), Blue Flame.
TELEVISION: The Night They Saved Christmas (exec. prod., s.p.), Cary Grant: A Celebration, Minnelli on Minnelli, The Wonderful Wizard of Oz. Panelist: To Tell the Truth (1991-92).

NIX, WILLIAM PATTERSON
Executive. b. Philadelphia, PA, April 10, 1948. e. Georgetown U., A.B., 1970; Antioch, M.A., 1971; Hofstra U. Sch. of Law, J.D., 1976; NYU Sch. of Law, LL.M., 1979. Formerly, v.p., Cartier, Frankfurt, Garbus, Klein & Selz, P.C., Entertainment & Media co. V.P. bus. affairs, NBA Properties Inc., NY. Prior to that, was sr. v.p. of both the Motion Picture Association of America and Motion Picture Export Assoc. of America. Chmn. of MPAA committee on copyright and literary property matters, and COO of film industry's intellectual property protection division (1976-91). Lifetime member, AMPAS.

NIXON, AGNES
Writer, Producer. b. Nashville, TN, Dec. 10, 1927. e. Northwestern Sch. of Speech, Catholic U. Landed 1st job writing radio serial dialogue (Woman in White, 1948-51), three days after graduating from college. Became a freelance writer for TV dramatic series. Guest writer, New York Times 1968-72, and TV Guide. Trustee, Television Conference Inst., 1979-82. Received National Acad. of Television Arts & Sciences' Trustee Award, 1981; Junior Diabetic Assn. Super Achiever Award, 1982; Communicator Award for American Women in Radio and Television, 1984. Gold Plate Award, American Acad. Achievement, 1993; inducted into TV Hall of Fame, 1993. Popular Culture Lifetime Achievement Award, 1995; Public Service Award, Johns Hopkins Hospital, 1995. Member, Int'l Radio & TV Society; Nat'l Acad. of TV Arts & Sciences; bd. of Harvard Foundation; The Friars Club.
TELEVISION: *Series writer:* Studio One, Philco Playhouse, Robert Montgomery Presents, Somerset Maugham Theatre, Armstrong Circle Theatre, Hallmark Hall of Fame, My True Story, Cameo Theatre, Search For Tomorrow, As The World Turns, Guiding Light, Another World. *Series creator-producer:* One Life to Live, All My Children, Loving. *Mini-Series:* The Manions of America.

NIXON, CYNTHIA
Actress. b. New York, NY, April 9, 1966. e. Barnard Coll. Started stage career at age 14.
THEATER: *B'way:* The Philadelphia Story (Theatre World Award), Hurlyburly, The Real Thing, The Heidi Chronicles, Angels in America: Millenium Aproaches/Perestroika, Indiscretions. *Off-B'way:* Moonchildren, Romeo and Juliet, The Balcony Scene, Servy N Bernice 4-Ever, On the Bum, The Illusion, The Scarlet Letter.
PICTURES: Little Darlings (debut, 1980), Tattoo, Prince of the City, I Am the Cheese, Amadeus, The Manhattan Project, Let It Ride, Addams Family Values, The Pelican Brief, Baby's Day Out, Marvin's Room.
TELEVISION: *Movies:* The Murder of Mary Phagan, The Love She Sought, Love Lies and Murder, Face of a Stranger. Specials: The Fifth of July, Kiss Kiss Dahlings, Tanner '88. *Guest:* The Equalizer, Gideon Oliver, Murder She Wrote.

NOBLE, PETER
Writer, Producer, Actor, TV personality. b. London, Eng., June 18; e. Hugh Myddelton Sch., Latymer Sch. Author several books on m.p. ind.; writer/host movie radio prog. for B.B.C. & Luxembourg (Film Time, Movie-Go-Round, Peter Noble's Picture Parade). Formed Peter Noble Productions, 1953; edit. Screen International, 1975; edit. Screen International Film & TV Yearbook, 1974. London Columnist for the Hollywood Reporter, 1967-75. Radio Show, 1989-90. Editor: British Film Year Book. AUTHOR: biographies of Bette Davis, Erich Von Stroheim, Ivor Novello, Orson Welles; I Know That Face, The Negro in Films.

PICTURES: Runaway Bus (prod. assoc.), To Dorothy a Son (asst. prod.), Fun at St. Fanny's (co-prod, s.p.), Three Girls in Paris (s.p.), Lost (assoc. prod.), Captain Banner (s.p.), Strange Inheritance (prod.).
TELEVISION: Find the Link, Other Screen, Film Fanfare, Movie Memories, Yakity Yak, Startime, Thank Your Lucky Stars, Juke Box, Jury, Simon Dee Show, Star Parade, Show Business, Who's Whose, Movie Magazine, The Big Noise, The Name Game, Line Up, Tea Break, Today, Anything You Can Do, Looks Familiar, Two's Company, Sounds Familiar, Electric Picture Show, Gossip, This Is Britain (cable series), Cannes Film Festival (cable), Kilroy, Good Afternoon New York (U.S.), Loose Ends, The Pete Murray Show, Cinema 2, Where Are They Now?, The Golden Gong (TV film), Elstree—The British Hollywood, Saturday Night at the Movies (series). Prod. consult.: On The Braden Beat, The Frost Program, Dee Time, Simon Dee Show, Movie Quiz (series), Musical Time Machine BBC2 series,
RADIO: BBC Star Sound, Radio Luxembourg, Film Focus, Newsnight, Looks Familiar Nationwide, Hotel TV Network, The Time of Your Life, Channel 4 News, Nationwide, The Colour Supplement (series);

NOIRET, PHILIPPE
Actor. b. Lille, France, Oct. 1, 1930. e. Centre Dramatique de l'Ouest. Company member of Theatre National Populaire 1951-63; nightclub entertainer before film debut in Agnes Varda's short, La Pointe Court. B'way debut Lorenzaccio (1958).
PICTURES: Gigi (debut, 1948), Olivia, Agence Matrimoniale, La Pointe Courte, Ravissante, Zazie dans le Metro, The Billionaire, Crime Does Not Pay, Therese Desqueyroux, Cyrano and D'Artagnan, None But the Lonely Spy, Death Where Is Thy Victory?, Monsieur, Les Copains, Lady L, La Vie de Chateau, Tender Scoundrel, The Night of the Generals, Woman Times Seven, The Assassination Bureau, Mr. Freedom, Justine, Topaz, Clerambard, Give Her the Moon, A Room in Paris, Murphy's War, A Time for Loving, Five-Leaf Clover, The Assassination, Sweet Deception, Poil de Carotte, The French Conspiracy, The Serpent, The Day of the Jackel, La Grande Bouffe, Let Joy Reign Supreme, The Old Gun, The Judge and the Assassin, A Woman at Her Window, Purple Taxi, Dear Inspector, Due Pezzi di Pane, Who Is Killing the Great Chefs of Europe?, Death Watch, Street of the Crane's Foot, A Week's Vacation, Heads or Tails, Three Brothers, Kill Birgitt Haas, Coup de Torchon, L'Etoile du Nord, Amici, Miei, Atto 2, L'Africain, A Friend of Vincents, Le Grand Carnival, Fort Saganne, Les Ripoux, Souvenirs, Next Summer, The Gold-Rimmed Glasses, No Downing Allowed, My New Partner, 'Round Midnight, Let's Hope It's a Girl, The 4th Power, The Thrill of Genius, The Secret Wife, Twist Again in Moscow, Masks, The Family Chouans!, IL Frullo del Passero, Young Toscanini, The Return of the Musketeers, Moments of Love, Cinema Paradiso, Life and Nothing But, Palermo Connection, My New Partner 2, Uranus, I Don't Kiss, The Two of Us, Especially on Sunday, The Postman, Grosse Fatigue.

NOLTE, NICK
Actor. b. Omaha, NB, Feb. 8, 1941. Attended 5 colleges in 4 yrs. on football scholarships, including Pasadena City Coll. and Phoenix City Coll. Joined Actors Inner Circle at Phoenix and appeared in Orpheus Descending, After the Fall, Requiem For a Nun. Did stock in Colorado. In 1968, joined Old Log Theatre in Minneapolis and after 3 yrs. left for New York, appearing at Cafe La Mama. Went to L.A. and did plays The Last Pad and Picnic, as well as several guest spots on TV series before big break in mini-series, Rich Man Poor Man as Tom Jordache.
PICTURES: Return to Macon County (debut, 1975), The Deep, Who'll Stop the Rain, North Dallas Forty, Heart Beat, Cannery Row, 48 HRS., Under Fire, Teachers, Grace Quigley, Down and Out in Beverly Hills, Extreme Prejudice, Weeds, Three Fugitives, New York Stories (Life Lessons), Farewell to the King, Everybody Wins, Q&A, Another 48 HRS, Cape Fear, The Prince of Tides (Golden Globe Award, Acad. Award nom.), The Player, Lorenzo's Oil, I'll Do Anything, Blue Chips, I Love Trouble, Jefferson in Paris, Mulholland Falls, Nightwatch, Mother Night.
TELEVISION: *Mini-Series:* Rich Man Poor Man. *Movies:* Winter Kill (pilot), The California Kid, Death Sentence, The Runaway Barge. *Guest:* Medical Center, Streets of San Francisco, The Rookies.

NOONAN, TOM
Actor, Writer. b. Greenwich, CT, Apr. 12, 1951. e. Yale.
THEATER: Buried Child (Off-B'way debut, 1978), Invitational Farmyard, The Breakers, Five of Us, Spookhouse, What Happened Was (also writer), Wifey (also writer).
PICTURES: Heaven's Gate, Wolfen, Eddie Macon's Run, Easy Money, The Man With One Red Shoe, F/X, Manhunter, The Monster Squad, Mystery Train, Robocop 2, Last Action Hero, What Happened Was (also dir., s.p.).

NORMAN, BARRY
Writer/presenter. b. London. Early career as show business
editor London Daily Mail; humorous columnist for The
Guardian. Entered TV as writer, presenter FILM 1972-81 and
1983-93. 1982, presenter Omnibus. Writer/host: The
Hollywood Greats and Talking Pictures. Radio work incl.:
Going Places, The News Quiz, Breakaway, The Chip Shop.
AUTHOR: The Hollywood Greats, Movie Greats, Film Greats,
Talking Pictures, 100 Best Films of the Century. Novels: A
Series of Defeats, Have a Nice Day, Sticky Wicket, The Bird
Dog Tapes.

NORRIS, CHUCK
Actor. r.n. Carlos Ray. b. Ryan, OK, Mar. 10, 1940. World mid-
dle weight karate champion 1968-74. Owner of LA karate
schools which led to film career.
PICTURES: The Wrecking Crew (debut, 1969), Slaughter in
San Francisco, Return of the Dragon, The Student Teachers,
Breaker! Breaker!, Good Guys Wear Black, Game of Death, A
Force of One, The Octagon, An Eye for an Eye, Silent Rage,
Forced Vengeance, Lone Wolf McQuade, Missing in Action,
Missing in Action 2, Code of Silence, Invasion U.S.A. (also co-
s.p.), Delta Force, Firewalker, Braddock: Missing in Action III
(also co-s.p.), Hero and the Terror, Delta Force II, The Hitman,
Sidekicks (also co-exec. prod.), Hellbound, Top Dog.
TELEVISION: Series: Chuck Norris's Karate Kommandos
(animated series, voice), Walker: Texas Ranger (also co-exec.
prod.). Special: The Ultimate Stuntman: A Tribute to Dar
Robinson (host), Wind in the Wire.

NORTH, SHEREE
Actress. r.n. Dawn Bethel. b. Los Angeles, CA, Jan. 17, 1933.
e. Hollywood H.S. Amateur dancer with USO at 11; prof. debut
at 13; many TV appearances
THEATER: B'way: Hazel Flagg (Drama Desk Award, Critics'
Award), I Can Get It For You Wholesale. Other: Madwoman of
Chaillot, ... And to My Daughter, Stepping Out, California
Dogfight, 6 Rms. Riv Vue, Turnstyle, Thursday Is a Good
Night, Dutchman, Private Lives, Irma La Douce, Bye Bye
Birdie, Your Own Thing, Can-Can, Two for the Seesaw,
Breaking Up the Act, etc. Also directed and produced several
productions.
PICTURES: Excuse My Dust, Here Come the Girls, Living It
Up, How to Be Very Very Popular, The Lieutenant Wore Skirts,
The Best Things in Life Are Free, Way to the Gold, No Down
Payment, In Love and War, Mardi Gras, Destination Inner
Space, Madigan, The Gypsy Moths, The Trouble With Girls,
Lawman, The Organization, Charley Varick, The Outfit,
Breakout, The Shootist, Telefon, Rabbit Test, Telefon, Cold
Dog Soup, Defenseless.
TELEVISION: Series: Big Eddie, I'm a Big Girl Now, Bay City
Blues. Guest: Hawaii 5-0, Kojak, Family, Archie Bunker's
Place, Murder She Wrote, Golden Girls, Matlock, Seinfeld,
Hunter, Magnum P.I., many others. Movies: Then Came
Bronson (pilot), Vanished, Rolling Man, Trouble Comes to
Town, Snatched, Maneater, Key West, Winter Kill, A Shadow
in the Streets, Most Wanted, The Night They Took Miss
Beautiful, A Real American Hero, Amateur Night at the Dixie
Bar and Grill, Women in White, Portrait of a Stripper, Marilyn:
The Untold Story, Legs, Scorned and Swindled, Jake
Spanner—Private Eye, Dead on the Money.

NOSSECK, NOEL
Director, Producer. b. Los Angeles, CA, Dec. 10, 1943.
Began as editor with David Wolper Prods; made documen-
taries; turned to features.
PICTURES: Director. Best Friends (also prod.), Youngblood,
Dreamer, King of the Mountain.
TELEVISION: Movies: Return of the Rebels, The First Time,
Night Partners, Summer Fantasies, Different Affair, Stark, A
Mirror Image, Roman Holiday, Full Exposure: The Sex Tapes
Scandal, Follow Your Heart, Opposites Attract, A Mother's
Justice, Without a Kiss Goodbye, Born Too Soon, French Silk,
Sister in Law, Down Out and Dangerous. Pilots: Aaron's Way,
Half 'n Half, Fair Game, Heaven Help Us.

NOURI, MICHAEL
Actor. b. Washington, DC, Dec. 9, 1945. e. Avon Old Farms,
Rollins Coll., Emerson Coll. Studied for theatre with Larry
Moss and Lee Strasberg. New York stage debut in Forty
Carats, 1969.
THEATER: Forty Carats, Victor/Victoria.
PICTURES: Goodbye Columbus (debut, 1969), Flashdance,
Gobots (voice), The Imagemaker, The Hidden, Chameleon,
Fatal Sky, Total Exposure, Black Ice, Fortunes of War, To the
Limit.
TELEVISION: Series: Beacon Hill, Search for Tomorrow, The
Curse of Dracula, The Gangster Chronicles, Bay City Blues,
Downtown, Love and War. Movies: Contract on Cherry Street,
Fun and Games, Secrets of a Mother and Daughter,
Sprague, Between Two Women, Rage of Angels: The Story
Continues, Quiet Victory: the Charlie Wedemeyer Story,
Shattered Dreams, Danielle Steel's Changes, In the Arms of a

Killer, Psychic, Exclusive, The Sands of Time, The Hidden 2,
Eyes of Terror, Between Love and Honor. Mini-Series: The
Last Convertible.

NOVAK, KIM
Actress. r.n. Marilyn Novak. b. Chicago, IL, Feb, 13, 1933. e.
Wright Junior Coll., Los Angeles City Coll. Started as model,
named World's Favorite Actress, Brussels World's Fair.
PICTURES: The French Line (debut, 1954), Pushover, Phffft!,
Five Against the House, Son of Sinbad, Picnic, The Man with
the Golden Arm, The Eddy Duchin Story, Jeanne Eagles, Pal
Joey, Vertigo, Bell Book and Candle, Middle of the Night,
Pepe, Strangers When We Meet, The Notorious Landlady,
Boys' Night Out, Of Human Bondage, Kiss Me Stupid, The
Amorous Adventures of Moll Flanders, The Legend of Lylah
Clare, The Great Bank Robbery, Tales That Witness Madness,
The White Buffalo, The Mirror Crack'd, Just a Gigolo, The
Children, Liebestraum.
TELEVISION: Series: Falcon Crest. Guest: Alfred Hitchcock
Presents (1985). Movies: Third Girl From the Left, Satan's
Triangle, Malibu.

NOVELLO, DON
Writer, Comedian, Actor. b. Ashtabula, OH, Jan. 1, 1943. e.
U. of Dayton, B.A., 1964. Best known as Father Guido
Sarducci on Saturday Night Live. Was advertising copy writer
before writing and performing on The Smothers Brothers
Comedy Hour (1975). Writer for Van Dyke and Company, and
writer-performer on Saturday Night Live 1978-80. Producer:
SCTV Comedy Network (1982) and performer-writer on B'way
in Gilda Radner—Live From New York (1979), as well as
filmed version (Gilda Live!). Recordings: Live at St. Douglas
Convent, Breakfast in Heaven. Author: The Lazlo Letters: The
Amazing Real-Life Actual Correspondence of Lazlo Toth,
American!, The Blade, Citizen Lazlo.
PICTURES: Gilda Live!, Head Office, Tucker: The Man and His
Dream, New York Stories (Life Without Zoe), The Godfather
Part III, Casper (cameo), One Night Stand, Jack.
TELEVISION: Cable specials: Fr. Guido Sarducci Goes to
College, The Vatican Inquirer—The Pope Tour.

NOYCE, PHILIP
Director. b. Griffith, New South Wales, Australia, Apr. 27,
1950. Began making films at school and university. Made first
short film at age 15, Better to Reign in Hell. In 1980, became
part-time mgr., Sydney Filmmaker's Co-operative and in 1973
was selected for Australian Nat'l Film School in Sydney, for
year-long training prog. which resulted in shorts, Good
Afternoon, Caravan Park, Castor and Pollux, God Knows Why
But It Works, and 60-minute film Backroads.
PICTURES: Backroads (also prod.., s.p.; Newsfront (also s.p.;
Australian Acad. Awards for best dir. & s.p., 1978), Heatwave
(also co-s.p.), Echoes of Paradise, Dead Calm, Blind Fury,
Patriot Games, Sliver (also cameo), Clear and Present
Danger.
TELEVISION: Mini-Series: Dismissal, Cowra Breakout.
Episodes: The Hitchhiker, Nightmare Cafe.

NUNN, BILL
Actor. b. Pittsburgh, PA. Teamed with friend Al Cooper as
member of comedy team Nunn and Cooper in nightclubs,
1980-83. On stage with various theatrical companies including
the Alliance, the Academy, Theatrical Oufit, Just Us Theatre.
THEATER: T-Bone and Weasel, Split Second, Home, A
Lesson From Aloes, A Soldier's Play, Macbeth, The River
Niger, Fences.
PICTURES: School Daze, Do the Right Thing, Def by
Temptation, Cadillac Man, Mo' Better Blues, New Jack City,
Regarding Henry, Sister Act, National Lampoon's Loaded
Weapon 1, The Last Seduction, Canadian Bacon, Things to
Do in Denver When You're Dead.
TELEVISION: Movie: The Littlest Victims. Specials: Native
Strangers, Dangerous Heart, War Stories, A Yankee in King
Arthur's Court. Guest: Fallen Angels.

NYKVIST, SVEN
Cinematographer. b. Moheda, Sweden, Dec. 3, 1922. e.
Stockholm Photog. Sch. Asst. cameraman 1941-44. Became
internationally known by photographing most of Ingmar
Bergman's pictures. Recipient of American Society of
Cinematographers Life Achievement Award, 1996.
PICTURES: Sawdust and Tinsel, The Virgin Spring, Winter
Light, Karin Mansdotter, The Silence, Loving Couples,
Persona, Hour of the Wolf, Cries and Whispers (Academy
Award, 1973), The Dove, Black Moon, Scenes from a
Marriage, The Magic Flute, Face to Face, One Day in the Life
of Ivan Denisovich, The Tenant, The Serpents' Egg, Pretty
Baby, Autumn Sonata, King of the Gypsies, Hurricane,
Starting Over, Willie and Phil, From the Life of the
Marionettes, The Postman Always Rings Twice, Cannery Row,
Fanny and Alexander (Academy Award, 1983), Swann in
Love, The Tragedy of Carmen, After the Rehearsal, Agnes of
God, Dream Lover, The Sacrifice, The Unbearable Lightness

of Being, Katinka, Another Woman, New York Stories (Oedipus Wrecks), Crimes and Misdemeanors, The Ox (dir., co-s.p. only), Chaplin, Sleepless in Seattle, What's Eating Gilbert Grape, With Honors, Kirsten Lavrandatter, Only You, Mixed Nuts, Something to Talk About, Confession.
TELEVISION: Movie: Nobody's Child.

O

O'BRIAN, HUGH
Actor. r.n. Hugh C. Krampe. b. Rochester, NY, Apr. 19, 1925. Raised in Chicago. e. Kemper Military Sch., U. of Cincinnati, UCLA. U.S. Marine Corps, where at age 18 he served as youngest drill instructor in Marine Corps history. Actor in stock cos. before film career. Founder, chmn. development: Hugh O'Brian Youth Foundation, 1958; Nat'l Chmn., Cystic Fibrosis Research Foundation 1969-74; Co-founder and pres. Thalians 1955-58; Founder Hugh O'Brian Annual Acting Awards at UCLA, 1962.
THEATER: B'way: Destry Rides Again, First Love, Guys and Dolls, Cactus Flower, The Decision. Regional: The Music Man, Rainmaker, Plaza Suite, On 20th Century, Stalag 17, Thousand Clowns, etc.
PICTURES: Young Lovers (debut, 1949), Never Fear, Rocketship X-M, The Return of Jesse James, Vengeance Valley, Fighting Coast Guard, Little Big Horn, On the Loose, The Cimarron Kid, Red Ball Express, The Battle at Apache Pass, Sally and Saint Anne, Son of Ali Baba, The Raiders, The Lawless Breed, Meet Me at the Fair, Seminole, Man from the Alamo, Back to God's Country, The Stand at Apache River, Saskatchewan, Fireman Save My Child, Drums Across the River, Broken Lance, There's No Business Like Show Business, White Feather, The Twinkle in God's Eye, Brass Legend, The Fiend Who Walked the West, Alias Jesse James, Come Fly with Me, Love Has Many Faces, In Harm's Way, Ten Little Indians, Ambush Bay, Africa--Texas Style!, Killer Force, The Shootist, Game of Death, Doin' Time on Planet Earth, Twins.
TELEVISION: Series: The Life and Legend of Wyatt Earp, Search. Specials: Dial M for Murder, A Punt a Pass and a Prayer, Going Home, Engagement Ring, Invitation to a Gunfighter, Reunion, Chain of Command, It's a Man's World, Wyatt Earp: Return to Tombstone. Movies: Wild Women, Harpy, Probe (Search), Murder on Flight 502, Benny & Barney: Las Vegas Undercover, Fantasy Island, Murder at the World Series, Cruise Into Terror, The Seekers, Gunsmoke: The Last Apache, The Gambler Returns: Luck of the Draw.

O'BRIEN, CONAN
Performer, Writer. b. Brookline, MA, Apr. 18, 1963. e. Harvard. Served two years as pres. of Harvard Lampoon before landing work as tv writer for The Simpsons, Saturday Night Live (Emmy Award, 1989). Prod. of pilot Lookwell. Series: Not Necessarily the News, NBC's Late Night With Conan O'Brien (Emmy nom., 1996).

O'BRIEN, MARGARET
Actress. r.n. Angela Maxine O'Brien. Los Angeles, CA, Jan. 15, 1938. Screen debut at 3 in Babes on Broadway (1941). Awarded special Academy Award as best child actress, 1944. Voted one of ten best money-making stars in Motion Picture Herald-Fame Poll 1945-46.
PICTURES: Babes on Broadway (debut, 1941), Journey for Margaret, Dr. Gillespie's Criminal Case, Lost Angel, Thousands Cheer, Madame Curie, Jane Eyre, The Canterville Ghost, Meet Me in St. Louis, Music for Millions, Our Vines Have Tender Grapes, Bad Bascomb, Three Wise Fools, Unfinished Dance, Tenth Avenue Angel, The Big City, The Secret Garden, Little Women, Her First Romance, Two Persons Eyes (Jap.), Agente S3S Operazione Uranio (It.), Glory, Heller in Pink Tights, Anabelle Lee, Diabolic Wedding, Amy, Sunset After Dark.
TELEVISION: Movies: Death in Space, Split Second to an Epitaph, Testimony of Two Men. Guest: Robert Montgomery Presents, Lux Video Theatre, Playhouse 90, Wagon Train, Studio One, U.S. Steel Hour, Dr. Kildare, Love American Style, Marcus Welby M.D.

O'BRIEN, VIRGINIA
Actress. b. Los Angeles, CA, Apr. 18, 1919. e. North Hollywood h.s. Singer, comedienne with a distinctive dead-pan delivery. On stage in Meet the People. 1990, performed at London Palladium.
PICTURES: Hullabaloo (debut, 1940), The Big Store, Lady Be Good, Ringside Maisie, Ship Ahoy, Panama Hattie, DuBarry Was a Lady, As Thousands Cheer, Meet the People, Two Girls and a Sailor, The Harvey Girls, Ziegfeld Follies, Till Clouds Roll By, The Showoff, Merton of the Movies, Francis in the Navy, Gus.

OBST, LYNDA
Producer. b. New York, NY, Apr. 14, 1950. e. Pomona Col., Columbia Univ. Former editor for New York Times Magazine,

1976-79; then exec. at Polygram Pictures, 1979-81; Geffen Films, 1981-83, co-prod. at Paramount, 1983-85; prod. for Walt Disney, 1986, before moving over to Columbia. Co-Author: Dirty Dreams (with Carol Wolper).
PICTURES: Flashdance (assoc. prod.). Producer: Adventures in Babysitting, Heartbreak Hotel, The Fisher King, This Is My Life. Exec. Prod.: Sleepless in Seattle.

O'CONNELL, JACK
Producer, Director, Writer. b. Boston, MA. e. Princeton U., Harvard Business Sch. After being a creative group head in all media and doing 500 tv commercials entered feature films working with Fellini on La Dolce Vita, then asst. dir. to Antonioni on L'Avventura.
PICTURES: Writer/Prod./Dir.: Greenwich Village Story, Revolution, Christa (aka Swedish Flygirls), Up the Girls Means Three Cheers for Them All, The Hippie Revolution.

O'CONNOR, CARROLL
Actor. b. New York, NY, Aug. 2, 1924. e. University Coll., Dublin; U. of Montana. Three years with Dublin's Gate Theatre, then N.Y.
THEATER: NY: Ulysses in Nighttown, Playboy of the Western World, The Big Knife, Brothers (also dir.), Home Front. Author: Ladies of Hanover Tower.
PICTURES: A Fever in the Blood (debut, 1961), Parrish, By Love Possessed, Lad: A Dog, Belle Sommers, Lonely Are the Brave, Cleopatra, In Harm's Way, What Did You Do in the War Daddy?, Hawaii, Not With My Wife You Don't, Warning Shot, Point Blank, Waterhole No. 3, The Devil's Brigade, For Love of Ivy, Death of a Gunfighter, Marlowe, Kelly's Heroes, Doctors' Wives, Law and Disorder.
TELEVISION: Series: All in the Family (4 Emmy Awards: 1972, 1977, 1978, 1979; later retitled Archie Bunker's Place), In the Heat of the Night (Emmy Award, 1989). Guest: U.S. Steel Hour, Armstrong Circle Theatre, Kraft Theatre, The Untouchables, Dr. Kildare, East Side/West Side, Gunsmoke, Wild Wild West, Party of Five, Mad About You, etc. Special: Of Thee I Sing. Movies: Fear No Evil, The Last Hurrah (also writer), Brass, Convicted, The Father Clements Story, In the Heat of the Night: A Matter of Justice (also co-exec. prod.), In the Heat of the Night: Who Was Geli Bendl? (also co-exec. prod.), In the Heat of the Night: By Duty Bound (also co-exec. prod.), In the Heat of the Night: Grow Old With Me (also co-exec. prod.).

O'CONNOR, DONALD
Actor. b. Chicago, IL, Aug. 28, 1925. In vaudeville with family and Sons o' Fun (Syracuse, N.Y.) before screen debut 1938 in Sing You Sinners; return to vaudeville 1940-41, then resumed screen career with What's Cookin'?, 1942. Entered armed services, 1943. Voted Star of Tomorrow, 1943; best TV performer by M.P. Daily poll, 1953.
PICTURES: Sing You Sinners (debut, 1938), Sons of the Legion, Men With Wings, Tom Sawyer—Private Detective, Unmarried, Death of a Champion, Million Dollar Legs, Night Work, On Your Toes, Beau Geste, Private Buckaroo, Give Out Sisters, Get Hep to Love, When Johnny Comes Marching Home, Strictly in the Groove, It Comes Up Love, Mr. Big, Top Man, Chip Off the Old Block, Patrick the Great, Follow the Boys, The Merry Monahans, Bowery to Broadway, This Is the Life, Something in the Wind, Are You With It?, Feudin' Fussin' and-a-Fightin', Yes Sir That's My Baby, Francis, Curtain Call at Cactus Creek, The Milkman, Double Crossbones, Francis Goes to the Races, Singin' in the Rain, Francis Goes to West Point, I Love Melvin, Call Me Madam, Francis Covers the Big Town, Walking My Baby Back Home, Francis Joins the WACS, There's No Business Like Show Business, Francis in the Navy, Anything Goes, The Buster Keaton Story, Cry for Happy, The Wonders of Aladdin, That Funny Feeling, That's Entertainment, Ragtime, Pandemonium, A Time to Remember, Toys.
TELEVISION: Series: The Colgate Comedy Hour (host: 1951-54; Emmy Award, 1954), The Donald O'Connor Texaco Show (1954-55), The Donald O'Connor Show (synd., 1968). Movies: Alice in Wonderland, Bandit and the Silver Angel. Guest: Dinah Shore, Hollywood Palace, Carol Burnett, Julie Andrews, Ellery Queen, The Love Boat, Highway to Heaven, Tales From the Crypt. Specials: The Red Mill, Hollywood Melody, Olympus 7-0000.

O'CONNOR, GLYNNIS
Actress. b. New York, NY, Nov. 19, 1955. Daughter of ABC News prod. Daniel O'Connor and actress Lenka Peterson. e. State U., NY at Purchase. Stage includes Domestic Issues (Circle Rep., NY, 1983), The Taming of the Shrew (Great Lakes Shakespeare Fest.), The Seagull (Mirror Rep.).
PICTURES: Jeremy (debut, 1973), Baby Blue Marine, Ode to Billy Joe, Kid Vengeance, California Dreaming, Those Lips Those Eyes, Night Crossing, Melanie, Johnny Dangerously.
TELEVISION: Series: Sons and Daughters. Mini-series: Black Beauty. Movies: The Chisholms, Someone I Touched, All Together Now, The Boy in the Plastic Bubble, Little Mo, My

Kidnapper, My Love, The Fighter, Love Leads the Way, Why Me?, Sins of the Father, The Deliberate Stranger, To Heal a Nation, Death in Small Doses, Past the Bleachers.

O'CONNOR, KEVIN J.
Actor. b. 1964. e. DePaul Univ.'s Goodman Sch. of Drama. On stage in Colorado Catechism (NY), El Salvador (Chicago).
PICTURES: One More Saturday Night, Peggy Sue Got Married, Candy Mountain, Signs of Life, Steel Magnolias, Love at Large, F/X 2, Hero, Equinox, No Escape, Color of Night, Virtuosity, Lord of Illusions, Canadian Bacon.
TELEVISION: *Movie:* The Caine Mutiny Court Martial. *Special:* Tanner 88. *Guest:* Birdland.

O'CONNOR, PAT
Director. b. Ardmore, Ireland, 1943. After working in London at odd jobs (putting corks in wine bottles, paving roads), came to U.S. e. UCLA, B.A. Studied film and TV at Ryerson Institute in Toronto. 1970, trainee prod., dir. with Radio Telefis Eireann. 1970-78 prod. and dir. over 45 TV features and current affairs documentaries. (The Four Roads, The Shankhill, Kiltyclogher, One of Ourselves, Night in Ginitia). A Ballroom of Romance won BAFTA Award (1981).
PICTURES: Cal (debut, 1984), A Month in the Country, Stars and Bars, The January Man, Fools of Fortune, Circle of Friends, Sacred Hearts.
TELEVISION: *Movie:* Zelda.

O'DONNELL, CHRIS
Actor. b. Winetka, IL, 1970.
PICTURES: Men Don't Leave (debut, 1990), Fried Green Tomatoes, School Ties, Scent of a Woman, The Three Musketeers, Blue Sky, Circle of Friends, Mad Love, Batman Forever, The Chamber, In Love and War.

O'DONNELL, ROSIE
Actress. b. Commack, NY, 1961. e. Dickinson Col., Boston Univ. Stand-up comic first gaining attention on series Star Search.
THEATER: Grease! (B'way debut, 1994).
PICTURES: A League of Their Own, Sleepless in Seattle, Another Stakeout, Car 54 Where Are You?, I'll Do Anything, The Flintstones, Exit to Eden, Now and Then, Beautiful Girls, Harriet the Spy.
TELEVISION: *Series:* Gimme a Break, Stand-Up Spotlight (host, exec. prod.), Stand by Your Man, The Rosie O'Donnell Show (host).

O'HARA, CATHERINE
Actress, Writer, Director. b. Toronto, Canada, Mar. 4, 1954. Professional debut in 1974 with Toronto's Second City. Co-founder of SCTV in 1976 (Emmy and Canadian Nellie Awards for writing).
PICTURES: Nothing Personal, Rock & Rule (voice), After Hours, Heartburn, Beetlejuice, Dick Tracy, Betsy's Wedding, Home Alone, Little Vegas, There Goes the Neighborhood, Home Alone 2: Lost in New York, The Nightmare Before Christmas (voice), The Paper, Wyatt Earp, A Simple Twist of Fate, Tall Tale, Last of the High Kings.
TELEVISION: *Series:* SCTV, Steve Allen Comedy Hour, SCTV Network 90. *Guest:* Trying Times (Get a Job), Comic Relief, Dream On (also dir.).

O'HARA, GERRY
Director, Writer. b. Boston-Lincs, England 1924. e. St. Mary's Catholic Sch., Boston. Junior Reporter Boston Guardian. Entered industry in 1942 with documentaries and propaganda subjects.
PICTURES: *Director:* That Kind of Girl (debut, 1963), Game for Three Lovers, Pleasure Girls (also s.p.), Maroc 7, Love in Amsterdam, All the Right Noises (also s.p.), Leopard in the Snow, The Bitch, Fanny Hill, The Mummy Lives (also co-s.p.). *Writer:* Ten Little Indians, Havoc in Chase County, Phantom of the Opera, De Sade's Nightmare, Sherlock Holmes and the Affair in Transylvania, Catherine the Great.
TELEVISION: The Avengers, Man in a Suitcase, Journey into the Unknown, The Professionals (story editor, writer), Special Squad (story consultant), Cats Eyes (exec. story editor), Operation Julie (writer; mini-series), Sherlock Holmes & The Leading Lady, Sherlock Holmes & The Incident at Victoria Falls (co-writer).

O'HARA, MAUREEN
Actress. r.n. Maureen FitzSimons. b. Dublin. Aug. 17, 1921. Abbey Sch. of Acting. Won numerous prizes for elocution. Under contract to Erich Pommer-Charles Laughton. Co-starred, Abbey & Repertory Theatre.
PICTURES: Kicking the Moon Around (debut, 1938), My Irish Molly, Jamaica Inn, The Hunchback of Notre Dame, A Bill of Divorcement, Dance Girl Dance, They Met in Argentina, How Green Was My Valley, To the Shores of Tripoli, Ten Gentlemen From West Point, The Black Swan, The Immortal Sergeant, This Land Is Mine, The Fallen Sparrow, Buffalo Bill, The Spanish Main, Sentimental Journey, Do You Love Me?, Miracle on 34th Street, Sinbad the Sailor, The Homestretch, The Foxes of Harrow, Sitting Pretty, Woman's Secret, Forbidden Street, Father Was a Fullback, Bagdad, Comanche Territory, Tripoli, Rio Grande, At Sword's Point, Flame of Araby, The Quiet Man, Kangaroo, Against All Flags, The Redhead From Wyoming, War Arrow, Fire Over Africa, The Magnificent Matador, Lady Godiva, Long Gray Line, Lisbon, Everything But the Truth, Wings of Eagles, Our Man in Havana, The Parent Trap, The Deadly Companions, Mr. Hobbs Takes a Vacation, McLintock!, Spencer's Mountain, The Battle of the Villa Fiorita, The Rare Breed, How Do I Love Thee?, Big Jake, Only the Lonely.
TELEVISION: *Movie:* The Red Pony, The Christmas Box. *Specials:* Mrs. Miniver, Scarlet Pimpernel, Spellbound, High Button Shoes, Who's Afraid of Mother Goose.

O'HERLIHY, DAN
Actor. b. Wexford, Ireland, May 1, 1919. e. National U. of Ireland (Bachelor of Architecture). Actor with Abbey Theatre, Dublin Gate, Longford Prod.; announcer on Radio Eireann; on Broadway in The Ivy Green.
PICTURES: Odd Man Out (debut, 1946), Kidnapped, Larceny, Macbeth, Iroquois Trail, The Blue Veil, The Desert Fox, The Highwayman, Soldiers Three, At Swords Point, Invasion U.S.A., Operation Secret, Actors and Sin, Sword of Venus, The Adventures of Robinson Crusoe (Acad. Award nom.), The Black Shield of Falworth, Bengal Brigade, The Purple Mask, The Virgin Queen, City After Midnight, Home Before Dark, Imitation of Life, The Young Land, Night Fighters (A Terrible Beauty), One Foot in Hell, The Cabinet of Caligari, Fail-Safe, The Big Cube, 100 Rifles, Waterloo, The Carey Treatment, The Tamarind Seed, MacArthur, Halloween III: The Season of the Witch, The Last Starfighter, The Whoopee Boys, Robocop, The Dead, Robocop 2.
TELEVISION: *Series:* The Travels of Jamie McPheeters, The Long Hot Summer, Hunter's Moon, Whiz Kids, Man Called Sloane, Twin Peaks. *Mini-series:* QB VII, Jennie: Lady Randolph Churchill, Nancy Astor. *Movies:* The People, Deadly Game, Woman on the Run, Good Against Evil, Love Cheat and Steal. *Guest:* The Equalizer, L.A. Law, Murder She Wrote, Ray Bradbury Theatre, Father Dowling. BBC: Colditz, The Secret Servant, Artemis, The Last Day, Jennie, Nancy Astor.

OHLMEYER, DONALD W., JR.
Executive, Producer, Director. b. New Orleans, LA, Feb. 3, 1945. e. U. of Notre Dame, B.A. (Communications), 1967. Producer and director at both ABC and NBC. Formed Ohlmeyer Communications Company, 1982 (diversified prod. and dist. of entertainment and sports prog.). Assoc. dir., ABC Sports, NY 1967-70; director, ABC Sports, 1971-72 (dir. 1972 Olympic Games); prod.: ABC Sports, NY 1972-77 (prod. and dir. 1976 Winter and Summer Olympics; prod. ABC's Monday Night Football, 1972-76); exec. prod.: NBC Sports, NY 1977-82 (exec. prod., 1980 Olympics, The World Series, The Super Bowl). Special Bulletin (exec. prod.), John Denver's Christmas in Aspen (exec. prod.). Chmn. and CEO, Ohlmeyer Communications Co., LA, 1982-present. 1993, named pres. NBC West Coast. Recipient of 14 Emmy Awards, Humanitas Prize, Award for Excellence, National Film Board. Member, Directors Guild of America.
TELEVISION: *Specials:* Heroes of Desert Storm (dir.), Disney's Christmas on Ice (dir.), Crimes of the Century (prod.). *Series:* Lifestories (dir./exec. prod.), Fast Copy (prod.). *Movies:* Cold Sassy Tree (exec. prod.), Crazy in Love (exec. prod.), Right to Die (exec. prod.).

O'KEEFE, MICHAEL
Actor. b. Larchmont, NY, April 24, 1955. e. NYU, AADA. m. singer Bonnie Raitt. Co-founder, Colonnades Theatre Lab, NY.
THEATER: *B'way:* Mass Appeal (Theatre World Award), Fifth of July. *Off-B'way:* Killdere (NYSF), Moliere in Spite of Himself, Christmas on Mars, Short Eyes. *Regional:* Streamers, A Few Good Men (tour).
PICTURES: Gray Lady Down (debut, 1978), The Great Santini (Acad. Award nom.), Caddyshack, Split Image, Nate and Hayes, Finders Keepers, The Slugger's Wife, Ironweed, Out of the Rain, Me and Veronica, Nina Takes a Lover, Three Lovers, Edie and Pen, Ghosts of Mississippi.
TELEVISION: *Series:* Against the Law, Roseanne. *Movies:* The Lindbergh Kidnapping Case, Friendly Persuasion, Panache, The Dark Secret of Harvest Home, A Rumor of War, Unholy Matrimony, Bridge to Silence, Disaster at Silo 7, Too Young to Die?, In the Best Interest of the Child, Fear, Incident at Deception Ridge, The People Next Door.

OLDKNOW, WIILIAM H.
Executive. b. Atlanta, GA, Sept. 3, 1924. e. U.S.C. Served in USNR from 1943-46. Pres., Sero Amusement Co., 1947-present (drive-in theatres, shopping centers, and commercial real-estate). Sole proprietor, Starlight Drive-in Theatre, Atlanta, GA. Chmn. and pres., De Anza Land & Leisure Corp.

OLDMAN, GARY
Actor. b. New Cross, South London, Eng., March 21, 1958. Won scholarship to Rose Bruford Drama College (B.A. Theatre Arts) after studying with Greenwich Young People's Theatre. Acted with Theatre Royal, York and joined touring theatre co. Then in 1980 appeared with Glasgow Citizens Theatre in Massacre at Paris, Chinchilla, Desperado Corner, A Waste of Time (also touring Europe and South America). Received Evening Standard Film Award for Best Newcomer for Sid and Nancy, 1986.
THEATER: London: Minnesota Moon, Summit Conference, Rat in the Skull, Women Beware Women, The War Plays, Real Dreams, The Desert Air, Serious Money (Royal Shakespeare Co.), The Pope's Wedding (Time Out's Fringe Award, best newcomer 1985-86; British Theatre Assc. Drama Mag. Award, Best Actor 1985).
PICTURES: Sid and Nancy (debut, 1986), Prick Up Your Ears, Track 29, We Think the World of You, Criminal Law, Chattahoochee, State of Grace, Rosencrantz and Guildenstern Are Dead, Exile, Before and After Death, JFK, Bram Stoker's Dracula, True Romance, Romeo Is Bleeding, The Professional, Immortal Beloved, Murder in the First, Dead Presidents, The Scarlet Letter, Basquiat.
TELEVISION: Remembrance, Meantime, Honest Decent and True, Rat in the Skull, The Firm, Heading Home, Fallen Angels.

OLIN, KEN
Actor, Director. b. Chicago, IL, July 30, 1954. e. Univ. of PA. m. actress Patricia Wettig. Studied acting with Warren Robertson and Stella Adler. Made Off-B'way deput in Taxi Tales, 1978.
PICTURES: Ghost Story, Queen's Logic, White Fang 2: Myth of the White Wolf (dir.).
TELEVISION: Series: The Bay City Blues, Hill Street Blues, Falcon Crest, thirtysomething (also dir.). Movies (actor): Women at West Point, Flight 90: Disaster on the Potomac, There Must Be a Pony, Tonight's the Night, Cop Killer, A Stoning in Fulham County, Goodnight Sweet Wife: A Murder in Boston, Telling Secrets, Nothing But the Truth. Movies (director): The Broken Cord, Doing Time on Maple Drive, In Pursuit of Honor. Guest: Murder She Wrote, Hotel, The Hitchhiker.

OLIN, LENA
Actress. b. Stockholm, Sweden, 1955. Member of the Royal Dramatic Theatre in Stockholm. Daughter of actor-director Stig Olin. m. director Lasse Hallstrom.
THEATER: NY: Miss Julie.
PICTURES: The Adventures of Picasso, Karleken, Fanny and Alexander, Grasanklingar, After the Rehearsal, A Matter of Life and Death, Friends, The Unbearable Lightness of Being, S/Y Joy (Gladjen), Enemies a Love Story (Acad. Award nom.), Havana, Mr. Jones, Romeo Is Bleeding, The Night and the Moment, Night Falls on Manhattan.

OLMI, ERMANNO
Director, Writer, Producer, Editor. b. Bergamo, Italy, July 24, 1931. e. Accademia d'Arte Drammatica, Milan. Worked as a clerk for an electric company Edisonvolta 1949-52, until 1952 when he began directing theatrical and cinematic activities sponsored by co. 1952-61, directed or supervised over 40 short 16mm and 35mm documentary films. 1959 first feature film, semi-doc. Time Stood Still. With other friends and Tullio Kezich formed prod. co., 22 December S.P.A., 1961. 1982, Helped found Hypothesis Cinema, a sch. for aspiring dirs.
PICTURES: Director/Writer: Time Stood Still (debut, 1959), The Sound of Trumpets, The Fiances (also prod.), And There Came a Man (A Man Named John), One Fine Day (also edit.), The Tree of the Wood Clogs (Cannes Film Fest. Award, 1978; also photog., edit.), Camminacammina (also photog., edit., design), Milano '83 (also photog., edit.), Long Live the Lady (also co-photog., edit.), Legend of the Holy Drinker (also edit.), Il Segreto Del Bosco Vecchio. Documenatries: Artigiani Veneti, Lungo Il Fiume.
TELEVISION: The Scavengers (also photog.), During the Summer (also photog., edit.), The Circumstance (also photog., edit.).

OLMOS, EDWARD JAMES
Actor. b. East Los Angeles, CA, February 24, 1947. e. East Los Angeles City Coll., CA State U. m. actress Lorraine Bracco. Started as rock singer with group Eddie James and the Pacific Ocean. By the early 1970s acted in small roles on Kojak and Hawaii Five-O. 1978 starred in Luis Valdez's musical drama Zoot Suit at Mark Taper Forum (L.A. Drama Critics Circle Award, 1978), later on B'way (Theatre World Award, Tony nom.), and in film version. Formed YOY Productions with director Robert Young. Numerous awards for humanitarian work.
PICTURES: Aloha Bobby and Rose (debut, 1975), Alambrista!, Virus, Wolfen, Zoot Suit, Blade Runner, The Ballad of Gregorio Cortez (also assoc. prod., composer and musical adaptor), Saving Grace, Stand and Deliver (Acad.

Award nom.; also co-prod.), Triumph of the Spirit, Talent for the Game, American Me (also dir., co-prod.), A Million to Juan, Mirage, My Family/Mi Familia, Roosters, Caught.
TELEVISION: Movies: Evening in Byzantium, 300 Miles for Stephanie, Menendez: A Killing in Beverly Hills, The Burning Season. Specials: Sequin, Y.E.S. Inc. Series: Miami Vice (Golden Globe & Emmy Awards, 1985; also dir. episodes). Mini-series: Mario Puzo's The Fortunate Pilgrim.

O'LOUGHLIN, GERALD STUART
Actor. b. New York, NY, Dec. 23, 1921. e. Blair Acad., Lafayette Col., U. of Rochester, Neighborhood Playhouse. U.S. Marine, WWII.
THEATER: B'way: Streetcar (ANTA series), Shadow of a Gunman, Dark at the Top of the Stairs, A Touch of the Poet, Cook for Mr. General, One Flew Over the Cuckoo's Nest, Calculated Risk, Lovers and Other Strangers. Off-B'way: Who'll Save the Plowboy (Obie Award), Harry Noon and Night, Machinal.
PICTURES: Lovers and Lollipops, Cop Hater, A Hatful of Rain, Ensign Pulver, A Fine Madness, In Cold Blood, Ice Station Zebra, Desperate Characters, The Organization, The Valachi Papers, Twilight's Last Gleaming, Frances, Crimes of Passion, City Heat, Quicksilver.
TELEVISION: Movies: The D.A.: Murder One, Murder at the World Series, Something for Joey, A Love Affair: The Eleanor and Lou Gehrig Story, Crash, Detour to Terror, Pleasure Palace, A Matter of Life and Death, Under Siege, Perry Mason: The Case of the Notorious Nun, Child's Cry, In the Arms of a Killer. Mini-Series: Wheels, Roots: The Next Generations, Blind Ambition, Women in White, The Blue and the Gray. Series: The Storefront Lawyers (Men at Law), The Rookies, Automan, Our House. Guest: Alcoa Premiere, Philco-Goodyear, Suspense, The Defenders, Ben Casey, Dr. Kildare, 12 O'Clock High, Going My Way, Naked City, Gunsmoke, Green Hornet, Mission Impossible, Mannix, Judd For The Defense, Hawaii 5-0, Cannon, Room 222, Charlie's Angels, M*A*S*H, Trapper John M.D., Fame, T.J. Hooker, Murder She Wrote, Highway to Heaven, Dirty Dancing, others.

OLSON, DALE C.
Executive. b. Fargo, ND, Feb. 20, 1934. e. Portland State Coll., OR. Owner, Dale C. Olson & Associates; formerly sn. v.p. & pres., m.p. div., Rogers & Cowan public relations. Journalist on Oregonian newspaper, West Coast editor, Boxoffice Magazine, 1958-60; critic and reporter, Daily Variety, 1960-66; dir. of publ., Mirisch Corp., 1966-68; Rogers & Cowan, 1968-85. Past pres., Hollywood Press Club, awarded Bob Yaeger and Les Mason award by Publicists Guild; v.p. Diamond Circle, City of Hope; delegate for U.S. to Manila International Film Festival. Chmn. public rltns. coordin. committee & member nat'l bd. of trustees, A.M.P.A.S., 1989-91. Chmn. Western Council, Actors Fund of America, 1991. On Nat'l Bd. of Trustees, 1992-present.

OLSON, JAMES
Actor. b. Evanston, IL, Oct. 8, 1930. e. Northwestern U.
THEATER: NY: The Young and the Beautiful, Romulus, The Chinese Prime Minister, J.B., Slapstick Tragedy, Three Sisters, Sin of Pat Muldoon, Winter's Tale, Of Love Remembered, Twelve Dreams.
PICTURES: The Sharkfighters, The Strange One, Rachel Rachel, Moon Zero Two, The Andromeda Strain, The Groundstar Conspiracy, The Mafu Cage, Ragtime, Amityville II: The Possession, Commando, Rachel River.
TELEVISION: Movies: Paper Man, Incident on a Dark Street, Manhunter, A Tree Grows in Brooklyn, The Sex Symbol, The Family Nobody Wanted, Someone I Touched, Man on the Outside, Strange New World, Law and Order, The Spell, Moviola: The Silent Years, Cave-In!, The Parade. Specials: Missiles of October, Vince Lombardi Story, Court-Martial of Geoge Armstrong Custer.

OLSON, NANCY
Actress. b. Milwaukee, WI, July 14, 1929. e. U. of Wisconsin, UCLA. No prof. experience prior to films.
PICTURES: Canadian Pacific (debut, 1949), Sunset Boulevard (Acad. Award nom.), Union Station, Mr. Music, Submarine Command, Force of Arms, Big Jim McLain, So Big, The Boy From Oklahoma, Battle Cry, Pollyanna, The Absent-Minded Professor, Son of Flubber, Smith!, Snowball Express, Airport 1975, Making Love.
TELEVISION: Series: Kingston: Confidential, Paper Dolls. Special: High Tor.

O'NEAL, RON
Actor. b. Utica, NY, Sept. 1, 1937. e. Ohio State U. Spent 9 yrs. at Karamu House in Cleveland (inter-racial theatre) from 1957 to 1966, acting in 40 plays. 1967-68 spent in N.Y. teaching acting in Harlem. Appeared in all-black revue 1968, The Best of Broadway, then in summer stock. Acted off-B'way in American Pastorale and The Mummer's Play. 1970 joined the

Public Theatre. Break came with No Place To Be Somebody, which won him the Obie, Clarence Derwent, Drama Desk and Theatre World Awards.
THEATER: Tiny Alice, The Dream of Monkey Mountain.
PICTURES: Move (debut, 1970), The Organization, Super Fly, Super Fly TNT (also dir., co-story), The Master Gunfighter, Brothers, A Force of One, When a Stranger Calls, The Final Countdown, St. Helens, Red Dawn, Mercenary Fighters, Hero and the Terror, Up Against the Wall (also dir.), Death House.
TELEVISION: Series: Bring 'em Back Alive, The Equalizer. Mini-Series: North and South. Movies: Freedom Road, Brave New World, Guyana Tragedy: The Story of Jim Jones, Sophisticated Gents, Playing with Fire, North Beach and Rawhide, As Summers Die.

O'NEAL, RYAN
Actor. r.n. Patrick Ryan O'Neal. b. Los Angeles, CA, April 20, 1941. Parents, screenwriter-novelist, Charles O'Neal, and actress Patricia Callaghan. Daughter is actress Tatum O'Neal; son is actor Griffin O'Neal. Boxer, L.A. Golden Gloves, 1956-57. Began career as stand-in, stunt man, then actor in Tales of the Vikings series, in Germany, 1959; freelanced in Hollywood.
PICTURES: The Big Bounce (debut, 1969), The Games, Love Story (Acad. Award nom.), Wild Rovers, What's Up Doc?, Paper Moon, The Thief Who Came to Dinner, Barry Lyndon, Nickelodeon, A Bridge Too Far, The Driver, Oliver's Story, The Main Event, So Fine, Green Ice, Partners, Irreconcilable Differences, Fever Pitch, Tough Guys Don't Dance, Chances Are, Faithful.
TELEVISION: Series: Empire, Peyton Place, Good Sports. Movies: Love Hate Love, Small Sacrifices, The Man Upstairs. Special: Liza Minnelli: A Triple Play. Guest: Dobie Gillis, Bachelor Father, Leave It to Beaver, My Three Sons, Perry Mason, The Larry Sanders Show. Pilot: 1775.

O'NEAL, TATUM
Actress. b. Los Angeles, CA, Nov. 5, 1963. Daughter of actors Ryan O'Neal and Joanna Moore. NY stage debut 1992 in A Terrible Beauty, followed by Adroscoggin Fugue.
PICTURES: Paper Moon (debut, 1973; Academy Award, best supporting actress), The Bad News Bears, Nickelodeon, International Velvet, Little Darlings, Circle of Two, Certain Fury, Little Noises.
TELEVISION: Movie: Woman on the Run: The Lawrencia Bembenek Story. Special: 15 and Getting Straight. Guest: Cher, Faerie Tale Theatre (Goldilocks and the Three Bears).

O'NEIL, THOMAS F.
Executive. b. Kansas City, MO, Apr. 18, 1915. e. Holy Cross Coll., 1933-37. Employed by General Tire and Rubber Co., 1937-41; U.S. Coast Guard, 1941-46; v.p., dir., Yankee Network, Boston, 1948-51; pres. chmn. of bd. RKO General, Inc., 1952. Arranged purchase RKO Radio by General Teleradio, Inc. from Howard Hughes, July, 1955; chairman of the Board, RKO General, Inc., dir., General Tire & Rubber Co.

O'NEILL, ED
Actor. b. Youngstown, OH, Apr. 12, 1946. e. Ohio Univ., Youngstown State. Taught social studies in Youngstown prior to becoming an actor. Made NY stage debut Off-Off-B'way in Requiem for a Heavyweight at SoHo Rep. Theatre. B'way debut in Knockout.
PICTURES: Deliverance, Cruising, The Dogs of War, Disorganized Crime, K-9, The Adventures of Ford Fairlane, Sibling Rivalry, Dutch, Wayne's World, Wayne's World 2, Blue Chips, Little Giants.
TELEVISION: Series: Married... With Children. Pilot: Farrell for the People. Movies: When Your Lover Leaves, The Day the Women Got Even, Popeye Doyle, A Winner Never Quits, Right to Die, Police School, The Whereabouts of Jenny, W.E.I.R.D. World.

O'NEILL, JENNIFER
Actress. b. Rio de Janeiro, Brazil, Feb. 20, 1949. e. Dalton Sch. Model before entering films. Spokeswoman: CoverGirl cosmetics. Pres., Point of View Productions and Management.
PICTURES: Rio Lobo, Summer of '42, Such Good Friends, The Carey Treatment, Glass Houses, Lady Ice, The Reincarnation of Peter Proud, Whiffs, Caravans, The Psychic, The Innocent, A Force of One, Cloud Dancer, Steel, Scanners, Committed, I Love N.Y., Love is Like That, Invasion of Privacy, The Gentle People.
TELEVISION: Series: Bare Essence, Cover Up. Movies: Love's Savage Fury, The Other Victim, Chase, Perry Mason: The Case of the Shooting Star, The Red Spider, Glory Days, Full Exposure: The Sex Tapes Scandal, Personals, Perfect Family, The Cover Girl Murders, Jonathan Stone: Threat of Innocence. Mini-Series: A.D.

ONTKEAN, MICHAEL
Actor. b. Vancouver, British Columbia, Canada, Jan. 24, 1946. e. U. of New Hampshire. Son of Leonard and Muriel Cooper Ontkean, actors. Acting debut at 4 with father's rep. theater. Child actor with Stratford Shakespeare Fest., CBC and Natl Film Bd. Attended coll. 4 years on hockey scholarship. Has performed with Public Theatre, NY, Willamstown Theatre Fest., Mark Taper Lab, The Kitchen, Soho.
PICTURES: The Peace Killers (debut, 1971), Pick Up on 101, Necromancy, Hot Summer Week, Slap Shot, Voices, Willie and Phil, Making Love, Just the Way You Are, The Allnighter, Maid to Order, Clara's Heart, Street Justice, Cold Front, Bye Bye Blues, Postcards From the Edge, Bayou Boy, The Toy Factory, Summer, Access All Areas, Le Sang des Autres, Cutting Loose, Square Deal, Rapture.
TELEVISION: Series: The Rookies, Twin Peaks. Movies: The Rookies (pilot), The Blood of Others, Kids Don't Tell, The Right of the People, Twin Peaks (pilot), Defense of a Married Man, In a Child's Name, Legacy of Lies, Whose Child Is This? The War for Baby Jessica, Vendetta 2: The New Mafia, Danielle Steel's Family Album, The Man Next Door, Man From the South.

OPHULS, MARCEL
Director, Writer. r.n. Hans Marcel Oppenheimer. b. Frankfurt-am-Main, Germany, Nov. 1, 1927. Son of German director Max Ophuls. e. Occidental Coll., U. of California, Berkeley, Sorbonne (philosophy). Family moved to France, 1932, then to Hollywood, 1941. Military service with Occupation forces in Japan, 1946; performed with theater unit, Tokyo. 1951 began working in French film industry as asst. dir., using name Marcel Wall. Asst. dir. on Moulin Rouge, Act of Love, Marianne de ma Jeunesse, Lola Montes. 1956-59, radio and TV story ed., West Germany. Later worked for French TV as reporter and dir. news mag. features. Dir. & wrote short film Henri Matisse. 1968 doc. dir. for German TV. 1975-78 staff prod. CBS News, then ABC News. MacArthur Fellowship 1991. Member of AMPAS.
PICTURES: Director/Writer: Love at 20 (dir. segment), Banana Peel, Fire at Will, Munich or Peace in Our Time, The Sorrow and the Pity (also prod.; Natl. Soc. of Film Critics, NY Film Critics & Prix de Dinard Awards, 1970), The Harvest at Mai Lai, A Sense of Loss, The Memory of Justice, Hotel Terminus--The Life and Times of Klaus Barbie (also prod.; Academy Award, Berlin Peace Prize, Cannes Jury Prize, 1988), The Troubles We've Seen (also prod.; Intl. Film Critics Prize, 1994).
TELEVISION: America Revisited, Two Whole Days, November Days.

OPOTOWSKY, STAN
Executive. b. New Orleans, LA, Apr. 13, 1923. e. Tulane U. Served in U.S. Marine Corps as combat corr. and later joined United Press, working in New Orleans, Denver, and New York. Published own weekly newspaper in Mississippi before returning to N.Y. to join New York Post as mgr. editor and traveling natl. corr. Is also cinematographer and film editor. Joined ABC News as TV assignment editor; named asst. assignment mgr. 1974 named dir. of operations for ABC News TV Documentaries. 1975 named dir. of TV News Coverage, ABC News.
TELEVISION: Author: The Big Picture, The Longs of Louisiana, The Kennedy Government, Men Behind Bars.

O'QUINN, TERRY
Actor. b. Michigan.
THEATER: B'way: Foxfire, Curse of an Aching Heart. Off-B'way: Richard III, Groves of Academy, Total Abandon. Regional: Streamers, Measure for Measure, The Front Page.
PICTURES: Heaven's Gate, Without a Trace, All the Right Moves, Places in the Heart, Mrs. Soffel, Mischief, Silver Bullet, SpaceCamp, The Stepfather, Black Widow, Young Guns, Pin, Stepfather 2, Blind Fury, The Rocketeer, Prisoners of the Sun, Company Business, The Cutting Edge, Amityville: A New Generation, Tombstone, Lipstick Camera.
TELEVISION: Movies: FDR: The Final Year, Prisoner Without a Name Cell Without a Number, Right to Kill, Unfinished Business, An Early Frost, Stranger on My Land, Women of Valor, When the Time Comes, Perry Mason: The Case of the Desperate Deception, Son of the Morning Star, The Last to Go, Deliver Them From Evil: The Taking of Alta View, Trial: The Price of Passion, Sexual Advances, Wild Card, The Good Fight, Born Too Soon, Visions of Murder, Heart of a Child, Don't Talk to Strangers, Justice in a Small Town, A Friend to Die For, Ray Alexander: A Menu for Murder.

ORBACH, JERRY
Actor. b. Bronx, NY, Oct. 20, 1935. e. U. of Illinois, Northwestern U. Trained for stage with Herbert Berghof and Lee Strasberg. N.Y. stage debut in Threepenny Opera, 1955.
THEATER: The Fantasticks (original cast, 1960), Carnival, The Cradle Will Rock, Guys and Dolls, Scuba Duba, Promises Promises (Tony Award, 1969), 6 Rms Riv Vu, Chicago, 42nd Street.
PICTURES: Cop Hater, Mad Dog Coll, John Goldfarb Please Come Home, The Gang That Couldn't Shoot Straight, A Fan's Notes, Foreplay (The President's Woman), The Sentinel,

Underground Aces, Prince of the City, Brewster's Millions, F/X, The Imagemaker, Dirty Dancing, Someone to Watch Over Me, Crimes and Misdemeanors, Last Exit to Brooklyn, I Love N.Y., A Gnome Named Norm, California Casanova, Dead Women in Lingerie, Out for Justice, Toy Soldiers (unbilled), Delusion, Delirious, Beauty and the Beast (voice), Straight Talk, Universal Soldier, Mr. Saturday Night, The Cemetery Club.
TELEVISION: Series: The Law and Harry McGraw, Law and Order. Guest: Shari Lewis Show, Jack Paar, Bob Hope Presents, Love American Style, Murder She Wrote, Kojak, Golden Girls, Hunter. Movies: An Invasion of Privacy, Out on a Limb, Love Among Thieves, In Defense of a Married Man, Broadway Bound, Quiet Killer. Mini-Series: Dream West.

ORMOND, JULIA
Actress. b. England, 1965. Studied acting at Webber Douglas Acad., London.
THEATER: The Rehearsal, Wuthering Heights, Arms and the Man, The Crucible, Faith Hope and Charity (London Drama Critics Award, 1989).
PICTURES: The Baby of Macon, Nostradamus, Legends of the Fall, First Knight, Captives, Sabrina.
TELEVISION: Mini-Series: Traffik. Movies: Young Catherine, Stalin.

ORTEGA, KENN
Director, Choreographer. b. Palo Alto, CA. e. American Conserv. Theatre, Canada Coll. Started acting at age 13. Earned several scholarships to dance academies in San Francisco Bay area. Regional theatre roles in Oliver, Hair, The Last Sweet Days of Isaac, before staging shows for rock band The Tubes. First major tv job choreographing Cher special. Directed/choreographed concerts and/or music videos for such performers as Michael Jackson, Kiss, Elton John, Cher, Rod Stewart, Diana Ross, Madonna, Billy Joel, Oingo Boingo, Miami Sound Machine, Pointer Sisters, Toto. Artistic dir. and choreographer, 1996 Centennial Olympic Games opening and closing ceremonies.
PICTURES: Director/Choreographer: Newsies, Hocus Pocus. Choreographer: The Rose (asst. to Toni Basil), Xanadu, One From the Heart, St. Elmo's Fire, Pretty in Pink, Ferris Bueller's Day Off, Dirty Dancing, Salsa (also assoc. prod.), Shag, To Wong Foo—Thanks for Everything–Julie Newmar.
TELEVISION: Series: Dirty Dancing (dir., choreog.), Hull High (dir., co-exec. prod., choreog.). Choreographed many specials including American Music Awards, Academy Awards, NAACP Awards, music specials starring Cher, Olivia Newton-John, Neil Diamond, Smokey Robinson, etc. Director: Second Noah.

O'SHEA, MILO
Actor. b. Dublin, Ireland, June 2, 1926. Member of Dublin Gate Theatre Co., 1944, before screen career.
THEATER: NY: Staircase, Dear World, The Comedians, A Touch of the Poet, Waiting For Godot (Brooklyn Acad. of Music), Mass Appeal, My Fair Lady, Corpse!, Meet Me in St. Louis, Remembrance (Off-B'way), Philadelphia Here I Come!, Alive Alive Oh! (alo co-writer), Mrs. Warren's Profession. London: Treasure Hunt, Glory Be, Hans Andersen, Corpse, Can-Can.
PICTURES: Carry on Cabby, Never Put It in Writing, Ulysses, Romeo and Juliet, Barbarella, The Adding Machine, The Angel Levine, Paddy, Sacco and Vanzetti, Loot, Theatre of Blood, Digby: The Biggest Dog in the World, It's Not the Size That Counts, Arabian Adventure, The Pilot, The Verdict, The Purple Rose of Cairo, The Dream Team, Opportunity Knocks, Only the Lonely, The Playboys, Rooney, Never Put It In Writing.
TELEVISION: Series: Once a Hero, Frasier. Mini-Series: QB VII, Ellis Island, The Best of Families. Movies/Specials: Two By Forsythe, Peter Lundy and the Medicine Hat Stallion, Portrait of a Rebel: Margaret Sanger, And No One Could Save Her, A Times for Miracles, Broken Vows, Angel in Green, Murder in the Heartland. Guest: The Golden Girls, Cheers, Who's the Boss, Beauty and the Beast, St. Elsewhere.

OSHIMA, NAGISA
Director, Writer. b. Kyoto, Japan, March 31, 1932. e. U. of Kyoto (law), 1954. Joined Shochiku Ofuna Studios in 1954 as asst. dir.; 1956 wrote film criticism and became editor-in-chief of film revue Eiga hihyo; 1959 promoted to director. 1962-65 worked exclusively in TV; 1962-64 made documentaries in Korea and Vietnam; 1975 formed Oshima Prods. 1976, his book of Realm of the Senses seized by police. With editor, prosecuted for obscenity, acquitted. Pres. of Directors Guild of Japan, 1980-present.
PICTURES: Dir./Writer: A Town of Love and Hope (debut, 1959), Cruel Story of Youth, The Sun's Burial, Night and Fog in Japan, The Catch (dir. only), The Christian Rebel, A Child's First Adventure, I'm Here Bellett, The Pleasures of the Flesh, Violence at Noon (dir. only), Band of Ninja (also co-prod.), Sing a Song of Sex (also co- prod.), Japanese Summer: Double Suicide (also co-prod.), Death By Hanging, Three

Resurrected Drunkards (A Sinner in Paradise), Diary of a Shinjuku Thief, Boy (dir. only), He Died After the War, The Ceremony, Dear Summer Sister, In the Realm of the Senses, Phantom Love, Empire of Passion (Phantom Love; also co-prod.), Merry Christmas Mr. Lawrence, Max My Love.

OSMOND, DONNY
Singer, TV Host. b. Ogden, UT, Dec. 9, 1957. Seventh of 9 children, he was fifth member of family to become professional singer. (Four brothers: Alan, Wayne, Merrill and Jay, were original members of Osmond Bros., who originally sang barbershop quartet.) Made debut at 4 on Andy Williams Show. Has had 12 gold albums. Was co-host with sister of Donny & Marie on TV.
THEATER: Little Johnny Jones, Joseph and the Amazing Technicolor Dreamcoat.
PICTURE: Goin' Coconuts.
TELEVISION: Series: The Andy Williams Show, Donny and Marie. Movie: The Wild Women of Chastity Gulch. Guest: The Jerry Lewis Show, Here's Lucy, The Love Boat.

OSMOND, MARIE
Singer, TV Host. b. Ogden, UT, Oct. 13, 1959. Began career at age of 3 on Andy Williams Show. Her first album, Paper Roses went gold. Appeared with brother Donny in feature film Goin' Coconuts.
TELEVISION: Series: Donny and Marie, Marie, Ripley's Believe It or Not (co-host), Maybe This Time. Movies: Gift of Love, I Married Wyatt Earp, Side By Side.

O'STEEN, SAM
Editor, Director. b. Nov. 6, 1923. Entered m.p. industry 1956 as asst. to editor George Tomassini on The Wrong Man. Became full editor in 1963 on Youngblood Hawke. Directorial debut with TV film A Brand New Life, 1972.
PICTURES: Youngblood Hawke, Kisses for My President, Robin and the 7 Hoods, Marriage on the Rocks, None But the Brave, Who's Afraid of Virginia Woolf?, Cool Hand Luke, The Graduate, Rosemary's Baby, The Sterile Cuckoo (spv. edit.), Catch-22, Carnal Knowledge, Portnoy's Complaint, The Day of the Dolphin, Chinatown, Sparkle (dir.), Straight Time, Hurricane, Amityville II: The Possession, Silkwood, Heartburn, Nadine, Biloxi Blues, Frantic, Working Girl, A Dry White Season (co-edit.), Postcards from the Edge, Regarding Henry, Wolf.
TELEVISION: Director: A Brand New Life, I Love You Goodbye, Queen of the Stardust Ballroom (DGA Award), High Risk, Look What's Happened to Rosemary's Baby, The Best Little Girl in the World, Kids Don't Tell.

O'SULLIVAN, KEVIN P.
Executive. b. New York, NY, April 13, 1928. e. Queens Coll., Flushing, NY. Associated with television 40 yrs., initially as a talent; later as businessman. Won first prize in Arthur Godfrey Talent Scouts competition in 1948. 1950-55 professional singer, actor on TV, in theatre, night clubs. 1955-57 on radio-TV promotion staff, Ronson Corp. 1958-61, salesman, Television Programs of America. 1961-67 dir. of program services, Harrington, Righter and Parsons. 1967 joined ABC Films, domestic sales as v.p. & gen. sales mgr. 1969 named v.p., gen. mgr. then pres., ABC Films, Inc.; 1970 made pres., ABC Int'l. TV, while retaining position as pres., ABC Films. 1973 became pres., Worldvision Enterprises, Inc., co. formed to succeed ABC Films when FCC stopped networks from TV program dist. Elected chmn. & CEO, Worldvision, 1982. Named pres., Great American Broadcasting Group, 1987. Resigned, 1988. Named pres., Kenmare Prods. Inc., 1988.

O'SULLIVAN, MAUREEN
Actress. b. Boyle, Ireland, May 17, 1911. Daughter is actress Mia Farrow. e. convents in Dublin, London; finishing sch., Paris. Discovered by dir. Frank Borzage; came to Hollywood in 1930 under contract to Fox.
THEATER: Never Too Late, The Front Page, No Sex Please, We're British, Mornings at Seven; regional theatre.
PICTURES: Song of My Heart (debut, 1930), Just Imagine, The Princess and the Plumber, A Connecticut Yankee, Skyline, The Big Shot, Tarzan the Ape Man, The Silver Lining, Skyscraper Souls, Strange Interlude, Payment Deferred, Tugboat Annie, Stage Mother, The Barretts of Wimpole Street, The Thin Man, Tarzan and His Mate, Hide-Out, David Copperfield, West Point of the Air, The Flame Within, Woman Wanted, Anna Karenina, Cardinal Richelieu, The Bishop Misbehaves, Tarzan Escapes, The Voice of Bugle Ann, The Devil Doll, A Day at the Races, The Emperor's Candlesticks, Between Two Women, My Dear Miss Aldrich, A Yank at Oxford, Hold That Kiss, Port of Seven Seas, The Crowd Roars, Spring Madness, Let Us Live, Tarzan Finds a Son, Sporting Blood, Pride and Prejudice, Maisie Was a Lady, Tarzan's Secret Treasure, Tarzan's New York Adventure, The Big Clock, Where Danger Lives, Bonzo Goes to College, All I Desire, Mission Over Korea, Duffy of San Quentin, The Steel

Cage, The Tall T, Wild Heritage, Never Too Late, The Phynx, Too Scared to Scream, Hannah and Her Sisters, Peggy Sue Got Married, Stranded.
TELEVISION: *Movies:* The Crooked Hearts, The Great Houdinis, With Murder in Mind, The Habitation of Dragons, Hart to Hart: Home is Where the Hart Is. *Guest:* Pros & Cons, many others. *Special:* Good Old Boy (Wonderworks).

O'TOOLE, ANNETTE
Actress. b. Houston, TX, April 1, 1953. e. UCLA.
PICTURES: Smile (debut, 1975), One on One, King of the Gypsies, Foolin' Around, Cat People, 48 HRS, Superman III, Cross My Heart, Love at Large, Andre (voice), Imaginary Crimes.
TELEVISION: *Movies:* The Girl Most Likely To..., The Entertainer, The War Between the Tates, Love For Rent, Stand By Your Man, Copacabana, Arthur Hailey's Strong Medicine, Broken Vows, Stephen King's IT, The Dreamer of Oz, White Lies, Kiss of a Killer, Love Matters, A Mother's Revenge, My Brother's Keeper. *Mini-Series:* The Kennedys of Massachusetts. *Specials:* Vanities, Best Legs in the Eighth Grade, Secret World of the Very Young, Unpublished Letters, On Hope.

O'TOOLE, PETER
Actor. b. Connemara, Ireland, Aug. 2, 1932. Studied at Royal Acad. of Dramatic Art. Early career with Bristol Old Vic. Partner with Jules Buck, Keep Films, Ltd. Autobiography: Loitering With Intent (1993).
THEATER: *London:* Major Barbara, Oh My Papa, The Long the Short and the Tall, Baal, Hamlet, Ride a Cock Horse, Macbeth, Man and Superman, Jeffrey Bernard is Unwell, Our Song. 1960, with the Stratford-on-Avon Company (The Taming of the Shrew, Merchant of Venice, etc). *Dublin:* Arms and the Man, Waiting for Godot. *Toronto:* Present Laughter, Uncle Vanya. B'way debut 1987: Pygmalion.
PICTURES: Kidnapped (debut, 1959), The Savage Innocents, The Day They Robbed the Bank of England, Lawrence of Arabia, Becket, Lord Jim, What's New Pussycat?, The Bible, How to Steal a Million, The Night of the Generals, Casino Royale (cameo), Great Catherine, The Lion in Winter, Goodbye Mr. Chips, Brotherly Love (Country Dance), Murphy's War, Under Milk Wood, The Ruling Class, Man of La Mancha, Rosebud, Man Friday, Foxtrot, Caligula, Power Play, Zulu Dawn, The Stunt Man, My Favorite Year, Supergirl, Creator, Club Paradise, The Last Emperor, High Spirits, On a Moonlit Night, Helena, Wings of Fame, The Nutcracker Prince (voice), The Rainbow Thief, Isabelle Eberhardt, King Ralph, Rebecca's Daughters, The Seventh Coin.
TELEVISION: *Movies:* Rogue Male (BBC), Svengali, Kim, Crossing to Freedom, Heaven & Hell: North and South Book III. *Specials:* Present Laughter, Pygmalion, The Dark Angel. *Series:* Strumpet City (BBC). *Mini-Series:* Masada.

OTWELL, RONNIE RAY
Theatre Executive. b. Carrollton, GA, Aug. 13, 1929. e. Georgia Inst. of Technology. Entered industry as mgr., Bremen Theatre, GA, 1950; dir. pub., adv., Martin Theatres, Columbus, GA, 1950-63; v.p.; dir. Martin Theatres of Ga., Inc., 1963, Martin Theatres of Ala., Inc., 1963; dir. Martin Theatres of Columbus, 1963; sr. v.p., Martin Theatres Companies, 1971.

OVERALL, PARK
Actress. b. Nashville, TN, March 15, 1957. Attended British boarding school, earned teaching degree, before turning to acting.
THEATER: *NY:* Biloxi Blues, Wild Blue, Only You, Loose Ends, Something About Baseball, Marathon '88.
PICTURES: Body Passion, Biloxi Blues, Mississippi Burning, Talk Radio (voice), Lost Angels, Kindergarten Cop, The Vanishing, House of Cards, Undercover Blues.
TELEVISION: *Series:* Empty Nest. *Movies:* Luck of the Draw: The Gambler Returns, Overkill: The Aileen Wuornos Story, Precious Victims, The Good Old Boys. *Pilot:* The Line.

OVITZ, MICHAEL
Talent Agent, Executive. b. Chicago, IL, Dec. 14, 1946. e. UCLA, 1968. Started as trainee at William Morris Agency before becoming agent, 1969-75. Co-founder of Creative Artists Agency, 1975; became chmn. and chief stock holder. 1995 named pres. The Walt Disney Company.

OWEN, BILL
Actor. r.n. Bill Rowbotham. b. Acton, Eng., Mar. 14, 1914.
PICTURES: The Way to the Stars (debut, 1945), School for Secrets, Daybreak, Dancing With Crime, Easy Money, When the Bough Breaks, My Brother's Keeper, Martha, Parlor Trick, The Roundabout, Trottie True, Once a Jolly Swagman, A Day to Remember, You See What I Mean, Square Ring, Rainbow Jacket, Ship That Died of Shame, Not so Dusty, Davy, Carve Her Name with Pride, Carry on Sergeant, Carry on Nurse, Night Apart, Shakedown, Hell Fire Club, Carry on Regardless, Carry on Cabby!, Secret of Blood Island, Georgy Girl,

Headline Hunters, O Lucky Man!, Kadoyng, In Celebration, When The Screaming Stopped, Comeback, Laughter House.
TELEVISION: *Series:* Last of the Summer Wine.

OWENSBY, EARL
Producer, Actor. b. North Carolina, 1935. Set up his own studio in Shelby, NC. Built new studio in Gaffney, SC, 1985.
PICTURES: Challenge, Dark Sunday, Buckstone County Prison, Frank Challenge—Manhunter, Death Driver, Wolfman, Seabo, Day of Judgment, Living Legend, Lady Grey, Rottweiler, Last Game, Hyperspace, Hit the Road Running, Rutherford County Line.

OXENBERG, CATHERINE
Actress. b. NY, NY, Sept. 21, 1961. Daughter of the exiled Princess Elizabeth of Yugoslavia, raised among intl. jet set with Richard Burton acting as her tutor. Modeled before making TV debut in The Royal Romance of Charles and Diana (1982).
PICTURES: The Lair of the White Worm, The Return of the Musketeers.
TELEVISION: *Series:* Dynasty, Acapulco H.E.A.T. *Movies:* The Royal Romance of Charles and Diana, Roman Holiday, Swimsuit, Trenchcoat in Paradise, Ring of Scorpio, K-9000, Charles & Diana: Unhappily Ever After, Rubdown, Treacherous Beauties.

OZ, FRANK
Puppeteer, Director, Performer. b. Hereford, Eng., May 25, 1944. r.n. Frank Oznowicz. Gained fame as creator and performer of various characters on Sesame Street and the Muppet Show (Fozzie Bear, Miss Piggy, Animal, Cookie Monster, Grover and Bert). V.P., Jim Henson Prods.
PICTURES: *Performer:* The Muppet Movie, The Blues Brothers, The Empire Strikes Back, The Great Muppet Caper (also prod.), An American Werewolf in London, The Dark Crystal (also co-dir.), Return of the Jedi, Trading Places, The Muppets Take Manhattan (also dir., co-s.p.), Spies Like Us, Labyrinth, Innocent Blood, The Muppet Christmas Carol (also exec. prod.), Muppet Treasure Island (voice). *Director only:* Little Shop of Horrors, Dirty Rotten Scoundrels, What About Bob?, Housesitter, The Indian in the Cupboard.
TELEVISION: *Series:* Sesame Street (3 Emmy Awards), The Muppet Show (Emmy Award, 1978), Saturday Night Live; various variety shows.

P

PAAR, JACK
Actor. b. Canton, OH, May 1, 1918. Radio announcer in Cleveland, Buffalo; served in U.S. Armed Forces, WWII; entertained in Pacific zone with 28th Special Service Div. On radio with own show, then quiz show Take It or Leave It. First host of The Tonight Show; various specials.
AUTHOR: I Kid You Not, My Sabre Is Bent, Three on a Toothbrush, P.S. Jack Paar.
PICTURES: Variety Time (debut, 1948), Easy Living, Walk Softly Stranger, Footlight Varieties, Love Nest, Down Among the Sheltering Palms.
TELEVISION: *Series:* Up to Paar (emcee, 1952), Bank on the Stars (emcee, 1953), The Jack Paar Show (1954), The Morning Show (1954), The Tonight Show (retitled The Jack Paar Show: 1957-62), The Jack Paar Program (1962-65), ABC Late Night (1973). *Specials:* Jack Paar Diary, Jack Paar Remembers, Jack Paar Is Alive and Well (also prod.), He Kids You Not.

PACINO, AL
Actor. b. New York, NY, Apr. 25, 1940. e. High Sch. for the Performing Arts, NY; Actors Studio, 1966; HB Studios, NY. Gained attention as stage actor initially at Charles Playhouse, Boston (Why Is a Crooked Letter, The Peace Creeps, Arturo Ui). Served as artistic dir. (with Ellen Burstyn), Actors Studio (1982-84).
THEATER: *NY:* The Indian Wants the Bronx (Obie Award), Does a Tiger Wear a Necktie? (Tony & Theatre World Awards, 1969), The Local Stigmatic, Camino Real, The Connection, Hello Out There, Tiger at the Gates, The Basic Training of Pavlo Hummel (Tony Award, 1977), Richard III, American Buffalo, Julius Caesar, Chinese Coffee, Salome, Hughie (also dir.).
PICTURES: Me Natalie (debut, 1969), The Panic in Needle Park, The Godfather, Scarecrow, Serpico, The Godfather Part II, Dog Day Afternoon, Bobby Deerfield, ... And Justice for All, Cruising, Author! Author!, Scarface, Revolution, Sea of Love, Dick Tracy, The Godfather Part III, Frankie and Johnny, Glengarry Glen Ross, Scent of a Woman (Academy Award, 1992), Carlito's Way, A Day to Remember, City Hall, Heat, Two Bits, Looking for Richard (also dir.), Donnie Brasco.

PACULA, JOANNA
Actress. b. Tomszowau, Poland, Jan. 2, 1957. Member of Polish National Theatre School. Model in Poland, France, then U.S. where she moved in early 1980's.

PICTURES: Gorky Park, Not Quite Paradise, Death Before Dishonor, The Kiss, Sweet Lies, Options, Marked for Death, Husbands and Lovers, Tombstone.
TELEVISION: *Series*: E.A.R.T.H. Force. *Movies*: Escape From Sobribor, Breaking Point, Not Like Us.

PAGE, ANTHONY
Director. b. Bangalore, India, Sept. 21, 1935. e. Oxford. Stage work includes Inadmissible Evidence, Waiting for Godot, A Patriot for Me, Look Back in Anger, Uncle Vanya, Mrs. Warren's Profession, Alpha Beta, Heartbreak House, Absolute Hell, etc.
PICTURES: Inadmissible Evidence (debut, 1968), Alpha Beta, I Never Promised You a Rose Garden, Absolution, The Lady Vanishes.
TELEVISION: *Specials*: Pueblo, The Missiles of October, The Parachute, Sheppey. *Movies*: Collision Course, F. Scott Fitzgerald in Hollywood, FDR—The Last Year, The Patricia Neal Story, Bill, Johnny Belinda, Grace Kelly, Bill—On His Own, Murder: By Reason of Insanity, Forbidden, Monte Carlo, Second Serve, Pack of Lies, Scandal in a Small Town, The Nightmare Years, Chernobyl: The Final Warning, Absolute Hell, Guests of the Emperor, Middlemarch.

PAGE, PATTI
Performer, Recording Artist. r.n. Clara Ann Fowler. b. Claremore, OK, Nov. 8, 1927. e. U. of Tulsa. Staff performer, radio stat. KTUL, Tulsa; Top recording star of the 1950's and 60's (The Tennessee Waltz, Cross Over the Bridge, How Much is That Doggie in the Window?, etc.). Appeared on CBS radio show. Author of Once Upon a Dream.
PICTURES: Elmer Gantry (debut, 1960), Dondi, Boys' Night Out.
TELEVISION: *Series* host: Music Hall, Scott Music Hall, The Patti Page Show, The Big Record, The Patti Page Olds Show. *Guest*: Appointment With Adventure, U.S. Steel Hour, Bachelor Father, etc.

PAGET, DEBRA
Actress. r.n. Debrahlee Griffin. b. Denver, CO, Aug. 19, 1933. e. Hollywood Prof. Sch. , also studied drama & dancing privately. Stage debut in Merry Wives of Windsor, 1946; in Jeanne D'Arc little theatre prod.
PICTURES: Cry of the City (debut, 1948), It Happens Every Spring, House of Strangers, Broken Arrow, Fourteen Hours, Bird of Paradise, Anne of the Indies, Belles on Their Toes, Les Miserables, Stars & Stripes Forever, Prince Valiant, Demetrius & the Gladiators, Princess of the Nile, Gambler from Natchez, White Feather, Seven Angry Men, Last Hunt, The Ten Commandments, Love Me Tender, The River's Edge, Omar Khayyam, From the Earth to the Moon, Why Must I Die?, Cleopatra's Daughter, Journey to the Lost City, The Most Dangerous Man Alive, Tales of Terror, The Haunted Palace.
TELEVISION: *Guest*: Steve Allen, Colgate Comedy Hour, Climax, Wagon Train, Rawhide, etc.

PAGETT, NICOLA
Actress. b. Cairo, Egypt, June 15, 1945. r.n. Nicola Scott. e. Royal Acad. of Dramatic Art. Appeared with Citizen's Rep. Theatre, Glasgow.
THEATER: Cornelia (debut, 1964, Worthing, U.K.), A Boston Story (London debut, 1968), A Midsummer Night's Dream, Widowers' Houses, The Misanthrope, A Voyage 'Round My Father, The Ride Across Lake Constance, Ghosts, The Seagull, Hamlet, The Marriage of Figaro, A Family and a Fortune, Gaslight, Yahoo, Old Times (L.A.).
PICTURES: Anne of the Thousand Days, There's a Girl in My Soup, Operation Daybreak, Oliver's Story, Privates on Parade.
TELEVISION: *Series*: Upstairs Downstairs. *Movies*: Frankenstein: The True Story, The Sweeney, Aren't We All, A Woman of Substance (mini-series), Anna Karenina.

PAIGE, JANIS
Actress r.n. Donna Mae Jaden. b. Tacoma, WA, Sept. 16, 1923. Sang with Tacoma Opera Co. Star of Tomorrow, 1947. Album: Let's Fall in Love. Owns and operates Ipanema, Janeiro, Rio-Cali, and Dindi Music Cos.
THEATER: Pajama Game, Remains to Be Seen, Here's Love, Mame, Alone Together.
PICTURES: Hollywood Canteen (debut, 1944), Of Human Bondage, Two Gals and a Guy, The Time the Place and the Girl, Two Guys from Milwaukee, Her Kind of Man, Cheyenne, Love and Learn, Always Together, Wallflower, Winter Meeting, One Sunday Afternoon, Romance on the High Seas, House Across the Street, The Younger Brothers, Mr. Universe, Fugitive Lady, Two Guys and a Gal, Silk Stockings, Please Don't Eat the Daisies, Bachelor in Paradise, The Caretakers, Welcome to Hard Times, The Dark Road (It.), Follow the Boys (Fr.).
TELEVISION: *Special*: Roberta (1958 and 1969). *Series*: It's Always Jan, Lanigan's Rabbi, Gun Shy, Baby Makes Five, Trapper John M.D, Capitol, General Hospital, Santa Barbara. *Guest*: Plymouth Playhouse, Alcoa Premiere, Columbo,

Banacek, Flamingo Road, St. Elsewhere. *Movies*: The Turning Point of Jim Malloy, Return of Joe Forrester, Lanigan's Rabbi (pilot), Valentine Magic on Love Island, Angel on My Shoulder, The Other Woman, No Man's Land.

PAINE, CHARLES F.
Executive. b. Cushing, TX, Dec. 23, 1920. e. Stephen F. Austin U. Pres. Tercar Theatre Company; pres., NATO of Texas, 1972-73. NATO board member, 1973 to present; Motion Picture Pioneers member; Variety Club of Texas member.

PAKULA, ALAN J.
Producer, Director. b. New York, NY, April 7, 1928. e. Yale U., B.A., 1948. Worked in Leland Hayward's office; asst. administrator, Warner Bros. cartoon dept, Prod. apprentice, MGM, 1950; prod. asst., Paramount 1951; prod. Paramount, 1955. Own prod. co., Pakula-Mulligan Prod. Stage prod. and m.p. dir. prod. 1988 received Eastman Award for Continued Excellence in M.P. Won London Film Critics Award for best director for Klute.
THEATER: Comes a Day, Laurette, There Must Be a Pony.
PICTURES: *Producer*: Fear Strikes Out, To Kill a Mockingbird, Love With the Proper Stranger, Baby the Rain Must Fall, Inside Daisy Clover, Up the Down Staircase, The Stalking Moon. *Director*: The Sterile Cuckoo, Klute (also prod.), Love and Pain and the Whole Damn Thing (also prod.), The Parallax View (also prod.), All the President's Men (NY Film Critics Award, 1976), Comes a Horseman, Starting Over (also prod.), Rollover, Sophie's Choice (also prod., s.p.), Dream Lover (also prod.), Orphans (also prod.), See You in the Morning (also prod., s.p.), Presumed Innocent, Consenting Adults (also prod.), The Pelican Brief (also prod., co-s.p.).

PALANCE, JACK
Actor. b. Lattimer, PA, Feb. 18, 1920. e. U. of North Carolina. Professional fighter; U.S. Air Corps.
THEATER: The Big Two, Temporary Island, The Vigil, A Streetcar Named Desire, Darkness at Head.
PICTURES: Panic in the Streets (debut, 1950), Halls of Montezuma, Sudden Fear (Acad. Award nom.), Shane (Acad. Award nom.), Flight to Tangier, Arrowhead, Second Chance, Man in the Attic, Sign of the Pagan, Silver Chalice, Kiss of Fire, Big Knife, I Died a Thousand Times, Attack!, Lonely Man, House of Numbers, The Man Inside, Ten Seconds to Hell, Battle of Austerliz, Sword of the Conqueror, The Mongols, Barabbas, Warriors Five, Contempt, Once a Thief, The Professionals, Torture Garden, Kill a Dragon, The Mercenary, Deadly Sanctuary, They Came to Rob Las Vegas, The Desperados, Che, Legion of the Damned, A Bullet for Rommel, The McMasters, Monte Walsh, Companeros, The Horsemen, Chato's Land, Oklahoma Crude, Craze, The Four Deuces, The Great Adventure, The Sensuous Nurse, Portrait of a Hitman, One Man Jury, Angel's Brigade, The Shape of Things to Come, Cocaine Cowboys, Hawk the Slayer, Without Warning, Alone in the Dark, Gor, Bagdad Cafe, Young Guns, Outlaw of Gor, Batman, Tango and Cash, City Slickers (Academy Award, best supporting actor, 1991), Solar Crisis, Cops and Robbersons, City Slickers II: The Legend of Curly's Gold, The Swan Princess (voice).
TELEVISION: *Specials*: Requiem for a Heavyweight (Emmy Award, 1957), Dr. Jekyll and Mr. Hyde, Twilight Zone: Rod Serling's Lost Classics: Where the Dead Are. *Movies*: Dracula, The Godchild, The Hatfields and the McCoys, Bronk (pilot), Last Ride of the Dalton Gang, The Ivory Ape, Golden Moment: An Olympic Love Story, Keep the Change, Buffalo Girls. *Series*: The Greatest Show on Earth, Bronk, Ripley's Believe It or Not (host).

PALCY, EUZHAN
Director. b. Martinique, 1957. e. Earned a degree in French lit., Sorbonne and a film degree from Vaugirard School in Paris. Began career working as TV writer and dir. in Martinique. Also made 2 children's records. In Paris worked as film editor, screenwriter and dir. of shorts. She received grant from French gov. to make 1st feature Sugar Cane Alley which cost $800,000 and won Silver Lion Prize at Venice Film Fest., 1983.
PICTURES: Sugar Cane Alley, A Dry White Season (also co-s.p.).

PALIN, MICHAEL
Actor, Writer. b. Sheffield, Yorkshire, England, May 5, 1943. e. Oxford. Performed there in The Birthday Party and in revue Hang Your Head Down and Die (also in West End prod., 1964). At Oxford met Terry Jones, began writing comedy together, incl. TV series The Frost Report. Became member of Monty Python's Flying Circus. On stage with troupe both in London and on B'way.
PICTURES: And Now for Something Completely Different (also co-s.p.), Monty Python and the Holy Grail (also co-s.p.), Jabberwocky, Life of Brian (also co-s.p.), Time Bandits, The Secret Policeman's Other Ball, Monty Python Live at the

Hollywood Bowl (also co-s.p.), The Missionary (also co-prod., s.p.), Monty Python's The Meaning of Life (also co-music, co-s.p.), A Private Function, Brazil, A Fish Called Wanda, American Friends (also co-s.p.), Fierce Creatures, The Wind In The Willows (voice).
TELEVISION: Do Not Adjust Your Set, The Frost Report, Monty Python's Flying Circus, Marty Feldman Comedy Machine, How To Irritate People, Pythons in Deutschland, Secrets, Ripping Yarns, Around the World in 80 Days, GBH, Pole to Pole.

PALMER, BETSY
Actress. b. East Chicago, IN, Nov. 1, 1929. e. DePaul U. Studied at Neighborhood Playhouse, HB Studio with Uta Hagen. On Broadway in The Grand Prize, South Pacific, Affair of Honor, Cactus Flower, Roar Like a Dove, Eccentricities of a Nightingale, Same Time Next Year and many regional prods.
PICTURES: Mister Roberts, The Long Gray Line, Queen Bee, The Tin Star, The Last Angry Man, Friday the 13th, Friday the 13th Part 2.
TELEVISION: All major live shows such as Studio One, U.S. Steel Hour, Kraft Theatre. Series: Masquerade Party (panelist), What's It For? (panelist), I've Got a Secret (panelist, 11 years), No. 96 (series), Candid Camera (host), The Today Show (host), Wifeline (host). Guest: As the World Turns, Murder She Wrote, Out of This World, Charles in Charge, Knots Landing, Newhart, Love Boat. Movies: Isabel's Choice, Windmills of the Gods, Goddess of Love, Still Not Quite Human, Columbo: Death Hits the Jackpot.

PALMER, GREGG
Actor. r.n. Palmer Lee. b. San Francisco, CA, Jan. 25, 1927. e. U. of Utah. U.S. Air Force, 1945-46; radio announcer, disc jockey; then to Hollywood.
PICTURES: Cimarron Kid, Battle at Apache Pass, Son of Ali Baba, Red Ball Express, Francis Goes to West Point, Sally and St. Anne, The Raiders, Back at the Front, Redhead From Wyoming, Column South, Veils of Bagdad, Golden Blade, The All American, Taza Son of Cochise, Magnificent Obsession, Playgirl, To Hell and Back, Creature Walks Among Us, Hilda Crane, Zombies of Mora Tau, Revolt of Fort Laramie, Rebel Set, Thundering Jets, Forty Pounds of Trouble, Night Hunt, The Undefeated, Chisum, Rio Lobo, Big Jake, Providenza (It.), Ci Risiamo Vero Providenza (It-Sp), The Shootist, The Man With Bogart's Face, Scream.
TELEVISION: Series: Run Buddy Run. Guest appearances incl: Wagon Train, Loretta Young, Wyatt Earp, Have Gun Will Travel, Sea Hunt, Roaring 20's, Mannix, The High Chaparral, Cannon, Baretta, Gunsmoke, etc. Movies: Mongo's Back in Town, Go West Young Girl, Hostage Heart, How the West Was Won, True Grit, Beggarman Thief, The Blue and the Gray (mini-series).

PALMER, PATRICK
Producer. b. Los Angeles, CA, Dec. 28, 1936. Began career with 10-year apprenticeship at Mirisch Company, involved in making of West Side Story, Seven Days in May, The Fortune Cookie, etc. 1966, began association with Norman Jewison, serving as assoc. prod. on The Landlord, Fiddler on the Roof, Jesus Christ Superstar, Rollerball, etc. 1972, prod., with Jewison, Billy Two Hats; exec. prod. on The Dogs of War.
PICTURES: Co-prod.: And Justice for All, Best Friends, Iceman, A Soldier's Story, Agnes of God, Children of a Lesser God, Moonstruck, Stanley & Iris, Mermaids, Paradise.

PALMINTERI, CHAZZ
Actor, Writer. b. Bronx, NY, May 15, 1951. e. Bronx Comm. Coll. NY stage in The Guys in the Truck (B'way), The King's Men, 22 Years, The Flatbush Faithful, A Bronx Tale (which he also wrote).
PICTURES: The Last Dragon (debut, 1985), Oscar, Innocent Blood, There Goes the Neighborhood, A Bronx Tale (also s.p.), Bullets Over Broadway (Acad. Award nom.), The Perez Family, The Usual Suspects, Faithful (also s.p.), Jade, Mulholland Falls, Diabolique.
TELEVISION: Movie: The Last Word.

PALTROW, BRUCE
Director, Producer, Writer. b. New York, NY, Nov. 26, 1943. e. Tulane U., B.F.A. m. actress Blythe Danner. Daughter is actress Gwyneth Paltrow. Has also produced stage plays.
PICTURE: A Little Sex (co-prod., dir.).
TELEVISION: Movies: Shirts and Skins (co-prod., writer), Ed McBain's 87th Precinct (dir.). Series: The White Shadow (creat. dir.), St. Elsewhere (exec. prod.-dir.), Tattinger's (exec. prod., dir., co-writer), Nick & Hillary (exec. prod.).

PALTROW, GWYNETH
Actress. b. Los Angeles, CA. p. actress Blythe Danner, prod. Bruce Paltrow. Family moved to NY when she was 11.
THEATER: Williamstown: Picnic, The Adventures of Huck Finn, Sweet Bye and Bye, The Seagull.
PICTURES: Shout (debut, 1991), Hook, Malice, Flesh and Bone, Mrs. Parker and the Vicious Circle, Jefferson in Paris, Moonlight and Valentino, Seven, The Pallbearer, Sydney, Emma.
TELEVISION: Movie: Cruel Doubt.

PANAMA, CHARLES A. (CHUCK)
Publicist, b. Chicago, IL, Feb. 2, 1925. e. Northwestern U., Beloit Coll., UCLA. Publicist, Los Angeles Jr. Chamber of Commerce; So. Calif. sports ed., Los Angeles bureau, INS; publicist, 20th Century-Fox Studios; adv.-pub. dir., Arcola Pics.; opened L.A. office, John Springer Associates; v.p. Jerry Pam & Assoc.; account exec., Rogers, Cowan & Brenner, Inc.; dir. m.p. div., Jim Mahoney & Assoc.; v.p. Guttman & Pam, Ltd.; asst. pub. dir., Twentieth TV. Owner, pres. Chuck Panama P.R.; winner 1990 Les Mason Award and 1993 Robert Yeager Award 1993, Publicists Guild of America.

PANAMA, NORMAN
Writer, Producer, Director. b. Chicago, IL, Apr. 12, 1914. Co-authored The Glass Bed (novel), and plays: A Talent for Murder, The Bats of Portobello.
PICTURES: Co-Writer: My Favorite Blonde, Happy Go Lucky, Star-Spangled Rhythm, Thank Your Lucky Stars, And the Angels Sing, Duffy's Tavern, Road to Utopia (Acad. Award nom.), Our Hearts Were Growing up, Monsieur Beaucaire, It Had to Be You, Mr. Blandings Builds His Dream House, Return of October, White Christmas, Li'l Abner, The Facts of Life. Co-Dir./Co-Writer (with Melvin Frank): The Reformer and the Redhead, Strictly Dishonorable, Callaway Went Thataway, Above and Beyond, Knock on Wood (Acad. Award nom. for s.p.), The Court Jester. Dir./Writer: The Road to Hong Kong, Not With My Wife You Don't, How to Commit Marriage, I Will I Will... for Now.
TELEVISION: Dir.: Barnaby and Me, The Stewardesses, Li'l Abner, Mrs. Katz and Katz (pilot), How Come You Never See Dr. Jekyll and Mr. Hyde Together?, Coffee Tea or Me.

PANKIN, STUART
Actor. b. Philadelphia, PA, Apr. 8, 1946. e. Dickinson Coll., Columbia U. Stage debut 1968 in The War of the Roses.
THEATER: NY: Timon of Athens, Tale of Cymbeline, Mary Stuart, The Crucible, Twelfth Night, Glorious Age, Wings, Gorky, Joseph and the Amazing Technicolor Dreamcoat, Three Sisters, The Inspector General.
PICTURES: Scavenger Hunt, Hangar 18, The Hollywood Knights, An Eye for an Eye, Earthbound, Irreconcilable Differences, The Dirt Bike Kid, Fatal Attraction, Love at Stake, Second Sight, That's Adequate, Arachnophobia, Mannequin 2 on the Move, The Vagrant, I Love Trouble, The Silence of the Hams, Squanto: A Warrior's Tale, Congo.
TELEVISION: Series: The San Pedro Beach Bums, No Soap Radio, Not Necessarily the News (ACE Award), Nearly Departed, Dinosaurs (voice). Movies: Valentine Magic on Love Island, Father & Scout, Down Out and Dangerous. Pilots: Car Wash, Wonderful World of Philip Malley. Guest: Night Court, Crazy Like a Fox, Golden Girls, Stingray, Family Ties, It's Garry Shandling's Show, Hooperman, Barney Miller. Special: Stuart Pankin (also co-exec. prod., co-writer).

PANTOLIANO, JOE
Actor. b. Jersey City, NJ, Sept. 12, 1954.
THEATER: NY: The Kitchen, The Off Season, The Death Star, Visions of Kerouac. Regional: One Flew Over the Cuckoo's Nest, Skaters, Brothers, Italian American Reconciliation (Dramalogue Award), Orphans (Dramalogue Award, Drama Critic Circle nomination), Pvt. Wars.
PICTURES: The Idolmaker, Monsignor, Risky Business, Eddie and the Cruisers, The Mean Season, The Goonies, Running Scared, La Bamba, The Squeeze, Amazon Women on the Moon, Empire of the Sun, The In Crowd, Midnight Run, Downtown, The Last of the Finest, Short Time, Zandalee, Used People, Three of Hearts, Goin' to Mexico, The Fugitive, Calendar Girl, Me and the Kid, Teresa's Tattoo, Baby's Day Out, Bad Boys, Congo, Steal Big Steal Little, Bound, The Immortals.
TELEVISION: Series: Free Country, The Fanelli Boys. Mini-Series: Robert F. Kennedy: His Life and Times, From Here to Eternity. Guest: Tales from the Crypt (ACE Award nomination), Amazing Stories, L.A. Law, The Hitchhiker. Movies: More Than Friends, Alcatraz: The Whole Shocking Story, Nightbreaker, Destination America, El Diablo, One Special Victory, Through the Eyes of a Killer, The Last (also co-assoc. prod.).

PAPAS, IRENE
Actress. b. Chiliomodion, Greece, Sept. 3, 1926. Entered dramatic school at 12. At 16 sang and danced in variety shows before debuting in Greek films, 1950. 1958 appeared with Greek Popular Theatre in Athens. Received Salonika Film Fest. Awards for the films Antigone, Electra.
THEATER: The Idiot, Journey's End, The Merchant of Venice, Inherit the Wind, That Summer, That Fall, Iphigenia in Aulis.
PICTURES: Lost Angels (debut, 1950), Dead City, The Unfaithful, Atilla the Hun, Theodora the Slave Empress, Whirlpool, Tribute to a Bad Man, Antigone, The Guns of Navarone, Electra, The Moon-Spinners, Zorba the Greek, We Still Kill the Old Way, The Desperate Ones, The Brotherhood, Anne of the Thousand Days, Z, A Dream of Kings, The Trojan Women, Roma Bene, Bambina, Mohammed: Messenger of

God, Iphigenia, Bloodline, (Christ Stopped at) Eboli, Lion of the Desert, Erendira, Into the Night, The Assisi Underground, Sweet Country, High Season, Chronicle of a Death Foretold, Island, Drums of Fire, Banquet, Zoe, Up Down and Sideways. TELEVISION: Moses the Lawgiver.

PARE, MICHAEL
Actor. b. Brooklyn, NY, Oct. 9, 1959. e. Culinary Inst. of America, Hyde Park, NY. Worked as chef and model before being discovered by ABC talent agent.
PICTURES: Eddie and the Cruisers (debut, 1983), Streets of Fire, The Philadelphia Experiment, Under Cover (Aust.), Space Rage, Instant Justice, The Women's Club, World Gone Wild, Eddie and the Cruisers II: Eddie Lives, Moon 44, Dragon Fight, Concrete War, The Closer, Into the Sun, Midnight Heat, First Light, Point of Impact, Village of the Damned, Bad Moon.
TELEVISION: Series: The Greatest American Hero, Houston Knights. Movie: Crazy Times.

PARISH, JAMES ROBERT
Film Historian, Executive. b. Cambridge, MA, Apr. 21, 1944. e. U. of PA (BBA, Phi Beta Kappa); U. of PA Law School (LLB). Member of NY Bar. Founder Entertainment Copyright Research Co., Inc. 1968-69, film reporter, Motion Picture Daily, weekly Variety. 1969-70, entertainment publicist, Harold Rand & Co. (NY). Currently marketing consultant in direct marketing industry, contributor to arts sections of major national newspapers and entertainment trade papers, series editor of show business books and author of over 85 books on the entertainment industry including: Hollywood's Great Musicals, Prostitution in Hollywood Films, Ghosts & Angels in Hollywood Films, Hollywood Songsters, Prison Pictures From Hollywood, Hollywood Baby Boomers, The Great Detective Pictures, The Great Cop Pictures, The Great Science Fiction Pictures II, Complete Actors TV Credits (1948-88), The Great Combat Pictures, Black Action Pictures From Hollywood, The Great Detective Pictures, The Great Western Pictures II: The Great Gangster Pictures II: The Great Spy Pictures II, Actors TV Credits, The Best of MGM, The Forties Gals, The Great American Movies Book, Hollywood Happiness, The Funsters, Hollywood on Hollywood, The Hollywood Beauties, Elvis!, The Great Science Fiction Pictures, The Child Stars, The Jeannette MacDonald Story, Great Movie Heroes, Liza!, The RKO Gals, Vincent Price Unmasked, The George Raft File, The Emmy Awards, Hollywood Death Book, Gays & Lesbians in Mainstream Cinema, Hollywood Celebrity Death Book (updated), Let's Talk: America's Favorite TV Talk Show Hosts, Today's Black Hollywood, Pirates and Seafaring Swashbucklers.

PARKER, ALAN
Director, Writer. b. Islington, London, England, Feb. 14, 1944. Worked way up in advertising industry from mail room to top writer and director of nearly 500 TV commercials between 1969-78.
PICTURES: Melody (s.p., 1968). Director: No Hard Feelings (also s.p.), Our Cissy (also s.p.), Footsteps (also s.p.), Bugsy Malone (also s.p.; Brit. Acad. Award for best s.p.), Midnight Express (Brit. Acad. Award), Fame, Shoot the Moon, Pink Floyd—The Wall, Birdy, Angel Heart, Mississippi Burning, Come and See the Paradise (also s.p.), The Commitments (also cameo; BAFTA Award for best dir., 1991), The Road to Wellville (also s.p., co-prod.), Evita.
TELEVISION: The Evacuees (Brit. Acad. Award).

PARKER, COREY
Actor. b. New York, NY, July 8, 1965. e. NYU.
THEATER: NY: Meeting the Winter Bike Rider (Off-B'way debut, 1984), Been Taken, The Bloodletters, The Semi-Formal.
PICTURES: Scream for Help (debut, 1984), Friday the 13th Part V: A New Beginning, Something Special, Nine 1/2 Weeks, Biloxi Blues, How I Got Into College, Big Man on Campus, White Palace.
TELEVISION: Series: Eddie Dodd, Blue Skies. Movies: Courage, At Mother's Request, Liz: The Elizabeth Taylor Story, A Mother's Prayer. Specials: Don't Touch, Teen Father, The Lost Language of Cranes. Pilot: Sons of Gunz. Guest: The Bronx Zoo, thirtysomething.

PARKER, ELEANOR
Actress. b. Cedarville, OH, June 26, 1922. In Cleveland play group; in summer stock Martha's Vineyard; at Pasadena Community Playhouse.
PICTURES: They Died With Their Boots On (debut, 1941), Buses Roar, Mysterious Doctor, Mission to Moscow, Between Two Worlds, The Very Thought of You, Crime By Night, Hollywood Canteen, Last Ride, Pride of the Marines, Never Say Goodbye, Of Human Bondage, Escape Me Never, Woman in White, Voice of the Turtle, It's a Great Feeling, Chain Lightning, Caged (Acad. Award nom.), Three Secrets, Valentino, Millionaire for Christy, Detective Story (Acad. Award nom.), Scaramouche, Above and Beyond, Escape from Fort

Bravo, Naked Jungle, Valley of the Kings, Many Rivers to Cross, Interrupted Melody (Acad. Award nom.), Man with the Golden Arm, King and Four Queens, Lizzie, Seventh Sin, A Hole in the Head, Home from the Hill, Return to Peyton Place, Madison Avenue, Panic Button, The Sound of Music, The Oscar, An American Dream, Warning Shot, Tiger and the Pussycat, Eye of the Cat, Sunburn.
TELEVISION: Series: Bracken's World. Movies: Maybe I'll Come Home in the Spring, Vanished, Home for the Holidays, The Great American Beauty Contest, Fantasy Island (pilot), The Bastard, She's Dressed to Kill, Once Upon a Spy, Madame X, Dead on the Money. Pilot: Guess Who's Coming to Dinner. Special: Hans Brinker. Guest: Buick Electra Playhouse, Kraft Suspense Theatre, The Man from U.N.C.L.E., Vega$, Hawaii 5-0, The Love Boat, Hotel, Murder She Wrote, etc.

PARKER, FESS
Actor. b. Fort Worth, TX, Aug. 16, 1924. e. USC. U.S. Navy, 1943-46; national co., Mr. Roberts, 1951.
PICTURES: Untamed Frontier (debut, 1952), No Room for the Groom, Springfield Rifle, Thunder Over the Plains, Island in the Sky, The Kid From Left Field, Take Me to Town, Them!, Battle Cry, Davy Crockett—King of the Wild Frontier (from Disney TV show), Davy Crockett and the River Pirates (from TV show), The Great Locomotive Chase, Westward Ho! the Wagons, Old Yeller, The Light in the Forest, The Hangman, Alias Jesse James (cameo), The Jayhawkers, Hell Is for Heroes, Smoky.
TELEVISION: Series: Mr. Smith Goes to Washington, Daniel Boone. Guest: Jonathan Winters, Walt Disney presents (Davy Crockett), Playhouse 90 (Turn Left at Mount Everest), Ed Sullivan, Danny Kaye Show, Phyllis Diller, Joey Bishop, Dean Martin, Red Skelton, Glen Campbell, Andy Williams, Vicki Lawrence. Movie: Climb an Angry Mountain.

PARKER, JAMESON
Actor. b. Baltimore, MD, Nov. 18, 1947. e. Beloit Coll. Professional stage debut in Washington Theatre Club production, Caligula. Acted with Arena Stage in DC; worked in dinner theatres and summer stock. Moved to N.Y., working in TV commercials and acted in play, Equus (Coconut Grove Playhouse).
PICTURES: The Bell Jar (debut, 1979), A Small Circle of Friends, White Dog, American Justice (also prod.), Prince of Darkness, Curse of the Crystal Eye.
TELEVISION: Series: Somerset, One Life to Live, Simon and Simon. Movies: Women at West Point, Anatomy of a Seduction, The Gathering Part II, The Promise of Love, Callie and Son, A Caribbean Mystery, Who Is Julia?, Spy, She Says She's Innocent, Dead Before Dawn, Simon & Simon: In Trouble Again.

PARKER, MARY-LOUISE
Actress. b. Ft. Jackson, SC, Aug. 2, 1964. e. Bard Coll. 1990, received Clarence Derwent Award for her work in the theatre.
THEATER: B'way: Prelude to a Kiss (Theatre World Award). Off-B'way: Hayfever, The Girl in Pink, Babylon Gardens, Throwing Your Voice, Four Dogs and a Bone. Regional: The Importance of Being Earnest, Up in Saratoga, The Miser, Hay Fever, The Night of the Iguana, The Age of Pie.
PICTURES: Signs of Life (debut, 1989), Longtime Companion, Grand Canyon, Fried Green Tomatoes, Mr. Wonderful, Naked in New York, The Client, Bullets Over Broadway, Boys on the Side, Reckless, Portrait of a Lady.
TELEVISION: Movies: Too Young the Hero, A Place for Annie.

PARKER, SARAH JESSICA
Actress. b. Nelsonville, OH, Mar. 25, 1965. Was dancer with Cincinnati Ballet and American Ballet Theatre. Professional debut at age 8 in TV special The Little Match Girl.
THEATER: NY: The Innocents, By Strouse, Annie (title role for 2 yrs.), To Gillian on Her 37th Birthday, The Heidi Chronicles, The Substance of Fire, Sylvia, How To Succeed In Business Without Really Trying, Once Upon A Mattress.
PICTURES: Rich Kids (debut, 1979), Somewhere Tomorrow, Footloose, Firstborn, Girls Just Want to Have Fun, Flight of the Navigator, L.A. Story, Honeymoon in Vegas, Hocus Pocus, Striking Distance, Ed Wood, Miami Rhapsody, If Lucy Fell, The Substance of Fire, First Wives Club, Extreme Measures, Mars Attacks!.
TELEVISION: Series: Square Pegs, A Year in the Life, Equal Justice. Specials: The Almost Royal Family, Life Under Water. Movies: My Body My Child, Going for the Gold: The Bill Johnson Story, A Year in the Life, The Room Upstairs, Dadah Is Death, Twist of Fate, The Ryan White Story, In the Best Interest of the Children, The Sunshine Boys.

PARKER, SUZY
Actress. r.n. Cecelia Parker. b. San Antonio, TX, Oct. 28, 1933. m. actor Bradford Dillman. e. schools in NY, FL. Began career at 17 as fashion model; becoming the highest paid fashion model and cover girl in U.S.; went to Paris under contract

to fashion magazine; film debut as model in Funny Face (1957); signed by 20th-Fox prod. chief Buddy Adler for part opposite Cary Grant in Kiss Them for Me.
PICTURES: Funny Face, Kiss Them For Me, Ten North Frederick, The Best of Everything, Circle of Deception, The Interns, Flight From Ashiya, Chamber of Horrors.

PARKES, WALTER F.
Producer, Writer. b. Bakersfield, CA. e. Yale, Stanford Univ. 1978 prod. & dir. documentary The California Reich which was nominated for Acad. Award.
PICTURES: WarGames (s.p.; Acad. Award nom.). *Producer*: Volunteers, Project X, True Believer, Awakenings (Acad. Award nom.), Sneakers (also co-s.p.).
TELEVISION: *Series*: Eddie Dodd (prod., writer). *Pilot*: Birdland (prod., writer).

PARKINS, BARBARA
Actress. b. Vancouver, British Columbia, Canada, May 22, 1943.
PICTURES: Valley of the Dolls, The Kremlin Letter, The Mephisto Waltz, Puppet on a Chain, Asylum, Shout at the Devil, Bear Island, Breakfast in Paris.
TELEVISION: *Series*: Peyton Place, Scene of the Crime. *Mini-Series*: Captains and the Kings. *Movies*: A Taste of Evil, Snatched, Law of the Land, Testimony of Two Men, Young Joe: The Forgotten Kennedy, Ziegfield: The Man and His Women, The Critical List, The Manions of America, Uncommon Valor, To Catch a King, Calendar Girl Murders, Peyton Place: The Next Generation, Jennie: Lady Randolph Churchill. *Guest*: G.E. Theatre, My Three Sons, Dr. Kildare, Gibbsville, Hotel, The Love Boat, Murder She Wrote. *Special*: Jennie.

PARKS, GORDON
Director, Writer, Photographer, Composer, Poet, Photojournalist. b. Fort Scott, KS, Nov. 30, 1912. From the age of 15 worked as piano player, bus boy, dining car waiter and prof. basketball player in MN before taking up photography in late 1930's. Awarded 1st Julius Rosenwald Fellowship in photog., 1942. Worked with Roy Stryker at Farm Security Admin., WWII Office of War Info. correspondent. Photo-journalist, Life Mag., 1949-68, editorial dir. (and founder) Essence Magazine 1970-73. Film debut 1961 with doc. Flavio (dir. and writer), followed by Diary of a Harlem Family (doc., Emmy Award). Winner of numerous awards including NAACP's Spingarn Medal and Kansas Governor's Medal of Honor, Nat'l Medal of Arts, 1988. Recipient of 23 honorary degrees in lit., fine arts, humane letters. Member of NAACP, AMPAS, PEN American Center, AFI, etc.
AUTHOR: The Learning Tree, A Choice of Weapons, A Poet and His Camera, Whispers of Intimate Things, In Love, Born Black, Moments Without Proper Names, Flavio, To Smile in Autumn, Shannon, Voices in the Mirror.
PICTURES: The Learning Tree (Library of Congress Nat'l Film Registry Classics honor, 1989), Shaft, Shaft's Big Score, Super Cops, Leadbelly.
TELEVISION: The Odyssey of Solomon Northup, Moments Without Proper Names, Martin.

PARKS, MICHAEL
Actor. b. Corona, CA, April 4, 1938.
PICTURES: Wild Seed (debut, 1964), Bus Riley's Back in Town, The Bible, The Idol, The Happening, The Last Hard Men, Sidewinder One, ffolkes, Hard Country, Savannah Smiles, Spiker, Club Life, The Return of Josey Wales (also dir.), Spiker, Arizona Heat, Nightmare Beach, Prime Suspect, The Hitman, Storyville, Death Wish 5: The Face of Death, Stranger by Night.
TELEVISION: *Series*: Then Came Bronson, The Colbys, Twin Peaks. *Movies*: Can Ellen Be Saved?, Savage Bees, Chase, Dangerous Affection, Gore Vidal's Billy the Kid, The China Lake Murders, Hart to Hart: Secrets of the Hart.

PARRETTI, GIANCARLO
Executive. b. Orvieto, Italy, Oct. 23, 1941. Hotelier in Sicily in the late 1970's. Managing dir. of Naples newspaper Diario, until 1981. 1987, purchased Cannon Group, renaming it Pathe Communications. 1990, company acquired MGM/UA, Communications. Resigned 1991.

PARSONS, ESTELLE
Actress. b. Marblehead, MA, Nov. 20, 1927. e. Connecticut Coll. for Women, Bachelor's degree in political science. Attended Boston U. Law Sch. Helped harvest crops in England with the Women's Land Army. Was active in politics; worked for the Committee for the Nation's Health in Wash. and the Republican Finance Committee in Boston. Was elected to public office in Marblehead, Mass. Joined NBC-TV's Today Show as prod. asst.; then writer, feature producer and commentator. Appeared in two Julius Monk revues, Jerry Herman's Nightcap.
THEATER: Happy Hunting, Whoop Up, Beg Borrow or Steal, Mrs. Dally Has a Lover (Theater World Award), Next Time I'll Sing to You (Obie Award), In the Summer House (Obie Award), Ready When You Are C.B., Malcolm, The Seven Descents of Myrtle, ...And Miss Reardon Drinks a Little, The Norman Conquests, Ladies of the Alamo, Miss Margarida's Way, Pirates of Penzance, The Unguided Missile, Threepenny Opera, Lincoln Center Repertory Theatre, Mahagonny, Forgiving Typhoid Mary, Shimada, The Shadow Box, Twice Removed.
PICTURES: Ladybug Ladybug (debut, 1963), Bonnie and Clyde (Academy Award, best supporting actress, 1967), Rachel Rachel (Acad. Award nom.), Don't Drink the Water, Watermelon Man, I Walk the Line, I Never Sang for My Father, Two People, For Pete's Sake, Foreplay (The President's Woman), Dick Tracy, The Lemon Sisters, Boys on the Side, That Darn Cat, Looking for Richard.
TELEVISION: *Mini-Series*: Backstairs at the White House. *Special*: The Front Page. *Guest*: All in the Family, Roseanne. *Movies*: Terror on the Beach, The Gun and the Pulpit, The UFO Incident, The Gentleman Bandit, Open Admissions, A Private Matter, The American Clock.

PARTON, DOLLY
Singer, Composer, Actress. b. Sevierville, TN, Jan. 19, 1946. Gained fame as country music singer, composer and radio and TV personality. Co-partner with Sandy Gallin, Sandollar Prods. *Author*: My Life and Other Unfinished Business (autobiography), Coat of Many Colors.
PICTURES: Nine to Five (debut, 1980; also wrote & sang title song), The Best Little Whorehouse in Texas (also wrote addtl. songs), Rhinestone (also songs), Steel Magnolias, Straight Talk (also songs), The Beverly Hillbillies.
TELEVISION: *Series*: Dolly (1976), Dolly (1987-88). *Guest*: Porter Wagoner Show, Cass Walker program, Bill Anderson Show, Wilbur Bros. Show. *Specials*: Kenny Dolly & Willie: Something Inside So Strong, A Tennessee Mountain Thanksgiving. *Movies*: A Smoky Mountain Christmas (also songs), Wild Texas Wind (also co-writer, co-prod.), Big Dreams & Broken Hearts: The Dottie West Story.

PASDAR, ADRIAN
Actor. b. Pittsfield, MA. E. Univ. of Central FL. Studied acting with People's Light and Theatre Co., Lee Strasberg Institute.
THEATER: *Regional*: The Glass Menagerie, Shadow Box, Hotters, Sorry Wrong Number, Cold Foot, Monkey's Paw.
PICTURES: Top Gun (debut, 1986), Streets of Gold, Solarbabies, Near Dark, Made in USA, Cookie, Vital Signs, Torn Apart, Just Like a Woman, The Pompatus of Love.
TELEVISION: *Series*: Profit. *Movies*: The Lost Capone, A Mother's Gift. *Special*: Big Time.

PASETTA, MARTY
Producer-Director. b. June 16, 1932. e. U. Santa Clara.
TELEVISION: AFI Salutes to Fred Astaire, John Huston, Lillian Gish, Alfred Hitchcock and Jimmy Stewart, Gene Kelly Special, Elvis Aloha From Hawaii, Oscar (17), Emmy (2) and Grammy (8) Award Shows, A Country Christmas (1978-81), The Monte Carlo Show, Texaco Star Theatre-Opening Night, Burnett Discovers Domingo, Disneyland's 30th Anniversary Celebration, 15 Years of Cerebral Palsy Telethons, A Night at the Moulin Rouge, Soap Opera Awards, An All-Star Celebration Honoring Martin Luther King, Disneyland's Summer Vacation Party, Disney's Captain EO Grand Opening, 15th Anniversary of Disney World; Beach Boys... 25 Years Together, Super Night at the Superbowl, 20th Anniversary of Caesars Palace, Paris by Night with George Burns, I Call You Friend Papal Spacebridge '87, Walt Disney World's Celebrity Circus, Las Vegas: An All-Star 75th Anniversary, Julio Iglesias—Sold Out, The Ice Capades with Kirk Cameron, American All-Star Tribute Honoring Elizabeth Taylor.

PASSER, IVAN
Director, Writer. b. Prague, Czechoslovakia, July 10, 1933. e. Film Faculty of Acad. of Musical Arts, Prague. 1961, asst. dir. to Milos Forman on Audition which led to scripting for Forman. 1969, moved to U.S., worked in NY as longshoreman while studying Eng. U.S. dir. debut: Born to Win, 1971.
PICTURES: *Writer*: Loves of a Blonde, A Boring Afternoon, Fireman's Ball. *Director*: Intimate Lighting (also s.p.), Born to Win, Law and Disorder, Crime and Passion, The Silver Bears, Cutter and Bone, Creator, Haunted Summer.
TELEVISION: *U.S.*: Faerie Tale Theatre. *Movies*: Fourth Story, Stalin, While Justice Sleeps, Kidnapped.

PASTER, GARY M.
Executive. b. St. Louis, MO, July 4, 1943. e. U. of MO, B.A.; UCLA, USC Graduate Sch. of Business. 1970, joined Burbank Studios as asst. to pres., treas.; 1976 v.p., admin. and chmn. of the exec. comm.; 1977 pres. Member: AMPAS, LA Film Dev. Council, Hollywood Radio & T.V. Society, Acad. of Television Arts and Sciences. Advisory bd., Kaufman Astoria Studios, N.Y.

PATINKIN, MANDY
Actor. b. Chicago, IL, Nov. 30, 1952. r.n. Mandel Patinkin. e. U. of Kansas, Juilliard Sch. (Drama Div.; 1972-74). m. actress

Kathryn Grody. In regional theatre before coming to New York where played with Shakespeare Festival Public Theater (Trelawny of the Wells, Hamlet, Rebel Women). Recordings: Mandy Patinkin, Dress Casual, Experiment.
THEATER: Savages, The Shadow Box (B'way debut), Evita (Tony Award, 1980), Henry IV, Part I (Central Park), Sunday in the Park With George (Tony nom.), The Knife, Follies in Concert, A Winter's Tale, Mandy Patinkin: Dress Casual (solo concert), The Secret Garden, Falsettos.
PICTURES: The Big Fix (debut, 1978), Last Embrace, French Postcards, Night of the Juggler, Ragtime, Daniel, Yentl, Maxie, The Princess Bride, The House on Carroll Street, Alien Nation, Dick Tracy, True Colors, Impromptu, The Doctor, The Music of Chance, Life With Mikey (cameo), Squanto: A Warrior's Tale.
TELEVISION: Series: Chicago Hope (Emmy Award, 1995). Guest: That Thing on ABC, That 2nd Thing on ABC, Taxi, Sparrow, Streets of Gold, Midnight Special. Movie: Charleston.

PATRIC, JASON
Actor. b. Queens, NY, June 17, 1966. Son of playwright-actor Jason Miller. Grandson of performer Jackie Gleason. Began professional career with Vermont's Champlain Shakespeare Festival.
THEATER: NY: Beirut. LA: Out of Gas on Lovers' Leap.
PICTURES: Solarbabies (debut, 1986), The Lost Boys, The Beast, Denial, After Dark My Sweet, Roger Corman's Frankenstein Unbound, Rush, Geronimo: An American Legend, The Journey of August King, Sleepers.
TELEVISION: Movie: Tough Love. Special: Teach 109.

PATRICK, C.L.
Theatre Executive. b. Honaker, VA, Dec. 6, 1918. Former pres. of Fuqua Industries which owned Martin Theatres and Gulf States Theatres. Prior to this was pres. and chairman of Martin Theatres. Presently chairman of board Carmike Cinemas, Inc.; v.p. Variety International; director, Will Rogers Institute; Motion Picture Pioneer of 1976; Recipient of: Sherrill Corwin Award, 1984; Salah Hassanein Humanitarian Award, ShowEast '88; Show South's Exhibitor of the Decade Award, 1990.

PATRICK, MICHAEL W.
Executive. b. Columbus, GA, May 17, 1950. e. Columbus Coll., B.S., 1972. Pres., CEO, Carmike Cinemas. 1989, assumed additional post of chief exec. Board of dir., Columbus Bank and Trust Co. Member: exec. comm., Will Rogers Institute; Variety Int'l; Motion Picture Pioneers.

PATTON, WILL
Actor. b. Charleston, SC, June 14, 1954. e. NC School of the Arts, 1975.
THEATER: NY: Tourists and Refugees #2 (La Mama E.T.C., Obie Award), Fool For Love (Obie Award), Goose and Tomtom (Public Theatre), A Lie of the Mind.
PICTURES: King Blank, Silkwood, Variety, Desperately Seeking Susan, After Hours, Chinese Boxes, Belizaire the Cajun, No Way Out, Stars and Bars, Wildfire, Signs of Life, Everybody Wins, A Shock to the System, The Rapture, Cold Heaven, In the Soup, The Paint Job, Romeo Is Bleeding, Natural Causes, Midnight Edition, Tollbooth, The Client, The Puppet Masters, Copycat, Johns.
TELEVISION: Movies: Kent State, Dillinger, A Gathering of Old Men, The Deadly Desire, In the Deep Woods, A Child Lost Forever, Taking the Heat, Judicial Consent. Series: Ryan's Hope, Search For Tomorrow.

PAULEY, JANE
TV Host, Journalist. b. Indianapolis, IN, Oct. 31, 1950. m. Doonesbury creator Garry Trudeau. e. Indiana U. Involved in Indiana state politics before joining WISH-TV, Indianapolis, as reporter. Co-anchored midday news reports and anchored weekend news reports. Co-anchor of nightly news at WMAQ-TV, NBC station in Chicago. Joined Today Show in October, 1976, as featured regular, prior to which had made guest appearances on that program; co-host until 1990. Began own series Real Life With Jane Pauley in 1991.

PAVAN, MARISA
Actress, r.n. Marisa Pierangeli. b. Cagliari, Sardinia, Italy, June 19, 1932. e. Torquato Tasso Coll. Twin sister of late actress Pier Angeli. Came to U.S. 1950.
PICTURES: What Price Glory? (debut, 1952), Down Three Dark Streets, Drum Beat, The Rose Tattoo (Acad. Award nom.), Diane, The Man in the Gray Flannel Suit, The Midnight Story, John Paul Jones, Solomon and Sheba, A Slightly Pregnant Man.

PAVLIK, JOHN M.
Executive. b. Melrose, IA, Dec. 3, 1939. e. U. of Minnesota, B.A., 1963. Reporter, Racine (WI) Journal-Times, San Bernardino (CA) Sun-Telegram, 1963-66; writer, News Bureau, Pacific Telephone, Los Angeles, 1966-68; asst. dir. of

publ. rltns., Association of Motion Picture and Television Producers, 1968-72; dir. of publ. rltns., 1972-78; v.p., 1978-79; exec. admin., Academy of Motion Picture Arts and Sciences, 1979-82; exec. dir., M.P. & TV Fund, 1982-88; consultant, 1988-89; dir. of endowment dev., Academy Foundation, 1989-present; member, bd. of dir., Permanent Charities Comm. of the Entertainment Industries, 1979-84; member, bd. of dir., Hollywood Chamber of Commerce, 1979-85; v.p., Los Angeles Film Dev. Committee, 1977-78, member, exec. council, 1974-85; special consultant, California Motion Picture Council, 1974-79; member, advisory board, Assn. of Film Commissioners int'l, 1988-present.

PAXTON, BILL
Actor. b. Fort Worth, TX, May 17, 1955. e. NYU. First professional job as set dresser for film Big Bad Mamma. Studied acting in NYC with Stella Adler. Dir. short films Fish Heads, Scoop (also s.p.)
PICTURES: Stripes, The Lords of Discipline, Mortuary, Streets of Fire, Impulse, The Terminator, Weird Science, Commando, Aliens, Near Dark, Pass the Ammo, Slipstream, Next of Kin, Back to Back, Brain Dead, The Last of the Finest, Navy SEALS, Predator 2, The Dark Backward, One False Move, The Vagrant, Trespass, Indian Summer, Boxing Helena, Future Shock, Monolith, Tombstone, True Lies, Apollo 13, The Last Supper, Twister, The Evening Star.
TELEVISION: Mini-Series: Fresno. Movies: Deadly Lessons, The Atlanta Child Murders, An Early Frost, Frank and Jesse. Guest: Miami Vice.

PAY, WILLIAM
UK Manager Quigley Publishing Co., Inc. b. London, England. Joined London office Quigley Publications. Served in RAF, 1941-46; rejoined Quigley; dir. Burnup Service Ltd., 1951; London news ed., Quigley Pub., 1955; dir., Quigley Pub. Ltd., 1961; appt. mgr. dir., 1963; mgr. dir., Burnup Company. Appt. Sec. British Kinematograph Sound & TV Society. Conference Co-ordinator biennial Intern. Film & TV Technology Conferences in U.K., 1975-87.

PAYMER, DAVID
Actor. b. Long Island, NY, Aug. 30, 1954. e. Univ. of Mich. First professional job with natl. company of Grease, which he later appeared in on B'way. Has also taught acting at UCLA and the Film Actor's Workshop, performed stand-up comedy and served as staff writer on The New Leave It to Beaver Show.
PICTURES: The In-Laws (debut, 1979), Airplane II: The Sequel, Best Defense, Irreconcilable Differences, Perfect, Howard the Duck, No Way Out, Crazy People, City Slickers, Mr. Saturday Night (Acad. Award nom.), Searching for Bobby Fischer, Heart and Souls, City Slickers II: The Legend of Curly's Gold, Quiz Show, City Hall, The American President, Unforgettable, Nixon.
TELEVISION: Series: The Commish. Movies: Grace Kelly, Pleasure, Cagney & Lacey: The Return, Cagney & Lacey: Together Again. Guest: Cagney & Lacy, The Paper Chase, Taxi, Cheers, L.A. Law, Hill Street Blues, Moonlighting, Murphy Brown. Special: In Search of Dr. Seuss.

PAYNTER, ROBERT
Cinematographer. b. London, England, Mar. 12, 1928. e. Mercer Sch. First job in industry at 15 years as camera trainee with Government Film Dept.
PICTURES: Hannibal Brooks (debut, 1969), The Games, Lawman, The Nightcomers, Chato's Land, The Mechanic, Scorpio, The Big Sleep, Superman, Firepower, The Final Conflict, Superman II, An American Werewolf in London, Superman III, Trading Places, The Muppets Take Manhattan, Into the Night, National Lampoon's European Vacation, Spies Like Us, Little Shop of Horrors, When the Whales Came, Strike It Rich, Get Back.

PAYS, AMANDA
Actress. b. Berkshire, England, June 6, 1959. m. actor Corbin Bernsen. Began as a model. Studied French, art and pottery at Hammersmith Polytechnic. Acting debut: Cold Room (HBO).
PICTURES: Oxford Blues, The Kindred, Off Limits, Leviathan, Exposure, Solitaire for Two.
TELEVISION: Series: Max Headroom, The Flash. Mini-Series: A.D. Movies: 13 at Dinner, The Pretenders, Parker Kane, Dead on the Money, The Thorn Birds: The Lost Years.

PAYSON, MARTIN D.
Executive. b. Brooklyn, NY, Jan. 4, 1936. e. Cornell U., NYU Sch. of Law, LLB, 1961. Practiced law privately before joining Warner Communications, Inc. as v.p. 1970. Later named exec. v.p., gen. counsel. 1987, appt. to 3-member office of pres., WCI. Was vice chmn. Time Warner Inc., until Dec. 1992. Retired.

PEAKER, E. J.
Actress, Singer, Dancer. r.n. Edra Jeanne Peaker. b. Tulsa, OK, Feb. 22. e. U. of New Mexico, U. of Vienna, Austria. Stage debut Bye, Bye Birdie

PICTURES: Hello Dolly! (debut, 1969), All American Boy, Private Roads, The Four Deuces, Graduation Day, Fire in the Night, I Can't Lose, Out of This World.
TELEVISION: *Series*: That's Life. *Guest*: The Flying Nun, That Girl, Love American Style, Odd Couple, Police Woman, Rockford Files, Get Christie Love, Houston Knights, Hunter, Quincy, Charlie's Angels, Six Million Dollar Man. *Movies*: Three's a Crowd, Getting Away From It All, Broken Promises (assoc. prod., writer).

PEARCE, CHRISTOPHER
Producer. b. Dursley, Eng. Nov. 19, 1943. Entered industry as gen. mgr. American Zoetrope. From 1982 to 1985 served as exec. in chg. of prod. for Cannon Films Inc. overseeing prod. on 150 films incl. That Championship Season, Runaway Train, Fool For Love and Barfly. 1987 became sr. v.p. and COO Cannon Group. Has since become pres. & CEO Cannon Pictures. TV movie: Coming Out of the Ice.

PEARCE, RICHARD
Director, Cinematographer. b. San Diego, CA, Jan. 25, 1943. e. Yale U., B.A. degree in Eng. lit., 1965. New School for Social Research, M.A., degree in political economics. Worked with Don Pennebaker and Richard Leacock on documentaries. Photographed Emile de Antonio's America Is Hard to See. In 1970 went to Chile where he dir., photographed and edited Campamento, an award-winning documentary.
PICTURES: As photographer (Academy Award winning documentaries): Woodstock, Marjoe, Interviews With My Lai Veterans, Hearts and Minds. *Director*: Heartland (debut, 1979), Threshold, Country, No Mercy, The Long Walk Home, Leap of Faith, A Family Thing.
TELEVISION: The Gardener's Son, Siege, No Other Love, Sessions, Dead Man Out, The Final Days.

PECK, GREGORY
Actor, Producer. r.n. Eldred Gregory Peck. b. La Jolla, CA, April 5, 1916. e. U. of California; Neighborhood Playhouse Sch. of Dramatics. Father of actors Tony and Cecilia Peck. On dramatic stage (The Doctor's Dilemma, The Male Animal, Once in a Lifetime, The Play's the Thing, You Can't Take It With You, The Morning Star, The Willow and I, Sons and Soldiers, etc.). Voted one of ten best Money-Making Stars Motion Picture Herald-Fame Poll, 1947, 1952. Co-prod. and starred in Big Country, for his company, Anthony Productions; prod. the Trial of the Catonsville Nine, The Dove (St. George Productions). Pres., Acad. M.P. Arts and Sciences, 1967-70. Founding mem., bd. mem. and chmn. American Film Inst. Recipient, Jean Hersholt Humanitarian Award, 1986. AFI Life Achievement Award, 1989. Voice of Florenz Ziegfeld in 1991 B'way musical The Will Rogers Follies.
PICTURES: Days of Glory (debut, 1944), The Keys of the Kingdom, The Valley of Decision, Spellbound, The Yearling, Duel in the Sun, The Macomber Affair, Gentleman's Agreement, The Paradine Case, Yellow Sky, The Great Sinner, Twelve O'Clock High, The Gunfighter, Only the Valiant, David and Bathsheba, Captain Horatio Hornblower, The World in His Arms, The Snows of Kilimanjaro, Roman Holiday, Night People, Man With a Million, The Purple Plain, The Man in the Gray Flannel Suit, Moby Dick, Designing Woman, The Bravados, The Big Country (also co-prod.), Pork Chop Hill (also prod.), Beloved Infidel, On the Beach, Guns of Navarone, To Kill a Mockingbird (Academy Award, 1962), Cape Fear (also prod.), How the West Was Won, Captain Newman M.D., Behold a Pale Horse (also prod.), John F. Kennedy: Years of Lightning—Day of Drums (narrator), Mirage, Arabesque, MacKenna's Gold, Stalking Moon, The Chairman, Marooned, I Walk the Line, Shootout, Billy Two Hats, The Omen, MacArthur (also prod.), The Boys from Brazil (also prod.), The Sea Wolves (also prod.), Amazing Grace and Chuck, Old Gringo, Other People's Money, Cape Fear (1991).
TELEVISION: *Mini-series*: The Blue and the Gray. *Movies*: The Scarlet and the Black (also prod.), The Portrait. *Special*: We the People 200: The Constitutional Gala, The First 50 Years.

PEDAS, JIM
Executive. b. Youngstown, OH. e. Thiel College. Opened Circle Theatre in Washington, D.C. in 1957 with brother Ted. 1984 formed Circle Releasing, serving as Secretary/Treasurer; Circle Films, serving as v.p. See Ted Pedas entry.

PEDAS, TED
Executive. b. Farrell, PA, May 6, 1931. e. Youngstown St. Univ., Wharton Sch. of Business at Univ. of Pa., Geo. Washington Univ. 1957, with brother Jim, opened Circle Theatre in Washington D.C. one of the first repertory houses. Circle/Showcase group of m.p. theatres expanded to over 80 quality screens before being sold in 1988. 1973-78, served on board of Cinema 5 in NY. 1984, Circle Releasing formed to distribute films with Ted serving as president. Releases include Blood Simple, The Navigator and the Killer. Circle Films has produced the Coen Brothers' Raising Arizona, Miller's Crossing, Barton Fink and Caught.

PEERCE, LARRY
Director. b. Bronx, NY. Father was late singer Jan Peerce.
PICTURES: One Potato Two Potato, The Big T.N.T. Show, The Incident, Goodbye Columbus, The Sporting Club, A Separate Peace, Ash Wednesday, The Other Side of the Mountain, Two Minute Warning, The Other Side of the Mountain—Part II, The Bell Jar (also exec. prod.), Why Would I Lie?, Love Child, Hard to Hold, Wired.
TELEVISION: *Movies*: A Stranger Who Looks Like Me, Love Lives On, I Take These Men, The Fifth Missile, Prison for Children, Queenie, Elvis and Me, The Neon Empire, The Court-Martial of Jackie Robinson, Child of Rage, Poisoned by Love: The Kern County Murders, Heaven & Hell: North and South Book III, A Burning Passion: The Margaret Mitchell Story, In Pursuit of Honor (co-exec. prod. only).

PENA, ELIZABETH
Actress. b. Cuba, Sept. 23, 1961. Moved to New York City in 1969 where she attended NY High School for Performing Arts. Off-B'way in Blood Wedding, Antigone, Romeo & Juliet, Act One & Only, Italian American Reconciliation.
PICTURES: El Super, Times Square, They All Laughed, Fat Chance, Crossover Dreams, Down and Out in Beverly Hills, La Bamba, Batteries Not Included, Vibes, Blue Steel, Jacob's Ladder, The Waterdance, Across the Moon, Free Willy 2: The Adventure Home, Fair Game, Dead Funny, Lone Star.
TELEVISION: *Series*: Tough Cookies, I Married Dora, Shannon's Deal. *Movies*: Fugitive Among Us, Roommates.

PENDLETON, AUSTIN
Actor. b. Warren, OH, Mar. 27, 1940. e. Yale Univ. Started acting with Williamstown Theatre Festival. Teaches acting at the Herbert Berghof Studio. Named artistic dir. of NY's Circle Rep. Theatre, 1995.
THEATER: *Actor*: Oh Dad Poor Dad Mama's Hung You in the Closet and I'm Feeling So Sad, Fiddler on the Roof, The Little Foxes, The Last Sweet Days of Isaac (NY Drama Critics & Outer Critics Circle Awards), Educating Rita, Doubles, The Sorrows of Frederick, Grand Hotel, Hamlet, Sophistry. *Director*: The Runner Stumbles, Say Goodnight Gracie, John Gabriel Borkman, The Little Foxes. *Author*: Booth, Uncle Bob.
PICTURES: Skidoo (debut, 1968), Catch-22, What's Up Doc?, Every Little Crook and Nanny, The Thief Who Came to Dinner, The Front Page, The Great Smokey Roadblock (The Last of the Cowboys), The Muppet Movie, Starting Over, Simon, First Family, My Man Adam, Off Beat, Short Circuit, Hello Again, Mr. & Mrs. Bridge, The Ballad of the Sad Cafe, True Identity, My Cousin Vinny, Charlie's Ear, Rain Without Thunder, My Boyfriend's Back, Searching for Bobby Fischer, Mr. Nanny, Greedy, Guarding Tess, Dangerous Minds, Two Much, Home for the Holidays, Sgt. Bilko.
TELEVISION: *Movie*: Don't Drink the Water. *Guest*: Miami Vice, The Equalizer.

PENN, ARTHUR
Director. b. Philadelphia, PA, Sept. 27, 1922. e. Black Mountain Coll., Asheville, NC; U. of Perugia, U. of Florence in Italy. Began as TV dir. in 1953, twice winner of Sylvania Award. Appeared in 1994 film Naked in New York.
THEATER: Two for the Seesaw, Miracle Worker (Tony Award, 1960), Toys in the Attic, All the Way Home, Golden Boy, Wait Until Dark, Sly Fox, Monday After the Miracle, Hunting Cockroaches.
PICTURES: The Left-Handed Gun (debut, 1958), The Miracle Worker (Acad. Award nom.), Mickey One (also prod.), The Chase, Bonnie and Clyde (Acad. Award nom.), Alice's Restaurant (Acad. Award nom.; also co-s.p.), Little Big Man, Visions of Eight (dir. segment: The Highest), Night Moves, The Missouri Breaks, Four Friends (also co-prod.), Target, Dead of Winter, Penn and Teller Get Killed (also prod.), Inside.
TELEVISION: *Movie*: The Portrait.

PENN, CHRISTOPHER
Actor. b. Malibu, CA. Son of director Leo Penn and actress Eileen Ryan. Brother of actor Sean Penn and musician Michael Penn. Studied acting with Peggy Feury.
PICTURES: Rumble Fish (debut, 1983), All the Right Moves, Footloose, The Wild Life, Pale Rider, At Close Range, Made in USA, Return From the River Kwai, Best of the Best, Mobsters, Leather Jackets, Reservoir Dogs, Best of the Best 2, The Pickle, The Music of Chance, True Romance, Short Cuts, Josh and S.A.M., Beethoven's 2nd, Imaginary Crimes, Fist of the Northstar, Under the Hula Moon, To Wong Foo—Thanks for Everything-Julie Newmar, Sacred Cargo, Mulholland Falls, The Boys Club, The Funeral.
TELEVISION: *Guest*: Magnum P.I., The Young Riders, North Beach, Rawhide, Chicago Hope.

PENN, SEAN
Actor, Director, Writer. b. Burbank, CA, Aug. 17, 1960. Son of actor-director Leo Penn and actress Eileen Ryan. Brother of actor Christopher Penn and musician Michael Penn. m. actress Robin Wright. e. Santa Monica H.S. Served as apprentice

for two years at Group Repertory Theatre, L.A. Acted in Earthworms, Heartland, The Girl on the Via Flaminia, etc. First prof appearance as guest star on TV's Barnaby Jones. On B'way in Heartland, Slab Boys. Also Hurlyburly (Westwood Playhouse, LA).
PICTURES: *Actor*: Taps (debut, 1981), Fast Times at Ridgemont High, Bad Boys, Crackers, Racing with the Moon, The Falcon and the Snowman, At Close Range, Shanghai Surprise, Colors, Judgment in Berlin, Casualties of War, We're No Angels, State of Grace, Carlito's Way, Dead Man Walking. *Dir./Writer*: The Indian Runner, The Crossing Guard (also co-prod.).
TELEVISION: *Movie*: The Killing of Randy Webster. *Guest*: Barnaby Jones. *Special*: Dear America (reader).

PENNEBAKER, D.A.
Director. b. Evanston, IL, July 15, 1925. r.n. Donn Alan Pennebaker. e. Yale U. Studied engineering, set up own electronics firm. Worked in advertising, before writing and directing documentaries, as well as experimental films. 1958 joined Richard Leacock, Willard Van Dyke and Shirley Clarke in equipment-sharing film co-op, Filmakers. 1960 joined Robert Drew operating out of Time Life with Leacock, Albert Maysles and others. Set up Leacock Pennebaker with Leacock and made several films that were blown up from 16mm to 35mm and released in theatres. Currently works with co-dir. and wife Chris Hegedus and son Frazer Pennebaker, continuing to film unscripted dramas of real events in cinema verite style. Dir. music videos for Suzanne Vega, Victoria Williams, Branford Marsalis, Randy Newman, etc.
PICTURES: Daybreak Express (1956), Opening in Moscow, Primary, David, Jane, Crisis, The Chair, On the Pole, Mr. Pearson, Don't Look Back, Monterey Pop, Beyond the Law, One P.M., Sweet Toronto, Maidstone, Ziggy Stardust and the Spiders from Mars, On the Pole, Town Bloody Hall, The Energy War, Dance Black America, Rockaby, Delorean, Happy Come Home, Depeche Mode, The Music Tells You, The War Room.

PEPLOE, MARK
Writer. b. Kenya. Sister is writer Clare Peploe. Raise in England and Italy. e. Magdalen Col., Oxford. Became researcher for documentary dept. of the BBC; then worked as research, writer and dir. for series Creative Persons.
PICTURES: The Pied Piper, The Passenger, The Babysitter, High Season, The Last Emperor (Academy Award, 1987), The Sheltering Sky, Afraid of the Dark (also dir.), Little Buddha.

PERAKOS, SPERIE P.
Executive. b. New Britain, CT, Nov. 12, 1915. e. Cheshire Acad., Yale U., Harvard Law Sch. Student mgr., Stanley-Warner Theatres, 1939-40; Perakos Theatres 1940 to present; Capt., U.S.A. Intelligence with 35 inf. division. Fellow, Pierson Coll., Yale, 1946-present; Yale Alumni Bd., 1949 to present; Yale Alumni Film Bd. 1952 to 1980; member Alumni Council for Yale Drama Sch.; past pres. Yale Club of New Britain, Conn.; dir. of Films & Filmings Seminars, Pierson Coll., Yale; prod. Antigone, 1962; pres. Norma Film Prod., Inc., 1962 to present. Past pres. and chmn. Yale's Peabody Museum Associates. Pres., Perakos Theatres, Conn. Theatre Circuit, Inc. Member, Exec. Board of Natl' Assn. of Theatre Owners, C.A.R.A.

PERENCHIO, ANDREW J.
Executive. b. Fresno, CA, Dec. 20, 1930. e. U. of California. Vice pres., Music Corp. of America, 1958-62; General Artists Corp., 1962-64; pres., owner, Chartwell Artists, Ltd., theatrical agency, Los Angeles, 1964; pres. & CEO, Tandem Productions, Inc., and TAT Communications Co., 1973-83, then became principal with Norman Lear in Embassy Communications. Held post of pres. & CEO of Embassy Pictures.

PEREZ, ROSIE
Actress. b. Brooklyn, 1964. Attended sch. in L.A. where she became a dancer on Soul Train; then choreographer for music videos and stage shows for such performers as Bobby Brown, The Boys, Diana Ross, LL Cool J, etc. Acting debut in Do the Right Thing.
PICTURES: Do the Right Thing (also choreog.; debut, 1989), White Men Can't Jump, Night on Earth, Untamed Heart, Fearless (Acad. Award nom.), It Could Happen to You, Somebody to Love, A Brother's Kiss.
TELEVISION: *Movie*: Criminal Justice. *Series*: In Living Color (choreographer). *Specials*: Rosie Perez Presents Society's Ride (exec. prod.), In a New Light: Sex Unplugged (co-host).

PERKINS, ELIZABETH
Actress. b. Forest Hills, Queens, NY, Nov. 18, 1960. Grew up in Vermont. After high school moved to Chicago to study at Goodman School of Drama. Two months after moving to NY in 1984, landed a role in the national touring co. of Brighton Beach Memoirs, later performing part on Broadway. Acted with

Playwright's Horizon, NY Ensemble Theater, Shakespeare in the Park and Steppenwolf Theatre Co. Appeared in short film Teach 109.
PICTURES: About Last Night... (debut, 1986), From the Hip, Big, Sweet Hearts Dance, Love at Large, Avalon, Enid Is Sleeping (Over Her Dead Body), He Said She Said, The Doctor, Indian Summer, The Flintstones, Miracle on 34th Street, Moonlight and Valentino.
TELEVISION: *Movie*: For Their Own Good.

PERKINS, MILLIE
Actress. b. Passaic, NJ, May 12, 1938. Was model when chosen by dir. George Stevens for starring role in The Diary of Anne Frank.
PICTURES: The Diary of Anne Frank (debut, 1959), Wild in the Country, Dulcinea, Ensign Pulver, Ride in the Whirlwind, The Shooting, Wild in the Streets, Cockfighter, Lady Cocoa, The Witch Who Came From the Sea, Table for Five, At Close Range, Jake Speed, Slam Dance, Wall Street, Two Moon Junction, The Pistol, Bodily Harm.
TELEVISION: *Series*: Knots Landing, Elvis. *Guest*: thirtysomething, Murder She Wrote, Our House, Jessie, Hart to Hart, Glitter, Wagon Train. *Movies*: A.D., The Thanksgiving Promise, Penalty Phase, Anatomy of an Illness, Shattered Vows, License to Kill, Strange Voices, Broken Angel, Best Intentions, The Other Love, Haunting Passion, A Gun in the House, Model Mother, Macbeth (cable tv), Call Me Anna, 72 Hours, Murder of Innocence. *Guest*: U.S. Steel Hour, Breaking Point.

PERKINS, ROWLAND
Executive. Vice-President, Creative Services, William Morris Agency, 1952-75. Founding President, Creative Artists Agency, 1975-95. Established The Rowland Perkins Company (a.k.a. Double Eagle Entertainment) in 1994 to develop and produce feature, network and cable films; television series and sepcials; Broadway shows, etc.

PERLMAN, RHEA
Actress. b. Brooklyn, NY, March 31, 1948. e. Hunter Coll. m. actor-dir. Danny DeVito. Co-founder Colonnades Theatre Lab., NY and New Street prod. co with Danny DeVito.
PICTURES: Love Child, My Little Pony (voice), Enid is Sleeping (Over Her Dead Body), Ted & Venus, Class Act, There Goes the Neighborhood, Canadian Bacon, Sunset Park, Matilda.
TELEVISION: *Series*: Cheers (4 Emmy awards: 1984, 1985, 1986, 1989), Pearl (co-exec. prod.). *Movies*: I Want to Keep My Baby!, Stalk the Wild Child, Having Babies II, Intimate Strangers, Mary Jane Harper Cried Last Night, Like Normal People, Drop-out Father, The Ratings Game, Dangerous Affection, A Family Again, To Grandmother's House We Go, A Place to Be Loved, Spoils of War. *Specials*: Funny You Don't Look 200, Two Daddies (voice), The Last Halloween.

PERLMAN, RON
Actor. b. New York, NY, April 13, 1950. While in high school, part of comedy team that played clubs. e. City U. of NY, U. of Minnesota, M.F.A. Joined Classic Stage Company, NY, for 2 years.
THEATER: *NY*: The Architect and the Emperor of Assyria (also toured Europe), American Heroes, The Resistible Rise of Arturo Ui, Tiebele and Her Demon, La Tragedie de Carmen, A Few Good Men.
PICTURES: Quest for Fire, The Ice Pirates, The Name of the Rose, Sleepwalkers, The Adventures of Huck Finn, Double Exposure, Romeo Is Bleeding, Crime and Punishment, Cronos, Fluke, The City of Lost Children, The Last Summer, The Island of Dr. Moreau.
TELEVISION: *Series*: Beauty and the Beast. *Movies*: A Stoning in Fulham County, Blind Man's Bluff, Original Sins.

PERLMUTTER, DAVID M.
Producer. b. Toronto, Canada, 1934. e. U. of Toronto. Pres., Quadrant Films Ltd.
PICTURES: The Neptune Factor, Sunday in the Country, It Seemed Like a Good Idea at the Time, Love at First Sight, Find the Lady, Blood and Guts, The Third Walker, Two Solitudes, Fast Company, Double Negative, Nothing Personal, Misdeal, Love.

PERMUT, DAVID A.
Producer. b. New York, NY, Mar. 23, 1954. In 1974, became pres., Diversified Artists Intl.; 1975, pres., Theatre Television Corp.; 1979, formed Permut Presentations, Inc., of which is pres. Production deals with Columbia Pictures (1979), Lorimar Productions (1981), Universal (1985), United Artists (1986), and New Line Cinema (1991).
PICTURES: Give 'Em Hell Harry, Fighting Back (exec. prod.), Blind Date, Richard Pryor—Live in Concert (exec. prod.), Dragnet, The Marrying Man, 29th Street, Captain Ron, Consenting Adults, The Temp, Three of Hearts, Surviving the Game, Trapped in Paradise, Eddie, Face Off.

TELEVISION: Mistress (sprv. prod.), Love Leads the Way (exec. prod.), Triumph of the Heart: The Ricky Bell Story (prod.), Breaking the Silence (prod.).

PERREAU, GIGI
Actress. r.n. Ghislaine Perreau. b. Los Angeles, CA, Feb. 6, 1941. e. Immaculate Heart H.S. & College. Many stage and TV guest appearances. Now teaching and directing. Among first 50 stars to be honored with star on Hollywood Walk of Fame.
PICTURES: Madame Currie (debut, 1943), Abigail, Dear Heart, Dark Waters, San Diego I Love You, Two Girls and a Sailor, The Master Race, The Seventh Cross, Mr. Skeffington, Yoland and the Thief, Voice of the Whistler, God Is My Co-Pilot, To Each His Own, Alias Mr. Twilight, High Barbaree, Song of Love, Green Dolphin Street, Family Honeymoon, Enchantment, Sainted Sisters, Roseanna McCoy, Song of Surrender, My Foolish Heart, Shadow on the Wall, For Heaven's Sake, Never a Dull Moment, Reunion in Reno, The Lady Pays Off, Weekend with Father, Has Anybody Seen My Gal, Bonzo Goes to College, There's Always Tomorrow, The Man in the Gray Flannel Suit, Dance With Me Henry, Wild Heritage, The Cool and the Crazy, Girls' Town, Tammy Tell Me True, Look in Any Window, Journey to the Center of Time, Hell on Wheels.
TELEVISION: Series: The Betty Hutton Show, Follow the Sun.

PERRINE, VALERIE
Actress. b. Galveston, TX, Sept. 3 1943. e. U. of Arizona. Was showgirl in Las Vegas before discovered by agent Robert Walker who got her contract with Universal Pictures.
PICTURES: Slaughterhouse 5 (debut, 1972), The Last American Hero, Lenny (NY Film Critics & Cannes Film Fest. Awards; Acad. Award nom.), W. C. Fields & Me, Mr. Billion, Superman, The Magician of Lublin, The Electric Horseman, Can't Stop the Music, Superman II, Agency, The Border, Water, Maid to Order, Reflections in a Dark Sky, Bright Angel, Boiling Point, Girl in the Cadillac, The Break.
TELEVISION: Movies: The Couple Takes a Wife, Ziegfeld: The Man and His Women, Marian Rose White, Malibu, When Your Lover Leaves, Sweet Bird of Youth, Un Casa a Roma, The Burning Shore. Series: Leo and Liz in Beverly Hills. Special: Steambath.

PERRY, LUKE
Actor. b. Fredricktown, OH, Oct. 11, 1966. r.n. Coy Luther Perry III. To LA then NY as teen to become actor, landing role on daytime serial Loving.
PICTURES: Terminal Bliss (debut, 1992), Scorchers, Buffy the Vampire Slayer, At Home With the Webbers (cameo), 8 Seconds, From the Edge, Christmas Vacation, Normal Life.
TELEVISION: Series: Loving, Another World, Beverly Hills 90210.

PERRY, SIMON
Producer, Writer. b. Farnham, Eng., Aug. 5, 1943. e. Cambridge Univ., 1965. Ent. ind. 1974. Early career in stage and television production. Prod. mini-budget feature Knots; prod. dir. Eclipse. Served on bureau staff of Variety. Ran the National Film Development Fund for two years. 1982 set up Umbrella Films to produce Another Time Another Place, Loose Connections, Nineteen Eighty Four, Hotel Du Paradis, Nanou, White Mischief, The Playboys, Innocent Lies. Chief exec. of British Screen Finance since 1991.

PERSKY, LESTER
Executive. b. New York, NY, July 6, 1927. e. Brooklyn Coll. Officer in U.S. Merchant Marine, 1946-48. Founder and pres. of own adv. agency, 1951-1964. Theatrical stage producer, 1966-69. 1973 creative director and co-owner Persky Bright Org. (owner-financier of numerous motion pictures for private investment group). Films: Last Detail, Golden Voyage of Sinbad, For Pete's Sake, California Split, The Man Who Would Be King, The Front, Shampoo, Hard Times, Taxi Driver, Missouri Breaks, Funny Lady, Gator, Bound for Glory, Sinbad and the Eye of the Tiger. Lester Persky Productions, Inc.
PICTURES: Producer: Fortune and Men's Eyes, Equus, Hair, Yanks.
TELEVISION: Mini-Series: Poor Little Rich Girl (Golden Globe Award, 1987), A Woman Named Jackie (Emmy Award, 1992), Liz: The Elizabeth Taylor Story.

PERSOFF, NEHEMIAH
Actor. b. Jerusalem, Israel, Aug. 2, 1919. e. Hebrew Technical Inst., 1934-37. Electrician, 1937-39; signal maint., N.Y. subway, 1939-41. Studied acting with Stella Adler and the Actors Studio. L.A. Critics Award 1971 for Sholem-Sholem Alecheim, and The Dybbuk. Has had exhibitions of his watercolor paintings in California, Florida.
THEATER: Sundown Beach, Galileo, Richard III, King Lear, Peter Pan, Peer Gynt, Tiger At the Gates, Colombe, Flahooly, Montserrat, Only in America. Tour: Fiddler on the Roof, Man of La Mancha, Oliver, Death of a Salesman (Stratford, Ont.), Peter Pan, I'm Not Rappaport, Sholem Aleichem (Drama Log & Bay Area Critics Circle Awards).

PICTURES: On the Waterfront, The Wild Party, The Harder They Fall, The Wrong Man, Men in War, This Angry Age, The Badlanders, Never Steal Anything Small, Al Capone, Some Like It Hot, Green Mansions, The Big Show, The Comancheros, The Hook, A Global Affair, Fate Is the Hunter, The Greatest Story Ever Told, The Power, The Money Jungle, Panic in the City, Mafia, The People Next Door, Mrs. Pollifax—Spy, Red Sky at Morning, Voyage of the Damned, In Search of Historic Jesus, Yentl, An American Tail (voice), The Last Temptation of Christ, Testament, Twins, The Dispossessed, An American Tail: Fievel Goes West (voice).
TELEVISION: Guest: Playhouse 90, Philco-Goodyear Show, Kraft, For Whom the Bells Tolls (Sylvania Award, 1958), Producers Showcase, Danger, You Are There, Untouchables, Route 66, Naked City, Wagon Train, Rawhide, Gunsmoke, Thriller, Hitchcock, Bus Stop, Five Fingers, Mr. Lucky, The Wild Wild West, I Spy, Columbo, Barney Miller, L.A. Law, Star Trek, Law and Order, Reasonable Doubts. Movies: Sadat, Adderly, The French Atlantic Affair.

PESCI, JOE
Actor. b. Newark, NJ, Feb. 9, 1943. Raised in Belleville, NJ. First show business job as child on TV's Star Time Kids. Worked as mason's laborer, restaurant owner, prior to becoming actor.
PICTURES: Death Collector, Raging Bull, I'm Dancing as Fast as I Can, Dear Mr. Wonderful (Ruby's Dream), Easy Money, Eureka, Once Upon a Time in America, Man on Fire, Moonwalker, Lethal Weapon 2, Betsy's Wedding, Goodfellas (Academy Award, best supporting actor, 1990), Home Alone, The Super, JFK, My Cousin Vinny, Tuti Dentro, Lethal Weapon 3, The Public Eye, Home Alone 2: Lost in New York, A Bronx Tale, Jimmy Hollywood, With Honors, Casino.
TELEVISION: Series: Half Nelson. Movies: Half Nelson (pilot), Backtrack. Guest: Tales From the Crypt (Split Personality).

PETERS, BERNADETTE
Actress. r.n. Bernadette Lazzara. b. New York, NY, Feb. 28, 1948. e. Quintano Sch. for Young Professionals, NY. Professional debut at age 5 on TV's Horn & Hardart Children's Hour, followed by Juvenile Jury and Name That Tune. Stage debut with N.Y. City Center production of The Most Happy Fella (1959).
THEATER: Gypsy (1961), This is Goggle, Riverwind, The Penny Friend, Curley McDimple, Johnny No-Trump, George M! (Theatre World Award), Dames at Sea (Drama Desk Award), La Strada, W.C. & Me, On the Town (1971 revival), Tartuffe, Mack and Mabel, Sally and Marsha, Sunday in the Park With George, Song and Dance (Tony, Drama Desk & Drama League Awards), Into the Woods, The Goodbye Girl.
PICTURES: Ace Eli and Rodger of the Skies (debut, 1973), The Longest Yard, W.C. Fields & Me, Vigilante Force, Silent Movie, The Jerk, Tulips, Pennies from Heaven, Heartbeeps, Annie, Slaves of New York, Pink Cadillac, Alice, Impromptu.
TELEVISION: Series: All's Fair. Mini-Series: The Martian Chronicles. Specials: George M, They Said It with Music, Party at Annapolis, Rich Thin and Beautiful (host), Faerie Tale Theatre, The Last Mile. Pilot: The Owl and the Pussycat. Movies: The Islander, David, Fall from Grace, The Last Best Year.

PETERS, BROCK
Actor. r.n. Brock Fisher. b. Harlem, NY, July 2, 1927. e. CCNY, U. of Chicago. Had numerous featured roles on and off B'way. in road and stock cos., nightclubs, TV. Toured with DePaur Infantry Chorus as bass soloist, 1947-50. Appeared in short film From These Roots.
THEATER: Porgy and Bess (debut, 1943), Anna Lucasta, My Darlin' Aida, Mister Johnson, King of the Dark Chamber, Othello, Kwamina, The Great White Hope (tour), Lost in the Stars, Driving Miss Daisy (Natl. Co.).
PICTURES: Carmen Jones (debut, 1954), Porgy and Bess, To Kill a Mockingbird, Heavens Above, The L-Shaped Room, The Pawnbroker, Major Dundee, The Incident, P.J., The Daring Game, Ace High, The MacMasters, Black Girl, Soylent Green, Slaughter's Big Rip-off, Lost in the Stars, Million Dollar Dixie Deliverance, Framed, Two-Minute Warning, Star Trek IV: The Voyage Home, Star Trek VI: The Undiscovered Country, Alligator II: The Mutation, The Importance of Being Earnest.
TELEVISION: Arthur Godfrey's Talent Scouts (debut, 1953), Series: The Young and the Restless. Guest: Eleventh Hour, It Takes a Thief, Mannix, Mod Squad. Mini-series: Seventh Avenue, Black Beauty, Roots: The Next Generations. Movies: Welcome Home Johnny Bristol, SST: Death Flight, The Incredible Journey of Doctor Meg Laurel, The Adventures of Huckleberry Finn, Agatha Christie's Caribbean Mystery, To Heal a Nation, Broken Angel, The Big One: The Great Los Angeles Earthquake, Highway Heartbreakers, The Secret. Specials: Challenge of the Go Bots (voice), Living the Dream: A Tribute to Dr. Martin Luther King. Co-prod.: This Far By Faith.

PETERS, JON
Producer. b. Van Nuys, CA, 1947. Started hair-styling business; built it into multimillion-dollar firm before turning film

producer. Formed Jon Peters Organization. 1980, joined with Peter Guber and Neil Bogart to form The Boardwalk Co. (dissolved 1981). Later Guber-Peters-Barris Company. 1989, became co-chairman of Columbia Pictures. Resigned, 1991.
PICTURES: A Star Is Born, Eyes of Laura Mars, The Main Event, Die Laughing, Caddyshack. *Co-Prod./Co-Exec. Prod. with Peter Guber:* An American Werewolf in London, Missing, Six Weeks, Flashdance, D.C. Cab, Vision Quest, Legend of Billie Jean, Clue, The Color Purple, Head Office, The Clan of the Cave Bear, Youngblood, The Witches of Eastwick, Innerspace, Who's That Girl, Gorillas in the Mist, Caddyshack II, Rain Man, Batman, Tango and Cash, The Bonfire of the Vanities, Batman Returns, This Boy's Life, With Honors, Money Train.
TELEVISION: *Movies:* Bay Coven (co-exec. prod.), Nightmare at Bitter Creek (exec. prod.).

PETERSEN, PAUL
Actor. b. Glendale, CA, Sept. 23, 1945. e. Valley Coll. Original Disney Mouseketeer (TV). Recorded hit songs She Can't Find Her Keys, and My Dad in 1962. In the late 1960's turned to writing beginning with a Marcus Welby script followed by paperback novels in 1970's. Author of book about Disney empire, Walt Mickey and Me (1977), and co-author of It's a Wonderful Life Trivia Book (1992). President and founder of A Minor Consideration, a support foundation for former kid actors with a current membership of 150 movie, tv and sports stars spanning the past 70 years.
PICTURES: Houseboat, This Could Be the Night, The Happiest Millionaire, Journey to Shiloh, A Time for Killing.
TELEVISION: *Series:* The Donna Reed Show. *Guest:* Playhouse 90, Lux Video Theatre, GE Theatre, The Virginian, Ford Theatre, Valentine's Day, Shindig. *Movies:* Something for a Lonely Man, Gidget Grows Up, Scout's Honor.

PETERSEN, WILLIAM
Actor. b. Chicago, IL, 1953. e. Idaho State U. Active in Chicago theatre; helped to found Ix, an ensemble acting group now called the Remains Theatre. Acted in Moby Dick, In the Belly of the Beast, A Streetcar Named Desire, etc. 1986, formed company with prod. Cynthia Chvatal called High Horse Prods.
THEATER: *NY:* Night of the Iguana.
PICTURES: To Live and Die in L.A., Manhunter, Amazing Grace and Chuck, Cousins, Young Guns II, Hard Promises (also co-prod.), Passed Away, Fear.
TELEVISION: *Movies:* Long Gone (HBO), Keep the Change (also co-prod.), Curacao. *Mini-Series:* The Kennedys of Massachusetts, Return to Lonesome Dove, The Beast.

PETERSEN, WOLFGANG
Director, Writer. b. Emden, Germany, Mar. 14, 1941. Career as asst. stage director at Ernst Deutsch Theatre in Hamburg before entering 4 year program at the German Film & TV Academy wher he directed for television and later theatrical films.
PICTURES: One of Us Two, Black and White Like Day and Night (also s.p.), The Consequence (also s.p.), Das Boot (The Boat; also s.p.; Acad. Award nom. for dir.), The Neverending Story (also s.p.), Enemy Mine, Shattered (also s.p., co-prod.), In the Line of Fire (also co-exec.prod.), Outbreak (also co-prod.).
TELEVISION: I Will Kill You Wolf (dir. debut 1970), Tatort (series), Smog (Prix Futura Award, 1975), For Your Love Only (also released theatrically), Scene of the Crime (series).

PETERSON, S. DEAN
Executive. b. Toronto, Canada, December 18, 1923. e. Victoria Coll., U. of Toronto. WWII service RCNVR; 1946 TV newsreel cameraman NBC; founded own prod. co. in 1947; incorporated Dordean Realty Limited to acquire new studios 1959; formed Peterson Productions Limited in 1957 to make TV commercials and sponsored theatrical shorts; formed Studio City Limited in 1965 to produce TV series and features acquiring an additional studio complex and backlot in Kleinberg, Ontario; 1972 formed SDP Communications Ltd. to package M.P. and TV; 1970 incorporated Intermedia Financial Services Limited to provide specialized financing and consultation to companies in M.P. and TV industries. Past-President Canadian Film and Television Production Assn., mbr. Variety Club, Tent 28; Canadian Society of Cinematographers; Directors Guild of America, Directors Guild of Canada, SMPTE.

PETERSON, RICHARD W.
Executive. b. Denver, CO, June 15, 1949. e. Col. Sch. of Broadcasting, Harper Coll. Joined Kennedy Theatres, Chicago, 1966. 1968 went with Great States Theatres (now Cineplex Odeon), Chicago. Was city mgr. of Crocker and Grove Theatres, Elgin, IL. 1973 joined American Automated Theatres, Oklahoma City, as dir. of adv., pub. Promoted to dir. of U.S. theatre operations. Worked for American International Pictures, Dallas, TX. Then moved to Dal Art Film Exchange

and B & B Theatres as general mgr.; 1987 took over 7 screens from McLendon and formed own co., Peterson Theatres, Inc, now operating 17 screens.

PETIT, HENRI-DOMINIQUE
Executive. b. Baden-Baden, Germany. e. Ecole Superieure de Physique et Chimie de Paris, Univ. of Paris. Joined Kodak 1975 as asst. mgr. of the Purchasing Division, Kodak Pathe, France. 1980, asst., then mgr. of Kodak Pathe Photofinishing Lab (1981). 1984, became bus. mgr. Business Information Systems and Corporate Accounts, Kodak Pathe. 1987, named bus. mgr. of Photofinishing Systems Division. 1989, appointed gen. mgr. and v.p. Motion Picture and Television Imaging, Europe/Africa/Middle East Region. Dec., 1992, named v.p. and gen. mgr. Motion Picture and Television Imaging.

PETRIE, DANIEL
Director. b. Glace Bay, Nova Scotia, Nov. 26, 1920. e. St. Francis Xavier U., Nova Scotia; Columbia U., MA, 1945; postgrad. Northwestern U. Broadway actor 1945-46. TV director from 1950. Son Daniel Petrie Jr. is a screenwriter; son Donald Petrie is a director.
THEATER: Shadow of My Enemy, Who'll Save the Plowboy?, Mornin' Sun, Monopoly, The Cherry Orchard, Volpone, A Lesson from Aloes.
PICTURES: The Bramble Bush (debut, 1960), A Raisin in the Sun, The Main Attraction, Stolen Hours, The Idol, The Spy With a Cold Nose, The Neptune Factor, Buster and Billie, Lifeguard, The Betsy, Resurrection, Fort Apache The Bronx, Six Pack, The Bay Boy (also s.p.; Genie Award), Square Dance (also prod.), Rocket Gibraltar, Cocoon: The Return, Lassie.
TELEVISION: *Movies:* Silent Night Lonely Night, A Howling in the Woods, A Stranger in Town, Moon of the Wolf, Trouble Comes to Town, Mousey, Returning Home, Eleanor and Franklin (Emmy Award, 1976), Sybil, Eleanor and Franklin: The White House Years (Emmy Award, 1977), Harry Truman, Plain Speaking (Emmy nom.), The Dollmaker (Emmy nom.), The Execution of Raymond Graham (Emmy nom.), Half a Lifetime, My Name is Bill W. (also prod.; Emmy nom.), Mark Twain and Me (also prod., Emmy Award), A Town Torn Apart (also prod., Emmy nom.), Kissinger and Nixon.

PETRIE, DONALD
Director. b. New York, NY. Son of dir. Daniel Petrie. Moved to LA as teenager, becoming tv actor. Attended American Film Inst. dir. program, where he made short film The Expert. Was then hired to dir. Mister Magic esisode of Amazing Stories.
PICTURES: Mystic Pizza (debut, 1988), Opportunity Knocks, Grumpy Old Men, The Favor, Richie Rich, The Associate.
TELEVISION: *Series episodes:* MacGyver, The Equalizer, L.A. Law. *Special:* Have You Tried Talking to Patty?

PETROU, DAVID MICHAEL
Writer, Producer, Public Relations Executive. b. Washington, DC, Nov. 3, 1949. e. U. of Maryland, B.A.; Georgetown U., M.A. Publicity assoc., Psychiatric Institutes of America, Washington, DC; 1971; assoc. dir. of publicity & film liaison, Random House, 1974; guest lecturer, screen writing & film production, The American University Consortium, Washington, DC, spring, 1980; Woodrow Wilson Fellowship, 1971. Entered industry in 1975. Joined Salkind Organization in chg. of literary projects. Worked in numerous production capacities on Crossed Swords, Superman, Superman II. 1977, exec. in chg. of literary development, Salkind. Wrote Crossed Swords (1978) and The Making of Superman. Co-authored screenplay, Shoot to Kill. 1978-79, promotional dev. on Time after Time for Warner Bros.; 1980-83, dir., special projects Joseph Kennedy Foundation. 1983-84, sr. edit. for entertainment, Regardie's Magazine; 1984-86, sr. exec., p.r. div., Abramson Associates; 1986-88, sr. v.p., Eisner, Held & Petrou, Inc., p.r. agency; 1988-present, pres. & COO, Eisner Petrou & Associates Inc. Baltimore-Wash., marketing communications agency. 1992, named chmn. of American Film Institute's Second Decade Council.

PETTET, JOANNA
Actress. b. London, England, Nov. 16, 1944. Raised in Canada. Studied acting at Neighborhood Playhouse in NY.
PICTURES: The Group (debut, 1966), The Night of the Generals, Casino Royale, Robbery, Blue, The Best House in London, Welcome to Arrow Beach (Tender Flesh), The Evil, An Eye for an Eye, Double Exposure, Sweet Country, Terror in Paradise.
TELEVISION: *Series:* Knots Landing. *Mini-Series:* Captains and the Kings. *Movies:* Footsteps, The Delphi Bureau, The Weekend Nun, Pioneer Woman, A Cry in the Wilderness, The Desperate Miles, The Hancocks, The Dark Side of Innocence, Sex and the Married Woman, Cry of the Innocent, The Return of Frank Cannon.

PETTY, LORI
Actress. b. Chattanooga, TN, 1965. Worked as graphic artist before turning to acting.

PICTURES: Cadillac Man, Point Break, A League of Their Own, Free Willy, Poetic Justice, In the Army Now, Tank Girl, The Glass Shield.
TELEVISION: *Series*: The Thorns, Booker, Lush Life.

PEYSER, JOHN
Producer, Director. b. New York, NY, Aug. 10, 1916. e. Colgate U., 1938. In TV ind. since 1939, with Psychological Warfare Div., ETO., W.W.II; pres. Peyser/Vance Productions, Woodland Hills, CA.
PICTURES: The Open Door, Kashmiri Run, Four Rode Out, Massacre Harbor.
TELEVISION: *Director*: Hawaii Five-O, Mannix, Movin On, Swiss Family Robinson, Bronk, Combat, Untouchables, Rat Patrol, Honeymoon with a Stranger.

PFEIFFER, MICHELLE
Actress. b. Santa Ana, CA, Apr. 29, 1957. Sister of actress Deedee Pfeiffer. While attending jr. coll. and working as supermarket checkout clerk, won Miss Orange County beauty contest. Began taking acting classes in L.A. Stage debut in L.A. prod. of A Playground in the Fall. NY Theatre debut 1989 in Twelfth Night (Central Park).
PICTURES: The Hollywood Nights (debut, 1980), Falling in Love Again, Charlie Chan and the Curse of the Dragon Queen, Grease 2, Scarface, Into the Night, Ladyhawke, Sweet Liberty, The Witches of Eastwick, Amazon Women on the Moon, Married to the Mob, Tequila Sunrise, Dangerous Liaisons (Acad. Award nom.), The Fabulous Baker Boys (NY, LA & & Natl. Society of Film Critics Awards; Acad. Award nom.), The Russia House, Frankie and Johnny, Batman Returns, Love Field (Acad. Award nom.), The Age of Innocence, Wolf, Dangerous Minds, Up Close and Personal, To Gillian On Her 37th Birthday.
TELEVISION: *Series*: Delta House, B.A.D. Cats. *Movies*: The Solitary Man, Callie and Son, Splendor in the Grass, The Children Nobody Wanted. *Specials*: One Too Many, Tales from the Hollywood Hills (Natica Jackson). *Guest*: Fantasy Island.

PHILLIPS, JULIA
Producer. b. Brooklyn, NY, April 7, 1944. e. Mt. Holyoke Coll. Production asst. at McCall's Magazine; later became textbook copywriter for Macmillan; story editor, Paramount; creative exec., First Artists Prods., NY. In 1970 with former husband, Michael Phillips and actor Tony Bill formed Bill/Phillips Productions to develop film projects. Author of You'll Never Eat Lunch in This Town Again (Random House, 1991).
PICTURES: Steelyard Blues, The Sting (Academy Award for Best Picture, 1973), Taxi Driver, The Big Bus, Close Encounters of the Third Kind, The Beat (co-prod.).

PHILLIPS, LESLIE
Actor, Producer. b. London, England, April 20, 1924. Early career as child actor. Ent. m.p. ind. 1935.
PICTURES: A Lassie From Lancashire (debut, 1935), The Citadel, Rhythm Serenade, Train of Events, The Woman With No Name (Her Paneled Door), Pool of London, The Galloping Major, Breaking the Sound Barrier, The Fake, The Limping Man, Time Bomb (Terror on a Train), The Price of Greed, Value for Money, The Gamma People, As Long as They're Happy, The Big Money, Brothers in Law, The Barretts of Wimpole Street, Just My Luck, Les Girls, The Smallest Show on Earth, High Flight, I Was Monte's Double, The Man Who Liked Funerals, The Angry Hills, Carry on Nurse, Ferdinand of Naples, This Other Eden, Carry on Teacher, Please Turn Over, The Navy Lark, Doctor in Love, Watch Your Stern, No Kidding (Beware of Children), Carry on Constable, Inn for Trouble, Raising the Wind, In the Doghouse, Very Important Persons, Crooks Anonymous, The Longest Day, The Fast Lady, Father Came Too, Doctor in Clover, You Must Be Joking, Maroc 7, Some Will Some Won't, Doctor in Trouble, The Magnificent 7 Deadly Sins, Not Now Darling, Don't Just Lie There Say Something!, Spanish Fly, Not Now Comrade, Out of Africa, Empire of the Sun, Scandal, Mountains of the Moon, King Ralph, Carry on Columbus, August, Caught In The Act.
TELEVISION: Our Man at St. Marks, Impasse, The Gong Game, Time and Motion Man, Reluctant Debutante, A Very Fine Line, The Suit, The Culture Vultures (series), Edward Woodward Show, Casanova 74 (series), Redundant—or the Wife's Revenge, You'll Never See Me Again, Mr. Palfrey of Westminister, Monte Carlo, Rumpole, Summers Lease, Chancer, Comic Strip, Who Bombed Birmingham, Life After Life, Thacker, Chancer II, The Oz Trial, Lovejoy, Boon, The Changeling, Bermuda Grace, Royal Celebration, Honey for Tea, House of Windsor, Two Golden Balls, Love on a Branch Line, Vanity Dies Hard, Edgar Wallace (Germany), Canterville Ghost, Woof, The Bill, The Pale Horse.

PHILLIPS, LOU DIAMOND
Actor. b. Philippines, Feb. 17, 1962. Raised in Corpus Christi, TX. e. U. of Texas, Arlington (BFA drama). Studied film technique with Adam Roarke, becoming asst. dir./instructor with the Film Actor's Lab, 1983-86. Regional theater includes: A

Hatful of Rain, Whose Life Is It Anyway?, P.S. Your Cat Is Dead, The Lady's Not for Burning, Doctor Faustus, Hamlet.
THEATER: *NY*: The King and I (Bdwy. debut, Tony nom.)
PICTURES: Angel Alley, Interface, Trespasses (also co-s.p.), Harley, La Bamba, Stand and Deliver, Young Guns, Dakota (also assoc. prod.), Disorganized Crime, Renegades, The First Power, A Show of Force, Young Guns II, Ambition (also s.p.), The Dark Wind, Shadow of the Wolf, Dangerous Touch (also dir.), Teresa's Tattoo, Sioux City (also dir.), Undertow, Boulevard, Courage Under Fire.
TELEVISION: *Movies*: Time Bomb, The Three Kings, Extreme Justice, The Wharf Rat. *Specials*: Avenue Z Afternoon, Wind in the Wire. *Guest*: Dallas, Miami Vice.

PHILLIPS, MICHAEL
Producer. b. Brooklyn, NY, June 29, 1943. e. Dartmouth Coll., B.A., 1965. NYU, Law Sch. J.D., 1968. Indep. m.p. prod. 1971.
PICTURES: Steelyard Blues, The Sting (Academy Award for Best Picture, 1973), Taxi Driver (Golden Palm Award at Cannes), The Big Bus, Close Encounters of the Third Kind, Heartbeeps, Cannery Row, The Flamingo Kid, Don't Tell Mom the Babysitter's Dead, Mom and Dad Save the World, Eyes of an Angel, The Companion.
TELEVISION: *Movie*: Jane's House.

PHILLIPS, MICHELLE
Actress. b. Long Beach, CA, June 4, 1944. r.n. Holly Michelle Gilliam. Daughter is actress-singer Chynna Phillips. Former member of The Mamas and the Papas. Co-wrote hit single California Dreamin'. Author: California Dreamin': The Story of The Mamas and the Papas (1986).
PICTURES: Monterey Pop, The Last Movie, Dillinger, Valentino, Sidney Sheldon's Bloodline, The Man With Bogart's Face, Savage Harvest, American Anthem, Let It Ride, Scissors, Army of One, Keep on Running.
TELEVISION: *Series*: Hotel, Knots Landing, Second Chances. *Mini-Series*: Aspen, The French Atlantic Affair. *Movies*: The Death Squad, The California Kid, The Users, Moonlight, Mickey Spillane's Mike Hammer: Murder Me Murder You, Secrets of a Married Man, Stark: Mirror Image, Assault and Matrimony, Trenchcoat in Paradise, Rubdown, Paint Me a Murder, Covenant. *Guest*: Owen Marshall, Matt Houston, The Fall Guy, Murder She Wrote, T.J. Hooker, Hotel, Fantasy Island, Love Boat, Burke's Law, Robin's Hood, Lois & Clark, Herman's Head, many others.

PHILLIPS, SIAN
Actress. b. Bettws, Wales. e. Univ. of Wales. Studied acting at RADA. London stage debut 1957 in title role in Hedda.
THEATER: Saint Joan, The Three Sisters, Taming of the Shrew, Duchess of Malfi, Lizard on the Rock, Gentle Jack, The Night of the Iguana, Ride a Cock Horse, Man and Superman, The Burglar, The Cardinal of Spain, Alpah Beta, Spinechiller, A Woman of No Importance, You Never Can Tell, Dear Liar, Pal Joey, Major Barbara, Gigi, Paris Match, Ghosts, Marlene, Painting Churches, Vanilla, Ghosts (Artist of the Year nom.), Marlene, many others. B'way debut 1994 in An Inspector Calls.
PICTURES: Becket, Young Cassidy, Laughter in the Dark, Goodbye Mr. Chips (NY Film Critics & Critics Circle Awards, 1969), Murphy's War, Under Milk Wood, Nijinsky, Clash of the Titans, Dune, The Doctor and the Devils, Valmont, The Age of Innocence, A Painful Case, House of America.
TELEVISION: *Mini-Series*: Shoulder to Shoulder, How Green Was My Valley (BAFTA Award), I Claudius (BAFTA & Royal TV Society Awards), Crime and Punishment, Tinker Tailor Soldier Spy, Vanity Fair. *Movies*: A Painful Case, Ewoks: The Battle for Endor, The Two Mrs. Grenvilles, Out of Time, Dark River. *Specials*: Off to Philadelphia in the Morning, Sean O'Casey, How Many Miles to Babylon?, Lady Windermere's Fan, Language and Landscape, Heartbreak House, Don Juan in Hell, Summer Silence, Shadow of the Noose, Snow Spider, The Quiet Man, The Sex Game, A Mind To Kill, Ivanhoe, Chestnut Soldier (BAFTA nom.).

PIALAT, MAURICE
Director, Writer. b. Cunlhat, Puy de Dome, France, Aug. 21, 1925. Worked as a painter and sometime actor before turning to film in 1952. Made a number of short films including L'Amour Existe (award winner Venice Film Fest., 1960). Worked in television before feature debut in 1967.
PICTURES: *Dir./Writer*: L'Enfance Nue (Naked Childhood; Prix Jean Vigo Award), We Will Not Grow Old Together, La Gueule Ouverte (also prod.), Passe ton Bac d'Abord (Graduate First), Loulou, A Nos Amours (also actor; Prix Louis Delluc Award), Police, Under Satan's Sun (also actor; Golden Palm Award, Cannes Festival), Van Gogh, Le Garcu.
TELEVISION: Janine, Maitre Galip, La Maison des Bois.

PICARDO, ROBERT
Actor. b. Philadelphia, PA, Oct. 27, 1953. e. Yale. Studied acting at Circle in the Square Theater School.
THEATER: *NY*: Sexual Perversity in Chicago, Gemini, Tribute.

PICTURES: The Howling, Star 80, Oh God You Devil, Explorers, Legend, Back to School, Munchies, Innerspace, Amazon Women on the Moon, Jack's Back, Dead Heat, The 'Burbs, 976-EVIL, Loverboy, Total Recall, Gremlins II, Samantha, Motorama, Matinee, Wagons East!
TELEVISION: Series: China Beach, The Wonder Years, Star Trek: Voyager. Movies: The Dream Merchants, The Violation of Sarah McDavid, Lois Gibbs and the Love Canal, Dixie: Changing Habits, The Other Woman, Runaway Daughters, White Mile.

PICCOLI, MICHEL
Actor. b. Paris, France, Dec. 27, 1925. r.n. Jacques Piccoli. Since his film debut in The Sorcerer in 1945 has had impressive career on the French stage and in films working for major French dirs. Renoir, Bunuel, Melville, Resnais, Clouzot, Godard as well as Hitchcock. Until 1957 was mgr. of Theatre Babylone in Paris. Formed prod. co. Films 66. Produced: Themroc (1972); La Faille; Les Enfants Gates.
PICTURES: The Sorcerer, Le Point du Jour, French Can Can, The Witches of Salem, Le Bal des Espiona, Gina, Le Doulos, Contempt, Diary of a Chambermaid, Lady L, La Guerre Est Finie, The Young Girls of Rochefort, Un Homme de Trop, Belle de Jour, La Chamade, Dillinger Is Dead, L'Invasion, The Milky Way, Topaz, The Things of Life, Ten Days' Wonder, The Discreet Charm of the Bourgeoisie, Themroc, Wedding in Blood, La Grande Bouffe, The Last Woman, Leonor, 7 Deaths by Prescription, The Weak Spot, F For Fairbanks, Mado, Todo Modo, Rene the Cane, Spoiled Children, Strauberg Is Here, The Fire's Share, Little Girl in Blue Velvet, The Savage State, The Sugar, The Bit Between the Teeth, La Divorcement, Leap into the Void, The Price for Survival, Atlantic City, The Prodigal Daughter, Beyond the Door, The Eyes The Mouth, Passion, A Room in Town, Will the High Salaried Workers Please Raise Their Hands!!!, The General of the Dead Army, La Passante, The Prize of Peril, Adieu Bonaparte, Dangerous Moves, Danger in the House, Long Live Life!, Success Is the Best Revenge, The Sailor 512, Departure, Return, Mon Beau-Frere a Tue Ma Soeur, The Nonentity, The Prude, Bad Blood, Undiscovered Country, Blanc de Chine, Le Peuple Singe (narrator), The French Revolution, May Fools, La Belle Noiseuse, The Children Thief, Archipelago, Punctured Life, Martha and I, Traveling Companion.

PICERNI, PAUL
Actor. b. New York, NY, Dec. 1, 1922. e. Loyola U., Los Angeles. U.S. Air Force 1943-46; head of drama dept. Mt. St. Mary's Coll., 1949-50.
PICTURES: Saddle Tramp, Breakthrough, Operation Pacific, The Tanks Are Coming, Force of Arms, I Was a Communist for the FBI, Mara Maru, Operation Secret, The Desert Song, She's Back on Broadway, House of Wax, The System, Shanghai Story, To Hell and Back, Bobby Ware Is Missing, Miracle in the Rain, Omar Khayyam, The Brothers Rico, Marjorie Morningstar, The Young Philadelphians, Strangers When We Meet, The Young Marrieds, The Scarface Mob, The Scalphunters, Che!, Airport, Kotch, Beyond the Poseidon Adventure.
TELEVISION: Series: The Untouchables. Guest: Philco Playhouse, Climax, Lux, Loretta Young Show, Desilu, Kojak, Mannix, Police Story, Lucy Special, Quincy, Alice, Trapper John M.D., Vegas, Fall Guy, Capitol, Hardcastle and McCormick, Matt Houston, Simon and Simon.

PICKER, DAVID V.
Executive. b. New York, NY, May 14, 1931. e. Dartmouth Coll., B.A., 1953. Father Eugene Picker, exec. Loew's Theatres. Ent. industry in 1956 as adv. pub. & exploitation liaison with sls. dept., United Artists Corp.; exec. v.p. U.A. Records; asst. to Max Youngstein, v.p.; v.p. U.A.; first v.p. UA; pres. 1969. Resigned 1973 to form own production co. 1976 joined Paramount Pictures as pres. of m.p. div.; v.p., Lorimar Productions; independent; 1987, pres. & COO, Columbia Pictures. Resigned.
PICTURES: Juggernaut, Lenny, Smile, Royal Flash, Won Ton Ton the Dog Who Saved Hollywood, The One and Only, Oliver's Story, Bloodline (prod.), The Jerk (prod.), Dead Men Don't Wear Plaid (prod.), The Man with Two Brains, Beat Street (prod.), The Appointments of Dennis Jennings (short, prod.), Stella (exec. prod.), Traces of Red, Leap of Faith, Matinee, The Saint of Fort Washington, The Crucible.

PICKMAN, JEROME
Executive. b. New York, NY, Aug. 24, 1916. e. St. John's U.; Brooklyn Law Sch. of St. Lawrence U., LL.B. Reporter N.Y. newspapers; U.S. Army World War II; Ad-pub exec. 20th-Fox, 1945-46; v.p., dir., adv. & pub., later v.p. domestic gen. sls. mgr., Paramount Pictures; sr. sls. exec. Columbia Pictures; pres. Motion Picture Div. of Walter Reade Org.; pres., Levitt-Pickman Film Corp.; sr. v.p., domestic distribution, Lorimar Productions; pres., Pickman Film Corp., Cineworld Enterprises Corp.; pres. Scotti Bros. Pictures Distribution, 1986. Consultant, various entertainment entities, legal and financial individuals and organizations.

PIERCE, DAVID HYDE
Actor. b. Albany, NY, Apr. 3, 1959. e. Yale U.
PICTURES: The Terminator, Moving Violations, Bright Lights Big City, Crossing Delancey, Rocket Gibraltar, The Fisher King, Little Man Tate, Sleepless in Seattle, Addams Family Values, Wolf, Nixon.
TELEVISION: Series: The Powers That Be, Frasier (Emmy Award, 1995; Emmy nom., 1996). Guest: Dream On, Crime Story, Spenser: For Hire, The OUter Limits.
THEATER: Off-B'way: Summer, That's It Folks, Donuts, Hamlet, The Moderati, The Cherry Orchard, Zero Positive, Much About Nothing, Elliot Loves. B'way: Beyond Therapy, The Heidi Chronicles. Regional: work with Long Wharf, Guthrie, Goodman, Doolittle Theatres.

PIERCE, FREDERICK S.
Executive. b. New York, NY, April 8, 1933. e. Bernard Baruch Sch. of B.A., City Coll. of New York. Served with U.S. Combat Engineers in Korean War. Associated with Benj. Harrow & Son, CAP, before joining ABC in 1956. Served as analyst in TV research dep.; prom. to supvr. of audience measurements, 1957, named mgr. next year. 1961 made dir. of research; 1962 dir. of research, sales dev. Named dir. of sales planning, sales devel. 1962; elec. v.p., 1964 and made nat. dir. of sales for TV. 1968 named v.p., planning; 1970 named asst. to pres.; 1972, named v.p., eng. ABC TV planning and devel. and asst. to pres. ABC TV, 1973. Named sr. v.p., ABC TV, 1974. Elected pres., ABC Television Division, 1974. Pres. & COO, ABC, Inc., 1983. Formed Frederick Pierce Co. and also Pierce/Silverman Co. with Fred Silverman, 1989.

PIERSON, FRANK
Producer, Director, Writer. b. Chappaqua, NY, May 12, 1925. e. Harvard U. Was correspondent for Time magazine before entering show business as story editor of TV series, Have Gun, Will Travel. Later served as both producer and director for show. Developed a number of properties for Screen Gems before writing theatrical screenplays.
PICTURES: Writer: Cat Ballou, The Happening, Cool Hand Luke, The Anderson Tapes, Dog Day Afternoon (Academy Award, 1975), In Country, Presumed Innocent. Director-Writer: The Looking Glass War, A Star Is Born, King of the Gypsies.
TELEVISION: Series: Nichols (prod.), Alfred Hitchcock Presents (1985; dir.). Movies: The Neon Ceiling (dir.), Haywire (co-writer), Somebody Has to Shoot the Picture (dir.; ACE Award, 1990), Citizen Cohn (dir.), Lakota Woman: Siege at Wounded Knee (dir.), Truman.

PIGOTT-SMITH, TIM
Actor. b. Rugby, England, May 13, 1946. e. U. of Bristol, B.A., Bristol Old Vic Theatre Sch., 1969. Acted with Bristol Old Vic, Royal Shakespeare Co. Artistic Director of Compass Theatre, 1989-93.
THEATER: Actor: As You Like It, Major Barbara, Hamlet, School for Scandal, Sherlock Holmes (B'way debut, 1974), Benefactors, Entertaining Strangers, The Winter's Tale, Antony and Cleopatra, Cymbeline, The Tempest, Jane Eyre, The Picture of Dorian Gray, Retreat. Director: Company, Royal Hunt of the Sun, Playing the Wife, Hamlet, The Letter, Retreat, Mary Stuart.
PICTURES: Aces High (debut, 1975), Man in a Fog, Sweet William, Richard's Things, Joseph Andrews, Clash of the Titans, Lucky Village, Victory, State of Emergency, The Remains of the Day.
TELEVISION: Dr. Who (debut, 1970). Mini-series: Winston Churchill: The Wilderness Years, The Jewel in the Crown. Movies: Eustace and Hilda, The Lost Boys, I Remember Nelson, Measure for Measure, Henry IV, Day Christ Died, The Hunchback of Notre Dame, Fame Is the Spur, Glittering Prizes, Dead Man's Folly, The Case of Sherlock Holmes (host), Life Story, Hannah, The True Adventures of Christopher Columbus, The Chief, Bullion Boys, The Shadowy Third, Calcutta Chronicles.

PIKE, CORNELIA M.
Executive. b. Holyoke, MA, 1933. e. Boston U. Sch. of Commun., BS Magna Cum Laude. Asst. Promotion & Publicity Dir. WNAC/WNAC-TV 1954-56, Boston, MA. Women's Director/On-air personality: WKNE Keene, NH 1957-60; WSMN Nashua, NH 1963-67; WHOB, Nashua, NH 1967-68. Mngr. Trade Winds Interior Design, Boston, MA 1979-81. Sls. Mngr./VP Pike Productions, Inc. 1981 to present. Company produces and markets trailers to exhibitors in U.S., UK, Germany, Australia and New Zealand. Alpha Epsilon Rho, Natl. Bdcstg. Soc. 1st VP, Variety Club of New England. Bd. dirs., Variety Club of New England. Life Patron, Variety Clubs International.

PIKE, JOHN S.
Executive. b. Cleveland, OH, Oct. 26, 1946. e. Univ. of Miami. Joined Paramount Pictures as v.p., video programming; promoted to sr. v.p., video prog. 1984, named sr. v.p., current net-

work programming; 1985, promoted to exec. v.p., Paramount Network TV. Appt. pres., Network TV and Intl. co-production, 1991.

PINCHOT, BRONSON
Actor. b. New York, NY, May 20, 1959. e. Yale U. Grew up in Pasadena. Studied acting at Yale. On NY stage in Poor Little Lambs, Zoya's Apartment.
PICTURES: Risky Business (debut, 1983), Beverly Hills Cop, The Flamingo Kid, Hot Resort, After Hours, Second Sight, Blame It on the Bellboy, True Romance, Beverly Hills Cop III, It's My Party, Courage Under Fire.
TELEVISION: Series: Sara, Perfect Strangers, The Trouble With Larry. Movie: Jury Duty—The Comedy. Mini-Series: Stephen King's The Langoliers.

PINSKER, ALLEN
Executive. b. New York, NY, Jan. 23, 1930. e. NYU. Mgr., Hempstead Theatre, 1950. 1954 joined Island Theatre Circuit as booker-buyer; named head buyer 1958. 1968 joined United Artists Eastern Theatres as film buyer; head buyer, 1969, v.p., 1970. Named v.p. United Artists Theatre Circuit, 1972. 1973 named UAET exec. v.p., member bd., 1974. Appt. pres. & COO, UA Communications, Inc., theatre division, 1987. 1987, named pres. and CEO, United Artists Theatre Circuit, Inc. and exec. v.p., United Artists Communications, Inc.; 1988, became member, bd. dir. United Artists Comm. Inc.

PINTER, HAROLD
Writer, Director, Actor. b. London, England, Oct. 10, 1930. Began career as actor then turned to writing and direction.
THEATER: The Dumb Waiter, Slight Ache, The Room, The Birthday Party, The Caretaker, The Homecoming, The Collection, Landscape, Silence, Old Times, No Man's Land, The Hothouse, Betrayal, One for the Road, Mountain Language, Party Time, Moonlight.
PICTURES: Writer: The Caretaker (The Guest), The Servant (also actor), The Pumpkin Eater, The Quiller Memorandum, Accident (also actor), The Birthday Party, The Go-Between, The Homecoming, Butley (dir. only), The Last Tycoon, The French Lieutenant's Woman, Betrayal, Turtle Diary (also actor), The Handmaid's Tale, Reunion, The Comfort of Strangers, The Trial.
TELEVISION: A Night Out, Night School, The Lover, Tea Party, The Basement, Langrishe Go Down, Heat of the Day.

PISANO, A. ROBERT
Executive. e. San Jose St. Univ., Boalt Hall School of Law at Univ. of CA, Berkeley. Was partner at law firm of O'Melveny & Myers prior to entering m.p. industry. 1985-91, exec. v.p. of Paramount Pictures serving as gen. counsel, member of office of chmn.; 1993, named exec. v.p. of MGM responsible for all business and legal affairs and labor relations.

PISCOPO, JOE
Actor, Comedian. b. Passaic, NJ, June 17, 1951. Stage appearances in regional and dinner theaters in South and Northeast. Worked as stand-up comic at the Improvisation and the Comic Strip clubs, NY 1976-80. Author: The Piscopo Tapes. Television debut as regular on Saturday Night Live, 1980.
PICTURES: American Tickler or the Winner of 10 Academy Awards (1976), King Kong, Johnny Dangerously, Wise Guys, Dead Heat, Sidekicks.
TELEVISION: Series: Saturday Night Live (1980-84). Guest: Comic Relief. Special: The Joe Piscopo Special (HBO). Movie: Huck and the King of Hearts.

PISIER, MARIE-FRANCE
Actress. b. Indochina, May 10, 1944. Began appearing in French films at age 17. Returned to school at Univ. of Paris for degrees in law and political science; continued to work in films.
PICTURES: Qui ose nous Accuser? (debut, 1961), Love at Twenty (Truffaut episode), La Mort d'un Tueur, Les Yeux cernes, Trans-Europe Express, Stolen Kisses, Celine and Julie Go Boating, French Provincial, Cousin Cousine, Serail, Barocco, The Other Side of Midnight, Love on the Run, Les Apprentis Sourciers, The Bronte Sisters, French Postcards, La Banquiere, Chanel Solitaire, Der Zauberberg (The Magic Mountain), Miss Right, Hot Touch, The Prize of Peril, The Silent Ocean, L'Ami de Vincent, Les Nanas, Parking, Blue Note, Why is My Mother in My Bed?
TELEVISION: U.S.: French Atlantic Affair, Scruples.

PITT, BRAD
Actor. b. Shawnee, OK, Dec. 18, 1963. r.n. William Bradley Pitt. Raised in Springfield, MO. Studied journalism at Univ. of MO at Columbia. Moved to L.A. to attend art school, instead studying acting with Roy London. Appeared in short film Contact.
PICTURES: Cutting Class (debut, 1989), Happy Together, Across the Tracks, Thelma & Louise, Cool World, Johnny

Suede, A River Runs Through It, Kalifornia, True Romance, The Favor, Interview With the Vampire. Legends of the Fall, Seven, Twelve Monkeys (Golden Globe, 1996), Sleepers, Devil's Own.
TELEVISION: Series: Another World, Glory Days. Movies: A Stoning in Fulham County, Too Young to Die, The Image. Guest: Dallas, Growing Pains, Head of the Class, Tales From the Crypt.

PIVEN, JEREMY
Actor. b. New York, NY. Raised in Chicago where parents ran Piven Theater Workshop. e. Drake Univ. Studied acting at Eugene O'Neill Theater Center, Natl. Theater of Great Britain, NYU. Eventually joined Chicago's Second City comedy troupe. Co-founded Chicago's New Criminals Theatre Company, 1988.
THEATER: Fear & Loathing in Las Vegas, Peacekeeper, Methusalen, Knuckle, Macbeth.
PICTURES: Lucas, One Crazy Summer, Say Anything, White Palace, The Grifters, Pay Dirt, The Player, Bob Roberts, Singles, Judgment Night, Twenty Bucks, Car 54 Where Are You?, Twogether, PCU, Miami Rhapsody, Dr. Jekyll and Ms. Hyde, Heat.
TELEVISION: Series: Carol and Company, The Larry Sanders Show, Pride and Joy. Pilots: Heads Will Roll, Ready or Not.

PLACE, MARY KAY
Actress, Writer. b. Tulsa, OK, Sept. 23, 1947. e. U. of Tulsa. Worked in production jobs and as Tim Conway's asst. for his TV show also as sect. for Norman Lear on Maude before starting to write for TV series (Mary Tyler Moore Show, Phyllis, Maude, M*A*S*H, etc.).
PICTURES: Bound For Glory (debut, 1976), New York New York, More American Graffiti, Starting Over, Private Benjamin, Modern Problems, Waltz Across Texas, The Big Chill, Smooth Talk, A New Life, Bright Angel, Captain Ron, Samantha, Teresa's Tattoo, Manny and Lo, Precious, Citizen Ruth.
TELEVISION: Series: Mary Hartman Mary Hartman (Emmy Award, 1977). Guest: All in the Family, Mary Tyler Moore Show, Fernwood 2-Night, Tonight Show, Saturday Night Live (host), thirtysomething. Movies: The Girl Who Spelled Freedom, Act of Love, For Love or Money, Out on the Edge, Just My Imagination, Telling Secrets, In the Line of Duty: The Pride of Vengeance. Specials: John Denver Special, Martin Mull's History of White People in America I & II, Portrait of a White Marriage, The Gift, Tales of the City, Leslie's Folly.

PLATT, OLIVER
Actor. b. 1962. Raised in Asia, Africa and Washington DC. e. Tufts Univ.
THEATER: Off-B'way: The Tempest, Moon Over Miami, Sparks in the Park, Urban Blight, Ubu, Elliot Loves.
PICTURES: Married to the Mob (debut, 1988), Working Girl, Crusoe, Flatliners, Postcards From the Edge, Beethoven, Diggstown, The Temp, Indecent Proposal, Benny & Joon, The Three Musketeers, Tall Tale, Funny Bones, Executive Decision, A Time to Kill.
TELEVISION: Movie: The Infiltrator.

PLESHETTE, SUZANNE
Actress. b. New York, NY, Jan. 31, 1937. e. H.S. for the Performing Arts, Finch Coll., Syracuse U. Broadway debut, Compulsion.
THEATER: The Cold Wind and the Warm, The Golden Fleecing, The Miracle Worker, Compulsion, Two for the Seesaw, Special Occasions.
PICTURES: The Geisha Boy (debut, 1958), Rome Adventure, 40 Pounds of Trouble, The Birds, Wall of Noise, A Distant Trumpet, Fate Is the Hunter, Youngblood Hawke, A Rage to Live, The Ugly Dachshund, Nevada Smith, Mister Buddwing, The Adventures of Bullwhip Griffin, Blackbeard's Ghost, The Power, If It's Tuesday This Must Be Belgium, Suppose They Gave a War and Nobody Came, Target Harry (How to Make It), Support Your Local Gunfighter, The Shaggy D.A., Hot Stuff, Oh God! Book II.
TELEVISION: Series: The Bob Newhart Show, Suzanne Pleshette Is Maggie Briggs, Bridges to Cross, Nightingales, The Boys Are Back. Movies: Wings of Fire, Along Came a Spider, Hunters Are for Killing, River of Gold, In Broad Daylight, Law and Order, Richie Brockelman: Missing 24 Hours, Kate Bliss and the Ticker Tape Kid, Flesh and Blood, For Love or Money, Fantasies, If Things Were Different, Help Wanted—Male, Dixie Changing Habits, Starmaker, One Cooks, The Other Doesn't, Legend of Valentino, Kojak The Belarus File, A Stranger Waits, Alone in the Neon Jungle, Leona Helmsley: The Queen of Mean, Battling for Baby, A Twist of the Knife.

PLESKOW, ERIC
Executive. b., Vienna, Austria, April 24, 1924. Served as film officer, U.S. War dept., 1946-48; entered industry in 1948 as asst. gen. mgr., Motion Picture Export Association, Germany; 1950-51, continental rep. for Sol Lesser Prods.; joined United

Artists in 1951 as Far East Sales Mgr.; named mgr., S. Africa, 1952; mgr., Germany, 1953-58; exec. asst. to continental mgr., 1958-59; asst. continental mgr., 1959-60; continental mgr., 1960-62; v.p. in charge of foreign distrib., 1962; exec. v.p. & CEO, Jan., 1973; pres. & CEO, Oct. , 1973. Resigned in 1978 to become pres. and CEO of Orion Pictures Co.; 1982, became pres. & CEO, Orion Pictures Corp; appointed chmn. of bd. 1991. Resigned 1992. Partner, Pleskow/Spikings Partnership, Beverly Hills, 1992-present. Prod., Beyond Rangoon.

PLIMPTON, MARTHA
Actress. b. New York, NY, Nov. 16, 1970. Daughter of actors Shelley Plimpton and Keith Carradine. Acting debut in film workshop of Elizabeth Swados's musical Runaways. At 11 gained recognition as model in Richard Avedon's commercials for Calvin Klein jeans. Also on stage in The Hagadah, Pericles, The Heidi Chronicles, Robbers, subUrbia, The Great Unwashed.
PICTURES: Rollover (debut 1981, in bit role), The River Rat, The Goonies, The Mosquito Coast, Shy People, Stars and Bars, Running on Empty, Another Woman, Parenthood, Stanley and Iris, Silence Like Glass, Samantha, Inside Monkey Zetterland, Josh and S.A.M., My Life's in Turnaround, Mrs. Parker and the Vicious Circle, The Beans of Egypt Maine, Last Summer in the Hamptons, Beautiful Girls, I Shot Andy Warhol, I'm Not Rappaport.
TELEVISION: *Movies*: Daybreak, Chantilly Lace.

PLOWRIGHT, JOAN
C.B.E. Actress. b. Scunthrope, Brigg, Lincolnshire, Eng., Oct. 28, 1929. m. late actor, Lord Laurence Olivier. Trained for stage at Laban Art of Movement Studio, 1949-50; Old Vic Theatre Sch. 1950-52; with Michel St. Denis, Glen Byam Shaw and George Devine. London stage debut The Duenna, 1954. Broadway debut The Entertainer, 1958. Won Tony Award in 1961 for A Taste of Honey. With Bristol Old Vic Rep., Royal Court, National Theatre in numerous classics and contemporary plays.
RECENT THEATER: Saturday Sunday Monday, The Seagull, The Bed Before Yesterday, Filumena, Enjoy, Who's Afraid of Virginia Woolf?, Cavell, The Cherry Orchard, The Way of the World, Mrs. Warren's Profession, Time and the Conways, If We Are Women.
PICTURES: Moby Dick (debut, 1956), Time Without Pity, The Entertainer, Uncle Vanya, Three Sisters, Equus, Brimstone and Treacle, Britannia Hospital, Wagner (tv in U.S.), Revolution, The Dressmaker, Drowning By Numbers, I Love You to Death, Avalon, Enchanted April (Acad. Award nom.), Last Action Hero, Dennis the Menace, A Pin for the Butterfly, The Summer House, Widow's Peak, A Pyromaniac's Love Story, Hotel Sorrento, The Scarlett Letter, Jane Eyre, Mr. Wrong, Surviving Picasso, 101 Dalmatians.
TELEVISION: Odd Man In, Secret Agent, School for Scandal, The Diary of Anne Frank, Twelfth Night, Merchant of Venice, Daphne Laureola, Saturday Sunday Monday, The Divider, Conquest of the South Pole, A Nightingale Sang, House of Bernarda Alba, Stalin, On Promised Land, A Place for Annie, The Return of the Native. *Pilot*: Driving Miss Daisy (U.S.).

PLUMMER, AMANDA
Actress. b. New York, NY, March 23, 1957. e. Middlebury Coll. Daughter of actors Christopher Plummer and Tammy Grimes.
THEATER: Artichokes, A Month in the Country, A Taste of Honey (Theatre World Award), Agnes of God (Tony Award, 1982), The Glass Menagerie, A Lie of the Mind, Life Under Water, You Never Can Tell, Pygmalion, The Milk Train Doesn't Stop Here Anymore.
PICTURES: Cattle Annie and Little Britches (debut, 1981), The World According to Garp, Daniel, The Hotel New Hampshire, Static, The Courtship, Made in Heaven, Prisoners of Inertia, Joe Versus the Volcano, California Casanova, The Fisher King, Freejack, So I Married an Axe Murderer, Needful Things, Nostradamus, Pulp Fiction, Pax, Butterfly Kiss, The Propechy, Drunks, Freeway.
TELEVISION: *Movies*: The Dollmaker, The Unforgivable Secret, Riders to the Sea, Miss Rose White (Emmy Award, 1992), The Sands of Time, Last Light, Whose Child Is This? The War for Baby Jessica. *Guest*: Outer Limits (Emmy Award, 1996). *Specials*: Gryphon, The Courtship. *Pilot*: True Blue.

PLUMMER, CHRISTOPHER
Actor. b. Toronto, Canada, Dec. 13, 1927. Daughter is actress Amanda Plummer. Stage & radio career began in Canada (French & English).
THEATER: toured U.S. in The Constant Wife; B'way debut in The Starcross Story, 1953. *B'way*: The Dark is Light Enough, Home Is the Hero, J.B., The Lark, The Good Doctor, Cyrano (Tony Award, 1974), Othello (Tony nom.), Macbeth, No Man's Land. *London*: leading actor, Royal Shakespeare Theatre, 1961-62, Becket (Evening Standard Award), Natl. Theatre, 1969-70. *Canada*: leading actor, Stratford Festival (6 yrs.).

PICTURES: Stage Struck (debut, 1958), Wind Across the Everglades, The Fall of the Roman Empire, The Sound of Music, Inside Daisy Clover, The Night of the Generals, Triple Cross, Oedipus the King, The High Commissioner (Nobody Runs Forever), The Battle of Britain, The Royal Hunt of the Sun, Lock Up Your Daughters, Waterloo, The Pyx, The Return of the Pink Panther, Conduct Unbecoming, The Man Who Would Be King, The Spiral Staircase, Aces High, Assassination at Sarajevo (The Day That Shook the World), The Assignment, The Disappearance, International Velvet, Murder by Decree, The Silent Partner, Hanover Street, Starcrash, RIEL, Highpoint, Somewhere in Time, Eyewitness, Being Different (narrator), The Amateur, Dreamscape, Ordeal by Innocence, Lily in Love, The Boy in Blue, The Boss' Wife, An American Tail (voice), Dragnet, Souvenir, Light Years (voice), Nosferatu in Venice, I Love N.Y., Shadow Dancing, Mindfield, Kingsgate, Red-Blooded American Girl, Where the Heart Is, Don't Tell Mom the Babysitter's Dead, Star Trek VI: The Undiscovered Country, Firehead, Rock-a-Doodle (voice), Money, Liar's Edge, Impolite, Malcolm X, Wolf, Dolores Claiborne, Twelve Monkeys.
TELEVISION: *Series*: Counterstrike. *Movies/Specials*: Hamlet at Elsinore (Emmy nom.), Don Juan in Hell (BBC), Little Moon of Alban, Prince and the Pauper, Jesus of Nazareth, Steiglitz and O'Keefe, Oedipus Rex, Omnibus, After the Fall, The Moneychangers (Emmy Award, 1977), Desperate Voyage, The Shadow Box, When the Circus Came to Town, Dial M for Murder, Little Gloria—Happy at Last, The Scarlet and the Black, The Thorn Birds, The Velveteen Rabbit, Crossings, A Hazard of Hearts, A Ghost in Monte Carlo, Young Catherine, Danielle Steel's Secrets, Stranger in the Mirror, Liar's Edge, Madeline (narrator; Emmy Award, 1994), Harrison Bergeron.

PODELL, ALBERT N.
Attorney. b. New York, NY, Feb. 25, 1937. e. Cornell U., U. of Chicago, NYU Sch. of Law. Non-fiction editor, Playboy magazine, 1959-60; dir. of photog. and m.p. reviewer Argosy magazine, 1961-64; Author: Who Needs a Road? Bobbs-Merrill, 1967; mng. edit., The Players Magazine, 1965-66; account exec. on 20th Century-Fox at Diener, Hauser, Greenthal, 1966-68; national advertising mgr., Cinema Center Films, 1969; account supervisor and creative dir. on Columbia Pictures at Charles Schlaifer, 1969-72; creator & dir. of Annual Motion Picture Advertising Awards sponsored by Cinema Lodge, B'nai B'rith. Attorney specializing in litigation, matrimonial law, rep. of performers (1976-present). Pres., 1990-95 Jean Cocteau Rep. Th. Chmn. of Trustees; 1980-90, Assn. for Development of Dramatic Arts. Pres., Far Above Films. Dir. & writer: A Class Above, The Class on the Cutting Edge, Lift the Chorus.

PODHORZER, MUNIO
Executive. b. Berlin, Germany, Sept. 18, 1911. e. Jahn-Realgymnasium, U. of Berlin Medical Sch. U.S. Army, 1943-47; pres. United Film Enterprises, Inc.; formerly secy.-treas. 86th St. Casino Theatre, N.Y.; former v.p. Atlantic Pictures Corp.; former pres. Casino Films, Inc.; former pres. Film Development Corp.; former rep. Export-Union of the German Film Ind.; former U.S. rep. Franco-London Film, Paris; former pres., Venus Productions Corp.; former U.S. rep. Atlas Int'l Film GmbH, Munich; former U.S. rep. Bavaria Atelier Gesellschaft U.S.; past rep. Israfilm Ltd., Tel-Aviv; past rep. Tigon British Film Prod., London; past rep. Elias Querejeta, P.C., Madrid; past rep. Equiluz Films, Madrid; past rep. Airport Cine, Haiti; Les Films Du Capricorne, Paris; Schongerfilm, German; Profilmes, Spain; Ligno, Spain; Films D'Alma, France; Intra Films, Italy. Member: Variety Club, Cinema Lodge, B'nai B'rith, Past Board of Governors IFIDA; past pres. CID Agents Assoc. Former gen. foreign sales mgr.; theatrical division of National Telefilm Associates; past rep. Barcino Films, S.A. Spain; Eagle Films Ltd., UK; Les Films Jacques Leitienne, France; Nero Film Classics, USA; Schongerfilm, Germany; Profilmes, S.A. Spain; VIP Ltd., Israel. Presently representing Atlas Film & AV, Germany; KFM Films, Inc. U.S.A.; Compagnie France Film, Canada; Cia. Iberoamerican de TV, S.A. Spain; Israel. Co-chmn., entertainment div., United Jewish Appeal, Federation of Jewish Philanthropies, 1981-83.

PODHORZER, NATHAN
Executive. b. Brody, Poland, Nov. 27, 1919. e. City Coll. of New York, Rutgers U., U. of Southern California. U.S. Army, 1942-46; documentary film prod., Israel, 1946-57; CEO, United Film Enterprises, Inc.

POE, STEPHEN
Executive. Began career as lawyer with Rutan & Tucker; 1976, joined 20th Century-Fox as prod. counsel; later v.p., business affairs. Turned to producing in 1982, first in association with Frank Mancuso Jr. Productions. 1986, acted as consultant and indep. prod. counsel for United Artists Pictures. 1987, joined CBS/Fox Video as sr. v.p. of acquisitions and programming.

POITIER, SIDNEY
Actor, Director. b. Miami, FL, Feb. 20, 1927. Raised in the Bahamas. m. actress Joanna Shimkus. e. Miami, FL. On stage with Amer. Negro Theatre in Days of Our Youth. Appeared in Army Signal Corps documentary From Whence Cometh My Help. Formed First Artists Prod. Co. Ltd., 1969, with Paul Newman and Barbra Streisand. *Autobiography*: This Life (1980). Recipient 1992 AFI Life Achievement Award.
THEATER: Strivers Road, You Can't Take It With You, Anna Lucasta (B'way debut, 1948), Lysistrata, Freight, A Raisin in the Sun.
PICTURES: No Way Out (debut 1950), Cry the Beloved Country, Red Ball Express, Go Man Go, Blackboard Jungle, Goodbye My Lady, Edge of the City, Something of Value, Band of Angels, Mark of the Hawk, The Defiant Ones, Virgin Island, Porgy and Bess, All the Young Men, A Raisin in the Sun, Paris Blues, Pressure Point, Lilies of the Field (Academy Award, 1963), The Long Ships, The Greatest Story Ever Told, The Bedford Incident, The Slender Thread, A Patch of Blue, Duel at Diablo, To Sir With Love, In the Heat of the Night, Guess Who's Coming to Dinner, For Love of Ivy, The Lost Man, They Call Me Mister Tibbs, Brother John, The Organization, Buck and the Preacher (also dir.), A Warm December (also dir.), Uptown Saturday Night (also dir.), The Wilby Conspiracy, Let's Do It Again (also dir.), A Piece of the Action (also dir.), Stir Crazy (dir. only), Hanky Panky (dir. only), Fast Forward (dir. only), Shoot To Kill, Little Nikita, Ghost Dad (dir. only), Sneakers.
TELEVISION: *Movies*: Separate But Equal, Children of the Dust, To Sir With Love II. *Guest*: Philco TV Playhouse, ABC Stage '67.

POLANSKI, ROMAN
Director, Writer. b. Paris, France, Aug. 18, 1933. m. actress Emmanuelle Seigner. Lived in Poland from age of three. Early career, art school in Cracow; Polish Natl. Film Acad., Lodz 1954-59. Radio Actor 1945-47; on stage 1947-53; asst. dir., Kamera film prod. group 1959-61. Co-founder Cadre Films, 1964. Wrote, dir. and acted in short films: Two Men and a Wardrobe, When Angels Fall, The Fat and the Lean, Mammals. On stage as actor in Amadeus (and dir., Warsaw & Paris), Metamorphosis (Paris, 1988). *Autobiography*: Roman (1984).
PICTURES: *Dir./Writer*: Knife in the Water (feature debut, 1962), Repulsion, Cul-de-Sac, The Fearless Vampire Killers or: Pardon Me But Your Teeth Are in My Neck (also actor), Rosemary's Baby, A Day at the Beach (s.p. only), Weekend of a Champion (prod. only), Macbeth (also prod.), What? (a.k.a. Che?; also actor), Chinatown (dir. & actor only), The Tenant (also actor), Tess, Pirates, Frantic, Bitter Moon, Death and the Maiden. *Actor only*: The Generation, The Magic Christian, Andy Warhol's Dracula, Back in the U.S.S.R., A Pure Formality, Grosse Fatigue.

POLEDOURIS, BASIL
Composer. b. Kansas City, MO, Aug. 21, 1945. e. Long Beach St. Univ., USC. While at USC composed music for short films by John Milius and Randal Kleiser. Became first American Film Institute intern.
PICTURES: Big Wednesday, Tintorera, Dolphin, The Blue Lagoon, Conan the Barbarian, Summer Lovers, House of God, Conan the Destroyer, Making the Grade, Red Dawn, Protocol, Flesh and Blood, Iron Eagle, Robocop, No Man's Land, Cherry 2000, Spellbinder, Split Decisions, Farewell to the King, Wired, The Hunt for Red October, Quigley Down Under, Flight of the Intruder, White Fang, Return to the Blue Lagoon, Harley Davidson & the Marlboro Man, Wind, Hot Shots Part Deux, Free Willy, Robocop 3, On Deadly Ground, Serial Mom, Lassie, The Jungle Book, Under Siege 2: Dark Territory, Free Willy 2: The Adventure Home, It's My Party, Celtic Pride.
TELEVISION: *Mini-Series*: Amerika, Lonesome Dove (Emmy Award, 1989). *Movies*: Congratulations It's a Boy, A Whale for the Killing, Fire on the Mountain, Amazons, Single Women Single Bars, Prison for Children, Misfits of Science, Island Sons, Intrigue, L.A. Takedown, Nasty Boys, Ned Blessing, Lone Justice, Danielle Steel's Zoya.

POLL, MARTIN H.
Producer. b. New York, NY, Nov. 24, 1926. e. Wharton Sch., U. of Pennsylvania. Pres. Gold Medal Studios (1956-61).
PICTURES: A Face in the Crowd, Middle of the Night, The Goddess, Butterfield 8, Love Is a Ball, Sylvia, The Lion in Winter, The Appointment, The Magic Garden of Stanley Sweetheart, The Man Who Loved Cat Dancing, Night Watch, Love and Death (exec. prod.); The Man Who Would Be King, The Sailor who Fell From Grace with the Sea, Somebody Killed Her Husband, Nighthawks, Gimme an F, Haunted Summer, My Heroes Have Always Been Cowboys.
TELEVISION: *Series*: Car 54 Where Are You? *Movies*: Arthur the King, Stunt Seven. *Mini-Series*: A Town Called Alice, The Dain Curse, Diana: Her True Story.

POLLACK, SYDNEY
Director, Producer. b. South Bend, IN, July 1, 1934. m. Claire Griswold. e. Neighborhood Playhouse. Assistant to Sanford Meisner at Neighborhood Playhouse. Appeared as actor on B'way in A Stone for Danny Fisher, The Dark is Light Enough. Dir. debut in 1960. Dir. play at UCLA, P.S. 193. Prepared the American version of The Leopard.
TELEVISION: *As actor*: Playhouse 90 (several segments), Shotgun Slade. *Dir.*: Ben Casey (15 episodes), The Game (Bob Hope-Chrysler Theatre; Emmy Award), Two is the Number. *Co-prod.* (movie): A Private Matter. *Exec. prod.* (series): Fallen Angels.
PICTURES: *Director*: The Slender Thread (debut, 1965), This Property Is Condemned, The Scalphunters, Castle Keep, They Shoot Horses Don't They? (also prod.), Jeremiah Johnson, The Way We Were (also prod.), The Yakuza (also prod.), Three Days of the Condor, Bobby Deerfield (also prod.), The Electric Horseman, Asence of Malice (also prod.), Tootsie (also prod., actor), Out of Africa (also prod.; Academy Awards for Best Picture & Director, 1985), Havana (also prod.), The Firm, Sabrina (also prod.). *Producer*: Songwriter, Bright Lights Big City, The Fabulous Baker Boys, Presumed Innocent. *Exec. Producer*: Honeysuckle Rose, White Palace, King Ralph, Dead Again, Leaving Normal, Searching for Bobby Fischer, Flesh and Bone, Sense and Sensibility. *Actor*: War Hunt, The Player, Death Becomes Her, Husbands and Wives.

POLLAK, KEVIN
Actor. b. San Francisco, CA, Oct. 30, 1958. Started doing stand-up comedy in the San Francisco Bay area, then continued in L.A. clubs.
PICTURES: Million Dollar Mystery (debut, 1987), Willow, Avalon, L.A. Story, Another You, Ricochet, A Few Good Men, The Opposite Sex and How to Live With Them, Indian Summer, Wayne's World 2, Grumpy Old Men, Reality Bites, Clean Slate, Miami Rhapsody, The Usual Suspects, Canadian Bacon, Casino, Nowhere Man, Chameleon, House Arrest, Grumpier Old Men, That Thing You Do!.
TELEVISION: *Series*: Coming of Age, Morton and Hayes. *Specials*: One Night Stand (also prod., writer), Stop With the Kicking (also prod., writer), The Seven Deadly Sins (also writer, dir.).

POLLAN, TRACY
Actress. b. New York, NY, June 22, 1960. m. actor Michael J. Fox.
THEATER: *B'way*: Jake's Women.
PICTURES: Promised Land, Bright Lights Big City, A Stranger Among Us.
TELEVISION: *Series*: Family Ties. *Movies*: For Lovers Only, Sessions, Trackdown: Finding the Goodbar Killer, A Good Sport, Dying to Love You, Children of the Dark.

POLLARD, MICHAEL J.
Actor. r.n. Michael J. Pollack. b. Passaic, NJ, May 30, 1939. e. Montclair Academy, Actors Studio.
THEATER: Comes a Day, Loss of Roses, Enter Laughing, Bye Bye Birdie, Leda Had a Little Swan, Our Town.
PICTURES: Adventures of a Young Man (debut, 1962), The Stripper, Summer Magic, The Russians Are Coming the Russians Are Coming, The Wild Angels, Caprice, Enter Laughing, Bonnie and Clyde (Acad. Award nom.), Jigsaw, Hannibal Brooks, Little Fauss and Big Halsy, The Legend of Frenchie King (Petroleum Girls), Dirty Little Billy, Between the Lines, Melvin and Howard, Heated Vengeance, America, The Patriot, The American Way (Riders of the Storm), Roxanne, Scrooged, Fast Food, Season of Fear, Next of Kin, Tango and Cash, Night Visitor, Sleepaway Camp 3, Why Me?, Dick Tracy, I Come in Peace, Joey Takes a Cab, The Art of Dying, Another You, Enid Is Sleeping (Over Her Dead Body), Split Second, The Arrival, Heartstopper, Arizona Dream, Motorama, Skeeter.
TELEVISION: *Series*: Leo and Liz in Beverly Hills. *Guest*: Alfred Hitchcock Presents (Anniversary Gift), Going My Way, Route 66, Here's Lucy, Mr. Novak, Honey West, I Spy, Lost in Space, Dobie Gillis, Get Christie Love, Star Trek, Simon & Simon, The Fall Guy, Gunsmoke, Guns of Paradise, The Young Riders, Nasty Boys. *Movies*: The Smugglers, Stuck With Each Other, Working Trash.

POLLEXFEN, JACK
Producer, Director, Writer. b. San Diego, CA, June 10, 1918. e. Los Angeles City Coll. Newspaperman, magazine writer, playwright: prod. for RKO, United Artists, Columbia, Allied Artists.
PICTURES: Son of Sinbad, At Swords Point, Secret of Convict Lake, Desert Hawk, Lady in the Iron Mask, Dragon's Gold, Problem Girls, Captive Women, Captain Kidd and the Slave Girl, Neanderthal Man, Captain John Smith and Pocahontas, Return to Treasure Island, Sword of Venus, Daughter of Dr. Jekyll, Monstrosity, Son of Dr. Jekyll, Mr. Big, Man from Planet X, Indestructible Man, Port Sinister, Treasure of Monte Cristo, Bulldog Drummond, Grey City.

POLLOCK, DALE
Producer. b. Cleveland, OH, May 18, 1950. e. Brandeis U., B.A. anthropology, San Jose State, M.S., mass communication.

Began journalistic career in Santa Cruz in early '70s, serving as reporter and film critic for Daily Variety, 1977-80. Joined Los Angeles Times as film writer, winning paper's Award for Sustained Excellence in 1984. 1985 left to take post with The Geffen Film Co. as executive in chg. creative development. Joined A&M Films as v.p. in chg. prod., 1986. Became pres., 1989. Author: Skywalking (about George Lucas).
PICTURES: The Beast (exec. prod.), The Mighty Quinn (exec. prod.). *Producer:* House of Cards, Worth Winning, Blaze, Crooked Hearts, A Midnight Clear, A Home of Our Own, S.F.W., Mrs. Winterbourne.

POLLOCK, THOMAS
Executive. b. 1943. In 1971, after 3 years as business mgr. for American Film Institute's film marketing wing, formed law firm Pollock Bloom, and Dekom with young filmmakers such as George Lucas and Matthew Robbins as clients. Served as chmn. Filmex, 1973-81. 1986, named chmn. MCA's Universal motion picture group., now vice chmn., MCA, Inc.

POLONSKY, ABRAHAM
Writer, Director. b. New York, NY, Dec. 5, 1910. e. CCNY, B.A.; Columbia Law Sch. Taught at City Coll. 1932 until war. Blacklisted from 1951-66.
AUTHOR: The Enemy Sea, The Discoverers, The World Above, The Season of Fear, Zenia's Way.
PICTURES: *Writer:* Golden Earrings, Body and Soul (also story), Force of Evil (also dir.), I Can Get It for You Wholesale, Odds Against Tomorrow, Madigan, Tell Them Willie Boy is Here (also dir.), Romance of a Horse Thief, Avalanche Express, Monsignor.

PONTECORVO, GILLO
Director. b. Pisa, Italy, Nov. 19, 1919. Younger brother of Prof. Bruno Pontecorvo, Harwell scientist who defected in 1950. Former photo-journalist. Worked as asst. dir., directed documentary shorts before feature debut in 1957.
PICTURES: Die Windrose (Giovanna episode), La Grande Strada Azzurra (The Long Blue Road; also co-s.p.), Kapo (also co-s.p.), The Battle of Algiers (also story; Acad. Award noms. as dir. & writer), Queimada! (Burn; also co-story), Ogro (The Tunnel; also co-s.p.).

PONTI, CARLO
Producer. b. Milan, Italy, Dec. 11, 1913. m. actress Sophia Loren. e. U. of Milan, 1934. Prod. first picture in Milan, Little Old World; prod. Lux Film Rome; prod. first of a series of famous Toto pictures, Toto Househunting.
PICTURES: A Dog's Life, The Knight Has Arrived, Musolino, The Outlaw, Romanticism, Sensuality, The White Slave, Europe 1951, Toto in Color, The Three Corsairs, The Gold of Naples, Ulysses, The Woman of the River, An American of Rome, Attila, La Strada, War and Peace, The Last Lover, The Black Orchid, That Kind of Woman, A Breath of Scandal, Heller in Pink Tights, Two Women, Boccaccio '70, Bluebeard, The Condemned of Altona, Marriage Italian Style, Casanova '70, Operation Crossbow, Doctor Zhivago, Lady L, Blow Up, More Than a Miracle, The Girl and the General, Sunflower, The Best House in London, Zabriskie Point, The Priest's Wife, Lady Liberty, White Sister, What?, Andy Warhol's Frankenstein, The Passenger, The Cassandra Crossing, A Special Day, Saturday Sunday Monday.
TELEVISION: Mario Puzo's The Fortunate Pilgrim (exec. prod.).

POOLE, FRANK S.
Executive. b. London, England, Oct. 11, 1913. e. Dulwich Coll., 1925-31. Ent. m.p. ind. 1931. Early career with Pathe Pictures, Twickenham Film Distributors, until joining 20th Century Fox as London branch office supervisor 1939. War service 1940-46. Rejoined Fox 1946-53; appt. Leed Branch mgr. 1954-59; supv. 1959-61; asst. sls. mgr., 1961 until joined Rank Film Distrib. as asst. sls. mgr. 1962; appt. sls. mgr. 1965, and to board as dir. of sls.; appt. gen. mgr. 1968; jnt. mng. dir. 1969; appt. mng. dir. 1970; appt. dir. Rank Overseas Film Dist. Ltd., 1972; appt. co-chmn Fox-Rank Distributors Ltd., 1972; appt. vice-chmn. Rank Film Distributors Ltd. 1977; 1975, elected to Committee of Cinema & TV Veterans; 1978, retired from Rank Organisation. Appt. chmn., Appeal Tribunal for the Film Industry, chmn., Grebelands Mgt. Committee & to exec. council of CTBF, 1979; assoc. Geoff Reeve & Associates. 1980, chmn. & mng. dir., Omandry Intl. Ltd. 1982 appointed film consultant U.K./Europe to the Alberta Government. Pres., Cinema & TV Veterans 1990-92.

POP, IGGY
Musician, Actor. b. MI, April 21, 1947. r.n. James Osterberg. Has recorded 16 albums with band the Stooges and solo.
PICTURES: *Actor:* Cry Baby, Hardware (voice only), Dead Man, The Crow: City of Angels. *Songs:* Rock 'N' Rule.

POPE OSBORNE, MARY
Executive. Pres., Author's Guild, Inc.

PORTER, DON
Actor. b. Miami, OK, Sept. 24, 1912. e. Oregon Inst. of Tech. Wide theatre work; then m.p, roles. U.S. Army, 3 yrs.

THEATER: The Best Man, Any Wednesday, Generation, Plaza Suite, The Price, How To Succeed in Business Without Really Trying, Harvey.
PICTURES: The Racket, The Savage, 711 Ocean Drive, Because You're Mine, Our Miss Brooks, Bachelor in Paradise, Youngblood Hawke, The Candidate, 40 Carats, Mame, White Line Fever.
TELEVISION: *Series:* Private Secretary, Ann Sothern Show, Gidget. *Guest:* Bionic Woman, Hawaii Five-O, Switch, Love Boat, Three's Company, The President's Mistress, The Murder That Wouldn't Die, The Last Song, Dallas, Old Money.

POST, TED
Producer, Director. b. Brooklyn, NY, March 31, 1918. Dir. many stage plays; dir. CBS-TV Repertoire Thea.; Producer-dir., NBC-TV Coney Island of the Mind. Directed Everyone Can Make Music.
TELEVISION: *Series:* Studio One, Ford Theatre, Playhouse of Stars, Alcoa Theatre, Gunsmoke, Rawhide, Twilight Zone, Wagon Train, Combat, Peyton Place, Alcoa, Defenders, Route 66, Baretta, Columbo. *Movies:* Night Slaves, Dr. Cook's Garden, Yuma, Five Desperate Women, Do Not Fold Spindle or Mutilate, The Bravos, Sandcastles, Girls in the Office, Diary of a Hitchhiker, Stagecoach. *Pilots:* Cagney & Lacey, Beyond Westworld, Steve Canyon, Perry Mason. *Mini-series:* Rich Man, Poor Man II (episode 3).
PICTURES: The Peacemaker (debut, 1956), The Legend of Tom Dooley, Hang 'em High, Beneath The Planet of the Apes, The Baby, The Harrad Experiment, Magnum Force, Whiffs, Good Guys Wear Black, Go Tell the Spartans, Nightkill, The Human Shield.

POSTER, STEVEN
Cinematographer. A.S.C. b. Chicago, IL, Mar. 1, 1944. e. L.A. Art Center Coll. Started as commercial cinematographer before moving into feature films. 2nd unit work includes: Close Encounters of the Third Kind, Blade Runner. 2nd v.p., American Society of Cinematographers.
PICTURES: Blood Beach, Dead and Buried, Spring Break, Strange Brew, Testament, The New Kids, The Heavenly Kid, Blue City, The Boy Who Could Fly, Aloha Summer, Someone to Watch Over Me, Big Top Pee-wee, Next of Kin, Opportunity Knocks, Rocky V, Life Stinks, The Cemetery Club.
TELEVISION: *Movies:* The Grass is Always Greener, The Cradle Will Fall, I'll Take Manhattan, Class of '65, Courage, Shanghai La Plaza, Roswell.

POSTLETHWAITE, PETE
Actor. b. Lancashire, England. Feb. 16, 1946.
THEATER: *RSC:* Every Man and His Humour, A Midsummer Night's Dream, MacBeth, King Lear, The Taming of the Shrew.
PICTURES: The Duellists, A Private Function, Distant Voices Still Lives, The Dressmaker, To Kill a Priest, Hamlet, Alien^3, The Last of the Mohicans, Waterland, In the Name of the Father (Acad. Award nom.), Anchoress, The Usual Suspects, James and the Giant Peach (voice), Dragonheart, When Saturday Comes.
TELEVISION: The Muscle Market, A Child From the South, Treasure Island (theatrical in U.K.), Martin Chuzzlewit.

POSTON, TOM
Actor. b. Columbus, OH, Oct. 17, 1927. Made B'way debut 1947 in Cyrano de Bergerac.
PICTURES: City That Never Sleeps (debut, 1953), Zotz!, The Old Dark House, Soldier in the Rain, Cold Turkey, The Happy Hooker, Rabbit Test, Up the Academy, Carbon Copy.
TELEVISION: *Movies:* The Girl The Gold Watch and Everything, Save the Dog!, A Quiet Little Neighborhood A Perfect Little Murder. *Series:* The Steve Allen Show (Emmy Award, 1959), Pantomime Quiz, To Tell the Truth, On the Rocks, We've Got Each Other, Mork and Mindy, Newhart, Grace Under Fire. *Guest:* Goodyear Playhouse, Phil Silvers Show, Password, The Defenders, Fame, The Love Boat, Dream On, etc.

POTTS, ANNIE
Actress. b. Nashville, TN, Oct. 28, 1952. e. Stephens Coll., MO, BFA. Amateur stage debut at 12 in Heidi. Then in summer stock; on road in Charley's Aunt, 1976. Serves on auxilliary bd. of MADD (Mothers Against Drunk Driving). Ambassador for Women for the Amer. Arthritis Fdn.
PICTURES: Corvette Summer (debut, 1978), King of the Gypsies, Heartaches, Ghostbusters, Crimes of Passion, Pretty in Pink, Jumpin' Jack Flash, Pass the Ammo, Who's Harry Crumb?, Ghostbusters II, Texasville, Breaking the Rules, Toy Story (voice).
TELEVISION: *Movies:* Black Market Baby, Flatbed Annie and Sweetie Pie, Cowboy, It Came Upon the Midnight Clear, Why Me?, Her Deadly Rival. *Series:* Goodtime Girls, Designing Women, Love & War, Dangerous Minds. *Guest:* Remington Steele, Magnum P.I., Twilight Zone.

POUND, LESLIE
Executive. b. London, Eng., Nov. 3, 1926. Entered industry in 1943 as reporter on British trade paper, The Cinema. Now,

Screen International. Following military service in India and Singapore returned to work for that publication until 1952 when joined Paramount pub. office in London on the The Greatest Show on Earth. Named dir. of adv./pub. in U.K. for Paramount. 1958, retained Paramount position when Cinema Int'l Corp. was formed. 1977, joined Lew Grade in ITC Entertainment as worldwide dir. of pub./adv. 1977, int'l pub. chief for Embassy Pictures in Los Angeles. 1982, named Paramount Pictures v.p., int'l mktg. for motion picture div., N.Y. 1983. Relocated to L.A. with mktg. div. as sr. v.p. Returned to London, 1993 as sr. v.p. International markets for Paramount Pictures.

POWELL, JANE
Actress, Singer. r.n. Suzanne Burce. b. Portland, OR, Apr. 1, 1929. m. pub. relations exec. Dick Moore. Had own radio program over KOIN, Portland; singer on nat'l networks; Star of Tomorrow, 1948. Autobiography: The Girl Next Door ... and How She Grew (1988). Video: Jane Powell's Fight Back With Fitness.
THEATER: Irene (B'way, 1974). After-Play (off-B'way, 1996). Toured nationally with South Pacific, Peter Pan, My Fair Lady, The Unsinkable Molly Brown, I Do I Do, Same Time Next Year, Chapter Two.
PICTURES: Song of the Open Road (debut, 1944), Delightfully Dangerous, Holiday in Mexico, Three Daring Daughters, A Date With Judy, Luxury Liner, Nancy Goes to Rio, Two Weeks With Love, Royal Wedding, Rich Young and Pretty, Small Town Girl, Three Sailors and a Girl, Seven Brides for Seven Brothers, Athena, Deep in My Heart, Hit the Deck, The Girl Most Likely, The Female Animal, Enchanted Island.
TELEVISION: Specials: Ruggles of Red Gap, Give My Regards to Broadway, Meet Me in St. Louis, Jane Powell Show. Series: Alcoa Theatre, Loving, As the World Turns. Guest: The Love Boat, Growing Pains, Murder She Wrote, others. Movies: The Letters, Mayday at 40,000 Feet. Host: The Movie Musicals (PBS).

POWELL, ROBERT
Actor. b. Salford, England, June 1, 1944. e. Manchester U. Stage work includes Tovarich.
PICTURES: Robbery (debut, 1967), Far From the Madding Crowd, Joanna, The Italian Job, Walk a Crooked Path, Secrets, Running Scared, Asylum, The Asphyx (Horror of Death), Mahler, Tommy, Oltre il Bene e il Male (Beyond Good and Evil), Cocktails for Three, The Thirty-Nine Steps, The Dilessi Affair, Harlequin (Dark Forces), Jane Austin in Manhattan, The Survivor, Imperative (Venice Film Fest. Award), The Jigsaw Man, What Waits Below, D'Annunio and I Down There in the Jungle, Romeo-Juliet (voice), The Sign of Command, Once on Chunuk Bar.
TELEVISION: Series: Doomwatch, Hannay, The First Circle. Mini-Series: Jesus of Nazareth. Movies/Specials: Shelley, Jude the Obscure, Mrs. Warren's Profession, Mr. Rolls & Mr. Royce, Looking for Clancy, The Four Feathers, The Hunchback of Notre Dame, Pygmalion, Frankenstein, Shaka Zulu, Merlin of the Crystal Cave, The Golden Years.

POWERS, MALA
Actress. r.n. Mary Ellen Powers. b. San Francisco, CA, Dec. 20, 1931. p. George and Dell Powers, latter, dramatic coach. e. Studied acting with Michael Chekhov. e. UCLA. Pasadena Playhouse in For Keeps, 1946, followed by Distant Isle; Actor's Lab, Hollywood; did considerable radio, theatre and tv work. Writer, narrator Children's Story, and Dial A Story (1979). Author: Follow the Star (1980), Follow the Year (1984). Teaches Michael Chekhov technique of acting.
PICTURES: Tough as They Come (debut, 1942), Outrage, Edge of Doom, Cyrano de Bergerac, Rose of Cimarron, City Beneath the Sea, City That Never Sleeps, Geraldine, The Yellow Mountain, Rage at Dawn, Bengazi, Tammy and the Bachelor, The Storm Rider, Death in Small Doses, The Colossus of New York, Sierra Baron, The Unknown Terror, Man on the Prowl, Flight of the Lost Balloon, Rogue's Gallery, Doomsday, Daddy's Gone-A-Hunting, Six Tickets to Hell.
TELEVISION: Series: Hazel, The Man and the City. Guest: Daniel Boone.

POWERS, C. F. (MIKE) JR.
Executive. b. San Francisco, CA, March 6, 1923. e. Park Coll., MO, Columbia U., N.Y., graduated U. of Oregon. Entered film business with P.R.C. in Portland, OR, 1947. Became Eagle Lion branch mgr. in Portland, 1950, and then United Artists. Moved to Seattle, WA as branch mgr. of 20th Century Fox, 1960. Was then western division mgr. for 20th Century Fox until 1967, then western division mgr. for Cinerama until 1973. Became exec. v.p., head film buyer for Robert L. Lippert Theatres, Transcontinental Theatres and Affiliated Theatres until 1978. Western div. mgr. Orion Pictures, 1982-4. Mike Powers Ent. (a buying and booking combine and indept. film distrib.). 1984-86 Western district mgr. Embassy Pictures. Became western division mgr. for Filmways Pictures. Past president of Catholic Entertainment Guild of Northern Calif.; past pres. of Variety Club Tent 32, San Francisco. Currently m.p. consultant to U.S. Federal Govt.

POWERS, STEFANIE
Actress. r.n. Stefania Federkiewicz. b. Hollywood, CA, Nov. 2, 1942. After graduation from Hollywood High signed by Columbia Studios.
PICTURES: Tammy Tell Me True (debut, 1962), Experiment in Terror, The Young Sinner, The Interns, If a Man Answers, McClintock!, Palm Springs Weekend, The New Interns, Love Has Many Faces, Die Die My Darling (Fanatic), Stagecoach, Warning Shot, The Boatniks, Crescendo, The Magnificent 7 Ride, Herbie Rides Again, Gone With the West, It Seemed Like a Good Idea at the Time, Escape to Athena, Invisible Stranger (The Astral Factor).
TELEVISION: Series: The Girl From U.N.C.L.E., Feather and Father Gang, Hart to Hart. Mini-series: Washington: Behind Closed Doors, Hollywood Wives. Movies: Five Desperate Women, Paper Man, Sweet Sweet Rachel, Hardcare, No Place to Run, Shootout in a One-Dog Town, Skyway to Death, Sky Heist, Return to Earth, Family Secrets (also prod.), A Death in Canaan, Nowhere to Run, Mistral's Daughter, Deceptions, At Mother's Request, Beryl Markham: A Shadow on the Sun (also co-prod.), She Was Marked for Murder, Love and Betrayal, When Will I Be Loved?, The Burden of Proof, Survive the Night, Hart to Hart Returns (also co-prod.), Hart to Hart: Home is Where the Hart Is, Hart to Hart: Crimes of the Hart (also co-prod.), Hart to Hart: Old Friends Never Die, The Good Ride, Good King Wenceslas, Hart to Hart: Secrets of the Hart, Hart to Hart: Til Death Do Us Hart.

PRENTISS, PAULA
Actress. r.n. Paula Ragusa. b. San Antonio, TX, March 4, 1939. m. actor-director Richard Benjamin. e. Northwestern U., Bachelor degree in drama, 1959. On stage in As You Like It, Arf!, The Norman Conquests, Love Letters, Secrets, Demons (Amer. Rep. Theatre, Cambridge, MA).
PICTURES: Where the Boys Are (debut, 1960), The Honeymoon Machine, Bachelor in Paradise, The Horizontal Lieutenant, Follow the Boys, Man's Favorite Sport?, The World of Henry Orient, Looking for Love, In Harm's Way, What's New Pussycat?, Catch-22, Move, Born to Win, Last of the Red Hot Lovers, Crazy Joe, The Parallax View, The Stepford Wives, The Black Marble, Saturday the 14th, Buddy Buddy, Mrs. Winterbourne.
TELEVISION: Series: He & She, Burke's Law. Movies: The Couple Takes a Wife, Having Babies II, No Room to Run (Australian), Friendships Secrets and Lies, Top of the Hill, Packin' It In, M.A.D.D.: Mothers Against Drunk Drivers.

PRESLE, MICHELINE
Actress. r.n. Micheline Chassagne. b. Paris, France, Aug. 22, 1922. e. Raymond Rouleau Dram. Sch. m.p. debut in Je Chante; on stage in Colinette. Am. Stram Gram, Spectacle des Allies; to U.S., 1945; Flea in Her Ear, Magic Circus, Who's Afraid of Virginia Woolf? (tour), Gigi, Nuit de Valognes, Boomerang, Adriana Mont, etc.
PICTURES: Jeunes Filles en Detresse, L'Histoire de Rire, La Nuit Fantastique, Felicie Nanteuil, Seul Amour, Faibalas, Boule de Suif, Jeux Sont Faix, Diable au Corps, Under My Skin, Some Kind of News, An American Guerilla in the Philippines, Adventures of Captain Fabian, Sins of Pompeii, House of Ricordi, Archipelago of Love, Thieves After Dark, Le Chien, At the Top of the Stairs, Le Jour de Rois. Fine Weather, But Storms Due Towards Evening, Confidences, Alouette, Je te plumerai, I Want to Go Home.
TELEVISION: The Blood of Others.

PRESLEY, PRISCILLA
Actress. b. Brooklyn, NY, May 24, 1945. Raised in Connecticut. e. Wiesbaden, West Germany where met and married Elvis Presley (1967-73). Studied acting with Milton Katselas, dance at Steven Peck Theatre Art School and karate at Chuck Norris Karate School. Formed a business, Bis and Beau, marketing exclusive dress designs. Became TV spokesperson for beauty products.
PICTURES: The Naked Gun: From the Files of Police Squad! (debut, 1988), The Adventures of Ford Fairlane, The Naked Gun 2 1/2: The Smell of Fear, Naked Gun 33 1/3: The Final Insult.
TELEVISION: Series: Those Amazing Animals (host, 1980-81), Dallas. Movies: Love is Forever, Elvis and Me (prod. only).

PRESSMAN, EDWARD R.
Producer. b. New York, NY. e. Fieldston Sch.; grad., Stanford U.; studied at London Sch. of Economics. Began career with film short, Girl, in collaboration with director Paul Williams in London. They formed Pressman-Williams Enterprises.
PICTURES: Prod.: Out of It, The Revolutionary, Dealing: or the Berkeley to Boston Forty Brick, Lost Bag Blues, Sisters, Badlands, Phantom of the Paradise, Despair (exec. prod.), Paradise Alley (exec. prod.), Old Boyfriends, Heartbeat (exec. prod.), The Hand, Conan the Barbarian (exec. prod.), Das Boot (exec. prod.), The Pirates of Penzance (exec. prod.), Crimewave (exec. prod.), Plenty (exec. prod.), Half Moon Street (exec. prod.), True Stories (exec. prod.), Good Morning

Babylon (exec. prod.), Masters of the Universe, Walker (exec. prod.), Wall Street, Cherry 2000 (exec. prod.), Paris By Night (exec. prod.), Talk Radio, Martians Go Home (exec. prod.), Blue Steel, Reversal of Fortune, To Sleep with Anger (exec. prod.), Waiting for the Light (exec. prod.), Homicide, Year of the Gun, Iron Maze (co-exec. prod.), Storyville, Bad Lieutenant, Hoffa, Dream Lover (exec. prod.), The Crow, Street Fighter, Judge Dredd (exec. prod.), City Hall, The Island of Dr. Moreau.

PRESSMAN, LAWRENCE
Actor. b. Cynthiana, KY, July 10, 1939. e. Kentucky Northwestern U. On B'way in Man in the Glass Booth, Play It Again, Sam, etc.
PICTURES: The Man in the Glass Booth, The Crazy World of Julius Vrooder, Hellstrom Chronicle, Shaft, Making It, Walk Proud, Nine to Five, Some Kind of Hero, The Hanoi Hilton, The Waterdance.
TELEVISION: Series: Mulligan's Stew, Doogie Howser M.D., Law and Order, N.Y.P.D. Blue. Movies: Cannon, The Snoop Sisters, The Marcus-Nelson Murder, Winter Kill, The First 36 Hours of Dr. Durant, Rich Man, Poor Man, Man from Atlantis, The Trial of Lee Harvey Oswald, The Gathering, Like Mom, Like Me, Blind Ambition, Little Girl Lost, Breaking Point, White Hot: The Mysterious Murder of Thelma Todd.

PRESSMAN, MICHAEL
Director, Producer. b. New York, NY, July 1, 1950. e. California Inst. of Arts. Comes from show business family; was actor in college.
PICTURES: Director: The Great Texas Dynamite Chase, The Bad News Bears Breaking Training, Boulevard Nights, Those Lips Those Eyes (also prod.), Some Kind of Hero, Doctor Detroit, Teenage Mutant Ninja Turtles II: The Secret of the Ooze, To Gillian On Her 37th Birthday.
TELEVISION: Movies: Like Mom, Like Me, The Imposter, The Christmas Gift, Final Jeopardy, Private Sessions, Haunted by Her Past, To Heal a Nation, Shootdown, The Revenge of Al Capone, Incident at Dark River, Man Against the Mob (also co-prod.), Joshua's Heart, Quicksand: No Escape.

PRESTON, FRANCES W.
Executive. Joined Broadcast Music Inc. in 1958. Pres. & CEO BMI, 1986-present.

PRESTON, KELLY
Actress. b. Honolulu, HI, Oct. 13, 1962. e. UCLA, USC. m. actor John Travolta.
PICTURES: Metalstorm: The Destruction of Jared-Syn (debut, 1983), Christine, Mischief, Secret Admirer, SpaceCamp, 52 Pick-Up, Amazon Women on the Moon, A Tiger's Tale, Love at Stake, Spellbinder, Twins, The Experts, Run, Only You, Love Is a Gun, Cheyenne Warrior, Waiting to Exhale, From Dusk Till Dawn, Citizen Ruth, Jerry Maguire.
TELEVISION: Series: For Love and Honor, Capitol. Movies: The Perfect Bride, The American Clock, Mrs. Munck. Guest: Quincy, Blue Thunder, Riptide.

PREVIN, ANDRE
Composer, Conductor. b. Berlin, Germany, Apr. 6, 1929. Composed and conducted over 50 m.p. scores. Music director, Pittsburgh Symphony Orchestra, & conductor emeritus of London Symphony Orchestra. Music Director, Royal Philharmonic Orch., 1985-89. Guest conductor of most major symphony orchestras in U.S. & Europe. Music dir., Pittsburgh Symphony 1972-81. Conductor, London Symphony, 1968-78. Conductor Emeritus London Symphony, 1992-present. Received Knighthood of British Empire in 1996.
PICTURES: Three Little Words, Cause for Alarm, It's Always Fair Weather, Bad Day at Black Rock, Invitation to the Dance, Catered Affair, Designing Woman, Silk Stockings, Gigi (Academy Award, 1958), Porgy and Bess (Academy Award, 1959), The Subterraneans, Bells Are Ringing, Pepe, Elmer Gantry, The Four Horsemen of the Apocalypse, One Two Three, Two for the Seesaw, Long Day's Journey Into Night, Irma LaDouce (Academy Award, 1963), My Fair Lady (Academy Award, 1964), Goodbye Charlie, Inside Daisy Clover, The Fortune Cookie, Thoroughly Modern Millie, Valley of the Dolls, Paint Your Wagon, The Music Lovers, Jesus Christ Superstar, Rollerball, One Trick Pony.

PRICE, FRANK
Executive. b. Decatur, IL, May 17, 1930. e. Michigan State U. following naval service. Joined CBS in N.Y. in 1951 as story editor and writer. Moved to Hollywood in 1953, serving as story editor first at Columbia and then NBC (Matinee Theatre). In 1958 joined Universal as an assoc. prod. and writer. In 1961 named exec. prod. of The Virginian TV series. Appt. exec. prod. of Ironside; later did It Takes a Thief and several World Premiere movies. 1964 named v.p. of Universal TV; 1971, sr. v.p.; 1974, pres. Also v.p., MCA, Inc. 1978 left to join Columbia as pres. of new company unit, Columbia Pictures Productions. In 1979 named chmn. & CEO of Columbia Pictures. In 1983

joined Universal: named chmn., motion picture group, pres. of Universal Pictures, and v.p. of MCA. In 1987 formed Price Entertainment Inc. as chmn. & CEO to produce movies and create TV shows for dist. through Columbia Pictures Entertainment. 1990, integrated Price Entertainment Inc., into Columbia and was named chairman. Resigned, 1991. Prod. tv movie The Tuskegee Airmen.

PRICE, RICHARD
Writer. b. Bronx, NY, Oct. 12, 1949. e. Cornell Univ., Columbia Univ.
AUTHOR: The Wanderers, Bloodbrothers, Ladies' Man, The Breaks, Clockers.
PICTURES: Cameos: The Wanderers, The Paper. Writer: The Color of Money (Acad. Award nom.; also cameo), Streets of Gold, New York Stories (Life Lessons; also cameo), Sea of Love, Night and the City (also cameo), Mad Dog and Glory (also exec. prod., cameo), Ethan Frome (exec. prod. only), Mad Dog and Glory (also exec. prod., cameo), Kiss of Death (also cameo), Clockers.

PRIES, RALPH W.
Executive. b. Atlanta, GA, August 31, 1919. Graduated Georgia Inst. of Technology. V.P., MEDIQ, Inc.; pres. MEDIQ/PRN Life Support Services, Inc.; past pres., Odgen Food Service Corp.; exec. comm. and bd., Firstrust Savings Bank and chmn. of audit comm.; Boards of St. Christopher's Hospital for Children, Moss Rehabilitation Hospital, United Hospital Corp., Philadelphia Heart Instit. Former intl pres., Variety Clubs Intl.; previously on bd. of Hahnemann U. and Hosp., chmn. of bd. Likoff Cardiovascular Instit., pres. Main Line Reform Temple, Wynnewood, PA.

PRIESTLEY, JASON
Actor. b. Vancouver, Canada, Aug. 28, 1969. First screen appearance as baby in 1969 film That Cold Day in the Park, in which his mother had bit part. Child actor in many Canadian TV commercials. First major U.S. acting job in 1986 TV movie Nobody's Child. Moved to L.A. in 1987. Theatre includes The Addict, The Breakfast Club.
TELEVISION: Series: Sister Kate, Beverly Hills 90210 (also co-prod.). Movies: Stacie (Canada), Nobody's Child, Teen Angel & Teen Angel Returns (Disney TV). Guest: Danger Bay (Canada), MacGyver, 21 Jump Street, Adventures of Beans Baxter, Quantum Leap.
PICTURES: The Boy Who Could Fly, Nowhere to Run, Watchers, Calendar Girl, Tombstone, Coldblooded.

PRIMUS, BARRY
Actor. b. New York, NY, Feb. 16, 1938. e. Bennington Coll., City Coll. of NY.
THEATER: The King and the Duke, The Nervous Set, Henry IV, Parts I and II, Creating the World, Teibele and the Demon, Lincoln Center Rep. (The Changling, After the Fall).
PICTURES: The Brotherhood, Puzzle of a Downfall Child, Been Down So Long It Looks Like Up to Me, Von Richtofen and Brown, Boxcar Bertha, The Gravy Train, New York New York, Avalanche, Autopsy, The Rose, Heartland, Night Games, Absence of Malice, The River, Down and Out in Beverly Hills, Jake Speed, SpaceCamp, Talking Walls, The Stranger, Big Business, Cannibal Women in the Avocado Jungle of Death, Torn Apart, Guilty by Suspicion, Mistress (dir., s.p. only), Night and the City.
TELEVISION: Series: Cagney and Lacey. Mini-Series: Washington Behind Closed Doors. Movies: Big Rose, Roger & Harry: The Mitera Target, Portrait of a Showgirl, Paper Dolls, I Want to Live, Heart of Steel, Brotherly Love, The Women of Spring Break. Guest: Law and Order.

PRINCE
Singer, Actor. r.n. Prince Rogers Nelson. b. Minneapolis, MN, June 7, 1958. Rock star and recording artist.
PICTURES: Purple Rain (also wrote songs; Acad. Award for best orig. song score, 1984), Under the Cherry Moon (also dir., s.p., songs), Sign O' the Times (also dir., songs), Batman (songs only), Graffiti Bridge (also dir., s.p., songs).

PRINCE, HAROLD
Director. b. New York, NY, Jan. 30, 1928. e. U. of Pennsylvania. Worked as stage mgr. for George Abbott on three shows, later co-produced, produced and/or directed the following: The Pajama Game (Tony Award), Damn Yankees (Tony Award), New Girl In Town, West Side Story, A Swim in the Sea, Fiorello! (Tony Award, Pulitzer Prize), Tenderloin, A Call on Kurpin, Take Her She's Mine, A Funny Thing Happened on the Way to the Forum (Tony Award), She Loves Me, The Matchmaker (revival), Fiddler on the Roof, Poor Bitos, Baker Street, Flora, The Red Menace, Superman, Cabaret (Tony Award), Zorba, Company, Follies, The Great God Brown, The Visit, Love for Love (the last three all revivals), A Little Night Music (Tony Award), Candide (Tony Award), Pacific Overtures, Side by Side by Sondheim, Some of My Best Friends, On the Twentieth Century, Evita (also London), Sweeney Todd (Tony Award 1979; also London),

Merrily We Roll Along, A Doll's Life, Play Memory, End of the World, Diamonds, Grind, Roza, Cabaret (revival), Phantom of the Opera (Tony Award, 1988; also London), Grandchild of Kings (dir. & adapt.), Kiss of the Spider Woman (Tony Award, 1993), Show Boat (Tony Award, 1995); and also directed the operas Ashmadei, Silverlake, Sweeney Todd, Candide and Don Giovanni for N.Y. City Opera, Girl of Golden West for Chicago Lyric Opera Co. and San Francisco Opera; Willie Stark for Houston Grand Opera; Madama Butterfly for Chicago Lyric Opera and Turandot for Vienna State Opera and Faust for Metropolitan Opera.
AUTHOR: Contradictions: Notes on Twenty-Six Years in the Theatre (1974).
PICTURES: Co-producer: The Pajama Game, Damn Yankees. Director: Something for Everyone, A Little Night Music.

PRINCE, WILLIAM
Actor. b. Nichols, NY, Jan. 26, 1913. With Maurice Evans, actor, 2 yrs.; radio announcer. On N.Y. stage, Ah, Wilderness; m.p. debut in 1943. Many TV credits.
THEATER: Guest in the House, Across the Board on Tomorrow Morning, The Eve of St. Mark, John Loves Mary, As You Like It, I Am a Camera, Forward the Heart, Affair of Honor, Third Best Sport, The Highest Tree, Venus at Large, Strange Interlude, The Ballad of the Sad Cafe, Mercy Street.
PICTURES: Destination Tokyo, Cinderella Jones, The Very Thought of You, Roughly Speaking, Objective Burma, Pillow to Post, Carnegie Hall, Dead Reckoning, Lust for Gold, Cyrano de Bergerac, Secret of Treasure Mountain, Macabre, Sacco and Vanzetti, The Heartbreak Kid, The Stepford Wives, Family Plot, Network, Rollercoaster, The Gauntlet, The Cat from Outer Space, The Promise, Bronco Billy, Love & Money, Kiss Me Goodbye, Movers and Shakers, Fever Pitch, Spies Like Us, Nuts, Vice Versa, Spontaneous Combustion, The Taking of Beverly Hills, The Paper.
TELEVISION: Series: The Mask, Justice, The American Girls. Mini-Series: Aspen, George Washington, War and Remembrance. Movies: Key West, Night Games, Murder 1 Dancer O, Found Money, The Portrait.

PRINCIPAL, VICTORIA
Actress. b. Fukuoka, Japan, Jan 3, 1950. Father was in U.S. air force. Went to New York to become model; studied acting privately with Jean Scott at Royal Acad. of Dramatic Art in London before moving to Hollywood. Worked as talent agent in the mid-1970's.
PICTURES: The Life and Times of Judge Roy Bean (debut, 1972), The Naked Ape, Earthquake, I Will I Will... for Now, Vigilante Force.
TELEVISION: Series: Dallas. Guest: Fantasy Island (pilot), Love Story, Love American Style, Greatest Heroes of the Bible. Movies: The Night They Stole Miss Beautiful, The Pleasure Palace, Last Hours Before Morning, Not Just Another Affair, Mistress, Naked Lie (also exec. prod.), Blind Witness (also exec. prod.), Sparks: The Price of Passion (also exec. prod.), Don't Touch My Daughter (also exec. prod.), The Burden of Proof, Seduction: Three Tales From the Inner Sanctum (also co-exec. prod.), Midnight's Child (exec. prod. only), Beyond Obsession, River of Rage: The Taking of Maggie Keene, Dancing in the Dark, The Abduction.

PRINE, ANDREW
Actor. b. Jennings, FL, Feb. 14, 1936. e. U. of Miami. m. actress Heather Lowe. Mem. Actors Studio. On stage in Look Homeward, Angel, A Distant Bell, Mrs. Patterson, Borak. Ahmanson Theatre, LA: Long Day's Journey into Night, The Caine Mutiny. South Coast Rep.: Goodbye Freddy.
PICTURES: The Miracle Worker, Advance to the Rear, Texas Across the River, Bandolero!, The Devil's Brigade, This Savage Land, Generation, Chisum, Riding Tall, Simon: King of the Witches, Barn of the Naked Dead (Terror Circus), One Little Indian, The Centerfold Girls, Grizzly, The Town That Dreaded Sundown, Winds of Autumn, High Flying Love, The Evil, Amityville II: The Possession, Playing with Fire, Eliminators, Chill Factor, The Big One, Life on the Edge, Double Exposure, Gettysburg, Inferno, Dark Dancer, Gathering Evidence, Without Evidence.
TELEVISION: Series: The Wide Country, The Road West, W.E.B., Dallas, Room for Two, Weird Science. Movies: And the Children Shall Lead, Roughing It, Callie & Son, The Deputies, Another Part of the Forest, Night Slaves, Split Second to an Epitaph, Along Came a Spider, Night Slaves, Wonder Woman, Law of the Land, Tail Gunner Joe, Last of the Mohicans, A Small Killing, Mind over Murder, M-Station Hawaii, Christmas Miracle in Caulfield, Young Abe Lincoln, U.S.A., Donner Pass: The Road to Survival, Mission of the Shark, Scattered Dreams: The Kathryn Messenger Story, The Avenging Angel. Mini-Series: V: The Final Battle.

PROCHNOW, JURGEN
Actor. b. Berlin, Germany, 1941. Studied acting at the Folkswangschule. In provinical theatre before making tv debut on the series Harbour at the Rhine River, 1970.

PICTURES: Zoff (debut, 1971), Zartlchket der Wolfe, The Lost Honor of Katharina Blum, The Consequence, Einer von uns Beiden, Das Boot (The Boat; Berlin Film Fest. Award), The Keep, Dune, Der Bulle und das Madchen, Killing Cars, Terminus, Beverly Hills Cop II, Devil's Paradise, The Seventh Sign, A Dry White Season, The Fourth War, The Man Inside, Twin Peaks: Fire Walk With Me, Body of Evidence, In the Mouth of Madness, Judge Dredd.
TELEVISION: Forbidden, Murder by Reason of Insanity, Danielle Steel's Jewels, The Lucona Affair, Love Is Forever, Robin Hood, The Fire Next Time.

PROSKY, ROBERT
Actor. b. Philadelphia, PA, Dec. 13, 1930. Won TV amateur talent search contest, leading to scholarship with American Theatre Wing. 23-year veteran with Washington's Arena stage. Taught acting and appeared in over 150 plays
THEATER: Death of a Salesman, Galileo, The Caucasian Chalk Circle, You Can't Take it With You, Our Town, The Price (Helen Hayes Award). B'way: Moonchildren, A View from the Bridge, Pale Horse Pale Rider, Arms and the Man, Glengarry Glen Ross (Tony nom.), A Walk in the Woods (Tony nom.). Off-B'way: Camping With Henry and Tom. Tours incl.: Our Town, Inherit the Wind, A Walk in the Woods (Soviet Union), After the Fall (Hong Kong).
PICTURES: Thief, Hanky Panky, Monsignor, The Lords of Discipline, Christine, The Keep, The Natural, Outrageous Fortune, Big Shots, Broadcast News, The Great Outdoors, Things Change, Loose Cannons, Gremlins II: The New Batch, Funny About Love, Green Card, Life in the Food Chain (Age Isn't Everything), Far and Away, Hoffa, Last Action Hero, Rudy, Mrs. Doubtfire, Miracle on 34th Street, The Scarlet Letter, Dead Man Walking.
TELEVISION: Series: Hill Street Blues, Lifestories (host). Movies: World War III, The Ordeal of Bill Carny, Lou Grant, The Adams Chronicles, Old Dogs, Into Thin Air, The Murder of Mary Phagan, Home Fires Burning, From the Dead of Night, Heist, Dangerous Pursuit, Johnny Ryan, Against the Mob, A Green Journey, The Love She Sought, Double Edge, Life on the High Wire, Teamster Boss: The Jackie Presser Story. Guest: Coach.

PROVINE, DOROTHY
Actress. b. Deadwood, SD, Jan. 20, 1937. e. U. of Washington. Retired from films in 1969.
PICTURES: The Bonnie Parker Story (debut, 1958), Live Fast Die Young, Riot in Juvenile Prison, The 30 Foot Bride of Candy Rock, Wall of Noise, It's a Mad Mad Mad Mad World, Good Neighbor Sam, The Great Race, That Darn Cat, One Spy Too Many, Kiss the Girls and Make Them Die, Who's Minding the Mint?, Never a Dull Moment.
TELEVISION: Series: The Alaskans, The Roaring 20's. Movie: The Sound of Anger.

PRYCE, JONATHAN
Actor. b. North Wales, June 1, 1947. e. Royal Acad. of Dramatic Art. Actor and artistic dir. of Liverpool Everyman Theatre Co.
THEATER: London: Comedians, Taming of the Shrew, Antony and Cleopatra, Tally's Folly, Hamlet (Olivier Award), Macbeth, The Seagull, Uncle Vanya, Miss Saigon (Olivier & Variety Club Awards), Oliver! NY: Comedians (Tony & Theatre World Awards, 1977), Accidental Death of an Anarchist, Miss Saigon (Tony & Drama Desk Awards, 1991).
PICTURES: Voyage of the Damned (debut, 1976), Breaking Glass, Loophole, The Ploughman's Lunch, Something Wicked This Way Comes, The Doctor and the Devils, Brazil, Haunted Honeymoon, Jumpin' Jack Flash, Man on Fire, Consuming Passions, The Adventures of Baron Munchausen, The Rachel Papers, Freddie as F.R.O. 7 (voice), Glengarry Glen Ross, The Age of Innocence, A Business Affair, Great Moments in Aviation, A Troll in Central Park (voice), Deadly Advice, Shopping, Carrington (Cannes Film Fest. Award, 1995), Evita.
TELEVISION: Comedians, Playthings, Partisans, For Tea on Sunday, Timon of Athens, Praying Mantis, Murder Is Easy, Daft as a Brush, Martin Luther Heretic, The Caretaker, Glad Day, The Man From the Pru, Roger Doesn't Live Here Anymore, Selling Hitler, Whose Line Is It Anyway?, Mr. Wroes Virgins, Barbarians at the Gate, Thicker Than Water.

PRYOR, RICHARD
Actor. b. Peoria, IL, Dec. 1, 1940. At age 7 played drums with professionals. Made NY debut as standup comic in 1963, leading to appearances on TV (Johnny Carson, Merv Griffin, Ed Sullivan). Co-wrote TV scripts for Lily Tomlin (Emmy Award, 1974) and Flip Wilson. Won Grammy Awards for albums That Nigger's Crazy, Is It Something I Said?, Bicentennial Nigger. Autobiography: Pryor Convictions and Other Life Sentences (1995).
PICTURES: The Busy Body (debut, 1967), The Green Berets, Wild in the Streets, The Phynx, You've Got to Walk It Like You Talk It Or You'll Lose That Beat, Dynamite Chicken, Lady Sings the Blues, Hit!, Wattstax, The Mack, Some Call It

Loving, Blazing Saddles (co-s.p. only), Uptown Saturday Night, Adios Amigo, The Bingo Long Traveling All-Stars and Motor Kings, Car Wash, Silver Streak, Greased Lightning, Which Way Is Up?, Blue Collar, The Wiz, California Suite, Richard Pryor—Live in Concert (also prod., s.p.), The Muppet Movie, Richard Pryor Is Back Live in Concert (also s.p.), Wholly Moses, In God We Trust, Stir Crazy, Bustin' Loose (also co-prod., co-s.p.), Richard Pryor Live on the Sunset Strip (also prod., s.p.), Some Kind of Hero, The Toy, Superman III, Richard Pryor Here and Now (also dir., s.p.), Brewster's Millions, Jo Jo Dancer Your Life Is Calling (also dir., prod., s.p.), Critical Condition, Moving, See No Evil Hear No Evil, Harlem Nights, Another You.
TELEVISION: Series: The Richard Pryor Show (1977), Pryor's Place. Guest: Wild Wild West, The Partridge Family, The Mod Squad, Chicago Hope. Movies: The Young Lawyers, Carter's Army.

PRYOR, THOMAS M.
Journalist. b. New York, NY, May 22, 1912. Joined NY Times, 1929; m.p. dept. 1931 as reporter, editor, asst. film critic; Hollywood bureau chief, corres., NY Times, 1951-59; editor, Daily Variety, 1959-88; 1988-90. Consultant to Variety & Daily Variety. 1990, retired.

PTAK, JOHN
Agent. b. San Diego, CA. Graduated UCLA film department, 1968. Theatre mgr. and booker for Walter Reade Organization and Laemmle Theatres, 1966-1969. Admin. exec. at American Film Institute's Center for Advanced Studies, 1969\-1971. International Famous Agency (ICM), 1971-1975, William Morris Agency, 1976-91, Creative Artists Agency, 1991-. Represents motion picture and television talent.

PULLMAN, BILL
Actor. b. Hornell, NY, Dec. 17, 1953. e. SUNY at Oneonta, Univ. of Mass. at Amherst.
THEATER: NY: Dramathon '84, Curse of the Starving Class. LA: All My Sons, Barabbas, Nanawatai, Demon Wine, Control Freaks.
PICTURES: Ruthless People (debut, 1986), Spaceballs, The Serpent and the Rainbow, Rocket Gibraltar, The Accidental Tourist, Cold Feet, Brain Dead, Sibling Rivalry, Bright Angel, Going Under, Newsies, A League of Their Own, Singles, Nervous Ticks, Sommersby, Sleepless in Seattle, Malice, Mr. Jones, The Favor, Wyatt Earp, While You Were Sleeping, Casper, Mr. Wrong, Independence Day.
TELEVISION: Movies: Home Fires Burning, Crazy in Love, The Last Seduction (also released theatrically).

PURCELL, PATRICK B.
Executive. b. Dublin, Ireland, Mar. 16, 1943. e. Fordham U., M.B.A., 1973. In pub. & acct., England, 1969-69; acct., Associated Hosp. Service, N.Y., 1968-70; joined Paramount Pictures, 1970; v.p., film., 1980-83; exec. v.p. chief fin. & admin. officer 1983-.

PURDOM, EDMUND
Actor. b. Welwyn Garden City, England, Dec. 19, 1924. e. St. Ignatius Coll., London. Played leads, character roles for Northampton Rep. Co., Kettering Rep., two seasons at Stratford-On-Avon; London stage in Way Things Go, Malade Imaginaire, Romeo and Juliet, played in Caesar and Cleopatra, Antony and Cleopatra, London and N.Y.
PICTURES: Titanic (debut, 1953), Julius Caesar, The Student Prince, The Egyptian, Athena, The Prodigal, The King's Thief, Strange Intruder, Trapped in Tangiers, The Cossacks, Herod the Great, The Loves of Salambo, Malaga (Moment of Danger), The Last of the Vikings, Nights of Rasputin, Lafayette, White Slave Ship, Queen of the Nile, Suleiman the Conqueror, The Comedy Man, The Beauty Jungle (Contest Girl), Last Ride to Santa Cruz, The Charge of the 7th, The Yellow Rolls Royce, Man With the Golden Mask, The Black Corsair, The Satanists, Evil Fingers, Frankenstein's Castle of Freaks, Night Child, Cursed Medallion, Mister Scarface, The New Godfathers, L'altra Donna, Ator the Fighting Eagle, Pieces, Don't Open Till Christmas (also dir.), After the Fall of New York, The Assissi Underground, Killer vs. Killer, Appointment in Trieste.
TELEVISION: Mini-Series: The Winds of War, The Scarlet and the Black. Movie: Sophia Loren: Her Own Story.

PURL, LINDA
Actress. b. Greenwich, CT, Sept. 2, 1955. Moved to Japan at age 2. Appeared in Japanese theatre, TV. e. Toho Geino Academy. Back to US in 1971. On stage in The Baby Dance (New Haven, NYC), Hedda Gabler, The Real Thing (Mark Taper), The Merchant of Venice (Old Globe Theatre), Romeo & Juliet, Doll's House.
PICTURES: Jory, Crazy Mama, W.C. Fields & Me, Leo and Loree, The High Country, Visiting Hours, Viper, Natural Causes.
TELEVISION: Series: The Secret Storm, Beacon Hill, Happy Days, Matlock, Under Cover, Young Pioneers, Robin's Hoods.

Movies: Eleanor and Franklin, Little Ladies of the Night, Testimony of Two Men, A Last Cry for Help, Women at West Point, Like Normal People, The Flame is Love, The Night the City Screamed, The Adventures of Nellie Bly, The Last Days of Pompeii, The Manions of America, Addicted to His Love, Spies Lies and Naked Thighs, Before the Storm, Spy Games, Danielle Steel's Secrets, Body Language, Accidental Meeting, Incident at Deception Ridge.

PUTTNAM, SIR DAVID
CBE: Hon. LL.D Bristol 1983; Hon. D. Litt, Leicester 1986. Hon. Litt. D., Leeds 1992. Knighted, 1995. Producer. b. London, England 1941. e. Michenden Sch. In advertising before joining VPS/Goodtimes Prod. Co. Dir. of Britain's National Film Finance Corp. (1980-85); Also served on Cinema Films Council and governing council of the British Acad. of Film & Television Arts. Officier dans L'Ordre des Arts et des Lettres, 1986. Chmn. National Film and Television Sch., 1988. Past Pres., Council for the Protection of Rural England; Fellow, Royal Soc. of Arts; Fellow, Royal Geographical Soc., Hon. Fellow, The Chartered Society of Designers. appt. Chmn. & CEO, Columbia Pictures. Resigned 1987. Received Eastman 2nd Century Award, 1988. 1988 formed a joint venture for his Enigma Productions Ltd. with Warner Bros., Fujisankei Comm. Gp. of Japan, British Satellite Broadcasting & Country Nat West to prod. 4 films. Appt. chmn. ITEL intl. TV dist. agency, 1989. Dir., Anglia Television Group and Survival Anglia. Dir., Chrysalis Group, PLC. V.P., BAFTA. Member, U.K. Arts Lottery Board. Founding pres., Atelier du Cinema Europeen. Member, European Commission's 'Think Tank' for audio-visual policy.
PICTURES: Melody, The Pied Piper, That'll Be The Day, Stardust, Mahler, Bugsy Malone, The Duellists, Midnight Express, Foxes, Chariots of Fire (Academy Award for Best Picture, 1981), Local Hero, Cal, The Killing Fields, The Mission, Defence of the Realm, Memphis Belle, Meeting Venus, Being Human, War of the Buttons, Le Confessional. Co-produced documentaries: Swastika, James Dean—The First American Teenager, Double-Headed Eagle, Brother Can You Spare a Dime?
TELEVISION: P'Tang Yang Kipperbang, Experience Preferred, Secrets, Those Glory Glory Days, Sharma and Beyond, Winter Flight, Josephine Baker, Without Warning: The James Brady Story, A Dangerous Man: Lawrence After Arabia, The Burning Season.

Q

QUAID, DENNIS
Actor. b. Houston, TX Apr. 9, 1954. Brother is actor Randy Quaid. m. actress Meg Ryan. e. U. of Houston. Appeared in Houston stage productions before leaving for Hollywood. On N.Y. stage with his brother in True West, 1984. Performer with rock band The Electrics; wrote songs for films The Night the Lights Went Out in Georgia, Tough Enough, The Big Easy. Formed Summers/Quaid Productions with producer Cathleen Summers, 1989.
PICTURES: Crazy Mama (debut, 1975), I Never Promised You a Rose Garden, September 30, 1955, Our Winning Season, Seniors, G.O.R.P., Breaking Away, The Long Riders, All Night Long, Caveman, The Night the Lights Went Out in Georgia, Tough Enough, Jaws 3-D, The Right Stuff, Dreamscape, Enemy Mine, The Big Easy, Innerspace, Suspect, D.O.A., Everybody's All-American, Great Balls of Fire, Postcards From the Edge, Come See the Paradise, Wilder Napalm, Undercover Blues, Flesh & Bone, Wyatt Earp, Hideaway (co-prod. only), Something to Talk About, Dragonheart.
TELEVISION: Movies: Are You in the House Alone?, Amateur Night at the Dixie Bar and Grill, Bill, Johnny Belinda, Bill: On His Own.

QUAID, RANDY
Actor. b. Houston, TX, Oct. 1, 1950. Brother is actor Dennis Quaid. Discovered by Peter Bogdanovich while still jr. at Drama Dept. at U. of Houston and cast in his Targets and The Last Picture Show, 1971. Off-B'way debut: True West (1983).
PICTURES: Targets (debut, 1968), The Last Picture Show, What's Up Doc?, Paper Moon, Lolly-Madonna XXX, The Last Detail (Acad. Award nom.), The Apprenticeship of Duddy Kravitz, Breakout, The Missouri Breaks, Bound for Glory, The Choirboys, Midnight Express, Three Warriors, Foxes, The Long Riders, Heartbeeps, National Lampoon's Vacation, The Wild Life, The Slugger's Wife, Fool for Love, The Wraith, Sweet Country, No Man's Land, Moving, Caddyshack II, Parents, Bloodhounds of Broadway, Out Cold, National Lampoon's Christmas Vacation, Martians Go Home!, Days of Thunder, Quick Change, Cold Dog Soup, Texasville, Freaked, The Paper, Major League 2, Bye Bye Love, The Last Dance, Independence Day, Kingpin.
TELEVISION: Movies: Getting Away From It All, The Great Niagara, The Last Ride of the Dalton Gang, To Race the Wind, Guyana Tragedy: The Story of Jim Jones, Of Mice and Men,

Inside the Third Reich, Cowboy, A Streetcar Named Desire, LBJ: The Early Years, Dead Solid Perfect, Evil in Clear River, Frankenstein, Roommates, Next Door, Ed McBain's 87th Precinct. *Series*: Saturday Night Live (1985-86), Davis Rules. *Special*: Dear America (reader).

QUIGLEY, MARTIN, JR.
Educator, Writer. b. Chicago, IL, Nov. 24, 1917. e. A.B. Georgetown U.; M.A., Ed. D., Columbia U. M.P. Herald, Oct. 1939; spcl. ed. rep., M.P. Herald & M.P. Daily, May, 1941; wartime work in U.S., England, Eire & Italy, Dec. 1941-Oct. 1945; assoc. ed., Quigley Pub., Oct. 1945; ed. M.P. Herald, July, 1949; also edit. dir. of all Quigley Pub., 1956; pres. Quigley Pub. Co., 1964; author, Great Gaels, 1944, Roman Notes, 1946, Magic Shadows—The Story of the Origin of Motion Pictures, 1948; Gov't. Relations of Five Universities, 1975; Peace Without Hiroshima, 1991; First Century of Film, 1995. Editor, New Screen Techniques, 1953; m.p. tech. section, Encyclopaedia Brit., 1956; co-author, Catholic Action in Practice, 1963. Co-author: Films in America, 1929-69, 1970. Pres., QWS, Inc., educational consultants, 1975-81. Adjunct professor of higher education, Baruch College Univ. City of New York 1977-1989; Teachers College, Columbia Univ., 1990. Village of Larchmont, N.Y., trustee, 1977-79; mayor, 1980-84. Board of trustees, American Bible Society, 1984-; Religious Education Ass'n., treasurer, 1975-80 & chairperson, 1981-84; Laymen's Nat'l. Bible Association, chmn. education committee, 1983-93; Will Rogers Institute, chmn. Health education committee, 1980-; Director, William J. Donovan Memorial Foundation, 1995-.

QUIGLEY, WILLIAM J.
Executive. b. New York, NY, July 6, 1951. e. Wesleyan U., B.A., 1973; Columbia U., M.S., 1983. From 1973 to 1974 was advt. circulation mgr. for Quigley Publishing Co. Taught school in Kenya in 1974; returned to U.S. to join Grey Advt. as media planner. 1975 joined Walter Reade Organization as asst. film buyer; promoted to head film buyer in 1977. Named v.p., 1982. In 1986 joined Vestron, Inc. as sr. v.p. to establish Vestron Pictures. Named pres., Vestron Pictures, 1987-89. In 1990 joined Fair Lanes Entertainment, Inc. as v.p. mktg. 1993, joined United Artists Theatre as sr. v.p., marketing & new business.
PICTURES: *Exec. prod.*: Steel Dawn, The Dead, Salome's Last Dance, The Unholy, Waxwork, Burning Secret, The Lair of the White Worm, Paint It Black, The Rainbow, Twister.

QUINLAN, KATHLEEN
Actress. b. Pasadena, CA, Nov. 19, 1954. Played small role in film, One Is a Lonely Number, while in high school.
THEATER: Taken in Marriage (NY Public Theatre; Theatre World Award), Uncommon Women and Others, Accent on Youth (Long Wharf, CT), Les Liaisons Dangereuses.
PICTURES: One Is a Lonely Number (debut, 1972), American Graffiti, Lifeguard, Airport '77, I Never Promised You a Rose Garden, The Promise, The Runner Stumbles, Sunday Lovers, Hanky Panky, Independence Day, Twilight Zone—The Movie, The Last Winter, Warning Sign, Wild Thing, Man Outside, Sunset, Clara's Heart, The Doors, Trial by Jury, Apollo 13.
TELEVISION: *Movies*: Can Ellen Be Saved?, Lucas Tanner (pilot), Where Have All the People Gone?, The Missing Are Deadly, The Abduction of St. Anne, Turning Point of Jim Malloy, Little Ladies of the Night, She's in the Army Now, When She Says No, Blackout, Children of the Night, Dreams Lost Dreams Found, Trapped, The Operation, Strays, An American Story, Stolen Babies, Last Light, Perfect Alibi.

QUINN, AIDAN
Actor. b. Chicago, IL, March 8, 1959. Raised in Rockwell, IL, also spent time in Ireland as a boy and following high sch. graduation. Returned to Chicago at 19, worked as tar roofer before debuting on Chicago stage in The Man in 605, followed by Scheherazade, The Irish Hebrew Lesson, Hamlet.
THEATER: Fool for Love (off-B'way debut), A Lie of the Mind, A Streetcar Named Desire (Theatre World Award).
PICTURES: Reckless (debut, 1984), Desperately Seeking Susan, The Mission, Stakeout, Crusoe, The Handmaid's Tale, The Lemon Sisters, Avalon, At Play in the Fields of the Lord, The Playboys, Benny & Joon, Blink, Mary Shelley's Frankenstein, Legends of the Fall, The Stars Fell on Henrietta, Haunted, Looking for Richard, Michael Collins.
TELEVISION: *Special*: All My Sons. *Movies*: An Early Frost, Perfect Witness, Lies of the Twins, A Private Matter.

QUINN, ANTHONY
Actor. b. Chihuahua, Mexico, Apr. 21, 1915. Came to U.S. as child. Brief stage work before bit roles in films. Autobiographies: The Original Sin (1972), One Man Tango (1995).
THEATER: *B'way*: A Streetcar Named Desire, Beckett, Zorba.
PICTURES: Parole (debut, 1936), Daughter of Shanghai, Last Train From Madrid, Partners in Crime, The Plainsman, Swing High Swing Low, Waikiki Wedding, The Buccaneer (1938),

Bulldog Drummond in Africa, Dangerous to Know, Hunted Men, King of Alcatraz, Tip-Off Girls, Island of Lost Men, King of Chinatown, Television Spy, Union Pacific, City for Conquest, Emergency Squad, Ghost Breakers, Parole Fixer, Road to Singapore, Blood and Sand, Bullets for O'Hara, Knockout, Manpower, The Perfect Snob, Texas Rangers Ride Again, They Died With Their Boots On, Thieves Fall Out, The Black Swan, Larceny Inc., Road to Morocco, Guadalcanal Diary, The Ox-Bow Incident, Buffalo Bill, Irish Eyes Are Smiling, Roger Touhy Gangster, Ladies of Washington, China Sky, Back to Bataan, Where Do We Go From Here?, California, Imperfect Lady, Sinbad the Sailor, Black Gold, Tycoon, The Brave Bulls, Mask of the Avenger, Viva Zapata! (Academy Award for Best Supporting Actor, 1952), The Brigand, The World in His Arms, Against All Flags, Ride Vaquero, City Beneath the Sea, Seminole, Blowing Wild, East of Sumatra, Long Wait, Magnificent Matador, Ulysses, Naked Street, Seven Cities of Gold, La Strada, Attila the Hun, Lust for Life (Academy Award for Best Supporting Actor, 1956), Wild Party, Man from Del Rio, The Hunchback of Notre Dame, Ride Back, The River's Edge, Wild is the Wind, The Buccaneer (1958; dir. only), Hot Spell, Black Orchid, Last Train From Gun Hill, Warlock, Portrait in Black, Heller in Pink Tights, Savage Innocents, The Guns of Navarone, Barabbas, Requiem for a Heavyweight, Lawrence of Arabia, Behold a Pale Horse, The Visit, Zorba the Greek (also assoc. prod.), High Wind in Jamaica, Marco the Magnificent, Lost Command, The 25th Hour, The Happening, Guns for San Sebastian, The Rover, The Magus, Shoes of the Fisherman, The Secret of Santa Vittoria, A Dream of Kings, A Walk in the Spring Rain, R.P.M., Flap, Across 110th Street (also exec. prod.), Deaf Smith and Johnny Ears, The Don Is Dead, The Destructors, The Inheritance, The Con Artists, Mohammad: Messenger of God, The Greek Tycoon, Caravans, The Passage, Lion of the Desert, High Risk, The Salamander, A Man of Passion, Stradivarius, Revenge, Ghosts Can't Do It, A Star for Two, Only the Lonely, Jungle Fever, Mobsters, Last Action Hero, Somebody to Love, A Walk in the Clouds.
TELEVISION: Much dramatic work in the early 1950s. *Series*: The City, American Playwrights Theater (host). *Movies*: Jesus of Nazareth, Treasure Island (Italian TV), Onassis: The Richest Man in the World, The Old Man and the Sea, This Can't Be Love, Hercules and the Amazon Women, Hercules and the Lost Kingdom, Hercules and the Circle of Fire, Gotti.

R

RABE, DAVID WILLIAM
Writer. b. Dubuque, IA, March 10, 1940. m. actress Jill Clayburgh. e. Loras Coll.
THEATER: The Basic Training of Pavlo Hummel (Obie Award, 1971), Sticks and Bones (Tony Award, 1971), The Orphan, In the Boom Boom Room, Streamers, Hurlyburly, Those the River Keeps.
PICTURES: I'm Dancing As Fast As I Can (also exec. prod.), Streamers, Casualties of War, State of Grace.
TELEVISION: *Special*: Sticks and Bones.

RABINOVITZ, JASON
Executive. b. Boston, MA, e. Harvard Coll., B.A. where elected to Phi Beta Kappa. Following WWII service as military intelligence captain with paratroops, took M.B.A. at Harvard Business Sch., 1948. Started in industry in 1949 as asst. to secty.-treas., United Paramount Theatres. Asst. controller, ABC, 1953; adm. v.p., ABC-TV, 1956; joined MGM as asst. treas., 1957; named MGM-TV gen. mgr.; director of business & financial affairs, 1958; treas. & chief financial officer, MGM, Inc., 1963; financial v.p. & chief financial officer, 1967. 1971 named exec. v.p. & dir. Encyclopedia Britannica Education Corp.; sr. v.p., American Film Theatre, 1974-75. Rejoined MGM as v.p./exec. asst. to the pres., 1976. Elected v.p. finance, 1979; promoted to sr. v.p., finance & corporate admin., MGM Film Co. & UA Prods. Resigned, 1984. Now film & TV consultant and indep. producer. Dir., Pacific Rim Entertainment, 1993-95.

RADIN, PAUL
Producer. b. New York, NY, Sept. 15, 1913. e. NYU. After college went in adv. Became v.p. in chg. of m.p. div. of Buchanan & Co. During WWII posted in Middle East as film chief for Office of War Information for that area. On return to U.S. assigned by Buchanan to ad campaign for Howard Hughes' The Outlaw. Turned to talent mgr., joining the Sam Jaffe Agency. Then joined Ashley-Famous Agency. Became exec. prod. for Yul Brynner's indep. prod. co. based in Switzerland, with whom made such films as The Journey, Once More with Feeling, Surprise Package.
PICTURES: Born Free, Living Free, Phase IV, The Blue Bird, The Ghost and the Darkness.
TELEVISION: The Incredible Journey of Dr. Meg Laurel, The Ordeal of Dr. Mudd, Crime of Innocence. *Series*: Born Free, The Wizard.

RADNITZ, ROBERT B.
Producer. b. Great Neck, NY, Aug. 9, 1924. e. U. of VA. Taught 2 years at U. of VA, then became reader for Harold Clurman; wrote several RKO This Is America scripts, then to Broadway where co-prod. The Frogs of Spring; prod. The Young and the Beautiful; to Hollywood working at United Artists, then as story consultant to Buddy Adler, head of prod., 20th Century-Fox, 1957-58. V.P., Producer Guild of America, 1982, 1984, 1985; bd. member, Producers Branch, AMPAS, last 4 yrs. First producer with retrospective at Museum of Modern Art, and first producer honored by joint resolution of both houses of Congress for his work, 1973. Pres. Robert B. Radnitz Productions, Ltd.
PICTURES: *Producer:* A Dog of Flanders (debut, 1960; first U.S. film to win Golden Lion Award at Venice Film Fest.), Misty, Island of the Blue Dolphins, And Now Miguel, My Side of the Mountain, The Little Ark, Sounder (Acad. Award nom.), Where the Lilies Bloom, Birch Interval, Sounder 2, A Hero Ain't Nothin' But a Sandwich, Cross Creek.
TELEVISION: Mary White (Emmy & Christopher Awards), Never Forget (ACE Award nom.).

RAFELSON, BOB
Producer, Director, Writer. b. New York, NY, Feb. 21, 1933. e. Dartmouth, B.A. (philosophy). Left NY in teens to ride in rodeos in AZ. Worked on cruise ship, then played drums and bass with jazz combos in Acapulco. 1953 won Frost Natl. Playwriting competition. Dir. his award-winning play at Hanover Experimental Theatre, N.H. After Army Service did program promotion for a radio station, was advisor for Shochiku Films, Japan, then hired by David Susskind to read scripts for Talent Assocs. Writer-assoc. prod., DuPont Show of the Month and Play of the Week (also script sprv.). Joined Screen Gems in California, developing program ideas for Jackie Cooper, then head of TV prod. arm of Columbia. Later formed BBS Productions with Burt Schneider and Steve Blauner. Appeared as actor in 1985 film Always.
PICTURES: *Co-Prod.* only: Easy Rider, The Last Picture Show, Drive He Said. *Director:* Head (debut, 1968; also co-prod., co-s.p.), Five Easy Pieces (also co-prod., co-story; Acad. Award noms. for picture & writing), The King of Marvin Gardens (also prod., co-s.p.), Stay Hungry (also co-prod., co-s.p.), The Postman Always Rings Twice (also co-prod.), Black Widow, Mountains of the Moon (also co-s.p.), Man Trouble.
TELEVISION: *Series:* The Monkees (1966-68, creator, writer, dir.; Emmy Award, 1967), Adapted 34 prods., Play of the Week. *Dir. music video:* All Night Long, with Lionel Ritchie.

RAFFERTY, FRANCES
Actress. b. Sioux City, IA, June 26, 1922. e. U. of California, premedical student UCLA. TV series, December Bride, Pete and Gladys.
PICTURES: Seven Sweethearts, Private Miss Jones, Girl Crazy, War Against Mrs. Hadley, Thousands Cheer, Dragon Seed, Honest Thief, Mrs. Parkington, Barbary Coast Gent, Hidden Eye, Abbott and Costello in Hollywood, Adventures of Don Coyote, Money Madness, Lady at Midnight, Old Fashioned Girl, Rodeo, Shanghai Story, Wings of Chance.

RAFFIN, DEBORAH
Actress. b. Los Angeles, CA, March 13, 1953. m. producer Michael Viner. Mother is actress Trudy Marshall. e. Valley Coll. Was active fashion model before turning to acting when discovered by Ted Witzer. Author: Sharing Christmas (Vols. I & II). Debut in 40 Carats (1973). Publisher Dove Books On Tape. Head of Dove Films, prod. co.
PICTURES: 40 Carats (debut, 1973), The Dove, Once Is Not Enough, God Told Me To (Demon), Assault on Paradise (Maniac!), The Sentinel, Touched by Love, Dance of the Dwarfs (Jungle Heat), Death Wish 3, Claudia, Scanners II, Morning Glory (also co-s.p.).
TELEVISION: *Series:* Foul Play. *Movies:* A Nightmare in Badham County, Ski Lift to Death, How to Pick Up Girls, Willa, Mind Over Murder, Haywire, For the Love of It, Killing at Hell's Gate, For Lovers Only, Running Out, Sparkling Cyanide, Threesome, The Sands of Time, A Perry Mason Mystery: The Case of the Grimacing Governor. *Mini-Series:* The Last Convertible, James Clavell's Noble House, Windmills of the Gods (also co-prod.). *Guest:* B.L. Stryker.

RAGLAND, ROBERT OLIVER
Composer. b. Chicago, IL, July 3, 1931. e. Northwestern U., American Conservatory of Music, Vienna Acad. of Music. Professional pianist at Chicago nightclubs. In U.S. Navy; on discharge joined Dorsey Bros. Orchestra as arranger. On sls. staff at NBC-TV, Chicago. 1970, moved to Hollywood to become composer for movies; has scored 67 feature films plus many TV movies and series segments. Has also written some 45 original songs.
PICTURES: The Touch of Melissa, The Yin and Yang of Mr. Go, The Thing with Two Heads, Project: Kill, Abby, Seven Alone, The Eyes of Dr. Chaney, Return to Macon County, The Daring Dobermans, Shark's Treasure, Grizzly, Pony Express Rider, Mansion of the Doomed, Mountain Family Robinson, Only Once in a Lifetime, Jaguar Lives, The Glove, Lovely But Deadly, "Q", The Day of the Assassin, A Time To Die, The Winged Serpent, Trial by Terror, The Guardian, Ten to Midnight, Dirty Rebel, Hysterical, Brainwaves, Where's Willie?, The Supernaturals, Nightstick, Messenger of Death, The Fifth Monkey, No Place to Hide, The Buffalo Soldiers, The Raffle, Morty, Crime and Punishment.
TELEVISION: Photoplay's Stars of Tomorrow, Wonder Woman, Barnaby Jones, Streets of San Francisco, High Ice, The Girl on the Edge of Town, The Guardian, etc.

RAILSBACK, STEVE
Actor. b. Dallas, TX, 1948. Studied with Lee Strasberg. On stage in Orpheus Descending, This Property Is Condemned, Cherry Orchard, Skin of Our Teeth, etc.
PICTURES: The Visitors, Cockfighter, Angela, The Stunt Man, Deadly Games, Turkey Shoot, The Golden Seal, Torchlight, Lifeforce, Armed and Dangerous, Blue Monkey, The Wind, Distortions, Deadly Intent, Alligator II: The Mutation, After-Shock, Private Wars, Forever, Calendar Girl, Nukie, Save Me.
TELEVISION: *Movies:* Helter Skelter, Good Cops Bad Cops, The Forgotten, Spearfield's Daughter, Sunstroke, Bonds of Love, Separated by Murder. *Mini-Series:* From Here to Eternity.

RAIMI, SAM
Director, Writer, Producer, Actor. b. Royal Oak, MI, Oct. 23, 1959. e. Michigan St. Univ. Formed Renaissance Pictures, Inc.
PICTURES: *Dir./Writer:* The Evil Dead, Crimewave, Evil Dead II, Darkman, Army of Darkness, The Quick and the Dead (dir. only). *Co-Producer:* Hard Target, Timecop. *Actor:* Spies Like Us, Thou Shalt Not Kill... Except, Maniac Cop, Miller's Crossing, Innocent Blood, Indian Summer, Intruder, The Hudsucker Proxy (also co-writer), The Flintstones.
TELEVISION: *Movies:* Journey to the Center of the Earth (actor), Mantis (prod., writer), Body Bags (actor), The Stand (actor). *Series:* American Gothic (exec. prod.).

RAJSKI, PEGGY
Producer. b. Stevens Point, WI. e. Univ. of Wisconsin. m. actor Josh Mostel. Began film career as prod. manager on John Sayles film Lianna, before becoming producer. Prod. of Bruce Springsteen music videos, incld. Glory Days which won American Video Award. Received 1994 Academy Award for short film Trevor.
PICTURES: The Brother From Another Planet, Matewan, Eight Men Out, The Grifters, Little Man Tate, Used People, Home for the Holidays.

RAKSIN, DAVID
Composer. b. Philadelphia, PA, Aug. 4, 1912. e. U. of Pennsylvania, studied music with Isadore Freed and Arnold Schoenberg. Composer for films, ballet, dramatic and musical comedy, stage, radio and TV, symphony orchestra and chamber ensembles. Arranger of music of Chaplin film, Modern Times; pres. Composers and Lyricists Guild of America, 1962-70; animated films include Madeline and The Unicorn in the Garden (UPA). Professor of Music and Urban Semester, U. of Southern California. Coolidge Commission from the Library of Congress: Oedipus Memneitai (Oedipus Remembers) for bass/baritone, 6-part chorus and chamber orchestra premiered there under dir. of composer, Oct. 1986. Pres., Society for the Preservation of Film Music, 1992. Recipient of ASCAP Golden Score Award for Career Achievement, 1992. Elected to ASCAP bd. of dirs., 1995.
PICTURES: Laura, Secret Life of Walter Mitty, Smoky, Force of Evil, Across the Wide Missouri, Carrie, Bad and the Beautiful, Apache, Suddenly, Big Combo, Jubal, Hilda Crane, Separate Tables, Al Capone, Night Tide, Too-Late Blues, Best of the Bolshoi (music for visual interludes), Two Weeks in Another Town, The Redeemer, Invitation to a Gunfighter, Sylvia, A Big Hand for the Little Lady, Will Penny, Glass Houses, What's the Matter With Helen?
TELEVISION: *Series:* Five Fingers, Life With Father, Father of the Bride, Ben Casey, Breaking Point. *Specials:* Journey, Tender is the Night, Prayer of the Ages, Report from America, The Olympics (CBC), The Day After, Lady in a Corner.

RALPH, SHERYL LEE
Actress. b. Waterbury, CT, Dec. 30, 1956. e. Rutgers U. Studied with Negro Ensemble Company in NYC.
THEATER: *NY:* Reggae, Dreamgirls. *LA:* Identical Twins From Baltimore.
PICTURES: A Piece of the Action (debut, 1977), Oliver and Company (voice), The Mighty Quinn, Skin Deep, To Sleep With Anger, Mistress, The Distinguished Gentleman, Sister Act 2: Back in the Habit, The Flintstones, White Man's Burden, Bogus.
TELEVISION: *Series:* Code Name: Foxfire, Search for Tomorrow, It's a Living, Designing Women, George. *Movies:* The Neighborhood, Sister Margaret and the Saturday Night Ladies, Luck of the Draw: The Gambler Returns, No Child of Mine. *Specials:* Happy Birthday Hollywood, Voices That Care, Story of a People: The Black Road to Hollywood (host).

RAMIS, HAROLD
Writer, Director, Actor, Producer. b. Chicago, IL, Nov. 21, 1944. e. Washington U., St. Louis. Assoc. ed. Playboy Mag. 1968-70; writer, actor, Second City, Chicago 1970-73; National Lampoon Radio Show, 1974-75.
PICTURES: National Lampoon's Animal House (co-s.p.), Meatballs (co-s.p.), Caddyshack (co-s.p., dir.), Stripes (co-s.p., actor), Heavy Metal (voice), National Lampoon's Vacation (dir.), Ghostbusters (co-s.p., actor), Back to School (co-s.p., exec. prod.), Club Paradise (co-s.p., dir.), Armed and Dangerous (exec. prod., co-s.p.), Baby Boom (actor), Caddyshack II (co-s.p.), Stealing Home (actor), Ghostbusters II (co-s.p., actor), Rover Dangerfield (co-story), Groundhog Day (dir., co-s.p., co-prod., actor), Airheads (actor), Love Affair (actor), Stuart Saves His Family (dir.), Multiplicity (dir., co-prod.).
TELEVISION: *Series*: SCTV (head writer, performer, 1976-78), Rodney Dangerfield Show (head writer, prod.). *Special*: Will Rogers—Look Back and Laugh (exec. prod.).

RAMPLING, CHARLOTTE
Actress. b. Sturmer, England, Feb. 5, 1946. e. Jeanne D'Arc Academie pour Jeune Filles, Versailles; St. Hilda's, Bushey, England.
PICTURES: The Knack... and How to Get It (debut, 1965), Rotten to the Core, Georgy Girl, The Long Duel, Sequestro di Persona (Island of Crime), The Damned, Target: Harry (How to Make It), Three, The Ski Bum, Corky, Addio Fratello Crrudele (Tis Pity She's a Whore), Asylum, The Night Porter, Giordano Bruno, Zardoz, Caravan to Vaccares, La Chair de L'orchidee, Farewell My Lovely, Foxtrot (The Other Side of Paradise), Yuppi-Du, Orca, Purple Taxi, Stardust Memories, The Verdict, Viva La Vie, Tristesse et Beaute, On ne Meurt que deux Fois (He Died With His Eyes Open), Angel Heart, Mascara, D.O.A., Max My Love, Rebus, Paris By Night, Helmut Newton: Frames from the Edge (doc.), Hammers Over the Anvil, Time is Money, Invasion of Privacy, Asphalt Tango.
TELEVISION: *BBC Series*: The Six Wives of Henry VIII, The Superlative Seven, The Avengers. *Movies*: Sherlock Holmes in New York, Mystery of Cader Iscom, The Fantasists, What's in it for Henry, Zinotchka, Infidelities, La Femme Abandonnee, Radetzky March, Murder In Mind, Samson Le Maqnifique, La Dernière Fête.

RAND, HAROLD
Executive. b. New York, NY, Aug. 25, 1928. e. Long Island U., B.S., 1948-50; CCNY, 1945-46. U.S. Army 1946-48; ent. m.p. ind. 1950, pub. dept. 20th-Fox; variety of posts incl. writer, trade press, newspaper contacts; joined Walt Disney's Buena Vista pub. mgr., 1957; pub. mgr. Paramount Pictures, 1959; formed own pub. rel. firm, 1961; dir. of pub. Embassy Picture Corp. 1962; dir. of world pub. 20th Century Fox 1962; resigned 1963; dir. of adv. & pub., Landau Co., 1963; dir. world pub., Embassy Pictures, 1964; est. Harold Rand & Co., Inc., 1966, pres. of p.r. & mktg. firm. Appt. mktg., dir., Kaufman Astoria Studios, 1984; elected v.p., 1985.

RANDALL, TONY
Actor. r.n. Leonard Rosenberg. b. Tulsa, OK, Feb. 26, 1920. e. Northwestern U. Prof. N.Y. debut as actor in Circle of Chalk; U.S. Army 1942-46; radio actor on many shows. Founder/Artistic Director of National Actors Theatre in NYC, 1991.
THEATER: Candida, The Corn is Green, Antony & Cleopatra, Caesar & Cleopatra, Inherit the Wind, Oh Men! Oh Women!, Oh Captain, The Sea Gull, The Master Builder, M. Butterfly, A Little Hotel on the Side, Three Men on a Horse, The Government Inspector, The Odd Couple (tour).
PICTURES: Oh Men! Oh Women! (debut, 1957), Will Success Spoil Rock Hunter?, No Down Payment, The Mating Game, Pillow Talk, The Adventures of Huckleberry Finn, Let's Make Love, Lover Come Back, Boys' Night Out, Island of Love, The Brass Bottle, 7 Faces of Dr. Lao, Send Me No Flowers, Fluffy, The Alphabet Murders, Bang Bang You're Dead, Hello Down There, Everything You Always Wanted to Know About Sex* But Were Afraid to Ask, Scavenger Hunt, Foolin' Around, The King of Comedy, My Little Pony (voice), It Had to Be You, That's Adequate, Gremlins 2: The New Batch (voice), Fatal Instinct.
TELEVISION: *Series*: One Man's Family, Mr. Peepers, The Odd Couple (Emmy Award, 1975), The Tony Randall Show, Love Sidney. *Guest*: TV Playhouse, Max Liebman Spectaculars, Sid Caesar, Dinah Shore, Playhouse 90, Walt Disney World Celebrity Circus. *Movies*: Kate Bliss and the Ticker Tape Kid, Sidney Shorr: A Girl's Best Friend, Off Sides, Hitler's SS: Portrait in Evil, Sunday Drive, Save the Dog!, The Odd Couple: Together Again.

RANSOHOFF, MARTIN
Executive. b. New Orleans, LA, 1927. e. Colgate U., 1949. Adv., Young & Rubicam, 1948-49; slsmn, writer, dir., Gravel Films, 1951; formed own co., Filmways, 1952; industrial films, commercials; formed Filmways TV Prods., Filmways, Inc.,

Filmways of Calif.; bd. chmn. Filmways, Inc. Resigned from Filmways in 1972 and formed own independent motion picture and television production company.
PICTURES: Boys' Night Out, The Wheeler Dealers, The Americanization of Emily, The Loved One, The Sandpiper, The Cincinnati Kid, The Fearless Vampire Killers, Don't Make Waves, Ice Station Zebra, Castle Keep, Hamlet (exec. prod.), Catch-22, The Moonshine War, King Lear, See No Evil, 10 Rillington Place, Fuzz, Save The Tiger, The White Dawn, Silver Streak (exec. prod.), Nightwing, The Wanderers, The Mountain Men, A Change of Seasons, American Pop, Hanky Panky, Class, Jagged Edge, The Big Town, Switching Channels, Physical Evidence, Welcome Home, Guilty as Sin.
TELEVISION: *Series*: Mister Ed, The Beverly Hillbillies, Petticoat Junction, Green Acres, The Addams Family.

RAPAPORT, MICHAEL
Actor. b. New York, NY, 1970. Started as stand-up comic appearing at Improv in LA before becoming actor.
PICTURES: Zebrahead, Point of No Return, Poetic Justice, Money for Nothing, True Romance, The Scout, Higher Learning, The Basketball Diaries, Kiss of Death, Mighty Aphrodite, The Pallbearer, A Brother's Kiss.

RAPHAEL, FREDERIC
Writer. b. Chicago, IL, Aug. 14, 1931. e. Charterhouse, St. John's Coll., Cambridge.
AUTHOR: The Earlsdon Way, The Limits of Love, A Wild Surmise, The Graduate Wife, The Trouble With England, Lindmann, Orchestra and Beginners, Like Men Betrayed, Who Were You With Last Night?, April June and November, Richard's Things, California Time, The Glittering Prizes, Sleeps Six & Other Stories, Oxbridge Blues & Other Stories, Heaven & Earth, Think of England and other stories, After the War, A Double Life, The Latin Lover and other stories, Old Scores. Biographies: Somerset Maugham and His World, Byron. Translations: (with Kenneth McLeish), Poems of Catullus The Oresteia. Essays: Cracks in the Ice, Of Gods and Men.
THEATER: From the Greek (1979), An Early Life.
PICTURES: Nothing But the Best, Darling (Academy Award, 1965), Two for the Road, Far from the Madding Crowd, A Severed Head, Daisy Miller, Richard's Things.
TELEVISION: The Glittering Prizes (Royal TV Society Writer Award 1976), Rogue Male, School Play, Something's Wrong, Best of Friends, Richard's Things, Oxbridge Blues (ACE Award, best writer), After the War, Byrow, The Man in the Brooks Brothers Shirt (also dir.; ACE Award best picture).

RAPHEL, DAVID
Executive. b. Boulogne-Seine, France, Jan. 9, 1925. e. university in France. Entered m.p. ind. as asst. to sales mgr. in France, 20th-Fox, 1950-51; asst. mgr. in Italy, 1951-54; mgr. in Holland, 1954-57; asst. to European mgr. in Paris, 1957-59; European mgr. for TV activities in Paris, 1959-61; Continental mgr. in Paris, 1961-64, transferred to NY as v.p. in chg. of intl. sales, 1964; named pres., 20th Century-Fox International, 1973. 1975, also appointed sr. v.p., worldwide marketing, feature film division, for 20th-Fox, (L.A.). 1976, joined ICM, appointed dir. general of ICM (Europe) headquartered in Paris. 1979 elected pres. ICM (L.A.) 1980, formed Cambridge Film Group Ltd.

RAPPER, IRVING
Director. b. London, Eng., Jan. 16, 1904. Stage prod. London: Five Star Final, Grand Hotel. NY: The Animal Kingdom, The Firebird, The Late Christopher Bean.
PICTURES: Shining Victory (debut, 1941), One Foot in Heaven, The Gay Sisters, Now Voyager, The Adventures of Mark Twain, Rhapsody in Blue, The Corn Is Green, Deception, The Voice of the Turtle, Anna Lucasta, The Glass Menagerie, Another Man's Poison, Forever Female, Bad for Each Other, The Brave One, Strange Intruder, Marjorie Morningstar, The Miracle, Joseph and His Brethren, Pontius Pilate, The Christine Jorgensen Story, Born Again, Justus.

RAPPOPORT, GERALD J.
Executive, Film Producer. b. New York, NY, Aug. 25, 1925. e. NYU. U.S. Marine Corps. Pres., Major Artists Representatives Corp., 1954-58; dir. of Coast Sound Services, Hollywood; 1959-61, pres., International Film Exchange Ltd.; 1960-91, CEO of IFEX Int'l; 1991-94, pres. CIFEX Corporation.

RASHAD, PHYLICIA
Actress-singer. b. Houston, TX, June 19, 1948. m. sportscaster Ahmad Rashad. Sister of Debbie Allen. e. Howard U., B.F.A., magna cum laude, 1970. NY School of Ballet. Acted under maiden name of Phylicia Ayers-Allen. Recording, Josephine Superstar (1979). Conceived (with Michael Peters) and appeared in revue Phylicia Rashad & Co. in 1989 in Las Vegas.
THEATER: Ain't Supposed to Die a Natural Death, The Duplex, The Cherry Orchard, The Wiz, Weep Not For Me, Zooman and the Sign, In an Upstate Motel, Zora, Dreamgirls, Sons and Fathers of Sons, Puppetplay, A Raisin in the Sun, Into the Woods, Jelly's Last Jam.

PICTURE: Once Upon A Time...When We Were Colored.
TELEVISION: *Series*: One Life to Live, The Cosby Show (People's Choice Award, NAACP Image Award, Emmy nom.), Cosby. *Movies*: Uncle Tom's Cabin, False Witness, Polly, Polly—Comin' Home!, Jailbirds, David's Mother, The Possession of Michael D. *Specials*: Nell Carter—Never Too Old to Dream, Superstars and Their Moms, Our Kids and the Best of Everything, The Debbie Allen Special, Hallelujah.

RATHER, DAN
News Correspondent, Anchor. b. Wharton, TX, Oct. 31, 1931. e. Sam Houston State Teachers Coll., BA journalism, 1953. Instructor there for 1 year. Graduate e.: U. of Houston Law School, S. Texas School of Law. Worked for UPI and Houston Chronicle. Radio: KSAM, Huntsville, KTRH, Houston. Joined CBS News in 1962 as chief of southwest bureau in Dallas. Transferred to overseas burs. (including chief of London Bureau 1965-66), then Vietnam before returning as White House corr. 1966. White House Correspondent, 1964-74. Covered top news events, from Democratic and Republican national conventions to President Nixon's trip to Europe (1970) and to Peking and Moscow (1972). Anchored CBS Reports, 1974-75. Presently co-editor of 60 minutes (since 1975) and anchors Dan Rather Reporting on CBS Radio Network (since 1977). Anchor for 48 Hours, 1988. Winner of numerous awards, including 5 Emmys. Anchorman on CBS-TV Evening News, 1981-. Books: The Palace Guard (1974); The Camera Never Blinks (1977); I Remember (1991); The Camera Never Blinks Twice (1994); Mark Sullivan's Our Times (editor, 1995).

RAUCHER, HERMAN
Writer. b. Apr. 13, 1928. e. NYU. Author of novels Watermelon Man, Summer of '42 and Ode to Billy Joe, adapted to films by him. Other novels inc. A Glimpse of Tiger, There Should Have Been Castles, Maynard's House.
PICTURES: Sweet November, Can Hieronymous Merkin Ever Forget Mercy Humppe and Find True Happiness?, Watermelon Man, Summer of '42, Class of '44, Ode to Billy Joe, The Other Side of Midnight.
TELEVISION: Studio One, Alcoa Hour, Goodyear Playhouse, Matinee Theatre, Remember When? (movie).

RAVETCH, IRVING
Writer, Producer. b. Newark, NJ, Nov. 14, 1920. e. UCLA. m. Harriet Frank, with whom he often collaborated.
PICTURES: *Writer*: Living in a Big Way, The Outriders, Vengeance Valley, Ten Wanted Men, The Long Hot Summer, The Sound and the Fury, Home from the Hill, The Dark at the Top of the Stairs, Hud (also co-prod.), Hombre (also co-prod.), The Reivers (also prod.), House of Cards (as James P. Bonner), The Cowboys, Conrack, Norma Rae, Murphy's Romance, Stanley and Iris.

RAYBURN, GENE
Performer, b. Christopher, IL, Dec. 22, 1917. e. Knox Coll., Galesburg, IL. NBC guide; with many radio stations in Baltimore, Philadelphia, NY; US Army Air Force, 1942-45; Rayburn and Finch Show, WNEW, NY, 1945-52; Gene Rayburn Show, NBC radio; TV shows: Many appearances as host-humorist on game shows, variety shows, drama shows. Also acted in summer stock; AFTRA, past pres. NY local; trustee on H&R Board for over 25 years.
THEATER: B'way: Bye Bye Birdie, Come Blow Your Horn.
TELEVISION: *Series*: The Name's the Same, Tonight (second banana), Make the Connection, The Steve Allen Show, The Steve Lawrence/Eydie Gorme Show (announcer), The Match Game, Dough Re Mi, The Sky's the Limit, Choose Up Sides, Tic Tac Dough, Play Your Hunch, Snap Judgment, Amateur's Guide to Love. *Guest*: The Love Boat, Fantasy Island.

RAYMOND, PAULA
Actress. r.n. Paula Ramona Wright, b. San Francisco, CA., Nov. 23, 1925. e. San Francisco Jr. Coll. Grad. Started career in little theatre groups, concerts, recitals, San Francisco; leading stage roles in Ah! Wilderness, Peter Pan, etc.; also sang lead coloratura rules in Madame Butterfly, Aidia, Rigoletto, Faust, etc.; ballerina with S.F. Opera Ballet; classical pianist; model, Meade-Maddick Photographers.
PICTURES: Racing Luck (debut, 1948), Rusty Leads the Way, Blondie's Secret, East Side West Side, Challenge of the Range, Adam's Rib, Devil's Doorway, Sons of New Mexico, Duchess of Idaho, Crisis, Grounds For Marriage, Inside Straight, The Tall Target, Texas Carnival, The Sellout, Bandits of Corsica, City That Never Sleeps, The Beast from 20,000 Fathoms, The Human Jungle, King Richard & the Crusaders, The Gun That Won the West, Hand of Death, The Flight That Disappeared, The Spy With My Face, Blood of Dracula's Castle, Five Bloody Graves.
TELEVISION: *Guest*: Perry Mason, 77 Sunset Strip, Wyatt Earp, Man from U.N.C.L.E., Maverick, The Untouchables, Bachelor Father, Bat Masterson, Temple Houston, Peter Gunn, many others.

RAYNOR, LYNN S.
Producer, Production Executive. b. Chicago, IL, Feb. 11, 1940. Produced West Coast premiere of The Balcony by Genet, The Crawling Arnold Review by Feiffer. Joined Television Enterprises, 1965; Commonwealth United, 1968 as business affairs exec. later prod. spvr. 1972 opened London branch of the Vidtronics Co. 1974, formed Paragon Entertainment & RAH Records. 1980-95, prod. of TV Movies and Mini-Series. Prod. & editor of 12 minute tv vignettes, A Hall of Fame Story.
PICTURE: Freejack.
TELEVISION: *Special*: Waiting for Godot. *Movies*: Marilyn: The Untold Story, The Execution, A Winner Never Quits, On Wings of Eagles, Stranger in My Bed, Hands of a Stranger, The High Price of Passion, The Kennedys of Massachusetts, Common Ground, Face of Love, The Rape of Doctor Willis, Quiet Killer, Love Honor & Obey: The Last Mafia Marriage, Tony & Nancy: The Inside Story, Tecumseh: The Last Warrior. *Series*: Camp Wilderness. *Pilot*: Murphy's Law.

REA, STEPHEN
Actor. b. Belfast, Northern Ireland, Oct. 31, 1948. e. Queens Univ. (BA in English Lit.). Started acting at Abbey Theatre in Dublin. Joined the Field Day Theatre Co. in 1980 in Londonderry, acting in or directing most of their productions. Also acted with Royal Natl. Theatre.
THEATER: Playboy of the Western World, Comedians, High Society, Endgame, Freedom of the City, Someone Who'll Watch Over Me (also B'way; Theatre World Award, Tony nom.).
PICTURES: Danny Boy (Angel), Loose Connections, The Company of Wolves, The Doctor and the Devils, The House, Life Is Sweet, The Crying Game (Acad. Award nom.), Bad Behavior, Angie, Princess Caraboo, Ready to Wear (Pret-a-Porter), Between the Devil and the Deep Blue Sea, Interview With A Vampire, All Men Are Mortal, Michael Collins, Last of the High Kings.
TELEVISION: Shadow of a Gunman, Fugitive, I Didn't Know You Cared, Professional Foul, The Seagull, Out of Town Boys, Calbe Williams, Joyce in June, The House, Four Days in July, Shergar, Scout, Lost Belongings, The Big Gamble, Not With a Bang, Saint Oscar, Hedda Gabler, Citizen X, Crime of the Century.

REAGAN, RONALD
Actor, Politician. b. Tampico, IL, Feb. 6, 1911. e. high school, Eureka Coll. m. former actress Nancy Davis. Wrote weekly sports column for a Des Moines, IA newspaper; broadcast sporting events. Signed as actor by Warner Bros. in 1937. In WWII 1942-45, capt., USAAF. Actor until 1966. Served as Governor, California, 1967-74. Businessman and rancher. Elected President of the United States, 1980. Re-elected, 1984. Autobiography: Where's the Rest of Me? (1965).
PICTURES: Love Is On the Air (debut, 1937), Hollywood Hotel, Sergeant Murphy, Swing Your Lady, Brother Rat, Going Places, Accidents Will Happen, Cowboy from Brooklyn, Boy Meets Girl, Girls on Probation, Dark Victory, Naughty but Nice, Hell's Kitchen, Code of the Secret Service, Smashing the Money Ring, Angels Wash Their Faces, Brother Rat and a Baby, Murder in the Air, Tugboat Annie Sails Again, Knute Rockne—All American, Santa Fe Trail, Angel From Texas, Nine Lives Are Not Enough, The Bad Man, International Squadron, Million Dollar Baby, Kings Row, Juke Girl, Desperate Journey, This Is the Army, Stallion Road, That Hagen Girl, The Voice of the Turtle, Night Unto Night, John Loves Mary, The Girl From Jones Beach, It's a Great Feeling (cameo), The Hasty Heart, Louisa, Storm Warning, The Last Outpost, Bedtime for Bonzo, Hong Kong, She's Working Her Way Through College, The Winning Team, Tropic Zone, Law & Order, Prisoner of War, Cattle Queen of Montana, Tennessee's Partner, Hellcats of the Navy, The Young Doctors (narrator), The Killers.
TELEVISION: *Series*: The Orchid Award (emcee), General Electric Theater (host, frequent star), Death Valley Days (host). *Guest*: Ford Theratre, Schlitz Playhouse of Stars, Lux Video Theatre, Startime.

REARDON, BARRY
Executive. b. Hartford, CT, Mar. 8, 1931. e. Holy Cross Col., Trinity Col. Began industry career with Paramount Pictures; named v.p.; left to join General Cinema Theatres Corp. as sr. v.p. Now with Warner Bros. as pres. of domestic distribution co.

REASON, REX
Actor. b. Berlin, Germany, Nov. 30, 1928. e. Hoover H.S., Glendale, CA. Worked at various jobs; studied dramatics at Pasadena Playhouse.
PICTURES: Storm Over Tibet, Salome, Mission Over Korea, Taza Son of Cochise, This Island Earth, Smoke Signal, Lady Godiva, Kiss of Fire, Creature Walks Among Us, Raw Edge, The Rawhide Trail, Under Fire, Thundering Jets, The Sad Horse, Yankee Pasha, Band of Angels, Miracle of the Hills.
TELEVISION: *Series*: Man Without a Gun, Roaring Twenties.

REDDY, HELEN
Singer. b. Melbourne, Australia, Oct. 25, 1942. Parents were producer-writer-actor Max Reddy and actress Stella Lamond. e. in Australia. Began career at age four as singer and had appeared in hundreds of stage and radio roles with parents by age of 15. Came to New York in 1966, subsequently played nightclubs, appeared on TV. First single hit record: I Don't Know How To Love Him (Capitol). Grammy Award, 1973, as best female singer of year for I Am Woman. Most Played Artist by the music operators of America: American Music Award 1974; Los Angeles Times Woman of the Year (1975); No. 1 Female Vocalist in 1975 and 1976; Record World, Cash Box and Billboard; named one of the Most Exciting Women in the World by International Bachelor's Society, 1976. Heads prod. co. Helen Reddy, Inc.
THEATER: B'way: Blood Brothers.
PICTURES: Airport 1975 (debut), Pete's Dragon.
TELEVISION: Series: The Helen Reddy Show (Summer, 1973), Permanent host of Midnight Special. Appearances: David Frost Show, Flip Wilson Show, Mike Douglas Show, Tonight Show, Mac Davis Show, Merv Griffin Show (guest host), Sesame Street, Live in Australia (host, 1988); Muppet Show, Home for Easter.

REDFORD, ROBERT
Actor, Director, Producer. b. Santa Monica, CA, Aug. 18, 1937. r.n. Charles Robert Redford. Attended U. of Colorado; left to travel in Europe, 1957. Attended Pratt Inst. and American Acad. of Dramatic Arts. Founded Sundance Film Institute, Park City, Utah, workshop for young filmmakers.
THEATER: B'way: Tall Story (walk on), The Highest Tree, Sunday in New York (Theatre World Award), Barefoot in the Park.
PICTURES: Actor: War Hunt (debut, 1962), Situation Hopeless But Not Serious, Inside Daisy Clover, The Chase, This Property is Condemned, Barefoot in the Park, Downhill Racer (also exec. prod.), Butch Cassidy and the Sundance Kid, Tell Them Willie Boy is Here, Little Fauss and Big Halsy, The Hot Rock, The Candidate (also co-exec. prod.), Jeremiah Johnson, The Way We Were, The Sting (Acad. Award nom.), The Great Gatsby, The Great Waldo Pepper, Three Days of the Condor, All The President's Men (also exec. prod.), A Bridge Too Far, The Electric Horseman, Brubaker, The Natural, Out of Africa, Legal Eagles, Havana, Sneakers, Indecent Proposal, Up Close and Personal. Exec. Producer: Promised Land, Some Girls, Yosemite: The Fate of Heaven (also narrator), The Dark Wind, Incident at Oglala (also narrator), Strawberry & Chocolate (presenter). Director: Ordinary People (Academy Award, 1980), The Milagro Beanfield War (also co-prod.), A River Runs Through It (also prod., narrator), Quiz Show (also prod.; NY Film Critics Award for Best Picture; Acad. Award noms. for picture & dir.).
TELEVISION: Guest: Maverick, Playhouse 90, Play of the Week (The Iceman Cometh), Alfred Hitchcock Presents, Route 66, Twilight Zone, Dr. Kildare, The Untouchables, The Virginian, The Defenders.

REDGRAVE, CORIN
Actor. b. London, England, July 16, 1939. e. Cambridge. p. late Sir Michael Redgrave and Rachel Kempson. Brother of Vanessa and Lynn Redgrave.
THEATER: On stage with England Stage Co.: A Midsummer Night's Dream, Chips with Everything. RSC: Lady Windermere's Fan, Julius Caesar, Comedy of Errors, Antony and Cleopatra. Young Vic: Rosmersholm.
PICTURES: A Man for All Seasons, The Deadly Affair, Charge of the Light Brigade, The Magus, Oh What a Lovely War, When Eight Bells Toll, Serail, Excalibur, Eureka, Between Wars, The Fool, In the Name of the Father, Four Weddings and a Funeral, Persuasion.
TELEVISION: I Berlioz, Measure for Measure, Persuasion, Henry IV, Circle of Deceit.

REDGRAVE, LYNN
Actress. b. London, England, Mar. 8, 1943. Sister of Vanessa and Corin Redgrave. p. late Sir Michael Redgrave and Rachel Kempson. m. dir.-actor-manager John Clark. Ent. m.p. and TV industries, 1962.
THEATER: NY: Black Comedy (B'way debut), My Fat Friend (1974), Mrs. Warren's Profession, Knock Knock, Misalliance, St. Joan, Twelfth Night (Amer. Shakespeare Fest), Sister Mary Ignatius Explains It All For You, Aren't We All?, Sweet Sue, A Little Hotel on the Side, The Master Builder, Shakespeare for My Father (also writer). LA: Les Liaisons Dangereuses.
PICTURES: Tom Jones (debut, 1963), Girl With Green Eyes, Georgy Girl (Acad. Award nom.), The Deadly Affair, Smashing Time, The Virgin Soldiers, Last of the Mobile Hot-Shots, Los Guerilleros (Killer From Yuma), Viva la Muerta—Tua! (Don't Turn the Other Cheek), Every Little Crook and Nanny, Everything You Always Wanted to Know About Sex* But Were Afraid to Ask, The National Health, The Happy Hooker, The Big Bus, Sunday Lovers, Morgan Stewart's Coming Home, Midnight, Getting It Right, Shine.

TELEVISION: BBC: Pretty Polly, Ain't Afraid to Dance, The End of the Tunnel, I Am Osango, What's Wrong with Humpty Dumpty, Egg On the Face of the Tiger, Blank Pages, A Midsummer Night's Dream, Pygmalion, William, Vienna 1900, Daft as a Brush, Not For Women Only, Calling the Shots. United States: Co-host: A.M. America. Movies: Turn of the Screw, Sooner or Later, Beggarman Thief, Gauguin the Savage, Seduction of Miss Leona, Rehearsal for Murder, The Bad Seed, My Two Loves, Jury Duty: The Comedy, What Ever Happened to Baby Jane? Mini-Series: Centennial. Series: House Calls, Teachers Only, Chicken Soup. Guest: The Muppet Show, Walking on Air, Candid Camera Christmas Special, Woman Alone, Tales From the Hollywood Hills: The Old Reliable, Death of a Son.

REDGRAVE, VANESSA
O.B.E. Actress. b. London, England, Jan. 30, 1937. p. Sir Michael Redgrave and Rachel Kempson. Sister of Lynn and Corin Redgrave. Mother of actresses Joely and Natasha Richardson. Early career with Royal Shakespeare Company. Appeared in documentary Tonight Let's All Make Love in London. Autobiography, 1994.
THEATER: Daniel Deronda, Cato Street, The Threepenny Opera, Twelfth Night, As You Like It, The Taming of the Shrew, Cymbeline, The Sea Gull, The Prime of Miss Jean Brodie, Antony & Cleopatra, Design for Living, Macbeth, Lady from the Sea, The Aspern Papers, Ghosts, Anthony and Cleopatra, Tomorrow Was War, A Touch of the Poet, Orpheus Descending, Madhouse in Goa, The Three Sisters, When She Danced, Maybe, Heartbreak House, Vita & Virginia.
PICTURES: Behind the Mask (debut, 1958), Morgan!: A Suitable Case for Treatment (Acad. Award nom.), A Man for All Seasons, Blow-Up, The Sailor From Gibraltar, Red and Blue, Camelot, The Charge of the Light Brigade, Isadora (Acad. Award nom.), Oh! What a Lovely War, The Sea Gull, A Quiet Place in the Country, Drop Out, The Trojan Women, La Vacanza, The Devils, Mary—Queen of Scots (Acad. Award nom.), Murder on the Orient Express, Out of Season, The Seven Percent Solution, Julia (Academy Award, best supporting actress, 1977), Agatha, Yanks, Bear Island, The Bostonians (Acad. Award nom.), Steaming, Wetherby, Prick Up Your Ears, Consuming Passions, Comrades, The Ballad of the Sad Cafe, Romeo-Juliet (voice), Howards End (Acad. Award nom.), Breath of Life, Sparrow, The House of the Spirits, Crime and Punishment, Mother's Boys, Great Moments in Aviation, Little Odessa, A Month by the Lake.
TELEVISION: Movies/Specials: A Farewell to Arms, Katherine Mansfield, Playing for Time (Emmy Award, 1981), My Body My Child, Wagner (theatrical in Europe), Three Sovereigns for Sarah, Peter the Great, Second Serve, A Man For All Seasons, Orpheus Descending, Young Catherine, What Ever Happened to Baby Jane?, They, Down Came a Blackbird. Guest: Faerie Tale Theatre (Snow White and the 7 Dwarfs).

REDSTONE, EDWARD S.
Exhibitor. b. Boston, MA, May 8, 1928. e. Colgate U., B.A., 1949; Harvard Grad. Sch. of Bus. Admin., M.B.A., 1952. v.p., treas., Northeast Drive-In Theatre Corp.; v.p., Theatre Owners of New England, 1962; chmn., advis. coms., mem. bd. dirs., TOA; gen. conven. chmn., joint convention TOA & NAC, 1962; pres. National Assn. of Concessionaires, 1963; chief barker. Variety Club of New England, 1963; pres., Theatre Owners of New England; gen. chmn., 35th annual reg. convention.

REDSTONE, SUMNER MURRAY
Entertainment Corporation Executive, Lawyer; b. Boston, MA, May 27, 1923. e. Harvard, B.A., 1944, LLB., 1947. Served to 1st Lt. AUS, 1943-45. Admitted to MA Bar 1947; U.S. Ct. Appeals 1st Circuit 1948, 8th Circuit 1950, 9th Circuit 1948; D.C. 1951; U.S. Supreme Ct. 1952; law sec. U.S. Ct. Appeals for 9th Circuit 1947-48; instr. U. San Francisco Law Sch. and Labor Management Sch., 1947; special asst. to U.S. Atty. General, 1948-51; partner firm Ford Bergson Adams Borkland & Redstone, Washington, D.C. 1951-54; exec. v.p. Northeast Drive-In Theatre Corp., 1954-68; pres. Northeast Theatre Corp.; chmn. bd., pres. & CEO, National Amusements, Inc.; chmn. bd., Viacom Int'l, Inc., 1987; asst. pres. Theatre Owners of America, 1960-63; pres. 1964-65; bd. chmn, National Assoc. of Theatre Owners, 1965-66. Member: Presidential Advisory Committee John F. Kennedy Center for the Performing Arts; chmn. Jimmy Fund, Boston 1960; chmn., met. div. Combined Jewish Philanthropies 1963; sponsor Boston Museum of Science; Trustee Children's Cancer Research Foundation; Art Lending Library; bd. of dirs. of TV Acad. of Arts and Sciences Fund; bd. dirs. Boston Arts Festival; v.p., exec. committee Will Rogers Memorial Fund; bd. overseers Dana Farber Cancer Institute; corp. New England Medical Center; Motion Picture Pioneers; bd. mem. John F. Kennedy Library Foundation; 1984-85; 1985-86 State Crusade Chairman American Cancer Society; Board of Overseers Boston Museum of Fine Arts; Professor, Boston U. Law Sch. 1982-83, 1985-86; Boston Latin School's Graduate of the Year, 1989; Acquired Viacom in 1987 which purchased

Paramount Communications in 1993. Member of exec. committe of the National Assoc. of Theatre Owners. Member, exec. bd., Combined Jewish Philanthropies. Judge of Kennedy Library Foundation. Founding trustee, American Cancer Society.
AWARDS: (Entertainment related) include: Communicator of the Year B'nai B'rith Communications, Cinema Lodge 1980; Man of the Year, Entertainment Industries div.; UJA-Federation, NY, 1988; Variety of New England Humanitarian Award, 1989; Motion Picture Pioneers Pioneer of the Year, 1991; Golden Plate Award American Acad. Achievement 32nd Annual Salute to Excellence Program; 1994, Man of the Year Award from MIPCOM, the Int'l Film and Programme Market for TV Video Cable and Satellite; 1995, Variety Club International Humanitarian Award; Hall of Fame Award, Broadcast & Cable Magazine, 1995.

REED, OLIVER

Actor. b. Wimbledon, England, Feb. 13, 1938. Nephew of late British dir. Sir Carol Reed. Dropped out of school in teens and worked as bouncer, boxer, taxi driver before first break on BBC-TV series The Golden Spur. Film debut as extra in Value for Money.
PICTURES: Value for Money (debut, 1955), Hello London, The Square Peg, The Captain's Table, Beat Girl (Wild for Kicks), The League of Gentlemen, The Angry Silence, The Two Faces of Dr. Jekyll (House of Fright), Sword of Sherwood Forest, His and Hers, No Love for Johnnie, The Bulldog Breed, The Rebel (Call Me Genius), Curse of the Werewolf, The Pirates of Blood River, Captain Clegg (Night Creatures), These Are the Damned, The Party's Over, The Scarlet Blade, Paranoic, The System (The Girl-Getters), The Brigand of Kandahar, The Trap, The Jokers, The Shuttered Room, I'll Never Forget What's 'is Name, Oliver!, The Assassination Bureau, Hannibal Brooks, Women in Love, Take a Girl Like You, The Lady in the Car with Glasses and a Gun, The Hunting Party, The Devils, Z.P.G., Sitting Target, Triple Echo, One Russian Summer, Dirty Weekend, Revolver (Blood in the Streets), Blue Blood, The Three Musketeers, Tommy, The Four Musketeers, Lisztomania (cameo), Ten Little Indians, Royal Flash, Sell Out, Blood in the Streets, Burnt Offerings, The Great Scout and Cathouse Thursday, Assault on Paradise (Ransom), Tomorrow Never Comes, Crossed Swords (The Prince and the Pauper), The Big Sleep, The Class of Miss MacMichael, Touch of the Sun, Dr. Heckyl & Mr. Hype, The Brood, Lion of the Desert, Condorman, Venom, The Great Question, Spasms, The Sting II, 99 Women, Two of a Kind, Black Arrow, Gor, Captive, Castaway, Dragonard, Fair Trade, The Return of the Musketeers, Hold My Hand I'm Dying, Fire With Fire, The Misfit Brigade, Rage to Kill, Skeleton Coast, Damnation Express, Captive Rage, The Adventures of Baron Munchausen, The Fall of the House of Usher, Master of Dragonard Hill, Outlaws, The Pit and the Pendulum, Panama, Severed Ties, Funny Bones.
TELEVISION: The Lady and the Highwayman, Treasure Island, A Ghost in Monte Carlo, Prisoner of Honor, Army, Return to Lonesome Dove.

REED, PAMELA

Actress. b. Tacoma, WA, Apr. 2, 1953. Ran day-care center and worked with Head Start children before studying drama at U. of Washington. Worked on Trans-Alaska pipeline. Off-Broadway showcases.
THEATER: Curse of the Starving Class (Off-B'way debut, 1978), All's Well That Ends Well (Central Park), Getting Out (Drama Desk Award), Aunt Dan and Lemon, Fools, The November People (Broadway debut), Sorrows of Stephen, Mrs. Warren's Profession, Getting Through the Night, Best Little Whorehouse in Texas, Fen, Standing on My Knees, Elektra.
PICTURES: The Long Riders (debut, 1980), Melvin and Howard, Eyewitness, Young Doctors in Love, The Right Stuff, The Goodbye People, The Best of Times, Clan of the Cave Bear, Rachel River, Chattahoochee, Cadillac Man, Kindergarten Cop, Passed Away, Bob Roberts, Junior.
TELEVISION: Series: The Andros Targets (TV debut, 1977), Grand, Family Album, The Home Court. Movies: Inmates—A Love Story, I Want To Live, Heart of Steel, Scandal Sheet, Caroline?, Woman With a Past, Born Too Soon, Deadly Whispers, The Man Next Door. Special: Tanner '88. Mini-Series: Hemingway. Guest: L.A. Law, The Simpsons (voice).

REES, ROGER

Actor. b. Aberystwyth, Wales, May 5, 1944. e. Camberwell Sch. of Art, Slade Sch. of Fine Art. Stage debut Hindle Wakes (Wimbledon, U.K., 1964). With Royal Shakespeare Co. from 1967. Starred in the title role The Adventures of Nicholas Nickleby (London and NY, Tony Award), also on stage in Hapgood (London, L.A.), Indiscretions (NY). Off-B'way in The End of the Day. Assoc. dir. Bristol Old Vic Theatre Co., 1986-present. Playwright with Eric Elice of Double Double and Elephant Manse.
PICTURES: Star 80 (debut, 1983), Keine Storung Bitte, Mountains of the Moon, If Looks Could Kill, Stop! Or My Mom Will Shoot, Robin Hood: Men in Tights, Sudden Manhattan.

TELEVISION: Movies: A Christmas Carol (released theatrically in Europe), Place of Peace, Under Western Eyes, Bouquet of Barbed Wire, Saigon: The Year of the Cat, Imaginary Friends, The Adventures of Nicolas Nickleby, The Comedy of Errors, Macbeth, The Voysey Inheritance, The Ebony Tower, The Finding, The Return of Sam McCloud, Charles & Diana: Unhappily Ever After, The Tower, The Possession of Michael D. Series: Cheers, Singles, M.A.N.T.I.S.

REESE, DELLA

Actress, Singer. b. Detroit, MI, July 6, 1932. r.n. Deloreese Patricia Early. e. Wayne St. Univ. As teen toured with Mahalia Jackson. Began recording in 1950's. Hit songs include Don't You Know.
PICTURES: Let's Rock!, Psychic Killer, Harlem Nights, The Distinguished Gentleman, A Thin Line Between Love and Hate.
TELEVISION: Series: The Della Reese Show, Chico and the Man, It Takes Two, Charlie & Company, The Royal Family, Touched by an Angel. Guest: The Ed Sullivan Show, Sanford and Son, The Rookies, McCloud, Welcome Back Kotter, The Love Boat, Night Court, The A-Team. Movies: The Voyage of the Yes, Twice in a Lifetime, The Return of Joe Forrester, Nightmare in Badham County. Mini-Series: Roots: The Next Generations.

REEVE, CHRISTOPHER

Actor. b. New York, NY, Sept. 25, 1952. e. Cornell U., B.A.; graduate work at Juilliard. Stage debut at McCarter Theatre in Princeton at age 9. B'way debut with Katharine Hepburn in A Matter of Gravity.
THEATER: NY: A Matter of Gravity, My Life, Fifth of July, The Marriage of Figaro, A Winter's Tale, Love Letters. LA: Summer and Smoke. Williamstown: The Front Page, Mesmer, Richard Corey, Royal Family, The Seagull, The Greeks, Holiday, Camino Real, John Brown's Body, Death Takes a Holiday, The Guardsman. Regional: The Irregular Verb to Love, Beggar's Opera, Troilus and Cressida, The Love Cure. London debut: The Aspern Papers.
PICTURES: Gray Lady Down (debut, 1978), Superman, Somewhere in Time, Superman II, Deathtrap, Monsignor, Superman III, The Bostonians, The Aviator, Street Smart, Superman IV: The Quest for Peace (also co-story), Switching Channels, Noises Off, Morning Glory, The Remains of the Day, Above Suspicion, Speechless, Village of the Damned.
TELEVISION: Series: Love of Life. Mini-Series: Kidnapped. Movies: Anna Karenina, The Great Escape II: The Untold Story, The Rose and the Jackal, Bump in the Night, Death Dreams, Mortal Sins, Nightmare in the Daylight, The Sea Wolf, Black Fox. Specials: Faerie Tale Theatre (Sleeping Beauty), The Last Ferry Home, Earth and the American Dream. Guest: Tales From the Crypt.

REEVES, KEANU

Actor. b. Beirut, Lebanon, Sept. 2, 1964. Lived in Australia and NY before family settled in Toronto. e. studied at Toronto's High School for the Performing Arts, then continued training at Second City Workshop. Made Coca-Cola commercial at 16. At 18 studied at Hedgerow Theatre in PA for summer. Professional debut on Hanging In, CBC local Toronto TV show. Toronto stage debut in Wolf Boy; later on stage in Romeo and Juliet, Hamlet.
PICTURES: Youngblood (debut, 1986), River's Edge, The Night Before, Permanent Record, The Prince of Pennsylvania, Dangerous Liaisons, Bill and Ted's Excellent Adventure, Parenthood, I Love You to Death, Tune in Tomorrow, Point Break, Bill and Ted's Bogus Journey, My Own Private Idaho, Bram Stoker's Dracula, Much Ado About Nothing, Freaked (cameo), Even Cowgirls Get the Blues, Little Buddha, Speed, Johnny Mnemonic, A Walk in the Clouds, Chain Reaction, Feeling Minnesota.
TELEVISION: Movies: Act of Vengeance, Under the Influence, Brotherhood of Justice, Babes In Toyland. Specials: I Wish I Were Eighteen Again, Life Under Water. Guest: The Tracey Ullman Show.

REEVES, STEVE

Actor. b. Glasgow, MT, Jan. 21, 1926. Delivered newspapers before winning body building titles Mr. Pacific, Mr. America, Mr. World, Mr. Universe. On stage in Kismet, The Vamp, Wish You Were Here.
PICTURES: Athena (debut, 1954), The Hidden Face, Jail Bait, Hercules, Hercules Unchained, Goliath and the Barbarians, The White Warrior, The Giant of Marathon, Morgan the Pirate, Thief of Baghdad, The Last Days of Pompeii, Duel of the Titans, The Trojan Horse, The Avenger (The Last Glories of Troy), The Slave (Son of Spartacus), The Shortest Day, Sandokan the Great, A Long Ride From Hell.

REHME, ROBERT G.

Executive. b. Cincinnati, OH, May 5, 1935. e. U. of Cincinnati. 1953, mgr., RKO Theatres, Inc., Cincinnati; 1961, adv. mgr., Cincinnati Theatre Co.; 1966, dir. of field adv., United Artists Pictures; 1969, named dir. of pub. and field adv./promotion,

Paramount Pictures; 1972, pres., BR Theatres and v.p., April Fools Films, gen. mgr. Tri-State Theatre Service; 1976, v.p. & gen. sls. mgr., New World Pictures; 1978, joined Avco Embassy Pictures as sr. v.p. & COO, then named exec. v.p.; 1979, named pres., Avco Embassy Pictures, Inc.; 1981, joined Universal Pictures as pres. of distrib. & marketing; 1982, named pres. of Universal Pictures; 1983, joined New World Pictures as co-chmn. & CEO; elected pres., Academy Foundation, 1988; pres. Foundation of Motion Picture Pioneers, 1989; 1st v.p., AMPAS; 1989, partner, Neufeld/Rehme prods. at Paramount; 1992, pres. of Academy of Motion Picture Arts & Sciences.
PICTURES: Patriot Games, Necessary Roughness, Gettysburg, Beverly Hills Cop III, Clear and Present Danger.

REID, BERYL
O.B.E. Actress. b. Hereford, England, June 17, 1920. Career in radio before London stage debut in revue, After the Show, 1951. Also on stage in The Killing of Sister George (London, NY, Tony Award), Spring Awakening, Campiello, Born in the Gardens, etc.
PICTURES: The Belles of St. Trinian's, The Extra Day, Trial and Error (The Dock Brief), Two-Way Stretch, Inspector Clouseau, Star!, The Killing of Sister George, The Assassination Bureau, Entertaining Mr. Sloane, The Beast in the Cellar, Dr. Phibes Rises Again, Psychomania, Father Dear Father, No Sex Please We're British, Joseph Andrews, Carry on Emmanuelle, Yellowbeard, The Doctor and the Devils, Didn't You Kill My Brother?
TELEVISION: Series: Educating Archie (BBC, 1952-56), Beryl Reid Says Good Evening, The Secret Diary of Adrian Mole. Mini-Series: Tinker Tailor Soldier Spy, Smiley's People. Movie: Duel of Hearts. Numerous specials.

REID, TIM
Actor. b. Norfolk, CA, Dec. 19, 1944. m. actress Daphne Maxwell. Started as half of comedy team of Tim and Tom in 1969, before becoming solo stand-up comedian. Published photo/poetry collection As I Find It, 1982.
PICTURES: Dead Bang, The Fourth War, Once Upon A Time...When We Were Colored.
TELEVISION: Series: Easy Does It... Starring Frankie Avalon, The Marilyn McCoo and Billy Davis Jr. Show, The Richard Pryor Show, WKRP in Cincinnati, Teachers Only, Simon and Simon, Frank's Place (also co-exec. prod.), Snoops (also co-exec. prod.). Guest: That's My Mama, Rhoda, What's Happening, Matlock. Movies: Perry Mason: The Case of the Silenced Singer, Stephen King's IT, Race to Freedom: The Underground Railroad (also co-exec. prod.), Simon & Simon: In Trouble Again. Special: Mastergate.

REILLY, CHARLES NELSON
Actor, Director. b. New York, NY, Jan. 13, 1931. e. U. of CT. On Broadway mostly in comedy roles before turning to TV and films. Recently directed stage plays.
THEATER: As actor: Bye Bye Birdie (debut), How to Succeed in Business Without Really Trying (Tony Award, 1962), Hello Dolly!, Skyscraper, God's Favorite. Acted in 22 off-B'way plays. Founded musical comedy dept. HB Studios. Conceived and dir.: The Belle of Amherst, Paul Robeson, The Nerd (dir.). Resident dir.: Burt Reynolds' Jupiter Theatre.
PICTURES: A Face in the Crowd, Two Tickets to Paris, The Tiger Makes Out, Cannonball Run II, Body Slam, All Dogs Go to Heaven (voice), Rock-a-Doodle (voice), A Troll in Central Park (voice).
TELEVISION: Series: The Steve Lawrence Show, The Ghost and Mrs. Muir, Dean Martin Presents The Golddiggers, Liddsville, Arnie, It Pays to Be Ignorant (1973-74), Match Game P.M., Sweethearts (game show host). Guest: Tonight Show (guest host), Dean Martin Show. Movies: Call Her Mom, The Three Kings, Bandit, Bandit Goes Country. Special: Wind in the Wire.

REILLY, MICHAEL
Executive. Pres., Variety Clubs International.

REINAUER, RICHARD
Executive. b. Chicago, IL, April 28, 1926. e. U. of Illinois, grad. 1952. Prod., dir., freelance, 1952-59; bus. mgr., asst. prod., Showcase Theatre Evanston, 1952; prod., dir., NBC, Chicago, 1953-55; film dir., Kling Studios, 1956; broadcast supvis. Foote Cone & Belding, 1956-59; dir., radio, TV & m.p., American Medical Assoc., 1959-64; pres., Communications Counselors, 1963-64; exec. dir., TV Arts & Sciences Foundation, 1964; pres., Acad. of TV Arts & Sciences, Chicago Chapter, 1970-72; assoc. prod. & asst. dir. Wild Kingdom & asst. to pres., Don Meier Prods., 1965-1988. Member: Illinois Nature Preserve Commission. Lifetime member: Acad. of TV Arts & Sciences, Pres. Pinewood Prods. Film Co. Communications consultant and advisor.

REINER, CARL
Actor, Director, Writer, Producer. b. New York, NY, March 20, 1922. Son is actor-director-writer Rob Reiner. Comedian on

B'way: Call Me Mr., Inside U.S.A., Alive and Kicking. Author (novels): Enter Laughing, All Kinds of Love, Continue Laughing. Playwright: Something Different.
PICTURES: Actor only: Happy Anniversary, Gidget Goes Hawaiian, It's a Mad Mad Mad Mad World, The Russians Are Coming the Russians Are Coming, Don't Worry We'll Think of a Title, A Guide for the Married Man, Generation, The End, The Spirit of '76. Writer-Actor: The Gazebo, The Thrill of It All (also co-prod.), The Art of Love. Director: Enter Laughing (also co-s.p.), The Comic (also s.p., actor), Where's Poppa?, Oh God! (also actor), The One and Only, The Jerk (also actor), Dead Men Don't Wear Plaid (also co-s.p., actor), The Man With Two Brains (also co-s.p.), All of Me, Summer Rental, Summer School (also actor), Bert Rigby You're a Fool (also s.p.), Sibling Rivalry, Fatal Instinct (also actor).
TELEVISION: Series: The Fashion Story, The Fifty-Fourth Street Revue, Eddie Condon's Floor Show, Your Show of Shows (also writer), Droodles (panelist), Caesar's Hour (also writer; 2 Emmy Awards for supporting actor, 1956, 1957), Sid Caesar Invites You, Keep Talking, Dinah Shore Chevy Show (writer), Take a Good Look (panelist), The Dick Van Dyke Show (also creator-prod.-dir.-writer; 5 Emmy Awards: writing: 1962, 1963, 1964, producing: 1965, 1966), Art Linkletter Show, The Celebrity Game (host), The New Dick Van Dyke Show (creator-prod.-writer), Good Heavens (also exec. prod.), Sunday Best (host). Movies: Medical Story, Skokie. Guest: Comedy Spot, Judy Garland Show, Burke's Law, That Girl, Night Gallery, Faerie Tale Theatre (Pinocchio), It's Garry Shandling's Show, Mad About You (Emmy Award, 1995). Special: The Sid Caesar-Imogene Coca-Carl Reiner-Howard Morris Special (Emmy Award for writing, 1967).
RECORDINGS: Carl Reiner and Mel Brooks, The 2000 Year Old Man, The 2001 Year Old Man, 2013 Year Old Man, Continue Laughing, A Connecticut Yankee in King Arthur's Court, Miracle on 34th Street, Jack and the Beanstalk, Aesop's Fables.

REINER, ROB
Actor, Director, Writer. b. New York, NY, March 6, 1947. Father is actor-writer-director-producer Carl Reiner. Worked as actor with regional theatres and improvisational comedy troupes. Wrote for the Smothers Brothers Comedy Hour. Breakthrough as actor came in 1971 when signed by Norman Lear for All in the Family. Directorial debut with This Is Spinal Tap, 1984. Co-founder of Castle Rock Entertainment.
PICTURES: Actor: Enter Laughing, Halls of Anger, Where's Poppa?, Summertree, Fire Sale, Throw Momma From the Train, Postcards From the Edge, The Spirit of '76, Sleepless in Seattle, Bullets Over Broadway, Mixed Nuts, Bye Bye Love. Director: This is Spinal Tap (also actor, co-s.p.), The Sure Thing, Stand by Me, The Princess Bride. Dir./Co-Prod.: When Harry Met Sally..., Misery, A Few Good Men (Acad. Award nom. for best picture; DGA nom.), North, The American President, Ghosts of Mississippi.
TELEVISION: Series: All in the Family (2 Emmy Awards: 1974, 1978), Free Country (also co-writer), Morton & Hayes (also co-creator, co-exec. prod.). Movies: Thursday's Game, More Than Friends (also co-writer, co-exec. prod.), Million Dollar Infield (also co-prod., co-writer). Guest: Gomer Pyle, Batman, Beverly Hillbillies, Room 222, Partridge Family, Odd Couple, It's Garry Shandling's Show. Special: But... Seriously (exec. prod.).

REINHOLD, JUDGE
Actor. b. Wilmington, DE, May 21, 1957. r.n. Edward Ernest Reinhold Jr. e. Mary Washington Coll., North Carolina Sch. of Arts. Acted in regional theatres including Burt Reynolds dinner theater in FL before signed to TV contract at Paramount.
PICTURES: Running Scared (debut, 1979), Stripes, Pandemonium, Fast Times at Ridgemont High, Lords of Discipline, Roadhouse 66, Gremlins, Beverly Hills Cop, Head Office, Off Beat, Ruthless People, Beverly Hills Cop II, Vice Versa, Rosalie Goes Shopping, Daddy's Dyin', Enid is Sleeping (Over Her Dead Body), Zandalee, Near Misses, Baby on Board, Bank Robber, Beverly Hills Cop III, The Santa Clause.
TELEVISION: Series: Secret Service Guy. Movies: Survival of Dana, A Matter of Sex, Promised a Miracle, Black Magic, Four Eyes and Six-Guns, Dad the Angel and Me, As Good as Dead, The Wharf Rat. Guest: Seinfeld. Specials: A Step Too Slow, The Willmar Eight, The Parallax Garden.

REISENBACH, SANFORD E.
Executive. e. NYU. Associated with Grey Advertising for 20 years; exec. v.p. and pres. of Grey's leisure/entertainment division in N.Y. In August, 1979, joined Warner Bros. as exec. v.p. in chg. of worldwide adv. & pub.; named pres., worldwide adv. & pub., 1985. Appt. exec. v.p. of marketing and planning, Warner Bros. Inc., 1988.

REISER, PAUL
Actor. b. New York, NY, Mar. 30, 1957. e. SUNY/Binghamton. Started performing as a stand-up comic in such clubs as Catch a Rising Star, the Improv, and the Comic Strip. Author: Couplehood (1994).

PICTURES: Diner (debut, 1982), Beverly Hills Cop, Aliens, Beverly Hills Cop II, Cross My Heart, Crazy People, The Marrying Man, Mr. Write, Bye Bye Love.
TELEVISION: Series: My Two Dads, Mad About You. Special: Paul Reiser—Out on a Whim. Guest: The Tonight Show, Late Night With David Letterman. Movies: Sunset Limousine, The Tower. Pilots: Diner, Just Married.

REISNER, ALLEN
Director. b. New York, NY.
PICTURES: The Day They Gave the Babies Away, St. Louis Blues, All Mine to Give.
TELEVISION: Movies/Specials: Captain and the Kings, Mary Jane Harper Cried Last Night, Your Money or Your Wife, To Die in Paris, The Clift, Skag, They're Playing Our Song, The Gentleman From Seventh Avenue, Escape of Pierre Mendes-France, Deliverance of Sister Cecelia, The Sound of Silence. Series: Murder She Wrote, Twilight Zone, Hardcastle & McCormick, Airwolf, The Mississippi, Hawaii Five-O, Blacke's Magic, Law and Harry McGraw, Playhouse 90, Studio One, Climax, United States Steel Hour, Suspense, Danger, etc.

REISS, JEFFREY C.
Executive. b. Brooklyn, NY, April 14, 1942. e. Washington U., St. Louis, B.A., 1963. Consultant at NYU and Manhattanville Coll. and instructor at Brooklyn Coll. before entering industry. Agent in literary dept. for General Artists Corp., 1966. Supervised development in NY of Tandem Prods. for Norman Lear, 1968. Produced off-B'way plays 1968-70. Dir. of program acquistion devel. for Cartridge TV, Inc. (mfg. of first home video cassette players-recorders), 1970-73. Joined ABC Entertainment as director of network feature films, 1973-75. Founder and pres., Showtime Pay TV Network, 1976-80. Co-founder, pres. & CEO, Cable Health Network, 1981-83. 1983, named vice chmn. & CEO, Lifetime Cable Network following Cable Health Network merger with Daytime. Chmn. of the board, pres. & CEO, Reiss Media Enterprises, Inc. 1984. Founder & chmn. of board, Request Television (pay-per-view svc.), 1985.

REISS, STUART A.
Set Decorator. b. Chicago, IL, July 15, 1921. e. L.A. High Sch., 1939. Property man, 20th-Fox, 1939-42; U.S. Army Air Corps, 1942-45; joined 20th-Fox as set decorator in 1945. Worked on over 30 tv shows and over 100 motion pictures, receiving 6 Academy Award noms. and 2 Oscars.
PICTURES: Titanic, How to Marry a Millionaire, Hell and High Water, There's No Business Like Show Business, Soldier of Fortune, The Seven Year Itch, Man in the Grey Flannel Suit, Teen Age Rebel, The Diary of Anne Frank (Academy Award, 1959), What a Way to Go, Fantastic Voyage (Academy Award, 1966), Doctor Doolittle, Oh God!, The Swarm, Beyond the Poseidon Adventure, Carbon Copy, All the Marbles, The Man Who Loved Women, Micki and Maude, A Fine Mess.

REITMAN, IVAN
Director, Producer. b. Komarno, Czechoslovakia, Oct. 26, 1946. Moved to Canada at age 4. e. McMaster U. Attended National Film Board's Summer Institute directing three short films including Orientation (1968) which received theatrical distribution. Produced Canadian TV show in 1970s with Dan Aykroyd as announcer.
THEATER: Prod.: The National Lampoon Show, The Magic Show, Merlin (also dir.).
PICTURES: Dir./Prod.: Foxy Lady (debut, 1971; also edit., music), Cannibal Girls, Meatballs (dir. only), Stripes, Ghostbusters, Legal Eagles (also co-story), Twins, Ghostbusters II, Kindergarten Cop, Dave, Junior. Prod. only: Columbus of Sex, They Came From Within (Shivers), Death Weekend (The House By the Lake), Rabid (co-exec. prod.), Blackout, National Lampoon's Animal House, Heavy Metal, Spacehunter: Adventures in the Forbidden Zone (exec. prod.), Big Shots (exec. prod.), Casual Sex? (exec. prod.), Feds (exec. prod.), Stop! Or My Mom Will Shoot, Beethoven (exec. prod.), Beethoven's 2nd (exec. prod.).
TELEVISION: Series: Delta House.

RELPH, MICHAEL
Producer, Director, Writer, Designer. 1942, became art dir. Ealing Studios then assoc. prod. to Michael Balcon on The Captive Heart, Frieda, Kind Hearts and Coronets, Saraband (also designed). Oscar nom.). 1948 appt. producer and formed prod/dir. partnership Basil Dearden (until 1972). 1971-76, Governor, Brit. Film Institute. Chairman BFI Prod. Board. Chairman Film Prod. Assoc. of G.B.; member Films Council.
PICTURES: For Ealing: The Blue Lamp (BFA Award, 1950), I Believe in You, The Gentle Gunman, The Square Ring, The Rainbow Jacket, Out of the Clouds, The Ship That Died of Shame, Davy, The Smallest Show on Earth (for Brit. Lion), Violent Playground (for Rank), Rockets Galore (Island Fling), Sapphire (BFA Award, 1959). 1960 Founder Dir. Allied Film Makers: Prod. The League of Gentlemen, Man in the Moon (co-s.p.), Victim, Life For Ruth (Walk in the Shadow). Also pro-

duced: Secret Partner, All Night Long, The Mind Benders, A Place To Go (s.p.), Woman of Straw (co-s.p.), Masquerade (co-s.p.), The Assassination Bureau (prod., s.p., designer), The Man Who Haunted Himself (prod., co-s.p.). 1978, exec. in chg. prod., Kendon Films, Ltd. Exec. prod., Scum, 1982. Co-prod., An Unsuitable Job for a Woman. 1984, exec. prod.: Treasure Houses of Britain; TV series, prod., Heavenly Pursuits, 1985-86; Gospel According to Vic (U.S.). Prod. Consultant: Torrents of Spring.

RELPH, SIMON
Producer. b. London, Eng., April 13, 1940. Entered industry 1961.
PICTURES: Reds (exec. prod.), The Return of the Soldier, Privates on Parade, The Ploughman's Lunch, Secret Places, Laughterhouse (exec. prod.), Wetherby, Comrades, Enchanted April (exec. prod.), Damage (coprod.), The Secret Rapture, Camilla, Look Me In The Eye, Blue Juice, The Slab Boys.

RELYEA, ROBERT E.
Producer, Executive. b. Santa Monica, CA, May 3, 1930. e. UCLA, B.S., 1952. In Army 1953-55. Entered industry in 1955; asst. dir. on The Magnificent Seven and West Side Story; assoc. prod. and 2nd unit dir. on The Great Escape; partnered with Steve McQueen as exec. prod. on Bullitt and The Reivers. 1979-82, exec. v.p. with Melvin Simon Prods. Served as exec. v.p. in chg. world wide prod., Keith Barish Prods. 1983-85. Served as sr. v.p. prod., Lorimar Prods. 1985-90. Named sr. v.p. features prod. management, Paramount Pictures Motion Picture Gp., 1989.
PICTURES: Exec. Prod.: Bullitt, The Reivers, Day of the Dolphin. Prod.: Love at First Bite, My Bodyguard, Porky's.

REMAR, JAMES
Actor. b. Boston, MA, Dec. 31, 1953. Studied acting at NY's Neighborhood Playhouse and with Stella Adler. Appeared on NY stage in Yo-Yo, Early Dark, Bent, California Dog Fight.
PICTURES: On the Yard (debut, 1979), The Warriors, Cruising, The Long Riders, Windwalker, Partners, 48 HRS, The Cotton Club, The Clan of the Cave Bear, Band of the Hand, Quiet Cool, Rent-a-Cop, The Dream Team, Drugstore Cowboy, Tales from the Darkside, Silence Like Glass, White Fang, Fatal Instinct, Blink, Renaissance Man, Miracle on 34th Street, Boys on the Side, Session Man (Academy Award, Best Action Short, 1991), Across the Moon, Judge Dredd (unbilled), The Quest, The Phantom, Robo-Warriors, Tale From The Darkside: The Movie, Wild Bill, Exquisite Tenderness, The Phantom.
TELEVISION: Movies: The Mystic Warrior, Desperado, Deadlock, Brotherhood of the Gun, Fatal Charm, Indecency. Guest: Hill Street Blues, Miami Vice, The Equalizer, The Hitchhiker, Tales From The Crypt.

REMBUSCH, MICHAEL J.
Executive. b. Indianapolis, IN, April 8, 1950. e. Ball State U. Son of Trueman T. Rembusch. Began working for father's circuit, Syndicate Theatres, Inc., in 1967. From 1970-80, managed various theatres in circuit. 1980-85, v.p., operations. 1985-90, acquired Heaston circuit (Indianapolis). Became pres., Syndicate Theatres, Inc. 1987-90, chmn. Indiana Film Commission. 1992 to present, pres., Theatre Owners of Indiana.

REMBUSCH, TRUEMAN T.
Exhibitor. b. Shelbyville, IN, July 27, 1909. f. Frank J. Rembusch, pioneer exhibitor. Inventor & manufacturer Glass Mirror Screen. e. U. of Notre Dame Sch. of Commerce, 1928. m. Mary Agnes Finneran. Ent. m.p. ind., 1928, servicing sound equip., father's circuit; became mgr., 1932; elect. bd. of dir., Allied Theatre Owners of Ind., 1936-45, pres. 1945-51, 1952-53; dir. chmn. Allied TV Committee, 1945-50; pres. Allied States Assn., 1950-51; 1952, named by Allied as one of tri-umvirate heading COMPO; 1953, named by Gov. of Indiana as dir. State Fair Board; elected chmn. Joint Com. on Toll TV, 1954; currently pres. Syndicate Theatres, Inc., Franklin, Ind; member, Notre Dame Club of Indianapolis (Man of Yr., 1961); BPOE, 4th Degree K of C, Meridian Hills Country Club, Marco Island Country Club. American Radio Relay League (amateur & commerce, licenses); OX5 Aviation Pioneers; awarded patent, recording 7 counting device, 1951; dir. Theatre Owners of Indiana; dir. to NATO; dir. NATO member ad hoc comm; 1972 chair., NATO Statistical Committee; 1976, NITE Award service to Independent Exhibition.

REMSEN, BERT
Actor. b. Glen Cove, NY, Feb. 25, 1925. e. Ithaca Coll.
PICTURES: Pork Chop Hill, Kid Galahad, Moon Pilot, Brewster McCloud, Thieves Like us, Baby Blue Marine, McCabe and Mrs. Miller, Sweet Hostage, California Split, Nashville, Tarantulas, Buffalo Bill and the Indians, A Wedding, The Rose, Uncle Joe Shannon, Carny, Borderline, Second Hand Hearts, Joni, Inside Moves, Looking to Get Out, The

Sting II, Lies, Independence Day, Code of Silence, Stand Alone, Eye of the Tiger, South of Reno, Remote Control, Vietnam Texas, Miss Firecracker, Daddy's Dyin'...Who's Got the Will?, Dick Tracy, Only the Lonely, Evil Spirits, The Player, The Bodyguard, Jack the Bear, Army of One, Maverick.
TELEVISION: *Series*: Gibbsville, It's a Living, Dallas. *Movies*: Who Is Julia?, The Awakening Land, Burning Rage, Crazy Times, Hobson's Choice, If Tomorrow Comes, Love For Rent, Mothers Against Drunk Driving, Little Ladies of the Night, Memorial Day, Maid for Each Other, There Was a Little Boy, In the Shadows Someone's Watching, Rise and Walk: The Dennis Byrd Story. *Guest*: Matlock, Jake and the Fatman. *Mini-Series*: Space.

RENO, JEAN
Actor. b. Casablanca, Morocco. To France in early 1970's to serve in French military. Began acting in Paris with theatre workshop, then established his own travelling acting company.
PICTURES: Claire de Femme, Le Dernier Combat, Subway, Signes Exterieurs de Richesse, Notre Histoire, I Love You, The Big Blue, La Femme Nikita, L'homme au Masque d'Or, L'Operation Corned Beef, Loulou Graffiti, The Professional (Leon), French Kiss, The Visitors (also s.p.), Beyond the Clouds.

RESNAIS, ALAIN
Director. b. Cannes, France, June 3, 1922. Began career as asst. dir. to Nicole Vedres on compilation of film for Paris 1900. During '50s worked as asst. editor and editor; experimented with making his own 16mm films. Directed or co-dir. several short films: Van Gogh, Gauguin, Guernica, The Statues Also Die, Night and Fog, etc.
PICTURES: Hiroshima Mon Amour (feature debut, 1959), Last Year at Marienbad, Muriel, La Guerre Est Finie (The War Is Over), Je t'Aime Je t'Aime (also co-s.p.), Stavisky, Providence, Mon Oncle d'Amerique, Life Is a Bed of Roses, L'Amour a Mort (Love Unto Death), Melo (also s.p.), I Want to Go Home, No Smoking.

RESNICK, JOEL H.
Executive. b. New York, NY, April 28, 1936. e. U. of PA, B.A., 1958; NY Law Sch. 1961, admitted to NY State Bar. 1962 received Masters of Law degree in taxation; 1961-66 served as associate with NY law firm, Phillips Nizer Benjamin Krim & Ballon; Was in-house counsel to United Artists Corp. 1967, joined UA as spec. asst. to the sr. v.p. & gen. mgr.; 1970, moved to American Multi-Cinema, Inc., Kansas City, as asst. to pres.; 1972, named v.p. in chg. development; 1976, promoted to v.p. in chg. film development; 1977, named exec. v.p.; 1983, elected exec. v.p. & dir., AMC Entertainment; 1984, appt. to office of pres. as chmn. & CEO, film mktg.; 1986, resigned to join Orion Pictures Distribution Corp. as pres.; has served as co-chmn. NATO trade practices comm. since 1979. 1982 elected pres., NATO; 1984, became chmn. NATO bd.; 1989, v.p. Foundation of Motion Picture Pioneers; 1990, resigned from Orion; pres., GKC Theatres, Springfield, IL, 1991-92; Cinemark Theatres, Intl. Development, 1994-.

REUBENS, PAUL (PEE-WEE HERMAN)
Actor, Writer. r.n. Paul Rubenfeld. Professional name Paul Reubens. b. Peekskill, NY, Aug. 27, 1952. Raised in Sarasota, FL. e. Boston U., California Inst. of the Arts (1976). Pee-wee character made debut, 1978 at Groundlings, improvisational theater, Los Angeles followed by The Pee-wee Herman Show, a live show which gave 5 months of sold-out performances at the L.A. rock club, Roxy, and was later taped for HBO special. Guest appearances on Late Night With David Letterman, The Gong Show, 227, Tonight Show, Mork & Mindy, Joan Rivers' The Late Show, and The Dating Game.
PICTURES: Midnight Madness, The Blues Brothers, Cheech & Chong's Next Movie, Cheech and Chong's Nice Dreams, Pandemonium, Meatballs Part II, Pee-wee's Big Adventure (also co-s.p.), Flight of the Navigator (voice), Back to the Beach, Big Top Pee-wee (also co-s.p., co-prod.), Batman Returns, Buffy the Vampire Slayer, Tim Burton's The Nightmare Before Christmas (voice), Dunston Checks In, Matilda.
TELEVISION: *Series*: Pee-wee's Playhouse (also creator, co-dir., co-writer, exec. prod.; 12 Emmy Awards). *Specials*: Pinocchio (Faerie Tale Theatre), Pee-wee Herman Show, Pee-wee's Playhouse Christmas Special (also exec. prod., co-dir. co-writer). *Guest*: Murphy Brown.

REVILL, CLIVE
Actor. r.n. Selsby. b. Wellington, New Zealand, Apr. 18, 1930. e. Rongotai Coll., Victoria U.
THEATER: Irma La Douce, The Mikado, Oliver, Marat/Sade, Jew of Malta, Sherry, Chichester Season, The Incomparable Max, Sherlock Holmes, Lolita, Pirates of Penzance, Mystery of Edwin Drood, My Fair Lady, Bandido.
PICTURES: Reach for the Sky, The Headless Ghost, Bunny Lake Is Missing, Once Upon a Tractor, Modesty Blaise, A Fine Madness, Kaleidoscope, The Double Man, Fathom, Italian

Secret Service, Nobody Runs Forever, Shoes of the Fisherman, Assassination Bureau, The Private Life of Sherlock Holmes, The Buttercup Chain, A Severed Head, Boulevard de Rhum, Avanti!, Escape to the Sun, Ghost in the Noonday Sun, The Legend of Hell House, The Little Prince, The Black Windmill, One of Our Dinosaurs Is Missing, Galileo, Matilda, Zorro the Gay Blade, Transformers (voice), Rumpelstiltskin, The Emperor's New Clothes, Mack the Knife, CHUD II: Bud the Chud, Frog Prince, Let Him Have It, Robin Hood: Men in Tights, Crime and Punishment, Arabian Knight (voice), The Wacky Adventures of Dr. Boris and Nurse Shirley, Dracula—Dead and Loving It!
TELEVISION: Chicken Soup with Barley, Volpone, Bam Pow Zapp, Candida, Platonov, A Bit of Vision, Mill Hill, The Piano Player, Hopcroft in Europe, A Sprig of Broome, Ben Franklin in Paris, Pinocchio, The Great Houdini, Show Business Hall of Fame, Feather and Father, Winner Take All, The New Avengers, Licking Hitler, Columbo, Centennial, A Man Called Sloane, Nobody's Perfect, Marya, Moviola, Diary of Anne Frank, Mikado, The Sorcerer, Wizards & Warriors, George Washington, Murder She Wrote, Faerie Tale Theatre, Twilight Zone, Newhart, Hunter, Star Trek, The Sea Wolf, Babylon 5, Fortune Hunter, The Preston Episodes (series), Murphy Brown.

REYNOLDS, BURT
Actor, Director. b. Waycross, GA, Feb. 11, 1936. Former Florida State U. football star; TV and film stunt performer. Won fame as actor on TV in series Riverboat. Founded the Burt Reynolds Dinner Theater in Jupiter, FL, 1979. *Autobiography*: My Life (1994).
THEATER: Mister Roberts (NY City Center), Look We've Come Through (B'way debut, 1956), The Rainmaker.
PICTURES: Angel Baby (debut, 1961), Armored Command, Operation CIA, Navajo Joe, Fade In, Impasse, Shark, Sam Whiskey, 100 Rifles, Skullduggery, Fuzz, Deliverance, Everything You Always Wanted To Know About Sex, Shamus, White Lightning, The Man Who Loved Cat Dancing, The Longest Yard, W.W. & The Dixie Dancekings, At Long Last Love, Hustle, Lucky Lady, Gator (also dir.), Silent Movie, Nickelodeon, Smokey and the Bandit, Semi-Tough, The End (also dir.), Hooper, Starting Over, Rough Cut, Smokey and the Bandit II, Cannonball Run, Paternity, Sharky's Machine (also dir.), The Best Little Whorehouse in Texas, Best Friends, Stroker Ace, Smokey and the Bandit III (cameo), The Man Who Loved Women, Cannonball Run II, City Heat, Stick (also dir.), Uphill All the Way (cameo), Heat, Malone, Rent-a-Cop, Switching Channels, Physical Evidence, Breaking In, All Dogs Go to Heaven (voice), Modern Love, The Player (cameo), Cop and a Half, The Maddening, Devil Inside, Meet Wally Sparks, Striptease, Mad Dog Time, Citizen Ruth.
TELEVISION: *Series*: Riverboat, Gunsmoke, Hawk, Dan August, Out of This World (voice), B.L. Stryker (also co-exec. prod.), Evening Shade (Emmy Award, 1991). *Movies*: Hunters Are for Killing, Run Simon Run, The Man Upstairs (co-exec. prod. only), The Man From Left Field (also dir.). *Host*: The Story of Hollywood. *Special*: Wind in the Wire. *Dir.*: Alfred Hitchcock Presents (1985).

REYNOLDS, DEBBIE
Actress. r.n. Mary Frances Reynolds. b. El Paso, TX, April 1, 1932. Daughter is actress Carrie Fisher. e. Burbank & John Burroughs H.S., Burbank, CA. With Burbank Youth Symphony during h.s.; beauty contest winner (Miss Burbank) 1948; signed by Warner Bros.; on stage in Personal Appearances, Blis-Hayden Theater. Voted Star of Tomorrow, 1952. *Autobiography*: Debbie: My Life (1988).
THEATER: B'way: Irene, Woman of the Year.
PICTURES: June Bride (debut, 1948), The Daughter of Rosie O'Grady, Three Little Words, Two Weeks With Love, Mr. Imperium, Singin' in the Rain, Skirts Ahoy, I Love Melvin, Give a Girl a Break, The Affairs of Dobie Gillis, Susan Slept Here, Athena, Hit the Deck, The Tender Trap, The Catered Affair, Bundle of Joy, Tammy and the Bachelor, This Happy Feeling, The Mating Game, Say One for Me, It Started with a Kiss, The Gazebo, The Rat Race, Pepe (cameo), The Pleasure of His Company, The Second Time Around, How the West Was Won, My Six Loves, Mary Mary, Goodbye Charlie, The Unsinkable Molly Brown (Acad. Award nom.), The Singing Nun, Divorce American Style, How Sweet It Is, What's the Matter with Helen?, Charlotte's Web (voice), That's Entertainment!, The Bodyguard (cameo), Heaven and Earth, That's Entertainment III, Mother.
TELEVISION: *Series*: The Debbie Reynolds Show, Aloha Paradise. *Movies*: Sadie and Son, Perry Mason: The Case of the Musical Murders, Battling for Baby. *Special*: Jack Paar Is Alive and Well.

REYNOLDS, GENE
Executive, Producer. b. Cleveland, OH, April 4, 1925. Acted from 1936-55. Executive producer of Room 222, Anna and the King, Karen. Producer of M*A*S*H, 1972-76. Currently pres., Director's Guild of America, Inc.

REYNOLDS, KEVIN
Director, Writer. b. 1950. e. Texas Marine Acad., Trinity Univ., Baylor Univ. (law degree), USC film school. Student film Proof led to offer to do expanded feature version subsequently retitled Fandango.
PICTURES: Red Dawn (co-s.p.). *Director:* Fandango (dir. debut, 1985; also s.p.), The Beast, Robin Hood: Prince of Thieves, Rapa Nui (also s.p.), Waterworld.

REYNOLDS, MARJORIE
Actress. r.n. Marjorie Goodspeed. b. Buhl, ID, Aug. 12, 1921. On screen as child actor in silent films. Resumed career during talkies billed as Marjorie Moore, then Reynolds, starting in 1937.
PICTURES: Scaramouche (debut, 1923), Revelation, College Humor (as Marjorie Moore), Wine Women and Song, Big Broadcast of 1936, Collegiate, College Holiday (1st billing as Marjorie Reynolds), Murder in Greenwich Village, Champagne Waltz, Western Trails, Mr. Wong in Chinatown, Sky Patrol, Enemy Agent, Robin Hood of the Precos, Dude Cowboy, Cyclone on Horseback, Up in the Air, The Great Swindle, Tillie the Toiler, Top Sergeant Mulligan, Holiday Inn, Star-Spangled Rhythm, Dixie, Ministry of Fear, Up in Mabel's Room, Three Is a Family, Duffy's Tavern, Bring on the Girls, Monsieur Beaucaire, Meet Me on Broadway, The Time of Their Lives, Heaven Only Knows, Bad Men of Tombstone, That Midnight Kiss, The Great Jewel Robbery, Customs Agent, Rookie Fireman, The Home Town Story, His Kind of Woman, No Holds Barred, Models Inc. (Call Girl), Mobs Inc., Juke Box Rhythm, The Silent Witness, … All the Marbles.
TELEVISION: *Series:* The Life of Riley.

REYNOLDS, SHELDON
Writer, Producer, Director. b. Philadelphia, PA, 1923. e. NYU. Radio-TV writer; programs include My Silent Partner, Robert Q. Lewis Show, We the People, Danger, Adventures of Sherlock Holmes (prod., dir., writer), Dick and the Duchess (prod., dir., writer), Foreign Intrigue (dir., prod., writer). TV Special: Sophia Loren's Rome (dir., writer). Movies: Foreign Intrigue (dir., prod., s.p.), Assignment to Kill (dir., s.p.).

REYNOLDS, STUART
Producer. b. Chicago, IL, March 22, 1907. e. Chicago law schools. Adv. exec., Lord and Thomas, BBDO. General Mills; sales exec. Don Lee-Mutual; formed Stuart Reynolds Prod., TV films. Now motion picture & TV program consultant.
TELEVISION: General Electric Theatre, Cavalcade of America, Your Jeweler's Showcase, Wild Bill Hickok. Producer and worldwide distributor of educational/training films; Eye of the Beholder.

RHAMES, VING
Actor. e. Juilliard Sch. of Drama.
THEATER: *B'way:* The Boys of Winter. *Off-B'way:* Map of the World, Short Eyes, Richard III, Ascension Day. *Europe:* Ajax.
PICTURES: Patty Hearst, Casualties of War, Jacob's Ladder, The Long Walk Home, Flight of the Intruder, Homicide, The People Under the Stairs, Stop! Or My Mom Will Shoot, Bound by Honor, Dave, The Saint of Fort Washington, Pulp Fiction, Drop Squad, Kiss of Death, Mission: Impossible, Striptease, Rosewood.
TELEVISION: *Series:* Another World. *Movie:* The Iran Project. *Special:* Go Tell It on the Mountain. *Guest:* Miami Vice, Spenser: For Hire, Tour of Duty, Crime Story.

RHODES, CYNTHIA
Actress, Dancer. b. Nashville, TN, Nov. 21, 1956. m. singer Richard Marx. Appeared on many TV specials, inc. Opryland USA, Music Hall America.
PICTURES: Xanadu, One From the Heart, Flashdance, Staying Alive, Runaway, Dirty Dancing, Curse of the Crystal Eye.

RHYS-DAVIES, JOHN
Actor. b. Salisbury, England, 1944. Grew up in Wales and East Africa. Began acting at Truro School in Cornwall at 15. e. U. of East Anglia where he founded school's dramatic society. Worked as teacher before studying at Royal Academy of Dramatic Art, 1969. Appeared in 23 Shakespearean plays.
PICTURES: The Black Windmill, Sphinx, Raiders of the Lost Ark, Victor/Victoria, Sahara, Sword of the Valiant, Best Revenge, King Solomon's Mines, In the Shadow of Kilimanjaro, Firewalker, The Living Daylights, Waxwork, Rising Storm, Indiana Jones and the Last Crusade, Young Toscanini, Journey of Honor, Unnameable II, The Seventh Coin, The Great White Hype.
TELEVISION: *Mini-series:* Shogun, James Clavell's Noble House, Riley, Ace of Spies, I, Claudius, War and Remembrance. *Movies:* The Little Match Girl, Sadat, Kim, The Naked Civil Servant, The Trial of the Incredible Hulk, Goddess of Love, The Gifted One, Great Expectations, Desperado, Secret Weapon, Before the Storm, Spy Games, Perry Mason: The Case of the Fatal Framing. *Series:* Under Cover, The Untouchables, Archaeology, Sliders.

RICCI, CHRISTINA
Actress. b. Santa Monica, CA, 1980. Raised in Long Island, NY, and Montclair, NJ. Started professional acting career in commercials.
PICTURES: Mermaids (debut, 1990), The Hard Way, The Addams Family, The Cemetery Club, Addams Family Values, Casper, Gold Diggers: The Secret of Bear Mountain, Now and Then, Last of the High Kings, The Ice Storm.

RICH, JOHN
Producer, Director. b. Rockaway Beach, NY, e. U. of Michigan, B.A., Phi Beta Kappa, 1948; M.A. 1949; Sesquicentennial Award, 1967; bd. of dir., Screen Dir. Guild of America, 1954-1960; v.p. 1958-1960, Founder-Trustee, Producers-Directors Pension Plan, chmn. of bd. 1965, 1968, 1970; treasurer, Directors Guild of America, 1966-67; v.p. 1967-72. Awards: Directors Guild Award, Most Outstanding Directorial Achievement, 1971. Christopher award: Henry Fonda as Clarence Darrow, 1975. NAACP Image Award, 1974; 2 Golden Globe Awards: All in the Family, 1972-73. DGA Robert B. Aldrich Award for 1992.
PICTURES: *Director:* Wives and Lovers, The New Interns, Roustabout, Boeing-Boeing, Easy Come Easy Go.
TELEVISION: *Director:* Academy Awards, The Dick Van Dyke Show, All in the Family (also prod.), Mr. Sunshine, Dear John, MacGyver.

RICH, LEE
Producer, Executive. b. Cleveland, OH, Dec. 10, 1926. e. Ohio U. Adv. exec.; resigned as sr. v.p., Benton & Bowles, to become producer for Mirisch-Rich TV, 1965 (Rat Patrol, Hey Landlord). Resigned 1967 to join Leo Burnett Agency. Left to form Lorimar Productions in 1969 and served as pres. until 1986 when left to join MGM/UA Communications as chmn. & CEO. Resigned 1988; signed 3-year deal with Warner Bros. setting up Lee Rich Prods. there. Twice named Television Showman of the Year by Publishers' Guild of Amer.
PICTURES: *Producer:* The Sporting Club, Just Cause, The Amazing Panda Adventure, Big Bully. *Executive Producer:* The Man, The Choirboys, Who Is Killing the Great Chefs of Europe?, The Big Red One, Hard to Kill, Innocent Blood, Passenger 57.
TELEVISION: *Exec. Prod.: Series:* The Waltons (Emmy Award, 1973), Dallas, Knots Landing, Against the Grain. *Mini-series:* The Blue Knight, Helter Skelter, Studs Lonigan. *Movies:* Do Not Fold Spindle or Mutilate, The Homecoming: A Christmas Story, The Crooked Hearts, Pursuit, The Girls of Huntington House, Dying Room Only, Don't Be Afraid of the Dark, A Dream for Christmas, The Stranger Within, Bad Ronald, The Runaway Barge, Runaways, Returning Home, Eric, Conspiracy of Terror, Widow, Green Eyes, Killer on Board, Desperate Women, Long Journey Back, Mary and Joseph: A Story of Faith, Mr. Horn, Some Kind of Miracle, Young Love, First Love, A Man Called Intrepid, Flamingo Road, Marriage Is Alive and Well, A Perfect Match, Reward, Skag, Killjoy, A Matter of Life and Death, Our Family Business, Mother's Day on Walton's Mountain, This is Kate Bennett, Two of a Kind, A Wedding on Walton's Mountain, A Day of Thanks on Walton's Mountain, Secret of Midland Heights, Face of Fear, Killer Rules.

RICHARD, SIR CLIFF
O.B.E. Singer, Actor. r.n. Harry Webb. b. India, Oct. 14, 1940. Ent. show business 1958 in TV series Oh Boy. Other TV includes Sunday Night at the London Palladium, several Cliff Richard Shows; top British Singer, 1960-71. Voted top box-office star of Great Britain, 1962-63, 1963-64. Twice rep. U.K. in Eurovision Song Contest. Innumerable platinum, gold and silver discs. 1989 became first UK artist to release 100 singles; voted top male vocalist of the 80's by UK Indept. TV viewers. Has made numerous videos. Knighted, 1995.
THEATER: Aladdin, Five Finger Exercise, The Potting Shed, Time.
PICTURES: Serious Charge (debut, 1959), Expresso Bongo, The Young Ones (Wonderful to Be Young), Summer Holiday, Wonderful Life (Swingers' Paradise), Finder's Keepers, Two a Penny, Take Me High (Hot Property).

RICHARDS, BEAH
Actress. b. Vicksburg, MS. e. Dillard U. On B'way in The Miracle Worker, A Raisin in the Sun, The Amen Corner (Theatre World Award), etc.
PICTURES: Take a Giant Step, The Miracle Worker, Gone Are the Days, In the Heat of the Night, Hurry Sundown, Guess Who's Coming to Dinner, The Great White Hope, Mahogany, Homer and Eddie, Drugstore Cowboy.
TELEVISION: *Series:* The Bill Cosby Show (1970), Sanford and Son, Frank's Place (Emmy Award, 1988), Hearts Afire. *Movies:* Footsteps, Outrage, A Dream for Christmas, Just an Old Sweet Song, Ring of Passion, Roots II—The Next Generation, A Christmas Without Snow, One Special Victory, Out of Darkness.

RICHARDS, DICK
Director, Producer, Writer. b. New York, NY, July 9, 1934. In U.S. Army as photo-journalist; work appeared in Life, Look, Time, Esquire, etc. Won over 100 int'l. awards, for commercials and photographic art work.
PICTURES: Director: The Culpepper Cattle Co. (also story), Rafferty and the Gold Dust Twins, Farewell My Lovely, March or Die (also co- prod., co-story), Death Valley, Tootsie (co-prod. only), Man Woman and Child, Heat.

RICHARDS, MICHAEL
Actor. b. Culver City, July 14, 1950. e. California Inst. of Arts. Work as stand-up comedian led to appearances on tv including regular stint on series Fridays. Acted on stage with San Diego Rep. Co.
THEATER: LA: The American Clock, Wild Oats.
PICTURES: Young Doctors in Love, Transylvania 6-5000, Whoops Apocalypse, UHF, Problem Child, Coneheads, So I Married an Axe Murderer, Airheads, Unstrung Heroes.
TELEVISION: Series: Fridays, Marblehead Manor, Seinfeld (2 Emmy Awards: 1993, 1994).

RICHARDSON, JOELY
Actress. b. London, Eng., January 9, 1965. Daughter of actress Vanessa Redgrave and director Tony Richardson, sister of actress Natasha Richardson. e. St. Paul's Girl's School, London; Pinellas Park H.S. (Florida), The Thacher Sch. (Ojai, CA), Royal Acad. of Dramatic Art. London stage: Steel Magnolias, Beauty and the Beast (Old Vic); also at Liverpool Playhouse, RSC.
PICTURES: Wetherby (debut, 1985 with mother), Drowning By Numbers, About That Strange Girl, King Ralph, Shining Through, Rebecca's Daughters, I'll Do Anything, Sister My Sister, Hollow Reed, Lochness, 101 Dalmations.
TELEVISION: Body Contact, Behaving Badly, Available Light, Heading Home, Lady Chatterly.

RICHARDSON, MIRANDA
Actress. b. Southport, England, 1958. Studied acting at the drama program at Bristol's Old Vic Theatre School. Began acting on stage, 1979. Appeared in Moving, at the Queen's Theatre and continued in All My Sons, Who's Afraid of Virginia Woolf?, The Life of Einstein in provincial theatres. Also A Lie of the Mind (London), The Changeling, Mountain Language.
PICTURES: Dance With a Stranger (debut, 1985), The Innocent, Empire of the Sun, Eat the Rich, Twisted Obsession, The Bachelor, Enchanted April, The Crying Game, Damage (BAFTA Award; Acad. Award nom.), Tom and Viv, Century, The Night and the Moment, Kansas City, The Evening Star.
TELEVISION: The Hard Word, Sorrel and Son, A Woman of Substance, After Pilkington, Underworld, Death of the Heart, The Black Adder (series), Die Kinder (mini-series), Sweet as You Are (Royal TV Society Award), Fatherland (Golden Globe Award).

RICHARDSON, NATASHA
Actress. b. London, Eng., May 11, 1963. m. actor Liam Neeson. Daughter of actress Vanessa Redgrave and director Tony Richardson; sister is actress Joely Richardson. e. Central Sch. of Speech and Drama. Appeared at the Leeds Playhouse in On the Razzle, Top Girls, Charley's Aunt. Performed A Midsummer Night's Dream and Hamlet with the Young Vic. 1985 starred with mother in The Seagull (London), also starred in the musical High Society. Won London Theatre Critics Most Promising Newcomer award, 1986. NY stage debut 1992 in Anna Christie.
PICTURES: Every Picture Tells a Story (debut, 1984). Gothic, A Month in the Country, Patty Hearst, Fat Man and Little Boy, The Handmaid's Tale, The Comfort of Strangers, The Favor the Watch and the Very Big Fish, Past Midnight, Widow's Peak, Nell.
TELEVISION: Ellis Island (mini-series), In a Secret State, The Copper Beeches (epis. of Sherlock Holmes), Ghosts, Suddenly Last Summer, Hostages, Zelda.

RICHARDSON, PATRICIA
Actress. b. Bethesda, MD, Feb. 23, 1951. e. Southern Methodist Univ.
THEATER: NY: Gypsy, Loose Ends, The Wake of Jamie Foster, The Collected Works of Billy the Kid, The Frequency, Vanities, The Miss Firecracker Contest, The Coroner's Plot, Fables for Friends. Regional: The Killing of Sister George, King Lear, The Philadelphia Story, Fifth of July, About Face.
PICTURES: Gas, C.H.U.D., You Better Watch Out, Lost Angels, In Country.
TELEVISION: Series: Double Trouble, Eisenhower and Lutz, FM, Home Improvement, Storytime (PBS). Movies: Hands of a Stranger, Parent Trap III. Guest: Love Sidney, Kate and Allie, The Cosby Show, Quantum Leap.

RICHMAN, PETER MARK
Actor. b. Philadelphia, PA, April 16, 1927. e. Philadelphia Coll. of Pharmacy & Science with Bachelor of Science Degree in Pharmacy. Previously acted as Mark Richman. Member of Actors Studio since 1954.

THEATER: B'way: End as a Man, Masquerade, A Hatful of Rain, The Zoo Story. Regional: Blithe Spirit, The Night of the Iguana, 12 Angry Men, Babes in Toyland, Funny Girl, The Best Man, Equus, The Rainmaker, 4 Faces (also author; Drama-Logue Best Performance Award, 1995).
PICTURES: Friendly Persuasion, The Strange One, The Black Orchid, Dark Intruder, Agent for H.A.R.M., For Singles Only, Friday 13th Part VIII—Jason Takes Manahattan, The Naked Gun 2 1/2: The Smell of Fear, Judgment Day (Manila).
TELEVISION: Series: Longstreet, Dynasty, Cain's Hundred, My Secret Summer (Berlin). Movies: House on Greenapple Road, Yuma, Mallory: Circumstantial Evidence, The Islander, Dempsey, Blind Ambition, City Killer, Bonanza: The Next Generation. Guest: Three's Company, Murder She Wrote, Star Trek: The Next Generation, Matlock, Beverly Hills 90210, and over 500 guest roles.

RICHMOND, TED
Producer. b. Norfolk, VA, June 10, 1912. e. MIT. Entered m.p. ind. as publicity dir., RKO Theatres; later mgr. Albany dist.; publ. dir. Fabian circuit, NY, Paramount upper NY state theats.; Grand Nat'l Pictures. Author Grand Nat'l series Trigger Pal, Six Gun Rhythm. Formed T. H. Richmond Prods., Inc., 1941. Formed Copa Prod. with Tyrone Power, 1954. Formed Ted Richmond Prod. Inc. for MGM release, 1959. Reactivated Copa Prod. Ltd., England, 1960.
PICTURES: Hit the Hay, The Milkman, Kansas Raiders, Shakedown, Smuggler's Island, Strange Door, Cimarron Kid, Bronco Buster, Has Anybody Seen My Gal, No Room for the Groom, Weekend with Father, The Mississippi Gambler, Desert Legion, Column South, Bonzo Goes to College, Forbidden, Walking My Baby Back Home, Francis Joins the Wacs, Bengal Brigade, Count Three and Pray, Nightfall, Abandon Ship, Solomon and Sheba, Charlemagne, Bachelor in Paradise, Advance to the Rear, Pancho Villa, Return of the 7, Red Sun, Papillon (exec. prod.), The Fifth Musketeer.

RICHTER, W. D.
Writer, Director. b. New Britain, CT, Dec. 7, 1945. e. Dartmouth Coll, B.A.; U. of Southern California Film Sch., grad. study.
PICTURES: Writer: Slither, Peeper, Nickelodeon, Invasion of the Body Snatchers, Dracula, Brubaker, All Night Long, Big Trouble in Little China, Needful Things, Home for the Holidays. Prod.-Dir.: Adventures of Buckaroo Banzai Across the Eighth Dimension, Late for Dinner.

RICKERT, JOHN F.
Executive. b. Kansas City, MO, Oct. 29, 1924. e. USC. Joined Universal Pictures in 1951; left in 1957 to start independent productions. 1960-68 handled indep. roadshow distribution (4-walling). 1969 formed Cineworld Corporation, natl. dist. co., of which he is pres. 1975-76 did tax shelter financing for 13 films. Currently involved in distribution, production packaging and intl. co-production as pres. of Coproducers Corp.

RICKLES, DON
Actor, Comedian. b. New York, NY, May 8, 1926. e. AADA.
PICTURES: Run Silent Run Deep, Rabbit Trap, The Rat Race, X: The Man With the X-Ray Eyes, Muscle Beach Party, Bikini Beach, Beach Blanket Bingo, Enter Laughing, The Money Jungle, Where It's At, Kelly's Heroes, Keaton's Cop, Innocent Blood, Casino, Toy Story (voice).
TELEVISION: Series: The Don Rickles Show (1968), The Don Rickles Show (1972), C.P.O. Sharkey, Foul-Ups Bleeps and Blunders, Daddy Dearest. Movie: For the Love of It. Guest: The Big Show, F Troop, Laugh-In, Kraft Music Hall, Dean Martin's Celebrity Roasts, Tales From the Crypt, many others.

RICKMAN, ALAN
Actor. b. London, England. Began as graphic designer before studying acting at RADA. Joined the Royal Shakespeare Co. where he starred in Les Liaisons Dangereuses; received Tony Award nomination for 1987 NY production.
THEATER: Commitments, The Last Elephant, The Grass Widow, Lucky Chance, The Seagull, As You Like It, Troilus and Cressida, Tango At the End of Winter, Hamlet.
PICTURES: Die Hard (debut, 1988), The January Man, Quigley Down Under, Closet Land, Truly Madly Deeply, Robin Hood: Prince of Thieves (BAFTA Award, 1991), Close My Eyes, Bob Roberts, Mesmer, An Awfully Big Adventure, Sense and Sensibility, Rasputin, Michael Collins.
TELEVISION: Series: The Barchester Chronicles (BBC). Specials: Smiley's People, Romeo and Juliet, Bonnie Prince Charley, Girls on Top. Guest: Fallen Angels (Murder Obliquely). Movie: Rasputin (Emmy Award, 1996).

RICOTTA, FRANK
Executive. Pres., Technicolor, Inc., Association of Cimena & Video Laboratories, Inc.

RIEGERT, PETER
Actor. b. New York, NY, Apr. 11, 1947. e. U. of Buffalo, B.A. Brief stints as 8th grade English teacher, social worker, and

aide de camp to politician Bella Abzug 1970, before turned actor, off-off B'way. Appeared with improvisational comedy group War Babies. Film debut in short, A Director Talks About His Film.
THEATER: Dance with Me (B'way debut), Minnie's Boys (as Chico Marx), Sexual Perversity in Chicago, Isn't it Romantic?, La Brea Tarpits, A Rosen By Any Other Name, The Nerd, Mountain Language/The Birthday Party, The Road to Nirvana.
PICTURES: National Lampoon's Animal House, Americathon, Head Over Heels, National Lampoon Goes to the Movies, Local Hero, City Girl, A Man in Love, Le Grand Carnaval, The Stranger, Crossing Delancey, That's Adequate, The Passport, A Shock to the System, The Object of Beauty, Beyond the Ocean, Oscar, The Runestone, Passed Away, Utz, The Mask, White Man's Burden, Coldblooded, Pie in the Sky.
TELEVISION: Specials: Concealed Enemies, The Hit List, W. Eugene Smith: Photography Made Difficult. Mini-Series: Ellis Island. Movies: News at Eleven, Barbarians at the Gate, Gypsy, The Infiltrator, Element of Truth. Series: The Middle Ages.

RIFKIN, RON
Actor. b. New York, NY, Oct. 31, 1939. e. NYU.
PICTURES: The Devil's 8 (debut, 1969), Flareup, Silent Running, The Sunshine Boys, The Big Fix, The Sting II, Husbands and Wives, Manhattan Murder Mystery, Wolf, Last Summer in the Hamptons, The Substance of Fire.
TELEVISION: Series: Adam's Rib, When Things Were Rotten, Husbands Wives & Lovers, One Day at a Time, Falcon Crest. Mini-Series: The Winds of War.
THEATER: B'way: Come Blow Your Horn, The Goodbye People, The Tenth Man. Off-B'way: Rosebloom, The Art of Dining, Temple, The Substance of Fire.

RIGG, DIANA
C.B.E. (1987). Actress. b. Doncaster, England, July 20, 1938. With the Royal Shakespeare Co. at Aldwych Theatre, 1962-64. Recent London stage: Follies, Medea (also B'way).
PICTURES: A Midsummer's Night Dream (debut, 1968), The Assassination Bureau, On Her Majesty's Secret Service, Julius Caesar, The Hospital, Theatre of Blood, A Little Night Music, The Great Muppet Caper, Evil Under the Sun, Snow White, A Good Man in Africa.
TELEVISION: Series: The Avengers, Diana, Mystery (host). Movies: In This House of Brede, Witness for the Prosecution, A Hazard of Hearts, Mother Love, Mrs. 'arris Goes to Paris, Running Delilah, Genghis Cohn, Danielle Steel's Zoya, The Haunting of Helen Walker. Specials: King Lear, Bleak House.

RINGWALD, MOLLY
Actress. b. Sacramento, CA, Feb. 16, 1968. Daughter of jazz musician Bob Ringwald; began performing at age 4 with his Great Pacific Jazz Band at 6 and recorded album, Molly Sings. Professional debut at 5 in stage play, The Glass Harp. Appeared in bit on TV's New Mickey Mouse Club, a West Coast stage production of Annie and in TV series, The Facts of Life, Off-B'way debut: Lily Dale (Theatre World Award, 1986).
PICTURES: Tempest (debut, 1982), P.K. and the Kid, Spacehunter: Adventures in the Forbidden Zone, Sixteen Candles, The Breakfast Club, Pretty in Pink, The Pick-Up Artist, For Keeps?, King Lear, Fresh Horses, Strike It Rich, Betsy's Wedding, Face the Music, Bastard Brood.
TELEVISION: Series: The Facts of Life, Townies. Movies: Packin' It In, Surviving, Women and Men: Stories of Seduction (Dust Before Fireworks), Something to Live For: The Alison Gertz Story. Mini-Series: The Stand.

RISHER, SARA
Executive. Chairperson of production, New Line Productions, Inc.

RISSIEN, EDWARD L.
Executive. b. Des Moines, IA. e. Grinnell Coll., Stanford U., B.A., 1949. Army Air Force, WWII. B'way stage, mgr., 1950-53; v.p., Mark Stevens Prods., 1954-56; prod., v.p., Four Star, 1958-60; prog. exec., ABC-TV, 1960-62; v.p., Bing Crosby Prods., 1963-66; v.p., Filmways TV Prods.; assoc. prod., Columbia, 1968-69; indept. prod., 1970; prod., WB, 1971; exec. v.p., Playboy Prods., 1972-80; consultant & indept. prod., 1981-82; sr. consultant, cable, Playboy Prods., 1982-85; pres., Playboy Programs, 1985-88; bd. of dirs.: Heritage Entertainment, Inc. 1985-88; indept. prod., 1989-present. Theatre producer in London: The School of Night.
PICTURES: Snow Job (prod.), Castle Keep (prod. exec.), The Crazy World of Julius Vrooder (prod.), Saint Jack (exec. prod.).
TELEVISION: Movies (exec. prod.): Minstrel Man, A Whale for the Killing, The Death of Ocean View Park, Big Bob Johnson, The Great Niagara, Third Girl from the Left, A Summer Without Boys.

RISSNER, DANTON
Executive. b. Brooklyn, NY, March 27, 1940. e. Florida So. Col. Began as agent with Ashley Famous (later Intl. Famous), 1967-69. 1969 joined Warner Bros. as v.p., chg. European prod.;

1970, moved to United Artists as v.p., chg. European prod.; 1973, named v.p. in chg. East Coast & European prod. for UA; 1975- 78, v.p. in chg. of world-wide prod.; 1981, exec. v.p., 20th Century-Fox.; 1984, joined UA as sr. v.p., motion pictures.
PICTURES: Prod.: Up the Academy, A Summer Story.
TELEVISION: Backfire (prod.).

RITCHIE, MICHAEL
Director. b. Waukesha, WI, Nov. 28, 1938. e. Harvard U. where he directed first production of Arthur Kopit's play, Oh Dad Poor Dad Mama's Hung You in the Closet and I'm Feeling So Sad. Professional career began as ass't. to Robert Saudek on Ford Foundation's Omnibus TV series. Later became assoc. prod. and then dir. on Saudek's Profiles in Courage series; dir. assignments on tv series. Appeared as actor in film Innocent Blood.
PICTURES: Downhill Racer (debut, 1969), Prime Cut, The Candidate, Smile (also prod., lyricist), The Bad News Bears, Semi-Tough, An Almost Perfect Affair (also co-s.p.), The Island, Divine Madness (also prod.), The Survivors, Fletch, Wildcats, The Golden Child, The Couch Trip, Fletch Lives, Diggstown, Cops and Robbersons, The Scout, The Fantasticks.
TELEVISION: Series: Profiles in Courage (also prod.), The Man from U.N.C.L.E., Run for Your Life, Dr. Kildare, The Big Valley, Felony Squad, The Outsider (pilot), The Sound of Anger. Movie: The Positively True Adventures of the Alleged Texas Cheerleader-Murdering Mom.

RITTER, JOHN
Actor. b. Burbank, CA, Sept. 17, 1948. Father was late Tex Ritter, country-western star. Attended Hollywood H.S. Began acting at USC in 1968. Appeared with college cast at Edinburgh Festival; later with Eva Marie Saint in Desire Under the Elms.
PICTURES: The Barefoot Executive (debut, 1971), Scandalous John, The Other, The Stone Killer, Nickelodeon, Americathon, Hero at Large, Wholly Moses, They All Laughed, Real Men, Skin Deep, Problem Child, Problem Child II, Noises Off, Stay Tuned, North, Slingblade.
TELEVISION: Movies: The Night That Panicked America, Leave Yesterday Behind, The Comeback Kid, Pray TV, In Love With an Older Woman, Sunset Limousine, Love Thy Neighbor, Letting Go, Unnatural Causes, A Smoky Mountain Christmas, The Last Fling, Prison for Children, Tricks of the Trade, My Brother's Wife, Stephen King's IT, The Dreamer of Oz, The Summer My Father Grew Up, Danielle Steel's Heartbeat, The Only Way Out, Gramps, The Colony, Unforgivable. Series: The Waltons, Three's Company (Emmy Award, 1984), Three's a Crowd, Hooper-man, Have Faith (exec. prod.), Anything But Love (exec. prod., also guest), Fish Police (voice), Hearts Afire.

RIVERA, CHITA
Actress, Dancer. b. Washington, DC, Jan. 23, 1933. r.n. Concita del Rivero. Trained for stage at American School of Ballet.
THEATER: Call Me Madam (1952), Guys and Dolls, Can-Can, Shoestring Revue, Seventh Heaven, Mr. Wonderful, Shinbone Alley, West Side Story, Bye Bye Birdie, Bajour, Sondheim: A Musical Tribute, Chicago, Hey Look Me Over, Merlin, The Rink (Tony Award, 1984), Jerry's Girls, Kiss of the Spider Woman (Tony Award, 1993).
PICTURE: Sweet Charity (1969).
TELEVISION: Series: The New Dick Van Dyke Show. Specials: Kennedy Center Tonight—Broadway to Washington!, Pippin, Toller Cranston's Strawberry Ice, TV Academy Hall of Fame, 1985. Movies: The Marcus-Nelson Murders, Mayflower Madam.

RIVERA, GERALDO
Journalist. b. New York, NY, July 4, 1943. e. U. of Arizona, Brooklyn Law Sch., 1969, Columbia Sch. of Journalism. Started legal career 1st as lawyer with Harlem Assertion of Rights Community Action for Legal Services 1968-70. Switched to journalism, joined WABC-TV, New York, 1970. Made several TV documentaries on such subjects as institutions for retarded, drug addiction, migrant workers, etc. Chmn., One-to-One Foundation. Winner 3 national and 4 local Emmys, George Peabody Award, 2 Robert F. Kennedy Awards. Appeared in film The Bonfire of the Vanities.
TELEVISION: Series: Geraldo Rivera: Good Morning America (contributor), Good Night America, 20/20, Gerald Show, Now It Can Be Told. Specials: The Mystery of Al Capone's Vault, American Vice: The Doping of a Nation, Innocence Lost: The Erosion of American Childhood, Sons of Scarface: The New Mafia, Murder: Live From Death Row, Devil Worship: Exposing Satan's Underground. Movie: Perry Mason: The Case of the Reckless Romeo.

RIVERS, JOAN
Actress, Writer, Director. r.n. Joan Molinsky. b. New York, NY, June 8, 1933. e. Barnard Coll. (Phi Beta Kappa). Formerly

fashion coordinator for Bond clothing stores. Performed comedy act in nightclubs, then with Second City 1961-62; TV debut: Johnny Carson Show, 1965; nat'l syndicated columnist, Chicago Tribune 1973-76; Hadassah Woman of the Year, 1983; Jimmy Award for Best Comedian 1981; Chair., National Cystic Fibrosis Foundation. 1978 created TV series Husbands Wives and Lovers.
AUTHOR: Having a Baby Can Be a Scream (1974), Can We Talk? (1983), The Life and Hard Times of Heidi Abramowitz (1984), Enter Talking (1986), Still Talking (1990).
THEATER: B'way: Fun City (also co-writer), Broadway Bound, Sally Marr... and Her Escorts (also co-writer).
PICTURES: The Swimmer, Rabbit Test (also dir., s.p.), The Muppets Take Manhattan, Spaceballs (voice), Serial Mom.
TELEVISION: Series: The Tonight Show (regular substitute guest host: 1983-86), The Late Show (host), The New Hollywood Squares, The Joan Rivers Show (morning talk show). Movies: How to Murder a Millionaire, Tears and Laughter: The Joan and Melissa Rivers Story.

ROBARDS, JASON
Actor. b. Chicago, IL, July 26, 1922. Served in Navy during WWII. Studied acting at Acad. of Dramatic Arts. Began with Children's World Theatre (1947), then stock radio parts, asst. stage mgr. and actor in Stalag 17, The Chase, D'Oyly Carte Opera Co., Stratford Ontario Shakespeare Fest. American Gothic, Circle in the Square.
THEATER: The Iceman Cometh (Obie Award, 1956), Long Day's Journey into Night (Theatre World Award), The Disenchanted (Tony Award, 1959), Toys in the Attic, Big Fish Little Fish, A Thousand Clowns, After the Fall, But for Whom Charlie, Hughie, The Devils, We Bombed in New Haven, The Country Girl, A Moon for the Misbegotten, Long Day's Journey Into Night (Brooklyn Acad. of Music, 1975; B'way, 1988), A Touch of the Poet, O'Neill and Carlotta, You Can't Take It With You, Ah Wilderness, A Month of Sundays, Established Price (Long Wharf), Love Letters, Park Your Car in Harvard Yard, No Man's Land.
PICTURES: The Journey (debut, 1959), By Love Possessed, Tender Is the Night, Long Day's Journey Into Night, Act One, A Thousand Clowns, A Big Hand for the Little Lady, Any Wednesday, Divorce American Style, The St. Valentine's Day Massacre, Hour of the Gun, The Night They Raided Minsky's, (Loves of) Isadora, Once Upon a Time in the West, Operation Snafu, The Ballad of Cable Hogue, Tora! Tora! Tora!, Fools, Julius Caesar, Johnny Got His Gun, Murders in the Rue Morgue, The War Between Men and Women, Pat Garrett and Billy the Kid, A Boy and His Dog, Mr. Sycamore, All the President's Men (Academy Award, best supporting actor, 1976), Julia (Academy Award, best supporting actor, 1977), Comes a Horseman, Hurricane, Raise the Titanic!, Caboblanco, Melvin and Howard, Legend of the Lone Ranger, Burden of Dreams, Max Dugan Returns, Something Wicked This Way Comes, Square Dance, Bright Lights Big City, The Good Mother, Dream a Little Dream, Parenthood, Quick Change, Reunion, Storyville, The Adventures of Huck Finn, The Trial, Philadelphia, The Paper, Little Big League, Crimson Tide.
TELEVISION: Specials: Abe Lincoln in Illinois, The Iceman Cometh, A Doll's House, Noon Wine, Belle of 14th Street, The House Without a Christmas Tree, For Whom the Bell Tolls, You Can't Take It With You, Hughie. Mini-Series: Washington: Behind Closed Doors. Movies: A Christmas to Remember, Haywire, F.D.R.: The Last Year, The Atlanta Child Murders, The Day After, Sakharov, Johnny Bull, The Long Hot Summer, Laguna Heat, Norman Rockwell's Breaking Home Ties, Inherit the Wind (Emmy Award, 1988), The Christmas Wife, The Perfect Tribute, Chernobyl: The Final Warning, An Inconvenient Woman, Black Rainbow, Mark Twain & Me, Heidi, The Enemy Within, My Antonia. Guest: Studio One, Philco Playhouse, Hallmark.

ROBARDS, SAM
Actor. b. New York, NY, December 16. m. actress Suzy Amis. Son of actors Jason Robards and Lauren Bacall. e. National Theater Institute and studied with Uta Hagen at H.B. Studios.
THEATER: Off-B'way: Album, Flux, Taking Steps, Moonchildren. Kennedy Center: Idiot's Delight and regional theater.
PICTURES: Tempest, Not Quite Paradise, Fandango, Bright Lights Big City, Bird, Casualties of War, The Ballad of Little Jo, Mrs. Parker and the Vicious Circle.
TELEVISION: Series: Movin' Right Along (PBS), TV 101, Get a Life! Movies: Jacobo Timerman: Prisoner Without a Name Cell Without a Number, Into Thin Air, Pancho Barnes.

ROBBINS, MATTHEW
Writer, Director. e. U. of Southern California Sch. of Cinema. Wrote early scripts in collaboration with Hal Barwood, Robbins branching out into directing also with Corvette Summer in 1978.
PICTURES: Writer: The Sugarland Express, The Bingo Long Traveling All-Stars and Motor Kings, Corvette Summer (also dir.), Dragonslayer (also dir.), Warning Sign, Batteries Not Included (also dir.), Bingo (dir. only).

ROBBINS, RICHARD
Composer. b. Boston, MA, Dec. 4, 1940. Bachelor of Music and Graduate Studies at New England Conservatory of Music. Received Frank Huntington Beebe Fellowship to Austria where he studied musicology, chamber music. Later became dir. of Mannes College of Music Preparatory School, N.Y. Has worked closely with James Ivory and Ismail Merchant. Also dir. doc. films Sweet Sounds, Street Musicians of Bombay. Awards: Best Score, Venice Film Festival for Maurice; Best Score, BFI Anthony Asquith Award for A Room With a View. Acad. Award nom. for Howards End.
PICTURES: The Europeans (supr. score), Jane Austen in Manhattan, Quartet, Heat and Dust, The Bostonians, A Room with a View, Maurice, Sweet Lorraine, My Little Girl, Slaves of New York, Mr. & Mrs. Bridge, The Ballad of the Sad Cafe, Howards End, The Remains of the Day, Jefferson in Paris.
TELEVISION: Love and Other Sorrows.

ROBBINS, TIM
Actor, Director. b. West Covina, CA, Oct. 16, 1958. Son of Greenwich Village folksinger, worked as actor while in high school. e. NYU. Transferred to UCLA theatre program appearing in guest roles on tv. 1981, co-founder and artistic dir., The Actors Gang, in L.A.; dir. them in and co-authored Alagazam: After the Dog Wars, Violence: The Misadventures of Spike Spangle—Farmer, Carnage: A Comedy (also prod. in NY).
PICTURES: Toy Soldiers (debut, 1984), No Small Affair, Fraternity Vacation, The Sure Thing, Top Gun, Howard the Duck, Five Corners, Bull Durham, Tapeheads, Miss Firecracker, Twister (cameo), Erik the Viking, Cadillac Man, Jacob's Ladder, Jungle Fever, The Player (Cannes Film Fest. Award, 1992), Bob Roberts (also dir., s.p., co-wrote songs), Short Cuts, The Hudsucker Proxy, The Shawshank Redemption, Ready to Wear (Pret-a-Porter), I.Q., Dead Man Walking (dir.).
TELEVISION: Movies: Quarterback Princess, Malice in Wonderland. Guest: Hardcastle and McCormick, St. Elsewhere, Hill Street Blues.

ROBERTS, CURTIS
Producer. b. Dover, England. e. Cambridge U. Child actor. England, Germany; numerous pictures for Rank Org.; prod. England, on Broadway in Gertie, Island Visit; co-prod. on Broadway, Horses in Midstream, Golden Apple, Tonight or Never; tour and NY The Journey. Recipient: Lawrence J. Quirk Photoplay Award 1990. Now pres., CGC Films, Munich.
AUTHOR: History of Summer Theatre, The History of Vaudeville, Other Side of the Coin, History of Music (Popular) 1900-70, History of English Music Halls, Latta, Then There Were Some, I Live to Love, Gabor the Merrier, I Live to Love II.
THEATER: Tours: Blithe Spirit, Showboat, Kiss Me Kate, Generation, The Camel Bell, Farewell Party, Twentieth Century, Great Sebastians, Goodbye Charlie, Time of the Cuckoo, Under Papa's Picture, Everybody's Gal, Divorce Me Darling, Gingerbread Lady, September Song, Same Time Next Year, Funny Girl, Pal Joey, South Pacific, It Girl, Fanny, Breaking Up the Act, Good, Good Friends, Together, I Remember Mama.
PICTURES: An Actress in Love, La Die, Hypocrite, Jet Over the Atlantic, The Vixen, Farewell Party, Polly's Return, Rain Before Seven, Halloween, Malaga, My Dear Children, Norma, The Lion's Consort, Whispers, Golden Idol, London Belongs To Me.
TELEVISION: Rendezvous, Deadly Species, Top Secret, The Ilona Massey Show, When In Rome, Ethan Frome, Black Chiffon, Illusion in Java (mini-series), Diamonds Don't Brun (mini-series).

ROBERTS, ERIC
Actor. b. Biloxi, MS, April 18, 1956. Father founded Actors and Writers Workshop in Atlanta, 1963. Sister is actress Julia Roberts. Began appearing in stage prods. at age 5. Studied in London at Royal Acad. of Dramatic Art, 1973-74. Returned to U.S. to study at American Acad. of Dramatic Arts. Stage debut in Rebel Women.
THEATER: Mass Appeal, The Glass Menagerie (Hartford Stage Co.), A Streetcar Named Desire (Princeton's McCarter Theater), Alms for the Middle Class (Long Wharf), Burn This (B'way debut; Theatre World Award).
PICTURES: King of the Gypsies (debut, 1978), Raggedy Man, Star 80, The Pope of Greenwich Village, The Coca Cola Kid, Runaway Train (Acad. Award nom.), Nobody's Fool, Rude Awakening, Blood Red, Best of the Best, The Ambulance, Lonely Hearts, Final Analysis, Best of the Best 2, By the Sword, Freefall, Babyfever, Love Is a Gun, The Specialist, Nature of the Beast, The Grave, Heaven's Prisoners, It's My Party, From the Edge, The Immortals, The Grave, Power 98, The Cable Guy, American Strays.
TELEVISION: Series: Another World. Specials: Paul's Case, Miss Lonelyhearts, Dear America (reader). Movies: To Heal a Nation, The Lost Capone, Descending Angel, Vendetta: Secrets of a Mafia Bride, Fugitive Among Us, Love Honor & Obey: The Last Mafia Marriage, Voyage, Love Cheat and Steal, Dark Angel.

ROBERTS, JULIA
Actress. b. Smyrna, GA, Oct. 28, 1967. r.n. Julie Roberts. Brother is actor Eric Roberts. Parents ran theater workshop in Atlanta. Moved to NY to study acting; modeled for the Click Agency before making prof. debut in brother's film Blood Red.
PICTURES: Blood Red (debut, 1986), Satisfaction, Mystic Pizza, Steel Magnolias (Acad. Award nom.), Pretty Woman (Acad. Award nom.), Flatliners, Sleeping With the Enemy, Dying Young, Hook, The Player, The Pelican Brief, I Love Trouble, Ready to Wear (Pret-a-Porter), Something to Talk About, Mary Reilly, Michael Collins, Everyone Says I Love You.
TELEVISION: Movie: Baja Oklahoma. Guest: Crime Story, Friends.

ROBERTS, PERNELL
Actor. b. Waycross, GA, May 18, 1930. e. U. of Maryland. Left college to begin working with summer stock companies, joining Arena Stage in Washington, DC in 1950. 1952 began appearing off-B'way (where he won a Drama Desk Award for Macbeth, 1957); made B'way debut in 1958 in Tonight in Samarkand.
PICTURES: Desire Under the Elms (debut, 1958), The Sheepman, Ride Lonesome, The Errand Boy (cameo), Four Rode Out, The Magic of Lassie.
TELEVISION: Series: Bonanza, Trapper John M.D., FBI: The Untold Stories (host). Movies: The Silent Gun, San Francisco International, The Bravos, Adventures of Nick Carter, Assignment: Munich, Dead Man on the Run, The Deadly Tower, The Lives of Jenny Dolan, Charlie Cobb: Nice Night for a Hanging, The Immigrants, The Night Rider, Hot Rod, High Noon Part II: The Return of Will Kane, Incident at Crestridge, Desperado, Perry Mason: The Case of the Sudden Death Payoff, Perry Mason: The Case of the All-Star Assassin, Donor. Mini-Series: Captains and the Kings, Centennial, Around the World in 80 Days.

ROBERTS, TONY
Actor. b. New York, NY, Oct. 22, 1939. e. Northwestern U.
THEATER: B'way: How Now Dow Jones, Don't Drink the Water, Play It Again Sam, Promises Promises, Barefoot in the Park, Absurd Person Singular, Sugar, Murder at the Howard Johnson's, They're Playing Our Song, Doubles, Arsenic and Old Lace, Jerome Robbins' Broadway, The Seagull, The Sisters Rosensweig, Victor/Victoria. Off-B'way: The Cradle Will Rock, The Good Parts, Four Dogs and a Bone. NY City Opera: Brigadoon, South Pacific. Dir: One of the All-Time Greats (Off-B'way).
PICTURES: Million Dollar Duck, Star Spangled Girl, Play It Again Sam, Serpico, The Taking of Pelham One Two Three, Lovers Like Us (Le Sauvage), Annie Hall, Just Tell Me What You Want, Stardust Memories, A Midsummer Night's Sex Comedy, Amityville 3-D, Key Exchange, Hannah and Her Sisters, Radio Days, 18 Again, Popcorn, Switch.
TELEVISION: Series: Rosetti and Ryan, The Four Seasons, The Lucie Arnaz Show, The Thorns. Movies: The Lindbergh Kidnapping Case, Girls in the Office, If Things Were Different, Seize the Day, Messiah on Mott Street, A Question of Honor, A Different Affair, Our Sons, Not in My Family, The American Clock, A Perry Mason Mystery: The Case of the Jealous Jokester. Guest: The Defenders, Phyllis, Storefront Lawyers, MacMillan, Trapper John M.D., Love American Style, Love Boat, Hotel.

ROBERTS, WILLIAM
Writer, Producer. b. Los Angeles, CA. e. U. of Southern California.
PICTURES: The Mating Game, The Magnificent Seven, The Wonderful World of the Brothers Grimm, Come Fly With Me, The Devil's Brigade, The Bridge At Remagen, One More Train to Rob, Red Sun, The Last American Hero, Posse, Ten to Midnight.
TELEVISION: Donna Reed Show (creator).

ROBERTSON, CLIFF
Actor, Writer, Director. b. La Jolla, CA, Sept. 9, 1925.
THEATER: Mr. Roberts, Late Love, The Lady and the Tiger, Ghosts of 87 (one-man show). B'way: The Wisteria Tree, Orpheus Descending (Theatre World Award), Love Letters.
PICTURES: Picnic (debut, 1955), Autumn Leaves, The Girl Most Likely, The Naked and the Dead, Gidget, Battle of the Coral Sea, As the Sea Rages, All in a Night's Work, Underworld USA, The Big Show, The Interns, My Six Loves, PT 109, Sunday in New York, The Best Man, 633 Squadron, Love Has Many Faces, Masquerade, Up From the Beach, The Honey Pot, The Devil's Brigade (also wrote), Charly (Academy Award, 1968), Too Late the Hero, J.W. Coop (also dir., s.p.), The Great Northfield Minnesota Raid, Ace Eli and Rodger of the Skies, Man on a Swing, Out of Season, Three Days of the Condor, Shoot, Obsession, Dominique, Fraternity Row (narrator), Class, Brainstorm, Star 80, Shaker Run, Malone, Wild Hearts Can't Be Broken, Wind, Renaissance Man, Dazzle, The Sunset Boys, Escape From L.A.

TELEVISION: Series: Falcon Crest. Guest: Philco-Goodyear, Studio One, Robert Montgomery Presents, The Game (Emmy Award, 1966), Batman. Movies: Man Without a Country, My Father's House, Washington: Behind Closed Doors, Dreams of Gold, Key to Rebecca, Henry Ford—The Man and the Machine, Dead Reckoning, Dazzle, The Last Best Days, Assignment Berlin. Special: Days of Wine and Roses (Playhouse 90). Also spokesman for AT&T.

ROBERTSON, DALE
Actor, Producer. r.n. Dayle Robertson. b. Harrah, OK, July 14, 1923. e. Oklahoma Military Coll. Prof. prizefighter; U.S. Army, 1942-45. Film debut as bit player. Voted Star of Tomorrow, M.P. Herald Fame Poll, 1951.
PICTURES: The Boy With Green Hair (debut, 1948), Flamingo Road, Fighting Man of the Plains, Caribou Trail, Two Flags West, Call Me Mister, Take Care of My Little Girl, Golden Girl, Lydia Bailey, Return of the Texan, The Outcasts of Poker Flat, O. Henry's Full House, The Farmer Takes a Wife, Devil's Canyon, The Silver Whip, City of Bad Men, The Gambler from Natchez, Sitting Bull, Son of Sinbad, Day of Fury, Dakota Incident, Hell Canyon Outlaws, Fast and Sexy, Law of the Lawless, Blood on the Arrow, Coast of Skeletons, The One-Eyed Soldier.
TELEVISION: Series: Tales of Wells Fargo, The Iron Horse, Death Valley Days, Dynasty, Dallas, J.J. Starbuck. Movies: Scalplock, Melvin Purvis: G-Man, Kansas City Massacre, Last Ride of the Dalton Gang. Guest: The Love Boat, Matt Houston, Murder She Wrote.

ROBERTSON, TIMOTHY B.
Executive. e. Univ of VA, Gordon-Conwell Thelogical Seminary, Columbia Univ. Manager of WXNE-TV in Boston, 1980-82; supervisor of Christian Broadcasting Network's tv facility; 1982-90, in charge of Middle East Television after purchase by CBN. Became President & CEO of International Family Entertainment Inc., holdings include The Family Channel, Cable Health Club, The Family Channel in the UK, MTM Entertainment Inc.

ROBINSON, BRUCE
Actor, Director, Writer. b. Kent, England, 1946. e. Central School of Speech and Drama. As actor appeared in 12 films but began writing novels and screenplays long before he gave up acting in 1975.
PICTURES: Actor: Romeo and Juliet (debut), The Story of Adele H. (last film as actor). Writer: The Killing Fields (Acad. Award nom.), Fat Man and Little Boy. Director-Writer: Withnail and I, How to Get Ahead in Advertising, Jennifer Eight.

ROBINSON, JAMES G.
Executive, Producer. e. Univ. of Maryland. Was prof. photographer and business entrepreneur prior to entering m.p. industry as co-prod. of The Stone Boy, and exec. prod. of Where the River Runs Black, Streets of Gold. Founded Morgan Creek Prods. in 1988, Morgan Creek Intl. in 1989, Morgan Creek Music Group in 1990, Morgan Creek Theatres and Morgan Creek International Theatres in 1992. Chairman and CEO of Morgan Creek.
PICTURES: Exec. Prod. for Morgan Creek: Young Guns, Skin Deep, Renegades, Enemies a Love Story, Nightbreed, Coupe de Ville, Young Guns II, The Exorcist III, Pacific Heights, Robin Hood: Prince of Thieves, Freejack, White Sands, The Last of the Mohicans, True Romance. Prod. for Morgan Creek: Stay Tuned, The Crush, Ace Ventura: Pet Detective, Major League II, Chasers, Trial by Jury, Silent Fall, Imaginary Crimes, A Walk in the Clouds, Big Bully, Ace Ventura: When Nature Calls, Two If By Sea.

ROBINSON, PHIL ALDEN
Director, Writer. b. Long Beach, NY, Mar. 1, 1950. e. Union Coll., Schenectady. Write and directed training films for Air Force, before writing two episodes for series Trapper John M.D.
PICTURES: Rhinestone (co-s.p.), All of Me (s.p., assoc. prod.). Dir./Writer: In the Mood, Field of Dreams, Sneakers.
TELEVISION: Series: Trapper John M.D. (writer), The George Burns Comedy Week (dir.)

ROCCO, ALEX
Actor. b. Cambridge, MA, Feb. 29, 1936.
PICTURES: Motor Psycho, St. Valentine's Day Massacre, Blood Mania, The Godfather, Slither, Detroit 9000, Friends of Eddie Coyle, The Outside Man, Stanley, Freebie and the Bean, Three the Hard Way, Rafferty and the Gold Dust Twins, Hearts of the West, Fire Sale, House Calls, Rabbit Test, Voices, Herbie Goes Bananas, The Stunt Man, Nobody's Perfekt, The Entity, Cannonball Run II, Stick, Gotcha!, P.K. and the Kid, Return to Horror High, Dream a Little Dream, Wired, The Pope Must Die.
TELEVISION: Series: Three for the Road, The Famous Teddy Z (Emmy Award, 1990), Sibs, The George Carlin Show. Movies: Hustling, The Blue Knight, A Question of Guilt, The

Grass is Always Greener Over the Septic Tank, Badge of the Assassin, Rock 'n' Roll Mom, The First Time, A Quiet Little Neighborhood A Perfect Little Murder, An Inconvenient Woman, Boris & Natasha, Love Honor & Obey: The Last Mafia Marriage, Robin Cook's Harmful Intent. *Mini-Series*: 79 Park Avenue.

RODDAM, FRANC
Director. b. Stockton, England, Apr. 29, 1946. Studied at London Film Sch. Spent two years as adv. copywriter/prod. with Ogilvy, Benson, Mather before joining BBC as documentary filmmaker. Founder of Union Pictures 1991.
PICTURES: Quadrophenia (also co-s.p.), The Lords of Discipline, Rain Forest (s.p. only), The Bride, Aria (sequence), War Party (also co-exec. prod.), K2.
TELEVISION: *Director*: The Family, Mini, Dummy. *Creator*: Aufwiedersehen Pet, Making Out, Masterchief, Harry.

RODRIGUEZ, ROBERT
Director, Writer, Producer, Editor. e. Univ. of TX. While in college created comic strip Los Hooligans. Made several short films including Bedhead which won several festival awards.
PICTURES: *Director/Writer*: El Mariachi (feature debut, 1993; also co-prod., story, photog., editor, sound), Desperado (also prod., editor), Four Rooms (segment), From Dusk Till Dawn (dir.).
TELEVISION: *Movie* (dir./writer): Roadracers.

ROEG, NICOLAS
Director, Cameraman. b. London, England. Aug. 15, 1928. m. actress Theresa Russell. Entered film industry through cutting rooms of MGM's British Studios, dubbing French films into English. Moved into prod. as clapper boy and part of photographer Freddie Young's crew at Marylebone Studios London, 1947. Next became camera operator (Trials of Oscar Wilde, The Sundowners). Had first experience as cameraman on TV series (Police Dog and Ghost Squad). Debut as director on Performance, co-directed with Donald Cammell. First solo dir. film, Walkabout.
PICTURES: *Cameraman*: The Miniver Story, The Trial of Oscar Wilde, The Sundowners, Lawrence of Arabia, Jazz Boat, Information Received, The Great Van Robbery. *Dir. of Photography*: The Caretaker, Dr. Crippen, Nothing But the Best, Masque of the Red Death, A Funny Thing Happened on the Way to the Forum, Fahrenheit 451, Far from the Madding Crowd, The Girl-Getters, Petulia. *Director-Cameraman*: Performance (co.-dir.), Walkabout. *Director*: Don't Look Now, The Man Who Fell To Earth, Bad Timing, Eureka, Insignificance, Castaway, Aria (sequence, also co-s.p.), Track 29, The Witches, Without You I'm Nothing (exec. prod. only), Cold Heaven.
TELEVISION: *Movies*: Sweet Bird of Youth, Heart of Darkness.

ROËVES, MAURICE
Actor, Director, Writer. b. Sunderland, England, Mar. 19, 1937. Ent. industry, 1964. Played Macduff to Alec Guinness's Macbeth, London stage. Early films: Ulysses, Oh! What a Lovely War, Young Winston, The Eagle Has Landed, Who Dares Wins. Dir. many stage plays.
THEATER: The Killing of Michael Malloy (Best Leading Actor Award, 1994).
PICTURES: Hidden Agenda, Last of the Mohicans, Judge Dredd.
TELEVISION: In *USA* and *UK* incl.: Scobie (series), The Gambler, Allergy, Magnum P.I., Remington Steele, Escape to Victoria, Inside the Third Reich, Journal of Bridgitte Hitler, Tutti Frutti, Unreported Incident, Bookie, North & South Part II, 919 Fifth Ave., Moses (mini-series).

ROGERS, CHARLES (BUDDY)
Actor. b. Olathe, KS, Aug. 13, 1904. e. U. of Kansas, and was trained for screen in Paramount Picture Sch. In armed services WWII. 1945 named v.p. & treas. Comet Prods., Inc. Assoc. prod. Sleep My Love, 1950, pres. PRB, Inc., prod. radio, video shows.
PICTURES: Fascinating Youth, So's Your Old Man, Wings, My Best Girl, Get Your Man, Abie's Irish Rose, The Lawyer's Secret, Road to Reno, Working Girls, This Reckless Age, Best of Enemies, Take a Chance, Dance Band, Old Man Rhythm, One in a Million, Let's Make a Night of It, This Way Please, Golden Hoofs, Mexican Spitfire's Baby, Sing for Your Supper, Mexican Spitfire at Sea, Mexican Spitfire Sees a Ghost, Don't Trust Your Husband, The Parson and the Outlaw, many others.

ROGERS, FRED
Television Host, Producer. b. Latrobe, PA, March 20, 1928. e. Rollins Coll., B.A., music composition, 1951; Pittsburgh Theol. Seminary, M. Div. 1962. 1951 served as asst. prod. of NBC-TV's The Voice of Firestone and NBC-TV Opera Theatre. Later promoted to network floor dir., supervising Your Lucky Strike Hit Parade, Kate Smith Hour, etc. 1953, joined WQED-TV in Pittsburgh, educational TV station, to handle programming. 1954 started Children's Corner series, writing, producing and per-

forming; it ran 7 years. 1963 was ordained minister of Presbyterian Church, dedicated to working with children and families through media. Same year introduced Mister Rogers on Canadian Broadcasting Corp. of 15-min. daily program. Ran for one year—was similar in content to present half-hour program, Mister Rogers' Neighborhood. 1964 programs were incorporated into larger, half-hour format on ABC affiliate in Pittsburgh. 1966, 100 programs acquired by Eastern Educational Network, broadcast in Pittsburgh, and seen for first time in other cities (and on some cable services) with underwriting by Sears & Roebuck Foundation. Mister Rogers' Neighborhood in its present format began on Feb. 19, 1968 on NET (now PBS). Program now carried over 300 PBS stations. Author of numerous fiction books for children and non-fiction books for adults; and albums and videos released by Family Communication. Also prod. 20 part PBS series Old Friends New Friends, interview/documentary format for adults, 1978-9. Produced Fred Rogers' Heroes (adult special for PBS). Recipient of 2 Emmy Awards, 2 Peabody Awards and over 25 honorary degrees from colleges and universities.

ROGERS, KENNY
Singer, Actor, Songwriter. b. Crockett, TX, Aug. 21, 1938. Country and western singer. Member Bobby Doyle Trio, Christy Minstrels, 1966-67; The First Edition 1967-76. On screen in Six Pack (1982).
TELEVISION: *Series*: McShane (NBC Friday Night Mystery). *Movies*: The Dream Makers, Kenny Rogers as The Gambler, Coward of the County, Kenny Rogers as the Gambler: The Adventure Continues, Wild Horses; Kenny Rogers as The Gambler Part III: The Legend Continues, Christmas in America, The Gambler Returns: Luck of the Draw, Real West, Rio Diablo, MacShayne: The Final Roll of the Dice, Gambler IV: Playing for Keeps, Big Dreams & Broken Hearts: The Dottie West Story. *Specials*: Kenny, Dolly & Willie: Something Inside So Strong, and numerous others. *Guest*: Dr. Quinn, Medicine Woman.

ROGERS, LAWRENCE H., II
Executive, b. Trenton, NJ, Sept. 6, 1921. e. Princeton U. 1942; U.S. Army, 1942-1946; with WSAZ, Huntington, WV, as radio & tv, v.p. & gen. mgr., 1949-55; WSAZ, Inc., pres., 1955-59; Taft Broadcasting Co., v.p., 1959-63; Taft Broadcasting Co., pres., 1963-76; cert., Harvard Business Sch., 1963; vice chmn., Hanna-Barbera Prods., LA, and Cinemobile Systems, Hollywood. Director: Cine Artists International, Hollywood; Theater Development Fund, NY. Author: Orlando Shoot-Out, 1990.

ROGERS, MIMI
Actress. b. Coral Gables, FL, Jan. 27, 1956.
PICTURES: Blue Skies Again (debut, 1983), Gung Ho, Street Smart, Someone to Watch Over Me, The Mighty Quinn, Hider in the House, Desperate Hours, The Doors, The Rapture, The Palermo Connection, The Player, White Sands, Dark Horse, Monkey Trouble, Far From Home: The Adventures of Yellow Dog, Bulletproof Heart, Reflections in the Dark, The Mirror Has Two Faces.
TELEVISION: *Series*: The Rousters, Paper Dolls. *Episodes*: Magnum, P.I., Hart to Hart, Quincy, M.E., Hill Street Blues, Tales From the Crypt. *Movies*: Divorce Wars, Hear No Evil, You Ruined My Life, Fourth Story, Deadlock, Ladykiller, Bloodlines: Murder in the Family, A Kiss to Die For.

ROGERS, PETER
Executive. b. Rochester, Eng., Feb. 20, 1916. e. Kings Sch., Rochester. Journalist and in theatre and BBC; joined G. W. H. Productions 1941 as script writer; with Gainsborough Studios; asst. scenario ed. to Muriel Box; assoc. prod.; personal asst. to Sydney Box 1949.
PICTURES: Dear Murderer, Holiday Camp, When the Bough Breaks, Here Come the Huggetts, Huggetts Abroad, Vote for Huggett, It's Not Cricket, Marry Me, Don't Ever Leave Me, Appointment with Venus (Island Rescue), The Clouded Yellow, The Dog and the Diamonds (Children's Film Found), Up to His Neck, You Know What Sailors Are, Cash on Delivery, To Dorothy A Son, Gay Dog, Circus Friends, Passionate Stranger, After the Ball, Time Lock, My Friend Charles, Chain of Events, Carry on Sergeant, Flying Scott, Cat Girl, Solitary Child, Carry On Teacher, Carry On Nurse, Carry On Constable, Please Turn Over, Watch Your Stern, The Tommy Steele Story, The Duke Wore Jeans, No Kidding, Carry On Regardless, Raising the Wind, Twice Around the Daffodils, Carry on Cruising, The Iron Maiden, Nurse on Wheels, Carry on Cabby, This Is My Street, Carry On Jack, Carry on Spying, Carry on Cleo, The Big Job, Carry on Cowboy, Carry on Screaming, Don't Lose Your Head, Follow that Camel, Carry on Doctor, Carry on Up the Khyber, Carry on Camping, Carry on Assault, Carry on Henry, Quest, Revenge, Carry on At Your Convenience, All Coppers Are..., Carry on Matron, Carry on Abroad, Bless This House, Carry on Girls, Carry on Dick, Carry on Behind, Carry on England, The Best of Carry On, Carry on Emmanuelle, Carry on Columbus.
TELEVISION: Ivanhoe (series), Carry on Laughing, Carry on Laughing, What a Carry On, Laugh With the Carry On's.

ROGERS, ROY
Actor. r.n. Leonard Slye. b. Cincinnati, OH Nov. 5, 1911. m.
actress-singer Dale Evans. Radio singer. Changed named to
Dick Wesson and formed singing group Sons of the Pioneers,
with which he made his film debut. Voted No. 1 Money-Making
Western Star in M.P. Herald-Fame, 1943-54 inclusive; also
voted one of ten best money-making stars in 1945, 1946.
Acting & prod. TV films, 1952 with wife, Dale Evans; one-hour
spectaculars, Chevy Show, 1959-60; contracted for several TV
specials and for nationwide appearances with Roy Rogers
touring show in Canada & U.S., 1962; state fairs, rodeos since
1962; TV series; Happy Trails with Roy and Dale (cable). Star
of 86 feature films and 104 TV episodes.
PICTURES: Way Up Thar (debut, 1935, as Dick Wesson),
Rhythm on the Range, Under Western Stars (1st billing as
Roy Rogers), The Old Barn Dance, Billy the Kid Returns,
Come On Rangers, Rough Riders, Round-Up, Frontier, Pony
Express, Southward Ho!, In Old Caliente, Wall Street Cowboy,
Heart of the Golden West, Sunset Serenade, Pals of the
Golden West, Son of Paleface, Alias Jesse James (cameo),
MacIntosh and T.J.
TELEVISION: Series: The Roy Rogers Show, The Roy Rogers
& Dale Evans Show.

ROGERS, THOMAS C.
Executive. e. Columbia Law School, Wesleyan Univ. 1981-86,
sr. counsel, U.S. House of Representatives Subcommittee on
Telecommunications, Consumer Protection and Finance;
Joined NBC in 1987 as v.p., policy and planning and business
development. 1988 became pres. of NBC Cable and Business
Development. 1992, also named exec. v.p. of NBC.

ROGERS, WAYNE
Actor. b. Birmingham, AL, April 7, 1933. e. Princeton U.
PICTURES: Odds Against Tomorrow (debut, 1959), The Glory
Guys, Chamber of Horrors, Cool Hand Luke, WUSA, Pocket
Money, Once in Paris, The Gig, The Killing Time, Ghosts of
Mississippi.
TELEVISION: Series: Edge of Night, Stagecoach West,
M*A*S*H, City of the Angels, House Calls, High Risk (host).
Movies: Attack on Terror: The FBI Versus the Ku Klux Klan,
Making Babies II, It Happened One Christmas, The Top of the
Hill, Chiefs, He's Fired She's Hired, The Lady from Yesterday,
American Harvest, Drop-Out Mother, One Terrific Guy,
Bluegrass, Passion and Paradise, Miracle Landing, The
Goodbye Bird. Mini-Series: Chiefs. Exec. prod.: Perfect
Witness, Age-Old Friends.

ROHRBECK, JOHN H.
Executive. e. Univ. of WA. 1967, account exec. for NBC Spot
Sales in San Francisco, then NY. 1969-78, with KNBC-TV in
mngmt. and sales, became station manager in 1976. 1978-84,
v.p. & gen. mngr. WRC-TV in Washington DC. Became pres. &
gen. mngr. of KNBC-TV in 1984. Named pres. of NBC
Television Stations, 1991. Also in charge of network's daytime
programming 1992-95.

ROHMER, ERIC
Director. Writer. r.n. Jean Maurice Scherer. b. Nancy, France,
April 4, 1920. Professor of literature. Film critic for La Gazette
du Cinema and its successor Cahiers du Cinema which he
edited, 1957-63. With Claude Chabrol wrote book on Alfred
Hitchcock as a Catholic moralist, 1957. 1959 directorial debut,
Le Signe du Lion. 1962 began a series of 6 Moral Tales; from
1980 with The Aviator's Wife began another series of 7 films
called Comedies and Proverbs. Staged Catherine de
Heilbronn in Nanterre, 1979.
PICTURES: Short films: Presentation ou Charlotte et Son
Steack (1961), La Boulangere de Monceau, Veronique et Son
Cancre, Nadja a Paris, Place de L'etoile, Une Etudiante d'au-
jourd'hui, Fermiere a Montfaucon. Feature films (dir. & s.p.):
Le Signe du Lion (The Sign of Leo; debut, 1959), La Carriere
de Suzanne, Six in Paris (episode), La Collectionneuse, My
Night at Maude's, Claire's Knee, Chloe in the Afternoon, The
Marquise of O, Perceval, The Aviator's Wife, Le Beau Mariage,
Pauline at the Beach, Full Moon in Paris, Summer, Boyfriends
and Girlfriends, Four Adventures of Reinette and Mirabelle
(also prod.), A Tale of Springtime, A Tale of Winter.
TELEVISION: Carl Dreyer, Le Celluloid et le Marbre, Ville
Nouvelle, Catherine de Heilbronn. Between 1964-69 directed
series of documentaries for French TV: Les Cabinets et Physique
du XVIII siecle, Les Metamorphoses du Paysage Industriel, Don
Quichotte, Edgar Poe, Pascal, Louis Lumiere, etc.

ROIZMAN, OWEN
Cinematographer. b. Brooklyn, NY, Sept. 22, 1936. e.
Gettysburg Col.
PICTURES: The French Connection, The Gang That Couldn't
Shoot Straight, Play It Again Sam, The Heartbreak Kid, The
Exorcist, The Taking of Pelham 1-2-3, The Stepford Wives,
Independence, Three Days of the Condor, The Return of the
Man Called Horse, Network, Straight Time, Sgt. Pepper's
Lonely Hearts Club Band, The Electric Horseman, The Black

Marble, True Confessions, Absence of Malice, Taps, Tootsie,
Vision Quest, I Love You to Death, Havana, The Addams
Family, Grand Canyon, Wyatt Earp, French Kiss.

ROLLE, ESTHER
Actress. b. Pompano Beach, FL, Nov. 8, 1922. e. New School
for Social Research. An original member of Negro Ensemble
Co. in NY. Has appeared both off and on B'way (in The Blacks,
Amen Corner, Blues for Mister Charlie, Don't Play Us Cheap,
Member of the Wedding) and in several TV series.
PICTURES: Nothing But a Man, Cleopatra Jones, P.K. and the
Kid, The Mighty Quinn, Driving Miss Daisy, House of Cards,
How to Make an American Quilt.
TELEVISION: Guest: N.Y.P.D., Like It Is, Darkroom, The
Winners, The Grand Baby. Series: One Life to Live, Maude,
Good Times. Movies: I Know Why the Caged Bird Sings,
Summer of My German Soldier (Emmy Award, 1979), A Raisin
in the Sun, Age-Old Friends, The Kid Who Loved Christmas,
To Dance With the White Dog. Mini-Series: Scarlett.

ROLLINS, HOWARD
Actor. b. Baltimore, MD, Oct. 17, 1950. e. Towson State Coll.
THEATER: NY: We Interrupt This Program, Traps, Streamers,
The Mighty Gents, Medal of Honor Rag, G.R. Point. Other
stage (London): I'm Not Rappaport, Othello (Statford,
Ontario).
PICTURES: Ragtime (debut, 1981; Acad. Award nom.), The
House of God, A Soldier's Story, On the Block, Drunks.
TELEVISION: Series: Our Street (PBS 1969-73), All My
Children, Wildside, In the Heat of the Night. Mini-series: King,
Roots: The Next Generation. Movies: My Old Man, Doctor's
Story, He's Fired, She's Hired, The Boy King, The Children of
Times Square. Johnnie Mae Gibson: FBI, With Murder in
Mind. Specials: Eliza: Our Story, Dear America: Letters Home
From Vietnam (reader).

ROLLINS, JACK
Producer. b. 1914. Co-founder of talent management firm
Rollins, Joffe, Mora and Brezner Inc. handling careers of
Woody Allen, Nichols and May, Robin Williams, Robert Klein,
David Letterman, Dick Cavett, Billy Crystal.
PICTURES: Co-prod./exec. prod. with Charles Joffe: Take the
Money and Run, Bananas, Everything You Always Wanted to
Know About Sex, Sleeper, Love and Death, The Front, Annie
Hall (Academy Award for Best Picture, 1977), Interiors,
Manhattan, Stardust Memories, Zelig, Broadway Danny Rose
(also actor), The Purple Rose of Cairo, Hannah and Her
Sisters, Radio Days, September, Another Woman, New York
Stories (Oedipus Wrecks), Crimes and Misdemeanors, Alice,
Shadows and Fog, Husbands and Wives, Manhattan Murder
Mystery, Bullets Over Broadway.
TELEVISION: Prod./exec. prod.: The Dick Cavett Show, Late
Night With David Letterman.

ROMAN, LAWRENCE
Writer. b. Jersey City, NJ, May 30, 1921. e. UCLA, 1943.
THEATER: Author: Under the Yum Yum Tree, P.S. I Love You,
Alone Together, Buying Out, Crystal, Crystal Chandelier
(prod. in Stockbridge, Mass), Coulda Woulda Shoulda (prod.
in Berlin, Germany), Moving Mountains (prod. in Berlin as
Grapes and Raisins).
PICTURES: Drums Across the River, Vice Squad, Naked Alibi,
One Desire, Man from Bitter Ridge, Kiss Before Dying,
Slaughter on Tenth Avenue, Under the Yum Yum Tree, The
Swinger, Paper Lion, Red Sun, A Warm December, McQ.
TELEVISION: Movies: Anatomy of an Illness, Badge of the
Assassin, Three Wishes for Jamie, Final Verdict, The Ernest
Green Story (Peabody Award).

ROMAN, RUTH
Actress. b. Boston, MA, Dec. 23, 1924. p. professionals. e.
Girls H.S.; Boston; Bishop Lee Dramatic Sch. Started career
with little theatre groups: New Eng. Repertory Co., Elizabeth
Peabody Players. Chicago Theatre includes Night of the
Iguana, Two for the Season (Sarah Siddons Award). Screen
debut in Universal serial, Queen of the Jungle.
PICTURES: Good Sam, Belle Starr's Daughter, The Window,
Champion, Barricade, Beyond the Forest, Always Leave Them
Laughing, Colt .45, Three Secrets, Dallas, Strangers on a
Train, Tomorrow is Another Day, Invitation, Lightning Strikes
Twice, Starlift, Mara Maru, Young Man With Ideas, Blowing
Wild, Far Country, Shanghai Story, Tanganyika, Down Three
Dark Streets, Joe Macbeth, Bottom of the Bottle, Great Day in
the Morning, Rebel in Town, Five Steps to Danger, Bitter
Victory, Desert Desperadoes, Look in Any Window, Miracle of
the Cowards (Spanish), Love Has Many Faces, Impulse, The
Killing Kind, The Baby, Day of the Animals, Echoes.
TELEVISION: Series: The Long Hot Summer, Knots Landing.
Guest: Naked City, Route 66, The Defenders, Breaking Point,
Eleventh Hour, Producers Showcase, Dr. Kildare, Murder She
Wrote, Cannon, Ironside. Movies: The Old Man Who Cried
Wolf, Incident in San Francisco, Go Ask Alice, Punch and
Jody, The Sacketts.

ROMERO, GEORGE A.
Director, Writer, Editor. b. New York, NY, 1940. e. Carnegie-Mellon Univ.
PICTURES: *Dir./Writer/Cameraman*: Night of the Living Dead (debut, 1968), There's Always Vanilla (The Affair), The Crazies (Code Name: Trixie), Jack's Wife (Hungry Wives; also edit.). *Director-Writer*: Martin (also edit., actor), Dawn of the Dead (dir. only), Knightriders, Creepshow (dir., co-edit. only), Day of the Dead (also edit.), Monkey Shines, Night of the Living Dead (s.p., co-exec. prod. only), Two Evil Eyes (The Facts in the Case of M. Valdemar), The Dark Half (also exec. prod.).
TELEVISION: Tales from the Dark Side (exec. prod., writer).

ROOKER, MICHAEL
Actor. b. Jasper, AL, 1955. e. Goodman School of Drama. Studied Japanese martial art of Aikido prior to establishing himself in Chicago theatre, where he appeared in Union Boys, The Crack Walker and Moon Children.
PICTURES: Streets of Fire (debut, 1984), Light of Day, Rent-a-Cop, Eight Men Out, Mississippi Burning, Sea of Love, Music Box, Henry: Portrait of a Serial Killer, Days of Thunder, JFK, The Dark Half, Cliffhanger, Tombstone, The Hard Truth, Mallrats, The Trigger Effect, Rosewood.
TELEVISION: *Movies*: Afterburn, Johnny & Clyde.

ROONEY, ANDREW A
Writer, Producer. b. Albany, NY, Jan. 14, 1919. e. Colgate U. Started career as writer at MGM 1946-7, then for Arthur Godfrey, Garry Moore, Sam Levenson, Victor Borge; wrote and produced documentaries, including Black History: Lost Stolen or Strayed (Emmy Award, 1969), An Essay on War, An Essay on Bridges, In Praise of New York City, Mr. Rooney Goes to Washington, etc. Regularly appears on 60 Minutes (CBS). Newspaper columnist for Tribune Syndicate, 1979-current.

ROONEY, MICKEY
Actor. r.n. Joe Yule, Jr. b. Brooklyn, NY, Sept. 23, 1920. Son of Joe Yule & Nell Carter, vaudeville performers. U.S. Army, WWII. In vaudeville as child with parents and others before m.p. debut and after; from age of 5 to 12 (1926-33) created screen version of Fontaine Fox newspaper comic character Mickey McGuire in series of short subjects (also billed as Mickey McGuire). Adopted name of Mickey Rooney, returned to vaudeville, then resumed screen career in features. Special Academy Award 1940 for Andy Hardy characterization; voted among first ten Money-Making Stars in M.P. Herald-Fame Poll: 1938-43. Autobiographies: i.e. (1965), Life is Too Short (1991). Novel: The Search for Sonny Skies (1994). Received honorary Academy Award, 1983.
THEATER: *B'way*: Sugar Babies, The Will Rogers Follies. *Regional*: W.C., Lend Me a Tenor.
PICTURES: Orchids and Ermine (feature debut, 1927), Emma, The Beast of the City, Sin's Pay Day, High Speed, Officer Thirteen, Fast Companions, My Pal the King, The Big Cage, The Life of Jimmy Dolan, The Big Chance, Broadway to Hollywood, The World Changes, The Chief, Beloved, I Like It That Way, Love Birds, Half a Sinner, The Lost Jungle, Manhattan Melodrama, Upperworld, Hide-Out, Chained, Blind Date, Death on the Diamond, The County Chairman, Reckless, The Healer, A Midsummer Night's Dream, Ah Wilderness, Riff-Raff, Little Lord Fauntleroy, The Devil is a Sissy, Down the Stretch, Captains Courageous, Slave Ship, A Family Affair, Hoosier Schoolboy, Live Love and Learn, Thoroughbreds Don't Cry, You're Only Young Once, Love is a Headache, Judge Hardy's Children, Hold That Kiss, Lord Jeff, Love Finds Andy Hardy, Boys Town, Stablemates, Out West With the Hardys, The Adventures of Huckleberry Finn, The Hardys Ride High, Andy Hardy Gets Spring Fever, Babes in Arms (Acad. award nom.), Judge Hardy and Son, Young Tom Edison, Andy Hardy Meets Debutante, Strike Up the Band, Andy Hardy's Private Secretary, Men of Boy's Town, Life Begins for Andy Hardy, Babes on Broadway, The Courtship of Andy Hardy, A Yank at Eton, Andy Hardy's Double Life, The Human Comedy (Acad. Award nom.), Girl Crazy, Thousands Cheer, Andy Hardy's Blonde Trouble, National Velvet, Love Laughs at Andy Hardy, Killer McCoy, Summer Holiday, Words and Music, The Big Wheel, Quicksand, He's a Cockeyed Wonder, The Fireball, My Outlaw Brother, The Strip, Sound Off, All Ashore, Off Limits, A Slight Case of Larceny, Drive a Crooked Road, The Atomic Kid (also prod.), The Bridges at Toko-Ri, The Twinkle in God's Eye, Francis in the Haunted House, The Bold and the Brave (Acad. Award nom.), Magnificent Roughnecks, Operation Mad Ball, Baby Face Nelson, Andy Hardy Comes Home, A Nice Little Bank That Should Be Robbed, The Last Mile, The Big Operator, Platinum High School, The Private Lives of Adam and Eve (also co-dir.), Breakfast at Tiffany's, King of the Roaring Twenties, Requiem for a Heavyweight, Everything's Ducky, It's a Mad Mad Mad Mad World, Secret Invasion, 24 Hours to Kill, The Devil in Love, Ambush Bay, How to Stuff a Wild Bikini, The Extraordinary Seaman, Skidoo, The Comic, 80 Steps to Jonah, The Cockeyed Cowboys of Calico County, Hollywood

Blue, B.J. Lang Presents (The Manipulator), Richard, Pulp, The Godmothers (also s.p., music), Ace of Hearts, Thunder County, That's Entertainment, Journey Back to Oz (voice), From Hong Kong With Love, Rachel's Man, Find the Lady, The Domino Principle, Pete's Dragon, The Magic of Lassie, The Black Stallion (Acad. Award nom.), Arabian Adventure, The Fox and the Hound (voice), The Emperor of Peru, The Black Stallion Returns, The Care Bears Movie (voice), Lightning the White Stallion, Erik the Viking, My Heroes Have Always Been Cowboys, Sweet Justice, The Legend of Wolf Mountain, Little Nemo (voice), Silent Night Deadly Night 5: The Toymaker, The Milky Life (La Vida Lactea), Revenge of the Red Baron, That's Entertainment III.
TELEVISION: *Series*: Hey Mickey, One of the Boys, The Black Stallion. *Many specials including*: Playhouse 90, Pinocchio, Eddie, Somebody's Waiting, The Dick Powell Theater. *Movies*: Evil Roy Slade, My Kidnapper My Love, Leave 'Em Laughing, Bill (Emmy Award, 1982), Senior Trip, Bill: On His Own, It Came Upon the Midnight Clear, Bluegrass, Home for Christmas, The Gambler Returns: Luck of the Draw. *Many guest appearances including*: The Golden Girls, The Judy Garland Show, Naked City, Wagon Train, Twilight Zone, The Lucy Show, Hollywood Squares, Night Gallery, The Love Boat.

ROOS, FRED
Producer. b. Santa Monica, CA, May 22, 1934. e. UCLA, B.A. Directed documentary films for Armed Forces Radio and Television Network. Worked briefly as agent for MCA and story editor for Robert Lippert Productions. Worked as casting dir. in 1960s and served as casting dir. on The Godfather, beginning longtime association with filmmakers Francis Coppola and George Lucas.
PICTURES: The Conversation, The Godfather Part II, Apocalypse Now, The Black Stallion, The Escape Artist (exec. prod.), The Black Stallion Returns, Hammett, One From the Heart, The Outsiders, Rumble Fish, The Cotton Club, One Magic Christmas, Seven Minutes in Heaven, Peggy Sue Got Married (special consultant), Barfly, Gardens of Stone (co-exec. prod.), Tucker: The Man and His Dream, New York Stories (Life Without Zoe), Wait Until Spring Bandini, The Godfather Part III, Hearts of Darkness: A Filmmaker's Apocalypse (exec. prod.), The Secret Garden, Radioland Murders, Jack (spec. consultant).
TELEVISION: *Series*: The Outsiders (exec. prod.). *Movie*: Montana.

ROSE, ALEX
Producer. r.n. Alexandra Rose. b. Jan. 20, 1946. e. U. of WI, BS. Started in m.p. distribution with Medford Films. Later became asst. sls. mgr. for New World Pictures.
PICTURES: *Co-prod.*: Drive-In, I Wanna Hold Your Hand, Big Wednesday, Norma Rae, Nothing in Common (solo prod.), Overboard (co-prod.), Quigley Down Under, Frankie and Johnny.
TELEVISION: Nothing in Common (co-exec. prod. with Garry Marshall), *Pilots*: Norma Rae, Just Us Kids.

ROSE, CHARLIE
Talk Show Host. b. Henderson, NC, Jan. 5, 1942. e. Duke Univ. (history, law). Was exec. prod. for Bill Moyers' Journal, 1975.
TELEVISION: *Series (host/anchor)*: A.M. Chicago, The Charlie Rose Show (NBC, 1979, 1981), CBS News Nightwatch, E.D.J. Entertainment Daily Journal (Personalities), Charlie Rose (synd; also exec. prod., editor). *Specials*: Public Debate With Charlie Rose, In Concert at the United Nations (host).

ROSE, REGINALD
Writer. b. New York, NY, Dec. 10, 1920. e. City Coll. of New York. Worked as clerk, publicist, Warner Bros.; adv. acct. exec., copy chief; U.S. Air Force, WWII; first TV play, Bus to Nowhere, 1951; since then numerous TV plays, Studio One, Playhouse 90. Creator of The Defenders, other programs.
PICTURES: Crime in the Streets, 12 Angry Men, Dino, Man of the West, The Man in the Net, Baxter, Somebody Killed Her Husband, The Wild Geese, The Sea Wolves, Whose Life Is It Anyway?, Wild Geese II, The Final Option.
TELEVISION: Dear Friends, Thunder on Sycamore Street, Tragedy in a Temporary Town, My Two Loves, The Rules of Marriage, Studs Lonigan, Escape from Sobibor.

ROSE, STEPHEN
Executive. Entered m.p. industry in 1964 with Columbia Pictures; named adv. dir. 1970 joined Cinema V Distributing, Inc. as dir. of adv.; left in 1971 to take post at Cinemation Industries, where was named v.p. and bd. member. 1975 joined Paramount Pictures as dir. of adv.; promoted to v.p./adv. 1979 formed Barrich Prods. with Gordon Weaver. 1982, rejoined Paramount as v.p., mktg; 1983, named v.p. of mktg. for Paramount; sr. v.p., mktg., 1983. Resigned in 1984 to form Barrich Marketing with Gordon Weaver.

ROSEANNE

Actress. b. Salt Lake City, UT, Nov. 3, 1952. Started performing in bars; prod. showcase for women performers, Take Back the Mike at U. of Boulder. 1983 won Denver Laff-Off. Moved to Los Angeles where performed at The Comedy Store, and showcased on TV special Funny and The Tonight Show. Has previously performed under the names Roseanne Barr, Roseanne Arnold. *Autobiographies:* My Life as a Woman (1989), My Lives (1994).
PICTURES: She-Devil (debut, 1989), Look Who's Talking Too (voice), Freddy's Dead, Even Cowgirls Get the Blues, Blue in the Face.
TELEVISION: *Series:* Roseanne (also co-exec. prod.; Peabody & Golden Globe Awards for Best Series; Emmy Award for Best Actress, 1993), The Jackie Thomas Show (co-exec. prod, guest), Tom (co-exec. prod.). *Specials:* Fast Copy, Rodney Dangerfield—It's Not Easy Bein' Me, Live From Minneapolis: Roseanne, Roseanne Arnold: Live From Trump Castle. *Movies:* Backfield in Motion, The Woman Who Loved Elvis (also co-exec. prod.).

ROSEN, ROBERT L.

Producer. b. Palm Springs, CA, Jan. 7, 1937. e. U. of Southern Calif.
PICTURES: French Connection II, Black Sunday, Prophecy, Going Ape, The Challenge, Courage (also dir.), Porky's Revenge, World Gone Wild, Dead-Bang (exec. prod.). *Exec. in chg. of prod.:* Little Big Man, Le Mans, The Reivers, Rio Lobo, Big Jake, Scrooge, Fourth War (Line Producer).
TELEVISION: Gilligan's Island, Hawaii Five-O, Have Gun Will Travel.

ROSENBERG, FRANK P.

Producer, Writer. b. New York, NY, Nov. 22, 1913. e. Columbia U., NYU. Joined Columbia 1929; writer m.p. novelizations & radio dramatizations; 1933, conceived and wrote script for first-ever ship-to-shore CBS network broadcast for Lady for a Day; exploit, mgr., 1941; apptd. national dir. adv., publicity, exploitation, Columbia Pictures, 1944. Pub. dir. M.P. Victory Loan, 1945; dir. pub. Columbia Pictures Studios, Hollywood, 1946. Resigned 1947 to enter production.
PICTURES: Man-Eater of Kumaon, Where the Sidewalk Ends (co-adapt.), The Secret of Convict Lake, Return of the Texan, The Farmer Takes a Wife, King of the Khyber Rifles, Illegal, Miracle in the Rain, The Girl He Left Behind, One-Eyed Jacks, Critic's Choice, Madigan, The Steagle (exec. prod.), The Reincarnation of Peter Proud, Gray Lady Down.
TELEVISION: Exec. prod. and prod. for Schlitz Playhouse programs during 1957-58; prod., The Troubleshooters; exec. prod., Arrest and Trial, 1963-64; exec. prod. Kraft Suspense Theatre, 1964-65; v.p. MCA Universal 1964-69; co-exec. prod., CBS tv movie Family of Strangers, 1993.

ROSENBERG, GRANT E.

Executive. b. San Francisco, CA, 1952. e. Univ. of Cal. at Davis. Started career in research dept., NBC; 1977, joined Paramount in research and later in development; 1984, v.p., dramatic dev.; then sr. v.p., dev., for TV group, Paramount. 1985, named sr. v.p., network TV for Walt Disney Pictures; 1988, named pres., Lee Rich Productions, TV div., and exec. prod. of Molloy TV series. 1990, writer, prod., Paramount TV. Series: MacGyver (writer), Star Trek: The Next Generation (writer), Time Trax (exec. prod., creator), Lois & Clark (writer, prod.). Writer, prod. for Warner Bros. TV.

ROSENBERG, RICHARD K.

Executive, Attorney. b. Paterson, NJ, Apr. 4, 1942. e. Indiana Univ. Corporation & intl. entertainment attorney for major corps. and celebrities. Formed RKR Entertainment Group in 1977 with subsidiaries RKR Releasing, RKR Artists and RKR Productions. Subsequently consolidated into RKR Pictures Inc. Author: Negotiating Motion Picture Contracts. Films include Alice Sweet Alice (Holy Terror), Hell's Angels Forever, Mother Lode, Best Revenge, The Wild Duck, Primary Motive, Fatal Past, Dutchman's Creek.

ROSENBERG, RICK

Producer. b. Los Angeles, CA. e. Los Angeles City Coll., UCLA. Started career in mail room of Columbia Pictures, then asst. to prod. Jerry Bresler on Major Dundee and Love Has Many Faces. Asst. to Col. v.p., Arthur Kramer. Was assoc. prod. on The Reivers and in 1970 prod. first feature, Adam at Six A.M., with Bob Christiansen, with whom co-prod. all credits listed below.
PICTURES: Adam at Six A.M., Hide in Plain Sight.
TELEVISION: Suddenly Single, The Glass House, A Brand New Life, The Man Who Could Talk to Kids, The Autobiography of Miss Jane Pittman, I Love You... Goodbye, Queen of the Stardust Ballroom, Born Innocent, A Death in Canaan, Strangers, Robert Kennedy and His Times, Kids Don't Tell, As Summers Die, Gore Vidal's Lincoln, Red Earth White Earth, Heist, A House of Secrets and Lies, The Last Hit, Heart of Darkness, Tad, Kingfish: A Story of Huey P. Long, Redwood Curtain.

ROSENBERG, STUART

Director, Producer. b. New York, NY, Aug. 11, 1927. e. NYU.
PICTURES: Murder, Inc. (co-dir.; debut, 1960), Question 7, Cool Hand Luke, The April Fools, Move (also co-exec. prod.), WUSA (also co-exec. prod.), Pocket Money, The Laughing Policeman (also prod.), The Drowning Pool, Voyage of the Damned, The Amityville Horror, Love and Bullets, Brubaker, The Pope of Greenwich Village, Let's Get Harry (under pseudonym Allan Smithee), My Heroes Have Always Been Cowboys.
TELEVISION: Numerous episodes of such series as The Untouchables, Naked City, The Defenders (Emmy Award, 1963), Espionage, Chrysler Theatre, Twilight Zone, Alfred Hitchcock Theater.

ROSENFELT, FRANK E.

Executive. b. Peabody, MA, Nov. 15, 1921. e. Cornell U., B.S.; Cornell Law Sch., L.L.B. Served as atty. for RKO Radio Pictures, before joining MGM in 1955 as member of legal dept. Appt. secty. in 1966. Named v.p., gen. counsel in 1969 and pres. in 1973. 1974-81, CEO, bd. chmn. & CEO, MGM; now vice chmn., MGM/UA Communications Co. Member: Bd. of Governors, Academy of M.P. Arts & Sciences for 9 years. Retired from MGM/UA in Aug. 1990, now consultant to MGM-Pathe Commun. Co.

ROSENFELT, SCOTT

Producer, Director. b. Easton, PA, Dec. 20, 1955. e. NYU.
PICTURES: *Producer:* Teen Wolf, Extremities, Russkies, Mystic Pizza, Big Man on Campus (co-prod.), Home Alone, Family Prayers (dir.).

ROSENFIELD, JONAS, JR.

Executive. b. Dallas, TX, June 29, 1915. e. U. of Miami, A.B. In U.S. Navy, WWII. Warner Bros. advertising copy dept., 1936-40; adv. mgr. Walt Disney, 1941; a founder & pres. N.Y. Screen Publicists Guild; adv. mngr. & dir., 20th Cent.-Fox, 1941-1950; v.p. Italian Films Export, 1950-55; v.p. in chg. adv. pub. expl. Columbia Pictures, 1955-63; v.p. worldwide adv., publ. and promotion, 20th Century-Fox, 1963-77; film mktg. consultant, 1977-78; lecturer in mktg., USC, 1978-79; v.p. in chg. of worldwide mktg., Melvin Simon Prods., 1979-1981; Filmways Pictures as exec. v.p., worldwide adv./pub. promo. 1982; lecturer adjunct, USC Sch. of Cinema & TV, 1982-84; pres. American Film Marketing Association, 1983 to present.

ROSENMAN, HOWARD

Producer. b. Brooklyn, NY, Feb. 1, 1945. e. Brooklyn Col. Asst. to Sir Michael Benthall on B'way show; prod., Benton & Bowles Agency; ABC-TV; RSO Prods. Co-pres., Sandollar Prods.; currently pres. Brillstein-Grey Motion Pictures.
PICTURES: Sparkle, The Main Event, Resurrection, Lost Angels, Gross Anatomy, True Identity, Father of the Bride, Shining Through, Straight Talk, A Stranger Among Us, Buffy the Vampire Slayer.
TELEVISION: *Movies:* Isn't It Shocking? Altogether Now, Death Scream, Virginia Hill, Killer Bees. *Specials:* Common Threads: Stories from the Quilt (co-exec. prod.), Tidy Endings.

ROSENMAN, LEONARD

Composer. b. New York, NY, Sept. 7, 1924.
PICTURES: East of Eden, Cobweb, Rebel Without a Cause, Edge of the City, The Savage Eye, The Chapman Report, Fantastic Voyage, Hellfighters, Beneath the Planet of the Apes, Barry Lyndon (Academy Award, 1975), Birch Interval, Race With the Devil, Bound For Glory (Academy Award, 1976), A Man Called Horse, The Car, September 30, 1955, The Enemy of the People, The Lord of the Rings, Promises in the Dark, Prophecy, Hide in Plain Sight, The Jazz Singer, Making Love, Miss Lonely Hearts, Cross Creek, Heart of the Stag, Star Trek IV: The Voyage Home, Robocop 2, Ambition.
TELEVISION: *Movies/Mini-Series:* Sybil (Emmy Award), Friendly Fire (Emmy Award), City in Fear, Murder in Texas, Vanished, The Wall, Miss Lonelyhearts, Celebrity, The Return of Marcus Welby MD, Heartsounds, First Steps, Promised a Miracle, Keeper of the City.

ROSENSTEIN, GERTRUDE

Director. b. New York, NY. e. Barnard Coll., B.A., Neighborhood Playhouse. exec. asst. to George Balanchine & Lincoln Kirstein, N.Y.C. Ballet. Assoc. with Gian Carlo Menotti, Festival of Two Worlds, Spoleto, Italy. Member of Emmy Awards committee. TV staff dir., NBC. Now freelance director, news programs, election coverage, music and dance programs, commercials. Governor, NY Television Academy.
TELEVISION: *Assoc. dir.:* NBC Opera, Emmy Awards, Kennedy Memorial Mass. *Dir.:* Concentration.

ROSENTHAL, BUD

Executive. b. Brooklyn, NY, Mar. 21, 1934. e. Brooklyn Coll., B.A., 1954, NYU. US Army, 1954-56; college correspondent, NY Times; ent. m.p. ind. as assoc. editor, Independent Film

Journal, 1957-59; joined Columbia Pictures publicity dept. as trade paper contact and news writer, 1959; newspaper and syndicate contact 1960; natl. publicity mngr., Columbia Pictures Corp., 1962-67; publ. dir., Anderson Tapes, Such Good Friends, The Blue Bird; story edit. and casting dir., Sigma Prods., 1972-75; associate prod., Broadway play, Full Circle, 1973; Warner Bros. project coordinator, Superman, Superman II, Superman III; project coordinator, Time Warner Presents The Earth Day Special, Warner Bros. Studios Rededication, Celebration of Tradition, 1990.
PICTURES: Something for Everyone (asst. prod.), Rosebud (assoc. prod.). Int'l mktg. co-ord. on films: Ghostbusters, Labyrinth, Batman, Boyz 'N the Hood, Addams Family, Batman Returns, A Few Good Men, Last Action Hero.

ROSENTHAL, JANE
Executive. b. Denver, CO. e. NYU. 1976-84, dir. of film for TV at CBS; 1984-87, v.p. prod. Disney; 1987-88, v.p. of TV & Mini-Series, Warners TV; 1988-93, exec. v.p., Tribeca Prods.; 1993-present, pres. of Tribeca Prods.; 1992-93, exec. prod. of series Tribeca. Producer of films Faithful, Marvin's Room.

ROSENTHAL, RICK
Director. b. New York, NY, June 15, 1949. e. Harvard, B.A. cum laude, 1971. Launched career as filmmaker-in-residence with New Hampshire TV Network. Moved to Los Angeles to study at American Film Institute where filmed Moonface, 1973.
PICTURES: Halloween II (debut, 1981), Bad Boys, American Dreamer, Russkies, Distant Thunder.
TELEVISION: Movies: Fire on the Mountain, Code of Vengeance, Secrets of Midland Heights, Nasty Boys, Devlin. Series: Life Goes On.

ROSENZWEIG, BARNEY
Producer. b. Los Angeles, CA, Dec. 23, 1937. e. USC, 1959. m. actress Sharon Gless.
PICTURES: Morituri (assoc. prod.), Do Not Disturb (assoc. prod.), Caprice (assoc. prod.), Who Fears the Devil (prod.).
TELEVISION: Prod.: Daniel Boone (series), Men of the Dragon, One of My Wives Is Missing, Charlie's Angels (series), Angel on My Shoulder, American Dream (pilot), John Steinbeck's East of Eden (mini-series; Golden Globe Award). Exec. prod.: Modesty Blasie (pilot), This Girl for Hire (movie), Cagney and Lacey (series; 2 Emmy Awards: 1985, 1986), The Trials of Rosie O'Neill (series), Christy (movie, series), Cagney & Lacey: The Return (movie), Cagney & Lacey: Together Again (movie), Cagney & Lacey: The View Through the Glass Ceiling (movie), Cagney & Lacey: True Convictions (movie).

ROSS, DIANA
Singer, Actress. b. Detroit, MI, Mar. 26, 1944. Formed musical group at age 14 with two friends, Mary Wilson and Florence Ballard. In 1960 they auditioned for Berry Gordy, head of Motown Record Corp. and were hired to sing backgrounds on records for Motown acts. After completing high school, the trio was named the Supremes and went on tour with Motor Town Revue. Over period of 10 yrs. Supremes had 15 consecutive hit records and once had five consecutive records in the number one spot on charts. In 1969 Diana Ross went on her own, appearing on TV and in nightclubs. Memoirs: Secrets of a Sparrow (1993).
PICTURES: Lady Sings the Blues (debut as actress, 1972; Acad. Award nom.), Mahogany, The Wiz.
TELEVISION: Movie: Out of Darkness (also co-exec. prod.). Specials: Diana! (also exec. prod. & writer), Motown 25: Yesterday Today Forever, Motown Returns to the Apollo, Diana's World Tour.

ROSS, HERBERT
Director. b. New York, NY, May 13, 1927. m. Lee Radziwill. e. studied dance with Doris Humphrey, Helene Platova, Caird Leslie. Trained for stage with Herbert Berghof, 1946-50. As B'way dancer in Laffing Room Only, Beggars Holiday, Bloomer Girl, Look Ma I'm Dancing, Inside U.S.A., and with the American Ballet Theatre. Resident choreographer 1958-59 ABT for Caprichos, Concerto in D, The Maids, Tristan, Thief Who Loved a Ghost. Ent. m.p. ind. as choreographer for Carmen Jones, The Young Ones, Summer Holiday (also dir. musical sequences), Inside Daisy Clover, Dr. Doolittle, Funny Girl (also dir. musical numbers). Exec. prod. on film Soapdish.
THEATER/OPERA: B'way Choreographer-Director: A Tree Grows in Brooklyn, The Gay Life, I Can Get It For You Wholesale, Tovarich, Anyone Can Whistle, Do I Hear a Waltz, On a Clear Day You Can See Forever, The Apple Tree, Finian's Rainbow, Wonderful Town. Dir.: Chapter Two, I Ought To Be in Pictures, Follies in Concert, Anyone Can Whistle (fundraiser for GMHC; Grammy nom.), La Bohème (L.A. & Dallas).
PICTURES: Goodbye Mr. Chips (debut, 1969), The Owl and the Pussycat, T.R. Baskin, Play It Again Sam, The Last of Sheila (also prod.), Funny Lady, The Sunshine Boys, The Seven Percent Solution (also prod.), The Turning Point (also prod.), The Goodbye Girl, California Suite, Nijinsky (also

prod.), Pennies from Heaven (also prod.), I Ought to Be in Pictures (also prod.), Max Dugan Returns (also prod.), Footloose, Protocol (also prod.), The Secret of My Success (also prod.), Dancers (also prod.), Steel Magnolias, My Blue Heaven (also prod.), True Colors (also prod.), Undercover Blues (also exec. prod.), Boys on the Side (also prod.).
TELEVISION: Choreographer: Series: Milton Berle Show (1952-57), Martha Raye Show, Bell Telephone Hour (also prod., dir.). Specials: Wonderful Town (also dir.), Meet Me in St. Louis, Jerome Kern Special, Bea Lillie and Cyril Ritchard Show (dir.), The Fantastiks, The Fred Astaire Special (1963, dir.).

ROSS, KATHARINE
Actress. b. Los Angeles, CA, Jan. 29, 1943. m. actor Sam Elliott. e. Santa Rosa Coll. Joined the San Francisco Workshop, appeared in The Devil's Disciple, The Balcony. TV debut, 1962 in Sam Benedict segment.
PICTURES: Shenandoah (debut, 1965), Mister Buddwing, The Singing Nun, Games, The Graduate (Golden Globe Award, Acad. Award nom.), Hellfighters, Butch Cassidy and the Sundance Kid, Tell Them Willie Boy is Here, Fools, Get to Know Your Rabbit, They Only Kill Their Masters, The Stepford Wives, Voyage of the Damned, The Betsy, The Swarm, The Legacy, The Final Countdown, Wrong Is Right, Daddy's Deadly Darling, Red-Headed Stranger.
TELEVISION: Movies: The Longest Hundred Miles, Wanted: The Sundance Woman, Murder by Natural Causes, Rodeo Girl, Murder in Texas, Marian Rose White, Shadow Riders, Travis McGee, Secrets of a Mother and Daughter, Conagher (also co-script). Guest: Ben Casey, The Bob Hope-Chrysler Theatre, The Virginian, Wagon Train, Kraft Mystery Theatre, The Lieutenant, The Road West. Series: The Colbys.

ROSS, KENNETH
Writer. b. London, Sept. 16, 1941. Entered m.p. industry 1970.
THEATER: The Raft, Under The Skin, Mr. Kilt & The Great I Am.
PICTURES: Brother Sun Sister Moon, Slag, The Reckless Years (also orig. story), Abelard & Heloise, The Day of the Jackal (So. Cal. M.P. Council Award; nom. for Writers' Guild, SFTA, and Golden Globes), The Devil's Lieutenant, The Odessa File (nom. for Writers' Guild Award), Quest (also orig. story), Black Sunday (Edgar Allen Poe Award, Mystery Writers of America, 1977), The Fourth War, Epiphany (also orig. story).
TELEVISION: The Roundelay, The Messenger.

ROSSELLINI, ISABELLA
Actress. b. Rome, Italy, June 18, 1952. Daughter of actress Ingrid Bergman and director Roberto Rossellini. Came to America in 1972. Worked as translator for Italian News Bureau. Taught Italian at New Sch. for Social Research. Worked 3 years on second unit assignments for journalist Gianni Mina and as NY corresp. for Ital. TV series, The Other Sunday. Model for Vogue, Harper's Bazaar, Italian Elle, Lancome Cosmetics.
PICTURES: A Matter of Time (debut 1976; with her mother), The Meadow, Il Pap'Occhio, White Nights, Blue Velvet, Tough Guys Don't Dance, Siesta, Red Riding Hood, Zelly and Me, Cousins, Les Dames Galantes, The Siege of Venice, Wild at Heart, Death Becomes Her, The Pickle, Fearless, Wyatt Earp, Immortal Beloved, The Innocent, Big Night.
TELEVISION: Movies: The Last Elephant, Lies of the Twins, The Crime of the Century. Guest: The Tracey Ullman Show. Specials: The Gift, Fallen Angels (The Frightening Frammis). Guest: Tales From the Crypt (You Murderer).

ROSSO, LEWIS, T.
Executive. b. Hoboken, NJ, Feb. 3, 1909. Ent. m.p. ind. 1930; prod. & mgt. for Consolidated Film Ind., 1930-44; Republic producer, 1944-50; prod. mgr., 1950-55; asst. sec'y & asst. treas., 1959; exec. asst. to exec. prod. mgr., 20th Century-Fox Films, 1960; plant mgr., Samuel Goldwyn Studios, 1961-71; exec. admin. asst. plant mgr., The Burbank Studios, 1972-88.

ROSSOVICH, RICK
Actor. b. Palo Alto, CA, August 28, 1957. e. Calif. St. Univ. Sacramento (art history). Studied acting with coach Vincent Chase.
PICTURES: The Lords of Discipline (debut, 1983), Losin' It, Streets of Fire, The Terminator, Fast Forward, Warning Sign, Top Gun, Let's Get Harry, The Morning After, Roxanne, Paint It Black, The Witching Hour, Spellbinder, Navy SEALS, Cognac, Tropical Heat, New Crime City.
TELEVISION: Series: MacGruder and Loud, Sons and Daughters, ER. Guest: Tales from the Crypt (The Switch). Special: 14 Going On 30. Movies: Deadly Lessons, The Gambler Returns: Luck of the Draw, Black Scorpion.

ROTH, BOBBY
Director, Writer, Producer.
PICTURES: The Boss' Son, Circle of Power, Independence Day, Heartbreakers.

TELEVISION: *Episodes:* Miami Vice, The Insiders, Crime Story. *Movies:* Tonight's the Night, The Man Who Fell to Earth, Dead Solid Perfect (dir., co-s.p.), Baja Oklahoma (dir., co-s.p.), The Man Inside.

ROTH, JOE
Executive, Producer, Director. b. New York, NY, 1948. Began career working as prod. assistant on commercials and feature films in San Francisco. Also ran the lights for improv group Pitchel Players. Moved with them to Los Angeles, and produced their shows incl. the $250,000 film Tunnelvision. 1987 co-founder of independent film prod. co. Morgan Creek Productions. 1989 left to become chairman of newly-formed Fox Film Corp., the theatrical film unit of 20th Century Fox Film Corp. Also named head of News Corp. unit. Resigned from Fox, 1993. Pres. & founder, Caravan Pictures, 1993. 1994, became chmn. Walt Disney Motion Pictures Group.
PICTURES: *Producer:* Tunnelvision, Cracking Up, Americathon, Our Winning Season, The Final Terror, The Stone Boy, Where the River Runs Black, Bachelor Party, Off Beat, Streets of Gold (also dir. debut), Tall Tale, Angels in the Outfield. *Exec. prod.:* Revenge of the Nerds II: Nerds in Paradise (also dir.), Young Guns, Dead Ringers, Skin Deep, Major League, Renegades, Enemies a Love Story, Pacific Heights, The Three Musketeers, Angie, I Love Trouble, Angels in the Outfield, A Low Down Dirty Shame, Houseguest, Tall Tale, While You Were Sleeping. *Dir.:* Coupe de Ville.

ROTH, PAUL A.
Executive. b. Asheville, NC, March 28, 1930. e. U. of North Carolina, A.B. political science, 1948-51; George Washington U. Law Sch., 1951-52. U.S. Army 1952-55. Dist. Mgr. Valley Enterprises, Inc. 1955-56; v.p. Roth Enterprises, Inc. 1956-65; pres. Roth Enterprises, Inc. 1965-present; pres., Valley Lanes Inc. 1975-present; v.p., CAPA Ltd. 1976-present; pres., Carolina Cinema Corp., 1980-present; pres., Thrashers Ocean Fries, 1987-present; dir. Riggs Bank of Maryland, 1984-93; pres. NATO of Virginia 1971-73; chmn. bd. NATO of Virginia, 1973-75; member National NATO Board, 1971-present; exec. comm. NATO of VA & MD, 1965-present; Variety Club Tent 11 Board Member 1959-65; pres. National NATO, 1973-75; chmn. National NATO bd. dir. 1975-77. Chmn., NATO Government Relations Committee, 1988-1996. member Foundation Motion Picture Pioneers, 1973-present; member & advisory committee, Will Rogers Hospital, 1973-present; trustee American Film Institute, 1973-75; Recipient: NATO Mid-Atlantic Exhibitor of the Year (1990), S.M. Hassanein Humanitarian Award at ShowEast (1991), ShoWester Award (1993).

ROTH, RICHARD A.
Producer. b. Beverly Hills, CA, 1943. e. Stanford U. Law Sch. Worked for L.A. law firm before beginning film career as lawyer and literary agent for Ziegler-Ross Agency. In 1970 left to develop s.p. Summer of '42 with Herman Raucher.
PICTURES: Summer of '42, Our Time, The Adventures of Sherlock Holmes' Smarter Brother, Julia, Outland, In Country, Havana.

ROTH, TIM
Actor. b. London, England, 1961. Started acting with various fringe theatre groups such as Glasgow Citizen's Theatre, The Oval House, and the Royal Court. Also on London stage in Metamorphosis.
PICTURES: The Hit, A World Apart, The Cook the Thief His Wife and Her Lover, Vincent & Theo, Rosencrantz and Guildenstern Are Dead, Jumpin at the Boneyard, Reservoir Dogs, Bodies Rest and Motion, Pulp Fiction, Rob Roy (BAFTA Award, 1995), Little Odessa, Captives, Hoodlums, Four Rooms, Everyone Say I Love You.
TELEVISION: *Specials/Movies* (BBC): Meantime, Made in Britain, Metamorphosis, Knuckle, Yellow Backs, King of the Ghetto, The Common Pursuit, Murder in the Heartland (U.S.), Heart of Darkness.

ROTHMAN, THOMAS E.
Executive. b. Baltimore, MD, Nov. 21, 1954. m. actress Jessica Harper. e. Brown U., B.A. 1976; Columbia Law Sch., J.D. 1980. Worked as law clerk with Second Circuit Court of Appeals 1981-82 before becoming partner at entertainment law firm, Frankfurt Garbus Klein & Selz 1982-87; 1987 joined Columbia Pictures as exec. v.p. and asst. to pres., named exec. prod. v.p. Left in 1989 to join Samuel Goldwyn Co. as pres. of worldwide production. Currently pres. of Fox Searchlight Films.
PICTURES: *Co-prod.:* Down By Law, Candy Mountain. *Exec. Prod.:* The Program.

ROTUNNO, GIUSEPPE
Cinematographer. b. Rome, Italy, March 19, 1923. Gained fame as leading cinematographer of Italian films working with Federico Fellini. Later worked in Hollywood.
PICTURES: Tosca, Monte Carlo Story, White Nights, The Naked Maja, On the Beach, Fast and Sexy, The Angel Wore Red, Five Branded Women, Rocco and His Brothers,

Boccaccio '70, The Leopard, The Organizer, Juliet of the Spirits, The Bible, Anizo, Candy, Spirits of the Dead, Fellini Satyricon, The Secret of Santa Vittoria, Carnal Knowledge, Fellini's Roma, Man of La Mancha, Amarcord, Love and Anarchy, Fellini's Casanova, All Screwed Up, End of the World in Our Usual Bed in a Night Full of Rain, Orchestra Rehearsal, All That Jazz, City of Women, Popeye, Rollover, Five Days One Summer, And the Ship Sails On, American Dreamer, Desire, Nothing Left to Do But Cry, The Red Sonja, Hotel Colonial, Julia and Julia, Rent-a-Cop, Rebus, Haunted Summer, The Adventures of Baron Munchausen, Regarding Henry, Once Upon a Crime, Wolf, The Night the Moment, Sabrina, La Sindrome di Stendhal.
TELEVISION: The Scarlet and the Black.

ROUNDTREE, RICHARD
Actor. b. New Rochelle, NY, July 9, 1942. e. Southern Illinos U. Former model, Ebony Magazine Fashion Fair; joined workshop of Negro Ensemble Company, appeared in Kongi's Harvest, Man Better Man, Mau Mau Room; played lead role in Philadelphia road company of The Great White Hope before film debut.
PICTURES: What Do You Say to a Naked Lady? (debut, 1970), Shaft, Embassy, Charley One-Eye, Shaft's Big Score, Embassy, Shaft in Africa, Earthquake, Diamonds, Man Friday, Portrait of a Hitman, Escape to Athena, Game for Vultures, An Eye for an Eye, Inchon, Q (The Winged Serpent), One Down Two to Go, The Big Score, Young Warriors, Killpoint, City Heat, Opposing Force, Jocks, Maniac Cop, Homer and Eddie, Angel III: The Final Chapter, The Party Line, Getting Even, American Cops, The Banker, Night Visitor, Crack House, Bad Jim, Lost Memories, Body of Influence, Deadly Rivals, Amityville: A New Generation, Gypsy Angels, Mind Twister, Seven, Once Upon A Time...When We Were Colored.
TELEVISION: *Series:* Shaft, Outlaws, Cop Files (host). *Movies:* Firehouse, The Fifth Missile, Christmas in Connecticut, Bonanza: The Return, Shadows of Desire, Bonanza: Under Attack. *Mini-Series:* Roots, A.D.

ROURKE, MICKEY
Actor. b. Schenectady, NY, Sept. 1956. Moved to Miami as a boy. Fought as an amateur boxer 4 years in Miami. Studied acting with Sandra Seacat while working as a nightclub bouncer, a sidewalk pretzel vendor and other odd jobs. Moved to LA, 1978. Debut: TV movie City in Fear (1978).
PICTURES: 1941 (debut, 1979), Fade to Black, Heaven's Gate, Body Heat, Diner (Natl. Society of Film Critics Award, 1982), Rumblefish, Eureka, The Pope of Greenwich Village, Year of the Dragon, 9-1/2 Weeks, Angel Heart, A Prayer for the Dying, Barfly, Homeboy (also wrote orig. story), Francesco, Johnny Handsome, Wild Orchid, Desperate Hours, Harley Davidson and the Marlboro Man, White Sands, F.T.W., Fall Time.
TELEVISION: *Movies:* City in Fear, Rape and Marriage: The Rideout Case, Act of Love, The Last Outlaw.

ROUSSELOT, PHILIPPE
Cinematographer. b. Meurthe-et-Moselle, France, 1945. e. Vaugirard Film Sch., Paris. Worked as camera assistant to Nestor Almendros on My Night at Maud's, Claire's Knee, Love in the Afternoon.
PICTURES: The Guinea Pig Couple, Adom ou le sang d'Abel, Paradiso, Pauline et l'ordinateur, Peppermint Soda, For Clemence, Cocktail Molotov, La Provinciale, A Girl From Lorraine, Diva (Cesar, Natl. Society of Film Critics, and Moscow Awards), The Jaws of the Wolf, The Moon in the Gutter, Thieves After Dark, The Emerald Forest, Therese (Cesar Award), Hope and Glory, Dangerous Liaisons, The Bear, We're No Angels, Too Beautiful for You, Henry and June, A River Runs Through It (Academy Award, 1992), Sommersby, Interview With the Vampire, Queen Margot.

ROWE, ROY
Exhibitor. b. Burgaw, May 29, 1905. e. U. of NC. Eng. instructor, private bus. coll., 1926-29; Publix Sch. for Mgrs., NY, 1930-31; mgr. theatres, Spartanburg, SC; Greensboro & Raleigh, NC; Warner Theatre, Pittsburgh, PA, 1931-34; city mgr. for Warner Theatres, Washington, PA, 1934-35; opened own theatres in NC 1935; member NC Senate, 1937, 1941, 1945, 1949, 1957, 1965; 1935-75, House of Rep., 1943; Major, Civil Air Patrol, WWII; pres. Carolina Aero Club, 1943-44; chmn. NC Aeronautics Comm., 1941-49; dir. Theatre Owners No. & So. Carolina 1943-45; pres., Theatre Owners of SC & NC 1944-45; pres., Assn. of Governing Boards of State Univs., 1964; Rowe Insurance Agency, 1967-69; Mem. Exec. Bd., U. of NC Trustees, 1969. Principal Clerk, NC Senate 1969-75. Owner-operator Rowe Amusement Co., Burgaw, NC. Retired.

ROWLAND, ROY
Director. b. New York, NY, Dec. 31, 1902. e. U. of Southern California, law. Script clerk; asst. dir.; asst. to late W. S. Van Dyke on Tarzan pictures; dir. of shorts, ``How to'' Benchley series; Crime Does Not Pay series; Pete Smith Specialties.

PICTURES: Think First, Stranger in Town, Lost Angel, Our Vines Have Tender Grapes, Tenth Avenue Angel, Night Patrol, Ski Soldier, Boys' Ranch, Romance of Rosy Ridge, Killer McCoy, Scene of the Crime, Outriders, Excuse My Dust, Two Weeks With Love, Bugles in the Afternoon, The 5000 Fingers of Dr. T, Affair with a Stranger, The Moonlighter, Witness to Murder, Rogue Cop, Many Rivers to Cross, Hit the Deck, Meet Me in Las Vegas, Slander, Somewhere I'll Find Him, Gun Glory, The Seven Hills of Rome, The Girl Hunters, Gunfighters of Casa Grande, They Called Him Gringo, Tiger of the Seven Seas, Thunder Over the Indian Ocean.

ROWLANDS, GENA
Actress. r.n. Virginia Cathryn Rowlands. b. Cambria, WI, June 19, 1934. e. U. of Wisconsin. Son is actor Nicholas Cassavetes. Came to New York to attend American Acad. of Dramatic Arts, where she met and married John Cassavetes. Made B'way debut as understudy and then succeeded to role of The Girl in The Seven Year Itch. Launched as star with part in The Middle of the Night, which she played 18 mos.
PICTURES: The High Cost of Loving (debut, 1958), Lonely Are the Brave, The Spiral Road, A Child Is Waiting, Tony Rome, Faces, Machine Gun McCain, Minnie and Moskowitz, A Woman Under the Influence (Acad. Award nom.), Two Minute Warning, The Brink's Job, Opening Night, Gloria (Acad. Award nom.), Tempest, Love Streams, Light of Day, Another Woman, Once Around, Ted and Venus, Night on Earth, The Neon Bible, Something to Talk About, Unhook The Stars.
TELEVISION: Movies: A Question of Love, Strangers: The Story of a Mother & Daughter, Thursday's Child, An Early Frost, The Betty Ford Story (Emmy Award, 1987), Montana, Face of a Stranger (Emmy Award, 1992), Crazy in Love, Silent Cries, Parallel Lives. Guest: The Philco TV Playhouse, Studio One, Alfred Hitchcock Presents, Dr. Kildare, Bonanza, The Kraft Mystery Theatre, Columbo. Series: Top Secret USA, 87th Precinct, Peyton Place.

ROWLEY, JOHN H.
Executive. b. San Angelo, TX, Oct. 6, 1917. e. U. of TX, 1935-39. Past pres., NATO of Texas; past Int'l Chief barker, Variety Clubs Int'l; past pres., TOA. Currently exec. dir. NATO of TX.

RUBEN, JOSEPH
Director. b. Briarcliff, NY, 1951. e. U. of Michigan, majoring in theater and film; Brandeis U., B.A. Interest in film began in high sch. Bought a Super-8 camera and filmed his first movie, a teenage love story. First feature, The Sister-in-Law, a low budget feature which he wrote and dir. in 1975.
PICTURES: Dir./Writer: The Sister-in-Law (also prod.), The Pom-Pom Girls (also prod.), Joy Ride, Our Winning Season. Dir.: G.O.R.P., Dreamscape (also co-s.p.), The Stepfather, True Believer, Sleeping With the Enemy, The Good Son, Money Train.
TELEVISION: Breaking Away (pilot), Eddie Dodd.

RUBIN, STANLEY
Producer, Writer. b. New York, NY, Oct. 8, 1917; ed. UCLA, 1933-37. Phi Beta Kappa. Writer for radio, magazines, pictures, 1937-41; U.S. Army Air Force, 1942-45; writer, prod., owner, Your Show Time, Story Theatre TV series; winner of 1st Emmy awarded to filmed series: The Necklace, 1949. Producer, RKO, 20th-Fox, U.I., MGM, Paramount, Rastar.
PICTURES: The Narrow Margin, My Pal Gus, Destination Gobi, River of No Return, Destry, Francis in the Navy, Behind the High Wall, Rawhide Years, The Girl Most Likely, Promise Her Anything, The President's Analyst, Revenge, White Hunter Black Heart (co-prod.).
TELEVISION: G.E. Theatre, Ghost and Mrs. Muir, Bracken's World, The Man and the City, Executive Suite. Movies: Babe (co-prod.; Golden Globe Award), And Your Name is Jonah, Don't Look Back: The Story of Satchel Page (Image Award), Escape From Iran: The Canadian Caper (exec. prod.).

RUBINEK, SAUL
Actor. b. Fohrenwold, Germany, July 2, 1948. Family moved to Canada when he was a baby. Acting debut at age 8 with local theatre groups. Founding member of the Toronto Free Stage Theatre.
PICTURES: Nothing Personal, Highpoint, Agency, Death Ship, Ticket to Heaven, Soup for One, Young Doctors in Love, By Design, Against All Odds, Martin's Day, Sweet Liberty, Taking Care, Wall Street, Obsessed, The Outside Chance of Maximillian Glick, The Bonfire of the Vanities, Man Trouble, Unforgiven, The Quarrel, True Romance, Undercover Blues, Death Wish V, Getting Even With Dad, I Love Trouble, Open Season, Nixon.
TELEVISION: Concealed Enemies, The Terry Fox Story, Clown White, Interrogation in Budapest, Woman on the Run, And the Band Played On, The Android Affair.

RUBINSTEIN, JOHN
Actor, Composer, Director. b. Los Angeles, CA, December 8, 1946. Son of concert pianist Arthur Rubinstein and dancer-writer Aniela Rubinstein. e. UCLA.

THEATER: Pippin (NY debut, 1972; Theatre World Award), Picture (Mark Taper, LA), Children of a Lesser God (Tony Award, Drama Desk, L.A. Drama Critics Awards, 1980), Fools, The Caine Mutiny Court-Martial, M. Butterfly, Kiss of the Spider Woman. Director: The Rover, Les Liaisons Dangereuses, Phantasie, Nightingale, The Old Boy.
PICTURES: Journey to Shiloh (debut, 1968), The Trouble With Girls, Getting Straight, The Wild Pack, Zachariah, The Car, The Boys From Brazil, In Search of Historic Jesus, Daniel, Someone to Watch Over Me, Another Stakeout, Mercy.
TELEVISION: Series: Family, Crazy Like a Fox. Guest: The Virginian, Ironside, Dragnet, Room 222, The Psychiatrist, The Mary Tyler Moore Show, Cannon, The Mod Squad, Nichols, Hawaii Five-O, Barnaby Jones, Policewoman, Barbary Coast, The Rookies, The Streets of San Francisco, Harry O, Vegas, The Class of '65, Movin' On, Stop the Presses, Wonder Woman, Lou Grant, Fantasy Island, The Quest, Quincy, Trapper John M.D., The Love Boat, Father Dowling, The Paper Chase, Murder She Wrote. Special: Triple Play—Sam Found Out. Movies: The Marriage Proposal, God Bless the Children, A Howling in the Woods, Something Evil, All Together Now, The Gift of the Magi, Roots: The Next Generations, Just Make Me an Offer, The French Atlantic Affair, Corey: For the People, Happily Ever After, Moviola, Skokie, The Mr. and Ms. Mysteries, Killjoy, Freedom to Speak, Someone's Killing the High Fashion Models; I Take These Men, M.A.D.D.: Mothers Against Drunk Driving, Liberace, Voices Within: The Lives of Truddi Chase, In My Daughter's Name, The American Clock. Director: A Matter of Conscience, Summer Stories: The Mall.
SCORES: Films: Paddy, Jeremiah Johnson, The Candidate, Kid Blue, The Killer Inside Me. Television: All Together Now, Emily, Emily, Stalk the Wild Child, Champions: A Love Story, To Race the Wind, The Ordeal of Patty Hearst, Amber Waves, Johnny Belinda, Secrets of a Mother and Daughter, Choices of the Heart, The Dollmaker, Family (Emmy nom.), The Fitzpatricks, The Mackenzies of Paradise Cove, The New Land, For Heaven's Sake, The Lazarus Syndrome, The City Killer, China Beach.

RUBINSTEIN, RICHARD P.
Producer, Executive. b. New York, NY, June 15, 1947. e. American U. B.S. 1969, Columbia U. MBA 1971. Pres. & CEO, New Amsterdam Entertainment, Inc.
PICTURES: Martin, Dawn Of The Dead, Knightriders, Creepshow, Day Of The Dead, Creepshow 2, Pet Sematary, Tales From the Darkside: The Movie.
TELEVISION: Exec. Prod.: Series: Tales From the Darkside, Monsters, Stephen King's Golden Years. Mini-Series: Stephen King's The Stand. Movies: The Vernon Johns Story, Precious Victims.

RUDDY, ALBERT S.
Producer. b. Montreal, Canada, March 28, 1934. e. U. of Southern California, B.S. in design, Sch. of Architecture, 1956. Exec. prod. of 1991 TV movie Miracle in the Wilderness.
PICTURES: The Wild Seed, Little Fauss & Big Halsey, Making It, The Godfather, The Longest Yard, Coonskin, Matilda, The Cannonball Run, Megaforce, Lassiter, Cannonball Run II, Farewell to the King, Paramedics, Speed Zone, Impulse, Ladybugs, Bad Girls, The Scout, Heaven's Prisoners.
TELEVISION: Series: Walker—Texas Ranger. Movies: Miracle in the Wilderness, Staying Afloat.

RUDIE, EVELYN
Actress, Singer, Songwriter. r.n. Evelyn Rudie Bernauer, b. Hollywood, Calif. March 28. e. Hollywood H.S., UCLA. At 19, after childstar career in TV and films, stage debut at Gallery Theatre in Hollywood as songwriter, musical dir.; choreographer and star performer: Ostrogoths and King of the Schnorrers. Currently producer, artistic dir., Santa Monica Playhouse; founder of own repertoire co. Received Emmy Nomination for first TV leading role, Eloise, Playhouse 90, 1956. Filmdom's Famous Fives critics award, 1958. Star on Hollywood's Walk of Fame.
PICTURES: Daddy Long Legs (debut, 1955). The Wings of Eagles, Gift of Love, Bye Bye Birdie.
TELEVISION: Hostess with the Mostess, Playhouse 90, Dinah Shore, Red Skelton Show, George Gobel Show, Omnibus, Matinee Theatre, Hitchcock Presents, Gale Storm Show, Jack Paar, Wagon Train, G.E. Theatre, 77 Sunset Strip, etc.

RUDIN, SCOTT
Executive. b. New York, NY, July 14, 1958. Began career as prod. asst. on B'way for producers Kermit Bloomgarden, Robert Whitehead; then casting director. 1984, became producer for 20th Century Fox; named exec. v.p. prod.; 1986, appt. pres. prod., 20th-Fox. Resigned 1987 becoming independent producer.
PICTURES: Prod.: I'm Dancing as Fast as I Can, Reckless, Mrs. Soffel, Flatliners (exec. prod.), Pacific Heights, Regarding Henry, Little Man Tate, The Addams Family, White Sands, Sister Act, Jennifer Eight, Life With Mikey, The Firm,

Searching for Bobby Fisher, Addams Family Values, Sister Act 2: Back in the Habit, Nobody's Fool, I.Q., Clueless, Sabrina, Up Close and Personal, Marvin's Room.
TELEVISION: Little Gloria... Happy at Last (exec. prod.).

RUDNER, RITA
Actress, Writer. b. Miami, FL, 1956. m. producer Martin Bergman. Was stage dancer then stand-up comic. Author: Naked Beneath My Clothing: Tales of a Revealing Nature, Rita Rudner's Guide to Men.
THEATER: Annie (B'way), Promises Promises, Follies, Mack and Mabel.
PICTURES: The Wrong Guys (debut, 1988), Gleaming the Cube, That's Adequate, Peter's Friends (also co-s.p.), A Weekend in the Country (also s.p.).
TELEVISION: Series: George Schlatter's Funny People (co-host). Specials: Women of the Night, One Night Stand: Rita Rudner, Rita Rudner: Born to Be Mild, The Rita Rudner Comedy Specials (also writer), Comic Relief, Rita Rudner: Married Without Children.

RUDOLPH, ALAN
Director, Writer. b. Los Angeles, CA, Dec. 18, 1943. Son of Oscar Rudolph, TV director of '50s and '60s. Made his screen debut in his father's The Rocket Man (1954). Began in industry doing odd jobs in Hollywood studios. 1969 accepted for Directors Guild assistant director's training program. Worked with Robert Altman as asst. dir. on California Split, The Long Goodbye and Nashville and co-writer on Buffalo Bill and the Indians.
PICTURES: Director: Welcome to L.A. (debut, 1977; also s.p.), Remember My Name (also s.p.), Roadie (also story), Endangered Species (also co-s.p.), Return Engagement, Songwriter, Choose Me (also s.p.), Trouble in Mind (also s.p.), Made in Heaven, The Moderns (also co-s.p.), Love at Large (also s.p.), Mortal Thoughts, The Player (actor only), Equinox (also s.p.), Mrs. Parker and the Vicious Circle (also co-s.p.).

RUEHL, MERCEDES
Actress. b. Queens, NY, 1950. Raised in Silver Spring, MD. e. College of New Rochelle, B.A. English lit. Worked for years in regional theater, mostly in classics.
THEATER: B'way: I'm Not Rappaport, Lost in Yonkers (Tony Award, 1991), The Shadow Box, The Rose Tattoo. Off-B'way: American Notes, The Marriage of Bette and Boo (Obie Award), Coming of Age in Soho, Other People's Money.
PICTURES: The Warriors (debut, 1979), Four Friends, Heartburn, Radio Days, 84 Charing Cross Road, The Secret of My Success, Leader of the Band, Big, Married to the Mob, Slaves of New York, Crazy People, Another You, The Fisher King (Academy Award, best supporting actress, 1991), Lost in Yonkers, Last Action Hero.
TELEVISION: Movie: Indictment: The McMartin Trial. Series: Frasier. Pilot: Late Bloomer. Guest: Our Family Honor. Special: On Hope.

RUGOLO, PETE
Composer, Arranger. b. Sicily, Italy, Dec. 25, 1915. To U.S., 1919. e. San Francisco State Coll., Mills Coll., Oakland. Armed Forces, 1942-46; pianist, arr. for many orch. including Stan Kenton. Conductor and arrang. for Nat King Cole, Peggy Lee, Harry Belafonte, many others. Received 3 Emmy Awards.
PICTURES: The Strip, Skirts Ahoy, Glory Alley, Latin Lovers, Easy to Love, Jack the Ripper, Foxtrot, Buddy Buddy, Chu Chu and the Philly Flash.
TELEVISION: Richard Diamond, The Thin Man, Thriller, The Fugitive, Run for Your Life, The Bold Ones, Leave It to Beaver, more than 25 movies.

RUIZ-ANCHIA, JUAN
Cinematographer. b. Bilbao, Spain. e. Escuela Official de Cinematografica, 1972. Worked on such Spanish prods. as 19/19, Cornica del Alba, Odd and Even, Soldier of Metal. Moved to L.A. Granted 2 yr. fellowship at American Film Inst. from which he graduated in 1981. First U.S. prod. was Reborn, 1982.
PICTURES: The Stone Boy, That Was Then This Is Now, Maria's Lovers, At Close Range, Where the River Runs Black, House of Games, Surrender, The Seventh Sign, Things Change, Lost Angels, The Last of the Finest, Dying Young, Naked Tango, Liebstraum, Glengarry Glen Ross, A Far Off Place, Mr. Jones, The Jungle Book, Two Bits.

RULE, JANICE
Actress. b. Cincinnati, OH, Aug. 15, 1931. e. Wheaton & Glenbard H.S., Glen Ellyn, IL. Received Phd in Clinical & Research Psychoanalysis, 1983. Dancer 4 yrs. in Chicago & New York nightclubs; stage experience in It's Great To Be Alive, as understudy of Bambi Lynn.
THEATER: Miss Liberty, Picnic (B'way debut, 1953), The Happiest Girl in the World.
PICTURES: Goodbye My Fancy (debut, 1951), Starlift, Holiday for Sinners, Rogue's March, A Woman's Devotion, Gun for a Coward, Bell Book and Candle, The Subterraneans,

Invitation to a Gunfighter, The Chase, Alvarez Kelly, Welcome to Hard Times, The Swimmer, The Ambushers, Doctors' Wives, Gumshoe, Kid Blue, 3 Women, Missing, Rainy Day Friends, American Flyers.
TELEVISION: Movies: Shadow on the Land, Trial Run, The Devil and Miss Sarah, The Word.

RUSH, BARBARA
Actress. b. Denver, CO, Jan. 4, 1927. e. U. of California. First stage appearance at age of ten, Loberto Theatre, Santa Barbara, CA, in fantasy, Golden Ball; won acting award in college for characterization of Birdie (The Little Foxes); scholarship, Pasadena Playhouse Theatre Arts Coll.
THEATER: A Woman of Independent Means, 40 Carats, Same Time Next Year, Steel Magnolias.
PICTURES: Molly (debut, 1950), The First Legion, Quebec, When Worlds Collide, Flaming Feather, Prince of Pirates, It Came From Outer Space, Taza—Son of Cochise, The Magnificent Obsession, The Black Shield of Falworth, Captain Lightfoot, Kiss of Fire, World in My Corner, Bigger Than Life, Flight to Hong Kong, Oh Men! Oh Women!, No Down Payment, The Young Lions, Harry Black and the Tiger, The Young Philadelphians, The Bramble Bush, Strangers When We Meet, Come Blow Your Horn, Robin and the 7 Hoods, Hombre, The Man, Superdad, Can't Stop the Music, Summer Lovers.
TELEVISION: Series: Saints and Sinners, Peyton Place, The New Dick Van Dyke Show, Flamingo Road. Movies: Suddenly Single, Cutter, Eyes of Charles Sand, Moon of the Wolf, Crime Club, The Last Day, Death on the Freeway, The Seekers, Flamingo Road (pilot), The Night the Bridge Fell Down.

RUSH, HERMAN
Executive. b. Philadelphia, PA, June 20, 1929. e. Temple U., Sales mgr., Official Films Inc., 1952-57. Headed Flamingo Telefilms, Inc. 1957-60; 1960-71, pres., tv div of Creative Mgt. Assoc.; pres., Herman Rush Assoc. Inc., 1971-77; 1977-78 chmn. bd., Rush-Flaherty Agency, Inc.; 1970 headed Marble Arch TV; 1980 named pres., Columbia TV; 1984, pres. of newly formed Columbia Pictures TV Group; 1986, chmn. of newly formed Coca-Cola Telecommunications, Inc.; 1988, chmn., Rush Entertainment Group; 1989, became creative consultant for CBN Producers Group; 1992, Katz/Rush Ent., partner; co-founder, dir. of Transactional Media, Informercial and Transactional Program Production Co.; 1993-94 exec. prod., Willard Scott's New Original Amateur Hour; 1994-95, exec. prod. Susan Powter Show; exec. prod. of The Montel Williams Show.

RUSH, RICHARD
Director, Producer, Writer. b. New York, NY, 1930.
PICTURES: Director: Too Soon To Love (also prod., s.p.), Of Love and Desire (also prod., s.p.), A Man Called Dagger, Fickle Finger of Fate, Thunder Alley, Hell's Angels on Wheels, Psych-Out (also s.p.), Savage Seven, Getting Straight (also prod.), Freebie and the Bean (also prod.), The Stunt Man (also prod., s.p.; Acad. Award nom. for best dir., s.p.), Air America (co-s.p.), Color of Night.

RUSSELL, CHUCK
Director. Asst. dir., and line prod. on many low-budget films for Roger Corman and Sunn Classics, including Death Race 2000.
PICTURES: Dreamscape (co-s.p., line prod.), Back to School (prod.), Nightmare on Elm Street III (dir., co-s.p.), The Blob (dir., co-s.p.), The Mask, Eraser.

RUSSELL, JANE
Actress. r.n. Ernestine Jane Russell. b. Bemidji, MN, June 21, 1921. e. Max Reinhardt's Theatrical Workshop & Mme. Ouspenskaya. Photographer's model.
PICTURES: The Outlaw (debut, 1943), Young Widow, The Paleface, His Kind of Woman, Double Dynamite, Macao, Son of Paleface, Montana Belle, Las Vegas Story, Road to Bali (cameo), Gentlemen Prefer Blondes, The French Line, Underwater, Gentlemen Marry Brunettes, Foxfire, Tall Men, Hot Blood, The Revolt of Mamie Stover, The Fuzzy Pink Nightgown, Fate Is the Hunter, Waco, Johnny Reno, Born Losers, Darker Than Amber.
TELEVISION: Series: Yellow Rose.

RUSSELL, KEN
Director, Producer, Writer. b. Southampton, England, July 3, 1927. e. Walthamstow Art Sch. Early career as dancer, actor, stills photographer, TV documentary film-maker. Ent. TV ind. 1959. Made 33 documentaries for BBC-TV. Also made numerous pop videos.
PICTURES: French Dressing, Billion Dollar Brain, Women in Love, The Music Lovers (also prod.), The Devils (also prod., s.p.), The Boy Friend (also prod., s.p.), Savage Messiah (also prod.), Mahler (also s.p.), Tommy (also prod., s.p.), Lisztomania (also s.p.), Valentino, Altered States, Crimes of Passion, Gothic, Aria (sequence), Salome's Last Dance (also

s.p., actor), The Lair of the White Worm (also prod., s.p.), The Rainbow (also prod., co-s.p.), The Russia House (actor only), Whore (also s.p.), Mindbender.
TELEVISION: The Secret Life of Sir Arnold Box, Lady Chatterly's Lover, Portrait of a Soviet Composer, Elgar, A House in Bayswater, Always on Sunday, The Debussy Film, Isadora Duncan, Dantes Inferno, Song of Summer—Delius, Dance of the Seven Veils. HBO: Dust Before Fireworks, Prisoner of Honor.

RUSSELL, KURT
Actor. b. Springfield, MA, March 17, 1951. Son of former baseball player-turned-actor Bing Russell (deputy sheriff on Bonanza). At 12 got lead in tv series The Travels of Jamie McPheeters (1963-64). Starred as child in many Disney shows and films. Professional baseball player 1971-73. Host, Kurt Russell Celebrity Shoot Out, 4-day hunting tournament.
PICTURES: It Happened at the World's Fair (debut, 1963), Follow Me Boys, The One and Only Genuine Original Family Band, The Horse in the Grey Flannel Suit, The Computer Wore Tennis Shoes, The Barefoot Executive, Fools' Parade, Now You See Him Now You Don't, Charley and the Angel, Superdad, The Strongest Man in the World, Used Cars, Escape from New York, The Fox and The Hound (voice), The Thing, Silkwood, Swing Shift, The Mean Season, The Best of Times, Big Trouble in Little China, Overboard, Tequila Sunrise, Winter People, Tango and Cash, Backdraft, Unlawful Entry, Captain Ron, Tombstone, StarGate, Executive Decision, Escape From L.A.
TELEVISION: Series: The Travels of Jamie McPheeters, The New Land, The Quest. Movies: Search for the Gods, The Deadly Tower, The Quest (pilot), Christmas Miracle in Caulfield U.S.A., Elvis, Amber Waves. Guest: The Fugitive, Daniel Boone, Gilligan's Island, Lost in Space, The F.B.I., Love American Style, Gunsmoke, Hawaii Five-O.

RUSSELL, THERESA
Actress. r.n. Theresa Paup. b. San Diego, CA, Mar. 20, 1957. m. dir.-cinematographer Nicolas Roeg. e. Burbank H.S. Began modeling career at 12. Studied at Actors' Studio in Hollywood.
PICTURES: The Last Tycoon (debut, 1976), Straight Time, Bad Timing/A Sensual Obsession, Eureka, The Razor's Edge, Insignificance, Black Widow, Aria, Track 29, Physical Evidence, Impulse, Whore, Kafka, Cold Heaven, The Grotesque.
TELEVISION: Mini-Series: Blind Ambition. Movie: Thicker Than Water.

RUSSO, JAMES
Actor. b. New York, NY, Apr. 23, 1953. e. NYU, where he wrote and starred in prize-winning short film Candy Store.
THEATER: NY: Welcome to Andromeda, Deathwatch, Marat/Sade, Extremities (Theatre World Award).
PICTURES: A Strange Is Watching (debut, 1982), Fast Times at Ridgemont High, Vortex, Exposed, Once Upon a Time in America, Beverly Hills Cop, The Cotton Club, Extremities, China Girl, The Blue Iguana, Freeway, We're No Angels, State of Grace, A Kiss Before Dying, My Own Private Idaho, Cold Heaven, Dangerous Game, Bad Girls, Donnie Brasco.
TELEVISION: Movie: The Secretary.

RUSSO, RENE
Actress. b. California, 1955. Raised in Burbank. Worked as top fashion model for Eileen Ford Agency prior to acting.
PICTURES: Major League (debut, 1989), Mr. Destiny, One Good Cop, Freejack, Lethal Weapon 3, In the Line of Fire, Outbreak, Get Shorty, Tin Cup, Ransom.
TELEVISION: Series: Sable.

RUTHERFORD, ANN
Actress. b. Toronto, Canada, Nov. 2, 1920. Trained by mother (cousin of Richard Mansfield); with parents in stock as child; later on Los Angeles radio programs. Screen debut, 1935.
PICTURES: Waterfront Lady (debut, 1935), Judge Hardy's Children, Of Human Hearts, A Christmas Carol, You're Only Young Once, Dramatic School, Love Finds Andy Hardy, Out West With the Hardys, The Hardys Ride High, Four Girls in White, Dancing Co-Ed, Andy Hardy Gets Spring Fever, Gone With the Wind, These Glamour Girls, Judge Hardy and Son, Wyoming, Pride and Prejudice, The Ghost Comes Home, Andy Hardy Meets Debutante, Washington Melodrama, Life Begins for Andy Hardy, Badlands of Dakota, Andy Hardy's Private Secretary, Whistling in the Dark, Orchestra Wives, The Courtship of Andy Hardy, Whistling in Dixie, Andy Hardy's Double Life, This Time for Keeps, Happy Land, Whistling in Brooklyn, Bermuda Mystery, Two O'Clock Courage, Bedside Manner, The Madonna's Secret, Murder in the Music Hall, Inside Job, The Secret Life of Walter Mitty, Operation Haylift, Adventures of Don Juan, They Only Kill Their Masters, Won Ton Ton the Dog Who Saved Hollywood.

RYAN, ARTHUR N.
Executive. Joined Paramount in N.Y. in 1967 as asst. treas; later made dir. of admin. and business affairs, exec. asst. to

Robert Evans and asst. scty. 1970 appt. v.p.-prod. adm. 1975 named sr. v.p. handling all prod. operations for Paramount's m.p. and TV divisions; 1976, asst. to the chmn. & CEO; chmn. & pres. Magicam, Inc.; chmn. Fortune General Corp.; chmn. Paramount Communications; co-chmn. of scholarship comm. of AMPAS; trustee of Univ. Film Study Center in Boston; joined Technicolor in 1976 as pres., COO & dir.; vice chmn., 1983-85; chmn. & CEO, 1985-; chmn. Technicolor Audio-Visual Systems International, Inc.; dir. Technicolor S.P.A.; dir. Technicolor, Film Intl.; and chmn. of exec. committee, Technicolor Graphics Services, Inc.; dir., Technicolor, Inc.; chmn., Technicolor Fotografica, S.A.; chmn. Technicolor Film Intl. Service Company, Inc.; dir. & deputy chmn. Technicolor Ltd.; chmn. & dir., The Vidtronics Company, Inc.; chmn. & CEO, Compact Video, Inc., 1984-; dir, Four Star Int'l., 1983-; dir., MacAndrews & Forbes, Inc. 1985-; Permanent charities committee of the Entertainment Industry; Hollywood Canteen Foundations. Vice-chmn. & dir., Calif. Inst. of Arts. Trustee: Motion Picture & Television Fund. 1985 named chmn., Technicolor.

RYAN, JOHN
Actor. b. New York, NY, July 30, 1936. e. City Coll. of NY.
THEATER: NY: Duet for Three, Sgt. Musgrave's Dance, Yerma, Nobody Hears a Broken Drum, The Love Suicide at Schofield Barracks, The Silent Partner, Twelve Angry Men, Medea.
PICTURES: The Tiger Makes Out (debut, 1967), A Lovely Way to Die, What's So Bad About Feeling Good?, Five Easy Pieces, The King of Marvin Gardens, The Legend of Nigger Charley, Cops and Robbers, Dillinger, Shamus, It's Alive, The Missouri Breaks, Futureworld, It Lives Again, The Last Flight of Noah's Ark, On the Nickel, The Postman Always Rings Twice, The Escape Artist, Breathless, The Right Stuff, The Cotton Club, Runaway Train, Avenging Force, Death Wish 4: The Crackdown, Delta Force II, Fatal Beauty, Three O'Clock High, Rent-a-Cop, Paramedics, City of Shadows, Best of the Best, White Sands, Hoffa, Star Time, Young Goodman Brown, Batman: Mask of the Phantasm (voice), Tall Tale, Bound.
TELEVISION: Series: Archer. Guest: M*A*S*H, Kojak, Starsky & Hutch, Matt Helm, Matt Houston, Miami Vice. Movies: Target Risk, Death Scream, Kill Me If You Can, A Killing Affair, Houston: The Legend of Texas, Blood River, Shooting Stars.

RYAN, MEG
Actress. b. Bethel, CT, Nov. 19, 1961. e. NYU. m. actor Dennis Quaid. Supported herself, while studying journalism at NYU, by making commercials. Auditioned for and won first prof. role as Candice Bergen's daughter in film Rich and Famous.
PICTURES: Rich and Famous (debut, 1981), Amityville 3-D, Top Gun, Armed and Dangerous, Innerspace, Promised Land, D.O.A., The Presidio, When Harry Met Sally, Joe Versus the Volcano, The Doors, Prelude to a Kiss, Sleepless in Seattle, Flesh & Bone, When a Man Loves a Woman, I.Q., French Kiss, Restoration, Courage Under Fire.
TELEVISION: Series: One of the Boys, As the World Turns (1982-84), Wild Side (Disney TV).

RYAN, MITCHELL
Actor. b. Louisville, KY, Jan. 11, 1928. Entered acting following service in Navy during Korean War. Was New York stage actor working off-B'way for Ted Mann and Joseph Papp; on B'way in Wait Until Dark. Member of Arena Stage group in Washington.
PICTURES: Monte Walsh, The Hunting Party, My Old Man's Place, High Plains Drifter, The Friends of Eddie Coyle, ElectraGlide in Blue, Magnum Force, Labyrinth, Winter People.
TELEVISION: Series: Chase, Executive Suite, Having Babies, The Chisholms, Dark Shadows, High Performance, King Crossings. Movies: Angel City, The Five of Me, Death of a Centerfold—The Dorothy Stratten Story, Uncommon Valor, Medea, Kenny Rogers as the Gambler—The Adventure Continues, Robert Kennedy & His Times, Fatal Vision, Favorite Son, The Ryan White Story, Margaret Bourke-White.

RYDELL, MARK
Director, Producer, Actor. b. March 23, 1934. e. Juilliard Sch. of Music. Studied acting with Sanford Meisner of NY Neighborhood Playhouse. Became member of Actors Studio. Was leading actor for six years on daytime CBS serial, As The World Turns. Made Broadway debut in Seagulls over Sorrento and film bow in Crime in the Streets. Went to Hollywood as TV director (Ben Casey, I Spy, Gunsmoke, etc.). Partner with Sydney Pollack in Sanford Prods., film, TV prod. co. Formed own production co., Concourse Productions.
PICTURES: Director: The Fox (debut, 1968), The Reivers, The Cowboys (also prod.), Cinderella Liberty (also prod.), Harry and Walter Go To New York, The Rose, On Golden Pond, The River, Man in the Moon (prod. only), For the Boys (also exec. prod.), Intersection (also co-prod.). Actor: Crime in the Streets, The Long Goodbye, Punchline, Havana.

RYDER, WINONA
Actress. b. Winona, MN, Oct. 29, 1971. r.n. Winona Horowitz. Grew up in San Francisco. At 7, moved with family to Northern

CA commune. At 13 discovered by talent scout during a performance at San Francisco's American Conservatory theatre, where she was studying, and given screen test.
PICTURES: Lucas (debut, 1986), Square Dance, Beetlejuice, 1969, Heathers, Great Balls of Fire, Welcome Home Roxy Carmichael, Edward Scissorhands, Mermaids, Night on Earth, Bram Stoker's Dracula, The Age of Innocence (Golden Globe Award; Acad. Award nom.), Reality Bites, The House of the Spirits, Little Women (Acad. Award nom.), How to Make an American Quilt, Boys, Looking for Richard, The Crucible.

S

SACKHEIM, WILLIAM B.
Producer, Writer. b. Gloversville, NY, Oct. 31, 1921. e. UCLA.
PICTURES: The Art of Love, The In-Laws (co-prod.), The Competition, First Blood (co-s.p.), The Survivors (prod.), No Small Affair (prod.), The Hard Way (prod.), Pacific Heights (prod.), White Sands (prod.).
TELEVISION: The Law (Emmy Award, 1975), Gideon Oliver (series, exec. prod.), Almost Grown (exec. prod.), The Antagonists (exec. prod.), The Human Factor (exec. prod.).

SACKS, SAMUEL
Attorney, Agent. b. New York, NY, March 29, 1908. e. CCNY, St. John's Law Sch., LL.B., 1930. Admitted Calif. Bar, 1943; priv. law practice, NY 1931-42; attorney, William Morris Agency, Inc., 1942; head of west coast TV business affairs, 1948-75; bd. of dir., Alliance of Television Film Producers, 1956-60; LA Copyright Society Treasurer, Beverly Hills Bar Assn., LA Bar Assn., American Bar Assn.; Academy of TV Arts & Sciences; Hollywood Radio & TV Society; counsel, entertainment field, Simon & Sheridan, 1975-89, Los Angeles Citizens' Olympic Committee; arbitrator for Screen Actors Guild, Assn. of Talent Agents and American Arbitration Assn.; bd. of dirs., Friars Club, 1991-95; Counsel for the Caucus for Producers, Writers & Directors, 1975-95.

SADLER, WILLIAM
Actor. b. Buffalo, NY, Apr. 13, 1950. e. SUNY, Cornell U. Made stage debut in title role in Hamlet for Colorado Shakespeare Fest. Also acted with La Jolla Playhouse, Yale Rep.
THEATER: NY: Ivanov (Off-B'way debut, 1975), Limbo Tales (Obie Award), Chinese Viewing Pavilion, Lennon, Necessary Ends, Hannah, Biloxi Blues (B'way debut, 1985; Clarence Derwent & Dramalogue Awards). Regional: Journey's End, A Mad World My Masters, Romeo and Juliet, Night Must Fall, etc.
PICTURES: Hanky Panky, Off Beat, Project X, K-9, Hard to Kill, Die Hard 2, The Hot Spot, Bill & Ted's Bogus Journey, Rush, Trespass, Freaked, The Shawshank Redemption, Tales From the Crypt Presents Demon Knight, Solo.
TELEVISION: Series: Private Eye. Movies: The Great Walendas, Charlie and the Great Balloon Race, Face of Fear, The Last to Go, Bermuda Grace. Guest: Hooperman, Roseanne, Dear John, Gideon Oliver, The Equalizer, In the Heat of the Night, Tales From the Crypt, Murphy Brown.

SAFER, MORLEY
News Correspondent. b. Toronto, Ont., 1931. e. U. of Western Ontario. Started as corresp. and prod. with Canadian Broadcasting Corp. Joined CBS News London Bureau 1964, chief of Saigon Bureau, 1965. Chief of CBS London bureau 1967-70. Joined 60 Minutes as co-editor in Dec., 1970.

SAFFLE, M. W. "BUD"
Executive. b. Spokane, WA, June 29, 1923. e. U. of Washington. In service 1943-46. Started in m.p. business as booker, 1948. Entire career with Saffle Theatre Service as buyer-booker; named pres. in 1970. Also pres. of Grays Harbor Theatres, Inc., operating theatres in Aberdeen, WA. Also operates drive-in in Centralia, WA. On bd. of NATO of WA for 15 yrs; pres. of same for 2 terms and secty.-treas. 6 yrs. Elected to National NATO bd. in 1972. Founder of Variety Tent 46, serving as chief barker three times.

SAGANSKY, JEFF
Executive. b. 1953. Joined CBS 1976 in bdcst. finance; 1977, NBC, assoc. in pgm. development.; 1977, mgr. film pgms.; 1978, dir. dramatic dev.; 1978, v.p., dev. David Gerber Co.; 1981, returned to NBC as series dev. v.p.; 1983, sr. v.p. series programming; 1985, joined Tri-Star Pictures as pres. of production; 1989 promoted to president of Tri-Star, later that year joined CBS as entertainment division president. Resigned, 1994.

SAGEBRECHT, MARIANNE
Actress. b. Starnberg, Germany, Aug. 27, 1945. In 1977 conceived revue Opera Curiosa, followed by stage role in Adele Spitzeder.
PICTURES: Die Schaukel (debut, 1983), Sugarbaby, Crazy Boys, Bagdad Cafe, Moon Over Parador, The War of the

Roses, Rosalie Goes Shopping, The Milky Life (La Vida Lactea), Dust Devil, Mona Must Die, Martha and I, Erotique, All Men Are Mortal.
TELEVISION: Movies: Herr Kischott, Eine Mutter Kampft un Ihren Sohn, My Lord.

SAGET, BOB
Actor. b. Philadelphia, PA, May 17, 1956. Started as stand-up comedian.
PICTURE: Critical Condition.
TELEVISION: Series: Full House, America's Funniest Home Videos (host). Movie: Father and Scout (also co-exec. prod.).

SAINT, EVA MARIE
Actress. b. Newark, NJ, July 4, 1924. e. Bowling Green State U., Ohio, Actors Studio. Radio, tv actress; on Broadway in Trip to Bountiful before film debut.
THEATER: Trip to Bountiful, The Rainmaker, Desire Under the Elms, The Lincoln Mask, Summer and Smoke, Candida, Winesburg Ohio, First Monday in October, Duet for One, The Country Girl, Death of a Salesman, Love Letters, The Fatal Weakness, On The Divide.
PICTURES: On the Waterfront (debut, 1954; Academy Award, best supporting actress), That Certain Feeling, Raintree County, Hatful of Rain, North by Northwest, Exodus, All Fall Down, 36 Hours, The Sandpiper, The Russians Are Coming the Russians Are Coming, Grand Prix, The Stalking Moon, Loving, Cancel My Reservation, Nothing in Common, Mariette in Ecstasy.
TELEVISION: Movies: Carol for Another Christmas, The Macahans, A Christmas to Remember, When Hell Was in Session, Fatal Weakness, Curse of King Tut's Tomb, Best Little Girl in the World, Splendor in the Grass, Malibu, Jane Doe, Love Leads the Way, Fatal Vision, The Last Days of Patton, A Year in the Life, Norman Rockwell's Breaking Ties, I'll Be Home for Christmas, Voyage of Terror: The Achille Lauro Affair, People Like Us (Emmy Award, 1991), Danielle Steel's Palomino, Kiss of a Killer, My Antonia, After Jimmy. Series: Campus Hoopla, One Man's Family, Moonlighting. Special: Our Town, First Woman President, Primary Colors: The Story of Corita.

SAINT JAMES, SUSAN
Actress. b. Los Angeles, CA, Aug. 14, 1946. r.n. Susan Miller. e. Connecticut Coll. for Women. Was model for 2 years; then signed to contract by Universal Pictures.
TELEVISION: Series: The Name of the Game (Emmy Award, 1969), McMillan & Wife, Kate and Allie. Movies: Fame Is the Name of the Game, Alias Smith and Jones, Once Upon a Dead Man, Magic Carpet, Scott Free, Night Cries, Desperate Women, The Girls in the Office, Sex and the Single Parent, S.O.S. Titanic, The Kid from Nowhere, I Take These Men. Special: A Very Special Christmas Party.
PICTURES: P.J., Where Angels Go... Trouble Follows, What's So Bad About Feeling Good?, Jigsaw, Outlaw Blues, Love at First Bite, How to Beat the High Cost of Living, Carbon Copy, Don't Cry It's Only Thunder.

ST. JOHN, JILL
Actress. r.n. Jill Oppenheim. b. Los Angeles, CA, Aug. 19, 1940. m. actor Robert Wagner. On radio series One Man's family. Television debut, A Christmas Carol, 1948.
PICTURES: Summer Love, The Remarkable Mr. Pennypacker, Holiday for Lovers, The Lost World, The Roman Spring of Mrs. Stone, Tender Is the Night, Come Blow Your Horn, Who's Minding the Store?, Who's Been Sleeping in My Bed?, Honeymoon Hotel, The Liquidator, The Oscar, Banning, Tony Rome, Eight on the Lam, The King's Pirate, Diamonds Are Forever, Sitting Target, The Concrete Jungle, The Act, The Player.
TELEVISION: Series: Emerald Point. Movies: Fame Is the Name of the Game, How I Spent My Summer Vacation, The Spy Killer, Foreign Exchange, Brenda Starr, Telethon, Hart to Hart (pilot), Rooster. Guest: Dupont Theatre, Fireside Theatre, Batman, The Love Boat. Mini-Series: Around the World in 80 Days.

SAJAK, PAT
TV Host. b. Chicago, IL, Oct. 26, 1946. e. Columbia Coll., Chicago. Broadcasting career began as newscaster for Chicago radio station. 1968 drafted into Army, where served 4 years as disc jockey for Armed Forces Radio in Saigon, Vietnam. Moved to Nashville, where continued radio career while also working as weatherman and host of public affairs prog. for local TV station. 1977 moved to LA to become nightly weatherman on KNBC. Took over as host of daytime edition of Wheel of Fortune and later the syndicated nighttime edition (4 Emmy nom.). 1989, The Pat Sajak Show.
PICTURE: Airplane II: The Sequel.
TELEVISION: Host: The Thanksgiving Day Parade, The Rose Parade.

SAKS, GENE
Director, Actor. b. New York, NY, Nov. 8, 1921. e. Cornell U. Attended dramatic workshop, New School for Social

Research. Active in off-Broadway in 1948-49, forming cooperative theatre group at Cherry Lane Theatre. Joined Actor's Studio, followed by touring and stock. Also appeared in live TV dramas (Philco Playhouse, Producer's Showcase). Directed many Broadway plays before turning to film direction with Barefoot in the Park (1967) President of SSDC.
THEATER: *B'way: Director.* Enter Laughing, Nobody Loves an Albatross, Generation, Half a Sixpence, Mame, A Mother's Kisses, Sheep on the Runway, How the Other Half Loves, Same Time Next Year, California Suite, I Love My Wife (Tony Award), Brighton Beach Memoirs (Tony Award), Biloxi Blues (Tony Award), The Odd Couple (1985), Broadway Bound, Rumors, Lost in Yonkers, Jake's Women. *Actor:* Middle of the Night, Howie, The Tenth Man, A Shot in the Dark, A Thousand Clowns.
PICTURES: *Director.* Barefoot in the Park, The Odd Couple, Cactus Flower, Last of the Red Hot Lovers, Mame, Brighton Beach Memoirs, A Fine Romance. *Actor:* A Thousand Clowns, Prisoner of Second Avenue, The One and Only, Lovesick, The Goodbye People, Nobody's Fool, I.Q.

SALANT, RICHARD S.
Executive. b. New York, NY, Apr. 14, 1914. e. Harvard Coll. A.B., 1931-35; Harvard Law Sch., 1935-38. Atty. Gen.'s Com. on Admin. Procedure, 1939-41; Office of Solicitor Gen., U.S. Dept. of Justice, 1941-43; U.S. Naval Res., 1943-46; assoc., Roseman, Goldmark, Colin & Kave, 1946-48; then partner, 1948-51; pres. CBS news div., 1961-64; v.p. special asst. to pres. CBS, Inc., 1951-61, 1964-66; pres., CBS news div., 1966; mem. bd. of dir., CBS, Inc. 1964-69; vice chmn., NBC bd., 1979-81; sr. adviser, 1981-83; pres. CEO, National News Council, 1983-84. Retired.

SALDANA, THERESA
Actress. b. Brooklyn, NY, Aug. 20, 1954. Following attack by stalker founded advocacy group Victims for Victims. *Author.* Beyond Survival, 1986.
PICTURES: Nunzio, I Wanna Hold Your Hand, Defiance, Raging Bull, Double Revenge, Angel Town.
TELEVISION: *Series:* The Commish. *Movies:* Sophia Loren: Her Own Story, Victims for Victims: The Theresa Saldana Story, Confessions of a Crime.

SALEH, ANGELIKA T.
Executive. Chmn., Angelika Films, Inc.

SALES, SOUPY
Comedian. r.n. Milton Hines. b. Franklinton, NC, Jan. 8, 1926. Was radio DJ before debuting with his own children show in Detroit, 1953. Program was picked up by ABC in 1955. Continued to perform on radio over the years.
PICTURES: Birds Do It, And God Spoke.
TELEVISION: *Series:* Soupy Sales (1955), Lunch With Soupy Sales, The Soupy Sales Show (1962), The Soupy Sales Show (1965-67), What's My Line (panelist), The Soupy Sales Show (1978-79), Sha Na Na. *Guest:* The Rebel, The Real McCoys, Route 66, The Beverly Hillbillies, Love American Style, The Love Boat, Wings.

SALHANY, LUCIE
Executive. Formerly chairman of Fox Broadcasting Co. Currently pres. & CEO, United Paramount Network.

SALKIND, ALEXANDER
Producer. b. Danzig/Gdansk, of Russian extraction, June 2, 1921. Grew up in Berlin where father, Miguel, produced films. Went to Cuba with father to assist him in film production. First solo venture a Buster Keaton comedy, 1945. Returned to Europe where made many pictures in Spain, Italy, France and Hungary. PICTURES: *Prod.:* Austerlitz, The Trial, Kill! Kill! (with Ilya Salkind), Bluebeard. *Exec. prod.:* The Light at the Edge of the World, The Three Musketeers, The Four Musketeers, The Prince and the Pauper, Superman, Supergirl, Santa Claus: The Movie, Christopher Columbus: The Discovery.
TELEVISION: Superboy.

SALKIND, ILYA
Producer. b. Mexico City, 1947. e. U. of London. Father is producer, Alexander Salkind. First film job as production runner on The Life of Cervantes for father. Was assoc. prod. on Light at the Edge of the World.
PICTURES: The Three Musketeers, The Four Musketeers, Superman, Superman II (exec. prod.), Supergirl (exec. prod.), Superman III (exec. prod.), Christopher Columbus: The Discovery.
TELEVISION: Superboy (exec. prod.).

SALKOW, SIDNEY
Director, Writer. b. New York, NY, June 16, 1911. e. City Coll. of New York, B.A.; Harvard Law Sch. Master of Fine Arts, USC. Stage dir. & prod. asst. number N.Y. dram. prods. (Dir. Bloodstream, Black Tower, etc.) and mgr. summer theatre.

From 1933 variously dialogue dir., assoc. dir., writer & dir. numerous pictures Paramount, Universal, Republic, Columbia, etc.; dir. number of pictures in Lone Wolf series (for Columbia), Tillie the Toiler, Flight Lieutenant, etc. In armed service, WWII. Head of film dept., CSUN, emeritus prof.
PICTURES: Millie's Daughter, Bulldog Drummond at Bay, Admiral Was a Lady, Fugitive Lady, Golden Hawk, Scarlet Angel, Pathfinder, Prince of Pirates, Jack McCall Desperado, Raiders of the 7 Seas, Sitting Bull, Robbers' Roost, Shadow of the Eagle, Las Vegas Shakedown, Toughest Man Alive, Chicago Confidential, Iron Sheriff, Great Sioux Massacre, Martin Eden.
TELEVISION: *Created, prod. dir.:* This Is Alice series for Desilu, Lassie, Fury, Wells Fargo series. Headed prod. for FF Prod. in Rome, 1967-71.

SALOMON, MIKAEL
Cinematographer. b. Copenhagen, Denmark, Feb. 24, 1945.
PICTURES: *Europe:* The Dreamers, Z.P.G., Three From Haparanda, The Five, Me and My Kid Brothers, The Owlfarm Brothers, Five on the Run, Magic in Town, 24 Hours With Ilse, Why?, Bedside Freeway, My Sister's Children Goes Astray, Around the World, Tumult, Welcome to the Club, Violets Are Blue, Tintomare, Tell It Like It Is Boys, Cop, Elvis Elvis, Hearts Are Trump, The Marksman, The Flying Devils, Peter von Scholten, The Baron, Once a Cop..., Early Spring, The Wolf at the Door. *U.S.:* Zelly and Me, Torch Song Trilogy, Stealing Heaven, The Abyss (Acad. Award nom.), Always, Arachnophobia, Backdraft, Far and Away, A Far Off Place (dir. only), Congo (2nd unit dir.), Judge Dredd (trailer dir.).
TELEVISION: *Movie:* The Man Who Broke 1,000 Chains (ACE Award). *Series:* Space Rangers (dir.) Also commercials for Mitsubishi, Nescafe, Converse, Mazda, etc.

SALZBURG, JOSEPH S.
Producer, Editor. b. New York, NY, July 27, 1917. Film librarian, then rose to v.p. in chg. of prod., Pictorial Films, 1935-42; civilian chief film ed. U.S. Army Signal Corps Photo Center, 1942-44; U.S. Army Air Forces, 1944-46; prod. mgr., Pictorial Films, 1946-50; prod. mgr. Associated Artists Prod., then M.P. for TV, 1950-51; org. m.p. prod. & edit. service for theatrical, non-theatrical & TV films 1951-56; prod. mgr., dir. of films oper., official Films. 1956-59; prod. sup. tech. dir. Lynn Romero Prod. features and TV; assoc. prod. Lynn Romero Prod. TV series, Counterthrust 1959-60; v.p., sec'y, B.L. Coleman Assoc., Inc. & Newspix, Inc. 1961; pres. National Production Assoc., Inc. 1960-1962, chief of production, UPI Newsfilm, 1963-66. Prod./account exec. Fred A. Niles Comm. Center, 1966. Appt. v.p., F.A. Niles Communications Centers Inc., N.Y., 1969. 1979 appointed in addition exec. producer & gen. mgr., F. A. Niles Communication centers Inc., N.Y. studio. 1989, elected mem. bd. dir., Florida Motion Pictures & Television Assn., Palm Beach area chap.; 1989 professor m.p. & TV prod. course at Palm Beach Comm. Coll.: Breaking into TV and Movie Making in South Florida.

SAMMS, EMMA
Actress. b. London, England, Aug. 28, 1960. Former fashion model. Has worked as commercial photographer for such magazines as Ritz, Metro, and Architectural Digest. Co-founder of charitable org. the Starlight Foundation.
PICTURES: Arabian Adventure (debut, 1979), The Shrimp on the Barbie, Delirious.
TELEVISION: *Series:* General Hospital, Dynasty, The Colbys. *Movies:* Goliath Awaits, Agatha Christie's Murder in Three Acts, The Lady and the Highwayman, A Connecticut Yankee in King Arthur's Court, Bejeweled, Shadow of a Stranger, Robin Cook's Harmful Intent, Treacherous Beauties. *Guest:* Hotel, The New Mike Hammer, Murder She Wrote, Newhart, My Two Dads.

SAMPSON, LEONARD E.
Exhibitor. b. New York, NY, Oct. 9, 1918. e. City Coll. of New York, B.B.A., 1939. Entered m.p. industry as stagehand helper and usher, Skouras Park Plaza, Bronx 1932-36; asst. mgr. Gramercy Park, 1937-38; mgr., 5th Avenue Playhouse, 1939-41; mgr., Ascot Bronx, 1941-42. In Army 1942-46. On return entered into partnership with cousin Robert C. Spodick in Lincoln, a New Haven art house. Organized Nutmeg Theatres in 1952 in assn. with Norman Bialek, operating 6 art and conventional theatres in Conn., mainly in Westport and Norwalk. Sold Nutmeg in 1968 to Robert Smerling (became Loews Theatres, now Sony Theatres). Built Groton, CT, Cinemas I & II in 1970 and Norwich, CT, Cinema I & II, 1976 and acquired Village Cinemas I, II & III, Mystic, in association with Spodick and William Rosen. Operated as Gemini Theatre Circuit. Acquired Westerly Cinema I, II & III, 1982. Sold Gemini Theatre Circuit to Hoyts Theatres, 1987. Retains partnership with Spodick in New Haven's York Sq., until 1996 when he became an inactive partner due to illness.

SAMUELSON, DAVID W.
F.R.P.S., F.B.K.S., B.S.C.: Executive. b. London, England, July 6, 1924. Son of early producer G.B. Samuelson. Joined

ind. 1941 with British Movietone News. Later film cameraman, 1947. Left Movietone 1960 to join family company, Samuelson Film Service Ltd. Dir., Samuelson Group Plc, 1958-84. Past president British Kinematograph Sound & TV Soc., Past Chmn, British Board of Film Classification, London Intl. Film Sch. Author: Hands On Manual for Cinematographer, Motion Picture Camera and Lighting Equipment, Motion Picture Camera Techniques, Motion Picture Camera Data, Samuelson Manual of Cinematography, Panaflex User's Manual and Cinematographers Computer Program. Currently consultant on technology film making, author, lecturer. Won Acad. Award for Engineering, 1980 and Acad. Award for Tech. Achievement, 1987.

SAMUELSON, PETER GEORGE WYLIE
Producer. b. London, England, October 16, 1951. e. Cambridge U., M.A., English literature. Early career as interpreter, production assistant, then prod. mgr. 1975, Return of the Pink Panther. 1979-85, exec. v.p., Interscope Communications, Inc. 1982-present, Intl. Pres., Starlight Foundation. 1986-present, pres., Film Associates, Inc. 1985-90 chmn., Samuelson Group, Inc. 1990-present, partner, Samuelson Prods. of Los Angeles and London.
PICTURES: Speed Merchants, High Velocity, One by One, Return of the Pink Panther, Santa Fe, A Man a Woman and a Bank, Revenge of the Nerds, Turk 182, Tom and Viv, Playmaker, The Gathering.

SAMUELSON, SIR SYDNEY
C.B.E., B.S.C., Hon. F.B.K.S., Executive. b. London, England, Dec. 7, 1925. e. Irene Avenue Council Sch., Lancing, Sussex. Early career as cinema projectionist, 1939-42; Gaumont British News, 1942-43; Royal Air Force, 1943-47; asst. cameraman, cameraman, director/cameraman until 1960; founded Samuelson Film Service, 1954; Trustee and chmn. board of management, British Acad. of Film and Television Arts (chmn. of Council 1973-76). Member (Pres. 1983-86; Trustee: 1982-89) Cinema and Television Benevolent Fund. Member of Executive, Cinema & Television Veterans (pres. 1980-81); assoc. member, American Society of Cinematographers. Hon. Tech. Adviser, Royal Naval Film Corp. Hon. member, Guild of British Camera Technicians, 1986 (now BECTU); Member, British Society of Cinematographers (governor, 1969-79; 1st vice pres., 1976-77), Hon. Mem. for Life, Assn. of Cinema & Television Technicians, 1990. Appointed first British Film Commissioner by U.K. government, 1991. Recipient of two British Academy Awards: Michael Balcon (1985), Fellowship (1993). Received knighthood for services to British Film Industry, 1995. Lifetime Honorary Fellowship, British Kinematograph, Sound & Television Society, 1995.

SANDA, DOMINIQUE
Actress. b. Paris, France, March 11, 1951. r.n. Dominique Varaigne. e. Saint Vincent de Paul, Paris. Was a popular model for women's magazines when cast by Robert Bresson as the tragic heroine in his Dostoyevsky adaptation Un Femme Douce (1968).
THEATER: Madame Klein, Les Liaisons Dangereuses, Un Mari Ideal, Carte Blanche de Dominique Sanda.
PICTURES: Un Femme Douce, First Love, The Conformist, The Garden of the Finzi-Contini, La Notte Dei Fiori, Sans Mobile Apparent, Impossible Object, Steppenwolf, Conversation Piece, 1900, L'Heritage, Le Berceau de Cristal, Damnation Alley, Au Dela du Bien et du Mal, Beyond Good and Evil, The Song of Roland, Utopia, The Navire Night, Travels on the Sly, Caboblanco, A Room in town, Dust of the Empire, The Way to Bresson, The Sailor 512, Corps et Biens, Les Mendiants, On a Moonlit Night, Warrior and Prisoners, Je Ne Vous Derangerai Plus, Moi La Pire De Toutes, Le Voyage, Emile Rosen, Henri Le Vert.
TELEVISION: The Sealed Train, La Naissance Du Jour, Il Decimo Clandestino, Voglia Di Vivere, Achille Lauro, Warburg, Comme Par Hazard, Non Siamo Soli, Albert Savarus, Der Lange Weg des Lukas B, The Lucona Affair, Nobody's Children, Brennendes Herz, Joseph.

SANDERS, JAY O.
Actor. b. Austin, TX, Apr. 16, 1953. e. SUNY/Purchase. First professional theatre experience with NY Shakespeare-in-the Park prods. of Henry V and Measure for Measure. Appeared in Abel's Sister for England's Royal Court Theatre.
THEATER: NY: Loose Ends, The Caine Mutiny Court-Martial, Buried Child, In Trousers, Geniuses, The Incredibly Famous Willy Powers, Heaven on Earth, Girls Girls Girls, King John, Saint Joan, Three Birds Alighting on a Field.
PICTURES: Starting Over (debut, 1979), Hanky Panky, Eddie Macon's Run, Cross Creek, Tucker: The Man and His Dream, The Prince of Pennsylvania, Glory, Just Like in the Movies, Mr. Destiny, V.I. Warshawski, Defenseless, Meeting Venus, JFK, Angels in the Outfield, Kiss of Death, Down Came a Blackbird, The Big Green.
TELEVISION: Series: Aftermash, Crime Story. Movies: The Day Christ Died, Living Proof: The Hank Williams Jr. Story, A Doctor's Story, Cold Sassy Tree, Hostages, State of Emergency, Nobody's Children. Special: The Revolt of Mother. Guest: Roseanne, The Young Riders, Spenser: For Hire, A

Man Called Hawk, Kate and Allie, Miami Vice, Northern Exposure, NY Undercover.

SANDERS, TERRY BARRETT
Producer, Director, Writer. b. New York, NY, Dec. 20, 1931. e. UCLA, 1951; Co-prod., photographed, A Time Out of War, 1954. Academy Award best two-reel subject, and won first prize Venice Film Festival, etc.; co-wrote The Day Lincoln Was Shot, CBS-TV; s.p. The Naked and the Dead; prod. Crime and Punishment—USA., prod., co-dir. War Hunt; prod. and dir. Portrait of Zubin Mehta for U.S.I.A. Assoc. dean, Film Sch., California Inst. of the Arts. Prod.-Dir.: Four Stones for Kanemitsu (Acad. Award nom.). Prod.-Dir.-Writer: Rose Kennedy: A Life to Remember (Acad. Award nom.) Professor, UCLA. Pres., American Film Foundation.
PICTURES: Maya Lin: A Strong Clear Vision (prod., Academy Award), Never Give Up: The 20th Century Odyssey of Herbert Zipper (prod., dir., Academy Award nom.).
TELEVISION: Prod./dir.: Hollywood and the Stars, The Legend of Marilyn Monroe, National Geographic Society specials, The Kids from Fame, Film Bios Kennedy Center Honors, Slow Fires, Lillian Gish: The Actor's Life for Me (Emmy Award).

SANDRICH, JAY
Director. b. Los Angeles, CA, Feb. 24, 1932. e. UCLA.
TELEVISION: Special: The Lily Tomlin Show (DGA Award, 1975). Movies: The Crooked Hearts, What Are Best Friends For?, For Richer For Poorer. Series: The Mary Tyler Moore Show (Emmy Awards: 1971, 1973), Soap, Phyllis (pilot), Tony Randall Show (pilot), Bob Newhart Show (pilot), Benson (pilot), Golden Girls (pilot), Empty Nest (pilot), The Cosby Show (Emmy Awards: 1985, 1986; DGA Award 1985).
PICTURE: Seems Like Old Times.

SANDS, JULIAN
Actor. b. Yorkshire, Eng. 1958. e. Central School of Speech and Drama, London 1979. Formed small theater co. that played in schools and youth clubs. Professional debut in Derek Jarman's short, Broken English and one-line part in Privates on Parade. Then opposite Anthony Hopkins in British TV series A Married Man (1981).
PICTURES: Privates on Parade (debut, 1982), Oxford Blues, The Killing Fields, After Darkness, The Doctor and the Devils, A Room with a View, Gothic, Siesta, Vibes, Wherever You Are, Manika: The Girl Who Lived Twice, Arachnophobia, Warlock, Night Sun, Impromptu, Naked Lunch, Wicked, Husbands and Lovers, Tale of a Vampire, Boxing Helena, Warlock: The Armageddon, Black Water, The Browning Version, Leaving Las Vegas.
TELEVISION: Series: A Married Man. Movies: Romance on the Orient Express, Harem, The Room, Murder By Moonlight, Grand Isle, Crazy in Love, Witch Hunt, The Great Elephant Escape.

SANDS, TOMMY
Singer. b. Chicago, IL, Aug. 27, 1937. e. Schools there and Houston, TX, Greenwood, LA. Father, Benny Sands, concert pianist. Started career as guitar player, singer when 5, at KWKH station, Shreveport. One of pioneers of rock music. First manager was Col. Tom Parker. Acting debut: Kraft TV show The Singin' Idol; recording contract won him million record sales of Teen Age Crush.
PICTURES: Sing Boy Sing, Mardi Gras, Love in a Goldfish Bowl, Babes in Toyland, The Longest Day, Ensign Pulver, None But the Brave, The Violent Ones.

SANFORD, ISABEL
Actress. b. New York, NY, Aug. 29, 1929. e. Textile H.S., Evander Childs H.S. Began acting in elementary school and continued through high school. Joined American Negro Theatre in the 1930's (then The Star Players) which disbanded in W.W.II. Later associated with YWCA project and off-B'way plays. B'way debut in The Amen Corner.
PICTURES: Guess Who's Coming to Dinner, The Young Runaways, Pendulum, The Comic, Stand Up and Be Counted, The New Centurions, Love at First Bite, South Beach, Original Gangstas.
TELEVISION: Series: All in the Family, The Jeffersons (Emmy Award, 1981). Movie: The Great Man's Whiskers. Guest: Fresh Prince of Bel Air, Roseanne, Hangin' With Mr. Cooper, Living Single, In the House, Fresh Prince of Bel Air, Lois & Clark, Cybill.

SAN GIACOMO, LAURA
Actress. b. New Jersey, 1962. e. Carnegie Melon Univ. m. actor Cameron Dye. Appeared Off-B'way in North Shore Fish, Beirut, The Love Talker, Italian American Reconciliation, Wrong Turn at Lungfish, Three Sisters.
PICTURES: Sex Lies and Videotape (debut, 1989), Pretty Woman, Vital Signs, Quigley Down Under, Once Around, Under Suspicion, Where the Day Takes You, Nina Takes a Lover, Stuart Saves His Family.
TELEVISION: Series: Just Shoot Me. Movie: For Their Own Good. Mini-Series: Stephen King's The Stand.

SANSOM, LESTER A.
Producer. b. Salt Lake City, UT, Apr. 24, 1910. e. U. of Utah. Radio singer under name of Jack Allen, 1930; ent. m.p. ind. in editorial dept., Fox Film Corp., 1931; served in U.S. Navy as head of film library, Washington, DC, 1942-45; head of edit. dept. & post-prod., Allied Artists, from 1953; assoc. prod. Skabenga; prod., co-writer, Battle Flame; assoc. prod. Hell to Eternity, exec. prod. The Thin Red Line, prod. Crack in the World; prod. Bikini Paradise, Battle of the Bulge, Custer of the West, Co-prod., Krakatoa—East of Java; exec. prod. 12+1.

SAPERSTEIN, DAVID
Writer, Director. b. Brooklyn, NY. e. Bronx H.S. of Science, CCNY, Film Institute, Chemical Engineering. 1960-80 wrote, prod. and dir. documentary films, TV commercials. Also wrote lyrics and managed rhythm and blues and rock 'n roll groups. Assoc. Professor NYU Graduate Film & TV. Has directed various music videos.Wrote libretto and lyrics for Blue PLanet Blue, Clowns and Cocoon: The Musical.
AUTHOR: Cocoon, Killing Affair, Metamorphosis, Red Devil, Funerama.
PICTURES: Cocoon (story), Killing Affair (dir., s.p.), Personal Choice (dir., s.p.), Fatal Reunion (s.p.), Queen of America (s.p.), Torch, Sara Deri, Hearts & Diamonds, Vets, Do Not Disturb, Point of Honor, Snatched, Jack in the Box, Schoolhouse, Roberto: The Roberto Clemente Story, Roamers, Joshua's Golden Band, Beyond the Stars (dir., s.p.), Bab's Labs (s.p.), Fighting Back (s.p.).
TELEVISION: The Vintage Years (pilot), Dance of the Athletes (dir., writer), Rodeo—A Matter of Style (dir., writer), Mama Sings, The Corky Project, OB/GYN (pilot).

SAPERSTEIN, HENRY G.
Executive. b. Chicago, IL, June 2, 1918. e. U. of Chicago. Theatre owner, Chicago, 1943-45; pres. Television Personalities, Inc., 1955-67, Mister Magoo, Dick Tracy, TV shows, 1960-62; 1960-67 Glen Films, Inc.; prod., All-Star Golf, 1958-62; prod. Championship Bowling, 1958-60; prod. Ding Dong School, 1959-60; pres. owner, UPA Pictures, Inc. Prod.: Mr. Magoo, Dick Tracy cartoon series, Mr. Magoo's Christmas Carol, T.N.T. Show, Turnon, Tune In Drop Out. Pres. Screen Entertainment Co., Benedict Pictures Corp., United Prod. of America; pres. H. G. Saperstein & Associates. Producer: The Vaudeville Thing; Tchaikovsky Competition, Gerald McBoing Boing Show.
PICTURES: Producer: Gay Purr-ee, What's Up Tiger Lily?, T-A-M-I, Swan Lake, Monster Zero, War of the Gargantuas, Hell in the Pacific.

SARA, MIA
Actress. b. Brooklyn, NY, 1968. Started doing TV commercials; landed role in soap opera, All My Children.
PICTURES: Legend (debut, 1986), Ferris Bueller's Day Off, The Long Lost Friend, Apprentice to Murder, A Row of Crows, Imagination, Any Man's Death, Shadows in the Storm, A Stranger Among Us, By the Sword, Timecop, The Pompatus of Love, The Maddening, Undertow, Bullet to Beijing, Black Day Blue Night.
TELEVISION: Movies: Queenie, Till We Meet Again, Daughter of Darkness, Blindsided, Call of the Wild, The Set Up. Special: Big Time. Guest: Alfred Hitchcock Presents.

SARAFIAN, RICHARD C.
Director. b. New York, NY. April 28, 1935. Studied medicine and law before entering film industry with director Robert Altman making industrial documentaries.
TELEVISION: Gunsmoke, Bonanza, Guns of Will Sonnet, I Spy Wild, Wild West; Maverick, Twilight Zone, Gangster Chronicles. Movies: Shadow on the Land, Disaster on the Coastline, Splendor in the Grass, A Killing Affair, Liberty, Golden Moment—An Olympic Love Story. As Actor: Foley Square (series).
PICTURES: Andy (debut, 1965), Run Wild Run Free, Ballad of a Badman, Fragment of Fear, Man in the Wilderness, Vanishing Point, Lolly Madonna XXX, The Man Who Loved Cat Dancing, The Next Man (also prod.), Sunburn, The Bear, Songwriter (actor only), Street Justice (also actor), Crisis 2050, Truk Lagoon.

SARANDON, CHRIS
Actor. b. Beckley, WV, July 24, 1942. e. U. of West Virginia. Mem. Catholic U.'s National Players touring U.S. in Shakespeare and Moliere. Acted with Washington, D.C. improvisational theater co. and Long Wharf. B'way debut, The Rothschilds.
THEATER: Two Gentlemen of Verona, Censored Scenes from King Kong, Marco Polo Sings a Solo, The Devil's Disciple, The Soldier's Tale, The Woods, Nick & Nora.
PICTURES: Dog Day Afternoon (debut, 1975; Acad. Award nom.), Lipstick, The Sentinel, Cuba, The Osterman Weekend, Protocol, Fright Night, Collision Course, The Princess Bride, Child's Play, Slaves of New York, Forced March, Whispers, The Resurrected, Dark Tide, The Nightmare Before Christmas (voice), Just Cause, Tales From the Crypt: Bordello of Blood, Edie and Pen.

TELEVISION: Series: The Guiding Light. Movies: Thursday's Game, You Can't Go Home Again, The Day Christ Died, A Tale of Two Cities, This Child Is Mine, Broken Promises, Liberty, Mayflower Madam, Tailspin: Behind the Korean Airliner Tragedy, The Stranger Within, A Murderous Affair: The Carolyn Warmus Story, David's Mother, When the Dark Man Calls.

SARANDON, SUSAN
Actress. r.n. Susan Tomaling. b. New York, NY, Oct. 4, 1946. e. Catholic U. Raised in Metuchen, New Jersey. Returned to New York to pursue acting, first signing with Ford Model Agency.
THEATER: NY: An Evening with Richard Nixon and..., A Coupla White Chicks Sitting Around Talking, Extremities.
PICTURES: Joe (debut, 1970), Lady Liberty, Lovin' Molly, The Front Page, The Great Waldo Pepper, The Rocky Horror Picture Show, Dragonfly (One Summer Love), Checkered Flag or Crash, The Last of the Cowboys (The Great Smokey Roadblock; also co-prod.), The Other Side of Midnight, Pretty Baby, King of the Gypsies, Something Short of Paradise, Loving Couples, Atlantic City (Acad. Award nom.), Tempest, The Hunger, The Buddy System, Compromising Positions, The Witches of Eastwick, Bull Durham, Sweet Hearts Dance, The January Man, A Dry White Season, Through the Wire (narrator), White Palace, Thelma & Louise (Acad. Award nom.), The Player, Light Sleeper, Bob Roberts, Lorenzo's Oil (Acad. Award nom.), The Client (Acad. Award nom.), Little Women, Safe Passage, The Celluloid Closet, Dead Man Walking (Academy Award), James and the Giant Peach (voice).
TELEVISION: Series: Search For Tomorrow. Guest: Calucci's Dept, Owen Marshall: Counsellor at Law. Specials: Rimers of Eldritch, June Moon, Who Am I This Time?, One Woman One Vote (narrator). Mini-Series: A.D. Movies: F. Scott Fitzgerald & the Last of the Belles, Mussolini: Decline and Fall of Il Duce, Women of Valor.

SARGENT ALVIN
Writer. b. Philadelphia, PA, Apr. 12, 1927. Began career as writer for TV, then returned to theatrical films.
PICTURES: Gambit (co-s.p.), The Stalking Moon, The Sterile Cuckoo, I Walk the Line, The Effect of Gamma Rays on Man-in-the-Moon Marigolds, Paper Moon (Acad. Award nom.), Love and Pain (and the Whole Damn Thing), Julia (Academy Award, 1977), Bobby Deerfield, Straight Time (co-s.p.), Ordinary People (Academy Award, 1980), Nuts (co-s.p.), Dominick and Eugene (co-s.p.), White Palace (co-s.p.), What About Bob? (co-story), Other People's Money, Hero (co-story), Bogus.
TELEVISION: Movies: Footsteps, The Impatient Heart. Series: The Naked City, Route 66, Ben Casey, Alfred Hitchcock Presents, The Nurses, Mr. Novak, Empire.

SARGENT, JOSEPH
Director. r.n. Giuseppe Danielle Sargente. b. Jersey City, NJ, July 25, 1925. e. studied theatre, New Sch. for Social Research 1946-49.
PICTURES: One Spy Too Many, The Hell With Heroes, Colossus: The Forbin Project, White Lightning, The Taking of Pelham One Two Three, MacArthur, Goldengirl, Coast to Coast, Nightmares, Jaws—The Revenge (also prod.).
TELEVISION: Special: The Spy in the Green Hat. Mini-series: The Manions of America, James Mitchener's Space. Movies: The Sunshine Patriot, The Immortal (pilot), The Man, Tribes, The Marcus-Nelson Murders (Emmy Award, 1973), Maybe I'll Come Home in the Spring (also prod.), The Man Who Died Twice, The Night That Panicked America, Sunshine (also prod.), Friendly Persuasion, Amber Waves, Hustling, Freedom, Tomorrow's Child, Memorial Day, Terrible Joe Moran, Choices of the Heart (also prod.), Space, Love Is Never Silent (Emmy Award, 1986), Passion Flower, Of Pure Blood, There Must Be a Pony, The Karen Carpenter Story, Day One, The Incident, Caroline? (Emmy Award, 1990), The Last Elephant, Never Forget, Miss Rose White (Emmy Award, 1992), Somebody's Daughter (also prod.), Skylark (also prod.), Abraham, World War II: When Lions Roared, My Antonia.

SARLUI, ED
Executive. b. Amsterdam, The Netherlands, Nov. 10, 1925. Owner, Peruvian Films, S.A.; pres., Radio Films of Peru, S.A.; pres. Bryant Films Educatoriana, S.A.; partner, United Producers de Colombia Ltd.; pres. Royal Film N.V.; pres., United Producers de Centroamerica, S.A.; pres. United Producers de Mexico, S.A.; pres., United Producers Int'l, Inc., Continental Motion Pictures, Inc. 1988, formed Cinema Corp. of America with Moshe Diamant and Elliott Kastner. Co-chmn. Epic Prods. Inc.
PICTURES: Exec. prod.: Full Moon in Blue Water, High Spirits, Teen Witch, Courage Mountain, Night Game.

SARNOFF, ROBERT W.
Executive. b. New York, NY, July 2, 1918. e. Harvard U., B.A., 1939; Columbia Law Sch. 1940. In office of Coordinator of

Info., Wash., DC, Aug. 1941; the U.S. Navy, Mar. 1942; asst. to publisher, Gardner Cowles, Jr., 1945; mem. of staff Look Mag., 1946, with NBC, 1948-65; pres., 1955-58; chmn. bd., 1958; bd. of dir. RCA, 1957; chmn bd. CEO, NBC, 1958-65; pres. RCA, 1966; CEO, 1968; bd. chmn., 1970-75; member, TV Pioneers, 1957; pres., 1952-53; International Radio & TV Society, Broadcasters Committee for Radio Free Europe, Am Home Products, Inc.; dir., of Business Committee for the Arts; chmn, past pres. council, Acad. of TV Arts & Sciences; formerly v.p. & bd. of dir., Acad. of TV Arts & Sciences Foundation.

SARNOFF, THOMAS W.
Executive. b. New York, NY, Feb. 23, 1927. e. Phillips Acad., Andover, MA, 1939-43, Princeton U., 1943-45, Stanford U. grad. 1948, B.S. in E.E.; Grad Sch. of Bus. Admin. 1948-49. Sgt., U.S. Army Signal Corps, 1945-46; prod. & sales, ABC-TV, Hollywood, 1949-50; prod. dept. MGM, 1951-52; asst. to dir. of finance and oper., NBC, 1952-54; dir. of prod. and bus. affairs, 1954-57; v.p. and bus. affairs, 1957-60; v.p. adm. west coast, 1960-62; v.p. west coast, 1962; exec. v.p. 1965-77; bd. of dir., NBC prods 1961-77; bd of dir. Hope Enterprises 1960-75; dir. NABCAT, Inc. 1967-75; dir. Valley County Cable TV, Inc. 1969-75; Pres. NBC Entertainment Corp. 1972-77; pres. Sarnoff International Enterprises, Inc. 1977-81; pres., Sarnoff Entertainment Corp., 1981-; pres., Venturetainment Corp. 1986-; past pres. Research Foundation at St. Joseph Hospital of Burbank; past pres. Permanent Charities of the Entertainment Ind.; past ch. bd. of trustees, National Acad. of TV Arts and Sciences. Pres. Acad. of TV Arts & Sciences Foundation 1990-.

SARRAZIN, MICHAEL
Actor. r.n. Jacques Michel Andre Sarrazin. b. Quebec, Canada, May 22, 1940. Began acting at 17 on CBC TV; signed by Universal, 1965.
PICTURES: Gunfight in Abilene (debut, 1967), The Flim-Flam Man, The Sweet Ride, Journey to Shiloh, A Man Called Gannon, Eye of the Cat, In Search of Gregory, They Shoot Horses Don't They?, The Pursuit of Happiness, Sometimes a Great Notion, Believe in Me, The Groundstar Conspiracy, Harry in Your Pocket, For Pete's Sake, The Reincarnation of Peter Proud, The Loves and Times of Scaramouche, The Gumball Rally, Caravans, Double Negative, The Seduction, Fighting Back, Joshua Then and Now, Captive Hearts, Mascara, Keeping Track, Malarek, Lena's Holiday, Bullet to Beijing.
TELEVISION: Movies: The Doomsday Flight, Frankenstein: The True Story, Beulah Land, Passion and Paradise. Guest: Chrysler Theatre, The Virginian, World Premiere.

SAUL, OSCAR
Writer. b. Brooklyn, NY, Dec. 26, 1912. e. Brooklyn Coll. 1932. Co-author play, Medicine Show; m.p. ed., U.S. Public Health Svce; numerous radio and TV plays. Wrote novel The Dark Side of Love.
PICTURES: Once Upon a Time, Strange Affair, Road House, Lady Gambles, Once More My Darling, Woman in Hiding, Secret of Convict Lake, A Streetcar Named Desire, Thunder on the Hill, Affair in Trinidad, Let's Do It Again (prod.), Helen Morgan Story, Joker is Wild, The Naked Maja, The Second Time Around, Major Dundee, The Silencers, Man and Boy.
TELEVISION: A Streetcar Name Desire, many others.

SAUNDERS, DAVID
Executive. Pres., Triumph Films, Inc.

SAUNDERS, WILLIAM
Executive. b. London, England, Jan. 4, 1923. e. left Upton House Central Sch. at 16. Served in British Eighth Army, 1941-47. Entered industry in 1947 as salesman with 20th Century Fox Film Co. in London; sales mgr., Anglo-Amalgamated Film Co., London, 1951-61; with Motion Picture Producers Assoc. of Amer. as sales dir. in Lagos, Nigeria, dist. Amer. feature films to West African countries, 1962-64; joined 20th Century Fox TV Intl., Paris as v.p. European TV sales, 1964-83; 20th Century TV Intl., Los Angeles as sr. v.p., 1983; named exec. v.p. 1987 and pres., 1988. Retired.

SAURA, CARLOS
Director. b. Huesca, Spain, January 4, 1932. e. educated as engineer. Worked as professional photographer from 1949. Studied at Instituto de Investigaciones y Experiencias Cinematograficos, Madrid, 1952-57 where he then taught from 1957-64 until being dismissed for political reasons. 1957-58 dir. shorts La tarde del domingo and Cuenca.
PICTURES: Director/Writer: Los Golfos (The Urchins), Lament for a Bandit, La Caza (The Hunt), Peppermint Frappe, Stress es Tres Tres, La Madriguera (The Honeycomb), The Garden of Delights, Anna and the Wolves, Cousin Angelica (Cannes Fest. jury prize, 1974), Cria! (Cannes Fest. jury prize, 1976), Elisa Vide Mia, Los ojos Vendados (Blindfold), Mama Turns 100, Hurry Hurry (Golden Bear, Berlin Fest., 1981),

Blood Wedding, Dulces Horas (Sweet Hours), Antonieta, Carmen, Los Zancos (The Stilts), El Amor Brujo (Love the Magician), El Dorado, The Dark Night, Ay Carmela!

SAVAGE, DAVID
Executive Producer, Advertising Executive, b. New York, NY, March 17, 1929. e. Rochester Inst. of Technology. In research development & testing div., Eastman Kodak Co., 2 yrs.; adv. mgr. asst. nat'l sales mgr., Official Films; org., film dept. mgr. WCBS-TV; dir. of film procurement, CBS; mgr. of film procurement, NBC; mgr. planning, merchandising, Recorded Tape Dept., RCA Records; promo. mgr., special products mktg. RCA Records Div.; program and marketing chmn. RCA SelectaVision group; v.p., operations, Wunderman, Rilotto, & Kline, 1970; pres., Response Industries, Inc., (direct response adv. agency), 1973 which became affiliate of McCann Erickson, and was sr. v.p. of McCann Erickson Pres., Mattel Direct Marketing, 1982; v.p. and man. dir., Foote Cene Belding, subsid. Knipp-Taylor USA, 1985.

SAVAGE, FRED
Actor. b. Highland Park, IL, July 9, 1976. e. Stanford Univ. While in kindergarten auditioned for commercial at local community center. Didn't get the job but called back by same dir. for two more tests. Chosen for Pac-Man vitamin ad which led to 27 on-camera TV commercials and 36 voice-over radio spots.
PICTURES: The Boy Who Could Fly, The Princess Bride, Vice Versa, Little Monsters, The Wizard.
TELEVISION: Series: Morningstar/Eveningstar, The Wonder Years. Movies: Convicted: A Mother's Story, Run Till You Fall, When You Remember Me, Christmas on Division Street, No One Would Tell. Special: Runaway Ralph. Guest: The Twilight Zone.

SAVAGE, JOHN
Actor. r.n. John Youngs. b. Old Bethpage, Long Island, NY, Aug. 25, 1949. Studied at American Acad. of Dramatic Arts. In Manhattan organized Children's Theatre Group which performed in public housing. Won Drama Desk Award for performance in One Flew Over the Cuckoo's Nest (Chicago & LA).
THEATER: Fiddler on the Roof, Ari, Siamese Connections, The Hostage, American Buffalo, Of Mice and Men.
PICTURES: Bad Company (debut, 1972), Steelyard Blues, The Killing Kind, The Sister in Law (also composed score), The Deer Hunter, Hair, The Onion Field, Inside Moves, Cattle Annie and Little Britches, The Amateur, Brady's Escape, Maria's Lovers, Salvador, Beauty and the Beast, Hotel Colonial, Soldier's Revenge, The Beat, Caribe, Do the Right Thing, Point of View, Any Man's Death, The Godfather Part III, Hunting, Primary Motive, My Forgotten Man, C.I.A. II: Target Alexa, Red Scorpion 2, Killing Obsession, Carnosaur 2, From the Edge, The Dangerous, Centurion Force, The Crossing Guard, White Squall, Where Truth Lies, American Strays.
TELEVISION: Series: Gibbsville. Movies: All the Kind Strangers, Eric (also wrote and performed songs), The Turning Point of Jim Malloy, Coming Out of the Ice, The Tender Age (The Little Sister), Silent Witness, The Nairobi Affair, Desperate, The Burning Shore, Daybreak, Shattered Image, Tom Clancy's Op Center. Special: Date Rape (Afterschool Special). Guest: Birdland, X Files, The Outer Limits.

SAVOCA, NANCY
Director. e. NYU film sch. m. prod.-writer Richard Guay. While in school directed and wrote short films Renata and Bad Timing. Received Haig P. Manoogian Award for filmmaking at 1984 NYU Student Film Festival. Made feature debut with True Love which won Grand Jury Prize at 1989 United States Film Festival.
PICTURES: True Love (also co-s.p.), Dogfight, Household Saints (also co-s.p.).

SAWYER, DIANE
News Correspondent, Anchor. b. Glasgow, KY, Dec. 22, 1945. m. director Mike Nichols. e. Wellesley Coll. Studied law before deciding on career in TV. Former Junior Miss winner and weather reporter on a Louisville TV station before arriving in Washington, 1970. Worked for Nixon Administration in press office from 1970-74; assisted Nixon in writing memoirs, 1975-78. Joined CBS News as reporter in Washington bureau in 1978; named correspondent in 1980. Served as CBS State Dept. correspondent 1980-81. Joined Charles Kuralt as co-anchor of the weekday editions of CBS Morning News in 1981; 1984-89 correspondent on 60 Minutes; 1989, signed by ABC News as co-anchor of Primetime Live news prog. with Sam Donaldson. 1994, co-anchor of Turning Point.

SAXON, JOHN
Actor. r.n. Carmine Orrico. b. Brooklyn, NY, Aug. 5, 1936.
PICTURES: Running Wild (debut, 1955), The Unguarded Moment, Rock Pretty Baby, Summer Love, The Reluctant Debutante, This Happy Feeling, The Restless Years, The Big

Fisherman, Cry Tough, Portrait in Black, The Unforgiven, The Plunderers, Posse from Hell, Mr. Hobbs Takes a Vacation, War Hunt, Evil Eye, The Cardinal, The Ravagers, The Cavern, The Appaloosa, Queen of Blood, Night Caller From Outer Space, For Singles Only, Death of a Gunfighter, Company of Killers, Joe Kidd, Enter The Dragon, Black Christmas, Mitchell, The Swiss Conspiracy, Strange Shadows in an Empty Room, Moonshine County Express, Shalimar, The Bees, The Glove, The Electric Horseman, Battle Beyond the Stars, Beyond Evil, Blood Beach, Cannibal in the Streets, Wrong Is Right, The Big Score, Nightmare on Elm Street, Prisioners of the Lost Universe, Fever Pitch, Nightmare on Elm Street 3: Dream Warriors, Criminal Act, Death House (also dir.), My Mom's a Werewolf, Aftershock, Blood Salvage, Hellmaster, Crossing the Line, Maximum Force, No Escape No Return, Jonathan of the Bears, Killing Obsession, Beverly Hills Cop III, Wes Craven's New Nightmare.
TELEVISION: *Series*: The Bold Ones (The New Doctors), Falcon Crest. *Movies*: The Doomsday Flight, Winchester 73, Istanbul Express, The Intruders, Snatched, Linda, Can Ellen Be Saved?, Planet Earth, Crossfire, Strange New World, Raid on Entebbe, The Immigrants, Golden Gate, Rooster, Prisoners of the Lost Universe, Payoff, Blackmail, Genghis Khan, Liz: The Elizabeth Taylor Story.

SAYLES, JOHN
Writer, Director, Editor, Actor. b. Schnectady, NY, Sept. 28, 1950. e. Williams Coll., B.S. psychology, 1972. Wrote two novels: Pride of the Bimbos, 1975 and Union Dues, 1978; also The Anarchist's Convention, collection of short stories and Thinking in Pictures: The Making of the Movie Matewan (1987). Wrote and directed plays off-B'way (New Hope for the Dead, Turnbuckle). Directed Bruce Springsteen music videos (Born in the U.S.A., I'm on Fire, Glory Days). Recipient of MacArthur Foundation Grant for genius.
PICTURES: Piranha (s.p., co-story, actor), Lady in Red (s.p.), Battle Beyond the Stars (story, s.p.), Return of the Secaucus Seven (dir., s.p., actor, edit.), Alligator (s.p., story), The Howling (co-s.p., actor), The Challenge (co-s.p.), Lianna (dir., s.p., actor, edit.), Baby It's You (dir., s.p.), The Brother from Another Planet (dir., s.p., edit., actor), Enormous Changes at the Last Minute (co-s.p.), The Clan of the Cave Bear (s.p.), Hard Choices (actor), Something Wild (actor), Wild Thing (s.p.), Matewan (dir., s.p., actor), Eight Men Out (dir., s.p., actor), Breaking In (s.p.), Little Vegas (actor), City of Hope (dir., s.p., edit., actor), Straight Talk (actor), Malcolm X (actor), Passion Fish (dir., s.p., edit.), Matinee (actor), My Life's in Turnaround (actor), The Secret of Roan Inish (dir., s.p., edit.), Lone Star (dir., s.p.).
TELEVISION: *Movies*: A Perfect Match, Unnatural Causes (actor, writer), Shannon's Deal (writer, creative consult.). *Special*: Mountain View (Alive From Off Center).

SCACCHI, GRETA
Actress. b. Milan, Italy, Feb. 18, 1960. e. England and Australia. Acted in Bristol Old Vic Theatre in England.
PICTURES: Das Zweiter Gesicht, Heat and Dust, The Coca Cola Kid, Burke & Wills, Defence of the Realm, A Man in Love, Good Morning Babylon, White Mischief, Paura e Amore (Fear and Love), Woman in the Moon, Presumed Innocent, Fires Within, Shattered, The Player, Turtle Beach, Desire, The Browning Version, Jefferson in Paris, Country Life, Cosi.
TELEVISION: *Mini-Series*: Waterfront (Australia). *Movies*: Ebony Tower, Dr. Fischer of Geneva, Camille, Rasputin (Emmy Award, 1996).

SCARWID, DIANA
Actress. b. Savannah, GA. e. St. Vincent's Acad. (Savannah), American Acad. of Dramatic Arts, Pace U., 1975. Member of National Shakespeare Conservatory (Woodstock, NY) and worked in regional theatres before moving to Hollywood 1976.
PICTURES: Pretty Baby (debut, 1978), Honeysuckle Rose, Inside Moves (Acad. Award nom.), Mommie Dearest, Rumble Fish, Strange Invaders, Silkwood, The Ladies Club, Psycho III, Extremities, Heat, Brenda Starr, Gold Diggers: The Secret of Bear Mountain, The Cure, The Neon Bible, Bastard Out of Carolina.
TELEVISION: *Mini-Series*: Studs Lonigan. *Movies*: In the Glitter Palace, The Possessed, Forever, Battered, Guyana Tragedy: The Story of Jim Jones, Desperate Lives, Thou Shalt Not Kill, A Bunny's Tale, After the Promise, Night of the Hunter, Simple Justice, Labor of Love: The Arlette Schweitzer Story, JFK: Reckless Youth, Truman. *Series*: The Outer Limits.

SCHAEFER, CARL
Media Consultant, Publicist, b. Cleveland, OH, Sept. 2, 1908. e. UCLA. Contr. to mag., including Vanity Fair, Hollywood Citizen-News, 1931-35; Warner Bros., 1935.; Huesped de Honor, Mexico, 1943; OSS WWII, 1944-45; Int'l Comt. AMPS, chmn. 1966-67; Italian Order of Merit, 1957; Chevalier de l'ordre de la Couronne, Belgium, 1963. Pres., Foreign Trade Assn. of Southern Calif., 1954; chmn. of bd., 1955; British-American C. of C., Dir., 1962; Chevalier French

Legion d'Honneur, 1955; Comm. Hollywood Museum; dir., intl. relations, Warner Bros. Seven Arts Int'l Corp., 1960; formed own firm, Carl Schaefer Enterprises, 1971. Dir. pub. rel., British-American Chamber of Commerce, 1971; dir. pub. rel. for Iota Intl. Pictures, 1971; dir. pub. rel. Lyric Films Intl., 1971; bureau chief (Hollywood) Movie/TV Marketing, 1971; man. dir., Intl. Festival Advisory Council, 1971; dir. pub. rel. & adv. Francis Lederer Enterprises Inc. (American National Acad. of Performing Arts, and Canoga Mission Gallery) 1974; West Coast rep. Angelika Films of N.Y. 1974, Hwd. rep Korwitz/Geiger Products. 1975-; Hwd. corresp. Movie News, S'pore, & Femina, Hong Kong, 1974-; member Westn. Publications Assn. 1975-; field rep. Birch Records 1975; Hollywood rep Antena Magazine, Buenos Aires; dir. pub. rel., Style Magazine. Coordinator Hollywood Reporter Annual Key Art Awards; coordinator Hollywood Reporter Annual Marketing Concept Awards; exec. comm. & historian ShoWest; Mem: National Panel of Consumer Arbitrators, 1985; Hollywood Corr., Gold Coast Times of Australia, 1986-87. Winner 1990 Key Art Award. Member: AMPAS, awarded certif. of Appreciation, 1962; charter member, Publicists Guild of America; pres. Pacific Intercollegiate Press Assn., while UCLA Daily Bruin Editor, 1930-31. Poetry anthologies, 1995-96, National Library of Poetry.

SCHAEFER, GEORGE
Director, Producer. b. Wallingford, CT, Dec. 16, 1920. e. Lafayette Coll., Yale Drama Sch. 1986, joined UCLA as chairman, Theatre Film TV; later assoc. Dean, now Emeritus Professor.
THEATRE: B'way:The Linden Tree; Man and Superman; Body Beautiful, Last of Mrs. Lincoln, G.I. Hamlet, Mixed Couples, The Heiress (revival), Idiot's Delight (revival), Teahouse of the August Moon, Write Me a Murder.
PICTURES: Pendulum, Generation, Doctors' Wives, Once Upon a Scoundrel, Macbeth, An Enemy of the People.
TELEVISION: *Director*: Hamlet, One Touch of Venus, The Corn Is Green, The Good Fairy, The Little Foxes, Little Moon of Alban (Emmy Award, 1959), Harvey, Macbeth (Emmy Award, 1961), The Magnificent Yankee (Emmy Award, 1965), Kiss Me Kate, Elizabeth the Queen (Emmy Award, 1968), A War of Children (Emmy Award, 1973), Pygmalion, F. Scott Fitzgerald, Blind Ambition, First You Cry, Our Town, Sandburg's Lincoln, The People vs. Jean Harris, A Piano for Mrs. Cimino, The Deadly Game, Children in the Crossfire, Right of Way, Stone Pillow, Mrs. Delafield Wants to Marry, Laura Lansing Slept Here, Let Me Hear You Whisper, The Man Upstairs.

SCHAFFEL, ROBERT
Producer. b. Washington, DC, March 2, 1944. Partner with Jon Voight in Voight-Schaffel Prods. Now heads Robert Schaffel Prods.
PICTURES: Gordon's War, Sunnyside, Lookin' to Get Out, Table for Five, American Anthem, Distant Thunder, Jacknife, Diggstown.

SCHATZBERG, JERRY
Director. b. New York, NY, June 26, 1927. e. student U. of Miami, 1947-48. Early career in photography as asst. to Bill Helburn 1954-56. Freelance still photographer and TV commercials dir. 1956-69. Contrib. photographs to several mags. incl. Life.
PICTURES: Puzzle of a Downfall Child (debut, 1970), The Panic in Needle Park, Scarecrow, Sweet Revenge (also prod.), The Seduction of Joe Tynan, Honeysuckle Rose, Misunderstood, No Small Affair, Street Smart, Reunion.
TELEVISION: *Movie*: Clinton and Nadine.

SCHEIDER, ROY
Actor. b. Orange, NJ, Nov. 10, 1932. e. Franklin and Marshall Coll. where he twice won the Theresa Helburn Acting Award. First professional acting in 1961 NY Shakespeare Festival prod. of Romeo and Juliet. Became member of Lincoln Center Repertory Co. and acted with Boston Arts Festival, American Shakespeare Festival, Arena Stage (Wash., DC) and American Repertory Co. Appeared in documentary In Our Hands.
THEATER: Richard III, Stephen D, Sergeant Musgrave's Dance, The Alchemist, Betrayal.
PICTURES: Curse of the Living Corpse (debut, 1964), Paper Lion, Star!, Stiletto, Loving, Puzzle of a Downfall Child, Klute, The French Connection (Acad. Award nom.), The Outside Man, The French Conspiracy, The Seven Ups, Sheila Levine is Dead and Living in New York, Jaws, Marathon Man, Sorcerer, Jaws 2, Last Embrace, All That Jazz (Acad. Award nom.), Still of the Night, Blue Thunder, 2010, Mishima (narrator), The Men's Club, 52 Pickup, Cohen and Tate, Listen to Me, Night Game, The Fourth War, The Russia House, Naked Lunch, Romeo Is Bleeding, Covert Assassin.
TELEVISION: *Movies*: Assignment Munich, Jacobo Timerman: Prisoner Without a Name Cell Without a Number, Tiger Town, Somebody Has to Shoot the Picture, Wild Justice. *Series*: seaQuest DSV. *Guest*: Hallmark Hall of Fame, Studio One, N.Y.P.D. *Special*: Portrait of the Soviet Union (host).

SCHEINMAN, ANDREW

Producer. b. 1948. e. Univ. of VA, law degree. Professional tennis player before entering film business as producer of three Charlton Heston films. Became one of 5 founding partners of Castle Rock Entertainment.
PICTURES: *Prod/Exec. Prod.*: The Mountain Man, The Awakening, Modern Romance, Mother Lode, The Sure Thing, Stand By Me, The Princess Bride, When Harry Met Sally..., Misery, A Few Good Men, North (also co-s.p.). *Director*: Little Big League.
TELEVISION: *Series*: Seinfeld (exec. prod.)

SCHELL, MARIA

Actress. b. Vienna, Austria, Jan. 5, 1926. Brother is actor Maximilian Schell. Made debut as teenager in Swiss film, Steinbruch (Quarry). Subsequently appeared in many British and American films.
PICTURES: Quarry (debut, 1941), Angel with the Trumpet, The Affairs of Dr. Holl, The Magic Box, Angelika, So Little Time, The Heart of the Matter, Der Traumende Mund (Dreaming Lips), The Last Bridge (Cannes Film Fest. Award, 1954), Angelika, The Rats, Napoleon, Gervaise (Venice Film Fest. Award, 1956), Liebe (Love), Rose Bernd, Le Notti Bianche (White Nights), Une Vie (End of Desire), The Brothers Karamazov, The Hanging Tree, Der Schinderhanners (Duel in the Forest), As the Sea Rages, Cimarron, The Mark, Only a Woman, La Assassin connait la Musique, Rendezvous in Trieste, Who Has Seen the Wind?, 99 Women, Devil By the Tail, Night of the Blood Monster, Lust in the Sun, The Odessa File, Voyage of the Damned, Folies Bourgeoises (The Twist), Superman, Just a Gigolo, 1919.
TELEVISION: *U.S.*: Heidi, Christmas Lilies of the Field, Inside the Third Reich, Martian Chronicles, Samson and Delilah.

SCHELL, MAXIMILIAN

Actor, Director. b. Vienna, Dec. 8, 1930. Sister is actress Maria Schell. e. Switzerland. Stage debut 1952. B'way debut in Interlock.
PICTURES: Children Mother and the General (debut, 1955), The Young Lions (U.S. debut, 1958), Judgment at Nuremberg (Academy Award, 1961), Five Finger Exercise, The Reluctant Saint, The Condemned of Altona, Topkapi, Return from the Ashes, The Deadly Affair, Counterpoint, The Desperate Ones, The Castle (also prod.), Krakatoa—East of Java, Simon Bolivar, First Love (also dir., co-s.p., co-prod.), Trotta (co-s.p.), Pope Joan, Paulina 1880, The Pedestrian (also dir., prod., s.p.), The Odessa File, The Man in the Glass Booth, End of the Game (also dir., co-prod., co-s.p.), St. Ives, The Day That Shook the World, A Bridge Too Far, Cross of Iron, Julia, Players, Avalanche Express, Together?, The Black Hole, Tales From the Vienna Woods (also prod., s.p.), The Chosen, Les Iles, Morgen in Alabama, Marlene (dir., s.p., interviewer), The Rose Garden, The Freshman, Labyrinth, An American Place, A Far Off Place, Little Odessa.
TELEVISION: Judgment at Nuremberg (Playhouse 90), The Fifth Column, The Diary of Anne Frank, Turn The Key Deftly, Phantom of the Opera, Heidi, The Assisi Underground, Peter the Great (mini-series), Young Catherine, Stalin, Miss Rose White, Candles in the Dark (also dir.).

SCHENCK, AUBREY

Producer. b. Brooklyn, NY, Aug. 26, 1908. e. Cornell U., NYU. With law firm of O'Brien, Driscoll & Raftery; buyer & attorney for Natl. Theatres, 1936; prod for 20th Century-Fox 1945; exec. prod. Eagle Lion 1946; contract prod. Universal Internatl. 1948; Aubrey Schenck Productions, Inc.
PICTURES: Shock, Johnny Comes Flying Home, Strange Triangle, Repeat Performance, T-Men, Mickey, It's a Joke Son, Trapped, Port of New York, Wyoming Man, Undercover Girl, Fat Man, Target Unknown; formed own co. to prod. War Paint, Beachhead. Also: Yellow Tomahawk, Shield for Murder, Big House, U.S.A., Crime Against Joe, Emergency Hospital, Ghost Town, Broken Star, Rebels in Town, Pharaoh's Curse, Three Bad Sisters, Fort Yuma, Desert Sands, Quincannon, Frontier Scout, Black Sleep, Hot Cars, War Drums, Voodoo Island, Revolt at Fort Laramie, Tomahawk Trail, Untamed Youth, Girl in Black Stockings, Bop Girl Goes Calypso, Up Periscope, Violent Road, Reckless, Frankenstein 1970, Wild Harvest, Robinson Crusoe On Mars, Don't Worry, Ambush Bay, Kill a Dragon, Impasse, More Dead Than Alive, Barquero, Daughters of Satan.
TELEVISION: Miami Undercover, series.

SCHEPISI, FRED

Producer, Director, Writer. b. Melbourne, Australia, Dec. 26, 1939. e. Assumption Col., Marist Bros. Juniorate, Marcellin Col. Assessed student films at Melbourne's Swinburne Inst. of Tech.; worked on gov. sponsored experimental Film Fund; made TV commercials. Founded The Film House prod. co. Dir. short film The Party.
PICTURES: *Director*: Libido (co-dir.), The Devil's Playground (also prod., s.p.), The Chant of Jimmie Blacksmith (also prod., s.p.), Barbarosa, Iceman, Plenty, Roxanne, A Cry in the Dark

(also co-s.p.; Australian Film Inst. Award for best dir. & s.p.). *Dir./Prod.*: The Russia House, Mr. Baseball, Six Degrees of Separation, I.Q.

SCHERICK, EDGAR J

Executive, Producer. b. New York, NY, Oct. 16, 1924. e. Harvard U.; elected to Phi Beta Kappa. Asst. dir. of radio and TV; assoc. media dir. and dir. of sports special events, Dancer-Fitzgerald-Sample ad agency, NY during 1950s. Introduced Wide World of Sports on TV through his co., Sports Programs, Inc. Was v.p. in chg. of network programming at ABC-TV. Pres. of Palomar Pictures Int'l. Now independent producer.
PICTURES: For Love of Ivy, The Birthday Party, Take the Money and Run, They Shoot Horses Don't They?, The Killing of Sister George, Ring of Bright Water, Jenny, Sleuth, The Heartbreak Kid, Law and Disorder, The Stepford Wives, I Never Promised You a Rose Garden, The Taking of Pelham One Two Three, American Success Company, I'm Dancing As Fast As I Can, Shoot the Moon, White Dog, He Makes Me Feel Like Dancin' (Academy Award, 1983), Reckless, Mrs. Soffel.
TELEVISION: The Man Who Wanted to Live Forever, The Silence, Circle of Children, Raid on Entebbe, Panic in Echo Park, Zuma Beach, An American Christmas Carol, The Seduction of Miss Leona, Revenge of the Stepford Wives, Hitler's SS, The High Price of Passion, The Stepford Children, Unholy Matrimony, Little Gloria... Happy at Last, On Wings of Eagles, Hands of a Stranger, Home Fires, He Makes Me Feel Like Dancin' (Emmy Award, 1983), Stranger on My Land (exec. prod.), And the Band Played On, The Kennedys of Massachusetts, Satin's Touch (exec. prod.), Phantom of the Opera, The Secret Life of Ian Fleming, Tyson.

SCHIAVELLI, VINCENT

Actor. b. Brooklyn, NY. e. NYU. On Stage in Hunting Cockroaches, Alphabetical Order, Angel City.
PICTURES: One Flew Over the Cuckoo' Nest, American Pop (voice), Chu Chu and the Philly Flash, Night Shift, Fast Times at Ridgemont High, The Adventures of Buckaroo Banzai Across the 8th Dimension, Amadeus, Cold Feet, Valmont, Homer and Eddie, Ghost, Waiting for the Light, Another You, Ted & Venus, Batman Returns, 3 Ninjas Knuckle Up, A Little Princess, Lord of Illusions.
TELEVISION: *Series*: The Corner Bar, Fast Times. *Movies*: Escape to Witch Mountain, The Whipping Boy.

SCHIFRIN, LALO

Composer. b. Buenos Aires, Argentina, June 21, 1932. Father was conductor of Teatro Colon in B.A. for 30 years. Schifrin studied with Juan Carlos Paz in Arg. and later Paris Cons. Returned to homeland and wrote for stage, modern dance, TV. Became interested in jazz and joined Dizzie Gillespie's band in 1962 as pianist and composer. Settled in L.A. Pres. Young Musicians Fed. Music; dir. and conductor, Paris Philharmonic 1987.
PICTURES: Rhino!, The Cincinnati Kid, The Liquidator, Once a Thief, Venetian Affair, Murderer's Row, Blindfold, Joy House, Cool Hand Luke, The President's Analyst, Sol Madrid, Where Angels Go--Trouble Follows, Coogan's Bluff, Hell in the Pacific, Bullitt, Beguiled, The Fox, The Brotherhood, Eye of the Cat, Kelly's Heroes, Hellstrom Chronicles, THX 1138, Dirty Harry, Joe Kidd, Prime Cut, Enter the Dragon, Charley Varrick, Magnum Force, Man on a Swing, The Four Musketeers, The Eagle Has Landed, Voyage of the Damned, Rollercoaster, Telefon, Nunzio, The Cat from Outer Space, The Manitou, Boulevard Nights, The Concorde: Airport '79, Love and Bullets, Serial, The Big Brawl, Brubaker, Escape to Athena, The Amityville Horror, The Nude Bomb, The Competition, When Time Ran Out, Caveman, Buddy, Buddy, The Seduction, A Stranger Is Watching, Amityville II: The Possession, The Sting II, The Osterman Weekend, Sudden Impact, The Mean Season, The New Kids, Doctor Detroit, Tank, The Silence at Bethany, The Fourth Protocol, The Dead Pool, Berlin Blues (also songs), Return From the River Kwai, Naked Tango, F/X 2, The Beverly Hillbillies, Scorpion Spring.
TELEVISION: Mission Impossible (theme), Mannix (theme), Petrocelli (theme), Hollywood Wives, A.D., Private Sessions, Foster and Laurie, Medical Center, Petrocelli, Starsky and Hutch, Earth Star Voyager, Princess Daisy, Falcon's Gold, Kung Fu: The Movie, Original Sin, The Neon Empire, Shakedown on Sunset Strip, Little White Lies, Face to Face, El Quixote, Danger Theatre (theme).

SCHILLER, FRED

Playwright, Screen & TV Writer. b. Vienna, Austria, Jan. 6, 1924. e. Columbia Univ. (B.A.). Awarded: New York Literary Prize for McCall magazine story Ten Men and a Prayer. Member of Dramatists' Guild and Writer's Guild of America. Formerly chief corresp. European Newspaper Feature Services. Honored by the U. of Wyoming and the American Heritage Center for literary achievements with a special Fred Schiller Collection for their library. Awarded the Honor Silver Cross by Austrian Govt., for literary achievements and for furthering cultural relations between Austria and U.S.

THEATER: Come On Up (U.S. key citiies , London), Anything Can Happen (London), Demandez Vicky (Paris), Finder Please Return (L.A., San Francisco, Madrid, Vienna), Finder Bitte Melden (Berlin, Baden-Baden, Vienna), The Love Trap.
TELEVISION: Wrote some 53 TV plays incl. The Inca of Perusalem, Demandez Vicky! for Paris and Finder Bitte Melden! for Austria.

SCHILLER, LAWRENCE J.
Producer, Director. b. New York, NY, Dec. 28, 1936. Photojournalist with Life Magazine & Saturday Evening Post, 1958-70; collaborated on numerous books including three by Norman Mailer: The Executioner's Song, Marilyn, and The Faith of Graffiti; also Muhammad Ali (with Wilfrid Sheed), Minamata (with Eugene Smith).
PICTURES: The Man Who Skied Down Everest (editorial concept & direction), Butch Cassidy & the Sundance Kid (conceived and executed special still montages & titles); The American Dreamer (prod., dir.).
TELEVISION: Prod.: Hey I'm Alive (also dir.), The Trial of Lee Harvey Oswald, The Winds of Kitty Hawk, Marilyn, The Untold Story, An Act of Love, Child Bride of Short Creek, The Executioner's Song (also dir.), Peter the Great, Margaret Bourke-White (also dir.).

SCHINE, G. DAVID
Executive. b. Gloversville, NY, Sept. 11, 1927. e. Harvard U., Pres., gen. mgr. Schine Hotels 1950-63. Film exhibitor until 1966 in New York, Ohio, Kentucky, Maryland, Delaware, and West Virginia. Exec. prod. of French Connection, 1971. Writer, prod., dir. of That's Action!, 1977. Chief Exec. officer of Schine Productions (production) and Epic Productions (distribution), Visual Sciences, Inc., High Resolution Sciences, Inc., and Studio Television Services, Inc.

SCHLAIFER, CHARLES
Executive. b. Omaha, NB, July 1, 1909. Reporter Daily News, World-Herald (Omaha). 1930 appt. adv. mngr. Paramount theatres, then Publix theatres in Omaha; then mngr. of Tri-State circuit, NE, Iowa; 1936-42 mng. dir. United Artists Theatres, San Francisco; advisor, nat'l adv., United Artists prods.; 1942 appt. adv. mgr. 20th Cent.-Fox; 1944, named asst. dir. adv., publicity & exploitation; 1945-49, v.p. & dir. of advertising, pub., exploitation and radio; 1949, resigned to establish own adv. agency becoming pres., Charles Schlaifer & Co., Inc.; chmn. advertising advisory council, MPAA; revised m.p. adv. code; permanent chmn. first MPAA public relations committee.

SCHLATTER, GEORGE
Producer, Director, Writer. b. Birmingham, AL, Dec. 31, 1932. m. former actress Jolene Brand. e. Pepperdine U. on football scholarship. First industry job was MCA agent in band and act dept. Then gen. mgr. and show producer Ciro's nightclub (where he met Dick Martin and Dan Rowan). Produced shows at Frontier Hotel and Silver Slipper, Las Vegas. Sang 2 seasons St. Louis Municipal Opera Co.
TELEVISION: Created: Laugh-In, Real People (3 Emmys, 27 nominations). Specials with: Goldie Hawn, Robin Williams, Shirley MacLaine, Doris Day, John Denver, Frank Sinatra, Jackie Gleason, Danny Thomas, Bob Hope, Milton Berle, Danny Kaye, George Burns, Dinah Shore, Lucille Ball, Goldie & Liza Together, Salute to Lady Liberty, Las Vegas 75th Anniversary, Speak Up America, Real Kids, Best of Times, Look At Us, Shape of Things, Magic or Miracle, Grammy Awards (first 5 years: also writer), series with Dinah Shore, Judy Garland, Bill Cosby, Steve Lawrence; also ABC American Comedy Awards (3 years), George Schlatter's Comedy Club, George Schlatter's Funny People, Beverly Hills 75th Anniversary, Humor and the Presidency, Frank Liza & Sammy... The Ultimate Event, Comedy Hall of Fame, She TV (series), Sinatra's 75th Birthday, The Best Is Yet to Come, Muhammad Ali's 50th Birthday, Welcome Home America, Laugh-In 25th Anniversary Reunion.

SCHLESINGER, JOHN
Director, Producer. b. London, England, Feb. 16, 1926. e. Oxford U., BBC dir. 1958-60: Wrote and dir. Terminus for British Transport Films (Golden Lion, best doc., Venice); The Class. Some episodes The Valiant Years series. Appeared as actor in films: Sailor of the King (1953), Pursuit of the Graf Spee, Brothers in Law, The Divided Heart, The Last Man to Hang, Fifty Years of Action (DGA doc.). Assoc. dir., National Theatre, London 1973-89. Recipient of 1995 BAFTA Fellowship.
THEATER: No Why (RSC), Timon of Athens (RSC), Days in the Trees (RSC), I and Albert, Heartbreak House (NT), Julius Caesar (NT), True West (NT).
PICTURES: A Kind of Loving (Berlin Golden Bear Award, 1961), Billy Liar, Darling (NY Film Critics Award), Far From the Madding Crowd, Midnight Cowboy (Academy Award, 1969), Sunday Bloody Sunday, Visions of Eight (sequence), The Day of the Locust, Marathon Man, Yanks, Honky Tonk Freeway,

The Falcon and the Snowman (also co-prod.), The Believers (also co-prod.), Madame Sousatzka (also co-s.p.), Pacific Heights (also cameo), The Innocent, Eye for an Eye.
TELEVISION: Separate Tables, An Englishman Abroad (BAFTA Award), The Lost Language of Cranes (actor only), A Question of Attribution (BAFTA Award), Cold Comfort Farm.
OPERA: Les Contes d'Hoffmann (Royal Opera House 1981; SWET award), Der Rosenkavalier, Un Ballo in Maschera (Salzburg Fest., 1989).

SCHLONDORFF, VOLKER
Director. b. Wiesbaden, Germany, March 31, 1939. m. dir.-actress Margarethe von Trotta. Studied in France, acquiring degree in political science in Paris. Studied at French Intl. Film Sch. (IDHEC) before becoming asst. to Jean-Pierre Melville, Alain Resnais, and Louis Malle.
PICTURES: Young Torless (debut, 1966; also s.p.), A Degree of Murder (also s.p.), Michael Kohlhass, Baal, The Sudden Fortune of the Poor People of Kombach, Die Moral der Ruth Halbfass, A Free Woman, The Lost Honor of Katharina Blum (also s.p.), Coup de Grace, The Tin Drum (also s.p.), Valeska Gert (also s.p.), Circle of Deceit, Swann in Love (also s.p.), The Handmaid's Tale, Voyager (also co-s.p.).
TELEVISION: Death of a Salesman, A Gathering of Old Men.

SCHLOSSBERG, JULIAN
Producer, Distributor, Director, Radio TV Host. b. New York, NY, Jan. 26, 1942. e. NYU. Joined ABC-TV network 1964 as asst. acct. rep.; named act. rep. 1965; 1966, joined Walter Reade Organization as asst. v.p. chg. of TV; 1969, moved to WRO Theatre Div.; 1970, joined faculty of School of Visual Arts; 1971 named v.p. of WRO Theatres; 1976, joined Paramount Pictures as v.p. in charge of feature film acquisition. Since 1978 pres. & owner of Castle Hill Productions; 1974, prod. & moderated An Evening with Joseph E. Levine at Town Hall, N.Y.; 1974-1980, host of radio show Movie Talk on WMCA (N.Y.), WMEX (Boston), WICE (Providence); 1982-83 host of syndicated TV show, Julian Schlossbergs' Movie Talk; producers' rep. for Elia Kazan, Dustin Hoffman, Elaine May, George C. Scott. Responsible for restored version of Orson Welles' Othello, re-released in 1992.
THEATER: It Had To Be You, An Evening with Nichols and May, Rainbow Room N.Y., Mr. Gogol and Mr. Preen, Damn Yankees, Death Defying Acts.
PICTURES: Going Hollywood: The War Years, Hollywood Uncensored, Hollywood Ghost Stories, No Nukes, Going Hollywood: The 30's, 10 From Your Show of Shows, In the Spirit, Bad Girls, Widow's Peak.
TELEVISION: Steve Allen's Golden Age of Comedy; All the Best, Steve Allen, Sex & Justice: The Anita Hill/Clarence Thomas Hearings, Slapstick Too, Elia Kazan: A Director's Journey.

SCHLOSSER, HERBERT S.
Executive. b. Atlantic City, NJ, April 21, 1926. e. Princeton U., Yale Law Sch. Joined law firm of Phillips, Nizer, Benjamin, Krim & Ballon, 1954; attorney, California National Productions (subsidiary of National Broadcasting Company) 1957; v.p. & gen. mgr., 1960; joined NBC-TV as director, talent & program admin., 1961; v.p., talent & program admin., 1962; v.p. programs, west coast, 1966-72; exec. v.p., NBC-TV, 1972; pres., 1973; pres. & COO, 1974-76; pres. & CEO, 1977-78; exec. v.p. RCA, 1978-85; sr. advisor, broadcasting & entertainment, Wertheim Schroder & Co., 1986.

SCHMIDT, WOLF
Producer, Distributor. b. Freiburg/Br., Germany, June 30, 1937. Came to U.S. 1962 as freelance journalist. Started producing in 1969, distributing independently since 1972. Now pres. Big Bearing Licensing Corp.
PICTURES: Prod./Exec. Prod.: Ski Fever, Stamping Ground, Young Hannah, Things Fall Apart, The Passover Plot, Run for the Roses, Ghost Fever, Defense Play, Riding the Edge, The Fourth War, Neon City, Extreme Justice, Silent Hunter.

SCHMOELLER, DAVID
Writer, Director. b. Louisville, KY, Dec. 8, 1947. e. Universidad de Las Americas, 1967-69, studied film and theater under Luis Bunuel and Alejandro Jodorowsky; U. of TX, B.A., M.A., 1969-74. Wrote and directed 7 short films while studying at college; won 27 intl. awards. In Hollywood spent 6 months working as intern to Peter Hyams on film, Capricorn One. Now heads own co., The Schmoeller Corp.
AUTHOR: The Seduction.
PICTURES: Tourist Trap (debut as dir.), The Seduction (dir., s.p.), Crawlspace (dir., s.p.). Writer: The Day Time Ended, The Peeper, Last Chance Romance, Thrill Palace, Warriors of the Wind (Eng. adaptation), Ghost Town (story). Director: Catacombs, Puppet Master, The Arrival, Netherworld, Catch the Wind (also s.p.).
TELEVISION: James at 15 (writer), Kid Flicks (cable; writer, prod.), Silk Stalkings (dir.), Renegades (dir.).

SCHNEER, CHARLES H.
Producer, b. Norfolk, VA, May 5, 1920. e. Columbia Coll. pres., Morningside Prods. Inc. & Pictures Corp.; 1956. Founded Andor Films 1974. Chmn., Acad. of MP Arts & Sciences, London Screening Committee.
PICTURES: *Prod.:* The 3 Worlds of Gulliver, The 7th Voyage of Sinbad, I Aim at the Stars, Face of a Fugitive, Good Day for a Hanging, Battle of the Coral Sea, Tarawa Beachhead, Mysterious Island, Jason and the Argonauts, First Men In The Moon, Half A Sixpence, Land Raiders, Valley of Gwangi, The Executioner, The Golden Voyage of Sinbad, Sinbad & The Eye of the Tiger, Clash of the Titans.

SCHNEIDER, DICK
Producer, Director. b. Cazadero, CA, Mar. 7. e. Univ. of the Pacific, Stockton, CA. US Navy, WWII. Has received 9 Emmy Awards.
TELEVISION: Dough Re Mi, Wide Wide World, Colgate Comedy Hour, Beatrice Lillie, Jackie Gleason, Henry Morgan Show, Kate Smith Show, Big Story, Treasury Men in Action, Doorway to Danger, Today Show, Home, Tonight Show, General Mills Circus, Princess Margaret's Wedding, Paris Summit Conference, Eleanor Roosevelt Specials, Something Special 61, At This Very Moment, Inauguration, Gemini, Papal Mass for all networks at Yankee Stadium, Orange Bowl, Jr. Miss Pageant, College Queen (Emmy Award), New Communication, Big Sur, Dream House, Who What or Where, Stars and Stripes, Post Parade, Salute to Sir Lew, NBC Star Salute, Rose Parade, UCP Telethons, Macy's Parade, People's Choice, Jeopardy, Photo Finish.

SCHNEIDER, JOHN
Actor. b. Mount Kisco, NY, Apr. 8, 1954. Active in drama club in high school in Atlanta. Worked as fashion model and played guitar singing own compositions in various Atlanta clubs. Active in local community theatre. Summer stock in New Hampshire. B'way debut 1991 in Grand Hotel.
PICTURES: Smokey and the Bandit, Million Dollar Dixie Deliverance, Eddie Macon's Run, The Curse, Cocaine Wars, Speed Zone, Ministry of Vengeance.
TELEVISION: *Series:* Dukes of Hazzard, Grand Slam, Second Chances, Heaven Help Us. *Specials:* John Schneider—Back Home, Wild Jack. *Movies:* Dream House, Happy Endings, Stagecoach, Christmas Comes to Willow Creek, Outback Bound, Gus Brown and Midnight Brewster, Highway Heartbreaker, Desperate Journey: The Allison Wilcox Story, Texas.

SCHNEIDER, PETER
Executive. President of feature animation, Walt Disney Pictures and Touchstone Pictures.

SCHNEIER, FREDERICK
Executive. b. New York, NY, May 31, 1927; e. NYU, 1951, bus. admin.; NYU Grad. Sch., M.B.A., 1953. Dir. sls. planning, Mutual Broadcasting System, 1947-53; media research dir., RKO Teleradio, 1953-55; RKO Teleradio Advisory Comm., 1955-56; exec. staff RKO Teleradio & dir., marketing services, 1956-58; exec. vice-pres., Showcorporation, 1958-71; v.p. TV programming, RKO General, 1972-1973; v.p., Hemdale Leisure Corp., 1973-79; Viacom Enterprises v.p., feature films, 1979; sr. v.p., program acquisitions & motion pictures, 1980-83; sr. v.p., acquisitions, Showtime/The Movie Channel, 1983-85; sr. v.p. program acquisitions, program enterprises, 1985-87; exec. v.p., programming; 1987-89; pres. & CEO, Viacom Pictures Inc., 1989-92; pres. & CEO, FSA Film Enterprises.

SCHOEFFLING, MICHAEL
Actor. b. Philadelphia, PA. e. Temple Univ.
PICTURES: Sixteen Candles (debut, 1984), Vision Quest, Sylvester, Bellizaire the Cajun, Let's Get Harry, Slaves of New York, Longtime Companion, Mermaids, Wild Hearts Can't Be Broken.

SCHOENFELD, LESTER
Executive. b. Brooklyn, NY, Dec. 6, 1916. e. CCNY, 1934-38. Asst. mgr., Randforce Amusement, 1936-38; mgr., Rugoff & Becker circuit, 1938-47; mgr., Golden & Ambassador Theatres, 1948; print & sales dept., Film Classics, 1948-50; chg. of theatrical, non-theatrical & TV dist., Brit. Info. Serv.; est. Lester A. Schoenfeld Films, 1958; Schoenfeld Films Distributing Corp., 1960.

SCHORR, DANIEL
Radio, Television News Correspondent. b. New York, NY, Aug. 31, 1916. e. City Coll. of New York. Started with various news services and newspapers. Joined CBS in 1953 as Washington correspondent; 1958, reopened CBS bureau in Moscow; 1958-60, roving assignment; 1960-1966, chief German Bureau; 1966-76, Washington Bureau; 1979, Public Radio and TV; 1980, sr. Washington correspondent for Cable News Network; 1985, sr. news analyst, National Public Radio.

SCHRADER, PAUL
Writer, Director. b. Grand Rapids, MI, July 22, 1946. m. actress Mary Beth Hurt. e. Calvin Coll. (theology & philosophy); Columbia U., UCLA, M.A., cinema. Served as film critic for L.A. Free Press and Cinema 1970-72. Former professor at Columbia U.
PICTURES: The Yakuza (co-s.p.), Taxi Driver (s.p.), Rolling Thunder (s.p.), Obsession (s.p.), Blue Collar (co-s.p., dir.), Hardcore (s.p., dir.), Old Boyfriends (co-s.p., exec. prod.), American Gigolo (s.p., dir.), Raging Bull (co-s.p.), Cat People (dir.), Mishima (co-s.p., dir.), The Mosquito Coast (s.p.), Light of Day (dir., s.p.), The Last Temptation of Christ (s.p.), Patty Hearst (dir.), The Comfort of Strangers (dir.), Light Sleeper (dir., s.p.), City Hall (co-s.p.).
TELEVISION: *Movie:* Witch Hunt (dir.).

SCHRODER, RICK
Actor. b. Staten Island, NY, April 13, 1970. Started modelling while only four months; did many TV commercials before theatrical film debut in The Champ, at age eight.
PICTURES: The Champ, The Last Flight of Noah's Ark, The Earthling, Apt Pupil, Across the Tracks, There Goes My Baby, Crimson Tide.
TELEVISION: *Series:* Silver Spoons. *Movies:* Little Lord Fauntleroy, Something So Right, Two Kinds of Love, A Reason to Live, Too Young the Hero, Terror on Highway 91, Out on the Edge, A Son's Promise, The Stranger Within, Blood River, My Son Johnny, Miles From Nowhere, Call of the Wild, To My Daughter with Love, Texas. *Mini-Series:* Lonesome Dove, Return to Lonesome Dove.

SCHROEDER, BARBET
Producer, Director. b. Teheran, Iran, Aug. 26, 1941. Critic for Cahiers du Cinema and L'Air de Paris, 1958-63. 1963: asst. to Jean-Luc Godard on Les Carabiniers. 1964: formed own prod. co. Les Films du Losange. As actor only: Paris vu par, La Boulangere de Monceau Roberte, Celline and Julie Go Boating, Beverly Hills Cop III, La Reine Margot.
PICTURES: *Producer:* La Boulangere de Monceau (26 mins.), La Carriere de Suzanne (52 mins.), Mediterrannee, Paris Vu Par, La Collectionneuse, Tu Imagines Robinson, My Night at Maud's, Claire's Knee, Chloe in the Afternoon, Out One (co-prod.), The Mother and the Whore (co-prod.), Celine and Julie Go Boating, Flocons D'Or, The Marquise of O, Roulette Chinoise (co-prod.), The American Friend (co-prod.), Le Passe-Montagne, The Rites of Death, Perceval Le Gallois, Le Navire Night, Le Pont du Nord, Mauvaise Conduite, Une Sale Historie. *Director & Producer:* More (1969), Sing-Sing (doc.), La Vallee, General Idi Amin Dada (doc.), Maitresse, Koko a Talking Gorilla (doc.), Charles Bukowski Tapes (doc.), Tricheurs, Barfly, Reversal of Fortune, Single White Female, Kiss of Death, Before and After (also prod.).

SCHUCK, JOHN
Actor. b. Boston, MA, Feb. 4, 1940. e. Denison (BA). Cabaret act: An Evening With John Schuck.
THEATER: *B'way:* Annie. *Off-B'way:* The Streets of NY, The Shrike. London: The Caine Mutiny. Regional incl. Long Day's Journey Into Night, As You Like It.
PICTURES: M*A*S*H, The Moonshine War, Brewster McCloud, McCabe and Mrs. Miller, Hammersmith Is Out, Blade, Thieves Like Us, Butch and Sundance: The Early Days, Just You and Me Kid, Earthbound, Finders Keepers, Star Trek VI: The Voyage Home, Outrageous Fortune, The New Adventures of Pippi Longstocking, My Mom's a Werewolf, Second Sight, Dick Tracy, Star Trek IV: The Undiscovered Country, Holy Matrimony, Pontiac Moon, Tales From the Crypt Presents Demon Knight.
TELEVISION: *Series:* McMillan and Wife, Holmes and Yoyo, Turnabout, The New Odd Couple, The Munsters Today. *Mini-Series:* Roots. *Movies:* Once Upon a Dead Man, Hunter, Till Death Us Do Part. *Guest:* Murder She Wrote, Time Trax, Deep Space Nine, many others.

SCHULBERG, BUDD WILSON
Writer. b. New York, NY, Mar. 27, 1914. son of B. P. Schulberg, prod. e. Dartmouth Coll. Publicist, Paramount Pictures, 1931; writer for screen from 1932. Armed services WWII. Syndicated newspaper columnist: The Schulberg Report.
AUTHOR: *Novels:* What Makes Sammy Run?, The Disenchanted, The Harder They Fall, On the Waterfront, Some Faces in the Crowd, Everything That Moves, Sanctuary V, Love Action Laughter and Other Sad Tales. *Non-fiction books:* Writers in America, Moving Pictures: Memories of a Hollywood Prince, Swan Watch, Loser and Still Champion: Muhammad Ali, Sparring With Hemingway and Other Legends of the Fight Game. *Short stories:* Some Faces In the Crowd, Love, Action, Laughter and Other Sad Tales
THEATER: The Disenchanted (with Harvey Breit, 1958), What Makes Sammy Run? (book for musical), On the Waterfront (with Stan Silverman).
PICTURES: A Star is Born (additional dial.), Nothing Sacred (add. dial.), Little Orphan Annie (co-s.p.), Winter Carnival (co-s.p. with F. Scott Fitzgerald), Weekend for Three (orig. and co-

s.p.), City Without Men (co-story), Government Girl (adapt.). Original s.p.: On the Waterfront (Academy Award, & Writers Guild Award, 1954), A Face in The Crowd, Wind Across the Everglades, Joe Louis: For All Time (doc., Cine Golden Eagle Award, 1985).
TELEVISION: *Teleplays*: What Makes Sammy Run?, Paso Doble, The Pharmacist's Mate, Memory In White, The Legend That Walks Lives A Man, A Question of Honor, A Table at Ciro's.

SCHULMAN, JOHN A.
Executive. b. Washington, D.C., June 13, 1946. e. Yale U., 1968; law degree from Boalt Hall, U. of California, Berkeley, 1972. Founding partner in Beverly Hills law firm, Weissmann, Wolff, Bergman, Coleman & Schulman in 1981 after nine years with firm of Kaplan, Livingston, Goodwin, Berkowitz & Selvin. Joined Warner Bros. 1984 as v.p. & gen. counsel; 1989 sr. v.p. and gen. counsel; 1991, exec. v.p. and gen. counsel.

SCHULTZ, DWIGHT
Actor. b. Baltimore, MD, Nov. 24, 1947. e. Townson St. Univ. Acted with Williamstown Theatre Fest. prior to NY stage work, incl. The Crucifer of Blood, The Water Engine, Night and Day.
PICTURES: The Fan, Alone in the Dark, Fat Man and Little Boy, The Long Walk Home, The Temp.
TELEVISION: *Series*: The A-Team, Star Trek: The Next Generation. *Movies*: Child of Rage, When Your Lover Leaves, Perry Mason: The Case of the Sinister Spirit, Perry Mason: The Case of the Musical Murder, A Woman With a Past, The Last Wish, A Killer Among Us, Victim of Love: The Shannon Mohr Story, Menendez: A Killing in Beverly Hills.

SCHULTZ, MICHAEL
Director, Producer. b. Milwaukee, WI, Nov. 10, 1938. e. U. of Wisconsin, Marquette U.
THEATER: The Song of the Lusitainian Bogey, Kongi's Harvest, Does a Tiger Wear a Necktie?, Operation Sidewinder, What the Winesellers Buy, The Cherry Orchard, Mulebone, Dream on Monkey Mountain.
PICTURES: *Director*: Together for Days, Honeybaby Honeybaby, Cooley High, Car Wash, Greased Lightning, Which Way Is Up?, Sgt. Pepper's Lonely Hearts Club Band, Scavenger Hunt, Carbon Copy, The Last Dragon, Krush Groove (also prod.), Disorderlies (also co-prod.), Livin' Large.
TELEVISION: *Specials*: To Be Young Gifted and Black, Ceremonies in Dark Old Men, For Us the Living, Fade Out: The Erosion of Black Images in the Media (documentary), Hollywood Follies, Travels With Father. *Series*: The Young Indiana Jones Chronicles, Picket Fences, Chicago Hope, Sisters. *Pilot*: Shock Treatment. *Movies*: Benny's Place, The Jerk Too, Timestalkers, Rock 'n' Roll Mom, Tarzan in Manhattan, Jury Duty, Dayo.

SCHUMACHER, JOEL
Director, Writer. b. New York, NY, Aug. 29, 1939. Worked as design and display artist for Henri Bendel dept. store NY while attending Parson's Sch. of Design. As fashion designer opened own boutique, Paraphernalia. Joined Revlon as designer of clothing and packaging before entering m.p. indus. as costume designer on Play It As It Lays, Sleeper, The Last of Sheila, Blume in Love, Prisoner of 2nd Avenue, Interiors.
PICTURES: *Writer*: Car Wash, Sparkle, The Wiz. *Director*: The Incredible Shrinking Woman (debut, 1981), D.C. Cab (also s.p.), St. Elmo's Fire (also s.p.), The Lost Boys, Cousins, Flatliners, Dying Young, Falling Down, The Client, Batman Forever, A Time to Kill, Batman & Robin.
TELEVISION: *Director*: *Movies*: The Virginia Hill Story (also writer), Amateur Night at the Dixie Bar & Grill (also writer). *Music video*: Devil Inside for rock group INXS (dir.). *Series*: 2000 Malibu Drive. *Exec. Prod.*: Slow Burn.

SCHWAB, SHELLY
Executive. Station mgr., WAGA-TV, Atlanta; various sls. & mgr. posts with CBS. Joined MCA, 1978, becoming exec. v.p., MCA-TV. 1986, appt. pres., MCA TV Enterprises, 1989 appt. pres. MCA TV.

SCHWARTZ, BERNARD
Producer. Brought to Hollywood by the late Howard Hughes to watch his film interests; Schwartz teamed with atty. Greg Bautzer to package movie deals for clients. Re-cut some of Buster Keaton's silent movies into documentary anthologies (The Golden Age of Comedy, When Comedy Was King, etc.). Subsequently made TV series, One Step Beyond, followed by The Wackiest Ship in the Army, Miss Teen International specials, etc. Named pres. Joseph M. Schenck Enterprises, for which he made Journey to the Center of the Earth, Eye of the Cat, A Cold Wind in August, I Passed for White, The Shattered Room, Trackdown. Presently partnered with Alan Silverman.
PICTURES: Coal Miner's Daughter (prod.), Road Games (exec. prod.) Psycho II (exec. prod.), St. Elmo's Fire (co-exec. prod.).
TELEVISION: Elvis and Me (co-exec. prod.).

SCHWARY, RONALD L.
Producer. b. Oregon, May 23, 1944. e. U. of Southern California. Started as movie extra before becoming asst. dir.; served as assoc. prod. on The Electric Horseman.
PICTURES: Ordinary People (Academy Award for Best Picture, 1980), Absence of Malice, Tootsie, A Soldier's Story, Batteries Not Included, Havana, Scent of a Woman, Cops and Robbersons, Sabrina.
TELEVISION: Tour of Duty.

SCHWARZENEGGER, ARNOLD
Actor. b. Graz, Austria, July 30, 1947. m. NBC reporter Maria Shriver. e. U. Wisconsin, B.A. Bodybuilding Titles: Junior Mr. Europe (at age 18), Mr. Universe (3 time winner), Mr. Olympia (7 times), Mr. Europe, Mr. World. Special Olympics weightlifting Coach (1989), Prison Weightlifting Rehabilitation Prog. Awards: Sportsman of the Year (1977, Assn. Physical Fitness Ctrs.), Golden Globe (best newcomer, 1977), ShoWest '85 Intl. Star., ShoWest Career Achievement Award, NATO Male Star of Yr. (1987).
AUTHOR: Arnold: The Education of a Bodybuilder, Arnold's Bodyshaping for Women, Arnold's Bodybuilding for Men, The Encyclopedia of Modern Bodybuilding, Arnold's Fitness for Kids (3 Vols.).
PICTURES: Hercules in New York (a.k.a. Hercules Goes Bananas; debut, 1970; billed as Arnold Strong), The Long Goodbye, Stay Hungry, Pumping Iron, The Villain, Scavenger Hunt, Conan the Barbarian, Conan the Destroyer, The Terminator, Red Sonja, Commando, Raw Deal, Predator, The Running Man, Red Heat, Twins, Total Recall, Kindergarten Cop, Terminator 2: Judgment Day, Beretta's Island (cameo), Dave (cameo), Last Action Hero (also exec. prod.), True Lies, Junior, Eraser, Jingle All the.Way, Batman and Robin.
TELEVISION: *Movie*: The Jayne Mansfield Story. *Special*: A Very Special Christmas Party (host). *Guest*: Streets of San Francisco. *Director*: Tales from the Crypt (The Switch), Christmas in Connecticut (movie).

SCHYGULLA, HANNA
Actress. b. Kattowitz, Germany, Dec. 25, 1943. Worked with Rainer Werner Fassbinder in Munich's Action Theater; a founder of the ``anti-theatre'' group. Made film debut in 1968 short Der Brautigam die Komodianten und der Zuhalter (The Bridegroom, the Comedienne and the Pimp).
PICTURES: Love Is Colder Than Death (feature debut, 1969), Gods of the Plague, Beware of a Holy Whore, The Merchant of Four Seasons, The Bitter Tears of Petra Von Kant, House by the Sea, Jail Bait, Effi Briest, The Marriage of Maria Braun, Berlin Alexanderplatz, Lili Marleen, The Night of Varennes, Passion, A Labor of Love, A Love in Germany, The Delta Force, The Future Is a Woman, Forever Lulu, Miss Arizona, The Summer of Ms. Forbes, Dead Again.
TELEVISION: *U.S.*: Rio das Mortes, Peter the Great, Barnum, Casanova.

SCIORRA, ANNABELLA
Actress. b. New York, NY, 1964. As teen studied acting at HB Studio; then AADA. Founded The Brass Ring Theatre Co. Won role of Sophia Loren's daughter in mini-series Fortunate Pilgrim.
THEATER: Orpheus Descending, Bus Stop, Three Sisters, Snow Angel, Cries and Shouts, Trip Back Down, Love and Junk, Stay With Me, Those the River Keeps.
PICTURES: True Love (debut, 1989), Internal Affairs, Cadillac Man, Reversal of Fortune, The Hard Way, Jungle Fever, The Hand That Rocks the Cradle, Whispers in the Dark, The Night We Never Met, Mr. Wonderful, Romeo is Bleeding, The Cure, The Addiction, The Innocent Sleep, The Funeral.
TELEVISION: *Mini-Series*: The Fortunate Pilgrim. *Movie*: Prison Stories: Women on the Inside.

SCOFIELD, PAUL
Actor. b. Hurstpierpoint, England, Jan. 21, 1922. Started acting at age 14.
THEATER: ADventure Story, Ring Round the Moon, Richard II, The Way of the World, Venice Preserved, Time Remembered, Hamlet, Power and the Glory, Family Reunion, Espresso Bongo, A Man For All Seasons (also B'way: Tony Award, 1962), Coriolanus, Don Armando, King Lear, Timon, Staircase, The Government Inspector, Hotel In Amsterdam, Uncle Vanya, The Captain of Kopernik, Rules of the Game, Savages, The Tempest, Volpone, The Family, Amadeus, Othello, Don Quixote, A Midsummer Night's Dream, I'm Not Rappaport, Heart-break House.
PICTURES: That Lady (debut, 1955), Carve Her Name With Pride, The Train, A Man for All Seasons (Academy Award, 1966), Tell Me Lies, King Lear, Bartleby, Scorpio, A Delicate Balance, 1919, When the Whales Came, Henry V, Hamlet, Utz, Quiz Show, London (narrator), The Crucible.
TELEVISION: *Movies*: Anna Karenina, The Attic: The Hiding of Anne Frank. *Specials*: The Male of the Species (Emmy Award, 1969), The Ambassadors, The Potting Shed, Martin Chuzzlewit, Little Riders, The Crucible.

SCOGGINS, TRACY
Actress. b. Galveston, TX, Nov. 13, 1959. Studied acting at H.B. Studies, Wynn Handman Studios. Appeared on stage in L.A. in The Sicilian Bachelor.
PICTURES: Some Kind of Hero, Toy Soldier, In Dangerous Company, The Gumshoe Kid, Watchers II, Time Bomb, Silhouette, Ultimate Desires, Alien Intruder, Demonic Toys, Dead On.
TELEVISION: *Series*: Renegades, Hawaiian Heat, The Colbys, Lois & Clark: The New Adventures of Superman. *Movies*: Twirl, Jury Duty, Dan Turner: Hollywood Detective, Jake Lassiter: Justice on the Bayou. *Pilots*: The Naturals, High Life, Unauthorized Biographies. *Guest*: Hotel, Crazy Like a Fox, Dallas, Magnum P.I., The Fall Guy, Mike Hammer, The Heights.

SCOLA, ETTORE
Director, Writer. b. Trevico, Italy, May 10, 1931. e. U. of Rome. Began career in 1947 as journalist; 1950, wrote for radio shows. Then made first film as script writer 1954; debut as director-writer, 1964. Has written 50 other scripts for other directors.
PICTURES: *Dir/Writer*: Let's Talk about Women (debut, 1964), La Congiuntura, Thrilling (segment: Il Vittimista), The Devil in Love, Will Your Heroes Find Their Friends Who Disappeared so Mysteriously in Africa?, Inspector Pepe, The Pizza Triangle, Rocco Papaleo, The Greatest Evening of My Life, We All Loved Each Other So Much, Down and Dirty, Signore e Signori Buonanotte (segment), A Special Day, Viva Italia! (segment), The Terrace, Passion d'Amore, La Nuit de Varennes, Le Bal, Macaroni, The Family, Splendor, What Time is It?, Le Capitain Fracassa, Mario Maria and Mario, Romanzo di un Giovane Povero

SCOLARI, PETER
Actor. b. New Rochelle, NY, Sept. 12, 1954.
PICTURES: The Rosebud Beach Hotel, Corporate Affairs, Ticks, Camp Nowhere, That Thing You Do!.
TELEVISION: *Series*: Goodtime Girls, Bosom Buddies, Baby Makes Five, Newhart, Family Album, Dweebs. *Movies*: Carpool, Amazon, Fatal Confession, The Ryan White Story. *Guest*: Remington Steele, The Love Boat, Family Ties, The New Mike Hammer, Trying Times (Death and Taxes), Fallen Angels (I'll Be Waiting).

SCORSESE, MARTIN
Writer, Director, Editor, Actor. b. New York, NY, Nov. 17, 1942. Began career while film arts student at NYU, doing shorts What's A Nice Girl Like You Doing in a Place Like This? (dir., s.p.), It's Not Just You Murray and The Big Shave. Other short films: Street Scenes, Italianamerican, American Boy, Mirror Mirror, Somewhere Down the Crazy River. *Dir*. 2 commercials for Armani. Currently campaigning for the preservation and restoration of historic films.
THEATER: The Act.
PICTURES: *Editor*: Woodstock, Medicine Ball Caravan, Unholy Rollers, Elvis on Tour. *Producer*: The Grifters, Mad Dog and Glory, Naked in New York (exec. prod.), Clockers. *Actor*: Cannonball, 'Round Midnight, Akira Kurosawa's Dreams, Guilty by Suspicion, Quiz Show, Search and Destroy (also co-exec. prod.). *Director*: Who's That Knocking at My Door? (also s.p., assoc. prod., actor), Boxcar Bertha (also actor), Mean Streets (also co-s.p., actor), Alice Doesn't Live Here Anymore, Taxi Driver (also actor), New York New York, The Last Waltz (also cameo), Raging Bull, The King of Comedy (also actor), After Hours (also cameo), The Color of Money, The Last Temptation of Christ, New York Stories (Life Lessons; also cameo), GoodFellas (also co-s.p.), Cape Fear, The Age of Innocence (also co-s.p., cameo), Casino (also co-s.p.).
TELEVISION: *Series episode*: Amazing Stories (dir.). *Special*: A Personal Journey With Martin Scorsese Through American Movies (dir. writer).

SCOTT, CAMPBELL
Actor. b. New York, NY, July 19, 1962. e. Lawrence Univ. Son of George C. Scott and Colleen Dewhurst. Studied with Geraldine Page and Stella Adler.
THEATER: *NY*: The Last Outpost, The Real Thing, Copperhead, The Queen and the Rebels, Hay Fever, A Man For All Seasons, Long Day's Journey Into Night, Measure for Measure, Pericles, On the Bum. *Regional*: Romeo and Juliet, Our Town, Gilette, School for Wives, Hamlet.
PICTURES: Five Corners (debut, 1988), From Hollywood to Deadwood, Longtime Companion, The Sheltering Sky, Dying Young, Dead Again, Singles, Mrs. Parker and the Vicious Circle, The Innocent, The Daytrippers, Big Night (also co-dir.).
TELEVISION: *Mini-Series*: The Kennedys of Massachusetts. *Guest*: Family Ties, L.A. Law. *Movie*: The Perfect Tribute.

SCOTT, GEORGE C.
Actor, Director. b. Wise, VA, Oct. 18, 1927. m. actress Trish VanDevere. Son is actor Campbell Scott. Served 4 years Marine Corps. e. U. of Missouri, appeared in varsity productions, summer stock, Shakespeare.

THEATER: *Off-B'way*: Richard III (Theatre World Award), As You Like It, Children of Darkness, General Seeger, Merchant of Venice, Desire Under the Elms, Antony and Cleopatra, Wrong Turn at Lungfish (also L.A.), Inherit the Wind (Tony nom.). *B'way*: Comes a Day, The Andersonville Trial, The Wall, The Little Foxes, Plaza Suite, Uncle Vanya, All God's Chillun Got Wings (dir.), Death of a Salesman (also dir.), Sly Fox, Present Laughter (also dir.), The Boys in Autumn, On Borrowed Time (also dir.).
PICTURES: The Hanging Tree (debut, 1959), Anatomy of a Murder, The Hustler, The List of Adrian Messenger, Dr. Strangelove: Or How I Learned to Stop Worrying and Love the Bomb, The Yellow Rolls Royce, The Bible, Not With My Wife You Don't, The Flim-Flam Man, Petulia, This Savage Land, The Last Run, The Hospital, The New Centurions, Rage (also dir.), Oklahoma Crude, The Day of the Dolphin, Bank Shot, The Savage Is Loose (also dir., prod.), The Hindenburg, Islands in the Stream, Crossed Swords, Movie Movie, Hardcore, The Changeling, The Formula, Taps, Firestarter, The Exorcist III, The Rescuers Down Under (voice), Malice, Angus.
TELEVISION: *Series*: East Side West Side, Mr. President, Traps. *Movies*: Jane Eyre, Fear on Trial, Oliver Twist, China Rose, A Christmas Carol, Choices, The Last Days of Patton, The Murders in the Rue Morgue, Pals, The Ryan White Story, Descending Angel, Finding the Way Home, Curacao, The Whipping Boy, In the Heat of the Night: A Matter of Justice, Tyson. *Mini-Series*: Mussolini--The Untold Story. *Guest*: DuPont Show of the Month, Playhouse 90, Hallmark Hall of Fame, Kraft Theatre, Omnibus, Armstrong Theatre, Play of the Week, NBC Sunday Showcase, Dow Hour of Great Mysteries, Esso Theatre. *Specials*: Power and the Glory, The Brass Bottle, The Savage Land, The Crucible, The Price (Emmy Award, 1971), Beauty and the Beast, The Andersonville Trial (dir.).

SCOTT, MARTHA
Actress. b. Jamesport, MO, September 22, 1914. e. U. of Michigan. In little theatres over U.S.; summer stock NY; on radio with Orson Welles; Broadway debut Our Town (1938), film debut in film adaptation of same. Became theater producer in 1968 with Henry Fonda and Alfred De Liagre at Kennedy Center and on B'way (Time of Your Life, First Monday in October).
THEATER: Our Town, Soldier's Wife, The Voice of the Turtle, The Number, The Male Animal, The Remarkable Mr. Pennypacker, Forty-Second Cousin, The Crucible.
PICTURES: Our Town (debut, 1940; Acad. Award nom.), The Howards of Virginia, Cheers for Miss Bishop, They Dare Not Love, One Foot in Heaven, In Old Oklahoma (The War of the Wildcats), Hi Diddle Diddle, So Well Remembered, Strange Bargain, When I Grow Up, The Desperate Hours, The Ten Commandments, Eighteen and Anxious, Sayonara, Ben-Hur, Charlotte's Web (voice), Airport 1975, The Turning Point, Doin' Time on Planet Earth.
TELEVISION: *Movies*: The Devil's Daughter, Thursday's Game, The Abduction of Saint Anne, Medical Story, Charleston, Father Figure, Summer Girl, Adam, Adam: His Song Continues, Love and Betrayal, Daughter of the Streets. *Mini-Series*: The Word, Beulah Land. *Guest*: Murder She Wrote, Hotel, A Girl's Life (pilot).

SCOTT, RIDLEY
Director, Producer. b. South Shields, Northumberland, Eng., Nov. 30, 1937. Brother is director Tony Scott. e. Royal College of Art, London. Joined newly formed Film Sch. First film: Boy on Bicycle (short). Won design scholarship in NY. Returned to London and joined BBC as set designer (Z-Cars, The Informer series). Directed almost 3,000 commercials in 18 years. Formed Percy Main Prods. Also mng. dir. of Ridley Scott Assocs.Exec. Prod. film Monkey Trouble, prod. of The Browning Version.
PICTURES: *Director*: The Duellists (debut, 1978), Alien, Blade Runner, Legend, Someone to Watch Over Me (also exec. prod.), Black Rain, Thelma & Louise (also prod.), 1492: Conquest of Paradise (also prod.), White Squall (also exec. prod.).

SCOTT, TONY
Director. b. Newcastle, England. Began career in TV commercials, being partnered with his brother Ridley in prod. co. Winner of numerous Clios, Gold & Silver Lions, and other awards. Entered m.p. industry 1972, directing half-hr. film, One of the Missing, for British Film Inst. and Loving Memory, 1-hr. feature for Albert Finney.
PICTURES: The Hunger (debut, 1983), Top Gun, Beverly Hills Cop II, Revenge, Days of Thunder, The Last Boy Scout, True Romance, Crimson Tide, The Fan.

SCOTT-THOMAS, KRISTIN
Actress. b. England. Lived in France since 18. e. Central School of Speech and Drama, London and Ecole Nationale

des Arts et Technique de Theatre in Paris. Stage debut in La Lune Declinante Sur 4 Ou 5 Personnes Qui Danse. Other theater work in Paris.
PICTURES: Djomel et Juliette, L'Agent Troube, La Meridienne, Under the Cherry Moon, A Handful of Dust, Force Majeure, Bille en tete, The Bachelor, Four Weddings and a Funeral, Bitter Moon, An Unforgettable Summer, The Confessional, Angels and Insects, The Pompatus of Love, Les Milles, Richard III.
TELEVISION: L'Ami D'Enfance de Maigret, Blockhaus, Chameleon/La Tricheuse (Aust.), Sentimental Journey (Germany), The Tenth Man, Endless Game, Framed, Body & Soul, Look at It This Way.

SCULLY, JOE
Talent Executive, Casting Director, Producer, Writer. b. Kearny, NJ, March 1, 1926. e. Goodman Memorial Theatre of the Art Inst. of Chicago, 1946. m. Penelope Gillette. Acted until 1951. CBS-TV, NY. Casting Dir., Danger, You Are There, Omnibus, The Web, 1951-56. Wrote The Little Woman for CBS Danger Anthology Series, 1954. 1956-60, CBS-TV, Associate Prod., Studio One, Dupont Show of the Month, Playhouse 90; 1962-64, Writer for CBS Repertoire Workshop anthology series; 1963-64, CBS Stations div. KNXT, prod., Repertoire Workshop; 1965-70 casting dir., 20th Century-Fox Films; 1970-74, indept. casting dir.; 1974-75 Universal TV, casting dir. Member, AMPAS since 1975; NBC-TV Manager, Casting & Talent; 1978, re-established Joe Scully Casting, indept. service to the industry. Founding member, CSA, 1982; 1983, casting dir., Walt Disney Pictures. 1991 published story in Emmy Magazine: 'Have You Ever... You Know?' Conducted AMPAS Seminar, 'The Casting Process in Motion Pictures.'
PICTURES: Hello Dolly, In Like Flint, Valley of the Dolls, Planet of the Apes, The Flim-Flam Man, Sounder, Lady Sings the Blues, Play It as It Lays, The Stone Killer, Parallax View, Lifeguard, Man in the Glass Booth, Middle Age Crazy, Death Wish II, Frankenweenie (short), North of Chiang Mai, Chained in Paradiso (video).
TELEVISION: Series: Peyton Place, Bonanza, Room 222, Nichols, Snoop Sisters, Columbo, Switch, McMillan & Wife, Tales of the Unexpected, Gone Are the Days (Disney Channel). Pilots: Julia, The Ghost and Mrs. Muir, The Bill Cosby Show. Movies: Thief, Missiles of October, Gone Are the Days, Earth II. Australian: Flair (mini-series), Ebb Tide (movie).

SEAGAL, STEVEN
Actor, Director, Producer, Writer. b. Lansing, MI, April 10, 1952. Became skilled at martial arts at an early age, studying Aikido. Lived in Japan for 15 yrs. where he opened a martial arts academy. Opened similar academy upon his return to U.S. in Los Angeles. Was martial arts choreographer/coordinator on film The Challenge.
PICTURES: Above the Law (debut, 1988; also co-prod., co-story), Hard to Kill, Marked for Death (also co-prod.), Out for Justice (also co-prod.), Under Siege (also co-prod.), On Deadly Ground (also dir., co-prod.). Under Siege 2: Dark Territory (also co- prod.), Executive Decision, The Glimmer Man.

SEAGROVE, JENNY
Actress. b. Kuala Lumpur, Malaysia. e. Bristol Old Vic. Theatre Sch. Stage debut 1979. Early TV: The Brack Report, The Woman in White, Diana. Recent stage: Jane Eyre, King Lear, Present Laughter, The Miracle Worker, Dead Guilty.
PICTURES: Moonlighting, Local Hero, Nate and Hayes, Appointment With Death, A Chorus of Disapproval, The Guardian, Bullseye!, Miss Beatty's Children.
TELEVISION: A Woman of Substance, Hold The Dream, In Like Flynn, Killer, Lucy Walker, Magic Moments, Some Other Spring, The Betrothed, Deadly Game, The Sign of Four, The Incident at Victoria Falls, A Shocking Accident.

SECOMBE, SIR HARRY
C.B.E.: Singer, Comedian, Actor. b. Swansea, Wales, Sept. 8, 1921. Awarded, C.B.E., 1963. Awarded Knight Bachelor, 1991. AUTHOR: Twice Brightly, Goon for Lunch, Katy and the Nurgla, Welsh Fargo, Goon Abroad, The Harry Secombe Diet Book, Harry Secombe's Highway, The Highway Companion. Autobiography: Arias and Raspberries.
THEATER: London: Pickwick (also NY), The Four Musketeers, The Plumber's Progress, Pickwick (revival: Chichester Fest., Sadlers Wells Theatre, natl. tour, 1993-95).
PICTURES: Hocus Pocus (debut, 1948), Helter Skelter, London Entertains, Penny Points to Paradise, Forces' Sweetheart, Down Among the Z Men, Svengali, Davy, Jet Storm, Oliver!, The Bed Sitting Room, Song of Norway, Rhubarb, Doctor in Trouble, The Magnificent Seven Deadly Sins, Sunstruck.
TELEVISION: Numerous appearances, incl. own series: Secombe and Friends, The Harry Secombe Show, Secombe with Music. Also special version, Pickwick. Presenter of Tyne Tees TV's Highway 1983-93; Presenter of BBC-TV Songs of Praise, 1995-96.

SEDGWICK, KYRA
Actress. b. New York, NY, Aug. 19, 1965. e. USC. m. actor Kevin Bacon.
THEATER: NY: Time Was, Dakota's Belly Wyoming, Ah Wilderness (Theatre World Award), Maids of Honor. LA: Oleanna.
PICTURES: War and Love, Tai-Pan, Kansas, Born on the Fourth of July, Mr. & Mrs. Bridge, Pyrates, Singles, Heart & Souls, Murder in the First, Something to Talk About, The Low Life, Losing Chase, Phenomenon.
TELEVISION: Movies: The Man Who Broke 1000 Chains, Women & Men II (In Love There Are No Rules), Miss Rose White, Family Pictures. Series: Another World. Guest: Amazing Stories. Specials: Cinder Ella: A Modern Fairy Tale, The Wide Net, Lemon Sky.

SEGAL, GEORGE
Actor. b. New York, NY, Feb. 13, 1934. e. Columbia U., B.A., 1955. Worked as janitor, ticket-taker, soft-drink salesman, usher and under-study at NY's Circle in the Square theatre. Acting debut: Downtown Theatre's revival of Don Juan. Formed a nightclub singing act with Patricia Scott. Record album of ragtime songs and banjo music: The Yama Yama Man. Dir. debut: Bucks County Playhouse prod. Scuba Duba.
THEATER: The Iceman Cometh (1956 revival), Antony and Cleopatra N.Y. Shakespeare Festival, Leave It to Jane, The Premise (satiric improv revue), Gideon, Rattle of a Simple Man, The Knack, Requiem for a Heavyweight, The Fourth Wall (regional).
PICTURES: The Young Doctors (debut, 1961), The Longest Day, Act One, The New Interns, Invitation to a Gunfighter, Ship of Fools, King Rat, Lost Command, Who's Afraid of Virginia Woolf? (Acad. Award nom.), The Quiller Memorandum, The St. Valentine's Day Massacre, Bye Bye Braverman, No Way to Treat a Lady, The Southern Star, The Bridge at Remagen, The Girl Who Couldn't Say No, Loving, The Owl and the Pussycat, Where's Poppa?, Born to Win, The Hot Rock, A Touch of Class, Blume in Love, The Terminal Man, California Split, Russian Roulette, The Black Bird, The Duchess and the Dirtwater Fox, Fun with Dick and Jane, Rollercoaster, Who Is Killing the Great Chefs of Europe?, Lost and Found, The Last Married Couple in America, Carbon Copy, Killing 'em Softly, Stick, All's Fair, Look Who's Talking, The Clearing, For the Boys, Look Who's Talking Now, Army of One, Direct Hit, Deep Down, Flirting With Disaster, The Cable Guy, The Feminine Touch, The Mirror Has Two Faces.
TELEVISION: Series: Take Five, Murphy's Law, High Tide. Specials: Death of a Salesman, Of Mice and Men, The Desperate Hours. Guest: The Nurses, Naked City, Alfred Hitchcock Presents. Movies: Trackdown: Finding the Goodbar Killer, The Cold Room, The Zany Adventures of Robin Hood, Not My Kid, Many Happy Returns, Endless Game, Taking the Heat, Following Her Heart.

SEGAL, MAURICE
Publicist. b. New York, NY, July 22, 1921. e. CCNY, 1937-41. Entered m.p. ind., adv. dept., 20th Fox, 1941-42; U.S. Army 1942-46; feature writer, publ. dept., 20th Fox, 1946; asst. to dir., adv., publ., Century Circuit, 1947; press book dept., Paramount, 1949; trade press rep. 1950; trade press rep. RKO Radio, 1952; resigned to join Richard Condon-Kay Norton, publicists, 1953; adv., pub. dept., U-I. 1954; asst. pub. mgr., United Artists 1957; Hollywood publ. coordinator, 1958; exec. in chg. of M.P. press dept., Universal City Studios, 1966; West Coast adv.-publ. dir., National Gen. Pictures, 1971; pres., Maurice E. Segal Co., 1974; dir., West Coast operations, Charles Schlaifer & Co., 1976; v.p., Max Youngstein Enterprises, 1979; exec. v.p., Taft Intl. Pictures, 1980; pres. Maurice E. Segal Co., 1982; pres. The Segal Company, 1987.

SEIDELMAN, ARTHUR ALLAN
Director, Producer, Writer. b. New York, NY, October 11. e. Whittier Coll., B.A.; UCLA, M.A. Former staff member, Repertory Theatre of Lincoln Center and Phoenix Theatre, NY.
THEATER: Dir.: LA: The Sisters, Gypsy Princess, The Beautiful People, Five Finger Exercise, The Purification, etc. Dir.: NY: Awakening of Spring, Hamp, Ceremony of Innocence, The Justice Box, Billy, Vieux Carre, The World of My America, Awake and Sing, The Four Seasons, Inherit the Wind, The Most Happy Fella, as well as numerous regional prods. and national tours.
PICTURES: Hercules in New York, Children of Rage (dir., s.p.), Echoes, The Caller, Rescue Me.
TELEVISION: Director: Family, Magnum, P.I., Murder She Wrote, Hill Street Blues, Trapper John M.D., Paper Chase, Knots Landing, Bay City Blues, Capitol News, WIOU, L.A. Law, FBI: The Untold Stories, Sweet Justice, Heaven Help Us, Amazing Grace. Movies: Which Mother is Mine? A Special Gift, Schoolboy Father, A Matter of Time, I Think I'm Having a Baby, Sin of Innocence, Kate's Secret, Ceremony of Innocence, Poker Alice, The People Across the Lake, Addicted to His Love, Kate's Secret, A Friendship in Vienna, A Place at the Table, An Enemy Among Us, Glory Years, Strange

Voices, A Taste of Honey, Look Away, False Witness, The Kid Who Loved Christmas, Body Language, Trapped in Space, Dying to Remember, Wing and a Prayer, Harvest of Fire, I Love Liberty..

SEIDELMAN, SUSAN
Director. b. near Philadelphia, PA, Dec.11, 1952. e. Drexel Univ. B.A. Worked at a UHF television station in Phila., NYU film school M.F.A. Debut: 28-min. student film And You Act Like One Too. Then dir. Deficit (short, funded by AFI), and Yours Truly, Andrea G. Stern.
PICTURES: Smithereens (dir., prod., co-s.p.; 1st Amer. indep. feature accepted into competition at Cannes Film Fest., 1982), Desperately Seeking Susan, Making Mr. Right, Cookie (also exec. prod.), She-Devil, The Dutch Master (short, Academy Award nom.).
TELEVISION: Confessions of a Suburban Girl (BBC; also writer, actress), The Barefoot Executive.

SEINFELD, JERRY
Comedian, Actor. b. Brooklyn, NY, Apr. 29, 1954. e. Queens Col. Stand-up comic; guested on such shows as The Tonight Show, Late Night With David Letterman. Received American Comedy Award for funniest male comedy stand-up, 1988. Author: Seinlanguage (1993).
TELEVISION: Series: Benson, Seinfeld (also co-creator, writer). Pilot: The Seinfeld Chronicles. Specials: Jerry Seinfeld—Stand-Up Confidential (also writer), Abott and Costello Meet Jerry Seinfeld (host).

SELBY, DAVID
Actor. b. Morgantown, WV. Feb. 5, 1941. e. West Virginia U. Acted in outdoor dramas in home state and did regional theatre elsewhere. Was asst. instructor in lit. at Southern Illinois U.
PICTURES: Night of Dark Shadows, Up the Sandbox, Super Cops, Rich Kids, Raise the Titanic, Rich and Famous, Dying Young, Intersection, Headless Body in Topless Bar.
TELEVISION: Series: Dark Shadows, Flamingo Road, Falcon Crest. Mini-Series: Washington: Behind Closed Doors. Movies: Telethon, The Night Rider, Love for Rent, Doctor Franken, King of the Olympics: The Lives and Loves of Avery Brundage, Grave Secrets: The Legacy of Hilltop Drive, Lady Boss. Guest: Kojak, Doogie Howser M.D.

SELF, WILLIAM
Producer. b. Dayton, OH, June 21, 1921. e. U. of Chicago, 1943. Prod.-dir., Schlitz Playhouse of Stars, 1952-56; prod., The Frank Sinatra Show, 1957; exec. prod., CBS-TV, The Twilight Zone, Hotel De Paree; 1960-61 exec. prod., 20th Century-Fox TV: Hong Kong, Adventures in Paradise, Bus Stop, Follow The Sun, Margie; v.p. in chg. of prod., 20th Century-Fox TV, 1962; exec. v.p., 1964; pres., Fox TV 1969; v.p. 20th Century Fox Film Corp., 1969; pres. of William Self Productions, Inc., partner, Frankovich/Self Productions; 1975; v.p., programs, Hollywood CBS TV Network, 1976; 1977, v.p. motion pictures for tv and miniseries, CBS TV; 1982, pres., CBS Theatrical Films; 1985, pres., William Self Prods. in association with CBS Prods; 1990, pres. Self Productions, Inc.
TELEVISION: Movies (exec. prod.): The Tenth Man (also prod.), Sarah Plain & Tall, Skylark.

SELIG, ROBERT WILLIAM
Exhibitor. b. Cripple Creek, CO, Feb., 1910. e. U. of Denver, 1932, B.A.; doctorate, 1959. 1932 joined advertising sales div., 20th Century Fox, Denver. Founding mem. Theatre Owners of Amer. and NATO. Consultant, Pacific Theatres. Lifetime Trustee, U. of Denver. Member Kappa Sigma, Omicron Delta Kappa, Beta Gamma Sigma; Nat'l Methodist Church Foundation; Past Pres., Theatre Association of California and CEO NATO of CA; board of directors Los Angeles Chamber of Commerce; founder NATO/ShoWest Conventions. Received NATO Sherrill C. Corwin Award, 1989.

SELLECCA, CONNIE
Actress. b. Bronx, NY, May 25, 1955. m. anchor-host John Tesh.
TELEVISION: Series: Flying High, Beyond Westworld, The Greatest American Hero, Hotel, P.S. I Luv U, Second Chances. Movies: The Bermuda Depths (debut, 1978), Flying High (pilot), Captain America II, She's Dressed to Kill, The Last Fling, International Airport, Downpayment on Murder, Brotherhood of the Rose, Turn Back the Clock, Miracle Landing, People Like Us, A House of Secrets and Lies (also co-exec. prod.), Passport to Murder, She Led Two Lives, A Dangerous Affair. Specials: The Celebrity Football Classic, Celebrity Challenge of the Sexes, Circus of the Stars.

SELLECK, TOM
Actor. b. Detroit, MI, Jan. 29, 1945. e. U. of Southern California. Grew up in Southern California, appearing in several commercials before being signed to 20th Century Fox. First acting job was on tv series Lancer.

PICTURES: Myra Breckenridge (debut, 1970), Midway, The Washington Affair, Coma, High Road to China, Lassiter, Runaway, Three Men and a Baby, Her Alibi, An Innocent Man, Quigley Down Under, Three Men and a Little Lady, Folks!, Christopher Columbus: The Discovery, Mr. Baseball.
TELEVISION: Series: Magnum P.I. (Emmy Award, 1984; also Golden Globe & People's Choice Awards). Movies: Most Wanted, Superdome, Returning Home, The Sacketts, The Concrete Cowboys, Divorce Wars, Louis L'Amour's The Shadow Riders, Broken Trust, Ruby Jean and Joe. Exec. prod.: Magnum P.I. (series), Revealing Evidence, The Silver Fox. Guest: The Young and the Restless, The Rockford Files, Friends

SELTZER, DAVID
Writer, Director. b. Highland Park, IL, 1940. m. flutist Eugenia Zukerman. e. Northwestern U. School for Film and Television. Moved to NY where worked on TV game show I've Got a Secret. Made short My Trip to New York. 1966 moved to LA to write for David Wolper's Incredible World of Animals. Then dir. and prod. Wolper documentaries. Worked as ghostwriter on film Willy Wonka and the Chocolate Factory.
PICTURES: Writer: The Hellstrom Chronicle, One Is a Lonely Number, The Omen, Damien: The Omen Part II, The Other Side of the Mountain, Six Weeks, Table for Five, Lucas (also dir.), Punchline (also dir.), Bird on a Wire, Shining Through (also dir., co-exec. prod.).
TELEVISION: National Geographic Specials (prod., dir., writer), William Holden in Unconquered Worlds (prod., dir., writer), The Underworld World of Jacques Cousteau. Movies (writer): The Story of Eric, Green Eyes, My Father's House, Larry.

SELTZER, WALTER
Executive. b. Philadelphia, PA, Nov. 7, 1914. e. U. of PA. Publicity Asst. for Warner Bros. Theatres, Philadelphia; Fox West Coast Theatres; with MGM 1936-39; Warner Bros., 1939-40; Columbia, 1940-41. Enlisted U.S. Marine Corp., 1941-44. Publ. dir., Hal Wallis, 1945-54; v.p. in chg. adv & pub., Hecht-Lancaster Orgn., 1954-56; assoc. prod., The Boss; partner, Glass-Seltzer, pub. rel. firm; v.p. & exec. prod, Pennebaker Production; 1982, v.p., M.P. & TV Fund; pres., WSP Inc. Bd. of trustees, v.p. 1980-87 of Motion Picture and TV Fund.
PICTURES: One-Eyed Jacks, Shake Hands With the Devil, Paris Blues, The Naked Edge, Man in the Middle, Wild Seed, War Lord, Beau Geste, Will Penny, Number One, Darker Than Amber, The Omega Man, Skyjacked, Soylent Green, The Cay, The Last Hard Men.

SEMEL, TERRY
Executive. b. New York, NY, Feb. 24, 1943. e. Long Island Univ., B.S. Accounting 1964. Warner Bros. sales trainee 1966. Branch mgr., Cleveland, Los Angeles. V.P. Domestic sls. mgr. for CBS, 1971-73. Buena Vista as v.p., gen. sls. mgr., 1973-5. 1975 went to Warner Bros. as pres. domestic sls. 1978 named exec. v.p. and COO WB Inc. Named pres., Warner Bros. & COO, 1980. Named Pioneer of the Year by Foundation of Motion Picture Pioneers, 1990.

SEMLER, DEAN
Cinematographer. b. Australia. Served as 2nd unit dir. and cameraman on the mini-series Lonesome Dove, Son of the Morningstar.
PICTURES: The Earthling, The Coca Cola Kid, The Road Warrior, Kitty and the Bagman, Razorback, Mad Max Beyond Thunderdome, The Coca-Cola Kid, Going Sane, The Lighthorsemen, Cocktail, Young Guns, Farewell to the King, K-9, Dead Calm, Impulse, Young Guns II, Dances With Wolves (Academy Award, 1990), City Slickers, The Power of One, Super Mario Bros., Last Action Hero, The Three Musketeers, The Cowboy Way, Waterworld.

SEMPLE, LORENZO, JR.
Writer.
THEATER: The Golden Fleecing (filmed as The Honeymoon Machine).
PICTURES: Fathom, Pretty Poison, Daddy's Gone A-Hunting (co-s.p.), The Sporting Club, The Marriage of a Young Stockbroker, Papillon (co-s.p.), Super Cops, The Parallax View (co-s.p.), The Drowning Pool (co-s.p.), Three Days of the Condor (co-s.p.), King Kong, Hurricane (and exec. prod.), Flash Gordon, Never Say Never Again, Sheena (co-s.p.), Never Too Young to Die.
TELEVISION: Series: Batman (1966). Movie: Rearview Mirror.

SENDREY, ALBERT
Music Composer, Arranger, Conductor. b. Chicago, IL, Dec. 26, 1921. e. Trinity Coll. Music, London, USC, Paris, & Leipzig Conservatories. Composer, arr., orch. for many plays, films and TV. On stage was pianist/conductor for Lauritz Melchior, Kathryn Grayson, Ray Bolger, Danny Kaye, Tony Martin, Buddy Ebsen. Numerous B'way productions, including Mary Martin's Peter Pan, Ginger Roger's Pink Jungle and Yul Brynner's Penelope.

PICTURES: *Orchestrations*: The Yearling, Three Musketeers, Father's Little Dividend, Duchess of Idaho, Royal Wedding, Easy to Love, Great Caruso, An American in Paris, Brigadoon, Guys and Dolls, Meet Me in Las Vegas, High Society, Raintree County, Ride the High Country, Hallelujah Trail, The Hook, The Comancheros, Nevada Smith, The Oscar, Thoroughly Modern Millie, Hello Down There, Private Navy of Sgt. O'Farrell, Bad Day at Black Rock (with Andre Previn), Undercurrent, Sea of GRass (with H. Stothart).
TELEVISION: *Comp. music*: Laramie, Wagon Train, Ben Casey, Wolper Documentaries, Americans Abroad, J. F. Kennedy Anthology, Young Man from Boston, High Chaparral, The Monroes, Ken Murray's Hollywood.

SERGENT, HERB
Executive. Pres., Writer Guild of America East, Inc.

SERNA, ASSUMPTA
Actress. b. Barcelona, Spain, Sept. 16, 1957. Abandoned plans to be a lawyer, making stage debut 1978 with anti-Franco theatre company.
PICTURES: Sweet Hours (debut, 1980), The Hunting Ground, Crime of Cuenca, Revolt of the Birds, Circle of Passions, Tin Soldier, Secret Garden, Extramuros, The Old Music, Lola, Matador, Ballad of Dogs, Lucky Ravi, La Brute, La Nuite de L'Ocean, What Belongs to Caesar, Neon Man, Wild Orchid, I the Worst of All, Rossini Rossini, Adelaide, Chain of Desire, Cracked Nut, Fencing Master, Green Henry, Nostradamus, Shortcut to Paradise, Belle al Bar, The Shooter.
TELEVISION: Valentina, First Brigade, Falcon Crest, Fur Elise, Drug Wars, Revolver, Sharpe, Day of Reckoning, Les Derniers Jours de la Victime.

SEYMOUR, JANE
Actress. r.n. Joyce Frankenberg. b. Hillingdon, England, Feb. 15, 1951. Dancer with London Festival Ballet at 13. On B'way in Amadeus (1980). British Repetory including Canterbury, Harrogate, Sussex, Windsor.
PICTURES: Oh! What a Lovely War (debut, 1968), The Only Way, Young Winston, Live and Let Die, Sinbad and the Eye of the Tiger, Battlestar Galactica, Oh Heavenly Dog, Somewhere in Time, Lassiter, Head Office, The Tunnel, The French Revolution, Keys to Freedom.
TELEVISION: *Series*: The Onedine Line, Dr. Quinn: Medicine Woman (Golden Globe, 1996). *Movies/Mini-Series*: Frankenstein: The True Story, Captains and the Kings, Benny and Barney: Las Vegas Undercover, Seventh Avenue, Killer on Board, The Four Feathers, The Awakening Land, Love's Dark Ride, Dallas Cowboys Cheerleaders, Our Mutual Friend, East of Eden, The Scarlet Pimpernal, Phantom of the Opera, The Haunting Passion, Dark Mirror, The Sun Also Rises, Obsessed with a Married Woman, Jamaica Inn, Crossings, War and Remembrance, The Woman He Loved, Onassis: The Richest Man in the World (Emmy Award, 1988), Jack the Ripper, Angel of Death, I Remember You, Memories of Midnight, Are You Lonesome Tonight?, Matters of the Heart, Sunstroke (also exec. prod.), Heidi, Praying Mantis (also co-exec. prod.), A Passion for Justice: The Hazel Brannon Smith Story (also co-exec. prod.). *Host*: The Heart of Healing.

SHABER, DAVID
Screenwriter. b. Cleveland, OH. e. Western Reserve U., Yale U., Taught at Allegheny Coll. and Smith Coll. in speech and drama dept. Prof. of screenwriting Columbia Univ. Film School. Contributor to Cosmopolitan, Life, Esquire; had several short stories in O'Henry prize collections. Also wrote dramas (Shake Hands with the Clown, The Youngest Shall Ask, Bunker Reveries, etc.). First screenplay was Such Good Friends for Otto Preminger.
PICTURES: The Last Embrace, The Warriors, Those Lips, Those Eyes, Night Hawks, Rollover, The Hunt for Red October (uncredited), Flight of the Intruder.

SHAFER, MARTIN
Executive. Pres., Castle Rock Pictures, a division of Castle Rock Entertainment.

SHAGAN, STEVE
Writer. b. New York, NY. Oct. 25, 1927. Apprenticed in little theatres, film lab chores, stagehand jobs. Wrote, produced and directed film short, One Every Second; moved to Hollywood in 1959. Was IATSE technician, working as grip, stagehand, electrician to support film writing. Also did freelance advertising and publicity; produced Tarzan TV show. In 1968 began writing and producing two-hour films for TV.
AUTHOR: Save the Tiger, City of Angels, The Formula, The Circle, The Discovery, Vendetta, Pillars of Fire, A Cast of Thousands.
PICTURES: *Writer*: Save the Tiger (also prod.; Acad. Award nom., WGA Award, 1973), W.W. and the Dixie Dancekings (exec. prod.), Hustle, Voyage of the Damned (co.-s.p.; Acad. Award nom.), Nightwing (co-s.p.), The Formula (also prod.), The Sicilian, Primal Fear (co-s.p.).

TELEVISION: *Writer-producer*: River of Mystery, Spanish Portrait, Sole Survivor, A Step Out of Line, House on Garibaldi Street (exec. prod.), John Gotti.

SHAIMAN, MARC
Composer, Arranger. b. Newark, NJ, Oct. 22, 1959. Moved to NY at 16 where he met Bette Milder; was arranger and lyricists for her stage shows and the album Thighs & Whispers. Wrote music for Saturday Night Live, musical material for Billy Crytsal for the Academy Awards. Prod. and arranger for several Harry Connick, Jr. albums. Appeared on stage in Harlem Nocturne.
PICTURES: Divine Madness (music dir., arranger), The Cotton Club (music sprv., arranger), Broadcast News (cameo), Big Business (music sprv., arranger), Beaches (arranger), When Harry Met Sally... (music sprv.), Misery (music), Scenes From a Mall (music, adapt., cameo), City Slickers (music), Hot Shots (cameo), For the Boys (music sprv., arranger, co-composer), The Addams Family (music, cameo, co-wrote song "Mamuschka"), Sister Act (music, adapt.), Mr. Saturday Night (music, cameo), A Few Good Men (music), Life With Mikey (music sprv.), Sleepless in Seattle (musical sprv., co-wrote song "With a Wink and a Smile"), Hocus Pocus (music prod.), Heart and Souls (music, cameo), For Love or Money (co-composer), Addams Family Values (music), Sister Act 2: Back in the Habit (music, adaptations), That's Entertainment III (music sprv.), City Slickers II: The Legend of Curly's Gold (music), North (music, cameo), Speechless, Stuart Saves His Family, Forget Paris.

SHALIT, GENE
Critic. b. New York, NY, 1932. e. U. of Illinois. Started as freelance writer; joined NBC Radio Network, working on Monitor, 1968. Has been book and film critic, sports and general columnist. Since 1973 has been featured regular on NBC Today Show. Edits newsletter Shalit's Sampler.

SHANDLING, GARRY
Actor, Comedian, Writer, Producer. b. Chicago, IL, Nov. 29, 1949. e. Univ. of AZ. Moved to LA where he became writer for such sitcoms as Sandford & Son, Welcome Back Kotter, Three's Company. Became stand-up comedian in nightclubs which led to appearances on The Tonight Show.
PICTURES: The Night We Never Met (debut, 1993), Love Affair, Mixed Nuts.
TELEVISION: *Series*: It's Garry Shandling's Show (also exec. prod., writer; ACE Awards for Best Series & Actor), The Larry Sanders Show (also co-exec. prod., co-creator, co-writer). *Specials*: Garry Shandling—Alone in Las Vegas (also writer, prod.), It's Garry Shandling's Show—25th Anniversary Special (also exec. prod., writer), Grammy Awards (host), Garry Shandling: Stand-Up (also writer). Guest: Tonight Show (also frequent guest host), Late Night With David Letterman.

SHANLEY, JOHN PATRICK
Writer, Director. b. New York, NY, 1950. e. NYU. Cameo appearance in 1988 film Crossing Delancey. Dir. and wrote short I am Angry.
THEATER: *Writer*: Rockaway, Welcome to the Moon, Danny and the Deep Blue Sea, Savage in Limbo, Dreamer Examines His Pillow. *Writer-Dir.*: Italian-American Reconciliation, Beggars in the House of Plenty, Four Dogs and a Bone.
PICTURES: *Writer*: Moonstruck (Academy Award & Writers Guild Award, 1987), Five Corners (also assoc. prod.), The January Man, Joe Versus the Volcano (also dir.), Alive, We're Back!, Congo.

SHAPIRO, ROBERT W.
Producer. b. Brooklyn, NY, March 1, 1938. e. USC. Joined William Morris Agency, Inc., 1958; dir. and head of motion picture dept., William Morris Agency (UK) Ltd., 1969; mng. dir., 1970; 1974 v.p., head int'l. m.p. dept.; 1977 joined Warner Bros. as exec. v.p. in chg. of worldwide production; 1981, named WB pres., theatrical production div. Resigned 1983 to produce films.
PICTURES: Pee-Wee's Big Adventure, Empire of the Sun (exec. prod.), Arthur 2 On the Rocks, There Goes My Baby, Dr. Jekyll and Ms. Hyde.
TELEVISION: *Movie*: The Summer My Father Grew Up.

SHARE, MICHAEL
Executive. Began career with Paramount Pictures 1974 as booker in Indianapolis; 1975-76 appt. salesman; 1976-77 sls. mgr. in Philadelphia; 1977, Cincinnati branch mgr.; 1980, Chicago branch mgr.; 1985, promoted to v.p., eastern div., Paramount.

SHARIF, OMAR
Actor. r.n. Michel Shahoub. b. Alexandria, Egypt, April 10, 1932. e. Victoria Coll., Cairo.; pres. of College Dramatic Society. Starred in 21 Egyptian (billed as Omar el Cherif or Omar Cherif) and two French films prior to English-language debut in Lawrence of Arabia. Left Egypt 1964. Champion contract bridge player. 1983 made rare stage appearance in The Sleeping Prince (Chichester, then West End).

PICTURES: The Blazing Sun (debut, 1954), Our Happy Days, La Chatelane du Liban, Goha, The Mameluks, Lawrence of Arabia (Acad. Award nom.), The Fall of the Roman Empire, Behold a Pale Horse, Marco the Magnificent, Genghis Khan, The Yellow Rolls-Royce, Doctor Zhivago, The Poppy Is Also a Flower, The Night of the Generals, More Than a Miracle, Funny Girl, Mackenna's Gold, The Appointment, Mayerling, Che!, The Last Valley, The Horsemen, The Burglars, The Right to Love (Brainwashed), The Tamarind Seed, The Mysterious Island of Captain Nemo, Juggernaut, Funny Lady, Crime and Passion, The Pink Panther Strikes Again (cameo), Ashanti, Bloodline, The Baltimore Bullet, Oh Heavenly Dog, Green Ice, Chanel Solitaire, Top Secret!, The Possessed, Paradise Calling, The Blue Pyramids, Keys to Freedom, Novice, Mountains of the Moon, Michelangelo and Me, Drums of Fire, Le Guignol, The Puppet, The Rainbow Thief, Journey of Love, Mother, 588 Rue Paradis.
TELEVISION: S*H*E, Pleasure Palace, The Far Pavilions, Peter the Great, Harem, Anastasia, Grand Larceny, Omar Sharif Returns to Egypt, The Mysteries of the Pyramids Live (host), Memories of Midnight, Mrs. 'arris Goes to Paris, Lie Down with Lions.

SHARP, ALAN
Writer. b. Glasgow, Scotland.
PICTURES: The Hired Hand, Ulzana's Raid, Billy Two Hats, Night Moves, The Osterman Weekend, Little Treasure (also dir.), Freeway, Cat Chaser (co-s.p.).
TELEVISION: Coming Out of the Ice.

SHATNER, WILLIAM
Actor. b. Montreal, Quebec, Mar. 22, 1931. e. McGill U. Toured Canada in various stock, repertory companies before U.S. tv debut in 1956. Author: TekWar, TekLords, TekLab, Tek Vengeance, TekSecret, Believe, Star Trek Memories (co-author with Chris Kreski), Star Trek Movie Memories (co-author with Kreski), The Return, Man O'War.
THEATER: NY: Tamburlaine the Great, The World of Susie Wong (Theatre World Award), A Shot in the Dark, L'Idiote.
PICTURES: The Brothers Karamazov (debut, 1958), Judgment at Nuremberg, The Explosive Generation, The Intruder, The Outrage, Incubus, White Comanche, Impulse, Big Bad Mama, The Devil's Rain, Kingdom of the Spiders, Land of No Return, Star Trek—The Motion Picture, The Kidnapping of the President, Visiting Hours, Star Trek II: The Wrath of Khan, Airplane II: The Sequel, Star Trek III: The Search for Spock, Star Trek IV: The Voyage Home, Star Trek V: The Final Frontier (also dir., orig. story), Bill & Ted's Bogus Journey (cameo), Star Trek VI: The Undiscovered Country, National Lampoon's Loaded Weapon 1, Star Trek: Generations.
TELEVISION: Series: For the People, Star Trek, Barbary Coast, T.J. Hooker, Rescue 911 (host), TekWar: The Series (also dir., co-exec. prod.). Movies: Sole Survivor, Vanished, Owen Marshall: Counselor at Law (pilot), The People, The Hound of the Baskervilles, Incident on a Dark Street, Go Ask Alice, The Horror at 37000 Feet, Pioneer Woman, Indict and Convict, Pray for the Wildcats, Barbary Coast (pilot), Perilous Voyage, The Bastard, Little Women, Crash, Disaster on the Coastliner, The Baby Sitter, Secrets of a Married Man, North Beach and Rawhide, Broken Angel, Family of Strangers, Columbo: Butterfly in Shades of Grey, TekWar (also dir., co-exec. prod.), TekLab, TekWar: TekJustice, Janek: A Silent Betrayal. Special: The Andersonville Trial, TekPower, TekMoney, Ashes of Money. Mini-Series: Testimony of Two Men.

SHAVELSON, MELVILLE
Writer, Director. b. Brooklyn, NY, April 1, 1917. e. Cornell U., 1937, A.B. Radio writer: We The People, Bicycle Party, 1937, Bob Hope Show, 1938-43, then screen writer; apptd. prod., Warner Bros, 1951. Conceived for TV: Make Room for Daddy, My World and Welcome To It. Author: book, How To Make a Jewish Movie, Lualda, The Great Houdinis, The Eleventh Commandment, Ike, Don't Shoot It's Only Me. Pres., Writers Guild of America, West, 1969-71, 1979-81, 1985-87; Pres., Writers Guild Foundation 1978-96.
PICTURES: Writer: The Princess and the Pirate, Wonder Man, The Kid From Brooklyn, Sorrowful Jones, It's a Great Feeling, The Daughter of Rosie O'Grady, Always Leave Them Laughing, Where There's Life, On Moonlight Bay, Double Dynamite, I'll See You in My Dreams, Room for One More (The Easy Way), April in Paris, Trouble Along the Way, Living It Up. Director-Writer: The Seven Little Foys (dir. debut, 1955), Beau James, Houseboat, It Started in Naples, The Five Pennies, On the Double, The Pigeon That Took Rome (also prod.), A New Kind of Love (also prod.), Cast a Giant Shadow (also prod.), Yours Mine and Ours, The War Between Men and Women, Mixed Company.
TELEVISION: Movies: The Legend of Valentino, The Great Houdinis, Ike, The Other Woman, Deceptions. Specials: Academy Awards, 1988, 1990 (writer).

SHAVER, HELEN
Actress. b. St. Thomas, Ontario, Canada, Feb. 24, 1951. e. Banff Sch. of Fine Arts, Alberta. Worked on stage and screen in Canada before coming to Los Angeles 1978.
THEATER: Tamara, Are You Lookin'? Ghost on Fire, A Doll's House, The Master Builder, The Hostage, Jake's Women (B'way debut; Theatre World Award).
PICTURES: Christina, Shoot, Starship Invasions, Outrageous!, High-Ballin', The Amityville Horror, In Praise of Older Women, Who Has Seen the Wind, Gas, Harry Tracy, The Osterman Weekend, Best Defense, Desert Hearts, The Color of Money, The Believers, The Land Before Time (voice), Walking After Midnight, Innocent Victim (Tree of Hands), Zebrahead, That Night, Dr. Bethune, Morning Glory, Change of Heart, Open Season, Born to Be Wild.
TELEVISION: Series: United States, Jessica Novak, WIOU. Movies: Lovey: Circle of Children II, Between Two Brothers, Many Happy Returns, The Park is Mine, Countdown To Looking Glass, No Blame, B.L. Stryker: The Dancer's Touch, Pair of Aces, Columbo: Rest in Peace Mrs. Columbo, Survive the Night, Poisoned By Love: The Kern County Murders, Trial & Error, The Forget-Me-Not Murders, Ride With the Wind, Without Consent, Janek: A Silent Betrayal. Guest: Ray Bradbury Theatre, Amazing Stories.

SHAW, MICHAEL M. (JOHN)
Executive. b. Ashland, KY, Jan. 10, 1945. e. Eastern KY Univ., Univ. of KY, Univ of MS. 1968-69, asst. booker, 20th Century Fox, Denver; 1969, head booker, Fox; 1970, salesman, Paramount Pictures, S.F.; 1970-71, head booker, sales Paramount L.A.; 1971-73, booker, Commonwealth Theatres; 1973, booker, McLendon theatres, Dallas; 1973-78, div. mngr. Mulberry Square Prods.; Dallas; 1978-79, branch mngr. Filmways Pictures, Dallas; 1980-82, owner, Sequoyah Cinema Svc.; Denver; 1983-87, head film buyer, Presidio Theatres, Austin; 1987-88, head film buyer, Santikos Theatres, San Antonio; 1988-present, pres./CEO, Film Bookiung Office Corp., Movieline Int'l, Dallas. Member: Motion Picture Pioneers, Variety Club.

SHAW, STAN
Actor. b. Chicago, IL, July 14, 1952. On stage received NAACP Image Award for West Coast premiere of Home, 1982.
PICTURES: The Bingo Long Travelling All-Stars and Motor Kings, Rocky, The Boys in Company C, The Great Santini, Tough Enough, Runaway, The Monster Squad, Harlem Nights, Fried Green Tomatoes, Body of Evidence, Rising Sun, Houseugest, Cutthroat Island, Daylight.
TELEVISION: Series: The Mississippi. Mini-Series: Roots: The Next Generations. Movies: Call to Glory, Maximum Security, The Gladiator, The Billionaire Boys Club, The Three Kings, The Court-Martial of Jackie Robinson, Lifepod. Guest: Starsky and Hutch, Wiseguy, Murder She Wrote, Hill Street Blues, Matlock.

SHAWN, WALLACE
Playwright, Actor. b. New York, NY, Nov. 12, 1943. Son of former New Yorker editor William Shawn. e. Harvard; Oxford U. Taught English in India on a Fulbright scholarship 1965-66. English, Latin and drama teacher, NY 1968-70.
THEATER: Writer: Our Late Night (1975, Obie Award), The Mandrake (translation, also actor), A Thought in Three Parts, Marie and Bruce, The Hotel Play, Aunt Dan and Lemon (also actor), The Fever (Obie Award, 1991; also actor). Opera: The Music Teacher (with Allen Shawn). Actor: The Master and Margarita, Chinchilla, Wifey.
PICTURES: Manhattan (debut, 1979), Starting Over, All That Jazz, Strong Medicine, Simon, Atlantic City, My Dinner With Andre (also co-s.p.), A Little Sex, Lovesick, The First Time, Deal of the Century, Strange Invaders, Saigon—Year of the Cat, Crackers, The Hotel New Hampshire, The Bostonians, Micki and Maude, Heaven Help Us, Head Office, The Bedroom Window, Radio Days, Prick Up Your Ears, Nice Girls Don't Explode, The Princess Bride, The Moderns, She's Out of Control, Scenes From the Class Struggle in Beverly Hills, We're No Angels, Shadows and Fog, Mom and Dad Save the World, Nickel and Dime, The Cemetery Club, Un-Becoming Age, The Meteor Man, Vanya on 42nd Street, Mrs. Parker and the Vicious Circle, A Goofy Movie (voice), Clueless, Canadian Bacon, Toy Story (voice), The Wife, House Arrest, All Dogs Go to Heaven II (voice).

SHAYE, ROBERT
Executive. b. Detroit, MI, Mar. 4, 1939. e. U. of Michigan, B.B.A.; Columbia U. Law. At 15 wrote, prod. dir. training film for father's supermarket staff. Later won first prize in Society of Cinematologists' Rosenthal Competition (best m.p. by American dir. under 25). Wrote, prod., dir., edited short films, trailers and TV commercials, including award-winning shorts, Image and On Fighting Witches (prod., dir.). Founded New Line Cinema 1967. Chmn. & CEO, New Line Cinema.
PICTURES: Prod./exec. prod.: Stunts, XTRO, Alone in the Dark, The First Time, Polyester, Critters, Quiet Cool, My Demon Lover, A Nightmare on Elm Street (also parts

2,3,4,5,6), The Hidden, Stranded, Critters 2, Hairspray, Heart Condition, Book of Love (dir.), Wes Craven's New Nightmare (also actor).
TELEVISION: Freddy's Nightmare: the Series (exec. prod.).

SHEA, JOHN
Actor. b. Conway, NH, April 14, 1949. Raised in MA. e. Bates Coll., ME, B.A. 1970; Yale Drama School, M.F.A. 1973. Worked as asst. dir. Chelsea Theater; taught part-time at Pratt Inst.
THEATER: Yentl (debut 1975, Off-B'way and B'way; Theatre World Award), Sorrows of Stephen, Long Day's Journey Into Night (Joseph Jefferson Award nom.), The Master and Margarita, Romeo and Juliet (Circle in the Sq.), American Days (Drama Desk Award), The Dining Room, End of the World (B'way), The Normal Heart (London, 1987), Animal Kingdom, Rosmersholm (La Mama), Impossible Spy (China's Golden Panda Award).
PICTURES: Hussy, Missing, Windy City (Best Actor Montreal Film Festival), A New Life, Unsettled Land, Honeymoon, Stealing Home, Freejack, Honey I Blew Up the Kid, A Weekend in the Country.
TELEVISION: Series: WIOU, Lois and Clark. Movies: The Nativity, Family Reunion, Coast to Coast (BBC), Hitler's S.S.: Portrait in Evil, A Case of Deadly Force, The Impossible Spy, Magic Moments, Baby M (Emmy Award), Do You Know the Muffin Man, Small Sacrifices, Notorious, Ladykiller, Justice in a Small Town, See Jane Run, Forgotten Sins. Mini-Series: The Last Convertible, Kennedy. Special: Leslie's Folly.

SHEAFF, DONALD J.
Executive. b. Oct. 23, 1925. e. U.of California at L.A., 1948; Pierce Coll., 1957. Served 4 yrs. during W.W.II in Navy Air Corps in South Pacific. 1946, joined Technicolor Motion Picture Div. in supervisory capacity; 1957, lab. supervisor, Lookout Mountain Air Force Station, handling Top Secret film for Air Force and Atomic Energy Commission; est. and org. the installation of Vandenberg Air Force Base Lab. facilities, which Technicolor designed; 1961 joined Panacolor Corp.; 1963, joined Pacific Title and Art Studio in charge of color control for special effects and titles; returned to Technicolor Corp. app't. Plant Mgr. of TV div., 1966; v.p. & gen. mngr. of the TV div., 1973; appt v.p. & gen. mgr., Motion Picture Division, 1976; mgr., special visual effects, Universal City Studios. Member: SMPTE, Nat'l Academy of Television Arts & Sciences. Has conducted scientific seminars for SMPTE.

SHEARER, HARRY
Writer, Actor. b. Los Angeles, CA, Dec. 23, 1943. e. UCLA (pol. science); grad. work in urban gov., Harvard. At 7 appeared on The Jack Benny Show. Worked as freelance journalist for Newsweek, L.A. Times and publ. articles in New West, L.A. Magazine and Film Comment. Also taught h.s. Eng. and social studies and worked in CA State Legislature in Sacramento. Founding mem. The Credibility Gap, co-wrote, co-prod. and performed on comedy group's albums (A Great Gift Idea, The Bronze Age of Radio). Co-wrote, co-prod. Albert Brooks' album A Star is Bought. Performed with group Spinal Tap. Host of Le Show, L.A. radio prog. Writer-cast mem. Saturday Night Live (1979-80 & 1984-85).
THEATER: Accomplice (Pasadena Playhouse).
PICTURES: Actor: Abbott and Costello Go to Mars (debut, as child, 1953), Cracking Up, Real Life (also co-s.p.), Animalympics (voice), The Fish That Saved Pittsburgh, Serial, One-Trick Pony, The Right Stuff, This is Spinal Tap (also co-s.p.), Plain Clothes, My Stepmother is an Alien (voice), Oscar, Pure Luck, Blood & Concrete, The Fisher King, A League of Their Own, Wayne's World 2, I'll Do Anything, Speechless.
TELEVISION: Series: Fernwood 2-Night (creative consultant), The Simpsons (voice), Harry Shearer's News Quiz. Specials: Likely Stories, It's Just TV, Paul Shaffer: Viva Shaf Vegas, Comedy Hour, Portrait of a White Marriage (also dir.), The Magic of Live, Spinal Tap Reunion (also co-writer).

SHEEDY, ALLY
Actress. r.n. Alexandra Sheedy. b. New York, NY, June 13, 1962. e. USC. m. actor David Lansbury. Daughter of literary agent Charlotte Sheedy. As child performed with American Ballet Theatre. At age 12 wrote children's book, She Was Nice to Mice; later wrote pieces for NY Times, Village Voice, Ms. Published book of poetry: Yesterday I Saw the Sun. Began acting in TV commercials at 15. Chicago Theatre in Wrong Turn at Lungfish; NY stage debut in Advice from a Caterpillar.
PICTURES: Bad Boys (debut, 1983), WarGames, Oxford Blues, The Breakfast Club, St. Elmo's Fire, Twice in a Lifetime, Blue City, Short Circuit, Maid to Order, Heart of Dixie, Betsy's Wedding, Only the Lonely, Home Alone 2: Lost in New York (cameo), Tattletale, The Pickle, Man's Best Friend, One Night Stand.
TELEVISION: Movies: The Best Little Girl in the World, The Violation of Sarah McDavid, The Day the Loving Stopped, Splendor in the Grass, Deadly Lessons, We Are the Children, Fear, The Lost Capone, Lethal Exposure, Chantilly Lace, Ultimate Betrayal, Parallel Lives, The Haunting of Seacliff Inn, The Tin Soldier. Guest: Hill Street Blues, St. Elsewhere.

SHEEN, CHARLIE
Actor. r.n. Carlos Irwin Estevez. b. Los Angeles, Sept. 3, 1965. Father is actor Martin Sheen. Brother of actors Emilio, Ramon and Renee Estevez. Made debut as extra in TV movie, The Execution of Private Slovik (starring father) and as extra in Apocalypse Now (also starring father).
PICTURES: Grizzly II—The Predator, Red Dawn, The Boys Next Door, Lucas, Ferris Bueller's Day Off, The Wraith, Platoon, Wisdom, Three for the Road, No Man's Land, Wall Street, Never on Tuesday, Young Guns, Eight Men Out, Major League, Beverly Hills Brats, Courage Mountain, Navy Seals, Men at Work, The Rookie, Cadence, Hot Shots!, National Lampoon's Loaded Weapon 1 (cameo), Hot Shots Part Deux!, DeadFall, The Three Musketeers, The Chase (also co-exec. prod.), Major League 2, Beyond the Law, Terminal Velocity, The Shadow Conspiracy, All Dogs Go to Heaven II (voice), The Arrival.
TELEVISION: Movies: Silence of the Heart, Backtrack.

SHEEN, MARTIN
Actor. r.n. Ramon Estevez. b. Dayton, OH, Aug. 3, 1940. Father of actors Emilio Estevez, Charlie Sheen, Ramon Estevez and Renee Estevez. Wrote play (as Ramon G. Estevez) Down the Morning Line (prod. Public Theatre, 1969). Emmy Award as dir., exec. prod. Babies Having Babies (1986).
THEATER: The Connection (debut, 1959 with the Living Theater), Women of Trachis, Many Loves, In the Jungle of Cities, Never Live Over a Pretzel Factory, The Subject Was Roses, The Wicked Crooks, Hamlet, Romeo and Juliet, Hello Goodbye, The Happiness Cage, Death of a Salesman (with George C. Scott), Julius Caesar, The Crucible.
PICTURES: The Incident (debut, 1967), The Subject Was Roses, Catch-22, No Drums No Bugles, Rage, Pickup on 101, Badlands, The Legend of Earl Durrand, The Cassandra Crossing, The Little Girl Who Lives Down the Lane, Apocalypse Now, Eagle's Wing, The Final Countdown, Loophole, Gandhi, That Championship Season, Enigma, Man Woman and Child, The Dead Zone, Firestarter, The Believers, Siesta, Wall Street, Walking After Midnight, Da (also co-exec. prod.), Judgment in Berlin (also exec. prod.), Beverly Hills Brats, Cold Front, Beyond the Stars, The Maid, Cadence (also dir.), JFK (narrator), Hear No Evil, Hot Shots Part Deux (cameo), Gettysburg, Trigger Fast, Hits!, Fortunes of War, Sacred Cargo, The Break, Dillinger & Capone, Captain Nuke and the Bomber Boys, Ghost Brigade, The Cradle Will Rock, Dead Presidents, Dorothy Day, Gospa, The American President, The War At Home.
TELEVISION: Series: As the World Turns. Movies: Then Came Bronson, Mongo's Back in Town, Welcome Home Johnny Bristol, That Certain Summer, Letters for Three Lovers, Pursuit, Catholics, Message to My Daughter, The Execution of Private Slovik, The California Kid, The Missiles of October, The Story of Pretty Boy Floyd, Sweet Hostage, The Guardian, The Last Survivors, Blind Ambition, The Long Road Home (Emmy Award, 1981), In the Custody of Strangers, Choices of the Heart, The Atlanta Child Murders, Consenting Adult, Shattered Spirits, News at Eleven, Out of the Darkness, Samaritan, Conspiracy: The Trial of the Chicago 8, No Means No (exec. prod. only), Nightbreaker (also exec. prod.), Guilty Until Proven Innocent, The Water Engine (voice), The Last P.O.W.?: The Bobby Garwood Story, A Matter of Justice, One of Her Own, Roswell. Mini-Series: Kennedy, Queen. Guest: Tales From the Crypt, Murphy Brown (Emmy Award, 1994). Narrator: Eyewitness (PBS).

SHEFFER, CRAIG
Actor. b. York, PA, 1960. e. East Stroudsberg Univ., PA. Started career in tv commercials; in soap operas One Life to Live. On NY stage in Fresh Horses, G.R. Point, Torch Song Trilogy (B'way & Off-B'way). Starred in IMAX film Wings of Courage.
PICTURES: That Was Then This Is Now (debut, 1985), Fire with Fire, Some Kind of Wonderful, Voyage of the Rock Aliens, Split Decisions, Nightbreed, Instant Karma (also exec. prod.), Blue Desert, Eye of the Storm, A River Runs Through It, Fire in the Sky, The Program, Sleep With Me, Roadflower, The Grave, Head Above Water.
TELEVISION: Series: The Hamptons. Movies: Babycakes, In Pursuit of Honor, The Desperate Trail.

SHEFFIELD, JOHN
Actor. b. Pasadena, CA, April 11, 1931. e. UCLA. Stage debut at 7 in On Borrowed Time. Created screen role of Tarzan's son in Tarzan Finds a Son, followed by 7 other entries in Tarzan series, and role of Bomba in Bomba series.
PICTURES: Babes in Arms, Tarzan Finds a Son, Lucky Cisco Kid, Little Orvie, Knute Rockne—All-American, Million Dollar Baby, Tarzan's Secret Treasure, Tarzan's New York Adventure, Tarzan Triumphs, Tarzan's Desert Mystery, Tarzan and the Amazons, Tarzan and the Leopard Woman, Tarzan and the Huntress, Roughly Speaking, Bomba the Jungle Boy, Bomba on Panther Island, Lost Volcano, Bomba and the Hidden City,

The Lion Huntress, Bomba and the Elephant Stampede, African Treasure, Bomba and the Jungle Girl, Safari Drums, The Golden Idol, Killer Leopard, Lord of the Jungle.
TELEVISION: *Series*: Bantu the Zebra Boy.

SHEINBERG, SIDNEY JAY
Executive. b. Corpus Christi, TX, Jan. 14, 1935. e. Columbia Coll., A.B. 1955; LL.B., 1958. Admitted to Calif. bar, 1958; assoc. in law U. of California Sch. of Law, Los Angeles, 1958-59; joined MCA, Inc, 1959; pres., TV div., 1971-74; exec. v.p., parent co., 1969-73. Named MCA pres. & chief oper. off., 1973. Resigned from position 1995 to form company The Bubble Factory to produce films for MCA.

SHELDON, DAVID
Producer, Director, Writer. b. New York, NY. e. Yale U. Sch. of Drama, M.F.A.; Principia Coll., B.A.; Actors Studio, directors unit. 1972-74 was exec. at American Int'l Pictures supervising development and production of 18 films include: Futureworld, Walking Tall, Dillinger, Sisters, Macon County Line, Reincarnation of Peter Proud, Slaughter, Dr. Phibes. *Prod./Dir.*, The Gateway Playhouse in NY where dir. over 50 plays and musicals. Started the Sheldon/Post Company in 1991 with Ira Post. *Exec. prod./writer* of Secret of a Small Town. Currently working with Orion on three tv series; with Kushner-Locke and the Larry Thompson Organization on movies; and with Merv Griffin Ent.
PICTURES: *Producer-Writer*: Grizzly, Sheba Baby, The Evil, Project: Kill. *Producer*: Just Before Dawn, Abby, Day of the Animals, The Manitou. *Director*: Lovely But Deadly. *Writer*: The Predator.

SHELDON, JAMES
Director. r.n. Schleifer. b. New York, NY. Nov. 12. e. U. of NC. Page boy, NBC; announcer-writer-dir., NBC Internat'l Div.; staff dir., ABC radio; staff prod. dir., Young & Rubicam; free lance prod. dir. of many programs live tape and film, N.Y. and Hollywood.
TELEVISION: *Series* (prod./ dir.): Mr. Peepers, Armstrong Circle Theatre, Robert Montgomery Presents, Schlitz Playhouse, West Point, Zane Grey Theatre, The Millionaire, Desilu Playhouse, Perry Mason, Twilight Zone, Route 66, Naked City, The Virginian, Alfred Hitchcock Presents, Fugitive, Espionage, Defenders, Nurses, Bing Crosby Show, Family Affair, Wonderful World of Disney, Man From UNCLE, Felony Squad, That Girl, Ironside, My World and Welcome To It, To Rome With Love, Owen Marshall, Room 222, Apple's Way, Love American Style, McMillan and Wife, Sanford and Son, Ellery Queen, Rich Man, Poor Man II, Family, MASH, Switch, Loveboat, Sheriff Lobo, Knots Landing, The Waltons, 240-Robert, Nurse, Dukes of Hazard, Todays F.B.I., McLain's Law, 7 Brides for 7 Brothers, Lottery, Partners in Crime, Jessie, Santa Barbara, Half Nelson, Stir Crazy, The Equalizer, Sledge Hammer, Cagney & Lacey. *Movies*: Gidget Grows Up, With This Ring, The Gossip Columnist.

SHELDON, SIDNEY
Writer, Director, Producer, Novelist. b. Chicago, IL, Feb. 11, 1917. e. Northwestern U.
AUTHOR: The Naked Face, The Other Side of Midnight, A Stranger in the Mirror, Bloodline, Rage of Angels, Master of the Game, If Tomorrow Comes, Windmills of the Gods, The Sands of Time, Memories of Midnight, The Doomsday Conspiracy, The Stars Shine Down, Nothing Lasts Forever, Morning Noon & Night.
THEATER: Redhead (Tony Award, 1959). Alice in Arms, Jackpot, Dream With Music, Merry Widow (revision), Roman Candle.
PICTURES: *Writer*: The Bachelor and the Bobbysoxer (Academy Award, 1947), Easter Parade, Annie Get Your Gun, Three Guys Named Mike, Dream Wife (also dir.), Remains to Be Seen, You're Never Too Young, Pardners, The Buster Keaton Story (also prod., dir.), The Birds and the Bees, Gambling Daughters, Dangerous Lady, Bill Rose's Jumbo. *Novels made into films*: The Naked Face, The Other Side of Midnight, Bloodline.
TELEVISION: *Series*: Patty Duke Show (creator), I Dream of Jeannie (creator, prod.), Nancy (creator, prod.), Hart to Hart (creator). *Novels made into Mini-Series/Movies*: Rage of Angels, Master of the Game, Windmills of the Gods, If Tomorrow Comes, Memories of Midnight, The Sands of Time, Stranger in the Mirror, Nothing Lasts Forever.

SHELLEY, CAROLE
Actress. b. London, England, Aug. 16, 1939. e. Arts Educational Sch., RADA.
THEATER: *NY*: The Odd Couple (debut, 1965), The Astrakhan Coat, Loot, Sweet Potato, Little Murders, Hay Fever, Absurd Person Singular (Tony nom.), The Norman Conquests, The Elephant Man (Tony Award, 1979), Twelve Dreams (Obie Award), The Misanthrope, Noises Off, Stepping Out (Tony nom.), What the Butler Saw, The Miser, Maggie and Misha, The Destiny of Me, Later Life, London Suite, Show Boat.

London: Simon and Laura (debut, 1955), New Cranks, Boeing-Boeing, Mary Mary, Lettice and Lovage. Also appearances with Shaw Festival, Stratford Fest., Amer. Shakespeare Fest., etc.
PICTURES: Give Us this Day (debut, 1949), Cure for Love, It's Great to Be Young, Carry on Regardless, Carry on Cabby, The Odd Couple, The Boston Strangler, The Aristocats (voice), Robin Hood (voice), The Super, Little Noises, Quiz Show, The Road to Wellville.
TELEVISION: *Series*: The Odd Couple. *Specials*: Coconut Downs, Gabby, A Salute to Noel Coward. *Movie*: Devlin. *Guest*: Brian Rix, Dickie Henderson Show, The Avengers.

SHELTON, RON
Writer, Director, Producer. b. Whittier, CA, Sept. 15, 1945. e. Westmont Coll., Santa Barbara, CA, 1967; U of Arizona, Tucson, AZ, 1974. For 5 years played second base for Baltimore Orioles farm team. Cleaned bars and dressed mannequins to support his art: painting and sculpture. A script he wrote, A Player to Be Named Later (which he later filmed himself as Bull Durham), attracted attention of dir. Roger Spottiswoode who directed his first two scripts.
PICTURES: The Pursuit of D. B. Cooper (assoc. prod.), Open Season (exec. prod.). *Writer*: Under Fire (also 2nd unit dir.), The Best of Times (also 2nd unit dir.), Bull Durham (also dir.), Blaze (also dir.), White Men Can't Jump (also dir.), Blue Chips (also co-exec. prod.), Cobb (also dir.), The Great White Hype (co-s.p.), Tin Cup (also prod., s.p.).

SHENSON, WALTER
Producer. b. San Francisco, CA. e. Stanford U., Calif.; Ent. m.p. ind. 1941; studio exec., writing, prod., prom. shorts, trailers, Columbia; sup. publ., expl., London, Columbia European production, 1955.
PICTURES: *Prod.*: The Mouse That Roared, A Matter of Who, The Mouse on the Moon, A Hard Day's Night, Help!, 30 Is a Dangerous Age Cynthia, Don't Raise the Bridge Lower the River, A Talent for Loving, Welcome to the Club (also dir.), The Chicken Chronicles, Reuben Reuben, Echo Park, Ruby Jean and Joe.

SHEPARD, SAM
Writer, Actor. r.n. Samuel Shepard Rogers. b. Fort Sheridan, IL, Nov. 5, 1943. Raised in California, Montana and South Dakota. Worked as stable hand, sheep shearer, orange picker in CA, a car wrecker in MA and musician with rock group Holy Modal Rounders. Lived near San Francisco, where, in addition to writing, ran a drama workshop at the U. of California at Davis. Recipient of Brandeis U. Creative Arts Citation, 1976, and American Acad. of Arts and Letters Award, 1975.
THEATER: *Playwright*: Icarus' Mother, Red Cross (triple bill— Obie Award, 1966), La Turista (Obie Award, 1967), Forensic and the Navigators, Melodrama Play, Tooth of Crime (Obie Award, 1973), Back Dog Beast Bait, Operation Sidewinder, 4-H Club, The Unseen Hand, Mad Dog Blues, Shaved Splits, Rock Garden, Curse of the Starving Class (Obie Award, 1978), Buried Child (Obie Award & Pulitzer Prize, 1979), True West, Fool For Love, A Lie of the Mind, Simpatico.
PICTURES: *Actor*: Renaldo and Clara (debut, 1978), Days of Heaven, Resurrection, Raggedy Man, Frances, The Right Stuff (Acad. Award nom.), Country, Fool for Love, Crimes of the Heart, Baby Boom, Steel Magnolias, Bright Angel, Defenseless, Voyager, Thunderheart, The Pelican Brief, Safe Passage. *Writer*: Me and My Brother (co-s.p.), Zabriskie Point (co-s.p.), Oh Calcutta! (contributor), Renaldo and Clara (co-s.p.), Paris Texas, Fool for Love, Far North (also dir.), Silent Tongue (also dir.).
TELEVISION: *Special*: Fourteen Hundred Thousand Blue Bitch (BBC). *Movie*: The Good Old Boys.

SHEPHERD, CYBILL
Actress, Singer. b. Memphis, TN, Feb. 18, 1950. e. Hunter Coll., NYU, USC. Was fashion model (won Model of the Year title, 1968) before acting debut in 1971. Debut record album, Cybill Does It... To Cole Porter, 1974, followed by Stan Getz: Mad About the Boy, Vanilla, Somewhere Down the Road.
PICTURES: The Last Picture Show (debut, 1971), The Heartbreak Kid, Daisy Miller, At Long Last Love, Taxi Driver, Special Delivery, Silver Bears, The Lady Vanishes, The Return, Chances Are, Texasville, Alice, Once Upon a Crime, Married to It.
TELEVISION: *Series*: The Yellow Rose, Moonlighting, Cybill (also co-exec. prod.; Golden Globe, 1996). *Movies*: A Guide for the Married Woman, Secrets of a Married Man, Seduced, The Long Hot Summer, Which Way Home, Memphis (also co-writer, co-exec. prod.), Stormy Weathers, Telling Secrets, There Was a Little Boy, Baby Brokers, For the Love of My Daughter, While Justice Sleeps, The Last Word.

SHEPHERD, RICHARD
Producer. b. Kansas City, MO, June 4, 1927. e. Stanford U. In U.S. Naval Reserve, 1944-45. Entered entertainment field as exec. with MCA, 1948, functioning in radio, TV, and m.p. fields

until 1956, with time out for U.S. Army, 1950-52. 1956 became head of talent for Columbia Pictures. 1962 joined CMA talent agency on its founding, becoming exec. v.p. in chg. of m.p. div.; 1972-74, exec. v.p. for prod. Warner Bros.; 1974 became indept. prod.; 1976 named MGM sr. vp. & worldwide head of theatrical prod. 1985 to present, partner in The Artists Agency.
PICTURES: Twelve Angry Men, The Hanging Tree, The Fugitive Kind, Breakfast at Tiffany's, Alex and the Gypsy, Robin and Marian, Volunteers, The Hunger.

SHER, LOUIS K.
Executive. b. Columbus, OH, Feb. 25, 1914. e. Ohio State U., 1933. Exec., Stone's Grills Co., 1934-37; owned & operated, Sher Vending Co., 1937-43. U.S. Army, 1943-46. V.p., Sons Bars & Grills, 1947-54; org. & pres. Art Theatre Guild, 1954; opened art theatres for first time in many cities, org. opera film series, film classic series and similar motion picture activities in many cities; org., Film Festival at Antioch Coll., 1960; pioneer in fighting obscenity laws in Ohio; operates 4 theatres in midwest and western states. Co-producer of the musical broadway production Shenandoah and American Dance Machine. Produced film, Deathmask.

SHERAK, THOMAS
Executive. b. Brooklyn, NY June 22, 1945. e. New York Community Coll., mktg. degree. 1967-69, US Army, Specialist E5 Sgt.; 1970, began career in m.p. industry, Paramount Pictures sls. dept.; 1974, R/C Theatres, booking dept.; 1977, joined General Cinema Theatres as district film buyer; 1978, promoted to v.p., films; 1982, promoted to v.p. head film buyer; 1983, joined 20th Century Fox as pres., domestic dist. & mktg.; 1985, pres., domestic dist.; 1986, president, domestic dist. & marketing. 1990-present, exec. v.p., 20th Century Fox.

SHERIDAN, JAMEY
Actor. b. Pasadena, CA, July 12, 1951. e. Univ. of CA, Santa Barbara.
THEATER: Off-B'way: Just a Little Bit Less Than Normal, The Arbor, One Wedding Two Rooms Three Friends. B'way: The Man Who Came to Dinner, Hamlet, Biloxi Blues, All My Sons (Tony nom.), Long Day's Journey Into Night, Ah Wilderness, The Shadow Box. Regional: Major Barbara, Loose Ends, Deathtrap, Homesteaders.
PICTURES: Jumpin' Jack Flash (debut, 1986), The House on Carroll Street, Distant Thunder, Stanley & Iris, Quick Change, Talent for the Game, All I Want for Christmas, A Stranger Among Us, Whispers in the Dark, White Squall.
TELEVISION: Series: Shannon's Deal, Chicago Hope. Movies: One Police Plaza, Shannon's Deal (pilot), A Mother's Courage: The Mary Thomas Story, Murder in High Places, My Breast, Spring Awakening, Killer Rules. Mini-Series: The Stand. Guest: The Doctors, Another World, St. Elsewhere, Spenser: For Hire, Picket Fences, The Equalizer.

SHERIDAN, JIM
Director, Writer. b. Dublin, Ireland, 1949. e. Univ Col. in Dublin, NYU Inst. of Films & TV. Started as director-writer at Lyric Theatre in Belfast and Abbey Theatre in Dublin; also at Project Arts Theatre (1976-80), NY Irish Arts Center (1982-87) as artistic director. Founded Children's Theatre Company in Dublin.
PICTURES: Dir.-Writer: My Left Foot, The Field, Into the West (s.p. only), In the Name of the Father.
THEATER: Writer: Mobile Homes, Spike in the First World War (Edinburgh Festival Fringe Award for best play, 1983).

SHERIDAN, NICOLLETTE
Actress. b. Worthing, Sussex, England, Nov. 21, 1963. Moved to LA in 1973. Became model in NYC before turning to acting.
PICTURES: The Sure Thing (debut, 1985), Noises Off, Spy Hard.
TELEVISION: Series: Paper Dolls, Knots Landing. Movies: Dark Mansions, Agatha Christie's Dead Man's Folly, Jackie Collins' Lucky/Chances, Deceptions, A Time to Heal, Shadows of Desire, Robin Cook's Virus.

SHERMAN, RICHARD M.
Composer, Lyricist, Screenwriter. b. New York, NY, June 12, 1928. e. Bard Coll., B.A., 1949. Info. & Educ. Br., U.S. Army, 1953-55. Songwriter, composer, Walt Disney Prods 1960-71, then freelance. With partner-brother Robert has won, 9 Acad. Award nom., 2 Grammys, 17 gold and platinum albums, 1st Prize, Moscow Film Fest. (for Tom Sawyer) and a star on Hollywood Walk of Fame. Have written over 500 pub. and recorded songs. Also wrote score for B'way musical Over Here (1974) and songs for Disney Theme Parks.
SONGS: Things I Might Have Been, Tall Paul, Christmas in New Orleans, Mad Passionate Love, Midnight Oil, The Ugly Bug Ball, You're Sixteen, That Darn Cat, The Wonderful Thing About Tiggers, It's a Small World, A Spoonful of Sugar, Supercalifragilistic, Feed the Birds, Let's Go Fly a Kite, Age of Not Believing, When You're Loved, Pineapple Princess, Let's Get Together, Maggie's Theme, Chim Chim Cheree (Academy

Award, 1964), Chitty Chitty Bang Bang, Hushabye Mountain, Winnie the Pooh, Fortuosity, Slipper and the Rose Waltz, many others. Comedy Album: Smash Flops.
PICTURES: Nightmare, The Cruel Tower, The Absent Minded Professor, The Parent Trap, Big Red, In Search of the Castaways, Moon Pilot, Bon Voyage, Legend of Lobo, Summer Magic, Miracle of the White Stallions, The Sword in the Stone, The Misadventures of Merlin Jones, Mary Poppins (2 Academy Awards for song & score, 1964), Those Calloways, The Monkey's Uncle, That Darn Cat, Follow Me Boys!, Winnie the Pooh, Monkeys Go Home!, Chitty Chitty Bang Bang, The Gnome-Mobile, The Jungle Book, The Happiest Millionaire, The One and Only Genuine Original Family Band, The Aristocats, Bedknobs & Broomsticks, Snoopy Come Home, Charlotte's Web, Beverly Hills Cop III, The Mighty Kong. Songs & S.P.: Tom Sawyer, The Slipper and the Rose, The Magic of Lassie, Huckleberry Finn, Little Nemo: Adventures in Slumberland.
TELEVISION: Wonderful World of Color, Bell Telephone Hour, Welcome to Pooh Corner, The Enchanted Musical Playhouse, The Timberwood Tales, Goldilocks, Harry Anderson's Sideshow.

SHERMAN, ROBERT B.
Composer, Lyricist, Screenwriter. b. New York, NY, Dec. 19, 1925. e. Bard Coll., B.A., 1949. U.S. Army, WWII, 1943-45 (purple heart). Songwriter, 1952-60; pres., Music World Corp., 1958; songwriter, composer, Walt Disney, 1971, then freelance. Hon. Phd., Lincoln Col, 1990. With partner-brother Richard Sherman, has won, 9 Acad. Award nom., 2 Grammys, 17 gold and platinum albums, 1st Prize, Moscow Film Fest. (for Tom Sawyer) and a star on Hollywood Walk of Fame. Have written over 500 pub. and recorded songs. Also wrote score for B'way musical Over Here (1974) and songs for Disney Theme Parks. (see Richard M. Sherman for co-writing credits.)

SHERMAN, SAMUEL M.
Producer, Director, Writer. b. New York, NY. e. CCNY, B.A. Entered m.p. ind. as writer, cameraman, film ed., neg. & sound cutter; nat'l mag. ed., Westerns Magazine 1959; pres., Signature Films; prod., dir., TV pilot, The Three Mesquiteers, 1960; prod., Pulse Pounding Perils, 1961; helped create, ed., dir., Screen Thrills Illustrated; exec. prod., Screen Thrills; v.p., Golden Age Films, 1962; prod., Joe Franklin's Silent Screen, 1963; NY rep., Victor Adamson Prods.; NY rep., Tal prods., Hlywd.; adv. & pub. Hemisphere Pictures; prod., writer, Chaplin's Art of Comedy, The Strongman; prod., Hollywood's Greatest Stuntman; story adapt., Fiend With the Electronic Brain; tech. consul., Hal Roach Studios, Music from the Land; 1968, NY rep. East West Pict. of Hollywood. 1968, N.Y. rep., Al Adamson Prods. of Hollywood; Ed.-in-chief, bk., The Strongman; pres., Independent-International Pictures Corp. (and tv div.); pres., Producers Commercial Productions, Inc. Chmn. of Creditors' Committee, Allied Artists Television Corp.; pres., Technovision Inc.; pres., Super Video, Inc.
PICTURES: Assoc. prod.: Horror of the Blood Monsters, Blood of Ghastly Horror. Prod., s.p.: Brain of Blood. Prod. supervisor: Dracula vs. Frankenstein. Exec. prod.: Angels, Wild Women, The Naughty Stewardesses (prod., s.p.), Girls For Rent, The Dynamite Brothers, Blazing Stewardesses (prod., s.p.), Cinderella 2000, Team-Mates (also story), Raiders of the Living Dead (dir., s.p.).

SHERMAN, VINCENT
Director. b. Vienna, GA, July 16, 1906. e. Oglethorpe U. B.A. Writer, actor, dialogue dir., then prod. dir.
PICTURES: The Return of Doctor X (debut, 1939), Saturday's Children, The Man Who Talked Too Much, Underground, Flight from Destiny, The Hard Way, All Through the Night, Old Acquaintance, In Our Time, Mr. Skeffington, Pillow to Post, Janie Gets Married, Nora Prentiss, The Unfaithful, Adventures of Don Juan, The Hasty Heart, The Damned Don't Cry, Harriet Craig, Goodbye My Fancy, Lone Star, Affair in Trinidad, Difendo il mio Amore, The Garment Jungle, The Naked Earth, The Young Philadelphians, Ice Palace, A Fever in the Blood, The Second Time Around, Cervantes (The Young Rebel).
TELEVISION: 35 episodes of Medical Center, Westside Medical, Baretta, Waltons, Doctors Hospital, Trapper John, Movies: The Last Hurrah, Women at West Point, The Yeagers (pilot), Bogey, The Dream Merchants, Trouble in High Timber Country, High Hopes—The Capra Years.

SHERRIN, NED
Producer, Director, Writer. b. Low Ham, Somerset, England, Feb. 18, 1931. Early career writing plays and musical plays. Prod., dir., ATV Birmingham, 1955-57; prod., Midlands Affairs, Paper Talk, etc. Joined BBC-TV 1957 and produced many TV talk programs. Novels: (with Caryl Brahms) Cindy-Ella or I Gotta Shoe (also prod. as stage play), Rappell 1910, Benbow Was His Name.
AUTHOR: Autobiography: A Small Thing Like a Earthquake. Anthology: Cutting Edge Theatrical Anecdotes. 1995, edit. of Oxford Dictionary of Humorous Quotations. Novel: Scratch an Actor. Diaries: Serrin's Year: 1995.

PICTURES: *Prod.*: The Virgin Soldiers (with Leslie Gilliat), Every Home Should Have One, Up Pompeii, Girl Stroke Boy (co-author with Caryl Brahms), Up the Chastity Belt, Rentadick, The Garnet Saga, Up the Front, The National Health, The Cobblers of Umbridge (dir. with Ian Wilson). *Actor*: Orlando.
TELEVISION: *England: Prod.*: Ask Me Another, Henry Hall Show, Laugh Line, Parasol. *Assoc. prod.*: Tonight series, Little Beggars. *Prod., creator. dir.*: Benbow Was His Name (co-author), Take a Sapphire (co-author), The Long Garden Party, The Long Cocktail Party. ABC of Britain revue, Not So Much a Programme—More a Way of Life. Appearances inc.: Your Witness, Quiz of The Week, Terra Firma, Who Said That, The Rather Reassuring Programme, Song by Song, Loose Ends Radio 4.

SHERWOOD, MADELEINE
Actress. b. Montreal, Canada, Nov. 13, 1922. e. Yale Drama Sch. Trained with Montreal Rep. and Actors Studio. Has dir. prods. at Actors Studio and regional theaters, as well as 2 AFI films Goodnight Sweet Prince and Sunday.
THEATER: The Crucible, Sweet Bird of Youth, Cat on a Hot Tin Roof, Invitation to a March, The Garden of Sweets, Camelot, Hey You, Light Man!, Brecht on Brecht, Night of the Iguana, Arturo Ui, Do I Hear a Waltz?, Inadmissible Evidence, All Over, Older People, Getting Out, The Suicide, Eclipse, Miss Edwina.
PICTURES: Baby Doll, Cat on a Hot Tin Roof, Parrish, Sweet Bird of Youth, The 91st Day, Hurry Sundown, Pendulum, Wicked Wicked, The Changeling, Resurrection, Teachers, An Unremarkable Life, Silence Like Glass.
TELEVISION: *Series*: The Flying Nun. *Mini-Series*: Rich Man Poor Man. *Movies*: The Manhunter, Nobody's Child, Palace Guard; many guest appearances.

SHIELDS, BROOKE
Actress. b. New York, NY, May 31, 1965. e. Princeton U. Honors in French Lit. Discovered at age 11 months by photographer Francesco Scavullo to pose in Ivory Soap ads.
THEATER: *Off-B'way*: The Eden Cinema; *B'way debut* 1994 in Grease! (Theatre World Award).
PICTURES: Alice Sweet Alice (Holy Terror/Communion; debut 1977), Pretty Baby, King of the Gypsies, Tilt, Wanda Nevada, Just You and Me Kid, The Blue Lagoon, Endless Love, Sahara, The Muppets Take Manhattan (cameo), Speed Zone (cameo), Back Street Dreams, Brenda Starr, An American Love (It.), The Seventh Floor, Freeway.
TELEVISION: *Movies*: The Prince of Central Park, Wet Gold, The Diamond Trap, I Can Make You Love Me: The Stalking of Laura Black; Nothing Lasts Forever; numerous specials. *Guest*: Friends. *Series*: Suddenly Susan.

SHIELDS, WILLIAM A.
Executive. b. New York, NY, 1946. e. El Camino Coll., California State Coll. at LA. Entered the motion picture industry in 1966 with Pacific Theatres, then MGM sales dept., L.A. and Denver, 1970; New World Pictures, 1972; 20th Century-Fox, Washington, 1973; NY district manager, 20th Century-Fox, 1973-75; joined Mann Theatres Corp. of California as head booker in 1975; gen. sls. mgr., Far West Films, 1977-79; joined Avco Embassy as Western div. mgr., promoted to asst. gen. sls. mgr., 1980; promoted to v.p.-gen. sls. mgr., 1981; 1983 joined New World Pictures as exec. v.p., worldwide mktg. & acquisitions; promoted to pres., worldwide sls. & mktg., 1985; 1987, pres. CEO, New World Intl.; 1989, joined Trans Atlantic Pictures as pres., CEO when company purchased assets of New World's feature film division. Sold ownership in Trans Atlantic and formed G.E.L. Prod. & Distrib., 1992. Exec. prod. Au Pair (1991); exec. in charge of prod. Death Ring (1992). Exec. prod. of Uninvited. Past chmn, American Film Mktg. Assn. (1987-91). Presently chmn. American Film Export Assn.

SHIFF, RICHARD
Executive. b. New York, NY, Mar. 3, 1942. e. Queens College, B.A., M.A., Brooklyn Col., P.D. Joined Warner Bros. as sales analyst, 1977. 1979 named dist. coordinator; 1980, asst. dir. sls. admin. 1982, promoted to post, dir. sls. admin. 1987, v.p., theatrical sls. operations.

SHIRE, DAVID
Composer. b. Buffalo, NY, July 3, 1937. m. actress Didi Conn. e. Yale U., 1959, B.A. Composer of theater scores: The Sap of Life, Urban Blight, Starting Here Starting Now, Baby, Closer Than Ever, Big. Emmy noms. Raid on Entebbe, The Defection of Simas Kudirka, Do You Remember Love? and The Kennedys of Massachusetts. Grammy Awards for Saturday Night Fever.
PICTURES: One More Train to Rob, Summertree, Drive, He Said; Skin Game, To Find a Man, Showdown, Two People, Steelyard Blues (adapt.), Class of '44, The Conversation, The Taking of Pelham 1-2-3, The Fortune, Farewell My Lovely, The Hindenburg, All the President's Men, The Big Bus, Harry and

Walter Go to New York, Saturday Night Fever (adapt. & add. music), Straight Time, The Promise (Acad. Award nom.), Old Boyfriends, Norma Rae (Academy Award for best song, It Goes Like It Goes, 1979), Only When I Laugh, The Night the Lights Went Out in Georgia, Paternity, The World According to Garp, Max Dugan Returns, Oh God You Devil, 2010, Fast Break, Return to Oz, Short Circuit, 'night Mother, Vice Versa, Monkey Shines, Bed and Breakfast, One Night Stand.
TELEVISION: *Series themes*: Sarge, McCloud, The Practice, Sirota's Court, Joe & Sons, Lucas Tanner, Alice, Tales of the Unexpected, Brewster Place, Room for Two. *Movies*: Priest Killer, McCloud, Harpy, Three Faces of Love, Killer Bees, Tell Me Where It Hurts, The Defection of Simus Kudirka, Three for the Road, Amelia Earhart, Something for Joey, Raid on Entebbe, The Storyteller, Promise, Mayflower Madam, Echoes in the Darkness, Jesse, God Bless the Child, Common Ground, The Clinic, Convicted, The Women of Brewster Place, I Know My First Name is Steven, The Kennedys of Massachusetts (mini-series), The Great Los Angeles Earthquake, The Boys, Sarah: Plain and Tall, Always Remember I Love You, Paris Trout, Four Eyes, Broadway Bound, Bed of Lies, Last Wish, Alison, Habitation of Dragons, Lily in Winter, Reunion, Serving in Silence, My Brother's Keeper, My Antonia, The Heidi Chronicles, The Man Who Wouldn't Die, Tecumseh: The Last Warrior, Almost Golden: The Jessica Savitch Story, many others.

SHIRE, TALIA
Actress. r.n. Talia Coppola. b. New York, NY, April 25, 1946. Raised on road by her father, arranger-conductor Carmine Coppola, who toured with Broadway musicals. After 2 yrs. at Yale Sch. of Drama she moved to L.A. where appeared in many theatrical productions. Brother is dir. Francis Ford Coppola. Started in films as Talia Coppola.
PICTURES: The Wild Racers, The Dunwich Horror, Gas-s-s-s, The Christian Licorice Store, The Outside Man, The Godfather, The Godfather Part II (Acad. Award nom.), Rocky (Acad. Award nom.), Old Boyfriends, Prophecy, Rocky II, Windows, Rocky III, Rocky IV, RAD, Lionheart (co-prod.), New York Stories (Life Without Zoe), Rocky V, The Godfather III, Bed and Breakfast, Cold Heaven, DeadFall, One Night Stand (dir. only).
TELEVISION: *Mini-Series*: Rich Man Poor Man. *Movies*: Foster and Laurie, Kill Me If You Can, Daddy I Don't Like It Like This, For Richer For Poorer, Chantilly Lace. *Special*: Please God I'm Only 17.

SHIVAS, MARK
Producer. e. Oxford.
PICTURES: *Producer*: Richard's Things, Moonlighting, A Private Function, The Witches. *Exec. Prod.*: Bad Blood, Truly Madly Deeply, Enchanted April, The Grass Arena, Memento Mori, The Snapper, Priest, An Awfully Big Adventure, Jude, The Van, Small Faces.
TELEVISION: Presenter of Cinema. *Producer*. The Six Wives of Henry VIII, Casanova, The Edwardians, The Evacuees, The Glittering Prizes, Abide With Me, Rogue Male, 84 Charing Cross Road, The Three Hostages, She Fell Among Thieves, Professional Foul, Telford's Change, On Giant's Shoulders, The Price, What If it's Raining?, The Story Teller. Now head of Films, BBC.

SHORE, HOWARD
Composer, Musician. Began career as musical director for Saturday Night Live.
PICTURES: Scanners, Videodrome, The Brood, The Fly, After Hours, Heaven, Belizaire the Cajun, Nadine, Moving, Big, Dead Ringers, The Lemon Sisters, An Innocent Man, Postcards From the Edge (musical numbers sprv.), The Silence of the Lambs, A Kiss Before Dying, Naked Lunch, Prelude to a Kiss, Single White Female, Sliver, Guilty as Sin, M. Butterfly, Mrs. Doubtfire, Philadelphia, Ed Wood, The Truth About Cats & Dogs, Striptease.
TELEVISION: Coca-Cola Presents Live: The Hard Rock.

SHORE, PAULY
Actor. b. Los Angeles, CA, 1968. Son of comedian Sammy Shore and nightclub owner Mitzi Shore. Worked as stand-up comedian at mother's club, the Comedy Store.
PICTURES: For Keeps? (debut, 1988), 18 Again!, Lost Angels, Phantom of the Mall, Wedding Band, Encino Man, Class Act, Son-in-Law, In the Army Now, Jury Duty, Bio-Dome.
TELEVISION: *Series*: Totally Pauly, Totally Different Pauly. *Special*: Pauly Does Dallas. *Movie*: Home By Midnight. *Guest*: 21 Jump Street, Married... with Children.

SHORT, MARTIN
Actor, Comedian, Writer. b. Toronto, Can., Mar. 26, 1950. e. McMaster U. Trained as social worker but instead performed on stage in Godspell as well as in revues and cabarets in Toronto, 1973-78, including a stint as a member of the Toronto unit of the Second City comedy troupe, 1977-78. Created

such characters as Ed Grimley, Jackie Rogers Jr. B'way debut 1993 in The Goodbye Girl (Theatre World Award; Tony nom.).
PICTURES: Lost and Found, The Outsider, Three Amigos!, Innerspace, Cross My Heart, Three Fugitives, The Big Picture, Pure Luck, Father of the Bride, Captain Ron, Clifford, The Pebble and the Penguin (voice), Father of the Bride Part 2, An Indian in the City, Mars Attacks!.
TELEVISION: Series: The Associates, I'm a Big Girl Now, SCTV Network (Emmy Award for writing, 1983), Saturday Night Live (1985- 86), The Completely Mental Misadventures of Ed Grimley (cartoon series), The Martin Short Show (also exec. prod., writer). Specials: All's Well That Ends Well, Really Weird Tales, Martin Short's Concert for the North Americas (SHO), Martin Short Goes Hollywood (HBO), The Show Formerly Known as the Martin Short Show (also exec. prod., co-writer). Movies: The Family Man, Sunset Limousine, Money for Nothing (BBC).

SHORT, THOMAS C.
Executive. International pres., International Alliance of Theatrical Stage Employees & Moving Picture Machine Operators of the U.S. and Canada (AFL-CIO-CLC).

SHOWALTER, MAX
Actor, Composer. r.n. Casey Adams. b. Caldwell, KS, June 2, 1917. e. Caldwell H.S.; Pasadena Playhouse. Composed background music for films: Vicki, Return of Jack Slade, B'way Harrigan 'n Hart (composer), Touch of the Child (lyricist-composer). Recordings incl. The Brementown Musicians, The Gold Dog (as narrator, composer, pianist and singer). On bd. of trustees: Eugene O'Neill Theatre Center, Natl. Theatre of the Deaf, Ivorytown Playhouse, Shoreline Alliance for the Arts. Gov's Bd.: Commission for the Arts.
THEATER: B'way: Knights of Song, Very Warm for May, My Sister Eileen, Showboat, John Loves Mary, Make Mine Manhattan, Lend an Ear, Hello Dolly!, The Grass Harp.
PICTURES: Always Leave Them Laughing (debut, 1949), With a Song in My Heart, What Price Glory?, My Wife's Best Friend, Niagara, Destination Gobi, Dangerous Crossing, Vicki, Night People, Naked Alibi, The Indestructible Man, The Return of Jack Slade, Never Say Goodbye, Bus Stop, Dragoon Wells Massacre, Down Three Dark Streets, Designing Woman, Female Animal, The Monster That Challenged the World, Voice In the Mirror, The Naked and the Dead, It Happened to Jane, Elmer Gantry, Return to Peyton Place, Summer and Smoke, The Music Man, Bon Voyage, My Six Loves, Move Over Darling, Sex and the Single Girl, Fate Is the Hunter, How to Murder Your Wife, Lord Love a Duck, A Talent for Loving, The Moonshine War, The Anderson Tapes, 10, Racing with the Moon, Sixteen Candles.

SHUE, ELISABETH
Actress. b. South Orange, NJ, Oct. 6, 1963. e. Harvard. Brother is actor Andrew Shue.
PICTURES: The Karate Kid (debut, 1984), Adventures in Babysitting, Link, Cocktail, Back to the Future Part II, Back to the Future Part III, The Marrying Man, Soapdish, Twenty Bucks, The Underneath, Leaving Las Vegas (Chicago Film Critics Award; Nat'l Film Critics Award), Trigger Effect.
TELEVISION: Series: Call to Glory. Movies: Charles and Diana, Double Switch, Hale the Hero, Blind Justice, Radio Inside.

SHULER-DONNER, LAUREN
Producer. b. Cleveland, OH. B.S. in film & bdcstg., Boston U. Began filmmaking career as ed. of educational films then camera-woman in TV prod., assoc. prod., story editor, creative affairs exec.; TV movie: Amateur Night at the Dixie Bar and Grill (prod.). Assoc. prod. on film Thank God It's Friday. Cameo in film Maverick.
PICTURES: Mr. Mom, Ladyhawke, St. Elmo's Fire, Pretty in Pink, Three Fugitives, The Favor, Radio Flyer, Dave, Free Willy, Free Willy 2: The Adventure Home, Assassins.

SHULL, RICHARD B.
Actor. b. Evanston, IL, Feb. 24, 1929. e. State U. of Iowa. B.A. drama, 1950., Kemper Mil. Sch. AA Humanities, 1986. U.S. Army, 1953. Armed Forces Korea Network. 1953-56, exec. asst. prod. Gordon W. Pollock Prods.; 1954-56 stage mgr. Hyde Park Playhouse; other prod. jobs and freelance stage mgr. and dir. 1950-70. NY stage debut in Wake Up Darling (1956), also in Minnie's Boys, Goodtime Charley (Tony nom.; Drama Desk nom.), The Marriage of Bette and Boo (Obie Award), One of the All-Time Greats, Ain't Broadway Grand, Victor Victoria.
PICTURES: The Anderson Tapes (debut, 1971), B.S. I Love You, Such Good Friends, Hail to the Chief, Slither, Sssss, Cockfighter, The Fortune, The Black Bird, Hearts of the West, The Big Bus, The Pack, Dreamer, Wholly Moses, Heartbeeps, Spring Break, Lovesick, Unfaithfully Yours, Splash, Garbo Talks, Tune in Tomorrow, Housesitter, For Love or Money, Trapped in Paradise, Cafe Society.

TELEVISION: Series: Diana, Holmes & Yoyo. Guest: Your Hit Parade (1950), Rockford Files, Good Times, Love American Style, Hart to Hart, Lou Grant. Movies: Ziegfeld: A Man and His Women, Studs Lonigan, Will There Really Be a Morning? The Boy Who Loved Trolls, Keeping the Faith, Seize the Day.

SHURPIN, SOL
Executive. b. New York, NY, Feb. 22, 1914. e. Pace Inst., 1936. Law stenog., 1932-33; Joe Hornstein, Inc., 1933-41; National Theatre Supply, 1941-48; purchased interest in Raytone Screen Corp., became v.p., 1948; pres., Raytone, 1952; pres., Technikote Corp., which succeeded Raytone Screen, 1956-present; sole owner, Technikote Corp., 1962.

SHUTT, BUFFY
Executive. e. Sarah Lawrence Col. Joined Paramount 1973 as sect. with N.Y. pub. staff; 1975, natl. mag. contact. 1978, named dir. of pub.; later exec. dir. of pub. Promoted 1980 to v.p., pub. & promo. Resigned to join Time-Life Films as v.p. East coast prod; returned to Paramount in 1981 as sr. v.p. & asst. to pres. of Motion Picture Group. 1984, appt. exec. v.p.-mktg. for M.P. Group, Paramount. 1985, appoint. pres. of mktg. 1986, resigned. Formed Shutt-Jones Communications, 1987, marketing consultancy with Kathy Jones. 1989, appt. marketing pres., Columbia Pictures & Tri-Star Pictures. 1991, mktg. pres. of TriStar.

SHYER, CHARLES
Director, Writer. b. Los Angeles, CA. e. UCLA. Was asst. dir. and prod. mgr. before becoming head writer for tv series The Odd Couple. First teamed with Nancy Meyers on Private Benjamin.
PICTURES: Writer: Smokey and the Bandit, House Calls, Goin' South, Private Benjamin (Acad. Award nom.; also prod.). Director-Writer: Irreconcilable Differences, Baby Boom, Father of the Bride, I Love Trouble, Father of the Bride Part II.

SIDARIS, ANDY
Producer, Director, Writer. b. Chicago, IL, Feb. 20, 1932. e. Southern Methodist U., B.A., radio-TV. Began television career in 1950 in Dallas, TX as a director at station WFAA-TV; now pres., The Sidaris Company. Won 8 Emmy Awards.
PICTURES: Dir.: Stacey, The Racing Scene, M*A*S*H (football sequences), Seven (also prod.). Dir.-Writer: Malibu Express (also prod.), Hard Ticket to Hawaii, Picasso Trigger, Savage Beach, Guns, Do or Die, Hard Hunted, Fit to Kill. Exec. Prod.: Enemy Gold, The Dallas Connection.
TELEVISION: Dir.: The Racers/Mario Andretti/Joe Leonard/Al Unser, ABC's Championship Auto Racing, ABC's NCAA Game of the Week, 1968 Summer Olympics: 1968 (Mexico City), 1972 (Munich), 1976 (Montreal), 1984 (L.A.), Winter Olympics: 1964 (Innsbruck), 1968 (Grenoble), 1976 (Innsbruck), 1980 (Lake Placid), 1988 (Calgary), Wide World of Sports, The Racers/Craig and Lee Breedlove, The Burt Reynolds Late Show, Kojak episode, Nancy Drew episodes.

SIDNEY, GEORGE
Director, Producer. b. New York, NY, Oct. 4, 1916. Son of L. K. Sidney, veteran showman and v.p. MGM, and Hazel Mooney, actress. From 1932 at MGM as test, second unit and short subjects dir. Won Academy Awards for shorts: Quicker 'n' a Wink (Pete Smith speciality), Of Pups and Puzzles (Passing Parade). In 1941 made feature dir. debut, MGM. Pres., Director's Guild of America, 16 yrs; spec. presidential assignment to Atomic Energy Commission and U.S. Air Force; 1961-66, pres., Hanna-Barbera Productions; Doctorate of Science Hanneman Medical University and Hospital. Member ASCAP. Pres., Directors, Inc., since 1969; v.p., Directors Foundation; v.p., D.W. Griffith Foundation; life mem., ACTT (England) and DGA. Directed U.N. special, Who Has Seen the Wind? Awarded Gold Medal for service to D.G.A. 1959, Doctorate from Collegio Barcelona 1989, Life Membership in D.G.A.
PICTURES: Free and Easy (debut, 1941), Pacific Rendezvous, Pilot No. 5, Thousands Cheer, Bathing Beauty, Anchors Aweigh, The Harvey Girls, Holiday in Mexico, Cass Timberlane, The Three Musketeers, The Red Danube, Key to the City, Annie Get Your Gun, Show Boat, Scaramouche, Young Bess, Kiss Me Kate, Jupiter's Darling, The Eddy Duchin Story, Jeanne Eagels (also prod.), Pal Joey, Who Was That Lady? (also prod.), Pepe (also prod.), Bye Bye Birdie, A Ticklish Affair, Viva Las Vegas (also co-prod.), The Swinger (also prod.), Half a Sixpence (also co-prod.).

SIDNEY, SYLVIA
Actress. b. New York, NY, Aug. 8, 1910. r.n. Sophia Kosow. e. Theatre Guild Sch. Prof. stage debut at age 16. NY debut 1927.
THEATER: Nice Women, Crossroads, Bad Girl, The Gentle People, Auntie Mame, Joan of Lorraine, Angel Street, Enter Laughing, Vieux Carre.
PICTURES: Broadway Nights (debut, 1927), Thru Different Eyes, City Streets, Ladies of the Big House, Confessions of a Co-Ed, An American Tragedy, Street Scene, The Miracle Man,

Merrily We Go to Hell, Make Me a Star (cameo), Madame Butterfly, Pick-Up, Jennie Gerhardt, Good Dame, Thirty Day Princess, Behold My Wife, Accent on Youth, Mary Burns—Fugitive, The Trail of the Lonesome Pine, Fury, Sabotage (A Woman Alone), You Only Live Once, Dead End, You and Me, One Third of a Nation, The Wagons Roll at Night, Blood on the Sun, Mr. Ace, The Searching Wind, Love From a Stranger, Les Miserables, Violent Saturday, Behind the High Wall, Summer Wishes Winter Dreams (Acad. Award nom.), Gold Told Me To (Demons), I Never Promised You a Rose Garden, Damien: Omen II, Corrupt, Hammett, Beetlejuice, Used People, Mars Attacks!.
TELEVISION: *Movies*: Do Not Fold Spindle or Mutilate, Death at Love House, Raid on Entebbe, The Gossip Columnist, FDR—The Last Year, The Shadow Box, A Small Killing, Come Along With Me, Having It All, Finnegan Begin Again, An Early Frost, Pals. *Specials*: Andre's Mother, The Witching of Ben Wagner. *Guest*: thirtysomething.

SIEMASZKO, CASEY
Actor. b. Chicago, IL, March 17, 1961. r.n. Kazimierz Siemaszko. e. Goodman Theatre School of Drama, Chicago.
PICTURES: Class (debut, 1983), Secret Admirer, Back to the Future, Stand By Me, Gardens of Stone, Three O'Clock High, Biloxi Blues, Young Guns, Breaking In, Back to the Future Part II, Of Mice and Men, Teresa's Tattoo, My Life's in Turnaround, Milk Money, The Phantom.
TELEVISION: *Movie*: Miracle of the Heart: A Boys Town Story.

SIGHVATSSON, SIGURJON (JONI)
Producer. b. Reykjavik, Iceland, June 15, 1952. e. Iceland Community Col, Univ. of Iceland. Came to U.S. in 1978. Also attended USC. Was film and music video prod. for Blue-Ice Prods. Founder and chairperson with Steve Golin of Propaganda Films.
PICTURE: *Assoc. Producer*: Hard Rock Zombies, American Drive-In. *Producer*: Private Investigations, The Blue Iguana, Kill Me Again, Fear Anxiety and Depression, Daddy's Dyin'... Who's Got the Will?, Wild at Heart, Truth or Dare, Ruby, A Stranger Among Us, Candyman, Kalifornia, Red Rock West, S.F.W., Lord of Illusions, Canadian Bacon.
TELEVISION: *Movie*: Memphis. *Specials*: Rock the Vote, Education First, Tales of the City. *Series*: Twin Peaks.

SIKKING, JAMES B.
Actor. b. Los Angeles, CA, March 5, 1934. e. UCLA, B.A. Theatre includes Waltz of the Toreadors, Plaza Suite, Damn Yankees, The Big Knife.
PICTURES: The Magnificent Seven, Von Ryan's Express, Chandler, The New Centurions, The Electric Horseman, Capricorn One, Ordinary People, Outland, The Star Chamber, Up the Creek, Star Trek III—The Search for Spock, Morons from Outer Space, Soul Man, Narrow Margin, Final Approach.
TELEVISION: *Series*: General Hospital, Turnabout, Hill Street Blues. Doogie Howser, M.D. *Movies*: The Jesse Owens Story, First Steps, Bay Coven, Brotherhood of the Rose, Too Good to be True, Desperado: Badlands Justice, Doing Time on Maple Drive, Jake Lassiter: Justice on the Bayou, In Pursuit of Honor, Tyson. *Mini-Series*: Around the World in 80 Days. *Specials*: Tales from the Hollywood Hills (Golden Land), Ollie Hopnoodle's Haven of Bliss.

SILLIPHANT, STIRLING
Executive, Writer. b. Detroit, MI, Jan. 16, 1918. e. USC, B.A., 1938. On pub. staff, Walt Disney Productions, Burbank 1938-41; 1941-42, exploit. & pub., Hal Horne Org. for 20th Century-Fox in NY & other key cities; 1942-43, asst. to Spyros P. Skouras. U.S. Navy, WWII. 1946, with 20th-Fox; in chg. special events and promotions, 1949; appt. Eastern pub. mgr. 1951.
PICTURES: *Prod.*: The Joe Louis Story, Shaft's Big Score (exec. prod.). *Writer*: Five Against the House (also co-prod.), The Nightfall, The Lineup, Village of the Damned, The Slender Thread, In the Heat of the Night (Academy Award, 1967), Charly, Marlowe, A Walk in the Spring Rain, The Liberation of L.B. Jones, Murphy's War, The New Centurions, The Poseidon Adventure, Shaft in Africa, The Towering Inferno, The Killer Elite, The Enforcer, Telefon, The Swarm, Circle of Iron, When Time Ran Out, Over the Top, Catch the Heat (also co-exec. prod.), The Grass Harp.
TELEVISION: *Series*: The Naked City, Route 66, Space, Golden Gate, Fly Away Home (also prod.). *Movies/Mini-Series*: Mussolini—The Untold Story, Pearl (also exec. prod.), Salem's Lot (also prod.), Welcome to Paradise (also exec. prod.), Travis McGee, The Three Kings (also prod.), Brotherhood of the Rose (exec. prod.), Day of Reckoning. (d. April 26, 1996)

SILVA, HENRY
Actor. b. Brooklyn, NY, 1928. Studied acting with Group Theatre, Actors Studio.
PICTURES: Viva Zapata!, Crowded Paradise, A Hatful of Rain, The Law and Jake Wade, The Bravados, Green Mansions, Cinderfella, Ocean's Eleven, Sergeants 3, The Manchurian Candidate, A Gathering of Eagles, Johnny Cool, The Secret Invasion, Hail Mafia, The Return of Mr. Moto, The Reward, The Hills Ran Red, The Plainsman, Matchless, Never a Dull Moment, The Animals, Man and Boy, The Italian Connection, The Kidnap of Mary Lou, Shoot, Thirst, Buck Rogers in the 25th Century, Love and Bullets, Virus, Alligator, Sharky's Machine, Wrong Is Right, Megaforce, Cannonball Run II, Lust in the Dust, Code of Silence, Alan Quartermain and the Lost City of Gold, Amazon Women on the Moon, Above the Law, Bulletproof, Dick Tracy, Fists of Steel, Trained to Kill, Possessed by the Night.
TELEVISION: *Movies*: Black Noon, Drive Hard Drive Fast, Contract on Cherry Street, Happy. *Series*: Buck Rogers in the 25th Century.

SILVER, CASEY
Executive. Pres., Universal Pictures, Inc.

SILVER, JOAN MICKLIN
Writer, Director. b. Omaha, NB, May 24, 1935. m. producer Raphael Silver. Daughter is dir. Marisa Silver. e. Sarah Lawrence Coll. Began career as writer for educational films. Original s.p., Limbo, purchased by Universal Pictures. In 1972 Learning Corp. of Am. commissioned her to write and direct a 30-min. film, The Immigrant Experience. Also wrote and directed two children's films for same co; dir. & wrote short film Bernice Bobs Her Hair. First feature was Hester Street, which she wrote and directed.
THEATER: *Director*: Album, Maybe I'm Doing It Wrong, A ... My Name is Alice, A ... My Name is Still Alice (co-conceived & co-dir. with Julianne Boyd).
PICTURES: *Director*: Hester Street (also s.p.), Between the Lines, On the Yard (prod.), Head Over Heels (also s.p.; retitled Chilly Scenes of Winter), Crossing Delancey, Loverboy, Big Girls Don't Cry... They Get Even.
TELEVISION: Finnegan Begin Again (dir.), The Nightingale: Faerie Tale Theatre (writer), Parole Board (Prison Stories): Women on the Inside), A Private Matter (dir.).

SILVER, JOEL
Producer. b. South Orange, NJ, July 14, 1952. e. NYU. Made first film, a short called Ten Pin Alley; moved to Los Angeles with job as asst. to Lawrence Gordon. Named pres., Lawrence Gordon Prods.; developed with Gordon and produced and marketed Hooper, The End, The Driver, The Warriors (also assoc. prod.). At Universal Pictures as prod. v.p.; supervising Smokey and the Bandit II. Honored 1990 as NATO/Showest's Producer of the Year. Appeared in 1988 film Who Framed Roger Rabbit.
PICTURES: Xanadu (co-prod.), Jekyll & Hyde ... Together Again (exec. prod.), 48 HRS., Streets of Fire, Brewster's Millions, Weird Science, Commando, Jumpin' Jack Flash, Lethal Weapon, Predator, Action Jackson, Die Hard, Road House, Lethal Weapon 2, The Adventures of Ford Fairlane, Die Hard 2, Predator 2, Hudson Hawk, Ricochet, The Last Boy Scout, Lethal Weapon 3, Demoliton Man, The Hudsucker Proxy, Richie Rich, Tales From the Crypt Presents Demon Knight (co-exec. prod.), Fair Game, Assassins, Executive Decision.
TELEVISION: Tales from the Crypt (exec. prod. & prod.; also dir. episode), Two Fisted Tales, Parker Can, W.E.I.R.D. World (co-exec. prod.).

SILVER, LEON J.
Executive. b. Boston, MA, March 25, 1918. e. USC, 1935-39. Independent prod. of short subjects, 1939; story analyst, Paramount, 1940; film writer, U.S. Army Pictorial Service, 1941-45; freelance writer, 1946; film writer. prod., U.S. Public Health Service, 1946-51; asst. chief, foreign film prod., U.S. Dept. of State, 1951-54; acting chief, domestic film prod., U.S. Information Agency, 1955; division chief, Worldwide Documentary Film & Television Product, U.S. Information Agency, 1968; 1978-79, sr. advisor IV, film production. Coordinator of TV & film, all Fed Govt. Agencies Private Industry under Exec. Office, pres. of U.S. 1980. Resigned, 1980. Now TV network writer-producer-novelist.

SILVER, MARISA
Director. b. New York, NY, April 23, 1960. Daughter of director Joan Micklin Silver and prod.-dir. Raphael Silver. e. Harvard U. where she directed short Dexter T. and edited doc. Light Coming Through: a Portrait of Maud Morgan.
PICTURES: Old Enough, Permanent Record, Vital Signs, He Said/She Said (co-dir.).
TELEVISION: *Co-dir.*: A Community of Praise (an episode of PBS series Middletown, 1982).

SILVER, RAPHAEL D.
Producer. b. Cleveland, OH, 1930. e. Harvard Coll. and Harvard Graduate Sch. of Business Adm. Is pres. of Middex Devel. Corp. 1973 formed Midwest Film Productions to produce Hester Street, written and directed by Joan Micklin Silver. Also distributed film independently. Also produced

Between the Lines. Exec. prod. of Crossing Delancey. Directed On the Yard and a Walk on the Moon. Currently pres. Silverfilm Prods. Inc.

SILVER, RON
Actor, Director. b. New York, NY, July 2, 1946. e. U. of Buffalo, St. John's U., Taiwan, M.A. Trained for stage at Herbert Berghof Studios and Actors Studio. N.Y. stage debut in Kasper and Public Insult, 1971. Elected pres. of Actors Equity Assn., 1991.
THEATER: El Grande de Coca Cola, Lotta, More Than You Deserve, Angel City (Mark Taper, LA), Hurlyburly, Social Security, Hunting Cockroaches, Speed-the-Plow (Tony & Drama Desk Award), Gorilla (Chicago, Jefferson Award nom.; N.YU. & L.A., Dramalogue Award), Friends, And, Broken Glass.
PICTURES: Tunnelvision, Welcome to L.A., Semi-Tough, Silent Rage, Best Friends, The Entity, Lovesick, Silkwood, Garbo Talks, Oh God! You Devil, Goodbye People, Eat and Run, Enemies A Love Story, Blue Steel, Reversal of Fortune, Mr. Saturday Night, Married to It, Timecop, Danger Zone, Deadly Takeover, Girl 6, The Arrival.
TELEVISION: Series: Mac Davis Show, Rhoda, Dear Detective, The Stockard Channing Show, Baker's Dozen, Chicago Hope. Movies: The Return of the World's Greatest Detective, Murder at the Mardi Gras, Betrayal, Word of Honor, Billionaire Boys Club, Fellow Traveler, Forgotten Prisoners: The Amnesty Files, Live Wire, Blindside, Lifepod (also dir.), Almost Golden: The Jessica Savitch Story, Billionaire Boys Club (Emmy nom.). Mini-Series: A Woman of Independent Means. Guest: Trying Times (Drive He Said), Hill Street Blues. Special: Loyalty and Betrayal: The Story of the American Mob (narrator).

SILVERMAN, FRED
Producer. b. New York, NY, Sept., 1937. e. Syracuse U., Ohio State U., master's in TV and theatre arts. Joined WGN-TV, indep. sta. in Chicago. Came to NY for exec. post at WPIX-TV, where stayed only six weeks. CBS-TV hired him as dir. of daytime programs. Named v.p., programs 1970. 1975 left CBS to become pres., ABC Entertainment. 1978, named pres. and CEO of NBC. Now Pres., Fred Silverman Company, Los Angeles.
TELEVISION: Prod./exec. prod.: Series: Perry Mason Movies, Matlock, In the Heat of the Night, Jake and the Fatman, Father Dowling Mysteries, Dick Van Dyke Mystery Movies. Movies: In the Heat of the Night: A Matter of Justice, Gramps, Diagnosis Murder, My Very Best Friend, Journey to Mars, Bonechillers & Bedtime Stories.

SILVERMAN, JONATHAN
Actor. b. Los Angeles, CA, Aug. 5, 1966. e. USC, NYU.
THEATER: NY: Brighton Beach Memoirs, Biloxi Blues, Broadway Bound. LA: The Illusion (Dramalogue Award), Pay or Play (Dramalogue Award), Sticks and Stones (Dramalogue Award).
PICTURES: Brighton Beach Memoirs (debut, 1986), Caddyshack II, Stealing Home, Weekend at Bernie's, Class Action, Breaking the Rules, Life in the Food Chain (Age Isn't Everything), Little Sister, Weekend at Bernie's II, Little Big League, Teresa's Tattoo, French Exit, At First Sight.
TELEVISION: Series: Gimme a Break, The Single Guy. Movies: Challenge of a Lifetime, Traveling Man, For Richer For Poorer, Broadway Bound, 12:01, Sketch Artist II: Hands That See.

SILVERSTEIN, ELLIOT
Director. b. Boston, MA, Aug. 3, 1927. e. Boston Coll., Yale U. Started career on television.
PICTURES: Belle Sommers (debut, 1962), Cat Ballou, The Happening, A Man Called Horse, Deadly Honeymoon, The Car (also co-prod.).
TELEVISION: Movies: Betrayed by Innocence, Night of Courage, Fight for Life, Rich Men Single Women. Series: Tales From the Crypt.

SILVERSTEIN, MAURICE
Executive. b. Syracuse, NY, March 1, 1912. Booker, salesman, MGM domestic dep't; International Dep't, MGM; supervisor Southeast Asia Hdqts. Singapore, MGM, 1938-42; OWI chief, film distribution for Europe, hdqts. London, during WWII; asst. sales supervisor, Far East, MGM; regional director, Latin America, 1947; liaison exec. to handle independent productions MGM, 1956; v.p., MGM International, 1957; first v.p., 1958; pres., MGM International, 1963; v.p., parent company, Metro-Goldwyn-Mayer Inc. in charge of foreign production, 1970; Silverstein Int'l Corp., pres.

SILVERSTONE, ALICIA
Actress. b. California, 1977. Made stage debut at Met Theater in Los Angeles in Carol's Eve. Starred in three Aerosmith videos including Cryin'. Formed own production co., First Kiss Prods.

PICTURES: The Crush (debut, 1993), The Babysitter, True Crime, Le Nouveau Monde, Hideaway, Clueless, Excess Baggage (also prod.).
TELEVISION: Movies: Torch Song, Shattered Dreams, The Cool and the Crazy. Guest: The Wonder Years.

SIMMONS, ANTHONY
Director, Writer. b. London, England. e. Grad. from the LSE with LL.B. Practiced briefly as a barrister before entering the industry as writer/director of documentaries, then commercials and feature films. Awards: Grand Prix (shorts), Venice, Grand Prix, Locarno; 2 Int. Emmys, various Intl. Awards for commercials. Publications: The Optimists of Nine Elms, A Little Space for Issie Brown.
PICTURES: Sunday By the Sea, Bow Bells, Time Without Pity (co- prod.), Four in the Morning, The Optimists, Black Joy, Little Sweetheart, Poison Candy.
TELEVISION: On Giant's Shoulders, Supergran and the Magic Ray, Harry Carpenter Never Said It Was Like This, Life After Death, Day After the Fair, Inspector Morse, Van de Valk, Inspector Frost, The Good Guys, 99-1.

SIMMONS, JEAN
Actress. b. London, England, Jan. 31, 1929. e. Aida Foster Sch., London. Screen debut 1944 at age 14. Voted one of top ten British money-making stars in M.P. Herald-Fame Poll, 1950-51. London stage: A Little Night Music. Awards: Cannes Film Festival Homage 1988, Italian Outstanding Film Achievement Award 1989, French Govt. Commandeur de L'Ordre des Arts des Lettres. 1990.
PICTURES: Give Us the Moon (debut, 1944), Mr. Emmanuel, Meet Sexton Blake, Kiss the Bride Goodbye, Sports Day, Caesar and Cleopatra, Way to the Stars, Great Expectations, Hungry Hill, Black Narcissus, Uncle Silas, The Women In the Hall, Hamlet (Acad. Award nom.), Blue Lagoon, Adam and Evelyne, Trio, So Long at the Fair, Cage of Gold, The Clouded Yellow, Androcles and the Lion (U.S. film debut, 1953), Angel Face, Young Bess, Affair with a Stranger, The Actress, The Robe, She Couldn't Say No, A Bullet Is Waiting, The Egyptian, Desiree, Footsteps in the Fog, Guys and Dolls, Hilda Crane, This Could Be the Night, Until They Sail, The Big Country, Home Before Dark, This Earth Is Mine, Elmer Gantry, Spartacus, The Grass Is Greener, All the Way Home, Life at the Top, Mister Buddwing, Rough Night in Jericho, Divorce American Style, The Happy Ending (Acad. Award nom.), Say Hello to Yesterday, Mr. Sycamore, Dominique, Going Undercover, The Dawning, How to Make an American Quilt.
TELEVISION: Movies & Specials: Heidi, Beggarman Thief, The Easter Promise, The Home Front, Golden Gate, Jacqueline Susann's Valley of the Dolls 1981, A Small Killing, Inherit the Wind, Great Expectations, Sensibility and Sense, The Laker Girls, Perry Mason: The Case of Lost Love, People Like Us, December Flower. Mini-Series: The Dain Curse, The Thorn Birds (Emmy Award, 1983), North and South Book II. Series: Dark Shadows (1991).

SIMMONS, MATTY
Producer. b. Oct. 3. As bd. chmn., National Lampoon, Inc. produced National Lampoon Radio Hour, National Lampoon Lemmings, National Lampoon Show. Resigned from National Lampoon Inc. 1989. Now heads Matty Simmons Productions.
PICTURES: National Lampoon's Animal House, National Lampoon's Vacation, National Lampoon Goes to the Movies, National Lampoon's Class Reunion, National Lampoon's European Vacation, National Lampoon's Christmas Vacation (exec. prod.).
TELEVISION: National Lampoon's Disco Beavers, National Lampoon's Class of '86 (exec. prod.), Delta House.

SIMON, MELVIN
Executive. b. New York, NY, Oct. 21, 1926. e. City Coll.of New York, B.B.A., 1949; graduate work at Indiana U. Law Sch. Owner and operator, in partnership with two brothers, of over 110 shopping centers in U.S. 1978 formed Melvin Simon Productions, privately owned corp., to finance films. Dissolved Co. in 1983.
PICTURES: Exec. Prod.: Dominique, Love at First Bite, When a Stranger Calls, The Runner Stumbles, Scavenger Hunt, Cloud Dancer, The Stunt Man, My Bodyguard, Zorro the Gay Blade, Chu Chu and the Philly Flash, Porky's, Porky's II—The Next Day, Uforia, Wolf Lake, Porky's Revenge.

SIMON, NEIL
Playwright, Screenwriter, Producer. b. Bronx, NY, July 4, 1927. e. NYU. U.S. Army Air Force, 1945-46. Wrote comedy for radio with brother, Danny, (Robert Q. Lewis Show and for Goodman Ace), also TV scripts for Sid Caesar, Red Buttons, Jackie Gleason, Phil Silvers, Garry Moore, Tallulah Bankhead Show. With Danny contributed to B'way revues Catch a Star (1955), and New Faces of 1956. Adapted most of own plays to screen.
THEATER: Playwright: Come Blow Your Horn, Little Me, Barefoot in the Park, The Odd Couple (Tony Award, 1965), Sweet Charity, The Star Spangled Girl, Plaza Suite, Promises

Promises, Last of the Red Hot Lovers, The Gingerbread Lady, The Prisoner of Second Avenue, The Sunshine Boys, The Good Doctor, God's Favorite, California Suite, Chapter Two, They're Playing Your Song, I Ought to Be in Pictures, Fools, Little Me (revised version), Brighton Beach Memoirs, Biloxi Blues (Tony Award, 1985), The Odd Couple (female version), Broadway Bound, Rumors, Lost in Yonkers (Pulitzer Prize, Tony Award, 1991), Jake's Women, The Goodbye Girl (musical), Laughter on the 23rd Floor, London Suite (Off-B'way). PICTURES: After the Fox, Barefoot in the Park (also assoc. prod.), The Odd Couple, The Out-of-Towners, Plaza Suite, Last of the Red Hot Lovers, The Heartbreak Kid, The Prisoner of Second Avenue, The Sunshine Boys, Murder by Death, The Goodbye Girl, The Cheap Detective, California Suite, Chapter Two, Seems Like Old Times, Only When I Laugh (also co-prod.), I Ought to Be in Pictures (also co-prod.), Max Dugan Returns (also co-prod.), The Lonely Guy (adaptation), The Slugger's Wife, Brighton Beach Memoirs, Biloxi Blues (also co-prod.), The Marrying Man, Lost in Yonkers. TELEVISION: Specials: The Trouble With People, Plaza Suite. Movie: Broadway Bound, Jake's Women.

SIMON, PAUL
Singer, Composer, Actor. b. Newark, NJ, Oct. 13, 1941. e. Queens Coll., BA; postgrad. Brooklyn Law Sch. Teamed with Art Garfunkel in 1964, writing and performing own songs; they parted in 1970. Reunited for concert in New York, 1982, which was televised on HBO. Songs: With Garfunkel incl.: Mrs. Robinson (Grammy Award), The Boxer, Bridge Over Troubled Water (Grammy Award). PICTURES: The Graduate (songs), Annie Hall (actor), One Trick Pony (s.p., actor, composer) TELEVISION: Specials: The Fred Astaire Show, The Paul Simon Special (Emmy Award), Home Box Office Presents Paul Simon, Graceland: The African Concert, Mother Goose Rock 'n' Rhyme, Paul Simon's Concert in the Park. Guest: Sesame Street. ALBUMS: with Garfunkel: Wednesday Morning 3 a.m., Sounds of Silence, Parsley, Sage, Rosemary and Thyme, The Graduate (Grammy Award), Bookends, Bridge Over Troubled Water (Grammy Award), Simon & Garfunkel's Greatest Hits, Concert in the Park. Solo: Paul Simon, There Goes Rhymin' Simon, Live Rhymin', Still Crazy After All These Years (Grammy Award), Greatest Hits, One Trick Pony, Hearts and Bones, Graceland (Grammy Award), Negotiations and Love Songs, The Rhythm of the Saints, Paul Simon's Concert in the Park.

SIMON, SIMONE
Actress. b. April 23, 1911, Marseilles, France. Played in many films in Europe, among them Les Beaux Jours, La Bete Humaine, and Lac aux Dames. On stage in Toi C'est Moi, and others. PICTURES: Girl's Domitory (U.S. debut, 1936), Ladies in Love, Seventh Heaven, All That Money Can Buy, Cat People, Tahiti Honey, Johnny Doesn't Live Here Any More, The Curse of the Cat People, Mademoiselle Fifi, Petrus, Temptation Harbor, La Ronde, Olivia (Pit of Loneliness), Le Plaisir (House of Pleasure), Double Destin, The Extra Day, La Femme en Bleu.

SIMPSON, DON
Producer. b. Anchorage, AL, Oct. 29, 1945. e. U. of Oregon, Phi Beta Kappa. Began career in industry as acct. exec. with Jack Woodel Agency, San Francisco, where supervised mktg. of Warner Bros. films. Recruited by WB in 1971 as mktg. exec. specializing in youth market; oversaw Woodstock, A Clockwork Orange, Billy Jack, etc. Co-writer on low-budget films, Aloha, Bobby and Rose and Cannonball. Joined Paramount as prod. exec. 1975; promoted 1977 to v.p., prod. Named sr. v.p. of prod., 1980; pres. of worldwide prod., 1981. Formed Don Simpson/Jerry Bruckheimer Prods. 1983, entering into exclusive deal with Paramount to develop and produce for m.p. and TV divisions. Company moved to Walt Disney in early 1990's. PICTURES: Co-writer: Aloha Bobby and Rose, Cannonball. Producer: Flashdance, Thief of Hearts, Beverly Hills Cop, Top Gun, Beverly Hills Cop II, Days of Thunder, The Ref, Bad Boys, Dangerous Minds. (d. January 19, 1996)

SIMPSON, GARRY
Producer, Director, Executive. b. Camden, MI, Feb. 16, 1914. e. Stanford U. Major shows with NBC-TV: Jimmy Durante Show, Armstrong Circle Theatre, Campbell Soundstage, Comedy Hour, Ford Festival, Chevrolet Tele-Theater, Ed Wynn Show, The World of Mr. Sweeney, Philco TV Playhouse, Wide Wide World, Ballet Theatre. Dir. of programming, Vermont State PBS Network and writer-prod. of documentary films. Awards: Peabody, NY Film & TV Fest., Chicago Film Fest., & 3 Emmys.

SIMPSON, O.J.
Actor. b. San Francisco, CA, July 9, 1947. r.n. Orenthal James Simpson. e. U. of Southern California. Was star collegiate and professional football player and winner of Heisman Trophy. Began sportscasting in 1969.

PICTURES: The Klansman (debut, 1974), The Towering Inferno, Killer Force, The Cassandra Crossing, Capricorn One, Firepower, Hambone & Hillie, The Naked Gun: From the Files of Police Squad, The Naked Gun 2 1/2: The Smell of Fear, Naked Gun 33 1/3: The Final Insult. TELEVISION: Mini-Series: Roots. Movies: A Killing Affair, Goldie and the Boxer (also exec. prod.), Detour to Terror (also exec. prod.), Goldie and the Boxer Go to Hollywood (also exec. prod.), Cocaine and Blue Eyes (also exec. prod.), Student Exchange. Prod.: High Five (pilot), Superbowl Saturday Night (host & co-prod.). Series: First and Ten (HBO), NFL Live (co-host).

SIMS, JOAN
Actress. b. Laindon, England, May 9, 1930. e. Trained at RADA. Early career in repertory and West End Theatre. PICTURES: Dry Rot, Off the Record, No Time for Tears, Just My Luck, The Naked Truth, The Captain's Table, Passport to Shame, Emergency Ward 10, Most of the Carry On films, Doctor in Love, Watch Your Stern, Twice Round the Daffodils, The Iron Maiden, Nurse on Wheels, Doctor in Clover, Doctor in Trouble, The Garnett Saga, Not Now Darling, Don't Just Lie There Say Something, Love Among the Ruins, One of Our Dinosaurs Is Missing, Till Death Us Do Part, The Way of the World, Deceptions, The Fool, My Good Friend, As Time Goes By, The Canterville Ghost. TELEVISION: Over 100 shows incl. Stanley Baxter Show, Dick Emery Show, Carry on Shows, Love Among the Ruins, Born and Bred, Worzel Gummidge, Ladykillers, Crown Court, Cockles, Fairly Secret Army, Tickle on the Tum, Miss Marple: A Murder Is Announced, Hay Fever, In Loving Memory, Drummonds, Farrington of the F.O., Dr. Who, On the Up (3 series), Boys From the Bush, Simon & the Witch, Children's TV, Boys From the Bush, Tender Loving Care, Canterville Ghost, My Good Friend, Smokescreen, As Time Goes By, Just William, Henrietta Wainthrop Investigates.

SINATRA, FRANK
Actor, Singer. b. Hoboken, NJ, Dec. 12, 1915. Sportswriter; then singer on radio various NY stations; joined Harry James orchestra, later Tommy Dorsey. Children: singer-actress Nancy Sinatra, singer-conductor Frank Sinatra Jr., producer Tina Sinatra. On screen as a band vocalist in Las Vegas Nights, Ship Ahoy, Reveille with Beverly. Special Academy Award 1945 for acting in The House I Live In, short subject on tolerance. Received Jean Hersholt Humanitarian Award, 1971. PICTURES: Las Vegas Nights (debut, 1941), Ship Ahoy, Reveille With Beverly, Higher and Higher (acting debut, 1943), Step Lively, Anchors Aweigh, Till the Clouds Roll By, It Happened in Brooklyn, The Miracle of the Bells, The Kissing Bandit, Take Me Out to the Ball Game, On the Town, Double Dynamite, Meet Danny Wilson, From Here to Eternity (Academy Award, best supporting actor, 1953), Suddenly, Young at Heart, Not as a Stranger, The Tender Trap, Guys and Dolls, The Man With the Golden Arm, Meet Me in Las Vegas (cameo), Johnny Concho (also prod.), High Society, Around the World in 80 Days, The Pride and the Passion, The Joker Is Wild, Pal Joey, Kings Go Forth, Some Came Running, A Hole in the Head, Never So Few, Can-Can, Ocean's Eleven, Pepe (cameo), The Devil at 4 O'Clock, Sergeants 3 (also prod.), The Road to Hong Kong (cameo), The Manchurian Candidate, Come Blow Your Horn, The List of Adrian Messenger, 4 for Texas, Robin and the 7 Hoods (also prod.), None But the Brave (also dir., prod.), Von Ryan's Express, Marriage on the Rocks, Cast a Giant Shadow, The Oscar (cameo), Assault on a Queen, The Naked Runner, Tony Rome, The Detective, Lady in Cement, Dirty Dingus Magee, That's Entertainment!, The First Deadly Sin (also exec. prod.), Cannonball Run II (cameo), Listen Up: The Lives of Quincy Jones. TELEVISION: Series: The Frank Sinatra Show (1950-52; 1957-58); numerous specials, and guest appearances, incl. Club Oasis, Anything Goes (1954), Hollywood Palace, Our Town (1955), Frank Sinatra: A Man and His Music (Emmy Award, 1965), Francis Albert Sinatra Does His Thing, Ol' Blue Eyes Is Back, Magnum P.I., Frank Liza & Sammy: The Ultimate Event, Sinatra: Concert for the Americas. Movies: Contract on Cherry Street, Young at Heart.

SINBAD
Actor. r.n. David Adkins. b. Benton Harbor, MI, Nov. 10, 1956. e. Univ. of Denver. Served in Air Force before becoming stand-up comic. Career was subsequently launched by appearances on tv series Star Search. PICTURES: Necessary Roughness (debut, 1991), Coneheads, The Meteor Man, Houseguest, First Kid (also co-exec. prod.), Jingle All the Way, Homeward Bound II: Lost in San Francisco, First Kid, Jingle All the Way. TELEVISION: Series: The Redd Foxx Show, A Different World, It's Showtime at the Apollo (host), The Sinbad Show (also exec. prod.). Specials: Sinbad: Brain Damaged, Afros and Bellbottoms, Take No Prisoners, Sinbad and Friends All the Way Live... Almost (also writer), Aliens for Breakfast. Guest: The Cosby Show, Saturday Night Live.

SINCLAIR, MADGE
Actress. b. Kingston, Jamaica, April 28, 1938. e. Shortwood Women's College. Worked in Jamaica as a teacher and in the insurance business before moving to NY. Chairwoman, Madge Walters Sinclair Inc., Caribbean Child Life Foundation. Awards: NAACP Image Award, 1981 and 1983, best actress in dramatic series, Trapper John M.D.; Drama-Logue Critics Award, 1986, Boseman & Lena; Mother of the Year Award, 1984. L.A. area Emmy Award, Look Away. Member: bd. of dir., Lost Angeles Theatre Center.
THEATER: Kumaliza (NYSF, debut, 1969), Iphigenia (NYSF, NY and with Young Vic, London), Mod Donna, Ti-Jean and His Brothers, Blood, Division Street (Mark Taper Forum), Boesman & Lena (LA Theatre Center), Tartuffe (L.A. Theatre Center), Stars in the Morning (LATC), Piano (LATC), Jacques and His Master (LATC), Trinity (New Federal Theatre).
PICTURES: Conrack (debut, 1974), Cornbread Earl & Me, Leadbelly, I Will I Wish… For Now, Convoy, Uncle Joe Shannon, Star Trek IV: The Voyage Home, Coming to America, The Lion King (voice).
TELEVISION: Series: Grandpa Goes to Washington, Trapper John M.D., O'Hara, Gabriel's Fire (Emmy Award, 1991; revamped as Pros & Cons), Me and the Boys. Guest: Madigan, Medical Center, The Waltons, Joe Forester, Doctor's Hospital, Executive Suite, Medical Story, Serpico, The White Shadow, All in the Family, Homeroom, Midnight Caller, Roseanne. Mini-Series: Roots, The Orchid House (Britain), Queen. Movies: I Love, You, Goodbye, One in a Million: The Ron LeFlore Story, I Know Why the Caged Bird Sings, High Ice, Jimmy B and Andre, Guyana Tragedy: The Story of Jim Jones, Victims, Look Away: The Emancipation of Mary Todd Lincoln, Divided We Stand, Jonathan: The Boy Nobody Wanted, The Man With 3 Wives. Special: A Century of Women.

SINDEN, DONALD
Actor. b. Plymouth, England, Oct. 9, 1923. Stage debut 1942 in fit-up shows; London stage includes There's a Girl in My Soup, The Relapse, Not Now Darling, King Lear, Othello, Present Laughter, Uncle Vanya, The School for Scandal, Two Into One, The Scarlet Pimpernel, Oscar Wilde, Major Barbara, Out of Order, Venus Observed, She Stoops to Conquer, Hamlet, That Good Night. B'way: London Assurance, Habeas Corpus. TV debut 1948.
PICTURES: Portrait From Life (The Girl in the Painting; debut, 1948), The Cruel Sea, Mogambo, A Day to Remember, You Know What Sailors Are, Doctor in the House, The Beachcomber, Mad About Men, An Alligator Named Daisy, Black Tent, Eyewitness, Tiger in the Smoke, Doctor at Large, Rockets Galore (Mad Little Island), The Captain's Table, Operation Bullshine, Your Money or Your Wife, The Siege of Sydney Street, Twice Around the Daffodils, Mix Me a Person, Decline and Fall, Villain, Rentadick, The Island at the Top of the World, That Lucky Touch, The Children, The Canterville Ghost.
TELEVISION: Bullet in the Ballet, Road to Rome, Dinner With the Family, Odd Man In, Love from Italy, The Frog, The Glove, The Mystery of Edwin Drood, The Happy Ones, The Comedy of Errors, The Wars of the Roses, The Red House, Blackmail, A Bachelor Gray, Our Man at St. Marks (3 series), The Wind in the Tall Paper Chimney, A Woman Above Reproach, Call My Bluff, Relatively Speaking, Father Dear Father, The 19th Hole, Seven Days in the Life of Andrew Pelham (serial), The Assyrian Rejuvenator, The Organization (serial), The Confederacy of Wives, Tell It to the Chancellor, The Rivals, Two's Company (4 series), All's Well That Ends Well, Never the Twain (11 series), Cuts.

SINGER, LORI
Actress. b. Corpus Christi, TX, Nov. 6, 1962. Brother is actor Marc Singer; father was symphony conductor Jacques Singer. Concert cellist while in teens. Won starring role in TV series Fame (1981).
PICTURES: Footloose (debut, 1984), The Falcon and The Snowman, The Man with One Red Shoe, Trouble in Mind, Summer Heat, Made in U.S.A., Warlock, Equinox, Sunset Grill, Short Cuts, F.T.W.
TELEVISION: Series: Fame, VR5. Movies: Born Beautiful, Storm and Sorrow. Special: Sensibility and Sense.

SINGER, MARC
Actor. b. Vancouver, B.C., Canada, Jan. 29. Brother of actress Lori Singer. Son of symphony conductor Jacques Singer. Trained in summer stock and regional theatre.
PICTURES: Go Tell the Spartans, If You Could See What I Hear, The Beastmaster, Born to Race, A Man Called Sarge, Watchers II, Body Chemistry, Dead Space, In the Cold of the Night, Beastmaster 2, Sweet Justice, The Berlin Conspiracy, Alien Intruder, Beastmaster 3.
TELEVISION: Series: The Contender, V, Dallas. Mini-Series: 79 Park Avenue, Roots: The Next Generation. Movies: Things in Their Season, Journey from Darkness, Something for Joey, Never Con a Killer, Sergeant Matlovich vs. the U.S. Air Force,

The Two Worlds of Jennie Logan, For Ladies Only, Paper Dolls, V, Her Life as a Man, V—The Final Battle, Deadly Game, The Sea Wolf.

SINGLETON, JOHN
Director, Writer. b. Los Angeles, CA, Jan. 6, 1968. Entered USC's Filmic Writing Program, where he received a Robert Riskin Writing Award and two Jack Nicholson Writing Awards. With debut feature Boyz N the Hood (1991) he became the first African-American and youngest person ever to be nominated for an Academy Award for Best Director. Appeared in film Beverly Hills Cop III.
PICTURES: Director-Writer: Boyz N the Hood (Acad. Award noms. for dir. & s.p.), Poetic Justice (also co-prod.), Higher Learning (also co-prod.), Rosewood.

SINGLETON, PENNY
Actress. r.n. Dorothy McNulty. b. Philadelphia, PA, September 15, 1908. e. Columbia U. First Broadway success came as top comedienne in Good News., exec. pres. AGVA.
PICTURES: Outside of Paradise, Swing Your Lady, Men Are Such Fools, Boy Meets Girl, Mr. Chump, Mad Miss Manton, Garden of the Moon, Secrets of an Actress, Hard to Get, 28 films in Blondie series (from Blondie, 1938, to Blondie's Hero, 1950), Rocket Busters, Go West Young Lady, Footlight Glamor, Young Widow, The Best Man, Jetsons: The Movie (voice).
TELEVISION: Series: The Jetsons (voice).

SINISE, GARY
Actor, Director. b. 1955. Co-founder and artistic dir. of Chicago's Steppenwolf Theatre Company, 1974.
THEATER: NY: Balm in Gilead, True West, The Caretaker, The Grapes of Wrath. Chicago: Of Mice and Men, Getting Out. Director: True West (Obie Award), Orphans, Buried Child.
PICTURES: Miles From Home (dir. only), A Midnight Clear, Of Mice and Men (also dir., co-prod.), Jack the Bear, Forrest Gump (Acad. Award nom.), The Quick and the Dead, Apollo 13, Albino Alligator, Ransom.
TELEVISION: Mini-Series: The Stand. Movies: Family Secrets, My Name is Bill W, The Final Days, Truman (Golden Globe Award). Director: Crime Story, thirtysomething, China Beach.

SIODMAK, CURT
Director, Writer. b. Dresden, Germany, Aug. 10, 1902. e. U. of Zurich. Engineer, newspaper reporter, writer in Berlin; novelist, including F.P.1 Does Not Answer, adapt. 1932 for Ufa. Originals and screenplays in France and England including France (Le Bal), Transatlantic Tunnel, GB.
PICTURES: Writer: Her Jungle Love (co-story), The Invisible Man Returns, Black Friday, The Ape, Aloma of the South Sea (co-story), The Wolf Man, Invisible Agent, Frankenstein Meets the Wolf Man, I Walked With a Zombie, Son of Dracula (co-story), The Mantrap, House of Frankenstein (story), The Climax, Shady Lady, The Beast with Five Fingers, Berlin Express (story), Tarzan's Magic Fountain, Four Days Leave, Bride of the Gorilla (also dir.), The Magnetic Monster (also dir.), Curucu—Beast of the Amazon (also dir.), Love Slaves of the Amazon (also dir., prod.), Riders to the Stars, Creature with the Atom Brain, Earth vs. the Flying Saucers.

SIZEMORE, TOM
Actor. b. Detroit, MI. e. Wayne St. Univ., Temple Univ.Stage incl. The Land of the Astronauts in NYC and D.C.
PICTURES: Lock Up, Rude Awakening, Penn and Teller Get Killed, Born on the Fourth of July, Blue Steel, Flight of the Intruder, Guilty by Suspicion, Harley Davidson and the Marlboro Man, A Matter of Degrees, Passenger 57, Watch It, Heart and Souls, True Romance, Striking Distance, Wyatt Earp, Natural Born Killers, Devil in a Blue Dress, Strange Days, Heat.

SKASE, CHRISTOPHER
Executive. b. Australia, 1946. Began career as reporter for Fairfax publication, Australian Financial Review. In 1970s set up investment company with about $20,000. Revived Australian TV Seven network in Melbourne and then in U.S. bought Hal Roach Studios and NY based prod.-dist. Robert Halmi which he merged into Qintex Entertainment. Qintex Entertainment produced TV mini-series Lonesome Dove.

SKELTON, RED
Actor, Comedian. r.n. Richard Skelton. b. Vincennes, IN, July 18, 1913. Joined medicine show at age 10; later in show boat stock, minstrel shows, vaudeville, burlesque, circus. On radio from 1936. Best Comedian, Best Comedy Writing). Received ATAS Governor's Award in 1986. Composer of music, writer of short stories and painter. Received Gorgas Gold Medal, 1995.
PICTURES: Having Wonderful Time (debut, 1939), Flight Command, Lady Be Good, The People vs. Dr. Kildare, Dr. Kildare's Wedding Day, Whistling in the Dark, Whistling in Dixie, Ship Ahoy, Maisie Gets Her Man, Panama Hattie, Du Barry Was a Lady, Thousands Cheer, I Dood It, Whistling in

Brooklyn, Bathing Beauty, Ziegfeld Follies, Merton of the Movies, The Fuller Brush Man, A Southern Yankee, Neptune's Daughter, The Yellow Cab Man, Three Little Words, The Fuller Brush Girl (cameo), Duchess of Idaho (cameo), Watch the Birdie, Excuse My Dust, Texas Carnival, Lovely to Look At, The Clown, Half a Hero, The Great Diamond Robbery, Susan Slept Here (cameo), Around the World in 80 Days (cameo), Public Pigeon No. 1, Ocean's Eleven (cameo), Those Magnificent Men in Their Flying Machines.
TELEVISION: *Series*: The Red Skelton Show (1951-71; Emmy Awards as Best Comedian: 1951; as writer: 1961).

SKERRITT, TOM
Actor. b. Detroit, MI, Aug. 25, 1933. e. Wayne State U., UCLA. Model for Guess? jeans ads.
PICTURES: War Hunt (debut, 1962), One Man's Way, Those Calloways, M*A*S*H, Wild Rovers, Fuzz, Run Joe Run, Big Bad Mama, Thieves Like Us, The Devil's Rain, La Madonna, The Turning Point, Up in Smoke, Ice Castles, Alien, Savage Harvest, The Silence of the North, A Dangerous Summer (The Burning Man), Fighting Back, The Dead Zone, Top Gun, Opposing Force (Hell Camp), SpaceCamp, Wisdom, Maid to Order, The Big Town, Poltergeist III, Steel Magnolias, Big Man on Campus, Honor Bound, The Rookie, Wild Orchid II: Two Shades of Blue, Poison Ivy, Singles, A River Runs Through It, Knight Moves.
TELEVISION: *Series*: Ryan's Four, Cheers, Picket Fences (Emmy Award, 1993). *Movies*: The Bird Men, The Last Day, Maneaters Are Loose!, The Calendar Girl Murders, Miles to Go, Parent Trap II, A Touch of Scandal, Poker Alice, Moving Target, Nightmare at Bitter Creek, The Heist, Red King White Knight, The China Lake Murders, Child of the Night, In Sickness and in Health, Getting Up and Going Home. *Director*: A Question of Sex (Afterschool Special), Picket Fences (3 episodes).

SKLAR, MARTY
Executive. Pres., Walt Disney Imagineering.

SKOLIMOWSKI, JERZY
Director, Writer. b. Lodz, Poland, May 5, 1938. e. Warsaw U., State Superior Film Sch., Lodz, Poland. Scriptwriter for Wajda's Innocent Sorcerers (also actor), Polanski's Knife in the Water and Lomnicki's Poslizg. Author: Somewhere Close to Oneself, Somebody Got Drowned.
PICTURES: *Director-Writer*: Identification Marks—None (also actor, edit., art dir.), Walkover (also actor, edit.), Barrier, The Departure, Hands Up (also actor), Dialogue, The Adventures of Gerard, Deep End, King Queen Knave (dir. only), The Shout, Circle of Deceit (actor only), Moonlighting (also prod., actor), Success Is the Best Revenge, The Lightship, White Nights (actor), Big Shots (actor), Torrents of Spring (also actor), 30 Door Key (also co-s.p., prod.), The Hollow Men (prod.).

SKYE, IONE
Actress. b. London, Eng., Sept. 4, 1971. r.n. Ione Skye Leitch. Daughter of folksinger Donovan (Leitch) and sister of actor Donovan Leitch. m. singer-actor Adam Horovitz. Raised in San Francisco, Connecticut, Los Angeles. Fashion photo of her in magazine led to audition for film River's Edge.
PICTURES: River's Edge (debut, 1987 as Ione Skye Leitch), Stranded, A Night in the Life of Jimmy Reardon, Say Anything..., The Rachel Papers, Mindwalk, The Color of Evening, Wayne's World, Gas Food Lodging, Samantha, Guncrazy, Four Rooms, Dream for an Insomniac.
TELEVISION: *Series*: Covington Cross. *Movies*: Napoleon and Josephine, Girls in Prison. *Specials*: It's Called the Sugar Plum, Nightmare Classics (Carmilla).

SLATER, CHRISTIAN
Actor. b. New York, NY, Aug. 18, 1969. Mother is NY casting dir. Mary Jo Slater; father Los Angeles stage actor Michael Hawkins. Made prof. debut at 9 in The Music Man starring Dick Van Dyke, natl. tour, then on B'way Also on B'way in Macbeth, A Christmas Carol, David Copperfield and Merlin. Off-B'way in Landscape of the Body, Between Daylight and Boonville, Somewhere's Better. Also summer theatre. Directed 1992 L.A. prod. of The Laughter Epidemic.
PICTURES: The Legend of Billie Jean (debut, 1985), Twisted, The Name of the Rose, Tucker: The Man and His Dream, Gleaming the Cube, Heathers, The Wizard, Tales from the Dark Side: The Movie, Beyond the Stars (Personal Choice), Young Guns II, Pump Up the Volume, Robin Hood: Prince of Thieves, Mobsters, Star Trek VI: The Undiscovered Country (cameo), Kuffs, FernGully... The Last Rainforest (voice), Where the Day Takes You, Untamed Heart, True Romance, Jimmy Hollywood, Interview With the Vampire, Murder in the First, Broken Arrow, Bed of Roses.
TELEVISION: *Soap operas*: One Life to Live, Ryan's Hope. *Specials*: Sherlock Holmes, Pardon Me for Living, The Haunted Mansion Mystery, Cry Wolf, The Edge (Professional Man). *Movies*: Living Proof: The Hank Williams Jr. Story, Desperate For Love.

SLATER, HELEN
Actress. b. New York, NY, Dec. 19, 1963. *Off-B'way*: Responsible Parties, Almost Romance.
PICTURES: Supergirl (debut, 1984), The Legend of Billie Jean, Ruthless People, The Secret of My Success, Sticky Fingers, Happy Together, City Slickers, A House in the Hills, Betrayal of the Dove, Lassie, The Steal.
TELEVISION: *Series*: Capital News. *Movies*: 12:01, Chantilly Lace, Parallel Lives.

SLATZER, ROBERT FRANKLIN
Writer, Director, Producer. b. Marion, OH, April 4, 1927. e. Ohio State U., UCLA, 1947. Radio news commentator sportscaster, wrote radio serials; adv. dir., Brush-Moore Newspapers; feature writer, Scripps-Howard Newspapers; adv. exec., The Columbus Dispatch; syn. columnist, NY Journal-American; wrote guest columns for Dorothy Kilgallen; author of western short stories and novels; wrote, dir., prod. industrial films, docs., sports specials and commercials; 1949-51, writer for Grand National Studios Prods, Monogram Pictures, Republic Studios, Eagle-Lion Films; 1951, publicist, Hope Enterprises; pub. dir., Paramount Pictures; 1952, personal mgr. to Marilyn Monroe, Ken Maynard, James Craig, Gail Russell and other stars; 1953, story editor and assoc. prod., Joe Palooka Productions; 1953-54, staff writer Universal Studios, RKO Radio Pictures, MGM, Columbia and Paramount; 1958, formed Robert F. Slatzer Productions; 1960, exec. in chg. of prod., Jaguar Pictures Corp.; 1963-65, pres., Slatzer Oil & Gas Co.; 1966-67, bd. dir., United Mining & Milling Corp.; 1970-74, exec., Columbia Pictures Corp.; 1974, resumed producing and financing features and television films; 1976, honored as Fellow, Mark Twain Inst.
AUTHOR: *Novels*: Desert Empire, Rose of the Range, Rio, Rawhide Range, The Cowboy and the Heiress, Daphne, Campaign Girl, Scarlet, The Dance Studio Hucksters, Born to be Wild, Single Room Furnished, The West is Still Wild, Gusher, The Young Wildcats. *Biographies*: The Life and Curious Death of Marilyn Monroe, The Life and Legend of Ken Maynard, Who Killed Thelma Todd?, The Duke of Thieves, Bing Crosby—The Hollow Man, Duke: The Life and Times of John Wayne, The Marilyn Files.
PICTURES: White Gold, The Obsessed, Mike and the Heiress, Under Texas Skies, They Came To Kill, Trail of the Mounties, Jungle Goddess, Montana Desperado, Pride of the Blue, Green Grass of Wyoming, The Naked Jungle, Warpaint, Broken Lance, Elephant Walk, South of Death Valley, The Big Gusher, Arctic Flight, The Hellcats, Bigfoot, John Wayne's No Substitute for Victory', Joniko-Eskimo Boy, Operation North Slope, Claws, Don't Go West, Mulefeathers, The Unfinished, Single Room Furnished, Viva Zapata, Inchon.
TELEVISION: The Great Outdoors, Adventures of White Arrow, Let's Go Boating, The Joe Palooka Story, Amos & Andy, I Am the Law, Files of Jeffrey Jones, Fireside Theatre, The Unser Story, Year of Opportunity, The Big Ones, Ken Maynard's West, Where are They Now?, The Groovy Seven, The Untouchables, The Detectives, Wild Wild West, Wagon Train, Playhouse 90, Highway Patrol, David Frost Special, Today Show, ABC News, 20/20, Inside Edition, The Reporters, Current Affair, The Geraldo Show, Hard Copy, Larry King Show, Marilyn and Me, The Marilyn Files.

SLAVIN, GEORGE
Writer. b. Newark, NJ, Mar. 2, 1916. e. Bucknell U., drama, Yale U. Has written over 300 TV episodes & pilots. WGA TV Award. Collected works at U. Wyoming. Received Stanford U, Maxwell Anderson Playwriting Award.
PICTURES: Intrigue, Woman on Pier 13, The Nevadan, Mystery Submarine, Peggy, Red Mountain, City of Bad Men, Weekend with Father, Thunder Bay, Rocket Man, Smoke Signal, Uranium Boom, Desert Sands, The Halliday Brand, Son of Robin Hood, Big House USA, Fighting Stallions.

SLOAN, JOHN R.
Producer. e. Merchiston Castle School, Edinburg, 1932-39; asst. dir. and prod. man. Warners, London, Hollywood; 1939-46, Army.
PICTURES: Sea Devils, The End of the Affair, Port Afrique, Abandon Ship, The Safecracker, Beyond this Place, The Killers of Kilimanjaro, Johnny Nobody, The Reluctant Saint, The Running Man, The Last Command, To Sir With Love, Fragment of Fear, Dad's Army, Lord Jim, No Sex Please, We're British, The Odessa File, Force 10 From Navarone, The Children's Story.

SLOCOMBE, DOUGLAS
Cinematographer. b. England, Feb. 10, 1913. Former journalist. Filmed the invasion of Poland and Holland. Under contract to Ealing Studios 17 years.
PICTURES: Dead of Night, The Captive Heart, Hue and Cry, The Loves of Joanna Godden, It Always Rains on Sunday, Saraband for Dead Lovers, Kind Hearts and Coronets, Cage of Gold, The Lavender Hill Mob, Mandy, The Man in the White Suit, The Titfield Thunderbolt, Man in the Sky, Ludwig II,

Lease on Life, The Smallest Show on Earth, Tread Softly, Stranger, Circus of Horrors, The Young Ones, The Mark, The L-Shaped Room, Freud, The Servant (BAFTA Award), Guns at Batashi, A High Wind in Jamaica, The Blue Max, Promise Her Anything, The Vampire Killers, Fathom, Robbery, Boom, The Lion in Winter, The Italian Job, The Music Lovers, Murphy's War, The Buttercup Chain, Travels With My Aunt (Acad. Award nom.), Jesus Christ Superstar, The Great Gatsby, Rollerball, Hedda, The Sailor Who Fell From Grace With the Sea, Nasty Habits, Julia (Acad. Award nom.), Close Encounters of the Third Kind (co-photog.), Caravans, Lost and Found, The Lady Vanishes, Nijinsky, Raiders of the Lost Ark (Acad. Award nom.), The Pirates of Penzance, Never Say Never Again, Indiana Jones and the Temple of Doom, Water, Lady Jane, Indiana Jones and the Last Crusade.
TELEVISION: Movie: Love Among the Ruins.

SMART, JEAN
Actress. b. Seattle, WA, Sept. 13, 1951. e. Univ. of WA. Member of Oregon Shakespeare Fest, 1975-77; also with Hartford Stage Co., Pittsburgh Public Theatre Co., Intiman Theatre Co.
THEATER: Regional: Equus, Much Ado About Nothing, A Moon for the Misbegotten, Terra Nova, Cat's Play, Saint Joan, A History of the American Film, Last Summer at Bluefish Cove (LA Drama Critics Circle, Dramalogue & LA Drama Desk Awards), Mrs. California, Strange Snow. NY: Last Summer at Bluefish Cove, Piaf (B'way debut, 1981).
PICTURES: Flashpoint (debut, 1984), Protocol, Fire With Fire, Project X, Mistress, Homeward Bound: The Incredible Journey.
TELEVISION: Series: Reggie, Teachers Only, Designing Women, High Society. Movies: Single Bars Single Women, A Fight for Jenny, A Seduction in Travis County, A Stranger in Town (also co-prod.), The Yarn Princess, The Yearling, A Stranger in Town. Specials: Piaf, Maximum Security, Royal Match, A Palce at the Table.

SMITH, CHARLES MARTIN
Actor, Director. b. Los Angeles, CA, Oct. 30, 1953. e. California State U. Father is animation artist Frank Smith.
PICTURES: The Culpepper Cattle Company (debut, 1972), Fuzz, The Spikes Gang, American Graffiti, Pat Garrett and Billy the Kid, Rafferty and the Gold Dust Twins, No Deposit No Return, The Hazing, The Buddy Holly Story, More American Graffiti, Herbie Goes Bananas, Never Cry Wolf (also co-wrote narration), Starman, Trick or Treat (also dir.), The Untouchables, The Experts, The Hot Spot, Deep Cover, Fifty-Fifty (also dir.), I Love Trouble, Perfect Alibi, Speechless, He Ain't Heavy.
TELEVISION: Series: Speed Buggy (voice). Guest: The Brady Bunch, Monte Nash, Baretta, Streets of San Francisco, Petrocelli, The Rookies, Grizzly Adams, Twilight Zone, Ray Bradbury Theatre, Outer Limits, L.A. Law, Picket Fences, Northern Exposure, Tales From the Crypt. Movies: Go Ask Alice, Law of the Land, Cotton Candy, Boris and Natasha (also dir.), And the Band Played On, Roswell. Special: Partners. Mini-Series: Streets of Laredo.

SMITH, DAVID R.
Archivist. b. Pasadena, CA, Oct. 13, 1940. e. Pasadena City Coll., A.A., 1960; U. of California, Berkeley, B.A. 1962, MLS 1963. Writer of numerous historical articles. Worked as librarian at Library of Congress, 1963-65 and as reference librarian, UCLA 1965-70 before becoming archivist for The Walt Disney Co. 1970-present. Exec. dir., The Manuscript Society, 1980-; member, Society of CA Archivists, Intl. Animated Film Society (ASIFA), Fellow of the Manuscript Society, 1993. Received service award, ASIFA, and award of distinction, Manuscript Soc, 1983. Co-Author: The Ultimate Disney Trivia Book (1992), Book 2 (1994), Disney A to Z: The Official Encyclopedia (1996).

SMITH, HOWARD K.
News commentator. b. Ferriday, LA, May 12, 1914. e. Tulane U., 1936; Heidelberg U., Germany; Oxford U., Rhodes scholarship. United Press, London, 1939; United Press Bureau, Copenhagen; United Press, Berlin, 1940; joined CBS News, Berlin corr., 1941. Reported on occupied Europe from Switzerland to 1944; covered Nuremberg trials, 1946; ret. to U.S., moderator, commentator or reporter, CBS Reports, Face the Nation, Eyewitness to History, The Great Challenge, numerous news specials (Emmy Award, 1960 for The Population Explosion). Sunday night news analysis. CBS News Washington corr., 1957; chief corr. & mgr., Washington Bureau, 1961; joined, ABC News, Jan. 1962. News and comment, ABC news. Anchorman and commentator, ABC Evening News. Author: Last Train from Berlin, 1942, The State of Europe, 1949. Washington, D.C.—The Story of Our Nation's Capital, 1967.

SMITH, HY
Executive. b. New York, NY, June 3, 1934. e. Baruch Sch., CCNY, B.B.A. Joined Paramount Pictures 1967, foreign ad.-pub coordinator; 1969, joined United Artists as foreign ad.-pub mgr.; named intl. ad.-pub dir., 1970; named v.p., intl. adv.-pub. 1976; v.p. worldwide adv., publ. & promo., 1978; 1981, named first v.p., adv./pub./promo; 1982, joined Rastar Films as v.p., intl. project director for Annie; 1983, joined United Intl. Pictures as sr. v.p., adv/pub, based in London. 1984, named sr. v.p., mktg. 1995, promoted to exec. v.p., mktg.

SMITH, JACLYN
Actress. b. Houston, TX, Oct. 26, 1947. Started acting while in high school and studied drama and psychology at Trinity U. in San Antonio. Appeared in many commercials as model.
PICTURES: The Adventurers, Bootleggers, Nightkill, Deja Vu.
TELEVISION: Series: Charlie's Angels, Christine Cromwell. Guest: McCloud, Get Christy Love, The Rookies. Movies: Probe (Switch), Charlie's Angels (pilot), Escape From Bogen County, The Users, Jacqueline Bouvier Kennedy, Rage of Angels, The Night They Saved Christmas, Sentimental Journey, Florence Nightingale, Rage of Angels: The Story Continues, Windmills of the Gods, The Bourne Identity, Settle the Score, Danielle Steel's Kaleidoscope, Lies Before Kisses, The Rape of Dr. Willis, In the Arms of a Killer, Nightmare in the Daylight, Love Can Be Murder, Cries Unheard: The Donna Yalich Story, Danielle Steel's Family Album.

SMITH, JAN
Exexcutive. Vice President, Disney Publishing & Mouseworks.

SMITH, JOSEPH P.
Executive. b. Brooklyn, NY, March 28, 1921. e. Columbia U. Started career Wall Street; joined RKO Radio Pictures, served in sales and managerial posts; exec. v.p., Lippert Productions, Hollywood; v.p., Telepictures, Inc.; formed and pres., Cinema-Vue Corp.; pres., Pathe Pictures, Inc., Pathe News, Inc.

SMITH, KURTWOOD
Actor. b. New Lisbon, WI, July 3, 1943. e. B.A. San Jose (1966), M.F.A. Stanford (1969). Starred in Oscar-nominated short 12:01 P.M.
THEATER: Plymouth Rock, The Price, Faces by Chekhov, Familiar Faces, Enemy of the People, The Debutante Ball (all in Calif.), The Lucky Spot (Williamston), Signature (Poughkeepsie), Hamlet, Taming of the Shrew, and over 20 other Shakespeare productions in CA.
PICTURES: Roadie (debut, 1980), Zoot Suit, Going Berserk, Staying Alive, Flashpoint, Robocop, Rambo III, True Believer, Dead Poets Society, Heart of Dixie, Quick Change, Oscar, Company Business, Star Trek VI: The Undiscovered Country, Shadows and Fog, The Crush, Heart and Souls, Fortress, Boxing Helena, Under Siege 2: Dark Territory, Last of the Dogmen, To Die For, Broken Arrow, A Time to Kill, Citizen Ruth, Precious.
TELEVISION: Series: The Renegades, The New Adventures of Beans Baxter, Big Wave Dave's. Movies: Murder in Texas, Missing Pieces, The Midnight Hour, International Airport, Deadly Messages, The Christmas Gift, Doorways, While Justice Sleeps. Mini-Series: North and South Book II, The Nightmare Years (Ace Award nom.). Guest: Stir Crazy, Stingray, Newhart, 21 Jump Street, It's Garry Shandling's Show, The Famous Teddy Z, Picket Fences.

SMITH, LANE
Actor. b. Memphis, TN, Apr. 29.
THEATER: NY: Visions of Kerouac, Brechtesgarten, Glengarry Glen Ross (Drama Desk Award).
PICTURES: Network, Honeysuckle Rose, Prince of the City, Frances, Purple Hearts, Red Dawn, Places in the Heart, Weeds, Prison, Race for Glory, Air America, My Cousin Vinny, The Mighty Ducks, The Distinguished Gentleman, Son-in-Law, The Scout.
TELEVISION: Series: V, Kay O'Brien, Good Sports, Good and Evil. Mini-Series: Chiefs. Movies: A Death in Canaan, Crash, The Solitary Man, Disaster on the Coastliner, City in Fear, Gideon's Trumpet, A Rumor of War, The Georgia Peaches, Mark I Love You, Dark Night of the Scarecrow, Prime Suspect, Thou Shalt Not Kill, Special Bulletin, Something About Amelia, Dress Gray, The Final Days, False Arrest, Duplicates. Specials: Displaced Person, Member of the Wedding.

SMITH, DAME MAGGIE
D.B.E. C.B.E. Actress. b. Ilford, England, Dec. 28, 1934. Early career Oxford Playhouse. With the Old Vic 1959-60. Also with Stratford Ontario Shakespeare Fest. 1975-78, & 1980. Received C.B.E. 1970; D.B.E., 1990.
THEATER: Twelfth Night (debut, 1952), Cakes and Ale, New Faces of 1956 (NY debut, as comedienne), Share My Lettuce, The Stepmother, What Every Woman Knows, Rhinoceros, The Rehearsal, The Private Ear, The Public Eye, Mary Mary, The Recruiting Officer, Othello, The Master Builder, Hay Fever, Much Ado About Nothing, Black Comedy, Miss Julie, Trelawney of the Wells, The Beaux Stratagem, The Three Sisters, Hedda Gabler, Design for Living (L.A.), Private Lives (London & NY), Slap, Peter Pan, As You Like It, Macbeth,

Night and Day (London & NY), Virginia, Way of the World, Lettice and Lovage (London & NY, Tony Award), The Importance of Being Earnest, Three Tall Women.
PICTURES: Nowhere to Go (debut, 1958), Go to Blazes, The V.I.P.s, The Pumpkin Eater, Young Cassidy, Othello, The Honey Pot, Hot Millions, The Prime of Miss Jean Brodie (Academy Award, BAFTA Award, 1969), Oh! What a Lovely War, Travels With My Aunt, Love and Pain and the Whole Damn Thing, Murder by Death, Death on the Nile, California Suite (Academy Award, best supporting actress, 1978), Clash of the Titans, Quartet, Evil Under the Sun, The Missionary, Better Late Than Never, A Private Function (BAFTA Award, 1985), Lily in Love, A Room with a View, The Lonely Passion of Judith Hearne, Romeo-Juliet (voice), Hook, Sister Act, The Secret Garden, Sister Act 2: Back in the Habit, Richard III.
TELEVISION: Much Ado About Nothing, Man and Superman, On Approval, Home and Beauty, Mrs. Silly, Bed Among the Lentils, Memento Mori, Suddenly Last Summer.

SMITH, ROGER
Actor, Producer. b. South Gate, CA, Dec. 18, 1932. m. actress-performer Ann Margret. e. U. of Arizona. Started career at age 7, one of the Meglin Kiddies, appearing at the Mayan Theater, Wilshire, Ebell. Sings, composes, American folk songs. Producer: Ann-Margret cabaret and theater shows.
PICTURES: No Time to Be Young, Crash Landing, Operation Madball, Man of a Thousand Faces, Never Steal Anything Small, Auntie Mame, Rogues Gallery.
TELEVISION: The Horace Heidt Show, Ted Mack Original Amateur Hour, 77 Sunset Strip (series), writer, ABC-TV.

SMITH, WILL
Actor, Singer. b. Philadelphia, PA, Sept. 25, 1968. Teamed with musician Jeff Townes as rap duo D.J. Jazzy Jeff & the Fresh Prince. Albums: Rock the House, He's the DJ I'm the Rapper, And in This Corner, Homebase. Recipient of 2 Grammy Awards.
PICTURES: Where the Day Takes You (debut, 1992), Made in America, Six Degress of Separation, Bad Boys, Independence Day, Men in Black.
TELEVISION: Series: Fresh Prince of Bel Air (also co-exec. prod.).

SMITH, WILLIAM
Actor. b. Columbia, MO, May 24, 1932. e. Syracuse, U., BA; UCLA, MA.
PICTURES: Darker Than Amber, C.C. and Company, The Losers, Run, Angel, Run, Blood and Guts, Seven, Fast Company, No Knife, Twilight's Last Gleaming, The Frisco Kid, Any Which Way You Can, Rumble Fish, Red Dawn, Eye of the Tiger, Commando Squad, Moon in Scorpio, Hell Comes to Frogtown, Maniac Cop, Red Nights, Nam, B.O.R.N., Action U.S.A., Deadly Breed, Evil Altar, Jungle Assault, L.A. Vice, Slow Burn, Terror in Beverly Hills, Hell on the Battleground, Forgotten Heroes, Instant Karma, Empire of Ash, Emperor of the Bronx.
TELEVISION: Mini-Series: Rich Man Poor Man. Series: Laredo, Rich Man Poor Man: Book II. Series: Laredo, Rich Man Poor Man: Book II, Hawaii 5-0, Wildside. Movies: The Over-the-Hill Gang, Crowhaven Farm, The Rockford Files (pilot), The Sex Symbol, Death Among Friends, Manhunter, The Rebels, Wild Times, The Jerk Too.

SMITROVICH, BILL
Actor. b. Bridgeport, CT, May 16, 1947. e. Univ. of Bridgeport, Smith Col. Studied acting at Actors and Directors Lab.
THEATER: B'way: The American Clock. Off-B'way: Never Say Die, Frankie and Johnny in the Claire de Lune, Seks. Regional: Requeim for a Heavyweight, Food from Trash, Of Mice and Men, The Love Suicide at Schofield Barracks.
PICTURES: A Little Sex, Without a Trace, Splash, Maria's Lovers, Key Exchange, Silver Bullet, Band of the Hand, Manhunter, A Killing Affair, Her Alibi, Renegades, Crazy People, Bodily Harm.
TELEVISION: Series: Crime Story, Life Goes On. Guest: Miami Vice. Movies: Born Beautiful, Muggable Mary, Gregory K, Labor of Love: The Arlette Schweitzer Story, Children of the Dark, Texas Justice.

SMITS, JIMMY
Actor. b. New York, NY, July 9, 1955. e. Brooklyn Coll., B.A.; Cornell U., M.F.A. Worked as community organizer before acting with NY Shakespeare Fest. Public Theater.
THEATER: Hamlet (NY Shakespeare Fest., 1983), Little Victories, Buck, The Ballad of Soapy Smith, Death and the Maiden.
PICTURES: Running Scared (debut, 1986), The Believers, Old Gringo, Vital Signs, Fires Within, Switch, Gross Misconduct, My Family/Mi Familia.
TELEVISION: Series: L.A. Law (Emmy Award, 1990), NYPD Blue (Golden Globe, 1996). Pilot: Miami Vice. Movies: Rockabye, The Highwayman, Dangerous Affection, Glitz, The Broken Cord, The Tommyknockers, The Cisco Kid, Solomon

and Sheba, The Last Word. Specials: The Other Side of the Border (narrator), Happily Ever After Fairy Tales: Cinderella, Hispanic Americans: The New Frontier (host).

SMOTHERS BROTHERS
Comedians, Singers.
SMOTHERS, DICK: b. New York, NY, Nov. 20, 1939. e. San Jose State College. Films: The Silver Bears (debut, 1978), Casino.
SMOTHERS, TOM: b. New York, NY, Feb. 2, 1937. e. San Jose State College. In films Get to Know Your Rabbit, The Silver Bears, There Goes the Bride, Serial, Pandemonium.
Began career as coffeehouse folk singers with a bit of comic banter mixed in. After success at some of hipper West Coast clubs, appeared on Jack Paar's Tonight Show, The Jack Benny Show and as regulars on Steve Allen's show, 1961. 1962-65 had a series of popular albums. After starring in a situation comedy show, they hosted their own variety program. On B'way in musical I Love My Wife. Both appeared in film Speed Zone.
TELEVISION: Series: The Steve Allen Show (1961), The Smothers Brothers Show (1965-66), The Smothers Brothers Comedy Hour (1967-69), The Smothers Brothers Show (1970), The Smothers Brothers Show (1975), Fitz and Bones, The Smothers Brothers Comedy Hour. Specials: The Smothers Brothers Reunion.

SNELL, PETER R. E.
Producer. b. Nov. 17, 1941. Entered industry 1967. Appt. head of prod. and man. dir. British Lion 1973. Joined Robert Stigwood group 1975. Returned to indep. prod., 1978; Hennessy. Appt. chief exec., Britannic Film & Television Ltd. 1985, purchased British Lion Film Prods., Ltd. from Thorn/EMI 1986-87. 1988: chmn. and chief executive British Lion.
PICTURES: Prod.: Winters Tale, Some May Live, A Month in the Country, Carnaby 68, Subterfuge, Julius Caesar, Goodbye Gemini, Antony and Cleopatra, The Wicker Man, Hennessy, Bear Island, Mother Lode, Lady Jane, Turtle Diary, A Prayer for the Dying.
TELEVISION: Exec. Prod.: A Man For All Seasons, Tears in the Rain, Treasure Island, The Crucifer of Blood. Prod.: Death Train, Nightwatch.

SNIDER, STACEY
Exuetive. President of production, TriStar Pictures (A Sony Pictures Entertainment Co., Inc.).

SNIPES, WESLEY
Actor. b. Bronx, NY, July 31, 1962. e. SUNY/Purchase. Performed with puppet theatre group called Struttin Street Stuff before landing NY stage work. Appeared in Michael Jackson video Bad.
PICTURES: Wildcats (debut, 1986), Streets of Gold, Critical Condition, Major League, Mo' Better Blues, King of New York, New Jack City, Jungle Fever, White Men Can't Jump, The Waterdance, Passenger 57, Boiling Point, Rising Sun, Demolition Man, Sugar Hill, Drop Zone, To Wong Foo—Thanks for Everything—Julie Newmar, Money Train, Waiting to Exhale, The Fan.
TELEVISION: Series: H.E.L.P. Special: Vietnam War Stories (ACE Award, 1989). Guest: Miami Vice.
THEATER: B'way: The Boys of Winter, Death and the King's Horsemen, Execution of Justice.

SNODGRESS, CARRIE
Actress. b. Chicago, IL, Oct 27, 1945. e. Northern Illinois U. and M.A. degree from the Goodman Theatre. Plays include All Way Home, Oh What a Lovely War, Caesar and Cleopatra and Tartuffe (Sarah Siddons Award, 1966), The Price, Vanities, The Curse of the Starving Class.
PICTURES: Rabbit Run (debut, 1970), Diary of a Mad Housewife (Acad. Award nom.), The Fury, The Attic, Homework, Trick or Treats, A Night in Heaven, Pale Rider, Rainy Day Friends, Murphy's Law, Blueberry Hill, The Chill Factor, Nowhere to Run, Across the Tracks, The Ballad of Little Jo, 8 Seconds, Blue Sky, White Man's Burden.
TELEVISION: Movies: The Whole World Is Watching, Silent Night Lonely Night, The Impatient Heart, Love's Dark Ride, Fast Friends, The Solitary Man, Nadia, The Rose and the Jackal, Woman With a Past, Rise & Walk: The Dennis Byrd Story. Guest: The Outsider, The Virginian, Judd for the Defense, Medical Center, Marcus Welby, M.D.

SNOW, MARK
Composer. b. Brooklyn, NY, 1946. e. Juilliard School of Music, 1968. As co-founder and member of New York Rock 'n' Roll Ensemble, appeared with the Boston Pops, at Carnegie Hall concerts and on the college circuit in the 1960s and 1970s.
PICTURES: Skateboard, Something Short of Paradise, High Risk, Jake Speed, Born to Be Wild.
TELEVISION: Series: The Rookies, Starsky and Hutch, The Gemini Man, Family, The San Pedro Beach Bums, The Love Boat, The Next Step Beyond, Vega$, Hart to Hart, When the

Whistle Blows, Dynasty, Falcon Crest, Strike Force, Cagney and Lacey, T.J. Hooker, The Family Tree, Lottery!, Double Trouble, Crazy Like a Fox, Hometown, The X-Files. *Miniseries*: Blood and Orchids. *Movies*: The Boy in the Plastic Bubble, Overboard, The Return of the Mod Squad, Angel City, Games Mother Never Taught You, John Steinbeck's Winter of Our Discontent, Packin' It In, I Married a Centerfold, Something About Amelia, Challenge of a Lifetime, California Girls, I Dream of Jeannie: Fifteen Years Later, Not My Kid, The Lady From Yesterday, Beverly Hills Cowgirl Blues, Acceptable Risks, News at Eleven, The Girl Who Spelled Freedom (Emmy nom.), Murder By the Book, A Hobo's Christmas, The Father Clements Story, Still Crazy Like a Fox, Cracked Up, Roman Holiday, Pals, Murder Ordained, Louis L'Amour's Down the Long Hills, The Saint, The Return of Ben Casey, Bluegrass, Alone in the Neon Jungle, Those She Left Behind, Stuck With Each Other, Settle the Score, Archie: To Riverdale and Back Again, Child of the Night, Dead Reckoning, Follow Your Heart, The Girl Who Came Between Them, The Little Kidnappers, Miracle Landing, When He's Not a Stranger, Opposites Attract, Crash: The Mystery of Flight 1501, In the Line of Duty: The Marla Hanson Story, A Woman Scorned: The Betty Broderick Story, Highway Heartbreaker, Deliver Them From Evil: The Taking of Alta View, An American Story, Telling Secrets, The Man With 3 Wives, Born Too Soon, In the Line of Duty: Ambush in Waco, Precious Victims, Scattered Dreams: The Kathryn Messenger Story, In the Line of Duty: The Price of Vengeance, Murder Between Friends, Moment of Truth: Cradle of Conspiracy, Substitute Wife, Down Out and Dangerous. *Specials*: Day-to-Day Affairs, Vietnam War Story.

SNYDER, BRUCE M.
Executive. b. New York, NY, July 1, 1946. e. Queens Coll. Began entertainment career with Paramount Pictures as a booker in San Francisco, 1968-69. Paramount sales, NY 1969-76. Became eastern div. mgr., 20th century Fox, 1976-80. New York sales mgr., American Cinema Releasing, 1980-82. Eastern div. mgr., Embassy Pictures, 1982-83. Eastern div. mgr., TriStar Pictures, 1984-85. General sales mgr., 20th Century Fox, 1985-89. Pres., domestic distribution, 20th Century Fox, 1989-present.

SNYDER, TOM
Newscaster, Host. b. Milwaukee, WI, May 12, 1936. e. Marquette U. First job in news dept. of WRIT, Milwaukee. Subsequently with WSAV-TV, Savannah; WAII-TV, Atlanta; KTLA-TV, Los Angeles; and KYW-TV, Philadelphia, before moving to KNBC in L.A. in 1970 as anchorman for weeknight newscast. Named host of NBC-TV's Tomorrow program in 1973 (Emmy Award), moved to NY in 1974, as anchorman of one-hour segment of NewsCenter 4. 1975, inaugurated the NBC News Update, one-minute weeknight prime time news spot. Host for Tomorrow talk show, Tom Snyder Show (ABC Radio), The Late Late Show With Tom Snyder.

SOADY, WILLIAM C.
Executive. b. Toronto, Canada, Oct. 7, 1943. Career with Universal Pictures started in 1970 when named Toronto branch mgr.; promoted to v.p. & gen. sls. mgr. of Universal Film (Canada) in 1971. Promoted to v.p. & gen. sls. mgr., Universal Pictures, 1981, in NY relocating to L.A. later that year. 1983 named pres. of Universal Pictures Distribution, new domestic dist. div. of Universal; resigned, 1988. Named exec. v.p. distrib., Tri-Star Pictures, 1988; pres. of distrib. , 1992.

SOAMES, RICHARD
Executive. b. London, England, June 6, 1936. Joined Film Finances Ltd. 1972; Appt. director Film Finances Ltd., 1977: Appt. man. dir. 1979. Appt. pres. Film Finances Canada Ltd. 1982: Appt. pres., Film Finances Inc. Also formed Doric Prods, Inc.
PICTURES: The Boss's Wife, The Principal, Honey I Shrunk the Kids, Tap.

SODERBERGH, STEVEN
Director, Writer, Editor. b. Atlanta, GA, Jan. 14, 1963. First major professional job was directing concert film for rock group Yes for Grammy-nominated video, 1986.
PICTURES: *Director-Editor*: Sex Lies and Videotape (debut, 1989; also s.p.; Cannes Fest. Palme d'Or Award; Acad. Award nom. for s.p.), Kafka, King of the Hill (also s.p.), Suture (exec. prod. only), The Underneath (also s.p.), Schizopolis (alos actor).
TELEVISION: *Series*: Fallen Angels (The Quiet Room).

SOKOLOW, DIANE
Executive. b. New York, NY. e. Temple U. m. Mel Sokolow. 1975, v.p., East Coast operations, for Lorimar; with Warner Bros. 1977-81; served as v.p. of East Coast production. Left to form The Sokolow Co. with husband, Mel, to produce films. 1982, returned to WB as v.p., East Coast prod. 1984, joined Motown Prods. as exec. v.p.; producer, MGM-UA 1986-87. Currently co-pres. Sokolow Co. with Mel Sokolow.
PICTURE: My Son's Brother (co-prod.).

TELEVISION: *Exec. Prod.*: Miles from Nowhere, Trial: The Price of Passion, Lady Against the Odds, Fallen Champ, Silent Cries.

SOLO, ROBERT H.
Producer. b. Waterbury, CT, Dec. 4, 1932. e. U. of Connecticut, BA. Early career as agent with Ashley-Famous; later production as exec. asst. to Jack Warner and Walter MacEwen at Warner Bros. 1971, named WB v.p., foreign production 1974, named exec. v.p., prod. at Burbank Studio. Now indep. prod.
PICTURES: Scrooge, The Devils (co-prod.), Invasion of the Body Snatchers, The Awakening, I the Jury, Bad Boys, Colors, Above the Law (exec. prod.), Winter People, Blue Sky, Car 54 Where Are You?, Body Snatchers.

SOLT, ANDREW W.
Producer, Writer, Director. b. London, Eng. December 13, 1947. e. UCLA.
PICTURES: Imagine: John Lennon, This is Elvis, It Came From Hollywood.
TELEVISION: Honeymooners' Reunion, The Muppets... A Celebration of 30 Years, Cousteau's Mississippi, Happy Birthday Donald Duck, America Censored, Remembering Marilyn, Great Moments in Disney Animation, ET & Friends, Disney's DTV, Heroes of Rock 'n Roll, Bob Hope's Christmas Tours, Disney Goes To The Oscars, Cousteau: Oasis In Space (series), Cousteau: Odyssey, Best of the Ed Sullivan Show (4 specials), The History of Rock 'n' Roll, Sesame Street's 25th Birthday Special, Grammy's Greatest Moments, TV Guide's 40th Anniversary Special, 25x5: The Continuing Adventures of the Rolling Stones, Andy Griffith Show Reunion, Cousteau: Search for Atlantis I&II, All My Children 25th Anniversary Special, Hunt for Amazing Treasure, Great Moments in Disney Animation.

SOMERS, SUZANNE
Actress. r.n. Suzanne Mahoney. b. San Bruno, CA, Oct. 16, 1946. e. Lone Mountain Sch., San Francisco Coll. for Women. Pursued modeling career; worked as regular on Mantrap, syndicated talk show. Did summer stock and theatrical films. *Author*: Touch Me Again, Keeping Secrets, Some People Live More Than Others, Wednesday's Children: Adult Survivors of Abuse Speak Out.
PICTURES: Bullitt (debut, 1968), Daddy's Gone A-Hunting, Fools, American Graffiti, Magnum Force, Yesterday's Hero, Nothing Personal, Serial Mom.
TELEVISION: *Series*: Three's Company, She's the Sheriff, Step by Step, The Suzanne Somers Show (talk). *Guest*: One Day at a Time, Lotsa Luck, The Rockford Files, Starsky & Hutch, The Rich Little Show, Battle of the Network Stars, Love Boat. *Movies*: Sky Heist, It Happened at Lakewood Manor (Ants), Happily Ever After, Zuma Beach, Rich Men Single Women, Keeping Secrets (also exec. prod.), Exclusive (also co-exec. prod), Seduced by Evil. *Mini-Series*: Hollywood Wives. *Specials*: Us Against the World, Suzanne, Suzanne Somers Presents: Showtime's Triple Crown of Comedy, Disney's Totally Minnie.

SOMMER, ELKE
Actress. r.n. Elke Schletz. b. Berlin, Germany, Nov. 5, 1940. Entered films in Germany, 1958.
PICTURES: Das Totenschiff (debut, 1958), Lampenfieber, The Day It Rained, Heaven and Cupid, Love the Italian Way, Why Bother to Knock? (English-language debut, 1961), Daniela by Night, Violent Ecstasy, Auf Wiedersehen, Cafe Oriental, Bahia de Palma, The Victors, Island of Desire, The Prize, Frontier Hellcat, Le Bambole (The Dolls), A Shot in the Dark, The Art of Love, The Money Trap, The Corrupt Ones, The Oscar, Boy Did I Get a Wrong Number, The Venetian Affair, Deadlier Than the Male, The Wicked Dreams of Paula Schultz, The Invincible Six, They Came to Rob Las Vegas, The Wrecking Crew, Baron Blood, Zeppelin, Percy, It's Not the Size That Counts (Percy's Progress), Ten Little Indians, The Swiss Conspiracy, Carry on Behind, House of Exorcism (Lisa and the Devil), Das Netz, The Astral Factor (Invisible Strangler), Thoroughbreds, I Miss You—Hugs and Kisses, The Prisoner of Zenda, A Nightingale Sang in Berkeley Square, The Double McGuffin, Exit Sunset Blvd., The Man in Pyjamas, Lily in Love, Death Stone, Himmelsheim, Neat and Tidy, Severed Ties.
TELEVISION: *Movies*: Probe, Stunt Seven, The Top of the Hill, Inside the Third Reich, Jenny's War, Anastasia: The Mystery of Anya. *Mini-Series*: Peter the Great.

SOMMER, JOSEF
Actor. b. Greifswald, Germany, June 26, 1934. Raised in North Carolina. e. Carnegie-Mellon U. Studied at American Shakespeare Festival in Stratford, CT, 1962-64. US Army, 1958-60. NY stage debut in Othello, 1970.
PICTURES: Dirty Harry (debut, 1971), Man on a Swing, The Front, Close Encounters of the Third Kind, Oliver's Story, Hide in Plain Sight, Absence of Malice, Reds, Rollover, Hanky Panky, Still of the Night, Sophie's Choice (narrator),

Independence Day, Silkwood, Iceman, Witness, D.A.R.Y.L., Target, The Rosary Murders, Chances Are, Dracula's Widow, Forced March, Bloodhounds of Broadway, Shadows and Fog, The Mighty Ducks, Malice, Cultivating Charlie, Nobody's Fool, Strange Days.
TELEVISION: *Series*: Hothouse, Under Cover. *Specials*: Morning Becomes Electra, The Scarlet Letter, Saigon. *Movies*: Too Far to Go, Doctor Franken, The Henderson Monster, Sparkling Cyanide, The Betty Ford Story, A Special Friendship, Bridge to Silence, The Bionic Showdown: The Six Million Dollar Man and the Bionic Woman, Money Power Murder, Spy Games, An American Story, Citizen Cohn, Hostages, The Enemy Within, Don't Drink the Water, The Minutes, Kansas, Letter to My Killer. *Mini-Series*: The Kennedys of Massachusetts, A Woman Named Jackie.

SONDHEIM, STEPHEN
Composer, Lyricist. b. New York, NY, March 22, 1930. e. Williams Coll. Writer for Topper TV series, 1953. Wrote incidental music for The Girls of Summer (1956), Invitation to a March (1961), Twigs (1971). Winner of 6 Grammy Awards: Cast Albums 1970, 1973, 1979, 1984, 1988 and song of the year 1975. Named Visiting Prof. of Contemporary Theater, Oxford U. 1990.
THEATER: *Lyrics only:* West Side Story, Gypsy, Do I Hear a Waltz? *Music and lyrics:* A Funny Thing Happened on the Way to the Forum, Anyone Can Whistle, Company (Tony Award, 1971), Follies (Tony Award, 1972), A Little Night Music (Tony Award, 1973), The Frogs, Candide (new lyrics for revival), Pacific Overtures, Sweeney Todd, (Tony Award, 1979), Merrily We Roll Along, Sunday in the Park with George (Pulitzer Prize, 1985), Into the Woods (Tony Award, 1988), Assassins, Passion (Tony Award, 1994). Theater anthologies of his songs: Side By Side By Sondheim; Marry Me a Little, You're Gonna Love Tomorrow, Putting It Together. *Play:* The Doctor Is In.
PICTURES: West Side Story (lyrics), Gypsy (lyrics), A Funny Thing Happened on the Way to the Forum (music, lyrics), The Last of Sheila (s.p.), Stavisky (score), A Little Night Music (music, lyrics), Reds (score), Dick Tracy (music, lyrics; Academy Award for best song: Sooner or Later, 1990).
TELEVISION: *Special:* Evening Primrose (music, lyrics; ABC Stage '67).

SONNENFELD, BARRY
Director, Cinematographer. b. 1953. Received Emmy Award for photography on series Out of Step.
PICTURES: *Cinematographer:* Blood Simple (debut, 1984), Compromising Positions, Raising Arizona, Three O'Clock High, Throw Momma From the Train, Big, When Harry Met Sally..., Miller's Crossing, Misery. *Director:* The Addams Family (debut, 1991), For Love or Money (also co-prod.), Addams Family Values (also cameo), Get Shorty (also exec. prod.).

SORVINO, PAUL
Actor. b. New York, NY, 1939. Daughter is actress Mira Sorvino.
THEATER: Bajour, An American Millionaire, The Mating Dance, King Lear, That Championship Season, Marlon Brando Sat Right Here.
PICTURES: Where's Poppa? (debut, 1970), The Panic in Needle Park, Made for Each Other, A Touch of Class, The Day of the Dolphin, The Gambler, Shoot It Black Shoot It Blue, I Will I Will... For Now, Oh God, Bloodbrothers, Slow Dancing in the Big City, The Brink's Job, Lost and Found, Cruising, Reds, I The Jury, That Championship Season, Off the Wall, Very Close Quarters, Turk 182, The Stuff, A Fine Mess, Vasectomy, Dick Tracy, GoodFellas, The Rocketeer, Life in the Food Chain (Age Isn't Everything), The Firm, Nixon, Romeo and Juliet.
TELEVISION: *Series*: We'll Get By, Bert D'Angelo: Superstar, The Oldest Rookie, Law and Order. *Mini-Series*: Seventh Avenue, Chiefs. *Movies*: Tell Me Where It Hurts, It Couldn't Happen to a Nicer Guy, Dummy, A Question of Honor, My Mother's Secret Life, With Intent to Kill, Surviving, Don't Touch My Daughter, The Case of the Wicked Wives, Parallel Lives, Without Consent. *Guest*: Moonlighting, Murder She Wrote. *Special:* The Last Mile.

SOTHERN, ANN
Actress. r.n. Harriet Lake. b. Valley City, ND, Jan. 22, 1909. e. Washington U. p. Annette Yde-Lake, opera singer. In m.p. since 1927. Star of 10 Maisie movies in series from 1939-47. Has recently become noted painter.
PICTURES: Broadway Nights (debut in bit part, 1927), Hearts in Exile, The Show of Shows, Hold Everything, Whoopee, Doughboys, Broadway Through a Keyhole, Let's Fall in Love, Melody in Spring, The Party's Over, The Hellcat, Blind Date, Kid Millions, Folies Bergere, Eight Bells, Hooray for Love, The Girl Friend, Grand Exit, You May Be Next, Hell Ship Morgan, Don't Gamble With Love, My American Wife, Walking on Air, The Smartest Girl in Town, Dangerous Number, Fifty Roads to Town, There Goes My Girl, Super Sleuth, Danger: Love at

Work, There Goes the Groom, She's Got Everything, Trade Winds, Hotel For Women, Maisie (and subsequent series of 9 other films), Fast and Furious, Joe and Ethel Turp Call on the President, Brother Orchid, Dulcy, Lady Be Good, Panama Hattie, Cry Havoc, Thousands Cheer, Three Hearts for Julia, April Showers, Words and Music, The Judge Steps Out, A Letter to Three Wives, Shadow on the Wall, Nancy Goes to Rio, The Blue Gardenia, Lady in a Cage, The Best Man, Sylvia, Chubasco, The Killing Kind, Golden Needles, Crazy Mama, The Manitou, The Little Dragons, The Whales of August (Acad. Award. nom).
TELEVISION: *Series*: Private Secretary, The Ann Sothern Show, My Mother The Car (voice of the car). *Movies*: The Outsider, Congratulations It's a Boy, A Death of Innocence, The Weekend Nun, The Great Man's Whiskers, A Letter to Three Wives. *Mini-Series*: Captains and the Kings.

SOUL, DAVID
Actor. r.n. David Solberg. b. Chicago, IL, Aug. 28, 1943.
PICTURES: Johnny Got His Gun, Magnum Force, Dog Pound Shuffle, The Hanoi Hilton, Appointment with Death, Pentathalon.
TELEVISION: *Series*: Here Come the Brides, Owen Marshall-Counselor at Law, Starsky and Hutch, Casablanca, Yellow Rose, Unsub. *Movies*: The Disappearance of Flight 412, Starsky and Hutch (pilot), Little Ladies of the Night, Salem's Lot, Swan Song (also co-prod.), Rage, Homeward Bound, The Manions of America, World War III, Through Naked Eyes, The Fifth Missile, Harry's Hong Kong, In the Line of Duty: The FBI Murders, Prime Target, So Proudly We Hail, Bride in Black, A Cry in the Wild, The Taking of Peggy Ann, Perry Mason: The Case of the Fatal Framing, Grave Secrets: The Legacy of Hilltop Drive.

SPACEK, SISSY
Actress. r.n. Mary Elizabeth Spacek. b. Quitman, TX, Dec. 25, 1949. m. director Jack Fisk. Cousin of actor Rip Torn. Attended acting classes in New York under Lee Strasberg. Had bit role in Andy Warhol's Trash. Worked as set decorator on films Death Game, Phantom of the Paradise.
PICTURES: Prime Cut (debut, 1972), Ginger in the Morning, Badlands, Carrie, Welcome to L.A., 3 Women, Heart Beat, Coal Miner's Daughter (Academy Award, 1980), Raggedy Man, Missing, The Man With Two Brains (voice), The River, Marie, Violets Are Blue, 'night Mother, Crimes of the Heart, The Long Walk Home, JFK, Hard Promises, Trading Mom, The Grass Harp.
TELEVISION: *Movies*: The Girls of Huntington House, The Migrants, Katherine, A Private Matter, The Good Old Boys, If These Walls Could Speak. *Special:* Verna: USO Girl. *Guest*: The Rookies, The Waltons.

SPACEY, KEVIN
Actor. b. South Orange, NJ, July 26, 1959. Raised in southern CA. e. L.A. Valley Coll., appearing in stage productions as well as stand-up comedy clubs, before attending Juilliard Sch. of Drama. Has appeared in numerous regional and repertory productions including Kennedy Center (The Seagull), Williamstown Theatre Fest. and Seattle Rep. Theatre, and with New York Shakespeare Fest.
THEATER: Henry IV Part I, The Robbers, Barbarians, Ghosts, Hurlyburly, Long Day's Journey into Night, National Anthems, Lost in Yonkers (Tony Award, 1991), Playland.
PICTURES: Heartburn (debut, 1986), Rocket Gibraltar, Working Girl, See No Evil Hear No Evil, Dad, A Show of Force, Henry and June, Glengarry Glen Ross, Consenting Adults, Iron Will, The Ref, Outbreak, Swimming With Sharks (also co-prod.), The Usual Suspects (Academy Award, Chicago Film Critics Award), Seven, Albino Alligator (dir.), A Time to Kill, Looking for Richard.
TELEVISION: *Specials*: Long Day's Journey into Night, Darrow. *Movies*: The Murder of Mary Phagan, Fall from Grace, When You Remember Me, Doomsday Gun. *Series*: Wiseguy, Tribeca. *Guest*: L.A. Law.

SPADE, DAVID
Actor. b. Birmingham, MI. Raised in Scottsdale, AZ. Performed stand-up comedy in clubs and colleges which led to debut on Saturday Night Live in 1990.
PICTURES: Light Sleeper (debut, 1982), Coneheads, Reality Bites, PCU, Tommy Boy, Black Sheep.
TELEVISION: *Series*: Saturday Night Live.

SPADER, JAMES
Actor. b. Boston, MA, Feb. 7, 1960. e. Phillips Academy. Studied acting at Michael Chekhov Studio.
PICTURES: Endless Love (debut, 1981), The New Kids, Tuff Turf, Pretty in Pink, Mannequin, Baby Boom, Less Than Zero, Wall Street, Jack's Back, The Rachel Papers, Sex Lies and Videotape (Cannes Fest. Award, 1989), Bad Influence, White Palace, True Colors, Storyville, Bob Roberts, The Music of Chance, Dream Lover, Wolf, Stargate, 2 Days in the Valley.

TELEVISION: *Series*: The Family Tree. *Movies*: Cocaine: One Man's Seduction, A Killer in the Family, Starcrossed, Family Secrets. *Pilot*: Diner.

SPANO, VINCENT
Actor. b. New York, NY, Oct. 18, 1962. While attending Stuyvesant H.S. made stage debut at 14 in The Shadow Box (Long Wharf and B'way).
THEATER: The Shadow Box, Balm in Gilead.
PICTURES: Over the Edge (debut, 1979), The Double McGuffin, The Black Stallion Returns, Baby It's You, Rumblefish, Alphabet City, Maria's Lovers, Creator, Good Morning Babylon, And God Created Woman, 1753: Venetian Red, High Frequency (Aquarium), Oscar, City of Hope, Alive, Indian Summer, The Ascent, The Tie That Binds.
TELEVISION: *Series*: Search for Tomorrow. *Movies*: The Gentleman Bandit, Senior Trip, Blood Ties, Afterburn.

SPEARS, JR., HAROLD T.
Executive. b. Atlanta, GA, June 21, 1929. e. U. of Georgia, 1951. With Floyd Theatres, Lakeland, FL, since 1953; now pres. Pres., Sun South Theatres, Inc., 1996.

SPECKTOR, FREDERICK
Executive. b. Los Angeles, CA, April 24, 1933. e. USC, UCLA. M.P. agent, Ashley Famous Agency, 1962-64; Artists Agency Corp., 1964-68; exec. M.P. dept., William Morris Agency, 1968-78; exec. Creative Artists Agency, 1978-present. Trustees Council, Education First, bd. of dirs., Amer. Jewish Committee. Bd. of dirs. for the ACLU and Center for Gun-Violence Prevention.

SPELLING, AARON
Executive. b. Dallas, TX, Apr. 22, 1928. Daughter is actress Tori Spelling. Was actor/writer before becoming producer at Four Star in 1957. Producer of series and tv movies: 1967, formed Thomas/Spelling Productions; 1969, formed his own co., Aaron Spelling Productions; 1972, partnered with Leonard Goldberg; then producer on his own company banner. and over 111 movies for television.
PICTURES: Mr. Mom (exec. prod.), Surrender, Three O'Clock High (exec. prod.), Cross My Heart (co-exec. prod.), Satisfaction (co-prod.), Loose Cannons, Soapdish.
TELEVISION: *Series*: The Mod Squad, The Rookies, Charlie's Angels, Fantasy Island, Starsky and Hutch, Hart to Hart, T.J. Hooker, Family, The Love Boat, Vega$, Dynasty, Matt Houston, Hotel, The Colbys, Life with Lucy, Nightingales, HeartBeat, Beverly Hills 90210, The Heights, Melrose Place, The Round Table, Winnetka Road, 7th Heaven. *Movies* (exec. prod./prod.): The Over-the-Hill Gang, Wake When the War Is Over, The Monk, The Pigeon, The Ballad of Andy Crocker, Say Goodbye Maggie Cole, Rolling Man, Shooting Stars, Dark Mirror, Making of a Male Model, The Three Kings, Nightingales, Day One (Emmy Award, 1989), Rich Men Single Women, The Love Boat: The Valentine Voyage, Jailbirds, Back to the Streets of San Francisco, Grass Roots, Terror on Track 9, A Stranger in the Mirror, And the Band Played On (Emmy Award, 1994), Jane's House, Green Dolphin Beat, many others.

SPENGLER, PIERRE
Producer. b. Paris, France, 1947. Went on stage at 15; returned to language studies at Alliance Franccaise. Entered film industry as production runner and office boy. Teamed for first time with friend Ilya Salkind on The Light at the Edge of the World, produced by Alexander Salkind.
PICTURES: Bluebeard, The Three Musketeers, The Four Musketeers, Crossed Swords, Superman, Superman II, Superman III, Santa Claus: The Movie, The Return of the Musketeers (tv in U.S.).

SPHEERIS, PENELOPE
Director. b. New Orleans, LA, 1945. e. UCLA. Film Sch., MFA.
PICTURES: Real Life (prod. only). Director: The Decline of Western Civilization (also prod., s.p.), Suburbia (also s.p.), The Boys Next Door, Summer Camp Nightmare (s.p. only), Hollywood Vice Squad, Dudes, The Decline of Western Civilization-Part II: The Metal Years, Wedding Band (actress only), Wayne's World, The Beverly Hillbillies, The Little Rascals, Black Sheep.
TELEVISION: Saturday Night Live (prod. only), Danger Theatre (co-creator, dir., co-writer). Movie: Prison Stories: Women on the Inside (New Chicks).

SPIEGEL, LARRY
Producer, Writer, Director. b. Brooklyn, NY. e. Ohio U. With CBS-TV; Benton & Bowles; Wells, Rich, Green; BBDO. Now heads Appledown Films, Inc.
PICTURES: Hail (s.p.), Book of Numbers (s.p.), Death Game (prod.), Stunts (prod.), Spree (dir., s.p.), Phobia (prod.), Remo Williams: The Adventure Begins (prod.), Dove against Death (prod.), The Sunchaser (prod.).
TELEVISION: *ABC Afterschool Specials*, Bear That Slept Through Christmas (writer), Never Fool With A Gypsy Ikon (writer), Planet of The Apes (animated; writer), Jan Stephenson Golf Video (prod.), Remo Williams (pilot ABC; prod.).

SPIELBERG, STEVEN
Director, Producer. b. Cincinnati, OH, Dec. 18, 1947. e. California State Coll. m. actress Kate Capshaw. Made home movies as child; completed first film with story and actors at 12 yrs. old in Phoenix. At 13 won film contest for 40-min. war movie, Escape to Nowhere. At 16 made 140-min. film, Firelight. At California State Coll. made five films. First professional work, Amblin', 20 min. short which led to signing contract with Universal Pictures at age 20. Formed own co. Amblin Entertainment, headquartered at Universal Studios. Received Irving G. Thalberg Memorial Award, 1987; American Film Institute Life Achievement Award, 1995. Parterned with David Geffen and Jeffrey Katzenberg formed film company DreamWorks, 1995.
PICTURES: *Director*: The Sugarland Express (debut, 1974; also story), Jaws, Close Encounters of The Third Kind (also s.p.; Acad. Award nom. for dir.), 1941, Raiders of the Lost Ark (Acad. Award nom.), E.T. The Extra-Terrestrial (also co-prod.; Acad. Award noms. for dir. & picture), Twilight Zone—The Movie (sequence dir.; also exec. prod.), Indiana Jones and the Temple of Doom, The Color Purple (also co-prod.; Acad. Award nom. for picture), Empire of the Sun (also co-prod.), Indiana Jones and the Last Crusade, Always (also co-prod.), Hook, Jurassic Park, Schindler's List (also co-prod.: Academy Awards for Best Director & Picture, 1993; DGA, Golden Globe & Natl. Society of Film Critics Awards for director; NY Film Critics, LA Film Critics, Natl. Board of Review. Natl. Society of Film Critics & Golden Globe Awards for picture), The Lost World. *Co-exec. prod.*: I Wanna Hold Your Hand, Used Cars, Continental Divide (exec. prod.), Poltergeist (co-prod., co-s.p.), Gremlins (also cameo), The Goonies (also story), Back to the Future, Young Sherlock Holmes, The Money Pit, An American Tail, Innerspace, Batteries Not Included, Who Framed Roger Rabbit, The Land Before Time, Dad, Back to the Future Part II, Joe Versus the Volcano, Back to the Future Part III, Gremlins 2: The New Batch, Arachnophobia, Cape Fear, An American Tail: Fievel Goes West (co-prod.), We're Back!: A Dinosaur's Story, The Flintstones, The Little Rascals, Casper (co-prod.), The Bridges of Madison County (co-prod.). *Actor only*: The Blues Brothers, Listen Up: The Lives of Quincy Jones.
TELEVISION: *Series* episodes (dir.): Columbo, Owen Marshall: Counsellor-at-Law, The Pyschiatrist. *Movies* (dir.): Night Gallery (episode dir.), Duel, Something Evil, Savage. *Exec. prod.*: Amazing Stories (series; also dir. of 2 episodes), Tiny Toon Adventures (series; Emmy Award, 1991), Class of '61 (movie), Family Dog (series), seaQuest DSV (series), Pinky and the Brain (series).

SPIKINGS, BARRY
Executive. b. Boston, England, Nov. 23, 1939. Ent. m.p. ind. 1973. Joint man. dir. British Lion Films Ltd., 1975. Appt. jnt. man. dir. EMI Films Ltd., 1977. 1979, appt. chmn. & chief exec., EMI Film & Theatre Corp.; chmn. & chief exec, EMI Films, Ltd., chmn. EMI Cinemas, Ltd.; chmn., Elstree Studios, Ltd.; chmn. EMI-TV Programs, Inc., 1980; appt. chmn. chief exec., EMI Films Group, 1982; 1985 Barry Spikings Productions Inc. (U.S.A.); 1985 became director Galactic Films Inc. (with Lord Anthony Rufus Issacs); 1986, acquired Embassy Home Entertainment from Coca Cola Co., renamed Nelson Entertainment Inc., appointed pres. and COO. 1992, Pleskow/Spikings Partnership, film prod. and distrib. partnership with Eric Pleskow.
PICTURES: *Prod.*: Conduct Unbecoming, The Man Who Fell to Earth, The Deer Hunter, Texasville, Beyond Rangoon. *Exec. prod.*: Convoy.

SPINER, BRENT
Actor. b. Houston, TX. Recorded solo album Ol' Yellow Eyes I Back.
THEATER: *NY*: The Seagull, The Three Musketeers, Sunday in the Park With George, Big River.
PICTURES: Stardust Memories, Rent Control, The Miss Firecracker Contest, Corrina Corrina, Star Trek: Generations, Independence Day, Phenomenon, Star Trek: First Contact.
TELEVISION: *Series:* Star Trek: The Next Generation (also dir. episode).

SPINETTI, VICTOR
Actor. b. South Wales, Sept. 2, 1933. e. Monmouth School. Entered industry in 1955. Appeared on Broadway in Oh! What a Lovely War winning 1965 Tony and Theatre World Awards.
THEATER: *London*: Expresso Bongo, Candide, Make Me an Offer, Oh What a Lovely War (also B'way), The Odd Couple, Cat Among the Pigeons, etc.
PICTURES: A Hard Day's Night, The Wild Affair, Help!, The Taming of the Shrew, The Biggest Bundle of Them All, Can Hieronymous Merkin Ever Forget Mercy Humppe and Find True Happiness?, Under Milk Wood, The Little Prince, The Return of the Pink Panther, Under the Cherry Moon, The Krays, The Princess and the Goblin (voice).
TELEVISION: The Magical Mystery Tour, Vincent Van Gogh, Paradise Club, The Attic.

SPIRA, STEVEN S.
Executive. b. New York, NY, Mar. 25, 1955. e. City Coll. of New York; Benjamin Cardozo Sch. of Law. Associated 10 years with N.Y. law firm, Monasch Chazen & Stream. 1984, joined 20th Century Fox as sr. counsel; 1985, to Warner Bros. Now WB sr. v.p., theatrical business affairs.

SPODICK, ROBERT C.
Exhibitor. b. New York, NY, Dec. 3, 1919. e. CCNY, 1940; ent. NYC m.p. ind. as errand boy Skouras Park Plaza, Bronx 1932-33; reel boy, asst. mgr., Loew's Theatres; mgr., Little Carnegie and other art theatres; exploitation man, United Artists. Acquired Lincoln, New Haven art house in 1945 in partnership with cousin Leonard E. Sampson; developed Nutmeg Theatre circuit, which was sold in 1968 to Robert Smerling. Beginning in 1970, built Groton, CT., Cinemas I and II; Norwich Cinemas I and II, Mystic Village Cinemas I, II and III, and Westerley Triple Cinemas in RI as Gemini Cinema Circuit in partnership with Sampson and William Rosen. Gemini sold to Interstate Theatres, 1986. With Sampson presently operates York Square I & II and The New Lincoln in New Haven. Pres., Allied of CT, 1962-64; Pres. NATO of Conn. 1968-73. Past Chmn. Exec. Comm., CT Ass'n of Theatre Owners, and still active member of Board of Directors in 1994.

SPOTTISWOODE, ROGER
Director. b. England. Film editor of TV commercials and documentaries before turning to direction.
PICTURES: *Editor*: Straw Dogs, The Getaway, Pat Garrett and Billy the Kid, Hard Times, The Gambler; Who'll Stop the Rain? (assoc. prod.), Baby: Secret of the Lost Legend (exec. prod.). Director: Terror Train (debut, 1980), The Pursuit of D.B. Cooper, Under Fire, The Best of Times, Shoot to Kill, Turner & Hooch, Air America, Stop Or My Mom Will Shoot.
TELEVISION: *Movies*: The Renegades, The Last Innocent Man, Third Degree Burn, And the Band Played On, Hiroshima. *Special*: Time Flies When You're Alive.

SPRADLIN, G.D.
Actor. b. Daylight Township, Garvin County, OK, Aug. 31, 1920. e. Univ. of Oklahoma-doctor of Juris Prudence (1948). Started career as lawyer, became Independent Oil Producer. Active in local politics before turning to acting. Joined Oklahoma Repertory Theatre in 1964.
PICTURES: Will Penny (debut, 1968), Number One, Zabriskie Point, Monte Walsh, Tora! Tora! Tora!, The Hunting Party, The Godfather Part II, MacArthur, One on One, North Dallas Forty, Apocalypse Now, The Formula, Wrong Is Right, The Lords of Discipline, Tank, The War of the Roses, Clifford, Ed Wood, Canadian Bacon.
TELEVISION: *Series*: Rich Man Poor Man Book II. *Mini-Series*: Space, Dream West, Nutcracker: Money Madness and Murder, Robert Kennedy and His Times, War and Remembrance. *Movies*: Dial Hot Line, Sam Hill: Who Killed the Mysterious Mr. Foster?, Oregon Trail, Maneaters Are Loose!, And I Alone Survived, Jayne Mansfield Story, Resting Place, Shoot First: A Cop's Vengeance, Telling Secrets.

SPRINGER, PAUL D.
Executive. e. Brooklyn Law Sch. Served as assoc. for NY law firm, Johnson and Tannebaum. Later with legal dept. of Columbia Pictures. 1970, joined Paramount Pictures N.Y. legal dept. 1970; promoted to v.p. Theatrical Distrib. Counsel, 1979; promoted to sr. v.p., chief resident counsel, 1987; promoted to sr. v.p., asst. general counsel responsible for all legal functions for Paramount's distribution and marketing depts. Mem., NY and California Bars.

SPRINGFIELD, RICK
Actor, Singer, Songwriter. b. Sydney, Australia, Aug. 23, 1949.
PICTURES: Battlestar Galactica, Hard to Hold (act., addl. music).
TELEVISION: *Series*: General Hospital, Human Target, High Tide. *Specials*: An Evening at the Improv, Countdown '81. *Movies*: Nick Knight, Dead Reckoning, In the Shadows Someone's Watching.

STACK, ROBERT
Actor. b. Los Angeles, CA, Jan. 13, 1919. e. U. of Southern California. In U.S. Armed Forces (Navy), W.W.II. Studied acting at Henry Duffy School of Theatre 6 mo. then signed a contract with Universal. National skeet champion at age 16. Autobiography: Straight Shooting (1980).
PICTURES: First Love (debut, 1939), When the Daltons Rode, The Mortal Storm, A Little Bit of Heaven, Nice Girl?, Badlands of Dakota, To Be or Not To Be, Eagle Squadron, Men of Texas, Fighter Squadron, A Date With Judy, Miss Tatlock's Millions, Mr. Music, The Bullfighter and the Lady, My Outlaw Brother, Bwana Devil, War Paint, Conquest of Cochise, Sabre Jet, The Iron Glove, The High and the Mighty, House of Bamboo, Good Morning Miss Dove, Great Day in the Morning, Written on the Wind (Acad. Award nom.), The Gift of Love, The Tarnished

Angels, John Paul Jones, The Last Voyage, The Caretakers, Is Paris Burning?, The Corrupt Ones, Action Man, Story of a Woman, A Second Wind, 1941, Airplane!, Uncommon Valor, Big Trouble, Transformers (voice), Plain Clothes, Caddyshack II, Dangerous Curves, Joe Versus the Volcano.
TELEVISION: *Series*: The Untouchables (Emmy Award, 1960), The Name of the Game, Most Wanted, Strike Force, Unsolved Mysteries (host), Final Appeal (host). *Guest*: Playhouse 90 (Panic Button). *Movies*: The Strange and Deadly Occurance, Adventures of the Queen, Murder on Flight 502, Most Wanted (pilot), Undercover With the KKK (narrator), Midas Valley, Perry Mason: The Case of the Sinister Spirit, The Return of Eliot Ness. *Mini-Series*: George Washington, Hollywood Wives.

STAHL, AL
Executive. b. July 3, 1916. Syndicated newspaper cartoonist; asst. animator, Max Fleischer, gag ed. Terrytoons; U.S. Signal Corps; opened own studios, 1946; prod. first animated TV cartoon show; pres., Animated Prod., prod. live and animated commercials; member of bd. NTFC. Developed and built first animation camera and stand, 1950. Designed and produced opening animation for The Honeymooners, The Electric Company, Saturday Night Live. Produced over 5,000 tv spots. Prod. 50 min. documentary War and Pieces for U.S. Army Commandy of War in the Gulf, 1991.

STAHL, NICK
Actor. b. Dallas, TX, 1980. Started acting at age 4.
PICTURES: The Man Without a Face (debut, 1993), Safe Passage, Tall Tale.
TELEVISION: *Movies*: Stranger at My Door, Woman With a Past, Incident in a Small Town.

STALLONE, SYLVESTER
Actor, Writer, Director. b. New York, NY, July 6, 1946. After high school taught at American Coll. of Switzerland instructing children of career diplomats, young royalty, etc. Returned to U.S. in 1967 and studied drama at U. of Miami, 1969. Came to New York to seek acting career, taking part-time jobs, including usher for Walter Reade Theatres. Then turned to writing, selling several TV scripts.
PICTURES: Party at Kitty and Studs (debut, 1970), Bananas, Rebel (A Man Called Rainbo), The Lords of Flatbush (also co-s.p.), The Prisoner of 2nd Avenue, Capone, Death Race 2000, Farewell My Lovely, Cannonball, Rocky (also s.p.; Acad. Award noms. for actor & s.p.), F.I.S.T. (also co-s.p.), Paradise Alley (also s.p., dir.), Rocky II (also s.p., dir.), Nighthawks, Victory, Rocky III (also s.p., dir.), First Blood (also co-s.p.), Staying Alive (cameo; also dir., prod., co-s.p.), Rhinestone (also co-s.p.), Rambo: First Blood Part II (also co-s.p.), Rocky IV (also dir., s.p.), Cobra (also s.p.), Over the Top (also co-s.p.), Rambo III (also co-s.p.), Lock Up, Tango and Cash, Rocky V (also s.p.), Oscar, Stop Or My Mom Will Shoot, Cliffhanger (also s.p.), Demolition Man, The Specialist, Judge Dredd, Assassins, Daylight.
TELEVISION: *Guest*: Kojak, Police Story, Dream On.

STAMOS, JOHN
Actor. b. Cypress, CA, Aug. 19, 1963. Landed role of Blackie Parrish on daytime serial General Hospital in 1982. Has toured with his own band John Stamos and the Bad Boyz.
THEATER: *B'way*: How to Succeed in Business Without Really Trying.
PICTURES: Never Too Young to Die, Born to Ride.
TELEVISION: *Series*: General Hospital, Dreams, You Again?, Full House. *Movies*: Daughter of the Streets, Captive, The Disappearance of Christina, Fatal Vows: The Alexandra O'Hara Story.

STAMP, TERENCE
Actor. b. London, England, July 23, 1938. Stage experience including Alfie on Broadway. Recent stage: Dracula, The Lady from the Sea, Airborne Symphony. *Autobiography*: Coming Attractions (1988).
PICTURES: Billy Budd (debut 1962; Acad. Award nom.), Term of Trial, The Collector (Cannes Film Fest. Award, 1965), Modesty Blaise, Far from the Madding Crowd, Poor Cow, Blue, Teorema, Spirits of the Dead, The Mind of Mr. Soames, A Season in Hell, Hu-Man, The Divine Nymph, Strip-Tease, Superman, Meetings with Remarkable Men, Together?, Superman II, Monster Island, Death in the Vatican, The Hit, The Company of Wolves, Link, Legal Eagles, The Sicilian, Wall Street, Young Guns, Alien Nation, Stranger in the House (also dir., co-s.p.), Genuine Risk, Beltenebros, The Real McCoy, The Adventures of Priscilla--Queen of the Desert, Mindbender.
TELEVISION: *Movie*: The Thief of Bagdad.

STANFILL, DENNIS C.
Executive. b. Centerville, TN, April 1, 1927. e. Lawrenceburg H.S.; U.S. Naval Acad., B.S., 1949; Oxford U. (Rhodes Scholar), M.A., 1953; U. of South Carolina, L.H.D. (hon.).

Corporate finance specialist, Lehman Brothers 1959-65; v.p. finance, Times Mirror Company, Los Angeles, 1965-69; exec. v.p. finance, 20th Century-Fox Film Corp., 1969-71, pres., 1971, chmn. bd./CEO, 1971-81; pres., Stanfill, Bowen & Co., venture capital firm, 1981-90; chmn. bd./CEO, AME, Inc., 1990-92; co-chmn. bd./co-CEO, MGM, 1992-93. Sr. advisor to Credit Lyonnais, 1993-95. Private Investments, 1995-.

STANG, ARNOLD
Performer, b. Chelsea, MA, Sept. 28, 1927. Radio, 1935-50; on B'way, in five plays and in m.p. and short subjects; guest appearances on TV shows. Much voice-over cartoon work. Starred in 36 shorts.
TELEVISION: *Series*: School House, Henry Morgan Show, Doc Corkle, Top Cat (voice), Broadside. *Guest*: Captain Video, Milton Berle, Danny Thomas, Perry Como, Ed Sullivan, Red Skelton, Frank Sinatra, Wagon Train, Jack Benny, Johnny Carson, December Bride, Playhouse 90, Batman, Bonanza, Bob Hope, Danny Kaye, Jackie Gleason, Emergency, Feeling Good, Chico & the Man, Super Jaws & Catfish, Busting Loose, Flying High, Robert Klein Specials, Tales from the Dark Side, True Blue, Cosby Show.
PICTURES: Seven Days Leave, My Sister Eileen, Let's Go Steady, They Got Me Covered, So This is New York, Double for Della, Return of Marco Polo, Spirit of '76, The Man with the Golden Arm, Dondi, The Wonderful World of the Brothers Grimm, It's a Mad Mad Mad Mad World, Pinocchio in Outer Space (voice), Alakazam the Great (voice), Hello Down There, Skidoo, The Aristocats (voice), Raggedy Ann & Andy (voice), Gang That Couldn't Shoot Straight, That's Life, Hercules in New York, Ghost Dad, Dennis the Menace, At The Cottonwood.

STANLEY, KIM
Actress. r.n. Patricia Reid. b. Tularosa, NM, Feb. 11, 1925. e. U. of NM. Began stage acting in college and later in stock. Worked as model in NY while training with Elia Kazan and Lee Strasberg at Actors Studio. In late 1960s and 1970s taught drama, Coll. of Santa Fe, NM.
THEATER: The Dog, Beneath the Skin (NY debut, 1948), Him, Yes Is For a Very Young Man, Montserrat, The House of Bernarda Alba, The Chase, Picnic (NY Drama Critics Award, 1953), The Traveling Lady, The Great Dreamer, Bus Stop, A Clearing in the Woods, A Touch of the Poet, A Far Country, Natural Affection, The Three Sisters.
PICTURES: The Goddess (debut, 1958), Seance on a Wet Afternoon (Acad. Award nom.), The Three Sisters, Frances (Acad. Award nom.), The Right Stuff.
TELEVISION: *Specials*: Clash by Night, The Travelling Lady, Cat on a Hot Tin Roof (Emmy Award, 1985). *Movie*: U.M.C. *Guest*: Ben Casey (A Cardinal Act of Mercy; Emmy Award, 1963).

STANTON, HARRY DEAN
Actor. b. West Irvine, KY, July 14, 1926. Acting debut at Pasadena Playhouse. Billed in early film appearances as Dean Stanton.
PICTURES: Revolt at Fort Laramie (debut, 1957), Tomahawk Trail, The Proud Rebel, Pork Chop Hill, The Adventures of Huckleberry Finn, A Dog's Best Friend, Hero's Island, The Man From the Diner's Club, Ride in the Whirlwind, The Hostage, A Time for Killing, Rebel Rousers, Cool Hand Luke, Day of the Evil Gun, The Miniskirt Mob, Kelly's Heroes, Cisco Pike, Two-Lane Blacktop, Face to the Wind (Cry for Me Billy), Pat Garrett and Billy the Kid, Dillinger, Where the Lilies Bloom, Cockfighter, Zandy's Bride, The Godfather Part II, Rafferty and the Gold Dust Twins, Rancho Deluxe, Farewell My Lovely, 92 in the Shade, Win Place or Steal, The Missouri Breaks, Straight Time, Renaldo and Clara, Alien, The Rose, Wise Blood, Death Watch, The Black Marble, Private Benjamin, Escape From New York, One From the Heart, Young Doctors in Love, Christine, Repo Man, Red Dawn, The Bear, Paris Texas, The Care Bears Movie (voice), One Magic Christmas, Fool for Love, UFOria, Pretty in Pink, Slamdance, Stars and Bars, Mr. North, The Last Temptation of Christ, Dream a Little Dream, Twister, The Fourth War, Stranger in the House, Wild at Heart, Man Trouble, Twin Peaks: Fire Walk With Me, Blue Tiger, Never Talk to Strangers, Down Periscope.
TELEVISION: *Movies*: Flatbed Annie & Sweetpie: Lady Truckers, I Want to Live, Payoff, Hostages, Against the Wall. *Special*: Hotel Room (Tricks).

STAPLETON, JEAN
Actress. r.n. Jeanne Murray. b. New York, NY. e. Wadleigh H.S. Summer stock in NH, ME, MA, and PA. Broadway debut in In the Summer House (1954). President, Advisory bd., Women's Research and Education Instit. (Wash., D.C.); bd.: Eleanor Roosevelt Val-kill, Hyde Park; trustee: Actors Fund of America.
THEATER: Harvey, Damn Yankees, Bells Are Ringing, Juno, Rhinoceros, Funny Girl, Arsenic and Old Lace (B'way and tour), Mountain Language/The Birthday Party (Obie Award), The Learned Ladies, Bon Appetit, The Roads to Home, Night

Seasons, Morning's at Seven, You Can't Take It With You, The Show-Off, The Mystery of Edwin Drood (natl. tour). and extensive regional work at the Totem Pole Playhouse, Fayetteville, PA, Pocono Playhouse, Mountain Home Pa; Peterborough Playhouse, N.H. and others. Operatic debut with Baltimore Opera Co. in Candide, then The Italian Lesson and Bon Appetit. Starred in San Jose Civic Light Opera Co.'s Sweeney Todd.
PICTURES: Damn Yankees (debut, 1958), Bells Are Ringing, Something Wild, Up the Down Staircase, Cold Turkey, Klute, The Buddy System, Michael.
TELEVISION: *Series*: All in the Family (3 Emmy Awards: 1971, 1972, 1978), Bagdad Cafe, Mrs. Piggle-Wiggle. *Movies*: Tail Gunner Joe, Aunt Mary, Angel Dusted, Isabel's Choice, Eleanor: First Lady of the World (Emmy nom.), A Matter of Sex, Dead Man's Folly, Fire in the Dark, The Habitation of Dragons, Ghost Mom. *Specials*: You Can't Take It With You, Grown-Ups (ACE nom.), Jack and the Beanstalk and Cinderella (Faerie Tale Theatre), Something's Afoot, Let Me Hear You Whisper, Mother Goose Rock 'n' Rhyme, Parallax Garden.

STAPLETON, MAUREEN
Actress. b. Troy, NY, June 21, 1925. e. Siena Col. Worked as a model and waitress while studying acting with Herbert Berghof in NY. Became member of Actors Studio. Broadway debut, 1946, in The Playboy of the Western World. *Autobiography*: A Hell of a Life (1995).
THEATER: *NY*: Antony and Cleopatra, Detective Story, The Bird Cage, The Rose Tattoo (Tony Award, 1951), The Emperor's Clothes, The Crucible, Richard III, The Seagull, 27 Wagons Full of Cotton, Orpheus Descending, The Cold Wind and the Warm, Toys in the Attic, The Glass Menagerie (1965 & 1975), Plaza Suite, Norman Is That You?, The Gingerbread Lady (Tony Award, 1971), The Country Girl, The Secret Affairs of Mildred Wild, The Gin Game, The Little Foxes. *LA*: Juno and the Paycock.
PICTURES: Lonelyhearts (debut, 1958; Acad. Award nom.), The Fugitive Kind, A View From the Bridge, Bye Bye Birdie, Airport (Acad. Award nom.), Plaza Suite, Interiors (Acad. Award nom.), Lost and Found, The Runner Stumbles, The Fan, On the Right Track, Reds (Academy Award, best supporting actress, 1981), Johnny Dangerously, The Cosmic Eye (voice), Cocoon, The Money Pit, Heartburn, Sweet Lorraine, Made in Heaven, Nuts, Doin' Time on Planet Earth (cameo), Cocoon: The Return, Passed Away, Trading Mom, The Last Good Time.
TELEVISION: *Series*: What Happened? (panelist, 1952), The Thorns. *Specials*: For Whom the Bell Tolls, Among the Paths to Eden (Emmy Award, 1968).*Movies*: Tell Me Where It Hurts, Queen of the Stardust Ballroom, Cat on a Hot Tin Roof, The Gathering, Letters From Frank, The Gathering Part II, The Electric Grandmother, Little Gloria--Happy at Last, Family Secrets, Sentimental Journey, Private Sessions, Liberace: Behind the Music, Last Wish, Miss Rose White.

STARGER, MARTIN
Producer, Executive. b. New York, NY, May 8, 1932. e. CCNY. Served in U.S. Army Signal Corp., where prod. training films. Joined BBDO, starting in TV prod. dept.; later made v.p. & assoc. dir. of TV. Joined ABC in 1966, as v.p. of programs, ABC-TV, East Coast. 1968, promoted to v.p. and natl prog. dir; 1969 named v.p. in chg. progr.; named pres., ABC Entertainment, 1972; 1975 formed & became pres. of Marstar Productions Inc., M.P. & TV prod. co.; 1978 formed Marble Arch Productions, of which he was pres. Formed Rule/Starger Co. with Elton Rule, 1988.
PICTURES: *Exec. prod./Producer*: Nashville, The Domino Principle, Movie/Movie, The Muppet Movie, Raise the Titanic, Saturn 3, The Great Muppet Caper, Hard Country, The Legend of the Lone Ranger, On Golden Pond, Sophie's Choice, Barbarosa, Mask.
TELEVISION: Friendly Fire (Emmy Award, 1979), Escape from Sobibor, Consenting Adult, Earth Star Voyager, Marcus Welby M.D., A Holiday Affair, The Return of Marcus Welby M.D., The Elephant Man, All Quiet on the Western Front.

STARK, RAY
Producer. e. Rutgers U. Began career after WWII as agent handling Red Ryder radio scripts, and later literary works for such writers as Costain, Marquand and Hecht. Publicity writer, Warner Bros. Joined Famous Artists Agency, where he represented such personalities as Marilyn Monroe, Kirk Douglas and Richard Burton; in 1957, resigned exec. position to form Seven Arts Prods. with Eliot Hyman, serving as exec. v.p. and head of production until 1966, when he left to take on personal production projects. Founded Rastar Prods. and Ray Stark Prods. Received Irving Thalberg Award from Acad. of M.P. Arts and Sciences 1980. TV production: Barbarians at the Gate.
PICTURES: The World of Susie Wong, The Night of the Iguana, This Property Is Condemned, Oh Dad Poor Dad Mama's Hung You in the Closet and I'm Feeling So Sad

Reflections in a Golden Eye, Funny Girl, The Owl and the Pussycat, Fat City, The Way We Were, Summer Wishes Winter Dreams, For Pete's Sake, Funny Lady, The Sunshine Boys, Robin and Marian, Murder by Death, The Goodbye Girl, Casey's Shadow, The Cheap Detective, California Suite, The Electric Horseman, Chapter Two, Seems Like Old Times, Annie, The Slugger's Wife, Nothing in Common, Brighton Beach Memoirs, Biloxi Blues, Steel Magnolias, Revenge, Lost in Yonkers.

STARR, MIKE
Actor. b. Queens, NY. e. Hofstra Univ. Theatre debut with Manhattan Punchline.
THEATER: NY: Requiem for a Heavyweight, The Guys in the Truck, Map of the World, Vesper's Ever.
PICTURES: Bushido Blade, Cruising, The Natural, The Last Dragon, Cat's Eye, The Money Pit, Violets Are Blue, Off-Beat, Collision Course, Five Corners, Funny Farm, Lean on Me, Blue Steel, Uncle Buck, Last Exit to Brooklyn, Miller's Crossing, GoodFellas, Billy Bathgate, Freejack, The Bodyguard, Mac, Mad Dog and Glory, Son of the Pink Panther, Cabin Boy, On Deadly Ground, The Hudsucker Proxy, Blown Away, Baby's Day Out, Trial by Jury, Ed Wood, Radioland Murders, Dumb & Dumber, A Pyromaniac's Love Story, Clockers, Two If By Sea.
TELEVISION: *Series:* Hardball. *Movies:* The Frank Nitti Story, Hot Paint, Stone Pillow. *Guest:* Kojak, Hawk, The Equalizer, Crime Story, Spenser: For Hire.

STARR, RINGO
O.B.E. Singer, Musician, Songwriter, Actor. r.n. Richard Starkey. b. Liverpool, England, July 7, 1940. m. actress Barbara Bach. Former member of The Beatles.
PICTURES: A Hard Day's Night (debut, 1964), Help!, Yellow Submarine (cameo), Candy, The Magic Christian, Let It Be, 200 Motels, Blindman, The Concert for Bangladesh, Lisztomania, The Last Waltz, Sextette, The Kids Are Alright, Caveman, Give My Regards to Broad Street, Water (cameo), Walking After Midnight.
TELEVISION: *Movies:* Princess Daisy, Alice in Wonderland. *Series:* Shining Time Station

STEADMAN, ALISON
Actress. b. Liverpool, England, Aug. 26, 1946. m. director Mike Leigh. Studied acting with East 15 Acting School.
THEATER: The Prime of Miss Jean Brodie, Hamlet, Wholesome Glory, The Pope's Wedding, The Anchor, The King, Abigail's Party, Joking Apart, Uncle Vanya, The Rise and Fall of Little Voice, Othello, The Plotters of Cabbage Patch Corner.
PICTURES: Kipperbang (debut, 1982), Champions, Number One, A Private Function, Clockwise, Stormy Monday, The Misadventures of Mr. Wilt, Shirley Valentine, Life Is Sweet, Blame It on the Bellboy.
TELEVISION: Virtuoso, The Singing Detective, The Finding, Hard Labour, Nuts in May, Throught the Night, Pasmore.

STEEL, DAWN
Executive. b. New York, NY, Aug. 19, 1946. m. producer Charles Roven. e. marketing student, Boston U. 1964-65, NYU 1966-67; sportswriter, Major League Baseball Digest and NFL/NY 1968-69; 1969-75, editor of Penthouse Magazine; Pres. Oh Dawn! merchandising co. 1979-80, v.p. merchandising Paramount Pictures; 1978-79, merchandising consult., Playboy NYC; 1980-83, v.p. prod. Paramount Pictures. Joined Columbia Pictures 1987 as president (first woman studio pres.), resigned 1990. Formed Steel Pictures for the Walt Disney Co., 1990. Prod. for Disney: Honey I Blew Up the Kid, Cool Runnings, Sister Act 2. Prod. for New Line: Angus. Recipient of Crystal Award (1989). Author: They Can Kill You... But They Can't Eat You (1993). Member: AMPAS, Amer. Film Inst. (bd. 1988-90), NOW Legal Defense Fund; 1993-present, member of dean's advisory bd. at UCLA Sch. of Theatre, Film & TV.

STEELE, BARBARA
Actress. b. Trenton Wirrall, England, Dec. 29, 1937. Studied to be painter prior to joining rep. cos. in 1957.
PICTURES: Bachelor of Hearts (debut, 1958), Sapphire, Your Money or Your Wife, Black Sunday, The Pit and the Pendulum, Revenge of the Mercenaries, The Horrible Dr. Hitchcock, 8 1/2, Danse Macabre (Castle of Blood), The Ghost, The Hours of Love, White Voices, Nightmare Castle, The Maniacs, Terror Creatures From the Grave, The She Beast, Young Torless, Crimson Cult, They Came From Within, Caged Heat, I Never Promised You a Rose Garden, Piranha, Pretty Baby, The Silent Scream.

STEELE, TOMMY
Performer. r.n. Tommy Hicks. b. London, Dec. 17, 1936. Early career Merchant Navy. 1956 first gained fame as successful pop singer. First TV and film appearances, 1957. Composed and sang title song for The Shiralee.

THEATER: Half a Sixpence, Hans Andersen, Singin' in the Rain, Some Like It Hot.
PICTURES: Kill Me Tomorrow (debut, 1957), The Tommy Steele Story (Rock Around the World), The Duke Wore Jeans, Tommy the Toreador, Light Up the Sky, It's All Happening (The Dream Maker), The Happiest Millionaire, Half a Sixpence, Finian's Rainbow, Where's Jack?
TELEVISION: Tommy Steele Spectaculars, Richard Whittington Esquire (Rediffusion), Ed Sullivan Show, Gene Kelly in NY NY, Perry Como Show, Twelfth Night, The Tommy Steele Hour, Tommy Steele in Search of Charlie Chaplin, Tommy Steele and a Show, Quincy's Quest.

STEENBURGEN, MARY
Actress. b. Newport, AR, Feb. 8, 1953. Graduated from Neighborhood Playhouse. Received honorary doctorate degrees from Univ. of Ark. at Little Rock and Hendrix Col. in Conway, AR. On B'way stage 1993 in Candida.
PICTURES: Goin' South (debut, 1978), Time After Time, Melvin and Howard (Academy Award, best supporting actress, 1980), Ragtime, A Midsummer Night's Sex Comedy, Cross Creek, Romantic Comedy, One Magic Christmas, Dead of Winter, End of the Line (also exec. prod.), The Whales of August, Miss Firecracker, Parenthood, Back to the Future Part III, The Long Walk Home (narrator), The Butcher's Wife, What's Eating Gilbert Grape, Philadelphia, Clifford, It Runs in the Family (My Summer Story), Pontiac Moon, My Family/Mi Familia, Powder, The Grass Harp, Nixon.
TELEVISION: *Series:* Ink (also co-exec. prod.). *Mini-Series:* Tender Is the Night. *Specials:* Faerie Tale Theatre (Little Red Riding Hood), The Gift. *Movie:* The Attic: The Hiding of Anne Frank. *Series:* Back to the Future (voice for animated series), Ink.

STEIGER, ROD
Actor. b. Westhampton, NY, Apr. 14, 1925. e. Westside H.S., Newark, NJ. Served in U.S. Navy, then employed in Civil Service; studied acting at N.Y. Theatre Wing Dramatic Workshop Actors' Studio; numerous TV plays; on Broadway in ANTA prod. of Night Music.
PICTURES: Teresa (debut, 1951), On the Waterfront, The Big Knife, Oklahoma!, The Court Martial of Billy Mitchell, Jubal, The Harder They Fall, Back From Eternity, Run of the Arrow, The Unholy Wife, Across the Bridge, Cry Terror, Al Capone, Seven Thieves, The Mark, World in My Pocket, 13 West Street, Convicts 4, The Longest Day, Hands Over the City, Time of Indifference, The Pawnbroker, The Loved One, Dr. Zhivago, And There Came a Man (A Man Called John), In the Heat of the Night (Academy Award, 1967), The Girl and the General, No Way to Treat a Lady, The Sergeant, The Illustrated Man, Three Into Two Won't Go, Waterloo, Happy Birthday Wanda June, Duck You Sucker! (A Fistful of Dynamite), The Heroes, Lolly Madonna XXX, Lucky Luciano, Mussolini: Dead or Alive (The Last Days of Mussolini), Hennessey, Dirty Hands, W.C. Fields and Me, Wolf Lake, F.I.S.T., Breakthrough (Sgt. Steiner), The Amityville Horror, Love and Bullets, Klondike Fever, The Lucky Star, Lion of the Desert, Cattle Annie and Little Britches, The Chosen, The Magic Mountain, Portrait of a Hitman (Jim Buck), The Naked Face, The Kindred, Catch the Heat, American Gothic, The January Man, Men of Respect, The Ballad of the Sad Cafe, Midnight Murders, Guilty as Charged, That Summer of White Roses, The Player, The Neighbor, The Last Tattoo, Black Water, The Specialist, Mars Attacks!.
TELEVISION: Many appearances in 1950s live TV including Marty. *Movies:* Jesus of Nazareth, Cook & Perry: The Race to the Pole, Sword of Gideon, Desperado: Avalanche at Devil's Ridge, Passion and Paradise, In the Line of Duty: Manhunt in the Dakotas, Sinatra, Tom Clancy's Op Center, Choices of the Heart: The Margaret Sanger Story, In Pursuit of Honor, Columbo: Strange Bedfellows. *Mini-Series:* Hollywood Wives. *Special:* Tales of the City.

STEINBERG, DAVID
Actor, Writer, Director. b. Winnipeg, Canada, Aug. 9, 1942. e. U. of Chicago; Hebrew Theological Coll. Member Second City troupe; comedian at comedy clubs: Mr. Kelly's Hungry i, Bitter End. Starred in London and B'way stage prods. B'way includes Little Murders, Carry Me Back to Morningside Heights.
PICTURES: *Actor:* The End, Something Short of Paradise. *Director:* Paternity, Going Berserk (also co.-s.p.).
TELEVISION: *Series:* Music Scene (writer, co-host), Tonight Show (guest host), David Steinberg Show. *Special:* Second City: 25 Years in Revue. *Director:* Newhart, The Popcorn Kid, Golden Girls, One Big Family, Faerie Tale Theatre, Richard Belzer Special, Baby on Board, Annie McGuire, Seinfeld, Mad About You, Evening Shade, Designing Women, and many commercials.

STEINBERG, HERB
b. New York, NY, July 3, 1921. e. City Coll. of New York, 1937-41. Capt. U.S. Army, 1942-46; pub. PRC, 1946, Eagle Lion,

1946-49, Paramount 1949; pub. mgr. 1951; expl. mgr., 1954; studio adv. & pub. dir., 1958; exec. chg. of spec. proj., press dept., Universal City Studio, 1963; v.p., Universal Studio Tours, 1971; 1974 v.p., MCA Recreation Services. Appt. to California Tourism Commission, Calif. Tourism Hall of Fame, 1984; consultant, MCA, Inc., 1987; bd. trustees, Motion Picture & TV Fund, 1987; bd. of trustees Hollywood Canteen Foundation, 1988; Communications dir. Alliance of Motion Picture & Television Producers.

STEINMAN, MONTE
Executive. b. New York, NY, May 18, 1955. e. Wharton Sch. of Univ. of PA. Joined Paramount Pictures 1980 as sr. financial analyst. Series of promotions followed, culminating in appt. as dir. of financial planning of Gulf & Western's Entertainment and Communications Group, 1984. 1985, named exec. dir., financial planning. 1990, joined Viacom Intl., as mgr. financial planning. 1993, dir. financial planning, MTV Networks. 1994, v.p. finance at MTV Networks.

STEMBLER, JOHN H.
Executive. b. Miami, FL, Feb. 18, 1913. e. U. of FL Law Sch., 1937. Asst. U.S. att., South. dist. of FL, 1941; U.S. Air Force, 1941-45; pres. Georgia Theatre Co., 1957; named chmn., 1983; NATO member exec. comm. and past pres.; Major Gen. USAF (Ret); past bd. chmn., National Bank of Georgia.

STEMBLER, WILLIAM J.
Executive. b. Atlanta, GA, Nov. 29, 1946. e. Westminster Sch., 1964; U. of FL, 1968; U. of GA Law Sch., 1971. 1st. lt. U.S. Army, 1971; capt., U.S. Army Reserve; resigned 1976. Enforcement atty., SEC, Atlanta office, 1972-73; joined Georgia Theatre Co., 1973; pres. 1983-86; joined United Artists Communications, Inc., 1986, as v.p.; Incorporated Value Cinemas 1988 and Georgia Theatre Co. II in 1991 as its chmn. & pres. Bd. of dir., & vice chmn., NATO; member, NATO OF GA & past-pres., 1983-85; Rotary Club of Atlanta, pres. 1991-92.

STEPHENS, ROBERT
Actor. b. Bristol, England, July 14, 1931. e. Esme Church School, Bradford. Made his stage debut at age 13; joined the Royal Court Company in 1956. Son is actor Toby Stephens.
THEATER: London: The Crucible, The Good Woman of Setzuan, The Country Wife, The Entertainer, Look After Lulu, The Wrong Side of the Park, Saint Joan, The Recruiting Officer, Royal Hunt of the Sun, The Beaux Stratagem, Armstrong's Last Goodnight, Apropos of Falling Sleet (also dir.), Murderer, Private Lives, King Lear. NY: Epitaph for George Dillon, Sherlock Holmes.
PICTURES: Circle of Deception (debut, 1961), A Taste of Honey, Pirates of Tortuga, Lisa (The Inspector), The Small World of Sammy Lee, Cleopatra, Morgan!, Romeo and Juliet, The Prime of Miss Jean Brodie, The Private Life of Sherlock Holmes, The Asphyx, Travels With My Aunt, Luther, The Duellists, The Shout, Empire of the Sun, Testimony, High Season, Wonderland (The Fruit Machine), Henry V, The Bonfire of the Vanities, The Pope Must Die, Afraid of the Dark, Chaplin, Searching for Bobby Fisher, The Secret Rapture, Century.
TELEVISION: Vienna 1900 (series), Parnell and O'Shea, Gangsters, Softly Softly, The Holocaust (series, Vienna), Eustace and Hilda, Voyage of Charles Darwin, Kean, Office Story, Friends in Space Society, Suez, Hesther for Example, The Executioner, Eden End, Year of the French, Box of Delights (series), By the Sword Divided, Hells Bells (series), War and Remembrance, Window Sir, Lizzies Pictures (series), Fortunes of War (series), Inspector Morse, Radical Chambers, Adam Bede.

STERLING, JAN
Actress. r.n. Jane Sterling Adriance. b. New Yor, NY, April 3, 1923. e. private tutors; Fay Compton Sch. of Dramatic Art, London. N.Y. stage debut: Bachelor Born.
THEATER: Panama Hattie, Present Laughter, John Loves Mary, Two Blind Mice, Front Page, Over 21, Born Yesterday, The November People.
PICTURES: Johnny Belinda (debut, 1948), Appointment with Danger, Mystery Street, Caged, Union Station, The Skipper Surprised His Wife, The Big Carnival (Ace in the Hole), The Mating Season, Rhubarb, Flesh and Fury, Sky Full of Moon, Pony Express, The Vanquished, Split Second, Alaska Seas, The High and the Mighty (Acad. Award nom.), Return From the Sea, Human Jungle, Women's Prison, Female on the Beach, Man with the Gun, 1984, The Harder They Fall, Slaughter on Tenth Avenue, Kathy O', The Female Animal, High School Confidential, Love in a Goldfish Bowl, The Incident, The Angry Breed, The Minx, First Monday in October.
TELEVISION: Series: You're in the Picture (panelist, 1961), Made in America, The Guiding Light (1969-70). Mini-Series: Backstairs at the White House. Movies: Having Babies, Dangerous Company, My Kidnapper My Love.

STERLING, ROBERT
Actor. r.n. William Sterling Hart. b. Newcastle, PA, Nov. 13, 1917. e. U. of Pittsburgh. m. Anne Jeffreys, actress. Daughter is actress Tisha Sterling. Fountain pen salesman, day laborer, clerk, industrial branch credit mgr., clothing salesman on West Coast; served as pilot-instructor U.S. Army Corps. 3 yrs.
PICTURES: The Amazing Mr. Williams (debut, 1939), Blondie Brings Up Baby, Blondie Meets the Boss, Only Angels Have Wings, Manhattan Heartbeat, Yesterday's Heroes, Gay Caballero, Penalty, I'll Wait for You, Get-Away, Ringside Maisie, Two-Faced Woman, Dr. Kildare's Victory, Johnny Eager, This Time for Keeps, Somewhere I'll Find You, Secret Heart, Roughshod, Bunco Squad, Sundowners, Show Boat, Column South, Voyage to the Bottom of the Sea, Return to Peyton Place, A Global Affair.
TELEVISION: Series: Topper, Love That Jill, Ichabod and Me. Movies: Letters from Three Lovers, Beggarman, Thief.

STERN, DANIEL
Actor, Director. b. Bethesda, MD, Aug. 28, 1957. e. H.B. Studios. Appeared in 1984 short film Frankenweenie.
PICTURES: Breaking Away (debut, 1979), Starting Over, A Small Circle of Friends, Stardust Memories, It's My Turn, One-Trick Pony, Honky Tonk Freeway, I'm Dancing As Fast As I Can, Diner, Blue Thunder, Get Crazy, C.H.U.D., Key Exchange, The Boss' Wife, Hannah and Her Sisters, Born in East L.A., D.O.A., The Milagro Beanfield War, Leviathan, Little Monsters, Friends Lovers and Lunatics, Coupe de Ville, My Blue Heaven, Home Alone, City Slickers, Home Alone 2: Lost in New York, Rookie of the Year (also dir.), City Slickers II: The Legend of Curly's Gold, Bushwhacked (also exec. prod.), Celtic Pride.
TELEVISION: Movies: Samson and Delilah, Weekend War, The Court-Martial of Jackie Robinson. Series: Hometown, The Wonder Years (narrator; also episode dir.).

STERN, EDDIE
Film buyer. b. New York, NY, Jan. 13, 1917. e. Columbia Sch. of Journalism. Head film buyer and booker, specializing in art theatres, for Rugoff and Becker, NY; Captain, USAF; joined Wometco Ent. in 1952 as asst. to film buyer; v.p. motion picture theatre film buying and booking, Wometco Enterprises, Inc. Retired from Wometco 1985. Now handling film buying and booking for Theatres of Nassau, Ltd.

STERN, EZRA E.
Attorney. b. New York, NY, Mar. 22, 1908. e. Southwestern U. 1930, LL.B. pres., Wilshire Bar Assn. Former legal counsel for So. Calif. Theatre Owners Assn. Member: Calif. State Bar; member, Int'l Variety Clubs; former chief barker, Variety Club So. Calif. Tent 25; pres., Variety Int'l Boys' Club; board of dir., Los Angeles Metropolitan Recreation & Youth Services Council; bd. of trustees, Welfare Planning Council, Los Angeles Region; former mem. Los Angeles Area Council, Boys' Club of America; pres., Variety International Boys' Club 1976-77 and 1979-80. Member bd., Will Rogers Inst., M.P. Pioneers. 1984, honored by Variety Boys and Girls Club as founder of youth recreational facility.

STERN, STEWART
Writer. b. New York, NY, Mar. 22, 1922. e. Ethical Culture Sch., 1927-40; U. of Iowa, 1940-43. Rifle Squad Leader, S/Sgt. 106th Inf. Div., 1943-45; actor, asst. stage mgr., The French Touch, B'way, 1945-46; dialogue dir. Eagle-Lion Studios, 1946-48. 1948 to date: screenwriter.
TELEVISION: Crip, And Crown Thy Good, Thunder of Silence, Heart of Darkness, A Christmas to Remember, Sybil (Emmy Award, 1977).
PICTURES: Teresa, Rebel Without a Cause, The Rack, The James Dean Story, The Outsider, The Ugly American, Rachel Rachel, The Last Movie, Summer Wishes Winter Dreams.

STERNHAGEN, FRANCES
Actress. b. Washington, DC, Jan. 13, 1930. e. Vassar Coll., drama dept.; Perry-Mansfield School of Theatre. Studied with Sanford Meisner at Neighborhood Playhouse, NY. Was teacher at Milton Acad. in MA. Acted with Arena Stage, Washington, DC, 1953-54.
THEATER: Thieves Carnival (off-B'way debut, 1955), The Skin of Our Teeth, The Carefree Tree, The Admirable Bashville, Ulysses in Night Town, Viva Madison Avenue!, Red Eye of Love, Misalliance, Great Day in the Morning, The Right Honorable Gentleman, The Displaced Person, The Cocktail Party, Cock-a-Doodle Dandy, Playboy of the Western World, The Sign in Sidney Brustein's Window, Enemies, The Good Doctor (Tony Award, 1974), Equus, Angel, On Golden Pond, The Father, Grownups, Summer, You Can't Take It With You, Home Front, Driving Miss Daisy, Remembrance, A Perfect Ganesh, The Heiress (Tony Award, 1995).
PICTURES: Up the Down Staircase (debut, 1967), The Tiger Makes Out, The Hospital, Two People, Fedora, Starting Over, Outland, Independence Day, Romantic Comedy, Bright Lights Big City, See You in the Morning, Communion, Sibling Rivalry, Misery, Doc Hollywood, Raising Cain.

TELEVISION: *Series*: Love of Life, Doctors, Golden Years, Under One Roof, The Road Home. *Movies*: Who'll Save Our Children?, Mother and Daughter: The Loving War, Prototype, Follow Your Heart, She Woke Up, Labor of Love: The Arlette Schweitzer Story, Reunion. *Guest*: Cheers, Tales From the Crypt, Outer Limits.

STEUER, ROBERT B.
Executive. b. New Orleans, LA, Nov. 18, 1937. e. U. of Illinois, & 1955-57; Tulane U., 1957-59, B.B.A. Booker-Southern D.I. circuit, New Orleans, 1959; assoc., prod., Poor White Trash; 1960; v.p. Cinema Dist. America, 1961; co-prod., Flesh Eaters, Common Law Wife, Flack Black Pussy Cat; partner, gen. mgr., radio station WTVF, Mobile, 1963; dir. special projects, American Intl. Pictures, 1967; so. div. sls. mgr., AIP, 1971; v.p. asst. gen. sls. mgr., AIP, 1974; partner, United Producers Organization, producing Screamers, 1977; v.p., sls., Ely Landau Org., 1979; v.p., gen. sls. mgr., Film Ventures Intl., 1981; exec. v.p. world-wide mktg., 1983; pres., FVI, 1986-89. 1987, exec. v.p. world-wide mktg. Film Ventures Intl; 1987-88 exec. prod. Operation: Take No Prisoners, Most Dangerous Women Alive, Tunnels, Criminal Act, Au Pair; 1989 sales consultant, 20th Century Fox, 1990-present, prods. rep.; When the Wales Came, China Cry, Twogether, Sweet and Short, Taxi to Soweto, and worldwide mktg., distrib. and sls. consultant to entertainment industry. Films incl. Bound and Gagged: A Love Story, Skin Art, Yankee Zulu.

STEVENS, ANDREW
Actor, Director, Writer, Producer. b. Memphis, TN, June 10, 1955. Mother is actress Stella Stevens. e. Antioch U., L.A., B.A. (psychology). L.A. stage includes Journey's End, Mass Appeal, Leader of the Pack, Billy Budd (also prod.), P.S. Your Cat is Dead, Bedroom (L.A. Drama Circle Critics Award). Pres., CEO Royal Oaks Entertainment Intl. Film Distributors.
PICTURES: *Actor*: Shampoo, Day of the Animals, Massacre at Central High, Las Vegas Lady, Vigilante Force, The Boys in Company C, The Fury, Death Hunt, The Seduction, Ten to Midnight, Scared Stiff, Tusks, Fine Gold, Deadly Innocents, Down the Drain, Eyewitness to Murder, The Ranch, The Terror Within, Blood Chase, Counterforce, The Terror Within II (also dir., s.p.), Red Blooded American Girl, Night Eyes (also s.p., prod.), Munchie, Double Threat, Night Eyes II (also s.p., prod.), Deadly Rivals, Night Eyes III (also s.p., dir.), Body Chemistry III (also prod.), Scorned (also dir.), Illicit Dreams (also dir.), Victim of Desire (prod. only), The Skateboard Kid 2 (also dir.), Body Chemistry 4 (prod. only), Hard Bounty (prod. only), Grid Runners (dir. only), Munchie Strikes Back. Producers: Victim of Desire, Body Chemistry 4, Starhunter, Cyber Zone, Masseuse, Virtual Desire, Alone in the Woods, Invisible Mom, Innocence Betrayed, Illicit Dreams 2, Over the Wire, Terminal Rush, Flash Frame (also dir.)
TELEVISION: *Series*: Oregon Trail, Code Red, Emerald Point N.A.S., Dallas. *Mini-Series*: Hollywood Wives, Once an Eagle. *Movies*: Beggarman Thief, The Rebels, The Bastard, The Last Survivors, The Oregon Trail, Secrets, Topper (also prod.), Women at Westpoint, Code Red, Miracle on Ice, Journey's End, Forbidden Love, Murder in Malibu (Columbo). *Special*: Werewolf of Woodstock. *Guest*: Adam-12, Apple's Way, The Quest, Police Story, Shazam, Hotel, Westside Medical, Murder She Wrote, Love Boat. *Director*: Swamp Thing (3 episodes), Silk Stalkings (2 episodes), General Hospital (3 eps), Walker—Texas Ranger, Marker.

STEVENS, CONNIE
Actress. r.n. Concetta Ann Ingolia. b. Brooklyn, NY, August 8, 1938. e. Sacred Heart Acad., Hollywood Professional Sch. Began career as winner of several talent contests in Hollywood; prof. debut, Hollywood Repertory Theatre's prod. Finian's Rainbow; B'way in Star Spangled Girl (Theatre World Award); recordings include: Kookie Kookie Lend Me Your Comb, 16 Reasons, What Did You Wanna Make Me Cry For, From Me to You, They're Jealous of Me, A Girl Never Knows.
PICTURES: Eighteen and Anxious (debut, 1957), Young and Dangerous, Dragstrip Riot, Rock-a-Bye Baby, The Party Crashers, Parrish, Susan Slade, Palm Springs Weekend, Two on a Guillotine, Never Too Late, Way ... Way Out, The Grissom Gang, The Last Generation, Scorchy, Sgt. Pepper's Lonely Hearts Club Band (cameo), Grease 2, Back to the Beach, Tapeheads, Love Is All There Is.
TELEVISION: *Movies*: Mister Jerico, Call Her Mom, Playmates, Every Man Needs One, The Sex Symbol, Love's Savage Fury, Scruples, Bring Me the Head of Dobie Gillis, Race with Destiny: The James Dean Story. *Series*: Hawaiian Eye, Wendy and Me, Kraft Music Halls Presents The Des O'Connor Show, Starting from Scratch.

STEVENS, CRAIG
Actor. r.n. Gail Shikles. b. Liberty, MO, July 8, 1918. Was married to late actress Alexis Smith. e. U. of Kansas. Played in coll. dramatics.
PICTURES: Affectionately Yours (debut, 1941), Law of the Tropics, Dive Bomber, Steel Against the Sky, Secret Enemies, Spy Ship, The Hidden Hand, Hollywood Canteen, Since You

Went Away, The Doughgirls, God Is My Co-Pilot, Roughly Speaking, Too Young to Know, Humoresque, The Man I Love, That Way With Women, Love and Learn, Night Unto Night, The Lady Takes a Sailor, Where the Sidewalk Ends, Blues Busters, The Lady From Texas, Drums in the Deep South, Phone Call from a Stranger, Murder Without Tears, Abbott and Costello Meet Dr. Jekyll Mr. Hyde, The French Line, Duel on the Mississippi, The Deadly Mantis, Buchanan Rides Alone, Gunn, S.O.B., La Truite (The Trout).
TELEVISION: *Guest*: Lux Video Theatre, Four Star Playhouse, Loretta Young Show, Schlitz Playhouse, Dinah Shore, Ernie Ford Shows, Chevy Show, Summer on Ice, The Millionaire, The Bold Ones. *Series*: Peter Gunn (1958-61), Man of the World (ATV England), Mr. Broadway, The Invisible Man, Dallas. *Movies*: The Killer Bees; The Cabot Connection, The Home Front, Supercarrier, Marcus Welby, M.D.-A Holiday Affair. *Mini-Series*: Rich Man Poor Man.
THEATER: Here's Love, King of Hearts, Plain and Fancy, Critics Choice, Mary Mary, Cactus Flower (natl. co.), My Fair Lady.

STEVENS, FISHER
Actor. b. Chicago, IL, Nov. 27, 1963. e. NYU. Artistic Director of Naked Angels Theatre Co. in NYC.
THEATER: *NY*: Torch Song Trilogy (Off-B'way & B'way), Brighton Beach Memoirs, A Perfect Ganesh, Carousel.
PICTURES: The Burning, Baby It's You, The Brother From Another Planet, The Flamingo Kid, My Science Project, Short Circuit, The Boss's Wife, Short Circuit 2, Point of View, Reversal of Fortune, The Marrying Man, Mystery Date, Bob Roberts, Hero, When the Party's Over, Super Mario Bros., Nina Takes a Lover, Only You, Hackers, Cold Fever.
TELEVISION: *Series*: Key West. *Guest*: Columbo. *Special*: It's Called the Sugar Plum.

STEVENS, GEORGE, JR.
Director, Writer, Producer. b. Los Angeles, CA, Apr. 3, 1932. Son of late director George Stevens. e. Occidental Coll., 1949-53, B.A. 1st Lieut. U.S. Air Force; TV dir., Alfred Hitchcock Presents, Peter Gunn, 1957-61; prod. asst. Giant Productions, 1953-54; prod. asst. Mark VII, Ltd., 1956-57; dir. M.P. Service, U.S. Information Agency 1962-67; chmn., U.S. deleg. to Film Festivals at Cannes (1962, 1964), Venice (1962, 1963), Moscow (1963); Founding director, American Film Institute, 1967-79; co-chmn., American Film Institute, 1979 to present.
PICTURES: The Diary of Anne Frank (assoc. prod.), The Greatest Story Ever Told (assoc. prod.), John F. Kennedy: Years of Lightning Day of Drums (prod.), America at the Movies (prod.), George Stevens: A Filmmaker's Journey (dir., s.p., prod.; 1988 WGA Award for TV broadcast).
TELEVISION: *Specials*: American Film Institute's Salutes (exec. prod./writer, 1973-; received 1975 Emmy Award as exec. prod. of The American Film Institue Salute to James Cagney), The Stars Salute America's Greatest Movies (exec. prod.), The Kennedy Center Honors (prod./writer, 1978-; Emmy Awards: 1984, 1986, 1989), America Entertains Vice Premier Deng (prod./writer), Christmas in Washington, (exec. prod./writer, 1982-), Movies: The Murder of Mary Phagan (co-writer, prod., 1988; Emmy Award for prod.; also Christopher & Peabody Awards), Separate But Equal (dir., writer, co-exec. prod.; Emmy Award for exec. prod.; also Christopher Award, Ohio State Award, Paul Selvin Award by the Writers Guild of America), George Stevens: D-Day to Berlin, The Kennedy Center Honors (co. prod., co-writer; Emmy Award, 1996).

STEVENS, STELLA
Actress, Director. b. Yazoo City, MS, Oct. 1, 1937. r.n. Estelle Eggleston. Mother of actor Andrew Stevens. e. Attended Memphis State U. Modeled in Memphis when she was discovered by talent scouts. Was briefly a term contract actress at 20th Century-Fox, later under exclusive contract to Paramount, then Columbia. *Director*: The American Heroine (feature length doc.), The Ranch (feature comedy).
PICTURES: Say One For Me (debut, 1959), The Blue Angel, Li'l Abner, Man Trap, Girls! Girls! Girls!, Too Late Blues, The Nutty Professor, The Courtship of Eddie's Father, Advance to the Rear, Synanon, The Secret of My Success, The Silencers, Rage, Where Angels Go Trouble Follows, How to Save a Marriage and Ruin Your Life, Sol Madrid, The Mad Room, The Ballad of Cable Hogue, A Town Called Hell, Slaughter, Stand Up & Be Counted, The Poseidon Adventure, Arnold, Cleopatra Jones and the Casino of Gold, Las Vegas Lady, Nickelodeon, The Manitou, Wacko, Chained Heat, The Longshot, Monster in the Closet, Down the Drain, Last Call, The Terror Within II, Eye of the Stranger, The Guest, Exiled in America, The Nutty Nut, Hard Drive, Molly & Gina, Body Chemistry 3: Point of Seduction, Illicit Dreams, The Granny.
TELEVISION: *Series*: Ben Casey, Flamingo Road, Santa Barbara. *Guest*: Bob Hope Bing Crosby Special, Frontier Circus, Johnny Ringo, Alfred Hitchcock, Love Boat, Highway to Heaven, Murder She Wrote, Martin Mull's White America, A Table at Ciros, In the Heat of the Night, Hotel, Night Court, Newhart, Dangerous Curves, The Commish, Burke's Law.

Movies: In Broad Daylight, Climb an Angry Mountain, Linda, The Day The Earth Moved, Honky Tonk, New Original Wonder Woman (pilot), Kiss Me Kill Me, Wanted the Sundance Woman, Charlie Cobb (pilot), The Night They Took Miss Beautiful, Murder in Peyton Place, The Jordan Chance, Cruise into Terror, New Love Boat (pilot), Friendship Secrets and Lies, Hart to Hart (pilot), The French Atlantic Affair, The Pendragon Affair (Eddie Capra Mystery pilot), Make Me an Offer, Children of Divorce, Twirl, Amazons, Women of San Quentin, No Man's Land, A Masterpiece of Murder, Fatal Confessions (Father Dowling pilot), Man Against The Mob, Jake Spanner: Private Eye. *Special*: Attack of the 5'2" Woman.

STEVENSON, CYNTHIA
Actress. b. Oakland, CA, Aug. 2, 1963. Raised in Washington, Vancouver.
THEATER: Ladies Room.
PICTURES: The Player, The Gun in Betty Lou's Handbag, Watch It, Forget Paris, Home for the Holidays.
TELEVISION: *Series*: My Talk Show, Bob, Hope and Gloria.

STEVENSON, JULIET
Actress. b. England, Oct. 30, 1956. e. RADA.
THEATER: Other Worlds, Measure for Measure, Breaking the Silence, Troilus and Cressida, As You Like It, Les Liaisons Dangereuses, Yerma, Hedda Gabler, On the Verge, Burn This, Death and the Maiden, Scenes From an Execution (LA), The Duchess of Malfi.
PICTURES: Drowning by Numbers (debut, 1988), Ladder of Swords, Truly Madly Deeply, The Trial, The Secret Rapture, Emma.
TELEVISION: The Mallens (TV debut), Maybury, Bazaar and Rummage, Life Story, Stanley, Out of Love, Antigone, Oedipus at Colonus, Living With Dinosaurs, Amy, The March, A Doll's House, The Politician's Wife.

STEVENSON, PARKER
Actor. b. Philadelphia, PA, June 4, 1952. e. Princeton U. m. actress Kirstie Alley. Began professional acting career by starring in film, A Separate Peace, while high school senior, having attracted attention through work on TV commercials.
PICTURES: A Separate Peace (debut, 1972), Our Time, Lifeguard, Stroker Ace, Stitches, Official Denial.
TELEVISION: *Series*: Hardy Boys Mysteries, Falcon Crest, Probe, Baywatch, Melrose Place. *Guest*: The Streets of San Francisco, Gunsmoke. *Mini-Series*: North & South Book II, All the Rivers Run. *Movies*: This House Possessed, Shooting Stars, That Secret Sunday, Baywatch: Panic at Malibu Pier, The Cover Girl and the Cop, Are You Lonesome Tonight?, Nighttide, Shadow of a Stranger, Official Denial, Not of This Earth.

STEWART, DOUGLAS DAY
Writer, Director.
PICTURES: *Writer*: The Blue Lagoon, An Officer and a Gentleman. *Director-Writer*: Thief of Hearts, Listen to Me.
TELEVISION: *Writer*: Boy in the Plastic Bubble, The Man Who Could Talk to Kids, Murder or Mercy.

STEWART, JAMES
Actor. b. Indiana, PA, May 20, 1908. e. Mercersburg Acad.; Princeton U. With Falmouth Stock Co., Cape Cod; on NY stage in Goodbye Again; stage mgr. for Camille with Jane Cowl (Boston). In films since 1935; joined U.S. Air Force 1942, commissioned Col. 1944. Retired as Brig. Gen. Voted one of top ten money-making stars, M.P. Herald-Fame poll, 1950, 1952, 1954, 1957; No. 1 Money-Making Star, 1955. 1968, Screen Actors Guild Award. Mem.: Bd. of Trustees, Princeton U. Trustee, Claremont Coll.; exec. bd. of Los Angeles Council of Boy Scouts of America; bd. of dirs., Project Hope. Honorary Academy Award, 1984. Author: Jimmy Stewart and His Poems (1989).
THEATER: Spring in Autumn, All Good Americans, Yellow Jack, Journey at Night, Harvey.
PICTURES: Murder Man (debut, 1935), Rose Marie, Wife vs. Secretary, Next Time We Love, Small Town Girl, Speed, The Gorgeous Hussy, Born to Dance, After the Thin Man, Seventh Heaven, The Last Gangster, Navy Blue and Gold, Of Human Hearts, You Can't Take It With You, Vivacious Lady, The Shopworn Angel, Made For Each Other, Ice Follies of 1939, Mr. Smith Goes to Washington (Acad. Award nom.), It's A Wonderful World, Destry Rides Again, The Shop Around the Corner, The Mortal Storm, No Time For Comedy, The Philadelphia Story (Academy Award, 1940), Come Live With Me, Pot O'Gold, Ziegfeld Girl, It's a Wonderful Life (Acad. Award nom.), Magic Town, Call Northside 777, On Our Merry Way (A Miracle Can Happen), Rope, You Gotta Stay Happy, The Stratton Story, Malaya, Winchester 73, Broken Arrow, Harvey (Acad. Award nom.), The Jackpot, No Highway in the Sky, The Greatest Show on Earth, Carbine Williams, Bend of the River, The Naked Spur, Thunder Bay, The Glenn Miller Story, Rear Window, The Far Country, Strategic Air Command, The Man From Laramie, The Man Who Knew Too Much, The

Spirit of St. Louis, Night Passage, Vertigo, Bell Book and Candle, Anatomy of a Murder (Acad. Award nom.), The FBI Story, The Mountain Road, X-15 (narrator), Two Rode Together, The Man Who Shot Liberty Valance, Mr. Hobbs Takes a Vacation, How the West Was Won, Take Her She's Mine, Cheyenne Autumn, Dear Brigitte, Shenandoah, The Flight of the Phoenix, The Rare Breed, Firecreek, Bandolero, The Cheyenne Social Club, Fool's Parade, That's Entertainment, The Shootist, Airport '77, The Big Sleep, The Magic of Lassie, Africa Mongotari (A Tale of Africa), An American Tail: Fievel Goes West (voice).
TELEVISION: *Series*: The Jimmy Stewart Show (1971-72), Hawkins (1973-74). *Movies*: Hawkins on Murder, Right of Way. *Special*: The Windmill, The Town With a Past, Let's Take a Trip, Flashing Spikes, Mr. Kreuger's Christmas.

STEWART, JAMES L.
Executive. e. U. of Southern California, B.A. in cinema-TV and M.B.A. in finance. Worked for two years in sales for CBS Radio Network-West Coast. Spent four years with MGM in promotion and marketing. With Walt Disney Prods. for 12 years, functioning in marketing, management and administrative activities; named v.p.-corp. relations & admin. asst. to pres. 1978 joined in formation of Aurora Pictures, as exec. v.p., secty., & COO.
PICTURES: *Exec. prod.*: Why Would I Lie?, The Secret of NIMH, Eddie and the Cruisers, Heart Like a Wheel, East of the Sun, West of the Moon, Maxie.

STEWART, MARILYN
Marketing & Public Relations Executive. b. New York, NY. e. Hunter Coll. Entered ind. as scty. then asst. to MGM dir. of adv. Left to become prom.-pub. dir. for Verve/Folkways Records; duties also included ar and talent scouting. In 1966 joined 20th-Fox as radio/tv pub. coordinator. In 1969 went to Para. Pictures as mag. pub. coordinator; 1970 named worldwide dir. of pub. for Para., including creation of overall mkt. concepts, becoming 1st woman to be appt. to that position at major co. Campaigns included Love Story and The Godfather. 1972 opened own consulting office specializing in m.p. marketing and p.r. Headquarters in NY; repr. in L.A. Has represented The Lords of Flatbush, Bang the Drum Slowly, The Kids Are Alright, Autumn Sonata, The Tin Drum, A Cry in the Dark, The Russia House, Filmex, Michael Moriarty, Arthur Hiller, Fred Schepisi, Volker Schlondorff, Hemdale Pictures, Lucasfilm.

STEWART, PATRICK
Actor. b. Mirfield, England, July 13, 1940. Trained at Bristol Old Vic Theatre School. Made professional stage debut 1959 in Treasure Island with Lincoln Rep. Co. at the Theatre Royal in Lincoln.
THEATER: *NY*: A Midsummer Night's Dream, A Christmas Carol, The Tempest. Numerous London theatre credits incl.: The Investigation, Henry V, The Caretaker, Body and Soul, Who's Afraid of Virginia Woolf?, Yonadab. Associate artist with Royal Shakespeare Co. since 1967; many appearances with them incl. Antony and Cleopatra for which he received the Olivier Award for Best Supporting Actor in 1979.
PICTURES: Hennessey, Hedda, Excalibur, The Plague Dogs (voice), Races, Dune, Lifeforce, Code Name: Emerald, Wild Geese II, The Doctor and the Devils, Lady Jane, L.A. Story, Robin Hood: Men in Tights, Gunmen, Star Trek: Generations, The Pagemaster (voice), Liberation (narrator), Jeffrey, Star Trek: First Contact.
TELEVISION: *Series*: Eleventh Hour (BBC), Maybury (BBC), Star Trek: The Next Generation. *Mini-Series*: I Claudius, Smiley's People. *Movies*: Little Lord Fauntleroy, Pope John Paul II, Death Train. *Special*: In Search of Dr. Seuss. *BBC Specials*: Oedipus Rex, Miss Julie, Hamlet, The Devil's Disciple, Tale of Eagles, The Artist's Story, Love Girl and the Innocent, Conrad, A Walk With Destiny, Alfred the Great, The Madness, When the Actors Come, Tolstoy: A Question of Faith, The Anatomist, The Mozart Inquest.

STIERS, DAVID OGDEN
Actor. b. Peoria, IL, Oct. 31, 1942. Guest conductor: 50 American orchestras incl. Chicago, San Diego, Dallas, Utah, and Chamber Orchestra of Baltimore. Resident conductor of Yaquina Chamber Orchestra in Oregon.
THEATER: *NY*: The Magic Show, Ulysses in Nighttown, The Three Sisters, Beggar's Opera, Measure for Measure.
PICTURES: Drive He Said, THX 1138, Oh God!, The Cheap Detective, Magic, Harry's War, The Man With One Red Shoe, Better Off Dead, Creator, Another Woman, The Accidental Tourist, Doc Hollywood, Beauty and the Beast (voice), Shadows and Fog, Iron Will, Bad Company, Pocahontas (voice), Steal Big Steal Little, Mighty Aphrodite, Meet Wally Sparks, The Hunchback of Notre Dame (voice).
TELEVISION: *Series*: Doc, M*A*S*H. *Movies*: Charlie's Angels (pilot), A Circle of Children, A Love Affair: The Eleanor and Lou Gehrig Story, Sgt. Matlovich Vs. the U.S. Air Force, Breaking Up is Hard to Do, Damien: The Leper Priest, The Day the Bubble Burst, Anatomy of an Illness, The First Olympics: Athens 1896, The Bad Seed, 5 Perry Mason Movies

(Shooting Star, Lost Love, Sinister Spirit, Avenging Ace, Lady in the Lake), Mrs. Delafield Wants to Marry, The Alamo: 13 Days to Glory, The Kissing Place, Final Notice, The Final Days, How to Murder a Millionaire, Wife Mother Murderer, The Last of His Tribe, Without a Kiss Goodbye. *Specials*: The Oldest Living Graduate, The Innocents Abroad, Mastergate. *Mini-Series*: North and South (also Book II).

STILLER, BEN
Actor, Director. b. New York, NY, 1966. Son of performers Jerry Stiller and Anne Meara. e. UCLA. Made short film parody of The Color of Money, called The Hustler of Money which landed him work on Saturday Night Live. Acting debut in 1985 B'way revival of The House of Blue Leaves.
PICTURES: Hot Pursuit, Empire of the Sun, Fresh Horses, Next of Kin, That's Adequate, Stella, Highway to Hell, Reality Bites (also dir.), Heavyweights, Get Shorty, Flirting With Disaster, The Cable Guy (also dir.).
TELEVISION: *Series*: Saturday Night Live (also writer), The Ben Stiller Show (also creator, dir., writer; Emmy Award as writer). *Specials*: House of Blue Leaves, Colin Quinn Back in Brooklyn (dir., writer). *Movie*: Working Trash.

STILLER, JERRY
Actor. b. New York, NY, June 8, 1929. m. actress Anne Meara. Son is actor Ben Stiller. With partner Meara gained recognition as comedy team in nightclubs, theatres and on tv, most notably The Ed Sullivan Show.
THEATER: *B'way*: The Ritz, Passione, Hurlyburly, Three Men on a Horse, What's Wrong With This Picture?
PICTURES: The Taking of Pelham One Two Three, Airport 1975, The Ritz, Nasty Habits, Those Lips Those Eyes, In Our Hands, Hot Pursuit, Nadine, Hairspray, That's Adequate, Little Vegas, Highway to Hell, The Pickle, Heavyweights.
TELEVISION: *Movies*: Madame X, The Other Woman, Seize the Day. Series: The Paul Lynde Show, Joe and Sons, Take Five With Stiller and Meara (synd), Tattingers, Seinfeld. *Guest*: L.A. Law, In the Heat of the Night, Homicide.

STING
Musician, Actor. r.n. Gordon Matthew Sumner. b. Newcastle-Upon-Tyne, England, Oct. 2, 1951. e. Warwick U. A schoolteacher before helping form rock group, The Police as songwriter, singer and bass player. Broadway debut, Threepenny Opera, 1989.
PICTURES: Quadrophenia, Radio On, The Great Rock 'n' Roll Swindle, The Secret Policeman's Other Ball, Brimstone and Treacle, Dune, The Bride, Plenty, Bring on the Night, Julia and Julia, Stormy Monday, The Adventures of Baron Munchausen, Resident Alien, The Music Tells You, The Grotesque.

STOCKWELL, DEAN
Actor. b. Hollywood, CA, Mar. 5, 1935. p. Harry and Betty Veronica Stockwell. Brother is actor Guy Stockwell. e. Long Island public schools and Martin Milmore, Boston. On stage in Theatre Guild prod. Innocent Voyage. Appeared on radio in Death Valley Days and Dr. Christian. Named in 1949 M.P. Herald-Fame Stars of Tomorrow poll; 1976 retired to Santa Monica as a licensed real estate broker but soon returned to acting.
PICTURES: Anchors Aweigh (debut, 1945), The Valley of Decision, Abbott and Costello in Hollywood, The Green Years, Home Sweet Homicide, The Mighty McGurk, The Arnelo Affair, The Romance of Rosy Ridge, Song of the Thin Man, Gentleman's Agreement, Deep Waters, The Boy With Green Hair, Down to the Sea in Ships, The Secret Garden, The Happy Years, Kim, Stars in My Crown, Kim, Cattle Drive, Gun for a Coward, The Careless Years, Compulsion, Sons and Lovers, Long Day's Journey Into Night, Rapture, Psych-Out, The Dunwich Horror, The Last Movie, The Loners, The Werewolf of Washington, Win Place or Steal (The Big Payoff), Won Ton Ton The Dog Who Saved Hollywood, Stick Fighter (South Pacific Connection), Tracks, She Came to the Valley, Alsino and the Condor, Sandino, Human Highway (also co-dir., s.p.), Wrong Is Right, To Kill a Stranger, Paris Texas, Dune, The Legend of Billie Jean, To Live and Die in L.A., Blue Velvet, Gardens of Stone, Beverly Hills Cop II, Banzai Runner, The Blue Iguana, Tucker: The Man and His Dream, Married to the Mob (Acad. Award nom.), Palais Royale, Limit Up, Buying Time, Time Guardian, The Player, Chasers, Mr. Wrong.
TELEVISION: *Series*: Quantum Leap. *Guest*: Miami Vice, Hart to Hart, Simon and Simon, The A-Team, Wagon Train, Twilight Zone, Playhouse 90, Bonanza, Hallmark Hall of Fame, Hunter, Police Story, Greatest Show on Earth. *Movies*: Paper Man, The Failing of Raymond, The Adventures of Nick Carter, The Return of Joe Forrester, Three for the Road, A Killing Affair, Born to Be Sold, Sweet Smell of Death (U.K.), The Gambler III: The Legend Continues, Son of the Morning Star, Backtrack, Shame, Fatal Memories, Bonanza: The Return, In the Line of Duty: The Price of Vengeance, Justice in a Small Town, The Innocent, Madonna: Innocence Lost, Deadline for Murder: From the Files of Edna Buchanan, Stephen King's The Langoliers. *Pilot*: Caught in the Act.

STODDARD, BRANDON
Executive. b. Brideport, CT, March 31, 1937. e. Yale U., Columbia Law Sch. Was program ass't. at Batton, Barton, Durstine and Osborn before joining Grey Advertising, where was successively, program operations supvr., dir. daytime programming, v.p. in chg. of TV, radio programming. Joined ABC in 1970; named v.p. daytime programs for ABC Entertainment, 1972; v.p. children's programs, 1973. Named v.p., motion pictures for TV, 1974; 1976 named v.p., dramatic programs and m.p. for TV; 1979, named pres., ABC Motion Pictures; 1985 appt. pres., ABC Entertainment. Resigned 1989 to head ABC Prods. unit to create and prod. series and movies for ABC and other networks.

STOLNITZ, ART
Executive. b. Rochester, NY, March 13, 1928. e. U. of Tennessee, LL.B., 1952. U.S. Navy Air Force. Legal dept., William Morris Agency, 1953, dir. business affairs, ZIV, 1959; dir. new program development, ZIV-United Artists, 1960; literary agent, MCA, 1961; dir. business affairs, Selmur Productions, Selmur Pictures, 1963; v.p. ABC Pictures, 1969; v.p. Metromedia Producers Corporation, 1970, executive v.p. Metromedia Producers Corporation; 1975 exec. v.p. and prod. Charles Fries Prods. 1976, prod. Edgar J. Scherick Productions; 1976-77 prod., Grizzly Adams (TV); 1977; v.p. business affairs, Warner Bros.-TV; 1980, sr. v.p., business affairs; 1990, exec. v.p. business & financial affairs, Lorimar; 1993, exec. v.p. business and financial affairs, Warner Bros. TV.

STOLOFF, VICTOR
Producer, Writer, Director, Editor. b. March 17, 1913. e. French Law U. Ac. Fines Arts. Prod. dir. writer of award winning documentaries (Warner Bros. release); Prod. dir. writer first U.S. film made in Italy, When in Rome; contract writer, dir. to Sidney Buchman, Columbia.
PICTURES: *Writer*: Volcano, The Sinner, Shark Reef, Journey Around the World. Of Love and Desire (also prod.), Intimacy (also prod., dir.), The Washington Affair (prod., dir.), The 300 Year Weekend (also dir.).
TELEVISION: Ford Theatre, Lloyd Bridges series, National Velvet, High Adventure with Lowell Thomas, *Prod.*: Hawaii Five-O. *Created* Woman of Russia (dir., writer); Audience (exec. prod., dir.).

STOLTZ, ERIC
Actor. b. Los Angeles, CA, 1961. Moved to American Samoa at age 3; family returned to California when he was 8. Spent 2 years at U. of Southern California in theatre arts; left to study with Stella Adler and later William Traylor and Peggy Feury. Stage work with an American rep. co. in Scotland in Tobacco Road, You're a Good Man Charlie Brown, Working. Off-B'way: The Widow Claire, The American Plan, Down the Road. Broadway debut Our Town (1988, Theatre World Award, Tony nom. & Drama Desk nom.), followed by Two Shakespearean Actors.
PICTURES: Fast Times at Ridgemont High (debut, 1982), Surf II, Running Hot, The Wild Life, The New Kids, Mask, Code Name: Emerald, Some Kind of Wonderful, Lionheart, Sister Sister, Haunted Summer, Manifesto, The Fly II, Say Anything, Memphis Belle, The Waterdance, Singles (cameo), Bodies Rest & Motion (also co-prod.), Naked in New York, Killing Zoe, Sleep With Me (also prod.), Pulp Fiction, Little Women, Rob Roy, Fluke, The Prophecy, Kicking and Screaming, Grace of My Heart, 2 Days in the Valley, Inside.
TELEVISION: *Movies*: The Grass Is Always Greener Over the Septic Tank, The Seekers, The Violation of Sarah McDavid, Paper Dolls, Thursday's Child, A Killer in the Family, Money, The Heart of Justice, Foreign Affairs, Roommates. *Specials*: Things Are Looking Up, Sensibility and Sense, Our Town. *Guest*: Mad About You.

STONE, ANDREW L.
Director, Producer, Writer. b. Oakland, CA, July 16, 1902. e. U. of CA. Ent. ind. 1918 at Universal San Francisco exch.; later author, prod., dir. series of pictures for Paramount; prod., dir. for Sono-Art; 1932-36 org. and oper. Race Night company. Formed Andrew Stone Prods., 1943. Co-prod. with wife Virginia beginning in 1958.
PICTURES: *Dir.*: Dreary House (debut, 1928; also prod.), Hell's Headquarters, The Girl Said No (also prod., story), Stolen Heaven (also prod., story), Say It in French (also prod.), The Great Victor Herbert (also prod., co-story), There's Magic in Music (also prod., co-story), Stormy Weather, Hi Diddle Diddle (also prod.), Sensations of 1945 (also prod., co-s.p.), Bedside Manner (also prod.), The Bachelor's Daughters (also prod., s.p.), Fun on a Weekend (also prod., s.p.), Highway 301 (also s.p.), Confidence Girl (also prod., story, s.p.), The Steel Trap (also story, s.p.), Blueprint for Murder (also story, s.p.), The Night Holds Terror (also prod., story), Julie (also s.p.). Dir./Co-Prod./Writer: Cry Terror, The Decks Ran Red, The Last Voyage, Ring of Fire, The Password Is Courage, Never Put It in Writing, The Secret of My Success, Song of Norway, The Great Waltz.

STONE, AUBRY
Executive. b. Charlotte, NC, Jan. 14, 1964. e. U. of NC-Chapel Hill. Joined Consolidated Theatres Inc. in 1987. Helped to found a new motion picyire exhibition business, consolidated Theatres/The Stone Group, 1990. V.P., Consolidates Theatres/The Stone Group, 1990-95. Assumed role of v.p./general mgr. in 1996. Bd. of dirs., NATO of NC & SC, 1991-present. Bd of dirs., National NATO, 1995-present; vice chmn., Programs & Services Committee, National NATO.

STONE, BURTON
Executive. b. Feb. 16, 1928; e. Florida Southern Coll. Was film ed., Hollywood Film Co. 1953-61; serv. mgr., sales mgr. and gen. mgr., Consolidated Film Inds., 1953-61; nat'l sales mgr., Movielab, 1961-63; pres., Allservice Film Laboratories, 1963-64; v.p. Technicolor, Inc., 1964-70. Pres., Precision Film Labs., 1965-76. Pres., Deluxe Laboratories, Inc., a wholly-owned subsidiary of 20th Century Fox, 1976-91. 1991, pres. Deluxe color, a sub of the Rank Org. Member: Board of directors, Will Rogers Foundation and Motion Picture Pioneers; member Acad. of Motion Picture Arts & Sciences, American Society of Cinematographers; awarded fellowship in Society of Motion Picture & Television Engineers; past pres., Association of Cinema & Video Laboratories; awarded fellowship in British Kinematograph, Sound & Television Society.

STONE, DEE WALLACE
Actress. r.n. Deanna Bowers. b. Kansas City, MO, Dec. 14, 1948. m. actor Christopher Stone. e. U. of Kansas, theater and education. Taught high school English. Came to NY to audition for Hal Prince and spent 2 years working in commercials and industrial shows. First break in Police Story episode.
PICTURES: The Stepford Wives (debut, 1975), The Hills Have Eyes, 10, The Howling, E.T. the Extra-Terrestrial, Jimmy the Kid, Cujo, Critters, Secret Admirer, Club Life, Shadow Play, The White Dragon, Alligator II: The Mutation, Popcorn, Rescue Me, Frighteners.
TELEVISION: Series: Together We Stand, Lassie, High Sierra Search and Rescue. Movies: The Sky's No Limit, Young Love First Love, The Secret War of Jackie's Girls, Child Bride of Short Creek, The Five of Me, A Whale for the Killing, Skeezer, Wait Til Your Mother Gets Home, Happy, I Take These Men, Hostage Flight, Sin of Innocence, Addicted to His Love, Stranger on My Land. Terror in the Sky, The Christmas Visitor, I'm Dangerous Tonight, Prophet of Evil: The Ervil LeBaron Story, Witness to the Execution, Search and Rescue, Moment of Truth: Cradle of Conspiracy, Huck and the King of Hearts. Guest: CHiPs.

STONE, MARIANNE
Actress. b. London, England. Studied Royal Acad. of Dramatic Art, West End debut in The Kingmaker, 1946.
PICTURES: Brighton Rock, Seven Days to Noon, The Clouded Yellow, Wrong Arm of the Law, Heavens Above, Stolen Hours, Nothing But the Best, Curse of the Mummy's Tomb, Hysteria, The Beauty Jungle, A Hard Day's Night, Rattle of a Simple Man, Echo of Diana, Act of Murder, Catch Us If You Can, You Must Be Joking, The Countess from Hong Kong, The Wrong Box, To Sir With Love, The Bliss of Mrs. Blossom, Here We Go Round the Mulberry Bush, Carry on Doctor, The Twisted Nerve, The Best House in London, Oh! What a Lovely War; The Raging Moon, There's a Girl in My Soup, All the Right Noises, Assault, Carry On at Your Convenience, All Coppers Are..., Carry on Girls, Penny Gold, The Vault of Horror, Percy's Progress, Confessions of a Window Cleaner, Carry on Dick, That Lucky Touch, Sarah, Carry on Behind, Confessions From a Holiday Camp, The Chiffy Kids, What's Up Superdoc?; The Class of Miss McMichael, The Human Factor, Dangerous Davies, Funny Money, Terry on the Fence, Carry on Laughing.
TELEVISION: Maigret, Bootsie and Snudge, Jimmy Edwards Show, Wayne and Schuster Show, Roy Hudd Show, Harry Worth Show, Steptoe and Son, Informer, Love Story, Father Dear Father, Bless This House, The Man Outside, Crown Court, Public Eye, Miss Nightingale, She, Little Lord Fauntleroy, The Secret Army (2 series), Shillingbury Tale, The Bright Side (series), Tickets for the Titanic (series), The Balance of Nature, Always, Hammer House of Mystery & Suspense, The Nineteenth Hole.

STONE, OLIVER
Director, Writer. b. New York, NY, Sept. 15, 1946. e. Yale U., NYU, B.F.A., 1971. Teacher in Cholon, Vietnam 1965-66. U.S. Infantry specialist 4th Class. 1967-68 in Vietnam (Purple Heart, Bronze Star with Oak Leaf Cluster honors).
PICTURES: Sugar Cookies (assoc. prod.), Seizure (dir., s.p., co-editor, 1974), Midnight Express (s.p.; Academy Award, 1978), The Hand (dir., s.p., cameo), Conan the Barbarian (co-s.p.), Scarface (s.p.), Year of the Dragon (co-s.p.), Salvador (dir., co-s.p., co-prod.), 8 Million Ways to Die (co-s.p.), Platoon (dir., s.p., cameo; Academy Award & DGA Award for Best Director, 1986), Wall Street (dir., co-s.p., cameo), Talk Radio (dir., co-s.p.), Born on the Fourth of July (dir., co-s.p., cameo;

Academy Award & DGA Award for Best Director, 1989), Blue Steel (co-prod.), Reversal of Fortune (co-prod.), The Doors (dir., co-s.p., cameo), Iron Maze (co-exec. prod.), JFK (dir., co-prod., co-s.p.), South Central (co-exec. prod.), Zebrahead (co-exec. prod.), Dave (actor), The Joy Luck Club (co-exec. prod.), Heaven and Earth (dir., co-prod., s.p.), Natural Born KIllers (dir., co-prod., co-s.p.), The New Age (exec. prod.), Nixon (dir., co-s.p., co-prod.) Chicago Film Critics Award), Killer: A Journal of Murder (co-exec. prod.), The People vs. Larry Flynt (prod.).
TELEVISION: Mini-Series: Wild Palms (co-exec. prod.). Movie: Indictment: The McMartin Trial (co-exec. prod.).

STONE, PETER
Writer. b. Los Angeles, CA, Feb. 27, 1930. Son of film prod. John Stone and screenwriter Hilda Hess Stone. e. Bard Col., B.A. 1951; Yale U, M.F.A., 1953. Won Mystery Writers of America Award for Charade, Christopher Award for 1776.
THEATER: Kean, Skyscraper, 1776 (Tony and NY Drama Critics Circle Awards, 1969), Two By Two, Sugar, Full Circle, Woman of the Year (Tony Award, 1981), My One and Only, Grand Hotel, Will Rogers Follies (Tony, Grammy and NY Drama Critics Circle Awards, 1991).
PICTURES: Charade, Father Goose (Academy Award, 1964), Mirage, Arabesque, The Secret War of Harry Frigg, Jigsaw, Sweet Charity, Skin Game, The Taking of Pelham One Two Three, 1776, The Silver Bears, Who Is Killing the Great Chefs of Europe?, Why Would I Lie?, Just Cause.
TELEVISION: Studio One, Brenner, Witness, Asphalt Jungle, The Defenders (Emmy Award, 1962). Androcles and the Lion, Adam's Rib (series), Ivan the Terrible (series), Baby on Board, Grand Larceny.

STONE, SHARON
Actress. b. Meadville, PA, March 10, 1958. e. Edinboro St. Univ. Started as model, appearing in several TV commercials.
PICTURES: Stardust Memories (debut, 1980), Deadly Blessing, Bolero, Irreconcilable Differences, King Soloman's Mines, Allan Quartermain and the Lost City of Gold, Cold Steel, Police Academy 4: Citizens on Patrol, Action Jackson, Above the Law, Blood and Sand, Beyond the Stars (Personal Choice), Total Recall, He Said/She Said, Scissors, Year of the Gun, Basic Instinct, Diary of a Hit Man, Where Sleeping Dogs Lie, Sliver, Last Action Hero (cameo), Intersection, The Specialist, The Quick and the Dead (also co- prod.), Casino (Golden Globe Award), The Last Dance, Diabolique.
TELEVISION: Series: Bay City Blues. Mini-Series: War and Remembrance. Movies: Not Just Another Affair, The Calendar Girl Murders, The Vegas Strip Wars, Tears in the Rain. Pilots: Mr. & Mrs. Ryan, Badlands 2005. Guest: T.J. Hooker, Magnu P.I., Roseanne.

STOPPARD, TOM
Writer, Director. b. Zlin, Czechoslovakia, July 3, 1937. r.n. Tomas Straussler. Playwright whose works include Rosencrantz and Guildenstern Are Dead, Jumpers, Travesties, The Real Thing, Hapgood, Arcadia.
PICTURES: The Romantic Englishwoman, Despair, The Human Factor, Squaring the Circle, Brazil, Empire of the Sun, The Russia House, Rosencrantz and Guildenstern Are Dead (also dir.), Billy Bathgate.

STORARO, VITTORIO
Cinematographer. b. Rome, Italy, June 24, 1940. Trained at Rome's Centro Sperimentale Cinematografia and began filming short films. His work as Bernardo Bertolucci's regular cinematographer won him an international reputation and award-winning work in Europe and America, including 3 Academy Awards.
PICTURES: Giovinezza Giovinezza (Youthful Youthful), The Conformist, The Spider's Stratagem, 'Tis Pity She's a Whore, Last Tango in Paris, Giordano Bruno, 1900, Submission, Agatha, Apocalypse Now (Academy Award, 1979), Luna, Reds (Academy Award, 1981), One From the Heart, Wagner, Ladyhawke, Captain Eo, Ishtar, The Last Emperor (Academy Award, 1987), Tucker: The Man and His Dream, New York Stories (Life Without Zoe), Dick Tracy, The Sheltering Sky, Tosca, Little Buddha, Roma! Imago Urbis, Flamenco, Taxi.

STOREY, FREDERICK
Executive. b. Columbus, GA, Nov. 12, 1909. e. Georgia Tech. Adv. staff Atlanta Journal, 1933-38; adv. staff C. P. Clark Adv. Agcy., 1938; partner 1940; U.S. Navy, 1941-46; staff Georgia Theatre Co., 1946; v.p. 1947-52. Founded Storey Theatres Inc., Atlanta, GA; 1952, now bd. chmn. emeritus (formerly pres.) of Georgia State Theatres; dir. numerous theatre cos.; v.p. dir., Motion Picture Theatre Owners of Georgia, Dist. Alumnus award, Georgia Tech, 1979.

STORKE, WILLIAM F.
Producer. b. Rochester, NY, Aug. 12, 1927. e. UCLA, B.A. 1948. In Navy, WWII. First position with NBC Hollywood guest relations staff, 1948. Moved to continuity acceptance dept. as

comm. editor. Prom. to asst. mgr, comm. spvr. before joining NBC West Coast sales dept., 1953. Transferred to N.Y. as prog. acct. exec., 1955; named administrator, participating prog. sales, 1957. Named dir., participating program sales, 1959. Named dir., program adm., NBC-TV, 1964; then elected v.p., program adm.; 1967 named v.p., programs, East Coast; 1968, appt. v.p., special programs, NBC-TV Network; 1979, pres., Claridge Group, Ltd.; exec. v.p. Entertainment Partners, Inc., N.Y., 1982-. Pres., Storke Enterprises Inc. 1988-.
TELEVISION: *Producer:* Oliver Twist, To Catch A King, A Christmas Carol, The Last Days of Patton, A Special Friendship, The Ted Kennedy Jr. Story, Buck James (series, exec. prod.), Old Man and the Sea, Hands of a Murderer (Sherlock Holmes).

STORM, GALE
Actress. r.n. Josephine Cottle. b. Bloomington, TX, April 5, 1922. Won Gateway to Hollywood talent contest while still in high school, in 1939. Also launched successful recording career. *Autobiography:* I Ain't Down Yet (1981).
PICTURES: Tom Brown's Schooldays (debut, 1939), Smart Alecks, Foreign Agent, Nearly Eighteen, Where Are Your Children?, Revenge of the Zombies, The Right to Live, Sunbonnet Sue, Swing Parade of 1946, It Happened on Fifth Avenue, The Dude Goes West, Stampede, The Kid From Texas, Abandoned, Between Midnight and Dawn, Underworld Story, Curtain Call at Cactus Creek, Al Jennings of Oklahoma, Texas Rangers, Woman of the North Country.
TELEVISION: *Series:* My Little Margie, Oh Susanna.

STOSSEL, JOHN
News Correspondent. b. 1947. e. Princeton U. Started as producer-reporter with KGW-TV in Portland, OR. Joined WCBS-TV in New York as investigative reporter and consumer editor, winning 15 local Emmy Awards. 1981 joined ABC-TV, appearing on Good Morning America and 20/20 as consumer editor. Also provides twice-weekly consumer reports on ABC Radio Information Network. Author: Shopping Smart (1982).

STOWE, MADELEINE
Actress. b. Los Angeles, CA, Aug. 18, 1958. e. USC. m. actor Brian Benben. Began acting at the Solari Theatre in Beverly Hills where she appeared in The Tenth Man.
PICTURES: Stakeout (debut, 1987), Tropical Snow, Worth Winning, Revenge, The Two Jakes, Closet Land, China Moon, Unlawful Entry, The Last of the Mohicans, Another Stakeout, Short Cuts, Blink, Bad Girls, Twelve Monkeys.
TELEVISION: *Series:* The Gangster Chronicles. *Movies:* The Nativity, The Deerslayer, Amazons, Blood and Orchids. *Mini-Series:* Beulah Land.

STRAIGHT, BEATRICE
Actress. b. Old Westbury, NY, Aug. 2, 1914. Trained in classics; won Tony award early in career for best actress in Arthur Miller's The Crucible.
THEATER: *NY:* King Lear, Twelfth Night, The Possessed, Land of Fame, Eastward in Eden, The Heiress (B'way & on tour), The Crucible (Tony Award), Phedra, Everything in the Garden, Ghosts, All My Sons. *Regional:* A Streetcar Named Desire, The Lion in Winter, Old Times.
PICTURES: Phone Call from a Stranger (debut, 1952), Patterns, The Nun's Story, Garden Party, Network (Academy Award, best supporting actress, 1976), The Promise, Bloodline, The Formula, Endless Love, Poltergeist, Two of a Kind, Power.
TELEVISION: *Series:* Beacon Hill, King's Crossing, Jack and Mike. *Mini-Series:* The Dain Curse, Robert Kennedy and His Times. *Specials:* The Borrowers, Faerie Tale Theatre (The Princess and the Pea). *Movies:* Killer on Board, Under Siege, Run Till You Fall, Chiller, People Like Us.

STRASBERG, SUSAN
Actress. b. New York, NY, May 22, 1938. e. NY. p. late Lee Strasberg, stage dir. & dir. of Actors Studio, and Paula Miller, actress. Off-B'way stage debut in Maya; followed by The Duchess and the Smugs, Romeo and Juliet, The Diary of Anne Frank (B'way; Theatre World Award), Time Remembered, Zeffirelli's Lady of the Camillias, Shadow of a Gunman, Agnes of God (tour). Author: Bittersweet. Also teaches acting.
PICTURES: The Cobweb (debut, 1955), Picnic, Stage Struck, Scream of Fear, Adventures of a Young Man, The High Bright Sun (McGuire Go Home!), The Trip, Psych-Out, Chubasco, The Name of the Game Is Kill, The Brotherhood, So Evil My Sister, Legend of Hillbilly John, And Millions Will Die, Rollercoaster, The Manitou, In Praise of Older Women, Sweet 16, The Delta Force, Bloody Birthday, Prime Suspect, The Runnin' Kind, Schweitzer, The Cherry Orchard.
TELEVISION: *Movies:* Marcus Welby M.D. (A Matter of Humanities), Hauser's Memory, Mr. & Mrs. Bo Jo Jones, SST-Death Flight, Beggarman, Thief, The Immigrants, Toma (pilot), Frankenstein, Rona Jaffe's Mazes and Monsters. *Series:* The Marriage, Toma. *Guest:* Murder She Wrote, Cagney and Lacy.

STRATHAIRN, DAVID
Actor. b. San Francisco, CA, 1949. e. Williams Col.
THEATER: Einstein and the Polar Bear, Blue Plate Special, Fen, I'm Not Rappaport, Salonika, A Lie of the Mind, The Birthday Party, Danton's Death, Mountain Language, L'Atelier, A Moon for the Misbegotten, Temptation.
PICTURES: Return of the Secaucus 7, Lovesick, Silkwood, Iceman, The Brother from Another Planet, When Nature Calls, Enormous Changes at the Last Minute, At Close Range, Matewan, Stars and Bars, Dominick and Eugene, Call Me, Eight Men Out, The Feud, Memphis Belle, City of Hope, Big Girls Don't Cry... They Get Even, A League of Their Own, Bob Roberts, Sneakers, Passion Fish, Lost in Yonkers, The Firm, A Dangerous Woman, The River Wild, Losing Isaiah, Dolores Claiborne, Mother Night.
TELEVISION: *Series:* The Days and Nights of Molly Dodd. *Movies:* Day One, Son of the Morning Star, Heat Wave, Judgment, Without Warning: The James Brady Story, O Pioneers!, The American Clock. *Guest:* Miami Vice, The Equalizer.

STRAUSS, PETER
Actor. b. Croton-on-Hudson, NY., Feb. 20, 1947. e. Northwestern U. Spotted by talent agent and sent to Hollywood. On stage at Mark Taper Theatre in Dance Next Door, The Dirty Man.
PICTURES: Hail Hero! (debut, 1969), Soldier Blue, The Trial of the Catonsville Nine, The Last Tycoon, Spacehunter: Adventures in the Forbidden Zone, Nick of Time.
TELEVISION: *Series:* Moloney. *Movies:* The Man Without a Country, Attack on Terror: The FBI Versus the Ku Klux Klan, Young Joe: The Forgotten Kennedy, The Jericho Mile (Emmy Award, 1979), Angel on My Shoulder, Heart of Steel, Under Siege, A Whale for the Killing, Penalty Phase, Proud Men, Brotherhood of the Rose, Peter Gunn, 83 Hours Till Dawn, Flight of Black Angel, Fugitive Among Us, Trial: The Price of Passion, Men Don't Tell, Thicker Than Blood: The Larry McLinden Story, The Yearling, Reunion, Texas Justice. *Mini-Series:* Rich Man Poor Man, Masada, Kane & Abel, Tender Is The Night.

STRAUSS, PETER E.
Executive. b. Oct. 7, 1940. e. Oberlin Coll., London Sch. of Economics, Columbia U. Sch. of Law, L.L.B., 1965. Vice pres., University Dormitory Dev. Co., 1965-68; v.p., Allart Cinema 16, 1968-69; v.p. prod., Allied Artists Pictures Corp., 1970; 1978-80, exec. v.p. Rastar Films; left to become independent as pres., Panache Prods., 1980-86. 1987, pres. & CEO of The Movie Group.
PICTURE: *Producer:* Best of the Best, Cadence, By the Sword, Best of the Best II, Best of the Best III.

STREEP, MERYL
Actress. r.n. Mary Louise Streep. b. Summit, NJ, June 22, 1949. e. Vassar. Acted for a season with traveling theater co. in VT. Awarded scholarship to Yale Drama School, 1972. NY stage debut: Trelawny of the Wells (1975) with New York Shakespeare Fest. Appeared in 1984 documentary In Our Hands.
THEATER: *Off-B'way:* 27 Wagons Full of Cotton (Theatre World Award), A Memory of Two Mondays, Secret Service, Henry V, (NY Shakespeare Fest.), Measure for Measure (NYSF), The Cherry Orchard, Happy End (B'way debut, 1977), The Taming of the Shrew (NYSF), Taken in Marriage, Alice in Concert, Isn't It Romantic?
PICTURES: Julia (debut, 1977), The Deer Hunter, Manhattan, The Seduction of Joe Tynan, Kramer vs. Kramer (Academy Award, best supporting actress, 1979), The French Lieutenant's Woman, Still of the Night, Sophie's Choice (Academy Award, 1982), Silkwood, Falling in Love, Plenty, Out of Africa, Heartburn, Ironweed, A Cry in the Dark, She-Devil, Postcards From the Edge, Defending Your Life, Death Becomes Her, The House of the Spirits, The River Wild, The Bridges of Madison County, Before and After, Marvin's Room.
TELEVISION: *Mini-Series:* Holocaust (Emmy Award, 1978). *Movie:* The Deadliest Season. *Specials* (PBS): Secret Service, Uncommon Women and Others, Age 7 in America (host).

STREISAND, BARBRA
Singer, Actress, Director, Producer. b. New York, NY, April 24, 1942. e. Erasmus H.S., Brooklyn. Son is actor Jason Gould. Appeared as singer in NY night clubs. NY stage debut: Another Evening with Harry Stoones (1961), followed by Pins and Needles. On Broadway in I Can Get It For You Wholesale, Funny Girl. Performed song Prisoner for 1978 film Eyes of Laura Mars. Appeared in 1990 documentary Listen Up.
PICTURES: Funny Girl (debut; Academy Award, 1968), Hello Dolly!, On a Clear Day You Can See Forever, The Owl and the Pussycat, What's Up Doc?, Up the Sandbox, The Way We Were (Acad. Award nom.), For Pete's Sake, Funny Lady, A Star Is Born (also co-composer, exec. prod.; Academy Award for best song: Evergreen, 1976), The Main Event (also co-prod.), All Night Long, Yentl (also dir., prod., co- s.p.), Nuts

(also prod., co-composer), The Prince of Tides (also dir., co-prod.; Acad. Award nom. for picture), The Mirror Has Two Faces (also dir.).

TELEVISION: *Specials*: My Name Is Barbra (Emmy Award, 1965), Color Me Barbra, The Belle of 14th Street, A Happening in Central Park, Barbra Streisand... And Other Musical Instruments, Putting It Together, One Voice, Barbra Streisand: The Concert (also co-prod.; 2 Emmy Awards, 1995). *Movie*: Serving in Silence: The Margarethe Cammermeyer Story (co-exec. prod. only). *Guest*: Ed Sullivan, Merv Griffin, Judy Garland Show, Saturday Night Live, Late Show With David Letterman.

STRICK, WESLEY
Writer. b. New York, NY, Feb. 11, 1954. e. UC at Berkeley, 1975. Was rock critic for magazines Rolling Stone, Cream, Circus.
PICTURES: True Believer, Arachnophobia, Cape Fear, Final Analysis, Batman Returns, Wolf, The Tie That Binds (dir.), The Saint (s.p.).
TELEVISION: *Series*: Eddie Dodd (pilot).

STRICKLAND, GAIL
Actress. b. Birmingham, AL, May 18. e. Florida St. Univ. NY Theatre includes Status Quo Vadis, I Won't Dance.
TELEVISION: *Series*: The Insiders, What a Country, Heartbeat. *Movies*: Ellery Queen, My Father's House, The Dark Side of Innocence, The Gathering, A Love Affair: The Eleanor and Lou Gehrig Story, The President's Mistress, Ski Lift to Death, Letters from Frank, King Crab, Rape and Marriage: The Rideout Case, A Matter of Life and Death, My Body My Child, Eleanor: First Lady of the World, Life of the Party: The Story of Beatrice, Starlight: The Plane That Couldn't Land, The Burden of Proof, Silent Cries, Spies, Barbara Taylor Bradford's Remember, A Mother's Prayer.
PICTURES: The Drowning Pool, Bittersweet Love, Bound for Glory, One on One, Who'll Stop the Rain, Norma Rae, Lies, Oxford Blues, Protocol, The Man in the Moon, Three of Hearts, When a Man Loves a Woman.

STRICKLYN, RAY
Actor. b. Houston, TX, October 8, 1928. e. U. of Houston. Official U.S. representative at Edinburgh Int'l Festival (1988); and Israel Intl. Festival (1989).
THEATER: The Climate of Eden (B'way debut; Theatre World Award). Tour: Stalag 17. Off-B'way: The Grass Harp, Confessions of a Nightingale (also LA, tour; LA Drama Critics, LA Weekly, Dramalogue, Oscar Wilde Awards). LA: Vieux Carre, Compulsion, The Caretaker, Naomi Court, Bus Stop.
PICTURES: The Proud and the Profane, Crime in the Streets, Somebody Up There Likes Me, The Catered Affair, The Last Wagon, Return of Dracula, 10 North Frederick, The Remarkable Mr. Pennypacker, The Big Fisherman, Young Jesse James, The Plunderers, The Lost World, Track of Thunder, Arizona Raiders, Dogpound Shuffle.
TELEVISION: *Movies*: Jealousy, Danielle Steel's Secrets, Hart to Hart Returns.

STRINGER, HOWARD
Executive. b. Cardiff, Wales. Feb. 19, 1942. e. Oxford U., B.A., M.A., modern history/international relations. Received Army Commendation Medal for meritorious achievement for service in Vietnam (1965-67). Joined CBS, 1965, at WCBS-TV, NY, rising from assoc. prod., prod. to exec. prod. of documentary broadcasts. Served as prod., dir. and writer of CBS Reports: The Palestinians (Overseas Press Club of America, Writers Guild Awards, 1974); The Rockefellers (Emmy Award, 1973). Won 9 Emmy Awards as exec. prod., prod., writer or dir: CBS Reports: The Boston Goes to China; CBS Reports: The Defense of the United States; CBS Evening News with Dan Rather: The Beirut Bombing; The Countdown Against Cancer; The Black Family. Exec. prod., CBS Reports; exec. prod., CBS Evening News with Dan Rather, 1981-84. Appointed exec. vice pres., CBS News Division, 1984; pres., CBS News, 1986; pres., CBS/Broadcast Group, 1988.

STRITCH, ELAINE
Actress. b. Detroit, MI, Feb. 2, 1926. e. studied acting with Erwin Piscator at the New Sch. for Social Research. Major career on stage. B'way debut 1946 in Loco.
THEATER: NY: Made in Heaven, Angel in the Wings, Call Me Madam, Pal Joey, On Your Toes, Bus Stop, Goldilocks, Sail Away, Who's Afraid of Virginia Woolf?, Wonderful Town, Company, Show Boat, A Delicate Balance (Tony Award nom.). *London*: Gingerbread Lady, Small Craft Warnings, Company.
PICTURES: The Scarlet Hour (debut, 1955), Three Violent People, A Farewell to Arms, The Perfect Furlough, Who Killed Teddy Bear?, Sidelong Glances of a Pigeon Kicker, The Spiral Staircase, Providence, September, Cocoon: The Return, Cadillac Man.
TELEVISION: *Series*: Growing Paynes (1948), Pantomine Quiz (regular, 1953-55, 1958), My Sister Eileen, The Trials of O'Brien, Two's Company (London), Nobody's Perfect (London;

also adapt.) The Ellen Burstyn Show. *Specials*: Company: the Making of the Album, Kennedy Center Tonight, Follies in Concert, Sensibility and Sense. Movies: The Secret Life of Archie's Wife, An Inconvenient Woman, Chance of a Lifetime. *Guest*: Law & Order (Emmy Award, 1993).

STROCK, HERBERT L.
Producer, Writer, Director, Film editor. b. Boston, MA, Jan. 13, 1918. e. USC, A.B., M.A. in cinema. Prof. of cinema, USC, 1941. Started career, publicity leg man, Jimmy Fidler, Hollywood columnist; editorial dept., MGM, 1941-47; pres., IMPPRO, Inc., 1955-59; assoc. prod.-supv. film ed., U.A.; director: AIP, Warner Bros. independent, Phoenix Films. Pres., Herbert L. Strock Prods. Lecturer at American Film Institute.
PICTURES: Storm Over Tibet, Magnetic Monster, Riders to the Stars, The Glass Wall. *Director*: Gog, Battle Taxi, Donovan's Brain, Rider on a Dead Horse, Devil's Messenger, Brother on the Run, One Hour of Hell, Witches Brew, Blood of Dracula, I Was a Teenage Frankenstein, The Crawling Hand; Soul Brothers Die Hard, Monstroids. *Writer-film editor*: Hurray for Betty Boop (cartoon). *Sound Effects editor* on Katy Caterpillar (cartoon feature). Editor: Night Screams, Detour. *Post-prod. spvr.*: King Kung Fu, Sidewalk Motel. *Co-director*: Deadly Presence. *Editor*: Snooze You Lose, Gramma's Gold, Distance, Fish Outta Water. *Prod/edit.*: The Visitors, Statistically Speaking.
TELEVISION: Highway Patrol, Harbor Command, Men of Annapolis, I Led Three Lives, The Veil, Dragnet, 77 Sunset Strip, Maverick, Cheyenne, Bronco, Sugarfoot, Colt 45, Science Fiction Thea., Seahunt, Corliss Archer, Bonanza, Hallmark Hall of Fame, The Small Miracle, Hans Brinker, The Inventing of America (specials); What Will We Say to a Hungry World (telethon), They Search for Survival (special), Flipper (series). *Documentaries*: Atlantis, Legends, UFO Journals, UFO Syndrome, Legend of the Lochness Monster, China-Mao to Now, El-Papa—Journey to Tibet. *Editor*: Peace Corps' Partnership in Health. *L.A. Dept. of Water & Power*: Water You Can Trust. Olympic Comm. Your Olympic Legacy—AAF.

STROLLER, LOUIS A.
Producer. b. Brooklyn, NY, April 3, 1942. e. Nicholas Coll. of Business Admin., BBA, 1963. Entered film business in 1963 doing a variety of jobs in local NY studios, and TV commercials. Unit manager on The Producers. Moved to L.A. in 1970s. First asst. dir. Charley, Take the Money and Run, Lovers and Other Strangers, They Might Be Giants, Man on a Swing, 92 in the Shade. Prod. mgr.: Mortadella, Sisters, Sweet Revenge, The Eyes of Laura Mars, Telefon. *Assoc. prod.*: Badlands, Carrie. The Seduction of Joe Tynan.
PICTURES: *Exec. prod. or prod.*: Simon, The Four Seasons, Venom, Eddie Macon's Run, Scarface, Sweet Liberty, Real Men, A New Life, Sea of Love, Betsy's Wedding, Back in the U.S.S.R., The Real McCoy, Carlito's Way, The Shadow, The Rock, Nothing to Lose.
TELEVISION: Half a Lifetime (exec. prod.; nom. 4 ACE Awards), Blue Ice.

STRONG, JOHN
Producer, Director, Writer, Actor. b. New York, NY, Dec. 3. e. U. of Miami, Cornell U., B.S., architectural engineering. Began acting in small role in film Duel in the Sun; on B'way in Annie Get Your Gun and understudy for James Dean in Immoralist. Appeared in many radio and TV serials, regular on Captain Video and the Video Ranger, later under contract as actor to Universal and Warner Bros. Member, Writers Guild America West, Directors Guild of America, Producers Guild of America, Dramatists Guild. Pres., Cinevent Corp.
PICTURES: Perilous Journey (exec. prod., s.p.), Eddie & the Cruisers (sprv. prod.), Heart Like a Wheel (sprv. prod.), For Your Eyes Only (s.p.), The Earthling (prod.), The Mountain Men (actor, prod.), Savage Streets (prod.), Steel Justice (prod.), Knights of the City (prod.), Garbage Pail Kids (sprv. prod.), Cop (sprv. prod.), Wild Thing (sprv. prod.), Summer Heat (sprv. prod.), Teen Wolf II (sprv. prod.), Atlantic Entertainment (sprv. prod.), Show of Force (prod., s.p.), Prime Directive (prod., s.p.), Sinapore Sling (prod., s.p.), Willie Sutton Story (prod.), Bandit Queen (prod.), Fatal Charm (exec. prod.), Colors of Love (prod.), Black Ice (dir., s.p.).
TELEVISION: The John Strong Show (host, exec. prod.), The Nurse (special, writer), McCloud (prod., writer), The Thrill of the Fall (prod.), Search (prod., writer, 2nd unit dir.), Outer Limits (exec. chg. prod.), Name of the Game (exec. chg. prod.), I Spy (writer), Love American Style (writer), All in the Family (writer), Changes (prod., dir., writer), Charlie's Angels (writer), Hawaii Five O' (writer).

STROUD, DON
Actor. b. Honolulu, Hawaii, Sept. 1, 1943. e. Kaimuki h.s. Was surfing champion, ranked 4th in the world.
PICTURES: Games, Madigan, Journey to Shiloh, What's So Bad About Feeling Good?, Coogan's Bluff, Bloody Mama, Explosion, Angel Unchained, Tick Tick Tick, Von Richtofen and Brown, Joe Kidd, Slaughter's Big Rip-Off, Scalawag,

Murph the Surf, The Killer Inside Me, The House by the Lake, The Choirboys, The Buddy Holly Story, The Amityville Horror, The Night the Lights Went Out in Georgia, Search and Destroy, Sweet Sixteen, Armed and Dangerous, Licence to Kill, Down the Drain, The Divine Enforcer, King of the Kickboxers, Cartel, Mob Boss, Street Wars, Frogtown, Deady Avenger, Danger Sign, Carnosaur II, Of Unknown Origin, Sudden Death, Dillinger and Capone, Twisted Justice, Two to Tango, Ghost Ship, Precious Find, Wild America.
TELEVISION: *Series*: Kate Loves a Mystery, Mike Hammer, The New Gidget, Dragnet. *Movies*: Split Second to an Epitaph, Something for a Lonely Man, DA: Conspiracy to Kill, Deadly Dream, Daughters of Joshua Cabe, Rolling Man, The Elevator, Return of Joe Forrester, High Risk, Katie: Portrait of a Centerfold, Out on a Limb, I Want to Live, Manhunters, Murder Me Murder You, The Alien Within, Sawbones, Barefoot in Paradise. *Special*: Hatful of Rain. *Guest*: Murder She Wrote, Quantum Leap, The FBI, Gunsmoke, Baywatch, Starsky and Hutch, The Mod Squad, Marcus Welby, Babylon 5, Walker: Texas Ranger, many others.

STRUTHERS, SALLY
Actress. b. Portland, OR, July 28, 1947. First tv appearance was as dancer on a Herb Alpert special. Appeared on Broadway stage in Wally's Cafe.
PICTURES: The Phynx, Five Easy Pieces, The Getaway.
TELEVISION: *Series*: The Summer Smothers (1970), The Tim Conway Comedy Hour, All in the Family (Emmy Awards: 1972, 1979), Pebbles and Bamm-Bamm (voice), Flintstones Comedy Hour (voice), Gloria, 9 to 5, Dinosaurs (voice). *Movies*: The Great Houdinis, Aloha Means Goodbye, Hey I'm Alive, Intimate Strangers, My Husband is Missing, And Your Name is Jonah, A Gun in the House, A Deadly Silence, In the Best Interests of the Children.

STUBBS, IMOGEN
Actress. b. Newcastle-upon-Tyne, 1961. Brought up in West London on sailing barge on the Thames. Grandmother was playwright Esther McCracken. e. Exeter Coll. First class degree at Oxford U. in English. Joined Oxford U. Dramatic Society appearing in revues and at Edinburgh Festival in play called Poison. Trained for stage at Royal Acad. of Dramatic Art. Prof. stage debut in Cabaret and The Boyfriend, in Ipswich. Acted with Royal Shakespeare Co. in The Two Noble Kinsmen, The Rover (promising newcomer critics award), Richard II, Othello, Heartbreak House, St. Joan, Uncle Vanya.
PICTURES: Privileged, A Summer Story, Nanou, Erik the Viking, True Colors, A Pin for the Butterfly, Sandra C'est la Vie, Jack & Sarah, Sense and Sensibility, Twelfth Night.
TELEVISION: The Browning Version, Deadline, The Rainbow, Fellow Traveller, After the Dance, Relatively Speaking, Othello, Anna Lee.

STULBERG, GORDON
Executive. b. Toronto, Canada, Dec. 17, 1927. e. U. of Toronto, B.A., Cornell Law Sch., LL.B. Was assoc. & member, Pacht, Ross, Warne & Bernhard; ent. m.p. ind. as exec. asst. to v.p., Columbia Pictures Corp., 1956-60; v.p. & chief studio admin. off., 1960-67; pres. of Cinema Center Films (div. of CBS) 1967-71; pres. 20th Century-Fox, 1971-75; 1980, named pres. & COO, PolyGram Pictures. Member of NY, Calif. bars, Chairman, American Interactive Media (Polygram subsidiary).

SUGAR, LARRY
Executive. b. Phoenix, AZ, May 26, 1945. m. Bonnie Sugar. e. Cheshire Acad., 1962; CSUN, B.A., 1967; U. of Southern Calif., J.D., 1971. Writer and co-author, Calif. Primary Reading Program, 1967-68. Joined Warner Bros. as dir., legal and corp. affairs, 1971-74; 20th Century Fox legal staff, 1974-77; co-owner with Bonnie Sugar, Serendipity Prods., 1977-81; named pres., intl., Lorimar Prods. 1981-84; exec. v.p., distribution, CBS 1984-85; exec. v.p. worldwide distribution, Weintraub Entertainment Group 1987-89; formed Sugar Entertainment, chmn., 1989-1991; pres. intl., Republic Pictures, Inc. 1991-93; pres. Larry Sugar Entertainment, 1993-.
PICTURES: *Exec. prod.*: Slapstick, Steel Dawn, Options, Damned River, Fatal Sky, Graveyard Shift, Shattered, Dark Horse, Family Prayers, The Plague, Boxing Helena. *Prod.*: With Deadly Intent, Annie O, Robin of Locksley.

SUGARMAN, BURT
Producer. b. Beverly Hills, CA, Jan. 4. e. U. of Southern California. Chmn. & CEO, GIANT GROUP, LTD., diversified co. traded on NYSE.
PICTURES: Kiss Me Goodbye, Extremities, Children of a Lesser God, Crimes of the Heart.
TELEVISION: Midnight Special, Switched on Symphony, The Mancini Generation, Johnny Mann's Stand Up and Cheer, etc.

SULLIVAN, REV. PATRICK J.
S.J., S.T.D.: Provost, Graduate Center at Tarrytown, Fordham U. b. New York, NY, March 25, 1920. e. Regis H.S.; Georgetown U., A.B., 1943; Woodstock Coll., M.A., 1944; Fordham U., 1945-47; S.T.L. Weston Coll., 1947-51; S.T.D. Gregorian U. (Rome), 1952-54. Prof. of Theology, Woodstock Coll., 1954-57; Consultor, Pontifical Commission for Social Communications, 1968-82; Exec. Dir., U.S. Catholic Conference, Film & Broadcasting Office, 1965-80; Fordham Univ. Grad Sch. of Business, Assoc. Dean 1982-83, Dean 1983-85.

SUNSHINE, ROBERT HOWARD
Publisher. b. Brooklyn, NY, Jan. 17, 1946. e. U. of RI; Brooklyn Law Sch., 1971. Admitted to NY State Bar, 1971. President of Pubsun Corp., owner of The Film Journal. Publisher of The Film Journal. Exec. dir., Theatre Equipment Association, 1979-present; sec. and exec. dir. Foundation of the Motion Picture Pioneers, 1975-present; exec. dir., Natl. Assoc. of Theatre Owners of NY State, 1985-present; Producer of Variety Telethon, 1985-present; coordinator and producer, Show East Convention; coordinator and prod., Cinema Expo Intl., Amsterdam, Holland; coordinator, m.p. CineAsia, Singapore.

SURTEES, BRUCE
Cinematographer. b. Los Angeles, CA, July 23, 1937. Son of cinematographer Robert L. Surtees.
PICTURES: The Beguiled, Play Misty for Me, Dirty Harry, The Great Northfield Minnesota Raid, Conquest of the Planet of the Apes, Joe Kidd, The Outfit, High Plains Drifter, Blume in Love, Lenny (Acad. Award nom.), Night Moves, Leadbelly, The Outlaw Josey Wales, The Shootist, Three Warriors, Sparkle, Big Wednesday, Movie Movie (segment: Baxter's Beauties of 1933), Dreamer, Escape from Alcatraz, Ladies and Gentlemen the Fabulous Stains, White Dog, Firefox, Inchon, Honkytonk Man, Bad Boys, Risky Business, Sudden Impact, Tightrope, Beverly Hills Cop, Pale Rider, Psycho III, Out of Bounds, Ratboy, Back to the Beach, License to Drive, Men Don't Leave, Run, The Super, The Crush, That Night. Corrina Corrina, The Stars Fell on Henrietta, The Substitute.

SUSCHITZKY, PETER
Cinematographer. Spent long time in Latin America as documentary cinematographer. Later made commercials in France, England and U.S. First feature was It Happened Here, 1962.
PICTURES: Over 30 features including: A Midsummer Night's Dream, Charlie Bubbles, Leo the Last, Privilege, That'll Be the Day, Lisztomania, The Rocky Horror Picture Show, All Creatures Great and Small (TV in U.S.), Valentino, The Empire Strikes Back, Krull, Falling in Love, In Extremis, Dead Ringers, Where the Heart Is, Naked Lunch, The Public Eye, The Vanishing, M. Butterfly, Immortal Beloved, Crash, Mars Attacks.

SUTHERLAND, DONALD
Actor. b. St. John, New Brunswick, Canada, July 17, 1935. Son is actor Kiefer Sutherland. e. U. of Toronto, B.A., 1956. At 14 became a radio announcer and disc jockey. Worked in a mine in Finland. Theatre includes: The Male Animal (debut), The Tempest (Hart House Theatre, U. of Toronto), Two years at London Acad. of Music and Dramatic Art. Spent a year and a half with the Perth Repertory Theatre in Scotland, then repertory at Nottingham, Chesterfield, Bromley and Sheffield.
THEATER: August for the People (London debut), On a Clear Day You Can See Canterbury, The Shewing Up of Blanco Posnet, The Spoon River Anthology, Lolita (B'way debut, 1981).
PICTURES: Castle of the Living Dead (debut, 1964), The World Ten Times Over, Dr. Terror's House of Horrors, Die Die My Darling (Fanatic), The Bedford Incident, Promise Her Anything, The Dirty Dozen, Billion Dollar Brain, Sebastian, Oedipus the King, Interlude, Joanna, The Split, M*A*S*H, Start the Revolution Without Me, Act of the Heart, Kelly's Heroes, Alex in Wonderland, Little Murders, Klute, Johnny Got His Gun, F.T.A. (also co-prod., co-dir., co-s.p.), Steelyard Blues (also exec. prod.), Lady Ice, Alien Thunder (Dan Candy's Law), Don't Look Now, S*P*Y*S, The Day of the Locust, End of the Game (cameo), Fellini's Casanova, The Eagle Has Landed, 1900, The Disappearance, The Kentucky Fried Movie, National Lampoon's Animal House, Invasion of the Body Snatchers, The Great Train Robbery, Murder by Decree, Bear Island, A Man a Woman and a Bank, Nothing Personal, Ordinary People, Blood Relatives, Gas, Eye of the Needle, Threshold, Max Dugan Returns, Crackers, Ordeal by Innocence, Heaven Help Us, Revolution, Wolf at the Door, The Rosary Murders, The Trouble with Spies, Apprentice to Murder, Lost Angels, Lock Up, A Dry White Season, Eminent Domain, Backdraft, Buster's Bedroom, JFK, Scream of Stone, Buffy the Vampire Slayer, Shadow of the Wolf, Benefit of the Doubt, Dr. Bethune (Bethune: The Making of a Hero), Younger and Younger, Six Degrees of Separation, Robert A. Heinlein's The Puppet Masters, Disclosure, Outbreak, Hollow Point, The Shadow Conspiracy, A Time to Kill.
TELEVISION: *Specials*: (British) Marching to the Sea, The Death of Bessie Smith, Hamlet at Elsinore, Gideon's Way, The Champions, Bethune (Canada), Give Me Your Answer True,

The Prize (narrator), People of the Forest: The Chimps of Gombe (narrator). *Guest*: The Saint, The Avengers. *Movies*: The Sunshine Patriot, The Winter of Our Discontent, Quicksand: No Escape, The Railway Station Man, The Lifeforce Experiment, Oldest Living Confederate Widow Tells All, Citizen X (Emmy Award, 1995; Golden Globe Award 1995). *Series*: Great Books (narrator).

SUTHERLAND, KIEFER
Actor. b. London, England, CA, Dec. 18, 1966. Son of actor Donald Sutherland and actress Shirley Douglas. Moved to Los Angeles at age 4, then to Toronto at 8. Debut with L.A. Odyssey Theatre at age 9 in Throne of Straw. Worked in local Toronto theater workshops before landing starring role in The Bay Boy (1984) for which he won Canadian Genie Award.
PICTURES: Max Dugan Returns (debut, 1983), The Bay Boy, At Close Range, Stand By Me, Crazy Moon, The Lost Boys, The Killing Time, Promised Land, Bright Lights Big City, Young Guns, 1969, Renegades, Flashback, Chicago Joe and the Showgirl, Flatliners, Young Guns II, The Nutcracker Prince (voice), Article 99, Twin Peaks: Fire Walk With Me, A Few Good Men, The Vanishing, The Three Musketeers, The Cowboy Way, Teresa's Tattoo, Eye for an Eye, Freeway, A Time To Kill.
TELEVISION: *Movies*: Trapped in Silence, Brotherhood of Justice, Last Light (also dir.), Dark Reflection (co-exec. prod. only). *Guest*: Amazing Stories (The Mission).

SUTTON, JAMES T.
Executive. b. California, Sept. 13. e. Columbia U. Film inspector, U.S. government; overseas m.p. service, WW II; co-owner, gen. mngr., Hal Davis Studios; hd. TV commercial div., Allan Sandler Films; Academy Art Pictures; pres., chmn. of bd., exec. prod., Royal Russian Studios, Inc., western hemisphere div.; pres. exec. prod. Gold Lion Prods., Inc.; pres. exec. prod. James T. Sutton-John L. Carpenter Prods.; pres., exec. dir., Airax Corp.; pres. of Skyax (div. of Airax).

SUZMAN, JANET
Actress. b. Johannesburg, South Africa, Feb. 9, 1939. e. Kingsmead Coll., U. of Witwatersrand. Trained at L.A.M.D.A. London stage debut in The Comedy of Errors. *Recent theater*: Another Time, Hippolytos, The Sisters Rosensweig. *Director*: Othello for Market Theatre and Channel 4 (TV), Death of a Salesman, A Dream of People, The Deep Blue Sea.
PICTURES: Nicholas and Alexandra (Acad. Award nom.), A Day in the Death of Joe Egg, The Black Windmill, Nijinsky, Priest of Love, The Draughtsman's Contract, And the Ship Sails On, A Dry White Season, Nuns on the Run, Leon the Pig Farmer.
TELEVISION: *Specials/Movies*: The Three Sisters, Hedda Gabler, The House on Garibaldi Street, The Zany Adventures of Robin Hood, Miss Nightingale, Macbeth, Mountbatten—Last Viceroy of India (series), The Singing Detective (series), Clayhanger (series), The Miser, Revolutionary Witness, Saint Joan, Twelfth Night, Master Class on Shakespearean Comedy, Inspector Morse, The Ruth Rendell Mysteries.

SVENSON, BO
Actor. b. Goteborg, Sweden, Feb. 13, 1941. e. UCLA, 1970-74. U.S. Marine Corps 1959-65.
PICTURES: Maurie (debut, 1973), The Great Waldo Pepper, Part 2: Walking Tall, Breaking Point, Special Delivery, Portrait of a Hitman, Final Chapter: Walking Tall, Our Man in Mecca, The Inglorious Bastard, North Dallas Forty, Virus, Night Warning, Thunder Warrior, Deadly Impact, Wizards of the Lost Kingdom, The Manhunt, The Delta Force, Choke Canyon, Heartbreak Ridge, War Bus 2, Silent Hero, Thunder Warrior II, White Phantom, Deep Space, Justice Done, The Train, Soda Cracker, Curse II: The Bite, Captain Henkel, Running Combat, Steel Frontier.
TELEVISION: *Series*: Here Come the Brides, Walking Tall. *Movies*: The Bravos, Frankenstein, You'll Never See Me Again, Hitched, Target Risk, Snowbeast, Gold of the Amazon Women, Jealousy.

SWAIM, BOB
Director, Writer. b. Evanston, IL, Nov. 2, 1943. e. Calif. State U, B.A.; L'Ecole Nationale de la Cinematographie, Paris, BTS 1969. American director who has often worked in France. Began career making shorts: Le Journal de M Bonnafous, Self Portrait of a Pornographer, Vive les Jacques. Received Cesar award French Acad. M.P., 1982; Chevalier des Arts et des Lettres 1985.
PICTURES: La Nuit de Saint-Germain-des-Pres (1977), La Balance, Half Moon Street, Masquerade, Atlantide, Da Costa, Parfum de Meurte, Femme de Passions.

SWANSON, DENNIS
Executive. e. Univ. of IL. B.A. in journalism, 1961, M.S. in communications/political science, 1966. 1966-67, news prod. & assignment mngr. for WGN radio & tv in Chicago; 1968-70, assign. edit. & field prod. for NBC news at WMAQ TV in Chicago; 1971-74, sportscaster and prod. WMAQ; worked for

TVN in Chicago and served as company's NY dir. of news division; 1976, became exec. prod. of KABC-TV in LA; 1981, appointed station mngr. KABC-TV; 1983, v.p. & gen. mngr. WLS-TV, Chicago; 1985, named pres. of ABC Owned TV Stations; 1986, became pres. of ABC Sports; 1990, pres., ABC Daytime and ABC Children's Programming.

SWANSON, KRISTY
Actress. b. Mission Viejo, CA, 1969. Signed with modeling agency at age 9, appearing in over 30 commercials. Acting debut at 13 on Disney series Dreamfinders.
PICTURES: Pretty in Pink, Ferris Bueller's Day Off, Deadly Friend, Flowers in the Attic, Diving In, Mannequin Two on the Move, Hot Shots, Highway to Hell, Buffy the Vampire Slayer, The Program, The Chase, Getting In (Student Body), Higher Learning, The Phantom.
TELEVISION: *Series*: Dreamfinders, Knots Landing, Nightingales. *Movies*: Miracle of the Heart: A Boys Town Story, Not Quite Human.

SWAYZE, PATRICK
Actor, Dancer. b. Houston, TX. Aug. 18, 1952. e. San Jacinto Col. m. actress-dancer Lisa Niemi. Son of choreographer Patsy Swayze (Urban Cowboy). Brother is actor Don Swayze. Began as dancer appearing in Disney on Parade on tour as Prince Charming. Songwriter and singer with 6 bands. Studied dance at Harkness and Joffrey Ballet Schs. On B'way as dancer in Goodtime Charley, Grease. Co-author of play Without a Word.
PICTURES: Skatetown USA (debut, 1979), The Outsiders, Uncommon Valor, Red Dawn, Grandview USA (also choreographer), Youngblood, Dirty Dancing (also co-wrote and sang She's Like the Wind), Steel Dawn, Tiger Warsaw, Road House, Next of Kin, Ghost, Point Break, City of Joy, Father Hood, Tall Tale, To Wong Foo—Thanks for Everything—Julie Newmar, Three Wishes.
TELEVISION: *Mini-Series*: North and South: Books I and II. *Movies*: The Comeback Kid, Return of the Rebels, The Renegades (pilot), Off Sides. *Series*: Renegades. *Guest*: M*A*S*H, Amazing Stories.

SWEENEY, D.B.
Actor. r.n. Daniel Bernard Sweeney. b. Shoreham, NY, 1961. e. NYU, 1984 B.F.A.
THEATER: *NY*: The Caine Mutiny Court-Martial (B'way), The Seagull: The Hamptons: 1990, Distant Fires (L.A.), among others.
PICTURES: Power (debut, 1986), Fire With Fire, Gardens of Stone, No Man's Land, Eight Men Out, Memphis Belle, Blue Desert, Sons, Leather Jackets, Heaven Is a Playground, The Cutting Edge, A Day in October, Hear No Evil, Fire in the Sky, Roommates.
TELEVISION: *Series*: Strange Luck. *Mini-Series*: Lonesome Dove. *Movies*: Out of the Darkness, Miss Rose White.

SWERLING, JO
Writer. b. Russia, Apr. 8, 1897. Newspaper & mag. writer; author vaude. sketches; co-author plays, The Kibitzer, Guys and Dolls (Tony Award, 1951).
PICTURES: The Kibitzer, Platinum Blonde, Washington Merry-Go-Round, Dirigible, Man's Castle, Whole Town's Talking, No Greater Glory, Pennies from Heaven, Double Wedding, Made for Each Other, The Westerner, Confirm or Deny, Blood and Sand, Pride of the Yankees, Lady Takes a Chance, Crash Dive, Lifeboat, Leave Her to Heaven, Thunder in the East.
TELEVISION: The Lord Don't Play Favorites.

SWERLING, JO, JR.
Executive, Producer. b. Los Angeles, CA, June 18, 1931. e. UCLA, 1948-51; California Maritime Acad., 1951-54. Son of writer Jo Swerling. Active duty US Navy 1954-56. Joined Revue Prods./Universal Television, 1957-81, as prod. coordinator, assoc. prod., prod., assoc. exec. prod., exec. prod., writer, director, actor; currently sr. v.p. and supervising prod., The Cannell Studios.
TELEVISION: *Series*: Kraft Suspense Theater (prod.), Run for Your Life (prod., writer, Emmy, nom.), The Rockford Files (prod., writer), Cool Million (prod.), Alias Smith & Jones (assoc. exec. prod.), Baretta (prod., Emmy nom.), City of Angels (exec. prod.), Toma (exec. prod.), Jigsaw (prod.), The Bold Ones (prod., writer), Lawyers (prod., writer). *Mini-series*: Captains and the Kings (prod., Emmy nom.), Aspen (prod.), The Last Convertible (exec. prod., dir.). *Movies* (prod.): This Is the West That Was, The Whole World Is Watching, The Invasion of Johnson County, The Outsider, Do You Take This Stranger, Burn the Town Down, The Three-Thousand Mile Chase, How to Steal an Airplane. Supervising prod., Stephen J. Cannell Productions: The Greatest American Hero, Quest, The A-Team, Hardcastle & McCormick, Riptide, The Last Precinct, Hunter, Stingray, Wiseguy, 21 Jump Street, J.J. Starbuck, Sonny Spoon, The Rousters, Unsub, Booker, Top of the Hill, Broken Badges, Dead End Brattigan, The Hat Squad, Traps, Profit.

SWIFT, LELA
Director.
TELEVISION: Studio One, Suspense, The Web, Justice, DuPont Show of the Week, Purex Specials For Women (Emmy Award) Dark Shadows, Norman Corwin Presents, ABC Late Night 90 min. Specials, ABC Daytime 90 min. Play Break, Ryan's Hope (Emmy Awards: 1977, 1979, 1980; Montior Awards: 1985, 1989), The Rope (A & E).

SWINK, ROBERT E.
Film Editor. b. Rocky Ford, CO, June 3, 1918. Joined editorial dept., RKO Radio, 1936; appt. film ed., 1941. In U.S. Army Signal Corps, 1944-45; supv. editor, Fox studio. Edited numerous productions.
PICTURES: Detective Story, Carrie, Roman Holiday, Desperate Hours, Friendly Persuasion, The Big Country, The Diary of Anne Frank, The Young Doctors, The Children's Hour, The Best Man, The Collector, How to Steal a Million, The Flim Flam Man, Funny Girl, The Liberation of L.B. Jones, The Cowboys, Skyjacked, Lady Ice, Papillion, Three the Hard Way, Rooster Cogburn, Midway, Islands in the Stream, Gray Lady Down, The Boys From Brazil, The In-Laws, Going in Style, Sphinx, Welcome Home.

SWIT, LORETTA
Actress. b. Passaic, NJ, Nov. 4, 1939. Stage debut in Any Wednesday. Toured in Mame for year. Arrived in Hollywood in 1971 and began TV career.
THEATER: Same Time Next Year, The Mystery of Edwin Drood (B'way), Shirley Valentine (Sarah Siddons Award).
PICTURES: Stand Up and Be Counted (debut, 1972), Freebie and the Bean, Race with the Devil, S.O.B., Beer, Whoops Apocalypse, Lords of Tanglewood.
TELEVISION: Series: M*A*S*H (Emmy Awards, 1980, 1982; also Genii, Silver Satellite & People's Choice Awards), Those Incredible Animals (host). Guest: Perry Como Show, Mac Davis, Dolly Parton, Bobby Vinton, etc. Movies: Hostage Heart, Shirts/Skins, The Last Day, Coffeeville, Valentine, Mirror Mirror, Friendships Secrets and Lies, Cagney & Lacey, Games Mother Never Taught You, Friendships Secrets & Lies, First Affair, The Execution, Dreams of Gold: The Mel Fisher Story, Hell Hath No Fury, A Killer Among Friends. Specials: 14 Going on 30, Best Christmas Pageant Ever, Texaco Salute to Broadway, It's a Bird It's a Plane It's Superman, Miracle at Moreaux, My Dad Can't Be Crazy Can He?, A Matter of Principal.

SWOPE, HERBERT BAYARD, JR.
Director, Producer, Commentator. b. New York, NY. e. Horace Mann Sch., Princeton U. U.S. Navy, 1941-46; joined CBS-TV as remote unit dir., 1946 directing many firsts in sportscasting; winner, Variety Show Management Award for sports coverage & citation by Amer. TV Society, 1948; joined NBC as dir., 1949; prod. dir., 1951; winner, 1952 Sylvania TV Award Outstanding Achievement in Dir. Technique; became exec. prod., NBC-TV in charge of Wide Wide World; film prod., 20th Century-Fox; 1960-62, exec. 20th-Fox TV; 1970-72 exec. at N.Y. Off-Track Betting Corp. 1973-74; v.p.; Walter Reade Organization, Inc.; 1975-76 producer-host, This Was TV, Growth of a Giant; 1976 to present commentator-interviewer, Swope's Scope (radio—WSBR-AM)); Critic's Views (TV: WTVJ, Ch. 5); Column: Now and Then (Palm Beach Pictorial).
THEATER: Dir./Co-Prod.: Step on a Crack, Fragile Fox, Fair Game for Lovers.
PICTURES: Producer: Hilda Crane, Three Brave Men, True Story of Jesse James, The Bravados, The Fiend Who Walked the West.
TELEVISION: Prod/Dir.: Lights Out, The Clock, The Black Robe, Robert Montgomery Presents, Arsenic and Old Lace, Climax, Many Loves of Dobie Gillis, Five Fingers.

SYKES, ERIC
O.B.E.: Writer, Comedian, Actor. b. Oldham, England, 1923. Early career as actor; 1948 wrote first three series, BBC's Educating Archie TV comedy series for Frankie Howerd, Max Bygraves, Harry Secombe. BBC panel show member. Sykes Versus TV, The Frankie Howerd Series. Longterm contract with ATV 1956. Own BBC series 1958-78, Sykes and A...
Specials: Silent Movies for TV, The Plank (also dir. & s.p.), If You Go Down Into the Woods Today, Rhubarb, It's Your Move, Mr. H Is Late, 19th Hole, The Big Freeze.
THEATER: Big Bad Mouse (tour: 1966-9 in America, Rhodesia, Australia, Canada), One Man Show (1982), Time and Time Again, Run for Your Wife, Two Into One, The 19th Hole, several pantomimes.
PICTURES: Watch Your Stern, Very Important Person, Invasion Quartet, Village of Daughters, Kill or Cure, Heavens Above, The Bargee, One Way Pendulum, Those Magnificent Men in Their Flying Machines, Rotten to the Core, The Liquidator, The Spy With The Cold Nose, Shalako, Monte Carlo or Bust, Theatre of Blood, Boys in Blue, Gabrielle and the Doodleman, Absolute Beginners, Splitting Heirs.

SYLBERT, ANTHEA
Executive. b. New York, NY, Oct. 6, 1939. e. Barnard Coll., B.A.; Parsons Sch. of Design, M.A. Early career in costume design with range of B'way (The Real Thing), off-B'way and m.p. credits (Rosemary's Baby, F.I.S.T., Shampoo, The Fortune, A New Leaf, The Heartbreak Kid. Two A.A. nominations for costume designs for Julia and Chinatown. Joined Warner Bros. in 1977, as v.p., special projects, acting as liaison between creative execs., prod. dept., and creative talent producing films for company. 1978, named v.p., prod. (projects included One Trick Pony, Personal Best, etc.). 1980 appointed v.p. prod., for United Artists, working on Jinxed, Still of the Night, Yentl, etc. 1982 became indept. prod. in partnership with Goldie Hawn (Hawn/Sylbert Movie Co.) producing Swing Shift, Protocol, Wildcats, Overboard, My Blue Heaven, Deceived, Crisscross, Something to Talk About. TV Movie: Truman.

SYMES, JOHN
Executive. e. Univ. of CA at Berkeley. Started at Paramount in tech. opts. dept. of Paramount's domestic tv distrib. div., then became mngr. of videotape opts., dir. of opts. Became sr. v.p. current programs for Paramount Network tv, then exec. v.p. crative affairs for same. Jan. 1994, became pres. of MGM Worldwide TV.

SYMS, SYLVIA
Actress. b. London, Dec. 3, 1934. e. Convent and Grammar Sch.
PICTURES: My Teenage Daughter (debut, 1956), No Time For Tears, The Birthday Present, Woman in a Dressing Gown, Ice Cold in Alex (Desert Attack), The Moonraker, Bachelor of Hearts, No Trees in the Street, Ferry to Hong Kong, Expresso Bongo, Conspiracy of Hearts, The Virgins of Rome, The World of Suzie Wong, Flame in the Streets, Victim, The Quare Fellow, The Punch and Judy Man, The World Ten Times Over, East of Sudan, Operation Crossbow, The Big Job, Hostile Witness, Danger Route, Run Wild Run Free, The Desperados, Asylum, The Tamarind Seed, Give Us Tomorrow, There Goes the Bride, Absolute Beginners, A Chorus of Disapproval, Shirley Valentine, Shining Through, Dirty Weekend.
TELEVISION: The Human Jungle (series), Something to Declare, The Saint (series), The Baron (series), Bat Out of Hell, Department in Terror, Friends and Romans, Strange Report, Half-hour Story, The Root of All Evil, The Bridesmaid, Clutterbuck, Movie Quiz, My Good Woman, Looks Familiar, Love and Marriage, The Truth About Verity, I'm Bob, He's Dickie, Blankety Blank, The Story of Nancy Astor, Give Us a Clue, Sykes, Crown Court, A Murder Is Announced, Murder at Lynch Cross, Rockcliffes Follies, Dr. Who, Countdown, Ruth Rendell Mystery, May to December, Intimate Contact, Thatcher the Final Days, Natural Lies, Mulberry, Peak Practice, Half the Picture, Original Sin.

SZABO, ISTVAN
Director. b. Budapest, Hungary, Feb. 18, 1938. e. Academy of Theatre and Film Art, Budapest, 1961. Debut Koncert (short, diploma film) 1961. Short films: Variations on a Theme, You, Piety, Why I Love It, City Map. Appeared in film Tusztortenet (Stand Off).
PICTURES: Age of Illusions (feature debut, 1964), Father, A Film About Love, 25 Fireman's Street, Premiere, Tales of Budapest, The Hungarians, Confidence (Silver Bear Award, Berlin Fest.), The Green Bird, Mephisto (Hungarian Film Critics Award; Academy Award, Best Foreign Film, 1982), Colonel Redl, Hanussen (also co-s.p.), Opera Europa, Meeting Venus.

SZWARC, JEANNOT
Director. b. Paris, France, Nov. 21, 1939.
PICTURES: Extreme Close-Up, Bug, Jaws II, Somewhere in Time, Enigma, Supergirl, Santa Claus, Honor Bound.
TELEVISION: Series: Ironside, To Catch a Thief, Kojak, Columbo, Night Gallery, Crime Club, True Life Stories, Twilight Zone (1986). Movies: Night of Terror, The Weekend Nun, The Devil's Daughter, You'll Never See Me Again, The Small Miracle, Lisa: Bright and Dark, A Summer Without Boys, Crime Club, Code Name: Diamond Head, Murders in the Rue Morgue, The Rockford Files: A Blessing in Disguise.

T

MR. T
Actor. r.n. Lawrence Tero. b. Chicago, IL, May 21, 1953. Professional bodyguard when hired by Sylvester Stallone in 1980 to play prizefighter in Rocky III.
PICTURES: Penitentiary II, Rocky III, D.C. Cab, Freaked.
TELEVISION: Series: The A Team, T & T. Movie: The Toughest Man in the World. Guest: Silver Spoons.

TAFFNER DONALD L.
Executive. b. New York, NY. e. St. Johns U. William Morris Agency, 1950-59; Paramount Pictures. 1959-63; D. L. Taffner Ltd., 1963-present.
TELEVISION: *Prod.*: Three's Company, Too Close For Comfort.

TAGAWA, CARY-HIROYUKI
Actor.
PICTURES: The Last Emperor, Spellbinder, Licence to Kill, The Last Warrior, Kickboxer 2, Showdown in Little Tokyo, American Me, Nemesis, Rising Sun, Picture Bride, Mortal Kombat, The Phantom.
TELEVISION: *Movies*: Mission of the Shark, Not of This World, Vestige of Honor, Murder in Paradise.

TAIT, CATHERINE
Executive. Exec. dir., The Independent Feature Project.

TAKEI, GEORGE
Actor. b. Los Angeles, CA, April 20, 1937. e. U. of California, UCLA. Professional debut in Playhouse 90 production while training at Desilu Workshop in Hollywood. Gained fame as Sulu in Star Trek TV series. *Author*: Mirror Friend Mirror Foe (novel), To the Stars (autobiography; 1994).
PICTURES: Ice Palace, A Majority of One, Hell to Eternity, PT 109, Red Line 7000, An American Dream, Walk Don't Run, The Green Berets, Star Trek: The Motion Picture, Star Trek II: The Wrath of Khan, Star Trek III: The Search for Spock, Star Trek IV: The Voyage Home, Star Trek V: The Final Frontier, Return From the River Kwai, Prisoners of the Sun, Star Trek VI: The Undiscovered Country, Live by the Fist, Oblivion.
TELEVISION: *Series*: Star Trek. *Movies*: Kissinger and Nixon, Space Cases, Star Trek Voyager. *Guest*: Perry Mason, Alcoa Premiere, Mr. Novak, The Wackiest Ship in the Army, I Spy, Magnum PI, Trapper John M.D., Miami Vice, Murder She Wrote, McGyver, Hawaiian Eye, Californian, Hawaii 5-O, My Three Sons, John Forsythe Show, Death Valley Days, Theatre in America, Game Night, Kung Fu: The Legend Continues.

TAMBLYN, RUSS
Actor b. Los Angeles, CA, Dec. 30, 1934. e. No. Hollywood H.S. West Coast radio shows; on stage with little theater group; song-and-dance act in Los Angeles clubs, veterans hospitals.
PICTURES: The Boy with Green Hair, Reign of Terror, Samson and Delilah, Gun Crazy, Kid from Cleveland, The Vicious Years, Captain Carey U.S.A., Father of the Bride, As Young As You Feel, Father's Little Dividend, Cave of Outlaws, Winning Team, Retreat Hell, Take the High Ground, Seven Brides for Seven Brothers, Deep in My Heart, Many Rivers to Cross, Hit the Deck, Last Hunt, Fastest Gun Alive, The Young Guns, Don't Go Near the Water, Peyton Place (Acad. Award nom.), High School Confidential, Tom Thumb, Cimarron, West Side Story, Wonderful World of the Brothers Grimm, How the West Was Won, Follow the Boys, The Haunting, Long Ships, Son of a Gunfighter, War of the Gargantuas, Scream Free, Dracula Vs. Frankenstein, Satan's Sadists, The Female Bunch, The Last Movie, Win Place or Steal, Murder Gang, Human Highway, Aftershock, Commando Squad, Cyclone, Necromancer, B.O.R.N., Phantom Empire, Bloodscream, Wizards of the Demon Sword, Desert Steel, Cabin Boy, Attack of the 60 Ft. Centerfold.
TELEVISION: *Series*: Twin Peaks. *Guest*: The Walter Winchell Show, ABC's Wide World of Entertainment, The Ed Sullivan Show, Gunsmoke, Name of the Game, Tarzan, Rags to Riches, Channing, Iron Horse, Perry Como Show, Love American Style, Grizzly Adams, Fame, Running Mates, Greatest Show on Earth, Burke's Law, Cade's County, The Quest, Quantum Leap, Babylon 5, Invisible Mom.

TAMBOR, JEFFREY
Actor. b. San Francisco, CA, July 8, 1944. e. San Francisco St. (BA), Wayne St. (MA). Acted with Seattle Rep., Actors Theatre of Louisville, Loeb Drama Ctr. (Harvard), Milwaukee Rep. Theatre, Acad. Festival Theatre (Chicago), Old Globe Theatre in San Diego, South Coast Rep. Theatre. B'way in Measure for Measure, Sly Fox.
PICTURES: And Justice for All, Saturday the 14th, Mr. Mom, The Man Who Wasn't There, No Small Affair, Three O'Clock High, Lisa, City Slickers, Life Stinks, Pastime, Article 99, Brenda Starr, Crossing the Bridge, At Home with the Webbers, Face Dancer, Under Pressure, A House in the Hills, Radioland Murders, Heavyweights, Big Bully, Learning Curves.
TELEVISION: *Series*: The Ropers, Hill Street Blues, 9 to 5, Mr. Sunshine, Max Headroom, Studio 5-B, American Dreamer, The Larry Sanders Show. *Movies*: Alcatraz: The Whole Shocking Story, A Gun in the House, The Star Maker, Take Your Best Shot, Cocaine: One Man's Seduction, Sadat, The Awakening of Candra, The Three Wishes of Billy Grier, The Burden of Proof, Honey Let's Kill the Neighbors, The

Countdown Has Begun. Mini-Series: Robert Kennedy & His Times. *Guest*: Three's Company, M*A*S*H, Barney Miller, Tales From the Crypt, The Golden Globe, Empty Nest, Doogie Howser M.D., Equal Justice, Murder She Wrote.

TANEN, NED
Executive. b. Los Angeles, CA, 1931. e. UCLA, law degree. Joined MCA, Inc. 1954; appt. v.p. in 1968. Brought Uni Records, since absorbed by MCA Records, to best-seller status with such artists as Neil Diamond, Elton John, Olivia Newton-John. First became active in theatrical film prod. in 1972. 1975 began overseeing feature prod. for Universal. 1976 named pres. of Universal Theatrical Motion Pictures, established as div. of Universal City Studios. Left in 1982 to become independent producer. 1985, joined Paramount Pictures as pres. of Motion Picture Group. Resigned 1988 to continue as sr. advisor at Paramount. Producer: Guarding Tess, Cops and Robbersons.

TANKERSLEY, ROBERT K.
Executive. b. Decatur, IL, July 31, 1927. In U.S. Navy, 1945-46; Marine Corps, 1949-55. With Natl. Theatre Supply as salesman in Denver 13 yrs. 1959-87, pres. Western Service & Supply, Denver, theatre equip. co.; 1960-87, mgr., Tankersley Enterprises theatre equip. Also was CEO of Theatre Operators, Inc., Bozeman, Mont. Member: Theatre Equipment Assn. (past pres.), National NATO Presidents Advisory Council; Rocky Mt. Motion Picture Assn. (past pres.), SMPTE, Motion Picture Pioneers, past chief barker, Variety Club Tent #37. Colorado, Wyoming NATO (past pres.) chmn.-elect Exhibitors West.

TAPLIN, JONATHAN
Producer. b. Cleveland, OH, July 18, 1947. e. Princeton U.
PICTURES: Mean Streets, The Last Waltz, Carny (exec. prod.), Grandview U.S.A. (co-exec. prod.), Under Fire, Baby, My Science Project, Until the End of the World, K2, To Die For (exec. prod.), Rough Magic (exec. prod.).
TELEVISION: Shelly Duvall's Faerie Tale Theatre (6 episodes), 1968: The 25th Anniversary, The Native Americans, The Prize.

TAPS, JONIE
Producer. Executive. Columbia Studio. Member of Friars Club, Hillcrest Country Club.
PICTURES: *Produced*: When You're Smiling, Sunny Side of Street, Sound Off, Rainbow Round My Shoulder, All Ashore, Cruisin' Down the River, Drive a Crooked Road, Three for the Show, Bring Your Smile Along, He Laughed Last, Shadow on the Window.

TARADASH, DANIEL
Writer, Director. b. Louisville, KY, Jan. 29, 1913. e. Harvard Coll., B.A., 1933; Harvard Law Sch., LL.B., 1936. Passed NY Bar, 1937; won nationwide playwriting contest, 1938; U.S. Army WWII. Pres. Screen Writers Branch, WGA, 1955-56; v.p., Writers Guild of America, West 1956-59; mem. Writers Guild Council, 1954-65; mem., bd. of govnrs. Motion Picture Acad. Arts & Sciences, 1964-74, 1990-93; v.p. 1968-70 and pres. 1970-73. Trustee, Producers-Writers Guild Pension plan 1960-73. chmn., 1965. Mem. Bd. of Trustees of American Film Institute 1967-69. WGA's Valentine Davies Award, 1971. Pres., Academy M.P. Arts & Sciences, 1970-73, mem. bd. trustees, Entertainment Hall of Fame Foundation. Mem., Public Media General Programs panel for the National Foundation for the Arts, 1975-85, 1992; Pres. Writers Guild of America, West, 1977-79. Natl. chmn., Writers Guild of America, 1979-81. WGA's Morgan Cox Award, 1988. WGA's Edmund H. North Founders Award 1991. Festival to present Taradash Screenwriting Award 1992-; USC retrospective and tribute, 1992. Writer of TV special Bogie. Recipient of the Writers Guild of America West Laurel Award, 1996.
PICTURES: Golden Boy, A Little Bit of Heaven, Knock on Any Door, Rancho Notorious, Don't Bother to Knock, From Here to Eternity (Academy Award 1953), Desiree, Storm Center (also dir., co-story), Picnic, Bell Book and Candle, The Saboteur Code Name—Morituri, Hawaii, Castle Keep, Doctors' Wives, The Other Side of Midnight.

TARANTINO, QUENTIN
Writer, Director, Actor, Producer. b. Knoxville, TN, March 27, 1963. Graduate of Sundance Institute Director's Workshop and Lab. With producer Lawrence Bender, formed production co. A Band Apart.
PICTURES: Past Midnight (assoc. prod., co-s.p.), Reservoir Dogs (dir., s.p., actor), True Romance (s.p.), Killing Zoe (co-exec. prod.), Natural Born Killers (story), Sleep With Me (actor), Pulp Fiction (dir., s.p., co-story, actor; Cannes Film Fest. Award for Best Film; LA Film Critics, NY Film Critics, Natl. Soc. of Film Critics, Chicago Film Critics & Independent Spirit Awards for dir. & s.p.; Academy Award & Golden Globe for s.p.; Natl. Bd. of Review Award for dir., 1994), Destiny Turns on the Radio (actor), Somebody to Love (actor),

Desperado (actor), Four Rooms (co-s.p., co-exec. prod.), From Dusk Till Dawn (s.p., actor, co-exec. prod.), Girl 6 (actor), Curdled (exec. prod.).
TELEVISION: *Guest*: The Golden Girls, All-American Girl. *Dir*: E/R (1 episode).

TARNOFF, JOHN B.
Producer. b. New York, NY, Mar. 3, 1952. e. UCLA, motion pictures & TV, 1973-74; Amherst Coll., B.A., 1969-73. Named field exec. with Taylor-Laughlin Distribution (company arm of Billy Jack Enterprises) 1974; left in 1975 to be literary agent with Bart/Levy, Inc.; later with Michael Levy & Associates, Paul Kohner/Michael Levy Agency; Headed TV dept., Kohner/Levy, 1979. Joined MGM as production exec., 1979; v.p., development, 1979-80; sr. v.p. production & devel., 1981-82; exec. v.p., Kings Road Prods., 1983-84; v.p., prod., Orion Pictures Corp., 1985; exec. prod., Out of Bounds, Columbia Pictures, 1986; v.p., prod., De Laurentiis Entertainment Group, 1987. Head of production, DeLaurentiis Entertainment, Australia, 1987-88. Exec. v.p. production, Village Roadshow Pictures, 1988-. *Exec. Prod.*: The Delinquents, Blood Oath.

TARSES, JAMIE
Executive. b. Pittsburgh, PA. e. Williams Coll. Worked as a casting director for Lorimar Productions. Joined NBC in Sept. 1987 as mgr., creative affairs for NBC Productions. In Dec. 1987, named mgr., current comedy programs, NBC Entertainment and was NBC's program exec. for such series as Cheers, Amen and A Different World. In 1988, named manager of comedy development. In 1995, promoted to s.v.p. of primetime series. In June of 1996, joined ABC Entertainment as President.

TARSES, JAY
Producer, Writer, Actor. b. Baltimore, MD, July 3, 1939. e. U. of Washington, degree in theater. Wrote and acted with little-theater co. in Pittsburgh, drove a truck in NY for Allen Funt's Candid Camera and worked in advertising and promotion for Armstrong Cork Co. in Lancaster, PA where he met Tom Patchett. Formed Patchett and Tarses, stand-up comedy team that played coffeehouse circuit in the late 1960s. Later two-some became TV writing team and joined writing staff of Carol Burnett Show winning Emmy in 1972.
PICTURES: *Co-s.p. with Patchett*: Up the Academy, The Great Muppet Caper, The Muppets Take Manhattan.
TELEVISION: As actor: *Series*: Make Your Own Kind of Music, Open All Night, The Days and Nights of Molly Dodd. *Specials*: Arthur Godfrey's Portable Electric Medicine Show, The Duck Factory. With Tom Patchett: The Bob Newhart Show (exec. prod., writer), The Tony Randell Show (creator, exec. prod., writer), We've Got Each Other (creator, exec. prod.), Mary (prod.), Open All Night (creator, prod., writer), Buffalo Bill (exec. prod., writer). *Solo*: The Days and Nights of Molly Dodd (creator, prod., writer), The "Slap" Maxwell Story (creator, prod., writer), Public Morals. *Pilots*: The Chopped Liver Brothers (exec. prod., writer), The Faculty (exec. prod., dir., writer).

TARTIKOFF, BRANDON
Executive. b. New York, NY, Jan. 13, 1949. e. Yale U. Started TV career in 1971 in promo. dept. of ABC affiliates in New Haven, CT Joined promo. staff at ABC affiliate in Chicago. In 1976 went to New York, with ABC-TV as mgr., dramatic development; moved to NBC Entertainment in Sept., 1977, as dir., comedy programs. In 1978 appt. v.p., programs, West Coast, NBC Entertainment; 1980, named pres. of that division. Pres. NBC Entertainment since 1980. Also heads own prod. co., NBC Productions. 1990, appointed chairman of NBC Entertainment Group. 1991, appointed chmn. of Paramount Pictures. Resigned from Paramount, Oct. 1992. Became chmn. of New World Entertainment, 1994. *Co-exec. prod. tv movie* Tom Clancy's Op Center.
PICTURES: Square Dance, Satisfaction.

TAVERNIER, BERTRAND
Director, Writer. b. Lyon, France, April 25, 1941. After 2 yrs. of law study, quit to become film critic for Cahiers du Cinema and Cinema 60. Asst. to dir. Jean-Pierre Melville on Leon Morin Priest (1961), also worked as film publicist. Wrote film scripts and a book on the Western and a history of American cinema. Partner for 6 yrs. with Pierre Rissient in film promotion company, during which time he studied all aspects of filmmaking. 1963: directed episode of Les Baisers. Pres., Lumiere Inst., Lyon. Book: 50 Years of American Cinema, Qu'est ce Qu'on Attend?, Amis Americains.
PICTURES: *Director-Co-writer*: The Clockmaker (L'Horloger de Saint-Paul), Let Joy Reign Supreme (Que La Fête Commence), The Judge and the Assassin (Le Judge et l'Assassin), Spoiled Children (also co-prod.), Deathwatch. *Dir./Co-Writer/Prod.*: A Week's Vacation, Clean Slate (Coup de Torchon; 11 César nom.), Oscar nom.), Mississippi Blues (co-dir. with Robert Parrish), A Sunday in the Country (Un

Dimanche a la Campagne; Best Direction Cannes, New york Critics Prize), 'Round Midnight, Beatrice (dir. co-prod. only), Life and Nothing But, Daddy Nostalgia, The Undeclared War (co-dir. with Patrick Rutman), L627, La Fille de D'Artagnan, L'Appat.
TELEVISION: Phillippe Soupault, October Country (co-dir. with Robert Parrish), Lyon, le regard interieur.

TAVIANI, PAOLO and VITTORIO
Directors, Writers. b. San Miniato, Pisa, Italy, (Paolo: Nov. 8, 1931; Vittorio: Sept. 20, 1929); e. Univ. of Pisa (Paolo: liberal arts; Vittorio: law). The two brothers always work in collaboration from script preparation through shooting and editing. 1950: With Valentino Orsini ran cine-club at Pisa. 1954: In collab. with Caesare Zavattini directed short about Nazi massacre at San Miniato. 1954-59: with Orsini made series of short documentaries (Curatorne e Montanara; Carlo Pisacane; Ville della Brianza; Lavatori della pietra; Pitori in cita; I Pazzi della domenica; Moravia, Cabunara). Worked as assistant to Rosellini, Luciano Emmer and Raymond Pellegrini. 1960: collaborated on an episode of Italy Is Not a Poor Country.
PICTURES (all by both): A Man for Burning (debut, 1962; co-dir. with Valentino Orsini), Matrimonial Outlaws (co-dir. with Orsini), The Subversives, Under the Sign of Scorpio, Saint Michael Had a Rooster, Allonsanfan, Padre Padrone (Cannes Film Fest.: Grand Prix & Critics International Prize, 1977), The Meadow, The Night of the Shooting Stars (1981, Best Director Award, Natl. Society of Film Critics; Special Jury Prize, Cannes), Kaos, Good Morning Babylon, The Sun Also Shines at Night, Fiorile.

TAYLOR, DELORES
Actress, Writer, Producer. b. Winner, SD, Sept. 27, 1939. e. U. of South Dakota, studying commercial art. m. Tom Laughlin. First TV experience was heading art dept. at RCA wholesale center in Milwaukee. Established first Montessori School in U.S. in Santa Monica for several yrs., with husband. Made feature film debut as actress in Billy Jack in 1971. Wrote s.p. with husband for that and sequels, The Trial of Billy Jack, Billy Jack Goes to Washington, under pseudonym Teresa Christina.
PICTURES: *Exec. Prod., Writer*: Proper Time, Young Sinners, Born Losers, The Master Gunfighter. *Exec. Prod., Writer, Actress*: Billy Jack, Trial of Billy Jack, Billy Jack Goes to Washington, Return of Billy Jack.

TAYLOR, DON
Actor, Director. b. Freeport, PA, Dec. 13, 1920. e. Pennsylvania State U. Appeared in Army Air Corps' Winged Victory on stage & screen.
PICTURES: *Actor*: The Human Comedy, Girl Crazy, Thousands Cheer, Swing Shift Maisie, Salute to the Marines, Winged Victory, The Red Dragon, Song of the Thing Man, The Naked City, For the Love of Mary, Battleground, Ambush, Father of the Bride, Target Unknown, Father's Little Dividend, Submarine Command, Flying Leathernecks, The Blue Veil, Japanese War Bride, Stalag 17, The Girls of Pleasure Island, Destination Gobi, Johnny Dark, Men of Sherwood Forest, I'll Cry Tomorrow, The Bold and the Brave, Lost Slaves of the Amazon, Ride the High Iron, The Savage Guns. *Director*: Everything's Ducky (debut, 1961), Ride the Wild Surf, Jack of Diamonds, Five Man Army, Escape From the Planet of the Apes, Tom Sawyer, Echoes of a Summer, The Great Scout and Cathouse Thursday, The Island of Dr. Moreau, Damien—Omen II, The Final Countdown.
TELEVISION: *Movies* (director): Something for a Lonely Man, Wild Women, Heat of Anger, Night Games, Honky Tonk, The Manhunter, Circle of Children, The Gift, The Promise of Love, Broken Promise, Red Flag: The Ultimate Game, Drop Out Father, Listen to Your Heart, September Gun, My Wicked Wicked Ways: The Legend of Errol Flynn, Secret Weapons, Going for the Gold: The Bill Johnson Story, Classified Love, Ghost of a Chance, The Diamond Trap.

TAYLOR, ELIZABETH
Actress. b. London, Eng., Feb. 27, 1932. e. Bryon House, London. When 3 years old danced before Princess Elizabeth, Margaret Rose. Came to U.S. at outbreak of WWII. *Author*: World Enough and Time (with Richard Burton; 1964), Elizabeth Taylor (1965), Elizabeth Takes Off (1988). Initiated Ben Gurion U.—Elizabeth Taylor Fund for Children of the Negev, 1982. Co-founded American Foundation for AIDS Research, 1985. Named Comdr. Arts & Letters (France) 1985, Legion of Honor, 1987. Established the Elizabeth Taylor AIDS Foundation in 1991. Developed various perfume products: Elizabeth Taylor's Passion, Passion Body Riches, Passion for Men, White Diamonds, Diamonds and Emeralds, Diamonds and Sapphires, Diamond and Rubies; 1993 launched Elizabeth Taylor Fashion Jewelry Collection. Recipient of AFI Life Achievement Award (1993), Jean Hersholt Humanitarian Award (1993).
THEATER: *B'way*: The Little Foxes (also London), Private Lives.

PICTURES: There's One Born Every Minute (debut, 1942), Lassie Come Home, Jane Eyre, White Cliffs of Dover, National Velvet, Courage of Lassie, Life with Father, Cynthia, A Date With Judy, Julia Misbehaves, Little Women, Conspirator, The Big Hangover, Father of the Bride, Father's Little Dividend, A Place in the Sun, Callaway Went Thataway (cameo), Love Is Better Than Ever, Ivanhoe, The Girl Who Had Everything, Rhapsody, Elephant Walk, Beau Brummel, The Last Time I Saw Paris, Giant, Raintree County, Cat on a Hot Tin Roof, Suddenly Last Summer, Scent of Mystery (cameo), Butterfield 8 (Academy Award, 1960), Cleopatra, The V.I.P.s, The Sandpiper, Who's Afraid of Virginia Woolf? (Academy Award, 1966), The Taming of the Shrew, Doctor Faustus, Reflections in a Golden Eye, The Comedians, Boom!, Secret Ceremony, The Only Game in Town, X Y and Zee (Zee and Company), Under Milk Wood, Hammersmith Is Out, Night Watch, Ash Wednesday, That's Entertainment!, The Driver's Seat, The Blue Bird, A Little Night Music, Winter Kills (cameo), The Mirror Crack'd, Genocide (narrator), Young Toscanini, The Flintstones.
TELEVISION: Movies: Divorce His/Divorce Hers, Victory at Entebbe, Return Engagement, Between Friends, Malice in Wonderland, There Must Be a Pony, Poker Alice, Sweet Bird of Youth. Mini-Series: North and South. Guest: Here's Lucy (1970 with Richard Burton), General Hospital (1981), All My Children (1983), Hotel. Specials: Elizabeth Taylor in London, America's All-Star Salute to Elizabeth Taylor.

TAYLOR, LILI
Actress. b. Chicago, 1967.
THEATER: NY: What Did He See, Aven U Boys. Regional: Mud, The Love Talker, Fun. Director: Collateral Damage.
PICTURES: Mystic Pizza (debut, 1988), Say Anything, Born on the Fourth of July, Bright Angel, Dogfight, Watch It, Household Saints, Short Cuts, Rudy, Arizona Dream, Mrs. Parker and the Vicious Circle, Ready to Wear (Pret-a-Porter), The Addiction, Cold Fever, Four Rooms, Things I Never Told You, I Shot Andy Warhol, Girl's Town, Ransom.

TAYLOR, MESHACH
Actor. b. Boston, MA, Apr. 11. e. Florida A & M Univ. Hosted Chicago TV show Black Life.
THEATER: Streamers, Sizwe Banzi is Dead, The Island, Native Son, Wonderful Ice Cream Suit, Bloody Bess, Sirens of Titan, Night Feast, Huckleberry Finn, Cops.
PICTURES: Damien: Omen II, The Howling, The Beast Within, Explorers, Warning Sign, One More Saturday Night, From the Hip, Mannequin, The Allnighter, House of Games, Welcome to Oblivion, Mannequin 2 on the Move, Class Act.
TELEVISION: Series: Buffalo Bill, Designing Women, Dave's World. Guest: Lou Grant, Barney Miller, Melba, Golden Girls, M*A*S*H, The White Shadow, What's Happening Now, ALF. Movies: An Innocent Man, How to Murder a Millionaire, Double Double Toil and Trouble, Virtual Seduction. Specials: Huckleberry Finn, The Rec Room.

TAYLOR, RENEE
Actress, Writer. b. New York, NY, March 19, 1935. Wife of actor Joseph Bologna, with whom she collaborates in writing. Their B'way plays include Lovers and Other Strangers, It Had to Be You. Stage actress: One of the All-Time Greats.
PICTURES: Actress: The Errand Boy, The Detective, The Producers, A New Leaf, Lovers and Other Strangers (also s.p.), Made for Each Other (also s.p.), Last of the Red Hot Lovers, Lovesick, It Had to Be You (also co-dir., co-s.p.), That's Adequate, White Palace, End of Innocence, Delirious, All I Want for Christmas, Forever.
TELEVISION: Writer: Acts of Love... and Other Comedies (Emmy Award, 1973), Paradise, Calucci's Department, The American Dream Machine, Bedrooms (Writers Guild Award, 1984), etc. Actress: Series regular: The Jack Paar Show, Mary Hartman Mary Hartman, Daddy Dearest, The Nanny. Movie: Woman of the Year (also co-writer).

TAYLOR, ROD
Actor. b. Sydney, Australia, Jan. 11, 1930. e. East Sydney Fine Arts Coll. Started out as artist then turned to acting on stage. Formed own company, Rodler, Inc., for TV-film production.
PICTURES: The Sturt Expedition (debut, 1951), King of the Coral Sea, Long John Silver, Top Gun, The Virgin Queen, Hell on Frisco Bay, World Without End, The Rack, Giant, The Catered Affair, Raintree County, Step Down to Terror, Separate Tables, Ask Any Girl, The Time Machine, Seven Seas to Calais, 101 Dalmatians (voice), The Birds, A Gathering of Eagles, The V.I.P.s, Sunday in New York, Fate is the Hunter, 36 Hours, Young Cassidy, Do Not Disturb, The Glass Bottom Boat, The Liquidator, Hotel, Chuka (also prod.), Dark of the Sun, High Commissioner (Nobody Runs Forever), The Hell with Heroes, Zabriskie Point, Darker Than Amber, The Man Who Had Power Over Women, The Heroes, The Train Robbers, Trader Horn, The Deadly Trackers, Hell River, Blondy, Picture Show Man, A Time To Die, On the Run, Close Enemy, Open Season, Point Deception.

TELEVISION: Movies: Powerkeg, Family Flight, The Oregon Trail, Cry of the Innocent, Jacqueline Bouvier Kennedy, Charles and Diana: A Royal Love Story, Outlaws, Danielle Steel's Palomino, Grass Roots. Series: Hong Kong, Bearcats, Masquerade, The Oregon Trail, Outlaws, Falcon Crest.

TAYLOR, RONNIE
Director of Photography. b. London, England, 1924. Ent. m.p. ind. 1941 at Gainsborough Studios
PICTURES: Tommy, The Silent Flute, Circle of Iron, Savage Harvest, Gandhi, High Road to China, The Hound of the Baskervilles, The Champions, Master of the Game (UK shoot), A Chorus Line, Foreign Body, Cry Freedom, Opera (Italy), The Experts, Sea of Love, Popcorn, The Rainbow Thief, Jewels, Age of Treason, The Steal, The Good King.

TAYLOR, JOHN RUSSELL
Writer, Critic. b. Dover, England, June 19, 1935. e. Cambridge U., B.A., 1956. Editor: Times Educational Supplement, London, 1959-60; film critic, The Times, London, 1962-73; art critic, 1978-; editor, Films and Filming, 1983-; prof., division of Cinema, USC, 1972-78. Member: London Film and TV Press Guild, London Critics Circle, NY Society of Cinematologists.
BOOKS: Joseph L. Mankiewicz: An Index, The Angry Theatre, Anatomy of a Television Play, Cinema Eye Cinema Ear, Shakespeare: A Celebration (cont.), New English Dramatists 8 (ed. & intr.), The Hollywood Musical, The Second Wave: Hollywood Dramatists for the 70s, Masterworks of the British Cinema, Directors and Directions: Peter Shaffer, Hitch, Cukor's Hollywood, Impressionism, Strangers in Paradise, Ingrid Bergman, Alec Guinness: A Celebration, Vivien Leigh, Hollywood 1940s, Portraits of the British Cinema.

TAYLOR-YOUNG, LEIGH
Actress. b. Washington, DC, Jan. 25, 1945. e. Northwestern U. B'way debut 1966 in Three Bags Full. Additional stage: The Beckett Plays (Off-B'way, LA), Knives, Sleeping Dogs.
PICTURES: I Love You Alice B. Toklas (debut, 1968), The Games, The Big Bounce, The Adventurers, The Buttercup Chain, The Horsemen, The Gang That Couldn't Shoot Straight, Soylent Green, Can't Stop the Music, Looker, Secret Admirer, Jagged Edge, Honeymoon Academy, Accidents.
TELEVISION: Series: Peyton Place, The Devlin Connection, The Hamptons, Dallas, Picket Fences (Emmy Award, 1994). Movies: Marathon, Napoleon and Josephine: A Love Story, Perry Mason: The Case of the Sinister Spirit, Who Gets the Friends, Bonnie and McCloud, Moment of Truth: Murder or Memory? Guest: Civil Wars, The Young Riders, Alfred Hitchcock Presents, Spenser for Hire, Evening Shade. Pilots: Ghostwriter, Houston Knights.

TEAGUE, LEWIS
Director. b. 1941. e. NYU. Editor and/or 2nd unit dir. on such films as Cockfighter, Crazy Mama, Death Race 2000, Avalanche, Fast Charlie: The Moonbeam Rider, The Big Red One.
PICTURES: Dirty O'Neil (co-dir.), Lady in Red (also editor), Alligator, Fighting Back, Cujo, Cat's Eye, The Jewel of the Nile, Collision Course, Navy SEALS.
TELEVISION: Series episodes: Alfred Hitchcock Presents, Daredevils, Shannon's Deal. Movies: T Bone N Weasel, Tom Clancy's Op Center.

TELLER, IRA
Executive, b. New York, NY, July 3, 1940. e. City Coll. of New York, & 1957-61; NYU Graduate Sch. of Arts, 1961-62. Publicist, Pressbook Dept., 20th Century Fox., 1961-62; asst. to adv. mgr., Embassy Pictures Corp., 1962-63; asst. adv. mgr., Columbia Pictures Corp., 1963; adv. mgr., Columbia Pictures Corp., 1964, 1964-65; asst. to chmn. of bd., Diener, Hauser, Greenthal Agy., 1966; adv. mgr., 20th Century-Fox, 1966-67; 1967, adv. dir. 20th Cent.-Fox.; dir. of adv., Nat'l General Pictures Corp., 1969; eastern dir., adv.-pub., 1972; national dir., adv-pub., 1973; Bryanston Distributors, Inc. v.p. adv.-pub., 1974; Cine Artists Pictures Corp. v.p. adv-pub., 1975; Lorimar Productions, v.p., adv.-marketing, 1976-77; 1977-present, pres. Ira Teller and Company, Inc.; This Is It, exec. prod.

TEMPLE, JULIEN
Director. b. London, England, Nov. 26, 1953. e. Cambridge, London's National Film School. Dir. many rock videos.
PICTURES: The Great Rock 'n' Roll Swindle (debut, 1979), The Secret Policeman's Other Ball, Undercover (also s.p.), Running Out of Luck (also s.p.), Absolute Beginners, Aria (segment: Rigoletto), Earth Girls Are Easy, Rolling Stones: At the Max (creative consultant).

TEMPLE (BLACK), SHIRLEY
Actress, Diplomat. b. Santa Monica, CA, April 23, 1928. In 1932 screen debut, Red Haired Alibi. In 1933 To the Last Man; then leading figure in series of Educational shorts called Baby

Burlesque and Frolics of Youth, until breakthrough role in Stand Up and Cheer, 1934, which resulted in career as child and teen star. Voted one of ten best Money-Making Stars in Motion Picture Herald-Fame Poll, 1934-39. As an adult, turned her attention to government and international issues. Republican candidate for U.S. House of Representatives, 1967. Rep. to 24th General Assembly of U.N. (1969-70). Special asst. to chmn., President's Council on the Environment (1970-72). U.S. Ambassador to Ghana (1974-76). Chief of Protocol, White House (1976-77); member of U.S. delegation on African Refugee problems, Geneva, 1981; 1987 made 1st honorary U.S. Foreign Service Rep. for State Dept.; 1989, appt. Ambassador to Czechoslovakia. *Autobiography:* Child Star (1988).
PICTURES: The Red-Haired Alibi (feature debut, 1932), To the Last Man, Out All Night, Mandalay, Carolina, Stand Up and Cheer, Baby Take a Bow, Now and Forever, Bright Eyes, Now I'll Tell, Change of Heart, Little Miss Marker, The Little Colonel, Our Little Girl, Curly Top, The Littlest Rebel, Captain January, Poor Little Rich Girl, Dimples, Stowaway, Wee Willie Winkle, Heidi, Rebecca of Sunnybrook Farm, Little Miss Broadway, Just Around the Corner, Little Princess, Susannah of the Mounties, The Blue Bird, Young People, Kathleen, Miss Annie Rooney, Since You Went Away, I'll Be Seeing You, Kiss and Tell, That Hagen Girl, Honeymoon, Bachelor and the Bobby-Soxer, Fort Apache, Mr. Belvedere Goes to College, Adventure in Baltimore, Story of Seabiscuit, Kiss for Corliss.
TELEVISION: *Series:* Shirley Temple's Storybook (host, performer).

TENNANT, VICTORIA
Actress. b. London, England, Sept. 30, 1953. e. Central Sch. of Speech & Drama. Daughter of ballerina Irina Baronova and talent agent Cecil Tennant.
THEATER: Love Letters (Steppenwolf), Getting Married (NY).
PICTURES: The Ragman's Daughter, Horror Planet (Inseminoid), Strangers Kiss, All of Me, The Holocraft Covenant, Best Seller, Flowers in the Attic, Fool's Mate, The Handmaid's Tale, L.A. Story, Whispers, The Plague.
TELEVISION: *Mini-Series:* Voice of the Heart, Winds of War, Chiefs, War and Remembrance, Act of Will, The Man from Snowy River. *Movies:* Maigret, Dempsey, Under Siege.

TESICH, STEVE
Writer. b. Titovo, Utice, Yugoslavia, Sept. 29, 1942. e. Indiana U., Columbia U. Came to U.S. at age 14. While doing graduate work in Russian literature at Columbia left to begin writing. Taken up by American Place Theatre which did his play, The Carpenters, in 1970.
THEATER: Division Street, Square One, The Speed of Darkness, and On the Open Road.
PICTURES: Breaking Away (Academy Award, 1979), Eyewitness, Four Friends, The World According to Garp, American Flyers, Eleni.
(d. July 1, 1996)

TETZLAFF, TED
Director. b. Los Angeles, CA, June 3, 1903. Joined camera dept. Fox Studios, became first cameraman; dir., 1940; served in U.S. Air Corps as a Major, WWII.
PICTURES: *Cameraman:* Enchanted Cottage, Notorious. *Dir.:* World Premiere, Riffraff, Fighting Father Dunne, Window, Johnny Allegro, Dangerous Profession, Gambling House, White Tower, Under the Gun, Treasure of Lost Canyon, Terror on a Train, Son of Sinbad, Seven Wonders of the World, The Young Land.

TEWKESBURY, JOAN
Writer, Director. b. Redlands, CA, April 8, 1936. e. USC. Student American Sch. Dance 1947-54. Was ostrich and understudy in Mary Martin's Peter Pan. Directed and choreographed Theatre prods. in L.A., London, Edinburgh Festival, Scotland. Taught dance and theory, American Sch. of Dance 1959-64; taught in theatre arts depts. of two universities: USC, Immaculate Heart. Became script supvr. for Robert Altman on McCabe & Mrs. Miller. *Off-B'way:* Cowboy Jack Street (writer, dir.). Teacher in film dept. UCLA. Sundance advisor, 1992-93; directors lab-writers lab. American Musical Theatre Festival in Philadelphia: Chippy (dir.).
PICTURES: Thieves Like Us (co.-s.p.), Nashville, (s.p.), Old Boyfriends (dir.), Hampstead Center (doc. of Anna Freud, writer, dir.), A Night in Heaven (s.p.), The Player (actress).
TELEVISION: *Series:* Alfred Hitchcock Presents (dir., writer), Elysian Fields (pilot; dir., writer, exec. prod.), Almost Grown (dir.), Shannon's Deal (dir., writer). *Movies:* The Acorn People (dir., s.p.), The Tenth Month (dir. - s.p.), Cold Sassy Tree (dir., s.p.), Sudie and Simpson (dir.), Wild Texas Wind (dir.), The Stranger (writer, dir.), On Promised Land (dir.).

THALHIMER, JR., MORTON G.
Former Theatre Executive. b. Richmond, VA, June 27, 1924. e. Dartmouth Coll., 1948, B.A.; U. of Virginia, 1959. Naval aviator in WWII. Joined Century Theatres as trainee 1948;

Jamestown Amusement, 1949-50. Past pres. Neighborhood Theatre, Inc. 1967-86. Charter member of Theatre Owners of America; past member and v.p. of NATO, served on finance comm. and Trade Practice comm. bd. member and past president of NATO of VA, 1973-75. Mem. Variety Club Int'l., Tent 11; patron life member, Variety Club of Israel, Tent 51.

THAXTER, PHYLLIS
Actress. b. Portland, ME, Nov. 20, 1919. e. St. Genevieve Sch., Montreal. Daughter is actress Skye Aubrey.
PICTURES: Thirty Seconds Over Tokyo (debut, 1944), Bewitched, Weekend at the Waldorf, Sea of Grass, Living in a Big Way, Tenth Avenue Angel, Sign of the Ram, Blood on the Moon, Act of Violence, No Man of Her Own, The Breaking Point, Fort Worth, Jim Thorpe_All American, Come Fill the Cup, She's Working Her Way Through College, Springfield Rifle, Operation Secret, Women's Prison, Man Afraid, The World of Henry Orient, Superman.
TELEVISION: *Movies:* Incident in San Francisco, The Longest Night, Three Sovereigns for Sarah. *Mini-Series:* Once an Eagle. *Guest:* Wagon Train, Alfred Hitchcock, Twilight Zone, Purex Specials For Women, Playhouse 90, The Fugitive, The Defenders, Murder She Wrote.

THEODORAKIS, MIKIS
Composer. b. Greece, 1925.
PICTURES: Eva, Night Ambush, Shadow of the Cat, Phaedra, Five Miles to Midnight, Zorba the Greek, The Day the Fish Came Out, The Trojan Women, State of Siege, Serpico, Iphigenia.

THEWLIS, DAVID
Actor. b. Blackpool, England, 1962. e. Guildhall School of Music and Drama, The Barbicon, London. First prof. job in breakfast food commercial.
PICTURES: Little Dorrit, Resurrected, Life Is Sweet, Afraid of the Dark, Damage, The Trial, Naked (Cannes Film Fest., NY Film Critics & Natl. Soc. of Film Critics Awards, 1993), Black Beauty, Restoration,Total Eclipse, Dragonheart, James and the Giant Peach (voice), The Island of Dr. Moreau.
TELEVISION: Only Fools and Horses, The Singing Detective, Filipino Dreamgirls, Prime Suspect, Dandelion Dead.

THIGPEN, LYNNE
Actress, Singer. b. Joliet, IL, Dec. 22, 1948.
THEATER: *NY:* Godspell, The Magic Show, But Never Jam Today, Tintypes, And I Ain't Finished Yet, Full Hookup, Balm in Gilead, A Month of Sundays, Fences, Boesman & Lena.
PICTURES: Godspell (debut, 1973), The Warriors, Tootsie, Streets of Fire, Sweet Liberty, Hello Again, Running on Empty, Lean on Me, Impulse, Article 99, Bob Roberts, The Paper, Naked in New York, Blankman, Just Cause.
TELEVISION: *Series:* Love Sidney, The News is the News, FM, All My Children, Where in the World is Carmen Sandiego? *Pilot:* Pottsville. *Guest:* The Equalizer, Gimme a Break, L.A. Law, Days and Nights of Molly Dodd, Roseanne, Frank's Place, The Cosby Show, Dear John, thirtysomething, Preston Episodes. *Movies:* Fear Stalk, Separate But Equal, A Mother's Instinct, Boys Next Door, Cagney & Lacey. *Pilot:* For the People, Those Two.

THINNES, ROY
Actor. b. Chicago, IL, April 6, 1938. Made tv debut as teen on DuPont Theatre, 1957.
PICTURES: Journey to the Far Side of the Sun, Charlie One-Eye, Airport 75, The Hindenburg, Rush Week.
TELEVISION: *Series:* General Hospital (1963-65), The Long Hot Summer, The Invaders, The Psychiatrist, From Here to Eternity, One Life to Live, Falcon Crest, Dark Shadows. *Movies:* The Other Man, The Psychiatrist: God Bless the Children, Black Noon, The Horror at 37000 Feet, The Norliss Tales, Satan's School for Girls, Death Race, The Manhunter, Secrets, Code Name: Diamond Head, Sizzle, The Return of the Mod Squad, Freedom, Dark Holiday, Blue Bayou, The Hand in the Glove, An Inconvenient Woman, Lady Against the Odds, Stormy Weathers. *Mini-Series:* From Here to Eternity, Scruples.

THOMAS, BETTY
Director, Actress. b. St. Louis, MO, July 27, 1949. e. Ohio U, Chicago Art Inst., Roosevelt U. Former member of Chicago's Second City improv group.
PICTURES: *Actress:* Tunnelvision, Chesty Anderson—U.S. Navy, Loose Shoes, Used Cars, Homework, Troop Beverly Hills, Jackson County Jail. *Director:* Only You, The Brady Bunch Movie.
TELEVISION: *Series:* Hill Street Blues (Emmy Award, 1985). *Movies:* Outside Chance, Nashville Grab, When Your Lover Leaves, Prison for Children. Director (series): Doogie Howser M.D., Dream On (Emmy Award, 1993), Hooperman, Mancuso FBI, Arresting Behavior, Couples. *Movie:* My Breast.

THOMAS, DAVE
Actor, Writer, Director. b. St. Catherines, Ontario, Canada, May 20, 1949. e. McMaster Univ.
PICTURES: Stripes (debut, 1981), Strange Bew (also co-dir., co-s.p.), My Man Adam, Sesame Street Presents Follow That Bird, Love at Stake, Nightflyers, Moving, The Experts (dir. only), Cold Sweat, Coneheads.
TELEVISION: Series (actor/writer): Second City TV, SCTV Network The New Show, The Dave Thomas Comedy Show (also exec. prod., dir.), Maniac Mansion, Grace Under Fire (actor only). Movies: Home to Stay, Just Me and You, The Canadian Conspiracy, Boris and Natasha, Ghost Mom (writer). Pilot: From Cleveland. Specials: Twilight Theatre, Martin Short Concert for the North, Dave Thomas: The Incredible Time Travels of Henry Osgood (also dir., exec. prod., writer), Andrea Martin: Together Again, Inside America's Totally Unsolved Lifestyles (also exec. prod., writer).

THOMAS, HARRY E.
Exhibitor. b. Monroe, LA, May 22, 1920. e. Louisiana State U., 1938-41. Psychological Branch of Army Air Force, 1942-46. Past pres., secy., and treas. of NATO of MS. Dir. of Design & Const. & Sec. Gulf State Theatres Inc. Retired 1978.

THOMAS, HENRY
Actor. b. San Antonio, TX, Sept. 8, 1971. Made film debut at the age of 9 in Raggedy Man, 1981. On stage in Artichoke, The Guardsman.
PICTURES: Raggedy Man (debut, 1981), E.T. The Extra-Terrestrial, Misunderstood, Cloak and Dagger, The Quest, Murder One, Valmont, Fire in the Sky, Legends of the Fall.
TELEVISION: Movies: Psycho IV: The Beginning, A Taste for Killing, Curse of the Starving Class, Indictment: The McMartin Trial. Special: The Steeler and the Pittsburgh Kid.

THOMAS, JAY
Actor. b. New Orleans, LA, July 12, 1948. Started as stand-up comedian before pursuing acting career in NY. Appeared on NY stage with Playwrights Horizons and Off-B'way in Isn't It Romantic? Also morning disc jockey on L.A. radio station KPWR-FM.
PICTURES: C.H.U.D., The Gig, Straight Talk, Mr. Holland's Opus.
TELEVISION: Series: Mork & Mindy, Cheers, Married People, Love & War. Guest: Murphy Brown (Emmy Award, 1991).

THOMAS, JEREMY
Producer. b. London, Eng., July 26, 1949. e. Millfield School. Son of dir. Ralph Thomas (Doctor comedies) and nephew of dir. Gerald Thomas (Carry On... comedies). Entered industry 1969. Worked as film edit. on Brother Can You Spare a Dime, 1974. Received Evening Standard Special Award for Outstanding Contribution to Cinema in 1990, BAFTA's Michael Balcon Award in 1991. Appointed chmn. of British Film Institute, 1992.
PICTURES: Mad Dog Morgan, The Shout, The Great Rock 'n' Roll Swindle, Bad Timing: A Sensual Obsession, Eureka, Merry Christmas Mr. Lawrence, The Hit, Insignificance, The Last Emperor (Academy Award, 1987), Everybody Wins, The Sheltering Sky, Let Him Have It (exec. prod.), Naked Lunch, Little Buddha.

THOMAS, LEO J.
Executive. b. Grand Rapids, MN. e. Univ. of MI, Univ. of IL. Started as research chemist in 1961 at Color Photog. Division of the Kodak Research Labs. 1967-70, head of Color Physics and Engingeering Lab; 1970-72, asst. head of Color Photog. Division; 1972-74, tech. asst. to dir. of the Research Labs; 1974, appointed sec. of Technical Affairs Committe. 1977, named dir. of Research Laboratories; later that year became v.p. of the company; 1978 elected sr. v.p. 1984, appointed gen. mgr. Life Sciences. 1988, v.p. Sterling Drug; 1989, gen. mgr. of Health Group; 1989, v.p. of Health Group; 1991, pres. of Imaging Group; 1994, exec. v.p. Eastman Kodak Company.

THOMAS, MARLO
Actress. b. Detroit, MI, Nov. 21, 1938. Daughter of late Danny Thomas. m. Phil Donahue. Brother is TV producer Tony Thomas. e. U. of Southern California. Started career with small TV roles, summer stock. Appeared in London stage prod. of Barefoot in the Park. Most Promising Newcomer Awards from both Fame and Photoplay for series That Girl. Conceived book, record and TV special Free to Be You and Me (Emmy Award, 1974).
THEATER: NY: Thieves, Social Security, The Shadow Box. Regional: Six Degrees of Separation.
PICTURES: Jenny, Thieves, In the Spirit.
TELEVISION: Series: The Joey Bishop Show, That Girl. Specials: Acts of Love and Other Comedies, Free To Be You and Me (also prod.; Emmy Award, 1974), The Body Human: Facts for Girls (Emmy Award, 1981), Love Sex... and Marriage (also exec. prod.; Free to Be a Family (host, exec. prod.;

Emmy Award, 1989). Movies: It Happened One Christmas (also co-prod.), The Lost Honor of Kathryn Beck (also exec. prod.), Consenting Adult, Nobody's Child (Emmy Award, 1986), Leap of Faith (co-exec. prod. only), Held Hostage: The Sis and Jerry Levin Story, Ultimate Betrayal, Reunion (also co-exec. prod.). Guest: Dobie Gillis, Zane Grey Theatre, Thriller.

THOMAS, PHILIP MICHAEL
Actor. b. Columbus, OH, May 26, 1949. e. Oakwood Coll.
PICTURES: Black Fist, Sparkle, Death Drug, The Wizard of Speed and Time.
TELEVISION: Series: Miami Vice. Movies: Toma, The Beasts Are on the Streets, This Man Stands Alone, Valentine, A Fight for Jenny, False Witness. Special: Disney's Totally Minnie, The Debbie Allen Special.

THOMAS, RALPH
Director. b. Hull, Yorkshire, England, Aug. 10, 1915. e. Tellisford Coll., Clifton and University Coll., London. Journalist in early career, entered m.p. ind. 1932 as film ed.; service with 9th Lancers, 1939-45; then film director.
PICTURES: Helter Skelter, Once Upon a Dream, Traveller's Joy, The Clouded Yellow, Appointment With Venus (Island Rescue), The Assassin (The Venetian Bird), A Day to Remember, Doctor in the House, Mad about Men, Above Us the Waves, Doctor at Sea, The Iron Petticoat, Checkpoint, Doctor at Large, Campbell's Kingdom, A Tale of Two Cities, The Wind Cannot Read, The 39 Steps, Upstairs and Downstairs, Conspiracy of Hearts, Doctor in Love, No Love for Johnnie, No My Darling Daughter, A Pair of Briefs, The Wild and the Willing, Doctor in Distress, Hot Enough for June (Agent 8 3/4), The High Bright Sun (McGuire Go Home!), Doctor in Clover, Deadlier Than the Male, Nobody Runs Forever (The High Commissioner), Some Girls Do, Doctor in Trouble, Percy, Quest for Love, The Love Ban, Percy's Progress (It's Not the Size That Counts), A Nightingale Sang in Berkeley Square, Pop Pirates.

THOMAS, RICHARD
Actor. b. New York, NY, June 13, 1951. e. Columbia U. Made TV debut at age 7 on Hallmark Hall of Fame special The Christmas Tree. That same year appeard on Brodawy in Sunrise at Campobello.
THEATER: Sunrise at Campobello, Everything in the Garden, Fifth of July, The Front Page, Love Letters, Square One, The Lisbon Traviata, Danton's Death, Richard II, Richard III.
PICTURES: Winning (debut, 1969), Last Summer, Red Sky at Morning, The Todd Killings, You'll Like My Mother, September 30, 1955, Battle Beyond the Stars.
TELEVISION: Series: One Two Three Go, As the World Turns, The Waltons (Emmy Award, 1973). Guest: Great Ghost Tales, Bonanza, Love American Style, Medical Center, Marcus Welby M.D., The F.B.I., Tales From the Crypt (Mute Witness to Murder), The Outer Limits. Movies: Homecoming, The Red Badge of Courage, The Silence, Getting Married, No Other Love, All Quiet on the Western Front, To Find My Son, Berlin Tunnel 21, Johnny Belinda, Living Proof: The Hank Williams Jr. Story, Hobson's Choice, The Master of Ballantrae, Final Jeopardy, Glory Glory, Go To the Light, Common Ground, Stephen King's IT, Mission of the Shark, Yes Virginia There Is a Santa Claus, Crash Landing: The Rescue of Flight 232, I Can Make You Love Me: The Stalking of Laura Black, Precious Victims, Linda, A Walton Thanksgiving Reunion, Death in Small Doses, A Walton Wedding, Down Out and Dangerous. Specials: A Doll's House, Give Us Barabbas, HMS Pinafore, Barefoot in the Park, Fifth of July, Andre's Mother.

THOMAS, ROBERT G.
Producer, Director. b. Glen Ridge, NJ, July 21, 1943. e. U. of Bridgeport, Fairleigh Dickinson U. Prod. educational film programs, 1962, WPKN-FM. Asst. stage mgr. Meadowbrook Dinner Theatre, 1963; 1964, began career as TV cameraman for NY stations. Worked both full-time and freelance for major TV and video tape studios. 1968, started Bob Thomas Productions, producing business/sales films and TV commercials. Has 8 awards from natl. film festivals; nominated for 5 Emmys for TV series called The Jersey Side he produced for WOR-TV. Inventor of Futurevision 2000 multi-imaging video system for conventions and exhibits and museums (American Museum of Natural History: Hall of Human Biology to be shown over 15 years). Inventor and pres. of Video Mail Marketing Inc., low cost, light weight paper board video cassettes for the direct mail video marketing industry. Shorts: Valley Forge with Bob Hope, New Jersey—200 Years, Road-Eo '77.
TELEVISION: The Jersey Side (talk/entertainment), Jersey People (weekly talk/entertainment prog.), Movies '89 (synd. film preview series).

THOMAS, ROBERT J. (BOB)
Columnist, Associated Press, Hollywood. b. San Diego, CA, Jan. 26, 1922. p. George H. Thomas, publicist. e. UCLA.

Joined Associated Press staff, Los Angeles, 1943; corr. Fresno, 1944; Hollywood since 1944. Writer mag. articles; appearances, radio; orig. story Big Mike.
AUTHOR: The Art of Animation, King Cohn, Thalberg, Selznick, Winchell—Secret Boss of California, The Heart of Hollywood, Howard—The Amazing Mr. Hughes, Weekend '33, Marlon—Portrait of the Rebel as an Artist, Walt Disney—An American Original, Bud and Lou—The Abbott and Costello Story, The Road to Hollywood (with Bob Hope), The One and Only Bing, Joan Crawford, Golden Boy: The Secret Life of William Holden, Astaire: The Man the Dancer, I got Rhythm—The Ethel Merman Story, Liberace, Clown Prince of Hollywood (Jack L. Warner), Disney's Art of Animation.

THOMOPOULOS, ANTHONY D.
Executive. b. Mt. Vernon, NY, Feb. 7, 1938. e. Georgetown U. Began career in broadcasting at NBC, 1959, starting as mailroom clerk and moving to radio division in prod. & admin. Shortly named to post in int'l division sales, involved with programming for stations and in dev. TV systems for other nations. Joined Four Star Entertainment Corp. as dir. of foreign sales, 1964; named v.p., 1965; exec. v.p., 1969; 1970 joined RCA SelectaVision Div. as dir. of programming; 1971 joined Tomorrow Entertainment as v.p.; 1973 joined ABC as v.p., prime-time programs in N.Y.; 1974, named v.p., prime-time TV creative operations, ABC Entertainment; 1975 named v.p. of special programs, ABC Entertainment; 1976 made v.p., ABC-TV, assisting pres. Frederick S. Pierce in supervising all activities of the division; 1978 named pres. of ABC Entertainment; 1983 promoted to pres., ABC Broadcast Group in chg. all TV & radio operations; 1986-88, pres. & COO, United Artists Corp.; independent prod. with Columbia, 1989.

THOMPSON, CAROLINE
Writer. b. Washington, DC, Apr. 23, 1956. e. Amherst Col., Harvard. Started as free-lance journalist. Wrote novel First Born, which led to screenwriting.
PICTURES: Edward Scissorhands (also assoc. prod.), The Addams Family, Homeward Bound: The Incredible Journey, The Secret Garden (also assoc. prod.), The Nightmare Before Christmas, Black Beauty (also dir.).

THOMPSON, EMMA
Actress. b. London, England, Apr. 15, 1959. e. Cambridge Univ. Daughter of actors Eric Thompson and Phyllida Law. Acted with the Footlights at the Edinburgh Fringe. At Cambridge co-wrote, co-produced, co-directed and co-starred in school's first all-female revue Woman's Hour, as well as solo show Short Vehicle.
THEATER: London: Me and My Girl, Look Back in Anger. Renaissance Theatre Company (World Tour): A Midsummer Night's Dream, King Lear.
PICTURES: Henry V, The Tall Guy, Impromptu, Dead Again, Howards End (Academy Award, BAFTA, NY Film Critics, LA Film Critics, Golden Globe, Nat'l Society of Film Critics & Nat'l Board of Review Awards for Best Actress of 1992), Peter's Friends, Much Ado About Nothing, The Remains of the Day (Acad. Award nom.), In the Name of the Father (Academy Award nom.), My Father the Hero (unbilled), Junior, Carrington, Sense and Sensibility (also s.p.; BAFTA Award, 1995; Academy Award, 1996; Writers Guild Award, 1996; Golden Globe Award, 1996).
TELEVISION: Series: Thompson (also writer). Mini-Series: Tutti Frutti, Fortunes of War (BAFTA Best Actress award). Specials: The Emma Thompson Special, The Winslow Boy, Look Back in Anger, Knuckle, The Blue Boy. Guest: Cheers.

THOMPSON, FRED (DALTON)
Actor. b. Sheffield, AL, Aug. 19, 1942. Raised in TN. e. Memphis St. U, Vanderbilt U, studying law. Was Federal prosecutor before going to DC to serve as minority counsel on the Senate Select Committe on Presidential Campaign Activies, which involved investigation of the Watergate scandal. Hired to serve as consultant on film Marie, then was asked to play himself in the movie, resulting in acting career. 1994 elected to U.S. senate as Republican representative from Tennessee.
Author: At That Point in Time (1975).
PICTURES: Marie (debut, 1985), No Way Out, Feds, Fat Man and Little Boy, The Hunt for Red October, Days of Thunder, Die Hard 2, Flight of the Intruder, Class Action, Necessary Roughness, Curly Sue, Cape Fear, Thunderheart, White Sands, Aces: Iron Eagle III, Born Yesterday, In the Line of Fire, Baby's Day Out.
TELEVISION: Movies: Bed of Lies, Keep the Change, Stay the Night, Day-O, Barbarians at the Gate.

THOMPSON, J. LEE
Director, Writer, Producer. b. Bristol, England, 1914. On Brit. stage as actor with Nottingham Rep. Co.; Playwright: Murder Without Crime, Cousin Simon, Curious Dr. Robson (collab.) Thousands of Summers, Human Touch. To films, 1934 as actor, then writer, before turning to directing.
PICTURES: Writer: The Middle Watch, For Them That Trespass. Director: Murder Without Crime, 1950; also story, s.p.), The Yellow Balloon (also s.p.), The Weak and the Wicked (also co-s.p.), For Better or Worse (also s.p.), As Long as They're Happy, An Alligator Named Daisy, Yield to the Night, The Good Companions (also co-prod.), Woman in the Dressing Gown (also co-prod.), Ice Cold in Alex (Desert Attack), No Trees in the Street (also co-exec. prod.), Northwest Frontier (Flame Over India), Tiger Bay, I Aim at the Stars, The Guns of Navarone, Cape Fear, Taras Bulba, Kings of the Sun, What a Way to Go!, John Goldfarb Please Come Home (also co-exec. prod.), Return From the Ashes (also prod.), Eye of the Devil, Mackenna's Gold, Before Winter Comes, The Chairman, Country Dance (Brotherly Love), Conquest of the Planet of the Apes, Battle for the Planet of the Apes, Huckleberry Finn, The Reincarnation of Peter Proud, St. Ives, The White Buffalo, The Greek Tycoon, The Passage, Caboblanco, Happy Birthday to Me, 10 to Midnight, The Evil That Men Do, The Ambassador, King Solomon's Mines, Murphy's Law, Firewalker, Death Wish IV: The Crackdown, Messenger of Death, Kinjite.
TELEVISION: A Great American Tragedy, The Blue Knight, Widow.

THOMPSON, JACK
Actor. r.n. John Payne. b. Sydney, Australia, Aug. 31, 1940. e. Queensland U. Joined drama workshop at school; first part was in TV soap opera as continuing character. 1988, appt. to bd. of Australian Film Finance Corp. Formed Pan Film Enterprises.
PICTURES: The Savage Wild, Outback (Wake in Fright), Libido, Petersen, A Sunday Too Far Away, Caddie, Scobie Malone, Mad Dog Morgan, The Chant of Jimmie Blacksmith, The Journalist, Breaker Morant, The Earthling, The Club, The Man From Snowy River, Bad Blood, Merry Christmas Mr. Lawrence, Flesh + Blood, Burke & Willis, Ground Zero, Waterfront, Turtle Beach, Wind, A Far Off Place, Deception, The Sum of Us, The Last Dance.
TELEVISION: The Last Frontier, A Woman Called Golda, Waterfront, The Letter, Beryl Markham: A Shadow on the Sun, Paradise, Last Frontier, Wreck of the Stinson, A Woman of Independent Means.

THOMPSON, LEA
Actress. b. Rochester, MN, May 31, 1961. m. director Howard Deutch. Danced professionally since age of 14; won scholarship to Pennsylvania Ballet Co., American Ballet Theatre, San Francisco Ballet. Gave up that career for acting, appearing in several commercials for Burger King. L.A. stage: Bus Stop, The Illusion.
PICTURES: Jaws 3-D (debut, 1983), All the Right Moves, Red Dawn, The Wild Life, Back to the Future, SpaceCamp, Howard the Duck, Some Kind of Wonderful, Casual Sex?, Going Undercover, The Wizard of Loneliness, Back to the Future Part II, Back to the Future Part III, Article 99, Dennis the Menace, The Beverly Hillbillies, The Little Rascals.
TELEVISION: Series: Caroline in the City. Movies: Nightbreaker, Montana, Stolen Babies, The Substitute Wife, The Unspoken Truth. Guest: Tales From the Crypt.

THOMPSON, SADA
Actress. b. Des Moines, IA, Sept. 27, 1929. e. Carnegie Inst. of Technology, Pittsburgh. First N.Y. stage appearance in Under Milk Wood. B'way incl. The Effect of Gamma Rays (Obie, Drama Desk, Variety Poll), Twigs (Tony Award, 1972), Saturday, Sunday, Monday. Recent theater: Real Estate, Any Given Day.
PICTURES: Pursuit of Happiness, Desperate Characters.
TELEVISION: Specials: Sandburg's Lincoln, Our Town, The Skin of Our Teeth, Andre's Mother, Painting Churches. Movies: The Entertainer, Princess Daisy, My Two Loves, Fatal Confession: A Father Dowling Mystery, Home Fires Burning, Fear Stalk, Indictment: The McMartin Trial. Series: Family (Emmy Award, 1978). Mini-Series: Queen.

THULIN, INGRID
Actress, Director. b. Solleftea, Sweden, Jan. 27, 1929. m. Harry Schein. Made acting debut at 18 at the Municipal Theatre in Norrkoping. Studied at Stockholm's Royal Dramatic Theatre. Worked with Malmo and Stockholm repertory. Appeared on Swedish stage in nearly 50 plays including Gigi, Peer Gynt, Two for the Seesaw, Twelfth Night, Miss Julie. Has directed plays and films in Stockholm. N.Y. stage debut, 1967: Of Love Remembered. Author: Somebody I Knew (1993).
PICTURES: Where the Wind Blows, Love Will Conqueror, Jack of Hearts, Foreign Intrigue, Wild Strawberries, Brink of Life (Cannes Film Fest. Award), The Magician, The Judge, The Four Horsemen of the Apocalypse, Winter Light, The Silence, Games of Desire, Return From the Ashes, La Guerre est Finie, Night Games, Adelaide, Hour of the Wolf, I a Virgin, The Ritual, The Damned, Cries and Whispers, A Handful of Love, La Cage, Moses, Madame Kitty, The Cassandra Crossing, Broken Sky, At the Rehearsal, Control, House of Smiles, Rabbit Face.

THURMAN, UMA
Actress. b. Boston, MA, Apr. 29, 1970. Named after a Hindu deity. Raised in Woodstock, NY and Amherst, MA where father taught Asian studies. Father's work took family to India where they lived three years. e. Professional Children's School, NY. Worked as model while still in high school.
PICTURES: Kiss Daddy Good Night (debut, 1988), Johnny Be Good, Dangerous Liaisons, The Adventures of Baron Munchausen, Where the Heart Is, Henry and June, Final Analysis, Jennifer Eight, Mad Dog and Glory, Even Cowgirls Get the Blues, Pulp Fiction (Acad. Award nom.), A Month by the Lake, The Truth About Cats and Dogs, Beautiful Girls, Batman and Robin.
TELEVISION: Movie: Robin Hood.

THURSTON, DONALD A.
Executive. b. Gloucester, MA, April 2, 1905. Chairman of the board, Broadcast Music, Inc.

TICOTIN, RACHEL
Actress. b. Bronx, NY, Nov. 1, 1958. Began career as dancer with the Ballet Hispanico of New York, before becoming a production assist. on such films as The Wanderers, Dressed to Kill and Raging Bull.
PICTURES: King of the Gypsies, Fort Apache: The Bronx, Critical Condition, Total Recall, One Good Cop, FX2, Falling Down, Natural Born Killers, Don Juan DeMarco, Steal Big Steal Little.
TELEVISION: Series: For Love and Honor, Ohara, Crime and Punishment. Movies: Love Mary, Rockabye, When the Bough Breaks, Spies Lies and Naked Thighs, Prison Stories: Women on the Inside, Keep the Change, From the Files of Joseph Wambaugh: A Jury of One, Thicker Than Blood: The Larry McLinden Story, Deconstructing Sarah.

TIERNEY, LAWRENCE
Actor. b. Brooklyn, NY, Mar. 15, 1919. Brother of actor Scott Brady. e. Manhattan Coll. Track athlete (natl. championship Cross Country Team, N.Y. Athletic Club). Stage actor before screen debut 1943.
PICTURES: The Ghost Ship (debut, 1943), Government Girl, Gildersleeve on Broadway, The Falcon Out West, Youth Runs Wild, Back to Bataan, Dillinger, Mama Loves Papa, Those Endearing Young Charms, Badman's Territory, Step By Step, San Quentin, The Devil Thumbs a Ride, Born to Kill, Bodyguard, Kill or Be Killed, Shakedown, The Hoodlum, The Bushwhackers, Best of the Bad Men, The Greatest Show on Earth, The Steel Cage, Female Jungle, Singing in the Dark, A Child Is Waiting, Custer of the West, Such Good Friends, Abduction, Andy Warhol's Bad, The Kirlian Witness, Never Pick Up a Stranger (Bloodrage), Gloria, Rosemary's Killer, Midnight, Prizzi's Honor, Stephen King's Silver Bullet, Murphy's Law, Tough Guys Don't Dance, The Offspring (From a Whisper to a Scream), The Horror Show, Wizards of the Demon Sword, Why Me?, City of Hope, The Runestone, Reservoir Dogs, A Kiss Goodnight, Junior.
TELEVISION: Movies: Terrible Joe Moran, Dillinger. Guest: Hill Street Blues, Star Trek: The Next Generation, Tales From the Dark Side, Hunter.

TIFFIN, PAMELA
Actress. r.n. Pamela Wonso. b. Oklahoma City, OK, Oct. 13, 1942. e. Hunter Coll., Columbia U., Loyola U, Rome Center. Studied acting with Stella Adler and Harold Clurman. Started modeling as a teenager.
THEATER: Dinner at Eight (Theatre World Award), Uncle Vanya.
PICTURES: Summer and Smoke (debut, 1961), One Two Three, State Fair, Come Fly with Me, For Those Who Think Young, The Lively Set, The Pleasure Seekers, Kiss the Other Sheik, The Hallelujah Trail, Harper, Paranoia, Viva Max!, The Godson, Giornata Nera per l'Ariete, Deaf Smith and Johnny Ears, Puntto e a Capo, Evil Fingers.

TIGHE, KEVIN
Actor. b. Los Angeles, CA, Aug. 13, 1944. e. Cal. State, B.A. in psychology; USC M.F.A. in performing arts. Served in U.S. Army, 1967-69. Received N.E.A. Director's Fellowship, Seattle Rep. Theatre, 1988-89.
PICTURES: The Graduate (debut, 1967), Matewan, Eight Men Out, K-9, Lost Angels, Road House, Another 48 HRS, Bright Angel, City of Hope, Newsies, School Ties, A Man in Uniform (Genie Award), Geronimo: An American Legend, What's Eating Gilbert Grape, Scorpion Spring, Jade, Race the Sun.
TELEVISION: Series: Emergency, Murder One. Guest: Tales From the Crypt (Cutting Cards). Movies: Better Off Dead, Betrayal of Trust, The Avenging Angel.

TILLY, JENNIFER
Actress. b. Harbour City, CA, 1958. Sister is actress Meg Tilly.
THEATER: One Shoe Off (Off-B'way debut, 1993; Theatre World Award).
PICTURES: No Small Affair, Moving Violations, Inside Out, He's My Girl, Johnny Be Good, Rented Lips, High Spirits, Far From Home, Let It Ride, The Fabulous Baker Boys, Made in

America, The Getaway, Bullets Over Broadway (Acad. Award nom.), Man With a Gun, Embrace of the Vampire, House Arrest, The Pompatus of Love, Bound, Bird of Prey, Edie and Pen, American Strays.
TELEVISION: Series: Shaping Up. Movie: Heads.

TILLY, MEG
Actress. b. Long Beach, CA, Feb. 14, 1960. Sister is actress Jennifer Tilly. Began acting and dancing in community theatrical prods. while in high school. To New York at 16; appeared on TV in Hill Street Blues. Author: Singing Songs (1994).
PICTURES: Fame (debut, 1980), Tex, Psycho II, One Dark Night, The Big Chill, Impulse, Agnes of God (Acad. Award nom.), Off Beat, Masquerade, The Girl in a Swing, Valmont, The Two Jakes, Leaving Normal, Body Snatchers, Sleep with Me.
TELEVISION: Series: Winnetka Road. Specials: The Trouble With Grandpa, Camilla (Nightmare Classics). Movies: In the Best Interest of the Child, Trick of the Eye. Guest: Fallen Angels (Dead-End for Delia).

TINKER, GRANT A.
Executive. b. Stamford, CT., Jan. 11, 1926. e. Dartmouth Coll., 1947. Joined NBC radio prog. dept. 1949. In 1954 with McCann-Erickson ad agency, TV dept. In 1958, Benton & Bowles Ad Agency, TV dept.; 1961-66 with NBC, v.p., programs, West Coast; v.p. in chg. of programming, NY, 1966-67; joined Universal Television as v.p., 1968-69; 20th-Fox, v.p., 1969-70. Became pres. MTM Enterprises, Inc. 1970. Named NBC bd. chmn. & CEO, 1981-86. Received ATAS Governor's Award in 1987. Formed indep. prod. co. G.T.G. Entertainment, 1988.

TISCH, LAURENCE A.
Executive. b. Brooklyn, NY, March 5, 1923. e. NYU, 1941; U. of Pennsylvania Wharton Sch., 1942; Harvard Law Sch., 1946. Pres. Tisch Hotels, Inc., 1950-59; pres. Americana Hotel, Inc., Miami Beach, 1956-59; Chmn. of bd. and co-chief executive officer of Loews Corp since 1960. Also chmn. of bd. of CNA Financial Corp since 1947. President and chief executive officer and chmn. of board, CBS since 1986.

TISCH, PRESTON ROBERT
Executive. b. Brooklyn, NY, April 29, 1926. e. Bucknell U., Lewisberg, PA, 1943-44; U. of Michigan, B.A., 1948. Pres. Loew's Corporation. Postmaster General of the U.S. 1986-1988. March, 1988 returned to Loews Corp. as president and co-chief executive. Elected member of bd. CBS Inc. 1988, 1994, position changed to co-chmn. & co-CEO of Loews Corp.

TISCH, STEVE
Producer. b. Lakewood, NJ, 1949. e. Tufts U. Son of Preston Tisch. Worked during school breaks for John Avildsen and Fred Weintraub. Signed upon graduation as exec. asst. to Peter Guber, then prod. head at Columbia Pictures. Entered producer ranks with Outlaw Blues, 1977, collaborating with Jon Avnet with whom formed Tisch/Avnet Prods. Alliance with Phoenix Entertainment 1988.
PICTURES: Outlaw Blues, Almost Summer, Coast to Coast, Risky Business, Deal of the Century, Soul Man, Big Business, Hot to Trot, Heart of Dixie, Heart Condition, Bad Influence, Forrest Gump (Academy Award for Best Picture, 1994), Corrina Corrina, The Long Kiss Goodnight (exec. prod.), Dear God, Wild America (exec. prod.).
TELEVISION: Homeward Bound, No Other Love, Prime Suspect, Something So Right, Calendar Girl Murders, The Burning Bed (exec. prod.), Call to Glory (series), Triple Cross, Silence of the Heart, In Love and War (sole prod.), Evil in Clear River, Dirty Dancing (series), Out on the Edge (exec. prod.), Judgment (exec. prod.), Lies of the Heart, The Vidiots (pilot), Victim of Love, Keep the Change, Afterburn (exec. prod.), Freshman Dorm (pilot & series), The People Next Door.

TOBACK, JAMES
Writer, Producer, Director. b. New York, NY, Nov. 23, 1944. e. Harvard U. Taught literature at City Coll. of New York; contributed articles and criticism to Harper's, Esquire, Commentary, etc. Wrote book Jim, on actor-athlete Jim Brown (1971). First screenplay, The Gambler, filmed in 1974.
PICTURES: Writer: The Gambler, Fingers (also dir.), Love and Money (also dir., prod.), Exposed (also dir., prod.), The Pick-Up Artist (also dir.), The Big Bang (also dir., actor), Alice (actor), Bugsy (also actor).

TOBOLOWSKY, STEPHEN
Actor. b. Dallas, TX, May 30, 1951. e. Southern Methodist Univ.
THEATER: Actor: Whose Life Is It Anyway?, Crimes of the Heart, Godspell, Three Sisters, The Glass Menagerie, Barabass, The Wake of Jamey Foster, The Wild Duck, No Scratch, The Miss Firecracker Contest, The Importance of Being Earnest, Purlie, Whispers in the Wind. Director: The

Miss Firecracker Contest, The Lucky Spot, The Bridgehead (Dramalogue Award), The Secret Rapture (Dramalogue Award), Our Town, The Debutante Ball.
PICTURES: Swing Shift, True Stories (co-s.p.), Nobody's Fool, Spaceballs, Mississippi Burning, Checking Out, Two Idiots in Hollywood (dir. & s.p.), Great Balls of Fire!, In Country, Breaking In, Bird on a Wire, Funny About Love, Welcome Home Roxy Carmichael, The Grifters, Thelma & Louise, Memoirs of an Invisible Man, Basic Instinct, Roadside Prophets, Single White Female, Sneakers, Where the Day Takes You, Sneakers, Hero, Groundhog Day, The Pickle, Calendar Girl, Josh and S.A.M., My Father the Hero, Radioland Murders, Murder in the First, Dr. Jekyll and Ms. Hyde, Power 98.
TELEVISION: Movies: Last Flight Out, Marla Hanson Story, Perry Mason: The Case of the Maligned Mobster, Tagget, Deadlock, Deadly Medicine, When Love Kills: The Seduction of John Hearn. Series: Against the Grain, Blue Skies, A Whole New Ballgame, Dweebs. Guest: Crazy Like a Fox, Designing Women, L.A. Law, Days and Nights of Molly Dodd, Seinfeld, Picket Fences, Chicago Hope, Hearts of the West, Baby Talk, Knots Landing, Falcon Crest.

TODD, BEVERLY
Actress, Director, Producer. b. Chicago, IL, July 11, 1953.
THEATER: NY: Carry Me Back to Morningside Heights, Black Visions. Producer: A Laugh a Tear: The Story of Black Humor in America, A Tribute to Ella Fitzgerald. Director: I Need a Man.
PICTURES: The Lost Man, They Call Me Mister Tibbs!, Brother John, Vice Squad, Homework, The Ladies Club, Happy Hour, Baby Boom, Moving, Clara's Heart, Lean on Me, The Class of '61.
TELEVISION: Series: Love of Life, Having Babies, The Redd Foxx Show. Mini-Series: Roots. Movies: Deadlock, The Ghost of Flight 401, Having Babies II, The Jericho Mile, Don't Look Back, A Touch of Scandal, A Different Affair. Guest: Magnum P.I., The Robert Guillaume Show, Falcon Crest, Quincy M.E., Hill Street Blues, Family, Benson, Lou Grant, A Different World. Special: Don't Hit Me Mom (Afterschool Special).

TODD, RICHARD
O.B.E. Actor. b. Dublin, Ireland, June 11, 1919. e. Shrewsbury. In repertory, 1937; founder-member, Dundee Repertory Theatre, 1939; distinguished war service, 1939-46; Dundee Repertory, 1946-48; screen debut, 1948; For Them That Trespass, 1948. 1970 Founder-Director Triumph Theatre Productions. Published autobiography, 1986, Volume II, 1989. Awarded O.B.E., 1993.
THEATER: An Ideal Husband, Dear Octopus. Co-founder, Triumph Theatre Prods., Ltd. plays since 1970: Roar Like a Dove, Grass Is Greener, The Marquise (U.S.). Sleuth (England and Australia). Murder by Numbers, The Hollow Crown (with RSC), Equus. On Approval, Quadrille, This Happy Breed, The Business of Murder (London), Intent to Kill, The Woman in Black, Beyond Reasonable Doubt, Sweet Revenge, Brideshead Revisited.
PICTURES: For Them That Trespass (debut, 1948), The Hasty Heart, Interrupted Journey, Stage Fright, Portrait of Clare, Lightning Strikes Twice (U.S.), Flesh and Blood, Story of Robin Hood, 24 Hours of a Woman's Life, The Venetian Bird, Sword and the Rose, Rob Roy, Les Secrets d'Alcove (Fr.), A Man Called Peter (U.S.), The Virgin Queen (U.S.), Dam Busters, D-Day the Sixth of June (U.S.), Marie Antoinette (Fr.), Yangtse Incident, Saint Joan, Chase a Crooked Shadow, The Naked Earth, Intent to Kill, Danger Within, Never Let Go, The Long the Short and the Tall, Don't Bother to Knock (also exec. prod.), The Hellions, The Longest Day, Crime Does Not Pay (Fr.), The Boys, The Very Edge, Death Drums Along the River, Battle of the Villa Fiorita, Operation Crossbow, Coast of Skeletons, The Love-Ins, Subterfuge, Dorian Gray, Asylum, The Sky is Falling, Number One of the Secret Service, The Big Sleep, House of the Long Shadows.
TELEVISION: Wuthering Heights, Carrington V.C., The Brighton Mesmerists, Beautiful Lies, The Boy Dominic, Murder She Wrote, Virtual Murder.

TOKOFSKY, JERRY H.
Executive. b. New York, NY, Apr. 14, 1936. e. NYU, B.S., journalism, 1956; New York Law, 1959. Entered William Morris Agency while at NYU 1953, working in night club dept. to live TV. Moved to Beverly Hills office, 1959. Entered m.p. div. WMA, 1960. Joined Columbia Pictures, as prod. v.p., 1963-70. Joined Paramount Pictures 1970 as prod. v.p. To MGM as prod. v.p., 1971. Now producer & exec. v.p., Zupnik Enterprises, Inc.
PICTURES: Producer: Where's Poppa, Born to Win, Paternity, Dreamscape, Fear City, Wildfire, Glengarry Glen Ross.

TOLKAN, JAMES
Actor. b. Calumet, MI, June 20, 1931. e. Univ. of Iowa. Trained with Stella Adler.
THEATER: NY: Abe Lincoln in Illinois, Once in a Lifetime, Three Sisters, The Cannibals, Mary Stuart, The Silent Partner, 42 Seconds from Broadway, Full Circle, Macbeth, Dream of a Blacklisted Actor, Jungle of Cities, Wings.

PICTURES: Stiletto, They Might Be Giants, The Friends of Eddie Coyle, Serpico, Love and Death, The Amityville Horror, Wolfen, Prince of the City, Author! Author!, Hanky Panky, Nightmares (voice), WarGames, Iceman, The River, Turk 182!, Flanagan, Back to the Future, Off Beat, Top Gun, Armed and Dangerous, Masters of the Universe, Made in Heaven, Viper, Split Decisions, True Blood, Second Sight, Back to the Future Part II, Family Business, Opportunity Knocks, Back to the Future Part III, Dick Tracy, Hangfire, Problem Child 2, Driving Me Crazy, Boiling Point.
TELEVISION: Series: Mary, The Hat Squad, Cobra. Movies: Little Spies, Leap of Faith, Weekend War, The Case of the Hillside Stranglers, Sketch Artist, Beyond Betrayal, Sketch Artist II: Hands That See. Guest: Remington Steele, Miami Vice, The Equalizer, Tales From the Crypt.

TOLKIN, MICHAEL
Writer, Director, Producer. b. New York, NY, Oct. 17, 1950. e. Middlebury Col, VT. Started as writer for LA Times, Village Voice, before becoming story editor on tv series Delta House. Novels: The Player (1988), Among the Dead (1992).
PICTURES: Writer: Gleaming the Cube, The Rapture (also dir.), The Player (also co-prod., actor; WGA Award, Acad. Award nom.), Deep Cover (also story), The New Age (also dir.).
TELEVISION: Movie: The Burning Season (co-writer).

TOMEI, MARISA
Actress. b. Brooklyn, NY, Dec. 4, 1964. e. Boston U.
THEATER: Beirut (L.A.). NY: Daughters (Theatre World Award), The Comedy of Errors, What the Butler Saw, Slavs!
PICTURES: The Flamingo Kid (debut, 1984), Playing for Keeps, Oscar, Zandalee, My Cousin Vinny (Academy Award, best supporting actress, 1992), Chaplin, Untamed Heart, Equinox, The Paper, Only You, The Perez Family, Four Rooms, A Brother's Kiss, Unhook the Stars.
TELEVISION: Series: As the World Turns, A Different World. Guest: Seinfeld. Movie: Parker Kane.

TOMLIN, LILY
Actress. r.n. Mary Jean Tomlin. b. Detroit, MI, Sept. 1, 1939. e. Wayne State U. (studied pre-med). Studied mime with Paul Curtis. Started inventing characters for comedy sketches in college, used them in cafe and night club dates in Detroit. 1965 went to NY performing skits on coffee-house circuit, landed job on The Garry Moore Show. Moved to L.A. where she appeared on The Music Scene. 1969, first appeared on Laugh-In TV series, gaining national attention with such characters as telephone operator Ernestine and child Edith Ann.
THEATER: Appearing Nitely (special Tony Award, 1977), The Search for Signs of Intelligent Life in the Universe (1985, on B'way and on tour; Tony Award).
PICTURES: Nashville (debut, 1975; NY Film Critics Award; Acad Award nom.), The Late Show, Moment by Moment, Nine to Five, The Incredible Shrinking Woman, All of Me, Big Business, The Search for Signs of Intelligent Life in the Universe, Shadows and Fog, The Player, Short Cuts, The Beverly Hillbillies, Blue in the Face, Getting Away With Murder, The Celluloid Closet (narrator), Flirting With Disaster.
TELEVISION: Series: The Music Scene (host, 1969), Rowan and Martin's Laugh-In (1969-73), Magic School Bus (voice for animated series), Murphy Brown. Specials: Lily (Emmy Award as writer, 1974), Lily Tomlin (Emmy Award as writer, 1976), The Paul Simon Special (Emmy Award as writer, 1978), Lily—Sold Out (also exec. prod.; Emmy Award as exec. prod., 1981), The Muppets Go to the Movies, Lily for President?, Live—and in Person, Funny You Don't Look 200, Free to Be... a Family, Edith Ann: A Few Pieces of the Puzzle (voice, exec. prod.), Edith Ann: Homeless Go Home (voice, exec. prod.). Movie: And the Band Played On. Guest: Homicide.
RECORDS: This Is a Recording (Grammy Award, 1971), Modern Scream, And That's the Truth, Lily Tomlin On Stage.

TOPOL
Actor. b. Tel-Aviv, Israel, Sept. 9, 1935. r.n. Chaim Topol.
THEATER: Fiddler on the Roof (London, 1967, 1994-95 also U.K. tour; NY 1989: Tony nom.; Canada & Japan tour) Chicester Fest. Theatre: Caucasian Chalk Circle, Romanov and Juliet, Othello, View From the Bridge.
PICTURES: Sallah, Cast a Giant Shadow, Before Winter Comes, A Talent for Loving, Fiddler on the Roof (Acad. Award nom.), Follow Me (The Public Eye), Galileo, Flash Gordon, For Your Eyes Only, Ervinka, A Dime Novel.
TELEVISION: Movies: House on Garibaldi Street, Queenie. Mini-Series: The Winds of War, War and Remembrance. Series (BBC): It's Topol, Topol's Israel.

TORME, MEL
Singer, Actor. b. Chicago, IL, Sept. 13, 1925. Singing debut at age of 4; won radio audition 1933; on radio; composed song Lament to Love; with Chico Marx's orchestra as drummer, arranger & vocalist 1942; served in U.S. Army, WWII; org. vocal group Meltones; many recordings; night club and con-

cert appearances. *Author*: The Other Side of the Rainbow: With Judy Garland on the Dawn Patrol (1970), It Wasn't All Velvet (1988), My Singing Teachers: Reflections on Singing Popular Music (1994).
PICTURES: Higher and Higher (debut, 1943), Pardon My Rhythm, Let's Go Steady, Janie Gets Married, Junior Miss, Night and Day, Good News, Words and Music, Duchess of Idaho, The Big Operator, Girls Town, Walk Like a Dragon, The Patsy, A Man Called Adam, The Land of No Return (Snowman), Daffy Duck's Quackbusters (voice), The Naked Gun 2 1/2: The Smell of Fear.
TELEVISION: Series: TV's Top Tunes, The Judy Garland Show (musical advisor, frequent guest), It Was a Very Good Year (host). Movie: Pray TV. *Guest*: Night Court.

TORN, RIP
Actor. r.n. Elmore Torn, Jr. b. Temple, TX, Feb. 6, 1931. e. Texas A & M U., U. of TX. Served in army. Signed as understudy for lead in Cat on a Hot Tin Roof on Broadway.
THEATER: Orpheus Descending, Sweet Bird of Youth (Theatre World Award), Daughter of Silence, Macbeth, Desire Under the Elms, Strange Interlude, Blues For Mr. Charlie, The Kitchen, The Deer Park (Obie Award), The Beard, The Cuban Thing, Dream of a Blacklisted Actor, The Dance of Death, Anna Christie.
PICTURES: Baby Doll (debut, 1956), A Face in the Crowd, Time Limit, Pork Chop Hill, King of Kings, Hero's Island, Sweet Bird of Youth, Critic's Choice, The Cincinnati Kid, One Spy Too Many, You're a Big Boy Now, Beach Red, Sol Madrid, Beyond the Law, Coming Apart, Tropic of Cancer, Maidstone, Slaughter, Payday, Crazy Joe, Birch Interval, The Man Who Fell to Earth, Nasty Habits, The Private Files of J. Edgar Hoover, Coma, The Seduction of Joe Tynan, Heartland, One Trick Pony, First Family, A Stranger is Watching, The Beastmaster, Jinxed, Airplane II: The Sequel, Cross Creek (Acad. Award nom.), Misunderstood, Songwriter, Flashpoint, City Heat, Summer Rental, Beer, Extreme Prejudice, Nadine, The Telephone (also dir.), Cold Feet, Hit List, Blind Curve, The Hunt for Red October, Defending Your Life, Silence Like Glass, Beautiful Dreamers, Hard Promises, Robocop 3, Dolly Dearest, Where the Rivers Flow North, Canadian Bacon, How to Make an American Quilt, Down Periscope.
TELEVISION: *Series*: The Larry Sanders Show (Emmy Awatd, 1996). *Movies*: The President's Plane Is Missing, Attack on Terror: The FBI vs. the Ku Klux Klan, Betrayal, Steel Cowboy, A Shining Season, Sophia Loren—Her Own Story, Rape and Marriage—The Rideout Case, Laguna Heat, When She Says No, The Execution, The Atlanta Child Murders, Manhunt for Claude Dallas, J. Edgar Hoover, The King of Love, April Morning, Sweet Bird of Youth, Pair of Aces, By Dawn's Early Light, Another Pair of Aces, My Son Johnny, Death Hits the Jackpot, T Bone N Weasel, A Mother's Right: The Elizabeth Morgan Story, Dead Ahead: The Exxon Valdez Disaster, She Stood Alone: The Tailhook Scandal, Letter to My Killer. *Mini-Series*: Blind Ambition, The Blue and the Gray, Heaven & Hell: North and South Book III, Heart of a Child.

TORNATORE, GIUSEPPE
Director. b. Bagheria, Sicily, Italy, 1956. Made directorial debut at age 16 with short film Il Carretto. 1978- 85, served as pres. of the CLTC filmmaking cooperative.
PICTURES: The Professor (debut, 1986), Cinema Paradiso, Everybody's Fine, The Blue Dog (segment), Especially on Sunday (segment), A Pure Formality.
TELEVISION: Portrait of a Thief, Metting With Francesco Rosi, Sicilian Writers and Films, Il Diario di Guttuso, Ethnic Minorities in Sicily (Salerno Film Fest. Prize), A Hundred Days in Palermo (also writer, 2nd unit dir.).

TOTTER, AUDREY
Actress. b. Joliet, IL, Dec. 20, 1918. In many stage plays. On radio 1939-44.
THEATER: Copperhead, Stage Door, Late Christopher Bean, My Sister Eileen.
PICTURES: Main Street After Dark (debut, 1944), Her Highness and the Bellboy, Dangerous Partners, The Sailor Takes a Wife, Adventure, The Hidden Eye, The Secret Heart, The Postman Always Rings Twice, Cockeyed Miracle, Lady in the Lake, Beginning or the End, Unsuspected, High Wall, The Saxon Charm, Alias Nick Beal, Any Number Can Play, Tension, The Set-Up, Under the Gun, The Blue Veil, Sellout, F.B.I. Girl, Assignment-Paris, My Pal Gus, Woman They Almost Lynched, Cruisin' Down the River, Man in the Dark, Mission Over Korea, Champ for a Day, Massacre Canyon, Women's Prison, A Bullet for Joey, Vanishing American, Ghost Diver, Jet Attack, Man or Gun, The Carpetbaggers, Harlow, Chubasco, The Apple Dumpling Gang Rides Again.
TELEVISION: *Series*: Cimarron City, Our Man Higgins, Medical Center (1972-76). *Movies*: The Outsider, U.M.C., The Nativity, The Great Cash Giveaway, City Killer. Guest: Murder, She Wrote.

TOWERS, CONSTANCE
Actress. b. Whitefish, MT, May 20, 1934. m. John Gavin, actor and former U.S. Ambassador to Mexico. e. Juilliard Sch. of Music. Stage work on Broadway and tour.
THEATER: B'way: Ari, Anya, Engagement Baby, The King and I (1977-79 opp. Yul Brynner). *Regional*: Steel Magnolias, Follies.
PICTURES: Horse Soldiers, Sergeant Rutledge, Fate Is the Hunter, Shock Corridor, Naked Kiss, Sylvester, Fast Forward, Nutty Nut, The Next Karate Kid, The Relic.
TELEVISION: *Series*: Love Is a Many Splendored Thing, VTV, Capitol, 2000 Malibu Road. *Mini-Series*: On Wings of Eagles, Sands of Time. *Guest*: Home Show, The Loner, Murder, She Wrote, Hour Mag, MacGyver, Designing Women, Midnight Caller, Matlock, Baywatch, Prince of Bel Air, Thunder in Paradise, L.A. Law, Civil Wars, Frasier, Robin's Nest, Caroline In the City, The Young & the Restless.

TOWERS, HARRY ALAN
Executive, Producer. b. London, England, 1920.
PICTURES: Sanders of the River (also s.p.), Code Seven Victim Five (also s.p.), City of Fear, Mozambique, Coast of Skeletons, Sandy the Seal, 24 Hours to Kill, The Face of Fu Manchu, Ten Little Indians, Marrakesh, Circus of Fear, The Brides of Fu Manchu, Sumuru, Five Golden Dragons, The Vengeance of Fu Manchu, Jules Verne's Rocket to the Moon, House of a Thousand Dolls, The Face of Eve, Blood of Fu Manchu, 99 Women, Girl From Rio, Marquis de Sade's Justine, Castle of Fu Manchu, Venus in Furs, Philosophy in the Boudoir, Eugenie, Dorian Gray, Count Dracula, The Bloody Judge. Black Beauty, Night Hair Child, The Call of the Wild, Treasure Island, White Fang, Death in Persepolis, Ten Little Indians, End of Innocence, Black Cobra, Black Velvet— White Silk, Night of the High Tide, King Solomon's Treasure, Shape of Things to Come, Klondike Fever, Fanny Hill, Frank and I, Black Venus, Christmas, Black Arrow, Pompeii, Love Circles, Lightning—The White Stallion, Gor, Outlaw of Gor, Dragonard, Skeleton Coast, Master of Dragonard Hill, Nam, Fire With Fire, Jekyll and Hyde, River of Death, Cobra Strike, The Howling IV: The Original Nightmare, Skeleton Coast, Edge of Sanity, Ten Little Indians, Platoon Leader, Captive Rage, American Ninja III: Blood Hunt, The Fall of the House of Usher, Edgar Allan Poe's Buried Alive, Phantom of the Opera, Oddball Hall, Terror of Manhattan, The Lost World, Return to the Lost World, Black Museum, Golden Years of Sherlock Holmes, The Mangler, Midnight in St. Petersburg, Bullet to Beijing (The Return of Harry Palmer), Cry the Beloved Country, China Bill, She, Stanley & Livingstone, The Zodiak Conspiracy.

TOWNE, ROBERT
Writer, Director, Producer. b. Los Angeles, CA, 1936. Raised in San Pedro. Was member of Warren Beatty's production staff on Bonnie and Clyde and contributed to that screenplay. Also uncredited, wrote Pacino-Brando garden scene in The Godfather; script doctor on Marathon Man, The Missouri Breaks and others.
PICTURES: *Writer*: The Last Woman on Earth (as Edward Wain), The Tomb of Ligeia, Villa Rides, The Last Detail, Chinatown (Academy Award, 1974), Shampoo (co-s.p.), The Yazuka (co-s.p.), Personal Best (also dir., prod.), Greystoke: The Legend of Tarzan (s.p., uncredited), Tequila Sunrise (also dir.), Days of Thunder, The Two Jakes, The Firm (co-s.p.), Love Affair (co-s.p.), Mission: Impossible (co-s.p.).

TOWNSEND, ROBERT
Actor, Producer, Director, Writer. b. Chicago, IL, Feb. 6, 1957. e.Illinois State U., Hunter Coll. Veteran of Experimental Black Actors Guild and Second City. TV commercials; stand-up comedy at NY Improvisation; taped Evening at the Improv.
PICTURES: *Actor*: Cooley High (debut, 1974), Willie and Phil, Streets of Fire, A Soldier's Story, American Flyers, Odd Jobs, Ratboy, Hollywood Shuffle (also prod., dir., co-s.p.), Eddie Murphy Raw (dir. only), The Mighty Quinn, That's Adequate, The Five Heartbeats (also dir., exec. prod., co-s.p.), The Meteor Man (also dir., s.p., co-prod.).
TELEVISION: *Series*: Another Page (PBS series), Townsend Television, The Parent 'Hood (also co-creator, co-exec. prod.). *Specials*: Robert Townsend and His Partners in Crime, Take No Prisoners: Robert Townsend and His Partners in Crime II (HBO). *Movies*: Women at West Point, Senior Trip!, In Love With an Older Woman.

TRAMBUKIS, WILLIAM J.
Executive. b. Providence, R.I., July 26, 1926. e. Mt. Pleasant Bus. Col. Began career as usher with Loew's in Providence, RI, 1941. Served 1943-46 with Navy Seabees. Recipient of Quigley Awards. Managed/supervised Loew's Theatres in several New England cities, Harrisburg, PA, Syracuse, Rochester, Buffalo, NY, Washington, DC, Richmond, Norfolk, VA, Toronto, Canada, Atlanta, GA. Appt. Loew's NorthEastern Division mgr. 1964, Loew's gen. mgr. 1975: v.p. in 1976; sr. v.p., 1985. Retired, 1987.

TRAVANTI, DANIEL J.
Actor. b. Kenosha, WI, March 7, 1940. e. U. of Wisconsin (B.A.), Loyola Marymount Univ. (M.A.), Yale Sch. of Drama. Woodrow Wilson fellow, 1961. Formerly acted as Dan Travanty. On stage in Twigs, Othello, I Never Sang for My Father, Only Kidding, The Taming of the Shrew, Les Liaisons Dangereuses, A Touch of the Poet, Antony & Cleopatra.
PICTURES: St. Ives, Midnight Crossing, Millenium, Megaville, Weep No More My Lady, Just Cause, Siao Yu, Who Killed Teddy Bear.
TELEVISION: Series: General Hospital, Hill Street Blues (Emmy Awards, 1981, 1982; Golden Globe Award, 1981), Missing Persons. Movies: The Love War, Adam, Aurora, Murrow, Adam: His Song Continues, I Never Sang for My Father, Fellow Traveler, Howard Beach: Making the Case for Murder, Tagget, Eyes of a Witness, The Christmas Stallion, In the Shadows Someone's Watching, My Name is Kate, Wasp Woman, A Case of Libel, To Sir With Love II.

TRAVIS, NANCY
Actress. b. New York, NY, Sept. 21, 1961. Raised in Baltimore, MD, and Farmingham, MA. e. NYU. Attended Circle-in-the-Square Theatre school. Acted with NY Amer. Jewish Theatre before landing role in touring prod. of Brighton Beach Memoirs.
THEATER: NY: It's Hard to Be a Jew, The Signal Season of Dummy Hoy, I'm Not Rappaport (B'way). Tour: Brighton Beach Memoirs. La Jolla Playhouse: My Children My Africa, Three Sisters.
PICTURES: Three Men and a Baby (debut, 1987), Married to the Mob, Eight Men Out, Internal Affairs, Loose Cannons, Air America, Three Men and a Little Lady, Passed Away, Chaplin, The Vanishing, So I Married an Axe Murderer, Greedy, Destiny Turns on the Radio, Fluke, Bogus.
TELEVISION: Series: Almost Perfect. Movies: Malice in Wonderland, Harem, I'll Be Home for Christmas, Body Language. Special: High School Narc (ABC Afterschool Special).

TRAVOLTA, JOHN
Actor. b. Englewood, NJ, Feb. 18, 1954. m. actress Kelly Preston. First stage role in Who Will Save the Plowboy? Did off-B'way prod. of Rain; then on Broadway in Grease (also on tour for 10 months), Over Here (with the Andrew Sisters).
PICTURES: The Devil's Rain (debut, 1975), Carrie, Saturday Night Fever (Acad. Award nom.), Grease, Moment by Moment, Urban Cowboy, Blow Out, Staying Alive, Two of a Kind, Perfect, The Experts, Look Who's Talking, Look Who's Talking Too, Shout, Eyes of an Angel, Look Who's Talking Now, Pulp Fiction (Acad. Award nom.), White Man's Burden, Get Shorty (Golden Globe winner), Broken Arrow, Phenomenon, Michael.
TELEVISION: Series: Welcome Back Kotter. Movies: The Boy in the Plastic Bubble, Chains of Gold, Boris & Natasha (cameo). Special: The Dumb Waiter. Guest: Emergency, Owen Marshall--Counselor at Law, The Rookies, Medical Center.

TREBOT, JEAN-PIERRE
Executive. Exec. dir., The Friars Club.

TREMAYNE, LES
Actor. b. London, England, Apr. 16, 1913. e. Northwestern U., Chicago Art Inst., Columbia U., UCLA. First professional appearance in British mp., 1916, with mother; stock, little theatres, vaudeville, 1925-40; entered radio field, 1930. Blue ribbon award for best perf. of the month for A Man Called Peter; dir. Hollywood Rep. Theatre, 1957; pres. Hollywood Actors' Council, 1951-58; chmn. Actors Div. workshop com. Acad. TV Arts & Sciences; mem.: The Workshop Comm. of the Hollywood M.P. & TV Museum Comm. One of 17 founding members, Pacific Pioneer Broadcasters; Life member, Actor's Fund; charter/founding mem. AFTRA, Chicago local. (delegate to most conventions since 1938). mem. Local, L.A, and Natl. AFTRA bds.
THEATER: Woman in My House, Errand of Mercy, You Are There, One Man's Family, Heartbeat Theatre, The First Nighter (lead 7 yrs.); on Broadway in Heads or Tails, Detective Story.
PICTURES: The Racket, Blue Veil, Francis Goes to West Point, It Grows on Trees, I Love Melvin, Under the Red Sea, Dream Wife, War of the Worlds, Susan Slept Here, Lieutenant Wore Skirts, Unguarded Moment, Everything But the Truth, Monolith Monsters, Perfect Furlough, North by Northwest, Say One for Me, The Gallant Hours, The Angry Red Planet, The Story of Ruth, The Fortune Cookie, Daffy Duck's Movie: Fantastic Island (voice), Starchaser (voice).
TELEVISION: Lux Video Theatre, 20th Century-Fox Hour, Navy Log, One Man's Family, Meet Mille, The Millionaire, The Whistler, Truth or Consequences, NBC Matinee, The Girl, O'Henry series, Rin Tin Tin, Bachelor Father, The Texan, Adventures of Ellery Queen, Court of Last Resort, Rifleman, State Trooper, Rescue 8, June Allyson-Dupont Show, Wagon Train, M Squad, Hitchcock Presents, Mr. Ed., Perry Mason.

TREVOR, CLAIRE
Actress. b. New York, NY, Mar. 8, 1910. e. American Acad. of Dramatic Arts; Columbia U. On Broadway in Party's Over, Whistling in the Dark, Big Two. On radio in Big Town for 4 yrs.
PICTURES: Life in the Raw (debut, 1933), The Last Trail, Mad Game, Jimmy and Sally, Hold That Girl, Baby Take a Bow, Elinore Norton, Wild Gold, Dante's Inferno, Spring Tonic, Navy Wife, Black Sleep, Human Cargo, My Marriage, The Song and Dance Man, To Mary—With Love, 15 Maiden Lane, Career Woman, Star for a Night, One Mile From Heaven, Time Out for Romance, Second Honeymoon, Big Town Girl, Dead End (Acad. Award nom.), King of Gamblers, The Amazing Dr. Clitterhouse, Walking Down Broadway, Valley of the Giants, Two of a Kind, I Stole a Million, Stagecoach, Allegheny Uprising, Dark Command, Texas, Honky Tonk, Street of Chance, The Adventures of Martin Eden, Crossroads, Woman of the Town, The Desperadoes, Good Luck Mr. Yates, Murder My Sweet, Johnny Angel, Crack-Up, The Bachelor's Daughters, Born to Kill, Raw Deal, The Babe Ruth Story, The Velvet Touch, Key Largo (Academy Award, best supporting actress, 1948), The Lucky Stiff, Borderline, Best of the Bad Men, Hard Fast and Beautiful, Hoodlum Empire, My Man and I, Stop You're Killing Me, The Stranger Wore a Gun, The High and the Mighty (Acad. Award nom.), Man Without a Star, Lucy Gallant, The Mountain, Marjorie Morningstar, Two Weeks in Another Town, The Stripper, How to Murder Your Wife, The Capetown Affair, Kiss Me Goodbye.
TELEVISION: Specials/Movies: If You Knew Elizabeth, Dodsworth (Emmy Award, 1957), No Sad Songs for Me, Ladies in Retirement, Breaking Home Ties. Guest: Alfred Hitchcock Presents, The Untouchables, Love Boat, Murder She Wrote.

TREXLER, CHARLES B.
Exhibitor. b. Wadesboro, NC, Feb. 8, 1916. 1937-48 was practicing CPA except for 2 yrs. in U.S. Army in WWII. Joined Stewart & Everett Theatres in 1948 as controller. 1953 named gen. mgr.; 1954, exec. v.p., treas.; 1962 named pres.; 1983, named bd. chmn.; former bd. chmn., NATO of North and South Carolina; v.p. & bd. mem., National NATO.

TRIKONIS, GUS
Director. b. New York, NY. Started career in chorus of West Side Story on B'way. Turned to directing, making low-budget weekenders (films shot in 12 days only on weekends).
PICTURES: Moonshine County Express, The Evil, Touched by Love, Take This Job and Shove It.
TELEVISION: Movies: The Darker Side of Terror, She's Dressed To Kill, Flamingo Road (pilot), Elvis and the Beauty Queen, Twirl, Miss All-American Beauty, Dempsey, First Affair, Malice in Wonderland, Love on the Run, Open Admissions, The Great Pretender. Mini-Series: The Last Convertible (co-dir.). Episode: Twilight Zone (1985).

TRINTIGNANT, JEAN-LOUIS
Actor. b. Aix-en-Provence, France, Dec. 11, 1930. m. Nadine Marquand, director. Theatre debut: 1951, To Each According to His Hunger. Then Mary Stuart, Macbeth (at the Comedie de Saint-Etienne). 1955 screen debut.
PICTURES: Si Tous Les Gars du Monde, La Loi des Rues, And God Created Woman, Club de Femmes, Les Liaisons Dangereuses, L'Estate Violente, Austerlitz, La Millieme Fenetre, Pleins Feux sur L'Assasin, Coeur Battant, L'Atlantide, The Game of Truth, Horace 62, Les Sept Peches Capitaux (7 Capital Sins), Le Combat dans L'Ile, The Easy Life, Il Successo, Nutty Naughty Chateau, Les Pas Perdus, La Bonne Occase, Mata-Hari, Meurtre a L'Italienne, La Longue Marche, Un Jour a Paris, Is Paris Burning?, The Sleeping Car Murders, A Man and a Woman, Enigma, Safari Diamants, Trans-Europ-Express, Mon Amour, Mon Amour, Un Homme a Abattre, La Morte Ha Fatto L'Uovo, Les Biches, Grand Silence, Z, Ma Nuit Chez Maud (My Night at Maud's), The Conformist, The Crook, Without Apparent Motive, The Outside Man, The French Conspiracy, Simon the Swiss, Agression, Les Violons du Bal, The Sunday Woman, Under Fire, La Nuit de Varennes, Long Live Life!, Next Summer, Departure, Return, The Man With the Silver Eyes, Femme Je Personne, Confidentially Yours, A Man and a Woman: 20 Years Later, La Vallee Fantome; Rendezvous, Bunker Palace Hotel, Three Colors: Red, The City of Lost Children, Fiesta.

TRIPP, STEVEN L.
Executive. b. Worthington, MN, Sept. 29, 1958. e. St. Cloud Community Coll. Managed local hometown theatres from 1978-82, then promoted to operation mgr., Tentelino Enterprises Circuit. Became general mgr. after Tentelino was purchased by Lakes & Rivers Cinemas in 1989. 1994-present, general mgr. and film buyer.

TRIPPLEHORN, JEANNE
Actress. b. Tulsa, OK, 1964. e. Julliard Sch. of Drama. On stage at NY's Public Theatre in The Big Funk, 'Tis Pity She's a Whore.
PICTURES: Basic Instinct (debut, 1992), The Night We Never Met, The Firm, Waterworld.
TELEVISION: Movie: The Perfect Tribute.

TRUMBULL, DOUGLAS
Cinematographer, Director, Writer. b. Los Angeles, CA, Apr. 8, 1942. Inventor Showscan Film process. Did Special Effects for Universal Studios attraction Back to the Future: The Ride; Luxor Live, Theatre of Time, In Search of the Obelisk. Director: Showscan short films New Magic, Let's Go, Big Ball, Leonardo's Dream, Night of the Dreams, Chevy Collector. Vice chmn., The Imax Corp.; pres. & CEO, Ridefilm Corp.; pres., Entertainment Design Workshop.
PICTURES: 2001: A Space Odyssey, Silent Running (also dir.), The Andromeda Strain, Close Encounters of the Third Kind, Star Trek: The Motion Picture, Blade Runner, Brainstorm (also dir., prod.).

TUBB, BARRY
Actor. b. Snyder, TX, 1963. Former rodeo star. Studied acting at Amer. Conservatory Theatre in SF.
THEATER: Sweet Sue (B'way), The Authentic Life of Billy the Kid.
PICTURES: Mask, The Legend of Billie Jean, Top Gun, Valentino Returns, Warm Summer Rain, Guilty By Suspicion.
TELEVISION: Series: Bay City Blues. Guest: Hill Street Blues. Movies: Consenting Adult, The Billionaire Boys Club, Without Her Consent. Mini-Series: Lonesome Dove, Return to Lonesome Dove.

TUCCI, STANLEY
Actor. b. Peekskill, NY. e. SUNY.
THEATER: B'way: The Misanthrope, Brighton Beach Memoirs, The Iceman Cometh. Moon Over Miami, Scapin, Dalliance, Balm in Gilead.
PICTURES: Who's That Girl, Monkey Shines, Slaves of New York, Fear Anxiety and Depression, The Feud, Quick Change, Men of Respect, Billy Bathgate, Beethoven, Prelude to a Kiss, The Public Eye, In the Soup, Undercover Blues, The Pelican Brief, It Should Happen to You, Mrs. Parker and the Vicious Circle, Kiss of Death, A Modern Affair, Big Night (also co-dir.).
TELEVISION: Series: The Street, Wiseguy, Murder One. Guest: Miami Vice, The Equalizer, thirtysomething, Equal Justice.

TUCKER, MELVILLE
Executive. b. New York, NY, Mar. 4, 1916. e. Princeton U. Asst. purchasing agent Consolidated Laboratories, N.Y., 1934-36; sound effects & picture ed., Republic Productions, Inc. 1936-8; then asst. production mgr. & first asst. dir., 1938-42; served in U.S. Army 1942-46; asst. prod. Republic 1946; assoc. producer, 1947-52; prod., Universal 1952-54; prod. exec. v.p., Universal, 1955-70; production exec. U-I, 1954-71; became prod.Verdon Prods., 1971.
PICTURES: Prod.: The Missourians, Thunder in God's Country, Rodeo King and the Senorita, Utah Wagon Train, Drums Across the River, Black Shield of Falworth, A Warm December, Uptown Saturday Night, Let's Do It Again, A Piece of the Action. Exec. prod.: Stir Crazy, Hanky Panky, Fast Forward.

TUCKER, MICHAEL
Actor. b. Baltimore, MD, Feb. 6, 1944. m. actress Jill Eikenberry. e. Carnegie Tech. Drama Sch. Worked in regional theater (Long Wharf, Washington's Arena Stage, Milwaukee Rep.) and with the NY Shakespeare Festival in Trelawney of the Wells, Comedy of Errors, Measure for Measure, The Merry Wives of Windsor. Also prod. revival of El Grande de Coca Cola (1986).
THEATER: Moonchildren, Modigliani, The Goodbye People, The Rivals, Mother Courage, Waiting for Godot, Oh What a Lovely War, I'm Not Rappaport (American Place Theatre).
PICTURES: A Night Full of Rain (debut, 1977), An Unmarried Woman, Eyes of Laura Mars, Diner, The Goodbye People, The Purple Rose of Cairo, Radio Days, Tin Men, Checking Out, For Love or Money, D2: The Mighty Ducks.
TELEVISION: Series: L.A. Law. Movies: Concealed Enemies, Vampire, Assault and Matrimony, Day One, Spy, Too Young to Die?, Casey's Gift: For Love of a Child, The Secret Life of Archie's Wife, In the Nick of Time, A Town Torn Apart. Specials: Love Sex... and Marriage, A Family Again, On Hope. Guest: Hill Street Blues.

TUCKERMAN, DAVID R.
Executive. b. Perth Amboy, NJ, Nov. 9, 1946. e. Monmouth Coll., F.L.U. 1967-70; B.S.B.A. Entered industry with A.I.T. Theatres, 1967; gen. mgr., Music Makers Theatres, 1973; v.p., Leigh Group, MMT, head film buyer, 1976; sr. v.p., MMT, 1980; Loews Film Buyer, 1986; Loews (now Sony) v.p. film, 1993. Member: SMPTE, Variety Int., MPBC, AFI, Motion Picture Pioneers.

TUGGLE, RICHARD
Director, Writer. b. Coral Gables, FL, Aug. 8, 1948. e. U. Virginia, B.A. 1970. Wrote screenplays before directorial debut with Tightrope, 1984.
PICTURES: Escape from Alcatraz (s.p.), Tightrope (dir., s.p.), Out of Bounds (dir.).

TUNE, TOMMY
Actor, Director, Choreographer, Dancer. b. Wichita Falls, TX, Feb. 28, 1939. e. Univ of Texas at Austin. Began professional career dancing in chorus of B'way shows (Baker Street, A Joyful Noise, How Now Dow Jones, etc.). Recipient of 9 Tony Awards.
THEATER: Performer: Seesaw, My One and Only, Bye Bye Birdie (tour), Tommy Tune Tonite! (B'way & tour). Director and/or choreographer: The Club, Cloud 9, The Best Little Whorehouse in Texas, Nine, A Day in Hollywood/A Night in the Ukraine, Stepping Out, My One and Only, Grand Hotel, The Will Rogers Follies.
PICTURES: Hello Dolly!, The Boy Friend.
TELEVISION: Series: Dean Martin Presents the Goldiggers; also numerous specials and Tony Award Shows.

TURMAN, LAWRENCE
Producer. b. Los Angeles, CA, Nov. 28, 1926. e. UCLA. In textile business 5 years, then joined Kurt Frings Agency; left in 1960 to form Millar-Turman Prods.
PICTURES: Prod.: The Young Doctors, I Could Go on Singing, The Best Man. Formed own prod. co., Lawrence Turman, Inc., to make The Flim-Flam Man, The Graduate, Pretty Poison (exec. prod.), The Great White Hope, The Marriage of a Young Stockbroker (also dir.), The Nickel Ride (exec. prod.), The Drowning Pool, First Love, Heroes, Walk Proud, Tribute, Caveman, The Thing, Second Thoughts (also dir.), Mass Appeal, The Mean Season, Short Circuit, Running Scared, Short Circuit 2, Full Moon in Blue Water, Gleaming the Cube, The Getaway, The River Wild.
TELEVISION: Co-prod. with David Foster: The Gift of Love, News at Eleven, Between Two Brothers. Prod.: The Morning After, She Lives, Unwed Father. Co-exec. prod.: Jesse.

TURNER, FREDERICK
Executive. b. London, England. Ent. m.p. ind. 1946. Early career with Eagle-Lion before transferring to Rank Overseas Film Distributors, then Rank Film Distributors. Became financial controller and appt. managing director 1981. Currently responsible for Film Investments and Distribution, UK and Overseas, covering all media.

TURNER, JANINE
Actress. r.n. Janine Gauntt. b. Lincoln, NE, Dec. 6, 1962. Raised in Texas. Studied dance, joined Forth Worth Ballet. Started modeling at age 15 in NYC, enrolled in Professional Children's School. First major acting job was on series Dallas. On stage in Full Moon and High Tide in the Ladies Room.
PICTURES: Young Doctors in Love, Knights of the City, Tai-Pan, Monkey Shines, Steel Magnolias, The Ambulance, Cliffhanger.
TELEVISION: Series: Behind the Screen, General Hospital (1982-83), Northern Exposure. Guest: The Love Boat, The A-Team, Mike Hammer.

TURNER, KATHLEEN
Actress. b. Springfield, MO, June 19, 1954. e. U. of Maryland, SMSU.
THEATER: B'way: Gemini, Cat on a Hot Tin Roof (Theatre World Award), Indiscretions. Regional: Camille (Long Wharf), A Midsummer Night's Dream (DC), Toyer (DC).
PICTURES: Body Heat (debut, 1981), The Man With Two Brains, Romancing the Stone, Crimes of Passion, A Breed Apart, Prizzi's Honor, The Jewel of the Nile, Peggy Sue Got Married (Acad. Award nom.), Julia and Julia, Switching Channels, Who Framed Roger Rabbit (voice), The Accidental Tourist, The War of the Roses, V.I. Warshawski, House of Cards, Undercover Blues, Serial Mom, Naked in New York, Moonlight & Valentino.
TELEVISION: Series: The Doctors. Movie: Friends at Last. Special: Dear America: Letters Home From Vietnam (reader). Director: Leslie's Folly.

TURNER, TED (ROBERT EDWARD)
Executive. b. Cincinnati, OH., Nov. 19, 1938. e. Brown U. m. actress Jane Fonda. Began career in Savannah in family's outdoor adv. business, selling space on billboards. Inherited co. in 1963 and in 1970 entered broadcasting with purchase of a failing TV station in Atlanta which he turned into WTBS, a "superstation" which in 1994 reached 95% of U.S. homes equipped with cable. 1980, established CNN a 24-hr. cable news service. Purchased MGM film library. Co-owner of two professional sports teams in Atlanta: Braves (baseball) and Hawks (basketball). Started Headline News, 1982; CNN International 1985; Turner Network Television 1988; Sportsouth, 1990; Cartoon Network in 1992; Turner Classic Movies, 1994; CNNfn Financial Network, 1995.

TURNER, TINA
Singer, Actress. r.n. Annie Mae Bullock. b. Brownsville, TX, Nov. 26, 1939. Previously married to Ike Turner and appeared with him on road in Ike and Tina Turner Revue. Many hit records. Autobiography: I Tina.

PICTURES: Gimme Shelter, Taking Off, Soul to Soul, Tommy, Sound of the City, Mad Max Beyond Thunderdome, What's Love Got to Do With It (vocals), Last Action Hero.
TELEVISION: *Special*: Tina—Live From Rio.

TURTURRO, JOHN
Actor. b. Brooklyn, NY, Feb. 28, 1957. e. SUNY/New Paltz; Yale Drama School, 1983. m. actress Katherine Borowitz. Worked in regional theater and off-B'way.
THEATER: Danny and the Deep Blue Sea (Obie & Theatre World Awards, 1985), Men Without Dates, Tooth of the Crime, La Puta Viva, Chaos and Hard Times, The Bald Soprano, Of Mice and Men, The Resistible Rise of Arturo Ui, Death of a Salesman (B'way debut, 1984).
PICTURES: Raging Bull (debut, 1980), Exterminator II, The Flamingo Kid, Desperately Seeking Susan, To Live and Die in L.A., Hannah and Her Sisters, Gung Ho, Off Beat, The Color of Money, The Sicilian, Five Corners, Do the Right Thing, Mo' Better Blues, State of Grace, Miller's Crossing, Men of Respect, Jungle Fever, Barton Fink (Cannes Film Fest. Award), Brain Donors, Mac (also dir., co-s.p.), Fearless, Being Human, Quiz Show, Search and Destroy, Clockers, Unstrung Heroes, Girl 6, Grace of My Heart.
TELEVISION: *Mini-Series*: The Fortunate Pilgrim. *Movie:* Backtrack.

TUSHINGHAM, RITA
Actress. b. Liverpool, England, March 14, 1942. Student at Liverpool Playhouse.
THEATER: The Giveaway, Lorna and Ted, Mistress of Novices, The Undiscovered Country, Mysteries.
PICTURES: A Taste of Honey (debut, 1961; BFA Award), The Leather Boys, A Place to Go, Girl With Green Eyes, The Knack... and How to Get It, Doctor Zhivago, The Trap, Smashing Time, Diamonds for Breakfast, The Guru, The Bed Sitting Room, Straight on Till Morning, The Case of Laura C., Where Do You Go From Here?, Situation, Instant Coffee, The Human Factor, Rachel's Man, The Slum Boy, The Black Journal, Bread Butter and Jam, Mysteries, Felix Krull, Spaghetti Thing, Dream to Believe, Flying, Seeing Red, The Housekeeper, Resurrected, Dante and Beatrice in Liverpool, Hard Days Hard Nights, Paper Marriage, Desert Lunch, An Awfully Big Adventure, The Boy From Mercury.
TELEVISION: *U.S.*: Green Eyes, Bread, Sunday Pursuit, Gutt Ein Journalist, Hamburg Poison.

TUTIN, DOROTHY
Actress. b. London, Eng., Apr. 8, 1930. e. St. Catherine's Sch. Bramley, Guildford (Surrey). Stage debut in The Thistle & the Rose, 1949.
THEATER: Much Ado About Nothing, The Living Room, I Am a Camera, The Lark, Wild Duck, Juliet, Ophelia, Viola, Portia, Cressida, Rosalind, The Devils, Once More With Feeling, The Cherry Orchard, Victoria Regina-Portrait of a Queen, Old Times, Peter Pan, What Every Woman Knows, Month in the Country, Macbeth, Antony and Cleopatra, Undiscovered Country, Reflections, After the Lions, Ballerina, A Kind of Alaska, Are You Sitting Comfortably?, Chalk Garden, Brighton Beach Memoirs, Thursday's Ladies, The Browning Version, A Little Night Music, Henry VIII, Party Time, The Seagull, Getting Married.
PICTURES: The Importance of Being Earnest, The Beggar's Opera, A Tale of Two Cities, Cromwell, Savage Messiah, The Shooting Party, Murder with Mirrors, Great Moments in Aviation, The Great Kandinsky.
TELEVISION: Living Room, Victoria Regina, Invitation to a Voyage, Antigone, Colombe, Carrington V.C., The Hollow Crown, Scent of Fear, From Chekhov With Love, Anne Boleyn in The Six Wives of Henry VIII, Flotsam and Jetsam, Mother & Son, South Riding, Willow Cabins, Ghosts, Sister Dora, The Double Dealer, The Combination, La Ronde, Tales of the Unexpected, 10 Downing Street, Life After Death, King Lear, Landscape, The Father, The Demon Lover, Robin Hood, All Creatures Great and Small, A Kind of Alaska, The Bill, Lease of Death, Anglo-Saxon Attitudes, Body and Soul, Jake's Progress, Indian Summer.

TWAINE, MICHAEL
Actor, Director. b. New York, NY, Nov. 1, 1939. e. Ohio State U. Served U.S. Army. While studying with Lee Strasberg, worked as private detective, school teacher. Made stage debut City Center, 1956, in Mr. Roberts. Became village coffee house and club comedian 1968 to 1972.
PICTURES: Marriage Italian Style (voice), American Soap, Blood Bath, F.I.S.T., Cheap Shots, Platoon (voice), Billy Bathgate (voice).
TELEVISION: The Silent Drum, Starsky & Hutch, Wonder Woman, Streets of San Francisco, Soap, Lou Grant, Diff'rent Strokes, Nurse, Stalk the Wild Child, The Courage and the Passion, Eischied, America's Most Wanted, Beyond the Universe.

TWIGGY
Actress. r.n. Leslie Hornby. b. London, England, Sept. 19, 1949. m. actor Leigh Lawson. At 17 regarded as world's lead-ing high fashion model. Made m.p. debut in The Boy Friend, 1971. Starred in many London West End Shows, including Cinderella and Captain Beaky Presents. 1983: on Broadway in musical, My One and Only.
PICTURES: The Boyfriend (debut, 1971), W, There Goes the Bride, The Blues Brothers, The Doctor and the Devils, Club Paradise, Madame Sousatzka, Istanbul.
TELEVISION: *Series*: Twiggy, Twiggy and Friends, Juke Box (U.S.), Princesses (U.S.). *Specials*: Pygmalion, Sun Child, Young Charlie Chaplin. *Movies*: The Diamond Trap, Body Bags.

TYLER, LIV
Actress. b. July, 1977. Daughter of musician Steven Tyler. Began as a model at age 14.
PICTURES: Silent Fall (debut), Empire Records, Heavy, Stealing Beauty, That Thing You Do!, Inventing the Abbotts.

TYRRELL, SUSAN
Actress. b. San Francisco, CA, 1946. Made first prof. appearance with Art Carney in summer theatre tour prod. of Time Out for Ginger. Worked in off-B'way prods. and as waitress in coffee house before attracting attention in Lincoln Center Repertory Co. prods. of A Cry of Players, The Time of Your Life, Camino Real.
THEATER: The Knack, Futz, Father's Day, A Coupla White Chicks Sitting Around Talking, The Rotten Life.
PICTURES: Shoot Out (debut, 1971), The Steagle, Been Down So Long It Looks Like Up to Me, Shoot Out, Fat City (Acad. Award nom.), Catch My Soul, Zandy's Bride, The Killer Inside Me, Islands in the Stream, Andy Warhol's Bad, I Never Promised You a Rose Garden, Another Man Another Chance, September 30, 1955, Racquet, Loose Shoes, Forbidden Zone, Subway Riders, Night Warning, Fast-Walking, Liar's Moon, Tales of Ordinary Madness, Fire and Ice (voice), Angel, The Killers, Avenging Angel, Flesh and Blood, The Chipmunk Adventure (voice), The Offspring, Big Top Pee-Wee, Tapeheads, The Underachievers, Far From Home, Cry-Baby, Motorama, Powder.
TELEVISION: *Series*: Open All Night. *Movies*: Lady of the House, Midnight Lace, Jealousy, Thompson's Last Run, Poker Alice, The Christmas Star, Windmills of the Gods. *Mini-Series*: If Tomorrow Comes.

TYSON, CICELY
Actress. b. New York, NY, Dec. 19, 1933. e. NYU. Studied at Actor's Studio. Former secretary and model. Co-founder, Dance Theatre of Harlem.
THEATER: The Blacks, Moon on a Rainbow Shawl, Tiger Tiger Burning Bright, The Corn Is Green.
PICTURES: A Man Called Adam (debut, 1966), The Comedians, The Heart Is a Lonely Hunter, Sounder (Acad. Award nom.), The Blue Bird, The River Niger, A Hero Ain't Nothin' But a Sandwich, The Concorde—Airport '79, Bustin' Loose, Fried Green Tomatoes, The Grass Harp.
TELEVISION: *Series*: East Side West Side, The Guiding Light, Sweet Justice. *Movies*: Marriage: Year One, The Autobiography of Miss Jane Pittman (Emmy Award, 1974), Just An Old Sweet Song, Wilma, A Woman Called Moses, The Marva Collins Story, Benny's Place, Playing with Fire, Acceptable Risks, Samaritan: The Mitch Snyder Story, The Women of Brewster Place, Heat Wave, The Kid Who Loved Christmas, Duplicates, When No One Would Listen, House of Secrets, Oldest Living Confederate Widow Tells All (Emmy Award, 1994). *Guest*: B.L. Stryker. *Special*: Without Borders (host). *Mini-Series*: Roots. *Pilot*: Clippers.

U

UGGAMS, LESLIE
Singer. b. New York, NY, May 25, 1943. e. Professional Children's Sch., grad., 1960. Juilliard Sch. of Music. Beg. singing career age 5. TV debut as Ethel Waters' niece on Beulah. Also on Johnny Olsen's TV kids at age 7, Your Show of Shows as singer, 1953; Recording artist for Columbia Records, Atlantic, Motown Wrote The Leslie Uggams Beauty Book (1962).
THEATER: Hallelujah Baby (Tony & Theatre World Awards, 1968), Her First Roman, Blues in the Night, Jerry's Girls, Anything Goes (natl. co. & Bdwy), Stringbean (Dallas), Into the Woods (Long Beach, CA).
PICTURES: Two Weeks in Another Town, Poor Pretty Eddie, Black Girl, Heartbreak Motel, Skyjacked, Sugar Hill.
TELEVISION: *Series*: Sing Along With Mitch, The Leslie Uggams Show (1969), Fantasy (Emmy Award, 1984). *Guest*: Beulah (1949), Kids and Company, Milton Berle Show, Name That Tune, Jack Paar Show, Garry Moore. *Mini-Series*: Roots, Backstairs at the White House. *Movie*: Sizzle. *Specials*: The Book of Lists (co-host). Fantasy (Emmy Award, 1983, host), I Love Men, 'S Wonderful, 'S Marvelous, 'S Gershwin, Sinatra and Friends, Placido Domingo Steppin' Out With the Ladies, Jerry Herman Tribute, Rooms for Improvement.
RADIO: Peter Lind Hayes-Mary Healy Show, Milton Berle, Arthur Godfrey, Star Time.

ULLMAN, TRACEY
Actress, Comedian, Singer. b. Hackbridge, England, Dec. 29, 1959. m. British TV prod. Allan McKeown. e. won a performance sch. scholarship at 12. Attended the Italia Conti School for 4 years. Soon after appeared on British TV and onstage in Grease and The Rocky Horror Picture Show. Also performed in improvisational play Four in a Million (1981) at the Royal Court Theatre, London (London Theatre Critics Award). Recorded gold-selling album You Broke My Heart in Seventeen Places. Appeared in music video They Don't Know. U.S. TV debut, The Tracey Ullman Show (debuted April, 1987).
THEATRE: NY: The Taming of the Shrew, The Big Love.
PICTURES: Give My Regards to Broad Street, Plenty, Jumpin' Jack Flash, I Love You to Death, Happily Ever After (voice), Robin Hood: Men in Tights, Household Saints, Bullets Over Broadway, Ready to Wear (Pret-a-Porter).
TELEVISION: Series: Three of a Kind (BBC), The Tracey Ullman Show (Emmy Awards, 1989, 1990), Tracey Takes On.... Specials: The Best of the Tracey Ullman Show (Emmy Award, 1990), Tracey Ullman: Takes on New York (Emmy Award, 1994), Tracey Ullman—A Class Act. Guest: Love & War (Emmy Award, 1993).

ULLMANN, LIV
Actress. b. Tokyo, Japan, of Norwegian parents, Dec. 16, 1939. Accompanied parents to Canada when WWII began and later returned to Norway. Was catapulted to fame in a succession of Swedish films directed by Ingmar Bergman. Author: Changing, Choices. Ambassador for UNICEF since 1980. Youngest person to date to receive the Order of St. Olav from the King of Norway. Recipient of 11 honorary doctorates.
THEATER: U.S.: A Doll's House, Anna Christie, I Remember Mama (musical), Ghosts, Old Times.
PICTURES: Fjols til Fjells (debut, 1957), The Wayward Girl, Tonny, Kort ar Sommaren, De Kalte Ham Skarven, Persona, Hour of the Wolf, Shame, The Passion of Anna, The Night Visitor, Cold Sweat, The Emigrants, Pope Joan, Cries and Whispers, Lost Horizon, Forty Carats, The New Land, Scenes From a Marriage, Zandy's Bride, The Abdication, Leonor, Face to Face, Couleur Chair, A Bridge Too Far, The Serpent's Egg, Autumn Sonata, Players (cameo), Richard's Things, The Wild Duck, Bay Boy, Dangerous Moves, Let's Hope It's a Girl, Gaby—A True Story. Moscow Adieu (Donatello Award, 1987), A Time of Indifference, La Amiga, The Rose Garden, Mindwalk, The Ox, The Long Shadow, Sophie (dir., co-s.p. only), Kristin Lavrandsdatter (dir., s.p. only).
TELEVISION: Lady From the Sea, Jacobo Timerman: Prisoner Without a Name Cell Without a Number.

UNDERWOOD, BLAIR
Actor. b. Tacoma, WA, Aug. 25, 1964. e. Carnegie-Mellon Univ. NY stage: Measure for Measure.
PICTURES: Krush Groove, Posse, Just Cause, Set It Off, The Eighth Day.
TELEVISION: Series: One Life to Live, Downtown, L.A. Law, High Incident. Movies: The Cover Girl and the Cop, Heat Wave, Murder in Mississippi, Father & Son: Dangerous Relations (also assoc. prod.), Soul of the Game, Mistrial. Guest: Scarecrow and Mrs. King, The Cosby Show, Knight Rider, 21 Jump Street.

UNDERWOOD, RON
Director. b. Glendale, CA, Nov. 6, 1953. e. USC, American Film Institute.
PICTURES: Tremors (also co-story), City Slickers, Heart and Souls, Speechless.
TELEVISION: The Mouse and the Motorcycle (Peabody Award), Runaway Ralph (Emmy nom.).

UNGER, ANTHONY B.
Executive, Producer. b. New York, NY, Oct. 19, 1940. e. Duke U., USC. Prod. ass't Third Man, TV series, 1961. v.p. Unger Productions, Inc., 1964; v.p. Landau-Unger Co., Inc., 1965; v.p. Commonwealth United Entertainment in London, 1968; pres., Unger Prods. Inc., 1978-present.
PICTURES: The Desperate Ones. The Madwoman of Chaillot. The Battle of Neretva, The Magic Christian, Julius Caesar, The Devil's Widow, Don't Look Now, Force Ten From Navarone, The Unseen, Silent Rage.

UNGER, STEPHEN A.
Executive. b. New York, NY, May 31, 1946. e. NYU, Grad. Film and Television Instit. Started as independent prod. and dist. of theatrical and TV films. 1978, joined Universal Pictures Intl. Sales as foreign sls. mgr.; named v.p. Universal Theatrical Motion Pictures in 1979, responsible for licensing theatrical or TV features not handled by U.I.P. in territories outside U.S. & Canada and worldwide acquisitions; 1980 joined CBS Theatrical Films as intl. v.p., sls.; 1982-88, pres., Unger Intl. Distributors, Inc.; 1988 joined Korn/Ferry Intl. as exec. v.p., worldwide entertainment div. Promoted to mng. dir., 1989-91. Joined Spencer Stuart Exec. Search Consultants as mng. dir., Worldwide Ent. Div. 1991.

URICH, ROBERT
Actor. b. Toronto, OH, Dec. 19, 1946. e. Florida State U., B.A., radio and TV communications; Michigan State U., M.A. Communications Mgmt. Appeared in university plays. Was sales account executive at WGN Radio, Chicago, before turning to stage acting (Ivanhoe Theatre, Chicago).
PICTURES: Magnum Force, Endangered Species, The Ice Pirates, Turk 182.
TELEVISION: Series: Bob & Carol & Ted & Alice, S.W.A.T., Soap, Tabitha, Vega$, Gavilan, Spenser For Hire, American Dreamer, Crossroads, National Geographic Explorers (host), It Had to Be You, Lazarus Man. Guest: The FBI, Gunsmoke, Kung Fu, Marcus Welby MD, The Love Boat. Movies: Killdozer, Vega$ (pilot), Leave Yesterday Behind, When She Was Bad, Fighting Back, Killing at Hell's Gate, Take Your Best Shot, Princess Daisy, Invitation to Hell, His Mistress, Scandal Sheet, Young Again, April Morning, The Comeback, She Knows Too Much, Murder By Night, Night Walk, Blind Faith, Spooner, A Quiet Little Neighborhood A Perfect Little Murder, Stranger at My Door, And Then She Was Gone, Survive the Savage Sea, Blind Man's Bluff (also co-prod.), Double Edge, Revolver, Deadly Relations, Spenser: Ceremony (also co-exec. prod.), Spenser: Pale Kings and Princes (also co-exec. prod.), Danielle Steel's A Perfect Stranger, Spenser: The Judas Goat, A Horse for Danny, She Stood Alone: The Tailhook Scandal. Mini-Series: Mistral's Daughter, Amerika, Lonesome Dove.

URMAN, MARK
Executive. b. New York, NY, Nov. 24, 1952. e. Union Coll., 1973; NYU, cinema, 1973-74. m. story analyst Deborah Davis. 1973, apprentice publicist, Universal Pictures; 1973-82, United Artists intl. dept. as assoc. publicist, sr. publicist and ultimately asst. to v.p. worldwide ad-pub.; 1982-84, dir., publicity and marketing, Triumph Films (Columbia/Gaumont); 1985-86, exec. dir. East Coast pub., Columbia Pictures; 1986-89, v.p. East Coast pub., Columbia Pictures. Joined Dennis Davidson Associates as v.p., 1989; promoted to sr.v.p., 1991. Member: Motion Picture Academy.

URQUHART, ROBERT
Actor, Writer. b. Scotland, October 16, 1922. e. George Heriots, Edinburgh. Served in Merchant Navy 1938-45; stage debut, Park Theatre, Glasgow; screen debut: You're Only Young Twice, 1951.
PICTURES: Isn't Life Wonderful, The House Of The Arrow, Knights of the Round Table, Happy Ever After (Tonight's the Night), Golden Ivory, The Dark Avenger, You Can't Escape, Yangtse Incident, Curse of Frankenstein, Dunkirk, The Trouble with Eve, Danger Tomorrow, Foxhole in Cairo, Murder in Mind, The Bulldog Greed, 55 Days At Peking, The Break, Murder at the Gallup, The Syndicate, The Limbo Line, The Looking Glass War, Brotherly Love (Country Dance), Playing Away, Restless Natives, Sharma and Beyond, P'Tang Bang Clipper Bang, Kitchen Toto, Testimony.
TELEVISION: Tamer Tamed, Infinite Shoeblack, Morning Departure, The Human Touch, The Iron Harp, Sleeping Clergyman, The Naked Lady, For Services Rendered, The Bright One, Jango, Murder Swamp, She Died Young, Plane Makers (series), Reporter, Inheritors (series); Mr. Goodall (series), The Nearly Man, The Button Man, Happy Returns, Endless-Aimless, Bleak House, The Queens Arms, Shostakovich. Writer: House of Lies, End of the Tether, Landfall, The Touch of a Dead Hand.

USLAN, MICHAEL E.
Producer, Writer. b. Bayonne, NJ, June 2, 1951. e. Indiana U., A.B., M.S., J.D. Wrote 12 books, including Dick Clark's 1st 25 Years of Rock 'n' Roll; 1976-80 atty. with United Artists; writer of syndicated comic strip Terry and the Pirates; produced with Benjamin Melniker.
PICTURES: Swamp Thing (prod.), The Return of Swamp Thing (exec. prod.), Batman Returns (exec. prod.), Batman: The Animated Movie (prod.), Batman Forever (exec. prod.), Batman & Robin (exec. prod.).
TELEVISION: Three Sovereigns for Sarah (exec. prod.), Dinosaucers (exec. prod., creator, writer), Swamp Thing (exec. prod. for both live-action and animated series), Fish Police (exec. prod.), South Korea cultural segments NBC Summer Olympics 1988 (exec. prod.), Television's Greatest Bits (prod., creator, writer), 1st National Trivia Quiz (prod., writer), Where in the World Is Carmen Sandiego? (animated, exec. prod.; Emmy Award), Robin Cook's Harmful Intent (exec. prod.), Little Orphan Annie's Very Animated Christmas (exec. prod., writer), remakes of The Kiss, The Sneeze, The Great Train Robbery, The Barbershop, Streetcar Chivalry, Smashing a Jersey Mosquito (prod., dir.).

USTINOV, SIR PETER
Actor, Writer, Director. b. London, Eng., Apr. 16, 1921. e. Westminster Sch. In Brit. Army, W.W.II. On Brit. stage from 1937. Screen debut 1941 in Brit. picture Mein Kampf, My Crimes. Awards: 3 Emmy Awards (Specials: Life of Samuel

Johnson, Barefoot in Athens, A Storm in Summer); Grammy Award for Peter and the Wolf; NY Critics Award and Donaldson Award for best foreign play (The Love of Four Colonels); British Critics Award (Romanoff and Juliet). Chancellor, Durham Univ., 1992. Received Britannia Award from BAFTA, 1992; Critics Circle Award, 1993; German Cultural Award, 1994; German Bambi, 1994; Rudolph Valentino Award, 1995.
THEATER: Romanoff and Juliet, N.Y., London; and 17 other plays. Dir., acted, Photo Finish; wrote, Life In My Hands, The Unknown Soldier and His Wife, Half Way Up The Tree, King Lear, Beethoven's Tenth, An Evening With Peter Ustinov.
PICTURES: Actor. The Goose Steps Out, One of Our Aircraft Is Missing, The Way Ahead (co-s.p.), School for Secrets (wrote, dir. & co-prod. only), Vice Versa (dir., s.p. only), Private Angelo (also adapt., dir., co-prod.), Odette, Quo Vadis (Acad. Award nom.), The Magic Box, Hotel Sahara, The Egyptian, Beau Brummell, We're No Angels, Lola Montez, The Spies, The Man Who Wagged His Tail, School for Scoundrels (adapt. only), The Sundowners, Spartacus (Academy Award, best supporting actor, 1960), Romanoff and Juliet (also prod., s.p.), Billy Budd (also prod., dir., s.p.), Topkapi (Academy Award, best supporting actor, 1964), John Goldfarb Please Come Home, Lady L. (also dir., s.p.), The Comedians, Blackbeard's Ghost, Hot Millions, Viva Max. Hammersmith Is Out (also dir.), Robin Hood (voice), One of Our Dinosaurs Is Missing, Logan's Run, Treasure of Matecumbe, Purple Taxi, The Last Remake of Beau Geste, Doppio Delitto, Death on the Nile, Ashanti, Charlie Chan and the Curse of the Dragon Queen, Grendel Grendel Grendel (voice), The Great Muppet Caper, Evil Under the Sun, Memed My Hawk (also dir., s.p.), Appointment with Death, Lorenzo's Oil, The Phoenix and the Magic Carpet.
RECENT TV: The Well Tempered Bach, 13 at Dinner, Deadman's Folly, Peter Ustinov's Russia, World Challenge, Murder in Three Acts, The Secret Identity of Jack the Ripper (host), Around the World in 80 Days, The Mozart Mystique, Ustinov on the Orient Express, Ustinov Meets Pavarotti, Inside the Vatican, The Old Curiosity Shop, Haydn Gala, An Evening With Sir Peter Ustinov, Paths of the Gods.

V

VACCARO, BRENDA
Actress. b. Brooklyn, NY, Nov. 18, 1939. e. Thomas Jefferson H.S., Dallas; studied two yrs. at Neighborhood Playhouse in N.Y. Was waitress and model before landing first B'way role in Everybody Loves Opal. Toured in Tunnel of Love and returned to N.Y. for role in The Affair.
THEATER: Everybody Loves Opal (Theatre World Award), Tunnel of Love (tour), The Affair, Children From Their Games, Cactus Flower (Tony Award, 1965), The Natural Look, How Now Dow Jones (Tony nom.), The Goodbye People (Tony nom.), Father's Day, The Odd Couple, Jake's Women.
PICTURES: Where It's At (debut, 1969), Midnight Cowboy, I Love My Wife, Summertree, Going Home, Once Is Not Enough (Acad. Award nom.), Golden Globe Award), Airport '77, House by the Lake (Death Weekend), Capricorn One, Fast Charlie the Moonbeam Rider, The First Deadly Sin, Zorro the Gay Blade, Supergirl, Water, Cookie, Heart of Midnight, Masque of the Red Death, Ten Little Indians, Lethal Games, Love Affair.
TELEVISION: Series: Sara, Dear Detective, Paper Dolls. Guest: The F.B.I., The Name of the Game, The Helen Reddy Show, The Shape of Things (Emmy Award, 1974), The Golden Girls, Columbo, Murder She Wrote, Flesh & Blood, Golden Girls (Emmy nom.), Civil Wars, Red Shoe Diaries, Friends. Movies: Travis Logan D.A., What's a Nice Girl Like You...?, Honor Thy Father, Sunshine, The Big Ripoff, Guyana Tragedy, The Pride of Jesse Hallam, The Star Maker, A Long Way Home, Deceptions, Julius and Ethel Rosenberg, Stolen: One Husband, Red Shoes Diaries, Following Her Heart.

VADIM, ROGER
Director, Writer. b. Paris, Jan. 26, 1928. r.n. Roger Vadim Plemiannikow. m. actress Marie-Christine Barrault. Appeared in films Rich and Famous, Into the Night.
PICTURES: Futures Vedettes (s.p.). Writer-Director: And God Created Woman, No Sun in Venice, The Night Heaven Fell, Les Liaisons Dangereuses, Blood and Roses, Please Not Now!, Seven Capital Sins (Pride segment), Love on a Pillow, Vice and Virtue (also prod.), Nutty Naughty Chateau, La Ronde (Circle of Love), The Game is Over (also prod.), Spirits of the Dead (Metzengerstein segment), Barbarella, Pretty Maids All in a Row, Helle, Ms. Don Juan, Night Games, Hot Touch, Surprise Party, Come Back, And God Created Woman (1988), The Mad Lover.
TELEVISION: Beauty and the Beast (Faerie Tale Theatre).

VAJNA, ANDREW
Executive. b. Budapest, Hungary, Aug. 1, 1944. e. UCLA. Launched career with purchase of m.p. theaters in Far East.

Founded Panasia Film Ltd. in Hong Kong. Exhibitor and dist. of feature films since 1970. Formed Carolco Service, Inc. (foreign sls. org.), with Mario Kassar 1976. Founder and Pres., American Film Mkt. Assn., 1982. Resigned from Carolco, 1989; formed independent production co., Cinergi Prods., 1989.
PICTURES: Exec. Prod.: The Deadly China Doll, The Silent Partner, The Changeling, Victory, The Amateur, First Blood, Superstition, Rambo: First Blood Part II, Angel Heart, Extreme Prejudice, Rambo III, Red Heat, Iron Eagle II, Deepstar Six, Johnny Handsome, Music Box, Mountains of the Moon, Total Recall, Air America, Narrow Margin, Jacob's Ladder, Medicine Man, Tombstone, Renaissance Man, Color of Night, Die Hard With a Vengeance, Judge Dredd, The Scarlet Letter, The Shadow Conspiracy, Nixon.

VALE, EUGENE
Writer. b. April 11, 1916. e. Zurich, Switzerland. m. Evelyn Wahl. Story and s.p., The Second Face, The Shattered Dream, 1954 SWG award nom., best written telefilm; The Dark Wave. 1957, m.p. academy award nominations.
PICTURES: A Global Affair, Francis of Assisi, The Bridge of San Luis Rey, A Family Scandal, The Thirteenth Apostle, Hold the Split Second.
TELEVISION: Four Star Playhouse, Fireside Theatre, 20th Century Fox Hour, Schlitz Playhouse, Hollywood Opening Night, NBC, Crusader, Lux Video Theatre, Danger, CBS, Chevron Theatre, Douglas Fairbanks, Pepsi Cola Playhouse, Waterfront, Christophers, Cavalcade of America, Hallmark Hall of Fame.
AUTHOR: The Technique of Screen & Television Writing, The Thirteenth Apostle, Chaos Below Heaven, Passion Play, Some State of Affairs.

VALENTI, JACK J.
Executive. b. Sept. 5, 1921. e. U. of Houston, B.A., 1946; Harvard U., M.B.A., bus. admin., 1948. Air force pilot in European theatre, W.W.II; adv. and pub. rel. exec. in Houston; special asst. and advisor to Pres. Lyndon B. Johnson, 1963-66, elected pres., Motion Picture Association of America, MPEA and AMPTP, since June, 1966. Named Motion Picture Pioneer of the Year, 1988.

VALENTINE, KAREN
Actress. b. Sebastopol, CA, May 25, 1947.
PICTURES: Forever Young Forever Free, Hot Lead and Cold Feet, The North Avenue Irregulars.
TELEVISION: Series: Room 222 (Emmy Award, 1970), Karen, Our Time (host). Guest: My Friend Tony, Hollywood Squares, Laugh-In, The Bold Ones, Sonny and Cher, Mike Hammer, Murder, She Wrote. Movies: Gidget Grows Up, The Daughters of Joshua Cabe, Coffee Tea or Me?, The Girl Who Came Gift-Wrapped, The Love Boat (pilot), Having Babies, Murder at the World Series, Return to Fantasy Island, Go West Young Girl, Muggable Mary: Street Cop, Money on the Side, Skeezer, Illusions, Jane Doe, Children in the Crossfire, He's Fired She's Hired, A Fighting Choice, Perfect People. Special: The Emancipation of Lizzie Stern (Afterschool Special).

VALLI, ALIDA
Actress. r.n. Alida von Altenburger. b. Pola, Italy, May 31, 1921. e. M.P. Acad., Rome (dramatics); m. Oscar de Mejo, pianist-composer. In Italian m.p.; won Venice Film Festival Award in Piccolo Mondo Antico (Little Old World); to U.S. in 1947, billed simply as Valli.
PICTURES: Vita Ricomincia, Giovanna; The Paradine Case, The Miracle of the Bells, The Third Man, Walk Softly Stranger, The White Tower, Lovers of Toledo, We the Women, Senso, The Stranger's Hand, The Outcry, The Night Heaven Fell, This Angry Age (The Sea Wall), The Horror Chamber of Dr. Faustus, The Long Absence, The Happy Thieves, The Castilian, Ophelia, Oedipus Rex, The Spider's Stratagem, Tender Dracula, La Jeu de Solitaire, The Cassandra Crossing, Suspiria, 1900, The Tempter, Luna, Inferno, Le Jupon Rouge, A Notre Regrettable Epoux, A Month by the Lake.

VALLONE, RAF
Actor. b. Turin, Italy, Feb. 17, 1916. e. U. of Turin. Former newspaper writer. Directed operas Norma, La Traviata, Adrianna in NY, San Francisco and Houston.
PICTURES: Bitter Rice (debut, 1949), Vendetta, Under the Olive Tree, Anna, Path of Hope, White Line, Rome 11 O'Clock, Strange Deception, Anita Garibaldi, Daughters of Destiny, Teresa Raquin, Riviera, The Secret Invasion. Two Women, El Cid, Phaedra, A View From the Bridge, The Cardinal, Harlow, Nevada Smith, Kiss the Girls and Make Them Die, The Desperate Ones, The Secret Invasion, The Italian Job, The Kremlin Letter, Cannon for Cordoba, A Gunfight, Summertime Killer, Rosebud, The Human Factor, That Lucky Touch, The Other Side of Midnight, The Devil's Advocate, The Greek Tycoon, An Almost Perfect Affair, A Time to Die, Lion of the Desert, The Godfather Part III.

TELEVISION: Fame (Hallmark Hall of Fame), Honor Thy Father, Catholics, The Scarlet and the Black, Christopher Columbus, Goya.

VAN ARK, JOAN
Actress. b. New York, NY. m. NBC news reporter John Marshall. e. Yale U of Drama. Began career in touring co., then on Broadway and in London in Barefoot in the Park. Also appeared on B'way with the APA-Phoenix Rep. Co. in the 1970s. As a runner has competed in 12 marathons, incl. Boston Marathon. On TV also created voices for animated series Spiderwoman, Thundarr and Dingbat, Dumb and Dumber, Santo Bugito and the Creeps and special Cyrano de Bergerac. Estee Lauder spokesperson.
THEATER: School for Wives (Tony Award nom.; Theatre World Award), The Rules of the Game (Theatre World Award). L.A.: Cyrano de Bergerac, Ring Around the Moon, Chemin de Fer, As You Like It (L.A. Drama Critics Award). Williamstown Theatre Fest.: Night of the Iguana, The Legend of Oedipus, Little Night Music. Off-B'way & L.A.: Love Letters, Three Tall Women.
PICTURES: Frogs, Dedication Day (dir. only).
TELEVISION: Series: Temperatures Rising, We've Got Each Other, Dallas, Knots Landing. Guest: The F.B.I., The Girl with Something Extra, Quark, Dallas, Quincy, Rockford Files, Rhoda. Co-host: Miss USA and Miss Universe Pageants, Battle of the Network Stars, Macy's Thanksgiving Parade, Tournament of Roses Parade. Movies: The Judge and Jake Wyler, Big Rose, Testimony of Two Men, Shell Game, The Last Dinosaur, Red Flag—The Ultimate Game, Glitter, Shakedown on the Sunset Strip, My First Love, Always Remember I Love You, The Grand Central Murders, Tainted Blood, In the Shadows Someone's Watching (also co-exec. prod.), Moment of Truth: A Mother's Deception, When the Dark Man Calls. Special: Boys Will Be Boys (also dir.).

VANCE, COURTNEY B.
Actor. b. Detroit, MI, Mar. 12, 1960. e. Harvard (B.A.), Yale Drama Sch. (M.A.).
THEATER: B'way: Fences (Theatre World & Clarence Derwent Awards; Tony nom.), Six Degrees of Separation (Tony nom.). Off-B'way: My Children My Africa (Obie Award), Romeo and Juliet, Temptation. Regional: A Lesson From Aloes, Rosencrantz and Guildenstern Are Dead, Hamlet, Butterfly, Jazz Wives Jazz Lives, Geronimo Jones.
PICTURES: Hamburger Hill, The Hunt for Red October, The Adventures of Huck Finn, Holy Matrimony, Panther, Dangerous Moves, The Last Supper, The Preacher's Wife.
TELEVISION: Movies: Percy and Thunder, Race to Freedom, Tuskegee Airmen, The Affair, Black Tuesday.

VAN DAMME, JEAN-CLAUDE
Actor. b. Brussels, Belgium, Apr. 1, 1961. r.n. Jean-Claude Van Varenberg. Former European karate champion, began studying martial arts at 11 yrs. old. Won the European Professional Karate Association's middleweight championship. As teen established the California Gym in Brussels; also worked as a model before coming to U.S. in 1981. Resumed career teaching martial arts before landing first film role.
PICTURES: No Retreat No Surrender, Bloodsport, Black Eagle, Cyborg, Kickboxer (also co-story), Death Warrant, Lionheart (also co-s.p., story), Double Impact (also co-prod., co-s.p., co-story, fight choreog.), Universal Soldier, Nowhere to Run, Last Action Hero (cameo), Hard Target, Timecop, Street Fighter, Sudden Death, The Quest (also dir. & story), Maximum Risk.

VAN DEVERE, TRISH
Actress. b. Englewood Cliffs, NJ, March 9, 1945. e. Ohio Wesleyan U. m. actor George C. Scott. On B'way in Sly Fox, Tricks of the Trade, etc.
PICTURES: The Landlord (debut, 1970), Where's Poppa?, The Last Run, One Is a Lonely Number, Harry in Your Pocket, The Day of the Dolphin, The Savage Is Loose, Movie Movie, The Changeling, The Hearse, Uphill All the Way, Hollywood Vice Squad, Messenger of Death.
TELEVISION: Movies: Stalk the Wild Child, Beauty and the Beast, Sharon: Portrait of a Mistress, Mayflower—The Pilgrim's Adventure, All God's Children, Haunted, Curacao.

VAN DOREN, MAMIE
Actress. r.n. Joan Lucille Olander. b. Rowena, SD, Feb. 6, 1933. e. Los Angeles H.S. Secy. law firm, L.A.; prof. debut as singer with Ted Fio Rita orch.; debuted in films as Joan Olander.
THEATER: Stock: Once in a Lifetime, Boy Meets Girl, Come Back Little Sheba.
PICTURES: His Kind of Woman (debut, 1951), Forbidden, The All-American, Yankee Pasha, Francis Joins the WACs, Ain't Misbehavin', The Second Greatest Sex, Running Wild, Star in the Dust, Untamed Youth, The Girl in Black Stockings, Teacher's Pet, Guns Girls and Gangsters, High School

Confidential, The Beat Generation, The Big Operator, Born Reckless, Girls' Town, The Private Lives of Adam and Eve, Sex Kittens Go to College, College Confidential, Vice Raid, The Sheriff Was a Lady, The Candidate, Three Nuts in Search of a Bolt, The Navy vs. the Night Monsters, Las Vegas Hillbillies, You've Got to Be Smart, Voyage to the Planet of the Prehistoric Women, The Arizona Kid, Boarding School (Free Ride).

VAN DYKE, DICK
Actor. b. West Plains, MO, Dec., 13, 1925. Brother is actor Jerry Van Dyke. Son is actor Barry Van Dyke. Served in USAF, WWII. After discharge from service, opened advertising agency in Danville, IL. Teamed with friend in nightclub act called Eric and Van, The Merry Mutes, and for 4 yrs. toured country doing a routine in which they pantomimed and lip-synched to records. 1953 hosted local TV show in Atlanta, then New Orleans. 1955 to NY as host of CBS Morning show.
THEATER: NY: The Girls Against the Boys (Theatre World Award), Bye Bye Birdie (Tony Award, 1961), The Music Man (revival).
PICTURES: Bye Bye Birdie (debut, 1963), What a Way to Go!, Mary Poppins, The Art of Love, Lt. Robin Crusoe USN, Divorce American Style, Fitzwilly, Chitty Chitty Bang Bang, Some Kind of a Nut, The Comic, Cold Turkey, The Runner Stumbles, Dick Tracy.
TELEVISION: Series: The Morning Show (host), CBS Cartoon Theatre (host), The Chevy Showroom, Pantomime Quiz, Laugh Line (emcee), The Dick Van Dyke Show (3 Emmy Awards: 1964, 1965, 1966), The New Dick Van Dyke Show, Van Dyke and Company (Emmy Award, 1977), The Carol Burnett Show, The Van Dyke Show, Diagnosis Murder. Movies: The Morning After, Drop-Out Father, Found Money, The Country Girl, Ghost of a Chance, Keys to the Kingdom, Daughters of Privilege, Diagnosis of Murder, The House on Sycamore Street, A Twist of the Knife. Pilot: Harry's Battles. Specials: The Dick Van Dyke Special, Dick Van Dyke and the Other Woman, Julie and Dick in Covent Garden, The Confessions of Dick Van Dyke, CBS Library: The Wrong Way Kid (Emmy Award, 1984), The Town Santa Forgot (narrator).

VAN DYKE, JERRY
Actor. b. Danville IL, July 27, 1931. Brother is actor Dick Van Dyke. Served in U.S. Air Force before becoming standup comic, banjo player in nightclubs. Guested on The Dick Van Dyke Show, playing Van Dyke's brother.
PICTURES: The Courtship of Eddie's Father (debut, 1963), McLintock!, Palm Springs Weekend, Love and Kisses, Angel in My Pocket, W.A.R.: Women Against Rape.
TELEVISION: Series: Picture This, The Judy Garland Show, My Mother the Car, Accidental Family, Headmaster, 13 Queens Boulevard, Coach. Mini-Series: Fresno. Movie: To Grandmother's House We Go. Pilots: My Boy Googie, You're Only Young Twice.

VANGELIS
Composer, Conductor. Full name: Vangelis Papathanassiou. b. Greece, March 23, 1943. Began composing as child, performing own compositions at 6. Left Greece for Paris by late 1960s. Composed and recorded his symphonic poem Faire que Ton Reve Soit Plus Long que la Nuit, and album Terra. Collaborated with filmmaker Frederic Rossif for whom composed La Cantique des Creatures. Moved to London then to Greece in 1989. Formed band Formynx in Greece; then Aphrodite's Child in Paris.
PICTURES: Chariots of Fire (Academy Award, 1981), Antarctica, Missing, Blade Runner, The Year of Living Dangerously, The Bounty, Wonders of Life, Wild and Beautiful, Nosferatu in Venice, Francesco, 1492: Conquest of Paradise, Bitter Moon.

VANOCUR, SANDER
News Commentator. b. Cleveland, OH, Jan. 8, 1928. e. Northwestern U. Began career as journalist on London staff of Manchester Guardian 1954-5; City staff, NY Times 1956-57. Joined NBC in 1957, hosting First Tuesday series. Resigned in 1971 to be correspondent of the National Public Affairs Center for PBS. TV Critic for Washington Post, 1975-7. In 1977 joined ABC News as v.p., special reporting units 1977-80. Chief overview corr. ABC news, 1980-81; sr. corr. 1981-present. Anchor: Business World.

VAN PALLANDT, NINA
Actress. b. Copenhagen, Denmark, July 15, 1932. e. USC. Returned to Denmark where she was married to Baron Frederik Van Pallandt with whom she appeared as folk singer throughout Europe, as well as making 3 films with him; went on world tour together before divorcing. Has appeared in New York as singer.
PICTURES: The Long Goodbye, Assault on Agathon, A Wedding, Quintet, American Gigolo, Cloud Dancer, Cutter and Bone, Asi Como Habian Sido, The Sword and the Sorcerer, Jungle Warriors, Time Out, O.C. and Stiggs.
TELEVISION: Movie: Guilty or Innocent: The Sam Shepherd Murder Case.

VAN PATTEN, DICK
Actor. b. New York, NY, Dec. 9, 1928. Sister is actress Joyce Van Patten. Father of actors James and Vincent Van Patten. Began career as child actor with B'way debut at 7 yrs., playing son of Melvyn Douglas in Tapestry in Gray.
THEATER: The Lady Who Came to Stay, O Mistress Mine, On Borrowed Time, Ah, Wilderness, Watch on the Rhine, The Skin of Our Teeth, Kiss and Tell, Mister Roberts, Thieves.
PICTURES: Reg'lar Fellers (debut, 1941), Psychomania, Charly, Zachariah, Making It, Joe Kidd, Soylent Green, Dirty Little Billy, Westworld, Superdad, The Strongest Man in the World, Gus, Treasure of Matecumbe, The Shaggy D.A., Freaky Friday, High Anxiety, Spaceballs, The New Adventures of Pippi Longstocking, Robin Hood: Men in Tights, A Dangerous Place.
TELEVISION: Series: Mama, The Partners, The New Dick Van Dyke Show, When Things Were Rotten, Eight Is Enough, WIOU. Guest: Arnie, The Rookies, Cannon, Banyon, The Little People, The Streets of San Francisco, Hotel, Growing Pains, Love Boat, Murder She Wrote. Specials: Jay Leno's Family Comedy Hour, A Mouse A Mystery and Me, 14 Going On 30. Movies: Hec Ramsey (pilot), The Crooked Hearts, The Love Boat (pilot), With This Ring, Diary of a Hitchhiker, Eight Is Enough Reunion, Going to the Chapel, An Eight Is Enough Wedding, Jake Spanner—Private Eye, The Odd Couple: Together Again, The Gift of Love.

VAN PATTEN, JOYCE
Actress. b. New York, NY, March 9, 1935. Brother is actor Dick Van Patten. Mother of actress Talia Balsam.
THEATER: NY: Spoon River Anthology, Same Time Next Year, The Supporting Cast, The Seagull, I Ought to Be in Pictures, Brighton Beach Memoirs, Murder at the Howard Johnson's, Rumors, Jake's Women.
PICTURES: Reg'lar Fellers (debut, 1941), Fourteen Hours, The Goddess, I Love You Alice B. Toklas, Making It, Something Big, Thumb Tripping, The Manchu Eagle Murder Caper Mystery, Mame, The Bad News Bears, Mikey and Nicky, The Falcon and the Snowman, St. Elmo's Fire, Billy Galvin, Blind Date, Trust Me, Monkey Shines.
TELEVISION: Series: The Danny Kaye Show, The Good Guys, The Don Rickles Show, Mary Tyler Moore Hour, Unhappily Ever After. Guest: Brooklyn Bridge. Movies: But I Don't Want to Get Married!, Winter Kill, The Stranger Within, Let's Switch, Winner Take All, To Kill a Cop, Murder at the Mardi Gras, The Comedy Company, Eleanor: First Lady of the World, Another Woman's Child, The Demon Murder Case, In Defense of Kids, Malice in Wonderland, Under the Influence, The Haunted, Maid for Each Other. Mini-Series: The Martian Chronicles. Special: Bus Stop.

VAN PEEBLES, MARIO
Actor, Director, Producer, Writer. b. Mexico D.F., Mexico, Jan. 15, 1957. Father is filmmaker Melvin Van Peebles. e. Columbia U., B.A. economics, 1980. Studied acting with Stella Adler 1983. Served as budget analyst for NY Mayor Ed Koch and later worked as a Ford model. Directed music videos for Kid Creole and the Coconuts, Nighttrain (also prod., cameo) and for film Identity Crisis. Appeared as child in father's film Sweet Sweetback's Baadasssss Song. Dir., prod., wrote and starred in short, Juliet, Exec. prod. of soundtracks for Posse and Gunmen.
THEATER: Waltz of the Stork (B'way debut, 1984), Take Me Along, The Legend of Deadwood Dick, Champeen, Friday the 13th.
PICTURES: The Cotton Club, Delivery Boys, Exterminator II, 3:15, Rappin' (also wrote and performed 5 songs), South Bronx Heroes, Heartbreak Ridge (also songs), Last Resort, Jaws: the Revenge, Hot Shot, Identity Crisis (also s.p.), New Jack City (also dir.), Posse (also dir.), Gunmen, Highlander: The Sorcerer, Panther (also dir., prod.), Jaws IV: The Revenge, Solo.
TELEVISION: Series: Sonny Spoon. Guest: L.A. Law, One Life to Live, The Cosby Show, The Pat Sajack Show (guest host), In Living Color, Living Single. Movies: The Cable Car Murder, Sophisticated Gents, Children of the Night (Bronze Halo Award), The Facts of Life Down Under, The Child Saver, Blue Bayou, Triumph of the Heart: The Ricky Bell Story, Stompin' at the Savoy, In the Line of Duty: Street War, Crosscurrents: Cable Car Murder, Full Eclipse. Specials: American Masters: A Glory of Ghosts (Emperor Jones, All God's Chillun), Third & Oak: The Pool Hall (CBS play), Strangers: Leave, Gang In Blue, Riot. Director: Sonny Spoon, 21 Jump Street, Top of the Hill, Wise Guy, Malcolm Takes a Shot (DGA nom.), Gabriel's Fire, Missing Persons.

VAN PEEBLES, MELVIN
Producer, Director, Writer, Composer, Editor, Actor. b. Chicago, IL, Aug. 21, 1932. e. Ohio Wesleyan U., 1953. Father of actor Mario Van Peebles. Was portrait painter in Mexico, cable car driver in San Francisco; journalist in Paris and (in 1970s) options trader on Wall Street. Dir. Funky Beat music video.
AUTHOR: Books: The Big Heart, A Bear for the FBI, Le Chinois de XIV, La Permission (Story of a Three Day Pass) La Fete a Harlem, The True American, Sweet Sweetback's Baadasssss Song, Just an Old Sweet Song, Bold Money, No Identity Crisis (co-author with Mario Van Peebles), Panther.
THEATER: B'way (writer, prod., dir.): Ain't Supposed to Die a Natural Death, Don't Play Us Cheap, Waltz of the Stork (also actor). Off-B'way: Champeen, Waltz of the Stork, Kickin the Science.
PICTURES: The Story of a Three-Day Pass (dir., s.p., music), Watermelon Man (dir., music), Sweet Sweetback's Baadasssss Song (prod., dir., s.p., edit., music, actor), Don't Play Us Cheap (prod., dir., s.p., edit., music), Greased Lightning (co-s.p.), America (actor), O.C. and Stiggs (actor), Jaws: The Revenge (actor), Identity Crisis (prod., dir., co-edit., actor), True Identity (actor), Boomerang (actor), Posse (actor), Last Action Hero (actor), Terminal Velocity (actor), Fist of the North Star (actor), Panther (s.p., actor, prod., co-edit.).
TELEVISION: Writer: Down Home, Just an Old Sweet Song, The Day They Came to Arrest the Book (Emmy Award). Actor: Taking Care of Terrific, Sophisticated Gents, Sonny Spoons (series). Director: Nipsey Russell at Harrah's, Vroom Vroom Vroom (also writer; German tv).
ALBUMS: Composer: Brer Soul, Watermelon Man, Sweet Sweetback's Baadasssss Song, As Serious as a Heart Attack, Don't Play Us Cheap, Ain't Suppose to Die a Natural Death, What the #*!% You Mean I Can't Sing, Ghetto Gothic.

VAN PRAAG, WILLIAM
Executive, Producer, Director, Writer, Editor, Advertising Consultant. b. New York, NY, Sept. 13, 1924. e. CREI, Columbia U. U.S. Army, 1942. Paramount, 1945; Brandt Bros. Prods., 1946; NBC, 1947; v.p. Television Features, 1948; devlpd. vidicon system in m.p. prod.; 1949; Started, pres., Van Praag Prod. Inc. 1951; formed Ernst-Van Praag, Inc. 1971, a communications and marketing counseling firm (NY, Brussels, Tokyo); pres., International Film, TV and A-V Producers Assn, 1969; creator of Van-O-Vision. Winner of commercial, short subject and feature theatrical awards. Author of Color Your Picture, Primer of Creative Editing, and Van Praag's Magic Eye. Past pres., Film Producer's Assn, mem. DGA, SAG, 771 IATSE, National Academy of TV Arts and Sciences, International Radio and TV Executive Society and Soc. of MP and TV Engineers.

VAN SANT, GUS
Director, Writer. b. Louisville, KY, 1952. Raised in Darien, CT, then moved to Oregon at age 17. e. Rhode Island Sch. of Design, where he studied painting. Went to L.A. in 1976, becoming prod. asst. to dir. Ken Shapiro. Made first low-budget film, Alice in Hollywood, which was never released. Later made commercials for NY ad agency before returning to film-making.
PICTURES: Mala Noche, Drugstore Cowboy (Natl. Soc. of Film Critics Awards for best dir. & s.p.; NY Film Critics & L.A. Film Critics Award for s.p.), My Own Private Idaho, Even Cowgirls Get the Blues, To Die For.

VARNEY, JIM
Actor. b. Lexington, KY, June 15, 1949. Studied acting at the Barter Theatre. Performed as stand-up comedian in NY and LA. Appeared in dinner theatre productions of Death of a Salesman, Camelot, Guys and Dolls, etc. During 1970's starred as Sgt. Glory in long running series of TV commercials. Became famous with character of Ernest P. Worrell in TV commercials beginning in 1980.
PICTURES: Ernest Goes to Camp, Ernest Saves Christmas, Fast Food, Ernest Goes to Jail, Ernest Scared Stupid, Wilder Napalm, The Beverly Hillbillies, Ernest Rides Again, Ernest Goes to School, Toy Story (voice).
TELEVISION: Series: The Johnny Cash Show (1976), Operation Petticoat, Pink Lady, Tom T.'s Pop Goes the Country, The Rousters, Hey Vern It's Ernest (Emmy Award, 1989). Guest: Fernwood 2-Night, Alice, America 2-Nite. Pilot: Operation Petticoat.

VAUGHN, ROBERT
Actor. b. New York, NY, Nov. 22, 1932. e. L.A. State coll., B.S. and M.A. Theatre Arts 1956; USC, Ph.D. Communications, 1970. Gained fame as Napoleon Solo in The Man From U.N.C.L.E. tv series. Author: Only Victims, 1972.
PICTURES: The Ten Commandments (debut, 1956), Hell's Crossroads, No Time to Be Young, Teenage Caveman, Unwed Mother, Good Day for a Hanging, The Young Philadelphians (Acad. Award nom.), The Magnificent Seven, The Big Show, The Caretakers, To Trap a Spy, The Spy With My Face, One Spy Too Many, The Glass Bottom Boat (cameo), The Venetian Affair, How to Steal the World, Bullitt, The Bridge at Remagen, If It's Tuesday This Must Be Belgium (cameo), The Mind of Mr. Soames, Julius Caesar, The Statue, Clay Pigeon, The Towering Inferno, The Babysitter, Lucifer Complex, Demon Seed (voice), Starship Invasions, Brass Target, Good Luck Miss Wycoff, Hangar 18, Sweet Dirty Tony, Battle Beyond the

Stars, Virus, S.O.B., Superman III, Black Moon Rising, The Delta Force, Rampage, Nightstick, Hour of the Assassin, Skeleton Coast, River of Death, Captive Rage, Nobody's Perfect, Fair Trade, Edgar Allan Poe's Buried Alive, That's Adequate, Blind Vision, C.H.U.D. II: Bud the Chud, Transylvania Twist, Going Under, Twilight Blue, Joe's Apartment.
TELEVISION: *Series*: The Lieutenant, The Man From U.N.C.L.E., The Protectors, Emerald Point N.A.S., The A-Team, Danger Theatre, As the World Turns. Mini-Series: Captains and the Kings, Washington: Behind Closed Doors (Emmy Award, 1978), Centennial, Backstairs at the White House, The Blue and the Gray, Evergreen. *Movies*: The Woman Hunter, Kiss Me Kill Me, The Islander, The Rebels, Mirror Mirror, Doctor Franken, The Gossip Columnist, City in Fear, Fantasies, The Day the Bubble Burst, A Question of Honor, Inside the Third Reich, Intimate Agony, The Return of the Man From U.N.C.L.E., International Airport, Murrow, Prince of Bel Air, Desperado, Perry Mason: The Case of the Defiant Daughter, Dark Avenger, Dancing in the Dark. BBC: One of Our Spies is Missing, The Spy in the Green Hat, The Karate Killers.

VELDE, JAMES R.
Executive. b. Bloomington, IL, Nov. 1, 1913. e. Illinois Wesleyan U. Entered m.p. ind. as night shipper Paramount ex. Detroit, 1934; then city salesman, office mgr. until joining Army, 1943, rejoining same ex. upon dischge., 1946; to Paramount, Washington as Baltimore city salesman, same yr.; br. mgr. Selznick Rel. Org. Pittsburgh, 1948; salesman Eagle-Lion Classics, Pittsburgh, 1949; br. mgr. ELC, Des Moines, 1949; br. mgr., ELC, Detroit, 1950; west coast dist. mgr., United Artists, April, 1951; Western div. mgr. UA, 1952; gen. sales mgr., 1956; v.p., 1958; dir., UA, 1968; sr. v.p., 1972. Retired, 1977. Worked with Ray Stark as advisor, 1978-83.

VEL JOHNSON, REGINALD
Actor. b. Queens, NY, Aug. 16, 1952. e. Long Island Inst. of Music and Arts, NYU.
THEATER: *NY*: But Never Jam Today, Inacent Black, World of Ben Caldwell, Staggerlee.
PICTURES: Wolfen (debut, 1981), Ghostbusters, The Cotton Club, Remo Williams, Armed and Dangerous, Crocodile Dundee, Die Hard, Turner & Hooch, Die Hard 2, Posse.
TELEVISION: *Series*: Perfect Strangers, Family Matters. *Movies*: Quiet Victory: The Charlie Wedemeyer Story, The Bride in Black, Jury Duty: The Comedy, Grass Roots, One of Her Own.

VENORA, DIANE
Actress. b. Hartford, CT, 1952. e. Juilliard Sch. (BFA degree). Member of Juilliard's Acting Company, Circle Repertory Co. and the Ensemble Studio Theatre.
THEATER: A Midsummer Night's Dream, Hamlet (New York Shakespeare Festival), Uncle Vanya (at La Mama), Messiah (Manhattan Theatre Club), Penguin Toquet, Tomorrow's Monday (Circle Rep), Largo Desolato, School for Scandal, The Seagull, A Man for All Seasons (Paramount Theatre Co.), Peer Gynt (Williamstown Fest.), The Winter's Tale, Hamlet (NYSF).
PICTURES: All That Jazz, Wolfen, Terminal Choice, The Cotton Club, F/X, Ironweed, Bird (NY Film Critics Award, 1988; Golden Globe nom.), Heat, Three Wishes, Surviving Picasso, The Subsitute, Romeo and Juliet.
TELEVISION: *Mini-Series*: A.D. *Movie*: Cook and Peary: The Race to the Pole. *Specials*: Getting There, Rehearsing Hamlet, Hamlet. *Guest*: Law and Order. *Series*: Thunder Alley, Chicago Hope.

VERDON, GWEN
Actress, Dancer, Choreographer. b. Culver City, CA, Jan. 13, 1925. Married to late dir.-choreographer Bob Fosse. Studied dancing with her mother, E. Belcher, Carmelita Marrachi, and Jack Cole.
THEATER: Bonanza Bound!, Magdalena (asst. choreographer to Jack Cole), Alive and Kicking, Can-Can (Donaldson & Tony Awards, 1954), Damn Yankees (Tony Award, 1956), New Girl in Town (Tony Award, 1958), Redhead (Tony Award, 1959), Sweet Charity, Children! Children!, Milliken's Breakfast Show, Damn Yankees (revival Westbury), Chicago, Dancin' (asst. choreographer, prod. sprv. road co.), Sing Happy (tribute to Kander and Ebb), Parade of Stars Playing the Palace (Actors' Fund benefit), Night of 100 Stars II (1985).
PICTURES: On the Riviera (debut, 1951), David and Bathsheba, The Mississippi Gambler, Meet Me After the Show, The Merry Widow, The I Don't Care Girl, Farmer Takes a Wife, Damn Yankees, The Cotton Club, Cocoon, Nadine, Cocoon: The Return, Alice, Marvin's Room.
TELEVISION: *Movies*: Legs, The Jerk Too, Oldest Living Confederate Widow Tells All. *Special*: Steam Heat. *Guest*: M*A*S*H, Fame, All My Children, Magnum P.I., The Equalizer, All is Forgiven, Dear John, Dream On, Homicide, many others.

VEREEN, BEN
Singer, Dancer, Actor. b. Miami, FL, Oct. 10, 1946. e. High School of Performing Arts.
THEATER: *NY*: Hair, Sweet Charity, Jesus Christ Superstar (Theatre World Award), Pippin (Tony Award, 1973), Grind.
PICTURES: Sweet Charity, Gasss, Funny Lady, All That Jazz, The Zoo Gang, Buy and Cell, Friend to Friend, Once Upon a Forest (voice).
TELEVISION: *Movies*: Louis Armstrong—Chicago Style, The Jesse Owens Story, Lost in London, Intruders. *Mini-Series*: Roots, Ellis Island, A.D. *Series*: Ben Vereen... Comin' at Ya, Ten Speed and Brown Shoe, Webster, Zoobilee Zoo, You Write the Songs (host), J.J. Starbuck, Silk Stalkings. *Specials*: Ben Vereen—His Roots, Uptown— A Tribute to the Apollo Theatre.

VERHOEVEN, PAUL
Director. b. Amsterdam, The Netherlands, July 18, 1938. e. U. of Leiden, Ph.D., (mathematics and physics) where he began making films.
PICTURES: Business Is Business, Turkish Delight, Keetje Tippel (Cathy Tippel), Soldier of Orange, Spetters, The Fourth Man, Flesh + Blood, Robocop, Total Recall, Basic Instinct, Showgirls, Starship Troopers.

VERNON, ANNE
Actress. r.n. Edith Antoinette Alexandrine Vignaud. b. Paris, Jan. 7, 1924. e. Ecole des Beaux Arts, Paris. Worked for French designer; screen debut in French films; toured with French theatre group; first starring role, Le Mannequin Assassine 1948. Wrote French cookbooks. Was subject of 1980 French TV film detailing her paintings, Les Peintres Enchanteurs.
PICTURES: Edouar et Caroline, Terror on a Train, Ainsi Finit La Nuit, A Warning to Wantons, Patto Col Diavolo, A Tale of Five Cities, Shakedown, Song of Paris, The Umbrellas of Cherbourg, General Della Rovere, La Rue L'Estrapade, Love Lottery, Therese and Isabelle.

VERNON, JOHN
Actor. b. Montreal, Canada, Feb. 24, 1932. r.n. Adolphus Raymondus Vernon Agopowicz. e. Banff Sch. of Fine Arts, Royal Acad. of Dramatic Art. Worked on London stage and radio. First film work as voice of Big Brother in 1984 (1956). Daughter is actress Kate Vernon.
PICTURES: 1984 (voice; debut, 1956), Nobody Waved Goodbye, Point Blank, Justine, Topaz, Tell Them Willie Boy is Here, One More Train to Rob, Dirty Harry, Fear Is the Key, Charley Varrick, W (I Want Her Dead), The Black Windmill, Brannigan, Sweet Movie, The Outlaw Josey Wales, Angela, A Special Day, The Uncanny, Golden Rendevzous, National Lampoon's Animal House, It Rained All Night the Day I Left, Crunch, Fantastica, Herbie Goes Bananas, Heavy Metal (voice), Airplane II: The Sequel, Chained Heat, Curtains, Savage Streets, Jungle Warriors, Fraternity Vacation, Doin' Time, Double Exposure (Terminal Exposure), Ernest Goes to Camp, Blue Monkey, Nightstick, Border Heat, Deadly Stranger, Dixie Lanes, Killer Klowns From Outer Space, Bail-Out, I'm Gonna Git You Sucka, Office Party, War Bus Commando, Mob Story, The Naked Truth.
TELEVISION: *Series*: Tugboat Annie (Canadian tv), Wojeck (Canadian tv), Delta House, Hail to the Chief. *Movies*: Trial Run, Escape, Cool Million, Hunter, The Questor Tapes, Mousey, The Virginia Hill Story, The Imposter, Swiss Family Robinson, The Barbary Coast, Matt Helm, Mary Jane Harper Cried Last Night, The Sacketts, The Blood of Others, Two Men (Can.), The Woman Who Sinned, The Fire Next Time, The Forget-Me-Not Murders. *Mini-Series*: The Blue and the Gray, Louisiana (Fr.). *Pilots*: B-Men, War of the Worlds. *Guest*: Tarzan, Kung Fu, Faerie Tale Theatre (Little Red Riding Hood), The Greatest American Hero, Fall Guy, Alfred Hitchcock Presents, Knight Rider, Tales From the Crypt, etc.

VERONA, STEPHEN
Director, Producer, Writer. b. Illinois, Sept. 11, 1940. e. Sch. of Visual Arts. Directed and wrote some 300 commercials (over 50 award-winners) before turning to feature films in 1972, which he wrote as well. Also dir. award-winning short subjects (featuring Barbra Streisand, The Beatles, Simon and Garfunkle and The Lovin' Spoonful). Also prod., dir. of Angela Lansbury's Positive Moves video. Is an artist whose works have been exhibited at numerous CA and NY galleries. Dir. Acad. Award nom. short subject, The Rehearsal, 1971.
PICTURES: *Director*: The Lords of Flatbush (prod., co-dir., co-s.p.), Pipe Dreams (also prod., s.p.), Boardwalk (also co-s.p.), Talking Walls (also s.p.).
TELEVISION: Class of 1966 (prod. designer, ani. dir.), Diff'rent Strokes, The Music People, Sesame Street, Take a Giant Step, Double Exposure, Flatbush Avenue (pilot, prod., co-s.p.).

VETTER, RICHARD
Executive. b. San Diego, CA, Feb. 24, 1928. e. Pepperdine Coll., B.A., 1950; San Diego State Coll., M.A., 1953; UCLA,

Ph.D., 1959. U.S. Navy: aerial phot., 1946-48, reserve instr., San Diego County Schools, 1951-54; asst. prof., audio-vis. commun., U.C.L.A., 1960-63. Inventor, co-dev., Dimension 150 Widescreen Process. 1957-63: formed D-150 Inc., 1963; exec. v.p. mem.: SMPTE, Technical & Scientific Awards Committee, AMPAS.

VICTOR, JAMES
Actor. r.n. Lincoln Rafael Peralta Diaz. b. Santiago, Dominican Republic, July 27, 1939. e. Haaren H.S., N.Y. Studied at Actors Studio West. On stage in Bullfight, Ceremony for an Assassinated Blackman, Latina, The Man in the Glass Booth, The M.C. (1985 Drama-Logue Critics, and Cesar best actor awards), I Gave You a Calendar (1983 Drama-Logue Critics Award), I Don't Have To Show You No Stinking Badges (1986 Drama-Logue Critics Award), The Rooster and the Egg. Member of Academy of Mo. Pic. Arts & Sciences, Actors Branch. Recipient of Cleo Award, 1975, for Mug Shot; L.A. Drama-Logue Critics Award, 1980, for Latina; Golden Eagle Award, 1981, for consistent outstanding performances in motion pictures.
PICTURES: Fuzz, Rolling Thunder, Boulevard Nights, Defiance, Losin' It, Borderline; Stand and Deliver.
TELEVISION: *Series*: Viva Valdez, Condo, I Married Dora, Angelica Mi Vida, The New Zorro, Murder She Wrote. Many appearances on specials. *Movies*: Robert Kennedy and His Times, Twin Detectives, Remington Steel, The Streets of L.A., I Desire, Second Serve, Grand Slam, Gunfighter's Moon. *Mini-Series*: Streets of Laredo.

VIGODA, ABE
Actor. b. New York, NYUU, Feb. 24, 1921.
PICTURES: The Godfather, The Don Is Dead, Newman's Law, The Cheap Detective, Vasectomy - A Delicate Matter, Plain Clothes, Look Who's Talking, Prancer, Joe vs. the Volcano, Sugar Hill, Jury Duty.
TELEVISION: *Series*: Dark Shadow, Barney Miller, Fish, One Life to Live. *Movies*: The Devil's Daughter, Tomaa, Having Babies, How to Pick Up Girls, Death Car on the Freeway. *Guest*: Mannix, Kojak, The Rookies, B.J. and the Bear, B.K. Stryker.

VINCENT, JR., FRANCIS T
Executive. b. Waterbury, CT, May 29, 1938. e. Williams Coll. B.A., 1960; Yale Law Sch. LL.B., 1963. Bar, CT 1963; NY, 1964; D.C. 1969. 1969-78, partner in law firm of Caplin & Drysdale, specializing in corporate banking and securities matters; 1978, assoc. dir. of, Division of Corporation Finance of Securities & Exchange Commission; exec. v.p. of the Coca-Cola Company and pres. & CEO of its entertainment business sector. Also chmn. & CEO of Columbia Pictures Industries, Inc.; appt. pres. CEO, 1978; mem. bd. of dir. of The Coca-Cola Bottling Co. of NY. 1987-88; rejoined law firm of Caplin & Drysdale, Washington, D.C., 1988. Trustee of Williams Coll. & The Hotchkiss Sch.

VINCENT, JAN-MICHAEL
Actor. b. Denver, CO, July 15, 1945. e. Ventura City (CA) Coll. as art major. Joined National Guard. Discovered by agent Dick Clayton. Hired by Robert Conrad to appear in his film, Los Bandidos. Signed to 6-mo. contract by Universal, for which made U.S. debut in Journey to Shiloh. Then did pilot TV movie for 20th-Fox based on Hardy Boys series of book. Originally called self Michael Vincent; changed after The Undefeated.
PICTURES: Los Bandidos (debut, 1967), Journey to Shiloh, The Undefeated, Going Home, The Mechanic, The World's Greatest Athlete, Buster and Billie, Bite the Bullet, White Line Fever, Baby Blue Marine, Vigilante Force, Shadow of the Hawk, Damnation Alley, Big Wednesday, Hooper, Defiance, Hard Country, The Return, The Last Plane Out, Born in East L.A., Enemy Territory, Hit List, Deadly Embrace, Demonstone, Hangfire, Raw Nerve, Alienator, Haunting Fear, Gold of the Samurai, The Divine Enforcer, Beyond the Call of Duty, Sins of Desire, Hidden Obsession, Xtro II, Deadly Avenger, Midnight Witness, Ice Cream Man, Abducted II: The Reunion.
TELEVISION: *Series*: Dangerous Island (Banana Splits Hour), The Survivors, Airwolf. *Movies*: Tribes, The Catcher, Sandcastles, Deliver Us From Evil, Six Against the Rock, Tarzan in Manhattan. *Mini-Series*: The Winds of War. *Guest*: Lassie, Bonanza.

VINCENT, KATHARINE
Actress. r.n. Ella Vincenti. b. St. Louis, MO, May 28, 1918.
THEATER: *B'way*: Love or Bust, Could She Tell?, Banners of 1939, Czarina Smith.
PICTURES: Peptipa's Waltz, Error in Her Ways, Stars and Stripes on Tour, Skin Deep, The Hungry, Voodoo Village, Welcome to Genoa, Unknown Betrayal, The Hooker, Study by M. Atget.
TELEVISION: The Untouchables, Moses the Lawgiver, Dolce Far Niente (mini-series, Roma).

VINER, MICHAEL
Producer, Writer. b. 1945. m. actress Deborah Raffin. e. Harvard U., Georgetown U. Served as aide to Robert

Kennedy; was legman for political columnist Jack Anderson. Settled in Hollywood, where worked for prod. Aaron Rosenberg, first as prod. asst. on three Frank Sinatra films; then asst. prod. on Joaquin Murietta. In music industry was record producer, manager, executive, eventually heading own division, at MGM. Debut as writer-producer in 1976 with TV special, Special of the Stars. Theatrical film debut as prod.-co-writer of Touched by Love, 1980. Television: Windmills of the Gods (exec. prod.). *Exec. Prod.*: Rainbow Drive; *Prod.*: Memories of Midnight. *President*: Dove Audio.

VITALE, RUTH
Executive. e. Tufts U., B.A.; Boston U., M.S. Prior to motion picture career, worked in advertising and media. Senior v.p., Vestron Pictures then s.v.p. of feature production at United Artists and management at Constantin Film Development before joining New Line as exec. v.p. of worldwide acquisitions. Currently pres., Fine Line Features, a wholly owned division of New Line Cinema.

VITTI, MONICA
Actress. r.n. Maria Luisa Ceciarelli. b. Rome, Italy, Nov. 3, 1933. Started acting in plays as teen, studying at Rome's Natl. Acad. of Dramatic Arts.
PICTURES: Ridere Ridere Ridere (debut, 1955), Smart Girls, L'Avventura, La Notte, L'Eclipse, Dragees du Poivre (Sweet and Sour), Three Fables of Love, The Nutty Naughty Chateau, Alta Infidelitata (High Infidelity), The Red Desert, Le Bambole (The Dolls), Il Disco Volante, Le Fate (The Queens), Modesty Blaise, The Chastity Belt (On My Way to the Crusades I Met a Girl Who...), Girl with a Pistol, La Femme Ecarlate, The Pizza Triangle, The Pacifist, Teresa la Ladra, Tosca, The Phantom of Liberty, Midnight Pleasures, My Loves, Duck in Orange Sauce, An Almost Perfect Affair, The Mystery of Oberwald, Tigers in Lipstick, The Flirt (also s.p.), When Veronica Calls, Secret Scandal (also dir., co- s.p.).

VOGEL, DAVID E.
Executive. President of Walt Disney Pictures.

VOIGHT, JON
Actor. b. Yonkers, NY. Dec. 29, 1938. e. Archbishop Stepinac H.S., White Plains, NY; Catholic U. of Amer., D.C. (B.F.A.) 1960; studied acting at the Neighborhood Playhouse and in private classes with Stanford Meisner, four yrs.
THEATER: *B'way*: The Sound of Music (debut, 1959), That Summer That Fall (Theatre World Award), The Seagull. *Off-B'way*: A View From the Bridge (1964 revival). *Regional*: Romeo & Juliet, A Streetcar Named Desire, Hamlet.
PICTURES: Hour of the Gun (debut, 1967), Fearless Frank, Midnight Cowboy, Out of It, Catch-22, The Revolutionary, Deliverance, All-American Boy, Conrack, The Odessa File, End of the Game, Coming Home (Academy Award, 1978), The Champ, Lookin' To Get Out (also co-s.p., prod.), Table for Five (also prod.), Runaway Train, Desert Bloom, Eternity, Heat, Rosewood.
TELEVISION: *Movies*: Chernobyl: The Final Warning, The Last of His Tribe, The Tin Soldier (also dir.), Convict Cowboy. *Mini-Series*: Return to Lonesome Dove. *Special*: The Dwarf (Public Broadcast Lab). *Guest*: Gunsmoke, Naked City, The Defenders, Coronet Blue, NYPD.

VON DER ESCH, LEIGH
Executive. President of the Utah Film Office, Association of Film Commissioners International.

VON SYDOW, MAX
Actor. b. Lund, Sweden, April 10, 1929. m. Keratin Olin, actress, 1951. Theatrical debut in a Cathedral Sch. of Lund prod. of The Nobel Prize. Served in the Swedish Quartermaster Corps two yrs. Studied at Royal Dramatic Theatre Sch. in Stockholm. Tour in municipal theatres. Has appeared on stage in Stockholm, London (The Tempest, 1988), Paris and Helsinki in Faust, The Legend and The Misanthrope. 1954 won Sweden's Royal Foundation Cultural Award. Appeared on B'way in Duet for One.
PICTURES: Bara en Mor (Only a Mother; debut, 1949), Miss Julie, Ingen Mans Kvinna, Ratten att Alska, The Seventh Seal, Prasten i Uddarbo, Wild Strawberries, Brink of Life, Spion 503, The Face, The Magician, The Virgin Spring, Brollopsdagen, Through a Glass Darkly, Nils Holgerssons Underbara Resa, Alskarinnen, Winter Light, 4x4, The Greatest Story Ever Told (English-language debut, 1965), The Reward, Hawaii, The Quiller Memorandum, Hour of the Wolf, Here Is Your Life, Svarta Palmkronor, Shame, Made in Sweden, The Kremlin Letter, The Passion of Anna, The Night Visitor, The Touch, The Emigrants, Appelbriget, I Hausbandet, Embassy, The New Land, The Exorcist, Steppenwolf, Egg! Egg!, Illustrious Corpses, Three Days of the Condor, The Ultimate Warrior, Foxtrot (The Other Side of Paradise), Cuore di Cane, Voyage of the Damned, Les Desert des Tartares, Exorcist II: The Heretic, March or Die, Black Journal, Brass Target, Gran Bolitto, Hurricane, Deathwatch, Venetian Lies, Flash Gordon,

Victory, She Dances Alone (voice), Conan the Barbarian, Flight of the Eagle, Strange Brew, Never Say Never Again, Target Eagle, Dreamscape, Dune, Code Name: Emerald, Hannah and Her Sisters, Duet for One, The Second Victory, The Wolf at the Door, Pelle the Conqueror (Acad. Award nom.), Katinka (dir.), Cellini: A Violent Life, Awakenings, A Kiss Before Dying, Until the End of the World, Zentropa (narrator), The Bachelor, The Best Intentions, The Ox, Father, Grandfather's Journey, Needful Things, The Silent Touch, Time Is Money, The Atlantic (narrator), Judge Dredd.
TELEVISION: *Movies/Mini-Series:* Samson and Delilah, Christopher Columbus, Kojak: The Belarus File, Brotherhood of the Rose, Hiroshima: Out of the Ashes, Red King White Knight, Radetzky March, Citizen X.

VON TROTTA, MARGARETHE
Director, Writer. b. Berlin, Germany, Feb. 21, 1942. e. Studied German and Latin literature in Munich and Paris. Studied acting in Munich and began career as actress. 1970 began collaborating on Schlondorff's films as well as acting in them.
PICTURES: *Actress:* Schrage Vogel, Brandstifter, Gotter der Pest, Baal, Der Amerikanische Soldat, The Sudden Wealth of the Poor People of Kombach (also co-s.p.), Die Moral der Ruth Halbfass, Strohfeuer (Free Woman; also co-s.p.), Desaster, Ubernachtung in Tirol, Coup de Grace (also co-s.p.). *Dir./ Co-s.p.:* The Lost Honor of Katharina Blum (co-dir., co-s.p., with Schlondorff), The Second Awakening of Christa Klages, Sisters or the Balance of Happiness, Marianne and Julianne, Heller Wahn (Sheer Madness), Rosa Luxemburg, Paura e Amore (Three Sisters), The African Woman, The Long Silence, The Promise (Years of the Wall).

VON ZERNECK, FRANK
Producer. b. New York, NY, Nov. 3, 1940. e. Hofstra Coll., 1962. Has produced plays in New York, Los Angeles and on national tour. Partner, von Zerneck/Sertner Films. Devised Portrait film genre for TV movies: Portrait of a Stripper, Portrait of a Mistress, Portrait of a Centerfold, etc. Past chmn. of California Theatre Council; former officer of League of Resident theatres; member of League of New York Theatres & Producers; Producers Guild of America; chmn's council, the Caucus for Producers, Writers and Directors; Board of Directors, Allied Communications, Inc. Museum of Radio & Television in NYC, Hollywood Television & Radio Society, Acad. of TV Arts & Sciences, Natl. Acad. of Cable Programming. Received American Film Institute Charles Fries Producer of the Year Award.
PICTURE: God's Lonely Man.
TELEVISION: 21 Hours at Munich, Dress Gray, Miracle on Ice, Combat High, Queenie, In the Custody of Strangers, The First Time, Baby Sister, Policewoman Centerfold, Obsessive Love, Invitation to Hell, Romance on the Orient Express, Hostage Flight. *Exec. prod.:* The Proud Men, Man Against the Mob, To Heal a Nation, Lady Mobster, Maybe Baby, Full Exposure: the Sex Tapes Scandal, Gore Vidal's Billy the Kid, Too Young to Die, The Great Los Angeles Earthquake, The Court-Martial of Jackie Robinson, White Hot: The Mysterious Murder of Thelma Todd, Survive the Savage Sea, Opposites Attract, Menu for Murder, Battling for Baby, Woman With a Past, Jackie Collins' Lady Boss, Danger Island, The Broken Chain, Beyond Suspicion, French Silk, The Corpse Had a Familiar Face, Robin Cook's Mortal Fear, Take Me Home Again, The Other Woman, Seduced and Betrayed, Robin Cook's Virus, The West Side Waltz, Crazy Horse, Robin Cook's Terminal, She Said No, Terror In the Family, My Son Is Innocent, Tornado!, Broder Music.

W

WADLEIGH, MICHAEL
Director. b. Akron, OH, Sept. 24, 1941. e. Ohio State U., B.S., B.A., M.A., Columbia Medical Sch.
PICTURES: Woodstock (dir.), Wolfen (dir., co-s.p.), Out of Order, The Village at the End of the Universe (dir., s.p.).

WAGGONER, LYLE
Actor. b. Kansas City, KS, April 13, 1935. e. Washington U., St. Louis, Was salesman before becoming actor with road co. prod. of Li'l Abner. Formed own sales-promo co. to finance trip to CA for acting career in 1965. Did commercials, then signed by 20th-Fox for new-talent school.
PICTURES: Love Me Deadly, Journey to the Center of Time, Catalina Caper, Surf II, Murder Weapon, Dead Women in Lingerie, Gypsy Angels.
TELEVISION: *Series:* The Carol Burnett Show, The Jimmie Rodgers Show, It's Your Bet (host), Wonder Woman. *Movies:* Letters from Three Lovers, The New Original Wonder Woman, The Love Boat II, The Gossip Columnist, Gridlock.

WAGNER, JANE
Writer, Director, Producer. b. Morristown, TN, Feb. 2, 1935. e. attended Sch. of Visual Arts, NY. Worked as designer for Kimberly Clark, created Teach Me Read Me sheets for Fieldcrest.

THEATER: *B'way:* Appearing Nitely (dir., co-writer), The Search for Signs of Intelligent Life in the Universe (dir., writer; NY Drama Desk Award & Special NY Drama Critics Award), both starring Lily Tomlin.
PICTURES: Moment by Moment (s.p., dir.), The Incredible Shrinking Woman (s.p., exec. prod.), The Search for Signs of Intelligent Life in the Universe (s.p., exec. prod.).
TELEVISION: *Specials:* J.T. (writer; Peabody Award), Lily (prod., co-writer; Emmy & WGA Awards, 1974), Lily Tomlin (prod., writer; Emmy Award for writing, 1976), People (prod., writer), Lily—Sold Out (exec. prod., co-writer; Emmy Award for producing, 1981), Lily for President? (exec. prod., co-writer), The Edith Ann Show (writer, exec. prod.).

WAGNER, LINDSAY
Actress. b. Los Angeles, CA, June 22, 1949. Appeared in school plays in Portland, OR; studied singing and worked professionally with rock group. In 1968 went to L.A. Signed to Universal contract in 1971.
PICTURES: Two People, The Paper Chase, Second Wind, Nighthawks, High Risk, Martin's Day, Ricochet.
TELEVISION: *Series:* The Bionic Woman (Emmy Award, 1977), Jessie, Peaceable Kingdom. *Guest:* The F.B.I., Owen Marshall: Counselor at Law, Night Gallery, The Bold Ones, Marcus Welby M.D., The Six Million Dollar Man. *Movies:* The Rockford Files (pilot), The Incredible Journey of Dr. Meg Laurel, The Two Worlds of Jennie Logan, Callie and Son, Memories Never Die, I Want to Live, Princess Daisy, Two Kinds of Love, Passions, This Child Is Mine, Child's Cry, Convicted, Young Again, Stranger in My Bed, The Return of the Six Million Dollar Man and the Bionic Woman, Student Exchange, Evil in Clear River, The Taking of Flight 847, Nightmare at Bitter Creek, From the Dead of Night, The Bionic Showdown: The Six-Million Dollar Man and the Bionic Woman, Shattered Dreams, Babies, Fire in the Dark, She Woke Up, Treacherous Crossing, To Be the Best, A Message From Holly, Nurses on the Line: The Crash of Flight 7, Danielle Steel's Once in a Lifetime, Bionic Ever After?, Fighting for My Daughter.

WAGNER, RAYMOND JAMES
Producer. b. College Point, NY, Nov. 3, 1925. e. Middlebury Coll., Williams Coll. Joined Young & Rubicam, Inc., as radio-TV commercial head in Hollywood, 1950-59. Head of pilot development, Universal Studios, 1960-65. V.p. of production (features) for MGM, 1972-79. Presently independent producer.
PICTURES: *Prod.:* Petulia, Loving (exec. prod.), Code of Silence, Rent-a-Cop, Hero and the Terror, Turner and Hooch, Run, Fifty Fifty.

WAGNER, ROBERT
Actor. b. Detroit, MI, Feb. 10, 1930. e. Saint Monica's H.S. m. actress Jill St. John. Signed to contract with 20th Century-Fox, 1950.
PICTURES: The Happy Years (debut, 1950), The Halls of Montezuma, The Frogmen, Let's Make It Legal, With a Song in My Heart, What Price Glory?, Stars and Stripes Forever, The Silver Whip, Titanic, Beneath the 12-Mile Reef, Prince Valiant, Broken Lance, White Feather, A Kiss Before Dying, The Mountain, Between Heaven and Hell, The True Story of Jesse James, Stopover Tokyo, The Hunters, In Love and War, Say One for Me, All the Fine Young Cannibals, Sail a Crooked Ship, The Longest Day, The War Lover, The Condemned of Altona, The Pink Panther, Harper, Banning, The Biggest Bundle of Them All, Don't Just Stand There, Winning, The Towering Inferno, Midway, The Concorde—Airport '79, Trail of the Pink Panther, Curse of the Pink Panther, I Am the Cheese, Delirious, The Player, Dragon: The Bruce Lee Story.
TELEVISION: *Series:* It Takes a Thief, Colditz (UK), Switch, Hart to Hart, Lime Street. *Movies:* How I Spent My Summer Vacation, City Beneath the Sea, The Cable Car Murder, Killer by Night, Madame Sin (also exec. prod.), Streets of San Francisco (pilot), The Affair, The Abduction of St. Anne, Switch (pilot), Death at Love House, Cat on a Hot Tin Roof, The Critical List, Hart to Hart (pilot), To Catch a King, There Must Be a Pony, Love Among Thieves, Windmills of the Gods, Indiscreet, This Gun for Hire, False Arrest, Daniel Steel's Jewels, Deep Trouble, Hart to Hart Returns (also co-exec. prod.), Hart to Hart: Home is Where the Hart Is, Hart to Hart: Crimes of the Hart, Hart to Hart: Old Friends Never Die, Parallel Lives, Hart to Hart: Secrets of the Heart. *Mini-Series:* Pearl, Around the World in 80 Days, Heaven & Hell: North and South Book III.

WAHL, KEN
Actor. b. Chicago, IL, Feb. 14, 1953. No acting experience when cast in The Wanderers in 1978.
PICTURES: The Wanderers (debut, 1979), Fort Apache The Bronx, Race to the Yankee Zephyr, Jinxed, The Soldier, Purple Hearts, The Omega Syndrome, The Taking of Beverly Hills (also co-exec. prod.), The Favor, Back in the U.S.A.
TELEVISION: *Movies:* The Dirty Dozen: The Next Mission, The Gladiator, Search for Grace, Wise Guy. *Series:* Double Dare, Wiseguy.

WAITE, RALPH
Actor. b. White Plains, NY, June 22, 1929. e. Bucknell U., Yale U. Social worker, publicity director, assistant editor and minister before turning to acting. Founder of the Los Angeles Actors Theatre.
THEATER: *B'way*: Hogan's Goat, The Watering Place, Trial of Lee Harvey Oswald. *Off-B'way*: The Destiny of Me, The Young Man From Atlanta. *Regional*: Hometown Heroes.
PICTURES: Cool Hand Luke, A Lovely Way to Die, Last Summer, Five Easy Pieces, Lawman, The Grissom Gang, The Sporting Club, The Pursuit of Happiness, Chato's Land, The Magnificent Seven Ride, Trouble Man, Kid Blue, The Stone Killer, On the Nickel (also dir., prod., s.p.), Crash and Burn, The Bodyguard, Cliffhanger, Sioux City, Homeward Bound II: Lost in San Francisco.
TELEVISION: *Series*: The Waltons, The Mississippi. *Movies*: The Secret Life of John Chapman, The Borgia Stick, Red Alert, Ohms, Angel City, The Gentleman Bandit, A Wedding on Waltons Mountain, Mother's Day on Waltons Mountain, A Day for Thanks on Waltons Mountain, A Good Sport, Crime of Innocence, Red Earth White Earth, A Walton Thanksgiving Reunion, Sin and Redemption, A Season of Hope, A Walton Wedding. *Mini-Series*: Roots.

WAITE, RIC
Cinematographer. b. Sheboygan, WI, July 10, 1933. e. Univ. of CO. Photographed more than 40 movies-of-the-week for TV, 1979-83.
PICTURES: The Other Side of the Mountain (debut, 1975), Defiance, On the Nickel, The Long Riders, The Border, Tex, 48 Hrs., Class, Uncommon Valor, Footloose, Red Dawn, Volunteers, Summer Rental, Brewster's Millions, Cobra, Adventures in Babysitting, The Great Outdoors, Marked for Death, Out for Justice, Rapid Fire, On Deadly Ground.
TELEVISION: Captains and the Kings (Emmy Award, 1977), Tail Gunner Joe (Emmy nom.), Huey P. Long (Emmy nom.), Revenge of the Stepford Wives, Baby Comes Home.

WAITS, TOM
Singer, Composer, Actor. b. Pomona, CA, Dec. 7, 1949. Recorded numerous albums and received Acad. Award nom. for his song score of One from the Heart. Composed songs for On the Nickel, Streetwise, Paradise Alley, Wolfen, American Heart, Dead Man Walking, Night on Earth (score). Featured songs in Smoke and Things to Do in Denver When You're Dead. Has starred in Chicago's Steppenwolf Theatre Co.'s Frank's Wild Years (also co-wrote, wrote the music) and Los Angeles Theatre Co.'s Demon Wine. Wrote songs and music for opera The Black Rider (1990). Co-wrote songs and music for opera Alice by Robert Wilson. Received Grammy Award for album, Blue Machine, 1992.
PICTURES: *As actor*: Paradise Alley, Poetry in Motion, The Outsiders, Rumble Fish, The Cotton Club, Down by Law (also music), Ironweed, Candy Mountain, Big Time (also co-s.p.), Cold Feet, Bearskin, On a Moonlit Night (music only), The Two Jakes, Queens Logic, The Fisher King, At Play in the Fields of the Lord, Bram Stoker's Dracula, Short Cuts.

WAJDA, ANDRZEJ
Director, Writer. b. Suwalki, Poland, March 6, 1926. e. Fine Arts Academy, Krakow, Poland, 1945-48; High School of Cinematography, Lodz, Poland, 1950-52. 1940-43, worked as asst. in restoration of church paintings. 1942, joined Polish gov. in exile's A.K. (Home Army Resistance) against German occupation. 1950-52, directed shorts (While You Sleep; The Bad Boy, The Pottery of Ilzecka) as part of film school degree; 1954, asst. dir. to Aleksander Ford on 5 Boys from Barska Street. 1981, concentrated on theatrical projects in Poland and film prods. with non-Polish studios. 1983, gov. dissolved his Studio X film prod. group. 1984, gov. demanded Wajda's resignation as head of filmmakers' assoc. in order to continue org.'s existence. 1989, appt. artistic dir. of Teatr Powszechny, official Warsaw theater. Also leader of the Cultural Comm. of the Citizen's Committee. 1989, elected senator. Short films: While You Sleep, The Bad Boy, The Pottery of Ilza, I Go to the Sun.
PICTURES: *Dir.-Writer*: A Generation (debut, 1957), Kanal, Ashes and Diamonds, Lotna, Innocent Sorcerers, Samson, Siberian Lady Macbeth (Fury Is a Woman), Love at 20 (Warsaw Poland episode), Ashes, Gates to Paradise, Everything for Sale, Hunting Flies, Landscape After the Battle, The Wedding, Promised Land, Shadow Line, Man of Marble, Without Anesthetic, The Girls From Wilko, The Orchestra Conductor, Man of Iron (Golden Palm Award, Cannes, 1981), Danton, A Love in Germany, Chronicle of Love Affairs, The Possessed, Korczak.
TELEVISION: Roly-Poly, The Birch Wood, Pilate and the Others, The Dead Class, November Night, Crime and Punishment.

WALD, MALVIN
Writer, Producer. b. New York, NY, Aug. 8, 1917. e. Brooklyn Coll., B.A., J.D. Woodland U. Coll. of Law; grad. work Columbia U., NYU, USC. Newspaper reporter and editor, publicist, social worker, radio actor. Screenplays and original stories for Columbia, 20th-Fox, UA, MGM, WB; U.S. Air Force; tech. sgt., wrote 30 doc. films for film unit; exec. prod., 20th Century Fox tv doc. unit, 1963-64; writer-prod., 1964-65; writer-prod., Ivan Tors Films, 1965-69; prof., USC Sch. of Cinema, Television, 1956-96; bd. of dir., Writer's Guild of America; 1983-85, Trustee, Writers Guild Foundation, edit. bd. WGA Journal, 1996; editorial bd., Creative Screenwriting, 1996; Acad. of Motion Picture Arts and Sciences, co-author of book, Three Major Screenplays. Contributor to books, American Screenwriters, Close-Ups, Henry Miller: A Book of Tributes, Tales From the Casting Couch. Published s.p., Naked City. Consultant, Natl. Endowment for Humanities and Corp. for Public Broadcasting. Visiting professor, Southern Illinois Univ., Univ of PA. Pre-selection judge, Focus writing awards. Media & prod. consultant, Apache Mountain Spirit (PBS); playwright, ANTA-West, Actors Alley, Rep. Theatre. Co-author, L.A. Press Club 40th Anniversary Show, 1987. Mag. articles published in Film Comment, Journal of Popular Film & TV, Journal of Writers Guild of America, American Heritage, Creative Screenwriting, Directors Guild Magazine, Hollywood: Then and Now, Writers Digest, 1991-. Shorts: An Answer, Employees Only (Acad. Award nom.), Boy Who Owned a Melephant (Venice Children's Film Fest. gold medal), Unarmed in Africa, The Policeman, James Weldon Johnson, Me an Alcoholic?, Problem Solving, Managerial Control, UFO—Fact or Fiction? Was admitted to Producers Guild Hall of Fame, 1996.
PICTURES: The Naked City (Acad. Award nom., best story), Behind Locked Doors, The Dark Past, Ten Gentlemen from West Point, The Powers Girl, Two in a Taxi, Undercover Man, Outrage, On the Loose, Battle Taxi, Man on Fire, Al Capone, Venus in Furs, In Search of Historic Jesus, Legend of Sleepy Hollow, Mysteries From Beyond Earth.
TELEVISION: Many credits including Playhouse 90, Marilyn Monroe, Hollywood: The Golden Years, The Rafer Johnson Story, D-Day, Project: Man in Space, Tales of Hans Christian Andersen, John F. Kennedy, Biography of A Rookie, Alcoa-Goodyear Hour, Climax, Shirley Temple Storybook, Life of Riley, Peter Gunn, Perry Mason, Dobie Gillis, Combat, Moonport (U.S.I.A.; prod., writer), Daktari (assoc. prod.) Primus, California Tomorrow (prod.), Mod Squad, Untamed World, Around the World of Mike Todd, The Billie Jean King Show, Life and Times of Grizzly Adams, Mark Twain's America, Greatest Heroes of the Bible, Littlest Hobo., Rich Little's You Asked For It, Hugh Hefner's Bunny Memories.

WALKEN, CHRISTOPHER
Actor. b. Astoria, NY, Mar. 31, 1943. Began career in off-B'way play J.B. billed as Ronnie Walken. Appeared in Madonna video Bad Girl.
THEATER: *NY*: Best Foot Forward (Clarence Derwent Award), Kid Champion (Obie Award), High Spirits (B'way debut, 1964), The Lion in Winter (Clarence Derwent Award). The Rose Tattoo (Theatre World Award), Hurlyburly (B'way), Him (also author). NY Shakespeare Festival: Coriolanus, Othello.
PICTURES: The Anderson Tapes (debut, 1971), The Happiness Cage, Next Stop Greenwich Village, The Sentinel, Annie Hall, Roseland, The Deer Hunter (Academy Award, best supporting actor, 1978), Last Embrace, Heaven's Gate, The Dogs of War, Shoot the Sun Down, Pennies from Heaven, Brainstorm, The Dead Zone, A View to a Kill, At Close Range, Deadline, The Milagro Beanfield War, Biloxi Blues, Puss in Boots, Homeboy, Communion, King of New York, The Comfort of Strangers, McBain, All-American Murder, Batman Returns, Mistress, Le Grand Pardon, Day of Atonement, True Romance, Wayne's World 2, A Business Affair, Pulp Fiction, Search and Destroy, The Prophecy, The Addiction, Wild Side, Things to Do in Denver When You're Dead, Nick of Time, The Funeral, Last Man Standing.
TELEVISION: *Movies*: Sarah: Plain and Tall, Skylark, Scam. *Special*: Who Am I This Time? *Guest*: Saturday Night Live.

WALKER, E. CARDON
Executive. b. Rexburg, ID, Jan. 9, 1916. e. UCLA, B.A. 1938. Four years officer, U.S. Navy. Started with Walt Disney Productions 1938; camera, story, unit director short subjects, budget control. Headed adv. & pub 1950. 1956, v.p. in chg. of adv. & sales. 1960 member bd. of dir. & exec. comm. 1965 v.p., mkt. 1967 exec. v.p. operations. 1968, exec. v.p. and chief operating officer; pres., 1971; 1976 pres. and chief executive officer; 1980, named bd. chmn. & chief executive officer; 1983-84, chmn. of exec. committee. Remains a board member.

WALKER, KATHRYN
Actress. b. Philadelphia, PA, Jan. 9. m. singer-songwriter James Taylor. e. Wells Coll., Harvard. Studied acting at London Acad. of Music and Dramatic Art on Fulbright Fellowship. Stage roles include part in Private Lives with Elizabeth Taylor and Richard Burton, and Wild Honey with Ian McKellen.
PICTURES: Slap Shot, Rich Kids, Neighbors, D.A.R.Y.L., Dangerous Game, Emma and Elvis.

TELEVISION: *Series*: Beacon Hill. *Movies*: The Winds of Kitty Hawk, Too Far to Go, FDR: The Last Year, A Whale for the Killing, Family Reunion, Special Bulletin, The Murder of Mary Phagan. *Mini-Series*: The Adams Chronicles (Emmy Award, 1976).

WALLACE, MIKE
TV Commentator, Interviewer. b. Brookline, MA, May 9, 1918. e. U. of Michigan, 1939. Night Beat, WABD, N.Y., 1956; The Mike Wallace Interview, ABC, 1956-58; newspaper col., Mike Wallace Asks, N.Y. Post, 1957-58; News Beat, WNTA-TV, 1959-61; The Mike Wallace Interview, WNTA-TV, 1959-61; Biography, 1962; correspondent, CBS News, 1963, CBS Radio; Personal Closeup, Mike Wallace at Large; Co-editor, 60 Minutes (Emmy Awards, 1971, 1972, 1973), CBS News, Host, 20th Century, 1994.

WALLACH, ELI
Actor. b. Brooklyn, NY, Dec. 7, 1915. m. actress Anne Jackson. e. U. of TX. Capt. in Medical Admin. Corps during WWII. After college acting, appeared in summer stock. Charter member of the Actors Studio.
THEATER: Skydrift (B'way debut, 1945), Antony & Cleopatra, The Rose Tattoo (Tony Award, 1951), Mademoiselle Colombe, Camino Real, The Teahouse of August Moon (also London), Major Barbara, Rhinoceros, Luv, Twice Around the Park, Cafe Crown, The Price, In Persons (Off-B'way), The Flowering Peach.
PICTURES: Baby Doll (debut, 1956; BFA Award), The Line Up, The Magnificent Seven, Seven Thieves, The Misfits, Hemingway's Adventures of A Young Man, How the West Was Won, The Victors, Act One, The Moonspinners, Kisses for My President, Lord Jim, Genghis Khan, How to Steal a Million, The Good the Bad and the Ugly, The Tiger Makes Out, How to Save a Marriage and Ruin Your Life, MacKenna's Gold, A Lovely Way to Die, Ace High, The Brain, Zigzag, The People Next Door, The Angle Levine, The Adventures of Gerard, Romance of a Horse Thief, Cinderella Liberty, Crazy Joe, Stateline Motel, Don't Turn the Other Cheek, The Sentinel, Nasty Habits, The Deep, The Domino Principle, Girlfriends, Movie Movie, Circle of Iron, Firepower, Winter Kills, The Hunter, The Salamander, Sam's Son, Tough Guys, Nuts, Funny, The Two Jakes, The Godfather Part III, Article 99, Mistress, Night and the City, Two Much, The Associate.
TELEVISION: *Series*: Our Family Honor. *Guest*: Studio One, Philco Playhouse, Playhouse 90, The Poppy Is Also a Flower (Emmy Award, 1967), Law & Order. *Movies*: Cold Night's Death, Indict and Convict, Seventh Avenue, The Pirate, Fugitive Family, Pride of Jesse Halam, Skokie, The Wall, Anatomy of an Illness, Murder: By Reason of Insanity, Something in Common, Executioner's Song, Christopher Columbus, Embassy, The Impossible Spy, Vendetta: Secrets of a Mafia Bride, Legacy of Lies, Teamster Boss: The Jackie Presser Story, Vendetta 2: The New Mafia.

WALLACH, GEORGE
Producer, Writer, Director. b. New York, NY, Sept. 25, 1918. e. SUNY-Westbury. Actor in theater & radio 1936-45; U.S. Navy 1942-45; supvr. radio-TV Div. of American Theatrical Wing 1946-48; dir., WNEW, 1946-48; prod./dir., Wendy Barrie Show, 1948-49; prod.-dir. for WNBC-WNBT, 1950; dir., news, spec. events WNBT-WNBC, 1951-52; prod. mgr., NBC Film Div. 1953-56, appt. TV officer, U.S.I.A., 1957. Film-TV officer American Embassy, Bonn, Germany, 1961. Film-TV officer American Embassy; Tehran, Iran, 1965-66; MoPix Prod. Officer, JUSPAO, American Embassy, Saigon, 1966; prod.-dir.-wr., Greece Today, 1967-68. Exec. prod.-dir., George Wallach Productions, spec. doc., travel, and industrial films, chairman, Film-TV Dept., N.Y. Institute of Photography, 1968-75; Prof. film-TV-radio, Brooklyn Coll., 1975-80; dir., special projects, Directors Guild of America 1978-88; presently international representative for Denver Film Festival, U.S. Contact for Moscow Film Festival, U.S. prod. for A Native of Beijing in NY, a series of 20 1 hr. programs for Beijing TV.
PICTURES: It Happened in Havana, Bwana Devil (assoc. prod., prod. mgr.).
TELEVISION: *NBC producer*: Inner Sanctum, The Falcon, His Honor Homer Bell, Watch the World. *Dir*.: Wanted.

WALSH, DYLAN
Actor. Raised in Africa, Indonesia, India, Washington D.C. e. Univ. of VA. On D.C. stage with Arena Stage and Studio Theatre, Heritage Rep. Co. Appearing in A Midsummer Night's Dream, Curse of the Starving Class, Romeo & Juliet, Death of a Salesman.
PICTURES: Where the Heart Is, Betsy's Wedding, Arctic Blue, Nobody's Fool, Congo, Eden.
TELEVISION: *Series*: Gabriel's Fire. *Guest*: Kate and Allie. *Movies*: Telling Secrets, Radio Inside.

WALSH, J.T.
Actor. b. San Francisco, CA. Did not begin acting until age 30, when he quit job in sales to join off-B'way theater co.

THEATER: Glengarry Glen Ross (Drama Desk Award), Rose, Last Licks, Richard III, Macbeth, Half a Lifetime, The American Clock.
PICTURES: Eddie Macon's Run, Hard Choices, Power, Hannah and Her Sisters, Tin Men, House of Games, Good Morning Vietnam, Things Change, Tequila Sunrise, Wired, The Big Picture, Dad, Crazy People, Why Me?, Narrow Margin, Misery, The Grifters, The Russia House, Backdraft, Defenseless, True Identity, Iron Maze, A Few Good Men, Hoffa, Sniper, National Lampoon's Loaded Weapon 1, Red Rock West, Needful Things, Morning Glory, Blue Chips, The Client, Miracle on 34th Street, Outbreak, The Low Life, Nixon, Executive Decision, The Babysitter, Black Day Blue Night.
TELEVISION: *Movies*: Little Gloria: Happy at Last, Jacobo Timerman: Prisoner Without a Name Cell Without a Number, Right to Kill, Tough Cookies, Windmills of the Gods, In the Shadow of a Killer, The American Clock, The Last Seduction, Against Their Will: Women in Prison, Crime of the Century. *Special*: Partners.

WALSH, M. EMMET
Actor. r.n. Michael Emmet Walsh. b. Ogdensburg, NY, Mar. 22, 1935. e. Clarkson Col. (B.B.A., 1958), Academy of Dramatic Arts (1959-61).
THEATER: *B'way*: Does the Tiger Wear a Necktie?, That Championship Season. *Off-B'way*: The Old Glory, The Outside Man, Death of the Well Loved Boy, Shepherds of the Shelf, Three From Column 'A', Are You Now or Have You Ever Been; also summer stock and regional theatre (Hometown Heroes).
PICTURES: Midnight Cowboy, Stiletto, Alice's Restaurant, End of the Road, Loving, The Traveling Executioner, Little Big Man, Cold Turkey, They Might Be Giants, Escape from the Planet of the Apes, Get to Know Your Rabbit, What's Up Doc?, Kid Blue, Serpico, The Gambler, The Prisoner of 2nd Avenue, At Long Last Love, Mikey and Nicky, Nickelodeon, Bound for Glory, Airport '77, Slap Shot, Straight Time, The Fish That Saved Pittsburgh, The Jerk, Brubaker, Raise the Titanic, Ordinary People, Back Roads, Reds, Cannery Row, The Escape Artist, Blade Runner, Fast-Walking, Silkwood, Scandalous, (Raw) Courage, The Pope of Greenwich Village, Grandview USA, Missing in Action, Blood Simple, Fletch, The Best of Times, Wildcats, Critters, Back to School, Raising Arizona, Harry and the Hendersons, No Man's Land, The Milagro Beanfield War, Sunset, Clean and Sober, Sundown: The Vampire in Retreat, The Mighty Quinn, Red Scorpion, Thunderground, War Party, Catch Me If You Can, Chattahoochee, Narrow Margin, White Sands, Killer Image, Equinox, The Naked Truth, The Music of Chance, Bitter Harvest, Wilder Napalm, Cops and Robbersons, Dead Badge, Probable Cause, The Child, Camp Nowhere, The Glass Shield, Panther, Free Willy 2: The Adventure Home, Criminal Hearts, Portraits of Innocence, Albino Alligator, The Killing Jar, A Time to Kill, Romeo & Juliet.
TELEVISION: *Series*: The Sandy Duncan Show, Dear Detective, Unsub. *Movies*: Sarah T.—Portrait of a Teenage Alcoholic, Crime Club, Invasion of Johnson County, Red Alert, Superdome, A Question of Guilt, No Other Love, The Gift, Skag, City in Fear, High Noon Part II, Hellinger's Law, Night Partners, The Deliberate Stranger, Resting Place, Broken Vows, Hero in the Family, The Abduction of Kari Swenson, Murder Ordained, Brotherhood of the Rose, Love and Lies, Fourth Story, Wild Card, Four Eyes and Six-Guns, From the Mixed-Up Files of Mrs. Basil E. Frankweiler. *Mini-Series*: The French-Atlantic Affair, East of Eden. *Guest*: Julia, Amy Prentiss, The Jimmy Stewart Show, Bonanza, All in the Family, Rockford Files, Baretta, The Waltons, Nichols, Starsky & Hutch, Amazing Stories, Twilight Zone, The Flash, Jackie Thomas Show, Tales From the Crypt, Home Improvement, The Outer Limits, Home Improvement, many others. *Pilot*: Silver Fox.

WALSTON, RAY
Actor. b. New Orleans, LA, Nov. 2, 1918. Stage debut in Houston, 1936. To NY where he appeared on stage in South Pacific, The Front Page, Me and Juliet, Damn Yankees (Tony Award, 1956).
PICTURES: Kiss Them For Me (debut, 1957), South Pacific, Damn Yankees, Say One for Me, Tall Story, The Apartment, Portrait in Black, Convicts Four, Wives and Lovers, Who's Minding the Store?, Kiss Me Stupid, Caprice, Paint Your Wagon, The Sting, Silver Streak, The Happy Hooker Goes to Washington, Popeye, Galaxy of Terror, Fast Times at Ridgemont High, O'Hara's Wife, Private School, Johnny Dangerously, RAD, From the Hip, O.C. and Stiggs, A Man of Passion, Blood Relations, Saturday the 14th Strikes Back, Paramedics, Ski Patrol, Blood Salvage, Popcorn, The Player, Of Mice and Men, House Arrest.
TELEVISION: *Series*: My Favorite Martian, Stop Susan Williams (Cliffhangers), Silver Spoons, Fast Times, Picket Fences (Emmy Awards, 1995 & 1996). *Guest*: You Are There, Producers Showcase, There Shall Be No Night, Studio One, Playhouse 90, Oh Madeline, Crash Course. *Movies*: Institute for Revenge, The Kid With the Broken Halo, The Fall of the

House of Usher, This Girl for Hire, The Jerk Too, Amos, Red River, I Know My First Name Is Steven, One Special Victory. *Mini-Series*: Stephen King's The Stand.

WALTER, JESSICA
Actress. b. Brooklyn, NY, Jan. 31, 1944. m. actor Ron Leibman. e. H.S. of the Performing Arts. Studied at Bucks County Playhouse and Neighborhood Playhouse. Many TV performances plus lead in series, For the People. Broadway debut in Advise and Consent, 1961. Also, Photo Finish (Clarence Derwent Award), Night Life, A Severed Head, Rumors.
PICTURES: Lilith (debut, 1964), The Group, Grand Prix, Bye Bye Braverman, Number One, Play Misty for Me, Goldengirl, Going Ape, Spring Fever, The Flamingo Kid, Tapeheads, Ghost in the Machine.
TELEVISION: *Series*: For the People, Love of Life, Amy Prentiss (Emmy Award, 1975), Bare Essence, Aaron's Way, Dinosaurs (voice), The Round Table. *Movies*: The Immortal (pilot), Three's a Crowd, They Call It Murder, Women in Chains, Home for the Holidays, Hurricane, Having Babies, Victory at Entebbe, Black Market Baby, Wild and Wooly, Dr. Strange, Secrets of Three Hungry Wives, Vampire, She's Dressed to Kill, Miracle on Ice, Scruples, Thursday's Child, The Return of Marcus Welby M.D., The Execution, Killer in the Mirror, Leave of Absence. *Mini-Series*: Wheels.

WALTER, TRACEY
Actor. b. Jersey City, NJ, Nov. 25.
PICTURES: Goin' South, Blue Collar, Hardcore, The Hunter, The Hand, Raggedy Man, Honkytonk Man, Timerider, Rumble Fish, Conan the Destroyer, Repo Man, At Close Range, Something Wild, Malone, Mortuary Academy, Married to the Mob, Under the Boardwalk, Out of the Dark, Batman, Homer and Eddie, Young Guns II, The Two Jakes, Pacific Heights, The Silence of the Lambs, City Slickers, Delusion, Amos and Andrew, Philadelphia, Mona Must Die, Destiny Turns on the Radio, Wild America, Road to Ruin, Dorothy Day, Junior, Amanda, Larger Than Life, Matilda.
TELEVISION: *Series*: Best of the West, On the Air. *Movies*: Ride With the Wind, In the Line of Duty: Kidnapped, Buffalo Girls, Bill On His Own, Mad Bull, Out of this World.

WALTERS, BARBARA
Broadcast Journalist. b. Boston, MA, Sept. 25, 1931. Daughter of Latin Quarter nightclub impressario Lou Walters. e. Sarah Lawrence Coll. Began working in TV after graduation. Joined The Today Show in 1961 as writer-researcher, making occasional on-camera appearances. In 1963, became full-time on camera. In April, 1974, named permanent co-host. Also hosted own synd. prog., Not for Women Only. In 1976, joined ABC-TV Evening News, (host, 1976-78), correspondent World News Tonight (1978); corresp. 20/20 (1979-present). Host of the Barbara Walters Specials (1979-present). Author: How to Talk with Practically Anybody About Practically Anything (1970). Recipient of numerous awards including Emmy, Media, Peabody. Named one of women most admired by American People in 1982 & -84 Gallup Polls. Inducted into the Television Academy Hall of Fame, 1990. 1994, co-anchor of Turning Point.

WALTERS, JULIE
Actress. b. Birmingham, England, Feb. 22, 1950. Trained for 2 years to be a nurse before studying drama at Manchester Polytechnic, followed by year at Granada's Stables Theatre. Joined Everyman Theatre, Liverpool. Also toured Dockland pubs with songs, dance and imitations.
THEATER: Breezeblock Park, Funny Perculiar, The Glad Hand, Good Fun, Educating Rita, Jumpers, Fool for Love, When I Was a Girl I Used to Scream and Shout, Frankie and Johnnie in the Claire de Lune, Macbeth, Having a Ball, The Rose Tattoo, Jumpers, Fool for Love, When I Was a Girl I Used to Scream and Shout, Frankie and Johnny.
PICTURES: Educating Rita (debut, 1983; Acad. Award nom.), She'll Be Wearing Pink Pyjamas, Car Trouble, Personal Services, Prick Up Your Ears, Buster, Mack the Knife, Killing Dad, Stepping Out, Wide Eyed and Legless, The Summer House, The Wedding Gift, Just Like a Woman, Sister My Sister.
TELEVISION: Unfair Exchanges, Talent, Nearly a Happy Ending, Family Man, Happy Since I Met You, The Secret Diary of Adrian Mole (series), Wood and Walters (series), Say Something Happened, Intensive Care, The Boys from the Black Stuff, Talking Heads, Victoria Wood As Seen on TV (series & special), The Birthday Party, Her Big Chance, Nearly a Happy Ending, Julie Walters & Friends (special), GBH (series), The All-Day Breakfast Show (special).

WANG, WAYNE
Director. b. Hong Kong, 1949. m. actress Cora Miao. e. came to U.S. to study photography at College of Arts and Crafts, Oakland, CA. With a Master's Degree in film and television, returned to Hong Kong. Worked on TV comedy series. First

dir. work, as asst. dir. for Chinese sequences of Golden Needle. First film was A Man, A Woman and a Killer. Won grant from AFI and National Endowment for the Arts, used to finance Chan is Missing (1982) which cost $22,000.
PICTURES: Chan is Missing (also s.p., editor, prod.), Dim Sum: A Little Bit of Heart (also prod., story), Slam Dance, Eat a Bowl of Tea, Life is Cheap... But Toilet Paper is Expensive (also exec. prod., story), The Joy Luck Club, Smoke, Blue in the Face (also co-s.p.).

WARD, DAVID S.
Writer, Director. b. Providence, RI, Oct. 24, 1947. Raised in Cleveland. e. Pomona Col. (BA), UCLA (MFA).
PICTURES: *Writer*: Steelyard Blues, The Sting (Academy Award, 1973), Cannery Row (also dir.), The Sting II, The Milagro Beanfield War (co-s.p.), Major League (also dir.), King Ralph (also dir.), Sleepless in Seattle (co-s.p.; Acad. Award nom.), The Program (also dir.), Major League 2 (dir., co-s.p.). *Director*: Major League II, Down Periscope.

WARD, FRED
Actor. b. San Diego, CA, 1943. Raised in Louisiana and Texas. Studied at Herbert Berghof Studio. Moved to Rome to work in experimental theatre. Returned to U.S. to appear on San Fransico stage with Sam Shepard's Magic Theatre in Inacoma and Angel City. Additional stage work in The Glass Menagerie, One Flew Over the Cuckoo's Nest, Domino Courts, Simpatico.
PICTURES: Escape From Alcatraz (debut, 1979), Tilt, Carny, Southern Comfort, Timerider, The Right Stuff, Silkwood, Uncommon Valor, Swing Shift, Uforia, Secret Admirer, Remo Williams: The Adventure Begins, Off Limits, Big Business, The Prince of Pennsylvania, Tremors, Miami Blues (also co-exec. prod.), Henry and June, Thunderheart, The Player, Bob Roberts, The Dark Wind, Equinox, Short Cuts, Naked Gun 33 1/3: The Final Insult, Two Small Bodies, The Blue Villa, Chain Reaction.
TELEVISION: *Movies*: Belle Starr, Noon Wine, Florida Straits, Cast a Deadly Spell, Backtrack, Four Eyes and Six-Guns. *Special*: Noon Wine (Amer. Playhouse).

WARD, RACHEL
Actress. b. London, 1957. m. actor Bryan Brown. Top fashion and TV commercial model before becoming actress. Studied acting with Stella Adler and Robert Modica. On stage in Sydney in A Doll's House, Hopping to Byzantium.
PICTURES: Night School (debut, 1981), The Final Terror, Sharky's Machine, Dead Men Don't Wear Plaid, Against All Odds, The Good Wife, Hotel Colonial, How to Get Ahead in Advertising, After Dark My Sweet, Christopher Columbus: The Discovery, Wide Sargasso Sea, The Ascent.
TELEVISION: *Mini-Series*: The Thorn Birds, Shadow of the Cobra (U.K.). *Movies*: Christmas Lillies of the Field, Fortress, And the Sea Will Tell, Black Magic, Double Jeopardy.

WARD, SELA
Actress. b. Meridian, MS, July 11, 1956.
PICTURES: The Man Who Loved Women, Rustler's Rhapsody, Nothing in Common, Steel Justice, Hello Again, The Fugitive.
TELEVISION: *Series*: Emerald Point N.A.S., Sisters (Emmy Award, 1994). *Movie*: Almost Golden: The Jessica Savitch Story.

WARD, SIMON
Actor. b. London, England, Oct. 19, 1941. Ent. ind. 1964.
PICTURES: If... (debut, 1969), Frankenstein Must Be Destroyed, I Start Counting, Quest for Love, Young Winston, Hitler—The Last Ten Days, The Three Musketeers, The Four Musketeers, Deadly Strangers. Aces High, Children of Rage, Battle Flag, The Chosen, Dominique, Zulu Dawn, La Sabina, The Monster Club, L'Etincelle, Supergirl, Leave All Fair, Double X, Wuthering Heights.
TELEVISION: Spoiled, Chips with Everything, The Corsican Brothers, All Creatures Great and Small, Dracula, Valley Forge, The Last Giraffe (Raising Daisy Rothschild), Around the World in 80 Days.

WARD, VINCENT
Director, Writer. b. New Zealand, 1956. e. Ilam Sch. of Art. At 21 dir. & co-wrote short film A State of Siege (Hugo Award, Chicago Film Fest.)
PICTURES: In Spring One Plants Alone (Silver Hugo, Chicago Film Fest.), Vigil (Grand Prix Awards, Madrid & Prades Film Fests), The Navigator (Australian Film Awards for Best Picture & Director), Alien^3 (story only), Map of the Human Heart.

WARDEN, JACK
Actor. b. Newark, NJ, Sept. 18, 1920. r.n. Jack Warden Lebzelter. Started with Margo Jones theatre in Dallas (rep. co.).
THEATER: *B'way*: Golden Boy, Sing Me No Lullaby, Very Special Baby, Cages (Obie Award), A View from the Bridge,

387

The Man in the Glass Booth, The Body Beautiful. *Repertory*: Twelfth Night, She Stoops to Conquer, The Importance of Being Earnest, Summer and Smoke, The Taming of the Shrew, etc.
PICTURES: You're in the Navy Now (U.S.S. Teakettle; debut, 1951), The Frogmen, The Man With My Face, Red Ball Express, From Here to Eternity, Edge of the City, 12 Angry Men, The Bachelor Party, Darby's Rangers, Run Silent Run Deep, The Sound and the Fury, That Kind of Woman, Wake Men When It's Over, Escape From Zahrain, Donovan's Reef, The Thin Red Line, Blindfold, Bye Bye Braverman, The Sporting Club, Summertree, Who Is Harry Kellerman?, Welcome to the Club, Billy Two Hats, The Man Who Loved Cat Dancing, The Apprenticeship of Duddy Kravitz, Shampoo (Acad. Award nom.), All the President's Men, The White Buffalo, Heaven Can Wait (Acad. Award nom.), Death on the Nile, The Champ, Dreamer, Beyond the Poseidon Adventure, And Justice for All, Being There, Used Cars, The Great Muppet Caper, Chu Chu and the Philly Flash, Carbon Copy, So Fine, The Verdict, Crackers, The Aviator, September, The Presidio, Everybody Wins, Problem Child, Problem Child 2, Passed Away, Night and the City, Toys, Guilty As Sin, Bullets Over Broadway, While You Were Sleeping, Things to Do in Denver When You're Dead, Mighty Aphrodite, Ed.
TELEVISION: *Series*: Mr. Peepers, Norby, The Asphalt Jungle, The Wackiest Ship in the Army, N.Y.P.D., Jigsaw John, The Bad News Bears, Crazy Like a Fox. *Guest*: Philco Goodyear Producer's Showcase, Kraft. *Movies*: The Face of Fear, Brian's Song (Emmy Award, 1972), What's a Nice Girl Like You...?, Man on a String, Lt. Schuster's Wife, Remember When, The Godchild, Journey From Darkness, They Only Come Out at Night, Raid on Entebbe, Topper, A Private Battle, Hobson's Choice, Helen Keller: The Miracle Continues, Hoover vs. The Kennedys, The Three Kings, Dead Solid Perfect, Judgment, Problem Child 3: Junior in Love. *Mini-Series*: Robert Kennedy and His Times, A.D.

WARNER, DAVID
Actor. b. Manchester, England, July 29, 1941. e. Royal Acad. of Dramatic Art. Made London stage debut in Tony Richardson's version of A Midsummer Night's Dream (1962). Four seasons with Royal Shakespeare Co. Theater includes Afore Night Comes, The Tempest, The Wars of the Roses, The Government Inspector, Twelfth Night, I Claudius.
PICTURES: Tom Jones (debut, 1963), Morgan!, The Deadly Affair, A King's Story (voice), Work Is a Four Letter Word, A Midsummer's Night Dream, The Bofors Gun, The Fixer, The Seagull, Michael Kolhaas, The Ballad of Cable Hogue, Perfect Friday, Straw Dogs, A Doll's House, From Beyond the Grave, Little Malcolm (and His Struggle Against the Eunuch), Mr. Quilp, The Omen, Providence, The Disappearance, Cross of Iron, Silver Bears, Nightwing, The Concorde—Airport '79, Time After Time, The 39 Steps, The Island, The French Lieutenant's Woman, Time Bandits, Tron, The Man With Two Brains, The Company of Wolves, Hansel and Gretel, My Best Friend Is a Vampire, Waxworks, Mr. North, Silent Night, Office Party, Hanna's War, Pulse Pounders, Keys to Freedom, Star Trek V: The Final Frontier, S.P.O.O.K.S., Tripwire, Mortal Passions, Teenage Mutant Ninja Turtles II: The Secret of the Ooze, Star Trek VI: The Undiscovered Country, Blue Tornado, Drive, Unnameable II, Dark at Noon, In the Mouth of Madness.
TELEVISION: *Movies*: S.O.S. Titantic, Desperado, A Christmas Carol, Hitler's SS—Portrait in Evil, Perry Mason: The Case of the Poisoned Pen, The Secret Life of Ian Fleming, Cast a Deadly Spell, The House on Sycamore Street, Perry Mason: The Case of the Skin-Deep Scandal, John Carpenter Presents Body Bags, Danielle Steel's Zoya. *Mini-Series*: Holocaust, Masada (Emmy Award, 1981), Marco Polo, Wild Palms. *Specials*: Love's Labour's Lost, Uncle Vanya.

WARNER, JULIE
Actress. b. New York, NY. e. Brown Univ., B.A. in Theatre Arts.
PICTURES: Doc Hollywood (debut, 1991), Mr. Saturday Night, Indian Summer, The Puppet Masters, Tommy Boy.
TELEVISION: *Series*: Pride and Joy. *Guest*: Star Trek: The Next Generation, 21 Jump Street, The Outsiders.

WARNER, MALCOLM-JAMAL
Actor. b. Jersey City, NJ, Aug. 18, 1970. Raised in Los Angeles. Was 13 years old when signed to play Bill Cosby's son on The Cosby Show.
THEATER: Three Ways Home (off-B'way debut, 1988).
PICTURE: Drop Zone (debut, 1994).
TELEVISION: *Series*: The Cosby Show (also dir. episode), Here and Now, Magic School Bus (voice), Malcolm & Eddie. *Movies*: The Father Clements Story, Mother's Day, Tyson. *Special*: Kids Killing Kids (host).

WARREN, GENE
Executive. b. Denver, CO, Aug. 12, 1916. Pres. of Excelsior Prods., prod. co. specializing in special effects and animation. Has headed 2 other cos. of similar nature over past 20 years, functioning at various times as prod., dir., studio prod. head

and writer. Producer-director of following shorts: The Tool Box, Suzy Snowflake, Santa and the Three Dwarfs, Land of the Midnight Sun and these documentaries/training films: Mariner I, Mariner III, Apollo, U.S. Navy titles. Special effects on theatrical features incl: Black Sunday, tom thumb, The Time Machine (Academy Award, 1960), The Wonderful World of the Brothers Grimm, 7 Faces of Dr. Lao, The Power, Legend of Hillybilly John. TV series include: The Man from Atlantis, Land of the Lost, Star Trek, Outer Limits, Twilight Zone, Mission Impossible. *TV Movie*: Satan's School for Girls.

WARREN, JENNIFER
Actress, Producer. b. New York, NY, Aug. 12, 1941. e. U. of Wisconsin, Madison, B.A. Graduate work at Wesleyan U. Studied acting with Uta Hagen at HB Studios. As part of AFI Women's Directing Workshop, directed Point of Departure, short film which received Cine Golden Eagle and Aspen Film Festival Awards. Formed Tiger Rose Productions, indep. film-TV prod. co., 1988. Exec. prod., You Don't Have to Die (Acad. Award, doc. short, 1989). Director: The Beans of Egypt Maine (1994). Recipient of 2 Spirit Awards.
THEATER: Scuba Duba (off-B'way debut, 1967), 6 RMS RIV VU (Theatre World Award), Harvey, P.S., Your Cat Is Dead, B'way: Saint Joan, Volpone, Henry V (Guthrie Theatre).
PICTURES: Night Moves (debut, 1975), Slapshot, Another Man Another Chance, Ice Castles, Fatal Beauty.
TELEVISION: *Series*: Paper Dolls. *Pilots*: Double Dare, Knights of the Kitchen Table. *Guest*: Kojak. *Movies*: Banjo Hackett: Roamin' Free, Shark Kill, First You Cry, Steel Cowboy, Champions: A Love Story, Angel City, The Choice, The Intruder Within, Freedom, Paper Dolls (pilot), Confessions of a Married Man, Amazons, Full Exposure: The Sex Tape Scandal. *Mini-Series*: Celebrity.

WARREN, LESLEY ANN
Actress. b. New York, NY, Aug. 16, 1946. Studied acting under Lee Strasberg. Big break came in Rodgers and Hammerstein's 1964 tv prod. of Cinderella, where she was seen by Disney scout. Broadway debut in 110 in the Shade (1963, Theatre World Award), followed by Drat! The Cat! Appeared in Aerosmith video Janie's Got a Gun.
PICTURES: The Happiest Millionaire (debut, 1967), The One and Only Genuine Original Family Band, Pickup on 101, Harry and Walter Go to New York, Victor/Victoria (Acad. Award nom.), A Night in Heaven, Songwriter (Golden Globe nom.), Choose Me, Race to the Yankee Zephyr, Clue, Burglar, Cop, Worth Winning, Life Stinks, Pure Country, Color of Night, Bird of Prey, Natural Enemy, The First Man, 79 Park Avenue (Golden Globe winner).
TELEVISION: *Series*: Mission: Impossible. *Mini-Series*: 79 Park Avenue, Pearl, Evergreen, Family of Spies, Joseph. *Movies*: Seven in Darkness, Love Hate Love, Assignment Munich, The Daughters of Joshua Cabe, The Letters, The Legend of Valentino, Betrayal, Portrait of a Stripper, Beulah Land, Portrait of a Showgirl, A Fight for Jenny, Apology, Baja Oklahoma (Ace Award nom.), A Seduction in Travis County, In Sickness and in Health, Willing to Kill: The Texas Cheerleader Story, A Mother's Revenge, Family of Spies (Emmy nom.), Murderous Intent, 27 Wagons Full of Cotton. *Specials*: The Saga of Sonora, It's a Bird It's a Plane It's Superman, A Special Eddie Rabbit, The Dancing Princess, 27 Wagons Full of Cotton (Ace Award nom.), Willie Nelson: Big Six-O.

WARRICK, RUTH
Actress. b. St. Joseph, MO, June 29, 1916. Started as radio singer. Autobiography: The Confessions of Phoebe Tyler (1980).
PICTURES: Citizen Kane (debut, 1941), Obliging Young Lady, The Corsican Brothers, Journey Into Fear, Forever and a Day, Perilous Holiday, The Iron Major, Secret Command, Mr. Winkle Goes to War, Guest in the House, China Sky, Song of the South, Driftwood, Daisy Kenyon, Arch of Triumph, The Great Dan Patch, Make Believe Ballroom, Three Husbands, Let's Dance, One Too Many, Roogie's Bump, Ride Beyond Vengeance, The Great Bank Robbery, Deathmask, The Returning.
TELEVISION: *Movie*: Peyton Place—The Next Generation. *Series*: Peyton Place, All My Children. *Guest*: Studio One, Robert Montgomery Presents, Lux Star Playhouse. *Special*: Sometimes I Don't Love My Mother.

WARZEL, PETER C.
Executive. b. Buffalo, NY, May 31, 1952. e. Univ. of Rochester, Canisius Col. Joined Tele-Communications Inc., 1982, also serving as v.p. of industrial relations at Community Tele-Communications Inc., a TCI subsidiary. 1988, became sr. v.p. of United Artists Entertainment Co.; 1990, promoted to pres. & CEO of United Artists Theatre Circuit. 1992, was party to management buy-out of UATC as pres. & COO.

WASHBURN, DERIC
Writer. b. Buffalo, NY. e.Harvard U., English lit. Has written number of plays, including The Love Nest and Ginger Anne.
PICTURES: Silent Running (co-s.p.), The Deer Hunter (co-s.p.), The Border, Extreme Prejudice.

WASHINGTON, DENZEL
Actor. b. Mt. Vernon, NY, Dec. 28, 1954. e. Fordham U., B.A., journalism. Studied acting with American Conservatory Theatre, San Francisco.
THEATER: When the Chickens Come Home to Roost (Audelco Award), Coriolanus, Spell #7, The Mighty Gents, Ceremonies in Dark Old Men, A Soldier's Play, Checkmates, Richard III.
PICTURES: Carbon Copy (debut, 1981), A Soldier's Story, Power, Cry Freedom (Acad. Award nom.), The Mighty Quinn, For Queen and Country, Glory (Academy Award, best supporting actor, 1989; Golden Globe Award), Heart Condition, Mo' Better Blues, Ricochet, Mississippi Masala, Malcolm X (NY Film Critics Award; Acad. Award nom.), Much Ado About Nothing, Philadelphia, The Pelican Brief, Crimson Tide, Virtuosity, Devil in a Blue Dress, Courage Under Fire, The Preacher's Wife.
TELEVISION: Movies: Wilma, Flesh and Blood, License to Kill, The George McKenna Story. Series: St. Elsewhere.

WASSERMAN, DALE
Writer, Producer. b. Rhinelander, WI, Nov. 2, 1917. Stage: lighting designer, dir., prod.; dir. for. attractions, S. Hurok; began writing, 1954. Founding member & trustee of O'Neill Theatre Centre; artistic dir. Midwest Playwrights Laboratory; member, Acad. M.P. Arts & Sciences; awards include Emmy, Tony, Critics Circle (Broadway), Outer Circle; Writers Guild.
PICTURES: Cleopatra, The Vikings, The Sea and the Shadow, Quick Before It Melts, Mister Buddwing, A Walk with Love and Death, Man of La Mancha.
TELEVISION: The Fog, The Citadel, The Power and the Glory, Engineer of Death, The Lincoln Murder Case, I Don Quixote, Elisha and the Long Knives, and others. PLAYS: Livin' the Life, 998, One Flew Over the Cuckoo's Nest, The Pencil of God, Man of La Mancha, Play With Fire, Shakespeare and the Indians, Mountain High, Western Star, Green.

WASSERMAN, LEW
Executive. b. Cleveland, OH, March 15, 1913. National dir. advertising and pub., Music Corporation of Amer. 1936-38; v.p. 1938-39; v.p. motion picture div. 1940; Chairman of the bd., Chief Executive Officer, MCA, Inc., Universal City, CA. Named chairman emeritus of MCA in 1995. Received Jean Hersholt Humanitarian Award, 1973; awarded Presidential Medal of Freedom, 1995.

WASSON, CRAIG
Actor. b. Ontario, OR, March 15, 1954. Also musician/songwriter.
THEATER: Godspell, All God's Chillun Got Wings, Death of a Salesman (also wrote incidental music), Jock, Children of Eden, M. Butterfly, Skin of Our Teeth, The Sisters (Pasadena Playhouse), etc. Wrote incidental music for prod. of The Glass Menagerie.
PICTURES: Rollercoaster, The Boys in Company C (also wrote and performed song Here I Am), Go Tell the Spartans, The Outsider, Carny, Schizoid, Ghost Story, Four Friends, Second Thoughts (also wrote and performed music), Body Double, The Men's Club, A Nightmare on Elm Street 3, The Trackers, Midnight Fear, Malcolm X, Bum Rap (also wrote and performed music).
TELEVISION: Series: Phyllis (also wrote and performed orig. songs), Skag, One Life to Live, The Tomorrow Man. Guest: M*A*S*H, Baa Baa Black Sheep, Rockford Files, Hart to Hart, L.A. Law, Kung Fu: The Legend Continues, Dr. Quinn Medicine Woman, Murder She Wrote. Movies: The Silence, Mrs. R's Daughter, Skag, Thornwell, Why Me?, Strapped, Trapped in Space, The Calvin Mire Story, The Becky Bell Story, The Sister in Law. Specials: A More Perfect Union, Innocents Abroad.

WATANABE, GEDDE
Actor. b. Ogden, UT, June 26. Trained for stage at American Conservatory Theatre, San Francisco. Appeared with N.Y. Shakespeare Fest. Shakespeare in the Park series and with Pan Asian Repertory Theatre, N.Y.
THEATER: Pacific Overtures (debut, as Tree Boy, B'way and on tour, 1976), Bullet Headed Birds, Poor Little Lambs, Dispatches, Music Lesson, Good Person.
PICTURES: Sixteen Candles (debut, 1984), Gremlins, Volunteers, Gung Ho, Vamp, UHF, Boys on the Side.
TELEVISION: Series: Gung Ho. Movie: Miss America: Behind the Crown.

WATERHOUSE, KEITH
Writer. b. Leeds, England, Feb. 6, 1929. Early career as journalist, novelist. Author of There is a Happy Land, Billy Liar, Jubb, The Bucket Shop. For m.p. ind. 1960.
PICTURES: Writer (with Willis Hall): Whistle Down the Wind, A Kind of Loving, Billy Liar, Man in the Middle, Pretty Polly, Lock Up Your Daughters, The Valiant, West Eleven.
TELEVISION: Series: Inside George Webley, Queenie's Castle, Budgie, Billy Liar, There is a Happy Land, Charters and Caldicott.

WATERS, JOHN
Director, Writer. b. Baltimore, MD, Apr. 22, 1946. First short film Hag in a Black Leather Jacket (1964) shot in Baltimore, as are most of his films. Other shorts include Roman Candles, Eat Your Makeup. Feature debut, Mondo Trasho. Appeared as actor in films Something Wild, Homer and Eddie. On tv in Homicide: Life on the Streets.
PICTURES: Director/Writer: Mondo Trasho (also prod., photo., edit.), Multiple Maniacs (also prod., editor, sound), Pink Flamingos (also prod., photo., edit.), Female Trouble (also photo., prod.), Desperate Living (also prod.), Polyester (also prod.), Hairspray (also co-prod., actor), Cry-Baby, Serial Mom.

WATERSTON, SAM
Actor. b. Cambridge, MA, Nov. 15, 1940. e. Yale U. Spent jr. year at Sorbonne in Paris as part of the Amer. Actors' Workshop run by American dir. John Berry. Broadway debut in Oh Dad Poor Dad ... (1963). Film debut, The Plastic Dome of Norma Jean (made 1965; unreleased). TV debut Pound (Camera Three). Has worked in New York Shakespeare Festival prods. since As You Like It (1963).
THEATER: N.Y. Shakespeare Festival: As You Like It, Ergo, Henry IV (Part I & II), Cymbeline, Hamlet, Much Ado About Nothing, The Tempest. Off-B'way: The Knack, La Turista, Waiting for Godot, The Three Sisters. B'way: The Paisley Convertible, Halfway Up the Tree, Indian, Hay Fever, The Trial of Cantonsville Nine, A Meeting by the River, Much Ado About Nothing (Drama Desk and Obie Awards), A Doll's House, Lunch Hour, Benefactors, A Walk in the Woods, Abe Lincoln in Illinois.
PICTURES: Fitzwilly, Three, Generation, Cover Me Babe, Mahoney's Estate, Who Killed Mary What's 'er Name?, Savages, The Great Gatsby, Journey Into Fear, Rancho Deluxe, Sweet Revenge, Capricorn One, Interiors, Eagle's Wing, Sweet William, Hopscotch, Heaven's Gate, The Killing Fields, Warning Sign, Hannah and Her Sisters, Just Between Friends, A Certain Desire, The Devil's Paradise, September, Welcome Home, Crimes and Misdemeanors, The Man in the Moon, Mindwalk, A Captive in the Land, Serial Mom, The Journey of August King (also co-prod.), The Shadow Conspiracy.
TELEVISION: Specials: Pound, Robert Lowell, The Good Lieutenant, Much Ado About Nothing, Oppenheimer, A Walk in the Woods. Movies: The Glass Menagerie, Reflections of Murder, Friendly Fire, Games Mother Never Taught You, In Defense of Kids, Dempsey, Finnegan Begin Again, Love Lives On, The Fifth Missile, The Room Upstairs, Terrorist on Trial: The United States vs. Salim Ajami, Gore Vidal's Lincoln, Lantern Hill, The Shell Seekers, Assault at West Point: The Court-Martial of Johnson Whittaker, David's Mother, The Enemy Within. Mini-Series: The Nightmare Years, The Civil War (voice). Series: Q.E.D., I'll Fly Away. Guest: Amazing Stories.

WATKIN, DAVID
Director of Photography. b. Margate, Eng., March 23, 1925. Entered British documentary industry in Jan., 1948. With British Transport Films as asst. cameraman, 1950 -55; as cameraman, 1955 -61. Feature film debut The Knack beginning long creative relationship with director Richard Lester.
PICTURES: The Knack... and How to Get It (debut, 1965), Help!, Marat/Sade, How I Won the War, The Charge of the Light Brigade, The Bed-Sitting Room, Catch-22, The Devils, The Boyfriend, The Homecoming, A Delicate Balance, The Three Musketeers, The Four Musketeers, Mahogany, To the Devil a Daughter, Robin and Marian, Joseph Andrews, Hanover Street, Cuba, That Summer, Endless Love, Chariots of Fire, Yentl, The Hotel New Hampshire, Return to Oz, White Nights, Out of Africa (Academy Award, 1985), Moonstruck, Sky Bandits, Masquerade, The Good Mother, Last Rites, Journey to the Center of the Earth, Memphis Belle, Hamlet, The Object of Beauty, Used People, This Boy's Life, Bopha!, Milk Money.

WAX, MORTON DENNIS
Public Relations Executive. b. New York, NY, March 13, 1932. e. Brooklyn Coll., 1952. President of Morton Dennis Wax & Assoc., Inc., p.r. and marketing firm servicing int'l creative marketplace, established 1956. Contrib. writer to Box Office Magazine, Film Journal. Recent articles: Creativity (Advertising Age), Rolling Stone's Marketing Through Music, Words & Music, Campaign Magazine, Songwriters Guild of America National Edition. As sect. of VPA, conceptualized int'l Monitor Award, an annual event, currently under auspices of ITS. Public relations counsel to London Int'l Advertising Awards. Member of The Public Relations Society of America, Nat'l Academy of TV Arts & Sciences, Nat'l Acadrmy of Recording Arts & Sciences, Publishers Publicity Association. Morton Dennis Wax & Assocs. in NY was awarded the first EPM Entertainment Marketing Cause Event Award for creating, developing and promoting a nat'l fund raising campaign to combat homelessness, called Brother Can You Spare a Dime Day.

WAYANS, DAMON
Actor, Writer, Producer. b. New York, NY, 1960. Brother is comedian-actor Keenen Ivory Wayans. Started as stand up comedian.
PICTURES: Beverly Hills Cop (debut, 1984), Hollywood Shuffle, Roxanne, Colors, Punchline, I'm Gonna Git You Sucka, Earth Girls Are Easy, Look Who's Talking Too (voice), The Last Boy Scout, Mo' Money (also s.p., co-exec. prod.), Last Action Hero (cameo), Blankman (also co-s.p., exec. prod.), Major Payne (also co-s.p., co-exec. prod.), The Great White Hype, Bulletproof.
TELEVISION: Series: Saturday Night Live (1985 -6), In Living Color (also writer). Special: The Last Stand? (HBO).

WAYANS, KEENEN IVORY
Actor, Director, Writer. b. NYC, June 8, 1958. e. Tuskegee Inst. Began as stand-up comic at The Improv in NYC and L.A. Brother is comedian-actor Damon Wayans.
PICTURES: Star 80 (debut, 1983), Hollywood Shuffle (also co-s.p.), Eddie Murphy Raw (co-prod., co-s.p. only), I'm Gonna Git You Sucka (also dir., s.p.), The Five Heartbeats (co-s.p. only), A Low Down Dirty Shame (also dir., s.p.), The Glimmer Man.
TELEVISION: Series: For Love and Honor, In Living Color (also exec. prod. & writer; Emmy Award 1990). Guest: Benson, Cheers, CHiPS, A Different World. Special: Partners in Crime (also co-writer).

WAYLAND, LEN
Actor. b. California, Dec. 28. e. Junior Coll., Modesto, CA. Wrote, prod. weekly radio series 1939-41, KPAS, KTRB, Calif. Service, radar navigator, 1941-45; theatre, Tobacco Road, 1946; 1973, formed Len Wayland Prods. for prod. of theatrical pictures and TV series. 1976-77: prod./dir.: Don't Let It Bother You. 1978, prod., dir., You're not there yet, for own co.
THEATER: A Streetcar Named Desire (B'way, tour), Heaven Can Wait, My Name Is Legion, Love of Four Colonels, Stalag 17, A Man For All Seasons.
TELEVISION: A Time to Live (serial), First Love, Armstrong Circle Theatre, Justice, Sgt. Bilko, Kraft Theatre; Dr. Weaver, From These Roots. Profiles in Courage, Dr. Kildare, Gunsmoke, Slattery's People, Ben Casey, A Noise in the World, Love Is a Many Splendored Thing; Dragnet, Outsider; Ironside, Name of the Game, The Bold Ones, Daniel Boone, The Virginian, Project U.F.O., Sam (series), The Blue and the Gray, Hunter, A-Team, Dallas, Amy on the Lips, Generations (serial).

WAYNE, JOEL
Executive. Began career with Grey Advertising; in 17 years won many awards (60 Clios, 25 N.Y. Art Director Club Awards, etc.). Was exec. v.p. & creative dir. of agency when left in 1979 to join Warner Bros. as v.p., creative adv. 1987, named sr. v.p., worldwide creative adv., then exec. v.p. worldwide creative adv. & publicity.

WAYNE, MICHAEL A.
Executive. r.n. Michael A. Morrison. b. Los Angeles, CA, Nov. 23, 1934. Father was late actor John Wayne. e. Loyola H.S.; Loyola U., B.B.A. Asst. dir., various companies, 1955-56; asst. dir., Revue Prods., 1956-57; pres. Batjac Prods. and Romina Prods., 1961.
PICTURES: Asst. to producer: China Doll, Escort West, The Alamo (asst. to prod.). Prod.: McLintock!, Cast Giant Shadow (co- prod.), The Green Berets, Chisum (exec. prod.), Big Jake, The Train Robbers, Cahill: U.S. Marshal, McQ (exec. prod.), Brannigan (exec. prod.).

WAYNE, PATRICK
Actor. b. Los Angeles, July 15, 1939. e. Loyola U, 1961, BS in biology. Father was late actor John Wayne. Made film debut at age 11 in Rio Grande with father.
PICTURES: The Long Gray Line, Mister Roberts, The Searchers, The Alamo, The Comancheros, McClintock, Donovan's Reef, Cheyenne Autumn, Shenandoah, An Eye for an Eye, The Green Berets, The Deserter, Big Jake, The Gatling Gun, Beyond Atlantis, The Bears and I, Mustang Country, Sinbad and the Eye of the Tiger, The People Time Forgot, Rustler's Rhapsody, Young Guns, Her Alibi, Blind Vengeance, Chill Factor.
TELEVISION: Series: The Rounders, Shirley. Movies: Sole Survivor, Yesterday's Child, Flight to Holocaust, The Last Hurrah, Three on a Date. Guest: Frank's Place.

WEATHERS, CARL
Actor. b. New Orleans, LA, Jan. 14, 1948. e. San Diego State Univ.
PICTURES: Bucktown (debut, 1975), Friday Foster, Rocky, Close Encounters of the Third Kind, Semi-Tough, Force Ten From Navarone, Rocky II, Death Hunt, Rocky III, Rocky IV, Predator, Action Jackson, Hurricane Smith, Happy Gilmore.
TELEVISION: Series: Fortune Dane, Tour of Duty, Street Justice, In the Heat of the Night. Movies: The Hostage Heart, The Bermuda Depths, Breaker, Dangerous Passion, In the Heat of the Night: A Matter of Justice, In the Heat of the Night: Who Was Geli Bendl?, In the Heat of the Night: By Duty Bound, Tom Clancy's Op Center, In the Heat of the Night: Grow Old With Me, The Defiant Ones. Director: Silk Stalkings (2 episodes), Renegade (1 episode).

WEAVER, DENNIS
Actor, Director. b. Joplin, MO, June 4, 1925. e. U. of Oklahoma, B.A., fine arts, 1948.
PICTURES: Horizons West (debut, 1952), The Raiders, The Redhead From Wyoming, The Lawless Breed, Mississippi Gambler, Law and Order, It Happens Every Thursday, Column South, The Man From the Alamo, The Golden Blade, The Nebraskan, War Arrow, Dangerous Mission, Dragnet, Ten Wanted Men, The Bridges at Toko-Ri, Seven Angry Men, Chief Crazy Horse, Storm Fear, Touch of Evil, The Gallant Hours, Duel at Diablo, Way... Way Out, Gentle Giant, Mission Batangas, A Man Called Sledge, What's the Matter With Helen?, Walking After Midnight.
TELEVISION: Series: Gunsmoke (Emmy Award, 1959), Kentucky Jones, Gentle Ben, McCloud, Stone, Emerald Point NAS, Buck James, Lonesome Dove. Movies: McCloud: Who Killed Miss USA?, The Forgotten Man, Duel, Rolling Man, Female Artillery, The Great Man's Whiskers, Terror on the Beach, Intimate Strangers, The Islander, Ishi: The Last of His Tribe, The Ordeal of Patty Hearst, Stone (pilot), Amber Waves, The Ordeal of Dr. Mudd, The Day the Loving Stopped, Don't Go to Sleep, Cocaine: One Man's Seduction, Bluffing It, Disaster at Silo 7, The Return of Sam McCloud (also co-exec. prod.), Greyhounds. Mini-Series: Centennial, Pearl. Special: Mastergate.

WEAVER, FRITZ
Actor. b. Pittsburgh, PA, Jan. 19, 1926. e. U. of Chicago.
THEATER: The Chalk Garden (Theatre World Award), Miss Lonelyhearts, All American, A Shot in the Dark, Baker Street, Child's Play (Tony, 1970), The Price, The Crucible, The Professional, etc.
PICTURES: Fail Safe (debut, 1964), The Guns of August (narrator), The Maltese Bippy, A Walk in the Spring Rain, Company of Killers, The Day of the Dolphin, Marathon Man, Demon Seed, Black Sunday, The Big Fix, Jaws of Satan, Creepshow, Power.
TELEVISION: Movies: The Borgia Stick, Berlin Affair, Heat of Anger, The Snoop Sisters, Hunter, The Legend of Lizzie Borden, Captains Courageous, The Hearst and Davies Affair, A Death in California, My Name is Bill W, Ironclads, Citizen Cohn, Blind Spot. Mini-Series: Holocaust, The Martian Chronicles, Dream West, I'll Take Manhattan.

WEAVER, SIGOURNEY
Actress. r.n. Susan Weaver. b. New York, NY, Oct. 8, 1949. e. Stanford U., Yale U. Daughter of Sylvester (Pat) Weaver, former NBC pres. Mother, actress Elizabeth Inglis (one-time contract player for Warner Bros.). After college formed working partnership with fellow student Christopher Durang for off-B'way improv. productions. First professional appearance on stage in 1974 in The Constant Wife with Ingrid Bergman. Formed Goat Cay Prods.
THEATER: Off-Off-B'way: The Nature and Purpose of the Universe. Off-B'way: Titanic/Das Lusitania Songspiel (also co-writer), Gemini, Marco Polo Sings a Solo, New Jerusalem, The Merchant of Venice, Beyond Therapy. B'way: Hurlyburly.
PICTURES: Madman (Israeli; debut, 1976), Annie Hall, Alien, Eyewitness, The Year of Living Dangerously, Deal of the Century, Ghostbusters, One Woman or Two, Aliens (Acad. Award nom.), Half Moon Street, Gorillas in the Mist (Acad. Award nom.), Working Girl (Acad. Award nom.), Ghostbusters II, Alien 3 (also co-prod.), 1492: Conquest of Paradise, Dave, Death and the Maiden, Jeffrey, Copycat, The Ice Storm.
TELEVISION: Series: The Best of Families (PBS), Somerset. Special: The Sorrows of Gin.

WEAVER, SYLVESTER L., JR.
Executive. b. Los Angeles, CA, Dec. 21, 1908. e. Dartmouth Coll. Daughter is actress Sigourney Weaver. CBS, Don Lee Network, 1932-35; Young & Rubicam adv. agency, 1935-38; adv. mgr., American Tobacco Co., 1938-47; v.p. Young & Rubicam, 1947-49; joined NBC as v.p., chg. TV, 1949; appt'd v.p. chg. NBC Radio & TV networks, 1952; vice-chmn. bd., NBC, 1953; pres. NBC, 1953; bd. chmn., 1955; as head of NBC during TV's formative years, Weaver is credited as the father of TV talk/service program, founding both Tonight and Today shows, also innovated the rotating multi-star anthology series, the Wide Wide World series and concept of TV "special;" Own firm, 430 Park Avenue., N.Y., 1956; chmn. of bd. McCann-Erickson Corp. (Intl.), 1959; pres., Subscription TV, Inc. Comm. Consultant in Los Angeles, CA and President, Weaver Productions, Inc. On magazine series Television: Inside and Out (1981-82). Author: The Best Seat in the House (1994). Awards: Emmy Trustees' and Governor's Award (1967) and Governor's Award (1983), TV Hall of Fame (1984), NAB Hall of Fame (1986), Dartmouth Lifetime Achievement Award, 1993.

WEBB, CHLOE
Actress. b. New York, NY. e. Boston Conservatory of Music and Drama. On stage with Boston Shakespeare Co., Goodman Theatre in Chicago and Mark Taper Forum, L.A.; improv. groups Imagination Theatre Co., Paul Sills Theatre.
THEATER: Forbidden Broadway (Off-B'way and L.A.), Addiction, Family Album, The Model Apartment (LA Critics Circle & Dramalogue Awards), House of Blue Leaves (Dramalogue Award), Twins, Heart Condition, The Belly of an Architect, Queens Logic, A Dangerous Woman, Love Affair.
TELEVISION: Series: Thicke of the Night. Special: Who Am I This Time? Movies: Lucky Day, Silent Cries. Mini-Series: Tales of the City. Guest: Remington Steele, China Beach (pilot).

WEBER, STEVEN
Actor. e. Purchase Col. Acted with Mirror Rep. Co. Off-B'way.
THEATER: NY: Paradise Lost, The Real Thing (B'way debut, 1985), Something About Baseball. Regional: Made in Bangkok, Come Back Little Sheba, Naked at the Coast, Death of a Salesman.
PICTURES: The Flamingo Kid, Flanagan, Hamburger Hill, Les Anges, Single White Female, The Temp, Jeffrey, Dracula: Dead and Loving It.
TELEVISION: Series: Wings. Mini-Series: The Kennedys of Massachusetts. Movies: In the Company of Darkness, In the Line of Duty: The Undercover Murders, Deception: A Mother's Secret, Betrayed by Love. Special: Pudd'nhead Wilson.

WEDGEWORTH, ANN
Actress. b. Abilene, TX, Jan. 21, 1935. e. U. of Texas. On stage in Thieves, Blues for Mr. Charlie, Chapter Two (Tony Award, 1978), etc.
PICTURES: Andy, Bang the Drum Slowly, Scarecrow, The Catamount Killing, Law and Disorder, Dragonfly (One Summer Love), Birch Interval, Thieves, Handle With Care, No Small Affair, Sweet Dreams, The Men's Club, Made in Heaven, A Tiger's Tale, Far North, Miss Firecracker, Steel Magnolias, Green Card, Love and a .45.
TELEVISION: Series: The Edge of Night, Another World, Somerset, Three's Company, Filthy Rich, Evening Shade. Movies: The War Between the Tates, Bogie, Elvis and the Beauty Queen, Killjoy, Right to Kill?, A Stranger Waits, Cooperstown, A Burning Passion: The Margaret Mitchell Story. Pilot: Harlan & Merleen.

WEILER, GERALD E.
Producer. b. Mannheim, Germany, May 8, 1928. e. Harvard, 1946-48; Columbia, B.S., 1949-51; New York U. Grad. Sch., 1951-53. Writer, WHN, N.Y. writer, sports ed., news ed., Telenews Prod., Inc., 1948-52; asst. to prod., Richard de Rochemont, Vavin, Inc., 1952; U.S. Army, 1953-55; v.p., Vavin Inc. 1955-73; President, Weiler Communications Inc. 1973. Winner, NY "Lotto" Lottery, 1988; retired 1989.

WEILL, CLAUDIA
Director. b. New York, NY 1947. e. Radcliffe, B.A., 1969. Teacher of acting, Cornish Institute, 1983; guest lecturer on film directing, NYU and Columbia U. Winner of Donatello Award, best director, 1979; Mademoiselle Woman of the Year, 1974; AFI Independent Filmmakers Grant, 1973. Worked as prod. asst. on doc., Revolution.
THEATER: An Evening for Merlin Finch (debut, 1975, Williamstown), Stillife, Found a Peanut, The Longest Walk.
PICTURES: Doc. shorts: This Is the Home of Mrs. Levant Grahame, Roaches' Serenade, Joyce at 34. Director: The Other Half of the Sky—A China Memoir (also photog., edit.), Girlfriends (also prod., story), It's My Turn.
TELEVISION: The 51st State, Sesame Street, Joyce at 34, The Great Love Experiment, thirtysomething. Movie: A Child Lost Forever.

WEINBLATT, MIKE
Executive. b. Perth Amboy, NJ, June 10, 1929. e. Syracuse U. Served in Army as counter-intelligence agent, mostly in Japan, 1952-53. Joined NBC in 1957; has headed two major TV network functions—talent/program admin. & sls.; joined network business affairs dept. in 1958 as mgr., business affairs, facilities operations; rose to post of director, pricing & financial services before moving to sales in 1962, as mgr., participating program sales; named v.p., eastern sales, NBC-TV, 1968; named v.p., talent & program admin., 1968; promoted to v.p. sales, 1973; 1975 named sr. v.p., sales; later became exec. v.p.; appointed exec. v.p. & gen. mgr. of NBC TV network, 1977; appointed Pres., NBC Entertainment, 1978; 1980, joined Showtime/Movie Channel as pres. & COO; 1984, pres., Multi Media Entertainment; 1990, chmn. Weinblatt Communications Co. Inc. 1991, mng. dir. Interequity Capital Corp.

WEINGROD, HERSCHEL
Writer, Producer. b. Milwaukee, WI, Oct. 30, 1947. e. U. of Wisconsin, 1965-69; London Film Sch., 1969-71.

PICTURES: Co-writer with Timothy Harris: Cheaper to Keep Her, Trading Places (BAFTA nom.), Brewster's Millions, My Stepmother Is An Alien, Paint It Black, Twins, Kindergarten Cop, Pure Luck, Falling Down (prod. only), Space Jam (co-s.p.).
TELEVISION: Street of Dreams (exec. prod.).

WEINSTEIN, BOB
Executive. With brother Harvey founded distribution company Miramax Films in 1979. Company branched into feature production in 1989 with film Scandal. Serves as Miramax co-chairman.
PICTURES: Light Years (Bob: prod., Harvey: dir. of U.S. version). Co-Executive Producers: Scandal, The Lemon Sisters, Hardware, A Rage in Harlem, The Miracle, Crossing the Line, The Night We Never Met, Benefit of the Doubt, True Romance, Into the West, Mother's Boys, Pulp Fiction, Ready to Wear (Pret-a-Porter), The Englishman Who Went Up a Hill But Came Down a Mountain, Smoke, The Crossing Guard, The Journey of August King, Last of the High Kings.

WEINSTEIN, HARVEY
Executive. With brother Bob founded distribution company Miramax Films in 1979. Company branched into feature production in 1989 with film Scandal. Serves as Miramax co-chairman. (For list of films see Bob Weinstein).

WEINSTEIN, PAULA
Producer. b. Nov. 19, 1945. e. Columbia U. Daughter of late prod. Hannah Weinstein. Raised in Europe. Partnered with Gareth Wigan in WW Productions at Warner Brothers. Started as theatrical agent with William Morris and ICM. With Warner Brothers, 1976-78 as production v.p.; left to go to 20th Century-Fox in same capacity; named Fox sr. v.p., worldwide prod; 1980, appointed v.p., prod., the Ladd Company; 1981, joined United Artists as pres., m.p. div.; 1983, began own prod. company at Columbia Pictures, also serving as a consultant for Columbia; 1987, joined MGM as exec. consultant; With late husband Mark Rosenberg formed Spring Creek Prods.
PICTURES: Prod.: A Dry White Season, The Fabulous Baker Boys, Fearless, Flesh and Bone, With Honors, Something to Talk About.
TELEVISION: TV Movies: The Rose and the Jackal, Citizen Cohn, Truman (Emmy Award, 1996).

WEINTRAUB, FRED
Executive, Producer. b. Bronx, NY, April 27, 1928. e. U. of PA, Wharton Sch. of Bus. Owner of The Bitter End Coffeehouse to 1971. Personal management, Campus Coffee House Entertain-ment Circuit; TV Production Hootenanny, Popendipity; syndicated TV show host: From The Bitter End; motion picture prod.; v.p., creative services, Warner Bros. 1969; exec. in chg. Woodstock; prod. motion pictures, Weintraub-Heller Productions, 1974; then Fred Weintraub Productions, which became Weintraub/Kuhn Prods. in 1990.
PICTURES: Enter the Dragon, Rage, Black Belt Jones, Truck Turner, Golden Needles, Animal Stars, Hot Potato, The Ultimate Warrior, Dirty Knights Work, Those Cuckoo Crazy Animals, Crash, Outlaw Blues, The Pack, The Promise, Tom Horn, Battle Creek Brawl, Force Five, High Road to China, Out of Control, Gymkata, Princess Academy, Born to Ride.
TELEVISION: My Father My Son (prod.), Triplecross. Produced: Trouble Bound, Dead Wrong, documentaries: JFK Assassination, The Bruce Lee Story.

WEINTRAUB, JERRY
Producer. b. New York, NY, Sept. 26, 1937. m. former singer Jayne Morgan. Sole owner and chmn. of Management Three, representing entertainment personalities, including John Denver, John Davidson, Frank Sinatra, Neil Diamond, etc. Also involved with Intercontinental Broadcasting Systems, Inc. (cable programming) and Jerry Weintraub/Armand Hammer Prods. (production co.). 1985, named United Artists Corp. chmn. Resigned, 1986. 1987: formed Weintraub Entertainment Group.
PICTURES: Nashville, Oh God!, Cruising, All Night Long, Diner, The Karate Kid, The Karate Kid Part II, The Karate Kid Part III, Pure Country, The Firm (actor), The Next Karate Kid, The Specialist.

WEINTRAUB, SY
Executive. b. New York, NY, 1923. e. U. of Missouri, B.A., journalism, 1947; graduate of American Theater Wing. Started career in 1949 forming with associates a TV syndication co., Flamingo Films, Inc., which merged with Associated Artists to form Motion Pictures for Television, Inc., largest syndicator at that time. Originated Superman and Grand Ol' Opry series for TV. 1958, bought Sol Lesser Prods., owners of film rights for Tarzan, and began producing and distributing Tarzan films through Banner Productions, Inc. Also formerly chmn. of bd. of Panavision, Inc.; bd. mem. and pres. of National General Television Corp., and pres. of KMGM-TV in Minneapolis. In 1978, named chmn. of Columbia Pictures Industries' new Film Entertainment Group, also joining office of the chief executive of CPI.

WEIR, PETER
Director, Writer. b. Sydney, Australia, Aug. 21, 1944. e. attended Scots Coll. and Sydney U. Briefly worked selling real estate, traveled to Eng. 1965. Entered Australian TV industry as stagehand 1967 while prod. amateur revues. *Dir. shorts*: Count Vim's Last Exercise, The Life and Times of Reverend Buck Shotte, Homeside, Incredible Floridas, What Ever Happened to Green Valley? 1967-73.
PICTURES: *Director*: Three to Go (debut, 1970; segment: Michael), The Cars That Ate Paris (also s.p., co-story; a.k.a. The Cars That Eat People), Picnic at Hanging Rock, The Last Wave (also s.p.), The Plumber (also s.p.; tv in Australia). Gallipoli (also story), The Year of Living Dangerously (also co-s.p.), Witness, The Mosquito Coast, Dead Poets Society, Green Card (also prod., s.p.), Fearless.

WEIS, DON
Director, Writer, Producer. b. Milwaukee, WI, May 13, 1922. e. USC. Started as dialogue dir. on such films as Body and Soul, The Red Pony, Champion, Home of the Brave, The Men.
PICTURES: Bannerline (debut, 1951), It's a Big Country (segment), Just This Once, You for Me, I Love Melvin, Remains to Be Seen, A Slight Case of Larceny, Half a Hero, The Affairs of Dobie Gillis, The Adventures of Haji Baba, Ride the High Iron, The Gene Krupa Story, Critic's Choice, Looking for Love, Pajama Party, Billie (also prod.), The King's Pirate, Did You Hear the One About the Traveling Saleslady?, Zero to Sixty.
TELEVISION: Dear Phoebe, The Longest Hundred Miles, It Takes a Thief, Ironside, M*A*S*H., Happy Days, Planet of the Apes, Bronk, Petrocelli, The Magician, Mannix, Night Stalker, Barbary Coast, Courtship of Eddie's Father, Starsky & Hutch, Hawaii Five-O, Chips, Charlie's Angels, Love Boat, Fantasy Island, Remington Steele, Hill St. Blues, Murphy's Law.

WEISS, STEVEN ALAN
Executive. b. Glendale, CA, Oct. 19, 1944. e. Los Angeles City Coll., A.A., 1964; USC, B.S., 1966; Northwestern U., B.S., 1967; LaSalle Extension U., J.D., 1970. U.S Navy-San Diego, Great Lakes, Vallejo & Treasure Island, 1966-67; shipyard liaison officer, Pearl Harbor Naval Shipyard, U.S. Navy, 1970; gen. mgr., Adrian Weiss Prods., 1970-74; organized Weiss Global Enterprises with Adrian Weiss 1974 for production, acquisition & distribution of films. Purchased with Tom J. Corradine and Adrian Weiss from the Benedict E. Bogeaus Estate nine features, 1974. Secty./treas. of Film Investment Corp. & Weiss Global Enterprises. (Cos. own, control or have dist. rights to over 300 features, many TV series, documentaries, etc.). Member of the Nat'l Assn. of TV Program Executive Int'l, National Cable TV Assn., American Film Institute.

WEISSMAN, MURRAY
Executive. b. New York, NY, Dec. 23. e. U. of Southern California. Asst. dir. of press info., CBS, 1960-66; mgr., TV press dept., Universal Studio, 1966-68; executive in charge of m.p. press dept., Universal Studios & asst. secy., Universal Pictures, 1968-76; marketing exec., Columbia Pictures, 1976-77; vice pres. of advertising & publicity, Lorimar Productions, 1977; vice pres., ICPR Public Relations Company, 1978-81; now principal, Weissman/Angellotti.

WEISWASSER, STEPHEN A.
Executive. e. Wayne St. Univ., John Hopkins Univ., Harvard Law School. Partner at Wilmer Cutler & Pickering law firm until he joined Capital Cities/ABC in 1986 as sr. v.p. Aug. 1993 became pres. of Capital Cities/ABC Multimedia Group until Oct. 1995. Nov. 1995, became pres. & CEO of Americast.

WEITZNER, DAVID
Executive. b. New York, NY, Nov. 13, 1938. e. Michigan State U. Entered industry in 1960 as member Columbia Pictures adv. dep't; later with Donahue and Coe as ass't exec. and Loew's Theatres adv. dep't; later with Embassy Pictures, adv. mgr.; dir. of adv. and exploitation for Palomar Pictures Corp.; v.p. in charge of adv., pub., and exploitation for ABC Pictures Corp.; v.p., entertainment/leisure div., Grey Advertising; v.p., worldwide adv., 20th Century Fox; exec. v.p. adv./pub./promo., Universal Pictures; exec. v.p., mktg. & dist., Embassy Pictures; 1985, joined 20th Century-Fox Films as pres. of mktg. 1987, pres., mktg., Weintraub Entertainment Group; 1988 joined MCA/Universal as pres. worldwide marketing, MCA Recreation Services.

WELCH, RAQUEL
Actress. r.n. Raquel Tejada. b. Chicago, IL, Sept. 5, 1940. e. La Jolla H.S. Theatre arts scholarship San Diego State Coll. Worked as model before landing bit parts in films. Broadway debut, Woman of the Year, 1981.
PICTURES: A House Is Not a Home (debut, 1964), Roustabout, Do Not Disturb, A Swingin' Summer, Fantastic Voyage, Shoot Loud Louder... I Don't Understand, One Million Years B.C., Fathom, The Oldest Profession, Bedazzled, The Biggest Bundle of Them All, Le Fate (The Queens),

Bandolero, Lady in Cement, 100 Rifles, Flare Up, The Magic Christian, Myra Breckinridge, Restless, Hannie Caulder, Kansas City Bomber, Fuzz, Bluebeard, The Last of Sheila, The Three Musketeers, The Four Musketeers, The Wild Party, Mother Jugs and Speed, Crossed Swords, L'Animal, Naked Gun 33 1/3: The Final Insult.
TELEVISION: *Specials*: Really Raquel, Raquel. *Movies*: The Legend of Walks Far Woman, Right to Die, Scandal in a Small Town, Trouble in Paradise, Tainted Blood, Judith Krantz's Torch Song, Hollyrock-a-Bye Baby (voice). *Guest*: Cher, The Muppet Show, Saturday Night Live.

WELD, TUESDAY
Actress. r.n. Susan Weld. b. New York, NY, Aug. 27, 1943. m. violinist Pinchas Zuckerman. e. Hollywood Professional Sch. Began modeling at 4 yrs.
PICTURES: Rock Rock Rock (debut, 1956), Rally 'Round the Flag Boys! The Five Pennies, Because They're Young, High Time, Sex Kittens Go to College, The Private Lives of Adam and Eve, Return to Peyton Place, Wild in the Country, Bachelor Flat, Soldier in the Rain, I'll Take Sweden, The Cincinnati Kid, Lord Love a Duck, Pretty Poison, I Walk the Line, A Safe Place, Play It As It Lays, Looking for Mr. Goodbar (Acad. Award nom.), Who'll Stop the Rain, Serial, Thief, Author! Author!, Once Upon a Time in America, Heartbreak Hotel, Falling Down.
TELEVISION: *Series*: The Many Loves of Dobie Gillis (1959-60). *Movies*: Reflections of Murder, F. Scott Fitzgerald in Hollywood, A Question of Guilt, Mother and Daughter: The Loving War, Madame X, The Winter of Our Discontent, Scorned and Swindled, Something in Common, Circle of Violence. *Special*: The Rainmaker.

WELLER, PETER
Actor. b. Stevens Point, WI, June 24, 1947. Acting since 10 years old. e. North Texas State U. Studied at American Acad. of Dramatic Arts with Uta Hagen. Member, Actor's Studio.
THEATER: Sticks and Bones (moved up from understudy, B'way debut), Full Circle, Summer Brave, Macbeth, The Wool-Gatherer, Rebel Women, Streamers, The Woods, Serenading Louie, Daddy Wolf.
PICTURES: Butch and Sundance: The Early Years (debut, 1979), Just Tell Me What You Want, Shoot the Moon, Of Unknown Origin, The Adventures of Buckaroo Banzai Across the 8th Dimension, Firstborn, Robocop, Shakedown, A Killing Affair, Leviathan, The Tunnel, Robocop 2, Cat Chaser, Naked Lunch, Fifty Fifty, Sunset Grill, The New Age, Screamers, Mighty Aphrodite, Beyond the Clouds.
TELEVISION: *Movies*: The Man Without a Country, The Silence, Kentucky Woman, Two Kinds of Love, Apology, Women & Men: Stories of Seduction (Dust Before Fireworks), Rainbow Drive, The Substitute Wife, The Road to Ruin, Decoy. *Guest*: Lou Grant, Exit 10. *Special*: Partners (also dir., co-writer).

WENDERS, WIM
Director, Writer. b. Dusseldorf, Germany, August 14, 1945. Studied film 1967-70 at Filmhochschule in Munich. Worked as film critic 1968-70 for Filmkritik and Die Suddeutsche Zeitung. 1967 made first short films (Schauplatze) and three others before first feature, Summer in the City.
PICTURES: *Director-Writer*: Summer in the City (debut, 1970; also prod., actor), The Scarlet Letter, The Goalie's Anxiety at the Penalty Kick, Alice in the Cities, Wrong Move (dir. only), Kings of the Road (also prod.), The American Friend, Lightning Over Water (also actor), Chambre 66 (dir., actor), Hammett (dir. only), The State of Things, Paris Texas (dir. only), I Played It for You (dir., actor only), Tokyo-Ga (also edit.), Wings of Desire (also prod.), Notebooks on Cities and Clothes (also photog.), Until the End of the World, Faraway So Close! (also prod.), Lisbon Story, Beyond the Clouds (co-dir. & co-s.p. with Michelangelo Antonioni) *Actor only*: Long Shot, King Kong's Faust, Helsinki Napoli All Night Long, Motion and Emotion.

WENDKOS, PAUL
Director. b. Philadelphia, PA, Sept. 20, 1926. e. Temple U., Columbia, the New School.
PICTURES: The Burglar, Tarawa Beachhead, Gidget, Face of a Fugitive, Battle of the Coral Sea, Because They're Young, Angel Baby, Gidget Goes to Rome, Miles to Terror, Guns of the Magnificent Seven, Cannon for Cordova, The Mephisto Waltz, Special Delivery.
TELEVISION: Hawaii 5-0 (pilot), Fear No Evil, The Brotherhood of the Bell, Travis Logan D.A., A Tattered Web, A Little Game, A Death of Innocence, The Delphi Bureau, Haunts of the Very Rich, Footsteps, The Strangers in 7-A, Honor Thy Father, Terror on the Beach, The Underground Man, The Legend of Lizzie Borden, Death Among Friends, The Death of Ritchie, Secrets, Good Against Evil, Harold Robbins' 79 Park Avenue, A Woman Called Moses, The Ordeal of Patty Hearst, Act of Violence, Ordeal of Doctor Mudd, A Cry for Love, The Five of Me, Golden Gate, Farrell for

the People, Cocaine: One Man's Seduction, Intimate Agony, The Awakening of Candra, Celebrity, Scorned and Swindled, The Execution, The Bad Seed, Picking Up the Pieces, Rage of Angels: The Story Continues, Sister Margaret and the Saturday Night Ladies, Six Against the Rock, Right to Die, The Taking of Flight 847: The Uli Derickson Story, The Great Escape II: The Untold Story (co-dir.), From the Dead of Night, Cross of Fire, Blind Faith, Good Cops Bad Cops, The Chase, White Hot: The Murder of Thelma Todd, Guilty Until Proven Innocent, The Trail, Bloodlines.

WENDT, GEORGE
Actor. b. Chicago, IL, Oct. 17, 1948. e. Rockhurst Col. Joined Second City's acting troupe in 1973. Appeared in NBC pilot Nothing but Comedy.
PICTURES: My Bodyguard, Somewhere in Time, Airplane II: The Sequel, Jekyll & Hyde Together Again, The Woman in Red, Dreamscape, Thief of Hearts, No Small Affair, Fletch, House, Gung Ho, Plain Clothes, Guilty by Suspicion, Forever Young, The Little Rascals, Man of the House.
TELEVISION: *Series*: Making the Grade, Cheers, The George Wendt Show. *Guest*: Alice, Soap, Taxi, Hart to Hart, Saturday Night Live, Seinfeld. *Movies*: Oblomov (BBC), The Ratings Game, Hostage for a Day, Columbo: Strange Bedfellows, Shame II: The Secret, Bye Bye Birdie.

WERNER, PETER
Producer, Director. b. New York, NY, Jan. 17, 1947. e. Dartmouth Coll., AFI. Received Academy Award for short subject, In the Region of Ice, 1976.
PICTURES: Don't Cry It's Only Thunder, No Man's Land.
TELEVISION: *Director*: Battered, William Faulkner's Barnburning, Moonlighting (Emmy & D.G.A. nom.), Aunt Mary, Women in Song, Outlaws (pilot), LBJ: The Early Years. Men (exec. prod., dir.; Emmy nom.), The Image (Ace Award), Hiroshima: Out of the Ashes (D.G.A. nom.), D.E.A. (pilot), Ned Blessing (pilot), Middle Ages (co-exec. prod.), Substitute Wife, The Four Diamonds, The Unspoken Truth, Almost Golden: The Jessica Savitch Story (D.G.A. nom.), Nash Bridges (pilot), For the Love of Zachary.

WERTHEIMER, THOMAS
Executive. b. 1938. e. Princeton U., B.A. 1960; Columbia U., LLB, 1963. V.p. business affairs subs. ABC 1964-72; joined MCA Inc, 1972; v.p. Universal TV dir.; corp. v.p. 1974 -83; exec. v.p. 1983-; chmn., MCA Television and Home Entertainment Groups.

WERTMULLER, LINA
Director, Writer. b. Rome, Italy, Aug. 14, 1928. m. sculptor-set designer Enrico Job. e. Acad. of Theatre, Rome, 1951. Began working in theatre in 1951; prod.-dir. avant-garde plays in Italy 1951-52; member puppet troupe 1952-62; actress, stage mgr., set designer, publicity writer, for theater, radio & TV, 1952-62. Began film career as asst. to Fellini on 8 1/2 in 1962. Following year wrote and directed first film, The Lizards. Had big TV success with series called Gian Burasca and then returned to theatre for a time. 1988, named Special Commissioner of Centro Sperimentale di Cinematografia. Was the first woman to be nominated for an Academy Award for Best Director (Seven Beauties, 1976).
PICTURES: *Director-Writer*: The Lizards (dir. debut, 1963), Let's Talk About Men, The Seduction of Mimi (Cannes Film Fest Award, 1972), Love and Anarchy, All Screwed Up, Swept Away... By an Unusual Destiny in the Blue Sea of August, Seven Beauties (Acad. Award noms. for dir. & s.p., 1976), The End of the World in Our Usual Bed in a Night Full of Rain, Blood Feud, A Joke of Destiny (Lying in Wait Around the Corner Like a Bandit), A Complex Plot About Women, Sotto Sotto (Softly Softly), Summer Night With Greek Profile Almond Eyes and a Scent of Basil, The Tenth One in Hiding, On a Moonlit Night, Saturday Sunday Monday, Ciao Professore!
TELEVISION: Rita the Mosquito, Il Decimo Clandestino (Cannes Fest. Award).

WEST, ADAM
Actor. b. Walla Walla, WA, Sept. 19, 1929. r.n. William West Anderson. e. Whitman Col. (B.A.), Stanford Univ. Appeared in interactive short film Ride for Your Life, and CD-ROM The Golden Nugget.
PICTURES: The Young Philadelphians, Geronimo, Soldier in the Rain, Tammy and the Doctor, Robinson Crusoe on Mars, The Outlaws Is Coming!, Mara of the Wilderness, Batman, The Girl Who Knew Too Much, Marriage of a Young Stockbroker, The Specialist, Hell River, Hooper, The Happy Hooker Goes to Hollywood, Blonde Ambition, One Dark Night, Young Lady Chatterly, Hell Raiders, Zombie Nightmare, Doin' Time on Planet Earth, Mad About You, John Travis: Solar Survivor, Maxim Xul, Night of the Kickfighter, The New Age, Not This Part of the World, Bigger Than Watermelon, An American Vampire Story.
TELEVISION: *Series*: The Detectives, Batman, The Last Precinct, Danger Theatre, The Clinic. *Movies*: The Eyes of Charles Sands, For the Love of It, I Take These Men, Nevada

Smith, Poor Devil, The Last Precinct. *Guest*: Hawaiian Eye, 77 Sunset Strip, Bonanza, The Outer Limits, Petticoat Junction, Bewitched, The Big Valley, Love American Style, Night Gallery, Mannix, Alice, Murder She Wrote, Hope and Gloria, Lois and Clark, Burke's Law, The Simpsons (voice), The Critic (voice), Batman (animated series; voice), Politically Incorrect, Weird Science, Rugrats (voice), Animaniacs (voice). *Pilots*: Lookwell, 1775, Reel Life, Doc Holliday, Burnett, Johnny Cinderella, Alexander the Great.

WEST, TIMOTHY
Actor. b. Yorkshire, England, Oct. 20, 1934. m. actress Prunella Scales. e. John Lyon Sch. Harow. Ent. ind. 1960. Began acting 1956 after two years as recording engineer. Worked in regional repertory, London's West End and for Royal Shakespeare Company. Dec., 1979 appointed artistic controller of Old Vic. Has directed extensively in the theatre.
PICTURES: Twisted Nerve, The Looking Glass War, Nicholas and Alexandra, The Day of the Jackal, Hedda, Joseph Andrews, The Devil's Advocate, Agatha, The Thirty Nine Steps, Rough Cut, Cry Freedom, Consuming Passions.
TELEVISION: Edward VII, Hard Times, Crime and Punishment, Henry VIII, Churchill and the Generals, Brass, The Monocled Mutineer, The Good Doctor Bodkin Adams, What the Butler Saw, Harry's Kingdom, The Train, When We Are Married, Breakthrough at Reykjavik, Strife, A Shadow on the Sun, The Contractor, Blore, m.p., Survival of the Fittest, Oliver Twist, Why Lockerbie, Framed, Smokescreen, Eleven Men Against Eleven, Cuts, The Place of the Dead.

WESTON, JAY
Producer. b. New York, NY, March 9, 1929. e. New York U. Operated own pub. agency before moving into film prod. In 1965 launched Weston Production; sold orig. s.p., the War Horses, to Embassy Pictures; acquired and marketed other properties. Became prod. story exec. for Palomar-ABC Pictures in 1967.
THEATER: Does a Tiger Wear a Necktie? (co-prod.).
PICTURES: For Love of Ivy (co-prod.), Lady Sings the Blues (co-prod.), W.C. Fields and Me, Chu Chu and the Philly Flash, Night of the Juggler, Buddy Buddy.
TELEVISION: Laguna Heat (exec. prod.).

WETTIG, PATRICIA
Actress. b. Cincinnati, OH, Dec. 4, 1951. m. actor Ken Olin. e. Temple Univ. Studied at Neighborhood Playhouse. Began acting career with NY's Circle Repertory Company appearing in The Wool Gatherer, The Diviners and A Tale Told. Other theatre work includes The Dining Room, Talking With (LA), Threads, Innocent Thoughts, My Mother Said I Never Should.
PICTURES: Guilty by Suspicion, City Slickers, Veronica & Me, City Slickers II: The Legend of Curly's Gold.
TELEVISION: *Series*: St. Elsewhere, thirtysomething (2 Emmy Awards), Courthouse. *Movies*: Silent Motive, Taking Back My Life: The Nancy Ziegenmeyer Story, Parallel Lives, Nothing But the Truth, Kansas. *Mini-Series*: Stephen King's The Langoliers.

WEXLER, HASKELL
Cinematographer, Director. b. Chicago, Feb. 6, 1922. Photographed educational and industrial films before features. Documentaries as cinematographer include: The Living City, The Savage Eye, T. for Tumbleweed, Stakeout on Dope Street, Brazil—A Report on Torture, Interviews With Mai Lai Veterans, Interview—Chile's President Allende, Introduction to the Enemy. Elected by AMPAS to Bd. of Governors, Cinematographers Branch. 1991, elected by AMPAS to bd. of govs., Cinematographers Branch; 1993, received lifetime achievement award from American Society of Cinematographers.
PICTURES: Studs Lonigan, Five Bold Women, The Hoodlum Priest, Angel Baby, A Face in the Rain, America America, The Best Man, The Bus (also dir., prod.), The Loved One (also co-prod.), Who's Afraid of Virginia Woolf? (Academy Award, 1966), In the Heat of the Night, The Thomas Crown Affair, Medium Cool (also dir., co-prod., s.p.), Trial of Catonsville Nine, American Graffiti, One Flew Over the Cuckoo's Nest, Bound for Glory (Academy Award, 1976), Coming Home, Days of Heaven (addit. photog.), No Nukes (also co-dir.), Second Hand Hearts, Richard Pryor: Live on the Sunset Strip, Lookin' to Get Out, The Man Who Loved Women, Matewan (Oscar nom.), Colors, Latino (dir., writer only), Three Fugitives, Blaze (Oscar nom.), Through the Wire, Other People's Money, Rolling Stones at the MAX, The Babe, The Secret of Roan Inish, Canadian Bacon, Mulholland Falls, Rich Man's Wife, IMAX: Mexico, Stakeout on Dope Street.

WHALEY, FRANK
Actor. b. Syracuse, NY, July 20, 1963. e. SUNY, Albany. With his brother formed rock band the Niagaras. Member of Malaparte Theatre Co. in NY.
THEATER: *NY*: Tigers Wild (debut, 1986), Face Divided, The Indian Wants the Bronx, The Years, Good Evening, Hesh, The Great Unwashed.

PICTURES: Ironweed (debut, 1987), Field of Dreams, Little Monsters, Born on the Fourth of July, The Freshman, Cold Dog Soup, The Doors, Career Opportunities, JFK, Back in the U.S.S.R., A Midnight Clear, Hoffa, Swing Kids, Pulp Fiction, I.Q., Swimming With Sharks, Homage, Cafe Society, Broken Arrow.
TELEVISION: *Specials*: Soldier Boys, Seasonal Differences. *Movies*: Unconquered, Flying Blind, Fatal Deception: Mrs. Lee Harvey Oswald, To Dance With the White Dog, The Desperate Trail. *Pilot*: Flipside. *Guest*: Spenser: For Hire, The Equalizer.

WHALLEY-KILMER, JOANNE
Actress. b. Manchester, England, Aug. 25, 1964. Began stage career while in teens including season of Edward Bond plays at Royal Court Theatre (Olivier Award nom.) and The Three Sisters, The Lulu Plays. *NY*: What the Butler Saw (Theatre World Award).
PICTURES: Dance with a Stranger, No Surrender, The Good Father, Willow, To Kill a Priest, Scandal, Kill Me Again, Navy SEALS, Crossing the Line, Shattered, Trial by Jury, A Good Man in Africa.
TELEVISION: The Singing Detective, A Quiet Life, Edge of Darkness, A Christmas Carol, Save Your Kisses, Will You Love Me Tomorrow, Scarlett.

WHEATON, WIL
Actor. r.n. Richard William Wheaton III. b. Burbank, CA, July 29, 1972. Began acting in commercials at age 7. Graduated L.A. Professional H.S., June, 1990.
PICTURES: The Secret of NIMH (voice), The Buddy System, Hambone and Hillie, The Last Starfighter, Stand by Me, The Curse, Toy Soldiers, December, The Liars' Club, Pie in the Sky.
TELEVISION: *Series*: Star Trek: The Next Generation. *Pilots*: Long Time Gone, 13 Thirteenth Avenue, The Man Who Fell to Earth. *Movies*: A Long Way Home (debut, 1981), The Defiant Ones, Young Harry Houdini, The Last Prostitute. *Specials*: The Shooting, My Dad Can't Be Crazy Can He?, Lifestories (A Deadly Secret). *Guest*: St. Elsewhere, Family Ties, Tales From the Crypt, Outer Limits.

WHITAKER, FOREST
Actor, Director. b. Longview, TX, July 15, 1961. Raised in Los Angeles. e. Pomona Col., studying music; USC, studying opera and drama. Prof. debut in prod. of The Beggar's Opera.
THEATER: Swan, Romeo and Juliet, Hamlet, Ring Around the Moon, Craig's Wife, Whose Life Is It Anyway?, The Greeks (all at Drama Studio London); School Talk (LA), Patchwork Shakespeare (CA Youth Theatre), The Beggar's Opera, Jesus Christ Superstar. *Dir.*: Look Back in Anger, Drums Across the Realm.
PICTURES: Tag: The Assassination Game (debut, 1982), Fast Times at Ridgemont High, Vision Quest, The Color of Money, Platoon, Stakeout, Good Morning Vietnam, Bloodsport, Bird (Cannes Film Fest. Award, 1988), Johnny Handsome, Downtown, Rage in Harlem (also co-prod.), Article 99, Diary of a Hit Man, Consenting Adults, The Crying Game, Bank Robber, Body Snatchers, Blown Away, Jason's Lyric, Ready to Wear (Pret-a-Porter), Smoke, Species, Waiting to Exhale (dir.only), Phenomenon.
TELEVISION: *Movies*: Hands of a Stranger, Criminal Justice, Last Light, Strapped (dir. only), Lush Life, The Enemy Within. *Guest*: Amazing Stories, Hill Street Blues, Cagney and Lacey, Trapper John M.D., The Fall Guy, Different Strokes. *Mini-Series*: North and South Parts I & II.

WHITE, BETTY
Actress. b. Oak Park, IL, Jan. 17, 1924. Graduated from Beverly Hills H.S. Performed on radio beginning in early 1940's on such shows as Blondie, The Great Gildersleeve, This Is Your FBI. Became local L.A. tv personality in early 1950's prior to starring in her first series to be seen nation-wide, Life With Elizabeth, in 1953. Was married to late tv host Allen Ludden. *Autobiography*: Here We Go Again: My Life in Television (1995).
PICTURE: Advise and Consent.
TELEVISION: *Series*: Life With Elizabeth, Make the Connection (panelist), Date With the Angels, The Betty White Show (1958), The Jack Paar Show, The Pet Set, The Mary Tyler Moore Show (2 Emmy Awards: 1975, 1976), Match Game P.M. (panelist), Liar's Club (panelist), The Betty White Show (1977-78), Just Men (host; Emmy Award, 1983), Mama's Family, The Golden Girls (Emmy Award, 1986), The Golden Palace, Bob, Maybe This Time. *Movies*: Vanished, With This Ring, The Best Place to Be, Before and After, The Gossip Columnist, Chance of a Lifetime. *Host*: Macy's Thanksgiving Parade for 10 yrs, Tournament of Roses Parade (20 yrs.). *Guest*: The Millionaire, U.S. Steel Hour, Petticoat Junction, The Odd Couple, Sonny and Cher, The Love Boat, Hotel, Matlock, The John Laroquette Show (Emmy Award, 1996), many others.

WHITE, JESSE
Actor. r.n. Jesse Weidenfeld. b. Buffalo, NY, Jan. 3, 1918. e. Akron, OH H.S. Did odd jobs, then salesman; radio, vaudeville, burlesque, nightclubs and little theatre work; Broadway

stage debut in Moon is Down, 1942; other shows include Harvey, Born Yesterday, etc. Played Maytag repairman on long-running tv commercial 1967-89.
PICTURES: Harvey (debut, 1950), Death of a Salesman, Callaway Went Thataway, Million Dollar Mermaid, Witness to Murder, Forever Female, Not as a Stranger, The Bad Seed, Back from Eternity, Designing Woman, Marjorie Morningstar, The Rise and Fall of Legs Diamond, A Fever in the Blood, Sail a Crooked Ship, It's Only Money, The Yellow Canary, It's a Mad Mad Mad Mad World, Looking For Love, A House Is Not a Home, Dear Brigitte, The Reluctant Astronaut, Bless the Beasts and Children, The Cat from Outer Space, Monster in the Closet, Matinee.
TELEVISION: *Series*: Private Secretary, The Danny Thomas Show, The Ann Sothern Show.

WHITE, LEONARD
Executive. Chairman & CEO, Orion Pictures Corporation.

WHITE, ROY B.
Executive, Exhibitor. b. Cincinnati, OH, July 30, 1926. e. U. of Cincinnati. Flight engineer, U.S. Air Force during WWII; sales department of 20th Century-Fox, 1949-52; began in exhibition, 1952; past pres., Mid-States Theatres; chmn. R. M. White Management, Inc.; past president, National Association of Theatre Owners, past Chairman of the Board, NATO, Board of Trustees—American Film Inst.; bd.of dirs. NATO of Ohio, Motion Picture Pioneers Foundation; Will Rogers Hospital, Nat'l. Endowment for Arts.

WHITELAW, BILLIE
C.B.E., D.Litt.: Actress. b. Coventry, England, June 6, 1932. Acted on radio and television since childhood. Winner of the TV Actress of the Year and 1972, Guild Award, Best Actress, 1960. British Acad. Award 1969; U.S. National Society of Film Critics Award best supp. actress, 1968. Evening News, Best Film Actress, 1977; best actress Sony Radio Radio Award 1987, 1989. 1988 Evening Standard Award for Best Actress.
THEATER: England Our England (revue), Progress to the Park, A Touch of the Poet, Othello; 3 yrs. with Natl. Theatre of Great Britain; Trelawney of the Wells, After Haggerty, Not I, Alphabetical Order, Footfalls, Molly, The Greeks, Happy Days, Passion Play, Rockaby (also in N.Y. and Adelaide Festival), Tales from Hollywood, Who's Afraid of Virginia Woolf?
PICTURES: The Fake (debut, 1953), Companions in Crime, The Sleeping Tiger, Room in the House, Small Hotel, Miracle in Soho, Gideon of Scotland Yard, Carve Her Name with Pride, Bobbikins, Mania, Hell Is a City, Make Mine Mink, No Love for Johnnie, Mr. Topaze (I Like Money), Payroll, The Devil's Agent, The Comedy Man, Charlies Bubbles, The Adding Machine, Twisted Nerve, Start the Revolution Without Me, Leo the Last, Eagle in a Cage, Gumshoe, Frenzy, Night Watch, The Omen, Leopard in the Snow, The Water Babies, An Unsuitable Job for a Woman, The Dark Crystal (voice), Tangier, Slayground, Shadey, The Chain, Murder Elite, Maurice, The Dressmaker, Joyriders, The Krays, Freddie as F.R.O.7 (voice), Deadly Advice.
TELEVISION: Over 100 leading roles including: No Trains to Lime Street, Lady of the Camelias, Resurrection, Beyond the Horizon, Anna Christie, You and Me, A World of Time, Dr. Jekyll and Mr. Hyde, Poet Game, Sextet (8 plays for BBC), Wessex Tales, The Fifty Pound Note, Supernatural (2 plays), Four plays by Samuel Beckett, Eustace and Hilda, The Oresteia of Aeschylus, The Haunted Man, Private Schultz, Jamaica Inn, Happy Days, Camille, Imaginary Friends, The Secret Garden, The Picnic, A Tale of Two Cities, The Fifteen Streets, Three Beckett plays, Lorna Doone, Duel of Love, A Murder of Quality, The Cloning of Joanna May, The Entertainer, Firm Friends, Skallagrigg.

WHITEMORE, HUGH
Writer. b. England, 1936. Studied acting at Royal Acad. of Dramatic Art. Has since written for television, film, theatre.
THEATER: Stevie, Pack of Lies, Breaking the Code, The Best of Friends, It's Ralph.
PICTURES: All Neat in Black Stockings, All Creatures Great and Small, Stevie, The Return of the Soldier, 84 Charing Cross Road, Utz, Jane Eyre.
TELEVISION: Cider With Rosie (Writers' Guild Award 1971), Elizabeth R (Emmy Award, 1971), Country Matters (Writers' Guild Award, 1972), Dummy (RAT—Prix Italia, 1979), Rebecca, All For Love, A Dedicated Man, Down at the Hydro, A Bit of Singing and Dancing, Concealed Enemies (Emmy & Neil Simon Awards, 1984), Pack of Lies, The Final Days, The Best of Friends, The Turn of the Screw.

WHITMAN, STUART
Actor. b. San Francisco, CA., Feb. 1, 1928. Army Corp. of Engineers (1945-1948); at Fort Lewis, WA; while in army, competed as light heavyweight boxer. Studied drama under G.I. Bill at Ben Bard Drama Sch. and L.A. City Coll. Performed in Heaven Can Wait and became member of Michael Chekhov Stage Society and Arthur Kennedy Group. Entered films in early 1950's. TV debut on 26 episodes of Highway Patrol.

PICTURES: When Worlds Collide, The Day The Earth Stood Still, Rhapsody, Seven Men From Now, War Drums, Johnny Trouble, Darby's Rangers, Ten North Frederick, The Decks Ran Red, China Doll, The Sound and the Fury, These Thousand Hills, Hound Dog Man, The Story of Ruth, Murder Inc., Francis of Assisi, The Fiercest Heart, The Mark (Acad. Award nom.), The Comancheros, Convicts 4, The Longest Day, The Day and the Hour (Fr./It.), Shock Treatment, Rio Conchos, Those Magnificent Men In Their Flying Machines, Sands of the Kalahari, Signpost to Murder, An American Dream, The Invincible Six, The Last Escape, Captain Apache (US/Sp.), Night Of The Lepus, Welcome To Arrow Beach (Tender Flesh), Crazy Mama, Call Him Mr. Shatter, Assault on Paradise (Maniac/Ransom), Mean Johnny Barrows, Las Vegas Lady, Eaten Alive!, Tony Saitta/Tough Tony (It.), Strange Shadows In An Empty Room, Ruby, The White Buffalo; Delta Fox, Thoroughbred (Run for the Roses), Oil (It. as Red Adair), La Murjer de la Tierra Caliente (Sp./It.); Guyana: Cult of the Damned, Cuba Crossing, Jamaican Gold, The Monster Club, Demonoid, Butterfly, Treasure of The Amazon, John Travis: Solar Survivor, Deadly Reactor, Moving Target, Mob Boss, Private Wars, Trail by Jury, Improper Conduct, Land of Milk and Honey.
TELEVISION: Series: Cimarron Strip, Shaunessy (pilot). Guest: The Crowd Pleaser (Alcoa-Goodyear), Highway Patrol, Dr. Christian, Hangman's Noose (Zane Grey), Walker Texas Ranger, Adventures of Brisco County Jr., Time Trax, Courthouse. Mini-Series: The Last Convertible, Hemingway. Movies: The Man Who Wanted to Live Forever, City Beneath the Sea, Revenge, The Woman Hunter, The Man Who Died Twice, Cat Creature, Go West Young Girl, The Pirate, Women in White, The Seekers, Condominium, Stillwatch, Once Upon a Texas Train, Wounded Heart.

WHITMORE, JAMES
Actor. r.n. James Allen Whitmore, Jr. b. White Plains, NY, Oct. 1, 1921. e. Yale U. In Yale Drama Sch. players; co-founder Yale radio station, 1942; U.S. Marine Corps, W.W.II; in USO, in American Wing Theatre school, in stock. Broadway debut in Command Decision, 1947.
THEATER: Give 'em Hell Harry, Will Rogers USA, Almost an Eagle.
PICTURES: The Undercover Man (debut, 1949), Battleground (Acad. Award nom.), The Asphalt Jungle, The Next Voice You Hear, Mrs. O'Malley and Mr. Malone, The Outriders, Please Believe Me, Across the Wide Missouri, It's a Big Country, Because You're Mine, Above and Beyond, The Girl Who Had Everything, All the Brothers Were Valiant, Kiss Me Kate, The Command, Them!, Battle Cry, The McConnell Story, The Last Frontier (Savage Wilderness), Oklahoma!, Crime in the Streets, The Eddie Duchin Story, The Deep Six, Face of Fire, Who Was That Lady?, Black Like Me, Chuka, Waterhole No. 3, Nobody's Perfect, Planet of the Apes, Madigan, The Split, Guns of the Magnificent Seven, Tora! Tora! Tora!, Chato's Land, The Harrad Experiment, Where the Red Fern Grows, Give 'em Hell Harry (Acad. Award nom.), The Serpent's Egg, Bully, The First Deadly Sin, The Adventures of Mark Twain (voice), Nuts, Old Explorers, The Shawshank Redemption.
TELEVISION: Series: The Law and Mr. Jones, My Friend Tony, Temperature's Rising. Movies: The Challenge, If Tomorrow Comes, I Will Fight No More Forever, Rage, Mark I Love You, Glory! Glory!, Sky High. Mini-Series: The Word, Celebrity, Favorite Son. Special: All My Sons.

WHITTON, MARGARET
Actress. b. Baltimore, MD, Nov. 30, 1950. Raised in Haddonfield, NJ. Has written articles for Village Voice, The National.
THEATER: NY: Nourish the Beast (Off-B'way debut, 1973), Another Language, The Art of Dining, Chinchilla, Othello, One Tiger to a Hill, Henry IV Part 1, Don Juan, Steaming, Aunt Dan and Lemon, Ice Cream/Hot Fudge. Regional: Hamlet, Camille, Time and the Conways, The House of Blue Leaves.
PICTURES: National Lampoon Goes to the Movies (debut, 1981), Love Child, The Best of Times, 9-1/2 Weeks, The Secret of My Success, Ironweed, Major League, Little Monsters, Big Girl Don't Cry... They Get Even, The Man Without a Face, Major League 2, Trial by Jury.
TELEVISION: Series: Search for Tomorrow, Hometown, A Fine Romance, Good and Evil. Special: Motherlove. Movies: The Summer My Father Grew Up, Menendez: A Killing in Beverly Hills.

WICKES, MARY
Actress. r.n. Mary Wickenhauser. b. St. Louis, MO. e. Washington U., St. Louis (A.B., D. Arts, Hon.); post-grad, UCLA. Lecturer, seminars on acting in comedy, Coll. of Wm. & Mary, Washington U. at St. Louis, Am. Conserv. Th. in S.F. Debut at Berkshire Playhouse, Stockbridge, MA. Bd. of dir., Med. Aux Center for Health Sciences, UCLA, 1977-1995; L.A. Oncologic Inst., 1987-1995.
THEATER: (B'way) Stage Door, Father Malachy's Miracle, The Man Who Came to Dinner, Jackpot, Hollywood Pinafore, Town House, Park Avenue, Oklahoma! (revival). Stock and regional

theatre at Mark Taper Forum, Ahmanson and Chandler Pavillion (L.A.), Berkshire Playhouse in Stockbridge, Cape Playhouse in Dennis (MA), Amer. Conservatory Theatre (San Francisco), and many others.
PICTURES: The Man Who Came to Dinner (debut, 1941), Now Voyager, Who Done It?, Mayor of 44th Street, How's About It?, Higher and Higher, Happy Land, Rhythm of the Islands, My Kingdom for a Cook, Decision of Christopher Blake, June Bride, Anna Lucasta, Petty Girl, I'll See You in My Dreams, On Moonlight Bay, The Story of Will Rogers, Young Man With Ideas, By the Light of the Silvery Moon, Half a Hero, The Actress, White Christmas, Proud Rebel, Dance With Me Henry, Don't Go Near the Water, It Happened to Jane, Sins of Rachel Cade, Cimarron (1961), The Music Man, Fate is the Hunter, Dear Heart, How to Murder Your Wife, The Trouble With Angels, The Spirit Is Willing, Where Angels Go Trouble Follows, Snowball Express, Touched By Love, Postcards from the Edge, Sister Act, Sister Act 2: Back in the Habit, Little Women, The Hunchback of Notre Dame (voice).
TELEVISION: Series: Halls of Ivy, Mrs. G Goes to College, Dennis the Menace, Doc, Sigmund and the Sea Monsters, Father Dowling Mysteries. Guest: Make Room for Daddy, Lucy Show, M*A*S*H, Wonderworks (The Canterville Ghost), Studio One (Mary Poppins, Miss Hargreaves, The Storm), Highway to Heaven, You Can't Take It With You, Murder She Wrote. Movies: The Monk, Willa.
(d. October 24, 1995)

WIDMARK, RICHARD
Actor. b. Sunrise, MN, Dec. 26, 1914. e. Lake Forest U. Was drama instructor, 1936, before going to NY where he acted on many radio dramas, then stage.
PICTURES: Kiss of Death (debut, 1947), Road House, Street With No Name, Yellow Sky, Down to the Sea in Ships, Slattery's Hurricane, Night and the City, Panic in the Streets, No Way Out, Halls of Montezuma, The Frogmen, Red Skies of Montana, Don't Bother to Knock, O. Henry's Full House, My Pal Gus, Destination Gobi, Pickup on South Street, Take the High Ground, Garden of Evil, Hell & High Water, Broken Lance, Prize of Gold, The Cobweb, Backlash, Run for the Sun, The Last Wagon, Saint Joan, Time Limit, The Law and Jake Wade, The Tunnel of Love, The Trap, Warlock, The Alamo, The Secret Ways, Two Rode Together, Judgment at Nuremberg, How the West Was Won, Flight from Ashiya, The Long Ships, Cheyenne Autumn, The Bedford Incident, Alvarez Kelly, The Way West, Madigan, Death of a Gunfighter, A Talent for Loving, The Moonshine War, When The Legends Die, Murder on the Orient Express, The Sell Out, To the Devil a Daughter, Twilight's Last Gleaming, The Domino Principle, Rollercoaster, Coma, The Swarm, Dinero Maldito, Bear Island, National Lampoon Goes to the Movies, Hanky Panky, Who Dares Wins, The Final Option, Against All Odds, True Colors.
TELEVISION: Series: Madigan. Movies: Vanished, Brock's Last Case, The Last Day, Mr. Horn, All God's Children, A Whale for the Killing, Blackout, A Gathering of Old Men, Once Upon a Texas Train, Cold Sassy Tree. Special: Benjamin Franklin.

WIESEN, BERNARD
Producer, Director, Writer, Executive. b. New York, NY. e. City Coll. of New York, B.A.; Pasadena Playhouse Coll. of Theatre, Master of Theatre Arts; Dramatic Workshop of New School.
THEATER: First Monday in October (B'way, co. prod).
PICTURES: Producer-Director: Fear No More. Asst. Dir.: The King and I, The Left Hand of God, The Rains of Ranchipur, To Catch a Thief, The Trouble with Harry.
TELEVISION: Director: How to Marry a Millionaire, Valentine's Day. Assoc. Prod.: Valentine's Day, Three on an Island, Cap'n Ahab, Sally and Sam. Assoc. Prod.: Daniel Boone. Producer/Director: Julia, Co-Producer-Director: The Jimmy Stewart Show. Prod. Exec.: Executive Suite (pilot). Exec. Paramount TV, director of current programming. Writer: Love 4 Love, The Grand Turk.

WIEST, DIANNE
Actress. b. Kansas City, MO, March 28, 1948. e. U. of Maryland. Studied ballet but abandoned it for theatre. Did regional theatre work (Yale Repertory, Arena Stage), performed with NY Shakespeare Festival, toured with American Shakespeare Co.
THEATER: Regional: Arena Stage (DC): Heartbreak House, Our Town, The Dybbuk, Inherit the Wind. Yale Rep.: Hedda Gabler, A Doll's House. NY: Ashes (NY debut, 1977, at Public Theatre), Agamemnon, Leave It to Beaver Is Dead, The Art of Dining (Obie & Theatre World Awards), Bonjour La Bonjour, Frankenstein (B'way), Three Sisters, Othello, Beyond Therapy, Other Places, Serenading Louie (Obie Award), After the Fall, Not About Heroes (dir.; also at Williamstown Fest.), Hunting Cockroaches, Square One, In the Summer House, Blue Light.
PICTURES: It's My Turn (debut, 1980), I'm Dancing as Fast as I Can, Independence Day, Footloose, Falling in Love, The Purple Rose of Cairo, Hannah and Her Sisters (Academy

Award, supporting actress, 1986), Radio Days, The Lost Boys, September, Bright Lights Big City, Parenthood (Acad. Award nom.), Cookie, Edward Scissorhands, Little Man Tate, Cops and Robbersons, The Scout, Bullets Over Broadway (Academy Award, best supporting actress, 1994; also Golden Globe, NY Film Critics, LA Film Critics, Natl. Board of Review Awards), Drunks, The Birdcage, The Associate.
TELEVISION: *Specials:* Zalman or the Madness of God, Out of Our Father's House. *Movies:* The Wall, The Face of Rage.

WIGAN, GARETH
Executive. b. London, England, Dec. 2, 1931. e. Oxford. Agent, MCA London; 1957; John Redway & Associates, 1960; co-founder, agent Gregson & Wigan Ltd., 1961; co-founder, agent London Intl., 1968; independent prod., 1970; v.p., creative affairs, 20th Century Fox, 1975; v.p., prod., Fox, 1976; v.p., The Ladd Co., 1979 -83. Company W.W. Prods. Currently exec. production consultant, Columbia Pictures.
PICTURES: Unman Wittering & Zigo, Running Scared.

WIHTOL, ARN S.
Executive. b. Millville, NJ, Sept. 4, 1944. e. San Jose State. Exec. v.p., international sales, Pacific International Enterprises.
PICTURES: *Production Exec., Co-Writer:* Mystery Mansion. Casting, *Controller:* Dream Chasers. *Producer's asst.:* Sacred Ground.

WILBY, JAMES
Actor. b. Rangoon, Burma, Feb. 20, 1958. Lived a nomadic childhood moving from Burma to Ceylon, then Jamaica and finally England. e. Durham U. Trained at Royal Acad. of Dramatic Art where he played Shakespearean roles and landed a part in Oxford Film Foundation's Privileged (1982). West End stage debut Another Country. Also acted in regional theater. 1988: The Common Pursuit.
PICTURES: Privileged (debut, 1982), Dreamchild, Maurice, A Handful of Dust, A Summer Story, Immaculate Conception, Howards End, The Chess Game, Une Partie d'Echec.
TELEVISION: Dutch Girls, A Tale of Two Cities, Mother Love, Tell Me That You Love Me, Adam Bede, Lady Chatterly, You Me and It, Crocodile Shoes.

WILDE, ARTHUR L.
Publicist. b. San Francisco, CA, May 27. S.F. Daily News; Matson Lines; pub. dept., Warner Bros., 1936; photo editor at Columbia Pictures, RKO Pictures, Universal Pictures; dir. exploitation, CBS; pub. dir., Hal Wallis Prod.; pub. dept., Paramount; pub., Hecht-Hill-Lancaster; v.p., Arthur Jacobs, public rel.; Blowitz-Maskell Publicity Agency; pub. dir., C. V. Whitney Pictures; gen. v.p., 1958; owner, pub.-ad. agency, The Arthur L. Wilde Co., 1961-65; freelance publicist, 1965-66; pub. rel. consultant, Marineland of Florida 1965; unit publicity dir., United Artists, National General, Paramount, 1966-69; freelance publicity, 1971; unit publicist, MGM, Paramount, United Artists, 1972-74; staff position; Features Publicity at Paramount Pictures, 1973. Freelance unit publicist again in 1976 at Universal, Paramount and Lorimar Productions. 1978-79, Columbia Pictures & Universal Studios; 1980, Marble Arch. Prods. & Northstar Intl. Pictures; 1981, studio pub. mgr. 20th Century-Fox; recently staff unit publicist for 20th-Fox; 1984-89; currently freelance unit publicist for feature films.

WILDER, BILLY
Director, Writer, Producer. r.n. Samuel Wilder. b. Austria, June 22, 1906. Newspaperman in Vienna and Berlin; then author of screen story People on Sunday (debut, 1929) followed by 10 other German films. including Emil and the Detectives (s.p.). Co-dir. French film Mauvaise Graine with Alexander Esway (also story), marking debut as director, 1933. To Hollywood 1934. Head of Film Section, Psych. Warfare Div., U.S. Army, 1945, American Zone, Germany. Recipient: American Film Institute Life Achievement Award, 1987; Irving Thalberg Memorial Award, 1988.
PICTURES: *U.S.: Co-Writer:* Adorable (co-story), Music in the Air, Lottery Lover, Champagne Waltz (co-story), Bluebeard's Eighth Wife, Midnight, Ninotchka, What a Life, Rhythm on the River (co-story), Arise My Love, Ball of Fire, Hold Back the Dawn. *Director/Co-Writer:* The Major and the Minor (U.S. dir. debut, 1942), Five Graves to Cairo, Double Indemnity, The Lost Weekend (Academy Awards for Best Director and Adapted Screenplay, 1945), The Emperor Waltz, A Foreign Affair, Sunset Boulevard (Academy Award for Best Original Story & Screenplay, 1950). *Director-Co-Writer-Producer:* Ace in the Hole (The Big Carnival), Stalag 17, Sabrina, The Seven Year Itch (dir. & co-s.p. only), The Spirit of St. Louis, Love in the Afternoon, Witness for the Prosecution (dir. & co-s.p. only), Some Like It Hot, The Apartment (Academy Awards for Best Picture, Director and Original Story & Screenplay, 1960), One Two Three, Irma La Douce, Kiss Me Stupid, The Fortune Cookie, The Private Life of Sherlock Holmes, Avanti!, The Front Page (dir. & co-s.p. only), Fedora, Buddy Buddy (dir. & co-s.p. only).

WILDER, GENE
Actor, Director, Writer. r.n. Jerry Silberman. b. Milwaukee, WI, June 11, 1935. e. U. of Iowa. Joined Bristol Old Vic company in England, became champion fencer; in NY, worked as chauffeur, fencing instructor, etc. before NY off-B'way debut in Roots. Co-founder of Gilda's Club, a cancer support center in Manhattan.
THEATER: *B'way:* The Complacent Lover, Mother Courage, Luv, One Flew Over the Cuckoo's Nest.
PICTURES: Bonnie and Clyde (debut, 1967), The Producers (Acad. Award nom.), Start the Revolution Without Me, Quackser Fortune Has a Cousin in the Bronx, Willy Wonka and the Chocolate Factory, Everything You Always Wanted to Know About Sex* But Were Afraid to Ask, Rhinoceros, Blazing Saddles, The Little Prince, Young Frankenstein (also co-s.p.), The Adventure of Sherlock Holmes' Smarter Brother (also dir., s.p.), Silver Streak, The World's Greatest Lover (also dir., s.p., prod.), The Frisco Kid, Stir Crazy, Sunday Lovers (also dir. & s.p.; episode: Skippy), Hanky Panky, The Woman in Red (also dir., s.p.), Haunted Honeymoon (also dir., s.p., prod.), See No Evil Hear No Evil (also co-s.p.), Funny About Love, Another You.
TELEVISION: *Series:* Something Wilder. *Specials:* The Man Who Refused to Die, Death of a Salesman (1966), The Scarecrow, Acts of Love—And Other Comedies, Annie and the Hoods, The Trouble With People, Marlo Thomas Special. *Movie:* Thursday's Game.

WILLENBORG, GREGORY H.
Producer. b. Miami, FL, Feb. 18, 1959. e. Geroge Washington U., B.B.A. 1981; UCLA M.B.A. Marketing & Strategic Planning 1983. During grad. school, worked at the political fundraising firm of Lynn, Bryan & Associates. In 1983, he formed Willenborg & Associates, a consulting grp. specializing in marketing and fundraising. Raised 25 million for the Bob Hope Cultural Center in Palm Desert, CA.
TELEVISION: America's Hope Awards (creator), America's Dance Awards (creator), America's Hope Award Honoring Bob Hope, America's All-Star Tribute to Elizabeth Taylor, Ray Charles: 50 Years in Music, An All-Star Tribute to Oprah Winfrey, Jerry Herman's Broadway at the Hollywood Bowl.

WILLIAMS, ANDY
Singer, Performer. b. Wall Lake, IA, Dec. 3, 1927. Sang as teen with brothers, performing on radio in Des Moines, Chicago, and Los Angeles. William Brothers were back up singers on Bing Crosby's hit recording of Swinging on a Star. Andy dubbed singing voice of Lauren Bacall in To Have and Have Not. Went solo after group disbanded in early 1950's.
PICTURES: Something to Sing About, I'd Rather Be Rich.
TELEVISION: *Series:* The College Bowl, Tonight (with Steve Allen; 1954-57), The Andy Williams and June Valli Show, The Chevy Showroom, The Andy Williams Show (1958), The Andy Williams Show (1962-67, 1969-71), The Andy Williams Show (synd.: 1976-77). *Specials:* Love Andy, Kaleidoscope Company, Magic Lantern Show Company, The NBC Kids Search for Santa, The NBC Kids Easter in Rome, many Christmas specials.

WILLIAMS, BERT
Executive, Actor. b. Newark, NJ, April 12, 1922. e. USC. Navy, 1942-45. Summer Stock, 1940-41; world's prof. diving champion, 1945-48; star diver, Larry Crosby, Buster Crabbe, Johnny Weismuller, Dutch Smith Shows, 1945-48; writer, asst. prod., Martin Mooney Prods., PRC, Goldwyn Studios; pres., Bert Prods., Bert Williams Motion Picture Producers and Distributors, Inc. Member, MP Academy of Fine Arts & TV Academy of Arts & Science. Masters Outdoor & Indoor National Diving, 1985-87, 89, 90. 1989 World Masters Diving Champion; 1990 & 1994 World Games Diving Champion.
THEATER: Cat on a Hot Tin Roof, Hamlet, Run From The Hunter, Sugar and Spice, Hope Is a Thing Called Feathers, 69 Below, Tribute.
PICTURES: *Actor:* Fort Apache, Rio Grande, American Bandito, Angel Baby; The Nest of the Cuckoo Birds (also prod., dir.), Around the World Under the Sea, Deathwatch 28 (s.p.), Gambit, No Secret, This Must Be the Last Day of Summer, Twenty Eight Watched (dir.), Adventure To Treasure Reef (prod., dir.), Knife Fighters (s.p.). Black Freedom; A Crime of Sex, The Masters (prod., dir.), Crazy Joe, Serpico, Lady Ice, The Klansman, Report to the Commissioner, Tracks, All the President's Men, From Noon Till Three, While Buffalo, Shark Bait (s.p.), The Big Bus, Wanda Nevada, Cuba Crossing, Sunnyside, Cuba, The Last Resort, The All Night Treasure Hunt. Tom Horn, Kill Castro, Midnight Madness, The All-American Hustler, 10 to Midnight, Police Academy 2, One More Werewolf Picture, Silent Scream, Murphy's Law, Cobra, Assassinations, Penitentiary III, Messenger of Death, Death Under the Rock, Innocent Blood, Public Access, Tropic of Desire, Duel at Pueblo Solo, Project Eliminators, No Secret, Usual Suspect.
TELEVISION: Flipper, Sea Hunt, Final Judgment, Project Eliminator, Speargun, Gentle Ben, The Law (pilot) and Police Story (actor), Get Christy Love, General Hospital, Columbo,

Brenner for the People, Mayday 40,000 Feet, Jigsaw John (Blue Knight episode), Police Woman, Chips, Mobil One, Street Killing, East of Eden, Rose for Emily, Brett Maverick, Today's F.B.I., The Judge, Fifth St. Gym (also prod., dir., s.p.; pilot), Helter Skelter, The Green Eyed Bear, The Amazing Howard Hughes, Mike Douglas Show, Johnny Carson Show, Tales from the Dark Side, The Last Car, This Is the Life, Deadly Intentions, Divorce Court, Man Who Broke 1000 Chains, Nightmare Classics (Eye of the Panther), Man from Atlantis, Land's End.

WILLIAMS, BILLY DEE
Actor. b. New York, NY, April 6, 1937. e. National Acad. of Fine Arts and Design. Studied acting with Paul Mann and Sidney Poitier at actor's workshop in Harlem. Was child actor in the Firebrand of Florence with Lotte Lenya; Broadway adult debut in The Cool World in 1961.
THEATER: A Taste of Honey, Hallelujah Baby, I Have a Dream, Fences.
PICTURES: The Last Angry Man (debut, 1959), The Out-of-Towners, The Final Comedown, Lady Sings the Blues, Hit!, The Take, Mahogany, The Bingo Long Travelling All-Stars and Motor Kings, Scott Joplin, The Empire Strikes Back, Nighthawks, Return of the Jedi, Marvin and Tige, Fear City, Number One with a Bullet, Deadly Illusion, Batman, The Pit and the Pendulum, Driving Me Crazy, Giant Steps, Alien Intruder.
TELEVISION: Series: The Guiding Light, Double Dare. Mini-Series: Chiefs. Movies: Carter's Army, Brian's Song, The Glass House, Christmas Lilies of the Field, Children of Divorce, The Hostage Tower, The Imposter, Courage, Oceans of Fire, The Right of the People, Dangerous Passion, The Jacksons: An American Dream, Marked for Murder, Percy & Thunder, Heaven & Hell: North and South Book III, Falling for You. Guest: The F.B.I., The Interns, Mission Impossible, Mod Squad, Dynasty, In Living Color.

WILLIAMS, CARA
Actress. r.n. Bernice Kamiat. b. Brooklyn, NY, June 29, 1925. e. Hollywood Professional Sch. Ent. ind., 20th Century Fox, child actress.
PICTURES: The Happy Land (debut, 1943), Something for the Boys, In the Meantime Darling, Boomerang!, Don Juan Quilligan, Sitting Pretty, The Saxon Charm, Knock on Any Door, The Girl Next Door, Monte Carlo Baby, The Great Diamond Robbery, Meet Me in Las Vegas, The Helen Morgan Story, Never Steal Anything Small, The Defiant Ones (Acad. Award nom.), The Man from the Diners' Club, Doctors' Wives, The White Buffalo.
TELEVISION: Series: Pete and Gladys, The Cara Williams Show, Rhoda. Guest: Alfred Hitchcock Presents, Desilu Playhouse, The Jackie Gleason Show, Henry Fonda Special.

WILLIAMS, CARL W.
Executive. b. Decatur, IL, March 9, 1927. e. Illinois State Normal U., B.S., 1949; UCLA, M.A., 1950. dir. adv. photo., Clark Equipment Co., 1951-54; film dir., WKAR-TV, E. Lansing, MI, 1954-56; Prod., dir., Capital Films, E. Lansing, MI, 1957; dir., A-V Laboratory, U.C.L.A., 1957-63; co-dev. Dimension 150 Widescreen process, 1957; formed D-150 Inc., 1963; Filbert Co., 1970, v.p., 1977; v.p., Cinema Equipment Sales of Calif., Inc., 1986; pres. 1992. Member: AMPAS, SMPTE, AFI.

WILLIAMS, CINDY
Actress. b. Van Nuys, CA., Aug. 22, 1947. e. Los Angeles City Coll. Appeared in high school and college plays; first prof. role in Roger Corman's film Gas-s-s-s. Made TV debut in Room 222 and had recurring role.
PICTURES: Gas-s-s-s (debut, 1970), Beware! the Blob, Drive He Said, The Christian Licorice Store, Travels With My Aunt, American Graffiti, The Conversation, Mr. Ricco, The First Nudie Musical, More American Graffiti, UFOria, Rude Awakening, Big Man on Campus, Bingo!, Father of the Bride II (co-prod. only), Meet Wally Sparks.
TELEVISION: Series: The Funny Side, Laverne and Shirley, Normal Life, Getting By. Guest: Barefoot in the Park, My World and Welcome to It, Love American Style, Nanny and the Professor, Getting Together, Lois and Clark. Movies: The Migrants, Helped Wanted: Kids, Save the Dog, Tricks of the Trade, The Leftovers, Perry Mason: The Case of the Poisoned Pen, Menu for Murder (Murder at the PTA Luncheon), Earth Angel, Escape From Terror: The Teresa Stamper Story. Special: The Laverne and Shirley Reunion. Pilot: Steel Magnolias, The Neighbors.

WILLIAMS, CLARENCE, III
Actor. b. New York, NY, Aug. 21, 1939. B'way stage: Slow Dance on the Killing Ground (Tony nom.; Theatre World Award), The Great Indoors, Night and Day.
PICTURES: Rituals, The End, Judgment, Road to Galveston, Purple Rain, 52 Pick-Up, Tough Guys Don't Dance, I'm Gonna Git You Sucka, My Heroes Have Always Been Cowboys, Deep Cover, Dead Fall, Sugar Hill, Tales From the Hood, The Immortals.

TELEVISION: Series: The Mod Squad. Guest: The Nasty Boys, Crazy Love, Miami Vice, Twin Peaks, Uptown Undercover, Cosby Mysteries. Movies: The Return of the Mod Squad, Against the Wall.

WILLIAMS, ELMO
Film Editor, Director, Producer. b. Oklahoma City, OK, Apr. 30, 1913. Film editor 1933-39, with British & Dominion Studio, England. Since then with RKO-Radio as film editor for numerous major productions; mgr., dir., 20th Century Fox Prods. Ltd. v.p., worldwide production, 20th Century-Fox Film 1971. President Ibex Films. Exec. v.p., Gaylord Prods., 1979; promoted to pres., worldwide prods.
PICTURES: High Noon (edit; Academy Award, 1952), Tall Texan (dir., edit.), The Cowboy (prod., dir., edit.), 20,000 Leagues Under the Sea (edit.), Apache Kid (dir.), The Vikings (2nd unit dir., film ed.), The Big Gamble (2nd Unit dir.), The Longest Day (assoc. prod.), Zorba the Greek (exec. prod.), Those Magnificent Men in Their Flying Machines (exec. prod.), The Blue Max (exec. prod.), Tora! Tora! Tora! (prod.), Sidewinder One (edit.), Caravans (edit.), Man Woman and Child (prod.).
TELEVISION: Tales of the Vikings (co-prod., dir.).

WILLIAMS, ESTHER
Actress, Swimmer. b. Los Angeles, CA, Aug. 8, 1923. e. USC. Swimmer at San Francisco World's Fair Aquacade; professional model. Signed to movie contract by MGM. Voted one of Top Ten Money-Making Stars in M.P. Herald-Fame poll, 1950.
PICTURES: Andy Hardy's Double Life (debut, 1942), A Guy Named Joe, Bathing Beauty, Thrill of a Romance, Ziegfeld Follies, The Hoodlum Saint, Easy to Wed, Fiesta, This Time for Keeps, On an Island With You, Take Me Out to the Ball Game, Neptune's Daughter, Pagan Love Song, Duchess of Idaho, Texas Carnival, Callaway Went Thataway (cameo), Skirts Ahoy!, Million Dollar Mermaid, Dangerous When Wet, Easy to Love, Jupiter's Darling, The Unguarded Moment, Raw Wind in Eden, The Big Show, The Magic Fountain, That's Entertainment III.
TELEVISION: Specials: Esther Williams in Cypress Gardens, Live From New York, Esther Williams Aqua Spectacular.

WILLIAMS, JO BETH
Actress. b. Houston, TX, 1953. m. director John Pasquin. e. Brown U. One of Glamour Magazine's top 10 college girls, 1969-70. Acted with rep. companies in Rhode Island, Philadelphia, Boston, Washington, DC, etc. Spent over two years in New York-based daytime serials, Somerset and The Guiding Light.
THEATER: Ladybird Blues (1979), A Coupla White Chicks Sitting Around Talking, Gardenia.
PICTURES: Kramer vs. Kramer (debut, 1979), Stir Crazy, The Dogs of War, Poltergeist, Endangered Species, The Big Chill, American Dreamer, Teachers, Desert Bloom, Poltergeist II, Memories of Me, Welcome Home, Switch, Dutch, Stop Or My Mom Will Shoot, Me Myself & I, Wyatt Earp.
TELEVISION: Movies: Fun and Games, The Big Black Pill, Feasting with Panthers, Jabberwocky, The Day After, Adam, Kids Don't Tell, Adam: His Song Continues, Murder Ordained, Baby M, My Name is Bill W, Child of the Night, Bump in the Night (co-exec. prod. only), Victim of Love, Jonathan: The Boy Nobody Wanted, Sex Love and Cold Hard Cash, Chantilly Lace, Final Appeal, Parallel Lives, Voices From Within, A Season of Hope. Series: Fish Police (voice), John Grisham's The Client.

WILLIAMS, JOHN
Composer. b. New York, NY, Feb. 8, 1932. e. UCLA, Juilliard Sch. Worked as session musician in '50s; began career as film composer in late '50s. Considerable experience as musical director and conductor as well as composer. Since 1977 conductor of Boston Pops.
PICTURES: I Passed for White, Because They're Young, The Secret Ways, Bachelor Flat, Diamond Head, Gidget Goes to Rome, The Killers, None But the Brave, John Goldfarb Please Come Home, The Rare Breed, How to Steal a Million, The Plainsman, Not with My Wife You Don't, Penelope, A Guide for the Married Man, Fitzwilly, Valley of the Dolls, Daddy's Gone A-Hunting, Goodbye Mr. Chips (music supvr. & dir.), The Reivers, Fiddler on the Roof (music. dir.; Academy Award, 1971). The Cowboys, Images, Pete 'n' Tillie, The Poseidon Adventure, Tom Sawyer (musc. supvr.), The Long Goodbye, The Man Who Loved Cat Dancing, The Paper Chase, Cinderella Liberty, Conrack, The Sugarland Express, Earthquake, The Towering Inferno, The Eiger Sanction, Jaws (Academy Award, 1975), Family Plot, The Missouri Breaks, Midway, Black Sunday, Star Wars (Academy Award, 1977), Raggedy Ann & Andy, Close Encounters of the Third Kind, The Fury, Jaws II, Superman, Meteor, Quintet, Dracula, 1941, The Empire Strikes Back, Raiders of the Lost Ark, Heartbeeps, E.T.: The Extra-Terrestrial (Academy Award, 1982), Yes Giorgio, Monsignor, Return of the Jedi, Indiana Jones and the Temple of Doom, The River, SpaceCamp, The

Witches of Eastwick, Empire of the Sun, The Accidental Tourist, Indiana Jones and the Last Crusade, Born on the Fourth of July, Always, Stanley & Iris, Presumed Innocent, Home Alone, Hook, JFK, Far and Away, Home Alone 2: Lost in New York, Jurassic Park, Schindler's List (Academy Award, 1993), Sabrina.
TELEVISION: Once Upon a Savage Night, Jane Eyre (Emmy Award), Sergeant Ryker, Heidi (Emmy Award), The Ewok Adventure. *Series themes:* Checkmate, Alcoa Premiere, Wide Country, Lost in Space, The Time Tunnel, NBC News Theme, Amazing Stories.

WILLIAMS, KENNETH S.
Executive. b. Tulsa, OK, Dec. 31, 1955. e. Harvard Coll., B.A. 1978; Columbia U., M.S. 1985. Began as team leader of Chase Manhattan's motion picture lending group 1978-81. Joined Sony Pictures Entertainment in Jan. 1982 as dir. of corporate finance, was promoted to assistant treas. Oct. 1982. He became treas. in Feb. 1984 and named a v.p. in Nov. 1984. Served as pres. & treas. of both Columbia PIctures Industries, Inc. and the Entertainment Business Sector of the Coca-Cola Co. (Sony Pictures previous parent co.), 1986-87. 1987-90, corporate v.p. & treas. of Sony Pictrues Entertainment and was then promoted to s.v.p., Corporate Operations. Was named exec. v.p. of Sony Picture Entertainment in Aug. 1995.

WILLIAMS, PAUL
Actor, Composer. b. Omaha, NE, Sept. 19, 1940. Began career at studios as set painter and stunt parachutist. Bit and character parts in commercials followed. Became song writer, collaborating briefly with Biff Rose and later with Roger Nichols, with whom wrote several best-sellers, including We've Only Just Begun, Rainy Days and Mondays, Just an Old-Fashioned Love Song.
PICTURES: *Actor:* The Loved One (debut, 1965), The Chase, Watermelon Man, Battle for the Planet of the Apes, Phantom of the Paradise (also songs), Smokey and the Bandit, The Cheap Detective, The Muppet Movie (also songs), Stone Cold Dead, Smokey and the Bandit II, Smokey and the Bandit 3, Zombie High, The Chill Factor, The Doors, Solar Crisis (voice), A Million to Juan, Headless Body in Topless Bar. *Songs for Films:* Cinderella Liberty, Bugsy Malone (also vocals), Lifeguard, A Star Is Born (co-composer; Academy Award for best song: Evergreen, 1976), One on One, The End, Agatha, Ishtar, The Muppet Christmas Carol, Headless Body in Topless Bar.
TELEVISION: *Series:* Sugar Time! (songs, music spvr.). *Movies (actor):* Flight to Holocaust, The Wild Wild West Revisted, Rooster, The Night They Saved Christmas, People Like Us, Hart to Hart Returns.

WILLIAMS, PAUL
Director. b. New York, NY, Nov. 12, 1943. e. Harvard (Phi Beta Kappa, 1965). First gained attention as director of film short, Girl, which won Golden Eagle award, made in collaboration with producer Edward R. Pressman, with whom he formed Pressman-Williams Enterprises which prod. Badlands, Phantom of the Paradise, etc. Now with Fulcrum Productions.
PICTURES: Out of It (also s.p.), The Revolutionary, Dealing: or the Berkeley-to-Boston Forty-Brick Lost-Bag-Blues (also s.p.), Nunzio, Miss Right (also story), The November Men (also actor), Mirage (also actor).

WILLIAMS, RICHARD
Producer, Painter, Film Animator. b. March, 1933, Toronto, Canada. Entered industry in 1955. Founded Richard Williams Animation Ltd. in 1962, having entered films by producing The Little Island (1st Prize, Venice Film Festival) in 1955. His company produces TV commercials for England, America, France and Germany, entertainment shorts and animated films. Designed animated feature titles/sequences for What's New Pussycat?, A Funny Thing Happened On The Way To The Forum, Casino Royale, The Charge of the Light Brigade, A Christmas Carol (Academy Award for best animated short, 1972), Who Framed Roger Rabbit (dir. of animation), Arabian Knight (dir., prod., co-s.p.). Awards: at Festivals at Venice, Edinburgh, Mannheim, Montreal, Trieste, Melbourne, West Germany, New York, Locarno, Vancouver, Philadelphia, Zagreb, Hollywood, Cork, Los Angeles. 1989, Academy Award, BAFTA Award, AMPAS Award, special effects, also Special Achievement Awards for work over 30 years, esp. Roger Rabbit by both BAFTA and AMPAS.

WILLIAMS, ROBIN
Actor, Comedian. b. Chicago, IL, July 21, 1951. e. Claremont Men's Coll. (CA), Coll. of Marin (CA), studying acting at latter. Continued studies at Juilliard with John Houseman in New York augmenting income as a street mime. As San Francisco club performer appeared at Holy City Zoo, Intersection, The Great American Music Hall and The Boardinghouse. In Los Angeles performed as stand-up comedian at The Comedy Store, Improvisation, and The Ice House. First TV appearance on 1977 Richard Pryor series followed by The Great American Laugh Off. Guest on Happy Days as extraterrestrial Mork from Ork, led to own series.

PICTURES: Can I Do It...Til I Need Glasses? (debut, 1977), Popeye, The World According to Garp, The Survivors, Moscow on the Hudson, The Best of Times, Club Paradise, Good Morning Vietnam (Acad. Award nom.), The Adventures of Baron Munchausen, Dead Poets Society (Acad. Award nom.), Cadillac Man, Awakenings, Dead Again, The Fisher King (Acad. Award nom.), Hook, Shakes the Clown, FernGully... The Last Rainforest (voice), Aladdin (voice), Toys, Mrs. Doubtfire (also co-prod.), Being Human, Nine Months, To Wong Foo—Thanks for Everything—Julie Newmar, Jumanji, Birdcage, Jack, Hamlet, Joseph Conrad's The Secret Agent.
TELEVISION: *Series:* The Richard Pryor Show (1977), Laugh-In (1977-78 revival; later aired as series in 1979), Mork and Mindy, Shakespeare: The Animated Tales (host). *Guest:* America Tonight, Ninety Minutes Live, The Alan Hamel Show. *Specials:* An Evening With Robin Williams, E.T. & Friends, Faerie Tale Theatre (The Frog Prince), Carol Carl Whoopi and Robin (Emmy Award, 1987), Free To Be... a Family, Dear America: Letters Home from Vietnam (reader), ABC Presents a Royal Gala (Emmy Award, 1988), In Search of Dr. Seuss. *Movie:* Seize the Day.

WILLIAMS, ROGER
Pianist, Concert, Film, TV Personality. b. Omaha, NE, Oct. 1, 1924. e. Drake U., Idaho State Coll. Hon. Ph.D. Midland and Wagner Colls. Served U.S. Navy WWII. Appeared as guest artist in number of films. Public debut on TV's Arthur Godfrey Talent Scouts and Chance of a Lifetime. Other TV appearances include Ed Sullivan, Hollywood Palace, Kraft Summer Series, Celanese Special. Recorded 75 Albums, Kapp (now MCA) Records, with sales over 15 million albums.

WILLIAMS, TREAT
Actor. r.n. Richard Williams. b. Rowayton, CT, Dec. 1, 1952. e. Franklin and Marshall Coll. Landed role on B'way in musical, Over Here! also played leading role in Grease on B'way.
THEATER: Over Here, Bus Stop (Equity Library Theatre), Once in a Lifetime, The Pirates of Penzance, Some Men Need Help, Oh Hell, Oleanna.
PICTURES: Deadly Hero (debut, 1976), The Ritz, The Eagle Has Landed, Hair, 1941, Why Would I Lie?, Prince of the City, The Pursuit of D. B. Cooper, Once Upon a Time in America, Flashpoint, Smooth Talk, The Men's Club, Dead Heat, Sweet Lies, Heart of Dixie, Night of the Sharks, Russicum, Beyond the Ocean, Where the Rivers Flow North, Hand Gun, Things to Do in Denver When You're Dead, Mulholland Falls, The Phantom.
TELEVISION: *Movies:* Dempsey, A Streetcar Named Desire, J. Edgar Hoover, Echoes in the Darkness, Third Degree Burn, Max and Helen, Final Verdict, Till Death Us Do Part, The Water Engine, Deadly Matrimony, Bonds of Love (also co-exec. prod), Parallel Lives, In the Shadow of Evil. *Mini-Series:* Drug Wars: The Camarena Story. *Specials:* The Little Mermaid (Faerie Tale Theatre), Some Men Need Help, Texan (also dir.), Edgar Allan Poe: Terror of the Soul. *Series:* Eddie Dodd, Good Advice. *Guest:* Tales From the Crypt.

WILLIAMS-JONES, MICHAEL
Executive. b. England, June 3, 1947. Joined United Artists as trainee, 1967; territorial mgr., South Africa, 1969; territorial mgr., Brazil, 1971; territorial mgr., England, 1976; appt. v.p., continental European mgr., 1978; sr. v.p. foreign mgr., 1979; 1982 joined United Intl. Pictures as sr. v.p. intl. sls., based in London. 1984, named pres. UIP motion picture group; 1986, named pres. & CEO. In Dec. 96, retired from UIP to create own production co., Merlin Angelsey U.K. Ltd.

WILLIAMSON, FRED
Actor, Director, Producer, Writer. b. Gary, IN, March 5, 1937. e. Northwestern U. Spent 10 yrs. playing pro football before turning to acting.
PICTURES: M*A*S*H (debut, 1970), Tell Me That You Love Me Junie Moon, The Legend of Nigger Charley, Hammer, Black Caesar, The Soul of Nigger Charley, Hell Up in Harlem, That Man Bolt, Crazy Joe, Three Tough Guys, Black Eye, Three the Hard Way, Boss Nigger, Bucktown, No Way Back (also dir., prod., s.p.), Take a Hard Ride, Adios Amigo, Death Journey (also dir., prod.), Joshua, Blind Rage, Fist of Fear Touch of Death, 1990: The Bronx Warriors, One Down Two to Go (also dir., prod., Vigilante, Warriors of the Wasteland, Deadly Impact, The Big Score (also dir.), The Last Fight (also dir.), Foxtrap (also dir., prod.), Warrior of the Lost World, Deadly Intent, Delta Force, Commando, Taxi Killer (prod.), Hell's Heroes, Three Days to a Kill (also dir., s.p.), Justice Done (also dir.), Soda Cracker (also dir., prod.), South Beach (also dir., prod.), Silent Hunter (also dir.), From Dusk Till Dawn, Original Gangstas (also prod.).
TELEVISION: *Series:* Julia, Monday Night Football, Half Nelson. *Guest:* Police Story, The Rookies, Lou Grant.

WILLIAMSON, NICOL
Actor. b. Hamilton, Scotland, Sept. 14, 1938. Has played many classical roles with Royal Shakespeare Co., including

Macbeth, Malvolio, and Coriolanus. Starred on Broadway in Inadmissible Evidence, Rex (musical debut), Macbeth, I Hate Hamlet. *London*: Jack.
PICTURES: Inadmissible Evidence (debut, 1968), The Bofors Gun, Laughter in the Dark, The Reckoning, Hamlet, The Jerusalem File, The Monk, The Wilby Conspiracy, Robin and Marian, The Seven Percent Solution, The Goodbye Girl (cameo), The Cheap Detective, The Human Factor, Excalibur, Venom, I'm Dancing as Fast as I Can, Return to Oz, Black Widow, The Exorcist III, Apt Pupil, The Advocate.
TELEVISION: *Movies*: Sakharov, Passion Flower. *Mini-Series*: Lord Mountbatten, The Word, Christopher Columbus. *Specials*: Of Mice and Men, Macbeth, I Know What I Meant.

WILLIAMSON, PATRICK
Executive. b. England, Oct. 1929. Joined Columbia Pictures London office 1944—career spanned advertising & publicity responsibilities until 1967 when appt. managing dir. Columbia Great Britain; also mng. dir. on formation of Columbia-Warner; promoted to exec. position in Columbia's home office, NY, 1973, and pres. of intl. optns. 1974; v.p., Coca-Cola Export Corp., 1983; exec. v.p. Columbia Pictures Industries, 1985; director, CPI, 1985; exec. v.p., Coca-Cola Entertainment Business Sector, 1987; promoted to special asst. to pres. & CEO of Coca-Cola Entertainment Business Sector, 1987; served on boards of Tri-Star Pictures, RCA/Columbia Home Video, RCA/Columbia Int'l. Video; 1987, named pres. Triumph Releasing Corp., a unit of Columbia Pictures Entertainment; Consultant to Sony Pictures Entertainment, 1989. 1994. dir. & co-founder, Sports Alliance Intl. TV.

WILLIS, BRUCE
Actor. b. Germany, March 19, 1955. m. actress Demi Moore. Moved to New Jersey when he was 2. After graduating high school, worked at DuPont plant in neighboring town. First entertainment work was as harmonica player in band called Loose Goose. Formed Night Owl Promotions and attended Montclair State Coll. NJ, where he acted in Cat on a Hot Tin Roof. *NY stage debut*: Heaven and Earth. Member of Barbara Contardi's First Amendment Comedy Theatre; supplemented acting work by doing Levi's 501 jeans commercials and as bartender in NY nightclub, Kamikaze. Appeared as extra in film The First Deadly Sin.
THEATER: Fool for Love.
PICTURES: Blind Date, Sunset, Die Hard, In Country, Look Who's Talking (voice), That's Adequate, Die Hard 2, Look Who's Talking Too (voice), The Bonfire of the Vanities, Mortal Thoughts, Hudson Hawk (also co-story), Billy Bathgate, The Last Boy Scout, The Player, Death Becomes Her, National Lampoon's Loaded Weapon 1 (cameo), Striking Distance, North, Color of Night, Pulp Fiction, Nobody's Fool, Die Hard With a Vengeance, Twelve Monkeys, Last Man Standing.
TELEVISION: *Series*: Moonlighting (Emmy Award, 1987). *Guest*: Hart to Hart, Miami Vice, Twilight Zone. *Special*: Bruce Willis: The Return of Bruno (also writer, prod.).

WILLIS, GORDON
Cinematographer. Acted two summers in stock at Gloucester, MA, where also did stage settings and scenery. Photographer in Air Force; then cameraman, making documentaries. In TV did commercials and documentaries.
PICTURES: End of the Road, Loving, The Landlord, The People Next Door, Little Murders, Klute, The Godfather, Bad Company, Up the Sandbox, The Paper Chase, The Parallax View, The Godfather Part II, The Drowning Pool, All the President's Men, Annie Hall, Interiors, September 30, 1955, Comes a Horseman, Manhattan, Stardust Memories, Pennies from Heaven, A Midsummer Night's Sex Comedy, Zelig, Broadway Danny Rose, The Purple Rose of Cairo, Perfect, The Money Pit, The Pick-Up Artist, Bright Lights Big City, Presumed Innocent, The Godfather Part III, Malice. *Director*: Windows (1980; debut).
TELEVISION: *Movie*: The Lost Honor of Kathryn Beck.

WILSON, ELIZABETH
Actress. b. Grand Rapids, MI, April 4, 1921.
THEATER: *B'way*: Picnic (debut, 1953), The Desk Set, The Tunnel of Love, Little Murders, Big Fish Little Fish, Sheep on the Runway, Sticks and Bones (Tony Award, 1972), Uncle Vanya, Morning's at Seven, Ah! Wilderness, The Importance of Being Earnest, You Can't Take It With You, A Delicate Balance. *Off-B'way*: Sheep on the Runway, Token in Marriage (Drama Desk Award), Three Penny Opera, Salonika, Ante Room, Eh?, All's Well That Ends Well. *Tour*: The Cocktail Hour.
PICTURES: Picnic (debut, 1955), Patterns, The Goddess, The Tunnel of Love, Happy Anniversary, A Child is Waiting, The Birds, The Tiger Makes Out, The Graduate, Jenny, Catch-22, Little Murders, Day of the Dolphin, Man on a Swing, The Happy Hooker, The Prisoner of Second Avenue, Nine to Five, The Incredible Shrinking Woman, Grace Quigley, Where Are the Children?, The Believers, Regarding Henry, The Addams Family, Quiz Show, Nobody's Fool.

TELEVISION: *Series*: East Side West Side, Doc, Morningstar/Eveningstar, Delta. *Movies*: Miles to Go Before I Sleep, Once Upon a Family, Million Dollar Infield, Sanctuary of Fear, Morning's at Seven, Nutcracker: Money Madness and Murder (Emmy nom.), Conspiracy of Love, Skylark, In the Best of Families: Marriage Pride & Madness, Bitter Blood, In the Best Families, Spring Awakening, Journey to Mars. *Mini-Series*: Queen, Scarlett. *Specials*: Patterns, Happy Endings, You Can't Take It With You. *Guest*: U.S. Steel Hour, Maude, All in the Family, Love Sidney, Murder She Wrote, The Boys Next Door.

WILSON, FLIP
Performer. r.n. Clerow Wilson. b. Newark, NJ, Dec. 8, 1933. Left school at 16 to join Air Force; played clubs in FL & Bahamas until 1965 when made guest appearance on NBC.
PICTURES: Uptown Saturday Night, Skatetown USA, The Fish That Saved Pittsburgh.
TELEVISION: *Series*: The Flip Wilson Show (Emmy Award for writing, 1971), People Are Funny (1984, host), Charlie & Co. *Guest*: That's Life, Sammy and Company, Love American Style, Here's Lucy, The Six Million Dollar Man, 227, etc. *Specials*: Flip Wilson Special (1969), Clerow Wilson and the Miracle of P.S. 114, Clerow Wilson's Great Escape, Pinocchio, Zora is My Name.

WILSON, HUGH
Producer, Director, Writer. b. Miami, FL, Aug. 21, 1943. e. Univ. of FL., 1965. Gained fame for creating, writing, producing and directing TV series, WKRP in Cincinnati, Frank's Place and The Famous Teddy Z. Feature film dir. debut with Police Academy (1984).
PICTURES: *Writer*: Stroker Ace, Down Periscope. *Director-Writer*: Police Academy, Rustler's Rhapsody, Burglar, Guarding Tess (also voice), Down Periscope (co-s.p.). *Dir.*: The First Wives Club.

WILSON, SCOTT
Actor. b. Atlanta, GA, 1942. Was college athlete on basketball scholarship when injured and had to leave school. Moved to L.A. and enrolled in local acting class.
PICTURES: In the Heat of the Night (debut, 1967), In Cold Blood, The Gypsy Moths, Castle Keep, The Grissom Gang, The New Centurions, Lolly Madonna XXX, The Great Gatsby, Twinkle Twinkle Killer Kane (The Ninth Configuration), The Right Stuff, The Aviator, On the Line, A Year of the Quiet Sun, Blue City, Malone, Johnny Handsome, The Exorcist III, Young Guns II, Femme Fatale, Pure Luck, Flesh and Bone, Geronimo: An American Legend, Tall Tale, Judge Dredd.
TELEVISION: *Movies*: Jesse, Elvis and the Colonel.

WINANS, CHARLES A.
Executive. Exec. dir., National Association of Concessionaires.

WINCER, SIMON
Director. b. Australia. Directed over 200 hours of dramatic programs for Australian TV, including Cash and Company, Tandarra, Ryan, Against the Wind, The Sullivans, etc. Exec. prod. of The Man from Snowy River, then the top-grossing theatrical film in Australia.
PICTURES: Snapshot (The Day After Halloween), Harlequin, Phar Lap, D.A.R.Y.L., The Lighthorsemen (also co.-prod.), Quigley Down Under, Harley Davidson and the Marlboro Man, Free Willy, Lightning Jack (also co-prod.), Operation Dumbo Drop, The Phantom.
TELEVISION: *Movies*: The Last Frontier, Bluegrass, Lonesome Dove (Emmy Award, 1989), The Girl Who Spelled Freedom. *Series*: The Young Indiana Jones Chronicles.

WINCHELL, PAUL
Actor, Ventriloquist. b. New York, NY, Dec. 21, 1922. e. Sch. of Industrial Arts. At 13 won first prize Major Bowes Radio Amateur Hour; signed by Ted Weems; created dummies Jerry Mahoney and Knucklehead Smiff. On radio as host of his own show in 1940's. In the news in 1975 as inventor of an artificial heart.
PICTURES: Stop! Look! and Laugh! (actor), Winnie the Pooh and the Blustery Day (short; voice), The Aristocats (voice), Which Way to the Front? (actor), Winnie the Pooh and Tigger Too (short; voice), The Fox and the Hound (voice).
TELEVISION: *Series*: The Bigelow Show, The Paul Winchell-Jerry Mahoney Spiedel Show (also prod., writer), Jerry Mahoney's Club House (also writer), What's My Name?, Circus Time (ringmaster), Toyland Express (also prod.), The Paul Winchell Show (1957-60), Banana Splits Adventure Hour (voice), Runaround. *Voices for series*: The Wacky Races, Cartoonsville, Dastardly and Mutley, Help It's the Hair Bear Bunch, Goober and the Ghost Chaser, The Oddball Couple, Clue Club, The C.B. Bears, Wheelie and the Chopper, Heathcliff and Marmaduke Show, The Smurfs, Winnie the Pooh Hour, various Dr. Seuss specials, Smurf specials. *Movie*: The Treasure Chest. *Guest*: Pat Boone Show, Polly Bergen Show, The Lineup, Candid Camera, The Beverly Hillbillies, 77 Sunset Strip, Donna Reed Show, Perry Mason, Dick Van Dyke Show, Lucy Show, Love American Style, Brady Bunch, many others.

WINCOTT, MICHAEL

Actor. b. Canada. Studied acting at Juilliard. NY stage incl. Talk Radio, States of Shock.

PICTURES: Wild Horse Hank (debut, 1979), Circle of Two, Ticket to Heaven, Curtains, The Sicilian, Talk Radio, Suffering Bastards, Bloodhounds of Broaway, Born on the Fourth of July, The Doors, Robin Hood: Prince of Thieves, 1492: Conquest of Paradise, The Three Musketeers, Romeo Is Bleeding, The Crow, Panther, Strange Days, Dead Man, Basquiat.

TELEVISION: Movies: Tragedy of Flight 103: The Inside Story. Guest: Miami Vice, Crime Story, The Equalizer. Special: High School Narc.

WINDOM, WILLIAM

Actor. b. New York, NY, Sept. 28, 1923.

PICTURES: To Kill a Mockingbird (debut, 1962), Cattle King, For Love or Money, One Man's Way, The Americanization of Emily, Hour of the Gun, The Detective, The Gypsy Moths, The Angry Breed, Brewster McCloud, Fool's Parade, Escape From the Planet of the Apes, The Mephisto Waltz, The Man, Now You See Him Now You Don't, Echoes of a Summer, Mean Dog Blues, Separate Ways, Last Plane Out, Grandview U.S.A., Prince Jack, Space Rage, Funland, Pinocchio and the Emperor of the Night (voice), Planes Trains and Automobiles, She's Having a Baby, Sommersby, Miracle on 34th Street.

TELEVISION: Series: The Farmer's Daughter, My World and Welcome to It (Emmy Award, 1970), The Girl With Something Extra, Brothers and Sisters, Murder She Wrote, Parenthood. Movies: Prescription: Murder, U.M.C., The House on Greenapple Road, Assault on the Wayne, Escape, A Taste of Evil, Marriage: Year One, The Homecoming, Second Chance, A Great American Tragedy, Pursuit, The Girls of Huntington House, The Day the Earth Moved, The Abduction of St. Anne, Journey from Darkness, Guilty or Innocent: The Sam Sheppard Murder Case, Bridger, Richie Brockelman: Missing 24 Hours, Hunters of the Reef, Portrait of a Rebel: Margaret Sanger, Leave 'Em Laughing, Side Show, Desperate Lives, The Rules of Marriage, Why Me?, Off Sides, Velvet, Surviving, There Must Be a Pony, Dennis the Menace, Chance of a Lifetime, Attack of the 50 Ft. Woman. Mini-Series: Once an Eagle, Seventh Avenue, Blind Ambition. Guest: Robert Montgomery Presents, Ben Casey, Lucy Show, The FBI, Gunsmoke, Partridge Family, That Girl, The Rookies, Streets of San Francisco, Barney Miller, Kojak, Police Woman, Love Boat, St. Elsewhere, Newhart, Night Gallery, Twilight Zone, many others.

WINDSOR, MARIE

Actress. r.n. Emily Marie Bertelsen. b. Marysvale, UT, Dec. 11, 1919. Winner of beauty contests, including Queen of Covered Wagon Days. Worked as telephone girl, dancing teacher. Trained for acting by Maria Ouspenskaya. Won Look Mag. Award, best supporting actress, 1957.

PICTURES: All-American Co-Ed (debut, 1941), Song of the Thin Man, Unfinished Dance, On an Island With You, Three Musketeers, Kissing Bandit, Force of Evil, Oupost in Morocco, Fighting Kentuckian, Beautiful Blonde From Bashful Bend, Frenchie, Dakota Lil, Little Big Horn, Two Dollar Bettor, Hurricane Island, The Narrow Margin, Japanese War Bride, The Jungle, The Sniper, The Tall Texan, The City That Never Sleeps, The Eddie Cantor Story, Trouble Along the Way, Cat Women of the Moon, Hell's Half Acre, The Bounty Hunter, No Man's Woman, Abbott & Costello Meet the Mummy, Swamp Women, Two Gun Lady, The Killing, The Unholy Wife, The Story of Mankind, Girl in Black Stockings, Parson and the Outlaw, Island Woman, Paradise Alley, The Day Mars Invaded Earth, Critics Choice, Mail Order Bride, Bedtime Story, Chamber of Horrors, Support Your Local Gunfighter, The Good Guys and the Bad Guys, One More Train To Rob, Cahill U.S. Marshall, The Outfit, Hearts of the West, Freaky Friday, Lovely But Deadly.

TELEVISION: Series: Supercarrier. Movies: Wild Women, Manhunter, Salem's Lot, J.O.E. and the Colonel.

WINFIELD, PAUL

Actor. b. Los Angeles, CA, May 22, 1940. e. attended U. of Portland 1957-59, Stanford U., L.A. City Coll. and UCLA. Inducted in Black Filmmakers Hall of Fame.

THEATER: Regional work at Dallas Theatre Center (A Lesson From Aloes), Goodman Theatre (Enemy of the People), Stanford Repertory Theatre and Inner City Cultural Center, L.A.; At Lincoln Center in The Latent Heterosexual, and Richard III. B'way: Checkmates, Othello, Merry Wives of Windsor.

PICTURES: The Lost Man (debut, 1969), R.P.M., Brother John, Sounder (Acad. Award nom.), Trouble Man, Gordon's War, Conrack, Huckleberry Finn, Hustle, Twilight's Last Gleaming, The Greatest, Damnation Alley, A Hero Ain't Nothin' But a Sandwich, High Velocity, Carbon Copy, Star Trek II—The Wrath of Khan, White Dog, On the Run, Mike's Murder, The Terminator, Blue City, Death Before Dishonor, Big Shots, The Serpent and the Rainbow, Presumed Innocent, Cliffhanger, Dennis the Menace, Original Gangstas, Mars Attacks!.

WINFREY, OPRAH

TV Talk Show Hostess, Actress, Producer. b. Kosciusko, MS, Jan. 29, 1954. e. Tennessee State U. Started as radio reporter then TV news reporter-anchor in Nashville. Moved to Baltimore in same capacity, later co-hosting successful morning talk show. Left for Chicago to host own show AM Chicago which became top-rated in only a month; expanded to national syndication in 1986. Formed own production co., Harpo Productions, Inc. in 1986 which assumed ownership and prod. of The Oprah Winfrey Show in 1988. Named Broadcaster of the Year by Intl. Radio and TV Soc., 1988. Purchased Chicago movie and TV production facility, 1988; renamed Harpo Studios. National Daytime Emmy Award, 1987, Outstanding Talk/Service Program Host.

PICTURES: The Color Purple (debut, 1985; Acad. Award nom.), Native Son, Throw Momma From the Train (cameo).

TELEVISION: Movies: The Women of Brewster Place (actress, co-exec. prod.), Overexposed (co-prod. only), There Are No Children Here. Series: The Oprah Winfrey Show (many Emmy Awards), Brewster Place (also exec. prod.). Special: Pee-wee's Playhouse Christmas Special.

WINGER, DEBRA

Actress. b. Cleveland, OH, May 16, 1955. e. California State U. Began career on TV series Wonder Woman.

PICTURES: Slumber Party (debut, 1977), Thank God It's Friday, French Postcards, Urban Cowboy, Cannery Row, An Officer and a Gentleman (Acad. Award nom.), Terms of Endearment (Acad. Award nom.), Mike's Murder, Legal Eagles, Black Widow, Made in Heaven, Betrayed, Everybody Wins, The Sheltering Sky, Leap of Faith, Wilder Napalm, A Dangerous Woman, Shadowlands (Acad. Award nom.), Forget Paris.

TELEVISION: Movie: Special Olympics. Guest: Wonder Woman, James at 16.

WINITSKY, ALEX

Producer. b. New York, NY, Dec. 27, 1924. e. NYU, BS, LLB, JD. In partnership as attorneys in L.A. for 20 years with Arlene Sellers before they turned to financing and later production of films.

PICTURES: Co-prod. with Sellers: End of the Game, The White Dawn, The Seven-Per-Cent Solution, Cross of Iron, Silver Bears, The Lady Vanishes, Cuba, Blue Skies Again, Irreconcilable Differences, Scandalous, Swing Shift, Bad Medicine, Stanley & Iris, Circle of Friends.

TELEVISION: Ford—The Man and the Machine.

WINKLER, HENRY

Actor, Producer, Director. b. New York, NY, Oct. 30, 1945. e. Emerson Coll., Yale Sch. of Drama, MA. Appeared with Yale Repertory Co.; returned to N.Y. to work in radio. Did 30 TV commercials before starring in The Great American Dream Machine and Masquerade on TV. Formed Winkler/Daniel Prod. Co. with Ann Daniel.

PICTURES: Actor: Crazy Joe (debut, 1974), The Lords of Flatbush, Heroes, The One and Only, Night Shift. Exec. Prod: The Sure Thing. Director: Memories of Me, Cop and a Half.

TELEVISION: Series (actor): Happy Days, Monty. Series (prod.): Ryans Four (co-prod.), Mr. Sunshine (co-exec. prod.), McGyver, A Life Apart. Guest: The Mary Tyler Moore Show, The Bob Newhart Show, The Paul Sand Show, Rhoda, Laverne & Shirley, The Larry Sanders Show. Specials: Henry Winkler Meets William Shakespeare, America Salutes Richard Rodgers, A Family Again (exec. prod.), Two Daddies (voice, exec. prod.). Movies: Katherine, An American Christmas Carol, Absolute Strangers, The Only Way Out, Truman Capote's One Christmas, A Child Is Missing. Director: A Smoky Mountain Christmas (movie), All the Kids Do It (also actor, exec. prod.; Emmy Award as exec. prod., 1985). Exec. prod.: Who Are the DeBolts and Where Did They Get 19 Kids?, Scandal Sheet, When Your Lover Leaves, Starflight, Second Start, Morning Glory (pilot), MacGyver: Lost Treasure of Atlantis, MacGyver: Trail to Doomsday.

WINKLER, IRWIN

Producer, Director. b. New York, NY, May 28, 1934. e. NYU.

PICTURES: Producer: Double Trouble, Blue, The Split, They Shoot Horses Don't They?, The Strawberry Statement, Leo the Last, Believe in Me, The Gang That Couldn't Shoot Straight, The Mechanic, The New Centurions, Up the Sandbox, Busting, S*P*Y*S, The Gambler, Breakout, Peeper,

(continued, left column top)

TELEVISION: Series: Julia, The Charmings, Wiseguy, 227. Movies: The Horror at 37,000 Feet, It's Good to Be Alive (The Fight), Green Eyes, Angel City, Key Tortuga, The Sophisticated Gents, Dreams Don't Die, Sister Sister, For Us the Living, Go Tell It on the Mountain, Under Siege, The Roy Campanella Story, Guilty of Innocence, Women of Brewster Place, Roots: The Gift, Back to Hannibal, Breathing Lessons, Tyson. Mini-Series: King, Backstairs at the White House, The Blue and the Gray, Roots: The Next Generations, Queen, Scarlett.

Rocky (Academy Award for Best Picture, 1976), Nickelodeon, New York New York, Valentino, Comes a Horseman, Uncle Joe Shannon, Rocky II, Raging Bull, True Confessions, Rocky III, Author! Author!, The Right Stuff, Rocky IV, Revolution, 'Round Midnight, Betrayed, Music Box, GoodFellas, Rocky V, The Juror. *Director*: Guilty by Suspicion (also s.p.), Night and the City, The Net (also co-s.p., co-prod.).

WINNER, MICHAEL
Producer, Director, Writer. b. London, Eng., Oct. 30, 1935. e. Cambridge U. Ent. m.p. ind. as columnist, dir., Drummer Films. *Presenter*: Michael Winner's True Crimes. *Actor*: For the Greater Good, Decadence, Calliope, Kenny Everett Show, The Full Wax, Birds of a Feather.
PICTURES: *Writer*: Man With A Gun. *Director-Writer*: Haunted England (also prod.), Shoot to Kill, Swiss Holiday, Climb Up the Wall, Out of the Shadow, Some Like It Cool, Girls Girls Girls, It's Magic, Behave Yourself, The Cool Mikado, You Must Be Joking, West 11 (dir. only). *Director/Producer*: The System (The Girl-Getters), I'll Never Forget What's 'is Name, The Jokers, Hannibal Brooks (also s.p.), The Games, Lawman, The Nightcomers, Chato's Land, The Mechanic (dir. only), Scorpio (also s.p.), The Stone Killer, Death Wish, Won Ton Ton the Dog Who Saved Hollywood, The Sentinel (also s.p.), The Big Sleep (also s.p.), Firepower (also s.p.), Death Wish II, The Wicked Lady (also s.p.), Scream for Help, Death Wish III (dir. only), Appointment With Death (also s.p.), A Chorus of Disapproval (also s.p.), Bullseye (also s.p.), Dirty Weekend (also s.p.).
TELEVISION: *Series*: White Hunter, Dick and the Duchess.

WINNINGHAM, MARE
Actress. b. Phoenix, AZ, May 16, 1959. TV debut at age 16 as a singer on The Gong Show. Debut solo album What Might Be released in 1992.
PICTURES: One-Trick Pony, Threshold, St. Elmo's Fire, Nobody's Fool, Made in Heaven, Shy People, Miracle Mile, Turner and Hooch, Hard Promises, Teresa's Tattoo, Wyatt Earp, The War, Georgia.
TELEVISION: *Mini-Series*: The Thorn Birds, Studs Lonigan. *Movies*: Special Olympics, The Death of Ocean View Park, Amber Waves (Emmy Award), Off the Minnesota Strip, The Women's Room, Freedom, A Few Days in Weasel Creek, Missing Children: A Mother's Story, Helen Keller: The Miracle Continues, Single Bars Single Women, Love Is Never Silent, Who is Julia, A Winner Never Quits, Eye on the Sparrow, God Bless the Child, Love and Lies, Crossing to Freedom, Fatal Exposure, She Stood Alone, Those Secrets, Intruders, Better Off Dead, Betrayed by Love, Letter to My Killer, The Deliverance of Elaine.

WINSTON, STAN
Makeup and Special Effects Artist. b. 1946. e. UofVA. Started in business in 1970 as apprentice to Robert Schiffer at makeup dept. of Walt Disney Studios. Established Stan Winston Studio in Van Nuys, CA.
PICTURES: W.C. Fields and Me, The Wiz, Dead and Buried, Heart Beeps, The Thing, The Entity, Something Wicked This Way Comes, The Terminator, Starman, Invaders From Mars, Aliens (Academy Award for Visual Effects, 1986), Predator, The Monster Squad, Alien Nation, Pumpkinhead (dir. debut), Leviathan, Predator 2, Edward Scissorhands, Terminator 2: Judgment Day (2 Academy Awards: Visual Effects and Makeup, 1991), A Gnome Named Gnorm (dir.), Batman Returns, Jurassic Park (Academy Award for Visual Effects, 1993), Interview With the Vampire, Tank Girl, Congo.
TELEVISION: *Movies*: Gargoyles (Emmy Award for Makeup, 1972), The Autobiography of Miss Jane Pittman (Emmy Award for Makeup, 1974), Roots. *Specials*: Masquerade, Pinocchio, An Evening With Diana Ross.

WINTER, ALEX
Actor. b. London, England, July 17, 1965. e. NYU. At age 4 began studying dance. Played opposite Vincent Price in St. Louis Opera production of Oliver! Co-founder of Stern-Winter Prods. Produced videos for Red Hot Chili Peppers, Human Radio, Ice Cube, etc. Co-directed TV special Hard Rock Cafe Presents: Save the Planet.
THEATER: *B'way*: The King and I (1977 revival), Peter Pan (1979 revival). *Off-B'way*: Close of Play.
PICTURES: Death Wish III, The Lost Boys, Haunted Summer, Bill & Ted's Excellent Adventure, Rosalie Goes Shopping, Bill & Ted's Bogus Journey, Freaked (also co-dir., co-s.p., co-prod.).
TELEVISION: *Movie*: Gaugin the Savage. *Series*: Idiot Box (also co-creator, co-dir., co-writer).

WINTERS, DAVID
Choreographer, Actor, Director. b. London, April 5, 1939. Acted in both Broadway and m.p. version of West Side Story (as A-rab). Directed and acted in number of TV shows. Choreography credits include films Viva Las Vegas, Billie, Send Me No Flowers, Tickle Me, Pajama Party, Girl Happy,

The Swinger, Made in Paris, Easy Come, Easy Go, The Island of Doctor Moreau, Roller Boogie, A Star is Born, Blame It on the Night. Was choreographer for TV series Hullabaloo, Shindig, Donny and Marie Osmond, The Big Show, and Steve Allen Show, and TV specials starring Joey Heatherton, Nancy Sinatra, Diana Ross, Raquel Welch, Ann Margret, Lucille Ball. Pres., A.I.P. Distribution, A.I.P. Productions and A.I.P. Home Video, 1989; formed Pyramid Distributors. Features incl.: Firehead, Raw Nerve, Center of the Web, Double Vision.

WINTERS, DEBORAH
Actress. b. Los Angeles, CA. e. Professional Children's Sch., New York; began studying acting at Stella Adler's with Pearl Pearson. at age 13 and Lee Strasberg at 16. Acting debut at age 5 in TV commercials. Casting dir.: Aloha Summer (asst.), Breakdancers From Mars (assoc. prod., casting dir.), Into the Spider's Web, The Hidden Jungle, Haunted, Broken Spur, Behind the Mask (also assoc. prod.).
PICTURES: Me Natalie, Hail Hero!, The People Next Door, Kotch, Class of '44, Blue Sunshine, The Lamp, The Outing.
TELEVISION: *Special*: Six Characters in Search of an Author. *Guest*: Matt Houston, Medical Center. *Movies*: Lottery, Gemini Man. Tarantulas: The Deadly Cargo, Little Girl Lost, Space City. *Mini-Series*: The Winds of War.

WINTERS, JONATHAN
Actor. b. Dayton, OH, Nov. 11, 1925. e. Kenyon Coll.; Dayton Art Inst., B.F.A. Disc jockey, Dayton and Columbus stations; night club comedian performing at Blue Angel and Ruban Bleu (NY), Black Orchid (Chicago), Flamingo, Sands, Riviera (Las Vegas), then on B'way in John Murray Anderson's Almanac. Author: Mouse Breath, Conformity and Other Social Ills, Winters Tales, Hang Ups (book on his paintings). Recorded 7 comedy albums. Won Grammy Award for "Crank Calls" comedy album, 1996.
PICTURES: Alakazam the Great! (voice), It's a Mad Mad Mad Mad World, The Loved One, The Russians Are Coming the Russians Are Coming, Penelope, Oh Dad Poor Dad Mama's Hung You in the Closet and I'm Feeling So Sad, Eight on the Lam, Viva Max, The Fish That Saved Pittsburgh, The Longshot, Say Yes, Moon Over Parador, The Flintstones, The Shadow, Arabian Knight (voice).
TELEVISION: *Series*: And Here's the Show, NBC Comedy Hour, The Jonathan Winters Show (1956-57), Masquerade Party (panelist), The Andy Williams Show, The Jonathan Winters Show (1967-69), Hot Dog, The Wacky World of Jonathan Winters, Mork and Mindy, Hee Haw, The Smurfs (voice of Papa Smurf), The Completely Mental Misadventures of Ed Grimley (voices), Davis Rules (Emmy Award, 1991), Fish Police (voice). *Guest*: Steve Allen Show, Garry Moore Show, Jack Paar, Omnibus, Twlight Zone, Bob Hope specials, Tonight Show, Hollywood Squares, many others. *Specials*: The Jonathan Winters Special, The Jonathan Winters Show (1964, 1965), Jonathan Winters Presents 200 Years of American Humor, 'Tis the Season to Be Smurfy (voice). *Movies*: Now You See It—Now You Don't, More Wild Wild West.

WINTERS, SHELLEY
Actress. r.n. Shirley Schrift. b. St. Louis, MO, Aug. 18, 1922. e. Wayne U. Clerked in 5 & 10 cent store; in vaudeville, chorus girl in night clubs; NY stage (Conquest, Night Before Christmas, Meet the People, Rosalinda, A Hatful of Rain, Girls of Summer, Minnie's Boys, One Night Stand of a Noisy Passenger. (Off-B'way). Autobiographies: Shelley Also Known as Shirley (1981), Shelley II: The Middle of My Century (1989).
PICTURES: What a Woman! (debut, 1943), Nine Girls, Sailor's Holiday, Knickerbocker Holiday, Cover Girl, A Double Life, Cry of the City, Larceny, Take One False Step, Johnny Stool Pigeon, The Great Gatsby, South Sea Sinner, Winchester '73, Frenchie, A Place in the Sun, He Ran All the Way, Behave Yourself, The Raging Tide, Phone Call From a Stranger, Meet Danny Wilson, Untamed Frontier, My Man and I, Tennessee Champ, Executive Suite, Saskatchewan, Playgirl, To Dorothy a Son (Cash on Delivery), Mambo, Night of the Hunter, I Am a Camera, Big Knife, Treasure of Pancho Villa, I Died a Thousand Times, The Diary of Anne Frank (Academy Award, best supporting actress, 1959), Odds Against Tomorrow, Let No Man Write My Epitaph, Young Savages, Lolita, Chapman Report, The Balcony, Wives and Lovers, Time of Indifference, A House Is Not a Home, A Patch of Blue (Academy Award, best supporting actress, 1965), The Greatest Story Ever Told, Harper, Alfie, Enter Laughing, The Scalphunters, Wild in the Streets, Buona Sera Mrs. Campbell, The Mad Room, How Do I Love Thee?, Bloody Mama, Flap, What's the Matter with Helen?, Who Slew Auntie Roo?, The Poseidon Adventure, Cleopatra Jones, Something to Hide, Blume in Love, Diamonds, Journey Into Fear, That Lucky Touch, Next Stop Greenwich Village, The Tenant, Tentacles, Pete's Dragon, King of the Gypsies, The Magician of Lublin, The Visitors, City on Fire, S.O.B., Over the Brooklyn Bridge, Ellie, Witchfire (also assoc. prod.), Deja Vu, Very Close Quarters, The Delta Force, The Order of Things, Purple People Eater, An

Unremarkable Life, Touch of a Stranger, Stepping Out, Weep No More My Lady, The Pickle, The Silence of the Hams, Heavy, Jury Duty, Portrait of a Lady.
TELEVISION: *Special*: Bob Hope Chrysler Theatre: Two Is the Number (Emmy Award, 1964). *Movies*: Revenge, A Death of Innocence, The Adventures of Nick Carter, The Devil's Daughter, Big Rose, The Sex Symbol, The Initiation of Sarah, Elvis, Alice in Wonderland, Mrs. Munck. *Mini-Series*: The French Atlantic Affair.

WINTMAN, MELVIN R.
Theatre Executive, b. Chelsea, MA. e. U. of Massachusetts, Northeastern U., J.D. Major, infantry, AUS, W.W.II. Attorney. Now consultant & dir., General Cinema Corp.; formerly exec. v.p., GCC and pres., GCC Theatres, Inc., Boston. Dir. Will Rogers Memorial Fund. Former pres. Theatre Owners of New England (1969-70); past dir. NATO (1969-70); treas., Nat'l Assoc. of Concessionaires (1960).

WISDOM, NORMAN
O.B.E. Actor, Singer, Comedian. Musical and legit. b. London, Eng., Feb. 4, 1915. Awarded Order of the British Empire (O.B.E.), 1995. Many London West End stage shows including royal command performances. New York Broadway shows include Walking Happy and Not Now Darling.
PICTURES: A Date With a Dream (debut, 1948), Meet Mr. Lucifer, Trouble in Store, One Good Turn, As Long as They're Happy, Man of the Moment, Up in the World, Just My Luck, The Square Peg, Follow a Star, There Was a Crooked Man, The Bulldog Breed, The Girl on the Boat, On the Beat, A Stitch in Time, The Early Bird, Press for Time, The Sandwich Man, The Night They Raided Minsky's, What's Good for the Goose, Double X.
TELEVISION: Androcles and the Lion.

WISE, ROBERT
Director, Producer. b. Winchester, IN, Sept. 10, 1914. e. Franklin Coll., Franklin, IN. Ent. m.p. ind. in cutting dept. RKO, 1933; sound cutter, asst. edit.; film edit., 1938; edited Citizen Kane, Magnificent Ambersons; 1944, became dir.; to 20th Century-Fox, 1949; ass'n Mirisch Co. independent prod. 1959; assn. MGM independent prod., 1962; assn. 20th Century Fox Independent Prod. 1963. Partner, Filmakers Group, The Tripar Group.
PICTURES: Curse of the Cat People (debut as co-dir., 1944), Mademoiselle Fifi, The Body Snatcher, A Game of Death, Criminal Court, Born to Kill, Mystery in Mexico, Blood on the Moon, The Set-Up, Three Secrets, Two Flags West, The House on Telegraph Hill, The Day the Earth Stood Still, The Captive City, Something for the Birds, Destination Gobi, The Desert Rats, So Big, Executive Suite, Helen of Troy, Tribute to a Bad Man, Somebody Up There Likes Me, Until They Sail, This Could Be the Night, Run Silent Run Deep, I Want to Live!, Odds Against Tomorrow (also prod.), West Side Story (co-dir., prod.), Academy Awards for Best Picture & Director, 1961), Two For the Seesaw, The Haunting (also prod), The Sound of Music (also prod.; Academy Awards for Best Picture & Director, 1965), The Sand Pebbles (also prod.), Star! (also prod.), The Andromeda Strain (also prod.), Two People (also prod.), The Hindenburg (also prod.), Audrey Rose, Star Trek: The Motion Picture, Wisdom (exec. prod. only), Rooftops.

WISEMAN, FREDERICK
Documentary Filmmaker, Producer, Director & Editor. b. Boston, MA, Jan. 1, 1930. e. Williams College, B.A., 1951; Yale Law Sch., L.L.B., 1954. Member: MA Bar. Private law practice, Paris, 1956-57. Lecturer-in-Law, Boston U. Law Sch., 1959-61; Russell Sage Fndn. Fellowship, Harvard U., 1961-62; research assoc., Brandeis U., dept. of sociology, 1962-66; visiting lecturer at numerous universities. Author: Psychiatry and Law: Use and Abuse of Psychiatry in a Murder Case (American Journal of Psychiatry, Oct. 1961). Co-author: Implementation (section of report of President's Comm. on Law Enforcement and Administration of Justice). Fellow, Amer. Acad. of Arts & Sciences, 1991; John D. and Catherine T. MacArthur Foundation Fellowship, 1982-87; John Simon Guggenheim Memorial Foundation Fellowship, 1980-81. Films are distributed through his Zipporah Films, located in Cambridge, MA. Awards include 3 Emmys, Peabody Award, Intl. Documentary Assn. Career Achievement Award, 3 Columbia Dupont Awards for Excellence in Broadcast Journalism, among others.
PICTURES: Titicut Follies, High School, Law and Order, Hospital, Basic Training, Essene, Juvenile Court, Primate, Welfare, Meat, Canal Zone, Sinai Field Mission, Manoeuvre, Model, Seraphita's Diary, The Store, Racetrack, Deaf, Blind, Multi-Handicapped, Adjustment and Work, Missile, Near Death, Central Park, Aspen, Zoo, High School II, Ballet, La Comedie Francaise.

WISEMAN, JOSEPH
Actor. b. Montreal, Canada, May 15, 1918.
THEATER: King Lear, Golden Boy, The Diary of Anne Frank,

Uncle Vanya, The Last Analysis, Enemies, Detective Story, Three Sisters, Tenth Man, Incident at Vickey, Marco Williams, Unfinished Stories, many others.
PICTURES: Detective Story (debut, 1951), Viva Zapata, Les Miserables, Champ for a Day, The Silver Chalice, The Prodigal, Three Brave Men, The Garment Jungle, The Unforgiven, Happy Thieves, Dr. No, Bye Bye Braverman, The Counterfeit Killer, The Night They Raided Minsky's, Stiletto, Lawman, The Valachi Papers, The Apprenticeship of Duddy Kravitz, Journey Into Fear, The Betsy, Buck Rogers in the 25th Century, Jaguar Lives.
TELEVISION: *Mini-Series*: QB VII, Masada, Rage of Angels. *Movies*: Pursuit, Murder at the World Series, Seize the Day, Lady Mobster. *Series*: Crime Story.

WITHERS, GOOGIE
Actress. b. Karachi, India, Mar. 12, 1917. Trained as a dancer under Italia Conti, Helena Lehmiski & Buddy Bradley; stage debut Victoria Palace in Windmill Man, 1929. Best Actress Award, Deep Blue Sea, 1954. Began screen career at 18. TV also. Theatrical tours Australia, Sun Award, Best Actress, 1974. Awarded officer of the Order of Australia (A.O.) 1980. U.S. ACE Cable award, best actress for Time After Time, 1988.
THEATER: *Britain*: Winter Journey, Deep Blue Sea, Hamlet, Much Ado About Nothing. *Australia*: Plaza Suite, Relatively Speaking, Beckman Place, Woman in a Dressing Gown, The Constant Wife, First Four Hundred Years, Roar Like a Dove, The Cherry Orchard, An Ideal Husband. *London*: Getting Married, Exit the King. *New York*: The Complaisant Lover. Chichester Festival Theatre and Haymarket, London, in The Circle, The Kingfisher, Importance of Being Earnest, The Cherry Orchard, Dandy Dick, The Kingfisher (Australia and Middle East), Time and the Conways (Chichester), School for Scandal (London), Stardust (UK tour). 1986: The Chalk Garden, Hay Fever, Ring Round the Moon, The Cocktail Hour (UK, Australian tour), High Spirits (Aus. tour), On Golden Pond (UK tour).
PICTURES: Haunted Honeymoon, Jeannie, One of Our Aircraft Is Missing, On Approval, Dead of Night, It Always Rains on Sunday, Miranda, Traveler's Joy, Night and the City, White Corridors, Lady Godiva Rides Again, Derby Day, Devil on Horseback, Safe Harbor, Nickel Queen, Country Life, Shine.
TELEVISION: *Series*: Within These Walls, Time After Time, *Movies*: Hotel Du Lac, Northanger Abbey, Ending Up.

WITHERS, JANE
Actress. b. Atlanta, GA, April 12, 1927. By 1934 attracted attention as child player on screen, after radio appearance in Los Angeles and experimental pictures parts, in 1934 in Fox production Bright Eyes, Ginger; thereafter to 1942 featured or starred in numerous 20th-Fox prod. Voted Money-Making Star M.P. Herald-Fame Poll, 1937, 1938. Starred as Josephine the Plumber in Comet tv commercials. TV Movie: All Together Now.
PICTURES: Handle With Care (debut, 1932), Bright Eyes, Ginger, This Is the Life, The Farmer Takes a Wife, Paddy O'Day, Pepper, Gentle Julia, Little Miss Nobody, Can This Be Dixie?, Wild and Woolly, The Holy Terror, Checkers, Angel's Holiday, Forty-Five Fathers, Always in Trouble, Rascals, Keep Smiling, Arizona Wildcat, Pack Up Your Troubles, Chicken Family Wagon, Boy Friend, Shooting High, High School, Youth Will Be Served, The Girl From Avenue A, Golden Hoofs, A Very Young Lady, Her First Beau, Small Town Deb, Young America, The Mad Martindales, Johnny Doughboy, The North Star, My Best Gal, Faces in the Fog, The Affairs of Geraldine, Danger Street, Giant, The Right Approach, Captain Newman M.D.

WITT, PAUL JUNGER
Producer. b. New York, NY, Mar. 20, 1941. e. Univ. of VA. Was assoc. prod., prod. and dir. for Screen Gems, starting in 1965; prod. for Spelling-Goldberg Prods., 1972; Prod.-exec. prod. for Danny Thomas Prods., 1973. With Tony Thomas became co-founder, exec. prod. of Witt/Thomas Prods., 1975.
PICTURES: Firstborn, Dead Poets Society, Final Analysis, Mixed Nuts.
TELEVISION: *Series*: Here Come the Brides, The Partridge Family, The Rookies, Soap, Benson, It's a Living, I'm a Big Girl Now, It Takes Two, Condo, Hail to the Chief, The Golden Girls (Emmy Awards: 1986, 1987), Beauty and the Beast, Empty Nest, Blossom, Good and Evil, Herman's Head, Nurses, Woops, Golden Palace, The John Larroquette Show, Brotherly Love, Minor Adjustments, Common Law, Pearl. *Movies*: Brian's Song (Emmy Award: 1972), No Place to Run, Home for the Holidays, A Cold Night's Death, The Letters, Blood Sport, Remember When, The Gun and the Pulpit, Satan's Triangle, Griffin and Phoenix, High Risk, Trouble in High Timber Country.

WOLF, DICK
Producer, Writer. b. New York, NY, Dec. 20, 1946. e. Univ. of PA. Started in advertising winning three Clio Awards for excellence.

PICTURES: *Prod./Writer:* Skateboard, Gas, No Man's Land, Masquerade (exec. prod., writer, actor), School Ties (story only).
TELEVISION: *Series (exec. prod.):* Miami Vice (also writer), Gideon Oliver (also writer), Christine Cromwell (also creator), Nasty Boys (also creator, writer), H.E.L.P. (also creator, writer), Law and Order (also creator, writer), Mann and Machine (also writer), The Human Factor, Crime and Punishment (also creator), South Beach (also creator), New York Undercover (also creator), The Wright Verdicts (also creator), FEDS (creator).

WOLF, EMANUEL L.
Executive b. Brooklyn, NY, Mar. 27, 1927. e. Syracuse U., B.A., 1950; Maxwell Sch., Syracuse U., M.A. 1952; Maxwell Scholar in Public Admin.-Economics; Chi Eta Sigma (Econ. Hon.). 1952-55. Management consultant, exec. office of Secretary of Navy & Dept. of Interior, Wash, DC, 1956; pres. E.L. Wolf Assocs., Washington, DC, 1961-65; Kalvex, Inc., treas: 1962, dir.: 1963, pres./chmn. of bd.: 1966; dir. Allied Artists Pictures Corp., 1965; chmn. of bd. Vitabath, Inc., Lexington Instruments, Pharmaceutical Savings Plan, Inc. (also pres.) Syracuse U.; corp. advisory bd., American Committee for the Weizmann Institute of Science (Bd. of Directors); pres. & chmn. of bd., Allied Artists Pictures Corp: 1976: pres., bd. chmn. & CEO, Allied Artists Industries Inc., created by Merger of Allied Artists Pictures Corp., Kalvex Inc. and PSP, Inc. 1985, formed indep. prod. co., Emanuel L. Wolf Prods.; 1986-90, pres. & chmn. of bd., Today Home Entertainment. 1991-present. Emanuel L. Wolf Prods., Inc. Chmn., Allied Artists Entertainment Group. Member, AMPAS.

WOLF, THOMAS HOWARD
TV News Exec. b. New York, NY, April 22, 1916. e. Princeton U., B.A., magna cum laude, 1937. Time & Life Mag. 1937-39; 1937-39 NEA (Scripps-Howard) 1940-46; European mgr., NEA, 1942-46. War correspondent, (ETO, MTO) NBC radio correspondent, Paris, 1944-45; co-owner, pres., Information Prod., Inc. founded 1951; co-owner, chmn. Butterfield & Wolf, Inc. founded 1955; prod. CBS series Tomorrow, 1960; exec. prod., CBS daily live Calendar Show, 1961-62; sr. prod., ABC News Report, 1963; exec. prod., ABC Scope, 1964-66. v.p. dir. of TV Documentaries, 1966; v.p., dir. of TV Public Affairs, 1974; dir. TV Cultural Affairs, 1976. Pres., Wolf Communications, Inc., 1981-; consultant Smithsonian Institution, 1981-88.

WOLFSON, RICHARD
Executive. b. New York, NY, Jan. 7, 1923. e. Harvard Coll., Yale Law Sch., 1945-47, law clerk to Justice Wiley Rutledge, U.S. Supreme Court. Law instructor at NYU Law Sch.; 1952, joined Wometco Ent. as counsel and asst. to pres.; named v.p. and dir. in 1959 and dir. in 1962; named exec. v.p. and general counsel in 1973; named chmn., exec. comm., 1976; retired from Wometco 1982.

WOLPER, DAVID L.
Producer. b. New York, NY, Jan. 11, 1928. m. Gloria Diane Hill. e. Drake U., U. of Southern California. Treas., Flamingo Films, 1948; merged with Associated Artist to form M.P. for TV, Inc., acting as v.p. in chg. of West Coast oper., 1950; v.p. reactivated Flamingo Films, 1954; also pres. Harris-Wolper Pictures, Inc.; pres. Wolper Prod. 1958; pres. Dawn Prod.; v.p. bd. dir. Metromedia, 1965; pres. Wolper Pictures Ltd. 1967; ch. of bd. Wolper Prod., Inc., 1967; pres. Wolper Pictures, 1968; pres. Wolper Productions, 1970; pres. & chmn. of bd. of dir. The Wolper Organization, Inc., 1971; consultant to Warner Bros. & Warner Communications. Pres., David L. Wolper Prods., Inc. 1977. Received Jean Hersholt Humanitarian Award, 1985; Intl. Documentary Assn. Career Achievement Award, 1988. Also received French Natl. Legion of Honor Medal, Lifetime Achievement Award from Producers Guild, Charles de Gaulle Centennial Medal.
PICTURES: Four Days in November, If It's Tuesday This Must Be Belgium, One Is a Lonely Number, The Hellstrom Chronicle, Willy Wonka and the Chocolate Factory, I Love My Wife, Visions of Eight, Birds Do It Bees Do It, This Is Elvis, The Man Who Saw Tomorrow, Imagine: John Lennon, Murder in the First.
TELEVISION: *Specials:* The Race For Space, The Making of the President (1960, 1964, 1968), National Geographic Society Specials (1965-68, 1971-75), The Rise and Fall of the Third Reich, The Undersea World of Jacques Cousteau (1967-68), George Plimpton specials (1970-72), American Heritage specials (1973-74), Primal Man specials (1973-75), Judgment specials (1974), Smithsonian Specials, Sandburg's Lincoln, The Man Who Saw Tomorrow, Opening & Closing Ceremonies: Olympic Games 1984, Liberty Weekend 1986, A Celebration of Tradition for Warner Bros, Here's Looking at You Warner Bros., Golf—The Greatest Game. *Series:* Story of..., Biography, Hollywood and the Stars, Men in Crisis, The March of Time (1965-66), Appointment With Destiny, Get Christie Love, Chico and the Man, Welcome Back Kotter,

Casablanca, Golf: Heroes of the Game. *Movies:* Say Goodbye, The 500 Pound Jerk, I Will Fight No More Forever, Victory at Entebbe, Agatha Christie's Murder Is Easy, What Price Victory, Roots: The Gift, When You Remember Me, The Betty Ford Story, Dillinger, The Plot to Kill Hitler, Murder in Mississippi, Bed of Lies, The Flood: Who Will Save Our Children?, Fatal Deception: Mrs. Lee Harvey Oswald. *Mini-Series:* Roots (Emmy Award, 1977), Roots: The Next Generations, (Emmy Award, 1979), Moviola (This Year's Blonde, The Scarlett O'Hara War, The Silent Lovers), The Thorn Birds, North & South, North & South Book II: Love & War, North & South Book III: Heaven & Hell, Napoleon & Josephine: A Love Story, Queen, Without Warning.

WONG, VICTOR
Actor. Was reporter in San Francisco's Chinatown, 1968-75, before working on stage at Joseph Papp's Public Theatre.
PICTURES: Dim Sum: A Little Bit of Heart, Year of the Dragon, Big Trouble in Little China, Shanghai Surprise, The Golden Child, Prince of Darkness, The Last Emperor, Eat a Bowl of Tea, Tremors, Life Is Cheap... But Toilet Paper Is Expensive, 3 Ninjas, The Joy Luck Club, The Ice Runner, 3 Ninjas Kick Back, 3 Ninjas Knuckle Up, The Stars Fell on Henrietta.
TELEVISION: *Series:* Search for Tomorrow. *Movies/Specials:* Night Song, Fortune Cookie, Paper Angel, Mild Bunch, Search, China Nights.

WOO, JOHN
Director. b. Guangzhou, China, 1948. e. Matteo Ricci Col, Hong Kong. Started making experimental 16 mm films in 1967. Joined film industry in 1969 as prod. asst. for Cathay Film Co., then asst. dir. 1971 joined Shaw Brothers working as asst. dir. to Zhang Che.
PICTURES: The Young Dragons (debut, 1973), The Dragon Tamers, Countdown in Kung Fu, Princess Chang Ping, From Riches to Rags, Money Crazy, Follow the Star, Last Hurrah for Chivalry, To Hell With the Devil, Laughing Times, Plain Jane to the Rescue, Sunset Warriors (Heroes Shed No Tears), The Time You Need a Friend, Run Tiger Run, A Better Tomorrow, A Better Tomorrow II, Just Heroes, The Killer, Bullet in the Head, Once a Thief, Hard Boiled, Hard Target (U.S. debut, 1993), Broken Arrow.

WOOD, ELIJAH
Actor. b. Cedar Rapids, IA, Jan. 28, 1981. Started in commercial modeling. Landed first acting job in Paula Abdul video Forever Your Girl.
PICTURES: Back to the Future Part II (debut, 1989), Internal Affairs, Avalon, Paradise, Radio Flyer, Forever Young, The Adventures of Huck Finn, The Good Son, North, The War, Flipper, The Ice Storm.
TELEVISION: *Movies:* Child of the Night, Day-O.

WOODARD, ALFRE
Actress. b. Tulsa, OK, Nov. 8, 1953. e. Boston U., B.A. Soon after graduation landed role in Washington, D.C. Arena Stage theater in Horatio, and Saved.
THEATER: A Christmas Carol, Bugs Guns, Leander Stillwell, For Colored Girls Who Have Considered Suicide/When the Rainbow Is Enuf, A Map of the World, A Winter's Tale, Two By South.
PICTURES: Remember My Name, Health, Cross Creek (Acad. Award nom.), Extremities, Scrooged, Miss Firecracker, Grand Canyon, The Gun in Betty Lou's Handbag, Passion Fish, Rich in Love, Heart and Souls, Blue Chips, Crooklyn, How to Make an American Quilt, Primal Fear, Star Trek: First Contact, Follow Me Home.
TELEVISION: *Series:* Tucker's Witch, Sara, St. Elsewhere. *Guest:* Palmerstown USA, What Really Happened to the Class of '65?, Hill Street Blues (Emmy Award, 1984), L.A. Law (Emmy Award, 1987). *Movies:* Freedom Road, Sophisticated Gents, Go Tell It on the Mountain, Sweet Revenge, Unnatural Causes, The Killing Floor, Mandela, A Mother's Courage: The Mary Thomas Story, Blue Bayou, Race to Freedom: The Underground Railroad, The Piano Lesson. *Specials:* For Colored Girls Who Haved Considered Suicide/When the Rainbow Is Enuf, Trial of the Moke, Words by Heart, Aliens for Breakfast.

WOODS, DONALD
Actor. b. Brandon, Manitoba, Canada, Dec. 2, 1906. e. UC Berkeley. Appeared in WB shorts Song of a Nation, and Star in the Night (Oscar winner, 1945).
THEATER: Holiday, Charley's Aunt, Dracula, Strange Interlude, Two for the Seesaw, Rosmersholm, One by One, Soldier, You Can't Take It With You, Twelfth Night, Assassination 1865, Perfect Gentleman, Kansas City Repertory.
PICTURES: A Tale of Two Cities, Story of Louis Pasteur, Anthony Adverse, Forgotten Girls, Love Honor and Oh Baby, I Was a Prisoner on Devil's Island, Watch on the Rhine, Bridge of San Luis Rey, Wonder Man, Roughly Speaking, Barbary Pirate, 13 Ghosts, Kissin' Cousins, Moment to Moment; many other films.

TELEVISION: G.E. Theatre, Wind from the South, Wagon Train, Thrillers, Sunset Strip, Ben Casey, Laramie, The Rebel, The Law and Mr. Jones, The Roaring 20's, Wild Wild West, Bonanza. *Series*: Tammy.

WOODS, JAMES
Actor. b. Vernal UT, Apr. 18, 1947. e. Massachusetts Inst. of Technology (appeared in 36 plays at MIT, Harvard and Theatre Co. of Boston). Left college to pursue acting career in New York.
THEATER: Borstal Boy (B'way debut, 1970), followed by Conduct Unbecoming (off-B'way, Obie Award), Saved, Trial of the Catonsville Nine, Moonchildren (Theatre World Award), Green Julia (off-B'way), Finishing Touches.
PICTURES: The Visitors (debut, 1971), Hickey and Boggs, The Way We Were, The Gambler, Distance, Night Moves, Alex and the Gypsy, The Choirboys, The Onion Field, The Black Marble, Eyewitness, Fast-Walking, Split Image, Videodrome, Against All Odds, Once Upon a Time in America, Cat's Eye, Joshua Then and Now, Salvador (Acad. Award nom.; Indept. Film Project Spirit Award, 1986), Best Seller, Cop (also co-prod.), The Boost, True Believer, Immediate Family, The Hard Way, Straight Talk, Diggstown, Chaplin, The Getaway, The Specialist, For Better or Worse, Casino, Nixon, Killer: A Journal of Murder, Ghosts of Mississippi.
TELEVISION: *Movies*: Footsteps, A Great American Tragedy, Foster and Laurie, F. Scott Fitzgerald in Hollywood, The Disappearance of Aimee, Raid on Entebbe, Billion Dollar Bubble, The Gift of Love, The Incredible Journey of Dr. Meg Laurel, And Your Name Is Jonah, Badge of the Assassin, Promise (Emmy & Golden Globe Awards, 1987), In Love and War, My Name is Bill W. (Emmy Award, 1989), Women & Men: Stories of Seduction (Hills Like White Elephants), The Boys, Citizen Cohn, Jane's House, Next Door, Curse of the Starving Class, Indictment: The McMartin Trial. *Specials*: All the Way Home, Crimes of Passion (host), Wildfire (host), Mobs and Mobsters (host), Fallen Angels. *Mini-series*: Holocaust. *Guest*: Kojak, Rockford Files, Streets of San Francisco, The Rookies, Police Story, Saturday Night Live, Dream On, The Simpsons (voice).

WOODWARD, EDWARD
O.B.E.: Actor, Singer. b. Croydon, England, June 1, 1930. e. Royal Acad. of Dramatic Art. As singer has recorded 11 LPs. 2 Gold Discs. Television Actor of the Year, 1969-70; also Sun Award, Best Actor, 1970-72. Has received 15 national & international awards.
THEATER: With Royal Shakespeare Company, 1958-59; Cyrano, 20 West End plays and musicals, including The Art of Living, The Little Doctor, A Rattle of a Simple Man (West End/B'way), The High Bid, The Male of the Species, High Spirits (B'way musical), The Best Laid Plans, On Approval, The Wolf, Richard III, The Assassin.
PICTURES: Where There's a Will (debut, 1955), Becket, File on the Golden Goose, Incense for the Damned, Young Winston, Sitting Target, Hunted, Wicker Man, Callan, Stand Up Virgin Soldiers, Breaker Morant, The Appointment, The Final Option (Who Dares Wins), Champions, King David, Mister Johnson, Deadly Advice.
TELEVISION: *Series*: Callan, Nice Work, The Equalizer (4 Emmy noms.), Golden Globe Award), Over My Dead Body, In Suspicious Cirumstances. *Movies/Specials*: Sword of Honour, Bassplayer and Blonde (mini-series), Saturday, Sunday, Monday, Rod of Iron, The Trial of Lady Chatterly, Wet Job–Callan Special, Churchill: The Wilderness Years, Blunt Instrument, Killer Contract, Arthur the King, Uncle Tom's Cabin, A Christmas Carol, Codename: Kyril, Hunted, The Man in the Brown Suit, Hands of a Murderer, World War II, Suspicious Circumstances, The Shamrock Conspiracy, Common as Muck, Harrison, Gulliver's Travels.

WOODWARD, JOANNE
Actress. b. Thomasville, GA, Feb. 27, 1930. m. Paul Newman. e. Louisiana State U. Studied at Neighborhood Playhouse Dramatic Sch. and the Actors Studio. Appeared in many TV dramatic shows.
THEATER: Picnic, The Lovers, Baby Want a Kiss, Candida, The Glass Menagerie (Williamstown, The Long Wharf), Golden Boy (dir., the Blue Light Theatre Company).
PICTURES: Count Three and Pray (debut, 1955), A Kiss Before Dying, Three Faces of Eve (Academy Award, 1957), No Down Payment, The Long Hot Summer, Rally 'Round the Flag Boys, The Sound and the Fury, The Fugitive Kind, From the Terrace, Paris Blues, The Stripper, A New Kind of Love, Signpost to Murder, A Big Hand for the Little Lady, A Fine Madness, Rachel Rachel (Acad. Award nom.), Winning, WUSA, They Might Be Giants, The Effect of Gamma Rays on Man-in-the-Moon Marigolds, Summer Wishes Winter Dreams (Acad. Award nom.), The Drowning Pool, The End, Harry and Son, The Glass Menagerie, Mr. and Mrs. Bridge (Acad. Award nom.), The Age of Innocence (narrator), Philadelphia.
TELEVISION: *Specials*: Broadway's Dreamers: The Legacy of The Group Theater (host, co-prod.; Emmy Award, 1990), Family Thanksgiving Special (dir. only). *Movies*: Sybil, Come

Back Little Sheba, See How She Runs (Emmy Award, 1978), A Christmas to Remember, The Streets of L.A., The Shadow Box, Crisis at Central High, Passions, Do You Remember Love? (Emmy Award, 1985), Foreign Affairs, Blind Spot (also co-prod.).

WOOLDRIDGE, SUSAN
Actress. b. London, England. e. Central Sch. of Speech & Drama/Ecole/Jacques LeCoq. Paris. Ent. ind. 1971.
THEATER: Macbeth, School for Scandal, Merchant of Venice, The Cherry Orchard, Look Back in Anger, 'night Mother, Map of the Heart.
PICTURES: The Shout, Butley, Loyalties, Hope and Glory, How to Get Ahead in Advertising, Bye Bye Blues, Twenty-One, Afraid of the Dark, Just Like a Woman, Butter.
TELEVISION: The Naked Civil Servant, John McNab, The Racing Game, The Jewel in the Crown, The Last Place on Earth, Hay Fever, Time and the Conways, Dead Man's Folly, The Devil's Disciple, The Dark Room, Pastoralcare, The Small Assassin, A Fine Romance, Ticket to Ride, Changing Step, Pied Piper, Crimestrike, Broke, Miss Pym's Day Out, An Unwanted Woman, The Humming Bird Tree, Inspector Alleyn Mysteries, Tracey Ullman Show, Bad Company, Under the Hammer, All Quiet on the Preston Front, Wycliffe, The Writing Game.

WOOLF, SIR JOHN
Knighted 1975. Producer. b. England, 1913. e. Institut Montana, Switzerland. Awarded U.S. Bronze star for service in WWII. Asst. dir. Army Kinematography, War Office 1944-45; Founder and chmn. Romulus Films Ltd, since 1948. Man dir. since 1967; chmn. since 1982 of British & American Film Holdings Plc; dir. First Leisure Corp. Plc since 1982. Co-founder and exec. dir., Anglia TV Group PLC, 1958-83. Member: Cinematograph Films Council, 1969-79; bd. of gov., Services Sound & Vision Corp (formerly Services Kinema Corp.) 1974-83; exec. council and trustee, Cinema and Television Benevolent Fund; Freeman, City of London, 1982; FRSA 1978. Received special awards for contribution to British film indust. from Cinematograph Exhibitors Assoc. 1969. and Variety Club of GB, 1974.
PICTURES: *Prod. by Romulus Gp.*: The African Queen, Pandora and the Flying Dutchman, Moulin Rouge, Beat the Devil, I Am a Camera, Carrington VC, The Bespoke Overcoat (short; Acad. Award, BAFTA Award), Story of Ester Costello, Room at the Top (BAFTA Award, best film, 1958), Wrong Arm of the Law, The L-Shaped Room, Term of Trial, Life at the Top, Oliver! (Acad. Award, Golden Globe, best film, 1968), Day of the Jackal, The Odessa File.
TELEVISION: *Prod. for Anglia TV incl.*: 100 Tales of the Unexpected, Miss Morrison's Ghosts, The Kingfisher, Edwin, Love Song.

WOPAT, TOM
Actor. b. Lodi, WI, Sept. 9, 1951. e. U. of Wisconsin. Left school to travel for two years with rock group as lead singer and guitarist. Spent two summers at Barn Theater in MI. Came to New York; *Off-B'way* in A Bistro Car on the CNR. *On B'way* in I Love My Wife, City of Angels, Guys and Dolls.
TELEVISION: *Series*: The Dukes of Hazzard, Blue Skies, A Peaceable Kingdom, Cybill. *Movies*: Christmas Comes to Willow Creek, Burning Rage, Just My Imagination.

WORKMAN, CHUCK
Director, Writer, Producer. b. Philadelphia, PA. June 5. e. Rutgers U., B.A.; Cornell U. Pres., International Documentary Assoc. 1987-88; Member: Directors Guild of America, National Board; Bd. mem.: Santa Monica Arts Fdn. Lecturer, U. of Southern California. Pres. Calliope Films, Inc. Winner Clio Award, 1969, 1970. Acad. Award, 1987.
THEATER: Bruno's Ghost (1981, writer, dir.), Diplomacy (writer, dir.), The Man Who Wore White Shoes (writer), Bloomers (writer).
PICTURES: Monday's Child (1967, editor), Traitors of San Angel (editor), The Money (dir., s.p.), Protocol (dir., media sequences), Stoogemania (dir., co-s.p.), Precious Images (Acad. Award, Best Live Action Short, 1986; Gold Hugo Award, Cannes Film Fest., N.Y. Film Fest.), Words (Best Short, Houston Fest., N.Y. Film Fest., 1988), Pieces of Silver, Superstar (dir.-prod.), The First 100 Years (dir., prod.).
DOCUMENTARIES: The Making of the Deep (prod., dir., writer), The Director and the Image (CINE Golden Eagle Award, 1980), The Game, The Best Show in Town (CINE Golden Eagle), And the Winner Is..., The Keeper of the Light.

WORONOV, MARY
Actress. b. Brooklyn, NY, Dec. 8, 1946. e. Cornell. On NY stage in In the Boom Boom Room (Theatre World Award).
PICTURES: The Chelsea Girls, Kemek: It's Controlling Your Mind, Sugar Cookies, Seizure, Cover Girl Models, Death Race 2000, Cannonball, Jackson County Jail, Hollywood Boulevard, Bad Georgia Road, Mr. Billion, The One and Only, The Lady in Red, Rock 'n' Roll High School, National Lampoon Goes to the

Movies, Angel of H.E.A.T., Heartbeeps, Eating Raoul, Get Crazy, Night of the Comet, Hellhole, My Man Adam, Nomads, Movie House Massacre, Chopping Mall, Terrorvision, Black Widow, Scenes From the Class Struggle in Beverly Hills, Let It Ride, Mortuary Academy, Dick Tracy, Watchers II, Warlock, Club Fed, Where Sleeping Dogs Lie, Motorama, Good Girls Don't, Hell-Rollers, Grief.
TELEVISION: *Movies*: In the Glitter Palace, Challenge of a Lifetime, Acting on Impulse.

WORTH, IRENE
Actress. b. Nebraska, June 23, 1916. e. UCLA. Formerly a teacher. B'way debut in The Two Mrs. Carrolls, after which went to London where made her home. Appeared with Old Vic and Royal Shakespeare Co.; returned to U.S. to appear on B'way in the Cocktail Party.
THEATER: Hotel Paradiso, Mary Stuart, The Potting Shed, Toys in the Attic, Tiny Alice (Tony Award, 1965), Sweet Bird of Youth (Tony Award, 1976), Cherry Orchard, Old Times Happy Days, Coriolanus (NY Shakespeare Fest), Lost in Yonkers (Tony Award, 1991).
PICTURES: One Night With You, Secret People, Orders to Kill (British Acad. Award, best actress), The Scapegoat, Seven Seas to Calais, King Lear, Nicholas and Alexander, Rich Kids, Eyewitness, Deathtrap, Fast Forward, Lost in Yonkers.
TELEVISION: The Lady from the Sea, The Duchess of Malfi, The Way of the World, Prince Orestes, Forbidden, The Big Knife, The Shell Seekers.

WORTH, MARVIN
Producer, Writer. b. Brooklyn, NY. Jazz promoter and manager before starting to write special material for Alan King, Buddy Hackett, Joey Bishop, Lenny Bruce and many others.
THEATER: Lenny (prod.).
PICTURES: *Writer*: Boys' Night Out, Three on a Couch, Promise Her Anything. *Producer*: Diabolique, Where's Poppa?, Malcolm X (documentary), Lenny, Fire Sale, The Rose, Up the Academy, Soup for One, Unfaithfully Yours, Rhinestone, Falling in Love, Less Than Zero, Patty Hearst, Running Mates, See No Evil, Hear No Evil, Flashback, Malcolm X.
TELEVISION: Steve Allen Show, Jackie Gleason, Ray Bolger's Washington Square, Chevy Shows, General Motors' 50th Anniversary Show, Milton Berle Show, Colgate Comedy Hour, Martha Raye Show, Polly Bergen Show, Ann Sothern Show, Judy Garland Show, Get Smart, others.

WOWCHUK, HARRY N.
Actor, Writer, Photographer, Producer, Executive. b. Philadelphia, PA. Oct. 16, 1948. e. Santa Monica City Coll., UCLA, theater arts, 1970. Started film career as actor, stunt-driver-photographer. T.V. and commercial credits include: TV Guide, Seal Test, Camel Cigarettes, Miller High Life, American Motors, Camera V, AW Rootbeer. Former exec. v.p. International Cinema, in chg. of prod. and distribution; V.P. J. Newport Film Productions; pres., United West Productions.
PICTURES: The Lost Dutchman, Las Vegas Lady, This Is a Hijack, Tidal Wave, Tunnel Vision, Incredible 2-Headed Transplant, Jug, Bad Charleston Charlie, Some Call It Loving, Summer School Teachers, Five Minutes of Freedom, Pushing Up Daisies, Money-Marbles-Chalk, The Models, Love Swedish Style, Up-Down-Up, Sunday's Child, Soul Brothers, Freedom Riders, Perilous Journey, Claws of Death, Georgia Peaches.

WOWCHUK, NICHOLAS
Executive, Producer, Writer, Editor, Financier. b. Philadelphia, PA. e. St. Basil's Coll., UCLA. Founder-publisher: All-American Athlete Magazine, Sports and Health Digest, The Spectator. Former sports writer: Phila. Evening Public Ledger; Phila. Daily Record; Phila. Inquirer. Founder & bd. chmn.: Mutual Realty Investment Co.; Mutual Mortgage Co., Beverly Hills, CA. President: Mutual General Films, Bev. Hills, CA; Abbey Theatrical Films, NY; Mutual Film Distribution Co.; Mutual Recording & Broadcasting Enterprises.
PICTURES: *Exec. Prod.*: Perilous Journey, The Incredible 2-Headed Transplant, Pushing Up Daisies, Money-Marbles-Chalk, Five Minutes of Freedom, The Campaign, Claws of Death. *Prod.*: Scorpion's Web, Pursuit, Brave Men, Sea of Despair, Cossacks in Battle, The Straight White Line, Tilt, Rooster, To Live... You Gotta Win.

WRAY, FAY
Actress. b. Alberta, Canada, Sept. 15, 1907. On stage in Pilgrimage Play, Hollywood, 1923; m.p. debut in Gasoline Love; thereafter in many m.p. from Paramount to 1930; then in films for various Hollywood and Brit. prod. Autobiography: On the Other Hand (1989).
PICTURES: Streets of Sin, The Wedding March, The Four Feathers, The Texan, Dirigible, Doctor X, The Most Dangerous Game, The Vampire Bat, The Mystery of the Wax Museum, King Kong, The Bowery, Madame Spy, The Affairs of Cellini, The Clairvoyant, They Met in a Taxi, Murder in Greenwich Village, The Jury's Secret, Smashing the Spy Ring, Navy

Secrets, Wildcat Bus, Adam Had Four Sons, Melody for Three, Not a Ladies' Man, Small Town Girl, Treasure of the Golden Condor, Queen Bee, The Cobweb, Hell on Frisco Bay, Crime of Passion, Rock Pretty Baby, Tammy and the Bachelor, Summer Love, Dragstrip Riot.
TELEVISION: *Series*: Pride of the Family. *Movie*: Gideon's Trumpet.

WRIGHT, AMY
Actress. b. Chicago, IL, Apr. 15, 1950. e. Beloit Col. Studied acting with Uta Hagen; 1976, joined Rip Torn's Sanctuary Theatre. B'way in Fifth of July, Noises Off, Mrs. Klein.
PICTURES: Not a Pretty Picture, Girlfriends, The Deer Hunter, Breaking Away, The Amityville Horror, Heartland, Wise Blood, Stardust Memories, Inside Moves, Off Beat, The Telephone, Crossing Delancey, The Accidental Tourist, Miss Firecracker, Daddy's Dyin', Deceived, Love Hurts, Hard Promises, Josh and S.A.M., Tom and Huck.
TELEVISION: *Movies*: Trapped in Silence, Settle the Score, To Dance With the White Dog. *Special*: Largo Desolato. *Pilot*: A Fine Romance.

WRIGHT, ROBERT C.
Executive. b. Rockville Center, NY, April 23, 1943. e. Coll. Holy Cross, B.A. history, 1965; U. of Virginia, LLB 1968. Mem. NY, VA, MA, NJ Bar. 1969, joined General Electric; lawyer in plastics div. Later moved into product & sls. management in plastics div. 1980, moved to Cox Cable as pres. Returned to GE 1983 heading small appliances div.; moved to GE Financial Services & GE Credit Corp. as pres., which posts he held when named head of NBC following purchase of NBC's parent RCA by GE. Pres. and CEO, National Broadcasting Co. (NBC), 1986-.

WRIGHT, ROBIN
Actress. b. Dallas, TX, 1966. m. actor Sean Penn. Was model at age 14 before making acting debut on tv series The Yellow Rose.
PICTURES: Hollywood Vice Squad (debut, 1986), The Princess Bride, Denial, State of Grace, The Playboys, Toys, Forrest Gump, The Crossing Guard, Moll Flanders.
TELEVISION: *Series*: Santa Barbara. *Pilot*: Home.

WRIGHT, TERESA
Actress. b. New York, NY, Oct. 27, 1918. e. Columbia H.S., Maplewood, NJ, 1938.
THEATER: *Tours*: Mary Mary, Tchin-Tchin, The Effect of Gamma Rays on Man-in-the-Moon Marigolds, Noel Coward in Two Keys, The Master Builder. *Regional*: Long Day's Journey into Night, You Can't Take It With You, All The Way Home, Wings. *NY*: Life with Father, Dark at the Top of the Stairs, I Never Sang for My Father, Death of a Salesman, Ah Wilderness!, Morning's at Seven (also London), On Borrowed Time.
PICTURES: The Little Foxes (debut, 1941), Pride of the Yankees, Mrs. Miniver (Academy Award, best supporting actress, 1942), Shadow of a Doubt, Casanova Brown, The Best Years of Our Lives, The Trouble With Women, Pursued, Imperfect Lady, Enchantment, The Capture, The Men, Something to Live For, California Conquest, Steel Trap, Count the Hours, The Actress, Track of the Cat, The Search for Bridey Murphy, Escapade in Japan, The Restless Years, Hail Hero, The Happy Ending, Roseland, Somewhere in Time, The Good Mother.
TELEVISION: *Specials*: The Margaret Bourke-White Story, The Miracle Worker, The Golden Honeymoon, The Fig Tree, A Century of Women. *Movies*: Crawlspace, The Elevator, Flood, Bill—On His Own, Perry Mason: The Case of the Desperate Deception.

WUHL, ROBERT
Actor, Writer. b. Union, NJ, Oct. 9, 1951. e. Univ. of Houston. Worked as stand-up comedian and joke writer. Was story editor on series Police Squad! Appeared in 1988 Academy Award winning short Ray's Male Heterosexual Dance Hall.
PICTURES: The Hollywood Knights (debut, 1980), Flashdance, Good Morning Vietnam, Bull Durham, Batman, Blaze, Wedding Band, Mistress, A Kiss Goodnight, Blue Chips, Cobb, Dr. Jekyll and Ms. Hyde, Open Season (also dir., s.p.).
TELEVISION: *Series*: Arliss. *Pilots*: Rockhopper, Sniff. *Guest*: Tales from the Crypt, Moonlighting, L.A. Law, Falcon Crest. *Specials*: The Big Bang (also dir.), Comic Relief IV, The Earth Day Special, The Real Deal. *Movie*: Percy & Thunder. *Writer*: Police Squad, Sledge Hammer, Grammy Awards (1987-89), Academy Awards (Emmy Award, 1991).

WYATT, JANE
Actress. b. New York, NY, Aug. 12, 1910. e. Miss Chapin's Sch., Barnard Coll. m. Edgar B. Ward. Joined Apprentice Sch., Berkshire Playhouse, Stockbridge, Mass. Understudied in Tradewinds and The Vinegar Tree. Appeared in Give Me Yesterday and the Tadpole. In 1933 succeeded Margaret Sullavan in Dinner at Eight.

THEATER: The Autumn Garden (NY), The Bishop Misbehaves, Conquest, Eveningsong, The Mad Hopes, Hope for the Best, The Joyous Season For Services Rendered, Driving Miss Daisy, Love Letters.
PICTURES: One More River (debut, 1934), Great Expectations, We're Only Human, The Luckiest Girl in the World, Lost Horizon, The Girl From God's Country, Kisses for Breakfast, Hurricane Smith, Weekend for Three, Army Surgeon, The Navy Comes Through, The Kansan, Buckskin Frontier, None But the Lonely Heart, Strange Conquest, The Bachelor's Daughters, Boomerang!, Gentleman's Agreement, Pitfall, No Minor Vices, Bad Boy, Canadian Pacific, Task Force, House By the River, Our Very Own, My Blue Heaven, The Man Who Cheated Himself, Criminal Lawyer, Interlude, Two Little Bears, Never Too Late, Treasure of Matecumbe, Star Trek IV: The Voyage Home.
TELEVISION: Series: Father Knows Best (1954-59; 3 Emmy Awards: 1957, 1958, 1959). Guest: Bob Hope Chrysler Theater, The Virginian, Wagon Train, U.S. Steel Hour, Bell Telephone Hour, Confidential For Women, My Father My Mother, Barefoot in the Park, The Ghost and Mrs. Muir, Here Come the Brides, Love American Style, Fantasy Island, Love Boat. Movies: Katherine, Tom Sawyer, Father Knows Best Reunion, A Love Affair, Amelia Earhart, Superdome, The Nativity, The Millionaire, Missing Children—A Mother's Story, Amityville: The Evil Escapes, Neighbors, Ladies of the Corridor, Star Trek.

WYMAN, JANE
Actress. r.n. Sarah Jane Fulks. b. St. Joseph, MO, Jan. 5, 1917. e. Univ. of MO. Started in show business as radio singer calling herself Jane Durrell. Debuted in films as bit player using her real name. Voted one of top ten money-making stars in M.P. Herald-Fame poll, 1954.
PICTURES: Cain and Mabel, Golddiggers of 1937, My Man Godfrey, King of Burlesque, Smart Blonde, Stage Struck, King and the Chorus Girl, Ready Willing and Able, Slim, The Singing Marine, Public Wedding, Mr. Dodd Takes the Air, The Crowd Roars, Brother Rat, Wide Open Faces, The Spy Ring, He Couldn't Say No, Fools for Scandal, Kid Nightingale, Tail Spin, Private Detective, Kid from Kokomo, Torchy Plays With Dynamite, Brother Rat and a Baby, An Angel From Texas, Gambling on the High Seas, Tugboat Annie Sails Again, My Love Came Back, The Body Disappears, Honeymoon for Three, Bad Men of Missouri, You're in the Army Now, Larceny, Inc., My Favorite Spy, Footlight Serenade, Princess O'Rourke, Doughgirls, Make Your Own Bed, Crime by Night, Hollywood Canteen, Lost Weekend, One More Tomorrow, Night and Day, The Yearling, Cheyenne, Magic Town, Johnny Belinda (Academy Award, 1948), A Kiss in the Dark, The Lady Takes a Sailor, It's a Great Feeling, Stage Fright, The Glass Menagerie, Three Guys Named Mike, Here Comes the Groom, Blue Veil, Starlift, Just for You, Story of Will Rogers, Let's Do It Again, So Big, Magnificent Obsession, Lucy Gallant, All That Heaven Allows, Miracle in the Rain, Holiday for Lovers, Pollyanna, Bon Voyage, How to Commit Marriage.
TELEVISION: Series: Fireside Theatre (The Jane Wyman Show), Summer Playhouse, Falcon Crest. Movies: The Failing of Raymond, The Incredible Journey of Dr. Meg Laurel.

WYMAN, THOMAS H.
Executive. b. 1931. Joined CBS, Inc. in 1980 as pres. & chief exec. Then chmn until 1986. Prior career as chief exec. of Green Giant Co.; became v. chmn. to 1988, of Pillsbury Co. when it acquired Green Giant in 1979.

WYNN, TRACY KEENAN
Writer. b. Hollywood, CA, Feb. 28, 1945. e. UCLA Theatre Arts Dept., BA in film/TV division, 1967. Fourth generation in show business: son of actor Keenan Wynn, grandson of Ed Wynn, great-grandson of Frank Keenan, Irish Shakespearean actor who made B'way debut in 1880.
PICTURES: The Longest Yard, The Drowning Pool (co-s.p.), The Deep (co. s.p.).
TELEVISION: Movies: The Glass House, Tribes (also assoc. prod.: Emmy & WGA Awards, 1971), The Autobiography of Miss Jane Pittman (Emmy Award & WGA Awards, 1974), Hit Lady (dir. only), Quest, Bloody Friday (also co-prod.), Capone in Jail, Carolina Skeletons.

Y

YABLANS, FRANK
Executive. b. Brooklyn, NY, Aug. 27, 1935. Ent. m.p. ind. as Warner Bros. booker, 1957. Warner Bros. salesman in N.Y., Boston, Milwaukee, Chicago, 1957-59. Milwaukee br. mgr. Buena Vista, 1959-66. Midwest sales mgr., Sigma III, 1966. Eastern sales mgr., 1967, sales v.p. 1968. V.P. general sales mgr., Paramount Pic. Corp., 1969; v.p.-dist., 1970; sr. v.p.-mkt., 1970; exec. v.p., 1971; named pres. 1971. 1975, became an indep. prod., his company called, Frank Yablans Presentations Inc. 1983, MGM/UA Entertainment Co. as bd. chmn. & chief oper. off. Held titles of bd. chmn. & CEO with both MGM and UA Corp when resigned, 1985. Same year teamed with PSO Delphi to form Northstar Entertainment Co.; 1986, non-exclusive deal with Empire Entertainment; 1988, non-exclusive 3-year deal with Columbia Pictures; 1989, pres. Epic Prods., pres., CEO Nova Intl. Films Inc.
PICTURES: Producer: Silver Streak (exec. prod.), The Other Side of Midnight, The Fury, North Dallas Forty (also co-s.p.), Mommie Dearest (also co-s.p.), Monsignor (co.-prod), Star Chamber, Kidco, Buy and Cell, Lisa, Congo (exec. prod.).

YABLANS, IRWIN
Executive. b. Brooklyn, NY, July 25, 1934. Began career in industry at WB in 1956 after two-yr. stint with U.S. Army in Germany. Held m.p. sales posts in Washington, DC, Albany, Detroit, Milwaukee and Portland. In 1962 joined Paramount as L.A. mgr.; in 1964 made western sales mgr. In 1972 entered production as assoc. prod. on Howard W. Koch's Badge 373. Pres. of Compass Int'l. Pictures. Exec. v.p., low budget films, Lorimar Productions. Resigned June, 1984. In 1985 named chmn., Orion Pictures Distributing Corp. 1988: named chmn. and CEO of newly formed Epic Pictures.
PICTURES: The Education of Sonny Carson. Exec. prod.: Halloween, Roller Boogie (also story), Fade To Black (also story), Seduction (prod.), Halloween II, Halloween III: Season of the Witch, Parasite, Tank, Hell Night, Prison Arena, Why Me?, Men at Work.

YATES, PETER
Producer, Director. b. Ewshoot, Eng., July 24, 1929. e. Royal Acad. of Dramatic Art. Ent. m.p. ind. as studio mgr. and dubbing asst. with De Lane Lea. Asst. dir.: The Entertainer, The Guns of Navarone, A Taste of Honey, The Roman Spring of Mrs. Stone. Stage dir.: The American Dream, The Death of Bessie Smith, Passing Game, Interpreters. Received Acad. Award noms. for Best Director/Picture (Producer): Breaking Away, The Dresser.
PICTURES: Summer Holiday, One Way Pendulum, Robbery (also co-s.p.), Bullitt, John and Mary, Murphy's War, The Hot Rock, The Friends of Eddie Coyle, For Pete's Sake, Mother Jugs and Speed (also prod.), The Deep, Breaking Away (also prod.), Eyewitness (also prod.), Krull, The Dresser (also prod.), Eleni, Suspect, The House on Carroll Street (also prod.), An Innocent Man, Year of the Comet (also co-prod.), Needful Things (exec. prod. only), Roommates, The Run of the Country (also co-prod.).
TELEVISION: Series: Danger Man (Secret Agent), The Saint.

YELLEN, LINDA
Producer, Director, Writer. b. New York, NY, July 13. e. Barnard Coll., B.A., Columbia U., M.F.A., Ph.D. Also lecturer Barnard Coll., Yale U., asst. professor, City U. of New York. Member: exec. council, DGA.
THEATER: Chantilly Lace (dir., prod., writer), Parallel Lives (dir., prod. writer).
PICTURES: The End of Summer (dir., prod., s.p.), Looking Up (prod., dir.), Prospera, Come Out Come Out, Everybody Wins (prod.).
TELEVISION: Movies: Mayflower: The Pilgrims' Adventure (prod.), Playing for Time (exec. prod.; Emmy, Peabody & Christopher Awards, 1980), Hardhat and Legs (prod.), The Royal Romance of Charles and Diana (exec. prod., co-writer), Prisoner Without a Name Cell Without a Number (prod., dir., co-writer; Peabody & WGA Awards), Liberace: Behind the Music (exec. prod.), Sweet Bird of Youth (exec. prod.), Rebound (dir., co-writer).

YORDAN, PHILIP
Writer. b. Chicago, IL, Apr. 1, 1914. e. U. of Illinois, B.A., Kent Coll. of Law, LL.D. Was attorney, then author, producer, playwright (Anna Lucasta). Began screen writing 1942 with collab. s.p. Syncopation.
PICTURES: Unknown Guest, Johnny Doesn't Live Here, When Strangers Marry, Dillinger (Acad. Award nom.), Whistle Stop, The Chase, Suspense, Anna Lucasta, House of Strangers, Edge of Doom, Detective Story (Acad. Award nom.), Mary Maru, Houdini, Blowing Wild, Man Crazy, Naked Jungle, Johnny Guitar, Broken Lance (Academy Award for story, 1954), Conquest of Space, Man from Laramie, Last Frontier, The Harder They Fall (also prod.), Men In War (also prod.), No Down Payment (also prod.), God's Little Acre (also prod. The Bravados, The Time Machine, The Day of the Outlaw, Studs Lonigan, King of Kings, El Cid, 55 Days at Peking, Fall of the Roman Empire, Battle of the Bulge, Royal Hunt of the Sun, Brigham, Cataclysm, Night Train to Terror, Satan's Warriors, Cry Wilderness, Bloody Wednesday (also prod.), The Unholy, Dead Girls Don't Dance (also prod.).

YORK, MICHAEL
Actor. r.n. Michael York-Johnson. b. Fulmer, England, March 27, 1942. Early career with Oxford U. Dramatic Society and National Youth Theatre; later Dundee Repertory, National Theatre. Chmn., California Youth Theatre. 1992 Autobiography: Accidentally on Purpose (Simon & Schuster).

THEATER: Any Just Cause, Hamlet, Ring Round the Moon (Los Angeles), Cyrano de Bergerac. B'way: Outcry, Bent, The Little Prince and the Aviator, Whisper in the Mind, The Crucible, Someone Who'll Watch Over Me, Nora.
PICTURES: The Taming of the Shrew, Accident, Red and Blue, Smashing Time, Romeo and Juliet, The Strange Affair, The Guru, Alfred the Great, Justine, Something for Everyone, Zeppelin, La Poudre D'Escampette, Cabaret, England Made Me, Lost Horizon, The Three Musketeers, Murder on the Orient Express, The Four Musketeers, Conduct Unbecoming, Logan's Run, Seven Nights in Japan, The Last Remake of Beau Geste, The Island of Dr. Moreau, Fedora, The Riddle of the Sands (also assoc. prod.), Final Assignment, The White Lions, The Weather in the Streets, Success Is the Best Revenge, Dawn, Lethal Obsession (Der Joker), The Return of the Musketeers, Phantom of Death, The Secret of the Sahara, Midnight Cop, The Wanderer, The Long Shadow, Wide Sargasso Sea, Rochade, Discretion Assured, The Shadow of a Kiss, Gospa.
TELEVISION: Specials: The Forsyte Saga, Rebel in the Grave, Jesus of Nazareth, True Patriot, Much Ado About Nothing. Series: Knots Landing. Guest: Seaquest, The Naked Truth, Babylon 5. Movies: Great Expectations, A Man Called Intrepid, The Phantom of the Opera, The Master of Ballantrae, Space, For Those I Loved, The Far Country, Dark Mansions, Sword of Gideon, Four Minute Mile, The Lady and the Highwayman, The Heat of the Day, Till We Meet Again, Night of the Fox, A Duel of Love, The Road to Avonlea, Charles Dickens' David Copperfield (voice), Fall from Grace, Tek War: Tek Lab, September, A Young Connecticut Yankee in King Arthur's Court, Not of This Earth, The Out of Towner, Danielle Steel's The Ring. Host: The Hunt for Stolen War Treasure, The Magic Paint Brush, Gardens of the World.

YORK, SUSANNAH
Actress. b. London, England, Jan. 9, 1941. Ent. TV 1959. Ent. films in 1960. Wrote two books: In Search of Unicorns and Lark's Castle.
THEATER: A Cheap Bunch of Flowers, Wings of the Dove, Singular Life of Albert Nobbs, Man and Superman, Mrs. Warren's Profession, Peter Pan, The Maids, Private Lives, The Importance of Being Earnest, Hedda Gabler (New York), Agnes of God, The Human Voice, Penthesilea, Fatal Attraction, The Apple Cart, Private Treason, Lyric for a Tango, The Glass Menagerie, A Streetcar Named Desire, September Tide. Produced The Big One, a variety show for peace, 1984.
PICTURES: Tunes of Glory (debut, 1960), There Was a Crooked Man, Greengage Summer (Loss of Innocence), Freud, Tom Jones, The Seventh Dawn, Sands of the Kalahari, Kaleidoscope, A Man for All Seasons, Sebastian, Duffy, The Killing of Sister George, Oh What a Lovely War, The Battle of Britain, Lock Up Your Daughters, They Shoot Horses Don't They? (Acad. Award nom.), Brotherly Love (Country Dance), Zee & Co. (X Y & Zee), Happy Birthday Wanda June, Images, The Maids, Gold, Conduct Unbecoming, That Lucky Touch, Sky Riders, The Silent Partner, Superman, The Shout, Falling in Love Again, The Awakening, Superman II, Loophole, Yellowbeard, Land of Faraway, Superman IV (voice), Prettykill, Bluebeard Bluebeard, A Summer Story, American Roulette, Diamond's Edge, Melancholia.
TELEVISION: The Crucible, The Rebel and the Soldier, The First Gentleman, The Richest Man in the World, Slaughter of St. Teresa's Day, Kiss On A Grass Green Pillow, Fallen Angels, Prince Regent, Second Chance, Betjeman's Briton, We'll Meet Again, Jane Eyre, A Christmas Carol, Star Quality, Macho, Return Journey, After the War, The Man From the Pru, The Haunting of the New, Devices and Desires, Boon, Little Women, Trainer.

YORKIN, BUD
Producer, Director. r.n. Alan Yorkin. b. Washington, PA, Feb. 22, 1926. e. Carnegie Tech.; Columbia U. U.S. Navy, 1942-45; Began career in TV in NBC's engineering dept. Moved into prod., first as stage mgr., then assoc. dir. of Colgate Comedy Hour (Martin and Lewis) and dir. of Dinah Shore Show. Formed Tandem Productions with Norman Lear; 1974 formed own production co.
PICTURES: Come Blow Your Horn (dir., co-prod., adapt.), Never Too Late (dir.), Divorce American Style (dir.), The Night They Raided Minsky's (exec. prod.), Inspector Clouseau (dir.), Start the Revolution Without Me (prod., dir.), Cold Turkey (exec. prod.), Thief Who Came to Dinner (prod., dir.), Deal of the Century (prod.), Twice in a Lifetime (prod., dir.), Arthur 2 on the Rocks (dir.), Love Hurts (prod., dir.), For the Boys (actor), Intersection (co-prod.).
TELEVISION: Series director: Songs at Twilight, Martin & Lewis Show, Abbott and Costello Show, Spike Jones Show, Tony Martin Show (also prod., writer), George Gobel Show, The Ford Show Starring Tennese Ernie Ford (also prod.). Specials (dir.): An Evening with Fred Astaire (Emmy Award, 1959), Another Evening with Fred Astaire, The Jack Benny Hour Specials (Emmy Award, 1960), Henry Fonda and the Family, We Love You Madly with Duke Ellington, TV Guide

Awards Show, Bobby Darin and Friends, Danny Kaye Special, Where It's At with Dick Cavett, Many Sides of Don Rickles, Robert Young and the Family, owner. Series co-prod.: All In The Family, Sanford and Son, Maude, Good Times, What's Happening!, Carter Country, Diff'rent Strokes, Archie Bunker's Place.

YOUNG, ALAN
Actor. r.n. Angus Young. b. North Shield, Northumberland, England, Nov. 19, 1919. First acted as monologist for 13 years in Canada; radio comedian 10 yrs. in Canada and U.S.; served in Canadian Navy as sub-lt. 1942-44; wrote, dir. and acted in comedy broadcasts. Author: Mister Ed and Me (1995).
PICTURES: Margie (debut, 1946), Chicken Every Sunday, Mr. Belvedere Goes to College, Aaron Slick from Punkin Crick, Androcles and the Lion, Gentlemen Marry Brunettes, Tom Thumb, The Time Machine, Baker's Hawk, The Cat from Outer Space, The Great Mouse Detective (voice), Duck Tales: The Movie (voice), Beverly Hills Cop III.
TELEVISION: Series: The Alan Young Show (Emmy Award, 1950), Saturday Night Revue, Mr. Ed, Coming of Age. Movies: Earth Angel, Hart to Hart: Home is Where the Hart Is.

YOUNG, BURT
Actor, Writer. b. New York, NY, April 30, 1940. Worked at variety of jobs (boxer, trucker, etc.) before turning to acting and joining Actor's Studio. Appeared in off-B'way plays which led to Hollywood career. On B'way in Cuba and His Teddy Bear.
PICTURES: Cinderella Liberty, Chinatown, The Gambler, Murph the Surf, The Killer Elite, Rocky (Acad. Award nom.), Twilight's Last Gleaming, The Choirboys, Convoy, Uncle Joe Shannon (also s.p.), Rocky II, Blood Beach, All the Marbles, Rocky III, Lookin' To Get Out, Amityville II: The Possession, Over the Brooklyn Bridge, Once Upon a Time in America, The Pope of Greenwich Village, Rocky IV, Back to School, Blood Red, Beverly Hills Brats, Last Exit to Brooklyn, Medium Rare, Betsy's Wedding, Wait Until Spring Bandini, Diving In, Backstreet Dreams, Rocky V, Bright Angel, Red American, Club Fed, Excessive Force.
TELEVISION: Series: Roomies. Guest: M*A*S*H, Baretta, Tales From the Crypt. Movies: The Great Niagara, Hustling, Serpico: The Deadly Game, Woman of the Year, Daddy I Don't Like It Like This (also s.p.), Murder Can Hurt You, A Summer to Remember, Double Deception, Vendetta 2: The New Mafia, Columbo: Undercover.

YOUNG, CHRIS
Actor. b. Chambersburg, PA, Apr. 28, 1971. Stage debut in college production of Pippin, followed by On Golden Pond.
PICTURES: The Great Outdoors (debut, 1988), Book of Love, December, The Runestone, Warlock: The Armageddon, PCU, Deep Down.
TELEVISION: Series: Max Headroom, Falcon Crest, Live-In, Married People. Pilot: Jake's Journey. Movies: Dance 'Til Dawn, Breaking the Silence, MacShayne: The Final Roll of the Dice, Runaway Daughters. Special: Square One. Guest: Crime & Punishment.

YOUNG, FREDDIE
O.B.E. Cinematographer. b. England, 1902. r.n. Frederick Young. Entered British film industry in 1917. Gaumont Studio Shepherd's Bush, London as lab asst. First picture as chief cameraman, 1927 then chief cameraman to Herbert Wilcox British & Dominions Studios Elstree Herts. Army capt. Army Film prod. group directing training films 3 yrs. Invalided out. Signed with MGM British 15 yrs. Also credited as F.A. Young. BAFTA Fellowship 1972, Prix D'Honeur (Lawrence of Arabia) O.B.E. 1970.
PICTURES: Victory 1918, A Peep Behind the Scenes, The Speckled Band, Goodnight Vienna, The Loves of Robert Burns, The King of Paris, White Cargo (first British talkie), Rookery Nook, A Cuckoo in the Nest, Canaries Sometimes Sing, A Night Like This, Plunder, Thark, On Approval, Mischief, Return of the Rat, The Happy Ending, Yes Mr. Brown, This'll Make You Whistle, That's a Good Girl, Nell Gwynne, Peg of Old Drury, The Little Damozel, Bitter Sweet, The Queen's Affair, Sport of Kings, A Warm Corner, The W Plan, Victoria the Great, Sixty Glorious Years, Goodbye Mr. Chips, Nurse Edith Cavell, The 49th Parallel, Contraband, Busman's Honeymoon, The Young Mr. Pitt, Caesar and Cleopatra, Escape, So Well Remembered, Edward My Son, The Conspirator, The Winslow Boy, Calling Bulldog Drummond, Ivanhoe, Knights of the Round Table, Mogambo, Invitation to the Dance, Bhowani Junction, The Barretts of Wimpole Street, The Little Hut, Indiscreet, I Accuse, Inn of the Sixth Happiness, Solomon and Sheba, Betrayed, Island in the Sun, Treasure Island, Lust for Life, Macbeth, Greengage Summer, Lawrence of Arabia (Academy Award, 1962), The Seventh Dawn, Lord Jim, The Deadly Affair, Rotten to the Core, Doctor Zhivago (Academy Award, 1965), You Only Live Twice, The Battle of Britain, Sinful Davey, Ryan's Daughter (Academy Award, 1970), Nicholas and Alexandra, The Asphyx, Luther, The Tamarind Seed, Permission to Kill, The

Blue Bird, Seven Nights in Japan, Stevie, Bloodline, Rough Cut, Richard's Things, Invitation to the Wedding, Sword of the Valiant.
TELEVISION: Great Expectations, The Man in the Iron Mask, Macbeth (Emmy Award, 1960), Ike: The War Years, Arthur's Hollowed Ground (director).

YOUNG, IRWIN
Executive. b. New York, NY. e. Perkiomen Sch., Lehigh U., B.S., 1950. Pres., Du Art Film Laboratories, Inc.

YOUNG, IRWIN W.
Executive. President of the Film Society of Lincoln Center.

YOUNG, KAREN
Actress. b. Pequonnock, NJ, Sept. 29, 1958. Trained at Image Theatre/Studio in NYC.
THEATER: A Lie of the Mind, 3 Acts of Recognition, Five of Us, Mud People.
PICTURES: Deep in the Heart (debut, 1983), Almost You, Birdy, 9-1/2 Weeks, Heat, Jaws the Revenge, Torch Song Trilogy, Criminal Law, Night Game, The Boy Who Cried Bitch, Hoffa, The Wife.
TELEVISION: Movies: The Execution of Raymond Graham, The 10 Million Dollar Getaway, The Summer My Father Grew Up.

YOUNG, LORETTA
Actress. r.n. Gretchen Young. b. Salt Lake City, UT, Jan. 6, 1913. e. Ramona Convent, Alhambra, CA, Immaculate Heart Coll. Hollywood. Family moved to Hollywood when she was 3 yrs. old; began acting as child. After small part in Naughty But Nice, lead in Laugh Clown, Laugh. Played in almost 100 films. Autobiography: The Things I Had to Learn (1962).
PICTURES: Laugh Clown Laugh (debut, 1928), Loose Ankles, The Squall, Kismet, I Like Your Nerve, The Devil to Pay, Platinum Blonde, The Hatchet Man, Big Business Girl, Life Beings, Zoo in Budapest, Life of Jimmy Dolan, Midnight Mary, Heroes for Sale, The Devil's in Love, She Had to Say Yes, A Man's Castle, The House of Rothschild, Bulldog Drummond Strikes Back, Born to Be Bad, Caravan, The White Parade, Clive of India, Call of the Wild, Shanghai, The Crusades, The Unguarded Hour, Private Number, Ramona, Ladies in Love, Love is News, Cafe Metropolis, Wife Doctor and Nurse, Second Honeymoon, Four Men and a Prayer, Suez, Kentucky, Three Blind Mice, Wife Husband and Friend, The Story of Alexander Graham Bell, Eternally Yours, The Doctor Takes a Wife, He Stayed for Breakfast, Lady from Cheyenne, The Men in Her Life, Bedtime Story, A Night to Remember, China, Ladies Courageous, And Now Tomorrow, Along Came Jones, The Stranger, The Perfect Marriage, The Farmer's Daughter (Academy Award, 1947), The Bishop's Wife, Rachel and the Stranger, The Accused, Mother Is a Freshman, Come to the Stable, Key to the City, Cause for Alarm, Half Angel, Paula, Because of You, It Happens Every Thursday.
TELEVISION: Series: The Loretta Young Show (1953-61; 3 Emmy Awards: 1954, 1956, 1959), The New Loretta Young Show (1962-63). Movies: Christmas Eve, Lady in a Corner.

YOUNG, ROBERT
Actor. b. Chicago, IL, Feb. 22, 1907. Acted at Pasadena Playhouse which led to film roles.
PICTURES: Black Camel (debut, 1931), The Sin of Madelon Claudet, Strange Interlude, The Kid From Spain, Today We Live, Men Must Fight, Hell Below, Tugboat Annie, Saturday's Millions, The Right to Romance, Carolina, Lazy River, The House of Rothschild, Spitfire, Paris Interlude, Whom the Gods Destroy, Death on the Diamond, The Band Plays On, Vagabond Lady, Calm Yourself, Red Salute, Remember Last Night?, West Point of the Air, The Bride Comes Home, It's Love Again, Secret Agent, 3 Wise Guys, The Bride Walks Out, Sworn Enemy, The Longest Night, Stowaway, Dangerous Number, Married Before Breakfast, The Emperor's Candlesticks, I Met Him in Paris, The Bride Wore Red, Navy Blue and Gold, Paradise for Three, Josette, The Toy Wife, Three Comrades, Rich Man Poor Girl, Shining Hour, Bridal Suite, Honolulu, Miracles For Sale, Maisie, Northwest Passage, The Mortal Storm, Florian, Western Union, Sporting Blood, Dr. Kildare's Crisis, The Trial of Mary Dugan, Lady Be Good, Married Bachelor, H.M. Pulham Esq., Joe Smith American, Cairo, Journey for Margaret, Slightly Dangerous, Claudia, Sweet Rosie O'Grady, The Canterville Ghost, The Enchanted Cottage, Those Endearing Young Charms, The Searching Wind, Claudia and David, Lady Luck, They Won't Believe Me, Crossfire, Relentless, Sitting Pretty, Adventure in Baltimore, That Forsyte Woman, Bride for Sale, And Baby Makes Three, The Second Woman, The Half-Breed, Goodbye My Fancy, Secret of the Incas.
TELEVISION: Series: Father Knows Best (2 Emmy Awards: 1956, 1957), Window on Main Street, Marcus Welby M.D. (Emmy Award, 1970). Movies: Marcus Welby M.D. (pilot; a.k.a. A Matter of Humanities), Vanished, All My Darling Daughters, My Darling Daughters' Anniversary, Little Women, The Return of Marcus Welby M.D., Marcus Welby M.D.: A Holiday Affair.

YOUNG, ROBERT M.
Director. b. New York, NY, Nov. 22, 1924. e. Harvard.
PICTURES: Nothing But a Man (prod., co-s.p.), The Plot Against Harry (co-prod., photog.), Short Eyes, Rich Kids, One-Trick Pony, The Ballad of Gregorio Cortez (also s.p. adapt.), Alambrista! (also s.p., photog.), Extremities, Saving Grace, Dominick and Eugene, Triumph of the Spirit, Talent for the Game, American Me (co-prod. only), Children of Fate (exec. dir. & exec. prod. only), Roosters, Caught.
TELEVISION: Specials: Sit-In, Angola—Journey to a War (Peabody Award), The Inferno (Cortile Cascino; also prod., writer, edit.), Anatomy of a Hospital, The Eskimo: Fight for Life (Emmy Award, 1971). Movie: Solomon and Sheba.

YOUNG, SEAN
Actress. b. Louisville, KY, Nov. 20, 1959. r.n. Mary Sean Young. e. Interlochen Arts Acad., MI, studied dance, voice, flute and writing. After graduating, moved to N.Y., worked as receptionist, model for 6 months and signed with ICM. Shortly after signing with ICM debuted in Jane Austen in Manhattan. On L.A. Stage in Stardust.
PICTURES: Jane Austen in Manhattan (debut, 1980), Stripes, Blade Runner, Young Doctors in Love, Dune, Baby: The Secret of the Lost Legend, No Way Out, Wall Street, The Boost, Cousins, Fire Birds, A Kiss Before Dying, Love Crimes, Once Upon a Crime, Hold Me Thrill Me Kiss Me, Forever, Fatal Instinct, Ace Ventura: Pet Detective, Even Cowgirls Get the Blues, Mirage, Dr. Jekyll and Ms. Hyde, The Proprietor.
TELEVISION: Special: Under the Biltmore Clock. Mini-Series: Tender Is the Night. Movies: Blood and Orchids, The Sketch Artist, Blue Ice, Witness to the Execution, Model by Day, Evil Has a Face, Everything to Gain.

YOUNGSTEIN, MAX E.
Executive. b. March 21, 1913. e. Fordham U. Member New York Bar. Motion picture consultant and indep. prod. Member, Producers Guild. Pres., Max E. Youngstein Enterprises. 1940-41, dir. adv. & pub., 20th Century Fox; later dir. studio special svcs.; asst. to pres. 1942-44, US Army Signal Corps. 1945, v.p. & gen. mgr., Stanley Kramer Prods. 1946-48, dir. adv. & pub., Eagle Lion Films; v.p. chg. adv. & pub. & prod. liaison. 1949-50, dir. adv. & pub., Paramount; mem. exec. comm. & v.p. & dir. dist. co. 1951-62, gen. v.p., partner, bd. mem., dir. adv. & pub., United Artists Corp. Formed UA Music Co. Pres., UA Records. 1977, consultant to Bart-Palevsky Prods. Advisor, Golden Harvest Films. Consultant, Rico-Lion. 1979, Shamrock Prods., Rank Film Distributors, Taft Bdcst. Co., Encore Prods., Bobrun Prods., Selkirk Films. 1980, named chmn. & CEO, Taft Int'l. Pictures. 1984, Consultant, Orion, 20th Century-Fox. 1985-86, pres., Great American Pictures. Consultant, H&M Trust, Color Systems Technology, Mickey Rooney Film Prods., Peachtree Prods.
PICTURES: Young Billy Young, Best of Cinerama, Man in the Middle, Fail Safe, The Money Trap, The Dangerous Days of Kiowa Jones, Welcome to Hard Times.

YULIN, HARRIS
Actor. b. Los Angeles, Nov. 5, 1937. On B'way in Watch on the Rhine, A Lesson from Aloes, etc. Founder of the Los Angeles Classic Theatre.
THEATER: The Little Foxes, Who's Afraid of Virginia Woolf?, Becket, The Entertainer, The Doctor's Dilemma, Night of the Iguana, School for Wives, Uncle Vanya, Tempest, Timon of Athens, The Seagull, Next Time I'll Sing to You (NY debut), Look Back in Anger, A Midsummer Night's Dream, King John, Hamlet, Julius Caesar, Tartuffe, Approaching Zanzibar, Henry V, The Visit (B'way), Arms and the Man, It's a Mad Mad World, Arts and Leisure. Dir. credits incl. Baba Goya, The Front Page, The Guardsman, Sheba, The Man Who Came to Dinner, Guns of Carrar, Cuba Si, Candida, Don Juan in Hell, Jitta's Atonement, etc.
PICTURES: End of the Road, Doc, The Midnight Man, Night Moves, Steel, Scarface, The Believers, Fatal Beauty, Candy Mountain, Bad Dreams, Judgement in Berlin, Another Woman, Ghostbusters II, Narrow Margin, Final Analysis, There Goes the Neighborhood, Clear and Present Danger, Stuart Saves His Family, The Baby-sitters Club, Looking for Richard, Multiplicity, Loch Ness.
TELEVISION: Specials/Movies: The Thirteenth Day--The Story of Esther, When Every Day Was the Fourth of July, Missiles of October, Conspiracy: Trial of the Chicago Seven, Last Ride of the Dalton Gang, Robert Kennedy and His Times, Tailspin: Behind the Korean Airlines Tragedy, Face of a Stranger, The Last Hit, Incident at Vichy, How the West Was Won, Truman. Series: WIOU, Frasier.

Z

ZAENTZ, SAUL
Producer. b. Passaic, NJ.
PICTURES: One Flew Over the Cuckoo's Nest (Academy Award for Best Picture, 1975), Three Warriors, The Lord of the

Rings, Amadeus (Academy Award for Best Picture, 1984), The Mosquito Coast (exec. prod.), The Unbearable Lightness of Being, At Play in the Fields of the Lord, The English Patient.

ZAILLIAN, STEVEN
Writer. Director. b. 1953.
PICTURES: The Falcon and the Snowman, Awakenings, Jack the Bear, Searching for Bobby Fischer (also dir.), Schindler's List (Academy Award, 1993; WGA & Golden Globe Awards), Clear and Present Danger (co-s.p.), Primal Fear.

ZANE, BILLY
Actor. b. Chicago, IL, 1966. Sister is actress Lisa Zane. Studied acting at American School in Switzerland. To Hollywood in 1984 landing small role in Back to the Future. On stage in American Music (NY), The Boys in the Backroom (Actors' Gang, Chicago).
PICTURES: Back to the Future (debut, 1985), Critters, Dead Calm, Back to the Future Part II, Megaville, Memphis Belle, Blood & Concrete: A Love Story, Billions, Femme Fatale, Sniper, Posse, Orlando, Flashfire, Tombstone, The Silence of the Hams, Cyborg Agent, Only You, Tales From the Crypt Presents Demon Knight, Reflections in the Dark, Danger Zone, The Phantom.
TELEVISION: Series: Twin Peaks. Movie: Brotherhood of Justice, The Case of the Hillside Stranglers, Lake Consequence, Running Delilah, The Set Up.

ZANUCK, LILI FINI
Producer, Director. b. Leominster, MA, Apr. 2, 1954. e. Northern VA Community Coll. Worked for Carnation Co. in LA prior to entering film business. Joined Zanuck/Brown Company in 1978 working in development and various phases of production; 1984-present, prod. Made directorial debut in 1991 with Rush. Named Producer of the Year (1985) by NATO, along with Richard D. Zanuck and David Brown; Producer of the Year (1989) by Producers Guild of America, with Zanuck.
PICTURES: Cocoon, Cocoon: The Return, Driving Miss Daisy (Academy Award, Golden Globe & Natl. Board of Review Awards for Best Picture 1989), Rush (dir.), Rich in Love, Clean Slate, Wild Bill, Mulholland Falls, The Double.

ZANUCK, RICHARD DARRYL
Executive. b. Los Angeles, CA, Dec 13, 1934. e. Stanford U. 1952-56. Father was exec. Darryl Zanuck. Story dept., 20th Century Fox, 1954; WD pub. dept., 1955; asst. to prod.: Island in the Sun, The Sun Also Rises, The Longest Day; v.p. Darryl F. Zanuck Prods.; first credit as prod. Compulsion (1959); president's prod. rep., 20th Century Fox Studio, 1963; v.p. charge prod.; 1968 Chmn. of Bd., Television div., 20th Century Fox, 1969 Pres., 20th Century Fox Film Corp. Joined Warner Bros., 1971, as sr. exec. v.p.; resigned 1972 to form Zanuck-Brown Production Company, Universal Pictures. Joined 20th Century-Fox, 1980-83. To Warner Bros., 1983. To MGM Entertainment, 1986. 1988, dissolved 16-year partnership with David Brown. Formed The Zanuck Company, 1989. Recipient: Irving Thalberg Award (1991).
PICTURES: Compulsion, The Chapman Report, Ssssssss, The Sting (Academy Award for Best Picture, 1973), The Sugarland Express, Willie Dynamite, The Black Windmill, The Girl from Petrovka, The Eiger Sanction, Jaws, MacArthur, Jaws 2, The Island, Neighbors, The Verdict, Cocoon, Target, Cocoon: The Return, Driving Miss Daisy (Academy Award for Best Picture, 1989), Rush, Rich in Love, Clean Slate, Wild Bill, Mulholland Falls.

ZEFFIRELLI, FRANCO
Director, Writer. b. Florence, Italy, Feb. 12, 1923. e. Florence Univ. Was stage director before entering film industry. Set designer 1949 -52 for Visconti plays (A Streetcar Named Desire, The Three Sisters). Worked as asst. dir. on La Terra Trema, Bellissima, Senso. Director of operas.
PICTURES: Director-Screenplay: The Taming of the Shrew (also co-prod.), Romeo and Juliet (also exec. prod.), Brother Sun Sister Moon, The Champ (dir. only), Endless Love (dir. only), La Traviata (also prod. design), Otello, Young Toscanini (dir., story), Hamlet, Jane Eyre.
TELEVISION: Mini-Series: Jesus of Nazareth.

ZELNICK, STRAUSS
Executive. b. Boston, MA, June 26, 1957. e. Wesleyan U. B.A., 1979 (Summa Cum Laude); Harvard Grad. School of Business Administration, M.B.A., 1983; Harvard Law School, J.D., 1983 (Cum Laude). 1983-86, v.p., international television sales, Columbia Pictures International Corp. 1988-89, pres. & chief operating officer, Vestron, Inc.; 1989-93, pres. & chief operating officer, Fox Film Corp. Became pres. & CEO of Bertelsman Music Group Entertainment in North America.

ZEMECKIS, ROBERT
Director, Writer. b. Chicago, IL, 1952. m. actress Mary Ellen Trainor. e. U. of Film Awards sponsored by M.P. Academy of Arts & Sciences, plus 15 intl. honors. Has film editing background, having worked as cutter on TV commercials in Illinois. Also cut films at NBC News, Chicago, as summer job. After schooling went to Universal to observe on set of TV series, McCloud. Wrote script for that series in collab. with Bob Gale. Turned to feature films, directing I Wanna Hold Your Hand and co-writing s.p. with Gale.
PICTURES: Director: I Wanna Hold Your Hand (also co-s.p.), Used Cars (also co-s.p.), Romancing the Stone, Back to the Future (also co-s.p.), Who Framed Roger Rabbit, Back to the Future II (also story), Back to the Future III (also story), Death Becomes Her (also co-prod.), Forrest Gump (Academy Award, Golden Globe & DGA Awards, 1994). Co-Writer: 1941, Trespass. Exec. Prod.: The Public Eye, Tales From the Crypt Presents Demon Knight, Frighteners, Tales From the Crypt Presents Bordello of Blood.
TELEVISION: Amazing Stories, Tales From the Crypt (exec. prod.; also dir., All Through the House, You Murderer).

ZENS, WILL
Producer, Director. b. Milwaukee, WI, June 26, 1920. e. Marquette U., USC, B.A., M.A. Wrote, produced and directed many TV shows. Formed Riviera Productions in 1960 to produce theatrical motion pictures.
PICTURES: Capture That Capsule, The Starfighters, To the Shores of Hell, Road to Nashville, Hell on Wheels, From Nashville with Music, Yankee Station, Help Me ... I'm Possessed!, Hot Summer in Barefoot County, The Fix, Truckin' Man, The Satan Crossing (dir., s.p.), Death on the Carrier, Terror in the Streets.
TELEVISION: Punch & Trudy, Your Police, Aqua Lung Adventures, Teletunes, Sunday Drive.

ZERBE, ANTHONY
Actor. b. Long Beach, CA, May 20, 1936. Studied at Stella Adler Theatre Studio.
THEATER: NY: Solomon's Child, The Little Foxes.
PICTURES: Cool Hand Luke, Will Penny, The Liberation of L.B. Jones, The Molly Maguires, The Call Me Mister Tibbs, Cotton Comes to Harlem, The Omega Man, The Life and Times of Judge Roy Bean, The Strange Vengeance of Rosalie, The Laughing Policeman, Papillon, The Parallax View, Farewell My Lovely, Rooster Cogburn, The Turning Point, Who'll Stop the Rain, The First Deadly Sin, The Dead Zone, Off Beat, Opposing Force, Private Investigation, Steel Dawn, Listen to Me, See No Evil Hear No Evil, Licence to Kill.
TELEVISION: Series: Harry-O (Emmy Award, 1976), The Young Riders. Movies: The Priest Killer, The Hound of the Baskervilles, Snatched, She Lives, The Healers, In the Glitter Palace, KISS Meets the Phantom of the Park, Attica, The Seduction of Miss Leona, Rascals and Robbers: The Secret Adventures of Tom Sawyer and Huck Finn, A Question of Honor, The Return of the Man from U.N.C.L.E., One Police Plaza. Mini-Series: Once an Eagle, Centennial, The Chisholms, George Washington, A.D.

ZIDE, LARRY M.
Executive. b. Flushing, NY, Oct. 16, 1954. 3rd generation in mp. industry. Started 1972 with American Intl. Pictures in sls. & adv.; 1973, named branch sls. mgr., Memphis. 1975, joined Dimension Pictures as print controller; 1978, formed Zica Films Co. serving m.p. industry; 1985, Zica merged with Filmtreat Intl. Corp; named pres., newly formed Filmtreat West Corp.

ZIDE, MICHAEL (MICKEY)
Executive. b. Detroit, MI, May 31, 1932. Joined m.p. industry with American Intl. Pictures as print controller; 1962, promoted to asst. gen. sls. mgr. Named v.p., special projects; 1970; 1972, joined Academy Pictures as v.p. of prod. Later went with Zica Film Co.; 1985, named exec. v.p., Filmtreat West Corp.

ZIEFF, HOWARD
Director. b. Chicago, IL. e. Art Center School in Los Angeles. Started as artist and photographer, working as newsreel photographer for L.A. TV station. Went to N.Y. to do still photography; became top photo artist in advertising. Turned to film direction with Slither.
PICTURES: Slither (debut, 1973), Hearts of the West, House Calls, The Main Event, Private Benjamin, Unfaithfully Yours, The Dream Team, My Girl, My Girl 2.

ZIFKIN, WALTER
Executive. b. July 16, 1936. New York, NY. e. UCLA, A.B., 1958; USC, LL.B., 1961. CBS legal dept., 1961-63; William Morris Agency 1963-present; exec. vice-pres.; 1989 also COO.

ZIMBALIST, EFREM, JR.
Actor. b. New York, NY, Nov. 30, 1923. Son of violinist Efrem Zimbalist and opera singer Alma Gluck. Daughter is actress Stephanie Zimbalist. e. Fay Sch., Southboro, MA; St. Paul's, Concord, NH; Yale. Studied drama, Neighborhood Playhouse. N.Y. Stage debut, The Rugged Path. Shows with American

Repertory Theatre; Henry VIII, Androcles and the Lion, What Every Woman Knows, Yellow Jack, Hedda Gabler, Fallen Angels. Co-prod., The Medium, The Telephone, The Consul. Gave up acting after death of his wife and served as asst. to father, Curtis Inst. of Music for 4 years. Returned to acting, stock co., Hammonton, NJ, 1954.
PICTURES: House of Strangers (debut, 1949), Bombers B-52, Band of Angels, The Deep Six, Violent Road, Girl on the Run, Too Much Too Soon, Home Before Dark, The Crowded Sky, A Fever in the Blood, By Love Possessed, The Chapman Report, The Reward, Harlow, Wait Until Dark, Airport 1975, Elmira, Hot Shots!, Batman: Mask of the Phantasm (voice).
TELEVISION: Series: Concerning Miss Marlowe (daytime serial), 77 Sunset Strip, The FBI, Hotel. Guest: Philco, Goodyear Playhouse, U.S. Steel Hour. Movies: Who Is the Black Dahlia?, A Family Upside Down, Terror Out of the Sky, The Best Place to Be, The Gathering Part II, Baby Sister, Shooting Stars. Host: You Are the Jury, The Tempest. Mini-Series: Scruples.

ZIMBALIST, STEPHANIE
Actress. b. New York, NY, Oct. 8. Father is actor Efrem Zimbalist Jr.; grandparents: violinist Efrem Zimbalist and soprano Alma Gluck; aunt is novelist Marcia Davenport.
THEATER: LA: Festival, The Tempest, American Mosaic, Love Letters, Baby Dance, The Crimson Thread, Ad Wars. Williamstown Theatre Festival: Barbarians, Summer and Smoke, Threepenny Opera. Tours: My One and Only, Carousel. Regional: The Philadelphia Story, The Cherry Orchard, The Baby Dance.
PICTURES: The Magic of Lassie, The Awakening.
TELEVISION: Series: Remington Steele. Mini-Series: Centennial. Movies: Yesterday's Child, In the Matter of Karen Ann Quinlan, The Gathering, The Long Journey Back, Forever, The Triangle Factory Fire Scandal, The Best Place to Be, The Baby Sitter, The Golden Moment—An Olympic Love Story, Elvis and the Beauty Queen, Tomorrow's Child, Love on the Run, A Letter to Three Wives, Celebration Family, The Man in the Brown Suit, Caroline?, Personals, The Killing Mind, The Story Lady, Some Kind of Love, Breaking the Silence, Sexual Advances, Jericho Fever, Incident in a Small Town, Voices From Within, The Great Elephant Escape, Whose Daughter Is She? Stop the World—I Want to Get Off, Dead Ahead.

ZIMMER, HANS
Composer. b. Germany. Member of the Buggles, producing hit song Video Killed the Radio Star. Pioneered use of digital synthesizers with computer technology and traditional orchestras. Establed Lillie Yard Studio in London. Received Grammy Award for best instrumental arragement with vocals and Golden Globe for best original score for The Lion King.
PICTURES: Burning Secret, A World Apart, Rain Man, Paperhouse, Wonderland, Black Rain, Driving Miss Daisy, Bird on a Wire, Days of Thunder, Pacific Heights, Green Card, Thelma & Louise, Backdraft, Radio Flyer, The Power of One, K-2, A League of Their Own, Toys, Younger and Younger, True Romance, Cool Runnings, I'll Do Anything, The House of the Spirits, Renaissance Man, The Lion King (Academy Award, 1994), Drop Zone, Crimson Tide, Nine Months, Something to Talk About, Beyond Rangoon, Muppet Treasure Island, Broken Arrow.
TELEVISION: Two Deaths.

ZINNEMANN, FRED
Director. b. Vienna, Austria, Apr. 29, 1907. e. Vienna U., law. Studied violin as a boy; after law, studied photographic technique, lighting & mechanics (Paris); asst. cameraman 1 yr. Berlin; came to U.S. 1929; extra in m.p. All Quiet on the Western Front, 1930; asst. to Berthold Viertel, script clerk & asst. to Robert Flaherty, 1931; dir. Mexican documentary The Wave, 1934; short subjects dir., MGM, winning Academy Award for That Mothers Might Live, 1938; feature dir. 1942: winner of first Screen Directors' Award 1948 with The Search. 4 N.Y. Film Critics Awards; 2 Director's Guild Annual Awards; 4 Acad. Awards, 9 Acad. Award noms., 3 Golden Globe Awards. Other awards: U.S. Congressional Life Achievement Award (1987), Gold Medal City of Vienna, Donatello Award (Italy), Order of Arts & Letters (France), Golden Thistle Award (Edinburgh, Scotland), etc. Fellowships: BAFTA and BFI. Director of Acad. Award winning short Benjy (for L.A. Orthopedic Hospital, 1951). 1994, John Huston Award from Artists Rights Foundation, hon. dr. lit. Univ. of Durham (England). Author: My Life in the Movies (Scribner, 1992).
PICTURES: Kid Glove Killer (debut, 1942), Eyes in the Night, The Seventh Cross, Little Mister Jim, My Brother Talks to Horses, The Search, Act of Violence, The Men, Teresa, High Noon (NY Film Critics Award, 1952), The Member of the Wedding, From Here to Eternity (Academy Award, DGA & NY Film Critics Award, 1953), Oklahoma!, A Hatful of Rain, The Nun's Story (NY Film Critics Award, 1959), The Sundowners (also prod.), Behold a Pale Horse (also prod.), A Man for All Seasons, (also prod.: Academy Awards for Best Picture & Director; also DGA & NY Film Critics Awards, 1966), The Day of the Jackal, Julia, Five Days One Summer (also prod.).

ZINNEMANN, TIM
Producer. b. Los Angeles, CA. e. Columbia U. Son of dir. Fred Zinnemann. Began career industry as film editor; then asst. dir. on 20 films. Production mgr. for 5 projects; assoc. prod. on The Cowboys and Smile. Produced Straight Time for Warners with Stanley Beck.
PICTURES: A Small Circle of Friends, The Long Riders, Tex, Impulse, Fandango, Crossroads, The Running Man, Pet Sematary (exec. prod.).
TELEVISION: The Jericho Mile.

ZISKIN, LAURA
Producer. e. USC Cinema School. Worked as game show writer, development exec. before joining Jon Peters' prod. co. where she worked on A Star is Born, Eyes of Laura Mars (assoc. prod.). Formed Fogwood Films with Sally Field. Became pres. of company Fox 2000 Pictures.
PICTURES: Murphy's Romance, No Way Out, D.O.A., The Rescue, Everybody's All American, Pretty Woman (exec. prod.), What About Bob?, The Doctor, Hero (also co-story), To Die For, Courage Under Fire.

ZITO, JOSEPH
Director. b. New York, NY, May 14, 1949. e. City Coll. of New York.
PICTURES: Abduction, The Prowler, Friday the 13th: The Final Chapter, Missing in Action, Invasion U.S.A., Red Scorpion.

ZSIGMOND, VILMOS
Cinematographer. b. Szeged, Hungary, June 16, 1930. e. National Film Sch. Began career photographing Hungarian Revolution of 1956. Later escaped from Hungary with friend Laszlo Kovacs, also a cinematographer. Winner of Academy Award and British Academy Award for cinematography, also several int'l and domestic awards as dir. of TV commercials.
PICTURES: The Time Travelers (1964), The Sadist, The Name of the Game Is Kill, Futz, Picasso Summer, The Monitors, Red Sky at Morning, McCabe and Mrs. Miller, The Hired Hand, The Ski Bum, Images, Deliverance, Scarecrow, The Long Goodbye, Cinderella Liberty, The Sugarland Express, The Girl From Petrovka, Sweet Revenge, Death Riders, Obsession, Close Encounters of the Third Kind (Academy Award, 1977), The Last Waltz, The Deer Hunter (BAFTA Award; Acad. Award nom.), Winter Kills, The Rose, Heaven's Gate, Blow Out, The Border, Jinxed, Table for Five, No Small Affair, The River (Acad. Award nom.), Real Genius, The Witches of Eastwick, Fat Man and Little Boy, The Two Jakes, Journey to Spirit Island, The Bonfire of the Vanities, The Long Shadow (dir.), Sliver, Intersection, Maverick (also actor), The Crossing Guard, Assassins, The Ghost and the Darkness.
TELEVISION: Flesh and Blood, Stalin (Emmy Award, ACE Award, ASC Award).

ZORADI, MARK
Executive. Began working for Disney in 1980, currently pres., Buena Vista International. Distributor of the Year, Cinema Expo International, 1996.

ZUCKER, DAVID
Producer, Director, Writer. b. Milwaukee, WI, Oct. 16, 1947. e. U. of Wisconsin, majoring in film. With brother, Jerry, and friend Jim Abrahams founded the Kentucky Fried Theatre in Madison in 1971 (moved theater to L.A. 1972); later wrote script for film of that name released in 1977.
PICTURES: The Kentucky Fried Movie (co-s.p., actor), Airplane! (co-s.p., co-dir., actor), Top Secret (co-dir., co-s.p., co-exec. prod.), Ruthless People (co-dir.), The Naked Gun: From the Files of Police Squad! (exec. prod., dir., co-s.p.), The Naked Gun 2 1/2: The Smell of Fear (dir., exec. prod., co-s.p., actor), Brain Donors (co-exec. prod.), The Naked Gun 33 1/3: The Final Insult (prod., co-s.p., actor), A Walk in the Clouds (co-prod.).
TELEVISION: Police Squad (series), Our Planet Tonight (special).

ZUCKER, JERRY
Producer, Director. Writer. b. Milwaukee, WI, Mar. 11, 1950. e. U. of Wisconsin, majoring in education. With brother, David, and friend Jim Abrahams founded the Kentucky Fried Theatre in Madison in 1970 and wrote script for film of that name released in 1977.
PICTURES: The Kentucky Fried Movie (co-s.p., actor), Rock 'n' Roll High School (2nd unit dir.), Airplane! (co-dir., co-s.p.), Top Secret (co-dir., co-s.p.), Ruthless People (co-dir.), The Naked Gun (exec. prod.), Ghost (dir.), The Naked Gun 2-1/2 (exec. co-prod.), Brain Donors (co-exec. prod.), My Life (co-prod.), Naked Gun 33-1/3 (co-exec. prod.), First Knight (dir.), A Walk in the Clouds (co-prod.).
TELEVISION: Series: Police Squad! (co-exec. prod., dir.; co-wrote first episode).

ZUGSMITH, ALBERT
Producer, Director, Writer. b. Atlantic City, NJ, April 24, 1910. e. U. of VA. Pres. Intercontinental Broadcasting Corp.; ed. publ. Atlantic City Daily World; v.p. Smith Davis Corp.; chmn of bd., Continental Telecasting Corp., Television Corp. of America; assoc. ed. American Press; pres. World Printing Co.; exec. CBS; pres. American Pictures Corp.; pres. Famous Players Int'l Corp.
PICTURES: *Producer*: Invasion USA, Top Banana, Female on the Beach, Raw Edge, Written on the Wind, Man in the Shadow, Red Sundown, Star in the Dust, Tarnished Angels, The Incredible Shrinking Man, The Girl in the Kremlin, The Square Jungle, Female on the Beach, Touch of Evil, Captive Women, Sword of Venus, Port Sinister, Paris Model, Slaughter on Tenth Avenue, The Female Animal (also story), High School Confidential, Night of the Quarter Moon, The Beat Generation, The Big Operator, Girls Town, Violated!, Platinum High School, Private Lives of Adam and Eve, Dondi (also dir., s.p.), College Confidential (also dir.), Confessions of an Opium Eater (also dir.), Sex Kitten Go to College (also dir., story), The Great Space Adventure, On Her Bed of Roses, Fanny Hill, The Rapist!, How to Break Into the Movies, Movie Star American Style: or LSA I Love You (dir., story, co- s.p.), The Chinese Room, Street Girl, The President's Girl Friend, The Phantom Gunslinger, Sappho Darling (s.p. only), Menage a Trois, Two Roses and a Goldenrod (dir., s.p. only), The Friendly Neighbors, Why Me God?, Tom Jones Rides Again.

ZUNIGA, DAPHNE
Actress. b. Berkeley, CA, 1962. e. UCLA.
PICTURES: Pranks (debut, 1982), The Dorm That Dripped Blood, The Initiation, Vision Quest, The Sure Thing, Modern Girls, Spaceballs, Last Rites, The Fly II, Gross Anatomy, Staying Together, Eight Hundred Leagues Down the Amazon. TELEVISION: *Movies*: Quarterback Princess, Stone Pillow, Prey of the Chameleon. *Series*: Melrose Place. *Guest*: Family Ties, Nightmare Classics (Eye of the Panther).

ZWICK, EDWARD
Writer, Producer, Director. b. Chicago, IL, Oct. 8, 1952. e. Harvard U., B.A., 1974; American Film Inst. Center for Advanced Film Studies, M.F.A., 1976. Editor and feature writer, The New Republic and Rolling Stone magazines, 1972-74. Author: Literature and Liberalism (1975). Formed Bedford Falls Production Co. with Special Bulletin collaborator Marshall Herskovitz.
PICTURES: *Director*: About Last Night... (debut, 1986), Glory, Leaving Normal, Legends of the Fall (also co-prod.), Courage Under Fire.
TELEVISION: *Series*: Family (writer, then story editor, dir., prod., Humanitas Prize Award, 1980), thirtysomething (co-exec. prod.; Emmy Award, 1988), Dream Street (exec. prod.). *Movies (dir.)*: Paper Dolls, Having It All, Extreme Close-Up (also co-exec. prod., co-story), Relativity. *Special*: Special Bulletin (dir., co-prod., co-story; 2 Emmy Awards, also DGA, WGA & Humanitas Prize Awards, 1983).

ZWICK, JOEL
Director. b. Brooklyn, NY, Jan. 11, 1942. e. Brooklyn Coll., B.A., M.A.
THEATER: Dance with Me, Cold Storage, Esther, Cafe La Mama.
PICTURE: Second Sight.
TELEVISION: *Series*: Laverne and Shirley, Mork and Mindy, It's a Living, America 2100, Goodtime Girls, Hot W.A.C.S. (also exec. prod.), Little Darlings, Joanie Loves Chachi, The New Odd Couple (also supv. prod.), Webster, Brothers (supv. prod.), Perfect Strangers (also pilot), Full House (also pilot), Getting By (also prod.). *Pilots*: Angie, Bosom Buddies, Struck by Lightning, Family Matters, Adventures in Babysitting, Morning Glory, Star of the Family, Up to No Good, Going Places, Hangin' With Mr. Cooper, Life Happens, On Our Own, Making Out, Nowhere Fast.

OBITUARIES

(OCT. 1, 1995 — SEPT. 30, 1996)

Martin Balsam	2/13/96	Patric Knowles	12/23/95
Saul Bass	4/25/96	Dorothy Lamour	9/22/96
Pandro S. Berman	7/13/96	Jenning Lang	5/29/96
Whit Bissell	3/8/96	Lash Larue	5/24/96
Vivian Blaine	12/9/95	Norm Levinson	9/26/97
Ralph Blane	11/13/96	Viveca Lindfors	10/25/95
Albert "Cubby" Broccoli	6/27/96	Jeffrey Lynn	12/1/96
George Burns	3/1/96	Guy Madison	2/6/96
Rosalind Cash	10/31/95	Louis Malle	11/23/95
Jesse Chinich	1/7/96	Walter Manley	1/20/96
Virginia Christine	7/24/96	Dean Martin	12/25/95
Rene Clement	3/17/96	Edward Dennis Martin	7/4/96
Claudette Colbert	7/30/96	Butterfly McQueen	12/22/95
Winston H. (Tony) Cox	9/21/96	Audrey Meadows	2/3/96
John Craven	11/24/95	Richard Morris	4/28/96
Saul David	6/7/96	Haing S. Ngor	3/3/96
Joanne Dru	9/10/96	David Opatoshu	4/30/96
Paul Eddington	11/4/95	Robert Parrish	12/4/95
Herb Edelman	7/21/96	Jon Pertwee	5/20/96
Vince Edwards	3/11/96	Tommy Rettig	2/13/96
William K. Everson	4/14/96	Jack Rose	10/20/95
Louise Fitch	9/11/96	Joe Seneca	8/15/96
Greer Garson	4/6/96	Stirling Silliphant	4/26/96
Bryant Haliday	7/28/96	Don Simpson	1/19/96
Margaux Hemingway	7/1/96	Terry Southern	10/29/95
Georg Heinemann	8/21/96	Lyle Talbot	3/3/96
Fred Hift	7/6/96	Steve Tesich	7/1/96
Harry Horwitz	9/21/96	Claire Townshend	12/19/95
Ross Hunter	3/10/96	Jamie Uys	1/29/96
Dorothy Jeakins	11/24/95	Jo Van Fleet	6/10/96
Ben Johnson	4/8/96	James R. Velde	7/24/96
Gene Kelly	2/2/96	Jack Weston	5/3/96
Frederick H. Kent	9/22/96	Mary Wickes	10/24/95
Krzystof Kieslowski	3/13/96	Joseph Youngerman	11/22/95

SERVICES

ADVERTISING & PUBLICITY SERVICES

A.C. COMMUNICATIONS
8489 W. Third St., #1096, Los Angeles, CA 90048. (213) 655-5833. FAX: (213) 655-5849.

AC & R ADVERTISING INC
16 E. 32 St., New York, NY 10016. (212) 685-2500. FAX: (212) 689-2258.
PRESIDENT
Alvin Chereskin

BOB ABRAMS AND ASSOCIATES
2030 Prosser Ave., Los Angeles, CA 90025. (310) 475-7739. FAX: (310) 475-7739.
Bob Abrams

AMMIRATI, PURIS & LINTAS INC.
100 Fifth Ave., New York, NY 10011. (212) 206-0500. FAX: (212) 337-9481.
CHAIRMAN
Ralph Ammirati

AUSTIN/SIMONS & ASSOCS.
P.O. Box 641523, Los Angeles, CA 90064. (310) 478-8900. FAX: (310) 478-8976.

N.W. AYER & PARTNERS
Worldwide Plaza, 825 Eighth Ave., New York, NY 10019-7498. (212) 474-5000. FAX: (212) 474-5400.
CHAIRMAN & CEO
Steve Dworkin
VICE CHAIRMAN
Dominick Rossi

BACKER, SPIELVOGEL, BATES WORLDWIDE INC.
405 Lexington Ave., 8th Fl., New York, NY 10174. (212) 297-7000.

BAKER, WINOKUR, RYDER
405 S. Beverly Dr., 5th fl., Beverly Hills, CA 90212. (310) 277-6200.
250 W. 57 St., #1610, New York, NY 10017. (212) 582-0700.

BBDO WEST
10960 Wilshire Blvd., # 1600, Los Angeles, CA 90024. (310) 444-4500. FAX: (310) 444-7581.

BBDO WORLDWIDE
1285 Avenue of the Americas, New York, NY 10019. (212) 459-5000.
CHAIRMAN
Allen Rosenshine

BENDER, GOLDMAN & HELPER
11500 W. Olympic Blvd., Suite 655, Los Angeles, CA 90064. (310) 473-4147. FAX: (310) 478-4727.
400 Madison Ave., New York NY 10017. (212) 371-0798. FAX: (212) 754-4380.

WALTER F. BENNETT COMMUNICATIONS
13355 Noel Rd., Suite 1815, Dallas, TX 75240. (214) 661-1122. FAX: (214) 980-0640.
PRESIDENT
Ted Dienert
CFO/COO
Benjamin C. Bell

BIEDERMAN, KELLY & SHAFFER INC.
475 Park Ave. South, New York, NY 10016. (212) 213-5500. FAX: (212) 213-4775.
CHAIRMAN
Barry Biederman

MARION BILLINGS PUBLICITY LTD,
250 W. 57 St., #2420, New York, NY 10107. (212) 581-4493.

RALPH BING ADVERTISING CO.
16109 Selva Dr., San Diego, CA 92128. (714) 487-7444.
PRESIDENT
Ralph Bing

MICHELLE BOLTON & ASSOCS.
100 S. Doheny Dr., #420, Los Angeles, CA 90048. (310) 273-4030. FAX: (310) 273-2640.

BOZELL, INC.
40 W. 23 St., New York, NY 10010. (212) 727-5000. FAX: (212) 645-9262.

CEO
Charles D. Peebler, Jr.

BROKAW COMPANY
9255 Sunset Blvd., #804, Los Angeles, CA 90069. (310) 273-2060. FAX: (310) 276-4037.

LEO BURNETT COMPANY, INC.
35 W. Wacker, Chicago, IL 60601. (312) 220-5959. FAX: (312) 220-6566.
CHAIRMAN
Richard Fizdale
CEO
William Lynch

BURSON-MARSTELLER
230 Park Ave. South, New York, NY 10003-1566. (212) 614-4000. FAX: (212) 598-6942.
CHAIRMAN
Harold Burson

CLEIN & WHITE
8584 Melrose Ave., 2nd fl., W. Hollywood, CA 90069. (310) 659-4141. FAX: (213) 659-3995.
33 W. 54th St., New York, NY 10019. (212) 247-4100.

COMMUNICATIONS PLUS INC.
102 Madison Ave. So., New York, NY 10016. (212) 686-9570.

D'ARCY, MASIUS, BENTON & BOWLES
1675 Broadway, New York, NY 10019-5809. (212) 468-3622. FAX: (212) 468-4385.
6500 Wilshire Blvd., Los Angeles, CA 90048. (213) 658-4500.
CEO
Roy J. Bostock
PRESIDENT
Clayton Wilmite

DENNIS DAVIDSON & ASSOCS. INC.
5670 Wilshire Blvd., Suite 700, Los Angeles, CA 90036. (213) 954-5858.
1776 Broadway, New York, NY 10019. (212) 246-0500.

DDB NEEDHAM WORLDWIDE INC.
437 Madison Ave., New York, NY 10022. (212) 415-2000. FAX: (212) 415-3591.
CHAIRMAN/CEO
Keith Reinhard
PRESIDENT, NY
Ken Kaes

SAMANTHA DEAN & ASSOCS.
36 W. 44 St., New York, NY 10036. (212) 391-2675.

DELLA FEMINA, TRAVISANO & PARTNERS
5900 Wilshire Blvd., #1900, Los Angeles, CA 90036. (310) 937-8540.

DENTSU, INC.
4751 Wilshire Blvd., #203, Los Angeles, CA 90010. (213) 939-3452. FAX: (213) 939-3857.

W. B. DONER & CO.
25900 Northwestern Highway, Southfield, MI 48075. (313) 354-9700. FAX: (313) 827-8448.
2305 N. Charles Street, Baltimore, MD 21218. (301) 338-1600.
PRESIDENT/COO
Alan Kalter

DOREMUS & COMPANY
200 Varick St., 11th & 12th fls., New York, NY 10014. (212) 366-3000. FAX: (212) 366-3632.
PRESIDENT
Carl Anderson
EXECUTIVE V.P., WORLDWIDE CREATIVE DIRECTOR
Rebecca Tudor-Foley

LARRY DORN ASSOCS. INC.
5820 Wilshire Blvd., Suite 306, Los Angeles, CA 90036. (213) 935-6266. FAX: (213) 935-9523.
Larry Dorn, Linda Dorn-Wallerstein, Lucy Kohn.

EARL, PALMER & BROWN
1710 East Franklin Street, Richmond, VA 23223. (804) 775-0700.
CHAIRMAN
Bill Bergman

EDELMAN PUBLIC RELATIONS WORLDWIDE
5670 Wilshire Blvd., #1500, Los Angeles, CA 90048. (213)
857-9100. FAX: (213) 857-9117.

EISAMAN, JOHNS & LAWS INC.
5700 Wilshire Blvd., 6th fl., Los Angeles, CA 90036. (213) 932-
1234. FAX: (213) 965-6134.

MAX EISEN
234 W. 44 St., New York, NY 10036. (212) 391-1072.

EVANS GROUP
110 Social Hall Ave., Salt Lake City, UT 84111. (801) 364-
7452. FAX: (801) 364-7484.
CHAIRMAN/CEO
Donald B. Kraft

FELDMAN PUBLIC RELATIONS
9220 Sunset Blvd., #230, Los Angeles, CA 90069. (310) 859-
9062. FAX: (310) 859-9563.

FOOTE, CONE & BELDING COMMUNICATIONS, INC.
101 East Erie Street, Chicago, IL 60611-2897. (312) 751-7000.
FAX: (312) 751-3501.
CHAIRMAN & CEO
Bruce Mason

B. D. FOX & FRIENDS, INC. ADVERTISING
1111 Broadway, Santa Monica, CA 90401. (310) 394-7150.
FAX: (310) 393-1569.
CEO
Brian D. Fox.

ALBERT FRANK GUENTHER LAW INC.
71 Broadway, New York, NY 10006. (212) 248-5200.
CHAIRMAN
Gary Goldstein
PRESIDENT
James H. Feeney

GS ENTERTAINMENT MARKETING GROUP
8721 Beverly Blvd., Los Angeles, CA 90048. (310) 358-8640.
FAX: (310) 289-1854.
Steven Zeller.

GELFOND, GORDON AND ASSOCIATES
11500 Olympic Blvd., Suite 350, Los Angeles, CA 90064. (310)
478-3600. FAX: (213) 477-4825.

GERBER ADVERTISING AGENCY
209 S.W. Oak St., Portland, OR 97204. (503) 221-0100. FAX:
(503) 228-7471.
PRESIDENT & CEO
Phil Stevens

GOLIN/HARRIS COMMUNICATIONS
500 N. Michigan Ave., Chicago, IL 60611. (312) 836-7100.
FAX: (312) 836-7170.
CHAIRMAN
Alvin Golin
PRESIDENT & CEO
Rich Jerntedt

FRANK GOODMAN
1776 Broadway, New York, NY 10019. (212) 246-4180.

GREY ADVERTISING, INC.
777 Third Ave., New York, NY 10017. (212) 546-2000. FAX:
(212) 546-1495.
CHAIRMAN & CEO
Edward H. Meyer

GREY ENTERTAINMENT & MEDIA
875 Third Ave., New York, NY 10022. (212) 303-2400.

GRISWOLD COMMUNICATIONS, INC.
101 Prospect Ave. West, Cleveland, OH 44115. (216) 696-
3400. FAX: (216) 696-3405.
CHAIRMAN, PRESIDENT & CEO
Patrick J. Morin

GUTTMAN ASSOCIATES
118 S. Beverly Dr., Suite 201, Beverly Hills, CA 90212. (310)
246-4600. FAX: (310) 246-4601.

HANSON & SCHWAM
2020 Ave. of Stars, Suite 410, Los Angeles, CA 90067. (310)
557-1199. FAX: (310) 557-9090.

HODES, BERNARD, ADV. INC.
555 Madison Ave., New York, NY 10022. (212) 758-2600. FAX:
(212) 751-6278.
PRESIDENT & CEO
Bernard S. Hodes

HUTCHINS/YOUNG & RUBICAM
400 Midtown Tower, Rochester, NY 14604. (716) 546-6480.
PRESIDENT & CEO
M.A. Sapos

JACOBS & GERBER INC.
731 N. Fairfax Ave., Los Angeles, CA 90046-7293. (213) 655-
4082. FAX: (213) 655-0195.
PRESIDENT & CEO
Albert B. Litewka

HENRY J. KAUFMAN & ASSOCIATES, INC.
2233 Wisconsin Ave. NW, Washington, DC 20007. (202) 333-
0700.
CHAIRMAN, PRESIDENT & CEO
Michael G. Carberry

KETCHUM COMMUNICATIONS, INC.
Six PPG Place, Pittsburgh, PA 15222. (412) 456-3500.
PRESIDENT, CHAIRMAN & CEO
Paul Alvarez

LANDIN MEDIA INC.
3033 N. 44 St., #375, Phoenix, AZ 85018-7229. (602) 553-
4080. FAX: (602) 553-4090.
PRESIDENT & CEO
Larry L. Cummings

LEE & ASSOCIATES
145 S. Fairfax Ave., Los Angeles, CA 90036. (213) 938-3300.
FAX: (213) 938-3305.

LEVINE, SCHNEIDER, PUBLIC RELATIONS CO.
8730 Sunset Blvd., Los Angeles, CA 90069. (310) 659-6400.
FAX: (310) 659-1309.

LEWIS & ASSOCIATES
3600 Wilshire Blvd., #200, Los Angeles, CA 90010. (213) 739-1000.

LINTAS: WORLDWIDE
One Dag Hammarskjold Plaza, New York, NY 10017-2203.
(212) 605-8000. FAX: (212) 935-2164.
CHAIRMAN & PRESIDENT
Spencer Plavoukos
CHAIRMAN & CEO
Kenneth L. Robbins

LIPPIN GROUP INC.
6100 Wilshire Blvd., #400, Los Angeles, CA 90048. (213) 965-
1990. FAX: (213) 965-1993.

MARCUS ADVERTISING INC.
Landmark Center, 25700 Science Park Dr., Cleveland, OH
44122. (216) 292-4700. FAX: (216) 831-6189.
CHAIRMAN & CEO
Donald M. Marcus

THE MARKETING GROUP
1411 Fifth St., #306, Santa Monica, CA 90401. (310) 393-
5505. FAX: (310) 393-1716.

MCCANN-ERICKSON
750 Third Ave., New York, NY 10017. (212) 697-6000. FAX:
(212) 867-5177.
CHAIRMAN & CEO
Robert L. James
PRESIDENT & COO
John J. Dooner

MELDRUM & FEWSMITH COMMUNICATIONS, INC.
1350 Euclid Ave., Cleveland, OH 44115. (216) 241-2141. FAX:
(216) 479-2437.
CHAIRMAN, CEO & CREATIVE DIRECTOR
Chris Perry

MOMENTUM INTERNATIONAL MARKETING
P.O. Box 5889, Sherman Oaks, CA 91413. (818) 752-4500.
FAX: (818) 752-4554.

MOROCH & ASSOCIATES
3625 N. Hall St., #1200, Dallas, TX 75219. (214) 520-9700.
FAX: (214) 520-6464.
CHAIRMAN
Tom Moroch

JULIAN MYERS PUBLIC RELATIONS
2040 Ave. of the Stars, 4th Fl., Century City, 90067. (213) 557-
1525. FAX: (213) 557-0133.

OGILVY & MATHER INC.
309 W. 49 St., New York, NY 10019. (212) 237-4000. FAX:
(212) 237-5123.
CHAIRMAN
Charlotte Beers

DALE C. OLSON & ASSOCS.
6310 San Vicente Blvd., #340, Los Angeles, CA 90048. (213)
932-6026. FAX: (213) 932-1989.

PMK INC.
955 Carrillo Dr., Suite 200, Los Angeles, CA 90048. (213) 954-
4000. FAX: (213) 954-4011.
1775 Broadway, New York, NY 10019. (212) 582-1111.

POLLACK PR MARKETING GROUP
2049 Century Park E., #2520, Los Angeles, CA 90067. (310) 556-4443. FAX: (310) 556-2350.
President: Noemi Pollock.

PORTER/NOVELLI
12100 Wilshire Blvd., #1800, Los Angeles, CA 90025. (310) 444-7000.

MYRNA POST ASSOCIATES
1650 Broadway, New York, NY10019. (212) 757-5021.

PUBLICITY WEST
2155 Ridgemont Dr., Los Angeles, CA 90046. (213) 654-3816. (818) 954-1951. FAX: (213) 654-6084.

ROGERS & COWAN
1888 Century Park East, Suite 500, Los Angeles, CA 90067-1709. (310) 201-8800. FAX: (310) 552-0412.
475 Park Ave. S., 32nd Fl., New York, NY 10016. (212) 779-3500.

ROSENFELD, SIROWITZ, HUMPHREY & STRAUSS ADVERTISING
111 Fifth Ave., New York, NY 10002. (212) 505-0200. FAX: (212)505-7309.
CO-CHAIRMEN & CEO's
Leonard Sirowitz, Harold Strauss

ROSKIN-FRIEDMAN ASSOCS., INC.
8425 W. 3rd St., #309, Los Angeles, CA 90048. (213) 653-5411. FAX: (213) 653-5474.
PRESIDENT
Monroe Friedman.
72 Reade St., New York, NY 10007. (212) 385-0005. FAX: (212) 385-0951.
PRESIDENT
Sheldon Roskin

ROSS ROY COMMUNICATIONS
100 Bloomfield Hills Pkwy., Bloomfield Hills, MI 48304. (313) 433-6000. FAX: (313): (313) 433-6421.
CHAIRMAN, PRESIDENT & CEO
Peter Mills

SAATCHI & SAATCHI ADVERTISING
375 Hudson St., New York, NY 10014-3620. (212) 463-2000. FAX: (212) 463-9855.
CHAIRMAN & COO
Harvey Hoffenberg
PRESIDENT & COO
Michael Keeshan

SAATCHI & SAATCHI/THE SAATCHI ENTERTAINMENT GROUP
3501 Sepulveda Blvd., Torrance, CA 90505. (310) 214-6000. FAX: (310) 214-6008.
DIRECTOR
Alfa Tate-O'Neill.

NANCY SELTZER & ASSOCS.
1775 Broadway, New York, NY 10019. (212) 307-0117.

SIMONS MICHELSON ZIEVE INC.
900 Wilshire Dr., Troy, MI 48084-1600. (313) 362-4242. FAX: (313) 362-2014.
CHAIRMAN
Morton Zieve

SUDLER & HENNESSEY INC.
1633 Broadway, New York, NY 10019. (212) 696-5800. FAX: (212) 969-5991.
CHAIRMAN, PRESIDENT & CEO
Willliam B. Gibson

TARGET & RESPONSE
420 N. Wabash Ave., Chicago, IL 60610. (312) 573-0500. FAX: (312) 573-0516.
PRESIDENT/GENERAL MANAGER
Lawrence Levis

TATHAM EURO RSCG
980 N. Michigan Ave., Chicago, IL 60611. (312) 337-4400. FAX: (312) 337-5930.
CHAIRMAN & CEO
Ralph Rydholm

J. WALTER THOMPSON COMPANY
466 Lexington Ave., New York, NY 10017. (212) 210-7000. FAX: (212) 210-6889.
CHAIRMAN & CEO
Burt Manning

TIERNEY & PARTNERS
200 S. Broad St., Philadelphia, PA 19102. (215) 790-4100. FAX: (215) 790-4363.
PRESIDENT & CEO
Brian P. Tierney
S.V.P., MEDIA DIRECTOR
William Melnick

TRACY-LOCKE ADVERTISING INC.
200 Crescent Ct., Dallas, TX 75250. (214) 969-9000.
PRESIDENT & CEO
Michael S. Rawlings

TUCKER WAYNE/LUCKIE & CO.
1100 Peachtree St., N.E., Suite 1800, Atlanta, GA 30309. (404) 347-8700. FAX: (404) 347-8800.
CHAIRMAN & CEO
Knox Massey, Jr.
PRESIDENT
Sidney L. Smith

MORTON D. WAX PUBLIC RELATIONS
1560 Broadway, New York, NY 10019. (212) 302-5360. FAX: (212) 302-5364. e-mail: 72124.250@compuserve.com
PRESIDENT
Morton D. Wax

WELLS, RICH, GREENE B.D.D.P. COMMUNICATIONS, INC.
9 W. 57 St., New York, NY 10019. (212) 303-5000. FAX: (212) 303-5040.
CHAIRMAN & CEO
Ken Olshan

WORLDWIDE INTELLIGENCE
9437 Santa Monica Blvd., #202, Beverly Hills, CA 90210. (310) 205-2828. FAX: (310) 205-2820.

YOUNG & RUBICAM INC.
285 Madison Ave., New York, NY 10017-6486. (212) 210-3000. FAX (212) 490-9073.
CHAIRMAN
Alexander S. Kroll
PRESIDENT & CEO
Peter A. Georgescu

ANIMATION

ABRAMS/GENTILE ENTERTAINMENT
244 W. 54th St., 9th Floor, New York, NY 10019. (212) 757-0700.
PRESIDENT
John Gentile

AMBLIMATION
(see Dreamworks)

ANGEL FILMS
967 Highway 40, New Franklin, MO 65274. (573) 698-3900.
PRESIDENT
William H. Hoehne, Jr.

ANIMOTION
501 W. Fayette St., Syracuse, NY 13204. (315) 471-3533. FAX: (315) 475-1969.
David Hicock, Larry Royer.

ATOMIX
1800 North Vine Street, Suite 310, Hollywood, CA 90028. (310) 962-4745.
PRESIDENT
Chris Mitchell

BAER ANIMATION COMPANY INC.
3765 Cahuenga Blvd. West, Studio City, CA 91604. (818) 760-8666. FAX: 818-760-9698.
PRESIDENT
Jane Baer

BAGDASARIAN PRODS.
1192 East Mountain Drive, Montecito, CA 93108. (805) 969-3349.
CEO
Ross Bagdasarian

BILL MELENDEZ PRODUCTIONS
439 N. Larchmont Ave., Los Angeles, CA 90004. (213) 463-4101.
PRESIDENT
Bill Melendez

BLUE SKY PRODUCTIONS, INC.
100 Executive Boulevard., Ossining, NY 10562. (914) 941-5260.
PRESIDENT
David Brown

BLUR STUDIO, INC.
1130 Abbot Kinney Blvd., Venice, CA 90291. (310) 581-8848.
EXECUTIVE PRODUCER
Cat Chapman

BOBTOWN
2003 Canyon Drive, Hollywood, CA 90068. (213) 462-6116.
PRESIDENT
John Lamb

BOHBOT ENTERTAINMENT
41 Madison Avenue, New York, NY 10010. (212) 213-2700.
PRESIDENT
Allen J. Bohbot

BROADWAY VIDEO DESIGN
1619 Broadway, 4th Floor, New York, NY 10019. (212) 333-0500.
VICE PRESIDENT
Peter Rosnick

BUZZCO ASSOCIATES INC.
33 Bleecker St., New York, NY 10012. (212) 473-8800. FAX: (212) 473-8891. e-mail: BUZZCO@aol.com
Candy Kugel

CALABASH PRODUCTIONS
657 West Ohio, Chicago, IL 60610. (312) 243-3433. FAX: 312-243-6227.
EXEUCTIVE PRODUCER
Monica Kendall

CALICO LTD.
9340 Eton Ave., Chatsworth, CA 91311-5879. (818) 407-5200. FAX: (818) 407-5323.
PRESIDENT & CEO
Tom Burton

THE CALVERT COMPANY
5050 Tujunga Ave., Suite 5, N. Hollywood, CA 91601. (818) 760-8700.
PRESIDENT
Fred Calvert

CELLULOID STUDIOS
2128 15th Street, Denver, CO 80202. (303) 595-3152.
EXECUTIVE PRODUCER
Olivier Katz

CHELSEA ANIMATION COMPANY
3035A W. Cary St., Richmond, VA 23221. (804) 353-0793.
PRESIDENT
John O'Donnell

CHIODO BROTHERS PRODUCTIONS, INC.
425 S. Flower St., Burbank, CA 91502. (818) 842-5656.
PRESIDENT
Stephen Chiodo

CHUCK JONES FILM PRODUCTIONS
4000 Warner Blvd., Bldg. 131, Burbank, CA 91522. (818) 954-2655.
Linda Jones Clough

CHURCHILL MEDIA
6917 Valjean Ave., Van Nuys, CA 91406-4716. (818) 778-1978.
DIRECTOR, PRODUCT DEVELOPMENT
George Holland

CINAR FILMS (U.S.) INC.
9350 Wilshire Blvd., Suite 400, Beverly Hills, CA 90212. (310) 285-7400. e-mail: CinarFilms@aol.com
V.P., DEVELOPMENT & PRODUCTION
Sam Wendel
1055 Rene Levesque Blvd. E., Montreal, Quebec, Canada H2L 4S5. (514) 843-7070. FAX: (514) 843-7080.
PRESIDENT
Ronald A. Weinberg

CINEPIX ANIMATION
900 Broadway, Suite 800, New York, NY 10003. (212) 995-9662. FAX: (212) 475-2284.
V.P., BUSINESS AFFAIRS
John J. Graves

CLASS 6 ENTERTAINMENT
6777 Hollywood Blvd., 7th Floor, Hollywood, CA 90028. (213) 465-0300.

EXECUTIVE PRODUCER
Reuben Frias

COFFEY/BALLANTINE
10202 W. Washington Blvd., SPP 3650, Culver City, CA 90232. (310) 280-6585.
PRESIDENT
Vanessa Coffey, Jim Coffey

COLOSSAL PICTURES
2800 3rd. St., San Francisco, CA 94107. (415) 550-8772.
PRESIDENT
Drew Takahashi

CORNELL/ABOOD
4400 Coldwater Canyon Ave., Suite 100, Studio City, CA 91604. (818) 508-1215.
ASSOCIATE PRODUCER
Karen Inwood

CURIOUS PICTURES
440 Lafayette, New York, NY 10003. (212) 674-1400.
EXECUTIVE PRODUCER
Richard Winkler

D'OCON FILMS
3694 Barham Blvd., Suite F-203, Los Angeles, CA 90068. (213) 878-6648.
MANAGING DIRECTOR
Robert Mitrani

DADDY-O PRODUCTIONS
6051 Alcott Ave., Van Nuys, CA 91401. (818) 782-1930.
Tom McLaughlin

DIC ENTERTAINMENT
202 N. Glen Oaks Blvd., Burbank, CA 91502. (818) 955-5400.
PRESIDENT
Andy Heyward

DREAMWORKS FEATURE ANIMATION
100 Universal City Plaza, Bldg. 601, Universal City, CA 91608. (818) 733-6000.
PRODUCTION CHIEF
Sandy Rabins

DREAMWORKS TELEVISION ANIMATION
(see address above). (818) 733-7500.
PRODUCTION CHIEF
Stephanie Graziano

ENCORE ENTERPRISES
25510 Stanford Ave., Suite 101, Valencia, CA 91355. (805) 295-0675.
PRESIDENT
Bill Hutton

ENOKI FILMS U.S.A., INC.
16501 Venture Blvd., Suite 606, Encino, CA 91436. (818) 907-6503.
Ricki Ames

FILM ROMAN, INC.
12020 Chandler Blvd., Suite 200, North Hollywood, CA 91607. (818) 761-2544.
PRESIDENT
Phil Roman

FLEISCHER STUDIOS, INC.
10160 Cielo Dr., Beverly Hills, CA 90210. (310) 276-7503.
PRESIDENT
Richard Fleischer

FLINT PRODUCTIONS INC.
1015 N. Orlando, Los Angeles, CA 90069. (213) 654-0503. FAX: (213) 848-9637.
Roger Flint

FOX ANIMATION STUDIOS
2747 E. Camelback Rd., Phoenix, AZ 85016. (602) 808-4600.
EXECUTIVE VICE PRESIDENT
Steve Brain

FRED WOLF FILMS
4222 W. Burbank Blvd., Burbank, CA 91505. (818) 846-0611.
PRESIDENT
Fred Wolf

GATEWAYS TO SPACE
5976 W. Las Positas, Suite 122, Pleasanton, CA 94588. (510) 847-2777.
PRESIDENT
Louis Karagochos

GRACIE FILMS
10202 W. Washington Blvd., Sidney Poitier Bldg., #2221, Culver City, CA 90232.
PRESIDENT
Richard Sakai

GREATEST TALES
22477 MacFarlane Dr., Woodland Hills, CA 90024. (310) 446-6000.
PRESIDENT
Fred Ladd

GROUP W PRODUCTIONS
10877 Wilshire Blvd., Los Angeles, CA 90024. (310) 446-6000.
PRESIDENT
Derk Zimmerman

GUNTHER-WAHL PRODUCTIONS
6345 Balboa Blvd., Suite 285, Encino, CA 91316. (818) 776-9200. FAX: 818-776-9293.
PRESIDENT
Michael Wahl

HALLMARK
1235 Avenue of the Americas, 21st Fl., New York, NY 10019. (212) 977-9001.
SENIOR VICE PRESIDENT
Joel Denton

HANNA-BARBERA PRODUCTIONS
3400 Cahuenga Blvd., Hollywood, CA 90068. (213) 851-5000.
PRESIDENT
Fred Seibert

HARVEY ENTERTAINMENT
100 Wilshire Blvd., 14th Fl., Santa Monica, CA 90401-1110. (310) 451-3377. FAX: (310) 458-6995.
PRESIDENT
Jeffrey Montgomery

HEARST ANIMATION PRODUCTIONS
1640 S. Sepulveda Blvd., Los Angeles, CA 90025. (310) 478-1700.
PRESIDENT
Wiliam Miller

HEART OF TEXAS PRODUCTIONS
2600 Dellana Lane, Suite 100, Austin, TX 78746. (512) 329-8262.
PRESIDENT
Don Smith

JIM HENSON PRODUCTIONS
c/o Raleigh Studios, 5358 Melrose Ave., West Bldg., 3rd Floor, Hollywood, CA 90038. (213) 960-4096.
PRESIDENT
Brian Henson

HUBLEY STUDIO
2575 Palisade Ave., Riverdale, NY 10463. (718) 543-5958.
Faith Hubley

HYPERION ANIMATION
111 N. Maryland Ave., Suite 200, Glendale, CA 91206. (818) 244-4704.
PRESIDENT
Tom Wilhite

I.N.I ENTERTAINMENT GROUP, INC.
11845 Olympic Blvd., Suite 1145W, Los Angeles, CA 90064. (310) 479-6755.
CEO
Irv Hollender

ICE TEA PRODUCTIONS
160 E. 38 St., #15-G, New York, NY 10016. (212) 557-8185.
Richard Durkin

IMAGINATION STUDIOS
11684 Ventura Blvd., Suite 144, Studio City, CA 91604. (310) 633-4230.
CEO
Dana Blanchard

THE INK TANK
2 W. 47th St., New York, NY 10036. (212) 869-1630.
EXECUTIVE PRODUCER
Brian O'Connell

ITC
9100 Wilshire Blvd., Suite 600 West, Beverly Hills, CA 90212. (310) 724-8100.
PRESIDENT
Jules Haimovitz

J.J. SEDELMAIER PRODUCTIONS, INC.
199 Main St., 10th Floor, White Plains, NY 10601. (914) 949-7979.
PRESIDENT
J.J. Sedelmaier

JETLAG PRODUCTIONS
15315 Magnolia Blvd., Suite 310, Sherman Oaks, CA 91403. (818) 385-3400.
PRESIDENT
Jean Chalopin

JUMBO PICTURES
75 Spring St., 6th Floor, New York, NY 10012. (212) 226-7890.
Jim Jinkins

KLASY-CSUPO, INC.
1258 N. Highland Ave., Hollywood, CA 90038. (213) 463-0145.
PRESIDENT
Terry Thoren

KOOKANOOGA TOONS
12754 Ventura Blvd., Suite D, Studio City, CA 91604. (818) 841-9900.
PRODUCTION MANAGER
Molly Bradford

THE KRISLIN COMPANY
23901 Calabasas Road, Suite 1501, Calabasas, CA 91302. (818) 222-0555.
PRESIDENT
Walt Kubiak

KURTZ & FRIENDS
2312 W. Olive Ave., Burbank, CA 91506. (818) 841-8188.
PRESIDENT
Bob Kurtz

L.A. ANIMATION
2920 W. Olive Ave., Burbank, CA 91505. (818) 563-2300.
PRESIDENT
Lyn Henderson

JERRY LIEBERMAN PRODUCTIONS
76 Laight Street, New York, NY 10013. (212) 431-3452. FAX: (212) 941-8976.
Jerry Lieberman

M3D PRODUCTIONS
18520 Arminta Dr., Van Nuys, CA 91406. (818) 785-6662.
PRESIDENT
Marcel Nottea

MARVEL FILMS ANIMATION
1440 S. Sepulveda Blvd., Los Angeles, CA 90025. (310) 444-8644. FAX: (310) 444-8168.
PRESIDENT
Avi Arad

MATINEE ENTERTAINMENT
345 N. Maple Dr., Suite 285, Beverly Hills, CA 90210. (310) 246-9044. FAX: (310) 246-9066.
PRESIDENT
Michael I. Yanover

MATTHEWS PRODUCTIONS
P.O. Box 74, Cedar Glen, CA 92321. (909) 867-5068.
PRODUCER
John Clark Matthews

MEDIAMAX PRODUCTIONS
9538 Brighton Way, Beverly Hills, CA 90210. (310) 285-0550.
PRESIDENT
Frederick Ittah

METROLIGHT STUDIOS
5724 W. 3rd St., Suite 400, Los Angeles, CA 90036-3078. (213) 932-0400.
PRESIDENT
James W. Kristoff

MGM ANIMATION
2500 Broadway St., Santa Monica, CA 90404. (310) 449-3795.
GENERAL MANAGER
Don Mirisch

MICHAEL SPORN ANIMATION, INC.
632 Broadway, 4th Floor, New York, NY 10012. (212) 228-3372.
PRESIDENT
Michael Sporn

MIKE YOUNG PRODUCTIONS
20315 Ventura Blvd., Suite B, Woodland Hills, CA 91364. (818) 999-0062.
PRESIDENT
Mike Young

MOON MESA MEDIA
P.O. Box 7848, Northridge, CA 91327. (818) 360-6224.
PRESIDENT
Sheryl Hardy

MORGAN CREEK PRODUCTIONS
4000 Warner Blvd., Bldg. 76, Burbank, CA 91522. (818) 954-4800.
Brian Robinson

MTM ENTERPRISES
12700 Ventura Blvd., Studio City, CA 91604. (818) 755-2400.
PRESIDENT
Tony Thomopolous

MTV ANIMATION
15 Columbus Circle, 40th Floor, New York, NY 10023. (212) 373-6710.
VICE PRESIDENT
John Andrews

MUSIVISION
195 E. 85th St., New York, NY 10028. (212) 860-4420.
Fred Kessler

NELVANA COMMUNICATIONS, INC.
4500 Wilshire Blvd., 1st Floor, Los Angeles, CA 90010. (213) 549-4222.
SENIOR VICE PRESIDENT
Toper Taylor

NEST ENTERTAINMENT
333 North Glenoaks Blvd., 3rd Floor, Burbank, CA 91502. (818) 846-9850.
SENIOR VICE PRESIDENT
Don Barrett

NEW WORLD ANIMATION
3340 Ocean Park Blvd., Santa Monica, CA 90405. (310) 444-8113.
PRESIDENT
Rick Unger

NICKELODEON
1440 S. Sepulveda Blvd., Los Angeles, CA 91607. (818) 753-3255.
VICE PRESIDENT
Mary Harrington

OPTICAM INC.
810 Navy St., Santa Monica, CA 90405. (310) 396-4665. FAX: (310) 452-0040.
Nancy Harris

OVATION/ANIMATION
9 Caccamo St., Westport, CT 06880. (203) 227-9346.
Art Petricone

PACIFIC DATA IMAGES
1111 Karlstad Drive, Sunnyvale, CA 94089. (408) 745-6755.
PRESIDENT
Carl Rosendahl

PERENNIAL PICTURES FILM CORP.
2102 E. 52nd St., Indianapolis, IN 46205. (317) 253-1519.
PRESIDENT
Jerry Reynolds

PIXAR ANIMATION STUDIOS
1001 W. Cutting Blvd., Point Richmond, CA 94804. (510) 236-4000.
EXECUTIVE VICE PRESIDENT
Ed Catmull

PLAYLIGHT PICTURES
1401 N. La Brea Ave., Hollywood, CA 90028. (213) 851-2112.
DIRECTOR
Ted Wooley

POLESTAR FILMS
231 W. 29th St., Suite 203, New York, NY 10001. (212) 268-2088.
Don Duga, Irra Verbitsky

PORCHLIGHT ENTERTAINMENT
11828 LaGrange Ave., Los Angeles, CA 90025. (310) 477-8400.
PRESIDENT
Bruce Johnson

QUARTER STAR PRODUCTIONS, INC.
7216 Park Rd., Charlotte, NC 28210. (704) 554-7127.
PRESIDENT
Patrick W. May

RED APPLE FILMS
14011 Ventura Blvd., Sherman Oaks, CA 91423. (818) 906-7299.
Boris Chacham

R/GREENBERG ASSOC. INC.
350 W. 39th St., New York, NY 10018. (212) 946-4000. FAX: (212) 946-4010.
Michael di Girolamo

RHYTHM N'HUES
5404 Jandy Place, Los Angeles, CA 90066. (310) 448-7500.
PRESIDENT
John Hughes

RICH ANIMATION STUDIOS
333 N. Glenoaks Blvd., 3rd Floor, Burbank, CA 91502. (818) 846-0166.
Tom Tobin

RICK REINERT PICTURES, INC.
32107 Lindero Canyon Rd., Suite 224, Westlake Village, CA 91361. (818) 889-8977.
PRESIDENT
Rick Reinert

RUBY-SPEARS PRODUCTIONS
710 S. Victory Blvd., Suite 201, Burbank, CA 91502. (818) 840-1234.
PRESIDENT
Joe Ruby

SABAN ENTERTAINMENT
10960 Wilshire Blvd., Suite 2400, Los Angeles, CA 90024. (310) 235-5100.
PRESIDENT
Haim Saban

7TH LEVEL
900 Allen Ave., Glendale, CA 91201. (818) 547-1955.
V.P., ANIMATION
Dan Kuenster

SHERWOOD ANIMATION
346 N. Kanan Rd., Suite 202, Agura Hills, CA 91304. (818) 879-1668.
David Egbert

SILVERLINE PICTURES
11846 Ventura Blvd., Suite 100, Studio City, CA 91604. (818) 752-3730.
PRESIDENT
Axel Munch

SINGLE FRAME FILMS
437-1/2 N. Genessee Ave., Los Angeles, CA 90036. (213) 655-2664.
Gary Schwartz

SKELLINGTON PRODUCTIONS
375 Seventh St., San Francisco, CA 94103. (415) 864-2846.
PRESIDENT
Henry Selick

SONY PICTURES IMAGEWORKS
10202 W. Washington Blvd., TriStar Bldg., Suite 207, Culver City, CA 90232. (310) 280-7600.
SENIOR VICE PRESIDENT
Bill Birrell

SPUMCO INC.
5625 Melrose Ave., Hollywood, CA 80038. (213) 462-2943.
PRESIDENT
John Kricfalusi

ST PRODUCTIONS
2041 Manning St., Burbank, CA 91505. (818) 846-3939. FAX: (818) 846-2530.

STARTOONS, INC.
P.O. Box 1232, Homewood, IL 60430. (708) 335-3535. FAX: (708) 339-3999.
EXECUTIVE PRODUCER
Christine McLenahan

STREAMLINE PICTURES
2908 Nebraska Ave., Santa Monica, CA 90404. (310) 998-0070.
PRESIDENT
Carl Macek

STRIBLING PRODUCTIONS
6528 Carnellia Ave., N. Hollywood, CA 91606. (818) 509-0748.
PRESIDENT
Mike Stribling

SUNBOW PRODUCTIONS
100 5th Ave., New York, NY 10011. (212) 886-4900. FAX: (212) 366-4242.
PRESIDENT
C.J. Kettler

TANDEM COMMUNICATIONS
9000 Sunset Blvd., Penthouse, Los Angeles, CA 90069. (310) 859-2941.
PRESIDENT
Joseph Perez

TAWEEL-LOOS & CO. ENTERTAINMENT
3965 Carpenter Ave., Studio City, CA 91604. (818) 760-2222.
George Taweel

TMS/KYOKUICHI CORPORATION
15760 Ventura Blvd., Suite 700, Encino, CA 91436. (818) 905-8881.
Andrew Berman

TOEI ANIMATION CO., LTD.
444 W. Ocean Blvd., Suite 1000, Long Beach, CA 90802. (310) 901-2444.
Mary Jo Winchester

TOON MAKERS, INC.
16007 Knapp St., North Hills, CA 91343. (818) 766-2460.
EXECUTIVE PRODUCER
Ricky Solotoff

THE TOONIVERSAL CO.
6324 Variel Ave., Suite 318, Woodland Hills, CA 91367. (818)
884-2374. FAX: 818-884-2259.
PRESIDENT
Igor Meglic

TURNER FEATURE ANIMATION
3330 Cahuenga Blvd., 2nd Floor, Los Angeles, CA 90068.
(213) 436-3100.
Michelle Lynskey

UNITED MEDIA
330 Primrose Rd., Suite 310, Burlingame, CA 94010. (415)
342-8284.
DIRECTOR
Lee Mendelson

UNIVERSAL CARTOON STUDIOS
100 Universal City Plaza, Universal City, CA 91608. (818)
777-1000.
PRESIDENT
Jeff Segal

UPA PRODUCTIONS OF AMERICA
14101 Valleyheart Dr., Sherman Oaks, CA 91423. (818)
990-3800.
PRESIDENT
Hank Saperstein

VIDE-U PRODUCTIONS
9976 Westwanda Dr., Beverly Hills, CA 90210. (310) 276-
5509. FAX: (310) 276-1183.
Bradley Freeman

WALT DISNEY FEATURE ANIMATION
500 S. Buena Vista Dr., Burbank, CA 91512. (818) 560-8000.
PRESIDENT
Peter Schneider

WALT DISNEY TELEVISION ANIMATION
(see address above)
PRESIDENT
Dean Valentine

WARNER BROS. FEATURE ANIMATION
500 N. Brand St. Glendale, CA 91203-1923. (818) 977-
7600.
PRESIDENT
Max Howard

WARNER BROS. TELEVISION ANIMATION
15303 Ventura Blvd., Suite 1200, Sherman Oaks, CA 91403.
(818) 977-8700.
PRESIDENT
Jean MacCurdy

WILL VINTON STUDIOS
1400 N. W. 22nd Ave., Portland, OR 97210. (503) 225-1130.
Will Vinton

WORLDWIDE SPORTS
345 North Maple Dr., Suite 285, Beverly Hills, CA 90210. (310)
246-9044.
PRESIDENT
Norman J. Singer

WSE FILMS, INC.
1700 Broadway, Suite 1202, Denver, CO 80290-1201. (303)
831-1275.
PRESIDENT
Norman J. Singer

ZEN ENTERTAINMENT
1323-A 3rd St. Promenade, Santa Monica, CA 90401.
(310) 451-1361.
Peter Keefe

CASTING SERVICES

BRAMSON & ASSOC.
7400 Beverly Blvd., Los Angeles, CA 90036. (213) 938-3595.
FAX: (213) 938-0852.

THE CASTING COMPANY
7461 Beverly Blvd., PH, Los Angeles, CA 90036-2704. (213)
938-0700.
Janet & Michael Hirshenson

CASTING SOCIETY OF AMERICA
6565 Sunset Blvd., Suite 306, Los Angeles, CA 90028. (213)
463-1925.

CENTRAL CASTING
1700 W. Burbank Blvd., Burbank, CA 91506. (818) 569-5200.
FAX: (818) 562-2786.

ENTERTAINMENT PARTNERS
3601 W. Olive Ave., 8th fl., Burbank, CA 91505. (818) 955-
6000. FAX: (818) 845-6507.

DANNY GOLDMAN & ASSOCIATES CASTING
1006 N. Cole Ave., Los Angeles, CA 90038. (213) 463-1600.
FAX: (213) 463-3139.

MEDIA CASTING
23391 Mulholland Dr., #477, Woodland, CA 91364. (800) 859-
8422.

NEW AGE CASTING
7471 Melrose Ave., #23, W. Hollywood, CA 90046-7551. (213)
782-6968.

PAGANO, BIALY, MANWILLER
c/o 20th Century Fox, 10201 W. Pico, Trailer 67, Los Angeles,
CA 90035. (213) 871-0051.

PRIME CASTING
7060 Hollywood Blvd., #1025, Hollywood, CA 90028. (213)
962-0377. FAX: (213) 465-1667.

RAINBOW CASTING
12501 Chandler Blvd., #206, N. Hollywood, CA 91607. (818)
752-2278. FAX: (818) 752-6580.
1282 Vallecita Dr., Santa Fe, NM 87501. (505) 268-9315. FAX:
(505) 255-9801.
Theresa Neptune

MARY JO SLATER CASTING
2401 Colorado, 3rd Fl., Santa Monica, CA 90404. (310) 449-
3695.

RON SMITH RON CELEBRITY LOOK-ALIKES
7060 Hollywood Blvd., #1215, Hollywood, CA 90028. (213)
467-3030. FAX: (213) 467-6720.

LYNN STALMASTER, & ASSOCIATES
5005 Sepulveda Blvd., Suite 600, Los Angeles, CA 90049.
(310) 552-0983.

VOICECASTER
1832 W. Burbank Blvd., Burbank, CA 91506-1348. (818) 841-
5300. FAX: (818) 841-2085.
MANAGER
Lisa Dyson

CONSULTANTS & TECHNICAL SERVICES

BENNER MEDICAL
(Medical consultants on set)
601 W. 26 St., New York, NY 10001. (212) 727-9815.

BIGGS-ADAMS
(Union Labor Consultant)
8019 Corbin Ave., Canoga Park, CA 91306. (818) 349-4057.
FAX: (818) 993-8642.

BOOZ, ALLEN & HAMILTON INC.
(Strategy, reorganization for companies)
101 Park Ave., New York, NY 10178. (212) 697-1900.

BROADCAST BUSINESS CONSULTANTS, LTD.
(Talent payment and residuals)
317 Madison Ave., New York, NY 10017. (212) 687-3525. FAX:
949-9143.

PAUL BRONSTON, M.D.
(Medical Adviser)
1 Jib St., #202, Marina Del Rey, CA 90292. (310) 301-9426.

CONSULTANTS FOR TALENT PAYMENT INC.
(Talent payment and residuals)
22 W. 27 St., New York, NY 10001. (212) 696-1100.

COUNCIL OF CONSULTING ORGANIZATIONS
521 Fifth Ave., 35th fl., New York, NY 10175. (212) 697-8262.

DALE SYSTEM INC.
1101 Stewart Ave., Garden City, NY 11530. (516) 794-2800.
FAX: (516) 542-1083.
250 W. 57 St., New York, NY 10107. (212) 586-1320.
PRESIDENT
Harvey M. Yaffe

CURT DECKERT ASSOCS. INC.
(Technical management consultants)

18061 Darmel Pl., Santa Ana, CA 92705. (714) 639-0746.
FAX: (714) 639-0746.

DEWITT MEDIA INC.
(Media consulting, advertising planning and buying)
460 Park Ave. S., 10th Fl., New York, NY 10106. (212) 545-0120.

IMERO FIORENTINO ASSOCIATES
(Lighting consultants)
33 W. 60 St., New York, NY 10023. (212) 246-0600. FAX: (212)
246-6408.
P.R. DIRECTOR
Angela Linsell

NINA FOCH STUDIOS
(Creative consultant)
P.O. Box 1884, Beverly Hills, CA 90213. (310) 553-5805. FAX:
(310) 553-6149.
Maud Valot

MARSHALL/PLUMB RESEARCH ASSOCIATES
(Legal research, script clearances)
4150 Riverside Dr., Suite 209, Burbank, CA 91505. (818) 848-
7071.

MIRIMAR ENTERPRISES
(Script consultants)
P.O. Box 4621, N. Hollywood, CA 91607. (818) 784-4177. FAX:
(818) 990-3439.
Mirk Mirkin

ROSS-GAFFNEY
(Assembling production crews)
21 W. 46 St., New York, NY 10036. (212) 719-2744.

SECOND LINE SEARCH
(Stock footage researchers)
1926 Bdwy., New York, NY 10023. (212) 787-7500.

COSTUME & PROP RENTALS

ABRAHAM RUGS GALLERY
525 N. La Cienega Blvd., Los Angeles, CA 90048. (310) 652-
6520. (800) 222-RUGS.

ADELE'S OF HOLLYWOOD
5034 Hollywood Blvd., Los Angeles, 90027. (213) 663-2231.
FAX: (213) 663-2232.

AGAPE UNIFORM CO.
3606 W. Washington Blvd., Los Angeles, CA 90018. (213) 731-
0621. FAX: (213) 731-0690.

AIM PROMOTIONS
Kaufman Astoria Studios, 34-12 36th St., Astoria, Queens, NY
11106. (718) 729-9288.

ALLAN UNIFORM RENTAL SERVICE INC.
121 E. 24 St., New York, NY 10010. (212) 529-4655.

WALTER ALLEN PLANT RENTALS
4996 Melrose Ave., Los Angeles, CA 90029-3738. (213) 469-
3621.

ALTMAN LUGGAGE
135 Orchard St., New York, NY 10002. (212) 254-7275.

AMERICAN COSTUME CORP.
12980 Raymer St., North Hollywood, CA 91605. (818) 764-
2239. FAX: (213) 765-7614.

ANIMAL MAKERS
2250 Turquoise, Newbury Park, CA 91320. (805) 499-9779.
FAX: (805) 499-3454.

ANIMAL OUTFITS FOR PEOPLE CO.
2255 Broadway, New York, NY 10024. (212) 877-5085.

ANTIQUARIAN TRADERS
9031 W. Olympic Blvd., Beverly Hills, CA 90211. (310) 247-
3900. FAX: (310) 247-8864.

399 Lafayette St., New York NY 10003. (212) 260-1200. FAX:
(212) 529-5320.

ANTIQUE & CLASSIC AUTOS
811 Union St., Brooklyn, NY 11215. (718) 788-3400.
Leonard Shiller

ANTIQUE & CLASSIC CAR RENTALS
611 1/2 W. Vernon Ave., Los Angeles, CA 90037. (213) 232-
7211.

ANTIQUE GUILD
8800 Venice Blvd., Los Angeles, CA 90034. (310) 838-3131.
FAX: (310) 287-2486.

ARENSON OFFICE FURNISHINGS
315 E. 62 St., New York, NY 10021. (212) 838-8880.

ARTS & CRAFTERS INC.
175 Johnson St., Brooklyn, NY 11201. (718) 875-8151.

BEDFELLOWS
12250 Ventura Blvd., Sherman Oaks, CA 91604. (818) 985-
0500. FAX: (818) 985-0617.

THE BRUBAKER GROUP
10560 Dolcedo Way, Los Angeles, CA 90077. (310) 472-4766.

BUENA VISTA STUDIOS
500 S. Buena Vista St., Burbank, CA 91521. (818) 560-1056.

CAL-EAST WIGS
232 S. Beverly Dr., #211, Beverly Hills, CA 90212. (310) 270-
4720.

CAMERA READY CARS
11161 Slater Ave., Fountain Valley, CA 92708. (714) 444-1700.

CARTHAY SET SERVICES
5907 West Pico Blvd., Los Angeles, CA 90038. (213) 938-
2101.

CENTRAL PROPERTIES
514 W. 49 St., 2nd Floor, New York, NY 10019. (212) 265-7767.

CENTRE FIREARMS CO, INC.
10 W. 37 St., New York, NY 10018. (212) 244-4040, (212) 244-4044. FAX: (212) 947-1233.

CINEMAFLOAT
1624 W. Ocean Front, Newport Beach, CA 92663. (714) 675-8888.

CLASSIC CARS LEASING CO.
500 Park Ave., New York, NY 10022. (212) 752-8080.

CLASSIC CAR SUPPLIERS
1905 Sunset Plaza Dr., W. Hollywood, CA 90069. (310) 657-7823.

CONTINENTAL SCENERY
7802 Clybourn Ave., Sun Valley, CA 91352. (818) 768-8075.

COOPER FILM CARS
132 Perry, New York, NY 10014. (212) 929-3909.

COSTUME ARMOUR INC.
2 Mill St., Cornwall, NY 12518. (914) 534-9120.

THE COSTUME PLACE
3117 Hamilton Way, Los Angeles, CA 90029. (213) 661-2597.

COSTUME RENTALS CO.
1149 Vanowen St., North Hollywood, CA 91605. (818) 753-3700. FAX: (818) 753-3737.

ELIZABETH COURTNEY COSTUMES
431 S. Fairfax Ave., 3rd fl., Los Angeles, CA 90036. (213) 937-0184.

CREATIVE COSTUME CO.
330 W. 38 St., New York, NY 10018. (212) 564-5552.

CUSTOM CHARACTERS
621 Thompson Ave., Glendale, CA 91201-2032. (818) 507-5940. FAX: (818) 507-1619.

DARROW'S FUN ANTIQUES
11011 First Ave., New York, NY 10021. (212) 838-0730.

DAVID'S OUTFITTERS, INC.
36 W. 20 St., New York, NY 10011. (212) 691-7388.

WALT DISNEY STUDIOS
500 S. Buena Vista St., Burbank, CA 91521. (818) 560-0044.

DOMSEY INTERNATIONAL SALES CORP.
431 Kent Ave., Brooklyn, NY 11211. (800) 221-RAGS. (718) 384-6000.

DOZAR OFFICE FURNITURE
9937 Jefferson Blvd., Culver City, CA 90232. (310) 559-9292. FAX: (310) 559-9009.

E. C. 2 COSTUMES
4019 Tujunga Ave., Studio City, CA 91604. (818) 506-7695. FAX: (818) 506-077

EASTERN COSTUME
7243 Coldwater Canyon, N. Hollywood, CA 91605. (818) 982-3611. FAX: (818) 503-1913.

EAVES-BROOKS COSTUME CO., INC.
21-07 41st Ave., Long Island City, NY 11101. (718) 729-1010.

ECLECTIC ENCORE PROPERTIES INC.
620 W. 26 St., 4th floor, New York, NY 10001. (212) 645-8880. FAX: (212) 243-6508.
James Gill

ELLIS MERCANTILE CO.
169 N. La Brea Ave., Los Angeles, CA 90036. (213) 933-7334. FAX: (213) 930-1268.

ENVIRION VISION
3074 Whaleneck Dr., Merrick, NY 11566. (516) 378-2250.

EXPENDABLE SUPPLY STORE
7830 N. San Fernando Rd., Sun Valley, CA 91352. (818) 767-5065. (213) 875-2409.

EYES ON MAIN
3110 Main St., #108, Santa Monica, CA 90405. (310) 399-3302. FAX: (310) 399-7682.

FANTASY COSTUMES
4649-1/2 San Fernando Rd., Glendale, CA 91204. (213) 245-7367.

FILMTRIX, INC.
P.O. Box 715, N. Hollywood, CA 91603. (818) 980-3700. FAX: (818) 980-3703. e-mail: FILMTRIX@aol.com
Kevin Pike

LARRY FIORITTO SPECIAL EFFECTS SERVICES
1067 E. Orange Grove, Burbank, CA 91501. (818) 954-9829.

FORMAL TOUCH ANTIQUE TUXEDO SERVICE
842 N. Fairfax Ave., Los Angeles, CA 90046. (213) 658-5553.

GARY GANG STABLES
13801 Gladstone, Sylmar, CA 91342. (818) 362-4648.

PETER GEYER ACTION PROPS & SETS
8235 Lankershim Blvd., Suite G, N. Hollywood, CA 91605. (818) 768-0070.

GLENDALE COSTUMES
746 W. Doran St., Glendale, CA 91203. (818) 244-1161. FAX: (818) 244-8576.

GLOBAL EFFECTS INC.
7119 Laurel Canyon Blvd., Unit 4, N. Hollywood, CA 91605. (818) 503-9273. FAX: (818) 503-9459.

GROSH SCENIC STUDIOS
4114 Sunset Blvd., Los Angeles, CA 90029. (213) 662-1134. FAX: (213) 664-7526.

HAND PROP ROOM, INC.
5700 Venice Blvd., Los Angeles, CA 90019. (213) 931-1534. FAX: (213) 931-2145.

HOLLYWOOD BREAKAWAY
15125-B Califa St., Van Nuys, CA 91411. (818) 781-0621.

HOLLYWOOD CENTRAL PROPS
9171 San Fernando Rd., Sun Valley, CA 91352. (818) 394-4504. FAX: (818) 394-4509.
V.P. & GENERAL MANAGER
Rick Caprarelli

HOLLYWOOD TOYS & COSTUMES
6562 Hollywood Blvd., Hollywood, CA 90028. (213) 465-3119.

HOUSE OF COSTUMES LTD.
166 Jericho Turnpike, Mineola, NY 11501. (516) 294-0170.

HOUSE OF PROPS
1117 Gower St., Hollywood, CA 90038. (213) 463-3166. FAX: (213) 463-8302.

IMAGE ENGINEERING, INC.
736 N. Reese Place, Burbank, CA 91506. (818) 840-1444.
Peter Chesney

IN COSTUME
37 W. 20 St., New York, NY 10011. (212) 255-5502.

INDEPENDENT STUDIO SERVICES
11907 Wicks St., Sun Valley, CA 91352. (818) 764-0840, (818) 768-5711.

INTERNATIONAL COSTUME
1423 Marcellina Ave., Torrance, CA 90501. (310) 320-6392. FAX: (310) 320-3054.

IWASAKI IMAGES OF AMERICA
(food replicas)
20460 Gramercy Pl., Torrance, CA 90501. (310) 328-7121. FAX: (310) 618-0876.

IZQUIERDO STUDIOS
118 W. 22 St., New York, NY 10011. (212) 807-9757.

KREISS COLLECTION
8619 Melrose Ave., Los Angeles, CA 90069-5010. (310) 657-3990.

KUTTNER PROP RENTALS INC.
56 W. 22 St., New York, NY 10010. (212) 242-7969. FAX: (212) 247-1293.
Barbara Guest

L.A. EYEWORKS
7407 Melrose Ave., Los Angeles, CA 90046. (213) 653-8255. FAX: (213) 653-8176.

LILLIAN COSTUME CO. OF L.I. INC.
226 Jericho Turnpike, Mineola, NY 11501. (516) 746-6060.

GENE LONDON STUDIOS
10 Gramercy Park So., New York, NY 10003. (212) 533-4105.

ELIZABETH LUCAS COLLECTION
1021 Montana Ave., Santa Monica, CA 90403. (310) 451-4058.

MERCURY NEON LIGHTING & SIGN UNLIMITED
104 E. 7 St., New York, NY 10009. (212) 473-NEON.

MODERN PROPS
5500 W. Jefferson Blvd., Los Angeles, CA 90016. (213) 934-3000. FAX: (213) 934-3155.

NATIONAL HELICOPTER SERVICE
16800 Roscoe Blvd., Van Nuys, CA 91406. (818) 345-5222.
FAX: (818) 782-0466.
Richard Hart, Helen Kosmala

A NEON SHOP
13026 Saticoy St., Unit 28, No. Hollywood, CA 91605. (818) 764-7181.

NICCOLINI ANTIQUES
19 W. 21 St., New York, NY 10010. (212) 243-2010. (800) 734-9974.

NIGHTS OF NEON
7442 Varna Ave., N. Hollywood, CA 91605. (818) 982-3592.
FAX: (818) 503-1090.

NORCOSTCO, INC.
3606 W. Magnolia Blvd., Burbank, CA 91505. (818) 567-0753.
FAX: (818) 567-1961.
GENERAL MANAGER
Wayne Thorton

OMEGA CINEMA PROPS
5857 Santa Monica, Blvd., Los Angeles, CA 90038. (213) 466-8201. FAX: (213) 461-3643.

ONE NIGHT AFFAIR GOWN RENTAL
2370 Westwood Blvd., #H, W. Los Angeles, CA 90064-2120.
(310) 474-7808. FAX: (310) 474-6543.

PALACE COSTUME COMPANY
835 N. Fairfax Ave., Los Angeles, CA 90046. (213) 651-5458.
FAX: (213) 658-7133.

PARAMOUNT COSTUME DEPARTMENT
5555 Melrose Ave., Hollywood, CA 90038. (213) 956-5288.
FAX: (213) 956-2342.

PARK PLACE STUDIO
4801 Penn Ave., Pittsburgh, PA 15224. (412) 363-7538. (800) 831-2410. FAX: (412) 363-4318.

PERIOD PROPS
235 W. Olive Ave., Burbank, CA 91502. (818) 848-PROP. (818) 41S-ERVE. FAX: (818) 843-4745.

PICTURE CARS, EAST, INC.
72 Huntington St., Brooklyn, NY 11231. (718) 852-2300.

PROPS DISPLAYS & INTERIORS, INC.
132 W. 18 St., New York, NY 10011. (212) 620-3840. FAX: (212) 620-5472.

PROPS FOR TODAY
330 W. 34th St. New York, NY 10001. (212) 244-9600. FAX: (212) 244-1053.

PROP MASTERS, INC.
912 W. Isabel St., Burbank, CA 91506. (818) 846-3915, (818) 846-3957. FAX: (818) 846-1278.

PROP SERVICES WEST INC.
915 N. Citrus Ave., Los Angeles, CA 90038. (213) 461-3371.
FAX: (818) 846-1278.

R/C MODELS
P.O. Box 6026, San Pedro, CA 90734. (310) 833-4700.

ROSCHU
7100 Fair Ave., N. Hollywood, CA 91605. (818) 503-9392.

RUBIE'S COSTUME CO., INC.
120-08 Jamaica Ave., Richmond Hill, Queens, NY 11418. (718) 846-1008.

SJACQUELINE SARTINO
953 N. Edinburgh Ave., Los Angeles, CA 90046. (213) 654-3326. FAX: (213) 656-6192.

SCENIC HIGHLIGHTS
4640 Sperry St., Los Angeles, CA 90039. (818) 956-3610.
FAX: (818) 956-3616.

SCHOEPFER STUDIOS
138 W. 31 St., New York, NY 10001. (212) 736-6939.

SONY PICTURES STUDIOS WARDROBE
10202 W. Washington Blvd., Culver City, CA 90232. (310) 280-7260.

STARBUCK STUDIO
162 W. 21 St., New York, NY 10011. (212) 807-7299.

STICKS & STONES
12990 Branford St., Suite M, Arleta, CA 91331. (818) 252-2088. FAX: (818) 252-2087.
Rob Burman, Jennifer E. McManus

STUDIO PICTURE VEHICLES
5418 Fair Ave., N. Hollywood, CA 91601. (818) 765-1201, (818) 781-4223. FAX: (818) 506-4789.

THE STUDIO WARDROBE DEPT.
1130 N. Highland, Los Angeles, CA 90038. (818) 781-4267.

TONY'S UNIFORMS
2527 W. Magnolia Blvd., Burbank, CA 91505. (818) 842-1494.

TRIANGLE SCENERY/DRAPERY/LIGHTING CO.
1215 Bates Ave., Los Angeles, CA 90029. (213) 662-8129.

TUXEDO CENTER
7360 Sunset Blvd., Los Angeles, CA 90046. (213) 874-4200.

20TH CENTURY PROPS
11651 Hart St., N. Hollywood, CA 91605-5802. (818) 759-1190. FAX: (818) 759-0081.

UNIVERSAL FACILITIES RENTAL
100 Universal City Plaza, #480-3, Universal City, CA 91608.
(818) 777-3000, (800) 892-1979. FAX: (818) 733-1579.

URSULA'S COSTUMES INC.
2516 Wilshire Blvd., Santa Monica, CA 90403. (310) 582-8230.
FAX: (310) 582-8233.

WESTERN COSTUME CO.
11041 Van Owen St., N. Hollywood, CA 91605. (818) 760-0902.

VISUAL SERVICES
40 W. 72 St., New York, NY 10023. (212) 580-9551.

WARNER BROS. STUDIOS
4000 Warner Blvd., Burbank, CA 91522. (818) 954-2923. FAX: (818) 954-2677.

WAVES
(Antique radios)
32 E. 13 St., New York, NY 10003. (212) 989-9284.

WEAPONS SPECIALISTS LTD.
33 Greene St., 1-W, New York, NY 10013. (212) 941-7696.
(800) 878-7696. FAX: (212) 941-7654.
Rick Washburn

WONDERWORKS
7231 Remmet Ave., #F, Canoga Park, CA 91303. (818) 992-8811. FAX: (818) 347-4330.

EDITING SERVICES

ABSOLUTE POST
2911 W. Olive Ave., Burbank, CA 91505. (818) 953-4820. FAX: (818) 845-9179.

ADVENTURE FILM & TAPE
1034 N. Seward St., Hollywood, CA 90038. (213) 460-4557.

ALTER IMAGE
1818 S. Victory Blvd., Glendale, CA 91201. (818) 244-6030.

ANIMATED PRODS., INC.
600 Broadway, New York, NY 10019. (212) 265-2942, (800) 439-1360.

ARCHIVE FILMS, INC.
530 W. 25 St., New York, NY 10001. (212) 620-3955. FAX: (212) 645-2137.
Eric Rachlis

ASTROFILM SERVICE
932 N. La Brea Ave., Los Angeles, CA 90038. (213) 851-1673.

AVAILABLE LIGHT LTD.
3110 W. Burbank Blvd., Burbank, CA 91505. (818) 842-2109.

AVID TECHNOLOGY
4000 W. Alameda Ave., Suite 400, Burbank, CA 91505. (818) 557-2520. FAX: (818) 557-2558.

JERRY BENDER EDITORIAL SERVICE, INC.
27 E. 39 St., New York, NY 10016. (212) 867-1515.

BEXEL CORP.
801 S. Main St., Burbank, CA 91506. (818) 841-5051.

BIRNS & SAWYER, INC.
1026 N. Highland Ave., Hollywood, CA 90038. (213) 466-8211. FAX: (213) 466-7049.

BIG SKY EDITORIAL
10 E. 40 St., Suite 1201, New York, NY 10016. (212) 683-4004.

BIG TIME PICTURE COMPANY, INC.
12210-1/2 Nebraska Ave., Los Angeles, CA 90025-3620. (310) 207-0921. FAX: (310) 826-0071.

CALIFORNIA COMMUNICATIONS INC.
6900 Santa Monica Blvd., Los Angeles, CA 90038. (213) 466-8511. FAX: (213) 466-8511. e-mail: Sales info@CCIPOST.com
Hope Schenk

CAMERA SERVICE CENTER INC.
625 W. 54 St., New York, NY 10019. (212) 757-0906.

B. CANARICK'S CO., LTD
50 E. 42 St., New York, NY 10017. (212) 972-1015.

CARTER, JOHN, ASSOCS., INC.
300 W. 55 St., #10-V, New York, NY 10019. (212) 541-7006.

MICHAEL CHARLES EDITORIAL
6 E. 45 St., New York, NY 10017. (212) 953-2490.

BOB CHENOWETH
1860 E. N. Hills Dr., La Habra, CA 90631. (310) 691-1652. FAX: (310) 690-8362.

CHRISTY'S EDITORIAL FILM SUPPLY, INC.
135 N. Victory Blvd., Burbank, CA 91502. (818) 845-1755. (213) 849-1148. FAX: (213) 849-2048.

CINE TAPE, INC.
241 E. 51 St., New York, NY 10022. (212) 355-0070.

COMPREHENSIVE SERVICE AV INC.
432 W. 45 St., New York, NY 10036. (212) 586-6161.

CONSOLIDATED FILM INDUSTRIES
959 Seward St., Hollywood, CA 90038. (213) 462-3161, (213) 960-7444. FAX: (213) 460-4885.

CREST NATIONAL FILM & VIDEOTAPE LABS
1000 N. Highland Ave., Hollywood, CA 90038. (213) 466-0624. FAX: (213) 461-8901.

CREW CUTS FILM & TAPE, INC.
25 W. 43 St., New York, NY 10017. (212) 371-4545.

THE CULVER STUDIOS
9336 W. Washington Blvd., Culver City, CA 90230. (310) 202-3396, (310) 836-5537. (310) 202-3272.

CUTTING EDGE ENTERPRISES
432 W. 45 St., New York, NY 10036. (212) 541-9664.

DJM FILMS, INC.
4 E. 46 St., New York, NY 10017. (212) 687-0111.

DAVID DEE'S EVEN TIME, LTD.
62 W. 45 St., New York, NY 10036. (212) 764-4700.

JEFF DELL & PARTNERS
241 E. 51 St., New York, NY 10022. (212) 371-7915. FAX: (212) 935-9539
Jeff Dell

DELTA PRODUCTIONS
3333 Glendale Blvd., Suite 3, Los Angeles, CA 90039. (213) 663-8754. FAX: (213) 663-3460.

DIRECTORS SOUND & EDITORIAL SERVICE
1150 W. Olive Ave., Burbank, CA 91506. (818) 843-0950. FAX: (818) 843-0357.

EAGLE EYE FILM CO.
10825 Burbank Blvd., N. Hollywood, CA 91601. (818) 506-6100. FAX: (818) 506-4313.

EASY EDIT
432 W. 45 St., New York, NY 10036. (212) 541-9664.

ECHO FILM SERVICES, INC.
4119 Burbank Blvd., Burbank, CA 91505. (818) 841-4114. FAX: (818) 841-5038.
Joe Melody, Russ Tinsley

EDIT DECISIONS, LTD.
311 W. 43 St., New York, NY 10036. (212) 757-4742. FAX: (212) 757-5258.
Harvey Kopel

THE EDITING COMPANY
8300 Beverly Blvd., Los Angeles, CA 90048. (213) 653-3570. FAX: (213) 653-8855.

EDITING CONCEPTS
214 E. 50 St., New York, NY 10022. (212) 980-3340.

THE EDITING MACHINE, INC.
630 Ninth Ave., New York, NY 10036. (212) 757-5420.

EDIT POINT POST PRODUCTION SYSTEMS
620 N. Victory Blvd., Burbank, CA 91502. (818) 841-7336. FAX: (818) 841-7378.

FILM CORE
849 N. Seward St., Hollywood, 90038. (213) 464-7303.

FILMSERVICE LABORATORIES, INC.
6325 Santa Monica Blvd., Los Angeles, CA 90038. (213) 464-5141.

FILM VIDEO ARTS INC.
817 Broadway, 2nd floor, New York, NY 10003-4797. (212) 673-9361.

525 POST PRODUCTION
6424 Santa Monica Blvd., Hollywood, CA 90038. (213) 466-3348. FAX: (213) 467-1589.

FOUR MEDIA CO.
2813 W. Alameda Ave., Burbank, CA 91505. (818) 840-7000. (800) 423-2277.

GRENADIER PRODS., INC.
220 E. 23 St., New York, NY 10010. (212) 545-0388.

ALAN GORDON ENTERPRISES, INC.
1430 Cahuenga Blvd., Hollywood, CA 90028. (213) 466-3561. FAX: (213) 871-2193.

HI-TECH RENTALS
2907 W. Olive Ave., Burbank, CA 91505. (213) 469-9000, (800) 954-3000. FAX: (818) 848-0112.
Andrew Bruce Overton

HOLLYWOOD FILM CO.
3294 E. 26th St., Los Angeles, CA 90023. (213) 462-3284. FAX: (213) 263-9665.

ROBERT HOROWITZ FILMS
321 W. 44 St., New York, NY 10036. (212) 397-9380.

J & R FILM CO., INC.
1135 Mansfield Ave., Los Angeles, CA 90038. (213) 467-3107. FAX (213) 466-2201.

J.P.C. VISUALS
11 E. 47 St., New York, NY 10017. (212) 223-0555.

J.R. PRODUCTIONS
738 Cahuenga Blvd., Hollywood, CA 90038. (213) 463-9836.

KESSER POST PRODUCTION
21 S.W. 15 Rd., Miami, FL 33129. (305) 358-7900. FAX: (305) 358-2209.

LASER-PACIFIC MEDIA CORP.
540 N. Hollywood Way, Burbank, CA 91505. (818) 842-0777. FAX: (818) 566-9834.

MAGNASYNC/MOVIELA CORP.
1141 N. Mansfield Ave., Los Angeles, CA 90038. (213) 962-0382.

MAGNO SOUND, INC.
729 Seventh Ave., New York, NY 10019. (212) 302-2505.

MAYSLES FILM INC.
250 W. 54 St., New York, NY 10019. (212) 582-6050.

WILLIAM MOFFIT ASSOCS.
747 N. Lake Ave., #B, Pasadena, CA 91104. (818) 791-2559. FAX: (818) 791-3092.

MONACO LABS & VIDEO
234 Ninth St., San Francisco, CA 94103. (415) 864-5350.

MONTAGE GROUP, LTD.
4116 W. Magnolia Blvd., #103, Burbank, CA 91505. (818) 955-8801. FAX: (818) 355-8808.
1 W. 85th St., New York, NY 10024. (212) 595-0400.
Jim Beaton

MOTION PICTURES ENTERPRISES, INC.
430 W. 45 St., New York, NY 10036. (212) 245-0969.

MOVIE TECH INC.
832 N. Seward St., Hollywood, CA 90038. (213) 467-8491, (213) 467-5423. FAX: (213) 467-8471.

P.A.T. FILM SERVICES
630 Ninth Ave., New York, NY 10036. (212) 247-0900.

PDR PRODUCTIONS, INC.
219 E. 44 St., New York, NY 10017. (212) 986-2020.

PALESTRINI FILM EDITING, INC.
575 Lexington Ave., New York, NY 10022. (212) 752-EDIT.

PARAMOUNT STUDIO GROUP
5555 Melrose Ave., Hollywood 90038. (213) 468-5000.

PELCO EDITORIAL INC.
757 Third Ave., New York, NY 10017. (212) 319-EDIT.

PHANTASMAGORIA PRODS.
111 Eighth Ave., New York, NY 10011. (212) 366-0909.

GLORIA PINEYRO FILM SERVICES CORP.
19 W. 21 St., New York, NY 10010. (212) 627-0707.

POST GROUP
6335 Homewood Ave., Los Angeles, CA 90028. (213) 462-2300.
c/o Walt Disney-MGM Studios, Roy O. Disney Production
Center, Lake Buena Vista, FL 32830. (407) 560-5600.

POST PLUS INC.
3301 Barham Blvd., Los Angeles, CA 90068. (213) 874-7110.

POST TIME
4640 Lankershim Blvd., #600, N. Hollywood, CA 90046. (213)
851-4123. FAX: (213) 851-9959.

PRECISION POST
1641 20th St., Santa Monica, CA 90404. (310) 829-5684. FAX:
(310) 453-9068.

PRODUCTIONS WEST
6311 Romaine St., Suite 4134, Los Angeles, CA 90038. (213)
464-0169. FAX: (213) 461-3841.

REBELEDIT
292 Madison Ave., 26th Floor, New York, NY 10017. (212) 686-
8622.

THE REEL THING, INC
7001 Melrose Ave., Hollywood, CA 90038. (213) 933-5701.
FAX: (213) 933-4908.

RICH ENTERPRISES CORP.
208 W. 30 St., New York, NY 10001. (212) 947-3943.

ROBERT RICHTER PRODS., INC.
330 W. 42 St., New York, NY 10036. (212) 947-1395.

ROSS-GAFFNEY, INC.
21 W. 46 St., New York, NY 10036. (212) 719-2744.

SOUND ONE CORP.
1619 Broadway, 8th floor, New York, NY 10019. (212) 765-4757.

SANDPIPER EDITORIAL SERVICE
298 Fifth Ave., New York, NY 10018. (212) 564-6643.

LEONARD SOUTH PRODS.
4883 Lankershim Blvd., N. Hollywood, CA 91601-2746. (818)
760-8383. FAX: (818) 766-8301.

SPECTRUM ASSOCS. INC.
536 W. 29 St., New York, NY 10001. (212) 563-1680.

SPLICE IS NICE
920 Broadway, New York, NY 10010. (212) 677-6007. FAX:
(212) 473-8164.
Dick Langenbach

STEENBECK INC.
9554 Vasser Ave., Chatsworth, CA 91311-4169. (818) 998-
4033. FAX: (818) 998-6992.
Bob Campos

STONE CUTTERS FILM & VIDEO
123 E. 54 St., #5-C, New York, NY 10022. (212) 421-9404.

SYNCROFILM SERVICES, INC.
72 W. 45 St., New York, NY 10036. (212) 719-2966.

TAKE 5 EDITORIAL SERVICES, INC.
9 E. 38 St., New York, NY 10016. (212) 683-6104.

TAPE HOUSE INC.
216 E. 45 St., New York, NY 10017. (212) 557-4949.

TAPESTRY PRODUCTIONS, LTD.
920 Broadway, New York, NY 10010. (212) 677-6007.

TELEVISION CENTER
6311 Romaine St., Los Angeles, CA 90038. (213) 464-6638.

TODD-AO STUDIOS
Please see listing under Sound, Post Production & Music.

UNIVERSAL FACILITIES RENTAL DIV.
100 Universal City Plaza, Universal City, CA 91608. (818) 777-
3000. FAX: (818) 777-2731. URL: http://www.mca.com/studio

VALKHN FILMS INC.
1650 Broadway, Suite 404, New York, NY 10019. (212) 586-
1603.

GARY WACHTER EDITORIAL, INC.
159 W. 53 St., New York, NY 10019. (212) 399-7770.

WARMFLASH PRODUCTIONS, INC.
630 Ninth Ave., New York, NY 10036. (212) 757-5969.

WARNER BROS. STUDIOS
4000 Warner Blvd., Burbank, CA 91522. (818) 954-6000.

WARNER HOLLYWOOD STUDIOS
1041 N. Formosa Ave., W. Hollywood, CA 90046. (213) 850-2500.

WILDWOOD FILM SERVICE
6855 Santa Monica Blvd., Suite 400, Los Angeles, CA 90038.
(213) 462-6388.

BILLY WILLIAMS ENTERPRISES
216 E. 45 St., New York, NY 10017. (212) 983-3348. FAX:
(212) 983-3349.
Bernadette Quinn

WOLLIN PRODUCTION SERVICES, INC.
666 N. Robertson Blvd., Los Angeles, CA 90069. (310) 659-
0175. FAX: (310) 659-2946.

WORLD CINEVISIONS SERVICES, INC.
321 W. 44 St., New York, NY 10036. (212) 265-4587.

FILM & VIDEO STOCK

**EASTMAN KODAK CO., PROFESSIONAL MOTION
IMAGING DIVISION**
Home Office: 343 State St., Rochester, NY 14608. (716)
724-4000.
6700 Santa Monica Blvd., Hollywood, CA, 90038. (213)
464-6131. FAX: (213) 468-1568.
1901 W. 22nd St., Oakbrook, IL 60521. (312) 654-5300.
360 W. 31st St., New York, NY 10001.

FUJI PHOTO FILM U.S.A., INC.
555 Taxter Rd., Elmsford, NY 10523. (914) 789-8100. (800)
755-3854.

ILFORD PHOTO, INC.
W. 70 Century Rd., Paramus, NJ 07653. (201) 265-6000.

3M AUDIO & VIDEO COLOR SYSTEMS DIVISION
3130 Damon Way, Burbank, CA 91505. (818) 843-5935.
(213) 726-6387. FAX: (213) 727-2142.
6023 S. Garfield Ave., Los Angeles, CA 90040. (213) 726-
6333. FAX: (213) 726-6562.

RESEARCH TECHNOLOGY, INC.
4700 Chase Ave., Lincolnwood, IL 60646. (847) 677-
3000.

STUDIO FILM & TAPE INC.
6674 Santa Monica Blvd., Hollywood, CA 90038. (213) 466-
8101, (800) 824-3130. FAX: (213) 466-6815.
630 Ninth Ave., New York, NY 10036. (212) 977-9330.

FILM PRESERVATION, PROCESSING, REPAIR & STORAGE

ACCUTREAT FILMS, INC.,
630 Ninth Ave., New York, NY 10036. (212) 247-3415.

AFD/PHOTOGRAD FILM COATING LAB
1015 N. Cahuenga Blvd., Hollywood, CA 90038. (213) 469-8141. FAX: (213) 469-1888.

ALLIED FILM & VIDEO SERVICES
1322 W. Belmont Ave., Chicago, IL 60657. (312) 348-0373. FAX: (312) 348-5669.
4 Dallas Communications Complex, 6305 N. O'Connor Rd., #111, Irving, TX 75039. (214) 869-0100.

ALPHA CINE LABORATORY INC.
307 W. 200 South, #4004, Salt Lake City, UT 84101. (801) 363-9465.
1001 Lenora St., Seattle, WA 98121. (206) 682- 8230, (800) 426-7016. FAX: (206) 682-6649.
Roberta Ukura, Bill Scott

AMERICAN ARCHIVES, INC.
2636 North Ontario, Burbank, CA 91504. (818) 558-6995. FAX: (818) 558-7791.

ARCHIVES FOR ADVANCED MEDIA
3205 Burton Ave., Burbank, CA 91504. (818) 848-9766.

ASTRO COLOR LAB
61 W. Erie St., Chicago, IL 60610. (312) 280-5500.

BARTCO CO.
924 N. Formosa, Hollywood, CA 90046. (213) 851- 5411.

BENTON FILM FORWARDING CO.
150 Great Southwest Pkwy., Atlanta, GA 30336. (404) 699-2020. FAX: (404) 699-5588.
Lucy Benton

BONDED FILM STORAGE
550 Main St., Fort Lee, NJ 07024. (201) 944-3700.

BRAMBLES INFORMATION MANAGEMENT
P.O. Box 128, Sun Valley, CA 91352. (800) 310-DATA. FAX: (818) 504-6918.
Reed E. Irvin

BROADCAST STANDARDS, INC.
2044 Cottner Ave., Los Angeles, CA 90025. (310) 312-9060.

CINE MAGNETICS FILM & VIDEO
298 Fifth Ave.,New York, NY 10016. (212) 564-6737.

CINE MOTION PICTURE SERVICE LABORATORIES, INC.
278 Babcock St., Boston, MA 02215. (617) 254-7882.

CINEFILM LABORATORY
2156 Faulkner Rd., N.E., Atlanta, GA 30324. (404) 633-1448, (800) 633-1448. FAX: (404) 633-3867.

CINESITE
1017 N. Las Palmas Ave., Suite 300, Hollywood, CA 90038. (212) 468-4400. FAX: (213) 468-4404.

CONSOLIDATED FILM INDUSTRIES (CFI)
959 N. Seward St., Hollywood, CA 90038. (213) 462-3161.

CONTINENTAL FILM LABS, INC.
1998 NE 150 St., N. Miami, FL 33181. (305) 949-4252, (800) 327-8396. FAX: (305) 949-3242.
Vincent Hogan
7675 Currency Drive, Orlando, FL 33181. (407) 856-8958. FAX: (407) 856-4070.
A. J. Robbins

CREST NATIONAL VIDEO FILM LABS
1141 N. Seward St., Hollywood, CA 90038. (213) 466-0624, (213) 462-6696. FAX: (213) 461-8901.

DELUXE LABORATORIES, INC.
1377 N. Serrano Ave., Hollywood, CA 90027. (213) 462-6171, (800) 2DE-LUXE.

DU ART FILM LABORATORIES
245 W. 55 St., New York, NY 10019. (212) 757-4580.

DELTA PRODUCTIONS
3333 Glendale Blvd., Suite 3, Los Angeles, CA 90039. (213) 663-8754. FAX: (213) 663-3460.

FILM CRAFT LAB., INC.
66 Sibley St., Detroit, MI 48201. (313) 962-2611.

FILM PRESERVE
2 Depot Plaza, #202-B, Bedford Hills, NY 10507. (914) 242-9838. FAX: (914) 242-9854.
Robert A. Harris

FILM TECHNOLOGY COMPANY INC.
726 N. Cole Ave., Hollywood, CA 90038. (213) 464-3456. FAX: (213) 464-7439.

FILMACK STUDIOS
1327 S. Wabash Ave., Chicago, IL 60605. (312) 427-3395, (800) FILMACK. FAX: (312) 427-4866.
Robert Mack

FILMLIFE INC. AMERICAN FILM REPAIR INSTITUTE
P.O. Box 604, Lake Worth, FL 33460. (941) 582-6700. FAX: (941) 582-3535.
Marvin A. Bernard

FILMTREAT INTERNATIONAL CORP.
42-24 Orchard St., Long Island City, NY 11101. (718) 784-4040. FAX: (718) 784-4677.
Y. W. Mociuk, Sam Borodinsky

FILMTREAT WEST CORP.
10810 Cantara St., Sun Valley, CA 91352. (818) 771-5390.

FORDE MOTION PICTURE LABS
306 Fairview Ave. N., Seattle, WA 98109. (206) 682-2510. (800) 682-2510.

FORT LEE FILM STORAGE & SERVICE
1 Mt. Vernon, St., Ridgefield Park, NJ 07660. (201) 440-6200. FAX: (201) 440-5799.
EXECUTIVE VICE PRESIDENT
Patricia Miller

FOTO-KEM FOTO-TRONICS, FILM-VIDEO LAB
2800 W. Olive Ave., Burbank, CA 91505. (818) 846-3101. FAX: (818) 841-2130.

FOTORAMA
1507 N. Cahuenga Blvd., Los Angeles, CA 90028. (213) 469-1578.

FOUR MEDIA COMPANY
2813 W. Alameda Ave., Burbank, CA 91505. (818) 840-7000. FAX: (818) 840-7195.

GUFFANTI FILM LABORATORIES INC.
630 Ninth Ave., New York, NY 10036. (212) 265-5530.

HIGHLAND LABS
840 Battery St., San Francisco, CA 94111. (415) 981-5010.

HOLLYWOOD FILM CO.
826 Seward St., Hollywood, CA 90038. (213) 462-1971, (213) 462-3284. FAX: (213) 263-9665.

HOLLYWOOD FILM & VIDEO INC.
6060 Sunset Blvd., Hollywood, 90028. (213) 464-2181. FAX: (213) 464-0893.

HOLLYWOOD VAULTS, INC.
Vault: 742 N. Seward St., Hollywood, 90038. (213) 461-6464. Office: 1780 Prospect Ave., Santa Barbara, CA 93103. (805) 569-5336. FAX: (805) 569-1657.

FRANK HOLMES LABORATORIES
6609 Santa Monica Blvd., Hollywood, CA 90038. (213) 461-8078.

INTERNATIONAL CINE SERVICES, INC.
920 Allen Ave., Glendale, CA 91201. (818) 242-3839. FAX: (818) 242-1566.

IRON MOUNTAIN RECORDS MANAGEMENT
6190 Boyle Ave., Vernon, CA 90058-3952. (213) 466-9271. FAX: (213) 467-8068.

LAB LINK, INC.
115 W. 45 St.,New York, NY 10036. (212) 302-7373.

LASER-PACIFIC MEDIA CORP.
809 N. Cahuenga Blvd., Hollywood, CA 90038. (213) 462-6266. FAX: (213) 464-3233.

KEN LIEBERMAN LABORATORIES INC.
118 W. 22 St., New York, NY 10011. (212) 633-0500. FAX: (212) 675-0500.
Ken Lieberman

LUCASFILM LTD.
P.O. Box 2009, San Rafael, CA 94912. (415) 662-1800.

MAGNO SOUND INC.
729 Seventh Ave., New York, NY 10019. (212) 302-2505. FAX: (212) 819-1282.

MAGNO VISUALS
115 W. 45 St., New York, NY 10036. (212) 575-5162, (212) 575-5159. FAX: (212) 719-1867.

METRO BUSINESS ARCHIVES
609 W. 51 St., New York, NY 10019. (212) 489-7890.

MILLENNIUM FILM WORK SHOP
66 E. 4 St., New York, NY 10003. (212) 673-0090.

MONACO LABORATORIES, INC.
234 Ninth St., San Francisco, CA 94103. (415) 864-5350.

MOTION PICTURE LABORATORIES, INC.
781 S. Main St., Memphis, TN 38106. (901) 774-4944, (800) 4MP-LMPL.

MULTI-LAB
1633 Maria St., Burbank, CA 91504. (213) 465-9970.

NATIONAL PHOTOGRAPHIC LABORATORIES
1926 W. Gray, Houston, TX 77019. (713) 527-9300. FAX: (713) 528-2584.

NEWELL COLOR LAB
221 N. Westmoreland Ave., Los Angeles, CA 90004. (213) 380-2980.

NEWSFILM & VIDEO LABORATORY, INC.
516 N. Larchmont Blvd., Hollywood, CA 90004. (213) 462-6814.

P.A.T. FILM SERVICES, INC.
630 Ninth Ave., New York, NY 10036. (212) 247-0900.

PACIFIC TITLE ARCHIVES
4800 San Vicente Blvd., Los Angeles, 90019. (213) 938-3711. FAX: (213) 938-6364.
David Weeden
561 Mateo St., Los Angeles, 90013. (213) 617-8650. FAX: (213) 617-7876.
10717 Vanowen St., N. Hollywood, 91605. (818) 760-4223. FAX: (818) 760-1704.
900 Grand Central Ave., Glendale, CA 91201. (818) 547-0090. FAX: (818) 548-7990.
Dan Gentile

PACIFIC TITLE & ART STUDIO
6350 Santa Monica Blvd., Los Angeles, CA 90038. (213) 464-0121.

PRODUCERS COLOR SERVICE
2921 E. Grand Blvd., Detroit, MI 48202. (313) 874-1112.

PRODUCERS FILM CENTER
948 N. Sycamore Ave., Hollywood, 90038. (213) 851-1122.

RGB COLOR LAB
816 N. Highland Ave., Los Angeles, CA 90038. (213) 469-1959.

SINA'S CUSTOM LAB
3136 Wilshire Blvd., Los Angeles, CA 90010. (213) 381-5161.

THE SITE
6918 Tujunga Ave., N. Hollywood, CA 91605. (818) 508-0505. FAX: (818) 508-5581.

SPECTRUM MOTION PICTURE LAB
399 Gundersen Dr., Carol Stream, IL 60188. (708) 665-4242, (800) 345-6522.

SPORTS FILM LAB
361 W. Broadway, South Boston, MA 02127. (617) 268-8388. FAX: (617) 268-8390.

TECHNICOLOR INC.
Professional Film Division, 4050 Lankershim Blvd., North Hollywood, CA 91608. (818) 769-8500.
321 W. 44 St., New York, NY 10036. (212) 582-7310.

TITRA FILM CALIFORNIA INC.
733 Salem St., Glendale, CA 91203. (818) 244-3663. FAX: (818) 244-6205.

TODD-AO/CHACE PRESERVATION SERVICES
201 S. Victory Blvd., Burbank, CA 91502. (818) 842-8346. FAX: (818) 843-8353.
MANAGING PARTNER
Robert Heiber

VALDHERE INC.
3060 Valleywood Dr., Dayton, OH 45429. (513) 293-2191.

VAN CHROMES CORP.
21 W. 46 St., New York, NY 10036. (212) 302-5700.

YALE LABS
1509 N. Gordon St., Los Angeles, CA 90028. (213) 464-6181.

FINANCIAL SERVICES

BANK OF AMERICA
Entertainment Industries Division, 2049 Century Park E., #300, Los Angeles, CA 90067. (310) 785-6050.

BANK OF CALIFORNIA
Entertainment Division, 9401 Wilshire Blvd., Beverly Hills, CA 90212. (310) 273-7200. FAX: (310) 273-9030.

BANK OF NEW YORK
530 Fifth Ave., New York, NY 10036. (212) 852-4099.

BANKERS TRUST
Media Division, 300 S. Grand Ave., Los Angeles, CA 90071. (213) 620-8200. FAX: (213) 620-8484.

BURNHAM COMPANY
474 Sylvan Ave., Englewood Cliffs, NJ 07632. (201) 568-9800, (212) 563-7000. FAX: (201) 568-5599.

CHASE MANHATTAN BANK, N.A.
Media & Communications Component, 1 Chase Manhattan Plaza, 5th floor, New York, NY 10081. (212) 552-2222. 552-4848.

CHEMICAL BANK
1800 Century Park E., #400, Los Angeles, CA 90067. (310) 788-5600.
Entertainment Industries Group, 277 Park Ave., New York, NY 10172. (212) 935-9935.

CITY NATIONAL BANK
Entertainment Division, 400 N. Roxbury Dr., Suite 400, Beverly Hills, CA 90210. (310) 550-5696.

COHEN INSURANCE
225 W. 34th St., New York, NY 10122. (212) 244-8075.

DE WITT STERN GROUP, INC.
420 Lexington Ave., New York, NY 10170. (212) 867-3550.

DELOITTE & TOUCHE
2029 Century Park E., #300, Los Angeles, CA 90067. (213) 551-6705.

FILM CAPITAL CORP.
P.O. Box 2465, Palm Springs, CA 92263-2465. (619) 778-7461. (800) 538-7997.

FILM FINANCES INC.
9000 Sunset Blvd., Suite 1400, Los Angeles, CA 90069. (310) 275-7323. FAX: (310) 275-1706.

FIRST CHARTER BANK
Entertainment Division, 265 N. Beverly Drive, Beverly Hills, CA 90210. (310) 275-2225.

FIRST INTERSTATE BANK OF CALIFORNIA
Entertainment Division, 9601 Wilshire Blvd., Beverly Hills, CA 90210. (310) 285-5768.

FIRST LOS ANGELES BANK
Entertainment Division, 9595 Wilshire Blvd., Beverly Hills, CA 90212. (310) 557-1211.

HILTON FINANCIAL GROUP, INC.
P.O. Box 2026, N. Hollywood, CA 91610-0026. (213) 851-6532. FAX: (213) 851-6532.

LEWIS HORWITZ ORGANIZATION
1840 Century Park East, Los Angeles, CA 90067. (310) 275-7171. FAX: (310) 275-8055.

IMPERIAL BANK
Entertainment Banking, 9777 Wilshire Blvd., Beverly Hills, CA 90212. (310) 338-3139.

INTERNATIONAL FILM GUARANTORS (FIREMAN'S FUNDINSURANCE CO.)
Entertainment Industry Div., 5750 Wilshire Blvd., Los Angeles, CA 90024. (213) 930-1910.

MARATHON NATIONAL BANK
11150 W. Olympia Blvd., W. Los Angeles, CA 90064. (310) 996-9100.

MERCANTILE NATIONAL BANK
1840 Century Park East, Los Angeles, CA 90067. (310) 277-2265.

THE MOTION PICTURE BOND COMPANY
1901 Avenue of the Stars, #2000, Los Angeles, CA 90067. (310) 551-0371. FAX: (310) 551-0518.

D. R. REIFF & ASSOCIATES
41 W. 83 St., New York, NY 10024. (212) 877-1099.

RICHMAR BROKERAGE
310 Northern Blvd., Great Neck, NY 11021. (718) 895-7151. (516) 829-5200.

RUBEN, ALBERT G., & CO.
48 West 25 St., 12 Floor, New York, NY 10010. (212) 627-7400.

UNION BANK
445 S. Figueroa, 15th fl., Los Angeles, CA 90071. (213) 236-5780.

WESTERN SECURITY BANK
Entertainment Division, 4100 W. Alameda Ave., Toluca Lake, CA 91505. (818) 843-0707.

MARKET RESEARCH SERVICES

ASI MARKET RESEARCH, INC.,
101 N. Brand Blvd., #1700, Glendale, CA 91203-2619. (818) 637-5600. FAX: (818) 637-5615.

AMERICAN MARKETING ASSOCIATION
6404 Wilshire Blvd., #1111, Los Angeles, CA 90048. (213) 655-1951. FAX: (213) 655-8627.

BRAMSON & ASSOCIATES
7400 Beverly Blvd., Los Angeles, CA 90036. (213) 938-3595. FAX: (213) 938-0852.

ROBERT A. BRILLIANT, INC.
13245 Riverside Dr., #530, Sherman Oaks, CA 91423. (818) 386-6600. FAX: (818) 990-9007.

CERTIFIED MARKETING SERVICES, INC. (CMS)
Route 9, Kinderhook, NY 12106. (518) 758-6405.

CINEMA CONSULTANTS GROUP
8033 Sunset Blvd., P.O. Box 93, Los Angeles, CA 90046-2427. (213) 650-5807. FAX: (213) 650-2006.
Michael Goldman

CINEMASCORE
8524 Sahara Blvd., P.O. Box 173, Las Vegas, NV 89117. (702) 255-9963.

CONSUMERS PERSPECTIVE
1456 Canfield Ave., Los Angeles, CA 90035. (310) 556-3006. FAX: (310) 556-3002.

DALE SYSTEM INC., THEATRE DIVISION
1101 Stewart Ave., Garden City, NY 11530. (516) 794-2800. FAX: (516) 542-1063.

ENTERTAINMENT DATA, INC.
8350 Wilshire Blvd., #210, Beverly Hills, CA 90210. (213) 658-8300.

EXHIBITOR RELATIONS CO., INC.
116 N. Robertson Blvd., #606, Los Angeles, CA 90048. (310) 657-2005. FAX: (310) 657-7283.

THE GALLUP ORGANIZATION
47 Hulfish St., Princeton, NJ 08542. (609) 924-9600.

HISPANIC ENTERTAINMENT SPECIALIST
3726 Laurel Canyon Blvd., Studio City, CA 91604. (818) 766-9100. FAX: (818) 766-9201.

IMAGE ANALYSTS ALL-MEDIA
P.O. Box 1587, Santa Monica, CA 90406. (310) 458-0503.

INTERNATIONAL RESEARCH & EVALUATION,
21098 IRE Control Ctr., Eagan, MN 55121-0098. (612) 888-9635. FAX: (612) 888-9124.
Rick Kenrick

MCCANN-ERICKSON INC.
6420 Wilshire Blvd., Los Angeles, CA 90048. (213) 655-9420.

MARKET RESEARCH CORP. OF AMERICA
819 S. Wabash, Chicago, IL 60605. (708) 480-9600.
2215 Sanders Road, Northbrook, IL 60062. (708) 480-9600.

MOMENTUM INTERNATIONAL
P.O. Box 5889, Sherman Oaks, CA 91413. (818) 752-4500. FAX: (818) 752-4554.

CHARLES A. MOSES
3211 W. Alameda Ave., Suite A, Burbank, CA 91505-4112. (818) 848-0513. FAX: (818) 848-4977.

A.C. NIELSEN COMPANY
150 N. Martingale Rd., Schaumburg, IL 60173. (708) 605-5000. 731 Wilshire Blvd., #940, Los Angeles, CA 90010. (213) 386-7316. FAX: (213) 386-7317.
299 Park Ave., New York, NY 10171. (212) 708-7500.

OPINION RESEARCH CORP.
P.O. Box 183, Princeton, NJ 08542-0183. (609) 924-5900.

JOAN PEARCE RESEARCH ASSOCS.
8111 Beverly Blvd., #308, Los Angeles, CA 90048. (213) 655-5464. FAX: (213) 655-4770.

PROFESSIONAL RESEARCH ASSOCIATES
913 California Ave., Suite A, Santa Monica, CA 90403. (310) 394-1650.

RADIO TV REPORTS
6255 Sunset Blvd., #1515, Los Angeles, CA 90028. (213) 466-6124.

R. SELTZER ASSOCIATES
15445 Ventura Blvd., #14, Sherman Oaks, CA 91413. (818) 888-8450. FAX: (818) 888-8446.

SINDLINGER & CO., INC.
405 Osborne St., Wallingford, PA 19086. (610) 565-0247.

JANET SNOW & ASSOCIATES
327 Reeves Dr., Beverly Hills, CA 90212. (310) 552-0082.

VIDEO MONITORING SERVICES OF AMERICA
6430 W. Sunset Blvd., #504, Los Angeles, CA 90028. (213) 993-0111.

SOUND SERVICES

A & J RECORDING STUDIOS, INC.
225 W. 57 St., New York, NY 10019. (212) 247-4860.

ADVANTAGE AUDIO
1026 Hollywood Way, Burbank, CA 91505. (818) 566-8555.

JOHN ERIC ALEXANDER MUSIC INC.
9 John Walsh Blvd., Suite 400, Peekskill, NY 10566. (914) 736-2829. FAX: (914) 736-3134.

ASSOCIATED PRODUCTION MUSIC
6255 Sunset Blvd., Suite 820, Hollywood, CA 90028. (213) 461-3211. FAX (213) 461-9102.

AUDIO EFFECTS COMPANY
1600 N. Western Ave., Hollywood 90027. (213) 469-3692.

THE AUDIO DEPARTMENT
119 W. 57 St., New York, NY 10019. (212) 586-3503.

WALLY BURR RECORDING
1126 Hollywood Way, Burbank, CA 91505. (818) 845-0500.

CORELLI-JACOBS RECORDING INC.
25 W. 45 St., New York, NY 10036. (212) 382-0220. FAX: (212) 382-0220.
Andrew Jacobs

CREATIVE MUSICAL SERVICES
13601 Ventura Blvd., #358, Sherman Oaks, CA 91423. (818) 385-1517. FAX: (818) 385-1266.
Dana Ferandelli

DISNEY-MGM STUDIOS
P.O. Box 10200, 1675 Buena Vista Blvd., Lake Buena Vista, FL 32830-0200. (407) 560-7299, (407) 560-5600.

DOLBY LABORATORIES, INC.
100 Potrero Ave., 94103. (415) 558-0200. Telex: 34409.
3375 Barham Blvd., Los Angeles, CA 90068. (213) 845-1880.
1350 Ave. of the Americas, 28th Floor, New York, NY 10019-4703. (212) 767-1700.

FIESTA SOUND
1655 S. Compton Ave., Los Angeles, CA 90021. (213) 748-2057. FAX: (213) 748-5388.
R. G. Robeson

JOHN HILL MUSIC
116 E. 37 St., New York, NY 10016. (212) 683-2273. FAX: (212) 683-2546.
Rosemary Rogers

THE HIT FACTORY, INC.
237 W. 54 St., New York, NY 10019. (212) 664-1000.

INTERLOCK AUDIO POST
6520 Sunset Blvd., Los Angeles, CA, 90028. (213) 469-3986. FAX: (213) 469-8507.
Lisa Pegnato

INTERSOUND, INC.
8746 Sunset Blvd., Los Angeles, CA 90069. (310) 652-3741. FAX: (310) 854-7290.
PRESIDENT
Kent Harrison Hayes

INTERWEAVE ENTERTAINMENT
22723 Berdon St., Woodland Hills, CA 91367. (818) 883-1920. FAX: (818) 883-9650.
VICE PRESIDENT
Lynne Weaver

KILLER MUSIC
3518 Cahuenga Blvd. West, Suite 108, Los Angeles, CA 90068. (213) 850-1966. FAX: (213) 850-3288.
Lori Colantuoni

LITTLE GEMSTONE MUSIC/24 CARAT PRODUCTIONS
P.O. Box 1703, Fort Lee, NJ 07024. (201) 488-8562.
Kevin D. Noel

LOOK INC.
168 5th Ave., New York, NY 10010. (212) 627-3500. FAX: (212) 633-1980.
Joanne Look

LUCASFILM LTD. (SPROCKET SYSTEMS, INC.)
P.O. Box 2009, San Rafael, CA 94912. (415) 662-1800.

LEE MAGID, INC.
P.O. Box 532, Malibu, CA 90265. (213) 463-5998. FAX: (310) 457-8891.

EDDY MANSON PRODUCTIONS, INC.
7245 Hillside Ave., Suite 216, Los Angeles, CA 90046-2329. (213) 874-9318. FAX: (213) 874-9338.

MOVIE TECH STUDIOS
832 N. Seward St., Hollywood, CA 90038. (213) 467-8491. FAX: (213) 467-8471.

NAMRAC MUSIC
15456 Cabrito Road, Van Nuys, CA 91406. (213) 873-7370.

PARAMOUNT RECORDING STUDIOS
6245 Santa Monica Blvd., Hollywood, CA 90038. (213) 465-4000. FAX: (213) 469-1905.

RYDER SOUND SERVICES, INC.
1161 Vine St., Hollywood, CA 90038. (213) 469-3511.

SOUND THINKING MUSIC RESEARCH
1534 N. Moorpark Rd., #333, Thousand Oaks, CA 91360. (805) 495-3306. FAX: (805) 495-3306.
Gary Ginell

SOUTHERN LIBRARY OF RECORDED MUSIC
4621 Cahuenga Blvd., Toluca Lake, CA 91602. (818) 752-1530. FAX: (818) 508-0213.
Roy Kohn

STUDIO M PRODUCTIONS UNLIMITED
4032 Wilshire Blvd., #403, Los Angeles, CA 90010. (213) 389-7372, (888) 389-7372. FAX: (213) 389-3299.
8715 Waikiki Station, Honolulu, HI 96830. (808) 734-3345, (888) 734-3345. FAX: (808) 734-3299.

SOUNDCASTLE RECORDING STUDIO
2840 Rowena Ave., Los Angeles, CA 90039. (213) 665-5201. FAX: (213) 662-4273.
Candace Corn

SUNSET SOUND RECORDERS
6650 Sunset Blvd., Hollywood, CA 90028. (213) 469-1186. FAX: (213) 465-5579.

TODD-AO/EDITWORKS
3399 Peachtree Rd. N.E., Suite 200, Atlanta, GA 303216. (404) 237-9977. FAX: (404) 237-3923.
PRESIDENT
Patrick Furlong

TODD-AO STUDIOS
900 N. Seward St., Hollywood, CA 90038. (213) 962-4000. FAX: (213) 466-2327.
PRESIDENT
Christopher Jenkins
4024 Radford St., Studio City, CA 91604. (818) 760-5069. FAX: (818) 760-5388.
SCORING STAGE MANAGER
Kirsten Smith

TODD-AO STUDIOS EAST
259 W. 54th St., New York, NY 10019. (212) 265-6225. FAX: (212) 247-5206.
PRESIDENT
Stephen Castellano

TODD-AO STUDIOS WEST
3000 Olympic Blvd., Bldg. One, Santa Monica, CA 90404. (310) 315-5000. FAX: (310) 315-5099.
PRESIDENT
Richard Hassanein

TOM THUMB MUSIC/ RUTH WHITE FILMS
Box 34485, Los Angeles, CA 90034. (310) 836-4678.
Ruth White

UNIVERSAL CITY STUDIOS
100 Universal City Plaza, Universal City, CA 91608. (818) 777-1000.

VOICES
16 E. 48 St., New York, NY 10017. (212) 935-9820. FAX: (212) 755-1150.
Richard Leonardi

WARNER BROS. STUDIOS
4000 Warner Blvd., Burbank, CA 91522. (818) 954-6000.
WARNER HOLLYWOOD STUDIOS, 1041 N. Formosa, Los Angeles, CA 90046. (213) 850-2500. FAX: (213) 850-2839.

WAVES SOUND RECORDERS
1956 N. Cahuenga Blvd., Hollywood, CA 90048. (213) 466-6141. FAX: (213) 466-3751.

WESTLAKE AUDIO
7265 Santa Monica Blvd., Los Angeles, CA 90046. (213) 851-9800. FAX: (213) 851-9386.

SID WOLOSHIN INC.
95 Madison Ave., New York, NY 10016. (212) 684-7222. FAX: (212) 689-5084.
Sid Woloshin, Carla Hill

SAUL ZAENTZ COMPANY FILM CENTER
2600 Tenth St., Berkeley, CA 94710. (510) 549-2500, (800) 227-0466. FAX: (510) 486-2015.

ZOUNDS, INC.
123 W. 18 St., New York, NY 10011. (212) 627-7700.

SPECIAL EFFECTS

A & A SPECIAL EFFECTS
7021 Hayvenhurst Ave., Van Nuys, CA 91406. (818) 909-6999.

AAFAB ENGINEERING
3112 Hermosa Ave., La Crescenta, CA 91214. (818) 249-9575.

ACCLAIM
12001 Ventura Pl., Suite 300, Studio City, CA 91604. (818) 752-5900. FAX: (818) 752-5917.

ACTION JETS F/X
6312 Hollywood Blvd., Suite 113, Hollywood, CA 90028-6269. (213) 769-4249.

ADVANCED CAMERA SYSTEMS
16117 Cohasset St., Van Nuys, CA 91406-2908. (818) 989-5222. FAX: (818) 994-8405.

ADVANCED FIRE & RESCUE SERVICES
10044 Columbus Ave., Mission Hills, CA 91345. (818) 837-7336. FAX: (818) 830-9221.
Craig Sanford, Mark Pedro

ALCONE COMPANY, INC
5-49 49th Ave., Long Island City, New York, NY 11011. (718) 361-8373.

ALL EFFECTS COMPANY, INC.
7915 Ajay Dr., Sun Valley, CA 91352. (818) 768-2000. FAX: (818) 768-2312.

DAVID ALLEN PRODUCTIONS
918 W. Oak St., Sun Valley, CA 91506. (818) 845-9270. FAX: (818) 567-4954.
David Allen

ALIAS/WAVEFRONT
11835 W. Olympic Blvd., Suite 350, Los Angeles, CA 90064. (310) 914-1566. FAX: (310) 914-1580. URL: www.aw.sgi.com

ALTERED ANATOMY, INC.
7125 Laurel Canyon Blvd., Suite A, North Hollywood, CA 91605. (818) 765-1192. FAX: (818) 765-5147.

ALTERIAN STUDIOS
1107 S. Mountain Ave., Monrovia, CA 91016. (818) 932-1488. FAX: (818) 932-1494.

AMALGAMATED DYNAMICS
21604 Marilla St., Chatsworth, CA 91311. (818) 882-8638. FAX: (818) 882-7327.

ANATOMORPHEX
8210 Lankershim, Suite 14, North Hollywood, CA 91605. (818) 768-2880. FAX: (818) 768-4808.
Robert Devine, James Clark

HOWARD A. ANDERSON CO.
100 Universal City Plaza, # 504-3, Universal City, CA 19608. (818) 777-2402.

ANIMUS FILMS
2 W. 47 St., New York, NY 10036. (212) 391-8716.

APA STUDIOS
230 W. 10 St., New York, NY 10014. (212) 929-9436.

ART F/X
3575 Caheunga Blvd. W., Suite 560, Los Angeles, CA 90068. (213) 876-9469.

ARTEFFEX
5419 Clean St., North Hollywood, CA 91601. (818) 506-5358. FAX: (818) 506-3171.

AVAILABLE LIGHT, INC.
1125 Flower St., Burbank, CA 91502. (818) 842-2109. FAX: (818) 842-0661.

BALSMEYER & EVERETT
230 W. 17 St., New York, NY 10011. (212) 627-3430.

BIFROST LASERFX
6733 Sale Ave., Wesy Hills, CA 91307. (818) 704-0423. FAX: (818) 704-0423.

BIGGER THAN LIFE INC.
1327 Fayette St., El Cajon, CA 92020. (800) 383-9980. FAX: (619) 449-8299.

BIOVISION
1580 California St., San Francisco, CA 94109. (415) 292-0333. FAX: (415) 292-0344.

BLACKSHEAR COMMUNICATIONS, INC.
6922 Hollywood Blvd., Suite 923, Hollywood, CA 90028. (213) 466-6412. FAX: (213) 466-1557.

BLACKSTONE MAGIK ENTERPRISES, INC.
12800 Puesta Del Sol, Redlands, CA 92373-7408.

BLUR STUDIO, INC.
1130 Abbot Kinney Blvd., Venice, CA 90291. (310) 581-8848. FAX: (310) 581-8850.
Cat Chapman

BODYTECH
13659 Victory Blvd., Suite 145, Van Nuys, CA 91401. (818) 385-0633.

BOSS FILM STUDIOS
13335 Maxella Ave., Marina Del Rey, CA 90292. (310) 823-0433. FAX: (310) 305-8576.

BRANAM ENTERPRISES, INC.
13335 Maxella Ave., Marina Del Rey, CA 90292. (818) 361-5030. FAX: (818) 361-8438.

BROOKLYN MODEL WORKS
60 Washington Ave., Brooklyn, NY 11205. (718) 834-1944. FAX: (718) 596-8934.
John Kuntzsch

THE BRUBAKER GROUP
10560 Dolcedo Way, Los Angeles, CA 90077. (310) 472-4766.

BUENA VISTA IMAGING
500 South Buena Vista St., Burbank, CA 91521-5073. (818) 560-5284. FAX: (818) 842-0532.
ohn Chambers.

BURMAN STUDIOS, INC.
4706 W. Magnolia Blvd., Burbank, CA 91505. (818) 980-6587. FAX: (818) 980-6589.

MICHAEL BURNETT PRODUCTIONS
8952 Glenoaks Blvd., Sun Valley, CA 91352. (818) 768-6103. FAX: (818) 768-6136.

CACIOPPO PRODUCTION DESIGN INC.
928 Broadway, Suite 1204, New York, NY 10010. (212) 777-1828. FAX: 212-777-1847.

CALICO ENTERTAINMENT
9340 Eton Ave., Chatsworth, CA 91311-5879. (818) 407-5200. FAX: (818) 407-5323.
PRESIDENT & CEO
Tom Burton

ADAMS R. CALVERT
17402 Chase St., Northridge, CA 91325. (818) 345-7703. FAX: (818) 365-0882.

CASTLE/BRYANT/JOHNSEN
210 N. Pass Ave., Suite 106, Burbank, CA 91505. (818) 557-7495. FAX: (818) 557-7498.

THE CHARACTER SHOP, INC.
9033 Owensmouth Ave., Canoga Park, CA 91304-1417. (818) 718-0094. FAX: (818) 718-0967.
Rick Lazzarini

CHARLEX, INC.
2 W. 45 St., New York, NY 10036. (212) 719-4600.

CHIODO BROS. PRODUCTIONS, INC.
425 S. Flower St., Burbank, CA 91502. (818) 842-5656. FAX: (818) 848-0891.

CIMMELLI INC.
16 Walter St., Pearl River, NY 10965. (914) 735-2090.

CINEMA ENGINEERING COMPANY
7243 Atoll Ave., Suite A, N. Hollywood, CA 91605-4105. (818) 765-5340. FAX: (818) 765-5349.

CINEMA NETWORK (CINENET)
2235 1st Ave., Suite 111, Simi Valley, CA 93065. (805) 527-0093. FAX: (805) 527-0305.

CINEMA RESEARCH CORP./ DIGITAL RESOLUTION
6860 Lexington Ave., Los Angeles, CA 90038. (213) 460-4111. FAX: (213) 469-4266.
V.P., MARKETING & SALES
Lena Evans

CINEMORPH EFFECTS GROUP
3123 Livonia Ave., Los Angeles, CA 90034. (310) 287-1674.

CINESITE DIGITAL FILM CENTER
1017 N. Las Palmas Ave., Suite 300, Hollywood, CA 90038.
(213) 468-4400. FAX: (213) 468-4404.

CINNABAR
1040 N. Las Palmas Ave., Hollywood, CA 90038. (213) 462-3737. Fax: (213) 462-0515.

COLLINS ENTERTAINMENT CONCEPTS CORP.
P.O. Box 292847, Kettering, OH 45429. (513) 293-0040. FAX: (513) 293-4431.

COMPOSITE IMAGE SYSTEMS
1144 N. Las Palmas Ave., Hollywood, CA 90038. (213) 463-8811.

THE COMPUTER FILM COMPANY
8522 National Blvd., Suite 103, Culver City, CA 92032. (310) 838-3456. FAX: (310) 838-1713.

CREATIVE CHARACTER ENGINEERING
7107 Gerald Ave., Van Nuys, CA 91406. (818) 901-0507. FAX: (818) 901-8417.

CREATIVE EFFECTS, INC.
760 Arroyo Ave., San Fernando, CA 91340-2222. (818) 365-0655. FAX: (818) 365-0651.

CRISWELL PRODUCTIONS
16535 Cualt St., Van Nuys, CA 91406. (818) 781-7739. FAX: (818) 781-7759.

CRUSE AND COMPANY, INC.
7000 Romaine St., Hollywood, CA 90038. (213) 851-8814. FAX: (213) 851-8788.

D'ANDREA PRODUCTIONS INC.
12 W. 37 St., New York, NY 10018. (212) 947-1211.

DAVE'S MARINE SERVICES INC.
1438 W. 14th St., Long Beach, CA 90813. (310) 437-4772. FAX: (310) 503-0848.

DAY SHADES
6859 Leetsdale Dr., Suite 202, Denver, CO 80224. (303) 399-8889. FAX: (303) 399-8881.
Craig T. Jones

DOM DE FILIPPO STUDIO, INC.
207 E. 37 St., New York, NY 10016. (212) 986-5444. FAX: 867-4220.

DE LA MARE ENGINEERING, INC.
1908 1st St., San Fernando, CA 91340-2610. (818) 365-9208. FAX: (818) 365-8775.

DESIGN FX CO.
936 N. Reese Place, Burbank, CA 91506. (818) 840-1444.

DIGISCOPE
6775 Centinela Ave., Stage 17, Culver City, CA 90230. (310) 574-5505. FAX: (310) 574-5509.

DIGITAL DOMAIN
300 Rose Ave., Venice, CA 90291. (310) 314-2800.

DIGITAL MAGIC COMPANY
3000 W. Olympic Blvd., Santa Monica, CA 90404. (310) 315-4720. FAX: (310) 315-4721.

DIRECT EFFECTS
31-00 47th Ave., Long Island City, NY 11101. (718) 706-6133. FAX: (718) 706-8026.
Tim Considine

WALT DISNEY IMAGINEERING
1401 Flower St., P.O. Box 25020, Glendale, CA 91221-5020. (818) 544-6500.

DREAM QUEST IMAGES
2635 Park Center Dr., Simi Valley, CA 93065. (805) 581-2671. FAX: (805) 583-4673.

DREAM THEATER
21345 Lassen Street, Suite 200, Chatsworth, CA 91311. (818) 773-4979. FAX: (818) 773-4970.
Darren Chuckru

DREAMLIGHT IMAGES, INC.
12700 Ventura Blvd., Studio City, CA 90038. (213) 850-1996. FAX: (213) 850-5318.

EASTERN OPTICAL EFFECTS
321 West 44th St., #401, New York, NY 10036. (212) 541-9220.

EDITEL
222 E. 44 St., New York, NY 10017. (212) 867-4600.
729 N. Highland Ave., Hollywood, CA 90038-3437. (213) 931-1821. FAX: (213) 931-7771.

E=MC2 INC.
621 E. Ruberta Ave., Suites 2, 3, 4, Glendale, CA 91201. (818) 243-2424. FAX: (818) 243-5126.
Bob Morgenroth

EFEX SPECIALISTS
43-17 37th St., Long Island City, NY 11101. (718) 937-2417.

EFILM
1146 N. Las Palmas, Hollywood, CA 90038. (213) 463-7041. FAX: (213) 465-7342.

EFFECTIVE ENGINEERING
6727 Flanders Dr., Suite 106, San Diego, CA 92121. (619) 450-1024. FAX: (619) 452-3241. e-mail: mlipsky@effecteng.com
Mark Lipsky

THE EFFECTS HOUSE
111 8th Ave., Suite 914, New York, NY 10011. (212) 924-9150. FAX: (212) 924-9193.

THE EFFECTSMITH
7831 Alabama Ave., Suite 19, Canoga Park, CA 91304. (818) 999-4560. FAX: (818) 999-4560.

ELECTRIC MACHINE ENTERTAINMENT
1930 Purdue Ave., Suite 6, Los Angeles, CA 90025. (310) 330-8841. FAX: (310) 477-1270.
Clive Milton

ELECTROFEX
1146 N. Central, Suite 231, Glendale, CA 91202. (818) 775-3838.

ENCORE VISUAL
702 Arizona Ave., Santa Monica, CA 90401. (310) 656-7663. FAX: (310) 656-7699.
Bob Coleman

ENERGY FILM LIBRARY
12700 Ventura Blvd., 4th flr, Studio City, CA 91604. (818) 508-1444, (800) IMAGERY. FAX: 818-508-1293.
Joan Sargent

EUE/SCREEN GEM PRINTS
222 E. 44 St., New York, NY 10017. (212) 867-4030.

FANTASY II FILM EFFECTS
504 S. Varney St., Burbank, CA 91502. (818) 843-1413. FAX: (818) 848-2824.

RUSS FARBER
19324 Oxnard St., Tarzana, CA 91356-1123. (818) 882-8220. FAX: (818) 708-8113.

FIM TECHNICAL SERVICES/SPECIAL EFFECTS
11118 Ventura Blvd., Studio City, CA 91604. (818) 508-1094.

FILMTRIX, INC.
P.O. Box 715, N. Hollywood, CA 91603. (818) 980-3700. FAX: (818) 980-3703.

FINE ART PRODUCTIONS/ RICHIE SURACI PICTURES
67 Maple St., Newburgh, NY 12550-4034. (914) 542-1585. FAX: (914) 561-5866. e-mail: Richie.Suraci@bbs.mhv.net
URL: http://www.geopages.com/Hollywood/1077

LARRY FIORITTO SPECIAL EFFECTS SERVICES
1067 E. Orange Grove Ave., Burbank, CA 91501. (818) 954-9828. FAX: (818) 954-9828.
Larry Fioritto

4-WARD PRODUCTIONS
2801 Hyperion Ave., Studio 104, Los Angeles, CA 90027. (213) 660-2430. FAX: (213) 660-2445.

F-STOP INC.
120 S. Buena Vista St., Burbank, CA 91505. (818) 843-7867.

FX ZONE
Jamboree Center, 1 Parl Plaza, 6th Floor, Irvine, CA 92714. (714) 852-7375. FAX: (714) 434-2776.
Jeff Miller

JOHN GATI FILM EFFECTS, INC.
6456 83rd Pl., Middle Village, NY 11379. (718) 894-5753.

PETER GEYER ACTION PROPS & SETS
8235 Lankershim Blvd., Suite G, North Hollywood, CA 91605. (818) 768-0070.

GILDERFLUKE & COMPANY
820 Thompson Ave., Suite 35, Glendale, CA 91202. (818) 546-1618. FAX: (818) 546-1619.

GLOBAL EFFECTS INC.
7119 Laurel Canyon Blvd., Unit 4, North Hollywood, CA 91605. (818) 503-9273. FAX: (818) 503-9459.

GLOBUS STUDIOS, INC.
44 W. 24 St., New York, NY 10010. (212) 243-1008.

GLOBAL EFECTS, INC.,
7119 Laurel Canyon Blvd., Unit 4, North Hollywood, CA 91605.
(818) 503-39273. FAX: (818) 503-9459.

R/GREENBERG ASSOCIATES
350 W. 39 St., New York, NY 10018. (212) 239-6767.

RICHARD HAAS PHOTO IMAGERY LTD.
P.O. Box 8385, Universal City, CA 91608. (818) 417-2064. FAX:
(818) 836-0817.

HANSARD ENTERPRISES INC.
P.O. Box 469, Culver City, CA 90232. (310) 840-5660. FAX:
(310) 840-5662.

HBO STUDIO PRODUCTIONS
120-A E. 23rd St., New York, NY 10010. (212) 512-7800. FAX:
(212) 512-7951.
Judy Glassman

JIM HENSON'S CREATURE SHOP
2821 Burton Ave., Burbank, CA 91504. (818) 953-3030. FAX:
(818) 953-3039.

HFWD VISUAL EFX
6666 Santa Monica Blvd., Hollywood, CA 90038. (213) 962-
2225. FAX: (213) 962-2220.

HILL PRODUCTION SERVICE INC.
6902 W. Sunset Blvd., Hollywood, CA 90028. (213) 463-1182.
FAX: (213) 463-2862.

HOLLYWOOD DIGITAL
6690 Sunset Blvd., Hollywood, CA 90028. (213) 465-0101.
FAX: (213) 469-8055.

HOLOGRAPHIC STUDIOS
240 E. 26 St., New York, NY 10010. (212) 686-9397.

HUNTER GRATZNER INDUSTRIES, INC.
4107 Redwood Ave., Los Angeles, CA 90088. (310) 578-9929.
FAX: (310) 578-7370.
Matthew Gratzner, Ian Hunter

ILLUSIONS
21205 Burton Ave., Burbank, CA 91504. (805) 296-0620. FAX:
9815) 296-9621.
Dave Simmons

IMAGE CREATORS INC.
2712 6th St., Santa Monica, CA 90405. (310) 392-3583. FAX:
(310) 396-6972.

IMAGE ENGINEERING INC.
736 N. Reese Place, Burbank, CA 91506. (818) 840-1444.

IMAGINE THAT
28064 Avenue, Unti K, Valencia, CA 91355.

INDUSTRIAL F/X PRODUCTIONS INC.
3522 Nobhill Dr., Sherman Oaks, CA 91423. (818) 501-1822.
FAX: (818) 501-4526.

INDUSTRIAL LIGHT & MAGIC (ILM)
P.O. Box 2459, San Rafael, CA 94912. (415) 258-2000.

INTERNATIONAL CREATIVE EFFECTS
401 S. Flower St., Burbank, CA 91502. (818) 840-8338. FAX:
(818) 840-8023.

INTROVISION INTERNATIONAL
1011 N. Fuller Ave., Hollywood, CA 90046. (213) 851-9262.
FAX: (213) 851-1649.

JEX FX
47 Paul Dr., #9, San Rafael, CA 94903. (415) 499-9477. FAX:
(415) 499-0911. e-mail: Gary@jexfx.com

STEVE JOHNSON'S X/FX INC.
8010 Wheatland Ave., Unit J, Sun Valley, CA 91352. (818) 504-
2177. FAX: (818) 504-2838.

THE JONES EFFECTS STUDIO
26007 Huntington Lane, Suite 9, Santa Clarita, CA 91355-
2746. (805) 294-9159. FAX: (805) 294-9689.
Andrew Jones

GENE KRAFT PRODUCTIONS
29 Calvados, Newport Beach, CA 92657. (714) 721-0609.
Gene Kraft

PETER KUNZ CO., INC.
55 Creek Rd., High Falls, NY 12440. (914) 687-0400.

LASER-PACIFIC MEDIA CORP.
540 N. Hollywood Way, Burbank, CA 91505. (818) 842-0777.
FAX: (818) 842-0776.
809 N. Cahuenga Blvd., Hollywood, CA 90038. (213) 463-6266.

LAZARUS LIGHTING DESIGN
4718 San Fernando Rd., Glendale, CA 91204-1825. (800) 553-
5554. FAX: (818) 956-3233.

ROBERT LEONARD PRODUCTIONS, INC.
P.O. Box 81440, Las Vegas, NV 89180. (702) 877-2449.

DANIEL LEVY
408 E. 13 St., New York, NY 10009. (212) 254-8964.

LEXINGTON SCENERY & PROPS
10443 Arminta St., Sun Valley, CA 91352-4109. (818) 768-
5768. FAX: (818) 768-4217.

LIBERTY STUDIOS, INC.
238 E. 26 St., New York, NY 10010. (212) 532-1865.

LINKER SYSTEMS
13612 Onkayha Circle, Irvine, CA 92720-3235. (714) 552-
1904. FAX: (714) 552-6985.

LIVE WIRE PRODUCTIONS
28729 S. Western, #209, Rancho Palos Verdes, CA 90275-
0800. (310) 831-6227. e-mail: LiveWirefx@aol.com

LOWTECH
11825 Major St., Suite 8, Culver City, CA 90230. (310) 398-
7094.

LUCASFILM, LTD.
(see Industrial Light & Magic)

LUMENI PRODUCTIONS, INC.
1632 Flower Street, Glendale, CA 91201-2357. (818) 956-
2200. FAX: (818) 956-3298.

MAGICRAFT
5722-A Union Pacific Ave., Commerce, CA 90022. (213) 724-
2279.

MAGICAL MEDIA INDUSTRIES, INC. (M.M.I.)
12031 Vose St., North Hollywood, CA 91605. (818) 765-6150.

MAKEUP & EFFECTS LABORATORIES, INC.
7110 Laurel Canyon Blvd., Unit E, N. Hollywood, CA 91605.
(818) 982-1483. FAX: (818) 982-5712.

MAKEUP & MONSTERS
18535 Devonshire Rd., Suite 109, Northridge, CA 91343. (818)
407-0197.

TODD MASTERS COMPANY
10312 Norris Ave., Unit D, Arleta, CA 91331. (818) 834-3000.

MATTE WORLD DIGITAL
24 Digital Dr., Suite 6, Novato, CA 94949. (415) 382-1929.
FAX: (415) 382-1999. email: info@matteworld.com
Krystyna Demkowicz

PAUL MANTELL STUDIO
16 Yale Ave., Jersey City, NJ 07304. (212) 966-9038.

MCCOURRY & ROBIN, INC.
22647 Ventura Blvd., Suite 240, Woodland Hills, CA 913643.
(818) 702-9544. FAX: (818) 386-2113.

MELROSE TITLES & OPTICAL EFFECTS
(213) 469-2070. FAX: (213) 469-7088.

METROLIGHT STUDIOS
5724 W. 3rd St., Suite 400, Los Angeles, CA 90016. (213) 932-
3344. FAX: (213) 932-8440.

MILLER IMAGING INTERNATIONAL, INC.
2718 Wilshire Blvd., Santa Monica, CA 90403. (310) 264-4711.
FAX: (310) 264-4717.

DAVID MILLER STUDIO
14141 Covello, Van Nuys, CA 91406. (818) 782-5615.

MODUS EFX PRODUCTIONS
11535 Tuxford St., Sun Valley, CA 91352. (818) 771-0016. FAX:
(818) 771-0017.

MOHAVE WEAPON SYSTEMS
P.O. Box 3821, Kingman, AZ 86402. (602) 565-3251.

MONSTER MECANIX
4319 Shitset Ave., Suite 3, Studio City, CA 91604.

MOTION ARTISTS, INC.
1400 N. Hayworth Ave., Suite 36, Los Angeles, CA 90046.
(213) 851-7737. FAX: (213) 851-7649.

MOVIE TECH STUDIOS
832 N. Seward St., Hollywood, CA 90038. (213) 467-8491.
FAX: (213) 467-8471.
Ewing M. "Lucky" Brown

NETWORK ART SERVICE
630 S. Mariposa St., Burbank, CA 91506. (818) 843-5078.
FAX: (818) 843-2528.

NOVOCOM
6314 Santa Monica Boulevard, Hollywood, CA 90038. (213) 461-
3688.

OBSCURE ARTIFACTS
8217 Lankershim Blvd., Suite 31, N. Hollywood, CA 91605.
(818) 767-8236. FAX: (818) 767-8236.

OCS/FREEZE FRAME/PIXEL MAGIC
10635 Riverside Dr., Toluca Lake, CA 91602. (818) 760-0862.
FAX: (818) 760-0483.
Ray McIntyre Jr., Dave Fiske

ONE UP
1645 N. Vine, Hollywood, CA 90028. (213) 957-9007.

JAMES O'NEIL & ASSOCIATES
725 N. Western Ave., Suite 109, Los Angeles, CA 90029. (213)
464-2995. FAX: (213) 464-2994.
Mandi Tinsley

OPTIC NERVE STUDIOS
9818 Glenoaks Blvd., Sun Valley, CA 91352. (818) 771-1007.
FAX: (818) 771-1009.

OPTICAL HOUSE, INC.
25 W. 45 St., New York, NY 10036. (212) 924-9150.

OWEN MAGIC SUPREME
734 N. McKeever Ave., Azusa, CA 91702. (818) 969-4519.
FAX: (818) 969-4614.

PACIFIC DATA IMAGES
1111 Karlstad Dr., Sunnyvale, CA 94089. (408) 745-6755. FAX:
(408) 745-6746.
3500 W. Olive Ave., Suite 980, Burbank, CA 91505. (818) 953-
7600. FAX: (818) 953-4191.
EXECUTIVE PRODUCER
Brad Lewis

PACIFIC TITLE & ART STUDIO
6350 Santa Monica Blvd., Los Angeles 90038. (213) 464-0121.
938-3711.

PACIFIC TITLE DIGITAL
5055 Wilshire Blvd., Suite 300, Los Angeles, CA 90036. (213)
938-8553. FAX: (213) 938-2836.

PENDLETON SYSTEMS, INC.
3710-A Foothill Blvd., Glendale, CA 91214. (818) 248-8310.
FAX: (818) 353-8428.

PERFORMANCE WORLD SPECIAL EFFECTS
416 S. Victory Blvd., Burbank, CA 91502. (818) 845-2704. FAX:
(818) 846-1145.
PRESIDENT
Jerry Williams

PERPETUAL MOTION PICTURES
24730 Tibbets Avenue, Suite 160, Valencia, CA 91355. (805)
294-0788. FAX: (815) 294-0786.
Richard Malzahn

PINNACLE EFX
2334 Elliot Ave., Seattle, WA 98121. (206) 441-9878. FAX:
(206) 728-2266.
EXECUTIVE PRODUCER
Karen Olcott

PLAYHOUSE PICTURES
1401 N. La Brea Ave., Hollywood, CA 90028-7505. (213) 851-
2112. FAX: (213) 851-2117.

POLAR TECHNOLOGIES USA
11419 Sunrise Gold Circle, Suite 2, Rancho Cordova, CA
95742. (916) 853-1111. FAX: (916) 853-9188.

PYROS PICTURES
1201 Dove St., Suite 550, Newport Beach, CA 92660. (714)
833-0334. FAX: (714) 833-8655.

QUANTEL
28 Thorndale Circle, Darien, CT 06820. (213) 656-3100. FAX:
(203) 656-3459.
Guy Walsingham

R/C MODELS
803 Channel St., San Pedro, CA 90731. (310) 833-4700. FAX:
(310) 833-9167.

RGA/LA
6526 Sunset Blvd., Los Angeles, CA 90028. (213) 957-6868.
FAX: (213) 957-9577.

RANDO PRODUCTIONS
1829 Dana St., Glendale, CA 91201. (818) 552-2900. FAX:
(818) 552-2388.

REEL EFX
5539 Riverton Ave., N. Hollywood, CA 91601. (818) 762-1710.

REELISTIC FX
21318 Hart St., Canoga Park, CA 91303. (818) 346-2484. FAX:
(818) 346-2710.

RHYTHM AND HUES
910 N. Sycamore Ave., Los Angeles, CA 90038. (213) 851-
6500. FAX: (213) 851-5505.

ROARING MOUSE ENTERTAINMENT
1800 Bridgegate St., Suite 204, Westlake Village, CA 91361.
(805) 373-8131. FAX: (805) 373-8133.

SAFARI ANIMATION & EFFECTS
10845 Van Owen St., Unit E, N. Hollywood, CA 91605. (805)
762-5203. FAX: (805) 762-3709.

SCENIC TECHNOLOGIES
4170 W. Harmon Ave., Suite 6, Las Vegas, NV 89103. (702)
876-1451. FAX: (702) 876-2795.
Robert Mealmear

SCHWARTZBERG & COMPANY
12700 Ventura Blvd., 4th Floor, Studio City, CA 91604. (818)
508-1833. FAX: (818) 508-1253.

SCREAMING MAD GEORGE, INC.
11750 Roscoe Blvd., Suite 11, Sun Valley, CA 91352. (818)
767-1631. FAX: (818) 768-3968.

SEE 3
2115 Colorado Ave., Santa Monica, CA 90404. (310) 264-
7970. FAX: (310) 264-7980.

SFX–STARLIGHT EFFECTS
923 N. Louise St., Suite C, Glendale, CA 91207. (818) 246-
5776. FAX: (818) 243-3308.

SIDESHOW PRODUCTIONS
31364 Via Colinas, Suite 106, Westlake Village, CA 90041.
(818) 259-0922.

SINGLE FRAME FILMS
437-1/2 N. Genesee Ave., Los Angeles, CA 90036. (213) 655-
2664.
Gary Schwartz

SLAGLE MINIMOTION, INC.
39 E. Walnut St., Pasadena, CA 91103. (818) 584-4088. FAX:
(818) 584-4099.

SOLDIERS OF LIGHT PRODUCTIONS
P.O. Box 16354, Encino, CA 91416-6354. (818) 345-3866. FAX:
(818) 345-1162.

ELAN SOLTES FX + DESIGN
3025 W. Olympic Blvd., Santa Monica, CA 90404-5001. (310)
315-2175. FAX: (310) 315-2176.

SONY PICTURES IMAGEWORKS
12020 W. Washington Blvd., Culver City, CA 90232. (310) 280-
7600. FAX: (310) 280-2342.

S.O.T.A. FX
7338 Valjean St., Van Nuys, CA 91406. (818) 780-1003. FAX:
(818) 780-4315.

SOUTHBAY MAKEUP FX STUDIOS
429 W. Laurel St., Suite A, Rancho Dominguez, CA 90220.
(310) 762-6057. FAX: (310) 490-0669.

SPECIAL EFFECTS SYSTEMS
26846 Oak Ave., Unit J, Canyon Country, CA 91351-2473.
(805) 251-1333. FAX: (805) 251-6619.

SPECIAL EFFECTS UNLIMITED, INC.
1005 Lillian Way, Los Angeles, CA 90038. (213) 466-3361.
FAX: (213) 466-5712.

SPECTAK PRODUCTIONS INC.
222 N. Sepulveda Blvd., Suite 2000, El Segundo, CA 90245.
(310) 335-2038.

STAGE 18
18 Leonard St., Norwalk, CT 06850. (203) 852-8185. FAX:
(203) 838-3126.

STICKS & STONES
12990 Branford St., Suite M, Arleta, CA 91331. (818) 252-
2088. FAX: (818) 252-2087.
Rob Burman, Jennifer E. McManus

DAVID STIPES PRODUCTIONS, INC.
685 Glenandale Ter., Glendale, CA 91206. (818) 243-1442.

STOKES/KOHNE ASSOCIATES, INC.
742 Cahuenga Blvd., Hollywood, CA 90038. (213) 469-8176.
FAX: (213) 469-0377.

STUDIO PRODUCTIONS
650 N. Bronson Ave., Suite 223, Hollywood, CA 90004. (213)
856-8048. FAX: (213) 461-4202.

SYNCHRONIC STUDIOS, INC.
535 Lipoa Pkwy., Suite 102, Kihei, Maui, HI 96753. (808) 875-
8600. FAX: (808) 875-8700.
Craig Robin

T&T OPTICAL EFFECTS
1619 1/2 S. Victory Blvd., Glendale, CA 91201. (818) 241-7407. FAX: (818) 241-7207.

THE TALKING LASER COMPANY
13248 Maxella Ave., Suite 261, Marina Del Rey, CA 90292-5671. (310) 822-6790. FAX: (310) 821-4010.

TECHNICREATIONS
2328 N. Batavia, Suite 106, Orange, CA 92665. (714) 282-8423. FAX: (714) 282-7853.

T.E.S.T. KREASHENS
26536 Golden Valley Rd., Suite 612, Saugus, CA 91350. (805) 251-6466. FAX: (805) 251-1153.

THIRD DIMENSION EFFECTS
330 N. Screenland Dr., Suite 138, Burbank, CA 91505. (818) 842-5665. FAX: (818) 842-9132.

3-D VIDEO
5240 Medina Rd., Woodland Hills, CA 91364-1913. (818) 592-0999. FAX: (818) 592-0987.

TITLE HOUSE INC.
738 N. Cahuenga Blvd., Los Angeles, CA 90038. (213) 469-8171. FAX: (213) 469-0377.

TODD-AO DIGITAL IMAGES
6601 Romaine St., Hollywood, CA 90038. (213) 962-4141. FAX: (213) 466-7903.
PRESIDENT
Brian Jennings

TRIBAL SCENERY
3216 Vanowen St., Burbank, CA 91505. (818) 558-4045.

TRI-ESS SCIENCES, INC.
1020 W. Chestnut St., Burbank, CA 91506. (818) 848-7838. FAX: (818) 848-3521.
Kim Greenfield

MIKE TRISTANO WEAPONS & SPECIAL EFFECTS
14431 Ventura Blvd., Suite 185, Sherman Oaks, CA 91423. (818) 888-6970. FAX: (818) 888-6447.

TRUE VIRTUAL REALITY
195 Sunset Hill Road, North Conway, NH 03860. (603) 356-7412. FAX: (603) 356-7412.

21ST CENTURY DIGITAL
3007 Washington Blvd., Marina Del Rey, CA 90292. (310) 574-1075.
Guerin "Gary" LaVaraque

TWO HEADED MONSTER
6161 Santa Monica Blvd., Suite 100, Los Angeles, CA 90038. (213) 957-5370. FAX: (213) 957-5371.

ULTIMATE EFFECTS
642 Sonora Ave., Glendale, CA 91201. (818) 547-4743.

VARITEL
3575 Cahuenga Blvd. W., Suite 675, Los Angeles, CA 90068. (213) 850-1165. FAX: (213) 850-6151.

THE VIDEO AGENCY
10900 Ventura Blvd., Studio City, CA 91604. (818) 505-8300. FAX: (818) 505-8370.

VIDEO DIMENSIONS INC.
6922 Hollywood Blvd., Suite 923, Hollywood, CA 90028. (213) 466-6412. FAX: (213) 466-1557.

VIEW STUDIOS INC.
6715 Melrose Ave., Hollywood, CA 90038. (213) 965-1270. FAX: (213) 965-1277.

VIEWPOINT DATA LABS
625 S. State Street, Orem, UT 84058. (801) 229-3000. FAX: (801) 229-3300.

VISIONART
3025 W. Olympic Blvd., Santa Monica, CA 90404. (210) 264-5566. FAX: (310) 264-6660.

VISUAL CONCEPT ENGINEERING
13300 Ralston Ave., Sylmar, CA 91342. (818) 367-9187. FAX: (818) 362-3490.
Peter Kuran

VISUAL IMPULSE PRODUCTIONS
10850 Wilshire Blvd., Suite 380, Los Angeles, CA 90024. (310) 441-2556. FAX: (310) 441-2558.

DON WAYNE MAGIC EFFECTS
10929 Hartsook St., N. Hollywood, CA 91601. (818) 763-3192. FAX: (818) 985-4953.

WILDFIRE ULTRAVIOLET VISUAL EFFECTS
11250 Playa Ct., Culver City, CA 90230-6150. (310) 398-3831. FAX: (310) 398-1871.
Richard Gleen

STAN WINSTON STUDIO
7032 Valjean Ave., Van Nuys, CA 91406. (818) 782-0870.

WONDERWORKS INC.
7231 Remmet Ave., Canoga Park, CA 91303. (818) 992-8811. FAX: (818) 347-4330.

WORKS NEW YORK, INC.
180 Varick St., New York, NY 10014. (212) 229-0741.

WORLDS, INC.
3160 W. Bayshore Rd., Palo Alto, CA 94303. (415) 813-5224. FAX: (415) 859-1130.

WUNDERFILM DESIGN
6690 Sunset Blvd., Hollywood, CA 90028-8116. (213) 466-1941. FAX: (213) 769-6095.

XAOS
600 Townsend St., Suite 271 E, San Francisco, CA 94103. (415) 558-9267. FAX: (415) 558-9160.
Helene Plotkin

Y.L.S. PRODUCTIONS
P.O. Box 34, Los Alamitos, CA 90720. (310) 430-2890. FAX: (310) 596-9563.

KEVIN YAGHER PRODUCTIONS
6615 Valjean Ave., Van Nuys, CA 91406. (818) 374-3210. FAX: 9818) 374-3214.

GENE YOUNG EFFECTS
517 W. Windsor Street, Glendale, CA 91204. (818) 243-8593.

Stock Shots

ACADEMY OF MOTION PICTURE ARTS & SCIENCES LIBRARY
333 S. La Cienega Blvd., Beverly Hills, CA 90211. (310) 247-3020, (310) 247-3000. FAX: (310) 657-5193.

AMERICAN FILM INSTITUTE LIBRARY
2021 N. Western Ave., Los Angeles, 90027. (213) 856-7600.

AMERICAN MUSEUM OF NATURAL HISTORY FILM ARCHIVES
Central Park West at 79th St., New York, NY 10024. (212) 769-5419.

AMERICAN STOCK PHOTOGRAPHY
6255 Sunset Blvd., #716, Los Angeles, CA 90028. (213) 469-3900. FAX: (213) 469-3909.

ARCHIVE FILMS
530 W. 25 St., New York, NY 10001. (212) 620-3955. FAX: (212) 645-2137.
V.P., SALES
Eric Rachlis

ASSOCIATED MEDIA IMAGES, INC.
650 N. Bronson, Suite 300, Los Angeles, 90004. (213) 871-1340. FAX: (213) 469-6048.

BRITANNICA FILMS
425 N. Michigan Ave., Chicago, IL 60611. (312) 347-7400, ext. 6512, (800) 554-9862.

BUDGET FILMS
4590 Santa Monica Blvd., Los Angeles, 90029. (213) 660-0187. FAX: (213) 660-5571.

BUENA VISTA STUDIOS
500 S. Buena Vista St., Burbank, 91521. (818) 560-1270.

CAMEO FILM LIBRARY, INC.
10760 Burbank Blvd., North Hollywood, 91601. (818) 980-8700. FAX: (818) 980-7113.
Steven Vrabel

CHERTOK ASSOCIATES, INC.
100 S. Main St., New City, NY 10956. (914) 639-4238. FAX: (914) 639-4239.

DICK CLARK MEDIA ARCHIVES, INC.
3003 W. Olive Ave., Burbank, CA 91505. (818) 841-3003. FAX: (818) 954-8609.

CLASSIC IMAGES
1041 N. Formosa Ave., W. Hollywood, CA 90046. (213) 850-2980, (800) 949-CLIP. FAX: (213) 850-2981.

CLIP JOINT FOR FILM
833-B N. Hollywood Way, Burbank, CA 91505. (818) 842-2525. FAX: (818) 842-2644.
Ken Kramer

COE FILM ASSOCIATES, INC.
65 E. 96 St.,New York, NY 10128. (212) 831-5355. FAX: (212) 645-0681.

LARRY DORN ASSOCS.
5820 Wilshire Blvd., #306, Los Angeles, 90036. (213) 935-6266. FAX: (213) 935-9523.

ENERGY FILM LIBRARY
12700 Ventura Blvd., Studio City, 91604. (818) 508-1444, (800) IMAGERY. FAX: (818) 508-1293.
Joan Sargent, Rafael Dalmua, Randy Gitsch.

FILE TAPE COMPANY
210 E. Pearson, Chicago, IL 60611. (312) 649-0599.

FILM & VIDEO STOCK SHOTS, INC.
10442 Burbank Blvd., N. Hollywood, CA 91601-2217. (818) 760-2098. FAX: (818) 760-3294. e-mail: stockshot@earthlink.net
URL: http://www.stockshots.com
PRESIDENT
Stephanie Siebart

FILM BANK
425 S. Victory Blvd., Burbank, 91502. (818) 841-9176.

THE FILM PRESERVE
2 Depot Plaza, #202-B, Bedford Hills, NY 10507. (914) 242-9838.

FISH FILMS FOOTAGE WORLD
4548 Van Noord Ave., Studio City, 91604-1013. (818) 905-1071. FAX (818) 905-0301.

GORDY COMPANY MEDIA LIBRARY
6255 Sunset Blvd., #1800, Los Angeles, CA 90028. (213) 856-3500. FAX: (213) 461-9526.

GREAT WAVES FILM LIBRARY
483 Mariposa Dr., Ventura, 93001-2230. (805) 653-2699.

GRINBERG FILM LIBRARIES, INC.
1040 N. McCadden Pl., Hollywood, CA 90038. (213) 464-7491. FAX: (213) 462-5352.
630 Ninth Ave., Suite 1200, New York, NY 10036. (212) 397-6200. FAX: (212) 262-1532.
Rich Sabreen

HALCYON DAYS PRODUCTIONS
1926 Broadway, #302, New York, NY10023. (212) 724-2626.

HOLLYWOOD NEWSREEL SYNDICATE INC.
1622 N. Gower St., Hollywood, 90028. (213) 469-7307. FAX: (213) 469-8251.

THE IMAGE BANK FILM & PHOTOGRAPHY LIBRARY
2400 Broadway, #220, Santa Monica, CA 90404. (310) 264-4850. FAX: (310) 453-1482.
111 Fifth Ave., New York, NY 10003. (212) 529-6793. FAX: (212) 529-8886.

IMAGEWAYS, INC.
412 W. 48 St., New York, NY 10036. (212) 265-1287.

INTERVIDEO INC.
10623 Riverside Dr., Toluca Lake, CA 91602. (818) 843-3633. (818) 569-4000. FAX: 843-6884.

JALBERT PRODUCTIONS, INC.
775 Park Ave., Huntington, NY 11743. (516) 351-5878. FAX: (516) 351-5875.
Carol Randel

KESSER STOCK LIBRARY
21 S.W. 15 Rd., Miami, FL 33129. (305) 358-7900.

KILLIAM SHOWS, INC.
500 Greenwich St., New York, NY 10013. (212) 925-4291.

CLAY LACY AVIATION INC.
7435 Valjean Ave., Van Nuys, 91406. (818) 989-2900. FAX: (818) 909-9537.

LIBRARY OF MOVING IMAGES
6671 Sunset Blvd., #1581, Hollywood, CA 90028. (213) 469-7499. FAX: (213) 469-7559.
Michael Yakaitis

MAC GILLIVRAY FREEMAN FILM & TAPE LIBRARY
P.O. Box 205, Laguna Beach, CA 92652. (714) 494-1055. FAX: (714) 494-2079.

MOONLIGHT PRODUCTIONS
3361 St. Michael Ct., Palo Alto, CA 94306. (415) 961-7440. FAX: (415) 961-7440.

MUSEUM OF MODERN ART FILM LIBRARY
11 W. 53 St., New York, NY 10019. (212) 708-9400.

NBC NEWS ARCHIVES
30 Rockefeller Plaza, New York, NY 10112. (212) 664-3797. FAX: (212) 957-8917. e-mail: ychin@nbc.com
Yuien Chin

NATIONAL GEOGRAPHIC FILM LIBRARY
1600 M St. NW, Washington, DC 20036. (202) 857-7659. FAX: (202) 429-5755.

NEWSREEL ACCESS SYSTEMS, INC.
50 E. 58 St., New York, NY 10155. (212) 826-2800.

PALISADES WILDLIFE LIBRARY
1205 S. Ogden Dr., Los Angeles, 90019. (213) 931-6186.

PARAMOUNT PICTURES STOCK FOOTAGE LIBRARY
5555 Melrose Ave., Hollywood, CA 90038. (213) 956-5510. FAX: (213) 956-1833.

PHOTO-CHUTING ENTERPRISES
12619 Manor Dr., Hawthorne, 90250-4313. (213) 678-0163.
Jean Boenish

PRELINGER ASSOC., INC.
430 W. 14 St., New York, NY 10014. (212) 633-2020.

PRODUCERS LIBRARY SERVICE
1051 N. Cole Ave., Hollywood, 90038. (213) 465-0572. FAX: (213) 465-1671.

PYRAMID MEDIA
2801 Colorado Ave., Santa Monica, 90404. (310) 828-7577. FAX: (310) 453-9083.
Pat Hamada

RETROSPECT FILM ARCHIVE
11693 San Vicente Blvd., #111, Los Angeles, CA 90049. (310) 471-1906. FAX: (310) 471-1430.

RON SAWADE CINEMATOGRAPHY.
P.O. Box 1310, Pismo Beach, CA 93448. (805) 481-0586. FAX: (805) 481-9752.

SECOND LINE SEARCH
1926 Broadway, New York, NY 10023. (212) 787-7500.

THE SOURCE STOCK FOOTAGE
738 N. Constitution Dr., Tucson, AZ 85748. (520) 298-4810. FAX: (520) 290-8831.
LIBRARY MANAGER
Don French

SPECTRAL COMMUNICATIONS
178 S. Victory Blvd., #106, Burbank, CA 91502. (818) 840-0111. FAX: (818) 840-0618.
Michael Povar

SPORTS CINEMATOGRAPHY GROUP
73 Market St., Venice, CA 90291. (310) 785-9100. FAX: (310) 396-7423.

STREAMLINE FILM ARCHIVES
432 Park Ave. S., New York, NY 10016. (212) 696-2616. FAX: (212) 696-0021.
Mark Trust

THE STOCK HOUSE
6922 Hollywood Blvd., Suite 621, Los Angeles, 90028. (213) 461-0061. FAX: (213) 461-2457.

TIMESCAPE IMAGE LIBRARY
12700 Ventura Blvd., 4th fl., Studio City, CA 91604. (818) 508-1444. FAX: (818) 508-1293.

TURNER ENTERTAINMENT CO.
10100 Venice Blvd., Culver City, 90232. (310) 558-7300.

20TH CENTURY FOX
P.O. Box 900, Beverly Hills, CA 90213. (310) 369-1000.

UCLA FILM & TELEVISION ARCHIVE
Commercial Services Division, 1015 N. Cahuenga Blvd.,
Hollywood, CA 90038. (213) 466-8559. FAX: (213) 461-6317.
Fonda Burrell

UNIVERSAL STUDIOS FILM LIBRARY
100 Universal City Plaza, Universal City, 91608. (818) 777-
3000. FAX: (818) 733-1579.

THE VIDEO AGENCY
10900 Ventura Blvd., Studio City, CA 91604. (818) 505-8300.
FAX: (818) 505-8370.
PRESIDENT
Jeffrey Goddard

VIDEO TAPE LIBRARY LTD.
1509 N. Crescent Heights Blvd. #2, Los Angeles, 90046. (213)
656-4330. FAX: (213) 656-8746. e-mail: vtl@earthlink.net
URL: http:/ www.videotapelibrary.com
Melody St. John, Peggy Shannon

WISH YOU WERE HERE FILM & VIDEO
1455 Royal Blvd., Glendale, CA 91207. (818) 243-7043. FAX:
(818) 241-1720.

WORLDWIDE TELEVISION NEWS
12401 W. Olympic Blvd., Los Angeles, CA 90064. (310) 826-
8133. FAX: (310) 826-6503.

STUDIO & EQUIPMENT SERVICES

ABC TELEVISION CENTER
4151 Prospect Ave., Los Angeles, CA 90027. (213) 557-7777.

ADVENTURE FILM STUDIOS
40-13 104 St., Queens, NY 11368. (718) 478-2639.

APOLLO THEATRE FOUNDATION, INC.
253 W. 125 St., New York, NY 10027. (212) 222-0992. FAX:
(212) 749-2743.
Charlotte Sutton

ATELIER CINEMA VIDEO STAGES
295 W. 4 St., New York, NY 10014. (212) 243-3550.

AVALON STAGES
6918 Tujunga Ave., N. Hollywood, CA 91605. (818) 508-0505.
FAX: (818) 508-5581.

BC STUDIOS
152 W. 25 St., New York, NY 10001. (212) 242-4065.

BIG VALLEY STAGE
7311 Radford Ave., No. Hollywood, CA 91605. (818) 340-1256.

BOKEN SOUND STUDIO
513 W. 54 St., New York, NY 10019. (212) 581-5507.

BREITROSE SELTZER STAGES, INC.
443 W. 18 St., New York, NY 10011. (212) 807-0664.

BROADWAY STUDIOS
25-09 Broadway, Long Island City, NY 11106. (718) 274-9121.

BURBANK MEDIA CENTER
2801 W. Olive Ave., Burbank, CA 91505. (818) 845-3531.

CBS STUDIO CENTER
4024 N. Radford Ave., Studio City, CA 91604. (818) 760-5000.
FAX: (818) 760-5048.

CBS TELEVISION CITY
7800 Beverly Blvd., Los Angeles, CA 90036. (213) 852-2345.

CFI (CONSOLIDATED FILM INDUSTRIES)
959 Seward St., Hollywood, CA 90038. (213) 960-7444. FAX:
(213) 460-4885.

THE CANNELL STUDIOS
7083 Hollywood Blvd., Hollywood, CA 90028. (213) 465-5800.
FAX: (213) 463-4987.

CARMAN PRODUCTIONS INC.
15456 Cabrito Rd., Van Nuys, CA 91406. (818) 787-6436. FAX:
(818) 787-3981.
Tom Skeeter

CAROLCO STUDIOS
1223 N. 23 St., Wilmington, NC 28405. (910) 343-3500.

CARTHAY STUDIOS, INC.
5907 W. Pico Blvd., Los Angeles, CA 90035. (213) 938-2101.
FAX: (213) 936-2769.

CECO INTERNATIONAL CORP.
440 W. 15 St., New York, NY 10011. (212) 206-8280. FAX:
(212) 727-2144.
Jody Baran

CHANDLER TOLUCA LAKE STUDIOS
11405 Chandler Blvd., No. Hollywood, CA 91601. (818) 763-
3650. FAX: (818) 990-4755.

CHAPLIN STAGE
1416 N. La Brea Ave., Hollywood, CA 90028. (213) 856-2682.
FAX: (213) 856-2795.
Bill Taylor

CHARLES RIVER STUDIOS
184 Everett St., Boston, MA 02134. (617) 787-4747.

CINE STUDIO
241 W. 54 St., New York, NY 10019. (212) 581-1916.

CINEMA SERVICES OF LAS VEGAS
4445 South Valley View Blvd., #7 & 8, Las Vegas, NV 89103.
(702) 876-4667. FAX: ((702) 876-4542.

CINEWORKS-SUPERSTAGE
1119 N. Hudson Ave., Los Angeles, CA 90038. (213) 464-
0296. FAX: (213) 464-1202.

THE COMPLEX
6476 Santa Monica Blvd., Hollywood, CA 90038. (213) 465-
0383, (213) 464-2124. FAX: (213) 469-5408.

COMTECH VIDEO PRODUCTIONS
770 Lexington Ave., New York, NY 10021. (212) 826-2935.
FAX: (212) 688-4264.
Ellen Zack

THE CULVER STUDIOS
9336 W. Washington Blvd., Culver City, CA 90230. (310) 202-
1234. FAX: (310) 202-3272.
Jack Kindberg

WALT DISNEY STUDIOS
500 S. Buena Vista St., Burbank, CA 91521. (818) 560-5151,
(818) 560-1000. FAX: (818) 560-1930.

WALT DISNEY/MGM STUDIOS
3300 N. Bonnett Creek Rd., Lake Buena Vista, FL 32830.
(407) 560-5353. (407) 560-6188.

DOM DE FILIPPO STUDIO
207 E. 37 St., New York, NY 10016. (212) 986-5444, (212)
867-4220.

EMPIRE BURBANK STUDIOS
1845 Empire Ave., Burbank, CA 91504. (818) 840-1400. FAX:
(818) 567-1062.
Robert Bagley, Don Buccola, Felix Girard

EMPIRE STAGES OF NY
25-19 Borden Ave., Long Island City, NY 11101. (718) 392-
4747.

ERECTER SET, INC.
1150 S. La Brea Ave., Los Angeles, CA 90019. (213) 938-
4762. FAX: (213) 931-9565.

FARKAS FILMS, INC.
385 Third Ave., New York, NY 10016. (212) 679-8212. FAX:
(212) 889-8354. URL: http://www.non-stop.com/farkas
F. E. Robinson

GMT STUDIOS
5751 Buckingham Parkway, Unit C, Culver City, CA 90230.
(310) 649-3733. FAX: (310) 216-0056.

GLENDALE STUDIOS
1239 S. Glendale Ave., Glendale, CA 91205. (818) 502-5300,
(818) 502-5500. FAX: (818) 502-5555.
Steven Makhanian

GLOBUS STUDIOS
44 W. 24 St., New York, NY 10011. (212) 243-1008.

GREAT SOUTHERN STUDIOS
15221 N.E. 21 Ave., N. Miami Beach, FL 33162. (305) 947-
0430.

GROUP W PRODUCTIONS
One Lakeside Plaza, 3801 Barham Blvd., Los Angeles, CA
90068. (213) 850-3800. FAX: (213) 850-3889.

HBO STUDIO PRODS.
120 E. 23 St., New York, NY 10010. (212) 512-7800.

HARPO STUDIOS
1058 W. Washington Blvd., Chicago, IL 60607. (312) 738-
3456.

HOLLYWOOD CENTER STUDIOS, INC.
1040 N. Las Palmas Ave., Los Angeles, CA 90038. (213) 860-
0000. FAX: (213) 860-8105.

HOLLYWOOD NATIONAL STUDIOS
6605 Eleanor Ave., Los Angeles, CA 90038. (213) 467-6272.

THE HOLLYWOOD STAGE
6650 Santa Monica Blvd., Los Angeles, CA 90038. (213) 466-
4393.

HORVATH & ASSOCIATES STUDIOS LTD.
95 Charles St., New York, NY 10014. (212) 741-0300.

INTER VIDEO, INC.
10623 Riverside Dr., Toluca Lake, CA 91602. (818) 843-3633,
(818) 569-4000. FAX: (818) 843-6884.

INTERSOUND INC.
8746 Sunset Blvd., Los Angeles, CA 90069. (310) 652-3741.
FAX: (310) 854-7290.

KCET STUDIOS
4401 W. Sunset Blvd., Los Angeles, CA 90027. (213) 953-
5258, (213) 666-6500. FAX: (213) 953-5496.

KAUFMAN ASTORIA STUDIOS
34-12 36th St., Astoria, NY 11106. (718) 392-5600. FAX: (718)
706-7733.

LIGHTING & PRODUCTION EQUIPMENT, INC.
1700 Marietta Blvd., Atlanta, GA 30318. (404) 352-0464.

MAGNO SOUND INC.
729 Seventh Ave., New York, NY10019. (212) 302-2505.

MELROSE STAGE
1215 Bates Ave., Los Angeles, CA 90029. (213) 660-8466.

MOLE-RICHARDSON CO.
937 N. Sycamore Ave., Los Angeles 90038. (213) 851-0111.

MORO-LANDIS
10960 Ventura Blvd., Studio City, CA 91604. (818) 753-5081.
FAX: (818) 752-1689.

MODERN TELECOMMUNICATIONS/MTI
1 Dag Hammarskjold Pl., New York, NY 10017. (212) 355-0510.

MOTHERS FILM STAGE
210 E. 5 St., New York, NY 10003. (212) 529-5097.

MOVIE TECH STUDIOS
832 N. Seward St., Hollywood, CA 90038. (213) 467-8491.
FAX: (213) 467-8471.

NBC TELEVISION
3000 W. Alameda Ave., Burbank, CA 91523. (818) 840-4444.

NATIONAL VIDEO CENTER/RECORDING STUDIOS, INC.
460 W. 42 St., New York, NY 10036. (212) 279-2000.

OCCIDENTAL STUDIOS
201 N. Occidental Blvd., Los Angeles, CA 90026. (213) 384-
3331. FAX: (213) 384-2684.

PARAMOUNT STUDIO GROUP
5555 Melrose Ave., Los Angeles, CA 90038. (213) 956-5000.

PATCHETT KAUFMAN ENTERTAINMENT
8621 Hayden Place, Culver City, CA 90232. (310) 838-7000.

PRIMALUX VIDEO PRODUCTION, INC.
30 W. 26 St., New York, NY 10010. (212) 206-1402. FAX: (212)
206-1826.
Judy Cashman

RALEIGH STUDIOS
5300 Melrose Ave., Los Angeles, CA 90038. (213) 466-3111.
FAX: (213) 871-5600.
Sharon Bode

REN-MAR STUDIOS
846 North Cahuenga Blvd., Los Angeles, CA 90038. (213) 463-
0808.

SANTA CLARITA STUDIOS
25135 Anza Dr., Santa Clarita, CA 91355. (805) 294-2000.
FAX: (805) 294-2020.

S.I.R. FILM STUDIOS, INC.
3322 La Cienega Pl., Los Angeles, CA 90016. (310) 287-3600.
FAX: (310) 287-3608.

SHINBONE ALLEY STAGE
680 Broadway, New York, NY 10012. (212) 420-8463.

SILVERCUP STUDIOS
42-25 21st St., Long Island City, NY 11101. (718) 784-3390,
(212) 349-9600.

SONY PICTURES STUDIOS
10202 W. Washington Blvd., Culver City, CA 90232. (310) 280-
6926.

SUNSET-GOWER STUDIOS LTD.
1438 N. Gower St., Los Angeles, CA 90028. (213) 467-1001.

TELETECHNIQUES, INC.
1 W. 19 St., New York, NY 10011. (212) 206-1475.

TELEVISION CENTER
6311 Romaine St., Los Angeles, CA 90038. (213) 464-6638.

3-G STAGE CORP.
236 W. 61 St., New York, NY 10023. (212) 247-3130.

TWENTIETH CENTURY FOX STUDIOS
10201 W. Pico Blvd., Los Angeles, CA 90035. (310) 369-1000.

UNITEL VIDEO SERVICES INC.
515 W. 57 St., New York, NY 10019. (212) 265-3600.

UNIVERSAL CITY STUDIOS
100 Universal City Plaza, Universal City, CA 91608. (818) 777-
3000.

UNIVERSAL STUDIOS FLORIDA
1000 Universal Studios Plaza, Orlando, FL 32819. (407) 363-8400.

VPS STUDIOS
800 N. Seward St., Hollywood, CA 90038. (213) 469-7244.
FAX: (213) 463-7538.

VANCO LIGHTING SERVICES
9561 Satellite Blvd., Orlando, FL 32837. (407) 855-8060. FAX:
(407) 855-8059.

VERITAS STUDIOS
527 W. 45 St., New York, NY 10036. (212) 581-2050.

VIDEO PLANNING INC.
250 W. 57 St., New York, NY 10019. (212) 582-5066.

VISUAL IMAGES UNLIMITED
1608 Mayflower, Unit A, Monrovia, CA 91016. (213) 994-
6119.
Mark Enzenauer

WTN-WORLDWIDE TV NEWS PRODS.
1995 Broadway, New York, NY 10023. (212) 362-4440. FAX:
(212) 446-1269.
MARKETING MANAGER
Earl Adams

WARNER BROS. INC.,
4000 Warner Blvd., Burbank, CA 91522. (818) 954-6000, (818)
954-923. FAX: (818) 954-4213.

WARNER HOLLYWOOD STUDIOS
1041 N. Formosa Ave., W. Hollywood, CA 90046. (213) 850-
2837. FAX: (213) 850-2839.

WHITEFIRE THEATRE, THE SOUNDSTAGE RENTAL
13500 Ventura Blvd., Sherman Oaks, CA 91423. (818) 990-
2324.

SUBTITLES & CAPTIONS

CAPTION CENTER
610 N. Hollywood Way, #350, Burbank, CA 91505. (818) 562-3344. FAX: (818) 562-3388.
125 Western Ave., Boston, MA 02134. (617) 492-9225. FAX: (617) 582-0590. URL: http://www.wgbh.org/caption
475 Park Ave. S., 10th fl., New York, NY 10016. (212) 223-4930. FAX: (212) 688-2181.

CAPTIONS, INC.
2479 Lanterman Terr., Los Angeles, CA 90039. (213) CAPTION.
2619 Hyperion Ave., Suite A, Los Angeles, CA 90027. (213) 227-8466.

CINETYP, INC.
843 Seward St., Hollywood, CA 90038. (213) 463-8569. FAX: (213) 463-4129.

CREST NATIONAL VIDEOTAPE FILM LABS
1000 N. Highland Ave., Hollywood, CA 90038. (213) 466-0624. 462-6696. FAX: (213) 461-8901.

DEVLIN VIDEO SERVICE
1501 Broadway, Suite 408, New York, NY 10036. (212) 391-1313.

FOREIGN LANGUAGE GRAPHICS
4303 N. Figueroa St., Los Angeles, CA 90065. (213) 224-8417. FAX: (213) 224-8446.

GLOBAL LANGUAGE SERVICES
2027 Las Lunas, Pasadena, CA 91107. (818) 792-0862, (818) 792-0576. FAX: (818) 792-8793.

HOMER AND ASSOCIATES, INC.
Sunset Gower Studios, 1420 N. Beachwood Dr., Hollywood, CA 90028. (213) 462-4710.

INTEX AUDIOVISUALS
9021 Melrose Ave., Suite 205, Los Angeles, CA 90069. (310) 275-9571. FAX: (310) 271-1319.

LINGUATHEQUE OF L.A.
13601 Ventura Blvd., #102, Sherman Oaks, CA 91423. (818) 995-8933. FAX: (818) 995-1228.
Eric Laufer

MASTERWORDS
1512 Eleventh St., #205, Santa Monica, CA 90401-2907. (310) 390-1033. FAX: (310) 394-7954.

NATIONAL CAPTIONING INSTITUTE
1443 Beachwood Dr., Hollywood, CA 90028. (213) 469-7000. FAX: (213) 957-5266.

P.F.M. DUBBING INTERNATIONAL
8306 Wilshire Blvd., Suite 947, Beverly Hills, CA 90211. (310) 936-7577. FAX: (310) 936-1691.

PACIFIC TITLE & ART STUDIO
6350 Santa Monica Blvd., Los Angeles, CA 90038. (213) 938-3711. FAX: (213) 938-6364.

JOY RENCHER'S EDITORIAL SERVICE
738 Cahuenga Blvd., Hollywood, CA 90038. (213) 463-9836. FAX: (213) 469-0377.

SOFTNI CORP/SDI SUBTITLING & DUBBING INTL.
11444 W. Olympic Blvd., 10th fl., Los Angeles, CA 90064. (310) 312- 9558. FAX: (310) 473-6052.

TITLE HOUSE INC.
738 N. Cahuenga Blvd., Los Angeles, CA 90038. (213) 469-8171. FAX: (213) 469-0377.

WORDS IN PICTURES
1028 S. Alfred, Los Angeles, CA 90035. (213) 655-9221. FAX: (213) 655-3350.

TALENT AGENCIES

ABRAMS ARTISTS & ASSOCS.
9200 Sunset Blvd., 11th Floor, Los Angeles, CA 90069. (310) 859-0625. FAX: (310) 276-6193.
420 Madison Ave., Suite 1400, New York, NY 10017. (212) 935-8980.

ABRAMS, RUBALOFF & LAWRENCE., INC.
8075 West 3rd, Suite 303, Los Angeles, CA 90048. (213) 935-1700. FAX: (213) 932-9901.

ACTORS GROUP AGENCY
8730 Sunset Blvd., Suite 220 W., Los Angeles, CA 90069. (310) 657-7113. FAX: (310) 657-1756.
157 W. 57 St., Suite 211, New York, NY 10019. (212) 245-2930. FAX: (212) 245-7096.
Pat House

THE AGENCY
1800 Avenue of the Stars, #400, Los Angeles, CA 90067. (310) 551-3000. FAX: (310) 551-1424.

AGENCY FOR THE PERFORMING ARTS
9000 Sunset Blvd., #1200, Los Angeles, CA 90069. (310) 273-0744. FAX: (310) 888-4242.
888 Seventh Ave., New York, NY10106. (212) 582-1500. FAX: (212) 245-1647.

AIMEE ENTERTAINMENT ASSOCIATION
1500 Ventura Blvd., Sherman Oaks, CA 91403. (818) 783-9115.

ALL-STAR TALENT AGENCY
7834 Alabama Ave., Canoga Park, CA 91304-4905. (818) 346-4313.
AGENT
Robert Allred

ALL TALENT AGENCY
2437 E. Washington Blvd., Pasadena, CA 91104. (818) 797-8202. FAX: (818) 791-5250.

CARLOS ALVARADO AGENCY
8455 Beverly Blvd., Suite 406, Los Angeles, CA 90048-3416. (213) 655-7978.

AMBROSIO/MORTIMER & ASSOCS.
9150 Wilshire Blvd., Suite 175, Beverly Hills, CA 90212. (310) 274-4274. FAX: (310) 274-9642.

AMERICAN-INT'L TALENT
303 W. 42 St., New York, NY 10036. (212) 245-8888. FAX: (212) 245-8926.

AMSEL, EISENSTADT & FRAZIER, INC.
6310 San Vicente Blvd., Suite 407, Los Angeles, CA 90048. (213) 939-1188. FAX: (213) 939-0630.

BEVERLY ANDERSON
1501 Broadway, New York, NY 10036. (212) 944-7773.

THE ARTISTS AGENCY
10000 Santa Monica Blvd., Suite 305, Los Angeles, CA 90067. (310) 277-7779. FAX: (310) 785-9338.

ARTIST NETWORK
8438 Melrose Pl., Los Angeles, CA 90039. (213) 651-4244. FAX: (213) 651-4699.
Debra Hope

ASSOCIATED BOOKING CORP.
1995 Broadway, New York, NY 10023. (212) 874-2400.

RICHARD ASTOR
250 W. 57th St., New York, NY 10107. (212) 581-1970

ATKINS & ASSOCS.
303 S. Crescent Heights Blvd., Los Angeles, CA 90048. (213) 658-1025.

BDP AND ASSOCS.
10637 Burbank Blvd., North Hollywood, 91601. (818) 506-7615.

BADGLEY/CONNOR
9229 Sunset Blvd., #311, Los Angeles, CA 90069. (310) 278-9313. FAX: (310) 278-4128.

BAUMAN, HILLER & ASSOCS.
5757 Wilshire Blvd., PH 5, Los Angeles, CA 90036. (213) 857-6666. FAX: (213) 857-0638.
250 W. 57 St., #2223, New York, NY 10019. 757-0098. FAX: (212) 489-8531.

J. MICHAEL BLOOM & ASSOC.
9255 Sunset Blvd., Suite 710, Los Angeles, CA 90069. (310) 275-6800. FAX: (310) 275-6941.
233 Park Ave. S., New York, NY 10003. (212) 529-6500. FAX: (212) 529-5838.

BENNETT AGENCY
150 S. Barrington Ave., Suite 1, Los Angeles, CA 90049. (310) 471-2251. FAX: (310) 471-2254.

BORINSTEIN ORECK BOGART AGENCY
8271 Melrose Ave., Suite 110, Los Angeles, CA 90046. (213) 658-7500. FAX: (213) 658-8866.

THE BRANDT COMPANY
15250 Ventura Blvd., #720, Sherman Oaks, CA 91403. (818) 783-7747. FAX: (818) 784-6012.
Geoffrey Brandt

KELLY BRESLER & ASSOCIATES
15760 Ventura Blvd., #1730, Encino, CA 91436. (818) 905-1155.

CURTIS BROWN, LTD.
606 N. Larchmont Blvd., #309, Los Angeles, CA 90004. (213) 473-5400.

CNA & ASSOCS.
1801 Avenue of the Stars, #1250, Los Angeles, CA 90067. (310) 556-4343. FAX: (310) 556-4633.

CAMDEN-ITG
822 S. Robertson Blvd., #200, Los Angeles, CA 90035. (310) 289-2700. FAX: (310) 286-2718.

WILLIAM CARROLL AGENCY
139 N. San Fernando Blvd., Suite A, Burbank, CA 91502. (818) 848-9948. FAX: (213) 849-2553.

CAVALERI & ASSOCIATES
405 Riverside Dr., Burbank, CA 91506. (818) 955-9300. FAX: (818) 955-9399.
Ray Cavaleri

CENTURY ARTISTS, LTD.
9744 Wilshire Blvd., Suite 308, Beverly Hills, CA 90212. (310) 273-4366.

THE CHASIN AGENCY
8899 Beverly Blvd., Suite 715, Los Angeles, CA 90048. (310) 278-7505. FAX: (310) 275-6685.

CINEMA TALENT AGENCY
8033 W. Sunset Blvd., #808. Los Angeles, CA 90046. (213) 656-1937. FAX: (213) 654-4678.

CIRCLE TALENT AGENCY
433 N. Camden Dr., #400, Beverly Hills, CA 90210. (310) 285-1585.

COMMERCIALS UNLIMITED, INC.
9601 Wilshire Blvd., #620, Los Angeles, CA 90210. (310) 888-8788. FAX: (310) 888-8712.

CONTEMPORARY ARTISTS LTD.
1427 Third St., #205, Santa Monica, CA 90401. (310) 395-1800.

CORALIE JR. AGENCY
4789 Vineland Ave., #100, N. Hollywood, CA 91602. (818) 766-9501.

THE CRAIG AGENCY
8485 Melrose Pl., Suite E, Los Angeles, CA 90069. (213) 655-0236. FAX: (213) 655-1491.

CREATIVE ARTISTS AGENCY
9830 Wilshire Blvd., Beverly Hills, CA 90212. (310) 288-4545. FAX: (310) 288-4800.

LIL CUMBER ATTRACTIONS AGENCY
6363 Sunset Blvd., Suite 807, Los Angeles, CA 90028. (213) 469-1919. FAX: (213) 469-4883.

CUNNINGHAM, ESCOTT, DIPENE & ASSOC.
10635 Santa Monica Blvd., #130, Los Angeles, CA 90025-4900. (310) 475-2111. FAX: (310) 475-1929.
257 Park Ave. South, Suite 900, New York, NY 10010. (212) 477-1666. FAX: (212) 979-2011.

DADE/SCHULTZ ASSOCS.
11846 Ventura Blvd., #101, Studio City, CA 91604. (818) 760-3100. FAX: (818) 760-1395.

DIAMOND ARTISTS AGENCY, LTD.
215 N. Barrington Ave., Los Angeles, CA 90049. (310) 472-7579. FAX: (310) 472-2687.

ENTERTAINMENT ENTERPRISES
1680 Vine St., Suite 519, Los Angeles, CA 90028. (213) 462-6001. FAX: (213) 462-6003.

FAVORED ARTISTS
122 S. Robertson Blvd., #202, Los Angeles, CA 90048. (310) 247-1040. FAX: (310) 247-1048.

WILLIAM FELBER
2126 Cahuenga Blvd., Los Angeles, CA 90068. (213) 466-7627.

LIANA FIELDS AGENCY
3325 Wilshire Blvd., #749, Los Angeles, CA 90010. (213) 487-3656.

FILM ARTISTS ASSOCIATES
7080 Hollywood Blvd., Suite 704, Los Angeles, CA 90028. (213) 463-1010. FAX: (213) 463-0702.

FIRST ARTISTS AGENCY
10000 Riverside Dr., Suite 10, Toluca Lake, CA 91602. (818) 509-9292. FAX: (818) 509-9295.

FLASHCAST/PETCAST
Centrum Towers, Ground Floor, 3575 Cahuenga Blvd. West, Universal City, CA 90068. (818) 760-7986, (800) 273-9008. FAX: (818) 760-6792.
Chris Adams, Richard Weiner

FLICK EAST-WEST TALENTS INC.
9057 Nemo St., Suite A, W. Hollywood, 90069. (310) 247-1777. FAX: (310) 858-1357.
Carnegie Hall Studio 1110, 881 Seventh Ave., New York, NY 10019. (212) 307-1850.

THE GAGE GROUP
9255 Sunset Blvd., Suite 515, Los Angeles, CA 90069. (310) 859-8777. FAX: (310) 859-8166.
315 W. 57 St., New York, NY 10019. 541-5250.

DALE GARRICK INTL. AGENCY
8831 Sunset Blvd., #402, Los Angeles, CA 90069. (310) 657-2661.

GEDDES AGENCY
1201 Greenacre Ave., Los Angeles, CA 90046-5707. (213) 878-1155. FAX: (213) 878-1150.

DON GERLER TALENT AGENCY
3349 Cahuenga Blvd. West, Suite 1, Los Angeles, CA 90068. (213) 850-7386.

THE GERSH AGENCY
232 N. Canon Dr., Beverly Hills, CA 90210. (310) 274-6611. FAX: (310) 274-3923.
130 W. 42 St., #1804, New York, NY 10036. (212) 997-1818.

GILLA ROOS LTD.
9744 Wilshire Blvd., #203, Beverly Hills, CA 90212. (310) 274-9356. FAX: (310) 274-3604.

GOLD/MARSHAK ASSOCIATES
3500 W. Olive, Suite 1400, Burbank, CA 91505. (818) 972-4300. FAX: (818) 955-6411.

GORFAINE/SCHWARTZ AGENCY
3301 Barham Blvd., #201, Los Angeles, CA 90068. (213) 969-1011. FAX: (213) 969-1022.

GROSSMAN & ASSOCIATES
211 S. Beverly Dr., Suite 206, Beverly Hills, CA 90212. (310) 550-8127.

HAMILBURG AGENCY
292 S. La Cienega, Suite 312, Beverly Hills, CA 90211. (310) 657-1501.

MICHAEL HARTIG
156 Fifth Ave., New York, NY 10010. (212) 929-1772.

BEVERLY HECHT AGENCY
8949 Sunset Blvd., Suite 203, Los Angeles, CA 90069. (310) 278-3544.

HENDERSON/ HOGAN AGENCY
247 S. Beverly Dr., #102, Beverly Hills, CA 90212. (310) 274-7815. 850 Seventh Ave., New York, NY 10019. (212) 765-5190.

IFA TALENT AGENCY
8730 Sunset Blvd., #490, Los Angeles, CA 90069. (310) 659-5522.

INNOVATIVE ARTISTS
1999 Ave. of the Stars, Suite 2850, Los Angeles, CA 90067-6082. (310) 553-5200. FAX: (310) 557-2211.
1776 Broadway, New York, NY 10019. (212) 315-4455. FAX: (212) 315-4455.

INTERNATIONAL CREATIVE MANAGEMENT
8942 Wilshire Blvd., Beverly Hills, CA 90211. (310) 550-4000. FAX: (310) 550-4108.
40 W. 57 St., New York, NY 10019. (212) 556-5600.

INTERNATIONAL TALENT GROUP
9000 Sunset Blvd., Los Angeles, CA 90069. (310) 247-0680.

JAN J. AGENCY
365 W. 34 St., New York, NY 10001. (212) 967-5265.

JORDAN, GILL & DORNBAUM
156 Fifth Ave., #711, New York, NY 10010. (212) 463-8455.

KAPLAN-STAHLER AGENCY
8383 Wilshire Blvd., #923, Beverly Hills, CA 90211. (213) 653-4483. FAX: (213) 653-4506.

KAZARIAN SPENCER & ASSOCS. INC.
11365 Ventura Blvd., #100, Studio City, CA 91604. (818) 769-9111. FAX: (818) 769-9840.

KELMAN/ARLETTA AGENCY
7813 Sunset Blvd., Los Angeles, CA 90046. (213) 851-8822. FAX: (213) 851-4923.

KOHNER AGENCY
9300 Wilshire Blvd., #555, Beverly Hills, CA 90212. (310) 550-1060. FAX: (310) 276-1083.

THE KOPALOFF COMPANY
1800 Avenue of the Stars, #400, Los Angeles, CA 90067. (310) 551-3000. FAX: (310) 277-9513.

THE KRAFT-BENJAMIN AGENCY
8491 Sunset Blvd., Suite 492, Los Angeles, CA 90069. (310) 652-6065. FAX: (310) 652-6146.

LUCY KROLL
390 West End Ave., New York, NY 10024. (212) 877-0627.

L.A. ARTISTS
606 Wilshire Blvd., #416, Santa Monica, CA 90401. (310) 395-9589.

L.A. TALENT
8335 Sunset Blvd., Los Angeles, CA 90069. (213) 656-3722. FAX: (213) 650-4272.

SUSAN LANE MODEL & TALENT
14071 Windsor Pl., Santa Ana, CA 92705. (714) 731-1420. FAX: (714) 731-5223.

LANTZ OFFICE
888 Seventh Ave., #2500, New York, NY 10106. (212) 586-0200.

LIONEL LARNER LTD.
119 W. 57 St., Suite 1412, New York, NY 10019. (212) 246-3105. FAX: (212) 956-2851.

LEVIN AGENCY
9255 Sunset Blvd., #400, W. Hollywood, 90069. (310) 278-0353.

ROBERT LIGHT AGENCY
6404 Wilshire Blvd., Suite 900, Los Angeles, CA 90048. (213) 651-1777. FAX: (213) 651-4933.

LYONS/SHELDON AGENCY
800 S. Robertson Blvd., #46, Los Angeles, CA 90069. (310) 652-8778.

MARGE MCDERMOTT
216 E. 39 St., New York, NY 10016. (212) 889-1583.

SANDRA MARSH MANAGEMENT
9150 Wilshire Blvd., #220, Beverly Hills, CA 90210. (310) 285-0303. FAX: (310) 285-0218.

MARTEL AGENCY
1680 N. Vine St., Suite 203, Los Angeles, CA 90028. (213) 461-5943. FAX: (213) 461-6350.

JOHNNIE MARTINELLI ATTRACTIONS
888 Eighth Ave., New York, NY 10019. (212) 586-0963.

MEDIA ARTISTS GROUP
8383 Wilshire Blvd., Suite 954, Beverly Hills, CA 90211-2408. (213) 658-5050.

MERIDIAN TALENT AGENCY
373 S. Robertson Blvd., Beverly Hills, CA 90211. (310) 652-7799. FAX: (310) 854-3966.
Arthur Braun

WILLIAM MORRIS AGENCY
151 El Camino Dr., Beverly Hills, 90212. (310) 274-7451. FAX: (310) 859-4462.
1350 Ave. of the Americas, New York, NY 10019. (212) 586-5100.

OMNIPROP INC. TALENT AGENCY WEST
10700 Ventura Blvd., 2nd fl., Studio City, 91604 (818) 980-9267. FAX: (818) 980-9371.

OPPENHEIM-CHRISTIE ASSOC.
13 E. 37 St., New York, NY 10016. (212) 213-4330.

FIFI OSCARD AGENCY
24 W. 40 St., New York, NY 10018. (212) 764-1100.

PARADIGM AGENCY
10100 Santa Monica Blvd., 25th fl., Los Angeles, CA 90067. (310) 277-4400.

PORTMAN ORGANZATION
8033 Sunset Blvd., #964, Los Angeles, CA 90046. (213) 871-8544. FAX: (708) 982-9383.

PREMIER TALENT AGENCY
3 E. 54 St., New York, NY 10022. (212) 758-4900. FAX: (212) 755-3251.

PREMIERE ARTISTS AGENCY
8899 Beverly Blvd., #102, Los Angeles, CA 90048. (310) 271-1414. FAX: (310) 205-3981.

PRIVILEGE TALENT AGENCY
8170 Beverly Blvd., Suite 204, Los Angeles, CA 90048. (213) 658-8781.

PROGRESSIVE ARTISTS AGENCY
400 S. Beverly Dr., Suite 216, Beverly Hills, CA 90212. (310) 553-8561.

THE ROBERTS COMPANY
10345 W. Olympic Blvd., PH, Los Angeles, CA 90064. (310) 552-7800. FAX: (310) 552-9324.

MARION ROSENBERG
8428 Melrose Pl., Suite B, Los Angeles, CA 90069. (213) 653-7383. FAX: (213) 653-9268.

THE SANDERS AGENCY LTD.
8831 Sunset Blvd., Suite 304, Los Angeles, CA 90069. (310) 652-1119. FAX: (310) 652-7810.
1204 Broadway, New York, NY 10001. (212) 779-3737.

IRV SCHECTER COMPANY
9300 Wilshire Blvd., #400, Beverly Hills, CA 90212. (310) 278-8070. FAX: (310) 278-6058.

SCHULLER TALENT
276 Fifth Ave., New York, NY 10001. (212) 532-6005.

DON SCHWARTZ & ASSOC.
6922 Hollywood Blvd., #508, Los Angeles, CA 90028. (213) 464-4366. FAX: (213) 464-4661.

SELECTED ARTISTS AGENCY
3900 W. Alameda Blvd., Suite 1700, Burbank, CA 91505. (818) 972-1747.

DAVID SHAPIRA ASSOCIATES, INC.
15301 Ventura Blvd., Suite 345, Sherman Oaks, CA 91403. (818) 906-0322. FAX: (818) 783-2562.

MICHAEL SLESSINGER & ASSOCS.
8730 Sunset Blvd., #220 West, Los Angeles, CA 90069. (310) 657-7113. FAX: (310) 657-1756.

SUSAN SMITH & ASSOCIATES
121 N. San Vicente Blvd., Beverly Hills, CA 90211. (310) 852-4777.

STONE/MANNERS AGENCY
8091 Selma Ave., Los Angeles, CA 90046. (213) 654-7575.

H. N. SWANSON
8523 Sunset Blvd., Los Angeles, CA 90069. (310) 652-5385.

TALENT GROUP INC.
9250 Wilshire Blvd., #208, Beverly Hills, CA 90212. (310) 273-9559. FAX: (310) 273-5147.

TALENT REPS., INC.
20 E. 53 St., New York, NY 10022. (212) 752-1835.

HERB TANNEN & ASSOC.
1800 N. Vine St., Suite 305, Los Angeles, CA 90028. (213) 466-6191. FAX: (213) 466-0863.

TWENTIETH CENTURY ARTISTS
15315 Magnolia Blvd., Suite 429, Sherman Oaks, 91403. (818) 788-5516.

UNITED TALENT AGENCY
9560 Wilshire Blvd., #500, Beverly Hills, CA 90212. (310) 273-6700. FAX: (310) 247-1111.

RUTH WEBB ENTERPRISES, INC.
13834 Magnolia Blvd., Sherman Oaks, CA 91423. (818) 905-7000. FAX: (213) 874-1860.
Scott Stander

BOB WATERS AGENCY
1501 Broadway, #705, New York, NY 10036. (212) 302-8787.

HANNS WOLTERS THEATRICAL AGENCY
10 W. 37 St., New York, NY 10018. (212) 714-0100. FAX: (212) 695-2385.

WRITERS & ARTISTS AGENCY
924 Westwood Blvd., Suite 900, Los Angeles, CA 90024. (310) 824-6300.
19 W. 44 St., #1000, New York, NY 10036. (212) 391-1112.

THEATRICAL TRAILERS

HOWARD A. ANDERSON, CO.
100 Universal City Plaza, #504-3, Universal City, CA 91608.
(818) 777-2402. FAX: (818) 733-1118.

AVAILABLE LIGHT LTD.
3110 W. Burbank Blvd., CA 91505. (818) 842-2109. FAX: (818)
842-0661.

BLOOMFILM
7722 W. Sunset Blvd., Los Angeles, CA 90046. (213) 850-
5575. FAX: (213) 850-7304.

CINEMA CONCEPTS THEATRE SERVICE COMPANY, INC.
2030 Powers Ferry Rd., Suite 214, Atlanta, GA 30339. (770)
956-7460, (800) SHOWADS. FAX: (770) 956-8358.
URL: http://www.cinemation.com

THE CREATIVE PARTNERSHIP, INC.
7525 Fountain Ave., Hollywood, CA 90046. (213) 850-5551.
FAX: (213) 850-0391.

CRUSE & CO.
7000 Romaine St., Hollywood, CA 90038. (213) 851-8814.
FAX: (213) 851-8788.

EAST END PRODUCTIONS
513 W. 54 St., New York, NY 10019. (212) 489-1865.

PABLO FERRO & ASSOCIATES
1756 N. Sierra Bonita Ave., Hollywood, CA 90046. (213) 850-
6193.

FILMACK STUDIOS
1327 S. Wabash Ave., Chicago, IL 60605. (312) 427-3395.
(800) FILMACK. FAX: (312) 427-4866.
Robert Mack

GLASS/SCHOOR FILMS
706 N. Citrus Ave., Los Angeles, CA 90038-3402. (213) 525-
1155. FAX: (213) 525-1156.

HOLLYWOOD NEWSREEL SYNDICATE INC.
1622 N. Gower St., Los Angeles, CA 90028. (213) 469-7307.
FAX: (213) 469-8251.

HOMER & ASSOCIATES, INC.
1420 N. Beachwood Dr., Hollywood, CA 90028. (213) 462-4710.

JKR PRODUCTIONS, INC.
12140 W. Olympic Blvd., Suite 21, Los Angeles, CA 90064.
(310) 826-3666.

KALEIDOSCOPE FILMS INC.
844 N. Seward St., Hollywood, CA 90038. (213) 465-1151.
FAX: (213) 871-1376.

LUMENI PRODUCTIONS
1632 Flower St., Glendale, CA 91201-2357. (818) 956-2200.
FAX: (818) 956-3298.

NATIONAL SCREEN SERVICE GROUP INC.
2001 S. La Cienega Blvd., Los Angeles, CA 90034. (310)
836-1505.
40 Rockwood Pl., Englewood, NJ 07631. (201) 871-7900.
1800 Baltimore Ave., Kansas City, MO 64108. (816) 842-5893.
FAX: (816) 842-4553.
MANAGER
Eric Allen

PIKE PRODUCTIONS, INC.
11 Clarke St., Box 300, Newport, RI 02840. (401) 846-8890.
FAX: (401) 847-0070.

QUARTERMOON PRODUCTIONS
12 Morand Lane, Wilton, CT 06897. (203) 762-2663. FAX:
(203) 762-0509.
Gary Balionis

JIM RUXIN
12140 W. Olympic Blvd., Suite 21, Los Angeles, CA 90064.
(310) 826-3666.

SILVER-GLAZER FILMS INC.
116 S. La Brea Ave., Los Angeles, CA 90036. (213) 935-2200.
FAX: (213) 935-2022.

SOUND SERVICES INC.
7155 Santa Monica Blvd., Los Angeles, CA 90046. (213) 874-
9344. FAX: (213) 850-7189.
Stuart Bartell

LEONARD SOUTH PRODUCTIONS
4883 Lankershim Blvd., N. Hollywood, CA 91601. (818) 760-
8383. FAX: (818) 760-8301.

HERBERT L. STROCK PRODUCTIONS
6311 Romaine Ave., Suite 7113, Los Angeles, CA 90038. (213)
461-1298.
Herbert L. Strock

VIDE-U PRODUCTIONS
9976 Westwanda Dr., Beverly Hills, CA 90210. (310) 276-5509.
FAX: (310) 276-1185.

U.S. State and City Film Commissions

ALABAMA
Michael Boyer
Alabama Film Office
401 Adams Ave.
Montgomery, AL 36130
(800) 633-5898, (205) 242-4195. FAX: (205) 242-2077
URL: http://www.telefilm-south.com/Alabama/Alabama.html

ALASKA
Mary Pignalberi, Coordinator
Alaska Film Office, Frontier Bldg.
3601 "C" St., Suite 700
Anchorage, AK 99503
(907) 269-8137. FAX: (907) 269-8136

ARIZONA
Linda Peterson Warren, Director
Arizona Film Commission
3800 N. Central Ave., Bldg. D
Phoenix, AZ 85012
(602) 280-1380, (800) 523-6695. FAX: (602) 280-1384

City of Phoenix Film Office
Luci Fontanilla Marshall, Program Manager
200 W. Washington, 10th fl.
Phoenix, AZ 85003
(602) 262-4850. FAX: (602) 534-2295

City of Scottsdale
Jan Horne, Film Liaison
3939 Civic Center Blvd.
Scottsdale, AZ 85251
(602) 994-2636. FAX: (602) 994-7780

City of Tucson
Tom B. Hilderband, Executive Director
Tucson Film Office
32 N. Stone Ave., #100
Tucson, AZ 85701
(602) 791-4000, (602) 429-1000. FAX: (602) 791-4963

ARKANSAS
Suzy Lilly, Manager of Film Services
AR Motion Picture Development Office
One State Capitol Mall, Suite 2C-200
Little Rock, AR 72201
(501) 682-7676. FAX: (501) 682-FILM
email: SLILLY@AIDC.STATE.AR.US

CALIFORNIA
Patti Stolkin Archuletta, Director
California Film Commission
6922 Hollywood Blvd., Suite 600
Hollywood, CA 90028
(213) 736-2465, (800) 858-4PIX. FAX: (213) 736-2465

City of Los Angeles
Jonathan Roberts, Director
Motion Picture/Television Division
6922 Hollywood Blvd., Suite 614
Hollywood, CA 90028
(213) 461-8614. FAX: (213) 847-5009

County of Los Angeles
Stephanie Leiner, Director
Entertainment Industry Dvlpmnt. Corp./
Los Angeles Film Office
6922 Hollywood Blvd., Suite 602
Los Angeles, CA 90028
(213) 957-1000. FAX: (213) 463-0613

City of Oakland
Jeanie Rucker
Oakland Film Office
505 14th St., #910
Oakland, CA 94612
(510) 238-2193. FAX: (510) 238-2227

City of San Diego
Cathy Anderson, Film Commissioner
San Diego Film Commission
402 W. Broadway, Suite 1000
San Diego, CA 92101
(619) 234-3456. FAX: (619) 234-0571

City of San Francisco
Robin Eickman, Director
San Francisco Film and Video Arts Commission
401 Van Ness Ave., Rm. 417
San Francisco, CA 94102
(415) 554-6244. FAX: (415) 554-6503

City of San Jose
Joe O'Kane, Executive Director
San Jose Film & Video Commission
333 W. San Carlos St., Suite 1000
San Jose, CA 95110
(408) 295-9600, (800) SAN-JOSE. FAX: (408) 295-3937
email: jokane@sanjose.org, URL: http://www.sanjose.org

Monterey County
Karen Nordstrand, Director
Monterey County Film Commission
P.O. Box 111
Monterey, CA 93942-0111
(408) 646-0910. FAX: (408) 655-9244, email: mryfilm@aol.com
URL: http://mry.infonet.com/MontereyFilmCommission/home.htm

Sonoma County
Sheree Green, Director
Sonoma County Film Liaison Office
5000 Roberts Lake Rd.
Rohnert Park, CA 94928
(707) 584-8100. FAX: (707) 584-8111

COLORADO
Michael Klein, Director
Colorado Motion Picture & TV Commission
1625 Broadway, Suite 1700
Denver, CO 80202
(303) 620-4500, (800) SCO-UTUS. FAX: (303) 620-4545

Boulder County
Shelly Helmerick
Boulder County Film Commission
P.O. Box 73
Boulder, CO 80306
(303) 442-1044, (800) 444-0447. FAX: (303) 938-8837

City of Colorado Springs
Paula Vickerman
Colorado Springs Film Commission
6 N. Teton, Suite 400
Colorado Springs, CO 80903
(719) 578-6943. FAX: (719) 578-6394, email: vickers@usa.net

CONNECTICUT
Bert Brown, Director
Connecticut Film Office
865 Brook St.
Rocky Hill, CT 06067
(860) 258-4339. FAX: (860) 258-4275

DELAWARE
Carol Myers
Delaware Film Office
99 Kings Highway, P.O. Box 1401
Dover, DE 19903
(800) 441-8846, (302) 739-4271. FAX: (302) 739-5749

DISTRICT OF COLUMBIA
Crystal Palmer Brazil, Director
Mayor's Office of TV & Film
717 12th St. NW, 10th fl.
Washington, D.C. 20005
(202) 727-6600. FAX: (202) 727-3787

FLORIDA
John Reitzammer
Florida Entertainment Commission
505 17 St.
Miami Beach, FL 33139
(305) 673-7468. FAX: (305) 673-7168

Fort Lauderdale Area/Broward County
Elizabeth Wentworth, Director
Motion Picture & TV Office
Broward Economic Development Council
200 E. Las Olas Blvd., Suite 1850
Fort Lauderdale, FL 33301
(305) 524-3113. FAX: (305) 524-3167

City of Jacksonville
Todd Roobin
Jacksonville Film & TV Office
128 E. Forsythe St., Suite 505
Jacksonville, FL 32202
(904) 630-2522. FAX: (904) 630-1485

Miami-Dade County
Jeff Peel, Director
Miami-Dade Office of Film, TV & Print
111 Northwest 1st Street, Suite 2510
Miami, FL 33128
(305) 375-3288. FAX: (305) 375-3266

Ocala/Marion County
Sue Sargent-Latham
Community Liaison
Ocala/Marion County Film Commission
Economic Development Council
110 E. Silver Springs Blvd.
Ocala, FL 34470
(904) 629-2757. FAX: (904) 629-1581

Orlando/Central Florida
Katherine Ramsberger, Director
Metro Orlando Film and Television Office
200 E. Robinson St., Suite 600
Orlando, FL 32801-1950
(407) 422-7159. FAX: (407) 843-9514
email: filminfo@film-orlando.org
URL: www.film-orlando.org

Palm Beach County
Chuck Eldred, Film Commission
Palm Beach County Film & Television Commission
1555 Palm Beach Lakes Blvd., Suite 414
West Palm Beach, FL 33401
(407) 233-1000, (800) 745-FILM. FAX: (407) 683-6857
URL: http://www.co.palmbeach.fl.us/film

GEORGIA
Norman Bielowicz, Director
Georgia Film & Videotape Office
285 Peachtree Center Avenue, NW, Suite 1000
Atlanta, GA 30303
(404) 656-3591. FAX: (404) 651-9063
email: Film@itt.state.ga.us
URL: http://www.Georgia-on-my-mind.org

HAWAII
Georgette T. Deemer, Manager
Hawaii Film Office
P.O. Box 2359
Honolulu, HI 96804
(808) 586-2570. FAX: (808) 586-2572

IDAHO
Peg Owens
Film Promotion, Idaho Film Bureau
700 W. State St., 2nd floor
Boise, ID 83720-2700
(208) 334-2470, (800) 942-8338. FAX: (208) 334-2631

ILLINOIS
Ron Ver Kuilen, Director
Illinois Film Office
100 W. Randolph, Suite 3-400
Chicago, IL 60601
(312) 814-3600. FAX: (312) 814-8874

City of Chicago
Richard M. Moskal, Director
Chicago Film Office
One North LaSalle, Suite 2165
Chicago, IL 60602
(312) 744-6415. FAX: (312) 744-1378

INDIANA
Jane Rulon, Director, Indiana Film Office
Indiana Department of Commerce
1 N. Capitol Ave., Suite 700
Indianapolis, IN 46204-2288
(317) 233-8829. FAX: (317) 233-6887
email: idoc70@indyvax.iupui.edu
URL: http://www.a1.com/derringer/filmcomm.html

IOWA
Wendol Jarvis
Iowa Film Office
200 E. Grand Ave.
Des Moines, IA 50309
(515) 242-4726, (800) 779-FILM. FAX: (515) 242-4859

KANSAS
Vicky Henley, Film Commissioner
Kansas Film Commission
700 SW Harrison St., Suite 1300
Topeka, KS 66603-3712
(913) 296-4927. FAX: (913) 296-6988, TTY: (913) 296-3487

KENTUCKY
Russ Slone
Kentucky Film Commission
Capitol Plaza Tower
500 Mero St., 22nd floor
Frankfort, KY 40601
(502) 564-FILM, (800) 345-6591. FAX: (502) 564-7588

LOUISIANA
Ed Lipscomb, III, Director
Louisiana Film Commission
P.O. Box 44320
Baton Rouge, LA 70804-4320
(504) 342-8150. FAX: (504) 342-7988
URL: http://www.doa.state.la.us/crt/filmvid.htm

City of New Orleans
Kimberly Carbo
New Orleans Film and Video Commission
1515 Poydras St.
New Orleans, LA 70112
(504) 565-8104. FAX: (504) 565-0801

MAINE
Lea Girardin, Director
Greg Gadberry, Location Specialist
Maine Film Office
Station 59
Augusta, ME 04333-0059
(207) 287-5703. FAX: (207) 287-8070
URL:http://www/state.me.us/deed/film/mainefilm.htm

MARYLAND
Michael Styer, Director
Maryland Film Office
217 E. Redwood St., 9th floor
Baltimore, MD 21202
(410) 767-6340, (800) 333-6632. FAX: (410) 333-0044

MASSACHUSETTS
Robin Dawson, Director
Massachusetts Film Office
10 Park Plaza, Suite 2310
Boston, MA 02116
(617) 973-8800. FAX: (617) 973-8810

MICHIGAN
Janet Lockwood
Michigan Film Office
201 N. Washington Sq.
Lansing, MI 48913
(517) 373-0638, (800) 477-3456. FAX: (517) 241-0593
email: lockwoodj@state.mi.us
URL: http://www.mjc.state.mi.us/mjc/business/filmoffice/index

MINNESOTA
Randy Adamsick, Kelly Pratt
Minnesota Film Board
401 N. Third St., Suite 460
Minneapolis, MN 55401
(612) 332-6493. FAX: (612) 332-3735

MISSISSIPPI
Ward Emling, Director
Mississippi Film Office
520 George St., P.O. Box 849
Jackson, MS 39205-0849
(601) 359-3297. FAX: (601) 359-5757

email: wemling%gw@decd.state.ms.us
URL: www.decd.state.ms.us

City of Columbus
Carolyn Denton, Director
Columbus Film Commission
P.O.Box 789
Columbus, MS 39703
(601) 329-1191, (800) 327-2686. FAX: (601) 329-8969

City of Natchez
Anne Mohon
Natchez Film Commission
P.O. Box 1485, Natchez, MS 39121
(601) 446-6345, (800) 647-6724. FAX: (601) 442-0814

MISSOURI
Kate Arnold-Schuck, Manager
Missouri Film Office
301 West High, Room 770, P.O. Box 118
Jefferson City, MO 65102
(573) 751-9050. FAX: (573) 751-7385
email: katnolds@mail.state.mo.us

MONTANA
Lonie Stimac, Director
Montana Film Office
1424 Ninth Ave.
Helena, MT 59620
(406) 444-3762, (800) 553-4563. FAX: (406) 444-4191
email: montanafilm@travel.mt.gov
URL: http://montanafilm.mt.gov

City of Billings
John Brewer
Billings Film Liaison Office
P.O. Box 31177
Billings, MT 59107
(406) 245-4111, (800) 711-2630. FAX: (406) 245-7333

City of Butte
Connie Kinney, Film Commissioner
Butte Film Liaison Office
2950 Harrison Ave.
Butte, MT 59701
(406) 494-5595

City of Great Falls and Northern Montana
Peggy Gentry
Great Falls Regional Film Liaison
710 First Ave. N.
Great Falls, MT 59401
(406) 761-4434, (800) 735-8535. FAX: (406) 761-6129

NEBRASKA
Laurie J. Richards
Nebraska Film Office
P.O. Box 94666
Lincoln NE 68509-4666
(402) 471-3797, (800) 228-4307. FAX: (402) 471-3026
email: laurier@ded2.ded.state.ne.us

City of Omaha/Douglas County
Julie Ginsberg
Omaha Film Commission
6800 Mercy Rd., Suite 202
Omaha, NE 68106
(402) 444-7736. FAX: (402) 444-4511

NEVADA
Robert Hirsch, Motion Picture Division/C.E.D.
Nevada Economic Development Commission
3770 Howard Hughes Pkwy., Suite 295
Las Vegas, NV 89109
(702) 486-7150, (702) 791-0839 (after hours and holidays)
FAX: (702) 486-7372

NEW HAMPSHIRE
Ann Kennard, Director
New Hampshire Film and Television Bureau
Box 1856, 172 Pembroke Rd.
Concord, NH 03302-1856
(603) 271-2598. FAX: (603) 271-2629

NEW JERSEY
Joseph Friedman
New Jersey Motion Picture and Television Commission
P.O. Box 47023, 153 Halsey St., 5th fl.
Newark, NJ 07101
(201) 648-6279. FAX: (201) 648-7350

NEW MEXICO
Linda Taylor Hutchison, Director
New Mexico Film Commission
1050 Old Pecos Trail
Santa Fe, NM 87503
(505) 827-7365, (800) 545-9871
URL: http://www.edd.state.nm.us

City of Albuquerque
Victoria Dye, Special Projects Manager
Albuquerque Film and Television Commission
Albuquerque Convention & Visitor's Bureau
P.O. Box 26866
Albuquerque, NM 87125
(505) 842-9918, (800) 733-9918. FAX: (505) 247-9101

NEW YORK
Pat Swinney Kaufman, Deputy Commissioner & Director
New York State Governor's Office for Motion Picture &
Television Development
633 Third Ave., 33rd floor
New York, NY 10017
(212) 803-2330. FAX: (212) 803-2339
email: erodgers@empire.state.ny.us

City of New York
Patricia Reed Scott, Commissioner
Mayor's Office of Film, Theatre & Broadcasting
1697 Broadway, 6th fl.
New York, NY 10019
(212) 489-6710. FAX: (212) 307-6237
URL: http://www.ci.nyc.ny.us/htwl/filmcomm.html

Nassau County
Debra Markowitz, Director
Nassau County Film Office
1550 Franklin Ave., Rm. 207
Mineola, NY 11501
(516) 571-4160. FAX: (516) 571-4161

Suffolk County
Thomas Junor, Commissioner
Suffolk County Motion Picture & TV Commission
220 Rabro Dr., Box 6100
Hauppage, NY 11788-0099
(516) 853-4800, (800) 762-GROW. FAX: (516) 853-4888

NORTH CAROLINA
William Arnold, Director
North Carolina Film Commission
430 N. Salisbury St.
Raleigh, NC 27611
(919) 733-9900, (800) 232-9227. FAX: (919) 715-0151

NORTH DAKOTA
North Dakota Film Office
604 E. Blvd., 2nd floor, Liberty Memorial Bldg.
State Capitol
Bismarck, ND 58505
(701) 328-2525, (800) 328-2871. FAX: (701) 328-4878

OHIO
Eve Lapolla, Manager
Ohio Film Bureau
77 S. High St., 29th Floor
Columbus, OH 43266-0101
(614) 466-2284, (800) 848-1300. FAX: (614) 466-6744

City of Cincinnati
Lori Holladay, Executive Director
Greater Cincinnati Film Commission
632 Vine St., Suite 1010
Cincinnati, OH 45202
(513) 784-1744. FAX: (513) 768-8963
email: gcfc@eos.net

OKLAHOMA
Mary Nell Clark, Director
Oklahoma Film Office
440 S. Houston, Suite 4
Tulsa, OK 74127
(800) 766-3456, (918) 581-2660. FAX: (918) 581-2244

OREGON
David Woolson, Executive Director
Oregon Film & Video Office
One World Trade Center
121 S.W. Salmon St., Suite 300A
Portland, OR 97204
(503) 229-5832. FAX: (503) 229-6869
email: shoot@oregonfilm.org

City of Portland
Nancy Blasi
Portland Film & Video Office
1220 S.W. Fifth Ave., Room 211
Portland, OR 97204
(503) 823-3030. FAX: (503) 823-3036

PENNSYLVANIA
Timothy D. Chambers, Director
Pennsylvania Film Office
Department of Commerce
200 N. 3rd St., Suite 901
Harrisburg, PA 17101
(717) 783-3456. FAX: (717) 772-3581

City of Philadelphia
Sharon Pinkenson, Executive Director
Greater Philadelphia Film Office
1600 Arch St., 12th Floor
Philadelphia, PA 19103
(215) 686-2668. FAX: (215) 686-3659
email: sharon@film.org
URL: http://www.film.org

RHODE ISLAND
Richardson Smith, Director
Rhode Island Film & TV Office
7 Jackson Walkway
Providence, RI 02903
(401) 277- 3456. FAX: (401) 277-2102

SOUTH CAROLINA
Isabel Hill, Director
South Carolina Film Office
P.O. Box 7367
Columbia, SC 29202
(803) 737-0490. FAX: (803) 737-3104

SOUTH DAKOTA
Gary Keller, Film Office Coordinator
South Dakota Film Commission
711 E. Wells Ave.
Pierre, SD 57501-3369
(605) 773-3301. FAX: (605) 773-3256
email: garyk@goed.state.sd.us

TENNESSEE
Marsha Blackburn, Executive Director
Tennessee Film, Entertainment & Music Commission
Rachel Jackson Bldg.
320 Sixth Ave. N., 7th floor
Nashville, TN 37243-0790
(615) 741-3456, (800) 251-8594. FAX: (615) 741-5829

Memphis & Shelby County
Linn Sitler, Executive Director
Memphis-Shelby Co. Film/Tape/Music Commission
Beale St. Landing
245 Wagner Pl., Suite 4
Memphis, TN 38103-3815
(901) 527-8300. FAX: (901) 527-8326

TEXAS
Tom Copeland, Executive Director
Texas Film Commission
P.O. Box 13246
Austin, TX 78711
(512) 463-9200. FAX: (512) 463-4114
email: film@governor.texas.gov

City of El Paso
Susie Gaines
El Paso Film Commission
One Civic Center Plaza
El Paso, TX 79901
(915) 534-0698, (800) 351-6024. FAX: (915) 532-2963

City of Houston
Rick Ferguson, Director
Houston Film Commission
801 Congress
Houston, TX 77002
(800) 365-7575, (713) 227-3100 x615
FAX: (713) 223-3816

City of Irving
Ellen Sandoloski Mayers, Director
Irving Texas Film Commission
6309 N. O'Connor Rd., Suite 222
Irving, TX 75039-3510
(214) 869-0303, (800) 247-8464. FAX: (214) 869-4609
email: itfc@airmail.net

Dallas/Fort Worth
Roger Burke
Dallas/Fort Worth Regional Film Commission
P.O. Box 610246
DFW Airport, TX 75261
(214) 621-0400, (800) 234-5699. FAX: (214) 929-0916

UTAH
Leigh von der Esch, Executive Director
Utah Film Commission
324 South State, Suite 500
Salt Lake City, UT 84114
(801) 538-8740, (800) 453-8824. FAX: (801) 538-8886

City of Moab
Bette L. Stanton, Executive Director
Moab To Monument Valley Film Commission
50 East Center, #1
Moab, UT 84532
(801) 259-6388. FAX: (801) 259-6399

Park City
Nancy V. Kolmer, Director
Park City Film Commission
P.O. Box 1630
Park City, UT 84060
(800) 453-1360. FAX: (801) 649-4132, (801) 649-6100

VERMONT
J. Gregory Gerdel, Director
Vermont Film Bureau
Agency of Development and Community Affairs
134 State St.
Montpelier, VT 05601-1471
(802) 828-33847. FAX: (802) 828-3233
email: ggerdel@dca.state.vt.us

VIRGINIA
Rita McClenny, Director
Virginia Film Office
901 E. Byrd St.
Richmond, VA 23219
(804) 371-8204. FAX: (804) 371-8177

WASHINGTON STATE
Christine Lewis, Manager
Washington State Film & Video Office
2001 6th Ave., Suite 2600
Seattle, WA 98121
(206) 464-7148. FAX: (206) 464-7722

WEST VIRGINIA
Mark McNabb, Director
West Virginia Film Office
State Capitol Complex
Building 6, Rm. 525
Charleston, WV 25305
(304) 558-2234. FAX: (304) 558-1189, (800) 982-3386

WISCONSIN
Stanley Solheim
Wisconsin Film Office
Department of Tourism
123 W. Washington Ave.
Madison, WI 53702-0001
(608) FILM-WIS. FAX: (608) 266-3403
email: ssolheim@mail.state.wi.us

WYOMING
Bill D. Lindstrom, Manager
Wyoming Film Office
Wyoming Travel Commission
Interstate 25 at College Dr.
Cheyenne, WY 82002-0660
(800) 458-6657 or (307) 777-7851. FAX: (307) 777-6904
email: blindstr@wyoming.com

City of Jackson Hole
Deborah Supowit, Director/Liaison
Jackson Hole Film Commission
P.O. Box E
Jackson, WY 83001
(307) 733-3316. FAX: (307) 733-5585

U.S. TERRITORIES & PROTECTORATES

PUERTO RICO

Puerto Rico Film Commission
355 F. D. Roosevelt Ave.
Fomento Bldg., Suite 106
San Juan, PR 00918
(787) 758- 4747, ext. 2250-2255. FAX: (787) 756-5706
URL: http://www.prfilm.com/

U.S. VIRGIN ISLANDS

Manny Centeno, Director
Film Promotion Office
78 Contant 1-2-3
St. Thomas U.S. VI 00804
(809) 774-8784, (809) 775-1444. FAX: (809) 774-4390

FEDERAL GOVERNMENT FILM & MEDIA SERVICES

EXECUTIVE DEPARTMENTS

DEPARTMENT OF AGRICULTURE
Video and Teleconference Division
Office of Public Affairs, 1614 South Bldg., USDA,
Washington, DC 20250-1300. (202) 720-6072. FAX: (202)
720-5773.
CHIEF OF DIVISION
Larry Quinn

DEPARTMENT OF COMMERCE
Audiovisual Section
Office of Public Affairs, 14th St., Rm. 5521, Washington, DC
20230. (202) 482-3263. FAX: (202) 482-2639.
SECTION CHIEF
Bob Nassiks
International Trade Administration
Office of Service Industries
Information Industries Division, 14th St. and Constitution
Ave., Rm. H-1114, Washington, DC 20230. (202) 482-4781.
FAX: (202) 482-2669.
SENIOR INTERNATIONAL TRADE SPECIALIST
John Siegmund
National Telecommunications and Information Administration
Main Commerce Bldg., 1401 Constitution Ave., Washington,
DC 20230. (202) 482-1840. FAX: (202) 482-1635.
ASST. SECRETARY, COMMUNICATIONS & INFORMATION
Larry Irving
National Technical Information Service
5282 Port Royal Rd., Springfield, VA 22161. (800) 553-6847.
FAX: (703) 321-8547.
DIRECTOR
Dr. Donald Johnson

DEPARTMENT OF DEFENSE
Special Assistant (Audiovisual)
Office of the Assistant Secretary of Defense (Public Affairs),
The Pentagon, Room 2E789, Washington, DC 20301. (703)
695-2936. FAX: (703) 695-1149.
HEAD OF DIVISION
Philip M. Strub
Broadcast-Pictorial Branch
Office of the Assistant Secretary of Defense (Public Affairs),
The Pentagon, Room 2E765, Washington, DC 20301. (703)
695-0168. FAX: (703) 697-3501.
BRANCH CHIEF
Jim Kout

MILITARY SERVICES
Secretary of the Air Force
Office of Public Affairs, Media Division, The Pentagon, Room
5C879, Washington, DC 20330-1000. (703) 697-2769. FAX:
(703) 614-7486.
CHIEF OF DIVISION
Lt. Col. Virginia Pribyla.
Secretary of the Army
Media Relations Division, Army Public Affairs, The Pentagon,
Room 2E641, Washington, DC 20310-1500, (703) 697-2564.
FAX: (703) 657-2159.
CHIEF OF DIVISION
Judith Johnston
Department of the Navy
Chief of Information, Audiovisual Entertainment, The
Pentagon, Room 2E352, Washington, DC 20350-1200. (703)
697-4627.
DIRECTOR
Robert Manning
Headquarters, U.S. Marine Corps
Media Branch Public Affairs Division, Code PAM, The
Pentagon, Washington, DC 20380. (703) 614-8010. FAX:
(703) 697-5362.
CHIEF OF BRANCH
Lt. Col. Pat Messer

DEPARTMENT OF EDUCATION
Office of Public Affairs
Audiovisual Division, 600 Independence Ave. SW, Rm. 2200,
Washington, DC 20202. (202) 401-1576. FAX: (202) 401-3130.
AUDIOVISUAL OFFICER
Greg Grayson
Office of Special Education and Rehabilitation Services
600 Independence Ave. SW, Washington, DC 20202. (202)
205-5465. FAX: (202) 205-9252.
BRANCH CHIEF, CAPTIONING
Ernie Hairston

DEPARTMENT OF ENERGY
Office of Public Affairs
Forrestal Bldg.,1000 Independence Ave. SW, CP41, Room
IE200, Washington, DC 20585. (202) 586-6250.
DIRECTOR OF INTERNAL COMMUNICATIONS
Chett Gray

DEPARTMENT OF HEALTH AND HUMAN SERVICES
Office of Public Affairs
200 Independence Ave. SW, Room 647D, Washington, DC
20201. (202) 690-7850. FAX: (202) 690-5673.
DIRECTOR OF COMMUNICATIONS
Jackie Nedell
Administration for Children & Family
370 L'Enfant Promenade SW, 7th floor, Washington, DC
20447. (202) 401-9215. FAX: (202) 205-9688.
DIRECTOR
Michael Kharfen
Health Care Financing Administration
200 Independence Ave. SW, Room 314G, Washington, DC
20201. (202) 690-6113. FAX: (202) 690-6262.
ADMINISTRATOR
Bruce Vladeck
Social Security Administration Office of Public Affairs
4200 West High Rise, 6401 Security Blvd., Baltimore, MD
21235. (401) 965-1720. FAX: (401) 965-3903.
DIRECTOR
Joan Wainwrithe

DEPARTMENT OF HOUSING AND URBAN DEVELOPMENT
Office of Public Affairs
HUD Bldg., 451 7th St. SW, Rm. 10132, Washington, DC
20410. (202) 708-0980. FAX: (202) 619-8153.
ASSISTANT SECRETARY
Jon Cowan

DEPARTMENT OF THE INTERIOR
Office of Public Information Audiovisual Programs
1849 C St. NW, Washington, DC 20240. (202) 501-9649.
FAX: (202) 208-64116.
MANAGER OF AUDIOVISUAL PROGRAMS
Steve Brooks

DEPARTMENT OF JUSTICE
Audiovisual Services
10th St. & Pennsylvania Ave., Rm. 1313, Washington, DC
20530. (202) 514-4387. FAX: (202) 514-6741.
SUPERVISOR
Joe Keyerleber

DEPARTMENT OF LABOR
Audiovisual and Photographic Services Branch
Audiovisual Division, 200 Constitution Ave. NW, N6311,
Washington, DC 20210. (202) 219-7910. FAX: (202) 219-4788.
DIRECTOR
Lionel White
EXECUTIVE PRODUCER
Stan Hankin

DEPARTMENT OF STATE

International Communications and Information Policy
Department of State, Rm. 4826, 2201 C St. NW, Washington, DC 20520. (202) 647-5727. FAX: (202) 647-5957.
DEPUTY ASST. SECRETARY
Ambassador Vonya B. McCann

Office of International Trade Control
Department of State, 1700 N. Lynn St., Rm. 200, Arlington, VA 22209. (703) 875-6644. FAX: (703) 0875-6647.
DIRECTOR OF STAFF
William Lowell

Office of Press Relations
Department of State, Rm. 2109-A, Washington, DC 20520. (202) 647-0874. FAX: (202) 647-0244.
DIRECTOR OF STAFF
John Dinger

DEPARTMENT OF TRANSPORTATION

Federal Highway Administration Audiovisual and Visual Aids
400 7th St. SW, Rm. 4429, HMS51, Washington, DC 20590. (202) 366-0481.
AUDIOVISUAL CHIEF
Colonel Giles

National Highway and Traffic Safety Administration
Public Affairs, Audiovisual Section, 400 7th St. SW, Rm. 5232, Washington, DC 20590. (202) 366-9550. FAX: (202) 366-5962.
PUBLIC AFFAIRS SPECIALIST
Tina Foley

U.S. Coast Guard Motion Picture & Television Liaison Office
11000 Wilshire Blvd., Room 10125, Los Angeles, CA 90024. (310) 235-7817. FAX: (310) 235-7851.
LIAISON OFFICERS
Cmdr. Dwight McGee, CWO Dan Dewell, CWO Lance Jones
U.S. Coast Guard Media Relations Branch
2100 2nd St. SW, Washington, DC 20593. (202) 267-1587. (202) 267-4307.
CHIEF OF DEPARTMENT
Lt. Cmdr. Pat Philbin
U.S. Coast Guard Audiovisual Branch, (202) 267-0923. FAX: (202) 267-4307.
AUDIOVISUAL SPECIALIST
Wayne Paugh

DEPARTMENT OF TREASURY

Office of Public Affairs
1500 Pennsylvania Ave. NW, Rm. 3442, Washington, DC 20220. (202) 622-2960. FAX: (202) 622-2808.
ASSISTANT SECRETARY
Howard Schloss

EXECUTIVE AGENCIES

ENVIRONMENTAL PROTECTION AGENCY

Audiovisual Division
401 M St. SW, North Conference, Washington, DC 20460. (202) 260-6735. FAX: (301) 585-7976.
DIRECTOR
Mawell Jama

FEDERAL COMMUNICATIONS COMMISSION

1919 M St. NW, Washington, DC 20554. (202) 418-0200. FAX: (202) 418-0999.
CHAIRMAN
Reed E. Hunt
COMMISSIONERS
James H. Quello, Andrew C. Barrett, Rachelle B. Chong, Susan Ness
CHIEF JUDGE, OFFICE OF ADMINISTRATIVE LAW JUDGES
Joesph Stirmer
GENERAL COUNSEL
William E. Kennard
MANAGING DIRECTOR
Andrew S. Fishel
CHIEF, MASS MEDIA BUREAU
Roy J. Steward
CHIEF, CABLE SERVICES BUREAU
Meredith Jones
CHIEF, COMMON CARRIER BUREAU
Kthleen M.H. Wallman

CHIEF, COMPLIANCE & INFORMATION BUREAU
Beverly G. Baker
DIRECTOR, OFFICE OF LEGISLATIVE & INT'L GOVER-MENTAL AFFAIRS
Judith L. Harris

Office of Public Affairs (202) 418-0500.
DEPUTY DIRECTOR, PUBLIC AFFAIRS
Maureen Pertino

FEDERAL TRADE COMMISSION

6th St. and Pennsylvania Ave. NW, Washington, DC 20580. (202) 326-2180. FAX: (202) 326-2050.
CHAIRMAN
Robert Pitofsky

LIBRARY OF CONGRESS

Copyright Office
Madison Bldg., Rm. 403, Washington, DC 20540. (202) 707-8350. FAX: (202) 707-8366.
REGISTER OF COPYRIGHTS
Marybeth Peters

Copyright Cataloging Division
Rm. 513. (202) 707-8040. FAX: (202) 707-8049.
CHIEF OF DIVISION
William Collins

Motion Picture, Collections Services,
Madison Bldg., Rm. 338, Washington, DC 20540. (202) 707-5840. FAX: (202) 707-2371.
CHIEF OF DIVISION
David Francis

NATIONAL AERONAUTICS & SPACE ADMINISTRATION

NASA Video Library
Code AP42, Bldg. 423, Johnson Space Center, Houston, TX 77058. (713) 483-2973. FAX: (713) 483-2848.
DIRECTOR
Jody Russel

NATIONAL ARCHIVES AND RECORDS ADMINISTRATION

Motion Picture Sound and Video Branch
7th St. & Pennslyvania Ave. NW, Room 2W, Washington, DC 20408. (202) 501-5449.
BRANCH CHIEF
Jack Saunders

Presidential Libraries Central Office
7th St. & Pennsylvania Ave. NW, Rm. 104, Washington, DC 20408. (202) 501-5700. FAX: (202) 501-5709.
ACTING DIRECTOR
Lewis Bellardo

NATIONAL ENDOWMENT FOR THE ARTS

Creation & Presentation—Media Arts Program
1100 Pennsylvania Ave. NW, Rm. 726, Washington, DC 20506. (202) 682-5452. FAX: (202) 682-5721.
MEDIA ARTS DIRECTOR
Brian O'Doherty

NATIONAL ENDOWMENT FOR THE HUMANITIES

Humanities Projects in Media
1100 Pennsylvania Ave. NW, Rm. 426, Washington, DC 20506. (202) 606-8278. FAX: (202) 606-8557.
PROGRAM OFFICER
James Dougherty

SECURITIES AND EXCHANGE COMMISSION

Division of Corporation Finance
450 5th St. NW, Washington, DC 20549. (202) 942-8088.
Radio, Television, and Telegraph
Rm. 3113. (202) 942-2800. FAX: (202) 942-9525.
ASSISTANT DIRECTOR
H. Christopher Owings
Motion Pictures
Rm. 3134. (202) 942-1800.
ASSISTANT DIRECTOR
James Daly

SMITHSONIAN INSTITUTION

Film Archives
Archives Division, National Air and Space Museum, Washington, DC 20560. (202) 357-3133. FAX: (202) 786-2835.
FILM ARCHIVIST
Mark Taylor

Telecommunications Office
National Museum of American History, Rm. BB40,
Washington, DC 20560. (202) 357-2984. FAX: (202) 357-1565.
DIRECTOR
Paul Johnson

U.S. INFORMATION AGENCY
Television and Film Service
601 D St. NW, Rm. 5000, Washington, DC 20547. (202) 501-
7806. FAX: (202) 501-6664.
DIRECTOR
Charles W. Fox

U.S. INTERNATIONAL TRADE COMMISSION
Office of the Secretary
500 E Street, Rm. 112, Washington, DC 20436. (202) 205-
2000. FAX: (202) 205-2104.
SECRETARY
Donna R. Koehnke

MILITARY FILM LIAISONS

ARMY CHIEF OF PUBLIC AFFAIRS
11000 Wilshire Blvd., Room 10104, Los Angeles, CA 90024-
3688. (310) 235-7621. FAX: (310) 473-8874.

CHIEF OF PUBLIC AFFAIRS
Lt. Col. Alfred Lott
TECHNICAL ADVISOR
Master Sgt. Grant Stombaugh
PUBLIC INFORMATION OFFICER
Kathy Canham Ross

MARINE CORPS PUBLIC AFFAIRS
11000 Wilshire Blvd., Room 10117, Los Angeles, CA 90024.
(310) 235-7272. FAX: (310) 235-7274.
OFFICER IN CHARGE
Major N. J. LaLuntas

U. S. AIR FORCE, MOTION PICTURE AND TELEVISION LIAISON OFFICE
11000 Wilshire Blvd., Room 10114, Los Angeles, CA 90024.
(310) 235-7522. FAX: (310) 235-7500.
CHIEF, ENTERTAINMENT LIAISON
Charles E. Davis

U. S. COAST GUARD, MOTION PICTURE AND TELEVISION OFFICE
11000 Wilshire Blvd., Los Angeles, CA 90024. (310) 235-
7817. FAX: (310) 235-7851.
LIAISON OFFICERS
Cmdr. Dwight McGee, CWO Dan Dewell, CWO Lance Jones

MOTION PICTURE COMPANIES

CORPORATE HISTORIES

MAJOR MOTION PICTURE CORPORATIONS

NON-THEATRICAL PRODUCERS

CORPORATE HISTORIES OF THE MAJOR MOTION PICTURE COMPANIES

Columbia Pictures/TriStar (Sony Pictures Entertainment, Inc.)

Columbia Pictures can trace its beginnings to the CBC Films Sales Co., formed in 1920 by Harry Cohn, Jack Cohn and Joe Brandt, all of whom had previously worked together at Universal Studios. CBC was set up to make a series of shorts known as Screen Snapshots, showing the off-screen activities of movie stars to publicize their current pictures. Soon the new company expanded to produce westerns and other comedy shorts and in 1922 produced its first feature, "More To Be Pitied Than Scorned." In 1924, the owners renamed their company Columbia Pictures.

Two years later, Columbia had advanced to the point where it began to open film exchanges of its own instead of selling films outright to theatres for a flat fee and established a studio with two stages and a small office building. Sam Briskin was hired as general manager. In 1929, it produced its first all-talking feature, "The Donovan Affair." This low-budget murder mystery was directed by Frank Capra. By this time, the company had opened a home office in New York where Jack Cohn functioned as vice president and treasurer, while Harry ran the production operation on the West Coast.

In 1931, Brandt sold his interest in Columbia and retired. The next year, Harry Cohn assumed the title of president, while retaining his post as production chief. In 1935, Columbia purchased a 40 acre ranch in Burbank for location filming (later expanded to 80 acres). The company's first big artistic success was in 1934 with Capra's "It Happened One Night," which was not only the top box office draw of 1934, but a winner of five major Academy Awards including Best Picture. Capra followed this with such hits as "Mr. Deeds Goes to Town" (1936), "Lost Horizon" (1937), "You Can't Take It With You" (1938) and "Mr. Smith Goes to Washington" (1939).

Throughout the 40's Columbia prospered and by the end of the decade, it could claim to be one of the industry's major studios. Unlike the other studios, Columbia did not own any theatres and was not affected by the industry's Consent Decrees which forced those studios to divest themselves of their exhibition properties. Commerical hits of the period included "Gilda" (1946), "The Jolson Story" (1946) and "Jolson Sings Again" (1949).

In 1951, Columbia diversified into television by forming Screen Gems, a wholly owned subsidiary set up to make programs and commercials. Founder Harry Cohn died in 1958. The successor management—headed by veterans of the company, Abe Schneider and Leo Jaffe—made major investments in British film production and released "Lawrence of Arabia" (1962), "A Man for All Seasons" (1966) and the musical "Oliver!" (1968). Other hits of the 60's were "Guess Who's Coming to Dinner" (1967) and "To Sir With Love" (1967). The success of these and others was attributable to Mike Frankovich, who became production head in 1954 and was succeeded by Stanley Schneider, whose father, Abe, headed the company at the time. Another son of Abe, Bert, and Bob Rafelson co-produced "Easy Rider" in 1969, one of the biggest hits in Columbia's history.

At the beginning of the 70's, Herbert Allen Jr., a former Wall Street banker, bought control of Columbia and took over as president and CEO. Allen brought in new management headed by Alan Hirschfield and David Begelman, who produced such hits as "Shampoo" (1975) and "Close Encounters of the Third Kind" (1977). Begelman's successor as production chief was Frank Price (who had previously headed Universal Television) and under his regime the company produced such successful films as "Kramer Vs. Kramer" (1979), "Tootsie" (1982) and "Ghostbusters" (1984). In 1982, Columbia was pur-chased by the Coca-Cola Company. Under its aegis Columbia, Home Box Office and CBS, Inc. joined forces to finance a new production company, TriStar Pictures. At the start, it was emphasized that the new company would be separate from Columbia, with TriStar using Columbia's distribution. Price departed in 1985 and in 1986 David Puttnam, an independent British producer, was signed as chairman. Succeeding him was Dawn Steel, who was named president. In 1989, TriStar was made a unit of Columbia Pictures with Jeff Sagansky, president of TriStar, reporting to Ms. Steel.

Columbia Pictures Entertainment was formed in 1987 by Coca-Cola to restructure its entertainment business. CPE consisted of two film production companies: Columbia Pictures and TriStar Pictures; two television arms: Columbia Pictures Television, Merv Griffin Enterprises and Loews Theatre Management Corp.

In September 1989, Columbia Pictures Entertainment was purchased by the Sony Corporation of Japan. Sony previously acquired CBS Records in 1987. Producers Jon Peters and Peter Guber were brought in as co-chairmen. In 1991, Peters resigned from his position as co-chairman, the company was renamed Sony Pictures Entertainment, Inc. and Mark Canton left Warner Bros. to become the new chairman of Columbia Pictures. In June 1994, Fred Bernstein was put in charge of the motion picture units at Columbia Pictures, TriStar Pictures, Sony Pictures Classics and Triumph Releasing Corporation. Later that summer, the marketing and distribution arms of these divisions were consolidated under the direction of Sid Ganis as president. In September 1994, Peter Guber announced his resignation as Sony chairman, with Alan J. Levine named as his successor. Sony was forced to write off $3.2 billion in 1995, but the Japanese parent company vowed to maintain its Hollywood commitment.

RECENT COLUMBIA RELEASES
1990: Awakenings, Lord of the Flies, Misery, Postcards From the Edge.
1991: Boyz N the Hood, City Slickers, My Girl, The Prince of Tides.
1992: Bram Stoker's Dracula, A Few Good Men, A League of Their Own, A River Runs Through It.
1993: The Age of Innocence, El Mariachi, Groundhog Day, In the Line of Fire, Last Action Hero, The Remains of the Day.
1994: Little Women, The Shawshank Redemption, Wolf.
1995: The Net, Sense and Sensibility.
1996: The Cable Guy, Donnie Brasco, The Fan, Multiplicity.

RECENT TRISTAR RELEASES
1990: Avalon, Look Who's Talking Too, Total Recall.
1991: Bugsy, The Doors, The Fisher King, Hook, Terminator 2: Judgment Day.
1992: Basic Instinct, City of Joy, Universal Soldier.
1993: Cliffhanger, Philadelphia, Sleepless in Seattle.
1994: Legends of the Fall, Mary Shelley's Frankenstein.
1995: Devil in a Blue Dress, Jumanji, Jury Duty.
1996: If Lucy Fell, Mrs. Winterbourne.

The Walt Disney Company

In 1923, Walt Disney set up an animation studio with his brother Roy. Five years later, he introduced his most famous creation, Mickey Mouse, in a cartoon called "Steamboat Willie." It was an immediate hit and Disney began his series of Silly Symphony cartoons, based on musical themes, the first of which was called "The Skeleton Dance." From 1929 through 1931, Disney distributed his products through Columbia Pictures. In 1932, distribution was through United Artists with about 20 cartoons per year—half of them featuring Mickey Mouse and the others in the Silly Symphony series.

Production cost of the cartoons was about $50,000 each. UA paid Disney 60% of rentals received from exhibitors, and his gross income at the time was in the neighborhood of one and a half million dollars per year.

Disney's contract with UA expired in 1937. He switched over to RKO for whom he produced his first feature-length cartoon, "Snow White and the Seven Dwarfs" followed by "Pinnochio" (1940), "Fantasia" (1940), "Dumbo" (1941), "Bambi" (1942), "Cinderella" (1950) and "Peter Pan" (1953), all released by RKO.

RKO's financial troubles, which led to its demise in 1958, caused Walt Disney Productions to break with it in 1953 and form its own national distribution unit, Buena Vista. Buena Vista's first release was "The Living Desert" (1953), winner of the Academy Award for feature documentary and an outgrowth of the True-Life Adventure shorts started in 1948. Disneyland in Anaheim, California, opened in 1955.

Rising costs in the production of animation films caused Disney to concentrate on live-action features, such as "20,000 Leagues Under the Sea" (1954) which took in over $11 million in domestic rentals, and "Mary Poppins" (1964) which made more than $45 million.

Walt Disney died in 1966. Roy Disney's death in 1971 left no surviving Disney family members at the studio's helm. Walt Disney World in Central Florida (near Orlando) opened in 1971. In 1983, Ron Miller, Walt's son-in-law, was made chief executive and started Touchstone Pictures, a subsidiary designed to make adult-oriented films. In 1984, Touchstone delivered "Splash." In the same year, a drive for new leadership was spearheaded by Roy Disney, son of Walt's brother of the same name. Frank Wells, former vice chairman of Warner Bros. and Michael Eisner, president of Paramount, were hired in 1984 with Eisner as chairman, Wells as president and Disney serving as vice chairman. Early in 1990, the Company announced a massive ten-year expansion agenda that would add hundreds of new rides and shows to its existing theme parks, and build additional attractions in Southern California and Florida. EuroDisneyland opened near Paris in 1992.

Disney continued to do well in its motion picture division with "Pretty Woman," "Dick Tracy" and new division Hollywood Pictures' "Arachnophobia" and "The Hand That Rocks the Cradle." The 1991 animated feature "Beauty and the Beast" took in over $145 million in the U.S., and became the first animated feature nominated for Best Picture. This success was followed by 1992's "Aladdin" which became the first Disney release to gross more than $200 million in the U.S. In 1993, Disney purchased the highly successful independent distributor Miramax, which would continue to operate as a separate company.

1994 saw the death of Frank Wells. "The Lion King" became the highest grossing film in Disney history. Jeffrey Katzenberg, crucial to the revitalization of the company's animation department, resigned as chairman to join Steven Spielberg and David Geffen in their own entertainment company, DreamWorks SKG. David Hoberman was named president of Disney's motion picture divisions. However, his departure after a mere eight months threw the weight of responsibilities over to new chairman of the motion picture group, Joe Roth. The year ended with Disney becoming the first distributor to achieve annual box office revenues of over $1 billion.

The big entertainment news of 1995 was the company's $19 billion purchase of Capital Cities/ABC. Michael Eisner named Creative Artists Agency chairman Michael Ovitz as president of the Walt Disney Company.

RECENT DISNEY RELEASES
1990: Arachnophobia, Dick Tracy, Green Card, Pretty Woman.
1991: Beauty and the Beast, Billy Bathgate, Father of the Bride, Scenes From a Mall.
1992: Aladdin, The Hand That Rocks the Cradle, The Mighty Ducks, Sister Act.
1993: Cool Runnings, The Nightmare Before Christmas, Tombstone, What's Love Got to Do With It.
1994: Ed Wood, The Lion King, Quiz Show, The Santa Clause, When a Man Loves a Woman.
1995: Crimson Tide, Dangerous Minds, Pocahontas, Mr. Holland's Opus, Toy Story, While You Were Sleeping.
1996: The Hunchback of Notre Dame, James and the Giant Peach, Ransom, The Rock.

RECENT MIRAMAX RELEASES
1993: Farewell My Concubine, Like Water for Chocalate.

1994: Bullets Over Broadway, The Crow, Pulp Fiction.
1995: The Englishman Who Went Up a Hill But Came Down a Mountain, Muriel's Wedding, The Postman, Priest.
1996: The Crow: City of Angels, Jane Eyre, Trainspotting.

Metro-Goldwyn-Mayer/ United Artists, Inc.

Metro-Goldwyn-Mayer, Inc. was originally founded by exhibitor Marcus Loew. In 1910, after several years of expansion, Loew organized Loew's Consolidated Enterprises, succeeded the next year by Loew's Theatrical Enterprises. In 1920, Loew's acquired the Metro Pictures Corporation, which later turned out such films as "The Prisoner of Zenda," "Scaramouche" and "The Four Horsemen of the Apocalypse."

In 1924, Loew and his associates, Nicholas and Joseph Schenck and Adolph Zukor acquired the Goldwyn Company (founded in 1917), and Loew's became the owner of the merged Metro-Goldwyn stock. Loew's then acquired Louis B. Mayer Pictures and the services of Mayer, Irving Thalberg and J. Robert Rubin. The company was renamed Metro-Goldwyn-Mayer.

In 1936 and 1937, legal control of the entire production and distribution organization was vested in Loew's, with Metro-Goldwyn-Mayer used merely as a trade name. On February 6, 1952, the consent decree against Loew's, Inc. provided a divorce between the producing and distributing phases of the corporation and its domestic exhibition activities and interests. Among notable pictures in the company's history have been "Ben Hur" (silent), "The Thin Man," "Mutiny on the Bounty," "Goodbye Mr. Chips," "Mrs. Miniver," "The Wizard of Oz," "Gone With the Wind," "Meet Me in St. Louis," "King Solomon's Mines," "Ben Hur" (sound), "Doctor Zhivago," "2001: A Space Odyssey" and many more.

In 1973, the company ceased its own distribution and licensed domestic distribution to United Artists and foreign distribution to CIC. In June 1980, the motion picture operations of MGM, Inc. were sold to stockholders as Metro-Goldwyn-Mayer Film Co. United Artists was purchased by the Metro-Goldwyn-Mayer Film Co. in 1981 with the former company becoming a wholly-owned subsidiary of the latter. In 1983, the name of the parent company was changed to MGM/UA Entertainment Co.

In 1986, Turner Broadcasting System purchased MGM/UA and sold the UA portion to Tracinda Corporation along with MGM motion picture and television production, distribution and the home entertainment division. The MGM lot and lab were sold by Turner to Lorimar-Telepictures. Turner retained only the MGM film library. During this period, MGM-UA produced "Moonstruck," "Rain Man" and "A Fish Called Wanda."

Pathe Communications Corporation acquired MGM/UA in November 1990 with Giancarlo Parretti as chairman. The new company was now renamed MGM-Pathe. In 1991, Parretti was removed as chairman with control given to Alan Ladd Jr., and MGM-Pathe was given a $145 million loan from Credit Lyonnais, allowing them to start film distribution after months of inactivity. Due to loans and transactions totalling $885 million, Pathe was $395 million in debt to Credit Lyonnais. In 1992, Credit Lyonnais bought up 98.5% of MGM, thereby officially disposing of Parretti. Following this move, the company was again renamed Metro-Goldwyn-Mayer, Inc. In July of 1993, Alan Ladd Jr. was replaced by former Paramount Pictures chairman Frank G. Mancuso. In 1994, the distribution arm was once again bearing the title MGM/UA and the revived studio had a major hit with the science-fiction film "Stargate." 1995 proved that Metro-Goldwyn-Mayer was again a major force with a number of critical and financial successes such as "Get Shorty" and "Leaving Las Vegas." Although "The Birdcage" was a big hit, in early 1996 MGM was the target of yet another bidding war.

RECENT MGM RELEASES
1990: Blue Steel.
1991: The Indian Runner, Thelma & Louise,
1992: The Cutting Edge, The Lover, Of Mice and Men.
1993: Benny & Joon, Body of Evidence, Six Degrees of Separation.
1994: Stargate, That's Entertainment III.
1995: Get Shorty, Goldeneye, Leaving Las Vegas.
1996: The Birdcage.

Orion Pictures

Orion Pictures was formed in 1978 by members of the Management Group, the company responsible for developing the film library of United Artists Corporation since 1951. The parent corporation, Filmways Inc., changed its name to Orion Pictures Corporation in 1982.

With distribution handled by Warner Bros., Orion released its first motion picture, "A Little Romance" in April 1979. Their first substantial hit, the Dudley Moore-Julie Andrews comedy "10," premiered that autumn. During their first 2 1/2 years Orion produced 23 films, the most successful of which was another Dudley Moore vehicle, "Arthur" (1981). In 1982, Orion formed its own distribution unit, scoring impressive box office returns on such films as "First Blood," "Terminator," "Back to School," "Throw Momma From the Train," and "Bull Durham." Orion won four Academy Awards for Best Picture in a seven year span: "Amadeus" (1984), "Platoon" (1986), "Dances With Wolves" (1990) and "The Silence of the Lambs" (1991). The Orion Classics unit was formed to handle specialized and foreign art house films.

Despite enormous box office revenues from "Dances With Wolves" and "The Silence of the Lambs," Orion was facing financial hardships in the 1990's as failed films drained away profits. The company officially declared bankruptcy in December 1991, with debts of $500 million. Several studio releases completed during that year were shelved until outside financing was available. Through a personal guarantee from its principal stockholder, John Kluge, Orion managed to reorganize. By 1993, Kluge owned 56% of the company. In 1992, both Arthur Krim, chairman of the board since 1978, and Eric Pleskow, who began as president and chief executive officer that same year, departed, the latter replaced by Leonard White.

In 1993, a joint venture with Metromedia Co. resulted in the creation of Orion Productions Co. with the idea of financing new films. Six older titles made little impact when finally released in 1994. As a result, Kluge implemented a merger of Orion and Metromedia with MCEG Sterling, Inc. and Actava Group under the name Metromedia International Group, Inc. During 1995, there were no new Orion Pictures releases although Orion Classics distributed a handful of films. In 1996, Orion seemed to be getting back on track with a number of new movies

RECENT ORION RELEASES
1990: Alice, Dances With Wolves, Mermaids, Robocop 2.
1991: The Silence of the Lambs.
1992: Love Field, Shadows and Fog.
1993: The Dark Half.
1994: Blue Sky, China Moon.
1996: The Arrival,The Substitute.

Paramount Pictures

Adolph Zukor formed the Engadine Corporation in 1912, which evolved into Famous Players Film Company. W. W. Hodkinson, from General Film Company, formed Paramount Pictures Corporation in 1914, distributing Zukor products and the products of the Jesse L. Lasky Feature Play Company and others. Famous Players-Lasky Corp. was incorporated in 1916. In 1917, twelve production companies merged with it and the corporation integrated production and distribution by acquiring a national distribution system through a merger with Artcraft Pictures and Paramount Pictures. Famous Players-Lasky began acquiring theatres in 1919 with Southern Enterprises, Inc. (135 theatres), followed in later years by New England Theatres, Inc. (50 theatres); the Butterfield Theatre Circuit (70 theatres) and Balaban & Katz (50 theatres). Theatres in the West and Midwest were acquired later.

Paramount's first great star was Mary Pickford. B.P. Schulberg was named head of production in 1925. In April 1927, the corporate name was changed to Paramount Famous Lasky Corporation, and in April of 1930, to Paramount Publix Corporation, which declared bankruptcy in 1933. Lasky and Schulberg left the company at this point. In 1935, it was reorganized under the name of Paramount Pictures. During this period, the studio's greatest asset was Mae West whose outrageous hits, "She Done Him Wrong" and "I'm No Angel," caused much furor among censors.

The company regained its footing in the late 1930's and

1940's with such popular stars as Bing Crosby, Bob Hope, Ray Milland and Dorothy Lamour, as well as high profile films from notable directors Ernst Lubitsch, Preston Sturges, Billy Wilder and Cecil B. DeMille. The 1940's saw such blockbuster hits as "For Whom the Bell Tolls," "Going My Way" and "Samson and Delilah." In 1949, as a result of the Consent Decree, Paramount split into two companies: Paramount Pictures Corp. for production and distribution, and United Paramount Theatres for theatre operation. After World War II, Paramount introduced a new process called VistaVision to compete with 20th Century Fox's CinemaScope. The first film in the process was the Bing Crosby-Danny Kaye hit musical "White Christmas" followed by Cecil B. DeMille's 1956 remake of "The Ten Commandments."

Paramount merged with Gulf & Western Industries in 1966, with Paramount as a subsidiary retaining its own management. Robert Evans was brought in as production head under Charles Bludhorn, head of Gulf & Western. Bludhorn expanded theatrical film production and increased the company's investment in TV production (an area Paramount had been slow to move into). Evans had great success with "Love Story" (1970) and two Francis Ford Coppola pictures, "The Godfather" (1972) and "The Godfather, Part II" (1974).

With the departure of Evans in 1975, the company moved ahead under Barry Diller as CEO and later under Frank Mancuso, promoted from v.p. of distribution to chairman of Paramount Pictures in 1984. The decade of the 1980's brought the company many successes including the "Star Trek" series, the "Indiana Jones" films, "Fatal Attraction," and "Top Gun." Ned Tanen left Universal Pictures to become president of Paramount. In 1989, Gulf and Western changed its name to Paramount Communications, Inc. Also in 1989, chairman Martin S. Davis sought to block the merger of Time, Inc. and Warner Communications, Inc. (see Warner Bros. history). His attempt was thwarted by the courts. Davis then began streamlining Paramount Communications in order to focus on entertainment and publishing.

In 1991, Mancuso was replaced by former NBC head Brandon Tartikoff, who resigned in 1992 to be replaced by Sherry Lansing. In the winter of 1994, Viacom Inc. purchased the company for $9.75 billion. Viacom head Sumner Redstone appointed Jonathan Dolgen, formerly of Sony, to oversee entertainment at both Paramount and Viacom. Earlier in 1994, the studio soared at the box office with "Forrest Gump" which became the highest grossing movie in Paramount history. In 1996, Viacom president and CEO Frank Biondi was dismissed with no replacement. That summer, "Mission: Impossible," a remake of the classic television show, became a smash hit, taking in $75 million over the six-day Memorial Day weekend.

RECENT PARAMOUNT RELEASES
1990: Ghost, The Godfather Part III, The Hunt for Red October.
1991: The Addams Family, Flight of the Intruder, The Naked Gun 2 1/2: The Smell of Fear.
1992: Juice, Patriot Games, Wayne's World.
1993: Addams Family Values, The Firm, Searching for Bobby Fischer, What's Eating Gilbert Grape.
1994: Clear and Present Danger, Forrest Gump, Naked Gun 33 1/3: The Final Insult.
1995: Braveheart, Clueless, Congo.
1996: Mission: Impossible, The Phantom, Star Trek: Resurrection Day.

Twentieth Century Fox

Twentieth Century Fox Film Corporation was started by William Fox, a pioneer in the arcade and nickelodeon business. Fox became a member of the exhibition firm of Fox, Moss and Brill and established the Greater New York Film Rental Company. In 1913, he organized the Box Office Attraction Company, acquiring the services of Winfield Sheehan. On February 1, 1915, the Fox Film Corporation was founded, combining production, exhibition and distribution under one name and with film exchanges in a dozen cities. In 1917, Fox Films moved into its Sunset Studio in Hollywood. In 1926, Fox introduced Movietone, a sound-on-film process developed by Theodore Case and Earl I. Sponable,.

In 1929, Fox began a series of reorganizations and financial deals, principally the purchase by Fox Films of Loew's, Inc. By order of the courts, Fox's ownership of Loew's was later dissolved and various banking interests acquired control of

Loew's. During these reorganizations, William Fox's connections with the company were discontinued. Sidney R. Kent became the company's president.

In 1935, The Fox Film Corporation merged with Twentieth Century Pictures, headed by Joseph M. Schenck, and the company assumed its present corporate name. This merger brought Darryl F. Zanuck into the company as vice-president in charge of production. Schenck became chairman of the board and continued in that position until his resignation in June 1942, when Wendell L. Wilkie took over the post. Zanuck remained as production head until 1956, when Buddy Adler succeeded him. Upon Adler's death, Robert Goldstein and then Peter G. Levathes took over studio reins. Spyros P. Skouras, a leading theatre operator, became president. On July 25, 1962, Darryl F. Zanuck was elected president and Skouras was named chairman of the board, a position he held until 1969. Richard D. Zanuck was named executive vice-president in charge of worldwide production. The Zanucks turned an ailing company into an industry leader. In 1969, Darryl Zanuck was made chairman of the board and chief executive officer and Richard Zanuck was made president.

In 1971, 20th Century-Fox Film Corporation weathered a trying proxy fight which had the resounding effect of giving the company added resolve. A new managerial team was elected by the Board of Directors which saw Dennis C. Stanfill succeeding Richard Zanuck as president of the company. Shortly thereafter, Stanfill was elevated to the position of chairman of the board of directors and the studio's chief executive officer. In 1972, Fox's East Coast offices were consolidated with the West Coast offices, placing distribution, publicity, advertising, promotion and general accounting under one roof.

In 1981, Fox merged with a company owned by Marvin Davis. In 1985, Davis sold the company to Rupert Murdoch's News Corporation and Fox, Inc. was formed, consolidating the principal operating units: Twentieth Century Fox Film Corporation, Fox Television Stations, Inc. and Fox Broadcasting Company. In the summer of 1989, a revamping was announced that signalled a new emphasis on motion pictures. The company appointed Joe Roth, an independent producer and director, as chairman of its major film-making unit and renamed it the Fox Film Corporation, marking the first time a film director had run a major studio since Ernst Lubitsch headed Paramount Pictures in 1935. Roth's first picture for Fox, "Die Hard 2," proved to be a hit in the summer of 1990. This was followed by the gigantic success of "Home Alone" which went on to become the 2nd highest grossing film in the studio's history following 1977's "Star Wars." At that time, the science-fiction epic had dethroned the company's previous record holder, "The Sound of Music."

Roth announced his resignation in December of 1992. His replacement, Peter Chernin, was a Fox television executive. In 1994, Fox released the James Cameron-Arnold Schwartzenegger film "True Lies" which reportedly cost in excess of $100 million to produce.

RECENT FOX RELEASES
1990: Die Hard 2, Edward Scissorhands, Home Alone.
1991: Barton Fink, The Commitments, Point Break, Sleeping With the Enemy.
1992: Hoffa, Home Alone 2: Lost in New York, The Last of the Mohicans, White Men Can't Jump.
1993: Hot Shots! Part Deux, Mrs. Doubtfire, Rising Sun.
1994: Nell, Speed, True Lies.
1995: Die Hard With a Vengeance, Mighty Morphin Power Rangers, Nine Months.
1996: Broken Arrow, Dead Drop, Independence Day.

Universal Pictures

Universal Pictures was formed in 1912, when exhibitor Carl Laemmle amalgamated Bison 101, Nestor, Powers and several other organizations, including his own Imp firm. Laemmle had earlier founded Laemmle Film Service and released his first Independent Motion Picture (Imp) Company feature "Hiawatha" in 1909. Universal launched the star system by hiring Florence Lawrence for $1,000 a week and billing her as "Queen of the Screen." Universal acquired a studio in 1914. In 1915, production was moved to its present site, Universal City. Contracted stars included Wallace Reid, Lon Chaney, Mary Pickford, Rudolph Valentino and Boris Karloff. "Foolish Wives" ("the first million-dollar feature"), "The Hunchback of Notre Dame," "All Quiet On the Western Front"

and others were filmed in the decades that followed. On March 16, 1920, Laemmle and R. H. Cochrane assumed complete control of the company.

In 1936, Universal named new management, with J. Cheever Cowdin as chairman of the board and Nate J. Blumberg as president beginning in 1938. Under the new management, Universal embarked upon the policy of developing star values and such stars as Deanna Durbin, Abbott & Costello, Maria Montez, Donald O'Connor and others were put under contract.

In 1946, the company underwent its second transformation, eliminating the production of all so-called "B" pictures, Westerns and serials. This followed a merger and acquisition of the assets of International Pictures Corp. of Leo Spitz and William Goetz, who became production heads and the Universal-International trademark emerged. Universal also completed a distribution deal with the J. Arthur Rank organization for the American distribution of British pictures produced by Rank. 1946 also saw the emergence of United World Pictures, a wholly-owned Universal subsidiary, to handle the production and distribution of non-theatrical films including the Bell and Howell Film Library and Castle Films.

1950 saw the resignation of Cowdin with Blumberg assuming full command. Alfred E. Daff, who had been foreign sales manager, assumed the top post in the foreign distribution set-up and then became director of world sales. In 1951, Decca Records acquired approximately 28% of Universal's common stock to make it the largest single stockholder in the company. In 1952, Decca Records became the controlling stockholder of Universal. Milton R. Rackmil, president of Decca Records, was made a member of the Universal board and subsequently elected president of Universal in July, 1952.

In 1962, MCA, Inc. consolidated with Decca and made Universal Pictures Company the theatrical film producing division of MCA, Inc. In 1964, the creation of the Universal City Studios image started with the separate motion picture and television arms. That same year, the company began its profitable Universal Studios Tour. In 1966, Universal Pictures became a division of Universal City Studios, Inc., a subsidiary of MCA, Inc. The company entered a successful period of high profile hits including "Thoroughly Modern Millie," "Airport," "American Graffiti," "The Sting," "Earthquake" and Steven Spielberg's "Jaws," which in 1975 became the highest grossing movie to that date.

In 1982, Universal released Steven Spielberg's "E.T.: The ExtraTerrestrial," which became the top-grossing film of all time, racking up over $228 million in film rentals in the domestic market alone. Other recent success have included the "Back to the Future" series, "Field of Dreams," "Born on the Fourth of July," and "Fried Green Tomatoes."

1990 saw two major events in the studio's recent history. A fire swept through the backlot in Universal City destroying acres of sets and causing millions of dollars worth of damage. MCA Inc. was purchased by the Matsushita Electrical Industrial Company for an estimated $6.6 billion, the most expensive sale of an American company to the Japanese in history. In 1993, Spielberg's "Jurassic Park" grossed over $300 million, placing it as the second highest grossing film of all time right behind "E.T." Spielberg was also responsible for "Schindler's List," the first black and white Academy Award winner for Best Picture in 33 years. Seagram Co. purchased 80% of MCA Inc. in 1995 for $5.7 billion, with Seagram's president & CEO Edgar Bronfman Jr. serving as acting chairman of the entertainment company. With this change of ownership, Lew Wasserman stepped down and was named chairman emeritus, and Sid Sheinberg ended his 22 year reign as president. In the summer of 1995, Universal released "Waterworld," which holds the dubious distinction of being the most expensive movie ever made, with estimates of its cost ranging as high as $175 million. In spite of critical drubbings and a lackluster domestic box-office, Waterworld went on to earn money for the company in the international market.

RECENT UNIVERSAL RELEASES
1990: Back to the Future Part III, Henry and June, Kindergarten Cop.
1991: Backdraft, Fried Green Tomatoes, Jungle Fever.
1992: Beethoven, Far and Away, Scent of a Woman.
1993: In the Name of the Father, Jurassic Park, Schindler's List.
1994: The Flintstones, Radioland Murders, The River Wild.

1995: Apollo 13, Babe, Casper, Waterworld.
1996: Dragonheart, Flipper, The Nutty Professor.

Warner Bros.

Warner Bros. Pictures, Inc. may be said to have its origins in the 90-seat Cascade Theatre set up by Harry Warner and his three brothers, Sam, Albert and Jack in New Castle, PA, in 1905. The brothers soon branched out into distribution, establishing film exchanges in Pennsylvania and Virginia. In 1913, they moved into film production with Warner Features. Warner Features' first production was 1918's "My Four Years in Germany." In 1920-22 they averaged only two or three features per year. Warner Bros. was incorporated in 1923 to produce as well as distribute and release 14 pictures, including the first of the famous Rin-Tin-Tin series. Scripts were written by Darryl F. Zanuck, an ambitious writer who soon worked his way up to become the company's production chief under Jack Warner. Harry was president; Albert, treasurer; and Sam shared production responsibilities with Jack. Zanuck stayed until 1933 and was succeeded by Hall Wallis, who held the post for the next decade.

In 1925, Warner acquired Vitagraph, Inc., which operated 34 exchanges in the U.S. and Canada, and two other concerns with foreign exchanges. That same year, the company began its experiments with sound, collaborating with Western Electric to produce a sound-on-disc process (called Vitaphone) for synchronized film sound. The first Vitaphone program premiered in August 1926, including some musical shorts and the feature "Don Juan" with John Barrymore backed by a full musical and sound-effects track. Owing to this success, the studio released the feature "The Jazz Singer" in October 1927, with dialogue and certain musical numbers in sound and in 1928, "the first 100% all-talking picture"—"Lights of New York," a one-hour feature that broke box office records. In 1927, Sam Warner died.

The new sound technology brought Warner Bros. to the forefront of the industry. It further expanded its theatre holdings and studio facilities, acquiring the Stanley Company of America theatre circuit in 1928, First National Pictures which had a 135-acre studio and back lot, along with exchanges and theatres, and a number of music publishing companies. Those acquisitions greatly helped in the production of the Warner Bros. musicals including "Forty-Second Street," the "Gold Diggers" series, "Footlight Parade" and others. Along with the other motion picture companies, Warner Bros. suffered in the early days of the Depression. Sales of some assets and theatres, along with drastic cuts in production costs, enabled the company to recover and to take advantage of the boom in the 1940's.

In 1953, the company completed the reorganization it was forced to undergo by the government's Consent Decree. Stockholders approved a plan to separate the company into two entities: the theatres were sold to Fabian Enterprises, Inc., and the company renamed Stanley Warner Corporation. The "new" production-distribution company remained Warner Bros. Pictures, Inc. In 1956, Harry and Albert sold their shares in the company to an investment group headed by Serge Semenenko and Charles Allen Jr. Jack retained his shares, remaining the largest single stockholder and becoming president of the company. The Warner pre-1948 film library of 850 features and 1,000 shorts was sold to United Artists in 1956.

On July 15, 1967, a subsidiary of Seven Arts Productions Limited (a Canadian-based company headed by Eliot Hyman) acquired substantially all the assets and business of Warner Bros. Pictures, Inc. The company subsequently was called Warner Bros.-Seven Arts Limited. In 1969, Warner Bros.-Seven Arts was acquired by Kinney National Service, Inc., headed by Steven J. Ross, and changed its name in 1971 to Warner Communications, Inc. The studio reverted to the original name of Warner Bros. and appointed Ted Ashley as studio chief. The studio's successes during this period included "Superman," "The Exorcist" and "All the President's Men." Robert A. Daly succeeded Ashley as Warner Bros. chairman and chief executive officer in 1980.

In 1989, Warner Communications was acquired by Time, Inc. in an $18 billion merger that created one of the largest communications and entertainment companies in the world. Time-Warner, as the new company is called, consists of Warner and its subsidiaries, Time Publishing, Home Box Office, Cinemax, HBO Video and American Television & Communications Corp. John Peters and Peter Guber were instrumental in aiding Warner to rebound from a two-year box office slump. In the summer of 1989, Peters and Guber produced "Batman," which brought in domestic rentals of over $150 million, making it the fourth top-grossing film of all-time to that date.

In early 1991, the company announced a partnership with several European entertainment companies to produce 20 films. Time–Warner continues to hold a 50% interest in Cinamerica Limited Partnership, a company that includes Mann Theatres and Festival Theatres in California, and Trans-Lux Theatres in the East. In October 1991, two Japanese companies, Toshiba Corp. and C. Itoh & Co., paid $500 million each for a combined 12.5% stake in the company. In May 1993, the company created a new division, Warner Bros. Family Entertainment, to release movies aimed at the children's market including the hit "Free Willy." In the autumn of 1995, Time–Warner began negotiations for the $7.3 billion purchase of the Turner Broadcasting System. These negotiations were the subject of intense FTC scrutiny in 1996, due to the 20% stake cable giant TCI held in Turner.

RECENT WARNER BROS. RELEASES

1990: GoodFellas, Reversal of Fortune, The Witches.
1991: JFK, New Jack City, Robin Hood.
1992: Batman Returns, The Bodyguard, Malcolm X, Unforgiven.
1993: Falling Down, Free Willy, The Fugitive.
1994: Ace Ventura: Pet Detective, Disclosure, Natural Born Killers.
1995: Ace Ventura: When Nature Calls, Batman Forever, The Bridges of Madison County, Outbreak.
1996: Eraser, Executive Decision, Mars Attacks!, A Time to Kill, Twister.

Motion Picture Corporations

See also, Index: Film Distributors in Key Cities, Non-Theatrical Motion Picture Companies, Exhbition Circuits & Services.

AMC ENTERTAINMENT, INC.
(For theatres listing see American Multi-Cinema, Inc. in theatre circuits section.)
106 W. 14th St., Kansas City, MO 64105. (816) 221-4000.
CHAIRMAN & CEO
Stanley H. Durwood
PRESIDENT
Edward D. Durwood
EXECUTIVE VICE PRESIDENT & COO
Philip M. Singleton
EXECUTIVE VICE PRESIDENT & CFO
Peter C. Brown

AMC FILM MARKETING, INC.
21700 Oxnard St., Suite 640, Woodland Hills, CA 91367. (818) 587-6400. FAX: (818) 587-6498.
AMC FILM MARKETING PRESIDENT
Richard M. Fay

ATA TRADING CORP.
(Distribution and production.)
50 W. 34 St., Suite 5C-6, New York, NY 10001. (212) 594-6460. FAX: (212) 594-6461.
PRESIDENT
Harold G. Lewis
VICE PRESIDENT
Susan Lewis

ALLIANCE COMMUNICATIONS
(Motion picture & television producer and distributor.)
301 N. Canon Dr., Suite 321, Beverly Hills, CA 90210. (310) 275-5501. FAX: (310) 275-5502. Toronto: (416) 967-1174.
CEO
Robert Lantos
PRESIDENT, ALLIANCE PICTURES
Anbras Hamori
INDEPENTDENT PRODUCER, ALLIANCE PICTURES
Lael McCall

AMAZING MOVIES
(Producer and distributor of feature films, worldwide.)
7471 Melrose Ave., Suite 7, Los Angeles, CA 90046. (213) 852-1396. FAX: (213) 658-7265. Organized 1984.
PRESIDENT
Douglas C. Witkins
V.P., BUSINESS AFFAIRS
Martin Ivada
DIRECTOR OF OPERATIONS
Koing Kouch

AMBLIN ENTERTAINMENT
100 Universal Plaza, Bungalow 477, Universal City, CA 91608. (818) 777-4600.
PRESIDENT
Walter F. Parkes

AMERICAN FILM DISTRIBUTORS
8490 W. Sunset Blvd., #701, Los Angeles, CA 90069. (310) 657-4506. FAX: (310) 657-3426.
PRESIDENT
Norbert Meisel

AMERICAN FILMWORKS
222 N. Canon Dr., Suite 201, Beverly Hills, CA 90210. (310) 288-0569. FAX: (310) 288-0578.
PRESIDENT
Bruce Gilbert

AMERICAN FIRST RUN STUDIOS
(Production and distribution.)
14225 Ventura Blvd., Sherman Oaks, CA 91423. (818) 981-4950. FAX: (818) 501-6224.
CHAIRMAN
Max Keller
PRESIDENT
Micheline Keller

AMERICAN PLAYHOUSE
(Produces films for theatrical distribution and public tv.)
1776 Broadway, 9th floor, New York, NY 10019-1990. (212) 757-4300. FAX: (212) 333-7552.
CHAIRMAN
Ward Chamberlain
MANAGING DIRECTOR & V.P.
Barbara Ludlum

AMERICAN ZOETROPE
916 Kearny St., San Francisco, CA 94133. (415) 788-7500. FAX: (415) 989-7910.
PRESIDENT
Fred Fuchs

APRICOT ENTERTAINMENT, INC.
(Feature film financing, studio rental and film production.)
940 N. Orange Dr., Hollywood, CA 90038-3197. (213) 469-4000. FAX: (213) 469-5809.
PRESIDENT
Naofumi Okamoto

AQUARIUS RELEASING INC./ AQUARIUS MEDIA CORPORATION
(Distribution, exhibition & production.)
The Technicolor Building, 321 W. 44th St., 9th fl., New York, NY 10036. (212) 245-8530. FAX: (212) 397-7701.
CEO
Terry Levene
SECRETARY-TREASURER
Sarie Berenstein
PUBLICITY & ADVERTISING DEPARTMENT
Wayne Weil

ARROW ENTERTAINMENT
135 W. 50 th St., Suite 1925, New York, NY 10020. (212) 258-2200.
PRESIDENT
Dennis Friedland
NATIONAL SALES MANAGER
Steve Fagan

ARTISTIC LICENSE FILMS
250 W. 57th St., #1620, New York, NY 10107. (212) 265-9119. FAX: (212) 251-8606.
PRESIDENT
Sande Zeig

ASTRON FILMS CORPORATION
(Writers, producers, directors, independent financiers of films.)
360 W. 22 St., New York, NY 10011. (212) 989-6089.
PRESIDENT & CHAIRMAN
Jack O'Connell
CREATIVE DIRECTOR
Patricia Kay Williams

AUGUST ENTERTAINMENT
838 N. Fairfax Ave., Los Angeles, CA 90046. (213) 658-8888. FAX: (213) 658-7654.
PRESIDENT
Gregory Cascante
EXECUTIVE VICE PRESIDENT & CFO
Elizabeth Davis
EXECUTIVE VICE PRESIDENTS
H. Michael Heuser
V.P., OPERATIONS
Eleanor Powell
V.P., OPERATIONS
Said Boudarga

AURORA PRODUCTIONS, INC.
8642 Melrose Ave., Suite 200, Los Angeles, CA 90069. (310) 854-6900. FAX: (310) 854-0583. Organized 1976.
PRESIDENT
William Stuart
WRITER, PRODUCER, PARTNER
Al Septien
WRITER, DIRECTOR, PARTNER
Turi Meyer
DIRECTOR, CREATIVE AFFAIRS
Palerma Pena

AVENUE PICTURES
(Motion picture and television production.)
11111 Santa Monica Blvd., Suite 2110, Los Angeles, CA 90025. (310) 996-6800. FAX: (310) 473-4376.

CHAIRMAN & CEO
Cary Brokaw
CFO
Sheri L. Halfon
DIRECTOR OF FEATURE DEVELOPMENT
Sandra Arber

AVNET-KERNER CO.

3815 Hughes Ave., Culver City, CA 90232. (310) 838-2500.
FAX: (310) 204-4208.
PRODUCERS
Jon Avnet
Jordan Kerner
SENIOR VICE PRESIDENTS, DEVELOPMENT &
PRODUCTION
Elizabeth Guber
Lisa Lindstrom

BALTIMORE PICTURES

c/o Warner Bros., 4000 Warner Blvd., Burbank, CA 91522.
(818) 954-2666. FAX: (818) 954-2693.
PRODUCER/DIRECTOR
Barry Levinson
EXECUTIVE PRODUCER
Peter Giuliano

KEITH BARISH PRODS.

9601 Wilshire, Suite 612, Beverly Hills, CA 90210. (310) 777-
0096.
CHAIRMAN
Keith Barish
VICE PRESIDENT
G. Evan Todd

BEACON PICTURES

c/o Warner-Hollywood Studios, 1041 N. Formosa Ave., Los
Angeles, CA 90046-6798. (213) 850-2651. FAX: (213) 850-
2613.
CHAIRMAN
Armyan Bernstein
PRESIDENT, PRODUCTION & DEVELOPMENT
Marc Abraham
EXECUTIVE VICE PRESIDENT
Thomas Bliss

BIG BEAR LICENSING CORP., INC.

(Motion picture production and foreign sales.)
12400 Wilshire Blvd., Suite 360, Los Angeles, CA 90025. (310)
820-5161. FAX: (310) 820-7683. Organized 1978.
PRESIDENT
Wolf Schmidt

BLUE RIDGE ENTERTAINMENT

(Motion picture production and international distribution.)
1640 S. Sepulveda, Suite #308, Los Angeles, CA 90025. (310)
444-0997. FAX: (310) 444-9166.
CHAIRMAN & CEO
Lamar Card
SENIOR VICE PRESIDENT
Eric Saltzgaber
DIRECTOR, ACQUISITIONS/PRODUCTION
Barbara Mannion

BOARDWALK ENTERTAINMENT

210 E. 39 St., New York, NY 10016. (212) 679-3800. FAX:
(212) 679-3816. email: Boardwalk@infohouse.com
CHAIRMAN
Fred Tarter
PRESIDENT
Alan Wagner

JERRY BRUCKHEIMER FILMS

1631 10th St., Santa Monica, CA 90403. (818) 560-7711. FAX:
(818) 848-6415.
PRODUCER
Jerry Bruckheimer
SENIOR VICE PRESIDENT
Chad Oman

BUENA VISTA PICTURES

(see The Walt Disney Company)

BURRUD PRODUCTIONS, INC.

16902 Bolsa Chica, #203, Huntington Beach, CA 92649. (714)
846-7174. FAX: (714) 846-4814.
PRESIDENT & CEO
John Burrud
VICE PRESIDENT IN CHARGE OF PRODUCTION
Linda Karabin-Hecomovich
VICE PRESIDENT BUSINESS AFFAIRS
Stanley Green

PRODUCER
Bill MacDonald
ASSOCIATE PRODUCER
Matt Craemer

CANNON PICTURES

P.O. Box 17198, Beverly Hills, CA 90209-3198. (310) 772-7764.
FAX: (310) 843-0919.
CHAPTER 11 TRUSTEE
John Hyde

CASTLE HILL PRODUCTIONS, INC.

1414 Ave. of the Americas, New York, NY, 10019. (212) 888-
0080. FAX: (212) 644-0956.
116 N. Robertson Blvd., Suite 505, Los Angeles, CA 90048.
(310) 652-5254. FAX: (310) 652-5595.
PRESIDENT
Julian Schlossberg
PRESIDENT, MARKETING & DISTRIBUTION
Mel Maron
VICE PRESIDENT
Milly Sherman
CONTROLLER
Yuk Yu
V.P., TELEVISION SALES
Barbara Karmel
DIRECTOR, THEATRICAL DISTRIBUTION
Ivory Harris
DIRECTOR, ADVERTISING/PUBLICITY/CLIENT SERVICES
David Wright
ASSISTANT TO THE PRESIDENT
Ruth Better

CASTLE ROCK ENTERTAINMENT

335 N. Maple Dr., Suite 135, Beverly Hills, CA 90210. (310)
285-2300. FAX: (310) 285-2345.
CHAIRMAN & CEO
Alan Horn
PRESIDENT, CASTLE ROCK TELEVISION
Glenn Padnick
PRESIDENT, CASTLE ROCK PICTURES
Martin Shafer
PRODUCER/DIRECTOR
Andrew Scheinman
PRODUCER/DIRECTOR
Rob Reiner
CHIEF OPERATING OFFICER
Gregory M. Paul
SENIOR V.P., BUSINESS AFFAIRS
Jess Wittenberg
CFO
Sue Fickenscher
PRESIDENT OF MARKETING, CASTLE ROCK PICTURES
Jim Frederick
SENIOR V.P., PUBLICITY & PROMOTION
John DeSimio
SENIOR V.P., PRODUCTION MANAGEMENT
Jeff Stott
PRESIDENT OF PRODUCTION, CASTLE ROCK PICTURES
Liz Glotzer
SENIOR V.P., TV PRODUCTION
Robin Green

CHARTOFF PRODUCTIONS

1250 Sixth St., Suite 101, Santa Monica, CA 90401. (310) 319-
1960. FAX: (310) 319-3469.
CEO & PRESIDENT
Robert Chartoff

CHERRY ALLEY PRODS.

225 Arizona Ave., Suite 350, Santa Monica, CA 90401. (310)
458-8886.
CEO
Goldie Hawn
PRESIDENT
Teri Schwartz
V.P., CREATIVE AFFAIRS
Jay Bernzweig

CINECOM ENTERTAINMENT GROUP, INC.

c/o October Films, Inc., 65 Bleeker St., 30th floor, New York,
NY 10012. (212) 539-4000. FAX: (212) 539-4099. Organized
1982.
PARTNERS
Amir J. Malin
John Schmidt
Bingham Ray
DIRECTOR OF SPECIAL PROJECTS
Linda Duchin
CORPORATE CONTROLLER
Daniel Lieblein

THE CINEMA GUILD

1697 Broadway, Suite 506, New York, NY 10019-5904. (212) 246-5522. FAX: (212) 246-5525. email: thecinema@aol.com
PRESIDENT
Philip S. Hobel
VICE PRESIDENT & GENERAL MANAGER
Gary Crowdus
VICE PRESIDENT
Mary Ann Hobel

CINEMAX MARKETING & DISTRIBUTION CORP.

(The Arthur Manson Organization—Marketing and distribution.) 1414 Avenue of the Americas, New York, NY 10019-2514. (212) 832-2806. FAX: (212) 832-2825.
PRESIDENT
Arthur Manson
ADMINISTRATIVE DIRECTOR
Norman Delaney

CINEPIX FILM PROPERTIES

900 Broadway, Suite 800, New York, NY 10003. (212) 995-9662. FAX: (212) 475-2284.
DIRECTOR, DEVELOPMENT
Lauren McLaughlin

CINERGI PRODS.

2308 Broadway, Santa Monica, CA 90404. (310) 315-6000. FAX: (310) 828-0443.
CHAIRMAN & CEO
Andrew Vajna

CINETEL FILMS, INC.

8255 Sunset Blvd., Los Angeles, CA 90046. (213) 654-4000. FAX: (213) 650-6400.
PRESIDENT & CEO
Paul Hertzberg
EXECUTIVE VICE PRESIDENT
Lisa Hansen
CFO
Nick Gorenc
DISTRIBUTION CONSULTANT
Milton Goldstein
V.P., CREATIVE AFFAIRS
Catalaine Knell
V.P., BUSINESS AFFAIRS
Benjamin R. Reder
V.P., INTERNATIONAL DISTRIBUTION
Marcy Rubin

CINETEL PICTURES
PRESIDENT
Lisa Hansen
V.P., PRODUCTION
Russ Markowitz

CINEVISTA, INC.

(Distribution and sales.)
1680 Michigan Ave., Suite 1106, Miami Beach, FL 33139. (305) 532-3400.
PRESIDENT
Rene Fuentes-Chao
NATIONAL SALES DIRECTOR
Giselle Everette
EDITOR-IN-CHIEF, CINEVISTA NEWS
Susan M. Alvarez

CIRCLE RELEASING CORP.

1101 23rd St., NW, Washington, D.C. 20037. (202) 331-3838. FAX: (202) 429-9043.
CO-CHAIRMAN
Ted Pedas
CO-CHAIRMAN
James Pedas
GENERAL MANAGER
George Pelecanos

HERMAN COHEN PRODUCTIONS/COBRA MEDIA, INC.

650 N. Bronson Ave., Suite 116, Hollywood, CA 90004. (213) 466-3388. email: 743-72.3433@compuserve.com
PRESIDENT
Herman Cohen
EXECUTIVE VICE PRESIDENT
Didier Chatelain

COLUMBIA PICTURES

(see Sony Pictures Entertainment, Inc.)

COMENT CORPORATION

(International film distribution company.)
1875 Century Park E., Suite 2130, Los Angeles, CA 90067. (310) 229-2430. FAX: (310) 229-2434.

PRESIDENT
Ira Smith
CEO
Stephen R. Greenwald
CFO & EXECUTIVE V.P.
Marvin N. Grossman
SENIOR V.P. OF ACQUISITIONS & DEVELOPMENT
Brenda J. Reiss
SENIOR V.P., INTERNATIONAL SALES & DISTRIBUTION
Andrea Miller

CONCORDE/NEW HORIZONS

11600 San Vicente Blvd., Los Angeles, CA 90049. (310) 820-6733. FAX: (310) 207-6826.
Studios: 600 S. Main St., Venice, CA 90291.
PRESIDENT
Roger Corman
EXECUTIVE VICE PRESIDENT
Julie Corman
V.P., DEVELOPMENT
Frannces Doel
V.P., PRODUCTION
Darin Stillman
SENIOR V.P., WORLDWIDE DISTRIBUTION
Pamela Abraham
V.P., DOMESTIC DISTRIBUTION
William H. Bromiley

CONTINENTAL FILM GROUP LTD.

1001 Park St., Sharon, PA 16146-3090. (412) 981-3456. FAX: (412) 981-2668. email: sultnat@aol.com
PRESIDENT & CEO
Amin Q. Chaudhri
VICE PRESIDENT IN CHARGE OF DEVELOPMENT
Asha N. Chaudhri
ASSISTANT TO THE PRESIDENT/CEO
Maraline A. Kubik
BOARD OF DIRECTORS
Amin Q. Chaudhri, Robert Holof

THOMAS CRAVEN FILM CORP.

5 W. 19 St., New York, NY 10011. (212) 463-7190. FAX: (212) 627-4761.
PRESIDENT
Michael Craven
VICE PRESIDENT
Ernest Barbieri

CREST FILM DISTRIBUTOR

116 N. Robertson Blvd., Suite 505, Los Angeles, CA 90048. (310) 652-8844. FAX: (310) 652-5595.
PRESIDENT
Jerry Percell

CROWN INTERNATIONAL PICTURES, INC.

8701 Wilshire Blvd., Beverly Hills, CA 90211. (310) 657-6700. FAX: (310) 657-4489.
PRESIDENT & CEO
Mark Tenser
SENIOR V.P., BUSINESS & LEGAL AFFAIRS
Scott Schwimer
V.P., INTERNATIONAL SALES
Herb Fletcher
V.P., FINANCE & ADMINISTRATION
James Boyd
CONTROLLER
Willie De Leon
DIRECTOR, INTERNATIONAL SALES
Beatriz Calfo
DIRECTOR, PUBLICITY & ADVERTISING
Lisa Agay
PRODUCER
Marilyn J. Tenser

CURB ENTERTAINMENT

3907 W. Alameda Ave., Suite 200, Burbank, CA 91505. (818) 843-8580. FAX: (818) 566-1719.
PRESIDENT
Carole Curb
CHAIRPERSON
Mike Curb

DAVIS ENTERTAINMENT CO.

2121 Ave. of the Stars, Suite 2900, Los Angeles, CA 90067. (310) 556-3550. FAX: (310) 556-3688.
CHAIRMAN
John A. Davis
PRESIDENT
David Friendly
V.P., PRODUCTION
Craig Berenson

DI NOVI PICTURES

3110 Main St., Suite 220, Santa Monica, CA 90405. (310) 581-1355. FAX: (310) 399-0499.
PRESIDENT
Denise Di Novi
PRESIDENT, PRODUCTION
Steve Rabiner
V.P., DEVELOPMENT
Pete Czernin

DIMENSION FILMS

(see Miramax Films)

THE WALT DISNEY COMPANY

500 S. Buena Vista St., Burbank, CA 91521. (818) 560-1000. FAX: (818) 840-5737. 500 Park Ave., New York, NY 10022. (212) 593-8900.
CHAIRMAN OF THE BOARD & CEO
Michael D. Eisner
PRESIDENT
Michael Ovitz
VICE CHAIRMAN OF THE BOARD
Roy E. Disney
EXECUTIVE V.P., STRATEGIC PLANNING & DEVELOPMENT
Lawrence P. Murphy
EXECUTIVE V.P., LAW & HUMAN RESOURCES/CHIEF OF CORPORATE OPERATIONS
Sanford Litvack
EXECUTIVE V.P., CORPORATE AFFAIRS
John F. Cooke
SENIOR V.P., CFO
Richard Nanula
V.P., PLANNING & CONTROL
John Garand
CORPORATE SECRETARY
Marsha L. Reed

WALT DISNEY STUDIOS
CHAIRMAN, WALT DISNEY STUDIOS
Joe Roth

THE WALT DISNEY MOTION PICTURES GROUP
500 South Buena Vista Street, Burbank, CA 91521. (818) 560-5151.
CHAIRMAN, MOTION PICTURE GROUP
Richard Cook
CHAIRMAN, BUENA VISTA TELEVISION
Walter Liss
EXECUTIVE V.P., BUSINESS & LEGAL AFFAIRS
Bernardine Brandis
EXECUTIVE V.P. & CFO
Robert Moore
SENIOR V.P., LEGAL AFFAIRS
Steve Bardwill
SENIOR V.P., BUSINESS & LEGAL AFFAIRS
Phillip Muhl

BUENA VISTA PICTURES DISTRIBUTION
3900 West Alameda Avenue, Tower Building, Suite 2400, Burbank, CA 91521-0021. (818) 567-5000.
PRESIDENT
Phil Barlow
SENIOR V.P., GENERAL COUNSEL
Robert Cunningham
SENIOR V.P., NON-THEATRICAL SALES, MARKETING & DISTRIBUTION
Linda Palmer
SENIOR V.P., OPERATIONS
Gary Weaver
SENIOR VICE PRESIDENT/GENERAL SALES MANAGER
Charles Viane
V.P., EAST/NEW YORK
Phil Fortune
V.P., FINANCE
Deborah Morrison
V.P., SOUTHWEST/DALLAS
Jim Nocella
V.P., WEST/LOS ANGELES
Pat Pade
V.P., MIDWEST/CHICAGO
Rick Rice
V.P., SOUTHEAST/ATLANTA
Rod Rodriguez

BUENA VISTA PICTURES DISTRIBUTION CANADA, INC.
1235 Bay Street, Suite 502, Toronto, Ontario, Canada M5R 3K4. (416) 964-9275.
SALES MANAGER, CANADA
Anthony Macina

BUENA VISTA PICTURES MARKETING
500 South Buena Vista Street, Burbank, CA 91521. (818) 560-1000.
PRESIDENT, WORLDWIDE MARKETING
John Cywinsk

SENIOR VICE PRESIDENTS, CREATIVE FILM SERVICES
Peter Adee
Oren Aviv
SENIOR V.P., MARKETING
Geoffrey Ammer
SENIOR V.P., MARKETING OPERATIONS
Brett Dicker
SENIOR V.P., CARAVAN PICTURES
Richard Ingber
SENIOR V.P., PUBLICITY
Terry Curtin
V.P., CREATIVE PRINT SERVICES
Glenn Garland
V.P., PRINT ADVERTISING
Alan Lobel
V.P. PUBLICITY, HOLLYWOOD PICTURES
Denise Greenawalt
V.P., FINANCE & ADMINISTRATION
Dean Hallett
V.P. PUBLICITY, TOUCHSTONE PICTURES
Lisa Halliday
V.P., RESEARCH
Dana Lombardo
V.P., EAST COAST PUBLICITY
Diana Loomis
V.P., CREATIVE FILM SERVICES
Constance Wells
V.P., FIELD MARKETING
Georgia O'Connor
V.P. PUBLICITY, WALT DISNEY PICTURES
Louise Spencer
V.P., MEDIA OPERATIONS
Nina Anderson
V.P., MEDIA
Krista Frudenfeld
V.P., MARKETING & SYNERGY
Mcihael Mendenhall
V.P., PROMOTIONS
Cherise McVicar

WALT DISNEY PICTURES AND TOUCHSTONE PICTURES
500 South Buena Vista Street, Burbank, CA 91521. (818) 560-1000.
PRESIDENT, FEATURE ANIMATION
Peter Schneider
PRESIDENT, TOUCHSTONE PICTURES
Donald De Line
PRESIDENT, WALT DISNEY PICTURES
David E. Vogel
EXECUTIVE V.P.
Susan Lyne
EXECUTIVE V.P., MOTION PICTURE PRODUCTION
Bruce Hendricks
SENIOR V.P., BUSINESS AFFAIRS
Robert J. DeBitetto
SENIOR V.P., FINANCE
William Clark
SENIOR V.P., LABOR RELATIONS
Robert W. Johnson
SENIOR V.P., MOTION PICTURE & TELEVISION POST-PRODUCTION
David McCann
SENIOR V.P., NEW TECHNOLOGY & DEVELOPMENT
Bob Lambert
SENIOR V.P., PRODUCTION
Ronald Lynch
SENIOR V.P., PRODUCTION
Art Repola
SENIOR V.P., PRODUCTION
Michael Stenson
SENIOR V.P., WALT DISNEY PICTURES
Bernie Goldman
SENIOR V.P., PRODUCTION, WALT DISNEY PICTURES
Michael Roberts
SENIOR V.P., TOUCHSTONE PICTURES
Jane Goldenring
SENIOR V.P. PRODUCTION, TOUCHSTONE PICTURES
Alexandra Schwartz
V.P. PRODUCTION, TOUCHSTONE PICTURES
Todd Garner
V.P. PRODUCTION, TOUCHSTONE PICTURES
Jordi Ross
V.P. PRODUCTION, TOUCHSTONE PICTURES
Christina Steinberg
V.P. PRODUCTION, WALT DISNEY PICTURES & TOUCHSTONE PICTURES
Whitney Green
PRESIDENT, MUSIC
Kathy Neroon
SENIOR V.P., MUSIC, BUSINESS & LEGAL
Scott Holzman
SENIOR V.P., MUSIC CREATIVE AFFAIRS
Matt Walker
SENIOR V.P., MUSIC CREATIVE AFFAIRS
Bill Green

EXECUTIVE V.P. FEATURE ANIMATION, DEVELOPMENT
Thomas Schumacher
SENIOR V.P. FEATURE ANIMATION, PRODUCTION
Tim Engel
SENIOR V.P. FEATURE ANIMATION, BUSINESS &
LEGAL AFFAIRS
Kevin W. Breen
V.P. FEATURE ANIMATION, COMMUNICATIONS
Jon Niermann
V.P. FEATURE ANIMATION, CREATIVE AFFAIRS
David Stainton
V.P. FEATURE ANIMATION, HUMAN RESOURCES
Marjorie Randolph
V.P. FEATURE ANIMATION, PRODUCTION
Kathleen Gavin
V.P. FEATURE ANIMATION, PRODUCTION
Sarah McArthur
V.P., PRODUCTION
Allison Breckner
V.P., PRODUCTION FINANCE
Paul Steinke
V.P., ADMINISTRATION & OPERATIONS,
FEATURE ANIMATION
Faith Raiguel
V.P., CASTING
Marcia S. Ross
V.P., CASTING
Gail Levin
V.P., FINANCE & PLANNING ANALYSIS,
FEATURE ANIMATION
Clark Spencer

BUENA VISTA PRODUCTIONS
500 South Buena Vista Street, Burbank, CA 91421. (818) 560-
2125. FAX: (818) 840-0543.
PRESIDENT, BUENA VISTA TELEVISION
Mort Marcus
SENIOR V.P., CURRENT PROGRAMMING
Mary Kellogg-Joslyn
SENIOR V.P., DEVELOPMENT
Mochael Davies
SENIOR V.P., BUENA VISTA PRODUCTIONS INT'L
David L. Simon
V.P., PRODUCTION
Screech Washington
V.P., PRODUCTION
Suzy Polse Unger

BUENA VISTA INTERNATIONAL
500 South Buena Vista Street, Burbank, California 91521 (818)
560-1000.
PRESIDENT
Mark Zoradi
SENIOR V.P., BUSINESS AFFAIRS & ACQUISITIONS
Jere Hausfater
SENIOR VICE PRESIDENT & GENERAL MANAGER
Lawrence Kaplan
SENIOR V.P., LATIN AMERICA & THE CARIBBEAN
Diego Lerner
V.P. & GENERAL MANAGER, GERMANY
Wolfgang Braun
V.P. & SWEDEN
Eric Broberg
V.P. & GENERAL MANAGER, U.K.
Danial Battsek
V.P., ASIA
Jeff Forman
V.P., MARKETING, JAPAN
Tateo Ikunaga
V.P. & GENERAL MANAGER, SOUTH KOREA
S.I. Kim
V.P., DISTRIBUTION
Anthony Marcohy
V.P., FINANCE
Ann Mather
V.P. & GENERAL MANAGER, AUSTRIA
Ferdinand Morawetz
V.P. & GENERAL MANAGER, ITALY
Sandro Pierotti
V.P., PUBLICITY
Teri Ritzer
V.P. DISTRIBUTION, EUROPE
Stuart Salter
V.P. & GENERAL MANAGER, SPAIN
Javier Vasallo
V.P. & GENERAL MANAGER, BENELUX
Paul Zonderland

BUENA VISTA VISUAL EFFECTS
500 South Buena Vista St., Burbank, CA 91421. (818) 560-2735.

WALT DISNEY AND TOUCHSTONE TELEVISION
500 South Buena Vista St., Burbank, CA 91521. (818) 560-5000.

BUENA VISTA TELEVISION
500 South Buena Vista St., Burbank, CA 91521. (818) 560-5000.

PRESIDENT
Walter C. Liss, Jr.

WALT DISNEY CONSUMER PRODUCTS
500 South Buena Vista Street, Burbank, CA 91521. (818) 560-
1000.
PRESIDENT
Barton K. Boyd
SENIOR V.P., ENTERTAINMENT
Caroline Mayer-Beuge

THE DISNEY CHANNEL
3800 West Alameda Avenue, Burbank, CA 91505. (818) 569-
7500.
PRESIDENT, THE DINEY CHANNEL & EXECUTIVE V.P., DIS-
NEY/ABC CABLE NETWORKS
Anne Sweeney
SENIOR V.P., ORIGINAL PROGRAMMING
Gary K. Marsh

BUENA VISTA HOME VIDEO
350 South Buena Vista Street, Burbank, CA 91521. (818) 560-
1000.
PRESIDENT, DOMESTIC HOME VIDEO
Ann Daly

BUENA VISTA INTERNATIONAL HOME VIDEO
350 South Buena Vista St., Burbank, CA 91521. (818) 560-1000.
PRESIDENT
Michael O. Johnson

HOLLYWOOD RECORDS
500 South Buena Vista St., Burbank, CA 91521. (818) 560-5670.
PRESIDENT
Bob Pfeifer
SENIOR VICE PRESIDENT
Richard Leher

WALT DISNEY RECORDS
500 South Buena Vista St., Burbank, CA 91521. (818) 560-1000.
VICE PRESIDENT
Mark Jaffe

WALT DISNEY IMAGINEERING
1401 Flower Street, Glendale, CA 91221. (818) 544-6500. FAX:
(818) 544-5080.
CHAIRMAN
Peter Rummell
VICE CHAIRMAN & PRINCIPAL CREATIVE EXECUTIVE
Marty Sklar
PRESIDENT
Ken Wong

WALT DISNEY PUBLISHING
500 South Buena Vista Street, Burbank, CA 91521. (818) 560-
1000;
114 Fifth Avenue, New York, NY 10011. (212) 633-4400.
V.P., DISNEY PUBLISHING & MOUSE WORKS (CA)
Jan Smith
EDITOR-IN-CHIEF, DISNEY ADVENTURES MAGAZINE (NY)
Phyllis Ehrlich
V.P. & PUBLISHER, DISNEY PRESS/HYPERION BOOKS FOR
CHILDREN & THE DISNEY PRESS (NY)
Elizabeth Gordon
V.P., DISNEY PUBLISHING (NY)
John Skipper
V.P., DISNEY MAGAZINE PUBLISHING (NY)
Jake Winebaum
V.P. & PUBLISHER, HYPERION BOOKS (NY)
Robert Miller

DELAURENTIIS COMMUNICATIONS
8670 Wilshire Blvd., 3rd fl., Beverly Hills, CA 90211. (310) 289-
6100. FAX: (310) 855-0562.
CHAIRMAN
Dino DeLaurentiis
PRESIDENT
Martha DeLaurentiis
V.P., PRODUCTION
Jonathan Fernandez

DISTANT HORIZON
8282 Sunset Blvd., Suite A, Los Angeles, CA 90046. (213) 848-
4140. FAX: (213) 848-4144. email: DistantH@ix.netcom.com
PRESIDENT
Anant Singh

DONNER/SHULER-DONNER PRODS.
c/o Warner Bros., 4000 Warner Blvd., Bldgs. 102 & 103, #4,
Burbank, CA 91522-0001. (818) 954-3611. FAX: (818) 954-
4908.
PRODUCER-DIRECTOR
Richard Donner
PRODUCER
Lauren Shuler-Donner
PRESIDENT
Richard Solomon

JEAN DOUMANIAN PRODS.

595 Madison Ave., Suite 2200, New York, NY 10022. (212) 486-2626. FAX: (212) 688-6236.
PRESIDENT
Jean Doumanian
VICE PRESIDENT
Letty Aronson

DREAMWORKS SKG

100 Universal City Plaza, Bldg. 477, Universal City, CA 91608. (818) 733-7000.
FOUNDERS
Steven Spielberg
Jeffrey Katzenberg
David Geffen

EASTMAN KODAK COMPANY

343 State St., Rochester, NY 14650. (716) 724-4000.
1901 W. 22nd St., Oakbrook, IL 60521-1283. (708) 218-5175.
6700 Santa Monica Boulevard, Hollywood, CA 90038. (213) 464-6131.
360 W. 31 St., New York, NY 10001. (212) 631-3450.
2800 Forest Lane, Dallas, TX 75234-7596. (214) 919-3444.
4 Concourse Parkway, Suite 300, Atlanta, GA 30328. (800) 800-8398.
CHAIRMAN, PRESIDENT & CEO
George M.C. Fisher
PRESIDENT, ENTERTAINMENT IMAGING GROUP
Joerg D. Agin
COO, PROFESSIONAL MOTION IMAGING
Richard P. Aschman
GENERAL MANAGER, DIGITAL MOTION IMAGING
Aidan P. Foley

EAST-WEST CLASSICS

(Distribution.) 225 Greenbank Ave., Piedmont, CA 94611-4131. (510) 655-6333. FAX: (510) 655-6580. Organized 1985.
CEO/OWNER
Audie E. Bock

EPIC PRODUCTIONS, INC.

4640 Lankershim Blvd., #600, North Hollywood, CA 91602. (818) 766-6888.
CEO
John Peters
V.P. & CONTROLLER
Carl Lau
LEGAL/BUSINESS AFFAIRS
Mark De Bacco
V.P., INTERNATIONAL SALES/ADMINISTRATION
Paul Woolley
V.P., DOMESTIC SALES/ADMINISTRATION
Sandy Lang

EXPANDED ENTERTAINMENT

(Distribution of animated shorts.)
30101 Agoura Ct., #110, Agoura Hills, CA 91301-2635. (818) 991-2884. FAX: (818) 991-3773. Telex: 247770 ANIM UR.
PRESIDENT
Terry Thoren
GENERAL MANAGER
Bill Buck

ROBERT EVANS COMPANY

c/o Paramount Studios, 5555 Melrose Ave., Lubitsch #117, Los Angeles, CA 90038-3197. (213) 956-8800. FAX: (213) 956-0070.
CHAIRMAN
Robert Evans
PRESIDENT
Christine Forsyth-Peters
V.P., PRODUCTION
Robin Guthie
V.P., CREATIVE AFFAIRS
Paul Sauer
DEVELOPMENT
Sherri Hopeman

EDWARD S. FELDMAN COMPANY

2600 W. Olive, Suite 748, Burbank, CA 91521-7257. (818) 972-3377. FAX: (818) 557-7256.
PRESIDENT
Edward S. Feldman
DEVELOPMENT
Susana Zepeda

FILM WORLD ENTERTAINMENTS INC./MIRACLE FILMS

(Film distribution.)
P.O. Box 2841, Los Angeles, CA 90078-2841. (818) 347-8601. FAX: (818) 347-8642.

PRESIDENT
Robert F. Burkhardt

FILMHAUS

(Film distribution.)
2255 W. Sepulveda Blvd., #204, Torrance, CA 90501. (310) 914-1776. FAX: (310) 320-8384.

FILMOPOLIS

11300 W. Olympic Blvd, Suite 625, Los Angeles, CA 90064. (310) 914-1776. FAX: (310) 914-1777.

FILMS AROUND THE WORLD, INC.

342 Madison Ave., Suite 812, New York, NY 10173. (212) 599-6040. FAX: (212) 838-9642.
PRESIDENT
Alexander W. Kogan, Jr.
VICE PRESIDENT
Barry Tucker

FINE LINE FEATURES

(see New Line Cinema)

FINNEGAN-PINKCHUK COMPANY

4225 Coldwater Canyon, Studio City, CA 91604. (818) 508-5614. FAX: (818) 985-3853.
EXECUTIVE PRODUCERS
Patricia Finnegan
William Finnegan
Sheldon Pinchuk

FIRST LOOK PICTURES/OVERSEAS FILM GROUP

(Film distribution and acquisition.)
8800 Sunset Blvd., Los Angeles, CA 90069. (310) 855-1199. FAX: (310) 855-0719.
CHAIRMAN
Robert Little
PRESIDENT
Ellen Little

FIRST RUN FEATURES

(Distributor of foreign films and documentaries.)
153 Waverly Place, New York, NY 10014. (212) 243-0600. FAX: (212) 989-7649.
PRESIDENT
Seymour Wishman
V.P., THEATRICAL SALES & MARKETING
Marc A. Mauceri
V.P., RETAIL HOME VIDEO SALES
Lisa Burkin

FORTY ACRES & A MULE FILMWORKS

124 Dekalb Ave., Brooklyn, NY 11217. (718) 624-3703.
PRESIDENT
Spike Lee
OFFICE MANAGER
Johanne Brown

DAVID FOSTER PRODS.

c/o The Mark of Zorro, Sony Pictures, 10202 W. Washington Blvd., Barrymore Bldg., Culver City, CA 90232. (310) 280-4635. FAX: (310) 280-2255.
PRODUCER
David Foster

4 CORNERS ENTERTAINMENT

(International distribution and production.)
636 N. Robertson Blvd., Los Angeles, CA 90069. (310) 657-2900. FAX: (310) 657-1479.
PRESIDENTS
Zac Reeder
Bryan Todd

FOUR POINT ENTERTAINMENT, INC.

(Television and motion picture production.)
89955 Beverly Blvd., Los Angeles, CA 90048. (310) 786-1600. FAX: (310) 247-2923.
OWNER/PRESIDENT
Michael Viner

FOX INC.

(Fox Inc. is the parent company of Fox Broadcasting Co., Fox Television Stations Inc., Twentieth Century Fox Film Corporation.)
P.O. Box 900, Beverly Hills, CA 90213. (310) 277-2211.
CHAIRMAN
Peter Chernin
PRESIDENT
William Mechanic

SENIOR EXECUTIVE VICE PRESIDENT
Tom Sherak
EXECUTIVE V.P., BUSINESS & LEGAL AFFAIRS
Greg Gelfan
SENIOR V.P., CFO
Simon Bax

TWENTIETH CENTURY FOX
PRESIDENT, TWENTIETH CENTURY FOX FILM PRODUCTION
Tom Rothman
PRESIDENT, DOMESTIC DISTRIBUTION
Bruce Snyder
PRESIDENT, FOX INTERNATIONAL THEATRICAL
Jim Gianopulous
PRESIDENT, MARKETING
Robert Harper
EXECUTIVE V.P., PRODUCTION
Dylan Sellers
EXECUTIVE V.P., PRODUCTION
Elizabeth Gabler
EXECUTIVE V.P., GENERAL SALES MANAGER
Richard Myerson
EXECUTIVE V.P., MARKETING, MEDIA & RESEARCH
Nancy Utley
EXECUTIVE V.P., DEPUTY GENERAL COUNSEL
Lyman Gronemeyer
EXECUTIVE V.P., LEGAL AFFAIRS
Robert Cohen
EXECUTIVE V.P., BUSINESS AFFAIRS
Steven Bersch
EXECUTIVE V.P., MUSIC
Robert Kraft
SENIOR V.P., PRODUCTION
Jon Landau
SENIOR V.P., PRODUCTION
Hutch Parker
SENIOR V.P., PRODUCTION
Sanford Panitch
SENIOR V.P., PRODUCTION
Jorge Saralcgui
SENIOR V.P., POST PRODUCTION
Theodore Gagliano
SENIOR V.P., PUBLICITY & PROMOTIONS
Jeffrey Godsick
SENIOR V.P., MARKETING/DISTRIBUTION
Bruce Pfander
SENIOR V.P., MARKETING & CREATIVE ADVERTISING
Anthony Sella
SENIOR V.P., MARKETING & CREATIVE ADVERTISING
Roland Mesa
SENIOR V.P., ACQUISITIONS
Cliff Werber
SENIOR V.P., LEGAL AFFAIRS-PRODUCTION
F. Jay Dougherty
SENIOR V.P., LEGAL AFFAIRS/ASSISTANT GENERAL COUNSEL
Michael Doodan
SENIOR V.P., BUSINESS AFFAIRS
Mark Resnick
SENIOR V.P., PERSONNEL
Leslee Perlstein
PRESIDENT, NORTH AMERICA, FOX HOME ENTERTAINMENT
Bob DeLellis
PRESIDENT INTERNATIONAL, HOME ENTERTAINMENT
Jeff Yapp
SENIOR V.P., BUSINESS & LEGAL AFFAIRS, FOX HOME ENTERTAINMENT
Laura Cook
SENIOR V.P., NORTH AMERICAN SALES, FOX HOME ENTERTAINMENT
Vincent Larinto
SENIOR V.P., OPERATIONS & ADMINISTRATION, FOX HOME ENTERTAINMENT
David Goldstein
V.P., MARKETING & DISTRIBUTION, FOX HOME ENTERTAINMENT
Michael Dunn
V.P., OPERATIONS, FOX HOME ENTERTAINMENT
Nadine Hall

HOME VIDEO
PRESIDENT, FOX VIDEO
Bob DeLellis

INTERNATIONAL
PRESIDENT, INTERNATIONAL TV
Mark Kaner
SENIOR V.P., INTERNATIONAL TV
Marion Edwards
EXECUTIVE V.P., INTERNATIONAL SALES & DISTRIBUTION
Julian Levin
SENIOR V.P., INTERNATIONAL MARKETING
Scott Neeson

SENIOR V.P., EUROPE/NEAR EAST & AFRICA
Jorge Canizares

FOX 2000
PRESIDENT
Laura Ziskin
EXECUTIVE VICE PRESIDENT
Kevin McCormick
SENIOR V.P., PRODUCTION
Alex Gartner

FOX FAMILY FILMS
PRESIDENT
Chris Meledandri

FOX SEARCHLIGHT
SENIOR V.P., PRODUCTION
Claudia Lewis
SENIOR V.P., MARKETING
David Dinerstein
SENIOR VICE PRESIDENT & GENERAL SALES MANAGER
James Naify

FOX ANIMATION STUDIOS
SENIOR V.P., GENERAL MANAGER
Steve Braun
PRODUCERS/DIRECTORS
Gary Goldman
Don Bluth

FOX INTERACTIVE
PRESIDENT
Jon Richmond
EXECUTIVE DIRECTOR, PRODUCT DEVELOPMENT
Paul Provenzano
DIRECTOR, BUSINESS & CREATIVE DEVELOPMENT
Scott Marcus

FOX LICENSING & MERCHANDISING
SENIOR V.P., WORLDWIDE PROMOTIONS
Steve Ross
SENIOR V.P., LEGAL & BUSINESS AFFAIRS
Jamie Samso
V.P., NATIONAL PROMOTIONS, FEATURE FILM & VIDEO
Michael Tomlin
V.P., WORLDWIDE PROMOTIONS & TELEVISION
Pierre Steele
V.P., LICENSING & MERCHANDISING
Michael Malone
V.P., FINANCE & ADMINISTRATION
Lisa Turchan

FOX STUDIO OPERATIONS
SENIOR V.P., FOX FILMED ENTERTAINMENT & FOX TELEVISION
Andy Setos

FOX STUDIO AUSTRALIA
PRESIDENT
Kim Williams

TWENTIETH CENTURY FOX TELEVISION
PRESIDENT
Peter Roth

FOX LORBER ASSOCIATES, INC.

(Motion picture and television distribution.)
419 Park Ave. South, 20th Floor, New York, NY 10016. (212) 686-6777. (212) 685-2625.
PRESIDENT & CEO
Richard Lorber
EXECUTIVE VICE PRESIDENT & GENERAL MANAGER, INTERNATIONAL SALES
Sheri Levine
EXECUTIVE VICE PRESIDENT & GENERAL MANAGER, HOME VIDEO
Michael Olivieri
SENIOR DIRECTOR, INTERNATIONAL SALES
Mickie Stienmann
DIRECTOR, INTERNATIONAL SALES
Krysanne Katsoolis
DIRECTOR, WORLDWIDE OPERATIONS
Cindy Banach
DIRECTOR, MARKETING & CREATIVE SERVICES
Kimberly Rubin
MANAGER, TELEVISION SALES & ACQUISITIONS, US & CANADA
Chris Peeler

FRIES ENTERTAINMENT, INC.

6922 Hollywood Blvd., Hollywood, CA 90028. (213) 466-2266. FAX: (213) 464-6082.
CHAIRMAN OF THE BOARD, PRESIDENT & CEO
Charles W. Fries
SENIOR V.P., PRODUCTION & DEVELOPMENT, THEATRICAL
Antony Ginnane

FULL MOON STUDIOS

3030 Andrita St., Los Angeles, CA 90065. (213) 341-5959.
FAX: (213) 341-5960.
CHAIRMAN OF THE BOARD & CEO
Charles Band
EXECUTIVE V.P., PRODUCTION
Albert Band
EXECUTIVE VICE PRESIDENT
Debra Dion

GENDECE FILM CO.

999 N. Doheny Dr., Suite 411, Los Angeles, CA 90069-3149.
(310) 271-8596. FAX: (213) 960-4735.
PARTNERS
Sam Firstenberg
Brian Gendece

GENERAL MEDIA INTERNATIONAL

(formerly Penthouse Films International)
277 Park Ave., New York, NY 10172. (212) 702-6000.
CHAIRMAN & CEO
Bob Guccione
VICE CHAIRMAN, PRESIDENT & COO
Kathy Kaeton
EXECUTIVE V.P. & CFO
Patrick Gavin

FREDERIC GOLCHAN PRODUCTIONS

9255 Doheny Rd., Suite 1106, Los Angeles, CA 90069. (310)
858-4939. emai: FGFilm@aol.com
2425 Olympic Blvd., 4th floor, Santa Monica, CA 90404. (310)
247-7317.
PRESIDENT
Frederic A. Golchan

GOLDEN HARVEST FILMS, INC.

9884 Santa Monica Blvd., Beverly Hills, CA 90212. (310) 203-
0722. FAX: (310) 556-3214.
V.P., PRODUCTION
Marlene Pivnick
COMPTROLLER
John W. Stuart

GOLDWYN ENTERTAINMENT COMPANY (A METROMEDIA ENTERTAINMENT GROUP COMPANY)

10203 Santa Monica Blvd., Suite 500, Los Angeles, CA 90067.
(310) 552-2255. FAX: (213) 284-8493.
CHAIRMAN & CEO
Samuel Goldwyn, Jr.
PRESIDENT & COO
Meyer Gottlieb
SENIOR V.P., BUSINESS AFFAIRS
Norman Flicker
SENIOR V.P., TREASURER & CFO
Hans W. Turner
SENIOR V.P., WORLDWIDE PRODUCTION
John Bard Manulis
V.P., PRODUCTION
Alison Rosenzweig
V.P., ACQUISITIONS
Rosanne Korenberg
V.P., TV PRODUCTION & DEVELOPMENT
Dan Smith

GORDON FILMS, INC.

119 W. 57 St., New York, NY 10019. (212) 757-9390. FAX:
(212) 757-9392.
PRESIDENT
Richard Gordon
VICE PRESIDENT
Joseph R. Cattuti
TREASURER
Richard Gordon

GOTHAM PICTURES

5333 McConnell Ave., Los Angeles, CA 90066. (310) 306-
0120. FAX: (310) 821-1012.
PARTNERS
Robert Greenhut
Rhonda Gunner

GRACIE FILMS

c/o Sony Film Corp., 10202 W. Washington Blvd., Culver City,
CA 90232. (310) 280-4222. FAX: (310) 280-1530.
PRESIDENT
Richard Sakai
PRODUCER-DIRECTOR
James L. Brooks

PRESIDENT, MOTION PICTURES
Bridget Johnson

GRAMERCY PICTURES

(Motion picture production and distribution.)
9247 Alden Dr., Beverly Hills, CA 90210. (310) 777-1960. FAX:
(310) 777-1966.
825 Eighth Ave., New York, NY 10019. (212) 333-8562. FAX:
(212) 333-1420.
PRESIDENT
Russell Schwartz
SENIOR V.P., PUBLICITY
Claudia Gray
V.P., DISTRIBUTION
Paul Rosenfeld
V.P., MARKETING
Steven Flynn

GREAT OAKS ENTERTAINMENT

500 S. Buena Vista St., Burbank, CA 91521.
COFOUNDERS
Richardo A. Mestres III
John Hughes

GREYCAT FILMS

3829 Delaware Lane, Las Vegas, NV 89109. (702) 737-0670.
FAX: (702) 734-3628. email: Greycat@aol.com
CO-PRESIDENTS
David Whitten
Suzanne Bowers Whitten

HKM FILMS

1641 North Ivar Ave., Hollywood, CA 90028. (213) 465-9191.
FAX: (213) 465-4203.
SENIOR V.P., CREATIVE AFFAIRS
Alexis Seely
DIRECTORS
Jesse Dylan
Graham Henman
Michael Karbelnikoff
Marco Brambilla
DEVELOPMENT
Patti Pagliei

HEADLINER PRODUCTIONS

(Motion picture producer and distributor.)
14717 Southwestern Ave., Gardena, CA 90249. (310) 327-
0729.
PRESIDENT
Dale Gasteiger Sr.

HOLLYWOOD PICTURES

(see The Walt Disney Company)

HOME BOX OFFICE

1100 Ave. of the Americas, New York, NY 10036. (212) 512-
1000.
2049 Century Park E., Suite 4100, Los Angeles, CA 90067.
(310) 201-9200.
PRESIDENT & COO
Jeff Bewkes

I.N.I. ENTERTAINMENT GROUP, INC.

11845 Olympic Blvd., Suite 1145, West Tower, Los Angeles,
CA 90064. (310) 479-6755. FAX: (310) 479-3475.
CHAIRMAN & CEO
Irv Holender
PRESIDENT & CFO
Michael Ricci

ICON PRODUCTIONS, INC.

(Motion picture production.)
4000 Warner Blvd., Burbank, CA 91522-0001. (818) 954-2960.
FAX: (818) 954-4212.
PRESIDENT
Bruce Davey
V.P., PRODUCTION
Steve McEveety

IMAGE ORGANIZATION, INC.

(International distribution of motion pictures, home video and
television.)
9000 Sunset Blvd., Suite 915, Los Angeles, CA 90069. (310)
278-8751. FAX: (310) 278-3967.
CHAIRMAN & CEO
Pierre David
CO-CHAIRMAN
Rene Malo (Montreal Office)
PRESIDENT
Lawrence Goebel

IMAGINE ENTERTAINMENT

(Motion picture development.)
1925 Century Park East, 23rd fl., Los Angeles, CA 90067.
(310) 277-1665. FAX: (310) 785-0107.
PRODUCER/PARTNER
Brian Grazer
DIRECTOR/PARTNER
Ron Howard
PRESIDENT OF PRODUCTION
Karen Kehela
EXECUTIVE VICE PRESIDENT
Michael Rosenberg
V.P., MOTION PICTURES
Michael Bostick
SENIOR V.P., ADMINISTRATION
Robin Barris

IMPERIAL ENTERTAINMENT CORP.

(Production, finance and distribution.)
4640 Lankershim Blvd., Suite 201, N. Hollywood, CA 91602.
(818) 762-0005. FAX: (818) 762-0006.
PRESIDENT
Sunil R. Shah
EXECUTIVE VICE PRESIDENT
Sundip R. Shah
EXECUTIVE V.P., PRODUCTION
Ash R. Shah
V.P., PRODUCTION
Eric Karson

INTERAMA, INC.

(Motion picture, non-theatrical and video distribution.)
301 W. 53rd St., Suite 19E, New York, NY 10019. (212) 977-4836. FAX: (212) 581-6582.
PRESIDENT
Nicole Jouve

INTERNATIONAL FILM CIRCUIT

(Motion picture distributor.)
P.O. Box 1151, Old Chelsea Station, New York, NY 10011. (212) 779-0660. FAX: (212) 779-9129. email: IFCPlanet@aol.com
PRESIDENT
Wendy Lidell

INTERSCOPE COMMUNICATIONS

10900 Wilshire Blvd., #1400, Los Angeles, CA 90024. (310) 208-8525. FAX: (310) 208-1764.
CHARIMAN & CEO
Ted Field
SENIOR PRODUCTION EXECUTIVE
Scott Kroopf
SENIOR VICE PRESIDENT
Michael Helfant

ISLAND PICTURES, INC.

(Producer-distributor.)
8920 Sunset Blvd., 2nd Floor, Los Angeles, CA 90069. (310) 276-4500. FAX: (310) 271-7840.
PRESIDENT
Mark Burg
SENIOR VICE PRESIDENTS, PRODUCTION
Todd Baker
Dan Genetti

ITALTOONS CORP.

32 W. 40 St., New York, NY 10018. (212) 730-0280. FAX: (212) 730-0313. email: Italtoon@ix.netcom.com
PRESIDENT
Giuliana Nicodemi
GENERAL MANAGER
Ken Priester
SALES & ACQUISITIONS
Luisa Rivosecchi

IXTLAN

(Motion picture production.)
201 Santa Monica Blvd., Suite 610, Santa Monica, CA 90401.
(310) 395-0525. FAX: (310) 395-1536. Ixxtlan@aol.com
PRESIDENT
Janet Yang
PRODUCER-DIRECTOR
Oliver Stone

JALEM PRODUCTIONS, INC.

(Motion picture production.)
141 El Camino, Suite 201, Beverly Hills, CA 90212. (310) 278-7750.
PRESIDENT
Jack Lemmon

VICE PRESIDENT
Connie McCauley

KENNEDY-MARSHALL COMPANY

c/o Raleigh Studios, 650 N. Bronson Ave., Clinton Bldg., Hollywood, CA 90004. (213) 960-4900. FAX: (213) 960-4922.
PRESIDENT, PRODUCTION
Jonathan A. Zimbert
V.P., PRODUCTION
Kathy Elliott
V.P., CREATIVE AFFAIRS
Phyllis Owens
PRODUCER
Kathleen Kennedy
PRODUCER-DIRECTOR
Frank Marshall

KINGS ROAD ENTERTAINMENT, INC.

1901 Ave. of the Stars, Suite 1545, Los Angeles, CA 90067.
(310) 552-0057. FAX: (310) 277-4468.
CHAIRMAN & CEO
Kenneth Aguado

KINO INTERNATIONAL CORP.

(Motion picture distribution.)
333 W. 39 St., Suite 503, New York, NY 10018. (212) 629-6880. URL: http://www.kino.com
PRESIDENT
Donald Krim
GENERAL MANAGER
Gary Palmucci

ARNOLD KOPELSON PRODS.

6100 Wilshire Blvd., Suite 1500, Los Angeles, CA 90048. (213) 932-0500. FAX: (213) 932-0238.
CHAIRMAN & CEO
Arnold Kopelson
CO-CHAIRPERSON & COO
Anne Kopelson

THE LADD COMPANY

(Motion picture production.)
c/o Paramount Pictures, 5555 Melrose Ave., Chevalier 117, Los Angeles, CA 90038. (213) 956-8203. FAX: (213) 862-1115.
PRESIDENT
Alan Ladd, Jr.
CREATIVE EXECUTIVE
Lisa Fielding

LARGO ENTERTAINMENT

(Foreign distribution company for motion pictures.)
2029 Century Park East, Suite 920, Los Angeles, CA 90067.
(310) 203-0055. FAX: (310) 203-0254.
CHAIRMAN/CEO
Barr Potter
EXECUTIVE VICE PRESIDENT
Peter Elson
SENIOR V.P., LEGAL & BUSINESS AFFAIRS
Bruce Vann
V.P., PRODUCTION & DISTRIBUTION SERVICES
Frank Isaac
V.P., AQUISITIONS
Kathleen Haase

LE STUDIO CANAL+

(Motion picture production.)
301 N. Canon Dr., Suite 228, Beverly Hills, CA 90210-4723.
(310) 247-0994. FAX: (310) 247-0998.
CHAIRMAN/PRESIDENT/CEO
Pierre Lescure
EXECUTIVE VICE PRESIDENT/GENERAL COUNSEL
Richard Garzilli
EXECUTIVE VICE PRESIDENT/CFO
Michael Meltzer

LEISURE TIME FEATURES

(Motion picture distribution.)
P.O. Box 1201, New York, NY 10009. (212) 267-4501.
PRESIDENT
Bruce Pavlow

LEVY-GARDNER-LAVEN PRODUCTIONS, INC.

9595 Wilshire Blvd., Suite 610, Beverly Hills, CA 90212. (310) 278-9820. FAX: (310) 278-2632.
PRESIDENT
Jules V. Levy
SECRETARY, TREASURER & VICE PRESIDENT
Arthur Gardner
VICE PRESIDENT
Arnold Laven

THE LEXINGTON GROUP LTD.

(Motion picture production and distribution.)
16 W. 16th St., New York, NY 10011. (212) 387-9348. FAX: (212) 691-2269.
CHAIRMAN & PRESIDENT
Michael S. Landes
EXECUTIVE V.P.
Michelle Landes

LIGHTMOTIVE, INC.

10351 Santa Monica Blvd., Suite 402, Los Angeles, CA 90025. (310) 282-0660. FAX: (310) 282-0990.
CHAIRMAN
Roland Joffe

LIGHTSTORM ENTERTAINMENT, INC.

919 Santa Monica Blvd., Santa Monica, CA 90401. (310) 656-6100. FAX: (310) 656-6102.
CHAIRMAN & CEO
James Cameron
PRESIDENT
Rae Sanchini
DIRECTOR OF DEVELOPMENT
Stacy Maes

LIVE ENTERTAINMENT

15400 Sherman Way, Suite 500, Van Nuys, CA 91406. (818) 908-0303. FAX: (818) 908-9539.
CEO
Roger Burlage
EXECUTIVE V.P., PRODUCTION & ACQUISITIONS
Paul Almond

LONGBOW PRODUCTIONS

4181 Sunswept Dr., Suite 100, Studio City, CA 91604-2335. (818) 762-6600. Longbow@ix.netcom.com
CHAIRMAN
Richard Kughn
PRESIDENTS
Ronnie D. Clemmer
Bill Pace

LUCASFILM, LTD.

(Motion picture and television production.)
P.O. Box 2009, San Rafael, CA 94912. (415) 662-1800.
Established in 1971.
CHAIRMAN OF THE BOARD & CEO
George W. Lucas, Jr.
PRESIDENT
Gordon Radley
V.P. & GENERAL MANAGER-LICENSING & THX
Howard Roffman
GENERAL MANAGER, THX
Monica Dashwood

LUCASARTS ENTERTAINMENT COMPANY

P.O. Box 10307, San Rafael, CA 94912. (415) 472-3400.
PRESIDENT
Jack Sorensen
DIRECTOR OF SALES & MARKETING
Mary Bihr

LUCAS DIGITAL, LTD.

P.O. Box 2459, San Rafael, CA 94912. (415) 258-2000.
PRESIDENT, INDUSTRIAL LIGHT & MAGIC
Jim Morris
V.P. & GENERAL MANAGER, SKYWALKER SOUND
Gloria Borders

MCA, INC.

100 Universal City Plaza, Universal City, CA 91608. (818) 777-1000. FAX: (818) 733-1506.
445 Park Ave., New York, NY 10022. (212) 759-7500.
PRESIDENT & CEO, SEAGRAM INC.
Edgar Bronfman, Jr.
CHAIRMAN & CEO
Frank A. Biondi, Jr.
PRESIDENT & COO
Ron Meyer
CONSULTING EXECUTIVES
George Smith
Lawrence D. Spungin
EXECUTIVE V.P., MCA & PRESIDENT, MCA ENTERPRISES
Charles S. Paul
EXECUTIVE V.P. & CFO
Bruce Hack
EXECUTIVE V.P., CORPORATE OPERATIONS
Howard Weitzman
EXECUTIVE V.P.
Sanford Climan
SENIOR V.P., CORPORATE COMMUNICATIONS & PUBLIC AFFAIRS
Deborah Rosen

SENIOR V.P. & GENERAL COUNSEL
Karen Randall
SENIOR V.P., REENGINEERING VALUE CREATION
Richard E. Baker
CHAIRMAN & CEO, MCA RECREATION
Ron Bension
CHAIRMAN, THE PUTNAM BERKLEY GROUP
Phyllis Grann
SENIOR V.P. & GENERAL MANAGER
Daniel E. Slusser
V.P., FINANCIAL OPERATIONS
David Hancock
V.P., IND. RELATIONS
Stuart Mandel
V.P. & CORPORATE SECRETARY
Michael Samuel
V.P., FOREIGN TAXES
H. Steven Gordon
V.P., CORPORATE DEVELOPMENT
Brian C. Mulligan
TREASURER
Pamela Cherney
VICE PRESIDENT & SECRETARY
Michael Samuel
V.P., FINANCIAL OPERATIONS
David Hancock
TREASURER
Pamela Cherney
BOARD OF DIRECTORS
Edgar Bronfman, Jr. (Acting Chairman), Samuel Bronfman II, Bruce L. Hack, Arnold M. Ludwick, Ron Meyer, Yasuo Nakamura, Thomas P. Pollock, Lew R. Wasserman (Chairman Emeritus)

PRINCIPAL SUBSIDIARIES & DIVISIONS

MCA MOTION PICTURE GROUP
Universal Pictures Production, Universal Pictures Marketing, Universal Pictures Distribution

MCA TELEVISION GROUP
Universal Television, MCA TV, MCA TV International, MCA Television Entertainment, MCA Family Entertainment Group

MCA HOME ENTERTAINMENT GROUP
MCA Home Video, MCA/Universal Home Video, Universal Pay Television, Universal Pictures Non-Theatrical, CIC Video Int'l, MCA Home Video Canada

MCA MUSIC ENTERTAINMENT GROUP
MCA Records, Uni Distribution (Records and Home Video), MCA Music Entertainment International, MCA Music Publishing, MCA Concerts, GRP Records, Geffen Records, Winterland Productions

MCA CONSUMER PRODUCTS GROUP
Spencer Gifts: Retail Stores, DAPY Stores.

MCA PUBLISHING GROUP: BOOK PUBLISHING
The Putnam Berkley Group, Berkley Publishing Group, Jove Publications, Putnam New Media

MCA DEVELOPMENT
Universal City Real Estate Development, MCA/Universal Real Estate Services, Universal CityWalk

MCA ENTERPRISES
MCA Enterprises International, Universal Interactive Studios, Universal Studios Japan

MCA RECREATION SERVICES GROUP
Universal Studios Hollywood, Universal Studios Florida, Victoria Station Restaurant

MCA/UNIVERSAL MERCHANDISING
MCA/Universal Animation Art, MCA Publishing Rights

UNIVERSAL PICTURES
(A division of Universal City Studios, Inc., subsidiary of MCA, Inc.)
100 Universal City Plaza, Universal City, CA 91608. (818) 777-1000. FAX: (818) 733-1440.
445 Park Ave., New York, NY 10022. (212) 759-7500. Cable: Unifilman.
CHAIRMAN, MOTION PICTURE GROUP
Casey Silver
EXECUTIVE V.P., MCA MOTION PICTURE GROUP
Lynwood Spinks
SENIOR V.P., MCA MOTION PICTURE GROUP
Ann Busby
SENIOR V.P., FINANCE
James Burk
EXECUTIVE V.P., LEGAL & BUSINESS AFFAIRS
Jon Gumpert
V.P., BUSINESS AFFAIRS
TBA

UNIVERSAL PICTURES PRODUCTION
PRESIDENT, PRODUCTION
Marc Platt

SENIOR V.P., PRODUCTION
Barry Isaacson
SENIOR V.P., PRODUCTION & FEATURE ANIMATION
Kate Barker
SENIOR V.P., MUSIC CREATIVE AFFAIRS
Harry Garfield
SENIOR V.P., PRODUCTION
Leonard Kornberg
SENIOR V.P., BUSINESS AFFAIRS
Robert W. Rubin
SENIOR V.P., FEATURE CASTING
Nancy Nayor
SENIOR V.P., PHYSICAL PRODUCTION
Don Zepfel
V.P., ACQUISITIONS
Matt Wall
V.P., PRODUCTION (EAST COAST)
Peter Arnoff
V.P., PRODUCTION
Anne Milder
V.P., MUSIC BUSINESS AFFAIRS
Phillip Cohen

UNIVERSAL PICTURES MARKETING
PRESIDENT, MARKETING
Buffy Shutt
EXECUTIVE VICE PRESIDENT
Kathy Jones
EXECUTIVE V.P., INTERNATIONAL MARKETING
Nadia Alves-Bronson
SENIOR V.P., CREATIVE ADVERTISING
William Loper
SENIOR V.P., MARKETING
Edward Egan
V.P., AUDIO VISUAL ADVERTISING
Mike Greenfeld
V.P., CREATIVE ADVERTISING OPERATIONS
Dan Wolfe
V.P., NATIONAL PUBLICITY
Stuart Zakim
SENIOR V.P., MEDIA & CO-OP ADVERTISING
Anthony Evergates-Price
V.P., NATIONAL PROMOTIONS
John Polwrek
V.P., PUBLICITY & PROMOTION/SPECIAL PROJECTS
Daniel Wheatcroft
V.P., PLANNING & FINANCE
Charlotte Reith
V.P., NATIONAL PUBLICITY
Alan Sutton

UNIVERSAL PICTURES DISTRIBUTION
PRESIDENT
Nikki Rocco
EXECUTIVE V.P., DISTRIBUTION]
TBA
V.P. & DIVISIONAL MANAGER
Dave Richoux
V.P. & DIVISIONAL MANAGER
Jack Finn
SENIOR V.P., NATIONAL SALES MANAGER
Nicholas C. Carpou
SENIOR V.P., NATIONAL SALES MANAGER
Mark T. Gaines
VICE PRESIDENT/GENERAL MANAGER UNIVERSAL FILMS CANADA
Eugene Amodeo
V.P., DIVISION MANAGER
Albert Quaedvlieg
V.P., PRINT CONTROL
Harold Goldberg
V.P., EXHIBITOR RELATIONS
Steve Ellman
DIRECTOR, SALES ADMINISTRATION
Gary Chang

DIVISION MANAGERS AND BRANCHES
100 Universal City Plaza, Universal City, CA 91608. (818) 777-4266. (Albany, Buffalo, Cincinnati, Salt Lake City, Denver).
MANAGER
Nicholas Carpou
8901 Beverly Blvd., Los Angeles, CA 90048. (213) 550-7461. (Los Angeles, Portland, Seattle, Philadelphia, Washington, D.C., Boston, New Haven, Puerto Rico).
MANAGER
Jack Finn
P.O. Box 5000, 6060 McDonough Dr., Norcross, GA 30091-5000. (404) 448-8032. (Atlanta, Charlotte, Jacksonville, Dallas, Kansas City, Memphis, New Orleans, Oklahoma City).
MANAGER
Mark Gaines
445 Park Avenue, New York, NY 10022. (212) 605-2828. (New York, Pittsburgh).
MANAGER
Albert Quaedvlieg

P.O. Box 8622, 618 Lamont Rd., Elmhurst, IL 60126. (708) 279-9200. (Chicago, Cleveland, Des Moines, Omaha, Detroit, Indianapolis, Milwaukee, Minneapolis, St. Louis, San Francisco.)
MANAGER
Dave Richoux

UNIVERSAL TELEVISION
PRESIDENT
Tom Thayer
EXECUTIVE V.P., BUSINESS AFFAIRS ADMINISTRATION
Susan Workman

MALIBU BAY FILMS

(Television and motion picture production.)
P.O. Box 17244, Beverly Hills, CA 90209-3244. (310) 278-5056.
FAX: (310) 278-5058.
PRESIDENT
Andrew Sidaris
OFFICERS
Arlene Sidaris, Drew Sidaris

MALPASO PRODS.

(Motion picture production.)
c/o Warner Bros., 4000 Warner Blvd., Burbank, CA 91522-0001. (818) 954-3367.
PRODUCER-DIRECTOR
Clint Eastwood
DIRECTOR, DEVELOPMENT
Melissa Rooker

THE MANHATTAN PROJECT, LTD.

(Motion picture production.)
888 7th Avenue, 30th Floor, New York, NY 10019. (212) 258-2541. FAX: (212) 258-2546.
PRESIDENT
David Brown
V.P., CREATIVE AFFAIRS
Kit Golden

THE MATTHAU COMPANY

(Motion picture production.)
1999 Ave. of the Stars, Suite 2100, Los Angeles, CA 90067. (310) 557-2727.
CHAIRMAN
Walter Matthau
CEO & PRESIDENT
Charles Matthau
CREATIVE EXECUTIVES
Richard Conner, Nina Kaye

MERCHANT IVORY PRODUCTIONS

250 W. 57 St., New York, NY 10107. (212) 582-8049.
PRESIDENT
James Ivory
V.P. & TREASURER (U.S.)
Ismail Merchant
EXECUTIVE PRODUCER
Donald Rosenfeld

METRO-GOLDWYN-MAYER, INC.

Headquarters: 2500 Broadway St., Santa Monica, CA 90404-3061. (310) 449-3000. FAX: (310) 449-3100.
1350 Avenue of the Americas, New York, NY 10019. (212) 708-0300. FAX: (212) 708-0337.
CHAIRMAN OF THE BOARD & CEO
Frank Mancuso
PRESIDENT, WORLDWIDE THEATRICAL DISTRIBUTION
Larry Gleason
PRESIDENT, MGM/UA TELECOMMUNICATIONS GROUP
Gary Marenzi
PRESIDENT, MGM WORLDWIDE TELEVISION
John P. Symes
PRESIDENT, MGM DOMESTIC TELEVISION DISTRIBUTION
Sid Cohen
PRESIDENT, WORLDWIDE MARKETING
Gerry Rich
PRESIDENT, MGM/UA HOME ENTERTAINMENT
Richard Cohen
PRESIDENT, MGM/UA MUSIC
Marsha Gleeman
EXECUTIVE VICE PRESIDENT
Michael S. Hope
EXECUTIVE VICE PRESIDENT
A. Robert Pisano
EXECUTIVE V.P., STRATEGY & DEVELOPMENT
Alan Cole-Ford
EXECUTIVE V.P. & GENERAL COUNSEL
David Johnson
EXECUTIVE V.P., CORPORATE AFFAIRS
William A. Jones
EXECUTIVE V.P., WORLDWIDE PUBLICITY
Susan Pile

EXECUTIVE V.P. & GENERAL MANAGER, MGM INTERACTIVE
Ronald Frankel
SENIOR V.P., LABOR RELATIONS
Benjamin B. Kahane
SENIOR V.P., ADMINISTRATION
Richard Parness
SENIOR V.P. & DEPUTY GENERAL COUNSEL
Mark Fleischer
SENIOR V.P. & DEPUTY GENERAL COUNSEL
Robert Brada
SENIOR V.P. & DEPUTY GENERAL COUNSEL
Rebecca Laurie Ford
SENIOR V.P. FINANCIAL OPERATIONS
Daniel J. Rosett
SENIOR V.P. FINANCIAL PLANNING & DEVELOPMENT
Charles E. Cohen
V.P., INFORMATION SERVICES
Kim Spenchian
V.P. & ASSISTANT SECRETARY
Maria Angeletti
V.P., TAXES
Deborah J. Arvesen
V.P., CORPORATE COMMUNICATIONS
Anne H. Corley
V.P., LABOR RELATIONS
Mark Crowley

MGM PICTURES
2500 Broadway St., Santa Monica, CA 90404 (310) 449-3000. FAX: (310) 449-3100.
PRESIDENT & CEO
Michael E. Marcus
SENIOR EXECUTIVE V.P., BUSINESS AFFAIRS
Frank Davis
EXECUTIVE V.P., BUSINESS AFFAIRS
Darcie Denkert
EXECUTIVE V.P., PRODUCTION
Robert E. Relyea
EXECUTIVE V.P., MGM PICTURES
Greg Foster
EXECUTIVE V.P., MGM PICTURES
David Ladd
SENIOR V.P., POST PRODUCTION
Gary Gerlich
SENIOR V.P., LABOR RELATIONS
Benjamin B. Kahane
SENIOR V.P. FINANCIAL OPERATIONS
Daniel J. Rosett
SENIOR V.P., PRODUCTION
Elisabeth Seldes
V.P. & ASSISTANT SECRETARY
Maria Angeletti
V.P., TAXES
Deborah J. Arvesen
V.P., PRODUCTION
Jeff Coleman
V.P., LABOR RELATIONS
Mark Crowley
V.P., PRODUCTION RESOURCES
Kathryn A. Findling
V.P., BUSINESS AFFAIRS ADMINISTRATION
Luba Keske
V.P., BUSINESS AFFAIRS
Marla E. Levine
V.P., BUSINESS AFFAIRS
Libby Pachares
V.P., DEVELOPMENT
Elizabeth Carroll
DIRECTOR, CREATIVE AFFAIRS
Kim Ciliberto

UNITED ARTISTS PICTURES
SENIOR EXECUTIVE V.P., BUSINESS AFFAIRS
Frank Davis
EXECUTIVE V.P., BUSINESS AFFAIRS
Darcie Denkert
EXECUTIVE V.P., PRODUCTION
Rebecca Pollack Parker
EXECUTIVE V.P., PRODUCTION
Robert E. Relyea
SENIOR V.P., PRODUCTION
Jeff Kleeman
SENIOR V.P., POST PRODUCTION
Gary Gerlich
SENIOR V.P., LABOR RELATIONS
Benjamin B. Kahane
SENIOR V.P. FINANCIAL OPERATIONS
Daniel J. Rosett
SENIOR V.P. FINANCIAL PLANNING & DEVELOPMENT
Charles E. Cohen
V.P. & ASSISTANT SECRETARY
Maria Angeletti
V.P., TAXES
Deborah J. Arvesen

V.P., PRODUCTION
Jeff Coleman
V.P., LABOR RELATIONS
Mark Crowley
V.P., PRODUCTION RESOURCES
Kathryn A. Findling
V.P., BUSINESS AFAIRS ADMINISTRATION
Luba Keske
V.P., BUSINESS AFFAIRS
Marla E. Levine
V.P., BUSINESS AFFAIRS
Libby Pachares
V.P., DEVELOPMENT
Dura Temple
V.P., DEVELOPMENT
James Middleton
DIRECTOR, CREATIVE AFFAIRS
Kim Ciliberto

THE MILTON I. MORITZ COMPANY, INC.
856 Malcolm Ave., Garden Suite, Los Angeles, CA, 90024. (310) 470-9122. FAX: (310) 475-5614.
PRESIDENT
Milton I. Moritz
VICE PRESIDENT
Neal A. Moritz

MIRACLE FILMS
P. O. Box 2841, Los Angeles, CA 90078-2841. (818) 347-8601. FAX: (818) 347-8642.
PRESIDENT
Robert F. Burkhardt

MIRAMAX FILMS CORP.
(Subsidiaries: Dimension Films, Shining Excalibur Pictures.)
375 Greenwich St., New York, NY 10013. (212) 941-3800. FAX: (212) 941-3949.
7920 Sunset Blvd., Los Angeles, CA 90046. (213) 969-2000. FAX: (213) 969-9840.
CHAIRMEN
Bob Weinstein
Harvey Weinstein
PRESIDENT, MARKETING
Mark Gill
PRESIDENT, INTERNATIONAL
Rick Sands
SENIOR V.P., INTERNATIONAL
David Linde
SENIOR EXECUTIVE V.P., PRODUCTION
Paul Webster
EXECUTIVE V.P., LEGAL & BUSINESS AFFAIRS
John Logigan
PRESIDENT, DISTRIBUTION
Jack Foley
EXECUTIVE V.P., PUBLICITY & PROMOTIONS
Marcy Granata
SENIOR V.P., PRODUCTION
Meryl Poster
SENRIOR V.P., PRODUCTION
Helena Echegoyen
V.P., PRODUCTION & FINANCE
John Hadity
SENIOR V.P., PHYSICAL PRODUCTION
Kevin Hayman
PRESIDENT, PRODUCTION & TELEVISION
Allen Sabinson
EXECUTIVE V.P., PRODUCTION & DEVELOPMENT
Jack Lechner
SENIOR V.P., PRODUCTION
Paul Rosenberg
SENIOR V.P., ACQUISITIONS
Eamonn Bowles
EXECUTIVE V.P., ACQUISITIONS
Trea Hoving
SENIOR V.P., ACQUISITIONS
Jeff Kurz

MIRISCH CORPORATION OF CALIFORNIA, THE
100 Universal City Plaza, Universal City, CA 91608-1002. (818) 777-1271. FAX: (818) 733-1422.
CHAIRMAN OF THE BOARD & CEO
Marvin E. Mirisch
PRESIDENT & CHIEF PRODUCTION OFFICER
Walter Mirisch

MODERN EDUCATION SERVICES
381 Park Avenue South, Suite 713, New York, NY 10016. (212) 696-5050. URL: http://www.modern.com
PRESIDENT
David A. Conway
VICE PRESIDENTS
Robert Treuber

MORGAN CREEK PRODUCTIONS

4000 Warner Blvd., Bldg. #76, Burbank, CA 91522. (818) 954-4800. FAX: (818) 954-4811. email: GSM1224@ix.netcom.com
CHAIRMAN/CEO
James G. Robinson
VICE CHAIRMAN/CHIEF OPERATING OFFICER/PRESIDENT, INTERNATIONAL
Gary Barber
V.P., WORLDWIDE PUBLICITY & PROMOTION
Linda Goldenberg
EXECUTIVE VICE PRESIDENT/V.P., INTERNATIONAL
Ken Shapiro
V.P., POST-PRODUCTION
Jody Levin
HEAD OF PRODUCTION
Bill Todman, Jr.
SENIOR V.P., PRODUCTION
Larry Katz

MOTION PICTURE CORP. OF AMERICA (A METROMEDIA ENTERTAINMENT GROUP COMPANY)

(Motion picture producer and distributor).
1401 Ocean Ave., #301, Santa Monica, CA 90401. (310) 319-9500. FAX: (310) 319-9501.
CO-PRESIDENT & TREASURER
Brad Krevoy
CO-PRESIDENT & SECRETARY
Steven B. Stabler
EXECUTIVE V.P.
Jeffrey Ivers
SENIOR V.P. & ASSISTANT SECRETARY
John W. Hester
EXECUTIVE V.P., PRODUCTION
Bradley Jenkel
EXECUTIVE V.P., PRODUCTION
Bradley Thomas
EXECUTIVe V.P., TELEVISION
Paul Frank
SENIOR V.P., PRODUCTION
John Bertolli

THE MOUNT/KRAMER COMPANY

5757 Wilshire Blvd., Suite 240, Los Angeles, CA 90036. (213) 525-3555. FAX: (213) 525-3599.
PARTNERS
Josh Kramer
Thomas Mount

THE MOVIE GROUP

(International distribution.)
1900 Ave. of the Stars, Suite 1425, Los Angeles, CA 90067. (310) 556-2830. FAX: (310) 277-1490.
PRESIDENT
Peter E. Strauss
SENIOR VICE PRESIDENTS
Jed Daly

NATIONAL FILM SERVICE, INC.

(For branch listings, see Film Distributors in Key Cities)
16830 Ventura Blvd., Suite 202, Encino, CA 91436. (818) 386-6650. FAX: (818) 386-6654.
PRESIDENT
Terry Kierzek
V.P., OPERATIONS
Patrick Benton
DIRECTOR, FINANCE
Jody Kelly
DIRECTOR, HUMAN RESOURCES
Patti Biglin
DIRECTOR, THEATRE SERVICES
Sean Lohan
DIRECTOR, ENTERTAINMENT SYSTEMS
Larry Riback
DIRECTOR, SALES & MARKETING
Sharon Scullion

NATIONAL LAMPOON

(Motion pictures & television production, magazine publishing.)
10850 Wilshire Blvd., Suite 1000, Los Angeles, CA 90024. (310) 474-5252. FAX: (310) 474-1219.
PRESIDENT & CEO
Jim Jimirro

NEUFELD/REHME PRODS.

c/o Paramount Pictures, 5555 Melrose Ave., Dressing #112, Hollywood, CA 90038-3197. (213) 956-4816. FAX: (213) 862-2571.
PRINCIPALS
Mace Neufeld
Bob Rehme

EXECUTIVE V.P., CREATIVE AFFAIRS & DEVELOPMENT
Nick Grillo
DIRECTOR, DEVELOPMENT
Susan Woods
EXECUTIVE V.P., PRODUCTION
Dan Rissner
V.P., PRODUCTION
Innes Weir

NEW LINE CINEMA CORPORATION

(Distribution & production)
888 Seventh Ave., 20th Fl., New York, NY 10106. (212) 649-4900. FAX: (212) 649-4966.
116 North Robertson Blvd., 2nd Fl., Los Angeles, CA 90048. (310) 854-5811.
4501 Circle 75 Parkway, Atlanta, GA 30339. (404) 952-0056.
6060 North Central Expressway, Dallas, TX 75206. (214) 696-0755.
CHAIRMAN & CEO
Robert Shaye
PRESIDENT & CHIEF OPERATING OFFICER
Michael Lynne
CFO
Stephen Abramson
PRESIDENT, PRODUCTION
Michael Deluca
PRESIDENT, HOME VIDEO
Stephen Einhorn
PRESIDENT, TELEVISION DISTRIBUTION
Robert Friedman
PRESIDENT, THEATRICAL DISTRIBUTION & MARKETING
Mitchell Goldman
PRESIDENT, INTERNATIONAL DISTRIBUTION
Rolf Mittweg
PRESIDENT, FINE LINE FEATURES
Ruth Vitale
EXECUTIVE V.P., FINANCE
Michael Spatt
SENIOR V.P., FINANCE
Tracy Adler
SENIOR V.P., BUSINESS DEVELOPMENT
James Rosenthal
SENIOR V.P., ROYALTY ACCOUNTING
Susannah Juni
V.P., TELEVISION & ANCILLARY ACCOUNTING
Frank Buquicchio
SENIOR V.P., ADMINISTRATION
Marsha Hook-Haygood
V.P., FINANCIAL OPERATIONS
David Eichler
V.P., CORPORATE ACCOUNTING
Raymond Landes
SENIOR V.P., INFORMATION SERVICES
Karen Zimmer

NEW LINE BUSINESS AFFAIRS

SENIOR VICE PRESIDENT
Judd Funk
PRESIDENT
Suzanne Rosencrans
EXECUTIVE VICE PRESIDENT
Benjamin Zinkin
SENIOR VICE PRESIDENT
Gary Stutman
VICE PRESIDENT
Avy Eschenasy
VICE PRESIDENT
Amy Gittleman
V.P., BUSINESS AFFAIRS ADMINISTRATION
Sonya Thompsen

NEW LINE PRODUCTIONS, INC.

CHAIRPERSON, PRODUCTION
Sara Risher
PRESIDENT, CREATIVE DEVELOPMENT
Michael De Luca
SENIOR V.P., TELEVISION PRODUCTION
Cindy Hornickel
SENIOR V.P., POST-PRODUCTION
Joseph Fineman
PRESIDENT, MUSIC
Toby Emmerich
EXECUTIVE V.P., PRODUCTION
Richard Saperstein
EXECUTIVE V.P., PRODUCTION
Carla Fry
SENIOR V.P., PRODUCTION
Mark Tusk
V.P., PRODUCTION
Lynn Harris
V.P., PRODUCTION
Jay Stern
V.P., PRODUCTION & DEVELOPMENT
Amy Henkels

V.P., POST-PRODUCTION SERVICES
Brent Kaviar
V.P., POST-PRODUCTION
Richard Keeley
V.P., POST-PRODUCTION
Sara King
V.P., FEATURE CASTING
Valerie McCaffrey
V.P., PRODUCTION FINANCE
Paul Prokop
V.P., PRODUCTION
Claire Rudnick-Polstein
V.P., MUSIC
Dana Sano

NEW LINE DISTRIBUTION, INC.
PRESIDENT, THEATRICAL DISTRIBUTION
Mitchell Goldman
SENIOR V.P., DISTRIBUTION, FINE LINE FEATURES
Steve Friedlander
EXECUTIVE V.P., SALES
Al Shapiro
SENIOR V.P., SALES ADMINISTRATION
David Keith
SENIOR V.P., SOUTHEASTERN DIVISION MANAGER
Don Osley
SENIOR V.P., SOUTHWEST DIVISION MANAGER
John Trickett
V.P., WESTERN DIVISION MANAGER
Lawrence Levy
V.P., MIDWESTERN DIVISION MANAGER
Scott Huneryager
V.P., EASTERN DIVISION MANAGER
Jonathan Beal
V.P., PRINT CONTROL
Gisela Corcoran

NEW LINE ACQUISITIONS
EXECUTIVE VICE PRESIDENT
Mark Ordesky

NEW LINE INTERNATIONAL RELEASING, INC.
PRESIDENT, INTERNATIONAL DISTRIBUTION
Rolf Mittweg
SENIOR V.P., SALES & ADMINISTRATION
Nestor Nieves
EXECUTIVE V.P., EUROPEAN SUPERVISOR
Camela Galano
V.P., INTERNATIONAL DISTRIBUTION
Ralpho Borgos
V.P., FINANCE
David Burkhardt
V.P., MARKETING
Teri Grochowski
V.P., SERVICING
William Spadafora

NEW LINE MARKETING, INC.
SENIOR V.P., MARKETING
Christina Kounelias
SENIOR V.P., FINANCE
Rob Kobus
EXECUTIVE V.P., MARKETING, FINE LINE FEATURES
Elizabeth Manne
EXECUTIVE V.P., MARKETING
Karen Hermelin
V.P., ADVERTISING, FINE LINE FEATURES
Brian Caldwell
PRESIDENT, MEDIA & CO-OP ADVERTISING
Christopher Pula
EXECUTIVE V.P., MEDIA & CO-OP ADVERTISING
Diana Charbanic
SENIOR V.P., PUBLICITY
Mary K. Donovan
V.P., NATIONAL PROMOTIONS
Mary Goss
V.P., FIELD & INTERACTIVE MARKETING
Elissa Greer
V.P., PUBLICITY, FINE LINE FEATURES
Marian Koltai-Levine
V.P., PUBLICITY
Michael Kramer
V.P., CORPORATE PUBLICITY
Steven Elzer
V.P., CO-OP ADVERTISING
Susan Russell
V.P., PHOTOGRAPHY
Helene Steel
DIRECTOR, MARKETING RESEARCH
Karen Brown

NEW LINE HOME VIDEO, INC.
PRESIDENT & CEO
Stephen Einhorn

NEW LINE TELEVISION
PRESIDENT, TELEVISION DISTRIBUTION
Robert Friedman

FINE LINE FEATURES
888 Seventh Ave., 20th fl., New York, NY 10106. (212) 649-4900.
PRESIDENT
Ruth Vitale
EXECUTIVE V.P., ACQUISITIONS
Jonathan Weisgal
V.P., PRODUCTION & ACQUISITIONS
Amy Lobowitz
V.P., PRODUCTION & ACQUISITIONS
Rachael Horovitz

NEW REGENCY PRODS.
4000 Warner Blvd., Burbank, CA 91522-0001. (818) 954-3044. FAX: (818) 954-3295.
OWNER
Arnon Milchan
PRESIDENT
Michael Nathanson
EXECUTIVE VICE PRESIDENT & COO
David Matalon
V.P., PHYSICAL PRODUCTION
Patrick Crowley
SENIOR V.P., PRODUCTION
Madeline Warren

NEW YORKER FILMS
(Motion picture distribution.)
16 W. 61 St., New York, NY 10023. (212) 247-6110. FAX: (212) 307-7855.
PRESIDENT
Daniel Talbot
VICE PRESIDENT
Jose Lopez

NOBLE PRODUCTIONS, INC.
1615 S. Crest Dr., Los Angeles, CA 90035-3315. (310) 552-2934. FAX: (310) 552-3508.
CHAIRMAN & PRESIDENT
Ika Panajotovic
VICE PRESIDENT
Elena Panajotovic

NORTHERN ARTS ENTERTAINMENT
(Motion picture producers and distributors.)
Northern Arts Studios, Williamsburg, MA 01096-0201. (413) 268-9301. FAX: (413) 268-9309.
CHAIRMAN
John Lawrence Re
PRESIDENT
David Mazor
V.P., ACQUISITIONS
Alison Brantley

NORTHERN LIGHTS ENTERTAINMENT
100 Universal City Plaza, Bldg. 489, Universal City, CA 91608. (818) 777-8080.
PRODUCER-DIRECTOR
Ivan Reitman
OPERATIONS MANAGER
Beth Cahn Kennedy

OCTOBER FILMS
(Motion picture producer and distributor.)
65 Bleecker St., 2nd fl., New York, NY 10012. (212) 539-4000. FAX: (212) 539-4099.
CO-MANAGING EXECUTIVES
Amir Malin
Bingham Ray
John Schmidt
DIRECTOR OF ACQUISITIONS
Susan Glatzer
CONTROLLER
Dan Lieblein

OMEGA ENTERTAINMENT, LTD.
(Production and distribution.)
8760 Shoreham Dr., Los Angeles, CA 90069. (310) 855-0516. FAX: (310) 652-2044. email: InhausP@aol.com
PRESIDENT & CEO
Nico Mastorakis
V.P., SALES
Carole Mishkind
EXECUTIVE VICE PRESIDENT
Isabelle Mastorakis Thompson
V.P., PRODUCTION
Christy L. Pokarney

ORION PICTURES CORPORATION (A METROMEDIA ENTERTAINMENT GROUP COMPANY)

1888 Century Park E., Los Angeles, CA 90067. (310) 282-0550. FAX: (310) 201-0798.
CHAIRMAN OF THE BOARD & CEO
John W. Kluge
VICE CHAIRMAN
Stuart Subotnick
PRESIDENT & CEO
Leonard White
SENIOR EXECUTIVE V.P., GENERAL COUNSEL & SECRETARY
John W. Hester
SENIOR EXECUTIVE V.P.
Silvia Kessel
SENIOR EXECUTIVE V.P.
Brad Krevoy
SENIOR EXECUTIVE V.P.
Steven Stabler
EXECUTIVE PRESIDENT & CFO
Cynthia Friedman
SENIOR V.P., BUSINESS & LEGAL AFFAIRS
Debra Roth
SENIOR V.P. & ASSISTANT SECRETARY
Arnold L. Wadler
V.P. & TREASURER
Gregory A. Arvensen
V.P., CORPORATE AUDIT & SPECIAL PROJECTS
Joseph P. Colleran
V.P., BUSINESS & LEGAL AFFAIRS
Barbara Custer
V.P., CREDIT
Peter Dublin
V.P. & CONTROLLER
Sandy Gong
V.P., CASH MANAGEMENT
Alberto Gonzalez
V.P., ADMINISTRATION
Cathy Houser
V.P., PRODUCTION MANAGEMENT
Julie Landau
V.P., MANAGEMENT INFORMATION SYSTEMS
Christine McKinnon
V.P., ACQUISITIONS
Sara Rose

ORION CLASSICS
SENIOR V.P., DISTRIBUTION
John (Jay) Peckos

ORION PICTURES INTERNATIONAL
PRESIDENT
Kathryn Cass
V.P., TELEVISION SALES & MANAGEMENT
Robert Davie
V.P., INTERNATIONAL SALES
Dean Shapiro
V.P., SALES & CONTRACT ADMINISTRATION
Rene Soraggi

ORION PICTURES DISTRIBUTION CORPORATION
CHAIRMAN OF THE BOARD, PRESIDENT
Leonard White
SENIOR EXECUTIVE V.P.
Brad Krevoy
SENIOR EXECUTIVE V.P.
Steve B. Stabler
EXECUTIVE V.P.
John W. Hester
EXECUTIVE V.P., MARKETING
John Hegeman
EXECUTIVE V.P., DISTRIBUTION
John (Jay) Peckos
SENIOR V.P. & CFO
Cynthia Friedman
V.P., NATIONAL FIELD PUBLICITY & PROMOTIONS
Marina Bailey
V.P., MARKETING
Robert Berney
V.P., NATIONAL PUBLICITY
Michael Lawson
V.P., POST PRODUCTION
Scott Mandell
V.P., MEDIA SERVICES
Denise Quon

BRANCH OFFICES
1888 Century Park East, Los Angeles, CA 90067. (310) 282-0550.
DIVISION MANAGER
Bob Wood
304 Park Ave. South, New York, NY 10010. (212) 505-0051.
DIVISION MANAGER
Sheila DeLoach

ORION TELEVISION ENTERTAINMENT
EXECUTIVE V.P., DOMESTIC TELEVISION DISTRIBUTION
Joseph D. Indelli

ORION HOME ENTERTAINMENT CORPORATION
CHAIRMAN OF THE BOARD & CEO
Leonard White
EXECUTIVE V.P.
Herbert N. Dorfman
SENIOR V.P., MARKETING
Susan Blodgett

ORION HOME VIDEO
PRESIDENT
Herbert N. Dorfman
V.P., SALES
Michael Katchman

ORION TELEVISION ENTERTAINMENT
EXECUTIVE V.P.
Joseph D. Indelli
V.P., DOMESTIC TV DISTRIBUTION
Mike Davis

ORR & CRUICKSHANK PRODS.

(Motion picture production.)
c/o Walt Disney Studios, 500 S. Buena Vista St., Animation 2G11, Burbank, CA 91521-1784. (818) 560-6423. FAX: (818) 566-7310.
PARTNERS
James Orr
Jim Cruickshank

OUTLAW PRODS.

(Motion picture production.)
c/o Warner Bros./Fuji TV, 827 N. Hilldale Ave., Los Angeles, CA 90069. (310) 777-2000. FAX: (310) 777-2010.
PRODUCERS
Robert Newmyer
Jeffrey Silver

OVERSEAS FILMGROUP, INC.

(see First Look Pictures)

EARL OWENSBY STUDIOS, INC.

(Motion picture production and development.)
1 Motion Picture Blvd., Shelby, NC 28150. (704) 487-0502. FAX: (704) 487-4763.
PRESIDENT & CEO
Earl Owensby
V.P., DEVELOPMENT
Debra Owensby
SECRETARY & TREASURER
Linda Comer

PAKULA PRODUCTIONS, INC.

(Motion picture and television production.)
330 W. 58 St., New York, NY 10019. (212) 664-0640. FAX: (212) 397-1344.
PRESIDENT
Alan J. Pakula

PARAMOUNT PICTURES

(see Viacom, Inc.)

TOM PARKER MOTION PICTURES

(Production & distribution .)
3941 S. Bristol, Suite 285, Santa Ana, CA 92704. (714) 545-2887. FAX: (714) 545-9775.
PRESIDENT
Tom Parker

PATHE PICTURES, INC.

(Producer and distributor.)
270 Madison Ave., 5th Fl., New York, NY 10016. (212) 696-0392. FAX: (212) 213-5498.
CHAIRMAN
Joseph P. Smith
VICE PRESIDENT
Charles Gegen
SECRETARY
James J. Harrington
TREASURER
James A. Griffith

PERMUT PRESENTATIONS

10866 Wilshire Blvd., Suite 1425, Los Angeles, CA 90024. (310) 441-8428. FAX: (310) 441-8433.
PRODUCER-PRESIDENT
David Permut
V.P., DEVELOPMENT
Steve Longi

MARTIN POLL FILMS, LTD.

(Motion picture and tv production.)
430 N. Maple Dr., Suite 207, Beverly Hills, CA 90210. (310) 273-0600. FAX: (310) 273-2307.
PRESIDENT
Martin Poll
EXECUTIVE VICE PRESIDENT
Shirley Mellner

POLYGRAM FILMED ENTERTAINMENT

(Motion picture production.)
9348 Civic Center Dr., Suite 300, Beverly Hills, CA 90210. (310) 777-7700. FAX: (310) 777-7709.
PRESIDENT/CEO
Michael Kuhn
CFO
Stuart Ells

OTTO PREMINGER FILMS, LTD.

(Motion picture and television production and distribution.)
17 Seth Canyon Dr., Mt. Kisco, NY 10549-9804. (914) 242-5112. FAX: (914) 666-4553.
PRESIDENT
Hope B. Preminger
VICE PRESIDENT
Valerie Robins

EDWARD R. PRESSMAN FILM CORP.

(Film production.)
445 N. Bedford Dr., PH, Beverly Hills, CA 90210. (310) 271-8383. FAX: (310) 271-9497.
PRESIDENT
Edward R. Pressman
V.P., PRODUCTION
Alessandro Camon
EXECUTIVE VICE PRESIDENT & COO
Neil Friedman

PRISM PICTURES CORPORATION

(Film production: cable, broadcast and syndication TV.)
1888 Century Park E., Suite 350, Los Angeles, CA 90067. (310) 277-3270. FAX: (310) 203-8036.
PRESIDENT
Barry Collier
CFO
Earl Rosenstein

PRODUCER'S DISTRIBUTION COMPANY

(Motion picture production and distribution.)
5400 Lindley Ave., #120, Encino, CA 91316. (818) 609-1074.
OWNER
Ray Axelrod

PRODUCERS ENTERTAINMENT

(Producer and distributor of motion pictures & television.)
9150 Wilshire Blvd., #205, Beverly Hills, CA 90212. (310) 285-0400. FAX: (310) 281-2585.
CHAIRMAN & CEO
Irwon Meyer

PROMARK ENTERTAINMENT GROUP

(International distribution and production.)
3599 Cahuenga Blvd. W., 3rd fl., Los Angeles, CA 90068. (213) 878-0404. FAX: (213) 878-0486. Promark@ix.netcom.com
PRESIDENT
Jonathan M. Kramer
V.P., INTERNATIONAL DISTRIBUTION
David T. Carson
V.P., PRODUCTION
Steve Beswick
DIRECTOR, INTERNATIONAL SALES
Julie McLaughlin
DIRECTOR, DISTRIBUTION
Danny St. Pierre
CFO
Al Haferkamp
ASSISTANT CONTROLLER
Scott Aaron

PROPAGANDA FILMS

940 N. Mansfield Ave., Los Angeles, CA 90038. (213) 462-6400. FAX: (213) 463-7874.
CO-FOUNDER
Steve Golin
PRESIDENT
Jim Tauber

RGH INTERNATIONAL FILM ENTERPRISES, INC.

8831 W. Sunset Blvd., Suite 300, Los Angeles, CA 90069. (310) 652-2893. FAX: (310) 652-6237.

PRESIDENT
Robert G. Hussong
EXECUTIVE ASSISTANT
Frank McClane
VICE PRESIDENT
Adriana Shaw

RKO PICTURES

1875 Century Park E., Suite 2140, Los Angeles, CA 90067. (310) 277-0707. FAX: (310) 284-8574.
551 Madison Ave., 14th fl., New York, NY 10022. (212) 644-0600. FAX: (212) 319-2610.
CHAIRMAN & CEO
Ted Hartley
VICE CHAIRMAN
Dina Merrill
V.P., RKO PRODUCTIONS
Carol Hamilton
DIRECTOR OF CREATIVE AFFAIRS, EAST COAST
Karen Glasser

CARL RAGSDALE ASSOCIATES, LTD.

(Producers.)
4725 Stillbrooke, Houston, TX 77035-4911. (713) 729-6530.
PRESIDENT
Carl V. Ragsdale
BRANCH OFFICES
4801 Mass. Ave., NW, Suite 400, Washington, DC 20016. (202) 364-0197;
EXECUTIVE PRODUCER IN CHARGE
Arthur Neuman
16036 Tupper St. Sepulveda, CA 91343. (213) 894-6291.
EXECUTIVE PRODUCER IN CHARGE
Frank Coghlan
Piazza Cairoli, 113 Roma, Italy 00186. (396) 654 5182.
EXECUTIVE PRODUCER IN CHARGE
Douglas R. Fleming

RAINBOW RELEASING

9165 Sunset Blvd., Suite 300, Los Angeles, CA 90069. (310) 271-0202. (310) 271-2753.
PRESIDENT
Henry Jaglom

RANKIN/BASS PRODUCTIONS

24 W. 55 St., New York, NY 10019. (212) 582-4017. (Producer.)
PRESIDENT & CEO
Arthur Rankin, Jr.
V.P., PRODUCTION & DEVELOPMENT
Peter Bakalian

MARTIN RANSOHOFF PRODUCTIONS, INC.

9460 Wilshire Blvd., Suite 415, Beverly Hills, CA 90212. (310) 274-4585. FAX: (310) 276-3093.
PRODUCER
Martin Ransohoff
VICE PRESIDENT
Bob Robinson

RASTAR PRODUCTIONS, INC.

c/o Sony Pictures Studios, 10202 W. Washington Blvd., Culver City, CA 90232. (310) 280-7871. FAX: (310) 280-2331.
CHAIRMAN OF THE BOARD
Ray Stark
PRESIDENT
Marykay Powell

REELTIME DISTRIBUTING CORP.

(Film production and distribution.)
353 W. 48 St., New York, NY 10036. (212) 582-5380. FAX: (212) 581-2731.
PRESIDENT
Roberta Findlay

REPUBLIC PICTURES ENTERTAINMENT

(see Spelling Entertainment)

RHAPSODY FILMS

(Film production and distribution.)
30 Charlton St., New York, NY 10014. (212) 243-0152.
PRESIDENT
Bruce Ricker

ROB-RICH FILMS, INC.

(Production and distribution of motion pictures.)
c/o Sidney Ginsberg, 4463 Winners Circle, Suite 1426, Sarasota, FL 34238. (941) 925-1672.
PRESIDENT
Sidney Ginsberg
V.P., SECRETARY & TREASURER
Nelly M. Ginsberg

ROCKET PICTURES

(Motion picture producers.)
9536 Wilshire Blvd., #410, Beverly Hills, CA 90212. (310) 550-3300. FAX: (310) 550-1126.
CHAIRMAN/PRESIDENT
Thomas J. Coleman

ROLLINS & JOFFE, INC.

860 Birchwood Dr., Los Angeles, CA 90024. (310) 278-7711. FAX: (310) 278-7719.
PRESIDENT
Charles Joffe
PRODUCER
Jack Rollins

ROXIE RELEASING

(Film distributors.)
3125 16th St., San Francisco, CA 94103. (415) 431-3611. FAX: (415) 431-2822. URL: http://www.roxie.com
PRESIDENT
Bill Banning

ROYAL PICTURES

(Motion picture distributor.)
19619 E. 17 Place, Aurora, CO 80011. (303) 367-4948.
GENERAL MANAGER
James Lowry
MARKETING DIRECTOR
Ron Gordon

SGE ENTERTAINMENT CORP.

12001 Ventura Place, Suite 404, Studio City, CA 91604. (818) 766-8500. FAX: (818) 766-7873.
CHAIRMAN
James M. Glickenhaus
PRESIDENT
Leonard Shapiro
EXECUTIVE VICE PRESIDENT
Alan Solomon

SANDOLLAR PRODUCTIONS, INC.

(Develops and produces projects for motion pictures.)
500 S. Buena Vista St., Animation 1D-10, Burbank, CA 91521. (818) 560-5820. FAX: (818) 566-7666.
OWNERS
Sandy Gallin
Dolly Parton

SCHWARTZBERG & COMPANY

(Film and commercial production.)
12700 Ventura Blvd., 4th fl., Studio City, CA 91604. (818) 508-1833. FAX: (818) 508-1293.
DIRECTOR
Louis Schwartzberg

SCREENVISION CINEMA NETWORK

(National screen advertising. A joint venture of Mediavision, Inc., Paris, France and F.T.T.L. Media Co., New York.)
597 5th Ave., New York, NY 10017. (212) 752-5774. FAX: (212) 752-0086.
6601 Center Dr. W., Suite 500, Los Angeles, CA 90045. (310) 342-8240.
400 Maple, Birmingham, MI 48009. (313) 433-3555.
PRESIDENT & CEO
Dennis Fogarty
SENIOR V.P., SALES
Anne-Marie Marcus
V.P., WEST
Nancy Kreider
V.P., EASTERN SALES
Debra Stein
V.P., MIDWEST SALES
Joelle Shandler

SEVENTH ART RELEASING

7551 Sunset Blvd., Suite 104, Los Angeles, CA 90046. (213) 845-1455. FAX: (213) 845-4717. email: sevnthart@aol.com
PRESIDENT & CEO
Jonathan Cordish
VICE PRESIDENT & COO
Udi Epstein
V.P., THEATRICAL DISTRIBUTION
Michael Gantman
V.P., INTERNATIONAL SALES
Maria Bjorkdahl
V.P., DEVELOPMENT
Stephen Kral

SHAPIRO GLICKENHAUS ENTERTAINMENT

(see SGE Entertainment)

SHINING EXCALIBUR PICTURES

(see Miramax Films)

SHOWSCAN ENTERTAINMENT

(Film production & entertainment/simulation attractions. For a listing of Showscan sites, see Specialized Exhibition section)
3939 Landmark St., Culver City, CA 90232. (310) 558-0150. FAX: (310) 559-7984.
PRESIDENT/CEO
William Soady
EXECUTIVE VICE PRESIDENT/CFO
Dennis Pope
VICE PRESIDENT/GENERAL COUNSEL
W. Tucker Lemon
V.P., PRODUCTION
Peter Henton

SILVER LION FILMS

(Motion picture production.)
715 Broadway, Suite 310, Santa Monica, CA 90401. (310) 393-9177. FAX: (310) 458-9372.
PRODUCERS
Lance Hool
Conrad Hool

SILVER PICTURES

(Motion picture production.)
c/o Warner Bros. Pictures, 4000 Warner Blvd., Bldg. 90, Burbank, CA 91522-0001. (818) 954-4490. FAX: (818) 954-3237. email: PamScan@aol.com
CHAIRMAN
Joel Silver
SENIOR V.P., PRODUCTION
Dan Cracchiolo

SILVERFILM PRODUCTIONS, INC.

(Motion picture production.)
510 Park Ave., #9B, New York, NY 10022. (212) 355-0282. FAX: (212) 421-8254.
PRESIDENT
Raphael Silver
VICE PRESIDENT
Joan Micklin Silver

SILVERSTEIN INTERNATIONAL CORP.

(Production and distribution of motion pictures.)
171 W. 57 St., New York, NY 10019. (212) 541-6620. FAX: (212) 586-0085. email: Silvintco@aol.com
PRESIDENT
Maurice Silverstein

SONY PICTURES ENTERTAINMENT, INC.

10202 W. Washington Blvd., Culver City, CA 90232. (310) 280-8000. FAX: (310) 204-1300.
3400 Riverside Dr., Burbank, CA 91505. (818) 972-7000. FAX: (818) 972-0234.
550 Madison Ave., New York, NY 10022. (212) 833-8500.
CORPORATE OFFICERS
PRESIDENT & COO
John Calley
CO-PRESIDENT
Jeff Sagansky
EXECUTIVE VICE PRESIDENT
Yuki Nozoe
EXECUTIVE VICE PRESIDENT
Robert Wynne
EXECUTIVE VICE PRESIDENT & CFO
Ted Howells, Jr.
EXECUTIVE VICE PRESIDENT
Kenneth Lemberger
EXECUTIVE VICE PRESIDENT
Dennis Miller
EXECUTIVE VICE PRESIDENT
Kenneth S. Williams
SENIOR V.P. & GENERAL COUNSEL
Ronald N. Jacobi
SENIOR V.P., CORPORATE COMMUNICATIONS & EXTERNAL AFFAIRS
Bruce Redditt
SENIOR VICE PRESIDENT
Lucy Wander-Perna
V.P. & TREASURER
Joe Kraft
VICE PRESIDENT
Robert M. Moses
ASSISTANT SECRETARY
Beth Berke
ASSISTANT SECRETARY
Robert Eichorn
ASSISTANT SECRETARY
Jared Jussim

COLUMBIA TRISTAR MOTION PICTURE COMPANIES
10202 W. Washington Blvd., Culver City, CA 90232. (310) 280-8000.
VICE CHAIRMAN
Lucy Fisher
PRESIDENT
Fred Bernstein

MARKETING
PRESIDENT, WORLWIDE MARKETING
Robert Levin
EXECUTIVE V.P., WORLDWIDE PUBLICITY
Edward Russell
SENIOR V.P., RESEARCH
Christine Birch
SENIOR V.P., MEDIA ADVERTISING
John Butkovich
SENIOR V.P., MARKETING
Joseph Foley
SENIOR V.P., PUBLICITY
Dennis P. Higgins
SENIOR V.P., NATIONAL PROMOTIONS
Diane Salerno
SENIOR V.P., FINANCE
Pat Walters
V.P., MEDIA
Debbie Bolsky
V.P., RESEARCH
Christine Birch
V.P., MARKETING, WORLDWIDE
Mimi Burri
V.P., PUBLICITY
Andre Caraco
V.P., SPECIAL PROJECTS
Carlotta Florio
V.P., PUBLICITY
Jamie Geller Hawtof
V.P., CREATIVE ADVERTISING
Josh Goldstine
V.P., PHOTOGRAPHIC SERVICES
Barbara Larkin
V.P., PUBLICITY
Susan Levin
V.P., PUBLICITY, EAST COAST
Ginny De Liagre
V.P., CREATIVE ADVERTISING
Dana Precious
V.P., CANADIAN MEDIA & COOP ADVERTISING
Donna Slack
V.P., NATIONAL FIELD OPERATIONS
Melanie Steele
V.P., CREATIVE ADVERTISING
Ricky Strauss
V.P., MEDIA RELATIONS, WORLDWIDE
Susan van der Werff

OTHER DEPARTMENTS
PRESIDENT, PRODUCTION ADMINISTRATION
Gary Martin
EXECUTIVE V.P., MUSIC
Burt Berman
EXECUTIVE V.P., POST-PRODUCTION
James Honore
SENIOR V.P., PRODUCTION ADMINISTRATION
Bill Ewing
SENIOR V.P., PRODUCTION ADMINISTRATION
Ray Zimmerman
V.P., MUSIC LICENSING
Monica Ciafardi
V.P., PRODUCTION ADMINISTRATION
Pete Corral
V.P., MUSIC ADMINISTRATION
Pam Lillig
V.P., PRODUCTION ADMINISTRATION
Kathy McDermott
V.P., POST PRODUCTION
Russ Paris
V.P., MUSIC ADMINISTRATION
Raul Perez

COLUMBIA PICTURES
10202 W. Washington Blvd., Culver City, CA 90232. (310) 280-8000. FAX: (310) 204-1300.

PRODUCTION
PRESIDENT
Barry Josephson
EXECUTIVE V.P., PRODUCTION
Gareth P. Wigan
EXECUTIVE V.P., PRODUCTION
Teddy Zee
SENIOR V.P., PRODUCTION
Kevin Jones
V.P., PRODUCTION
Michael Costigan
V.P., PRODUCTION
Doug Belgrad

OTHER DEPARTMENTS
EXECUTIVE V.P., BUSINESS AFFAIRS & OPS.
Bryan Lee
SENIOR V.P., BUSINESS AFFAIRS
Alan Krieger
SENIOR V.P., LEGAL AFFAIRS
Roger Toll
V.P., LEGAL AFFAIRS
Deb Bruenell
V.P., BUSINESS AFFAIRS, CONTRACT ADMINISTRATION
Thomas Stack
V.P., BUSINESS AFFAIRS
Marci Wiseman
V.P., BUSINESS AFFAIRS
Mark Wyman

TRI STAR PICTURES
(A Sony Pictures Entertainment Company)
10202 West Washington Blvd., Culver City, CA 90232. (310) 280-7700. FAX: (310) 280-1577.
PRESIDENT
Robert Cooper

PRODUCTION
PRESIDENT, PRODUCTION
Stacey Snider
EXECUTIVE V.P., PRODUCTION
Christopher Lee
SENIOR V.P., PRODUCTION
Amy Baer
V.P. PRODUCTION
Rob Levine

OTHER DEPARTMENTS
EXECUTIVE V.P., LEGAL AFFAIRS
Liz Aschenbrenner
EXECUTIVE V.P., BUSINESS AFFAIRS
Robert Geary
EXECUTIVE VICE PRESIDENT
Paul Smith
SENIOR V.P., BUSINESS AFFAIRS
Jon Gibson
SENIOR V.P., BUSINESS AFFAIRS
Gary A. Hirsch
SENIOR V.P., BUSINESS AFFAIRS
John Levy
SENIOR V.P., POST PRODUCTION
Sol Lomita
V.P., LEGAL AFFAIRS
Luis Allen
V.P., LEGAL ADMINISTRATION
Cassandra Barbour
V.P., BUSINESS AFFAIRS ADMINISTRATION
Mark Horowitz
V.P., LEGAL AFFAIRS
Andrea Levitt

SONY PICTURES CLASSICS
550 Madison Ave., 8th floor, New York, NY 10022. (212) 833-8833.
CO-PRESIDENTS
Michael Barker
Tom Bernard
Marcie Bloom
V.P., LARGE FORMAT SALES
Marc Katz
V.P., OPERATIONS
Grace Murphy

TRIUMPH FILMS
10202 W. Washington Blvd., Culver City, CA 90232. (310) 280-8000.
PRESIDENT
David Saunders
SENIOR V.P., MARKETING
Gary Shapiro
V.P., ACQUISITIONS & BUSINESS AFFAIRS
Philip Breen
V.P., MARKETING
Pam Rodi

SONY PICTURES RELEASING
10202 W. Washington Blvd., Culver City, CA 90232. (310) 280-8000.
PRESIDENT
Jeffrey Blake
EXECUTIVE V.P. & GENERAL SALES MANAGER
Pat Notaro
SENIOR V.P. & ASSISTANT GENERAL SALES MANAGER
David Garel
SENIOR V.P., OPERATIONS & ADMINISTRATION
Mark L. Zucker
V.P., EASTERN DIVISION MANAGER
Jim Amos
V.P., SALES ADMINISTRATION
Craig Bartlet
V.P., WESTERN/CANADIAN DIVISION MANAGER
Rory Bruer

V.P., BRANCH ADMINISTRATION
Al Cameron
V.P., EXHIBITOR RELATIONS
Ted Hatfield
V.P., PRINT OPERATIONS
Mike Jones
V.P., FINANCIAL ADMINISTRATION
Eileen Loomis
V.P., MIDWEST DIVISION MANAGER
Jack Simmons
GENERAL MANAGER, CANADA
Michael Skewes
V.P., DISTRIBUTION SERVICES
Conrad K. Steely
V.P., SOUTHERN/MIDWEST DIVISION MANAGER
Terry Tharpe
V.P., SOUTHERN DIVISION MANAGER
Sherman Wood
V.P., NON-THEATRICAL SALES, TRAILER PLACEMENT
Martin Zeidman

COLUMBIA TRISTAR FILM DISTRIBUTORS INT'L
10202 W. Washington Blvd., Culver City, CA 90232. (310) 280-8000.
PRESIDENT
Duncan Clark
EXECUTIVE VICE PRESIDENT
S. Anthony Manne
SENIOR V.P., SALES & DISTRIBUTION
Ralph Alexander, Jr.
SENIOR V.P., WORLDWIDE MARKETING
Nigel Clark
SENIOR V.P., LATIN AMERICA
Giovanni Gentili
SENIOR V.P., EUROPE, MIDDLE EAST & AFRICA
Lester McKeller
V.P., MARKETING
Mimi Burri
V.P., SALES & DISTRIBUTION
Jimmy Katz
V.P., CREATIVE ADVERTISING
Sal Ladestro
V.P., INTERNATIONAL PRINT SERVICES
Beverly Starr
VICE PRESIDENT/ASSISTANT CONTROLLER
Reid Sullivan
V.P., PUBLICITY & PROMOTIONS
Susan van der Werff
V.P., MARKETING, LATIN AMERICA
Vittorio Tamburini
V.P., SOUTHEAST ASIA, AUSTRALIA & NEW ZEALAND
Peter Wilkinson

SONY TELEVISION ENTERTAINMENT
10202 W. Washington,.Culver City, CA 90232. (310) 280-8000.
PRESIDENT
Jon Feltheimer
EXECUTIVE VICE PRESIDENT
Andy Kaplan

COLUMBIA TRISTAR TELEVISION
9336 W. Washington Blvd., Culver City, CA 90232. (310) 202-1234.
PRESIDENT
Eric Tannenbaum
EXECUTIVE V.P.
Helene Michaels

COLUMBIA TRISTAR TELEVISION DISTRIBUTION
10202 W. Washington Blvd., Culver City, CA 90232. (310) 280-8000.
PRESIDENT
Barry Thurston
EXECUTIVE V.P., PLANNING & OPERATIONS
David Mumford

COLUMBIA TRISTAR INTERNATIONAL TELEVISION
10202 W. Washington Blvd., Culver City, CA 90232. (310) 280-8000.
PRESIDENT—INTERNATIONAL, SONY TELEVISION ENTERTAINMENT
Nicholas Bingham
PRESIDENT, CTIT
Michael Grindon

COLUMBIA TRISTAR HOME VIDEO
10202 W. Washington Blvd., Culver City, CA 90232. (310) 280-8000.
PRESIDENT
Ben Feingold

SONY PICTURES STUDIOS
10202 W. Washington Blvd., Culver City, CA 90232. (310) 280-8000.

THE CULVER STUDIOS
9336 W. Washington Blvd., Culver City, CA 90232. (310) 202-1234.

PRESIDENT, STUDIO OPERATIONS & ADMINISTRATION
Arnold Shupak
EXECUTIVE V.P., STUDIO OPERATIONS
Jack Kindberg
V.P., STUDIO OPERATIONS, SONY PICTURES STUDIOS
Barbara Francuz
V.P., STUDIO OPERATIONS, THE CULVER STUDIOS
Jan Kelly

SONY PICTURES STUDIOS POST PRODUCTION FACILITIES
EXECUTIVE V.P., POST PRODUCTION FACILITIES
Michael Kohut
V.P., SOUND, VIDEO & PROJECTION
Richard Branca
V.P., THEATRICAL & TV SOUND EDITORIAL
Tom McCarthy

SONY PICTURES STUDIOS IMAGEWORKS
9050 W. Washington Blvd., Culver City, CA 90232. (310) 840-8000.
PRESIDENT
Ken Ralston
SENIOR V.P. & CHIEF TECHNOLOGY OFFICER
Lincoln Hu
SENIOR V.P., CREATIVE AFFAIRS
Tim McGovern
SENIOR V.P., BUSINESS AFFAIRS
Mary O'Hare
SENIOR V.P., TECHNOLOGY & DIGITAL PRODUCTION
Bill Schultz
V.P., PREVISUALIZATION & MULTIMEDIA
Frank Foster
VICE PRESIDENT
Debbie Denise
V.P., PRODUCTION
Ralph Horian
V.P., ANIMATION PRODUCTION ADMINISTRATION
Barry Weiss
EXECUTIVE PRODUCER, COMMERCIAL DIVISION
Tracy Hauser

SONY SIGNATURES
10202 W. Washington Blvd., Culver City, CA 90232. (310) 280-7788.
2 Bryant St., 3rd Fl., San Francisco, CA 94105. (415) 247-7400.
PRESIDENT & CEO
Dell Furano
EXECUTIVE V.P., MARKETING
Mark Coopersmith
SENIOR V.P., ARTIST RELATIONS/EVENT MERCHANDISING
Daniel Cooper
SENIOR V.P., WORLDWIDE LICENSING/MERCHANDISING
Kimberly LaPadula-Scardino
SENIOR V.P. & MANAGING DIRECTOR
Andrew Rich
V.P., DOMESTIC SALES
Anita Frazier
V.P., MARKETING
Madelyn Hammond
V.P., LICENSING & MARKETING
Steven Roberts
V.P., RETAIL SALES & PROMOTIONS
Juli Riddles

SPECTROMEDIA ENTERTAINMENT
(Motion picture and television production.)
P.O. Box 2397, Oxnard, CA 93034-2397. (805) 984-3525.
PRESIDENT
William Byron Hillman
VICE PRESIDENT
Henry Hiller
SECRETARY
Kristy Kay
TREASURER
Los Vallow
ACQUISITIONS
Rob Hill

SPELLING ENTERTAINMENT INC./REPUBLIC ENTERTAINMENT
(Development and production of television & motion pictures.)
Wilshire Court, 5700 Wilshire Blvd., 5th floor, Suite 575, Los Angeles, CA 90036. (213) 965-5700. FAX: (213) 965-5895.
CHAIRMAN OF THE BOARD & CEO
Aaron Spelling
PRESIDENT & CEO
Steven R. Berrard
EXECUTIVE VICE PRESIDENT
Tom Carson
EXECUTIVE VICE PRESIDENT
Peter Bachmann
EXECUTIVE VICE PRESIDENT
Ron Castell
REPUBLIC PICTURES PRESIDENT & CEO
Robert W. Sigman

SPIKINGS ENTERTAINMENT

335 North Maple Dr., Suite 135, Beverly Hills, CA 90210. (310) 888-3525. FAX: (310) 888-3511.
PRESIDENT, OWNER
Barry P. Spikings

STAR GLOBE PRODUCTIONS

(Feature film and video production.)
1901 Avenue of the Stars, 18th Floor, Los Angeles, CA 90067. (310) 553-5541.
PRESIDENT
C. K. Hobson
VICE PRESIDENT
Terence Hobson
TREASURER
Jerry Mosley

STRAND RELEASING

(Motion picture distribution and production.)
1460 4th St., Suiite 302, Santa Monica, CA 90401. (310) 395-5002. FAX: (310) 395-2502. email: strand@strandrel.com
CO-PRESIDENTS
Jon Gerrans
Marcus Hu
Mike Thomas

STREAMLINE PICTURES

(Distribution of animated films.)
2908 Nebraska Ave., Santa Monica, CA 90404. (310) 998-0070. FAX: (310) 998-1145.
PRESIDENT
Carl Macek

TARA RELEASING

(Film marketing and distribution.)
124 Belvedere St., Suite 5, San Rafael, CA 94901-4707. (415) 454-5838. FAX: (415) 454-5977. email: TaraFilm@aol.com
PRESIDENT
Guy Cables

TAURUS ENTERTAINMENT CO.

Sunset Gower Studios, Bldg. 50, 1420 N. Beachwood Dr., Box 2, Hollywood, CA 90028. (213) 993-7355. FAX: (213) 993-7316.
CHAIRMAN
Stanley Dudelson
PRESIDENT & CEO
James Dudelson
PRESIDENT & COO
Robert Dudelson

TAURUS FILM CO.

8033 Sunset Blvd., Box #93, Los Angeles, CA 90046. (213) 650-5646. FAX: (213) 650-2006.
DIRECTOR
Michael F. Goldman

TELEMATED MOTION PICTURES

(Producer, non-theatrical films.)
137 S.W. 54 St., Cape Coral, FL 33914. (941) 542-9131.
PRESIDENT & PRODUCER-DIRECTOR
Saul Taffet

BOB THOMAS PRODUCTIONS, INC.

(Motion picture and television producer.)
60 E. 42 St., New York, NY 10165. (212) 221-3602. FAX: (201) 335-0098.
2 Franklin Ct., Montville, NJ 07045. (201) 335-9100.
PRESIDENT
Robert G. Thomas

THUNDER RIVER PICTURES

3960 Ince Blvd., Culver City, CA 90232. (310) 836-9977. FAX: (310) 836-5501.
PRESIDENT & CEO
Sarah Duvall

THE STEVE TISCH CO.

3815 Hughes Ave., Culver City, CA 90232-2715. (310) 838-2500. FAX: (310) 204-2713.
PRESIDENT
Steve Tisch
FEATURE DEVELOPMENT
Kearie Peak

THE TODD-AO CORPORATION

(For Sound, Editing, Special Effects, Film Presevation & Repair sub-divisions, please see the Services Section of this book).
172 Golden Gate Ave., San Francisco, CA 94102. (415) 928-3200.

514 Via De La Valle #300-A, Solana Beach, CA 92075. (619) 793-6901. FAX: (619) 793-1154.
CEO
Salah M. Hassanein
CO-CHAIRMEN
Robert A. Naify
Marshall Naify
VICE CHAIRMAN
Buzz Knudson
SENIOR V.P. & DIRECTOR
Christopher Jenkins
SENIOR V.P. & DIRECTOR
J.R. DeLang
VICE PRESIDENT & TREASURER
Silas Cross
VICE PRESIDENT & CONTROLLERS
Coburn Haskell
SECRETARY
Dan R. Malstrom

TOUCHSTONE PICTURES

(see Walt Disney Company)

TOWNHOUSE FILMS, INC.

411 E. 53 St., PHC, New York, NY 10022. (212) 838-8113. FAX: (212) 838-1127.
PRESIDENT
Romano Vanderbes
PRODUCTION
John Maddocks
Jim Hunter

TRANSATLANTIC ENTERTAINMENT

(Film and television production and distribution.)
10351 Santa Monica Blvd., Suite 211, Los Angeles, CA 90025. (310) 772-7300. FAX: (310) 772-0610. email: transat@general.net
CHAIRMAN OF THE BOARD
Robert M. Bennett
PRESIDENT & CEO
Paul Rich
SENIOR V.P., INTERNATIONAL SALES & ACQUISITIONS
Rena Ronson

TRISTAR PICTURES

(see Sony Pictures Entertainment.)

TRIBECA PRODUCTIONS

(Feature film production; affiliated with TriStar Pictures.)
375 Greenwich St., New York, NY 10013. (212) 941-4040. FAX: (212) 941-4044.
PRESIDENT
Jane Rosenthal

TRIDENT RELEASING

(Sales agents for motion pictures and television.)
8401 Melrose Pl., 2nd Floor, Los Angeles, CA 90069. (213) 655-8818. email: Trifilm@primenet.com
URL: http://www.trifilm.com
PRESIDENTS
Jean Ovrum
Victoria Plummer

TRIMARK PICTURES

(a division of Trimark Holdings, Inc.)
2644 30th St., Santa Monica, CA 90405. (310) 314-2000. FAX: (310) 392-0252.
CHAIRMAN & ACTING CEO
Mark Amin
SENIOR VICE PRESIDENT
Barry Barnholtz
SENIOR V.P., INTERNATIONAL SALES
Sergio Aguero
SENIOR V.P., DOMESTIC DISTRIBUTION
Tim Swain
V.P., PRODUCTION
Andrew Hersh
V.P., PRODUCTION
Phillip Goldfine
V.P., MARKETING
Gina Draklich
V.P., PUBLICITY
David Bowers

TRITON PICTURES

9000 Sunset Blvd., Suite 711, Los Angeles, CA 90069. (310) 275-7779. FAX: (310) 275-7334.
PRESIDENT & CEO
Jonathan Dana
SENIOR V.P., MARKETING & DISTRIBUTION
Robert Berney

EXECUTIVE VICE PRESIDENT
Jeff Ivers
SENIOR V.P., ACQUISITIONS & DEVELOPMENT
Robert Rock

TRIUMPH RELEASING CORPORATION

(see entry under Sony Pictures Entertainment, Inc.)

TROMA ENTERTAINMENT, INC.

(Producer and distributor.)
733 Ninth Ave., New York, NY 10019. (212) 757-4555. FAX:
(212) 399-9885. URL: http://Troma.com/home
650 N. Bronson, Suite 103, Los Angeles, CA 90004. (213) 960-
4012. FAX: (213) 960-4013.
PRESIDENT
Lloyd Kaufman
VICE PRESIDENT
Michael Herz
DIRECTOR, LOS ANGELES OPERATIONS
David Schultz

TWENTIETH CENTURY FOX FILM CORPORATION

(see Fox, Inc.)

UPA PRODS. OF AMERICA

14101 Valleyheart Dr., Suite 200, Sherman Oaks, CA 91423.
(818) 990-3800. FAX: (818) 990-4854.
CHAIRMAN & CEO
Henry G. Saperstein

UNITED ARTISTS PICTURES

(see Metro-Goldwyn-Mayer Inc.)

UNITED FILM ENTERPRISES, INC.

120 W. Park Ave., Suite 3-F, Long Beach, NY 11561. (516)
431-2687. FAX: (516) 431-2805.
CHIEF OPERATING EXECUTIVE
Nathan Podhorzer

UNIVERSAL PICTURES

(see MCA, Inc.)

VANGUARD FILMS

(Television and film production.)
135 E. 65 St., 4th Floor, New York, NY 10021. (212) 517-4333.
FAX: (212) 734-3609.
PRESIDENT
John H. Williams
VICE PRESIDENT
Charles Hobson

VIACOM, INC.

1515 Broadway, New York, NY 10036, (212) 258-6000, FAX:
(212) 258-6175.
15 Columbus Circle, New York, NY 10023-7780. (213) 373-
7000. FAX: (212) 373-8228.
CHAIRMAN OF THE BOARD OF VIACOM, INC./CHAIRMAN,
PRESIDENT & CEO OF NATIONAL AMUSEMENTS
Sumner M. Redstone
CHAIRMAN & CEO, VIACOM ENTERTAINMENT GROUP
Jonathan Dolgen

PARAMOUNT PICTURES

5555 Melrose Ave., Los Angeles, CA 90038-3197. (213) 956-
5000.
EXECUTIVE V.P., PARAMOUNT PICTURES
William Bernstein
EXECUTIVE V.P., CHIEF FINANCIAL & ADMINISTRATIVE
OFFICER
Patrick B. Purcell
SENIOR V.P., PLANNING
Mark Badagliacca
SENIOR V.P. & TREASURER
Alan J. Bailey
SENIOR V.P., HUMAN RESOURCES
William A. Hawkins
SENIOR V.P., INDUSTRIAL RELATIONS
Stephen Koppekin
SENIOR V.P. & GENERAL COUNSEL
Rebecca L. Prentice
SENIOR V.P. & GENERAL COUNSEL
J. Jay Rakow
SENIOR V.P., FINANCE
Stephen P. Taylor
SENIOR V.P., INFORMATION SYSTEMS
H. Edgar Trainor
V.P., INFORMATION PROCESSING/INFORMATION SYSTEMS
S.R. (Stan) Balcomb
V.P., GROUP ACCOUNTING
Chact S. Chu
V.P., CONTRACT ACCOUNTING
Carmen Desiderio

V.P., ADMINISTRATION
Rosemary DiPietra
V.P. & ASSOCIATE GENERAL COUNSEL
David C. Friedman
V.P., SYSTEMS DEVELOPMENT
Brent Greenspan
V.P., LEGAL & HUMAN RESOURCES
Louis Gutierrez
V.P., RESIDUALS
Kathleen Hoops
V.P., FINANCIAL PLANNING
Stephanie Love
V.P., FINANCE
Michael Masters
V.P., MOTION PICTURE PLANNING
Steve Nagan
V.P., EMPLOYEE RELATIONS, LEGAL SERVICES
Rina Roselli
V.P., MOTION PICTURE CONTROLLER
Carolyn F. Scott
EXECUTIVE DIRECTORS, SYSTEMS DEVELOPMENT &
INFORMATION SYSTEMS
Diana Nall Browne
Bonnie Hill
EXECUTIVE DIRECTOR, SYSTEMS PLANNING &
INFORMATION SYSTEMS
Joseph D. Giles
EXECUTIVE DIRECTOR, GROUP FINANCIAL REPORTING
Stephen Hendry
EXECUTIVE DIRECTOR, EMPLOYMENT, DEVELOPMENT &
HUMAN RESOURCES
Timothy M. McDonald
EXECUTIVE DIRECTOR, LABOR RELATIONS
Louis Shore
EXECUTIVE DIRECTOR, CONTRACT ACCOUNTING
Vicente P. Ching

MOTION PICTURE GROUP

CHAIRMAN
Sherry Lansing
VICE CHAIRMAN
Barry London
PRESIDENT, WORLDWIDE MARKETING
Arthur Cohen
PRESIDENT, WORLDWIDE VIDEO
Eric Doctorow
PRESIDENT, PRODUCTION
John Goldwyn
PRESIDENT, DOMESTIC DISTRIBUTION
Wayne Lewellen
PRESIDENT, WORLDWIDE PAY TELEVISION
Jack Waterman
SENIOR V.P., BUSINESS AFFAIRS
Rochel Blachman
SENIOR V.P., BUSINESS AFFAIRS
Richard Fowkes
SENIOR V.P., LEGAL AFFAIRS
Karen Magid
SENIOR V.P., MUSIC LEGAL AFFAIRS
Linda Wohl
V.P., LEGAL
Alan Heppel
V.P., MUSIC BUSINESS AFFAIRS
Kevin Koloff
V.P., CREDITS & TITLES
Claudia Martin
V.P., INTELLECTUAL PROPERTIES
Scott Martin
V.P., INTERNATIONAL (London)
Michael O'Sullivan
V.P., BUSINESS AFFAIRS
Steven Plum
V.P., MUSIC PRODUCTION
Linda Springer

DOMESTIC DISTRIBUTION DIVISION, MOTION PICTURE GROUP

PRESIDENT, DISTRIBUTION
Wayne Lewellen
EXECUTIVE V.P., GENERAL SALES MANAGER
Gino Campagnola
EXECUTIVE V.P., SALES OPERATIONS
Steve Rapaport
SENIOR V.P., ASSISTANT GENERAL COUNSEL
Paul Springer
VICE PRESIDENT SOUTHERN DIVISION
Royce Brimage
V.P., EASTERN DIVISION
Mike Share
V.P., WESTERN DIVISION
Clark Woods
EXECUTIVE V.P., CANADIAN DIVISION
Chris Sullivan
V.P., SALES ADMINISTRATION
John Hersker

DOMESTIC BRANCHES AND MANAGERS, MOTION PICTURE GROUP

EASTERN
1633 Broadway, 11th Floor, New York, NY 10019.
DISTRICT MANAGER, NEW YORK
Pam Araujo
SALES MANAGER, BUFFALO/ALBANY
Steve Toback
BRANCH MANAGER, WASHINGTON, D.C./CLEVELAND
Claudia Ungar
BRANCH SALES MANAGER, BOSTON/NEW HAVEN
Tom Molen
BRANCH SALES MANAGER, PHILADELPHIA/PITTSBURGH
Jim Orr
BRANCH MANAGER, DETROIT/CINCINNATI/INDIANAPOLIS
Bruce Placke

SOUTHERN
12222 Merit Drive, Suite 1700, Dallas, TX 75251.
BRANCH MANAGER, DALLAS/NEW ORLEANS/OKLAHOMA CITY/MEMPHIS
Don Wallace
BRANCH SALES MANAGER, ATLANTA
Jeffrey Greenspun
BRANCH SALES MANAGER, JACKSONVILLE
Bob Mueller
BRANCH SALES MANAGER, CHARLOTTE/ DES MOINES
Buddy Williams
BRANCH SALES MANAGER, KANSAS CITY/ST. LOUIS
Jeremy Devine

PUERTO RICO
Miramar Plaza Building, 954 Ponce de Leon Avenue, Suite 201, San Juan, PR 00907.
BRANCH SALES MANAGER
Nestor Rivera

WESTERN
15260 Ventura Boulevard, Suite 1140, Sherman Oaks, CA 91403.
BRANCH MANAGER, LOS ANGELES
Bob Box
BRANCH MANAGER, CHICAGO/SAN FRANCISCO
Bob Weiss
BRANCH SALES MANAGER, DENVER/SALT LAKE CITY/MINNEAPOLIS
Jackie Rouleau
BRANCH SALES MANAGER, SEATTLE/PORTLAND/MILWAUKEE
John Slama

CANADA
146 Bloor Street West, Toronto, Ontario, Canada M5S 1M4.
BRANCH SALES MANAGER, TORONTO
Bob Cowan
BRANCH SALES MANAGER, CALGARY/VANCOUVER
Philip May
BRANCH SALES MANAGER, ST. JOHN/WINNIPEG
Jean White

MONTREAL
1255 University Street, Suite 921, Montreal, Quebec, Canada H3B 3W4.
BRANCH SALES MANAGER
Lise Bertrand

HOME VIDEO DIVISION, MOTION PICTURE GROUP
PRESIDENT, WORLDWIDE VIDEO
Eric Doctorow
EXECUTIVE V.P., SALES & MARKETING
Jack Kanne

MARKETING DIVISION, MOTION PICTURE GROUP
PRESIDENT, WORLDWIDE MARKETING
Arthur Cohen
EXECUTIVE V.P., NATIONAL ADVERTISING/ PROMOTION
Thomas Campanella
EXECUTIVE V.P., CREATIVE ADVERTISING
James P. Gibbons
EXECUTIVE V.P., MARKETING/CREATIVE AFFAIRS
Nancy Goliger
EXECUTIVE V.P., WORLDWIDE PUBLICITY
Cheryl Boone Isaacs
EXECUTIVE V.P., CREATIVE AVERTISING
Lucia Ludovico
SENIOR V.P., CREATIVE ADVERTISING
Bryan Allen
SENIOR V.P., CREATIVE SERVICES/AUDIO-VISUAL
Jim Gibbons
SENIOR V.P., CREATIVE ADVERTISING
Maren Moebius
SENIOR V.P., NATIONAL PUBLICITY
Blaise J. Noto
SENIOR V.P., CREATIVE ADVERTISING
William Rus

SENIOR V.P., MEDIA DIRECTOR
Susan Wrenn
V.P., MARKETING ADMINSTRATION
Leslie H. Anderson
V.P., PROMOTIONS
Lisa Di Marzio
V.P., SPECIAL PROJECTS
Allison Jackson
EXECUTIVE DIRECTOR, PRINT PRODUCTION
John Barry
EXECUTIVE DIRECTOR, MARKETING ADMINISRATION & MEDIA
Fred Manny
EXECUTIVE DIRECTOR, NATIONAL PUBLICITY
Greg Brilliant
EXECUTIVE DIRECTOR OF PLANNING, NATIONAL ADVERTISING
Suki Yamashita
EXECUTIVE DIRECTOR, NATIONAL ADVERTISING
Eric Greenwald
EXECUTIVE DIRECTOR, NATIONAL PROMOTIONS
Susan M. Kelly
EXECUTIVE DIRECTORS, PUBLICITY
Cecelia Horwitch
John Rentsch
EXECUTIVE DIRECTOR, CREATIVE ADVERTISING
Shaylee Dunn
EXECUTIVE DIRECTOR, SPOT BROADCASTING
Nicky Shapiro

PRODUCTION DIVISION, MOTION PICTURE GROUP
PRESIDENT, PRODUCTION
John Godlwyn
EXECUTIVE V.P., PRODUCTION
Michelle Manning
EXECUTIVE V.P., PRODUCTION
Karen Rosenfelt
SENIOR V.P., FEATURE PRODUCTION MANAGEMENT
Fred T. Gallo
SENIOR V.P., MUSIC
Harlan Goodman
SENIOR V.P., PRODUCTION
Donald Granger
SENIOR V.P., PRODUCTION
Thomas K. Levine
V.P., CASTING
Deborah Aquila
V.P., TELEVISION MUSIC
David Grossman
V.P., CREATIVE AFFAIRS
Bradley Kessell
V.P., MUSIC
Linda Springer
V.P., MUSIC CLEARANCE
Eldridge Walker
EXECUTIVE DIRECTOR, MUSIC PRODUCTION & CREATIVE AFFAIRS
Steve Londo
EXECUTIVE DIRECTOR, PRODUCTION BUDGETING & ESTIMATING
Brain Wensel

POST-PRODUCTION DIVISION, MOTION PICTURE GROUP
EXECUTIVE V.P., POST-PRODUCTION
Paul Haggar
V.P., POST-PRODUCTION
John Wiseman
EXECUTIVE DIRECTOR, POST-PRODUCTION FACILITIES
John Bloechle
EXECUTIVE DIRECTOR, WORLDWIDE TECHNICAL FACILITIES
Laverne Williams

PARAMOUNT DIGITAL ENTERTAINMENT
V.P. & EXECUTIVE PRODUCER
Leonard Washington

PARAMOUNT STUDIO GROUP
PRESIDENT
Earl Lestz
SENIOR V.P., VIDEO OPERATIONS
Tom Bruehl
SENIOR V.P., FACILITIES OPERATIONS
Rae Ann Del Pozzo
SENIOR V.P., BACKLOT OPERATIONS
Richard Nelson
V.P., PLANNING & DEVELOPMENT/PUBLIC AFFAIRS
Christine Essel
V.P., STUDIO PROTECTION
Thomas G. Hays
V.P., STUDIO ADMINISTRATION
Larry A. Owens
V.P., PLANNING & CONSTRUCTION
Michael Romano
V.P., LEGAL SERVICES
Nathan Smith

PARAMOUNT TELEVISION GROUP
CHAIRMAN, PARAMOUNT TELEVISION GROUP & VIACOM
TELEVISION GROUP
Kerry Mc Cluggage
EXECUTIVE V.P., TELEVISION GROUP
Steven Goldman
EXECUTIVE V.P., TELEVISION GROUP
Richard D. Lindheim

PARAMOUNT DOMESTIC TELEVISION DIVISION
PRESIDENT
Steven Goldman
PRESIDENT, DISTRIBUTION
Joel P. Berman
PRESIDENT, MARKETING
Meryl Cohen

PARAMOUNT INTERNATIONAL TELEVISION
PRESIDENT
Bruce Gordon

PARAMOUNT NETWORK TELEVISION
PRESIDENT
Garry Hart

FAMOUS MUSIC PUBLISHING
10635 Santa Monica Blvd., #300, Los Angeles, CA 90025.
CHAIRMAN & CEO
Irwin A. Robinson
PRESIDENT
Ira Jaffe
EXECUTIVE V.P., ADMINISTRATION/NY
Sidney Herman

VIACOM NEW MEDIA
EXECUTIVE V.P. & GENERAL MANAGER
Paul Meyer

VIACOM CONSUMER PRODUCTS
PRESIDENT
Andrea Hein
V.P., SALES
Howard Berk
V.P., MERCHANDISING & LICENSING
Elizabeth Dambriunas
V.P., BUSINESS
Michael Goldman
V.P., MERCHANDISING
Terri Helton
V.P., MARKETING
Neil Newman
V.P., DOMESTIC LICENSE
Debbi Petrasek
V.P., INTERNATIONAL LICENSING
Jonathon Zill

CINEAMERICA THEATRES L.P.
EXECUTIVE V.P. & CFO
Ken Crowe
EXECUTIVE V.P. & COO
Ben Littlefield

WARNER BROS. INC.

(A subsidiary of Time Warner, Inc.)
75 Rockefeller Plaza, New York, NY 10019. (212) 484-8000.
640 Fifth Ave., New York, NY 10019. (212) 903-5500.
4000 Warner Blvd., Burbank, CA 91522. (818) 954-6000.
CHAIRMAN OF THE BOARD & CO-CEO, WB & WARNER
MUSIC
Robert A. Daly
CHAIRMAN OF THE BOARD & CO-CEO, WB & WARNER
MUSIC
Terry Semel
EXECUTIVE V.P. & COO
Barry A. Meyer
EXECUTIVE V.P., BUSINESS & ACQUISITIONS
James R. Miller
EXECUTIVE V.P., INTERNATIONAL THEATRICAL
ENTERPRISES
Richard J. Fox
EXECUTIVE V.P., CORPORATE PROJECTS
Charles D. McGregor
EXECUTIVE VICE PRESIDENT & TREASURER
Edward Romano
EXECUTIVE V.P., MARKETING & PLANNING
Sanford E. Reisenbach
EXECUTIVE VICE PRESIDENT & GENERAL COUNSEL
John Schulman
SENIOR V.P., TV PUBLICITY, PROMOTION & PUBLIC
RELATIONS
Barbara S. Brogliatti
SENIOR V.P., WW CORPORATE PROMOTIONS
Robert Schneider
ASSISTANT TO CHAIRMAN & VICE PRESIDENT,
CORPORATE SERVICES
Marisa O'Neil

WARNER BROS. THEATRICAL PRODUCTION
CO-PRESIDENT, WORLDWIDE THEATRICAL PRODUCTION
Lorenzo Di Bonaventura
CO-PRESIDENT, WORLDWIDE THEATRICAL PRODUCTION
Bill Gerber
EXECUTIVE V.P., PRODUCTION
Robert Guralnick
EXECUTIVE V.P., WORLDWIDE FEATURE PRODUCTION
Steven Papazian
EXECUTIVE V.P., PRODUCTION
Tom Lasally
SENIOR V.P., PRODUCTION
William Young
SENIOR V.P., PRODUCTION
Diana Rathburn
V.P., PRODUCTION
Jennifer Perrini
V.P., PRODUCTION
Michael Andreen
V.P., PRODUCTION
Lionel Wigram
V.P., FEATURE PRODUCTION
Mark Scoon
V.P., CREATIVE AFFAIRS
Courtney Valenti
SENIOR V.P., WORLDWIDE CO-PRODUCTIONS &
ACQUISTIONS
Clifford L. Werber
PRODUCTION EXECUTIVE, FEATURE PRODUCTIONS
Christopher Defaria
PRODUCTION EXECUTIVE, FEATURE PRODUCTIONS
Bill Draper
EXECUTIVE PRODUCTION MANAGER
Phil Rawlins
EXECUTIVE PRODUCTION MANAGER
Lynn Morgan
DIRECTOR, STORY DEPARTMENT
Teresa Wayne
STORY SUPERVISOR
Diane Bellis
SENIOR V.P., TALENT
Marion Dougherty
V.P., POST PRODUCTION
Fred Talmage
V.P., POST PRODUCTION
Marc Solomon
V.P., FEATURE ESTIMATING
Amy Rabins

FEATURE ANIMATION
PRESIDENT, FEATURE ANIMATION
Max Howard
SENIOR V.P., OPERATIONS, FEATURE ANIMATION
Michael Laney
SENIOR V.P., PRODUCTION
Amy Pell
SENIOR V.P., CREATIVE AFFAIRS
Dalisa Cooper Cohen
V.P., FEATURE ANIMATION, LONDON DIVISION
John McKenna
V.P., BUSINESS & LEGAL AFFAIRS
Amanda Seward
V.P., TECHNOLOGY
Wendy Aylsworth
DIRECTOR, ANIMATION RESOURCES
Kay Salz
PRODUCERS
Tim Hauser
Ron Tippe

WARNER BROS. ANIMATION
15503 Ventura Blvd., Sherman Oaks, CA 91403.
SENIOR V.P. & GENERAL MANAGER
Jean MacCurdy
V.P., PRODUCTION
Kathleen Helppie
DIRECTOR, CLASSIC ANIMATION
Lorri Bond

ADVERTISING & PUBLICITY
4000 Warner Blvd., Burbank, CA 91522. (818) 954-6000.
PRESIDENT
Robert G. Friedman
EXECUTIVE V.P., WORLDWIDE CREATIVE ADVERTISING
PROJECTS
Joel Wayne
EXECUTIVE V.P., SPECIAL PROJECTS
Joe Hyams
SENIOR V.P., WORLDWIDE THEATRICAL MARKETING
RESEARCH
Richard Del Belso
SENIOR V.P., WORLDWIDE CREATIVE ADVERTISING
Chris Carlisle
SENIOR V.P., WORLDWIDE PUBLICITY & PROMOTION
Charlotte Kandel

SENIOR V.P., WORLDWIDE ADVERTISING & PUBLICITY
Dawn Taubin
V.P., CREATIVE ADVERTISING
Lori Drazen
V.P., WORLDWIDE MEDIA
Lynn Whitney
V.P., PUBLICITY
John Dartigue
V.P., PUBLICITY
Nancy Kirkpatrick
V.P., NATIONAL PUBLICITY
Carl Samrock
V.P., NATIONAL FIELD ACTIVITIES
Stuart Gottesman
V.P., CO-OPERATIVE ADVERTISING
Richard Kallet
V.P., ADMINISTRATION
Dennis Tange
V.P., THEATRICAL MARKETING RESEARCH
Daniel P. Rosen
V.P., EAST COAST ADVERTISING & PUBLICITY
Don Buckley
V.P., INTERNATIONAL MARKETING RESEARCH
Barbara Shuler
V.P., WORDWIDE PROMOTIONS
Barbara DeGroot
DIRECTOR, NATIONAL PUBLICITY
Mark Reina
DIRECTOR, WEST COAST PUBLICITY
Vivian Boyer
DIRECTOR, PUBLICITY
Diane Gursky
DIRECTOR OF MEDIA CONTRACTS & CONTROL
Louise Hays
DIRECTOR OF MEDIA
Sandy Finkel
DIRECTOR OF GRAPHIC ARTS
Kirk Freeman
DIRECTOR, WORLDWIDE ADVERTISING & PUBLICITY SER-
VICES
Elizabeth Maffei
DIRECTOR, INTERNATIONAL MEDIA
Jan Herbert
MANAGER, INTERNATIONAL PROMOTIONS
Christina George
MANAGER, DOMESTIC PROMOTIONS
Rulivia Lee Wong
MANAGER, FILM & TAPE, T.V. ADVERTISING & PUBLICITY
SERVICES
Bruce Szeles
MANAGER, EAST COAST PUBLICITY
Willa Clinton
SENIOR PUBLICIST, RADIO & TV PUBLICITY
Lisa St. Amand
SENIOR PUBLICIST, PHOTO EDITOR
Jess M. Garcia
SENIOR PUBLICIST, PHOTO EDITOR
Diane Sponsler
SENIOR PUBLICIST, ASSISTANT TO NANCY KIRKPATRICK
Larry Anreder
SENIOR PUBLICIST, ASSISTANT TO JOHN DARTIGUE
Marilyn Nelson
SENIOR PUBLICIST, PROMOTIONS
Ron Chan
SENIOR PUBLICIST, WRITER
Stacy Ivers
STAFF PUBLICIST, NY
Sandy Thompson
STAFF PUBLICIST, NY
Catherine Ortiz
THE IDEA PLACE
V.P., BROADCAST ADVERTISING
Bruce Brewer
V.P., CREATIVE ADVERTISING
Dale Spina
TRAILER EDITOR
Norman Schubert
TRAILER EDITOR
Ritchie Sax
TRAILER EDITOR
Reid Martin
WARNER BROS. DOMESTIC DISTRIBUTION
PRESIDENT
D. Barry Reardon
EXECUTIVE V.P., DOMESTIC THEATRICAL DISTRIBUTION
Daniel R. Fellman
SENIOR V.P., DOMESTIC THEATRICAL DISTRIBUTION
Jeff Goldstein
SENIOR V.P., ADMINISTRATION
Howard Welinsky
V.P., SYSTEMS & DEVELOPMENT
Don Tannenbaum

V.P., SALES OPERATIONS
Richard A. Schiff
V.P., PRINT CONTROL
Nancy Sams
DIRECTOR OF NON-THEATRICAL SALES
Bill Grant
DIRECTOR, EXHIBITOR RELATIONS
Kelly O'Connor
MIDWESTERN DIVISION MANAGER
Shirley Becker
WESTERN DIVISION MANAGER
Scott Foreman
MANAGER, EXHIBITOR SERVICES
Corey Carr
**WARNER BROS. INTERNATIONAL THEATRICAL
DISTRIBUTION**
PRESIDENT, INTERNATIONAL THEATRICAL DISTRIBUTION
DIVISION
Edward Frumkes
SENIOR V.P. THEATRICAL DISTRIBUTION FOR EUROPE,
MIDDLE EAST & AFRICA
Xavier Marchand
SENIOR V.P., EUROPEAN ADVERTISING & PUBLICITY
Julian Senior
SENIOR V.P., INTERNATIONAL THEARICAL OPERATIONS
Angelina Speare
SENIOR V.P., BUSINESS DEVELOPMENT FOR ASIA PACIFIC
REGION
Ellen Eliasoph
V.P. & SUPERVISOR, LATIN AMERICAN REGION
Redo Farah
V.P., BUSINESS AFFAIRS
Eric Senat
V.P., INTERNATIONAL OPERATIONS
Veronica Kwan-Rubinek
DIRECTOR, INTERNATIONAL THEATRICAL DISTRIBUTION
& WARNER ASIA
Ivan Cheah
DIRECTOR, INTERNATIONAL PUBLICITY
Juliana Olinka
MANAGER, INTERNATIONAL ADVERTISING & PUBLICITY
Francine Velarde
MANAGER, INTERNATIONAL ADVERTISING & PUBLICITY
BUDGETING
Yolanda Exparza
SENIOR PUBLICIST, INTERNATIONAL
Mary Stuart Geoffries
SENIOR PUBLICIST, INTERNATIONAL
Helen Rhodes
WARNER BROS. ADMINISTRATION
SENIOR V.P., INDUSTRIAL RELATIONS
Alan H. Raphael
SENIOR V.P., WORLDWIDE HUMAN RESOURCES
Adrienne J. Gary
SENIOR V.P., CHIEF INFORMATION TECHNOLOGY
OFFICER
James L. Halsey III
V.P., HUMAN RESOURCES & OPERATIONS
Theodore C. Newman
V.P., HUMAN RESOURCES
Sharon Feldman
V.P., LABOR RELATIONS
Jay R. Ballance
V.P., CASTING ADMINISTRATION
Pat Hopkins
V.P., CREDIT & TITLE ADMINISTRATION
Norma Fuss
WARNER BROS. BUSINESS AFFAIRS
SENIOR V.P., THEATRICAL BUSINESS AFFAIRS
Steve Spira
V.P., BUSINESS AFFAIRS
Dan Furie
V.P., BUSINESS AFFAIRS
Patti Connolly
V.P., BUSINESS AFFAIRS
Virginia Tweedy
WARNER BROS. THEATRICAL LEGAL
SENIOR V.P. & GENERAL COUNSEL, THEATRICAL LEGAL
Jeremy Williams
V.P. & DEPUTY GENERAL COUNSEL, THEATRICAL LEGAL
Sheldon Presser
V.P. & ASSOCIATE GENERAL COUNSEL
Mary Biebel
V.P. & SENIOR EMPLOYMENT COUNSEL
Judith D. Cooper
V.P. & SENIOR EMPLOYMENT COUNSEL
Julie B. Yanow
SENIOR V.P., SPECIAL PROJECTS
Stephen Ross
V.P., THEATRICAL LEGAL
Jack Sattinger

ASSOCIATE GENERAL COUNSEL
Donna Josephson
V.P., ANTI-PIRACY
Molly Kellogg
V.P., EAST COAST COUNSEL
Stephen R. Langenthal
SENIOR THEATRICAL COUNSEL
Sherri Ralph
SENIOR MOTION PICTURE COUNSEL
Marshall Silverman
DIRECTOR OF LEGAL AFFAIRS-THEATRICAL
Michele Moore

WARNER BROS. MUSIC
PRESIDENT, MUSIC
Gary Le Mel
SENIOR V.P., MUSIC
Doug Frank
V.P., MUSIC ADMINISTRATION
Bill Schrank
V.P., BUSINESS AFFAIRS, MUSIC
Keith Zajic
DIRECTOR OF MUSIC ADMINISTRATION
Richard C. Harris

WARNER BROS. TECHNICAL OPERATIONS
SENIOR V.P.
Chris Cookson
V.P., FINANCE
Mitzy Barreto
V.P., TELEVISION DISTRIBUTION SERVICES
Richard Aycock
V.P. & GENERAL MANAGER, CALIFORNIA VIDEO CENTER
Marian Stevens
V.P., PRESERVATION/ARCHIVING
Pamela Tarrabe
DIRECTOR, VIDEO SERVICES
Tad Marburg

WARNER BROS. DIGITAL STUDIOS
SENIOR V.P.
Tim Sarnoff
V.P., PRODUCTION
Ellen Somers
V.P. & SENIOR VISUAL EFFECTS SUPERVISOR
Michael Fink
DIRECTOR, TECHNOLOGY
George Joblove
CO-LEAD, SOFTWARE TECHNOLOGY
Yun-Chen Sung
CO-LEAD, SOFTWARE TECHNOLOGY
Hiroyuki Miyoshi
HEAD OF PHYSICAL INTEGRATION
Jeffrey Platt

WARNER BROS. ACCOUNTING
V.P. & ASST. CORPORATE CONTROLLER
Michael Goodnight
V.P. & ASSISTANT CORPORATE CONTROLLER
Taylor E. Metters
V.P., PARTICIPATIONS & RESIDUALS
Michael G. Edwards
V.P., PARTICIPATIONS
Dorothy C. Barber
V.P., RESIDUALS MANAGEMENT
Robin R. Sikora
V.P., FINANCIAL INVESTMENTS
Robert Fisher
V.P., FINANCIAL REPORTING
Katherine R. Tracy
V.P., PRODUCTION ACCOUNTING
Lawrence W. Schneider
V.P., PAYROLL SERVICES
Phillip T. Dunne

WARNER HOME VIDEO
PRESIDENT, HOME VIDEO
Warren N. Lieberfarb
EXECUTIVE V.P., INTERNATIONAL
Ed Byrnes
EXECUTIVE V.P., NORTH AMERICA
James Cardwell

WARNER BROS. REAL ESTATE PLANNING & PUBLIC AFFAIRS
SENIOR V.P., REAL ESTATE PLANNING & PUBLIC AFFAIRS
Dan Garcia
V.P., REAL ESTATE OPERATIONS
John Matthews
V.P., GOVERNMENTAL AFFAIRS
Mee H. Lee
COMMUNITY RELATIONS & MINORITY SMALL BUSINESS
Kathy Jones-Irish
MANAGER, REAL ESTATE DEVELOPMENT
Marley Gann

V.P., STUDIO & PRODUCTION AFFAIRS
Lisa Rawlins
DIRECTOR, STUDIO & PRODUCTION AFFAIRS
Michael Walbrecht

WARNER BROS. STUDIOS FACILITIES
4000 Warner Boulevard, Burbank, CA 91522. (818) 954-6000. FAX: (818) 954-4213.
PRESIDENT
Gary Credle
EXECUTIVE V.P., STUDIOS FACILITIES
Jon Gilbert
SENIOR V.P.& GENERAL MANAGER, WARNER HOLLYWOOD STUDIOS
Norman Barnett
SENIOR V.P., PRODUCTION SERVICES
Ron Stein
SENIOR V.P., POST PRODUCTION SERVICES
Curt Behlmer
V.P., POST PRODUCTION SERVICES
Barry Snyder
V.P., STUDIO DESIGN & CONSTRUCTION SERVICES
Kirk Solomon
V.P., HUMAN RESOURCES
Jo Ann Black
V.P., LEGAL AFFAIRS
Jeff Nagler
DIRECTOR, STUDIO SERVICES
Gene Dresdow
DIRECTOR, CONSTRUCTION SERVICES & STUDIO FACILITIES
Jason Parker
DIRECTOR OF FINANCIAL PLANNING
T.J. Majauskas

WARNER BROS. WORLDWIDE CONSUMER PRODUCTS
PRESIDENT
Dan Romanelli
SENIOR VICE PRESIDENT
Randy Blotky
V.P., INTERNATIONAL
John Heinritz
V.P., PROPERTY DEVELOPMENT & WORLDWIDE PUBLICITY
Michael Peikoff
DIRECTOR, INTERNATIONAL
Kim Sudhalter
DIRECTOR, PUBLIC RELATIONS
Monica Bouldin

WARNER BROS. WORLDWIDE RETAIL
3550 W. Olive Ave., Burbank, CA 91505.
PRESIDENT
Peter Starrett
SENIOR V.P., WORLDWIDE RETAIL OPERATIONS
Dennis Adomaitis
SENIOR V.P., STUDIO STORES
Barry Gilbert
SENIOR V.P. & GENERAL MANAGER, RETAIL MERCHANDISE
Linda Postell
V.P., MARKETING & PUBLIC RELATIONS
Karine Joret
GALLERY MARKETING SUPERVISOR
Catherine Wittick

WARNER BROS. INTERNATIONAL THEATRE CO.
PRESIDENT
Millard Ochs

WARNER BROS. RECREATION ENTERPRISES
PRESIDENT
Nicholas Winslow
V.P., ADMINISTRATION & BUSINESS DEVELOPMENT
Kelly Eppich
SENIOR V.P., DESIGN & CONSTRUCTION
Rolf Roth
V.P., AUDIO & VISUAL PRODUCTION
Jim House

WARNER BROS. PAY-TV, CABLE & NETWORK FEATURES
75 Rockefeller Plaza, New York, NY 10019. (212) 484-8000. FAX: (212) 397-0728.
PRESIDENT
Edward Bleier

WARNER BROS. TELEVISION
4000 Warner Blvd., Burbank, CA 91522. (213) 843-6000, FAX: (818) 954-4539; 75 Rockefeller Plaza, New York, NY 10019. (212) 484-8000.
PRESIDENT
Tony Jonas

TIME TELEPICTURES TELEVISION
3500 W. Olive Ave., #1000, Burbank, CA 91505. (818) 972-0777.
V.P., CURRENT PROGRAMMING
David Goldberg

TELEPICTURES PRODUCTIONS
3500 W. Olive, Suite #1000, Burbank, CA 91505. (818) 972-0778.
PRESIDENT
Jim Paratore
INTERNATIONAL OFFICES, DISTRIBUTORS & MANAGERS
ARGENTINA
Tucuman 1938, Buenos Aires 1050. Tel:(541) 372 6094. FAX: (541) 11 2030.
GENERAL MANAGER
Anibal Codebo
ADVERTISING & PUBLICITY MANAGER
Erin McCrea Steele
AUSTRALIA
Village Roadshow Corp. Ltd., 206 Bourke St., Melbourne VIC 3001. Tel: (613) 9667 6666. FAX: (613) 9663 1972. Telex: AA 32502.
MANAGING DIRECTOR
Graham Burke
AUSTRIA
Warner Bros. GMBH, Zieglergasse 10, Vienna A-1070. Tel: (431) 523 8626. FAX: (431) 523 8626 31.
GENERAL MANAGER
Wilhelm Geike
BELGIUM
Warner Bros., Boulevard Brand Whitlock 42, Brussels 1200. Tel: (322) 735 4242. FAX: (322) 735 4919.
GENERAL MANAGER
Jacques Dubois
BOLIVIA
c/o Manfer Films, SRL, Avenida Montes 768, 4to. Piso, Edificio Giovanni de Col, La Paz. Tel: (5912) 37 6834. FAX: (5912) 39 1158.
MANAGING DIRECTOR
Licnio Manay
BRAZIL
Fox-Warner Brazil, Rua Calcados dos Cravos 141, Centro Commercial Alphaville, Barueri, Sao Paolo CEP 06543-00. Tel: (5511) 7295 5999. FAX: (5511) 7295 1143.
GENERAL MANAGER
Marcos de Oliviera
BULGARIA
c/o Alexandra Films, 89 Oborishte St., 4th & 5th Floors, Sofia 1505. Tel: (3592) 467 566. FAX: (3592) 943 3230.
MANAGING DIRECTOR
Stefan Minchev
CHILE
Associacion Fox/Warner, Huerfanos 786, Oficina 210, Santiago. Tel: (562) 633 2503. FAX: (562) 639 7921.
MANAGER
Arthur Ehrlich
CHINA
Warner New Asia, c/o The Shangri-La Hotel, Room 365, 29 Zizhuyan Rd., Beijing 100081. Tel: (8610) 6846 0695. FAX: (8610) 6846 0694.
WARNER REPRESENTATIVE
Lihui Zhang
COLOMBIA
c/o Elephant Joseph & CIA Ltda, Calle 96 No. 12-10, Santafe De Bogota. Tel: (571) 610 2041. FAX: (571) 610 2020.
PRESIDENT
Jaime Joseph
CROATIA
c/o Kinemayografi Zagreb, Tuskanac 1, 41000 Zagreb. Tel: (3851) 426 305. FAX: (3851) 426 531.
MANAGING DIRECTOR
Davor Kovacevic
CYPRUS
c/o Islanders Overseas Ltd., Gregoris Afxentiou Ave., Avensia Court 3, Flats 201, 202 & 204, P.O. Box 87, 6300 Larnaca. Tel: (3574) 627 320. FAX: (3574) 628 921.
MANAGING DIRECTOR
Elias Antypas
CZECH REPUBLIC
c/o Scriba/Gemini Films, S.R.O. V Jame 1, 11000 Prague 1. Tel: (422) 2416 2471. FAX: (422) 2422 6562.
MANAGING DIRECTOR
Jitka Jerabkova
DENMARK
Warner & Metronome Film APS, Sondermarksvej 16, DK-2500 Copenhagen/Valby. Tel: (45) 3646 8822. FAX: (45) 3644 0604.
GENERAL MANAGER
Loke Havn
ECUADOR
c/o Productora Filmica Nacional, Del Ecuador C. Ltda., Cordova #1015 y 9 de Octubre, Guayaquil. Tel: (5934) 564 455. FAX: (5934) 561 877.

MANAGER
Carlos Espinosa
EGYPT
c/o United Motion PIctures, 7, 26 July Street, P.O. Box 923, Cairo. Tel: (202) 591 2477. FAX: (202) 591 2829.
MANAGING DIRECTOR
Antoine Zeind
ESTONIA
c/o Motion Picture Distribution of Estonia, Parnu mnt. 45, Tallinn EE0001. Tel: (3726) 313569. FAX: (3726) 313671.
MANAGER
Aldo Tammsaar
FINLAND
Warner Bros. Finland Oy, Kaisaniemenkatu 1B A 69, Helsinki 00100. Tel: (3580) 58400 806. FAX: (3580) 58400 810.
MANAGER
Aune Turja
FRANCE
Warner Bros. Inc., 67, Avenue De Wagram, Paris 75017. Tel: (331) 4401 4999. FAX: (331) 4763 4515.
DIRECTOR
Steve Rubin
ADVERTISING & PUBLICITY MANAGER
Sybill Mellion
GERMANY
Warner Bros. Film GmbH, Hans Henny Jahnn Weg 35, D-22085, Hamburg. Tel: (4940) 22 6500. FAX: (4940) 22 650 109.
GENERAL MANAGER
Willi Geike
PUBLICITY DIRECTOR
Christoph Liedke
GREECE
c/o Victor G. Michaelides A.E. Co., 96 Akadimias Street, GR 10677 Athens. Tel: (301) 382 3801. FAX: (301) 380 3611. Telex: 215083.
MANAGING DIRECTOR
George V. Michaelides
HOLLAND
Warner Bros. (Holland), 1803 DeBoelelaan 16 3H, 1083 HJ Amsterdam. Tel: (3120) 541 1211. FAX: (3120) 644 9001.
MANAGING DIRECTOR
Jean Heijl
HONG KONG
Warner Bros. (Far East) Inc., 7th Floor, 100 Canton Rd., Tsimshatsui, Kowloon. Tel: (852) 2376 3963. FAX: (852) 2376 1302.
GENERAL MANAGER
Jenny Li
HUNGARY
c/o Intercom, Bacskai u. 28-36, Budapest 1145. Tel: (361) 467 1400. FAX: (361) 252 2736.
MANAGING DIRECTOR
George Mihaly
ICELAND
c/o Samfilm, Alfabakka 8, 109 Rekjavik. Tel: (354) 587 8900. FAX: (354) 587 8910.
MANAGING DIRECTOR
Arni Samuelsson
INDIA
Warner Bros. (Far East) Inc., Eros Cinema Bldg., 42 M. Karve Rd., Bombay 400020. Tel: (9122) 285 6557. FAX: (9122) 285 0984.
MANAGING DIRECTOR
Blaise J. Fernandes
INDONESIA
c/o P.T. Satyra Perkasa Esthetika Film, Suite 703, Room #1, Subentra Bank Bldg., J1, Gatot Subroto Kav. 21, Jakarta 12930. Tel: (6221) 522 0080. FAX: (6221) 522 0081.
WARNER REPRESENTATIVE
Kurt Reider (based in Singapore)
IRELAND
Warner Bros. Distributors Ltd., Russell House, Russell Court St. Stephans Green, Dublin 2. Tel: (3531) 478 4000. FAX: (3731(478 4572.
MANAGING DIRECTOR
Maj-Britt Kirchner (based in England)
ISRAEL
c/o Noah Films, 10 Glickson St., 3rd Floor, Tel Aviv 63567. Tel: (9723) 6200 221. FAX: (9723) 6202 435.
MANAGING DIRECTOR
Chilik Michaeli
ITALY
Warner Bros. Italia S.p.A., Via Varese, 16/B, 00185 Rome. Tel: (396) 448 891. FAX: (396) 446 2981
MANAGING DIRECTOR
Paolo Ferrari

JAMAICA
Russgram Investments Ltd. (Distributor), 1A South Camp Rd., Kingston. Tel: (809) 928 1240. FAX: (809) 928 5632.
OWNER
Douglas Graham

JAPAN
Warner Bros. Theatrical Distribution Japan, 1-2-4 Hamamatsucho, Minato-ku, Tokyo 105. Tel: (813) 5472 8000. FAX: (813) 5472 8031.
MANAGING DIRECTOR
William Ireton

KOREA
Warner Bros. Korea, Inc., M Building, 6th floor, 221-5 Nonhyun-Dong, Kangnam-ku, Seoul, Korea 135-010. Tel: (822) 547 0181. FAX: (822) 547-8396.
GENERAL MANAGER
Hyo-Sung Park

LATVIA
c/o Blatic Cinema SIA, KR Barona Iela 31, LV-1011 Riga. Tel: (371) 728 3990. FAX: (371) 783 0520.
MANAGING DIRECTOR
Atis Amolins

LEBANON
c/o Joseph Chacra & Son, Kazandjian Bldg., Horsh Tabet, Shamoun St., Sin El-Fil. Tel: (9611) 480 312. FAX: (9611) 495 745.
OWNER
Joseph Chacra

MALAYSIA
Warner Bros (Far East) Inc., 24 Jalan Padang Walter Grenier, Off Jalan Imbi, 55100 Kuala Lumpur. Tel: (603) 242 3669. FAX: (603) 248 9670.
GENERAL MANAGER
Kurt Reider (based in Singapore)

MEXICO
Warner Bros. (Mexico), c/o Videocione, S.A. de C.V., America No. 173, Col. Parque San Andres, Coyoacan, 04040 Mexico D.F.. Tel: (525) 549 3100. FAX: (525) 549 2911.
WARNER REPRESENTATIVE
Mike Moraskie

NEW ZEALAND
c/o Roadshow Film Distributors (N.Z.) Ltd., P.O.Box 68246, Newton, Auckland. Tel: (649) 377 9669. FAX: (649) 377 9449.
GENERAL MANAGER
Robert Crockett
MARKETING MANAGER
Gunther Behrendt

NORWAY
Oscarsgate 55, Oslo N-0258. Tel: (47) 2204 9110. FAX: (47) 2204 9157
GENERAL MANAGER
Jon Narvestad

PAKISTAN
c/o Zeray Entertainment, Hotel Metropole, Suite 209, Karachi. Tel: (9221) 567 1613. FAX: (9221) 568 0671.
PRESIDENT
Ray Hafeez

PANAMA
Warner Bros. (South) Inc., Avenida Balboa, Centro Commercial Balboa Plaza, Quinto Piso, Oficina 504, Panama. Tel: (507) 264 2606. FAX: (507) 263 9161.
MANAGER
Miquel Joseph

PERU
Warner Bros. (South) Inc./20th Century Park, Av. Canaval Y Moreyra, No. 290, #21, San Isidro, Lima 27. Tel: (5114) 412 568. FAX: (5114) 412 568.
GENERAL MANAGER
Julio Noriega

PHILIPPINES
Warner Bros. (Far East Inc.), PPL Bldg., Room 311, 1000 United Nations Ave., Central P.O. Box 2489, Metro Manila 2801. Tel: (632) 526 5741. FAX: (632) 521 2673.
GENERAL MANAGER
Jose Alonte

POLAND
Warner Bros. Poland, 02-508 Warszawa, ul. Pulawska, 37/39. Tel: (4822) 495959. FAX: (4822) 493598.
MANAGING DIRECTOR
Arkadiusz Praglowski

PORTUGAL
Columbia TriStar & Warner Filmes De Portugal Limitada, Rua Barata Salguiero 30-6 Dt., 1200 Lisbon. Tel: (3511) 316 0968. FAX: (3511) 316 1548.
GENERAL MANAGER
Antonio Avelar Gomes

PUERTO RICO
Warner Bros. (South) Inc.,Edificio Pesquera, Calle Del Parque 601, Ofna 605, Santurce 00910. Tel: (809) 725 5795. FAX: (809) 725 7275.
ACTING GENERAL MANAGER
Redo Farah

ROMANIA
c/o Ecran XXI Romania S.R.L., Blvd. Carol 1 no. 51 (fost Republicii 51), Et. 1, Apt. 7, Sector 2, Bucharest. Tel: (401) 614 8846. FAX: (401) 312 5095.
MANAGING DIRECTOR
Mihai Duta

SINGAPORE
Warner Bros. (Far East) Inc., 112 Middle Rd. 04-02, Midland House, Sinapore 0718. Tel: (65) 337 5060. FAX: (65) 339 1709. Telex: 22151.
GENERAL MANAGER
Kurt Rieder

SLOVAK REPUBLIC
c/o Gemini Film, P.O. Box 124, Stefanikova 47, 81000 Bratislava 1. Tel: (427) 391127. FAX: (427) 396361.
MANAGING DIRECTOR
Anton Drobny

SLOVENIA
c/o Ljubljanski Kinematografi, Nazorjeva 2, 1000 Ljubljana. Tel: (38661) 219 564. FAX: (38661) 219 524.
GENERAL MANAGER
Marjan Gabrijelcic

SOUTH AFRICA
c/o United International Pictures (South Africa), Castrol House, 7 Junction Ave., Parktown, 2193 Johannesburg. Tel: (2711) 484 4215. FAX: (2711) 484 3339.
MANAGING DIRECTOR
Roger LeComber

SPAIN
Warner Espanola S.A., Manuel Montilla 1, 28016 Madrid. Tel: (341) 350 6200. FAX (341) 345 1948.
WARNER REPRESENTATIVE
Edouard Weinberg

SWEDEN
Warner Bros. Sweden AB, Hornsbruksgatan 19, 3rd floor, S-117 34 Stockholm. Tel: (468) 658 1050. FAX: (468) 658 6482.
GENERAL MANAGER
Peter Jansson

SWITZERLAND
Studerweg 3, CH-8802 Kilchberg. Tel: (411) 715 5911. FAX: (411) 715 3451.
MANAGING DIRECTOR
Michael Hangartner

TAIWAN
Warner Bros. (Far East) Inc., 1/3 F, #24, Section 2, 24 Kai Feng St.,Taipei 100. Tel: (8862) 311 0159. FAX: (8862) 311 8526.
GENERAL MANAGER
Oliver Chen

THAILAND
Warner Bros. (Far East) Inc./Twentieth Century-Fox Thailand, Inc., 315 Silom Rd., 6th Floor, Room 603, Bangkok 10500; Tel: (662) 233 0920. FAX: (662) 236 4834.
GENERAL MANAGER
Philip Lau

TRINIDAD
U.I.P. Corp. (Distributor), Film Center, St. James, Port of Spain. Tel: (809) 622 4671. FAX: (809) 622 2517.
MANAGING DIRECTOR
Mausley Ellis

TURKEY
Warner Bros. Film & Video San. Tic. A.S., Topcu Cad, Uygun uis Merkezi 2/6, 80090 Taksim, Istanbul. Tel: (90212) 237 2000. FAX: (90212) 237 29600.
MANAGING DIRECTOR
Haluk Kaplanoglu

UNITED KINGDOM
Warner Bros. Distributors Ltd., 135 Wardour St., London WIV 4AP. Tel: (4471) 734 8400. FAX: (4471) 437 5521.
MANAGING DIRECTOR
Maj-Britt Kirchner
DIRECTOR OF SALES
Mike Boyce

URUGUAY
Horacio Hermida Limitada, Soriance 1263, Montevideo. Tel: (5982) 903 044. FAX: (5982) 921 677.
OWNER
Horacio D. Hermida

VENEZUELA

c/o Distribuidora Difox C.A., Avenida Las Palmas, Edificio Teatro Las Palmas, 4o Piso, Caracas 1050. Tel: (582) 782 2922. FAX: (582) 7881 7586.
WARNER REPRESENTATIVE
Augusto Bogni

WARNER HOLLYWOOD STUDIOS

1041 N. Formosa Ave., West Hollywood, CA 90046. (213) 850-2500. FAX: (213) 850-2650.
V.P. & GENERAL MANAGER
Norman C. Barnett
V.P. STUDIO OPERATIONS
Donald Daves
V.P., TECHNICAL OPERATIONS
Curt Belhmer
V.P. & CONTROLLER
Donald Putrimas

MD WAX/COURIER FILMS

(Distributor.)
1560 Broadway, Suite 907, New York, NY 10036. (212) 302-5360. FAX: (212) 302-5364. email: 72124.250@compuserve.com
PRESIDENT
Morton D. Wax

WEST GLEN COMMUNICATONS, INC.

(Producer and distributer of 35mm short subjects.)
1430 Broadway, New York, NY 10018. (212) 921-2800. FAX: (212) 944-9055.
PRESIDENT
Stanley Zeitlin
THEATRICAL DISTRIBUTION MANAGER
Cathy Boje

WINKLER FILMS, INC.

(Producer.)
211 S. Beverly Dr., #200, Beverly Hills, CA 90212. (310) 858-5780. FAX: (310) 858-5799.
CEO, PRODUCER/DIRECTOR
Irwin Winkler
PRESIDENT
Rob Cowan
EXECUTIVE ASSISTANT
Lisa Steen

WOLPER ORGANIZATION INC., THE

4000 Warner Blvd., Burbank, CA 91522. (818) 954-1707. FAX: (818) 954-4380.
CHAIRMAN
David L. Wolper
PRESIDENT
Mark M. Wolper
SENIOR VICE PRESIDENT
Auriel K. Sanderson
V.P., DEVELOPMENT
Marci Pool

WORKING TITLE FILMS

(Film production.)
9348 Civic Center Dr., Suite 100, Beverly Hills, CA 90210. (310) 777-1970. FAX: (310) 777-1970.
CHAIRMEN
Tim Bevan
Eric Fellner

WORLD WIDE PICTURES

1201 Hennepin Ave., Minneapolis, MN 55403. (612) 338-3335. FAX: (612) 338-3029.
CHAIRMAN
Billy Graham
SECRETARY
John R. Corts
ACTING DIRECTOR OF OPERATIONS
Barry Werner

WORLDVIEW ENTERTAINMENT INC.

The Killiam Collection, 500 Greenwich St., New York, NY 10013. (212) 925-4291. FAX: (212) 925-2314.
CHAIRMAN/CEO
Sandra J. Birnhak
PRESIDENT
Glenn E. Shealey

SAUL ZAENTZ FILM CENTER

2600 Tenth St., Berkeley, CA 94710. (510) 486-2100. FAX: (510) 486-2115.
PRESIDENT
Saul Zaentz
DIRECTOR OF OPERATIONS
Steve Shurtz

THE ZANUCK COMPANY

(Production of theatrical motion pictures.)
202 N. Canon Dr., Beverly Hills, CA 90210. (310) 274-0261. FAX: (310) 273-9217. Organized 1989.
PARTNERS
Richard D. Zanuck
Lili Fini Zanuck

ZEITGEIST FILMS LTD.

(Distribution of independent films.)
247 Centre St., 2nd fl., New York, NY 10013. (212) 274-1989. FAX: (212) 274-1644. email: zeitgeist@tunanet.com
CO-PRESIDENTS
Emily Russo
Nancy Gerstman

ZUCKER BROTHERS PRODS.

(Motion picture production.)
1351 Fourth St., Suite 300, Santa Monica, CA 90401. (310) 656-9200. FAX: (310) 656-9220.
PRESIDENT-PRODUCER
Gil Netter
PRODUCERS-DIRECTORS
David Zucker
Jerry Zucker

NON-THEATRICAL
MOTION PICTURE COMPANIES

Following is a list of producers, distributors and film libraries handling educational, entertainment and advertising pictures for non-theatrical distribution to schools, clubs, civic organizations, and teaching groups, as well as television.

THE AHERN GROUP
2160 Rockrose Ave., Baltimore, MD 21211. (410) 462-1550. FAX: (410) 462-1551.

CAMERON PRODUCTIONS
222 Minor Ave. N., Seattle, WA 98109-5436. (206) 623-4103. FAX: (206) 623-7256.
e-mail: cameron.productions@worldnet.att.net

CAROUSEL FILMS, INC.
260 Fifth Ave., New York, NY 10001. (212) 683-1660, (800) 683-1660. FAX: (212) 683-1662. e-mail: carousel@pipeline.com

CAVALCADE PRODUCTIONS, INC.
P.O. Box 2480, Nevada City, CA 95959-1948. (916) 265-0370. FAX: (916) 265-0370.

CIFEX CORPORATION
One Peconic Hills Ct., Southampton, NY 11968-1618. (516) 283-4795, (212) 582-4318. FAX: (516) 283-9454.

CONTINENTAL FILM PRODUCTIONS CORP.
4220 Amnicola Highway, P.O. Box 5126, Chattanooga, TN 37406. (423) 622-1193. FAX: (423) 629-0853. e-mail: cfpc@chattanooga.net

THOMAS CRAVEN FILM CORPORATION
5 W. 19 St., 3rd floor, New York, NY 10011-4216. (212) 463-7190. FAX: (212) 627-4761.

CUSTOM FILMS/VIDEO, INC.
11 Cob Dr., Westport, CT 06880. (203) 226-0300. FAX: (203) 227-9435.

WALT DISNEY, NON-THEATRICAL
3900 W. Alameda Ave., Suite 2477, Burbank, CA 91521-0021. (818) 567-5058. FAX: (818) 972-9447.

WILLIAM DITZEL PRODUCTIONS
1505 E. David Rd., Dayton, OH 45429. (513) 298-5381.

EBBETS FIELD PRODUCTIONS, LTD.
P.O. Box 42, Wykagyl Station, New Rochelle, NY 10804. (914) 636-1281.

EDWARD FEIL PRODUCTIONS
4614 Prospect Ave., Cleveland, OH 44103. (216) 881-0040.

FILMS FOR EDUCATORS/FILMS FOR TV
420 E. 55th St., Suite 6-U, New York, NY 10022. (212) 486-6577. FAX: (212) 980-9826.

FILMS INCORPORATED
National Sales Office: 5547 N. Ravenswood Ave., Chicago, IL 60640. (312) 878-2600, (800) 323-4222, ext. 42.

GOLDSHOLL FILM GROUP
420 Frontage Rd., Northfield, IL 60093. (708) 446-8300. FAX: (708) 446-8320.

HANNA-BARBERA CARTOONS
3400 Cahuenga Blvd., Hollywood, CA 90068. (213) 851-5000. FAX: (213) 969-1201.

HARDCASTLE FILMS & VIDEO
7319 Wise Ave., St. Louis, MO 63117. (314) 647-4200. FAX: (314) 647-4201.

HURLOCK CINE-WORLD, INC.
Box 34619, Juneau, AK 99803-4619. (907) 789-3995.

IFEX FILMS/IFEX INTERNATIONAL
159 W. 53 St., Suite 19-B, New York, NY 10019-6050. (212) 582-4318. FAX: (212) 956-2257.

IVY FILM
P.O. Box 18376, Ashville, NC 28814. (704) 285-9995.

HUGH & SUZANNE JOHNSTON, INC.
16 Valley Rd., Princeton, NJ 08540. (609) 924-7505.

WALTER J. KLEIN COMPANY, LTD.
6311 Carmel Rd., Box 472087, Charlotte, NC 28247-2087. (704) 542-1403. FAX: (704) 542-0735.

MRC FILMS
P.O. Box 697, Plainview, NY 11803. (212) 730-7705.

LEE MENDELSON FILM PRODUCTIONS, INC.
1440 Chapin Ave., Burlingame, CA 94010. (415) 342-8284. FAX: (415) 342-6170.

MODERN TALKING PICTURE SERVICE, INC.
5000 Park St. N., St. Petersburg, FL 33709-2200. (813) 541-7571. FAX: (813) 546-9323.

BYRON MORGAN ASSOCIATES
P.O. Box 1293, Lake Arrowhead, CA 92352-1293. (909) 337-3219. FAX: (909) 337-6218.

NFL FILMS, INC.
330 Fellowship Rd., Mt. Laurel, NJ 08054. (609) 778-1600.

NATIONAL TELEVISION NEWS
13691 W. Eleven Mile Rd., Oak Park, MI 48237. (810) 541-1440.

PACE FILMS, INC.
411 E. 53rd St., New York, NY 10022. (212) 755-5486.

PENFIELD PRODUCTIONS, INC.
35 Springfield St., Agawam, MA 01001. (413) 786-4454.

PILOT PRODUCTIONS, INC.
2123 McDaniel Ave., Evanston, IL 60201-2126. (708) 328-3700. FAX: (708) 328-3761.

PLAYHOUSE PICTURES
1401 N. La Brea Ave., Hollywood, CA 90028. (213) 851-2112. FAX: (213) 851-2117.

ROSS ROY COMMUNICATIONS
100 Bloomfield Hills Pkwy., Bloomfield Hills, MI 48304. (810) 433-6000.

SNAZELLE FILMS
155 Fell St., San Francisco, CA 94102. (415) 431-5490. FAX: (415) 552-9474.

SNYDER FILMS & VIDEO
1419 First Ave. S., Fargo, ND 58103. (701) 293-3600.

SWAIN FILM & VIDEO
1185 Cattleman Rd., Sarasota, FL 34232. (941) 371-2360. FAX: (941) 377-1459.

SWANK MOTION PICTURES, INC.
201 S. Jefferson Ave., St. Louis, MO 63103. (314) 534-6300. FAX: (314) 289-2187.

TFI
619 W. 54th St., New York, NY 10019-3591. (212) 708-0550. FAX: (212) 977-9458.

T.H.A. MEDIA DISTRIBUTORS LTD.
1200 W. Pender St., Suite #307, Vancouver, B.C., Canada V6E 2S9. (604) 687-4215. e-mail: tha@thamedia.com

TR PRODUCTIONS, INC.
1031 Commonwealth Ave., Boston, MA 02215-1094. (617) 783-0020. FAX: (617) 783-4844.

TEL-AIR INTEREST, INC.
1755 N.E. 149th St., Miami, FL 33181. (305) 944-3268. FAX: (305) 944-1143.

TRANS WORLD FILMS, INC.
332 S. Michigan Ave., Chicago, IL 60604-4382. (312) 922-1530, (800) 432-2241. FAX: (312) 427-4550.

ROBERT WARNER PRODUCTIONS
P.O. Box 880, East Hampton, NY 11937-0701. (516) 324-1050.

WEST GLEN COMMUNICATIONS, INC.
1430 Broadway, New York, NY 10018. (212) 921-2800. FAX: (212) 944-9055.

WEXLER FILM PRODUCTIONS, INC.
801 N. Seward St., Los Angeles, CA 90038-3601. (213) 462-6671. FAX: (213) 462-6349.

FEATURE FILMS

MAJOR, INDEPENDENT & FOREIGN FEATURES
(OCTOBER 1, 1995—SEPTEMBER 30, 1996)

Ace Ventura: When Nature Calls

A Warner Bros. release of a James G. Robinson presentation of a Morgan Creek production. Director: Steve Oedekerk. Producer: James G. Robinson. Camera: Donald E. Thorin. Editor: Malcolm Campbell. Screenplay: Oedekerk. Running time: 92 minutes. PRAA rating: PG-13. Release date: November, 17, 1995.

Cast: Jim Carrey, Ian McNeice, Simon Callow, Maynard Eziashi, Bob Gunton, Sophie Okonedo, Tommy Davidson, Adewale, Adrew Steele, Bruce Spence.

Across the Sea of Time

A Columbia pictures and Sony New Technologies presentation. Director: Stephen Low. Producer: Low. Screenplay: Andrew Gellis. Camera: Andrew Kitzanuk. Editor: James Lahti. In Imax 3-D color. Release date: October 20, 1995.

Cast: Peter Reznik, John Mcdonough, Avi Hoffman, Victor Steinbach, Peter Boyden, Philip Levy, Abby Lewis, Donald Trump.

Alaska

A Columbia Pictures release of a Castle Rock Entertainment production. Producers: Carol Fuchs, Andy Brug. Co-rpoducer: Gordon Mark. Director: Fraser S. Heston. Screenplay: Burg, Scott Myers. Camera: Tony Westman. Editor: Rob Kobrin. Music: Reg Powell. Running time: 104 minutes. MPAA rating: PG.

Cast: Thora Brich, Vincent Kartheiser, Dirk Benedict, Charlton Heston, Duncan Fraser, Gordon Tootoosis.

All Dogs Go To Heaven 2

MGM/UA release of an MGM Family Entertainment presentation of a Metro-Goldwyn-Mayer Animation production. Producers: Paul Sabella, Jonathan Dern, Kelly Ward, Mark Young. Directors: Sabella, Larry Leker. Screenplay: Arne Olsen, Ward, Young, from a story by Ward, Young. Editor: Tony Garber. Music: Mark Watters. Animation Director: Todd Waterman. Running time: 82 minutes. MPAA rating: G. Release date: March 29, 1996.

Cast: (voices), Charlie Sheen, Sheena Easton, Dom DeLuise, Ernest Borgnine, George Hearn, Bebe Neuwirth, Wallace Shawn.

The American President

A Columbia release of a Castle Rock Entertainment and Universal Pictures presentation of a Wildwood production. Director: Rob Reiner. Producer: Reiner. Camera: John Seale. Screenplay: Aaron Sorkin. Editor: Robert Leighton. In Panavision Widescreen Technicolor. Running time: 113 minutes. MPAA rating: PG-13. Release date: November 17, 1995.

Cast: Michael Douglas, Annette Bening, Martin Sheen, Michael J. Fox, David Paymer, Samantha Mathis, John Mahoney, Richard Dreyfuss.

The Arrival

An Orion release of a Live Entertainment presentation of a Steelwork Films/Thomas G. Smith production. Produced by Thomas G. Smith, Jim Steel. Director-Writer: David Twohy. Camera: Hiro Narita. Editor: Martin Hunter. Music: Arthur Kempel. In color, Panavision. Running time: 109 minutes. MPAA rating: PG-13. Release date: May 23, 1996.

Cast: Charlie Sheen, Ron Silver, Lindsay Crouse, Teri Polo, Richard Schiff, Tony T. Johnson, Leon Rippy, Buddy Joe Hooker.

Assassins

A Warner Bros release of a Silver Pictures production in association with Donner/Schuler -Donner Prods. Producers: Richard Donner, Joel Silver, Bruce Evans, Raynold Godeon, Andrew Lazar, Jim Van Wyck. Director: Richard Donner. Screenplay: Andy Wachowski, Larry Wachowski. Camera: Vilmos Zsigmond. Editor: Richard Marks. Music: Mark Mancina. Running time: 132 minutes. MPAA rating: R. Release date: October 6, 1995.

Cast: Sylvester Stallone, Antonio Banderas, Julianne Moore, Anatoly Davydov.

Balto

A Universal Pictures release of an Amblin Entertainment film. Producer: Steve Hickner. Director: Simon Wells. Screenplay: Cliff Ruby, Elana Lesser, David Steven Cohen, Roger S.H. Schulman based on a story by Ruby, Lesser. Animated. MPAA rating: G. Release date: December 24, 1995.

Voice Cast: Kevin Bacon, Bridget Fonda, Bob Hoskins, Phil Collins.

Before and After

A Hollywood Pictures release. Producers: Barbet Schroder, Susan Hoffman. Director: Schroder. Screenplay: Ted Tally based on the book by Rosellen Brown. Camera: Luciano Tovoli. Editor: Lee Percy. Music: Howard Shore. Running time: 108 minutes. MPAA rating: PG-13. Release date: February 22, 1996.

Cast: Meryl Streep, Liam Neeson, Edward Furlong, Julia Weldon, Alfred Molina.

Big Bully

A Warner Bros. release of a James G. Robinson presentation of a Morgan Creek production in association with Lee Rich Prods. Producers: Lee Rich, Gary Foster. Director: Steve Minor. Screenplay: Mark Steven Johnson, Camera: Daryn Okada. Editor: Marshall Harvey. Music: David Newman. Production Designer: Ian Thomas. Running time: 93 minutes. MPAA rating: PG. Release date: January 26, 1996.

Cast: Rick Moranis, Tom Arnold, Julianne Philips, Carol Kane, Don Knotts.

Bio-Dome

An MGM Pictures presentation in association with the Motion Picture Corporation of America of a Brad Krevoy & Steve Sabler, Weasel Productions and 3 Arts Entertainment production. Producers: Brad Jenkel, Krevoy, Stabler. Director: Jason Bloom. Screenplay: Kip Koenig, Scott Marcano based on a story Adam Leff, Mitchell Peck, Jason Blumenthal. Camera: Phedon Papamichael. Music: Andrew Gross. MPAA rating: PG-13. Release date: January 12, 1995.

Cast: Pauly Shore, Stephen Baldwin, William Atherton, Joey Adams, Kylie Minogue.

The Birdcage

An MGM/UA release of a United Artists presentation. Producer: Mike Nichols. Director: Nichols. Screenplay: Elaine May, based on the stage play "La Cage aux Folles" by Jean Poiret and the script by Francis Veber, Edouard Molinaro, Danon, Poiret. Camera: Emmanuel Lubezki. Editor: Arthur Schmidt. In Technicolor. Running time: 119 minutes. MPAA rating: R. Release date: March 8, 1996.

Cast: Robin Williams, Gene Hackman, Nathan Lane, Dianne Wiest, Hank Azaria, Christina Baranski, Dan Futterman, Calista Flockhart.

Black Sheep

A Paramount release of a Lorne Michaels production. Producer: Michaels. Director: Penelope Spheeris. Screenplay: Fred Wolf. Camera: Daryn Okada. Editor: Ross Albert. Music: William Ross. Production Design: Peter Jamison. In Deluxe color. Running time: 87 minutes. MPAA rating PG-13. Release date: February 2, 1996.

Cast: Chris Farley, David Spade, Tim Matheson, Christine Ebersole, Gary Busey, Grant Heslov, Timothy Carhart, Bruce McGill.

Bogus

A Warner Bros. release of a Regency Enterprise presentation of a Yorktown/New Regency production. Producer: Norman Jewison, Arnon Milchan, Jeff Rothberg. Executive producers: Michael Nathanson, Patrick Markey, Gayle Fraser-Baigleman. Director: Jewison. Screenplay: Alvin Sargent, story by Rothberg, Frances X. McCarthy. Camera: David Watkin. Editor: Stephen Rifkin. Music: Mark Shaiman. Running tim: 11 minutes. MPAA rating: PG. Release date: August 30, 1996.

Cast: Whoopi Goldberg, Gerard Depardieu, Haley Joel Osmet, Denis Mercier, Nany Travis, Ute Lemper.

Bottle Rocket

A Sony Pictures release of a Columbia Pictures presentation of a Gracie Films/Boyle-Taylor production. Producers: Polly Platt, Cynthia Hargrave. Director: Wes Anderson. Screenplay: Owen C. Wilson, Anderson. Camera: Robert Yeoman. Editor: David Moritz. Music: Mark Mothersbaugh. In Technicolor. Running time: 95 mins. MPAA rating: R. Release date: February, 1996.

Cast: Owen C. Wilson, Luk Wilson, Robert Musgrave, Andrew Wilson, Lumi Cavazos, James Caan, Teddy Wilson, Jim Ponds.

Boys

A Buena Vista release of a Touchstone Pictures presentation of an Interscope Communications/Polygram Filmed Entertainment production. Producers: Peter Frankfurt, Paul Feldsher, Erica Huggins. Director: Stacy Cochran. Screenplay: Cochran, based on the short story "Twenty Minutes" by James Salter. Camera: Robert Elswit. Editor: Camilla Toniolo. Music: Stewart Copeland. Running time: 89 minutes. MPAA rating: PG-13. Release date: May 8, 1996.

Cast: Winona Ryder, Lukas Haas, Skeet Ulrich, John C. Reilly, Bill Sage, James LeGros.

Broken Arrow

A 20th Century Fox release of a Mark Gordon production in association with WCG Entertainment. Producers: Mark Gordon, Bill Badalato. Co-producer: Allison Lyon Segan. Director: John Woo. Screenplay: Graham Yost. Camera: Peter Levy. Editors: John Wright, Steve

Mirkovich, Joe Hutshing. Music: Hans Zimmer. In Deluxe color, Panavision widescreen. Running time: 108 minutes. MPAA rating: R. Release date: February 14., 1996.

Cast: Christian Slater, John Travolta, Samantha Mathis, Delroy Lindo, Bob Gunton, Frank Whaley, Howie Long, Vondie Curtis-Hall.

Bulletproof

A Universal Pictures release of a Bernie Brillstein-Brad Grey/Robert Simonds/Gold-Miller production. Producer: Robert Symonds. Executive producers: Grey, Brillstein, Sandy Wernick, Eric L. Gold. Co-producers: Ira Shuman, Jack Giarraputo. Director: Ernest Dickerson. Screenplay: Joe Gayton, Lewis Colick; story by Gayton. Camera: Steven Bernstein. Editor: George Folsey Jr. Music: Elmer Bernstein. Released August 28, 1996. MPAA rating: R. Running time: 84 Min.

Cast: Damon Wayans, Adam Sandler, James Caan, Kristen Wilson, James Farentino, Jeep Swenson, Bill Nunn, Mark Roberts.

The Cable Guy

A Sony Pictures Entertainment release of a Columbia Pictures presentation of a Bernie Brillstein/Brad Grey and Licht/Mueller Film Corp. production. Producers: Andrew Licht, Jeffrey A. Mueller, Judd Apatow. Director: Ben Stiller. Screenplay: Lou Holtz, Jr. Camera: Robert Brinkman. Editor: Steven Weisberg. Music: John Ottman. In Technicolor, widescreen. Running time: 95 minutes. MPAA Rating: PG-13. Release date: June 6, 1996.

Cast: Jim Carrey, Matthew Broderick, Leslie Mann, Jack Black, George Segal, Diane Baker, Ben Stiller, Eric Roberts.

Carpool

A Warner Bros. release of a Regency Enterprises presentation of an Arnon Milchan production. Producers: Milchan, Michael Nathanson. Executive producer: Fitch Cady. Director: Arthur Hiller. Screenplay: Don Rhymer. Camera: David M. Walsh. Editors: William Reynolds, L. James Langlois. Music: John Debney. Running time: 90 minutes. MPAA rating: PG. Release date: August 23, 1996.

Cast: Tom Arnold, David Paymer, Rhea Perlman, Rod Steiger, Kim Coastes, Leigh Cook, Mikey Kovar, Mocah Gardener.

Casino

A Universal Pictures and Syalis D.A. and Legende Enterprises present a De Fina/Cappa production of a Martin Scorsese picture. Producer: Barbara De Fina. Director: Martin Scorsese. Screenplay: Nicholas Pileggi, Scorsese, based on the book by Pileggi. Camera: Robert Richardson. Editor: Thelma Schoonmaker. MPAA Rating: R. Release date: November, 22, 1995.

Cast: Robert De Niro, Joe Pesci, Sharon Stone, Alan King, Don Rickles, Kevin Pollack, James Woods.

Celtic Pride

A Buena Vista release of a Hollywood Pictures presentation in association with Caravan Pictures. Producer: Roger Birnbaum. Director: Tom deCherchio. Screenplay: Judd Apatow, based on a story by Apatow, Colin Quinn. Camera: Oliver Wood. Editor: Hubert De La Bouillerie. Music: Basil Poledouris. Running time: 90 minutes. MPAA rating: PG-13. Release date: April 19, 1996.

Cast: Damon Wayans, Daniel Stern, Dan Aykroyd, Gail O'Grady.

Chain Reaction

A 20th Century Fox release of a Zanuck Co./Chicago Pacific Entertainment/Arne L. Schmidt production. Producers: Arne L. Schmidt, Andrew Davis. Director: Davis. Screenplay: J.F. Lawton, Michael Bortman, based on a story by Schmidt, Rick Seaman, Josh Friedman. Camera: Frank Tidy. Editors: Donald Brochu, Dov Hoenig, Schmidt. Music: Jerry Goldsmith. In Astrolab color, Panavision widescreen. Running time: 106 minutes. MPAA Rating: PG-13. Release date: July 25, 1996.

Cast: Keanu Reeves, Morgan Freeman, Rachel Weisz, Fred Ward, Kevin Dunn, Brian Cox, Joanna Cassidy.

The Chamber

A Universal release of an Imagine Entertainment presentation of a Brian Grazer/Davis Entertainment production. Producers: John Davis, Brian Grazer, Ron Howard. Executive Producers: David Friendly, Rick Kidney, Karen Kehela. Director: James Foley. Screenplay: William Goldman, Chris Reese, based on the novel by John Grisham. Cinematography: Ian Baker. Editor: Mark Warner. Music: Carter Burwell. MPAA Rating: R. Release date: Oct. 11, 1996. Running time: 100 Min.

Cast: Chris O'Donnell, Gene Hackman, Faye Dunaway, Robert Prosky, Raymond Barry, Bo Jackson, Lela Rochon, David Marshall Grant

City Hall

A Sony Pictures Entertainment release of a Columbia Pictures/Castle Rock Entertainment presentation of an Edward R. Pressman/Ken Lipper production. Producers: Pressman, Lipper, Charles Mulvehill, Harold Becker. Director: Becker. Screenplay: Lipper, Paul Schrader, Nicholas Pileggi, Bo Goldman. Camera: Michael Seresin. Editor: Robert C. Jones. In Technicolor. Running time: 111 minutes. MPAA rating: R. Release date: February 9, 1996.

Cast: Al Pacino, John Cusack, Bridget Fonda, Danny Aiello, Martin Landau, David Paymer, Tony Franciosa, Richard Schiff.

Copycat

A Warner Bros. release of a Regency Entrprises presentation of an Arnon Milchan production. Producers: Arnon Milchan & Mark Tarlov. Director: Jon Amiel. Screenplay: Ann Biderman & Jay Presson, based

on a story by David Madsen. Camera: Laszlo Kovacs. Music: Christopher Young. Editors: Alan Heim & Jim Clark. Running Time: 123 minutes. MPAA rating: R. Release date: October 27, 1995.

Cast: Sigourney Weaver, Holly Hunter, Dermot Mulroney, William McNamara, Will Patton, John Rothman, J. E. Freeman, Harry Connick Jr.

Courage Under Fire

A 20th Century Fox release of a Davis Entertainment/Joseph M. Singer production. Producers: John Davis, Joseph M. Singer, David T. Friendly. Director: Edward Zwick. Screenplay: Patrick Sheane Duncan. Camera: Roger Deakins. Editor: Steven Rosenblum. Music: James Horner. In Deluxe Color. Running time: 115 minutes. MPAA Rating: R. Release date: June 20, 1996.

Cast: Denzel Washington, Meg Ryan, Lou Diamond Phillips, Michael Moriarty, Matt Damon, Bronson Pinchot, Seth Gilliam, Regina Taylor.

The Craft

A Columbia release of a Douglas Wick production. Producer: Wick. Director: Andrew Fleming. Screenplay: Peter Filardi, Fleming, based on Filardi's story. Camera: Alexander Gruszynski. Editor: Jeff Freeman. Music: Graeme Revell. Running time: 100 minutes. MPAA rating: R. Release date: May 3, 1996.

Cast: Robin Tunney, Fairuza Balk, Neve Campbell, Rachel True, Skeet Ulrich, Helen Shaver.

Cutthroat Island

A Metro-Goldwyn-Mayer and Mario Kassar presentation of a Carolco/Forge production in association with Laurence Mark productions and Beckner/Gorman productions. Producers: Laurence Mark, Joel B. Michaels, James Gorman, Renny Harlin. Director: Harlin. Screenplay: Robert King, Marc Norman based on the story by Michael Frost Beckner, Gorman, Bruce A. Evans, Roynold Gideon. Music: John Debney. MPAA rating: PG-13. Release date: December 29, 1995.

Cast: Geena Davis, Matthew Modine, Frank Langella, Maury Chakin, Patrick Malahide, Stan Shaw.

D3: The Mighty Ducks

A Buena Vista release of a Walt Disney Picture presentation of an Avnet/Kerner production. Producers: Jordan Kerner, Jon Avnet. Executive Producers: Steven Brill, C. Tad Devlin. Director: Robert Lieberman. Screenplay: and story, Steven Brill, Jim Burstein, based on characters created by Brill. Cinematography: David Hennings. Editors: Patrick Lussier, Colleen Halsey. Music: J.A.C. Redford. MPAA Rating: PG. Release date: Sept. 28, 1996. Running time: 104 Min.

Cast: Emilio Estevez, Jeffrey Nordling, Joshua Jackson, David Selby, Heidi Kling, Joss Ackland, Elden Ryan Ratliff, Shaun Weiss.

Dead Presidents

A Buena Vista release of a Hollywood Pictures presentation in association with caravan Pictures of a Uniworld Entertainment production. Producers: the Hughes Brothers. Directors: the Hughes Brothers. Screenplay: Michael Henry Brown, story Allen and Albert Hughes, Brown. Camera: Lisa Rinzler. Editor: Dan Lebental. Music: Danny Elfman. Running time: 119 minutes. MPAA rating: R. Release date: October 13, 1995.

Cast: Larenz Tate, Keith David, Chris Tucker, N'Bushe Wright, Freddy Rodriguez, Rose Jackson, Michael Imperioli.

Diabolique

A Warner Bros. release of a James G. Robinson presentation of a Morgan Creek production in association with Marvin Worth Productions. Producers: Robinson, Worth. Director: Jeremiah Chechik. Screenplay: Don Roos. Camera: Peter James. Editor: Carol Littleton. Music: Randy Edelman. MPAA rating: R. Release date: March 22, 1996.

Cast: Sharon Stone, Isabelle Adjani, Chazz Palminteri, Kathy Bates, Spalding Gray, Allen Garfield, Adam Hann-Byrd.

Down Persicope

A 20th Century Fox release of a Robert Lawrence production. Producer: Lawrence. Director: David S. Ward. Screenplay: Hugh Wilson, Andrew Kurtzman, Eliot Wald, story by Wilson. Camera: Victor Hammer. Editors: Wiliam Anderson, Armen Minasian. Music: Randy Edelman. In Deluxe color. Running time: 92 minutes. MPAA rating: R. Release date: March 8, 1996.

Cast: Kelsey Grammar, Lauren Holly, Rob Schneider, Rip Torn, Harry Dean Stanton, William H. Macy, Ken Hudson Campbell.

Dracula: Dead And Loving It

A Sony Pictures Entertainment release from Columbia Pictures of a Castle Rock Entertainment of a Brooksfilms production. Producer: Mel Brooks. Director: Brooks. Screenplay: Brooks, Rudy de Luca, Steve Haberman based on a story by Haberman, De Luca. Camera: Michael D. O'Shea. Editor: Adam Weiss. Music: Hummie Mann. In Technicolor. Running time: 90 minutes. MPAA rating: PG-13. Release date: December 29, 1995.

Cast: Leslie Nielsen, Peter MacNichol, Steven Weber, Amy Yasbeck, Lysette Anthony, Harvey Korman, Mel Brooks, Mark Blankfield, Megan Cavanaugh.

Dragonheart

A Universal Release of a Raffaella De Laurentiis production. Producer: Dino De Laurentiis. Director: Rob Cohen. Screenplay: Charles Edward Pogue, based on a story by Patrick Read Johnson, Pogue. Camera: David Eggby. Editor: Peter Amundson. Music: Randy Edelman. In Deluxe color, Panavision widescreen. Running time: 103 minutes. MPAA Rating: PG-13. Release date: May 23, 1996.

Cast: Dennis Quaid, David Thewlis, Pete Postlethwaite, Dina Meyer, Julie Christie, Sean Connery.

Dunston Checks In

A 20th Century Fox release of a Joe Wizan/Todd Black production. Producers: Wizan, Black. Director: Ken Kwapis. Screenplay: John Hopkins, Bruce Graham, based on a story by Hopkins. Camera: Peter Collister. Editor: Jon Pol. Music: Miles Goodman. In Deluxe color. Running time: 88 minutes. MPAA rating: PG. Release date: January 5, 1996.
Cast: Jason Alexander, Faye Dunaway, Eric Lloyd, Rupert Everett, Graham Sack, Paul Reubens.

Ed

A Univeral release of a Longview Entertainment presentation. Producer: Rosalie Swedlin. Director: Bill Couturie. Screenplay: David Mickey Evans, story by Ken Richards, Janus Cercone. Camera: Alan Caso. Editor: Robert K. Lambert. Music: Stephen D. Endelman. Running time: 94 minutes. MPAA rating: PG. Release date: March 12, 1996.
Cast: Matt LeBlanc, Jayne Brook, Bill Cobbs, Jack Warden.

Eddie

A Buena Vista release of a Hollywood Pictures presentation of a David Permut production in association with Polygram Filmed Entertainment/Island Pictures. Producers: David Permut, Mark Burg. Director: Steve Rash. Screenplay: Jon Connolly, Davaid Ioucka, Eric Champnela, Keith Mitchell, Steve Azcharias, Jeff Buhai. Camera: Victor Kemper. Editor: Richard Halsey. Music: Stanley Clarke. In Technicolor. Running time: 100 minutes. MPAA rating: PG-13. Release date: May 28, 1996.
Cast: Whoopie Goldberg, Frank Langella, Dennis Farina, Richard Jenkins, Lisa Ann Walter, John Benjamin Hickey, John Salley.

Eraser

A Warner Bros. release of an Arnold Kopelson production. Producers: Arnold Kopelson, Anne Kopelson. Director: Charles Russel. Screenplay: Tony Puryear, Walon Green, from a story by Puryear, Green, Michael S. Chernuchin. Camera: Adam Greenberg. Editor: Michael Tronick. Music: Alan Silvestri. In Technicolor, Panavision widescreen. Running time: 115 minutes. MPAA Rating: R. Release date: June 11, 1996.
Cast: Arnold Schwarzenegger, James Caan, Vanessa Williams, James Coburn, Robert Pastorelli, James Crownwell, Danny Nucci.

Escape From L.A.

A Paramount release of a Debra Hill production presented in association with Rysher Entertainment. Producers: Debra Hill, Kurt Russell. Director: John Carpenter. Screenplay: Carpenter, Hill, Russell, based on characters created by Carpenter, Nick Castle. Camera: Gary B. Kibbe. Editor: Edward A. Warschilka. Music: Shirley Walker. Running time: 100 minutes. MPAA rating: R. Release date: August 9, 1996.
Cast: Kurt Russell, Stacy Keach, Steve Buscemi, Peter Fonda, Cliff Robertson, Valeria Golino, Pam Grier, A.J. Langer.

Executive Decision

A Warner Bros. release of a Silver Pictures production. Producer: Joel Silver. Director: Stuart Baird. Screenplay: Jim thomas, John Thomas. Camera: Alex Johnson, Don Burgess. Editors: Dallas Pruitt, Frank J. Urioste. Music: Jerry Goldsmith. In Technicolor. Running time: 132 minutes. MPAA rating: R. Release date: March 6, 1996.
Cast: Kurt Russell, Halle Berry, John Leguizamo, Steven Seagal, Oliver Platt, Joe Morton, David Suchet, B.D. Wong, J.T. Walsh.

Extreme Measures

A Sony Pictures Entertainment release of a Columbia/Castle Rock presentation of a Simian Films production. Producer: Elizabeth Hurley. Executive Producer: Andrew Scheinman. Co-producer, Chris Bingham. Director: Michael Apted. Screenplay: Tony Gilroy, based on the novel by Michael Palmer. Cinematography: John Bailey. Editor: Rick Shaine. Music: Danny Elfman. MPAA Rating: R. Release date: Oct. 4, 1996. Running time: 84 Min.
Cast: Hugh Grant, Gene Hackman, Sarah Jessica Parker, David Morse, Bill Nunn, Debra Monk, Paul Guilfoyle, John Toles-Bey.

Eye For An Eye

A Paramount Pictures presentation of a Michael I. Levy production. Producer: Michael I. Levy. Co-Producer: Michael Polaire. Director: John Schlesinger. Screenplay: Amanda Silver, Rick Jaffa based on the novel by Erika Holzer. Music: James Newton Howard. Running time: MPAA rating: R. Release date: January 12, 1996.
Cast: Sally Field, Kiefer Sutherland, Ed Harris, Beverly D'Angelo, Joe Mantegna.

Fair Game

A Warner Bros. Release of a Silver Pictures Production. Director: Andrew Sipes. Producer: Joel Silver. Screenplay: Charlie Fletcher, based on the novel by Paula Gosling. Camera: Richard Bowan. Music: Mark Mancina. Running time: 90 minutes. MPAA rating: R. Release date: November 3, 1995.
Cast: William Baldwin, Cindy Crawford, Steven Berkoff, Christopher McDonald.

A Family Thing

A Universal Artists Pictures presentation of a Todd Black & Randa Haines /Butchers Run Films production. Producers: Robert Duvall, Black, Haines. Director: Richard Pearce. Screenplay: Billy Bob

Thornton, Tom Epperson. Camera: Fred Charles Gross. Editor: Mark Warner. Music: Charles Gross. Running time: 109 minutes. MPAA rating: PG-13. Release date: March 23, 1996.
Cast: Robert Duvall, James Earl Jones, Michael Beach, Irma P. Hall, Grace Zabriskie.

The Fan

A Sony Pictures Entertainment release of a TriStar and Mandalay Entertainment presentation of a Wendy Finerman and Scott Free production. Producer: Finerman. Executive Producers: Bill Unger, James W. Skotchdopole, Barrie M. Osborne. Co-producer: Margaret French Isaacy. Director: Tony Scot. Screenplay: Phoef Sutton, based upon the novel by Peter Abrahams. Cinematography: (Technicolor, Panavision widescreen) Darius Wolski. Editor: Christian Wagner, Claire Simpson. Music: Hans Zimmer. MPAA Rating: R. Release date: August 12, 1996. Running time: 117 Min.
Cast: Robert DeNiro, Wesley Snipes, Ellen Barkin, John Leguizamo, Benicio DelToro, Patti D'Arbanville-Quinn, Chris Mulkey.

Father of The Bride II

A Buena Vista release of a Touchstone Pictures presentation of a Sandy Gallin production of a Nancy Meyers/Charles Shyer film. Producer: Meyers. Co-Producers: Cindy Williams, Bruce A. Block. Director: Shyer. Screenplay: Meyers, Shyer. Camera: William A. Fraker. Production designer: Linda DeScenna. Editor: Steven A. Rotter. Music: Alan Silvestri. Running time: 106 minutes. MPAA rating: PG. Release date: December, 8, 1995.
Cast: Steve Martin,. Dinae Keaton, Martin Short, Kimberly Williams, George Newbern, Kieran Culkin, B.D. Wong.

Fear

A Univeral Pictures release of an Imagine Entertainment presentation of a Brian Grazer production of a James Foley film. Producers: Grazer, Ric Kidney. Director: Foley. Screenplay: Christopher Crowe. Camera: Thomas Kloss. Production designer: Alex McDowell. Editor: Davod Brenner. Music: Carter Burwell. Running time: 98 minutes. MPAA rating: R. Release date: April 12, 1996.
Cast: Mark Wahlberg, Reese Witherspoon, William Petersen, Amy Brenneman, Alyssa Milano, Christopher Gray.

First Kid

A Buena Vista—Walt Disney—Caravan production. Producers: Roger Brinbaum, Riley Kathryn Ellis. Executive producers: Sinbad, Dale De La Torre, Tim Kelleher. Director: David Mickey Evans. Screenplay: Kelleher. Camera: Anthony B. Richmond. Editor: Harry Keramidas. Music: Richard Gibbs. Running time: 101 minutes. MPAA rating: PG.
Cast: Sinbad, Brock Pierce, RoBert Guillaume, Timothy Busfield.

The First Wives Club

A Paramount Pictures release of a Scott Rudin production. Producer: Rudin. Executive Producers: Ezra Swerdlo, Adam Schroeder. Co-producer: Thomas Imperato. Director: Hugh Wilson. Screenplay: Robert Harling, based on the novel by Olivia Goldsmith. Cinematography: Donald Thorin. Editor: John Bloom. Music: Marc Shaiman. MPAA Rating: PG. Release date: Sept. 11, 1996. Running time: 102 Min.
Cast: Goldie Hawn, Bette Midler, Diane Keaton, Maggie Smith, Sarah Jessica Parker, Dan Hedaya, Stockard Channing, Elizabeth Berkley, Marcia Gay Harden, Bronson Pinchot, Rob Reiner.

Fled

An MGM/UA release of an MGM presentation of a Frank Mancuso, Jr. production. Producer: Frank Mancuso, Jr. Director: Kevin Hooks. Screenplay: Preston A. Whitmore II. Camera: Matthew F. Leonetti. Editors: Richard Nord, Joseph Gutowski. Music: Graeme Revell. In Deluxe color. Running time: 98 minutes. MPAA Rating: R. Release date: July 9, 1996.
Cast: Laurence Fishburne, Stephen Baldwin, Salma Hayek, Will Patton, Robert John Burke, Robert Hooks, Victor Rivers, David Dukes.

Flipper

A Universal release, presented with the Bubble Factory, of an American Film/Perry Katz production. Producers: Katz, James J. McNamara. Director: Alan Shapiro. Screenplay: Shapiro, based upon the motion picture screenplay by Arthur Weiss and story by Ricou Browning, Jack Cowden. Camera: Bill Butler. Editor: Peck Prior. Music: Joel McNeely. Running time: 96 minutes. MPAA rating: PG. Release date: May 10, 1996.
Cast: Elijah Wood, Paul Hogan, Chelsea Field, Isaac Hayes.

Fly Away Home

A Columbia Pictures release. Producers: John Veitch, Carol Baum. Executive producer: Sandy Gallin. Director: Carol Ballard. Screenplay: Robert Rodat, Vince McKewin, based on the autobiography by Bill Lishman. Camera: Caleb Dechanel. Editor: Nicholas C. Smith. Music: Mark Isham. Running time: 110 minutes. MPAA rating: PG.
Cast: Jeff Daniels, Anna Paquin, Dana Delany, Terry Kinney.

The Frighteners

A Universal release of a Robert Zemeckis presentation of a Wingnut Films production. Producers: Jamie Selkirk, Peter Jackson. Director: Jackson. Screenplay: Fran Walsh, Jackson. Camera: Alun Bollinger, John Blick. Editor: Jamie Selkirk. Music: Danny Elfman. In Film Unit color, Film Facilities Ltd. widescreen. Running time: 109 minutes. MPAA Rating: R. Release date: July 11, 1996.
Cast: Michael J. Fox, Tini Alvarado, Peter Dobson, John Astin, Jeffrey Combs, Dee Wallace Stone, Jake Busey, Chi McBride.

Get on the Bus

A Sony Pictures Entertainment release from Columbia Pictures of a 15 Black Men production in association with 40 Acres & A Mule Filmworks. Producers: Reuben Cannon, Bill Borden, Barry Rosenbush. Executive producer: Spike Lee. Director: Spike Lee. Screenplay: Reggie Rock Bythewood. Cinematography: Elliot Davis. Editor: Leander T. Sales. Music: Terence Blanchard. MPAA Rating: R. Release date: Oct. 2, 1996. Running time: 120 Min.

Cast: Richard Belzer, DeAundre Bonds, Andre Braugher, Thomas Jefferson Byrd, Gabriel Casseus, Albert Hall, Hill Harper.

Get Shorty

An MGM Release of a Jersey Films Production. Producers: Danny DeVito Michael Shamber & Stacy Sher. Co-Producer: Graham Place. Director: Barry Sonnenfeld. Screenplay: Scott Frank, based on the novel by Elmore Leonard. Music: John Lurie. Release date: October 20, 1995.

Cast: John Travolta, Gene Hackman, Danny DeVito, Rene Russo, Delroy Lindo.

The Ghost and the Darkness

A Paramount Pictures release of a Constellation Films presentation of a Douglas/Reuther production. Producers: Gale Anne Hurd, Paul Radinm A. Kitman Ho. Executive Producers: Michael Douglas, Steven Reuther. Co-producer: Grant Hill. Director: Stephen Hopkins. Screenplay: William Goldman. Cinematography: Vilmos Zsigmond. Editors: Robert Brown, Steve Mirkovich. Music: Jerry Goldsmith. MPAA Rating: R. Release date: Oct. 11, 1996. Running time: 109 Min.

Cast: Michael Douglas, Val Kilmer, Tom Wilkinson, John Kani, Bernard Hill, Brian McCardle, Henry Cele, Om Puri, Emily Mortimer.

Glimmer Man

A Warner Bros. release of a Seagal/Nasso production. Producers: Steven Seagal, Julius R. Nasso. Executive producer: Michael Rachmil. Director: John Gray. Screenplay: Kevin Brodbin. Cinematography: Rick Botha. Editor: Donn Cambern. Music: Trevor Rabin. Technicolor. Panavision widescreen. MPAA Rating: R. Release date: Oct. 2, 1996. Running time: 84 Min.

Cast: Steven Seagal, Keenan Ivory Wayans, Bob Gundton, Brian Cox, Michelle Johnson, John Jackson, Stephen Tobolowsky.

Gold Diggers: The Secret of Bear Mountain

A Universal Pictures Releaseof a Bregamn/Deyhle Production. Director: Kevin James Dobson. Producers: Martin Bregman, Rolf Deyhle, Michael S. Bregman. Executive Producer: Louis A. Stroller. Screenplay: Barry Glesser. Camera: Ross Berryman. MPAA rating: PG.

Cast: Anna Chlumsky, Christina Ricci, Polly Draper, Brian Kerwin, Diana Scarwid, David Keith, Amy Kirk, Betty Phillips, Jay Brazeau.

GoldenEye

A United Artists release. Producers: Michael G. Wilson, Barbara Broccoli. Director: Martin Campbell. Screenplay: Jeffrey Caine, Bruce Feirstein. Story: Michael France. Camera: Phil Meheux. Editor: Terry Rawlings. Music: Eric Serra. MPAA rating: PG-13. Release date: November 17, 1995.

Cast: Pierce Brosnan, Sean Bean, Izabella Scorupco, Famke Janssen, Joe Don Baker.

The Great White Hype

A 20th Century Fox release of an Atman Entertainment/Fred Berner Films production. Producers: Berner, Joshua Donen. Director: Reginald Hudlin. Screenplay: Tony Hendra, Ron Shelton. Camera: Ron Garcia. Editor: Earl Watson. Music: Marcus Miller. Running time: 90 minutes. MPAA Rating: R. Release date: May 10, 1996.

Cast: Samuel L. Jackson, Jeff Goldblum, Peter Berg, Jon Lovitz, Corbin Bernsen, Cheech Marin, Damon Wayans.

Grumpier Old Men

A Warner Bros. presentation of a John David/Lancaster Gate production. Producers: John David, Richard C. Berman. Director: Howard Deutch. Co-Producer: George Folsey, Jr. Screenplay: Mark Steven Johnson. Camera: Tak Fujimoto. Music: Alan Silvestri. Production Design: Gary Frutkoff. Running time: 100 minutes. MPAA rating: PG-13. Release date: December 22, 1995.

Cast: Jack Lemmon, Walter Matthau, Ann-Margret, Sophia Loren, Kevin Pollak, Daryl Hannah.

Happy Gilmore

A Universal Pictures presentation of a Bernie Brillstein-Brad Grey/Robert Simonds production. Producer: Simonds. Director: Dennis Dugan. Screenplay: Tim Herlihy, Adam Sandler. Camera: Arthur Albert. Editor: Jeff Gourson. Music: Mark Mothersbaugh. Production Designers: Perry Andelin Blake, William Heslup. MPAA rating: PG-13. Release date: February 16, 1996.

Cast: Adam Sandler, Christopher MacDonald, Julie Bowen, Carl Weathers.

Harriet the Spy

A Paramount release, in association with Nickelodeon Movies, of a Rastar production. Producer: Marykay Powell. Director: Bronwen Hughes. Screenplay: Douglas Petrie, Theresa Rebeck, based on Greg Taylor and Julie Talen's adaptation of the novel by Louise Fitzhugh. Camera: Francis Kenny. Editor: Debra Chiate. Music: Jamshied Sharifi. Production Designer: Lester Cohen. Art Director: Paul Austerberry. In Deluxe color. Running time: 101 minutes. MPAA Rating: PG. Release date: June 19, 1996.

Cast: Michelle Trachtenberg, Rosie O'Donnell, Vanessa Lee Chester, Gregory Smith, J. Smith-Cameron, Robert Joy, Eartha Kitt.

Heat

A Warner Bros. release of a Forward Pass Production in association with New Regency Productions. Producers: Michael Mann, Arnon Milchan, Art Linson. Director: Michael Mann. Screenplay: Mann. Camera: Dante Spinotti. Production design: Neil Spisak. Editors: Dov Hoenig, Pasquale Buba, William Goldenberg, Tom Rolf. Music: Elliot Goldenthal. Running time: 169 minutes. MPAA rating: R. Release date: December 22, 1995.

Cast: Al Pacino, Robert De Niro, Val Kilmer, Jon Voight, Tom Sizemore, Diane Venora, Amy Brenneman, Ashley Judd, Mykelti Williamson, Wes Studi.

Home for the Holidays

A Paramount Pictures and Polygram Filmed Entertainment Release of an Egg Pictures Production. Director: Jodie Foster. Producers: Peggy Rajski, Jodie Foster. Camera: Lajos Koltai. Screenplay: W.D. Richter, based on a short story by Chris Radant. MPAA rating: PG-13. Release date: November 3, 1995.

Cast: Holly Hunter, Robert Downey, Jr., Anne Bancroft, Dylan McDermott, Geraldine Chaplin, Steve Guttenberg, Claire Danes, Cynthia Stevenson, Charles Durning.

Homeward Bound II: Lost in San Francisco

A Buena Vista release of a Walt Disney Pictures production. Producer: Barry Jossen. Co-producers: James Pentecost, Justis Greene. Director: David R. Ellis. Screenplay: Chris Hauty, Julie Hickson, based on characters from "The Incredible Journey" by Sheila Burnford. Camera: Jack Conroy. Editors: Peter E. Berger, Michael A. Stevenson. Animal Coordinator: Gary Gero. In Technicolor. Running time: 88 minutes. MPAA rating: G. Release date: March 6, 1996.

Cast: Robert Hays, Kim Greist, Veronica Lauren, Kevin Chevalia, Max Perlich. Voices: Michael J. Fox, Sally Field, Ralph Waite, Sinbad.

House Arrest

An MGM/UA release in association with Rysher Entertainment. Executive producer: Keith Samples. Producers: Judith A. Polone, Harry Winer. Director: Winer. Screenplay: Michael Hitchcock. CameraL Ueli Steiger. Editor: Ronald Roose. Music: Bruce Broughton. Running time: 108 minutes. MPAA rating: PG. Release date: August 14, 1996.

Cast: Jamie Lee curtis, Kevin Pollak, Jennifer Tilly, Christopher McDonald, Sheila McCarthy, Wallace Shawn, Ray Wlaston.

How to Make an American Quilt

A Universal Pictures release of an Amblin Entertainment production. Director: Jocelyn Moorhouse. Producers: Sarah Pillsbury and Midge Sanford. Screenplay: Jane Anderson, based on the novel by Whitney Otto. Music: Thomas Newman. Music Supervision: Tim Sexton. MPAA rating: PG-13. Release date: October 27, 1995.

Cast: Ellen Burstyn, Winona Ryder, Maya Angelou, Kate Capshaw, Loren Dean, Alfre Woodard, Kate Nelligan, Anne Bancroft, Samantha Mathis, Dermot Mulroney, Rip Torn.

The Hunchback of Notre Dame

A Buena Vista release of a Walt Disney Pictures presentation. Producer: Don Hahn. Directors: Gary Trousdale, Kirk Wise. Animation screenplay: Tab Murphy, Irene Mecchi, Bob Tzudiker, Noni White, Jonathan Roberts. Animation story by Murphy based on the novel "Notre Dame de Paris" by Victor Hugo. Score and music: Alan Menken. Lyrics: Stephen Schwartz. Editor: Ellen Keneshea. Art Director: David Goetz. In Technicolor. Running time: 86 minutes. MPAA Ratings: G. Release date: June 11, 1996.

Cast (voices): Tom Hulce, Demi Moore, Heidi Mollenhauer, Tony Jay, Kevin Kline, Paul Kandel, Jason Alexander, Charles Kimbrough.

If Lucy Fell

A Sony Pictures Entertainment release of a TriStar presentation of a Motion Picture Corp. of America production. Producers: Brad kevoy, Steve Stabler, Brad Jenkel. Director: Eric Schaeffer. Screenplay: Schaeffer, based on a story by Schaeffer, Tony Spiridakis. Camera: Ron Fortunato. Editor: Sue Graef. Music: Marry Me Jane, with Amanda Kravet, Charles Pettis. Production Designer: Ginger Tougas. In Technicolor. Running time: 94 minutes. MPAA rating: R. Release date: January 20, 1996.

Cast: Sarah Jessica Parker, Eric Schaeffer, Ben Stiller, Elle Macpherson, James Rebhorn, Dominic Luchese.

Independence Day

A 20th Century Fox release of a Centropolis Entertainment production. Producer: Dean Devlin. Director: Roland Emmerich. Screenplay: Devlin, Emmerich. Camera: Karl Walter Lindenlaub. Editor: David Brenner. Music: David Arnold. Production Designers: Oliver Scholl, Patrick Tatopoulos. Art Director: Jim Teegarden. In Deluxe color, Super 35 Panavision widescreen. Running time: 145 minutes. MPAA Rating: PG-13. Release date: June 25, 1996.

Cast: Will Smith, Bill Pullman, Jeff Goldblum, Mary McDonnell, Judd Hirsch, Margaret Colin, Randy Quaid, Robert Loggia, James Rebhorn, Harvey Fierstein, Adam Baldwin.

It Takes Two

A Warner Bros. release of a Rysher Entertainment presentation of an Orr & Cruikshank production in association with DualStar Productions. Producers: James Orr, Jim Cruikshank. Director: Andy Tennant. Screenplay: Deborah Dean Davis. Camera: Kenneth D. Zunder. Editor: Roger Bondelli. MPAA rating: PG. Release date: November 22, 1995.

Cast: Kirstie Alley, Steve Guttenberg, Mary-Kate and Ashley Olsen, Philip Bosco, Jane Sibbett.

It's My Party

An MGM/UA release of a UA presentation of an Opala production. Producers: Joel Thurm, Randal Kleiser. Director: Randal Kleiser. Camera: Bernd Heinl. Editor: Ila Von Hasperg. Music: Basil Poledouris. Production Designer: Clark Hunter. In Deluxe color. Running time: 110 minutes. MPAA rating: R. Release date: January, 1996.

Cast: Eric Roberts, Gregory Harrison, Lee Grant, Marlee Matlin, Paul Regina, Margaret Cho, Bronson Pinchot, Geroge Segal.

Jack

A Buena Vista release of a Hollywood Pictures presentation of an american Zoetrope/Great Oaks production. Producers: Ricardo Mestres, Fred Fuchs, Francis Ford Coppola. Director: Coppola. Screenplay: James DeMonaco, Gary Nadeau. Camera: John Toll. Editor: Barry Malkin. Music: Michael Kamen. Production Designer: Dean Tavoularis. In Foto-Kem color; Technicolor prints. Running time: 113 minutes. MPAA Rating: PG-13. Release date: July 25, 1996.

Cast: Robin Williams, Diane Lane, Brian Kerwin, Fran Drescher, Bill Cosby, Michael McKean, Don Novello, Allan Rich.

Jade

A Paramount release of a Robert Evans and an Adelson/Baumgarten production. Director: William Friedkin. Producers: Robert Evans, Craig Baumgarten, Gary Adelson. Screenplay: Joe Eszterhas. Camera: Andrej Bartkowiak. Editor: Augie Hess. Running time: 95 minutes. MPAA rating: R. Release date:

Cast: David Caruso, Linda Fiorentino, Chazz Palminteri, Michael Biehn, Richard Crenna, David Hunt, Angie Everhart, Kevin Tighe.

James And The Giant Peach

A Buena Vista release of a Walt Disney Pictures presentation in association with Allied Filmmakers. Producers: Denise Di Novi, Tim Burton. Director: Henry Selick. Screenplay: Karey Kirkpatrick, Jonathan Roberts, Steve Bloom, based on the book by Roald Dahl. Camera: Pete Kozachik, hiro Narita. Editor: Stan Webb. Music: Randy Newman. Animation Supervisor: Paul Berry. Running time: 80 minutes. MPAA rating: PG. Release date: April 5, 1996.

Cast: (Voice) Simon Callow, Richard Dreyfuss, Jane Leeves, Joanna Lumley, Susan Sarandon, Pete Postlethwaite, David Thewlis.

Joe's Apartment

A Warner Bros. release of a Geffen Pictures presentation of an MTV production. Producers: Diana Phillips, Bonni Lee. Director-Writer: John Payson. Camera: Peter Deming. Editor: Peter Frank. Music: Carter Burwell. Production Designer: Carol Spier. In color. Running time: 80 minutes. MPAA rating: PG-13. Release date: July 25, 1996.

Cast: Jerry O'Connell, Megan Ward, Jim Sterling, Shiek Mahmud-Bey, Jim Turner, Sandra Denton, Robert Vaughn, Don Ho, David Huddelson.

Jumanji

A TriStar release of an Interscope Communications/Teitler Film Production of a Joe Johnston film. Producers: Scott Kroopf, William Teitler. Director: Joe Johnston. Screenplay: Jonathan Hensleigh, Greg Taylor, Jim Strain, based on the book by Chris Van Allsburg. Camera: Thomas Ackerman. Production design: James Bissell. Editor: Robert Dalva. Music: James Horner. Running time: 100 minutes. MPAA rating: PG. Release date: December 20, 1995

Cast: Robin Williams, Bonnie Hunt, Jonathan Hyde, Kirsten Dunst, Bradley Pierce, Bebe Neuwirth, David Alan Grier.

The Juror

A Columbia Pictures release of an Irwin Winkler Production. Producers: Winkler, Rob Cowan. Director: Brian Gibson. Screenplay: Ted Tally, based on the book by George Dawes green. Camera: Jamie Anderson. Editor: Robert Reitano. Music: James Newton Howard. In Technicolor. Running time: 116 minutes. MPAA rating: R. Release date: January 26, 1996.

Cast: Demi Moore, Alec Baldwin, Joeph Gordon-Levitt, Anne Heche, James Gandolfini, Lindsay Course, Tony Lo Bianco, Michael Constatine.

Kazaam

A Buena Vista release of a Touchstone Pictures presentation of an Interscope Communications/Polygram Filmed Entertainment production. Producers: Scott Kroopf, Paul M. Glaser, Bob Engelman. Director: Glaser. Screenplay: Christian Ford, Roger Soffer, from a story by Glaser. Camera: Charles Minsky. Editor: Michael E. Polokow. Music: Christopher Tyng. In Technicolor. Running time: 93 minutes. MPAA Rating: PG. Release date: July 15, 1996.

Cast: Shaquille O'Neal, Francis Capra, Ally Walker, Marashall Manesh, James Acheson, Fawn Reed, John Costelloe.

Kids In The Hall: Brain Candy

A Paramount release of a Lakeshore Entertainment presentation of a Lorne Michaels production. Producers: Barnaby Thompson, Richard S. Wright. Director: Kelly Makin. Screenplay: Norm Hiscock, Bruce McCulloch, Kevin McDonald, Mark McKinney, Scott Thompson. Camera: David Makin. Editor: Christopher Cooper. Music: Craig Northey. Running time: 88 minutes. MPAA rating: R. Release date: April 18, 1996.

Cast: David Foley, Bruce McCulloch, Kevin McDonald, Mark McKinney, Scott Thompson, Janeane Garofalo.

Kingpin

An MGM/UA release of a Rysher Entertainmetn presentation of a Motion Picture Corp. of America production. Directors: Peter Farrelly, Bobby Farrelly. Producers: Brad Krevoy, Steve Stabler, Bradley

Thomas. Screenplay: Barry Fanaro, Mort Nathan. Camera: Mark Irwin. Editor: Christopher Greenbury. Music: Freedy Johnston. In Foto-Kem color. Running time: 113 minutes. MPAA Rating: PG-13. Release date: June 14, 1996.

Cast: Woody Harrleson, Randy Quaid, Vanessa Angel, Bill Murray, Chris Elliot, William Jordan, Richard Tyson.

Last Dance

A Buena Vista release of a Touchstone Pictures presentation of a Steven Haft production. Producer: Haft. Director: Bruce Beresford. Screenplay: Ron Koslow. Story: Haft, Koslow. Camera: Peter James. Editor: John Bloom. Music: Mark Isham. Production Design: John Stoddart. Running time: 103 minutes. MPAA rating: R. Release date: April 26, 1996.

Cast: Sharon Stone, Rob Morrow, Randy Quaid, Peter Gallagher, Jack Thompson, Jayne Brook.

Leaving Las Vegas

An MGM/UA release of a United Artists/Lumiere Pictures production. Producers: Lila Cazes & Annie Stewart. Director & Writer: Mike Figgis, based on the novel by John O'Brien. Camera: Declan Quinn. Music: Figgis. Editor: John Smith. Running time: 112 minutes. MPAA rating: R. Release date: October 27, 1995.

Cast: Nicholas Cage, Elisabeth Shue, Julian Sands, Valerie Golino, Richard Lewis, Laurie Metcalf, Lou Rawls.

Matilda

A Sony Pictures Entertainment release from TriStar Pictures of a Jersey Films production. Producers: Danny DeVito, Michael Shamberg, Stacey Sher, Liccy Dahl. Director: DeVito. Screenplay: Nicholas Kazan, Robin Swicord, based on the novel by roald Dahl. Camera: Stefan Czapsky. Editors: Lynzee Klingman, Brent White. Music: David Newman. In Technicolor. Running time: 93 minutes. MPAA Rating: PG. Release date: July 12, 1996.

Cast: Mara Wilson, Danny DeVito, Rhea Perlman, Paul Reubens, Tracey Walter, Brian Levinson, Kira Spencer Hesser, Kiami Davael.

Maximum Risk

A Sony Pictures Entertainment release of a Columbia Pictures presentation of a Roger Birnbaum/Moshe Diamant production. Producer: Diamant. Executive producer: Birnbaum. Co-producer: Jason Clark. Director: Ringo Lam. Screenplay: Larry Ferguson. Cinematography: Alexander Gruszynski. Editor: Bill Pankow. Music: Robert Folk. Deluxe color, Panavision widescreen. MPAA Rating: R. Release date: Sept. 8, 1996. Running time: 100 Min.

Cast: Jean Claude Van Damme, Natasha Henstridge, Zach Grenier, Jean Hugues Anglade, Paul Ben Victor, Frank Senger.

Mission: Impossible

A Paramount Pictures release. Executive producer: Paul Hitchcock. Producers: Tom Cruise, Paula Wagner. Director: Brian De Palma. Screenplay: David Koepp, Robert Towne, story by Koepp, Steven Zaillian based on the television series created by Bruce Geller. Camera: Stephn H. Burum. Editor: Paul Hirsch. Music: Danny Elfman. Running time: 111 minutes. MPAA rating: PG-13.

Cast: Tom Cruise, Jon Voight, Emmanuelle Beart, Herny Czerny, Jean Reno, Ving Rhames, Vanessa Redgrave, Kristin Scott-Thomas.

Moll Flanders

An MGM/UA release of a Metro-Goldwyn-Mayer Pictures presentation, in association with Spelling Films, of a Trilogy Entertainment Group production. Producers: John Watson, Richard B. Lewis, Pen Densham. Director-Writer: Densham. Story based on the character from the novel by Daniel Defoe. Camera: David Tattersall. Editors: Neil Travis, James R. Symons. Music: Mark Mancina. In Deluxe color, Panavision widescreen. Running time: 123 minutes. MPAA Rating: PG-13. Release date: May 21, 1996.

Cast: Robin Wright, Morgan Freeman, Stockard Channing, John Lynch.

Money Train

A Columbia Pictures presentation of a Peter Entertainment production of a Joseph Burden film. Producers: Jon Peters, Neil Canton. Director: Joseph Ruben. Screenplay: Doug Richardson, David Loughery, based on the story by Richardson. Camera: John W. Lindley. Editors: Geroge Bowers, Bill Pankow. MPAA rating: R. Release date: November 17, 1995.

Cast: Wesley Snipes, Woody Harrelson, Jennifer Lopez, Robert Blake, Chris Cooper.

Mother

A Paramount release of a Scott Rudin production. Producers: Rudin, Herb Nanas. Director: Albert Brooks. Screenplay: Brooks, Monica Johnson. Cinematography: Lajos Koltai. Editor: Harvey Rosenstock. Music: Marc Shaiman. Deluxe color. Release date: Sept. 7, 1996. Running time: 104 Min.

Cast: Albert Brooks, Debbie Reynolds, Rob Morrow, Lisa Kudrow, John C. McGinley, Isabel Glasser, Peter White

Mr. Holland's Opus

A Buena Vista release from Hollywood Pictures of an Interscope Communications/Polygram Filmed Entertainment production in association with the Charlie Mopic Co. Producers: Ted Field, Michael Nolin, Robert W. Cort. Director: Stephen Herek. Screenplay: Patrick Sheane Duncan. Camera: Oliver Wood. Editor: Trudy Ship. Music: Michael Kamen. Music Sueprvisor: Sharon Boyle. In Technicolor, Panavision. Running time: 142 minutes. MPAA rating: PG. Release date: January 3, 1996.

Cast: Richard Dreyfuss, Glenne Headley, Jay Thomas, Olympia Dukakis, W.H. Macy, Alicia Witt, Jean Louisa Kelly, Nicholas John Renner, Joseph Anderson, Anthony Natale.

Mr. Wrong

A Buena Vista release of a Touchstone Pictures presentation of a Mandeville Films/Marty Katz production. Producer: Katz. Director: Nick Castle. Screenplay: Chris Matheson, Kerry Ehrin, Craig Muson. Camera: John Schwartzman. Editor: Patrick Kennedy. Music: Craig Safan. Production Designer: Doug Kraner. Running time: 96 minutes. MPAA rating: PG-13. Release date: February 16, 1996.

Cast: Ellen deGeneres, Bill Pullman, Joan Cusack, Dean Stockwell, Joan Plowright, John Livingston, Robert Goulet, Ellen Cleghorne.

Mrs. Winterbourne

A TriStar release of an A7M Films production. Producers: Dale Pollock, Ross Canter, Oren Koules. Director: Richard Benjamin. Screenplay: Phoef Sutton, Lisa-Marie Radano, based on the novel "I Married a Dead Man" by Cornell Woolrich. Camera: Alex Nepomniaschy. Editors: Jacqueline Cambas, William Fletcher. Music: Patrick Doyle. Running time: 104 minutes. MPAA rating: PG-13. Release date: April 18, 1996.

Cast: Shirley MacLaine, Ricki Lake, Brendan Fraser, Miguel Sandoval, Loren Dean, Peter Gerety.

Mulholland Falls

An MGM/UA release of an MGM presentation in association with Largo Entertainment and the Zanuck Co. Producers: Richard D. Zanuck, Lili Fini Zanuck. Director: Lee Tamahori. Screenplay: Pete Dexter, story by Dexter, Floyd Mutrux. Camera: Haskell Wexler. Editor: Sally Menke. Music: Dave Grusin. Running time: 107 minutes. MPAA rating: R. Release date: April 26, 1996.

Cast: Nick Nolte, Melanie Griffith, Chazz Palminteri, Michael Madsen, Chris Penn, Treat Williams, Jennifer Connelly, Daniel Bladwin, Andrew McCarthy,John Malkovich, Bruce Dern.

Multiplicity

A Sony Pictures Entertainment release of a Columbia Pictures presentation of a Trevor Albert production. Producers: Trevor Albert, Harold Ramis. Director: Harold Ramis. Screenplay: Chris Miller, Mary Hale, Lowell Ganz, Babaloo Mandel, based on the short story by Miller. Camera: Laszlo Kovacs. Editors: Pem Herring, Craig Herring. Music: George Fenton. In Technicolor, Panavision widescreen. Running time: 117 minutes. MPAA Rating: PG-13. Release date: July 1, 1996.

Cast: Michael Keaton, Andie MacDowell, Harris Yulin, richard Masur, Eugene Levy, Ann Cusack, John de Lancie, Brian Doyle.

Muppet Treasure Island

A Walt Disney Pictures presentation from Jim Henson Productions of a Brian Henson film. Producers: Martin G. Baker and Brian Henson. Director: Brain Henson. Camera: John Fenner. Screenplay: Jerry Juhl, Kirk R. Thatcher, James V. Hart, suggested by the story by Robert Louis Stevenson. Editor: Michael Jablow. Music: Hans Zimmer. Song Composers: Barry Mann, Cynthia Weil. Running time: 98 minutes. MPAA rating: G. Release date: February 16, 1996.

Cast: Tim Curry, Kevin Bishop, Billy Connolly, Jennifer Saunders; (voices): Steve Whitmire, Frank Oz, Dave Goelz, Jerry Nelson.

Nick of Time

A Paramount release. Producer: John Badham. Executive producer: D.J. Caruso. Director: Badham. Screenplay: Patrick Sheane Duncan. Camera: Roy H. Wagner. Editor: Frank Morriss. Music: Arthur B. Rubinstein. DeLuxe color. Running time: 89 minutes. MPAA rating: R. Release date: December, 13, 1995.

Cast: Johnny Depp, Christopher Walken, Charles S. Dutton, Peter Strauss, Roma Maffia, Gloria Reuben, Marsha Mason, Courtney Chase.

Nixon

A Buena Vista release from Hollywood Pictures of an Andrew G. Vajna presentation of an Illusion Entertainment Group/Cinergi production. Producers: Clayton Townsend, Oliver Stone, Stone. Screenplay: Stephen J. Rivele, Christopher Wilkinson, Stone. Camera: Robert Richardson. Editors: Brian Berdan, Hank Corwin. In Technicolor, B&W, Panavision. Running time: 190 minutes. MPAA rating: R. Release date: December 15, 1995.

Cast: Anthony Hopkins, Joan Allen,. Powers Boothe, Ed Harris, Bob Hoskins, E.G. Marshall, David Paymer, David Hyde Pierce, Paul Sorvino, Mary Steenburgen, J.T. Walsh, James Woods.

The Nutty Professor

A Universal Release of an Image Entertainment presentation. Producers: Brian Grazer, Russel Simmons. Director: Tom Shadyac. Screenplay: David Sheffield, Barry W. Blaustein, Shadyac, Steve Oedekerk, based on the motion picture written by Jerry Lewis and Bill Richmond. Camera: Julio Macat. Editor: Don Zimmerman. Music: David Newman. In Deluxe Color. Running time: 95 minutes. MPAA Rating: PG-13. Release date: June 11, 1996.

Cast: Eddie Murphy, Jada Pinkett, James Coburn, Larry Miller, Dave Chappelle, John Ales.

Original Gangstas

An Orion release of a Po'Boy production. Producer: Fred Williamson. Director: Larry Cohen. Screenplay: Aubrey Rattan. Camera: Carlos Gonzalez. Editors: David Kern, Peter B. Ellis. Music: Vladimir Horunzy. Running time: 98 minutes. MPAA rating: R. Release date: April 2, 1996.

Cast: Fred Williamson, Jim Brown, Pam Grier, Paul Winfield.

Othello

A Columbia Pictures release of a Castle Rock Entertainment presentation of a Dakota Films/Imminent Films production. Producers: Luc Roeg, David Barron,. Director: Oliver Parker. Camera: David Johnson. Production design: Tim Harvey. Editor: Tony Lawson. Music: Charlie Mole. Costumes: Caroline Harris. Running time: 124 minutes. MPAA rating: R. Release date: December 22, 1995.

Cast: Laurence Fishburne, Irene Jacob, Kenneth Branagh, Nathaniel Parker, Michael Maloney, Anna Patrick.

The Phantom

A Paramount release, presented in association with Robert Evans and the Ladd Co., of a Village Roadshow production. Producers: Robert Evans, Alan Ladd, Jr. Director: Simon Wincer. Screenplay: Jeffrey Boam, based on characters created by Lee Falk. Camera: David Burr. Editor: O. Nicholas Brown. Music: David Newman. In Deluxe color, Panavision, widescreen. Running time: 100 minutes. MPAA Rating: PG. Release date: June 5, 1996.

Cast: Billy Zane, Kristy Swanson, Treat Williams, Catherine Zeta-Jones, James Remar, Cary-Hiroyuki Tagawa, Samantha Eggar, Patrick McGoohan.

Phenomenon

A Buena Vista release of a Touchstone Pictures presentation of a Barbara Boyle and Michael Taylor production. Producers: Barbara Boyle, Michael Taylor. Director: Jon Turteltaub. Screenplay: Gerald DiPego. Camera: Phedon Papamichael. Editor: Bruce Green. Music: Thomas Newman. In Foto-Kem color, Technicolor prints; Panavision widescreen. Running time: 124 minutes. MPAA Rating: PG. Release date: June 17, 1996.

Cast: John Travolta, Robert Duvall, Forest Whitaker, Kyra Sedgewick.

Powder

A Buena Vista release of a Hollywood Pictures presentation in association with Caravan Pictures of a Roger Birnbaum/Daniel Grodnik production. Producers: Roger Birnbaum and Daniel Grodnik. Director & Writer: Victor Salva. Camera: Jerzy Zielinski. Music: Jerry Goldsmith. Editor: Dennis M. Hill. Running time: 111 minutes. MPAA rating: PG-13. Release date: October 27, 1995.

Cast: Mary Steenburgen, Sean Patrick Flannery, Lance Henriksen, Jeff Goldblum, Brandon Smith, Branford Tatum, Susan Tyrrell.

Primal Fear

A Paramount release presented in association with Rysher Entertainment of a Gary Lucchesi production. Producer: Lucchesi. Director: Gregory Hoblit. Screenplay: Steve Shagan, Ann Biderman, based on the novel by Willliam Diehl. Camera: Michael Chapman. Editor: David Rosenbloom. Music: James Newton Howard. Running time: 129 minutes. MPAA rating: R. Release date: March 29, 1996.

Cast: Richard Gere, Laura Linney, John Mahoney, Alfre Woodard, Frances McDormand, Edward Norton, Andre Braugher.

The Proprietor

A Warner Bros. release of a Merchant Ivory production. Producers: Humbert Balsan, Donald Rosenfeld. Executive Producers: Paul Bradley, Osman Eralp. Director: Ismail Merchant. Screenplay: Jean-Marie Besset, George Trow. Cinematography: Larry Pizer. Editor: William Webb. Music: Richard Robbins. MPAA Rating: R. Release date: Oct. 1, 1996. Running time: 102 Min.

Cast: Jeanne Moreau, Sean Young, Sam Waterston, Christopher Cazenove, Nell Carter, Jean Pierre Aumont, Austin Pendelton.

The Quest

A Universal release of an MDP Worldwide presentation of a Moshe Diamant production. Producer: Diamant. Director: Jean Claude Van Damme. Screenplay: Stuart Klein, Paul Mones. Story: Frank Dux, Van Damme. Camera: David Gribble. Editor: John F. Link. Music: Randy Newman. Running time: 93 minutes. MPAA rating: PG-13. Release date: April 26, 1996.

Cast: Jean Claude Van Damme, Roger Moore, James Remar, Janet Gunn, Jack McGee, Abdel Qissi.

Race The Sun

A Sony Pictures release of a TriStar Pictures presentation of a Morrow/Heus production. Producers: Richard Heus, Barry Morrow. Director: Charles T. Kanganis. Screenplay: Morrow. Camera: David Burr. Editor: WEndy Greene Bricmont. Music: Graeme Revell. Running time: 99 minutes. MPAA rating: PG. Release date: March 14, 1996.

Cast: Halle Berry, James Belushi, Casey Affleck, Eliza Dushku.

The Rich Man's Wife

A Buena Vista release of a Hollywood Pictures presentation in association with Caravan Pictures. Producers: Roger Birnbaum, Julie Bergman Sender. Executive producer: Jennifer Ogden. Director: Amy Holden Jones. Screenplay: Holden Jones. Cinematography: Haskell Wexler. Editor: Wendy Greene Bricmont. Music: John Frizzell. Music: James Newton Howard. MPAA Rating: R. Release date: Sept. 11, 1996. Running time: 94 Min.

Cast: Halle Berry, Christoper McDonald, Clive Owen, Peter Greene, Charles Hallahan, Frankie Faison, Clea Lewis.

Richard III

An MGM/UA release of a United Artists Pictures presentation with the participation of British Screen of a Bayly/Pare production developed in association with First Look Pictures. Producers: Lisa Katselas Pare, Stephen Bayly. Director: Richard Loncraine. Screenplay: Ian McKellen,

Loncraine, based on a stage production by Richard Eyre of the play by William Shakespeare. Camera: Peter Biziou. Editor: Paul Green. Music: Trevor Jones. In Technicolor. Running time: 105 minutes. MPAA rating: R. Release date: December 28, 1995.

Cast: Ian McKellen, Annette Bening, Jim Broadbent, Robert Downey Jr., Nigel Hawthorne, Kristin Scott Thomas, Maggie Smith, John Wood.

The Rock

A Buena Vista release of a Hollywood Pictures presentation of a Don Simpson and Jerry Bruckheimer production. Producers: Don Simpson, Jerry Bruckheimer. Director: Michael Bay. Screenplay: David Weisberg, Douglas S. Cook, Mark Rosner, based on a story by Weisberg, Cook. Camera: John Schwartzzman. Editor: Richard Francis-Bruce. Music: Nick Glennie-Smith. Hans Zimmer. Production Designer: Michael White. Art Director: Ed McAvoy. In Technicolor, Panavision widescreen. Running time: 136 minutes. MPAA Rating: R.

Cast: Sean Connery, Nicholas Cage, Ed Harris, Michael Biehn, William Forsythe, David Morse, John Spencer, John C. McGinley.

Sabrina

A Paramount Pictures release in association with Constellation Films of a Mirage/Scott Rudin/Sandollar production of a Sydney Pollack Film. Producers: Rudin, Pollack. Director: Pollack. Screenplay: Barbara Benedeck, David Rayfiel, based on the film written by Billy Wilder, Samuel Taylor, Ernest Lehman from the play by Taylor. Camera: Guiseppe Rotunno. Editor: Frederic Steinkamp. Music: John Williams. Running time: 127 minutes. MPAA rating: R. Release date: December 15, 1995.

Cast: Harrison Ford, Julia Ormond, Greg Kinnear, Nancy Marchand, John Wood, Richard Crenna, Angie Dickinson, Lauren Holly.

The Scarlet Letter

A Buena Vista release from Hollywood Pictures of an Andrew G. Vajna presentation of a Lighmotive/Allied Stars/Cinergi/Moving Pictures production. Director: Roland Joffe. Producers: Joffe, Vajna. Co-producer: Robert Colesberry. Screenplay: Douglas Day Stewart, freely adapted from the novel by Nathaniel Hawthorne. Camera: Alex Thomson. Editor: Thom Noble. Running time: 135 minutes, MPAA rating: R. Release date:

Cast: Gary Oldman, Robert Duval, Demi Moore, Joan Plowright, Amy Wright, Robert Prosky, Edward Hardwick.

Sense and Sensibility

A Columbia release of a Mirage production. Producer: Lindsay Doran. Co-producers: James Schamus, Laurie Borg. Director: Ang Lee. Screenplay: Emma Thompson, based on the novel by Jane Austen. Camera: Michael Coulter. Editor: Tim Squyres. Art Direction: Philip Elton. In technicolor. Running Time: 135 minutes. MPAA rating: PG. Release date: December , 1995.

Cast: Emma Thompson, Alan Rickman, Kate Winslet, hugh Grant, James Fleet, Harriet Walter, Gemma Jones, Elizabeth Spriggs.

Sgt. Bilko

A Universal release of an Imagine Entertainment presentation of a Brian Grazer production. Producer: Grazer. Director: Jonathan Lynn. Screenplay: Andy Breckman, based on the television series created by Nat Hiken. Camera: Peter Sova. Editor: Tony Lombardo. Music: Alan Silvestri. Running time: 94 minutes. MPAA rating: PG. Release date: March 27, 1996.

Cast: Steve Martin, Dan Ackroyd, Phil Hartman, Glenne Headly.

Solo

A Sony Pictures Entertainment release of a Triumph Films presentation of an Orpheus Films-John Flock production in association with Can Peebles Films. Producers: Joseph Newton Cohen, Flock. Co-producers: Jose Ludlow, Gina Resnick. Director: Norberto barba. Screenplay: David Corley, based on the novel "Weapon" by Robert Mason. Camera: Chris Walling. Editor: Scott Conrad. Music: Christopher Frank. Running time: 94 minutes. MPAA rating: PG-13. Release date: August 22, 1996.

Cast: Mario Van Peebles, Barry Corbin, Bill Sadler, Adrien Brody, Seidy Lopez, Abraham Verduzco.

The Spitfire Grill

A Colmbia Pictures release of a Castle Rock Entertainment presentations. Executive producer: Warren G. Stitt. ProducerL Forrest Murray. Co-producers: Edward E. Vaughan, Marci Liroff. Director: Lee David Zlotoff. Screenplay: Zlotoff. Camera: Robert Draper. Editor: Margie Goodspeed. Music: James Horner. Running time: 111 minutes. MPAA Rating: R. Release date: September 6, 1996.

Cast: Alison Elliott, Ellen Burstyn, Marcia Gay Harden, Will Patton, Kieran Mulroney, Gallard Sartain.

Spy Hard

A Buena Vista release of a Hollywood Pictures prsentation of a Friedberg/Draizin/Konvitz production. Producers: Rick Friedberg, Doug Draizin, Jeffrey Konvitz. Director: Rick Friedberg. Screenplay: Friedberg, Dick Chudnow, Jason Friedberg, Aaron Seltzer, from a story by Jason Friedberg, Seltzer. Camera: John R. Leonetti. Editor: Eric Sears. Music: Bill Conti. In Technicolor. Running time: 80 minutes. MPAA Rating: PG-13. Release date: May 20, 1996.

Cast: Leslie Nielsen, Nicollette Sheridan, Charles Durning, Marcia Gay Harden, Barry Bostwick, John Ales, Andy Griffith, Elya Baskin.

Strange Days

A Twentieth Century Fox presentation of a Lightstorm Entertainment producrtion of a Kathryn Bigelow Film. Producers: James Cameron,

Steven-Charles Jaffe. Director: Kathryn Bigelow. Screenplay: Cameron, Jay Cocks based on a story by Cameron. Camera: Matthew F. Leonetti. Editor: Howard Smith. Music: Graeme Revell. Production Design: Lilly Kilvert. MPAA rating: R. Release date: October, 20, 1995.

Cast: Ralph Fiennes, Angela Bassett, Juliette Lewis, Tom Sizemore, Vincent D'Onofrio, Michael Wincott.

Striptease

A Sony Pictures Entertainment release from Columbia Pictures of a Castle Rock Entertainment presentation of a Lobell/Berman production. Producer: Mike Lobell. Director-Writer: Andrew Bergman, based on the book by Carl Hiaasen. Camera: Stephen Goldblatt. Editor: Anne V. Coates. Music: Howard Shore. In Technicolor. Running time: 115 minutes. MPAA Rating: R. Release date: June 19, 1996.

Cast: Demi Moore, Armand Assante, Ving Rhames, Robert Patrick, Burt Reynolds, Paul Guilfoyle, Jerry Grayson, Rumer Willis.

The Substitute

An Orion Pictures release of a Live Entertainment presentation of a Dinamo/H2 production. Producers: Morrie Eisenmann, Jim Steele. Director: Robert Mandel. Screenplay: Roy Frumkes, Rocco SImonello, Alan Ormsby. Cameria: Bruce Surtees. Editor: Alex Mackie. Music: Gary Chang. Running time: 114 minutes. MPAA rating: R. Release date: April 15, 1996.

Cast: Tom Berenger, Ernie Hudson, Diane Venora, Marc Anthony, William Forsythe.

Sudden Death

A Universal release of a Signature/Baldwin Cohen production in association with Imperial Entertainment. Producers: Moshe Diamant, Howard Baldwin. Director: Peter Hyams. Screenplay: Gene Quintano, based on a story by Karen Baldwin. Camera: Hyams. Editor: Steven Kemper. In Deluxe color. Running time: 110 minutes. MPAA rating: R. Release date: December 22, 1995.

Cast: Jean Claude Van Damme, Powers Boothe, Raymond J. Barry, Whittni Wright, Ross Malinger, Dorian Harewood, Kate McNeil.

Sunset Park

A Sony release of a TriStar presentation of a Jersey Films production in association with Daniel A. Paulson Prods. Producers: Danny DeVito, Michael Shamberg, Paulson. Director: Steve Gomer. Screenplay: Set Zvi Rosenfeld, Kathleen McGhee-Anderson. Camera: Robbie Greenberg. Editor: Arthur Coburn. Music: Miles Goodman, Kay Gee. Running time: 99 minutes. MPAA rating: R. Release date: April 26, 1996.

Cast: Rhea Perlman, Fredro Starr, Carol Kane, Terrence Dashon Howard, Camille Saviola.

Surviving Picasso

A Warner Bros. release of a Merchant Ivory/Wolper production. Executive producers: Donald Rosenfeld, Paul Bradley. Producers: Ismail Merchant, David L. Wolper. Co-producer: Humbert Balsan. Directed: James Ivory. Screenplay: Ruth Prawwer Jhabvala. Camera: Tony Pierce-Roberts. Editor: Andrew Marcus. Music: Richard Robbins. Production Design: Luciana Arrighi. Costume Design: Carol Ramsey. MPAA Rating: NR. Released Sept. 4, 1996. Running time: 123 Min.

Cast: Anthony Hopkins, Natascha McElhone, Julianne Moore, Joss Ackland, Peter Eyre, Diane Venora, Joan Plowright.

Sweet Nothing

A Warner Bros. release of a Concrete Films production. Executive producer: Mark Ross. Producers: Rick Bowman, Gary Winick. Co-producer: Richie Vetter. Director: Winick. Screenplay: Lee Drysdale. Camera: Makoto Waranabe. Editor: Niels Mueller. Music: Steven M. Stern. Running time: 90 minutes. MPAA rating: R.

Cast: Michael Imperioli, Mira Sorvino, Paul Calderon.

Tales Fom the Crypt Presents Bordello of Blood

A Universal release. Producer: Gilbrt Adler. Executive producers: Richard Donner, David Giler, Walter Gill, Joel Silver, Robert Zemeckis. Co-producers: A.L. Katz, Alexander Collett. Director: Adler. Screenplay: A.L. Katz, Adler, from a story by Bob Glae, Zemeckis. Camera: Tom Priestly. Editor: Stephen Lovejoy. Music: Chris Boardman. Running time: 87 minutes. MPAA rating: R. Release date: August 14, 1996.

Cast: Dennis Miller, Erika Eleniaki, Angie Everhart, Chris Sarandon, Corey Feldman, Aubrey Morris, William Sadler.

That Thing You Do

A 20th Century Fox release of a Clinica Estetico production in association with Claudius Base. Producers: Gary Goetzman, Jonathan Demme, Edward Saxon. Director: Tom Hanks. Screenplay: Hanks. Cinematography: Tak Fujimoto. Editor: Richard Chew. Music: Howard Shore. MPAA Rating: PG. Release date: Oct. 4, 1996. Running time: 110 Min.

Cast: Liv Tyler, Johnathon Schaech, Steve Zahn, Ethan Embry, Tom Hanks, Chris Ellis, Peter Scolari, Rita Wilson, Chris Isaak, Kevin Pollak.

A Time To Kill

A Warner Bros. release presented in association with Regency Enterprises of an Arnon Milchan production. Producers: Arnon Milchan, Michael Nathanson, Hunt Lowery, John Grisham. Director: Joel Schumacher. Screenplay: Akiva Goldman, based on the novel by John Grisham. Camera: Peter Menzies, Jr. Editor: William Steinkamp. Music: Elliot Goldenthal. In Technicolor, Panavision widescreen. Running time: 150 minutes. MPAA rating: R. Release date: June 21, 1996.

Cast: Sandra Bullock, Samuel L. Jackson, Matthew McConaughey, Kevin Spacey, Brenda Fricker, Oliver Platt, Charles S. Dutton, Ashley Judd, Patrick McGoohan, Donald Sutherland, Kiefer Sutherland.

Tin Cup

A Warner Bros. release, presented in association with Regency Enterprises. of a Gary Foster production. Producers: Gary Foster, Ron Shelton. Director: Shelton. Screenplay: John Norville, Shelton. Camera: Russell Boyd. Editors: Paul Seydor, Kimberly Ray. Music: William Ross. Production Designer: James Bissell. Art Director: Gae Buckley. In Technicolor, Panavision widescreen. Running time: 133 minutes. MPAA Rating: R. Release date: July 29, 1996.

Cast: Kevin Costner, Rene Russo, Cheech Marin, Linda Hart, Don Johnson, Dennis Burkley, Rex Linn, Lou Myers, Richard Lineback.

Tom and Huck

A Buena Vista release of a Walt Disney Pictures presentation. Producers: Laurence Mark, John Baldecchi. Director: Peter Hewitt. Screenplay: Stephen Sommers, David Loughery, based on the novel "The Adventures of Tom Sawyer" by Mark Twain. Cinematogrpahy: Bobby Bukowski. Editor: David Freeman. Music: Stephen Endelman. In Foto-Kem color. Running time: 92 minutes. MPAA rating: PG. Release date: December 29, 1995.

Cast: Jonathan Taylor Thomas, Brad Renfro, Eric Schweig, Charles Rocket, Amy Wright, Michael McShane, Marian Seldes.

Toy Story

A Buena Vista Pictures release of a Walt Disney picture. Director: John Lasseter. Producers: Ralph Guggenheim, Bonnie Arnold. Screenplay: Joss Whedon, Andrew Stanton, Joel Cohen, Alex Sokolow, based on an original story by Lasseter. Supervising Technical Director: William Reeves. Supervising Animator: Pete Docter. Editor: Robert Gordon, Lee Unkrich. Animated. Running time: 81 minutes. MPAA rating: G. Release date: November 24, 1995.

Voice Cast: Tom Hanks, Tim Allen, Don Rickles, Jim Varney, Wallace Shawn, John Ratzenberger, Annie Potts, John Morris.

Trees Lounge

An Orion Pictures release of a Live Entertainment presentation. Producers: Brad Wayman, Chris Hanely. Director: Steve Buscemi. Screenplay: Buscemi. Camera: Lisa Rinzler. Editor: Kate Williams. Music: Evan Lurie. Running time: 94 minutes. MPAA rating: R. Release date: October 11, 1996.

Cast: Steve Buscemi, Elizabeth Bracco, Anthony LaPaglia, Debi Mazar, Chloe Sevigny, Daniel Baldwin.

The Truth Abouth Cats & Dogs

A 20th Century Fox release of a Noon Attack production. Producer: Cari-Esta Albert. Director: Michael Lehmann. Screenplay: Audrey Wells. Camera: Robert Brinkman. Editor: Stephen Semel. Music: Howard Shore. Running time: 97 minutes. MPAA rating: PG-13. Release date: April 26, 1996.

Cast: Uma Thurman, Janeane Garofalo, Ben Chaplin, Jamie Foxx.

12 Monkeys

A Universal Pictures and Atlas/Classico presentation of an Atlas Entertainment production of a Terry Gilliam film. Producer: Charles Roven. Director: Terry Gilliam. Screenplay: David Peoples, Janet Peoples, inspired by the film "La Jetee" written by Chris Marker. Camera: Roger Pratt. Editor: Mick Audsley. Production Design: Jeffrey Beecroft. Music: Paul Buckmaster. MPAA rating: R. Release date: January 5, 1996.

Cast: Bruce Willis, Madeleine Stowe, Brad Pitt, Christopher Plummer.

Twister

A Warner Bros. release of a Warner Bros. and Universal presentation of an Amblin Entertainment production. Producers: Kathleen Kennedy, Ian Bryce, Michael Crichton. Director: Jan De Bont. Screenplay: Michael Crichton, Anne-Marie Martin. Camera: Jack N. Green. Editor: Michael Kahn. Music: Mark Mancina. Special Effects: Industrial Light & Magic. Running time: 114 minutes. MPAA rating: PG-13. Release date: May 10, 1996.

Cast: Helen Hunt, Bill Paxton, Cary Elwes, Jami Gertz, Lois Smith.

2 Days In the Valley

An MGM/UA release from MGM of a Rysher Entertainment presentation of a Redemption production. Producers: Jeff Wald, Herb Nanas. Execfutive Producers: Keith Samples, Tony Amatullo. Co-producer: Jim Burke. Director: John Herzfeld. Screenplay: Herzfeld. Camera: Oliver Wood. Editors: Jim Miller, Wayne Wahrman. Music: Anthony Marinello. MPAA Rating: R. Release date: Oct. 4, 1996. Running time: 107 minutes.

Cast: Danny Aiello, Jeff Daniels, Teri Hatcher, James Spader, Glenne Headly, Peter Horton, Eris Stoltz, Marsha Mason.

Two If By Sea

A Warner Bros. release of a James G. Robinson presentation of a Morgan Creek production of a Bill Bennett film. Producer: James G. Robinson. Director: Bill Bennett. Screenplay: Denis Leary, Mike Armstrong based on a story by Denis Leary, Armstrong, Ann Lembeck. Camera: Andrew Lesnie. Editor: Bruce Green. Music: Nick Glennie-Smith, Paddy Maloney. MPAA rating: R. Release date: January 5, 1996.

Cast: Sandra Bullock, Denis Leary, Stephen Dillane, Yaphet Kotto.

Two Much

A Bunea Vista release. Producer: Christina Huete. Director: Fernando Trueba. Screenplay: Fernando and David Trueba, nased on the novel by Donald E. Westlake. Camera: Jose Luis Alcaine. Editor: Nena Bernard. Music: Michel Camilo. Running time: 118 minutes. MPAA rating: PG-13. Release date: March 15, 1996.

Cast: Antonio Banderas, Melanie Griffith, Daryl Hannah, Danny Aiello, Joan Cusack, Eli Wallach, Austin Pendleton.

Unforgettable

An MGM release of a Dino de Lurentiis presentation of a John Dahl film. Producers: Dino de Laurentiis, Martha de Laurentiis. Director: John Dahl. Screenplay: Bill Geddie. Music: Christopher Young. MPAA rating: R. Release date: February 23, 1996.

Cast: Ray Liotta, Linda Fiorentino, Peter Coyote, Christopher MacDonald, David Paymer.

Up Close and Personal

A Buena Vista release of a Touchstone Pictures presentation in association with cinergi Pictures Entertainment of an Avnet/Kerner production. Producers: Jon Avnet, David Nicksay, Jordan Kerner. Director: Avnet. Screenplay: Joan Didion, John Gregory Dunne, suggested by the book "Golden Girl" by Alanna Nash. Camera: Karl Walter Lindenlaub. Editor: Debra Neil-Fisher. Music: John Newman. In Technicolor. Running time: 124 minutes. MPAA rating: PG-13. Release date: March 8, 1996.

Cast: Robert Redford, Michelle Pfeiffer, Stockard Channing, Joe Mantegna, Kate Nelligan, Glenn Plummer, James Rebhorn, Dedee Pfeiffer.

Vampire in Brooklyn

A Paramount Pictures Release of an Eddie Murphy Production. Producers: Eddie Murphy & Mark Lipsky. Director: Wes Craven. Screenplay: Charles Murphy, Michael Lucker & Christopher Parker, based on an a story by Eddie Murphy, Vernon Lynch Jr. & Charles Muphy. Camera: Mark Irwin. Music: J. Peter Robinson. Editor: Patrick Lussier. Running time: 103 minutes. MPAA rating: R. Release date: October 27, 1995.

Cast: Eddie Murphy, Angela Bassett, Allen Payne, Kadeem Hardison, John Witherspoon, Zakes Mokae, Joanna Cassidy, Simbi Khali.

A Very Brady Sequel

A Paramount release of a Ladd Co./Sherwood Schwartz production. Producers: Sherwood Schwartz, Lloyd J. Schwartz, Alan Ladd Jr. Co-producers: Michael Fottrell, Kelliann Ladd. Director: Arlene Sanford. Screenplay: Harry Elfont, Deborah Kaplan, James Berg, Stan Zimmerman. Story: Elfont, Kaplan, based on characters created by Sherwood Schwartz. Cinematography: Mac Ahlberg. MPAA Rating: PG-13. Release date: August 13, 1996. Running time: 89 Min.

Cast: Shelley Long, Gary Cole, Tim Matheson, Christopher Daniel Barnes, Christine Taylor, Paul Sutera, Jennifer Elise Cox.

Waiting To Exhale

A Twentieth Century Fox presentation of a Deborah Schindler/Ezra Swerdlow film. Producers: Swerdlow, Schindler. Director: Forest Whitaker. Screenplay: Terry McMillan, Ronald Bass based on the novel by Terry McMillan. Editor: Richard Chew. Camera: Toyomichi Kurita. Production Design: David Gropman. Running time: 122 minutes. MPAA rating: R. Release date: December 22, 1995.

Cast: Whitney Houston, Angela Bassett, Lela Rochon, Loretta Devine, Gregory Hines, Dennis Haysbert, Mykelti Williamson, Wesley Snipes.

The War At Home

A Buena Vista release of a Touchstone Pictures presentation in association with the Motion Picture Corp. of America and Avatar Entertainment. Producers: Brad Krevoy, Emilio Estevez, Steve Stabler, James Duff. Executive Producer: Tracie Graham Rice. Co-executive producer: Chad Oman. Director: Emilio Estevez. Screenplay: Duff, based upon his play "Homefront." Camera: Peter Levy. Editor: Craig Bassett. Music: Basil Poledouris. Release date: October 11, 1996. Running time: 119 minutes.

Cast: Emilio Estevez, Kathy Bates, Charlie Sheen, Kimberly Williams, Carla Gugino, Geoffrey Blake.

White Squall

A Buena Vista Pictures release of a Hollywood Pictures presentation in association with Largo Entertainment of a Scott Free production. Producers: Mimi Polk Gitlin, Rocky Lang. Director: Ridley Scott. Screenplay: Todd Robinson. Camera: Hugh Johnson. Editor: Gerry Hambling. Music: Jeff Rona. In Technicolor. Running time: 127 minutes. MPAA rating: PG-13. Release date: January 26, 1996.

Cast: Jeff Bridges, Caroline Goodall, John Savage, Scott Wolf, Jeremy Sisto, Ryan Phillipe, Balthazar Getty.

Wild Bill

An MGM/UA release from United Artists of a Zanuck Co. production. Producers: Richard D. Zanuck, Lili Fini Zanuck. Co-producer: Gary Daigler. Director: Walter Hill. Screenplay: Hill, based on the play "Fathers and Sons" by Thomas Babe, and the novel "Deadwood" by Pete Dexter. Camera: Lloyd Ahern. Editor: Freeman Davies. Deluxe color/B&W. Running time: 97minutes. MPAA rating: R.

Cast: Jeff Bridges, Ellen Barkin, John Hurt, Diane Lane, David Arquette, Christina Applegate, Bruce Dern, James Gammon.

Independent U.S. Films

(October 1, 1995—September 30, 1996)

Many of the following films have been released in a limited fashion at film festivals or other similar venues but have not yet been nationally distributed. Directors are in parenthesis.

A Business Affair
CASTLE HILL (R) December, 1995. (Charlotte Brandstrom) Christopher Walken, Carole Bouquet, Jonathan Pryce.

A Perfect Candidate
SEVENTH ART. April, 1996. (R.J. Cutler) Documentary.

The Addiction
OCTOBER. (R) October, 1995. (Abel Ferrara) Lili Taylor, Christopher Walken, Annabella Sciorra.

Albino Alligator
MIRAMAX. August, 1996. (Kevin Spacey) Matt Dillion, Faye Dunaway, Gary Sinise.

Alchemy
SENECA FALLS. October, 1995. (Suzanne Myers) Rya Kihlsetd, Jeff Webster, D.V. de Vincentis.

All Over Me
FINE LINE. July 16, 1996. (Alex Sichel) Alison Folland, Tara Subkoff, Cole Hauser.

All's Fair in Love and War
STAR LAND ENTERTAINMENT. August 1996. (Sartaj Khan) Khan, Miki O'Brien, Bill Trillo, William Night.

American Buffalo
SAMUEL GOLDWYN. (R) October, 1996. (Michael Corrente), Dustin Hoffman, Dennis Franz, Sean Nelson.

American Job
BLUEMARK. January, 1996. (Chris Smith) Randy Russell, Tom Wheeler, Matt Collier, Charlie Smith.

American Purgatory:
90 Days Behind the Wire of Guantanamo USNB
NINETY MILES. October, 1995. (Rafael Oller) Documentary.

American Strays
CANNED PICTURES. April 16, 1996. (Michael Covert) Jennifer Tilly, Eric Roberts, John Savage.

Ancestors in the Americas: Coolies, Sailors, Settlers
CENTER FOR EDUCATIONAL TELECOMM. February, 1996. (Loni Ding) Documentary.

Angels and Insects
SAMUEL GOLDWYN. November, 1995. (Philip Haas) Mark Rylance, Kristin Scott Thomas, Patsy Kensit.

Anne Frank Remembered
SONY PICTURES CLASSICS. (PG) January, 1996. (Jon Blair), Kenneth Brabagh, Glenn Close, Miep Gies.

Apocalypse Bop
OL' BAIT SHOP PRODS. April, 1996. (Andrew Osborne) Scott Von Doviak, Bryant Marshall, Holly Harris.

August
SAMUEL GOLDWYN. April, 1996. (Anthony Hopkins) Hopkins, Kate Burton, Leslie Phillips, Kate Burton, Gawn Grainger.

The Babysitter
SPELLING (R) November, 1995. (Guy Ferland) Alicia Silverstone, J.T. Walsh, Lee Garlington, Nicky Katt.

Bandwagon
PAMLICO. January, 1996. (John Schultz) Kevin Corrigan, Steve Parlavecchio, Lee Holmes.

Barb Wire
GRAMERCY. (R) May, 1996. (David Hogan) Pamela Anderson Lee, Temuera Morrison, Victoria Rowell, Udo Kier.

Basquiat
MIRAMAX. (R) July 10, 1996. (Julian Schnabel) Jeffrey Wright, Michael Wincott, Benicio Del Toro, David Bowie.

Battle Over Citizen Kane, the
WGBH. January, 1996. (Thomas Lennon and Michael Epstein) Documentary.

Beautiful Girls
MIRAMAX. (R) February, 1996. (Ted Demme) Matt Dillon, Noah Emmerich, Annabeth Gish, Lauren Holly, Uma Thurman, Timothy Hutton, Rosie O'Donnell, Max Perlich, Martha Plimpton, Natalie Portman, Mira Sorvino.

Bed of Roses
NEW LINE. (PG) February, 1996. (Michael Goldenberg) Christian Slater, Mary Stuart Masterson, Pamela Segall.

Belly Talkers
MIRAMAX. January, 1996. (Sandra Luckow) Documentary.

Big Night
RYSHER. January, 1996. (Stanley Tucci, Campbell Scott) Minnie Driver, Ianholm, Osabella Rossellini.

The Big Squeeze
FIRST LOOK PICTURES. June 7, 1996. (Marcus De Leon) Peter Dobson, Lara Flynn Boyle, Luca Bercovici.

Bitter Sugar (Azucar Amarga)
AZUCAR FILMS. February, 1996. (Leon Ichaso) Rene Lavan. Mayte Vilan, Miguel Guttierez.

Black Day Blue Night
CAPELLA INTERNATIONAL. (R) November, 1995. (J.S. Cardone) Gil Bellows, Michelle Forbes, Mia Sara, J.T. Walsh.

Black & White: A Love Story
A WOMAN UNDER THE INFLUENCE PRODS. February, 1996. (Susanna Lo) Katherine Donahue, Kenny Ranson, Alicia Hoge.

Black Is . . . Black Ain't
TARA. October, 1995 (Marlon Riggs) Angela Davis, Bell Hooks, Barabara Smith, Cornel West.

Blood and Wine
FOX SEARCHLIGHT. Sept., 1996. (Bob Rafelson) Jack Nicholson, Stephen Dorff, Jennifer Lopez.

Blue in the Face
MIRAMAX. (R) November, 1995. (Wayne Wang, Paul Auster) Harvey Keitel, Victor Argo, Giancarlo Esposito.

Bound
GRAMERCY. (R) October, 1996. (Larry and Andy Wachowski) Jennifer Tilly, Gina Gershon, Joe Pantoliano,.

Box of Moonlight
LARGO ENTERTAINMENT. August, 1996. (Tom DiCillo) John Turturro, Sam Rockwell, Catherine Keeler.

Buckminster Fuller: Thinking Out Loud
SIMON & GOODMAN PICTURE CO. January, 1996. (Karen Goodman, Kirk Simon) Documentary. Color/B&W.

Cadillac Ranch
DAVIS ENTERTAINMENT. January, 1996. (Lisa Gottlieb) Renee Humphrey, Christopher Lloyd.

Carried Away
FINE LINE. January, 1996. (Bruno Barreto) Dennis Hopper, Amy Irving, Amy Locane, Julie Harris, Gary Busey, Hal Holbrook.

Carrington
GRAMERCY. (R) November, 1995. (Christopher Hampton) Emma Thompson, Jonathan Pryce.

Casa Hollywood
CASA HOLLYWOOD. June 29, 1996. (Mark Decker) Estuardo Volty, Michael Banks, Lisa Cobano.

Cashing In
PENDULUM. February, 1996. (Anne Rose Dremman) Paul Ruehl, Cassidy Phillips, John Serge, Brian Wankum.

Catwalk
ARROW. January, 1996. (Robert Leacock, Milton Moses Ginsberg) Christy Turlington. Documentary.

Caught
CINEHAUS/DUART/CIRCLE. January, 1996. (Robert M. Young) Edward James Olmos, Maria Conchita Alonso.

The Celluloid Closet
SONY PICTURES CLASSICS. (R) March, 1996. (Rob Epstein, Jeffery Friedman) Documentary with Tony Curtis, Tom Hanks, Susan Sarandon, Shirley Maclaine, Whoopi Goldberg.

Chalk
TENDERLOIN ACTION GROUP/PACIFIC RIM MEDIA. April, 1996. (Rob Nillson) Kevin Han Yee, Don Bajema, Johnnie Reese.

Childhood's End
PLAINVIEW PICTURES. August, 1996. (Jeff Lipsky) Cameron Foord, Heather Gottlieb, Sam Trammell.

Chocolate Babies
OPEN CITY FILMS. July 21, 1996. (Stephen Winter) Gregg Ferguson, Dudley Findlay, Jr. Jon Lee.

Cold Comfort Farm
GRAMERCY. (PG) May, 1996. (John Schlesinger), Kate Beckinsdale, Eileen Atkins, Ian McKellen.

Cold Fever
ARTISTIC LICENSE FILMS. (NR) April, 1996. (Fridrik Thor Fridriksson), Masatoshi Nagase, Lili Taylor, Fisher Stevens.

Color of a Brisk and Leaping Day
JIM STARK/ANTARCTIC. January, 1996. (Christopher Munch) Peter Alexander, Michael Stipe, Jeri Arredondo.

Comfortably Numb
QUARTET. September, 1995. (Henri Barges) Catherine Ussel, Phillipe Spiteri, Marc Duret.

Conjure Women
REBEKAH. September, 1995. (Demetria Royals) Documentary.

The Continued Adventures of Reptile Man (And His Faithful Sidekick Tadpole)
CINEMA ARTS, Paris. May 11, 1996. (Stewart Schill) Tony Curtis, Arye Gross, Ally Walker.

Crimetime
TRIMARK. August, 1996. (George Sluizer) Stephen Baldwin, Pete Postlethwaite, Sadie Frost, Gerladine Chaplin, Karen Black, Marianne Faithfull.

Crosscut
PAVLIC-RAIMONDI. October, 1995. (Paul Raimondi) Costas Mandylor, Megan Gallagher, Casey Sander.

The Crossing Guard
MIRAMAX. (R) November, 1995. (Sean Penn) Jack Nicholson, Angelica Houston, Robin Wright, David Morse.

The Crow II: City of Angels
MIRAMAX/DIMENSION. (R) August, 1996. (Tim Pope), Vincent Perez, Richard Brooks, Mia Kirschner, Iggy Pop.

Cry, The Beloved Country
MIRAMAX. (PG-13) December, 1995. (Darrell James Roodt) James Earl Jones, Richard Harris, Charles S. Dutton, Vusi Kunene.

Curdled
MIRAMAX. (R) September, 1996. (Reb Braddock) William Baldwin, Angela Jones, Bruce Ramsay, Barry Corbin.

Cutting Loose
LEAPFROG. January, 1996. (Susan Todd & Andrew Young) Documentary.

Dadetown
KHXT. September 1995. (Russ Hexter) Bill Harrison, David Phelps, Jim Pryor, Jonathan Shafer.

The Darien Gap
NOMAD. January, 1996. (Brad Anderson) Lyn VBaus, Sandi Carroll.

Davy Jones' Locker
JACOBY. December, 1995. (Joseph Jacoby) Bil Baird's Marionettes.

The Daytrippers
March, 1996. (Greg Mottola) Hope Davos, Pat McNamara, Anne Meara, Parker Posey, Stanley Tucci, Campbell Scott.

Dead Man
MIRAMAX. (R) May, 1996. (Jim Jarmusch), Johnny Depp, Gary Farmer, Lance Henriksen, Iggy Pop, Crispin Glover, Gabriel Byrne, John Hurt, Robert Mitchum, Mili Avital.

Dead Man Walking
GRAMERCY. (R) December, 1995. (Tim Robbins) Susan Sarandon, Sean Penn, Robert Prosky.

The Delicate Art Of The Rifle
CAMBRAI LIBERATION COLLECTIVE. March, 1996. (D.W. Harper) David Grant, Stephen Grany, John Kessel.

Demolition High
SUNSET FILMS INTL. (L.A.) May 11, 1996. (Jim Wynorski) Corey Haim, Alan Thicke, Jeff Kober.

Deseret
December, 1995. (James Benning) Documentary.

The Destiny of Marty Fine
ONE-TWO PRDS. March, 1996. (Michael Hacker) Alan Gelfant, James LeGros, Catherine Keener.

Dog Run
C&P PRODS. April, 1996. (D. Ze'ev Gilad) Brian Marc, Craid DuPlessis, Lisa Ristorucci, Elizabeth Horsburgh.

Don't Be A Menace To South Central While Drinking Your Juice In The Hood
MIRAMAX. (R) January, 1996. (Paris Barclay) Shawn Wayans, Marlon Wayans.

The Doom Generation
TRIMARK (R) November , 1995. (

Dream For An Insomniac
TRITONE PRODS. April, 1996. (Tiffanie DeBartolo) Ione Skye, Jennifer Aniston, Seymour Cassel, Mackenzie Austin.

Drinking Games
VILLAGE IDIOT PLAYHOUSE PRODS. March, 1996. (Joseph Lawson) Christian Leffler, Dinah Leffert, Geoffrey L. Smith.

Driven
PALISADES PICTURES. August, 1996. (Michael Paradies Shoob) Tony Todd, Whip Hubley, Chad Lowe.

Drop Dead Rock
SPAZZ-O PRODS. March, 1996. (Adam Dubin) Adam Ant, Deborah Harry, Ian Maynard, Shelly Mars.

Ed's Next Move
BLUEHAWK. January, 1996. (John Walsh) Matt Ross, Calliope Thorne, Kevin Carroll.

Eden
WATER STREET. January, 1996. (Howard Goldberg) Joanna Going, Dylan Walsh, Sean Patrick Flannery.

Edie & Pen
PACIFIC SHORE MEDIA, Los Angeles. May, 1996. (Matthew Irmas) Stockard Channing, Jennifer Tilly, Scott Glenn.

Entertaining Angels: The Dorothy Day Story
PAULIST PICTURES. (PG-13) Sept., 1996. (Michael Ray Rhodes) Moira Kelly, Martin Sheen, Melinda Dillon.

Everything Relative
BIG SISTERS. January, 1996. (Sharon Pollack) Ellen McLaughlin, Olivia Negron, Stacey Nelkin.

Faithful
NEW LINE. (R) February, 1996. (Paul Mazursky) Cher, Chazz Palminteri, Ryan O'Neal, Amber Smith.

Fallout
SHOWCASE ENTERTAINMENT. August, 1996. (Robert Palumbo) Claire Beckman, Mark Deakins, David Wasson.

Fargo
GRAMERCY. (R) February, 1996. (Ethan Coen) Steve Buscemi, William H. Macy, Peter Stormare, Frances McDermott.

Farmer & Chase
ARROW. October, 1995. (Michael Seltzman) Todd Field, Ben Gazzara, Lara Flynn Boyle, Ron Kaell.

Feeling Minnesota
FINE LINE. (R) September, 1996. (Steven Baigelman) Keanu Reeves, Vincent D'Onofrio, Cameron Diaz.

Female Perversions
OCTOBER. January, 1996. (Susan Streifeld) Tilda Swinton, Amy Madigan, Karen Sillas, Laila Robins.

The Feminine Touch
MIRACON PICTURES. April, 1996. (Conrad Janis) Paige Turco, Dirk Benedict, Janis, George Segal, Bo Hopkins.

Fetishes
ITEL, London. June 14, 1996. (Nick Broomfield) Documentary.

Fiddlefest
FOUR OAKS. October, 1995. (Lana Miller) Documentary.

Fire On the Mountain
GAGE & GAGE. January, 1996. (Beth Gage, George Gage) Documentary.

Flipping
MON FRERE. January, 1996. (Gene Mitchell) David Amos, David Proval, Keith David, Shant Benjamin.

Flirt
TRUE FICTION. September, 1995. (Hal Hartley) Bill Sage,, Parker Posey, Dwightt Ewell, Elina Lowensohn, Miho Nikaidoh, Toshizo Fujisawa.

Flirting With Disaster
MIRAMAX. (R) March, 1996. (David O. Russell) Patricia Arquette, Tea Leoni, Alan Alda, Ben Stiller, Mary Tyler Moore.

Follow Me Home
January, 1996. (Peter Bratt) Jesse Borrego, Benjamin Bratt, Clavin Levels, Alfre Woodard.

Four Rooms
MIRAMAX. (Allison Anders, Alexandre Rockwell, Robert Rodriguez, Quentin Tarantino) Tim Roth, Valeria Golino, Madonna, Lili Taylor, Jennifer Beals.

Foxfire
SAMUEL GOLDWYN. July 10, 1996. (Annette Haywood-Carter) Hedy Burress, Angelina Jolie, Jenny Lewis.

Frankie Starlight
FINE LINE. (R) September, 1995. (Michael Lindsay-Hogg) Annie Parillaud, Matt Dillon, Gabriel Byrne.

Freeway
KUSHNER-LOCKE. January, 1996. (Matthew Bright) Kiefer Sutherland, Brooke Shileds, Reese Witherspoon, Dan Hedaya, Amanda Plummer.

Fresh Kill
STRAND. January, 1996. (Shu Lea Cheang) Sarita Choudhury, Erin McMurtry, Abraham Lim.

French Exit
CINEVILLE. September 1995. (Daphna Kastner) Madchen Amick, Jonathan Silverman, Molly Hagan, Vince Grant, Kurt Fuller.

Frisk
STRAND. (NC-17) March, 1996. (Todd Verow) Michael Gunther, Craig Chester, Parker Posey, Alexis Arquette.

From Dusk Till Dawn
DIMENSION. (R) January, 1996. (Robert Rodriguez) Harvey Keitel, George Clooney, Quentin Tarantino, Juliette Lewis, Cheech Marin, Kelly Preston.

The Funeral
OCTOBER FILMS. (R) August, 1996. (Abel Ferrara) Christopher Walken, Chris Penn, Vincent Gallo.

Galgameth
GALAXY INTL. May 12, 1996. (Sean McNamara) Devin Oatway, Sean McNamara, Stephen Macht.

Garbage
PBFM/VOIX. September, 1995. (Peter Byck) Derich Wittliff, Byck.

Gay Cuba
CUBA'S FELIX VARELA CENTER. August, 1996. (Sonja de Vries) Documentary.

Georgia
MIRAMAX. (R) December, 1995. (Lilli Grosbard) Jennifer Jason Leigh, Mare Winningham.

Girl 6
FOX SEARHCLIGHT. (R) March 1996. (Spike Lee) Theresa Randle, Spike Lee, Peter Berg, Naomi Campbell, John Turturro.

Girl's Town
OCTOBER. January, 1996. (Jim McKay) Lili Taylor, Anna Grace, Bruklin Harris, Aunjanue Ellis.

God's Lonely Man
ST. FRANCES OF ASSISI. January, 1996. (Francis Von Zerneck) Michael Wyle, Heather McComb, Justine Bateman, Paul Dooley.

Grace of My Heart
GRAMMERCY PICTURES. (R) September, 1996. (Allison Anders) Illeana Douglas, Matt Dillon, Eric Stoltz.

The Grass Harp
FINE LINE. September, 1996. (Charles Matthau) Sissy Spacek, Walter Matthau, Jack Lemmon, Piper Laurie, Mary Steenburgen, Nell Carter, Charles Durning, Piper Laurie.

The Grave
KUSHNER-LOCKE. January, 1996. (Jonas Pate) Craig Sheffer, Garbielle Anwar, Josh Charles, Max perlich, Anthony Michael Hall, Eric Roberts, Keith David.

Gray's Anatomy
INDEPENDENT FILM CHANNEL. Sept., 1996. (Steven Soderbergh) Spalding Gray.

Green Plaid Shirt
VICIOUS CIRCLE. July, 1996. (Richard Natale) Gregory Phelan, Kevin Spirtas, Richard Israel.

Grind
KODIAK. April, 1996. (Chris Kentis) Adrienne Shelly, Billy Crudup, Paul Schulze, Frank Vincent, Saul Stein.

Gumby: The Movie
ARROW. (G) December, 1995. (Art Clokey) Animation.

A Gun For Jennifer
CONSPIRACY FILMS. August, 1996. (Todd Morris) Deborah Twiss, Benja Kay, Freida Hoops, Rene Alberta.

Guns on the Clackamas
October, 1995. (Bill Plympton) Keith Scales, Michael Thomas Parks, Danny Bruno, William Tate.

Guy
POLYGRAM FILM INTERNATIONAL. September, 1996. (Michael Lindsay-Hogg) Vincent D'Onofrio, Hope Davis, Kimber Riddle.

Habit
GLASS EYE PIX. April, 1996. (Larry Fessenden) Fessenden, Meredith Snaider, Aaron Beall, Patricia Coleman.

Harlem Diary: Nine Voices of Resilience
DISCOVERY. October, 1995. (Jonathan Sacks) Jermaine Ashwood, Michael Cousins, Christina Head.

Headless Body in Topless Bar
NORTHERN ARTS. February, 1996. (James Bruce) Jennifer MacDonald, Raymond J. Barry, Paul Williams, Taylor Nichols.

Heavy
CFP DISTRIBUTION. (NR) May, 1996. (James Mangold), Pruitt Taylor Vince, Shelley Winters, Deborah Harry, Evan Dando.

Hellraiser: Bloodline
DIMENSION/TRANS ATLANTIC ENT. (R) March 1996. (Alan Smithee) Bruce Ramsay, Valentina Vargas.

The Hemp Revolution
TARA. December, 1995. (Anthony Clarke) Documentary.

Hitting the Ground
LIVING PICTURES. January, 1996. (David P. Moore) Neal Huff, Anney Giobbe, Rik Walter, Daintry Jensen.

Homage
ARROW. October, 1995

Hustler White
STRAND RELEASING. January, 1996. (Bruce LaBruce) Tony Ward, LaBruce, Kevin P. Scott.

Hype
HELVEY/PRAY. January, 1996. (Doug Pray) Documentary.

I Crave Rock & Roll
VISTA PACIFIC. June 12, 1996. (Carmen Santa Maria) Carmen Santa Maria, Julie Gray, Jon Rashad Kamal.

I Shot Andy Warhol
SAMUEL GOLDWYN. January, 1996. (Mary Harron) Lili Taylor, Jared Harris, Lothaire Bluteau, Martha Plimpton, Stephen Dorff, Jill Hennessy, Donovan Leitch.

I Was a Jewish Sex Worker
PHILIP B. ROTH. June 28, 1996. (Philip B. Roth) Documentary.

Illtown
SHOOTING GALLERY. September, 1996. (Nick Gomez) Michael Rapaport, Lili Taylor, Adam Trese.

Infinity
FIRST LOOK PICTURES. September, 1996. (Matthew Broderick) Matthew Broderick, Patricia Arquette, Peter Riegert.

Inn Trouble!
FEARLESS PRODS. June 27, 1996. (Cristina Rey) Christina Rey, Stephani Shope, Melissa Aronson.

Inside
SHOWTIME. April, 1996. (Arthur Penn) Eric Stoltz, Nigel Hawthorne, Louis Gossett Jr., Ian Roberts.

Invasion of Privacy
SENATOR, London. May 13, 1996. (Anthony Hickox) Mili Avital, Jonathan Schaech, Naomi Campbell.

The Island of Dr. Moreau
New Line. (PG-13) August 20, 1996. (John Frankenheimer) Marlon Brando, Val Kilmer, David Thewlis, Fairuza Balk, Ron Perlman, Marco Hofschneider.

It's Elementary: Talking About Gay Issues in School
WOMEN'S EDUCATIONAL MEDIA. May 20, 1996. (Debra Chasnoff) Documentary.

Jack & Sarah
POLYGRAM. (R) March, 1996. (Tim Sullivan) Richard E. Grant, Samantha Mathis, Judi Dench. Ian McKellen.

Jane: An Abortion Service
ITVS. (Kate Kirtz, Nell Lundy) Documentary.

Jane Eyre
MIRAMAX. April, 1996. (Franco Zeffirelli) William Hurt, Charlotte Gainsbourg, Joan Plowright, Anna Paquin, Gerladine Chaplin, Elle McPherson.

Jane Street
BEADS & TRINKETS PRODS. June, 1996. (Charles Merzbacher) Mark Berlin, Jane Jensen, Christa Kirby.

Jenipapo
BOKU/RAVINA/DUETO. September, 1995. (Monique Gardenberg) Patrick Bauchau, Marilia Pera.

Joe & Joe
LITTLE HORSE THIEF. November, 1995. (David Wall) David Wysocki, Sean Patrick Brennan, Tracy Griffith.

Johns
FIRST LOOK/OVERSEAS FILMGROUP. January, 1996. (Scott Silver) Lukas Haas, David Arquette, Arliss Howard, Elliot Gould.

Joint Adventure
ELECTRIC MOUNTAIN. October, 1995. (John Foran) James Brinkley, David Haley, Biz Lyon.

The Journey of August King
MIRAMAX. (PG) November, 1995. (John Duigan) Jason Patric, Thandie Newton, Larry Drake, Sam Waterston.

The Keeper
RADA. January, 1996. (Joe Brewster) Giancarlo Esposito, Regina Taylor, Isaach de Bankole.

Kicking & Screaming
TRIMARK. (R) November, 1995.

Kids of Survival
The Art And Life of Tim Rollins & K.O.S.
GELLER/GOLDFINE PRODS. April, 1996. Documentary.

Killer: A Journal of Murder
OLIVER STONE/SPELLING FILMS. January, 1996. (Tim Metcalfe) James Woods, Robert Sean Leonard, Lili Taylor.

Kiss & Tell
FILMWORKS, Burbank. May, 1996. (Jordan Alan) Lewis Arquette, Richmond Arquette, Justine Bateman.

Land of Milk and Honey
SHOWCASE. September, 1995. (Joseph Destein) Richard Panebiance, Lumi Cavazos, Roxana Zal.

Last Call
FUSION/WEINY/WOODWARD. October, 1995. (Rich Wilkes) Ben Afflek, French Stewart, Sam Rockwell.

Last Man Standing
NEW LINE. (R) September, 1996. (Walter Hill) Bruce Willis, Christopher Walken, Bruce Dern.

Last Summer In The Hamptons
RAINBOW FILM. September, 1995. (Henry Jaglom) Victoria Foyt, Viveca Lindfors, Martha Plimpton, Roddy McDowall, Ron Rifkin.

The Last Supper
VAULT. October, 1995. (Stacy Title) Cameron Diaz, Ron Eldard, Annabeth Gish, Jonathan Penner, Courtney B. Vance.

Late Bloomers
ONE MIND. January, 1996. (Julia Dyer, Gretchen Dyer) Connie Nelson, Dee Hennigan, Gary Carter.

Lawnmower Man 2: Beyond Cyberspace
NEW LINE. (PG-13) January, 1996. (Farhad Mann) Patrick Bergen, Matt Frewer, Austin O'Brien.

A Leap of Faith
PARALLEL. January, 1996. (Jennifer McShane, Tricia Regan) Documentary.

The Limits of Thermal Travelling
BLUESTORM INTERNATIONAL. October, 1995. (Mark Bender) David Jacob Ryder, Cullen Douglas, Robin Krasny.

Listen
Orion Pictures. Sept., 1996. (Gavin Wilding) Brooke Langton, Sarah Buxton, Gordon Currie.

Lone Star
SONY PICTURES CLASSICS. (R) March, 1996. (John Sayles) Chris Cooper, Elizabeth Pena, Joe Morton, Kris Kristofferson.

The Long Kiss Goodnight
NEW LINE. (R) October, 1996. (Renny Harlin) Geena Davis, Samuel L. Jackson, G.D. Spradlin, Patrick Malahide.

Looking for Richard
FOX SEARCHLIGHT. January, 1996. (Al Pacino) pacino, Harris Yulin, Penelope Allen, Alec Baldwin, Kevin Spacey, Winona Ryder, Aidan Quinn, Estelle Parsons.

Loser
EDGE CINEMA. March, 1996. (Kirk Harris) Harris, Jonathan Chaus, Norman Saleet, Peta Wilson.

Losing Chase
SHOWTIME. January, 1996. (Kebin Bacon) Helen Mirren, Kyra Sedgwick, Beau Bridges, Michael Yarmush.

Love Is All There Is
TRIDENT. May 10, 1996. (Renee Taylor) Lainie Kazan, Joseph Bologna, Barbara Carrera.

Lover's Knot
SHOWCASE ENTERTAINMENT. May 11, 1996. (Peter Shaner) Bill Campbell, Jennifer Grey, Tim Curry.

Man of the Year
SEVENTH ART. February, 1996. (Dirk Shafer) Shafer, Vivan Paxton, Michael Ornstein, Bill Brochtrup.

Mallrats
GRAMERCY. (R) September, 1995. (Kevin Smith) Shannen Doherty, Jeremy London, Jason Lee.

Man With A Gun
OCTOBER. October, 1995. (David Wyles) Michael Madsen, Jennifer Tilly, Gary Busey, Robert Loggia.

Man With a Plan
BELLWEATHER FILMS. May 21, 1996. (John O'Brien) Fred Tuttle, Joe Tuttle, Bruce Lyndes.

Manny & Lo
SONY CLASSICS. January, 1996. (Lisa Krueger) Mary Kay Place, Scarlett Johansson, Aleksa Palladino.

Me & My Matchmaker
WEXLER'S WORLD. January, 1996. (Mark Wexler) Documentary.

Mercy
INJOSHO. October, 1995. (Richard Shephard) John Rubinstein, Amber Kain, Sam Rockwell, Jane Lanier.

Message to Love
CASTLE MUSIC. February, 1996. (Murray Lerner) Documentary.

A Midwinter's Tale
CASTLE ROCK. February, 1996. (Kenneth Branagh) Richard Briers, Hetta Charnely, Joan Collins.

Mighty Aphrodite
MIRAMAX. (R) October, 1995. (Woody Allen) F. Murray Abraham, Allen, Claire Bloom, Mira Sirvino.

A Modern Affair
TRIBE. September, 1995. (Vern Oakley) Lisa Eichhorn, Stanley Tucci, Tammy Grimes, Robert Joy.

Mojave Moon
INITIAL ENTERTAINMENT GROUP. (R) May 13, 1996. (Kevin Dowling) Danny Aiello, Anne Archer, Angelina Jolie.

A Month By The Lake
MIRAMAX. (PG) September, 1995. (John Irvin) Vanessa Redgrave, James Fox, Uma Thurman.

Mr. Speckman's Boat
CINEQUANON PICTURES INTL. May 14, 1996. (John Huddles) Jennifer Connelly, Edward Atterton, Jim True.

Mr. Wrong
TOUCHSTONE. (PG-13) February, 1996. (Nick Castle) Ellen DeGeneres, Bill Pullman, Joan Cusack, Dean Stockwell, Joan Plowright.

Mugshot
MORTAL FILMS. April, 1996. (Matt Mahurin) Robert Knepper, Michael Williams, Robert Walker, Belinda Becker.

My Dubious Sexdrive
SEAMLESS. October, 1995. (Lucy Phillips, Glen Scantlebury) Samantha Pendse, Ian Spencer.

My Father's Garden
MIRANDA PRODS. January, 1996. (Miranda Smith) Documentary.

Mystery Science Theater 3000
GRAMERCY. (PG-13) April, 1996. (Jim Mallon) Michael J. Nelson, Trace Beaulieu, Kevin Murphy.

The Next Step
WAVELENGHT. March, 1996. (Christian Faber) Rick Negron, Kristin Moreau, Denise Faye.

Never Met Picasso
MIGHTY REEL. June, 1996. (Stephen Kijak) Margot Kidder, Alexis Arquette, Georgia Ragsdale.

Normal Life
FINE LINE. January, 1996. (John McNaughton) Ashley Judd, Luke Perry, Bruce Young, Jim True, Dawn Maxey.

Notes From Underground
WALKOW-GRUBER/RENEGADE. October, 1995. (Gary Alan Walkow) Henry Czerny, Sheryl Lee, Eammon Roche, Charlie Stratton, Geoffrey Rivas.

The November Men
NORTHERN ARTS. November, 1995. (Paul Williams) Leslie Bevis, James Andronica, Baeu Starr.

Now and Then
NEW LINE. (PG-13) October, 1995. (Lesli Linka) Christina Ricci, Thora Birch, Gaby Hoffman.

Nowhere Fast
CHILD HOODS. February, 1996. (Cinque Lee) Darnell Martin, Addison Cook, Gloria Toyum Park.

Once Upon A Time...When We Were Colored
REPUBLIC (NR) January, 1996. (Tim Reid) Al Freeman, Jr., Phylicia Rashad, Polly Bergen, Richard Roundtree.

One Way Out
ARROW PICTURES. April, 1996. (Kevin Lynn) Jack Swaltney, Jeff Monahan, Isabel Gillies, Annie Golden.

Other Voices, Other Rooms
GOLDEN EYE. October, 1995. (David Rocksavage) Lothaire Bluteau, Anna Thompson, David Speck.

Painted Hero
IRS. (R) November, 1995. (Terry Benedict) Dwight Yokam, Michelle Joyner, Bo Hopkins, John Getz.

The Pallbearer
Miramax. (PG-13) May, 1996. (Matt Reeves) David Schwimmer, Gwyneth Paltrow, Michael Rapaport, Toni Collette, Carol Kane.

Palookaville
PLAYHOUSE INTERNATIONAL. (R) Septmber, 1995. (Alan Taylor) William Forsythe, Vincent Gallo, Frances McDormand.

Paradise Lost:
The Child Murders at Robin Hood Hills
HBO. January, 1996. (Joe Berlinger) Documentary.

Personal Belongings
STEVEN BOGNAR. January, 1996. (Steven Bognar) Documentary.

Persuasion
SONY PICTURE CLASSICS. (PG) September, 1995. (Roger Michell)

Phantom Pain
WHITE STREAK. June 21, 1996. (Neil Matsumoto) Tina Alexis, Scott Reda, Holly Woodland.

Phat Beach
ORION. August 1, 1996. (Doug Ellin) Jermaine (Huggy) Hopkins, Brian Hooks, Gregg Vance.

The Plutonium Circus
GREYCAT. February, 1996. (George Whittenberg Ratliff) Documentary.

Poco Loco
SIGNS OF LIFE. October, 1995. (Deborah Koons) Susan Brecht, George Castillo, Sandra Chapin.

The Portrait of a Lady
GRAMMERCY. September, 1996. (Jane Campion) Nicole Kidman, John Malkovich, Barbara Hershey.

Power 98
WARNERVISION FILMS. April, 1996. (Jaime Hellman) Eric Roberts, Jason Gedrick, Jennie Garth, Larry Drake.

Precious
MIRAMAX. January, 1996. (Alexander Payne) Laura Dern, Swoosie Kurtz, Kurtwood Smith, Mary Kay Place.

Prey of the Jaguar
UNITED FILM DISTRIBUTORS. May 12, 1996. (David DeCoteau) Maxwell Caulfield, Linda Blair, Stacey Keach.

Pterodactyl Woman from Beverly Hills
PTERO PICTURES. January, 1996. (Phillipe Mora) Beverly D'Angelo, Brad Wilson, Moon Zappa.

Raging Angels
MARK BORDE FILMS. (R) November, 1995. (Alan Smithee) Sean Patrick Flannery, Dianne Ladd, Monet Mazur.

Raising Heroes
DOPELGANGER FILMS. June 24, 1996. (Douglas Langway) Troy Sostillio, Henry White, Edmond Sorel.

Ratchet
RATCHET PRODS. Sept., 1996. (John Johnson) Tom Gilroy, Margaret Welsh.

Reckless
GOLDWYN. September, 1995. (Norman Rene) Mia Farrow, Scott Glenn, Mary Luois Parker, Tony Goldwyn, Eileen Brennan, Stephen Dorff, Ginacarlo Esposito.

Red Ribbon Blues
RED RIBBON. Septmber, 1995. (Charles Winkler) Paul Mercurio, Debi Mazar, RuPaul, John Epperson.

The Reggae Movie
UNITED ARTISTS THEATRES. May 2, 1996. (Randy Rovins) Documentary.

Rescuing Desire
PILGRIMS 4. May 16, 1996. (Adam Rodgers) Melinda Mullins, Tamara Tunie, Caitlin Dulany.

Restoration
MIRAMAX. (R) December, 1995. (Michael Hoffman) Robert Downey, Jr., Sam Neill, David Thewlis, Polly Walker, Meg Ryan, Hugh Grant.

Riot
PM ENTERTAINMENT GROUP. May 10, 1996. (Joseph Merhi) Gary Daniels, Sugar Ray Leonard, Paige Rowland.

Ripe
C&P PRODS. April, 1996. (Mo Ogrodnik) Monica Keena, Daisy Eagan, Gordon Currie, Ron Brice.

Rhythm Thief
STRAND. (NR) November 1995. (Matthew Harrison) Jason Andrews, Eddie Daniels, Kevin Corrigan.

Road Movie
WARNER BROS. RECORDS. September, 1996. (Peter Care) Documentary with R.E.M.

Robert Altman's Jazz '34:
Remembrances of Kansas City Swing
SANDCASTLE 5/CIBY 2000. Sept., 1996. (Robert Altman) Harry Belafonte.

The Rolling Stones Rock and Roll Circus
ABKCO/ROLLING STONES. SEPT., 1996. (Michael Lindsay Hogg) The Rolling Stones.

Rude Awakening
S.P.B. FILMS. March, 1996. (Steve Bilich) Denia Ridley, John Ellison, Glen B. Svendrowski, Euan McDonald.

Sacred Hearts
AMERICAN MONGREL.October, 1995. (Patrick O'Connor) Kelly Fritz, Doug Hubbel, Marlene May.

Schizopolis
POINT 406 LTD. May 18, 1996. (Steven Soderbergh) Steven Soderbergh, Betsy Brantley, David Jensen.

Scorpion Spring
ANANT SINGH/DISTANT HORIZON. October, 1995. (Brian Cox) Alfred Molina, Patrick McGaw, Esai Morales, Ruben Blades.

Screamers
TRIUMPH. (R) September, 1995. (Christian Duguay) Peter Weller, Roy Dupus, Charles Powell, Jennifer Rubin.

The Search for One-Eyed Jimmy
NORTHERN ARTS. (R) June 10, 1996. (Sam Henry Kass) Nick Turturro, Steve Buscemi, Michael Baldalucco.

Seeking the Cafe Bob
CALICO DOG PRODS. April 20, 1996. (Jeff Stolhand) Christian Zimmerman, Michael Dalman, Roger Harrell.

Serpent's Lair
KUSHNER-LOCKE (R) October, 1995. (Jeffrey Reiner) Jeff Fahey, Lisa B., Heather Medway, Anthony Palermo.

Shady Grove
DREAM HOME PICTURES. March, 1996. (Christian Moore) Richard (Dicko) Mather, Amy Grappell, Jubal Clark, Lina Haltman.

She's The One
FOX SEARCHLIGHT. (R) September, 1996. (Edward Burns), Jennifer Aniston, Maxine Bahns, Cameron Diaz, John Mahoney.

Shotgun Freeway: Drives Through Lost L.A.
SHOTGUN. December, 1995. (Morgan Neville, Harry Pallenberg) Documentary.

Shut Yer Mouth!
WORD OF MOUTH! March, 1996. (Fraser Bresnahan) Colleen Quinn, Michael Louis Wells, Ben Bode.

Sister Island
WILLIAM MORRIS AGENCY. June, 1996. (Avery Crounse) Kathleen York, Karen Black, Erin Buchanan.

Skin & Bone
FILM RESEARCH UNIT. June 22, 1996. (Everett Lewis) b. Wyatt, Alan Boyce, Garret Scullin.

Sling Blade
MIRAMAX. August, 1996. (Billy Bob Thornton) Billy Bob Thornton, Dwight Yoakam, J.T. Walsh.

Soul In The Hole
HBO. January, 1996. (Danielle Gardner) Documentary.

Special Effects
NOVA/WGBH BOSTON. June 28, 1996. (Ben Burtt) Documentary.

Spirits Rising
RAMONA S. DIAZ. April, 1996. (Diaz) Documentary narrated by William Consul.

Squeeze
MIRAMAX. (R) April, 1996. (Robert Patton-Spruill) Tyrone Burton, Eddie Cutanda, Phuong Duong, Geoffrey Rhue.

Staccato Purr Of The Exhaust
SKUNKBOY INK. January, 1996. (L.M. Meza) Ron Garcia, Michelle Beauchamp, Dennis Brooks, Kristina Haddad.

Stealing Beauty
FOX SEARCHLIGHT. June, 1996. (Bernardo Bertolucci) Liv Tyler, Sinead Cusack, Donal McCann, Jeremy Irons, Jean Marais.

Stonewall
STRAND RELEASING. (NR) July, 1996. (Nigel Finch) Guillermo Diaz, Frederick Weller, Duane Boutte.

Street Corner Justice
Sunset Films International. Sept., 1996. (Chuck Bail) Marc Singer, Steve Railsback, Kim Lankford.

Struggles In Steel
ITVS. January, 1996. (Tony Buba, Raymond Henderson) Documentary. Color/B&W.

The Stupids
NEW LINE. (PG) August, 1996. (John Landis) Tom Arnold, Jessica Lundy, Bug Hall, Alex McKenna, Jenny McCarthy.

The Substance of Fire
MIRAMAX. October, 1996. (Daniel Sullivan) Ron Rifkin, Sarah Jessica Parker, Tony Goldwyn, Timothy Hutton.

Sudden Manhattan
April, 1996. (Adrienne Shelly) Shelly, Tim Guinee, Roger Rees, Louis Lasser.

Swingers
MIRAMAX. Sept., 1996. (Doug Liman) John Favreay.

Switchblade Sisters
MIRAMAX. (R) (Jack Hill) Robbie Lee, Joanne Nail, Monica Gayle.

Sydney
SAMUEL GOLDWYN. January, 1996. (Paul Thomas Anderson) Philip Baker Hall, Gwyneth Paltrow, Samuel L. Jackson, John C. Reilly.

Synthetic Pleasures
CAIPIRINHA. September, 1995. (Iara Lee) Documentary.

Tattoo Boy
GOTHAM/OREGON.October, 1995. (Larry Turner) C.J. Barkus, Amanda Tirey, Matthew James.

Theodore Rex
NEW LINE CINEMA. June 27, 1996. (Jonathan Betuel) Whoopi Goldberg, Armin Mueller-Stahl, Juliet Landau.

A Thin Line Between Love And Hate
NEW LINE. (R) April, 1996. (Martin Lawrence) Lawrence, Lynn Whitfield, Regina King, Bobby Brown, Della Reese.

Things To Do In Denver When You're Dead
MIRAMAX. (R) December, 1995. (Gary Fleder) Andy Garcia, Christopher Walken, Treat Wiliams.

Things I Never Told You
EDDIE SAETA/CARBO FILMS. April, 1996. (Isabel Coixet) Lili Taylor, Andrew McCarthy, Debi Mazar, Alexis Arquette.

This is Cuba
ASPECT RATIO/UNA CHICA ENT. February, 1996. (Chris Hume) Documentary

Three Wishes
SAVOY. (PG) October, 1995. (Martha Coolidge) Patrick Swayze, Mary Elizabeth Mastranonio, Seth Mumy.

Throwing Down
NIGHT LIGHT. October, 1995. (Lawrence O'Neill) Jeffrey Donovan, Kevin Pinassi, Colleen Werthmann.

Timeless
TGOM. July 11, 1996. (Chris Hart) Peter Byrne, Melissa Duge, Michael Griffiths.

'Til Christmas
GOOD MACHINE. May 14, 1996. (Jon Sherman) Dan Futterman, Susan Floyd, Nadia Dajani.

The Toilers and The Wayfarers
OUTSIDER. December, 1995. (Keith Froelich) Matt Klemp, Ralf Schirg, Andrew Woodhouse, Michael Glen.

Total Eclipse
FINE LINE. (R) November, 1995. (Agnieska Holland) Leonardo DiCaprio, David Thewlis, Dominique Blanc.

Trailer Camp
ARTISTIC LICENSE. January, 1996. (Jenni Olson) Compilation.

Traps
FILMOPOLIS. December, 1995. (Pauline Chan) Saaskia reeves, Robert Reynolds, Jacqueline McKenzie.

The Trigger Effect
GRAMERCY. (R) June 4, 1966. (David Koepp) Kyle MacLachlan, Elisabeth Shue, Dermot Mulroney.

Tromeo & Juliet
TROMA, NY. May 13, 1996. (Lloyd Kaufman) Will Keenan, Jane Jensen, Debbie Rochon.

Troublesome Creek: A Midwestern
WEST CITY. January, 1996. (Jeanne Jordan) Documentary.

Twilight Highway
SHOOTING GALLERY. November, 1995. (Laurie Taylor-Williams) Sandy Baron, D.V. De Vincentis.

Twisted
DONS QUIXOTE. July 1, 1996. (Seth Michael) David Norona, Keivyn McNeil Graves, Anthony Crivelo.

Two Bits
MIRAMAX. August, 1996. (James Foley) Jerry Barone, Mary Elizabeth Mastrantonio, Al Pacino, Joe Grifasi, Joanna Merlin.

Voices
AVENUE PICTURES. September, 1995. (Malcolm Clarke) Jeremy Northam, Tushka Bergen, Allan Corduner, Hilton Mcrae.

Waiting for Guffman
SONY PICTURES CLASSICS. August, 1996. (Christoper Guest) Christopher Guest, Eugene Levy, Fred Willard.

Walking and Talking
MIRAMAX. January, 1996. (Nicole Holofcener) Catherine Keener, Anne Heche, Todd Field.

Wallace & Gromit
NORTHERN ARTS. April, 1996. Animated.

The Watermelon Woman
DANCING GIRLS PROD. February 25, 1996. (Cheryl Dunye) Guin Turner, Valerie Walker, Lisa Marie Bronson.

Welcome Says The Angel
SILVER SHADOW. February, 1996. (Phillipe Dib) Jon Jacobs, Ayesha Hauer, Leroy Jones, Marian O'Brien.

Welcome to the Dollhouse
SUBURBAN PICTURES. September, 1995. (Todd Solondz) Heather Matarazzo, Daria Kalinina, Matthew Faber, Angela Pietropinto, Bill Buell.

When Night Is Falling
OCTOBER (NC-17) November, 1995. (Patricia Rozema) Rachael Crawford, Pascale Bussieres, Henry Czerny.

When We Were Kings
UFA NON-FICTION/USA January, 1996. (Leon Gast) Documentary.

Where Truth Lies
SILVERLINE PICS. April, 1996. (William H. Molina) John Savage, Kim Cattral, Malcolm McDowell, Cadice Daly.

White Man's Burden
SAVOY. (R) October, 1995. (Desmond Nakano) John Travolta, Harry Belafonte, Kelly Lynch, Margaret Avery.

The Whole Wide World
KUSHNER-LOCKE. January, 1996. (Dan Ireland) Vincent D'Onofrio, Renee Zellweger, Harve Presnell.

Who Is Henry Jaglom?
CALLIOPE. December, 1995. (Alex Rubin, Jeremy Workman) Documentary.

Wild Bill: Hollywood Maverick
TURNER. January, 1996. (Todd Robinson) Documentary.

Wings of Courage
SONY PICTURES CLASSICS. (G) February, 1996. (Jean-Jacques Annaud), Craig Sheffer, Ton Hulce, Elizabeth McGovern, Val Kilmer; IMAX 3-D.

The Winner
NORTSAR/MDP WORLDWIDE. September, 1996. (Alex Cox) Vincent D'Onofrio, Rebecca DeMornay, Delroy Lindo, Frank Whaley, Michael Madsen.

Without Evidence
MFD LTD. March, 1996. (Gill Dennis) Scott Plank, Anna Gunn, Andrew Prine, Angelina Jolie, Paul Perri.

Women Outside
THIRD WORLD NEWSREEL. February, 1996. (JT Takagi) Documentary.

Work
DISTRICT PICTURES. March, 1996. (Rachel Reichmann) Cynthia Kaplan, Sonja Sohn, Peter Sprague.

FOREIGN INDEPENDENT RELEASES, 1995-96

Many of the following films have been released in a limited fashion at film festivals or other similar venues but have not yet been nationally distributed. Directors are in parenthesis.

Acropole
GREEK FILM CENTER, Athens. May, 1996. Greek-Bulgarian-Italian-German. (Pantelis Voulgaris) Lefteris Voyatzis, Stavros Paravas, Constanatine Tzoumas.

The Adventures of Pinocchio
NEW LINE CINEMA. June, 1996. British-French-German. (Steve Barron) Martin Landau, Jonathan Taylor Thomas, Genevieve Bujold.

Un Air De Famille
CANAL PLUS. May, 1996. French. (Cedric Klapisch) Jean-Pierre Bacri, Agnes Jaoui, Jean-Pierre Darroussin.

Alfred
SANDREWS. December, 1995. Swedish. (Vilgot Sjoman) Sven Wollter, Rita Russek, Judit Danyi.

All of Them Witches
VIDEOCINE. June, 1996. Mexican. (Daniel Gruener) Susana Zabaleta, Alejandro Tommasi, Delia Casanova.

All Things Fair
COLUMBIA/TRISTAR. October, 1995. Swedish. (Bo Widerberg) Johan Widerberg, Marika Lagerkrantz.

Anna Oz
STUDIO CANAL PLUS. September, 1996. French-Italian-Swiss. (Eric Rochant) Charlotte Gainsbourg, Gerard Lanvin, Sami Bouajila.

Antonia's Line
FIRST LOOK. October, 1995. Dutch. (Marleen Gorris) Willeke Van Amerooy, Els Dottermans, Jan Decleir.

The Apprentices
GALA FILM. November, 1995. French. (Pierre Salvadori) Francois Cluzet, Guillaume Depardieu.

The Art of Remembrance: Simon Wiesenthal
RIVER LIGHTS PICTURES. May, 1996. German. Documentary. (Johanna Heer, Werner Schmeidel)

At Full Gallop
TOR FILM STUDIO. May, 1996. Polish. (Krzysztof Zanussi) Maja Komorowska, Bartosz Obuchowicz.

Au Petit Marguery
FILMS DU LOSANGE. November, 1995. French. (Laurent Benegui) Stephane Audran, Michel Aumont.

August Vacation (Ferie D'Agosto)
CECCHI GORI. April, 1996. Italian. (Paolo Virzi) Silvio Orlando, Sabrina Ferilli, Ennio Fantastichini.

Autumn In Paradise
SONET. December, 1995. Swedish. (Richard Hobert) Mona Malm, Sven Lindberg, Goran Stangertz.

Autumn Sun (Sol de Otono)
EDUARDO MIGNOGNA & ASSOCIADOS. September, 1996. Argentine. (Eduardo Mignogna) Norma Aleandro, Jorge Luz.

B. Love: Colder Than Death
SCARABEE FILMS, Paris. March, 1996. French-Turkish-Swiss. (Canan Gerede) Bennu Gerede, Kadir Inanir, Aysegul Unsal.

Back of Beyond
TOURIST FILMS. November, 1995. Australian. (Michael Robertson) Paul Mercurio, Colin Friels.

Background Noise
LUCKY RED DISTRIBUZIONE. April, 1996. Italian. (Claudio Camarca) Francesco Dominedo, Francesco Meoni, Guiditta Del Vecchio.

Bastard Brood (Enfants De Salaud)
UFD (France) April, 1996. French. (Tonie Marshall) Anemone, Nathalie Baye, Molly Ringwald.

Beaumarchais
ALLIANCE. August, 1996. French. (Edourd Molinaro) Fabrice Luchini, Sandrine Kerlain, Michel Serrault.

Beautiful Mystery
NEK. February, 1996; originally released 1983. Japanese. (Genji Nakamura) Tatuya Nagatomo, Kei Shiyuto, Ren Osugi.

Body Without Soul
MIROFILM. June, 1996. Czech Republic. Documentary (Wiktor Grodecki)

The Boy From Mercury
LE STUDIO CANAL PLUS, Paris. June, 1996. Irish-French-British. (Martin Duffy) James Hickey, Rita Tushingham, Tom Courtenay.

The Boys Club
LE MONDE ENTERTAINMENT, Toronto. May, 1996. Canadian. (John Fawcett) Chris Penn, Dominic Amprogna, Devon Sawa.

Brilliant Lies
VILLAGE ROADSHOW. April, 1996. Australian. (Richard Franklin) Gia Carides, Anthony LaPaglia, Zoe Carides.

Broken English
SONY PICTURES CLASSICS. August, 1996. New Zealand. (Gregor Nicholas) Aleksandra Vujcic, Julian Arahanga.

Brother of Sleep
SONY PICTURES CLASSICS. (R) October, 1996. Austrian. (Joseph Vilsmaier) Andre Eisermann, Dana Vavrova.

Bruno's Waiting in the Car
ITALIAN INTL. FILM. April, 1996. Italian. (Duccio Camerini) Nancy Brilli, Antonello Fassari, Leo Gullotta.

Buenos Aires Vice Versa
MGI INTL. May, 1996. Argentine-Dutch. (Alejandro Agresti) Vera Fogwill, Fernan Miras, Mirta Busnelli.

The Butterfly Effect
UIP, Spain. January, 1996. Spanish-French. (Fernando Colomo) Maria Barranco, Coque Malla, James Fleet.

By The Dawn's Early Light
DANISH FILM INSTITUTE WORKSHOP. June, 1996. Danish. (Knud Vesterkov) Documentary.

Camping Cosmos
BRUSSELS AVE. May, 1996. Belgian. (Jan Bucquoy) Jean-Henri Compere, Fanny Hanciaux, Eve Ferrari.

Caught in the Act
MIDSUMMER FILMS, London. May, 1996. British. (Mark Greenstreet) Sara Crowe, Annette Badland, Nadia Sawalha.

Cemetary Man
OCTOBER FILMS. (R) April, 1996. Italian-French-British. (Michele Soavi) Rupert Everett, Francois Hadji-Lazaro, Anna Falchi.

Chacun cherche son chat
MALO FILMS. August, 1996. French. (Cedric Klapisch)

A Chef in Love
UGC. May, 1996. French-Georgian. (Nana Djordjadze) Pierre Richard, Micheline Presle.

Christmas Vacation
FILMAURO. December, 1995. Italian. (Neri Parenti) Luke Perry, Massimo Baldi, Christian diSica.

Chungking Express
MIRAMAX/ROLLING THUNDER. (PG-13) Chinese. (Wong Kar Wei) Brigitte Lin, Tony Leung.

City of Lost Children
SONY PICTURES CLASSICS. (R) October, 1995. French. (Jean-Pierre Jeunet) Ron Perlman, Daniel Emilfork, Jean-Louis Trintignant, Domninique Pinon.

Close Shave
MKL. March, 1996. French. (Etienne Dhaene) Jean-Marc Barr, Anemone, Olivia Bonamy.

The Confessions Of An Innocent Man
CINEXPORT. April, 1996. French. (Jean-Pierre Ameris) Bruno Putzulu, Elisabeth Depardieu, Michele Laroque.

Corisco and Dada
GRUPO NOVO DE CINEMA ETV. May, 1996. Brazilian. (Rosemberg Cariry) Chico Dias, Dira Paes.

Cosi
MIRAMAX. April, 1996. Autralian. (Mark Joffe) Ben Mendelsohn, Barry Otto, Toni Collette, Greta Scacchi, Paul Mercurio.

The Crusade of Anne Buridan
LOLISTAR. December, 1995. (Judith Cahen) Cahen, Joel Luecht.

A Cry In The Night
CFP DISTRIB. April, 1996. Canadian. (Jean Beaudry) Pierre Curzi, Felix-Antoine Leroux, Louise Richer.

Dating the Enemy
PANDORA FILM. May, 1996. Australian. (Megan Simpson Huberman) Claudia Karvan, Guy Pearce, Matt Day.

Delphine 1—Yvan 0
AMLF, Paris. June, 1996. French. (Dominique Farrugia) Julie Gayet, Serge Hazanavicius, Dominique Farrugia.

Desire
AMLF (France) March, 1996. French. (Bernard Murrat) Jean-Paul Belmondo, Fanny Arant, Beatrice Dalle.

Diary Of A Seducer
GEMINI FILMS. December, 1995. French. (Daniele Dubroux) Chiara Mastroianni, Melvil Poupaud.

Diary Of A Young Fool (Memoire D'Un Jeune Con)
MKL. January, 1996. French. (Patrick Aurignac) Christophe Hemon, Francois Perier, Daniel Russo, Aurignac, Alexandra London, Emanuelle Seigner.

Different For Girls
BBC FILMS. January, 1996. (Richard Spence) Steven Mackintosh, Rupert Graves, Saskia Reeves.

Drifting Clouds
CHRISTA SAREDI, Zurich. May, 1996. Finnish. (Aki Kaurismaki) Kati Outinen, Kari Vaananen, Elina Salo.

A Drifting Life
CENTRAL MOTION PICTURE CORP. May, 1996. Taiwanese. (Lin Cheng-sheng) Lee Kang-sheng, Vicky Wei, Grace Chen.

Drowning
SHANGHAI FILM STUDIO. November, 1995. Chinese. (Hu Xueyang) Xueyang, Saren Gaowa, Yang Ming.

Earth
SOGEPAQ INTL. May, 1996. Spanish. (Julio Medem) Carmelo Gomez, Emma Suarez, Karra Elejalde.

Elective Affinities
SACIS. May, 1996. French-Italian. (Paolo and Vittorio Taviani) Isabelle Huppert, Jean-Hugues Anglade, Fabrizio Bentivoglio.

The Elephant Master
CIBY. December, 1995. French-Spanish. (Patrick Grandperret) Erwan Baynaud, Jacques Dutrone.

Emma
MIRAMAX. June, 1996. British. (Douglas McGrath) Gwyneth Paltrow, Jeremy Northam, Toni Collette.

The Emperor's Shadow
OCEAN FILM, Hong Kong. May, 1996. Hong Kong-China. (Zhou Xiaowen) Jiang Wen, Ge You, Xu Qing.

Encore
PARIS-NEW YORK PRODUCTION. French. (Pascal Bonitzer) Jacky Berroyer, Valeria Bruni-Tedeschi, Natacha Regnier.

Erotic Tales II
REGINA ZIEGLER. December, 1995. German. (Cinzia TH Torrini, Nicolas Roeg, Janusz Makewski)

Escoriandoli
ADRIANA CHIESA ENT. September, 1996. Italian. (Antonio Rezza) Isabel Ferrari, Valeria Golino, Claudia Gerrini.

Exquisite Tenderness
GUILD FILM. November, 1995. U.S.-German. (Carl Schenkel) Isabel Glasser, James Remar, Sean Haberle.

Fall Out
MKL. June, 1996. French. (Jean-Denis Robert) Stanislas Crevillen, Laure Duthilleul, Pierre-Arnaud Crespeau.

The Father
FARABI CINEMA FOUNDATION, Tehran. May, 1996. Iranian. (Majid Majidi) Mohammad Kasebi, Parivash Nazarieh, Hassan Sadeghi.

The Ferry
VILNIS KALNAELLIS. May, 1996. Latvian. Documentary. (Laila Pakalnina)

Few Of Us
MERCURE. May, 1996. Portuguese-French-German-Lithuanian. (Sharunas Bartas) Katerina Golubeva, Sergei Tulayev, Piotr Kishteev.

The Fishing Net
November, 1995. Sri Lankan. (H.D. Premaaratne) Anosha Sonali, Jackson Anthony, W. Jayasiri.

A Fistful of Fingers
BLUE DOLPHIN. November, 1995. British. (Edgar Wright) Graham Low, Martin Curtis, Oliver Evans.

Flame
BLACK & WHITE FILM CO. May, 1996. Zimbabwean. (Ingrid Sinclair) Marian Kunonga, Ulla Mahaka, Norman Madawo.

The Flower of My Secret
SONY PICTURES CLASSICS. (R) April, 1996. Spanish-French. (Pedro Amaldovar) Marisa Paredez, Juan Echanove.

Follow Your Heart (Va' Dove Ti Porta II Cuore)
FILMAURO. January, 1996. Italian-French-German. (Cristina Comencini) Virna Lisi, Margherita Buy, Galatea Ranzi.

For Want of Sun
PIERRE GRISE. June, 1996. French. (Christophe Blanc) Jean-Jacques Benhamou, Sara Haxaire, Christian Baltauss.

Forgotten Silver
PANDORA FILM, Paris. May, 1996. New Zealand. (Peter Jackson) Sam Neill, Leonard Maltin, Harvey Weinstein.

Frankenstein and Me
MALOFILM INTL. April, 1996. Canadian. (Robert Tinnell) Jamieson Boulanger, Burt Reynolds, Louise Fletcher.

French Twist
MIRAMAX ZOE. (R) January, 1996. French. (Josiane Balasko) Victoria Abril, Balasko, Alain Chabat.

Full Speed
POLYGRAM FILM. April, 1996. French. (Gael Morel) Elodie Bouchez, Stephane Rideau, Pascal Cervo.

Le Garcu
PAN-EUROPEENNE. October, 1995. French. (Maurice Pialat) Gerard Depardieu, Geralding Pailhas.

Ghost In The Shell
MANGA ENTERTAINMENT LTD. April, 1996. Japanese. (Mamoru Oshii) Animated.

The Gingko Bed
GOLDEN NETWORK, HONG KONG/MORE IN GROUP, SEOUL. South Korean. May, 1996. (Jacky Kang) Han Suk-kyu, Shim Hae-jin, Jin Hee-kyung.

The Girl of the Silence
FILM-MAKERS. November, 1995. Japanese. (Genjiro Arato) Mami Nakamura, Kaori Momoi.

The Graduates
WARNER ITALIA. December, 1995. Italian. (Leonardo Pieraccioni) Rocco Papaleo, Gianmarco Tognazzi.

The Grand Dukes
BAC FILMS. January, 1996. January, 1996. (Patrice Leconte) Phillipe Noiret, Michel Blanc.

Gypsy Soul
ALTAFILMS (Spain) January, 1996. (Chuz Gutierrez) Amara Carmona, Pedro Alonso, Peret, Rafael Alvarez. Loles Leon.

Half Spirit: Voice Of The Spider
QUARTET. September, 1995. French. (Henri Barges) Catherine Ussel, Phillipe Spiteri, Marc Duret.

Happiness Is In The Field
BAC FILMS. December, 1995. French. (Etienne Chatiliez) Michel Serrault, Eddy Mitchell.

Hard Core Logo
CFP INTL. May, 1996. Canadian. (Bruce McDonald) Hugh Dillon, Keith Callum Rennie, John Pyper-Ferguson.

Haru
CINEQUANON, Paris/Tokyo. May, 1996. Japanese. (Yoshimitsu Morita) Eri Fukatsu, Masaki Uchino, Naho Toda.

Haunted
OCTOBER. November, 1995. British. (Lewis Gilbert) Aidan Quinn, Kate Beckinsdale, Anthony Andrews.

Hi Cousin!
LEONOR FILMS. May, 1996. French-Algerian-Belgian-Luxembourgian. (Merzak Allouache) Gad Elmaleh, Mess Hattou, Magaly Berdy.

Hollow Reed
SCALA. January, 1996. (Angela Pope) Martin Donovan, Joely Richardson, Ian Hart, Jason Flemyng, Sam Bould.

Honeymoon Trips
WARNER BROS. ITALIA. December, 1995. Italian. (Carlo Verdone) Claudia Gerini, Cinzia Mascoli.

Horseman on the Roof
MIRAMAX/ZOE. (R) French. (Jean-Paul Rappeneau) Juliette Binoche, Olivier Martinez, Isabelle Carre, Francois Cluzet.

Intimate Relations
FOX SEARCHLIGHT. June, 1996. British-Canadian. (Philip Goodhew) Julie Walters, Rupert Graves, Laura Sadler.

Iron Eagle IV
NORSTAR. January, 1996. Canadian. (Sidney J. Furie) Louis Gossett Jr, Al Waxman, Jason Cadieux.

Ivo the Genius
UIP. October, 1995. Italian. (Alessandro Benvenuti) Benvenuti, Francesca Neri, Davide Bechini.

Jude
POLYGRAM. June, 1996. British. (Michael Winterbottom) Christopher Eccleston, Kate Winslet.

Kansas City
FINE LINE. (R) June, 1996. French-U.S. (Robert Altman) Jennifer Jason Leigh, Miranda Richardson, Harry Belafonte.

Kids Return
OFFICE KITANO. May, 1996. Japanese. (Takeshi Kitano) Masanobu Ando, Ken Kaneko.

Killer Tongue
SOGEPAQ INTL., Madrid. May, 1996. Spanish-British. (Alberto Sciamma) Melinda Clarke, Jason Durr, Robert Englund.

The Kingdom
OCTOBER. November, 1995. Swedish. (Lars Von Trier) Ernst Hugo Jaregard, Kirsten Rolffes, Ghita Norby, Udo Kier.

Kolya
MIRAMAX. September, 1996. Czech-British-French. (Jan Sverak) Zdenek Sverak, Andrej Chalimon, Libuse Safrankova.

Law of the Frontier
UIP, Spain. January, 1996. Spanish. (Adolfo Aristarain) Pere Ponce, Achero Manas, Aitana Sanchez-Gijon.

Living Dream
CELESTIAL MEDIA ORGANIZATION. May, 1996. Chinese. (Hu Xueyang) Jindao Xinxin, Zhang Mengxi, Chang Rong.

Loch Ness
GRAMERCY. February, 1996. British. (John Henderson) Ted Danson, Joely Richardson, Ian Hom.

Looking For Paradise
MEDUSA, Italy. December, 1995. Italian. (Mario Monicelli) Margherita Buy, Lello Arena, Philippe Noiret.

Loose Ends
LUNA-FILM GmbH. June, 1996. German. (Sandra Nettlebeck) Regula Grauwiller, Jasmin Tabatabai, Natascha Bub.

The Lost Garden:
The Life and Cinema of Alice Guy-Blanche
NATIONAL FILM BOARD OF CANADA. Canadian. (Marquise LePage) Documentary.

Love Case
SMART EGG PICTURES. May, 1996. Italian. (Riccardo Sesani) Stephane Ferrara, Marina Giulia Cavalli, Maria Luisa Tadeo.

Love Story With Cramps
CECCHI GORI, Italy. January, 1996. Italian. (Pino Quartullo) Sergio Rubini, Chiara Caselli, Debora Caprioglio, Rosella Falk.

Lulu
ALLIANCE. May, 1996. Canadian. (Srinivas Krishna) Kim Lieu , Clark Johnson, Michael Rhoades.

Lumiere and Company
CINETEVE. November, 1995. French-Spanish-Swedish. (Sarah Moon) Documentary.

Les Lumiere De Berlin
LES FILMS DU LOSANGE. July, 1996. German. (Wim Wenders) Udo Kier, Nadine Buttner, Christoph Merg.

Lust and Revenge
SEAWELL FILMS, Paris. March, 1996. Australian. (Paul Cox) Nicholas Hope, Gosia Dobrowolska, Claudia Karvan.

Macadam Tribe
MERCURE DISTRIBUTION. May, 1996. Zairian-French. (Jose Laplaine) Lydia Ewande, Hassane Kouyate, Sidy Camara.

Madame Butterfly
FILMS DU LOSANGE. December, 1995. French. (Frederic Mitterand) Ying Huang, Richard Troxell.

Making A Film For Me Is Living
October, 1995. Italian. (Enrica Antonioni) Documentary.

The Making of The Mahatma
NFDC, Bombay. May, 1996. Indian-South African. (Shyam Benegal) Rajit Kapur, Pallavi Joshi, Keith Stevenson.

The Mandarin
GRUPO NOVO DE CINEMA ETV. May, 1996. Brazilian. (Julio Bressane) Fernando Eiras, Giulia Gam, Gal Costa.

Mayor Oedipus
LATINA, Mexico. May, 1996. Colombian-Mexican-Spanish. (Jorge Ali Triana) Jorge Perugorria, Angela Molina, Francisco Rabal.

Men Of The Port (Les Hommes Du Port)
LES FILM DU CYCLONE. April, 1996. Swiss-French. (Alain Tanner) Documentary.

Mistaken Identity
ALLEGRO. February, 1996. Canadian. (Gilles Noel) Michel Cote, Macha Grenon, Paul Doucet.

Moebius
UNIVERSIDAD DE CINE. September, 1996. Argentine. (Gustavo Mosquera & students of the Universidad de Cine) Guillermo Angelelli, Roberto Carnaghi.

The Monster
CFP DISTRIBUTION. April, 1996. Italian. (Roberto Benigni) Benigni, Michel Blanc, Nicoletta Braschi.

Moon Lake
GREEN FOREST ADVERTISEMENT CO. May, 1996. Taiwanese. (Hu Chen-hsiang) Wang Yu-wen, Shaw Chwan-yeong, Jan Jye-shiun.

Motel
CINEMA LIBRE. November, 1995. Canadian. (Pascal Maeder) Anna Papdakos, Jerry Snell, Carlo d'Orlando.

Mouth to Mouth
MIRAMAX. November, 1995. Spanish. (Manual Gomez Periera) Javier Bardem, Aitana Sanchez-Gijon.

Mr. Reliable: A True Story
POLYGRAM. May, 1996. Australian. (Nadia Tass) Colin Friels, Jacqueline McKenzie, Paul Sonkkila.

La Murciaiola
CIANCARELLI ART. April, 1996. Italian-U.S. (Olivia Ciancarelli) Odetta Ciancarelli, Carolina Bracci.

Murmuring
DOCU FACTORY VISTA. March, 1996. South Korean. (Byun Young-joo) Documentary.

My Favorite Season (Ma Saison Préférée)
FILMOPOLIS. April, 1996. French. (André Téchiné) Catherine Deneuve, Daniel Auteuil.

My Friend Joe
PORTMAN ENTERTAINMENT GROUP, London. June, 1996. Irish-German. (Chris Bould) Schuyler Fisk, John Cleere, Stephen McHattie.

My Last Man
GAVIOLA PRODS. May, 1996. Chilean. (Tatiana Gaviola) Claudia DiGirolamo, Willy Semler, Liliana Garcia.

My Summer Vacation
ORTON PRODS. May, 1996. Canadian. (Sky Gilbert) Clinton Walker, Christofer Williamson.

The Nest (Ligdza)
TRIS FILM STUDIO. April, 1996. Latvian. (Aivars Freimanis) Leonids Locenieks, Dace Bonate.

Never Ever
TRIMARK PICTURES. September, 1996. U.S.-British. (Charles Finch) Sandrine Bonnaire, Jane March, Charles Finch.

Next Year ... We'll Go to Bed By Ten
SACIS INTL. June 8, 1996. Italian. (Angelo Orlando) Angelo Orlando, Ricky Memphis, Ninetto Davoli

Nico Icon
ROXIE. January, 1996. German. (Susanne Ofteringer) Documentary.

No Sex Last Night
PIERRE GRISE (France) French-U.S. (Sophie Calle) Documentary.

Nobody Loves Me
COBRA. November, 1995. (Doris Dorrie) Maria Schrader, Pierre Sanoussi-Bloiss, Michael Von Ua.

Nobody Will Speak of Us When We're Dead
FLAMENCO. January, 1996. Spanish. (Augustin Diaz Yanes) Victoria Abril, Federico Luppi, Pilar Bardem.

Not Me!
MALOFILM INTL., Montreal. May, 1996. Canadian. (Pierre Gang) Louise Portal, Isabelle Pasco, Patrice Godin.

Nueba Yol
KIT PARKER/D'PELICULA. February, 1996. Dominican. (Angel Muniz) Lusito Marti, Caridad Ravelo, Raul Carbonell.

The Ogre
UGC D.A. August, 1996. German-French-British. (Volker Schlondorff) John Malkovich, Armin Mueller-Stahl, Marianne Sagebrecht, Gottfried John.

1-900
ZETGEIST. October, 1995. Dutch. (Theo van Gogh) Ariane Schulter, Ad Van Kempen.

Once Upon A Time...This Morning
FIVE STARS. February, 1996. Thai. (Bhandit Rittakol) Jintara Sukkapat, Satisuk Phromisi. Martang Jantranee.

One And A Half
MEDIA ASIA. December, 1995. Hong Kong. (Lawrence Ah Mon) Zhang Fengyi, Carrie Ng, Paul Chen.

Oskar And Jack
JANE BALFOUR FILMS. April, 1996. German. (Frauke Sandig) Documentary.

Parental Guidance
LES CINEMAS DE LA ZONE, Paris. May, 1996. French. (Lucile Hadzihalilovic) Sandra Sammartino, Michel Trillot, Denise Schropfer.

Perfect Love!
FLACH PYRAMIDE INTL. May, 1996. French. (Catherine Breillat) Isabelle Renauld, Francis Renaud, Laura Saglio.

Persuasion
SONY PICTURES CLASSICS. (PG) October, 1995. British. (Roger Michell) Ciaran Hinds, Amanda Root.

Pictures Of The Soul
ADAGIO SRL. October, 1995. Argentinian. (Diego Musiak) Jorge Diez, Maria Lura Leon, China Zorilla.

The Postwoman
VILNIS KALNAELLIS. May, 1996. Latvian. Documentary. (Laila Pakalnina)

Prisoners of War
LAB 80. June, 1996. Italian. (Yervant Gianikian, Angela Ricci Lucchi) (Documentary)

Private Lives
NEW LIFE. May, 1996. Icelandic. (Thrainn Bertelsson) Gottskalkur Dagur, Dora Takefusa, Olafur Egilsson.

The Promise
SEAWELL FILMS, Paris. May, 1996. Belgian-French-Luxembourgian. (Jean-Pierre Dardenne) Jeremie Renier, Olivier Gourmet, Assita Ouedraogo.

Quicksand
LES FILMS DE LA LIANE. April, 1996. French. (Paul Carpita) Beppe Clericci, Daniel San Pedro, Ludiuine Vaillet.

Rainbow
FIRST INDEPENDENT. July, 1996. Canadian-British. (Bob Hoskins) Dan Aykroyd, Saul Rubinek, Terry Finn.

Rainbow for Rimbaud
MICHELE RAY-GAVRAS. June, 1996. French. (Jean Teule) Laure Marsac, Robert MacLeod, Bernadette Lafont.

Red Blooded 2
SC ENTERTAINMENT, Toronto. May, 1996. Canadian. (David Blyth) Kari Salin, Kristoffer Ryan Winters, Burt Young.

Red Cherry
MOONSTONE INT'L. January, 1996. Chinese. (Ye Ying) Guo Ke-Yu, Xiu Xiao-Li, Vladimir Mizmiroff.

Redeem Her Honor
STAR CINEMA. November, 1995. Filipino. (Marilou Diaz Albaya) Sharmaine Arnaiz, Chin Chin Gutierrez.

Regular Guys
BUENA VISTA INTL. May, 1996. German. (Rolf Silber) Christoph M. Ohrt, Carin C. Tietze, Tim Bergmann.

Rendezvous in Paris
ARTIFICIAL EYE. August, 1996. French. (Eric Rohmer) Clara Bellar, Antoine Basler, Serge Renko.

Ridicule
POLYGRAM (France) April, 1996. French. (Patrice Leconte) Charles Berling, Jean Rochefort, Fanny Ardant.

Sahara
ROADSHOW. June, 1996. Australian-U.S. (Brian Trenchard-Smith) James Belushi, Jerome Ehlers, Paul Empson.

Salt in the Wound
FERNANDO COLOMO/MANDALA. May, 1996. Spanish-Argentine. (Alberto Lecchi) Juanjo Puigcorbe, Karra Elejalde, Dario Grandinetti.

A Saturday on Earth
AFMD. May, 1996. French. (Diane Bertrand) Elsa Zylberstein, Eric Caravaca.

Savages
MEDUSA, Italy. January, 1996. Italian. (Carlo Vanzina) Enzo Greggio, Cinzia Leone, Leo Gullotta.

The Scream of the Silk
PRESIDENT FILMS, Paris. April, 1996. French-Swiss-Belgian. (Yvon Marciano) Marie Trintignant, Sergio Castellitto, Anemone.

Sebastian
MEFISTO FILM/MIRAMAR/NORDISK FILM. June, 1996. Norwegian-Swedish. (Svend Wam) Hampus Bjorck, Nicolai Cleve Broch, Ewa Froling.

The Second Time
LUCKY RED. November, 1995. Italian-French. (Mimmo Calopresti) Nanni Moretti, Valeria Bruni Tedeschi.

Secrets & Lies
FILM FOUR. June, 1996. French-British. (Mike Leigh) Timothy Spall, Brenda Blethyn, Phyllis Logan.

Seize The Day (Uz)
BONTONFILM (Czech R.) April, 1996. Czech. (Zdenek Tyc) Radek Holub, Barbora Hrzanova.

Select Hotel
CLIMAX, Paris. April, 1996. French. (Laurent Bouhnik) Julie Gayet, Jean-Michel Fete, Serge Blumental.

Shall We Dance
DAIEI/NTV NETWORK/HAKUHODO/NIPPAN. May, 1996. Japanese. (Masayuki Suo) Koji Yakusyo, Tamiyo Kusakari, Naoto Takenaka.

Shanghai Triad
SONY PICTURES CLASSICS. (R) January, 1996. Chinese. (Zhang Yimou)

Shine
RONIN, Aus. January, 1996. Australian-British. (Scott Hicks) Armin Mueller-Stahl, Noah Taylor, Lynn Redgrave, John Gielgud, Nicholas Bell.

The Shooter
DIMENSION. January, 1996. British-U.S.-Spanish-Czech. (Ted Kotcheff) Dolph Ludgren, Maruschka Detmers.

Shut Up and Listen!
NORDIC SCREEN DEVELOPMENT. May 16, 1996. Norwegian. (Erik Gustavson) Bjorn Floberg, Kjersti Holmen, Keve Hjelm.

A Single Girl
CINEA. November, 1995. French. (Benoit Jacquot) Virginie Ledoyen, Benoit Magimel, Vera Briole.

The Size of Watermelons
NORSTAR ENTERTAINMENT, Toronto. May, 1996. Canadian. (Kari Skogland) Paul Rudd, Donal Logue, Marissa Ribisi.

Somebody Up There Likes Me
LONG SHOW PICTURES. June, 1996. Hong Kong. (Patrick Leung) Aaron Kwok, Carmen Lee, Sammo Hung.

The Spirit And Mystery of Flamenco
CINEMATHEQUE DE LA DANSE. April, 1996. Spanish. Antonio, Pilar Lopez and the Ballet Espanol.

Star Maker
MIRAMAX. March, 1996. Italian. (Giuseppe Tornatore) Serio Castellitto, Tiziana Lodato.

Strangers in Beijing (Hun Zai Beijing)
SOUTHERN FILM CO. April, 1996. Chinese. (He Qun) Zhang Guoli, Ju Xuem, Xi Meijuan.

A Summer's Tale
LES FILMS DU LOSANGE, Paris. May, 1996. French. (Eric Rohmer) Melvil Poupaud, Amanda Langlet, Aurelia Nolin.

The Super-Wife
ATLAS INTL. Munich. June, 1996. German. (Soenke Wortmann) Veronica Ferres, Joachim Krol, Thomas Heinze.

Supercop
MIRAMAX/DIMENSION. (R) July, 1996. Chinese. (Stanley Tong) Jackie Chan, Michelle Khan, Maggie Cheung.

Tears of Stone
TELEPICTURE MARKETING, London. May, 1996. Icelandic. (Hilmar Oddsson) Throstur Leo Gunnarsson, Ruth Olafsdottir, Heinz Bennent.

301, 302
MORNING CALM. September, 1995. South Korean. (Chul-Soo Park) Eun-Jin Pang, Sin-Hye Hwang.

Thieves
STUDIO CANAL PLUS. May, 1996. French. (Andre Techine) Daniel Auteuil, Catherine Deneuve, Laurence Cote.

Things I Never Told You
EDDIE SAETA/CARBO FILMS. February, 1996. U.S.-Spanish. (Isabel Coixet) Lili Taylor, Andrew McCarthy, Debi Mazar, Alexis Arquette.

Three Brothers
AMLF. January, 1996. French. (Didier Bourdon, Bernard Campan) Bourdon, Campan, Pascal Legitimus.

Three Lives and Only One Death
GEMINI FILMS. May, 1996. French. (Raoul Ruiz) Marcello Mastroianni, anna Galiena, Marisa Paredes.

'Til Death Do Us Part
AGAT FILMS. November, 1995. French. (Robert Guediguian) Ariane Ascaride, Jacques Boudet.

The Time of Yellow Grass (Vremya Jholtoi Travy)
TADJIKFILM STUDIO. April, 1996. Tajakistani. (Mairiam Yusupova) R. Makarov.

Timisoara: December 1989
SAHIAFILM. September, 1995. Romanian. (Bose O. Pastina) Documentary, B&W.

To Have and To Hold
SOUTHERN STAR GROUP. April, 1996. Australian. (John Hillcoat) Tcheky Karyo, Rachel Griffiths, Steve Jacobs.

Too Late
MKL MK2 DIFFUSION. May, 1996. French-Romanian. (Lucian Pintilie) Razvan Vasilescu, Cecilia Barbora, Victor Rebengiuc.

Trainspotting
MIRAMAX. (R) January, 1996. British. (Danny Boyle) Ewan McGregor, Ewen Bremmer, Jonny Lee Miller.

Traps
FILMOPOLIS. December, 1995. Australian. (Pauline Chan) Sami Frey, Saskia Reeves, Jacqueline McKenzie.

Traveling Companion (Compagna Di Viaggio)
ISTITUTO LUCE. April, 1996. Italian. (Peter Del Monte) Michel Piccoli, Asia Argento, Lino Capolicchio.

Tree of Blood
MERCURE DISTRIBUTION. May, 1996. French-Guinea Bissau-Tunisian-Portuguese. (Flora Gomes) Ramiro Naka, Edna Evora, Adma Kouyate.

Trojan Eddie
FILM FOUR INT'L. August, 1996. British. (Gillies MacKinnon) Richard Harris, Stephen Rea, Brendan Gleeson, Angeline Ball.

True Blue
MIRAMAX. September, 1996. British. (Ferdinand Fairfax) Johan Leysen, Dominic West, Dylan Baker, Gerladine Somerville.

Twelfth Night
FINE LINE. (PG) September, 1996. British-U.S. (Trevor Nunn) Helena Bonham Carter, Richard E. Grant, Nigel Hawthorne, Ben Kingsley, Imelda Staunton, Imogen Stubbs.

Two Dads and One Mom
AMLF. May, 1996. French. (Jean-Marc Longval) Arielle Dombasle, Smain, Antoine de Caunes.

Two Friends
MILESTONE FILMS. April, 1996. Autralian. (Jane Campion) Kris Bedenko, Emma Coles, Kris McQuade. (originally debuted in 1986)

The Typewriter, the Rifle & the Movie Camera
BRITISH FILM INSTITUTE/INDEPENDENT FILM CHANNEL. January, 1996. (Adam Simon) Documentary.

The Unpredictable Nature of The River
CANAL PLUS. November, 1995. French. (Bernard Giraudeau) Giraudeau, Richard Bohringer, Anna Galiena.

Visit to a Green Planet (La Belle Verte)
STUDIO CANAL PLUS. August, 1996. French. (Coline Serreau) Serreau, Vincent Lindon, Philippine Leroy-Beaulieu.

The Visitors
MIRAMAX. (R) July, 1996. French. (Jean-Marie Poire) Christian Clavier, Jean Reno, Valerie Lemercier.

Vivid
SC ENTERTAINMENT, Toronto. May, 1996. Canadian. (Evan Georgiades) Stephen Shellen, Kari Salin, Ilene Kristen.

Vol-Au-Vent
WINCHESTER FILMS & TV SALES. June, 1996. British. (John McKenzie) Dennis Waterman, Julia McKenzie, Lisa Coleman.

The War Between Us
ATLANTIS. February, 1996. Canadian. (Anne Wheeler) Shannon Lawson, Mieko Ouchi, Robert Wisden, Ian Tracey.

The Waste Land
ILLUMINATIONS TELEVISION. May, 1996. British. (Deborah Warner) Fiona Shaw.

Watari-Gawa: The River of Reconciliation
WATARI-GAWA. February, 1996. Japanese. (Duk-Chui Kim, Yasduyuki Moli) Documentary.

The White Balloon
OCTOBER. January, 1996. Iranian. (Jafar Panahi) Aida Mohammadkhani, Mohsen Kalifi, Anna Boukowska.

The White Feast (Bely Praznik)
MOSFILM STUDIO. April, 1996. Russian. (Vladimir Naumov) Innokenti Smoktunovsky.

The Wind in the Willows
GOOD TIMES. January, 1996. British. (Dave Unwin) Voices: Alan Bennett, Michael Palin, Rik Mayall.

When Saturday Comes
GUILD FILM. February, 1996. British. (Maria Giese) Sean Bean, Emily Lloyd, Pete Postlethwaite.

When the Stars Meet the Sea
MERCURE DISTRIBUTION. May, 1996. French. (Raymond Rajaonarivelo) Jean Rabenjamina, Barbara Razanajao.

Who Is The Monster...You Or Me?
DAVID A. HESS PRODS. German. September, 1995. Documentary.

The Whole of the Moon
CFP INTL., Montreal. April, 1996. New Zealand-Canadian. (Ian Mune) Toby Fisher, Nikki Si'Ulepa, Pascale Bussieres.

Will It Snow At Christmas?
OGNON PICTURES, Paris. May, 1996. French. (Sandrine Veysset) Daniel Duval, Jessica Martinez, Alexandre Roger.

Wives III
NORSK FILMDISTRIBUSJON. May, 1996. Norwegian. (Anja Breien) Froydis Armand, Katja Medboe, Anne Marie Ottersen.

Workaholic
CONCORDE/CASTLE ROCK TURNER. May, 1996. German. (Sharon von Wietersheim) Christiane Paul, Tobias Moretti, Ralf Bauer.

X,Y
AFMD (France) January, 1996. French-Belgian. (Jean-Paul Lielenfeld) Clementine Celarie, Patrick Braoude, Jenny Cleve.

Yesterday's Wine
CHINA FILM EXPORT & IMPORT CORP., Beijing. May, 1996. Chinese. (Xia Gang) Liu Yan, Shao Bing, Guo Yuan.

Youth Without God
CANAL PLUS DISTRIBUTION. April, 1996. French-Belgium. (Catherine Corsini) Marc Barbe, Roland Amstuz, Samuel Dupuy.

Yuri
DAVID LAMPING CO. May, 1996. South Korean. (Yoonho Yang) Shinyang Park, Eunjung Lee, Youngdong Moon.

Zone 39
BEYOND FILMS. May, 1996. Australian. (John Tatoulis) Peter Phelps, Caroline Bock, William Zappa.

FEATURE FILMS

1990 – 1995

FEATURE FILMS

In the following listings, the distributor is followed by the release date, country of origin, the director (in parentheses), and cast. For feature films released from 1980 - 1989, please see the 1996 edition of the Motion Picture Almanac.

ABOVE THE RIM
NEW LINE CINEMA. March, 1994. (Jeff Pollack), Duane Martin, Leon, Tonya Pinkins.

ACCOMPANIST, THE
SONY CLASSICS. December, 1993. French. (Claude Miller), Richard Bohringer, Elena Safonova.

ACE VENTURA, PET DETECTIVE
WARNER BROS. February, 1994. (Tom Shadyac), Jim Carrey, Courteney Cox, Sean Young.

ACES: IRON EAGLE III
NEW LINE/7 ARTS. June, 1992. (John Glen), Louis Gossett, Jr., Rachel McLish, Horst Buccholz.

ACLA
INFRAFILMS/SACIS. December, 1993. Italian (Aurelio Grimaldi), Francesco Cusimano, Tony Sperandeo.

ACROSS THE TRACKS
ACADEMY ENT./DESERT PRODS. February, 1991. (Sandy Tung), Rick Schroder, Brad Pitt, Carry Snodgress.

ACT OF PIRACY
BLOSSOM. March, 1990. (John "Bud" Cardos), Gary Busey, Belinda Bauer, Ray Sharkey.

ADAM'S RIB
OCTOBER. May, 1992. Russian. (Vyacheslav Krishtofovich), Inna Churikova, Svetlana Ryabova, Maria Golubkina.

ADDAMS FAMILY, THE
PARAMOUNT. November, 1991. (Barry Sonnenfeld), Anjelica Huston, Raul Julia, Christopher Lloyd.

ADDAMS FAMILY VALUES
PARAMOUNT. November, 1993. (Barry Sonnenfeld), Anjelica Huston, Raul Julia, Joan Cusack.

ADJUSTER, THE
ORION CLASSICS. May, 1992. Canadian. (Atom Egoyan), Elias Koteas, Arsinee Khanjian, Maury Chaykin.

ADVENTURES OF FORD FAIRLANE, THE
20TH CENTURY FOX. July, 1990. (Renny Harlin), Andrew Dice Clay, Wayne Newton, Priscilla Presley.

ADVENTURES OF HUCK FINN, THE
BUENA VISTA. April, 1993. (Stephen Sommers), Elijah Wood, Courtney Vance, Jason Robards.

ADVENTURES OF PRISCILLA, QUEEN OF THE DESERT, THE
GRAMERCY. August, 1994. Australian. (Stephan Elliott), Terence Stamp, Hugo Weaving, Guy Pearce.

ADVOCATE, THE
MIRAMAX. August, 1994. British. (Leslie Megahey), Colin Firth, Lysette Anthony, Ian Hol.

AFFENGEIL
FIRST RUN FEATURES. July, 1992. German. (Rosa von Praunheim), Lotte Huber, Rosa von Praunheim, Helga Sloop.

AFRAID OF THE DARK
FINE LINE. July, 1992. British. (Mark Peploe), James Fox, Fanny Ardant, Ben Keyworth.

AFTER DARK, MY SWEET
AVENUE. August, 1990. (James Foley), Jason Patric, Rachel Ward, Bruce Dern.

AGE OF INNOCENCE, THE
COLUMBIA. September, 1993. (Martin Scorsese), Daniel Day-Lewis, Michelle Pfeiffer, Winona Ryder.

AILEEN WURONOS:
THE SELLING OF A SERIAL KILLER
STRAND. February, 1994. (Nick Broomfield), Documentary.

AIR AMERICA
TRISTAR. August, 1990. (Roger Spottiswoode), Mel Gibson, Robert Downey, Jr., Nancy Travis.

AIR UP THERE, THE
BUENA VISTA. January, 1994. (Paul M. Glaser), Kevin Bacon, Charles Gitonga Maina, Yolanda Yazquez.

AIRBORNE
WARNER BROS. September, 1993. (Rob Bowman), Shane McDermott, Seth Green, Brittany Powell.

AIRHEADS
20TH CENTURY FOX. August, 1994. (Michael Lehmann), Brendan Fraser, Steve Buscemi.

AKIRA KUROSAWA'S DREAMS
WARNER BROS. August, 1990. Japanese. (Akira Kurosawa), Mitsunori Isaki, Mieko Harada, Martin Scorsese.

ALADDIN
BUENA VISTA. November, 1992. (John Musker, Ron Clements), Animated.

ALAN & NAOMI
TRITON. January, 1992. (Sterling VanWagenen), Lukas Haas, Vanessa Zaoui, Michael Gross.

ALBERTO EXPRESS
MK2. October, 1992. French-Italian. (Arthur Joffe), Sergio Castellitto, Nino Manfredi, Marie Trintignant.

ALEX
CORALIE. March, 1992. Portuguese. (Teresa Villaverde), Ricardo Colares, Vincent Gallo, Teresa Roby.

ALICE
ORION. December, 1990. (Woody Allen), Mia Farrow, Joe Mantegna, William Hurt, Alec Baldwin.

ALIEN³
20TH CENTURY FOX. May, 1992. (David Fincher), Sigourney Weaver, Charles S. Dutton, Charles Dance.

ALIVE
BUENA VISTA. January, 1993. (Frank Marshall), Ethan Hawke, Josh Hamilton, Vincent Spano.

ALL I WANT FOR CHRISTMAS
PARAMOUNT. November, 1991. (Robert Lieberman), Harley Jane Kozak, Ethan Randall, Thora Birch.

ALL THE VERMEERS IN NEW YORK
STRAND. May, 1992. (Jon Jost), Emmanuelle Chaulet, Katherine Bean, Grace Phillips.

ALLIGATOR EYES
CASTLE HILL. November, 1990. (John Feldman), Annabelle Larsen, Roger Kabler.

ALMA'S RAINBOW
PARADISE PLUM. June, 1994. (Ayoka Chenzira), Victoria Gabriela Platt, Kim Weston-Moran, Mizan Nunes.

ALMOST AN ANGEL
PARAMOUNT. December, 1990. (John Cornell), Paul Hogan, Elias Koteas, Linda Kozlowski.

AMATEUR
SONY CLASSICS. (R) April, 1995. (Hal Hartley), Isabelle Huppert, Martin Donovan, Elina Lowensohn.

AMAZING PANDA ADVENTURE, THE
WARNER BROS. August 1995. (Christopher Cain), Stephen Lang, Ryan Slater, Yi Ding, Huang Fei.

AMAZON
CABRIOLET. February, 1992. Brazilian-Finnish. (Mika Kaurismaki), Robert Davi, Rae Dawn Chong, Kari Vaananen.

AMBITION
MIRAMAX. May, 1991. (Scott D. Goldstein), Lou Diamond Phillips, Clancy Brown, Cecilia Peck.

AMERICAN BLUE NOTE
PANORAMA ENT. November, 1990. (Ralph Toporoff), Peter MacNicol, Carl Capotorto.

AMERICAN CYBORG
CANNON. January, 1994. (Boaz Davidson), Joe Lara, Nicole Hansen, John Ryan.

AMERICAN DREAM
PRESTIGE. March, 1992. (Barbara Kopple), Documentary.

AMERICAN FABULOUS
FIRST RUN FEATURES. October, 1992. (Reno Dakota), Jeffrey Strouth.

AMERICAN FRIENDS
CASTLE HILL. April, 1993. British. (Tristam Powell), Michael Palin, Connie Booth, Trini Alvarado.

AMERICAN HEART
TRITON. May, 1993. (Martin Bell), Jeff Bridges, Edward Furlong, Lucinda Jenney.

AMERICAN KICKBOXER
CANNON. February, 1991. South African. (Frans Nel), John Barrett, Keith Vitali, Terry Norton.

AMERICAN ME
UNIVERSAL. March, 1992. (Edward James Olmos), Edward James Olmos, William Forsythe, Pepe Serna.

AMERICAN NINJA 4: THE ANNIHILATION
CANNON. March, 1991. (Cedric Sundstrom), Michael Dudikoff, David Bradley, James Booth.

AMERICAN SUMMER, AN
CASTLE HILL. June, 1991. (James Slocum), Michael Landes, Brian Austin Green, Amber Susa.

AMERICAN TAIL: FIEVEL GOES WEST, AN
UNIVERSAL. November, 1991. (Phil Nibbelink, Simon Wells), Animated.

AMONGST FRIENDS
FINE LINE. July, 1993. (Rob Weiss), Steve Parlavecchio, Joseph Lindsey, Patrick McGraw.

AMOS & ANDREW
COLUMBIA. March, 1993. (E. Max Frye), Nicolas Cage, Samuel L. Jackson, Dabney Coleman, Brad Dourif.

ANCHORESS
INT'L FILM CIRCUIT. May, 1994. British. (Chris Newby), Natalie Morse, Eugene Bervoets, Pete Postlethwaite.

... AND GOD SPOKE
LIVE ENT. (R) September, 1994. (Arthur Borman), R.C. Bates, Michael Riley, Stephen Rappaport, Soupy Sales.

AND YOU THOUGHT YOUR PARENTS WERE WEIRD
TRIMARK. November, 1991. (Tony Cookson), Marcia Strassman, Joshua Miller, Edan Gross.

ANDRE
PARAMOUNT. August, 1994. (George Miller), Keith Carradine, Tina Majorino, Chelsea Field.

ANGELS IN THE OUTFIELD
BUENA VISTA. July, 1994. (William Dear), Danny Glover, Joseph Gordon Levitt, Christopher Lloyd.

ANGIE
BUENA VISTA. March, 1994. (Martha Coolidge), Geena Davis, Stephen Rea, James Gandolfini.

ANGUS
NEW LINE CINEMA. (PG-13) September, 1995. (Patrick Read Johnson), Charlie Talbert, Kathy Bates, George C. Scott.

ANOTHER 48 HRS.
PARAMOUNT. June, 1990. (Walter Hill), Eddie Murphy, Nick Nolte, Brion James.

ANOTHER STAKEOUT
BUENA VISTA. July, 1993. (John Badham), Richard Dreyfuss, Emilio Estevez, Rosie O'Donnell.

ANOTHER YOU
TRISTAR. July, 1991. (Maurice Phillips), Gene Wilder, Richard Pryor, Mercedes Ruehl.

ANTIGONE/RITES FOR THE DEAD
ASA COMMUNICATIONS. November, 1990. (Amy Greenfield), Amy Greenfield, Bertram Ross.

ANTONIA & JANE
MIRAMAX. October, 1991. British. (Beeban Kidron), Imelda Staunton, Saskia Reeves, Iain Cuthbertson.

ANY MAN'S DEATH
INI ENTERTAINMENT. May, 1990. (Tom Clegg), John Savage, William Hickey, Mia Sara.

APEX
REPUBLIC. March, 1994. (Phillip J. Roth), Richard Keats, Mitchell Cox, Lisa Ann Russell.

APOLLO 13
UNIVERSAL. June, 1995. (Ron Howard), Tom Hanks, Kevin Bacon, Bill Paxton, Ed Harris, Gary Sinise, Kathleen Quinlan.

ARABIAN KNIGHT
MIRAMAX. (G) August, 1995. (Richard Williams), Animated.

ARACHNOPHOBIA
BUENA VISTA. July, 1990. (Frank Marshall), Jeff Daniels, Harley Jane Kozak, John Goodman.

ARCHANGEL
ZEITGEIST. March, 1991. Canadian. (Guy Maddin), Kyle McCulloch, Kathy Marykuca. B&W.

ARCHITECTS, THE
INDEPENDENT. October, 1993. German. (Peter Kahane), Kurt Naumann, Rita Feidmeier, Uta Eisold.

ARCHITECTURE OF DOOM, THE
FIRST RUN FEATURES. October, 1991. German-Swedish. (Peter Cohen), Documentary.

ARIEL
KINO. August, 1990. Finnish. (Aki Kaurismaki), Turo Pajalo, Susanna Haavisto.

ARIZONA DREAM
WARNER. September, 1994. (Emir Kusturica), Johnny Depp, Jerry Lewis, Faye Dunaway, Lili Taylor.

ARMY OF DARKNESS
UNIVERSAL. February, 1993. (Sam Raimi), Bruce Campbell, Embeth Davidtz, Marcus Gilbert.

ART DECO DETECTIVE
TRIDENT. September, 1994. (Philippe Mora, Bruce Critchley), John Dennis Johnston, Stephen McHattie, Brion James.

ART FOR TEACHERS OF CHILDREN
ZEITGEIST. August, 1995. (Jennifer Montgomery), Caitlin Grace McDonnell, Duncan Hannah, Coles Burroughs. B&W.

ARTICLE 99
ORION. March, 1992. (Howard Deutch), Ray Liotta, Kiefer Sutherland, Kathy Baker.

ASPEN EXTREME
BUENA VISTA. January, 1993. (Patrick Hasburg), Paul Gross, Peter Berg, Finola Hughes.

AT PLAY IN THE FIELDS OF THE LORD
UNIVERSAL. December, 1991. (Hector Babenco), Tom Berenger, Kathy Bates, Aidan Quinn, John Lithgow.

AT THE CROSSROADS:
JEWS IN EASTERN EUROPE TODAY
ARTHUR CANTOR FILMS. February, 1991. (Oren Rudavsky, Yale Strom), Documentary.

AT THE MAX
BLC GROUP/IMAX CORP. October, 1991. (Julien Temple), The Rolling Stones.

ATLANTIS
MILESTONE. December, 1993. French. (Luc Besson), Documentary.

AVALON
TRISTAR. October, 1990. (Barry Levinson), Aidan Quinn, Armin Mueller Stahl, Elijah Wood.

AWAKENINGS
COLUMBIA. December, 1990. (Penny Marshall), Robert De Niro, Robin Williams, Julie Kavner.

AWFULLY BIG ADVENTURE, AN
FINE LINE. (R) July, 1995. British. (Mike Newell), Alan Rickman, Hugh Grant, Georgina Cates.

AY, CARMELA!
PRESTIGE. February, 1991. Spanish. (Carlos Saura), Carmen Maura, Andres Pajares, Gabin Diego.

B

BAB EL OUED CITY
JANE BALFOUR FILMS. June, 1995. Algerian. (Merzak Allouache), Nadia Kaci, Mohammed Ourdache, Hassan Abdou.

BABE
UNIVERSAL. August, 1994. (Chris Noonan), James Cromwell, Magda Szubanski.

BABE, THE
UNIVERSAL. April, 1992. (Arthur Hiller), John Goodman, Kelly McGillis, Trini Alvarado.

BABY'S DAY OUT
20TH CENTURY FOX. July, 1994. (Patrick Read Johnson), Joe Mantegna, Lara Flynn Boyle.

BABYFEVER
RAINBOW. April, 1994. (Henry Jaglom), Frances Fisher, Eric Roberts, Victoria Foyt, Matt Salinger.

BABYSITTER'S CLUB, THE
COLUMBIA, BEACON. August, 1995. (Melanie Mayron), Schuyler Fisk, Bre Blair, Rachael Leigh Cook.

BACK IN THE U.S.S.R.
20TH CENTURY FOX. February, 1992. (Deran Sarafian), Frank Whaley, Natalya Negoda, Roman Polanski.

BACK TO BACK
CONCORDE. January, 1990. (John Kincade), Bill Paxton, Todd Field, Apolonia Kotero.

BACK TO THE FUTURE PART III
UNIVERSAL. May, 1990. (Robert Zemeckis), Michael J. Fox, Christopher Lloyd, Mary Steenburgen.

BACK TO THE PROMISED LAND
BLUE PRODS. April, 1993. Israeli. (Madeleine Ali), Documentary.

BACKBEAT
GRAMERCY. April, 1994. British. (Iain Softley), Stephen Dorff, Sheryl Lee, Ian Hart.

BACKDRAFT
UNIVERSAL. May, 1991. (Ron Howard), Kurt Russell, William Baldwin, Robert De Niro.

BACKSTREET DREAMS
VIDMARK. September, 1990. (Rupert Hitzig), Jason O'Malley, Brooke Shields, Burt Young.

BAD BEHAVIOUR
OCTOBER. September, 1993. British. (Les Blair), Stephen Rea, Sinead Cusack, Philip Jackson.

BAD BOYS
COLUMBIA. April, 1995. (Michael Bay), Martin Lawrence, Will Smith, Tea Leoni, Tcheky Karyo.

BAD COMPANY
BUENA VISTA. January, 1995. (Damian Harris), Ellen Barkin, Laurence Fishburne, Frank Langella.

BAD GIRLS
CASTLE HILL. January, 1994. (Amos Kollek), Amos Kollek, Marla Sucharetz, Mari Nelson.

BAD GIRLS
20TH CENTURY FOX. April, 1994. (Jonathan Kaplan), Madeleine Stowe, Andie MacDowell, Mary Stuart Masterson.

BAD INFLUENCE
TRIUMPH. March, 1990. (Curtis Hanson), Rob Lowe, James Spader, Lisa Zane.

BAD LIEUTENANT
ARIES. November, 1992. (Abel Ferrara), Harvey Keitel, Frankie Thorn, Paul Hipp.

BAIL JUMPER
ANGELIKA. April, 1990. (Christian Faber), Eszter Balint, B.J. Spalding, Tony Askin.

BALLAD OF LITTLE JO, THE
FINE LINE. August, 1993. (Maggie Greenwalt), Suzy Amis, Ian McKellen, David Chung.

BALLAD OF THE SAD CAFE, THE
ANGELIKA. May, 1991. (Simon Callow), Vanessa Redgrave, Keith Carradine, Cork Hubbert.

BALLET
ZIPPORAH. March, 1995. (Frederick Wiseman), Documentary.

BALLOT MEASURE 9
ZEITGEIST. June, 1995. (Heather MacDonald), Documentary.

BANDIT QUEEN
ARROW. June, 1995. Hindi. (Shekhar Kapur), Seema Biswas, Nirmal Pandey, Manoj Bajpai.

BANK ROBBER
I.R.S. December, 1993. (Nick Mead), Patrick Dempsey, Lisa Bonet, Judge Reinhold.

BAR GIRLS
ORION CLASSICS. (R) April, 1995. (Marita Giovanni), Nancy Allison Wolfe, Liza D'Agostino, Camilla Griggs.

BARAKA
GOLDWYN. September, 1993. (Ron Fricke), Non-narrative images.

BARCELONA
FINE LINE. July, 1994. (Whit Stillman), Taylor Nichols, Chris Eigeman, Tushka Bergen.

BARJO
MYRIAD PICTURES. July, 1993. French. (Jerome Boivin), Anne Brochet, Richard Bohringer, Hippolyte Girardot.

BARROCO
INT'L FILM CIRCUIT. January, 1991. Spain/Cuba (Paul LeDuc), Francisco Rabal, Angela Molina.

BARTON FINK
20TH CENTURY FOX. August, 1991. (Joel Coen), John Turturro, John Goodman, Michael Lerner.

BASIC INSTINCT
TRISTAR. March, 1992. (Paul Verhoeven), Michael Douglas, Sharon Stone, George Dzundza.

BASKET CASE 2
SHAPIRO GLICKENHAUS. March, 1990. (Frank Henenlotter), Kevin Van Hentenryck, Annie Ross.

BASKET CASE 3: THE PROGENY
SHAPIRO GLICKENHAUS. February, 1992. (Frank Henenlotter), Annie Ross, Kevin Van Hentenryck.

BASKETBALL DIARIES, THE
NEW LINE. (R) April, 1995. (Scott Kalvert), Leonardo DiCaprio, Mark Wahlberg, Lorraine Bracco.

BATMAN FOREVER
WARNER BROS. June, 1995. (Joel Schumacher), Val Kilmer, Tommy Lee Jones, Jim Carrey, Nicole Kidman.

BATMAN: MASK OF THE PHANTASM
WARNER BROS. December, 1993. (Eric Radomski, Bruce W. Timm), Animated.

BATMAN RETURNS
WARNER BROS. June, 1992. (Tim Burton), Michael Keaton, Danny DeVito, Michelle Pfeiffer.

BEANS OF EGYPT, MAINE, THE
I.R.S. (R) November, 1994. (Jennifer Warren), Martha Plimpton, Rutger Hauer, Kelly Lynch.

BEASTMASTER 2: THROUGH THE PORTAL OF TIME
NEW LINE CINEMA. August, 1991. (Sylvio Tabet), Marc Singer, Kari Wuhrer, Wings Hauser.

BEAUTY AND THE BEAST
BUENA VISTA. November, 1991. (Gary Trousdale, Kirk Wise), Animated.

BEBE'S KIDS
PARAMOUNT. July, 1992. (Bruce Smith), Animated.

BECAUSE OF THE WAR
NURIT PRICE. March, 1991. Israeli. (Orna Ben Dor Niv), Documentary.

BECOMING COLETTE
CASTLE HILL. November, 1992. German-U.S. (Danny Huston), Mathilda May, Klaus Maria Brandauer, Virginia Madsen.

BED & BREAKFAST
HEMDALE. August, 1992. (Robert Ellis Miller), Roger Moore, Colleen Dewhurst, Talia Shire.

BEEKEEPER, THE
MK2. May, 1993. Greek. (Theo Angelopoulous), Marcello Mastroianni, Nadia Mourouzi, Serge Reggiani.

BEETHOVEN
UNIVERSAL. April, 1992. (Brian Levant), Charles Grodin, Bonnie Hunt, Dean Jones.

BEETHOVEN'S 2ND
UNIVERSAL. December, 1993. (Rod Daniel), Charles Grodin, Bonnie Hunt, Nicholle Tom.

BEFORE SUNRISE
COLUMBIA. January, 1995. (Richard Linklater), Ethan Hawke, Julie Delpy.

BEFORE THE RAIN
GRAMERCY. February, 1995. Macedonian-British-French. (Milcho Manchevski), Katrin Cartlidge, Rade Serbedzija.

BEGOTTEN
THEATRE OF MATERIAL. June, 1991. (E. Elias Merhige), Brian Salzberg, Donna Dempsey. B&W.

BEING HUMAN
WARNER BROS. May, 1994. British-U.S. (Bill Forsyth), Robin Williams, John Turturro, Anna Galiena.

BELLE EPOQUE
SONY CLASSICS. February, 1994. Spanish. (Fernando Trueba), Fernando Fernan Gomez, Jorge Sanz, Maribel Verdu.

BELLY OF AN ARCHITECT, THE
HEMDALE. May, 1990. British (Peter Greenaway), Brian Dennehy, Chloe Webb, Lambert Wilson.

BENEFIT OF THE DOUBT
MIRAMAX. July, 1993. (Jonathan Heap), Donald Sutherland, Amy Irving, Graham Greene.

BENNY & JOON
MGM. April, 1993. (Jeremiah Hechik), Johnny Depp, Mary Stuart Masterson, Aidan Quinn.

BERKELEY IN THE SIXTIES
P.O.V. THEATRICAL FILMS. September, 1990. (Mark Kitchell), Documentary.

BERLIN JERUSALEM
JANE BALFOUR FILMS. March, 1991. French-Israeli. (Amos Gitai), Lisa Dreuzer, Rivka Neuman.

BEST INTENTIONS, THE
GOLDWYN. July, 1992. Swedish. (Bille August), Samuel Froler, Pernilla August, Max von Sydow.

BEST OF THE BEST 2
20TH CENTURY FOX. March, 1993. (Robert Radler), Eric Roberts, Phillip Ree, Christopher Penn.

BETSY'S WEDDING
BUENA VISTA. June, 1990. (Alan Alda), Alan Alda, Madeline Kahn, Molly Ringwald.

BETTY
MK2. August, 1993. French. (Claude Chabrol), Marie Trintignant, Stephane Audran, Jean-Francois Garreau.

BETWEEN HEAVEN AND EARTH
ARROW. October, 1993. French. (Marion Mansel), Carmen Maura, Jean-Pierre Cassel, Didier Bezace.

BETWEEN THE TEETH
TODO MUNDO. February, 1994. (David Byrne), David Byrne, 10 Car Pile Up.

BEVERLY HILLBILLIES, THE
20TH CENTURY FOX. October, 1993. (Penelope Spheeris), Jim Varney, Lily Tomlin, Cloris Leachman.

BEVERLY HILLS COP III
PARAMOUNT. May, 1994. (John Landis), Eddie Murphy, Judge Reinhold, Hector Elizondo.

BEYOND RANGOON
COLUMBIA. August, 1995. (John Boorman), Patricia Arquette, Frances McDormand, U Aung Ko.

BHAJI ON THE BEACH
FIRST LOOK. May, 1994. British. (Gurinder Chadha), Kim Vithana, Jimmi Harkishin, Sarita Khajuria.

BIG BAD JOHN
MAGNUM ENT. February, 1990. (Burt Kennedy), Jimmy Dean, Jack Elam, Ned Beatty.

BIG BANG, THE
TRITON. May, 1990. (James Toback), Emma Astner, Missy Body, Eugene Fodor.

BIG DIS, THE
OLYMPIA. June, 1990. (Gordon Eriksen, John O'Brien), James Haig, Kevin Haig. B&W.

BIG GIRLS DON'T CRY... THEY GET EVEN
NEW LINE CINEMA. May, 1992. (Joan Micklin Silver), Hillary Wolf, David Strathairn, Margaret Whitton.

BIG GREEN, THE
BUENA VISTA. September, 1995. (Dennis Bishop), Olivia D'Abo, Steve Guttenberg, Jay O. Saunders.

BIG MAN ON CAMPUS
VESTRON. February, 1990. (Jeremy Paul Kagan), Allan Katz, Corey Parker, Cindy Williams.

BIKINI ISLAND
CURB/ESQUIRE. July, 1991. (Anthony Markes), Holly Floria, Alicia Anne.

BILL & TED'S BOGUS JOURNEY
ORION. July, 1991. (Pete Hewitt), Keanu Reeves, Alex Winter, William Sadler.

BILLY BATHGATE
BUENA VISTA. November, 1991. (Robert Benton), Dustin Hoffman, Loren Dean, Nicole Kidman.

BILLY MADISON
UNIVERSAL. February, 1995. (Tamra Davis), Adam Sandler, Darren McGavin, Bridgette Wilson.

BINGO
TRISTAR. August, 1991. (Matthew Robbins), Cindy Williams, David Rasche, Robert J. Steinmiller, Jr.

BIRD ON A WIRE
UNIVERSAL. May, 1990. (John Badham), Mel Gibson, Goldie Hawn, David Carradine.

BITTER MOON
FINE LINE. March, 1994. French-British. (Roman Polanski), Peter Coyote, Emmanuelle Seigner, Hugh Grant.

BLACK BEAUTY
WARNER BROS. July, 1994. (Caroline Thompson), Sean Bean, David Thewlis, Andrew Knott.

BLACK CAT
HEADLINER. October, 1993. Hong Kong. (Stephen Shin), Jade Leung, Simon Yam, Thomas Lam.

BLACK DIAMOND RUSH
WARREN MILLER ENT. October, 1993. (Kurt Miller, Peter Speek), Documentary.

BLACK LIZARD
CINEVISTA. September, 1991. Japanese, 1968. (Kinji Fukasaku), Akihiro Maruyama, Isao Kimura.

BLACK RAIN
ANGELIKA. February 1990. Japanese. (Shohei Imamura), Yoshiko Tanaka, Kazuo Kitmamura.

BLACK ROBE
GOLDWYN. October, 1991. Canadian-Australian. (Bruce Beresford), Lothaire Bluteau, Aden Young, Sandrine Holt.

BLAME IT ON THE BELLBOY
BUENA VISTA. March, 1992. British. (Mark Herman), Dudley Moore, Bryan Brown, Patsy Kensit.

BLANK CHECK
BUENA VISTA. February, 1994. (Rupert Wainwright), Brian Bonsall, Karen Duffy, Miguel Ferrer.

BLANKMAN
COLUMBIA. August, 1994. (Mike Binder), Damon Wayans, David Alan Grier, Robin Givens.

BLAST 'EM
SILENT FICTION FILMS. July, 1992. Canadian. (Joseph Blasioli), Documentary.

BLESSING
STARR VALLEY. April, 1995. (Paul Zehrer), Melora Griffis, Carlin Glynn, Guy Griffis.

BLIND FURY
TRISTAR. March, 1990. (Phillip Noyce), Rutger Hauer, Brandon Call, Terry O'Quinn.

BLINK
NEW LINE CINEMA. January, 1994. (Michael Apted), Madeleine Stowe, Aidan Quinn, Laurie Metcalf.

BLOOD & CONCRETE
I.R.S. September, 1991. (Jeffrey Reiner), Billy Zane, Jennifer Beals, Darren McGavin.

BLOOD IN THE FACE
FIRST RUN FEATURES. February, 1991. (Anne Bohlen, Kevin Rafferty, James Ridgeway), Documentary.

BLOOD OF HEROES, THE
NEW LINE CINEMA. February, 1990. (David Peoples), Rutger Hauer, Joan Chen.

BLOOD SALVAGE
PARAGON ARTS. May, 1990. (Tucker Johnston), Danny Nelson, Lori Birdsong, John Saxon.

BLOODFIST II
CONCORDE. October, 1990. (Andy Blumenthal), Don Wilson, Rina Reyes.

BLOODFIST III: FORCED TO FIGHT
CONCORDE. January, 1992. (Francis Sassone), Don "The Dragon" Wilson, Richard Roundtree, Gregory McKinney.

BLOWBACK
NORTHERN ARTS. August, 1991. (Marc Levin), Bruce McCarty, Jane Hamper, Eddie Figueroa.

BLOWN AWAY
MGM. July, 1994. (Stephen Hopkins), Jeff Bridges, Tommy Lee Jones, Lloyd Bridges.

BLUE
MIRAMAX. December, 1993. Polish-French. (Krzyzstof Kieslowksi), Juliette Binoche, Benoit Regent.

BLUE
ZEITGEIST. April, 1994. British. (Derek Jarman), John Quentin, Nigel Terry, Tilda Swinton.

BLUE CHIPS
PARAMOUNT. February, 1994. (William Friedkin), Nick Nolte, Mary McDonnell, Shaquile O'Neal.

BLUE KITE, THE
KINO. April, 1994. Dutch-Hong Kong. (Tian Zhuangzhuang), Zhang Wenyo, Chen Xiaoman, Lu Liping.

BLUE SKY
ORION. September, 1994. (Tony Richardson), Jessica Lange, Tommy Lee Jones, Powers Boothe, Amy Locane.

BLUE STEEL
MGM/UA. March, 1990. (Kathryn Bigelow), Jamie Lee Curtis, Ron Silver, Clancy Brown.

BLUE VILLA, THE
NOMAD. September, 1995. Belgian. (Alain Robbe Grillet), Fred Ward, Arielle Dombasle, Charles Tordjman.

BOB ROBERTS
PARAMOUNT. September, 1992. (Tim Robbins), Tim Robbins, Giancarlo Esposito, Ray Wise, Gore Vidal.

BODIES, REST & MOTION
FINE LINE. April, 1993. (Michael Steinberg), Phoebe Cates, Eric Stoltz, Bridget Fonda.

BODY CHEMISTRY
CONCORDE. March, 1990. (Kristine Peterson), Marc Singer, Lisa Pescia, Mary Crosby.

BODY OF EVIDENCE
MGM. January, 1993. (Uli Edel), Madonna, Willem Dafoe, Joe Mantegna, Anne Archer.

BODY PARTS
PARAMOUNT. August, 1991. (Eric Red), Jeff Fahey, Lindsay Duncan, Brad Dourif.

BODY SNATCHERS
WARNER BROS. January, 1994. (Abel Ferrara), Gabrielle Anwar, Terry Kinney, Meg Tilly, Billy Wirth.

BODYGUARD, THE
WARNER BROS. November, 1992. (Mick Jackson), Kevin Costner, Whitney Houston, Gary Kemp.

BONFIRE OF THE VANITIES, THE
WARNER BROS. December, 1990. (Brian DePalma), Tom Hanks, Bruce Willis, Melanie Griffith.

BOOK OF DAYS
STUTZ CO. February, 1990. (Meredith Monk), Gerd Wameling, Lucas Hoving.

BOOK OF LOVE
NEW LINE CINEMA. February, 1991. (Robert Shaye), Chris Young, Keith Coogan, John Cameron Mitchell.

BOOMERANG
PARAMOUNT. July, 1992. (Reginald Hudlin), Eddie Murphy, Robin Givens, Halle Berry.

BOPHA!
PARAMOUNT. September, 1993. (Morgan Freeman), Danny Glover, Malcolm McDowell, Alfre Woodard.

BORN TO BE WILD
WARNER BROS. March, 1995. (John Gray), Will Horneff, Helen Shaver, Peter Boyle.

BORN TO RIDE
WARNER BROS. May, 1991. (Graham Baker), John Stamos, John Stockwell, Teri Polo.

BORN YESTERDAY
BUENA VISTA. March, 1993. (Luis Mandoki), Melanie Griffith, John Goodman, Don Johnson.

BORROWER, THE
CANNON. August, 1991. (John McNaughton), Tom Towles, Rae Dawn Chong, Antonio Fargas.

BOSNA!
ZEITGEIST. November, 1994. Bosnian-French. (Bernard Henri Levy, Alain Ferrari), Documentary.

BOUND & GAGGED: A LOVE STORY
NORTHERN ARTS. October, 1993. (Daniel Appleby), Ginger Lynn Allen, Chris Denton, Elizabeth Saltarrelli.

BOUND BY HONOR (BLOOD IN, BLOOD OUT)
BUENA VISTA. January, 1993. (Taylor Hackford), Damian Chapa, Jesse Borrego, Benjamin Bratt.

BOXING HELENA
ORION CLASSICS. September, 1993. (Jennifer Lynch), Julian Sands, Sherilyn Fenn, Bill Paxton.

BOY WHO CRIED BITCH, THE
PILGRIMS 3 CORP. October, 1991. (Juan Jose Campanella), Harley Cross, Karen Young, Jesse Bradford.

BOYS LIFE
STRAND. September, 1994. (Brian Sloan, Raoul O'Connell, Robert Lee King), Josh Weinstein, Raoul O'Connell, Matt Nolan.

BOYS OF ST. VINCENT'S, THE
ALLIANCE. June, 1994. Canadian. (John N. Smith), Henry Czerny, John Morina, Sebastian Spence.

BOYS ON THE SIDE
WARNER BROS. February, 1995. (Herbert Ross), Whoopi Goldberg, Mary Louise Parker, Drew Barrymore.

BOYZ N THE HOOD
COLUMBIA. July, 1991. (John Singleton), Cuba Gooding, Jr., Ice Cube, Laurence Fishburne.

BRADY BUNCH MOVIE, THE
PARAMOUNT. February, 1995. (Betty Thomas), Shelley Long, Gary Cole, Michael McKean, Christine Taylor.

BRAIN DONORS
PARAMOUNT. April, 1992. (Dennis Dugan), John Turturro, Mel Smith, Bob Nelson.

BRAINSCAN
TRIUMPH. April, 1994. (John Flynn), Edward Furlong, T. Ryder Smith, Frank Langella.

BRAM STOKER'S DRACULA
COLUMBIA. November, 1992. (Francis Ford Coppola), Gary Oldman, Winona Ryder, Anthony Hopkins, Keanu Reeves.

BRANCHES OF THE TREE, THE
ERATO FILMS. April, 1992. Indian-French. (Satyajit Ray), Ajit Benerjee, Maradan Benerjee, Soumitra Chatterjee.

BRAVEHEART
PARAMOUNT. May, 1995. (Mel Gibson), Mel Gibson, Sophie Marceau, Patrick McGoohan, James Cosmo.

BREAK, THE
TRIMARK. (PG-13), September, 1995. (Lee H. Katzin), Vince Van Patten, Martin Sheen, Ben Jorgensen.

BREAKING THE RULES
MIRAMAX. October, 1992. (Neal Israel), Jason Bateman, C. Thomas Howell, Jonathan Silverman.

BREATH OF LIFE, A
SURF FILM. January, 1993. Italian. (Beppe Cino), Franco Nero, Vanessa Redgrave, Lucrezia Lante Della Rovere.

BRENDA STARR
TRIUMPH. April, 1992. (Robert Ellis Miller), Brooke Shields, Timothy Dalton, Tony Peck.

BRIDE OF RE-ANIMATOR
50TH ST. FILMS. February, 1991. (Brian Yuzna), Jeffrey Combs, Bruce Abbott, Kathleen Kinmont.

BRIDGES OF MADISON COUNTY, THE
WARNER BROS. June, 1995. (Clint Eastwood), Clint Eastwood, Meryl Streep, Annie Corley, Victor Slezak.

BRIEF HISTORY OF TIME, A
TRITON. August, 1992. British. (Errol Morris), Stephen Hawking.

BRIGHT ANGEL
HEMDALE. June, 1991. (Michael Fields), Dermot Mulroney, Lili Taylor, Sam Shepard.

BROKEN JOURNEY, THE
FILMHAUS. May, 1995. Indian. (Satyajit Ray), Soumitra Chatterji, Sadhu Meher, Subhalakshmi Munshi.

BRONX TALE, A
SAVOY. September, 1993. (Robert De Niro), Robert De Niro, Chazz Palminteri, Lilo Brancato.

BROTHER MINISTER:
THE ASSASSINATION OF MALCOLM X
X-CEPTIONAL PRODS. January, 1995. (Jack Baxter, Jefri Almuhammed), Documentary.

BROTHER'S KEEPER
CREATIVE THINKING. September, 1992. (Joe Berlinger, Bruce Sinofsky), Documentary.

BROTHERS McMULLEN, THE
20TH CENTURY FOX. August, 1995. Irish. (Edward Burns), Edward Burns, Mike McGlone, Jack Mulcahy.

BROWNING VERSION, THE
PARAMOUNT. October, 1994. (Mike Figgis), Albert Finney, Greta Scacchi, Matthew Modine, Julian Sands.

BUFFY THE VAMPIRE SLAYER
20TH CENTURY FOX. July, 1992. (Fran Rubel Kazui), Kristy Swanson, Donald Sutherland, Luke Perry.

BUGSY
TRISTAR. December, 1991. (Barry Levinson), Warren Beatty, Annette Bening, Harvey Keitel, Ben Kingsley.

BULLETPROOF HEART
KEYSTONE. (R) March, 1995. (Mark Malone), Mimi Rogers, Anthony LaPaglia, Peter Boyle.

BULLETS OVER BROADWAY
MIRAMAX. (R) October, 1994. (Woody Allen), John Cusack, Dianne Wiest, Chazz Palminteri, Jennifer Tilly.

BURNT BY THE SUN
SONY CLASSICS. April, 1995. Russian-French. (Nikita Mikhalkov), Nikita Mikhalkov, Ingeborga Dapkounaite.

BUSHWHACKED
20TH CENTURY FOX. August, 1995. (Greg Beeman), Daniel Stern, Jon Polito, Brad Sullivan, Ann Dowd.

BUTCHER'S WIFE, THE
PARAMOUNT. October, 1991. (Terry Hughes), Demi Moore, Jeff Daniels, George Dzundza.

BUTTERSCOTCH AND CHOCOLATE
LANG & ASSOCS. October, 1992. (Nate Grant), Rickey Hendon, Tony Alcantar.

BY THE SWORD
MOVIE GROUP. May, 1993. (Jeremy Kagan), F. Murray Abraham, Eric Roberts, Mia Sara.

BYE BYE BLUES
CIRCLE. March, 1990. Canadian. (Anne Wheeler), Rebecca Jenkins, Luke Reilly, Michael Ontkean.

BYE BYE LOVE
20TH CENTURY FOX. March, 1995. (Sam Weisman), Matthew Modine, Paul Reiser, Randy Quaid, Janeane Garofalo, Rob Reiner.

CB4
UNIVERSAL. March, 1993. (Tamra Davis), Chris Rock, Allen Payne, Deezer D., Chris Elliott.

CABEZA DE VACA
CONCORDE. May, 1992. Mexican-Spanish. (Nicolas Eshevarria), Juan Diego, Daniel Gimenez Cacho.

CABIN BOY
BUENA VISTA. January, 1994. (Adam Resnick), Chris Elliott, James Gammon, Brian Doyle-Murray.

CADENCE
NEW LINE CINEMA. January, 1991. (Martin Sheen), Charlie Sheen, Martin Sheen, Laurence Fishburne.

CADILLAC MAN
ORION. May, 1990. (Roger Donaldson), Robin Williams, Tim Robbins, Pamela Reed.

CAFE AU LAIT
NEW YORKER. August, 1994. French. (Mathieu Kassovitz), Julie Mauduech, Hubert Kounde, Mathieu Kassovitz.

CAGE/CUNNINGHAM
CUNNINGHAM DANCE FOUNDATION. December, 1991. (Elliot Caplan), Documentary.

CALENDAR
ZEITGEIST. March, 1994. Armenian-Canadian-German. (Atom Egoyan), Arsinee Khanjian, Ashot Adamian.

CALENDAR GIRL
COLUMBIA. September, 1993. (John Whitesell), Jason Priestley, Gabriel Olds, Jerry O'Connell.

CAMILLA
MIRAMAX. (PG-13) December, 1994. Canadian-British. (Deepa Mehta), Jessica Tandy, Bridget Fonda, Elias Koteas.

CAMP AT THIAROYE, THE
NEW YORKER. September, 1990. French. (Ousmane Sembene, Thierno Faty Sow), Ibrahima Sane, Sijiri Bakaba.

CAMP NOWHERE
BUENA VISTA. August, 1994. (Jonathan Prince), Christopher Lloyd, Jonathan Jackson, Wendy Makkena.

CANADIAN BACON
GRAMERCY. (PG) September, 1995. (Michael Moore), Alan Alda, John Candy, Kevin Pollak, Rip Torn.

CANDYMAN
TRISTAR. October, 1992. (Bernard Rose), Virginia Madsen, Tony Todd, Xander Berkeley.

CANDYMAN: FAREWELL TO THE FLESH
GRAMERCY. (R) March, 1995. (Bill Condon), Tony Todd, Kelly Rowan, Timothy Carhart.

CAPE FEAR
UNIVERSAL. November, 1991. (Martin Scorsese), Robert De Niro, Nick Nolte, Jessica Lange, Juliette Lewis.

CAPTAIN RON
BUENA VISTA. September, 1992. (Thom Eberhardt), Kurt Russell, Martin Short, Mary Kay Place.

CAPTIVE IN THE LAND, A
NORKAT. January, 1993. Soviet-U.S. (John Berry), Sam Waterston, Aleksandr Potapov.

CAR 54, WHERE ARE YOU?
ORION. January, 1994. (Bill Fishman), David Johansen, John C. McGinley, Fran Drescher.

CAREER OPPORTUNITIES
UNIVERSAL. March, 1991. (Bryan Gordon), Frank Whaley, Jennifer Connelly, Dermot Mulroney.

CAREFUL
ZEITGEIST. August, 1993. Canadian. (Guy Maddin), Kyle McCulloch, Gosia Dobrowolska, Sarah Neville.

CARLITO'S WAY
UNIVERSAL. November, 1993. (Brian De Palma), Al Pacino, Sean Penn, Penelope Ann Miller.

CARMEN MIRANDA: BANANAS IS MY BUSINESS
INT'L. CINEMA. July, 1995. Brazilian-U.S. (Helena Solberg), Erick Barreto, Leticia Monte.

CARNOSAUR
CONCORDE. May, 1993. (Adam Simon), Diane Ladd, Raphael Sbarge, Jennifer Runyon.

CARO DIARIO
FINE LINE. September, 1994. Italian-French. (Nanni Moretti), Nanni Moretti, Renato Carpentieri, Valerio Magrelli.

CASPER
UNIVERSAL. May, 1995. (Brad Silberling), Christina Ricci, Bill Pullman, Eric Idle, Cathy Moriarty.

CASSANDRA CAT
CESKOSLOVENSKY FILMEXPORT. July, 1990 (release of 1963 film), Czechoslovak. (Vojtech Jasný), Jan Werich, Emilie Vasáryová.

CASTLE OF CAGLIOSTRO, THE
STREAMLINE. July, 1992. Japanese. (Hayao Miyazaki), Animated.

CEMETERY CLUB, THE
BUENA VISTA. February, 1993. (Bill Duke), Ellen Burstyn, Olympia Dukakis, Diane Ladd, Danny Aiello.

CENTER OF THE WEB
A.I.P. STUDIO. May, 1992. (David A. Prior), Robert Davi, Charlene Tilton, Tony Curtis.

C'EST LA VIE
GOLDWYN. November, 1990. French. (Diane Kurys), Nathalie Baye, Richard Berry, Julie Bataille.

CHAIN OF DESIRE
MAD DOG PICTURES. June, 1993. (Temistocles Lopez), Malcolm McDowell, Linda Fiorentino, Tim Guinee.

CHAMELEON STREET
NORTHERN ARTS. April, 1991. (Wendell B. Harris, Jr.), Wendell B. Harris, Jr., Angela Leslie.

CHAPLIN
TRISTAR. December, 1992. (Richard Attenborough), Robert Downey Jr., Geraldine Chaplin, Kevin Kline, Diane Lane.

CHASE, THE
20TH CENTURY FOX. March, 1994. (Adam Rifkin), Charlie Sheen, Kristy Swanson, Henry Rollins.

CHASERS
WARNER BROS. April, 1994. (Dennis Hopper), Tom Berenger, William McNamara, Erika Eleniak.

CHATTAHOOCHEE
HEMDALE. April, 1990. (Mick Jackson), Gary Oldman, Dennis Hopper, Pamela Reed.

CHEAP SHOTS
HEMDALE/SELECT. November, 1991. (Jeff Ureless), Louis Zorich, David Patrick Kelly, Mary Louise Wilson.

CHEATIN' HEARTS
TRIMARK. July, 1993. (Rod McCall), Sally Kirkland, James Brolin, Kris Kristofferson.

CHEYENNE WARRIOR
CONCORDE. July, 1994. (Mark Griffiths), Kelly Preston, Pato Hoffman, Bo Hopkins.

CHICAGO JOE AND THE SHOWGIRL
NEW LINE CINEMA. July, 1990. British. (Bernard Rose), Kiefer Sutherland, Emily Lloyd, Patsy Kensit.

CHILDREN OF THE CORN II
DIMENSION. January, 1993. (David Price), Terence Knox, Paul Scherrer, Rosalind Allen.

CHILD'S PLAY 2
UNIVERSAL. November, 1990. (John Lafia), Alex Vincent, Christine Elise, Jenny Agutter.

CHINA CRY
PENLAND CO. November, 1990. (James E. Collier), Julia Nickson-Soul, Russell Wong, James Shigeta.

CHINA MOON
ORION. March, 1994. (John Bailey), Ed Harris, Madeleine Stowe, Charles Dance.

CHINA, MY SORROW
MILESTONE. January, 1993. Chinese. (Dai Sijie), Guo Liang Yi, Tieu Quan Nghieu.

CHOPPER CHICKS IN ZOMBIETOWN
TRIAX. March, 1990. (Dan Hoskins), Jamie Rose, Catherine Carlen.

CHRISTOPHER COLUMBUS—THE DISCOVERY
WARNER BROS. August, 1992. (John Glen), George Corraface, Marlon Brando, Tom Selleck.

CIAO, PROFESSORE!
MIRAMAX. July, 1994. Italian. (Lina Wertmuller), Paolo Bonacelli, Pier Francesco Borruto, Esterina Carloni.

CINEMA PARADISO
MIRAMAX. February, 1990. Italian. (Giuseppe Tornatore), Philippe Noiret, Jacques Perrin.

CIRCLE OF FRIENDS
SAVOY. (PG-13) March, 1995. Irish. (Pat O'Connor), Minnie Driver, Chris O'Donnell, Geraldine O'Rawe.

CIRCUITRY MAN
SKOURAS. August, 1990. (Steve Lovy), Jim Metzler, Dennis Christopher, Dana Wheeler Nicholson.

CITY OF HOPE
GOLDWYN. October, 1991. (John Sayles), Vincent Spano, Joe Morton, Tony Lo Bianco, Todd Graff.

CITY OF JOY
TRISTAR. April, 1992. British-French. (Roland Joffé), Patrick Swayze, Om Puri, Pauline Collins.

CITY SLICKERS
COLUMBIA. June, 1991. (Ron Underwood), Billy Crystal, Daniel Stern, Bruno Kirby, Jack Palance.

CITY SLICKERS II:
THE LEGEND OF CURLY'S GOLD
COLUMBIA. June, 1994. (Paul Weiland), Billy Crystal, Daniel Stern, Jon Lovitz, Jack Palance.

CITY UNPLUGGED
FILMHAUS. June, 1995. Estonian. (Ilkka Jarvilaturi), Peeter Oja, Ivo Uukkivi, Milena Gulbe

CITY ZERO
IFEX. March, 1991. Soviet. (Karen Shakhnazarov), Leonid Filatov, Oleg Basilashvili.

CLAIRE OF THE MOON
DEMI MONDE. October, 1992. (Nicole Conn), Trisha Todd, Karen Trumbo, Faith McDevitt.

CLASS ACT
WARNER BROS. June, 1992. (Randall Miller), Christopher "Kid" Reid, Christopher "Play" Martin.

CLASS ACTION
20TH CENTURY FOX. March, 1991. (Michael Apted), Gene Hackman, Mary Elizabeth Mastrantonio, Colin Friels.

CLASS OF 1999
TAURUS ENTERTAINMENT. May, 1990. (Mark L. Lester), Bradley Gregg, Malcolm McDowell, Traci Lind.

CLASS OF NUKE 'EM HIGH PART 2:
SUBHUMANOID MELTDOWN
TROMA. April, 1991. (Eric Louzil), Brick Bronsky, Lisa Gaye.

CLEAN, SHAVEN
STRAND. April, 1995. (Lodge H. Kerrigan), Peter Greene, Jennifer MacDonald, Robert Albert.

CLEAN SLATE
MGM. May, 1994. (Mick Jackson), Dana Carvey, Valeria Golino, James Earl Jones.

CLEAR AND PRESENT DANGER
PARAMOUNT. August, 1994. (Phillip Noyce), Harrison Ford, Willem Dafoe, Anne Archer.

CLEARCUT
NORTHERN ARTS. August, 1992. Canadian. (Richard Bugajski), Ron Lea, Graham Greene, Michael Hogan.

CLERKS
MIRAMAX. (R) October, 1994. (Kevin Smith), Brian O'Halloran, Jeff Anderson, Marilyn Ghigliotti. B&W

CLIENT, THE
WARNER BROS. July, 1994. (Joel Schumacher), Susan Sarandon, Tommy Lee Jones, Brad Renfro.

CLIFFHANGER
TRISTAR. May, 1993. (Renny Harlin), Sylvester Stallone, John Lithgow, Michael Rooker.

CLIFFORD
ORION. April, 1994. (Paul Flaherty), Martin Short, Charles Grodin, Mary Steenburgen.

CLOCKERS
UNIVERSAL. September, 1995. (Spike Lee), Harvey Keitel, John Turturro, Delroy Lindo, Mekhi Phifer.

CLOSE MY EYES
CASTLE HILL. November, 1991. British. (Stephen Poliakoff), Alan Rickman, Clive Owen, Saskia Reeves.

CLOSE TO EDEN
MIRAMAX. October, 1992. Russian. (Nikita Mikhalkov), Bayaertu Badema, Vladimir Gostukhin.

CLOSET LAND
UNIVERSAL. March, 1991. (Radha Bharadwaj), Madeleine Stowe, Alan Rickman.

CLOWNHOUSE
TRIUMPH. July, 1990. (Victor Salva), Nathan Forrest Winters, Brian McHugh.

CLUELESS
PARAMOUNT. July, 1995. (Amy Heckerling), Alicia Silverstone, Stacey Dash, Brittany Murphy, Dan Hedaya, Paul Rudd.

COBB
WARNER BROS. December, 1994. (Ron Shelton), Tommy Lee Jones, Robert Wuhl, Lolita Davidovitch.

COLD HEAVEN
HEMDALE. May, 1992. (Nicolas Roeg), Theresa Russell, Mark Harmon, James Russo.

COLD MOON
GAMUONT. April, 1992. French. (Patrick Bouchitey), Jean Francois Stevenin, Patrick Bouchitey, Jean Pierre Bisson.

COLDBLOODED
I.R.S. (R) September, 1995. (M. Wallace Wolodarsky), Jason Priestley, Peter Riegert, Kimberly Williams.

COLIN NUTLEY'S HOUSE OF ANGELS
SONY PICTURES CLASSICS. August, 1993. Swedish. (Colin Nutley), Helena Bergstrom, Rikard Wolff, Sven Wollter.

COLONEL CHABERT
OCTOBER. December, 1994. French. (Yves Angelo), Gérard Depardieu, Fanny Ardant, Fabrice Luchini.

COLOR ADJUSTMENT
CALIFORNIA NEWSREEL. January, 1992. (Marlon T. Riggs), Documentary.

COLOR OF NIGHT
BUENA VISTA. August, 1994. (Richard Rush), Bruce Willis, Jane March, Ruben Blades, Andrew Lowery.

COMBINATION PLATTER
ARROW. November, 1993. (Tony Chan), Jeff Lau, Colleen O'Brien, Colin Mitchell, Kenneth Lu.

COME SEE THE PARADISE
20TH CENTURY FOX. December, 1990. (Alan Parker), Dennis Quaid, Tamlyn Tomita, Sab Shimono.

COMEDY'S DIRTIEST DOZEN
ISLAND. October, 1990. (Lenny Wong), Tim Allen.

COMING OUT UNDER FIRE
ZEITGEIST. July, 1994. (Arthur Dong), Documentary. Brian Thompson, Kathy Shower.

COMMITMENTS, THE
20TH CENTURY FOX. August, 1991. British. (Alan Parker), Robert Arkins, Johnny Murphy, Andrew Strong, Angeline Ball.

COMPANY BUSINESS
MGM. September, 1991. (Nicholas Meyer), Gene Hackman, Mikhail Baryshnikov, Kurtwood Smith.

COMPLEX WORLD
HEARTBREAK HITS. November, 1990. (James Wolpaw), Stanley Matis, Dan Von Bargen, Dan Welch.

CONEHEADS
PARAMOUNT. July, 1993. (Steve Barron), Dan Aykroyd, Jane Curtin, Michael McKean.

CONGO
PARAMOUNT. June, 1995. (Frank Marshall), Dylan Walsh, Laura Linney, Ernie Hudson, Tim Curry.

CONGRESS OF PENGUINS, THE
ARIANE FILM. January, 1995. Swiss. (Hans Ulrich Schlumpf), Documentary.

CONJUGAL BED, THE
LEISURE TIME. July, 1994. Romanian. (Mircea Daneliuc), Gheorghe Dinica, Coca Bloos, Valentin Teodosiu.

CONSENTING ADULTS
BUENA VISTA. October, 1992. (Alan J. Pakula), Kevin Kline, Mary Elizabeth Mastrantonio, Kevin Spacey.

CONVICTION, THE
INT'L FILM CIRCUIT. May, 1994. Italian-French. (Marco Bellocchio), Vittorio Mezzogiorno, Claire Nebout.

CONVICTS
M.C.E.G. December, 1991. (Peter Masterson), Robert Duvall, Lukas Haas, James Earl Jones.

COOK, THE THIEF, HIS WIFE & HER LOVER, THE
MIRAMAX. April, 1990. British. (Peter Greenaway), Helen Mirren, Michael Gambon, Alan Howard.

COOL AS ICE
UNIVERSAL. October, 1991. (David Kellogg), Vanilla Ice, Kristin Minter, Michael Gross.

COOL RUNNINGS
BUENA VISTA. October, 1993. (Jon Turteltaub), Leon, Doug E. Doug, Rawle D. Lewis, John Candy.

COOL WORLD
PARAMOUNT. July, 1992. (Ralph Bakshi), Kim Basinger, Brad Pitt, Gabriel Byrne.

COP AND A HALF
UNIVERSAL. April, 1993. (Henry Winkler), Burt Reynolds, Norman D. Golden II, Ray Sharkey, Ruby Dee.

COPS AND ROBBERSONS
TRISTAR. April, 1994. (Michael Ritchie), Chevy Chase, Jack Palance, Dianne Wiest, David Barry Gray.

CORMORANT, THE
BBC/PUBLIC TH. April, 1995. British. (Peter Markham), Ralph Fiennes, Helen Schlesinger, Thomas Williams.

CORPORATE AFFAIRS
CONCORDE. October, 1990. (Terence H. Winkless), Peter Scolari, Mary Crosby, Chris Lemmon.

CORRINA, CORRINA
NEW LINE CINEMA. August, 1994. (Jessie Nelson), Whoopi Goldberg, Ray Liotta, Tina Majorino.

COUNTESS, THE
INT'L FILM CIRCUIT. January, 1991. Bulgaria. (Peter Popzlatev), Svetlana Yancheva, Itzhak Fintsi, Peter Popyordanov.

COUNTRY LIFE
MIRAMAX. (PG-13) July, 1995. Australian. (Michael Blakemore), Sam Neill, Greta Scacchi, John Hargreaves.

COUPE DE VILLE
UNIVERSAL. March, 1990. (Joe Roth), Patrick Dempsey, Daniel Stern, Alan Arkin.

COURAGE MOUNTAIN
TRIUMPH. February, 1990. (Christopher Leitch), Juliette Caton, Leslie Caron, Charlie Sheen.

COUSIN BOBBY
CINEVISTA. May, 1992. (Jonathan Demme), Documentary.

COW, THE
CZECH TV/PUBLIC TH. February, 1995. Czech. (Karyl Kachyna), Radek Holub, Alena Mikulova.

COWBOY WAY, THE
UNIVERSAL. June, 1994. (Gregg Champion), Woody Harrelson, Kiefer Sutherland, Dylan McDermott.

COWS (Vacas)
PUBLIC THEATRE. June, 1994. Spanish. (Julio Medem), Manuel Blasco, Emma Suarez, Carmelo Gomez.

CRACKDOWN
CONCORDE. January, 1991. (Louis Morneau), Cliff De Young, Robert Beltran, Jamie Rose.

CRAZY PEOPLE
PARAMOUNT. April, 1990. (Tony Bill), Dudley Moore, Daryl Hannah, Paul Reiser.

CRIME BROKER
A-PIX. (R) September, 1994. Australian. (Ian Barry), Jacqueline Bisset, Masaya Kato.

CRIMSON TIDE
BUENA VISTA. May, 1995. (Tony Scott), Denzel Washington, Gene Hackman, George Dzundza.

CRISSCROSS
MGM. May, 1992. (Chris Menges), Goldie Hawn, Arliss Howard, David Arnott, Keith Carradine.

CRONOS
OCTOBER. March, 1994. Mexican. (Guillermo Del Toro), Federico Luppi, Ron Perlman, Claudio Brook.

CROOKED HEARTS
MGM. May, 1991. (Michael Bortman), Vincent D'Onofrio, Jennifer Jason Leigh, Peter Berg.

CROOKLYN
UNIVERSAL. May, 1994. (Spike Lee), Alfre Woodard, Delroy Lindo, Zelda Harris.

CROSS MY HEART (La Fracture du Myocarde)
MK2. April, 1991. French. (Jacques Fansten), Sylvain Copans, Nicolas Parodi, Cecilia Rouaud.

CROSSING THE BRIDGE
BUENA VISTA. September, 1993. (Mike Binder), Josh Charles, Jason Gedrick, Stephen Baldwin.

CROSSING THE LINE (The Big Man)
MIRAMAX. August, 1991. British. (David Leland), Liam Neeson, Joanne Whalley-Kilmer, Ian Bannen.

CROW, THE
MIRAMAX. May, 1994. (Alex Proyas), Brandon Lee, Ernie Hudson, Michael Wincott.

CRUDE OASIS, THE
MIRAMAX. (R) July, 1995. (Alex Graves), Jennifer Taylor, Aaron Shields, Robert Peterson.

CRUMB
SONY CLASSICS. April, 1995. (Terry Zwigoff), Documentary.

CRUSH
STRAND. September, 1993. New Zealand. (Alison MacLean), Marcia Gay Harden, Donogh Rees, Caitlin Bossley.

CRUSH, THE
WARNER BROS. April, 1993. (Alan Shapiro), Cary Elwes, Alicia Silverstone, Jennifer Rubin.

CRY BABY
UNIVERSAL. April, 1990. (John Waters), Johnny Depp, Amy Locane, Polly Bergen, Ricki Lake.

CRY IN THE WILD, A
CONCORDE. June, 1990. (Mark Griffiths), Jared Rushton, Pamela Sue Martin.

CRYING GAME, THE
MIRAMAX. November, 1992. British. (Neil Jordan), Stephen Rea, Forest Whitaker, Miranda Richardson.

CUP FINAL
FIRST RUN FEATURES. August, 1992. Israeli. (Eran Riklis), Moshe Ivgi, Muhamad Bacri, Suheil Haddad.

CURE, THE
UNIVERSAL. April, 1995. (Peter Horton), Joseph Mazzello, Brad Renfro, Annabella Sciorra.

CURE SHOW, THE
I.R.S. October, 1993. (Aubrey Powell, Leroy Bennett), The Cure.

CURFEW
NEW YORKER. December, 1994. Dutch-Palestinian. (Rashid Masharawai), Salim Daw, Na'ila Zayaad, Younis Younis.

CURLY SUE
WARNER BROS. October, 1991. (John Hughes), James Belushi, Alisan Porter, Kelly Lynch.

CUTTING EDGE, THE
MGM. March, 1992. (Paul M. Glaser), D.B. Sweeney, Moira Kelly, Roy Dotrice.

CYRANO DE BERGERAC
ORION CLASSICS. November, 1990. French. (Jean Paul Rappeneau), Gérard Depardieu, Anne Brochet, Vincent Perez.

D

D2: THE MIGHTY DUCKS
BUENA VISTA. March, 1994. (Sam Weisman), Emilio Estevez, Kathryn Erbe, Michael Tucker, Jan Rubes.

DADDY NOSTALGIA
AVENUE. April, 1991. French. (Bertrand Tavernier), Dirk Bogarde, Jane Birkin, Odette Laure.

DADDY'S DYIN'... WHO'S GOT THE WILL?
MGM/UA. May, 1990. (Jack Fisk), Beau Bridges, Beverly D'Angelo, Keith Carradine, Tess Harper.

DANCES WITH WOLVES
ORION. November, 1990. (Kevin Costner), Kevin Costner, Mary McDonnell, Graham Greene.

DANGEROUS GAME
MGM. November, 1993. (Abel Ferrara), Harvey Keitel, Madonna, James Russo.

DANGEROUS MINDS
BUENA VISTA. August, 1995. (John N. Smith), Michelle Pfeiffer, George Dzundza, Courtney B. Vance.

DANGEROUS WOMAN, A
GRAMERCY. December, 1993. (Stephen Gyllenhaal), Debra Winger, Barbara Hershey, Gabriel Byrne.

DANZON
SONY PICTURES CLASSICS. September, 1992. Mexican. (Maria Novaro), Maria Rojo, Carmen Salinas, Blanca Guerra.

DAREDREAMER
LENSMAN CO. February, 1990. (Barry Caillier), Tim Noah, Alyce LaTourelle.

DARK AT NOON
SIDERAL PRODS. August, 1993. French-Argentine. (Raul Ruiz), John Hurt, Didier Bourdon, David Warner.

DARK BACKWARD, THE
GREYCAT FILMS. July, 1991. (Adam Rifkin), Judd Nelson, Bill Paxton, Wayne Newton.

DARK HALF, THE
ORION. April, 1993. (George A. Romero), Timothy Hutton, Amy Madigan, Michael Rooker.

DARK HORSE
REPUBLIC. July, 1992. (David Hemmings), Ed Begley Jr., Mimi Rogers, Ari Meyers.

DARK OBSESSION (Diamond Skulls)
CIRCLE. June, 1991. British. (Nick Broomfield), Gabriel Byrne, Amanda Donohoe, Douglas Hodge.

DARKMAN
UNIVERSAL. August, 1990. (Sam Raimi), Liam Neeson, Frances McDormand, Colin Friels.

DAUGHTERS OF THE DUST
KINO INT'L. January, 1992. (Julie Dash), Cora Lee Day, Alva Rodgers, Adisa Anderson.

DAVE
WARNER BROS. May, 1993. (Ivan Reitman), Kevin Kline, Sigourney Weaver, Frank Langella, Charles Grodin.

DAY THE SUN TURNED COLD, THE
KINO. April, 1995. Chinese. (Yim Ho), Siqin Gowa, Tuo Zhong Hua, Ma Jing Wu.

DAYS OF THUNDER
PARAMOUNT. June, 1990. (Tony Scott), Tom Cruise, Robert Duvall, Nicole Kidman.

DAZED AND CONFUSED
GRAMERCY. September, 1993. (Richard Linklater), Jason London, Joey Lauren Adams, Anthony Rapp.

DEAD AGAIN
PARAMOUNT. August, 1991. (Kenneth Branagh), Kenneth Branagh, Emma Thompson, Derek Jacobi.

DEAD–ALIVE
TRIMARK. February, 1993. New Zealand. (Peter Jackson), Timothy Balme, Diana Penalver, Elizabeth Moody.

DEAD FLOWERS
OAK ISLAND. April, 1993. Austrian. (Peter Ily Huemer), Kate Valk, Thierry van Werveke, Tana Schanzara.

DEAD FUNNY
CINEPIX. (R) July, 1995. (John Feldman), Andrew McCarthy, Elizabeth Pena, Paige Turco.

DEAD MEN DON'T DIE
TRANS ATLANTIC. September, 1991. (Malcolm Marmorstein), Elliott Gould, Melissa Anderson, Mabel King.

DEAD RINGER
OGDEN AVE. July, 1991. (Allan Nicholls), Meat Loaf, Josh Mostel, MacIntyre Dixon.

DEAD SPACE
CONCORDE. January, 1991. (Fred Gallo), Marc Singer, Laura Tate.

DEAD WOMEN IN LINGERIE
AFI USA. November, 1991. (Erica Fox), John Romo, Jerry Orbach, Dennis Christopher.

DEADFALL
TRIMARK. October, 1993. (Christopher Coppola), Michael Biehn, Sarah Trigger, Nicolas Cage.

DEADLY CURRENTS
NORMANDIE. October, 1992. Canadian. (Simcha Jacobovici), Documentary.

DEATH AND THE MAIDEN
FINE LINE. (R) December, 1994. French-British-U.S. (Roman Polanski), Sigourney Weaver, Ben Kingsley, Stuart Wilson.

DEATH BECOMES HER
UNIVERSAL. July, 1992. (Robert Zemeckis), Meryl Streep, Goldie Hawn, Bruce Willis.

DEATH WARRANT
MGM/UA. September, 1990. (Deran Sarafian), Jean Claude Van Damme, Robert Guillaume, Cynthia Gibb.

DEATH WISH V: THE FACE OF DEATH
TRIMARK. January, 1994. Canadian. (Allan A. Goldstein), Charles Bronson, Lesley Anne Down, Michael Parks.

DECEIVED
BUENA VISTA. September, 1991. (Damian Harris), Goldie Hawn, John Heard, Ashley Peldon.

DECEMBER
I.R.S. December, 1991. (Gabe Torres), Wil Wheaton, Chris Young, Balthazar Getty, Brian Krause.

DECEMBER BRIDE
WAX/COURIER. September, 1994. Irish. (Thaddeus O'Sullivan), Saskia Reeves, Donal McCann, Ciaran Hinds.

DECEPTION
MIRAMAX. October, 1993. (Graeme Clifford), Liam Neeson, Andie MacDowell, Viggo Mortensen.

DEEP BLUES
AFI USA. November, 1991. (Robert Mugge), Junior Kimbrough, Jessie Mae Hemphill.

DEEP COVER
NEW LINE CINEMA. April, 1992. (Bill Duke), Laurence Fishburne, Jeff Goldblum, Victoria Dillard.

DEF BY TEMPTATION
TROMA. March, 1990. (James Bond III), James Bond III, Cynthia Bond, Kadeem Hardison.

DEFENDING YOUR LIFE
WARNER BROS. March, 1991. (Albert Brooks), Albert Brooks, Meryl Streep, Rip Torn.

DEFENSELESS
7 ARTS/NEW LINE CINEMA. August, 1991. (Martin Campbell), Barbara Hershey, Sam Shepard, Mary Beth Hurt.

DELICATESSEN
MIRAMAX. April, 1992. French. (Jean Pierre Jeunet, Marc Caro), Marie-Laure Dougnac, Jean Claude Dreyfus, Dominique Pinon.

DELIRIOUS
MGM. August, 1991. (Tom Mankiewicz), John Candy, Mariel Hemingway, Dylan Baker, Emma Samms.

DELIVERED VACANT
ISLET. May, 1993. (Nora Jacobson), Documentary.

DELTA FORCE 2
MGM/UA. August, 1990. (Aaron Norris), Chuck Norris, Billy Drago, John P. Ryan.

DELUSION
I.R.S. MEDIA. June, 1991. (Carl Colpaert), Jim Metzler, Jennifer Rubin, Kyle Secor.

DEMOLITION MAN
WARNER BROS. October, 1993. (Marco Brambilla), Sylvester Stallone, Wesley Snipes, Sandra Bullock.

DEMONSTONE
FRIES. March, 1990. (Andrew Prowse), Jan Michael Vincent, R. Lee Ermey.

DENNIS THE MENACE
WARNER BROS. June, 1993. (Nick Castle), Walter Matthau, Mason Gamble, Joan Plowright.

DESIRE & HELL AT SUNSET MOTEL
TWO MOON RELEASING. April, 1992. (Allen Castle), Sherilyn Fenn, Whip Hubley, David Hewlett.

DESIRE: SEXUALITY IN GERMANY, 1910–1945
MAYAVISION. June, 1990. British. (Stuart Marshall), Documentary.

DESPERADO
COLUMBIA. August, 1995. (Robert Rodriguez), Antonio Banderas, Joaquim de Almeida, Salma Hayek.

DESPERATE HOURS
MGM. October, 1990. (Michael Cimino), Mickey Rourke, Anthony Hopkins, Mimi Rogers.

DESPERATE REMEDIES
MIRAMAX. May, 1994. New Zealand. (Stewart Main, Peter Wells), Jennifer Ward Lealand, Kevin Smith, Lisa Chappell.

DESTINY TURNS ON THE RADIO
SAVOY. (R) April, 1995. (Jack Baran), James LeGros, Dylan McDermott, Quentin Tarantino.

DEVIL IN A BLUE DRESS
TRISTAR. September, 1995. (Carl Franklin), Denzel Washington, Jennifer Beals, Tom Sizemore.

DEVIL, PROBABLY, THE
NEW YORKER. November, 1994. French. (Robert Bresson), Antoine Monnier, Tina Irissari, Henri de Maublanc.

DIALOGUES WITH MADWOMEN
LIGHT/SARAF. August, 1994. (Allie Light), Documentary.

DIAMOND'S EDGE (JUST ASK FOR DIAMOND)
CASTLE HILL. November, 1990. British. (Stephen Bayly), Colin Dale, Dursley McLinden, Susannah York.

DIARY OF A HIT MAN
VISION INT'L. May, 1992. (Roy London), Forest Whitaker, Sherilyn Fenn, Sharon Stone.

DICE RULES
7 ARTS. May, 1991. (Jay Dubin), Andrew Dice Clay.

DICK TRACY
BUENA VISTA. June, 1990. (Warren Beatty), Warren Beatty, Madonna, Al Pacino, Charlie Korsmo.

DIE HARD 2
20TH CENTURY FOX. July, 1990. (Remy Harlin), Bruce Willis, Bonnie Bedelia, Franco Nero.

DIE HARD WITH A VENGEANCE
20TH CENTURY FOX. May, 1995. (John McTiernan), Bruce Willis, Jeremy Irons, Samuel L. Jackson.

DIGGSTOWN
MGM. August, 1992. (Michael Ritchie), James Woods, Louis Gossett, Jr., Bruce Dern.

DIPLOMATIC IMMUNITY
FRIES ENT. April, 1991. (Peter Maris), Bruce Boxleitner, Billy Drago, Tom Breznahan.

DIRTY MONEY
NORTHERN ARTS. May, 1995. (James Bruce), Frederick Deane, Timothy Patrick Cavanaugh, Biff Yeager.

DISCLOSURE
WARNER BROS. December, 1994. (Barry Levinson), Michael Douglas, Demi Moore, Donald Sutherland.

DISTINGUISHED GENTLEMAN, THE
BUENA VISTA. December, 1992. (Jonathan Lynn), Eddie Murphy, Lane Smith, Sheryl Lee Ralph.

DISTURBED
LIVE ENTERTAINMENT. November, 1990. (Charles Winkler), Malcolm McDowell, Geoffrey Lewis, Priscilla Pointer.

DIVINE OBSESSION
PANORAMA ENTERTAINMENT. March, 1990. (Yuri Sivo), Brian Benben, Deborah Farentino.

DIVING IN
SKOURAS. September, 1990. (Strathford Hamilton), Matt Adler, Burt Young, Matt Lattanzi.

DJEMBEFOLA
INTERAMA. September, 1993. French. (Laurent Chevalier), Documentary.

DO OR DIE
MALIBU BAY. June, 1991. (Andy Sidaris), Pat Morita, Erik Estrada, Dona Speir.

DOC HOLLYWOOD
WARNER BROS. August, 1991. (Michael Caton Jones), Michael J. Fox, Julie Warner, Barnard Hughes.

DOCTOR, THE
BUENA VISTA. July, 1991. (Randa Haines), William Hurt, Elizabeth Perkins, Christine Lahti.

DOG TAGS
CINEVEST ENTERTAINMENT. February, 1990. (Romano Scavolini), Clive Wood, Baird Stafford.

DOGFIGHT
WARNER BROS. September, 1991. (Nancy Savoca), River Phoenix, Lili Taylor, Richard Panebianco.

DOLORES CLAIBORNE
COLUMBIA. March, 1995. (Taylor Hackford), Kathy Bates, Jennifer Jason Leigh, Christopher Plummer.

DON JUAN DEMARCO
NEW LINE CINEMA. (PG-13), April, 1995. (Jeremy Leven), Marlon Brando, Johnny Depp, Faye Dunaway.

DON JUAN, MY LOVE
IFEX. July, 1991. Spanish. (Antonio Mercero), Juan Luis Galiardo, Maria Barranco, Loles Leon.

DON'T TELL HER IT'S ME
HEMDALE. September, 1990. (Malcolm Mowbray), Steve Guttenberg, Shelley Long, Jami Gertz.

DON'T TELL MOM THE BABYSITTER'S DEAD
WARNER BROS. June, 1991. (Stephen Herek), Christina Applegate, Joanna Cassidy, Keith Coogan.

DOORS, THE
TRISTAR. March, 1991. (Oliver Stone), Val Kilmer, Meg Ryan, Frank Whaley, Kyle MacLachlan.

DOUBLE DRAGON
GRAMERCY. (PG-13) November, 1994. (James Yukich), Robert Patrick, Mark Dacascos, Scott Wolf.

DOUBLE EDGE
CASTLE HILL. September, 1992. Israeli-U.S. (Amos Kollek), Faye Dunaway, Amos Kollek, Mohammad Bakri.

DOUBLE HAPPINESS
FINE LINE. (PG-13) July, 1995. Canadian. (Mina Shum), Sandra Oh, Alannah Ong, Stephen Chang.

DOUBLE IMPACT
COLUMBIA. August, 1991. (Sheldon Lettich), Jean Claude Van Damme, Geoffrey Lewis, Alan Scarfe.

DOUBLE LIFE OF VERONIQUE, THE
MIRAMAX. November, 1991. French-Polish. (Krzysztof Kieslowski), Irene Jacob, Halina Gryglaszewska.

DOUBLE THREAT
PYRAMID. December, 1992. (David A. Prior), Sally Kirkland, Andrew Stevens, Richard Lynch.

DOWNTOWN
20TH CENTURY FOX. January, 1990. (Richard Benjamin), Anthony Edwards, Forest Whitaker, David Clennon.

DR. BETHUNE
TARA. September, 1993. Canadian. (Phillip Borsos), Donald Sutherland, Helen Mirren, Helen Shaver.

DR. CALIGARI
STEINER. May, 1990. (Stephen Sayadian), Madeleine Reynal, Fox Harris.

DR. GIGGLES
UNIVERSAL. October, 1992. (Manny Coto), Larry Drake, Holly Marie Combs, Cliff De Young.

DR. JEKYLL AND MS. HYDE
SAVOY. (PG-13) August, 1995. (David F. Price), Tim Daly, Sean Young, Lysette Anthony.

DRAGON: THE BRUCE LEE STORY
UNIVERSAL. May, 1993. (Rob Cohen), Jason Scott Lee, Lauren Holly, Robert Wagner.

DREAM AND MEMORY
C&A PRODS. May, 1994. Chinese. (Ann Hu), Bing Yang, Shao Bing, Li Wei.

DREAM DECEIVERS
FIRST RUN FEATURES. August, 1992. (David Van Taylor), Documentary.

DREAM LOVER
GRAMERCY. May, 1994. (Nicholas Kazan), James Spader, Madchen Amick, Bess Armstrong.

DREAM MACHINE, THE
INT'L. CREATIVE EXCHANGE. September, 1991. (Lyman Dayton), Corey Haim, Evan Richards, Jeremy Slate.

DREAMING OF RITA
FIRST RUN. April, 1995. Swedish. (Jon Lindstrom), Per Oscarsson, Marika Lagercrantz, Philip Zanden.

DRIVE
MEGAGIANT ENT. July, 1992. (Jeffery Levy), David Warner, Steven Antin, Dedee Pfeiffer.

DRIVING ME CRAZY
MOTION PICTURE CORP. OF AMER. November, 1991. (Jon Turtletaub), Thomas Gottschalk, Billy Dee Williams, Milton Berle.

DRIVING ME CRAZY
FIRST RUN FEATURES. March, 1990. British. (Nick Broomfield), André Heller, Mercedes Ellington.

DROP DEAD FRED
NEW LINE CINEMA. May, 1991. (Ate De Jong), Phoebe Cates, Rik Mayall, Marsha Mason.

DROP SQUAD
GRAMERCY. (R) October, 1994. (D. Clark Johnson), Eriq La Salle, Vondie Curtis Hall, Ving Rhames.

DROP ZONE
PARAMOUNT. December, 1994. (John Badham), Wesley Snipes, Gary Busey, Yancy Butler, Michael Jeter.

DROWNING BY NUMBERS
PRESTIGE. April, 1991. British. (Peter Greenaway), Joan Plowright, Juliette Stevenson, Bernard Hill.

DUCK TALES:
THE MOVIE—TREASURE OF THE LOST LAMP
BUENA VISTA. August, 1990. (Bob Hathcock), Animated.

DUMB AND DUMBER
NEW LINE. (PG-13) December, 1994. (Peter Farrelly), Jim Carrey, Jeff Daniels, Lauren Holly.

DUNE WARRIORS
CONCORDE. January, 1991. (Cirio H. Santiago), David Carradine, Rick Hill, Luke Askew.

DUTCH
20TH CENTURY FOX. July, 1991. (Peter Faiman), Ed O'Neill, Ethan Randall, JoBeth Williams.

DYING YOUNG
20TH CENTURY FOX. June, 1991. (Joel Schumacher), Julia Roberts, Campbell Scott, Vincent D'Onofrio.

EAR, THE
INT'L. FILM EXCHANGE. March, 1992. Czech. (Karel Kachyna), Radoslav Brzobahaty, Jirina Bohdalova.

EAT DRINK MAN WOMAN
GOLDWYN. August, 1994. Taiwanese. (Ang Lee), Sihung Lung, Kuei Mei Yang, Chien Lien Wu.

EATING
INT'L RAINBOW. November, 1990. (Henry Jaglom), Nelly Alard, Mary Crosby, Frances Bergen.

ECHOES FROM A SOMBER EMPIRE
NEW YORKER. July, 1992. German-French. (Werner Herzog), Documentary.

ED AND HIS DEAD MOTHER
I.R.S. November, 1993. (Jonathan Wacks), Steve Buscemi, Ned Beatty, Miriam Margolyes.

ED WOOD
BUENA VISTA. September, 1994. (Tim Burton), Johnny Depp, Martin Landau, Sarah Jessica Parker, Bill Murray.

EDWARD SCISSORHANDS
20TH CENTURY FOX. December, 1990. (Tim Burton), Johnny Depp, Dianne Wiest, Winona Ryder.

EDWARD II
FINE LINE FEATURES. March, 1992. British. (Derek Jarman), Steven Waddington, Kevin Collins, Andrew Tiernan.

EFFICIENCY EXPERT, THE
MIRAMAX. November, 1992. Australian. (Mark Joffe), Anthony Hopkins, Ben Mendelsohn, Toni Collette.

8 SECONDS
NEW LINE CINEMA. February, 1994. (John G. Avildsen), Luke Perry, Stephen Baldwin, James Rebhorn.

EL MARIACHI
COLUMBIA. February, 1993. (Robert Rodriguez), Carlos Gallardo, Consuelo Gomez, Reinol Martinez.

ELLIOT FAUMAN, Ph.D.
TAURUS ENTERTAINMENT. March, 1990. (Ric Klass), Randy Dreyfuss, Jean Kasem.

EMINENT DOMAIN
TRIUMPH. April, 1991. Canadian-Israeli-French. (John Irvin), Donald Sutherland, Anne Archer, Paul Freeman.

EMMA AND ELVIS
NORTHERN ARTS. October, 1992. (Julia Reichert), Kathryn Walker, Mark Blum, Jason Duchin.

EMPIRE RECORDS
WARNER BROS. September, 1995. (Allan Moyle), Anthony LaPaglia, Rory Cochrane, Johnny Whitworth.

ENCHANTED APRIL
MIRAMAX. July, 1992. British. (Mike Newell), Josie Lawrence, Miranda Richardson, Joan Plowright.

ENCHANTMENT, THE
HERALD ACE/NIPPON HERALD. May, 1992. Japanese. (Chun'Ichi Nagaskai), Kumiko Akiyoshi, Masao Kusakari, Kiwako Harada.

ENCINO MAN
BUENA VISTA. May, 1992. (Les Mayfield), Sean Astin, Brendan Fraser, Pauly Shore.

ENCOUNTER AT RAVEN'S GATE
HEMDALE. January, 1990. Australian. (Rolf de Heer), Steven Vidler, Celine Griffin.

END OF INNOCENCE, THE
SKOURAS. December, 1990. (Dyan Cannon), Dyan Cannon, John Heard, George Coe.

END OF OLD TIMES, THE
IFEX. January, 1992. Czech. (Jiri Menzel), Josef Abraham, Marian Labuda, Jaromir Hanzlik.

ENDLESS SUMMER II, THE
NEW LINE CINEMA. June, 1994. (Bruce Brown), Documentary.

ENEMY UNSEEN
TRIAX ENTERTAINMENT. January, 1990. (Elmo DeWitt), Vernon Wells, Angela O'Neil.

ENGLISHMAN WHO WENT UP A HILL
BUT CAME DOWN A MOUNTAIN, THE
MIRAMAX. (PG-13) May, 1995. British. (Christopher Monger), Hugh Grant, Tara Fitzgerald, Colm Meaney.

EQUINOX
I.R.S. June, 1993. (Alan Rudolph), Matthew Modine, Lara Flynn Boyle, Marisa Tomei.

ERMO
ARROW. May, 1995. Chinese. (Zhou Xiaowen), Alia, Liu Peiqi, Ge Zhijun.

ERNEST GOES TO JAIL
BUENA VISTA. April, 1990. (John Cherry), Jim Varney, Gailard Sartain, Bill Byrge.

ERNEST RIDES AGAIN
EMSHELL. November, 1993. (John R. Cherry III), Jim Varney, Ron K. James, Linda Kash.

ERNEST SCARED STUPID
BUENA VISTA. October, 1991. (John Cherry), Jim Varney, Eartha Kitt, Austin Nagler.

EROTIQUE
GROUP 1/ODYSSEY. April, 1995. U.S.-German. (Lizzie Borden, Monika Truet, Clara Law), Kamela Lopez Dawson, Bryan Cranston.

ESPECIALLY ON SUNDAY
MIRAMAX. August, 1993. Italian. (Giuseppe Tornatore), Philippe Noiret, Ornella Muti, Bruno Ganz.

ETERNITY
PAUL ENTERTAINMENT. October, 1990. (Steven Paul), Jon Voight, Armand Assante, Eileen Davidson.

ETHAN FROME
MIRAMAX. March, 1993. (John Madden), Liam Neeson, Patricia Arquette, Joan Allen.

EUROPA, EUROPA
ORION CLASSICS. June, 1991. German-Russian-Polish. (Agnieszka Holland), Marco Hofschneider, Rene Hofschneider, Julie Delpy.

EVE OF DESTRUCTION
ORION. January, 1991. (Duncan Gibbins), Gregory Hines, Renee Soutendijk, Michael Greene.

EVEN COWGIRLS GET THE BLUES
FINE LINE. May, 1994. (Gus Van Sant), Uma Thurman, Lorraine Bracco, John Hurt, Rain Phoenix.

EVERY OTHER WEEKEND
MK2. June, 1991. French. (Nicole Garcia), Nathalie Baye, Joachim Serreau, Felicie Pasotti.

EVERYBODY WINS
ORION. January, 1990. (Karel Reisz), Nick Nolte, Debra Winger, Will Patton.

EVERYBODY'S FINE
MIRAMAX. May, 1991. Italian. (Giuseppe Tornatore), Marcello Mastroianni, Michele Morgan, Marino Cenna.

EXCESSIVE FORCE
NEW LINE CINEMA. May, 1993. (Jon Hess), Thomas Ian Griffith, Charlotte Lewis, James Earl Jones.

EXECUTION PROTOCOL, THE
FIRST RUN. April, 1993. British. (Stephen Trombley), Documentary.

EXECUTIONERS
RIM FILMS. June, 1995. Hong Kong. (Johnny To, Ching Siu Tung), Michelle Khan, Anita Mui, Maggie Cheung.

EXIT TO EDEN
SAVOY. (R) October, 1994. (Garry Marshall), Dana Delany, Paul Mercurio, Rosie O'Donnell, Dan Aykroyd.

EXORCIST III, THE
20TH CENTURY FOX. August, 1990. (William Peter Blatty), George C. Scott, Brad Dourif, Ed Flanders.

EXOTICA
MIRAMAX. (R) March, 1995. Canadian. (Atom Egoyan), Bruce Greenwood, Mia Kirshner, Don McKellar.

EXPOSURE
MIRAMAX. October, 1991. Brazilian. (Walter Salles, Jr.), Peter Coyote, Tcheky Karyo, Amanda Pays.

EXTRAMUROS
FRAMELINE. June, 1991. Spanish. (Miguel Picazo), Carmen Maura, Mercedes Sampietro, Assumpta Serna.

EYE OF THE STRANGER
SILVER LAKE. September, 1993. (David Heavener), David Heavener, Martin Landau, Sally Kirkland.

F/X 2
ORION. May, 1991. (Richard Franklin), Bryan Brown, Brian Dennehy, Rachel Ticotin.

FALLING DOWN
WARNER BROS. February, 1993. (Joel Schumacher), Michael Douglas, Robert Duvall, Barbara Hershey.

FALLING FROM GRACE
COLUMBIA. February, 1992. (John Mellencamp), John Mellencamp, Mariel Hemingway, Kay Lenz.

FALSE IDENTITY
RKO PICTURES. June, 1990. (James Keach), Stacy Keach, Genevieve Bujold.

FAMILY PRAYERS
ARROW. March, 1993. (Scott Rosenfelt), Joe Mantegna, Anne Archer, Paul Reiser.

FAMINE–33
INDEPENDENT. December, 1993. Ukranian. (Oles Yanchuk), Halyna Sulyma, Georgi Morozuik. B&W.

FAMINE WITHIN, THE
DIRECT CINEMA. July, 1991. (Katherine Gilday), Documentary.

FAR AND AWAY
UNIVERSAL. May, 1992. (Ron Howard), Tom Cruise, Nicole Kidman, Thomas Gibson.

FAR FROM HOME:
THE ADVENTURES OF YELLOW DOG
20TH CENTURY FOX. January, 1995. (Phillip Borsos), Jesse Bradford, Bruce Davison, Mimi Rogers.

FAR OFF PLACE, A
BUENA VISTA. March, 1993. (Mikael Salomon), Reese Witherspoon, Ethan Randall, Sarel Bok.

FAR OUT MAN
NEW LINE CINEMA. May, 1990. (Tommy Chong), Tommy Chong, C. Thomas Howell, Shelby Chong.

FARAWAY, SO CLOSE!
SONY CLASSICS. December, 1993. German. (Wim Wenders), Otto Sander, Nastassja Kinski, Peter Falk.

FAREWELL MY CONCUBINE
MIRAMAX. October, 1993. Hong Kong. (Chen Kaige), Leslie Cheung, Zhang Fengyi, Gong Li.

FARINELLI
SONY CLASSICS. (R) March, 1995. Belgian. (Gerard Corbiau), Stefano Dionisi, Erico Lo Verso, Jeroen Krabbe.

FATAL INSTINCT
MGM. October, 1993. (Carl Reiner), Armand Assante, Kate Nelligan, Sherilyn Fenn, Sean Young.

FATHER
NORTHERN ARTS. July, 1992. Australian. (John Power), Max von Sydow, Carol Drinkwater, Julia Blake.

FATHER HOOD
BUENA VISTA. August, 1993. (Darrell James Roodt), Patrick Swayze, Sabrina Lloyd, Brian Bonsall, Halle Berry.

FATHER OF THE BRIDE
BUENA VISTA. December, 1991. (Charles Shyer), Steve Martin, Diane Keaton, Kimberly Williams.

FATHERS AND SONS
PACIFIC PICTURES. November, 1992. (Paul Mones), Jeff Goldblum, Rory Cochrane, Rocky Carroll.

FAUST
FILM FORUM. October, 1994. French-Czech-British-German. (Jan Svankmajer), Petr Cepek.

FAVOR, THE
ORION. April, 1994. (Donald Petrie), Harley Jane Kozak, Elizabeth McGovern, Bill Pullman, Brad Pitt.

FAVOR, THE WATCH AND THE VERY BIG FISH, THE
TRIMARK. May, 1992. British. (Ben Lewin), Bob Hoskins, Natasha Richardson, Jeff Goldblum.

FEAR OF A BLACK HAT
GOLDWYN. June, 1994. (Rusty Cundieff), Mark Christopher Lawrence, Larry B. Scott, Rusty Cundieff.

FEARLESS
WARNER BROS. October, 1993. (Peter Wier), Jeff Bridges, Isabella Rossellini, Rosie Perez, Tom Hulce.

FEDERAL HILL
TRIMARK. (R) December, 1994. (Michael Corrente), Nicholas Turturro, Anthony De Sando, Libby Langdon. B&W

FEED
ORIGINAL CINEMA. October, 1992. (Kevin Rafferty, James Ridgeway), Documentary.

FEMALE MISBEHAVIOR
FIRST RUN. April, 1993. German. (Monika Truet), Documentary.

FERNGULLY... THE LAST RAINFOREST
20TH CENTURY FOX. April, 1992. (Bill Kroyer), Animated.

FEUD, THE
CASTLE HILL. May, 1990. (Bill D'Elia), Rene Auberjonois, Scott Allegrucci, Ron McLarty.

FEW GOOD MEN, A
COLUMBIA. December, 1992. (Rob Reiner), Tom Cruise, Jack Nicholson, Demi Moore, Kevin Bacon.

FIELD, THE
AVENUE. December, 1990. Irish. (Jim Sheridan), Richard Harris, Sean Bean, John Hurt.

FIFTH MONKEY, THE
COLUMBIA. October, 1990. French-Brazilian-U.S. (Eric Rochat), Ben Kingsley, Silvia De Carvalho.

FIFTY FIFTY
CANNON. February, 1993. (Charles Martin Smith), Peter Weller, Robert Hays, Ramona Rahman.

FINAL ANALYSIS
WARNER BROS. February, 1992. (Phil Joanou), Richard Gere, Kim Basinger, Eric Roberts, Uma Thurman.

FINAL APPROACH
TRIMARK. December, 1991. (Eric Steven Stahl), James B. Sikking, Hector Elizondo, Madolyn Smith.

FINAL IMPACT
PM ENTERTAINMENT. February, 1992. (Joseph Merhi), Lorenzo Lamas, Kathleen Kinmont, Michael Worth.

FINE ROMANCE, A
CASTLE HILL. September, 1992. Italian. (Gene Saks), Julie Andrews, Marcello Mastroianni.

FINZAN
CALIFORNIA NEWSREEL. March, 1992. Malian Bambara. (Cheik Oumar Sissoko), Diarrah Sanogo, Oumar Namory Keita, Balla Moussa Keita.

FIORILE
FINE LINE. February, 1994. Italian. (Paolo and Vittorio Taviani), Claudio Bigagli, Galatea Ranzi.

FIRE IN THE SKY
PARAMOUNT. March, 1993. (Robert Lieberman), D.B. Sweeney, Robert Patrick, James Garner.

FIREBIRDS
BUENA VISTA. May, 1990. (David Green), Nicolas Cage, Tommy Lee Jones, Sean Young.

FIREHEAD
PYRAMID DISTRIB. January, 1991. (Peter Yuval), Christopher Plummer, Chris Lemmon, Martin Landau.

FIRES WITHIN
MGM. June, 1991. (Gillian Armstrong), Jimmy Smits, Greta Scacchi, Vincent D'Onofrio.

FIRM, THE
PARAMOUNT. June, 1993. (Sydney Pollack), Tom Cruise, Gene Hackman, Jeanne Tripplehorn, Holly Hunter.

FIRST DATE
PETER WANG FILMS. June, 1991. Taiwanese. (Peter Wang), Chang Shi, Li Xing Wen, Shi Jun.

FIRST KNIGHT
COLUMBIA. July, 1995. (Jerry Zucker), Sean Connery, Richard Gere, Julia Ormond, Ben Cross.

FIRST POWER, THE
ORION. April, 1990. (Robert Resnikoff), Lou Diamond Phillips, Tracy Griffith, Jeff Kober.

FISHER KING, THE
TRISTAR. September, 1991. (Terry Gilliam), Robin Williams, Jeff Bridges, Mercedes Ruehl, Amanda Plummer.

FIST OF THE NORTH STAR
STREAMLINE. October, 1991. Japanese. (Toyoo Ashida), Animated.

FIVE HEARTBEATS, THE
20TH CENTURY FOX. March, 1991. (Robert Townsend), Robert Townsend, Michael Wright, Harry J. Lenix.

FLAMING EARS
WOMEN MAKE MOVIES. January, 1993. Austrian. (Angela Hans Scheirl, Dietmar Schipek, Ursula Puerrer), Susanna Heilmayr, Ursula Puerrer.

FLASHBACK
PARAMOUNT. February, 1990. (Franco Amurri), Dennis Hopper, Kiefer Sutherland, Carol Kane.

FLATLINERS
COLUMBIA. August, 1990. (Joel Schumacher), Kiefer Sutherland, Julia Roberts, Kevin Bacon.

FLESH AND BONE
PARAMOUNT. November, 1993. (Steve Kloves), Dennis Quaid, Meg Ryan, James Caan.

FLEX
TRIAX. May, 1990 (Pat Domenico), Harry Grant, Lorin Jean Vail.

FLIGHT OF THE INNOCENT
MGM. October, 1993. Italian. (Carlo Carlei), Manuel Colao, Francesca Neri, Jacques Perrin.

FLIGHT OF THE INTRUDER
PARAMOUNT. January, 1991. (John Milius), Danny Glover, Willem Dafoe, Brad Johnson.

FLINTSTONES, THE
UNIVERSAL. May, 1994. (Brian Levant), John Goodman, Rick Moranis, Elizabeth Perkins, Rosie O'Donnell.

FLOUNDERING
STRAND. November, 1994. (Peter McCarthy), James LeGros, Sy Richardson, Ethan Hawke, John Cusack.

FLUKE
MGM/UA. June, 1995. (Carlo Carlei), Matthew Modine, Nancy Travis, Eric Stoltz, Ron Perlman.

FOLKS!
20TH CENTURY FOX. May, 1992. (Ted Kotcheff), Tom Selleck, Don Ameche, Anne Jackson.

FOOLS OF FORTUNE
NEW LINE CINEMA. September, 1990. British. (Pat O'Connor), Mary Elizabeth Mastrantonio, Iain Glen, Julie Christie.

FOR A LOST SOLDIER
STRAND. May, 1993. Dutch. (Roeland Kerbosch), Maarten Smit, Andrew Kelley, Jeroen Krabbe.

FOR LOVE OR MONEY
UNIVERSAL. October, 1993. (Barry Sonnenfeld), Michael J. Fox, Gabrielle Anwar, Anthony Higgins.

FOR SASHA
MK2. June, 1992. French. (Alexandre Arcady), Sophie Marceau, Richard Berry, Fabien Orcier.

FOR THE BOYS
20TH CENTURY FOX. November, 1991. (Mark Rydell), Bette Midler, James Caan, George Segal.

FORBIDDEN DANCE, THE
COLUMBIA. March, 1990. (Greydon Clark), Laura Herring, Jeff James, Richard Lynch.

FORBIDDEN LOVE:
THE UNASHAMED STORIES OF LESBIAN LIVES
WOMEN MAKE MOVIES. August, 1993. Canadian. (Aerlyn Weissman, Lynne Fernie), Documentary.

FORBIDDEN QUEST, THE
ZEITGEIST. January, 1994. Dutch. (Peter Delpeut), Joseph O'Conor, Roy Ward.

FORCE OF CIRCUMSTANCE
UPFRONT. June, 1990. (Liza Bear), Borbala Major, Jessica Stutchbury.

FOREIGN STUDENT
GRAMERCY. July, 1994. French. (Eva Sereny), Marco Hofschneider, Robin Givens, Charles S. Dutton.

FOREVER ACTIVISTS: STORIES FROM THE
VETERANS OF THE ABRAHAM LINCOLN BRIGADE
TARA. June, 1991. (Judith Montell), Documentary.

FOREVER MARY
CINEVISTA. April, 1991. Italian. (Marco Risi), Michele Placido, Alessandro di Sanzo, Claudio Amendola.

FOREVER YOUNG
WARNER BROS. December, 1992. (Steve Miner), Mel Gibson, Elijah Wood, Jamie Lee Curtis.

FORGET PARIS
COLUMBIA. May, 1995. (Billy Crystal), Billy Crystal, Debra Winger, Joe Mantegna, Cynthia Stevenson.

FORREST GUMP
PARAMOUNT. July, 1994. (Robert Zemeckis), Tom Hanks, Robin Wright, Gary Sinise, Sally Field.

FORTRESS
DIMENSION. September, 1993. Australian-U.S. (Stuart Gordon), Christopher Lambert, Kurtwood Smith.

FOUR WEDDINGS AND A FUNERAL
GRAMERCY. March, 1994. British. (Mike Newell), Hugh Grant, Andie MacDowell, Simon Callow, David Bower.

1492: CONQUEST OF PARADISE
PARAMOUNT. October, 1992. (Ridley Scott), Gérard Depardieu, Armand Assante, Michael Wincott.

FOURTH WAR, THE
NEW AGE RELEASING. March, 1990. (John Frankenheimer), Roy Scheider, Jurgen Prochnow.

FRANCOIS TRUFFAUT: STOLEN PORTRAITS
MYRIAD PICTURES. July, 1994. French. (Serge Toubiana, Michel Pascal), Documentary.

FRANKENHOOKER
SHAPIRO GLICKENHAUS. June, 1990. (Frank Henenlotter), James Lorinz, Patty Mullen.

FRANKIE AND JOHNNY
PARAMOUNT. October, 1991. (Garry Marshall), Al Pacino, Michelle Pfeiffer, Kate Nelligan, Nathan Lane.

FRAUDS
LIVE/J&M. September, 1993. Australian. (Stephan Elliott), Phil Collins, Hugo Weaving, Josephine Byrnes.

FREAKED
20TH CENTURY FOX. October, 1993. (Tom Stern, Alex Winter), Alex Winter, Randy Quaid, Megan Ward.

FREDDIE AS F.R.O. 7
MIRAMAX. August, 1992. British. (Jon Acevski), Animated.

FREDDY'S DEAD: THE FINAL NIGHTMARE (3–D)
NEW LINE CINEMA. September, 1991. (Rachel Talalay), Robert Englund, Lisa Zane, Lezlie Deane.

FREE WILLY
WARNER BROS. July, 1993. (Simon Wincer), Jason James Richter, Lori Petty, August Schellenberg.

FREE WILLY 2: THE ADVENTURE HOME
WARNER BROS. July, 1995. (Dwight Little), Jason James Richter, August Schellenberg, Michael Madsen.

FREEJACK
WARNER BROS. January, 1992. (Geoff Murphy), Emilio Estevez, Mick Jagger, Rene Russo.

FREEZE–DIE–COME TO LIFE
IFEX. December, 1990. Soviet. (Vitaly Kanevski), Pavel Nazarov, Dinara Drukarova. B&W.

FRENCH KISS
20TH CENTURY FOX. May, 1995. (Lawrence Kasdan), Meg Ryan, Timothy Hutton, Kevin Kline, Jean Reno.

FRESH
MIRAMAX. August, 1994. (Boaz Yakin), Sean Nelson, Giancarlo Esposito, Samuel L. Jackson.

FRESHMAN, THE
TRISTAR. July, 1990. (Andrew Bergman), Marlon Brando, Matthew Broderick, Penelope Ann Miller.

FRIDAY
NEW LINE. (R) April, 1995. (F. Gary Gray), Ice Cube, Chris Tucker, Nia Long.

FRIED GREEN TOMATOES
UNIVERSAL. December, 1991. (Jon Avnet), Kathy Bates, Mary Stuart Masterson, Jessica Tandy, Mary Louise Parker.

FROM HOLLYWOOD TO HANOI
INDEPT. July, 1993. (Tiana Thi Thanh Nga), Documentary.

FROM RUSSIA WITH ROCK
INT'L. FILM CIRCUIT. December, 1990. Soviet. (Marjaana Mykkanen), Documentary.

FROSH: NINE MONTHS IN A FRESHMAN DORM
HORIZON UNLIMITED. October, 1994. (Dan Geller, Dayna Goldfine), Documentary.

FROZEN ASSETS
RKO. October, 1992. (George Miller), Shelley Long, Corbin Bernsen, Larry Miller.

FUGITIVE, THE
WARNER BROS. August, 1993. (Andrew Davis), Harrison Ford, Tommy Lee Jones, Jeroen Krabbe.

FULL FATHOM FIVE
CONCORDE. August, 1990. (Carl Franklin), Michael Moriarty, Maria Rangel, Diego Bertie.

FULL MOON IN NEW YORK
SHIOBU FILM CO. June, 1990. Chinese. (Stanley Kwan), Sylvia Chang, Maggie Cheung.

FUN
INDEPT./FILM FORUM. April, 1995. (Rafael Zelinsky), Alicia Witt, Renee Humphrey, William R. Moses.

FUN DOWN THERE
FRAMELINE. June, 1990. (Roger Stigliano), Michael Waite, Nickolas B. Nagourney.

FUNNY ABOUT LOVE
PARAMOUNT. September, 1990. (Leonard Nimoy), Gene Wilder, Christine Lahti, Mary Stuart Masterson.

FUNNY BONES
BUENA VISTA. March, 1995. (Peter Chelsom), Oliver Platt, Jerry Lewis, Leslie Caron, George Carl.

G

GAME, THE
AQUARIUS RELEASING. April, 1990. (Curtis Brown), Curtis Brown, Richard Lee Ross.

GARDEN, THE
INT'L FILM CIRCUIT. January, 1991. U.K. (Derek Jarman), Tilda Swinton, Johnny Mills, Philip MacDonald, Spencer Lee.

GARDEN OF SCORPIONS
LEN FILM. March, 1993. Russian. (Oleg Kovalov). Compilation.

GAS FOOD LODGING
I.R.S. July, 1992. (Allision Anders), Brooke Adams, Ione Skye, Fairuza Balk.

GATE II
TRIUMPH. February, 1992. (Tibor Takacs), Louis Tripp, Simon Reynolds, Pamela Segall.

GENUINE RISK
I.R.S. RELEASING. December, 1990. (Kurt Voss), Terence Stamp, Peter Berg, Michelle Johnson.

GEORGE BALANCHINE'S THE NUTCRACKER
WARNER BROS. October, 1993. (Emile Ardolino), Darci Kistler, Macaulay Culkin, Jessica Lynn Cohen.

GEORGE'S ISLAND
NEW LINE CINEMA. October, 1991. Canadian. (Paul Donovan), Ian Bannen, Sheila McCarthy, Nathaniel Moreau.

GERMANY YEAR 90 NINE ZERO
BRAINSTORM. January, 1995. French-German. (Jean Luc Godard), Eddie Constantine, Hanns Zischler, Claudia Michelsen.

GERMINAL
SONY CLASSICS. December, 1993. French. (Claude Berri), Gérard Depardieu, Miou-Miou.

GERONIMO: AN AMERICAN LEGEND
COLUMBIA. December, 1993. (Walter Hill), Jason Patric, Wes Studi, Gene Hackman, Matt Damon.

GET THEE OUT
FIRST RUN FEATURES. January, 1993. Russian. (Dimitri Astrakhan), Otar Mengvinetukutsey, Elena Anisimova.

GETAWAY, THE
UNIVERSAL. February, 1994. (Roger Donaldson), Alec Baldwin, Kim Basinger, Michael Masden, James Woods.

GETTING EVEN WITH DAD
MGM. June, 1994. (Howard Deutch), Macaulay Culkin, Ted Danson, Glenne Headly.

GETTYSBURG
NEW LINE CINEMA. October, 1993. (Ronald E. Maxwell), Tom Berenger, Jeff Daniels, Martin Sheen.

GHOST
PARAMOUNT. July, 1990. (Jerry Zucker), Patrick Swayze, Demi Moore, Whoopi Goldberg.

GHOST DAD
UNIVERSAL. June, 1990. (Sidney Poitier), Bill Cosby, Kimberly Russell, Denise Nicholas.

GHOST IN THE MACHINE
20TH CENTURY FOX. December, 1993. (Rachel Talalay), Karen Allen, Wil Horneff, Chris Mulkey.

GHOSTS CAN'T DO IT
TRIUMPH. June, 1990. (John Derek), Bo Derek, Anthony Quinn, Don Murray.

GIRLFRIEND FROM HELL
AUGUST ENT. April, 1991. (Daniel M. Peterson), Liane Curtis, Dana Ashbrook, Lezlie Deane.

GIVING, THE
NORTHERN ARTS. November, 1992. (Eames Demetrios), Jeremiah Pollock, Lee Hampton, Flor Hawkins.

GLADIATOR
COLUMBIA. March, 1992. (Rowdy Herrington), James Marshall, Brian Dennehy, Cuba Gooding Jr.

GLASS SHIELD, THE
MIRAMAX. (PG-13) June, 1995. (Charles Burnett), Michael Boatman, Lori Petty, Ice Cube.

GLENGARRY GLEN ROSS
NEW LINE CINEMA. September, 1992. (James Foley), Al Pacino, Jack Lemmon, Ed Harris.

GO FISH
GOLDWYN. June, 1994. (Rose Troche), Guinevere Turner, V.S. Brodie, T. Wendy McMillan.

GODFATHER PART III, THE
PARAMOUNT. December, 1990. (Francis Ford Coppola), Al Pacino, Andy Garcia, Talia Shire, Diane Keaton.

GODS MUST BE CRAZY II, THE
COLUMBIA. April, 1990. Botswana. (Jamie Uys), N!xau, Lena Farugia.

GOLDEN BOAT, THE
STRAND. June, 1991. (Paul Ruiz), Federico Muchnik, Michael Kirby.

GOLDEN BRAID
CABRIOLET. December, 1991. Australian. (Paul Cox), Chris Haywood, Gosia Dobrowolska, Paul Chubb.

GOLDEN GATE
GOLDWYN. January, 1994. (John Madden), Matt Dillon, Joan Chen, Bruno Kirby, Stan Egi.

GOOD MAN IN AFRICA, A
GRAMERCY. (R) September, 1994. (Bruce Beresford), Colin Friels, Sean Connery, John Lithgow.

GOOD SON, THE
20TH CENTURY FOX. September, 1993. (Joseph Ruben), Macaulay Culkin, Elijah Wood, Wendy Crewson.

GOOD WOMAN OF BANGKOK, THE
ROXIE. November, 1991. Australian. (Dennis O'Rourke), Documentary.

GOODFELLAS
WARNER BROS. September, 1990. (Martin Scorsese), Robert De Niro, Ray Liotta, Joe Pesci, Paul Sorvino.

GOOFY MOVIE, A
BUENA VISTA. April, 1995. (Kevin Lima), Bill Farmer, Jason Marsden, Jim Cummings, Kellie Martin.

GORDY
MIRAMAX. (G) November, 1994. (Mark Lewis), Doug Stone, Michael Roescher, Kristy Young.

GORILLA BATHES AT NOON
INDEPT./PUBLIC TH. March, 1995. German-Russian. (Dusan Makavejcu), Svetozar Cvetkovic, Anita Manic. B&W/Color.

GRAFFITI BRIDGE
WARNER BROS. November, 1990. (Prince), Prince, Morris Day, Jerome Benton & The Time.

GRAND CANYON
20TH CENTURY FOX. December, 1991. (Lawrence Kasdan), Kevin Kline, Danny Glover, Steve Martin, Mary McDonnell.

GREAT DAY IN HARLEM, A
CASTLE HILL. February, 1995. (None credited), Documentary.

GREEDY
UNIVERSAL. March, 1994. (Jonathan Lynn), Michael J. Fox, Kirk Douglas, Nancy Travis.

GREEN CARD
BUENA VISTA. December, 1990. French-Australian. (Peter Weir), Gérard Depardieu, Andie MacDowell, Bebe Neuwirth.

GREMLINS 2: THE NEW BATCH
WARNER BROS. June, 1990. (Joe Dante), Zach Galligan, John Glover, Phoebe Cates.

GRIEF
STRAND. March, 1994. (Richard Glatzer), Craig Chester, Jackie Beat, Alexis Arquette, Illeana Douglas.

GRIFTERS, THE
MIRAMAX. December, 1990. (Stephen Frears), John Cusack, Anjelica Huston, Annette Bening.

GRIM PRAIRIE TALES
COE HAN FILMS. August, 1990. (Wayne Coe), Brad Dourif, James Earl Jones, Marc McClure.

GROSSE FATIGUE
MIRAMAX. (R) July, 1995. French. (Michel Blanc), Michael Blanc, Carole Bouquet, Phillipe Noiret.

GROUNDHOG DAY
COLUMBIA. February, 1993. (Harold Ramis), Bill Murray, Andie MacDowell, Chris Elliott.

GRUMPY OLD MEN
WARNER BROS. December, 1993. (Donald Petrie), Jack Lemmon, Walter Matthau, Ann-Margaret.

GUARDIAN, THE
UNIVERSAL. April, 1990. (William Friedkin), Jenny Seagrove, Dwier Brown, Carey Lowell.

GUARDING TESS
TRISTAR. March, 1994. (Hugh Wilson), Shirley MacLaine, Nicolas Cage, Austin Pendleton.

GUELWAAR
NEW YORKER. April, 1993. Senegalese-French. (Ousmane Sembene), Omar Seck, Ndiawar Diop, Isseu Niang.

GUILTY AS CHARGED
I.R.S. January, 1992. (Sam Irvin), Rod Steiger, Lauren Hutton, Zelda Rubinstein.

GUILTY AS SIN
BUENA VISTA. June, 1993. (Sidney Lumet), Rebecca De Morany, Don Johnson, Jack Warden, Stephen Lang.

GUILTY BY SUSPICION
WARNER BROS. March, 1991. (Irwin Winkler), Robert De Niro, Annette Bening, George Wendt.

GUMSHOE KID, THE
SKOURAS. February, 1990. (Joe Manduke), Jay Underwood, Tracy Scoggins.

GUN IN BETTY LOU'S HANDBAG, THE
BUENA VISTA. August, 1992. (Allan Moyle), Penelope Ann Miller, Eric Thal, Alfre Woodard.

GUNMEN
DIMENSION. February, 1994. (Mario Van Peebles), Mario Van Peebles, Christopher Lambert, Patrick Stewart.

GUNS
MALIBU BAY FILMS. November, 1990. (Andy Sidaris), Erik Estrada, Dona Spier, Roberta Vasquez.

H–2 WORKER
FIRST RUN FEATURES. November, 1990. (Stephanie Black), Documentary.

HACKERS
MGM/UA. September, 1995. (Iain Softley), Johnny Lee Miller, Angelina Jolie, Fisher Stevens, Lorraine Bracco.

HAIRDRESSER'S HUSBAND, THE
TRITON. June, 1992. French. (Patrice Leconte), Jean Rochefort, Anna Galiena, Roland Bertin.

HALF JAPANESE: THE BAND WHO WOULD BE KING
INDEPENDENT. October, 1993. (Jeff Feuerzeig), Half Japanese.

HALLOWEEN: THE CURSE OF MICHAEL MYERS
DIMENSION. (R) September, 1995. (Joe Chappelle), Donald Pleasence, Mitch Ryan, Mariann Hagen.

HAMLET
WARNER BROS. December, 1990. British. (Franco Zeffirelli), Mel Gibson, Glenn Close, Alan Bates, Paul Scofield.

HAND THAT ROCKS THE CRADLE, THE
BUENA VISTA. January, 1992. (Curtis Hanson), Annabella Sciorra, Rebecca De Mornay, Matt McCoy.

HANDMAID'S TALE, THE
CINECOM. March, 1990. (Volker Schlondorff), Natasha Richardson, Faye Dunaway, Aidan Quinn.

HANGFIRE
MOTION PICTURE CORP. OF AMERICA. January, 1991. (Peter Maris), Brad Davis, Jan Michael Vincent, Kim Delaney.

HANGIN' WITH THE HOMEBOYS
NEW LINE CINEMA. May, 1991. (Joseph B. Vasquez), Doug E. Doug, Mario Joyner, John Leguizamo.

HANS CHRISTIAN ANDERSEN'S THUMBELINA
WARNER BROS. March, 1994. (Don Bluth, Gary Goldman), Animated.

HAPPILY EVER AFTER
FIRST NATIONAL. May, 1993. (John Howley), Animated.

HAPPY TOGETHER
SEYMOUR BORDE & ASSOC. May, 1990. (Mel Damski), Patrick Dempsey, Helen Slater.

HARD PROMISES
COLUMBIA. January, 1992. (Martin Davidson), Sissy Spacek, William Petersen, Brian Kerwin.

HARD TARGET
UNIVERSAL. August, 1993. (John Woo), Jean Claude Van Damme, Lance Henriksen, Yancy Butler.

HARD TO KILL
WARNER BROS. February, 1990. (Bruce Malmuth), Steven Seagal, Kelly Le Brock, Bill Sadler.

HARD WAY, THE
UNIVERSAL. March, 1991. (John Badham), Michael J. Fox, James Woods, Stephen Lang.

HARD–BOILED
GOLDEN PRINCESS/MILESTONE. April, 1993. Hong Kong. (John Woo), Chow Yun-fat, Bowie Lam, Philip Chan.

HARMS CASE, THE
INT'L FILM CIRCUIT, October, 1992. Yugoslavia (Slobodan Pesic), Franco Lasic, Damjana Luthar, Milica Tomic.

HARLEY DAVIDSON AND THE MARLBORO MAN
MGM. August, 1991. (Simon Wincer), Mickey Rourke, Don Johnson, Daniel Baldwin.

HARVEST, THE
ARROW. November, 1993. (David Marconi), Miguel Ferrer, Leilani Sarelle, Henry Silva, Harvey Fierstein.

HAUNTING OF MORELLA, THE
CONCORDE. February, 1990. (Jim Wynorksi), David McCallum, Nicole Eggert.

HAVANA
UNIVERSAL. December, 1990. (Sydney Pollack), Robert Redford, Lena Olin, Alan Arkin, Raul Julia.

HAWK, THE
CASTLE HILL. December, 1993. British. (David Hayman), Helen Mirren, George Costigan, Rosemary Leach.

HE SAID/SHE SAID
PARAMOUNT. February, 1991. (Ken Kwapis, Marisa Silver), Kevin Bacon, Elizabeth Perkins, Nathan Lane.

HEAR MY SONG
MIRAMAX. December, 1991. British-Irish. (Peter Chelsom), Ned Beatty, Adrian Dunbar, Shirley Anne Field.

HEAR NO EVIL
20TH CENTURY FOX. March, 1993. (Robert Greenwald), Marlee Matlin, D.B. Sweeney, Martin Sheen.

HEARING VOICES
PHOENIX INT'L. November, 1991. (Sharon Greytak), Erika Nagy, Stephen Gatta, Tim Ahern.

HEART AND SOULS
UNIVERSAL. August, 1993. (Ron Underwood), Robert Downey, Jr., Kyra Sedgwick, Charles Grodin.

HEART CONDITION
NEW LINE CINEMA. February, 1990. (James D. Parriott), Bob Hoskins, Denzel Washington, Chloe Webb.

HEARTS OF DARKNESS: A FILMMAKER'S APOCALYPSE
TRITON. November, 1991. (Fax Bahr), Documentary.

HEAVEN AND EARTH
TRITON. February, 1991. Japanese. (Haruki Kadokawa), Takaai Enoki, Masahiko Tsugawa.

HEAVEN & EARTH
WARNER BROS. December, 1993. (Oliver Stone), Hiep Thi Le, Tommy Lee Jones, Joan Chen, Haing S. Ngor.

HEAVEN IS A PLAYGROUND
NEW LINE CINEMA. October, 1991. (Randall Field), D.B. Sweeney, Michael Warren, Richard Jordan.

HEAVEN'S A DRAG
FIRST RUN. June, 1995. British. (Peter Mackenzie Litten), Thomas Arklie, Ian Williams, Tony Slattery.

HEAVENLY CREATURES
MIRAMAX. (R) November, 1994. New Zealand. (Peter Jackson), Melanie Lynskey, Kate Winslet, Sarah Peirse.

HEAVYWEIGHTS
BUENA VISTA. February, 1995. (Steven Brill), Aaron Schwartz, Tom McGowan, Ben Stiller, Shaun Weiss.

HELAS POUR MOI
CINEMA PARALLEL. March, 1994. Swiss-French. (Jean Luc Goddard), Gérard Depardieu, Laurence Masliah, Bernard Verley.

HELLRAISER III: HELL ON EARTH
DIMENSION. September, 1992. (Anthony Hickox), Doug Bradley, Terry Farrell, Paula Marshall.

HENRY AND JUNE
UNIVERSAL. October, 1990. (Philip Kaufman), Fred Ward, Uma Thurman, Maria de Medeiros, Richard E. Grant.

HENRY: PORTRAIT OF A SERIAL KILLER
GREYCAT FILMS. January, 1990. (John McNaughton), Michael Rooker, Tracy Arnold, Tom Towles.

HERMAN
RKO. November, 1992. Norwegian. (Erik Gustavson), Anders Danielson Lie, Frank Robert, Elisabeth Sand.

HERO
COLUMBIA. October, 1992. (Stephen Frears), Dustin Hoffman, Geena Davis, Andy Garcia.

HEXED
COLUMBIA. January, 1993. (Alan Spencer), Arye Gross, Claudia Christian, Adrienne Shelly.

HIDDEN AGENDA
HEMDALE. November, 1990. British. (Ken Loach), Frances McDormand, Brian Cox, Brad Dourif.

HIDEAWAY
TRISTAR. March, 1995. (Brett Leonard), Jeff Goldblum, Christine Lahti, Alicia Silverstone, Jeremy Sisto.

HIGH HEELS
MIRAMAX. December, 1991. Spanish. (Pedro Almodovar), Victoria Abril, Marisa Paredes, Miguel Bose.

HIGH LONESOME: THE STORY OF BLUEGRASS MUSIC
TARA. April, 1994. (Rachel Liebling), Documentary.

HIGH SCHOOL II
ZIPPORAH. July, 1994. (Frederick Wiseman), Documentary.

HIGHER LEARNING
COLUMBIA. January, 1995. (John Singleton), Omar Epps, Kristy Swanson, Michael Rapaport, Ice Cube.

HIGHLANDER: THE FINAL DIMENSION
DIMENSION. (R) January, 1995. Canadian-U.S. (Andy Morahan), Christopher Lambert, Mario Van Peebles.

HIGHLANDER 2: THE QUICKENING
INTERSTAR. November, 1991. (Russell Mulcahy), Christopher Lambert, Sean Connery, Virginia Madsen.

HIGHWAY PATROLMAN
FIRST LOOK. November, 1993. Mexican. (Alex Cox), Roberto Sosa, Bruno Bichir, Vanessa Bauche.

HIGHWAY 61
SKOURAS. April, 1992. British-Canadian. (Bruce McDonald), Valerie Buhagiar, Don McKellar, Earl Pastko.

HIGHWAY TO HELL
HEMDALE. March, 1992. (Ate De Jong), Patrick Bergin, Adam Storke, Chad Lowe.

HITMAN, THE
CANNON. October, 1991. (Aaron Norris), Chuck Norris, Michael Parks, Al Waxman.

HOCUS POCUS
BUENA VISTA. July, 1993. (Kenny Ortega), Bette Midler, Sarah Jessica Parker, Kathy Najimy, Omri Katz.

HOFFA
20TH CENTURY FOX. December, 1992. (Danny DeVito), Jack Nicholson, Danny DeVito, Armand Assante.

HOLD ME, THRILL ME, KISS ME
MAD DOG PICTURES. July, 1993. (Joel Hirshman), Adrienne Shelly, Sean Young, Max Parrish.

HOLLYWOOD MAVERICKS
ROXIE RELEASING. September, 1990. (Florence Dauman), Documentary.

HOLY MATRIMONY
BUENA VISTA. April, 1994. (Leonard Nimoy), Patricia Arquette, Joseph Gordon Levitt, Armin Mueller Stahl.

HOME ALONE
20TH CENTURY FOX. November, 1990. (Chris Columbus), Macaulay Culkin, Joe Pesci, Daniel Stern.

HOME ALONE 2: LOST IN NEW YORK
20TH CENTURY FOX. November, 1992. (Chris Columbus), Macaulay Culkin, Joe Pesci, Brenda Fricker.

HOME OF OUR OWN, A
GRAMERCY. November, 1993. (Tony Bill), Kathy Bates, Edward Furlong, Soon-Teck Oh.

HOMEWARD BOUND: THE INCREDIBLE JOURNEY
BUENA VISTA. February, 1993. (DuWayne Dunham), Ben, Rattler, Tiki, Robert Hays.

HOMICIDE
TRIUMPH. October, 1991. (David Mamet), Joe Mantegna, William H. Macy, Natalija Nogulich.

HONEY, I BLEW UP THE KID
BUENA VISTA. July, 1992. (Randal Kleiser), Rick Moranis, Marcia Strassman, Robert Oliveri.

HONEYMOON ACADEMY
TRIUMPH. May, 1990. (Gene Quintano), Kim Cattrall, Robert Hays, Leigh Taylor Young.

HONEYMOON IN VEGAS
COLUMBIA. August, 1992. (Andrew Bergman), Nicolas Cage, James Caan, Sarah Jessica Parker.

HOOK
TRISTAR. December, 1991. (Steven Spielberg), Dustin Hoffman, Robin Williams, Julia Roberts.

HOOP DREAMS
FINE LINE. (PG-13) October, 1994. (Steve James), Documentary.

HORSEPLAYER, THE
GREYCAT FILMS. July, 1991. (Kurt Voss), Brad Dourif, Sammi Davis, M.K. Harris.

HOT SHOTS!
20TH CENTURY FOX. July, 1991. (Jim Abrahams), Charlie Sheen, Lloyd Bridges, Cary Elwes.

HOT SHOTS! PART DEUX
20TH CENTURY FOX. May, 1993. (Jim Abrahams), Charlie Sheen, Lloyd Bridges, Richard Crenna, Valeria Golino.

HOT SPOT, THE
ORION. October, 1990. (Dennis Hopper), Don Johnson, Virginia Madsen, Jennifer Connelly.

HOTEL SORRENTO
CASTLE HILL. May, 1995. Australian. (Richard Franklin), Joan Plowright, Caroline Goodall.

HOURS AND TIMES, THE
ANTARCTIC. April, 1992. (Christopher Munch), David Angus, Ian Hart. B&W.

HOUSE OF CARDS
MIRAMAX. June, 1993. (Michael Lessac), Kathleen Turner, Tommy Lee Jones, Asha Menina.

HOUSE OF THE SPIRITS, THE
MIRAMAX. April, 1994. German-Danish-Portuguese. (Bille August), Jeremy Irons, Meryl Streep, Glenn Close.

HOUSE PARTY
NEW LINE CINEMA. March, 1990. (Reginald Hudlin), Christopher Reid, Robin Harris.

HOUSE PARTY 2
NEW LINE CINEMA. October, 1991. (Doug McHenry), Christopher Martin, Tisha Campbell, Martin Lawrence.

HOUSE PARTY 3
NEW LINE CINEMA. January, 1994. (Eric Meza), Christopher Reid, Christopher Martin, David Edwards.

HOUSEGUEST
BUENA VISTA. January, 1995. (Randall Miller), Sinbad, Phil Hartman, Kim Greist, Stan Shaw.

HOUSEHOLD SAINTS
FINE LINE. September, 1993. (Nancy Savoca), Tracey Ullman, Vincent D'Onofrio, Lili Taylor.

HOUSESITTER
UNIVERSAL. June, 1992. (Frank Oz), Steve Martin, Goldie Hawn, Dana Delany.

HOW TO BE LOUISE
VENUS DE MYLAR PRODS. September, 1990. (Anne Flournoy), Lea Floden, Bruce McCarthy.

HOW TO MAKE LOVE TO A NEGRO WITHOUT GETTING TIRED
ANGELIKA. June, 1990. French. (Jacques W. Benoit), Issach De Bankole, Maka Kotto.

HOW U LIKE ME NOW
SHAPIRO GLICKENHAUS. March, 1993. (Darryl Roberts), Darnell Williams, Salli Richardson, Daniel Gardner.

HUDSON HAWK
TRISTAR. May, 1991. (Michael Lehmann), Bruce Willis, Danny Aiello, Andie MacDowell.

HUDSUCKER PROXY, THE
WARNER BROS. March, 1994. (Joel Coen), Tim Robbins, Jennifer Jason Leigh, Paul Newman.

HUGH HEFNER: ONCE UPON A TIME
I.R.S. October, 1992. (Robert Heath), Documentary.

HUMAN SHIELD, THE
CANNON. May, 1992. (Ted Post), Michael Dudikoff, Tommy Hinkley, Hana Azoulay-Hasfari.

HUNT FOR RED OCTOBER, THE
PARAMOUNT. March, 1990. (John McTiernan), Sean Connery, Alec Baldwin, Scott Glenn.

HUNTED, THE
UNIVERSAL. February, 1995. (J.F. Lawton), Christopher Lambert, John Lone, Joan Chen.

HUNTING
SKOURAS. February, 1992. Australian. (Frank Howson), John Savage, Kerry Armstrong, Jeffrey Thomas.

HUSBANDS AND WIVES
TRISTAR. September, 1992. (Woody Allen), Woody Allen, Judy Davis, Mia Farrow, Sydney Pollack.

HYENAS
KINO. August, 1995. Senegalese. (Friedrich Durrenmatt), Mansour Diouf, Ami Diakhate.

I

I.Q.
PARAMOUNT. December, 1994. (Fred Schepisi), Tim Robbins, Meg Ryan, Walter Matthau, Stephen Fry.

I AM CUBA
MILESTONE. March, 1995. Cuban-Russian, 1964. (Mikhail Kalatozov), Documentary. B&W.

I AM MY OWN WOMAN
CINEVISTA. April, 1994. German. (Rosa von Praunheim), Lothar Berfelde, Ichgola Androgyn, Jens Taschner.

I CAN'T SLEEP
NEW YORKER. August, 1995. French. (Claire Denis), Katerina Golubeva, Richard Courcet, Vincent Dupont.

I COME IN PEACE
TRIUMPH. September, 1990. (Craig R. Baxley), Dolph Lundgren, Brian Benben, Betsy Brantley.

I DON'T BUY KISSES ANYMORE
SKOURAS. February, 1992. (Robert Marcarelli), Jason Alexander, Nia Peeples, Lainie Kazan.

I DON'T WANT TO TALK ABOUT IT
SONY CLASSICS. (PG-13) September, 1994. Argentine. (Maria Luisa Bemberg), Marcello Mastroianni, Luisina Brando, Alejandra Podesta.

I JUST WASN'T MADE FOR THESE TIMES
PALOMAR. August, 1995. (Don Was), Documentary.

I LIKE IT LIKE THAT
COLUMBIA. October, 1994. (Darnell Martin), Lauren Velez, Jon Seda, Jesse Borrego, Lisa Vidal, Griffin Dunne.

I LOVE YOU TO DEATH
TRISTAR. April, 1990. (Lawrence Kasdan), Kevin Kline, Joan Plowright, William Hurt, River Phoenix.

I LOVE TROUBLE
BUENA VISTA. June, 1994. (Charles Shyer), Julia Roberts, Nick Nolte, Saul Rubinek.

I ONLY WANT YOU TO LOVE ME
BAVARIA. April, 1994. German ('76 film). (Rainer Werner Fassbinder), Vitus Zeplichal, Elke Aberle.

I, THE WORST OF ALL
FIRST RUN. September, 1995. Argentine. (Maria Luisa Bemberg), Assumpta Serna, Dominque Sanda.

I'LL DO ANYTHING
COLUMBIA. February, 1994. (James L. Brooks), Nick Nolte, Albert Brooks, Whittni Wright, Julie Kavner.

I'LL LOVE YOU FOREVER... TONIGHT
HEADLINER PRODS. July, 1993. (Edgar Michael Bravo), Paul Marius, Jason Adams, David Poynter. B&W.

ICE RUNNER, THE
BORDE. November, 1993. (Barry Samson), Edward Albert, Victor Wong, Olga Kabo.

ICICLE THIEF, THE
ARIES. August, 1990. Italian. (Maurizio Nichetti), Maurizio Nichetti, Caterina Sylos Labini.

IF LOOKS COULD KILL
WARNER BROS. March, 1991. (William Dear), Richard Grieco, Linda Hunt, Roger Rees.

IL LADRO DI BAMBINI (Stolen Children)
GOLDWYN. March, 1993. Italian. (Gianni Amelio), Enrico LoVerso, Valentina Scalici, Florence Darel.

IMAGES OF THE WORLD AND THE INSCRIPTION OF WAR
GOETHE HOUSE. November, 1991. German. (Harum Farocki), Documentary.

IMAGINARY CRIMES
WARNER BROS. October, 1994. (Anthony Drazen), Harvey Keitel, Fairuza Balk, Kelly Lynch, Chris Penn.

IMMORTAL BELOVED
COLUMBIA. December, 1994. (Bernard Rose), Gary Oldman, Jeroen Krabbe, Isabella Rossellini.

IMPORTANCE OF BEING EARNEST, THE
ECLECTIC CONCEPTS. May, 1992. (Kurt Baker), Wren T. Baker, Daryl Roach, Chris Calloway.

IMPORTED BRIDEGROOM, THE
ASA COMMUNICATIONS. March, 1990. (Pamela Berger), Gene Troobnick, Avi Hoffman.

IMPROMPTU
HEMDALE. April, 1991. (James Lapine), Judy Davis, Hugh Grant, Bernadette Peters, Mandy Patinkin.

IMPROPER CHANNELS
CROWN INT'L. May, 1992. Canadian. (Eric Till), Alan Arkin, Mariette Hartley, Monica Parker.

IMPULSE
WARNER BROS. April, 1990. (Sondra Locke), Theresa Russell, Jeff Fahey, George Dzundza.

IN ADVANCE OF THE LANDING
CINEPLEX ODEON. January, 1993. Canadian. (Dan Curtis), Documentary.

IN CUSTODY
SONY CLASSICS. April, 1994. Indian. (Ismail Merchant), Shashi Kapoor, Om Puri, Shabana Azmi.

IN THE ARMY NOW
BUENA VISTA. August, 1994. (Daniel Petrie, Jr.), Pauly Shore, Lori Petty, David Alan Grier.

IN THE BLOOD
WHITE MOUNTAIN. April, 1990. (George Butler), Documentary.

IN THE HEAT OF PASSION
CONCORDE. January, 1992. (Rodman Flender), Sally Kirkland, Nick Corri, Jack Carter.

IN THE LAND OF THE DEAF
INT'L. FILM CIRCUIT. September, 1994. French. (Nicolas Philibert), Documentary.

IN THE LINE OF FIRE
COLUMBIA. July, 1993. (Wolfgang Petersen), Clint Eastwood, John Malkovich, Rene Russo.

IN THE MOUTH OF MADNESS
NEW LINE CINEMA. (R) February, 1995. (John Carpenter), Sam Neill, Julie Carmen, Jurgen Prochnow.

IN THE NAME OF THE FATHER
UNIVERSAL. December, 1993. Irish. (Jim Sheridan), Daniel Day-Lewis, Pete Postlethwaite, Emma Thompson.

IN THE SHADOW OF THE STARS
FIRST RUN FEATURES. August, 1991. (Irving Sarah, Allie Light), Documentary.

IN THE SOUP
TRITON. October, 1992. (Alexandre Rockwell), Steve Buscemi, Seymour Cassel, Jennifer Beals. B&W.

IN THE SPIRIT
CASTLE HILL. April, 1990. (Sandra Seacat), Marlo Thomas, Elaine May, Peter Falk.

INCIDENT AT OGLALA
MIRAMAX. May, 1992. (Michael Apted), Documentary, narrated by Robert Redford.

INCREDIBLY TRUE ADVENTURE OF TWO GIRLS IN LOVE, THE
FINE LINE. (R) June, 1995. (Maria Maggenti), Laurel Holloman, Nicole Parker, Kate Stafford.

INDECENT PROPOSAL
PARAMOUNT. April, 1993. (Adrian Lyne), Robert Redford, Demi Moore, Woody Harrelson.

INDIAN IN THE CUPBOARD, THE
PARAMOUNT. July, 1995. (Frank Oz), Hal Scardino, Litefoot, Lindsay Crouse, Richard Jenkins.

INDIAN RUNNER, THE
MGM. September, 1991. (Sean Penn), David Morse, Viggo Mortensen, Valeria Golino.

INDIAN SUMMER
BUENA VISTA. April, 1993. (Mike Binder), Alan Arkin, Elizabeth Perkins, Bill Paxton, Vincent Spano.

INEVITABLE GRACE
SILVERSTAR. September, 1994. (Alex Canawati), Maxwell Caulfield, Jennifer Nicholson, Tippi Hedren.

INKWELL, THE
BUENA VISTA. April, 1994. (Matty Rich), Larenz Tate, Joe Morton, Suzzanne Douglas, Glynn Turman.

INNER CIRCLE, THE
COLUMBIA. December, 1991. (Andrei Konchalovsky), Tom Hulce, Lolita Davidovich, Bob Hoskins.

INNOCENT, THE
MIRAMAX. (R) September, 1995. British. (John Schlesinger), Anthony Hopkins, Isabella Rossellini, Campbell Scott.

INNOCENT BLOOD
WARNER BROS. September, 1992. (John Landis), Ann Parillaud, Robert Loggia, Anthony LaPaglia.

INSIDE MONKEY ZETTERLAND
I.R.S. August, 1993. (Jefery Levy), Steven Antin, Patricia Arquette, Tate Donovan.

INSTANT KARMA
MGM/UA. April, 1990. (Roderick Taylor), Craig Sheffer, David Cassidy, Chelsea Noble.

INTERGIRL
UNIV. OF MN. FILM CENTER. January, 1992. Russian-Swedish. (Pyotr Todorovski), Elena Yakovleva, Tomas Laustiola.

INTERNAL AFFAIRS
PARAMOUNT. January, 1990. (Mike Figgis), Richard Gere, Andy Garcia, Nancy Travis.

INTERSECTION
PARAMOUNT. January, 1993. (Mark Rydell), Richard Gere, Sharon Stone, Lolita Davidovich.

INTERVIEW WITH THE VAMPIRE
WARNER BROS. November, 1994. (Neil Jordan), Tom Crusie, Brad Pitt, Antonio Banderas, Stephen Rea.

INTERVISTA
CASTLE HILL. November, 1992. Italian. (Federico Fellini), Sergio Rubini, Maurizio Mein, Anita Ekberg.

INTO THE SUN
TRIMARK. January, 1992. (Fritz Kiersch), Anthony Michael Hall, Michael Paré, Deborah Maria Moore.

INTO THE WEST
MIRAMAX. September, 1993. Irish. (Mike Newell), Gabriel Byrne, Ellen Barkin, Ciaran Fitzgerald.

IRON AND SILK
PRESTIGE. February, 1991. (Shirley Sun), Mark Salzman, Pan Qingfu.

IRON MAZE
CASTLE HILL. November, 1991. Japanese-U.S. (Hiroaki Yoshida), Jeff Fahey, Bridget Fonda, Hiroaki Murakami.

IRON WILL
BUENA VISTA. January, 1994. (Charles Haid), Mackenzie Astin, Kevin Spacey, David Ogden Stiers.

IT COULD HAPPEN TO YOU
TRISTAR. July, 1994. (Andrew Bergman), Nicolas Cage, Bridget Fonda, Rosie Perez.

IT RUNS IN THE FAMILY
MGM. September, 1995. (Bob Clark), Charles Grodin, Kieran Culkin, Mary Steenburgen, Christian Culkin.

IT'S ALL TRUE:
BASED ON AN UNFINISHED FILM BY ORSON WELLES
PARAMOUNT. October, 1993. French-U.S. (Richard Wilson, Myron Meisel, Bill Krohn), Documentary.

IT'S HAPPENING TOMORROW
SACIS. April, 1994. Italian. (Daniele Luchetti), Paolo Hendel, Giovanni Guidelli, Ciccio Ingrassia.

IT'S PAT
BUENA VISTA. August, 1994. (Adam Bernstein), Julia Sweeney, David Foley, Charles Rocket.

IVAN AND ABRAHAM
NEW YORKER. March, 1994. French-Yiddish-Polish. (Yolande Zauberman), Roma Alexandrovitch. B&W.

J

JFK
WARNER BROS. December, 1991. (Oliver Stone), Kevin Costner, Sissy Spacek, Tommy Lee Jones, Kevin Bacon.

J.L.G. by J.L.G.
INDEPT./PUBLIC TH. January, 1995. French. (Jean Luc Godard), Documentary.

JACK BE NIMBLE
CINEVISTA. June, 1994. New Zealand. (Garth Maxwell), Alexis Arquette, Sarah Smuts Kennedy, Bruno Lawrence.

JACK THE BEAR
20TH CENTURY FOX. April, 1993. (Marshall Herskovitz), Danny DeVito, Robert J. Steinmiller, Jr., Gary Sinise.

JACOB'S LADDER
TRISTAR. November, 1990. (Adrian Lyne), Tim Robbins, Elizabeth Pena, Danny Aiello.

JACQUOT
SONY CLASSICS. June, 1993. French. (Agnes Varda), Philippe Maron, Edouard Joubeaud, Laurent Monnier.

JAMON JAMON
ACADEMY ENT. September, 1993. Spanish. (Bigas Lunas), Penelope Cruz, Anna Galiena, Javier Bardem.

JAR, THE
ARTISTIC LICENSE. September, 1995. Iranian. (Ebrahim Foruzesh), Behzad Khodaveisi, Fatemeh Azrah.

JASON GOES TO HELL: THE FINAL FRIDAY
NEW LINE CINEMA. August, 1993. (Adam Marcus), John D. LeMay, Kane Hodder, Allison Smith.

JASON'S LYRIC
GRAMERCY. (R) September, 1994. (Doug McHenry), Allen Payne, Jada Pinkett, Bokeem Woodbine, Forest Whitaker.

JEFFERSON IN PARIS
BUENA VISTA. March, 1995. (James Ivory), Nick Nolte, Greta Scacchi, Jean Pierre Aumont, Simon Callow.

JEFFREY
ORION CLASSICS. (R) August, 1995. (Christopher Ashley), Peter Weber, Patrick Stewart, Michael T. Weiss.

JENNIFER EIGHT
PARAMOUNT. November, 1992. (Bruce Robinson), Andy Garcia, Uma Thurman, Lance Henriksen.

JERKY BOYS, THE
BUENA VISTA. February, 1995. (James Melkonian), Johnny Brennan, Kamal Ahmed, Alan Arkin.

JESUS OF MONTREAL
ORION CLASSICS. May, 1990. Canadian-French. (Denys Arcand), Lothaire Bluteau, Catherine Wilkening.

JETSONS: THE MOVIE
UNIVERSAL. July, 1990. (David Michener), Animated.

JIMI HENDRIX AT THE ISLE OF WIGHT
ORIGINAL CINEMA. July, 1991. (Murray Lerner), Jimi Hendrix.

JIMMY HOLLYWOOD
PARAMOUNT. March, 1994. (Barry Levinson), Joe Pesci, Christian Slater, Victoria Abril.

JIT
NORTHERN ARTS. March, 1993. Zimbabwe. (Michael Raeburn), Dominic Makuvachuma, Sibongile Nene.

JOE VERSUS THE VOLCANO
WARNER BROS. March, 1990. (John Patrick Shanley), Tom Hanks, Meg Ryan, Lloyd Bridges.

JOEY BREAKER
SKOURAS. May, 1993. (Steven Starr), Richard Edson, Cedella Marley, Fred Fondren.

JOEY TAKES A CAB
BANDWAGON PRODS. June, 1991. (Albert Band), Lionel Stander, Kathleen Freeman.

JOHANNA D'ARC OF MONGOLIA
WOMEN MAKE MOVIES. May, 1992. West German. (Ulrike Ottinger), Delphine Seyrig, Xu Re Huar, Irm Hermann.

JOHN LURIE AND THE LOUNGE LIZARDS LIVE IN BERLIN
TELECOM JAPAN. September, 1992. Japanese. (Garret Linn), Documentary.

JOHNNY MNEMONIC
TRISTAR. May, 1995. (Robert Longo), Keanu Reeves, Dolph Lundgren, Takeshi, Ice-T, Dina Meyer, Udo Kier.

JOHNNY STECCHINO
NEW LINE CINEMA. October, 1992. Italian. (Roberto Benigni), Roberto Benigni, Nicoletta Braschi, Paolo Bonacelli.

JOHNNY SUEDE
MIRAMAX. August, 1992. (Tom DiCillo), Brad Pitt, Alison Moir, Calvin Levels.

JOSH AND S.A.M.
COLUMBIA. November, 1993. (Billy Weber), Jacob Tierney, Noah Fleiss, Martha Plimpton.

JOURNEY OF HOPE
MIRAMAX. April, 1991. Swiss. (Xavier Koller), Necmettin Cobanoglu, Nur Surer, Emin Sivas.

JOURNEY TO SPIRIT ISLAND
GRIFFIN FILM ASSOCS. May, 1990. (Laszlo Pal), Bettina, Marie Antoinette Rodgers.

JOY LUCK CLUB, THE
BUENA VISTA. September, 1993. (Wayne Wang), Tsai Chin, Kieu Chinh, Lauren Tom, Tamlyn Tomita.

JU DOU
MIRAMAX. March, 1991. Chinese. (Zhang Yimou), Gong Li, Li Baotian, Li Wei.

JUDAS PROJECT, THE
RS ENTERTAINMENT. February, 1993. (James H. Barden), John O'Banion, Ramy Zada, Jeff Corey.

JUDGE DREDD
BUENA VISTA. June, 1995. (Danny Cannon), Sylvester Stallone, Armand Assante, Rob Schneider, Jurgen Prochnow, Max von Sydow.

JUDGMENT NIGHT
UNIVERSAL. October, 1993. (Stephen Hopkins), Emilio Estevez, Cuba Gooding Jr., Stephen Dorff.

JUICE
PARAMOUNT. January, 1992. (Ernest Dickerson), Omar Epps, Tupac Shakur, Jermaine Hopkins.

JULIA HAS TWO LOVERS
SOUTH GATE ENT. March, 1991. (Bashar Shbib), Daphna Kastner, David Duchovny, David Charles.

JUMPIN AT THE BONEYARD
20TH CENTURY FOX. September, 1992. (Jeff Stanzler), Tim Roth, Alexis Arquette, Danitra Vance.

JUNGLE FEVER
UNIVERSAL. June, 1991. (Spike Lee), Wesley Snipes, Annabella Sciorra, Anthony Quinn, Ossie Davis.

JUNIOR
UNIVERSAL. November, 1994. (Ivan Reitman), Arnold Schwarzenegger, Danny DeVito, Emma Thompson.

JUPITER'S WIFE
ARTISTIC LICENSE. August, 1995. (Michel Negroponte), Documentary.

JURASSIC PARK
UNIVERSAL. June, 1993. (Steven Spielberg), Sam Neill, Laura Dern, Richard Attenborough, Jeff Goldblum.

JURY DUTY
TRISTAR. April, 1995. (John Fortenberry), Pauly Shore, Stanley Tucci, Abe Vigoda, Brian Doyle Murray.

JUST ANOTHER GIRL ON THE I.R.T.
MIRAMAX. March, 1993. (Leslie Harris), Ariyan Johnson, Kevin Thigpen, Ebony Jerido.

JUST CAUSE
WARNER BROS. February, 1995. (Arne Glimcher), Sean Connery, Laurence Fishburne, Blair Underwood.

JUST LIKE A WOMAN
GOLDWYN. July, 1994. British. (Christopher Monger), Julie Walters, Adrian Pasdar, Paul Freeman.

JUST LIKE IN THE MOVIES
CABRIOLET. September, 1990. (Bram Towbin, Mark Halliday), Jay O. Sanders, Alan Ruck.

K

K2
PARAMOUNT. May, 1992. British. (Franc Roddam), Michael Biehn, Matt Craven, Raymond J. Barry.

KAFKA
MIRAMAX. December, 1991. (Steven Soderberg), Jeremy Irons, Theresa Russell, Joel Grey, Ian Holm. B&W/Color.

KALIFORNIA
GRAMERCY. September, 1993. (Dominic Sena), Brad Pitt, Juliette Lewis, David Duchovny.

KEATON'S COP
CANNON. March, 1990. (Bob Burge), Lee Majors, Abe Vigoda.

KICKBOXER 2
TRIMARK. June, 1991. (Albert Pyun), Sasha Mitchell, Peter Boyle.

KID IN KING ARTHUR'S COURT, A
BUENA VISTA. August, 1995. (Michael Gottlieb), Thomas Ian Nichols, Joss Ackland, Art Malik.

KIDS
EXCALIBUR. July, 1995. (Larry Clark), Leo Fitzpatrick, Justin Pierce, Yakira Peguero.

KIKA
OCTOBER. May, 1994. Spanish. (Pedro Almodovar), Veronica Forque, Peter Coyote, Victoria Abril.

KILLING ZOE
OCTOBER. August, 1994. (Roger Roberts Avary), Eric Stoltz, Julie Delpy, Jean-Hughes Anglade.

KILL–OFF, THE
CABRIOLET. October, 1990. (Maggie Greenwald), Loretta Gross, Jackson Sims.

KINDERGARTEN COP
UNIVERSAL. December, 1990. (Ivan Reitman), Arnold Schwarzenegger, Penelope Ann Miller, Pamela Reed.

KING JAMES VERSION
FIRST RUN FEATURES. September, 1991. (Robert Gardner), Christina Braggs, Joan Pryor, Ellwoodson Williams.

KING OF NEW YORK
NEW LINE CINEMA. September, 1990. Italian-U.S. (Abel Ferrara), Christopher Walken, Laurence Fishburne, David Caruso.

KING OF THE BEGGARS
RIM. November, 1993. Chinese. (Gordon Chan), Stephen Chiau, Chang Min, Ng Man Tat.

KING OF THE HILL
GRAMERCY. August, 1993. (Steven Soberbergh), Jesse Bradford, Jeroen Krabbe, Lisa Eichhorn.

KING RALPH
UNIVERSAL. February, 1991. (David S. Ward), John Goodman, Peter O'Toole, John Hurt.

KINGDOM OF ZYDECO, THE
MUGSHOT. June, 1994. (Robert Mugge), Documentary.

KISS BEFORE DYING, A
UNIVERSAL. April, 1991. (James Dearden), Matt Dillon, Sean Young, Max von Sydow.

KISS ME A KILLER
CONCORDE. April, 1991. (Marcus De Leon), Julie Carmen, Robert Beltran.

KISS OF DEATH
20TH CENTURY FOX. April, 1995. (Barbet Schroeder), David Caruso, Nicholas Cage, Samuel L. Jackson.

KKK BOUTIQUE AIN'T JUST REDNECKS, THE
INDEPT./PUBLIC TH. March, 1995. (Camille Billops, James V. Hatch), Documentary.

KNIGHT MOVES
INTERSTAR. January, 1993. (Carl Schenkel), Christopher Lambert, Diane Lane, Tom Skerritt.

KORCZAK
NEW YORKER. April, 1991. Polish. (Andrzej Wajda), Wojtek Pszoniak, Ewa Dalkowska, Piotr Kozlowski.

KRAYS, THE
MIRAMAX. November, 1990. British. (Peter Medak), Gary Kemp, Martin Kemp, Billie Whitelaw.

KUFFS
UNIVERSAL. January, 1992. (Bruce A. Evans), Christian Slater, Tony Goldwyn, Milla Jovovich.

L

L.627
KINO. July, 1994. French. (Bertrand Tavernier), Didier Bezace, Jean Paul Comart, Cecile Garcia Fogel.

L.A. STORY
TRISTAR. February, 1991. (Mick Jackson), Steve Martin, Victoria Tennant, Richard E. Grant.

L'ANGE
FIRST RUN FEATURES. March, 1991. French. (Patrick Bokanowski), Maurice Baquet, Jean Marie Bon.

L'ENFER
MK2. October, 1994. French. (Claude Chabrol), Emmanuelle Beart, Francois Cluzet, Nathalie Cardone.

L'ETAT SAUVAGE
INTERAMA. January, 1990. French (Francis Girod), Marie Christine Barrault, Claude Brasseur.

LA BELLE NOISEUSE
MK2. October, 1991. French. (Jacques Ribette), Michel Piccoli, Jane Birkin, Emmanuelle Beart.

LA CHASSE AUX PAPILLONS
NEW YORKER. October, 1993. French-German-Italian. (Otar Iosseliani), Narda Blanchet, Pierrett Pompom Bailhache.

LA DISCRETE
MK2. August, 1992. French. (Christian Vincent), Fabrice Muchini, Judith Henry, Maurice Garrel.

LA FEMME NIKITA
GOLDWYN. March, 1991. French. (Luc Besson), Anne Parillaud, Jean-Hughes Anglade, Jeanne Moreau.

LA SCORTA
FIRST LOOK. May, 1994. Italian. (Ricky Tognazzi), Claudio Amendola, Enrico Lo Verso, Carlo Cecchi.

LA TIGRA
INT'L FILM CIRCUIT. January, 1991. Ecuador (Camilo Luzuriaga), Lissette Cabrera, Rosanna Iturralde, Veronica Garcia.

LA VIE DE BOHEME
KINO. July, 1993. French-Finnish. (Aki Kurasmaki), Matti Pellonpaa, Evelyn Didi, Andre Wilms.

LABYRINTH OF PASSION
CINEVISTA. January, 1990. Spanish. (Pedro Almodovar), Cecilia Roth, Imanol Arias, Antonio Banderas.

LADYBIRD, LADYBIRD
GOLDWYN. December, 1994. British. (Ken Loach), Crissy Rock, Vladimir Vega, Ray Winstone.

LADYBUGS
PARAMOUNT. March, 1992. (Sidney J. Furie), Rodney Dangerfield, Jackée, Jonathan Brandis.

LAIBACH: VICTORY UNDER THE SUN
INT'L FILM CIRCUIT. October, 1992. Yugoslavia (Goran Gajic).

LAMB
CAPITOL ENT. February, 1995. British, 1986. (Colin Gregg), Liam Neeson, Hugh O'Connor, Ian Bannen.

LAMBADA
WARNER BROS. March, 1990. (Joel Silberg), J. Eddie Peck, Melora Hardin, Shabba-Doo.

LANDSCAPE IN THE MIST
NEW YORKER. September, 1990. Greek. (Theo Angelopoulos), Michalis Zeke, Tania Palaiologou.

LARKS ON A STRING
IFEX. February, 1991. Czechoslovakian, 1969. (Jiri Menzel), Vaclav Neckar, Rudolf Hrusinsky.

LASER MAN, THE
ORIGINAL CINEMA. March, 1990. (Peter Wang), Marc Hayashi, Tony Leung.

LASSIE
PARAMOUNT. July, 1994. (Daniel Petrie), Thomas Guiry, Helen Slater, Jon Tenney, Lassie.

LAST ACTION HERO
COLUMBIA. June, 1993. (John McTiernan), Arnold Schwarzenegger, Austin O'Brien, Charles Dance.

LAST BOY SCOUT, THE
WARNER BROS. December, 1991. (Tony Scott), Bruce Willis, Damon Wayans, Chelsea Field.

LAST BUTTERFLY, THE
ARROW. August, 1993. Czech. (Karel Kachyna), Tom Courtenay, Brigitte Fossey, Ingrid Held.

LAST CALL AT MAUD'S
MAUD'S PROJECT. March, 1993. (Paris Poirier), Documentary.

LAST DAYS OF CHEZ NOUS, THE
FINE LINE. February, 1993. Australian. (Gillian Armstrong), Lisa Harrow, Bruno Ganz, Kerry Fox.

LAST EXIT TO BROOKLYN
CINECOM. May, 1990. W. German-U.S. (Uli Edel), Stephen Lang, Jennifer Jason Leigh, Burt Young.

LAST GOOD TIME, THE
GOLDWYN. April, 1995. (Bob Balaban), Armin Mueller Stahl, Olivia d'Abo, Maureen Stapleton.

LAST KLEZMER, THE
INDEPENDENT. August, 1994. (Yale Strom), Documentary.

LAST OF THE DOGMEN
SAVOY. (PG) September, 1995. (Tab Murphy), Tom Berenger, Barbara Hershey, Steve Reevis.

LAST OF THE FINEST
ORION. March, 1990. (John Mackenzie), Brian Dennehy, Joe Pantoliano, Bill Paxton.

LAST OF THE MOHICANS, THE
20TH CENTURY FOX. September, 1992. (Michael Mann), Daniel Day-Lewis, Madeleine Stowe, Russell Means.

LAST PARTY, THE
TRITON. August, 1993. (Mark Benjamin, Marc Levin), Robert Downey, Jr.

LAST SEDUCTION, THE
OCTOBER. October, 1994. (John Dahl), Linda Fiorentino, Peter Berg, Bill Pullman. (Premiered on Showtime in July '94.)

LATCHO DROM
SHADOW DISTRIB. July, 1994. French. (Tony Gatlif), Documentary.

LATE FOR DINNER
COLUMBIA. September, 1991. (W.D. Richter), Brian Wimmer, Peter Berg, Marcia Gay Harden.

LAWNMOWER MAN, THE
NEW LINE CINEMA. March, 1992. (Brett Leonard), Jeff Fahey, Pierce Brosnan, Jenny Wright.

LAWS OF GRAVITY
RKO. August, 1992. (Nick Gomez), Adam Trese, Peter Greene, Edie Falco.

LEAGUE OF THEIR OWN, A
COLUMBIA. July, 1992. (Penny Marshall), Tom Hanks, Geena Davis, Lori Petty, Madonna.

LEAP OF FAITH
PARAMOUNT. December, 1992. (Richard Pearce), Steve Martin, Debra Winger, Lukas Haas, Lolita Davidovich.

LEATHERFACE: TEXAS CHAINSAW MASSACRE III
NEW LINE CINEMA. January, 1990. (Jeff Burr), Kate Hodge, Ken Foree, Viggo Mortensen.

LEAVING NORMAL
UNIVERSAL. April, 1992. (Edward Zwick), Christine Lahti, Meg Tilly, Patrika Darbo.

LEGEND OF WOLF MOUNTAIN
HEMDALE. November, 1992. (Craig Clyde), Bo Hopkins, Mickey Rooney, Robert Z'Dar.

LEGENDS OF THE FALL
TRISTAR. December, 1994. (Edward Zwick), Brad Pitt, Anthony Hopkins, Aidan Quinn, Julia Ormond.

LEMON SISTERS, THE
MIRAMAX. August, 1990. (Joyce Chopra), Diane Keaton, Carol Kane, Kathryn Grody.

LENINGRAD COWBOYS GO AMERICA
ORION CLASSICS. November, 1990. Finnish. (Aki Kaurismaki), Matti Pellonpaa, Heikki Keskinen.

LEOLO
FINE LINE FEATURES. April, 1993. French. (Jean Claude Lauzon), Gilbert Sicotte, Maxime Collin, Ginette Reno.

LEON THE PIG FARMER
CINEVISTA. September, 1993. British. (Vadim Jean, Gary Sinyor), Mark Frankel, Janet Suzman, Brian Glover.

LEPRECHAUN
TRIMARK. January, 1993. (Mark Jones), Warwick Davis, Jennifer Aniston, Ken Olandt.

LEPRECHAUN 2
TRIMARK. April, 1994. (Rodman Flender), Warwick Davis, Charlie Heath, Shevonne Durkin.

LET HIM HAVE IT
NEW LINE CINEMA. December, 1991. British. (Peter Medak), Chris Eccleston, Paul Reynolds, Tom Courtenay.

LETHAL WEAPON 3
WARNER BROS. May, 1992. (Richard Donner), Mel Gibson, Danny Glover, Joe Pesci, Rene Russo.

LETTER TO THE NEXT GENERATION
NEW DAY. May, 1990. (James Klein), Documentary.

LETTERS FROM THE PARK
FOX/LORBER. January, 1990. Cuban. (Tomas Futierrez), Victor Laplace, Ivonne Lopez.

LIABILITY CRISIS
FILMHAUS. June, 1995. (Richard Brody), Mirjana Jokovic, Jim Helsinger, Sheri Meg Seidman.

LIE DOWN WITH DOGS
MIRAMAX. (R) June, 1995. (Wally White), Wally White, James Sexton, Randy Becker.

LIEBESTRAUM
MGM. September, 1991. (Mike Figgis), Kevin Anderson, Pamela Gidley, Kim Novak.

LIFE AND TIMES OF ALLEN GINSBERG, THE
FIRST RUN. February, 1994. (Jerry Aronson), Documentary.

LIFE IS A LONG QUIET RIVER
MK2 PRODS. July, 1990. French. (Etienne Chatiliez), Benoit Magimel, Helene Vincent.

LIFE IS CHEAP ... BUT TOILET PAPER IS EXPENSIVE
SILVERLIGHT. August, 1990. Chinese. (Wayne Wang), Chan Kim Wan, Spencer Nakasako, Victor Wong.

LIFE IS SWEET
OCTOBER. October, 1991. British. (Mike Leigh), Alison Steadman, Jim Broadbent, Jane Horrocks.

LIFE ON A STRING
KINO. January, 1992. German-Japanese-British-Mandarin. (Chen Kaige), Liu Zhongyuan, Huang Lei.

LIFE ON THE EDGE
FESTIVAL ENT. June, 1992. (Andrew Yates), Jeff Perry, Jennifer Holmes, Andrew Prine.

LIFE STINKS
MGM. July, 1991. (Mel Brooks), Mel Brooks, Lesley Ann Warren, Jeffrey Tambor.

LIFE WITH MIKEY
BUENA VISTA. June, 1993. (James Lapine), Michael J. Fox, Christina Vidal, Nathan Lane.

LIGHT SLEEPER
FINE LINE. August, 1992. (Paul Schrader), Willem Dafoe, Susan Sarandon, Dana Delany.

LIGHTNING JACK
SAVOY. March, 1994. Australian. (Simon Wincer), Paul Hogan, Cuba Gooding Jr., Beverly D'Angelo.

LIKE WATER FOR CHOCOLATE
MIRAMAX. February, 1993. Mexican. (Alfonso Arau), Lumi Cavazos, Marco Leonardi, Pegina Torne.

LIMITE
MOMA. August, 1992. Brazilian, 1932. (Mario Peixoto), Silent. B&W.

LINGUINI INCIDENT, THE
ACADEMY ENTERTAINMENT. May, 1992. (Richard Shepard), Rosanna Arquette, David Bowie, Eszter Balint.

LION KING, THE
BUENA VISTA. June, 1994. (Roger Allers, Rob Minkoff), Animated.

LIONHEART
UNIVERSAL. January, 1991. (Sheldon Lettich), Jean Claude Van Damme, Harrison Page, Deborah Rennard.

LIPSTICK CAMERA
TRIBORO. March, 1994. (Mike Bonifer), Brian Wimmer, Ele Keats, Corey Feldman.

LIQUID DREAMS
NORTHERN ARTS. April, 1992. (Mark Manos), Candice Daly, Richard Steinmetz, Juan Fernandez.

LISA
MGM/UA. April, 1990. (Gary Sherman), Cheryl Ladd, Staci Keanan, D. W. Moffett.

LISTEN UP: THE LIVES OF QUINCY JONES
WARNER BROS. October, 1990. (Ellen Weissbrod), Documentary.

LITTLE BIG LEAGUE
COLUMBIA. June, 1994. (Andrew Scheinman), Luke Edwards, Timothy Busfield, John Ashton.

LITTLE BUDDHA
MIRAMAX. May, 1994. (Bernardo Bertolucci), Keanu Reeves, Chris Isaak, Bridget Fonda, Ying Ruocheng.

LITTLE GIANTS
WARNER BROS. October, 1994. (Duwayne Dunham), Rick Moranis, Ed O'Neill, John Madden.

LITTLE MAN TATE
ORION. October, 1991. (Jodie Foster), Jodie Foster, Dianne Wiest, Adam Hann Byrd, Harry Connick, Jr.

LITTLE NEMO: ADVENTURES IN SLUMBERLAND
HEMDALE. August, 1992. Japanese. (Masami Hata, William T. Hurtz), Animated.

LITTLE NOISES
MONUMENT PICTURES. April, 1992. (Jane Spencer), Crispin Glover, Tatum O'Neal, Rik Mayall.

LITTLE ODESSA
FINE LINE. (R) May, 1995. (James Gray), Tim Roth, Maximilian Schell, Edward Furlong.

LITTLE PRINCESS, A
WARNER BROS. May, 1995. (Alfonso Cuaron), Liesel Matthews, Eleanor Bron, Liam Cunningham.

LITTLE RASCALS, THE
UNIVERSAL. August, 1994. (Penelope Spheeris), Travis Tedford, Bug Hall, Brittany Ashton Holmes.

LITTLE VEGAS
I.R.S. RELEASING. November, 1990. (Perry Land), Anthony John Denison, Catherine O'Hara, Ann Francis.

LITTLE WOMEN
COLUMBIA. December, 1994. (Gillian Armstrong), Winona Ryder, Gabriel Byrne, Trini Alvarado.

LIVIN' LARGE
GOLDWYN. September, 1991. (Michael Schultz), Terrence "T.C." Carson, Lisa Arrindell, Blanche Baker.

LIVING END, THE
OCTOBER. August, 1992. (Gregg Araki), Mike Dytri, Craig Gilmore, Darcy Marta.

LIVING IN OBLIVION
SONY CLASSICS. (R) July, 1995. (Tom DiCillo), Steve Buscemi, Catherine Keener, Dermot Mulroney.

LIVING PROOF: H.I.V. AND THE PURSUIT OF HAPPINESS
FIRST RUN. February, 1994. (Kermit Cole), Documentary.

LIVING TO DIE
PM ENTERTAINMENT. September, 1990. (Wings Hauser), Wings Hauser, Darcy DeMoss, Asher Brauner.

LOBSTER MAN FROM MARS
ELECTRIC PICTURES. February, 1990. (Stanley Sheff), Tony Curtis, Deborah Foreman.

LOCKED UP TIME
ZEITGEIST. May, 1992. German. (Sibylle Schonemann), Documentary. B&W.

LONDON
ZEITGEIST. September, 1994. British. (Patrick Keiller), Documentary.

LONDON KILLS ME
FINE LINE. August, 1992. British. (Hanif Kureishi), Justin Chadwick, Steven Mackintosh, Fiona Shaw.

LONELY WOMAN SEEKS LIFE COMPANION
IFEX. March, 1990. Russian, (Vyacheslav Krishtofovich), Irina Kupchenko, Aleksandr Zbruyev.

LONG DAY CLOSES, THE
SONY CLASSICS. May, 1993. British. (Terence Davies), Leigh McCormack, Marjorie Yates, Anthony Watson.

LONG WALK HOME, THE
MIRAMAX. December, 1990. (Richard Pearce), Sissy Spacek, Whoopi Goldberg, Dwight Schultz.

LONG WEEKEND (O' DESPAIR)
DESPERATE PICTURES. June, 1990. (Gregg Araki), Bretton Vail, Maureen Dondanville.

LONGTIME COMPANION
SAMUEL GOLDWYN. May, 1990. (Norman Rene). Campbell Scott, Bruce Davison, Mark Lamos.

LOOK WHO'S TALKING NOW
TRISTAR. November, 1993. (Tom Ropelewski), John Travolta, Kirstie Alley, Olympia Dukakis.

LOOK WHO'S TALKING TOO
TRISTAR. December, 1990. (Amy Heckerling), John Travolta, Kirstie Alley, Elias Koteas.

LOOSE CANNONS
TRISTAR. February, 1990. (Bob Clark), Gene Hackman, Dan Aykroyd, Dom DeLuise.

LORD OF ILLUSIONS
MGM/UA. August, 1995. (Clive Barker), Scott Bakula, Kevin J. O'Connor, Famke Janssen.

LORD OF THE FLIES
COLUMBIA. March, 1990. (Harry Hook), Balthazar Getty, Chris Furrh, Danuel Pipoly.

LORENZO'S OIL
UNIVERSAL. December, 1992. (George Miller), Nick Nolte, Susan Sarandon, Zack O'Malley Greenburg.

LOSING ISAIAH
PARAMOUNT. March, 1995. (Stephen Gyllenhaal), Jessica Lange, Halle Berry, David Strathairn.

LOST PROPHET
ROCKVILLE PICTURES. June, 1992. (Michael de Avila), James Burton, Zandra Huston, Drew Morone. B&W.

LOST WORDS, THE
FILM CRASH. September, 1994. (Scott Saunders), Michael Kaniecki, Bob McGrath, Zelda Gergel.

LOVE AFFAIR
WARNER BROS. October, 1994. (Glenn Gordon), Warren Beatty, Annette Bening, Katharine Hepburn.

LOVE AFTER LOVE
RAINBOW. July, 1994. French. (Diane Kurys), Isabelle Huppert, Bernard Giraudeau, Hippolyte Girardot.

LOVE AND A .45
TRIMARK. (R) November, 1994. (C.M. Talkington), Gil Bellows, Renee Zellweger, Rory Cochrane, Jeffrey Combs.

LOVE AND HUMAN REMAINS
SONY CLASSICS. (R) June, 1995. Canadian. (Denys Arcand), Thomas Gibson, Cameron Bancroft, Ruth Marshall.

LOVE AND MURDER
HEMDALE/SOUTHPAW. November, 1991. Canadian. (Steven Hilliard Stern), Todd Waring, Kathleen Lasky, Ron White.

LOVE AT LARGE
ORION. March, 1990. (Alan Rudolph), Tom Berenger, Elizabeth Perkins, Anne Archer.

LOVE CRIMES
MILLIMETER FILMS. January, 1992. (Lizzie Borden), Sean Young, Patrick Bergen, Arnetia Walker.

LOVE FIELD
ORION. December, 1992. (Jonathan Kaplan), Michelle Pfeiffer, Dennis Haysbert, Stephanie McFadden.

LOVE OR MONEY
HEMDALE. January, 1990. (Todd Hallowell), Timothy Daly, Michael Garin, Kevin McCarthy.

LOVE POTION NO. 9
20TH CENTURY FOX. November, 1992. (Dale Launer), Tate Donovan, Sandra Bullock, Mary Mara.

LOVE WITHOUT PITY
ORION CLASSICS. May, 1991. French. (Eric Rochant), Hippolyte Girardot, Mireille Perrier, Yvan Attal.

LOVE YOUR MAMA
HEMDALE. March, 1993. (Ruby L. Oliver), Carol E. Hall, Audrey Morgan, Andre Robinson.

LOVER, THE
MGM. October, 1992. French. (Jean Jacques Annaud), Jane March, Tony Leung, Frederique Meininger.

LOVERS
ARIES. March, 1992. Spanish. (Vicente Aranda), Victoria Abril, Jorge Sanz, Maribel Verdu.

LOW DOWN DIRTY SHAME, A
BUENA VISTA. November, 1994. (Keenen Ivory Wayans), Wayans, Charles S. Dutton, Jada Pinkett.

LUNA PARK
NORTHERN ARTS. January, 1994. Russian. (Pavel Lounguine), Oleg Borisov, Andrei Goutine, Natalya Yegorova.

LUNATIC, THE
TRITON. February, 1992. (Lol Creme), Julie T. Wallace, Paul Campbell, Reggie Carter.

M

M. BUTTERFLY
WARNER BROS. October, 1993. (David Cronenberg), Jeremy Irons, John Lone, Barbara Sukowa.

MAC
GOLDWYN. February, 1993. (John Turturro), John Turturro, Michael Badalucco, Carl Capotorto.

MACK THE KNIFE
21ST CENTURY FILMS. February, 1990. (Menahem Golan), Raul Julia, Richard Harris, Julia Migenes.

MAD DOG AND GLORY
UNIVERSAL. March, 1993. (John McNaughton), Robert De Niro, Uma Thurman, Bill Murray, David Caruso.

MAD LOVE
BUENA VISTA. May, 1995. (Antonia Bird), Chris O'Donnell, Drew Barrymore, Matthew Lillard.

MADAME BOVARY
GOLDWYN. December, 1991. French. (Claude Chabrol), Isabelle Huppert, Jean Francois Balmer, Christophe Malavoy.

MADE IN AMERICA
WARNER BROS. May, 1993. (Richard Benjamin), Whoopi Goldberg, Ted Danson, Will Smith.

MADHOUSE
ORION. February, 1990. (Tom Ropelewski), John Larroquette, Kirstie Alley, Alison LaPlaca.

MADNESS OF KING GEORGE, THE
GOLDWYN. December, 1994. British. (Nicholas Hytner), Nigel Hawthorne, Helen Mirren, Ian Holm, Rupert Graves.

MAGIC IN THE WATER
TRISTAR. August, 1995. (Rick Stevenson), Mark Harmon, Joshua Jackson, Harley Jane Kozak.

MAGICAL WORLD OF CHUCK JONES, THE
WARNER BROS. May, 1993. (George Daugherty), Documentary.

MAHABHARATA, THE
MK2. April. 1990. British-French. (Peter Brook), Robert Langton Lloyd, Antonin Stahly Vishwanadan.

MAJOR PAYNE
UNIVERSAL. March, 1995. (Nick Castle), Damon Wayans, Karyn Parsons, William Hickey, Albert Hall.

MAJOR LEAGUE 2
WARNER BROS. March, 1994. (David S. Ward), Charlie Sheen, Tom Berenger, Corbin Bernsen.

MALCOLM X
WARNER BROS. November, 1992. (Spike Lee), Denzel Washington, Angela Bassett, Al Freeman Jr., Spike Lee.

MALICE
COLUMBIA. October, 1993. (Harold Becker), Alec Baldwin, Nicole Kidman, Bill Pullman.

MALINA
INDEPENDENT. September, 1993. German. (Werner Schroeter), Isabelle Huppert, Mathieu Carriere, Can Togay.

MAMA, THERE'S A MAN IN YOUR BED
MIRAMAX. April, 1990. French. (Coline Serreau), Firmine Richard, Pierre Vernier.

MAMA ROMA
MILESTONE. January, 1995. Italian, 1962. (Pier Paolo Pasolini), Anna Magnani, Ettore Garofalo, Franco Citti.

MAMBO KINGS, THE
WARNER BROS. February, 1992. (Arne Glimcher), Armand Assante, Antonio Banderas, Cathy Moriarty.

MAN BITES DOG
ROXIE RELEASING. January, 1993. Belgian-French. (Remy Belvaux), Benoit Poelvoorde, Remy Belvaux, Andre Bonzel.

MAN CALLED SARGE, A
CANNON. February, 1990. (Stuart Gillard), Gary Kroeger, Marc Singer.

MAN IN THE MOON, THE
MGM. October, 1991. (Robert Mulligan), Reese Witherspoon, Jason London, Sam Waterston.

MAN IN UNIFORM, A
ALLIANCE. June, 1994. Canadian. (David Wellington), Tom McCamus, Brigitte Bako, Kevin Tighe.

MAN INSIDE, THE
NEW LINE CINEMA. October, 1990. (Bobby Roth), Jurgen Prochnow, Peter Coyote, Nathalie Baye.

MAN OF NO IMPORTANCE, A
SONY CLASSICS. (R) December, 1994. British. (Suri Krishnamma), Albert Finney, Brenda Fricker, Michael Gambon, Tara Fitzgerald.

MAN OF THE HOUSE
BUENA VISTA. March, 1995. (James Orr), Chevy Chase, Jonathan Taylor Thomas, Farrah Fawcett.

MAN TROUBLE
20TH CENTURY FOX. July, 1992. (Bob Rafelson), Jack Nicholson, Ellen Barkin, Beverly D'Angelo.

MAN WITHOUT A FACE, THE
WARNER BROS. August, 1993. (Mel Gibson), Mel Gibson, Nick Stahl, Margaret Whitton.

MAN WITHOUT A WORLD, THE
MILESTONE. September, 1992. (Eleanor Antin), Pier Marton, Christine Berry, Anna Henriques. B&W.

MAN'S BEST FRIEND
NEW LINE CINEMA. November, 1993. (John Lafia), Ally Sheedy, Lance Henriksen, Robert Costanzo.

MANGLER, THE
NEW LINE CINEMA. (R) March, 1995. (Tobe Hooper), Robert Englund, Ted Levine, Daniel Matmor.

MANHATTAN BY NUMBERS
INDEPENDENT. November, 1994. (Amir Naderi), Jonh Wojda, Branislav Tomich, Mary Chang.

MANHATTAN MURDER MYSTERY
TRISTAR. August, 1993. (Woody Allen), Diane Keaton, Woody Allen, Alan Alda, Anjelica Huston.

MANNEQUIN TWO ON THE MOVE
20TH CENTURY FOX. May, 1991. (Stewart Raffill), William Ragsdale, Kristy Swanson, Meshach Taylor.

**MANUFACTURING CONSENT:
NOAM CHOMSKY AND THE MEDIA**
ZEITGEIST. March, 1993. Canadian. (Mark Achbar, Peter Witonik), Documentary.

MAP OF THE HUMAN HEART
MIRAMAX. April, 1993. British-French-Australian-Canadian. (Vincent Ward), Jason Scott Lee, Anne Parillaud, Patrick Bergin.

MARKED FOR DEATH
20TH CENTURY FOX. October, 1990. (Dwight H. Little), Steven Seagal, Basil Wallace, Keith David.

MARQUIS
A.Y. ALLIGATOR. July, 1991. Belgian-French. (Henri Xhonneux), Philippe Bizot, Bien de Moor.

MARRIED TO IT
ORION. March, 1993. (Arthur Hiller), Stockard Channing, Robert Sean Leonard, Ron Silver.

MARRYING MAN, THE
BUENA VISTA. April, 1991. (Jerry Rees), Alec Baldwin, Kim Basinger, Robert Loggia, Fisher Stevens.

MARTHA & ETHEL
SONY CLASSICS. (G) February, 1995. (Jyll Johnstone), Documentary.

MARTHA AND I
CINEMA FOUR. March, 1995. German. (Jiri Weiss), Marianne Sagebrecht, Michel Piccoli, Vaclov Chalupa.

MARTIANS GO HOME
TAURUS ENTERTAINMENT. April, 1990. (David Odell), Randy Quaid, Margaret Colin, Anita Morris.

MARY SHELLEY'S FRANKENSTEIN
TRISTAR. November, 1994. (Kenneth Branagh), Kenneth Branagh, Robert De Niro, Helena Bonham Carter.

MASALA
STRAND. March, 1993. Canadian. (Srinivas Krishna), Saeed Jaffrey, Zohra Segal, Sakina Jaffrey.

MASK, THE
NEW LINE CINEMA. July, 1994. (Chuck Russell), Jim Carrey, Cameron Diaz, Peter Riegert.

MATCH FACTORY GIRL, THE
KINO INT'L. November, 1992. Finnish. (Aki Kaurismaki), Kati Outinen, Elina Salo, Esko Nikkari.

MATINEE
UNIVERSAL. January, 1993. (Joe Dante), John Goodman, Omri Katz, Cathy Moriarty, Simon Fenton.

MATTER OF DEGREES, A
FOX/LORBER. September, 1991. (W. T. Morgan), Arye Gross, Judith Hoag, Tom Sizemore, Bruce Norris.

MAVERICK
WARNER BROS. May, 1994. (Richard Donner), Mel Gibson, Jodie Foster, James Garner.

MAY FOOLS
ORION CLASSICS. June, 1990. French. (Louis Malle), Michel Piccoli, Miou-Miou, Michel Duchaussoy.

MAZEPPA
MK2. December, 1993. French. (Bartabas), Miguel Bose, Bartabas, Brigitte Marty.

McBAIN
SHAPIRO GLICKENHAUS. September, 1991. (James Glickenhaus), Christopher Walken, Michael Ironside, Maria Conchita Alonso.

ME AND THE KID
ORION. October, 1993. (Dan Curtis), Danny Aiello, Alex Zuckerman, Joe Pantoliano, Cathy Moriarty.

ME AND THE MOB
ARROW. September, 1994. (Frank Rainone), James Lorinz, Tony Darrow, Vinny Pastore.

ME AND VERONICA
ARROW. September, 1993. (Don Scardino), Elizabeth McGovern, Patricia Wettig, Michael O'Keefe.

MEDICINE MAN
BUENA VISTA. February, 1992. (John McTiernan), Sean Connery, Lorraine Bracco, Jose Wilker.

MEET THE APPLEGATES
TRITON. February, 1991. (Michael Lehmann), Ed Begley Jr., Stockard Channing, Dabney Coleman.

MEET THE FEEBLES
GREYCAT. February, 1995. New Zealand. (Peter Jackson), Puppets.

MEETING VENUS
WARNER BROS. November, 1991. British. (Istvan Szabo), Glenn Close, Niels Arestrup, Erland Josephson.

MEIN KRIEG
LEISURE TIME. April, 1993. German. (Harriet Eder, Thomas Kufus), Documentary.

MEMOIRS OF A RIVER
CASTLE HILL. March, 1992. Hungarian-French. (Judit Elek), Sandor Gaspar, Pal Hetenyi, Andras Stohl.

MEMOIRS OF AN INVISIBLE MAN
WARNER BROS. February, 1992. (John Carpenter), Chevy Chase, Daryl Hannah, Sam Neill.

MEMORIES OF A MARRIAGE (Waltzing Regitze)
NORDISK FILM. January, 1991. Danish. (Kaspar Rostrup), Frits Helmuth, Mikael Helmuth.

MEMPHIS BELLE
WARNER BROS. October, 1990. British. (Michael Caton Jones), Matthew Modine, Eric Stoltz, D.B. Sweeney, Harry Connick Jr.

MEN AT WORK
TRIUMPH. August, 1990. (Emilio Estevez), Charlie Sheen, Emilio Estevez, Leslie Hope.

MEN DON'T LEAVE
WARNER BROS. February, 1990. (Paul Brickman), Jessica Lange, Arliss Howard, Chris O'Donnell, Charlie Korsmo.

MEN IN LOVE
CRYSTAL CLEAR COMMUNICATIONS. January, 1990. (Marc Huestis), Doug Self, Joe Tolbe.

MEN OF RESPECT
COLUMBIA. January, 1991. (William Reilly), John Turturro, Katherine Borowitz, Dennis Farina.

MENACE II SOCIETY
NEW LINE CINEMA. May, 1993. (The Hughes Brothers), Tyrin Turner, Jada Pinkett, Larenz Tate.

MERIDIAN (Kiss of the Beast)
JGM ENTERPRISES. April, 1990. (Charles Band), Sherilyn Fenn, Malcolm Jamieson.

MERMAIDS
ORION. December, 1990. (Richard Benjamin), Cher, Bob Hoskins, Winona Ryder.

METAL AND MELANCHOLY
ARIEL. April, 1995. Spanish-Dutch. (Heddy Honigmann, Peter Delpeut), Documentary.

METEOR MAN, THE
MGM. August, 1993. (Robert Townsend), Robert Townsend, Marla Gibbs, James Earl Jones.

METROPOLITAN
NEW LINE CINEMA. August, 1990. (Whit Stillman), Carolyn Farina, Edward Clements, Christopher Eigeman.

MI VIDA LOCA (MY CRAZY LIFE)
SONY CLASSICS. July, 1994. (Allison Anders), Agel Aviles, Seidy Lopez, Jacob Vargas.

MIAMI BLUES
ORION. April, 1990. (George Armitage), Fred Ward, Alec Baldwin, Jennifer Jason Leigh.

MIAMI RHAPSODY
BUENA VISTA. January, 1995. (David Frankel), Sarah Jessica Parker, Gil Bellows, Antonio Banderas.

MIDNIGHT CLEAR, A
INTERSTAR. April, 1992. (Keith Gordon), Ethan Hawke, Arye Gross, Frank Whaley, Gary Sinise.

MIDNIGHT DANCERS
FIRST RUN. July, 1995. Filipino. (Mel Chionglo), Alex Del Rosario, Grandong Cervantes, Lawrence David.

MIDNIGHT EDITION
SHAPIRO GLICKENHAUS. April, 1994. (Howard Libov), Will Patton, Michael DeLuise, Sarabeth Tucek.

MIGHTY DUCKS, THE
BUENA VISTA. October, 1992. (Stephen Herek), Emilio Estevez, Lane Smith, Heidi Kling.

MIGHTY MORPHIN POWER RANGERS: THE MOVIE
20TH CENTURY FOX. June, 1995. (Brian Spicer), Karen Ashley, Johnny Yong Bosch, Steve Cardenas.

MILK MONEY
PARAMOUNT. August, 1994. (Richard Benjamin), Melanie Griffith, Ed Harris, Michael Patrick Carter.

MILLER'S CROSSING
20TH CENTURY FOX. September, 1990. (Joel Coen), Gabriel Byrne, Marcia Gay Harden, Albert Finney.

MILLION TO JUAN, A
GOLDWYN. May, 1994. (Paul Rodriguez), Paul Rodriguez, Ruben Blades, Polly Draper.

MINA TANNENBAUM
NEW YORKER. March, 1995. French. (Martine Dugowson), Romane Bohringer, Elsa Zylberstein, Florence Thomassin.

MINBO—OR THE GENTLE ART OF JAPANESE EXTORTION
NORTHERN ARTS. October, 1994. Japanese. (Juzo Itami), Nobuko Miyamoto, Akira Takarada, Yasuo Daichi.

MINDWALK
TRITON. October, 1991. (Bernt Capra), Liv Ullman, Sam Waterston, John Heard.

MIRACLE, THE
MIRAMAX. July, 1991. British. (Neil Jordan), Beverly D'Angelo, Donald McCann, Niall Byrne.

MIRACLE ON 34TH STREET
20TH CENTURY FOX. November, 1994. (Les Mayfield), Richard Attenborough, Elizabeth Perkins.

MIRROR, MIRROR
ORPHANS ENTERTAINMENT. September, 1990. (Marina Sargenti), Karen Black, Rainbow Harvest.

MISADVENTURES OF MR. WILT, THE
SAMUEL GOLDWYN CO. June, 1990. British (Michael Tuchner), Griff Rhys Jones, Mel Smith.

MISERY
COLUMBIA. November, 1990. (Rob Reiner), James Caan, Kathy Bates, Lauren Bacall.

MISPLACED
SUBWAY FILMS. October, 1990. (Louis Yansen), John Cameron Mitchell, Viveca Lindfors, Elzbieta Czyzewska.

MISSISSIPPI MASALA
SAMUEL GOLDWYN CO. February, 1992. (Mira Nair), Denzel Washington, Sarita Choudhury, Roshan Seth.

MISTER JOHNSON
AVENUE. March, 1991. British. (Bruce Beresford), Pierce Brosnan, Maynard Eziashi, Edward Woodward.

MISTRESS
RAINBOW/TRIBECA. August, 1992. (Barry Primus), Robert Wuhl, Martin Landau, Robert De Niro.

MIXED NUTS
TRISTAR. December, 1994. (Nora Ephron), Steve Martin, Madeleine Kahn, Robert Klein, Anthony LaPaglia.

MO' BETTER BLUES
UNIVERSAL. August, 1990. (Spike Lee), Denzel Washington, Joie Lee, Wesley Snipes.

MO' MONEY
COLUMBIA. July, 1992. (Peter MacDonald), Damon Wayans, Marlon Wayans, Stacey Dash.

MOBSTERS
UNIVERSAL. July, 1991. (Michael Karbelnikoff), Christian Slater, Patrick Dempsey, Richard Grieco.

MODEL COUPLE, THE
INDEPT. November, 1990. French. (William Klein), Anemone, Andre Dussolier.

MODERN LOVE
SVS/TRIUMPH. April, 1990. (Robby Benson), Robby Benson, Karla DeVito, Burt Reynolds.

MOM AND DAD SAVE THE WORLD
WARNER BROS. July, 1992. (Greg Beeman), Teri Garr, Jeffrey Jones, Jon Lovitz.

MONEY FOR NOTHING
BUENA VISTA. September, 1993. (Ramon Menendez), John Cusack, Debi Mazar, Michael Madsen.

MONEY MAN
MILESTONE. January, 1993. (Philip Hass), Documentary.

MONEYTREE, THE
BLACK SHEEP FILMS. April, 1992. (Alan Dienstag), Christopher Dienstag, Robbi Collins, Richard Roughgarden.

MONKEY TROUBLE
NEW LINE CINEMA. March, 1994. (Franco Amurri), Thora Birch, Harvey Keitel, Mimi Rogers.

MONSIEUR HIRE
ORION CLASSICS. April, 1990. French. (Patrice Leconte), Michel Blanc, Sandrine Bonnaire.

MONSTER IN A BOX
FINE LINE FEATURES. May, 1992. (Nick Broomfield), Spalding Gray.

MONTH BY THE LAKE, A
MIRAMAX. (R) September, 1995. British. (John Irvin), Vanessa Redgrave, Edward Fox, Uma Thurman.

MOONLIGHT AND VALENTINO
GRAMERCY. (R) September, 1995. (David Anspaugh), Elizabeth Perkins, Kathleen Turner, Whoopi Goldberg.

MORNING GLORY
ACADEMY ENT. September, 1993. (Steven Hilliard Stern), Christopher Reeve, Deborah Raffin, Lloyd Bochner.

MORTAL KOMBAT
NEW LINE CINEMA. (PG-13) August, 1995. (Paul Anderson), Linden Ashby, Cary Hiroyuki Tagawa, Christopher Lambert.

MORTAL PASSIONS
MGM/UA. January, 1990. (Andrew Lane), Zach Galligan, Krista Errickson.

MORTAL THOUGHTS
COLUMBIA. April, 1991. (Alan Rudolph), Demi Moore, Glenne Headley, Bruce Willis.

MOTHER'S BOYS
DIMENSION. March, 1994. (Yves Simoneau), Jamie Lee Curtis, Peter Gallagher, Luke Edwards.

MOTORAMA
TWO MOON RELEASING. January, 1993. (Barry Shils), Jordan Christopher Michael, Martha Quinn, Susan Tyrrell.

MOUNTAINS OF THE MOON
TRISTAR. February, 1990. (Bob Rafelson), Patrick Bergin, Iain Glen, Richard E. Grant.

MOVING THE MOUNTAIN
OCTOBER. April, 1995. (Michael Apted), Documentary.

MR. AND MRS. BRIDGE
MIRAMAX. November, 1990. (James Ivory), Paul Newman, Joanne Woodward, Robert Sean Leonard.

MR. BASEBALL
UNIVERSAL. October, 1992. (Fred Schepisi), Tom Selleck, Ken Takakura, Aya Takanashi.

MR. DESTINY
BUENA VISTA. October, 1990. (James Orr), James Belushi, Michael Caine, Linda Hamilton.

MR. FROST
TRIUMPH. November, 1990. British-French. (Philippe Setbon), Jeff Goldblum, Kathy Baker, Alan Bates.

MR. HOOVER & I
TURIN FILM. April, 1990. (Emile DeAntonio), Documentary.

MR. JONES
TRISTAR. October, 1993. (Mike Figgis), Richard Gere, Lena Olin, Anne Bancroft, Delroy Lindo.

MR. NANNY
NEW LINE CINEMA. October, 1993. (Michael Gottlieb), Hulk Hogan, Sherman Hemsley, Austin Pendleton.

MR. SATURDAY NIGHT
COLUMBIA. September, 1992. (Billy Crystal), Billy Crystal, David Paymer, Helen Hunt, Julie Warner.

MR. UNIVERSE
ZEITGEIST. March, 1990. Hungarian. (György Szomjas), Laszlo Szabo, Mickey Hargitay.

MR. WONDERFUL
WARNER BROS. October, 1993. (Anthony Minghella), Matt Dillon, Annabella Sciorra, Mary Louise Parker.

MR. WRITE
SHAPIRO GLICKENHAUS. May, 1994. (Charlie Loventhal), Paul Reiser, Jessica Tuck, Doug Davidson.

MRS. DOUBTFIRE
20TH CENTURY FOX. November, 1993. (Chris Columbus), Robin Williams, Sally Field, Pierce Brosnan.

MRS. PARKER AND THE VICIOUS CIRCLE
FINE LINE. (R) November, 1994. (Alan Rudolph), Jennifer Jason Leigh, Campbell Scott, Matthew Broderick.

MUCH ADO ABOUT NOTHING
GOLDWYN. May, 1993. British. (Kenneth Branagh), Kenneth Branagh, Robert Sean Leonard, Emma Thompson.

MUHAMMAD ALI, THE GREATEST
FILMS PARIS. November, 1990. (William Klein), Documentary.

MUNCHIE
CONCORDE. May, 1992. (Jim Wynorski), Loni Anderson, Andrew Stevens, Jaime McEnnan.

MUPPET CHRISTMAS CAROL, THE
BUENA VISTA. December, 1992. (Brian Henson), Michael Caine, The Muppets.

MURDER IN THE FIRST
WARNER BROS. January, 1995. (Marc Rocco), Christian Slater, Kevin Bacon, Gary Oldman.

MURDER MAGIC
METROPOLIS. May, 1994. (Windell Williams), Ron Cephas Jones, D. Ruben Green, Collette Wilson.

MURIEL'S WEDDING
MIRAMAX. (R) March, 1995. Australian. (P.J. Hogan), Toni Collette, Rachel Griffiths, Bill Hunter.

MUSIC OF CHANCE, THE
I.R.S. June, 1993. (Philip Haas), Mandy Patinkin, James Spader, M. Emmet Walsh.

MUSIC TELLS YOU, THE
PENNEBAKER ASSOCS. June, 1992. (Chris Hegedus, D. A. Pennebaker), Branford Marsalis.

MUTE WITNESS
SONY CLASSICS. (R) September, 1995. British. (Anthony Waller), Marina Sudina, Evan Richards, Fay Ripley.

MY BLUE HEAVEN
WARNER BROS. August, 1990. (Herbert Ross), Steve Martin, Rick Moranis, Joan Cusack.

MY BOYFRIEND'S BACK
BUENA VISTA. August, 1993. (Bob Balaban), Andrew Lowery, Traci Lind, Austin Pendleton, Paul Dooley.

MY COUSIN VINNY
20TH CENTURY FOX. March, 1992. (Jonathan Lynn), Joe Pesci, Marisa Tomei, Ralph Macchio.

MY FAMILY, MI FAMILIA
NEW LINE. (R) May, 1995. (Gregory Nava), Jimmy Smits, Esai Morales, Eduardo Lopez Rojas.

MY FATHER, THE HERO
BUENA VISTA. February, 1994. (Steve Miner), Gérard Depardieu, Katherine Heigl, Dalton James.

MY FATHER'S COMING
TARA RELEASING. November, 1991. German. (Monika Treut), Alfred Edel, Shelley Kastner, Annie Sprinkle.

MY FATHER'S GLORY
ORION CLASSICS. June, 1991. French. (Yves Robert), Philippe Caubere, Nathalie Roussel.

MY GIRL
COLUMBIA. November, 1991. (Howard Zieff), Dan Aykroyd, Jamie Lee Curtis, Anna Chlumsky, Macaulay Culkin.

MY GIRL 2
COLUMBIA. February, 1994. (Howard Zieff), Anna Chlumsky, Dan Aykroyd, Jamie Lee Curtis, Austin O'Brien.

MY HEROES HAVE ALWAYS BEEN COWBOYS
GOLDWYN. March, 1991. (Stuart Rosenberg), Scott Glenn, Kate Capshaw, Ben Johnson, Balthazar Getty.

MY LIFE
COLUMBIA. November, 1993. (Bruce Joel Rubin), Michael Keaton, Nicole Kidman, Haing S. Ngor.

MY LIFE AND TIMES WITH ANTONIN ARTAUD
LEISURE TIME. July, 1995. French. (Gerard Mordillat), Sami Frey, Marc Barbe, Julie Jezequel.

MY LIFE'S IN TURNAROUND
ARROW. June, 1994. (Eric Schaeffer, Donald Lardner Ward), Eric Schaeffer, Donald Lardner Ward, John Sayles.

MY MOTHER'S CASTLE
ORION CLASSICS. July, 1991. French. (Yves Robert), Julien Ciamaca, Philippe Caubere.

MY NEIGHBOR TOTORO
TROMA. May, 1993. Japanese. (Hayao Miyazaki), Animated.

MY NEW GUN
I.R.S. October, 1992. (Stacy Cochran), Diane Lane, James LeGros, Stephen Collins.

MY OWN PRIVATE IDAHO
NEW LINE CINEMA. September, 1991. (Gus Van Sant), River Phoenix, Keanu Reeves, James Russo.

MY UNCLE'S LEGACY
IFEX. June, 1990. Serbo-Croatian. (Krsto Papic), Davor Janjic, Alma Prica.

MYSTERY DATE
ORION. August, 1991. (Jonathan Wacks), Ethan Hawke, Teri Polo, B.D. Wong, Brian McNamara.

MYSTERY OF RAMPO, THE
GOLDWYN. May, 1995. Japanese. (Kazuyoshi Okuyama), Masahiro Motoki, Naoto Takenaka, Michiko Hada.

N

NADJA
OCTOBER. (R) August, 1995. (Michael Almereyda), Elina Lowensohn, Peter Fonda, Suzy Amis, Martin Donovan. B&W.

NAKED
FINE LINE. December, 1993. British. (Mike Leigh), David Thewlis, Lesley Sharp, Katrin Cartlidge, Greg Cruttwell.

NAKED GUN 2½: THE SMELL OF FEAR
PARAMOUNT. June, 1991. (David Zucker), Leslie Nielsen, Priscilla Presley, Robert Goulet.

NAKED GUN 33 1/3: THE FINAL INSULT
PARAMOUNT. March, 1994. (Peter Segal), Leslie Nielsen, Priscilla Presley, O.J. Simpson, Fred Ward.

NAKED IN NEW YORK
FINE LINE. April, 1994. (Dan Algrant), Eric Stoltz, Mary Louise Parker, Tony Curtis, Ralph Macchio.

NAKED KILLER
RIM. March, 1995. Hong Kong. (Clarence Fok), Simon Yam, Chingmy Yau, Carrie Ng.

NAKED LUNCH
20TH CENTURY FOX. December, 1991. British-Canadian. (David Cronenberg), Peter Weller, Judy Davis, Ian Holm.

NAKED OBSESSION
CONCORDE. January, 1991. (Dan Golden), William Katt, Rick Dean, Maria Ford.

NAKED TANGO
NEW LINE CINEMA. August, 1991. Argentinian-U.S. (Leonard Schrader), Vincent D'Onofrio, Mathilda May, Esai Morales.

NARROW MARGIN
TRISTAR. September, 1990. (Peter Hyams), Gene Hackman, Anne Archer, James B. Sikking.

NASTY GIRL, THE
MIRAMAX. October, 1990. German. (Michael Verhoeven), Lena Stolze, Monika Baumgartner. Color/B&W.

NATIONAL LAMPOON'S LOADED WEAPON 1
NEW LINE CINEMA. February, 1993. (Gene Quintano), Emilio Estevez, Samuel L. Jackson, Jon Lovitz.

NATIONAL LAMPOON'S SENIOR TRIP
NEW LINE CINEMA. (R) September, 1995. (Kelly Makin), Matt Frewer, Valeri Mahaffey, Thomas Chong.

NATURAL BORN KILLERS
WARNER BROS. August, 1994. (Oliver Stone), Woody Harrelson, Juliette Lewis, Robert Downey Jr.

NATURAL HISTORY OF PARKING LOTS, THE
STRAND. October, 1990. (Everett Lewis), Charlie Bean, B. Wyatt.

NAVY SEALS
ORION. July, 1990. (Lewis Teague), Charlie Sheen, Michael Biehn, Rick Rossovich.

NECESSARY ROUGHNESS
PARAMOUNT. September, 1991. (Stan Dragoti), Scott Bakula, Hector Elizondo, Robert Loggia.

NEEDFUL THINGS
COLUMBIA. August, 1993. (Fraser Heston), Max von Sydow, Ed Harris, Bonnie Bedelia, J.T. Walsh.

NEIL SIMON'S "LOST IN YONKERS"
COLUMBIA. May, 1993. (Martha Coolidge), Mercedes Ruehl, Richard Dreyfuss, Irene Worth, Brad Stoll.

NELL
20TH CENTURY FOX. December, 1994. (Michael Apted), Jodie Foster, Liam Neeson, Natasha Richardson.

NEMESIS
IMPERIAL. January, 1993. (Albert Pyun), Olivier Gruner, Tim Thomerson, Cary Hiroyuki Tagawa.

NET, THE
COLUMBIA. July, 1995. (Irwin Winkler), Sandra Bullock, Jeremy Northam, Dennis Miller, Diane Baker.

NEVER LEAVE NEVADA
CABRIOLET. April, 1991. (Steve Swartz), Steve Swartz, Rodney Rincon. B&W.

NEVERENDING STORY II: THE NEXT CHAPTER, THE
WARNER BROS. February, 1991. German. (George Miller), Jonathan Brandis, Kenny Morrison, Clarissa Burt.

NEW AGE, THE
WARNER BROS. September, 1994. (Michael Tolkin), Peter Weller, Judy Davis, Patrick Bauchau, Adam West.

NEW JACK CITY
WARNER BROS. March, 1991. (Mario Van Peebles), Wesley Snipes, Ice T, Mario Van Peebles, Judd Nelson.

NEW JERSEY DRIVE
GRAMERCY. (R) April, 1995. (Nick Gomez), Sharron Corley, Gabriel Casseus, Saul Stein.

NEWSIES
BUENA VISTA. April, 1992. (Kenny Ortega), Christian Bale, Robert Duvall, David Moscow, Trey Parker.

NEXT KARATE KID, THE
COLUMBIA. August, 1994. (Christopher Cain), Noriyuki "Pat" Morita, Hilary Swank, Michael Ironside.

NIGHT AND DAY
INT'L FILM CIRCUIT. December, 1992. French. (Chantal Ackerman), Guilaine Londez, Thomas Langmann, Francois Negret.

NIGHT AND THE CITY
20TH CENTURY FOX. October, 1992. (Irwin Winkler), Robert De Niro, Jessica Lange, Alan King, Jack Warden.

NIGHT ANGEL
FRIES ENT. September, 1990. (Dominique Othenin Girard), Isa Anderson, Karen Black, Debra Feuer.

NIGHT OF THE DEMONS 2
REPUBLIC. May, 1994. (Brian Trenchard Smith), Cristi Harris, Bobby Jacoby, Merle Kennedy.

NIGHT OF THE LIVING DEAD
COLUMBIA. October, 1990. (Tom Savini), Tony Todd, Patricia Tallman, Tom Towles.

NIGHT OF THE WARRIOR
TRIMARK. June, 1991. (Rafal Zielinski), Lorenzo Lamas, Anthony Geary, Arlene Dahl.

NIGHT ON EARTH
FINE LINE. May, 1992. (Jim Jarmusch), Gena Rowlands, Giancarlo Esposito, Roberto Benigni, Winona Ryder.

NIGHT WE NEVER MET, THE
MIRAMAX. April, 1993. (Warren Leight), Matthew Broderick, Annabella Sciorra, Kevin Anderson.

NIGHTBREED
20TH CENTURY FOX. February, 1990. (Clive Barker), Craig Sheffer, David Cronenberg.

1991: THE YEAR PUNK BROKE
TARA. November, 1992. (Dave Markey), Documentary.

NINA TAKES A LOVER
TRIUMPH. March, 1995. (Alan Jacobs), Laura San Giacomo, Paul Rhys, Michael O'Keefe.

NINE MONTHS
20TH CENTURY FOX. July, 1995. (Chris Columbus), Hugh Grant, Julianne Moore, Tom Arnold, Joan Cusack.

NITRATE KISSES
STRAND. April, 1993. (Barbara Hammer), Documentary.

NO ESCAPE
SAVOY. April, 1994. (Martin Campbell), Ray Liotta, Lance Henriksen, Stuart Wilson, Kevin Dillon.

NO FEAR, NO DIE
ART LOGIC. August, 1992. French. (Claire Denis), Isaach de Bankole, Alex Descas, Jean Claude Brialy.

NO MERCY
INCA FILMS. September, 1995. Spanish. (Francisco J. Lombardi), Diego Bertie, Adriana Davila, Jorge Chiarella.

NO PICNIC
GREAT JONES FILM GROUP. July, 1990. (Philip Hartman), David Brisbin, Myoshin.

NO SECRETS
I.R.S. MEDIA. May, 1991. (Dezso Magyar), Adam Coleman Howard, Amy Locane, Traci Lind.

NO SKIN OFF MY ASS
STRAND. November, 1991. Canadian. (Bruce LaBruce), Bruce LaBruce, Klaus Von Brucker, G. B. Jones.

NOBODY'S FOOL
PARAMOUNT. December, 1994. (Robert Benton), Paul Newman, Jessica Tandy, Bruce Willis, Melanie Griffith.

NOBODY'S PERFECT
MOVIESTORE ENT. February, 1990. (Robert Kaylor), Chad Lowe, Gail O'Grady.

NOIR ET BLANC
GREYCAT FILMS. May, 1991. French. (Claire Devers), Francis Frappat, Jacques Martial.

NOISES OFF
BUENA VISTA. March, 1992. (Peter Bogdanovich), Michael Caine, Carol Burnett, John Ritter, Christopher Reeve.

NORTH
COLUMBIA. July, 1994. (Rob Reiner), Elijah Wood, Jon Lovitz, Bruce Willis, Alan Arkin.

NORTHERNERS, THE
INDEPENDENT. November, 1993. Dutch. (Alex van Warmerdam), Leonard Lucieer, Jack Vouterse.

NOSTRADAMUS
ORION CLASSICS. (R) September, 1994. British-German. (Roger Christian), Tcheky Karyo, Amanda Plummer, F. Murray Abraham.

NOT WITHOUT MY DAUGHTER
MGM. January, 1991. (Brian Gilbert), Sally Field, Alfred Molina, Sheila Rosenthal.

NOTEBOOKS ON CITIES AND CLOTHES
CONNOISSEUR. October, 1991. German. (Wim Wenders), Documentary.

NOTHING BUT TROUBLE
WARNER BROS. February, 1991. (Dan Aykroyd), Chevy Chase, Demi Moore, John Candy, Dan Aykroyd.

NOWHERE TO RUN
COLUMBIA. January, 1993. (Robert Harmon), Jean Claude Van Damme, Rosanna Arquette, Kieran Culkin.

NUNS ON THE RUN
20TH CENTURY FOX. March, 1990. British. (Jonathan Lynn), Eric Idle, Robbie Coltrane. Camille Coduri.

NUTCRACKER PRINCE, THE
WARNER BROS. November, 1990. Canadian. (Paul Schibli), Animated.

OAK, THE
MK2. January, 1993. Romanian. (Luican Pintilie), Maia Morgenstern, Razuan Vasilescu, Victor Rebengiuc.

OBJECT OF BEAUTY, THE
AVENUE. April 1991. British. (Michael Lindsay Hogg), John Malkovich, Andie MacDowell.

OBLIVION
FULL MOON. (R) January, 1995. (Sam Irvin), Richard Joseph Paul, Jackie Swanson, Andrew Divoff.

OF MICE AND MEN
MGM. October, 1992. (Gary Sinise), John Malkovich, Gary Sinise, Ray Walston, Sherilynn Fenn.

OKOGE
CINEVISTA. April, 1993. Japanese. (Takehiro Nakajima), Misa Shimizu, Takehiro Murata, Takeo Nakahara.

OLD EXPLORERS
TAURUS. September, 1990. (William Pohlad), Jose Ferrer, James Whitmore, Jeffrey Gadbois.

OLD LADY WHO WALKED IN THE SEA, THE
CFP. September, 1995. French. (Laurent Heynemann), Jeanne Moreau, Michael Serrault, Luc Thuillier.

OLEANNA
GOLDWYN. November, 1994. (David Mamet), William H. Macy, Debra Eisenstadt.

OLIVIER, OLIVIER
SONY CLASSICS. February, 1993. French. (Agnieszka Holland), François Cluzet, Brigitte Rouan, Gregoire Colin.

OLYMPIC SUMMER, THE
NEW YORKER. August, 1994. German. (Gordian Maugg), Jost Gerstein, Verena Plangger. B&W.

ON DEADLY GROUND
WARNER BROS. February, 1994. (Steven Seagal), Steven Seagal, Michael Caine, Joan Chen.

ON THE BRIDGE
DIRECT CINEMA. October, 1993. (Frank Perry), Frank Perry.

ONCE AROUND
UNIVERSAL. January, 1991. (Lasse Halstrom), Richard Dreyfuss, Holly Hunter, Danny Aiello.

ONCE UPON A CRIME
MGM. March, 1992. (Eugene Levy), John Candy, James Belushi, Sean Young, Cybill Shepherd.

ONCE UPON A FOREST
20TH CENTURY FOX. June, 1993. (Charles Grosvenor), Animated.

ONCE UPON A TIME IN CHINA
GOLDEN HARVEST. May, 1992. Hong Kong. (Tsui Hark), Jet Li, Yuen Biao, Jacky Cheung.

ONCE UPON A TIME IN CHINA PART 2
GOLDEN HARVEST. September, 1993. Hong Kong. (Tsui Hark), Jet Li, Rosamund Kwan, Mok Siucheung.

ONCE WERE WARRIORS
FINE LINE. (R) February, 1995. New Zealand. (Lee Tamahori), Rena Owen, Temuera Morrison, Mamaengaroa KerrBell.

ONE FALSE MOVE
I.R.S. May, 1992. (Carl Franklin), Bill Paxton, Cynda Williams, Billy Bob Thornton.

ONE GOOD COP
BUENA VISTA. May, 1991. (Heywood Gould), Michael Keaton, Rene Russo, Anthony LaPaglia.

ONE HAND DON'T CLAP
RHAPSODY FILMS. August, 1991. (Kavery Dutta), Documentary.

1-900
ZEITGEIST. September, 1995. Dutch. (Theo van Gogh), Ariane Schluter, Ad van Kempen.

1000 PIECES OF GOLD
GREYCAT. May, 1991. (Nancy Kelly), Rosalind Chao, Chris Cooper, Dennis Dun.

ONLY THE BRAVE
FIRST RUN. May, 1995. Australian. (Ana Kokkinos), Elena Mandalis, Dora Kaskanis, Maude Davey.

ONLY THE BRAVE
SCORPIO. August, 1994. Dutch. (Sonia Herman Dolz), Documentary.

ONLY THE LONELY
20TH CENTURY FOX. May, 1991. (Chris Columbus), John Candy, Ally Sheedy, Maureen O'Hara.

ONLY THE STRONG
20TH CENTURY FOX. August, 1993. (Sheldon Lettich), Mark Dacascos, Stacey Travis, Geoffrey Lewis.

ONLY YOU
TRISTAR. October, 1994. (Norman Jewison), Marisa Tomei, Robert Downey, Jr., Bonnie Hunt, Billy Zane.

OPEN DOORS
ORION CLASSICS. March, 1991. Italian. (Gianni Amelio), Gian Maria Volonte, Ennio Fantastichini.

OPERATION DUMBO DROP
BUENA VISTA. July, 1995. (Simon Wincer), Danny Glover, Ray Liotta, Denis Leary, Doug E. Doug.

OPPORTUNITY KNOCKS
UNIVERSAL. March, 1990. (Donald Petrie), Dana Carvey, Robert Loggia, Todd Graff.

OPPOSITE SEX, THE (AND HOW TO LIVE WITH THEM)
MIRAMAX. March, 1993. (Matthew Meshekoff), Arye Gross, Courteney Cox, Kevin Pollak.

ORLANDO
SONY CLASSICS. June, 1993. British-Russian-French-Dutch. (Sally Potter), Tilda Swinton, Billy Zane, Lothaire Bluteau.

OSCAR
BUENA VISTA. April, 1991. (John Landis), Sylvester Stallone, Peter Riegert, Vincent Spano, Tim Curry.

OTHELLO
ROCKBOTTOM/UPTOWN FILMS. November, 1990. (Ted Lange), Ted Lange, Hawthorne James, Mary Otis.

OTHER PEOPLE'S MONEY
WARNER BROS. October, 1991. (Norman Jewison), Danny DeVito, Gregory Peck, Penelope Ann Miller.

OUT FOR JUSTICE
WARNER BROS. April, 1991. (John Flynn), Steven Seagal, William Forsythe, Jerry Orbach.

OUT ON A LIMB
UNIVERSAL. September, 1992. (Francis Veber), Matthew Broderick, Jeffrey Jones, Heidi Kling.

OUTBREAK
WARNER BROS. March, 1995. (Wolfgang Petersen), Dustin Hoffman, Renee Russo, Morgan Freeman.

OUTSIDE CHANCE OF MAXIMILLIAN GLICK, THE
SOUTH GATE ENTERTAINMENT. January, 1990. Canadian. (Allan A. Goldstein), Noam Zylberman, Fairuza Balk.

OVEREXPOSED
CONCORDE. March, 1990. (Larry Brand), Catherine Oxenberg, David Naughton.

OVERSEAS
ARIES. November, 1991. French. (Brigitte Rouan), Nicole Garcia, Marianne Basler, Brigitte Rouan.

OX, THE
CASTLE HILL/FIRST RUN FEATURES. August, 1992. Swedish. (Sven Nykvist), Stellan Skarsgård, Ewa Fröling, Liv Ullman.

P

PCU
20TH CENTURY FOX. April, 1994. (Hart Bochner), Jeremy Piven, Chris Young, David Spade.

PACIFIC HEIGHTS
20TH CENTURY FOX. September, 1990. (John Schlesinger), Matthew Modine, Melanie Griffith, Michael Keaton.

PAGEMASTER, THE
20TH CENTURY FOX. November, 1994. (Joe Johnston), Macauley Culkin, Christopher Lloyd, Ed Begley Jr.

PAINTING THE TOWN
PADDED CELL. May, 1992. (Andrew Behar), Richard Osterwell.

PALOMBELLA ROSSA
INT'L FILM CIRCUIT. January, 1991. Italian. (Nanni Moretti), Nanni Moretti, Silvio Orlando, Mariella Valentini.

PANAMA DECEPTION, THE
EMPOWERMENT PROJECT. July, 1992. (Barbara Trent), Documentary.

PANTHER
GRAMERCY. (R) May, 1995. (Mario Van Peebles), Kadeem Hardison, Bokeem Woodbine, Courtney B. Vance.

PAPER, THE
UNIVERSAL. March, 1994. (Ron Howard), Michael Keaton, Glenn Close, Marisa Tomei, Robert Duvall.

PAPER MASK
CASTLE HILL. November, 1991. British. (Christopher Morahan), Paul McGann, Amanda Donohoe, Frederick Treves.

PAPER WEDDING, A
CAPITOL ENT. June, 1991. French Canadian. (Michel Brault), Genevieve Bujold, Manuel Aranguiz.

PARADISE
BUENA VISTA. September, 1991. (Mary Agnes Donoghue), Don Johnson, Melanie Griffith, Elijah Wood.

PARIS, FRANCE
ALLIANCE. February, 1994. Canadian. (Gerard Ciccoritti), Leslie Hope, Peter Outerbridge, Victor Ertmanis.

PARIS IS BURNING
OFF WHITE PRODS. March, 1991. (Jennie Livingston), Documentary.

PARTY GIRL
FIRST LOOK. (R) June, 1995. (Daisy von Scherler Mayer), Parker Posey, Guillermo Diaz, Omar Townsend.

PASSED AWAY
BUENA VISTA. April, 1992. (Charlie Peters), Bob Hoskins, Pamela Reed, Maureen Stapleton.

PASSENGER 57
WARNER BROS. November, 1992. (Kevin Hooks), Wesley Snipes, Bruce Payne, Alex Datcher.

PASSION FISH
MIRAMAX. December, 1992. (John Sayles), Mary McDonnell, Alfre Woodard, David Strathairn.

PASSION TO KILL, A
APIX/RYSHER. (R) November, 1994. (Rick King), Scott Bakula, Chelsea Field, Sheila Kelley, France Nuyen.

PASTIME
MIRAMAX. August, 1991. (Robin B. Armstrong), William Russ, Glenn Plummer, Noble Willingham.

PATRIOT GAMES
PARAMOUNT. June, 1992. (Phillip Noyce), Harrison Ford, Patrick Bergin, Anne Archer, Sean Bean.

PAUL BOWLES: THE COMPLETE OUTSIDER
FIRST RUN. September, 1994. (Catherine Warnow, Regina Weinreich), Documentary.

PAUL McCARTNEY'S GET BACK
NEW LINE CINEMA. October, 1991. British. (Richard Lester), Documentary.

PEACEMAKER
FRIES. May, 1990. (Kevin S. Tenney), Robert Forster, Lance Edwards, Robert Davi.

PEBBLE AND THE PENGUIN, THE
MGM/UA. April, 1995. (Russel Boland), Martin Short, Annie Golden, Tim Curry, James Belushi (voices). Animated.

PELICAN BRIEF, THE
WARNER BROS. December, 1993. (Alan J. Pakula), Julia Roberts, Denzel Washington, Sam Shepard.

PEOPLE UNDER THE STAIRS, THE
UNIVERSAL. November, 1991. (Wes Craven), Brandon Adams, Everett McGill, Wendy Robie.

PEREZ FAMILY, THE
GOLDWYN. (R) May, 1995. (Mira Nair), Marisa Tomei, Alfred Molina, Anjelica Huston, Chazz Palminteri.

PERFECT MURDER, THE
MERCHANT IVORY PRODS. March, 1990. British-Indian. (Zafar Hai), Naseeruddin Shan, Stellan Skarsgård.

PERFECT WEAPON, THE
PARAMOUNT. March, 1991. (Mark DiSalle), Jeff Speakman, John Dye, Mako.

PERFECT WORLD, A
WARNER BROS. November, 1993. (Clint Eastwood), Kevin Costner, Clint Eastwood, Laura Dern, T.J. Lowther.

PERFECTLY NORMAL
4 SEASONS ENT. February, 1991. Canadian. (Yves Simoneau), Robbie Coltrane, Michael Riley, Deborah Duchene.

PERMANENT VACATION
ANTHOLOGY FILMS. September, 1990 (release of 1980 film). (Jim Jarmusch), Chris Parker, Leila Gastil.

PERSUASION
SONY CLASSICS. (PG) September, 1995. British. (Roger Michell), Amanda Root, Ciaran Hinds, Susan Fleetwood.

PET SEMATARY II
PARAMOUNT. August, 1992. (Mary Lambert), Edward Furlong, Anthony Edwards, Clancy Brown.

PETER'S FRIENDS
GOLDWYN. December, 1992. British. (Kenneth Branagh), Hugh Laurie, Kenneth Branagh, Emma Thompson.

PHANTOM OF THE OPERA, THE
HIRSCHFELD PRODS. June, 1991. (Darwin Knight), David Staller, Elizabeth Walsh.

PHILADELPHIA
TRISTAR. December, 1993. (Jonathan Demme), Tom Hanks, Denzel Washington, Jason Robards.

PHILADELPHIA EXPERIMENT 2, THE
TRIMARK. November, 1993. (Stephen Cornwell), Brad Johnson, Marjean Holden, Gerrit Graham.

PIANO, THE
MIRAMAX. November, 1993. Australian-New Zealand-French. (Jane Campion), Holly Hunter, Harvey Keitel.

PICKLE, THE
COLUMBIA. April, 1993. (Paul Mazursky), Danny Aiello, Dyan Cannon, Clotilde Courau.

PICTURE BRIDE
MIRAMAX. (PG-13) April, 1995. (Kayo Hatta), Youki Kudoch, Akira Takayama, Tamlyn Tomita.

PICTURES FROM A REVOLUTION
KINO INT'L. May, 1992. (Susan Meiselas, Richard O. Rogers, Alfred Guzzetti), Documentary.

PIT AND THE PENDULUM, THE
JGM/FULL MOON. May, 1991. (Stuart Gordon), Lance Henriksen, Rona De Ricci, Jonathan Fuller.

PIZZA MAN
MEGALOMANIA PRODS. December, 1991. (J.D. Athens), Bill Maher, Annabelle Gurwitch, David McKnight.

PLAYBOYS, THE
GOLDWYN. April, 1992. Irish. (Gillies MacKinnon), Albert Finney, Aidan Quinn, Robin Wright.

PLAYER, THE
FINE LINE. April, 1992. (Robert Altman), Tim Robbins, Greta Scacchi, Whoopi Goldberg, Fred Ward.

PLOT AGAINST HARRY, THE
NEW YORKER. January, 1990. (made 1969). (Michael Roemer), Martin Priest, Ben Lang. B&W.

POCAHONTAS
BUENA VISTA. June, 1995. (Mike Gabriel, Eric Goldberg), Animated.

POETIC JUSTICE
COLUMBIA. July, 1993. (John Singleton), Janet Jackson, Tupac Shakur, Regina King.

POINT BREAK
20TH CENTURY FOX. July, 1991. (Kathryn Bigelow), Patrick Swayze, Keanu Reeves, Gary Busey.

POINT OF NO RETURN
WARNER BROS. March, 1993. (John Badham), Bridget Fonda, Gabriel Byrne, Dermot Mulroney.

POISON
ZEITGEIST. April, 1991. (Todd Haynes), Larry Maxwell, Susan Norman, Scott Renderer.

POISON IVY
NEW LINE CINEMA. May, 1992. (Katt Shea), Sara Gilbert, Drew Barrymore, Tom Skerritt.

POLICE ACADEMY: MISSION TO MOSCOW
WARNER BROS. August, 1994. (Alan Metter), George Gaynes, Michael Winslow, David Graf.

POLICE STORY III: SUPERCOP
PACIFIC FILMS. October, 1993. Chinese. (Stanley Tong), Jackie Chan, Michelle Yeoh, Maggie Cheung.

PONTIAC MOON
PARAMOUNT. November, 1994. (Peter Medak), Ted Danson, Mary Steenburgen, Ryan Todd, Eric Schweig.

POPCORN
STUDIO THREE. February, 1991. (Mark Herrier), Jill Schoelen, Tom Villard, Tony Roberts.

POPE MUST DIE, THE
MIRAMAX. August, 1991. British. (Peter Richardson), Robbie Coltrane, Beverly D'Angelo, Herbert Lom.

POSITIVE
FIRST RUN FEATURES. May, 1990. W. German. (Rosa von Praunheim), Documentary.

POSSE
GRAMERCY. May, 1993. (Mario Van Peebles), Mario Van Peebles, Charles Lane, Stephen Baldwin.

POSTCARDS FROM AMERICA
STRAND. July, 1995. (Steve McLean), Jim Lyons, Michael Tighe, Michael Imperioli.

POSTCARDS FROM THE EDGE
COLUMBIA. September, 1990. (Mike Nichols), Meryl Streep, Shirley MacLaine, Dennis Quaid, Gene Hackman.

POSTMAN, THE
MIRAMAX. (PG) June, 1995. Italian-French. (Michael Radford), Massimo Troisi, Philippe Noiret.

POWER OF ONE, THE
WARNER BROS. March, 1992. (John G. Avildsen), Stephen Dorff, Armin Mueller, Morgan Freeman.

PRAYER OF THE ROLLERBOYS
CASTLE HILL. August, 1991. (Rick King), Corey Haim, Patricia Arquette, Christopher Collet.

PRAYING WITH ANGER
CINEVISTA/UNAPIX. September, 1993. Indian. (M. Night Shyamalan), M. Night Shyamalan, Mike Muthu.

PREDATOR 2
20TH CENTURY FOX. November, 1990. (Stephen Hopkins), Danny Glover, Gary Busey, Ruben Blades.

PRELUDE TO A KISS
20TH CENTURY FOX. July, 1992. (Norman Rene), Alec Baldwin, Meg Ryan, Sydney Walker, Patty Duke.

PRESUMED INNOCENT
WARNER BROS. July, 1990. (Alan J. Pakula), Harrison Ford, Raul Julia, Bonnie Bedelia.

PRETTY WOMAN
BUENA VISTA. March, 1990. (Garry Marshall), Richard Gere, Julia Roberts, Hector Elizondo.

PRIEST
MIRAMAX. (R) March, 1995. British. (Antonia Bird), Linus Roache, Tom Wilkinson, Cathy Tyson.

PRIMARY MOTIVE
BLOSSOM PICTURES. July, 1992. (Daniel Adams), Judd Nelson, Justine Bateman, John Savage.

PRIME TARGET
BORDER/HERO FILMS. September, 1991. (David Heavener), David Heavener, Tony Curtis, Isaac Hayes.

PRINCE BRAT AND THE WHIPPING BOY
GEMINI/JONES. (G) September, 1995. (Syd McCartney), Nic Knight, Truan Munro, George C. Scott.

PRINCE OF TIDES, THE
COLUMBIA. December, 1991. (Barbra Streisand), Nick Nolte, Barbra Streisand, Blythe Danner.

PRINCES IN EXILE
FRIES ENT. February, 1991. Canadian. (Giles Walker), Zachary Ansley, Stacie Mistysyn.

PRINCESS AND THE GOBLIN, THE
HEMDALE. June, 1994. British-Hungarian. (Joszef Gemes), Animated.

PRINCESS CARABOO
TRISTAR. September, 1994. (Michael Austin), Phoebe Cates, Jim Broadbent, Wendy Hughes, Kevin Kline.

PRISONER OF ST. PETERSBURG, THE
INDEPT. November, 1990. Soviet/German. (Ian Pringle), Noah Taylor, Katja Teichmann. B&W.

PRISONERS OF THE SUN (Blood Oath)
SKOURAS. July, 1991. Australian. (Stephen Wallace), Bryan Brown, George Takei, Terry O'Quinn.

PRIVILEGE
ZEITGEIST. January, 1991. (Yvonne Rainer), Alice Spivak, Novella Nelson.

PROBLEM CHILD
UNIVERSAL. July, 1990. (Dennis Dugan), John Ritter, Jack Warden, Amy Yasbeck.

PROBLEM CHILD 2
UNIVERSAL. July, 1991. (Brian Levant), John Ritter, Jack Warden, Laraine Newman.

PROGRAM, THE
BUENA VISTA. September, 1993. (David S. Ward), Craig Sheffer, James Caan, Halle Berry, Omar Epps.

PROFESSION: NEO–NAZI
DRIFT. May, 1995. German. (Winfried Bonengal), Documentary.

PROFESSIONAL, THE
COLUMBIA. November, 1994. (Luc Besson), Jean Reno, Gary Oldman, Natalie Portman, Danny Aiello.

PROMISE, THE
FINE LINE. (R) September, 1995. German. (Margarethe von Trotta), Corinna Harfouch, August Zirner.

PROOF
FINE LINE. March, 1992. Australian. (Jocelyn Moorhouse), Hugo Weaving, Genevieve Picot, Russell Crowe.

PROPHECY, THE
DIMENSION. (R) September, 1995. (Gregory Widen), Christopher Walken, Elias Koteas, Eric Stoltz, Virginia Madsen.

PROS AND CONS OF BREATHING, THE
LEISURE TIME. June, 1995. (Robert Munic), Joey Lauren Adams, Phillip Brock, Joey Dedeo.

PROSPERO'S BOOKS
MIRAMAX. November, 1991. British-Dutch. (Peter Greenaway), John Gielgud, Michael Clark, Michel Blanc.

PUBLIC EYE, THE
UNIVERSAL. October, 1992. (Howard Franklin), Joe Pesci, Barbara Hershey, Stanley Tucci.

PUERTO RICAN MAMBO, THE (NOT A MUSICAL)
CABRIOLET FILMS. March, 1992. (Ben Model), Luis Caballero.

PULP FICTION
MIRAMAX. (R) October, 1994. (Quentin Tarantino), John Travolta, Samuel L. Jackson, Uma Thurman, Bruce Willis.

PUMP UP THE VOLUME
NEW LINE CINEMA. August, 1990. (Allan Moyle), Christian Slater, Annie Ross, Ellen Greene.

PUPPET MASTER
JGM ENTERPRISES. January, 1990. (David Schmoeller), Paul LeMat, Irene Miracle.

PURE COUNTRY
WARNER BROS. October, 1992. (Christopher Cain), George Strait, Lesley Ann Warren, Isabel Glasser.

PURE FORMALITY, A
SONY CLASSICS. (PG-13) May, 1995. French. (Giuseppe Tornatore), Gérard Depardieu, Roman Polanski.

PURE LUCK
UNIVERSAL. August, 1991. (Nadia Tass), Martin Short, Danny Glover, Sheila Kelley.

PUSHING HANDS
CFP. June, 1995. Chinese. (Ang Lee), Sihung Lung, Lai Wang, Bo Z. Wang.

PYROMANIAC'S LOVE STORY, A
BUENA VISTA. April, 1995. (Joshua Brand), William Baldwin, John Leguizamo, Sadie Frost, Erik Eleniak.

Q&A
TRISTAR. April, 1990. (Sidney Lumet), Nick Nolte, Timothy Hutton, Armand Assante.

QUEENS LOGIC
NEW LINE CINEMA. February, 1991. (Steve Rash), Kevin Bacon, Joe Mantegna, John Malkovich.

QUEEN MARGOT
MIRAMAX. (R) December, 1994. (Patrice Chereau), Isabelle Adjani, Daniel Auteuil, Jean-Hugues Anglade.

QUICK AND THE DEAD, THE
TRISTAR. February, 1995. (Sam Raimi), Sharon Stone, Gene Hackman, Leonardo DiCaprio, Russell Crowe.

QUICK CHANGE
WARNER BROS. July, 1990. (Howard Franklin, Bill Murray), Bill Murray, Geena Davis, Randy Quaid.

QUIGLEY DOWN UNDER
MGM. October, 1990. (Simon Wincer), Tom Selleck, Alan Rickman, Laura San Giacomo.

QUIZ SHOW
BUENA VISTA. September, 1994. (Robert Redford), John Turturro, Rob Morrow, Ralph Fiennes.

RADIO FLYER
COLUMBIA. February, 1992. (Richard Donner), Elijah Wood, Lorraine Bracco, Joseph Mazzello.

RADIO STORIES
INDEPENDENT. November, 1993. Spanish. (1955 film). (Jose Luis Saez de Heredia), Francisco Rabal, Margarita Andrey.

RADIOLAND MURDERS
UNIVERSAL. October, 1994. (Mel Smith), Mary Stuart Masterson, Brian Benben, Stephen Toblowsky.

RAGE IN HARLEM, A
MIRAMAX. May, 1991. (Bill Duke), Forest Whitaker, Gregory Hines, Robin Givens.

RAGGEDY RAWNEY, THE
L.W. BLAIR PRODS. February, 1990. British. (Bob Hoskins), Bob Hoskins, Dexter Fletcher.

RAIN KILLER, THE
CONCORDE. September, 1990. (Ken Stein), Ray Sharkey, David Beecroft, Michael Chiklis.

RAIN WITHOUT THUNDER
ORION CLASSICS. February, 1993. (Gary Bennett), Betty Buckley, Jeff Daniels, Frederic Forrest.

RAINING STONES
NORTHERN ARTS. March, 1994. British. (Ken Loach), Bruce Jones, Julie Brown, Gemma Phoenix.

RAISE THE RED LANTERN
ORION CLASSICS. March, 1992. Hong Kong-Chinese-Mandarin. (Zhang Yimou), Gong Li, Ma Jingwu, He Califei.

RAISING CAIN
UNIVERSAL. August, 1992. (Brian DePalma), John Lithgow, Lolita Davidovich, Steven Bauer.

RAMBLING ROSE
NEW LINE CINEMA. October, 1991. (Martha Coolidge), Laura Dern, Robert Duvall, Lukas Haas, Diane Ladd.

RAMBLIN' GAL
AQUARIUS. June, 1991. (Roberto Monticello, Lu Ann Horstman Person), Deborah Strang, Andrew Krawetz.

RAMPAGE
MIRAMAX. October, 1992. (William Friedkin), Michael Biehn, Alex McArthur, Nicholas Campbell.

RAPA NUI
WARNER BROS. September, 1994. (Kevin Reynolds), Jason Scott Lee, Esai Morales, Sandrine Holt.

RAPID FIRE
20TH CENTURY FOX. August, 1992. (Dwight H. Little), Brandon Lee, Powers Boothe, Nick Mancuso.

RAPTURE, THE
NEW LINE CINEMA. October, 1991. (Michael Tolkin), Mimi Rogers, David Duchovny, Patrick Bauchau.

RASPAD
MK2. April, 1992. Soviet. (Mikhail Belikov), Sergei Shakurov, Tatiana Kochemasova.

RAW NERVE
A.I.P. STUDIOS. May, 1991. (David A. Prior), Glenn Ford, Ted Prior, Sandahl Bergman.

READY TO WEAR (PRET–A–PORTER)
MIRAMAX. (R) December, 1994. (Robert Altman), Sophia Loren, Tim Robbins, Julia Roberts, Stephen Rea.

REAL McCOY, THE
UNIVERSAL. September, 1993. (Russell Mulcahy), Kim Basinger, Val Kilmer, Terence Stamp.

REALITY BITES
UNIVERSAL. February, 1994. (Ben Stiller), Winona Ryder, Ethan Hawke, Ben Stiller, Steve Zahn, Janeane Garofalo.

REASON TO BELIEVE, A
CASTLE HILL. (R) September, 1995. (Douglas Tirola), Allison Smith, Jay Underwood, Danny Quinn.

RECOLLECTIONS OF THE YELLOW HOUSE
INVICTA. February, 1994. Portuguese. (Joao Cesar Monteiro), Manuela de Freira, Joao Cesar Monteiro.

RED
MIRAMAX. December, 1994. Polish. (Krzysztof Kieslowski), Irene Jacob, Jean-Louis Trintignant, Frederique Feder.

RED FIRECRACKER, GREEN FIRECRACKER
OCTOBER. April, 1995. Hong Kong. (He Ping), Ning Jing, Wu Gang, Zhao Xiaoruli.

RED ROCK WEST
ROXIE. January, 1994. (John Dahl), Nicolas Cage, Dennis Hopper, Lara Flynn Boyle.

RED SURF
ARROWHEAD ENT. June, 1990. (H. Gordon Boos), George Clooney, Doug Savant.

REF, THE
BUENA VISTA. March, 1994. (Ted Demme), Denis Leary, Judy Davis, Kevin Spacey.

REFLECTING SKIN, THE
PRESTIGE. June, 1991. British. (Philip Ridley), Viggo Mortensen, Lindsay Duncan, Jeremy Cooper.

REFLECTIONS IN THE DARK
CONCORDE. (R) April, 1995. (Jon Purdy), Mimi Rogers, Billy Zane, John Terry.

REFRIGERATOR, THE
AVENUE D. September, 1992. (Nicholas Tony Jacobs), Julia Mueller, David Simonds, Angel Caban.

REGARDING HENRY
PARAMOUNT. July, 1991. (Mike Nichols), Harrison Ford, Annette Bening, Bill Nunn, Mikki Allen.

REGGAE MOVIE, THE
TRIMEDIA. (PG-13) September, 1995. (Randy Rovins), Documentary.

REMAINS OF THE DAY, THE
COLUMBIA. November, 1993. British-U.S. (James Ivory), Anthony Hopkins, Emma Thompson, Christopher Reeve.

RENAISSANCE MAN
BUENA VISTA. June, 1994. (Penny Marshall), Danny DeVito, Gregory Hines, Lilo Brancato.

REPOSSESSED
NEW LINE CINEMA. September, 1990. (Bob Logan), Linda Blair, Leslie Nielsen, Ned Beatty.

REQUIEM FOR DOMINIC
HEMDALE. April, 1991. Austrian. (Robert Dornhelm), Felix Mitterer, Victoria Schubert.

RESCUE ME
CANNON. December, 1993. (Arthur Allan Seidelman), Michael Dudikoff, Stephen Dorff, Ami Dolenz.

RESCUERS DOWN UNDER, THE
BUENA VISTA. November, 1990. (Hendel Butoy, Mike Gabriel), Animated.

RESERVOIR DOGS
MIRAMAX. October, 1992. (Quentin Tarantino), Harvey Keitel, Tim Roth, Michael Madsen.

RESIDENT ALIEN
GREYCAT. October, 1991. (Jonathan Nossiter), Documentary.

RESISTANCE
ANGELIKA. November, 1994. Australian. (Paul Elliott, Hugh Keays Byrne), Lorna Lesley, Jennifer Claire, Bobby Noble.

RETURN OF SUPERFLY, THE
TRITON PICTURES. November, 1990. (Sig Shore), Nathan Purdee, Margaret Avery, David Groh.

RETURN OF THE LIVING DEAD 3
TRIMARK. October, 1993. (Brian Yuzna), Mindy Clarke, J. Trevor Edmond, Kent McCord.

RETURN TO THE BLUE LAGOON
COLUMBIA. August, 1991. (William A. Graham), Milla Jovovich, Brian Krause, Lisa Pelikan.

REUNION
CASTLE HILL. March, 1991. French-German-British. (Jerry Schatzberg), Jason Robards, Christien Anholt, Samuel West.

REVENGE
COLUMBIA. February, 1990. (Tony Scott), Kevin Costner, Anthony Quinn, Madeleine Stowe.

REVERSAL OF FORTUNE
WARNER BROS. October, 1990. (Barbet Schroeder), Jeremy Irons, Glenn Close, Ron Silver.

REVOLUTION!
NORTHERN ARTS. November, 1991. (Jeff Kahn), Christopher Renstrom, Kimberly Flynn, Georg Osterman.

RHAPSODY IN AUGUST
ORION CLASSICS. December, 1991. Japanese. (Akira Kurosawa), Sachiko Murase, Hisashi Igawa, Richard Gere.

RICH GIRL
STUDIO THREE FILM CORP. May, 1991. (Joel Bender), Jill Schoelen, Don Michael Paul, Paul Gleason.

RICH IN LOVE
MGM. March, 1993. (Bruce Beresford), Albert Finney, Kathryn Erbe, Kyle MacLachlan, Ethan Hawke.

RICHIE RICH
WARNER BROS. December, 1994. (Donald Petrie), Macauley Culkin, John Larroquette, Edward Herrman.

RICOCHET
WARNER BROS. October, 1991. (Russell Mulcahy), Denzel Washington, John Lithgow, Ice T.

RIFF-RAFF
FINE LINE FEATURES. February, 1993. British. (Ken Loach), Robert Carlyle, Emer McCourt, Jimmy Coleman.

RIFT
CURB ENT. June, 1995. (Edward S. Barkin), William Sage, Timothy Cavanaugh, Jennifer Bransford.

RIKYU
CAPITOL ENT. January, 1991. Japanese. (Hiroshi Teshigahara), Rentaro Mikuni, Tsutomu Yamazaki.

RISING SUN
20TH CENTURY FOX. July, 1993. (Philip Kaufman), Sean Connery, Wesley Snipes, Tia Carrere, Harvey Keitel.

RISK
SEVENTH ART. October, 1994. (Deirdre Fishel), Karen Sillas, David Ilku, Molly Price.

RIVER OF GRASS
STRAND. August, 1995. (Kelly Reichardt), Lisa Bowman, Larry Fessenden, Dick Russell.

RIVER RUNS THROUGH IT, A
COLUMBIA. October, 1992. (Robert Redford), Craig Sheffer, Brad Pitt, Tom Skerritt.

RIVER WILD, THE
UNIVERSAL. September, 1994. (Curtis Hanson), Meryl Streep, Kevin Bacon, David Strathairn.

RIVERBEND
PRISM ENTERTAINMENT. March, 1990. (San Firstenberg), Steve James, Margaret Avery.

ROAD SCHOLAR
SAMUEL GOLDWYN. July, 1993. (Roger Weisberg), Andrei Codrescu.

ROAD TO WELLVILLE, THE
COLUMBIA. October, 1994. (Alan Parker), Anthony Hopkins, Matthew Broderick, Bridget Fonda, John Cusack, Dana Carvey.

ROADSIDE PROPHETS
FINE LINE FEATURES. March, 1992. (Abbe Wool), John Doe, Adam Horovitz, David Anthony Marshall.

ROB ROY
MGM/UA. April, 1995. (Michael Caton Jones), Liam Neeson, Jessica Lange, John Hurt, Tim Roth.

ROBERT A. HEINLEN'S THE PUPPET MASTERS
BUENA VISTA. October, 1994. (Stuart Orne), Donald Sutherland, Eric Thal, Julie Warner, Keith David.

ROBIN HOOD: MEN IN TIGHTS
20TH CENTURY FOX. July, 1993. (Mel Brooks), Cary Elwes, Richard Lewis, Roger Rees.

ROBIN HOOD: PRINCE OF THIEVES
WARNER BROS. June, 1991. (Kevin Reynolds), Kevin Costner, Morgan Freeman, Alan Rickman.

ROBOCOP 2
ORION. June, 1990. (Irvin Kershner), Peter Weller, Nancy Allen, Tom Noonan.

ROBOCOP 3
ORION. November, 1993. (Fred Dekker), Robert John Burke, Nancy Allen, Rip Torn.

ROBOT CARNIVAL
STREAMLINE. February, 1991. Japanese. (Various directors), Animated.

ROBOT JOX
TRIUMPH. November, 1990. (Stuart Gordon), Gary Graham, Anne-Marie Johnson, Paul Koslo.

ROCK HUDSON'S HOME MOVIES
COUCH POTATO INC. April, 1993. (Mark Rappaport), Documentary.

ROCK-A-DOODLE
SAMUEL GOLDWYN CO. April, 1992. (Don Bluth), Animated.

ROCK SOUP
Z FILMS. April, 1992. (Lech Kowalski), Documentary.

ROCKETEER, THE
BUENA VISTA. June, 1991. (Joe Johnston), Bill Campbell, Jennifer Connelly, Alan Arkin, Timothy Dalton.

ROCKULA
CANNON. February, 1990. (Luca Bercovici), Dean Cameron, Toni Basil, Susan Tyrrell.

ROCKY V
MGM/UA. November, 1990. (John G. Avildsen), Sylvester Stallone, Talia Shire, Burt Young.

RODRIGO D: NO FUTURE
KINO INT'L. January, 1991. Colombian-Spanish. (Victor Manuel Gaviria), Ramiro Menese, Carlos Maria Resrepo.

ROGER CORMAN'S FRANKENSTEIN UNBOUND
20TH CENTURY FOX. November, 1990. (Roger Corman), John Hurt, Raul Julia, Jason Patric.

ROMEO & JULIA
KAUFMAN FILMS. February, 1992. (Kevin Kaufman), Bob Koherr, Ivana Kane, Patrick McGuinness.

ROMEO IS BLEEDING
GRAMERCY. February, 1994. (Peter Medak), Gary Oldman, Lena Olin, Annabella Sciorra, Juliette Lewis.

ROMPER STOMPER
ACADEMY ENT. June, 1993. Australian. (Geoffrey Wright), Russell Crowe, Daniel Pollock, Jacqueline McKenzie.

ROOKIE, THE
WARNER BROS. December, 1990. (Clint Eastwood), Clint Eastwood, Charlie Sheen, Raul Julia, Sonia Braga.

ROOKIE OF THE YEAR
20TH CENTURY FOX. July, 1993. (Daniel Stern), Thomas Ian Nichols, Gary Busey, Daniel Stern.

ROOMMATES
BUENA VISTA. Match, 1995. (Peter Yates), Peter Falk, D.B. Sweeney, Julianne Moore, Jan Rubes.

ROOSTERS
IRS. July, 1995. (Robert M. Young), Edward James Olmos, Sonia Braga, Maria Conchita Alonso.

ROSALIE GOES SHOPPING
FOUR SEASONS ENTERTAINMENT. February, 1990. W. German. (Percy Adlon), Marianne Sagebrecht, Brad Davis, Judge Reinhold.

ROSENCRANTZ & GUILDENSTERN ARE DEAD
CINECOM. February, 1991. British. (Tom Stoppard), Gary Oldman, Tim Roth, Richard Dreyfuss.

ROUGE OF THE NORTH
GREYCAT. December, 1991. Chinese. (Fred Tan), Hsia Wen Shi, Msu Ming, Kao Chich.

ROUTE ONE/USA
INTERAMA. November, 1990. (Robert Kramer), Documentary.

ROVER DANGERFIELD
WARNER BROS. August, 1991. (Jim George, Bob Seeley), Animated.

ROY COHN/JACK SMITH
STRAND. August, 1995. (Jill Godmilow), Ron Vawter.

RUBIN & ED
I.R.S. May, 1992. (Trent Harris), Crispin Glover, Howard Hesseman, Karen Black.

RUBY
TRIUMPH. March, 1992. (John Mackenzie), Danny Aiello, Sherilyn Fenn, Arliss Howard.

RUBY IN PARADISE
OCTOBER. October, 1993. (Victor Nunez), Ashley Judd, Bentley Mitchum, Todd Field.

RUDY
TRISTAR. October, 1993. (David Anspaugh), Sean Astin, Charles S. Dutton, Ned Beatty.

RUDYARD KIPLING'S THE JUNGLE BOOK
BUEN VISTA. December, 1995. (Stephen Sommers), Jason Scott Lee, Cary Elwes, Lena Headey, Sam Neill.

RUN
BUENA VISTA. Feburary, 1991. (Geoff Burrowes), Patrick Dempsey, Kelly Preston, Ken Pogue.

RUN OF THE COUNTRY, THE
COLUMBIA. September, 1995. British. (Peter Yates), Albert Finney, Matt Keeslar, Victoria Smurfit.

RUN OF THE HOUSE
ZOO PRODS. LTD. May, 1992. (James M. Felter), Alan Edwards, Lisa-Marie Felter, Harry A. Winter.

RUNESTONE, THE
HYPERION PICTURES. February, 1992. (Willard Carroll), Peter Riegert, Joan Severance, Alexander Gudonov.

RUSH
MGM. December, 1991. (Lili Fini Zanuck), Jason Patric, Jennifer Jason Leigh, Sam Elliott.

RUSSIA HOUSE, THE
MGM. December, 1990. (Fred Schepisi), Sean Connery, Michelle Pfeiffer, Roy Scheider.

SAFE
SONY CLASSICS. (R) June, 1995. (Todd Haynes), Julianne Moore, Xander Berkeley, Peter Friedman.

SAFE PASSAGE
NEW LINE. (PG-13) December, 1994. (Robert Allan Ackerman), Susan Sarandon, Sam Shepard, Robert Sean Leonard.

SAINT OF FORT WASHINGTON, THE
WARNER BROS. November, 1993. (Tim Hunter), Matt Dillon, Danny Glover, Rick Aviles.

SALMONBERRIES
ROXIE. March, 1994. German. (Percy Adlon), K.D. Lang, Rosel Zech, Chuck Connors.

SAMANTHA
ACADEMY ENT. November, 1992. (Stephen La Rocque), Martha Plimpton, Dermot Mulroney, Hector Elizondo.

SAMBA TRAORE
NEW YORKER. September, 1993. Burkina Faso. (Idrissa Ouedraogo), Bakary Sangare, Mariam Kaba.

SANDLOT, THE
20TH CENTURY FOX. April, 1993. (David Mickey Evans), Tom Guiry, Mike Vitar, Karen Allen, James Earl Jones.

SANKOFA
MYPHEDUH. April, 1994. German-Ghanian-Burkina Faso-U.S. (Haile Gerima), Oyafunmike Ogunlano.

SANTA CLAUSE, THE
BUENA VISTA. November, 1994. (John Pasquin), Tim Allen, Judge Reinhold, Wendy Crewson.

SARAFINA!
BUENA VISTA. September, 1992. French-British-South African. (Darrell James Roodt), Leleti Khumalo, Whoopi Goldberg, Miriam Makeba.

SATAN
RUSSIMPEX. June, 1992. Russian. (Viktor Aristov), Sergei Kuprianov, Svetlana Bragarnik, Veniamin Malotschevski.

SATIN SLIPPER, THE
CANNON GROUP. September, 1994. French-Portuguese. (Manoel de Oliveira), Luis Miguel Cintra, Anne Consigny, Patricia Barzyk.

SAVAGE NIGHTS
GRAMERCY. February, 1994. French-Italian. (Cyril Collard), Cyril Collard, Romane Bohringer, Carlos Lopez.

SAVE AND PROTECT
INT'L. FILM CIRCUIT. July, 1992. Russian. (Aleksandr Sokurov), Cecile Zervudacki, Robert Vaab.

SCANNERS II: THE NEW ORDER
TRITON. June, 1991. Canadian. (Christian Duguay, David Hewlett), Yvan Ponton, Deborah Raffin.

SCENES FROM A MALL
BUENA VISTA. February, 1991. (Paul Mazursky), Bette Midler, Woody Allen.

SCENT OF A WOMAN
UNIVERSAL. December, 1992. (Martin Brest), Al Pacino, Chris O'Donnell, James Rebhorn.

SCENT OF GREEN PAPAYA, THE
FIRST LOOK. January, 1994. Vietnamese. (Tran Anh Hung), Tran Nu Yen Khe, Lu Man San, Truong Thi Loc.

SCHINDLER'S LIST
UNIVERSAL. December, 1993. (Steven Spielberg), Liam Neeson, Ben Kingsley, Ralph Fiennes. B&W.

SCHOOL TIES
PARAMOUNT. September, 1992. (Robert Mandel), Brendan Fraser, Matt Damon, Andrew Lowery, Chris O'Donnell.

SCISSORS
DDM FILM CORP. March, 1991. (Frank De Felitta), Sharon Stone, Steve Railsback, Ronny Cox.

SCOUT, THE
20TH CENTURY FOX. September, 1994. (Michael Ritchie), Albert Brooks, Brendan Fraser, Dianne Wiest.

SEARCH AND DESTROY
OCTOBER. April, 1995. (David Salle), Griffin Dunne, Illeana Douglas, Christopher Walken.

SEARCH FOR SIGNS OF INTELLIGENT LIFE IN THE UNIVERSE, THE
ORION CLASSICS. September, 1991. (John Gailey), Lily Tomlin.

SEARCHING FOR BOBBY FISCHER
PARAMOUNT. August, 1993. (Steven Zaillian), Max Pomeranc, Joe Mantegna, Ben Kingsley, Joan Allen.

SECOND BEST
WARNER BROS. September, 1994. British. (Chris Menges), William Hurt, Chris Cleary Miles, Keith Allen.

SECOND CIRCLE, THE
INT'L. FILM CIRCUIT. January, 1992. CIS. (Alexander Sokurov).

SECRET ADVENTURES OF TOM THUMB, THE
ZEITGEIST. April, 1994. British-French. (Dave Borthwick), Animation.

SECRET FRIENDS
BRIARPATCH. February, 1992. British. (Dennis Potter), Alan Bates, Gina Bellman, Frances Barber.

SECRET GARDEN, THE
WARNER BROS. August, 1993. (Agnieszka Holland), Kate Maberly, Heydon Prowse, Maggie Smith.

SECRET RAPTURE, THE
CASTLE HILL. April, 1994. British. (Howard Davies), Juliet Stevenson, Joanne Whalley Kilmer, Penelope Whilton.

SECUESTRO: A STORY OF A KIDNAPPING
INDEPENDENT. January, 1994. Colombian-Spanish. (Camila Motta), Documentary.

SEPARATE LIVES
TRIMARK. (R) September, 1995. (David Madden), James Belushi, Linda Hamilton, Vera Miles.

SERIAL MOM
SAVOY. April, 1994. (John Waters), Kathleen Turner, Sam Waterston, Ricki Lake, Mink Stole.

SEVEN
NEW LINE CINEMA. (R) September, 1995. (David Fincher), Morgan Freeman, Brad Pitt, Gwyneth Paltrow.

SEVENTH COIN, THE
HEMDALE. September, 1993. Israeli. (Dror Soref), Peter O'Toole, Navin Chowdhry, Alexandra Powers.

SEX AND ZEN
GOLDEN HARVEST. August, 1993. Hong Kong. (Michael Mak), Amy Yip, Isabella Chow, Lawrence Ng.

SEX, DRUGS AND DEMOCRACY
RED HAT PRODS. February, 1995. (Jonathan Blank), Documentary.

SEX, DRUGS, ROCK & ROLL
AVENUE. September, 1991. (John McNaughton), Eric Bogosian.

SEX IS
OUTSIDER PRODS. May, 1993. (Marc Huestis), Documentary.

SEX OF THE STARS, THE
FIRST RUN FEATURES. October, 1994. Canadian. (Paule Baillargeon), Denis Mercier, Marianne Coquelicot Mercier.

S.F.W.
GRAMERCY. (R) January, 1995. (Jefery Levy), Stephen Dorff, Reese Witherspoon, Jack Noseworthy.

SHADOW, THE
UNIVERSAL. July, 1994. (Russell Mulcahy), Alec Baldwin, John Lone, Penelope Ann Miller.

SHADOW OF ANGELS
ALBATROS/ARTCOFILM. March, 1992. German. (Daniel Schmid), Ingrid Craven, Rainer Werner Fassbinder.

SHADOW OF CHINA
NEW LINE CINEMA. March, 1991. Japanese. (Mitsuo Yanagimachi), John Lone, Koichi Sato, Sammi Davis.

SHADOW OF THE WOLF
TRIUMPH. March, 1993. French-Canadian. (Jacques Dorfmann), Lou Diamond Phillips, Toshiro Mifune.

SHADOWLANDS
SAVOY. December, 1993. British. (Richard Attenborough), Anthony Hopkins, Debra Winger.

SHADOWS AND FOG
ORION. March, 1992. (Woody Allen), Woody Allen, Mia Farrow, John Cusack, Lily Tomlin. B & W.

SHADOWZONE
JGM ENTERPRISES. January, 1990. (J.S. Cardone), Louise Fletcher, David Beecroft.

SHAKES THE CLOWN
I.R.S. March, 1992. (Bobcat Goldthwait), Bobcat Goldthwait, Julie Brown, Paul Dooley.

SHAKING THE TREE
CASTLE HILL. January, 1992. (Duane Clark), Arye Gross, Gale Hansen, Courteney Cox.

SHAKMA
QUEST ENT. October, 1990. (Hugh Parks, Tom Logan), Christopher Atkins, Amanda Wyss, Roddy McDowall.

SHALLOW GRAVE
GRAMERCY. (R) February, 1995. Scottish. (Danny Boyle), Kerry Fox, Christopher Eccleston, Ewan McGregor.

SHATTERED
MGM. October, 1991. (Wolfgang Petersen), Tom Berenger, Bob Hoskins, Greta Scacchi.

SHAWSHANK REDEMPTION, THE
COLUMBIA. September, 1994. (Frank Darabont), Tim Robbins, Morgan Freeman, Bob Gunton.

SHE'S BEEN AWAY
BBC. December, 1990. British. (Peter Hall), Peggy Ashcroft, James Fox, Geraldine James.

SHE LIVES TO RIDE
ARTISTIC LICENSE. July, 1995. (Alice Stone), Documentary.

SHELTERING SKY, THE
WARNER BROS. December, 1990. British-Italian. (Bernardo Bertolucci), Debra Winger, John Malkovich, Campbell Scott.

SHINING THROUGH
20TH CENTURY FOX. January, 1992. (David Seltzer), Michael Douglas, Melanie Griffith, Liam Neeson.

SHIPWRECKED
BUENA VISTA. March, 1991. Norwegian. (Nils Gaup), Stian Smestad, Gabriel Byrne, Louisa Haigh.

SHOCK TO THE SYSTEM, A
CORSAIR PICTURES. March, 1990. (Jan Egleson), Michael Caine, Elizabeth McGovern, Swoosie Kurtz.

SHORT CUTS
FINE LINE. October, 1993. (Robert Altman), Matthew Modine, Jack Lemmon, Lily Tomlin, Tim Robbins.

SHORT TIME
20TH CENTURY FOX. May, 1990. (Gregg Champion), Dabney Coleman, Matt Frewer, Teri Garr.

SHOUT
UNIVERSAL. October, 1991. (Jeffrey Hornaday), James Walters, John Travolta, Heather Graham.

SHOW, THE
SAVOY. (R) August, 1995. (Brian Robbins), Concert Documentary.

SHOW OF FORCE, A
PARAMOUNT. May, 1990. (Bruno Barreto), Amy Irving, Lou Diamond Phillips, Andy Garcia.

SHOWDOWN IN LITTLE TOKYO
WARNER BROS. August, 1991. (Mark L. Lester), Dolph Lundgren, Brandon Lee, Tia Carrere.

SHOWGIRLS
MGM/UA. September, 1995. (Paul Verhoeven), Elizabeth Berkley, Kyle MacLachlan, Gina Gershon.

SIBLING RIVALRY
COLUMBIA. October, 1990. (Carl Reiner), Kirstie Alley, Bill Pullman, Carrie Fisher, Scott Bakula.

SIDE OUT
TRISTAR. March, 1990. (Peter Israelson), C. Thomas Howell, Peter Horton, Courtney Thorne Smith.

SIDEKICKS
TRIUMPH. April, 1993. (Aaron Norris), Jonathan Brandis, Chuck Norris, Beau Bridges.

SILENCE = DEATH
FIRST RUN FEATURES. May, 1990. W. German. (Rosa von Praunheim), Documentary.

SILENCE OF THE LAMBS, THE
ORION. February, 1991. (Jonathan Demme), Jodie Foster, Anthony Hopkins, Scott Glenn, Ted Levine.

SILENT FALL
WARNER BROS. October, 1994. (Bruce Beresford), Richard Dreyfuss, Linda Hamilton, John Lithgow.

SILENT TONGUE
TRIMARK. February, 1994. (Sam Shepard), Richard Harris, Alan Bates, River Phoenix, Dermot Mulroney.

SILENT TOUCH, THE
CASTLE HILL. November, 1993. British-Polish-Danish. (Krzysztof Zanussi), Max von Sydow, Lothaire Bluteau.

SILK ROAD, THE
TRIMARK. January, 1992. Japanese. 1988. (Junya Sato), Koichi Sato, Toshiyuki Nishida.

SILVERLAKE LIFE: THE VIEW FROM HERE
ZEITGEIST. March, 1993. (Tom Joslin, Peter Friedman), Documentary.

SIMPLE MEN
FINE LINE FEATURES. October, 1992. (Hal Hartley), Robert Burke, William Sage, Karen Sillas.

SIMPLE TWIST OF FATE, A
BUENA VISTA. September, 1994. (Gillies MacKinnon), Steve Martin, Gabriel Byrne, Catherine O'Hara.

SINGLE WHITE FEMALE
COLUMBIA. August, 1992. (Barbet Schroeder), Bridget Fonda, Jennifer Jason Leigh, Steven Weber.

SINGLES
WARNER BROS. September, 1992. (Cameron Crowe), Campbell Scott, Bridget Fonda, Kyra Sedgwick, Matt Dillon.

SIOUX CITY
I.R.S. (PG-13) September, 1994. (Lou Diamond Phillips), Lou Diamond Phillips, Salli Richardson, Melinda Dillon.

SIRENS
MIRAMAX. March, 1994. Australian-British. (John Duigan), Tara Fitzgerald, Hugh Grant, Elle McPherson.

SISTER ACT
BUENA VISTA. May, 1992. (Emile Ardolino), Whoopi Goldberg, Maggie Smith, Harvey Keitel, Kathy Najimy.

SISTER ACT 2: BACK IN THE HABIT
BUENA VISTA. December, 1993. (Bill Duke), Whoopi Goldberg, Kathy Najimy, Barnard Hughes.

SISTER MY SISTER
7TH ART. June, 1995. British. (Nancy Meckler), Julie Walters, Joely Richardson, Jodhi May.

SIX DEGREES OF SEPARATION
MGM. December, 1993. (Fred Schepisi), Stockard Channing, Will Smith, Donald Sutherland.

SKI PATROL
TRIUMPH. January, 1990. (Richard Correll), Roger Rose, T. K. Carter, Martin Mull.

SKI SCHOOL
MOVIESTORE ENT. January, 1991. Canadian. (Damian Lee), Dean Cameron, Tom Breznahan, Patrick Labyorteaux.

SLACKER
ORION CLASSICS. July, 1991. (Richard Linklater), Richard Linklater, Rudy Basquez.

SLEAZY UNCLE, THE
QUARTET. February, 1991. Italian. (Franco Brusati), Vittorio Gassman, Giancarlo Giannini, Andrea Ferreol.

SLEEP WITH ME
MGM/UA. September, 1994. (Rory Kelly), Eric Stoltz, Meg Tilly, Craig Sheffer, Adrienne Shelly.

SLEEPING CAR, THE
TRIAX ENT. February, 1990. (Douglas Curtis), David Naughton, Judie Aronson.

SLEEPING WITH THE ENEMY
20TH CENTURY FOX. February, 1991. (Joseph Ruben), Julia Roberts, Patrick Bergin, Kevin Anderson.

SLEEPLESS IN SEATTLE
TRISTAR. June, 1993. (Nora Ephron), Tom Hanks, Meg Ryan, Ross Malinger, Rosie O'Donnell.

SLINGSHOT, THE
SONY CLASSICS. June, 1994. Swedish. (Ake Sandgren), Jesper Salen, Stellan Skarsgard, Basia Frydman.

SLIVER
PARAMOUNT. May, 1993. (Phillip Noyce), Sharon Stone, William Baldwin, Tom Berenger.

SLUMBER PARTY MASSACRE III
CONCORDE. September, 1990. (Sally Mattison), Keely Christian, Brittain Frye.

SMALL TIME
PANORAMA. November, 1991. (Norman Loftis), Richard Barboza, Carolyn Kinebrew, Scott Ferguson.

SMOKE
MIRAMAX. (R) June, 1995. (Wayne Wang), Harvey Keitel, William Hurt, Forest Whitaker.

SNAPPER, THE
MIRAMAX. November, 1993. British. (Stephen Frears), Colm Meaney, Tina Kellegher, Ruth McCabe.

SNEAKERS
UNIVERSAL. September, 1992. (Phil Alden Robinson), Robert Redford, Sidney Poitier, River Phoenix.

SNIPER
TRISTAR. January, 1993. (Luis Llosa), Tom Berenger, Billy Zane, J. T. Walsh.

SO I MARRIED AN AXE MURDERER
TRISTAR. July, 1993. (Thomas Schlamme), Mike Myers, Nancy Travis, Anthony LaPaglia.

SOAPDISH
PARAMOUNT. June, 1991. (Michael Hoffman), Sally Field, Kevin Kline, Robert Downey Jr., Whoopi Goldberg.

SOCIETY
ZECCA CORP. February, 1992. (Brian Yuzna), Bill Warlock, Connie Danese, Ben Slack.

SOFIE
ARROW. May, 1993. Danish, 1993. (Liv Ullmann), Karen Lise Mynster, Ghita Norby, Erland Josephson.

SOLOVKI POWER
MOSFILM. January, 1991. Soviet. (Marina Goldovskaya), Documentary.

SOMETHING TO TALK ABOUT
WARNER BROS. August, 1995. (Lasse Hallstrom), Julia Roberts, Dennis Quaid, Robert Duvall, Kyra Sedgwick.

SOMETHING TO DO WITH THE WALL
FIRST RUN FEATURES. February, 1991. (Marilyn Levine, Ross McElwee), Documentary.

SOMMERSBY
WARNER BROS. February, 1993. (Jon Amiel), Richard Gere, Jodie Foster, Bill Pullman.

SON–IN–LAW
BUENA VISTA. July, 1993. (Steve Rash), Pauly Shore, Carla Gugino, Lane Smith.

SON OF THE PINK PANTHER
MGM. August, 1993. (Blake Edwards), Robert Benigni, Herbert Lom, Claudia Cardinale.

SON OF THE SHARK
7TH ARTS. March, 1995. French-Belgian. (Agnes Merlet), Ludovic Vandendaele, Erick DaSilva, Sandrine Blancke.

SONNY BOY
TRIUMPH. October, 1990. (Robert Martin Caroll), David Carradine, Brad Dourif, Paul L. Smith.

SOULTAKER
ACTION INT'L. PICTURES. October, 1990. (Michael Rissi), Joe Estevez, Vivian Schilling.

SOUTH CENTRAL
WARNER BROS. September, 1992. (Steve Anderson), Glenn Plummer, Byron Keith Minns, Lexie D. Bigham.

SPACE AVENGER
MANLEY PRODS. May, 1990. (Richard W. Haines), Robert Prichard, Mike McCleric.

SPACE IS THE PLACE
RHAPSODY. September, 1993. (John Coney), Sun Ra.

SPACED INVADERS
BUENA VISTA. April, 1990. (Patrick Read Johnson), Douglas Barr, Royal Dano, Ariana Richards.

SPANKING THE MONKEY
FINE LINE. July, 1994. (David O. Russell), Jeremy Davies, Alberta Watson, Carla Gallo.

SPEAKING PARTS
ZEITGEIST. February, 1990. Canadian (Atom Egoyan), Michael McManus, Arsinee Khanjian.

SPECIALIST, THE
WARNER BROS. October, 1994. (Luis Llosa), Sylvester Stallone, Sharon Stone, James Woods, Eric Roberts.

SPECIES
MGM/UA. July, 1995. (Roger Donaldson), Ben Kingsley, Michael Madsen, Alfred Molina, Forrest Whitaker.

SPEECHLESS
MGM. December, 1994. (Ron Underwood), Michael Keaton, Geena Davis, Christopher Reeve, Bonnie Bedelia.

SPEED
20TH CENTURY FOX. June, 1994. (Jan De Bont), Keanu Reeves, Dennis Hopper, Sandra Bullock.

SPIRIT OF 76, THE
COLUMBIA. October, 1990. (Lucas Reiner), David Cassidy, Olivia D'Abo, Geoff Hoyle.

SPLIT
JANE BALFOUR. September, 1993. (Andrew Weeks, Ellen Fisher Turk), Documentary.

SPLIT SECOND
INTERSTAR. May, 1992. British. (Tony Maylam), Rutger Hauer, Kim Cattrall, Michael J. Pollard.

SPONTANEOUS COMBUSTION
TAURUS ENTERTAINMENT. February, 1990. (Tobe Hooper), Brad Dourif, Cynthia Bain.

SQUANTO: A WARRIOR'S TALE
BUENA VISTA. October, 1994. (Xavier Koller), Adam Beach, Sheldon Peters Wolfchild, Eric Schweig.

STAGES
PAUL THOMPSON FILMS. November, 1990. (Randy Thompson), Ron Reid, Dan Lishner.

STANLEY & IRIS
MGM/UA. February, 1990. (Martin Ritt), Jane Fonda, Robert De Niro, Swoosie Kurtz.

STAR TIME
NORTHERN ARTS. April, 1993. (Alexander Cassini), John P. Ryan, Michael St. Gerard, Maureen Teefy.

STAR TREK GENERATIONS
PARAMOUNT. November, 1994. (David Carson), Patrick Stewart, Malcolm McDowell, William Shatner.

STAR TREK VI:
THE UNDISCOVERED COUNTRY
PARAMOUNT. December, 1991. (Nicholas Meyer), William Shatner, Leonard Nimoy, Christopher Plummer.

STARGATE
MGM. October, 1994. (Roland Emmerich), Kurt Russell, James Spader, Jaye Davidson, Viveca Lindfors.

STARS FELL ON HENRIETTA, THE
WARNER BROS. September, 1995. (James Keach), Robert Duvall, Aidan Quinn, Frances Fisher.

STARTING PLACE
INTERAMA. April, 1995. French-Vietnamese. (Robert Kramer), Documentary.

STATE OF GRACE
ORION. September, 1990. (Phil Joanou), Sean Penn, Ed Harris, Gary Oldman, Robin Wright.

STATION, THE
ARIES. January, 1992. Italian. (Sergio Rubini), Sergio Rubini, Margherita Buy, Ennio Fantastichini.

STAY TUNED
WARNER BROS. August, 1992. (Peter Hyams), John Ritter, Pam Dawber, Jeffrey Jones.

STEAL AMERICA
TARA RELEASING. April, 1992. (Lucy Phillips), Clara Bellino, Charlie Homo, Diviana Ingravallo.

STEEL & LACE
FRIES/PARAGON ARTS. November, 1990. (Ernest Farino), Clare Wren, Bruce Davison, David Naughton.

STEAL BIG, STEAL LITTLE
SAVOY. (PG-13), September, 1995. (Andrew Davis), Andy Garcia, Rachel Ticotin, Alan Arkin.

STEFANO QUANTESTORIE
ITALTOONS. November, 1994. Italian. (Maurizio Nichetti), Maurizio Nichetti, James Spencer Thierree.

STELLA
BUENA VISTA. February, 1990. (John Erman), Bette Midler, Trini Alvarado, John Goodman, Stephen Collins.

STEPHEN KING'S GRAVEYARD SHIFT
PARAMOUNT. October, 1990. (Ralph S. Singleton), David Andrews, Stephen Macht, Brad Dourif.

STEPHEN KING'S SLEEPWALKERS
COLUMBIA. April, 1992. (Mick Garris), Brian Krause, Alice Krige, Mädchen Amick.

STEPPING OUT
PARAMOUNT. October, 1991. (Lewis Gilbert), Liza Minnelli, Shelley Winters, Ellen Greene, Bill Irwin.

STONE COLD
COLUMBIA. May, 1991. (Craig R. Baxley), Brian Bosworth, Lance Henriksen, William Forsythe.

STOP! OR MY MOM WILL SHOOT
UNIVERSAL. February, 1992. (Roger Spottiswoode), Sylvester Stallone, Estelle Getty, JoBeth Williams.

STORY OF BOYS AND GIRLS, THE
ARIES. August, 1991. Italian. (Pupi Avati), Felice Andreasi, Angiola Baggi, Davide Bechini.

STORY OF QIU JU, THE
SONY CLASSICS. April, 1993. Chinese-Mandarin. (Zhang Yimou), Gong Li, Lei Lao Sheng, Liu Pei Qi.

STORYVILLE
20TH CENTURY FOX. August, 1992. (Mark Frost), James Spader, Jason Robards, Joanne Whalley Kilmer.

STRAIGHT OUT OF BROOKLYN
SAMUEL GOLDWYN CO. May, 1991. (Matty Rich), George T. Odom, Lawrence Gilliard Jr.

STRAIGHT TALK
BUENA VISTA. April, 1992. (Barnet Kellman), Dolly Parton, James Woods, Griffin Dunne.

STRAND: UNDER THE DARK CLOTH
KINO. December, 1991. Canadian. (John Walker), Documentary.

STRANGER, THE
NATL. FILM DEVELOPMENT. May, 1992. Indian. (Satyajit Ray), Deepankar De, Mamata Shankar, Utpal Dutt.

STRANGER AMONG US, A
BUENA VISTA. July, 1992. (Sidney Lumet), Melanie Griffith, Eric Thal, John Pankow.

STRANGERS IN GOOD COMPANY
FIRST RUN/CASTLE HILL. May, 1991. Canadian. (Cynthia Scott), Alice Diabo, Constance Garneau.

STRAPLESS
MIRAMAX. May, 1990. British. (David Hare), Blair Brown, Bruno Ganz, Bridget Fonda.

STRAWBERRY AND CHOCOLATE
MIRAMAX. January, 1995. Cuban. (Tomas Guiteerz Alea), Juan Carlos Tabio, Jorge Perugorria, Vladimir Cruz.

STREET ASYLUM
ORIGINAL CINEMA. April, 1990. (Greggory Brown), Wings Hauser, Alex Cord, G. Gordon Liddy.

STREET FIGHTER
UNIVERSAL. December, 1994. (Steven E. de Souza), Jean Claude Van Damme, Raul Julia, Ming-Na Wen.

STREET HUNTER
CDGP/21ST CENTURY FILMS. November, 1990. (John A. Gallagher), Steve James, Reb Brown, John Legiuzamo.

STREET KNIGHT
CANNON. March, 1993. (Albert Magnoli), Jeff Speakman, Christopher Neame, Lewis Van Bergen.

STREET OF NO RETURN
THUNDER FILMS. August, 1991. French-Portuguese. (Samuel Fuller), Keith Carradine, Valentina Vargas, Bill Duke.

STREET SOLDIERS
ACADEMY ENTERTAINMENT. March, 1991. (Lee Harry), Jun Chong, Jeff Rector.

STREETS
CONCORDE. January, 1990. (Katt Shea Ruben), Christina Applegate, David Mendenhall, Kay Lenz.

STRICTLY BALLROOM
MIRAMAX. February, 1993. Australian. (Baz Luhrmann), Paul Mercurio, Tara Morice, Bill Hunter.

STRICTLY BUSINESS
WARNER BROS. November, 1991. (Kevin Hooks), Tommy Davidson, Halle Berry, Joseph C. Phillips.

STRICTLY PROPAGANDA
FIRST RUN. October, 1993. German. (Wolfgang Kissel), Documentary.

STRIKE IT RICH
MILLIMETER. January, 1990. British. (James Scott), Robert Lindsay, Molly Ringwald, John Gielgud.

STRIKING DISTANCE
COLUMBIA. September, 1993. (Rowdy Herrington), Bruce Willis, Sarah Jessica Parker, Dennis Farina.

STRIP JACK NAKED
FRAMELINE. June, 1991. British. (Ron Peck), Documentary.

STUART SAVES HIS FAMILY
PARAMOUNT. April, 1995. (Harold Ramis), Al Franken, Laura San Giacomo, Vincent D'Onofrio.

SUBURBAN COMMANDO
NEW LINE CINEMA. October, 1991. (Burt Kennedy), Hulk Hogan, Christopher Lloyd, Shelley Duvall.

SUGAR HILL
20TH CENTURY FOX. February, 1994. (Leon Ichaso), Wesley Snipes, Michael Wright, Theresa Randle.

SUM OF US, THE
GOLDWYN. March, 1995. Australian. (Kevin Dowling), Geoff Burton), Jack Thompson, Russell Crowe, John Polson.

SUMMER HOUSE, THE
GOLDWYN. December, 1993. British. (Waris Hussein), Jeanne Moreau, Joan Plowright, Julie Walters.

SUMMER VACATION: 1999
NEW YORKER. March, 1990. Japanese. (Shusuke Kaneko), Eri Miyajima, Temeke Otakara.

SUNDAY'S CHILDREN
CASTLE HILL. April, 1994. Swedish. (Daniel Bergman), Henrik Linnos, Thommy Berggen, Lena Enare.

SUPER, THE
20TH CENTURY FOX. October, 1991. (Rod Daniel), Joe Pesci, Vincent Gardenia, Madolyn Smith Osborne.

SUPER 8 1/2
STRAND. March, 1995. Canadian. (Bruce La Bruce), Bruce La Bruce, Liza LaMonica, Chris Teen.

SUPER MARIO BROS.
BUENA VISTA. May, 1993. (Rocky Morton, Annabel Jankel), Bob Hoskins, John Leguizamo, Dennis Hopper.

SUPERSTAR: THE LIFE AND TIMES OF ANDY WARHOL
ARIES FILMS. February, 1991. (Chuck Workman), Documentary.

SURE FIRE
STRAND. October, 1993. (Jon Jost), Tom Blair, Robert Ernst, Kristi Hager.

SURF NINJAS
NEW LINE CINEMA. August, 1993. (Neal Israel), Ernie Reyes Jr., Rob Schneider, Leslie Nielsen.

SURVIVING THE GAME
NEW LINE CINEMA. April, 1994. (Ernest Dickerson), Ice T, Rutger Hauer, Gary Busey, F. Murray Abraham.

SUTURE
GOLDWYN. March, 1994. (Scott McGehee, David Siegel), Dennis Haysbert, Mel Harris, Sab Shimono. B&W.

SWAN LAKE–THE ZONE
ZEITGEIST. September, 1991. Soviet-Swedish-Canadian-U.S. (Yuri Illienko), Viktor Solovyov.

THE SWAN PRINCESS
NEW LINE CINEMA. (G) November, 1994. (Richard Rich), Animated.

SWEET TALKER
7 ARTS/NEW LINE CINEMA. May, 1991. Australian. (Michael Jenkins), Bryan Brown, Karen Allen, Bill Kerr.

SWEETIE
AVENUE. January, 1990. Australian. (Jane Campion), Genevieve Lemon, Karen Colston.

SWIMMING WITH SHARKS
TRIMARK. (R) April, 1995. (George Huang), Kevin Spacey, Frank Whaley, Michelle Forbes.

SWING KIDS
BUENA VISTA. March, 1993. (Thomas Carter), Robert Sean Leonard, Christian Bale, Frank Whaley.

SWITCH
WARNER BROS. May, 1991. (Blake Edwards), Ellen Barkin, Jimmy Smits, JoBeth Williams.

SWOON
FINE LINE FEATURES. September, 1992. (Tom Kalin), Daniel Schlachet, Craig Chester, Ron Vawter. B&W.

T

TAIGA
NEW YORKER. March, 1993. Mongolian. (Ulrike Ottinger). Documentary.

TAKING OF BEVERLY HILLS, THE
COLUMBIA. October, 1991. (Sidney J. Furie), Ken Wahl, Matt Frewer, Harley Jane Kozak.

TAKING CARE OF BUSINESS
BUENA VISTA. August, 1990. (Arthur Hiller), James Belushi, Charles Grodin, Anne DeSalvo.

TALE OF SPRINGTIME, A
ORION CLASSICS. July, 1992. French. (Eric Rohmer), Anne Teyssedre, Hugues Quester, Florence Darel.

TALE OF THE WIND, A
CAPI FILMS. January, 1991. Dutch-French. (Joris Ivens, Marceline Loridan), Joris Ivens, Han Zenxiang.

TALE OF WINTER, A
MK2. April, 1994. French. (Eric Rohmer), Charlotte Very, F. Van Dren Driessche, Michel Voletti.

TALENT FOR THE GAME
PARAMOUNT. April, 1991. (Robert M. Young), Edward James Olmos, Lorraine Bracco, Jeff Corbett.

TALES FROM THE CRYPT PRESENTS DEMON KNIGHT
UNIVERSAL. January, 1995. (Ernest Dickerson), Billy Zane, William Sadler, Jada Pinkett, Brenda Bakke.

TALES FROM THE DARKSIDE: THE MOVIE
PARAMOUNT. May, 1990. (John Harrison), Christian Slater, Rae Dawn Chong, Deborah Harry.

TALES FROM THE HOOD
SAVOY. (R) May, 1995. (Rusty Cundieff), Clarence Williams III, Joe Torry, Wings Hauser, Corbin Bernsen.

TALKING TO STRANGERS
BALTIMORE. December, 1991. (Rob Tregenza), Ken Gruz, Marvin Hunter, Dennis Hunter.

TALKIN' DIRTY AFTER DARK
NEW LINE CINEMA. August, 1991. (Topper Carew), Martin Lawrence, Jedda James, Mark Curry.

TALL GUY, THE
MIRAMAX. September, 1990. British. (Mel Smith), Jeff Goldblum, Emma Thompson, Rowan Atkinson.

TALL TALE
BUENA VISTA. March, 1995. (Jeremiah Chechik), Nick Stahl, Patrick Swayze, Scott Glenn, Oliver Platt.

TANGO PLAYER, THE
DEFA STUDIOS. November, 1993. German. (Roland Graf), Michael Gwisdek, Corinna Harfouch.

TANK GIRL
MGM/UA. March, 1995. (Rachel Talalay), Lori Petty, Malcolm McDowell, Ice-T, Naomi Watts.

TATIE DANIELLE
PRESTIGE. May, 1991. French. (Etienne Chatiliez), Tsilla Chelton, Catherine Jacob, Isabelle Nanty.

TAXI BLUES
MK2. January, 1991. Soviet-French. (Pavel Lounguine), Piotr Mamonov, Piotr Zaitchenko.

TED & VENUS
DOUBLE HELIX. December, 1991. (Bud Cort), Bud Cort, Jim Brolin, Kim Adams, Carol Kane.

TEENAGE MUTANT NINJA TURTLES
NEW LINE CINEMA. March, 1990. (Steve Barron), Judith Hoag, Elias Koteas.

TEENAGE MUTANT NINJA TURTLES II: THE SECRET OF THE OOZE
NEW LINE CINEMA. March, 1991. (Michael Pressman), Paige Turco, David Warner, Michelan Sisti.

TEENAGE MUTANT NINJA TURTLES III
NEW LINE CINEMA. March, 1993. (Stuart Gillard), Elias Koteas, Paige Turco, Sab Shimono.

TEMP, THE
PARAMOUNT. February, 1993. (Tom Holland), Timothy Hutton, Lara Flynn Boyle, Faye Dunaway.

TEMPTATION OF A MONK
NORTHERN ARTS. December, 1994. Chinese. (Clara Law), Joan Chen, Wu Hsinkuo, Zhang Fengyi.

TEREZIN DIARY
FIRST RUN FEATURES. June, 1991. (Dan Weissman), Documentary.

TERMINAL BLISS
CANNON. March, 1992. (Jordan Alan), Timothy Owen, Luke Perry, Estee Chandler.

TERMINAL CITY RICOCHET
FESTIVAL FILMS. February, 1991. Canadian. (Zale Dalen), Peter Breck, Jello Biafra.

TERMINAL VELOCITY
BUENA VISTA. September, 1994. (Deran Serafian), Charlie Sheen, Nastassja Kinski, James Gandolfini.

TERMINATOR 2: JUDGMENT DAY
TRISTAR. July, 1991. (James Cameron), Arnold Schwarzenegger, Linda Hamilton, Robert Patrick.

TERMINI STATION
NORTHERN ARTS. May, 1991. Canadian. (Allan King), Colleen Dewhurst, Megan Follows, Gordon Clapp.

TERRITORY, THE
INT'L FILM CIRCUIT. August, 1990. French. (Raul Ruiz), Isabelle Weingarten, Rebecca Pauly.

TERROR 2000
LEISURE TIME. November, 1994. German. (Christoph Schlingensief), Peter Kern, Margit Carstensen, Udo Kier.

TERROR WITHIN II, THE
CONCORDE. January, 1991. (Andrew Stevens), Andrew Stevens, Stella Stevens, Chick Vennera.

TETSUO: THE IRON MAN
ORIGINAL CINEMA. April, 1992. Japanese, 1989. (Shinya Tsukamoto), Tomoroh Taguchi, Nobu Kanaoko, Shinya Tsukamoto.

TEXAS TENOR: THE ILLINOIS JACQUET STORY
RHAPSODY FILMS. November, 1992. (Arthur Elgort), Documentary.

TEXASVILLE
COLUMBIA. September, 1990. (Peter Bogdanovich), Jeff Bridges, Cybill Shepherd, Timothy Bottoms.

THANK YOU AND GOODNIGHT!
ARIES FILMS. January, 1992. (Jan Oxenberg), Documentary.

THAT NIGHT
WARNER BROS. August, 1993. (Craig Bolotin), C. Thomas Howell, Juliette Lewis, Eliza Duschku.

THAT'S ADEQUATE
SOUTH GATE ENTERTAINMENT. January, 1990. (Harry Hurwitz), Tony Randall, James Coco, Bruce Willis.

THAT'S ENTERTAINMENT! III
MGM. May, 1994. (Bud Friedgen, Michael J. Sheridan), Gene Kelly, Cyd Charisse, Lena Horne, Howard Keel.

THELMA AND LOUISE
MGM. May, 1991. (Ridley Scott), Susan Sarandon, Geena Davis, Harvey Keitel, Brad Pitt.

THERE GOES MY BABY
ORION. September, 1994. (Floyd Mutrux), Dermot Mulroney, Rick Schroder, Kelli Williams, Noah Wyle.

THERE GOES THE NEIGHBORHOOD
PARAMOUNT. November, 1992. (Bill Phillips), Jeff Daniels, Catherine O'Hara, Dabney Coleman.

THERE'S NOTHING OUT THERE
VALKHN FILM. January, 1992. (Rolfe Kanefsky), Craig Peck, Wendy Bednarz, Mark Collver.

THEREMIN: AN ELECTRONIC ODYSSEY
ORION CLASSICS. (PG-13) August, 1995. (Steven M. Martin), Documentary.

THIEVES QUARTET
HEADLINER. June, 1994. (Joe Chappelle), Phillip Van Lear, Joe Guastaferro, Michele Cole.

THING CALLED LOVE, THE
PARAMOUNT. August, 1993. (Peter Bogdanovich), River Phoenix, Samantha Mathis, Dermot Mulroney.

THINK BIG
CONCORDE. March, 1990. (Jon Turteltaub), Peter Paul, David Paul, Martin Mull.

THIRTY-TWO SHORT FILMS ABOUT GLENN GOULD
GOLDWYN. April, 1994. Canadian. (Francois Girard), Colm Feore, Katya Lada, Don McKellar.

35 UP
GOLDWYN. January, 1992. British. (Michael Apted), Documentary.

THIS BOY'S LIFE
WARNER BROS. April, 1993. (Michael Caton Jones), Robert De Niro, Ellen Barkin, Leonardo DiCaprio.

THIS IS MY LIFE
20TH CENTURY FOX. February, 1992. (Nora Ephron), Julie Kavner, Samantha Mathis, Dan Aykroyd.

3 A LA MODE
MIRAMAX. August, 1994. French. (Remy Duchemin), Jean Yanne, Ken Higelin, Florence Darel.

THREE MEN AND A LITTLE LADY
BUENA VISTA. November, 1990. (Emile Ardolino), Tom Selleck, Steve Guttenberg, Ted Danson.

THREE MUSKETEERS, THE
BUENA VISTA. November, 1993. (Stephen Herek), Kiefer Sutherland, Chris O'Donnell, Charlie Sheen.

3 NINJAS
BUENA VISTA. August, 1992. (Jon Turtletaub), Victor Wong, Michael Treanor, Max Elliott Slade.

3 NINJAS KICK BACK
TRISTAR. May, 1994. (Charles T. Kanganis), Victor Wong, Max Elliott Slade, Sean Fox.

3 NINJAS KNUCKLE UP
TRISTAR. March, 1995. (Simon S. Sheen), Victor Wong, Charles Napier, Michael Treanor, Max Elliot Slade.

THREE OF HEARTS
NEW LINE CINEMA. April, 1993. (Yurek Bogayevicz), William Baldwin, Kelly Lynch, Sherilyn Fenn.

THREESOME
TRISTAR. April, 1994. (Andrew Fleming), Stephen Baldwin, Lara Flynn Boyle, Josh Charles.

THROUGH THE OLIVE TREES
MIRAMAX. (G) February, 1995. Iranian. (Abbas Kiarostami), Tahereh Ladania, Mohamad Ali Kershavarz.

THROUGH THE WIRE
ORIGINAL CINEMA. April, 1990. (Nina Rosenblum), Documentary.

THUNDERHEART
TRISTAR. April, 1992. (Michael Apted), Val Kilmer, Sam Shepard, Graham Greene.

TIE-DIED: ROCK-AND-ROLL'S MOST DEADICATED FANS
I.S.A. (R) September, 1995. (Andrew Behar), Documentary.

TIE ME UP! TIE ME DOWN!
MIRAMAX. April, 1990. Spanish. (Pedro Almodovar), Victoria Abril, Antonio Banderas.

TIE THAT BINDS, THE
BUENA VISTA. September, 1995. (Wesley Strick), Daryl Hannah. Keith Carradine, Moira Kelly, Vincent Spano.

TIGRERO: A FILM THAT WAS NEVER MADE
ARROW. December, 1994. Finnish-German-Brazilian. (Mika Kaurismaki), Samuel Fuller, Jim Jarmusch.

TILAI
NEW YORKER. October, 1990. Burkina Faso. (Idrissa Ouedraogo), Rasmane Ouedraogo, Ina Cisse.

TIM BURTON'S THE NIGHTMARE BEFORE CHRISTMAS
BUENA VISTA. October, 1993. (Henry Selick), Stop-action animation.

TIME INDEFINITE
FIRST RUN FEATURES. May, 1993. (Ross McElwee) Documentary.

TIME OF THE GYPSIES
COLUMBIA. February, 1990. Serbo-Croatian. (Emir Kusturica), Davor Dujmovic, Bora Todorovic.

TIME WILL TELL
I.R.S. May, 1992. British. (Delcan Lowney), Documentary.

TIMEBOMB
MGM. September, 1991. (Avi Nesher), Michael Biehn, Patsy Kensit, Tracy Scoggins, Robert Culp.

TIMECOP
UNIVERSAL. September, 1994. (Peter Hyams), Jean Claude Van Damme, Mia Sara, Ron Silver.

TITO AND ME
KINO. August, 1993. Yugoslav-French. (Goran Markovic), Dimitrie Vojnov, Lozar Ristovski.

TO DIE FOR
COLUMBIA. September, 1995. (Gus Van Sant), Nicole Kidman, Matt Dillon, Joaquin Phoenix, Casey Affleck.

TO LIVE
SAMUEL GOLDWYN.November, 1994. Chinese. (Zhang Yimou), Ge You, Gong Li, Niu Ben.

TO RENDER A LIFE
AGEE FILM PROJ. November, 1992. (Ross Spears), Documentary.

TO SLEEP WITH ANGER
SAMUEL GOLDWYN CO. October, 1990. (Charles Burnett), Danny Glover, Paul Butler, Mary Alice.

TO WONG FOO, THANKS FOR EVERYTHING! JULIE NEWMAR
UNIVERSAL. September, 1995. (Beeban Kidron), Wesley Snipes, Patrick Swayze, John Leguizamo.

TOGETHER ALONE
FRAMELINE. September, 1992. (P.J. Castellaneta), Todd Stites, Terry Curry. B&W.

TOKYO DECADENCE
NORTHERN ARTS. April, 1993. Japanese. (Ryu Murakami), Miho Nikaido, Tenmei Kano, Yayoi Kusama.

TOM AND JERRY: THE MOVIE
MIRAMAX. July, 1993. (Phil Roman), Animated.

TOM & VIV
MIRAMAX. (R) December, 1994. British. (Brian Gilbert), Willem Dafoe, Miranda Richardson, Rosemary Murphy.

TOMBSTONE
BUENA VISTA. December, 1993. (George P. Cosmatos), Kurt Russell, Val Kilmer, Dana Delany, Michael Biehn.

TOMMY BOY
PARAMOUNT. March, 1995. (Peter Segal), Chris Farley, David Spade, Brian Dennehy, Bo Derek, Rob Lowe.

TOO BEAUTIFUL FOR YOU
ORION CLASSICS. March, 1990. French. (Bertrand Blier), Gérard Depardieu, Josiane Balasko, Carole Bouquet.

TOO MUCH SUN
NEW LINE CINEMA. January, 1991. (Robert Downey), Andrea Martin, Eric Idle, Robert Downey, Jr.

TOP DOG
MGM/UA. April, 1995. (Aaron Norris), Chuck Norris, Clyde Kusatsu, Michele Lamar Richards.

TORN APART
CASTLE HILL. April, 1990. (Jack Fisher), Adrian Pasdar, Cecilia Peck, Barry Primus.

TORRENTS OF SPRING
MILLIMETER. February, 1990. Italian-French. (Jerzy Skolimowski), Timothy Hutton, Nastassja Kinski.

TOTAL RECALL
TRISTAR. June, 1990. (Paul Verhoeven), Arnold Schwarzenegger, Rachel Ticotin, Sharon Stone.

TOTALLY F**D UP**
STRAND. August, 1994. (Gregg Araki), James Duval, Roko Belic, Susan Behshid.

TOTO LE HEROS
TRITON. March, 1992. Belgian-French-German. (Jaco Van Dormael), Michel Bouguet, Jo De Backer, Thomas Doget.

TOUS LES MATINS DU MONDE
(ALL THE MORNINGS OF THE WORLD)
OCTOBER FILMS. November, 1992. French. (Alain Corneau), Jean Pierre Marielle, Gerard Depardieu, Anne Brochet.

TOUCH OF A STRANGER
RAVENSTAR PICTURES. September, 1990. (Brad Gilbert), Shelley Winters, Anthony Nocerino.

TOUKI–BOUKI
INT'L. FILM CIRCUIT. February, 1991. French-Senegalese. (Djibril Diop Mambety), Magaye Niang, Mareme Niang.

TOYS
20TH CENTURY FOX. December, 1992. (Barry Levinson), Robin Williams, Joan Cusack, Michael Gambon.

TOY SOLDIERS
TRISTAR. April, 1991. (Daniel Petrie, Jr.), Sean Astin, Wil Wheaton, Keith Coogan, Louis Gossett, Jr.

TRACES OF RED
GOLDWYN. November, 1992. (Andy Wolk), James Belushi, Lorraine Bracco, Tony Goldwyn.

TRADING MOM
TRIMARK. May, 1994. (Tia Brelis), Sissy Spacek, Anna Chlumsky, Aaron Michael Metchik, Maureen Stapleton.

TRAPPED IN PARADISE
20TH CENTURY FOX. December, 1994. (George Gallo), Nicolas Cage, Jon Lovitz, Dana Carvey.

TREMORS
UNIVERSAL. January, 1990. (Ron Underwood), Kevin Bacon, Fred Ward, Finn Carter.

TRESPASS
UNIVERSAL. December, 1992. (Walter Hill), Bill Paxton, William Sadler, Ice T, Ice Cube.

TRIAL BY JURY
WARNER. September, 1994. (Heywood Gould), Joanna Whalley-Kilmer, Armand Assante, Gabriel Byrne.

TRIAL, THE
ANGELIKA. November, 1993. British. (David Jones), Kyle MacLachlan, Alfred Molina, Anthony Hopkins.

TRIPLE BOGEY ON A PAR 5 HOLE
POE PRODS. March, 1992. (Amos Poe), Eric Mitchell, Daisy Hall, Jesse McBride.

TRIPWIRE
NEW LINE CINEMA. January, 1990. (James Lemmo), Terence Know, David Warner.

TROLL IN CENTRAL PARK
WARNER BROS. October, 1994. (Don Bluth, Gary Goldman), Animated.

TRUE BELIEVERS:
THE MUSICAL FAMILY OF ROUNDER RECORDS
DAKIN. April, 1995. (Robert Mugge), Documentary.

TRUE COLORS
PARAMOUNT. March, 1991. (Herbert Ross), John Cusack, James Spader, Imogen Stubbs, Mandy Patinkin.

TRUE IDENTITY
BUENA VISTA. August, 1991. (Charles Lane), Lenny Henry, Frank Langella, Charles Lane.

TRUE LIES
20TH CENTURY FOX. July, 1994. (James Cameron), Arnold Schwarzenegger, Jamie Lee Curtis, Bill Paxton.

TRUE ROMANCE
WARNER BROS. September, 1993. (Tony Scott), Christian Slater, Patricia Arquette, Dennis Hopper.

TRULY, MADLY, DEEPLY
GOLDWYN. May, 1991. British. (Anthony Minghella), Juliette Stevenson, Alan Rickman, Michael Maloney.

TRUST
FINE LINE/NEW CINEMA. July, 1991. (Hal Hartley), Adrienne Shelly, Martin Donovan, Merritt Nelson.

TRUSTING BEATRICE
CASTLE HILL. January, 1993. (Cindy Lou Johnson), Mark Evan Jacobs, Irene Jacob, Charlotte Moore.

TRUTH OR DARE
MIRAMAX. May, 1991. (Alek Keshishian), Madonna.

TSAHAL
NEW YORKER. January, 1995. Israeli-French. (Claude Lanzmann), Documentary.

TUNE, THE
OCTOBER FILMS. September, 1992. (Bill Plympton), Animated.

TUNE IN TOMORROW
CINECOM. October, 1990. (Jon Amiel), Barbara Hershey, Keanu Reeves, Peter Falk.

TURTLE BEACH
WARNER BROS. May, 1992. Australian. (Stephen Wallace), Greta Scacchi, Joan Chen, Jack Thompson.

TWENTY BUCKS
TRITON. October, 1993. (Keva Rosenfeld), Brendan Fraser, Linda Hunt, Christopher Lloyd, Elisabeth Shue.

TWENTY–ONE
TRITON. October, 1991. British. (Don Boyd), Patsy Kensit, Jack Shepherd, Patrick Ryecart.

29TH STREET
20TH CENTURY FOX. November, 1991. (George Gallo), Danny Aiello, Anthony LaPaglia, Lainie Kazan.

TWIN PEAKS: FIRE WALK WITH ME
NEW LINE CINEMA. August, 1992. (David Lynch), Sheryl Lee, Moira Kelly, Ray Wise.

TWIST
TRITON. August, 1993. Canadian. (Ron Mann), Documentary.

TWISTED JUSTICE
SEYMOUR BORDE. March, 1990. (David Heavener), David Heavener, Erik Estrada.

TWISTED OBSESSION
IVE. (R) August, 1990. French-Italian. (Fernando Trueba), Jeff Goldblum, Miranda Richardson, Anemone.

TWO EVIL EYES
TAURUS. October, 1991. Italian. (George Romero, Dario Argento), Adrienne Barbeau, Harvey Keitel, Madeleine Potter.

TWO JAKES, THE
PARAMOUNT. August, 1990. (Jack Nicholson), Jack Nicholson, Harvey Keitel, Meg Tilly.

TWO SMALL BODIES
CASTLE HILL. April, 1994. German. (Beth B.), Fred Ward, Suzy Amis.

TWOGETHER
BORDE. February, 1994. (Andre Chiaramonte), Nick Cassavetes, Brenda Bakke, Jeremy Piven.

U

UN COEUR EN HIVER (A HEART IN WINTER)
OCTOBER. June, 1993. French. (Claude Sautet), Daniel Auteuil, Emmanuelle Beart, André Dussollier.

UNBECOMING AGE
CASTLE HILL. April, 1993. (Deborah Ringel), Diane Salinger, John Calvin, Wallace Shawn.

UNBELIEVABLE TRUTH, THE
MIRAMAX. July, 1990. (Hal Hartley), Adrienne Shelly, Robert Burke, Christopher Cooke, Gary Sauer.

UNBORN, THE
CONCORDE. April, 1991. (Rodman Flender), Brooke Adams, Jeff Hayenga, James Karen, K Callan.

UNCLE MOSES
NATL CTR FOR JEWISH FILM. November, 1991. Yiddish. (Origianally released 1932). (Sidney Goldin, Aubrey Scotto), Maurice Schwartz, Zvee Scooler. B&W.

UNDER ONE ROOF
CASTLE HILL. March, 1994. Portuguese. (Paulo Thiago), Norma Bengell, Maria Zilda Bethlem.

UNDER SIEGE
WARNER BROS. October, 1992. (Andrew Davis), Steven Seagal, Tommy Lee Jones, Gary Busey.

UNDER SIEGE 2: DARK TERRITORY
WARNER BROS. July, 1995. (Geoff Murphy), Steven Seagal, Eric Bogosian, Katherine Heigl, Everett McGill.

UNDER SUSPICION
COLUMBIA. February, 1992. British. (Simon Moore), Liam Neeson, Laura San Giacomo, Kenneth Cranham.

UNDERCOVER BLUES
MGM. September, 1993. (Herbert Ross), Kathleen Turner, Dennis Quaid, Fiona Shaw.

UNDERNEATH, THE
GRAMERCY. (R) April, 1995. (Steven Soderbergh), Peter Gallagher, Alison Elliott, William Fichtner.

UNDERTOW
CAPSTONE. September, 1992. (Thomas Mazziotti), Peter Dobson, Burtt Harris, Greg Mullavey.

UNFORGETTABLE SUMMER, AN
MK2. November, 1994. French-Romanian. (Lucian Pintilie), Kristin Scott Thomas, Claudiu Bleont, Olga Tudorache.

UNFORGIVEN
WARNER BROS. August, 1992. (Clint Eastwood), Clint Eastwood, Gene Hackman, Morgan Freeman, Richard Harris.

UNIVERSAL SOLDIER
TRISTAR. July, 1992. (Roland Emmerich), Jean Claude Van Damme, Dolph Lundgren, Ally Walker.

UNLAWFUL ENTRY
20TH CENTURY FOX. June, 1992. (Jonathan Kaplan), Kurt Russell, Ray Liotta, Madeleine Stowe.

UNSTRUNG HEROES
BUENA VISTA. September, 1995. (Diane Keaton), John Turturro, Andie MacDowell, Michael Richards.

UNTAMED HEART
MGM. February, 1993. (Tony Bill), Christian Slater, Marisa Tomei, Rosie Perez.

UNTIL THE END OF THE WORLD
WARNER BROS. December, 1991. German-French-Australian. (Wim Wenders), William Hurt, Solveig Dommartin, Jeanne Moreau, Max Von Sydow.

UNZIPPED
MIRAMAX. (R) August, 1995. (Douglas Keeve), Documentary.

URANUS
PRESTIGE. August, 1991. French. (Claude Berri), Philippe Noiret, Gérard Depardieu, Michel Blanc.

USED PEOPLE
20TH CENTURY FOX. December, 1992. (Beeban Kidron), Shirley MacLaine, Marcello Mastroianni, Kathy Bates.

USUAL SUSPECTS, THE
GRAMERCY. (R) August, 1995. (Bryan Singer), Gabriel Byrne, Kevin Spacey, Chazz Palminteri, Giancarlo Esposito, Stephen Baldwin, Kevin Pollack.

UTZ
FIRST RUN FEATURES. February, 1993. British-Italian-German. (George Sluizer), Armin Muller Stahl, Brenda Fricker.

V. I. WARSHAWSKI
BUENA VISTA. July, 1991. (Jeff Kanew), Kathleen Turner, Jay O. Sanders, Charles Durning.

VAGRANT, THE
MGM. May, 1992. (Chris Walas), Bill Paxton, Michael Ironside, Colleen Camp, Marc McClure.

VALLEY OF ABRAHAM
INDEPENDENT. December, 1993. Portuguese-French-Swiss. (Manoel de Oliveira), Leonor Silveira, Cecil Sanz De Alba.

VAN GOGH
SONY CLASSICS. October, 1992. French. (Maurice Pialat), Jacques Dutronc, Alexandra London.

VANISHING, THE
TARA. October, 1990. Dutch. (George Sluizer), Bernard Pierre Donnadieu, Gene Bervoets.

VANISHING, THE
20TH CENTURY FOX. February, 1993. (George Sluizer), Jeff Bridges, Keifer Sutherland, Nancy Travis.

VANYA ON 42ND STREET
SONY CLASSICS. (PG) October, 1994. (Louis Malle), Wallace Shawn, Julianne Moore, Brooke Smith, Larry Pine.

VEGAS IN SPACE
TROMA. December, 1993. (Phillip R. Ford), Doris Fish, Miss X, Ginger Quest.

VENICE/VENICE
RAINBOW. October, 1992. (Henry Jaglom), Nelly Alard, Henry Jaglom, Suzanne Bertish.

VERONICO CRUZ
CINEVISTA. January, 1990. Argentinian-British. (Miguel Pereira), Juan Jose Camero, Gonzalo Morales.

VERTICAL REALITY
WARREN MILLER. October, 1994. (Kurt Miller, Peter Speek), Documentary.

VERY OLD MAN WITH ENORMOUS WINGS, A
ORIGINAL CINEMA. December, 1990. Spanish. (Fernando Birri), Fernando Birri, Asdrubal Melendez.

VIA APPIA
STRAND. August, 1992. German. (Jochen Hick), Peter Senner, Yves Jansen, Guilherme de Padua.

VIETNAM, TEXAS
TRIUMPH. June, 1990. (Robert Ginty), Robert Ginty, Haing S. Ngor.

VILLAGE OF THE DAMNED
UNIVERSAL. April, 1995. (John Carpenter), Christopher Reeve, Kirstie Alley, Linda Kozlowski.

VINCENT & THEO
HEMDALE. November, 1990. French-British. (Robert Altman), Tim Roth, Paul Rhys, Johanna Ter Steege.

VIRTUOSITY
PARAMOUNT. August, 1995. (Brett Leonard), Denzel Washington, Kelly Lynch, Russell Crowe.

VISION OF LIGHT
KINO INT'L. April, 1993. (Arnold Glassman, Todd McCarthy, Stuart Samuels), Documentary.

VITAL SIGNS
20TH CENTURY FOX. April, 1990. (Marisa Silver), Adrian Pasdar, Diane Lane, Jimmy Smits.

VOICES FROM THE FRONT
FRAMELINE. March, 1992. (Robyn Hutt), Documentary.

VOLERE, VOLARE
FINE LINE FEATURES. February, 1993. Italian. (Maurizio Nichetti, Guido Manuli), Maurizio Nichetti, Angela Finocchiaro.

VOYAGER
CASTLE HILL. January, 1992. German-French. (Volker Schlondorff), Sam Shepard, Julie Delpy, Barbara Sukowa.

VOYEUR
PRESTIGE. August, 1991. Dutch. (Alex Van Warmerdam), Alex Van Warmerdam, Olga Zuiderhoek.

WAGONS EAST!
TRISTAR. August, 1994. (Peter Markle), John Candy, Richard Lewis, John C. McGinley.

WAIT FOR ME IN HEAVEN
MD WAX/COURIER. October, 1990. Spanish. (Antonio Mercero), Jose Soriano, Chus Lampreave.

WAIT UNTIL SPRING, BANDINI
ORION CLASSICS. June, 1990. Belgian-French-Italian. (Dominique Deruddere), Joe Mantegna, Faye Dunaway.

WAITING FOR THE LIGHT
TRIUMPH. November, 1990. (Christopher Monger), Shirley MacLaine, Teri Garr, Clancy Brown.

WALK IN THE CLOUDS, A
20TH CENTURY FOX. August, 1995. (Alfonse Arau), Keanu Reeves, Aitana Sanchez-Gijon, Anthony Quinn.

WALKING DEAD, THE
SAVOY. (R) February, 1995. (Preston A. Whitmore II), Allen Payne, Eddie Griffin, Joe Morton.

WAR, THE
UNIVERSAL. November, 1994. (Jon Avnet), Elijah Wood, Kevin Costner, Mare Winningham, Lexi Randall.

WAR OF THE BUTTONS
WARNER BROS. September, 1995. (John Roberts), Gregg Fitzgerald, John Coffey, Colm Meaney.

WAR ROOM, THE
OCTOBER. November, 1993. (D.A. Pennebaker), Documentary.

WARLOCK
TRIMARK. January, 1991. (Steve Miner), Julian Sands, Richard E. Grant, Lori Singer.

WARLOCK: THE ARMAGEDDON
TRIMARK. September, 1993. (Tony Hickox), Julian Sands, Chris Young, Paula Marshall.

WATCH IT
SKOURAS. March, 1993. (Tom Flynn), Peter Gallagher, Lili Taylor, John C. McGinley.

WATERDANCE, THE
SAMUEL GOLDWYN CO. May, 1992. (Neal Jimenez, Michael Steinberg), Eric Stoltz, Helen Hunt, Wesley Snipes.

WATERLAND
FINE LINE FEATURES. October, 1992. British. (Stephen Gyllenhaal), Jeremy Irons, Ethan Hawke, Sinead Cusack.

WATERWORLD
UNIVERSAL. July, 1995. (Kevin Reynolds), Kevin Costner, Dennis Hopper, Jeanne Tripplehorn, Tina Majorino.

WAX, OR THE DISCOVERY OF TELEVISION AMONG THE BEES
JASMINE TEA. August, 1992. (David Blair), David Blair, Meg Savlov.

WAYNE'S WORLD
PARAMOUNT. February, 1992. (Penelope Spheeris), Mike Myers, Dana Carvey, Rob Lowe.

WAYNE'S WORLD 2
PARAMOUNT. December, 1993. (Stephen Surjik), Mike Myers, Dana Carvey, Christopher Walken.

WE'RE BACK: A DINOSAUR'S STORY
UNIVERSAL. November, 1993. (Dick Zondag, Ralph Zondag, Phil Nibblink, Simon Wells), Animated.

WEDDING BAND
I.R.S. MEDIA. March, 1990. (Daniel Raskov), William Katt, Joyce Hyser.

WEDDING BANQUET, THE
GOLDWYN. August, 1993. (Ang Lee), Ah Leh Gua, Sihung Lung, Mitchell Lichtenstein.

WEDDING GIFT, THE
MIRAMAX. July, 1994. British. (Richard Loncraine), Julie Walters, Jim Broadbent, Thora Hird.

WEEKEND AT BERNIE'S II
TRISTAR. July, 1993. (Robert Klane), Andrew McCarthy, Jonathan Silverman, Barry Bostwick.

WEININGER'S LAST NIGHT
CINEPOOL/WEGA FILM. July, 1991. Austrian. (Paulus Manker), Paulus Manker, Hilde Sochor.

WELCOME HOME ROXY CARMICHAEL
PARAMOUNT. October, 1990. (Jim Abrahams), Winona Ryder, Jeff Daniels, Laila Robbins.

WELCOME TO OBLIVION
CONCORDE. February, 1990. (Augusto Tomayo), Dack Rambo, Meshach Taylor.

WE'RE TALKIN' SERIOUS MONEY
CINETEL. May, 1992. (James Lemmo), Dennis Farina, Leo Rossi, Fran Drescher.

WES CRAVEN'S NEW NIGHTMARE
NEW LINE CINEMA. (R) October, 1994. (Wes Craven), Robert Englund, Heather Langenkamp, Miko Hughes, John Saxon.

WHAT ABOUT BOB?
BUENA VISTA. May, 1991. (Frank Oz), Bill Murray, Richard Dreyfuss, Julie Hagerty.

WHAT HAPPENED WAS...
GOLDWYN. September, 1994. (Tom Noonan), Noonan, Karen Sillas.

WHAT'S EATING GILBERT GRAPE
PARAMOUNT. December, 1993. (Lasse Hallstrom), Johnny Depp, Leonardo DiCaprio, Juliette Lewis.

WHAT'S LOVE GOT TO DO WITH IT
BUENA VISTA. June, 1993. (Brian Ibson), Angela Bassett, Laurence Fishburne, Vanessa Bell Calloway.

WHEN A MAN LOVES A WOMAN
BUENA VISTA. April, 1994. (Luis Mandoki), Andy Garcia, Meg Ryan, Lauren Tom, Tina Majorino.

WHERE
WHERE PRODS. September, 1991. Hungarian-U.S. (Gabor Szabo), Renata Satler. B&W.

WHERE ANGELS FEAR TO TREAD
FINE LINE FEATURES. February, 1992. British. (Charles Sturridge), Helena Bonham Carter, Rupert Graves, Judy Davis.

WHERE THE DAY TAKES YOU
NEW LINE CINEMA. September, 1992. (Marc Rocco), Dermot Mulroney, Sean Astin, Balthazar Getty, Lara Flynn Boyle.

WHERE THE HEART IS
BUENA VISTA. February, 1990. (John Boorman), Dabney Coleman, Uma Thurman, Joanna Cassidy.

WHERE THE RIVERS FLOW NORTH
CALEDONIA. January, 1994. (Jay Craven), Rip Torn, Tantoo Cardinal, Bill Raymond, Michael J. Fox.

WHISPERS IN THE DARK
PARAMOUNT. August, 1992. (Christopher Crowe), Annabella Sciorra, Jamey Sheridan, Alan Alda.

WHILE YOU WERE SLEEPING
BUENA VISTA. April, 1995. (Jon Turtletaub), Sandra Bullock, Bill Pullman, Peter Gallagher, Peter Boyle.

WHITE
MIRAMAX. June, 1994. Polish. (Krzysztof Kieslowski), Zbigniew Zamachowski, Julie Delpy, Janusz Gajos.

WHITE FANG
BUENA VISTA. January, 1991. (Randal Kleiser), Ethan Hawke, Klaus Maria Brandauer, Seymour Cassel.

WHITE FANG 2: THE MYTH OF THE WHITE WOLF
BUENA VISTA. April, 1994. (Ken Olin), Scott Bairstow, Charmaine Craig, Al Harrington.

WHITE GIRL, THE
TONY BROWN PRODS. February, 1990. (Tony Brown), Troy Beyer, Taimak.

WHITE HUNTER, BLACK HEART
WARNER BROS. September, 1990. (Clint Eastwood), Clint Eastwood, Jeff Fahey, George Dzundza.

WHITE MEN CAN'T JUMP
20TH CENTURY FOX. March, 1992. (Ron Shelton), Wesley Snipes, Woody Harrelson, Rosie Perez.

WHITE PALACE
UNIVERSAL. October, 1990. (Luis Mandoki), Susan Sarandon, James Spader, Eileen Brennan.

WHITE SANDS
WARNER BROS. April, 1992. (Roger Donaldson), Willem Dafoe, Mary Elizabeth Mastrantonio, Mickey Rourke.

WHO'S THE MAN?
NEW LINE CINEMA. April, 1993. (Ted Demme), Doctor Dre, Ed Lover, Badja Djola.

WHOLE TRUTH, THE
CINEVISTA. October, 1992. (Dan Cohen, Jonathan Smythe), Dyan Kane, Dan Cohen, Jim Willig.

WHORE
TRIMARK. October, 1991. (Ken Russell), Theresa Russell, Antonio Fargas, Benjamin Mouton.

WHY ME?
TRIUMPH. April, 1990. (Gene Quintano), Christopher Lambert, Christopher Lloyd, Kim Greist.

WICKED CITY
STREAMLINE. October, 1993. Japanese. (Carl Macek), Animated.

WIDE SARGASSO SEA
FINE LINE. April, 1993. Australian. (John Duigan), Karina Lombard, Nathaniel Parker, Rachel Ward.

WIDOW'S PEAK
FINE LINE. May, 1994. British. (John Irvin), Mia Farrow, Joan Plowright, Natasha Richardson.

WIGSTOCK: THE MOVIE
GOLDWYN. June, 1995. (Barry Shils), Documentary.

WILD AT HEART
GOLDWYN. August, 1990. (David Lynch), Nicolas Cage, Laura Dern, Willem Dafoe.

WILD HEARTS CAN'T BE BROKEN
BUENA VISTA. May, 1991. (Steve Miner), Gabrielle Anwar, Michael Schoeffling, Cliff Robertson.

WILD ORCHID
TRIUMPH. April, 1990. (Zalman King), Mickey Rourke, Jacqueline Bisset, Carre Otis.

WILD REEDS, THE
STRAND. May, 1995. French. (Andre Techine), Elodie Bouchez, Gael Morel, Stephane Rideau.

WILD WEST
GOLDWYN. November, 1993. British. (David Attwood), Naveen Andrews, Sarita Choudhury, Ronny Jhutti.

WILD WHEELS
TARA RELEASING. August, 1992. (Harrold Blank), Documentary.

WILDER NAPALM
TRISTAR. August, 1993. (Glenn Gordon Caron), Debra Winger, Dennis Quaid, Arliss Howard.

WIND
TRISTAR. September, 1992. (Carroll Ballard), Matthew Modine, Jennifer Grey, Cliff Robertson.

WINDOW SHOPPING
WORLD ARTISTS. April, 1992. French. (Chantal Akerman), Miriam Boyer, John Berry, Delphine Seyrig.

WINDOW TO PARIS
SONY CLASSICS. February, 1995. French-Russian. (Yuri Mamin), Agnes Soral, Sergei Dontsov, Viktor Mikhailov.

WINTER IN LISBON, THE
CASTLE HILL. March, 1992. Spanish-French-Portuguese. (Jose Antonio Zorrilla), Dizzy Gillespie, Christian Vadim.

WISECRACKS
ALLIANCE. June, 1992. Canadian. (Gail Singer), Documentary.

WISHMAN
CURB ESQUIRE. July, 1993. (Michael Marvin), Paul LeMat, Geoffrey Lewis, Brion James.

WITCHES, THE
WARNER BROS. February, 1990. (Nicolas Roeg), Anjelica Huston, Jasen Fisher, Mai Zetterling.

WITH HONORS
WARNER BROS. April, 1994. (Alex Keshishian), Joe Pesci, Brendan Fraser, Moira Kelly, Josh Hamilton.

WITHOUT YOU I'M NOTHING
M.C.E.G. May, 1990. (John Boskovich), Sandra Bernhard, Joe Doe.

WITTGENSTEIN
ZEITGEIST. September, 1993. British. (Derek Jarman), Karl Johnson, Michael Gough, Clancy Chassay.

WOLF
COLUMBIA. June, 1994. (Mike Nichols), Jack Nicholson, Michelle Pfeiffer, James Spader.

WOMAN, HER MEN AND HER FUTON, A
INTERPERSONAL FILMS. July, 1992. (Mussef Sibay), Jennifer Rubin, Lance Edwards, Michael Cerveris.

WOMAN HUMAN DEMON
JASMINE TEA. September, 1992. Chinese. (Huang Shuqin), Xu Houli, Li Baotian.

WOMAN'S TALE, A
ORION CLASSICS. December, 1991. Australian. (Paul Cox), Sheila Florance, Gosia Dobrowolska, Norman Kaye.

WOMEN FROM THE LAKE OF SCENTED SOULS
YELLOW LINE. February, 1994. Chinese. (Xie Fie), Siquin Gaowa, Wu Yujuan, Lei Luosheng.

WOMEN'S STORY
INT'L FILM CIRCUIT. January, 1991. Chinese. (Peng Xiaolian), Zhong Wenrong, Song Ruhui, Zhang Min.

WONDERFUL HORRIBLE LIFE OF LENI RIEFENSTAHL, THE
KINO. March, 1994. German-British-French. (Ray Muller), Documentary.

WOODEN MAN'S BRIDE, THE
ARROW. February, 1995. Chinese. (Huang Jianxin), Chang Shih, Wang Lan, Ku Paoming.

WORLD AND TIME ENOUGH
STRAND. August, 1995. (Eric Mueller), Matt Guidry, Gregory G. Giles, Kraig Swartz.

WRESTLING ERNEST HEMINGWAY
WARNER BROS. December, 1993. (Randa Haines), Robert Duvall, Richard Harris, Shriley MacLaine.

WYATT EARP
WARNER BROS. June, 1994. (Lawrence Kasdan), Kevin Costner, Dennis Quaid, Gene Hackman.

Y

YEAR OF THE COMET
COLUMBIA. April, 1992. (Peter Yates), Penelope Ann Miller, Tim Daly, Louis Jourdan.

YEAR OF THE GUN
TRIUMPH. November, 1991. (John Frankenheimer), Andrew McCarthy, Valeria Golino, Sharon Stone.

YEN FAMILY, THE
FUJISANKEI COMMUN. INT'L. August, 1991. Japanese. (Yojiri Takita), Kaori Momoi, Takeshi Kaga.

YOU SO CRAZY
GOLDWYN. April, 1994. (Thomas Schlamme), Martin Lawrence.

YOUNG GUNS II
20TH CENTURY FOX. August, 1990. (Geoff Murphy), Emilio Estevez, Lou Diamond Phillips, Christian Slater.

YOUNG SOUL REBELS
PRESTIGE. November, 1991. British. (Isaac Julien), Valentine Nonyela, Mo Sesay, Dorian Healy.

Z

ZEBRAHEAD
TRIUMPH. October, 1992. (Anthony Drazan), Michael Rapaport, N'Bushe Wright, Ray Sharkey.

ZENTROPA
PRESTIGE. May, 1992. Danish-French-German-Swedish. (Lars Von Trier), Jean Marc Barr, Barbara Sukowa, Udo Kier.

ZERO PATIENCE
CINEVISTA. March, 1994. Canadian. (John Greyson), John Robinson, Normand Fauteux, Dianne Heatherington.

ZOMBIE AND THE GHOST TRAIN
FIRST RUN. August, 1994. Finnish. (Mika Kaurismaki), Silu Sepala, Marjo Leinonen, Matti Pellonpaa.

EXHIBITION

THEATRE CIRCUITS

INDEPENDENT THEATRES

THEATRES IN MAJOR MARKETS

EXHIBITOR ORGANIZATIONS

BUYING & BOOKING SERVICES

FILM DISTRIBUTORS IN KEY CITIES

THEATRE EQUIPMENT & SERVICES

CONCESSION SUPPLIERS

THEATRE CIRCUITS

These listings are for companies operating within the United States and its territories and possessions. Certain corporate listings may contain foreign theatre listings. Circuits in Canada are in the section on Canada. Number of screens and total theatre/screen counts have been provided by the circuits, reported from other sources or have been calculated by Quigley Publishing. This listing covers 23,014 screens.

ABSHER ENTERPRISES, INC.

5 theatres, 23 screens.
295 North Arnold Ave., Prestonburg, KY 41653. (606) 886-6397.
OWNER
J. Absher
KENTUCKY—GOODY: South Side Theatre 5; PIKEVILLE: Plaza Cinemas 2, Riverfill 10 Cinemas; PRESTONBURG: Strand 2 Theatre; SOMERSET: Showplace Cinemas 4.

ACKERMAN THEATRES

11 theatres, 33 screens.
163 Amsterdam Ave., Suite 149, New York, NY 10023. (212) 595-2141. FAX: (212) 595-2979.
PRESIDENT
Meyer Ackerman
VICE PRESIDENT
J. Robert Tolchin
TREASURER
Corey Greenberg
SECRETARY
Brian Ackerman
NEW YORK—NEW YORK CITY: Eastside Playhouse, 86th St. East Twin, 57th St. Playhouse, 68th St. Playhouse, Village East Cinemas; STATEN ISLAND: Hylan Plaza 5-plex, Staten Island 14-Plex; WESTCHESTER: Cinema 100 Twin, Rye Ridge Twin, Fine Arts, Westchester Mall Cinemas.

ACT III THEATRES

128 theatres, 710 screens.
919 S.W. Taylor, Suite 900, Portland, OR 97205. (503) 221-0213. FAX: (503) 228-5032.
PRESIDENT & CFO
Walt Aman
V. P. & HEAD FILM BUYER
Bob Lenihan
V. P., FILM SETTLEMENTS
Bill Spencer
V. P., OPERATIONS
Timothy G. Wood
V. P., REAL ESTATE & FACILITIES
Tim Reed
NATIONAL CONCESSIONS & PURCHASING MANAGER
Robert Perkins III
V. P., FINANCE
Wade Canning
NATIONAL DIR. MARKETING, PUBLICITY & PROMOTION
Randy Blaum
Santikos/Presidio Theatres
DIVISIONAL MANAGER
Mark Reis
TEXAS—AUSTIN: Arbor, Lakecreek, Lakehills, Lincoln, Northcross, Riverside, Southwood, Village, Westgate 3, Westgate 8; SAN ANTONIO: Northwest 14, Galaxy 14, Ingram Square 8, Windsor Mall, Century South, Mission D.I., Westlakes, Embassy 14, Crossroads, Bandera, Nakoma, Rolling Oaks, Fiesta 16.
Luxury Theatres
DIVISIONAL MANAGER
Steve Guffey
ALASKA—ANCHORAGE: Denali, Fireweed, Totem; FAIRBANKS: Goldstream, KENAI: Kambe.
IDAHO—COEUR D'ALENE: Coeur d'Alene, Showboat V; LEWISTON: Orchards Tri Cinemas, Liberty.
NEVADA—HENDERSON: Sunset Station; LAS VEGAS: Texas Station, Boulder Station.
OREGON—ALBANY: Albany; BEAVERTON: Valley Tri, Westgate; BEND: Pilot Butte Cinema, Bend Tri Cinemas, Mountain View Cinemas; COOS BAY: Egyptian; CORVALLIS: Ninth Street, Whiteside; EUGENE: Cinema World, McDonald, Movieland; GRANTS PASS: Rogue, Redwood D.I.; GRESHAM: Gresham Quad; HILLSBORO: Evergreen Parkway; HOOD

RIVER: Trail; McMINNVILLE: McMinnville; NORTH BEND: Pony IV Cinemas; OREGON CITY: Hilltop; PORTLAND: Broadway Metroplex, Clackamas, Eastgate, 82nd Ave. Cinemas, Foster D.I., Fox, Guild, Hollywood Cinemas, Jantzen Cinemas, Lloyd Cinemas, Lloyd Mall Cinemas, Mall 205 Cinemas, Music Box, Rose Moyer, Southgate, Tigard, Washington Square Cinemas; ROSEBURG: Garden Valley, Harvard Tri Cinemas, Starlite; SALEM: Keizer Cinemas, Lancaster Mall Cinemas, Movieland, Southgate Cinemas; SPRINGFIELD: Springfield; WILSONVILLE: Town Center.
WASHINGTON—ABERDEEN: Southshore Mall Cinemas, Harbor D.I.; AUBURN: Cinema 17 Super; BELLINGHAM: Bellis Fair Mall, Sehome, Sunset Square; BREMERTON: Redwood Plaza; CENTRALIA: Fox; CHEHALIS: Cinema 3; EVERETT: Everett; KELSO: Three Rivers; KENNEWICK: Columbia Center, Clearwater; KENT: Kent Cinemas; ISSAQUAH: Issaquah; LACEY: Lacey; LONGVIEW: Longview, Triangle; OLYMPIA: Olympia Mall, State; PUYALLUP: Hilltop Cinema, Puyallup; REDMOND: Bella Bottega; RENTON: Renton 13; RICHLAND: Uptown, Metro; SEATTLE: Alderwood, Alderwood Village, Crossroads, Mountlake 9, Parkway; SILVERDALE: Silverdale Cinemas; SPOKANE: East Sprague, East-Side, Fox, Lincoln Heights, Lyons, Newport, North Division; VANCOUVER: Cascade Park, Hazel Dell, Vancouver Mall, Vancouver Plaza.

ALLEN THEATRES, INC.

23 theatres, 68 screens.
P.O. Drawer 1500, 208B West Main St., Farmington, NM 87401. (505) 325-9313. FAX: (505) 326-2647.
PRESIDENT
Larry F. Allen
VICE PRESIDENT
Lane E. Allen
SECRETARY-TREASURER
Boyd F. Scott
FILM BUYER
Larry F. Allen
COLORADO—CORTEZ: Fiesta Twin, Arroyo D.I.
NEW MEXICO—ALAMOGORDO: Cinema 5; CARLSBAD: Mall Cinema 3; CLOVIS: Hilltop Twin, North Plains 4; FARMINGTON: Allen, Allen 8, Apache Twin D.I., Cameo, Centennial Twin, Animas Cinema IV; GALLUP: Aztec 5, Rio West Twin; HOBBS: Broadmoor, Cinema 5; LAS CRUCES: Video 4, Rio Grande, Cinema 8; PORTALES: Tower Twin; ROSWELL: Cinema 4, Del Norte Twin, Plains Park Twin.

AMERICAN MULTI-CINEMA, INC.

240 theatres, 1950 screens.
(An AMC Entertainment Corp.) 106 West 14th St., Suite 1700, Kansas City, MO 64105. (816) 221-4000.
CHAIRMAN, CEO & PRESIDENT
Stanley H. Durwood
EXECUTIVE V.P. & COO
Philip M. Singleton
EXECUTIVE V.P. & CFO
Peter C. Brown
AMC FILM MARKETING PRESIDENT
Richard M. Fay
DIVISION OFFICES
American Multi-Cinema, Inc., Northside Square, 29399 U.S. Highway 19 North, Suite 320, Clearwater, FL 34621.
American Multi-Cinema, Inc., Main St., Plaza 10000, Suite 503; Voorhees, NJ 08043.
American Multi-Cinema, Inc., Suite 1020, Two Century Plaza, 2049 Century Park East,Los Angeles CA, 90067.
ARIZONA—CHANDLER: Laguna Village 10; GLENDALE: Gateway Village 10; MESA: Fiesta Village 6, Sunvalley 10, Three Fountains 4; PHOENIX: Ahwautukee 24, Arrowhead 14, Bell Plaza 8, Metro Village 8, Town & Country 6; TEMPE: Lakes 6; TUCSON: El Con 6, Valencia 4.
CALIFORNIA—BAKERSFIELD: Stockdale 6; BEVERLEY HILLS: Fine Arts 1; BURBANK: Burbank 14, Media Center 8,

Media Center 6; CERRITOS: Alondra 6; CHINO: Chino Town Square 10; COLMA: Serramonte 6; ENCINITAS: Wiegand Plaza 8; FULLERTON: Fullerton 10; HAWTHORNE: Hawthorne 6; HERMOSA BEACH: Hermosa Beach 6; INDUSTRY: Puente East 4, Puente West 6, Puente Plaza 10; LA JOLLA: La Jolla 12; LONG BEACH: Marina Pacifica 6, Pine Square 16; LOS ANGELES: Century 14; MILPITAS: Milpitas 10; MONTEBELLO: Montebello 10; NORWALK: Norwalk 20; ONTARIO: Ontario Mills 30; ORANGE: Orange 6; PASADENA: Old Pasadena 8; SAN BERNARDINO: Commercenter 6; SAN DIEGO: Mission Valley 20; SAN FRANCISCO: Kabuki 8; SAN JOSE: Oakridge 6, Town & Country 1; SANTA ANA: Mainplace 6; SANTA MONICA; Santa Monica 7; SANTEE: Santee Village 8; SUNNYVALE: Sunnyvale 6; TORRANCE: Rolling Hills 6; VALLEJO: Vallejo Plaza 6; VICTORVILLE: Victor Valley 10: WOODLAND HILLS: Promenade 16.
COLORADO—AURORA: Buckingham Square 4, Buckingham Village 6, Seven Hills 10; COLORADO SPRINGS: Tiffany Square 6; DENVER: Tiffany Plaza 6, Tivoli 12; GLENDALE: Colorado Plaza 6; LITTLETON: Southbridge 8; WESTMINSTER: Westminster Mall 6, Westminster 5.
DELAWARE—NEWARK: Cinema Center 3; WILMINGTON: Concord 2.
DISTRICT OF COLUMBIA—WASHINGTON, DC: Union Station 9.
FLORIDA—ALTAMONTE SPRINGS: Interstate 6;BOCA RATON: Mizner Park 8; BRANDON: Regency Square 20; CLEARWATER: Clearwater 5, Countryside 6, Tri-City 8; COCONUT GROVE: Cocowalk 16; DAVIE: Ridge Plaza 8; DAYTONA: Volusia Square 8; DAYTONA BEACH: Daytona 6; FORT LAUDERDALE: Coral Ridge 10; FORT MYERS: Merchants Crossing 16; GAINESVILLE: Oaks 6, Oaks 4; HOLLYWOOD: Sheridan 12; HOLLYWOOD BEACH: Oceanwalk 10; JACKSONVILLE: Regency Mall 8, Regency Square 6; LAKE BUENA VISTA: Pleasure Island 10; LAKELAND: Merchants Walk 10; LEESBURG: Lakes 12; MERRITT ISLAND: Merritt Square 1-6, Merritt Square 7-12; MIAMI: Fashion Island 16; Kendall 10, Mall of the Americas 14, Omni 6, Omni 4, South Dade 8, ORANGE PARK: Orange Park 5; ORLANDO: Celebration 2, Fashion Village 8; SARASOTA: Sarasota 1/6, Sarasota 7/12; SEMINOLE: Seminole 8; ST. PETERSBURG: Crossroads 8, Tyrone Square 6; TALLAHASSEE: Tallahassee 20; TAMPA: Horizon Park 4, Old Hyde Park 7, Twin Bays 4, Varsity 8; WEST PALM BEACH: Cross Country 8.
GEORGIA—ALPHARETTA: Mansell Crossing 14; ATLANTA: Galleria 8, Market Square 16, Phipps Plaza 14; KENNESHAW: Cobb Place 8; LAWRENCEVILLE: Colonial 18; TUCKER: Northlake Festival 8.
ILLINOIS—CARBONDALE: University Place 8; HOFFMAN ESTATES: Barrington Square 6; NAPERVILLE: Ogden Mall 6.
KANSAS—OVERLAND PARK: Oak Park Mall 6, Oak Park Plaza 6.
LOUISIANA—BOSSIER CITY: Bossier 6; METAIRIE: Galleria 8; SHREVEPORT: St. Vincent 6.
MARYLAND—GREENBELT: Academy 8, Academy 6; LAVALE: Country Club 6; NEW CARROLLTON: Carrollton 6; OXON HILL: Rivertowne 12; SILVER SPRING: City Place 10.
MASSACHUSETTS—HADLEY: Hampshire 6, Mountain Farms 4.
MICHIGAN—BLOOMFIELD: Maple 3; DETROIT: Bel-Air Centre 10; FARMINGTON HILLS: Old Orchard 3; GROSSE POINT WOODS: Woods 6; HARPER WOODS: Eastland 5, Eastland 2; LANSING: Elmwood 8; LIVONIA: Laurel Park 10; MADISON HEIGHTS: Abbey 8; OAK PARK: Towne 4; OKEMOS: Meridian 1/4, Meridian 5/8, Meridian 6; ROCHESTER: Hampton 4; SOUTHFIELD: Southfield 12; STERLING HEIGHTS: Sterling Center 10; TAYLOR: Southland 4; WEST BLOOMFIELD TOWNSHIP: Americana West 6.
MISSOURI—HAZELWOOD: Village 6; INDEPENDENCE: Independence 20; KANSAS CITY: Bannister Square 6, Crown Center 6, Metro North 1/6, Metro 7/12, Ward Parkway 22; LEE'S SUMMIT: Summit 6; ST. ANN: Northwest Square 10; ST. CHARLES: Regency 8; ST. LOUIS: Esquire 7, Crestwood Plaza 10, Galleria 6.
NEBRASKA—OMAHA: Westroads 6, Westwoods 2.
NEW JERSEY—DELRAN: Millside 4; DEPTFORD: Deptford 8; LAWRENCEVILLE: Quaker Bridge 4; MARLTON: Marlton 8; MORRISTOWN: Headquarters 10; ROCKAWAY: Rockaway 1/6, Rockaway 7/12; VINELAND: Vineland 4.
NEW YORK—AMHERST: Maple Ridge 8; CHEEKTOWAGA: Como 8.
NORTH CAROLINA—CHARLOTTE: Carolina Pavilion 22.
OHIO—COLUMBUS: Eastland Center 8, Eastland Plaza 6, Lennox 24; DUBLIN: Dublin Village 18; WESTERVILLE: Westerville 6.
OKLAHOMA—NORMAN: Robinson Crossing 10; OKLAHOMA CITY: Memorial Square 8, Northwest 8.
PENNSYLVANIA—ALLENTOWN: Tilghman Plaza 8; BEN-SALEM: Woodhaven 10; DOYLESTOWN: Barn 5; EASTON: 25th St. Cinema 4; HARRISBURG: Colonial Commons 9; LANCASTER: Eden 2; WONDERLAND 4; MECHANICSBURG: Hampden Center 8; MEDIA: Granite Run 8; PHILADELPHIA: Andorra 8, Olde City 2, Orleans 8; QUAKERTOWN: Quakertown 6; SPRINGFIELD: Marple 10; SPRINGHOUSE: 309 Cinema 9; WARRINGTON: Bucks County Twin; WAYNE: Anthony Wayne 2, WESTCHESTER: Painters Crossing 9; WHITEHALL: Plaza 2; YORK: York 4.

TEXAS—ARLINGTON: Forum 6, Green Oaks 8; DALLAS: Glen Lakes 8, Grand 24, Prestonwood 5; FT. WORTH: Hulen Village 10, Palace 9, Sundance 11; HIGHLAND PARK: Highland Park Village 4; HOUSTON: Almeda East 5, Commerce Park 8, Deerbrook Expansion 6, Festival 6, Greens Crossing 6, Meyer Park 16, North Oaks 6, Town & Country 10, Westchase 5, Willowbrook 10; HUMBLE: Deerbrook 18, Deerbrook 8; IRVING: Irving 8; MESQUITE: Towne Crossing 8; PLANO: Central Park 7; SAN ANTONIO: Rivercenter 9.
VIRGINIA—ARLINGTON: Courthouse Plaza 8; FALLS CHURCH: Skyline 12, HAMPTON: Coliseum 4, Newmarket 4; NEWPORT NEWS: Patrick Henry 7; NORFOLK: Circle 4; VIRGINIA BEACH: Lynnhaven 8; WOODBRIDGE: Potomac Mills 15.
WASHINGTON—FEDERAL WAY: Center Plaza 6, SeaTac 6; TACOMA: Narrows Plaza 8.
PORTUGAL—PORTO: Arrabida 20.

APEX CINEMAS

5 theatres, 24 screens.
4818 Yuma St., N.W., Washington, DC 20016. (202) 244-7700. FAX: (202) 363-4680.
PRESIDENT & OWNER.
Ron Goldman
MARYLAND—ANNAPOLIS: Annapolis Mall 4, Annapolis Harbour 9, Eastport Twin; PRINCE FREDERICK: Calvert Village 5; WHEATON: Aspen Hill 4.

ASSOCIATED THEATRES OF KENTUCKY

7 theatres, 35 screens.
4050 Westport Rd., Suite 201, Louisville, KY 40207. (502) 893-8811. FAX: (502) 894-8823.
PRESIDENT
Henry I. Saag
V.P. & TREASURER
John D. Saag
DIRECTOR OF OPERATIONS
Karen Cosson
INDIANA—MADISON: Madison 6, Jasper 3.
KENTUCKY—LOUISVILLE: Dixie Dozen 12, Oldham 8, South Park D.I., Vogue.
WEST VIRGINIA—WESTON: Weston 4.

B & B THEATRES

26 Theatres, 88 Screens.
Box 171, 112 West 2nd, Salisbury, MO 65281. (816) 388-5219.
Kansas Office: Box 388, 202 S. Washington, Iola, KS 66749. (316) 365-5701.
OWNERS
Elmer Bills, Bob Bagby, Sterling Bagby
KANSAS—ARKANSAS CITY: Buford Cinema 3; CHANUTE: Chanute Cinema 2; COFFEYVILLE: Coffeyville Cinema 2; EL DORADO: El Dorado Embassy 2; INDEPENDENCE: Independence Cinema 4; IOLA: Iola Cinema 2; Iola 54 D.I.; McPHERSON: McPherson Cinema 4; PARSONS: Parsons Cinema 3; RUSSELL: Russell Dream Cinema; WINFIELD: Winfield Cinema 3.
MISSOURI—BOLIVAR: Cinema 4; BROOKFIELD: Cedar Cinema; CARROLLTON: Carrollton Uptown Theatre; CARTHAGE: Carthage Cinema 2; FESTUS: Festus 8; FULTON: Fulton Cinema 2; HANNIBAL: Hannibal Cinema 5; LEBANON: Ritz 4; LIBERTY: Cinema 8; MARSHALL: Marshall Cinema 3; MOBERLY: Moberly Cinema, State 2; MONETT: Plaza 5; SALISBURY: Salisbury Lyric; WAYNESVILLE: Cinema 5.
OKLAHOMA—PONCA CITY: Plaza Twin.

BLUMENFELD SAN FRANCISCO THEATRES

8 theatres, 13 screens.
1521 Sutter St., San Francisco, CA 94109. (415) 563-6200. FAX: (415) 563-6210.
CHIEF EXECUTIVE
Allan Blumenfeld
BOOKER & SUPERVISION
Robert Blumenfeld
PURCHASING AGENT
Nathan Blumenfeld
ADVERTISING
Max Blumenfeld
CALIFORNIA—FAIRFAX: Fairfax; LARKSPUR: Lark; SAN JOSE: Meridian 6; SAN FRANCISCO: Regency 1, Regency 2, Royal, Alhambra, Castro.

CDB THEATRES

5 theatres, 21 screens.
Drawer B, Beckley, WV 25802-2854. (304) 255-4036. FAX: (304) 252-0526.
OWNER
Curtis McCall

WEST VIRGINIA—BECKLEY: Crossroads Cinema 6, Showplace Cinemas 7; FAIRLEA: Seneca Showcase 2; RAINELLE: Curdanbri Twin Cinemas; SUMMERSVILLE: Merchants Walk Cinemas 4.

CAMERA CINEMAS

4 theatres, 10 screens.
P.O. Box 720728, San Jose, CA 95172. (408) 998-3022
CALIFORNIA—LOS GATOS: Los Gatos Cinema 2; SAN JOSE: Camera One Theatre 2, Camera Three Theatre, Towne Theatre 3.

CANAD CINEMAS THEATRES

7 theatres, 49 screens.
1279 South Willow Street, Manchester, NH 03103. (603) 623-6348. FAX: (603) 623-3606.
CHAIRMAN
Frank G. Adam
PRESIDENT
Joan C. Canavan
VICE PRESIDENT
Mark T. Adam
FILM BUYER
Martin Goldman
NEW HAMPSHIRE—BEDFORD: Bedford Mall Cinema; CONCORD: Loudon Road 10; HOOKSET: Cental Park; MANCHESTER: South Willow Street Cinemas 9; NASHUA: Nashua Mall; PORTSMOUTH: Lafayette Road Cinemas 5; SOMERSWORTH: Tri-City Plaza 4.

CARMIKE CINEMAS

566 theatres, 2469 screens.
Home Office: 1301 First Ave., P.O. Box 391, Columbus, GA 31902-0391. (706) 576-3400. FAX: (706) 576-3441.
CHAIRMAN
C. L. Patrick, Sr.
PRESIDENT & CEO
Michael W. Patrick
V. P., FINANCE, TREASURER & CFO
John O. Barwick III
V. P. FILM
Anthony J. Rhead
V. P & GENERAL MANAGER
Fred Van Noy
V. P., DEVELOPMENT
P. Lamar Fields
V. P., INFO SYSTEMS & SECRETARY
Larry M. Adams
V. P., CONCESSIONS & ASST. SECRETARY
H. Madison Shirley
V. P., ADVERTISING
Marilyn Grant
V. P., TECHNICAL
Jim Davis
HUMAN RESOURCES DIRECTOR
Sadie Harper
ALABAMA—ANNISTON: Carmike, Plaza; AUBURN: Cinema; BIRMINGHAM: Carmike, Colonade, Bama; CULLMAN: Town Square; DECATUR: Century; DOTHAN: Circle West; FLORENCE: Capri, Hickory Hills; GADSDEN: Gadsden Mall; MOBILE:, Bel Air, Dauphin, Village, Carmike, Springfield, Movies; MONTGOMERY: Carmike, Easdale, Movies, Twin Oaks; OPELIKA: Carmike; PRATTVILLE: Movies; MUSCLE SHOALS: Cinema; PHENIX CITY: Phenix; SYLACAUGA: Plaza; TALLADEGA: Martin; TUSCALOOSA: Bama.
ARKANSAS—FT. SMITH: Carmike; LITTLE ROCK: Carmike; N. LITTLE ROCK: Carmike.
COLORADO—ASPEN: Stage; COLORADO SPRINGS: Chapel Hills, Citadel, Carmike; DURANGO: Gaslight; FT. COLLINS: Creger Plaza, University, Carmike; GREELEY: Cinema; GRAND JUNCTION: Carmike; STEAMBOAT SPRINGS: Chief Plaza, Ski Time Square Cinema.
FLORIDA—BRADENTON: Arcadia, Cortez; BRANDON: Brandon, Plitt; BROOKSVILLE: Brooksville; CLEARWATER: Countryside, Main Street; JACKSONVILLE: Baymeadows, Mandarin Corner; LAKE WALES: Lake Wales; LAKELAND: Palm Cinema; LARGO: Ulmerton Cinema; OCALA: Ocala Springs; ORLANDO: Hoffner Corner, University; PANAMA CITY: Panama City, Carmike; PENSACOLA: Carmike, Mariner; PLANT CITY: Lake Waldon Cinema; SEBRING: Fairmont Cinema, Lakeshore Cinema; SOUTH DAYTONA: Big Tree; TALLAHASSEE: Mugs & Movies; TAMPA: Hillsboro, Main Street, University Collection; TARPON SPRINGS: Tarpon Springs; WINTERHAVEN: Boulevard, Continental Mugs & Movies.
GEORGIA—ALBANY: Georgia, Carmike; AMERICUS: Cinema; ATHENS: Cinema; ATHENS: Georgia Square I, Georgia Square II; CALHOUN: Martin; CARTERSVILLE: Plaza; COLUMBUS: Carmike, Columbus Square, Peachtree, Plaza; CONYERS: Conyers; CORDELE: Martin; CUMMING: Cumming; DALTON: Carmike; DORAVILLE: Friday Plaza; DOUGLAS: Martin; DOUGLASVILLE: Douglasville, Douglasville Exchange; DUBLIN: Cinema, Westgate; DULUTH: Mall Corners; FITZGERALD:

Capri; FT. OGLETHORPE: Southgate; GRIFFIN: Griffin; LA GRANGE: LaGrange; MARIETTA: Merchants, Town Center; MILLEDGEVILLE: Carmike; MORROW: Southlake Festival, Southlake Plaza; PEACHTREE CITY: Westpark; ROSWELL: Brannon Square, Holcomb Woods; SAVANNAH: Carmike; SNELLVILLE: Snellville; STATESBORO: Cinema; STOMNE MOUNTAIN: Stone Mountain; TIFTON: Tifton.
IDAHO—BLACKFOOT: Plaza; BOISE: 5 Mile Plaza; CHUBBUCK: Starlite; IDAHO FALLS: Rio Theatre, Yellowstone; MOSCOW: Kenworthy, Nuart, University; POCATELLO: Alameda; REXBURG: Holiday, Westwood.
ILLINOIS—COLLINSVILLE: Petite; GALESBURG: Cinema; MACOMB: Cinema.
IOWA—CEDAR RAPIDS: Carmike, Collins Rd., Lindale Mall, Stage, Westdale; COUNCIL BLUFFS: Mall of the Bluffs; DES MOINES: Carmike, Cobblestone, Fleur, Forum, River Hills, Sierra, Southridge, Valley, Value Cinema, Westwood; DUBUQUE: Cinema Center, Kennedy Mall.
KENTUCKY—BOWLING GREEN: Plaza, Greenwood, Martin; HOPKINSVILLE: Martin; LEXINGTON: Carmike; MADISONVILLE: Martin.
LOUISIANA—ALEXANDRIA: Alexandria; LAFAYETTE: Acadiana; LAKE CHARLES: Prien Lake; SLIDELL: North Shore.
MARYLAND—HAGERSTOWN: Theatres; OCEAN CITY: Gold Coast, Sun & Surf.
MICHIGAN—HOUGHTON: Copper; MARQUETTE: Delft.
MINNESOTA—ALBERT LEA: Mall; AUSTIN: Oak Park, Sterling; COON RAPIDS: Springbrook; FOREST LAKE: Forest Lake; HUTCHINSON: State; NEW ULM: Cinema; ROBBINSDALE: Terrace; ROCHESTER: Apache, Barclay, Cinema, Galleria; WILMAR: Midco; WINONA: Cinema.
MONTANA—BILLINGS: Carmike, Cine, Rimrock, World West; BOZEMAN: Campus Square, Ellen, Rialto; BUTTE: Plaza; GREAT FALLS: Cinema, Twilite, Village; HELENA: Circus, Gaslight; MISSOULA: Cinema, Village.
NEBRASKA—GRAND ISLAND: Conestoga, Island; HASTINGS: Imperial; OMAHA: Orchard.
NEW MEXICO—ARTESIA: Cinema.
NEW YORK—ALLEGANY: Carmike.
NORTH CAROLINA—ASHEBORO: Cinema; ASHEVILLE: Mall; BOONE: Chalet, Apalachian; CAROLINA BEACH: Cinema; CARY: Waverly Place; CHAPEL HILL: Ram; CHARLOTTE: University, Town Cinema; DUNN: Plaza; DURHAM: Carmike, Wynnsong, Willowdale; EDEN: Kingsway; FAYETTEVILLE: Westwood, Bordeaux; FOREST CITY: Cinema; GASTONIA: East Ridge; GOLDSBORO: Berkely; GREENSBORO: Circle; GREENVILLE: Capri, Park, Plaza, Buccaneer; HAVELOCK: Cinema; HICKORY: Terrace; HIGH POINT: Capri, Carmike; JACKSONVILLE: Cardinal, Northwoods, Bryn Mawr, Carmike, Cinema; KINSTON: Plaza; LAURINBURG: Cinema; LENOIR: Westgate; LEXINGTON: Cinema; LINCOLNTON: Cinema; MATTHEWS: Festival; MOREHEAD: Morehead, Cinema; MORGANTON: Studio, Mimosa; NEW BERN: Cinema; NORTH WILKSBORO: Westpark, Mall; RALEIGH: Blueridge, Six Forks, Tower, Merchant, Carmike; ROANOKE RAPIDS: Cinema; ROCKINGHAM: Plaza; ROCKY MOUNT: Cardinal, Golden East, Englewood, Oakwood; SANFORD: Kendale; SHELBY: Cinema, Mall; Southern Pines; SOUTHERN PINES: Cinema, Town & Country; STATESVILLE: Gateway, Newtowne; WASHINGTON: Cinema; WILMINGTON: Cinema, Ind. Mall; WILSON: Parkwood, Gold Park; WINSTON-SALEM: Carmike, Market Place, Reynolda.
NORTH DAKOTA—BISMARCK: Midco, Plaza; DEVILS LAKE: Lake; GRAND FORKS: Midco, Columbia, Plaza; DICKSON: Cinema; MINOT: Cine North, Cine South.
OHIO—ASHTABULA: Mall; EAST LIVERPOOL: Skyview; FINDLAY: Findlay, Palace; MANSFIELD: Kingsgate; MT. VERNON: Colonial; ST. CLAIRSVILLE: Mall; SANDUSKY: Plaza; STEUBENVILLE: Cinema.
OKLAHOMA—ARDMORE: Carmike; BARTLESVILLE: Eastland, Penn; CUSHING: Dunkin; ELK CITY: Westland; ENID: Oakwood, Video; LAWTON: Video, Carmike; MUSKOGEE: Cinema; PONCA CITY: North Park; SHAWNEE: Cinema, Hornbeck; STILLWATER: Carmike, Satellite.
PENNSYLVANIA—ALTOONA: Park Hills, Carmike; BEAVER FALLS: Plaza; BUTLER: Clearview; CHAMBERSBURG: Southgate, Cinema; CHAMBERSBURG: Southgate, Cinema; DUBOIS: Cinema; EDINBORO: Village; ERIE: Cinema World, Eastway, Plaza; GREENSBURG: Cinema, Greensburg, Greengate; HANOVER: Cinemas; HUMMELS WHARF: Sunbury; INDIANA: Cinema, Regency; IRWIN: Norwin; KITTANING: Cinema; LEBANON: Cinema; LATROBE: Laurel; MONACA: Movies; OIL CITY: Cranberry; PITTSBURGH: Crnberry, Galleria, Village, Southland, Monroeville, Rainbow, Maxisaver; POTTSTOWN: Coventry; POTTSVILLE: Cinema; READING: Fairgrounds, Wyomissing; SHARON: Hermitage; STATE COLLEGE: Cinema I, Cinema II, State, The Movies; UNIONTOWN: Carmike, Cinema; VANDERGRIFT: Cinema; WARREN: Cinema; WASHINGTON: Cinema, Mall.
SOUTH CAROLINA—AIKEN: Cinema; CHARLESTON: Carmike, Ultravision; CHESTER: Cinema; CLEMSON: Astro; COLUMBIA: Carmike, Wynnsong; FLORENCE: Magnolia; GREENVILLE: Carmike; GREENWOOD: Apollo, Cross Creek; HARTSVILLE:

Cinema; LAURENS: Oak; MT. PLEASANT: Carmike; MYRTLE BEACH: Myrtle, Briarcliff, Dunes, Broadway at the Beach; N. MYRTLE BEACH: Ocean; ORANGEBURG: Camelot, Cinema; ROCK HILL: Carmike; SPARTANBURG: Carmike, Wynnsong; SUMTER: Cinema, Movies, Palmetto; SURFSIDE: Deerfield.
SOUTH DAKOTA—ABERDEEN: Midco; RAPID CITY: Carmike, Rushmore; SIOUX FALLS: Carmike, Empire, West Mall.
TENNESSEE—ATHENS: Plaza; CHATTANOOGA: East Ridge, Four Square, North Gate, Wynnsong; CLARKSVILLE: Carmike, Cinema,Martin; CLEVELAND: Carmike, Village; CROSSVILLE: Capri; DYERSBURG: Martin; COOKEVILLE: Higland, Varsity; COOL SPRINGS: Galleria; FRANKLIN: Williamson Square; GREENVILLE: Capri; JOHNSON CITY: Johnson City; KINGS-PORT: Fort Henry, Martin, Terrace; KNOXVILLE: Carmike, Commons, Movies; LAFOLETTE: Movies; LEBANON: Martin; MARYVILLE: Foothills; MORRISTOWN: Capri, College Square; MURFREESBORO: Carmike, Stone Rivers; NASHVILLE: Belcourt, Fountain Square, Carmike, Hermitage, Bell Forge, Bellevue, Rivergate, Cinema North, Cinema South, Lionshead, Bell, Wynnsong; SPRINGFIELD: Springfield.
TEXAS—ABILENE: AMARILLO: Cinema; BEAUMONT: Colonade; BORGER: Morley; COLLEGE STATION: Post Oak, Cinema; CONROE: Woodcreek; DENTON: Cinema; GREEN-VILLE: Rolling Hills; JACKSONVILLE: Cinema; LAKE JACK-SON: Brazos, Cinema; LONGVIEW: North Loop, Martin, Carmike; LUFKIN: Town Square, Cinema, Angelina; NACODOCHES: Carmike I, Carmike II; ORANGE: Cinema; PLAINVIEW: Granada; PORT ARTHUR: Mall; SILSBEE: Pines; TYLER: Southloop, Times Square; WACO: Cinema, Waco Square; WICHITA FALLS: Century City, Cinema, Sikes.
UTAH—LOGAN: Cache Valley; OGDEN: City Square, Riverdale; OREM: Carrilon; PROVO: Academy, Central Square; SALT LAKE CITY: Cottonwood, Creekside, Flick, Plaza, Villa, Carmike.
VIRGINIA—BRISTOL: Bristol; CHARLOTTESVILLE: Carmike, Terrace; DANVILLE: Riverside, Plaza; LYNCHBURG: Carmike, River Ridge; NEWPORT NEWS: Beechmont; ROANOKE: Tanglewood, Valley View; SALEM: Salem Valley; WILLIAMS-BURG: Carmike, Williamsburg Crossing; WINCHESTER: Appleblossom, Cinema Center.
WASHINGTON—PULLMAN: Cordova, Old Post Office.
WEST VIRGINIA—BARBOURSVILLE: Huntington Mall; BLUE-FIELD: Cinema, Blue Prince; CLARKSBURG: Meadowbrook; HUNTINGTON: Huntington; MORGANTOWN: Warner, Mall.
WISCONSIN—APPLETON: Fox River; BELOIT: Prairie; DELE-VAN: Delevan; EAU CLAIRE: Oak Wood; GREEN BAY: Bay; LACROSSE: Valley; LAKE GENEVA: Geneva; MADISON: University; MARSHFIELD: Marshfield; RICE LAKE: Rice Lake; STEVENS POINT: Stevens Point; SUPERIOR: Mariner; WAUSAU: Wausau.
WYOMING—CASPER: Eastridge, Beverly; CHEYENNE: Frontier, Cole Square; JACKSON: Teton; LARAMIE: Wyo Theatre; ROCK SPRINGS: White Mountain.

CENTRAL STATES THEATRE CORP.

26 theatres, 75 screens.
505 Fifth Ave., Insurance Exchange Bldg., Des Moines, IA 50309. (515) 243-5287.
PRESIDENT & TREASURER
Myron Blank
V. P., ASSISTANT SECRETARY
Jacqueline Blank
GENERAL MANAGER
Arthur Stein, Jr.
SECRETARY, ASSISTANT TREASURER
R. D. Jackson
IOWA—AMES: Century 3, Mall 2, Varsity 2; CEDAR FALLS: Cinema 4, Hillcrest D.I.; COUNCIL BLUFFS: Drive-In; DES MOINES: S.E. 14th St. D.I.; FORT DODGE: Cinema 4; CENTER-VILLE: Majestic; CHARLES CITY: Charles; CLINTON: Capri III, Cinema I; IOWA CITY: Coral 4, Englert 2, Cinema 2, Campus 3; MASON CITY: Cinema V, Drive-In; NEWTON: Capitol 2; OTTUMWA: Capri V; FAIRFIELD: CoEd 2.
NEBRASKA—COLUMBUS: Center 6; FREMONT: Cinema 3; KEARNEY: World 2, Drive-In; NORFOLK: Cinema 3.

CENTURY THEATRES

65 theatres, 475 screens reported.
150 Golden Gate Ave., San Francisco, CA 94102. (415) 885-8400.
PRESIDENT
Raymond W. Syufy
SENIOR EXECUTIVE V. P.
Joseph Syufy
EXECUTIVE V. P., BUSINESS AFFAIRS
Mike Plymesser
EXECUTIVE V. P., FILMS & ADVERTISING
David Shesgreen
EXECUTIVE V. P., CORPORATE DEVELOPMENT
Greg Rutkowski
ARIZONA—GLENDALE: Glendale 9 D.I.; TEMPE: Scottsdale 6 D.I.; TUCSON: Century Gateway 12, Century Park 12.
CALIFORNIA—BURLINGAME: Hyatt Cinema Triplex, Burlingame 4 D.I.; CARSON: Southbay 6 D.I.; CITRUS

HEIGHTS: Cinedome 9; CONCORD: Solano 2 D.I.; DALY CITY: Geneva 4 D.I.; FREMONT: Cinedome 8; MOUNTAIN VIEW: Century Cinema 16; NAPA: Cinedome 8 Complex; NEWARK: Cinedome 7-plex; NORTH HOLLYWOOD: Century 8; OAKLAND: Century 8; ORANGE: Cinedome 11, City Center 4, Stadium 8 D.I.; PINOLE: Century 10 Complex; PLEASANT HILL: Century 5-plex; REDWOOD: Century Park 12; SACRAMENTO: Capitol 4-plex, State 6-plex, Sacramento 6 D.I., 49er 6 D.I., Century 14 Complex; SALINAS: Century Park 7, Northridge 8-plex; SAN FRANCISCO: Cinema 21, Empire 3, Presidio; SOUTH SAN FRANCISCO: Century Plaza 8; SAN JOSE: Century Almaden 5, Century 21, Century 22 Triplex, Century 23 Twin, Century 24 Twin, Century 25 Twin, Century Berryessa 10, Capitol 6 D.I., Capitol 16; UNION CITY: Union City 6 D.I.; VALLEJO: Cinedome 8; VENTURA: Century 8.
NEVADA—HENDERSON: Cinedome 12; LAS VEGAS: Century Desert 12; Cinedome 12, Las Vegas D.I.; Redrock 11; RENO: Century 11, Cine Old Towne Triplex; SPARKS: El Rancho 4 D.I.
NEW MEXICO—ALBUQUERQUE: Albuquerque 6 D.I.
UTAH—SALT LAKE CITY: Century 21-23 Triplex, Century 24-29 Twin.

CHAKERES THEATRES

25 theatres, 63 screens.
State Theatre Bldg., 222 N. Murray, Box 1200, Springfield, OH 45501. (513) 323-6447. FAX: (513) 325-1100.
PRESIDENT & CEO
Michael H. Chakeres
VICE PRESIDENT & COO
Philip H. Chakeres
VICE PRESIDENT
Harry N. Chakeres
DIRECTOR OF ADVERTISING
Paul Ramsey
COMPTROLLER
Elden L. Paden
KENTUCKY—FRANKFORT: Brighton Park Cinemas 1 & 2, Franklin Square Cinemas 6; LEXINGTON/WINCHESTER: Skyvue D.I. 1 & 2; MOREHEAD: University Cinema 3.
OHIO—BELLFONTAINE: Bellefontaine 8; CELINA: Celina Cinema 5, Lake D.I.; DAYTON: Kettering Cinemas 1 & 2, Melody 49 D.I. 1 & 2, Belmont Auto; FAIRBORN: Fairborn Cinemas 1 & 2, Skyborn D.I.; NEW CARLISLE: Park Layne D.I.; PORTSMOUTH: Scioto Breeze D.I. 1 & 2; SIDNEY: Sidney Cinemas 1-3; SPRINGFIELD: Cinemas 10, Upper Valley Mall Cinemas 5, Melody Cruise-In 1 & 2; URBANA: Urbana Cinemas 1 & 2; WILMINGTON: Plaza Cinemas 5, Wilmington D.I.

CINAMERICA CORPORATION (MANN THEATRES)

68 theatres, 401 screens.
P.O. 20077, Encino, CA 91416-0077; 16530 Ventura Blvd., Suite 500, Encino, CA, 91436. (818) 784-6266. FAX: (818) 784-8717.
PRESIDENT & CEO
Charles Goldwater
EXECUTIVE V. P., FINANCE
Ken Crowe
EXECUTIVE V. P., REAL ESTATE & DEVELOPMENT
Ben Littlefield
V. P., FILM
Denise Gurin
EXECUTIVE DIRECTOR, FILM
Alan Davy
V.P., CONSTRUCTION & DEVELOPMENT
Bruce Coleman
EXECUTIVE DIRECTOR, THEATRE DEVELOPMENT
Dan Griesmer
EXEC. DIRECTOR, THEATRE OPERATIONS PROGRAMS
Cindy Cronkhite
EXECUTIVE DIRECTOR, CONCESSIONS OPERATIONS
Wally Helton
DIRECTOR, REAL ESTATE
David Lichterman
EXECUTIVE DIRECTOR, MARKETING & PUBLICITY
Rich Given
ALASKA—ANCHORAGE: University 6-plex; EAGLE RIVER: Valley River 6-plex.
ARIZONA—TUCSON: Park Mall 4-plex.
CALIFORNIA—AGOURA HILLS: Agoura Hills 8; ARROYO GRANDE: Festival 10-plex; BAKERSFIELD: Crest Drive-In Twin; CITY OF INDUSTRY: Puente Hills 6; CLOVIS: Regency 6-plex; CULVER CITY: Culver Plaza 6; FRESNO: Festival 6-plex, Fig Garden 4-plex; GLENDALE: Exchange 8, Glendale Mann 9; GLEN-DORA: Glendora 6; GRANADA HILLS: Mann 9; HAYWARD: Festival 9-plex; HOLLYWOOD: Chinese 3; LA JOLLA: University Towne Center 6-plex; LARKSPUR: Festival 4-plex; MANHATTAN BEACH: Manhattan Village 6; MARTINEZ: Contra Costa 5-plex; MODESTO: Festival 10-plex; MONROVIA: Huntington Oaks 6-plex; NATIONAL CITY: Plaza Bonita 6-plex; OCEANSIDE: El Camino 8-plex; PASADENA: Hastings Ranch Triplex; SAN DIEGO: Grove 9, Cinema 21, Hazard Center 7, Round

Bernardo 6-plex, Sports Arena 6-plex, Valley Circle; SAN RAMON: Crow Canyon 6-plex; SANTA FE SPRINGS: Santa Fe Springs 8; SANTA MONICA: Criterion 6; SIMI VALLEY: Sycamore Plaza 6; STOCKTON: Festival 4-plex, Regency 4-plex; TARZANA: Valley West 9-plex; THOUSAND OAKS: Janss Marketplace 9-plex; TORRANCE: Del Amo 9; VALENCIA: Mann 10-plex; VENTURA: Buenaventura 6-plex; VISALIA: Fox Triplex, Sequoia 12; WALNUT CREEK: Festival 5-plex; WESTLAKE: Northranch 8; WESTWOOD: Bruin, Mann 4-plex, National, Plaza, Regent, Village, Festival.
COLORADO—ARVADA: Olde Towne 14; AURORA: Aurora Plaza 6; BOULDER: Arapahoe Village 4, Crossroads 6; DENVER: Cherry Creek 8, Tamarac Square 6-plex; ENGLEWOOD: Arapahoe East 4-plex; LAKEWOOD: Green Mountain 6-plex, Union Square 6-plex, LITTLETON: Bowles Crossing 12, Festival 6, Southwest Plaza 5-plex; LOUISVILLE: Colony Square 12; NORTHGLENN: Northglenn 6-plex.

CINEMA ENTERTAINMENT CORP.

15 theatres, 92 screens.
Box 1126, St. Cloud, MN 56302. (320) 251-9131. FAX: (320) 251-1003.
PRESIDENT
Robert A. Ross
GENERAL MANAGER
Edward Villata
VICE PRESIDENT
Anthony D. Tillemans
SECRETARY
David M. Ross
TREASURER
George R. Becker
BOOKER
Stanley McCulloch
IOWA—WATERLOO: Crossroads 10.
MINNESOTA—BEMIDJI: Amigo 7; BRECKENRIDGE: Cinema 4; DULUTH: Cinema 8, Lakes 8; FARIBAULT: Cinema 6; ST CLOUD: Crossroads 6, Parkwood 8, Cinema Arts 3; MOORHEAD: Safari 7; VIRGINIA: Cinema 6.
NORTH DAKOTA—FARGO: West Acres 5, West 3, Century 7.
WISCONSIN—HUDSON: Southside Cinema 4.

CINEMACAL ENTERPRISES, INC.

9 theatres, 38 screens.
1130 Burnett Ave., Suite J, P.O. Box 27848, Concord, CA 94527. (510) 685-6650. FAX: (510) 685-6507.
PRESIDENT & CEO
Dale Davison
V. P. & HEAD FILM BUYER
Lou Lencioni III
V.P., OPERATIONS
Ron Dunning
V.P., FINANCE
Sue Sherer
V.P., ADVERTISING
Maurice L'Estrange
ADMINISTRATIVE ASSISTANT
Pat Petersen
CALIFORNIA—CARMEL: Crossroads 2; MONTEREY: Galaxy 6; MORGAN HILL: Cinema 6, Granada 2; PACIFIC GROVE: Lighthouse 4; SAN BRUNO: Tanforan 4; STOCKTON: Royal 4, Sherwood Plaza 2; VACAVILLE: Galaxy 8.

CINEMAGIC USA

5 theatres, 17 screens.
1300 Fulton Building, 107 Sixth St., Pittsburgh, PA 15222. (412) 232-3015.
PRESIDENT & CEO
Richard Stern
DIRECTOR, THEATRE OPERATIONS
Vincent F. Porco
FILM BUYER
Arlene S. Wiener
PENNSYLVANIA—PITTSBURGH: Bellevue 2, Denis 4, Hollywood, Manor 4, Squirrel Hill 6.

CINEMARK USA, INC.

169 U.S. theatres, 1444 U.S. screens; Canada- 2 theatres, 24 screens; Mexico- 11 theatres, 114 screens; Chile- 2 theatres, 19 screens; TOTAL: 184 theatres, 1601 screens.
7502 Greenville Ave., Suite 800, Dallas, TX 75231. (214) 860-0823. FAX: (214) 696-3946. Buying & Booking Office: (214) 692-1425, 692-1471, 692-1419. FAX: (214) 696-1834.
CHAIRMAN & CEO
Lee Roy Mitchell
PRESIDENT
Alan Stock
EXECUTIVE V. P.
Tandy Mitchell
V. P., FILM LICENSING
Jerry Brand

V. P., OPERATIONS
Robert Carmony
V. P. & GENERAL COUNSEL
Gary Gibbs
PRESIDENT, 2 DAY VIDEO
Walter Hebert
DIRECTOR CORPORATE DEVELOPMENT
Randy Hester
DIRECTOR, CONSTRUCTION
Don Harton
PRESIDENT, CINEMARK DE MEXICO
Ken Higgins
V.P., REAL ESTATE
Margaret Richards
CFO
Jeff Stedman
DIRECTOR OF DESIGN
Pam Taylor
PRESIDENT, CINEMARK INTERNATIONAL
Tim Warner
DIRECTOR, MIS
Philip Wood
ARIZONA—KINGMAN: The Movies 4.
ARKANSAS—CONWAY: Cinema 6; NORTH LITTLE ROCK: Tandy 10.
CALIFORNIA—CATHEDRAL CITY: Movies 10; CHICO: Movies 8; CHINO: Movies 8; DANVILLE: Blackhawk Movies 7; HANFORD: Movies 4, Movies 8 Hanford Mall; HEMET: Holiday Cinema III; LANCASTER: Movies 1-4, Movies 5-7, Movies West, Movies 12; PALMDALE: Movies 8; REDDING: Movies 8, Movies 10; TRACY: Movies 14; VICTORVILLE: Movies 7, Movies 10; WOODLAND: County Fair Movies 5; YUBA CITY: Yuba City 8.
DELAWARE—WILMINGTON: Movies 10.
FLORIDA—ORLANDO: Movies 12; TALLAHASSEE: Movies 8.
GEORGIA—FAYETTEVILLE: Movies 10.
ILLINOIS—BRADLEY: Movies 10; JOLIET: Movies 8, Movies 10.
INDIANA—CLARKSVILLE: Greentree Cinema 4, Greentree Cinema 10; INDIANAPOLIS: Greenwood Movies 8, Washington Market Movies 8; MISHAWAKA: Movies 10.
KANSAS—OVERLAND PARK: Movies 10.
KENTUCKY—ASHLAND: Cinema 10; LEXINGTON: Lexington Green 8, Man o' War 8, Movies 10; LOUISVILLE: Village 8; PADUCAH: Kentucky Oaks 12; RICHMOND: Cinema 8.
LOUISIANA—MONROE: Cinema III, Cinema 10.
MICHIGAN—LIVONIA: Terrace Cinema 4, ROSEVILLE: Macomb Mall Cinema 4; SOUTHFIELD: Tel-Ex Cinema 4; WARREN: Movies 16.
MINNESOTA—MANKATO: Movies 8.
MISSISSIPPI—TUPELO: Movies 8.
NEBRASKA—OMAHA: Movies 8- Stockyards.
NEW JERSEY—SOMERDALE: Somerdale Movies 8.
NEW MEXICO—ALBUQUERQUE: Movies 8, Movies West 8.
NEW YORK—ROCHESTER: Brighton Movies 10; TOWN OF GATES: Movies 16.
NORTH CAROLINA—ASHEBORO: Rudolph Cinema 5; GREENSBORO: Brassfield Cinema 10; MATTHEWS: Movies 10; SALISBURY: Salisbury Mall Cinema 6.
OHIO—ALLIANCE: Carnation Cinema 5; BOWLING GREEN: Woodland Mall Cinema 5; CANTON: Movies 4; COLUMBUS: Movies 10; Movies 12; GAHANNA: Movies 16; HILLIARD: Movies 12; MANSFIELD: Cinema 10; NORTH CANTON: Movies 10; ONTARIO: Richland Cinema III; PIQUA: Miami Valley Cinema 4; SANDUSKY: Cinemark Movies 10; WILLOUGHBY HILLS: Loehman's Plaza Movies 10; WOOSTER: Movies 10; YOUNGSTOWN: Movies 8; ZANESVILLE: Cinema 10.
OKLAHOMA—ADA: North Hills 6; BROKEN ARROW: Cinema 8; SAND SPRINGS: Cinema 8; TULSA: Movies 8.
OREGON—MEDFORD: Cinema 4, Cinema 5; SPRINGFIELD: Movies 12; WHITE CITY: White City 6.
PENNSYLVANIA—EDWARDSVILLE: West Side Mall Movies 10; ERIE: Millcreek Cinema 6, Millcreek Cinema 3, Movies 17.
SOUTH CAROLINA—SUMMERVILLE: Movies 8 Ladson Oakbrook II.
TENNESSEE—OAK RIDGE: Oak Ridge Movies 8; OLIVER SPRINGS: Tri-County Cinema 3.
TEXAS—AMARILLO: Bell Plaza Cinema 4; AUSTIN: Dollar Cinema 8; BAY CITY: Cinema 4; BIG SPRING: Movies 4; BROWNSVILLE: Movies 8, Northpark Plaza 3,Sunrise III; CARROLTON: Movies 8; COLLEGE STATION: Hollywood Movies 16; CONROE: Pine Hollow 6; CLEBURNE: Cinema 6; CORISCANA: Cinema IV; CORPUS CHRISTIE: Corpus Christie 16 Dollar Cinemas 7; DALLAS: Cinemark 17, Skillman Cinema 6; FORT WORTH: Wedgewood 4; GARLAND: Hollywood USA 15; GRAND PRAIRIE: Moviesa 16; GRAPEVINE: Tinseltown 17; HARLINGEN: Cinema Triple, Cinemark Valle Vista 3, Commerce Twin, Movies 10; HOUSTON: Bear Creek 6, Eastway 4, NW Village Cinema 6; KATY: Mason Park 8; KINGSVILLE: Cinema I & II; LANCASTER: Movies 8; LAREDO: Movies 12; LEWISVILLE: Movies 12; LUBBOCK: Movies 4 Slide Road, Movies 16; MC ALLEN: Main Place 6; Movies 17; MC KINNEY Movies 14; MESQUITE: Big Town Cinema 9; N. Richmond Hills: Movies 8; PARIS: Cinemas I & II; PASADENA: Movies 16, Southmore 6; PFLUGERVILLE: Movies 12; PHARR: Movies 8;

PLAINVIEW: Town Centre Movies 6; PLANO: Movies 10; ROCK-WALL: Rockwall 8; ROSENBERG: Rosenberg 8; ROUND ROCK: Movies 8; SAN ANTONIO: Dollar Movies 16, Movies 9 McCreeless Mall; SHERMAN: Cinema 7, Discount Cinema 4, Midway Movies 5; STEPHENVILLE: Cinema 6; TEXARKANA: Movies 12; TEXAS CITY: Movies 12; VICTORIA: Cinema IV, Playhouse Cinema 4, Salem Cinema 6: WESLACO: Palm Plaza 2; WOODLANDS: The Woodlands 17.
UTAH—LAYTON: Layton Hills 6, Movies 10; OGDEN: Newgate 4; PARK CITY: Village Cinema 3; PROVO: Movies 10; SALT LAKE CITY: Sugarhouse Movies 10; SANDY: Movies 9; WEST VALLEY: Valley Fair 9.
VIRGINIA—CHESAPEAKE: Movies 10; LYNCHBURG: Movies 10.
WISCONSIN—MILWAUKEE: Movies 10.
CANADA
ALBERTA—EDMONTON: Cinema City 12, Movies 12.
CENTRAL AMERICA
MEXICO—ACAPULCO: Oceanic 2000 Movies 8; AGUAS-CALIENTES: Expo Movies 10, CHIHUAHUA: Plaza Hollywood Movies 12; HERMOSILLO: Cinemark Movies 10; IRAPUATO: Jacarandas Plaza Movies 10; JUAREZ: Plaza Del Camino Movies 10; MEXICO CITY: Centtro Cultural Movies 12, Pedregal Plaza Cinemark 10; MONTEREY: Plaza Le Fe 10; QUERTARO: Movies 12; REYNOSA: Plaza Del Rio Movies 10.
SOUTH AMERICA
CHILE—SANTIAGO: Cinemark 12; TALCAHUANO: Plaza Del Trebol 7.

CINEMA USA

9 theatres, 24 screens.
702 Park Ave., Suite 203, P.O. Box 1270, Norton VA 24273. (504) 679-3311. FAX: (540) 679-5773.
PRESIDENT & CEO
Jeffrey G. Kiser
EXECUTIVE V. P.
Jack L. Wagner, Jr.
OPERATIONS MANAGER
Clinton B. Griffin
DIVISION MANAGER, WESTERN REGION
Russell E.Kress
DIVISION MANAGER, EASTERN REGION
G. Todd Dillon
MEDIA & PROMOTION MANAGER
Michael Solomon
OFFICE MANAGER
Susie Peters
TENNESSEE—ROGERSVILLE: Cinemas USA East Gate 4.
VIRGINIA—DALE CITY: Dale 2; FALLS CHURCH: Loehmanns 2; HAMPTON: Riverdale 3; NORFOLK: Little Creek 3; PORTSMOUTH: Plaza 3; RADFORD: Radford 2; ROANOKE: Cinemas USA Crossroads 2, Towers 3.

CINEPLEX ODEON CORPORATION (U.S.)

189 U.S. theatres, 869 U.S. screens; 128 Canadian theatres, 619 Canadian screens; TOTAL: 317 theatres, 1488 screens.
1303 Yonge Street, Toronto, Ontario M4T 2Y9. (416) 323-6600
CHAIRMAN
Senator E. Leo Kolber
PRESIDENT & CEO
Allen Karp
SENIOR V. P. & HEAD FILM BUYER
Michael McCartney
EXECUTIVE V.P., MARKETING & COMMUNICATIONS
Howard Lichtman
EXECUTIVE V. P. & CFO
Ellis Jacobs
EXECUTIVE V. P.
Robert Tokio
EXECUTIVE V.P., OPERATIONS, NORTH AMERICA
Irwin Cohen
V.P., PUBL. & PROMO., N. A. THEATRE OPERATIONS
Jerry Bulger
EXECUTIVE V.P., CORPORATE AFFAIRS, & SECRETARY
Michael Herman
SR. V. P. FINANCE & M. I. S. , THEATRES
Jeffrey Kent
V. P. FILM, CENTRAL & WESTERN DIVISIONS
Shauna King
SENIOR V.P., ADVERTISING
William Snelling
V.P., OPERATIONS, NORTH AMERICA
Dan McGrath
V.P., MERCHANDISING
Ken Prue
Regional Cineplex Odeon U.S. Executive Offices
LOS ANGELES: 1925 Century Park East, Suite 300, Los Angeles, CA 90067. (310) 551-2500.
NEW YORK: 241 East 34th Street, New York, NY 10016. (212) 679-2000.
CHICAGO: 70 E. Lake St., Suite 1600, Chicago, IL 60601-5905. (312) 726-5300.
WASHINGTON, D.C.: 1101 23rd Street N.W., Washington, D.C. 20037. (202) 331-7471.

HOUSTON: 1450 West Gray, Houston, TX 77019. (713) 524-8731.
SEATTLE: 18421 Alderwood Mall Blvd., Lynnwood, WA 98036. (206) 771-9011.
ARIZONA—TUCSON: Catalina 6, Crossroads 6, El Dorado 6, Foothills 7.
CALIFORNIA—DALY CITY: Plaza 2; LOS ANGELES: Beverly Center 13, Century Plaza 4, Fairfax Triple, Showcase, Universal City 18; MARINA DEL REY: Marina Marketplace 6; SANTA MONICA: Broadway 4; RICHMOND: Hilltop 8; SAN FRANCISCO: Northpoint.
DISTRICT OF COLUMBIA—WASHINGTON: Cinema Avalon 2, Dupont 5, Embassy, Wisconsin Ave. 6, MacArthur 3, Outer Circle 2, Tenley 3, Uptown, West End 7, Janus 3, Foundry 7, Mazzia Galleria 3, Cinema.
IDAHO—BOISE: Egyptian, 86th St. Marketplace 2, Northgate 6, Towne Square 6; NAMPA: Nampa Cinemas 6.
ILLINOIS—ARLINGTON HEIGHTS: Ridge 8, Town & Country 6; AURORA: Fox Valley 10, West Plaza 3, Westridge Court 8; BLOOMINGDALE: Stratford Square 8, Bloomingdale Court 6; CALUMET CITY: River Oaks 12; CARPENTERSVILLE: Springhill Mall 6; CHICAGO: Bricktown Square 6, Broadway Lakeshore, Biograph 3, Burnham Plaza 5, Chestnut Station 5, Chicago Ridge 6, Commons 4, Lincoln Village 3, Lincoln Village 6, McClurg 3, Plaza 3, 900 North Michigan 2, Water Tower 7, 600 N. Michgan 9, Navy Pier Imax 3-D; DOWNERS GROVE: Grove Cinemas 6; HOMEWOOD: Diana 4; NILES: Golf Mill 3, Golf Glen 6; NORTH RIVERSIDE: North Riverside Theatres 6; OAKBROOK: Oakbrook 3, Oakbrook 4; ORLAND PARK: Orland Square 10; SCHAUMBURG: One Schaumburg 9; Woodfield 9; SKOKIE: Gardens at Old Orchard 7; ST. CHARLES: Foxfield 4, St. Charles 3; VERNON HILLS: Hawthorn Quad, Rivertree Court 8; WHEATON: Rice Lake 10.
MARYLAND—BOWIE: Market Place 6; GAITHERSBURG: Rio 14 Cinemas, Lakeforest 5; St. Charles Towne 9; KENSINGTON: White Flint 5; MARLOW HEIGHTS: Marlow 6; WALDORF: Waldorf North 4, Waldorf South 5; WHEATON: Wheaton Plaza 4.
MINNESOTA—EDINA: Edina 4, Yorktown 3; MINNEAPOLIS: Skyway 6; MINNETONKA: Ridge Square 3, Westwind 3; PLYMOUTH: Willow Creek 8; ST. LOUIS PARK: Knollwood 4.
NEW JERSEY—BLOOMFIELD: Royal Twin; CRANFORD: Cranford Twin; JERSEY CITY: Newport Centre 11; MENLO PARK: Menlo Park 12; MILLBURN: Millburn Twin; PARAMUS: Paramus Rte. 17 3, Paramus Rt. 4 10; RIDGEWOOD: Warner Quad; UNION: Union Twin.
NEW YORK—NEW YORK CITY: BROOKLYN: Cinema III, Metropolitan 4, Alpine 7, Fortway 5, Kenmore Quad, Kings Plaza Quad, Kingsway 5; MANHATTAN: 23rd Street West 3, Baronet, Coronet, Ziegfield, 34th St., Manhattan Twin, Waverly Twin, National Twin, Greenwich Twin, Carnegie Hall 2, Metro 2, Regency, Chelesea 9, Park & 86th 2, 62nd & Broadway, 1st & 62nd, Beekman, Olympia Twin, Plaza, Worldwide Cinemas 6, 59th St. East; FRESH MEADOWS: Meadows 7, City Cinema 5; HUNTINGTON: Shore Quad, Whitman; LAKE GROVE: Smithhaven Mall Theatre 4; LAWRENCE: Lawrence Triplex; NANUET: Nanuet 5-plex; ROCKVILLE CENTER: Fantasy 5, Rockville Twin; GLEN COVE: Glen Cove 6; PORT WASHINGTON: Soundview 6, Islip Cinema 3, Hampton Arts Twin, Mattituck 8.
TEXAS—BAYTOWN: Cinema 6, Goosecreek Cinema 6, Plitt Cinema 4, HOUSTON: Plitt 5, West Oaks 7, Presidio Square 6, River Oaks 12, Sharpstown Center 8, Spectrum 9; TEMPLE: Cinema 5, Plitt 6.
UTAH—MIDVALE: Family Center 4; NORTH SALT LAKE CITY: Trolley North 3; ODGEN: Cinedome 2, Wilshire 3; OREM: University 4; SALT LAKE CITY: Broadway 4, Crossroads 3, Holladay Center 6, Midvalley Cinemas 6, Trolley Corners 3, Trolley Square Mall 4; SANDY: Southtowne Centre 10.
VIRGINIA—ALEXANDRIA: Old Town 2; ARLINGTON: Shirlington 7; FAIRFAX: Fair City Mall 6; LAKERIDGE: Tackett's Mills 4; MANASSAS: Manassas Mall 7; VIENNA: Fairfax Square 8.
WASHINGTON—BELLEVUE: Factoria 8, John Danz; KIRKLAND: Kirkland Parkplace 6, Lakewood 6, Totem Lake 3; LYNWOOD: Grand Cinemas Alderwood 8, SEATTLE: Cinerama, City Center Cinemas 2, Lewis & Clark 7, Newmark Square 5, Northgate, Oak Tree 6, South Center, Uptown 3; TACOMA: Tacoma Central 6, Tacoma Mall Twin, Tacoma South 5, Tacoma West 5.

CINESTAR THEATRES, INC.

4 theatres, 8 screens.
P. O. Box 7248, Atlanta, GA 30357. (404) 875-2540. FAX: (404) 875-2014.
PRESIDENT
Donald L. Furr
V.P., TREASURER
David O. Bond
GEORGIA—CONYERS: Salem Gate Twin Cinema;THOMSON: Thomson Twin, WARNER ROBINS: Rama Twin.
TENNESSEE—CLEVELAND: Cinema 1 & 2.

CITY CINEMAS

10 theatres, 26 screens.
1001 Third Ave., New York, NY 10022. (212) 758-5600. FAX: (212) 832-1457.
CHAIRMAN
James J. Cotter
PRESIDENT & CEO
Robert Smerling
V. P. & GENERAL MANAGER
Richard Eininger
NEW YORK—NEW YORK CITY: Angelika Film Center, Cinema 1, Cinema 2, Cinema 3rd Ave., Eastside Playhouse, 86th St. East 1 & 2, Murray Hill 4, 68th St. Playhouse, Sutton 1 & 2, Village East Cinemas 7.

CLARK THEATRES

6 theatres, 47 screens.
P.O. Box 570, Enterprise, AL 36331. (334) 347-1129.
OWNER
Mack Clark, Jr.
ALABAMA—ANDALUSIA: Martin Twin Cinema; ENTERPRISE: Cinema I & II, Cinema III & IV, College Cinema 1, 2 & 3; OZARK: Twin Cinemas 2; TROY: Pike 3.

CLASSIC CINEMAS

15, theatres, 60 screens.
603 Rogers St. Downers Grove, IL 60515. (708) 968-1600. FAX: (708) 968-1626. (A division of Tivoli Enterprises, Inc.)
PRESIDENT
Willis Johnson
VICE PRESIDENT
Christopher Johnson
SECRETARY
Shirley Johnson
ILLINOIS—CARPENTERSVILLE: Cinema 12; DOWNERS GROVE: Tivoli, Tivoli South; ELGIN: Casino 3; ELK GROVE VILLAGE: Elk Grove 2; ELMHURST: York 5; FOX LAKE: Fox Lake 5; FREEPORT: Lindo 6; HANOVER PARK: Tradewinds 2; KANKAKEE: Meadowview 3, Paramount 5; OAK PARK: Lake 7; PARK FOREST: Park Forest 5; ST. CHARLES: Arcada; WOODSTOCK: Woodstock 2.

CLEARVIEW CINEMA CORP.

13 theatres, 47 screens.
7 Waverly Place, Madison, NJ 07940 (201) 377-4646. FAX (201) 377-4303.
PRESIDENT
A. Dale Mayo
V. P. OPERATIONS
Paul Kay
TREASURER
Sueanne H. Mayo
FILM BUYER.
Rose Devery
Craig Zeltner
NEW JERSEY—BERNARDSVILLE: Cinema 3; CHESTER: Chester Twin; CLIFTON: Allwood 6; EMERSON: Emerson Cinema 4; MADISON: Madison Cinema 4; MANASQUAN: Algonquin Arts, WASHINGTON TOWNSHIP: Washington Township Cinema 3.
NEW YORK—BALDWIN: Grand Ave. Cinema 2; BEDFORD: Bedford Cinemas 2; MT. KISCO: Mt. Kisco Cinemas 5; NEW CITY: New City Cinemas 6; NEW HYDE PARK: Herricks Cinemas 2; PORT WASHINGTON: Port Washington Cinemas 7.

COBB THEATRES

70 theatres, 593 screens.
Executive Office: 924 Montclair Road, Birmingham, AL 35213. (205) 591-2323. FAX: (205) 591-7715. Booking Office: 5485 Beltline Rd., Suite 230, Dallas TX 75240. (214) 404-9888. FAX: (214) 404-9892.
PRESIDENT
R. M. Cobb
EXECUTIVE V. P., SECRETARY & TREASURER
J. R. Cobb
SENIOR V. P. . OPERATIONS
Gary Golden
SENIOR V. P., OPERATIONS
Ricky Thomas
V.P., CONTROLLER
Judith Blank
V.P., REAL ESTATE
Wes Cline
V.P., ADVERTISING
Bob Zeitz
V.P., CONSTRUCTION
Rod Curlette
V. P., CONCESSIONS & MARKETING
Lee De Fore

V. P., PROJECTION & SOUND
Bob Wall
BOOKING OFFICE FILM BUYERS
Jim Ellis, Kevin Keller, Mike Cieminski
District 1 Mike McMaken, 924 Montclair Rd., Birmingham AL 35213. (205) 591-2323.
ALABAMA—BIRMINGHAM: Brook Highland 10, Centerpoint 6, Galleria 10, Festival 18, Hoover Square 6, Wildwood 14; HUNTSVILLE: Cinema Center 8, Madison Square 12, Hollywood 16; JASPER: Movies 4; SELMA: Cahaba Twin; TUSCALOOSA: Fox 12.
ARKANSAS—FAYETTEVILLE: Fiesta Square 10; ROGERS: Mall 6.
MISSISSIPPI—JACKSON: Metro Center 4.
District 2 (West Florida)- Bill Koontz, P. O. Box 6906, Fort Myers FL 32902. (941) 936-0831. FAX: (941) 936-7097.
FLORIDA—BRADENTON: Bradenton 8, DeSoto Square 6, Oakmont 8; CAPE CORAL: Coralwood 10; FT. MYERS: Edison 8, Bell Tower 18; LARGO: Largo Mall 8; NAPLES: Pavilion 10, Hollywood 20, Towne Centre 6; PINELLAS PARK: Pinella 3, Pinellas 6; PORT CHARLOTTE: Cinema Centre 8; PORT RICHEY: Embassy 6, Hollywood 18; SARASOTA: Crossing 10, Gulfgate 8, Parkway 8; SPRINGHILL: Springhill 8; TAMPA: Eastlake 3, Northdale 6, University 4.
District 3 (East & Central Florida)- Rob Kurrus, P. O. Box 310, Melbourne FL 32902. (407) 676-4273.
FLORIDA—BELLEVIEW: Belleview Twin; FT. PIERCE: Sabal Palm 6; KISSIMMEE: Osceola Square 12; LAKE WALES: Eagle Ridge 12; MELBOURNE: Oaks 10, Roxy 10; OCALA: Boulevard 6; ORLANDO: Southchase 7; PALM BAY: Palm Bay 10; SAINT AUGUSTINE: Mall 6; STUART: Martin Square 3, Regency Square 8; VERO BEACH: Galaxy 12; WINTER HAVEN: Springlake 10.
District 4 (Southeast Florida)- Gary McMakren, Sawgrass 18, 2600 NW 136th, Sunrise FL 33323. (305) 846-9116. FAX: (305) 846-8852.
FLORIDA—BAY HARBOR: Bay Harbor 4; BOCA RATON: Shadowood 12; BOYNTON BEACH: Boynton 8; GREEN ACRES CITY: Lakeworth 8; HOLLYWOOD: Oakwood 18; JUPITER: Jupiter 14; KEY WEST: Cinema 6; MIAMI: Mayfair 10, Miller Square 8, University 4, Kendall 9; MIAMI BEACH: Byron Carlyle 7; MIAMI LAKES: Miami Lakes 10; SUNRISE: Sawgrass 18.

COMING ATTRACTIONS, INC.

9 theatres, 48 screens.
P.O. Box 1240, Ashland, OR 97520-0055. (503) 488-1021. FAX: (503) 482-9290.
OWNER
John C. Schweiger
CALIFORNIA—CRESCENT CITY: Crescent City Cinema 6.
OREGON—ASHLAND: Varsity 5; FLORENCE: Florence 4; FOREST GROVE: Cinema 7; GRANT'S PASS: Movies 6 East, Movies 6 West; KLAMATH FALLS: Pelican 6; ROSEBURG: Cinema 7.
WASHINGTON—SNOHOMISH: Snohomish 3.

CONSOLIDATED AMUSEMENT CO., LTD.

21 theatres, 83 screens.
P.O. Box 30548, Honolulu, HI 96820. (808) 847-1985. FAX: (808) 847-9270. (A subsidiary of Pacific Theatres).
HAWAII—ISLAND OF HAWAII: HILO: Prince Kuhio Twin; Waiakea Triplex; KONA: Hualalai Triplex; ISLAND OF OAHU: Aikahi Twin, Cinerama, Kahala 8-Plex, Kam D.I. Twins, Kapiolani, Kapolei 16-plex, Koko Marina Twin, Kuhio Twin, Marina Twin, Mililani 5-Plex, Pearlridge 4-plex, Pearlridge West 12-Plex, Varsity Twin, Waikiki Twin, Waikiki 3; ISLAND OF MAUI: Maui Theatre, Kaahumanu 6-plex, Kukui Mall 4-Plex.

CROWN CINEMA CORPORATION

43 theatres, 173 screens.
406 West 34th St., Kansas City, MO 64111. (816) 753- 2355. FAX: (816) 931-6021.
PRESIDENT
Richard M. Durwood
CONTROLLER
Brent Hudson
HEAD FILM BUYER
Hal McClure
SECRETARY
Jackie Dixon
DIRECTOR OF OPERATIONS
Harold Sawtelle
DIRECTOR OF MARKETING
Keith Durwood
KANSAS—EMPORIA: Petite Twin 2; GARDEN CITY: Sequoyah 6, State; GREAT BEND: Village 3; HUTCHINSON: Cinema Twin, Mall 4, Mall 8; JUNCTION CITY: Westside 4; LAWRENCE: Cinema Twin, Hillcrest 5, Varsity; LEAVENWORTH: Landing 4; LIBERAL: Southgate 4; TOPEKA: Gage 4, West Ridge 8, West Ridge Mall 6; WICHITA: Cinema East 6, Cinema West 4, Towne East 6, Towne West 5.
MISSOURI—CHILLICOTHE: Ben Bolt; COLUMBIA: Campus 2, Cinema, Mall 4; JEFFERSON CITY: Ramada 4, Capital 4;

JOPLIN: Joplin 6; KANSAS CITY: Blue Ridge East 5, Blue Ridge West 6, Blue Springs 8, Chouteau 4, Red Bridge 4, Seville 4, Truman Corners 4, Watts Mill 4; ROLLA: Forum 2, Uptown; ST. JOSEPH: Hillcrest 4, Plaza 8; WARRENSBURG: Campus 2. **OHIO**—HEATH: Indian Mound 6; NEWARK: Newark 4.

CROWN THEATRES

10 theatres, 43 screens.
64 N. Main St., South Norwalk, CT 06854. (203) 846-8800. FAX: (203) 846-9828.
PRESIDENT
Daniel M. Crown
EXECUTIVE V. P. & COO
Milt Daly
EXECUTIVE V. P. & CFO
David Clifford
DIRECTOR OF OPERATIONS
Chris Dugger
CONTROLLER
Catherine Nonnenmacher
DIRECTOR ADVERTISING
Steve Gould
DIRECTOR OF SPECIAL PROJECTS
Thomas Becker
CONNECTICUT—DANBURY: Cine 3, Cinema 2; GREENWICH: Plaza 3; NORWALK: Sono Regent 8; STAMFORD: Landmark Square 9, Avon 2, Ridgway 2; TRUMBULL: Triple 3, Marquis 10. **NEW YORK**—NEW YORK CITY: Gotham.

DEANZA LAND & LEISURE CORP.

7 theatres, 28 screens.
1615 Cordova St., Los Angeles, CA 90007. (213) 734-9951.
PRESIDENT
William H. Oldknow
GENERAL MANAGER
Joseph Pietroforte
ARIZONA—TUSCON: DeAnza 4.
CALIFORNIA—POMONA: Mission 4; RUBIDOUX: Rubidoux 2; SAN DIEGO: South Bay 3; VAN BUREN: Van Buren 3.
GEORGIA—ATLANTA: Starlight 6.
UTAH—SALT LAKE CITY: Redwood 6.

DICKINSON OPERATING CO., INC. (D.B.A. DICKINSON THEATRES)

36 theatres, 155 screens reported.
5913 Woodson Road, Mission, KS 66202. (913) 432-2334. FAX: (913) 432-9507.
PRESIDENT & BOARD CHAIRMAN
Wood Dickinson
BOARD CHAIRMAN EMERITUS
Georgia Dickinson
VICE PRESIDENT
Scott Dickinson
V.P., COMMUNITY RELATIONS
Patti Dickinson
TREASURER/ASSISTANT SECRETARY
Steve Taul
CFO & ASSISTANT SECRETARY
Steve Krueger
V. P. & HEAD FILM BUYER
Frank Torchia
KANSAS—EMPORIA: Flinthills 8; HAYS: Fox 2; LAWRENCE: Dickinson Cinema 6; LEAVENWORTH: Plaza Cinema 6; NEWTON: Fox; OLATHE: Olathe Landing 8; OVERLAND PARK: Glenwood 4, SouthGlen 12; PITTSBURG: Mall Cinema 4; SALINA: Central Mall 4, Midstates 2, Sunset Plaza 2; SHAWNEE: Westglen 12; TOPEKA: Fox Whitelakes 4; WICHITA: Mall Cinema 1, Mall Cinema 3, Northrock 6.
MISSOURI—BELTON: Belton Cinema 8; BRANSON: Tablerock 4; COLUMBIA: Biscayne 3, Forum 8; GLADSTONE: Gladstone 4; INDEPENDENCE: Noland Fashion Square 4; JOPLIN: Eastgate Cinema 5, Northpark 2, Northpark Mall 5; KANSAS CITY: Antioch 2, Dickinson Cinema 6, Plaza 3; ST. JOSEPH: Trail; SPRINGFIELD: Century 21, Dickinson 8, Fremont 3, Town & Country 6, Tower, Northtown 4; WEBB CITY: Webb City D.I.
OKLAHOMA—MUSKOGEE: Arrowhead Mall Cinema 6; WEATHERFORD: Showest 3, Vesta.

DIPSON THEATRES, INC.

12 theatres, 28 screens.
210 Main St. East, Room 111, 2nd Floor, Batavia, NY 14020; P.O. Box 579, Batavia, NY 14021. (716) 343-2700.
PRESIDENT
Bernard Clement
VICE PRESIDENT
William Gilliland
VICE PRESIDENT
Michael Clement
SECRETARY TREASURER
Bonnie Clement

NEW YORK—BATAVIA: Cinemas I & II, Mall I & II; BUFFALO: Amherst 3, North Park Cinema, Eastern Hills; ELMIRA: Elmira I, II, & III, Heights; HORNELL: Cinemas Three; LAKEWOOD: Chautauqua Mall Cinemas I & II, Lakewood Cinema 6; SALAMANCA: Cinema I & II.
PENNSYLVANIA—BRADFORD: Cinemas I & II.

DOUGLAS THEATRES

14 theatres, 53 screens.
P.O. Box 81848, Lincoln NE 68501. (402) 474-4909.
NEBRASKA—BELLEVUE: South Cinema 7, Southroads 4; LINCOLN: Cinema Twin, East Park 3, Douglas 3, Edgewood 3, Lincoln 3, Plaza 4, Stuart; OMAHA: Cinema Center Complex 8, Maplewood Twin, Q Cinema 9, Park 4, Millard 4.

EASTERN FEDERAL CORP.

22 theatres, 138 screens.
901 East Boulevard, Charlotte, NC 28203-5203. (704) 377-3495. FAX: (704) 358-8427.
PRESIDENT
Ira S. Meiselman
V.P. & TREASURER
Paul E. Lloyd
SECRETARY
George Royster
FILM BUYER
Curtis Fainn
V. P., OPERATIONS
Scott Baldwin
ADVERTISING COORDINATOR
Nancy Herron
FLORIDA—TALLAHASSEE: Miracle 5, Oak Lake 6; GAINESVILLE: Royal Park 1, 2, 3 & 4; ORLANDO: Conway 1 & 2; PANAMA CITY: Regency 11; FORT MYERS: South Pointe 6; FORT WALTON BEACH: Sun Plaza 4; PORT ORANGE: Port Orange 6; PORT ST. LUCIE: Village Green 6; TALLAHASSEE: Movies at Governor's Square 12.
NORTH CAROLINA—CHARLOTTE: Delta 6, Movies 8, Regency 4, Manor 1 & 2, Park 51-6; CHAPEL HILL: Movies at Timberlyne 5, Plaza 3; CORNELIUS: Movies at the Lake 12; LUMBERTON: Town & Country 1, 2, 3 & 4; WINSTON-SALEM: North Point 5.
SOUTH CAROLINA—COLUMBIA: The Movies at Polo Road 8; MT. PLEASANT: Movies at Mt. Pleasant 10.

EDWARDS THEATRES

76 theatres, 436 screens.
300 Newport Center Drive, Newport Beach, CA 92660. (714) 640-4603. FAX: (714) 721-7170.
PRESIDENT & CHIEF OPERATING OFFICER
James Edwards III
CHAIRMAN
James Edwards, Sr.
EXECUTIVE V. P.
Joan Edwards Randolph
DIRECTOR OF OPERATIONS
Don C. Barton
V. P. & CHIEF ADMIN. OFFICER
Frank Haffar
CHIEF CORP. EXECUTIVE SECRETARY
Marcella Sheldon
CALIFORNIA—ALHAMBRA: Alhambra Place 5, Atlantic Palace 10; ANAHEIM: Anaheim Hills 8; AZUSA: Azusa D.I., Foothill Center 10; BREA: Brea Plaza 4; CAMARILLO: Camarillo 12; CARLSBAD: La Costa 6; CERRITOS: Cerritos Town Center 10; CORONA: Corona 11, Corona Westend 8; COSTA MESA: Cinema Costa Mesa, Cinema Center 4, Harbor Twin, Mesa, South Coast Plaza 1 & 2, South Coast Village 3, Town Center 4, Triangle Square 8; DEL MAR: Del Mar Highlands 8, Flowerhill 4; EL MONTE: El Monte Cinemas 5; EL TORO: El Toro Cinema 5, Saddlebrook 1-2-3, Saddlebrook 4-5-6; ESCONDIDO: Carousel 6, Vineyard Twin; FONTANA: Fontana 8; FOUNTAIN VALLEY: Fountain Valley Twin, Family 4; HUNTINGTON BEACH: Huntington Twin, Charter Centre 5, Lido, Pierside 6; IRVINE: University Cinema 6, Westpark 8, Woodbridge 5; LAGUNA BEACH: South Coast Laguna 2; LAGUNA HILLS: Laguna Hills Mall; LAGUNA NIGUEL: Ocean Ranch 7, Rancho Niguel 8; LA MIRADA: Gateway Plaza 5; LAVERNE: Laverne 12; MISSION VIEJO: Mission Viejo Mall 3, Trabuco Hills 5; MONTEREY PARK: Monterey Mall 3; MORENO VALLEY: Towngate 8; NEWPORT BEACH: Island 7, Newport Cinema 3; POWAY: Poway Cinemas 10; RANCHO CALIFORNIA: Rancho California 10; RANCHO CUCAMONGA: Rancho Cucamonga 6, Terra Vista Town Center 6; SAN DIEGO: Mira Mesa 4, Mira Mesa 7; SAN JUAN CAPISTRANO: Franciscan Plaza 5; SAN LUIS OBISPO: Fremont/Mission 4, Madonna Plaza 5; SAN MARCUS: San Marcos 5; SANTA ANA: Bristol IV, Hutton Center 8; SANTA CLARITA: Valencia Town Center 10; SANTA MARIA: Santa Maria Cinemas 10; SIMI VALLEY: Mountaingate Plaza 7, Simi Valley 10; STANTON: Village Center 6; TEMPLE CITY: Temple Cinema 4; TUSTIN: Tustin Market Place 6; UPLAND: Mountain Green 4, Upland 8 Cinemas; WEST PARK: Paseo West Park; WESTMINSTER: Westminster Twin, Westminster 10, Westminster Mall 4.

ENTERTAINMENT MANAGEMENT CORP.

7 theatres, 44 screens.
807 Washington St., Stoughton, MA 02072. (617) 341- 2800.
FAX: (617) 341-4170.
PRESIDENT
Bill Hanney
DIRECTOR OPERATIONS
Keith Ash
DISTRICT MANAGER
Mike Harmon
ADMINISTRATOR
Joan Overstreet
PUBLIC ADMINISTRATOR
Teresa Abbett
MARKETING & CONCESSIONS
Cassandra Cast
MASSACHUSETTS—BUZZARDS BAY: Buzzards Bay Cinemas 4; EAST BRIDGEWATER: Cinema 6; SCITUATE: Scituate Playhouse 4; SHARON: Cinema 8; SOUTH DENNIS: Cinema 12; STOUGHTON: Stoughton Cinema Pub.
RHODE ISLAND—EAST PROVIDENCE: Cinemas 10.

FIRST INTERNATIONAL THEATRES

25 theatres, 105 screens reported.
4200 W. 83rd Street, Suite 206, Prairie Village, KS 66207. (913) 341-7910. FAX (913) 341-6826.
OWNERS
Ron Leslie, Morgan Creek & Svenska Bio
PRESIDENT & CEO
Ron D. Leslie
REGIONAL MGRS.
Phil Blakey
Tom Woolery
FILM BUYER
John Shaw

FLOYD THEATRES

6 theatres.
4226 Old Highway 37, P.O. Box 1528, Lakeland, FL 33802. (813) 646-2436. FAX: (813) 647-2721.
PRESIDENT
Harold T. Spears, Jr.
FLORIDA—LAKELAND: Silvermoon D.I.; LOCKHART: Rimar D.I.; SANFORD: Movieland D.I.; ST. PETERSBURG: 28th St. D.I.; TARPON SPRINGS: Midway D.I.; WINTER GARDEN: Starlite D.I.

FOX THEATRES CORP.

4 theatres, 25 screens.
825 Berkshire Blvd, Wyomissing, PA, 19610. (610) 374-4904.
FAX: (610) 374-7121.
PRESIDENT
Donald M. Fox
DIRECTOR, THEATRE OPERATIONS
William E. Yergey
OFFICE MANAGER
Wendy D. Moore
FLORIDA—POMPANO BEACH: Fox Festival 8; SUNRISE: Fox Sunrise 8.
MARYLAND—OCEAN CITY: Fox White Marlin 5.
PENNSYLVANIA—READING: Fox East 4.

FRANK THEATRES, INC.

25 theatres, 151 screens.
P.O. Box 33, Pleasantville, NJ 08232.
NEW JERSEY—ABSECON: Absecon 12; ATLANTIC CITY: Towne 16, Point 4; CAPE MAY: Cape May 6; CAPE MAY COURT HOUSE: Bayshore 8; HAMMONTON: Pike 12; LONG BEACH ISLAND & MANAHAWKIN: Harbor Twin, Colony 4, Beach 4, Colonial 4, Manahawkin 12; MAY'S LANDING: Hamilton 8; NORTH CAPE MAY: Cape May 8; OCEAN CITY: Moorlyn 4, Strand 5, Village 5; PENNSVILLE: Penn 8; STONE HARBOR: Harbor 5; VENTNOR: Ventnor 5; VINELAND: Landis 5; WILDWOOD AREA: Strand 4, Ocean Twin, Shore 4, Beach Twin (Cape May), Penn Twin (Pennsville).

FRIDLEY THEATRES

39 theatres, 72 screens.
1321 Walnut St. Des Moines, IA 50309. (515) 282-9287.
IOWA—ALGONA: Algona; ANKENY: Paramount 5; ATLANTIC: Frederick 2; BOONE: Boone; CARROLL: Carroll 2; CENTERVILLE: Lake Center 2; CHEROKEE: American; CLARION: Clarion; CLARINDA: Caprice; CRESTON: Strand; DECORAH: Viking 3; EMMETSBURG: Riviera; ESTHERVILLE: Grand 3; GRINNELL: Cinema; HUMBOLDT: Humota; INDIANOLA: Paramount 3; IOWA FALLS: Metropolitan 2; JEFFERSON: Sierra; KNOXVILLE: Village 2, LAKE CITY: Capri; MANCHESTER: Castle; MARSHALLTOWN: Orpheum 2, Plaza 5; MT. PLEASANT: Temple 2; MUSCATINE: Plaza 4, Riviera; NEVADA:

Camelot; OELWEIN: Paramount 2; OSKALOOSA: Penn Centre Twin; PELLA: Holland; PERRY: Grand 3; RED OAK: Grand; SHENANDOAH: Page; SPENCER: Spencer 3; STORM LAKE: Vista 3; WASHINGTON: State; WEBSTER CITY: Webster.
NEBRASKA—GRAND ISLAND: Grand; HASTINGS: Rivoli 3; MC COOK: Cinema 3.

GKC THEATRES

42 theatres, 208 screens.
500 First National Bank Bldg., Springfield IL 62701. (217) 753-0018.
CHAIRMAN & PRESIDENT
George G. Kerasotes
EXECUTIVE V. P. OPERATIONS
Dale J. Garvey
EXECUTIVE V.P., FINANCE
Marshall N. Selkirk
EXECUTIVE V.P., FILM
Daniel J. Rogers
EXECUTIVE V.P., PURCHASING.
Roger Ford
ARIZONA—TUSCON: American Cinemas 6;
ILLINOIS—BLOOMINGTON/NORMAL: University Cinemas 8, College Hills Cinemas 4, Parkway Cinemas 8; CHAMPAIGN: Coed Cinemas 4, Country Fair Cinemas 7, Market Place Cinemas 4, Urbana Cinemas 2; DECATUR: Hickory Point 12, Northgate 3; DEKALB: Campus Cinemas 4, Carrol Cinemas 4, DeKalb Cinemas 4; KEWANEE: Wanee Cinemas 2; LASALLE: Illinois Valley Cinemas 2, Showplace Cinemas 2; LINCOLN: Lincoln Cinemas 4; MORRIS: Morris Cinemas 2; OTTAWA: Roxy Cinemas 6; PEORIA: Landmark Mall Cinemas 12, Metro Cinemas 4, Westlake Cinemas 4; PERU: Peru Mall Cinemas 6; PONTIAC: Crescent Cinemas 2; PRINCETON: Apollo Cinemas 2; STERLING: Sterling Cinemas 2; STREATOR: Majestic Cinemas 2. WASHINGTON: Sunnyland Cinemas 10.
INDIANA—ELKHART: Concord Cinemas 2, Encore Park Cinemas 8.
MICHIGAN—ALPENA: State Cinemas 2; BATTLE CREEK: Towne Cinemas 8; BIG RAPIDS: Big Rapids Cinemas 4; FORT GRATIOT: Birchwood Cinemas 10; HILLSDALE: Dawn Cinema; LUDINGTON: Lyric Cinema 4; MARQUETTE: Royal Cinemas 10, SAGINAW: Fashion Square Cinemas 10; TRAVERSE CITY: Grand Traverse Cinemas 9, State Cinemas 2; WILLIAMSBURG:Traverse Bay Cinemas 2.

GENERAL CINEMA THEATRES

193 theatres, 1179 screens.
(A subsidiary of GC Companies, Inc.)
1280 Boylston St., Chestnut Hill, MA 02167. (617) 277-4320.
FAX: (617) 277-8875.
PRESIDENT & CEO
Paul Del Rossi
EXECUTIVE V. P. & COO
William Doeren
SENIOR V. P,. DEVELOPMENT
Poston Tanaka
SENIOR V. P., OPERATIONS
Frank Stryjewski
V. P,. FILM-EAST
Alan DeLemos
V. P,. FILM-WEST
Ben Barbosa
V. P., ENTERTAINMENT MARKETING
Ellen Aub
V.P., THEATRE MARKETING
Page Thompson
V.P., FINANCE
Jim Burnham
V.P., CONSTRUCTION
John Townsend
V.P., HUMAN RESOURCES
Daniel Stravinski
V. P. BUSINESS SERVICES
Manny Laetao
CALIFORNIA—COLTON: Rancho 6; DUBLIN: Dublin Place 6; FAIRFIELD: Solano Mall 6; FREMONT: Fremont Hub 8; HAYWARD: Southland 5; LOS ANGELES: Avco 4, Beverly Connection 6, Fallbrook 7, Glendale Central 5, Hollywood Galaxy 6, Santa Anita 4, Sherman Oaks 2; MONTCLAIR: Montclair Plaza 5; REDONDO BEACH: Galleria at South Bay 6; SACRAMENTO: Birdcage Walk 6; SAN MATEO: Hillsdale 4.
DELAWARE—WILMINGTON: Christiana Mall 5.
FLORIDA—FT. LAUDERDALE: Coral Square 8, Deerfield Mall 8, Fountains 8, The Galleria 4, Mission Bay Plaza 8, Pembroke Pines 8; MIAMI: Cinema 10 at Miracle Center, Hialeah 8, Intracoastal 8, Riviera 5; ORLANDO: Altamonte 8, Altamonte Mall 2, Colonial Promenade 6, Fashion Square 6, Lake Mary Centre 8; WEST PALM BEACH: PGA 6.
GEORGIA—ATLANTA: Akers Mill Square 4, Gwinnett Place 6, Hairston Village 8, Merchants Walk 8, Perimeter Mall 4, Sandy Springs 8, AUGUSTA: Regency Exchange 8.
ILLINOIS—CHICAGO: Deerbrook 4, Ford City 14, Lincoln Mall 3,

Northbrook Court 14, Randhurst 16, Woodgrove Festival 6, Yorktown 6; WAUKEGAN: Lakehurst 12.
INDIANA—GARY: Griffith Park 2, Ridge Plaza 2, Southlake Mall 9; INDIANAPOLIS: Castleton Square 3, Clearwater Crossing 12, Eastgate Mall 6, Glendale 3, Greenwood Park 7, Lafayette Square 5; SOUTH BEND: University Park East 6, University Park West 3; VALPARISO: County Seat 6.
LOUISIANA—NEW ORLEANS: Esplanade Mall 9, Lakeside 5.
MAINE—PORTLAND: Maine Mall 7.
MARYLAND—BALTIMORE: Columbia City 3, Security Square 8, Towson Commons 8.
MASSACHUSETTS—BOSTON: Braintree 10, Burlington 10, Chestnut Hill 5, Framingham 14, Hanover Mall 4, Northshore 3; N. DARTMOUTH: North Dartmouth Mall 8; TYNGSBORO: Tyngsboro 6.
MICHIGAN—DETROIT: Canton 6, Novi Town Center 8; KALAMAZOO: Maple Hill Mall 3; LANSING: Lansing Mall West 6.
MINNESOTA—MINNEAPOLIS: Centennial Lakes 8, Mall of America 14, Northtown 4, Shelard Park 5; ST. PAUL: Burnhaven 8, Har Mar 11.
NEW JERSEY—BRIDGEWATER: Bridgewater Commons 7; CAMDEN: Deptford Mall 6; SOMERSET: Rutgers 6; TOMS RIVER: Ocean County Mall 3; TRENTON: Mercer Mall 7; WATCHUNG: Blue Star 4; WEST ORANGE: Essex Green 3.
NEW MEXICO—ALBUQUERQUE: Park Square 3, San Mateo 8.
NEW YORK—BRONX: Bay Plaza 13; BUFFALO: Market Arcade 8, McKinley Mall 6, Thruway Mall 8, University 8, Walden Galleria 12; NIAGARA FALLS: Summit Park 6; ROCHESTER: Marketplace 7, Pittsford Plaza 6; YONKERS: Central Plaza 4.
NORTH CAROLINA—CHARLOTTE: South Park 3, Tower Place Festival 8; FAYETTEVILLE: Cross Creek Mall 3, Cross Pointe 6; GREENSBORO: Four Seasons Town Centre 4; RALEIGH: Pleasant Valley Promenade 7; WINSTON-SALEM: Hanes Mall 4.
OHIO—AKRON: Chapel Hill Mall 5, Plaza at Chapel Hill 8, West Market Plaza 7; CANTON: Canton Centre 8; CLEVELAND: Erie Commons 8, Parmatown 5, Ridge Park Square 8, Westgate Mall 6, Westwood Town Center 6; COLUMBUS: Northland 8, Westland 8; ELYRIA: Midway Mall 8.
OKLAHOMA—OKLAHOMA CITY: Brixton Square 8, Crossroads 8, Penn Square Mall 10, Quail Springs 6; TULSA: Eastland Mall 6, Eton Square 6, Woodland Hills 6.
PENNSYLVANIA—ALLENTOWN: Lehigh Valley Mall 8; PHILADELPHIA: Franklin Mills 10, Northeast 4, Plymouth Meeting 2; SCRANTON: Viewmont Mall 5; WILKES-BARRE: Wyoming Valley Mall 7.
RHODE ISLAND—PROVIDENCE: Lincoln Mall 4, Warwick Mall 3.
SOUTH CAROLINA—CHARLESTON: Citadel Mall 6, Northwoods Mall 8; COLUMBIA: Bush River Mall 8, Columbia Mall 8.
TENNESSEE—MEMPHIS: Hickory Ridge Mall 4, Mall of Memphis 5, Raleigh 6.
TEXAS—AUSTIN: Great Hills 8, Highland 10; DALLAS: Carrollton Centre 6, Collin Creek 6, Furneaux Creek 7, Galleria 5, Irving Mall 7, Northpark East 2, Northpark West 2, Prestonwood 4, Richardson 6, Town East 6, Town East Mall 5; EL PASO: Cielo Vista Mall 10, The Park 6, Sunland Park Mall 6; FT. WORTH: Arlington Park 8, Central Park 8, Cinema V, North Hills 7, Ridgmar Town Square 6; HOUSTON: Baybrook Mall 4, Copperfield 6, Deerbrook Commons 6, Greenspoint Mall 5, Gulfgate Mall 4, Meyerland 8, Point NASA 6, West Oaks Central 6, Willowbrook Mall 6; MIDLAND: Midland Park Mall 4, North Park 4.
VIRGINIA—NORFOLK: Janaf Plaza 8; SPRINGFIELD: Springfield Mall 10.
WASHINGTON—EVERETT: Everett Mall 10; FEDERAL WAY: Gateway Center 8; RENTON: Renton Village 8; SEATTLE: Aurora 3; SILVERDALE: Kitsap Mall 8; TACOMA: Lincoln Plaza 8.

GENERAL THEATRES CO.

6 theatres, 16 screens.
23811 Chagrin Blvd., Beachwood, OH 44122. (216) 464-4366. FAX: (216) 464-4368.
PRESIDENT
Leonard L. Mishkind
GENERAL MANAGER
Norman Barr
OHIO—CLEVELAND: Detroit Twin, Parma Triple, Berea Triple, Southgate 5; ORRVILLE: Orr Twin; TIFFIN: Tiffin Drive In.

GEORGIA THEATRE COMPANY II

16 theatres, 94 screens.
2999 Piedmont Road, Atlanta, GA 30305. (404) 264-4542. FAX: (404) 233-8184.
CHAIRMAN & PRESIDENT
William J. Stembler
VICE-CHAIRMAN
John H. Stembler
SECRETARY & TREASURER
Dennis P. Merton
V. P., CONCESSIONS
John H. Stembler, Jr.

V. P., OPERATIONS
C. M. Harris
V.P., FILM
Clifford "Kip" Smiley, Jr.
FLORIDA—LANTANA: Value Cinemas Atlantis 6; NORTH LAUDERDALE: Valley Cinemas N. Lauderdale 6.
GEORGIA—ATHENS: Beechwood 8; AUGUSTA: Columbia Square 4, Evans Cinemas 12; BRUNSWICK: Lanier 5, Movies at Glynn Place 8; COVINGTON: Newton Twin; MARIETTA: Park 12 Cobb; MARTINEZ: Columbia Square 4; MOULTRIE: Moultrie Twin; ST. MARY'S: Kings Bay 6; ST. SIMONS ISLAND: Island Cinema 7; STATESBORO: College Cinemas 2; THOMASVILLE: Gateway 7; VALDOSTA: Ashley Cinema 8, Movies at Valdosta Mall 6; WAYCROSS: Mall Cinema 7.

GOODRICH QUALITY THEATERS, INC.

17 theatres, 129 screens.
4417 Broadmoor S.E., Kentwood, MI 49512. (616) 698-7733. FAX: (616) 698-7720.
PRESIDENT & SECRETARY
Robert Emmett Goodrich
V. P. & GENERAL MANAGER
William T. McMannis
CFO
Ross Pettinga
FILM BUYER
Wanda J. Holst
MARKETING MANAGER
Lisa Cooper
CONTROLLER
Ronald B. Muscott
OPERATIONS MANAGER
Martin S. Betz
MICHIGAN DISTRICT MANAGER
Reed L. Simon
INDIANA/ILLINOIS DISTRICT MANAGER
Matthew Johnson
INDIANA—ANDERSON: Applewood 9; LAFAYETTE: Eastside 10, Market Square 2.
ILLINOIS—BATAVIA: Randall 14; CHAMPAIGN: Savoy 14; PEORIA: Willow Knolls 14.
MICHIGAN—ANN ARBOR: Ann Arbor 2; BATTLE CREEK: West Columbia 7; BAY CITY: Bay City 6, Hampton 6; CADILLAC: Cadillac 5; HOLLAND: Holland 7; JACKSON: Jackson 8; LOWELL: Lowell 5; PORT HURON: Krafft 8; SAGINAW: The Quad, Saginaw 8.

GREATER HUNTINGTON THEATRE CORP.

5 theatres, 20 screens reported.
P.O. Box 1957, Huntington, WV 25720. (304) 523-0185.
CHAIRMAN
Jack S. Hyman
PRESIDENT
Derek Hyman
VICE PRESIDENT
Joshua Hyman

GUETSCHOFF THEATRES

7 theatres, 52 screens.
P.O. Box 313, 130 N. Main, Cambridge, MN 55008. (612) 689-2900. FAX: (612) 444-6401.
OWNER, PRESIDENT & FILM BUYER
Robert Guetschoff
OWNER & V. P
Deborah Zeise
OWNER & V. P
JoAnn Sprino
OWNER, SECY. & TREASURER
Richard Guetschoff
MINNESOTA—APPLE VALLEY: Apple Valley 6; CAMBRIDGE: Cinema 5; ELK RIVER: Elk River Cinema 10; HASTINGS: Hastings Theatre 8; ROSEVILLE: Roseville 4; ROSEMOUNT: Rosemount 8; SHAKOPEE: Shakopee Town 11

HARKINS THEATRES

18 theatres, 117 screens.
8350 E. McDonald, Suite 2, Scottsdale, AZ 85250. (602) 955-2233. FAX: (602) 443-0950.
PRESIDENT & OWNER
Dan Harkins
VICE PRESIDENT
Wayne Kullander
SECRETARY & TREASURER
Karen Harkins
FILM BUYER
Lou Lencioni
ADVERTISING
Kelly Maloney
ASSISTANT TO THE PRESIDENT
Jere Gabriel

DISTRICT MANAGERS
Timothy Spain (East)
Michael Bowers (West)
CONTROLLER
Greta Newell
ENGINEERING
Kirk Griffin
ARIZONA—PHOENIX: Arcadia 8, Bell Tower 8, Bell Towne Centre 4, Camelview Luxury 5, Camelback Mall 3, Centerpoint Luxury 11, Christown 5, Cine Capri, Cornerstone 6; Fashion Square 7; Fiesta 5, Paradise Valley Mall 7, Poca Fiesta 4, Sedona Luxury 6, Shea-North Scottsdale 14, Southwest 8, Tri-City 5, Westride Mall 6.

HOLLYWOOD THEATRES

17 theatres, 105 screens.
2911 Turtle Creek Blvd., Suite 1150, Dallas, TX 75219. (214) 522-8686. FAX: (214) 520-2323.
PRESIDENT
Thomas W. STEPHENSON, JR.
VICE PRESIDENT & CFO
Jeff Lightfoot
THEATRE OPERATIONS
Brad Wardlow
Todd Hecht
Debbie Faubion
Scott Gunn
FILM BUYER
Carri Irby
BOOKER
Susan Hodge
OKLAHOMA—BARTLESVILLE: Movies 6; SHAWNEE: Movies 6.
TEXAS—BROWNWOOD: Movies 4; BURLESON: Movies 8; COMMERCE: Cinema 3; DALLAS: Medallion 5, Northtown 6; FORT WORTH: Cinema 8; GRAPEVINE: Movies 8; LANCASTER: Cinema 7; LONGVIEW: Movies 9; MIDLAND: Movies 4; ODESSA: Cinema 7; PEARLAND: Westside Cinema 6; SAN ANGELO: Movies 4; TYLER: Movies 6; WACO: Lacy-Lakeview.

HOYTS CINEMAS CORPORATION

93 theatres, 638 screens.
One Exeter Plaza, Boston, MA 02116-2836. (617) 267-2700. FAX: (617) 262-0707.
CEO
Peter Ivany
PRESIDENT & COO
Roger Eaton
CFO
Terence Moriarity
SENIOR V. P., FILM
Carl Bertolino
SENIOR V. P., OPERATIONS & MARKETING
Alan Johnson
SENIOR V. P., CONSTRUCTION & TECHNICAL
Daniel Viera
SENIOR V. P., DEVELOPMENT
Harold Blank
SENIOR V. P., INTERNATIONAL BUSINESS DEVELOPMENT
Kevin Healy
CONNECTICUT—DAYVILLE: Dayville 3; MANCHESTER: East Manchester Cinemas 6; ENFIELD: Cine Enfield 8; GROTON: Groton Cinemas 6; HARTFORD: Cine 4; MADISON: Madison Cinemas 2; MERIDEN: Meriden Cinemas 10; MYSTIC: Mystic Village Cinemas 3; NEW CANAAN: Playhouse 2; NORWICH: Norwich Cinemas 2; SAYBROOK: Saybrook Cinemas 2, Saybrook Cinemas 4; STRATFORD: Cinemas 6; WATERBURY: Mall View Plaza 10; WATERFORD: Waterford Cinemas 9; WILLIMANTIC: Jillson Sq. 6.
MAINE—AUBURN: Auburn Plaza 10; AUGUSTA: Cinema 10; BANGOR: Bangor Cinemas 10; BIDDEFORD: Cine 8; BRUNSWICK: Cinema 10; ELLSWORTH: Maine Coast Cinemas 2; PORTLAND: Clarks Pond Cinema 8, Nickelodeon Cinemas 6; PRESQUE ISLE: Presque Isle Cinemas 8; WATERVILLE: Cinema Center 6.
MARYLAND—FREDERICK: Francis Scott Key 3, Frederick Towne Mall 2, Westridge Mall 6; LAUREL: Laurel Lakes 12, Laurel 6; SALISBURY: The Center at Salisbury 10, Movies 8; WESTMINSTER: Cranberry Mall Cinemas 9.
MASSACHUSETTS—ACTON: Acton Cinemas 4; BERLIN: Solomon Pond Cinemas 15; FRANKLIN: Franklin Cinemas 6; GREAT BARRINGTON: Mahaiwe Theatre; GREENFIELD: Greenfield 6; HARWICH: Harwich Cinemas 6; HYANNIS: Airport Cinema 8, Cape Cod Mall Cinema 1 & 2, Cape Cod Mall Cinema 3 & 4; MASHPEE: Mashpee Cinemas 6; MILFORD: Milford Cinema 3 Centre 495; NORTH ADAMS: North Adams 6; NORTH FALMOUTH: Nickelodeon 5; PITTSFIELD: Berkshire Mall 10; PLYMOUTH: Independence Mall 14; SALISBURY: Cinema 95 6; TAUNTON: Silver City Galleria 10, Taunton Cinemas 8; WESTBOROUGH: Westborough Cinemas 12.
MICHIGAN—MONROE: Frenchtown Square Mall 8.
NEW HAMPSHIRE—KEENE: Keene Cinema 6; PORTSMOUTH: Newington Mall Cine 12.

NEW YORK—ALBANY: Cine 10, Crossgates 30; AUBURN: Finger Lakes Cinema 4; CLIFTON PARK: Clifton Country Mall 6; CORNING: Painted Post 8; DUNKIRK: Dunkirk 8; EAST GREENBUSH: Rensselaer Cinemas 8; ELMIRA: Arnot Mall 10; GLENS FALLS: Aviation 7, Route 9 Cinemas 5; ITHACA: Ithaca Cinemas 10; KINGSTON: Hudson Valley Mall 6; LATHAM: Latham Mall 10; NEWBURGH: Newburgh Cinema 10; ONEONTA: South Side Mall 4; PLATTSBURGH: Champlain Center 8; POUGHKEEPSIE: Galleria Cinema 12, South Hills Mall Cine 8; ROCHESTER: Cine Greece 8; SARATOGA: Saratoga Cinemas 6, Wilton Mall 8; SYRACUSE: Camillus 10, Carousel Center Mall 14, Fayetteville 6, Great Northern 6, Shoppintown 4; UTICA: Riverside Mall 8, Sangertown Square 9; WATERTOWN: Salmon Run Mall 8, Stateway Plaza 4.
OHIO—CLEVELAND: Tower City 11; LANCASTER: River Valley 10; NEW PHILADELPHIA: New Town Mall 8.
RHODE ISLAND—WESTERLY: Westerly Cinemas 4.
VERMONT—BURLINGTON: Cinema 9, Showcase 5, Ethan Allen 4, Century Plaza 3; NEWPORT: Showplace 3.

KENT THEATRES, INC.

9 theatres, 62 screens.
2870 University Blvd. W., Jacksonville, FL 32217. (904) 731-9616. FAX: (904) 739-2752. Booking Office: 4407 Highlands Dr., McKinney, TX 75070. (214) 529- 6535
CHAIRMAN AND SECRETARY
Norma F. Kent
PRESIDENT
J. Cleveland Kent
GENERAL COUNSEL & DIRECTOR
John B. Kent
V. P. & GENERAL MANAGER OF OPERATIONS
Michael Spivey
V. P., FINANCE, ASST. SECRETARY & TREASURER
Norma K. Lockwood
V. P., COMPTROLLER & ASST. TREASURER
Robert M. Fulford
ASSISTANT TREASURER
Norma L. Johnson
ASSISTANT TREASURER
William G. Lockwood, Jr.
ASSISTANT SECRETARY
JoAnn F. Green
FLORIDA—ATLANTIC BEACH: Atlantic 8; GAINESVILLE: Plaza 3; JACKSONVILLE: St. Johns 8; JACKSONVILLE BEACH: Pablo 9; LAKELAND: Lakeland Square 10; NEPTUNE BEACH: Neptune 3; TALLAHASSEE: Cinema 2.
GEORGIA—CARROLTON: Mall 8.
SOUTH CAROLINA—COLUMBIA: Capitol 8.

KERASOTES THEATRES

95 theatres, 404 screens.
Kerasotes Building, 104 N. 6th Street, Springfield, IL 62701. (217) 788-5200. FAX: (217) 788-5207.
PRESIDENT & CEO
Anthony L. Kerasotes
EXECUTIVE V. P. & COO
Dean L. Kerasotes
HEAD FILM BUYER
Pat Rembusch
CFO
Roger Hurst
DIRECTOR OF REAL ESTATE
Robert Gallivan
MIS DIRECTOR
John Ketchum
GENERAL MANAGER
John G. Miller
ASSISTANT GENERAL MANAGER/OPERATIONS
Tim Johnson
DIRECTOR, TECHNICAL SERVICES & PURCHASING
Fred Walraven
ADVERTISING MANAGER
Kelly Johnson
ILLINOIS—ALTON: Eastgate 6; BELLEVILLE: Quad 4, Ritz 3; BENTON: Toler Cinema 2; BOLINGBROOK: Showplace 12; CANTON: Garden 2; CARBONDALE: Varsity 3, Fox Eastgate 3; CENTRALIA: Illinois 2; CHARLESTON: Will Rogers 2; CHILLICOTHE: Town 2; DANVILLE: Times, Village Mall Cinema 6; GALESBURG: West 2, Sandburg Mall 2; GRANITE CITY: Nameoki 2; HARRISBURG: Cinema 4; HIGHLAND: Lory 2; JACKSONVILLE: Times 2, Illinois 2; JERSEYVILLE: Stadium 2; LKE IN THE HILLS: Lake in the Hills 12; MACOMB: Illinois 2; MARION: Town & Country 4, Illinois Center 8; MATTOON: Showplace 8; MONMOUTH: Rivoli 2; MT. VERNON: Showplace 8; MURPHYSBORO: Liberty; PARIS: Paris 2; PEKIN: Pekin Mall Cinema 2; QUINCY: Adams Cinema 2, Quincy Mall 3, Quincy Showcase 6; RANTOUL: Wings Cinema 2; ROCKFORD: Showplace 16; Cherryvale 3, Cherryvale mall 4, Colonial Village 5, North Towne 6, Machesney Park 10; ROXANA: Cine; SALEM: Salem 2; SPRINGFIELD: Fox Town & Country 2, Esquire 4, Showplace 8, White Oaks Cinema 5, Parkway Pointe 8; TAYLORVILLE: Cinema 2; VERNON HILLS: Showplace 8.

INDIANA—ANDERSON: Showplace 4, Mounds Mall 2; BLOOM-INGTON: Showplace 11, Von Lee 3, College Mall Cinema 4; COLUMBUS: Columbus Center Cinema 5, Commons 2, Showplace 8; FORT WAYNE: Gateway 3; KOKOMO: Kokomo Mall Cinema 8, Markland Mall Cinema 5; LA PORTE: La Porte Cinema 4; MARION: Movies 4, Park Mall 2; MICHIGAN CITY: Dunes Plaza Cinema 6, Marquette 3; MUNCIE: Cinema 7, Muncie Mall Cinema 3, Northwest Plaza Cinema 8; NEW CAS-TLE: Castle; PERU: Eastwood Cinema 2; PRINCETON: Princeton 4; RICHMOND: Cinema 11, Mall Cinema 2; SALEM: Hoosier Cinema 2; SCHEREVILLE: Showplace 16; SOUTH BEND: Town & Country 3, Scottsdale 6; TERRE HAUTE: Honey Creek 3, Towne South Cinema 3; VINCENNES: Plaza 2, Showplace 3; WASHINGTON: Indiana 2.
IOWA—KEOKUK: Plaza Cinema 3.
MISSOURI—CAPE GIRARDEAU: Broadway Theatre, Town Plaza Cinema 3; DEXTER: Town & Country 2; FARMINGTON: Showplace 4; FLAT RIVER: Movies 2; KENNETT: Cinema; POPLAR BLUFF: Rodgers 2, Mansion Mall Cinema 2; SULLI-VAN: Meramec Cinema 2.
OHIO—HAMILTON: Showplace 8.

JANE M. KLOTZ BOOKING

5 theatres, 6 screens.
9801 Tribonian Drive, Fort Washington, MD 20744-5713. (301) 567-1775 (also FAX #).
BOOKER & OWNER
Jane M. Klotz
VIRGINIA—ABINGDON: Moonlite D.I.; LEXINGTON: Hull's; ONANCOCK: Roseland; RICHLANDS: Richlands Mall Two.
WEST VIRGINIA—WHITE SULPHUR SPRINGS: Greenbrier.

KRIKORIAN PREMIER THEATRES, INC.

2 theatres, 11 screens.
Pier Plaza Business Park, 119 W. Torrance Blvd., Suite 1, Redondo Beach, CA 90277. (310) 318-3363. FAX: (310) 376-8541.
PRESIDENT
George Krikorian
CONTROLLER
Pam Weatherly
DIRECTOR OPERATIONS
Neal Myer
FILM BUYER, ALAMO THEATRE SERVICES
Lou Lencioni
CALIFORNIA—LA HABRA: La Habra Cinema 4; LA MIRADA: La Mirada Cinema 7.

LAEMMLE THEATRES

8 theatres, 24 screens.
11523 Santa Monica Blvd., Los Angeles, CA 90025. (310) 478-1041. FAX: (310) 478-4452.
CHIEF OFFICERS
Robert and Gregory Laemmle
CALIFORNIA—BEVERLY HILLS: Music Hall 3; ENCINO: Town Center 5; LOS ANGELES: Grande 4; PASADENA: Esquire, Colorado; SANTA MONICA: Monica 4-plex; WEST HOLLY-WOOD: Sunset 5; WEST LOS ANGELES: Royal.

LAKES & RIVERS CINEMAS

8 theatres, 38 screens.
3989 Central Avenue NE, Box 48, Columbia Heights, MN 55421. (612) 781-8858. FAX: (612) 781-8044.
PRESIDENT
James H. Payne
SECRETARY & CASHIER
Shiloy Ziemann
GENERAL MANAGER, FILM BUYER
Steve Tripp
MINNESOTA—DETROIT LAKES: Washington Square 5; FAIR-MONT: Fair Lakes 5; FERGUS FALLS: Westridge Twin; OEWA-TONNA: Cedar Mall 6; REDWING: Redwing 5; WORTHINGTON: Northland 5.
SOUTH DAKOTA—WATERTOWN: Watertown 5.
WISCONSIN—ST. CROIX FALLS: Falls 5.

LANDMARK THEATRE CORPORATION

52 theatres, 140 screens.
Home Office: 2222 S. Barrington Ave., Los Angeles, CA 90064. (310) 473-6701. FAX: (310) 477-3066
PRESIDENT
Stephen A. Gilula
SENIOR V. P., FILM
Bert Manzari
SENIOR V. P., OPERATIONS & ACQUISITIONS
Paul S. Richardson
V. P , ADMINISTRATION
Janet Hughes
V. P. MARKETING
Cary Jones

CALIFORNIA—BELMONT: Belmont Arts 3; BERKELEY: Act 1 & 2, Albany Twin 2, California Theatre 3, Piedmont Theatre 3, Shattuck Cinemas 8, U.C. Berkeley; CORONA DEL MAR: Port; LOS ANGELES: Goldwyn Pavilion Cinemas IV, Nuart, NuWilshire 2; MENLO PARK: Park, Guild; PALO ALTO: Aquarius 2, Varsity, Palo Alto Square 2; SACRAMENTO: Tower 3 Sacramento Inn 3,; SAN DIEGO: Cove, Guild, Hillcrest 5, Ken, Park; SAN FRANCISCO: Bridge, Clay, Embarcadero Center 5, Gateway, Lumiere 3, Opera Plaza 4; SOUTH PASADENA: Rialto.
COLORADO—DENVER: Chez Artiste 3, Esquire 2, Mayan 3.
LOUISIANA—NEW ORLEANS: Prytania, Canal Place Cinemas 4.
MASSACHUSSETTS—CAMBRIDGE: Kendall Square 9.
MINNESOTA—MINNEAPOLIS: Lagoon 5, Uptown.
OHIO—CLEVELAND: Centrum 3.
TEXAS—DALLAS: Inwood 3; HOUSTON: River Oaks 3.
WASHINGTON—SEATTLE: Broadway Market 4, Crest Cinema Center 4, Egyptian, Guild 45th Theatre 2, Harvard Exit 2, Metro Cinemas 10, Neptune, Seven Gables, Varsity 3.
WISCONSIN—MILWAUKEE: Downer 2, Oriental 3.

JACK LOEKS THEATRES

12 theatres, 58 screens.
1400 28th Street, S.W., Grand Rapids, MI 49509. (616) 532-6302. FAX: (616) 532-3660.
CHAIRMAN & CEO
John D. Loeks
PRESIDENT & COO
John D. Loeks, Jr.
EXECUTIVE V. P.
Ron van Timmeren
V. P., OPERATIONS
Roger Lubs
TREASURER
Nancy Hagan
MICHIGAN—GRAND HAVEN: Grand; GRAND RAPIDS: Studio 28 (20 screen), Alpine 4; KALAMAZOO: Plaza 2, Eastowne 5; MT. PLEASANT: Cinema 4, Ward, Broadway; MUSKEGON: Cinema 12, Getty 4 D.I., New Plaza 1 & 2; ST JOSEPH: Southtown Twin Theatre.

LOEKS STAR THEATRES

8 theatres, 94 screens.
(Loeks Michigan Theatres, Inc., general partner, and Star Theatres, Inc., general partner.) 3020 Charlevoix Dr. S.E., Grand Rapids, MI 49546. (616) 940-0866. FAX: (616) 940-0046.
PRESIDENT, LOEKS MICHIGAN
Barrie Loeks
CHAIRMAN, LOEKS MICHIGAN
James Loeks
COO & EXECUTIVE V. P.
Kenyon Shane
V. P., OPERATIONS
Robert Kleinhans
CONTROLLER
Jay Laninga
V. P., TECHNICAL
Jon Karell
ADVERTISING AND PROMOTION
Krystal Bylund
MICHIGAN—CLINTON TOWNSHIP: Star Gratiot 16; GRAND RAPIDS: Star Grand Rapids 18; HOLLAND: Star Holland 8; LIN-COLN PARK: Star Lincoln Park 14; MADISON HEIGHTS: Star John R 10; ROCHESTER HILLS: Star Rochester Hills 10, Star Winchester 8; TAYLOR: Star Taylor 10.

LOGAN LUXURY THEATRES CORP.

4 theatres, 9 screens.
209 N. Lawler St., Mitchell, SD 57301. (605) 996-9022. FAX: (605) 996-9241.
PRESIDENT
Jeff Logan
VICE PRESIDENT
Linda Logan
BOOKER
Jim Wilson
SOUTH DAKOTA—HURON: Huron Cinema 3; MITCHELL: Roxy Cinema 4, Starlite D.I., State.

M.I. THEATRES

14 theatres, 99 screens.
One Seine Court, Suite. 316, New Orleans, LA 70114. (504) 367-8421.
PRESIDENT
Charles Funk
FILM BUYER
A. J. Roquevert
OFFICE MANAGER
Carol Spirolo
FLORIDA—MARGATE: Movies 8 Margate.
LOUISIANA—BASTROP: Washington Square 4; BOGALUSA: Trackside 5; CHALMETTE: Chalmette Cinema 9; KENNER:

Cinema City 8; LA PLACE: Movies 6; LAFAYETTE: VMovies 4; MARRERO: Oakridge Cinema 5; METAIRIE: Panorama 6; MONROE: Eastgate Cinema 6; NEW ORLEANS: Movies 5 at the Plaza, Uptown Square 2; SHREVEPORT: Cinema City 7.
OKLAHOMA—OKLAHOMA CITY: Northpark Cinema 7; YUKON: Dollar Movies 5.
TEXAS—MISSOURI CITY: Missouri Cinema 6; NASH: Cinema City 6.

MJR THEATRES, INC.

10 theatres, 57 screens.
13671 West Eleven Mile Road, Oak Park, MI 48237. (810) 548-8282. FAX: (810) 548-4706.
PRESIDENT
Michael R. Mihalich
V. P., FILM BUYER
Candi Mihalich
V. P., OPERATIONS
Dennis Redmer
MICHIGAN—ADRIAN: Cinema Adrian 8; ALLEN PARK: Allen Park 5; ANN ARBOR: Fox Village 4; LIVONIA: Livonia Mall Cinema 3; ROYAL OAK: Main Art Theatre 3, Brighton Cinemas 9, Chesterfield Crossing Cinema 12; WATERFORD: Waterford Twin 1 & 2, Waterford Eleven.

MALCO THEATRES, INC.

31 theatres, 135 screens.
5851 Ridgeway Center Parkway, Memphis, TN 38120. (901) 761-3480. FAX: (901) 681-2044.
BOARD CHAIRMAN
M. A. Lightman
BOARD CHAIRMAN
Richard L. Lightman
PRESIDENT
Stephen P. Lightman
VICE PRESIDENT
Bill Blackburn
V. P. & SECRETARY
Herbert R. Levy
V. P., ADVERTISING
Robert Levy
V. P., OPERATIONS
Jimmy Tashie
VICE PRESIDENT
John Lightman
ARKANSAS—BLYTHEVILLE: Malco Trio; FAYETTEVILLE: Mall Twin, Razorback Six; FORT SMITH: Mall Trio, Malco Quartet, Malco Twin, JONESBORO: Malco Cinema 10, Plaza Twin; ROGERS: Malco Twin; SPRINGDALE: Springdale Twin.
KENTUCKY—OWENSBORO: Mall Twin, Plaza Twin, Owensboro Cinema 8.
MISSISSIPPI—COLUMBUS: Cinema 3, Malco Twin, Mall, Varsity Twin; TUPELO: Tupelo Cinema 10.
MISSOURI—SIKESTON: Malco Trio, Mall.
TENNESSEE—JACKSON: Malco Cinema 8; MEMPHIS: Winchester Court 8, Germantown Cinema 9, Highland Quartet, Bartlett Cinema 10; Malco's Ridgeway 4, Southwest Twin D.I., Summer Quartet D.I., Appletree 12, Forest Hill Cinema 8.

MANN THEATRES, INC.

20 theatres, 87 screens.
704 Hennepin Ave., Minneapolis, MN 55403. (612) 332-3303. FAX: (612) 332-3305.
PRESIDENT
Stephen Mann
VICE PRESIDENT
Benjie Mann
FILM BUYER & BOOKER
Stephen Mann
Neil O'Leary
MINNESOTA—BRAINERD: Westgate Cinema 10, Westport 3; EAGAN: Eagan Cinema 9; GRAND RAPIDS: Central Square Cinema 3; HOPKINS: Hopkins Cinema 6; HIBBING: Irongate Cinema 3; MAPLE GROVE: Cinema 10; MINNEAPOLIS: Apache 6, Boulevard 2, Suburban World, Village 4; ST. LOUIS PARK: St. Louis Park Cinema 6; ST. PAUL: Cina 5, Cottage View D.I., Galtier 4, Grandview 2, Highland 2, Signal Hills 5; STILLWATER: Mall 5.

MARCH THEATRES

5 theatres, 10 screens.
P.O. Box 509, Spirit Lake, IA 51360. (712) 332-2784.
PRESIDENT & FILM BUYER
Jack P. March
VICE PRESIDENT
Jane March
SECRETARY & TREASURER
Peter March
IOWA—LE MARS: Royal I, II & II; SPIRIT LAKE: Royal.
NEBRASKA—WAYNE: Twin.

SOUTH DAKOTA—VERMILLION: Coyote Twin 1, 2 & 3, Vermillion.

MARCUS THEATRES CORPORATION

41 theatres, 331 screens.
250 E. Wisconsin Ave., Suite 1650, Milwaukee, WI 53202-4222. (414) 272-5120. FAX: (414) 272-0189.
CHAIRMAN
Steve Marcus
PRESIDENT
Bruce J. Olson
EXECUTIVE V. P. & FILM BUYER
Michael Kominsky
V. P. & BOOKER
Michael Ogrodowski
V. P. & FILM BOOKER
Rick Neals
VICE PRESIDENT
Don Perkins
VICE PRESIDENT
Mark Gramz
ILLINOIS—ADDISON: Marcus 20; CHICAGO HEIGHTS: Western Heights 11; GURNEE: Gurnee 20; ORLAND PARK: Marcus 10.
WISCONSIN—APPLETON: Hollywood 10, Marc 3, Valley Fair 10; BEAVER DAM: Wisconsin 4; CEDARBURG: Rivoli; GREEN BAY: Bay Park Square 12, Marc 8, Stadium 4; LA CROSSE: Cinema 4, King 3; MADISON: Eastgate 14, Point 10, Southtown 5, Westgate 3, West Towne 3, Point 10; MENOMONEE FALLS: Marcus 14; MILWAUKEE AREA: South Shore 13, North Shore 11, Marc 5, Northtown 8, Prospect 3, Skyway 6, Southtown 6, Tosa, Westown 10, West Point 8, Delafield 12, Value 6, Value 8; NEENAH: Neenah; NEW BERLIN: Ridge Cinema 12; OSHKOSH: Cinema 10; RACINE: Regency Mall 8, Westgate 5; RIPON: Campus; SHEBOYGAN: Marc 10; STEVENS POINT: Campus 4; WAUSAU: Crossroads 4.

MELROSE ASSOCIATES, INC.

15 theatres, 45 screens.
120 Fulton St., Boston, MA 02109. (617) 523-2900.
PRESIDENT
Steve Manasian
MAINE—AUGUSTA: State Street 5; BRUNSWICK: Cooks Corner 4; WESTBROOK: Cine City 5.
MASSACHUSETTS—CHELMSFORD: Route 3 Cinemas 6; NORTH ATTLEBORO: Tri-Boro Twin; NORTH WILBRAHAM: Parkway D.I.; RAYNHAM: Chalet Twin, Route 24 Twin Cinemas; SHREWSBURY: Edgemere D.I.
NEW HAMPSHIRE—GILFORD: Lake Region Twin Cinema; NORTH CONWAY: Mt. Vally Mall Cinema 4.
RHODE ISLAND—NEWPORT: Newport D.I. PROVIDENCE: Four Seasons Cinema 5; SMITHFIELD: Apple Valley Cinemas 4; WAKEFIELD: Campus Cinema.

METROPOLITAN THEATRES CORP.

26 theatres, 116 screens (28 in joint ventures).
8727 West Third St., Los Angeles CA 90048. (310) 858-2800 FAX: (310) 858-2860.
PRESIDENT
Bruce C. Corwin
EXECUTIVE V. P.
Allen Gilbert
V. P., FILM MARKETING
Allen Stokes
V. P., FINANCE
Candace Crawford
V. P., OPERATIONS & CONCESSIONS
Deborah Clark
SENIOR V. P., FILM BUYER.
Mike Doban
CALIFORNIA—DUBLIN: Dublin 6 (joint venture with Enea Bros.); INDIO: Metro 8; LIVERMORE: Vine Twin (joint venture with Enea Bros.); LOS ANGELES: Campus, Fiesta Twin, Olympic, Orpheum, Panorama Twin, Park Twin, State; PALM DESERT: Cinema 3, Town Center Cinema 10; PALM SPRINGS: Courtyard 10; PLEASANTON: Galaxy 8 (joint venture with Enea Bros.); SANTA BARBARA-GOLETA: Arlington Center for the Performing Arts, Cinema Twin, Fairview Twin, Fiesta 5, Granada 3, Metro 4, Pasa Nuevo 4, Plaza de Oro Twin, Riviera; SIMI VALLEY: Simi D.I. PALMDALE: Antelope Valley 10.
COLORADO—LOVELAND: Metrolux 12 (joint venture with Trans-Lux).

MILGRAM THEATRES, INC.

28 theatres, 52 screens.
G.S.B. Bldg., Belmont & City Line Aves., Suite 412, Bala Cynwyd, PA 19004. (215) 664-3900. FAX: (215) 664-3903.
PRESIDENT
William Milgram
EXECUTIVE V. P.
Henry Milgram

V. P. & FILM BUYER
Robert Milgram
NEW JERSEY—BAYVILLE: Friendly Twin; GLASSBORO: Glassboro; MT. EPHRAIM: Harwan; NORTHFIELD: Tilton 6; PITMAN: Broadway; PRINCETON: East Windsor Twin.
NEW YORK—ENDICOTT: $1.50 Twin.
PENNSYLVANIA—ALLENTOWN: Broad, Valley; EPHRATA: Main 2; HAZELTON: Churchill 7; HUNTINGDON: Cinema 5, Village; LAKE HARMONY: Galleria; LEWISBURG: Campus; LEWISTOWN: Midway D.I.; LOCK HAVEN: Roxy; MARIETTA: Marietta; MT. POCONO: Casino; NEW CUMBERLAND: West Shore; NEW HOLLAND: Ritz; MUNCY: Ritz, PHILADELPHIA: Merlin, Yeadon; PHOENIXVILLE: Colonial; SCRANTON: Ritz; THORNDALE: Thorndale; WILKES BARRE: Gateway Cinemas 6.

MINI THEATRES

53 theatres, 143 screens.
534 Broadhollow Rd., Suite 430, Melville, NY 11747. (516) 293-3456. FAX: (516) 293-3490.
PARTNERS
Marty Goldman
Harold S. Lager
CONNECTICUT—CANAAN: Colonial; SPRINGDALE: State Cinema.
MASSACHUSETTS—FAIRHAVEN: Cinema Six; MARTHA'S VINEYARD: Capawock, Island, Strand; RAYNHAM: Bijou Twin; SOUTH HADLEY: Tower Twin.
NEW HAMPSHIRE—HOOKSETT: Cinema 12; LACONIA: Colonial 5; MANCHESTER: South Willow St. Cinema Nine; NASHUA: Nashua Mall 8; PORTSMOUTH: Cinema 4 5; WEIRS BEACH: Weirs Twin D.I.
NEW YORK—ALBANY: Madison Cinema; ALEXANDRIA BAY: Bay D.I.; AVERILL PARK: Hollywood D.I.; CANANDAIGUA: Movie Time 10; CANTON: American; CHATHAM: Crandell Cinema; COBBLESKILL: Park; GLENS FALLS: Glen Twin D.I.; HANCOCK: Capitol Cinema; LAKE PLACID: Palace Triple; LITTLE FALLS: Valley Twin; LOWVILLE: Town Hall, Valleybrook D.I.; MALONE: Plaza; MASSENA: Massena, 56 Auto D.I.; NORTH HOOSICK: Hatheway D.I.; OGDENSBURG: Cinema Twin; OLD FORGE: Strand; ONEIDA: Glenwood Movieplex 7; POTSDAM: Roxy Twin; SARANAC LAKE: Berkeley Twin; TANNERSVILLE: Orpheum; THOUSAND ISLAND: Thousand Island Cinema; TUPPER LAKE: State; UNADILLA: Unadilla D.I.
PENNSYLVANIA—JOHNSTOWN: New Westwood Plaza Twin.
RHODE ISLAND—NARRAGANSETT: Pier Cinema Twin.
SOUTH CAROLINA—CHARLESTON: Charleston South, Windmere Twin.
VERMONT—BURLINGTON: Century Plaza Three, Merrill's Cinema Nine, Merrills Showcase 5, Ethan Allen Quad; NEWPORT: Showplace Cinema Three; RUTLAND: Plaza Cinema Twin, Studio Cinema Twin, Westway Quad.

MOVIE CITY

4 theatres, 20 screens.
P.O. Box 315, Atlantic Highlands, NJ 07716. (908) 291-0099. FAX: (908) 291-0939.
PRESIDENT
Edward Grant
VICE PRESIDENT
Howard Grant
TREASURER
Mildred Grant
SECRETARY
Jane Fabrici
NEW JERSEY—EAST BRUNSWICK: Movie City 6; EDISON: Movie City 6; TEANECK: Movie City 3; WOODBRIDGE: Movie City 5.

MOVIE ENTERTAINMENT CORP. (MAGIC THEATRES)

5 theatres, 37 screens reported.
155 S. Livingston Ave., Suite 4, Livingston, NJ 07039. (201) 535-1227. FAX: (201) 535-1228.
PRESIDENT
Jeffrey Davidson
NEW JERSEY—BERGENFIELD: Bergenfield Cinema 5; CLOSTER: Closter Cinemas 4; JERSEY CITY: Hudson Mall 4-plex; LIVINGSTON: Colony 3; SOUTH PLAINFIELD: Hadley Center Cinemas 11-plex; TENAFLY: Tenafly Theatre 4.

MOVIE ONE THEATRES, INC.

6 theatres, 30 screens reported.
109 N. Oregon, Suite 1106, El Paso TX, 79901. (915) 532-7675. FAX. (915) 544-8327.
OWNER & PRESIDENT
Lana Plasko
FILM BUYER & CEO
Ernst Plasko

MOYER THEATRES

5 theatres, 23 screens.
1953 N.W. Kearney, Portland, OR 97209. (503) 226-2735. FAX: (503) 295-1210.
PRESIDENT & COO
Larry Moyer
V. P., FINANCE
Chris Moyer
V. P., OPERATIONS.
Larry Moyer, Jr.
OREGON—EUGENE: West 11th Movieland 6; PORTLAND: Rose Moyer Cinemas 6; WILSONVILLE: Grand Parkway 3.
WASHINGTON—VANCOUVER: Vancouver Mall Cinema 4; OLYMPIA: Capitol Mall Cinema 4.

MULONE THEATRES

4 theatres, 24 screens.
100 Highland Ave., Cheswick PA 15024. (412) 274-6646.
PRESIDENT
Nick Mulone
PENNSYLVANIA—PITTSBURGH: Waterworks Cinema 10; HARMAR: Harmar Cinemas 6; CHESWICK: Cheswick Quads; SPRUER: Cinema 356 4.

MUVICO THEATERS

6 theatres, 53 screens.
3101 North Federal Highway, 6th Floor, Fort Lauderdale, FL 33306. (954) 564-6550. FAX: (954) 564-6553.
PRESIDENT
A. Hamid Hashemi
SENIOR V. P.
Robert Caleffe
FLORIDA—BOCA RATON: Muvico Town Center 7; CASSELBERRY: Muvico Lake Howell 8; HIALEAH: Muvico Hialeah 14; ORLANDO: Muvico Republic Square 8; PALM HARBOR: Muvico Palm Harbor 10; POMPANO: Muvico Pompano 6.

NATIONAL AMUSEMENTS, INC.

95 U.S. theatres, 858 U.S. screens; 11 U.K. theatres, 143 U.K. screens; 4 South American theatres, 50 South American screens; Total: 110 theatres, 1,051 screens.
200 Elm St., P.O. Box 9126, Dedham, MA 02026. (617) 461-1600. FAX: (617) 326-1306.
CHAIRMAN OF BOARD & PRESIDENT
Sumner M. Redstone
EXECUTIVE V. P.
Sheri E. Redstone
SENIOR V. P., FINANCE & TREASURER
Jerome Magner
SENIOR V. P., OPERATIONS
William J. Towey
SENIOR V. P., ADVERTISING & PUBLICITY
Edgar A. Knudson
SENIOR V. P., FILM BOOKING
George Levitt
SENIOR V. P. & GENERAL COUNSEL
Thaddeus Jankowski
V. P., REAL ESTATE
William J. Moscarelli
V. P,. FILM BOOKING
Mark Walukevich
V. P., CONCESSIONS
James Hughes
V. P., CONSTRUCTION
Peter J. Brady
V. P., OPERATIONS, FOREIGN
John Bilsborough
V. P., OPERATIONS, U.S.A
James J. Murray
V. P. MIS
Stephen Sohles
CONNECTICUT—BERLIN: Showcase 12; BRIDGEPORT: Showcase 12; EAST HARTFORD: Showcase 14; EAST WINDSOR: Showcase 12; FAIRFIELD: Fairfield Cinemas 9; MILFORD: Showcase 5, Milford 4-plex; NEWINGTON: Newington 3; NORTH HAVEN: Showcase Cinemas 8; ORANGE: Showcase 8; SOUTHINGTON: Showcase 12.
ILLINOIS—MILAN: Showcase 11; MOLINE: Super Saver 6.
INDIANA—RIVER FALLS: River Falls 10.
IOWA—DAVENPORT: Showcase 10.
KENTUCKY—ERLANGER: Showcase 9; FLORENCE: Cinemas 9; LOUISVILLE: Showcase 13, Stonybrook Cinemas 10.
MASSACHUSETTS—ALLSTON: Allston Cinemas 2; BROOKLINE: Circle Cinemas 7; DEDHAM: Showcase Cinemas 12; LAWRENCE: Showcase Cinemas 12; NORTH ATTLEBORO: Showcase Cinemas 12; QUINCY: Quincy Cinemas 8; REVERE: Showcase 14; SEEKONK: Showcase 10; SHREWSBURY: White City 3; SPRINGFIELD: Springfield Cinemas 14; WEST SPRINGFIELD: Showcase Cinemas 14; WOBURN: Showcase 14; WORCESTER: Showcase 4, Webster Square 2, Worcester North 14.

MICHIGAN—ANN ARBOR: Showcase 14; AUBURN HILLS: Showcase 14; CANTON: Showcase Cinemas 18; DEARBORN: Dearborn 8; EAST LANSING: Super Cinemas 12; FLINT: Genesee Valley 6; Showcase 12 (West), Showcase 14 (East); GRAND RAPIDS: Showcase 10; HARPER WOODS: Beacon East 4; PONTIAC: Showcase 12; STERLING HEIGHTS: Showcase 15; WESTLAND: Quo Vadis 6, Showcase 8.
NEW HAMPSHIRE—SALEM: Salem Tri.
NEW JERSEY—ATCO: Multiplex 14; HAZLET: Hazlet Multiplex 12; NEWARK: All Jersey Multiplex 14; SAYERVILLE: Amboy Multiplex 14.
NEW YORK—BRONX: Concourse Plaza 10, Whitestone Multiplex 14; COMMACK: Commack Multiplex 15; FARMINGDALE: Farmingdale Multiplex 14; HAWTHORNE: All Westchester Sawmill Multiplex 10; HICKSVILLE: Broadway Multiplex 12; MEDFORD: Brookhaven Multiplex 14; VALLEY STREAM: Green Acres 6, Sunrise Multiplex 14; YONKERS: Cross County 10.
OHIO—CINCINNATI: Eastgate Mall 7, I-275 Cinemas 4, Kenwood Towne Center 5, Northgate Cinemas 7, Showcase Cincinnati 12, Showcase King's Island 12, Showcase Springdale 9, Showcase Western Hills 12, Tri County Cinemas 5; DAYTON: Beaver Creek 7, Centerville 6, Cinema North 5, Dayton Mall 5, Showcase Cross Pointe 12, Showcase Huber Heights 12; TOLEDO: Franklin Mall 6, Franklin Park 5, Northtowne 5, Showcase 5, Southwyck 3, Super Cinemas 10.
PENNSYLVANIA—PITTSBURGH: Showcase East 10, Showcase West 12, Showcase North 11, Supersaver 8.
RHODE ISLAND—GREENVILLE: Apple Valley 8; WARWICK: Showcase 12.
VIRGINIA—ALEXANDRIA: Mt. Vernon Multiplex 10; CENTREVILLE: Centreville Multiplex 12; MERRIFIELD: Lee Highway Multiplex 14; RESTON: Reston Multiplex 11.
UNITED KINGDOM
ENGLAND—BIRMINGHAM: Showcase 12; BRISTOL: Showcase 14; COVENTRY: Showplace 12; DERBY: Showcase 11; LEEDS: Showcase 14; LIVERPOOL: Showcase 12; MANCHESTER: Showcase 14; NOTTINGHAM: Showcase 13; PETERBOROUGH: Showcase 13; TEESSIDE: Showcase 14; WALSALL: Showcase 12.
SCOTLAND—GLASGOW: Showcase Cinemas (East) 13, Showcase Cinemas (West) 14, Showcase Cinemas 14.
SOUTH AMERICA
ARGENTINA—CORDOBA: Cinemas Showcase 12; HAEDO: Cinemas Showcase 14.
CHILE—SANTIAGO: Cinemas Showcase 10, Cinemas Showcase 14.

NORET THEATRES

8 theatres, 25 screens.
2726 82nd St., Lubbock, TX 79423. (806) 745-1693. FAX: (806) 745-0952.
TEXAS—AMARILLO: Showplace 4; AUSTIN: Showplace 6; LA MESA: The Movies 1 & 2; LUBBOCK: Cinema West, Showplace 6, Winchester Twin; SAN ANGELO: Village Cinema 1 & 2; SNYDER: Cinema 1 & 2.

B. L. NUTTER THEATRES

7 theatres, 9 screens.
P. O. Box 44, Putnam, CT 06260. (401) 568-6428.
PRESIDENT & TREASURER
Bruce L. Nutter
V. P. & ASSISTANT GENERAL MANAGER
Christine E. Nutter
CONNECTICUT—HARTFORD: Colonial; PUTNAM: Royale Deluxe Theatre I & II.
MASSACHUSETTS—PALMER: Imperial Cinema; SPENCER: Imperial Cinema; WINCHENDON: Capitol.
RHODE ISLAND—PROVIDENCE: New Imperial Art Cinema; WEST GLOCESTER: Cold Springs Theatre I & II.

P & G THEATRES

7 theatres, 18 screens.
2300 Shonefield Rd., Suite 204, Silver Spring, MD 20902. (301) 949-4761.
OWNER
P. Sanchez
HEAD BOOKER
Pat Curtis
OFFICE MANAGER
Le Pham
MARYLAND—CAMP SPRINGS: Andrews Manor 2; CHESTERTOWN: Chestertown 5; GAITHENSBURG: Montgomery Village 3; GREENBELT: Old Greenbelt; LAUREL: Laurel Towne Center 2; RIVERDALE: Riverdale Plaza; SILVER SPRING: Flower Theatre 4.

PACIFIC THEATRES

40 theatres, 217 screens.
120 North Robertson Boulevard, Los Angeles, CA 90048. (310) 657-8420. FAX: (310) 855-9837, (310) 652-2439. (also owns Consolidated Amusement, Hawaii)

BOARD CHAIRMAN
Michael R. Forman
CEO
Christopher Forman
PRESIDENT
Jerome A. Forman
CFO
John Hunter
EXECUTIVE V. P., OPERATIONS
Jay Swerdlow
EXECUTIVE V. P., HEAD FILM BUYER & DIR. MARKETING
Chan Wood
Drive-in Theatres
CALIFORNIA—CHATSWORTH: Winnetka 6; FRESNO: Woodward Park 4; GARDENA: Vermont Triplex; CITY OF INDUSTRY: Vineland 4-plex; LONG BEACH: Los Altos Triplex; PICO RIVERA: Fiesta 4; VAN NUYS: Van Nuys 3; VENTURA: 101 Triplex; WESTMINSTER: Hi-Way 39 4.
Walk-in Theatres
CALIFORNIA—CARMEL MOUNTAIN: Carmel Mountain 12; CITY OF COMMERCE: Commerce 7; CORTE MADERA: Cinema; EAGLE ROCK: Eagle Rock 4; HOLLYWOOD: El Capitan, Pacific's Cinerama Dome; HUNTINGTON PARK: Warner 2; LA JOLLA: La Jolla Village 4; LAKEWOOD: Lakewood Center 4, Lakewood Center South 9, Regency 8; LA MESA: Grossmont Center 8, Grossmont Trolley 8 Cinemas; MANHATTAN BEACH: Beach Cities Cinemas 16; MILL VALLEY: Sequoia Twin; NORTHRIDGE: Northridge 10; NOVATO: Rowland Plaza; ONTARIO: Ontario 10; OXNARD: Carriage Square 5; PASADENA: Hastings 8; PETALUMA: Petaluma 8; SAN BERNARDINO: Inland Cinema 5; SAN DIEGO: Cinerama 6, Clairemont Twin; SAN RAFAEL: Regency 6, Northgate Cinemas 15; SAUSALITO: Marin 3; SHERMAN OAKS: Pacific 4; SWEETWATER: Sweetwater 9; WESTWOOD: Crest; WOODLAND HILLS: Topanga 3.

PATRIOT CINEMAS, INC., THE

4 theatres, 19 screens.
350 Lincoln St., Hingham, MA 02043. (617) 749-7963. FAX: (617) 749-7974.
PRESIDENT
Philip J. Scott
VICE PRESIDENT
David A. Kiolbasa
VICE PRESIDENT
Edith L. Scott
BOOKER
Peter Wright
OFFICE MANAGER & TREASURER
David A. Scott
MASSACHUSETTS—FALMOUTH: Falmouth Mall Cinemas 6; HINGHAM: Loring Cinema; NORTH WEYMOUTH: Harborlight Cinemas 10; SOUTH WEYMOUTH: Cameo Theatres 2.

PEACHES/MOVIE PALACE

5 theatres, 9 screens.
P. O. Box 2180, Casper, WY 82601.
IDAHO—IDAHO FALLS: Paramount Triplex.
WYOMING—CASPER: America, Rialto; CHEYENNE: Lincoln; RAWLINS: Movies Triplex.

PIEDMONT THEATRES

8 theatres, 35 screens.
3700 South Blvd., Charlotte, NC 28217. (704) 527-7200.
PRESIDENT
Jerry L. Theimer
NORTH CAROLINA—BOONE: Flick 2; CHARLOTTE: Tryon Mall 4-plex, Queen Park 6-plex Indoor; CONCORD: Clearsprings 6; FAYETTEVILLE: Sycamore 5; GASTONIA: Watertower 4.
SOUTH CAROLINA—CHARLESTON: Fox IV.
VIRGINIA—LYNCHBURG: Fort Cinema 4-plex.

PLITT AMUSEMENT CO.

9 theatres, 34 screens.
9059 90th St. N.W., P.O. Box 2339, Oak Harbor, WA 98277. (206) 675-0746. FAX: (206) 675-9402.
Los Angeles Office: 1801 Century Park E., Suite 1225, Los Angeles, CA 90067, (213) 553-2364. FAX: (213) 201-9164.
PRESIDENT
Raymond C. Fox
V. P. & DIRECTOR OF OPERATIONS
Sam M. Plitt
V. P., SECRETARY TREASURER
Sandra J. Andre
WASHINGTON—ELLENSBURG: Liberty 3; MOSES LAKE: Lake Cinema 4; MT. VERNON: Cinema 5, College Tri 3; OAK HARBOR: Plaza 3; SUNNYSIDE: Eastway 3; WALLA WALLA: Jefferson Park 3, Plaza Twin 2, Poplar Street 3.

POLSON THEATRES

9 theatres, 9 screens.
P.O. Box 999, Polson, MT 59860. (406) 883-5603.

IDAHO—SALMON: Roxy Cinema.
MONTANA—DILLON: Big Sky Cinemas; GLASGOW: Valley Cinemas; HAVRE: Havre Cinemas; POLSON: Showboat Cinemas; PRAIRIE: Prairie Cinemas; RONAN: Entertainer Cinemas; WHITEFISH: Mountain Cinemas.

QUEENS CIRCUIT MANAGEMENT CORP.

3 theatres, 10 screens.
P.O. Box 120, Corona A Station, Corona, NY 11368-2395. (718) 478-9200.
FILM BUYER & GENERAL MANAGER
Orlando Mendoza
NEW YORK—CORONA: Plaza Twin; JACKSON HEIGHTS: Jackson Triplex; RIDGEWOOD: Ridgewood 5-plex.

R/C THEATRES MANAGEMENT CORP.

27 theatres, 130 screens.
(An Etmac Co.) 231 West Cherry Hill Ct., Box 1056, Reisterstown, MD 21136-1056. (410) 526-4774. FAX: (410) 526-6871.
PRESIDENT & CEO
Irwin R. Cohen
PRESIDENT OF OPERATIONS
J. Wayne Anderson
PRESIDENT OF FILM
Scott R. Cohen
V. P., OPERATIONS
David G. Phillips
V. P., FINANCE
Richard A. Hershel
V. P., FILM
Jan S. Anderson
DIVISION MANAGERS
Philip Ridenour (MD, PA)
Barry L. Wiseman (Southeast VA, NC)
John C. Epperly (Southwest VA)
MARYLAND—ARBUTUS: Hollywood 4 Cinema; EASTON: Easton Movies 4; ELDERSBURG: Carrolltowne Movies 6; FROSTBURG: Frostburg Cinema 3; HAGERSTOWN: Hagerstown Movies 10, Long Meadow Triple Cinema; REISTERSTOWN: Village Cinema 3.
NORTH CAROLINA—COROLLA: Corolla 4; KITTY HAWK: Kitty Hawk 2; NAGS HEAD: Cineplex 4, Outer Banks 2; SOUTHERN SHORES: Market Place 2.
PENNSYLVANIA—CARLISLE: Mall Cinema 8; GETTYSBURG: Majestic Cinema 3.
VIRGINIA—BLACKSBURGH: Capri Twin; CHRISTIANSBURG: New River Valley Mall 8; COVINGTON: Covington Movies 3; CULPEPER: Regal Twin Cinema; FREDERICKSBURG: Movies of Fredericksburg 10, Spotsylvania Mall 4, Virginians Cinema 4; LEESBURG: Tally Ho Twin Cinema; LEXINGTON: State Cinema 3; NORFOLK (Naval Base): Main Gate 10; STAFFORD: Aquia Town Center Movies 10; VIRGINIA BEACH: Columbus Movies 12; WAYNESBORO: Wayne Twin Cinema.

RTC THEATRES & ASSOCIATES

5 theatres, 6 screens.
805 Fletcher Lane, Hayward, CA 94544. (510) 886- 7727. FAX: (510) 886-7751.
PRESIDENT
Lawrence E. Martin
VICE PRESIDENT
Ralph Martin
CFO
Paul Martin
CALIFORNIA—SAN LEANDRO: Bal; VISALIA: Visalia, Mooney D.I. 1 & 2; SALINAS: Fox; SAN FRANCISCO: Tower.

REGAL CINEMAS, INC.

156 theatres, 1282 screens.
7132 Commercial Park Dr., Knoxville, TN 37918. (615) 922-1123. FAX: (615) 922-6739.
PRESIDENT chairman
Michael L. Campbell
EXECUTIVE V. P.
Gregory Dunn
EXECUTIVE V. P. & CFO
Lewis Frazer
SENIOR V. P., FILM & ADVERTISING
Robert Engel
SENIOR V. P., REAL ESTATE & DEVELOPMENT
Keith Thompson
V. P., EQUIPMENT & PURCHASING
R. Neal Melton
V. P., ENTERTAINMENT CENTERS & FOOD SERVICES
Robert J. Del Moro
V. P., OPERATIONS, NORTH
Michael Kivett
V. P., OPERATIONS, SOUTH
Leon Hurst

V. P. & CONTROLLER
Susan Seagraves
V. P., TECHNICAL SERVICES
Roger Frazee
V. P., MANAGEMENT INFORMATION SYSTEMS
J. E. Henry
V. P., ADVERTISING
Kip Daley
V. P., CONSTRUCTION
Ronald Kooch
HEAD FILM BUYER
Judd Parker
DIRECTOR, TRAINING & SAFETY
Tony Griffin
DIRECTOR, CONSTRUCTION
Ray Dunlap
DIRECTOR, OPERATIONAL SUPPORT SERVICES
Jan Frazee
DIRECTOR, SPECIAL ACCOUNTING PROJECTS
Mark Monroe
DIRECTOR, MARKETING & PUBLIC RELATIONS
Mike Levesque
DIRECTOR, PROJ. DEVEL.–ENTERTAINMENT CENTERS
Dean Duncan
DIRECTOR, HUMAN RESOURCES
Debbie Robertson
DIRECTOR, LEASING
John Roper
PROMOTIONS MANAGER
Jennifer Bohlken
CONCESSION ACCOUNTING MANAGER
Susan D. Milam
ASSISTANT CONTROLLER
Lisa Depew
ASSISTANT CONTROLLER
Joseph Marlowe
ALABAMA—DECATUR: Gateway 4, River Oaks 8; GADSEN: Rainbow 8.
CALIFORNIA—DIAMOND BAR: Diamond Bar 8; EL CAJON: El Cajon 8; HEMET: Hemet 12; LAKE ELSINORE: Lake Elsinore 8; RANCHO PALOS VERDES: Terrace 6; ROLLING HILLS ESTATES: Peninsula 8; SAN BERNARDINO: Del Rosa 8; WHITTIER: Whittwood 10.
DELAWARE—NEWARK: Peoples Plaza 13.
FLORIDA—CORAL SPRINGS: Coral Springs 6; DELRAY BEACH: Delray 18; GAINESVILLE: Regal 14; INVERNESS: Citrus 6; JACKSONVILLE: Beach Boulevard 12, Regal 10; LAKE MARY: Regal 10; MIAMI: California Club 6; ORLANDO: UC 7; ORMOND BEACH: Ormond Beach 12; PENSACOLA: Cordova 3, Cordova Mall 4; TAMPA: Britton 8.
GEORGIA—ATLANTA: Twelve Oaks 4; AUGUSTA: Augusta Village 12; AUSTELL: Austell Road 10; COLLEGE PARK: National 7; KENNESAW: Town 12; LAWRENCEVILLE: Town Center 10; LITHONIA: Covington Square 8; MACON: Macon Mall 4, Rivergate 14; MARIETTA: Regal 10, Delk 10; NORCROSS: Peachtree 10; RIVERDALE: Riverdale 10; SAVANNAH: Eisenhower 6, Victory Square 9; SNELLVILLE: Snellville Oaks 14; UNION CITY: Shannon 7.
INDIANA—CARMEL: Village Park 12; FORT WAYNE: Coldwater Crossing 8, Coventry 13, Georgetown 1 & 2, Glenbrook 3, Holiday 1 & 2, Holiday 6, Northwood Park 2; INDIANAPOLIS: Shilo Crossing 8.
KENTUCKY—FLORENCE: Turfway Park 10.
LOUISIANA—BOSSIER CITY: Bossier Corners 9; SHREVEPORT: South Park Mall 8.
MARYLAND—FREDERICK: Holiday 2.
NEW JERSEY—BURLINGTON: Burlington 14; MARLBORO: The Movies 8; TURNERSVILLE: Cross Keys 12.
NEW YORK—CICERO: Cicero 13/Funscape; VICTOR: East View Mall 13/Funscape.
NORTH CAROLINA—ASHEVILLE: Hollywood 4; BOONE: Regal 7; FAYETTEVILLE: Omni 8; GREENSBORO: Regal 7; HIGHPOINT: Oak Hollow Mall 7; MOUNT AIRY: Mayberry 5; WILSON: Regal 7.
OHIO—AKRON: Akron 10, Montrose 8, Interstate Park 14; BROOK PARK: Brookgate 5; BRUNSWICK: Hickory Ridge 8; CHILLICOTHE: Regal 6, Shawnee Square 4; CINCINNATI: Central Parke 11; CLEVELAND HEIGHTS: Severance 8; DEFIANCE: Northtowne 9; DELAWARE: Delaware Square 5; GARFIELD HEIGHTS: Garfield Mall 5; HUDSON: Hudson 10; LIMA: Eastgate 4, Lima Center 3, Regal 7; LORAIN: Sheffield Centre 10; MARIETTA: Lafayette Center 7; MARION: Southland 7; MAYFIELD HEIGHTS: Mayfield Heights Cinema 10; MENTOR: Great Lakes Mall 9; MIDDLEBURG HEIGHTS: Middleburg Heights 12; MIDDLETOWN: Towne East 5; NILES: Boulevard Centre 14, Movie World 6; NORTH OLMSTED: Great Northern 7; SOLON: Solon Commons 10; TIFFIN: Tiffin 4; WESTLAKE: Westlake Promenade 11; YOUNGSTOWN: Cinema South 10.
OKLAHOMA—EDMOND: Kickingbird 8; OKLAHOMA CITY: Windsor Hills 10.
PENNSYLVANIA—BUTLER: Moraine Pointe Plaza 10; CONSHOHOCKEN: Plymouth Meeting 14; EXTON: Lionville 12; HUNTINGDON VALLEY: Huntingdon Valley 14; PHILADELPHIA: Center City 12, YORK: Queensgate 10.

SOUTH CAROLINA—AIKEN: Aiken Mall 8; COLUMBIA: Regal 7; GREENVILLE: Pelham Road 10; MURRELS INLET: Inlet Square 7; MYRTLE BEACH: Pottery 6; NORTH CHARLESTON: North Charleston 10; ROCK HILL: Galleria Mall 8; SPARTANBURG: Converse 6, Westgate Mall 8.
TENNESSEE—CHATTANOOGA: Hamilton Place 9, Hamilton Place 10-17; HENDERSONVILLE: Indian Lake 10; HERMITAGE: Courtyard 8; HIXSON: Northgate Crossing 6; JACKSON: Jackson 10; KNOXVILLE: Downtown West 8, East Towne Crossing 8, East Towne Mall 7, Farragut Towne Square 10; NASHVILLE: Bellevue Cinema 12, Nippers Corner 10; TULLAHOMA: Tullahoma 8.
VIRGINIA—CHARLOTTESVILLE: Downtown Mall 6, Greenbriar 2, Seminole Square 4; CHESAPEAKE: Greenbriar 4; Greenbriar 13/Funscape; CHESTER: Chester 6; COLONIAL HEIGHTS: Southpark 6; FARMVILLE: Longwood Village 3; FRANKLIN: Armory Drive 3; GLEN ALLEN: Virginia Center 14; HARRISONBURG: Harrinburg 3, Valley Mall 4; MIDLOTHIAN: Genito Forest 9; NEWPORT NEWS: Kiln Creek 14, Newmarket 1-4; PETERSBURG: Crater 8; RICHMOND: Cloverleaf Mall 8, Ridge 7, Westhampton 2, Willow Lawn 4; SOUTH HILL: South Hill 2; STAUNTON: Staunton Mall 6; STERLING: Countryside 14; VIRGINIA BEACH: Pembroke Mall 8.
WASHINGTON—PORT ORCHID: South Sound 10.
WEST VIRGINIA—PARKERSBURG: Towne Square 6; VIENNA: Grand Central Mall 5.

REGENCY CARIBBEAN CINEMAS

20 U.S. theatres, 109 U.S. screens; 7 Dominican Republic theatres, 22 Dominican screens; TOTAL: 27 theatres, 131 screens.
1512 Fernandez Juncos Ave., 3rd floor, San Juan, PR 00910. (809) 727-7137.
PRESIDENT
Victor Carrady
VICE PRESIDENT
Robert Carrady
DOMINICAN REPUBLIC—LA ROMANA: Papagayo; SANTO DOMINGO, Cinema Centro 9, Diana, Manzana 2, Max, Santiago, Broadway 7.
PUERTO RICO—BAYAMON: Rio Hondo 10; CAGUAS: Plaza Centro 5; GUAYNABO: Cinema 4, Guaynabo 3; PONCE: Plaza Del Caribe 6, Ponce 3; SAN JUAN: Fine Arts 3, Metro 3, Fajardo 6, Humacao 5, Yauco 4, Aquadilla 6, Isabela 4, Carolina 10, Montehiedra 14; TRUJILLO ALTO: Trujillo Alto 3. GUAYAMA: Guayama 6; ARECIBO: Arecibo 7.
U.S. VIRGIN ISLANDS—ST. THOMAS: Four Winds 4, Cinema 3.

ROGERS CINEMA, INC.

5 theatres, 21 screens reported.
1813 S. Koddis, P.O. Box 280, Marshfield, WI 54449. (715) 387-2566. FAX: (715) 387-2165.
OWNER & PRESIDENT
Paul J. Rogers
OWNER & V. P.
John V. Koran

SCHULMAN THEATRES, INC.

7 theatres, 22 screens.
2000 East 29th St., Bryan, TX 77806.
TEXAS—BRYAN: Manor East III, Schulman Six; COLLEGE STATION: Plaza Three; CROCKETT: Ritz; PALESTINE: Schulman 2; WACO: Schulman 5, Ivy Twin Cinema.

SIGNATURE THEATRES

9 theatres, 48 screens.
(Formerly Harris Theatres) 1600 Broadway, Suite 250, Oakland, CA 94612. (510) 268-9498. FAX: (510) 268-9843.
OWNER, CHAIRMAN, & PRESIDENT
Philip Harris III
OWNERS
Philip Harris, Sr. & Douglas Stephens
FILM BUYER
Chris Aaronson
CALIFORNIA—DAVIS: Cinema 2, Holiday 6; MODESTO: Briggsmore 7, Vintage Faire 4; OAKLAND: Jack London Cinema 4; SANTA CRUZ: Santa Cruz 9; STOCKTON: Holiday 8; VISALIA: Tower Plaza 3, Visalia Cinema.

SOCAL CINEMAS, INC.

15 theatres, 33 screens.
13 Corporate Plaza, Newport Beach, CA 92660. (714) 640-2370.
PRESIDENT
Bruce Sanborn
GENERAL MANAGER
Gary Richardson
CALIFORNIA—ANAHEIM HILLS: Cinemapolis 13; BLUE JAY VILLAGE: Blue Jay Cinema 4; CARLSBAD: Plaza Camino Real Cinema 4; LAGUNA HILLS: Laguna Hills Mall Cinema 3; LOS ANGELES: University Cinema 3; MORENO VALLEY: Canyon Springs Cinema 7; OCEANSIDE: Town & Country Cinema 3; RIVERSIDE: Canyon Crest Cinema 9, Marketplace Cinema; TEMECULA: Temeku Cinema 7, Tower Cinema 7; WEST COVINA: Fox Theatre 3, Eastland Theatre 5, Wescove Cinema 3; SAN LUIS OBISPO: Downtown Center Cinema 7.

SONY THEATRE MANAGEMENT CORP.

143 theatres, 949 screens (includes one IMAX screen).
(A Sony Retail Entertainment Company). 711 Fifth Ave., New York, NY 10022-3109. (212) 833-6200.
PRESIDENT, SONY RETAIL ENTERTAINMENT
Lawrence J. Ruisi
CHAIRMEN
Barrie Lawson Loeks
Jim Loeks
EXECUTIVE V. P., FILM BUYING
Travis Reid
EXECUTIVE V. P. & GENERAL COUNSEL
Seymour Smith
EXECUTIVE V. P., DEVEL., REAL ESTATE & CONST.
Joyce Storm
SENIOR V. P., CORPORATE DEVEL. & ADMINISTRION
Dorian Brown
SENIOR V. P., OPERATIONS
Michael P. Norris
SENIOR V. P., FINANCE
John Walker
V.P. & DEPUTY GENERAL COUNSEL
David Badain
V. P., REAL ESTATE
Kenneth B. Benjamin
V. P., FILM BUYING
Steve Bunnell
V. P., PERSONNEL & ADMINISTRATION
Peter Fournier
V. P., CONCESSIONS
Fred Gable
V. P., ADVERTISING & PUBLICITY
Marc Pascucci
V. P., FILM
David Tuckerman
V. P. & CONTROLLER
Joseph Sparacio
V. P., CONSTRUCTION
Cary Spiegel
V.P., MIS
Jim Fagerstrom
CALIFORNIA—LOS ANGELES: Magic Johnson Theatres 12.
CONNECTICUT—BRISTOL: Bristol 8; DANBURY: Danbury 10; FAIRFIELD: Community 1 & 2; GREENWICH: Greenwich 1 & 2; TORRINGTON: Holiday 6; WESTPORT: Fine Arts 1 & 2, Fine Arts 3, Post Cinema.
GEORGIA—ATLANTA: Magic Johnson Theatre 12.
ILLINOIS—CHICAGO: Double Drive-In 3, Esquire 6, Fine Arts 4, Hyde Park 4, Pipers Alley 4, Webster Place 11; CICERO: Bel-Air Drive-In 3; CRESTWOOD: Sony Crestwood 12; EVANSTON: Evanston 5; EVERGREEN: Evergreen 4; HILLSIDE: Hillside Mall 3, Hillside Square 6; LANSING: River Run 8; NORRIDGE: Norridge 10; ROLLING MEADOWS: Rolling Meadows 9; SKOKIE: Old Orchard 4; STREAMWOOD: Streamwood 14.
INDIANA—INDIANAPOLIS: Cherry Tree 10, College Park 10, Greenwood 9, Lafayette Square 8, Norgate 4; MERRILLVILLE: Merrillville 10, Y & W Drive-In 3.
KENTUCKY—ASHLAND: Midtown 3; LEXINGTON: Fayette 3, Lexington Mall 2, North Park 10, Southpark 6.
MARYLAND—BALTIMORE: Greenspring 3, Northpoint 4, Rotunda 2; BEL AIR: Campus Hills 7, Hartford Mall 2; BELTSVILLE: Centerpark 8; COLUMBIA: Columbia Palace 9; CROFTON: Crofton 4; GERMANTOWN: Germantown 6; GLEN BURNIE: Glen Burnie 7; LEXINGTON PARK: Lexington Park 6; OWINGS MILLS: Valley Centre 9; PASADENA: Jumpers 7 Cinema; TIMONIUM: Timonium 3, Yorkridge 4; WHEATON: Wheaton Plaza 11.
MASSACHUSETTS—BOSTON: Copley Place 11, Nickelodeon 5, Cheri 4; CAMBRIDGE: Janus, Harvard Square 5, Fresh Pond 10; DANVERS: Liberty Tree Mall 2, Cinema City Danvers 6; FALL RIVER: Harbour Mall 8; LEOMINSTER: Leominster 12; NATICK: Natick 6; SOMERVILLE: Assembly Square 12.
NEW HAMPSHIRE—CONCORD: Merrimack 6; LEBANON: Lebanon 6.
NEW JERSEY—BRICK: Cinema Center 5, Circle 5; EAST BRUNSWICK: Route 18 Twin; EAST HANOVER: East Hanover Metroplex 12; EATONTOWN: Monmouth Mall 15; EDGEWATER: Showboat Quad; FREEHOLD: Freehold Metroplex 8, Freehold Cinemas 6; MOUNTAINSIDE: Mountainside 10; NEWARK: Newark Metroplex 6; NEW BRUNSWICK: New Brunswick 18; RAMSEY: Interstate Twin; RED BANK: Red Bank 2; RIDGEFIELD PARK: Ridgefield Park 12; SECAUCUS: Plaza 8, Meadow 6; TOMS RIVER: Seacourt 10, Dover 2; WAYNE: Wayne 14.
NEW YORK—BAYSHORE: South Shore Mall 2; BAYSIDE: Bay Terrace 6; BUFFALO: West Seneca 15; ELMHURST: Elmwood 4;

ELMIRA: Elmira 3; FOREST HILLS: Trylon 1; GARDEN CITY: Roosevelt Field 8; JOHNSON CITY: Oakdale Mall 3; LEVITTOWN: Nassau Metroplex 10; NEW YORK: Tower East 1, New York Twin, Astor Plaza 1, Orpheum 7, 84th Street 6, State (inside Virgin Records megastore), 34th Street Showplace 3, Village 7, 19th Street 6, Paris, Lincoln Square 12 (includes Sony IMAX); MIDDLETOWN: Middletown 10, Galleria Metroplex 16; ROCHESTER: Pittsford, Pittsford Twin, Towne Quad; SCHENECTADY: Mowhawk Mall 7, Rotterdam Square 6; STONYBROOK: Stonybrook 3; VESTAL: Town Square Mall 9; WEBSTER: Webster 12; WESTBURY: Roosevelt Raceway 10.
OHIO—CLEVELAND: East 8, Cedar Center 2; COLUMBUS: Continent 9, Westerville 2; DAYTON: Salem Avenue 3, Beaver Valley 6.
PENNSYLVANIA—STROUDSBURG: Stroud Mall 7.
TEXAS—ARLINGTON: Lincoln Square 10, 20 & 287 Six; DALLAS: Cityplace 14, Keystone Park 16, Park Central 4; FORT WORTH: City View 8; HOUSTON: Fountains 18, Memorial City 8, Easton Commons 8, Southpoint 5-plex; MEADOWS: Southwest 6; PLANO: Preston Park 6, Chisholm 5; SPRING: Spring 10; WEBSTER: Bay Area 6.
VIRGINIA—ARLINGTON: Pentagon City 6; HERNDON: Worldgate 9; McLEAN: Tysons Corner 8.

STANDARD THEATRES, INC.

5 theatres, 16 screens.
19065 North Hills Dr., P.O. Box 632, Brookfield, WI 53008-0632. (414) 784-1450.
PRESIDENT
John F. Ling
WISCONSIN—BELOIT: Prairie Cinema 5; DELAVAN: Delavan Twin; GREEN BAY: Bay Triple; LAKE GENEVA: Geneva 4; MILWAUKEE: 41 Twins Outdoor.

SUPER SAVER CINEMA LTD.

29 theatres, 219 screens.
109 North Oregon, Suite 1000, El Paso, TX 79912. (915) 532-1943. FAX: (915) 542-2945.
PRESIDENT & CEO
Lloyd Curley
COO
Lynn Hunt
CFO
Bill Husby
ASSISTANT V. P., THEATRE OPERATIONS
Lois Hufnagel
MAINTENANCE & CONSTRUCTION
Lonnie Gillman
CONCESSIONS & MARKETING DIRECTOR
Kathi Gillman
PURCHASING MANAGER
Mark Cabral
ARIZONA—MESA: Superstation Springs 8, Town Center 8; PHOENIX: Bell Rd. 8, Palm Glen 8.
CALIFORNIA—FREEMONT: Gateway Plaza 7; NORWALK: Norwalk Square 8; POMONA: Indian Hills 8; SEAL BEACH: Rossmoor 7.
COLORADO—ARVADA: Arlington Square 8; AURORA: Aurora Plaza 8; COLORADO SPRINGS: Citadel 8; DENVER: Bear Valley 8; THORNTON: Pinnacle 8.
FLORIDA—MIAMI: Westbird 8.
NEBRASKA—OMAHA: Westwood 8.
NEW YORK—BUFFALO: Elmwood 8.
OHIO—CINCINNATI: Biggs 8, Forest Fair 8; COLUMBUS: Glengary 8, Brice Outlet 8.
OKLAHOMA—OKLAHOMA CITY: Lakeshore 8, Mall 31 7, Shields Plaza 8; TULSA: Mall 31 7.
TEXAS—LEWISVILLE: Lewisville 10.
WISCONSIN—MILWAUKEE: Budget Cinema 6; GREENFIELD: Budget Cinema 6; MADISON: East Town Cinema 4, Market Square 5.

SYNDICATE THEATRES, INC.

6 theatres, 6 screens.
55-1/2 E. Court Street, Franklin, IN 46131. (317) 736-7144. FAX (317) 736 4126.
CHAIRMAN
Trueman T. Rembusch
PRESIDENT
Michael Rembusch
TREASURER
Mary Agnes Rembusch
BOOKER
Nancy Gilliland
INDIANA—BATESVILLE: Gibson; FRANKLIN: Artcraft; HUNTINGTON: Huntington, Huntington D.I.; WABASH: Eagles, 13-24 D.I.

TEGTMEIER ASSOCIATES, INC.

5 theatres, 13 screens.
P.O.Box 776, Menlo Park, CA 94026. (415) 324-4335. FAX (415) 324-4336.

CALIFORNIA—FAIRFIELD: Chief Cinemas 4, Fairfield 1 & 2; LAKEPORT: Lakeport Auto Movies, Lakeport Twin; VACAVILLE: Vaca Valley 4.

THEATRE MANAGEMENT, INC.

10 theatres, 38 screens.
P.O. Box 2076, Deland, FL 32721. (904) 736-6830. FAX: (904) 738-2596.
FLORIDA—DELAND: Deland Cinema, Victoria Square 6; NEW SMYRNA: Beacon 8; MELBOURNE: Payless Sarno 6; ORANGE CITY: Showcase 2; PALM CITY: Martin Downs 4.
PENNSYLVANIA—BUTLER: Penn Twin, Pioneer D.I., CLARION: Clarion Theatres 4; MEADVILLE: Meadville 4.

TRAD-A-HOUSE CORPORATION (O'NEIL THEATRES)

18 theatres, 166 screens.
1926 C Corporate Square Dr., Slidell, LA 70458. (504) 641-4720. FAX: (504) 641-5726.
PRESIDENT
Tim O'Neil, Jr.
VICE PRESIDENT
Tim O'Neil III
SECRETARY & TREASURER
Betty O'Neil
OFFICE OPERATIONS
C. Jean Johnson
FIELD OPERATIONS
Steven L. Moss
ALABAMA—FOLEY: Riviera Cinema 12.
FLORIDA—DESTIN: Destin Cinema 10; HOLLYWOOD: Taft-Hollywood Plaza Cinema 12. PANAMA CITY BEACH: Edgewater Cinema 10.
GEORGIA—ATLANTA: Northeast Plaza Cinema 12; DECATUR: Avondale Mall Cinema 16; DULUTH: Outlet Mall Cinema 12.
LOUISIANA—COVINGTON: Holiday Cinema 10; CROWLEY: Crowley Cinema 4; MANDEVILLE: Causeway Cinema 4; SLIDELL: The Movies 8.
MISSISSIPPI—HATTIESBURG: Broadacres Cinema 6; PICAYUNE: River Ridge Cinema 4; WAVELAND: Choctow Cinema 4.
NEW HAMPSHIRE—LONDONDERRY: Appletree Cinema 8.
TENNESSEE—FRANKLIN: Watson Glen Cinema 10; MADISON: Old Hickory Cinema 16.
TEXAS—DALLAS: Westend Cinema 8.

UNITED ARTISTS THEATRE CIRCUIT, INC.

414 theatres, 2380 screens.
9110 E. Nichols Ave., Suite 200, Englewood, CO 80112. (303) 792-3600.
CHAIRMAN & CEO
Stewart D. Blair
EXECUTIVE V. P. & CFO
Kurt Hall
EXECUTIVE V. P., DEVELOPMENT
Hal Cleveland
EXECUTIVE V. P., INTERNATIONAL DEVELOPMENT
Thomas C. Elliot
EXECUTIVE V. P., INTERNATIONAL DEVELOPMENT
Joseph R. Crotty
EXECUTIVE V. P., FILM
Bob Capps
EXECUTIVE V. P., CONCESSIONS
Bruce Taffet
EXECUTIVE V. P., OPERATIONS
Dennis Daniels
EXECUTIVE V. P., NEW BUSINESS
Jim Ruybal
EXECUTIVE V. P. & GEN'L COUNSEL
Gene Hardy
SENIOR V. P., MIS
Judy Paquet
SENIOR V. P., MARKETING AND NEW BUSINESS
Bill Quigley
SENIOR V. P., TAX
Steven Koets

REGIONAL OFFICES
Western: 21700 Oxnard St., Suite 1000,, Woodland Hills CA 91367
Eastern: 3521 US Route 1, Princeton, NJ 08540
540 Madison Ave., 30th fl., New York, NY 10022
2 South 69th St., Upper Darby, PA 19082
Central: 1900 S. Central Expressway, Dallas, TX 75215
ARIZONA—CHANDLER: East Valley Mall; GLENDALE: Bell Park Cinemas 6; MESA: Valvista 10; PHOENIX: Metro Park 8, Westridge Park 6, Christown Mall Cinema 6; SCOTTSDALE: Sonora Village 10, UA 5 Scottsdale, UA Scottsdale Pavillion 11.
ARKANSAS—LITTLE ROCK: UA Cinema 150 I, UA Cinema City 7, UA Park Plaza 7; MAGNOLIA: Cameo 3; NORTH LITTLE ROCK: Cinema 8.

CALIFORNIA—APTOS: Aptos Twin 2; BAKERSFIELD: UA Bernards Street, UA Movies 6, UA East Hills; BERKELEY: UA 7 Berkeley; BREA: Marketplace 8, UA Movies 4; BUENA PARK: UA Buena Park 8; CAMARILLO: UA Mission Oaks 8; CAMPBELL: UA Pruneyard 3; CAPITOLA: 41st Avenue Playhouse 3; CERRITOS: UA Cerritos Mall 4, UA Cerritos Twin 2; CHICO: El Rey, Senator 4, Valley Plaza 3; CITRUS HEIGHTS: Greenback 6, Sunrise 4; CLOVIS: UA 8 Clovis, UA Sierra Vista; COMA: Metro Center; EMERYVILLE: UA Emery Bay 10; ESCONDIDO: UA 8 Escondido; FRESNO: Broadway Faire 10, Movies 4, Manchester Mall Cinema 2, UA Northgate Cinemas 4; GRANADA HILLS: UA Movies 7; GRASS VALLEY: Del Oro 3, Grass Valley Cinema 2; HAYWARD: UA Hayward 6; LA CANADA: UA La Canada Flintridge; LAKEWOOD: UA Lakewood 6; LONG BEACH: UA Movies Long Beach 6; LOS ANGELES: Westwood 5; MARINA DEL REY: UA 6 Marina Del Rey; MERCED: UA 4 Merced, UA Regency Merced 7; MONTCLAIR: $ Town Center; MONTEREY: UA State Monterey 3; NORTH HOLLYWOOD: Valley Plaza; PASADENA: Pasadena Marketplace; REDDING: Cascade 4; REDWOOD CITY: UA Cinema 6; RIVERSIDE: UA Park Sierra 6; Tyler Cinema 4; ROHNERT PARK: Empire 4; SACRAMENTO: Arden Fair 6, Laguna Village, UA Downtown Plaza 7; SAN DIEGO: Glasshouse 6, Horton Plaza 7; SAN FRANCISCO: UA Cinema Stonestown 2, Alexandria 3, Coronet 1, UA Galaxy 4, Metro 1, Vogue 1; SAN JOSE: San Jose Pavillion 6; SANTA CRUZ: Del Mar, Rio, UA Riverfront 2; SANTA MARIA: UA Movies 3; SANTA ROSA: Santa Rosa 6, UA 5 Santa Rosa, Coddingtown 4; THOUSAND OAKS: UA 5 Thousand Oaks; TORRANCE: Del Amo 6; WOODLAND HILLS: UA 6 Warner Center.

COLORADO—ARVADA: Cooper 5; AURORA: Cooper 5; BOULDER: Flatirons, Village 4; COLORADO SPRINGS: Hancock Plaza 4, Cinema 70 3-plex, Academy 6, Broadmoor Theatre; DENVER: Continental; ENGLEWOOD: UA Greenwood Plaza; FORT COLLINS: Campus West Twin 2, Foothills Twin 2, Arbor Cinema 4; GRAND JUNCTION: Colorado West 4, Teller Arms Twin 2; GREELEY: Cooper Twin 2, Greeley Mall Twin 2, Bittersweet 4-plex; LITTLETON: Cooper 7; LONGMONT: Movies 3-Plex, Courtyard 4-plex; LOVELAND: Orchards Twin 2; PUEBLO: Pueblo Mall 3, Cinema Twin 2; THORNTON:Thornton Town Center 10.

CONNECTICUT—DARIEN: UA Darien Playhouse 10.

FLORIDA—APOPKA: Movies at Wekiva 8; BOCA RATON: Town Center Boca Raton 7; BOYNTON BEACH: Boynton Beach 9; CASSELBERRY: UA Movies at Lake Howell 8; CLEARWATER: Movies at Clearwater 8; DAYTONA BEACH: Volusia 6 Cinemas; HIALEAH: Movies at Hialeah 5; JACKSONVILLE: Regency Square 12, The Movies at Orange Park 7, Movies at Mandarin Landing 8; JENSEN BEACH: Movies at Treasure Coast 6; LAKE CITY: Cinema 90 6; LAUDERHILL: Movies at Lauderhill 13; MARY ESTHER: Santa Rosa 3; MIAMI: Movies at the Falls 7; OCALA: Cinemas West 5; ORANGE CITY: MVS Market Place 8; ORLANDO: Florida Mall 7, Movies at Republic Sq.; PALM BEACH GARDENS: Promenade Plaza 8; PEMBROKE PINES: Movies at Pembroke Pines 9; PENSACOLA: University 11; PINELLAS PARK: UA Pinellas Park 12; POMPANO BEACH: UA Movies 6; SANFORD: Seminole Town Center; TALLAHASSEE: Capitol 6; TAMPA: Mission Bell 8; TITUSVILLE: UA Searstown Mall 10; WEST PALM BEACH: Mall Cinema 4, Movies at River Bridge 8, Wellington Market Place, UA Okee Square 8.

GEORGIA—ALPHARETTA: UA North Point Market 8; ATLANTA: CNN Cinemas 6, Lenox Square Theatres 4, Midtown 8, Perimeter Pointe, Tara Theatre; AUGUSTA: Masters Cinemas 7; DECATUR: South Dekalb 4; DULUTH: Gwinnett Mall 12; GRIFFIN: Parkwood Cinemas 4; MACON: Riverside Cinemas 4; MORROW: Southlake 8; NORCROSS: Greens Corner Cinemas 5; ROME: Litchfield Cinemas 4; SAVANNAH: Abercorn 6, Tara 4, UNION CITY: Shannon 8; WARNER ROBINS: Parkway Cinemas 5.

IDAHO—BOISE: Overland Park 3, Plaza Twin 2; IDAHO FALLS: UA Cinemas 4.

INDIANA—INDIANAPOLIS: Circle Center Starport 9, UA Eagle Highlands.

LOUISIANA—ALEXANDRIA: Westgate Cinema 8; BATON ROUGE: Essen Mall Cinema 6, Bon Marche Theatre 15, Siegen Village 10; HOUMA: Plaza Cinema 4, Houma Twin 2, Southland Cinema 4; KENNER: UA 8; LAFAYETTE: Ambassador 10; Northgate Cinema 8, Westwood Theatre 1; LAKE CHARLES: Oak Park 6, UA Lake Charles; LEESVILLE: Lee Hills Cinema 6; MARRERO: Belle Promenade 14; NEW IBERIA: Bayou Landing 6; NEW ORLEANS: Eastlake Plaza 8, Village Aurora Cinemas 6; OPELOUSAS: Vista Village 4.

MARYLAND—BALTIMORE: Golden Ring 9, Movies at Harbor Park 9, UA Westview; BETHESDA: UA Bethesda 10; GLEN BURNIE: Movies at Marley Station 8.

MICHIGAN—ANN ARBOR: Briarwood Cinemas 7; BENTON HARBOR: Fairlaine Theatre; DEARBORN: Fairlane 10; FARMINGTON: UA West River; GRAND RAPIDS: Movies at Woodland 8, North Kent Theatrel 8; KALAMAZOO: West Main 7; NOVI: 12 Oaks 5; PORTAGE: Movies at Crossroads 10; STERLING HEIGHTS: Lakeside Mall Cinema 4; TROY: Movies at Oakland Mall 5.

MINNESOTA—BROOKLYN CENTER: Movies at Brookdale 8; BURNSVILLE: UA Burnsville I, UA Burnsville 2; DULUTH: Movies at Miller Hill 3; EDEN PRAIRIE: UA 5 Eden Prairie West, Eden Prairie II East 4; MAPLEWOOD: UA 6 Maplewood, Maplewood Two 6; MINNEAPOLIS: Saint Anthony Main 5;

ROSEVILLE: Movies at Pavillon Place 7; WOODBURY: UA Woodbury 10.

MISSISSIPPI—BILOXI: Biloxi 10; Surfside Cinema 4; BROOKHAVEN: Westbrook Cinema 4; CLINTON: Clinton 10; FLOWOOD: UA Parkway Place; GAUTIER: Singing River 4, Singing River 5; GREENVILLE: Cinema I-82 4, Plaza Twin 2; GREENWOOD: Highland Park 3; HATTIESBURG: Cloverleaf Mall 3, UA Turtle Creek 9; JACKSON: Ellis Isle 4; LAUREL: Sawmill Square 5; McCOMB: Camelia Cinema 4; MERIDIAN: College Park Cinema 3, R & S Cinema 5; NATCHEZ: Natchez Mall Cinema 4; OXFORD: Cinema 4; RIDGELAND: Movies at Northpark Mall 10; VICKSBURG: Pemberton Square 4.

MISSOURI—KANSAS CITY: Bannister Mall 5.

NEVADA—HENDERSON: UA Green Valley Cinema 8; LAS VEGAS: Sunrise 7, Cinema 8; SPARKS: Sparks Cinemas 1 & 2.

NEW JERSEY—LAWRENCEVILLE: Eric Lawrenceville; MIDDLETOWN: UA 7 Middletown; MOORESTOWN: Moorestown Mall; PENNSAUKEN: Eric Pennsauken 5; PRINCETON: Movies at Princeton Market Fair 9; SEWELL: UA Washington Township 14; TOTOWA: Cinema 46 3; UPPER MONTCLAIR: Bellevue 3; WAYNE: Wayne 4; WESTFIELD: Rialto; WESTWOOD: Movies at Pascack 4.

NEW MEXICO—ALBUQUERQUE: Coronado 6, Del Norte 4, Montgomery Plaza 5, UA Four Hills 12, UA at High Ridge 8, Winrock 6; SANTA FE: UA Lensic Theatres, UA De Vargas Center 6, UA North Theatre 6, UA South Theatre.

NEW YORK—BABYLON: Babylon LI 3; BAYSIDE: Bayside 4; BRONX: Interboro Bronx 4; BRONXVILLE: Bronxville 3; BROOKLYN: Marboro Brooklyn 4, Movies at Brooklyn Sheepshead 9; CORAM: Coram 12; DOUGLASTON: Movieworld Douglaston 7; EASTHAMPTON: Easthampton 5; EAST MEADOW: Meadowbrook LI 6; FLUSHING: UA Quartet Flushing 4; FOREST HILLS: Midway 4 Queens, Forest Hills 2, Continental 1 & 2 2, Continental 3 (1); GREAT NECK: Squire Great Neck 3; LARCHMONT: Larchmont Playhouse; LINDENHURST: Lindenhurst; LONG ISLAND CITY: Astoria 6; LYNBROOK: Lynbrook 6; MAMARONECK: Mamaroneck Playhouse 4; MANHASSET: Manhasset 3; MASSAPEQUA: Sunrise Massapequa 9; MOHEGAN: UA Westchester Mall 4; NEW CITY: Cinema 304 2; NEW YORK: Criterion Cinema 7, Gemini 2, UA Cinema East Theatre; NORTHPORT: Northport; OZONE PARK: Crossbay I 3, Crossbay II 7; PATCHOGUE: Movies at Patchogue 13; SMITHTOWN: Smithtown; SOUTHAMPTON: Southampton Theatre 5; SPRING VALLEY: Spring Valley 11; STATEN ISLAND: Hylan Plaza, Movies at Staten Island 10; WESTBURY: Westbury D.I. 3; WESTHAMPTON BEACH: Westhampton 1; WOODBURY: UA Cinema 150; YONKERS: Movieland Yonkers 6; YORKTOWN HEIGHTs: Jefferson Valley 8.

NORTH CAROLINA—ALBEMARLE: Eastgate 5; ASHEVILLE: Beaucatcher, Biltmore Square Cinemas 4; CARY: Imperial 4; CONCORD: Carolina Mall 8; GASTONIA: Litchfield Cinemas 4; GOLDSBORO: Litchfield Cinemas 4; HENDERSONVILLE: 4 Seasons 4; HICKORY: Crown Cinemas 6; LUMBERTON: Cinema IV; RALEIGH: UA Mission Valley 5; WILMINGTON: College Road 6.

OKLAHOMA—LAWTON: Cache Cinemas 8; MIDWEST CITY: Heritage Park 3, Heritage Plaza 5; NORMAN: Village 6-plex; OKLAHOMA CITY: UA Almonte 6; TULSA: Fontana 6, Parklane 2, UA Promenade 4, UA Annex 7.

PENNSYLVANIA—ALLENTOWN: Allentown 5; ARDMORE: Ardmore 2; BRYN MAWR: Bryn Mawr; CAMP HILL: Camp Hill Twin PA 2, UA 6 Capital Ct; EASTON: Easton 6; FAIRLESS HILLS: Penn Jersey 3; FEASTERVILLE: Feasterville 4; FRACKVILLE: Schuylkill 4; FRAZER: Frazer 2; HARRISBURG: Eric Colonial Park Mall; HOLMES: Eric Macdade Mall 4; JENKINTOWN: Baederwood 2; KING OF PRUSSIA: Eric Plaza 2, Eric King 2, Eric Queen 4; LANCASTER: Pacific Lancaster 4; LANGHORNE: UA Oxford Valley 10; MONTGOMERYVILLE: Eric Montgomeryville 7; MUNCY: Lycoming 4; PHILADELPHIA: UA Theatres at Cheltenham Square 8, Grant Plaza, Sameric 4, Chestnut Hill 2, Riverview Plaza 11; SCRANTON: UA Scranton 8, UA Steamtown Mall; UPPER DARBY: UA Theatres at 69th Street; WILLIAMSPORT: Loyal Plaza 5; WYNNEWOOD: Eric Wynnewood; YORK: Delco Plaza York 9, Movies at York Mall 2.

SOUTH CAROLINA—ANDERSON: Market Place 6, Anderson Mall 2; FLORENCE: Capri 3, Julia 4; GREENVILLE: Bijou 5, Haywood Cinemas 10; N. CHARLESTON: Aviaton Ave 8.

TEXAS—ABILENE: UA Cinema 10; AMARILLO: UA Amarillo 6, Westgate 6 Mall; ARLINGTON: UA Bowen 8; BEAUMONT: Phelan 6; BEDFORD: UA Bedford 10; CEDAR PARK: Starport at Lakeline Mall; CORPUS CHRISTI: Cinema 4, Padre Staples Mall 6, UA Cinema 6; DALLAS: Galaxy, UA Cine Theatre 1 & 2, Walnut Hill 6, Prestonwood 5, UA Plaza & Park Lane 8, UA South 8; DENTON: UA Golden Triangle 4, UA Golden Triangle Mall 5; EL PASO: $ Northgate 2, Towne East 4, Basset 6; FT WORTH: Hulen 10, Las Vegas Trail 8; GARLAND: UA North Star 8; GRAND PRAIRIE: Grand Prairie; HURST: Northeast Mall 6; LAREDO: Plaza 3, UA Del Norte 4; LEWISVILLE: UA Lakepointe 10; MESQUITE: Town East 4; MIDLAND: UA 4; MINERAL WELLS: UA Cinemas 3; ODESSA: Northpark 6, Winwood 3, UA Permian 4; PLANO: Berkeley Square 4; PORT ARTHUR: UA Cinema 6; SAN ANGELO: Southwest 7 Cinema, UA Sunset 4; SWEETWATER: Texas 1 & 2.

VIRGINIA—FAIRFAX: Movies at Fair Oaks 8, UA Fairfax Towne Center 10; RICHMOND: Midlothian 6, West Tower 6, Chesterfield Mall 9; VIRGINIA BEACH: UA 5 Lynnhaven 5, Lynnhaven Mall 11, UA Kempsriver 7.
WEST VIRGINIA—CHARLESTON: Kanawha 9; TEAYS: Putnam Village 3.
WASHINGTON—SEATTLE: UA Cinema 150 2.
PUERTO RICO—CAROLINA: UA Carolina 6; SAN JUAN: UA Cinema 150 San Juan 5; SANTURCE: Paramount 3.
ASIA
HONG KONG—CAUSEWAY BAY: UA Times Square 4; HONG KONG: UA Queensway 4; KOWLOON: Kowloon City Plaza 2, Bonds Plaza 2; UA Shatin 6, UA Wampoa 1 & 2.
SINGAPORE—SINGAPORE: UA Cinemas at Bugis Junction 3.
SOUTH AMERICA
ARGENTINA—BUENOS AIRES: Cineplex Lavalle 3, Cine Trocadero 6, UA Savoy 4.

WALLACE THEATER CORPORATION

25 theatres, 109 screens.
3375 Koapaka Street, Suite 345, Honolulu HI 96819. (808) 836-6055;
PRESIDENT & CEO
Scott C. Wallace
GENERAL MANAGER
Brett Havlik
CORPORATE CONTROLLER
Denise Wong
AREA MANAGER
Russell Cook
AREA MANAGER
Todd Blumhoff
DIRECTOR, SPECIAL PROJECTS
David Lyons
AMERICAN SAMOA—NU'UULI: Nu'uuli Place Cinemas.
CALIFORNIA—BARSTOW: New Barstow Station Cinema; MALIBU: New Malibu Theatre; SACRAMENTO: Florin Family Savings Theatre; SANTA MARIA: Town Center Cinemas; SANTA PAULA: Santa Paula 7 Theatres; SOUTH LAKE TAHOE: New Lakeside Theatre, New Stateline Cinema, New Tahoe Cinema.
GUAM—TAMUNING: Gibson 14.
HAWAII—HILO: Kress Cinemas; HONOLULU: Restaurant Row 9 Theatres; KAILUA: Kailua Cinemas, Enchanted Lake Cinemas, Keolu Center Cinemas; WAIANAE: Nanakuli Cinemas; LAHAINA: Wharf Cinemas, Front Street Theatres; KAILUA-KONA: Kona Marketplace Cinemas; KAUAI: Coconut Marketplace; LAIE: Laie Cinemas.
NEVADA—CARSON CITY: New Movies 4, Frontier Plaza Theatre, New Cinema 50, New Greenbrae 8 Theatre, Florin Family Theatre.

WEHRENBERG THEATRES, INC.

32 theatres, 202 screens.
1215 Des Peres Road, St. Louis, MO 63131. (314) 822-4520. FAX: (314) 822-8032.
PRESIDENT
Ronald P. Krueger
EXECUTIVE V. P.
John Louis
V. P. & CFO
Charles Nicks
FILM BUYER
Doug Whitford
DIRECTOR OF FACILITIES.
Bill Menke
ARIZONA—FLAGSTAFF: Flag East Twin, Flagstaff Mall Twin, Greentree 3, Orpheum, University Plaza 3; PRESCOTT: Frontier Village 10, Plaza West Twin, Marina Twin.
ILLINOIS—ALTON: Alton Twin; FAIRVIEW HEIGHTS: St. Clair 10 Cine, O'FALLON: O'Fallon 15.
MISSOURI—CAPE GIRARDEAU: West Park 4 Cine; OSAGE BEACH: Osage Village 5 Cine; ST. LOUIS: St. Charles 10 Cine, Chesterfield 4, Cine, Eureka 6, Clarkson 6, Lindbergh 8 Cine, Mid Rivers 6 Cine, Kenrick 8, Creve Coeur 3, Westport 2, Des Peres 14 Cine, Ronnie's 8 Cine, Halls Ferry 14 Cine, Shady Oak Theatre, North Twin D.I., Union Station 10 Cine, Keller 8 Cine, North West Plaza 8; SPRINGFIELD: Battlefield 6 Cine, Campbell 16.

WESTERN MASSACHUSETTS THEATRES, INC.

7 theatres, 16 screens.
265 State St., Springfield, MA 01103. (413) 737-4347.
PRESIDENT
Ronald I. Goldstein
MASSACHUSETTS—AMHERST: Amherst Cinema; CHICOPEE: Rivoli; GREENFIELD: Garden 7; NORTHAMPTON: Calvin; SPRINGFIELD: Bing; WARE: Casino 2.
VERMONT—BRATTLEBORO: First Cinema 3.

YAKIMA THEATRES, INC.

4 theatres, 23 screens.
P.O. Box 50, Yakima, WA 98907. (509) 248-1360. FAX: (509) 453-3074.
PRESIDENT
Michael M. Mercy
VICE PRESIDENT
Earl Braden
WASHINGTON—WENATCHEE: Columbia Cinema 5-plex; YAKIMA: Mercy 6-plex, Uptown Plaza 4, Yakima Cinema 8-plex.

INDEPENDENT THEATRES

Drive-in theatres are indicated by an asterisk. In the case of drive-ins, seats refers to car capacity.

Name	Address	City & Zip	Owner	Seats	Screens
ALABAMA					
Mall Garden 1 & 2	850 Highway 431 So. #3	Albertville 35950	Hammonds-Lawler		1
Playhouse Cinemas	722 Cherokee Road	Alexander City 35010	H. Legg		2
Eastern Shore Cinema	P.O. Box 1091	Daphne 36526			1
Davis Theatre of Dothan	P.O. Box 1689	Dothan 36302	Davis Theatres		1
Hamilton Theatres Damar	P.O. Box 117	Fort Payne 35967	David Hamilton		1
Dixie Theatre	Box 246	Haleyville 35565	J. Gunter		1
*Hayala Drive-in	P.O. Box 246	Haleyville 35565	J. Gunter		1
Locke Theatre	233 Commerce	Jackson 36545	M. Denton		1
Montevallo Twin	605 Main Street	Montevallo 35115	C.Love		1
*Kings Drive-in	Route 7	Russellville 35653	A.King	200	1
ALASKA					
Capri Cinema	3425 E. Tudor Road	Anchorage 99507	Silver Screen Mgmt.Corp.	90	1
Cyrano's Cinema	413 D St.	Anchorage 99501	Silver Screen Mgmt.Corp.	35	1
Homer Family Theatre	Corner	Homer 99603			1
20th Century	222 Front St.	Juneau 99801	Gross-Alaska Theatres		2
Twin Theatres		Juneau 99801	Gross-Alaska Theatres		2
Coliseum Twin Theatre	405 Mission St.	Ketchikan 99901	Gross-Alaska Theatres		2
Orpheum Theatre	102 Center St.	Kodiak 99615	Ina Fletcher		1
Liberty Theatre	305 Adams	Seward 99664	W. E. Fletcher		1
Coliseum Theatre	315 Lincoln St.	Sitka 99835	Gross-Alaska Theatres		1
Orca Theatres	Red Diamond	Soldotna 99669			2
Mat-Su Family Theatre	2430 Parks Hwy	Wasilla 99654			3
ARIZONA					
Movieola Theatre	1389 East Hwy. 89A	Cottonwood 86326	D. Olds	252	1
Valley West Cinema 5	5720 W. Hayward	Glendale 85301	V.W. Operating Co.		5
Cinema Theatre	2130 McCulloch Blvd.	Lake Havasu City 86403	K. Standal	250	1
Payson Picture Show	213 E. Cedar Lane	Payson 85541	L. Bevell		1
Royal Palm Cinemas	4025 N.Central	Phoenix 85012	Royal Palm Partners		1
Cinema	1914 W. Thatcher Blvd.	Safford 85546	Fountain Cinemas Inc.		2
University Dollar Theatre	8485 E. McDonald Dr. #366	Scottsdale 85250	K. Griffin		1
R & M Cinema	300 E. Wilcox	Sierra Vista 85635	M. Kroft	590	3
Royal Palms Theatres, Inc.	1825 E. Elliot Rd.	Tempe 85284			1
Airedale Cinemas		Yuma			2
ARKANSAS					
Landers Theatre	332 E. Main	Batesville 72501	P. Landers		1
Melba Theatre	115 W. Main St.	Batesville 72501	D. Reynolds		1
Main Theatre	P.O.Box 386	Berryville 72616	K. Clark		1
Savage Theatre	P.O.Box 388	Booneville 72927	J. McNutt		1
Garden Oaks Twin Cinema	Garden Oaks Shopping Ctr.	Camden 71701	Union Cinema Corp.	500	2
*DeQueen Drive-In	P.O.Box 920	DeQueen 71832	D. Stearns		1
El Dorado Cinema	1936 Northwest Ave.	El Dorado 71730	Union Cinema Corp.	980	3
*112 Drive-In	Highway 112	Fayetteville 72702	J. Terry		1
Broadway Twin Cinema	1101 East Broadway	Forrest City 72335	Victor & Ann Vaccaro	440	2
Marcus Twin Cinemas	P.O.Box 430	Hope 71801	D. Murphy		2
*Kenda Drive-In	P.O.Box 355	Marshall 72650	K. Sanders		1
*Stone Drive-In Theatre	P.O.Box 59	Mountain View 72560	Bobby Thompson	300	1
*Howard Auto Drive-In	P.O.Box 835	Nashville 71852	J. Paul & C. Johnston		1
Plaza Twin Cinema, Inc.	P.O.Box 1206	Paragould 72540	L. Miller		2
Pickwood 7 Cinemas	P.O.Box 218	Russellville 72801	J. Lowrey		7
Spring Cinema	P.O.Box 598	Siloam Springs 72761	D. Smith		9
Spring Dale Cinema	2804 W. Sunset Ave.	Spring Dale 72767			2
Stuttgart Twin Cinemas	806 W.2nd St.	Stuttgart 72160	Bill Gardner	346	2
Scott Theatre	P.O.Box 657	Waldron 72958	K. Hines		1
CALIFORNIA					
Niles Theater	127 S. Main	Alturas 96101	F. Ertle	449	1
Brookhurst 4	2299 W. Ball Rd.	Anaheim 92804			4
Stamm Theatres, Inc.	114 G. Street	Antioch 94509	G. Stamm		2
Arcata & Minor Theatre	1036 G Arc.	Arcata 95521	David Phillips		4
Century Cinema	6905 El Camino Real	Atascadero 93422			1
Fox Cineplex Theatres	60 West Ramsey	Banning 92220	Cinema Showcase Inc.	525	3
Pacific Film Archive	2625 Durant Ave.	Berkeley 94720	Univ. of California		1
Bishop Twin Theatre	237 N. Main St.	Bishop 93514	B. Hilborn	540	2
Camarillo Cinemas 3	390 N. Lantana St.	Camarillo 93010	Chealin Inc.		3
Plaza 4 Theatres	2501 Winchester Blvd.	Campbell 95008	J. Gunsky		4

Name	Address	City & Zip	Owner	Seats	Screens
Capitola Theatre	120 Monterey Ave.	Capitola 95010	A. Jacobs	500	1
Plaza Cinema	2822 State St.	Carlsbad 92008	R. Normandin		10
Plaza Theatre	4916 Carpinteria Ave.	Carpinteria 93013	P. Wheeler		1
*Ceres Drive-in	P.O. Box 35	Ceres 94307	Maestri		1
Chula Vista 10		Chula Vista			10
Vogue Theatre	226 Third Ave.	Chula Vista 91910	P. Upham		1
Clearlake Cinema	Box 2586	Clearlake 95422	J. Wilder		2
Colfax Cinema	P.O. 577	Colfax 95713	Wendell Jacob	240	1
Capri Theatre	1653 Willow Pass Rd.	Concord 94520	D. Cooper	700	3
Rodgers Theatre	1217 Solano St	Corning 96021	P. Bridgeford		1
Redwood Theatres Inc.	5725 Paradise Dr., #350	Corte Madera 94925	Richard Mann		(12)
Oaks Theatres	21275 Stevens Creek	Cupertino 95014	San Carlos Cinemas	732	5
Family Twin Cinema	9823 Walker	Cypress 90630	V. Chang		2
Avenue Theatre	11022 Downey Ave.	Downey 90241	E. Chang		1
Dublin Cinema, Inc.	6670 Armador Plaza Rd.	Dublin 94568			1
*Aero Drive-in	1470 East Broadway	El Cajon 92021	Don Johnson		1
Crest Theatre	723 Main St.	El Centro 92243	Gallery Cinemas USA Inc.	920	3
Fox Theatre	139 S. 7th St.	El Centro 92243	Gallery Cinemas USA Inc.	792	3
Old Town Music Hall	140 Richmond St.	El Segundo 90245			1
La Paloma Theatre	471 First St.	Encinitas 92024	Allen Largent	400	1
Avery Memorial Theatre	430 Main St.	Etna 96027	J. Reynolds		1
Fall River Theatre	P.O. Box 211	Fall River Mill 96028	McAllister Enterprises	250	1
*Bel Air Drive-in	15895 Valley Blvd.	Fontana 92335	B. Poynter		1
Family Four	17161 Brookhurst St.	Fountain Valley 92708	J. Randolph		4
Garberville Theatre	766 Redwood Drive	Garberville 95440	S. Burke		1
Gardena Theatres		Gardena			1
Gilroy Theatre Company	1624 Calabreses Way	Gilroy 95020			1
Pacific Regency Theatre	417 N. Brand Blvd.	Glendale 91204	Satalino		1
Hanford Theatre	326 N. Irwin	Hanford 93230	J. Humason	1055	1
Metro 4		Hanford	Culver Cinemas		4
Movies 1-4 Theatres	136 N. 11th Avenue	Hanford 93232	Entertainment Centers		4
Raven Theatre	115 North St.	Healdsburg 95448	Straylight Inc.	1200	5
Hemet Theatre	220 E. Florida Ave.	Hemet 92343			1
Highland 3 Theatres	5604 N. Figueroa	Highland Park 90042	A. Akarakian		3
Los Feliz Theatre	1822 N. Vermont Ave.	Hollywood 90027			1
Metro 8		Indio			8
Star Theatre	145 N. First Street	La Puente 91744	M. Tocoline		1
Grove Theatre	242 S. Elmwood	Lindsay 93247	M.R. "Mel" Wardean		1
Gemini Twin Cinema	1028 N. H Street	Lompoc 93436	Los Padres Theatres		2
Art Theatre	2025 E. 4th Street	Long Beach 90812	H. Linn		1
Ackerman Grand Ballroom	308 Westwood Blvd.	Los Angeles 90024	UCLA Campus Events	1200	1
Eagle Theatre	4884 Eagle Rock Blvd.	Los Angeles 90041	Cinema Showcase Inc.	700	1
Four Star Theatre	5112 Wilshire Blvd.	Los Angeles 90036			1
New Beverly Cinema	7165 Beverly Blvd	Los Angeles			1
Silent Movie	611N. Fairfax Ave.	Los Angeles			1
Trans-Lux Southwest	6201 Sunset Blvd.	Los Angeles 90028			1
UCLA Melnitz Theatre	405 Hilgard Ave.	Los Angeles 90024	UCLA Thtr, Film, TV	270	1
Valley Cinema	P.O. Box 967	Manteca 95336	E. Fonseca		4
*Marysville Drive-in	5575 Chestnut Road	Marysville 95901	R. Golding	474	1
Bay Theatre	464 Morro Bay Blvd.	Morro Bay 93442	J. Jannopoulos		1
Bay Theatre	330 National Avenue	National City 92050	R. Topete		1
Peppertree Cinema 5	10155 Reseda Blvd.	Northridge 91324	Livingston		5
Grand Lake Theatres	3200 Grand Ave	Oakland 94610	Rennaisance Rialto, Inc.		2
Paramount Theatre	2025 Broadway	Oakland 94612	City of Oakland	2998	1
Ojai Playhouse	145 East Ojai Avenue	Ojai 93023	K.Al Awar		1
Seavue Twin Cinemas	520 Palmetto	Pacifica 94044	B. Rau		2
Stanford	221 University Ave.	Palo Alto 94301			1
Pine Ridge Theatre	5990 Foster Road	Paradise 95969	Harrison		1
Perris Theatre	279 South D Street	Perris 92370	City of Perris	500	1
Phoenix Theatre	205 Washington Street	Petaluma 94952	K. Frankel		1
Arena Theatre	214 Main	Point Arena 95468	R. Earlygrow		1
Porter 3 Theatres	36 E. Mill Avenue	Porterville 93258	W. Ward		3
*Porterville Drive-in	P.O. Box 990	Porterville 93257	Vermay Corp	550	2
Poway Theatre	12845 Poway Rd., #204	Poway 92064	P. Upham	300	1
Town Hall Theatre	469 Main Street	Quincy 95971	Town Hall Theatres Inc.	287	1
Ramona Twin Cinemas	626 Main Street	Ramona 92065	Cook/Long	360	2
*Redding Drive-in	897 North Market Street	Redding 96049	R. Golding	600	1
State 3		Red Bluff	Redwood Theatres, Inc.		3
Tarantino's Theatres, Inc.	355 Palomar St.	Redwood City 94062	J. Tarantino	847	2
Ridgecrest Cinemas	1631 Triangle Drive	Ridgecrest 93555	C. McGee		1
Mission Grove Plaza 4		Riverside			4
Harding Plaza Cinema	212 Harding Blvd.	Roseville 95678	Korte/Bentz	241	1
Crest Theatre	1013 K Street	Sacramento 95814	L. Garcia-Heberger	975	1
*Skyview Drive-in	N. Sandburn	Salinas 93902	N. Martins		1
Sterling Cinemas	2373 N. Sterling Ave.	San Bernardino 92404	American Family Theatres		6
Century Cinemas	4370 54th Street	San Diego 92115	B. Stinson		4
Canyon Theatre	165 N.San Dimas Canyon	San Dimas 91773	Gene Harvey	600	1
Four Star Theatre	2200 Clement St.	San Francisco 94121	Tillamook		1
Gateway Theatre	215 Jackson Street	San Francisco 94111	C.Marishita		1
New Strand Theatre	1127 Market Street	San Francisco 94103	Red Victorian Movie House	143	1
Red Vic Movie House	1727 Haight Street	San Francisco 94117	W. Banning		1
Roxie Theatre	3110 16th Street	San Francisco 94103	H. Ho		2
St. Francis 1 & 2 Theatres	965 Market Street	San Francisco 94103	Aphrodite, Inc.	900	1
York Theatre	2789 24th Street	San Francisco 94110	J. Gunsky		2
Almaden Twin Theatre	5655 Gallup Dr.	San Jose 95118	J. Gunsky	1989	7
Campbell Plaza Theatre	P.O. Box 6395	San Jose 95150	J. Borges		1
*Capitol Drive-In	3630 Hillcap Ave.	San Jose 95136	J. Dee	700	2
Cine Mexico Theatre	1191 E.Santa Clara Street	San Jose 95116	L. Rodkey		1
Palm Theatre	817 Palm Street	San Luis Obispo 93401	J. Schwenterley	400	2
*Sunset Drive-in	255 Elks Lane	San Luis Obispo 93401			1
Nickelodeon Theatres	210 Lincoln Street	Santa Cruz 95060			4

569

Name	Address	City & Zip	Owner	Seats	Screens
* Skyview Drive-in 1-2	2260 Soquel Drive	Santa Cruz 95062	N. Martins	1062	2
Aero Theatre	1328 Montana Avenue	Santa Monica 90403	S. Allen	650	1
San Carlos Cinemas	2425 Cleveland Ave.	Santa Rosa 95403			1
* Santee Drive-in	10990 Woodside Avenue	Santee 92071	Santee Drive-In Inc.		2
Scotts Valley 5	222 Mt. Hermon Road	Scotts Valley 95060	G. Culver		5
Bay Theatre	340 Main Street	Seal Beach 90740	Loderhouse Enterprises		1
Sebastopol 5		Sebastopol 95472			5
State Theatre	770 E Colorado Blvd.	South Pasadena 91106		845	1
Stanton Theatre	11300 Beach Blvd.	Stanton 90680	R. Anthony		1
Sierra Theatre	P.O. Box 31	Susanville 96130	C. Smith		2
Eagle Theatre	18653 Ventura Blvd.	Tarzana 91356	Susan Frydrych		1
Melody 1 & 2 Theatre	1792 Moorpark Road	Thousand Oaks 91360	Chealin, Inc.		2
* Smith Ranch Drive-in	4584 Adobe Rd.	Twentynine Palms 92277	A. Clemons		1
Whittier Village 3	7038 Greenleaf Ave.	Whittier 90602			3
Zion Canyon Theatre	130 N. Butte St.	Willows 95988			1
State 1, 2, & 3		Woodland	Redwood Theatres		3

COLORADO

Name	Address	City & Zip	Owner	Seats	Screens
Grove Theatre	Box 1327	Alamosa 81101	Murphy		1
Rialto Theatre	Box 1327	Alamosa 81101	Murphy		1
Isis Theatre	Box 180	Aspen 81612	D. Linza	387	1
Sands Theatre	211 Clayton	Brush 80723	J. Machetta		1
Crystal Theatre	427 Main Street	Carbondale 81623	R. Ezra		1
Wells Theatre	170 S. 1st	Cheyenne Wells 80810	K. Thyne	306	1
Majestic Theatre	P.O. Box 307	Crested Butte 81224	Crested Butte Cinema Inc.		3
* Big Sky Drive-in	452 Main St.	Delta 81416	S. Dewsnup		1
Lake Twin Cinema	154 Dillon Mall	Dillon 80435	D. Virgak		2
* Rocket Drive-in	P.O. Box 3181	Durango 81301	Scales Family	300	1
Plains Theatre	P.O. Box 755	Eads 81036	J. Gardner	321	1
Stanley Village Cinemas	543 Big Thompson Hwy	Estes Park 80517	Stanley Pratt	437	3
Flager Theatre	Box 216	Flager 80815	Arthena Witt	260	1
* Holiday Twin Drive-in 1-2	P.O. Box 1822	Fort Collins 80522	W. Webb		2
Reel Theatres Inc.	204 S. College	Fort Collins 80524	R. Garner		1
Cover Theater	314 Main	Fort Morgan 80701	M. Boehm	300	2
* Valley Drive-in	19937 U.S. Hwy 34	Fort Morgan 80701	M. Boehm	276	1
Springs Theatre	915 Grand Avenue	Glenwood Springs 81601	J. Buxman		1
Two Bux Limited	915 Grand Ave.	Glenwood Springs 81601	J. Buxman		1
Cinema 25	1204 North 25th Street	Grand Junction 81501	J.Houle		1
Dynasty East Corp.	P.O. Box 1113	Greeley 80632	Michael Smaha		1
Flicka 1 & 2 Theatres	Box 276	Gunnison 81230	L. Steele		2
Chaka Theatre	Box 328	Julesburg 80737	W. CollinsDe Castro		1
Moutaineer Movie Theatre.	P.O. Box 280	Lake City 81235	P. Virden	120	1
Lincoln Theatre	245 E. Ave.	Limon 80828	M. Steele		1
Southglenn Cinemas 7	6840 Race St.	Littleton 80122	R. Miller	1100	7
Colony Square Theatres		Louisville			3
Metroloux Theatre		Loveland			1
* Star Drive-in	2830 West U.S. 160	Monte Vista 81144	G. Kelloff	150	1
Vali 3 Theatre	2839 West U.S. 160	Monte Vista 81144	G. Kelloff	500	3
* Star Drive-in	P.O. Box 86	Montrose 81401	G. De Vries		1
Liberty Theatre	418 Main St.	Pagosa Springs 81147	D. Wood	166	1
Rifle Creek Theatre	132 E. 4th	Rifle Creek 81650	Pratt		1
Carlos Beaubien Theatre	401 Church Pl.	San Luis 81152	C. Attencio	118	1
Capitol Theatre	P.O. Box 34	Springfield 81073	R. Ruby	310	1
* Kar Vu Drive-in	Hwy 287	Springfield 81073	R. Ross	165	1
Fox Twin Theatre	P.O.Box 471	Sterling 80751	Jack South		2
* Starlight Twin Drive-in	P.O.Box 471	Sterling 80751	Jack South		2
Moon Theatre	P.O. Box 6	Stratton 80836	M. Koons	206	1
Fox Theatre	23 W. Main, Box 788	Trinidad 81082	Salma & Marie Sawaya		2
Cascade Village Theatre	P.O. Box 1152	Vail 81658	S. Lindstrom		1
Crossroads Cinema		Vail			1
Silver Screen Cinema, Inc.	P.O. Box 3397	Winter Park 80482	C. Craig	210	1
Gold Hill Twin Cinemas	615 N. Midland Ave.	Woodland Park 80866	Stanley Pratt	330	2
Yuma Theatre	311 S. Albany St.	Yuma 80759	H. Long		1

CONNECTICUT

Name	Address	City & Zip	Owner	Seats	Screens
Cine 1-2-3-4	P.O.Box 522	Branford 06405	Joseph Soffer		4
Downtown Studio Cinema.	275 Fairfield Ave.	Bridgeport 06603	G. Christ		1
Cinestudio Theatre	300 Summit St.	Hartford 06106	Film Society	489	1
State Twin Theatre	100 Main St.	Jewett City 06351	R. Nethercote	480	2
Capitol Theatre	26 Daniel St.	Milford 06460	M. Arjo		1
Cine 1-2-3-4	371 Middletown Ave.	New Haven 06513		700	4
Bank Street Theatre	48 Bank St.	New Milford 06776	Bank St. Entrps.		2
Newington Theatre	40 Cedar St.	Newington 06111	C. Tolis.		1
Edmond Town Hall Theatre	45 Main St.	Newtown 06470	Town of Newtown	560	1
* Pleasant Valley Drive-In	P.O.Box 45 Rte. 181	Pleasant Valley 06063	B. Miller	250	1
Sono Cinema	15 Washington St.	South Norwalk 06854	J. Bedusa	300	1
* Mansfield Drive-In Theatre	228 Willimantic Rd.	Storrs 06226	M. Jungden		3
Village Cinema Theatre	118 Suffield Village	Suffield 06078	J. Coatti		2
Elm 1 & 2	924 South Quaker Lane	West Hartford 06110	CT Theatre Circuit	945	2
Forest Theatre	2 Forest Rd.	West Haven 06516	Terrazzano		1

DELAWARE

Name	Address	City & Zip	Owner	Seats	Screens
Atlantic Theatres	29 Midway Shopping Ctr	Rehoboth Beach 19971	Atlantic Theatres		1

DISTRICT OF COLUMBIA

Name	Address	City & Zip	Owner	Seats	Screens
AFI Theatre	Kennedy Center	Washington 20036	American Film Institute		1
Biograph Theatre	2819 M Street NW	Washington 20007	Rubin/Poryles	270	1

Name	Address	City & Zip	Owner	Seats	Screens
Circle Company	1101 23rd Street NW	Washington 20037	Theodore & James Pedas		1
Key Theatre	1222 Wisconsin Ave. NW	Washington 20007	S. Levy		4

FLORIDA

Name	Address	City & Zip	Owner	Seats	Screens
Vance Theatre	115 N. 6th St.	Chipley 32428	Luis Valencia	300	1
Teatro Avante	235 Alcazar Ave.	Coral Gables 33134	N. Chediak		1
Crestview Triplex Theatre	P.O. Box 55	Crestview 32536	E. Neutzling		3
Festival Theatre	3215 South U.S.	Fort Pierce 34982	R. Landy		2
Gateway Cinema IV	1820 E. Sunrise Blvd.	Ft. Lauderdale 33304	Mitchell Dreier		4
Mercede Cinema 4	1870 N. University Dr.	Ft. Lauderdale 33322	Mitchell Dreier		4
*Fort Lauderdale Drive-in	3121 West Sunrise Blvd.	Ft. Lauderdale 33311	P. Henn		6
Tringas Theatres, Inc.	P.O. Box 970	Ft. Walton Beach 32549	J. Tringas	818	4
Cinema & Cafe	P.O.Box 140598.	Gainesville 32614-0598	Gainesville Entertainment		1
Eagle Ridge 12		Lake Wales			12
Inverrary 3 Theatres	6004 Royal Poincana Blvd	Lauderhill 33313	M. Wurtzburg		3
Enzian Theatre	1300 S. Orlando Ave.	Maitland 32751	C. Tiedtke	250	1
Intracoastas Cinemas		Miami			1
Marti Triplex Theatres	420 S.W. 8th Ave.	Miami 33130	E. Capote		3
Miracle Theatre	280 Miracle Mile	Miami 33134			1
Palm Plaza Twin Cinema	1147 E. John Sims Pkwy.	Niceville 32578	J. Smith	400	2
Starlite Theatre	12564 N.E. 14th Avenue	North Miami 33161			1
*Ocala Drive In Theatre	4850 South Pine Avenue	Ocala 34480	Williams & Tomlinson	300	1
Casa Apava		Palm Beach	T. H. Frassrand		1
Showcase Cinema III, Inc	229 St. Joe Plaza Drive	Palm Coast 32137	D. Denk		3
Silver Screen	P.O.Box 10145	Pensacola 32524	R. Estrada		4
"Walk In" Perry Cinemas	P.O. Box 838	Perry 32347	Holly Longley	393	3
Cinema 4	3251 N. Federal Way	Pompano Beach 33064	Lockwood & McKinnon		4
Island Cinema	P.O. Box 381	Sanibel 33957	S. Kaplan		2
Carolina Movies	2504 Wilkinson Rd.	Sarasota 34231			1
Burns Ct. Cinema	P.O. Box 3378	Sarasota 34230	S. Morris	500	3
*301 Drive-in	U.S. 301	Starke 32091	V. Sparks		1
Florida Theatre	101 W. Call Street	Starke 32091	V. Sparks		2
Tampa Pitcher Show	14416 N. Dale Mabry	Tampa 33618	Tampa Pitcher Show		1
Aloma Cinema	2155 Aloma Avenue	Winter Park 32792	K. Stults		1
Zephyrhills Cinema 6	6848 Gall Blvd.	Zephyrhills 34541			1

GEORGIA

Name	Address	City & Zip	Owner	Seats	Screens
Abrams Alps Cinema	Alps Shopping Ctr.	Athens 30604	Alps Cinema Inc.	300	1
Buford Highway Twin	5805 Buford Highway	Atlanta 30340			2
Cinema & Grill	7270 Roswell Rd.	Atlanta 30350	Cinema & Drafthouse Inc.	450	2
Cinevision Theatre		Atlanta			1
Fox Theatre	660 Peachtree Street	Atlanta 30305	Atlanta Landmarks		1
Garden Hills Cinema	2835 Peachtree Rd.	Atlanta 30305			1
Plaza Theatre	1049 Ponce de Leon Ave.	Atlanta 30306	G. Lefont		3
Blue Ridge Twin Cinema	P.O. Box 1022	Blue Ridge 30513	R. McNelley	400	2
*Swan Drive-in	P.O. Box 275	Blue Ridg 30513	J. Jones		1
Zebulon Theatre	207 N. Broad Street	Cairo 31728	Judge Larry Bearden	450	1
*Commerce Drive-in	2367 Hwy 4415	Commerce 30529	N. Smith		1
East Towne Twin Cinema	East Towne	East Ellijay 30540	R. McNelley	400	2
The Theatre	206 Century Center	Hazlehurst 31539	W. Thompson	186	1
Brice Cinema City	Hwy 84	Hinesville 31313	Pal Amusement Co.		2
Jackson Cinema	1314 Brookwood Avenue	Jackson 30233	D. Ralph		2
Main Street Theatre	188 S. Main St.	Jasper 30143	S. Middendorf		1
The Movies Square		Rome 30161	G. Smith		6
Village Theatres, Inc.	836 Turner McCall Blvd.	Rome 30162	G. Smith		4
Civic Cinema	Box 407	Swainsboro 30401	B. Sowell		1
Ritz Theatre	112 S. Church Street	Thomastown 30286	Odom/Brown		1
Brice Cinema	1101 E. 1st St.	Vidalia 30474	Pal Amusement Co.		1
New Pal Theatre		Vidalia 30474	Pal Amusement Co.		1

IDAHO

Name	Address	City & Zip	Owner	Seats	Screens
Flicks Twin	646 Fulton St.	Boise 83702	C. Skinner	291	2
Rex Theatre	Rt. 4 Box 626	Bonners Ferry 83805	L. Mace		1
Linden 3 Theatres	P.O. Box 1223	Caldwell 83605	David L. Cornwell	700	3
*Coeur D Alene Drive-in	No. 3555 Government Way	Coeur D. Alene 83814	T. Moyer		1
*Spud Drive-in	231 South Hwy 33	Driggs 83422	R. Wood	150	1
Spud Too!	190 N. Main	Driggs 83422	R.Wood	144	1
Gooding Theatre	841 Main St.	Gooding 83330	R.Ward	400	1
Rex Theatre	2122 E. 1750 S	Gooding 83330	T. Dye		1
Blue Fox Theatre	Box 370	Grangeville 83530	A. Wagner		1
*Sky Vu Drive-in	3000 S. Yellowsone Hwy	Idaho Falls 83401	K. Ellis		1
Magic Lantern Cinema	Box 238	Ketchum 83340	R. Kessler		1
Valley Theatre	54 N. Main St.	Malad 83252	M. Evans		1
Micro Moviehouse	230 W. Third St.	Moscow 83843	Suto/Ball		1
*Parma Motor-Vu	P.O. Box 338	Parma 83660	Cornwell		1
Pond Student Union Thtr	Idaho State University	Pocatello 83209	D. DeTienne	425	1
*Sunset Drive-in	P.O. Box 5397	Pocatello 83201	R. Morris		1
Idanha Theatre	75 S. Main St.	Soda Springs 83201	J. Bowen		2
Interstate Amusements	P.O. Box T	Twin Falls 83301	Interstate Amusements		1
Ace Theatres	P.O.Box 258	Wendell 83355	John & Kathy Eickhof	267	2

ILLINOIS

Name	Address	City & Zip	Owner	Seats	Screens
Aledo Opera House Thtr	108 S.E. Second Avenue	Aledo 61231	R. Maynard	500	1
Rodgers Theatre	119 W. Vienna	Anna 62906	M. McSparin	325	1
*Hi-Lite 30 Drive-In	9 S. 307 Hill Ave.	Aurora 60504	Parkside Inc.	700	1
Hi-Lite 30 Indoor Theatre	9 S. 307 Hill Ave.	Aurora 60504	Parkside Inc.	900	1
Paramount Arts Centre	23 E. Galena Blvd.	Aurora 60506	Aurora Civic Center	1888	1

Name	Address	City & Zip	Owner	Seats	Screens
Catlow Theatre	116 W. Main Street	Barrington 60010	E. Skehan		1
Tradewinds	1452 Irving Park Rd.	Bartlett 60103			2
*B.A.C. Skyview	403 E. Main	Belleville 62220	B.A.C. Theatres		1
B.A.C. Theatre	403 E. Main St.	Belleville 62220	B.A.C. Theatres		2
Lincoln Theatre	103 E. Main Street	Belleville 62220	R. Wright		3
Bensenville Theatre	9 S. Center St.	Bensenville 60106			2
*Avon Drive-in	Route 50	Breese 62230	Gramann		1
Buffalo Grove	1000 Lake Cook Rd.	Buffalo Grove 60089	Chicago Area Theatres	1225	5
Marvel Cinema	228 W. Main Street	Carlinville 62626	N. Paul		2
400 Theatre	6746 N. Sheridan Rd.	Chicago 60626	Entertainment Group		2
Adelphi Theatre	7074 N. Clark Street	Chicago 60626	Lakshmi Films USA, Ltd.	850	1
Brew & View Inc.	222 N. Lasalle St., #450	Chicago 60611	B & B Theatre Mgmt Inc.	2692	6
Davis Theatre	4614 N. Lincoln Avenue	Chicago 60625	F & F Mgt.		4
Heart Theatre	4741 N. Magnolia Ave.	Chicago 60640	J. Johns		1
Logan	Milwaukee at Kedzie Ave	Chicago			4
Music Box	3733 N. Southport	Chicago 60613			1
Patio Theatre	6008 Irving Park Blvd.	Chicago 60634	A. Kouvalis		2
Portage Theatre	4050 N. Milwaukee	Chicago 60641			1
3 Penny	2424 Lincoln	Chicago			2
Village Theatre	1548 N. Clark Street	Chicago 60610	Taylor	650	4
W. Hts Cinema I-VIII	1301 Hilltop	Chicago Heights 60411	M. Crescenzo		8
Olympic Theatre	6131 W. Cermak Road	Cicero 60650	G. Nikolopas		1
Des Plaines	1476 Minter Ave.	Des Plaines 60016			2
Dolton Cinema	14112 Chicago Rd.	Dolton 60419	B. Ivy	550	1
Grand Theatre	220 E. Main Street	Duquoin 62832			2
Elgin Fox	450 Shepard St.	Elgin 60123	Mainstreet Theatres, Inc.		3
Palace Theatre	122 W. Main, Box 753	Elmwood 61529	V. Reynolds		1
Town Theatre	120 E. North	Flora 62839	J. Philips		1
Fox Lake Theatre		Fox Lake			3
*Harvest Moon Drive-in	Rte 47 South	Gibson City 60936	Michael Harroun		1
Canna Theatre	110 E. Chestnut	Gillespie 62033	L. Pianfetti	268	1
Glenwood Theatre	183 Rd. & Halsted Sts.	Glenwood 60425	Barcikowski & Schlaffer		5
Harlem Corners 5		Harlem Corners			4
Highland Park	445 Central Ave.	Highland Park 60035			1
Hinsdale Theatre	7823 Eleanor	Hinsdale 60514			1
Lorraine Theatre	24-326 Main Street	Hoopeston 60942	A. Nelson		3
La Grange Theatre	84 S. La Grange Rd.	La Grange 60525	Bischof		2
Illinois Vall. Cinema 1 & 2	700 First Street	La Salle 61301	J. Hurley		2
Rhyan Management Co.	755 South Rand Road	Lake Zurich 60047			3
*53 Drive-In Management	6 Briarwood Lane	Lincolnshire 60069	J. Kohlberg		2
Cinema Mgmt Corp.	6 Briarwood Lane	Lincolnshire 60069	J. Kohlberg	765	4
Northgate	North Ave & I-355	Lombard			4
Morton Grove Theatre	7300 Dempster Ave.	Morton Grove 60053	F & F Mgt.		4
Mundelein Cinema	155 N. Seymour	Mundelein 60060	L. Marubio		1
State Theatre	153 W. Elm Street	Nashville 62263	Nashville Theatre Corp.	360	1
*Fairview Drive-in	Route #5	Newton 62448	D. Boldrey		1
Roseland Theatre	127 S. Locust St.	Pana 62557	R. Tanner		1
Pickwick Theatre	5 S. Prospect Avenue	Park Ridge 60068	D. Vlahakis	2114	5
Salem Theatre	Box 487	Salem 62881	L. Cluster		1
Springfield Theatre Centre	101 E. Lawrence Ave.	Springfield 62704	R. Schmidt		1
Sycamore Theatre	420 W. State St.	Sycamore 60178	T. Burnidge	800	3
Bremen Theatre	Brementowne	Tinley Park 60477			4
Liberty Theatre	Box 93	Vandalia 62471	G. Carroll	550	1
Gem Theatre	17 N. Main Street	Villa Grove 61956	K. Kleinschmidt	286	1
Wheaton Theatre	123 N. Hale	Wheaton 60187	T. Loftus	720	4
Wilmette Theatres	1122 Central Avenue	Wilmette 60091	Mark Stern		1
Hinsdale Theatre	7823 Eleanor	Willowbrook 60514	Gregory Szymski		2
Mar Theatre	121 S. Main Street	Wilmington 60481	C. Smith		1
Countryside Cinema 1 & 2	550 Countryside Drive	Yorkville 60560	National Care, Inc.		2

INDIANA

Name	Address	City & Zip	Owner	Seats	Screens
Strand Theatre	P.O. Box 39	Angola 46703	D. Thompson		1
Brokaw 1 & 2 Theatres	711 Calvary Lane	Angola 46703	Mary Roberts		2
Northway Cinemas 1 & 2	P.O. Box 388	Auburn 46706	David L. John	420	2
Brookville Theatre & Video	16 W. Fifth	Brookville 47012	M. Klenke		1
Woodland Theatres	2330 E. 116th St.	Carmel 46032	CTS Heaston Theatres		2
Times Theatre	616 N. Central	Connersville 47331	Elmer DeWitt		1
Crown Theatre	19 N. Court Street	Crown Point 46307	J. Paunicka		2
Showplace Cinemas	1801 Morgan Center	Evansville 47715			2
Embassy Theatre	1107 S. Harrison Street	Fort Wayne 46802	Embassy Theatre Found.	2727	1
*Georgetown Drive-in	8200 State Road 64	Georgetown 47122	B. Powell	300	1
Northgate Cinema	1021 N. State	Greenfield 46140	A. Strahl		1
Calumet Theatre	5622 Calumet Ave.	Hammond 46320	T. Myjewski		1
*Starlite Drive-in Theatre	P.O. Box 17	Harrodsburg 47434	C. Stewart	400	1
Art Theatre	230 Main St./PO Box 31	Hobart 46342	E. Prusiecki	525	2
Greenbriar Twin	1289 W. 86th St.	Indianapolis 46260	CTS Heaston Theatres		2
S. KeystoneCinema I & II	44044 S. Keystone Ave.	Indianapolis 46227	CTS Heaston Theatres		2
Twin Drive-In East & West	3000 Southeastern Rd.	Indianapolis 46203	Wisper & Wetsman, Inc.		2
Vogue Theatre	6259 N. College Avenue	Indianapolis 46220	S. Ross	600	1
Strand Theatre	221 S. Main St.	Kendallville 46755	David L. John	600	2
*Melody Drive-In Theatre	R.R. 3, Box 7444	Knox 46534	F. Heise		1
Avon Theatre	216 N. Lebanon St.	Lebanon 46052			2
State Theatre 1 & 2	321 E. Market Street	Logansport 46947	W. Ritchie	725	2
Cinema 37 Theatres	1910 Morton Avenue	Martinsville 46151	C. Martens	352	1
*Mechanicsburg Drive-in	Route 1	Mechanicsburg 46071	Professional Book Co.	250	1
*Monticello Drive-in	P.O. Box 251	Monticello 47960	J. Eubanks	470	1
Twin Lakes 1 & 2 Theatre	107 Main St.	Monticello 47960	C. Ryan		2
Mooresville Cinema	11 S. Carlisle	Mooresville 46158	J. Perry	280	1
Majestic Theatre	20 Public Square	Nelsonville 45764	E. Edwards	214	1
Rees Cinema	100 N. Michigan Street	Plymouth 46563	J. Housouer		1

Name	Address	City & Zip	Owner	Seats	Screens
* Tri Way Drive-in	Old Road 31 North	Plymouth 46563	J. Housouer		1
Ritz Theatre	200 N.Meridan St.	Portland 47371	M. Volpe		1
Times Cinema 1 & 2	618 Main Street	Rochester 46975	K. Hoff	234	2
* Holiday Drive-In	Jct 231 & 66	Rockport 47635	D. Mosely	900	4
Scott Theatre	10675 Lake Rd.	Scottsburg 47170	P. West	450	1
Jackson Park Cinemas	P.O. Box 762	Seymor 47274	Bowman & Cartmel	443	2
Cinema A B & C	P.O. Box 277	Shelbyville 46176	Elmer DeWitt		3
* Skyline Drive-In	East Michigan Rd.	Shelbyville 46176	Elmer DeWitt	400	1
Tivoli Theatre	26 N. Washington St	Spencer 47460	WR Theatres	300	1
Pickwick Theatre	108 W. Main Street	Syracuse 46567	D. Wright		1
Diana Theatre	137 E. Jefferson	Tipton 46072	J. Paikos	404	1
* Forty-Niner Drive-In	North State Road 49	Valparaiso 46383	B. Shinabarger	428	1
Lake 1 & 2 Theatres	P.O. Box 976	Warsaw 46580	Lake Theatre		2
* Warsaw Drive-in	2180 E. Old Rd. #30	Warsaw 46580	Lake Theatre		1
Isis Theatre	Box 362	Winamac 46996	W. Doty	300	1

IOWA

Name	Address	City & Zip	Owner	Seats	Screens
Opera House	115 Benton Ave, E	Albia 52531	D. Walker	500	1
Rose Theatre and Video	318 Broadway	Audubon 50025	R. Kirk Wiges	275	1
Iowa Theatre	107 S. Washington	Bloomfield 52537	Davis County Council	300	1
Clarion Theatre	P.O. Box 68	Clarion 50525	D. Anderson		1
American Theatre	1101 Nodaway St.	Corning 50841	C. Ambrose		1
Wayne Theatre	P.O. Box 32	Corydon 50060	Wayne Theatre Committee	256	1
Cresco Theatre	115 Second Ave, W.	Cresco 52136-0376	LaVern R. Buttjer	463	1
Varsity Theatre	1207 25th Street	Des Moines 50311	Bev Mahon	472	1
Opera Theatre	716 Sixth Avenue	Dewitt 52742	D. Prichard	238	1
Circle Theatre	108 Main Street	Elkader 52043	D. Wellendorf		1
Forest Theatre	215 N. Clark	Forest City 50436	G. Gary Compston		1
Grand Theatre & Video	238 Public Square	Greenfield 50849	Main Street Theatres, Inc.	400	1
Harlan Theatre	621 Court Street	Harlan 51537	A. Woodraska		1
Mills Entertainment	216 W. Main Street	Lake Mills 50450	A. Skellenger	251	1
Coliseum	700 College Ave.	Lamoni 50140	Graceland College		1
South Central IA Theatre	208 N. Main St.	Leon 50144			1
Skyline Drive-In	321 E. Market St	Logansport 46947	W. Ritchie	500	2
Castle Theatre	112 E. Main	Manchester 52057	D. Voy		1
* 61 Drive-in	P.O. Box 857	Maquoketa 52060	D. Voy	180	1
Pioneer Theatre	P.O. Box 555	Milford 51351	Crystal Theatres Ltd.		1
Odeum	123 2nd St. SW	Mount Vernon 52314			1
* Valle Drive-In	P.O. Box 1243	Newton 50208	Perry Th. Co.		1
Iowa Theatre	Box 245	Onawa 51040	F. Rash		1
Watts Theatre	P.O. Box 58	Osage 50461	Paul Bunge		1
Lyric Theatre	118 S. Fillmore Street	Osceola 50213	R. Clark		1
Wonderland Theatre	110 S. Main	Paullina 51046	Coppaullina	180	1
Iowa Theatre	923 Third Avenue	Sheldon 51201	D. Dummett	206	1
Story Theatre	512 Broad Street	Story City 50248	Todd Thorson	388	1
Hardacre Theatre	Box 271	Tipton 52772	S. Clark	375	1
Traer Chamber Theatre	516 Second Avenue	Traer 50675	Chamber of Commerce	180	1
Rialto Theatre	P.O. Box 82	Villisca 50864	M. Lapley		1

KANSAS

Name	Address	City & Zip	Owner	Seats	Screens
Plaza Theatre	408 N.W. Second	Abilene 67410	C. Strowig		1
Royal Movie Theatre Inc.	612 Commercial Street	Atchison 66002	K. Nagel		2
Augusta Theatre	Box 608	Augusta 67010	Augusta Arts Council	0	1
Mainstreet Theatre	117 West Main	Beloit 67420	J. Weide	657	1
Midland Theatre	212 W. 8th Street	Coffeyville 67337	P. Richardson	250	1
* Tal's Midland-Tal's Drive-In	P.O. Box 667	Coffeyville 67337	P. Richardson		2
Colby Theatres	355 N. Franklin Ave.	Colby 67701	D. Phillips		2
Ritz Theatre	222 Fairway Dr.	Council Grove 66846			1
Derby Cinema	824 Nelson Drive	Derby 67037	R. Jones	200	1
* Star Vu Drive-in	PO Box 565	El Dorado 67042	S. Fowler	300	1
Fredonia Cinema	407 N. 6th	Fredonia 66736			1
Fox Twin Cinema	113 S. Main	Ft. Scott 66701	J. Novak	350	2
Arrow Twin Theatres	729 Oregon	Hiawatha 66434	C. Holthaus		2
Midway Theatre	217 A N. Pomeroy	Hill City 67642	S. Schulz		1
* Boulevard Drive-in	1051 Merriam Lane	Kansas City 66103	W. Neal		1
Jarvis Theatre	P.O. Box 401	Ness City 67560	D. Jarvis	160	1
Sunflower Theatre	P.O. Box 6	Oberlin 67749	J. Sullivan		1
Majestic Theatre	724 4th St.	Phillipsburg 67661	Paula J. Hackett		2
Scott City Uptown Theatre	420 Main	Scott City 67871	D. Kite		1
Strand Theatre	Box 84	Sharon Springs 67758	R. Koons	200	1
Center Theatre	217 S. Main St.	Smith Center 66967	Center Theaters Inc.	209	1
Regent Theatre	114 W. Lincoln	Wellington 67152	K. Brown		1
* Landmark Twin Drive-in	3900 South Hydraulic	Wichita 67216	Landmark Theatres Inc.	1300	2
Palace East Cinemas		Wichita	American Entertainment		2
Warren 10	P.O.Box 782560	Wichita 67278	American Entertainment		10

KENTUCKY

Name	Address	City & Zip	Owner	Seats	Screens
* Tri-City Drive-in	Hwy 231 South	Beaver Dam 42320	D. Moseley		1
Corbin Cinemas 1-4	P.O. Box 172	Corbin 40701	Carnahan-Hu		1
New Pastime Theatre	128 E.Shelby St.	Falmouth 41040	M. Goldberg		1
Cinema 1-3 Theatres	P.O. Box 445	Glasgow 42141	W. Aspley		3
Old Orchard Cinemas	1800 Cinema Dr.	Henderson 42420	J. Scott		5
Oldham 8		La Grange			8
Regency Cinema 7	1868 Highway 192 West	London 40741	Michael D. Hensley	1252	7
* Cardinal Drive-in	P.O. Box 473	Mayfield 42066	D. Jones		1
Mayfield Twin Cinema	P.O. Box 473	Mayfield 42066	D. Jones		2
* Judy Drive-in	Rt 11 Maysville Rd.	Mount Sterling 40353	K. Sargent	300	1
Cheri V Theatre	1008 Chestnut.	Murray 42071	Murray Theatres	800	5

Name	Address	City & Zip	Owner	Seats	Screens
*Bourbon Drive-in	P.O. Box 409	Paris 40361	E. Earlywine		1
*Buccaneer Drive-in	2435 Lexington Rd.	Richmond 40475	H. Roaden		1
*Mountain View Drive-In	1327 E. College Ave.	Stanton 40380	D. Baker		2
Towne Cinema	Main St.	West Liberty 41472	L. Franklin	200	1
*New Dixie Drive-In	P.O.Box 179	Williamsburg 40769	Byrd	225	1

LOUISIANA

Name	Address	City & Zip	Owner	Seats	Screens
Lafitte Cinema 4	P.O. Box 429	Abbeville 70510	F.& R. deGraauw	650	4
Dollar Cinemas 6	3820 Alexandria Mall Dr.	Alexandria 71301	Joy's Theatres		6
MacArthur Village 6	1427 Dorchester	Alexandria 71303	Carlton H.Mann	1420	6
Broadmoor Theatre	9810 Florida Blvd.	Baton Rouge 70815	Ogden Theatres	1000	4
Lake Cinema	P.O. Box 87	Berwick 70342	A. Lasseigne		1
Jet Cinema	P.O. Box 2080	Galland 70345	Jet Cinema, Inc.		2
Dollar Cinemas 4	109 Auditorium Pl.	Lafayette 70503	Joy's Theatres		4
Many Twin Cinema	P.O. Box 1568	Many 71449	J. Cole		2
Lakeside Theatres, Inc	2805 Edenborn Ave	Metairie 70002	C. Johnson & W. Terral	1616	4
Parkway Cinema 4	1011 Keyser Avenue	Natchitoches 71457	Don Theatres		4
Delta Theatres, Inc.	2238 S. Salcedo St.	New Orleans 70125	R. Brunet		3
Gulf States Theatres	510 O'Keefe Avenue	New Orleans 70113	T.G. Solomon		1
Village Cinema	P.O. Box 457	Ruston 71270	Don Theatres		2
Quail Creek Cinema 7	2919 Valley View	Shreveport 71108	Joy's Theatres		4

MAINE

Name	Address	City & Zip	Owner	Seats	Screens
Criterion Theatre	P.O. Box 242	Bar Harbor 04609	B. Johnson		1
Casablanca	23 Cross Street	Bethel 04217	H. Merrill		6
Magic Lantern Theatre	PO Box 328	Bridgton 04009	Down East Inc.	250	2
Eveningstar Cinema	149 Maine St.	Brunswick 04011		126	1
State Cinema	79 Main Street	Calais 04619	F. Freda		3
Bayview Street Cinema	10 Bayview St.	Camden	W. D. Ford		1
Lincoln Theatre	Elm Street	Damariscotta 04543	Mid-coast Shop. Ctr.	240	1
Grand Auditorium	P.O. Box 941	Ellsworth 04605	George Wojtasik		1
Century Theatre	8 Hall Street	Fort Kent 04743	Ouellette		1
Temple Twin Theatre	Market Square	Houlton 04730	J. Lyford		2
The Movie Mill	35 Canal St.	Lewiston 04240	L. Morin		2
Lincoln Theatre	87 Main Street	Lincoln 04457	P. Quirion	300	1
Fox Cinema Theatre	1 Fox Street	Madawaska 04756	R. Pelletiee		1
Temple Theatre	PO Box 296 Temple Ave.	Ocean Park 04063	Ocean Park Assn.	500	1
Leavitt Theatre	P.O. Box 351	Ogunquit 03907	P. Clayton		1
Ogunquit Square Theatre	P.O. Box 144	Ogunquit 03907	G. Cookson		1
Pittsfield Community	P.O. Box 579	Pittsfield 04967	Town of Pittsfield	279	1
Movies on Exchange St.	10 Exchange Street	Portland 04101	S. Halpert	145	2
Sanford Twin Cinema	277A Main Street	Sanford 04073	RPW Theatres		2
Skowhegan Cinema	Box 522	Skowhegan 04976	C. Perry		1
Railroad Sq. Cinema	Box 945	Waterville 04903	RSC	250	2
*Prides Corner Drive-in	651 Bridgton Rd Rt 302	Westbrook 04092	A. Tevanian		1

MARYLAND

Name	Address	City & Zip	Owner	Seats	Screens
*Bengies Drive-in	3417 Eastern Blvd	Baltimore 21220	D.E. Vogel	750	1
Charles Theatre	1711 N. Charles Street	Baltimore 21201	S. Levy		1
Hillendale Cinemas	1045 Taylor Ave.	Baltimore 21286	T. Kefaber		1
Patterson	3136 Eastern	Baltimore 21224	F. Durkee		2
Perry Hall Movies	Belair & Ebenezer Rds.	Baltimore 21128			5
Premiere Discount Cine	8632 Liberty Rd.	Baltimore	Liberty Theatres		4
Senator Theatre	5904 York Rd.	Baltimore 21212	T. Kefaber		1
Southside Movies 4	Fort Ave.	Baltimore 21230			4
Westview Theatre	6026 Balt. Natl. Pike	Baltimore 21228	G. Brehm		10
Bethesda Theatre	7719 Wisconsin Avenue	Bethesda 20814	P. Carney	400	1
*Bel Air Drive-in	P.O.Box 111	Churchville 21028	R. Wagner		1
Hoff Theatre	Stamp Student Union	College Park 21228	Univ. of Maryland	700	1
Maryland Theatre	21 S. Potomac St.	Hagerstown 21740	MD Theatre Assn.		2
Mid Towns Cinemas	Rt. 135 Mid Towns Plaza	Oakland 21550	L. Holler		9
Olney 9 Cinemas	18167 Town Center Drive	Olney 20832	Holiday Prods. Inc.		1
Liberty Cinema	8632 Liberty	Randallstown 21133	T. Herman		2
Riverdale Theatre	5617 Riverdale Road	Riverdale 20840	P. Sanchez	600	

MASSACHUSSETTS

Name	Address	City & Zip	Owner	Seats	Screens
Agawam Family Theatres	P.O.Box 462	Agawam 01001	Robert McQuade		1
Amherst Theatre	30 Amity Street	Amherst 01002	R. Goldstein		1
Capitol Theatre	204 Mass Ave.	Arlington 02174			6
Regent Theatre	7 Medford Street	Arlington 02174	H. Capra		1
Studio Cinema Theatre	376 Trapelo Road	Belmont 02178	S. Myerson		1
Cabot Street Cinema	286 Cabot Street	Beverly 01915	W. Bull		1
Larcom Theatre	13 Wallis Street	Beverly 01915	Abracadabra Ltd.		3
Billerica Flick	Billerica Mall	Billerica	Flick Theatres		1
Museum of Fine Arts	465 Huntington Ave.	Boston 02176	James Gould		1
South Windermere	715 Boylston St.	Boston 02116	R. Wedge		6
Brockton East Cinemas	758 Crescent St.	Brockton 02402	J. Freed		2
Coolidge Crnr Moviehouse	290 Harvard Ave.	Brookline 02146	Running Arts, Inc.	250	1
Brattle Theatre	40 Brattle Street	Cambridge 02138		1700	8
*Route 3 Cinema	308 Chelmsford St.	Chelmsford 01824	Carpenter		1
Rivoli Theatre	41 Springfield Street	Chicopee 01013	R. Goldstein		1
Last Strand	58 High St.	Clinton	P. Safiol & H. Himmel		1
Cape Cinema	Rte. 6A	Dennis 02638			1
Dedham Comm. Theatre		Dedham			2
Island Theatre	P.O. Box 98	Edgartown 02539	R. Lockwood		1
Franklin Zoetrope	34 E. Central St.	Franklin 02038	Lucinda R. Cleary	500	3
Gardner 1 & 2 Theatres	34 Parker Street	Gardner 01440	M. Fideli		2

Name	Address	City & Zip	Owner	Seats	Screens
* Mohawk Drive-In	Airport Rd.	Gardner 01440	M. Fideli		1
Lexington Flick	1794 Mass. Ave.	Lexington 02173	Flick Theatres		2
Lowell Flick	205 Cabot St.	Lowell 01854	Flick Theatres		3
Warwick Cinema	117 Pleasant St.	Marblehead 01945	Thomas A. McNulty	500	2
Fine Arts Theatre I, II & III.	19-21 Summer Street	Maynard 01754		670	3
* Mendon Drive-In	45 Milford St.	Mendon 01756			1
Elm Draughthouse	35 Elm Street	Milbury 01527	R. McCrohon		1
Dreamland Theatre	P.O.Box 1092	Nantucket 02554	Juan Garusky Rubin	500	1
Zeiterion Theatre	684 Purchase Street	New Bedford 02740	R. Freedman		1
Star Theatres	P.O. Box 34	Newton 02165		985	6
West Newton Cinemas	1296 Washington St.	Newton 02165			6
Triboro Cinemas		North Attleboro 02760			10
Harborlight Mall Cinemas..	Route 3A	North Weymouth			10
Pleasant St. Theatre	27 Pleasant St.	Northampton 01060	R. Pini	189	2
Westboro Theatre Corp.	56 Brewer St.	Northboro 01532			1
Art Cinema	Commercial St.	Provincetown			2
Little Art Cinema	13 Broadway	Rockport 01966	A. Morton		6
Salem Flick	Museum Place Mall	Salem	Flick Theatres		2
* Edgemere Drive-In	Route 20	Shrewsbury 01545	Route 20 Associates	1600	1
Casino Theatre	P.O. Box 315	Siasconset 02564	Siaconset Casino Ass.	250	1
Somerville Theatre	55 Davis Sq.	Somerville 02144			1
Wellfleet Cinema	P.O.Box 900	South Wellfleet 02663	Spring Brook Center	1000	4
Cameo Theatre	Columbian Square	South Weymouth			1
* Tri Town Drive-In Theatre	52 S. Nelson Road	Sterling Junction 01565			1
* Wellfleet Drive-In	P.O.Box 900	Wellfleet 02663	Spring Brook Center	700	1
West Newton Cine 1-2-3	1296 Washington Street	West Newton 02165	D. Bramante		3
Westboro Cinema	18 Lyman Street	Westboro 01581	A. Edmonds	372	2
Images Cinema	50 Spring Street	Williamstown 01267	D. Fisher	191	1
Wollaston Theatre	4 Beale Street	Wollaston 02170	A. Chandler	1050	1

MICHIGAN

Name	Address	City & Zip	Owner	Seats	Screens
Chesterfield Cinemas 3	33125 Mile Rd.	Anchor Bay 48047	Aloha Entertainment	600	3
Bohm Theatre		Albion			1
Michigan Theater	603 E. Liberty Street	Ann Arbor 48104	Michigan Theat. Fdtn.	1710	1
State Theatre	233 S. State St.	Ann Arbor 48104	Aloha Entertainment	700	2
State Theatre	913 Washington Ave.	Bay City 48708	Tim S. O'Brien	800	1
Beaverton Gem Theatre	120 Ross Street	Beaverton 48612	Hank Huckins	320	1
Bellaire Theatre	219 N. Bridge	Bellaire 49615	L. Dawson	300	1
* Cherry Bowl Drive-In	P.O.Box C	Beulah 49617	Thomas Kenney		1
New Birmingham Theatre..		Birmingham			3
Boyne Cinema Theatre	216 S. Lake Street	Boyne City 49712	T. Toomey		1
Cass Theatre	6464 Main Street	Cass City 48726	R. Hendrick	490	1
Eaton Theatres	235 S. Cochran	Charlotte 48813	Rick & Myra Dedoph	750	2
* Cheboygan Drive-In	1122 Shore Dr.	Cheboygan 49721	R.J. Theatres, Inc.		1
Clio Cinema	2151 W. Vienna Rd.	Clio 48420	Gary Geiger		1
* Capri Drive-In	1455 W. Chicago Rd.	Coldwater 49036	J. Magocs	1200	1
Ford-Tel	23830 Ford Rd.	Dearborn Heights 48126	Robert Sloan	750	2
Norwest Theatre	17630 Grand River	Detroit 48227	Robert Sloan	950	2
Rennaissance Theatre	400 Renaissance Ctr.	Detroit 48243	Rennaisance Ctr.Ventures..		1
Eastwood Theatre	21145 Gratiot Ave.	East Detroit 48021	I. Belinsky		1
Willow Creek 8		Escanaba 49829	Thomas Theatre Group		8
Farmington Civic 2	33332 Grand River	Farmington 48336	H & H Theatres		2
* U.S.Twin 23 Drive-In	G5200 Fenton Rd.	Flint 48507	Warrington		2
Community Theatre	52 Carrington	Harbor Beach 48441	J. Swartz		1
Alco Theatre	P.O. Box 547	Harrisville 48740	J. Swise et.al.	320	1
Heart Theatre	19 Main St.	Hartford 49057	J. Johns		1
Cinema 4	213 W. State Street	Hastings 49058	Debra Dorsey	955	4
Hillman Theatre	430 N. State	Hillman 49746	W. Watkins		1
* Cherry Bowl Drive-In	9812 Honor Hwy.	Honor 49640	T. Kenney	300	1
Copper Theatre	510 Shelden Avenue	Houghton 49931	Jim Payne		1
Pines Theatre	4673 Houghton Lake Drive	Houghton Lake 48629	C. Huddy		1
The Howell Theatre	315 E. River	Howell 48843	Wisper & Wetsman, Inc.	530	1
Braumart Twin Cinemas	P.O.Box 887	Iron Mountain 49801	James Andes		2
Plaza Cinema Theatre	U.S. #2 West	Iron River 49935	L. Anceli		1
Butler Theatre Company	119 S. Main Street	Ishpeming 49849	E. Wales		1
Michigan Theatre		Jackson			1
Keego Twin	3040 Orchard Lake Rd.	Keego Harbor 48320			2
Odeon Southside	3500 S. Cedar Street	Lansing 48910	Odeon Corp.	460	4
Odeon Theatre	300 N. Clipper Street	Lansing 48912	Frank Leahey	178	1
Pix Theatre	172 W. Nepessing St.	Lapeer 48446	Wisper & Wetsman, Inc.		1
Cinema I & 2	P.O. Box 261	Manistique 49854	William Giles		2
Delft 1 & 2 Theatres	139 W. Washington Street	Marquette 49855			1
Bogar Theatre		Marshall			1
Studio M	5201 Bay City Rd.	Midland 48642	J. Rapanos		3
Denniston Cinema 3	6495 N. Monroe Street	Monroe 48161	J. Sterling	900	3
Rex Theatre	235 W. Main St.	Morenci 49256	E. Chase	225	1
Tahqua-Land Theatre	212 S. Newberry Ave.	Newberry 49868	F. Dunkeld		1
Gaslight Cinema	302 Petoskey St.	Petoskey 49770	L. Dawson	980	5
Penn Theatre	P.O. Box 537	Plymouth 48170	Bonny S. Smith	670	1
Tri-City 8	P.O.Box 109	Quinnesec 49876	Thomas Theatre Group		8
Showboat Theatre	13800 Sibley Rd.	Riverview 48192	Aloha Entertainment	950	5
Rogers Theatre	245 N. Third Street	Rogers City 49779	R. Vogelheim	400	1
Court Street Theatre	1216 Court Street	Saginaw 48602	L. Eischer		1
* Hi-Way Drive-In	2887 E. Sanick	Sandusky 48471	S. Fetting	200	1
Sanilac Theatre	31 E. Lincoln	Sandusky 48471	S. Fetting	361	1
Berkley Theatre Company	28400 Northwestern Pkwy	Southfield 48034			1
Tivoli Theatre	302 Railroad Street	Stephenson 49887			1
Bay Theatre	214 St. Joseph	Suttons Bay 49682	R. Bahle	285	1
Riviera Theatre	50 N. Main Street	Three Rivers 49093	J. Went	388	1
Moore Theatre	8189 Verlynda St.	Watervliet 49098			

Name	Address	City & Zip	Owner	Seats	Screens
*Ford Wyoming Drive-In	P.O.Box 220	Wayne 48184	Ford-Wyoming Inc.	2600	8
State-Wayne	35310 Michigan Ave.	Wayne 48184			4
Clarkston Cinema Corp.	33290 W. Fourteen Mi Rd	West Bloomfield 48322	P. Glatz & C. Slemer	166	1
West Branch Cinema	210 W. Houghton	West Branch 48661	West Branch Cinema, Inc.		1
Milford Cinema	8580 Cooley Beach Drive	White Lake 48386	Tom Henn		1
Rullis Sun Thatre	112 S. Kalamazoo	White Pigeon 49099	J. Herring	360	1

MINNESOTA

Name	Address	City & Zip	Owner	Seats	Screens
Orpheum Theatre	305 W. Main St.	Ada 56510	T. Rocker		1
Rialto Theatre	220 Minnesota Ave. North	Aitkin 56431			1
Midway Mall Cinema 7	2910 S. Broadway St.	Alexandria 56308	Tentelino Enterprises	1160	7
Anoka Cinema	420 E. Main	Anoka 55303	Continental Cinema	424	2
Lido Theatre	309 W. Main St.	Arlington 55307	M. Curtis & C. Bergstad	330	1
Tacora Theatre	Box 142	Aurora 55705	D. Rudolph	300	1
De Marce Theatre	1320 Atlantic Avenue	Benson 56215	L. Demarce		1
Blackduck	Main Street	Blackduck 56630	R. Moore	150	1
*65 Hi Drive-In	10100 Central Ave. NE	Blaine	I. Braverman		1
Brookdale Cinemas	58012 Shingle Creek Pkwy.	Brooklyn Center	B. Copeland		4
Buffalo Cinema	100 NE 1st Ave.	Buffalo 55313	Cinema Business Corp.	510	3
BurnsvilleCinema Cafe	1725 W. Burnsville Pkwy.	Burnsville	Brian Minnette		1
Canby Theatre	109 St. Olaf Ave. N.	Canby 56220	Brenda Alley	600	2
Chaska 4	511 Walnut	Chaska 55318	M. Deleuhry		4
Premiere 4	904 Hwy 33 South	Cloquet 55720	R. Stowell	720	4
Heights Theatre	3951 Central Ave NE	Columbia Heights	Classic Theatres Corp.	448	1
Comet Theatre	River St. & Second Ave.	Cook 55723	J. & D. Lawson		1
Cottage Grove 3	7280 S.E. Point Douglas	Cottage Grove	Classic Theatres		3
Grand Theatres 1 & 2	124 E. 2nd Street	Crookston 56716	J. Hiller.		2
Delano Theatre West	West Hwy 12	Delano 55328	Muller Family Theatres		5
East Bethel Theatre	187th & Hwy 65	East Bethel	Muller Family Theatres		10
State Theatre	238 E. Sheridan St.	Ely 55731	Ronald Forsman	300	1
Excelsior Dock	26 Water St.	Excelsior 55331	H. Arendt		3
Lesdan Theatre	105 W. First Street	Fosston 56542	J. Winter		1
*75 Hi Drive-In		Hallock			1
JEM Theatre	Rte 1 Box 137	Harmony 55939	M. Fishbaugher & S.Ryden	250	1
Cine 1-2 Theatres	1319 Third Street	International Falls 56649	R. Hanover	612	2
State Theatre	600 2nd St.	Jackson 56143	J. Matuska		1
Kee Theatre	100 N. Main	Kiester 56751			1
*Vali Hi Drive-In	11260 Hudson Blvd	Lake Elmo 55042	R. O'Neil		1
LeSueur Theatre	209 S. Main	LeSueur 56058	J. Edwards	274	1
Hollywood	210 N. Sibley Ave.	Litchfield 55355	P. Schoell	90	1
Falls	115 1st Street SE	Little Falls 56345			3
*Long Drive-In	Hwy 71 N.	Long Prairie 56347	C. & L. Meier		1
Palace Theatre	104 E. Main St.	Luverne 56156	M. DeBates	441	1
Madelia	117 W. Main St.	Madelia 56062	Everett Christensen	290	1
Grand Theatre	310 6th St.	Madison 56256	MG Entertainment	400	2
Marshall 6	230 W. Lyon	Marshall 56258	S. Hiller	966	6
Milaca Theatre	160 S. Central	Milaca 56353	B. Gorecki		1
Oak Street Cinema	309 Oak St. E.	Minneapolis 55414	R. Cowgill	360	1
Parkway Theatre	4814 Chicago Ave.	Minneapolis 55417	W. Irvine	628	1
Riverview Theatre	3800 42nd Ave. So.	Minneapolis 55406	Classic Theaters Corp	800	1
Plaza Theatre	Southtown	Montevideo 56265	R. Vonderhaar		3
Monticello Theatres	137 Broadway St. E.	Monticello 55362	Muller Family Theatres		4
Lake Theatre	Fourth & Elm	Moose Lake 55767	W. Lower	350	1
Morris	12 E. 6th Street	Morris 56267	Curt Barber		1
Cinema Cafe	2749 Winnetka Ave. N	New Hope 55427	Brian Minnette	420	3
North Branch 5	628 Main St.	North Branch 55056			5
Southgate Cinema 3	960 Main St.	Northfield 55057	R. Thompson		3
Park Theatre	107 S. Main St.	Park Rapids 56470	J. Wasche	427	2
Koronis Cinema 1 & 2	209 Washburne Ave.	Paynesville 56362	P. Schoell	210	2
Comet Theatre	247 First Ave. S.	Perham 56573	D. Quincer	300	1
Quarry Twin	204 E. Main St.	Pipestone 56164	Duane Hess		2
Strand 2	128 5th Ave. N.	Princeton 55371			1
Redwood Falls Twin	230 E. 2nd St.	Redwood Falls 56283	D. Paul		2
Roso Theatre	310 Main Ave. N.	Roseau 56751			1
Vogue	309 N. Commercial	Sandstone 55072	J. Petersen		1
Main Street Theatre	319 N. Main	Sauk Centre 56378	R. Douvier	480	3
Sherburn Theatre	116 N. Main	Sherburn 56171	Harold Anderson		1
St. James Cinema	505 1st Ave. So.	St. James			1
Staples Cinema	204 4th St. NE	Staples 56479	G. Rosenthal		1
Galaxy Twin	Box 337	Thief River Falls 56701	Hickerson		2
Cozy Theatre	223 Jefferson St.	Wadena 56482	D. Quincer		1
*Sky Vu Drive In		Warren	S. Novak		1
Flame Theatre	125 S. Broadway	Wells			1
White Bear TownshipThtr	I-35E & County Rd. J	White Bear	Muller Family Theatres		14
State Theatre	926 4th Ave	Windom 56101	E. Christian		1
State Theatre	88-96 E. Fourth St.	Zumbrota 55992	R.& C. Hawley	269	1

MISSISSIPPI

Name	Address	City & Zip	Owner	Seats	Screens
Star Theatre	600 S. Beach Blvd.	Bay St. Louis 39520	W. Schulz	250	1
Silver Screen	2650 Beach Blvd.	Biloxi 39531	Pensacola Silver Screen		4
Norwood Village Cinema	P.O. Box 3028	Gulfport 39505	C. & R.Triggs		1
DeVille Cinema, Inc.	5100 I-55 North 39211	Jackson 39236	W. Collins	527	1
Broadcountry Cinema 3	227 SW 2nd Ave.	Magee 39111	B. McCall	463	3
Cine Theatre	125 E. Bankhead Street	New Albany 38652	H. Stephens	450	1
Hoka Cinema	304 S. 14th	Oxford 38655	R. Shapiro		1
Trace Theatre	728 Main Street	Port Gibson 39150	E. Doss		1
New Dixie Theatre	106 S. Main St.	Ripley 38663	D. Wells		1
Tobie Twin Cinema	218 E. Main Street	Senatobia 38668	P. Maxey		2
Starkville Theatres Inc.	705 1/2 Highway 12 East	Starkville 39759	Alan Riekhof	798	5

Name	Address	City & Zip	Owner	Seats	Screens
Plaza Twin Cinema	P.O. Box 688	Yazoo City 39194	G. Twiner	390	2

MISSOURI

Name	Address	City & Zip	Owner	Seats	Screens
Princess Theatre	1110 Sunshine Dr.	Aurora 65605	Shelby J. Ruble		1
* Sunset Drive-In	1601 E. Church	Aurora 65605	David L. Marks	230	1
* Highway 65 Drive-In	P.O.Box 174	Buffalo 65622	De Jarnette	200	1
Crest Cinema 2 & Video	112 N. Washington	Clinton 64735	Robert Follmer	450	2
Cross Keys Cinema	110 Cross Keys S/C	Florissant 63033			2
Englewood Theatre	10917 Winner Rd	Independence 64052		670	1
* Twin Drive-In 1 & 2	Kentucky Rd.	Independence 64050	Twin DI Theatres		1
* I 70 Drive-In	8701 U.S. Hwy 40	Kansas City 64129	Stone Enter.		4
* 63rd Street Drive-In		Kansas City			2
Petite 3 Cinemas	2020 N. Baltimore	Kirksville 63501	B. Collier		3
* Barco Drive-In	57 SE 25th Lane	Lamar 64759	B. Felts	400	1
Star Theatre	268 N. Jefferson	Lebanon 65536	Charles Burton	400	1
* Macon Drive-In	32506 US Hwy 63 S.	Macon 63552	Dan Arnold		1
Royal Theatre	29197 Kendall Rd.	Macon 63552	T. Davison	400	1
Carlanco Enterprises	P.O. Box 551	Mexico 65265	C. Ruble	1220	6
Strand Theatre	308 South Hickory	Mount Vernon 65712	C. Ruble		1
Twin Fox Theatre	110 S. Main Street	Nevada 64772	J. Novak	332	3
Civic Theatre	635 3rd Street	Osceola 64776	M. & T. Hampton	340	1
St. Andrews Cinema	2025 Golfway	St. Charles 63301	Beta Theatre Co.		1
Avalon Theatre	4225 S. Kings Hwy.	St. Louis 63109	C. Tsvis		1
Hi-Pointe Theatre	1001 McCausland Avenue	St. Louis 63117	G. James	500	1
Kirkwood Cinema	338 S. Kirkwood Rd.	St. Louis 63122	Harmon & Sara Mosely	400	1
The Tivoli	6350 Delmar Blvd.	St. Louis 63130			1
State Fair Cinemas	P.O. Box 189	Sedalia 65302	Marge Wagernecht		1
* Owen Drive-In Theatre	P.O. Box 223	Seymour 65746	H. Owen	75	1
* Mo. Outdoor Theatre, Inc.	P.O. Box 2261	Springfield 65801			1
Palace 8		Springfield	American Entertainment		8
Theatre Associates, Inc.	#7 Plaza, Suite A	Troy 63379		808	4
Roxy Theatre & Video	325 N. Van Buren	Warsaw 65335	Robert Follmer	190	2
Cinema 1 Plus 1 Plus 1	1900 Hwy. 100 E.	Washington 63090	D. Mittler	673	3
Glass Sword Cinema 3	Route 1, Box 37	West Plains 65775	G. York		3

MONTANA

Name	Address	City & Zip	Owner	Seats	Screens
Washoe Theatre	305 Main Street	Anaconda 59711	J. Lussy		1
* Silver Bow Drive-In	Silver Bow Interchange	Butte 59701	M. Hansen	500	2
Roxy Theatre	Box 782	Choteau 59422	L. Schilling	380	1
* Midway Drive-In	Hwy 2 & 40	Columbia Falls 59912	Anderson Theatres		1
Orpheum Theatre	P.O. Box/#7, 4th St., S.E	Conrad 59425	Larcon Theatres	320	1
State Theatre	111 East Main	Cut Bank 59427	Larcon Theatres	380	1
Rialto Theatre	418 Main	Deer Lodge 59722	H. Hansen	700	1
Big Sky Cinema I & II	560 N. Montana Street	Dillon 59725	H. Pickerill	472	2
Madison Theatre	115 Main Street	Ennis 59729	Armitage	250	1
Roxy Theatre	981 Main Street	Forsyth 59327	N. Blakesley		1
Terry's II Theatres	620 Second Ave. S.	Glasgow 59230	P. Terry		2
Rose Theatre	P.O. Box 851	Glendive 59330	Lewis Moore	480	1
Northgate Theatres, Inc.	P.O. Box 157	Hamilton 59840			1
Centre Cinema & Video	Box 437	Hardin 59034	D. Smith	256	1
Harlo Theatre	20 N. Central	Harlowton 59036	Booster Club	140	1
Gateway Cinema	1275 Hwy 2 West	Kalispell 59901	Anderson Theatres		6
Liberty Theatre	120 1st Ave. East	Kalispell 59901	Anderson Theatres		1
Strand Theatre	120 2nd St. East	Kalispell 59901	Anderson Theatres		1
Laurel Movie Haus	Box 546	Laurel 59044	T. Kilpatrick	253	1
* Westernaire Drive-In	219 West Main	Lewiston 59457	J. Campbell	195	1
Judith Theatre	219 West Main	Lewistown 59457	J. Campbell	400	1
Dome Theatre	602 Mineral	Libby 59923	L. & E.Huber	480	1
* Libby Drive-In	6024 Mineral Ave.	Libby 59923	L. & E.Huber		1
Empire Twin	106 North 2nd Street	Livingston 59047	George Hancock		2
Villa & Grand Theatres	P.O. Box 820	Malta 59538	Rosetta & Garry Adams		1
Montana Theatres	P.O. Box 671	Miles City 59301	Robert Johnson	670	1
Crystal Theatre	515 S. Higgins	Missoula 59801	J. Laakso	160	1
* Go West Drive-in	P.O. Box 7277	Missoula 59807	Wilma Amusements		1
Orpheum Theatre	119 S. Main Street	Plentywood 59254	G. Nielsen		1
* Sunset Theatre	414 E. Boundway	Plentywood 59254	G. Nielsen		1
Roxy Theatre	189 Main St.	Shelby 59474	Larcon Theatres	400	1
Center Theatre	Box 1113	Sidney 59270	B. Suckstorff	476	1
Strand Theatre	P.O. Box 700	Superior 59872	Jensen Enterprises	300	1
Strand Theatre	P.O. Box 783	White Sulphur Sprng 59645	T. Barth	162	1
Mountain Cinemas	P.O. Box 1491	Whitefish 59937	H. Pickerill		2
Star Theatre	25 W. Legion	Whitehall 59759	H. Hansen	350	1

NEBRASKA

Name	Address	City & Zip	Owner	Seats	Screens
* Pineview Drive-In Theatre	HC65 Box 190	Ainsworth 69210	David Cole		1
Royal Theatre	HC65 Box 190	Ainsworth 69210	D. Cole		1
Geju Theatre	P.O. Box 738	Alliance 69301	Gerald Bullard		1
Blair Twin Theatre	South Highway 30	Blair 68008	Frederick		2
State Theatre	P.O.Box 263	Central City 68826	K. Blodgett		1
Center 4		Columbus			4
Star Theatre	321 Center Avenue	Curtis 69025	Star Theatres, Inc.	200	1
Rialto II Theatre	160 N. Ninth Street	Geneva 68361	City of Geneva	300	1
Sun Theatre	421 West Avenue	Holdrege 68949	F. Bahm	444	1
Imperial Theatre	P.O. Box 637	Imperial 69033	City of Imperial	180	1
Joyo Theatre	Box 29138	Lincoln 68529	D. Montgomery	313	1
Pioneer 3 Theatre	110 S.11th St.	Nebraska City 68410	Main Street Theatres, Inc.	750	3
Dundee Theatre		Omaha			1
Ritz Theatre	134 S. 6th St.P.O.Box 127	Plattsmouth 68048	Main Street Theatres, Inc	200	1

Name	Address	City & Zip	Owner	Seats	Screens
Rivoli Theatre	533 Main Street	Seward 68434	J. Wisehart	300	1
Carlin Theatre	P.O. Box 28	Spalding 68665	P. Carlin	276	1
Twin Theatre	310 Main Street	Wayne 68787	J. March	356	2

NEVADA

Fallon Theatre	71 S. Maine Street	Fallon 89406	R. Erickson		2
Meadowdale Theatres	P.O. Box 6	Gardnerville 89410	W. Tomerlin		2
Cactus Theatre	P.O. Box 1252	Hawthorne 89415	M. Rogers	210	1
Four Star Theatre	5303 E. Twain Ave.	Las Vegas 89122	E. Glass		1
Gold Coast Twin		Las Vegas			2

NEW HAMPSHIRE

Bear Island Restorations	RFD 1 Box 99M	Centre Harbor 03226	D. Leavitt	350	2
Cinema 93 Theatre	12 Loudon Road	Concord 03301	B. Steelman	330	1
Concord Theatre	18 1/2 S. Main St.	Concord 03301			1
The Majestic	36 Main St.	Conway 03818	J. Quirk		1
Spinelli Cinemas	400 Central Ave.	Dover 03820	Michael Spinelli		1
Hampton Cinema Six	P.O. Box 1259	Hampton 03842	K. Tinios		6
Drennan Hall Cinema		Keene	Keene State University		1
*Midway Drive-In	Box 594	Littleton 03561	R. Morneau		1
Cinema 8	Appletree Mall	Londonderry 03053	Eastern Shores Cinemas	2100	8
*Milford Drive-in 1 & 2	Rt. 101A	Milford 03055	Scharmett Corp.		2
Scenic Theatre	21 Depot Street	Pittsfield 03263	A. Dame		1
Plymouth Theatre	39 South Main Street	Plymouth 03264	D. Leavitt		2
Town Hall Theatre	P.O. Box 7	Wilton 03086	D. Markaverich		1
*Northfield Drive-In	Northfield Rd.	Winchester 03470	M. Shakaer	450	1
*Meadows Drive-In	P.O. Box 44 Route 135	Woodsville 03785	L. Tegu	400	1

NEW JERSEY

Strathmore Twin	Rt. 34	Aberdeen 07747			2
Lincoln Cinema Five	832 Kearney Ave.	Arlington 07032	S. Papas		5
Cinemas 1-2-3	82 First Avenue-Box 269	Atlantic Highlands 07716	L. Edwards	600	3
Berkley Cinema	450 Springfield Ave.	Berkeley Heights 07922	S. Goldstein	346	1
Brook Cinema	10 Hamilton St.	Bound Brook 08805	I. Muthu		1
Cinema 23 Fiveplex	State Hwy. No. 23	Cedar Grove 07009	Kin-Mall Cinemas		5
Chatham	641 Shunpike Road	Chatham 07928			1
Chester Twin Cinemas	Chester Spngs. Shop. Ctr.	Chester 07930			2
Allwood Sixplex	96 Market St.	Clifton 07012			6
Dunellen	458 North Ave.	Dunnellen 08812			1
Elmora	144 Elmora	Elizabeth 07202			0
Liberty Twin Theatre	1121 Elizabeth Ave.	Elizabeth 07201	F. Bravo	600	2
Emerson Quad Theatre	346 Kinderkamack	Emerson 07630	Sanders		4
Hyway Theatres	2260 Broadway	Fair Lawn 07410			5
Cinema Plaza	Hwy. 202 & 31	Flemington 08822			6
Galaxy Theatre	7000 Blvd. East	Guttenberg 07093	Page	450	3
Mall Twin Cinema	Route No. 57	Hackettstown 07840			2
Hawthorne Theatre	300 Lafayette Ave.	Hawthorne 07506	J. Sayegh		5
Hoboken Cinemas #1-2	5 Marine View Plaza	Hoboken 07030	V. Orjelick		2
Castle Twin	1115 Clinton Avenue	Irvington 07109			2
Kendall Park Cinema	3560 Route 27	Kendall Park 08824			7
Kin-Mall Theatres	25 Kinnelon Rd.	Kinnelon 07405	Kin-Mall Cinemas		8
Meadtown	Route 23 South	Kinnelon 07405	Kin-Mall Cinemas		1
Linden Fiveplex Cinemas	400 N. Wood Avenue	Linden 07036	Kin-Mall Cinemas		5
Maplewood Theatre	155 Maplewood Ave.	Maplewood 07040		945	4
Clairidge Triple Cinema	486 Bloomfield Ave.	Montclair 07042	P. Petersen		3
Lumberton Cinema	Rt. 38 Eayerstown Rd.	Mt. Molly 08060	D. Saunders		3
Newton Twin	234 Spring	Newton 07110	P. Vivian		2
Galleria Cinemas	1502 Route 35 S.	Ocean Township			10
Cinema 35 Theatre	65 West Route 4	Paramus 07652	Hudson Amusements		1
Broadway Theatre	South Broadway	Pitman 08071	C. Platt		1
Colonial Twin	245 Wanague Ave.	Pompton Lakes 07442			2
Ramsey Cinema	125 E. Main St.	Ramsey 07446	P. Vivian		1
Broad Street Cinema	58 Broad St.	Red Bank 07701			1
Rialto	172 Main Street	Ridgefield Park 07660	Nissimdjiji	500	1
Montgomery Ctr Theatre	Highway #206	Rocky Hill 08558	R. Piechota		6
New Park Theatre	23 Westfield Ave. W.	Roselle Park 07204	TLN Corp.	975	5
William Center Twin	One Williams Plaza	Rutherford 07070	Williams/Meadowlands	532	2
Sparta Theatre	25 Centre	Sparta 07871			2
Five Points Cinema	327 Chestnut St.	Union 07083	Jem Theatres	350	2
Summit Quadplex	1214 Summit Ave.	Union City 07087	Andrew Dai	600	4
Washington Twin Cinema	163 E. Washington	Washington 07882			3
West Milford Cinema	West Milford		Magic Cinemas		1
Mayfair Theatre	6405 Park Ave.	West New York 07093	Hong Sheng Co. Inc.		3
Rialto 3	250 E. Broad St.	Westfield 07090			3
Westfield Twin	138 Central Ave.	Westfield 07090	D. Horn	635	2
Hanover Twin Cinema	Sykesville Road	Wrightstown 08562	T. Miller		2

NEW MEXICO

Lobo Theatre Inc.	3013 Central Ave, NE	Albuerque 87106	J. Ciccarello		1
*Sunset Drive-In	1700 Arenal Rd. S.W.	Albuquerque 87105	D. Armino		1
Cuba Cinema	Box 1537	Cuba 87013	J. Hodovance	200	1
Deming Cinema 3	P.O.Box 1001e	Deming 88031	C. Childers	568	3
Kiva Theatre	1111 Seventh Street	Las Vegas 87701	Malcom Neal	250	1
Coronado Theatre	324 E. Second	Lordsburg 88045	W. Gavin		1
Pecos Theatre	219 4th Street	Santa Rosa 88435	R. Sanchez	200	1
El Rio Theatre	P.O. Box 147	Truth or Consequence 87901	J. Whetzel		1

Name	Address	City & Zip	Owner	Seats	Screens
NEW YORK					
Madison Theatre	1036 Madison Ave.	Albany 12208	B. Rosenblatt		1
Spectrum Cinemas	290 Delaware Avenue	Albany 12209	Spectrum Cinema Corp.		3
*Orleans Drive-In	Route 31	Albion 14411	W. Baker	2435	1
Transit Drive-In Theatre	804 Sweet Home Road	Amherst 14226	Macy J.Cohen		4
*Hollywood Drive-In	RR 4 Box 44	Averill Park 12018	F. Fisher	300	1
Bellmore Movies	222 Pettit Ave.	Bellmore 11710	Henry & Ann Stampfel	480	1
Mid Island Theatre	4045 Hempstead Tpke.	Bethpage L.I. 11714	M. Abrams		1
Cameo Theatre	63 Main Street	Brewster 10509	W. Quinn		2
New American Quad	1450 East Avenue	Bronx 10461			4
New Riverdale Twin	5683 Riverdale Ave.	Bronx 10471		412	2
Brooklyn Heights Twin	70 Henry St.	Brooklyn 11201	Bklyn Bridge Cinemas	400	2
Canarsie Triplex	9310 Avenue L	Brooklyn 11236			3
Cobble Hill Fiveplex	265 Court St.	Brooklyn 11231			5
Commodore Twin Theatre	329 Broadway	Brooklyn 11211	J. Crespi		2
New Kent Twin	1170 Coney Island Avenue	Brooklyn 11230	E. Steinberg		2
Plaza Twin Cinema	314 Flatbush Avenue	Brooklyn 11226	R. Ardala		2
Community	373 Main St.	Catskill 12414	T. Thornton	734	2
*Border Drive-In	Route 9	Champlain 12919	A. Bruce		1
Chester 6	Rte 17 N	Chester 10918			6
Pine Cinema	1850 Route 112	Coram 11727	S. Epstein		4
*Hi-Way D.I.	Rte. 9W	Coxsackie 12051	Morris Klein		1
R H Theatre, Inc.	195 Colabaugh Pond Road	Croton-on Hudson 10520	Diana Horn		1
*Delevan Drive-In	Route 16	Delevan 14042	G. Mendola		1
State Theatre	148 Front St.	Deposit 13754	Deposit Comm. Theatre		1
$1.50 Theatre	111 W. Main St.	Endicott 13760	Ronda Fitzsimmons		1
Zurich Cinema Corp.	5181 Brockway Lane	Fayetteville 13066	Conrad Zurich		1
Movies 4	Dutchess Mall	Fishkill 12524	Lockwood & McKinnon		4
N. Shore Towers Cinema	272-40 Grand Cent. Park	Floral Park 11005	J. Aidela		1
Main Street Quad	7266 Main St.	Flushing 11367			4
Franklin	989 Hempstead Turnpike	Franklin Square 13057	WSA Theatres	800	6
*Greenville Drive-In	Route #32	Greenburgh 12083	Greenville Eleven		1
Village Cinema	211 Front Street	Greenport 11944	Village Cinema Circuit		4
*Hathaway's Drive-In	P.O. Box 211	Greenwich 12834	Karl & Liz Pingree		1
Hamilton Cinema	7 Lebanon Street	Hamilton 13346	A. Shepherd	300	1
Village Cinema Seven	145 N. Franklin Ct.	Hempstead 11550	Village Cinema Circuit		7
Fairview Cinema 3	Fairview	Hudson 12534	Morris Klein		3
Hunter	Main St.	Hunter 12442	T. Thornton	229	1
*Hyde Park Drive-In	Rte. 9	Hyde Park 12538			1
Roosevelt Fourplex	11 Caywood Place	Hyde Park 12538			4
Cinemapolis 1 & 2	171 E. State St.	Ithaca 14850	L. Cohen & R. Szanyi	289	2
Cornell Cinema	104 Willard Straight	Ithaca 14853	Cornell Univ.	760	2
Fall Creek Pictures	1201 N. Tioga St.	Ithaca 14850	L. Cohen & R. Szanyi	300	3
Hudson Valley Mall Sixplex	6 Hudson St	Kingston 12401			6
Palace	26 Main St.	Lake Placid 12946	Reg. Clark	572	3
Liberty Triplex	P.O.Box 525	Liberty 12754	J. Illiparampil	900	3
*Transit Drive-In	6655 Transit Rd.	Lockport 14094	M. Cohen	900	1
Park Avenue Twin	179 E. Park Ave.	Long Beach 11561	Henry & Anne Stampfel	280	2
Malverne Twin Cinema	350 Hempstead Ave.	Malverne 11565	Henry & Anne Stampfel	620	2
Mattituck Twin Theatre	Route 25 Mattituck	Mattituck 11952	Puma		2
*Middletown Drive-In	R.D. 4	Middletown 10940	ABK Theatres		2
The Moviehouse	Main St.	Millerton 12546	Movies Millerton Inc.	429	3
Monroe	Millpond Parkway	Monroe 10950			1
Mall Quad	Route 42	Monticello 12701	Vacation Cinemas		4
New Paltz Quad	Rte. 299 New Paltz Plaza	New Paltz 12516	Al Bell		4
Angelika 57th	225 W. 57th St.	New York 10019	Angelika Film Centers		1
Anthology Film Archives	32 2nd Ave.	New York 10003			1
Cinema Village 12th Street	22 E. 12th Street	New York 10003	Cinemart Cinema Corp.	300	1
Eastside Playhouse	919 3rd Ave.	New York 10022			1
Embassy 1	Broadway & 46th Sts.	New York 10036	Guild Enterprises	500	1
Embassy 2-3-4	701 7th Ave.	New York 10036	Guild Enterprises	1057	3
Film Forum	209 W. Houston Street	New York 10014	Film Forum	472	3
Guild Theatre	Rockefeller Plaza	New York 10020	Guild Enterprises	450	1
Harlem Victoria 5	235 W. 125th St.	New York 10027	Harlem Redevelopment Co.		5
Lincoln Plaza Cinemas 6	30 Lincoln Plaza	New York 10023	New York Cinemas	1100	6
New Coliseum	701 W. 181st St.	New York 10033			4
Nova Theatre	3589 Broadway	New York 10031	J. Nova		2
Quad Cinema	34 W. 13th St.	New York 10011	Maurice Kanbar	575	4
Walter Reade Theatre	Lincoln Center	New York 10023	Film Soc. Lincoln Center		1
Cinema East	Rte. 59	Nyack 10960			2
Oceanside Twin Theatre	2743 Long Beach Rd.	Oceanside 11572	Henry & Anne Stampfel	500	2
Strand Theatre	P.O. Box 681	Old Forge 13420	Robert Card		1
*Allegany Drive-In	P.O.Box 606	Olean 14760	Bordanaro Bros. Theatres		1
Cinema Twin Theatres	NY St. Rts. Big N Shp.	Oneida 13421	Zurich		2
Showcase Cinema	11 Elm Street	Oneonta 13820	Harold deGraw		1
*El Rancho Drive-In	Rte. #5	Palatine Brdg. 13428	Hallmark		1
West Wayne Theatre	170 Stafford Rd.	Palmyra 14522	R. Kommer	294	1
Central Theatre	East Central Ave	Pearl River 10965			1
*Silver Lake Drive-In	P.O.Box 26	Perry 14530	J. Stefanon	400	1
Port Jefferson Twin	Rt. 112	Port Jefferson 11776			2
Port Washington 7-Plex	116 Main St.	Port Washington 11050	G.G. Theatres	1405	7
Cinema 8	Galleria Mall	Poughkeepsie 12701			8
SUNY Film Series	Campus Center N.	Purchase 10577	State Univ.		1
Cinemart Twin	106-03 Metropolitan Ave.	Queens 11375	Cinemart Cinema Corp.	950	2
*Glen Twin Drive-In	P.O.Box 4079	Queensbury 12804	J. Gardner		2
Lyceum Theatre	139 S. Broadway	Red Hook 12571	Al Bell		2
Drake Theatre	62-90 Woodhaven Blvd.	Rego Park 11374			7
Upstate Films	26 Montgomery St.	Rhinebeck 12572	S. Leiber		2
Cinema Theatre	957 S. Clinton Avenue	Rochester 14620	J. Morreale		2
Film City Cinema Theater	957 S. Clinton Ave.	Rochester 14620	J. Morreale		1

Name	Address	City & Zip	Owner	Seats	Screens
Little Theatre	240 East Avenue	Rochester 14604	W. Coppard	678	5
Surfside Twin Theatre	103-22 Rockaway Beach Blv	Rockaway Park 11694	H.Elgart		2
Rosendale Theatre	Main Street	Rosendale 12472	A. Cacchio	300	1
Roslyn Trio Theatre	20 Tower Place	Roslyn 11576	Levinson		3
Sag Harbor Cinema	Main Street	Sag Harbor L.I. 11963	G. Mallow		1
Orpheum Theatre	P.O.Box 113	Saugerties 12477	Thomas Thornton	423	3
Sayville Triplex	Railroad Ave.	Sayville 11782		850	3
Royal Cinema Corp., The	P.O. Box 9207	Schenectady 12309	J. DiSalvatore		1
Southampton Cinemas	43 Hill Street	Southampton L.I. 11968	H. Karlin		3
Atrium Cinemas	680 Arthur Kill Road	Staten Island 10308	Bernard Goldberg		6
Lafayette Theatre	Lafayette Ave.	Suffern 10901			1
Center Twin Theatre	42-17 Queens Blvd.	Sunnyside 11104	S. Epstein		2
Genesee Theatre	2182 W. Genesee St.	Syracuse 13215	Danlin Corp.		1
Westcott Cinema	524 Westcott St.	Syracuse 13202	Westcott Cinema Inc.	575	1
State Theatre	Park St.	Tupper Lake 12986	J.S. Cinema		1
Fitzgerald Entertainment	5 Irving Pl.	Utica 13501	M. Fitzgerald		1
Walton	30 Gardiner St.	Walton 13850	P & P Enterprises		1
* Warwick Drive-In	Rte 94	Warwick 10990	ABK Theatres		3
South Bay Cinemas	495 Montauk Hwy.	West Babylon 11704	JHL Assoc.		4
West Islip Cinemas	444 Union Blvd.	West Islip 11795	WITC Corp.	400	2
Salisbury Theatre	610 Old Country Road	Westbury 11590	Salisbury Thea. Corp.		1

NORTH CAROLINA

Name	Address	City & Zip	Owner	Seats	Screens
Andrews Twin Cinema		Andrews 28901	R. McNelley	400	2
* Belmont Drive-In	314 McAdenville Road	Belmont 28012	W. Lawing		1
* Bessemer City Drive-In	Box 664	Bessemer City 28016	R. Stinette		1
Terrace Theatre	Huffman Mill Rd.	Burlington 27215	H. Bennett	982	5
Yancey 1 & 2 Theatre	19 Main St.	Burnsville 28714	B. Mandala		2
Varsity Theatres	123 E. Franklin St.	Chapel Hill 27514	C.H. Cinema Corp.	555	2
Arboretum Cinema 10	8008 Providence Rd.	Charlotte 28277	Consolidated Theatres		10
Ruby Cinemas	P.O. Box 557	Franklin 28734	R.E.I.Cinemas	725	3
Graham Cinema	119 N. Main St.	Graham 27253	T.Matthews		1
Carolina Theatre	310 S. Greene St.	Greensboro 27401	United Arts Council	1091	1
* Raleigh Road Outdoor	P.O. Box 1412	Henderson 27536	E. Lyles	265	1
Westchester Cinema	2200 Westchester Drive	High Point 27262	Cinema Development Co.		1
Highlands Theatre	Box 725	Highlands 28741	Schiffi		1
Gem Theatre	111 W. First St.	Kannapolis 28081	Rutledge	912	2
Countryside Cinema/MSP	631 N. Main Street	Kenersville 27284	D. Clark		3
Center Theatre	P.O. Box 3365	Lenoir 28655			1
Louisburg Theatre	109 W. Nash St.	Louisburg 27549	W. Pernell	372	2
Ye Olde Pioneer Theatre	111 Budleigh St.	Manteo 27954	H. Creef	315	1
Mars Theatre	P.O. Box 1290	Mars Hill 28754	Edwards & Fender	365	1
Union Square Cinemas	911 Dickerson Blvd.	Monroe 28110	Consolidated Theatres		8
* Bright Leaf Drive-In	P.O.Box 1348	Mt. Airy 27030			1
Henn Theatre	P.O. Box 398	Murphy 28906	P. Henn	400	1
Tryon Theatre	127 Trade St.	Tryon 28782	B. Flood	350	1
* Waynesville Drive-In	Box 77	Waynesville 28786	J. Clark		1
Cinema III Theatres	627 S. Madison	Whitsville 28472	J. Fisher	350	3

NORTH DAKOTA

Name	Address	City & Zip	Owner	Seats	Screens
Ash Theatre	P.O. Box 444	Ashley 58413	L. Schnabel	198	1
Bijou Theatre	82 S.E. First	Beach 58621	L. Walz	300	1
Grand Theatres	1486 Interstate Loop	Bismarck 58501	J. Brekke		3
Fargo Theatre	314 Broadway	Fargo 58108	Fargo Theatre Mgmt. Co.	870	1
Strand I & II	P.O. Box 72	Grafton 58237	Red River Film Group	425	2
Central Cinema Theatre	810 Lincoln Ave.	Harvey 58341	Harvey Youth Activities	200	1
Cinema Twin	Highway 200 East	Hazen 58545	L. Keim	400	2
Bison Twin Theatres	Buffalo Mall	Jamestown 58401	L. Keim	430	2
Cinema Twin	Jamestown Mall	Jamestown 58401	L. Keim	500	2
Roxy Theatre	714-Third Street	Langdon 58249	J. Dunford		1
Delchar Theatre	20 W. Main	Mayville 58257	S. Larson		1
Rockford Theatre	8 North 8th Street	New Rockford 58356	Caulfield, Johnson		1
Page Theatre	P.O. Box 141	Page 58064	Page Jaycees		1
Curt's Theatre	106 Main Avenue	Rolla 58367	C. Bonn		1
* Lake Park Drive-In	307 Main St.	Willston 58807	J. Snyder		1

OHIO

Name	Address	City & Zip	Owner	Seats	Screens
Mount Union Theatre	1745 S. Union Street	Alliance 44601	P. Honaker		1
* Magic City Drive-In	5602 S.Cleveland Massilon.	Barberton 44203	G. Greive	700	1
West Theatre	1017 Wooster Rd. West	Barberton 44203	G. Greive	700	1
Detroit Theatre	23811 Chagrin Blvd.	Beachwood 44122	N. Barn		2
Movies at Southgate	23811 Chagrin Blvd.	Beachwood 44122	N. Barn		3
Midway Theatre & Video.	210 West Plane Street	Bethel 45106	D. Brooks		1
Brunswick Cinema	1480 Pearl Road	Brunswick 44212	P. Pyros		1
Bryan Theatre	140 South Lyn Street	Bryan 43506	M. Sobieck	400	3
Belden Village Cinemas	6404 Market St.	Canton 44718	E. Pollak		4
Circle Mall Cinemas	3911 Everhard Rd. N.W.	Canton 44718	H. Poulos		4
Palace Theatre	605 N. Market Street	Canton 44702	Canton Palace Assn.	1514	1
Geauga Cinema	101 Water Street	Chardon 44024	Dolan		1
* Mayfield Road Drive-In	P.O.Box 368	Chardon 44026	Maisano		1
Court		Cincinnati	Holiday Amusement Co.		1
Emery Theatre	1112 Walnut Street	Cincinnati 45210	Univ. of Cincinnati	1376	1
Hollywood Cinema 1 & 2	1600 Central Parkway	Cincinnati 45210	Holiday Amusement Co.		2
Real Movies	719 Race St.	Cincinnati	Telkamp Theatres		2
Telkamp Theatres, Inc.	3118 Harrison Avenue	Cincinnati 45211	J. Telkamp		2
Circle Cinema, Inc.	117 Pinckney Street	Circleville 43113	P. Greene & S. Dettra	458	2
Cleveland Cinemas	6200 SOM Center Rd. C-20	Cleveland 44139	Cleveland Cinemas		1
Cleveland Cinematheque	11141 East Blvd.	Cleveland 44106	Cleveland Institute Art	700	2

580

Name	Address	City & Zip	Owner	Seats	Screens
Cleveland Museum of Art	11150 East Blvd.	Cleveland 44106	Cleveland Museum of Art	920	2
Lakeshore 1-3 Theatre	22624 Lakeshore Blvd.	Cleveland 44123	Saluan		3
Lee Cedar Theatre	2163 Lee Rd.	Cleveland 44118			1
Graceland Cinema 1&2	230 Graceland Blvd.	Columbus 43214	G. Ackerman		2
Palace Theatre	55 E. State Street	Columbus 43215	K. LeVegue		1
*South Drive-In 1 & 2	865 King Ave.	Columbus 43212	Rainbow Ent.		2
New Neon Movies	130 E. 5th St.	Dayton	Telkamp Theatres		1
MNC's Valentine 1 & 2	602 Clinton Street	Defiance 43512	M. Sobieck	700	2
Colony Theatre	Box 31	Gallipolis 45631	H. Wheeler		1
Garrettsville Twin 1 & 2	8001 State St.	Garrettsville 44231	Naft Enterprises	474	2
*Ranch Drive-In	P.O. Box 7	Greenfield 45123	Teicher Theatres Inc.		1
Wayne Cinema 2	538 Broadway	Greenville 45331	Teicher Theatres Inc.		2
*Holiday Drive-In	1816 Old Oxford Rd.	Hamilton 45013	Holiday Amusement Co.		2
Cinema West	509 Main Street	Hamilton 45013	B. Schuler		2
Markay Theatre	Main Street	Jackson 45640	Jackson Bact. Inc.		2
Elder Theatre	106 W. Pike St.	Jackson Center 45334	R. Miller	400	1
Plaza 1 & 2	University Shpg. Ctr.	Kent 44240	Ohio Movies		2
Duncan Theatre	110 N. Main St.	Killbuck 44637	Entertainment Enterprises		1
Duerson Theatres, Inc.	335 Overlook Dr.	Lancaster 43130	W.F. Duerson		1
*Skyview Drive-In	315 Timberlane Dr.	Lancaster 43130	C. Crum	400	1
Frontier Theatres	2100 Harding Hwy	Lima 45804	R. Heitmeyer		4
Palace Theatre	617 Broadway	Lorain 44052	G.M. Handyside	1399	1
Renaissance Theatre	138 Park Ave. W.	Mansfield 44902	Kelly Johnson	1406	1
*Sunset Drive-In	4018 State Rte 309	Mansfield 44907	H. Nusbaum		1
*Starlite Drive-In	1889 State Rte 127	Maria Stein 45860	E. Hyman		1
McArthur Twin Cinema	112 N. Market St.	McArthur 45651	D. Burton	255	2
Opera House Theatre	15 W. Main St.	McConnellsville 43756	G. Finley		1
Crescent Theatre	47 N. Hanover St.	Minster 45865	Robert Knostman		1
Capitol Theatre	22 W. High St.	Mt.Gilead 43338	Joseph A. Bash	199	1
Lake Cinemas 8	6404 Market Avenue N	North Canton 44721	Alexander Square Assoc.		1
Multiplex	14333 U.S. 33 South	Nelsonville 45764	E. Edwards		10
*Auto Rama Twin Drive-In	33395 Lorain Rd.	North Ridgeville 44039	T. Sherman	1200	2
*Starview Drive-In	2883 US Hwy 20W	Norwalk 44857	S.Steel		1
Towne & Country Theatre	55 E. Main St.	Norwalk 44857	T & C Players	900	1
Princess 4 Theatres Inc.	P.O. BOX 386	Oxford 45056			1
Cinema 20	1469 Mentor Ave.	Painseville 44077	Hall/Ryan		1
*Memphis Drive-In	30799 Pinetree Road	Pepper Pike 44124	R.Winter		3
Vogel Theatres	1098 E. State St.	Salem 44460	J. Vogel		3
*Sandusky Drive-In	P.O. Box 550	Sandusky 44870	Seitz Amusements	350	1
Sandusky State Theatre	103 Columbus Ave.	Sandusky 44870	Sandusky State Theatres	1575	1
*Auto-Vue Drive-In	P.O. Box 92	Sidney 45365	Negelspach		1
St. Mary's Theatre	119 W. Spring St.	St.Mary's 45885	R. Knotsman		1
*Winter Drive-In 1 & 2	Route 43	Steubenville 43952	Skirball		1
Strongsville Cinema 1 & 2	14781 Pearl Rd.	Strongsville 44136	A. Goisios		2
Ritz Theatre	30 S. Washington	Tiffin 44883	Tiffin Theatres Inc.	1000	1
Fox Theatre	3725 Williston Rd.	Toledo 43619	JR Denniston Theatre Co.	725	2
Great Eastern Theatre Co.	3540 Secor Road, #205	Toledo 43606	James Walter		1
Mayflower Twin	11 W. Main	Troy 45373	Teicher Theatres Inc.		2
*Ridgeway Drive-In	10721 West Ridge Rd.	Van Wert 45891	J. Boyd	350	1
*Van Del Drive-In	19986 E. Ridge Road	Van Wert 45891	J. Boyd	350	1
*Blue Sky Drive-In	959 Broad St.	Wadsworth 44261	G. Greive	600	1
Great Oaks Cinema	179 Great Oaks Trail	Wadsworth 44281	G. Grieve	600	2
*Elm Road Twin Drive-In	1895 Elm Road	Warren 44446	M. Hreno		2
*Pymatuning Lake Drive-In	8980 Inverrarry Dr. SE	Warren 44003	Mary Ann Hirtz		1
*Star Auto	1150 N. Shoop Ave.	Wauseon 43567	R. Wyse		1
Wheelersburg Cinema	8805 Ohio River Rd.	Wheelersburg 45694	W. Duerson		6
Austin Town Cinema	617 Duke Circle	Youngstown 44515			1
Uptown Theatre	38 W. Hylda Ave.	Youngstown 44507	S. Foster		1

OKLAHOMA

Name	Address	City & Zip	Owner	Seats	Screens
Rialto 1 & 2 Theatres	516 Flynn St.	Alva 73717	J. Jones		2
Pastime Theatre	201 N. High	Antlers 74523	G. Poole		1
Camelot Theatre	P.O. Box 836	Boise City 73933	J. James		1
H & S Theatre	816 Manvel	Chandler 74834	H. Wakely		1
Rook Theatre	P.O. Box 530	Cheyenne 73628	G. Kirk		1
Southland Twin Theatre	P.O. Box 427	Chickasha 73534	M. Wells	416	2
Palace Theatre	P.O. Box 427	Duncan 73534	M. Wells	525	1
Royal Theatre	109 N. Main St.	Fairview 73737	J. Adamson	150	1
*Beacon Drive-In	P.O. Box 337	Guthrie 73044	J. Marsh Powell	264	1
Ortman Theatre	Box 37	Hennessey 73742	G. Ortman		1
89er Theatre	113 N. Main	Kingfisher 73750	D. Collier		1
*Chief Drive-In Theatre	P.O. Box 427	Nennekah 73534	M. Wells	200	1
Crystal Theatre	401 W. Broadway	Okemah 74859	M. Smyth		1
McConnell Theatre	P.O. Box 40	Okmulgee 74447	McConnel Theatres	840	4
Royal Twin Theatre	119 E. Paul	Pauls Valley 73075	M. Brewer		2
*Tee Pee Drive-In	Hwy. 66 West	Sapulpa 74066	J. Malone		1
*Tahlequah Drive-In	HC 11, Box 34	Tahlequah 74464	Dennis Ukena	250	1
Lakeside Triple Theatres	P.O. Box 571	Woodward 73801	D. Terry		3

OREGON

Name	Address	City & Zip	Owner	Seats	Screens
Varsity Theatre	P.O. Box 1240	Ashland 97520		900	5
Eltrym Theatre	1809 First St.	Baker City 97814	Western Amusement		1
Aloha Theatre	18295 SW Tualatin Vly Hwy	Beaverton 97006	Family Theatre		1
*Frontier Drive-In	28569 Redwood Hwy	Cave Junction 97523	L. Musil		1
Egyptian Theatre	229 S. Broadway	Coos Bay 97420	Toni McSwain	1000	3
Fox Theatre	166 SE Mill St.	Dallas 97338	Fox Enterprises		1
*Motor Vu Drive-In	315 S.E. Fir Villa	Dallas 97338	Fox Enterprises		1
Opera House	P.O.Box 657	Elgin 97827	C. McLaughlin		1
OK Theatre	208 W. Main	Enterprise 97828	R. Ford		1

Name	Address	City & Zip	Owner	Seats	Screens
Bijou Theatre	492 E. 13th Ave.	Eugene 97401	M. Lamont		2
Mt. Hood Theatre	401 E. Powell Blvd.	Gresham 97030			1
Wilderness Theatre	P.O. Box 309	John Day 97845	D. Elliott	258	1
Pelican Cinemas 6		Klamath Falls	Redwood Theatres, Inc.		6
Lake Twin Cinema	106 N. State St.	Lake Oswego 97034			3
Alger Theatre	Box 31	Lakeview 97630	R. Alger		1
Kuhn Theatre	668 Main	Lebanon 97355	Fox Enterprises		1
Bijou Theatre	Box 354	Lincoln City 97367	J. Mace	177	1
Centre 1 & 2 Theatre	Box 449	Ontario 97914	H. Matthews	600	2
Pix Theatre	358 S. Oregon St.	Ontario 97914	J. Ross		1
*Oregon City Drive-in	18955 S. South End Rd.	Oregon City 97503			1
Cinema Tri-Plex Theatre	P.O. Box 430	Pendleton 97801	L. Spiess		3
Avalon 1 & 2 Theatre	3451 S.E. Belmont St.	Portland 97214	J. McKee		2
Cinema 21	616 NW 21st Ave.	Portland 97209			1
Cinemagic	2021 SE Hawthorne Blvd.	Portland 97214			1
Clinton Street Theatre	2522 Clinton St.	Portland 97202	A & E Productions, Inc.	240	1
Joy Theatre	11959 SW Pacific Hwy.	Portland 97223	Family Theatre		1
Laurelhurst Theatre	2735 E. Burnside St.	Portland 97214			5
Milwaukie Tri Cinema	11011 SE Main St.	Portland 97222	Family Theatre		1
Moreland Theatre	6712 SE Milwaukee Ave.	Portland 97202			1
Mt. Tabor Theatre & Pub.	4811 S.E. Hawthorne	Portland 97215	S. Philip Braun	100	1
New St. Johns Theatre	8704 N. Lombard St.	Portland 97203		1	
Roseway Theatre	7229 NE Sandy Blvd.	Portland 97213		1	
Salem Cinema	445 High S.E.	Salem 97308	L. Miles	165	1
Sherwood Oriental Theatre	125 N.W. First St.	Sherwood 97140	Rothschild/Stoller		1
Palace Theatre	P.O. Box 176	Silverton 97381	Paulson & Rasmussen	480	1
Star Cinema	350 N. Third Ave.	Stayton 97383	J. Lane	427	1
Cascade Cinema	1410 W.6th St./POB 1146	The Dalles 97058	Bruce Humphreys		2
Joy Theatre	11959 S.W. Pacific Hwy.	Tigard 97223	Kerchinsky		1
Tualatin Twin Cinema	8345 SW Nyberg Rd.	Tualatin 97062	Family Theatre		2
*Woodburn Drive-In	1970 Molalla Hwy.	Woodburn 97071	Fox Enterprises		1

PENNSYLVANIA

Name	Address	City & Zip	Owner	Seats	Screens
19th Street Theatrre	525 N. 19th St.	Allentown 18104	Civic Little Theatres	500	1
Franklin	425 Tilghman St.	Allentown 18103	A. Moffa	479	1
Pitt Theatre	P.O. Box 246	Bedford 15522	John Cessna	400	1
Berwick Theatre	108 E. Front St.	Berwick 18603	M. Trautman		1
Boyd Theatre	30 Bethlehem Plaza	Bethlehem 18018	Valley Theatres	1040	1
Capitol Twin Theatre	E. Main St.	Bloomsburg 17815.	M. Trautman		2
Cinema Center	1879 New Berwick Hwy	Bloomsburg 17815.	M. Trautman		8
State Theatre	61 N. Reading Ave.	Boyertown 19512	R. Ritner	320	1
*Malden Drive-In	380 Old National Pike	Brownsville 15417.	A. Shashura		1
Rialto Theatre	105 E. Main Street	Canton	Bradford Cty Reg.Art	175	1
*Circle Drive-In	12 Salem Avenue	Carbondale 18407	Michael Delfino		1
Ritz Twin Theatres	111 E. Market St.	Clearfield 16830	R. Knepp		2
Columbia Drive-In	338 Union Street	Columbia 17512	J. McBride		1
*Dependable Drive-In	9 Clinton Rd.	Coraopolis 15108			2
Coudersport Theatre	Main Street	Coudersport 16915	J. Rigas		1
*Harr's Drive-In	185 Logan Rd.	Dillsburg 17019.	V. Harr		1
Foxmoor Cinemas	Foxmoor S/C Box 6M	E. Stroudsburg 18301		1000	5
Gateway Cinema Center	75 S. Wyoming Avenue	Edwardsville 18704.	Cinemette	1640	6
*Peninsula Twin Drive-In	303 Peninsula Drive	Erie 16505	Cinemette		2
*Route 222 Drive-In	Rte. 222	Fleetwood 19522	Jeff Mattox	300	1
Glen Theatre	37 Manchester St.	Glen Rock 17327	F. Strausbaugh	150	1
*Sky-Vu Drive In		Graty	M. Trautman		1
The Movies	1154 Main St.	Hellertown 18055.	E. Koffler		1
Hershey Lodge Cinema	15 E. Caracas Ave.	Hershey 17033	Herco, Inc.		1
Huntingdon Cinema	717 Washington Street.	Huntingdon 16652	D. Peoples	629	5
Merlin Theatre	212 Old York Td.	Jenkintown 19046.	P. Merlin		1
Country Amusements Co.	Richland Mall	Johnston 15901			1
*Family Drive-In Theatre	Route 6 East	Kane 16735	F. Holmes		1
Strand Cinemas I & II	32 N. Whiteoak Street	Kutztown 19530	P. Angstadt		2
Campus Theatre	413 Market Street	Lewisburg 17837	J. Stiefel	650	1
Ligonier Theatre	210 W. Main Street.	Ligonier 15658	John & Betty Horrell		1
*Port Drive-In	Rd. #1	Linden 17744	J. Farruggio		2
Roxy Theatre	314 E. Main Street	Lock Haven 17745	J. Stiefel	450	1
Marietta Theatre	130 W. Market Street.	Marietta 17547.	D. Kalmbach		1
Tri State 1-2 Theatres.	1023 Pennsylvania Ave.	Matamoras 18336	M. Tonkin		2
*Tri-State Drive-In	1023 Pennsylvania Ave.	Matamoras 18336	M. Tonkin		1
*Twin Hi-Way D.I.	Moon Run Road.	McKee's Rocks 15136	Mini Cinemas Inc.		2
Eastland Theatre		McKeesport 15132.			2
Elks Theatre	Emaus & Union Sts.	Middletown 17057.	J. Crist	378	1
Colonnade Theatre	Center Street	Millersburg 17061	M. Trautman		1
Pump n Pantry Theatre	RR6, Box 6028.	Montrose 18801			1
Casino Theatre	Rte 611, Pocono Blvd.	Mt. Pocono 18344	G. Litz.	300	1
Narberth Theatre	129 N. Narberth Avenue.	Narberth 19072	Narberth Theatre Inc.		1
*Skyline Drive-In	1707 Maple Ave.	New Castle 16105	Ohio Movies		1
Ritz Theatre.	132 E. Main Street	New Holland 17557	R. Peters		3
Newtown Theatre	120 N. State Street	Newtown 18940	M. Farruggio	419	1
*Cumberland Drive-In	Route 1	Newville 17241	D. Mowery		1
Roxy Theatre	2004 Main Street	Northampton 18067	Roxy Mgt. Co.	561	1
*Shankweiler Drive-In	Rd. 1	Orefield 18069	R. Malkames		1
Posel Theatres	212 Walnut Street	Philadelphia 19106			1
Ritz Five	214 Walnut St.	Philadelphia 19106			5
Ritz at the Bourse	Fourth St.	Philadelphia 19106			5
Colonial Theatre	227 Bridge St.	Phoenixville 19460	S. LaRosa		1
*Pine Grove Drive-In.	Rte 443	Pine Grove 17963	Jeff Mattox	1100	1
Beehive Big Screen	3807 Forbes Ave.	Pittsburgh 15213	S. Zumoff.		1
Oaks Cinema	310 Allegheny River Blvd.	Pittsburgh 15139			1
Plaza 2	4765 Liberty Ave	Pittsburgh 15224	Mini Cinemas Inc.		2

Name	Address	City & Zip	Owner	Seats	Screens
Regent Square	1035 S. Braddock St.	Pittsburgh 15218			1
Rex Theatre	1602 E. Carson St.	Pittsburgh 15203			1
Holiday Entertainment	212 N. Springwood Place	Port Matelda 16870			1
Sayre Theatre	205 S. Elmer Avenue	Sayre 18840	Bradford Cty Reg.Art	175	1
Ritz Courtyard Cinema	222 Wyoming Avenue	Scranton 18503	A. Clay	586	1
Sellersville Cinema	24W Temple Avenue	Sellersville 18960	David Maclay	385	1
Victoria Theatre	46 W. Independence Street	Shamokin 17872	Jeff Mattox	2000	1
Broad Theatre	24 W. Broad St.	Souderton 18964	M. Kerver		1
Glen Theatre	RD 1 Box 1121	Spring Grove 17362	F. Strasbaugh		1
* Temple Drive-In	1670 N. Atherton St.	State College 16801	Eds Discount		1
Keystone Theatre	601 Main St.	Towanda 18848	Bradford Cty Reg.Art	500	1
Tremont Theatre	135 E. Main Street	Tremont 17891	P. Knapp		1
Majestic Theatre	29 W. Broad St.	W. Hazleton 18201	G. Litz	650	1
* Bucks County Drive-In	401 Easton Rd.	Warrington 18976			1
Watson Theatre	131 Main Street	Watsonville 17777	R. Whistler	490	1
Waynesburg Theatre	40 W. High Street	Waynesburg 15370	R. Kuger		1
Arcadia Theatre	50 Main Street	Wellsboro 16901	Wellsboro Hotel Co.	600	1
* Wysox Family Drive-In	Route 6	Wysox 18854	Douglas McInko		1

RHODE ISLAND

Name	Address	City & Zip	Owner	Seats	Screens
Park Cinemas I, II & III	848 Park Ave.	Cranston 02910	Eastern Cinemas	770	3
Pier Cinema 1 & 2 Theatre	Pier Village Marketplace	Narragansett 02882	Piyush Patel	430	2
Jane Pickens Theatre	49 Touro Road	Newport 02840	J. Jarvis		1
SSC Opera Hse Cinemas	19 Touro Street	Newport 02840	Eastern Cinemas		3
* Rustic Drive-In	146 Eddie Dowling Hwy.	No. Smithfield 02876	C.B.B. Enterprises	500	3
Avon Cinema Theatre	260 Thayer Street	Providence 02906	E. Dulgarian		1
Cable Car Cinema	204 S. Main Street	Providence 02906	R. Bilodeau		1
Castle Inc.	1039 Chalkstone Avenue	Providence 02908	A. Bilodeau		3
Meadowbrook Cinema	2452 Warwick Avenue	Warwick 02889	B. Vanasse		3

SOUTH CAROLINA

Name	Address	City & Zip	Owner	Seats	Screens
Marquis Theatres Inc.	P.O. Box 3561	Anderson 29624			1
Plaza 8 Theatres	U.S. Hwy. 21 & 170	Beaufort 29902	P. Trask		5
Little Theatre	506 Dekalb Street	Camden 29020	G. Coan		1
Midland Theatres, Inc.	P.O. Box 66	Camden 29020	G. Coan		1
South Windmere Cinema	96 Folly Rd.	Charleston 29407		390	2
Dutch Square Theatre	P.O.Box 79	Columbia 29202	Paul Roth		3
Fuller Theatre Company	P.O.Box 210365	Columbia 29221	Jack Fuller		1
Easley Cinemas 6	P.O. Box 1548	Easley 29640	R.E.I. Cinemas	1368	6
Island Theatre	Coligny Plaza	Hilton Head Island 29928	W. Harn		1
Main Street Cinemas	3000 Main Street	Hilton Head Island 29926	W. Harn		3
Crown Twin Theatre	Westgate Shopping Center	Lancaster 29720	D. Watson		2
Pastime Pavillion Cinemas	929 N. Lake Dr.	Lexington 29072	Consolidated Theatres		6
Seneca Cinemas 6	P.O.Box 557	Seneca 29679	R.E.I. Cinemas	1318	6

SOUTH DAKOTA

Name	Address	City & Zip	Owner	Seats	Screens
Strand Theatre	703 Main, P.O.Box 129	Britton 57430	Thomas Farber	300	1
Showcase Cinema 1-2-3	P.O. Box 77	Brookings 57006	State Theatres		3
Dakota Cinema	Box 101	Bryant 57221	L. Klungseth	195	1
State Theatre	108 S. Main	Chamberlain 57325	J. Buche	215	1
Dells Theatre	511 4th Street	Dell Rapids 57022	J. King	400	1
Lyric Theatre	805 G Avenue	Eureka 57437	D. Lapka	297	1
Crystal Theatre	402 West Pipestone Ave.	Flandreau 57028			1
Twin State Theatre	P.O. Box 930	Huron 57350			1
West Twin 1-2 Theatres	Hwy 34	Madison 57042	Prostrollo		2
Inland Theatre	Box 608	Martin 57551	P. Nelson		1
Mill Theatres 1-2-3	318 S. Main Street	Milbank 57252	N. Bagaus	336	3
Mac Theatre	P.O.Box 217	Mobridge 57601	Ron Maier	550	1
* Pheasant Drive-In	Box 217	Mobridge 57601	Ron Maier		1
State 1-2-3	123 W. Capitol Ave.	Pierre 57501	State Theatres		3
Elks Theatre	P.O. Box 3327	Rapid City 57709	Doug Andrews	605	1
Cinema Theatre	P.O. Box 37, 718 Main St.	Redfield 57469	Tom & Letha Gallup	376	1
* Pheasant City Drive-In	P.O.Box 37	Redfield 57469	Tom & Letha Gallup	200	1
Flicka Theatres	P.O. Box 280	Spearfish 57783	Steele Theatres		1
* Winner Drive-In	P.O. Box 562	Winner 57580	H. Fast		1

TENNESSEE

Name	Address	City & Zip	Owner	Seats	Screens
American Cinema Twin	Whiteway Shopping Center	Athens 37303	P. Goddard		2
* Midway Drive-In	2133 Highway 30 E	Athens 37303	T. Epps		1
Hollywood Cinema 20	6711 Stage Rd.	Bartlett 38135	Ajay Inc.		20
Cinema 1 & 2 Theatre	Box 3206	Cleveland 37311	C. Benton		2
Shady Brook Cinema	P.O. Box 419	Columbia 38402	H. Vinson		6
* Broadway Drive-In	3020 Highway 70 W	Dickson 37055	Armstrong		1
* Dunlap Drive-In	Box 178	Dunlap 37327	L. Boston		1
Bonnie Kate Theatre	115 S. Sycamore St.	Elizabethton 37643	L. Policky	390	2
* Stateline Drive-In	Route 8 Box 598	Elizabethton 37643	Andrew Wetzel II		1
Cinema 1 & 2	Box 100	Erwin 37650	J. Hendren	390	2
Lincoln Twin Theatres	Box 604	Fayetteville 37334	C. Freehauf	541	2
* Sumner Drive-In	1401 Nashville Pike	Gallatin 37066	H. Smith		1
Halls Cinema 7	3800 Neal Road	Knoxville 37918	John D. Wallace		1
Tennessee Theatre	604 S. Gay Street	Knoxville 37902	Dick Bdcstg. Co.	1500	1
Terrace Twin Theatres	315 Mohican Drive	Knoxville 37901	J. Simpson	400	2
Cumberland Amusement	P.O. Box 111	McMinnville 37110			1
Cinema Showcase 12	5117 Old Summer Road	Memphis 38122	Ajay Inc.	2400	12
Campus Twin Theatre	726 S. Tennessee Blvd.	Murfreesboro 37130	H. Christian		1
* Woodzo Drive-In	Box 87	Newport 37821	H. Smith		1
Paris Theatres	P.O. Box 42	Paris 38242	Loren & Larry Smith	434	2

Name	Address	City & Zip	Owner	Seats	Screens
Southgate Cinemas	411 Florence Road	Savannah 38372	Gary Adams		3
Reel Theatres Corporation	P.O.Box 4218	Sevierville 37862	W. Holt		7
Capri Twin Theatre	201 Depot St.	Shelbyville 37160			2
Fair Theatre & Lobby Video	112 E. Market Street	Somerville 38608	N. Fair	365	1
* Sparta Drive-In	Box 187	Sparta 38583	Mid. Tenn. Amusements.		1
Flexer Theatres, Inc.	P.O. Box 330	Waverly 37185			1
* Valley Drive-In	P.O. Box 330	Waverly 37185	N. Flexer		1
* Cross Roads Drive-In	R.F.D. 2	Whitwell 37397	R. Reeves		1
* Family Drive-In	Box 523	Winchester 37398	Cumberland Theatres		1

TEXAS

Name	Address	City & Zip	Owner	Seats	Screens
Paramount Theatre	352 Cypress Street	Abilene 79601	Paramount Comm.		1
* Park Drive-In	P.O. Box 3654	Abilene 79601	J. Mitchell		1
* Buckhorn Drive-In	Box 1170	Alice 78332	Noret Theas.		1
Rangra Theatres	109 E. Holland	Alpine 79830	A. Rangra	375	2
Cinema IV Theatres	Athens Center	Athens 75751	Mitchell Theatres		4
Gateway Cinema	3684 College Dr.	Beaumont 77701	Foothills Entertainment	1100	2
Parkdale Cinema	4455 Dowlen Rd.	Beaumont 77706	Foothills Entertainment	1200	3
Plaza Theatre	119 N. Buffalo	Canton 75103	T. Honea		1
Carthage Twin Cinema	1120 W. Panola	Carthage 75633	D. Bates.		2
Film Society TX A & M	Box J-1	College Station 77844	Texas A&M Univ.	3150	2
Marshall Cinema 3	P.O. Box P	Daingerfield 75638	Walter Bass	600	3
Morris Twin Cinema	P.O. Box P	Daingerfield 75638	Walter Bass	460	2
Mission Theatre	409 Denrock	Dalhart 79022	D. Gilbert	450	1
* Astro 3 Drive-In	3141 Walton Walker	Dallas 75211	Tri-State Theatres		3
Casa Linda 4 Theatres	150 Casa Linda Plaza	Dallas 75218	Peterson Theatres	937	4
Cinema 1 & 2	7622 Queensferry	Dallas 75248	El Rey, Inc.		1
Cinemore 7	6060 N. Central Expwy	Dallas 75206	GMCI		7
Evelyn Twin Theatre	P.O. Box 476	Dumas 79029	R. Nies		2
Eagle Pass Cinema 3	455 Bibb Street	Eagle Pass 78852	C. Brill		3
Majestic Theatre	P.O. Box 705	Eastland 76448	Eastland Fine Arts	825	1
* Ascarate Drive-In	6701 Delta Dr.	El Paso 79905	D. Pierce.		1
Pioneer Theatre	P.O.Box 334	Falfurrias 78355	G. Vela.		1
* Mansfield 1 & 2 Drive-In	2935 E. Seminary Dr.	Fort Worth 76119	J. Mitchell		2
Seventh Street Theatre	3128 W. Seventh Street.	Fort Worth 76107	B.Milligan		1
Ganado Theatre	Rt. 1 Box 32	Ganado 77962	A. Svoboda	200	1
Walnut Twin Theatre	3310 W. Walnut	Garland 75042	D. Christenson	514	2
National Theatre	526 Oak	Graham 76450	D. Scott		2
* Brazos Drive-In	W. Pearl	Granbury 76048	Johnson		1
Texan Theatre, Inc.	110 South Bell Street	Hamilton 76531	L. Little, P. & M. Jordan	300	1
Showplace 3		Harker Heights	John Treadwell	650	3
Briargrove III Theatres	6100 Westheimer	Houston 77057	Dollar Cinema		1
Garden Oaks	3732 N. Shepherd Drive	Houston 77018	Zarzana Theatres		1
Cinema 1-2-3 Theatres	Univ. Hts. Shopping Ctr.	Huntsville 77340	G. Palmer		3
Chateau 3 Theatre	P.O. Box 150517	Irving 75017	Meagher	1200	3
Texan Theatre	648 E. Main St.	Junction 76849	J. Evans		1
4 Star Cinema	1607 Hiway 2595	Kilgore 75602	Foothills Entertainment		1
Cinema 4	2100 SW S.Young Dr.	Killeen 76543	John Treadwell	1109	4
Northside Cinema	Rancier	Killeen 76543	John Treadwell	2440	10
Cinema I & II Theatres	310 This Way	Lake Jackson 77566	J. Huebel	600	2
Lake I & II Theatres	3 Circle Way	Lake Jackson 77566	J. Huebel	850	2
Fain Theatre	Box 1171	Livingston 77351	P. O'Bryan		1
Texan Theatre	P.O. Box 251	Livingston 77351	T. White		1
Caprock Entertainment	2726 82nd Street	Lubbock 79423			1
Marble Theatre	218 Main St.	Marble Falls 78654	G. Spitzer		1
Marshall Twin Cinema	1901 E. Travis	Marshall 75670	Walter Bass		2
Cinemore 4	4400 Midland Dr.	Midland 79707			1
South Side Theatre	P.O. Box 612	Mt. Pleasant 75455			1
Cinema 1 & 2 Theatre	3330 W. Bowling Lane	Orange 77636			2
Plestex Theatre	P.O. Box 24	Pleasanton 78064	G. Talley		3
Twin Dolphin Cinemas	P.O. Box 989	Port Lavaca 77979	D. Walraven	460	2
Cinema 35 Theatre	P.O. Box 634	Rockport 78382	Dinger		1
Roma Theatre	P.O. Box 131	Roma 78584	E. Ramirez		1
Palace Twin Theatre	314 S. Austin Street	Seguin 78155	Mrs.G.Roscoe		2
Island Cinema	P.O. Box 3530	So. Padre Island 78597	Deborah Marcum		1
Lyric Theatre	111 Main	Spearman 79081	Alton Ellsworth	375	1
Cinema Four	P.O. Box 8246	The Woodlands 77387	Carlton H.Mann	1160	4
Plaza Twin Theatre	1717 Cumberland	Vernon 76384	S. Barton	848	2
Cole Theatre	608 Perth	Victoria 77904			1
Buffalo Creek 4 Theatre	210 W. Franklin	Waxahachie 75165	Jerry Camp	626	4
Weatherford Theatres	111 College St.	Weatherford 76086	A.B. Cinema		4
Majestic Theatre	136 W.N.Commerce	Wills Point 75169	K.Lybrand		1

UTAH

Name	Address	City & Zip	Owner	Seats	Screens
Towne Cinemas 1 & 2	120 W. Main St.	American Fork 84003	R. Vance		2
Wayne Theatre	Box 205	Bicknell 84715	S. Brinkerhoff	315	1
Gateway Cinemas 8	206 South 625 West	Bountiful 84010	R. Miller	1400	8
Queen Theatre	460 W. 500 South	Bountiful 84010	R. Miller	500	1
Capitol Theatre I & II	53 S. Main St.	Brigham City 84302	R. Walker		2
Cedar Cinemas	P.O. Box 366	Cedar City 84721			1
T & T Twin Theatre	420 E. Topaz Blvd.	Delta 84624	C. Tolbert		2
Towne Theatre	21 N. Main.	Ephraim 84627	R. Anderson	414	1
Avon Theatre	94 S. Main St.	Heber 84032	S. Zimmerman		1
Kanab Theatre	29 W. Center	Kanab 84741	P. Roundy		1
Cinemas 5	4140 West 5415 South.	Kearns 84118	R. Miller	800	5
Utah Theatre	18 W. Center St.	Logan 84321	K. Hansen		1
Slickrock Cinemas 3	580 Kane Creek Blvd.	Moab 84532	J. Buxman	500	3
The Movies	P.O. Box 489	Monticello 84535	G. Young		1
* Basin Drive-In Theatre	680 N. State	Mt. Pleasant 84647	R. Anderson	200	1

Name	Address	City & Zip	Owner	Seats	Screens
Cinedome North Theatre	1481 W. Riverdale Rd.	Ogden 84403	D. Tulles		1
Country Club Theatre	3930 Washington Blvd.	Ogden 84403	J. Cuculich		1
*Motor Vu Drive-In	5368 So. 1050 West	Ogden 84403	Ritz Mgt. Corp.	250	1
*North Star Drive-In	2131 N. Highway 89	Ogden 84404	W. Webb		2
Scera Theatre	745 S. State St.	Orem 84057	Scera Corp.		1
*Timpanagos Drive-In	614 N. 1200 W.	Orem 84057	W. Bunting		1
Huish Theatre	98 W. Utah Ave.	Payson 84651	P. Mower		1
Walker Cinemas 4	1776 S. Highway 89	Perry 84302	R. Walker		4
Varsity Theatre	Rm. 218 Bldg. ELWC	Provo 84602	Brigham Young Univ.	415	1
Roosevelt Twin Theatre	P.O. Box 2139	Roosevelt 84066	J. Chasel		2
Avalon Theatre	3605 S. State	Salt Lake City 84115	A. Proctor	500	1
Olympus Starship	3900 S. Wasatch Blvd.	Salt Lake City 84121	R. Miller	750	2
Sandy Starship	9400 S. 800 East	Salt Lake City 84070	R. Miller	1150	5
*Valley View Drive-In	3646 View Crest Crcl.	Salt Lake City 84117	W. Webb	700	1
Main Family Theatre	141 N. Main	Smithfield 84335	K. Hansen		1
Main Street Movie	165 North Main Street	Spanish Fork 84660	D. Dunn	312	1
*Art City Drive-In	720 North Main	Springfield 84663	W. Webb		1
*Pioneer Twin Drive-In	97 S. 1300 E.	Springfield 84663	M. Cox		2
Ritz Theatre	107 N. Main St.	Tooele 84074	Ritz Mgt. Corp.	750	2
*Sunset Drive-In	Box 910	Vernal 84078	Shiner Bros.		1
Sunset Theatre	P.O. Box 910	Vernal 84078	Shiner Bros.		1
Tri Cinema Theatre	P.O. Box 910	Vernal 84078	Shiner Bros.		3
*Valley Vu Drive-In	3560 S. 4800 West	West Valley City 84120	W. Webb		1

VERMONT

Cinema 1-2-3 Theatre	Rt. 67 A	Bennington 05201	G. Couture		2
*Randall Drive-In	Rte 12	Bethel 05032	Osterberg	180	1
Nickelodeon 6 Plex	222 College St.	Burlington 05401	J. Tranum		6
*Fairlee Drive-In	Rte 5, Box 31	Fairlee 05045	R. Herb	350	1
Bijou Theatre	General Delivery	Lake Elmore 05657	J. McKinley		1
Capitol Theatre	93 State St.	Montpelier 05602	F. Bashara		5
Savoy Theatre	26 Main St.	Montpelier 05602	R. Winston		1
Elray Theatre	26 Main St.	Springfield 05156	R. Ellis	300	2
Welden Theatre 3	17 Prospect St.	St. Albans 05478	P. Gamache	500	3
Catamount Arts Center	60 Eastern Ave.	St. Johnsbury 05819		100	1
Star Theatre	18 Eastern Ave.	St. Johnsbury 05819	Recreation Inc.		1
Stowe Cinema 3-plex	Box 1287	Stowe 05672	V. Buonano	355	3

VIRGINIA

Fox Chase Cinema	4621 Duke St.	Alexandria 22304	Rubin/Porykes	620	3
Arlington Cinema	2903 Columbia Pike	Arlington 22204			1
Idle Hour Theatre	P.O. Box 245	Belle Haven 23306	R. Pase	400	1
*Hull's Drive-In Theatre	1407 Cedar Ave.	Buena Vista 24416	S. Hull		1
Palace Theatre	303 Mason Ave.	Cape Charles 23310	T. Savage		1
Jefferson Theatre	110 E. Main St.	Charlottesville 22902	Hawes C. Spencer		2
Movies Palace	110 E. Main St.	Charlottesville 22901	Hawes C. Spencer	550	2
Vinegar Hill Theatre	Box 642/ 220 W. Market St.	Charlottesville 22902	A. Porotti	220	1
Lee Cinema	1215 E. Lee Highway	Chillhowie 24319	J. Maxey		2
Coeburn Theatres, Inc.	P.O. Box 860	Coeburn 24230			1
Ballou Park 4 Theatre	150 Tunstall Rd.	Danville 24546	William Headley		4
University Mall Theatres	10659 Braddock Rd.	Fairfax 22032	M. O'Meara		3
*Fork Union Drive-In	Route 612	Fork Union 23055	F. White		1
Royal Theatres	117 East Main St.	Front Royal 22630	Royal Cinemas		1
Hillside Cinema #1-2	Box 449 Rt. 14	Gloucester 23061	Jennings/Mullins		2
Grundy Comm.Center	P.O. Box 2688	Grundy 24614	Town of Grundy	409	1
Henrico Theatre	305 E. Nine Mile Rd.	Highland Springs 23075	C. Horne		1
Page Theatre	33 E. Main St.	Luray 22825	J. Spencer		2
Martinsville Theatre	215 Church Street	Martinsville 24112	Brown's Inc.		2
Movie Town, Inc.	P.O. Box 2067, SR 825	Martinsville 24113	Henry C. Wall, Sr.		2
Mountain Entertainment	P.O. Box 1270	Norton 24273			1
Roseland Theatre	48 Market St./P.O. 178	Onancock 23417	Onancock Theatre Corp.	349	1
Century Theatres of VA	P.O. Box 6526	Portsmouth 23703	F. Schoenfeld		1
Commmodore Theatre	421 High St.	Portsmouth 23704	F. Schoenfeld	538	1
*Central Drive-In Theatre	Blackwood	Pound 24279	J. Kiser		1
Radford Theatre	1043 Norwood St.	Radford 24141	F. Kirk	509	1
Richland Mall Twin Theatres	P.O. Box 1440	Richlands 24641	K. Davis		2
Hippodrome Theatre	528 N. Second St.	Richmond 23219	J. Stalling		1
*Plaza Drive-In Theatre	4730 N. Southside Plaza	Richmond 23224	Brock A.Summs		1
Cinema 1 & 2 Inc.	Rt 2, Box 336, Hwy 58 E.	South Boston 24592	M. Day	450	2
Daw Theatre	P.O. Box 1025	Tappahannock 22560	W. Cleaton	396	1
Tazewell Cinema II, Inc.	P.O. Box 60	Tazewell 24651	D. Dunford		3
Cinema Cafe	758 Independence Blvd.	Virginia Beach 23455			1
Williamsburg Theatre	424 Duke of Gloucester St.	Williamsburg 23185	Col. Williamsburg Fdn.	538	1
Community Theatre	P.O.Box 268	Woodstock 22664	Dalke's Theatres Inc.	610	3
*Family Drive-In	P.O.Box 268	Woodstock 22664	Dalke's Theatres, Inc.	490	2
Davidson Theatres, Inc.	P.O. Boc 559	Wytheville 24382	R. Herring		3

WASHINGTON

I.C.U. Theatres	3813 168th St. NE	Arlington 98223	A Theatre Near You, Inc.		1
Olympic Theatre	107 N. Olympic Ave.	Arlington 98223	Norma Pappas	300	1
*White Elephant Drive-In 1	502 State St.	Centralia 98531	W. Slusher		2
*Auto View Drive-In	112 North Main St.	Colville 99114	Jest Theatres		1
Sunset Theatre	P.O. Box 827	Connell 99326	Dirk & Jeri Reinauer	372	1
Village Cinema	515 River Dr.	Coulee Dam 99116	K. Waltermyer, L. Crabtree	230	1
Edmonds Theatre	415 Main St.	Edmonds 98020	Aeries II, Inc.	300	1
Roxy Theatre	P.O. Box 214	Newport 99156	Gladys Bishop		1
*Blue Fox Dri-Vin	1403 Monroe Landing Rd.	Oak Harbor 98277	D. Bratt		1
Omak Theatre	Box W	Omak 98841	L. Lassila		1

Name	Address	City & Zip	Owner	Seats	Screens
Seeley Theatre	P.O. Box 887	Pomeroy 99347	Lucck & Compt.		1
Plaza Twin Theatre	820 Bay St.	Port Orchard 98366	P.O. Improvement Corp.	325	2
* Rodeo Triplex Drive-In	7369 State Hwy. 3 S. W.	Port Orchard 98366	Jack & Cindy Ondracek		3
Rose Theatre	235 Taylor Street	Port Townsend 98368	Rocky Friedman	241	2
* Wheel In Motor Movie	210 Theatre Rd.	Port Townsend 98368	R. Wiley	150	1
* Big Bear Drive-In	P.O. Box 25	Poulsbo 98370	J. Lilquist		1
Liberty Theatre	116 W. Main St.	Puyallup 98371			1
Ritz Theatre	107 E. Main St.	Ritzville 99169	D. Gesche		1
Roslyn Theatre	101 Dakota St.	Roslyn 98941	J. Donaldson	91	1
Grand Illusion Cinema	1403 N.E. 50th St.	Seattle 98105			1
Market Theatre	1428 Post Alley	Seattle 98101	A. Broroder		1
Franklin Plaza Theatre	517 W. Franklin St.	Shelton 98584	R. Nye	445	2
Blue Mouse Theatre	2611 N. Proctor	Tacoma 98407	Blue Mouse Assoc.	325	1
Liberty Theatre Inc.	857 142 St. So.	Tacoma 98444	W. Dunwoody		1
Cascade Park Cinemas	S.E. 411 Chkalov Dr.	Vancouver 98684	J. Thrift		4
* Liberty Theatre Drive-In	P.O.Box 2506	Wenatchee 98807	Sun Basin		2
Liberty Cinemas	P.O.Box 2506	Wentachee 98807	Sun Basin	3692	13
* Country Drive-In	8301 Tieton Drive	Yakima 98908	J. Anderson	650	2
* Fruitvale Drive-In Triple	P.O. Box 1551	Yakima 98901	W .Davidson		3

WEST VIRGINIA

Name	Address	City & Zip	Owner	Seats	Screens
* Pipe Stem Drive-In		Athens 25873	R. Warden		1
Star Theatre	Rt. 3, Box 191	Berkeley Springs 25411	Mozier/Soronen	325	1
Kanawha Theatre	601 57th St. NE.	Charleston 25304	D. Corder		1
* Craigsville Drive-In		Craigsville 26205	J. Hanna	225	1
Seneca Showcase 1 & 2	Rt. 219 Greenbriar Mall	Lewisburg 24901	C. McCall		2
Capitol Theatre	401 Stratton St.	Logan 25601	A. Defobio		1
Berkley Plaza Seven	Berkeley Place Shpng. Ctr .	Martinsburg 24134	E. Costolo, Jr.		7
Strand Theatre	Fifth & Jefferson St.	Moundsville 26041	Ramser		1
Valley Cinema 3	249 N. State Rte 2	New Martinsville 26155	Brent Pauley	627	3
Jungle Drive-In	RR 1	Parkersburg 26101	C. Westbrook		1
Cherry River Cinema	Cherry River Shopping Pl.	Richwood 26261	J. Chapman		1
Shepherdstown Opera Hse	131 W. German St.	Shepherdstown 25443	Rusty Berry	150	1
Robey Theatre	318 Main St.	Spencer 25276	M. Burch	400	1
* Valley Drive-In	P.O. Box 188	St. Albans 25177	W.Erwin		1
Cinderella Theatre	P.O. Box 220	Williamson 25661	S.Kapourales		1

WISCONSIN

Name	Address	City & Zip	Owner	Seats	Screens
* 1329 Drive-In	P.O. Box 86	Abbotsford 54405	D.& L.Hodd	250	1
Abby Theatre	P.O. Box 86	Abbotsford 54405	D.& L.Hodd	386	1
Adams Theatre	157 S. Main Street	Adams 53910	A. Davidson		1
Towne Movie House	524 2nd St.	Algoma 54201	Dean Paulik	150	1
Amery Theatre	228 N. Keller Avenue	Amery 54001	M. Schanon	266	1
Palace Theatre	825 Fifth Avenue	Antigo 54409	Suick Theatre Co.		3
Bay Theatre	420 Main Street	Ashland 54806	A. Bergman		1
Al Ringling Theatre	136 Fourth Avenue	Baraboo 53913	Al Ringling Theatre Inc.	800	1
Blaine Theatre	102 East Oak	Boscobel 53805	J. Thiele	365	1
Ruby Isle Theatre	2205 N. Calhoun Road	Brookfield 53005		825	6
Value Cinema	20075 Water Tower Blvd.	Brookfield			1
West Point Cinemas	20241 W. Bluemound Road	Brookfield 53045			1
Movies Northridge	7700 W. Brown Deer Road	Brown Deer 53223			1
Plaza Theatre	448 Milwaukee Avenue	Burlington 53105	Stephen & Dana Lind		1
Norton Cinema 1 Theatre	26 N. Madison Street	Chilton 53014	J. Norton	200	1
Falls Cinema & Video	7 East Spring Street	Chippewa Falls 54729			1
Cornell Theatre	Box 325	Cornell 54732	J. Harvatine		1
Isle Theatre	1345 2nd Ave.	Cumberland 54829	D. Long	230	2
De Pere Theatre	417 George	De Pere 54115	N. LeGros		1
Dodge Theatre	205 N. Iowa Street	Dodgeville 53533	J.B labaum	300	1
Conway Theatres	218 E. Wall Street	Eagle River 54521	S.Conway		3
Cameo Twin	315 Barstow	Eau Claire	Gene Grengs		2
* Gemini Drive-In Theatre	1830 Brackett Ave.	Eau Claire 54701	Gene Grengs		1
London Square 6	3109 Mall Drive	Eau Claire	Gene Grengs		6
Elroy Theatre	122 Main Street	Elroy 53929			1
Forest Mall Cinemas	755 W. Johnson	Fond du Lac 54935			1
Retlaw Theatre	23 S. Main Street	Fond du Lac 54935			1
Brown Port Theatre	8617 N.Prt.	Fox Point 53217			1
* 41 Twin Outdoor Theatre	7701 S. 27th St.	Franklin 53131			2
West Pitcher Show	405 W. Walnut St.	Green Bay 54303	J. Routhieaux		1
Hartford Theatre	2941 Hwy 83 South	Hartford 53027	Gregory Ehlenbach		1
Park Theatre, Inc.	116 East First St.	Hayward 54843	D. Williamson		4
Southside Cinema 4	1920 Crestview Drive	Hudson 54016			3
Mall Cinemas	2500 Milton Ave.	Janesville 53545	B. Porchetta		1
Park Place Cinemas	319 Milwaukee Street	Janesville 53545			7
Rock Theatres	1620 Newport Ave.	Janesville 53547	B. Porchetta		5
* Hiway 18 Drive-In	Hwy 18	Jefferson 53549	Mescop Inc.		1
Fort Theatre	W5421 Riverhill Drive	Johnson Creek 53038	Richard A. Clifton		1
Cinema 1-5	7310 57th Avenue	Kenosha 53140			5
* Keno Family Drive-In	9102 Sheridan Rd.	Kenosha 53143	Minnie Spheeris	200	1
Market Square Theatres	8600 Sheridan Rd.	Kenosha 53719	Square Duck Corp	692	4
Hollywood Theatre	123 5th Avenue South	La Crosse 54601			1
Rivoli Theatre, Inc.	123 North 4th Street	LaCrosse 54602			1
* Sparta Hwy 16 Drive In	1507 Nakamis Avenue	LaCrosse 54603	G. Mueller		1
Miner Theatre	116 E. Miner Avenue	Ladysmith 54848	T. Lovely		1
Grantland Theater	218 S. Madison	Lancaster 53813	Star Cinemas	350	2
East Towne Cinemas	96 East Towne Mall	Madison 53704			1
Barrymore Theatre	2090 Atwood	Madison 53704	Schenks-Atwood Rev. Corp	1468	1
Fredric March /WI Un.Thtr.	800 Langdon Street	Madison 53706	Univ. of WI		1
Hilldale Theatre	702 N. Midvale Blvd.	Madison 53705	Madison 20th Theatres	747	2
Majestic Theatre	115 King St.	Madison 53703	Madison 20th Theatres		1

Name	Address	City & Zip	Owner	Seats	Screens
Orpheum Theatre	216 State St.	Madison 53705	Madison 20th Theatres	2050	2
Rogers Cinema	P.O. Box 280	Marshfield 54449			1
Cinema North I & II	910 W. Broadway	Medford 54451	Cinema North Ltd.		2
Cinema North	203 N. Lake Ave.	Medford 54555	Cinema North Ltd.		1
* Starlite Outdoor Theatre	P.O.Box 256	Menomonee Falls 53051			1
State Theatre	639 Broadway	Menomonie 54751			4
North Shore Cinemas	11700 N. Port Washington	Mequon 53092			6
Cosmo Theatre	813 E. Main Street	Merrill 54452	O. Settele	500	2
Avalon Theatre	2473 S. Kinnickinnic	Milwaukee 53207	E. Levin	1300	1
Budget Cinemas-North	7222 W. Good Hope	Milwaukee 53203	B.C., Inc.		2
Budget Cinemas South	4475 S. 108th	Milwaukee 53228	B.C., Inc.		7
Loomis Road Cinemas	3555 South 27th Street	Milwaukee 53221			1
Mill Road Theatres	6530 North 76th Street	Milwaukee 53223			1
Modjeska Theatre	1134 W. Mitchell Street	Milwaukee 53204	S. Johnson	1000	2
Movies 10	Southgate Mall	Milwaukee 53215			1
* Skyway Drive-In	4901 S. Howell Ave.	Milwaukee 53207	Mescop Inc.		1
Spring Mall Cinemas	4200 South 76th Street	Milwaukee 53220			1
Times Cinema	5905 W. Vliet St.	Milwaukee 53208	E. Levin	440	1
Villa Theatre	3610 W. Villard Avenue	Milwaukee 53209			1
South Towne Cinemas	2305 W. Broadway	Monona 53713			1
* Sky Vue Drive-In	P.O. Box 297	Monroe 53566	R. Goetz		1
Montello Theatre	30 E. Montello St.	Montello 53949	Paul & Donna Sveum		1
Cedar Creek Cinemas	10101 Market Street	Mosinee 54455			1
Parkland Twin Theatre	S74 W17000 Janesville Rd.	Muskego 53150	Cathy Zmudzinski	350	2
Grand Theatre	319 N. Water Street	New London 54961			1
South Shore Cinemas	7261 South 13th Street	Oak Creek 53154			1
Value Cinema	6912 South 27th Street	Oak Creek 53154	Nancy Berchem		1
Capitol Cinemas 12	Hwy 16 & J	Pewaukee	Wildwood Cinema		12
Cinema North 1 & 2	P.O.Box 7	Phillips 54555	D. Deda		2
Avalon Theatre	95 E. Main St.	Platteville 53818	Jim & Patti Blabaum		1
Portage Theatre	P.O. Box 426	Portage 53901	J. McWilliams		1
Star Cinema	P.O. Box 317	Prairie du Chien 53821	A.G.T.Ent/Star Theatres	750	6
Bonham Theatre & Video	564 Water St.	Prairie du Sac 53578	S. Edelstein		3
Badger Theatre	548 Vine St.	Reedsburg 53959	Elmer V. Kreuger	392	1
Star Cinema	P.O.Box 164	Reedsburg 53959	Star Cinemas	750	6
State 1-4 Cinemas	110 North Brown	Rhinelander 54501	Mike Rouman		4
Center Cinema Theatre	192 S. Central Ave.	Richland Center 53581	William & Lisa Muth		2
Falls Theatre	P.O.Box 26	River Falls 54022	S. McCulloch		1
Soo Theatres	534 Ashmun	Sault Ste. Marie 49783	J. Haller & S. Harrington	600	2
Shawano Cinema 1 & 2	1494 W. Green Bay Street	Shawano 54166			2
* Skyway Drive In	9990 Highway 57	Sister Bay 54234			1
K-M Cinemas	730 E. Washington Street	Slinger 53086			1
* Hiway 61 Drive-In		Sparta 54656		750	6
Palace Theatre	238 Walnut Street	Spooner 54801	G. Clayton		1
Cinema Cafe	255 E. Main Street	Stoughton 53589	D. Lange		1
Donna Theatre	P.O. Box 289	Sturgeon Bay 54235	G. Goebel		2
Norton Bargain Cinema	17 W. Wisconsin Ave.	Tomahawk 54487	J. Norton	300	1
Town Cinemas	302 East Main Street	Watertown 53094			1
Rosa Theatre	218 S.Main St.	Waupaca 54981	O. Settele	300	2
Tosa Theatre	6825 W. North Avenue	Wauwatosa 53213			1
Southtown Cinemas 6	2867 South 108th Street	West Allis 53227			6
Chalet Cinema	P.O. Box 403	Wisconsin Dells 53965			1
* Dells Drive-In	P.O. Box 383	Wisconsin Dells 53965	D. Legros	200	1
Lakeland Cinemas	Hwy. 51	Woodruff 54568	Conway Theatre	500	3

WYOMING

Name	Address	City & Zip	Owner	Seats	Screens
Flick Theatre	Box 314	Big Piney 83113	C. Smith		1
Big Horn Cinemas	P.O.Box 365	Cody 82414			1
Cody Theatre	1251 Sheridan Ave.	Cody 82414	R. Beaverson & G. Greck		1
Mesa Theatres	P.O. Box 144	Douglas 82633	R. Sack		1
Valley Cinemas 4	P.O.Box 1442	Evanston 82931	D. Coleman		4
Sky Hi Theatres		Gillette 82716	L. Steele		2
Jackson Hole Cinema	P.O.Box 3681	Jackson 83001	F. Lundy	1192	6
Gabel Theatres	855 S. 9th Street	Lander 82520	Darrell Gabel		1
* Drive-In	P.O. Box 815	Lovell 82431	L. Bischoff		1
Hyart Theatre	P.O. Box 815	Lovell 82431	H. Bischoff		1
* Vali Drive-In	1070 Road 9	Powell 82435	A. Mercer	190	1
Vali Twin Cinema Theatre	204 N. Bent	Powell 82435	A. Mercer	596	2
Movies 3	1720 Edinburgh	Rawlins 82301	R. Pryde		3
Reel Theatre		Rock Springs 82901	K. Hiatt		1
Centennial Twin Theatres	36 E. Alger Street	Sheridan 82801	R. Campbell		2
* Skyline Drive-In	Box C	Sheridan 82801	R. Campbell		1
Ritz Theatre	309 Arapahoe	Thermopolis 82443	D. Kraske	192	1
Wyoming Theatre II	126 E. 20th Avenue	Torrington 82240	R. Heyl	426	2
Cinema West Theatre	Box 576	Wheatland 82201	S. Reichhardt		1

MAJOR THEATRES WITHIN MAJOR NORTH AMERICAN MARKETS

The following chart presents by key metropolitan cities circuit theatres and independent theatres arranged is descending order of market size, alphabetically by town and within each town alphabetically by circuit name and theatre name. Market areas are those covered by key city television and radio stations, cable markets and to some extent, newspapers. Independent theatres in selected markets have been chosen to represent those theatres which premiere independent and foreign releases.

New York

Ackerman Theatres

East Side Playhouse	New York	NY
86th St. East Twin	New York	NY
57th St. Playhouse	New York	NY
68th St. East Playhouse	New York	NY
Village East	New York	NY
Hylan Plaza 5-Plex	Staten Island	NY
Staten Island 10-Plex	Staten Island	NY
Ryeridge Twin	Rye	NY
Fine Arts	Westchester	NY
Westchester Malls Cinema	Westchester	NY
Cinema 100 Twin	White Plains	NY

American Multi Cinema

Deptford 8	Deptford	NJ
Headquarters 10	Morristown	NJ
Rockaway 12	Rockaway	NJ
Maple Ridge 8	Amherst	NY

Cineplex

Royal Twin	Bloomfield	NJ
Cranford Twin	Cranford	NJ
Newport Centre 11	Jersey City	NJ
Menlo Park 12	Menlo Park	NJ
Milburn Twin	Milburn	NJ
Paramus Rt. #17 3	Paramus	NJ
Paramus Rt. #4 10	Paramus	NJ
Warner Quad	Ridgewood	NJ
Union Twin	Union	NJ
Alpine 7	Brooklyn	NY
Cinema III	Brooklyn	NY
Fortway 5	Brooklyn	NY
Kenmore Quad	Brooklyn	NY
Kings Plaza Quad	Brooklyn	NY
Kingsway 5-plex	Brooklyn	NY
Metro 4	Brooklyn	NY
City Cinema 5	Fresh Meadows	NY
Meadows 7	Fresh Meadows	NY
Glen Cove 6	Glen Cove	NY
Shore Quad	Huntington	NY
Smithaven 4	Lake Grove	NY
Whitman	Huntington	NY
Lawrence Triple	Lawrence	NY
Nanuet 5-plex	Nanuet	NY
23rd Street 3	New York	NY
34th St.	New York	NY
59th St. East	New York	NY
62nd & Broadway	New York	NY
Baronet	New York	NY
Beekman	New York	NY
Carnegie Hall 2	New York	NY
Chelsea 9	New York	NY
Coronet 2	New York	NY
Greenwich Twin	New York	NY
Manhattan Twin	New York	NY
Metro 2	New York	NY
National Twin	New York	NY
Olympia Twin	New York	NY
Park & 86th 2	New York	NY
Plaza	New York	NY
Regency	New York	NY
Waverly Twin	New York	NY
Worldwide Cinemas 6	New York	NY
Ziegfeld	New York	NY
Hampton Arts Twin	Port Washington	NY
Islip Cinema 3	Port Washington	NY
Mattituck 8	Port Washington	NY
Soundview 6	Port Washington	NY
Fantasy 5	Rockville Center	NY
Rockville Twin	Rockville Center	NY

City Cinemas

Angelika 6	New York	NY
Cinema 1	New York	NY
Cinema 2	New York	NY
Cinema 3rd Ave	New York	NY

Eastside Playhouse	New York	NY
86th St. East 1 & 2	New York	NY
Murray Hill 4	New York	NY
68th Street Playhouse	New York	NY
Sutton 1 & 2	New York	NY
Village East 7	New York	NY

Clearview Cinema

Cinema 3	Bernardsville	NJ
Chester Twin	Chester	NJ
Allwood 6	Clifton	NJ
Emerson Cinema 4	Emerson	NJ
Madison Cinema 4	Madison	NJ
Algonquin Arts	Manasquan	NJ
Washington Township 3	Washington Township	NJ
Grand Ave. 2	Baldwin	NY
Bedford Cinemas	Bedford	NY
Mt. Kisco Cinemas 5	Mt. Kisco	NY
New City Cinema 6	New City	NY
Herricks Cinemas 2	New Hyde Park	NY
Cinemas 7	Port Washington	NY

General Cinema

Bridgewater Commons 7	Bridgewater	NJ
Rutgers 6	Somerset	NJ
Ocean County Mall 3	Toms River	NJ
Blue Star 4	Watchung	NJ
Essex Green 3	West Orange	NJ
Bay Plaza 13	Bronx	NY
Central Plaza 4	Yonkers	NY

Hoyts

Galleria Cinema 12	Poughkeepsie	NY
South Hills Cine 8	Poughkeepsie	NY

Magic Theatres

Cinema 5	Bergenfield	NJ
Cinemas 4	Closter	NJ
Hudson Mall 4-plex	Jersey City	NJ
Colony 3	Livingston	NJ
Hadley Center 11	South Plainfield	NJ
Tenafly Theatre 4	Tenafly	NJ

Movie City

Movie City 6	East Brunswick	NJ
Movie City 6	Edison	NJ
Movie City 3	Teaneck	NJ
Movie City 5	Woodbridge	NJ

National Amusement

Multiplex 12	Hazlet	NJ
Multiplex 14	Newark	NJ
Amboy Multiplex 14	Sayerville	NJ
Concourse Plaza 10	Bronx	NY
Whitestone Multiplex 14	Bronx	NY
Commack Multiplex 15	Commack	NY
Sawmill 10	Hawthorne	NY
Broadway 12	Hicksville	NY
Brockhaven Multiplex 14	Medford	NY
Green Acres 6	Valley Stream	NY
Sunrise Multiplex 14	Valley Stream	NY
Cross Country 10	Yonkers	NY

Sony

Danbury 10	Danbury	CT
Greenwich 2	Greenwich	CT
Cinema Center 5	Brick	NJ
Circle 5	Brick	NJ
Route 18 (2)	East Brunswick	NJ
Metroplex 12	East Hanover	NJ
Monmouth Mall	Eatontown	NJ
Showboat 4	Edgewater	NJ
Freehold 6	Freehold	NJ
Freehold Metroplex 8	Freehold	NJ
Mountainside 10	Mountainside	NJ
Newark Metroplex 6	Newark	NJ
New Brunswick 18	New Brunswick	NJ
Interstate 2	Ramsey	NJ
Red Bank 2	Red Bank	NJ

Ridgefield Park 12	Ridgefield	NJ
Meadow 6	Secaucus	NJ
Plaza 8	Secaucus	NJ
Dover 2	Toms River	NJ
Seacourt 10	Toms River	NJ
Wayne 14	Wayne	NJ
South Shore 2	Bayshore	NY
Bay Terrace 6	Bayside	NY
Elmwood 4	Elmhurst	NY
Trylon	Forest Hills	NY
Roosevelt Field 8	Garden City	NY
Nassau Metroplex 10	Levittown	NY
Galleria Metroplex 10	Middletown	NY
Middletown 10	Middletown	NY
19th Street East 6	New York	NY
84th Street 6	New York	NY
Astor Plaza 1	New York	NY
Lincoln Sq. 12	New York	NY
New York 2	New York	NY
Orpheum 7	New York	NY
Paris	New York	NY
34th St. Showplace 3	New York	NY
Sony IMAX	New York	NY
Sate	New York	NY
Tower East 1	New York	NY
Village 7	New York	NY
Stonybrook 3	Stonybrook	NY
Roosevelt Raceway 12	Westbury	NY

United Artists

Playhouse 10	Darien	CT
Eric Lawrenceville	Lawrenceville	NJ
Middletown 7	Middletown	NJ
UA Wash.Twnshp. 14	Sewell	NJ
Cinema 46 (3)	Totowa	NJ
Bellevue Montclair 3	Upper Montclair	NJ
Wayne 4	Wayne	NJ
Rialto	Westfield	NJ
Movies 4	Westwood	NJ
Babylon 3	Babylon	NY
Bayside 4	Bayside	NY
Interboro Bronx 4	Bronx	NY
Bronxville 3	Bronxville	NY
Brooklyn Sheepshead 9	Brooklyn	NY
Marboro Brooklyn 4	Brooklyn	NY
Coram 12	Coram	NY
Movieworld 7	Douglaston	NY
Meadowbrook 6	East Meadow	NY
Easthampton 5	Easthampton	NY
Quartet Flushing 4	Flushing	NY
Continental 2	Forest Hills	NY
Continental 3	Forest Hills	NY
Forest Hills 2	Forest Hills	NY
Midway 4 Queens	Forest Hills	NY
Squire Great Neck 3	Great Neck	NY
Larchmont Playhouse	Larchmont	NY
Lindenhurst	Lindenhurst	NY
Astoria 6	Long Island City	NY
Lynbrook 4	Lynbrook	NY
Playhouse 4	Mamaroneck	NY
Manhasset 3	Manhasset	NY
Sunrise Massapequa 9	Massapequa	NY
Cinema 304 2	New City	NY
Criterion Center 7	New York	NY
Gemini 2	New York	NY
UA East Theatre	New York	NY
North Point	North Point	NY
Crossbay I 3	Ozone Park	NY
Crossbay II 7	Ozone Park	NY
Movies 13	Patchogue	NY
Smithtown	Smithtown	NY
Southampton 5	Southampton	NY
Spring Valley 11	Spring Valley	NY
Hylan Plaza	Staten Island	NY
Staten Island 10	Staten Island	NY
Westbury D.I. 3	Westbury	NY
Westhampton 1	Westhampton	NY
UA Cinema 150	Woodbury	NY
Movieland Yonkers 6	Yonkers	NY
Jefferson Valley 8	Yorktown Heights	NY

Independent Theatres

Angelika 57	New York	NY
Cinema Village	New York	NY
Film Forum 4	New York	NY
Quad Cinema	New York	NY

Los Angeles

American Multi-Cinema

Fine Arts I	Beverly Hills	CA
Burbank 14	Burbank	CA
Media Center 6	Burbank	CA
Media Center 8	Burbank	CA
Alondra 6	Cerritos	CA
Town Square 10	Chino	CA
Serramonte 6	Colma	CA
Fullerton 10	Fullerton	CA
Hawthorne 6	Hawthorne	CA
Hermosa Beach 6	Hermosa Beach	CA
Puente East 4	Industry	CA
Puente West 6	Industry	CA
Puente Plaza 10	Industry	CA
Marina Pacifica 6	Long Beach	CA
Pine Square 16	Long Beach	CA
Century City 14	Los Angeles	CA
Milpitas 10	Milpitas	CA
Montebello 10	Montebello	CA
Norwalk 20	Norwalk	CA
Ontario Mills 30	Ontario	CA
Old Pasadena 8	Pasadena	CA
Orange 6	Orange	CA
Commercenter 6	San Bernardino	CA
Main Place 6	Santa Ana	CA
Santa Monica 7	Santa Monica	CA
Rolling Hills 6	Torrance	CA
Victor Valley 10	Victorville	CA
Promenade 16	Woodland Hills	CA

Century Theatres

Southbay 6 D.I.	Carson	CA
Century 7	North Hollywood	CA
Cinedome 11-plex	Orange	CA
City Center 4	Orange	CA
Stadium 8 D.I.	Orange	CA
Century 8	Ventura	CA

Cinamerica

Agoura Hills 8	Agoura Hills	CA
Puente Hills 6	Industry	CA
Culver Plaza 6	Culver City	CA
Exchange 8	Glendale	CA
Glendora 6	Glendora	CA
Mann 9	Granada Hills	CA
Chinese 3	Hollywood	CA
Manhattan Village 8	Manhattan Beach	CA
Huntington Oaks 6-plex	Monrovia	CA
Hasting Ranch Triplex	Pasadena	CA
Sante Fe Springs 8	Santa Fe Springs	CA
Criterion 6	Santa Monica	CA
Sycamore Plaza 6	Simi Valley	CA
Valley West 9-plex	Tarzana	CA
Janss 9-plex	Thousand Oaks	CA
Del Amo 9	Torrance	CA
Mann Tenplex	Valencia	CA
Buenventura 6-plex	Ventura	CA
Bruin	Westwood	CA
Festival	Westwood	CA
Mann 4-plex	Westwood	CA
National	Westwood	CA
Plaza	Westwood	CA
Regent	Westwood	CA
Village	Westwood	CA

Cinemark

Movies 10	Cathedral City	CA
Movies 8	Chino	CA
Movies 12	Lancaster	CA
Movies 5-7	Lancaster	CA
Movies 1-4	Lancaster	CA
Movies West	Lancaster	CA
Movies 8	Palmdale	CA
Movies 10	Victorville	CA
Movies 7	Victorville	CA

Cineplex

Beverly Center 13	Los Angeles	CA
Century Plaza 4	Los Angeles	CA
Fairfax Triple	Los Angeles	CA
Showcase	Los Angeles	CA
Universal City 18	Los Angeles	CA
Marina Marketplace 6	Marina Del Rey	CA
Broadway 4 Cinemas	Santa Monica	CA

Edwards

Alhambra Palace 5	Alhambra	CA
Atlantic Palace 10	Alhambra	CA
Anaheim Hills Festival 8	Anaheim	CA
Azusa D.I.	Azusa	CA
Foothill Center 13	Azusa	CA
Brea Plaza 4	Brea	CA
Camarillo 12	Camarillo	CA
La Costa 6	Carlsbad	CA
Cerritos 10	Cerritos	CA
Corona 11	Corona	CA
Corona West End 8	Corona	CA
Cinema Costa Mesa	Costa Mesa	CA
Cinema Center 4	Costa Mesa	CA
Harbor Twin	Costa Mesa	CA
Mesa	Costa Mesa	CA
South Coast Plaza 1 & 2	Costa Mesa	CA
South Coast Village 3	Costa Mesa	CA
Triangle Sq. 8	Costa Mesa	CA
Town Center 4	Costa Mesa	CA
El Monte Cinemas	El Monte	CA
Saddleback 1-2-3	El Toro	CA
Saddleback 4-5-6	El Toro	CA
El Toro Cinema 5	El Toro	CA
Fontana 8	Fontana	CA
Family 4	Fountain Valley	CA
Fountain Valley Twin	Fountain Valley	CA
Charter Centre	Huntington Beach	CA
Huntington Pierside	Huntington Beach	CA

Huntington Twin	Huntington Beach	CA
Lido	Huntington Beach	CA
Westpark 8	Irvine	CA
University 6	Irvine	CA
Woodbridge 5	Irvine	CA
South Coast 2	Laguna Beach	CA
Laguna Hills Mall 3	Laguna Hills	CA
Ocean Ranch Cinema 7	Laguna Niguel	CA
Rancho Niguel 8	Laguna Niguel	CA
Gateway Plaza 5	La Mirada	CA
Laverne 12	Laverne	CA
Mission Viejo 3	Mission Viejo	CA
Trabuco Hills 5	Mission Viejo	CA
Monterey Mall 3	Monterey Park	CA
Towngate 8	Moreno Valley	CA
Island 7	Newport Beach	CA
Newport Cinema 3	Newport Beach	CA
Rancho California 10	Rancho California	CA
Rancho Cucamonga 6	Rancho Cucamonga	CA
Town Center	Rancho Cucamonga	CA
Franciscan Plaza 5	San Juan Capistrano	CA
Bristol IV	Santa Ana	CA
Hutton Center 8	Santa Ana	CA
Valencia 10	Santa Clarita	CA
Mountaingate Plaza 7	Simi Valley	CA
Simi Valley 10	Simi Valley	CA
Village Center 6	Stanton	CA
Temple 4	Temple City	CA
Market Place 6	Tustin	CA
Upland 8	Upland	CA
Mountain Green 4	Upland	CA
Mall 4	Westminister	CA
Twin	Westminister	CA
Westminster 10	Westminister	CA

General Cinema

Rancho 6	Colton	CA
Avco 4	Los Angeles	CA
Beverly Connection 6	Los Angeles	CA
Fallbrook 7	Los Angeles	CA
Glendale Central 5	Los Angeles	CA
Hollywood Galaxy 6	Los Angeles	CA
Santa Anita 4	Los Angeles	CA
Sherman Oaks 2	Los Angeles	CA
Montclair Plaza 8	Montclair	CA
Galleria 6	Redondo Beach	CA

Laemmle

Music Hall 3	Beverly Hills	CA
Town Center 5	Encino	CA
Grande 4	Los Angeles	CA
Colorado	Pasadena	CA
Esquire	Pasadena	CA
Monica 4-plex	Santa Monica	CA
Sunset 5	West Hollywood	CA
Royal	West Los Angeles	CA

Landmark

Port	Corona Del Mar	CA
Goldwyn Pavilion 4	Los Angeles	CA
NuWilshire 2	Los Angeles	CA
Nuart	Los Angeles	CA
Rialto	South Pasadena	CA

Metropolitan

Campus	Los Angeles	CA
Fiesta Twin	Los Angeles	CA
Olympic	Los Angeles	CA
Orpheum	Los Angeles	CA
Panorama	Los Angeles	CA
Park 1 & 2	Los Angeles	CA
State	Los Angeles	CA
Cinema 3	Palm Desert	CA
Town Center Cinema 10	Palm Desert	CA
Courtyard 10	Palm Springs	CA
Antelope Valley 10	Palmdale	CA
Arlington Center	Santa Barbara	CA
Cinema 1 & 2	Santa Barbara	CA
Fairview 1 & 2	Santa Barbara	CA
Fiesta 5	Santa Barbara	CA
Granada 1 2 & 3	Santa Barbara	CA
Metro 4	Santa Barbara	CA
Plaza de Oro 1 & 2	Santa Barbara	CA
Riviera	Santa Barbara	CA
Simi D.I.	Simi Valley	CA

Pacific

Winnetka 6	Chatsworth	CA
Commerce 7	City of Commerce	CA
Vineland 4-plex D.I.	City of Industry	CA
Eagle Rock 4	Eagle Rock	CA
Vermont Triplex D.I.	Gardena	CA
El Capitan	Hollywood	CA
Pacific's Cinerama Dome	Hollywood	CA
Warner 2	Huntington Park	CA
Lakewood Center Four	Lakewood	CA
Lakewood Center South 9	Lakewood	CA
Regency 8	Lakewood	CA
Los Altos Triplex D.I.	Long Beach	CA
Beach Cities 16	Manhattan Beach	CA
Northridge 10	Northridge	CA
Ontario 10	Ontario	CA

Carriage Square 5	Oxnard	CA
Hastings 8	Pasadena	CA
Inland Cinema 5	San Bernardino	CA
Pacific 4	Sherman Oaks	CA
Van Nuys 3 D.I.	Van Nuys	CA
101 Triplex D.I.	Ventura	CA
HiWay 39 4 D.I.	Westminster	CA
Crest	Westwood	CA
Topanga 3	Woodland Hills	CA

Regal

Diamond Bar Cinema	Diamond Bar	CA
El Cajon Cinema 8	El Cajon	CA
Hemet 12	Hemet	CA
Lake Elsinore 8	Lake Elsinore	CA
Terrace Cinema 6	Rancho Palos Verdes	CA
Peninsula Cinema 9	Rolling Hills Estates	CA
Del Rosa Cinema 8	San Bernardino	CA
Whittwood Cinema 10	Whitter	CA

SoCal

Cinemapolis 13	Anaheim Hills	CA
Blue Jay Cinema 4	Blue Jay Village	CA
Laguna Hills Mall Cinema 3	Laguna Hills	CA
University Cinema 3	Los Angeles	CA
Canyon Springs Cinema 7	Moreno Valley	CA
Canyon Crest Cinema 9	Riverside	CA
Marketplace Cinema	Riverside	CA
Fox Theatre 3	West Covina	CA
Eastland Theatre 5	West Covina	CA
Wescove Cinema 3	West Covina	CA

Sony Theatres

Magic Johnson 12	Los Angeles	CA

United Artists

Marketplace 8	Brea	CA
UA Movies 4	Brea	CA
Buena Park 8	Buena Park	CA
Cerritos 4	Cerritos	CA
UA Twin Cerritos	Cerritos	CA
Colma Cinema 6	Colma	CA
Granada Hills 7	Granada Hills	CA
UA La Canada Flintridge	La Canada	CA
Lakewood 6	Lakewood	CA
Movies Long Beach 6	Long Beach	CA
Westwood 5	Los Angeles	CA
Marina Del Rey 6	Marina Del Rey	CA
Town Center 6	Montclair	CA
Valley Plaza 6	North Hollywood	CA
Pasadena Marketplace 6	Pasadena	CA
UA Park Sierra 6	Riverside	CA
Tyler Cinema 4	Riverside	CA
Thousand Oaks 5	Thousand Oaks	CA
Del Amo 6	Torrance	CA
UA 6 Warner Center	Woodland Hills	CA

Independent Theatres

UCLA Melnitz	Los Angeles	CA
Monica 4-plex	Santa Monica	CA

Chicago
American Multi Cinema

Barrington Square 6	Hoffman Estates	IL
Ogden Mall 6	Naperville	IL

Cineplex

Ridge Cinemas 8	Arlington Heights	IL
Town n' Country 6	Arlington Heights	IL
Fox Valley 10	Aurora	IL
West Plaza 3	Aurora	IL
Westridge Court 8	Aurora	IL
Stratford Square 8	Bloomingdale	IL
Bloomingdale Court 6	Bloomingdale	IL
River Oaks 12	Calumet City	IL
Springhill Mall 6	Carpentersville	IL
900 North Michigan 2	Chicago	IL
600 North Michigan 9	Chicago	IL
Biograph 3	Chicago	IL
Bricktown Square 6	Chicago	IL
Broadway (Lakeshore)	Chicago	IL
Burnam Plaza 5	Chicago	IL
Chestnut Station 5	Chicago	IL
Chicago Ridge 6	Chicago	IL
Commons 4	Chicago	IL
Lincoln Village 3	Chicago	IL
Lincoln Village 6	Chicago	IL
McClurg 3	Chicago	IL
Navy Pier Imax 3-D	Chicago	IL
Plaza 3	Chicago	IL
Water Tower 7	Chicago	IL
Grove Cinemas 6	Downer's Grove	IL
Diana 4	Homewood	IL
Golf Glen 6	Niles	IL
Golf Mill 3	Niles	IL
North Riverside 6	North Riverside	IL
Oakbrook 3	Oakbrook	IL
Oakbrook Mall 4	Oakbrook	IL
Orland Square 10	Orland Park	IL
Foxfield 4	St. Charles	IL

St. Charles 3	St. Charles	IL
One Schaumberg 9	Schaumberg	IL
Woodfield 9	Schaumburg	IL
Gardens 7	Skokie	IL
Hawthorne Quad	Vernon Hills	IL
Rivertree Court 8	Vernon Hills	IL
Rice Lake 10	Wheaton	IL

Classic Cinemas

Cinema 12	Carpentersville	IL
Tivoli	Downer's Grove	IL
Tivoli South	Downer's Grove	IL
Casino 3	Elgin	IL
Elk Grove 2	Elk Grove Vill.	IL
York 5	Elmhurst	IL
Fox Lake 5	Fox Lake	IL
Tradewinds 2	Hanover Park	IL
Meadowview 3	Kankakee	IL
Paramount 3	Kankakee	IL
Lake 4	Oak Park	IL
Park Forest 4	Park Forest	IL
Arcada	St. Charles	IL
Woodstock 2	Woodstock	IL

GKC

Campus Cinemas 4	Dekalb	IL
Carrol Cinemas 4	Dekalb	IL
Dekalb Cinemas 4	Dekalb	IL
Cinemas 2	Lasalle	IL
Showplace Cinemas 2	Lasalle	IL
Morris Cinemas 2	Morris	IL
Roxy Cinemas 6	Ottawa	IL
Peru Mall Cinemas 6	Peru	IL
Crescent Cinemas 2	Pontiac	IL
Majestic Cinemas 2	Streator	IL

General Cinema

Deerbrook 4	Chicago	IL
Ford City 14	Chicago	IL
Lincoln Mall 3	Chicago	IL
Northbrook Court 14	Chicago	IL
Randhurst 4	Chicago	IL
Woodgrove Festival 6	Chicago	IL
Yorktown 6	Chicago	IL
Lakehurst 12	Waukegan	IL
Griffith Park 2	Gary	IN
Ridge Plaza 2	Gary	IN
Southlake Mall 9	Gary	IN
University Park East 6	South Bend	IN
University Park West 3	South Bend	IN
County Seat 6	Valparaiso	IN

Kerasotes

Showplace 12	Bolingbrook	IL
Lake in the Hills 12	Lake in the Hills	IL
Showplace 8	Vernon Hills	IL
La Porte Cinema 4	La Porte	IN
Dunes Plaza Cinema 6	Michigan City	IN
Marquette 3	Michigan City	IN
Scottsdale Mall 6	South Bend	IN
Town & Country 3	South Bend	IN

Sony

Double Drive-In 3	Chicago	IL
Esquire 6	Chicago	IL
Fine Arts 4	Chicago	IL
Hyde Park 4	Chicago	IL
Pipers Alley 4	Chicago	IL
Webster 8	Chicago	IL
Bel-Air Drive-In 3	Cicero	IL
Cedarwood 12	Crestwood	IL
Evanston 5	Evanston	IL
Evergreen 4	Evergreen	IL
Hillside Mall 3	Hillside	IL
Hillside Square 6	Hillside	IL
River Run 8	Lansing	IL
Norridge 10	Norridge	IL
Rolling Meadows 9	Rolling Meadows	IL
Old Orchard 4	Skokie	IL
Streamwood 14	Streamwood	IL
Merrillville 10	Merrillville	IN
Y&W Drive-In 3	Merrillville	IN

Independent Theatres

Davis Art	Chicago	IL
Facets Multimedia	Chicago	IL
Willmette	Wilmette	IL

Philadelphia

American Multi-Cinema

Cinema Center 3	Newark	DE
Concord 2	Wilmington	DE
Millside 4	Delran	NJ
Quaker Bridge 4	Lawrenceville	NJ
Marlton 8	Marlton	NJ
Vineland 4	Vineland	NJ
Tilghman Plaza 8	Allentown	PA
Woodhaven 10	Ben Salem	PA
Hampden Center 8	Mechanicsburg	PA
Barn 5	Doylestown	PA
Granite Run 8	Media	PA
Andorra 8	Philadelphia	PA
Olde City 2	Philadelphia	PA
Orleans 8	Philadelphia	PA
Quakertown 6	Quakertown	PA
Anthony Wayne 2	Wayne	PA
Marple 10	Springfield	PA
309 Cinema 9	Springhouse	PA
Bucks County Twin	Warrington	PA
Painters Crossing 9	West Chester	PA
Plaza 2	Whitehall	PA

General Cinema

Christiana Mall 5	Wilmington	DE
Deptford Mall 6	Camden	NJ
Mercer Mall 7	Trenton	NJ
Lehigh Valley Mall 8	Allentown	PA
Franklin Mills 10	Philadelphia	PA
Northeast 4	Philadelphia	PA
Plymouth Meeting 2	Philadelphia	PA

Milgram

Glassboro	Glassboro	NJ
Harwan	Mount Ephraim	NJ
Tilton 6	Northfield	NJ
Broadway	Pitman	NJ
East Windsor Twin	Princeton	NJ
Broad Valley	Allentown	PA
Ritz	Muncy	PA
Ritz	New Holland	PA
Merlin	Philadelphia	PA
Yeadon	Philadelphia	PA
Colonial	Phoenixville	PA
Thorndale	Thorndale	PA

Regal

Plymouth Meeting 14	Conshohocken	PA
Lionville 12	Exton	PA
Center City 12	Philadelphia	PA

United Artists

Eric Pennsauken 5	Pennsauken	NJ
Princeton Market Fair 9	Princeton	NJ
Allentown 5	Allentown	PA
Ardmore 2	Ardmore	PA
Easton 6	Easton	PA
Penn Jersey 3	Fairless Hills	PA
Frazer 2	Frazer	PA
Eric Macdale Mall 4	Holmes	PA
Baederwood 2	Jenkintown	PA
Eric King 2	King of Prussia	PA
Eric Plaza 2	King of Prussia	PA
Eric Queen 4	King of Prussia	PA
Eric Montgomeryville 7	Montgomeryville	PA
Cheltenham Square 8	Philadelphia	PA
Chestnut Hill 2	Philadelphia	PA
Grant Square	Philadelphia	PA
Riverview Plaza	Philadelphia	PA
Sameric 4	Philadelphia	PA
Movies at 69th St.	Upper Darby	PA
Eric Wynnewood	Wynnewood	PA

Independent Theatres

Ritz	Philadelphia	PA

San Francisco-Oakland

American Multi-Cinema

Kabuki 8	San Francisco	CA
Oakridge 6	San Jose	CA
Town & Country 1	San Jose	CA
Sunnyvale 6	Sunnyvale	CA
Vallejo Plaza 6	Vallejo	CA

Blumenfeld Theatres

Fairfax	Fairfax	CA
Lark	Larkspur	CA
Meridian 6	San Jose	CA
Regency 1	San Francisco	CA
Regency 2	San Francisco	CA
Royal	San Francisco	CA
Alhambra	San Francisco	CA
Castro	San Francisco	CA

Century Theatres

Burlingame 4 D.I.	Burlingame	CA
Hyatt Cinema Triplex	Burlingame	CA
Solano Twin 2 D.I.	Concord	CA
Geneva 4 D.I.	Daly City	CA
Cinedome 8	Fremont	CA
Century Cinema 16	Mountain View	CA
Cinedome 8-plex	Napa	CA
Cinedome 7-plex	Newark	CA
Century 8	Oakland	CA
Century 10 plex	Pinole	CA
Century 5-plex	Pleasant Hill	CA
Century Park 12	Redwood City	CA
Century Park 7	Salinas	CA
Northridge 8-plex	Salinas	CA
Cinema 21	San Francisco	CA
Empire 3	San Francisco	CA

Presidio	San Francisco	CA
Capitol 6 D.I.	San Jose	CA
Century 21	San Jose	CA
Century 22 Triplex	San Jose	CA
Century 23 Twin	San Jose	CA
Century 24 Twin	San Jose	CA
Century 25 Twin	San Jose	CA
Century Almaden 5	San Jose	CA
Century Berryessa 10	San Jose	CA
Century Plaza 8	South San Francisco	CA
Union City 6 D.I.	Union City	CA
Cinedome 8	Vallejo	CA

Cinamerica
Festival 9-plex	Hayward	CA
Festival 4-plex	Larkspur	CA
Contra Costa 5-plex	Martinez	CA
Crow Canyon 6-plex	San Ramon	CA
Festival 5-plex	Walnut Creek	CA

Cinemacal
Cinema 6	Morgan Hill	CA
Granada 2	Morgan Hill	CA
Tanforan 4	San Bruno	CA
Galaxy 8	Vacaville	CA

Cineplex
Plaza 2	Daly City	CA
Hilltop 8	Richmond	CA
Northpoint	San Francisco	CA

General Cinema
Dublin Place 6	Dublin	CA
Solano Mall 6	Fairfield	CA
Fremont Hub 8	Fremont	CA
Southland 5	Hayward	CA
Hillsdale 4	San Mateo	CA

Landmark
U.C. Berkeley	Berkeley	CA
Act 1 & 2	Berkeley	CA
Albany Twin	Berkeley	CA
California 3	Berkeley	CA
Piedmont 3	Berkeley	CA
Shattuck 8	Berkeley	CA
Guild	Menlo Park	CA
Park	Menlo Park	CA
Aquarius 2	Palo Alto	CA
Palo Alto Square 2	Palo Alto	CA
Varsity	Palo Alto	CA
Bridge	San Francisco	CA
Clay	San Francisco	CA
Embarcadero Center 5	San Francisco	CA
Gateway	San Francisco	CA
Lumiere	San Francisco	CA
Opera Plaza	San Francisco	CA

Pacific
Cinema	Corte Madera	CA
Sequoia Twin	Mill Valley	CA
Rowland	Novato	CA
Petaluma 8	Petaluma	CA
Northgate 15	San Rafael	CA
Regency 6	San Rafael	CA
Marin 3	Sausalito	CA

Signature Theatres
Cinema 2	Davis	CA
Holiday 6	Davis	CA
Briggsmore 7	Modesto	CA
Vintage Faire 4	Modesto	CA
Jack London Cinema 4	Oakland	CA
Santa Cruz 9	Santa Cruz	CA
Holiday 8	Stockton	CA
Tower Plaza 3	Visalia	CA
Visalia Cinema	Visalia	CA

Tegtmeier Associates, Inc.
Chief Cinemas 4	Fairfield	CA
Fairfield 1&2	Fairfield	CA
Lakeport Auto Movies	Lakeport	CA
Lakeport Twin	Lakeport	CA
Vaca Valley 4	Vacaville	CA

United Artists
Aptos Twin 2	Aptos	CA
Berkeley 7	Berkeley	CA
Pruneyard 3	Campbell	CA
41st Avenue Playhouse 3	Capitola	CA
Movies at Emery Bay 10	Emeryville	CA
Hayward 6	Hayward	CA
UA Cinema 6	Redwood City	CA
Empire 4	Rohnert Park	CA
Alexandria 3	San Francisco	CA
Cinema Stonestown 2	San Francisco	CA
Coronet 1	San Francisco	CA
Galaxy 4	San Francisco	CA
Metro	San Francisco	CA
Vogue	San Francisco	CA
Del Mar	Santa Cruz	CA
Rio	Santa Cruz	CA
UA Riverfront 2	Santa Cruz	CA

Coddingtown 4	Santa Rosa	CA
UA Santa Rosa 5	Santa Rosa	CA
Santa Rosa 6	Santa Rosa	CA

Independent Theatres
Pacific Film Archive	Berkeley	CA
Red Vic	San Francisco	CA
Roxie	San Francisco	CA

Boston
General Cinema
Braintree 10	Boston	MA
Burlington 10	Boston	MA
Chestnut Hill 5	Boston	MA
Framingham 14	Boston	MA
Hanover Mall 4	Boston	MA
Northshore 3	Boston	MA
Tyngsboro 6	Tyngsboro	MA

Hoyts
Acton Cinemas 4	Acton	MA
Franklin Cinemas 6	Franklin	MA
Harwich Cinemas 6	Harwich	MA
Airport Cinema 8	Hyannis	MA
Cape Cod Mall Cinema 1 & 2	Hyannis	MA
Cape Cod Mall Cinema 3 & 4	Hyannis	MA
Milford Cinema Centre 495	Milford	MA
Independence Mall 14	Plymouth	MA

Landmark
Kendall Square 9	Cambridge	MA

Melrose
Route 3 Cinemas 6	Chelmsford	MA
Tri-boro Twin	North Attleboro	MA
Route 24 Twin Cinemas	Raynham	MA

National Amusement
Allston 2	Allston	MA
Circle 7	Brookline	MA
Showcase 12	Dedham	MA
Showcase 10	Lawrence	MA
Showcase 12	North Attleboro	MA
Quincy Cinemas 8	Quincy	MA
Showcase 14	Revere	MA
Showcase 14	Woburn	MA

Sony
Cheri 4	Boston	MA
Copley Place 11	Boston	MA
Nickelodeon 5	Boston	MA
Fresh Pond 10	Cambridge	MA
Harvard Square 5	Cambridge	MA
Janus 1	Cambridge	MA
Danvers 6	Danvers	MA
Liberty Tree 2	Danvers	MA
Natick 6	Natick	MA

Independent Theatres
Brattle Theatre	Cambridge	MA

Washington-Baltimore-Arlington
American Multi-Cinema
Union Station 9	Washington	DC
Academy 6	Greenbelt	MD
Academy 8	Greenbelt	MD
Carollton 6	New Carrollton	MD
Rivertowne 12	Oxon Hill	MD
City Place 10	Silver Spring	MD
Courthouse Plaza 8	Arlington	VA
Potomac Mills 15	Dale City	VA

Cineplex
Avalon 2	Washington	DC
Cinema	Washington	DC
Dupont 5	Washington	DC
Embassy	Washington	DC
Janus 3	Washington	DC
Foundry 7	Washington	DC
Mazza Galleria 3	Washington	DC
MacArthur Theatre 3	Washington	DC
Outer Circle 2	Washington	DC
Tenley 3	Washington	DC
Uptown	Washington	DC
West End 7	Washington	DC
Wisconsin Avenue 6	Washington	DC
Marketplace 6	Bowie	MD
Rio 14 Cinemas	Gaithersberg	MD
St. Charles Town 9	Gaithersberg	MD
Lake Forest 5	Gaithersburg	MD
White Flint 5	Kensington	MD
Marlow 6	Marlow Heights	MD
Waldorf North 4	Waldorf	MD
Waldorf South 5	Waldorf	MD
Wheaton Plaza 4	Wheaton	MD
Old Town 2	Alexandria	VA
Shirlington 7	Arlington	VA
Fair City Mall 6	Fairfax	VA

Skyline 12	Falls Church	VA
Manassas Mall 7	Manassas	VA
Fairfax Sq. 8	Vienna	VA
Potomac Malls 15	Woodbridge	VA

General Cinema

Columbia City 3	Baltimore	MD
Security Square 8	Baltimore	MD
Towson Commons 8	Baltimore	MD
Springfield Mall 10	Springfield	VA

Hoyts

Francis Scott Key 3	Frederick	MD
Frederick Town Mall 2	Frederick	MD
Westridge Mall 6	Frederick	MD
Laurel 6	Laurel	MD
Laurel Lakes 12	Laurel	MD
Cranberry Malls Cinemas 9	Westminster	MD

R/C

Hollywood 4	Arbutus	MD
Carrolltowne Movies 6	Eldersburg	MD
Village Cinema 3	Reisterstown	MD
Regal Twin	Culpepper	VA
Movies 10	Fredericksburg	VA
Spotsylvania Mall 4	Fredericksburg	VA
Virginians Cinema 4	Fredericksburg	VA
Tally Ho Twin Cinema	Leesburg	VA
Aquia Town Movies 10	Stafford	VA

Sony

Greenspring 3	Baltimore	MD
Northpoint 4	Baltimore	MD
Rotunda 2	Baltimore	MD
Campus Hills 7	Bel Air	MD
Hartford 2	Bel Air	MD
Center Park 8	Beltsville	MD
Palace 9	Columbia	MD
Germantown 6	Germantown	MD
Glen Burnie 7	Glen Burnie	MD
Valley Centre 9	Owings Mills	MD
Jumpers 7	Pasadena	MD
Timonium 3	Timonium	MD
Yorkridge 4	Timonium	MD
Wheaton Plaza 11	Wheaton	MD
Pentagon City 6	Arlington	VA
Worldgate 9	Herndon	VA
Tysons 8	McLean	VA

United Artists

Golden Ring 9	Baltimore	MD
Movies at Harbor Park 9	Baltimore	MD
UA Westview	Baltimore	MD
UA Bethesda 10	Bethesda	MD
Marley Station 9	Glen Burnie	MD
Movies at Fair Oaks 8	Fairfax	VA
UA Towne Center 10	Fairfax	VA

Independent Theatres

AFI Theatre	Washington	DC
Biograph Theatre	Washington	DC
Key Theatre	Washington	DC

Dallas-Forth Worth

American Multi-Cinema

Forum 6	Arlington	TX
Green Oaks 8	Arlington	TX
Glen Lakes 8	Dallas	TX
Grand 24	Dallas	TX
Prestonwood 5	Dallas	TX
Hulen Village 10	Ft. Worth	TX
Sundance 11	Ft. Worth	TX
Irving 8	Irving	TX
Towne Crossing 8	Mesquite	TX
Central Park 7	Plano	TX

Carmike

Cinema	Denton	TX
Rolling Hills	Greenville	TX
Cinema	Jacksonville	TX
Northloop	Longview	TX
Martin	Longview	TX
Angelina	Lufkin	TX
Cinema	Lufkin	TX
Town Square	Lufkin	TX
Carmike I	Nacodoches	TX
Carmike II	Nacodoches	TX
Southloop 4	Tyler	TX
Times Square 5	Tyler	TX
Cinema	Waco	TX
Waco Square 6	Waco	TX
Century City	Wichita Falls	TX
Cinema	Wichita Falls	TX
Sikes	Wichita Falls	TX

Cinemark

Movies 8	Carrollton	TX
Cinema 6	Cleburne	TX
Cinema 4	Corsicana	TX
Cinemark 17	Dallas	TX

Skillman Cinema 7	Dallas	TX
Wedgwood 4	Ft. Worth	TX
Hollywood USA 15	Garland	TX
Movies 16	Grand Prairie	TX
Tinseltown 17	Grapevine	TX
Movies 8	Lancaster	TX
Movies 12	Lewisville	TX
Movies 14	McKinney	TX
Big Town Cinema 9	Mesquite	TX
Movies 8	N. Richland Hills	TX
Cinemas I & II	Paris	TX
Movies 10	Plano	TX
Rockwall 8	Rockwall	TX
Cinema 4	Sherman	TX
Cinema 7	Sherman	TX
Midway Movies 5	Sherman	TX
Cinema 6	Stephenville	TX

General Cinema

Carrollton Centre 6	Dallas	TX
Collin Creek 6	Dallas	TX
Furneaux Creek 7	Dallas	TX
Galleria 5	Dallas	TX
Irving Mall 7	Dallas	TX
Northpark East 2	Dallas	TX
Northpark West 2	Dallas	TX
Prestonwood 4	Dallas	TX
Richardson 6	Dallas	TX
Town East 6	Dallas	TX
Town East Mall 5	Dallas	TX
Arlington Park 8	Ft. Worth	TX
Central Park 8	Ft. Worth	TX
Cinema 5	Ft. Worth	TX
North Hills 7	Ft. Worth	TX
Ridgmar Town Square 6	Ft. Worth	TX
Cinema 5	Temple	TX
Plitt 6	Temple	TX

Hollywood Theatres

Movies 4	Brownwood	TX
Movies 8	Burleson	TX
Cinema 3	Commerce	TX
Medallion 5	Dallas	TX
Cinema 8	Ft. Worth	TX
Movies 8	Grapevine	TX
Cinema 7	Lancaster	TX
Movies 9	Longview	TX
Movies 6	Tyler	TX
Lacy-Lakeview	Waco	TX

Landmark

Inwood 3	Dallas	TX

Sony

20 & 287 (6)	Arlington	TX
Lincoln Square 10	Arlington	TX
Cityplace 14	Dallas	TX
Keystone Park 16	Dallas	TX
Park Central 4	Dallas	TX
Cityview 8	Fort Worth	TX
Chisholm 5	Plano	TX
Preston Park 6	Plano	TX

United Artists

Bowen 8	Arlington	TX
Bedford 10	Bedford	TX
Cinema 1 & 2	Dallas	TX
Galaxy	Dallas	TX
Park Lane 8	Dallas	TX
Prestonwood 5	Dallas	TX
UA South 8	Dallas	TX
Walnut Hill 6	Dallas	TX
Golden Triangle 4	Denton	TX
Golden Triangle Mall 5	Denton	TX
Hulen 10	Ft. Worth	TX
Las Vegas Trail 8	Ft. Worth	TX
North Star 8	Garland	TX
Grand Prairie	Grand Prairie	TX
Northeast Mall 6	Hurst	TX
Lakepointe 10	Lewisville	TX
Town East 6	Mesquite	TX
Cinemas 1, 2 & 3	Mineral Wells	TX
Berkeley Square 8	Plano	TX

Detroit

American Multi-Cinema

Maple 3	Bloomfield	MI
Bel-Air Centre 10	Detroit	MI
Old Orchard 3	Farmington Hills	MI
Woods 6	Grosse Pointe Woods	MI
Eastland 7	Harper Woods	MI
Eastland 2	Harper Woods	MI
Elmwood 8	Lansing	MI
Laurel Park 10	Livonia	MI
Wonderland 6	Livonia	MI
Abbey 8	Madison Heights	MI
Towne 4	Oak Park	MI
Meridian 1-4	Okemos	MI
Meridian 5-8	Okemos	MI
Meridian 6	Okemos	MI

Hampton 4	Rochester	MI
Southfield City 12	Southfield	MI
Sterling Center 10	Sterling Heights	MI
Southland 4	Taylor	MI
Americana West 6	W. Bloomfield	MI

Cinemark

Cinema 4	Livonia	MI
Cinema 4	Roseville	MI
Cinema 4	Southfield	MI
Movies 16	Warren	MI

General Cinema

Canton 6	Detroit	MI
Novi Town Center 8	Detroit	MI
Lansing Mall West 6	Lansing	MI

Goodrich

Ann Arbor 2	Ann Arbor	MI
Kraft 8	Port Huron	MI

Loeks Star

Star Gratiot 16	Clinton Township	MI
Star Lincoln Park 8	Lincoln Park	MI
Star John R 10	Madison Hts.	MI
Star Rochester Hills 10	Rochester Hills	MI
Star Winchester 8	Rochester Hills	MI
Star Taylor 10	Taylor	MI

MJR Theatres

Allen Park 5	Allen Park	MI
Fox Village 4	Ann Arbor	MI
Livonia Mall Cinema 3	Livonia	MI
Main Art Theatre 3	Royal Oak	MI
Brighton Cinemas 9	Royal Oak	MI
Chesterfield Crossing Cinema 12	Royal Oak	MI
Waterford Twin 1&2	Waterford	MI
Waterford 11	Waterford	MI

National Amusement

Showcase 14	Ann Arbor	MI
Showcase 14	Auburn Hills	MI
Showcase 18	Canton	MI
Dearborn 8	Dearborn	MI
Super Cinemas 12	East Lansing	MI
Genesee Valley 6	Flint	MI
Showcase 12	Flint	MI
Showcase 14	Flint	MI
Beacon East 4	Harper Woods	MI
Showcase 12	Pontiac	MI
Showcase 15	Sterling Heights	MI
Quo Vadis 6	Westland	MI
Showcase 8	Westland	MI

United Artists

Briarwood Cinema 7	Ann Arbor	MI
Fairlane 10	Dearborn	MI
West River	Farmington	MI
12 Oaks 5	Novi	MI
Movies Lakeside 4	Sterling Heights	MI
Oakland 5	Troy	MI

Atlanta

American Multi-Cinema

Mansell 14	Alpharetta	GA
Galleria 8	Atlanta	GA
Market Square 16	Atlanta	GA
Phipps Plaza 12	Atlanta	GA
Cobb Place 14	Kenneshaw	GA
Colonial 18	Lawrenceville	GA
Festival 8	Tucker	GA

Carmike

Cinema	Athens	GA
Georgia Square I	Athens	GA
Georgia Square II	Athens	GA
Conyers	Conyers	GA
Douglasville	Douglasville	GA
Douglasville Exchange	Douglasville	GA
Griffin Cinema	Griffin	GA
Plaza Twin	Cartersville	GA
Cumming	Cumming	GA
Friday Plaza	Doraville	GA
Mall Corners	Duluth	GA
La Grange	La Grange	GA
Merchant's	Marietta	GA
Towne Centre Village	Marietta	GA
Southlake Festival	Morrow	GA
Southlake Plaza	Morrow	GA
West Park Walk	Peachtree City	GA
Brannon Square	Roswell	GA
Holcomb Woods	Roswell	GA
Snellville	Snellville	GA
Stone Mountain	Stone Mountain	GA

Cinemark

Movies 10	Fayetteville	GA

General Cinema

Akers Mill Square 4	Atlanta	GA
Gwinnett Place 6	Atlanta	GA
Hairston Village 8	Atlanta	GA
Merchants Walk 8	Atlanta	GA
Perimeter Mall 4	Atlanta	GA
Sandy Springs 8	Atlanta	GA

Georgia Theatre Company II

Beechwood 8	Athens	GA
Lanier 5	Brunswick	GA
Movies at Glynn Place 8	Brunswick	GA
Newton Twin	Covington	GA
Park 12	Marietta	GA
Columbia Square 4	Martinez	GA
Moultrie Twin	Moultrie	GA
Kings Bay 6	St. Mary's	GA
Gateway 7	Thomasville	GA
Ashley Cinema 8	Valdosta	GA
Movies at Valdosta Mall 6	Valdosta	GA
Mall Cinema 7	Waycross	GA

Regal

Twelve Oaks 4	Atlanta	GA
Austell Road 10	Austell	GA
National 7	College Park	GA
Town 12	Kennesaw	GA
Town Center 10	Lawrenceville	GA
Covington Sq. 8	Lithonia	GA
Regal 10	Marietta	GA
Delk 10	Marietta	GA
Peachtree 10	Norcross	GA
Riverdale 10	Riverdale	GA
Oaks 14	Snellville	GA
Shannon 7	Union City	GA

Sony

Magic Johnson 12	Atlanta	GA

United Artists

North Point Market 8	Alpharetta	GA
CNN Cinemas 6	Atlanta	GA
Lenox Square Theatres 6	Atlanta	GA
Midtown 8	Atlanta	GA
Perimeter Pointe	Atlanta	GA
Tara Theatre	Atlanta	GA
South Dekalb 4	Decatur	GA
Gwinnett Mall 12	Duluth	GA
Parkwood Cinemas 3	Griffin	GA
Riverside 4	Macon	GA
Southlake 8	Morrow	GA
Greens Corner Cinemas 5	Norcross	GA
Cinemas 4	Rome	GA
Shannon 8	Union City	GA

Houston

American Multi-Cinema

Highland Park Village 4	Highland Park	TX
Alameda East 5	Houston	TX
Commerce Park 8	Houston	TX
Deerbrook Expansion 6	Houston	TX
Festival 6	Houston	TX
Greens Crossing 6	Houston	TX
Meyer Park 14	Houston	TX
North Oaks 6	Houston	TX
Town & Country 10	Houston	TX
Westchase 5	Houston	TX
Willowbrook 10	Houston	TX
Deerbrook 8	Humble	TX
Deerbrook 18	Humble	TX

Carmike

Colonnade Four	Beaumont	TX
Morley	Borger	TX
Cinema 3	College Station	TX
Post Oak	College Station	TX
Woodcreek Four	Conroe	TX
Brazos Mall Triple	Lake Jackson	TX
Cinema 4	Lake Jackson	TX
Cinema Twin	Orange	TX
Mall	Port Arthur	TX
Pines	Silsbee	TX

Cinemark

Cinema 4	Bay City	TX
Hollywood Movies 16	College Station	TX
Pine Hollow 6	Conroe	TX
Bear Creek 6	Houston	TX
Cinema 6	Houston	TX
Eastway 6	Houston	TX
Mason Park 8	Katy	TX
Movies 16	Pasadena	TX
Southmore 6	Pasadena	TX
Rosenberg 8	Rosenberg	TX
Movies 12	Texas City	TX
Cinema 4	Victoria	TX
Playhouse Cinema	Victoria	TX
Cinema 6	Victoria	TX

Cineplex

Cinema 6	Baytown	TX
Goose Creek Cinema 6	Baytown	TX

Plitt Cinema 4	Baytown	TX
Cinema 7 West Oaks	Houston	TX
Plitt 5	Houston	TX
Presidio Square 6	Houston	TX
River Oaks 12	Houston	TX
Sharpstown Center 8	Houston	TX
Spectrum 9	Houston	TX

General Cinema

Baybrook Mall 4	Houston	TX
Central 6	Houston	TX
Copperfield 6	Houston	TX
Deerbrook Commons 6	Houston	TX
Greenspoint Mall 5	Houston	TX
Gulfgate Mall 4	Houston	TX
Meyerland 8	Houston	TX
Point NASA 6	Houston	TX
West Oaks Central 6	Houston	TX
Willowbrook Mall 6	Houston	TX

Landmark

River Oaks 3	Houston	TX

Sony

Easton Commons 8	Houston	TX
Fountains 18	Houston	TX
Memorial City 8	Houston	TX
South Point 5-Plex	Houston	TX
Spring 10	Spring	TX

United Artists

Phelan 6	Beaumont	TX
Cinema 6	Port Arthur	TX

Seattle-Tacoma

American Multi-Cinema

Center Plaza 6	Federal Way	WA
Sea Tac 6	Federal Way	WA
Narrows Plaza 8	Tacoma	WA

Act III

Harbor D.I.	Aberdeen	WA
Southshore Mall Cinemas	Aberdeen	WA
Cinema 17	Auburn	WA
Redwood Plaza Quad	Bremerton	WA
Fox	Centralia	WA
Cinema 3	Chehalis	WA
Everett 9	Everett	WA
Issaquah	Issaquah	WA
Kent VI Cinemas	Kent	WA
Lacey	Lacey	WA
State	Olympia	WA
Hilltop Cinema	Puyallup	WA
Puyallup	Puyallup	WA
Bella Bottega	Redmond	WA
Renton 13	Renton	WA
Alderwood	Seattle	WA
Alderwood Village	Seattle	WA
Crossroads	Seattle	WA
Mountlake 9	Seattle	WA
Parkway	Seattle	WA
Silverdale Cinemas	Silverdale	WA

Cineplex

Factoria 8	Bellevue	WA
John Danz	Bellevue	WA
Kirkland Park Place 6	Kirkland	WA
Lakewood 6	Kirkland	WA
Totem Lake 3	Kirkland	WA
Grand Cinemas Alderwood 8	Lynnwood	WA
Cinerama	Seattle	WA
City Centre Cinemas 2	Seattle	WA
Lewis & Clark 7	Seattle	WA
Newmark Square 5	Seattle	WA
Northgate	Seattle	WA
Oak Tree 6	Seattle	WA
South Centre	Seattle	WA
Uptown 3	Seattle	WA
Tacoma Central 6	Tacoma	WA
Tacoma Mall Twin	Tacoma	WA
Tacoma South Cinemas 5	Tacoma	WA
Tacoma West 5	Tacoma	WA

General Cinema

Everett Mall 10	Everett	WA
Gateway Center 8	Federal Way	WA
Renton Village 8	Renton	WA
Aurora 3	Seattle	WA
Kitsap Mall 6	Silverdale	WA
Lincoln Plaza 8	Tacoma	WA

Landmark

Broadway Market 4	Seattle	WA
Crest Cinema Center 4	Seattle	WA
Egyptian	Seattle	WA
Guild 45th Theatre 2	Seattle	WA
Harvard Exit 2	Seattle	WA
Metro Cinemas 10	Seattle	WA
Neptune	Seattle	WA
Seven Gables	Seattle	WA
Varsity 3	Seattle	WA

Regal

South Sound 10	Point Orchid	WA

United Artists

UA Cinema 150 Twin	Seattle	WA

Cleveland

Carmike

Kingsgate 4	Mansfield	OH
Plaza 8	Sandusky	OH

Cinemark

Cinema 5	Alliance	OH
Movies 4	Canton	OH
Cinema 10	Mansfield	OH
Movies 10	Sandusky	OH
Movies 10	Willoughby	OH
Movies 10	Wooster	OH

General Cinema

Chapel Hill Mall 5	Akron	OH
Plaza 8	Akron	OH
West Market Plaza 7	Akron	OH
Canton Centre 8	Canton	OH
Erie Commons 8	Cleveland	OH
Parmatown 5	Cleveland	OH
Ridge Park Square 8	Cleveland	OH
Westgate Mall 6	Cleveland	OH
Westwood Town Center 6	Cleveland	OH
Midway Mall 8	Elyria	OH

General Theatre Company

Berea Triple	Cleveland	OH
Detroit Twin	Cleveland	OH
Parma Triple	Cleveland	OH
Southgate 5	Cleveland	OH
Orr Twin	Orrville	OH
Tiffin D.I.	Tiffin	OH

Hoyts

Tower City 11	Cleveland	OH

Regal

Akron 10	Akron	OH
Montrose 8	Akron	OH
Interstate Park 14	Akron	OH
Brookgate 8	Brook Park	OH
Hickory Ridge 8	Brunswick	OH
Severance 8	Cleveland	OH
Garfield 5	Garfield	OH
Hudson 10	Hudson	OH
Eastgate 4	Lima	OH
Sheffield Center 10	Lorain	OH
Cinema 10	Mayfield Heights	OH
Great Lakes 9	Mentor	OH
Middleburgh Heights 12	Middleburgh Heights	OH
Great Northern 7	North Olmstead	OH
Solon Commons 10	Solon	OH
Westlake Promenade 11	Westlake	OH

Sony

Cedar Center 2	Cleveland	OH
East 8	Cleveland	OH

Minneapolis-St. Paul

Carmike

Mall 3	Albert Lea	MN
Oak Park	Austin	MN
Sterling	Austin	MN
Spring Brook 4	Coon Rapids	MN
Forest Lake	Forest Lake	MN
State Triple	Hutchinson	MN
Cinema 4	Mankato	MN
Mall 4	Mankato	MN
Cinema 3	New Ulm	MN
Cameo 3	Owatonna	MN
Chief 3	Red Wing	MN
Terrace 3	Robbinsdale	MN
Apache 4	Rochester	MN
Barclay Square 6	Rochester	MN
Cinema 3	Rochester	MN
Galleria 6	Rochester	MN
Kandi 4	Willmar	MN
Cinema 4	Winona	MN

Cinemark

Movies 8	Mankato	MN

Cineplex

Edina 4	Edina	MN
Yorktown 3	Edina	MN
Skyway 6	Minneapolis	MN
Ridge Square 3	Minnetonka	MN
Westwind 3	Minnetonka	MN
Willow Creek 8	Plymouth	MN
Knollwood 4	St. Louis Park	MN

General Cinema

Centennial Lakes 8	Minneapolis	MN
Mall of America 14	Minneapolis	MN
Northtown 4	Minneapolis	MN
Shelard Park 5	Minneapolis	MN
Southtown 2	Minneapolis	MN
Burnhaven 8	Saint Paul	MN
Har Mar 11	Saint Paul	MN

Guetschoff Theatres

Apple Valley 6	Apple Valley	MN
Cinema 5	Cambridge	MN
Elk River Cinema 10	Elk River	MN
Hastings 8	Hastings	MN
Rosemount 8	Rosemount	MN
Roseville 4	Roseville	MN
Shakopee Town 11	Shakopee	MN

Lakes & Rivers Cinemas

Washington Square 5	Detroit Lakes	MN
Fair Lakes 5	Fairmont	MN
Westridge Twin	Fergus Falls	MN
Redwing 5	Redwing	MN

Landmark

Uptown	Minneapolis	MN
Lagoon 5	Minneapolis	MN

Mann

Eagan Cinema 9	Eagan	MN
Hopkins Cinema 6	Hopkins	MN
Cinema 10	Maple Grove	MN
Apache 6	Minneapolis	MN
Boulevard 2	Minneapolis	MN
Suburban World	Minneapolis	MN
Village 4	Minneapolis	MN
Cinema 6	St. Louis Park	MN
Cina 5	Saint Paul	MN
Cottage View D.I.	Saint Paul	MN
Galtier 4	Saint Paul	MN
Grandview 2	Saint Paul	MN
Highland 2	Saint Paul	MN
Maple Leaf D.I.	Saint Paul	MN
Signal Hills 5	Saint Paul	MN
Mall 5	Stillwater	MN

United Artists

Brookdale 8	Brooklyn Center	MN
UA Burnsville I	Burnsville	MN
UA Burnsville II	Burnsville	MN
Eden Prairie East 4	Eden Prairie	MN
Eden Prairie West 5	Eden Prairie	MN
Maplewood	Maplewood	MN
UA 6 Maplewood	Maplewood	MN
Saint Anthony Main 5	Minneapolis	MN
Movies at Pavillon l7	Roseville	MN
UA Woodbury 10	Woodbury	MN

Miami-Ft. Lauderdale-West Palm Beach

American Multi-Cinema

Mizner Park 8	Boca Raton	FL
Cocowalk 16	Coconut Grove	FL
Ridge Plaza 8	Davie	FL
Coral Ridge 10	Fort Lauderdale	FL
Sheridan 12	Hollywood	FL
Oceanwalk 10	Hollywood Beach	FL
Kendall 10	Miami	FL
Mall of the Americas 14	Miami	FL
Marina 8	Miami	FL
Omni 4	Miami	FL
Omni 6	Miami	FL
South Dade 8	Miami	FL
Fashion Island 16	Miami	FL
Cross Country 8	West Palm Beach	FL

Cobb

Bay Harbor 4	Bay Harbor	FL
Shadowood 12	Boca Raton	FL
Belleview Twin	Belleview	FL
Boynton 8	Boynton Beach	FL
Sabal Palm 6	Ft. Pierce	FL
Lakeworth 8	Green Acres City	FL
Oakwood 18	Hollywood	FL
Jupiter 14	Jupiter	FL
Cinema 6	Key West	FL
Kendall 9	Miami	FL
Mayfair 10	Miami	FL
Miller Square 8	Miami	FL
University 7	Miami	FL
Byron Carlyle	Miami Beach	FL
Miami Lakes 10	Miami Lakes	FL
Martin Square	Stuart	FL
Regency Square 10	Stuart	FL
Sawgrass 18	Sunrise	FL
Galaxy 12	Vero Beach	FL

General Cinema

Coral Square 8	Fort Lauderdale	FL
Deerfield Mall 8	Fort Lauderdale	FL
Fountains 8	Fort Lauderdale	FL
Galleria 4	Fort Lauderdale	FL
Mission Bay Plaza 8	Fort Lauderdale	FL
Pembroke Pines 8	Fort Lauderdale	FL
Cinema 10	Miami	FL
Hialeah 8	Miami	FL
Intracoastal 8	Miami	FL
Riveria 5	Miami	FL
PGA 6	West Palm Beach	FL

Georgia Theatre Company II

Value Cinemas Atlantis 6	Lantana	FL
Valley Cinemas N. Lauderdale 6	North Lauderdale	FL

Regal

Coral Springs 8	Coral Springs	FL
Delray 18	Delray Beach	FL
California Club 6	Miami	FL

United Artists

Town Center 7	Boca Raton	FL
Boynton Beach 9	Boynton Beach	FL
Movies at Hialeah 14	Hialeah	FL
Treasure Coast 6	Jensen Beach	FL
Movies at Lauderhill 13	Lauderhill	FL
Movies at the Falls 7	Miami	FL
Promenade Plaza 8	Palm Beach	FL
Movies 6	Pompano Beach	FL
Mall Cinema 4	West Palm Beach	FL
River Bridge 8	West Palm Beach	FL
Okee Square 8	West Palm Beach	FL
Wellington Market Place	West Palm Beach	FL

Tampa-St. Petersburg

American Multi-Cinema

Regency 20	Brandon	FL
Clearwater 5	Clearwater	FL
Countryside 6	Clearwater	FL
Tri-City 8	Clearwater	FL
Merchants Walk 10	Lakeland	FL
Crossroads 8	Saint Petersburg	FL
Tyrone Square 6	Saint Petersburg	FL
Sarasota 12	Sarasota	FL
Seminole 8	Seminole	FL
Horizon Park 4	Tampa	FL
Old Hyde Park 7	Tampa	FL
Twin Bays 4	Tampa	FL
Varsity 6	Tampa	FL

Carmike

Arcadia 2	Bradenton	FL
Cortez 2	Bradenton	FL
Brandon 2	Brandon	FL
Plitt	Brandon	FL
Countryside Village	Clearwater	FL
Main Street	Clearwater	FL
Lake Wales 2	Lake Wales	FL
Palm Cinema	Lakeland	FL
Ulmerton Cinema	Largo	FL
Hillsboro West	Tampa	FL
Main Street	Tampa	FL
University Collection	Tampa	FL
Tarpon Springs	Tarpon Springs	FL

Cobb

Bradenton 8	Bradenton	FL
DeSoto Square 6	Bradenton	FL
Oakmont 8	Bradenton	FL
Coralwood 10	Cape Coral	FL
Eagle Ridge 12	Lake Wales	FL
Largo Mall 8	Largo	FL
Embassy 6	Port Richey	FL
Hollywood 18	Port Richey	FL
Crossing 10	Sarasota	FL
Gulfgate 8	Sarasota	FL
Parkway 8	Sarasota	FL
Eastlake 3	Tampa	FL
Northdale 6	Tampa	FL
University Square 4	Tampa	FL
Springlake 10	Winter Haven	FL

Muvico

Lake Howell 8	Casselberry	FL

Regal

Citrus 6	Inverness	FL
Cordova 3	Pensacola	FL
Cordova Mall 4	Pensacola	FL
Britton 8	Tampa	FL

United Artists

Movies at Lake Howell 8	Casselberry	FL
Movies at Clearwater 8	Clearwater	FL
Cinema 90 (6)	Lake City	FL
Santa Rosa 3	Mary Esther	FL
Cinemas West 5	Ocala	FL
Pembroke Pines 9	Pembroke Pines	FL
University 11	Pensacola	FL
Pinellas Park 12	Pinellas Park	FL
Seminole Town Center	Sanford	FL
Capitol 6	Tallahassee	FL
Mission Bell 8	Tampa	FL
Searstown Mall 10	Titusville	FL

Phoenix

American Multi-Cinema

Laguna Village 10	Chandler	AZ
Gateway Village 10	Glendale	AZ
Fiesta Village 6	Mesa	AZ
Sunvalley 10	Mesa	AZ
Three Fountains 4	Mesa	AZ
Ahwautukee 24	Phoenix	AZ
Arrowhead 14	Phoenix	AZ
Bell Plaza 8	Phoenix	AZ
Metro Village 6	Phoenix	AZ
Town & Country 6	Phoenix	AZ
Lakes 6	Tempe	AZ

Century Theatres

Glendale 9 D.I.	Glendale	AZ
Scottsdale 6 D.I.	Tempe	AZ

Harkins

Arcadia 8	Phoenix	AZ
Bell Tower 8	Phoenix	AZ
Bell Towne Centre 8	Phoenix	AZ
Camelview Luxury 5	Phoenix	AZ
Camelback Mall 3	Phoenix	AZ
Centerpoint Luxury 11	Phoenix	AZ
Christown 5	Phoenix	AZ
Cine Capri	Phoenix	AZ
Cornerstone 6	Phoenix	AZ
Fashion Square 7	Phoenix	AZ
Fiesta 5	Phoenix	AZ
Paradis Valley Mall 7	Phoenix	AZ
Poca Fiesta 4	Phoenix	AZ
Sedona Luxury 6	Phoenix	AZ
Shea N. Scottsdale 14	Phoenix	AZ
Southwest 8	Phoenix	AZ
Tri-City 5	Phoenix	AZ
Westride Mall 6	Phoenix	AZ

Super Saver

Superstation Springs 8	Mesa	AZ
Town Center 8	Mesa	AZ
Bell Road 8	Phoenix	AZ
Palm Glen 8	Phoenix	AZ

United Artists

Chandler Park 10	Chandler	AZ
Bell Park Cinemas 6	Glendale	AZ
Valvista 10	Mesa	AZ
Metro Park 8	Phoenix	AZ
Christown Mall Cinemas 6	Phoenix	AZ
Westridge Park 6	Phoenix	AZ
Pavillion 11	Scottsdale	AZ
Scottsdale 5	Scottsdale	AZ
Sonora Village 10	Scottsdale	AZ

Wehrenberg

Frontier Village 10	Prescott	AZ
Marina Twin	Prescott	AZ
Plaza West	Prescott	AZ

Denver

American Multi-Cinema

Buckingham Square 4	Aurora	CO
Buckingham Village 6	Aurora	CO
Seven Hills 10	Aurora	CO
Tiffany Square 6	Colorado Springs	CO
Tiffany Plaza 6	Denver	CO
Tivoli 12	Denver	CO
Colorado Plaza 6	Glendale	CO
Southbridge 8	Littleton	CO
Westminster 5	Westminster	CO
Westminster Mall 6	Westminster	CO

Carmike

Stage	Aspen	CO
Carmike	Colorado Springs	CO
Chapel Hill 9	Colorado Springs	CO
Citadel Terrace 6	Colorado Springs	CO
Carmike	Ft. Collins	CO
Creger Plaza 4	Ft. Collins	CO
University	Ft. Collins	CO
Cinema	Greeley	CO

Cinamerica

Old Town 14	Arvada	CO
Aurora Plaza 6	Aurora	CO
Arapahoe Village 4	Boulder	CO
Crossroads 6	Boulder	CO
Cherry Creek 8	Denver	CO
Tamarac Square 6-plex	Denver	CO
Arapahoe East 4-plex	Englewood	CO
Green Mountain 6-plex	Lakewood	CO
Union Square 6-plex	Lakewood	CO
Bowles Crossing 12	Littleton	CO
Festival 6	Littleton	CO
Southwest Plaza 5-plex	Littleton	CO
Colony Square 12	Louisville	CO
Northglenn 6-plex	Northglenn	CO

Landmark

Chez Artiste 3	Denver	CO
Esquire 2	Denver	CO
Mayan 3	Denver	CO

Metropolitan

Metrolux 12	Loveland	CO

Super Saver

Arlington Square 8	Arvada	CO
Aurora Plaza 8	Aurora	CO
Citadel 8	Colorado Springs	CO
Bear Valley 8	Denver	CO
Pinnacle 8	Thornton	CO

United Artists

Cooper 6	Arvada	CO
Cooper 5	Aurora	CO
Flatirons	Boulder	CO
Village 4	Boulder	CO
Academy 6	Colorado Springs	CO
Broadmoor	Colorado Springs	CO
Cinema 70 3-Plex	Colorado Springs	CO
Hanock Plaza 4	Colorado Springs	CO
Continental	Denver	CO
Greenwood Plaza	Englewood	CO
Arbor Cinema 4	Fort Collins	CO
Campus West Twin 2	Fort Collins	CO
Foothills Twin 2	Fort Collins	CO
Bittersweet 4-Plex	Greeley	CO
Cooper Twin 2	Greeley	CO
Greeley Mall Twin 2	Greeley	CO
Cooper 7	Littleton	CO
Courtyard 4-Plex	Longmont	CO
Movies 3-Plex	Longmont	CO
Orchards Twin 2	Loveland	CO
Cinema Twin 2	Pueblo	CO
Pueblo Mall 3	Pueblo	CO
Thorton Town Center 10	Thorton	CO

Pittsburgh

Carmike

Plaza	Beaver Falls	PA
Clearview 4	Butler	PA
Cinema	Greensburg	PA
Greensburg	Greensburg	PA
Greengate Mall Triple	Greensburg	PA
Cinema	Indiana	PA
Regency	Indiana	PA
Laurel 30	Latrobe	PA
Movie World 7	Monaca	PA
Monroeville Mall Four	Monroeville	PA
Cranberry	Pittsburgh	PA
Galleria	Pittsburgh	PA
Maxisaver	Pittsburgh	PA
Rainbow	Pittsburgh	PA
South Hills Village	Pittsburgh	PA
Southland 9	Pittsburgh	PA
Cinema 19	Washington	PA
Washington Mall 8	Washington	PA

Cinemagic

Bellevue 2	Pittsburgh	PA
Denis 4	Pittsburgh	PA
Hollywood	Pittsburgh	PA
Manor 4	Pittsburgh	PA
Squirrel Hill 6	Pittsburgh	PA

Mulone Theatres

Waterworks Cinema 10	Pittsburgh	PA
Harmar Cinemas 6	Harmar	PA
Cheswick Quads	Cheswick	PA
Cinema 356 4	Spruer	PA

National Amusement

Showcase East 10	Pittsburgh	PA
Showcase North 11	Pittsburgh	PA
Showcase West 12	Pittsburgh	PA
Supersaver 8	Pittsburgh	PA

St. Louis

American Multi-Cinema

Village 6	Hazelwood	MO
Northwest 10	St. Ann	MO
Regency 8	St. Charles	MO
Crestwood 10	St. Louis	MO
Esquire 7	St. Louis	MO
Galleria 6	St. Louis	MO

B & B Theatres

Festus 8	Festus	MO
Cinema 2	Fulton	MO

Kerasotes

Eastgate 6	Alton	IL
Quad	Belleville	IL
Ritz 3	Belleville	IL
Nameoki 2	Granite City	IL

Lory 2	Highland	IL
Stadium 2	Jerseyville	IL
Broadway Theater	Cape Girardeau	MO
Town Plaza Cinema 5	Cape Girardeau	MO
Movies 2	Flat River	MO
Meramec Cinema 2	Sullivan	MO

Wehrenberg

Alton Twin	Alton	IL
St. Clair 10 Cine	Fairview Heights	IL
West Park 4 Cine	Cape Girardeau	MO
Battlefield 6 Cine	Springfield	MO
Campbell 16	Springfield	MO
Chesterfield 4	St. Louis	MO
Cine	St. Louis	MO
Clarkson 6	St. Louis	MO
Creve Coeur 3	St. Louis	MO
Des Peres 14 Cine	St. Louis	MO
Eureka 6	St. Louis	MO
Halls Ferry 14	St. Louis	MO
Keller 8 Cine	St. Louis	MO
Kenrick 8	St. Louis	MO
Lindbergh 8 Cine	St. Louis	MO
Mid River 6 Cine	St. Louis	MO
North Twin D.I.	St. Louis	MO
North West Plaza 8	St. Louis	MO
Ronnie's 8 Cine	St. Louis	MO
Shady Oak Theatre	St. Louis	MO
St. Charles 10 Cine	St. Louis	MO
Union Station 10 Cine	St. Louis	MO
Westport 1 & 2	St. Louis	MO

Sacramento-Stockton

Century Theatres

Cinedome 9	Citrus Heights	CA
49er 6 D.I.	Sacramento	CA
Capitol 4-plex	Sacramento	CA
Century 14 Complex	Sacramento	CA
Sacramento 6 D.I.	Sacramento	CA
State 6-plex	Sacramento	CA

Cinamerica

Festival Tenplex	Modesto	CA
Festival 4-plex	Stockton	CA
Regency 4-plex	Stockton	CA

Cinemacal

Royal 4	Stockton	CA
Sherwood Plaza 2	Stockton	CA

Cinemark

County Fair Movies 5	Woodland	CA
Yuba City 8	Yuba	CA

Landmark

Tower 3	Sacramento	CA
Sacramento Inn 3	Sacramento	CA

United Artists

Sunrise 4	Citrus Heights	CA
UA The Movies 6	Citrus Heights	CA
Del Oro Grass Valley 3	Grass Valley	CA
Grass Valley Cinemas 2	Grass Valley	CA
UA Merced 4	Merced	CA
Regency Merced 7	Merced	CA
Arden Fair 6	Sacramento	CA
UA Downtown Plaza 7	Sacramento	CA

Orlando-Daytona Beach

American Multi-Cinema

Interstate 6	Altamonte Springs	FL
Volusia Square 8	Daytona	FL
Daytona 6	Daytona Beach	FL
Oaks 10	Gainesville	FL
Pleasure Island 10	Lake Buena Vista	FL
Merritt Square 1-6 & 7-12	Merritt Island	FL
Orange Park 5	Orange Park	FL
Celebration 2	Orlando	FL
Fashion Village 8	Orlando	FL

Carmike

Eustis 2	Eustis	FL
Baymeadows	Jacksonville	FL
Mandarin	Jacksonville	FL
Hoffner Centre	Orlando	FL
Palatka 2	Palatka	FL
Big Tree	South Daytona	FL
Boulevard 3	Winterhaven	FL
Mugs & Movies	Winterhaven	FL
University	Winter Park	FL

Cobb

Osceola Square 12	Kissimmee	FL
Oaks 10	Melbourne	FL
Roxy 10	Melbourne	FL
Southchase 7	Orlando	FL
Palm Bay 10	Palm Bay	FL

Eastern Federal

Royal Park 4	Gainesville	FL
Conway 1 & 2	Orlando	FL
Port Orange 6	Port Orange	FL

General Cinema

Altamonte 8	Orlando	FL
Altamonte Mall 2	Orlando	FL
Colonial Promenade 6	Orlando	FL
Fashion Square 6	Orlando	FL
Lake Mary Centre 8	Orlando	FL

Regal Cinemas

Litchfield 10	Gainesville	FL
Beach Boulevard 12	Jacksonville	FL
Litchfield 10	Jacksonville	FL
The Avenues Mall	Jacksonville	FL
UC 6 (7)	Orlando	FL

United Artists

Movies at Wekiva	Apopka	FL
Volusia 1-3	Daytona Beach	FL
Mandarin Landing 8	Jacksonville	FL
Regency Square 12	Jacksonville	FL
The Movies at Orange Sq. 7	Jacksonville	FL
Market Place 8	Orange City	FL
Florida Mall 7	Orlando	FL
Movies at Republic Square	Orlando	FL

Portland, OR

Act III

Albany	Albany	OR
Valley Tri	Beaverton	OR
Westgate	Beaverton	OR
Ninth Street	Corvallis	OR
White Side	Corvallis	OR
Gresham Quad	Gresham	OR
Evergreen Parkway	Hillsboro	OR
Trail Twin	Hood River	OR
McMinnville	McMinnville	OR
Hilltop	Oregon City	OR
82nd Ave. Cinemas	Portland	OR
Broadway Metroplex	Portland	OR
Clackamas	Portland	OR
Eastgate	Portland	OR
Foster D.I.	Portland	OR
Fox	Portland	OR
Guild	Portland	OR
Hollywood Cinemas	Portland	OR
Jantzen Cinemas	Portland	OR
Lloyd Cinemas	Portland	OR
Lloyd Mall Cinemas	Portland	OR
Mall 205 Cinemas	Portland	OR
Music Box	Portland	OR
Rose Moyer	Portland	OR
Southgate	Portland	OR
Tigard	Portland	OR
Washington Square Cinemas	Portland	OR
Keizer Tri Cinemas	Salem	OR
Lancaster Mall Cinemas	Salem	OR
Movieland	Salem	OR
Southgate Cinemas	Salem	OR
Town Center	Wilsonville	OR
Three Rivers	Kelso	WA
Longview	Longview	WA
Triangle	Longview	WA
Cascade Park	Vancouver	WA
Hazel Dell	Vancouver	WA
Vancouver Mall	Vancouver	WA
Vancouver Plaza 10	Vancouver	WA

Coming Attractions

Florence 4	Florence	OR
Cinema 7	Forest Grove	OR

Indianapolis

Cinemark

Greenwood Corners Mov. 8	Indianapolis	IN
Washington Market Mov. 8	Indianapolis	IN

General Cinema

Castleton Square 3	Indianapolis	IN
Clearwater Crossing 12	Indianapolis	IN
Eastgate Mall 6	Indianapolis	IN
Glendale 3	Indianapolis	IN
Greenwood Park 7	Indianapolis	IN
Lafayette Square 5	Indianapolis	IN

Goodrich

Applewood 9	Anderson	IN
Eastside 10	Lafayette	IN
Market Square 2	Lafayette	IN

Kerasotes

Mounds Mall 2	Anderson	IN
Showplace 4	Anderson	IN
College Cinema Mall 4	Bloomington	IN
Showplace 11	Bloomington	IN

Von Lee 3	Bloomington	IN
Cinema8	Kokomo	IN
Markland Mall Cinema5	Kokomo	IN
Dollar Cinema 7	Muncie	IN
Muncie Mall Cinema 3	Muncie	IN
Northwest Plaza Cinema 8	Muncie	IN

Sony

Cherry Tree 10	Indianapolis	IN
College Park 10	Indianapolis	IN
Greenwood 9	Indianapolis	IN
Lafayette Square 8	Indianapolis	IN
Norgate 4	Indianapolis	IN

United Artists

Circle Center Starport 9	Indianapolis	IN
Eagle Highlands	Indianapolis	IN

Hartford-New Haven

Hoyts

Dayville 3	Dayville	CT
East Manchester Cinemas 6	East Manchester	CT
Cine Enfield 8	Enfield	CT
Cinemas 6	Groton	CT
Cine 4	Hartford	CT
Madison Cinemas 2	Madison	CT
Meriden Cinemas 10	Meriden	CT
Mystic Village Cinemas 3	Mystic	CT
Playhouse 2	New Canaan	CT
Norwich Cinemas 2	Norwich	CT
Saybrook Cinemas 2	Saybrook	CT
Saybrook Cinemas 4	Saybrook	CT
Cinemas 6	Stratford	CT
Mall View Plaza 10	Waterbury	CT
Naugatuck Valley Mall 4	Waterbury	CT
Waterford Cinemas 9	Waterford	CT
Jillson Square 6	Willimantic	CT

National Amusement

Showcase 12	Berlin	CT
Showcase East 14	Hartford	CT
Milford 4-plex	Milford	CT
Showcase 5	Milford	CT
Newington 3	Newington	CT
Showcase 8	North Haven	CT
Showcase 8	Orange	CT

Sony

Bristol 8	Bristol	CT
Community 2	Fairfield	CT
Holiday 6	Torrington	CT
Fine Arts 1 & 2	Westport	CT
Fine Arts 3	Westport	CT
Post 1	Westport	CT

San Diego

American Multi-Cinema

Wiegand Plaza 8	Encinitas	CA
La Jolla 12	La Jolla	CA
Mission Valley 20	San Diego	CA

Cinamerica

University Town 6-plex	La Jolla	CA
Plaza Bonita 6-plex	National City	CA
El Camino 8-plex	Oceanside	CA
Cinema 21	San Diego	CA
Grove 9	San Diego	CA
Hazard Center 7	San Diego	CA
Rancho Bernardo 6-plex	San Diego	CA
Sports Arena 6-plex	San Diego	CA
Valley Circle	San Diego	CA

Cinemark

Cinema 3	Hemet	CA
Movies 10	Hemet	CA

Edwards

Del Mar Highlands 8	Del Mar	CA
Flower Hill 4	Del Mar	CA
Carousel 6	Escondido	CA
Vineyard Twin	Escondido	CA
Poway Cinemas 10	Poway	CA
San Marcos 5	San Marcos	CA
Santa Maria Cinemas 10	Santa Maria	CA
Mira Mesa 4	San Diego	CA
Mira Mesa 7	San Diego	CA

Landmark

Cove	San Diego	CA
Guild	San Diego	CA
Hillcrest 5	San Diego	CA
Ken	San Diego	CA
Park	San Diego	CA

Pacific

La Jolla Village 4	La Jolla	CA
Grossmont Center 8	La Mesa	CA
Grossmont Trolley 8	La Mesa	CA

Cinerama 6	San Diego	CA
Clairemont Twin	San Diego	CA

SoCal

Plaza Camino Real Cinema 4	Carlsbad	CA
Town & Country Cinema 3	Oceanside	CA
Temeku Cinema 7	Temecula	CA
Tower Cinema 2	Temecula	CA

United Artists

Escondido 8	Escondido	CA
Glasshouse 6	San Diego	CA
Horton Plaza 7	San Diego	CA

Charlotte - Greensboro - Winston Salem

American Multi-Cinema

Carolina Pavillion 22	Charlotte	NC

Carmike

Cinema Twin	Asheboro	NC
Town Cinema 6	Charlotte	NC
University 6	Charlotte	NC
Eastride 4	Gastonia	NC
Circle 6	Greensboro	NC
Terrace 4	Hickory	NC
Capri Triple	High Point	NC
Carmike 8	High Point	NC
Cinema 4	Lexington	NC
Cinema 4	Lincolnton	NC
Festival 10	Matthews	NC
Plaza Twin	Rockingham	NC
Kendale Twin	Sanford	NC
Cinema 4	Southern Pines	NC
Town & Country Twin	Southern Pines	NC
Gateway 4	Statesville	NC
Newtowne Twin	Statesville	NC
Marketplace 6	Winston-Salem	NC
Reynolds Triple	Winston-Salem	NC
Carmike 10	Winston-Salem	NC

Cinemark

Cinema 5	Asheboro	NC
Brassfield 10	Greensboro	NC
Movies 10	Matthews	NC
Mall Cinema 6	Salisbury	NC

Eastern Federal

Delta 6	Charlotte	NC
Manor 1 & 2	Charlotte	NC
Movies 8	Charlotte	NC
Park 51-6	Charlotte	NC
Regency 4	Charlotte	NC
Movies at the Lake	Cornelius	NC
North Point 5	Winston-Salem	NC

General Cinema

South Park 3	Charlotte	NC
Tower Place Festival 8	Charlotte	NC
Four Seasons Town 4	Greensboro	NC
Hanes Mall 4	Winston-Salem	NC

United Artists

Eastgate 5	Albemarle	NC
Carolina Mall 8	Concord	NC
Litchfield Cinemas 4	Gastonia	NC
Crown Cinemas 6	Hickory	NC

Cincinnati

Chakeres

Belmont Auto	Dayton	OH
Kettering Cinemas 1 & 2	Dayton	OH
Melody 49 D.I. 1 & 2	Dayton	OH
Fairborn Cinemas 1 & 2	Fairborn	OH
Skyborn D.I.	Fairborn	OH
Park Layne D.I.	New Carlisle	OH
Sidney Cinemas 1-3	Sidney	OH
Plaza Cinemas 5	Wilmington	OH
Wilmington D.I.	Wilmington	OH

National Amusement

Showcase 9	Erlanger	KY
Eastgate Mall 7	Cincinnati	OH
I-275 Cinemas 4	Cincinnati	OH
Kenwood Towne Center 5	Cincinnati	OH
Northgate Cinemas 7	Cincinnati	OH
Showcase 12	Cincinnati	OH
Tri County Cinemas 5	Cincinnati	OH
Showcase Western Hills 12	Cincinnati	OH
Centerville 6	Centerville	OH
Beaver Creek 7	Dayton	OH
Cinema North 5	Dayton	OH
Cross Pointe 12	Dayton	OH
Dayton Mall 8	Dayton	OH
Showcase 12	Huber Heights	OH
Showcase 9	Springdale	OH

Sony

Salem Ave 3	Dayton	OH
Beaver Valley 6	Dayton	OH

Raleigh-Durham

Carmike

Ram Triple	Chapel Hill	NC
Carmike 7	Durham	NC
Willowdale 8	Durham	NC
Wynnsomg 10	Durham	NC
Berkely 4	Goldsboro	NC
Carmike 7	Raleigh	NC
Six Forks 6	Raleigh	NC
Tower Twin	Raleigh	NC
Waverly Place	Raleigh	NC
Merchants 6	Raleigh	NC
Cardinal Triple	Rocky Mount	NC
Englewood Twin	Rocky Mount	NC
Golden East 4	Rocky Mount	NC
Oakwood Twin	Rocky Mount	NC
Gold Park Twin	Wilson	NC
Parkwood Triple	Wilson	NC

Eastern Federal

Plaza 3	Chapel Hill	NC
Movies at Timberlyne 6	Chapel Hill	NC

General Cinema

Cross Creek Mall 3	Fayetteville	NC
Cross Pointe 6	Fayetteville	NC

United Artists

Imperial 4	Cary	NC
Litchfield Cinemas 4	Goldsboro	NC
Mission Valley 5	Raleigh	NC

Milwaukee

Carmike

Prairie 5	Beloit	WI
Delavan 2	Delavan	WI
Geneva 4	Lake Geneva	WI
University Sq. 4	Madison	WI

Landmark

Downer 2	Milwaukee	WI
Oriental 3	Milwaukee	WI

Marcus

Wisconsin 4	Beaver Dam	WI
Rivoli	Cedarburg	WI
Eastgate 14	Madison	WI
Point 10	Madison	WI
Southtown 5	Madison	WI
West Towne 3	Madison	WI
Westgate 3	Madison	WI
Delafield 12	Milwaukee	WI
Marc 5	Milwaukee	WI
North Shore 10	Milwaukee	WI
Northtown 8	Milwaukee	WI
Prospect 3	Milwaukee	WI
Skyway 6	Milwaukee	WI
South Shore 13	Milwaukee	WI
Southtown 6	Milwaukee	WI
Tosa	Milwaukee	WI
Value 6	Milwaukee	WI
Value 8	Milwaukee	WI
Westown 10	Milwaukee	WI
Regency Mall 6	Racine	WI
Westgate 5	Racine	WI
Marc 10	Sheboygan	WI

Kansas City

American Multi-Cinema

Indian Springs South 6	Kansas City	KS
Oak Park 12	Overland Park	KS
Independence 20	Independence	MO
Bannister Square 6	Kansas City	MO
Crown Center 6	Kansas City	MO
Metro North 12	Kansas City	MO
Ward Parkway 20	Kansas City	MO
Summit 4	Lee's Summit	MO

B B Theatres

Cinema 8	Liberty	MO

Crown

Cinema Twin	Lawrence	KS
Hillcrest 5	Lawrence	KS
Varsity	Lawrence	KS
Landing 4	Leavenworth	KS
Gage 4	Topeka	KS
West Ridge 8	Topeka	KS
West Ridge Mall 6	Topeka	KS
Blue Ridge East 5	Kansas City	MO
Blue Ridge West 6	Kansas City	MO
Blue Springs 8	Kansas City	MO
Chouteau 4	Kansas City	MO
Red Bridge 4	Kansas City	MO
Seville 4	Kansas City	MO
Truman Corners 4	Kansas City	MO
Watts Mill 4	Kansas City	MO

Hillcrest 4	St. Joseph	MO
Plaza 8	St. Joseph	MO
Campus 2	Warrensburg	MO

Dickinson

Dickinson Cinema 6	Lawrence	KS
Olathe Landing 8	Olathe	KS
Glenwood 4	Overland Park	KS
South Glen 12	Overland Park	KS
Gladstone 4	Gladstone	MO
Noland Fashion Square 6	Independence	MO
Antioch 2	Kansas City	MO
Dickinson Cinema 6	Kansas City	MO
Plaza 3	Kansas City	MO
Trail	St. Joseph	MO

United Artists

Trailridge 3	Shawnee	KS
Bannister Mall 5	Kansas City	MO

Nashville

Carmike

Carmike 8	Clarksville	TN
Cinema 5	Clarksville	TN
Martin 4	Clarksville	TN
Martin Triple	Lebanon	TN
Carmike 6	Murfreesboro	TN
Stone River 6	Murfreesboro	TN
Belcourt Twin	Nashville	TN
Bellevue 4	Nashville	TN
Bell Forge 10	Nashville	TN
Bell Road Triple	Nashville	TN
Carmike 6	Nashville	TN
Cinema North	Nashville	TN
Cinema South 4	Nashville	TN
Fountain Sq. 14	Nashville	TN
Hermitage 4	Nashville	TN
Lions Head Five	Nashville	TN
Rivergate 8	Nashville	TN
Springfield	Springfield	TN

Regal

Indian Lakes 10	Hendersonville	TN
Courtyard 8	Hermitage	TN
Nippers Corner 10	Nashville	TN
Bellevue 12	Nashville	TN

Columbus

American Multi-Cinema

Eastland Center 8	Columbus	OH
Eastland Plaza 6	Columbus	OH
Lennox 24	Columbus	OH
Village 18	Dublin	OH
Westerville 6	Westerville	OH

Carmike

Movies 16	Gahanna	OH
Movies 12	Hilliard	OH
Colonial Twin	Mt. Vernon	OH

Chakeres

Cinemas 10	Springfield	OH
Melody Cruise-In 2	Springfield	OH
Upper Valley 5	Springfield	OH

Cinemark

Movies 12	Columbus	OH
Movies 10	Columbus	OH
Cinema 10	Zanesville	OH

Crown

Indian Mound 6	Heath	OH
Newark 4	Newark	OH

General Cinema

Northland 8	Columbus	OH
Westland 8	Columbus	OH

Sony

Continent 9	Columbus	OH
Westerville 2	Columbus	OH

Greenville
Salt Lake City-Ogden

Carmike

Cache Valley	Logan	UT
City Square 4	Ogden	UT
Riverdale 4	Ogden	UT
Cottonwood 4	Salt Lake City	UT
Creeksides 3	Salt Lake City	UT
Flick 2	Salt Lake City	UT
Plaza 5400 Six	Salt Lake City	UT
Villa 1	Salt Lake City	UT

600

Century Theatres

Century 21-23 Triplex	Salt Lake City	UT
Century 24-29 Twin	Salt Lake City	UT

Cinemark

Layton Hills 6	Layton	UT
Movies 10	Layton	UT
Newgate 4	Ogden	UT
Holiday Village Cinema 3	Park City	UT
Movies 8	Provo	UT
Movies 10	Salt Lake City	UT
Movies 9	Sandy	UT
Valley Fair 9	West Valley City	UT

Cineplex

Family Center 4	Midvale	UT
Trolley North 3	North Salt Lake City	UT
Cinedome 2	Ogden	UT
Wilshire 3	Ogden	UT
University 4	Orem	UT
Broadway 6	Salt Lake City	UT
Crossroads 3	Salt Lake City	UT
Holladay Center 6	Salt Lake City	UT
Midvalley Cinemas 6	Salt Lake City	UT
Trolley Corners 3	Salt Lake City	UT
Trolley Square Mall 4	Salt Lake City	UT
SouthTowne Centre 10	Sandy	UT

San Antonio

Act III

Arbor	Austin	TX
Lakecreek	Austin	TX
Lakehills	Austin	TX
Lincoln	Austin	TX
Northcross	Austin	TX
Riverside	Austin	TX
Southwood	Austin	TX
Westgate 3	Austin	TX
Westgate 8	Austin	TX
Village	Austin	TX
Bandera	San Antonio	TX
Century South	San Antonio	TX
Crossroads	San Antonio	TX
Embassy 14	San Antonio	TX
Galaxy 14	San Antonio	TX
Ingram Square 8	San Antonio	TX
Mission D.I.	San Antonio	TX
Nakoma 8	San Antonio	TX
Northwest 14	San Antonio	TX
Rolling Oaks 6	San Antonio	TX
Westlakes	San Antonio	TX
Windsor Mall 5	San Antonio	TX

American Multi Cinema

Rivercenter 9	San Antonio	TX

Cinemark

Movies 12	Pflugerville	TX
Movies 8	Round Rock	TX
Movies 9	San Antonio	TX
Movies 16	San Antonio	TX

General Cinema

Great Hills 8	Austin	TX
Highland 10	Austin	TX

Grand Rapids-Battle Creek-Kalamazoo

GKC Theatres

Towne Cinemas 8	Battle Creek	MI
Lyric Cinema 4	Ludington	MI

General Cinemas

Maple Hill Mall 3	Kalamazoo	MI

Goodrich

W. Columbia 7	Battle Creek	MI
Holland 7	Holland	MI
Jackson 8	Jackson	MI

Loeks Star

Grand Rapids 18	Grand Rapids	MI
Holland 8	Holland	MI

National Amusements

Showcase 10	Grand Rapids	MI

United Artists

Benton Harbor 5	Benton Harbor	MI
North Kent Mall 8	Grand Rapids	MI
Woodland 8	Grand Rapids	MI
West Main 7	Kalamazoo	MI
Movies at Portage 10	Portage	MI

Buffalo-Niagara Falls

American Multi-Cinema

Como 8	Cheektowaga	NY
Holiday 6	Cheektowaga	NY

General Cinema

Market Arcade 8	Buffalo	NY
Mckinley Mall 6	Buffalo	NY
Thruway Mall 8	Buffalo	NY
University 8	Buffalo	NY
Walden Galleria 12	Buffalo	NY
Summit Park 6	Niagara Falls	NY
Marketplace 7	Rochester	NY
Pittsford Plaza 6	Rochester	NY

Sony

Pittsford 1	Rochester	NY
Pittsford 2	Rochester	NY
Towne Quad	Rochester	NY
Webster 12	Webster	NY

Norfolk-Virginia Beach

American Multi-Cinema

Coliseum 4	Hampton	VA
Newmarket 4	Hampton	VA
Patrick Henry 7	Newport News	VA
Circle 10	Norfolk	VA
Lynnhaven 8	Virginia Beach	VA

Carmike

Beechmont Twin	Newport News	VA
Carmike Four	Williamsburg	VA
Williamsburg Crossing 7	Williamsburg	VA

Cinemark

Movies 10	Chesapeake	VA
Movies 10	Lynchburg	VA

R/C

Columbus Movies 12	Virginia Beach	VA

Regal

Chester 6	Chester	VA
Greenbrier 4	Chesapeake	VA
Southpark 6	Colonial Height	VA
Armory Drive 3	Franklin	VA
Kiln Creek 14	Newport News	VA
Newmarket 4	Newport News	VA
Cloverleaf 8	Richmond	VA
Ridge 7	Richmond	VA
Westhampton 2	Richmond	VA
Willow Lawn 4	Richmond	VA
Virginia Beach 12	Virginia Beach	VA

United Artists

Chesterfield Mall 5	Richmond	VA
Midlothian 6	Richmond	VA
West Tower 6	Richmond	VA
Kempsriver 7	Virginia Beach	VA
UA Lynnhaven 5	Virginia Beach	VA
Lynhaven Mall 11	Virginia Beach	VA

New Orleans

General Cinema

Esplanade Mall 9	New Orleans	LA
Lake Side 5	New Orleans	LA

Landmark

Canal Place Cinemas 4	New Orleans	LA
Prytania	New Orleans	LA

M.I. Theatres

Washington Square 4	Bastrop	LA
Trackside 5	Bogalusa	LA
Chalmette Cinema 9	Chalmette	LA
Cinema City 2	Kenner	LA
Movies 4	Lafayette	LA
Movies 5	La Place	LA
Oakridge Cinema 9	Marrero	LA
Panorama 6	Metairie	LA
Eastgate Cinema 6	Monroe	LA
Movies 5 at the Plaza	New Orleans	LA
Uptown Square 4	New Orleans	LA

United Artists

Bon Marche 11	Baton Rouge	LA
Essen Mall Cinema 6	Baton Rouge	LA
Siegen Village 10	Baton Rouge	LA
Houma Twin 2	Houma	LA
Plaza Cinema 4	Houma	LA
Southland Cinema 4	Houma	LA
Eastlake Plaza 8	New Orleans	LA
Village Aurora Cinemas 6	New Orleans	LA

Memphis

General Cinema
Hickory Ridge Mall 4	Memphis	TN
Mall of Memphis 5	Memphis	TN
Raleigh 6	Memphis	TN

Malco
Appletree 12	Memphis	TN
Bartlett Cinema 10	Memphis	TN
Forest Hill Cinema 8	Memphis	TN
Germantown Cinema 9	Memphis	TN
Highland Quartet	Memphis	TN
Malco Trio	Memphis	TN
Ridgeway 4	Memphis	TN
Southwest Twin D.I.	Memphis	TN
Summer Quartet D.I.	Memphis	TN
Winchester Court 8	Memphis	TN

Oklahoma City

American Multi-Cinema
Robinson Crossing 6	Norman	OK
Memorial Square 8	Oklahoma City	OK
Northwest 8	Oklahoma City	OK

Carmike
Dunkin	Cushing	OK
Oakwood 5	Enid	OK
Video Twin	Enid	OK
Carmike	Lawton	OK
Video Triple	Lawton	OK
Carmike 6	Stillwater	OK
Satellite Twin	Stillwater	OK

General Cinema
Brixton Square 8	Oklahoma City	OK
Crossroads 8	Oklahoma City	OK
Penn Square Mall 10	Oklahoma City	OK
Quail Springs 6	Oklahoma City	OK

Hollywood Theatres
Movies 6	Bartlesville	OK
Movies 6	Shawnee	OK

M.I. Theatres
Northpark Cinema 7	Oklahoma City	OK
Dollar Movies 5	Yukon	OK

United Artists
Cache Cinemas 8	Lawton	OK
Heritage Park 3	Midwest City	OK
Heritage Plaza 5	Midwest City	OK
Village 6-Plex	Norman	OK
Almonte 6-plex	Oklahoma City	OK

Harrisburg-Lancaster

American Multi-Cinema
Colonial Commons	Harrisburg	PA
Eden 2	Lancaster	PA
Wonderland 4	Lancaster	PA
York 4	York	PA

Milgram
Main 2	Ephrata	PA
Campus	Lewisburg	PA
Midway D.I.	Lewistown	PA
West Shore	New Cumberland	PA
Marietta	Marietta	PA

United Artists
Camp Hill Twin 2	Camp Hill	PA
UA 6 Capitol Ct.	Camp Hill	PA
Eric Colonial Park Mall	Harrisburg	PA
Pacific Lancaster 4	Lancaster	PA
Delco Plaza 9	York	PA
Movies at York Mall 2	York	PA

Providence-New Bedford

General Cinema
No. Dartmouth Mall 8	North Dartmouth	MA
Lincoln Mall 4	Providence	RI
Warwick Mall 3	Providence	RI

Hoyts
Mashpee Cinemas 6	Mashpee	MA
Silver City Galleria 10	Taunton	MA
Taunton Cinemas 8	Taunton	MA

Melrose
Newport D.I.	Newport	RI
Four Seasons Cinema 5	Providence	RI
Apple Valley Cinemas 4	Smithfield	RI
Campus Cinema	Wakefield	RI

Mini
Bijou	Fairhaven	MA
Cinema 6	Fairhaven	MA
Pier Cinema Twin	Narragansett	RI

National Amusement
Showcase 10	Seekonk	MA
Showcase 12	Warwick	RI

Sony
Harbour Mall 8	Fall River	MA
Somerville 12	Somerville	MA

Albuquerque-Santa Fe

Century
Albuquerque 6 D.I.	Albuquerque	NM

Cinemark
Movies 8	Albuquerque	NM
Movies West 8	Albuquerque	NM

General Cinemas
Park Square 3	Albuquerque	NM
San Mateo 8	Albuquerque	NM

United Artists
Coronado 6	Albuquerque	NM
Del Norte 4	Albuquerque	NM
Montomery Plaza 5	Albuquerque	NM
Four Hills 12	Albuquerque	NM
High Ridge 8	Albuquerque	NM
Winrock 6	Albuquerque	NM
UA Lensic Theatres	Santa Fe	NM
UA De Vargas Center 6	Santa Fe	NM
UA North Theatre 6	Santa Fe	NM
UA South Theatre	Santa Fe	NM

Scranton - Wilkes Barre

General Cinema
Viewmont Mall 5	Scranton	PA
Wyoming Mall 7	Wilkes Barre	PA

Milgram
Churchill 7	Hazleton	PA
Ritz	Scranton	PA
Gateway Cinema 6	Wikes Barre	PA

Sony Theatres
Stroud Mall 7	Stroudsburg	PA

United Artists
UA Scranton 8	Scranton	PA
UA Steamtown Mall	Scranton	PA

Louisville

Chakeres
Brighton Park Cinemas 2	Frankfort	KY
Franklin Square Cinema 6	Frankfort	KY
University Cinema	Morehead	KY

Cinemark
Village 8	Louisville	KY
Cinema 8	Richmond	KY

National Amusement
Showcase 13	Louisville	KY
Stonybrook Cinemas 10	Louisville	KY

THEATRES IN THE TOP CANADIAN MARKETS

Toronto

Cineplex

410 & 7 Centre 4	Brampton	ON
Centennial 3	Brampton	ON
Cinemas 3	Brantford	ON
Market Square 3	Brantford	ON
Odeon 2	Brantford	ON
Cineplex 6	Burlington	ON
Showcase Cinema 6	Burlington	ON
Twin Cinema	Cambridge	ON
Stone Road Mall 5	Guelph	ON
Centre Mall 8	Hamilton	ON
Upper James Place 7	Hamilton	ON
Hyland 1	Kitchener	ON
Fairway Center 7	Kitchener	ON
Frederick Mall 2	Kitchener	ON
Erin Mills 5	Mississauga	ON
South Common Mall 7	Mississauga	ON
Niagara Square 3	Niagara Falls	ON
Oakville Mews 5	Oakville	ON
Elgin Mills 10	Richmond Hill	ON
Promenade 6	Richmond Hill	ON
Fairview Mall 5	St. Catharines	ON
Pendale 2	St. Catharines	ON
Promenade 6	Thornhill	ON
Canada Square 8	Toronto	ON
Carlton 9	Toronto	ON
Eaton Center 17	Toronto	ON
Fairview 6	Toronto	ON
Finch 3	Toronto	ON
Humber 2	Toronto	ON
Hyland 2	Toronto	ON
Madison 5	Toronto	ON
Market Square 6	Toronto	ON
Scarborough Town Ctr.12	Toronto	ON
Sherway 9	Toronto	ON
Varsity 2	Toronto	ON
Warden Woods 8	Toronto	ON
Woodbine Center 6	Toronto	ON
Woodside 3	Toronto	ON
York 2	Toronto	ON
Waterloo 1	Waterloo	ON
Seaway 2	Welland	ON
Champlain Mall 6	Whitby	ON

Famous Players

Gateway 6	Brampton	ON
Burlington Mall 3	Burlington	ON
Jackson Square 6	Hamilton	ON
Lime Ridge Cinema 4	Hamilton	ON
Capitol 2	Kitchener	ON
Kings College 4	Kitchener	ON
Markville 4	Markham	ON
Square One 4	Mississauga	ON
Sussex Centre 4	Mississauga	ON
Glenway 5	Newmarket	ON
Town Centre 6	Oakville	ON
Centre 8	Oshawa	ON
Town Centre 3	Pickering	ON
Parkway 6	Richmond Hill	ON
Lincoln Mall 3	St. Catharines	ON
Pen Centre 3	St. Catharines	ON
Fiesta Mall 4	Stoney Creek	ON
Bayview Village 4	Toronto	ON

Capitol	Toronto	ON
Cedarbrae 8	Toronto	ON
Centerpoint 3	Toronto	ON
Cumberland 4	Toronto	ON
Eglinton	Toronto	ON
Hollywood North	Toronto	ON
Hollywood South	Toronto	ON
Plaza 2	Toronto	ON
Runnymede 2	Toronto	ON
Sheraton Center 2	Toronto	ON
Sheridan 4	Toronto	ON
Skyway 6	Toronto	ON
Uptown 3	Toronto	ON
Uptown Backstage 2	Toronto	ON
Victoria Terrace 6	Toronto	ON
Westwood 3	Toronto	ON
Yorkdale 6	Toronto	ON

Montreal

Cineplex

Berri 5	Montreal	QC
Centreville 9	Montreal	QC
Cote de Neiges 7	Montreal	QC
Cremazie	Montreal	QC
Dauphin 2	Montreal	QC
Decarie Square 2	Montreal	QC
Desjardins 4	Montreal	QC
Egyptien 3	Montreal	QC
Le Fauborg 4	Montreal	QC
Le Nouvel Elysee 2	Montreal	QC
Capital	Sherbrooke	QC

Famous Players

Centre Eaton 6	Montreal	QC
Loew's 5	Montreal	QC
Palace 6	Montreal	QC
Parisien 7	Montreal	QC
Versailles 6	Montreal	QC
Carrefour de L'Estrie 3	Sherbrooke	QC
Cine du Parc 3	Sherbrooke	QC

Vancouver

Cineplex

Station Square 5	Burnaby	BC
Pinetree 6	Coquitlam	BC
Richport Town Center 2	Richmond	BC
Granville 7	Vancouver	BC
Oakridge 3	Vancouver	BC
Park & Tilford 6	Vancouver	BC
Odeon 3	Victoria	BC

Famous Players

Station Square 7	Burnaby	BC
Eagle Ridge 6	Coquitlam	BC
Willowbrook 6	Langley	BC
Esplanade 6	North Vancouver	BC
Richmond Centre 6	Richmond	BC
Guildford 4	Surrey	BC
Capitol 6	Vancouver	BC
Vancouver Centre 2	Vancouver	BC
Capitol 6	Victoria	BC
University 4	Victoria	BC

EXHIBITOR ORGANIZATIONS

NATIONAL ASSOCIATION OF CONCESSIONAIRES

(Organized 1944.)
35 E. Wacker Dr., Chicago, IL 60601. (312) 236-3858. FAX: (312) 236-7809.
EXECUTIVE DIRECTOR
Charles A. Winans
PRESIDENT
David Scoco
PRESIDENT ELECT
Norman Chesler
CHAIRMAN OF THE BOARD
Bill Rector
DIRECTOR, COMMUNICATIONS
Susan Cross
VICE PRESIDENTS
Gary Horvath, Norman Chesler, Peter Leyh, Nancy Pantuso
TREASURER
Skip Stefansen
DIRECTORS, DIVERSIFIED OPERATORS
Gary Waechter, Randy Ziegler
DIRECTOR, THEATRE CONCESSION OPERATORS
Bruce Taffett
DIRECTOR, EQUIPMENT MANUFACTURERS
Dan Gallery
DIRECTOR, SUPPLIERS
Bruce Proctor
DIRECTOR, JOBBER/DISTRIBUTOR
Libby Mauro
DIRECTORS-AT-LARGE
Chris Bigelow, Phil Blavat, Mark Duffy, Jim Conlan, Phil Noyes, R. Evan Gordon Jr., David Tomber
REGIONAL VICE PRESIDENTS
Jeff Dodge, John Evans, Jr., Dan Gray, Frank Liberto, Luella Pappas, Robert Perkins, Bill Wells
LIFETIME HONORARY MEMBERS, BOARD OF DIRECTORS
Louis L. Abramson, Larry Blumenthal, Nat Buchman, Sydney Spiegel, Van Myers
COUNCIL OF PAST PRESIDENTS
Andrew S. Berwick, Jr., Shelley Feldman, Doug Larson, Julian Lefkowitz, Jack Leonard, Philip L. Lowe, Phillip M. Lowe, Edward S. Redstone, Vernon B. Ryles, Jr., Vince Pantuso

NATIONAL ASSOCIATION OF THEATRE OWNERS, INC.

4605 Lankershim Blvd., Suite 340, N. Hollywood, CA 91602. (818) 506-1778. FAX: (818) 506-0269.
PRESIDENT
William F. Kartozian
CHAIRMAN OF THE BOARD
Pete Warzel
CHAIRMAN OF THE FINANCE COMMITTEE & TREASURER
Irwin R. Cohen
SECRETARY
Jerome Gordon
EXECUTIVE DIRECTOR
Mary Ann Grasso
BOARD OF DIRECTORS
EXECUTIVE COMMITTEE: Walt Aman (Portland, OR), Michael Campbell (Knoxville, TN), Irwin R. Cohen (Reisterstown, MD), Roger Eaton (Boston, MA), Jerome Forman (Los Angeles, CA), Steve Gilula (Los Angeles, CA), Charles Goldwater (Encino, CA), Jerome Gordon (Hampton, VA), Peter Ivany (Sydney, Australia), Allen Karp (Toronto, Canada), Barrie Lawson Loeks (New York, NY), Lee Roy Mitchell (Dallas, TX), Shari Redstone (Dedham, MA), Paul Roth (Silver Spring, MD), Philip Singleton (Kansas City, MO), William Stembler (Atlanta, GA), Pete Warzel (Denver, CO)
DIRECTORS-AT-LARGE: Meyer Ackerman (New York, NY), Walter Aman (Portland, OR), J. Wayne Anderson (Reisterstown, MD), Thomas Becker (Norwalk, CT), Byron Berkley (Kilgore, TX), Myron Blank (Des Moines, IA), Matt Brandt (Los Angeles, CA), Tobey Brehm (Ellicott, MD), H. Donald Busch (Philadelphia, PA), Michael Campbell (Knoxville, TN), Michael Chakeres (Springfield, OH), Hal Cleveland (Englewood, CO), Irwin A. Cohen (Toronto, Canada), Irwin R. Cohen (Reisterstown, MD), Scott Cohen (Reisterstown, MD), Bruce Corwin (Los Angeles, CA), Ken Crowe (Encino, CA), Dennis Daniels (Engelwood, CO), Scott Dickinson (Mission, KS), Richard Durwood (Kansas City, MO), Roger Eaton (Boston, MA), Andrea Edmonds (Northboro, MA), Mike Edmonds (Northboro, MA), James Edwards (Atlanta, GA), Jerome Forman (Los Angeles, CA), Donald Fox (Wyomissing, PA), Richard Fox (Boca Raton, FL), A. Alan Friedberg (Boston, MA), Jack Fuller, Jr. (Columbia, SC), Darrell Gabel (Lander, WY), Robyn Gabel (Lander, WY), Steve Gilula (Los Angeles, CA), Bernard Goldberg (New York, NY), Marvin J. Goldman (Washington, DC), Charles Goldwater (Encino, CA), Robert Goodrich (Kentwood, MI), Jerome Gordon (Hampton, VA), Malcolm Green (Boston, MA), W. D. Gross (Juneau, AK), Larry Hanson (Marshfield, WI), Dan Harkins (Scottsdale, AZ), Philip Harris (Oakland, CA), Derek Hyman (Huntington, WV), Allen Karp (Toronto, Canada), Beth Kerasotes (Springfield, IL), George Kerasotes (Springfield, IL), Edgar Knudson (Dedham, MA), Ronald Krueger (St. Louis, MO), Barrie Lawson Loeks (New York, NY), Ron Leslie (Prairie Village, KS), Howard Lichtman (Toronto, Canada), Richard Lightman (Memphis, TN), Ben Littlefield (Encino, CA), Jack Loeks (Grand Rapids, MI), Jim Loeks (New York, NY), John Loeks Jr. (Grand Rapids, MI), Jerome Magner (Dedham, MA), T. M. Manos (Greensburg, PA), Steve Marcus (Milwaukee, WI), Mike Mercy (Yakima, WA), Lee Roy Mitchell (Dallas, TX), Larry Moyer (Portland, OR), Richard Orear (Kansas City, MO), Sperie Perakos (New Britain, CT), Ayron Pickerill (Polson, MT), Bob Pinkston (Englewood, CO), William J. Quigley (Englewood, CO), Shari Redstone (Dedham, MA), Sumner Redstone (Dedham, MA), Joel Resnick (Shawnee Mission, KS), Larry Roper (Twin Falls, ID), Paul Roth (Silver Spring, MD), John Rowley (Dallas, TX), Bruce Sanborn (Newport Beach. CA), Philip Singleton (Kansas City, MO), Robert Smerling (New York, NY), Seymour Smith (New York, NY), T. G. Soloman (New Orleans, LA), Arthur Stein (Des Moines, IA), William Stembler (Atlanta, GA), John Stembler, Sr. (Atlanta, GA), Alan Stock (Dallas, TX), Herman Stone, Sr. (Charlotte, NC), R.K. Tankersley (Denver, CO), William Towey (Dedham, MA), John Treadwell (Dallas, TX), Peter Walch (Switzerland), Tim Warner (Dallas, TX), Pete Warzel (Denver, CO), Roy B. White (Cincinnati, OH), Russell Wintner (Pepper Pike, OH)

ARIZONA THEATRE OWNERS ASSOCIATION

8485 E. MacDonald Dr., #366, Scottsdale, AZ 85250. (602) 991-3307.
PRESIDENT
Krista Griffin

NATO OF CALIFORNIA/NEVADA

116 N. Robertson Blvd., Suite 708, Los Angeles, CA 90048. (310) 652-1093. FAX: (310) 657-4758.
PRESIDENT
Tim C. Warner

NATO OF COLORADO AND WYOMING

855 S. 9th, Lander, WY 82520. (307) 332-4437.
Darrell Gabel (Wyoming)

CONNECTICUT ASSOCIATION OF THEATRE OWNERS

164 E. Center St., Manchester, CT 06040. (203) 649-1092. FAX: (203) 643-4897.
PRESIDENT
Steve Menschell

NATO OF DISTRICT OF COLUMBIA

P.O. Box 1830, Hampton, VA 23669. (804) 722-5275. FAX: (804) 722-5276.
PRESIDENT
Ted Pedas

NATO OF FLORIDA

c/o Muvico Theatres, 255 Commercial Blvd., Suite 200, Lauderdale by the Sea, FL 33308. (305) 493-7700.
PRESIDENT
Jon C. Wray, Sr.

NATO OF GEORGIA

c/o LeFont Theatres, Inc., 550 Pharr Rd., N.E., Ste. 202, Atlanta, GA 30305. (404) 261-1070. FAX: (404) 261-8877.
PRESIDENT
George Lefont

NATO OF IDAHO

P.O. Box "T", Twin Falls, ID 83301. (208) 734-2402.
PRESIDENT
Larry Roper

NATO OF ILLINOIS

603 Rogers St., Downers Grove, IL 60515. (708) 968-1600. FAX: (708) 968-1626.
PRESIDENT
Willis Johnson

THEATRE OWNERS OF INDIANA
6919 E. 10th Street, Indianapolis, IN 46219. (317) 357-3660.
PRESIDENT
Michael Rembusch

**UNITED MOTION PICTURE ASSOCIATION OF
KANSAS & MISSOURI**
8900 Stateline Rd., Ste. 357, Leawood, KS 66206. (913) 381-5555. FAX: (913) 381-5552.
PRESIDENT
Deryl Smith

NATO OF KENTUCKY
P.O. Box 716, Radcliff, KY 40159. (502) 769-1501.
PRESIDENT
Ike Boutwell

LOUISIANA ASSOCIATION OF THEATRE OWNERS
2805 Edenborn Ave., Metairie, LA 70002. (504) 888-5338.
PRESIDENT
Charles Funk

NATO OF MARYLAND
P.O. Box 1830, Hampton, VA 23669. (804) 722-5275. FAX:
(804) 722-5276.
PRESIDENT
Scott Cohen

MID-ATLANTIC NATO
(Maryland, Virginia, Washington D.C.)
P.O. Box 1830, Hampton, VA 23669. (804) 722-5275. FAX:
(804) 722-5276.
EXECUTIVE DIRECTOR
Jerome Gordon

MONTANA ASSOCIATION OF THEATRE OWNERS
P.O. Box 157, Hamilton, MT 59840. (406) 363-2336.
PRESIDENT
Rusty Eitel

THEATRE OWNERS OF NEW ENGLAND
One Exeter Plaza, 6th fl., Boston, MA 02116-2836. (617) 424-TONE. FAX: (617) 267-2143.
EXECUTIVE DIRECTOR
Carl Goldman

NATO OF NEW JERSEY
101 Pompton Ave., c/o Cinema 23 Fiveplex, Cedar Grove, NJ 07009. (201) 492-2277. FAX: (201) 492-5617.
PRESIDENT
Jesse Sayegh

NATO OF NEW YORK STATE
244 West 49th St., Suite 200, New York, NY 10019. (212) 246-6460. FAX: (212) 265-6248.
EXECUTIVE DIRECTOR
Robert H. Sunshine

NATO OF NORTH & SOUTH CAROLINA
5970 Fairview Rd., Suite 518, Charlotte, NC 28210. (704) 554-1695. FAX: (704) 554-1696.
PRESIDENT
Aubrey Stone

NATO OF NORTH CENTRAL STATES
3508 France Ave. N., Minneapolis, MN 55422. (612) 521-0776.
FAX: (612) 521-0580.
PRESIDENT
Larry Kirschenmann

NATO OF OHIO
14 Troy Rd., Suite 124, Delaware, OH 43015. (614) 881-5541.
FAX: (614) 881-5390.
EXECUTIVE DIRECTOR
Belinda Judson

UNITED THEATRE OWNERS OF OKLAHOMA
P.O. Box 54484, Oklahoma City, OK 73154.
PRESIDENT
Marsh Powell

NATO OF PENNSYLVANIA
111 Chestnut Street, Philadelphia, PA 19106. (215) 592-8326.
FAX: (215) 592-7061.
PRESIDENT
H. Donald Busch

NATO OF TEXAS
12201 Merit Dr., Suite 720, Dallas, TX 75251. (214) 387-3588.
FAX: (214) 404-8041.
PRESIDENT
Randy Hester

NATO OF VIRGINIA
P.O. Box 1830, Hampton, VA 23669. (804) 722-5275. FAX:
(804) 722-5276.
PRESIDENT
Richard Herring

**MOTION PICTURE EXHIBITORS OF
WASHINGTON & ALASKA**
P.O. Box 2714, Kirkland, WA 98083. (206) 823-9456. FAX:
(206) 823-2022.
PRESIDENT
Michael Mercy

NATO OF WISCONSIN & UPPER MICHIGAN
759 N. Milwaukee St., Suite 421, Milwaukee, WI 53202. (414) 271-5935. FAX: (414) 271-8819.
EXECUTIVE DIRECTOR
Wayne J. Painter

THEATRE EQUIPMENT ASSOCIATION
244 W. 49 St., New York, NY 10019. (212) 246-6460. FAX:
(212) 265-6428.
PRESIDENT
Ioan Allen
VICE PRESIDENT
Tim Reed
SECRETARY
Jerry Van de Rydt
TREASURER
Dan Taylor
EXECUTIVE DIRECTOR
Robert Sunshine
CHAIRMAN OF THE BOARD
John Wilmers

BUYING AND BOOKING SERVICES

ASHURST AGENCY
215 Huntcliff Court, Fayetteville, GA 30214. (770) 461-9851.
FAX: (770) 719-1565.
OWNER
Annette Ashurst

BENDHEIM BOOKING-BUYING SERVICE
1510 East Ridge Rd., P.O. Box 71270, Richmond, VA 23255.
(804) 282-0303. FAX (804) 282-1565.
PRESIDENT & CEO
Frank Novak Jr.
FILM BUYER
Robert Tessier

CALIFORNIA BOOKING
Box 11, Agoura, CA 91301. (818) 991-8593. FAX: (818) 991-8898.
OWNER
Carol Combs

CAPITOL SERVICE
10624 N. Port Washington, Mequon, WI 53092. (414) 241-4545. FAX: (818) 241-4301.
OWNER
Dean Fitzgerald

CAROLINA BOOKING SERVICE
250 Cabarrus Ave. W., P.O. Box 994, Concord, NC 28026.
(704) 788-3366.
OWNER
Bill Cline

CINEMA BOOKING SVC. OF NEW ENGLAND
P.O. Box 827, Needham, MA 02199. (617) 986-2122. e-mail:
stadav@aol.com
PRESIDENT
Stanton Davis

CINEMA MANAGEMENT
Box 990311, Boston, MA 02199-0311. (617) 247-2216. FAX:
(617) 266-1918. e-mail: cinmanage@aol.com
OWNER
Richard Myerson

CINEMA SERVICE
6060 N. Central Expwy., #638, Dallas, TX 75206. (214) 692-7555 . FAX: (214) 692-7559.
PRESIDENT
Tim Patton

CINEMA SERVICE, INC.
15840 Ventura Blvd., Suite 308, Encino, CA 91436. (818) 995-8737.
PRESIDENT
Ennis Adkins

CINEMA SERVICES FILM BOOKING
Roxbury Mall, Box 654, Succasunna, NJ 07876. (201) 584-8160.
OWNER
Craig Zeltner
BOOKER
Mary Shefford

CLARK THEATRE SERVICE, INC.
325 Huron Ave. Suite B, Port Huron, MI 48060. (810) 982-9935. FAX: (810) 982-9947.
PRESIDENT
Robert Hines
VICE PRESIDENT
Patrick Sammon

COMPLETE BOOKING SERVICE
4 Woodlawn Green, Suite 150, Charlotte, NC 28217. (704)
522-0777. FAX: (704) 525-6344.
OWNER
Gary Vanderhorst

CONTINENTAL FILM SERVICE
526 B St., Suite A, Santa Rosa, CA 95401. (707) 523-1592.
FAX: (707) 523-4024.
OWNER
Richard Gambogi

CO-OPERATIVE THEATRES OF OHIO, INC.
6263 Mayfield Rd., Suite 214, Mayfield Heights, OH 44124.
(216) 461-2700. FAX: (216) 461-6411.
PRESIDENT
John Knepp
BOOKER
Frances Volan

CREATIVE ENTERTAINMENT CONSULTANTS
1600 Broadway, Suite 601, New York, NY 10019. (212) 333-7770. FAX: (212) 333-7904.
PRESIDENT
Larry Lapidus
EXECUTIVE VICE PRESIDENT
Nick Guadagno

COUCH BOOKING SERVICE
Box 763302, Dallas, TX 75376. (214) 330-9976.
OWNER
Leon A. Couch

DALRYMPLE THEATRE SERVICE
4208 Overlook Drive, Bloomington, MN 55437. (612) 888-0041.
OWNER
Don Dalrymple

EPPERSON THEATRE SERVICE
104 Mimosa Way, Box 1484, Mesquite, NV 89024. (702) 346-3514.
OWNER
Dick Epperson

EDDY G. ERICKSON BOOKING SERVICE
3405 Jubilee Trail, Dallas, TX 75229. (214) 352-3821.
OWNER
Eddy G. Erickson

FILM BOOKING OFFICE
9441 LBJ Freeway, #507, Dallas, TX 75243. (214) 234-6192.
FAX: (214) 234-8571.
PRESIDENT
John Shaw
SENIOR V.P. & HEAD FILM BUYER
Edward M. Kershaw
V.P. & HEAD BOOKER
Kathy Dixon

FILM SERVICE THEATRE GROUP
3487 W. 2100, South #204, Salt Lake City, UT 84119. (801)
973-3227. FAX: (801) 973-3364.
PRESIDENT
David Sharp

FLORIN-CREATIVE FILM SERVICES
125 North Main Street, Port Chester, NY 10573. (914) 937-1603. FAX: (914) 937-8496.
PRESIDENT
Steven Florin

FORMAN & UNITED THEATRES
Box 1649, Bothell, WA 98041. (206) 488-0944. FAX: (206) 488-9318.
OWNER
Michael Forman

GUYETT BOOKING SERVICE
P.O. Box 6346, Shawnee Mission, KS 66206. (913) 648-5189.
FILM BUYER & BOOKER
Harold P. Guyett

INDEPENDENT FILM SERVICES
8900 State Line Rd., Suite 405, Leawood, KS 66206. (913)
381-5555. FAX: (913) 381-5552.
OWNER
Bradford Bills

INDEPENDENT THEATRE BOOKING SERVICE
4523 Park Road, #A-105, Charlotte, NC 28209. (704) 529-1200.
FILM BUYER
Steve Smith

INDEPENDENT THEATRE SERVICE
5225 Touhy Avenue, Skokie, IL 60077. (708) 675-8232.
OWNER
Della M. Gallo

JANE M. KLOTZ BOOKING
9801 Tribonian Drive, Fort Washington, MD 20744. (301) 567-1775. FAX: (301) 567-1775.
OWNER & BOOKER
Jane M. Klotz

LESSER THEATRE SERVICE
110 Greene Street, Suite 802, New York, NY 10012. (212) 925-4776. FAX: (212) 941-6719.
PRESIDENT
Ron Lesser
FILM BUYER
Rob Lawinski

MJR THEATRE SERVICE, INC.
13691 West Eleven Mile Rd., Oak Park, MI 48237. (810) 548-
8282. FAX: (810) 548-4706.
PRESIDENT
Michael R. Mihalich

MARCUS THEATRES CORPORATION
250 E. Wisconsin Avenue, Milwaukee, WI 53202. (414) 272-
5120. FAX: (414) 272-0872.
PRESIDENT
Bruce Olson
EXECUTIVE VICE PRESIDENT/FILM BUYER
Michael Kominsky

MCCULLOCH THEATRE SERVICE
704 Hennepin Avenue, Minneapolis, MN 55403. (612) 333-
2281.
OWNER
Stan McCulloch

MESCOP, INC.
P.O. Box 303, Sussex, WI 53089. (414) 251-6808.
PRESIDENT & BUYER
James Florence
BOOKERS
Patricia B. Florence, Steve Rottler

MINI THEATRES
534 Broadhollow Rd., Suite 430, Melville, NY 11747. (516)
293-FILM. FAX: (516) 293-3490.
PARTNERS
Harold S. Lager, Marty Goldman

MORRIS PROJECTS, INC.
P.O. Box 3378, Sarasota, FL 34230. (941) 364-8662. FAX:
(941) 364-8478. e-mail: sfsfilm@gate.net
PRINCIPAL
Sue Morris

MOTION PICTURE COUNSELING
1010 B Street, #210, San Rafael, CA 94901. (415) 459-3456.
OWNER
Ron Litvin

NORRIS BOOKING AGENCY
P.O. Box 8824, Jacksonville, FL 32239. (904) 641-0019.
OWNER
Rex Norris

NORTHWEST DIVERSIFIED ENTERTAINMENT
2819 First Avenue, Suite 240, Seattle, WA 98121. (206) 441-5380.
PRESIDENT
Benjamin L. Hannah
FILM BUYERS
Victoria Hawker, Bruce Goodnow, John Teegarden

PREFERRED BOOKING SERVICE
1601 Harrison Avenue, Cincinnati, OH 45214. (513) 921-8266.
FAX: (513) 921-8206
OWNER
Fred Schweitzer

PHILBIN CINEMA SERVICE INC.
4700 S. 900 E., Suite 9B, Salt Lake City, UT 84117. (801) 263-
3725.
OWNER
Tom Philbin

PROFESSIONAL SERVICE FOR BOOKING/BUYING FILM
37 Norman Drive, Framingham, MA, 01701. (508) 872-9389.
OWNER
Henry Scull

R/C THEATRES BOOKING SERVICE
231 West Cherry Hill Ct., Box 1056, Reistertown, MD 21136.
(410) 526-4774. FAX: (410) 526-6871.
PRESIDENT
Irwin R. Cohen
FILM NEGOTIATOR
Scott R. Cohen

SENIOR BOOKER
Jan S. Anderson

ROXY MANAGEMENT COMPANY, INC.
2004 Main Street, Northampton, PA 18067. (610) 262-7699.
FAX: (610) 262-6459.
PRESIDENT
Richard C. Wolfe
VICE PRESIDENT
Lee J. Stein

SAFFLE UNITED THEATRE SERVICE
P.O. Box 1649, Bothell, WA 98041. (208) 488-0944. FAX: (206)
488-9318.
BOOKER
Dorothea Mayes

THEATRE MANAGEMENT ASSOC.
53 Carlton Pl., Passaic, NJ 07055. (201) 471-3002. FAX: (201)
471-3004.
PRESIDENT
Rudy DeBlasio
VICE PRESIDENT
Rick Sullivan

THEATRE SERVICE NETWORK
P.O. Box 190, 211 S. Bridge St., Yorkville, IL 60560. (708) 553-
0588. FAX: (708) 553-0594.
PRESIDENT
Buck Kolkmeyer
VICE PRESIDENT
Steve Felperin

TRIANGLE THEATRE SERVICE, INC.
1170 Broadway, New York, NY 10001. (212) 679-6400. FAX:
(212) 679-6461.
OWNER
Richard Dollinger

TRI-STATE THEATRE SERVICE, INC.
Film Arts Building, 636 Northland Blvd., Cincinnati, OH 45240.
(513) 851-5700. FAX: (513) 851-5708.
PRESIDENT
Phil Borack
VICE PRESIDENT
Barry Steinberg

TURBYFILL BOOKING SERVICE
P.O. Box 16126, Jacksonville, FL 32216. (904) 725-7590.

TWIN STATES BOOKING SERVICE
3600 Johnny Cake Lane, Charlotte, NC 28226. (704) 554-
5949.
OWNER
R.T. Belcher

VIKING FILM SERVICE
1228 Wagon Wheel Road, Hopkins, MN 55343. (612) 933-
7271.
BOOKER & BUYER
John R. Kelvie

VONDERHAAR CINEMA MARKETING
P.O. Box 222, Osseo, MN 55369. (612) 422-8535. FAX: (612)
422-8236.
OWNER
Mike Vonderhaar

WALKER THEATRE SERVICE
350 South 400 East, #222W, Salt Lake City, UT 84111. (801)
521-0335.
OWNER
Barry Walker

WILSON THEATRE SERVICE
22035 167th St., Big Lake, MN 55309. (612) 263-3800.
OWNER
Jim Wilson

FILM DISTRIBUTORS IN KEY CITIES

Following is a listing of distributors in key cities. Those marked with an asterisk are 16mm film distributors.

ALBANY

NATIONAL FILM SERVICE, INC.
24 N. Third St. (rear), Albany, NY 12204-1621. (518) 434-1289.
FAX: (518) 426-3501.

ATLANTA

BUENA VISTA DISTRIBUTION CO.
1190 W. Druid Hill Dr., Suite T-75, Atlanta, GA 30329. (404)
634-6525.

NATIONAL FILM SERVICE, INC.
150 Great Southwest Pkwy., Atlanta, GA 30336-2300. (404)
699-2020. FAX: (404) 699-5588.

NEW LINE CINEMA DISTRIBUTION, INC.
4501 Circle 75 Parkway, # A1270, Atlanta, GA 30339. (404)
952-0056.

BOSTON

BUENA VISTA DISTRIBUTION CO.
990 Washington St., #123, Dedham, MA 02026. (617) 461-
0870.

CINE RESEARCH ASSOC.
32 Fisher Avenue, Roxbury, MA 02161. (617) 442-9756.

CINEMA BOOKING SERVICE OF NEW ENGLAND
PO Box 827, Needham, MA 02192. (617) 986-2122.

CINEMA FILM CONSULTANTS INC.
PO Box 331, Boston, MA 02199. (617) 437-7050.

LOCKWOOD/McKINNON COMPANY, INC.
45 Walpole St., Norwood, MA 02062. (617) 769-8900.

NATIONAL FILM SERVICE, INC.
20-30 Freeport Way, Dorchester, MA 02122-2832. (617) 288-
1600. FAX: (617) 288-7481.

UNIVERSAL FILM EXCHANGES, INC.
44 Winchester St., Boston, MA 02116. (617) 426-8760.

WARNER BROS. DISTRIBUTING CORP.
45 Braintree Hill, Office Park 301, Braintree, MA 02184. (617)
848-2550.

ZIPPORAH FILMS,
1 Richdale Ave. #4, Cambridge, MA 02140. (617) 576-3603.

BUFFALO

NATIONAL FILM SERVICE, INC.
108 Gruner Rd., Buffalo, NY 14227-1071. (716) 897-0467.
FAXL (716) 897-0761.

BUTTE

NATIONAL FILM SERVICE, INC.
150 West Parkmont, Butte, MT 59072-3466. (406) 494-3434.
FAX: (406) 494-5598.

CHARLOTTE

CAROLINA BOOKING SERVICE
250 Cabarrus Ave., Concord, NC 28202. (704) 788-3366.

CAROLINA FILM SERVICE INC.
522 Penman St., Charlotte, NC 28203. (704) 333-2115.

NATIONAL FILM SERVICE, INC.
522 Penman St., Charlotte, NC 28230-0845. (704) 333-2115.
FAX: (704) 343-0162.

WARNER BROS. DISTRIBUTING CORP.
8144 Walnut Hill Lane, Suite 500, Dallas, TX 75231. (214) 360-
3041. FAX: (214) 696-1154.

CHICAGO

BEACON FILMS
1560 Sherman Ave., #100, Evanston, IL 60201. (800) 323-
5448.

BUENA VISTA DISTRIBUTION CO. INC.
9700 W. Higgins Rd., Des Plaines, IL 60018. (708) 696-0900.

***FILMS INCORPORATED**
5547 N. Ravenswood Ave., Chicago, IL 60640. (312) 878-2600,
(800) 323-4222.

NATIONAL FILM SERVICE, INC.
4343 S. Tripp St., Chicago, IL 60632-4318. (312) 254-8100.
FAX: (312) 254-0421.

PARAMOUNT FILM DISTRIBUTING CO.
8750 W. Bryn Mawr Ave., Chicago, IL 60631. (312) 380-4560.

***TRANS-WORLD FILMS**
332 S. Michigan Ave., Chicago, IL 60604. (312) 922-1530.

CINCINNATI

C. J. RUFF FILM DISTRIBUTING CO.
1601 Harrison Ave., Cincinnati, OH 45214. (513) 921-8200.

NATIONAL FILM SERVICE, INC.
421 Bauer St., Cincinnati, OH 45214-2898. (513) 621-4240.
FAX: (513) 621-4242.

CLEVELAND

NATIONAL FILM SERVICE, INC.
1625 E. 45th St., Cleveland, OH 44103-2316. (216) 431-9491.
FAX: (216) 431-6791.

DALLAS

BUENA VISTA DISTRIBUTION
10000 N. Central Expressway, #850, Dallas, TX 75231. (214)
363-9494.

MGM/UA DISTRIBUTION CO.
3 Forest Plaza, 12221 Merit Drive, #1610, Dallas, TX 75251.
(214) 387-1500.

NATIONAL FILM SERVICE, INC.
2500 S. Harwood St., Dallas, TX 75215. (214) 421-5411. FAX:
(214) 421-7021.

NEW LINE CINEMA DISTRIBUTION, INC.
6060 N. Central Expwy., # 602, Dallas, TX 75206. (214) 696-
0755.

ORION PICTURES DISTRIBUTION CORP.
7557 Rambler Rd., Suite 670, Dallas, TX 75231. (214) 363-
7600.

PARAMOUNT FILM DISTRIBUTING CORP.
12222 Merit Dr., Suite 1700, Dallas, TX 75251. (214) 387-
4400.

SONY PICTURES RELEASING
12770 Merit Dr., #702, Dallas, TX 75251. (214) 770-4220.

TWENTIETH CENTURY FOX FILM CORP.
12001 N. Central Exp. #650, Dallas, TX 75243. (214) 392-0101.

UNIVERSAL FILM EXCHANGE, INC.
7502 Greenville Ave., Dallas, TX 75231. (214) 360-0022.

WARNER BROS. DISTRIBUTING CORP.
8144 Walnut Hill Lane, Suite 500, Dallas, TX 75231. (214) 360-
3041. FAX: (214) 696-1154.

DENVER

CREST DISTRIBUTING CO.
1443 Larimer, Denver, CO 80202. (303) 571-5569.

NATIONAL FILM SERVICE, INC.
5355 Harrison St., Denver, CO 80216-2439. (303) 296-3793.
FAX: (303) 296-3794.

DES MOINES

NATIONAL FILM SERVICE, INC.
3123 Delaware Ave., Des Moines, IA 50316-0371. (515) 265-1469. FAX: (515) 262-9718.

DETROIT

NATIONAL FILM SERVICE, INC.
9855 Harrison St., Romulus, MI 48174. (313) 946-4641.

HONOLULU

PACIFIC MOTION PICTURE CO. LTD.
470 N. Nimitz Hwy., Honolulu, HI 96817. (808) 531-1117.

INDIANAPOLIS

NATIONAL FILM SERVICE, INC.
6245 Morenci Trail, Indianapolis, IN 46268. (317) 329-4132.
FAX: (317) 293-1932.

JACKSONVILLE

CLARK FILM CO., INC.
1405 University Blvd., Jacksonville, FL 32211. (904) 744-4500.
FAX: (904) 745-0078.

NATIONAL FILM SERVICE, INC.
2208 W. 21st St., Jacksonville, FL 32209-4111. (904) 355-5447. FAX: (904) 632-1342.

KANSAS CITY

NATIONAL FILM SERVICE, INC.
1717 No. Topping St., Kansas City, MO 64120-1225. (816) 483-5209. FAX: (816) 483-9741.

LOS ANGELES

*BUDGET FILMS
4590 Santa Monica Blvd., Los Angeles, CA 90029. (213) 660-0187.

BUENA VISTA PICTURES DISTRIBUTION CO. INC.
3900 W. Alameda Ave., Suite 2431, Burbank, CA 91521-0021.
(818) 567-5000.

*BUENA VISTA PICTURES DISTRIBUTION—NON-THEATRICAL
3900 West Alameda Avenue, Suite 2400, Burbank, CA 91521-0021. (818) 567-5058. FAX: (818) 557-0797.
S.V.P., NON-THEATRICAl DISTRUBUTION
Linda Palmer.

CORI FILMS DISTRIBUTORS
2049 Century Park E., #780, Los Angeles, CA 90067. (310) 557-0173.

CREST FILM DISTRIBUTORS
116 N. Robertson Blvd., Los Angeles, CA 90052. (310) 652-8844.

CROWN INTERNATIONAL PICTURES, INC.
8701 Wilshire Blvd., Beverly Hills, CA 90211. (310) 657-6700.
FAX: (310) 657-4489.

*DIRECT CINEMA
P.O. Box 10003, Santa Monica, CA 90410. (310) 636-8200.
FAX: (3100 636-8228. e-mail: directcinema@ATTMAIL.com

*EM GEE FILM LIBRARY
6924 Canby Ave., Suite 103, Reseda, CA 91335. (818) 881-8110. FAX: (818) 981-5506. e-mail: mglass@worldnet.att.net

FINE LINE FEATURES DISTRIBUTION, INC.
116 N. Robertson Blvd., Suite 200, Los Angeles, CA 90048.
(310) 854-5811.

*SAMUEL GOLDWYN COMPANY, INC.
10203 Santa Monica Blvd., Los Angeles, CA 90067. (310) 552-2255.

LEGACY RELEASING
1800 N. Highland Ave., Suite 311, Hollywood, CA 90028. (213) 461-3936. FAX: (213) 461-5287.

MGM/UA DISTRIBUTION CO.
11111 Santa Monica Blvd., Los Angeles, CA 90025. (310) 444-1500.

NATIONAL FILM SERVICE, INC.
8401 Slauson Ave., Pico Rivera, CA 90660-0097. (313) 949-9397. FAX: (313) 942-1822.

NEW LINE CINEMA DISTRIBUTION, INC.
16027 Ventura Blvd., # 506, Encino, CA 91436. (818) 380-7300. FAX: (818) 995-6049.

ORION PICTURES DISTRIBUTION CORP.
1888 Century Park E., Suite 416, Century City, CA 90067.
(310) 282-0550.

PARAMOUNT FILM DIST. CORP.
15260 Ventura Blvd., Suite 1140, Sherman Oaks, CA 91403.
(818) 789-2900.

PYRAMID FILMS
2801 Colorado Ave., Santa Monica, CA 90404. (310) 828-7577, (800) 421-2304.

*REPUBLIC PICTURES CORPORATION
12636 Beatrice St., Los Angeles, CA 90066. (310) 306-4040.

SAVOY PICTURES
2425 Olympic Blvd., 6th fl., Santa Monica, CA 90404. (310) 247-7930. FAX: (310) 247-7929.

SONY RELEASING CORP.
3400 Riverside Dr., Burbank, CA 91505. (818) 972-0496.

*SONY PICTURES RELEASING
10202 West Washington Blvd., Suite 2119, Culver City, CA 90232. (310) 280-4485.

TOHO COMPANY LTD.
2029 Century Park E., Suite 1150, Los Angeles, CA 90067.
(310) 277-1081.

TWENTIETH CENTURY FOX FILM CORP.
6320 Canoga Ave., #430, Woodland Hills, CA 91367. (818) 702-7282.

UNIVERSAL FILM EXCHANGE
8901 Beverly Blvd., Los Angeles, CA 90048. (310) 550-7461.

WARNER BROS. DISTRIBUTING CORP.
15821 Ventura Blvd., #525, Encino, CA 91436. (818) 784-7494.

MEMPHIS

NATIONAL FILM SERVICE, INC.
3931 Homewood Rd., Memphis, TN 38181. (901) 794-6601.
FAX: (901) 795-8766.

MIAMI

CINEVISTA, INC.
1680 Michigan Ave., Suite 1106, Miami Beach, FL 33139.
(305) 532-3400. (305) 532-3400. FAX: (305) 532-0047.

MILWAUKEE

NATIONAL FILM SERVICE, INC.
333 N. 25th St., Milwaukee, WI 53233-2590. (414) 344-0300.
FAX: (414) 344-2828.

MINNEAPOLIS

NATIONAL FILM SERVICE, INC.
245 2nd Ave. N., Minneapolis, MN 55401-1621. (612) 332-2203. FAX: (612) 333-0939.

NEW HAVEN

NATIONAL FILM SERVICE, INC.
90 Woodmont Rd., Milford, CT 06460-0958. (203) 878-1465.
(203) 877-5811.

NEW ORLEANS

NATIONAL FILM SERVICE, INC.
2411 Edenborn Ave., Metairie, LA 70001. (504) 833-5552.
FAX: (504) 833-5553.

NEW YORK

*BIOGRAPH ENTERTAINMENT
2 Depot Plaza #202-B, Bedford Hills, NY 10507. (914) 242-9838.

BUENA VISTA DISTRIBUTION CO.
500 Park Ave., New York, NY 10022. (212) 735-5420.

*CAROUSEL FILM, INC.
241 E. 34 St., New York, NY 10016. (212) 683-1660.

*CINEMA GUILD
1697 Broadway, New York, NY 10019. (212) 246-5522.

*CORINTH FILMS
34 Gansevoort St., New York, NY 10014. (212) 463-0305.

*FILM-MAKERS COOPERATIVE
175 Lexington Ave., New York, NY 10016. (212) 889-3820.

FINE LINE FEATURES DISTRIBUTION, INC.
888 Seventh Ave., 20th fl., New York, NY 10106. (212) 649-4900.

*FIRST RUN/ICARUS
153 Waverly Place, New York, NY 10004. (212) 243-0600.

INDEPENDENT INTERNATIONAL PICTURES CORP.
223 State Hwy. #18, East Brunswick, NJ 08816. (201) 249-8982.

INDEPENDENT FEATURE PROJECT
104 W. 29th St., 12th floor, New York, NY 10001. (212) 465-8200. URL: http://www.ifp.org
e-mail: IFPNY@aol.com

*INTERAMA
301 W. 53rd St., Suite 19E, New York, NY 10019. (212) 977-4836.

ITALTOONS CORP.
32 W. 40 St., New York, NY 10018. (212) 730-0280. FAX: (212) 730-0313. URL: http://www.Italtoons.com

*KINO INTERNATIONAL
333 W. 39th St., Suite 503, New York, NY 10018. (212) 629-6880.

MGM DISTRIBUTION CO.
1350 Ave. of the Americas, New York, NY 10019. (212) 708-0300.

MARVIN FILMS, INC.
2 Heitz Pl., Hicksville, NY 11801. (516) 931-3456.

MIRAMAX FILMS
375 Greenwich St., New York, NY 10013. (212) 941-3800.

*MUSEUM OF MODERN ART FILM LIBRARY
11 W. 53rd St., New York, NY 10019. (212) 708-9433.

NATIONAL FILM SERVICE, INC.
902 East Hazelwood Ave., Rahway, NJ 07065-5608. (908) 396-9100. FAX: (908) 396-4595.

NEW LINE CINEMA DISTRIBUTION, INC.
888 Seventh Ave., 20th fl., New York, NY 10106. (212) 649-4900. FAX: (212) 649-4966.

*NEW YORKER FILMS
16 W. 61st St., New York, NY 10023. (212) 247-6110.

ORION PICTURES DISTRIBUTION CORP.
304 Park Ave. S., New York, NY 10010. (212) 505-0051.

PARAMOUNT FILM DISTRIBUTING CORP.
1515 Broadway, New York, NY 10036. (212) 258-6000.

THIRD WORLD NEWSREEL
(also 16mm). 335 W. 38 St., 5th floor, New York, NY 10018. (212) 947-9277. FAX: (212) 594-6417. Dir., Distribution: Veena Cabreros-Sud.

TOHO INTERNATIONAL
1501 Broadway, New York, NY 10036. (212) 391-9058.

SONY PICTURES RELEASING
550 Madison Avenue, New York, NY 10022. (212) 833-8500.

TWENTIETH CENTURY FOX FILM CORP.
1211 Ave. of the Americas, 3rd Fl., New York, NY 10036. (212) 556-2490.

UNIVERSAL FILM EXCHANGE
445 Park Ave., New York, NY 10022. (212) 759-7500.

WARNER BROS. DISTRIBUTING CORP.
75 Rockefeller Plaza, 14th floor, New York, NY 10019. (212) 484-6203.
DIVISION MANAGER
Robert Miller

OKLAHOMA CITY

NATIONAL FILM SERVICE, INC.
809 S. West 7th St., Oklahoma City, OK 73109. (405) 235-2553. FAX: (405) 235-2554.

OMAHA

MODERN SOUND
1402 Howard St., Omaha, NE 68102. (402) 341-8476.

NATIONAL FILM SERVICE, INC.
1441 N. 11th St., Omaha, NE 68102. (402) 342-6576. FAX: (402) 342-1930.

PHILADELPHIA

NATIONAL FILM SERVICE, INC.
130 Ferry Ave., Camden, NJ 08104. (609) 962-6800. FAX: (609) 962-6051.

PITTSBURGH

NATIONAL FILM SERVICE, INC.
Bldg. 16, Nichol Ave. IV, McKees Rocks, PA 15136. (412) 771-2665. (412) 771-6394.

PORTLAND

NATIONAL FILM SERVICE, INC.
16 N.E. Lawrence, Portland, OR 97232. (503) 234-6202. FAX: (503) 234-6224.

ST. LOUIS

NATIONAL FILM SERVICE, INC.
3974 Page Ave., St. Louis, MO 63113-3432. (314) 371-6572. FAX: (314) 371-6574.

SALT LAKE CITY

NATIONAL FILM SERVICE, INC.
190 N. 640 W., N. Salt Lake, UT 84054. (801) 292-7626. FAX: (801) 292-7785.

*SWANK MOTION PICTURES
2720 Walnut Pl., St. Louis, MO 63103. (314) 534-6300.

SAN FRANCISCO

KIT PARKER FILMS
(also 16mm). P.O. Box 16022, Monterey, CA 93942. (408) 393-0303, (800) 538-5838.

NATIONAL FILM SERVICE, INC.
701 Bradford Way, Union City, CA 94587-3605. (510) 471-9400. FAX: (510) 471-8447.

SEATTLE

NATIONAL FILM SERVICE, INC.
214 21st St., S.E., Auburn, WA 98002. (206) 939-1533. FAX: (206) 735-9219.

NORTHWEST DIVERSIFIED ENTERTAINMENT
2819 First, #210, Seattle, WA 98121. (206) 441-5380.

WASHINGTON, DC

*CAPITOL ENTERTAINMENT
4818 Yuma St. NW, Washington, DC 20016. (202) 363-8800.

*CIRCLE RELEASING
1101 23 St., Suite 225, Washington, DC 20037. (202) 429-9044.

KEY THEATRE ENTERPRISES
1325-1/2 Wisconsin Ave., NW, Washington, DC 20007. (202) 965-4401. FAX: (202) 965-4416.

NATIONAL FILM SERVICE, INC.
15113 Old Marlboro Pike, Upper Marlboro, MD 20772-3129. (301) 952-1322. FAX: (301) 627-0532.

THEATRE EQUIPMENT AND SERVICES

ADMISSIONS SYSTEMS, TICKET ISSUING EQUIPMENT AND TICKETS

AAMI-TDS (THEATRON)
P.O. Box 4142, Seal Beach, CA 90740. (310) 434-1627.
FAX: (310) 434-9948. Larry Benson

AUTOMATICKET, A DIVISION OF CEMCORP
110 Industry Lane, P.O. Box 296, Forest Hill, MD 21050-
1638. (410) 879-3022. FAX: (410) 838-8079.
V.P., OPERATIONS
Gorman White Jr.

DILLINGHAM TICKET COMPANY
781 Ceres Ave., Los Angeles, CA 90021-1515. (213) 627-
6916. FAX: (213) 623-2758. Michael O'Keefe

GLOBE INFORMATION SYSTEMS
5405 Cypress Center Drive, #100, Tampa, FL 33609.
(813) 289-3611. FAX: (813) 289-3072. Cathy Gerrard

GLOBE TICKET AND LABEL COMPANY
300 Constance Dr., Warminster, PA 18974-2815. (813)
289-3611. FAX: (813) 289-3072. Sheri Green

ICON INTERNATIONAL
World Trade Center, 3600 Port of Tacoma Road, Tacoma,
WA 98424. (206) 926-8075. FAX: (206) 926-8076. Gary
Brown

IN-TOUCH TECHNOLOGIES
P.O. Box 20411, New York, NY 10017-0004. (212) 697-
4600. Jay Maller

KELMAR SYSTEMS, INC.
284 Broadway, Huntington Station, NY 11746-1497. (516)
421-1230. FAX: (516) 421-1274. Andrew Marglin

NATIONAL TICKET COMPANY
P.O. Box 547, Shamokin, PA 17872-0547. (717) 672-
2900, (800) 829-0829. FAX: (800) 829-0888, (717) 672-
2999.

PACER/CATS
355 Inverness Drive S., Englewood, CO 80112-5816.
(303) 649-9818. FAX: (303) 643-3814. Del Banjo

PREMIER SOUTHERN TICKET CO.
7911 School Road, Cincinnati, OH 45249. (800) 331-
2283. FAX: (513) 489-6867.

READY THEATRE SYSTEMS
8189 Verlyna Drive, Watervliet, MI 49098. (800) 676-
9393. FAX: (616) 463-4542.

TICKETPRO SYSTEMS
4921 Albermarle Rd., Suite 203, Charlotte, NC 28205.
(800) 552-0313. FAX: (704) 567-2821. John Shaw.

WELDON, WILLIAMS & LICK, INC.
P.O. Box 168, Fort Smith, AR, 72902-0168. (501) 783-
4113. FAX: (501) 783-7050. Jerry Hendricks

ARCHITECTURE, CONSTRUCTION AND DESIGN

EAST COAST THEATER DESIGN
P.O. Box 499, Washingtonville, NY 10992. (914) 496-
9125. FAX: (914) 496-1692. Harvey Berg

FOREST BAY CONSTRUCTION COMPANY
3070 Lawson Blvd., Oceanside, NY 11572. (516) 763-
4800. FAX: (516) 763-3061. Robert Beacher

GLATZ-JACOBSEN THEATRE DESIGN CONSULTANTS, INC.
9961 W. 86th Place, Arvada, CO 80005-1210. (303) 421-
9516. FAX: (303) 421-9516. Chris Jacobsen

HENRY ARCHITECTS, INC.
2125 Western Avenue, #200, Seattle, WA, 98121. (206)
448-6265. FAX: (206) 448-5856. Rob Henry

LARGO CONSTRUCTION
555 Street Rd., Bensalem, PA 19020. (215) 245-0300,
(800) 272-2432. FAX: (215) 638-7933.
Jeffrey W. Spence

M.B.C. CONSTRUCTION, INC.
9 Circle Lane, Roslyn Heights, NY 11577. (516) 741-
4900. FAX: (516) 621-2874. Scott Cadiff

MHB DESIGN GROUP, INC.
985 Parchment S.E., Grand Rapids, MI 49546. (616) 942-
1870. FAX: (616) 942-2057. Richard A. Murphy

TK ARCHITECTS
106 W. 11th St., Suite 1900, Kansas City, MO 64105.
(816) 842-7552. FAX: (816)-842-1302. Tamra Knapp.
Garden Studios, 11-15 Betterton, London WC2H 9BP,
England. (44 171) 470-8882. FAX: (44 171) 470-8883.
William Slusher

CARPETING

DURKAN PATTERNED CARPET
405 Virgil Drive, Dalton, GA 30720. (706) 278-7037. FAX:
(706) 226-0630. Pat Durkan

KONETA MATTING DIVISION
7090 Lunar Dr., Wapakoneta, OH 45895. (419) 739-4200.
FAX: (419) 739-4247.

MASLAND CARPETS, INC.
P.O. Box 11467, Mobile, Al 36671. (800) 633-0468. FAX:
(334) 675-5808. Robert Munisteri

MILLIKEN CARPET
201 Lukken Industrial Drive West, LaGrange, GA 30240.
(706) 880-5359. FAX: (706) 880-5888. Becky Frazier

PATCRAFT COMMERCIAL CARPET
P.O. Box 1527, Dalton, GA 30722-1527. (706) 517-0075.
FAX: (706) 517-3110. Doug Enck

CONCESSION EQUIPMENT AND DESIGN

ALL STAR CARTS AND VEHICLES, INC.
1565 Fifth Industrial Ct., Bayshore, NY 11706. (800) 831-
3166. FAX: (516) 666-1319. Mark Weiner

C. CRETORS & CO.
3243 N. California Avenue, Chicago, IL 60618. (800) 228-
1885. FAX: (312) 588-2171. Van Neathery

CARTS OF COLORADO, INC.
P.O. Box 16249, 5750 Holly Street, Commerce City, CO
80022. (303) 288-1000. FAX: (303) 286-8539. Daniel
Gallery

CONCESSION SUPPLY CO.
1016 Summit Street, Toledo, OH 43697. (419) 241-7711.
Robert Brockway

GOLD MEDAL PRODUCTS
223 World Headquarters Building, 2001 Dalton Ave.,
Cincinnati, OH 45214. (513) 381-1313.
V.P., SALES
John Evans, Jr.

IMI CORNELIUS INC.
One Cornelius Place, Anoka, MN 55303. (800) 238-3600.
FAX: (612) 422-3226. Ray Ouliette

JARCO INDUSTRIES
98 Park Ave., Babylon, NY 11702-1709. (516) 422-9005.
FAX: (516) 422-9005. Jeffrey Stein

JET SPRAY CORP.
P.O. Box 8250, Norwood, MA 02062. (617) 769-7500.
FAX: (617) 769-2368. Tim Donlon.

KRISPY KIST MACH. CO.
120 S. Halsted St., Dept. M-1, Chicago, IL 60661. (312)
733-0900. FAX: (312) 733-3508.

LANCER CORPORATION, INC.
235 W. Turbo, San Antonio, TX 78216. (210) 344-3071.
Dennis Stout

P.P.R. ENTERPRISES
(Concession design) 1523-L West Struck Avenue,
Orange, CA 01923. (508) 777-1900, (508) 750-2089.

PRIME TICKET, INC.
11540 B-Hwy 17 By-Pass, Frontage Road, Murrells Inlet,
SC 29576. (803) 651-3138, (800) 385-3148. FAX: (803)
651-3173. Todd Hensley

PROCTOR COMPANIES
10497 W. Centennial Rd., Littleton, CO 80127-4218.
(303) 973-8989. FAX: (303) 973-8884. (Also concession
design). Everett Hughes

ROUNDUP FOOD EQUIPMENT
1045 W. National Avenue, Addison, IL 60101. (800) 253-
2991. FAX: (312) 543-0359.

SANI SERV
2020 Production Drive, Indianapolis, IN 46241. (317)
247-0460.

SCOTSMAN ICE SYSTEMS
775 Corp. Wood Pkwy., Vernon Hills, IL 60061. (708) 215-
4550. FAX: (708) 913-9644.

SERVER PRODUCTS, INC.
P.O. Box 530, Menomonee Falls, WI 53052. (800) 558-
8722. FAX: (414) 251-2688.

STAR MANUFACTURING INTERNATIONAL
9325 Olive Blvd., St. Louis, MO 63132. (314) 994-0880.
FAX: (314) 994-0406.

STEIN INDUSTRIES
22 Sprague Ave., Amityville, NY 11701-0536. (516) 789-
2222. FAX: (516) 789-8888. Andrew Stein

WILSHIRE CORPORATION
2401 N. Palmer Drive, Schaumburg, IL 60196. (708) 397-
4600. FAX: (703) 397-0250. Robert Wonder

DISPLAY

Internal and external signs, marquee letters, electronic
displays and poster cases.

BASS INDUSTRIES
380 N.E. 67th St., Miami, FL 33138-6024. (305) 751-
2716, (800) 346-8575. FAX: (305) 756-6165. Robert
Baron

BUX-MONT SIGNS
221 Horsham Road, Horsham, PA 19044. (215) 675-
1040. FAX: (215) 675-4443. William Sweigart

CHANGE-AD LETTER CO.
20954 Currier Road, Walnut, CA 91789. (909) 598-1996.
FAX: (909) 598-2251. Beverly Cobb

DAKTRONICS, INC.
331 32nd Avenue, Brookings, SD 57006. (605) 697-4700.
FAX: (605) 697-4700. Frank Kurtenbach

DATA DISPLAY USA, INC.
95 Hoffman Lane, Suite K, Central Islip, NY 11722-5012.
(516) 342-9455. FAX: (516) 234-9463. Robert Destefano

DURA ENGRAVING CORP.
48-15 32nd Place, Long Island City, NY 11101. (718)
706-6400. Art Forst

EAST COAST SIGN ADV., INC.
5058 Rt. 13 North, at the PA Turnpike, Bristol, PA 19007.
(215) 781-8500. FAX: (215) 781-0400. Steven Weiler

FAST-AD, INC.
224 S. Center Street, Santa Ana, CA. 92703. (714) 835-
9353. FAX: (714) 835-4805. Guy Barnes

GEMINI, INC.
103 Mensing Way, Cannon Falls, MN 55009. (800) 533-
0520. FAX: (507) 263-4887. Bill Frederickson

IMAGE NATIONAL
444 E. Amity Rd., Boise, ID, 83707. (208) 345-4020.
Linda Knigh

MOVIEAD CORP.
475 Ramblewood Drive, Coral Spring, FL 33071. (305)
344-7705. FAX: (305) 344-7821. Emil Noah

POBLOCKI AND SONS
620 S. 1st St., Milwaukee, WI 53204-1607. (414) 453-
4010. Ray Poblocki

READERVISION, INC.
119 Brookstown Avenue, Winston-Salem, NC 27101.
(910) 721-2375. FAX: (910) 721-2382.

SUNNYWELL DISPLAY SYSTEMS
730 Stimson Avenue, City of Industry, CA 91745. (818)
369-7359. FAX: (818) 369-5739.

WAGNER ZIP CHANGE, INC.
3100 Hirsch St., Melrose Park, IL 60160. (708) 681-4100.
Gary Delaquila

FURNISHINGS

Draperies, acoustic wall and ceiling panels, stanchions,
decorative fixtures, beverage holders, etc.

AVL SYSTEMS, INC.
5540 S.W. 6th Place, Ocala, FL 34474. (800) ACUSTIC.
FAX: (352) 854-1278. J. Philip Hale

BRASS SMITH, INC.
3880 Holly Street, Denver, CO 80207. (800) 662-9595.
FAX: (303) 296-2320. Joe Martin

**BREJTFUS ENTERPRISES, INC., A DIVISION OF
CINACOUSTICS**
410 S. Madison Drive, Suite #1, Tempe, AZ, 85281. (602)
731-9899, (800) 264-9190. FAX: (602) 731-9469. Michael
Regan

CADDY CUPHOLDER C/O MTS
7667 Cahill Rd., Minneapolis, MN 55439-2750. (612)
828-0030. FAX: (612) 829-0166. Peter Bergin

CINE COASTERS, INC.
250 26th Street, Suite 204, Santa Monica, CA 90402.
(800) 882-8269. FAX: (310) 451-3583. Richard Katz

CROWN INDUSTRIES, INC.
155 North Park Street, East Orange, NJ 07017. (800)
GO-CROWN. FAX: (201) 672-7536. Carmen Ware

CY YOUNG INDUSTRIES, INC.
1270 N. Winchester & KC Road, Olathe, KS 66061. (800)
729-0756. FAX: (913) 780-0756. Carrie Young

DURAFORM/DIVISION OF CENTURY PLASTICS, INC.
1435 S. Fanta Fe Avenue, Compton, CA 90221. (310)
761-1640. FAX: (310) 761-1646. Betty Prosser

ECONO-PLEAT/EASTWEST CARPET
2664 S. La Cienega Blvd, Los Angeles, CA 90034-2604.
(310) 559-7847. FAX: (310) 559-6357. Larry Sperling

GOLTERMAN & SABO, INC.
5901 Elizabeth, St. Louis, MO 63110. (314) 781-1422.
FAX: (314) 781-3836. Ned Golterman

KOALA CORP.
4390 McMenemy St., St. Paul, MN, 55127-6004. (800)
666-0363. FAX: (612) 490-1859. Rick Robbins

LAVI INDUSTRIES
27810 Hopkins Ave., Valencia, CA 91355-3409. (800)
624-6225. FAX: (800) 257-4938. K. Tom Anderson

LAWRENCE METAL PRODUCTS, INC.
P.O. Box 400, Bay Shore, NY 11706-0779. (516) 666-
0300. FAX: (516) 666-0336. Stephen Lawrence

LIBERTY THEATRICAL DECOR
P.O. Box 2122, Castro Valley, CA 94546-0122. (510) 889-
6945. FAX: (510) 889-6408. Don Nethercott

MANKO FABRICS CO., INC.
50 W. 36th St., New York, NY 10018-8002. (212) 695-
7470. FAX: (212) 563-0840. Norman Manko

NOVELTY SCENIC STUDIOS
40 Sea Cliff Ave., Glen Cove, NY 11542-3601. (718) 895-
8668. FAX: (516) 674-2213. Leslie Kessler

O'BRIEN PARTITION COMPANY
5301 E. 59th Street, Kansas City, MO 64130. (800) 821-3595. FAX: (816) 363-7034.

S & K THEATRICAL DRAPERIES
7313 Varna Ave., North Hollywood, CA 91605-4009. (818) 503-0596, (818) 503-0599.

SCULPTURED WALL ORNAMENTAL
1210 4th Street, Berkeley, CA 94710. (510) 526-4090. FAX: (510) 524-2608.

SOUNDFOLD INTERNATIONAL
P.O. Box 292125, Dayton, OH 45429. (513) 293-2671. FAX: (513) 293-9542. Thomas Miltner

TRIANGLE SCENERY DRAPERY & LIGHTING
1215 Bates Ave., Los Angeles, CA 90029-2203. (213) 662-8129. FAX: (213) 662-8120. Terry Miller

TROY SOUND CONTROL SYSTEM
3420 South Malt Ave., Commerce, GA 90040. (800) 987-3306.

LIGHTING

APPLIED LIGHTING SYSTEMS
407 Old County Rd., Belmont, CA 94002-2547. (415) 595-5496. FAX: (415) 595-5197. Rodolfo Luppi

ATLAS SPECIALTY LIGHTING
7304 N. Florida Avenue, Tampa, FL 33604. (813) 238-6481. FAX: (813) 238-6656. Ralph Felton Jr.

AURA LIGHTING PRODUCTS
(Low voltage lighting) 779 North Benson Ave., Upland, CA 91786-5836. (909) 985-3864, (800) 942-8880. FAX: (909) 985-5938. Rolando Flores

CELESTIAL LIGHTING
14009 Dinard Ave., Santa Fe Springs, CA 90670. (800) 233-3563. FAX: (310) 802-2882. Adam Lamar

DAVID TYSON LIGHTING, INC.
4549 St. Augustine Road, Suite 24, P.O. Box 1932, Callahan, FL 32011. (800) 385-3148. FAX: (800) 385-4149. Donna Tyson

DECOLITE PRODUCTS
21610-3 Lassen Street, Chatsworth, CA 91311. (818) 772-4594. FAX: (818) 772-2458. Herb Beatus

EAST COAST LAMP SALES, INC.
8 Vernon Valley Road, East Northport, NY 11731. (516) 754-5655. FAX: (516) 754-2213. Thomas Kelly

ILLUMILITE, INC.
19215 Parthenia Street, Suite A, Northridge, CA 91324. (818) 886-6306. FAX: (818) 886-6308. Jana DeWitt

LEHIGH ELECTRIC PRODUCTS CO.
6265 Hamilton Blvd., Allentown, PA 18106. (610) 395-3386. FAX: (610) 395-7735. Lloyd Jones

LIGHTING AND ELECTRONIC DESIGN
1111 West Avenue L-12, Suite B, Lancaster, CA 93534. (800) 700-5483. FAX: (805) 736-5488. Janie Lynn

LIGHTWORKS
3345 W. Hunting Park Ave., Philadelphia, PA 19132. (215) 223-9200. FAX: (215) 227-7332. Peter Altman

LINSEY-FAIRBANKS, INC.
1670 Maywood Ave., Upland, CA 91786-1729. (909) 982-0467. George Mackey

MICA LIGHTING CO., INC.
717 S. State College Blvd., #L, Fullerton, CA 92631. (714) 738-8448. FAX: (714) 738-7748. Gayle Sweet

PASKAL LIGHTING
6820 Romaine St., Los Angeles, CA 90038-2433. (213) 466-5233. FAX: (213) 466-1071.

TEMPO INDUSTRIES, INC.
2022-C S. Grand Ave., Santa Ana, CA 92705. (714) 641-0313. FAX: (714) 641-0944

TIVOLI INDUSTRIES, INC.
1513 East St., Gertrude Place, Santa Ana, CA 92711. (714) 957-6101. FAX: (714) 957-1501.

VISTA MANUFACTURING, INC.
(Theatre Aisle lighting) FM 2449 E., Ponder, TX 76259. (817) 479-2787. FAX: (817) 479-8139. Rick Guhr

PROJECTION EQUIPMENT

Bulbs, projectors, and projection booth accessories.

AVASK
75 West Forest Ave., Englewood, NJ 07631. (201) 567-7300. FAX: (201) 569-6285. Leslie Kaplan

BALLANTYNE OF OMAHA/STRONG INT'L
4350 McKinley St., Omaha, NE, 68112. (402) 453-4444. FAX: (402) 453-7238. John Wilmers, Ray Boegner

CHINA FILM EQUIPMENT CORP.
189 Gentry Street, Pomona, CA 91767. (909) 392-2247. FAX: (909) 596-5289. Alan Richmond

CHRISTIE, INC.
10550 Camden Dr., Cypress, CA 90630-4600. (714) 236-8610. FAX: (714) 229-3185.
V.P., SALES & MARKETING
Jack Kline

CINEMA FILM SYSTEMS/RENTEC, INC.
791 N. Benson Ave., Upland, CA 91786-5836. (909) 931-9318. FAX: (909) 949-8815. Ron Offerman, Dick Niccum
3840 South Helena St., Aurora, CO 80013-2506. (303) 699-7477. FAX: (303) 680-6071. "TC" Costin

CINEMECCANICA U.S., INC.
13130 56th Court, Suite 608, Clearwater, FL 34620. (813) 573-3011. FAX: (813) 572-0136. Tom Brenner

EDW. H. WOLK CO., INC.
921 S. Jefferson, Chicago, IL 60607. (312) 939-2720. FAX: (312) 939-0654. Norm Lauterbach

GOLDBERG BROTHERS, INC.
8000 E. 40th Avenue, Denver, CO 80207. (303) 321-1099. FAX: (303) 388-0749. Victoria Adams

HANOVIA
100 Chestnut St., Newark, NJ 07105-1192. (201) 589-4300. FAX: (201) 589-4430. Dennis Priscandero

INTERNATIONAL CINEMA EQUIPMENT
100 N.E. 39th St., Miami, FL 33137-3632. (305) 573-7339. FAX: (305) 573-8101. Steven Krams

KINOTONE, DIVISION OF ARRIFLEX
617 Route 303, Blauvelt, NY 10913. (914) 353-1400. FAX: (914) 425-1250. John Galucci

KNEISLEY ELECTRIC
2501 Lagrange St., Toledo, OH 43608-2301. (419) 241-1219. FAX: (419) 241-9920. Harry Ewell

LAVEZZI PRECISION, INC.
999 Regency Dr., Glendale Heights, IL 60139-2281. (630) 582-1238. FAX: (630) 582-1238.

MARBLE COMPANY, INC.
P.O. Box 160030, Nashville, TN 37216-0030. (800) 759-5905. FAX: (615) 227-7008. Ronald Purtee

NEUMADE PRODUCTS CORP.
200 Connecticut Ave., Norwalk, CT, 06854-1940. (203) 866-7600. FAX: (203) 866-7522. Jeff Buchanan

OPTICAL DATA CORP.
1300 Optical Dr., Azusa, CA 91702. (818) 969-3344. FAX: (818) 812-9608.

OSRAM SYLVANIA, INC.
(Xenon lamps) P.O. Box 3305, Brentwood, TN 37024. (800) 394-0363. FAX: (615) 661-4710. John Dawsey

PIONEER TECHNOLOGY, INC.
1021 N. Lake St., Burbank, CA 91502. (818) 842-7165. FAX: (818) 842-0921. Don Stults

PLASTIC REEL CORP. OF AMERICA
Brisbin Ave., Lyndhurst, NJ 07071. (201) 933-5100. Frank Giglio

SCHNEIDER CORPORATION OF AMERICA
400 Crossways Park Dr., Woodbury, NY 11797-2032. (516) 496-8500. FAX: (516) 496-8524. Dwight Lindsey

SPECIAL-OPTICS (HEYER SCHULTZ DIV.)
315 Richauel Mine Road, Whirton, NJ 07885. (201) 785-4015. FAX: (201) 322-7407. James Waters

SYSTEMS & PRODUCTS ENGINEERING CO.
709 N. 6th St., Kansas City, KS 66101-3031. (913) 321-3978. FAX: (913) 321-7439. George Higginbotham

TECCON ENTERPRISES LTD.
686 Cliffside Drive, P.O. Box 38, San Dimas, CA 91773. (909) 592-2408.

TECO
1122 Industrial Drive, Mathews, NC 28105. (704) 847-4455. FAX: (704) 845-1709.

XETRON DIVISION/NEUMADE PRODUCTS
10 Saddle Rd., Cedar Knolls, NJ 07927-1901. (201) 267-8200. FAX: (201) 267-4903. Mark Smith

SCREENS AND FRAMES

HURLEY SCREEN CORP., A SUBSIDIARY OF CEMCORP
110 Industry Lane, P.O. Box 296, Forest Hill, MD 21050. (410) 838-0036. FAX: (410) 838-8079.
V.P., OPERATIONS
Gorman H. White, Jr.

KLIPSCH PROFESSIONAL
149 N. Industrial Park Rd., Hope, AR 71801. (501) 777-0693. FAX: (501) 777-0593. Chuck Mulhearn

NICK MULONE & SONS, INC.
100 Highland Ave., Cheswick, PA 15024. (412) 274-3221. FAX: (412) 274-4808. Nick Mulone

SELBY PRODUCTS, INC.
(Drive-in screens) P.O. Box 267, Richfield, OH 44286-0267. (800) 647-6224. FAX: (216) 659-4112. Jerry Selby

STEWART FILMSCREEN CORP.
1161 Sepulveda Blvd., Torrance, CA 90502-2797. (310) 326-1422. FAX: (310) 326-6870. Don Stewart

TECHNIKOTE CORPORATION
63 Seabring St., Brooklyn, NY 11231-1697. (718) 624-6429. FAX: (718) 624-0129. Mitchell M.Schwam

SEATING

AMERICAN DESK MANUFACTURING
2600 West Avenue G, P.O. Box 6107, Temple, TX 76502. (817) 773-1776. FAX: (817) 773-7370. Gary Knight

AMERICAN SEATING CO.
901 Broadway Ave. NW, Grand Rapids, MI 49504-4499. (616) 732-6895. FAX: (616) 732-6446. Ed Yates

ASSIGNED SEATING & MANUFACTURING GROUP, INC.
102 California Ave., City of Industry, CA 91744-4321. (818) 333-4464. FAX: (818) 968-5316. Chuck Kaplan

CALIFORNIA SEATING & REPAIR CO., INC.
12455 Branford Street, Suite 21B, Arleta, CA 91331. (818) 890-7328. FAX: (805) 581-0226. Tim McMahan

HAYES EQUIPMENT & SUPPLY CO., INC.
P.O. Box 29, Syracuse, NY 13211. (315) 432-8183. Jack Hayes

HUSSEY SEATING COMPANY
Dyer St., N. Berwick, ME, 03906. (207) 676-2271. FAX: (207) 676-2222. Jim Chadbourne

IRWIN SEATING COMPANY
P.O. Box 2429, Grand Rapids, MI 49501-2429. (616) 784-2621. FAX: (616) 784-5819. Don Winkels

SEATING CONCEPTS, INC.
4901-600 Morena Blvd., San Diego, CA 92117. (619) 581-5715. FAX: (619) 581-5725.

SOUND EQUIPMENT

Amplifiers, sound reinforcement, speakers and encoding devices. Companies noted with a * supply assistive listening systems.

ASC THEATRE EQUIPMENT SALES
P.O. Box 851625, Richardson, TX 75085-1625. (214) 437-2160. FAX: (214) 437-2138. Roy Lisenbe

ALTEC LANSING CORP.
10500 W. Reno Ave., P.O. Box 26105, Oklahoma City, OK 73127-7100. (405) 324-5311. FAX: (405) 324-8981. John Sexton

ASHLY AUDIO, INC.
847 Holt Rd., Webster, NY 14580-9103. (716) 872-0010, (800) 828-6308. FAX: (716) 872-0739. Bob French

*ASSOCIATED HEARING INSTRUMENTS
6976 Market St., Upper Darby, PA 19082-2308. Daniel Libby

*AUDEX, ASSISTIVE LISTENING SYSTEMS
710 Standard Street, Longview, TX 75604. (800) 237-0716. FAX: (800) AUDEX-74. Kelly Green

BGW SYSTEMS, INC.
13130 Yukon Avenue, Hawthorne, CA 90250. (310) 973-8090, (800) 468-AMPS. FAX: (213) 676-6713. Joe DeMeo

CARDINAL SOUND & MOTION PICTURE SYSTEM, INC.
10219 Southard Drive, Beltsville, MD 20705-2126. (301) 595-8811. FAX: (301) 595-5985. Catherine Rockman

CERWIN-VEGA
555 E. Easy Street, Simi Valley, CA 93065. (818) 896-0777. Rich Mandella

*CHAPARRAL COMMUNICATIONS, INC.
2450 North First Street, San Jose, CA 95131-1191. (408) 435-1530. FAX: (408) 435-1429. Howard B. Koch

CINEMA EQUIPMENT, INC.
1375 N.W. 97th Avenue, Suite 12, Miami, FL 33172. (305) 594-0570. FAX: (305) 592-6970. William Younger

COMMUNITY LIGHT & SOUND, INC.
333 East Fifth Street, Chester, PA 19013. (215) 876-3400. FAX: (215) 874-0190. Janine Masten

COMPONENT ENGINEERING CO.
3601 Gilman Ave W., Seattle, WA 98199-2339. (206) 284-9171. FAX: (206) 286-4462. Sam Chavez

CREST AUDIO, INC.
100 Eisenhower Dr., Paramus, NJ 07652-1401. (201) 909-8700. FAX: (201) 909-8744. John V. Lee

CROWN INTERNATIONAL
P.O. Box 1000, Elkhart, IN 46515. (219) 294-8000. FAX: (219) 294-8329. Jim Beattie

DIGITAL TECHNOLOGY SYSTEMS, INC.
249 S. Highway 101, #435, Solana Beach, CA 92075. (619) 270-3354. FAX: (619) 634-3725. Ronald Vale

DIGITAL THEATER SYSTEMS
31336 Via Colinas, #101, Westlake Village, CA 91362-3903. (818) 706-3525. FAX: (818) 706-1868. Walter Browski

DOLBY LABORATORIES
100 Potrero Ave., San Francisco, CA 94103-4813. (415) 558-0200. FAX: (415) 863-1373. Sabine Gonzalez

EPRAD, INC.
P.O. Box 73, Rossford, OH 43460-0073. (419) 666-3266. FAX: (419) 666-6534. Ted Stechschulte

FRAZIER, INC.
Route 3, Box 319, Morrilton, AR 72110-9532. (501) 727-5543. FAX: (501) 727-5402. J. E. Mitchell

HAFLER PROFESSIONAL
546 S. Rockford Drive, Tempe, AZ, 85281. (800) 366-1619. FAX: (602) 894-1528. Rick Gentry

HIGH PERFORMANCE STEREO
64 Bowen St., Newton, MA, 02159-1820. (617) 244-1737. FAX: (617) 244-7350. John Allen

JBL PROFESSIONAL
8500 Balboa Blvd., Northridge, CA 91325-3503. (818) 893-8411. FAX: (818) 787-0788. Brad Lunde

KINETICS NOISE CONTROL
6300 Irelan Place, Dublin, OH 43017-3257. (614) 889-0480. FAX: (614) 889-0540. Jill Skaggs

KINTEK, INC.
P.O. Box 9143, Waltham, MA, 02254-9143. (617) 894-6111. FAX: (617) 647-4235. Sarah Fuller

LUCASFILM LTD./THX DIVISION
P.O. Box 2009, San Rafael, CA 94912-2009. (415) 662-1900. FAX: (415) 662-2734. Monica Dashwood

MTS NORTHWEST SOUND, INC.
7667 Cahill Rd., Minneapolis, MN 55439-2749. Jerry van de Rydt

MARK IV CINEMA SYSTEM/ELECTRO-VOICE
600 Cecil St., Buchanan, MI 49107-1799. (616) 695-6831. FAX: (616) 695-1304. Chris Alfiero

MISCO-MINNEAPOLIS SPEAKER COMPANY
3806 Grand Avenue South, Minneapolis, MN, 55409. (612) 825-1010. Dan Ohlgre

NADY SYSTEMS, INC.
(Wireless microphones) 6701 Bay Street, Emeryville, CA 94608. (510) 652-2411. FAX: (510) 652-5075. Howard Zimmerman

PHONIC EAR
3880 Cypress Drive, Petaluma, CA 94954. (707) 769-1110. FAX: (707) 769-9624.

PROJECTED SOUND, INC.
(Drive-in sound equipment) 469 Avon Ave., Plainfield, IN 46168-1001. (317) 839-4111. FAX: (317) 839-2476. Tom Hilligoss

QSC AUDIO PRODUCTS
1675 Macarthur Blvd., Costa Mesa, CA 92626-1440. (714) 754-6175. FAX: (714) 754-6174. Barry Ferrell

RGM INDUSTRIES, INC.
3342 Lillian Blvd., Titusville, FL 32780. (407) 269-4720.

SENNHEISER ELECTRONIC CORP.
6 Vista Dr., Old Lyme, CT 06371. (860) 434-9190. FAX: (860) 434-1759. Joe Ciandelli

SMART THEATRE SYSTEMS
5945 Peachtree Corners E, Norcross, GA 30071-1337. (404) 449-6698. FAX: (404) 449-6728. Norman Schneider

SONY CINEMA PRODUCTS CORP.
10202 Washington Blvd., Culver City, CA 90232-3119. (310) 280-5777. FAX: (310) 280-2024. Dan Taylor

SOUND ASSOCIATES, INC.
424 West 45th Street, New York, NY 10036. (212) 757-5679. FAX: (212) 265-1250.

ULTRA STEREO LABS
18730 Oxnard St., #208, Tarzana, CA 91356-1455. (818) 609-7405. FAX: (818) 609-7408. Felicia Cashin

*WILLIAMS SOUND CORP.
10399 W. 70th Street, Eden Prairie, MN, 55344. (612) 943-2252. FAX: (612) 943-2174.

OTHER THEATRE SUPPLIES AND SERVICES

ALCOPS INCORPORATED
(Security services) 6701 West 64th Street, Overland Park, KS 66202. (913) 362-0104. FAX: (913) 362-5859. Mickey Gitlin

AMPAC THEATRE CLEANING SERVICES
(Theatre cleaning) P.O. Box 421, Monterey, CA 93942. (408) 372-3728. FAX: (408) 373-3490. Arnold Meltzer

AUTOMATIC DEVICES CO.
(Theatre equipment) 2121 S. 12th St. Allentown, PA 18103-4751. (610) 797-6000. John Samuels

BARTCO CO.
(Film cleaning) 924 N. Formosa, Hollywood, CA 90046. (213) 851-5411. LeRoy Bartels

BERN LEVY ASSOCIATES
(Lens cleaning) 21 Bowling Circle, Palmyra, VA 22963. (804) 589-2171. FAX: (804) 589-2172. Bern Levy

BOB WELLS THEATRE PAINTING
(Theatre painting) 1823 Cordova Ave., Cincinnati, OH 45239-4963-(513) 522-9026. Bob Wells

CREST-TALMADGE SALES
(Janitorial supplies) 1590 Rollins Road, Burlingame, CA 94010. (415) 692-7378. FAX: (415) 692-8059. Mark Talmadge

DALE SYSTEM, INC.,THEATRE DIVISION
(Security services) 1101 Stewart Ave, Garden City, NY 11530-4808. (516) 794-2800. FAX: (516) 542-1063. Helen Robin

DATA QUEST INVESTIGATIONS LTD.
(Security services) 15 Springvale Avenue, Boston, MA, 02132. (800) 292-9797. FAX: (617) 323-0054. Tracey Bubas

HANOVER UNIFORM COMPANY
(Uniforms) 529 W. 29th St., Baltimore, MD 21211-2988. (800) 541-9709. FAX: (410) 235-6071. John Mintz

HARRAH'S THEATRE EQUIPMENT CO.
(Theatre equipment) 25613 Dollar St., Unit 1, Hayward, CA 94544-2535. (510) 881-4989. FAX: (510) 881-0448. Jerry Harrah

INDIANA CASH DRAWER COMPANY
(Theatre equipment) P.O. Box 236, Shelbyville, IN 46176-0236. (317) 398-6643. Phil Stephens

LENNOX INDUSTRIES
(Air-conditioning) P.O. Box 799900, Dallas, TX 75379. (214) 497-5076. FAX: (214) 497-5112. Frank Cuevas

MCALLISTER ASSOCIATES, INC.
(Computer Systems) 247 Main St., Reading, MA 01867. (617) 942-0700. FAX: (617) 942-0240. David Zaltman

MAGTECH ENVIRONMENTAL INC.
(Seat cleaning) 710 Season Heather Ct., Ballwin, MO 63021. (314) 394-0414. Don Waldman

MIRACLE EQUIPMENT CO.
(Playground equipment) P.O. Box 420, Monett, MO 65708-0420. (417) 274-6917. FAX: (417) 235-3551.

MODULAR HARDWARE
(Restroom equipment) P.O. Box 35398, Tuscon, AZ 85740. (800) 533-0042. FAX: (800) 533-7942. Robert Hoch

NATIONAL CINEMA SUPPLY CORP.
(Theatre equipment) 8406 Sunstate St., Tampa, FL 33634. (813) 884-7909. FAX: (813) 884-0544. Syndi Graham

NOVAR CONTROLS CORP.
(Air-conditioning) 3200 W. Market St., Suite 106, Akron, OH 44333-3324. (216) 745-0074. FAX: (216) 745-7401. Mike Tindall

PRIORITY MANUFACTURING, INC.
(Uniforms) 571 N.W. 29th Street, Miami, FL 33127. (305) 576-3000.

RMS SERVICE AND ELECTRONICS, INC.
(Theatre maintenance) 250 West 49th Street, Suite 403, New York, NY 10019. (212) 586-4900. FAX: (212) 586-5069. Roger Getzoff

REYNOLDS & REYNOLDS
(Insurance) The Plaza, Suite 200, 300 Walnut St., Des Moines, IA 50309. (800) 767-1724. FAX: (515) 243-6664. Sandra Bell

SCHULT DESIGN AND DISPLAY
(Theatre equipment) 13910 Century Lane, Grandview, MO 64030-3920. (816) 966-8998. FAX: (816) 966-0990. Jeffrey Schult

THEATRE SERVICES
(Cleaning services) P.O. Box 835932, Richardson, TX 75083-5932. (214) 690-0615. FAX: (214) 699-7355. Alvin Wigington

THEATRE SPECIALTY CO. INC.
(Theatre cleaning) P.O. Box 5091, Loveland, CO 80538. (970) 669-5407. FAX: (970) 669-1829.

CONCESSION SUPPLIERS

This listing features food productsand other food-related consumable suppliers (disposable paper products, etc.).

AMERICAN CHICLE
201 Tabor Road, Morris Plains, NJ, 07950. (201) 540-3900.
FAX: (201) 540-4200.

AMERICAN INTERNATIONAL CONCESSION PRODUCTS CORP.
P.O. Box 379, Malverne, NY, 11565. (516) 420-1868. FAX:
(516) 420-4042.

AMERICAN LICORICE COMPANY
2477 Liston Way, Union City, CA, 94587. (510) 487-5500. FAX:
(510) 487-2517.

AMERICAN POPCORN COMPANY
P.O. Box 178, Sioux City, IA, 51102. (712) 239-1232. FAX:
(712) 239-1268.

BAGCRAFT CORPORATION OF AMERICA
3900 West 43rd Street, Chicago, IL, 60632. (773) 254-8000.
FAX: (773) 254-8204.

BANNER CANDY MFG. CORP.
700 Liberty Avenue, Brooklyn, NY, 11208. (718) 647-4747.
FAX: (718) 647 7192.

BIL MAR FOODS, INC.
8300 96th Avenue, Zeeland, MI, 49464. (800) 654-3650. FAX:
(616) 875-7591.

BOYD COFFEE COMPANY
19730 NE Sandy Blvd., Portland, OR, 97230. (503) 666-4545.
FAX: (503) 669-2223.

BRAD BARRY CO.
1245 E. Watson Center Rd, Bldg A, Carson, CA, 90745. (310)
522-8848. FAX: (310) 522-8844.

BREWED AWAKENING / GODIVA CHOCOLATES
24 E. 22nd Street, New York, NY, 10010. (212) 674-3724. FAX:
(212) 533-0519.

CARGILL
P.O. Box 5693, Minneapolis, MN 55440. (612) 742-6627. FAX:
(612) 742-5503.

CENTRAL SOYA
1946 West Cook Rd., Ft. Wayne, IN 46818. (800) 788-6336.
FAX: (219) 425 5753.

CHINA MIST TEA COMPANY
7435 E. Tierra Buena Lane, Scottsdale, AZ 85260. (800) 242-
8807. FAX: (602) 443-8384.

J.G. CLARK COMPANY/SOUTHFIELD CARTON COMPANY
1171 West Center St,. Marion, OH 43302. (800) 274-4882.
FAX: (800) 538 2594.

THE COCA-COLA COMPANY
One Coca-Cola Plaza, Atlanta, GA 30313. (404) 676-8622.
FAX: (404) 676-3605.

COCA-COLA CO. FOODS DIV.
P.O. Box 2079, Houston, TX 77252. (713) 888-5000. FAX: 888-
5959.

COLFAX, INC.
36 Colfax Street, Pawtucket, RI 02860. (800) 556-6777. FAX:
(401) 724-4313.

COMSTOCK MICHIGAN FRUIT FOODSERVICE
P.O. Box 20670, Rochester, NY 14602. (716) 383-1070. FAX:
(716) 383-8337.

DART CONTAINER CORPORATION
500 Hogsback Road, Mason, MI 48854. (800) 248-5960. FAX:
(517) 676-3883.

DREYER'S/EDY'S GRAND ICE CREAM
5929 College Avenue, Oakland, CA 94618. (510) 601-4459.
FAX: (510) 450-4625.

DUBUQUE FOODS, INC.
2040 Kerper Blvd., Dubuque, IA 52004. (319) 588-5501. FAX:
(319) 583-8643.

DURO BAG
10 East Merrick Road, Valley Stream, NY 11580. (800) 451-
7816. FAX: (516) 825-2792.

EISENBERG GOURMET BEEF FRANKS
3531 N. Elston Avenue, Chicago, IL 60618. (773) 588-2882.
FAX: (773) 588-0510.

ELLIS POPCORN COMPANY, INC.
101 East Poplar Street, Murray, KY 42071. (502) 753-5451.
FAX: (502) 753-7002.

EURO-AMERICAN BRANDS, INC.
15 Prospect Street, Paramus NJ 07652. (201) 368-2624. FAX:
(201) 368-2512.

THE FOREIGN CANDY COMPANY, INC.
451 Black Forest Road, Hull, IA 51239. (800) 831-8541. FAX:
(712) 439-1434.

GEHL'S GUERNSEY FARMS, INC.
P.O. Box 1004, Germantown, WI 53022-8204. (414) 251-8570.
FAX: (414) 251-9318.

HERMAN GOELITZ CANDY CO., INC.
2400 N. Watney Way, Fairfield, CA 94533. (707) 428-2800.
FAX: (707) 423-4436.

GREAT BRANDS OF EUROPE/ EVIAN WATERS OF FRANCE
500 W. Putnam Ave., Greenwich, CT 06830. (203) 629-3642.
FAX: (203) 629-7961.

GREAT WESTERN PRODUCTS COMPANY
30290 US Highway 72, Hollywood, AL 35752. (800) 239-2143.
FAX: (205) 574-2116.

HAAGEN-DAZS
17043 Green Drive, Industry, CA 91745. (818) 964-5797. FAX:
(818) 965-3889.

HARIBO OF AMERICA, INC.
1825 Woodlawn Drive, Suite 204, Baltimore, MD 21207. (410)
265-8890. FAX: (410) 265-8898.

HERSHEY FOODS
19 E. Chocolate Ave., Hershey, PA 17033. (717) 534-4007.
FAX: (717) 534-7694.

J & J SNACK FOODS
5353 Downey Road, Vernon, CA 90058. (213) 581-0171. FAX:
(213) 583-4732.

JUDSON-ATKINSON CANDY CO.
P.O. Box 830046, San Antonio, TX 78283. (800) 962-3984.
FAX: (210) 222-8498.

JUICY WHIP, INC.
15845 Business Center Dr., Irwindale, CA, 91706. (818) 338-
5339. FAX: (818) 814-8016.

JUST BORN, INC.
P.O. Box 1158, Bethlehem, PA 18016. (800) 6J-BEANS. FAX:
(800) 543-4981.

KRAFT FOODS / OSCAR MAYER FOODS CORPORATION
P.O. Box 19532, Irvine, CA, 92715. (714) 453-3645. FAX: (714)
453-3610.

L&H INDUSTRIES
1100 Quail Street, Suite 205, Newport Beach CA, 92660. (714)
851-0424. FAX: (714) 851-8540.

LETICA CORP., MAUI CUP DIVISION
52585 Dequinder Road, Rochester, MI 48307. (810) 652-0557.
FAX: (810) 652-0577.

M&M / MARS
800 High Street, Hackettstown, NJ 07840. (908) 852-1000.
FAX: (908) 850-2734.

METRO GOOD TIME FOODS
48839 Kato Road, Fremont, CA 94539. (510) 490-3434. (510)
226-9758.

METROPOLITAN CONCESSIONS INDUSTRIES
9950 Mission Mill Rd., Whittier, CA 90601. (310) 695-0541.
FAX: (310) 695-6796.

MORRISON FARMS POPCORN
RR 1, Box A, Clearwater, NE 68726. (402) 887-5335. FAX:
(402) 887-4709.

MULTI FOODS SPECIALTY DISTRIBUTION
1 Denver Highlands, Suite 200, Denver, CO 80231. (800) 880-9900.

NATIONAL ICEE CORP.
800 Dutch Sq. Blvd., Suite 131, Columbia, SC 29210. (803) 772-6363. FAX: (803) 731-0597.

NESTLE FOOD COMPANY
2 Summit Park Drive, Suite 300, Independence, OH 44131. (216) 573-6715. FAX: (216) 372-6715.

NEW ENGLAND CONFECTIONARY
254 Massachusetts Avenue, Cambridge, MA 02139. (617) 876-4700. FAX: (617) 876-2356.

ODELL'S
1325 Airmotive Way, Suite 290, Reno, NV 89502. (702) 323-8688. FAX: (702) 323-6532.

PEPSI-COLA COMPANY
1 Pepsi Way, Somers, NY 10589. (914) 767-7814. FAX: (914) 767-1195.

POPT TIME
P.O. Box 2, Lake View, IA 51450. (712) 657-8561.

PROMOTION IN MOTION CO., INC./ FERRARA PAN CANDY CO.
3 Reuten Drive, Closter, NJ 07624. (201) 784-5800. FAX: (201) 784-1010.

QUAKER BEVERAGE (SNAPPLE, GATORADE)
321 N. Clark St., Chicago, IL 60610. (312) 222-6421. FAX: (312) 222 7411

RAMSEY POPCORN CO., INC.
5645 Clover Valley Rd. NW, Ramsey, IN 47166. (812) 347-2441. FAX: (812) 347 3336.

RICOS PRODUCTS/LIBERTO SPECIALTY
621 S. Flores, San Antonio, TX 78204. (210) 222-1415. FAX: (210) 226-6453.

RIO SYRUP COMPANY, INC.
2311 Chestnut Street, St. Louis, MO 63103. (800) 325-7666. FAX: (314) 436-7707.

SQUARE H BRANDS
2731 S. Soto Street, Los Angeles, CA 90023. (213) 267-4600. FAX: (213) 261-7350.

STAR SNACKS
2640 Market St., San Diego, CA 92102. (619) 231 2617. FAX: (619) 231 2985.

SUNMARK SPECIAL MARKETS
8155 New Hampshire Ave., St. Louis, MO 63123. (314) 832-7575. FAX: (314) 832-6813.

SWEETHEART CUP CO.
10100 Reistertown Rd., Owings Mills, MD 21117. (410) 363-1111.

TASTE OF NATURE
400 S. Beverly Drive, #214, Beverly Hills, CA 90212. (310) 276-2927. FAX: (310) 278-9509.

TENNECO PACKAGING
14505 Proctor Ave, Industry, CA 91746. (818) 968 3801. FAX: (818) 961-9625.

TOOTSIE ROLL INDUSTRIES, INC.
7401 South Cicero Ave., Chicago, IL 60629. (800) 877-7655, (312) 838-3430. FAX: (312) 838-3569.

VICTOR PRODUCTS CO.
P.O Box 7910, Richmond, VA 23223. (804) 643-9091. FAX: (804) 648-3601.

VOGEL POPCORN CO.
2301 Washington Street, Hamburg, IA 51640. (800) 831-5818. FAX: (712) 382-1357.

WEAVER POPCORN COMPANY, INC.
130 Main Street, Van Buren, IN 46991. (800) 227-6159. FAX: (317) 934-4052.

W.N.A./CUPS ILLUSTRATED, INC.
2155 W. Longhorn Drive, Lancaster, TX 75134. (800) 334-CUPS. FAX: (972) 224 3067.

WORD POPCORN CO.
P.O. Box 466, Hollywood, AL 35752. (800) 633-5091. FAX: (205) 574-2116.

WRIGHT POPCORN & NUT CO.
150 Potrero Ave., San Francisco, CA 94103. (415) 861-0912. FAX: 415 861 6745.

WYANDOT, INC.
135 Wyandot Avenue, Marion, OH 43302. (614) 383-4031. FAX: (614) 382-5584.

ZENITH SPECIALTY BAG COMPANY, INC.
17625 E. Railroad Street, Industry, CA 91748. (818) 912-2481. FAX: (818) 810-5136.

SCREENING ROOMS

All major studios, producers and distributors have screening rooms at their home offices in Hollywood and New York for their own use. Most also have screening room facilities at local distribution offices.

ACADEMY OF MOTION PICTURE ARTS & SCIENCES:
ACADEMY LITTLE THEATER & SAMUEL GOLDWYN THEATRE
8949 Wilshire Blvd., 3rd Floor, Beverly Hills, CA 90211-1972. (310) 247-3000. FAX: (213) 859-9619.

ACADEMY PLAZA THEATRE
5230 Lankershim Blvd., N. Hollywood, CA 91601. (818) 761-0458. FAX: (818) 766-7484.

CHARLES AIDIKOFF SCREENING ROOM
150 S. Rodeo Dr., #140, Beverly Hills, CA 90212. (310) 274-0866.

AMERICAN FILM INSTITUTE
2021 N. Western Ave., Los Angeles, CA 90027. (213) 856-7600. FAX: (213) 467-4578.

BEVERLY HILLS SCREENING INC.
8949 Sunset Blvd., Suite 201, Beverly Hills, CA 90069. (310) 275-3088.

BIG TIME PICTURE COMPANY
122101-1/2 Nebraska Ave., Los Angeles, CA 90025. (310) 207-0921. FAX: (310) 826-0071.

BROADWAY SCREENING ROOM
1619 Broadway, 5th Floor, New York, NY 10019. (212) 307-0990.

CINE-METRIC THEATRE INC.
290 Madison Ave., New York, NY 10017. (212) 922-0910.

CINEVISION CORP.
3300 Northeast Expwy., Bldg. 2, Atlanta 30341. (404) 455-8988. FAX: (404) 455-4066.

DICKINSON OPERATING CO.
5913 Woodson Rd., Mission, KS 66202. (913) 432-2334.

DIRECTORS GUILD OF AMERICA
7920 W. Sunset Blvd., Los Angeles, CA 90046. (310) 289-2000. FAX: (310) 289-2029.

EXPLORATORIUM, MCBEAN THEATER
3601 Lyon St., San Francisco, CA 94123. (415) 563-7337.

HARPO STUDIOS INC.
1058 W. Washington, Chicago, IL 60607. (312) 633-1000.

HOLLY-VINE SCREENING ROOM
6253 Hollywood Blvd., Suite 1210, Los Angeles, CA 90028. (213) 462-3498.

HOLLYWOOD NEWSREEL SYNDICATE, INC.
1622 N. Gower St., Los Angeles, CA 90028. (213) 469-7307. FAX: (213) 469-8251.

MAGNO PREVIEW THEATRE
1600 Broadway, New York, NY 10019. (212) 302- 2505.

MAGNO SOUND SCREENING ROOM
729 Seventh Ave., New York, NY 10019. (212) 302-2505.

MARCUS THEATRES
250 E. Wisconsin Ave., Milwaukee, WI 53202-4222. (414) 272-512.

NAVESYNC SOUND
513 W. 54 St., New York, NY 10019. (212) 246-0100.

OCCIDENTAL STUDIOS
201 N. Occidental Blvd., Los Angeles, CA 90026. (213) 384-3331. FAX: (213) 384-2684.

PACIFIC FILM ARCHIVE
2625 Durant Ave., Berkeley, CA 94720-2250. (510) 642-1412.

RALEIGH STUDIOS
650 N. Bronson Ave., Los Angeles, CA 90004. (213) 466-3111.

GLENN ROLAND FILMS
P.O. Box 341408, Los Angeles, CA 90024. (310) 475-0937. FAX: (310) 475-0939.

TECHNICOLOR
321 W. 44 St., New York, NY 10036. (212) 582-7310.

TODD-AO STUDIOS EAST
259 W. 54 St., New York, NY 10019. (212) 265-6225.

BRUNO WALTER AUDITORIUM
Lincoln Center, Amsterdam Ave. at 65th St., New York, NY 10023. (212) 870-1680.

WARNER BROS. STUDIOS
4000 Warner Blvd., Burbank, CA 91522. (818) 954-6000, 954-2923. FAX: (818) 954-2677.

WRITERS GUILD DOHENY PLAZA THEATER
135 S. Doheny Dr., Beverly Hills, CA 90211. (310) 550-1000, 205-2502.

SAUL ZAENTZ CO. FILM CENTER
2600 Tenth St., Berkeley, CA 94710. (510) 549-2500.

SPECIALTY EXHIBITION

For the definition of this section, specialty exhibitors show non-theatrical films, usually in a proprietary format and occasionally involving mechanical simulations in conjuction with the film, to non-theatrical audiences (usually museum-goers and amusement park attendees). However, traditional exhibitors are installing limited numbers of specialty screens in multiplexes. Films are usually much shorter than traditional theatrical releases.

IMAX CORPORATION

Imax leases IMAX projection systems and distributes films to specially designed theatres worldwide.
45 Charles Street East, 5th Floor,Toronto, Ontario, Canada M4Y 1S2. (416) 960- 8509. FAX (416) 960-8596.
Subsidiaries: Ridefilm Entertainment, Sonics Associates, David Keighley Productions/70MM Inc.
CHAIRMAN
Bradley J. Wechsler
VICE CHAIRMAN
Richard L. Gelfond
PRESIDENT & CEO
Robert J. Corrigan
PRESIDENT RIDEFILM CORP.
Douglas Trumbull
U.S. IMAX THEATRES
(Most American IMAX theatres are independently owned and operated. Theatres marked with an asterisk have IMAX 3D capability.)
ALABAMA—HUNTSVILLE: Spacedome Theatre- U.S. Space and Rocket Center.
ARKANSAS—LITTLE ROCK: Aerospace Education Centre.
ARIZONA—SCOTTSDALE: IMAX Theatre; TUSAYAN: Grand Canyon IMAX Theatre.
CALIFORNIA—IRVINE: Edwards IMAX 3D*; LOS ANGELES: California Museum of Science and Industry, Universal Studios; SAN DIEGO: Reuben H. Fleet Space Theatre; SANTA CLARA: Great Adventure*; SAN FRANCISCO: Sony IMAX 3D*.
COLORADO—DENVER: Denver Museum of Natural History.
CONNECTICUT—NORWALK: IMAX Theatre at the Maritime Center.
WASHINGTON, D.C.—Langley Theatre at the Smithsonian Institute.
FLORIDA—FORT LAUDERDALE: Museum of Discovery and Science; KENNEDY SPACE CENTER: Spaceport USA Theatres 1 & 2; ORLANDO: Epcot Center-Disney World, Universal Studios; TAMPA: Museum of Science and Industry.
GEORGIA—ATLANTA: The Fernback Museum of Natural History.
HAWAII—HONOLULU: Hawaii IMAX Theatre; LAIE: Polynesian Cultural Center.
ILLINOIS—CHICAGO: Cineplex Odeon Navy Pier Imax 3-D*, Museum of Science and Industry; GURNEE: Six Flags*.
KANSAS—HUTCHINSON: Cosmosphere Theatre.
KENTUCKY—LOUISVILLE: Louisville Science Center.
LOUISIANA—NEW ORLEANS: New Orleans Aquarium.
MARYLAND—BALTIMORE: Maryland Science Center.
MASSACHUSETTS—BOSTON: Museum of Science.
MICHIGAN—DETROIT: Detroit Science Center.

MINNESOTA—SHAKOPEE: Valleyfair Amusement Park; SAINT PAUL: Science Museum of Minnesota.
MISSOURI—BRANSON: Ozarks Discovery IMAX Theatre; KANSAS CITY: Kansas City Zoo.
MONTANA—WEST YELLOWSTONE: Yellowstone IMAX Theatre.
NEBRASKA—HASTINGS: Hastings Museum.
NEVADA—LAS VEGAS: Caesar's Palace.
NEW MEXICO—ALAMOGORDO: The Space Center.
NEW JERSEY—JERSEY CITY: Liberty Science Center.
NEW YORK—NEW YORK: Sony IMAX*, Museum of Natural History; SYRACUSE: Discovery Center.
NORTH CAROLINA—CHARLOTTE: Discovery Place.
OHIO—CINCINNATI: Museum Center; DAYTON: U.S. Air Force Museum; SANDUSKY: Cedar Point Amusement Center.
OREGON—PORTLAND: Oregon Museum of Science and Industry.
PENNSYLVANIA—PHILADELPHIA: Franklin Institute Science Museum; PITTSBURGH: Carnegie Science Center.
TENNESSEE—MEMPHIS: Pink Palace Museum.
TEXAS—DALLAS: Science Place; FORT WORTH: Fort Worth Museum of Science and Industry; GALVESTON: Moody Gardens*; HOUSTON: Houston Museum of Natural Science, Space Center Houston; LUBBOCK: Science Spectrum; SAN ANTONIO: Rivercenter.
VIRGINIA—HAMPTON: Air and Space Center; RICHMOND: Science Museum.
WASHINGTON—SEATTLE: Omnidome, Pacific Science Center; SPOKANE: Riverfront Park.

SHOWSCAN ENTERTAINMENT

3939 Landmark St., Culver City, CA 90232-2315. (310) 558-0150. FAX: (310) 559-7984.
PRESIDENT & CEO
William C. Soady
CALIFORNIA—UNIVERSAL CITY: CineMania at Universal CityWalk.
INDIANA—INDIANAPOLIS: United Artists Circle Center.
MARYLAND—BALTIMORE: Golden Ring.
MASSACHUSETTS—BOSTON: Jillian's Billiard Club; FRAMINGHAM: General Cinemas at Shoppers World.
MISSISSIPPI—BILOXI: Boomtown.
NEVADA—LAS VEGAS: Excalibur Hotel & Casino; STATELINE: Buffalo Bill's; VERDI: Boomtown Hotel & Casino.
NEW YORK—NIAGARA FALLS: Niagara State Park; SYRACUSE: Funscape.
TEXAS—AUSTIN: Lakeline Mall; DALLAS: Jupiter Road, United Artists Northpark; SAN ANTONIO: Presidio Plaza.
VIRGINIA—CHESAPEAKE: Regal Cinemas Funscape.

MOTION PICTURE ORGANIZATIONS

PRODUCER, DISTRIBUTOR, EXHIBITOR, VARIETY & FILM CLUBS

GUILDS & UNIONS

PRODUCER-DISTRIBUTOR, VARIETY & FILM CLUBS

ACADEMY OF MOTION PICTURE ARTS AND SCIENCES
(Organized June, 1927. Membership 5,127.)
8949 Wilshire Blvd., Beverly Hills, CA 90211. (310) 247-3000.
Library: 333 S. La Cienega Blvd., Beverly Hills, CA 90211.
(310) 247-3020.
PRESIDENT
Arthur Hiller
FIRST VICE PRESIDENT
Sid Ganis
VICE PRESIDENTS
Arthur Hamilton, Fay Kanin
TREASURER
Robert Rehme
SECRETARY
Roddy McDowell
EXECUTIVE DIRECTOR
Bruce Davis
LEGAL COUNSEL
John B. Quinn
BOARD OF GOVERNORS
Saul Bass, Carl Bell, Curt R. Behlmer, Charles Bernstein, John
A. Bonner, Robert F. Boyle, Bruce Broughton, Martha Coolidge,
Robert A. Daly, Allen Daviau, Linwood G. Dunn, Richard
Edlund, Sid Ganis, Conrad L. Hall, Don Hall, Arthur Hamilton,
Arthur Hiller, Cheryl Boone Isaacs, Norman Jewison, Fay
Kanin, Hal Kanter, Kathleen Kennedy, Howard W. Koch, Marvin
Levy, William C. Littlejohn, Carol Littleton, Karl Malden, Marvin
Narch, Roger L. Mayer, Roddy McDowall, Gregory Peck, Frank
R. Pierson, Robert Rehme, Arthur Scmidt, Bill Taylor, Frank J.
Urioste, Haskell Wexler, Albert Wolsky, Richard D. Zanuck

ALLIANCE OF MOTION PICTURE AND TELEVISION PRODUCERS
(Membership: Major studios, independent production compa-
nies and film processing laboratories.)
15503 Ventura Blvd., Encino, CA 91436-3140. (818) 995-3600.
PRESIDENT
J. Nicholas Counter III
S.V.P., LEGAL & BUSINESS AFFAIRS
Carol A. Lombardini
CFO
Kathy Grotticelli
V.P., LEGAL AFFAIRS
Helayne Antler

AMERICAN CINEMATHEQUE
(Organized 1984. Celebrates the moving picture in all its forms
through public film and video exhibition.)
c/o Hollywood Roosevelt Hotel, 7000 Hollywood Blvd., 3rd Fl.,
Hollywood, CA 90028. (213) 466-3456. FAX: (213) 461-9737.
Program Information: (213) 466-FILM.
CO-CHAIRMEN
Peter J. Dekoim, Mike Medavoy
PRESIDENT
Sigurjon Sighvatsson
EXECUTIVE DIRECTOR
Barbara Zicka Smith
CHAIRMAN EMERITUS
Sydney Pollack
BOARD OF DIRECTORS
Charles Champlin, Robert Cort, David Geffen, Lawrence
Gordon, Brian Grazer, Buck Henry, Godfrey Isaac, Leonard
Levy, Barry London, David Morse, Peter Morton, George E.
Moss, Lenore Nelson, Sanford P. Paris, Michael John Pittas,
Elisabeth Pollon, Dennis Pope, Arnold Rifkin, Joe Roth, Henry
Shields, Jr., Bette L. Smith, Rosalie Swedlin, Saul Zaentz.

THE AMERICAN FILM INSTITUTE
(A national trust dedicated to preserving the heritage of film and
television.)
The John F. Kennedy Center for the Performing Arts,
Washington, DC 20566. (202) 828-4000. FAX: (202) 659-1970.
2021 N. Western Ave., P.O. Box 27999, Los Angeles, CA
90027. (213) 856-7600. FAX: (213) 467-4578.
DIRECTOR
Jean Firstenberg
DEPUTY DIRECTOR
James Hindman

BOARD OF TRUSTEES
CHAIRMAN
Fred Pierce
CO-CHAIRMAN
George Stevens, Jr.
PRESIDENT
Charlton Heston
VICE CHAIRMEN
Charles W. Fries, Howard Stringer, Liener Temerlin
HONORARY TRUSTEE
Jack Nicholson
BOARD MEMBERS: Merv Adelson, Debbie Allen, Jon Avnet,
Jeanine Basinger, Robert M. Bennett, Jeff Berg, James
Billington, Richard Brandt, Mark Canton, Alfred A. Checchi,
Peter Chernin, Martha Coolidge, Robert A. Daly, Suzanne de
Passe, John DiBiaggio, Jean Firstenberg, Michael Forman,
Richard Frank, Stephen D. Frankfurt, Michael Fuchs, Ina
Ginsburg, Suzanne Lloyd Hayes, Lawrence Herbert, Gale Ann
Hurd, Robert Iger, Gene F. Jankowski, Robert L. Johnson, Fay
Kanin, Lawrence Kasdan, Jerry Katzman, Sherry Lansing,
Marsha Mason, Ron Meyer, Michael Nesmith, Mace Neufeld,
Daniel Petrie, Tom Pollock, Kelly Rose, Jill Sackler, Vivian
Sobchack, Steven Spielberg, Helen Stansbury, Charles
Steinberg, Brandon Tartikoff, Anthony Thomopoulos, Jack
Valenti, Irwin Winkler, Robert Wise, David L. Wolper, Robert C.
Wright, Bud Yorkin

AMERICAN FILM MARKETING ASSN.
(Organized 1980. Membership: 126 companies engaged in the
sale of independently produced films to the international mar-
ket. Sponsors the American Film Market in the spring.)
10850 Wilshire Blvd., 9th Floor, Los Angeles, CA 90024. (310)
446-1000. FAX: (310) 446-1600.
CHAIRMAN OF BOARD
Pamela Pickering
PRESIDENT
Jonas Rosenfield
VICE CHAIRMAN
John Hyde, Lawrence Safir, Frederick Schneier
VICE CHAIRMAN, FINANCE
Ann Oliver
VICE CHAIRMAN, SECRETARY
Lorin Brennan
EXECUTIVE VICE PRESIDENT
Timothy Kittleson
SENIOR VICE PRESIDENT
Jonathon Wolf
BOARD OF DIRECTORS 1996-97:
Rob Aft (Alliance MDP Worldwide), Herb Fletcher (Crown
International Pictures, Inc.), Gene George (Green Communica-
tions), Lawrence Goebel (Image Organization, Inc.), Michael
Goldman (Cinema Consultants Group), Lewis Horwitz (Lewis
Horwitz Org.), Penny Karlin (Dire Straits Prods.), Norman B.
Katz (The Nor Kat Company, Ltd.), Lloyd Kaufman (Troma,
Inc.), Robert Little (Overseas Filmgroup, Inc.), Liz Mackiewicz
(Prism Pictures), James Marrinan (Marrinan Multimedia),
Robert Meyers (Village Roadshow), Andrew Milner (The
Samuel Goldwyn Company), Kathy Morgan (Kathy Morgan
International), Barbara Mudge (New World Ent.), Nestor Nieves
(New Line Cinema Corporation), Leonard Shapiro (SGE
Entertainment Corporation), June Shelley (MoviCorp
Holdings), Peter Wetherell (Full Moon Entertainment)
MEMBER COMPANIES:
ABC Distribution Co., 825 Seventh Ave., 5th Fl., New York, NY
10019.
ADN Associates Ltd., 8 Cleveland Gardens, London W2 6HA
U.K.
Alliance Communications Corporation, 920 Yonge Street, Suite
400, Toronto, Ontario M4W 3C7, Canada.
Allied Vision Ltd., Avon House, The Glassworks, 3-4 Ashland
Place, London, WIM 3JH, U.K.
American First Run, 14225 Ventura Blvd., Sherman Oaks, CA
91423.
Arista Films Inc., 16027 Ventura Blvd., #206, Encino, CA 91436.
Atlas International, Rumfordstrasse 29-31, 80469 Munich,
Germany.
Australian Film Commission, 8 West St., N. Sydney, NSW 2060,
Australia.

Australian Film Finance Corp. Pty. Ltd., 130 Elizabeth St., GPO Box 3886, Sydney, NSW 2001, Australia.

Bank of America NT & SA, 2049 Century Park East, Suite 300, Los Angeles, CA 90067.

Banque Paribas, 2029 Century Park E., #3900, Los Angeles, CA 90067.

Beyond Films Ltd., 1875 Century Park E., Suite 1300, Los Angeles, CA 90067.

Big Bear Licensing Corp., 12400 Wilshire Blvd., Suite 360, Los Angeles, CA 90025.

Blue Ridge Entertainment, 10490 Santa Monica Blvd., Los Angeles, CA 90025.

Broadstar Entertainment Corp., 6464 Sunset Blvd., PH1130 Hollywood, CA 90028.

Capella International Inc., 9242 Beverly Boulevard, Suite 280, Beverly Hills, CA 90210-3710.

Chemical Bank, 1800 Century Park East, Suite 400, Los Angeles, CA 90067.

CineTelFilms Inc., 8255 W. Sunset Blvd., Los Angeles, CA 90046-2432.

Cinetrust Entertainment Corp., 2121 Ave. of the Stars, 6th floor, Los Angeles, CA 90067.

Cinevest Entertainment, 450 Seventh Ave., #2702, New York, NY 10123.

Concorde-New Horizons Corp., 11600 San Vicente Blvd., Los Angeles, CA 90049.

Cori International: Film & Television, 19 Albermarle St., London W1, U.K.

Credit Lyonnais Bank Nederland, Coolsingel 49, 3012 AA Rotterdam, Netherlands.

Crown International Pictures Inc., 8701 Wilshire Blvd., Beverly Hills, CA 90211.

Curb Organization, 3907 W. Alameda Ave., Suite 102, Burbank, CA 91505.

Davian Int'l Ltd., 144 Boundry St., 1st fl., Kowloon, Hong Kong.

De Nationale Investeringsbank N.V., Carnegieplein 4, P.O. Box 380, 2501 BH The Hague, Netherlands.

Dino DeLaurentiis Communications, 8670 Wilshire Blvd., Beverly Hills, CA 90211.

Distant Horizon Ltd., 84-86 Regent St., #508, London WIR 5PF U.K.

Film Four International, 60 Charlotte St., London WIP 2AX U.K.

Film World Entertainment/Miracle Films, 6311 Romaine St., #7309, Hollywood, CA 90038.

Filmark International Ltd., Garley Bldg., #1401, 233-239 Nathan Rd., Kowloon, Hong Kong.

Filmexport Group SRL, Via Polonia 7-9, 00198 Rome, Italy.

Film Four International, 60 Charlotte St., London W1P 2AX, U.K.

Films Guernsey, Limited, c/o F.I.L.M.S., 40 Queen Anne's Gate, London SW1H 9AP, England, U.K.

First Charter Bank, 265 N. Beverly Dr., Beverly Hills, CA 90210.

Fries Distribution Co., 6922 Hollywood Blvd., Hollywood, CA 90028.

Full Moon Studios, 3030 Andrita St., Los Angeles, CA 90065.

GEL Distribution, 11075 Santa Monica Blvd., #250, Los Angeles, CA 90025.

Goldcrest Films & TV, 65/66 Dean St., London W1V 6PL U.K.

Golden Harvest/Golden Comm., 8 King Tung St., Hammer Hill Rd., Kowloon, Hong Kong.

Samuel Goldwyn Company, 10203 Santa Monica Blvd., #500, Los Angeles, CA 90067.

Grand Am Ltd., 6649 Odessa Ave., Van Nuys, CA 91406.

Green Communications Inc., 3407 W. Olive Ave., Burbank, CA 91505.

Hemdale Pictures Corp., 7966 Beverly Blvd., Los Angeles, CA 90048.

Hills Entertainment Group, Lappersveld 68, Hilversum, 1213 VB, Netherlands.

IFD Films & Arts Ltd., Suite 1208, 12th fl., 233-239 Nathan Rd., Kowloon, Hong Kong.

I.N.I. Entertainment Group Inc., 11150 Olympic Blvd., Suite #700, Los Angeles, CA 90064.

I.R.S. Media International, 3939 Lankershim Blvd., Universal City, CA 91604.

ITC Entertainment Group, 12711 Ventura Blvd., 3rd fl., Studio City, CA 91604.

Imperial Bank Entertainment Industries Group, 9777 Wilshire Boulevard, 4th Floor, Beverly Hills, CA 90212.

Internationale Nederlanden Bank, N.V., Postbus 1800, Locatie Code HE0401, Amsterdam 1000 BV, Netherlands.

Inter-Ocean Film Sales Ltd., 6100 Wilshire Blvd., #1500, Los Angeles, CA 90048.

J & M Entertainment, 1289 Sunset Plaza Dr., Los Angeles, CA 90069.

Largo Entertainment, 10201 W. Pico Blvd., Los Angeles, CA 90035.

The Robert Lewis Company, 8755 Shoreham Drive, #303, Los Angeles, CA 90069.

Lone Star Pictures Int'l, 4826 Greenville Ave., Dallas, TX 75206.

M.C.E.G./Sterling Entertainment, 1888 Century Park East, Suite 1777, Los Angeles, CA 90067.

Majestic Films & Television, P.O. Box 13, Gloucester Mansions, Cambridge Circus, London WC2H 8XD, England, U.K.

Manifesto Film Sales, 10 Livonia St., 3rd Floor, London W1V 3PH, England, U.K.

Mark Damon Productions Inc., 1875 Century Park East, Suite 450, Los Angeles, CA 90067.

Marquee Entertainment Inc., 9044 Melrose Avenue, 3rd Floor, Los Angeles, CA 90069.

Mayfair Entertainment Int'l, 13 Tottenham Mews, London W1P 9PJ, England, U.K.

Melrose Entertainment Inc., 8383 Wilshire Blvd., Beverly Hills, CA 90211.

Mercantile National Bank, 1840 Century Park East, 3rd Floor, Los Angeles, CA 90067.

Miramax Int'l, 7920 Sunset Blvd., Suite 230, Los Angeles, CA 90046.

Moonstone Entertainment, 9242 Beverly Blvd., Suite 230, Beverly Hills, CA 90210-3710.

Morgan Creek International Inc., 1875 Century Park E., #200, Los Angeles, CA 90067.

Motion Picture Corp. of America, 1401 Ocean Ave., 3rd fl., Santa Monica, CA 90401.

The Movie Group Inc., 1900 Ave. of the Stars, #1425, Los Angeles, CA 90067.

The Movie House Sales Co. Ltd., Regal Chambers, 51 Bancroft Hitchin, Hertfordshire, SG5 7LL, England, U.K.

New Line Cinema Corp., 116 N. Robertson, Suite 200, Los Angeles, CA 90048.

New World Int'l Entertainment, 1440 S. Sepulveda Blvd., Los Angeles, CA 90025-3458.

New Zealand Film Commission, P.O. Box 11-546, 36 Allen St., Wellington, New Zealand.

Noble Productions, 1615 South Crest Drive, Los Angeles, CA 90035.

The Norkat Co. Ltd., 280 S. Beverly Dr., #306, Beverly Hills, CA 90212.

Norstar Entertainment, 86 Bloor St. W., #400, Toronto, Ontario M5S 1M5 Canada.

North American Releasing, 808 Nelson St., #2105, Vancouver, BC V6Z 2H2, Canada.

Odyssey Distributors Ltd., 6500 Wilshire Blvd., #400, Los Angeles, CA 90048.

Omega Entertainment Ltd., 8760 Shoreham Drive, Los Angeles, CA 90069.

Overseas Filmgroup Inc., 8800 Sunset Blvd., #302, Los Angeles, CA 90069.

P.C. Films Corp., 60 E. 42nd St., #2320, New York, NY 10165.

Pandora Cinema, 23 Avenue de Neuilly, Paris 75116, France.

Penta Int'l Ltd., 8 Queen St., London W1X 7PH, England, U.K.

Playpont Films Ltd., 1-2 Ramilies St., London WIV 1DF, U.K.

Promark Entertainment Group, The Promark Center West, 3599 Cahuenga Blvd. W, #300, Los Angeles, CA 90068.

Puzon Creative Entertainment, 462 Regina Blvd., Escolta, Manila, 3679 Phillipines.

Rank Film Distributors, 127 Wardour St., London W1V 4AD U.K.

Rapi Films, Cikini 217, Jakarta, Indonesia.

Reel Movies International Inc., 8235 Douglas Ave., #770, Dallas, TX 75225.

Republic Pictures Int'l, 12636 Beatrice St., Los Angeles, CA 90066.

SC Entertainment Int'l, 434 Queen St. E., Toronto, Ont. M5A IT5 Canada.

SCE Inc., 434 Queen St. E., Toronto, Ontario M5A IT5 Canada.

SGE Entertainment Corp., 12001 Ventura Place, #404, Studio City, CA 91604.

Saban Pictures Int'l, 4000 W. Alameda Ave., Burbank, CA 91505.

Safir Films Ltd., 49 Littleton Rd., Harrow, Middlesex HA1 3SY, U.K.

The Sales Company, 62 Shaftesbury Ave., London W1V 7AA, U.K.

Showcase Entertainment Inc., Warner Center, 21800 Oxnard St., #150, Woodland Hills, CA 91367.

Silver Star Film Corp., 1102 N. Screenland Dr., Burbank, CA 91505.

Smart Egg Pictures, 62 Brompton Rd., London SW3 1BW, U.K.

Spelling Films International, 5700 Wilshire Blvd., #575, Los Angeles, CA 90036.

Starway Int'l Corp., 2100 Century Park West, Los Angeles, CA 90067.

Summit Entertainment L.P., 2308 Broadway, Santa Monica, CA 90404.

Sunny Film Inc., No. 2 USJ4/16, Subang Jaya, 47600 Petaling Jaya, Malaysia.

Trans Atlantic Entertainment, 10351 Santa Monica Boulevard, Suite 200, Los Angeles, CA 90025.

Trimark Pictures, 2644 30th St., Santa Monica, CA 90405.

Troma Inc., 733 Ninth Ave., New York, NY 10019.

Turner Pictures Worldwide, 1888 Century Park East, 12th Floor, Los Angeles, CA 90067.

21st Century Film Corp., 11080 N. Olympic Blvd., Los Angeles, CA 90064.

Viacom Pictures Inc., 10 Universal Plaza, 31st fl., Universal City, CA 91608.

Vine Int'l Pictures, 21 Great Chapel St., London W1V 3AQ U.K.

West Side Studios, 10726 McCune Ave., Los Angeles, CA 90034.

World Films Inc., 8920 Sunset Blvd., 2nd fl., Los Angeles, CA 90069.
World Media Sales, 662 West Huntington Dr., Suite 518, Monrovia, CA 91016.

AMERICAN HUMANE ASSOCIATION
(Organized 1877. Liaison with the television and motion picture industry as supervisors of animal action in television and motion picture production.)
15503 Ventura Blvd., Encino, CA 91436. (818) 501-0123.
National Headquarters: 63 Inverness Dr. E., Englewood, CO 80112. (303) 792-9900.
NATIONAL PRESIDENT
Charles Granoski
VICE PRESIDENT
Loretta Kowal
TREASURER
Timothy O'Brien
DIRECTOR, L.A. OFFICE
Betty Denny Smith

AMERICAN SOCIETY OF COMPOSERS, AUTHORS AND PUBLISHERS (ASCAP)
(Organized February 13, 1914. Membership: 39,000 Music Writers, 18,000 Publishers.)
One Lincoln Plaza, New York, NY 10023. (212) 621-6000. FAX: (212) 724-9064.
7920 Sunset Blvd., Suite 300, Hollywood, CA 90046. (213) 883-1000. FAX: (213) 883-1049.
PRESIDENT & CHAIRMAN
Marilyn Bergman
VICE PRESIDENTS
Cy Coleman, Jay Morgenstern
SECRETARY
Arthur Hamilton
TREASURER
Arnold Broido
COUNSEL
I. Fred Koenigsberg
COO
John A. LoFrumento
DIRECTOR OF MEMBERSHIP
Todd Brabec
SOUTHERN REGIONAL EXECUTIVE DIRECTOR
Connie Bradley, ASCAP, Two Music Square W., Nashville, TN 37203

ASIAN CINEVISION, INC.
(A not-for-profit organization dedicated to encouraging Asian and Asian-American media arts.)
32 East Broadway, New York, NY 10002. (212) 925-8685. FAX: (212) 925-8157.
EXECUTIVE DIRECTOR
Bill J. Gee

ASSOCIATION OF CINEMA & VIDEO LABORATORIES, INC.
(Organized 1953. Publishes *ACVL Handbook.*)
7095 Hollywood Blvd., #751, Hollywood, CA 90028.
Correspondence only, no phone number.
PRESIDENT
Frank Ricotta, Technicolor, Inc.
FIRST VICE PRESIDENT
George Hutchison, Consolidated Film Industries
SECOND VICE PRESIDENT
Jim George, Deluxe Laboratories
TREASURER
Richard Vedvick, Forde Motion Picture Labs
SECRETARY
Robert Smith, Duart Film Laboratories

ASSOCIATION OF FILM COMMISSIONERS INTERNATIONAL
(Organized 1975. Acts as a liaison between the visual communications industry and local governments or organizations to facilitate on-location production, to stimulate economic benefit for member governments.)
c/o Utah Film Commission, 324 South State, Suite 500, Salt Lake City, UT 84114. (801) 538-8681. FAX: (801) 538-8778.
PRESIDENT
Leigh von der Esch, Utah Film Office
FIRST VICE PRESIDENT
Linda Taylor Hutchinson, New Mexico Film Commission
SECOND VICE PRESIDENT
Isabel Hill, South Carolina Film Office
SECRETARY
Linda Peterson Warren, Arizona Film Commission
TREASURER
Eve Lapolla, Ohio Film Commission
BOARD OF DIRECTORS
Luci Marshall (Phoenix Film Office), Frank Miller (Sedona Film Commission), Paul Mingard (Northern Screen Commission), Loni Stimac (Montana Film Commission), Gail Thomson (Ontario Film Development Corp.)

ASSOCIATION OF INDEPENDENT VIDEO & FILMMAKERS, INC.
(A national membership organization dedicated to the growth of independent media.Publishes *The Independent Magazine.*)
625 Broadway, New York, NY 10012. (212) 473-3400.
EXECUTIVE DIRECTOR
Ruby Lerner
DIRECTOR OF PROGRAMS & SERVICES
Pamela Calvert
EDITOR
Pat Thompson
MANAGING EDITOR
Michele Shapiro
BOARD OF DIRECTORS
Joe Berlinger, Melissa Burch, Loni Ding, Barbara Hammer, Ruby Lerner, James Klein, Diane Markrow, Meni Matias, Robb Moss, Robert Richter, James Schamus, Norman Wang, Burton Wiess

BMI (BROADCAST MUSIC, INC.)
320 W. 57 St., New York, NY 10019. (212) 586-2000. FAX: (212) 582-5972.
8730 Sunset Blvd., 3rd fl. West, Los Angeles, CA 90069. (310) 659-9109.
10 Music Square E., Nashville, TN 37203. (615) 401-2000.
79 Marylebone Rd., London NW1 5HN, England. (44) 171 935-8517.
CHAIRMAN OF THE BOARD
Donald A. Thurston
PRESIDENT & CEO
Frances W. Preston
S.V.P. & GENERAL COUNSEL
Marvin Berenson
S.V.P., FINANCE & ADMINISTRATION & CFO
Fred Willms
S.V.P., PERFORMING RIGHTS, WRITER & PUBLISHER RELATIONS
Del Bryant
V.P., CORPORATE RELATIONS
Robbin Ahrold
S.V.P., INTERNATIONAL
Ekke Schnabel
S.V.P. & SPECIAL COUNSEL
Theodora Zavin
S.V.P., LICENSING
John M. Shaker
V.P., INFORMATION TECHNOLOGY
Bob Barone
V.P. & CONTROLLER
Thomas Curry
V.P., NASHVILLE
Roger Sovine
V.P., WRITER & PUBLISHER RELATIONS, CALIFORNIA
Rick Riccobono
V.P., WRITER & PUBLISHER RELATIONS, NEW YORK
Charles S. Feldman
V.P., GENERAL LICENSING
Tony Annastas
V.P., HUMAN RESOURCES & SECRETARY
Edward W. Chapin
V.P., EUROPEAN WRITER & PUBLISHER RELATIONS
Philip R. Graham
V.P., RESEARCH & INFORMATION
John Marsillo
V.P., TELECOMMUNICATIONS
Larry Sweeney

COMMUNICATION COMMISSION OF THE NATIONAL COUNCIL OF THE CHURCHES OF CHRIST IN THE USA
475 Riverside Dr., Room 856, New York, NY 10115. (212) 870-2574. FAX: (212) 870-2030.
CHAIRMAN
Eric Shafer
DIRECTOR OF ELECTRONIC MEDIA
David W. Pomeroy

COUNCIL ON INTERNATIONAL NON-THEATRICAL EVENTS (CINE)
(Organized 1957. CINE selects and enters tv documentaries, theatrical short subjects, educational, religious, scientific film and tv products in 120 international film & video competitions.)
1001 Connecticut Ave. NW, Suite 638, Washington, DC 20036. (202) 785-1136. (202) 785-1137. FAX: (202) 785-4114.
PRESIDENT
Dr. Frank Frost
CHAIRMAN
Alan Rettig
EXECUTIVE DIRECTOR
Christine Reilly

FILM SOCIETY OF LINCOLN CENTER
(Organized 1969. Sponsors The New York Film Festival and
publishes *Film Comment* magazine.)
70 Lincoln Center Plaza, New York, NY 10023-6595. (212)
875-5610. FAX: (212) 875-5636.
URL: http://www.filmline.com
CHAIRMAN
Roy L. Furman
PRESIDENT
Irwin W. Young
EXECUTIVE DIRECTOR
Joanne Koch
EXECUTIVE PRODUCER, PROGRAMMING
Wendy Keys
PROGRAM DIRECTOR
Richard Pena

**THE FOUNDATION OF THE MOTION PICTURE
PIONEERS, INC.**
244 W. 49 St., Suite 200, New York, NY 10019. (212) 247-
3178. FAX: (212) 265-6428.
PRESIDENT
Tom Sherak
CHAIRMAN OF BOARD
Daniel R. Fellman
EXECUTIVE VICE PRESIDENT
Dick Cook
VICE PRESIDENTS
Jeff Blake, Jerry Forman, Larry Gleason, Mitch Goldman, Allen
Karp, Barrie Lawson Loeks, Wayne Lewellen, Hank Lightstone,
Fred Mound, Michael Patrick.
TREASURER
Travis Reid
SECRETARY
Robert Sunshine

**FRENCH FILM OFFICE/UNIFRANCE FILM
INTERNATIONAL**
(Organized 1956. Promotes French films in U.S.)
745 Fifth Ave., Suite 1512, New York, NY 10151. (212) 832-
8860. FAX: (212) 755-0629.
EXECUTIVE DIRECTOR FOR THE U.S.
Catherine Verret

FRENCH CONSULATE–AUDIOVISUAL DEPARTMENT
10990 Wilshire Blvd., #300, Los Angeles, CA 90024. (310)
479-0643. FAX: (310) 479-8331.
DIRECTOR
Laurent Danielou

FRIARS CLUB
57 E. 55 St., New York, NY 10022. (212) 751-7272.
ABBOT
Frank Sinatra
DEAN
Freddie Roman
PRIOR
Robert W. Sarnoff
SCRIBE
Frank Military
TREASURER
David B. Cornstein
EXECUTIVE DIRECTOR
Jean-Pierre L. Trebot
DIRECTOR OF SPECIAL EVENTS
David W. Tebet
HONORARY OFFICERS
ABBOT EMERITUS
Milton Berle
SCRIBE EMERITUS
Red Buttons
PROCTOR
Buddy Hackett
HERALD
Paul Anka
MONITOR
Alan King
HISTORIAN
Bernard M. Kamber
MONK
Robert Merrill
SAMARITAN
Norman King
BIOGRAPHER
Joey Adams
SQUIRE
Henny Youngman
KNIGHT
Gene Baylos
KNIGHT
Tom Jones

ARCHIVIST
James W. Grau

FRIARS CLUB OF CALIFORNIA, INC.
(Organized 1947.)
9900 Santa Monica Blvd., Beverly Hills, CA 90212. (213) 553-
0850. FAX: (310) 286-7906.
CHAIRMAN
Steve Allen
PRESIDENT
Irwin M. Schaeffer
FIRST VICE PRESIDENT
Edward G. Lewis
SECOND VICE PRESIDENT
Norman Edell
SECRETARY
Albert Mayo
TREASURER
Gary G. Cohen
ASSISTANT SECRETARY/TREASURER
David Daar
PUBLIC RELATIONS
Michael Saltzman

THE INDEPENDENT FEATURE PROJECT
(Organized 1979. Non-profit organization which provides infor-
mation and support services to independent filmmakers.)
104 W. 29 St., 12th floor, New York, NY 10001-5310. (212)
465-8200. FAX: (212) 465-8525. URL: http://www.ifp.org
EXECUTIVE DIRECTOR
Catherine Tait
DEPUTY DIRECTOR
Michelle Byrd
MARKETING DIRECTOR
Valerie Sheppard
BOARD OF DIRECTORS
Stephanie Allain (Pres., Production, Jim Henson Pictures),
Doro Bachrach (Pres., The Noon Wine Co.), Michael Barker
(Co-Pres., Sony Pictures Classics), Herbert Beigel (Pres.,
Beigel Entertainment Corp.), Richard Brick (Silo Cinema, Inc.),
Ralph Donnelly (President, Cinema Connection), Douglas
Durst (Pres., The Durst Organization), Nely Galan (Pres.,
Galan Entertainment), Maggie Greenwald (Dal Vero Pictures,
Inc.), Ted Hope (Co-Pres., The Good Machine, Inc.), Peter
Howe (Partner, Ernst & Young), Tom Kalin (Principal, Vachon
Productions, Inc.), Spike Lee (40 Acres & A Mule), Jeff Lipsky
(Plainview Pictures, Inc.), Richard Pena (Program Dir., Film
Soc. of Lincoln Ctr.), Richard P. Rubinstein (Chairman & CEO,
New Amsterdam Entertainment Inc.), Sandra Schulberg
(Playhouse Int'l Pictures, Inc.), Thomas Selz (Frankfurt,
Garbus, Klein & Selz), Nancy Sher (Media Consultant),
Raphael Silver (Chairman, Silverfilm Productions), John Sloss
(Sloss Law Office), Nancy Tennenbaum (Nancy Tenenbaum
Films), Irwin Young (Chairman, DuArt Film Laboratories Inc.).

INDEPENDENT FEATURE PROJECT/WEST
(Organized 1980. Publishes *Filmmaker: The Magazine of
Independent Film*, a co-publication of IFP/West & IFP.)
1625 Olympic Blvd., Santa Monica, CA 90404. (310) 392-8832.
FAX: (310) 392-6792.
PRESIDENT
Barbara Boyle
VICE PRESIDENT
Theodore Thomas
PROGRAMMING
Jesse Beaton
TREASURER
Caldecot Chubb
EXECUTIVE DIRECTOR
Dawn Hudson
BOARD OF DIRECTORS
Stephen K. Bannon, Peter Broderick, Julie Carmen, Laura
Anne Edwards, Carl Franklin, Geoff Gilmore, Michael Helfant,
Gale Anne Hurd, Jeff Kleeman, Carol Munday Lawrence,
Jeanne Lucas, Peggy Rajski, Charles Ries, Sara Risher, Tom
Rothman, Midge Sanford, Vickie Thomas, Jonathon Wacks,
Janet Yang.

INTERNATIONAL DOCUMENTARY ASSOCIATION
(Organized 1982.)
1551 S. Robertson Blvd., Suite 201, Los Angeles, CA 90035-
4257. (310) 284-8422. FAX: (310) 785-9334. e-mail: idf@net-
com.com
PRESIDENT
Lisa Leeman
VICE PRESIDENT
Ann Hassett
SECOND VICE PRESIDENT
Steven Roche
SECRETARY
Richard L. Samuels

624

TREASURER
Mitchell Block
EXECUTIVE DIRECTOR
Betsy A. McLane
BOARD OF DIRECTORS
Mitchell Block, Nicholas Clapp, Carol L. Fleisher, Lyn Goldfarb,
David Haugland, Carol Munday Lawrence, Lisa Leeman, Lynne
Littman, Tom Neff, Steven Ogden, Steven Roche, Bram Roos,
Richard L. Samuels, Lance Webster, Lance A. Williams.
REGIONAL MEMBERS: John Alonzo (Mobile), Henry Hampton
(Boston), Richard Kilbnerg (New York), Len McClure (Hong
Kong), Michael Rabiger (Chicago), Harry Rasky (Toronto),
Robert Richter (New York), Andre Singer (London), Marc Weiss
(New York), Frederick Wiseman (Boston)

JAPAN SOCIETY/FILM CENTER
(Organized 1907. Promotes Japanese culture through exhibit-
ing Japanese films and films on Japan.)
333 E. 47 St., New York, NY 10017. (212) 832-1155. FAX:
(212) 755-6752.
DIRECTOR, FILM CENTER
Dr. Kyoko Hirano
FILM PROGRAM ASSISTANT
Robert Lazzaro

MOTION PICTURE AND TELEVISION FUND
23388 Mulholland Drive, Woodland Hills, CA 91364. (818) 876-
1888.
Bob Hope Health Center, 335 N. LaBrea Ave., Los Angeles,
CA 90036. (213) 634-3850.
Toluca Lake Health Center, 4323 Riverside Dr., Burbank, CA
91505, (818) 556-2700.
Westside Health Center, 1950 Sawtelle Blvd., Suite 130, Los
Angeles, CA 90025. (310) 996-9355.
Samuel Goldwyn Foundation Children's Center, 2114 Pontius
Ave., Los Angeles, CA 90025, (310) 445-8993.
CHAIRMAN
Roger H. Davis
VICE CHAIRMAN
Chester L. Migden, Frank I. Davis, Janet Leigh Brandt,
Marshall Wortman
TREASURER
Roger L. Mayer
SECRETARY
Irma Kalish
PRESIDENT/CEO
William F. Haug
V.P., PROFESSIONAL SERVICES
Timothy M. Lefevre, M.D.
CFO
Frank Guarrera

MOTION PICTURE ASSOCIATION OF AMERICA, INC./
MOTION PICTURE ASSOCIATION
15503 Ventura Blvd., Encino, CA 91436. (818) 995-6600. FAX:
(818) 382-1799. Anti-Piracy Hot Line: 1-800-NO-COPYS.
1600 I Street NW, Washington, D.C. 20006. (202) 293-1966.
FAX: (202) 293-7674.
PRESIDENT & CEO
Jack Valenti
EXECUTIVE VICE PRESIDENT & COO
William M. Baker
SENIOR VICE PRESIDENTS
Fritz Attaway, Simon Barsky, William Billick, John J. Collins,
Bethlyn Hand, William Murray
VICE PRESIDENTS
Anthony J. Adamski, John Clynick, Allen Cooper, Barbara
Dixon, Paul Egge, Robert Franklin, Matthew Gerson, Marsha
Kessler, Walid Nasser, Vans Stevenson, Nancy Thompson
California Office:
EXECUTIVE V.P. & COO/MPAA PRESIDENT & CEO
William M. Baker
V.P. & DIRECTOR, WORLDWIDE ANTI-PIRACY
Anthony J. Adamski
V.P., FINANCE WORLDWIDE ANTI-PIRACY
John Clynick
DEPUTY, FINANCE WORLDWIDE ANTI-PIRACY
Mark Howe
DEPUTY DIRECTOR/SPECIAL COUNSEL WORLWIDE
ANTI-PIRACY
Gregory P. Goeckner
DIRECTOR, U.S.A. ANTI-PIRACY OPERATIONS
Ed Pistey
DIRECTOR, LEGAL OPERATIONS, U.S.A. ANTI-PIRACY
Crossan Andersen
WASHINGTON OFFICE:
PRESIDENT & CEO
Jack Valenti
S.V.P., GOVERNMENT RELATIONS
Fritz Attaway

S.V.P., DOMESTIC LEGAL & TAX
Simon Barsky
V.P., CONGRESSIONAL AFFAIRS
Matthew Gerson
V.P., TRADE & FEDERAL AFFAIRS
Bonnie Richardson
V.P., NEW TECHNOLOGY
Allen R. Cooper
V.P., CABLE COPYRIGHT COLLECTION DISTRIBUTION
Marsha Kessler
V.P., PUBLIC AFFAIRS
Barbara Dixon
V.P., ADMINISTRATION
Nancy Thompson
COUNSEL STATE LEGISLATION
Karin Newman
V.P., STATE LEGISLATION
Vans Stevenson
DIRECTOR, DOMESTIC CABLE COPYRIGHT COMPILATION
Sandra Pope
DIRECTOR INTERNATIONAL COPYRIGHT
Jane Saunders
DIRECTOR, PUBLIC AFFAIRS
Richard Taylor
DIRECTOR, ADMINISTRATION
Kathy Grant

REGIONAL OFFICES—WORLDWIDE ANTI-PIRACY
ASIA-PACIFIC OPERATIONS:
REGIONAL DIRECTOR
Lowell Strong
EUROPE, MIDDLE EAST & AFRICA ANTI-PIRACY
OPERATIONS:
DIRECTOR
Tim Kuik
S.V.P. & GENERAL COUNSEL
William Billick
V.P., LEGAL AFFAIRS
Walid Nasser
SENIOR COUNSEL
Axel aus der Muhlen
SENIOR INTERNATIONAL TAX COUNSEL
Barbara Rosenfeld
COUNSEL
Lisa Wilske
S.V.P. & CFO
John J. Collins
DIRECTOR, ACCOUNTING
Tom Igner
DIRECTOR, FINANCE
Don McLellan
S.V.P., ADMINISTRATION
Bethlyn J. Hand
DIRECTOR, BENEFITS
Nancy Nolan
DIRECTOR, OFFICE ADMINISTRATION
Marilyn Gordon
S.V.P., INT'L THEATRICAL, TV & HOME VIDEO/DEPUTY COO
William Murray
ASSISTANT V.P., DIRECTOR, TELEVISION
Kelley Nichols
DIRECTOR, INT'L THEATRICAL
Lisa Mundt
DIRECTOR, PROJECT DEVELOPMENT
Ana Crescioni

WORLDWIDE MARKET RESEARCH:
VICE PRESIDENT WORLDWIDE MARKET RESEARCH
Robert Franklin
DIRECTOR, WORLDWIDE MARKET RESEARCH
Lori Bushman
TITLE REGISTRATION BUREAU
Mitchell Schwartz, Director

CLASSIFICATION & RATING ADMINISTRATION:
CHAIRMAN
Richard M. Mosk
VICE CHAIRMAN
Joan Graves

ADVERTISING ADMINISTRATION
DIRECTOR
Bethlyn J. Hand
ASSOCIATE DIRECTOR
Marilyn Gordon

INTERNATIONAL OFFICES—MPA
SENIOR VICE PRESIDENT, BRUSSELS
Harlan Moen
VICE PRESIDENTS, BRUSSELS
Frank Tonini, Jane Albrecht

VICE PRESIDENT, LATIN AMERICA
Steve Solot
SENIOR VICE PRESIDENT, AUSTRALIA & ASIA
Michael Connors
VICE PRESIDENT, AUSTRALIA & ASIA
Jeff Hardee
SENIOR VICE PRESIDENT, ROME
Marc Spiegel
NATIONAL DIRECTOR, MONTREAL
Norman Quimet
VICE PRESIDENT, MONTREAL
Millard Roth
LEGAL MANAGER LMLA OPERATIONS
Nathan Knight
DIRECTOR EUROPEAN AFFAIRS
Michael Bartholomew

MUSEUM OF MODERN ART, DEPARTMENT OF FILM AND VIDEO
(Organized May, 1935.)
11 W. 53 St., New York, NY 10019. (212) 708-9600. FAX: (212) 708-9531.
CHIEF CURATOR
Mary Lea Bandy
CURATOR & COORDINATOR OF EXHIBITIONS
Laurence Kardish
CIRCULATING FILM LIBRARIAN
William Sloan
MANAGER OF FILM COLLECTIONS
Stephen Higgins
ASSOCIATE RESEARCHER
Charles Silver

NATIONAL ASSOCIATION OF THEATRE OWNERS, INC.
(For a complete list of state and regional NATO offices and Directors-At-Large please see the exhibition section.)
4605 Lankershim Blvd., Suite 340, N. Hollywood, CA 91602. (818) 506-1778. FAX: (818) 506-0269.
PRESIDENT
William F. Kartozian
CHAIRMAN OF THE BOARD
Pete Warzel
CHAIRMAN OF THE FINANCE COMMITTEE
Irwin R. Cohen
TREASURER
Irwin R. Cohen
SECRETARY
Jerome Gordon
EXECUTIVE DIRECTOR
Mary Ann Grasso
BOARD OF DIRECTORS
EXECUTIVE COMMITTEE: Walt Aman (Portland, OR), Michael Campbell (Knoxville, TN), Irwin R. Cohen (Reisterstown, MD), Roger Eaton (Boston, MA), Jerome Forman (Los Angeles, CA), Steve Gilula (Los Angeles, CA), Charles Goldwater (Encino, CA), Jerome Gordon (Hampton, VA), Peter Ivany (Sydney, Australia), Allen Karp (Toronto, Canada), Barrie Lawson Loeks (New York, NY), Lee Roy Mitchell (Dallas, TX), Shari Redstone (Dedham, MA), Paul Roth (Silver Spring, MD), Philip Singleton (Kansas City, MO), William Stembler (Atlanta, GA), Pete Warzel (Denver, CO)

NATIONAL BOARD OF REVIEW OF MOTION PICTURES, INC.
(Organized March, 1909. Publisher of *Films in Review*, sponsor of the NBR Awards.)
P.O. Box 589, New York, NY 10021. (212) 628-1594.
PRESIDENT
Inez S. Glucksman
VICE PRESIDENT
Ross Claiborne
EDITOR
Robin Little

NATIONAL MUSIC PUBLISHERS' ASSOCIATION, INC./ THE HARRY FOX AGENCY, INC.
(NMPA represents music publishing companies. The Harry Fox Agency was founded in 1927 and represents more than 15,000 music publishers, also serving as an information source, clearing house and monitoring service for licensing music copyrights.)
711 Third Ave., 8th fl., New York, NY 10017. (212) 370-5330. FAX: (212) 953-2584. URL: http://www.nmpa.org
PRESIDENT & CEO
Edward P. Murphy
V.P., LICENSING
Yoshio Inomata
V.P., FINANCE
Bernard Kerner

NEW YORK WOMEN IN FILM & TELEVISION
(Organized in 1977.)
274 Madison Ave., Suite 1202, New York, NY 10016-0701. (212) 679-0870. FAX: (212) 679-0899.
PRESIDENT
Harlene Freezer
V.P., DEVELOPMENT
Sandra Colony
V.P., PROGRAMMING
Lisa Hackett Stafford
V.P., SPECIAL EVENTS
Karen L. King
SECRETARY
Barbara Goodman
TREASURER
Debra Kozee
BOARD OF DIRECTORS
Marsha Brooks, Kathy Demerit, Alma Derricks, Marlene Freezer, Barbara Goodman, Linda Kahn, Debra Kozee, Karen King, Valerie Light, Susan Margolin, Wanda McGill, Eileen Newman, Marquita Pool-Eckert, Marcie Setlow, Dana Thrush, Vivian Treves, Charlette Van Doren, Ellen Zalk.
LEGAL COUNSEL
Marsha Brooks
EXECUTIVE DIRECTOR
Raquel R. Levin
CHAPTERS
Atlanta, Baltimore, Boston, Chicago, Dallas, Denver, Los Angeles, Orlando, Savannah, Seattle, Washington, D.C., Jamaica, London, Melbourne, Montreal, Paris, Sydney, Toronto, Vancouver

PERMANENT CHARITIES COMMITTEE OF THE ENTERTAINMENT INDUSTRIES
(Supports community-wide charities.)
11132 Ventura Blvd., Suite 401, Studio City, CA 91604-3156. (818) 760-7722. FAX: (818) 760-7898.
CHAIRMAN OF THE BOARD
Earl Lestz
PRESIDENT & CEO
Lisa Paulsen
FIRST VICE PRESIDENT
Harry J. Floyd
SECOND VICE PRESIDENT
Roger L. Mayer
SECRETARY
T. J. Baptie
TREASURER
Robert S. Colbert, CPA
V.P., ADMINISTRATION
Marilyn Augustine
V.P., COMMUNICATIONS & CORPORATE RELATIONS
Danielle M. Guttman

SESAC, INC.
(A music licensing organization.)
55 Music Square East, Nashville, TN 37203. (800) 826-9996.
CHAIRMEN
Freddie Gershon, Stephen Swid, Ira Smith
PRESIDENT & COO
Bill Velez

SOCIETY OF COMPOSERS & LYRICISTS
400 South Beverly Dr., Suite 214, Beverly Hills, CA 90212. (310) 281-2812. FAX: (818) 990-0601.
PRESIDENT
Richard Bellis
VICE PRESIDENT
Brad Fiedel
SECRETARY/TREASURER
Bruce Babcock
ADVISORY BOARD
Alan Bergman, Marilyn Bergman, Elmer Bernstein, Bill Conti, Jerry Goldsmith, James Newton Howard, Quincy Jones, Peter Matz, Alan Menken, David Raksin, Lalo Schifrin, Marc Shaiman, Howard Shore, Alan Silvestri, Patrick Williams, Hans Zimmer
BOARD OF DIRECTORS
Charles Bernstein, Steven Bramson, Jane Brockman, Bruce Broughton, John Cacavas, Alf Clausen, James Di Pasquale, Brad Fiedel, Dan Foliart, Jerry Grant, Ron Grant, Arthur Hamilton, Lee Holdridge, Ron Ramin, Alex Shapiro, Dennis Spiegel, Mark Watters, Gary Woods

SOCIETY OF MOTION PICTURE AND TELEVISION ENGINEERS
(Organized 1916. Membership: 9,700.)
595 W. Hartsdale Ave., White Plains, NY 10607-1824. (914) 761-1100. FAX: (914) 761-3115.
PRESIDENT
Stanley N. Baron
PAST PRESIDENT
Irwin Young
EXECUTIVE VICE PRESIDENT
David L. George

V.P., ENGINEERING
Kenneth P. Davies
V.P., EDITORIAL
Peter A. Dare
V.P., FINANCE
Charles H. Jablonski
V.P., CONFERENCE
Edward P. Hobson II
SECRETARY/TREASURER
Richard L. Thomas
EXECUTIVE DIRECTOR
Lynette Robinson
DIRECTOR, MARKETING
John Izzo, Jr.

**UNITED STATES CATHOLIC CONFERENCE,
DEPARTMENT OF COMMUNICATION—OFFICE
FOR FILM & BROADCASTING**
Suite #1300, 1011 First Ave., New York, NY 10022. (212) 644-1894. FAX: (212) 644-1886.
DIRECTOR, OFFICE FOR FILM & BROADCASTING
Henry Herx

VARIETY CLUBS INTERNATIONAL
(Organized October 10, 1927. Membership: 15,000.)
1560 Broadway, Suite 1209, New York, NY 10036. (212) 704-9872. FAX: (212) 704-9875.
PRESIDENT
Michael Reilly
IMMEDIATE PAST PRESIDENT
John Ratclif
INTERNATIONAL CHAIRMAN
Monty Hall, O.C.
PAST PRESIDENTS
Jarvis Astaire, Robert R. Hall, Q.C., Salah M. Hassanein, Eric D. Morley, Ralph W. Pries, Stanley J. Reynolds, Burton Robbins, John H. Rowley, Michael Samuelson, Joseph Sinay
VICE PRESIDENTS
Maureen Arthur, Peter J. Barnett, Vincent Catarella, Tom Fenno, Michael Forman, Frederick M. Friedman, Anthony Hasham, Fred Levin, Graham Mapp, A. M., Julia Morley, George Pitman, Marsha Rae Ratcliff, Jody Reynolds, Bruce Rosen, Frank Strean, John R. Weber.
PRESIDENT'S COUNCIL
Samuel Z. Arkoff, Monty Berman, MBE, Trevor Chinn, CVO, Philip Isaacs, Lou Lavinthal, Frank Mancuso, Hank Milgram, Carl L. Patrick, Ric R. Roman, Zollie Volchok.
TREASURER
Bernard Myerson
INTERNATIONAL COUNSELOR
Robert R. Hall, Q.C.
AMBASSADORS
Jeffrey Archer, Beatrice Arthur, Alvin Blechman, Fran Blechman, Sydney Chertkoff, Michael Caine, Sean Connery, Peter Drummond, Walter Dunn, Douglas Fairbanks, Jr., Ilene Graf, Hortense Grant, C.K. Greidinger, Norm Griesdorf, Paul Hogan, Harry Horowitz, Dick Jacobson, Leo Jaffe, David Lapidus, Peter Legge, Michael Lemberg, Hank Lightstone, Milton H. London, Dame Vera Lynn, Pauline McFetridge, Roger Moore, John Nerich, Jeffry Newman, Gregory Peck, Emma Samms, Shirley Schwartz, Neil Sinclair, Bene Stein, Barbara Stewart, Gina Tolleson, Chaim Topal, Jackie Trent.
LIFE BOARD MEMBER
Edward Shafton
EXECUTIVE DIRECTOR
Mania Boyder
MEDICAL ADVISORS
John Gay, M.D., Dr. Ian B. Kern, MF, BS, FRCS, FRACS, Michael A. LaCorte, M.D., Ronald Pennock, M.D., Steven Phillips, M.D., Prof. C. Eric Stroud, FRCP, DCH, Robert H. Zeff, M.D.
INTERNATIONAL PRESS GUY
Dennis Davidson

VARIETY CLUB TENTS
TENT No. 1: Variety Club of Pittsburgh, Pittsburgh Engineers Building, 337 Fourth Ave., Pittsburgh, PA 15222. (412) 281-1163.
TENT No. 4: Variety Club of St. Louis, 1000 Des Peres Rd., #120, St. Louis, MO 63131. (314) 821-8184.
TENT No. 5: Variety Club of Detroit, Cranbrook Centre, 30161 Southfield Rd., #301, Southfield, MI 48076. (310) 258-5511.
TENT No. 7: Variety Club of Buffalo, 195 Delaware Ave., Buffalo, NY 14202. (716) 854-7577.
TENT No. 8: Variety Club of Greater Kansas City, 8340 Mission Rd., Ste. B4, Kansas City, MO 66206. (913) 341-2315.
TENT No. 10: Variety Club of Indiana, 716 N. Munsee, Indianapolis, IN, 46260. (317) 244-8984.
TENT No. 12: Variety Club of Minnesota, 391 E. River Rd., Minneapolis, MN 55455. (612) 624-6900.
TENT No. 13: Variety Club of the Delaware Valley, Warwick Hotel, 3rd Fl., 17th & Locust, Philadelphia, PA 19103. (215) 735-0803.

TENT No. 14: Variety Club of Wisconsin, 212 W. Wisconsin, Rm. 420, Milwaukee, WI 53203. (414) 298-9991.
TENT No. 15: Variety Club of Iowa, 505 Fifth Ave., #310, Des Moines, IA 50309. (515) 243-4660.
TENT No. 16: Variety Club of Nebraska, 9100 F. Street, Omaha, NE 68127. (402) 331-4313.
TENT No. 17: Variety Club of Northern Texas, 6060 N. Central Expwy., #543, Dallas, TX 75206. (214) 368-7449.
TENT No. 20: Variety Club of Memphis, P.O. Box 1523, Memphis, TN 38111. (901) 323-2220.
TENT NO. 21: Variety Club of Atlanta, 2030 Powers Ferry Road, # 214, Atlanta, GA 30339. (404) 956-7461.
TENT No. 22: Variety Club of Oklahoma, P.O. Box 26203, Oklahoma City, OK 73126. (405) 946-9277.
TENT No. 23: Variety Club of New England, P.O. Box 130, Boston, MA 02258. (617) 969-2660.
TENT No. 25: Variety Club of Southern California, 8455 Beverly Blvd., #303., Los Angeles, CA 90048. (213) 655-1547.
TENT No. 26: Variety Club of Illinois, 101 W. Grand Ave., Suite 400, Chicago, IL 60601. (312) 822-0660.
TENT No. 27: Variety Club of Grand Rapids, P.O. Box 2293, Grand Rapids, MI 49501. (616) 458-1246.
TENT No. 28: Variety Club of Ontario, The King Edward Hotel, 37 King St. East, Suite 300, Toronto, Ont. M5C 2E9 Canada. (416) 367-2828.
TENT No. 29: Variety Club of Mexico, Liga Periferico Sur 4903, Col. Parques Del Pedregal, Mexico City, Mexico C.P. 14010. (525) 665-4246.
TENT No. 32: Variety Club of Northern California, 582 Market St., Suite 101, San Francisco, CA 94104. (415) 781-3894.
TENT No. 34: Variety Club of Houston, 3701 Kirby, #1090, Houston, TX 77098. (713) 524-2878.
TENT No. 35: Variety Club of New York, 244 W. 49 St., Room 200, New York, NY 10019. (212) 247-5588.
TENT No. 36: Variety Club of Great Britain, 326 High Holborn, London, WC1V 7AW. (171) 611-3888.
TENT No. 37: Variety Club of Colorado, c/o United Artists, 9110 E. Nichols Ave., #200, Englewood, CO 80112. (303) 792-8766.
TENT No. 39: Variety Club of Southern Nevada, 301 E. Fremont-Sundance Hotel, 12th fl., Las Vegas, NV 89101. (702) 382-7692.
TENT No. 41: Variety Club of Ireland, Room 25, Central Hotel Chambers, Dame Court, Dublin 2, Ireland. 31-671-8469.
TENT No. 45: Variety Club of New Orleans, 4132 S. Carrolton Ave., New Orleans, LA 70119. (504) 486-3255.
TENT No. 46: Variety Club of the Pacific Northwest, 825 15th Ave., Seattle, WA 98122. (206) 328-8005.
TENT No. 47: Variety Club of British Columbia, 1250 Homer St., Vancouver, B.C. V6B 2Y5 Canada. (609) 669-2313.
TENT No. 50: Variety Club of Hawaii, 1370 Kapiolani Blvd., 103A, Honolulu, HI 96814. (808) 955-5106.
TENT No. 51: Variety Club of Israel, 26 Yimiyahu St., Tel Aviv, 62594 Israel. (23) 546-7715.
TENT No. 52: Variety Club of Jersey, Maufant Variety Youth Centre, Grand Route de St. Martin, Jersey, St. Saviodor, JE3 6JB Channel Islands. (1534) 856-937.
TENT No. 54: Soleil d'Enfance, 46 Rue de Seine, Paris, France 75006. (44) 07-2828.
TENT No. 56: Variety Club of Australia, Private Bag 1044, Rozelle, N.S.W., 2039 Australia. (2) 555-1977.
TENT No. 58: Variety Club of Manitoba, 611 Wellington Crescent, Winnipeg, R3M 0A7 Manitoba, Canada. (204) 284-3911.
TENT No. 60: Variety Club of Utah, 5200 Emigration Canyon, Salt Lake City, UT 84108. (801) 582-0700.
TENT No. 61: Variety Club of Southern Alberta, #202 Sony Bldg., 110 Eleven Ave. S.E., Calgary, Alberta, T3B 3B5, Canada. (403) 264-9041.
TENT No. 63: Variety Club of Northern Alberta, 10712 176th St., Edmonton, Alberta T5S 1G7 Canada. (403) 448-9544.
TENT No. 65: Variety Club of Palm Beach, 2785 So. Ocean Blvd., Ste. 200, Unit 7, Palm Beach, FL 33480. (407) 586-7123.
TENT No. 66: Variety Club of the Desert, 1043 So. Palm Canyon Drive, Palm Springs, CA 92262. (619) 320-1177.
TENT No. 68: Variety Club of New Zealand, P.O. Box 17276, 290 Great South Rd., Greenlane, Auckland 5, New Zealand. (649) 520-4111.
TENT No. 70: Variety Club of Orlando, 3956 Towne Center Blvd., #203, Orlando, FL 32837. (407) 422-5437.
TENT No. 71: Variety Club of Ottawa, 703-150 Metcalf St., Ottawa, Ontario K2P 1P1 Canada. (613) 567-5437.
TENT No. 72: Variety Club of South Dakota, 824 Day Avenue, Sioux Falls, SD 57103. (605) 336-1100.
TENT No. 73: Variety Club Caribbean (Barbados), Pemberton Hotel, St. James, Barbados. (808) 422-5555.
TENT No. 74: Variety Club of Western Australia, 7 Thomas St., Subiaco, Western Australia 6008, P.O. Box 534 West Perth, Western Australia 6872. (09) 388-3480.

WILL ROGERS MEMORIAL FUND

785 Mamaroneck Ave., White Plains, NY 10605. (914) 761-5550. FAX: (914) 761-1513.
PRESIDENT
Stewart Blair
EXECUTIVE VICE PRESIDENT
Jeff Blake
CHAIRMAN OF THE BOARD
Fred Mound
HONORARY CHAIRMEN
Salah M. Hassanein, Bernard Myerson, Frank G. Mancuso, Burton Stone
TREASURER
Thomas Elefante
SECRETARY
Seymour H. Smith
EXECUTIVE DIRECTOR
Martin Perlberg

WOMEN IN COMMUNICATIONS, INC.

(Organized 1909.)
10605 Judicial Dr., #A-4, Fairfax, VA 22030. (703) 359-9000. FAX: (703) 359-0603.
PRESIDENT
Carol Fenstermacher
BRANCHES
187 chapters

WOMEN IN FILM

(Organized 1973.)
6464 Sunset Blvd., #530, Hollywood, CA 90028. (213) 463-6040. FAX: (213) 463-0963.
PRESIDENT EMERITUS—FOUNDER
Tichi Wilkerson-Kassel
PRESIDENT
Joan Hyler
EXECUTIVE DIRECTOR
Harriet Silverman

Guilds and Unions

ACTORS' EQUITY ASSOCIATION
(AAAA-AFL-CIO-CLC)
(Organized May 26, 1913. Membership: 38,000.)
165 W. 46 St., New York, NY 10036. (212) 869-8530. FAX: (212) 719-9815.
235 Pine St., #1100, San Francisco, CA 94104.
6430 Sunset Blvd., Hollywood, CA 90028.
203 N. Wabash Ave., Chicago, IL 60601.
PRESIDENT
Ron Silver
FIRST VICE PRESIDENT
Patrick Quinn
SECOND VICE PRESIDENT
Richard Warren Pugh
THIRD V.P. & EASTERN REGIONAL V.P.
Donald Christy
CENTRAL REGIONAL V.P.
Madeleine Fallon
WESTERN REGIONAL V.P.
Carol Swarbrick
EASTERN REGIONAL V.P.
Arne Gundersen
SECRETARY & TREASURER
Conard Fowkes
COUNSEL
Spivak, Lipton, Watanabe, Spivak (NY)
Taylor, Roth, Bush & Geffner (L.A.)

AMERICAN CINEMA EDITORS
(Organized November 28, 1950. Membership: 400.)
1041 N. Formosa Ave., W. Hollywood, CA 90046. (213) 850-2900. FAX: (213) 850-2922.
PRESIDENT
Tom Rolf
VICE PRESIDENT
Bill Gordian
SECRETARY
George Hirely
TREASURER
Jack Tucker

AMERICAN FEDERATION OF MUSICIANS
(AFL-CIO)
(Organized October, 1896. Membership: 150,000.)
1501 Broadway, New York, NY 10036. (212) 869-1330. FAX: (212) 764-6134.
PRESIDENT
Steve Young
VICE PRESIDENT
Tom Lee, 4400 MacArthur Blvd. NW, Washington, DC 20001.
CANADIAN VICE PRESIDENT
Ray Petch, 75 The Donway West, Suite 1010, Don Mills, Ontario, Canada M3C 2E9.
SECRETARY-TREASURER
Stephen R. Sprague
EXECUTIVE BOARD
Thomas C. Bailey, Ray Hair, Bill Moriarity, Tim Shea, Kenneth B. Shirk

AMERICAN GUILD OF MUSICAL ARTISTS, INC.
(AFL-CIO, AAAA)
(Organized 1936. Membership: 5,500.)
1727 Broadway, New York, NY 10019-5284. (212) 265-3687. FAX: (212) 262-9088.
PRESIDENT
Gerald Otte
FIRST VICE PRESIDENT
Michael Byars
SECOND VICE PRESIDENT
Pamela Smith
TREASURER
William Cason
NATIONAL EXECUTIVE SECRETARY
Louise J. Gilmore
ADMINISTRATOR FOR DANCE
Alexander Dubae
COUNSEL
Becker, London & Kossow
MEMBERSHIP SUPERVISOR
Carol Caldwell
FINANCIAL SECRETARY
Grace Pedro

DIRECTOR OF PUBLIC RELATIONS
Michael Rubino
CANADA: Christopher Marston, 260 Richmond St. E., Toronto, Ontario M5A 1P4. (416) 867-9165. CHICAGO: Barbara J. Hillman, Cornfield & Feldman, 343 S. Dearborn St., 13th Floor, Chicago, IL 60604. (312) 922-2800. NEW ENGLAND: Robert M. Segal, 11 Beacon St., Boston, MA 02108. (617) 742-0208. NEW ORLEANS: Rosemary LeBoeuf, 4438 St. Peter St., New Orleans, LA 70119. (504) 486-9410. NORTHWEST: Carolyn C. Carpp, 11021 NE 123rd Lane, Apt. C114, Kirkland, WA 98034. (206) 820-2999. PHILADELPHIA: Gail Lopez-Henriquez, 400 Market St., Philadelphia, PA 19106. (215) 925-8400. PITTSBURGH: Frank Kerin, 223 Thompson Run, Pittsburgh, PA 15232. (412) 798-0550. SAN FRANCISCO: Harry Polland, Donald Tayer, Ann Sebastian, 235 Pine St., Suite 1100, San Francisco, CA 94104. (415) 986-4060. TEXAS: Benny Hopper, 3915 Fairlakes Dr., Dallas, TX 75228. (214) 279-4720. WASHINGTON DC: Eleni Kallas, 16600 Shea Lane, Gaithersburg, MD 20877. (301) 869-8266.

AMERICAN GUILD OF VARIETY ARTISTS
(AAAA AFL-CIO)
(Organized July 14, 1939. Registered Membership: 78,000. Active Membership: 5,000.)
184 Fifth Ave., New York, NY 10010. (212) 675-1003.
4741 Laurel Canyon Blvd., #208, N. Hollywood, CA 91607. (818) 508-9984. FAX: (818) 508-3029.
HONORARY FIRST VICE PRESIDENT
Rip Taylor
HONORARY THIRD VICE PRESIDENT
Gloria DeHaven
PRESIDENT
Rod McKuen
SECRETARY-TREASURER
Frances Gaar
REGIONAL VICE PRESIDENTS
Emelise Aleandri, Bobby Brookes, Ron Chisholm, David Cullen, John Eaden, Bobby Faye, Doris George, Wayne Hermans, Elaine Jacovini-Gonella, Deedee Knapp-Brody, Eddie Lane, Tina Marie, Angela Martin, Scott Senatore, Dorothy Stratton, Susan Streater, Dorothy Zuckerman

AMERICAN SOCIETY OF CINEMATOGRAPHERS, INC.
1782 N. Orange Dr., Hollywood, CA 90028. (213) 876-5080. FAX: (213) 882-6391.
PRESIDENT
Victor J. Kemper
FIRST VICE PRESIDENT
Woody Omens
SECOND VICE PRESIDENT
Steven Poster
THIRD VICE PRESIDENT
Allen Daviau
SERGEANT AT ARMS
Richard C. Glouner
TREASURER
Howard A. Anderson, Jr.
SECRETARY
John Bailey
ART DIRECTORS
Local 876 (See IATSE)

ASSOCIATED ACTORS AND ARTISTS OF AMERICA
(AAAA)-AFL-CIO
(Organized July 18, 1919. Membership: 90,000.)
165 W. 46 St., New York, NY 10036. (212) 869-0358. FAX: (212) 869-1746.
PRESIDENT
Theodore Bikel
VICE PRESIDENTS
Kendall Orsatti, Thomas Jamerson, Bruce York, Rod McKuen, Seymour Rexite
TREASURER
John Sucke

ASSOCIATED MUSICIANS OF GREATER NEW YORK
LOCAL 802 AFM (NEW YORK)
(Organized August 27, 1921. Membership: 15,000.)
322 W. 48 St., New York, NY 10036-1308. (212) 245-4802. FAX: (212) 489-6030.
PRESIDENT
William Moriarty

FINANCIAL VICE PRESIDENT
Mary Landolfi
RECORDING VICE PRESIDENT
Erwin Price

ASSOCIATION OF TALENT AGENTS

(Organized April, 1937. Official organization of talent agents in Hollywood.)
9255 Sunset Blvd., Suite 318, Los Angeles, CA 90069. (310) 274-0628. FAX: (310) 274-5063. e-mail: agentassoc@aol.com
EXECUTIVE DIRECTOR
Karen Stuart
FIRST VICE PRESIDENT
Sandy Bresler
VICE PRESIDENTS
Sid Craig
T. J. Escott
Sheldon Sroloff
Sonjia Warren Brandon
SECRETARY & TREASURER
Martin Gage

AUTHORS' GUILD, INC.

(Membership: 6,500.)
330 W. 42 St., 29th Floor, New York, NY 10036-6902. (212) 563-5904. FAX: (212) 564-8363.
PRESIDENT
Mary Pope Osborne
VICE PRESIDENT
Sidney Offit
SECRETARY
Letty Cottin Pogrebin
TREASURER
Paula J. Giddings
EXECUTIVE DIRECTOR
Robin Davis Miller

AUTHORS LEAGUE OF AMERICA, INC., THE

(Membership: 15,000.)
Authors League, 330 W. 42 St., 29th Floor, New York, NY 10036. (212) 564-8350.
PRESIDENT
Garson Kanin
VICE PRESIDENT
Robert Anderson
SECRETARY
Eve Merriam
TREASURER
Gerold Frank
ADMINISTRATOR
Robin Davis Miller

BROADCASTING STUDIO EMPLOYEES

LOCAL 782 (See IATSE)

CATHOLIC ACTORS GUILD OF AMERICA

(Organized April, 1914. Membership: 700.)
1501 Broadway, Suite 510, New York, NY 10036. (212) 398-1868.
PRESIDENT
William J. O'Malley
TREASURER
Martin Kiffel

DIRECTORS GUILD OF AMERICA, INC. (DGA)

7920 Sunset Blvd., Los Angeles, CA 90046. (310) 289-2000. FAX: (213) 289-2029.
110 W. 57 St., New York, NY 10019. (212) 581-0370.
400 N. Michigan Ave., Suite 307, Chicago, IL 60611. (312) 644-5050.
2410 Hollywood Blvd., Hollywood, FL 33020. (305) 927-3338.
PRESIDENT
Gene Reynolds
NATIONAL VICE PRESIDENT
Jane Schimel
VICE PRESIDENTS
Martha Coolidge, Max A. Schindler, Jack Shea, Nancy Littlefield, Robert Butler, Larry Auerbach
SECRETARY & TREASURER
Sheldon Leonard
EXECUTIVE DIRECTOR
Glenn J. Gumpel

DRAMATISTS GUILD, INC., THE

234 W. 44 St., New York, NY 10036. (212) 398-9366. FAX: (212) 944-0420.
PRESIDENT
Peter Stone
VICE PRESIDENT
Terrence McNally
SECRETARY
Arthur Kopit

TREASURER
Richard Lewine
EXECUTIVE DIRECTOR
Richard Garmise
COUNSEL
Cahill, Gordon & Reindel
DIRECTOR OF MEMBERSHIP
Todd Neal

EPISCOPAL ACTORS GUILD OF AMERICA, INC.

(Organized 1926. 750 members.)
1 E. 29 St., New York, NY 10016. (212) 685-2927.
PRESIDING BISHOP
The Right Reverend Edmond L. Browning
BISHOP OF NEW YORK
The Right Reverend Richard F. Grein
PRESIDENT
Barnard Hughes
VICE PRESIDENTS
Rev. Norman J. Catir, Jr., Warden of the Guild
Edward Crimmins
Joan Fontaine
Peter Harris
Cliff Robertson
Joan Warren

EXHIBITION EMPLOYEES

LOCAL 829 (See IATSE)

FILM EXCHANGE EMPLOYEES, BACK ROOM, LOCALS (IATSE)

(See IATSE)

FILM EXCHANGE EMPLOYEES, FRONT OFFICE

LOCAL F-45 (See IATSE)

FIRST AID EMPLOYEES

LOCAL 767 (IATSE) (See IATSE)

HOLLYWOOD FILM & BROADCASTING LABOR COUNCIL

(Organized September, 1947.)
11365 Ventura Blvd., Suite 315, Studio City, CA 91604-3148. (818) 762-9995. FAX: (818) 762-9997.
PRESIDENT
Steve Allen
VICE PRESIDENTS
Nick Long
Ken Orsatti
SECRETARY-TREASURER
H. O'Neil Shanks

INTERNATIONAL ALLIANCE OF THEATRICAL STAGE EMPLOYEES & MOVING PICTURE MACHINE OPERATORS OF THE U.S. AND CANADA (AFL-CIO, CLC)

(Organized nationally, July 17, 1893; internationally, October 1, 1902. The Alliance comprises approximately 800 local unions covering the United States, Canada and Hawaii.)
1515 Broadway, Suite 601, New York, NY 10036-5741. (212) 730-1770. FAX: (212) 921-7699.
INTERNATIONAL PRESIDENT
Thomas C. Short
GENERAL SECRETARY & TREASURER
Michael W. Proscia
FIRST VICE PRESIDENT
John J. Nolan
SECOND VICE PRESIDENT
John J. Ryan
THIRD VICE PRESIDENT
Edward C. Powell
FOURTH VICE PRESIDENT
Nick Long
FIFTH VICE PRESIDENT
Daniel J. Kerins
SIXTH VICE PRESIDENT
Rudy N. Napoleone
SEVENTH VICE PRESIDENT
Carmine A. Palazzo
EIGHTH VICE PRESIDENT
Jean Fox
NINTH VICE PRESIDENT
Ben F. Lowe
TENTH VICE PRESIDENT
Timothy Magee
ELEVENTH VICE PRESIDENT
James Wood
INTERNATIONAL TRUSTEES
Ada S. Philpot, Thomas M. Riley, Michael J. Sullivan
AFL-CIO DELEGATES
Stephen R. Flint, Nancy Manganelli-Bues
CLC DELEGATE
C. Gus Bottas

PRODUCTION

AFFILIATED PROPERTY CRAFTSMEN LOCAL 44 (IATSE-AFL-CIO), HOLLYWOOD
11500 Burbank Blvd. N. Hollywood, CA 91605. (818) 769-2500.
FAX: (818) 769-1739.
SECRETARY
Walter Keske

ART DIRECTORS, LOCAL 876 (IATSE) HOLLYWOOD
11365 Ventura Blvd., #315, Studio City, CA 91604. (818) 762-9995. FAX: (818) 762-9997.
SECRETARY
Bernard P. Cutter

COSTUME DESIGNERS GUILD LOCAL 892
13949 Ventura Blvd., Suite 309, Sherman Oaks, CA 91423. (818) 905-1557. FAX: (818) 905-1560.
SECRETARY
Barbara Inglehart

FIRST AID EMPLOYEES, LOCAL 767 (IATSE), LOS ANGELES
2611 Taffrail Lane, Oxnard CA 93035-1766. (805) 984-7918. FAX: (310) 523-3691.
SECRETARY
Eddie R. Clark

INTERNATIONAL PHOTOGRAPHERS OF THE MOTION PICTURE INDUSTRIES (CAMERAMEN) IPMPI LOCAL 666, CHICAGO
111 W. Jackson Blvd., Suite 1060, Chicago, IL 60604. (312) 341-0966. FAX: (312) 341-1373.
SECRETARY
Larry Gianneschi

MOTION PICTURE COSTUMERS, LOCAL 705 (IATSE), HOLLYWOOD
1427 N. La Brea Ave., Hollywood, CA 90028. (213) 851-0220. FAX: (213) 851-9062.
SECRETARY
Mort Schwartz

MOTION PICTURE CRAFTS SERVICE LOCAL 727 (IATSE), HOLLYWOOD
13949 Ventura Blvd., Suite 310, Sherman Oaks, CA 91423. (818) 385-1950. FAX: (818) 385-1057.
SECRETARY
David J. Schwartz

MOTION PICTURE AND VIDEO EDITORS GUILD, LOCAL 776 (IATSE), LOS ANGELES
7715 Sunset Blvd., #220, Hollywood CA 90046. (213) 876-4770. FAX: (213) 876-0861.
SECRETARY
Diane Adler

MOTION PICTURE & VIDEO TAPE EDITORS, LOCAL 771 (IATSE), NEW YORK
165 W. 46 St., Suite 900, New York, NY 10036. (212) 302-0771. FAX: (212) 302-1091.
SECRETARY
Damian Begley

MOTION PICTURE SCREEN CARTOONISTS, LOCAL 839 (IATSE), HOLLYWOOD
4729 Lankershim Blvd., N. Hollywood, CA 91602-1864. (818) 766-7151. FAX: (818) 506-4805.
SECRETARY
Jerffrey Massie

MOTION PICTURE SCRIPT SUPERVISORS AND PRODUCTION OFFICE COORDINATORS, LOCAL 161
80 Eight Ave., 14th fl., New York, NY 10011. (212) 647-7300. FAX: (212) 647-7317.
SECRETARY
Linda Haftel

MOTION PICTURE SET PAINTERS, LOCAL 729 (IATSE), HOLLYWOOD
11365 Ventura Blvd., Suite 202, Studio City, CA 91604-3138. (818) 984-3000. FAX: (818) 760-8237.
SECRETARY
Carmine A. Palazzo

MOTION PICTURE STUDIO ELECTRICAL TECHNICIANS, LOCAL 728 (IATSE)
14629 Nordhoff St., Panorama City, CA 91402. (818) 891-0728. FAX: (818) 891-5288.
SECRETARY
Dean Bray

MOTION PICTURE STUDIO ART CRAFTSMEN, (ILLUSTRATORS AND MATTE ARTISTS) LOCAL 790 (IATSE), HOLLYWOOD
13949 Ventura Blvd., Suite 301, Sherman Oaks, CA 91423. (213) 784-6555. FAX: (818) 784-2004.

SECRETARY
Camille Abbot

MOTION PICTURE STUDIO GRIPS, LOCAL 80 (IATSE), HOLLYWOOD
2520 W. Olive, Burbank, CA 91505. (818) 526-0100. FAX: (818) 526-0719.
SECRETARY
Partik Hoff

MOTION PICTURE STUDIO MECHANICS, LOCAL 476 (IATSE), CHICAGO
6309 N. Northwest Hwy., Chicago, IL 60631. (312) 775-5300. FAX: (312) 775-2477.
SECRETARY
J. Paul Oddo

MOTION PICTURE STUDIO TEACHERS AND WELFARE WORKERS, LOCAL 884 (IATSE) HOLLYWOOD
P.O. Box 461467, Los Angeles, CA 90046. (213) 650-3792.
SECRETARY
Judith M. Brown

PAINTERS & SCENIC ARTISTS, LOCAL 921 (IATSE) NEW ENGLAND AREA
P.O. Box 1686, Jamaica Plain, MA 02130. (617) 269-8567. FAX: (617) 269-4715.
SECRETARY
Mary E. Hopkins

PRODUCTION OFFICE COORDINATORS & ACCOUNTANTS GUILD LOCAL 717
13949 Ventura Blvd., Suite 306, Sherman Oaks, CA 91403. (818) 906-9986. FAX: (818) 990-8287.
SECRETARY
David J. Schwartz

PUBLICISTS, LOCAL 818 (IATSE), HOLLYWOOD
13949 Ventura Blvd., Suite 302, Sherman Oaks, CA 91423. (818) 905-1541.
SECRETARY
Gaye Ann Bruno

RADIO AND TELEVISION SOUND EFFECTS, LOCAL 844 (IATSE), NEW YORK
Box 637, Ansonia Station, New York, NY 10023. (212) 456-3220.
SECRETARY
Karen Johnson

SCENIC & TITLE ARTISTS, LOCAL 816 (IATSE) LOS ANGELES
13949 Ventura Blvd., Suite 308, Sherman Oaks, CA 91423. (818) 906-7822. FAX: (818) 906-0481.
SECRETARY
Lisa Frazza

SCRIPT SUPERVISORS, LOCAL 871 (IATSE), HOLLYWOOD
P.O. Box 6110, Burbank, CA 91510-6110. (818) 782-7063. FAX: 9818) 782-5483.
SECRETARY
Marilyn Giardino-Zych

SET DESIGNERS AND MODEL MAKERS, LOCAL 847 (IATSE), HOLLYWOOD
13949 Ventura Blvd., Suite 301, Sherman Oaks, CA 91423. (818) 784-6555. FAX: (818) 784-2004.
SECRETARY
Suzanne Feller-Otto

STORY ANALYSTS, LOCAL 854 (IATSE), HOLLYWOOD
13949 Ventura Blvd., Suite 300, Sherman Oaks, CA 91423. (818) 784-6555. FAX: (818) 784-2004.
SECRETARY
Calvin T. Yocum

STUDIO MECHANICS, LOCAL 52 (IATSE), NEW YORK
326 W. 48 St., New York, NY 10036. (212) 399-0980. FAX: (212) 315-1073.
SECRETARY
Robert F. Reilly

STUDIO MECHANICS, LOCAL 485 (IATSE) TUCSON
P.O. Box 5705, Tucson, AZ 85704-5705. (602) 579-0088. FAX: (602) 579-0089.
SECRETARY
Rose Lujan

STUDIO MECHANICS, LOCAL 477 (IATSE) N. MIAMI
8025 N.W. 36 St., Suite 303, Miami, FL 33166. (305) 594-8585. FAX: (305) 597-9278.
SECRETARY
Norman Zuckerman

STUDIO MECHANICS, LOCAL 479 (IATSE) ATLANTA
P.O. Box 78757, Atlanta, GA 30357. (404) 607-7773. FAX: (404) 367-0240.
SECRETARY
Suzanne L. Carter

STUDIO MECHANICS, LOCAL 812 (IATSE) DETROIT
20017 Van Dyke, Detroit, MI 48234. (313) 368-0825. FAX:
(313) 368-1151.
SECRETARY
Timothy F. Magee

STUDIO MECHANICS, LOCAL 480 (IATSE) SANTA FE
P.O. Box 8481, Albuquerque, NM 87198-0481. (505) 265-1500.
FAX: (505) 266-7155.
SECRETARY
Ryan Blank

STUDIO MECHANICS, LOCAL 209 (IATSE) OHIO
1468 West 9th St., Room 435, Cleveland, OH 44113. (216)
621-9537.FAX: (216) 621-3518.
SECRETARY
Peter Lambros

STUDIO MECHANICS, LOCAL 484 (IATSE) TEXAS
440 Louisiana, Suite 480, Houston, TX 77002. (713) 229-8357.
FAX: (713) 229-8138.
SECRETARY
Janelle V. Flanagan

**TELEVISION BROADCASTING STUDIO
EMPLOYEES, LOCAL 794 (IATSE), NEW YORK**
P.O. Box 154, Lenox Hill Sta., New York, NY 10021. (516) 724-
4815. FAX: (516) 724-4815.
SECRETARY
Cerena Gourdine

**THEATRICAL WARDROBE ATTENDANTS,
LOCAL 769 (IATSE), CHICAGO**
1220 Hawkins Ct., Bartlett, IL 60103. (708) 289-4568. FAX:
(708) 289-4568.
SECRETARY
Cheryl Ryba

**THEATRICAL WARDROBE ATTENDANTS,
LOCAL 768 (IATSE), LOS ANGELES**
13949 Ventura Blvd., Suite 307, Sherman Oaks, CA 91423.
(818) 789-8735. FAX: (818) 905-6297.
SECRETARY
Mary Seward

**THEATRICAL WARDROBE UNION, LOCAL 764 (IATSE),
NEW YORK**
151 W. 46 St., 8th fl., New York, NY 10036. (212) 221-1717.
FAX: (212) 302-2324.
SECRETARY
James Roberts

DISTRIBUTION

**FILM EXCHANGE EMPLOYEES, BACK ROOM, LOCAL
B-61 (IATSE), LOS ANGELES**
120 S. San Fernando Blvd., Suite 461, Burbank, CA 91502.
(818) 242-2184. FAX: (805) 533-2113.
SECRETARY
Lyn Moon

**COMBINED FILM EXCHANGE EMPLOYEES, FRONT
OFFICE, LOCAL F-45 (IATSE), CHICAGO**
92 Park Justice, Chicago, IL 60658. (708) 839-1024.

**MOTION PICTURE HOME OFFICE AND FILM EXCHANGE
EMPLOYEES, LOCAL H-63 (IATSE), NEW YORK**
P.O. Box 1018, Cornell Station, Bronx, NY 10473. (718) 893-
6655. FAX: (718) 893-4664.

*In addition to the above, there are 34 locals of Back Room
Employees and 29 locals of Front Office Employees in the
other exchange cities.*

EXHIBITION

**AMUSEMENT AREA EMPLOYEES, LOCAL B-192 (IATSE),
LOS ANGELES**
3518 Cahuenga Blvd. West, Suite 206, Los Angeles, CA
90068. (213) 849-1826.

EXHIBITION EMPLOYEES, LOCAL 829 (IATSE), NEW YORK
150 E. 58 St., New York, NY 10022. (212) 752-4427. FAX:
(212) 826-2275.
SECRETARY
John V. McNamee, Jr.

**PROJECTIONISTS & VIDEO TECHNICIANS, LOCAL 110
(IATSE), CHICAGO**
230 W. Monroe St., Suite 2511, Chicago, IL 60606. (312) 443-
1011. FAX: (312) 443-1012.
SECRETARY
Albin C. Brenkus

OPERATORS LOCAL 150 (IATSE), LOS ANGELES
1545 N. Verdugo Rd., Suite 9, Glendale, CA 91208. (818) 240-
5644. FAX: (818) 240-6196.

SECRETARY
Teri L. McClintock

**PROJECTIONISTS & VIDEO TECHNICIANS LOCAL 306
(IATSE), NEW YORK**
723 Seventh Ave., 11th Fl., New York, NY 10019. (212) 764-
6270. FAX: (212) 302-6369.
SECRETARY
Joel Deitch

STAGE EMPLOYEES, LOCAL 4 (IATSE), BROOKLYN
2917 Glenwood Rd., Brooklyn, NY 11210. (718) 252-8777.
FAX: (718) 421-5605.
SECRETARY
William Meems

STAGE EMPLOYEES, LOCAL 2 (IATSE), CHICAGO
20 N. Wacker Dr., Suite 722, Chicago, IL 60606. (312) 236-
3457. FAX: (312) 236-0701.
SECRETARY
Thomas J. Cleary

STAGE EMPLOYEES, LOCAL 33 (IATSE), LOS ANGELES
1720 W. Magnolia Blvd., Burbank, CA 91506-1871. (818) 841-
9233. FAX: (818) 567-1138.
SECRETARY
Joseph F. Doucette, Jr.

STAGE EMPLOYEES, LOCAL 1 (IATSE), NEW YORK
320 W. 46 St., New York, NY 10036. (212) 333-2500. FAX:
(212) 586-2437.
SECRETARY
Frank Dwyer

THEATRE EMPLOYEES, LOCAL B-46 (IATSE), CHICAGO
230 W. Monroe St., Suite 2511, Chicago, IL 60606. (312) 443-
1011. FAX: (312) 443-1012.
SECRETARY
Al Cimino

**THEATRE EMPLOYEES, LOCAL B-183 (IATSE),
NEW YORK**
319 W. 48 St., New York, NY 10036. (212) 586-9620. FAX:
(212) 586-7106.
SECRETARY
Mary A. Huff

**TREASURERS AND TICKET SELLERS, LOCAL 750
(IATSE), CHICAGO**
446 N. Edgewood, LaGrange Park, IL 60525. (708) 579-9381.
FAX: (708) 352-9085.
SECRETARY
Michael Keenan

**TREASURERS AND TICKET SELLERS, LOCAL 857
(IATSE), LOS ANGELES**
13949 Ventura Blvd., Suite 303, Sherman Oaks, CA 91423.
(818) 990-7107. FAX: (818) 990-8287.
SECRETARY
Deirdre Floyd

**TREASURERS AND TICKET SELLERS, LOCAL 751
(IATSE), NEW YORK**
1500 Broadway, Rm. 2011, New York, NY 10036. (212) 302-
7300. FAX: (212) 944-8687.
SECRETARY
Michael Charnee

**INTERNATIONAL BROTHERHOOD OF ELECTRICAL
WORKERS (AFL-CIO, CFL)**
(Organized November 28, 1891. Membership: over 1 million.)
1125 15th St. NW, Washington, DC 20005. (202) 833-7000.
INT'L PRESIDENT
John J. Barry
INT'L SECRETARY
Jack Moore
INT'L TREASURER
Thomas Van Arsdale
DISTRICT OFFICES
ALABAMA: Wade H. Gurley, No. 2 Metroplex Dr., Suite 304,
Birmingham, AL 35209-6899. CALIFORNIA: S. R. McCann,
150 N. Wiget Lane, Suite 100, Walnut Creek, CA 94598-2494.
CANADA: Ken Woods, 45 Sheppard Ave. East, Suite 401,
Willowdale, Ont. M2N 5Y1. IDAHO: Jon Walters, 330 Shoup
Ave., Suite 204, P.O. Box 51216, Idaho Falls, ID 83405. ILLI-
NOIS: James P. Conway, 2200 S. Main St., Suite 303,
Lombard, IL 60148. MASSACHUSETTS: Paul A. Loughran,
Batterymarch Park, Quincy, MA 02169. NY: Edwin D. Hill, 16
Computer Dr. West, Suite C, Albany, NY 12205. MISSOURI:
Ray Edwards, 300 S. Jefferson, Suite 300, Springfield, MO
65806. OHIO: Paul J. Witte, 7710 Reading Rd., Suite 9,
Cincinnati, OH 45237. OKLAHOMA: Orville A. Tate, Jr., 4400
Will Rogers Pkwy., #309, Oklahoma City, OK 73108. TEN-
NESSEE: Carl Lansden, 500 Franklin Bldg., Suite 500,
Chattanooga, TN 37411.

IBEW, LOCAL 349 (FILM)
1657 N.W. 17th Ave., Miami, FL 33135. (305) 325-1330.
BUSINESS MANAGER
Art Fernandez
IBEW, LOCAL 40 (FILM)
5643 Vineland Ave., North Hollywood, CA 91601. (818) 762-4239.
BUSINESS MANAGER
Tim Dixon

INTERNATIONAL SOUND TECHNICIANS OF THE MOTION PICTURE BROADCAST AND AMUSEMENT INDUSTRIES
LOCAL 695 (See IATSE)

LABORATORY TECHNICIANS
LOCALS 683, 702 and 780 (See IATSE)

MAKE-UP ARTISTS & HAIR STYLISTS
LOCALS 706 and 798 (See IATSE)

MOTION PICTURE COSTUMERS
LOCAL 705 (See IATSE)

MOTION PICTURE CRAFTS SERVICE
LOCAL 727 (See IATSE)

MOTION PICTURE & VIDEO EDITORS
LOCALS 771 and 776 (See IATSE)

MOTION PICTURE HOME OFFICE EMPLOYEES
LOCAL H-63 (See IATSE)

MOTION PICTURE SCREEN CARTOONISTS
LOCALS 839 (See IATSE)

MOTION PICTURE SET PAINTERS
LOCAL 729 (See IATSE)

MOTION PICTURE STUDIO ELECTRICAL TECHNICIANS
LOCAL 728 (See IATSE)

PRODUCERS GUILD OF AMERICA
(Organized 1950. Membership: 400.)
400 S. Beverly Dr., Suite 211, Beverly Hills, CA 90212. (310) 557-0807. FAX: (310) 557-0436.
PRESIDENT
Leonard B. Stern
VICE PRESIDENT
Robert B. Radnitz
SECRETARY
Joel Freeman
TREASURER
Gary Nardino
EXECUTIVE DIRECTOR
Charles B. FitzSimons

PROFESSIONAL MUSICIANS, LOCAL 47, (AFM,AFL-CIO)
(Organized October 30, 1894. Membership: 10,000.)
817 Vine St., Hollywood, CA 90038. (213) 462-2161. FAX: (213) 461-5260.
PRESIDENT
Bill Peterson
SECRETARY
Serena Kay Williams
TREASURER
Richard Totusek
TRUSTEES
Hal Espinosa, Vince Trombetta, Abe Most
DIRECTORS
William (Buddy) Collette, Art Davis, Vince DiBari, Lyle (Spud) Murphy, Jay Rosen, Ann Stockton

PROJECTIONISTS, IATSE & MPMO LOCALS
(See IATSE)

PUBLICISTS GUILD, INC.
LOCAL 818 (See IATSE)

RADIO & TELEVISION SOUND EFFECTS
LOCAL 844 (See IATSE)

SCENIC ARTISTS
LOCAL 816 (See IATSE)

SCREEN ACTORS GUILD (AAAA-AFL-CIO)
(Organized July 1933. Membership: 88,000.)
5757 Wilshire Blvd., Los Angeles, CA 90036. (213) 465-4600. FAX: (213) 856-6603.
PRESIDENT
Richard Masur
VICE PRESIDENT
Sumi Haru

THIRD VICE PRESIDENT
Paul Hecht
FOURTH VICE PRESIDENT
Mel Boudrot
FIFTH VICE PRESIDENT
Mary Seibel
SIXTH VICE PRESIDENT
Scott DeVenney
TREASURER
F.J. O'Neil
NATIONAL EXECUTIVE DIRECTOR
Ken Orsatti
ASSOCIATE NATIONAL EXECUTIVE DIRECTOR
John McGuire
DIRECTOR, COMMUNICATIONS
Katherine Moore
COUNSEL
Leo Geffner
DIRECTOR, FINANCE
Gerald Wilson
DIRECTOR OF ADMINSTRATION
Clinta Dayton
DISTRICT OFFICES
ARIZONA: John McGuire, 1616 East Indian School Rd., Suite 330, Phoenix, AZ 85016. (602) 265-2712. MASSACHUSETTS: 11 Beacon St., Rm. 512, Boston, MA 02108. (617) 742-2688. ILLINOIS: 75 E. Wacker Dr., 14th Fl., Chicago, IL 60601. (312) 372-8081. COLORADO: 950 South Cherry Street, Suite 502, Denver, CO 80222. (303) 757-6226. DALLAS: 6060 N. Central Expressway, #302, LB 604, Dallas, TX 75206. (214) 363-8300. MICHIGAN: 28690 Southfield Rd., #290 A&B, Lathrup Village, MI 48076. (810) 559-9450. FLORIDA: 7300 N. Kendall Dr., #620, Miami, FL 33145. (305) 444-7677. GEORGIA: 455 E. Paces Ferry Rd., NE, #334, Atlanta, GA 30305. (404) 239-0131. HAWAII: 949 Kapiolani Boulevard, Suite 105, Honolulu, HI 96814. (808) 596-0388. HOUSTON: 2650 Fountainview, Suite 326, Houston, TX 77057. (713) 972-1806. NEW YORK: 1515 Broadway, 44th Floor, New York, NY 10036. (212) 944-1030. PENNSYLVANIA: 230 South Broad Street, 10th Floor, Philadelphia, PA 19102. (215) 545-3150. SAN DIEGO: 7827 Convoy Court, #400, San Diego, CA 92111. (619) 278-7695. SAN FRANCISCO: 235 Pine St., 11th fl., San Francisco, CA 94104. (415) 391-7510. TENNESSEE: P.O. Box 121087, Nashville, TN 37212. (615) 327-2958. WASHINGTON DC/BALTIMORE: 5480 Wisconsin Avenue, Suite 201, Chevy Chase, MD 20815. (301) 657-2560.

SCREEN COMPOSERS OF AMERICA
2451 Nichols Canyon Rd., Los Angeles, CA 90046-1798. (213) 876-6040. FAX: (213) 876-6041.
PRESIDENT
Herschel Burke Gilbert
VICE PRESIDENT
John Parker
SECRETARY
Frank DeVol
TREASURER
Nathan Scott

SCREEN WRITERS' GUILD, INC.
(See Writers Guild of America)

SCRIPT SUPERVISORS
LOCAL 871 (See IATSE)

SET DESIGNERS AND MODEL MAKERS
LOCAL 847 (See IATSE)

SOCIETY OF MOTION PICTURE ART DIRECTORS
LOCAL 876 (See IATSE)

THE SONGWRITERS GUILD OF AMERICA
1500 Harbor Blvd., Weehawken, NJ 07087-6732. (201) 867-7603. FAX: (201) 867-7335.
1560 Broadway, Room 1306, New York, NY 10036. (212) 768-7902. FAX: (212) 768-9048.
6430 Sunset Blvd., Suite 1011, Hollywood, CA 90028. (213) 462-1108. FAX: (213) 462-5430.
1222 16th Avenue South, Suite 25, Nashville, TN 37212. (615) 329-1782. FAX: (615) 329-2623.
PRESIDENT
George David Weiss
EXECUTIVE DIRECTOR
Lewis M. Bachman

STAGE EMPLOYEES
LOCALS 1, 2, 4 and 33 (See IATSE)

STORY ANALYSTS
LOCAL 854 (See IATSE)

STUDIO GRIPS
LOCAL 80 (See IATSE)

STUDIO MECHANICS
LOCALS 52 and 476 (See IATSE)

STUDIO PROJECTIONISTS
LOCAL 165 (See IATSE)

STUDIO PROPERTY CRAFTSMEN
LOCAL 44 (See IATSE)

STUNTMEN'S ASSOCIATION
(Organized 1961.)
4810 Whitsett Ave., North Hollywood, CA 91607. (818) 766-
4334. (213) 462-2301.
PRESIDENT
Carl Ciarfalio

THEATRE AUTHORITY, INC.
(Organized May 21, 1934.)
16 E. 42 St., Suite 202, New York, NY 10017-6907. (212) 682-
4215. FAX: (212) 682-8407.
EXECUTIVE DIRECTOR
Helen Leahy
PRESIDENT
Jane Powell
FIRST VICE PRESIDENT
John H. Sucke
SECOND VICE PRESIDENT
Terry Walker
THIRD VICE PRESIDENT
Robert J. Bruyr
FOURTH VICE PRESIDENT
Rod McKuen
RECORDING SECRETARY
Thomas H. Jamerson
TREASURER
Joan Greenspan
REPRESENTATIVE
Francis Garr
ADVISORY COMMITTEE
Julie Andrews, Harry Belafonte, Theodore Bikel, Joey Bishop,
Ellen Burstyn, Billy Davis Jr., Patty Duke, Richard Dysart,
Barbara Feldon, Joan Fontaine, John Forsythe, Robert Goulet,
Charlton Heston, Jerome Hines, Bob Hope, Barnard Hughes,
Jack Jones, Alan King, Werner Klemperer, Angela Lansbury,
Jerry Lewis, Patti Lupone, Marilyn McCoo, Ed McMahon,
Estelle Parsons, Gregory Peck, Jane Powell, Tony Randall, Lou
Rawls, Debbie Reynolds, Tony Roberts, Frank Sinatra, Barbra
Streisand, Nancy Wilson

THEATRE EMPLOYEES
LOCALS B-46 and B-183 (See IATSE)

THEATRICAL WARDROBE ATTENDANTS
LOCALS 764, 768 and 769 (See IATSE)

TREASURERS AND TICKETSELLERS
LOCALS 750, 751 and 857 (See IATSE)

WRITERS GUILD OF AMERICA, EAST, INC.
555 W. 57 St., New York, NY 10019. (212) 767-7800. FAX: (212)
582-1909.
PRESIDENT
Herb Sargent
VICE PRESIDENT
Claire Labine
SECRETARY & TREASURER
Jane C. Bollinger
EXECUTIVE DIRECTOR
Mona Mangan

WRITERS GUILD OF AMERICA, WEST, INC.
7000 W. Third St., Los Angeles, CA 90048. (310) 550-1000.
FAX: (310) 550-8185.
PRESIDENT
Brad Radnitz
VICE PRESIDENT
Dan Petrie, Jr.
SECRETARY & TREASURER
John Wells
EXECUTIVE DIRECTOR
Brian Walton

TRADE PUBLICATIONS

QUIGLEY PUBLISHING COMPANY
Publishers of International Motion Picture Almanac (Annual), International Television and Video Almanac (Annual) and Quigleys Entertainment Industry Reference CD-ROM. 159 W. 53 St., New York, NY 10019. (212) 247-3100. FAX: (212) 489-0871. email: QUIGLEYPUB@aol.com
PRESIDENT AND PUBLISHER
Martin Quigley
VICE PRESIDENT
Katherine D. Quigley
EDITOR & VICE PRESIDENT
James D. Moser
MANAGING EDITOR
Tracy Stevens
EDITORIAL ASSISTANT
Alicia Ocana

LONDON BUREAU
William Pay, Manager and London Editor. 15 Samuel Rd., Langdon Hills, Basildon, Essex SS16 6E, England. (01 268) 417-055.

CANADIAN BUREAU
Patricia Thompson, Editor. 1430 Yonge St., Suite 214, Toronto, Ont. M4T 1Y6 Canada.

FOREIGN CORRESPONDENTS
GREECE: Rena Velissariou, 32, Kolokotroni Str., Aguia Paraskevi, Attikis, Athens. 153 42, Greece. (65) 67 665.
INDIA: B. D. Garga, 11 Verem Villas, Reis Magos, Bardez, Goa 403114 India. FAX: (91 832) 43433.
PAKISTAN: A.R. Slote, P.O. Box 7426, Karachi, 74400, Pakistan.

INTERNATIONAL MOTION PICTURE ALMANAC
(Annual) 159 W. 53 St., New York, NY 10019. (212) 247-3100. FAX: (212) 489-0871. email: QUIGLEYPUB@aol.com
EDITOR
James D. Moser
MANAGING EDITOR
Tracy Stevens
BRITISH EDITOR
William Pay
CANADIAN EDITOR
Patricia Thompson

INTERNATIONAL TELEVISION & VIDEO ALMANAC
(Annual) 159 W. 53 St., New York, NY 10019. (212) 247-3100. FAX: (212) 489-0871. email: QUIGLEYPUB@aol.com
EDITOR
James D. Moser
MANAGING EDITOR
Tracy Stevens
BRITISH EDITOR
William Pay
CANADIAN EDITOR
Patricia Thompson

QUIGLEY'S ENTERTAINMENT INDUSTRY REFERENCE
(CD-ROM, Annual) 159 W. 53 St., New York, NY 10019. (212) 247-3100. FAX: (212) 489-0871. email: QUIGLEYPUB@aol.com
PUBLISHER
Martin S. Quigley
EDITORS
Tracy Stevens
James D. Moser
EDITOR
BRITISH EDITOR
William Pay
CANADIAN EDITOR
Patricia Thompson

ACADEMY PLAYERS DIRECTORY
(Tri-Annual)
Academy of Motion Picture Arts & Sciences, 8949 Wilshire Blvd., Beverly Hills, CA 90211-1972. (310) 247-3000. FAX: (310) 550-5034.
EDITOR
Keith W. Gonzales

ADVERTISING AGE
(Weekly)
740 N. Rush St., Chicago, IL 60611. (312) 649- 5200. 220 E. 42 St., New York, NY 10017. (212) 210-0100.
CHAIRMAN
Mrs. G. D. Crain
PUBLISHING DIRECTOR
Joe Cappo

PUBLISHER
Ed Erhardt
PRESIDENT & EDITOR-IN-CHIEF
Rance Crain

THE AMERICAN CINEMATOGRAPHER
(Monthly)
Published by American Society of Cinematographers, Inc., P.O. Box 2230, Hollywood, CA 90078. (213) 969-4333. FAX: (213) 876-4973.
EDITOR
Stephen Pizzello
ASSOCIATE EDITOR
David E. Williams
ASSISTANT EDITOR
Andrew O. Thompson
CIRCULATION MANAGER
Saul Molina

AMERICAN PREMIERE MAGAZINE
(Bi-monthly)
8421 Wilshire Blvd., Penthouse, Beverly Hills, CA 90211. (213) 852-0434.
PUBLISHER & EDITOR
Susan Royal
ASSISTANT EDITOR
Dawn Brooks

ANNUAL INDEX TO MOTION PICTURE CREDITS
(Annual compilation of feature film credits)
c/o Academy of Motion Picture Arts and Sciences, 8949 Wilshire Blvd., Beverly Hills, CA 90211. (310) 247-3000. FAX: (310) 859-9619.
EXECUTIVE DIRECTOR
Bruce Davis
EDITOR
Byerly Woodward

AV GUIDE: THE LEARNING MEDIA NEWSLETTER
(Monthly)
380 Northwest Highway, Des Plaines, IL 60016-2282. (847) 298-6622. FAX: (847) 390-0408.
PUBLISHER
H. S. Gillette
EDITOR
Natalie Ferguson
CIRCULATION DIRECTOR
Linda Lambdin

BILLBOARD
(Weekly)
5055 Wilshire Blvd., Los Angeles, CA 90036-4396. (310) 525-2300. FAX: (213) 525-2394.
1515 Broadway, New York, NY 10036. (212) 764-7300. FAX: (212) 536-5358.
49 Music Square W., Nashville, TN 37203. (615) 321-4290. FAX: (615) 327-1575.
806 15 St., NW, Washington, D.C. 20005. (202) 783-3282. FAX: (202) 737-3833.
23 Ridgmount St., 3rd fl., London WC1E 7AH. (01 71) 323-6686. FAX: (01 71) 631-0428.
PRESIDENT & PUBLISHER
Howard Lander
EDITOR-IN-CHIEF
Timothy White
MANAGING EDITOR
Susan Nunziata
ASSOCIATE PUBLISHER, MARKETING & SALES
Gene Smith

BOXOFFICE
6640 Sunset Blvd., #100, Hollywood, CA 90028. (213) 465-1186. FAX: (213) 465-5049. Published by RLD Communications, Inc., 203 N. Wabash Ave., Chicago, IL 60605
PUBLISHER
Robert L. Deitmeier
EDITOR-IN-CHIEF
Ray Greene
NATIONAL AD DIRECTOR
Robert Vale

BROADCASTING & CABLE—THE NEWS WEEKLY OF TELEVISION AND RADIO
(Weekly)
1705 DeSales St., NW, Washington, DC 20036. (202) 659-2340. FAX: (202) 429-0651.
245 W. 17 St., New York, NY 10011. (212) 645-0067. FAX: (212) 337-7028.

5700 Wilshire Blvd., #120, Los Angeles, CA 90036. (213) 549-4100. FAX: (213) 937-4240.
PUBLISHER
Peggy Conlon
SENIOR VICE PRESIDENT & EDITOR
Donald V. West

CELEBRITY SERVICE INTERNATIONAL
Publisher of Celebrity Bulletin (daily).and Celebrity Service International Contact Book (annual).
1780 Broadway, New York, NY 10019. (212) 757-7979. FAX: (212) 397-4626.
8833 Sunset Blvd., Los Angeles, CA 90069. (310) 652-1700. FAX: (310) 652-9244.
EDITOR, CELEBRITY BULLETIN (NY)
Bill Murray
EDITOR, CELEBRITY BULLETIN (LA)
Todd Longwell
EDITORS, CELEBRITY SERVICE INTERNATIONAL CONTACT BOOK
Vicki Bagley, Mark Kerrigan

COMING ATTRACTIONS
(Monthly)
Connell Communications Inc., 86 Elm St., Peterborough, NH 03458. (603) 924-7271. FAX: (603) 924-7013.
PUBLISHER
Kathy Morris

CINEFEX
(Quarterly)
P.O. Box 20027, Riverside, CA 92516.
PUBLISHER
Don Shay
EDITOR
Jody Duncan

COSTUME DESIGNERS GUILD DIRECTORY
(Annual)
c/o Costume Designers Guild, 13949 Ventura Blvd., #309, Sherman Oaks, CA 91423. (818) 905-1557. FAX: (818) 905-1560.

DAILY VARIETY
(Daily)
5700 Wilshire Blvd., Suite 120, Los Angeles, CA 90036. (213) 857-6600. FAX: (213) 857-0494.
SPECIAL EDITIONS EDITOR
Steven Gaydos
MANAGING EDITOR
Jonathan Taylor
NATIONAL SALES MANAGER
Charles Koones
PRODUCTION MANAGER
Bob Butler

EDITOR & PUBLISHER
(Weekly)
11 W. 19 St., New York, NY 10011. (212) 675- 4380. FAX: (212) 929-1259.
PRESIDENT & EDITOR
Robert U. Brown
MANAGING EDITOR
John P. Consoli

ELECTRONIC MEDIA
(Weekly.)
740 N. Rush St., Chicago, IL 60611, (312) 649- 5293. FAX: (312) 649-5465.
VICE PRESIDENT, PUBLISHER & EDITORIAL DIRECTOR
Ron Alridge
EDITOR
P. J. Bednarski

ELECTRONICS
(Monthly)
Penton Publishing, 1100 Superior Ave., Cleveland, OH 44114. (216) 696-7000.
PUBLISHER/EDITOR
Jonah McLeod

ELECTRONICS NOW
(Monthly)
500 Bi-County Blvd., Farmingdale, NY 11735. (516) 293-3000. FAX: (516) 293-3115. url: http://www.gernsback.com
PUBLISHER
Larry Steckler
EDITOR
Carl Laron

FILM & VIDEO MAGAZINE
(Monthly)
Organized 1983. 8455 Beverly Blvd., #508, Los Angeles, CA 90048-3416. (213) 653-8053. FAX: (213) 653-8053.

ASSOCIATE PUBLISHER/EDITOR
Paula Swartz
ASSOCIATE PUBLISHER
Debbie Vodenos
SENIOR EDITOR
Collen O'Mara
ASSOCIATE EDITORS
Cristina Clapp
ASSISTANT EDITOR
Debbie Sweeney
NATIONAL SALES DIRECTOR
Steven Rich

FILM JOURNAL, THE
(Monthly)
244 W. 49 St., Suite 200, New York, NY 10019. (212) 246-6460. FAX: (212) 265-6428.
PUBLISHER-EDITOR
Robert H. Sunshine
ASSOCIATE PUBLISHER
Jimmy Sunshine
MANAGING EDITOR
G. Kevin Lally
ASSOCIATE EDITORS
Ed Kelleher, Mitch Neuhauser
ASSISTANT EDITOR
Glenn Slavin
DIRECTOR OF ADVERTISING/SALES
Jim Merck
WEST COAST EDITOR
Myron Meisel
CIRCULATION MANAGER
Michelle Lederkramer

FILM QUARTERLY
(Quarterly)
University of California Press, 2120 Berkeley Way, Berkeley, CA 94720. (510) 601-9070. FAX: (510) 601-9036.
EDITOR
Ann Martin
Published by University of California Press

FILMS IN REVIEW
P.O. Box 589, New York, NY 10021. (212) 628-1594.
EDITOR
Robin Little

HOLLYWOOD CREATIVE DIRECTORY
(Annual)
3000 Olympic Blvd., Santa Monica, CA 90404. (310) 315-4815.
e-mail: hcd@hollyvision.com

THE HOLLYWOOD REPORTER
(Daily)
5055 Wilshire Blvd., Los Angeles, CA 90036. (213) 525-2000, (213) 525-2068 (editorial). FAX: (213) 525-2377 (editorial), (213) 525-2189 (advertising), (213) 957-5766 (special issues).
1515 Broadway, New York, NY, 10036. (212) 536-5344, (212) 536-5325 (editorial). FAX: (212) 536-5345.
PUBLISHER & EDITOR-IN-CHIEF
Robert J. Dowling
EDITOR
Alex Ben Block
MANAGING EDITOR
Glenn Abel
BUREAUS:
806 15th St., N.W., # 421, Washington, DC 20005. (202) 737-2828. FAX: (202) 737-3833.
1515 Broadway, New York, NY, 10036. (212) 536-5344, (212) 536-5325. FAX: (212) 536-5345.
23 Ridgmount St., London WC1E 7AH England. (01 71) 323-6686. FAX: (01 71) 323-2314, (01 71) 323-2316.

I.A.T.S.E. OFFICIAL BULLETIN
(Quarterly)
1515 Broadway, Suite 601, New York, NY 10036. (212) 730-1770. FAX: (212) 921-7699.
EDITOR
Michael W. Proscia
ASSISTANT EDITOR
Karen Pizzuto

IN MOTION FILM & VIDEO PRODUCTION MAGAZINE
(Monthly)
Phillips Business Information, 1201 Seven Locks Rd., Suite 300, Potomac, MD 20854. (301) 340-1520.
PUBLISHER
David Durham
EDITOR
Allison Dollar

INTERNATIONAL DOCUMENTARY
1551 S. Robertson Blvd., Suite 201, Los Angeles, CA 90035. (310) 284-8422. FAX: (310) 785-9334.
EDITOR
Diana Rico

INTERNATIONAL PHOTOGRAPHER
(Monthly)
7715 Sunset Blvd., Suite 300, Hollywood, CA 90046. (213) 876-0160.
PUBLISHER
International Photographers Guild
EDITOR-IN-CHIEF
George Spiro Dibie, ASC
EDITOR
Suzanne R. Lezotte

JOURNAL OF THE SYD CASSYD ARCHIVES ACADEMY OF TELEVISION ARTS & SCIENCES/HOLLYWOOD REPORT
(Quarterly)
917 S. Tremaine, Hollywood 90019, CA. (213) 939-2345.
Founded 1946.
FOUNDER
Syd Cassyd

MILLIMETER
(A monthly magazine covering the motion picture and television production industries.)
122 E. 42 St., #900, New York, NY 10168. (212) 309-7650.
Fax: (212) 867-5893.
5300 Melrose Ave., # 219E, Hollywood, CA 90038. (213) 960-4050. FAX: (213) 960-4059.
PUBLISHER
Sam Kintzer
EDITOR
Bruce Stockler

PACIFIC COAST STUDIO DIRECTORY
(3 times per year)
P.O. Box V, Pine Mountain, CA 93222-4921. (805) 242-2722.
FAX: (805) 242-2724.
PUBLISHER
Jack Reitz

PERFORMANCE MAGAZINE
(Weekly)
2049 Century Park E., Suite 1100, Los Angeles, CA 90067.
(310) 552-3118. FAX: (310) 286-1990.
PUBLISHER
Don Waitt
L.A. SENIOR EDITOR
Stann Findelle
MANAGING EDITOR
Jane Cohen

PRODUCER'S MASTERGUIDE
(Annual)
60 E. 8th St., 31st Floor, New York, NY 10003. (212) 777-4002.
FAX: (212) 777-4101. url: http://www.producers.masterguide.com
PUBLISHER
Shmuel Bension

REEL DIRECTORY, THE
(Annual)
P.O. Box 866, Cotati, CA 94931. (707) 584-8083.
PUBLISHER & EDITOR
Bonnie Carroll

SMPTE JOURNAL (SOCIETY OF MOTION PICTURE AND TELEVISION ENGINEERS)
(Monthly)
595 West Hartsdale Ave., White Plains, NY 10607. (914) 761-1100. FAX: (914) 761-3115.
EDITOR
Jeffrey B. Friedman
DIRECTOR OF MARKETING & COMMUNICATIONS
John Izzo

SCREEN ACTOR/CALL SHEET
(Bi-Monthly)
5757 Wilshire Blvd., Los Angeles, CA 90036. (213) 549-6652.
FAX: (213) 549-6656.

SHOOT
(Weekly)
1515 Broadway, New York, NY 10036. (212) 764-7300. FAX: (212) 536-5321.
5055 Wilshire Blvd., Los Angeles, CA 90036. (213) 525-2262.
FAX: (213) 525-0275.
Merchandise Mart Plaza, #936, Chicago, IL 60654. (312) 464-8555. FAX: (312) 464-8550.
PUBLISHER
Roberta Griefer
EDITOR
Peter Caranicas

TV GUIDE
(Weekly)
News America Publications, Inc., 100 Matsonford Rd., Radnor, PA 19088. (215) 293-8500.
EDITOR-IN-CHIEF
Steven Reddicliffe
PRESIDENT/CEO
Joseph F. Barletta
PUBLISHER/SENIOR VICE PRESIDENT
Mary G. Berner
MANAGING EDITOR-PROGRAMMING
Elisabeth Bacon
EXECUTIVE EDITOR-NATIONAL EDITORIAL
Barry Golson

TAPE/DISC BUSINESS
(Monthly)
Knowledge Industry Publications, Inc., 701 Westchester Ave., White Plains, NY 10604-3098. (914) 328-9157. FAX: (914) 328-9093.
EDITOR
Patricia Casey
CIRCULATION DIRECTOR
Jeff Hartford

TELEVISION & CABLE FACTBOOK
(Annual)
Warren Publishing, Inc., 2115 Ward Court, N.W., Washington, DC 20037. (202) 872- 9200. FAX: (202) 293-3435.
EDITOR & PUBLISHER
Albert Warren
MANAGING EDITOR
Michael C. Taliaferro
EDITORIAL DIRECTOR
Mary Appel

TELEVISION DIGEST WITH CONSUMER ELECTRONICS
(Weekly)
Warren Publishing, Inc., 2115 Ward Court, N.W., Washington, DC 20037. (202) 872-9200. FAX: (202) 293-3435.
EDITOR & PUBLISHER
Albert Warren
EDITORIAL DIRECTOR
David Lachenbruch
EXECUTIVE EDITOR
Dawson B. Nail
SENIOR EDITOR & EXECUTIVE PUBLISHER
Paul Warren
SENIOR EDITOR & ASSOCIATE PUBLISHER
Daniel Warren

TELEVISION INDEX
40-29 27th St., Long Island City, NY 11101-3869, (718) 937-3990.
EDITOR & PUBLISHER
Jonathan Miller

TELEVISION QUARTERLY
(Quarterly)
National Academy of Television Arts & Sciences, 111 W. 57 St., New York, NY 10019. (212) 586-8424.
EDITOR
Richard Pack
ADVERTISING
Trudy Wilson

VARIETY
(Weekly)
Reed Publishing, Inc., 249 W. 17 St., 4th fl., New York, NY 10011. (212) 645-0067. FAX: (212) 337-6977.
5700 Wilshire Blvd., Suite #120, Los Angeles, CA 90036, (213) 857-6600. FAX: (213) 857-0494.
1483 Chain Bridge Rd., McLean, VA 22101, (703) 448-0510. FAX: (703) 827-8214.
P.O. Box 535, Lake Bluff, IL, 60044, (708) 615-9742, FAX: (708) 615-9743.
33 Champs Elysees, 75008 France. Phone (33-1) 43-55-07-43.
Lungotevere Flaminio 22, Rome 00196. (39-6) 361-3103.
34/35 Newman St., W1P 3PD England, (44-01 71) 637-3663.
Madrid: Phone (34-1) 576-4262.
Sydney, Australia: Phone: (61-2) 372-5577.
CHAIRMAN/CEO
Robert L. Krakoff
VICE PRESIDENT, PUBLISHING OPERATIONS
Gerard A. Byrne
EDITORIAL DIRECTOR
Peter Bart
MANAGING EDITORS
Elizabeth Guider, Jonathan Taylor
EUROPEAN EDITOR
Adam Dawtrey

VARIETY'S ON PRODUCTION
5700 Wilshire Blvd., Suite 120, Los Angeles, CA 90036. (213) 857-6600. FAX: (213) 549-4184.e-mail: onprodmag@aol.com
PUBLISHER
Jerry Brandt

VIDEO

(Consumer magazine covering home theatre, audio, video, and multimedia hardware and software.)
Published by Hachette Filipacchi Magazines, Inc., 1633 Broadway, 45th Floor, New York, NY 10019. (212) 767-6020. FAX: (212) 767-5615. email: VideoMag@aol.com
GROUP PUBLISHER
Tony Catalaro
EDITOR-IN-CHIEF
Bill Wolfe

VIDEO BUSINESS

(Weekly)
Chilton Publications, 825 Seventh Ave., New York, NY 10019. (212) 887-8400.
PUBLISHER
John Gaffney
EDITOR
Bruce Apar
ADVERTISING DIRECTOR
Stacy Kelly
ADVERTISING SALES
Andi Elliott, Linda Buckley

VIDEO STORE MAGAZINE

(Weekly)
201 E. Sandpointe Ave., Ste. 600, Santa Ana, CA 92707. (714) 513-8400, (800) 854-3112. FAX: (714) 513-8403.
PRESIDENT OF PUBLICATIONS
Brian Nairn
GROUP VICE PRESIDENT
Glenn Rogers
PUBLISHER
Don Rosenberg
EDITOR IN CHIEF
Thomas K. Arnold
ASSOCIATE PUBLISHER
Anne Sadler
MARKET RESEARCH DIRECTOR
Judith McCourt

VIDEO SYSTEMS MAGAZINE

(Monthly)
9800 Metcalf Ave., Overland Park, KS 66212-2215. (913) 341-1300. FAX: (913) 967-1898.
PUBLISHER
Dennis Triola
GROUP VICE PRESIDENT
Cameron Bishop
MARKETING DIRECTOR
Tom Brick
AD PRODUCTION COORDINATOR
Pat Eisenman

VIDEO WEEK

(Weekly)
Warren Publishing, Inc. 2115 Ward Court N.W., Washington, DC 20037-1213. (202) 872-9200. FAX: (202) 293-3435.

VIDEOGRAPHY MAGAZINE

(Monthly)
2 Park Ave., Suite 1820, New York, NY 10016. (212) 779-1919. FAX: (212) 213-3484.
PUBLISHER
Paul Gallo
EDITOR
Brian McKernan

WHO'S WHO IN THE MOTION PICTURE INDUSTRY/WHO'S WHO IN TELEVISION

(Semi-Annual)
Packard Publishing, P.O. Box 2187, Beverly Hills, CA 90213. (310) 275-6531. FAX: (818) 501-7392. e-mail: rodpub@aol.com

PUBLISHER & EDITOR
Rodman W. Gregg

GREAT BRITAIN

BROADCAST

(Published weekly).
EMAP Media Ltd., 33-39 Bowling Green Lane, London, EC1R ODA. (01 71) 837 9263. FAX: (01 71) 837 8250.
EDITOR
Mike Jones

EYEPIECE

Journal of the Guild of British Camera Technicians, 5-11 TauntonRoad, Metropolitan Centre, Greenford, Middx., UB6 8UQ. (01 81) 578 9243. FAX: (01 81) 575 5972.
EDITORS
Kerry Anne-Burrows, Charles Hewitt
ADVTG. CONSULTANT
Ron Bowyer

IMAGE TECHNOLOGY

Journal of the British Kinematograph, Sound and Television Society. M6-M14 Victoria House, Vernon Place, London, WC1B 4DF. England. (01 71) 242-8400. FAX: (01 71) 405 3560.
MANAGING EDITOR
John Gainsborough

MOVING PICTURES

(Published weekly) 1 Richmond Mews, London W1V 5AG. (01 71) 287-0070. FAX: (01 71) 287-9637.
EDITORS
Sara Squire
Damon Wise

SCREEN INTERNATIONAL EUROGUIDE

(Annual directory for the motion picture and television industry in Europe).
Published by EMAP Media, 33-39 Bowling Green Lane, London EC1R 0DA, England. (01 71) 837-1212. FAX: (01 71) 278-4003.
EDITOR IN CHIEF
Oscar Moore

TELEVISUAL

(Published monthly).
Centaur Group, St. Giles House, 50 Poland St., London, W1V 4AX. (01 71) 439 4222. FAX: (01 71) 287 0768.
PUBLISHER
Tim Macpherson
EDITOR
Mundy Ellis

CANADA

FILM CANADA YEARBOOK

1430 Yonge St., Suite 214, Toronto, ON, M4T 1Y6. (416) 696-2382. FAX: (416) 696-6496.
EDITOR
Patricia Thompson

FRANCE

LE FILM FRANCAIS

(Weekly French motion picture trade magazine)
103 Blvd. St. Michel, Paris, France, 75005. (143) 29 4090. FAX: (143) 29 1405.
PUBLISHER
Claude Pommereau
EDITOR
Marie-Claude Arbaudie

MOTION PICTURE AND TELEVISION INFORMATION
RESEARCH AND DATA ANALYSIS COMPANIES

CERTIFIED REPORTS INC. (CRI) EAST
7 Hudson St., Kinderhook NY 12106. (518) 758-6400. FAX:
(518) 758-6451. (Theatre checking open, blind and trailer
checking nationwide.)
CHAIRMAN OF BOARD
Jack J. Spitzer
PRESIDENT
Bill Smith
EXECUTIVE VICE PRESIDENT
Bryan Zweig
VICE PRESIDENT
Frank Falkenhainer
VICE PRESIDENT, ADMINISTRATION & FINANCE
Michael F. Myers

CERTIFIED REPORTS INC. (CRI) WEST
9846 White Oak Ave., Suite 202, Northridge CA 91325. (818)
727- 0929. FAX: (818) 727-7426.
VICE PRESIDENT
Elizabeth Stevens

ENTERTAINMENT DATA INC.
8350 Wilshire Blvd., Suite 210, Beverly Hills CA 90211. (213)
658-8300. BRANCHES: Los Angeles, Washington DC, San
Francisco, New York, Dallas, Chicago, Toronto, Atlanta,
London, Munich.
(Provides daily box-office information for exhibition and distrib-
ution. On-line access to data.)
PRESIDENT
Marcy Polier
SENIOR VICE PRESIDENT
Philip Garfinkle

EXHIBITOR RELATIONS CO., INC.
116 N. Robertson Blvd., Suite 606, Los Angeles CA 90048.
(310) 657-2005. FAX: (310) 657-7283.
PRESIDENT
John N. Krier

THE GALLUP ORGANIZATION
47 Hulfish St., Princeton, NJ 08542. (609) 924-9600.

HANOVER SECURITY REPORTS
952 Manhattan Beach Blvd., Suite 250, Manhattan Beach CA
90266. (310) 545-9891. (800) 634-5560. FAX: (310) 545-7690.
EXECUTIVE VICE PRESIDENT
Nancy Stein

INTERNATIONAL RESEARCH & EVALUATION,
21098 IRE Control Ctr., Eagan, MN 55121-0098. (612) 888-
9635. FAX: (612) 888-9124.
Rick Kenrick

PAUL KAGAN ASSOCIATES, INC.
126 Clock Tower Place, Carmel CA 93923-8734. (408) 624-
1536. FAX: (408) 625-3225. (Research and analysis of entertainment, communications and media industries.)
PRESIDENT
Paul Kagan

KINDERHOOK RESEARCH, INC.
P.O. Box 589, Kinderhook NY 12106. (518) 758-1492. FAX:
(518) 758-9896. (Distributor/ exhibitor open and blind checking.
housekeeping/integrity surveys. industry research.)
PRESIDENT
Andrea Koppel

MARKET RESEARCH CORP. OF AMERICA
819 S. Wabash, Chicago, IL 60605. (708) 480-9600.
2215 Sanders Road, Northbrook, IL 60062. (708) 480-9600.

MCCANN-ERICKSON INC.
6420 Wilshire Blvd., Los Angeles, CA 90048. (213) 655-9420.

A.C. NIELSEN COMPANY
150 N. Martingale Rd., Schaumburg, IL 60173. (708) 605-5000.
731 Wilshire Blvd., #940, Los Angeles, CA 90010. (213) 386-
7316. FAX: (213) 386-7317.
299 Park Ave., New York, NY 10171. (212) 708-7500.

The Industry in Great Britain and Ireland

The Year in Review

Production, Distribution & Services Companies

Financial Services

Studio Facilities

Costume Suppliers

Public Relations & Marketing

Trade Publications

Equipment & Services

Exhibition Circuits

Trade & Government Organisations

British Year in Review

Cinema attendance figures for 1995 were 116 million. This showed a 7 million ticket decline from the previous year, the first time in a decade that such a decline was recorded. Nevertheless, the early months of 1996 showed a recovery with the best attendance in 20 years with audiences averaging 2.81 million per week, an increase of 31% over the previous year. A variety of reasons have been cited for the 1995 fall-off, with the main reason being the simultaneous release of attractive products making it difficult for exhibition to take full advantage of the films. For a period of five months, there were no movies that caught the imagination of the public in large numbers followed by the hottest summer since 1976. Also, the recently introduced National Lottery has undoubtedly had an influence with a larger proportion of the leisure pound being spent on gambling. However, this was partially compensated for by the government allocating £70 million to British film production and a further £10 million to distribution and exhibition.

There are now 1,695 screens in the UK at 470 sites. Total admissions for the first quarter of 1996 were 32.2 million with an average revenue per admission of £3.04. Payment for film hire amounted to £42.7 million. Average revenue per screen for the same period was nearly £60,000.

American films, as always, dominated British screens. In 1995 Batman Forever grossed £20 million, Casper £16.1 million, Goldeneye £14.8 million, Apollo 13 £11.9 million and Braveheart £11.4 million. The table below shows the top films for the first half of 1996.

In spite of the lower than anticipated revenues of the past year, it is an indication of the industry's faith in the future that American and British groups have all announced new development and refurbishing plans together with the building of multiplexes. In the coming year, Virgin will concentrate on the expansion of its 37 multiplex sites involving a link with the Virgin Megastores. ABC plans to develop high street cinemas and 17 multiplex sites in the next three years. In addition to Virgin and ABC, other groups, such as Odeon, UCI, Cine UK, National Amusements and Warners, have continuous reinvestment plans. The Rank Organisation now operates 337 Odeon screens at 73 UK locations.

British studios, thanks to continued American investment, albeit with limited government support, had a reasonably successful year. Rank, for example, had 22 features and television productions made at its Pinewood Studios. Further, in mid 1996, ITV announced that it will invest £100 million over the next ten years to make British features.

Competition for the cinema from television, home video and cable remains fierce. Commenting on the current position in Cinema Exhibitor's Association annual report, chief executive John Wilkinson said, "Exhibitors jealously guard the six months exclusive theatrical window for the release of movies into cinemas. We believe that the voluntarily recognised window for exclusive theatrical release is a benefit to the studios, distributors and other down-stream media for the delivery of film to the public. Unfortunately, certain distributors unilaterally decided that a number of films should be released to the video market within six months to catch, in particular, the Christmas market. This breach was of great concern to CEA members especially as the majority of films had been major summer releases." These developments were raised with the Society of Film Distributors and it was agreed that if a distributor wishes to release a film within the six month theatrical exclusivity window, he would first contact the CEA. As a matter of principle, it was agreed by all parties that the window would be adhered to. It is hoped that this voluntary accord will satisfy those member who have been seeking the enactment of legally defined windows as favoured by the majority of European exhibitors.

The British Board of Film Classification reported that film submissions had risen significantly in recent years. In the last year under review 373 features were passed for cinema exhibition together with 36 short films, 348 trailers and 196 advertisements. Despite some public concern about Hollywood standards, there was a preponderance of family films. The BBFC said that 86 of the submitted films were untranslated Asian films intended for Britain's ethnic minorities. This represents a growing market in Britain. According to the BBFC, some of these films were of a high standard and it is a pity that they were not made available to a wider audience.

Confirming the trend towards mainsteam values, editing was needed in 21 features, 5.6% of the total, the lowest figure for many years. Most of the cuts were required of films targeted at the family audience and were made at the request of the distributors who wished to reach a wider audience. The BBFC's strict policy on violence accounted for ten of the 21 cut films. Others which might have been viewed as problematic due to violence had already been trimmed in order to achieve the desired American rating.

The BBFC certification is as follows: 'U'–suitable for all; 'PG'–parental guidance; '12'–suitable for children over 12; '15'–suitable for persons of 15 years and over; '18'–suitable only for persons of 18 years and over; 'R18'–restricted, to be supplied only in licensed sex shops to persons of not less than 18 years.

National Cinema Day, celebrating a century of cinema, proved a huge success with over 1 million people taking advantage of the £1 ticket price on Sunday, June 3, 1996. With a total attendance figure of 1.1 million, it was a significant increase over the average Sunday attendance of 400,000. Due to this success, National Cinema Day may become an annual event.

All this good news means that the industry is confident of its future but that it must continue to strive to achieve that "more than twice a year visit to the pictures" for the average moviegoer.

—WILLIAM PAY

Top Box Office Films by Circuit, January – June 1996

Odeon (Rank)	Virgin Cinemas	UCI
Toy Story	Toy Story	Toy Story
Seven	Seven	Seven
Jumanji	Babe	Babe
Sense and Sensibility	Heat	Trainspotting
Trainspotting	Jumanji	Sense and Sensibility
Dangerous Minds	Trainspotting	Heat
The Bridcage	Ace Ventura — When Nature Calls	Get Shorty
Father of the Bride Part II	Sense and Sensibility	Twelve Monkeys
Broken Arrow	Twelve Monkeys	Ace Ventura — When Nature Calls
Twelve Monkeys	Get Shorty	

Overseas Transactions of the Film & Television Industry
In £ million

	1991	1992	1993	1994
Total Receipts	586	657	788	938
Total Payments	517	525	588	753
Net Receipts	69	132	200	185

Source: Governmental Statistical Service

Overseas Transactions: Net Receipts from Film Companies
In £ million

	1987	1988	1989	1990	1991	1992	1993	1994
Receipts less Payments	107	42	59	68	107	172	88	29

Source: Governmental Statistical Service

Overseas Transactions of Film Companies by Area
In £ million

	1987	1988	1989	1990	1991	1992	1993	1994
Receipts [1]								
EC	76	74	81	1014	154	182	95	134
Other Western Europe	17	12	20	21	24	29	18	20
North America	137	97	120	169	100	115	190	225
Other Developed Countries	16	29	26	28	39	44	22	17
Rest of the World	17	19	15	17	29	30	20	29
Total	264	230	263	334	346	400	345	426
Payments [2]								
EC	51	41	52	75	81	54	68	81
Other Western Europe	2	2	2	2	3	5	3	4
North America	91	138	129	169	124	151	157	295
Other Developed Countries	3	4	7	7	10	5	5	7
Rest of the World	10	3	14	13	21	13	24	10
Total	157	188	204	266	239	228	257	397

1 Sums receivable from overseas residents/companies
2 Sums payable to overseas residents/companies
Source: Governmental Statistical Service

Film Companies: 1994 Receipts

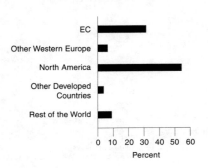

Film Companies: 1994 Payments

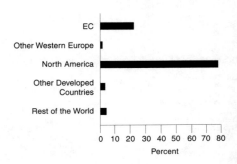

GB Cinema Exhibitors Statistics

		Sites	Screens	Total # of admissions	Gross box office	Rental fees	Revenue per admission	Revenue per screen
		number	number	millions	£ million	£ million	£	£ thousand
Quarterly:								
1995	Q1p	467	1,620	23.8	70.8	23.6	2.98	44.4
	Q2p	458	1,598	19.0	55.3	16.6	2.92	34.8
	Q3p	460	1,619	28.5	81.47	30.7	2.52	50.5
	Q4p	451	1,624	26.8	79.3	27.6	2.96	49.2
1996	Q1p	470	1,695	32.2	97.7	42.7	3.04	59.6
Annual Totals:								
1989		481	1,177	85.5	169.5	64.9	1.98	147.4
1990		496	1,331	78.6	187.7	69.5	2.39	143.8
1991		537	1,544	88.9	229.7	78.5	2.58	152.4
1992		480	1,547	89.4	243.7	81.9	2.73	153.6
1993	p	495	1,591	99.3	271.3	95.9	2.73	171.0
1994	p	487	1,597	106.1	291.4	105.2	2.75	183.8
1995	p	458	1,598	98.0	286.8	98.5	2.92	178.9

p = provisional
Source: Central Statistical Office.

Analysis of UK Cinemas by Screens

	Sites	%	Screens	%
Single Screens	321	46	321	17
2 Screens	114	16	228	12
3 Screens	109	16	327	17
4 Screens	41	6	168	9
5 Screens	25	4	125	7
6 Screens	24	3	144	8
7 Screens	9	1	63	3
8 Screens	10	1	80	4
9 Screens	8	1	72	4
10 Screens	18	3	180	9
11 Screens	3	-	33	2
12 Screens	8	1	96	5
13 Screens	2	-	26	1
14 Screens	4	1	56	3
Total	696	100	1919	100

Source: Cinema Advertising Association

Analysis of U.K. Cinemas by Seating Capacity

	1-500	501-1,000	1,001-1,500	1,501-2,000	2,000+
Single Screens	253	60	6	4	1
2 Screens	199	25	2	2	-
3 Screens	272	50	2	2	-
4 Screens	154	13	1	-	-
5 Screens	110	14	1	-	-
6 Screens	134	8	1	1	-
7 Screens	60	3	-	-	-
8 Screens	80	-	-	-	-
9 Screens	70	2	-	-	-
10 Screens	179	1	-	-	-
11 Screens	32	1	-	-	-
12 Screens	94	2	-	-	-
13 Screens	25	1	-	-	-
14 Screens	56	-	-	-	-
Total	1,718	180	16	7	1

Source: Cinema Advertising Association

U.K. Circuit Breakdown

	Sites	Screens
Cannon/MGM/Virgin	114	394
Odeon Cinemas	76	340
UCI	26	232
Showcase	11	143
Warner	15	135
Apollo	21	62
Cinema & General (Belfast)	11	38
Robin Cinemas	17	34
Caledonian	6	13
Panton (Coronet)	5	11
Bloom Theatres (Mainline)	6	10
Hoare Circuit	5	9
Service Cinemas	7	7
Curzon Cinemas	5	5
Graves Cinemas	4	5
Cinema Ltd. (Artificial Eye)	3	4
Independents	406	594
Total	738	2,036

U.K. Multiplexes

	Sites	Screens	% of Total U.K. Screens
1985	1	10	1
1986	2	18	1
1987	5	44	4
1988	14	137	10
1989	14	137	10
1990	42	393	24
1991	58	516	30
1992	64	564	31
1993	70	625	34
1994	76	683	36
1995	83	732	37

Note: £650 million has been invested in new state-of-the-art cinemas since 1985 largely sustaining the industry's growth. A further 45 multiplex sites are currently in development.

Source: Cinema Advertising Association

PRODUCTION, DISTRIBUTION & SERVICE COMPANIES

AARDMAN ANIMATIONS
Gas Ferry Road, Bristol, BS1 6UN. Tel: 0117 9848845. FAX: 0117 9848486.
CONTACT
Michael Rose

A1 ENTERTAINMENT
16a South Parade, Chiswick, London, W4. Tel: 0181 742 1975. FAX: 0181 742 1980.

ADN ASSOCIATES/HOLLYWOOD CLASSICS
8 Cleveland Gardens, London, W2 6HA. Tel: 0171 262 4646. FAX: 0171 262 3242.
CONTACTS
Pano AlaFouzo, Joe Dreier, John Flynn (USA)

AGFA-GEVAERT LTD. (MOTION PICTURE DIVISION)
27 Great West Road, Brentford, Middlesex, TW8 9AX. Tel: 0181 231 4310. FAX: 0181 231 4315.

ABBEY FILMS LTD.
Film House, 35 Upper Abbey Street, Dublin 1, Ireland. Tel: Dublin 8723922. FAX: 8723687.
DIRECTORS
K. Anderson, L. Ward, A. Ryan

ALL AMERICAN LEISURE GROUP INC.
Production Office: 6 Woodland Way, Petts Wood, Kent BR5 1ND. Tel: 01689 871535. Fax: 01689 871519. Corporate Office: Suite 1, 370 Minorca Avenue, Coral Gables, (MIAMI) FL 33134. Tel: (305) 443-5444. FAX: (305) 443-4446.
CONTACT
Bachoo Sen

ALLIED VISION LTD.
3-4 Ashland Place, London, W1M 3JH. Tel: 0171 224 1992. Telex: 22721 HGENTS. FAX: 0171 224 0111.
MANAGING DIRECTOR
Peter McRae

AMY INTERNATIONAL PRODUCTIONS
2a Park Ave., Wraysbury, Middx. TW19 5ET. Tel: 01784 483131/483288. FAX: 01784 483812.
DIRECTORS
Simon MacCorkindale, Susan George

ANDOR FILMS LTD.
8 Ilchester Place, London, W14 8AA. Tel: 0171 602 2382. FAX: 0171 602 1047.
MANAGING DIRECTOR
Charles H. Schneer (U.S.)

ANGELS & BERMANS
119 Shaftesbury Avenue, London, WC2H 8AE. Tel: 0171 836 5678. FAX: 0171 240 9527 and 40 Camden Street, London, NW1 OEN. Tel: 0171 387 0999. FAX: 0171 383 5603.
CONTACTS
Tim Angel, Jonathan Lipman, Richard Green, Ron Mawbey

ANGLE FILMS LIMITED
25 Blenheim Crescent, London, W11 2EF. Tel: 0171 229 6034. FAX: 0171 727 8498.

ANTELOPE FILMS LTD.
2 Bloomsbury Place, London, WC1A 2QA. Tel: 0171 209 0099. FAX: 0171 209 0098.
CONTACT
Mick Csaky

ANVIL FILM POST PRODUCTION LTD.
Denham Studios, North Orbital Road, Denham, Uxbridge, Middlesex, UB9 5HL. Tel: 01895 833522. Telex: 934704. FAX: 01895 835006.
CONTACTS
Ken Somerville, C. Eng. M.I.E.R.E., Alan Snelling

ARROW FILM DISTRIBUTORS
18 Walford Road, Radlett WD7 8LE, Berkshire. Tel: 1923 858 306. FAX: 1923 859 673.

ARTIFICIAL EYE FILM CO.
13 Soho Square, London W1V 5FB. Tel: 0171 437 2552. FAX: 0171 437 2992.
CONTACT
Pamela Engel

ARTS COUNCIL OF ENGLAND
14 Great Peter Street, London, SW1P 3NQ. Tel: 0171 973 6443. FAX: 0171 973 6581.

HEAD OF FILM, VIDEO & BROADCASTING DEPARTMENT
Rodney Wilson

RICHARD ATTENBOROUGH PRODUCTIONS LTD.
Beaver Lodge, The Green, Richmond, Surrey, TW9 1NQ. Tel: 0181 940 7234. Telex: 266446 BAPUG. FAX: 0181 940 4741.
DIRECTORS
Lord Richard Attenborough, CBE, The Lady Attenborough, J.P., Richard Blake, Claude Fielding

AUSTRALIAN FILM COMMISSION
Victory House, 99-101 Regent Street, London, WIR 7HB. Tel: 0171 734 9383. FAX: 0171 434 0170.
DIRECTOR OF MARKETING
Sue Murray

AUTOCUE LTD.
Autocue House, 265 Merton Road, London, SW18 5JS. Tel: 0181 870 0104. FAX: 0181 874 3726.
CONTACTS
Mick Gould, Sarah Lewis

AVTON COMMUNICATIONS AND ENTERTAINMENT, INC.
19 Watford Road, Radlett, Herts., WD7 8LF. Tel: 0192385 3255. FAX 01923855757.
CONTACT
Tony Klinger

JANE BALFOUR FILMS LTD.
Burghley House, 35 Fortress Road, London, NW5 1AD. Tel: 0171 267 5392. FAX: 0171 267 4241.
CONTACT
Mary Barlow

BEACONSFIELD FILMS LTD.
52 Queen Anne Street, London, W1M 9LA. Tel: 0171 935 1186.
DIRECTORS
Peter Rogers, Mrs. B. E. Rogers, G. E. Malyon

BFI FILM & VIDEO LIBRARY
21 Stephen Street, London, W1P 1PL. Tel: 0171 255 1444. FAX: 0171 436 7950.
HEAD OF DISTRIBUTION SERVICES
Heather Stewart

BLUE DOLPHIN FILM DISTRIBUTORS LTD.
(Blue Dolphin Film Productions Ltd.)
40 Langham Street, London, W1N 5RG. Tel: 0171 255 2494. FAX: 0171 580 7670.
CONTACT
Joseph D'Morais

BOP MOTION PICTURES LTD.
6 Woodland Way, Petts Wood, Kent BR5 IND. Tel: 01689 871535/871519. FAX: 01689 871519.
DIRECTORS
Bachoo Sen, John C. Broderick

BORDEAUX FILMS INTERNATIONAL LTD.
22 Soho Square, London, W1V 5FJ. Tel: 0181 959 8556. FAX: 0181 959 0555.
MANAGING DIRECTOR
K. Barakat
CONTACT
Melanie Young

SYDNEY BOX ASSOCIATES, LTD.
52 Queen Anne Street, London, W1M 9LA. Tel: 0171 935 1186.
DIRECTORS
Mrs. B. E. Rogers, G. E. Malyon

MARY BREEN-FARRELLY PRODUCTIONS LTD.
Ardmore Studios, Herbert Road, Bray Co. Wicklow, Ireland. Tel: Dublin 286 2971. Fax: Dublin 286 6637.
CONTACT
Mary Breen-Farrelly

BRIGHT STAR
Reuters Television Ltd., 40 Cumberland Avenue, London, NW10 7EH. Tel: 0181 965 7733. Telex: 22678. FAX: 0181 965 0620.

BRITISH LION
Pinewood Studios, Pinewood Road, Iver, Bucks., SL0 0NH. Tel: 01753 651 700. FAX: 01753 656 391.
CHAIRMAN & CHIEF EXECUTIVE
Peter R. E. Snell

BRITISH MOVIETONEWS LTD.
North Orbital Road, Denham, Nr. Uxbridge, Middlesex, UB9 5HQ. Tel: 01895 833071. FAX: 01895 834893.
MANAGING DIRECTOR
Barry S. Florin
LIBRARIAN
Barbara Heavens

BRITISH SKY BROADCASTING LTD.
Grant Way, Isleworth, Middx. TW7 5QD. Tel: 0171 705 3000. FAX: 0171 705 3030.
CHIEF EXECUTIVE & MANAGING DIRECTOR
Sam Chisholm
MARKETING DIRECTOR
Jim Hytner

BRITISH SCREEN FINANCE LTD.
14-17 Wells Mews, London, W1P 3FL. Tel: 0171 323 9080. FAX: 0171 323 0092.
CHIEF EXECUTIVE
Simon Perry

BRITISH UNIVERSITIES FILM & VIDEO COUNCIL
55 Greek St., London, W1V 5LR. Tel: 0171 734 3687. FAX: 0171 287 3914.
DIRECTOR
Murray Weston

BROUGHTON HOUSE
6-8 Sackville St., 3rd fl., London W1X 1DD. Tel: 0171 287 4601. FAX: 0171 287 9652.

BUENA VISTA PRODUCTIONS LTD.
Beaumont House, Kensington Village, Avonmore Road, London, W14 8TS. Tel: 0171 605 2400. FAX: 0171 605 2597.
MANAGING DIRECTOR
David Simon

CFS CONFERENCE CENTRE LTD.
22-25 Portman Close, Baker Street, London, W1H 9JH. Tel: 0171 486 2881. Telex: 24672. FAX: 0171 486 4152.

CAPITOL FILMS LTD.
15 Portland Place, London, W1N 3AA. Tel: 0171 872 0154. FAX: 0171 636 6691.
CONTACTS
Sharon Harel, Jane Barclay

CARLTON COMMUNICATIONS PLC
15 St. George Street, London, W1R 9DE. Tel: 0171 499 8050. FAX: 0171 895 9575.
CHAIRMAN
Michael Green
MANAGING DIRECTOR
June de Holler

CASTLE COMMUNICATIONS PLC
A29 Barwell Business Park, Leatherhead Road, Chessington, Surrey KT9 2NY. Tel: 0181 974 1021. FAX: 0181 974 2674.
CHAIRMAN
Terry Shand
MANAGING DIRECTOR
Geoff Kempin

CASTLE ROCK INTERNATIONAL
8 Queen Street, London, W1X 7PH. Tel: 0171 409 3532. FAX: 0171 499 9885/4120.
PRESIDENT
Masamo Grassni
V.P., MARKETING & PUBLICITY
Lindsey Shide

CASTLE TARGET INTERNATIONAL
(Castle Premier Releasing Ltd.)
A29 Barwell Business Park, Leatherhead Road, Chessington, Surrey KT9 2NY. Tel: 0181 974 1021. FAX: 0181 974 2674.

CATTERMOUL FILM SERVICE
(Cecil Cattermoul Ltd.)
69 New Oxford Street, London, WC1A 1DG. Tel: 0171 379 4361 and 0171 379 4038. Telex: 268312 WESCOM G ATTN. CATTERMOUL. FAX: 071 240 4895.
DIRECTOR
Marina Cattermoul (Mrs.)

CAZENZA PRODUCTIONS LTD.
57 Great Cumberland Place, London W1H 7LJ. Tel: 0171 402 8858. FAX: 0171 262 4143.
CONTACT
Ann Zahl

CHARGEURS PRODUCTIONS LTD.
Kent House, Market Place, London, W1N 8AR. Tel: 0171 323 5151. FAX: 0171 636 7594.
CONTACT
Timothy Burrill

CHEERLEADER PRODUCTIONS
62 Chiswick High Road, Chiswick, London W4 15Y. Tel: 0171 995 7778. FAX: 0171 995 7779.

ROGER CHERRILL LTD.
65-66 Dean Street, London, W1V 6PL. Tel: 0171 437 7972. FAX: 0171 437 6411.
CONTACT
Brian Hickin

CHRYSALIS MULTIMEDIA
The Chrysalis Building, 13 Bramley Road, London, W1O 6SP. Tel: 0171 221 2213. FAX: 0171 221 6337.
CONTACT
Jo Wood

CI BY SALES
14 Curzon St., London, W1Y 7FH. Tel: 0171 333 8877. FAX: 0171 493 2443.
CONTACT
Wendy Palmer

CINE-LINGUAL SOUND STUDIOS LTD.
27/29 Berwick Street, London, W1V 3RF. Tel: 0171 437 0136. FAX: 0171 439 2012.
DIRECTORS
A. Anscombe, P. J. Anscombe, M. Anscombe, D. J. Old, D. J. Newman

CINEMA SEVEN PRODUCTIONS LTD.
Pinewood Studios, Iver Heath, Bucks, SL0 0NH. Tel: 01753 651700. FAX: 01753 652525.
DIRECTORS
Cassian Elwes, George Pappas
CONTACT
Chantal Ribeiro

CINEMA VERITY PRODUCTIONS LTD.
The Mill House, Millers Way, 1a Shepherds Bush Road, London, W6 7NA. Tel: 0181 749 8485. FAX: 0181 743 5062.
EXECUTIVE PRODUCER
Verity Lambert

CINESOUND EFFECTS LIBRARY LTD.
Imperial Studios, Maxwell Road, Elstree Way, Boreham Wood, Herts. Tel: 0181 953 5837. FAX: 0181 207 1728.
CONTACTS
Mike Rogers, Angela Marshall

CINE-U.K. LTD.
Sutherland House, 5/6 Argyll St., London W1V 1AD. Tel: 0171 494 1394. FAX: 0171 734 1443.
MANAGING DIRECTOR
Steve Wiener

BRIAN CLEMENS ENTERPRISES LTD.
Park Farm Cottage, Ampthill, Beds. Tel: 01525 402215. FAX: 01525 402954.

CLIP JOINT
(Film Archive Library)
4 Aldred Road, London NW6 IAN. Tel: 0171 794 3666. FAX: 0171 431 4132.

COLSTAR INTERNATIONAL
11 Wythburn Place, London W1H 5WL. Tel: 0171 437 5725. FAX: 0171 706 1704.

COLUMBIA PICTURES CORPORATION LTD.
19-23 Wells Street, London W1P 4DH. Tel: 0171 580 2090. Telex: 263392 COLPIC G. FAX: 0171 528 8980.
DIRECTORS
Nicholas Bingham, Martin Blakstad, Lester McKellar, J. Edward Shugrue (USA)

COLUMBIA TRI-STAR FILMS (UK)
19/23 Wells Street, London, W1P 4DH. Tel: 0171 580 2090. Telex: 263392 COLPIC G. FAX: 0171 436 0323.
MANAGING DIRECTOR, UK
Carmen Menegazzi

COLUMBIA TRI-STAR FILMS (IRELAND)
54 Middle Abbey St., Dublin, Ireland. Tel: 01 38 72 4151.
BRANCH MANAGER
Gerry Mulcahy

COMPLETION BOND CO., INC.
Pinewood Studios, Iver, Bucks., SL0 0NH. Tel: 01753 651700, 01753 652099.
CONTACT
John L. Hargreaves

CONTEMPORARY FILMS
24 Southwood Lawn Road, Highgate, London, N6 5SF. Tel: 0181 340 5715. FAX: 0181 348 1238.
CONTACT
Kitty Cooper

CORI FILM DISTRIBUTORS
19 Albemarle Street, London, W1X 3HA. Tel: 0171 493 7920. FAX: 0171 493 8088.
CONTACTS
Marie Hoy, Bob Jenkins

CREWS EMPLOYMENT AGENCY
111 Wardour Street, London, W1V 4AY. Tel: 0171 437 0350/0810/0721. FAX: 0171 494 4644.
CONTACTS
Lynda Loakes, Shirley Hinds

CURZON FILM DISTRIBUTORS LTD.
38 Curzon Street, London, W1Y 8EY. Tel: 0171 465 0565. Telex: 21612. FAX: 0171 499 2018.
DIRECTORS
R. C. Wingate, G. Biggs, D. Kiernan, J. Gamble, R. Cossey

CYGNET LTD.
Communications Business Centre, Blenheim Road, High Wycombe, Bucks., HP12 3RS. Tel: 0194 450541. FAX: 0194 462154.
MANAGING DIRECTOR
D. N. Plunket

DE LANE LEA SOUND CENTRE
75 Dean Street, London, W1V 5HA. Tel: 0171 439 1721. FAX: 0171 437 0913.
CONTACT
Richard Paynter

DELUXE FILM LABORATORIES
(A subsidiary of the Rank Organisation PLC)
1377 North Serrano Ave., Hollywood, CA 90027. Tel: 001 213 462 6171. FAX: 001 213 461 0608.
PRESIDENTS & CHIEF EXECUTIVE OFFICERS
Cyril Drabinsky
Bud Stone

DELUXE LABORATORIES CANADA
(A subsidiary of the Rank Organisation PLC)
Film House Laboratory, 380 Adelaide Street West, Toronto, Ontario M5V 1R7, Canada. Tel: 0101 416 364 4321. FAX: 0101 416 364 3601.
PRESIDENT & CEO
Cyril Drabinsky

DIGITAL FILM
5 D'Arblay Street, London, W1V 3FD. Tel: 0171 434 3100. FAX: 0171 287 3191.
CONTACT
Matthew Holben

WALT DISNEY COMPANY LTD.
Beaumont House, Kensington Village, Avonmore Road, London, W14 8TS. Tel: 0171 605 2400. FAX: 0171 605 2593.
MANAGING DIRECTOR
Etienne de Villiers

DISTANT HORIZON LTD.
84-86 Regent Street, London, W1R 5PF. Tel: 0171 734 8690. FAX: 0171 734 8691.

DOLBY LABORATORIES INC.
Interface Park, Wootton Bassett, Wiltshire, SN4 8QJ. Tel: 01793 842100. FAX: 01793 842101.
CONTACT
Catherine Unwin

DOLPHIN INTERNATIONAL FILM DISTRIBUTORS LTD.
70-71 New Bond Street, London, W1Y 9DE. Tel: 071 493 8811. FAX: 071 491 2094.

DRUMMER FILMS LTD.
14 Haywood Close, Pinner, Middx. HA5 3LQ. Tel: 0181 866 9466. FAX: 0181 866 9466.
PRODUCER & MANAGING DIR.
Martin M. Harris

DUCK LANE FILM PRODUCTIONS LTD.
8 Duck Lane, London, W1V 1FL. Tel: 0171 439 3912. FAX: 0171 437 2260.
DIRECTOR
Rigby Andrews

EATON FILMS
10 Holbein Mews, Lower Sloane Street, London SW1W 8NN. Tel: 0171 823 6173. FAX: 0171 823 6017.
CONTACTS
Judith Bland, Liz Cook

ECO LTD.
9-10 Westgate Street, Cardiff, CF1 1DA, Wales. Tel: 01222 373321. FAX: 01222 341391.
CONTACT
John Cross

EDUCATIONAL AND TELEVISION FILMS, LTD.
247a Upper Street, London, N1 IRU. Tel: 0171 226 2298.
GENERAL MANAGER
Stanley Forman

ELECTRIC PICTURES
15 Percy Street, London W1P 9FD. Tel: 0171 636 1231. FAX: 0171 636 1675.

ENGLISH FILM CO. (EXPORTS) LTD.
6 Woodland Way, Petts Wood, Kent BR5 IND. Tel: 01689 871535. FAX: 01689 871519.

CONTACT
Bachoo Sen

ENIGMA PRODUCTIONS
13-15 Queen's Gate Place Mews, London, SW7 5BG. Tel: 0171 581 0238.
CHAIRMAN
David Puttnam
MANAGING DIRECTOR
Steve Norris

ENTERTAINMENT FILM DISTRIBUTORS LTD.
27 Soho Square, London, W1V 5FL. Tel: 0171 439 1606. Telex: 262428 ENTVIF. FAX: 0171 734 2483.
DIRECTORS
Michael L. Green, Trevor H. Green, Nigel G. Green

EON PRODUCTIONS, LTD.
138 Piccadilly, London, W1V 9FH. Tel: 071 493 7953. Cables: Brocfilm, London, W1. FAX: 071 408 1236.
DIRECTORS
M. G. Wilson, J. Higgins, MBE

EUREKA LOCATION MANAGEMENT
51 Tonsley Hill, London, SW18 1BW. Tel: 0181 870 6569. FAX: 0181 871 2158.
HEAD OF OPERATIONS
Suzannah Holt

EUROPA FILMS LTD.
Registered Office: Park House 158/160, Arthur Road, Wimbledon Park, London, SW19.
DIRECTORS
Hugh Stewart, Michael M. Stewart

EUSTON FILMS
Pinewood Studios, Iver Heath, Bucks, SL0 0NH. Tel: 01753 654321. FAX: 01753 650222.
CONTACT
John Hambley

EYELINE FILM FACILITIES/VIDEO 77 LTD.
77 Dean Street, London, W1V 6LP. Tel: 0171 734 3391. Telex: 265361. FAX: 0171 437 2095.
DIRECTORS
Harold Orton, Jacki Roblin

F.I.L.M.S. LTD.
2 Savile Row, London W1X 1AF. Tel: 0171 434 0340. FAX: 0171 434 0442.
DIRECTORS
Jorge Gallegos, Adrian Scrope

FTS BONDED
Heston Industrial Estate, Aerodrome Way, Cranford Lane, Hounslow, Middlesex, TW5 9QN. Tel: 0181 897 7973. Telex: 21747 FILMBO G. FAX: 0181 897 7979.
SALES DIRECTOR
John Reeves

FILM AND GENERAL PRODUCTIONS LTD.
10 Pembridge Place, London, W2 4XB. Tel: 0171 221 1141. FAX: 0171 792 1167.
DIRECTORS
Clive Parsons, Davina Belling, Richard Whatmore

FILM FOUR INTERNATIONAL
124 Horseferry Road, London, SW1P 2TX. Tel: 0171 396 4444. FAX: 0171 3068361.
DIRECTOR OF SALES
Bill Stephens
FILM SALES MANAGER
Heather Playford-Denman

FILM BOOKING OFFICES LTD.
211 The Chambers, Chelsea Harbour, London, SW10 OXF. Tel: 0171 734 5298. FAX: 0171 352 4182.
DIRECTORS
B. G. Sammes, F. B. Perham

FILM FINANCES LTD.
1/11 Hay Hill, Berkeley Square, London, W1X 7LF. Tel: 0171 629 6557. FAX: 0171 491 7530. Telex: 298060;
U.S. Office: Suite 1400, 9000 Sunset Boulevard, Los Angeles, CA 90069, U.S.A. Tel: (310) 275-7323. FAX: (310) 275-1706.
DIRECTORS
Richard M. Soames (Pres. Film Finances Inc.), Graham J. Easton

FILMARKETEERS LTD.
81 Piccadilly, London, W1V 9HB. Tel: 0171 491 2767. Telex: 299565. FAX: 0171 629 1803.
DIRECTORS
S. Shorr, I. Hamaoui

FILMVERHUURKANTOOR DE DAM B.V.
59 Warwick Square, London, SW1V 2AL. Tel: 0171 233 6034. FAX: 0171 233 6036.
CONTACT
Moses Rothman

FIRST INDEPENDENT FILMS LTD.
69 New Oxford St., London, WC1A 1DG. Tel: 0171 528 7767. FAX: 0171 528 7770.
MANAGING DIRECTOR
Michael Myers

FIRST LEISURE CORPORATION
7 Soho Street, London, W1V 5FA. Tel: 0171 437 9727. FAX: 0171 439 0088.
CHAIRMAN
Lord Rayne
CONTACT
D. W. Wright

BRYAN FORBES LTD.
Seven Pines, Wentworth, Surrey. FAX: 01344 845174.

MARK FORSTATER PRODUCTIONS LTD.
Suite 66, Pall Mall Deposit, 124-128 Barlby Road, London, W1O 6BL. Tel: 0181 964 1888. FAX: 0181 960 9819.
DIRECTOR
Mark Forstater

FOUR STAR FILMS LTD.
52 Queen Anne Street, London, W1M 9LA. Tel: 0171 935 1186.
DIRECTORS
N. Butt, G. Golledge

FOWLER-CHAPMAN CO. LTD., THE
28 Saint Mary le Park Court, Albert Bridge Road, London, SW11 4PJ. Tel: 0171 223 0034. FAX: 0189 278 4023.
MANAGING DIRECTOR
Roy Fowler

FOXWELL FILM PRODUCTIONS LTD.
8 Alexander Place, London, SW7 2SF.
DIRECTORS
Ivan Foxwell, A. G. Cotterell

FRONTROOM FILMS LTD.
1 The Barton, Mill Road, Countess Wear, Exeter, Devon EX2 6LD. Tel: 01392 70985. FAX: 01392 431405.
CONTACTS
John Davies, Robert Smith

FUJI PHOTO FILM (UK) LTD.
Fuji Film House, 125 Finchley Road, Swiss Cottage, London, NW3 6JH. Tel: 0171 586 5900. FAX: 0171 722 4259.
MANAGING DIRECTOR
S. Takekoshi

GFD COMMUNICATIONS LTD.
Unit 15a, Parkmore Ind. Est. Long Mile Road, Dublin 12, Ireland. Tel: Dublin 01 569500. FAX: 01 569342.
DIRECTORS
C. M. Anderson, R. J. Whitty

G.H.W. PRODUCTIONS LTD.
52 Queen Anne Street, London, W1M 9LA. Tel: 0171 935 1186.
DIRECTORS
Peter Rogers, Betty E. Box, O.B.E., G. E. Malyon

GAINSBOROUGH (FILM & TV) PICTURES LTD.
8 Queen Street, Mayfair, London, W17 XPH. Tel: 0171 049 1925. FAX: 0171 408 2042.

GALA FILM DISTRIBUTORS LTD.
26 Danbury St., Islington, London, N18JU. Tel: 0171 226 5085. FAX: 0171 226 5897.
MANAGING DIRECTOR & CHIEF EXECUTIVE
Kenneth Rive

GANNET FILMS LTD.
Eton Cottage, 88 Gresham Road, Staines, Middx. TW18 2AE. Tel: 01784 453912.
DIRECTORS
Bob Kellett, Anne Kellett
SECRETARY
B.C. Stebbings

GARRETT, JAMES, & PARTNERS LTD.
25 Bruton Street, London, W1X 7DB. Tel: 0171 499 6452. Telex: 261163. FAX: 0171 409 1797.
DIRECTORS
J. L. M. P. Garrett (Chmn.), M. Gilmour (Managing), D. T. Cromwell (Production Dir.), M. Garrett

GENERAL SCREEN ENTERPRISES
Highbridge Estate, Oxford Road, Uxbridge, Middlesex, UB8 1LX. Tel: 01895 231931. FAX: 01895 235335.
DIRECTOR & GENERAL MANAGER
Fred Chandler

WILLIAM GILBERT ASSOCIATES LTD.
16 Brook Mews North, London W23 BW. Tel: 0171 258 3620. FAX: 0171 723 5100. Telex: 264826 RKOINT G.
DIRECTORS
William G. Gilbert (Managing), M. Gilbert

GINGER FILMS PRODUCTIONS LTD.
39-41 Hanover Steps, St. Georges Fields, Albion Street, London, W2 2YG. Tel: 44 0171 402 7543. Telex: 896559 GECOMS G. FAX: 44 0171 262 5736.
CONTACT
Brian Jackson

GLOBAL ENTERTAINMENT MANAGEMENT LTD.
22 Wadsworth Road, Perivale, Middx. NB6 7JD. Tel: 0181 991 5051. FAX: 0181 998 3521.
CHIEF EXECUTIVE
Claude Heilman
DIRECTOR
P. Kotak

GOLDCREST FILMS AND TELEVISION LTD.
65-66 Dean Street, London, W1V 6PL. Tel: 0171 437 8696. Telex: 267458 GOLDCR. FAX: 0171 437 4448.
CHIEF EXECUTIVE
John Quested

SAMUEL GOLDWYN COMPANY
St. George's House, 14-17 Wells Street, London, W1P 3FP. Tel: 0171 436 5105. FAX: 0171 580 6520.
CONTACT
Diana Hawkins

GRADE COMPANY
8 Queen Street, London, W1X 7PH. Tel: 0171 409 1925. FAX: 0171 408 2042.
CONTACT
Lord Grade

GRANADA GROUP PLC
36 Golden Square, London, W1R 4AH. Tel: 0171 734 8080. Telex: 27937. FAX: 0171 734 8080.
DIRECTORS
Alex Bernstein (Chairman), G. J. Robinson (Chief Executive), C. L. Allen, J. Ashworth, A. W. Clements, I. A. Martin, J. C. Orr, H. E. Staunton, G. J. Parrott, FCIS, G. M. Wallace

GUILD FILM DISTRIBUTION LTD.
Kent House, 14-17 Market Pl., Great Titchfield St., London W1N 8AR. Tel: 0171 323 5151. FAX: 0171 631 3568.
CONTACTS
Alexis Lloyd, Nick Hill

HAMMER FILM PRODUCTIONS LTD.
Millennium Studios, Elstree Way, Herts. WD6 1SF. Tel: 0181 207 401. FAX: 0181 905 1127.
DIRECTORS
Roy Skeggs, Andrew Mitchell

HAMMERWOOD FILM PRODUCTIONS
6 North Street Quadrant, Brighton, BN1 3FA. Tel: 01273 748353. FAX: 01273 822247.

HANDMADE FILMS (DISTRIBUTORS) LTD.
15 Golden Square, London, W1R 2AG. Tel: 0171 434 3122. FAX: 0171 434 3143.
DIRECTORS
Denis O'Brien, Gareth Jones

HARKNESS HALL LTD.
Gate Studios, Station Road, Boreham Wood, Herts., WD6 1DQ. Tel: 0181 953 3611. Cables: Screens, London. Tel: 0181 207 3657. FAX: 441 207 3657.

HEMDALE COMMUNICATIONS LTD.
21 Albion Street, London, W2 2AS. Tel: 0171 724 1010. FAX: 0171 724 9168.
CONTACT
John Smattcombe

JIM HENSON PRODUCTIONS
1 (B) Downshire Hill, Hampstead, London, NW3 1NR. Tel: 0171 431 2818. FAX: 0171 431 3737.
CONTACTS
Duncan Kenworthy, Angus Fletcher, Martin Baker

HIGH POINT FILMS & TELEVISION LTD.
25 Elizabeth Mews, London, NW3 4UH. Tel: 0171 586 3686. FAX: 0171 586 3117.
MANAGING DIRECTOR
Carey Fitzgerald

HIT ENTERTAINMENT PLC
The Pump House, 13-16 Jacobs Well Mews, London, W1H SPD. Tel: 0171 224 1717. FAX: 0171 224 1719.
MANAGING DIRECTOR
Peter Orton

GERARD HOLDSWORTH PRODUCTIONS LTD.
140 Buckingham Palace Road, London, SW1W 95A. Tel: 0171 824 8770. FAX: 0171 824 8762.
DIRECTORS
P. H. Filmer-Sankey, A. M. V. Brunker

IAC FILM SALES
No. 1 Elysium Gate, 126 New Kings Road, London, SW6 4LZ. Tel: 0171 731 8719. FAX: 0171 731 8721.
MANAGING DIRECTOR
Guy Collins
DIRECTOR OF SALES
Penny Wolf

ICA PROJECTS
12 Carlton House Terrace, London, SW1Y 5AH. Tel: 0171 930 0493. FAX: 0171 873 0051.
CONTACT
Simon Field

ITV NETWORK ACQUISITIONS
ITV Network Centre, 200 Gray's Inn Road, London, WCIX 8X2. Tel: 0171 843 8120. Telex: 262988. FAX: 0171 843 8160.
CONTROLLER OF ACQUISITIONS
Pat Mahoney

ITV NETWORK CENTRE
200 Gray's Inn Road, London WC1X 8HF. Tel: 0171 843 8000. FAX: 0171 843 8158.
CHIEF EXECUTIVE
Andrew Quinn
NETWORK DIRECTOR
Marcus Plantin

INIMITABLE LTD.
Greenman, Highmoor, Henley-on-Thames, Oxfordshire RG9 5DH. Tel: 01491 641140. FAX: 01491 641080.
CONTACT
Gerry Anderson

INITIAL FILMS & TV LTD.
74 Black Lion Lane, Hammersmith, London, W6 9BE. Tel: 0181 741 4500. FAX: 0181 741 9416.
CONTACT
Malcolm Gerrie

ISLAND PICTURES
22 St. Peters Square, London, W6 9NW. Tel: 0181 741 1511.

J & M ENTERTAINMENT
2 Dorset Square, London, NW1 6PU. Tel: 0171 723 6544. Telex: 298538. FAX: 0171 724 7541.
CONTACTS
Julia Palau, Michael Ryan

BRIAN JACKSON FILMS LTD.
39-41 Hanover Steps, St. Georges Fields, Albion Street, London, W2 2YG. Tel: 0171 402 7543. Telex: 896559 GECOMS G. FAX: 0171 262 5736.
CONTACT
Brian Jackson

JARAS ENTERTAINMENTS LTD.
Broughton House, 3rd fl., 6-8 Sackville St., London W1X 1DD. Tel: 0171 287 4601. FAX: 0171 287 9652.

KAVUR PRODUCTIONS LTD.
14 Lownes Square, London, SW1X 9HB. Tel: 0171 235 4602. FAX: 0171 235 5215.

KENILWORTH FILM PRODUCTIONS LTD.
Newhouse, Mersham, Ashford, Kent TW2S 6NQ. Tel: 01233 503636. FAX: 01233 502244.
DIRECTORS
Lord Brabourne, Richard Goodwin

KETTLEDRUM FILMS LTD.
37 Connaught Square, London, W2. Tel: 0171 262 0077.

KODAK LIMITED
Professional Motion Imaging, Kodak House, P.O. Box 66, Station Road, Hemel Hempstead, Herts., HP1 1JU. Tel: 01442 61122. FAX: 01442 844458.
DIRECTOR & GENERAL MANAGER
John Parsons-Smith
NATIONAL SALES MANAGER
Denis Kelly

LIBERTY FILMS
4th Floor, The Forum, 74-80 Camden Street, London, NW1 0JL. Tel: 0171 387 5733. FAX: 0171 383 95368.
CONTACTS
Teresa Kelleher, John Kelleher

LIGHTWORKS EDITING SYSTEMS LTD.
31-32 Soho Square, London, W1V 6AP. Tel: 0171 494 3084. FAX: 0171 437 3570.

LIMELIGHT FILMS
3 Bromley Place, London, W1P 5HB. Tel: 0171 255 3939. FAX: 0171 436 4334.
CONTACT
Sally Woodward

LONDON FILM PRODUCTIONS LTD.
Kent House, 14-17 Market Place, Great Titchfield Street, London, W1N 8AR. Tel: 0171 323 5251. FAX: 0171 436 2834.
CONTACT
Andrew Luff

LONDON INDEPENDENT PRODUCERS LTD.
52 Queen Anne Street, London, W1M 9LA. Tel: 0171 935 1186.
DIRECTORS
William MacQuitty, Mrs. B. E. MacQuitty, Ralph Thomas, Leonora Dossett

LUCIDA PRODUCTIONS LTD.
53 Greek Street, London, WIV 5LR. Tel: 0171 437 1140. FAX: 0171 287 5335.
DIRECTORS
Paul Joyce, Chris Rodley

LUMIERE PICTURES LTD.
(Please see UGC UK Ltd.)

MTM ARDMORE STUDIOS LTD.
Herbert Road, Bray, Co. Wicklow, Ireland. Tel: Dublin 862971. FAX: Dublin 861894. Telex: 91504 PATT E1.

MTV EUROPE
Hawley Crescent, London NW1 8TT. Tel: 0171 284 7777. FAX: 0171 284 7788.
DIRECTOR OF CORPORATE COMMUNICATIONS
Monique Amaudry

MAINLINE PICTURES
37 Museum Street, London, WC1A 1LP. Tel: 0171 242 5523. FAX: 0171 430 0170.
MANAGING DIRECTOR
Romaine Hart

MAJESTIC FILMS AND TELEVISION INTERNATIONAL
P.O. Box 13, Gloucester Mansions, Cambridge Circus, London, WC2H 8XD. Tel: 0171 836 8630. FAX: 0171 836 5819. Telex: 46601 BTGKA G.
CHIEF EXECUTIVE
Guy East

MANAGEMENT COMPANY ENTERTAINMENT GROUP INC.
Portobello Dock, 328 Kensal Road, London W10 5XJ. Tel: 0171 968 8888. FAX: 0171 968 8537.

MAYFAIR CINEMAS & THEATRES UK LTD.
110 St. Martin's Lane, London, WC2N 4AD. Tel: 0171 867 1131.

MEDIA RELEASING DISTRIBUTORS LTD.
27 Soho Square, London, W1V 5FL. Tel: 0171 437 2341. Telex: 943763 CROCOM G (MRD). FAX: 0171 734 2483.
DIRECTORS
Trevor H. Green, J. Green

MEDUSA COMMUNICATIONS LTD.
Regal Chambers, 51 Bancroft, Hitchin, Herts., SG5 1LL. Tel: 01462 421818. FAX: 01462 420393.
CHAIRMAN
David Hodgins
EXECUTIVE DIRECTOR
Stephen Rivers

MERCHANT IVORY PRODUCTIONS
46 Lexington Street, London W1P 3LH. Tel: 0171 437 1200. FAX: 0171 734 1579.
CONTACTS
Ismail Merchant, James Ivory

MERSHAM PRODUCTIONS LTD.
Newhouse, Mersham, Ashford, Kent. TW25 6NQ. Tel: 01233 503636. FAX: 01233 502244.
DIRECTORS
Lord Brabourne, Michael-John Knatchbull, Richard Goodwin

METRO TARTAN LTD.
79 Wardour Street, London, WIV 3TH. Tel: 0171 734 8508. FAX: 0171 287 2112.

METROCOLOUR LONDON LTD.
91-95 Gillespie Road, London, N5 1LS. Tel: 0171 226 4422; 22 Soho Square, London, W1V 5FL. Tel: 0171 437 7811. FAX: 0171 359 2353.
DIRECTORS
K. B. Fraser (Managing), D. A. Compton, C. P. Smith, C. Young, M. Hillier, E. Senat

METROPOLIS MEDIA
P.O. Box 2875, London, W6 O2X. Tel: 0181 563 7989. FAX: 0181 563 8867.
CHIEF EXECUTIVE
Tony Stephens

MIRACLE COMMUNICATIONS LTD.
69 New Oxford Street, London, WC1A 1DG. Tel: 0171 379 5006. FAX: 0171 528 7772.

MIRAMAX FILMS (UK)
Prominent Studios, 68A Delancey Street, London, NW1 7RY. Tel: 0171 284 0242. FAX: 0171 267 9666.
CONTACT
Anne Greenhalgh

MOLLIKO FILMS (LONDON) LTD.
16-18 New Bridge Street, London, EC4V 6AU. Tel: 0171 262 0638. Cables: Umeshmalik, London, EC4.
CHAIRMAN & MANAGING DIRECTOR
Umesh Mallik, B.A., India
DIRECTOR-PRODUCTION
Bina Chatterjee (Miss)
GENERAL MANAGER IN INDIA
P.C. Mallik, BSC, B.L.
SCRIPT EDITOR
Janet Bennett

MOVING PICTURE COMPANY
25 Noel Street, London, W1V 3RD. Tel: 0171 434 3100. FAX: 0171 437 3951.
CONTACT
David Jeffers

MUSEUM OF THE MOVING IMAGE
South Bank, Waterloo, London, SE1 8XT. Tel: 0171 928 3535. FAX: 0171 815 1378.
CURATOR
Leslie Hardcastle, OBE

N.F.H. LTD.
37 Ovington Square, London, SW3 1LJ. Tel: 0171 584 7561. FAX: 0171 589 1863.
MANAGING DIRECTOR
Norma Heyman

NAMARA LTD.
51 Beak Street, London, W1R 3LF. Tel: 0171 437 9524. FAX: 0171 734 1844.
EXECUTIVE PRODUCER
Naim Attallah

NATIONAL FILM BOARD OF CANADA
1 Grosvenor Square, London, WIX OAB. Tel: 0171 258 6480. FAX: 0171 258 6532.
CONTACT
Jane Taylor

NATIONAL SCREEN
15 Wadsworth Road, Greenford, Middlesex, UB6 7JN. Tel: 0181 998 2851. FAX: 0181 997 0840; 2 Wedgwood Mews, 12-13 Greek Street, London, W1V 6BH. Tel: 0171 437 4851. FAX: 0171 287 0328.
DIRECTORS
John Mahony, Brian Mcmail, Norman Darkins

NELSON ENTERTAINMENT
8 Queen Street, London, W1X 7PH. Tel: 0171 493 3362. FAX: 0171 409 0503. Telex: 8950483 NELSON G.

NEW WORLD TRANS ATLANTIC PICTURES (UK) LTD.
27 Soho Square, London, W1V 5FL. Tel: 0171 434 0497. FAX: 0171 434 0490.

OASIS FILM DISTRIBUTION
155-157 Oxford Street, London, W1R 1TB. Tel: 0171 734 7477. FAX: 0171 734 7470.
MANAGING DIRECTOR
Peter Buckingham

ODEON CINEMAS LTD.
(A subsidiary of the Rank Organisation PLC.)
439-445 Godstone Road, Whyteleafe, Surrey. Tel: 088362 3355. FAX: 01883 626717. Telex: 262305 088362 6044.
54 Whitcomb Street, London, WC2H 7DN. Tel: 0171 839 6373. FAX: 0171 321 0357.
MANAGING DIRECTOR
Hugh Corrance
BOOKING EXECUTIVE
Michael Archibald
MARKETING EXECUTIVE
Stuart Francis

OPTICAL FILM EFFECTS LTD.
Pinewood Studios, Iver Heath, Bucks., SL0 0NH. Tel: 01753 655486. Telex: 847505 Pinew G. FAX: 01753 656844.
DIRECTORS
R. W. Field, R. A. Dimbleby

OVERVIEW FILMS LTD.
16 Brook Mews North, London, W2 3BW. Tel: 0171 258 3620. FAX: 0171 723 5100. Telex: 2 64826 RKOINT 6.
CONTACT
William G. Gilbert

OXFORD SCIENTIFIC FILMS
Lower Road, Long Hanborough, Oxon OX8 8LL. Tel: 0993 881881. FAX: 0993 882808.
10 Poland Street, London, W1. Tel: 0171 494 0720. FAX: 0171 287 9125.
MANAGING DIRECTOR
Karen Goldie-Morrison

PALOMAR PICTURES INTERNATIONAL (UK) LTD.
5 Chancery Lane, Clifford's Inn, London, EC4A 1BU.

DAVID PARADINE PRODUCTIONS LTD.
5 St. Mary Abbots Place, Kensington, London, W86LS. Tel: 0171 371 3111. FAX: 0171 602 0411.

PARALLAX PICTURES
Denmark Street, London, WC2H 8LS. Tel: 0171 836 1478. FAX: 0171 497 8062.
DIRECTOR
Ken Loach

PARAMOUNT BRITISH PICTURES LTD.
Twickenham Film Studios Ltd., The Barons, St. Margaret's, Twickenham, Middx. TW1 2AW. Tel: 0181 892 4477. Telex: 8814497. FAX: 0181 891 0168.

PARAMOUNT PICTURES (UK) LTD.
UIP House, 45 Beadon Road, Hammersmith, London, W6 0EG. Tel: 0181 563 4220. FAX: 0181 563 4266.
SENIOR V.P., INTERNATIONAL MARKETING
Leslie Pound

PARK ENTERTAINMENT LTD.
Mortlake Court, 28 Sheen Court, London, SW14 8LW. Tel: 0181 876 0207. FAX: 0181 876 4686.

PEARL & DEAN LTD.
Woolverstone House, 61-62 Berners Street, London, WIP 3AE. Tel: 0171 636 5252. FAX: 0171 637 3191.
MANAGING DIRECTOR
Peter Howard Williams

PHOENIX FILMS LTD.
6 Flitcroft St., London WC2 8DJ. Tel: 0171 836 5000. FAX: 0171 836 3060.
DIRECTORS
Lewis More O'Ferrall, Alan Taylor

PINEWOOD STUDIOS LTD.
(A subsidiary of the Rank Organisation PLC. Film and TV studios; goods and services relating to the manufacture of cinematograph and television films.)
Pinewood Road, Iver, Buckinghamshire SL0 0NH. Tel: (Iver) 651700. Telex: 847505. FAX: 01753 656844.
MANAGING DIRECTOR
Steve Jaggs

PLATO FILMS LTD.
247a Upper Street, London, N1 1RU. Tel: 0171 226 2298.
GENERAL MANAGER
Stanley Forman

POLYGRAM FILMED ENTERTAINMENT
8 St. James Square, London, SW1 4JV. Tel: 0171 747 4000. FAX: 0171 747 4499.
CONTACT
Stuart Till

POLYGRAM FILM INTERNATIONAL
76 Oxford St., London W1N 0HQ. Tel: 0171 307 1300. FAX: 0171 307 1355.
PRESIDENT
Aline Perry

PORTMAN PRODUCTIONS
Advance House, 105 Ladbroke Grove, London W11 1PG. Tel: 0171 468 3400. FAX: 0171 468 3499.
CONTACT
Victor Glynn

PORTMAN ZENITH GROUP LTD.
43-45 Dorset Street, London, W1H 4AB. Tel: 0171 224 3344. FAX: 0171 224 1057.
DIRECTORS
Victor Glynn, John Hall, John Sivers, Simon Cox, Andrew Warren, Richard Leworthy, Scott Meek, Dorothy Berwin, Ivan Rendall

PORTOBELLO PICTURES
42 Tavistock Road, London W1I 1AW. Tel: 0171 379 5566. FAX: 0171 379 5599.
EXECUTIVE PRODUCER/DIRECTOR
Eric Abraham

POST OFFICE FILM & VIDEO UNIT
(Archival Material) 130 Old Street, London EC1V 9PQ. Tel: 0171 320 7125. FAX: 0171 320 7209.
CONTACT
Alma Headland

PROMINENT FEATURES LTD.
Prominent Studios, 68A Delancey Street, London, NW1 7RY. Tel: 0171 284 0242. FAX: 0171 284 1004.
DIRECTORS
Steve Abbott, Terry Gilliam, Eric Idle, Anne James, Terry Jones, Michael Palin

PYTHON (MONTY) PICTURES LTD.
Prominent Studios, 68A Delancey Street, London, NW1 7RY. Tel: 0171 284 0242. FAX: 0171 284 1004.
DIRECTORS
John Cleese, Terry Gilliam, Eric Idle, Terry Jones, Michael Palin

Q FILM PRODUCTIONS LTD.
Rosehill House, Rose Hill, Nr. Burnham, Bucks. SL1 8NN. Tel: 0168 605129.
DIRECTORS
I. E. L. Shand, D. J. Bennet, F. Shand

QUIGLEY PUBLICATIONS
15 Samuel Road, Langdon Hills, Basildon, Essex, SS16 6EZ. Tel: 01268 417055.
UK MANAGER
William Pay

QWERTYUIOP PRODUCTIONS LTD.
118-120 Wardour Street, London, W1 4BT. Tel: 0171 437 3224. FAX: 0171 437 3674.
MANAGING DIRECTOR
David Land

RANK BRIMAR LTD.
(A subsidiary of the Rank Organisation PLC.).
Greenside Way, Middleton, Manchester M24 1SN. Tel: 0161 681 7072. Telex: 665326. FAX: 0161 682 3818.
MANAGING DIRECTOR
Dr. Richard Fenby

RANK CINTEL LTD.
(A subsidiary of the Rank Organisation PLC. Manufacturer of telecine equipment for broadcast and film/tape transfer.) Watton Road, Ware, Hertfordshire SG12 OAE. Tel: 01920 463939. Telex: 81415. FAX: 01920 460803.
MANAGING DIRECTOR
Jack R. Brittain

RANK FILM DISTRIBUTORS LTD.
(A subsidiary of the Rank Organisation PLC. Distribution of cinematograph films.)
127 Wardour Street, London, W1V 4AD. Tel: 0171 437 9020. Telex: 262556. FAX: 0171 434 3689.
MANAGING DIRECTOR
Frederick Turner

RANK FILM LABORATORIES LTD.
(A subsidiary of the Rank Organisation PLC. Processing of colour and black and white film for cinema and television.)
North Orbital Road, Denham, Uxbridge, Middlesex, UB9 5HQ. Tel: 01895 832323. FAX: 01895 833617. Telex: 934704.
MANAGING DIRECTOR
Trevor McCurdie
DIRECTOR OF SALES
David Dowler

THE RANK ORGANISATION PLC
6 Connaught Place, London, W2 2EZ. Tel: 0171 706 1111. Telex: 263549. FAX: 0171 262 9886.
DIRECTORS
Sir Denys Henderson (Chairman), Andrew Teare (Managing Director and Chief Executive), Dr. David V. Atterton, James Daly, Michael Jackaman, Anthony W. Stenham, Douglas M. Yates, Nigel V. Turnbull (Finance Director), J. F. Garrett, Peter J. Jarvic, Hugh R. Jenkins.

RANK PRECISION INDUSTRIES LTD.
(A subsidiary of the Rank Organisation PLC)
Watton Road, Ware, Herts, SG12 OAE. Tel: 01920 3929. FAX: 01920 461137.

RANK TAYLOR HOBSON LTD.
(A subsidiary of the Rank Organisation PLC. Manufacturer of precision measurement equipment, professional cine lenses.)
P.O. Box 36, 2 New Star Road, Thurmaston Lane, Leicester LE3 7JQ. Tel: 01533 763771. Telex: 342338. FAX: 01533 740167.
MANAGING DIRECTOR
Richard Freeman

RANK VIDEO SERVICES AMERICA INC.
(A subsidiary of the Rank Organisation PLC)
Corporate Centre, 540 Lake Cook Road, Suite 200, Deerfield, Illinois 60015, U.S.A. Tel: (708) 291 1150. FAX: (708) 480 6077.
PRESIDENT & CEO
David Cuyler

RANK VIDEO SERVICES LTD.
(A subsidiary of the Rank Organisation PLC. Operation of video and broadcast facilities and video cassette duplication.)
Phoenix Park Great West Road, Brentford, Middlesex, TW8 9PL. Tel: 0181 568 4311. Telex: 22345. FAX: 0181 847 4032.
MANAGING DIRECTOR
Peter Pacitti

RECORDED PICTURE CO. LTD.
8-12 Broadwick St., London, W1V 1FH. Tel: 0171 439 0607. FAX: 0171 434 1192.
DIRECTORS
Jeremy Thomas, Hercules Bellville, Chris Auty

RED ROOSTER FILM & TELEVISION ENTERTAINMENT
29 Floral Street, London, WC2E 9DP. Tel: 0171 379 7727. FAX: 0171 379 5756.
CHIEF EXECUTIVE
Linda James

REDIFFUSION FILMS LTD.
P.O. Box 451, Buchanan House, 3 St. James's Square, London, SW1Y 4LS. Tel: 0171 925 0550. Telex: 919673. Cables: Rediffuse. FAX: (Group 3) 0171 839 7135.

REUTERS TELEVISION LTD.
40 Cumberland Avenue, London, NW10 7EH. Tel: 0181 965 7733. FAX: 0181 965 0620.
DIRECTOR
Enrique Jara
HEAD OF NEWS
Stephen Claypole

PETER ROGERS PRODUCTIONS LTD.
Pinewood Studios, Iver Heath, Bucks. SL0 0NH. Tel: 01753 651700. FAX: 01753 656844.
DIRECTORS
Peter Rogers, B. E. Rogers, G. E. Malyon

ROMULUS FILMS LTD.
214, The Chambers, Chelsea Harbour, London, SW10 0XF. Tel: 0171 376 3791. FAX: 0171 352 7457.
DIRECTORS
Sir John Woolf (Chairman), J. C. Woolf, M.A. (Executive Director), Lady Woolf, C. E. Fielding

ROYAL SOCIETY FOR THE PROTECTION OF BIRDS (RSPB)
Film and Video Unit, The Lodge, Sandy, Beds. SG19 2DL. Tel: 01767 680551. Telex: 82469 RSPB. FAX: 01767 692365.
FILM & VIDEO MANAGER
Colin Skevington

SAFIR FILMS LTD.
49 Littleton Road, Harrow, Middx. HA1 3SY. Tel: 0181 423 0763. FAX: 0181 423 7963.
CONTACT
Lawrence Safir

SALAMANDER FILM PRODUCTIONS LTD.
Seven Pines, Wentworth, Surrey. FAX: 01344 845174.
DIRECTORS
Bryan Forbes, Nanette Forbes, John L. Hargreaves

SALES COMPANY, THE
62 Shaftesbury Ave., London, W1V 7AA. Tel: 0171 434 9061. FAX: 0171 494 3293.
CONTACT
Alison Thompson

SCIMITAR FILMS LTD.
6-8 Sackville Street, London, W1X 1DD. Tel: 0171 734 8385. FAX: 0171 602 9217.
DIRECTORS
Michael Winner, M.A. (Cantab), John Fraser, M.A. (Oxon), M.Phil

SCOTT FREE ENTERPRISES LTD.
6-10 Lexington St., London, W1R 36S. Tel: 0171 437 7426.

SETAN A STUDIOS LTD.
Ardmore Studios, Herbert Road, Bray, Co. Wicklow, Ireland. Tel: Dublin 286 2971. FAX: Dublin 286 1894.
CONTACT
Tracey Richardson

SHAND PICTURES LTD.
Rosehill House, Rose Hill Nr. Burnham, Bucks SL1 8NN. Tel: 0168 605129.
DIRECTORS
I. E. L. Shand, D. J. Bennett, F. Shand

SHEPPERTON STUDIOS
Studios Road, Shepperton, Middx. TW17 0QD. Tel: 01932 562611. FAX: 01932 568989.
CONTACT
Paul Oliver

SIEGE PRODUCTIONS LTD.
17 Adam's Row, London, W1. Tel: 0171 493 44412.
MANAGING DIRECTOR
Peter Fetterman

SKREBA FILMS LTD.
5a Noel St., London, W1V 3RB. Tel: 0171 437 6492. FAX: 0171 437 0644.

SMART EGG PICTURES
62 Brompton Road, London, SW3 1BW. Tel: 0171 581 1841. Telex: 27786 GZOM G. FAX: 0171 581 8998.
CONTACT
Tom Stoberg

SOVEREIGN PICTURES INC.
10 Greek Street, London, W1V 5LE. Tel: 0171 494 1010. FAX: 0171 494 3949. Telex: 261564 SOVE G.

STIGWOOD, ROBERT, ORGANISATION LTD.
118-120 Wardour Street, London. Tel: 0171 437 2512. Telex: 264267.
DIRECTORS
Robert Stigwood, David Land, David Herring

STRAND LIGHTING LTD.
(A subsidiary of the Rank Organisation PLC)
Grant Way, off Syon Lane, Isleworth, Middx. TW7 5QD. Tel: 0181 560 3171. FAX: 0181 490 0002.
MANAGING DIRECTOR
Christopher Waldron

TKO COMMUNICATIONS LTD.
P.O. Box 130, Hove, East Sussex, BN3 6QV. Tel: 01273 550088. FAX: 01273 540969.
DIRECTORS
J. S. Kruger, R. Kruger

TARGET INTERNATIONAL LTD.
A-29 Barwell Business Park, Leatherhead Road, Chessington Castle, Surrey KT9 2NY. Tel: 0181 974 1021. FAX: 0181 974 2674.
CHAIRMAN
Terry Shand
MANAGING DIRECTOR
Geoffrey Kerpin

TARTAN FILMS LTD.
40 Bernard St., London, WC1N 1LG. Tel: 0171 837 3377. FAX: 0171 833 4102.
CONTACT
Hamish McAlpine

TECHNICOLOR LTD.
(Subsidiary of Carlton Communication PLC.)
Bath Road, West Drayton, Middlesex, UB7 0DB. Tel: 0181 759 5432; Telegraphic and Cable Address: Technicolor, West Drayton. FAX: 0181 897 2666.
DIRECTORS
Ashley Hopkins (Mng. Dir. & CEO), S. T. Baxter, D. Abdoo, G. Filardi (Italy).

TELEFILM CANADA
22 Kingly Court, London, W1R 5LE. Tel: 0171 437 8308. FAX: 0171 734 8586.
INTERIM DIRECTOR
Bill Niven

TILIRIS FILM PRODUCTIONS
13A Fitzgeorge Ave., London W14 0SY. Tel: 0171 602 2824. FAX: 0171 371 4709.

TRING ENTERTAINMENTS
Twickenham Film Studios, St. Margarets, Twickenham, TW1 2AW, Middx. Tel: 0181 892 4477. FAX: 0181 891 5574.
DIRECTORS
Maurice Landsberger, Nabil Daou

TROY FILMS, LTD.
Film Rights Ltd., Hammer House, 113 Wardour Street, London, W1V 4EH. Tel: 0171 437 7151.
DIRECTORS
Michael Anderson, Maurice Lambert

TURNER INTERNATIONAL
19-22 Rathbone Place, London, W1P 1DF. Tel: 0171 637 6900.
CONTACT
Howard Karshan

TWENTIETH CENTURY FOX FILM CO. LTD.
20th Century House, 31-32 Soho Square, London, W1V 6AP. Tel: 0171 437 7766. FAX: 0171 434 2170.
DIRECTORS
S. Moore, P. Livingstone

TWICKENHAM FILM STUDIOS LTD.
St. Margarets, Twickenham, Middlesex, TW1 2AW. Tel: 0181 892 4477. FAX: 0181 891 0168.
CONTACT
G. Humphreys

UGC UK LTD.
(Formerly Lumiere Pictures Ltd.)
24 av Charles de Gaulle, 92522 Neuilly-sur-Seine, France. Tel: 33146 404400. FAX: 33146 243728.
CHAIRMAN
Alain Sussfeld
EXECUTIVE V.P. (UK)
Louisa Dent

UNION PICTURES
36 Marshall Street, London, W1V 1LL. Tel: 0171 287 5100. FAX: 0171 287 3770.
DIRECTORS
Brad Adams, Franc Roddam, Geoff Deeham
CONTACT
Richard Kalms

UNITED ARTISTS SCREEN ENTERTAINMENT LTD.
84-86 Regent Street, London, W1R 5PF. Tel: 0171 915 1717. FAX: 0171 915 1702.
DIRECTORS
Trevor Fetter, Brian Yell
CONTACT
Paul Hudson

UNITED CINEMAS INTERNATIONAL UK LTD.
Lee House, 90 Great Bridgewater Street, Manchester, MI 5JW. Tel: 0161 455 4000. FAX: 0161 455 4079.
MANAGING DIRECTOR
Steve Knibbs

UNITED INTERNATIONAL PICTURES
(A subsidiary of United International Pictures B.V., Postbus 9255, 1006 AG Amsterdam, The Netherlands.)
UIP House, 45 Beadon Road, Hammersmith, London, W6 0EG. Tel: 0181 741 9041. Telex: 8956521. FAX: 0181 748 8990.
PRESIDENT & CEO
Michael Williams-Jones
SENIOR V.P., GENERAL COUNSEL
Brian Reilly
SENIOR V.P., MARKETING
Hy Smith

SENIOR V.P., FINANCE & ADMINISTRATION
Peter Charles
SENIOR V.P., INTERNATIONAL SALES
Andrew Cripps
V.P., PUBLICITY
Anne Bennett
V.P., PROMOTIONS
Mark deQuervain
V.P., SALES, LATIN AMERICA
Michael Murphy
V.P., SALES, EUROPE
Tony Themistocleous
SENIOR EXEC./GENERAL MANAGER—PAY-TV GROUP
Andrew Kaza

UNITED INTERNATIONAL PICTURES (UK)
Mortimer House, 37-41 Mortimer Street, London, W1A 2JL. Tel: 0171 636 1655. FAX: 0171 637 4043 (Mng. Dir.). FAX: 0171 636 4118 (Accounts/Sales). FAX: 0171 323 0121 (Publicity).
MANAGING DIRECTOR
Christopher Hedges
DIRECTOR OF MARKETING
Ken Green

UNIVERSAL PICTURES LTD.
c/o UIP House, 45 Beadon Rd., Hammersmith, London, W6 0EG. Tel: 0181 563 4329. FAX: 0181 563 4331.

VICTOR FILMS COMPANY
2B Chandos Street, London, W1M 0EH. Tel: 0171 636 6620. FAX: 0171 636 6620.
MANAGING DIRECTOR
Vic Bateman

VIDEO COLLECTION INTERNATIONAL
36 Caxton Way, Watford Herts, WD1 8VF. Tel: 01923 55558.

VIRGIN CINEMAS LTD.
Adelaide House, 626 High Road., Chiswick, London W4 5RY. Tel: 0181 987 5000. FAX: 0181 742 2998.
COMMERCIAL DIRECTOR
Margaret Taylor
BOOKING MANAGER
Joe Nunes

VISUAL PROGRAMME SYSTEMS LTD.
Sardinia House, 52 Lincoln's Inn Fields, London, WC2A 2L2. Tel: 0171 405 0438. FAX: 0171 831 9668.
CONTACT
Bernard Gilinsky

WALPORT INTERNATIONAL LTD.
(Subsidiary of Novo Communications)
15 Park Road, London, NW1 6XH. Tel: 0171 258 3977. FAX: 0171 723 9568.
DIRECTORS
C. Preuster, S. Campion

WARNER BROS. DISTRIBUTORS LTD.
135 Wardour Street, London, W1V 4AP. Tel: 0171 437 5600. Telex: 22653. FAX: 0171 465 4869.
DIRECTORS
R. Fox, C. Young, E. Savat, W. Duband, C. Lima

WARNER BROS. OPERATIONAL DIVISION
135 Wardour Street, London, W1V 4AP. Tel: 0171 734 8400. FAX: 0171 437 2950.
MANAGING DIRECTOR
Maj-Britt Kirchner

WARNER BROS. PRODUCTIONS LTD.
Warner Suite, Pinewood Studios, Iver Heath, Bucks., SL0 0NH. Tel: 01753 654545.
DIRECTORS
R. D. Button (Managing), E. H. Senat, A. R. Parsons

WELBECK FILM DISTRIBUTORS, LTD.
52 Queen Anne Street, London, W1M 9LA. Tel: 0171 935 1186.
DIRECTORS
Mrs. B. E. Rogers, R. P. Thomas, J. Thomas

WEST ONE FILM PRODUCERS LTD.
c/o Cooper Murray, Princess House, 50-60 Eastcastle Street, London, W1A 4BY. Tel: 0171 436 4773. FAX: 0171 436 1889.
DIRECTOR
Anthony Simmons

MICHAEL WHITE PRODUCTIONS LTD.
13 Duke St., St. James', London, SW1Y 6DB. Tel: 0171 839 3971. FAX: 0171 839 3836.
DIRECTORS
Michael S. White, Louise M. White

WORLD FILM SERVICES LTD.
Pinewood Studios, Iver Heath, Bucks, SL0 0NH. Tel: 01753 656501. FAX: 01753 656475.
CONTACT
Richard Dalton

WORKING TITLE FILMS LTD.
1 Water Lane, Kentish Town Road, London, NW1 8NZ. Tel: 0171 911 6100. Telex: 914106. FAX: 0171 911 6150/1.
CONTACTS
Tim Bevan, Eric Fellner

WORLD FILM SERVICES LTD.
12-14 Argyll Street, London, W1V 1AB. Tel: 0171 734 3536. FAX: 0171 437 4098.
DIRECTORS
John Heyman (Chairman), John Chambers (Managing), Michael Simkins

WORLDMARK PRODUCTIONS LTD.
The Old Studio, 18 Middle Row, London, W10 5AT. Tel: 0181 960 3251. FAX: 0181 960 6150.

DIRECTORS
Drummond Challis, David Wooster

WORLD WIDE GROUP LTD.
21-25 St. Anne's Court, London, W1V 3AW. Tel: 0171 434 1121. FAX: 0171 734 0619.
CONTACTS
R. King, R. Townsend, M. Rosenbaum, C. Courtenay Taylor

YOUNG, CHRISTOPHER, FILMS LTD.
102 Brandon Street, London, SE17 1AL. Tel: 0171 708 0820.

ZENITH GROUP
43-45 Dorset Street, London W1H 4AB. Tel: 0171 224 2440. FAX: 0171 224 3194.
DIRECTOR OF PRODUCTION
Scott Meek

FINANCIAL SERVICES

ARTS COUNCIL FILMS
14 Great Peter Street, London, SW1P 3NQ. Tel: 0171 973 6454. FAX: 0171 973 6581.

BARCLAYS BANK PLC
The Media Section, Barclays Business Centre, 27 Soho Square, London, W1A 4WA. Tel: 0171 439 6851. FAX: 0171 434 9035.

BRITISH & COMMONWEALTH MERCHANT BANK PLC
62 Cannon Street, London, EC4N 6AE. Tel: 0171 248 0900. FAX: 0171 528 8444. Telex: 884040 BCMB G.

BRITISH SCREEN FINANCE LTD.
14-17 Wells Street, London, W1P 3FL. Tel: 0171 323 9080. FAX: 0171 323 0092.

COMPLETION BOND COMPANY INC.
Pinewood Studios, Iver Heath, Bucks. SL0 0NH. Tel: 01753 651700. FAX: 01753 655697.

CONSOLIDATED ARTISTS
Strachans Somerville, Phillips Street, St. Helier, Jersey, Channel Islands. Tel: 01534 71505. FAX: 01534 23902.

CONTRACTS INTERNATIONAL LTD.
13-14 Golden Square, London, W1R 3AG. Tel: 0171 287 5800. FAX: 0171 287 3779. Telex: 295835.

ERNST & YOUNG
Beckett House, 1 Lambeth Palace Road, London, SE1 7EU. Tel: 0171 928 2000. FAX: 0171 401 2136.

EUROPEAN SCRIPT FUND
39C Highbury Place, London, N5 1QP. Tel: 0171 226 9903. FAX: 0171 354 2706.

ILM FINANCES LTD.
1-11 Hay Hill, Berkeley Square, London, W1X 7LF. Tel: 0171 629 6557. Telex: 298060 FILFIN G. FAX: 0171 491 7530.

FILM TRUSTEES LTD.
Swan House, 52 Poland Street, London, W1V 3DF Tel: 0171 439 8541. FAX: 0171 495 3223. Telex: 23788.

FILMAKER COMPLETION (UK) LTD.
Millard House, Cutler Street, London, E1 7DJ. Tel: 0171 283 3951. Telex: 8956132 ROBTAY G. FAX: 0171 621 0140.

INTERNATIONAL COMPLETION INC.
Pinewood Studios, Pinewood Road, Iver Heath, Bucks. SL0 0NH. Tel: 01753 651 700. FAX: 01753 656 564.

INVESTORS LEASE MANAGEMENT GROUP
Economist's Bldg., 268 St. James St., London, SW1A 1HA. Tel: 0171 839 2336. FAX: 0171 930 3793.

J & M ENTERTAINMENT
2 Dorset Square, London, NW1 6PU. Tel: 0171 723 6544. FAX: 0171 724 7541.

KMPG PEAT MARWICK
1 Puddle Dock, Blackfriars, London, EC4V 3PD. Tel: 0171 236 8000. FAX: 0171 248 6552.

GUINNESS MAHON & CO. LTD.
32 St. Mary at Hill, London, EC3P 3AJ. Tel: 0171 623 9333. FAX: 0171 283 4811.

MANDEMAR FINANCE LTD.
113-117 Wardour St., London W1V 3TD. Tel: 0171 434 9729. FAX: 0171-734 4970.

MEDIA GUARANTORS INTERNATIONAL INC.
38 Dover St., London, W1X 3PB. Tel: 0171 491 7311. FAX: 0171 493 6729.

SAMUEL MONTAGU & CO. LTD.
10 Lower Thames Street, London EC3R 6AE. Tel: 0171 260 9000. FAX: 0171 488 1630.

MOTION PICTURE GUARANTORS LTD.
Production Centre, 40-44 Clipstone St., London, W1P 7EA. Tel: 0171 323 3220. FAX: 0171 637 2590.

ONE WORLD COMMUNICATIONS
1 Wardour Mews, London, W1V 3FF. Tel: 0171 437 8381.

PARMEAD INSURANCE BROKERS LTD.
Artillery House, 35 Artillery Lane, London, E1 7LR. Tel: 0181 467 8656.

PERFORMANCE GUARANTEES LTD.
113-117 Wardour St., London, W1V 3TD. Tel: 0171 434 9729. FAX: 0171 734 4970.

PIERSON, HELDRING & PIERSON
99 Gresham Street, London, EC2V 7PH. Tel: 0171 696 0500. FAX: 0171 600 1732. Telex: 885119.

PRODUCTION PROJECTS FUND, BFI
29 Rathbone Place, London, W1P 1AG. Tel: 0171 636 5587. FAX: 0171 780 9456.

RUBEN SEDGWICK INSURANCE SERVICES
Pinewood Studios, Pinewood Road, Iver, Bucks. SL0 0NH. Tel: 01753 654 555. FAX: 01753 653 152.

SCOTTISH FILM PRODUCTION FUND
74 Victoria Crescent Road, Glasgow, G12 9JN. Tel: 0141 337 2526. FAX: 0141 337 2562.

SPECTRUM ENTERTAINMENT GROUP PLC
The Pines, 11 Putney Hill, London, SW15 6BA. Tel: 0181 780 2525. FAX: 0181 780 1671. Telex: 262433.

STOY HAYWARD
8 Baker Street, London, W1M 1DA. Tel: 0171 486 5888. FAX: 0171 487 3686. Contact: Carl Williams.

TOUCHE ROSS
Hill House, 1 Little New Street, London, EC4A 3TR. Tel: 0171 936 3000. FAX: 0171 538 8517.

UBA LTD.
Pinewood Studios, Pinewood Road, Iver Heath, Bucks. SL0 0NH. Tel: 01753 656699. FAX: 01753 656844.

UNITED MEDIA LTD.
2nd fl., Broadwick House, 8-12 Broadwick St., London, W1V 4EQ. Tel: 0171 434 3501. FAX: 0171 734 8893.

WASA FILM FINANCE CORP. LTD.
49 Park Lane, London, W1V 4EQ. Tel: 0171 491 2822. FAX: 0171 493 3710.

WILLIS WRIGHTSON LONDON LTD.
Willis Wrightson House, Wood Street, Kingston-upon-Thames, Surrey KT1 1UG. Tel: 0171 860 6000. Telex: 929606. FAX: 0181 943 4297.

BRITISH AND IRISH STUDIO FACILITIES AND LABORATORIES

Studio Facilities

ABBEY ROAD STUDIOS
3 Abbey Road, St. John's Wood, London, NW8 9AY. Tel: 0171 286 1161. FAX: 0171 289 7527.

ANVIL FILM AND RECORDING GROUP LTD.
Denham Studios, North Orbital Road, Denham, Nr. Uxbridge, Middlesex, UB9 5HH. Tel: 01895 833522. Telex: 934704 FAX: 01895 833617.

ARDMORE STUDIOS LTD.
Herbert Road, Bray, Co. Wicklow, Ireland. Tel: Dublin 286 2971. FAX: Dublin 286 1894. Contact: Kevin Moriarty.

BRAY STUDIOS
Windsor Road, Windsor, Berks. SL4 5UG. Tel: 01628 22111. FAX: 01628 770381. Contact: Karen Jones.

CENTRAL TELEVISION STUDIOS
Lenton Lane, Nottingham NG7 2NA. Tel: 01602 863322. FAX: 01602 435142. Contact: Nic Beeby.

DE LANE LEA SOUND CENTRE
75 Dean Street, London, W1V 5HA. Tel: 0171 439 1721. FAX: 0171 437 0913. Contact: Richard Paynter.

EALING STUDIOS
Ealing Green, Ealing, London, W5 5EP. Tel: 0181 567 6655. FAX: 0181 758 8579. Contact: Bernie Pearson.

FOUNTAIN TELEVISION
128 Wembley Park Drive, Wembley, Middx., HA9 8HQ. Tel: 0181 900 1188. FAX: 0181 900 2860. Contact: Brianan Dolan.

HALLIFORD FILM STUDIOS LTD.
Manygate Lane, Shepperton, Middlesex, TW17 9EG. Tel: 0932 226341. FAX: 0932 246336. Studio Manager: Allan d'Aguiar.

HILLSIDE STUDIOS
Merry Hill Road, Bushey, Watford, WD2 1DR. Tel: 0181 950 7919 FAX: 0181 950 1437. Contact: Dave Hillier.

LIMEHOUSE (LIMEHOUSE TELEVISION LTD.)
The Trocadero, 19 Rupert Street, London, W1V 7FS. Tel: 0171 287 3333. FAX: 0171 287 1998. Contact: A. Goddard.

PINEWOOD STUDIOS
Iver, Bucks. SL0 0NH. Tel: 01753 651700. FAX: 01753 656844. Managing Director: Steve Jaggs.

SHEPPERTON STUDIOS
Studios Road, Shepperton, Middlesex, TW17 0QD. Tel: 01932 562611. FAX: 01932 568989. Contact: Paul Olliver.

TEDDINGTON STUDIOS
Broom Road, Teddington Lock, Middx. TW11 9NT. Tel: 0181 977 3252. FAX: 0181 943 4050. Contact: Steve Gunn.

TWICKENHAM
St. Margarets, Twickenham, Middx., TW1 2AW. Tel: 0181 892 4477. FAX: 0181 891 0168. Contact: G. Humphreys.

JOHN WOOD SOUND LTD.
St. Martin's Studios, Greenbank Road, Ashton-upon-Mersey, Sale, Cheshire, M33 5PN. Tel: 0161 905 2077. FAX: 0161 905 2382. Contact: John Wood.

Film and Video Services

BUCKS MOTION PICTURE LABORATORIES LTD.
714 Banbury Avenue, Slough, Berks., SL1 4LH. Tel: 01753 576611. FAX: 01753 691762.
Roger Cherrills, 65-66 Dean Street, London, W1V 5HD. Contacts: Harry Rushton, Mike Bianchi.

COLOUR FILM SERVICES LTD.
10 Wadsworth Road, Perivale, Greenford, Middx. UB6 7JX. Tel: 0181 998 2731. FAX: 0181 997 8738. Telex: 24672.
22-25 Portman Close, London, W1A 4BE. Tel: 0171 486 2881. Telex: 24672.

FILMATIC LABORATORIES LTD.
16 Colville Road, London, W11 2BS. Tel: 0171 221 6081. FAX: 0171 229 2718. Chairman & Managing Director: D. L. Gibbs.

METROCOLOR LONDON LTD.
91/95 Gillespie Road, Highbury, London, N5 1LS. Tel: 0171 226 4422. Managing Director: K. B. Fraser.
22 Soho Square, London, W1V 5FL. Tel: 0171 437 7811. FAX: 0171 359 2353.

RANK FILM LABORATORIES
North Orbital Road, Denham, Uxbridge, Middlesex, UB9 5HQ. Tel: 01895 832323. Telex: 934704. FAX: 01895 833617. Contact: David Dowler.

RANK VIDEO SERVICES LTD.
Phoenix Park, Great West Road, Brentford, Middlesex, TW8 9PL. Tel: 0181 568 4311. Telex: 22345. FAX: 0181 847 4052. Managing Director: Peter Pacitti.

SOHO IMAGES GROUP LTD.
8-14 Meard Street, London, W1V 3HR. Tel: 0171 437 0831. FAX: 0171 734 9471. Managing Director: Ray Adams.

TECHNICOLOR LTD.
Bath Road, West Drayton, Middlesex, UB7 0DB. Tel: 0181 759 5432. FAX: 0181 897 2666. Managing Director: Ashley Hopkins.

COSTUME SUPPLIERS

ANGELS & BERMANS
119 Shaftesbury Avenue, London, WC2H 8AE. Tel: 0171 836 5678. FAX: 0171 240 9527. Contacts: Tim Angel, Jonathan Lipman.
40 Camden Street, London, NW1 0EN. Tel: 0171 387 0999. FAX: 0171 383 5603. Contacts: Tim Angel, Richard Green, Ron Mawbey.

ARMS & ARCHERY
The Coach House, London Road, Ware, Herts, SG12 9QU. Tel: 01920 460335. FAX: 01920 461044. Contact: Terry Goulden.

CARLO MANZI RENTALS
32-33 Liddell Road, London, NW6 2EW. Tel: 0171 625 6391. FAX: 0171 625 5386.

COSPROP LTD.
26-28 Rochester Place, London, NW1 9JR. Tel: 0171 485 6731. FAX: 0171 485 5942. Contact: Bernie Chapman.

THE COSTUME STUDIO
6 Penton Grove, Off White Lion Street, London, N1 9HS. Tel: 0171 388 4481. FAX: 0171 837 5326. Contact: Rupert Clive, Richard Dudley.

Public Relations, Publicity and Marketing Services

BLUE DOLPHIN FILMS
40 Langham Street, London, W1N 5RG. Tel: 0171 255 2494. FAX: 0171 580 7670.

CORBETT & KEENE
122 Wardour St., London W1V 3TD. Tel: 0171 494 3478. FAX: 0171 734 2024.

CONSOLIDATED COMMUNICATIONS MANAGEMENT
1-5 Poland Street, London, W1V 3DG. Tel: 0171 287 2087. FAX: 0171 734 0772.

NAMARA COWAN LTD.
45 Poland Street, London, W1V 3DF. Tel: 0171 434 3871. Telex: 919034. FAX: 0171 439 6489.

CREATIVE PARTNERSHIP
19 Greek Street, London W1V. Tel: 0171 439 7762. FAX: 0171 437 1467.

DENNIS DAVIDSON ASSOCIATES LTD.
Royalty House, 72-74 Dean Street, London, W1V 5HB. Tel: 0171 439 6391. Telex: 24148 DADASS G. FAX: 0171 437 6358.

CLIFFORD ELSON PUBLICITY LTD.
223 Regent Street, London, W1R 7DG. Tel: 0171 495 4012. FAX: 0171 495 4175.

EDELMAN PUBLIC RELATIONS
Kings Gate House, 536 Kings Road, London, SW10 0TE. Tel: 0171 835 1222. FAX: 0171 351 7676.

FEREF ASSOCIATES LTD.
14-17 Wells Mews, London, W1A 1ET. Tel: 0171 580 6546. FAX: 0171 631 3156.

MARGARET GARDNER CONSULTANTS
17 Onslow Square, London, SW7 3NJ. Tel: 0171 584 6700. FAX: 0171 581 9823.

SUE HYMAN ASSOCIATES LTD.
70 Chalk Farm Road, London, NW1 8AN. Tel: 0171 485 8489. FAX: 0171 267 4715.

IMPRESSION MEDIA & PUBLIC RELATIONS
Premier House, 77 Oxford St., London, W1R 1RB. Tel: 0171 439 1188. FAX: 0171 734 8367.

INTERMARK PUBLIC RELATIONS LTD.
91 Regent Street, London, W1R 7TB. Tel: 0171 937 1284. FAX: 0171 734 1014.

JAC PUBLICITY & MARKETING CONSULTANTS LTD.
36 Great Queen Street, Covent Garden, London, WC2B 5AA. Tel: 0171 430 0211. FAX: 0171 430 0222.

CAROLYN JARDINE PUBLICITY
2nd fl., 3 Richmond Bldgs., London, W1V 5EA. Tel: 0171 287 6661. FAX: 0171 437 0499.

RICHARD LAVER PUBLICITY
3 Troy Court, High Street Kensington, London, W8 7RA. Tel: 0171 937 7322. FAX: 0171 937 8670.

MEDIA RELATIONS LTD.
Glen House, 125 Old Brompton Road, London SW7 3RP. Tel: 0171 835 1000. FAX: 0171 373 0265.

PEARTREE ASSOCIATES LTD.
Cloister Court, 22 Farringdon Lane, London, EC1R 3AV. Tel: 0171 250 0292. FAX: 0171 250 3031.

ROGERS & COWAN INTERNATIONAL
43 King Street, Covent Garden, London, WC2E 8RJ. Tel: 0171 411 3000. FAX: 0171 411 3020. Contacts: Phillip Symes, Brian Daly.

JUDY TARLO ASSOCIATES
100 Ebury Street, London, SW1W 9QD. Tel: 0171 824 8815. FAX: 0171 823 6195.

PETER THOMPSON ASSOCIATES
134 Great Portland Street, London, W1N 5PH. Tel: 0171 436 5991. FAX: 0171 436 0509.

TOWN HOUSE PUBLICITY
45 Islington Park Street, London, N1 1QB. Tel: 0171 226 7450. FAX: 0171 359 6026.

WINSOR BECK PUBLIC RELATIONS
Network House, 29-39 Stirling Road, London, W3 8DJ. Tel: 0181 993 7506. FAX: 0181 993 8276.

Trade Publications

BROADCAST
Published weekly by EMAP Media Ltd., 33-39 Bowling Green Lane, London, EC1R 0DA. Tel: 0171 505 8035. FAX: 0171 505 8050.
EDITOR
Mike Jones

EYEPIECE
Journal of the Guild of British Camera Technicians, 5-11 Taunton Road, Metropolitan Centre, Greenford, Middx., UB6 8UQ. Tel: 0181 578 9243. FAX: 0181 575 5972.
EDITORS
Charles Hewitt, Kerry Anne Burrows

IMAGE TECHNOLOGY
Journal of the British Kinematograph, Sound and Television Society. 67-71 Victoria House, Vernon Place, London, WC1B 4DA. Tel: 0171 242 8400. FAX: 0171 405 3560.
MANAGING EDITOR
Jim Slater

MOVING PICTURES
Published weekly. 1 Richmond Mews, London W1V 5AG. Tel: 0171 287 9637.
EDITORS
Sara Squire, Damon Wise

SCREEN DIGEST
Published monthly by Screen Digest Ltd., 37 Gower Street, London, WC1E 6HH. Tel: 0171 580 2842. FAX: 0171 580 0060.

EDITORIAL CHAIRMAN
John Chittock, O.B.E.
EDITOR
David Fisher

SCREEN INTERNATIONAL
Published weekly by EMAP Media. 33-39 Bowling Green Lane, London, EC1R 0DA. Tel: 0171 505 8101. FAX: 0171 505 8117.
EDITOR
Boyd Farrow

THE SPOTLIGHT
7 Leicester Place, London, WC2H 7BP. Tel: 0171 437 7631. FAX: 0171 437 5881. email: info@spotlite.demon.co.uk
PUBLISHERS
Nigel Seale, Emma Seale
EDITOR
Christine Barry

TELEVISUAL
Published monthly by The Centaur Group. St. Giles House, 50 Poland Street, London, W1V 4AX. Tel: 0171 439 4222. FAX: 0171 287 0768.
EDITOR
Mundy Ellis
PUBLISHER
Roger Beckett

BRITISH-BASED EQUIPMENT COMPANIES AND SERVICES

ABEKAS COX ELECTRONICS
Hanworth Trading Estate, Feltham TW13 6DH. Tel: 0181 894 5622. FAX: 0181 898 0298.

ACMADE INTERNATIONAL LTD.
Shepperton Studios, P.O. Box 64, Studios Road, Shepperton, Middx. TW17 0QD. Tel: 01932 562611. FAX: 01932 568414.

ADVENT COMMUNICATIONS LTD.
Watermeadow House, Watermeadow Chesham, Bucks. HP5 1LF. Tel: 01494 774400. Telex: 838870 G.

AEG-TELEFUNKEN (UK) LTD.
217 Bath Road, Slough, Berks. SL1 4AW. Tel: 2872101.

AGFA-GEVAERT LTD., MOTION PICTURE DIVISION
27 Great West Road, Brentford, Middlesex TW8 9AX. Tel: 0181 231 4310. FAX: 0181 231 4315.

AKG ACOUSTICS LTD.
191 The Vale, London, W3 7QS. Tel: 0181 749 2042.

AMEK SYSTEMS AND CONTROLS LIMITED
Islington Mill, James Street, Salford M3 5HW. Tel: 0161 834 6747. Telex: 668127.

AMPEX INTERNATIONAL
Acre Road, Reading, RG2 0QR. Tel: 01734 875200. FAX: 01734 866693.

AMS NEVE PLC
Billington Road, Burnley, Lancs. BB11 5ES. Tel: 01282 57011. FAX: 01282 39542.

AMSTRAD PLC
Brentwood House, 169 Kings Road, Brentwood, Essex. CM14 4EF. Tel: 01277 228888.

ARRI (G.B.) LTD.
The Movie House, 1-3 Airlinks, Spitfire Way, Heston, Middlesex. Tel: 0181 848 8881. FAX: 0181 561 1312.

ASTON ELECTRONIC DEVELOPMENTS LTD.
125 Deepcut Bridge Road, Deepcut, Camberley, Surrey. Tel: 012516 6221.

AUDIENCE SYSTEMS LTD.
Wahington Road, West Wilts. Trading Estate, Westbury, Wilts. BA13 4JP. Tel: 01373 865050.

AUDIO ENGINEERING LTD.
33 Endell St., London, WCZ. Tel: 0171 836 9373.

AUDIO SYSTEMS COMPONENTS LTD.
1 Comet House, Calleva Park, Aldermaston, Reading, Berks. RG7 4QW. Tel: 017356 79565. FAX: 017356 71000.

AUDIX BROADCAST
Station Road, Wenden, Saffron Walden, Essex, CB11 4LG. Tel: 01799 542 220. FAX: 01799 541 248.

AUDIO KINETICS
Kinetic House, Theobald St., Boreham Wood, Herts. Tel: 0181 953 8118.

AVS BROADCAST
Venture House, Davis Road, Chessington, Surrey KT9 1TT. Tel: 0181 391 5678. FAX: 0181 391 5409. Telex: 267439 AVS.

AV DISTRIBUTORS (LONDON) LTD.
21-22 St. Albans Place, Upper Street, Islington Green, London N1 0NX. Tel: 0171 226 1508.

BAL COMPONENTS LTD.
Bermuda Road, Nuneaton, Warwickshire, CV10 7QF. Tel: 01203 341111. Telex: 311563.

DAVID BAYLISS LTD.
Telegraph House, Royal Crescent Formby L37 6BT. Tel: 017048 79686. FAX: 017048 78608.

BAUCH SYSTEMS
49 Theobald Street, Boreham Wood, Herts. WD6 4RZ. Tel: 0181 953 0091. Telex: 27502. FAX: 0181 847 5803.

BELL THEATRE SERVICES LTD.
9-17 Park Royal Road, London, NW10 7LQ. Tel: 0181 963 0354. FAX: 0181 963 0622.

BLITZ VISION
Unit 2, 5 Garnet Close, Grecaine Estate, Watford, Herts., WD2 4JL. Tel: 01923 819401.

ROBERT BOSCH LTD.
Broadwater Park, Denham, Uxbridge, Middx. UB9 5HJ. Tel: 01895 73750. FAX: 01895 73055.

BOSE (UK) LTD.
Trinity Trading Estate, Sittingbourne, Kent, ME10 2PD. Tel: 01795 75341. FAX: 01795 27227.

BOSTON INSULATED WIRE (UK) LTD.
1 Canbury Park Road, Kingston-upon-Thames, Surrey. Tel: 0181 546 3384.

BRABURY ELECTRONICS LTD.
Smirham Bridge, Hungerford, Berks. RG17 1OQU. Tel: 014 886 5511.

C.A.T.S. (UK) LTD.
Eagle House, 108-110 Jermyn Street, London, SW1Y 6HB. Tel: 0171 930 2294.

CFS EQUIPMENT LTD.
10 Wadsworth Road, Perivale, Greenford, Middx. UB6 7JX. Tel: 0181 998 2731. FAX: 0181 997 8738. Telex: 24672.

CP CASES
Worton Hall Industrial Estate, Worton Road, Isleworth, Middx. TW7 6ER. Tel: 0181 568 1881. FAX: 0181 568 1141.

CALDER EQUIPMENT LTD.
Batford Mill Industrial Estate, Lower Luton Rd., Harpenden, Herts. AL5 5BZ. Tel: 015827 64331.

CAMERON VIDEO SYSTEMS LTD.
Burnfield Road, Glasgow G46 7TH, Scotland. Tel: 0141 633 0077. FAX: 0141 633 1745.

CANFORD AUDIO
Crowther Road, Washington, Tyne & Wear NE38 0BW. Tel: 0191 415 0205. Telex: 538202 CANFRD G. FAX: 0191 416 0392.

CANON (U.K.) LTD.
TV Products Dept., Canon House, 2 Manor Rd., Wallington, Surrey, SM6 0BW. Tel: 0181 773 3173. FAX: 0181 773 2851.

CARLTON COMMUNICATIONS PLC
15 St. George Street, London, W1R 9DE. Tel: 0171 499 8050. FAX: 0171 895 9575.

CEL ELECTRONICS LTD.
Chroma House, Shire Hill, Saffron Walden, Essex CB11 3AQ. Tel: 01799 23817. Telex: 817807 CHROMA G. FAX: 01799 280181.

BILL CHEW ASSOCIATES
61-71 Collier Street, London, N1 9BE. Tel: 0171 278 8924. FAX: 0171 278 0337.

CHRIS JAMES & CO. LTD.
Unit 7, North Western Commercial Centre, 75 Broadfield Lane, York Way, London, NW1 9YJ. Tel: 0171 284 2221.

CINE-EUROPE LTD.
7 Silver Road, White City Industrial Park, Wood Lane, London, W12 75G. Tel: 0181 743 6762. FAX: 0181 749 3501.

CINEMA SUPPLY AND DESIGN (UK) LTD.
13 Carters Lane, Kiln Farm, Milton Keynes. MK11 3ER. Tel: 01908 260666. FAX: 01908 567 989.

CINEVIDEO LTD.
7 Silver Road, White City Industrial Park, Wood Lane, London W12 7SG. Tel: 0181 743 3839. Telex: 915 282 CINEGP G. FAX: 0181 749 3501.

CONVERGENCE EDITING
(A division of Paltex International)
7 Airlinks, Spitfire Way, Heston, Middx. TW5 9NR. Tel: 0181 759 3891. FAX: 0181 561 1122.

COX ASSOCIATES LTD.
Cox House, Amberley Way, Hounslow, Middlesex TW4 6BH. Tel: 0181 570 8283. Telex: 946441 COXAL G.

CROMA RESEARCH LTD.
Croma House, North Way, Walworth Industrial Estate, Andover, Hants. SP10 5AZ. Tel: 01264 332132. Telex: 477407.

DESISTI LIGHTING (UK) LTD.
15 Old Market Street, Thetford, Norfolk IP24 2EQ. Tel: 01842 752909. FAX: 01842 753746.

DOLBY LABORATORIES INC.
Interface Park, Wootton Bassett, Wiltshire, SN4 8QJ. Tel: 01793 842100. FAX: 01793 842101.

PHILLIP DRAKE ELECTRONICS LTD.
37 Broadwater Road, Welwyn Garden City, Herts. AL7 3AX. Tel: 01707 333866. Telex: 25415 DRAKE G.

EDRIC AUDIO VISUAL LTD.
34-36 Oak End Way, Gerrards Cross, Bucks. SL9 8BR. Tel: 012813 84646/86521.

EDS PORTAPROMPT LTD.
Lane End Road Sands, High Wycombe, Bucks. HP12 4JQ. Tel: 01494 450414. Telex: 848314 CHACOM G. ATTN EDS. FAX: 01494 37591.

ELECTROSONIC LTD.
Hawley Mill, Hawley Rd., Dartford, Kent DA2 75Y. Tel: 01322 222211.

ELF AUDIO VISUAL LTD.
836 Yeovil Road, Trading Estate, Slough, Berks. Tel: 75 36123.

ENGLISH ELECTRIC VALVE COMPANY LIMITED
Chelmsford, Essex CM1 2QU. Tel: 01245 493493.

FILM CLINIC
8-14 Meard Street, London, W1V 3HR. Tel: 0171 734 9235. FAX: 0171 734 9471.

FILM STOCK CENTRE
68-70 Wardour Street, London, W1V 3HP. Tel: 0171 734 0038.

FILMLAB SYSTEMS INTERNATIONAL LTD.
P.O. Box 297, Stokenchurch, High Wycombe HP14 3RH. Tel: 01494 485271. FAX: 01494 483079.

FUJI PHOTO FILM (UK) LTD.
Fuji Film House, 125 Finchley Road, Swiss Cottage, London, NW3 6JH. Tel: 0171 586 5900. Telex: 8812995. FAX: 0171 722 4259.

FUTURE FILM DEVELOPMENTS
11 The Green, Brill, Aylesbury HP18 9RU. Tel: 01844 238444. FAX: 01844 238106.

GE THORN LAMPS LTD.
Miles Road, Mitcham, Surrey CR4 3YX. Tel: 0181 640 1221. FAX: 0181 640 9760.

GEC CABLE SYSTEMS
P.O. Box 53, Copesewood, Coventry CV3 1HJ. Tel: 01203 433184. Telex: 31361 GECTEL G.

GEC (LAMPS AND LIGHTING) LTD.
P.O. Box 17, East Lane, Wembley, Middlesex HA9 7PG. Tel: 0181 904 4321.

GML
143-145 Cardiff Road, Reading, Berks. RG1 8JF. Tel: 01734 584948. Telex: 847109 GUNML G.

GORDON AUDIO VISUAL LTD.
28 Market Place, Oxford Circus, London W1N 8PH. Tel: 0171 580 9191.

GTE LIGHTING LTD.
Otley Rd., Charleston, Shipley, West Yorkshire. Tel: 01274 595921.

G2 SYSTEMS
5 Mead Lane, Farnham, Surrey GU9 7DY. Tel: 01252 737151. FAX: 01252 737147.

HARKNESS HALL LTD.
The Gate Studios, Station Road, Boreham Wood, Herts. WD6 1DQ. Tel: 0181 953 3611. FAX: 0181 207 3657. Int'l FAX: 44 1 207 3657.

HARMAN (AUDIO) UK LTD.
Mill Street, Slough, Berks SL2 500. Tel: 01753 76911. FAX: 01753 35306.

HAYDEN LABORATORIES LTD.
Chiltern Hill, Chalfont St. Peter, Bucks. 9UG. Tel: 01753 888447. FAX: 01753 880109.

HITACHI DENSHI (UK) LTD.
13-14 Garrick Industrial Centre, Irving Way, Hendon, London, NW9 6A2. Tel: 0181 202 4311. FAX: 0181 202 2451.

HOLMES PHOTOGRAPHIC (LOWEL)
Unit 3, Kennet Enterprise Centre, Charnham Lane, Hungerford, Berks. RG17 0EY. Tel: 01488 85244. FAX: 01488 85248.

I.C. EQUIPMENT LTD.
Unit 1-3, The Robert Elliot Center, 1 Old Nichol Street, Shoreditch, London, E2 7HR. Tel: 0171 739 4800. FAX: 0171 729 2554.

ICON SOFTWARE
Icon House, 376-378 Chiswick High Road, London, W4 5TF. Tel: 0181 742 8770. FAX: 0181 742 8772.

IKEGAMI ELECTRONICS
61 High Street, Kingston-upon-Thames, Surrey, KT1 1LO. Tel: 0181 546 7772. Telex: 897005 ITC G.

INTERACT SYSTEMS LTD.
185 Ebberns Road, Hemel Hempstead, Herts, HP3 9RD. Tel: 01442 254110. FAX: 01442 232011.

INTERNATIONAL VIDEO CORPORATION (UK) LTD.
10 Portman Road, Reading, Berks, RG3 1JR. Tel: 01734 585421.

JVC PROFESSIONAL PRODUCTS (UK) LTD.
Alperton House, Bridgewater Road, Wembley, Middx. HA0 1EG. Tel: 0181 902 8812. FAX: 0181 900 0941.

JEMANI LTD.
Southampton House, 192-206 York Road, Battersea, London, SW11 3SA. Tel: 0171 924 3887. FAX: 0171 228 0451.

KINLOCH, IAN P., AND COMPANY LTD.
3 Darwin Close, Reading, Berkshire, RG2 0TB. Tel: 01734 311030. Telex: 846787 IPK CO.

KODAK LTD.
Professional Motion Imaging, P.O. Box 66, Kodak House, Station Road, Hemel Hempstead, Herts. HP1 1JU. Tel: 01442 61122. FAX: 01442 844458.

LEE LIGHTING LTD.
Wycombe Road, Wembley, Middx., HA0 1QD. Tel: 0181 900 2900.

LEE FILTERS LTD.
Walworth Industrial Estate, Andover, Hants. SP10 5AN Tel: 01264 366245. FAX: 01264 355058.

LIGHTWORKS EDITING SYSTEMS LTD.
38 Soho Square, London, W1V GLE. Tel: 0171 494 3084. FAX: 0171 437 3570.

LONDON EDITING MACHINES LTD.
Twickenham Studios, St. Margarets, Twickenham, Middx., TW1 2AW. Tel: 0181 892 4477.

MALHAM PHOTOGRAPHIC EQUIPMENT LTD.
65-67 Malham Road, London, SE23 1AJ. Tel: 0181 699 0917. FAX: 0181 699 4291.

MARCONI COMMUNICATION SYSTEMS LTD.
Marconi House, New Street, Chelmsford, Essex CM1 1PL. Tel: 01245 353221.

MITCHELL CAMERAS
Wycombe Road, Wembley, Middx. HA0 1QN. Tel: 0181 903 7933. FAX: 0181 902 3273.

NEILSON-HORDELL LTD.
11 Central Trading Estate, Staines, Middlesex TW18 4UU. Tel: 01784 456456. FAX: 01784 459657.

OPTEX
22-26 Victoria Road, New Barnet, Herts. EN4 9PF. Tel: 0181 441 2199. FAX: 0181 449 3646.

OSRAM (GEC) LTD.
P.O. Box 17, East Lane, Wembley, Middlesex HA9 7PG. Tel: 0181 904 4321.

OTARI ELECTRIC (UK) LTD.
22 Church Street, Slough, Berks, SL1 1PT. Tel: 01753 822381. FAX: 01753 83707.

P.A.G. FILM LTD. & P.A.G. POWER LTD.
565 Kingston Road, London SW20 85A. Tel: 0181 543 3131.

PANASONIC BROADCAST EUROPE
107-109 Whitby Road, Slough, Berks. SL1 3DR. Tel: 01753 521626. FAX: 01753 512673.

PANAVISION U.K.
Wycombe Rd., Stonebridge Park, Wembley, Middx. HA0 1QN. Tel: 0181 903 7933. FAX: 0181 902 3273.

PANDORA'S OTHER BOX LTD.
208A Main Road, Sutton-at-Hone, Dartford, Kent DA4 9HP. Tel: 01322 866 245.

PEC VIDEO
2-4 Dean Street, London W1V 5RN. Tel: 0171 437 4633. FAX: 0171 287 0492.

PERFECTONE PRODUCTS SA.
Ladbroke Films Ltd., 4 Kensington Park Gardens, London, W11 3HB. Tel: 0171 727 3541.

PHILIPS LIGHTING LTD.
City House, 420-430 London Road, Croydon, Surrey CR9 3QR. Tel: 0181 689 2166. FAX: 0181 665 5102.

PHOTOMEC (LONDON) LTD.
Valley Road Industrial Estate, St. Albans, Herts, AL3 6NU. Tel: 01727 501711. FAX: 01727 43991.

QUANTEL
31 Turnpike Road, Newbury, Berks. RG13 2NE. Tel: 01635 48222. FAX: 01635 31776.

RPS BROADCAST FACILITIES
10 Giltway, Giltbrook, Nottingham NG16 2GN. Tel: 01602 384103.

RTI (UK) LTD.
Unit 6, Swan Wharf Business Centre, Waterloo, Middx. UB8 2RA. Tel: 01895 52191. FAX: 01895 74692.

RADAMEC EPO LTD.
Bridge Road, Chertsey, Surrey, KT16 8LJ. Tel: 01932 561181. FAX: 01932 568775. Telex: 929945 RADEPO G.

RANK CINTEL
Watton Road, Ware, Hertfordshire SC12 0AE. Tel: 01920 463939. FAX: 01920 460803.

RANK FILM LABORATORIES LTD.
North Orbital Road, Denham, Uxbridge, Middlesex UB9 5HQ. Tel: 01895 832323. Telex: 934704. FAX: 01895 833617.

RANK TAYLOR HOBSON LTD.
P.O. Box 36, 2 New Star Rd., Leicester LE4 7JQ. Tel: 01533 763771. FAX: 01533 740167.

RANK VIDEO SERVICES LTD.
Phoenix Park, Great West Road, Brentford, Middlesex TW8 9PL. Tel: 0181 568 4311. Telex: 22345. FAX: 0181 847 4032.

PHILIP RIGBY AND SONS LTD.
14 Creighton Avenue, Muswell Hill, London, N10 1NU. Tel: 0181 883 3703. FAX: 0181 444 3620.

RONFORD-BAKER ENGINEERING CO. LTD.
Braziers, Oxhey Lane, Watford, Herts. WD1 4RJ. Tel: 0181 428 5941. FAX: 0181 428 4743.

ROSCOLAB LTD.
Blanchard Works, Kangley Bridge Road, Sydenham, London SE26 5AQ. Tel: 0181 659 2300. FAX: 0181 659 3153.

SAMUELSON FILM SERVICE LONDON LTD.
21 Derby Rd., Metropolitan Centre, Greenford, Middx. UB6 8UQ. Tel: 0181 578 7887. FAX: 0181 578 2733.

MICHAEL SAMUELSON LIGHTING LTD.
Pinewood Studios, Iver Heath, Bucks. SL0 0NH. Tel: 01753 631133. FAX: 01753 630485.

SCREEN SUBTITLING SYSTEM LTD.
The Old Rectory, Church Lane, Claydon, Ipswich, Suffolk, IP6 0EG. Tel: 01473 831700.

SCREENTECH
23 Wrotham Road, Gravesend, Kent DA11 0PA. Tel: 01474 333111. FAX: 01474 328184. Telex: 966475 VACORP.

SELTECH/SONDOR
Bourne End Business Centre, Cores End Road, Bourne End, Bucks. SL8 5AT. Tel: 016285 29131. FAX: 016285 27468.

SHURE ELECTRONICS LTD.
Eccleston Road, Maidstone, Kent, ME15 6AU. Tel: 01622 59881.

SIGMA FILM EQUIPMENT LTD.
Unit K, Chantry Lane Industrial Estate, Storrington, West Sussex, RH20 4AD. Tel: 01903 743382. FAX: 01903 745038.

SOHO IMAGES GROUP LTD.
8-14 Meard Street, London, W1V 3HR. Tel: 0171 437 0831. FAX: 0171 734 9471.

SNELL AND WILCOX LTD.
57 Jubilee Road, Waterlooville, Hants, P07 7RF. Tel: 01705 241252.

SOLID STATE LOGIC
Begbroke, Oxford OX5 1RU. Tel: 01865 842300. FAX: 01865 842118.

SONY BROADCAST INTERNATIONAL
Jay Close, Viables, Basingstoke, Hants. RG22 4SB. Tel: 01256 55011. FAX: 01256 474585.

SOUND ASSOCIATES LTD.
56 Ayres Street, London, SW1 1EU. Tel: 0171 403 5348. FAX: 0171 403 5394.

SPACEWARD MICROSYSTEMS LTD.
The Old School, Haddenham, Cambridge CB6 3XA. Tel: 01353 741 222.

STRAND LIGHTING
Grant Way (off Syon Lane) Isleworth, Middlesex TW7 5QD. Tel: 0181 560 3171. FAX: 0181 490 0002.

SURVEY & GENERAL INSTRUMENT CO. LTD.
Fircroft Way, Edenbridge, Kent TN8 6HA. Tel: 01732 864111. Telex: 95527 OPTSLS G.

SYLVANIA LIGHTING
Otley Road, Charlestown Shipley, West Yorkshire, BD17 7SN. Tel: 01274 595921.

SYSTEM VIDEO LTD.
Venture House, Davis Rd., Chessington, Surrey KT9 1TT. Tel: 0181 391 5678. FAX: 0181 391 5522.

TECHNOVISION CAMERAS LTD.
Unit 4, St. Margarets Business Centre, Drummond Place, Twickenham, Middlesex TW1 1JN. Tel: 0181 891 5961. FAX: 0181 744 1154.

TELEFEX LTD.
1 Brentford Business Centre, Commerce Road, Brentford, Middx. Tel: 0181 569 9595.

THOMSON VIDEO EQUIPMENT (UK)
18 Horton Road, Datchet, Berks. Tel: 01753 681 122. FAX: 01753 681 196.

TOPHAM FILM & ENG. LTD.
316-318 Latimer Road, London, W1O 6QN. Tel: 0181 960 0123.

3M UNITED KINGDOM PLC
3M House, P.O. Box 1, Bracknell, Berkshire RG12 1JU. Tel: 01344 58571.

VALIANT ELECTRICAL WHOLESALE CO.
20 Lettice Street, Fulham, London SW6. Tel: 0171 736 8115. FAX: 0171 731 3339.

VAN DIEMEN FILMS LTD.
Bridge House, Branksome Park Road, Camberley, Surrey, GU15 2AQ. Tel: 01276 61222. FAX: 01276 61549.

VARIAN TVT LTD.
(Subsidiary of Varian Associates Inc. of California)
P.O. Box 41, Coldhams Lane, Cambridge CB1 3JU. Tel: 01223 245115. Telex: 81342 VARTVT G. FAX: 01223 214632.

VG ELECTRONICS LTD.
Theaklen Drive, Hastings, East Sussex, TN34 1YQ. Tel: 01424 446888. Telex: 957357 VGELEC. FAX: 01424 435699.

VINTEN BROADCAST LTD.
Western Way, Bury St. Edmunds, Suffolk IP33 3TB. Tel: 01284 752121. FAX: 01284 750560.

VISTEK ELECTRONICS LTD.
Unit C, Wessex Road, Bourne End, Bucks. SL8 5DT. Tel: 016285 31221. FAX: 846077.

WESTAR SALES & SERVICES LTD.
Unit 7, Cowley Mill Trading Estate, Longbridge Way, Uxbridge, Middlesex UB8 2YG. Tel: 01895 34429. Telex: 8954 169.

WILMAC LTD.
Pine Lodge, Gannock Park, Deganwy, Conwy, Gwynedd. LL31 9P2. Tel: 01895 83757.

WINSTED
Units 3/4, Wassage Way, Hampton Lovett Industrial, Estate, Droitwich WR9 1ONX. Tel: 01905 770276. Telex: 334007 WINSTD G.

MEL WORSFOLD LTD.
66 Carlyle Rd., Ealing, London, W5 4BL. Tel: 0181 568 7884. FAX: 0181 569 8846.

WOTAN LAMPS LTD.
1 Gresham Way, Durnsford Road, London, SW19 8HU. Tel: 0181 947 1261. FAX: 0181 947 5132.

ZONAL LTD.
Holmethorpe Avenue, Redhill, Surrey, RH1 2NX. Tel: 01737 767171. FAX: 01737 767610.

EXHIBITION CIRCUITS

ABBEY FILMS LTD.
135 Upper Abbey Street, Dublin 1. Tel: Dublin 723922. FAX: Dublin 723687. Managing Director: Leo Ward.

APOLLO LEISURE GROUP
424 Woolton Road, Liverpool L25 6JQ. Tel: 0151 708 6672. Contacts: G. S. Lipson, J. Merryweather.

CAC LEISURE PLC.
P.O. Box 21m, 23-25 Huntley St., Inverness, Scotland 1VI 1LA. Tel: 01463 237611. Contacts: I. Cluley, P. Perrins.

CINE-UK LTD.
Sutherland House, 5/6 Argyll St., London, W1V 1AD. Tel: 0171 494 1394. FAX: 0171 734 1443. Managing Director: Steve Wiener.

FOCUS CINEMAS LTD.
147-149 Wardour Street, London, W1V 3TB. Tel: 0171 434 1961.

GALLERY CINEMAS
Nightingale House, 65 Curzon Steet, London, W1Y 7PE. Tel: 0171 629 9642.

KINE SUPPLIES (BIRMINGHAM) LTD.
Regal Buildings, Augusta Place, Leamington Spa CV32 5EP. Tel: 01926 22157.

MGM CINEMAS LTD.
84-86 Regent Street, London, W1R 5PA. Tel: 0171 915 1717. FAX: 0171 734 8410.

NATIONAL AMUSEMENTS (UK)
Showcase Cinema, Redfield Way, Lenton, Nottingham, NG7 2UW. Tel: 01159 862508. Contact: J. Bilsborough.
200 Elm Street, Dedham, MA 02026, U.S.A. Tel: (617) 461 1600. Contact: Ira A. Korff.

ODEON CINEMAS
439-445 Godstone Road, Whyteleafe, Surrey, CR3 0YG. Tel: 01883 623 355. Telex: 262 305. FAX: 01883 626717.
54 Whitcomb Street, London, WC2H 7DN. Tel: 0171 839 6373. FAX: 0171 321 0357. Managing Director: Hugh Corrance. Contacts: Mike Archibald, Barry Keward.

RECORDED CINEMAS
155-157 Oxford St., London, W1R 1TB. Tel: 0171 734 7477.

UNITED CINEMAS INTERNATIONAL UK
Lee House, 90 Great Bridgewater Street, Manchester, M1 5JW. Tel: 0161 455 4000. FAX: 0161 455 4079. Managing Director: Steve Knibbs.

VIRGIN CINEMAS LTD.
Adelaide Hous, 626 High Rd., Chiswick, London W4 5RY. Tel: 0181 987 5000. FAX: 0181 742-2998. Booking Manager: Joe Nunes.

WARNER BROS. THEATRES UK
3rd fl. S., Weels POint, 79 Wells St., London, W1P 3RD. Tel: 0171 437 5600. Contacts: S. Wiener, P. Dobson.

Central London Cinemas

BARBICAN CENTRE CINEMA
Silk Street, Barbican, London, EC2Y 8DS. Tel: 0171 638 4141.

CANNON EDGWARE ROAD
Edgware Road NW1. Tel: 0171 723 5901.

CORONET NOTTINGHILL GATE
103 Notting Hill Gate, London, W11 3LB. Tel: 0171 727 6705.

CURZON MAYFAIR
Curzon Street W1. Tel: 0171 499 3737.

CURZON PHOENIX
Charing Cross Road WC1. Tel: 0171 240 9661.

CURZON WEST END
Shaftesbury Avenue W1. Tel: 0171 439 4805.

EMPIRE LEICESTER SQUARE
Leicester Square WC2. Tel: 0181 200 0200.

ICA CINEMA
The Mall, London, SW1Y 5A11. Tel: 0171 930 0493. FAX: 071 873 0051.

LUMIERE
St. Martin's Lane WC2. Tel: 0171 836 0691.

MGM BAKER STREET
Marylebone Road NW1. Tel: 0171 935 9772.

MGM COVENTRY STREET
13 Coventry Street, London, W1V 7FE. Tel: 0171 434 0034.

MGM CHELSEA
Kings Road SW3. Tel: 0171 352 5096.

MGM FULHAM ROAD
Fulham Road SW10. Tel: 0171 370 2636/0265.

MGM HAYMARKET
Haymarket SW1. Tel: 0171 839 1528.

MGM OXFORD STREET
Oxford Street W1. Tel: 0171 636 0310.

MGM PANTON STREET
SW1. Tel: 0171 930 0632.

MGM PICCADILLY
Piccadilly W1. Tel: 0171 437 3561.

MGM SHAFTESBURY AVENUE
Shaftesbury Avenue W1. Tel: 0171 836 8861/8606.

MGM TOTTENHAM COURT ROAD
Tottenham Court Road W1. Tel: 0171 636 6148.

MGM TROCADERO
London, W1. Tel: 0171 434 0031.

MINEMA
45 Knightsbridge, SW3. Tel: 0171 235 4225.

MEZZANINE LEICESTER SQUARE
Leicester Square, WC2. Tel: 0171 930 6111.

ODEON HAYMARKET
Haymarket W1. Tel: 0171 839 7697.

ODEON HIGH STREET KENSINGTON
Kensington High Street W8. Tel: 0171 602 6644.

ODEON LEICESTER SQUARE
Leicester Square WC2. Tel: 0171 930 6111.

ODEON LEICESTER SQUARE THEATRE
Leicester Square WC2. Tel: 0171 930 5252/7615.

ODEON MARBLE ARCH
Marble Arch W1. Tel: 0171 723 2011.

PLAZA
Lower Regent Street W1. Tel: 0181 200 0200.

PREMIERE SWISS CENTRE
Leicester Square WC2. Tel: 0171 439 4470.

PRINCE CHARLES
Leicester Square WC2. Tel: 0171 437 8181.

RENOIR
Brunswick Square WC1. Tel: 0171 837 8402.

SCREEN ON THE GREEN
Islington Green N1. Tel: 0171 226 3520.

WARNER WEST END
Leicester Square WC2. 0171 439 0791.

WHITELEYS UCI BAYSWATER
Queensway W2. Tel: 0171 229 4149.

BRITISH TRADE ORGANISATIONS AND GOVERNMENT UNITS

AMALGAMATED ENGINEERING & ELECTRICAL UNION (EETPU SECTION)
Hayes Court, West Common Road, Bromley, BR2 7AU. Tel: 0181 462 7755. FAX: 0181 462 4959.
GENERAL SECRETARY
Paul Gallagher

THE ARTISTES ASSOCIATION (GREAT BRITAIN)
54 Keyes House, Dolphin Square, London, SW1V 3NA. Tel: 0171 834 0515. FAX: 0171 821 0261.
PRESIDENT
Kenneth Earle
SECRETARY
Ivan Birchall

ASSOCIATION OF PROFESSIONAL RECORDING SERVICES LTD.
2 Windsor Square, Silver Street, Reading, Berks. RG1 2TH. Tel: 01734 756218. FAX: 01734 756216.
CHIEF EXECUTIVE
Philip Vaughan

BRITISH ACADEMY OF FILM AND TELEVISION ARTS
195 Piccadilly, London, W1V 0LN. Tel: 0171 734 0022. FAX: 0171 734 1792.
PRESIDENT
H.R.H. The Princess Royal
VICE PRESIDENT
David Puttnam, C.B.E.
CHAIRMAN
Edward Mirzoeff, C.V.O.
CHIEF EXECUTIVE
Harry Manley

BRITISH ACTORS' EQUITY ASSOCIATION
(Incorporating the Variety Artistes' Federation)
Guild House, Upper St. Martin's Lane, London, WC2 9EG. Tel: 0171 379 6000. FAX: 0171 379 7001.
PRESIDENT
Jeffry Wickham
GENERAL SECRETARY
Ian McGarry
VICE PRESIDENTS
Dave Eager, Helen Lambert

BRITISH BOARD OF FILM CLASSIFICATION
3 Soho Square, London, W1V 6HD. Tel: 0171 439 7961. FAX: 0171 287 0141.
PRESIDENT
Earl of Harewood, KBE
DIRECTOR
James Ferman

BRITISH FEDERATION OF FILM SOCIETIES
21 Stephen Street, London, W1P 1PL. Tel: 0171 255 1444. FAX: 0171 255 2315.

BRITISH FILM DESIGNERS GUILD
Tel: 0171 286 6716. FAX: 0171 286 6716.
EXECUTIVE CONSULTANT
John French

BRITISH KINEMATOGRAPH, SOUND AND TELEVISION SOCIETY
(Publisher of the BKSTS Journal, "Image Technology" and Cinema Technology.)
M6-M14 Victoria House, Vernon Place, London, WC1B 4DF. Tel: 0171 242 8400. FAX: 0171 405 3560.
EXECUTIVE DIRECTOR
Anne Fenton

BRITISH MUSIC INFORMATION CENTRE
(Reference library of works by 20th Century British composers.)
10 Stratford Place, London, W1N 9AE. Tel: 0171 499 8567. FAX: 0171 499 4795.
CENTRE MANAGEMENT
Tom Morgan/Matthew Greenall

BRITISH SOCIETY OF CINEMATOGRAPHERS LTD.
Tree Tops, 11 Croft Road, Chalfont St. Peter Gerrards Cross, Bucks., SL9 9AE. Tel: 01753 888052. FAX: 01753 891486.
PRESIDENT
Robin Vidgeon
SECRETARY & TREASURER
Frances Russell

BRITISH VIDEO ASSOCIATION LTD.
167 Great Portland Street, London, W1M 5FD. Tel: 0171 436 0041. FAX: 0171 436 0043.
DIRECTOR GENERAL
Mrs Lavinia Carey

BROADCASTING ENTERTAINMENT CINEMATOGRAPH AND THEATRE UNION
111 Wardour Street, London, W1V 4AY. Tel: 0171 437 8506. FAX: 0171 437 8268.

CENTRAL CASTING LTD.
(Licensed annually by the Dept. of Employment)
162-170 Wardour Street, London, W1V 3AT. Tel: 0171 437 1881. FAX: 0171 437 2614.
DIRECTORS
R. McCallum, T. Burrill, G. Smith, M. O'Sullivan, J. Sargent, B.T. Yeoman, J. Woodward

CHILDREN'S FILM & TELEVISION FOUNDATION LTD.
Elstree Studios, Boreham Wood, Herts., WD6 1JG. Tel: 0181 953 0844. FAX: 0181 207 0860.
CHIEF EXECUTIVE & SECRETARY
Stanley T. Taylor, FCIS

CINEMA ADVERTISING ASSOCIATION LTD.
127 Wardour Street, London, W1V 4NL. Tel: 0171 439 9531. FAX: 0171 439 2395.
SECRETARY
Bruce Koster

CINEMA AND TELEVISION VETERANS
166 The Rocks Road, East Malling, Kent. ME19 6AX. Tel: 01732 843291.
PRESIDENT
Robert Bennett
SECRETARY
K.M. Morgan

CINEMA AND TELEVISION BENEVOLENT FUND
22 Golden Square, London, W1R 4AD. Tel: 0171 437 6567. FAX: 0171 437 7186.
EXECUTIVE DIRECTOR
P. J. C. Ratcliffe, O.B.E.
APPEALS & PUBLIC RELATIONS OFFICER
Sandra Bradley

CINEMA EXHIBITORS' ASSOCIATION
22 Golden Square, London, W1R 3PA. Tel: 0171 734 9551. FAX: 0171 734 6147.

OFFICERS
President—Stan Fishman, c/o CEA.
Vice-Presidents—N. Kilby, Robins Cinemas, 13 New Rd, London, WC2 N4LF. Tel: 0171 497 3320. M. J. Vickers, Reeltime Entertainment, 6 Ryders Avenue, Westgate-on-Sea, Kent CT8 8LN. Tel: 01843 834609. J. Merryweather, Apollo Leisure (UK) Ltd., 199 Glenfield Rd., Leicester LE3 6DL. Tel: 01257 471102. G. B. Henshaw, Cine City, Wilmslow Road, Withington, Manchester M20 9BG. Tel: 0161 445 0368.
Immediate Past President—R. C. Warbey, c/o CEA.
Honorary Treasurer—B. J. F. Bull, Circle Cinemas, 1 Teamans Rd., Morganstown, Radyr, Wales. Tel: 01222 522606.
Chief Executive—John Wilkinson, CEA, 22 Soho Square, London, W1R 3PA. Tel: 0171 734 9551. FAX: 0171 734 6147.

DELEGATES
Birmingham, Midlands & North Staffordshire Branch—M. P. Jervis, Kings Cinema Screens 1, 2, 3, Kings Square, West Bromwich, Staffs. Tel: 0121 553 0030. Deputy—S. Clarke, Victoria Playhouse Group, 8 Gate Lane, Sutton Coldfield, West Midlands. B73 5TT. Tel: 0121 355 2330.
Devon, Cornwall & West of England Branch—P. J. Hoare, Alexandra Theatre, Newton Abbott, Devon. Tel: 01626 65368. R. Lambert, Studio Cinema, High Street, Colefield, W. Midlands B73 5TT. Tel: 01594 893 3311. D. Williams, Regal Cinema, The Platt, Wadebridge, Cornwall, PL27 7AD. Tel: 01208 812791.
London Regional Branch—M. J. Vickers, Reeltime Entertainment, 6 Ryders Avenue, Westgate-on-Sea, Kent CT8 8LN. (01843 834609). B. Tonks, Regal Cinema, High Street, Cranleigh, Surrey, GU6 8RT. Tel: 01483 272373. D. Dowson, Coronet Cinema, Notting Hill Gate, London W11 3LB. Tel: 0171 221 0123). N. Waring, Plaza Cinema, Station Road West, Oxted, Surrey RH8 9AE. Tel: 01883 712567.
Manchester & Northern Counties Branch—G. B. Henshaw, Cine City, Wilmslow Road, Withington, Manchester M20 9BG.

Tel: 0161 445 0368. J. S. Downs, Cosmo Leisure Group, Central Hall, 62/4 Market Street, Stalybridge, Cheshire SK15 2AB. Tel: 0161 338 7953.
Scottish Branch—D.M. Cameron, Dominion Cinema, Newbattle Terrace, Morningside, Edinburgh. Tel: 0131 447 2660.
South Wales & Monmouthshire Branch—B.J.F. Bull, 1 Teamans Row, Morganstown Radyr, Cardiff. Tel: 01495 522606.
Wessex Branch—H. King, The Little Theatre, St. Michael's Place, Bath, Avon BA1 1SF Tel: 0171 435 7207.

CIRCUIT DELEGATES
National Amusements (UK) Ltd.—200 Elm Street, Dedham, Massachussetts 02026, USA Tel: 001 617 461 1600. Showcase Cinema, Redfield Road, Lenton, Nottingham NG7 2UW. Tel: 011 59 862 508. J. Bilsborough (USA), D. Short (Nottingham).
Odeon Cinemas—54 Whitcomb Street, London WC2H 7DN. Tel: 0171 839 6373. 439-445 Godstone Road, Whyteleafe, Surrey, CR3 0YG. Tel: 01883 623 355. M. Archibald, H. Corrance, B. Keward, M. Walker, N.J.A. Pidgeon, D. Morton, A. Robertshaw, D. Robertson.
United Cinemas International (UK)—Lee House, 90 Great Bridgewater Street, Manchester M1 5JW. Tel: 0161 455 4000.
Warner Bros. Theatres (UK)—3rd fl. S., Wells Point, 79 Wells St., London W1P 3RD. P. Dobson, M. Angell, D. Cownty.
Apollo Leisure Group—G. Lipson, 424 Woolton Road, Liverpool L25 6AQ. Tel: 0151 708 6672. P. Gregg, Boar's Hill, P.O. Box 16, Oxford OX1 5JB. Tel: 01865 730 066. J. Merryweather, 199 Glenfield Road, Leicester LE3 6DL. Tel: 01257 471 012. D. Hutchinson, Fox Hill House, Wains Lane, Read, Burnley BB12 7QY. Tel: 01282 774 269.
CAC Leisure PLC—P. Perrins, P.O. Box 21, 23-25 Huntly Street, Inverness IV1 1LA, Scotland. Tel: 01463 237 611. I. Cluley, 16 Locarno Road, Acton, London, W3 6RG. Tel: 0181 993 1511. J. Davidson, 203B High Street, Elgin IV1 1DT Tel: 01343 549 100.
Robins Cinemas—13 New Row, London WC2N 4LF. Tel: 0171 497 3320. B. Freedman, N. Kilby.
Virgin Cinemas Ltd.—626 High Rd., Chiswick, London W4 5RY. Tel: 0181 987 5000. J. Carrol, K. Pullinger.

CEA BRANCH SECRETARIES
Birmingham, Midlands & North Staffordshire
Victoria Playhouse Group, 8 Gate Lane, Sutton Coldfield, West Midlands, B73 5TT. Tel: 0121 355 5032. S. W. Clarke.
Devon, Cornwall & West of England
6 Elmside, Willand Old Village, Nr. Cullompton, Devon EX15 2RN. Tel: 01884 333 98. G. Vearncombe.
London Regional
CEA Head Office, 22 Golden Square, London W1R 3PA. Tel: 0171 734 9661. FAX: 0171 734 6147.
Manchester & Northern Counties
Cheshire County Cinemas Ltd., Plaza Buildings, Witton Street, Northwich, Cheshire CW9 5EA Tel: 01606 483 75. R.I. Godfrey.
Scottish Branch
30-34 Reform Street, Dundee, Fife DD1 1RJ. Tel: 01382 229 222. N.J.A. Robertson, Messrs. Blackadder, Reid, Johnston.
South Wales & Monmouthshire
Scala Cinema, Pontypool, Gwent. Tel: 01495 756 038. S. Reynolds.
Wessex
Odeon Cinema, Westover Road, Bournemouth, Dorset BH1 2BZ. Tel: 01202 557 627.

COMPOSERS' GUILD OF GREAT BRITAIN
34 Hanway Street, London, W1P 9DE. Tel: 0171 436 0007. FAX: 0171 436 1913.
PRESIDENT
Sir Peter Maxwell Davies, C.B.E.
GENERAL SECRETARY
Heather Rosenblatt

CRITICS' CIRCLE
(Film Section)
CHAIRMAN
George Perry, 7 Ruehampton Lane, London, SW15 5LS.
HON. SECRETARY
John Marriott, 73 Hornsey Lane, Highgate, London, N6 5LQ.

DIRECTORS GUILD OF GREAT BRITAIN
15-19 Great Titchfield Street, London, W1P 7FB. Tel: 0171 436 8646. FAX: 0171 436 8626.
CONTACT
David Litchfield

EDINBURGH AND LOTHIAN SCREEN INDUSTRIES OFFICE
Filmhouse, 88 Lothian Road, Edinburgh EH3 9BZ, Scotland. Tel: 0131 228 5960. FAX: 0131 228 5967.
CONTACTS
George Carlaw, Ros Davis

EUROPEAN SCRIPT FUND
39c Highbury Place, London, N5 1QP. Tel: 0171 226 9903. FAX: 0171 354 2706.

FEDERATION AGAINST COPYRIGHT THEFT (FACT)
7 Victory Business Centre, Worton Road, Isleworth, Middx., TW7 6ER. Tel: 0181 568 6646. FAX: 0181 560 6364.
DIRECTOR GENERAL
R. Dixon

FILM ARTISTES' ASSOCIATION
(Trade Union No. 1990), F.A.A. House, 61 Marloes Road, London, W8 6LE. Tel: 0171 937 4567. FAX: 0171 937 0790.
GENERAL SECRETARY
Roy Hodges

FILM CENSOR'S OFFICE
16 Harcourt Terrace, Dublin 2, Republic of Ireland. Tel: 01 676 1985.
CONTACT
Sheamus Smith

FILM INSTITUTE OF IRELAND
Irish Film Centre, 6 Eustace Street, Dublin 2, Republic of Ireland. Tel: 01 679 5744. FAX: 01 677 8755.
DIRECTOR
Sheila Pratschke

GUILD OF BRITISH CAMERA TECHNICIANS
5-11 Taunton Road, Metropolitan Centre, Greenford, Middx., UB6 8UQ. Tel: 0181 578 9243. FAX: 0181 575 5972.
CONTACT
Maureen O'Grady

GUILD OF BRITISH FILM EDITORS
Travair, Spurlands End Road, Great Kingshill, High Wycombe, Bucks., HP15 6HY. Tel: 01494 712313. FAX: 01494 863563.
HON. SECRETARY
Alfred E. Cox
HON. TREASURER
Gillian Dearberg

GUILD OF FILM PRODUCTION EXECUTIVES
Pinewood Studios, Iver, Bucks. Tel: 01753 651700.
PRESIDENT
Stuart Lyons
HON. SECRETARY
Hugh Attwooll

GUILD OF FILM PRODUCTION ACCOUNTANTS AND FINANCIAL ADMINISTRATORS
Pinewood Studios, Pinewood Road, Iver, Bucks. SL0 0NH. Tel: 01753 656473. FAX: 01753 656850.
PRESIDENT
Mike Smith
CONTACT
Ann Runeckles

INDEPENDENT FILM DISTRIBUTORS' ASSOCIATION
c/o Connoisseur Video Ltd., 10A Stephen Mews, London, W1A 0AX. Tel: 0171 957 8957. FAX: 0171 957 8968.

INTERNATIONAL ANIMATED FILM ASSOCIATION
61 Railwayside, Barnes, London, SW13 0PQ. Tel: 0181 878 4040. FAX: 0181 675 8499.
VICE PRESIDENT
Pat Raine Webb

INTERNATIONAL ASSOCIATION OF BROADCASTING MANUFACTURERS
4B, High St., Burnham, Slough SL1 7JH. Tel: 01628 667633. FAX: 01628 665882.
CHAIRMAN
Tom McGann
SECRETARY
Claude Guillaume
TREASURER
Dan Anco
ADMINISTRATOR
Alan Hirst
SECRETARIAT
Ken Walker

INTERNATIONAL VISUAL COMMUNICATION ASSOCIATION (IVCA)
Bolsover House, 5-6 Clipstone Street, London, W1P 7EB. Tel: 0171 580 0962. FAX: 0171 436 2606.
CHIEF EXECUTIVE
Jamie Neil

IRISH ACTORS EQUITY GROUP
Liberty Hall, Dublin 1, Republic of Ireland. Tel: 8740081. FAX: 8743691.
GROUP SECRETARY
Gerard Browne

MECHANICAL-COPYRIGHT PROTECTION SOCIETY LTD. (MCPS)
Elgar House, 41 Streatham High Road, London, SW16 1ER. Tel: 0181 769 4400. FAX: 0181 769 8792. Telex: 946792 MCPS G.
CUSTOMER SERVICES ADVISOR
Malcolm Carruthers

MUSICIANS' UNION
60-62 Clapham Road, London, SW9 0JJ. Tel: 0171 582 5566.
FAX: 0171 582 9805.
GENERAL SECRETARY
Dennis Scard

PACT LTD.
(Producers Alliance for Cinema and Television)
Gordon House, Greencoat Place, London, SW1P 1PH. Tel: 0171
233 6000. FAX: 0171 233 8935.
CHIEF EXECUTIVE
John Woodward
MEMBERSHIP OFFICER
Martin Hart

THE PERFORMING RIGHT SOCIETY LTD. (PRS)
29-33 Berners Street, London, W1P 4AA. Tel: 0171 580 5544.
Telex: 892678 PRSLONG. FAX: 0171 631 4138.
GENERAL MANAGER
John Axon
PUBLIC AFFAIRS CONTROLLER
Terri Anderson

THE PERSONAL MANAGERS' ASSN. LTD.
Rivercroft, One Summer Road, East Molesey, Surrey KT8 9LX.
Tel: 0181 398 9796. FAX: 0181 398 9796.
SECRETARY
Angela Adler

ST. PAUL BOOK AND MEDIA CENTRE
5A-7 Royal Exchange Square, Glasgow, G1 3AH, Scotland. Tel:
0141 226 3391.

SCREEN ADVERTISING WORLD ASSOCIATION LTD.
103A Oxford Street, London, W1R 1TF. Tel: 0171 734 7621.
SECRETARY GENERAL
Charles Sciberras

SOCIETY OF FILM DISTRIBUTORS LTD.
22 Golden Square, London, W1R 3PA. Tel: 0171 437 4383. FAX:
0171 734 0912.
PRESIDENT
James Higgins, M.B.E.
GENERAL SECRETARY
D.C. Hunt
SFD COUNCIL MEMBERS
Artificial Eye Film Co. Ltd., Buena Vista Int'l (UK) Ltd., Columbia
Tri-Star Films UK, Film Four Distributors Ltd., First Independent
Films Ltd., Entertainment Film Dist. Ltd., Gala Film Dist., Guild
Film Dist. Ltd., Metro Tartan, Polygram Filmed Entertainment
(UK) Ltd., Rank Film Dist. Ltd., Twentieth Century Fox Film Co.
Ltd., United International Pictures (UK), Warner Bros.
Distributors Ltd.

SOUND & COMMUNICATIONS INDUSTRIES FEDERATION
4-B High Street, Burnham, Slough SL1 7JH. Tel: 01 628 667633.
FAX: 01 628 665882.
CHIEF EXECUTIVE
Ken Walker, M.B.E.

VARIETY CLUB OF GREAT BRITAIN
(Tent No. 36)
326 High Holbron, London, WC1V 7AW. Tel: 0171 611 3888.
FAX: 0171 611 3892.
PRESS GUY
Bill Hagerty

THE WRITERS' GUILD OF GREAT BRITAIN
430 Edgware Road, London, W2 1EH. Tel: 0171 723 8074. FAX:
0171 706 2413.
PRESIDENT
Rosemary Anne Sisson
HON. TREASURER
Gary Hopkins
GENERAL SECRETARY
Alison Gray

Government Divisions On Film Affairs

AUSTRALIAN FILM COMMISSION
2nd Floor, Victory House, 99-101 Regent Street, London,
W1R 7HB. Tel: 0171 734 9383. FAX: 0171 434 0170.

BRITISH COUNCIL EVENTS SECTION
Film, TV and Video Department, 11 Portland Place, London,
W1N 4EJ. Tel: 0171 389 3063/4. FAX: 0171 389 3041. Telex:
8952201 BRICON G.
FESTIVALS OFFICERS
Kevin Franklin, Satwant Gill
OTHER EVENTS
Geraldine Higgins, Jo Maurice

THE BRITISH DEFENCE FILM LIBRARY
SSVC Chalfont Grove, Chalfont St. Peter, Gerrerds Cross,
Bucks, SL9 8TN. Tel: 01494 878278. FAX: 01494 878007.
PATRON
H.R.H. The Princess Margaret
MANAGING DIRECTOR
Air Vice Marshall David Crwys-Williams, CB FIPM, FIMGT,
RAR
FILM & VIDEO DEPARTMENT
Renate Foster

BRITISH FILM INSTITUTE (BFI)
(The BFI's divisions and departments include: BFI on the South
Bank (National Film Theatre, Museum of the Moving Image and
London Film Festival); Research (Research and Education, Book
Publishing and "Sight and Sound" magazine); the National Film
and Television Archive; Exhibition and Distribution; Library and
Information Services; Planning Unit; BFI Production.)
21 Stephen Street, London, W1P 1PL. Tel: 0171 255 1444.
FAX: 0171 436 7950. Telex: 27624 BFILDNG.
CHAIRMAN
Jeremy Thomas
DIRECTOR
Wilf Stevenson

BRITISH FILM COMMISSION
70 Baker Street, London, W1M 1DJ. Tel: 0171 224 5000. FAX:
0171 224 1013.
COMMISSIONER
Sir Sydney Samuelson
CHIEF EXECUTIVE
Andrew Patrick
MARKETING MANAGER
Amanda Sparks
INFORMATION MANAGER
Joanna Dewar Gibb
PRESS & P.R. OFFICER
Tina McFarling

BRITISH SCREEN ADVISORY COUNCIL
93 Wardour Street, London, W1V 3TE. Tel: 0171 413 8009.
FAX: 0171 734 5122.
CHAIRMAN
Lord Attenborough
DEPUTY CHAIRMEN
Michael Deeley, John Howkins, Colin Leventhal
DIRECTOR
Fiona Clarke-Hackslor

CENTRAL OFFICE OF INFORMATION
Hercules Road, London, SE1 7DU. Tel: 0171 928 2345. FAX:
0171 261 8874.
DIRECTOR OF FILMS, TELEVISION & RADIO DIVISION
Malcolm Nisbet

**DEPARTMENT OF NATIONAL HERITAGE BROADCASTING
AND MEDIA DIVISION**
Room 203, 2-4 Cockspur Street, London, SWIY 5DH. Tel:
0171 211 6000. FAX: 0171 211 6210.
CONTACT
Paul Wright

LONDON FILM COMMISSION
c/o Carnival Films, 12 Raddington Rd., Ladbroke Grove,
London, W10 5TG. Tel: 0181 968 0968. FAX: 0181 968
0177.
CONTACT
Christabel Alberty

NATIONAL FILM AND TELEVISION SCHOOL
Beaconsfield Studios, Station Road, Beaconsfield, Bucks.,
HP9 1LG. Tel: 01494 671234. FAX: 01494 674042.
DIRECTOR
Henning Camre

THE SERVICES SOUND & VISION CORPORATION
Chalfont Grove, Chalfont St. Peter, Gerrards Cross, Bucks.,
SL9 8TN. Tel: 01494874. FAX: 0149487 2982.
PATRON
H.R.H. The Princess Margaret
BOARD OF MANAGEMENT CHAIRMAN
Gen. Sir Geoffrey Howlett, K.B.E. M.C.
MANAGING DIRECTOR
Air Vice Marshal David Crwys-Williams, CB FIPM, FIMGT, RAR (Ret'd)
ASSISTANT DIRECTOR, MARKETING
Renate Foster
PURCHASING MANAGER
Anne Eva

The Industry
in Canada

Year in Review

Production Companies

Production Services

Distribution Companies

Exhibition Circuits

Trade Associations

Government Agencies

CANADIAN YEAR IN REVIEW

Famous Players Inc., in April 1996, announced major upgrades and additions to its theatre chain operations, plus an ambitious new project. "Our expansion plans call for the addition of 250 screens over the next three years," says President Joseph Peixoto. John Bailey, CEO, adds, "We are not merely getting larger, we are also getting better." At mid-1996, Famous operated a total of 106 locations with 480 screens. With headquarters in Toronto, it is part of the entertainment operations of Viacom Inc.

In Ontario, its Burlington 8-plex will boast eight wall-to-wall screens and 1,920 seats. The Lambton cinema in Sarnia will expand by four screens and 800 seats to a 9-screen complex of 2,079 seats with wall-to-wall screens and digital sound technology, automated ticketing machines and video games. In New Brunswick, a new theatre in Moncton will be the largest in that city and will house eight screens and 1,920 seats. The new cinemas in Burlington and Moncton are designed to encompass wall-to-wall screens, digital sound technology, infrared systems for the hard of hearing and handicapped access. Among other features are the use of bank cards at automated ticketing machines for both ticket and concession combos, interactive video kiosks to record customer feedback, video game arcades and a birthday party room. In May, Famous Players announced another upgrade—the addition of five screens to Polson Place Cinemas in Vernon, British Columbia, making it a state-of-the-art 7-screen complex with 2,000 seats. These four cinemas were scheduled to open in November 1996. On July 19, 1996 Famous Players' President Peixoto opened Westhills Cinema in Calgary, Alberta, declaring that it was "the first of our new high concept theatres to open in Canada." In addition to being the largest cinema complex in Western Canada (10 large screens and 2,730 seats), Westhills boasts the country's first Tech-Town." Tech-Town houses 12 state-of-the-art video games inside a glowing futuristic spaceship which opens onto the multi-purpose theatre lobby.

Famous Players and Menkes Developments have unveiled plans for a 350,000 square-foot Citywalk Entertainment Centre, an innovative new complex in the city of North York, Ontario, devoted to lifestyle and leisure activities and anchored by a 10-screen cinema multiplex. A new concept and a first for Metro Toronto, the three-story Citywalk will feature a major bookstore, music store, computer & electronics retailer, high-tech interactive entertainment, plus a mix of restaurants to appeal to all pockets and tastes. The third-floor cinema will have stadium seating and, says Famous President Joseph Peixoto, "This flagship complex will guarantee every moviegoer an unobstructed view." The project is scheduled for completion in the spring of 1998 at a cost of approx. $C50 million. Ticket prices at Famous Players theatres remain steady with a top price of $C8, and lower before 6 pm. on weekends. There are also discounts on weekday matinees.

Cineplex Odeon Corporation owns and operates motion picture theatres, related food service concessions and complementary theater entertainment businesses in the U.S. and six Canadian provinces. It is the largest exhibitor in Canada with, at mid-1996, 618 screens in 128 theatres principally serving the major metropolitan areas. Seventy-nine percent of its Canadian screens are in the top 10 Canadian markets.

The Corporation's 1995 Annual Report showed that its Canadian theatres reported a decrease in box office revenue of 5.8% for that year compared to 1994. This was the result of a drop in attendance of 4.0% and a decrease in box office revenue per patron of 1.8%. The fourth quarter of 1995 showed box office revenue down 8.7% compared to the same quarter for 1994. This was a result of a decrease in attendance of 5.7% and revenue per patron declining 3.0%. The Corporation experienced the worst first quarter in attendance and box office revenue since 1988. This was primarily attributed to the lack of commercially viable film product, fundamental to attracting patrons. Canadian concession revenue decreased in 1995 by 2.8% compared to 1994, reflecting an increase in concession revenue per patron of 1.2% offset by the drop in attendance of 4.0%. In the fourth quarter of 1995, concession revenue was down 5.2% comprising a decrease in attendance of 5.7% and an increase in concession revenue per patron of 0.5%. President & CEO Allen Karp reported that the primary thrust of the Corporation's future strategy is to "increase its revenue and generating cash flow by developing and building approximately 500 additional screens in target markets..." However, the report of Cineplex Odeon Corporation for the six months ending June 20, 1996 showed better performance. The Canadian theatres reported admission revenue increased over this period by 11.5% compared to the same period in 1995. This gain was the result of a 13.2% surge in attendance and a 1.7% increase in box office revenue per patron. Concession revenue was up by 16.1% compared to the same period in 1995, reflecting both the improved attendance and a 2.9% increase in concession revenue per patron.

At mid-1996, Cineplex Canadian admission prices for adults in major cities were $C8.50 on Friday and Saturday nights, $C8.00 on other nights, and $C4.25 in smaller venues. A 'Cinesave' adult admission of $C4.25 applies on Tuesdays across the country and in the province of Québec only, on Tuesdays and Wednesdays. There are also special concessions for children and seniors.

Johnny Mnemonic (Alliance Productions) won the 1995 Golden Reel Award for the dramatic feature which achieved the highest gross box office—a respectable $C3.3—in Canadian theatres. Two notable Canadian releases were Robert LePage's Le Confessional and Margaret's Museum starring Helena Bonham Carter. Canadian films selected for the 1996 Toronto International Film Festival included a gala presentation of David Wellington's adaptation of the Stratford (Ontario) Festival's production of Eugene O'Neill's Long Day's Journey Into Night, and the latest features from established directors such as Deepa Mehta's Fire, John Greyson's Lillies, Peter Lynch's Project Grizzly, Srinivas Krishna's Lulu, Bruce LaBruce/Rick Castro's Hustler White, Colin Strayer's Rod Serling—Writer and Pierre Hébert's La Plante Humaine. A number of short film directors had first features showcased including Lynne Stopkewich's Kissed, Pierre Gang's Sous-sol, Paul DiStefano's Trouble, Michael McNamara's The Cockroach That Ate Cincinnati, Denis Langlois's L'escorte, Magnus Isacsson's documentary Power, Robin Schlaht's Moscow Summer, Colleen Murphy's Shoemaker and Ileana Pietrobruno's Cat Swallows Parakeet and Speaks!. U.S. films which did well at the Canadian box office include Apollo 13, Ace Ventura: When Nature Calls, Casper, The Hunchback of Notre Dame, Mission: Impossible, Pocohontas, A Time to Kill, Tin Cup, Toy Story and Twister.

— PATRICIA THOMPSON

Canadian Box Office Statistics

This latest information released by Statistics Canada, a federal government agency, is based upon new survey processes for 1994-95, and covers movie theatres and drive-ins, including chains and 268 independently operated theatres.
Number of theatres/screens: There were 582 regular motion picture theatres (598 in 1992-93) plus 77 drive-in theatres (88 in 1992-93), for a total of 659 theatres (686 in 1992-93). Though the number of theatres decreased by about 3% to 582, of which 355 were operated by chains, the number of regular theatre screens grew by almost 2% to 1,682 (1,613 in 1992-93). Drive-in theatres had an average of 1.6 screens per theatre, almost unchanged from the total of 1,742 from the previous year.
Box Office: Renewed interest in the big-screen experience, and large, multi-screen theatres with comfortable seats, digital sound and video games, along with special seat pricing on Tuesdays, and other discounts, attracted teenagers and families. Thus, attendance at movie theatres and drive-ins appears to be showing a steady growth reaching a seven-year high in 1994-95, and all provinces (except Manitoba which remains unchanged) recorded increased admissions. Attendance at movie theatres rose 4% to 81.1 million, and drive-in attendance hit a four-year high of 2.7 million, up 9% over 1993-94. Chain-operated theatres, including drive-ins, had an average attendance of 181,840, about four times the average attendance of independent theatres (47,260). On average, each Canadian went to the movies nearly three times during the year 1994-95, and people in Alberta and British Columbia were the keenest moviegoers.
Profit Margin: In 1994-95, companies continued to close unprofitable theatres and to turn many in urban centres into multi-screen houses. Another move was to reduce employment costs; movie theatres had 2.0 full-time employees per theatre, down 15% from the previous year. Part-time employees per movie theatre also dropped 8% to 13.3. Chain and independent theatres had revenues of $568.2 million, a 5% increase over 1993-94, and profits rose 7% to $C62.6 million. Chain profits were up nearly 8%; independents 6%. However, drive-in profits fell 9%, and reported an 30% increase in number of full-time employees per drive-in to 2.2, with an average 2% drop in part-time staff to 10.42.

663

PRODUCTION COMPANIES

ABATON PICTURES, INC.
185 Grace St., Toronto, ON, M6G 3A7. (416) 537-2641. FAX: (416) 588-8125
PRESIDENT
Ian McDougall

ABS PRODUCTIONS LIMITED
196 Joseph Zatzman Dr., Dartmouth, NS, B3B 1N4. (902) 468-4336. FAX: (902) 468-4341
PRESIDENT
Robert G. Sandoz
TECHNICAL DIRECTOR
A. J. McKay

ACCENT ENTERTAINMENT CORPORATION
207 Adelaide St. E., Ste. 300, Toronto, ON, M5A 1M8. (416) 867-8700. FAX: (416) 867-1764.
Susan Cavan

THE ACE FILM CO.
1152 Mainland St., Ste. 400, Vancouver, BC, V6B 4X2. (604) 682-0001. FAX: (604) 682-7346.
EXECUTIVE PRODUCER
Parker Jefferson

ACPAV
1050 boul. René-Lévesque est, bureau 200,Montréal, QC, H2L 2L6. (514) 849-2281. FAX: (514) 849-9487.
PRODUCERS
Marc Daigle, René Gueissaz, Bernadette Payeur

ALLAN KING ASSOCIATES LIMITED
965 Bay St., #2409, Toronto, ON, M5S 2A3. (416) 964-7284. FAX: (416) 964-7997
PRESIDENT
Allan King

ALLEGRO FILMS INC.
2187 rue Lariviére, Montréal, QC, H2K 1P5. (514) 529-0320. FAX: (514) 529-0328.
Tom Berry, Franco Battista

ALLIANCE COMMUNICATIONS CORPORATION
121 Bloor St. E., Ste.1400, Toronto, ON, M4W 3M5. (416) 967-1174. FAX: (416) 960-0971.
5 Place Ville Marie, Ste. 1435, Montréal, QC, H3B 2G2. (514) 878-2282. FAX: (514) 878-2419.
1199 W. Hastings., Ste. 1221, Vancouver, BC, V6E 3T5. (604) 687-3798. FAX: (604) 687-3958
301 North Canon Dr., Ste. 321, Beverly Hills, CA 90210. (310) 275-5501. FAX: (310) 275-5502.
40 rue Bayard, 75008 Paris, France. 011 331 58 83 18 00. FAX: 011 331 53 83 18 01.
Block 1, Unit H, Shannon Business Park, Shannon, Co. Clare, Ireland. 01 353 61 47 23 29. FAX: 011 353 61 47 22 28
CHAIRMAN & CEO
Robert Lantos
EXECUTIVE V.P., PRODUCTION
Michael Weisbarth

ARGUS FILM PRODUCTIONS INC.
3924 Blantyre Pl., N. Vancouver, BC, V7G 2G5. (604) 929-5355. FAX: (604) 929-5341
Bob Ennis

ARK FILMS INC.
1140 Homer St., Ste. 308, Vancouver, BC, V6B 2X6. (604) 689-1555. FAX: (604) 689-1631.
PRESIDENT
Alan Morinis

ARTO-PELLI MOTION PICTURES INC.
18 Gloucester Lane, 3rd Fl., Toronto, ON, M4Y 1L5. (416) 928-0164. FAX: (416) 928-3399
PRODUCER
Stavros C. Stavrides

ARVI'S PRODUCTION COMPANY
9408 148 St., Edmonton, AB, T5R 1A6. Tel & FAX: (403) 481-1798.
Arvi Liimatainen

ASKA FILM PRODUCTIONS INC.
1600 ave. de Lorimier, Ste. 211, Montréal, QC, H2K 3W5. (514) 521-7103. FAX: (514) 521-6174.
Claude Gagnon, Yuri Yoshimura-Gagnon

ASSOCIATED PRODUCERS
110 Spadina Ave., Ste. 1001, Toronto, ON, M5V 2K4. (416) 504-6662. FAX: (416) 504-6667.
Elliott Halpern, Simcha Jacobovici

ASTERISK PRODUCTIONS LTD.
977 Hampshire Rd., Victoria, BC, V8S 4S3. (604) 598-1256. FAX: (604) 598-1299. e-mail: asterisk@islandnet.com
David Springbett, Heather MacAndrew

ASTRAL ENTERTAINNMENT GROUP
(An Astral Communications Company) 2100 rue Ste-Catherine ouest, bur. 900, Montréal, QC, H3H 2T3. (514) 939-5000. FAX: (514) 939-1515.
33 Yonge St., Ste. 1020, Toronto, ON, M5E 1S9. (416) 956-2000. FAX: (416) 956-2020
PRESIDENT & C.O.O.
Sidney Greenberg
SENIOR VICE-PRESIDENT
Stephen Greenberg

ATLANTIS FILMS LIMITED
65 Heward Ave., Toronto, ON, M4M 2T5. (416) 462-0246. FAX: (416) 462-0254.
Michael MacMillan, Seaton McLean, Ted Riley
227 Broadway, Ste. 300, Santa Monica, CA 90401. (310) 576-7719. FAX: (310) 576-0799.
Peter Sussman

BARNA-ALPER PRODUCTIONS INC.
366 Adelaide St. W., Ste. 700, Toronto, ON, M5V 1R9. (416) 979-0676. FAX: (416) 976-7476.
Laszlo Barna, Tom Perlmutter, Laura Lightbown, Vibika Bianchi

BEACON GROUP INVESTMENTS LTD.
1285 W. Pender St., 9th Fl., Vancouver, BC, V6E 4B1. (604) 684-6440. FAX: (604) 684-9272.
PRESIDENT & CEO
A. Grant Allen

BEAVER CREEK PICTURES
6 Springwood Cr., Unionville, ON, L3R 3Z9. (905) 477-3821. FAX: (905) 470-0410.
PRODUCER & DIRECTOR
Conrad Beaubien
EXECUTIVE PRODUCERS
Jane Beaubien, Eric Douglas

BLOKLAND PICTURES CORPORATION
217 St. George St., Unit 44, Toronto, ON, M5R 3S7. (416) 975-9259. FAX: (416) 975-8214.
PRODUCER & DIRECTOR
Jim Blokland

BLUE SKY COMMUNICATIONS INC.
10022 103 St., 3rd Fl., Edmonton, AB, 5TJ 0X2. (403) 944-0340. FAX: (403) 428-0651.
PRODUCERS
Kate Holowach, Norm Fassbender

BLUE SKY PRODUCTIONS INC.
1605 Wilmot Pl., Victoria, BC, V8R 5S3. Tel. & FAX: (604) 370-1108.
Lloyd Chesley, James Fry, Jeffrey Fuhr

BONGARD FILMS INC.
59 Mutual St., Toronto, ON, M5B 2A9. (416) 368-4593.
PRODUCER & DIRECTOR
Ralph Bongard
POST-PRODUCTION
Bob Buchan, cfe

BOOTLEG FILMS
188 Spadina Ave., Ste. 705, Toronto, ON, M5T 3A4. (416) 703-3546. (416) 703-3599.
Milan Cheylov, Lori Lansens

BRAVURA PRODUCTIONS LTD.
1 Benvenuto Pl., Ste. 220, Toronto, ON, M5V 2L1. (416) 964-7490.
PRESIDENT
Bruce Martin

BREAKTHROUGH FILMS AND TELEVISION INC.
179 Mavety St., Toronto, ON, M6P 2M1. (415) 766-6588. FAX: (416) 769-1436.
DIRECTORS & PRODUCERS
Ira Levy, Peter Williamson

BRIAN AVERY AUDIO
65 Hilton Ave., Toronto, ON, M5R 3E5. (416) 538-3103.
Brian Avery

BRIAN BOBBIE PRODUCTIONS LTD.
1007 Broadview Ave., Toronto, ON, M4K 2S1. (416) 467-9595. FAX: (416) 467-9782.
Brian Bobbie, Janice Bobbie

BRIDGE FILM PRODUCTIONS INC.
44 Charles St. W., Ste. 2518, Toronto, ON, M4Y 1R7. (416) 927-0663.
Brigitte Berman

BUFFALO GAL PICTURES INC.
180 Market Ave. E., Ste. 200, Winnipeg, MB, R3B 0P7. (204) 942-3568. FAX: (204) 943-4716.
PRODUCER
Phyllis Laing

CALGARY TELEVISION CENTRE
222 23 St. N.E., Calgary, AB, T2E 7N2. (403) 235-7733,800-661-8374.
Kim Corrigall

CAMBIUM FILM & VIDEO PRODUCTIONS LTD.
18 Dupont St., Toronto, ON, M5R 1V2. (416) 964-8750. FAX: (416) 964-1980.
EXECUTIVE PRODUCER
Arnie Zipursky

CAMERA ONE FILMS LIMITED
2150 Suphur Springs Dr., R.R.#1, Ridgeville, ON, L0S 1M0. (905) 892-3077.
PRODUCER & DIRECTOR
Elias Petras

CANAMEDIA PRODUCTIONS LTD.
125 Dupont St., Toronto, ON, M5R 1V4. (416) 324-9190. FAX: (416) 972-6261.
PRESIDENT
Les Harris

CANNELL PRODUCTION SERVICES INC.
555 Brooksbank Ave., N. Vancouver, BC, V7J 3S5. (604) 983-5000. FAX: (604) 983-5198.
V. P. & GENERAL MANAGER
Stephen Sassen

CAROL REYNOLDS PRODUCTIONS INC.
2 Bloor St. W., Ste. 1740, Toronto, ON, M4W 3E2. (416) 926-1661. FAX: (416) 926-1668.
PRESIDENT
Carol Reynolds

CASSAR FILMWORKS INC.
4 Large Ct., Brampton, ON, L6S 5V2. (905) 451-3596. FAX: (905) 451-4168.
PRESIDENT
John Cassar, csc, DGC, DGA

CATALYST ENYTERTAINMENT INC.
495 Wellington St. W., Ste. 212, Toronto, ON, M5V 1G1. (416) 591-6767. FAX: (416) 591-6764.
CEO
Charles Falzon

CHAMPLAIN PRODUCTIONS INC.
4 Westmount Sq., Ste. 200, Westmount, QC, H3Z 2S6. (514) 933-1161. FAX: (514) 933-1706.
CHAIRMAN
Adrien Pouliot
PRESIDENT
Ghislain St-Pierre
GENERAL MANAGER
François Garcia

CHECK-HIT-OUT PRODUCTIONS
3726 blvd. St-Laurent, Montréal, QC, H2X 2V8. (514) 843-4725. FAX: (514) 843-4631.
Claude Chamberlan
550 La Guardia Pl., New York, NY 10021. Tel. & FAX: (212) 925-1575

CHRISTOPHER CHAPMAN LTD.
415 Merton St., Toronto, ON, M4S 1B4. (416) 487-3005.
PRESIDENT
Christopher Chapman

CHUMCITY
299 Queen St. W., Toronto, ON, M5V 1Z5. (416) 591-5757. FAX: (416) 340-7005.
PRESIDENT & EXECUTIVE PRODUCER
Moses Znaimer
PRESIDENT: CHUM TV
Ron Waters

CINAK LTEE
C.P. 360, Bedford, QC, J0J 1A0. (514) 248-3295.
PRESIDENT
Jean Pierre Lefebvre

CINAR FILMS INC.
1055 boul. Ste-André, Ste. 900, Montréal, QC, H2L 4S5. (514) 843-7070. FAX: (514) 843-7080.
Ron Weinberg, Micheline Charest

CINEFLIX INC.
5505 St-Laurent Blvd., Ste. 4104, Montréal, QC, H2T 1S6. (514) 278-3140. FAX: (514) 270-3165.
Glen Salzman

CINEGRAPHE PRODUCTIONS
2717 Morgan, Sainte-Foy, QC, G1W 4R9. (418) 652-3345. FAX: (418) 652-3353.
Nicholas Kinsey, Andrée Tousignant

CINE-GROUPE J.P. INC.
1151 Alexandre-DeSève, Montréal, QC, H2L 2T7.
TV SERIES CONTACTS
Jacques Pettigrew, Hubert Gariepy

CINEMA ESPERANCA INTERNATIONAL INC.
96 Spadina Ave., Ste. 301, Toronto, ON, M5V 2J6. (416) 703-5000. FAX: (416) 703-5002.
PRESIDENT & CEO
André Bennett

CHAIR & CONTROLLER
Maria Pimentel

CINEMAGINAIRE
5505 boul. Saint-Laurent, Ste. 3005, Montreal, QC, H2T 1S6. (514) 272-5505. FAX: (514) 272-9841.
PRESIDENT & PRODUCER
Denise Robert

CINEPIX INC.
8275 rue Mayrand, Montréal, QC, H4P 2C8. (514) 342-2340. FAX: (514) 342-1922.
CHAIRMAN
J. Dunning
PRESIDENT
A. Link

CINEROUTES PRODUCTIONS
259 Erskine Ave., Toronto, ON, M4P 1Z6. (416) 486-4830.
Anthony Azzopardi

CINEVIDEO PLUS
2100 rue Ste-Catherine ouest, Ste. 810, Montréal, QC, H3H 2T3. (514) 937-7986. FAX: (514) 937-8332.
PRÉSIDENTE & DIRECTEUR GÉNÉRAL
Justine Héroux

CITADEL FILMS LIMITED
1652 Barrington St., Halifax, NS, B3J 2A2. (902) 421-1326. FAX: (902) 423-0484.
PRESIDENT
Barry Cowling

CITE AMERIQUE CINEMA TELEVISION
5800 boul. St-Laurent, Montreal, QC, H2T 1T3. (514) 278-8080. FAX: (514) 278-4000.

CLEARWATER FILMS LIMITED
1255 Yonge St., Ste. 100, Toronto, ON, M4T 1W6. (416) 929-7232. FAX: (416) 929-7225.
PRESIDENT
G. Chalmers Adams

COCHRAN ENTERTAINMENT INC.
1820 Hollis St., Ste. 300, Halifax, NS B3J 1W4. (902) 421-9777. FAX: (902) 425-8659. e-mail: hello@cochran.com
PRESIDENT
Andrew Cochran
MANAGER OF DEVELOPMENT
Maureen Wheller

ANNETTE COHEN PRODUCTIONS
25 Imperial St., #500, Toronto, ON, M5P 1C1. (416) 483-8018. FAX: (416) 483-9763.
PRESIDENT
Annette Cohen

CONTINUITIES
41 Park Hill Rd., Toronto, ON, M6C 3N2. (416) 787-3496.
PRODUCER, DIRECTOR & PROJECT DEVELOPMENT
Ambrose Roche

CO-PRODUCERS FUND OF CANADA LIMITED
49 Don River Blvd., Toronto, ON, M2N 2M8. Tel. & FAX: (416) 222-8491.
PRESIDENT
Tad Jaworski, MFA, RCA

CRESCENT ENTERTAINMENT
177 W. 7th Ave., Vancouver, BC, V5Y 1L8. (604) 668-8300. FAX: (604) 668-8304.
PRESIDENT
Harold Tichenor

CRONE FILMS LTD.
8175 Pasco Rd., W. Vancouver, BC, V7W 2T5. (604) 921-6500.
Robert Crone csc
5341 Monteverdi Pl., W. Vancouver, BC V7W 2W8. (604) 921-6554. (416) 365-1471.
David Crone

CURLCOM INC.
7 Avon Ct., Whitby, ON, L1N 3H2. (905) 428-6466. FAX: (905) 666-8316.
PRESIDENT
E. G. (Ted) Curl

CYCLOPS COMMUNICATIONS CORPORATION
44 Gibson Ave., Toronto, ON, M5R 1T5. (416) 926-8981. FAX: (416) 926-9878.
PRESIDENT
Samuel C. Jephcott

DAMBERGER FILM & CATTLE CO.
R.R. 5, Tofield, AB, T0B 4J0.Tel. & FAX: (403) 662-3380.
PRODUCER, WRITER & DIRECTOR
Francis Damberger

DAVID MACKAY LTD.
67 Mowat Ave., Ste. 531, Toronto, ON, M6K 3E3. (416) 538-7625. FAX: (416) 538-3775.
David Mackay

DEVINE ENTERTAINMENT CORP.
2 Berkeley St., Ste. 504, Toronto, ON, M5K 2W3. (416) 364-2282. FAX: (416) 364-1440.
David Devine, Richard Mozer

DOMINO FILM & TELEVISION INTERNATIONAL LTD.
4002 Grey Ave., Montréal, QC, H4A 3P1. (514) 484-0446. FAX: (514) 484-0468.
66 Roxborough St. E., Ste. 402, Toronto, ON, M4W 1V7. (416) 323-0900. FAX: (416) 975-1942.

DOOMSDAY STUDIOS LIMITED
212 James St., Ottawa, ON, K1R 5M7. (613) 230-9769. FAX: (613) 230-6004.
Ramona MacDonald

DORMONT STUDIOS INC.
75 Orchard Park Blvd., Toronto, ON, M4L 3E3. (416) 698-4482. Los Angeles: (310) 457-1104. Vancouver: (604) 730-0860. Montréal: (514) 631-4291.
Peter Benison csc

EGO FILM ARTS
80 Niagara St., Toronto, ON, M5V 1C5. (416) 365-2137. FAX: (416) 369-9093.
DIRECTOR & PRODUCER
Atom Egoyan
CONTACT
Simone Urdl

EPITOME PICTURES INC.
935 Queen St. E., Toronto, ON, M4M 1J6. (416) 466-6170. FAX: (416) 466-5896.
Linda Schuyler

EQUUS FILM PRODUCTIONS INC.
174 Fulton Ave., Toronto, ON, M4K 1Y3. (416) 429-7399.
Keith Lock, Leslie Padorr

EXCALIBUR PICTURES INC.
2105-808 Nelson St., Vancouver, BC, V6Z 2H2. (604) 681-2165. FAX: (604) 681-5538.
PRESIDENT
Lloyd A. Simandl

LA FABRIQUE D'IMAGES LIMITEE
318 rue Sherbrooke est, Montréal, QC, H2X 1E6. (514) 282-1505. FAX: (514) 282-8784.
PRODUCERS
Denis Martel, Christiane Hamelin, Michel Raymond, Claude Landry, Louis Morin, Christiane Ciupka
DIRECTORS
Jacques Fournier, Marc S. Grenier, Michel Poulette, Jean-François Pouliot, Karim Waked, François Gingras, Jim Donovan, Jane-Michel Ravon

FILM CREW PRODUCTIONS
2345 Smith St., Regina, SK, S4P 2P7. (306) 777-0160. FAX: (306) 352-8558.
PRODUCER
Clark Donnelly
PRODUCER
Jack Tunnicliffe

FILMLINE INTERNATIONAL INC.
410 St. Nicolas, Ste. 600, Montréal, QC, H2Y 2P5. (514) 288-5888. FAX: (514) 288-8083.
Nicolas Clermont

THE FILM WORKS LTD.
194 Sherbourne St., #1, Toronto, ON, M5A 2R7. (416) 360-7968. FAX: (416) 360-8569.
Eric Jordan, Paul Stephens, Victor Solnicki

FISHTALES PRODUCTIONS
300 Westmoreland Ave., Toronto, ON, M6H 3A5. Tel. & FAX: (416) 588-1832.
Honey Fisher

FOREFRONT ENTERTAINMENT GROUP
700-402 West Pender St., Vancouver, BC, V6B 1T6. (604) 682-7910. FAX: (604) 682-8583. e-mail: 75031.1011@compuserve.com
PRODUCERS
Helena Cynamon, Gillian Lindsay, Teri Woods McArter, Mickey Rogers

FRIDAY STREET PRODUCTIONS
1274 May St., Victoria, BC, V8V 2T2. (604) 380-6656. FAX: (604) 380-6670.
PRESIDENT
Hilary Jones-Farrow

FRONT ROW COMMUNICATIONS INC.
410-2446 York Ave., Vancouver, BC, V6K 1E1. (604) 739-7501.
PRODUCER
Stephen Benoit

FUNDAMENTALLY FILM INC.
349 St. Clair Ave. W., Ste. 107, Toronto, ON, M5P 1N3. (416) 928-1992. FAX: (416) 928-0614.
Ron Singer, Joe Green

GALAFILM
402 Notre Dame est, Montreal, QC, H2Y 1C8. (514) 987-9972. e-mail: agelbart@galafilm.ca
PRESIDENT
Arnie Gelbart

GENESIS COMMUNICATIONS CORP.
Box 888, Gibsons, BC, V0N 1V0. (604) 886-3639. FAX: (604) 886-3508.

PRESIDENT & PRODUCER
Robert Nichol

GREAT NORTH PRODUCTIONS INC.
11523 100 Ave., #012, Edmonton, Alta. T5K 0J8. (403) 482-2022. FAX: (403) 482-3036.
Patricia Phillips

BARRY GREENWALD
242 Delaware Ave., Toronto, ON, M6H 2T6. (416) 536-0655.

GROUNDSTAR ENTERTAINMENT CORP.
918 16 Ave. N.W., Ste. 4001, Calgary, AB, T2M 0K3. (403) 284-2889. FAX: (403) 282-7797.
PRODUCER & DIRECTOR
David Winning
7336 Santa Monica Blvd., Ste. 710, Los Angeles, CA 90046. (213) 960-5708. FAX: (213) 654-5206.

HBW FILM CORP.
1725 10th Ave. S.W., Stes. 301 & 302H, Calgary, AB T3C 0K1. (403) 228-1900. FAX: (403) 228-1110. e-mail: hbwflmtv@agt.net
PRINCIPAL
Helene B. White

HEARTLAND MOTION PICTURES INC.
2345 Smith St., Regina, SK, S4P 2P7. (306) 777-0888. FAX: (306) 352-8558.
Stephen Onda

HEARTSTAR PRODUCTIONS LTD.
63 Polson St. Toronto, ON, M5A 1A4. (416) 778-8612. FAX: (416) 778-8617. Los Angeles: (213) 650-4383. FAX. (213) 650-5734.
PRESIDENT & PRODUCER
John Danylkiw

HENRY LESS PRODUCTIONS INC.
27 Government Rd., Toronto, ON, M8X 1V6. (416) 236-5004.
Henry Less, Debra Gjendem, Wenda Thomson

HIGH ROAD PRODUCTIONS INC.
235 Carlaw Ave., Ste. 603, Toronto, ON, M4M 2S5. (416) 461-3089. FAX: (416) 466-8423.
Paul Jay, Joan Hutton

HOBEL-LEITERMAN PRODUCTIONS LTD.
6 Birch Ave., Toronto, ON, M4V 1C8. (416) 968-0577.
Douglas Leiterman, Beryl Fox

HUMEWOOD COMMUNICATIONS CORPORATION
62 Humewood Dr., Toronto, ON, M6C 2W4. (416) 658-2929. FAX: (416) 658-3176.
PRESIDENT
Dan Johnson

IMAGEX LTD.
6073 Coburg Rd., Halifax, NS, B3H 1Z1. (902) 422-4000. FAX: (902) 422-4427.
PRESIDENT
Christopher Zimmer

IMAX CORPORATION
(For a listing of the Imax theatres in the U.S., see the specialty Exhibition section.)
45 Charles St. E., Toronto, ON, M4Y 1S2. (416) 960-8509. FAX: (416) 960-8596.
CHAIRMAN
Bradley J. Wechsler
PRODUCERS
Graeme Ferguson, Roman Koiter, Sally Dundas, Toni Myers
Technology Centre, 2525 Speakman Dr., Sheridan Park, Mississauga, ON, L5K 1B1. (905) 855-1379. FAX: (905) 855-2606.
MANAGER, FILM TECHNOLOGY
Gord Harris

INDEPENDENT PICTURES INC.
18 Gloucester Lane, 4th Fl., Toronto, ON, M4Y 1L5 . (416) 960-6310. FAX: (416) 960-8463.
PRESIDENT
Peter O'Brian

INSIGHT PRODUCTION COMPANY LTD.
489 King St. W., Ste. 401, Toronto, ON, M5V 1L3. (416) 596-8118. FAX: (416) 596-8270.
EXECUTIVE PRODUCER
John M. Brunton

INTERCOM FILMS LIMITED
1231 Yonge St., Ste. 200, Toronto, ON, M4T 2T8. (416) 923-9008.
PRESIDENT
Gilbert W. Taylor

INTERNATIONAL MOVIE FINANCE INC.
14th Fl. Park Place, 66 Burrard St., Vancouver, BC, V6C 2X8. (604) 687-3250. FAX: (604) 687-6155.
PRESIDENT
Lyn Vince

INTERNATIONAL ROCKETSHIP LTD.
1778 West 2nd Ave., Vancouver, BC V6J 1H6. (604) 738-1778. FAX: (604) 7380-0009.
PRODUCER
Michael van den Bos

INVESTIGATIVE PRODUCTIONS INC.
490 Adelaide St. W., Ste. 302, Toronto, ON, M5V 1T2. (416) 703-5580. FAX: (416) 703-1691.
PRESIDENT
Peter Raymont

JAMS PRODUCTIONS INC.
1262 Don Mills Rd., Ste.203, Don Mills, ON, M3B 2W7. (416) 449-4844. FAX: (416) 449-4843.
Alan J. Schwarz

JOHN MCGREEVY PRODUCTIONS
36 Roxborough St. E., Toronto, ON, M4W 1V6. (416) 922-8625. FAX: (416) 922-8624.
PRESIDENT
John McGreevy

JOHN M. ECKERT PRODUCTIONS LIMITED
385 Carlton St., Toronto, ON, M5A 2M3. (416) 960-4961.
John M. Eckert

KATHERINE SMALLEY PRODUCTIONS
368 Brunswick Ave., Toronto, ON, M5R 2Y9. (416) 961-8907. FAX: (416) 324-8253.
PRESIDENT
Katherine Smalley

KEG PRODUCTIONS LTD.
1231 Yonge St., Ste. 201, Toronto, ON, M4T 2T8. (416) 924-2186. FAX: (416) 924-6115.
PRESIDENT
Ralph C. Ellis
MANAGING DIRECTOR
R. Stephen Ellis

KERRIGAN PRODUCTIONS INC.
3471 ave. Hingston, Montréal, QC, H4A 2J5. (514) 486-1365.
DIRECTOR
Bill Kerrigan

KONO FILMS LTD.
81 Claremont Ave., Winnipeg, Man. R2H 1W1. (204) 237-5649. FAX: (204) 237-1563.
PRESIDENT
Charles Konowal

KRIZSAN FILM PRODUCTIONS
23 Fairbanks St., Dartmouth, NS, B3A 1B9. Tel. & FAX: (902) 466-8689. Cell: (902) 4567-0948.
Les Krizsan, Corinne Lange

LAURON PRODUCTIONS LTD.
56 Shaftesbury Ave., Toronto, ON, M4T 1A3. (416) 967-6503. FAX: (416) 967-1292.
Ronald Lillie, William Johnston

LAWRENCE HERTZOG PRODUCTIONS LIMITED
62 Charles St. E., Toronto, ON, M4Y 1T1. Tel. &. FAX: (416) 531-4670.

LINDISFARNE PRODUCTIONS INC.
3627-114 A St., Edmonton, AB, T6J 1N2. Tel. &. FAX: (403) 434-6348. Pager: (403) 497-6046.
WRITER & PRODUCER
Fred Keating

LINDUM FILMS INC.
67 Marjory Ave., Toronto, ON, M4M 2Y2. (416) 461-2305. FAX: (416) 461-4311.
WRITER, DIRECTOR & PRODUCER
Peter Blow

LORENZO ORZARI PRODUCTIONS
5135 Jean Talon E., CP 704, Montréal, QC, H1S 2Z5. (514) 329-5412.
WRITER, PRODUCER & DIRECTOR
Lorenzo Orzari

MAC PRODUCTIONS INC.
2169 Denise Rd., Mississauga, ON, L4X 1H9. (905) 270-7616.
EXECUTIVE PRODUCER
Michael A. Charbon

MAKIN' MOVIES INC.
843 Manning Ave., Toronto, ON, M6G 2X1. (416) 534-5077.
Maureen Judge, Martin Waxman

MALOFILM PRODUCTION INC.
3575 boul. St-Laurent, bur. 650, Montréal, QC, H2X 2T7. (514) 844-4555. FAX: (514) 844-6227.
CHAIRMAN OF THE BOARD
René Malo
PRESIDENT
Yves Dion
2221 Yonge St., Ste. 100, Toronto, ON, M4S 2B4. (416) 480-0453. FAX: (416) 480-0501.

MARINER PRODUCTIONS
695 Logan Ave., 2nd Fl., Winnipeg, MB, R3E 1M5. (204) 992-2420. FAX: (204) 992-2421.
VICE-PRESIDENT
Martin Russell
EXECUTIVE PRODUCER
Robb Mavins

MASSEY PRODUCTIONS LTD.
249 East St. James Rd., N. Vancouver, BC, V7N 1L3. (604) 990-9044. FAX: (604) 990-9066.
Raymond Massey

MAX FILMS INC.
5200 Henri-Julien, Montréal, QC, H2T 1R8. (514) 276-4499. FAX: (514) 276-6544.
Roger Frappier

MAXIMA FILM CORPORATION
70 East Beaver Creek Rd., Unit 19, Richmond Hill, ON, L4B 3B2. (905) 882-9600. FAX: (906) 882-9605.
John Stoneman, B.Sc., M.Sc., csc

MICHAEL MILLS PRODUCTIONS LIMITED
4492 Ste-Catherine W., Montréal, QC, H3Z 1R7. (514) 931-7117. FAX: (514) 931-7099.
PRESIDENT
Michael Mills

MINDS EYE PICTURES
1212A Winnipeg St., Regina, SK S4R 1J6. (306) 359-7618. FAX: (306) 359-3466. e-mail: mindseye@sasknet.sk.ca
CHAIRMAN & CEO
Kevin DeWalt

MOONDOG VISUAL PRODUCTIONS
179C DeGrassi St., Toronto, ON, M4M 2K8. (416) 778-5073. FAX: (416) 778-1659. Pager: (416) 374-1966.
Shannon Farr, John Tran

MY COUNTRY PRODUCTIONS INC.
21 Sackville St., Toronto, ON, M5A 3E1. (416) 868-1972.
Pierre Berton, Elsa Franklin

NELVANA LIMITED
32 Atlantic Ave., Toronto, ON, M6K 1X8. (416) 588-5571. FAX: (416) 588-5588.
PRODUCERS
Patrick Loubert, Michael Hirsh, Clive Smith

NEMESIS PRODUCTIONS
22 Bishop St., Toronto, ON, M5R 1N2. (416) 323-0577. FAX: (416) 515-7934.
Jacques Holender

NEOFILMS
5162 boul. St-Laurent, Ste. 200, Montréal, QC, H2T 1R8. e-mail: neomodus@login.net
PRODUCERS
Philippe Dussault, Christian Gagne

NEW COMMUNICATION CONCEPTS LTD.
5-23260 Dyke Rd., Richmond, BC V6V 1E2. (604) 520-0272. FAX: (604) 526-3351.
PRESIDENT
Keith Cutler

NORSTAR ENTERTAINMENT INC.
86 Bloor St.W., 5th Fl., Toronto, ON, M5S 1M5. (416) 961-6278. FAX: (416) 961-5608.
PRESIDENT, CHAIRMAN & CEO
Peter R. Simpson

NORTH AMERICAN PICTURES LTD.
808 Nelson St., #2105, Vancouver, BC, V6Z 2H2. (604) 681-2165. FAX: (604) 681-5538.
PRESIDENT
Lloyd A. Simandl

NORTHERN LIGHTS ENTERTAINMENT CORP.
302-1132 Hamilton St., Vancouver, BC, V6B 2S2. (604) 684-2888. FAX: (604) 681-3299.
Werner Aellen, Bill Aylesworth

NORTHERN NATIVE PUBLIC BROADCASTING INC.
Box 204, Birch Hills, SK, S0J 0G0. (306) 749-2578. FAX: (306) 749-3112.
PRESIDENT
Patrick Wolfe

NORTHERN OUTLAW PRODUCTIONS INC.
628 Indian Rd., Toronto, ON, M6P 2C6. (416) 767-9091. FAX: (416) 767-9488.
Peter Gentile

NORTHLAND PICTURES
Box 549, Adelaide Stn., Toronto, ON, M5C 2J6. (416) 251-5659. FAX: (416) 251-4786.
Colin Strayer

NORTHSTAR ENTERTAINMENT
904 Winnington Ave., Ottawa, ON, K2B 5C7. (613) 729-3157. FAX: (613) 596-1867.
PRODUCER & DIRECTOR
Bryan Michael Stoller

OCCHIO VERO PRODUCTIONS INC.
80 Lime Dr., Woodbridge, ON, L4L 5N2. (905) 851-9250. e-mail: biagi@passport.ca
Roberto Biagi

OCTOBER FILMS INC.
67 Brookfield St., Toronto, ON, M6J 3A8.. (416) 532-6253.
Bruno Lazaro Pacheco

OPEN CITY PRODUCTIONS LTD.
54 Mansfield Ave., Toronto, ON, M6J 2B2. (416) 532-6892.
PRESIDENT
Andrew Johnson

THE ORIGINAL MOTION PICTURE COMPANY
56 The Esplanade, Ste.213, Toronto, ON, M5E 1A7. (416) 368-4039. FAX: (416) 368-4906. e-mail: sifilms@inforamp.net
John Board

OWL TELEVISION
179 John St., Ste. 500, Toronto, ON, M5T 3G5. (416) 971-5275.
FAX: (416) 971-5294.
EXECUTIVE PRODUCER
Annabel Slaight

PACIFIC MOTION PICTURES
45 Dunlevy Ave., Vancouver, BC, V6A 3A3. (604) 683-8811.
FAX: (604) 683-4868.
CEO
Tony Allard
PRÉSIDENT
Matthew O'Connor

PARAGON ENTERTAINMENT CORPORATION
119 Spadina Ave., Ste. 900, Toronto, ON, M5V 2L1. (416)
977-2929. FAX: (416) 977-8247.
CHAIRMAN & CEO
Jon Slan
PRESIDENT & COO
Richard Borchiver

PARALLEL FILMS INC.
7677 French St., Vancouver, BC, V6P 4V5. (604) 263-6729.
FAX: (604) 263-7784.
Andrew McLean, Linda McLean

THE PARTNERS' FILM COMPANY LIMITED
53 Ontario St., Toronto, ON, M5A 2V1. (416) 869-3500. FAX:
(416) 869-3365.
GENERAL MANAGER & PRESIDENT
Donald McLean

PAT FERNS PRODUCTIONS LTD.
207 Adelaide St. E., Ste. 200, Toronto, ON, M5A 1M8. (416) 362-
1950. FAX: (416) 362-1951.
PRESIDENT
W. Paterson Ferns

PATTERSON-PARTINGTON TV PRODUCTIONS
206 Laird Dr., Ste. 200, Toronto, ON, M4G 3W4. (416) 696-9633.
FAX: (416) 696-9640.
Carol Patterson, Lawrence Partington

PBG PUBLIC BROADCASTING GROUP INC.
1418-133 A St., Surrey, BC, V4A 6A2. (604) 535-8265. FAX:
(604) 535-8265.
Jack McGaw
10 Balsam Ave., Toronto, ON, M4E 3B4. (416) 694-6619. FAX:
(416) 694-4303.
Ian McLeod

PETER GERRETSEN PRODUCTIONS LTD.
118 Castlefield Ave., Toronto, ON, M4R 1G4. (416) 484-9671.
WRITER & DIRECTOR
Peter Gerretsen
PRODUCER
Patricia Gerretsen

PETER HITCHCOCK PRODUCTIONS INC.
17 Poplar Plains Rd., Toronto, ON, M4V 2M7. (416) 921-1021.
PRODUCER & DIRECTOR
Peter Hitchcock

PETERSEN PRODUCTION,S INC.
314 W. Pender St., 3rd Fl., Vancouver, BC, V6B 1T3. (604) 669-
8890. FAX: (604) 662-8013. e-mail: ppi@res.com
PRESIDENT
Curtis Petersen

PICTURE PLANT LTD.
P.O. Box 2465, Stn. M,Halifax, NS, B3J 3E8. (902) 423-3901.
FAX: (902) 422-5704.
PRESIDENT
William MacGillivray

PLAYING WITH TIME INC.
935 Queen St. E., Toronto, ON, M4M 1J6. (416) 466-6170. FAX:
(416) 466-5896.
EXECUTIVE OFFICERS
Kit Hood, Linda Schuyler

POINTS EAST PRODUCTIONS INC.
557 N. River Rd., Charlottetown, PEI, C1A 1J7. (902) 892-7359.
FAX: (902) 368-3798.
PRODUCER
Jack McAndrew

PORTFOLIO FILM & TELEVISION
344 Bloor St. W., Ste. 402, Toronto, ON, M5S 3A7. (416) 920-
8119. FAX: (416) 920-6070.
CO-PRESIDENTS
Lisa Olfman, Joy Rosen

PRODUCER'S NETWORK & LIGHTSCAPE INC.
Cinevillage, Ste. B-216 & Ste. 206, 65 Heward Ave., Toronto,
ON, M4M 2T5. (416) 462-9741. FAX: (416) 462-3236.
Philip Jackson, David Dior

LES PRODUCTIONS CLAUDE HEROUX
4542 boul. Décarie, Montréal, QC, H3X 2H5. (514) 738-3737.
FAX: (514) 488-2862.
Claude Héroux

PRODUCTIONS GRAND NORD QUEBEC INC.
La Maison Premier Plan, Ste. 391, 1600 ave de Lorimier,
Montréal, QC, H2K 3W5. (514) 521-7433. FAX: (514) 522-3013.
Ian McLaren

LES PRODUCTIONS LA FETE INC.
225 est, rue Roy, Ste 203, Montréal, QC, H2W 1M5. (514)
848-0417. FAX: (514) 848-0064.
Kevin Tierney

LES PRODUCTIONS POINT DE MIRE
154 Laurier Ave. W., Ste. 302, Montréal, QC, H2T 2N7. (514)
278-8922. FAX: (514) 278-8925.
PRESIDENT
Lise Payette

PRODUCTIONS PAX
3781 de Bullion, Montréal, QC, H2W 2C9. (514) 844-7077. FAX:
(514) 844-2265.
Tanya Tree

LES PRODUCTIONS PRISMA INC.
1035 ave. Laurier ouest, 3iéme étage, Montréal, QC, H2V 2L1.
(514) 277-6686. FAX: (514) 277-8910.
PRESIDENT
Claude Godbout

PROGRAMMED COMMUNICATIONS LIMITED
1155 Metcalfe, Ste. 2121,Montréal, QC, H3B 2V6. (514) 397-
9091. FAX: (514) 397-9345.
James L. Muir

PRV PRODUCTIONS/RELEASING INC.
125 Dupont St., 2nd Fl., Toronto, ON, MR 1V4. (416) 975-9768.
FAX: (416) 972-6261.
PRESIDENT
Bill Nemtin

QUEST FILM PRODUCTIONS LTD.
1272 Redpath Cr., Montréal, QC, H3G 2K1. (514) 849-7921.
PRESIDENT
Paul Almond

RAYMOND INTERNATIONAL
238 Davenport Rd., Ste. 122, Toronto, ON, M5R 1J6. (416) 485-
3406. FAX: (416) 487-3820.
PRESIDENT
Bruce Raymond

REBELFILMS, INC.
494 Euclid Ave., #3, Toronto, ON, M6G 2S9. (416) 963-8692.
FAX: (416) 588-6300.
Jeremy Podeswa

RED SNAPPER FILMS LTD.
2125 Brunswick St., Halifax, NS, B3K 2Y4. (902) 422-2427. FAX:
(902) 492-2125.
PRODUCER & DIRECTOR
Lulu Keating

RHOMBUS MEDIA INC.
489 King St. W., Ste. 102, Toronto, ON, M5V 1L3. (416)
971-7856. FAX: (416) 971-9647.
Niv Fichman, Barbara Willis Sweete, Larry Weinstein, Sheena
Macdonald

RICHMOND HOUSE LTD.
33 Howard St., Toronto, ON, M4X 1J6. (416) 961-0555. FAX:
(416) 961-4234.
Damian Lee

RIFFRAFF FILMS INC.
60 Millbrook Cr. , Toronto, ON, M4K 1H4. (416) 469-8063.
Alexandra Raffé

ROGER PYKE PRODUCTIONS LTD.
58 Cartier Cres., Richmond Hill, ON, L4C 2N2. (905) 884-5957.
FAX: (905) 884-0951. Cell: (416) 315-6352. e-mail: rpyke@msn.
com
PRESIDENT
Roger Pyke

ROSE FILMS INC.
C.P. 40, Saint-Paul d'Abbotsford, QC, J0E 1A0. (514) 379-5304.
FAX: (514) 379-5742.
Claude Fournier, Marie-José Raymond

R.S.M. PRODUCTIONS INTERNATIONALES INC.
720 Montpellier, Ste. 912, Ville St. Laurent, QC, H4L 5B5. (514)
748-2678. FAX: (514) 748-7560.
PRODUCER & DIRECTOR
Rafik M. Murad

RUDY INC.
Corporate Office: 40 Glengarry Ave., Toronto, ON, M5M 1C9.
Production Office: 31 Lawrence Ave. W., Toronto, ON, M5M 1A3.
(416) 489-7115. FAX: (416) 489-7760.
Rudy Buttignol, Howard Hutton

SAJO PRODUCTIONS INC.
Box 888, Gibsons, BC, VON 3M6. (604) 886-3639. FAX: (604)
266-5499.
PRESIDENT
Robert Nichol

SALISH PARK PRODUCTIONS
4230 Salish Dr , Vancouver, BC, V6N 3M6. (604) 266-4993. FAX:
(604) 266-5499.
Les Weinstein

SALTER STREET FILMS
2507 Brunswick St., Halifax, NS, B3K 2Z5. (902) 4320-1577.
FAX: (902) 425-8260. e-mail: salter@salter.com
PRESIDENT
Paul Donovan

VICE-PRESIDENT
Michael Donovan
SARRAZIN/COUTURE PRODUCTIONS INC.
42 Bernard Ave., Toronto, ON, M5R 1R2. (416) 324-9254. FAX: (416) 324-1262.
Pierre Sarrazin, Suzette Couture
SCHULZ FILMS INC.
400 Walmer R., East Tower, Ste. 2323, Toronto, ON, M5P 2X7. (416) 961-2001. FAX: (416) 961-2003.
Bob Schulz, Sam Jephcott, Madeline Thompson, Jean-Yves David
SDA PRODUCTIONS LTEE.
1425 ouest boul. René-Lévesque, 10e étage, Montréal, QC, 3G 1T7, (514) 866-1761. FAX: (514) 866-0331.
PRÉSIDENT
François Champagne
SHANE LUNNY PRODUCTIONS INC.
560 Beatty St., Ste. 305, Vancouver, B.C. V6B 2L3. (604) 669-0333. FAX: (604) 662-7500.
PRESIDENT
Shane Lunny
SKOGLAND FILMS LTD.
53 Ontario St., Toronto, ON, M5A 2V1. (416) 481-4187. FAX: (416) 481-8095. L.A.: (310) 301-0560.
DIRECTOR
Kari Skogland
SLEEPING GIANT PRODUCTIONS
151 John St., Ste. 511, Toronto, ON, M5V 2T2. (416) 351-9240. FAX: (416) 351-9241.
CEO & EXECUTIVE PRODUCER
Jim Hanley
SOMA: FILM & VIDEO
P.O. Box X-26, Bowen Island, BC, V0N 1G0. (604) 947-0044. FAX: (604) 947-0049.
PRESIDENT
Deepak Sahasrabudhe
SOUND VENTURE PRODUCTIONS
126 York St., Ste. 219, Ottawa, ON, K1N 5T5. (613) 241-5111. FAX: (613) 241-5010. e-mail: bregmans@magi.com
EXECUTIVE PRODUCER
Neil Bregman
SPECTRUM FILMS
Box 358, Stn. B, Toronto, ON, M5T 2W2. Tel. & Fax: (416) 504-4340.
Holly Dale, Janis Cole
SPHINX PRODUCTIONS
24 Mercer St., Toronto, ON, M5V 1H3. (416) 971-9131. FAX: (416) 971-6014. e-mail: mann@voyagerco.com
Ron Mann
STRONG MEDICINE PRODUCTIONS
358 Danforth Ave., Ste. 65022, Toronto, ON, M4K 3Z2. Tel. &. FAX: (416) 469-5925.
PRODUCER & DIRECTOR
Tina Petrova
SULLIVAN ENTERTAINMENT INC.
110 Davenport Rd., Toronto, ON, M5R 3R3. (416) 921-7177. FAX: (416) 921-7538.
President
Kevin Sullivan
SUNRISE FILMS LIMITED
352 Walmer Rd., Toronto, ON, M5R 2Y4. (416) 929-7900. FAX: (416) 929-9900.
Paul Saltzman
TAMARAC FILMWORKS LTD.
3812 W. 12 Ave., Vancouver, BC, V6R 2W9. (604) 224-1992. FAX: (604) 224-1980.
PRODUCER, WRITER & DIRECTOR
Alyson Drysdale
TELESCENE COMMUNICATIONS INC.
5510 Ferrier St., Montréal, QC, H4P 1M2. (514) 737-5512. FAX: (514) 737-7945.
PRÉSIDENT
Robin Spry

THREE BLONDES INC.
72 Rusholme Rd., Toronto, ON, M6R 3H6. (416) 537-8348. FAX: (416) 534-6542.
Annette Mangaard
TRIANGLE FILMS
1303 Greene Ave., Ste. 300, Westmount, QC, H3Z 2A7. (514) 846-1940. FAX: (416) 846-1550.
PRESIDENT
Debbie Travis
GENERAL MANAGER
Hans Rosenstein
TRICORD FILM & TELEVISION CORP.
141 Drakefield Rd., Markham, ON, L3P 1G9. (905) 472-0535. FAX: (905) 472-0448.
Karen Pascal
TRIPTYCH MEDIA INC.
56 The Esplanade, Ste. 505, Toronto, ON, M5E 1A7. (416) 955-8866. FAX: (416) 955-8867.
Louise Garfield, Anna Stratton, Robin Cass
TWIN DRAGON FILM PRODUCTIONS LTD.
6347 Yonge St., North York, ON, M2M 3X7. (416) 229-1280. FAX: (416) 229-2425.
PRESIDENT
Michael McNamara
VICE PRESIDENT
Martin McNamara
VINTAGE VISUALS
1133 Harwood St., #302, Vancouver, BC, V6E 1R9. (604) 688-5985.
George C. Koller, Wendy M. Ennion
WACKO ENTERTAINMENT CORPORATION
46 Stan Wright Industrial Park, P.O. Box 1651, Jasper, AB, T0E 1E0. (403) 852-4728. FAX: (403) 852-4702.
PRESIDENT
Wendy Wacko
WATER STREET PICTURES LTD.
111 Water St., Ste. 204, Vancouver, BC, V6B 1A7. (604) 681-6543. FAX: (604) 681425. e-mail: omni@mindlink.bc.ca
PRESIDENT & EXECUTIVE PRODUCER
Michael Chechik
WHEELER-HENDREN ENTERPRISES LTD.
212 Sunset Dr., Saltspring Island, B.C. V8K 1L4. Tel. & FAX: (604) 737-0632.
PRODUCER, DIRECTOR & WRITER
Anne Wheeler
ASSOCIATE PRODUCER
Garth Hendren
WHY NOT PRODUCTIONS INC.
P.O. Box 980, Stn. A, Toronto, ON, M5W 1G5. (416) 597-0059. FAX: (416) 597-0550.
PRESIDENT
Barbara Barde
YALETOWN PRODUCTIONS
1431 Howe St., Vancouver, BC, V6M 1H8. (604) 669-3453. FAX: (604) 669-5149.
PRESIDENT & EXECUTIVE PRODUCER
Mike Collier
YELLOWKNIFE FILMS INC.
5021 53rd St., Box 2562, Yellowknife, NT X1A 2P9. (403) 873-8610. FAX: (403) 873-9405.
Alan Booth, Charles Laird
YORKTOWN PRODUCTIONS LTD.
18 Gloucester Lane, Toronto, ON, M4Y 1L5. (416) 923-2787. FAX: (416) 923-8580.
PRESIDENT
Norman Jewison
ZAMARIA PRODUCTIONS
R.R. 4, Shelburne, ON, L0N 1S8. (519) 925-1400. FAX: (519) 925-1422. e-mail: csamaria@acs.ryerson.ca
PRESIDENT
Charles Zamaria

STUDIO FACILITIES, POST-PRODUCTION, LABS, SOUND TRANSFER & MIXING

STUDIO FACILITIES

ALLARCOM STUDIOS
5305 Allard Way, Edmonton, AB, T6H 5B8. (403) 436-1250. FAX: (403) 438-8495.
CONTACT
Doug Steeden

THE ANNEX STUDIOS LTD.
174 Bedford Rd. , Toronto, ON, M5R 2K9. (416) 922-8270. FAX: (416) 922-7100.
PRESIDENT
Ed Zemla

CINESPACE STUDIOS
345 Carlaw Ave., Ste. 200, Toronto, ON, M4M 2T1. (416) 406-4000. FAX: (416) 469-5975.
CONTACTS
Sherrie Cameron, Nick Mirkopoulos

CINEVILLAGE
65 Heward Ave., Bldg. C, Toronto, ON, M4M 2T5. (416) 461-8750. FAX: (416) 466-9612.
CONTACT
Renato Dumlao

NORTH SHORE STUDIOS
555 Brooksbank Ave., N. Vancouver, BC, V7J 3S5. (604) 983-5555. FAX: (604) 983-5554.
GENERAL MANAGER
Peter Leitch

STUDIOASIS MEDIA CORPORATION
793 Pharmacy Ave., Toronto, ON, M1L 3K2. (416) 285-1111. FAX: (416) 285-9617.
STUDIO MANAGER
Gord Brodie

STUDIO G
P.O.Box 3500, Stn. C, Montréal, QC, H2L 4Z3. (514) 526-2881. FAX: (514) 526-3740.

23 FPS
23 Fraser Ave., Toronto, ON, M4K 1Y7. (416) 535-3522. FAX (416) 535-1041.
STUDIO MANAGER
Jim Hardie

WALLACE AVENUE STUDIOS INC.
258 Wallace Ave., Toronto, ON, M6P 3M9. (416) 537-3471. FAX: (416) 532-3132.
VICE PRESIDENT & MARKETING
Lillyann D. Goldstein
STUDIO MANAGER
Jody Gale

POST-PRODUCTION

CALGARY TELEVISION CENTRE (CICT)
222 23rd. St. N.E., Calgary, AB, T2E 7N2. (403) 235-7733, 800-661-8374.
Kim Corrigall

CENTRE DE MONTAGE ELECTRONIQUE (CME)
1600 est boul. de Maisonneuve, Montréal, QC H2L 4P2. (514) 598-2938. FAX: (514) 526-3417.
CONTACT
Claude Fournier

CINAR STUDIOS
1207 rue St. André, Montréal, QC H2L 3S8. (514) 843-7070. FAX: (514) 843-7080.
Ron Weinberg, Micheline Charest

CINE-BYTE IMAGING INC.
543 Richmond St. W., Ste. 200, P.O. Box 107, Toronto, ON, M5V 2L4. (416) 504-1010. FAX: (416) 504-9910.
PRESIDENT
Alan Bak
MARKETING MANAGER
Dennis Berardi

CINE GROUPE POST PRODUCTION
1151 Alexandre-DeSéve, Montréal, QC, H2l 2T7. (514) 524-7567. FAX: (514) 524-1997.

COMMUNICAPTION CANADA
511 King St. W., Ste. 301, Toronto, ON, M5V 1K4. (415) 598-4613. FAX: (416) 591-6661.
CONTACT
Jeff Reinke

THE DAILY POST VIDEO
103 Walnut Ave., Toronto, ON, M5V 2S1. (416) 504-3348. FAX: (416) 504-5596.
CONTACT
Sarah Brooks

GASTOWN POST & TRANSFER
50 W. 2nd Ave., Vancouver, BC V5Y 1B3. (604) 872-7000. FAX: (604) 872-2106.
PRESIDENT & CEO
Tom Locke

LABORATOIRE KINECO INC.
608 Côte de l'Aqueduc, C.P.368, Québec, QC, G1K 6W8. (418) 527-1742. FAX: (418) 527-6822
Pierre Rochette

MCCLEAR PATHE RECORDING AND POST-PRODUCTION STUDIOS
225 Mutual St., Toronto, ON, M5B 2B4. (416) 977-9740. FAX: (416) 977-7147.
STUDIO MANAGER
Pamela Brookes

OFF'N ONLINE/SOUNDHOUSE VIDEO & AUDIO POST PRODUCTION
Off'N Online: 511 King St. W., Ste. 301, Toronto, ON, M5V 1K4. (416) 591-1143.
Soundhouse: 409 King St. W., Ste. 300, Toronto, ON, M5V 1K1. (416) 598-2260. FAX: (416) 598-1496.
PRESIDENT
Bill Cooke Jr.

PRISMA-LIGHT LTD.
762 Queen St. W. , Toronto, ON, M6J 1E9. (416) 504-4321 . FAX: (416) 863-6913.
V.P. PRODUCTION
Les Zawadzki

ZAZA SOUND PRODUCTIONS LTD.
322 Dufferin St., Toronto, ON, M6K 1Z6. (416) 534-4211. FAX: (416) 534-9520.
Paul Zaza, John Gare

LABORATORIES, SOUND TRANSFER & MIXING

ALPHA CINE SERVICE
A division of Tegra Industries Inc., 916 Davie St., Vancouver, BC, V6Z 1B8. (604) 688-7757. FAX: (604) 688-0127.
PRODUCTION MANAGER
Bryn Dix

ASTRALTECH INC.
An Astral Communications Company, 2100 rue Sainte-Catherine ouest, Montréal, QC H3H 1M6. (514) 939-5060. FAX: (514) 939-5070.
PRESIDENT AND GENERAL MANAGER
Hubert Harel

BLACK & WHITE FILM FACTORY
317 Adelaide St. W., Main Fl., Toronto, ON, M5V 1P9. (416) 593-0367. FAX: (416) 971-8389.
Dragan Stojanovic, Sebastjian Henrickson

BROCK SOUND POST AUDIO
576 Manning Ave., Toronto, ON, M6G 2V9. (416) 534-7464. FAX: (416) 538-2563.
MANAGEMENT
Brock Fricker

COMFORT SOUND RECORDING STUDIO
26 Soho St., Ste.390, Toronto, ON, M5T 1Z7. (416) 593-7992. FAX: (416) 593-7301.
PRODUCER & MANAGER
Bernie Walsh

DELUXE TORONTO
Laboratory, 380 Adelaide Ste. W., Toronto, ON, M5V 1R7. (416) 364-4321.
SR.VICE PRESIDENT & GENERAL MANAGER
Des Henry
Sound Studios, 424 Adelaide St.E., Toronto, ON, M5A 1N4. (416) 364-4321.
SR. VICE PRESIDENT & GENERAL MANAGER
Tom Allwood

THE FINE PRINT
77 Mowat Ave., Toronto, ON, M6K 3E3. (416) 596-8310 . FAX: (416) 596-1149.
Hratch Keoshkerian

GASTOWN FILM LABS
52 W. 2nd Ave., Vancouver, BC V5Y 1B3. (604) 875-9600. FAX:
(604) 875-1347.
GENERAL MANAGER
Dave Hardon
MANTA EASTERN SOUND
311 Adelaide St. E., Toronto, ON, M5A 1N2. (416) 863-9316.
FAX: (416) 863-1448.
VICE PRESIDENT & GENERAL MANAGER
Kevin Evans
MASTER'S WORKSHOP
A division of Magnetic Enterprises Inc. , 306 Rexdale Blvd., Unit
7, Rexdale, ON, M9W 1R6. (416) 741-1312. FAX: (416) 741-1894.
GENERAL MANAGER
Bob Predovich
MEDALLION/PFA FILM & VIDEO
111 Peter St., 9th Fl., Toronto, ON, M5V 2H1. (416) 593-0556.
FAX: (416) 593-7201.
VICE-PRESIDENT
Joe Scrivo
REAL TO REEL SOUND STUDIOS
379 Shuter St., Toronto, ON, M5A 1X3. (416) 360-7836. FAX:
(416) 360-8302.
ENGINEER & MANAGER
Neil Splitter
SONOLAB INC.
1500 Papineau St., Montréal, QC H2K 4L9. (514) 527-8671.
FAX: (514) 526-1871.

GENERAL MANAGER
Pierre Mercier
SOUNDMIX LTD.
22 Boston Ave., Toronto, ON, M4M 2T9. (416) 461-2550. FAX:
(416) 461-9709.
Steve Mayhew, David Cooke
SOUND TECHNIQUES
181 Carlaw Ave., Toronto, ON, M4M 2S1. (416) 778-4973.
PRESIDENT
Larry Johnson
SPENCE-THOMAS AUDIO POST
329B King St. E., Toronto, ON, M5A 1K6. (416) 361-6383. FAX:
(416) 361-2970.
PRESIDENT
Patrick Spence-Thomas
SPOT FILM AND VIDEO
23 Fraser Ave., Toronto, ON, M6K 1Y7. (416) 535-3522. FAX:
(416) 535-1041.
PRODUCTION MANAGER
Jim Hardie
STUDIO SAINT-CHARLES
85 Grant St., Longueuil, QC J4H 3H4. (514) 674-4927, (514)
527-8671. FAX: (514) 526-1871.
CONTACT
Lucie Bourbonniére

DISTRIBUTION COMPANIES

ACTION FILM LIMITEE
467 est boul. St-Joseph, Montréal, QC, H2J 1J8. (514)
845-5572. FAX: (514) 286-2313.
André Monette
ADFILMS
250 Merton St., Ste. 403, Toronto, ON, M4S 1B1. (416)
483-3551. FAX: (416) 483-2401.
PRESIDENT
Fred T. Stinson
ALLIANCE RELEASING
5 place Ville Marie, Ste. 1435, Montréal, QC, H3B 2G2. (514)
878-2282. FAX: (514) 878-2419.
PRESIDENT
Victor Loewy
920 Yonge St., Ste. 500, Toronto, ON, M4W 3C7. (416)
967-1141. FAX: (416) 967-4358.
ASKA FILM DISTRIBUTION INC.
1600 ave. de Lorimier, Ste.211, Montréal, QC, H2K 3W5. (514)
521-0623. FAX: (514) 521-6174.
Claude Gagnon
ASTRAL DISTRIBUTION GROUP
An Astral Communications Company. 33 Yonge St., Ste. 1020
Toronto, ON, M5E 1S9. (416) 956-2000. FAX: (416) 956-2020.
PRESIDENT
Irving Ivers
ATLANTIS RELEASING INC.
Cinevillage, 65 Heward Ave., Toronto, ON, M4M 2T5. (416)
462-0246. FAX: (416) 462-0254.
CONTACT
Ted Riley
AUDIO CINE FILM
8462 Sherbrooke E., Montréal, QC, H1L 1B2. (514) 493-8887.
FAX: (514) 493-9058. (800) 289-8887.
CONTACT
Christian Bergeron
BAYVIEW FILMS DISTRIBUTION INC.
8 Mandel Cr., Willowdale, ON, M2H 1B9. (416) 362-5890, (416)
223-0716. FAX: (416) 362-1218.
PRESIDENT
Orval Fruitman
BBS PRODUCTIONS INC.
9 Channel Nine Ct., Scarborough, ON, M1S 4B5. (416) 299-
2000. FAX: (416) 299-2067.
VP & GENERAL MANAGER
Suzanne Steeves
BELLEVUE FILM DISTRIBUTORS LIMITED
40 Lesmill Rd., Don Mills, ON, M3B 2T5. (416) 449-9322
PRESIDENT
Herbert S. Mathers
VICE-PRESIDENT
H. Paul Wroe

BONDED SERVICES INTERNATIONAL LIMITED
781 King St. W., Toronto, ON, M5V 1N4. (416) 368-1740. FAX:
(416) 368-7075.
VICE-PRESIDENT
Dan Armstrong
BRIGHTSTAR DISTRIBUTION
100 Yonge St., Ste. 1205, Toronto, ON, M5C 2W1. (416) 362-
5890. FAX: (416) 362-1218.
BUENA VISTA PICTURES DISTRIBUTION CANADA, INC.
1235 Bay St., Ste. 901, Toronto, ON, M5R 3K4. (416) 964-9275.
FAX: (416) 964-8537. (800) 263-2853.
CANADIAN DIVISION MANAGER
Anthony Macina
CANAMEDIA PRODUCTIONS LTD.
125 Dupont St., Toronto, ON, M5R 1V4. (416) 324-9190. FAX:
(416) 972-6261.
PRESIDENT
Les Harris
CFP DISTRIBUTION INC.
2 Bloor St.W., Ste. 1901, Toronto, ON, M4W 3E2. (416) 944-
0104. FAX: (416) 944-2212.
8275 rue Mayrand, Montréal, QC, H4P 2C8. (514) 342-2340.
FAX: (514) 342-1922.
PRESIDENT & CEO
André Link
EXECUTIVE VP
Jeff Sackman
CINAR FILMS INC.
1055 rue St-André, Ste. 900, Montréal, QC, H2L 3S8. (514) 843-
7070. FAX: (514) 843-7080.
Micheline Charest, Ron Weinberg, Louise Fournier, Theresa
Holst
CINEMA ESPERANCA INTERNATIONAL INC.
96 Spadina Ave., Ste. 301, Toronto, ON, M5V 2J6. (416) 703-
5000. FAX: (416) 703-5002.
PRESIDENT & CEO
André Bennett
CINEPLEX ODEON FILMS CANADA
1303 Yonge St., Toronto, ON, M4T 2Y9. (416) 323-6600. FAX:
(416) 323-6711. Cable: CINELAW.
SENIOR VP
Bryan Gliserman
COLUMBIA TRISTAR FILMS OF CANADA
1300 Yonge St., Ste. 200, Toronto, ON, M4T 2W3. (416)
922-5740.
CANADIAN GENERAL MANAGER
Michael Skewes
BRANCH MANAGER
Michael Brooker
Branches: 522 11th. Ave. S.W., Ste.202, Calgary, AB, T2R 0C8.
(403) 262-8711.
2388 est rue Beaubien, Montréal, QC, H2G 1N2. (514) 376-8551.

CREATIVE EXPOSURE
2236 Queen St. E., Toronto, ON, M4E 1G2. (416) 690-0775.
FAX: (416) 690-0755.
PRESIDENT
Tom Litvinskas
CRESWIN FILM DISTRIBUTORS LTD.
18 Corwin Cr., Downsview, ON, M3H 2A1. (416) 633-9079. FAX:
(416) 638-5282.
PRESIDENT
Larry Rittenberg
DISTRIBUTION CINE GROUP
1151 Alexandre-DeSève, Montréal, QC, H2L 2T7. (514) 524-
7567. FAX: (514) 524-1997.
CONTACT
Hubert Gariépy
FILMS TRANSIT INC.
402 est rue Notre-Dame, Montréal, QC, H2Y 1C8. (514)
844-3358. FAX: (514) 844-7298.
PRESIDENT
Jan Roefekamp
FIRST ONTARIO FILM DISTRIBUTORS INC.
2 Bloor St. W., Ste. 1901, Toronto, ON, M4W 3E2. (416) 944-
0104. FAX: (416) 944-2212.
PRESIDENT
Jeff Sackman
FRANCE FILM COMPANY INC./COMPAGNE FRANCE FILM
505 est rue Sherbrooke, Ste. 2401, Montréal, QC, H2L 4N3.
(514) 844-0680.
PRÉSIDENT, DIRECTEUR GÉNÉRAL
Pierre René
JASMINE TEA FILMS INC.
83 Rameau Dr., Unit 5, Willowdale, ON, M2H 1T6. (416) 493-
3584. FAX: (416) 493-9117.
PRESIDENT
Russell Chan
KALEIDOSCOPE ENTERTAINMENT INC.
23 Lesmill Rd., Ste. 300, Don Mills, ON, M3B 3P6. (416)
443-9200. FAX: (416) 443-8685.
PRESIDENT
F.J. Braun
VICE-PRESIDENT
Randy H. Zalken
K FILMS AMERIQUE
55 ouest Mont-Royal, bur. 205, Montréal, QC, H2T 2S5. (514)
849-2477. FAX: (514) 849-5859.
PRÉSIDENT
Louis Dussault
MALOFILM DISTRIBUTION INC.
3575 boul. St-Laurent, bur. 650, Montréal, QC, H2X 2T7. (514)
844-4555. FAX: (514) 844-1471.
PRÉSIDENT DU CONSEIL
René Malo
2221 Yonge St., Ste. 400, Toronto, ON, M4S 2B4. (416) 480-
0453. FAX: (416) 480-0501.
VICE-PRESIDENT, DISTRIBUTION
Peter Wertelecky
MGM/UA DISTRIBUTION COMPANY
720 King St. W., Ste.611, Toronto, ON, M5V 2T3. (416) 703-9579
VP & CANADIAN GENERAL MANAGER
Don Popow
666 Sherbrooke St. W., Ste. 1002, Montréal, QC, H3A 1E7. (514)
284-5113.
BRANCH MANAGER
Robert Montplaisir
NORSTAR RELEASING
86 Bloor St. W., 4th Fl., Toronto, ON M5S 1M5. (416) 961-6278.
FAX: (416) 961-5608.
PRESIDENT, CHAIRMAN & CEO
Peter R. Simpson
NORTH AMERICAN RELEASING INC.
808 Nelson St., Ste. 2105, Vancouver, BC, V6Z 2H2. (604) 681-
2165. FAX: (604) 681-5538.
Lloyd A Simandl, A. William Smyth
PARAGON-INTERNATIONAL
119 Spadina Ave., Ste. 900, Toronto, ON, M5V 2L1. (416) 595-
6300. FAX: (416) 977-0489.
SENIOR V.P.
Kirstine Layfield
PARAMOUNT PICTURES CANADA
146 Bloor St. W., Toronto, ON, M5S IM4. (416) 969-9901. FAX:
(416) 922-0287.

PRESIDENT
Gino Campagnola
1255 University Ave., Ste. 912, Montréal, QC, H4A 2J1. (514)
866-2010. FAX: (514) 866-2411.
PICTURE PLANT RELEASING LTD.
P.O. Box 2465, Stn. M, Halifax, NS, B3J 3E8. (902) 423-3901.
FAX: (902) 422-5704.
PRESIDENT
William D. MacGillivray
POLYGRAM FILMED ENTERTAINMENT
80 Citizen Ct., Unit 1, Markham, ON, L6G 1A7. (905) 940-9700.
FAX: (905)940-5556.
PRESIDENT
Darryl Iwai
THE ROKE ENTERTAINMENT GROUP
522 11th. Ave. S.W., Calgary, AB, T2R 0C8. (403) 264-4660.
FAX: (403) 264-6571.
Hector Ross, Frank Kettner, Syd Sniderman, Lloyd Fedor
SATURDAY PLAYS LIMITED
965 Bay St., Ste. 2409, Toronto, ON, M5S 2A3. (416) 964-7284.
FAX: (416) 964-7997.
PRESIDENT
Allan King
SOVCAN FILMS INC.
1204 est rue Ste-Catherine, Montréal, QC, H2L 2G9. (514) 525-
4616. FAX: (414) 521-1793.
PRESIDENT
Claire Costom
SULLIVAN ENTERTAINMENT INC.
110 Davenport Rd., Toronto, ON, M5R 3R3. (416) 921-7177.
FAX: (416) 921-7538.
PRESIDENT
Trudy Grant
TRIANGLE FILMS
1303 Greene Ave., Ste. 100, Westmount, QC, H3Z 2A7. (514)
846-1940. FAX: (514) 846-1550.
PRESIDENT
Debbie Travis
GENERAL MANAGER
Hans Rosenstein
TWENTIETH CENTURY FOX FILM CORPORATION
33 Bloor St. E., Ste. 1106, Toronto, ON, M4W 3H1. Sales: (416)
921-0001. Advertising: (416) 515-3367. Publicity: (416) 515-
3365. FAX: (416) 921-9062. (800) 668-9927
VICE PRESIDENT & GENERAL MANAGER
Doris J. Payne
UNIVERSAL FILMS CANADA
MCA Bldg., 2450 Victoria Pk. Ave., Willowdale, ON, M2J 4A2.
(416) 491-3000. FAX: (416) 491-2857.
VICE-PRESIDENT & GENERAL MANAGER
Eugene Amodeo
Branches: 2450 Victoria Pk. Ave., Willowdale, ON, M2J 4A2.
TORONTO/ST.JOHN BRANCH MANAGER
Peter Doody
CALGARY/VANCOUVER/WINNIPEG BRANCH MANAGER
Gail Shiffman
10500 Côte-de-Liesse, Ste 145, Lachine, QC, H8T 1A4. (514)
636-4886.
MANAGER, 35MM
Jean Paul Hurtubise
VIACOM ENTERPRISES CANADA
146 Bloor St. W., Toronto, ON, M5S 1M4. (416) 969-7119.
VICE-PRESIDENT & GENERAL MANAGER
Alastair Banks
WARNER BROS. ENTERTAINMENT INC.
4576 Yonge St., 2nd Fl., North York, ON, M2N 6N4. (416) 250-
8384. FAX: (416) 250-1898. (Advertising). FAX: (416) 250-8930.
(Sales).
PRESIDENT & CANADIAN DIVISION MANAGER
Philip R. Carlton
Branch: 9900 Cavendish, Ste. 205, Ville Saint-Laurent, QC, H4M
2V2. (514) 333-6400. FAX: (514) 333-1460.
MANAGER
Francine Loranger
WINNIPEG FILM GROUP DISTRIBUTION OFFICE
304-100 Arthur St., Winnipeg, MB R3B 1H3. (204) 942-6795.
FAX: (204) 942-6799.
CONTACT
Terry Coles

CHIEF EXHIBITION CIRCUITS

CAPRICE ENTERTAINMENT LIMITED
963 Granville St., 2nd Fl., Vancouver, BC, V6Z 1L3. (604) 683-8038. FAX: (604) 683-8077.
PRESIDENT
Terry Weir
HEAD BOOKER & FILM BUYER
Dene Joyal
BRITISH COLUMBIA—CAMPBELL RIVER: Caprice Showcase. (5); COURTENAY: Caprice Showcase (5), Palace (1); Delta: Caprice Showcase (1); DUNCAN: Caprice (4); LANGFORD: Caprice Showcase (3); Nanaimo: Caprice Showcase (2), Roxy (2); Newton: Caprice Showcase (4); VANCOUVER: Caprice Showcase (1), Paradise (1); W. VANCOUVER: Caprice Park Royal (3); White Rock: Caprice Rialto (2).

CINEPLEX ODEON CORPORATION
1303 Yonge St., Toronto, ON, M4T 2Y9. (416) 323-6600. FAX: (416) 323-6677. Cable: CINELAW.
CHAIRMAN
Senator E. Leo Kolber
PRESIDENT & CHIEF EXECUTIVE OFFICER
Allen Karp
EXECUTIVE VICE-PRESIDENT & CHIEF FINANCIAL OFFICER
Ellis Jacob
EXECUTIVE VICE-PRESIDENT
Robert J. Tokio
EXECUTIVE VICE-PRESIDENT, MARKETING & COMMUNICATIONS
Howard Lichtman
EXECUTIVE VICE-PRESIDENT, CORPORATE AFFAIRS & SECRETARY
Michael Herman
EXECUTIVE VICE-PRESIDENT, OPERATIONS
Irwin Cohen
SENIOR VICE-PRESIDENT, BUSINESS AFFAIRS & CORPORATE CONTROLLER
James Vassos
SENIOR VICE-PRESIDENT, HEAD FILM BUYER
Michael McCartney
SENIOR VICE-PRESIDENT, TAXATION & TREASURER
Stephen F. Brown
SENIOR VICE-PRESIDENT
Sam DiMichele
NORTH AMERICAN THEATRES DIVISION:
SENIOR VICE-PRESIDENT, FILM, CANADA
Eric Bauman
SENIOR VICE-PRESIDENT & GENERAL MANAGER, QUÉBEC
Claude Chabot
SENIOR VICE-PRESIDENT, ADVERTISING
Bill Snelling
VICE-PRESIDENT, PUBLICITY & PROMOTIONS
Jerry Bulger
VICE-PRESIDENT, FILM & DEVELOPMENT
Michael Kennedy
SENIOR VICE-PRESIDENT, FINANCE, THEATRES & M.I.S.
Jeffrey Kent
VICE-PRESIDENT, ASSISTANT HEAD FILM BUYER, U.S.
Shauna Young
VICE-PRESIDENT, OPERATIONS, NORTH AMERICA
Dan McGrath
ALBERTA—CALGARY: Cineplex Esso Plaza. (9), Corral Drive-In (4), Eau Claire Market (5), London Town Square (6), Marlborough (3), North Hill (1), Northland Village (5), Showcase Grand (2), Southland (4), Westbrook (3); EDMONTON: Capitol (4), Eaton Centre (9), Twin Drive-In (2), West Mall 6 (6), West Edmonton Mall 8 (8), Westmount (4), Whitemud Crossing (6) LETHBRIDGE: Park Place (6), ST. ALBERT: Cineplex Village Tree (12).
BRITISH COLUMBIA—BURNABY: Station Square (5); CLEARBROOK: Clearbrook (6); COQUITLAM: Pinetree (6); KAMLOOPS: Odeon (4); NORTH DELTA: Scott 72 (4); PRINCE GEORGE: Odeon (3); RICHMOND: Richport (3); SURREY: Hillcrest Drive-In (1); VANCOUVER: Granville (7), Oakridge (3), Park & Tilford (5); VICTORIA: Odeon (3).
MANITOBA—WINNIPEG: Garrick (4), Grant Park (4), Odeon Drive-In (1).
ONTARIO—BRAMPTON: Centennial (3), 410 & 7 Centre (4); BRANTFORD: Cinemas 3 (3), Odeon (2); BURLINGTON: Cineplex (6), Showcase (6); CAMBRIDGE: Twin (2); COBOURG: Northumberland Mall (3); FONTHILL: Can-View Drive-In (4); GUELPH: Stone Road Mall (5); HAMILTON: Centre Mall (4), Upper James Place (7); KINGSTON: Cataraqui (6); KITCHENER: Fairway Centre (7), Frederick Mall (2), Hyland (1); LONDON: Galleria (6), Huron Market Place (6), Westmount (2); MISSISSAUGA: Erin Mills (5), South Common Mall (7); NIAGARA

FALLS: Niagara Square (3); OAKVILLE: Oakville Mews (5); OTTAWA: Kanata (4), Orleans Town Centre (6), St Laurent (5), Somerset (1), Vanier (7), Westgate (3), World Exchange (7); RICHMOND HILL: Elgin Mills (10), Hillcrest (5); ST. CATHARINES: Fairview Mall (1), Pendale (2); SARNIA: Odeon (2); SUDBURY: Odeon (2); THORNHILL: Promenade (6); THUNDER BAY: Cineplex (8), Cumberland (5), Victoria (2); TORONTO: Canada Square (8), Carlton (9), Eaton Centre (17), Fairview (6), Finch (3), Humber (2), Hyland (3), Madison (5), Market Square (6), Scarborough Town Centre (12), Sherway (9), Varsity (2), Warden Woods (8), Woodbine Centre (6), Woodside (3), York (2); WATERLOO: Waterloo (1); WELLAND: Seaway (2); WHITBY: Champlain Mall (6); WINDSOR: Glade Place (3), Odeon (1), Palace (4).
QUEBEC—BEAUPORT: Beauport Drive-In (3); BOUCHERVILLE: Cinema 6 (6) (partnership), Odeon Drive-In (2); BROSSARD: Odeon (6); CAP-AUX-MEULES: Chateauguay Drive-In (3); CHICOUTIMI: Place du Royaume (3); LASALLE: Place la Salle (12); LAVAL: Carrefour (6), Cinema 2000 (2), Les Galleries Laval (8), Laval Drive-In (4); LONGUEUIL: Place Longueuil (2); MONTREAL: Berri (5), Centreville (9), Côte de Neiges (7), Cremazie (1), Dauphin (2), Decarie Sq. (2), Desjardins (4), Egyptien (3), Le Faubourg (4), Le Nouvel Elysee (2) (partnership); POINTE-CLAIRE: Pointe-Claire (6); POINTE DU LAC: Trois-Rivieres Drive-In (2); QUEBEC: De Paris (3), Place Charest (8); ST NICHOLAS: de la Colline Drive-In (2); SHERBROOKE: Capital (1); TRACY: Tracy Drive-In (1); WESTMOUNT: Atwater (3).
SASKATCHEWAN—REGINA: Coronet (6); SASKATOON: Pacific (4), Towne (2).

EMPIRE THEATRES LIMITED
610 East River Rd., New Glasgow, NS B2H 3S8. (902) 755-7620. FAX: (902) 755-7640. e-mail: empir eng@fox.nstn.ca
PRESIDENT
Stuart G. Fraser
Regional Office: 650 Portland St., Dartmouth, NS B2W 6A3. (902) 434-4114. FAX: (902) 434-6933. e-mail: empire da@www.atcon.com
DIRECTOR OF MARKETING
Dean S. Leland
NEW BRUNSWICK—FREDERICTON: Nashwaaksis (2), Plaza (4); SAINT JOHN: Exhibition Cinema (7), King Square (1).
NEWFOUNDLAND—CORNER BROOK: Millbrook (2); ST JOHN'S: Avalon Mall (5), Empire Cinemas (6).
NOVA SCOTIA—AMHERST: Paramount (3); BEDFORD: Empire (6), BRIDGEWATER: Southshore (3); DARTMOUTH: Empire 6 (6); HALIFAX: Oxford (1); NEW GLASGOW: Aberdeen Mall (4), Empire Drive-In (1); SYDNEY: Empire Cinemas (8); TRURO: Centennial (3); YARMOUTH: Yarmouth (3).
PRINCE EDWARD ISLAND—CHARLOTTETOWN: Charlottetown Mall (8).

FAMOUS PLAYERS INC.
146 Bloor St. W., Toronto, ON, M5B 1P3. (416) 969-7800. FAX: (416) 964-3924.
PRESIDENT
Joseph Peixoto
EXECUTIVE VICE-PRESIDENT
John Bailey
EXECUTIVE VICE-PRESIDENT & TREASURER
Ton Kars
V.P., GENERAL COUNSEL & SECRETARY
Michael Scher
V.P., OPERATIONS
Brian Holberton
V.P., MARKETING
Roger Harris
V.P. & CONTROLLER
Belen Croutch
V.P., FILM
Joe Strebinger
V.P., BUSINESS PLANNING & LOGISTICS
Damien Cheng
DIRECTOR, CONCESSIONS & MARKETING
Stuart Pollock
COMMUNICATIONS COORDINATOR, PUBLIC RELATIONS & GENERAL INFORMATION
Josephine Starodub
ALBERTA—CALGARY: Banker's Hall. (5), Market Mall (8), South Centre (7), Sunridge (5), Westhills (10); EDMONTON: Gateway (8), Londonderry (2), Paramount (1), West Mall (5), Westmount Centre (4); LETHBRIDGE: Centre Cinema (2), Paramount (2); RED DEER: Park Plaza (7).
BRITISH COLUMBIA—BURNABY: Station Square (7); COQUITLAM: Eagle Ridge (4); KELOWNA: Orchard Park (5); LANGLEY: Willowbrook (6); NORTH VANCOUVER: Esplanade 6 (6); PRINCE RUPERT: Prince Rupert (3); RICHMOND:

Richmond Centre (6); SURREY: Guildford (4); VANCOUVER: Capitol (6), Dunbar (1), Vancouver Centre (2); VERNON: Polson Place (2); VICTORIA Capitol (6), University (4).
MANITOBA—WINNIPEG: Garden City (2), Kildonan Place (6), Northstar (2), Portage Place (3), St. Vital (6).
NEW BRUNSWICK—MONCTON: Paramount (2); SAINT JOHN: Paramount (2).
NOVA SCOTIA—DARTMOUTH: Penhorn(5); HALIFAX: Park Lane (8).
ONTARIO—BELLEVILLE: Quinte Mall (2); BRAMPTON: Gateway (6), BRANTFORD: Market Square (3); BURLINGTON: Burlington Mall (3); GLOUCESTER: Gloucester 5 (5); HAMILTON: Jackson Square (6), Lime Ridge (4); KINGSTON: Capitol (7); KITCHENER: Capitol (2), Kings College (4); LONDON: Capitol (2), Famous Players (6); Famous Players Wellington (8); MARKHAM: Markville (4); MISSISSAUGA: Square One (4), Sussex Centre (4); NEWMARKET: Glenway (5); OAKVILLE: Town Centre (6); OSHAWA: Centre 8 (8); OTTAWA: Airport Drive-In (3), Britannia (6), Britannia Drive-In (2), Capitol Square (3), Place de Ville (2), Rideau Centre (3); PICKERING: Town Centre (3); RICHMOND HILL: Parkway (4); ST. CATHARINES: Lincoln Mall (3), Pen Centre (3); SARNIA: Lambton 5 (5); STONEY CREEK: Fiesta Mall (4); SUDBURY: City Centre (3), Super Mall (3); THUNDER BAY: Capitol (2); TORONTO: Bayview Village (4), Capitol (1), Cedarbrae (8), Centrepoint (3), Cumberland (4), Eglinton (1), Hollywood North & South (2), Plaza (2), Runnymede (2), Sheraton Centre (2), Sheridan (4), Skyway 6 (6), Uptown (3), Uptown Backstage (2), Victoria Terrace (6), Westwood (3), Yorkdale (6); WINDSOR: Devonshire (3), Parkway (5); WOODBRIDGE: 400 Drive-In (3), 7 & 27 Drive-In (2).
QUEBEC—DORVAL: Dorval (4); GATINEAU: Les Promenades (4); GREENFIELD PARK: Greenfield Park (3); Famous Players Greenfield Park (8); LASALLE: Carrefour Angrignon (10); LAVAL: Cinéma Laval (12); MONTREAL: Centre Eaton (6), Ciné du Parc (3), Loew's (5), Palace (6), Parisien (7), Versailles (6); POINTE-CLAIRE: Famous Players 8 (8); QUEBEC CITY: Les Galéries Capitale (6); STE. FOY: Ste. Foy (3), SHERBROOKE: Carrefour de l'Estrie (3).
SASKATCHEWAN—REGINA: Cornwall Centre (4); SASKATOON: Capitol Four (4), Midtown (2).

FESTIVAL CINEMAS
2236 Queen St. E., Toronto, ON, M4E 1G2. (416) 690-0667. FAX: (416) 690-0755.
PRINCIPALS
Tom Litvinskas, Jerry Szczur
ONTARIO—TORONTO: Bloor (1), Fox (1) Kingsway (1), Paradise (1), Revue (1).

LANDMARK CINEMAS OF CANADA LTD.
522 11th.Ave. S.W., 4th Fl., Calgary, AB, T2R 0C8. (403) 262-4255. FAX: (403) 266-1529.
DIRECTORS
Hector H. Ross, Philip H. May, Frank Kettner, Charles D. K. May, Barry Myers, Brian F. McIntosh
CHAIRMAN
Hector H. Ross
PRESIDENT
Brian F. McIntosh
SECRETARY
Philip H. May
VICE-PRESIDENTS
Frank Kettner
CHARLES D. K. MAY
Barry Myers.
OPERATIONS MANAGER
D.C.. (Chuck) Bradley
MANAGER, FILM BUYING & BOOKING
Kevin Norman
MANAGER, ADVERTISING & CREATIVE SERVICES
Donald D. Langkaas
MANAGER, MARKETING & PROMOTION
Gordon Imlach
ACCOUNTING MANAGER
Ian Harwood
ADMINISTRATION MANAGER
Sherry Chappell
OPERATIONS
Geoff Linquist
Kevin Graham
ALBERTA—AIRDRIE: Roxy Theatre. (2); BANFF: Lux Cinema Centre (4); BROOKS: Oasis Theatre (1); CALGARY: Globe Cinema (2); CAMROSE: Bailey Theatre (1); DRUMHELLER: Napier Theatre (1); EDMONTON: Jasper Cinema Centre (2), Stardust Drive-In (2); EDSON: Nova Theatre (1); GRANDE PRAIRIE: Jan Cinema (3), Prairie Cinema Centre (2); HINTON: Roxy Theatre (1); MEDICINE HAT: Monarch Theatre (1), Towne Cinema Centre (3); REDCLIFF: Gemini Drive-In (1); RED DEER: Uptown Cinema Centre (4); SHERWOOD PARK: Sword & Shield Cinema Centre (4); STETTLER: Jewel Theatre (1).
BRITISH COLUMBIA—ABBOTSFORD: Towne Cinema Centre (7); CHILLIWACK: Paramount Theatre (2); CRANBROOK:

Armond Theatre (2); DAWSON CREEK: Centre Cinema (1); FORT ST JOHN: Lido Theatre (1); KAMLOOPS: Northills Theatre (1), Paramount Theatre (2); KELOWNA: Paramount Theatre (3), Uptown Cinema (2); NANAIMO: Avalon Cinemas (3), The Bay Theatre (2); PENTICTON: Pen-Mar Cinema Centre (4); PORT ALBERNI: Paramount Theatre (1); PRINCE GEORGE: Coronet Theatre (2); VERNON: Towne Theatre (1); VICTORIA: Vic Theatre (1).
MANITOBA—BRANDON: Strand Theatre (1) Towne Cinema (1); SELKIRK: Garry Theatre (1); WINNIPEG: Towne 8 (8).
SASKATCHEWAN—REGINA: Cinema 6 Drive-In (1), WEYBURN: Soo Theatre (1); YORKTON: Tower Theatre (1).
YUKON—WHITEHORSE: Qwanlin Cinema Centre (2) Yukon Cinema Centre (2).

MAGIC LANTERN THEATRES
14306 115 Ave., P.O.Box 3707, Stn. D, Edmonton, AB, T5L 4J7. (403) 482-1611. FAX: (403) 482-3520.
PRESIDENT
Tom Hutchinson
SECRETARY
Bill Booth
ALBERTA—EDMONTON: Garneau (1); PEACE RIVER: Cinema 72 (2); ST PAUL: Elite (1); SPRUCE GROVE: Magic Lantern (1); WHITECOURT: Vista (1).
BRITISH COLUMBIA—FERNIE: Vogue (1).
NORTH WEST TERRITORY—YELLOWKNIFE: Capitol (3).
SASKATCHEWAN—NORTH BATTLEFORD: Capitol (1), Frontier Twin (2).

ONTARIO THEATRE GROUP
672 Mt. Pleasant Rd., Toronto, ON, M4S 2N3. (416) 481-1186.
PRESIDENT
Norman Stern
SECRETARY-TREASURER
Peter Sorok;
ACCOUNTING
Wendy Ciampaglia
ADMINISTRATION & BOOKING
Shellie Goldberg
ADVERTISING & CONCESSIONS
Cindy Morris
FILM OPERATIONS
Dale Doody
THEATRE OPERATIONS
Dudley Dumond
ONTARIO—BELLEVILLE: Bellestar (3); BROCKVILLE: Parkedale (2); CORNWALL: Brookdale (3); GEORGETOWN: Cinema (3); HAMILTON: Westdale (1); INGLESIDE Colonial Drive-In (1); NORTH BAY: Champlain (4), Gateway (1); OWEN SOUND: Owen Sound Cinema (5); PEMBROKE: Algonquin (4); PETERBOROUGH: Lansdowne (6) Trent (2); SAULT STE. MARIE: Station Cinema (5); TORONTO: Regent (1).

STINSON THEATRES LTD.
Box 142, Barrie, ON, L4M 4S9. (705) 726-8190. (705) 721-9579.
PRESIDENT
Robert Stinson
BOOKER & BUYER
Cathy Watson
ONTARIO—BARRIE: Barrie Triple Drive-In (3), Imperial (8); CHATHAM: Cinema Six (6); COLLINGWOOD: Cinema Four (4), Collingwood Drive-In (1); HUNTSVILLE: Capitol (2), Huntsville Drive-In (1); ORANGEVILLE: Uptown (2); ORILLIA: Orillia Cinema Four (4); OWEN SOUND: Twin Drive-In (1); TIMMINS: Cinema Six (6).

TARRANT ENTERPRISES LIMITED
56 Charles St., Newmarket, ON, L3Y 3V9. (905) 898-4072. FAX: (905) 898-7629.
PRESIDENT
June Tarrant
ONTARIO—GUELPH: 3-Star (6); NEWMARKET: Film Factory (6); PICKERING: MoVIPlex 9 (9); ST. THOMAS: Capitol (3); TRENTON: Centre (3).

INDEPENDENT BOOKING

ATLANTIC THEATRE SERVICES LTD.
P.O. Box 2419, 114 Dresden Ave., Saint John, NB E2L 3V9.. (506) 696-6618.. FAX: (506) 696-4472.
INDEPENDENT BOOKING & THEATRE SERVICES LTD.
61 Renwick Ave., Cambridge, ON, N3C 2T5. Tel. & FAX: (519) 658-6920.
PRESIDENT
Eric Ball
PRAIRIE ALLIED BOOKING ASSOCIATION
(A division of Theatre Agencies Ltd.) 522 11th Ave. S.W., Calgary, AB, T2R 0C8;. (403) 264-4660 FAX: (403) 264-6571. Frank Kettner, Ellen Smeltzer, Donna Campbell
WEST COAST THEATRE SERVICE LTD.
401-788 Beatty St., Vancouver, BC, V6B 1A2. (604) 669-4738. FAX: (604) 669-9640.
Hector H. Ross, Doug Isman

FILM CARRIERS

EMERY WORLDWIDE
Pearson International Airport, P.O. Box 251, Toronto, ON, L5P 1B1. Information: (905) 676-0488. Sales & Information: (905) 676-8872. FAX: (905) 673-5761
SALES MANAGER
Barbara Williams
Branches: Calgary: (403) 221-1981. Dorval: (514) 636-1333. Edmonton: (403) 890-4475, Halifax: (902) 873-3545. London: (519) 452-0088. Ottawa: (613) 733-9650. Regina: (306) 352-9046. Saskatoon: (306) 931-1110. Vancouver: (604) 273-9077. Winnipeg: (204) 775-2676.

RUSSELL A. FARROW LIMITED
5397 Eglinton Ave. W., Ste. 220, Etobicoke, ON, M9C 5K6. (416) 622-3777. FAX: (416) 622-2217.
5200 Miller Rd., Ste. 2040, Vancouver International Airport, Richmond, BC, V7B 1K5. (604) 270-3131. FAX: (604) 270-9741

MAVETY FILM DELIVERY
40 Lesmill Rd., Don Mills, ON, M3B 2T5. (416) 447-5169.
GENERAL MANAGER
Jim Matsumoto

SAMEDAY RIGHT-O-WAY
6555 Northwest Dr., Mississauga, ON, L4V 1K2. (905) 676-1888. (Pickup): (905) 677-9722. (Customer Service)
VICE PRESIDENT & GENERAL MANAGER
Bob Brogan

VICTORIA FILM SERVICES LIMITED
40 Lesmill Rd., Don Mills, ON, M3B 2T5. (416) 449-8597.
PRESIDENT
Paul Wroe
CANADIAN GENERAL MANAGER
Jim Matsumoto
Branches: 1644 W. 75th Ave., Vancouver, BC, V6P 6G2. (604) 263-2551. Manager: Rick Williston.
3904 1st St. N.E., Calgary, AB, T2E 3E3. (403) 276-6696. Manager: Susan Piotrowski.
2315 Logan Ave., Winnipeg, MB R2R 2S7. (204) 633-1203. Manager: Ben Adleman.
708 rue Walnut, Montréal, QC, H4C 2M4. (514) 931-6212. Manager: Marie-Claude Boudreau.
55 Bentley St., St. John, NB E2K 1B2. (506) 634-1018. Manager: Kevin McDermott.

TRADE ASSOCIATIONS

ACADEMY OF CANADIAN CINEMA AND TELEVISION
158 Pearl St., Toronto, ON, M5H 1L3. (416) 591-2040. FAX: (416) 591-2157.
3375 boul. St-Laurent, bur. 709, Montréal, QC, H2X 2T7. (514) 849-7448. FAX: (514) 849-5069.
1385 Homer St., Vancouver, BC, V6B 2S2. (604) 684-4528. FAX: (604) 684-4574.
1652 Barrington St., Halifax, NS, B3J 2A2. (902) 425-0489. FAX: (902) 425-8851.
Los Angeles Division. (800) 644-5194.
CHAIR
Ann Medina
NATIONAL VICE-CHAIRMAN
David Cronenberg
CEO
Maria Topalovich

ACTRA PERFORMERS GUILD (CLC, FIA)
National Office, 2239 Yonge St., Toronto, ON, M4S 2B5. (416) 489-1311. FAX: (416) 489-1435.
NATIONAL EXECUTIVE DIRECTOR
Stephen Waddell. (Toronto)
NATIONAL PRESIDENT
Brian Gromoff

ASSOCIATION DES PRODUCTEURS DE FILMS ET DE TELEVISION DU QUEBEC (APFTQ)
740 St-Maurice, bur. 201, Montréal, QC, H3C 1L5. (514) 397-8600. FAX: (514) 392-0232.
PRESIDENTE & DIRECTRICE-GENERALE
Louise Baillargeon

THE ASSOCIATION OF CANADIAN FILM CRAFTSPEOPLE. (ACFC)
Head Office: Cinevillage, 65 Heward Ave., Ste. 105, Toronto, ON, M4M 2T5. (416) 462-0211. FAX: (416) 462-3248.
BUSINESS MANAGER
Ray Stringer
63 Albert St., Ste. 302, Winnipeg, MB R3B 1G4. (204) 943-1866. FAX: (204) 943-1860.
CONTACT
Nancy Jakubic
555 Brooksbank Ave., N.Vancouver, BC, V7J 3S5. (604) 983-5450. FAX: (604) 983-5451.
CONTACT
Brenda Collins

ASSOCIATION QUEBECOISE DES REALISATEURS ET REALISATRICES DE CINEMA ET DE TELEVISION
1600 De Lorimier, bur. 122, Montréal, QC, H2K 3W5. (514) 527-2197, (514) 521-1984. Poste 436. FAX: (514) 527-7699.
PRESIDENT
François Côté

CANADIAN ACTORS' EQUITY ASSOCIATION
260 Richmond St. E., 2nd Fl. Toronto, ON, M5A 1P4. (416) 867-9165. FAX: (416) 867-9246.
EXECUTIVE DIRECTOR
Susan Wallace

CANADIAN ASSOCIATION OF FILM DISTRIBUTORS AND EXPORTERS
62 Humewood Dr., Toronto, ON, M6C 2W4. (416) 658-2929. FAX: (416) 658-3176.

PRESIDENT & CEO
Dan Johnson

CANADIAN CABLE TELEVISION ASSOCIATION
360 Albert St., Ste. 1010, Ottawa, ON, K1R 7X7. (613) 232-2631. FAX: (613) 232-2137.
PRESIDENT & CEO
Richard Stursberg

CANADIAN FILM & TELEVISION PRODUCTION ASSOCIATION (CFTPA)
175 Bloor St. E., North Tower, Ste. 806, Toronto, ON, M4W 3R8. (416) 927-8942. FAX: (416) 922-4038.
116 Albert St., Ste. 303, Ottawa, ON, K1P 5G3. (613) 233-1444. FAX: (613) 233-0073.
Producers Branch, 1431 Howe St., Vancouver, BC, V6Z 1R9. (604) 682-8619 FAX. (604) 684-9294
CHAIRMAN
Tom Berry
PRESIDENT
Elizabeth McDonald

CANADIAN INDEPENDENT FILM CAUCUS (CIFC)
189 Dupont St., Toronto, ON, M5R 1V6. (416) 920-9989. FAX: (416) 968-9092.
CO-CHAIRS
Barri Cohen, Barry Greenwald
EXECUTIVE DIRECTOR
Debbie Nightingale

CANADIAN MOTION PICTURE DISTRIBUTORS ASSOCIATION (CMPDA)
22 St. Clair Ave.E., Toronto, ON, M4T 2S4. (416) 961-1888. FAX: (416) 968-1016.

CANADIAN PICTURE PIONEERS
21 Dundas Sq., Ste. 906, Toronto, ON, M5B 1B7. (416) 368-1139. FAX: (416) 368-1130.
PRESIDENT
Philip R. Carlton
VICE-PRESIDENT
Cathy Watson

CANADIAN SOCIETY OF CINEMATOGRAPHERS. (CSC)
235 Carlaw Ave., Ste. 603, Toronto, ON, M4M 2S5. (416) 466-5013. FAX: (416) 266-3996.
PRESIDENT
Joan Hutton, csc

CANADIAN WOMEN IN COMMUNICATIONS
372 Bay St., Ste. 1900, Toronto, ON, M5H 2W9. (416) 363-1880, (800) 361-2978. FAX: (416) 363-1882.
EXECUTIVE DIRECTOR
Beverley A. Dales

CASTING DIRECTORS OF CANADA (CDC)
366 Adelaide St., Toronto, ON, M5A 3X9. (416) 866-8339. FAX. (416) 866-8049.
CO-CHAIR
Jann Stefoff, Deirdre Bowen

DIRECTORS GUILD OF CANADA
National Office: 387 Bloor St. E., Ste. 401, Toronto, ON, M4W 1H7. (416) 972-0098. Vancouver: (604) 688-2976. Calgary: (403) 244-3456. Toronto: (416) 351-8200. Montréal: (514) 844-4084. Halifax: (902) 492-3424.
PRESIDENT
Allan King

675

THE GUILD OF CANADIAN FILM COMPOSERS
Canadian Music Centre, 20 St. Joseph St., Toronto, ON, M4Y 1J9. (416) 961-6601.
PRESIDENT
Paul Hoffert

THE MOTION PICTURE FOUNDATION OF CANADA
22 St. Clair Ave. E., Ste. 1603, Toronto, ON, M4T 2S4. (416) 961-1888. Telecopier: (416) 968-1016.

MOTION PICTURE THEATRE ASSOCIATIONS OF CANADA
1303 Yonge St., Ist Flr. Toronto, ON, M4T 2Y9. (416) 323-7214. FAX: (416) 323-6633.
EXECUTIVE DIRECTOR
Dina Lebo
PRESIDENT
Cathy Watson

SOCAN/SOCIETY OF COMPOSERS, AUTHORS AND MUSIC PUBLISHERS OF CANADA
41 Valleybrook Dr., Don Mills, ON, M3B 2S6. (416) 445-8700, (800) 55 SOCAN.
GENERAL MANAGER
Michael Rock

UNION DES ARTISTES
1290 rue Saint-Denis, 6e étage, Montréal, QC, H2X 3J7. (514) 288-6682. FAX: (514) 288-7150.
PRESIDENT
Serge Turgeon
DIRECTEUR-GENERALE
Jean-Robert Choquet
Section de Toronto: (416) 485-7670. FAX: (416) 485-9063.
Marco Dufour
Section de Hull-Ottawa: (819) 778-2658. FAX: (819) 770-8678.
Denise Marleau
Section de Québec: (418) 523-4241. FAX: (418) 523-4241. FAX: (418) 523-0168.
Chantal Latour

WRITERS GUILD OF CANADA (WGC)
35 McCaul St., Ste. 300, Toronto, ON, M5T 1V7. (416)979-7907. FAX: (416) 979-9273. (800) 567-9974
EXECUTIVE DIRECTOR
Maureen Parker

GOVERNMENT AGENCIES

FEDERAL

THE NATIONAL FILM BOARD OF CANADA
Head Office: 179 Rideau St., Ottawa, ON, K1A 0M9
Operational Headquarters: 3155 Côte de Liesse Rd., Ville Saint-Laurent, QC, H4N 2N4.
Postal address: P.O. Box 6100, Stn. Centre-Ville, Montréal, QC, H3C 3H5. (514) 283-9000. FAX: (514) 283-8971
GOVERNMENT FILM COMMISSIONER AND CHAIRPERSON OF THE NATIONAL FILM BOARD OF CANADA
Sandra Macdonalld. (514) 283-9244.
DIRECTOR GENERAL, ENGLISH PROGRAM
Barbara Janes. (514) 283-9501.
DIRECTOR GENERAL, FRENCH PROGRAM
Claude Bonin. (514) 283-9285.
SENIOR DIRECTOR GENERAL, ADMINISTRATION & OPERATIONS
Gilles Roy. (514) 283-9029.
DIRECTOR GENERAL, SERVICES & TECHNOLOGICAL BRANCH
Robert Forget. (514) 283-9149.
DIRECTOR, PLANNING, EVALUATION AND AUDIT
Claude Parent. (514) 283-9134.
DIRECTOR, INTERNATIONAL PROGRAM
Joanne Leduc. (514) 283-9439.
DIRECTOR, CORPORATE AFFAIRS
Laurie Jones. (613) 992-3615.
DIRECTOR, HUMAN RESOURCES
Guy Gauthier. (514) 283-9108.
SECRETARY TO THE BOARD OF TRUSTEES
Jean-Claude Mahé. (514) 283-2905.
ENGLISH PROGRAM BRANCH PRODUCTION CENTRES
ATLANTIC CENTRE: 5475 Spring Garden Rd., 2nd Fl., Halifax, NS, B3J 1G2. (902) 426-1739. Head: Marilyn Belec.
ONTARIO CENTRE: 150 John St., Toronto, ON, M5V 3C3. (416) 973-3012. Interim Head: Louise Lore.
PRAIRIE CENTRE: 245 Main St., Winnipeg, MB, R3C 1A7. (204) 983-2818. Head: Ches Yetman.
NORTH WEST CENTRE: Canada Place, 9700 Jasper Ave., Ste. 120, Edmonton, AB, T5J 4C3. (403) 495-3015. Head: Graydon McCrea.
PACIFIC CENTRE: 1045 Howe St., Ste. 100, Vancouver, BC, V6Z 2B1. (604) 666-5410. Head: Erik Eriksen.
U.S. OFFICE: 1251 Avenue of the Americas, 16th Fl., New York, NY 10020. (212) 283-9441

STATISTICS CANADA
Education, Culture and Tourism Division, Culture Section, R. H. Coats Bldg., 17th Fl., Ottawa, ON, K1A 0T6. (613) 951-6862.
DIRECTOR
Sange de Silva

TELEFILM CANADA
HEAD OFFICE: Tour de la Banque Nationale, 600 ouest de la Gauchetière, 14e étage, Montréal, QC, H3B 4L8. (514) 283-6363. FAX: (514) 283-8212.
OFFICES: 2 Bloor St.W., 22nd Fl., Toronto, ON, M4W 3E2. (416) 973-6436. FAX (416) 973-8606.
5523 Spring Garden Rd., Ste.206, Box 27, Halifax, NS, B3J 3T1. (902) 426-8425. FAX: (902) 426-4445.
350-375 Water St., Vancouver, BC, V6B 5C6. (604) 666-1566, FAX: (604) 666-7754.

BOARD OF DIRECTORS
CHAIRMAN
Robert Dinan Q.C
VICE-CHAIRMAN
André Provost
MEMBERS
Walter Gray, Nancy-Gay Rotstein, Marcelle Lean, Sandra Macdonald (Government Film Commissioner).
EXECUTIVE DIRECTOR
François Macerola
LEGAL ADVISOR, CORPORATE AFFAIRS
John Pelletier
DIRECTOR, CANADIAN OPERATIONS
Peter Katadotis

MONTREAL
DIRECTOR, OPERATIONS QUÉBEC
Louis Laverdière
DIRECTOR, CORE BUSINESS UNIT—FEATURE FILMS
Myrianne Pavlovic
DIRECTOR, CORE BUSINESS UNIT—TELEVISION
Joëlle Levis
PROJECT CO-ORDINATOR
Diane Ste-Marie

TORONTO
DIRECTOR, OPERATIONS
Bill House
DIRECTOR, CORE BUSINESS UNIT—-TELEVISION
Karin Franklin
DIRECTOR, CORE BUSINESS UNIT—-FEATURE FILMS
Shane Kinnear
PROJECT CO-ORDINATOR
Helen Paul

VANCOUVER
DIRECTOR, OPERATIONS WESTERN REGION
John Taylor
DIRECTOR, CORE BUSINESS UNIT—-TELEVISION
Janine Boyd
DIRECTOR, CORE BUSINESS UNIT—-FEATURE FILMS
Gretchen Doyle
PROJECT COORDINATOR
Colleen MacDonald

HALIFAX
DIRECTOR, OPERATIONS ATLANTIC REGION
Ralph Holt
DIRECTOR, STRATEGIC DEVELOPMENT AND PLANNING
Noel Cormier
DIRECTOR, RESEARCH AND POLICIES
Guy de Repentigny
DIRECTOR, FINANCES
Danny Chalifour
CONTROLLER
Lisa Scardocchio
ASSISTANT DIRECTOR, FINANCES
(temporary assignment) Carolle Brabant
MANAGER, CO-PRODUCTIONS
Deborah Drisdell
DIRECTOR, ADMINISTRATION AND HUMAN RESOURCES
Marcel Choquette
DIRECTOR, INFORMATION SYSTEMS
Gilles Gagné

MANAGER, SYSTEM DEVELOPMENT AND OFFICE
AUTOMATION
François Laurin
MANAGER, MATERIAL RESOURCES
Johanne Laurin
INTERIM DIRECTOR, COMMUNICATIONS, PUBLIC AFFAIRS
AND FESTIVALS
Francine Lavoie
DIRECTOR, FESTIVALS BUREAU
Jean Lefebvre

PROVINCIAL

ALBERTA
ALBERTA COMMUNITY DEVELOPMENT
227 Legislature Bldg., Edmonton, AB, T5K 2B6. (403) 427-4928.
MINISTER
Hon. Gary G. Mar
ARTS, RECREATION & LIBRARIES BRANCH, COMMUNITY & CITIZENSHIP SERVICES DIVISION
5th Fl. Beaver House, 10158 103 St., Edmonton, AB, T5J 0X6.
(403) 427-6315. FAX: (403) 422-9132.
DIRECTOR
Dr. Clive Padfield
ALBERTA FILM COMMISSION
Economic Development & Tourism, 12th Fl., Commerce Place,
10155 102 St., Edmonton, AB, T5J 4L6. (403) 427-2005. FAX:
(403) 427-5924.
FILM COMMISSIONER
Lindsay Cherney
ALBERTA FOUNDATION FOR THE ARTS
5th Fl. Beaver House, 10158 103 St., Edmonton AB, T5J 0X6.
(403) 427-9968. FAX: (403) 422-1162.
EXECUTIVE DIRECTOR
Dr. Clive Padfield
CALGARY ECONOMIC DEVELOPMENT AUTHORITY
Calgary Film Services, P.O. Box 2100, Stn. M, #6, Calgary, AB,
T2P 2M5. (403) 268-1485. FAX: (403) 268-1946.
DIRECTOR, FILM SERVICES
Murray Ord
BRITISH COLUMBIA
MINISTRY OF SMALL BUSINESS, TOURISM AND CULTURE
Cultural Industries, Cultural Services Branch, 800 Johnson St.,
5th Fl., Victoria, BC, V8V 1X4. (604) 356-2136.
Lindsay Allen
BRITISH COLUMBIA FILM COMMISSION
601 W. Cordova St. Vancouver, BC, V6B 1G1. (604) 660-2732.
FAX: (604) 660-4790.
DIRECTOR
Peter Mitchell
MANAGER, LOCATION & PRODUCTION SERVICES
Mark DesRochers
BRITISH COLUMBIA FILM FUND
2225 W. Broadway, Vancouver, BC, V6K 2E4. (604) 736-7997.
FAX (604) 736-7290.
PRESIDENT & CEO
Wayne Sterloff
VICTORIA AND VANCOUVER ISLAND FILM COMMISSION
(A Division of the Greater Victoria Chamber of Commerce), 525
Fort St., Victoria, BC, V8W 1E8. (604) 386-3976.
FILM COMMISSIONER
David B. Mills

MANITOBA
MANITOBA FILM & SOUND DEVELOPMENT CORPORATION
333-93 Lombard Ave., Winnipeg, MB, R3B 3B1. (204) 947-2040.
FAX: (204) 956-5261.
GENERAL MANAGER
Carole Vivier
NEW BRUNSWICK
N.B. FILM & VIDEO COMMISSION
Tourism/Recreation/Heritage, P.O. Box 6000, Fredericton, NB,
E3B 5H1. (506) 453-2553. FAX: (506) 453-2416.
NEWFOUNDLAND
GOVERNMENT OF NEWFOUNDLAND
Cultural Affairs, P.O. Box 1854, St.John's, NF, A1C 5P9. (709)
729-3650. FAX: (709) 729-5952.
NOVA SCOTIA
GOVERNMENT OF NOVA SCOTIA
Dept. of Education, Cultural Affairs Division, P.O. Box 456,
Halifax, NS, B3J 2R5. (902) 424-6389.
CULTURAL INDUSTRIES OFFICER
Peggy Walt
NOVA SCOTIA FILM DEVELOPMENT CORPORATION
1724 Granville St., Halifax, NS B3J 1X5. (902) 424-7177. FAX:
(902) 424-0617. Location Services. (902) 424-7185. FAX: (902)
424-0563.
Helen Wickwire Foster
ONTARIO
MINISTRY OF CITIZENSHIP, CULTURE AND RECREATION
77 Bloor St.W., 6th Fl., Toronto, ON, M7A 2R9. (416) 325-6200
MINISTER
Hon. Marilyn Mushinski
DEPUTY MINISTER
Naomi Alboim
Culture Division: Assistant Deputy Minister: Jane Marlatt. (416)
314-7262; Cultural Policy Branch Director: Robert Montgomery.
(416) 314-7115.
ONTARIO FILM DEVELOPMENT CORPORATION
175 Bloor St.E., North Tower, Ste.300. Toronto, ON, M4W 3R8.
(416) 314-6858. FAX: (416) 314-6876.
QUEBEC
MONTREAL FILM & TV COMMISSION
413 St-Jacques, 4th Fl., Montréal, QC, H2Y 1N9. (514) 872-
2883. FAX: (514) 872-3409.
FILM COMMISSIONER
André Lafond
SOCIETE DE DEVELOPPEMENT DES ENTREPRISES CULTURELLES (SODEC)
1755 boul. René Lévesque est, bur. 200, Montréal, QC, H2K
4P6. (514) 873-7768. FAX (514) 873-4388.
SASKATCHEWAN
THE SASKATCHEWAN FILM AND VIDEO DEVELOPMENT CORPORATION (SASKFILM)
2445 13th Ave., Ste. 340, Regina, SK, S4P OW1. (306) 347-
3456. FAX: (306) 359-7768.
GENERAL MANAGER
Mark Prasuhn
YUKON
YUKON FILM COMMISSION
P.O. Box 2703, Whitehorse, YT, Y1A 2C5. (403) 667-5400. FAX:
(403) 667-3546.
COMMISSIONER
Patty Howlett

THE WORLD MARKET

ASSOCIATIONS, ORGANIZATIONS, PRODUCERS, DISTRIBUTORS & EXHIBITORS BY COUNTRY

THE INDUSTRY IN
FOREIGN COUNTRIES

The following is a list of companies, associations and organizations in alphabetical order by country. All country code and city code numbers appear within parenthesis before the telephone numbers. Statistics, when available, are for 1995 unless noted otherwise.

THE WORLD MARKET

Estimates show that films can earn close to two thirds of their grosses in the foreign market. According to a box-office survey, in 1995, the top 100 feature films grossed $9.15 billion dollars worldwide (including the U.S.). Die Hard With a Vengeance, Batman Forever, Apollo 13 and Pocahontas each grossed over $300 million.

THE EUROPEAN UNION

Members of the European Parliament voted to tighten quotas on non-European Union films and television programming, reserving 51% of the market for European products. The building of new multiplexes across Europe seems to be increasing the demand for films with local production gaining a new focus. In the former Communist bloc nations, piracy of products is still epidemic. In addition, American studios are filming more big budget films in Europe.

SOUTHEAST ASIA

It remains to be seen if the 1997 takeover of Hong Kong by the People's Republic of China will affect the production of Chinese-language films in the former British colony. Strained relations between Taiwan and the PRC may cause some problems as well. Meanwhile, Australia seems to be the center of the new Southeast Asian marketplace.

ARGENTINA

Population: 34.2 million
No. of Screens: 280
Ticket Price: $7.00
DISTRIBUTORS
COLUMBIA TRISTAR FILMS OF ARGENTINA, INC.
Ayacucho 533/37, 1026 Buenos Aires. Tel: (541) 954 3820. FAX: (541) 954 3819. General Manager: Oscar Scarinci.
DISTRIFILMS S. A.
Lavalle 1860, 1051 Capital Federal, Buenos Aires. Tel: (541) 371 3438. FAX: (541) 374 9250. President: Luis Albert Scalella.
UNITED INTERNATIONAL PICTURES
Ayacucho 520, 1026 Buenos Aires. Tel: (541) 373 0261. FAX: (541) 111 303. Manager: Juan Manuel Fascetto.
WARNER BROS.
Tucuman 1938, 1050 Buenos Aires. Tel: (541) 372 6094. FAX: (541) 111 3030. General Manager: Anibal Codebo.

AUSTRALIA

Population: 18.3 million.
Number of Screens: 1,137.
Admissions (1995): 70 million.
Box Office Gross (1995): $353 million (up 6% over 1994).
Feature Production (1995): $85 million (32 films).
Top ten films of 1995: Batman Forever, Casper, Dumb and Dumber, Forrest Gump, Apollo 13, Die Hard With a Vengeance, Braveheart, Babe, While You Were Sleeping, Ace Ventura: When Nature Calls.
Adopted native son Mel Gibson won Academy Awards for Best Picture and Best Director for "Braveheart" and George Miller's family film "Babe" was a huge success worldwide and gathered an Oscar nomination for best picture. 20 Australian-produced films were scheduled for release in 1996. Major films such as "The Phantom" and "The Island of Dr. Moreau" are being filmed in Australia. The Australian Film Commission has set up a $4.5 million fund for financing smaller films.
Australia continues to be the dominant force in the Southeast Asian distribution and exhibition industry. All three of Australia's

major exhibitors (Hoyt's, Village Roadshow and Greater Union) continued adding theatres and increasing their number of screens. In addition, Village Roadshow announced that they were planning to build screens in Continental Europe, most notably in Greece, Italy, Hungary and the Czech Republic, and in Asian countries including Thailand, Malaysia and Vietnam.
FILM COMMISSIONS
AUSTRALIAN FILM COMMISSION
Level 4, 150 William Street, Woolloomooloo NSW 2011. Tel: (612) 951 6444. FAX: (612) 357 3737. email: info@afc. gov. au URL: www. afc. gov. au
AUSTRALIAN FILM FINANCE CORP.
Bob Campbell, G. P. O. Box 3886, Sydney NSW 2001, 130 Elizabeth St., Sydney NSW 2001. Tel: (612) 268 2555. FAX: (612) 264 8551.
FILM AUSTRALIA
101 Eton Road, Lindfield NSW 2070, Level 12. Tel: (612) 413 8777. FAX: (612) 416 5672.
DISTRIBUTORS AND PRODUCERS
ALL MEDIA INTERNATIONAL
643 Chapel St., South Yarra 3141, Victoria. Tel: (613) 926 3637. FAX: (613) 824 0370.
ANJOHN INTERNATIONAL
19/151 Bayswater Rd., Rushcutters Bay 2011, NSW. Tel: (612) 361 6536. FAX: (612) 361 6521.
ARTISTRALIA (FILM EXCHANGE SERVICES)
Australia House, 155 Clairebrook Rd., Perth 6000, Western Australia. Tel: (619) 227 1577. FAX: (619) 227 1516.
ATLANTA FILM INTERNATIONAL
95 James Cook Drive, Kings Langley, 2147 NSW. Tel: (612) 838 9210. FAX: (612) 674 5028.
ATLANTIS RELEASING
Suite 4, 65 Military Rd., Neutral Bay 2089, NSW. Tel: (612) 953 2999. FAX: (612) 953 3248.
AUSTRALIAN FILM INSTITUTE DISTRIBUTION
49 Eastern Rd., South Melbourne 3205, Victoria. Tel: (613) 696 1844. FAX: (613) 696 7972.
AUSTRALIAN VISUAL PRODUCTIONS
Unit 1, 17 Grosvenor St., Neutral Bay 2096, NSW. Tel: (612) 953 8877. FAX: (612) 953 6221.
AUSTRALIAN WORLD ENTERTAINMENT
202 Tynte St., North Adelaide 5006, South Australia. (618) 267 3644. FAX: (618) 267 3996.
BEYOND FILMS
1st Floor, 53 55 Brisbane St., Surry Hills 2010, NSW. Tel: (612) 281 1266. FAX: (612) 281 9220.
CINEMA CENTRE GROUP
Bunda St., Canberra 2601, ACT. (616) 295 9644. FAX: (616) 295 9694.
COLIN MCLENNAN AND ASSOCIATES
13 Napier St., North Sydney 2060, NSW. Tel: (612) 955 5122. FAX: (612) 957 3550.
COLUMBIA TRISTAR FILM DISTRIBUTORS INTERNATIONAL
42-26 Longueville Rd., Lane Cove, NSW, 2066. Tel: (612) 911 3377. FAX: (612) 418 6270. Vice President: Peter Wikinson.
D. L. TAFFNER AUSTRALIA
Unit 20, Greenwich Square, 130-134 Pacific Highway, Greenwich 2065, NSW. Tel: (612) 439 5699. FAX: (612) 439 4501.
DENDY FILMS
34 Louisa Rd., Birchgrove 2041, NSW. Tel: (612) 810 8733. FAX: (612) 810 3228.
DISCOVERY INTERNATIONAL
P. O. Box 550, Malvern 3144, Victoria. Tel: (613) 563 9344. FAX: (613) 563 9885.
FILM AUSTRALIA
Eaton Rd., Linfield 2070, NSW. Tel: (612) 413 8777. FAX: (612) 416 5672.
HOYTS FOX COLUMBIA TRI-STAR FILMS
490 Kent St., Sydney 2000, NSW. Tel: (612) 261 7800. FAX: (612) 283 2191.

M. C. STUART AND ASSOCIATES
88 Highett St., Richmond 3121, Victoria. Tel: (613) 429 8666.
FAX: (613) 429 1839.
MCA
1st Floor, MCA Universal House, 23 Pelican Street, Sydney
2010, NSW. Tel: (612) 267 9844. FAX: (612) 264 1742.
NEW VISION FILM DISTRIBUTORS
2nd Floor, 254 Bay St., Port Melbourne 3207, Victoria. Tel:
(613) 646 5555. FAX: (613) 646 2411.
OPEN EYE (FILM & TV)
1/87 Bent St., North Sydney 2060, NSW. Tel: (612) 954 3626.
FAX: (612) 959 3253.
OTHER FILM DISTRIBUTION
89 High St., Northcote 3070, Victoria. Tel: (613) 489 1741.
FAX: (613) 481 5618.
PACIFIC LINK COMMUNICATIONS
2A Eltham St., Gladesville 2111, NSW. Tel: (612) 817 5055.
FAX: (612) 879 7297.
PALACE ENTERTAINMENT
1/101 Union St., North Sydney 2060, NSW. Tel: (612) 954
3323. FAX: (612) 954 3306.
PARAMOUNT PICTURES
Suite 3209, Australia Square, Sydney 2000, NSW. Tel: (612)
247 9367. FAX: (612) 251 3251.
POLYGRAM FILMED ENTERTAINMENT
3 Munn Reserve, Sydney 2000. Tel: (612) 207 0500. FAX: (612)
241 1497. Richard Sheffield MacClure.
PREMIUM FILMS
92 Bay St., Port Melbourne 3207, Victoria. Tel: (613) 645 1612.
FAX: (613) 645 1591.
QUALITY FILMS
405-411 Sussex St., Sydney 2000, NSW. Tel: (612) 212 2313.
FAX: (612) 281 1460.
QUANTAS
14 Bourke Rd., Mascot 2020, NSW. Tel: (612) 691 1069. FAX:
(612) 691 1865.
**R. A. BECKER AND CO/FREEMANTLE INTERNATIONAL
PRODUCTIONS**
4/21 Chandos St., St. Leonards 2065, NSW. Tel: (612) 438
3377. FAX: (612) 439 1827.
REID AND PUSKAR
44 Moruben Rd., Mosman 2088, NSW. Tel: (612) 969 2077.
FAX: (612) 960 4971.
SHARMILL FILMS
Suite 4, 200 Toorak Rd., South Yarra 3141, Victoria. Tel: (613)
826 9077. FAX: (613) 826 1935.
UNITED INTERNATIONAL PICTURES
208 Clarence St., Sydney 2000, NSW. Tel: (612) 264 7444.
FAX: (612) 264 3203. Manager: Michael Selwyn.
VALKYRIE FILMS
166 Glebe Point Rd., Glebe 2037, NSW. Tel: (612) 552 2456.
FAX: (612) 552 2457.
VILLAGE ROADSHOW CORPORATION
4th Fl, 235 Pyrmont St., Pyrmont 2009, NSW. Tel: (612) 552
8600. FAX: (612) 552 2510.
VIRGIN VISION AUSTRALIA
99 Victoria St., Potts Point 2011, NSW. Tel: (612) 368 1700.
THE WALT DISNEY COMPANY
149 Castlereagh St., Sydney 2000, NSW. Tel: (612) 268 942.
FAX: (612) 264 1289.
WARNER BROTHERS AUSTRALIA
Level 22, 8-20 Napier St., North Sydney, NSW. Tel: (612) 957
3899. FAX: (612) 956 7788. Contact: Fiona Curtis.
WORLD VISION ENTERPRISES
2nd Floor, 5-13 Northcliff St., Milsons Point 2061, NSW. Tel:
(612) 922 4722. FAX: (612) 955 8207.

EXHIBITORS
HOYTS CORPORATION PTY. LTD.
(152 screens) Level 6, 505 George St., Sydney 2000, NSW.
Tel: (612) 261 7777. FAX: (612) 261 7897.
VILLAGE ROADSHOW CORPORATION
(150 screens) 4th Fl, 235 Pyrmont St., Pyrmont 2009, NSW.
Tel: (612) 552 8600. FAX: (612) 552 2510.

AUSTRIA

Population: 7.9 million.
Screens: 391.
Admissions: 13.0 million (1995).
Ticket Price: $6.24.
Theatre grosses: $80.9 million.
Top Five Films of 1995: The Lion King, Forrest Gump,
Casper, Disclosure, While You Were Sleeping.
Austria, like other European countries, has seen a boom in
construction of multiplexes. In 1994, Austria was home to 42
mulitplex screens. Towards the end of 1996, new construction
had brought that number to 74. Admissions rose by one million
in 1995, a staggering 8% increase, due largely to the popularity of American blockbusters, several German films that were
widely attended and the quality of the new theaters.

ASSOCIATIONS & ORGANIZATIONS
AKTION FILM
(Austrian Section of the International Center of Films for
Children and Young Children), Neubaugasse 25, Vienna A-
1070. Tel: (431) 523 2437. FAX: (431) 523 3971.
**ARGE OSTERREICHISCHES DREHBUCHAUTOREN-
DREHBUCHFORUM WIEN**
Stiftgasse 6, Vienna A-1070. (431) 526 8503 500. FAX: (431)
526 8503 550.
ART DIRECTORS & COSTUME DESIGNERS ASSOCIATION
Siegelgasse 1/16, Vienna A-1030. (431) 523 6085. FAX: (431)
523 6085.
**ASIFA-AUSTRIA (INTERNATIONAL ANIMATED FILM
ASSOCIATION)**
Huttelberggasse 75/1, Vienna A-1140. (431) 914 7797. FAX:
(431) 712 0392.
ASSOCIATION OF AUSTRIAN FILM DIRECTORS
Spittelberggasse 3, Vienna A-1070. Tel: (431) 526 0006. FAX:
(431) 426 0006 16.
ASSOCIATION OF AUSTRIAN FILM JOURNALISTS
Speisinger Strasse 4, Vienna A-1130. Tel: (431) 804 3561.
FAX: (431) 804 1720.
ASSOCIATION OF AUSTRIAN FILM PRODUCERS
Speisinger Strasse 121-127, Vienna A-1230. Tel: (431) 888
9622.
ASSOCIATION OF DISTRIBUTORS
Wiener Hauptstrasse 63, P. O. Box 327, Vienna A-1045. Tel.:
(431) 50105 3011. FAX: (431) 50206 376.
AUSTRIA FILMMAKERS CO-OPERATIVE
Wahringer Str. 59, Vienna A-1090. Tel: (431) 408 7627. FAX:
(431) 408 7627.
AUSTRIAN ASSOCIATION OF CINEMATOGRAPHERS (AAC)
Karlsplatz 5, Künstlerhaus, Vienna A-1010. Tel: (431) 713
6611. FAX: (431) 587 9665.
AUSTRIAN FILM COMMISSION–AFC
Stiftgasse 6, Vienna A-1070. Tel: (431) 526 3323 200. FAX:
(431) 526 6801.
AUSTRIAN FILM FUND
Stiftgasse 6, Vienna A-1070. Tel: (431) 526 9730 406. FAX:
(431) 526 9730 440.
AUSTRIAN FILM INSTITUTE
Stiftgasse 6, Vienna A-1070. Tel: (431) 523 9730 400. FAX:
(431) 526 9730 440.
AUSTRIAN SOCIETY OF SOUND ENGINEERS
Natteregasse 4, Laxenburg A-2361. Tel: (43) 2236 71307. FAX:
(43) 2236 71307.
FEDERATION OF AUSTRIAN FILM PRODUCERS
Neubaugasse 25, Vienna A-1070. Tel: (431) 523 7437. FAX:
(431) 526 4302/3.
NATIONAL TOURIST OFFICE
Margaretenstrasse 1, Vienna A-1040. Tel: (431) 588 660. FAX:
(431) 588 660.
AUDIENCE RESEARCH
**AUSTRIAN SOCIETY FOR FILM SCIENCES,
COMMUNICATION & MEDIA STUDIES**
Rauhensteingasse 6, Vienna A-1010. Tel: (431) 512 9936. FAX:
(431) 513 5330. email: oegfkm@cybertron.at
DISTRIBUTORS
**AKTION FILM (AUSTRIAN SECTION OF THE
INTERNATIONAL CENTER OF FILMS FOR CHILDREN AND
YOUNG PEOPLE)**
Neubaugasse 25, Vienna A-1070. Tel: (431) 523 2437. FAX:
(431) 523 3971.
ALPHA FILM
Neubaugasse 4, Vienna A-1070. Tel: (431) 523 7660. FAX:
(431) 523 7660.
AUSTRIA FILMMAKERS CO-OPERATIVE
Wahringer Strasse 59, Vienna A-1090. Tel: (431) 408 7627.
FAX: (431) 408 3871.
BUENA VISTA INTERNATIONAL (BVI)
Hermanngasse 18, Vienna A-1071. Tel: (431) 526 9467. FAX:
(431) 526 9468 5.
CENTFOX FILM GMBH
Neubaugasse 35, Vienna A-1070. Tel: (431) 932 2629. FAX:
(431) 526 7297.
CINESTAR
Opernring 19, Vienna A-1010. Tel: (431) 587 8406. FAX: (431)
587 5711.
CLASSIC-FILM
Magaretenstrasse 24, Vienna A-1040. Tel: (431) 319 6386.
COLUMBIA TRISTAR
Wallgasse 21, Vienna A-1060. Tel: (431) 597 1515. FAX: (431)
597 1516.
CONSTANTIN FILM
Siebensterngasse 37, Vienna A-1070. Tel: (431) 521 2850.
FAX: (431) 521 2860.
CZERNY FILM
Lorgasse 17, Vienna A-1150. Tel: (431) 982 0249. FAX: (431)
982 4081.

EINHORN FILM
Unterfeld Strasse 29, P.O. Box 158, Bludenz A-6700. Tel: (4355) 526 7034. FAX: (4355) 526 3674.
EPO FILM PRODUCTIONS
Edelsinn Strasse 58, Vienna A-1120. Tel: (431) 812 3718. FAX: (431) 812 3718 9.
FILMHAUS STOBERGASSE
Stobergasse 11-15, Vienna A-1050. Tel: (431) 545 3244. FAX: (431) 545 3244.
FILMLADEN
Mariahilferstrasse 58, Vienna A-1070. Tel: (431) 523 4362. FAX: (431) 526 4749.
FLEUR FILM
Stadlgasse 2, Enns A-4470. Tel: (431) 7223 2670. FAX: (431) 7223 2406.
INDEPENDENT MOVIES
Paracelsusgasse 19-21, Gablitz A-3003. Tel: (432) 231 4629.
JUPITER FILM
Neubaugasse 36, Vienna A-1070. Tel: (431) 521 270. FAX: (431) 523 8253.
OEFRAM FILM
Neubaugasse 36, Vienna A-1070. Tel: (431) 523 7611. FAX: (431) 523 3709.
POLYFILM VERLEIH
Margaretenstrasse 78, Vienna A-1050. Tel: (431) 581 3900 20. FAX: (431) 581 3900 39.
SMILE FILM
Lange Gasse 52/2/20, Vienna A-1080. Tel: (431) 408 9843. FAX: (431) 408 9843.
STADTKINO FILMVERLEIH
Spittelberggasse 3, Vienna A-1070. Tel: (431) 522 4814. FAX: (431) 522 4815.
TOP FILM
Lindengasse 56, Vienna A-1070. Tel: (431) 526 1919. FAX: (431) 526 1918.
UNITED INTERNATIONAL PICTURES
Neubaugasse 1, P.O. Box 280, Vienna A-1071. Tel: (431) 523 4631. FAX: (431) 526 7548.
WARNER BROS.
Zieglergasse 10, Vienna A-1072. Tel: (431) 523 8626. FAX: (431) 523 8626 31.
WEGA FILM
Hagelingasse 13, Vienna A-1140. Tel: (431) 982 5742 0. FAX: (431) 982 5833.

PRODUCERS
ADI MAYER FILM
Lindengasse 65, Vienna A-1070, Tel: (431) 523 4788. FAX: (431) 526 6673.
AICHHOLZER FILM PRODUCTION
Mariahilferstrasse 58, Vienna A-1070. Tel: (4310) 523 4081. FAX: (431) 526 4749.
ALLEGRO FILM PRODUCTIONS
Krummgasse 1A, Stg. 1, Vienna A-1030. Tel: (431) 712 5036. FAX: (431) 712 5036 20.
ARION FILM
Wuerzburgergasse 11, Vienna A-1130. Tel: (431) 804 2000.
CINE CARTOON
Haydngasse 5, Vienna A-1060. Tel: (431) 597 4162 12. FAX: (431) 597 4162 20.
CINE-FILM PRODUCTION
Speisingerstrasse 234, Vienna A-1238. Tel: (431) 889 3366. FAX: (431) 889 2831.
CINECOOP FILM PRODUCTIONS
Mariahilferstrasse 1B, Vienna A-1060. Tel: (431) 587 6735. FAX: (431) 587 6735 20.
CINEDOC FILM PRODUCTION
Hauslabgasse 6-10/1, Vienna A-1050. Tel: (431) 545 6645 90. FAX: (431) 545 6645 90.
CINEMERCURY
Hietzinger Kai 169, Vienna A-1130. Tel: (431) 876 3066. FAX: (431) 876 3099.
DEGN FILM
Konstanze Webergasse 3, Salzburg A-5020. Tel: (43662) 831 992. FAX: (43662) 822 688.
DOR FILM PRODUCTION
Neulerchenfelderstrasse 12, Vienna A-1160. Tel: (431) 403 2138. FAX: (431) 402 2139.
EXTRA FILM
Grosse Neugasse 44/24, Vienna A-1040. Tel: (431) 581 7896. FAX: (431) 587 2743.
FILM & CO.
Lainzerstrasse 71, Vienna A-1170. Tel: (431) 877 7875. FAX: (431) 877 7876.
GOESS FILM & MEDIA
Metternichgasse 2/8, Vienna A-1090. Tel: (431) 713 3905. FAX: (431) 713 2827.

INTERSPOT
Lainzerstrasse 121, Vienna A-1130. Tel: (431) 804 8363. FAX: (431) 804 8363 10.
LOTUS FILM
Sechshauserstrasse 83, Vienna A-1150. Tel: (431) 892 8808. FAX: (431) 892 8809 11.
MICHAEL PILZ FILM
Teschnergasse 37, Vienna A-1180. Tel: (431) 402 3392. FAX: (431) 408 4649.
MUNGO FILM
Munichreiterstrasse 18, Vienna A-1130. Tel: (431) 876 3600. FAX: (431) 876 3646.
NEUE STUDIO FILM
Hietzinger Hauptstrasse 11, Vienna A-1130. Tel: (431) 877 6253. FAX: (431) 877 3564.
ODELGA FILM PRODUCTIONS
Landhausgasse 2.37, Vienna A-1010. Tel: (431) 535 0433. FAX: (431) 532 8496.
PAMMER FILM
Neubaugasse 1, Vienna A-1070. Tel: (431) 523 9191. FAX: (431) 523 9192.
PAN FILM
Obkirchergasse 41, Vienna A-1070. Tel: (431) 321 4033. FAX: (431) 325 7169.
PPM FILMPRODUCTIONS
Lerchenfelderstrasse 136, Vienna A-1080. Tel: (431) 408 1630 0. FAX: (431) 408 9243.
SATEL FILM
Computerstrasse 6, Vienna A-1101. Tel: (431) 661 1090. FAX: (431) 667 5650.
SCHOENBRUNN FILM
Neubaugasse 1, Vienna A-1070. Tel: (431) 523 2265. FAX: (431) 523 9568.
SK FILM
Salzachstrasse 15A, Salzburg A-5026. Tel: (43662) 625 969. FAX: (43662) 625 969 22.
STAR FILM
Konstanze Webergasse 3, Salzburg A-5020. Tel: (43662) 831 992. FAX: (43662) 822 688.
TEAM FILM PRODUCTION
Waaggasse 5, Vienna A-1040. Tel: (431) 587 2542 0. FAX: (431) 587 2542 27.
TERRA FILM
Lienfeldergasse 39, Vienna A-1160. Tel: (431) 484 1101 0. FAX: (431) 484 1101 27.
WEGA FILM
Hagelingasse 13, Vienna A-1140. Tel: (431) 982 5742 0. FAX: (431) 982 5833.

EXHIBITORS
UCHTSPIELTHEATER/CONSTANTIN FILM
Siebensterngasse 37, Vienna A-1070. Tel: (431) 521 280. FAX: (431) 521 2860.
WIENER STADTHALLE KIBA
Vogelweidplatz 14, 1150 Vienna. Tel: (431) 322 954 90. FAX: (431) 322 742 206.

BELGIUM

Population: 10.1 million.
Screens: 409.
Admissions: 21.2 million.
Average Ticket Price: $5.52.
Theater Grosses: $117.0 million.
Top Ten Films of 1995: Die Hard With A Vengeance, Les Anges Gardiens, Disclosure, Pocahontas, Outbreak, Casper, Farinelli, Bad Boys, The Shawshank Redemption, The Lion King.
Of the 409 screens in Belgium, almost 150 of those are megaplex sites. Led by Decatron, the country's leading exhibitor commanding a 50% share, theaters are modern and comfortable. Such amenities, in conjunction with the continuing dominance of U.S. blockbusters, yielded almost a 3 million increase in admissions in 1995.

ASSOCIATIONS & ORGANIZATIONS
APEC
Association for the Promotion of Belgian Cinema in Education, 73 Ave. de Coccinelles, Brussels B-1170. Tel: (322) 672 9459.
ASSOCIATION OF DIRECTORS AND PRODUCERS
109 Rue du Fort, Brussels B-1060. Tel: (322) 534 3152. FAX: (322) 534 7637.
CINEMATHEQUE ROYALE DE BELGIQUE
23 Rue Ravenstein, Brussels B-1000. Tel: (322) 507 8370. FAX: (322) 513 1272.
EUROPEAN ACADEMY FOR FILM & TELEVISION
69 Rue Verte, Brussels B-1210. Tel: (322) 218 6607. FAX: (322) 217 5572.
FEDERATION DES CINEMAS DE BELGIQUE
10-12 Ave. L'Montmarts, Brussels B-1140. Tel: (322) 705-0670. FAX: (322) 705-0664.

MINISTERIE VAN DE VLAAMSE GEMEENSCHAP
ADMINISTRATIE KUNST BESTUUR MEDIA
29-31 Kolonienstraat, Brussels B-1000. Tel: (322) 510 3565.
FAX: (322) 510 3651.
MUSEE DU CINEMA/FILMMUSEUM
9 Baron Horta St., Brussels B-1000. Tel: (322) 507 8370. FAX:
(322) 513 1272.
POUR LE CINEMA BELGE
12 Rue Paul-Emile Janson, Brussels B-1050. Tel: (322) 649
5969. FAX: (322) 649 3340.

DISTRIBUTORS AND PRODUCERS
ALAIN KEYTSMAN PRODUCTION
159 Berkendaelstraat, Brussels B-1060. Tel: (322) 347 5710.
FAX: (322) 347 2462.
ALCYON FILMS
89 Rue de Lorrian, Brussels B-1210. Tel: (322) 426 7981. FAX:
(322) 426 7981.
ALTERNATIVE FILMS
10 Place Colignon, Brussels B-1030. Tel: (322) 242 1930. FAX:
(322) 242 0180.
BEECK TURTLE
27F Van Den Bosschestraat, Lennik B-1750. Tel: (322) 582
8318. FAX: (322) 582 8318.
BUENA VISTA INTERNATIONAL
Chausee Romaine, 468 Romeinsesteenweg, 1853
Grimbergen, Brussels. Tel: (322) 263 1700. FAX: (322) 263
1797.
CINELIBRE
270 Chaussee de Haecht, Brussels B-1030. Tel: (322) 245
8700. FAX: (322) 216 2575.
COLUMBIA TRISTAR FILMS
38 Rue Souveraine Opperstraat, Brussels B-1050. Tel: (322)
512 3914. FAX: (322) 514 1975.
CONCORDE FILM
Terhulpsesteenweg 130, Brussels B-1050. Tel: (322) 675 2050.
FAX: (322) 675 3076.
IMAGE CREATION
92 Rue Colonel Bourg, Brussels B-1040. Tel: (322) 733 3451.
FAX: (322) 732 6666.
INDEPENDENT FILMS
1 Doornveld, Box 42, Zellik-Asse B-1731. Tel: (322) 463 1130.
FAX: (322) 466 9460.
KINEPOLIS FILMS DISTRIBUTION
Eeuwfesstlaan 20, Brussels B-1020. Tel: (322) 478 0450. FAX:
(322) 479 6060.
PROGRES CLUB
243 Rue Royale, Brussels B-1210. Tel: (322) 218 0960. FAX:
(322) 218 4354.
UNITED INTERNATIONAL PICTURES
288 Rue Royale, Brussels B-1210. Tel: (322) 218 5206. FAX:
(322) 218 7933.
WARNER BROS. BELGIUM
42 Boulevard Brand Whitlock, Brussels B-1200. Tel: (322) 735
4242. FAX: (322) 735 4919.

EXHIBITORS
KINEPOLIS SA/DECATRON NV
1 Eeufeestlaan, Brussels B-1020. Tel: (322) 478 0450. FAX:
(322) 478 0450.
STUDIO THEATRE CHAIN
25 Brabanconnestraat, Leuven B-3000. Tel: (3216) 202 895.
FAX: (3216) 200 3287.
SUPER CLUB
110 Van Kerckhovenstraat, Bornem B-2880. Tel: (323) 890
4811. FAX: (323) 890 4800.
UGC BELGIQUE
8 Ave. de la Toison d'Or, Brussels B-1060. Tel: (322) 513 7945.
FAX: (322) 511 8556.

BOLIVIA

Population: 7.9 million.
DISTRIBUTORS
MANFER FILMS S.R.L.
Ave. Montes 768, 4th floor, Box 4709, La Paz. Tel: (5912) 376
834. FAX: (5912) 391 158.
WAZA FILMS
(Agent for UIP), Edificio Caraas-2do. piso, Avenida 16 de Julio
No. 1456, Casilla 2613, La Paz. Tel: (5912) 354 635. FAX:
(5912) 354 054.
MARKET RESEARCH
REN
Guachalla, Casilla 9773, La Paz. Tel/FAX: (5912)376 992.
Telex: 3317 guatec BV.

BRAZIL

Population: 160.7 million.
Number of Screens: 1,550.
Admissions (1995): 85 million.
Average Ticket Price: $4.29
Feature Production (1995): 20 films.
As the Brazilian economy continues to rebound, the future
looks bright for the film industry. The Brazilian film, O
Quatrilho, which was nominated for an Academy Award for
Best Foreign Film, was the highest grossing film ever in that
country with revenues of over $10 million. Until 1990, the
industry was run by Embrafilme, a government agency. Since
its divestment, both production and box office revenues have
suffered considerably. In 1995, only 5 films were produced in
Brazil. In 1996 that figure rose to 20. This is still a marked
decrease compared to the 1970's when over 100 films per year
were produced. To improve matters, the government has
offered a federal tax incentive plan that will provide up to 15%
in cost reduction to filmmakers. In addition, local governments
are offered the opportunity for co-productions with financial
inducements. The government is also permitting monies to be
raised for film financing through the sale of stock in exchange
for shareholder participation. Regional film commissions are
also being formed to galvanize the industry.
DISTRIBUTORS & PRODUCERS
C.E.F. REPRESENTACOES
(Agent for Columbia Tristar), Rua Aarao Reis 538, S/206
Centro, 3012000-000 Belo Horizonte, Mias Gerais. Tel: (5531)
273 2093.
COLUMBIA TRISTAR
Av. Rio Branco, 277-Sobrejola 101-Centro, 20040-009 Rio de
Janeiro. Tel: (5521) 262 0722. FAX: (5521) 262 0675.
DISTRIBUIDORA DE FILMES WERMAR
Rua General Bento Martins 268, 90010-080 Porto Alegre, Rio
Grande de Sul. Tel: (5551) 228 6275.
FOX/WARNER BROS. FILM DO BRASIL
Calcada dos Cravos 141, Centro Commercial Alphaville,
06453-000 Barueri, Sao Paulo. Tel: (5511) 725 5999. FAX:
(5511) 725 0767.
SETIMA ARTE SERVICOS
Av. Barbosa Lima, 149 S/102, Centro, 50030-330 Recife-
Pernambuco. Tel: (5581) 224 3732.
UNITED INTERNATIONAL PICTURES
Rue Desbargado, Viriato 16, CEP 20030-090, Rio de Janeiro.
Tel: (5521) 210 2400. FAX: (5521) 220 9491. Manager: Jorge
Peregrino.
WARNER BROS. (SOUTH)
Rua Senador Dantas 19-10 Andar, 20031-200 Rio de Janiero.
Tel: (5521) 282 1322. FAX: (5521) 262 0195.

CHILE

Population: 14.1 million, (Santiago: 4.9 million).
DISTRIBUTORS AND PRODUCERS
ARTHUR EHRLICH
Huerfanos 786, Suite 210, Santiago. Tel: (562) 633 2503 FAX:
(562) 639 7921. Rep. for: Twentieth Century Fox
CHILE INC./WARNER BROS. (SOUTH) INC.
(Columbia Pictures, Tri-Star, Hollywood Pictures, Touchstone
Pictures, Orion), Chilefilms, La Capitana 1200, Las Condes—
Santiago. Tel: (562) 220 3086
CINE CHILE S. A.
(umbrella org. of the Association of Producers), Huerfanos 878,
Suite 918, Santiago. Tel: (562) 633 3948. FAX: (562) 632 5342
FILMOCENTRO
Gerona 3450, Santiago. Tel: (562) 225 2203. FAX: (562) 209
1671. Producer: Eduardo Larrain.
SILVIO CAIOZZI PRODUCTIONS
Federico Froebel 1755, Santiago. Tel: (562) 209 9031. FAX:
(562) 204 8988. Pres.: Silvio Caiozzi.
UNITED INTERNATIONAL PICTURES
Huerfanos 786, Office 808, Casilla 3462, Santiago. Tel: (562)
639 5005. FAX: (562) 633 0562. Manager: Mario Cuevas.

EXHIBITORS
CONATE S. A.
La Capitana 1200, Las Condes—Santiago. Tel: (562) 220 3086
CINEMARK CHILE S. A.
La Capitana 1200, Las Condes—Santiago. Tel: (562) 246
3510. FAX: (562) 246 3504
LOCATION SERVICES
FILM & TELEVISION COMMISSION OF CHILE
Alan Hootnick, Clasificador 125, Santiago. Tel: (562) 537 8438.
FAX: (562) 531 4908.

CHINA

Population: 1.2 billion.
Number of Screens: 3,100 fixed screens, 180,000 factory based screens and outdoor theatres.
Admissions: 5 billion.
Average Ticket Price: varies by province, $.47–$1.20.
Domestic Feature Production: 150 films.
Top Domestic Film of 1995: In the Heat of the Sun.

From a peak of 14 billion admissions in 1992, theatre attendance in China has dwindled, mostly due to the availability and popularity of pirated videotapes. In 1995 however, revenues bounced 15%, climbing to $213 million. This revival was lead by Shanghai which posted an estimated distribution income of $24.1 million. United International has signed a distribution agreement to bring in "Goldeneye", "Apollo 13" and an unnamed Hong Kong made action-adventure. Meanwhile, the Ministry of Radio, Film and Television was newly created out of several other agencies. This new ministry will oversee film-making and partially subsidize production at the country's 30 film studios. Around 150 feature films were produced in China in 1995, with around 80% of the combined cost of $27 million being financed by investors outside3 the film industry. There are an increasing number of independent film-makers in China, encouraged by the new willingness of other industry sectors to invest in a highly profitable business.With the takeover of Hong Kong by mainland China set for 1997, the enormous output of the island's movie studios will be added to the nation's film figures. For the 1.2 billion people in China, there are about 200 films shown per year, including 50-60 imported features. In ongoing talks with the U.S., China has pledged to crack down on piracy of movies, videos and other entertainment media. China has also pledged to promote domestic films by allowing no more than one-third of screen time to be devoted to foreign products. In 1995, ten Hollywood films accounted for more than 75% of screen playdates.

ASSOCIATIONS & ORGANIZATIONS
CHINA FILM EXPORT & IMPORT CORPORATION
25 Xin Wai St., Beijing 100088. Tel: (861) 225-4488. FAX: (861) 225-1044.
CHINA FILM-MAKERS' ASSOCIATION
22 Beisanhuan Donglu, Beijing 100013. Tel: (861) 421-9977. FAX: (861) 421-1870.

DISTRIBUTOR
SONY PICTURES ENTERTAINMENT BEIJING
Suite 189, Beijing Asia Jinjiang Hotel, 8 Xinzhong Xi Je, Gongti Bei Lu, Beijing 100027. Tel: (861) 508 9869. FAX: (861) 500 7335.

COLOMBIA

Population: 36.2 million.
DISTRIBUTORS
AMERICAN FILMS
Av. 2C Norte No, 24 N 40, Cali. Tel: (5723) 685 792.
COLUBIA TRISTAR FILMS OF COLOMBIA
Carrera 13A, No. 97-23, Bogota. Tel: (571) 610 0149. FAX: (571) 610 0125.
ELEPHANT JOSEPH & CIA
(Agent for Warner Bros.), Calle 96 No. 12-10, Santafe de Bogota, D.C. Tel: (571) 610 2142. FAX: (571) 610 2060.
FERRADA HIJOS
Calle 34 No. 26-46 Local 3, Bucaranga. Tel: (5773) 453 129. FAX: (5773) 453 126.
L.D. FILMS
Calle 23 No. 5-85 Interior 201, Bogota. Tel: (571) 341 7285. FAX: (571) 286 5960.
PROGRAFILMS
Carrera 53 No. 59-77, Edificio Royal Films, Barranquilla. Tel: (5753) 318 520.
UNITED INTERNATIONAL PICTURES
Calle 77 No. 15-09 Paratado Aereo 3450, Bogota. Tel: (571) 256 2139. FAX: (571) 218 6089. Manager: Maitland Pritchett.

CROATIA

Population: 4.6 million.
DISTRIBUTORS AND PRODUCERS
BLITZ FILM & VIDEO
Sv Mateja 121-04, Zagreb 10000. Tel: (3851) 687 541. FAX: (3851) 692 814.
CONTINENTAL FILM
Sostariceva 10, Zagreb 10000. Tel: (3851) 421 312. FAX: (3851) 428 247.
JADRAN FILM DD
Oporovecka 12, Zagreb 10000. Tel: (3851) 298 7222. FAX: (3851) 251 394.

KINEMATOGRAFI
(UIP), Tuskanac 1, Zagreb 41000. Tel: (3851) 426 305. FAX: (3851) 426 531. Contact: Davor Koracevic.
MOVIE PRODUCTION
Frankopanska 3, Osijek 31000. Tel: (38531) 559 704. FAX: (38531) 559 730.
ORLANDO FILM
Nasicka 14, Zagreb 10000. Tel: (2851) 334 587. FAX: (3851) 170 167.
POLYBROS
Draganicka 19, Zagreb 10000. Tel: (3851) 563 236. FAX: (3851) 563 236.
ZAUDER FILM
Jablanicka 1, Zagreb 10040. Tel: (3851) 245 724. FAX: (3851) 245 973.

CZECH REPUBLIC

Population: 10.4 million (1.5 million in Prague).
Number of Screens: 1,845.
Average Ticket Price: $0.69.
Admissions: 21.9 million.
Domestic Feature Production: 22 films.
Top Five Domestic Films of 1995: Once There Was A Policeman, Dance Teacher, The Battle of Colours, Playgirl, How to Deserve the Princess.
Top Ten Films of 1995: Forrest Gump, The Specialist, Waterworld, Die Hard With A Vengeance, The Mask, Dumb and Dumber, Time Cop, The Lion King, Apollo 13, Interview With A Vampire.

The Czech Republic was the first country in Eastern Europe to privatize the exhibition industry when the state operator, Filmovy Podnik was dissolved in 1995. Multikino, Kappel and Bontonfilm have joined to open the country's first multiplex, Kino 2005. Yet, in spite of the changes, including modernization of theaters and a greater breadth of film releases, Czech box office admissions have continued to lag.

ASSOCIATIONS & ORGANIZATIONS
AUTHORS' PRODUCTION AND DISTRIBUTION
P. O. Box 60, Prague 10 10100. Tel: (422) 729 204. FAX: (422) 725 453.
CZECH FILM SOCIETY
Novotneho Lavka 5, Prague 1 11000. Tel: (422) 298 138.
FILMOVY PODNIK HL. M. PRAHY
Vodickova 30, Prague 1 11000. Tel: (422) 242 16010. FAX: (422) 242 26497.
FILMOVY PRUMYSL (EQUIPMENT)
Krizeneckeho Nam. 322, Prague 5. Tel: (422) 294 510. FAX: (422) 542 539.
FITES-UNION OF TV AND FILM
Pod Nuselskymi Schody 3, Prague 2 12000. Tel: (422) 691 0310. FAX: (422) 691 1375.
MINISTRY OF CULTURE
Valdstejnske Nam 4, Prague 1 11000. Tel: (422) 513 1111. FAX: (422) 536 322.
SLOVENSKA POZICOVNA FILMOV
Priemyselna 1, Bratislava 82460. Tel: (427) 211 301. FAX: (427) 215 685.

DISTRIBUTORS AND PRODUCERS
AVED
Wenzigova 15, Prague 12000. Tel: (422) 299 290. FAX: (422) 297 137.
BONTON FILMS
Nardoni Trida 28, Prague 1 11000. Tel: (422) 2422 7644. FAX: (422) 2422 5263.
CINEMART
Nardoni Trida 28, Prague 1 11121. Tel: (422) 2422 7202. FAX: (422) 2110 5234.
FALCON FILM
Stroupenznickeho 6, Prague 5 15000. Tel: (422) 538 085. FAX: (422) 533 194.
FILMEXPORT PRAGUE
Na Moranhi 5, Prague 5 12800. Tel: (422) 293 275. FAX: (422) 293 312.
GEMINI FILMS
V Jame 1, Prague 1 11000. Tel: (422) 2416 2142. FAX: (422) 2422 6562.
GUILD ENTERTAINMENT (FILM DISTRIBUTION)
V Jame 5, Prague 1 11000. Tel: (422) 2421 5738. FAX: (422) 2422 6385.
GUILD ENTERTAINMENT FILM AND VIDEO
Krliprovo Nam-3, Prague 6. Tel: (422) 328 094. FAX: (422) 311 8852.
HEART OF EUROPE
Mala Stepanska 3, Prague 2 12000. Tel: (422) 292 144. FAX: (422) 292 144.

HEUREKA
Litevska 8, Prague 10 11174. Tel: (422) 6731 5219. FAX: (422) 6731 5221.
LUCERNA FILM
Narodni Trida 28, Prague 111 21. Tel: (422) 2422 7644. FAX: (422) 422 2563.
NATIONAL PRODUCTION
Krizeneckeho Nam 322, Prague 5 15252. Tel: (422) 692 7291. FAX: (422) 2451 0628.
SPACE FILM
Karlovo Namesti 19, 12000 Prague 2. Tel: (422) 249 12937. FAX: (422) 249 11370.
EXHIBITOR
MULTIKINO 93
Plackeho 8, Prague 1. Tel: (422) 261 134. FAX: (422) 261 134.

DENMARK

Population: 5.2 million.
Screens: 309.
Admissions: 10.3 million.
Box Office Gross: $95.9 million.
Average Ticket Price: $6.39.
Domestic Feature Production: 14 films.
Top Five Domestic Films of 1995: Dad's Bright Idea, Final Hour, The Monkey and the Sea, Bodyswitch, Just A Girl.
Top Ten Films of 1995: Die Hard With A Vengeance, Dumb and Dumber, Pocahontas, The Bridges of Madison County, Forrest Gump, The Lion King, Outbreak, The Mask, Nine Months, Apollo 13. In early 1996, Nordisk Film bought the remaining half of MGM-Nordisk Film Biografer theater chain, restoring its full ownership. Nordisk is the largest exhibitor in Denmark, with a 65% share of the Copenhagen market, and 40% of the country as a whole, operating 45 theaters with 8,000 seats. Admissions in 1995-96 were down 4%, but gross revenues remained steady due to a hike in ticket prices.

ASSOCIATIONS & ORGANIZATIONS
DANISH FILM DISTRIBUTORS ASSOCIATION
Bulowsvej 50A, Fredericksberg DK-1870. Tel: (45) 3536 5616. FAX: (45) 3135 5758. Director: Anne-Grete Wezelenburg.
DANISH FILM INSTITUTE
Miels Hemmingsensgade 20, Bh3, Copenhagen K DK-1153. (45) 3315 6760. FAX: (45) 3391 5242.
DANISH FILM MUSEUM
Store Sondervoldstraede 4, Copenhagen DK-1419. Tel: (45) 3157 6500. FAX: (45) 3154 1312.
DANISH FILM WORKSHOP
Versterbrogade 24, Copenhagen DK-1620. Tel: (45) 3124 1624. FAX: (45) 3124 4419.
DANISH PRODUCERS' ASSOCIATION
Kroprinsensgade (B 3, Copenhagen K DK-1114. Tel: (45) 3314 0311. FAX: (45) 3314 0365.
FILM KONTAKT NORD
Skindergade 29 A, Copenhagen DK-1159. Tel: (45) 3311 5152. FAX: (45) 3311 2152.
NORDIC FILM/TV SOCIETY
c/o MGM Nordisk Film Biografer, Axeltorv 9, Copenhagen DK-1609. Tel: (45) 3314 76906. FAX: (45) 3314 7979.

DISTRIBUTORS AND PRODUCERS
AB COLLECTION
Hirsemarken 3, Farum DK-3520. Tel: (45) 4499 6200. FAX: (45) 4295 1786.
ALL RIGHT FILM DISTRIBUTION
Indiakaj 12, Copenhagen DK-2100. Tel: (45) 3543 4000. FAX: (45) 3543 4008.
BUENA VISTA INTERNATIONAL
Ostergade 24B, 3rd floor, Copenhagen K DK-1100. Tel: (45) 3312 0800. FAX: (45) 3312 4332.
CAMERA FILM
Mikkel Bryggergade 8, Copenhagen K DK-1460. Tel: (5) 3313 6112. FAX: (45) 3315 0882.
CINNAMON FILM
Brandts Passage 15, Odense C DK-5000. Tel: (45) 6612 1716. FAX: (45) 6612 8082.
CONSTANTIN APS
Skelbaekgade 1, Copenhagen V DK-1717. Tel: (45) 3325 2424. FAX: (45) 3325 0707.
DAN INA FILM
Huset, Radhusstraede 13, 2. floor, Copenhagen DK-1466. Tel: (45) 33 324077. FAX: (45) 33 325077.
DIVA FILMS
Osterbrogade 48, Copenhagen O DK-2100. Tel: (45) 3142 1488. FAX: (45) 3142 1489.
EGMONT AUDIO VISUAL
Skelbaekgade 1, Copenhagen V DK-1717. Tel: (45) 3325 4000. FAX: (45) 3123 0488.
FOX FILM
Skelbaekgade 1, 3, Copenhagen V DK-1717. Tel: (45) 3325 4000. FAX: (45) 3123 0488.

HUSETS BIOGRAF
Huset, Radhusstraede 13, 2nd floor, Copenhagen K DK-1466. Tel: (45) 3315 2002. FAX: (45) 3332 5077.
KRAK VIDEO
Virumsgardvej 21, Virum DK-2830. Tel: (45) 4583 6600. FAX: (45) 4583 1011.
NORDSIK FILM ACQUISITION
Skelbaekgade 1, Copenhagen DK-1717. Tel: (45) 3123 2488. FAX: (45) 3123 0488. email: nikki@inet.uni-c.dk
PATHE-NORDISK
Skelbaekgade 1, Copenhagen DK-1717. Tel: (45) 3123 2488.
REGINA FILM IMPORT
Bregnegaardsvej 7, Charlottenlund DK-2920. Tel: (45) 3962 9640.
SAGA FILM INTERNATIONAL
Soendergada 5, Hjorring DK-9800. Tel: (45) 9892 2199. FAX: (45) 9890 0439.
SCALA FILM
Centrumpladsen, P.O. Box 215, Svendborg DK-5700. Tel: (45) 6221 8866. FAX: (45) 6221 0821.
SCANBOX DANMARK A/S
Hirsemarken 3, Farum DK-3520. Tel: (45) 4499 6200. FAX: (45) 4295 1786.
SFC
Vestergade 27, Copenhagen P DK-1456. Tel: (45) 3313 2686. FAX: (45) 3313 0243.
UNITED INTERNATIONAL PICTURES
Haunchvej 13, Frederiksberg C DK-1825. Tel: (45) 3131 2330. FAX: (45) 3123 3420.
WARNER & METRONOME FILM
Sondermarksvej 16, Copenhagen, Valby DK-2500. Tel: (45) 3646 8822. FAX: (45) 3644 0604.
ZENTROPA PRODUCTION
Ryesdage 106A, Copenhagen DK-2100. Tel: (45) 3142 4233. FAX: (45) 3142 4299.

EXHIBITORS
BIOGRAFEN & FOLKETEATRET
Jaegergaardsgade 68, Aarhus C DK-8000. Tel: (45) 8612 4301. FAX: 8612 4389.
FILM HOUSE DENMARK
Vognmagergade 10, Copenhagen DK-1120. Tel: (45) 3393 1914. FAX: (45) 3393 1912.
HUSETS BIOGRAF
Huset, Radhusstraede 13, 2nd floor, Copenhagen K DK-1466. Tel: (45) 3315 2002. FAX: (45) 3332 5077.
NORSDISK FILM BIOGRAFER
Axeltorv 9, Copenhagen DK-1609. Tel: (45) 3314 7606. FAX: (45) 3332 7505. CEO: Morten Anker Nielsen.
PALADS TEATRET
Tordenskjoldsgade 21, Aarhus N DK-8200. Tel: (45) 8616 8898. FAX: (45) 8616 8838.
PATHE-NORDISK
Skelbaekgade 1, Copenhagen DK-1717. Tel: (45) 3123 2488.

EGYPT

Population: 62.3 million.
Average ticket price: Varies from E£3.00 to E£7.00.
FREE FILM CENTERS
THE CATHOLIC FILM CENTER
9, Adly St., Cairo.
THE AMERICAN CENTER
Part of the American Embassy, Cairo.
THE BRITISH CENTER
Part of the British Embassy, Cairo.
Both the American and British Centers have film libraries.
CENTER CULTURAL FRANCE
One al Al Mounira, Cairo, and at Hiliopolice.
PRINCIPAL PRODUCTION COMPANIES & DISTRIBUTORS
ARTIST UNITY
Farid Shawki 16, Adly St., Cairo
AFLAM FARID SHAWKI
Farid Shawki 36, Sherif St., Cairo.
AFLAM GALAL
Nader Galal 85, Ramses St., Cairo.
ALAMIA T. V. & CINEMA
Hussein Kalla-41, Guizira Elwosta, Zamalek, Cairo.
AFLAM MISR ALAMIA
Yousef Shahin 35, Champion St., Cairo.
BADIE SOBHI
Badie Sobhi 12, Soliman Elhalabi St., Cairo.
EL-LEITHY FILMS
Ihab El-Leithy 37, Kasr El-Nil St., Cairo.
GAMAL EL-LEITHY
Gamal El-Leithy 11, Saray El-Azbakia St., Cairo.
MANAR FILM
Atef Ibrahim, 11, Saray El-Azbakia St., Cairo.

TAMIDO FILM
Medhat Sherif 4, Zaki St., Orabi, Cairo.
NASR FILM
Mohamed Hassan 33, Orabi St., Cairo.
KASR EL-NIL INTERNATIONAL AHMED SAMI
(Ahmed Sami & Co.) 4, Hussein Almimar St., Kasr El Nil,
Cairo, Tel. (202) 574 5416. FAX: (202) 291 8059.
CENTRAL FILM
Nagib Spiro, 85, Ramses St., Cairo.
MISR EL-ARABIA
Wasef Faiez 12, Soliman Elhalabi St., Cairo.
HANY FILM
Zaki Guirges 4, Soliman Elhalabi St., Cairo.
SOAT EL-FANN
D. Abdel Wahab 16, Adly St., Cairo.
OSIRIS FILM
Omran Ali 87, Ramses St., Cairo.
MASR EL-GUIDIDA
Salah Kharma, 36, Orabi St., Cairo.
DISTRIBUTORS AND PRODUCERS
MGM
35 Talaat Harb St., Cairo. Tel: (202) 393 3897. FAX: (202) 392
7998. Manager: Fouad Nader.
TWENTIETH CENTURY FOX IMPORT CORP.
11 Saray el Ezbekieh, Box 693, Cairo. Tel: (202) 591 2477.
FAX: (202) 591 2829. Manager: Zagloul Gad El Karim Salama.
UNITED MOTION PICTURES
(Licensee for Warner Bros.), 7 26th of July St., P.O. Box 923,
Cairo. Tel: (202) 591 2477. FAX: (202) 591 2829. Manager:
Antoine Zeind.

FINLAND

Population: 5.0 million.
Number of Screens: 326.
Admissions: 4.2 million.
Box Office Gross: $36.3 million.
Average Ticket Price: $9.01.
After Portugal and Greece, Finland has the lowest rate of cinema attendance per capita in Europe. 1995 admissions declined
by 14%, perhaps due to the increase in ticket price. Local films
are losing out at the box office to the U.S. blockbusters and
releases from other European countries. In 1994, they accounted for only 4% of revenues.

ASSOCIATIONS & ORGANIZATIONS
ASSOCIATION OF FINNISH FILM DIRECTORS
Suomen Elokuva Ohjaajalitto SELO, PI 116, Helsinki 00171.
Tel: (3580) 632 108.
ASSOCIATION OF FINNISH FILM WORKERS
Soumen Elokuvaja Videotyontekijain, Litto Set, Metritullinkatu
33, Helsinki 00170. Tel: (3580) 135 6370. FAX: (3580) 135
6658.
ASSOCIATION OF INDEPENDENT PRODUCERS
Suomen Audiovisuaalisen Alan Tuottajatm SATU, Kanavaranta
3 D 31, Helsinki 00160. Tel: (3580) 622 1690. FAX: (3580) 622
1860.
**AVEK—THE PROMOTION CENTRE FOR AUDIOVISUAL
CULTURE IN FINLAND**
Hietaniemenkatu 2, Helsinki 00100. Tel: (3580) 446 411. FAX:
(3580) 446 414.
CENTRAL ORGANISATION OF FINNISH FILM PRODUCERS
Kaisaniemenkatu 3 B 29, Helsinki 00100. Tel: (3580) 636 305.
FAX: (3580) 176 689.
FINNISH FILM CHAMBER
Kaisaniemenkatu 3 B 29, Helsinki 00100. (3580) 636 305.
FINNISH FILM CONTACT
Annakatu 13 B 11, Helsinki 00120. Tel: (3580) 645 126. FAX:
(3580) 641 736.
FINNISH FILM FOUNDATION
Kanavakatu 12, Helsinki 00160. Tel: (3580) 622 0300. FAX:
(3580) 6220 3050.
FINNISH SOCIETY OF CINEMA
Lonnrotink 35D, Helsinki 00180. Tel: (3580) 645 126. FAX:
(3580) 645 127.
STATE COMMITTEE FOR CINEMA
Valion elokuvataidetoimikunta PL 293, Helsinki 00171. Tel:
(3580) 134 171. FAX: (3580) 624 313.

DISTRIBUTORS AND PRODUCERS
ALFA PANORAMA FILM & VIDEO
Laipattie 5, Helsinki 00880. Tel: (3580) 759 2600. FAX: (3580)
755 5460.
ARISTA FILM
Pohjoisranta 11, Box 24, Pori 28100. Tel: (35839) 633 4433.
FAX: (35839) 633 4433.
AXEL FILM
Maneesikatu 1-3 J, Helsinki 00170. Tel: (3580) 278 1996.

BUENORAMA PICTURES
Purimiehenkatu 27, Helsinki 00150. Tel: (3580) 2709 0490.
FAX: (3580) 622 3855.
CINEMA MONDO
Unioninkatu 10, Helsinki 00130. Tel: (3580) 629 528. FAX:
(3580) 631 450.
DADA-FILMI
Kolmas Linja 5, Helsinki 00530. Tel: (3580) 737 788. FAX:
(3580) 730 734. email: rile@dada.pp.fi
EL-KO FILMS
Kavallvagen 23A, Grankulla 02700. Tel: (3580) 505 2600.
ERIKSSON ENTERTAINMENT
Kaisaniemenkatu 2B, Helsinki 00100. Tel: (3580) 1311 9377.
FAX: (3580) 1311 9444.
EUROPA VISION
Koivuvaarankuja 2, Vantaa 01641. Tel: (3580) 852 711. FAX:
(3580) 853 2183.
FINNKINO OY
Koivuvaarankuja 2, Vantaa 01641. Tel: (3580) 131 191. FAX:
(3580) 1311 9300.
KINOFINLANDIA
Maunnkatuoiu 2, Helsinki 00170. Tel: (3580) 278 1783. FAX:
(3580) 278 1763.
KINOSCREEN/KINOPRODUCTION
Katajanokantuu 6, Helsinki 00160. Tel: (3580) 663 217. FAX:
(3580) 662 048.
KOSMOFILMI
Steinbackinkatu 8A, Helsinki 00250. Tel: (3580) 477 3587. FAX:
(3580) 477 3583.
MIO-FILM
Hiidentie 1 A 7, Oulu 90550. Tel: (35881) 314 1732. FAX:
(35881) 314 1730.
OULUN ELEKUVAKESKUS
Torikatu 8, Oulu 90100. Tel: (35881) 881 1292. FAX: (35881)
881 1290.
SENSO FILMS
Uudenmaankatu 13D, Helsinki 00120. Tel: (3580) 602 810.
FAX: (3580) 602 292.
TALENT HOUSE
Tallberginkatu 1 A, loc. 141, Helsinki 00180. Tel: (3580) 685
2227. FAX: (3580) 685 2229.
UNITED INTERNATIONAL PICTURES OY
Kaisaniemenkatu 1C 98, Helsinki 00100. Tel: (3580) 662 166.
FAX: (3580) 665 005.
URANIA FILM
Hiidentie 1 A 7, Oulu 90550. Tel: (35881) 881 1291. FAX:
(35881) 881 1290.
WALHALLA
P.O. Box 1134, Helsinki 00101. Tel: (3580) 1311 9365. FAX:
(3580) 637 023.
WARNER BROTHERS FINLAND OY
Kaisaniemenkatu 1B A 69, Helsinki 00100. Tel: (3580) 638 953.
FAX: (3580) 638 161.

EXHIBITORS
CINEMA MONDO
Unioninkatu 10, Helsinki 00130. Tel: (3580) 629 528. FAX:
(3580) 631 450.
ESPOO CINE FILM FESTIVAL
P.O. Box 95, Espoo 02101. Tel: (3580) 466 599. FAX: (3580)
466 458.
FINNKINO
Koivuvaarankuja 2, Vantaa 01640. Tel: (3580) 131 191. FAX:
(3580) 1311 9300.

FRANCE

Population: 58.1 million.
Screens: 4,367.
Admissions: 129.7 million.
Average Ticket Price: $6.29.
Theater Grosses: $900 million.
Domestic Feature Production: 97 films.
Top Ten Domestic Films of 1995: Un indien dans la ville, Les
Anges gardiens, Gazon maudit, Alisa, Le Hussard sur le toit, Le
Bonheur est dans le pre, La Haine, Les Trois freres, La Cite des
enfants perdus, Nelly et Monsieur Arnaud.
Top Ten Films of 1995: Un indien dans la ville, Les Anges gardi-
ens, Pocahontas, Gazon maudit, Die Hard With A Vengeance, 101
Dalmations, Stargate, The Lion King, Elisa, Le Hussard sur le toit.
France is the only country in Europe in which cinema admissions per head have never fallen below two per year. However,
unlike 1994 in which only one French film appeared in the top
ten films of the year, 1995 saw five domestic productions in the
list of top theatrical grosses. In 1995, French films accounted for
36% of gross box office, while U.S. films were flat at 54% of market share, the same figure as 1994. The French government has
passed a new law restricting cinemas to no more than 2,000
seats. This is a major setback to exhibitors planning multiplexes
in France and wishing to take advantage of economies of scale.

France is home to almost 800 multplex screens currently, with more planned for 1997 although admissions have not increased since 1994, and some industry analysts feel that the exhibition industry is near a saturation point.

ASSOCIATIONS & ORGANIZATIONS

ACADEMIE DES ARTS ET TECHNIQUES DU CINEMA
19 Ave. du President Wilson, Paris 75116. Tel: (331) 4723 7233. FAX: (331) 4070 0291.

ATELIERS DU CINEMA EUROPEEN
(European Film Studio), 68 Rue de Rivoli, Paris 75004. Tel: (331) 4461 8830. FAX: (331) 4461 8840.

AUXITEC
(SOCIETE AUXILIAIRE POUR LE CINEMA ET LA TV)
1bis Ave. du Roi Albert, Cannes 06400. Tel: (3393) 940777. FAX: (3393) 438895.

BUREAU DE LIAISON EUROPEEN DU CINEMA
c/o FIADF, 43 Blvd. Malesherbes, Paris 75008. Tel: (331) 4266 0532. FAX: (331) 4266 9692.

CENTRE FRANCAIS DU COMMERCE EXTERIEUR
10 Ave. d'Iena, Paris Cedex 16 75783. Tel: (331) 4073 3000. FAX: (331) 4073 3979.

CENTRE NATIONAL DE LA CINEMATOGRAPHIE
12 Rue Lubeck, Paris 75016. Tel: (331) 4434 3440. FAX: (331) 4755 0491.

CHAMBRE SYNDICALE DES PRODUCTEURS & EXPORTATEURS DE FILMS FRANCAIS
5 Rue de Cirque, Paris 75008. Tel: (331) 4225 7063. FAX: Tel: (331) 4225 9427.

CICCE
(European Committee Film Industries Commission), 5 Rue du Cirque, Paris 75008. Tel: (331) 4225 7063. FAX: (331) 4225 9427.

CONSEIL SUPERIEUR DE L'AUDIOVISUEL (CSA)
39-43 Quai Andre-Citroen, Paris Cedex 15 75015. Tel: (331) 4058 3800. FAX: (331) 4579 0006.

EUROPA CINEMAS
54 Rue Beaubourg. Paris 3 75003. Tel: (331) 4271 5370. FAX: (331) 4271 4755.

FEDERATION INTERNATIONALE DES ASSOCIATIONS DE DISTRIBUTEURS DE FILMS
43 Blvd. Malesherbes, Paris 75008. Tel: (331) 4266 0532. FAX: (331) 4266 9692.

FEDERATION NATIONALE DES CINEMAS FRANCAIS (FNCF)
10 Rue de Marignan, Paris 75008. Tel: (331) 4359 1676. FAX: (331) 4074 0864.

FEDERATION NATIONALE DES DISTRIBUTEURS DE FILMS
43 Blvd. Malesherbes, Paris 75008. Tel: (331) 4266 0532. FAX: (331) 4266 9692.

FEDERATION OF THEATRE, CINEMA & AUDIOVISUAL UNIONS
14-16 Rue des Lilias, Paris 75015. Tel: (331) 4240 1495. FAX: (331) 4240 9020.

INSTITUT NATIONAL DE L'AUDIOVISUEL
4 Ave. de l'Europe, Bry-Sur-Marne 94366. Tel: (331) 4983 2000. FAX: (331) 4983 3195.

INTERNATIONAL FEDERATION OF FILM PRODUCERS
33 Champs Elysées, Paris 75008. Tel: (331) 4225 6214. FAX: (331) 4256 1652.

INTERNATIONAL FEDERATION OF INDEPENDENT FILM PRODUCERS
50 Ave. Marceau, Paris 75008. Tel: (331) 4723 7030. FAX: (331) 4256 1652.

INTERNATIONAL UNION OF CINEMAS
10 Rue de Marignan, Paris 75008. Tel: (331) 4359 1676. FAX: (331) 4074 0864.

MINISTERE DES AFFAIRES ETRANGERES
244 Blvd. St. Germaine, Paris 75007. Tel: (331) 4317 9662. FAX: (331) 4317 9242.

SESAM
16 Place de la Fontaine, Aux Lions, Paris 19 75920. Tel: (331) 4715 4905. FAX: (331) 4715 4974.

SOCIETE DES REALISATEURS DE FILMS (SRF)
215 Rue de Faubourg-Honoré, Paris 75008. Tel: (331) 4563 9630. FAX: (331) 4074 0796.

UNION DES PRODUCTEURS DE FILMS
1 Place des Deux Ecus, Paris 75001. Tel: (331) 4028 0138. FAX: (331) 4221 1700.

UNIFRANCE FILM INTERNATIONAL
4 Villa Bosquet, Paris 75007. Tel: (331) 4753 9580. FAX: (331) 4705 9655.

DISTRIBUTORS AND PRODUCERS

AAA DISTRIBUTION
12bis Rue Keppler, Paris 75011. Tel: (331) 4475 7070. FAX: (331) 4705 4554.

LES ACACIAS CINE AUDIENCE
33 Rue Berger, Paris 75008. Tel: (331) 4256 4903. FAX: (331) 4256 0865.

AGENCE DU COURT METRAGE
2 Rue de Toqueville, Paris 75017. Tel: (331) 4380 0365. FAX: (331) 4267 5971.

A.I.L.O. PRODUCTIONS
9 Rue Fontaine, St. Denis 93200. Tel: (331) 4813 0666. FAX: (331) 4813 0632.

AMLF
10 Rue Lincoln, Paris 75008. Tel: (331) 4076 9100. FAX: (331) 4225 1289.

ARCHEO PICTURES
9 Rue René Boulanger, Paris 75010. Tel: (331) 4240 4899. FAX: (331) 4239 9413.

FARIANE FILMS
15 Rue de Colonel Pierre Avia, Paris 75015. Tel: (331) 4662 1777. FAX: (331) 4662 1797.

ARP
75 Ave. des Champs Elysées, Paris 75008. Tel: (331) 4359 4330. FAX: (331) 4563 8337.

ARTEDIS CINEMA ARTS ENTERTAINMENT
44 Rue du Colisee, Paris 75008. Tel: (331) 4256 2275. FAX: 33 1 4256 1087.

A.S.P.
23 Rue Raynouard, Paris 75016. Tel: (331) 4224 5050. FAX: (331) 4224 6642.

BAC FILMS
5 Rue Pelouze, Paris 75008. Tel: (331) 4470 9230. FAX: (331) 4470 9070.

CELLULOID DREAMS
24 Rue Lamartine, 75009 Paris. Tel: (331) 4970 0370. FAX:(331) 4970 0371.

CIBY DISTRIBUTION
90 Ave. des Champs Elysées, Paris 75008. Tel: (331) 4421 6417. FAX: (331) 4421 6435.

CINEMADIS FILMS
78 Ave. des Champs Elysées, Paris 75008. Tel: (331) 4562 8287. FAX: (331) 4289 2198.

COLUMBIA TRISTAR FILMS
131 Ave. de Wagram, Paris 75017. Tel: (331) 4440 6220. FAX: (331) 4440 6201.

CONNAISSANCE DU CINEMA
22 Rue du Pont Neuf, Paris 75001. Tel: (331) 4013 0722. FAX: (331) 4026 2544.

CYTHERE FILMS
34 Ave. des Champs Elysées, Paris 75008. Tel: (331) 4289 0767. FAX: (331) 4256 0773.

DIAPHANA DISTRIBUTION
24 Rue de Paradis, Paris 75010. Tel: (331) 4479 9292. FAX: (313) 4246 5448.

EUROCINE
33 Ave. des Champs Elysées, 75008 Paris. Tel: (331) 4225 6492. FAX: (331) 4225 7338.

LES FILM DE L'ATALANTE
100 Rue Monfletard, Paris 75005. Tel: (331) 4287 0202. FAX: (331) 4287 0189.

LES FILMS DU LOSANGE
26 Ave. Pierre 1er de Serfie, Paris 75116. Tel: (331) 4720 5412/ 4443 8715. FAX: (331) 4952 0640.

LES FILMS NUMBER ONE
16 Ave. Hoche, Paris 75008. Tel: (331) 4563 4402. FAX: (331) 4289 1921.

FILMS SANS FRONTIERES
70 Blvd. de Sebastopol, Paris 75003. Tel: (331) 4277 2184. FAX: (331) 4277 4266.

LES FILMS SINGULIER
20 Rue Michelet, Montreuil 93100. Tel: (331) 4287 5908. FAX: (331) 4287 0189.

GAUMONT
30 Ave. Charles de Gaulle, Neuilly-sur-Seine 92200. Tel: (331) 46 43 20 00. FAX: (331) 46 43 21 68.

GAUMONT/BUENA VISTA INTERNATIONAL
5 Rue du Clisée, Paris 75008. Tel: (331) 4643 2000. FAX: (331) 4643 2047.

LES GRANDS FILMS CLASSIQUES
49 Ave. Theophile Gautier, Paris 75016. Tel: (331) 45 24 43 24. FAX: (331) 45 25 49 73.

HAUT ET COURT
5 Passage Piver, Paris 75011. Tel: (331) 4338 5300. FAX: (331) 4338 3872.

JECK FILM
5 Rue René Boulanger, Paris 75010. Tel: (331) 42 40 78 00. FAX: (331) 48 03 02 64.

K—FILMS
15 Rue Saintonge, Paris 75003. Tel: (331) 4274 7016. FAX: (331) 4274 7024.

LOGOS
24 Ave. du Recteur Poincare, Paris 75016. Tel: (331) 46 47 97 48. FAX: (331) 46 47 97 58.

METROPOLITAN FILMEXPORT
1 Rue Lord Byron, Paris 75008. Tel: (331) 4563 4560. FAX: (331) 4563 7731.
MK2
55 Rue Traversiere, Paris 75012. Tel: (331) 4467 3000. FAX: (331) 4341 3230.
OUTSIDER DIFFUSION
63 Rue Pascal, Paris 75013. Tel: (331) 43 35 81 74. FAX: (331) 47 07 10 49.
POINT DU JOUR
38 Rue Croix des Petits Champs, Paris 75001. Tel: (331) 47 03 40 00. FAX: (331) 47 03 39 48.
POLYGRAM FILM DISTRIBUTION
107 Blvd. Periere, Paris 75017. Tel: (331) 4415 6666. FAX: (331) 4764 3638.
PRETTY PICTURES
9 Rue Charlot, Paris 75003. Tel: (331) 4029 0044. FAX: (331) 4029 0121.
PYRAMIDE DISTRIBUTION
6 Rue Catulle Mendes, Paris 75017. Tel: (331) 42 67 44 66. FAX: (331) 42 67 80 28.
QUINTA COMMUNICATIONS
16 Ave. Hoche, Paris 75008. Tel: (331) 4076 04540. FAX: (331) 4256 6921.
REVCOM INTERNATIONAL/LES FILMS ARIANE
15 Rue du Colonel Pierre Avia, Paris 75015. Tel: (331) 4662 1777. FAX: (331) 4662 1797.
REZO FILMS
52 Rue Charlot, Paris 75003. Tel: (331) 4027 8525. FAX: (331) 4027 0887.
STUDIO—CANAL PLUS
6 Blvd. de la Republique, Boulogne-Billancourt Cedex 95214. Tel: (331) 4610 1200. FAX: (331) 4610 1220.
TWENTIETH CENTURY FOX
8 Rue Bellini, Paris 75116. Tel: (331) 4434 6000. FAX: (331) 4434 6105.
U.F.D.
2 Ave.nue de Montaigne, Paris 75008. Tel: (331) 5367 1717. FAX: (331) 5367 1700.
UNITED INTERNATIONAL PICTURES
1 Rue Meyerbeer, Paris 75009. Tel: (331) 4007 3838. FAX: (331) 47472 5716.
WARNER BROS.
67 Ave. de Wagram, Paris 75017. Tel: (331) 4401 4999. FAX: (331) 4763 4515.

EXHIBITORS
GAUMONT
30 Ave. Charles de Gaulle, Neuilly-sur-Seine 92200. Tel: (331) 4643 2021. FAX: (331) 4643 2033.
PATHE CINEMA
5 Blvd. Malesherbes, Paris 75008. Tel: (331) 4924 4333. FAX: (331) 4924 4350. Director: Jerome Seydoux.
UGC
24 Ave. Charles de Gaulle, Neuilly-sur-Seine 92200. Tel: (331) 4640 4430. FAX: (331) 4624 3728.

STUDIOS
ACME FILMS
24-26 Rue Paul Fort, Paris 75014. Tel: (331) 4543 6657. FAX: (331) 4542 6159.
BOULOGNE-BILLANCOURT
2 Rue de Silly, Boulogne 92100. Tel: (331) 4605 6569. FAX: (331) 4825 2347.
CAIMAN
30 Blvd. de la Bastille, Paris 75012. Tel: (331) 4344 1122. FAX: (331) 4344 7930.
PARIS STUDIO BILLANCOURT
50 Quai du Point-du-Jour, Boulogne-Billancourt 9200. Tel: (331) 4609 9324. FAX: (331) 4620 2471.
STUDIOS LA VICTORINE COTE D'AZUR
16 Ave. Edouard Grinda, Nice 06200. Tel: (3393) 725 454. FAX: (3393) 719 173.

GERMANY

Population: 81.3 million.
Screens: 3,901.
Admissions: 124.5 million (down 6% from 1994).
Box Office Gross: $787.1 million.
Average Ticket Price: $5.93.
Domestic Feature Production: 70 films.
Top Five Domestic Films of 1995: Der bewegte Mann, Stadtgespraech, Keiner liebt mich, Schlafes Bruder, Rennschwein Rudi Russel.
Top Ten Movies of 1995: While You Were Sleeping, Casper, Die Hard With A Vengeance, Stargate, Waterworld, Disclosure, Apollo 13, Pocahontas, Outbreak, Dumb & Dumber.
Three German films, "Stille Nacht", "Nur aus Liebe", and "Peanuts-Die Bank zahlt alles", distributed by the German arms of American studios Disney and Warner, performed less well than expected. Comedy "Maennerpension" became the third German film to win the Gold Screen, awarded to films with admissions over 3 million. On the whole, German-produced comedies seem to be more successful domestically than the traditionally produced heavier fare. In 1995, Hollywood films accounted for more than 83% of admissions in Germany, the highest share ever. The German government's film subsidies, totaling over $167 million annually, are increasingly being aimed at market-oriented productions.The German film industry's official self-censorship board (the FSK) maintains a five-tiered rating system: for all ages, for 6+, for 12+, for 16+, and for 18+ only. The more restrictive ratings are being imposed more for violence than for other matters. An additional rating can insist that certain films not be shown on religious holidays.
United Cinemas International and Warner Bros International Theaters are the only international exhibitors to have established a presence in Germany and have both undertaken massive building programs. Indeed, there seems to be a cinema boom in Germany with six new complexes planned in the Mannheim, Magdeburg and Augsburg areas in the next year. However, there are only enough ticket buyers in each of these areas to support one multiplex. The German Cinema Association reports that there are now 24 multiplexes under construction with another 45 pending and that the number of screens in Germay will rocket from the current 3,901 to 5,000 by the 1999. Competition for box office revenue in Germany will be fierce with that level of saturation, and some industry experts estimate that at least 800 screens will close, bringing the number back to around 4,000. UFA Theatres remains the country's leading theater operator with 87 screens, closely followed by Flebbe, who expect to have increased their presence to over 80 screens by the beginning of 1997.

ASSOCIATIONS & ORGANIZATIONS
BERLIN PROVINCIAL FILM SERVICE
Bismarckstrasse 80, 1000 Berlin 12. Tel: (4930) 313 80 55.
GERMAN INSTITUTE FOR FILM INFORMATION
Schaumainkai 41, Frankfurt am Main 60596. Tel: (4969) 617 045. FAX: (4969) 620 060.
GERMAN INSTITUTE FOR FILM INFORMATION/FILM ARCHIVE
Kreuzbergerring 56, Wiesbaden 65205. Tel: (49611) 723 310. FAX: (49611) 723 318.
INSTITUTE FOR FILM AND THE VISUAL ARTS IN EDUCATION
Bavariafilmplatz 3, Geiselgaskig 82031. Tel: (4989) 64971. FAX: (4989) 649 7300.

DISTRIBUTORS AND PRODUCERS
ALHAMBRA FILMVERLEIH
Friedrich Ebertstrasse 12, Dusseldorf 40120. Tel: (49211) 352 972.
ARSENAL FILMVERLEIH STEFAN PAUL KG
Neue Strasse 2, Tuebingen 72012. Tel: (497071) 92960. FAX: (497071) 929611.
ATLAS FILM UND AV GMBH & CO. KG
Ludgeristrasse 14-16, Duisburg 47057. Tel: (49203) 378 6222. FAX: (49203) 362 482.
ATLAS INTERNATIONAL
Rumfordstrasse 29-31, Munich D-80469. Tel: (4989) 227 525. FAX: (4889) 224 332.
BAUER FILMVERLEIH-KINO UND GASTRONOMIE
Schmiedingstrasse 19, Postfach 100329, Dortmund 4600. Tel: (49231) 148 078.
BAVARIA FILM GMBH
Bavariafilmplatz 7, Geiselgasteig, Munich D-82031. Tel: (4989) 6499 2681. FAX: (4989) 6499 2240.
BEATE UHSE INTERNATIONAL
Gutenbergstrasse 12, Flensburg 24941. Tel: (49461) 996 6221.
BOJE BUCK PRODS./DELPHI FILM
Kantstrasse 12a, Berlin 10623. Tel: (4930) 313 2200, (4930) 312 6070. FAX: (4930) 312 9996.
BUENA VISTA INTERNATIONAL
P.O. Box 800329, Munich D-81603. Tel: (4989) 9934 0270. FAX: (4989) 9934 0139.
CAPELLA (SEE CONNEXION)
CENTRAL FILMVERTRIEB
(Represents Senator Filmverleih & Jugendfilm), Uhlandstrasse 179/180, Berlin 10263. Tel: (4930) 8842 8570. FAX: (4930) 8842 8512.
CINE INTERNATIONAL
Leopoldstrasse 18, Munich D-80802. Tel: (4989) 391 025. FAX: (4989) 331 089.
CINEMA FILMVERLEIH
Braystrasse 20, Munich D-811677. Tel: (4989) 472 061. FAX: (4989) 474 736.
CINEPOOL
Sonnenstrasse 21, Munich D-80331. Tel: (4989) 5587 6188. FAX: (4989) 5587 6188.

CINEVOX
Bavariafilmplatz 7, Gruenwald 82031. Tel: (4989) 641 8000.
FAX: (4989) 649 3288.

COLUMBIA TRISTAR FILM
8 Ickstattstrasse 1, Munich D-80469. Tel: (4989) 230 370. FAX:
(4989) 264 380. Sales: Gerd Bender.

CONCORDE—CASTLE ROCK/TURNER FILMVERLEIH
Rosenheimer Strasse 143b, Munich D-81671. Tel: (4989) 450
6100. FAX: (4989) 4506 1010.

CONNEXION IMPULS CI-VERTRIEBSGEM
Rothembaumchausee 80c, Hamburg 20148. Tel: (4940) 419
9750. FAX: (4940) 419 9799.

CONSTANTIN FILM
Kaiserstrasse 39, Munich D-80801. Tel: (4989) 386 090. FAX:
(4989) 386 9242.

CONTACT FILMVERLEIH
Huttenstrasse 40, Dusseldorf 14000. Tel: (49211) 374 024.
FAX: (49211) 374 025.

DAZU FILM BONN
c/o Daniel Zuta Filmproduktion, Kaiserstrasse 39, Frankfurt am
Main D-60329. Tel: (4869) 253 735. FAX: (4989) 239 058.

ENDFILM
Am Vogelherd 4, Bach D-93090. Tel: (4994) 823 377. FAX:
(4994) 823 378.

FILMWELT—PROKINO VERLEIHGEMEINSCHAFT
Ismaninger Strasse 51, Munich D-81675. Tel: (4989) 418 0010.
FAX: (4989) 4180 0143.

FUTURA/FILMVERLAG DER AUTOREN
Rambergstrasse 5, Munich 80799. Tel: (4989) 381 7000. FAX:
(4989) 381 70020.

GERMANIA FILMVERLEIH
Blissestrasse 38-40, Berlin 10713. Tel: (4930) 821 3072.

HIGHLIGHT FILMVERLEIH
Herkomerplatz 2, Munich D-80000. Tel: (4989) 9269 6602.
FAX: (4989) 981 543.

HVW FOCUS FILMVERTRIEB
Wurmtalstrasse 125, Munich D-81375. Tel: (4989) 740 9411.
FAX: (4989) 740 9319.

JUGENDFILM VERLEIH GMBH
Reichstrasse. 15, Berlin D-14052. Tel: (4930) 300 6970. FAX:
(4930) 3006 9711.

KERYX FILM
Immenried 97, Kisslegg D-88353. Tel: (497563) 8372 8147.
FAX: (497563) 8372 8217.

KINOWELT FILMVERLEIH
Pfisterstrasse 11, Munich 80331. Tel: (4989) 296 963. FAX:
(4989) 221 491.

KIRCHGROUP
Robert-Burklestrasse 2, Ismaning W-8045. Tel: (4989) 9508
8323. FAX: (4989) 9508 8330.

KLASING
Siekerwass 21, Bielefeld 33602. Tel: (49521) 5590. FAX:
(49521) 559 113.

KORA FILMVERLEIH
Leopoldstrasse 65, 8000 Munich 40. Tel: (4989) 334 409.

KUCHENREUTHER FILM GMBH
Film Theater Verleih Produktion, Leopoldstrasse 80, Munich
80802. Tel: (4989) 332 224. FAX: (4989) 333 742.

MERCATOR FILMVERLEIH
Postfach 101950, Bielefeld 33519. (49521) 124 061. FAX:
(49521) 131 010.

NEUE CONSTANTIN FILM
Kaiserstrasse 39, Munich 80801. Tel: (4989) 386 090. FAX:
(4989) 3860 9242.

NEW VISION VIDEO
Hoerkomerplatz 2, Munich 81679. Tel: (4989) 9269 6601. FAX:
(4989) 981 543.

PANDORA FILM
Hamburger Allee 45, Frankfurt 60486. Tel: (4969) 779 094.
FAX: (4969) 707 4033.

PROGRESS FILMVERLEIH
Burgstrasse 27, Berlin 10178. Tel: (4930) 280 5110. FAX:
(4930) 282 9157.

RING FILMVERLEIH
Schwalbenstrasse 13, Ottobrunn 85521. Tel: (4989) 609 4141.
FAX: (4989) 609 9696.

SCOTIA INTERNATIONAL
Possartstrasse 14, Munich 81679. Tel: (4989) 413 0900. FAX:
(4989) 470 6320.

SELLENG FILMAGENTUR
Lietzenburgerstrasse 51, Berlin 1000. Tel: (4930) 213 6788.

TIME MEDIENVERTRIEBS
Nymphenburgerstrasse 158, Munich D-80634. Tel: (4989) 160
923. FAX: (4989) 162 056. Distribution: Annette Niehues.

TOBIS FILMKUNST GMBH & CO.
Pacelliallee 47, Berlin 14175. Tel: (4930) 839 0070. FAX:
(4930) 890 0765.

TWENTIETH CENTURY FOX OF GERMANY
Hainer Weg 37-53, 70 Frankfurt am Main D-60599. Tel: (4969)
609 020. FAX: (4969) 627 715.

UNITED INTERNATIONAL PICTURES
Hahnstrasse 31-35, Frankfurt am Main D-60528, Tel: (4969)
669 8190. FAX: (4969) 666 6509. Manager: Paul Steinshulte.
Lietzenburger Strasse 51, Berlin 10789. Tel: (4930) 211 2063.
FAX: (4930) 213 3148.

WARNER BROS. FILM
Hans-Henry-Jahn-Weg 35, Hamburg D-22085. Tel: (4940) 227
1250. FAX: (4940) 2271 2519. Sales: Hans Hermann Schopen.

WILD OKAPI FILM VERLEIH VERTRIEB
Kreuzbergstrasse 43, Berlin 10965. Tel: (4930) 785 0376. FAX:
(4930) 785 9620.

EXHIBITORS

BLUE MOVIE
Gutenbert 12, Flensburg 24941. Tel: (49461) 996 6247. FAX:
(49461) 96265.

BROADWAY KINO
Ehrenstrasse 11, Cologne 50672. Tel: (49221) 925 6570. FAX:
(49221) 9257 5714.

CADILLAC
Rosenkavalierplatz 12, Munich 81925. Tel: (4989) 912 000.
FAX: (4989) 916 390.

CITY KINO
Schwanthalerstrasse 7, Munich 80331. Tel: (4989) 598 749.
FAX: (4989) 550 2171.

COLM FILMTHEATERBETRIEBE
Alte Poststrasse 3, Stuttgart 70197. Tel: (49711) 650 400. FAX:
(49711) 657 2530.

DELPHI FILMVERLEIH
Kantstrasse 12a, Berlin 10623. Tel: (4930) 313 2200. FAX:
(4930) 313 9996.

ERASMUS KINOVERWALTUNG
Grimmstrasse 30A, Stuttgart 70197. Tel: (49711) 650 400. FAX:
(49711) 657 2530.

FILMTHEATERBETRIEBE BERLIN
Schuchardtweg 9B, Berlin 14109. Tel: (4930) 805 4829. FAX:
(4930) 805 5258.

FILMTHEATERBETRIEBE GEORGE REISS
Sophienstrasse 1, Munich 803333. Tel: (4989) 552 1650.
FAX: (4989) 5521 6525.

FLEBBE FILMTHEATER/FLEBBE GROUP
Bellevue 7, Hamburg 22301. Tel: (4940) 270 9570. FAX:
(4940) 279 5173.

FWU FILM INSTITUTE
Bavaria Film Platz 3, Gruenwald 82131. Tel: (4989) 64970.
FAX: (4989) 649 7360.

GILDE DEUTSCHES FILMKUNSTTHEATER
Waldseerstrasse 3, Biberach/Riss 884000. Tel: (4973) 517
2331. FAX: (4973) 511 3764.

HANSEATER FILMTHEATERBETRIEBE
Kurfuerstendamm 33, Berlin 10719. Tel: (4930) 883 6086.
FAX: (4930) 883 6520.

KINOCENTER OTTOBRUNN
Ottostrasse 72, Ottobrunn 85521. Tel: (4989) 609 4141.
FAX: (4989) 609 9696.

KRUGMANN & WEISCHERMUNDSBURGER
Hamburgerstrasse 152, Hamburg 22083. Tel: (4940) 291
111. FAX: (4940) 291 117.

KUCHENREUTHER FILM
Sonnenstrasse 22, Munich 80331. Tel: (4989) 596 717.
FAX: (4989) 596 286.

LISELOTTE JAEGER FILMTHEATERBETRIEBE
Holzgraben 26, Frankfurt 60313. Tel: (4969) 285 205. FAX:
(4969) 281 957.

NEUE CONSTANTIN KINOBETRIEBE
Kaiserstrasse 39, Munich 80801. Tel: (4989) 386 090. FAX:
(4989) 3860 9166.

OLYMPIC/HIENZ RIECH & SOHN
Graf Adolfstrasse 96, Dusseldorf 40210. Tel: (49211) 169 060.
FAX: (49211) 169 0633.

PALAST/SCHMID & THEILE
Lautenschlagerstrasse 3, Stuttgart 70173. Tel: (49711) 225
750. FAX: (49711) 225 7599.

POTSDAM FILM MUSEUM
Martsall, Potsdam 14467. Tel: (49331) 271 810. FAX: (49331)
271 8126.

ROLF THEILE FILMTHEATERBETRIEBE
Holdgestrasse 12, Darmstadt 6100. Tel: (49615) 129 780. FAX:
(49615) 129 7832.

ROYAL PALAST
Goetheplatz 2, Munich 80337. Tel: (4989) 533 956. FAX: (4989)
530 9618.

UCI
Bongardstrasse 16-18, Bochum 44787. Tel: (49234) 60536.
FAX: (49234) 64199.

UFA THEATER
Graf Adolfstrasse 96, Dusseldorf 40210. Tel: (49211) 169 060.
FAX: (49211) 169 0633. Director: Volker Reich.
WARNER BROS. FILM KINOBETRIEBE
Will-Brandt-Allee 55, Glesenkirchen 45879. Tel: (49209) 787
230.
YORCK KINO
Rankestrasse 31, Berlin 10789. Tel: (4930) 211 1087. FAX:
(4930) 211 9799.

GREECE

Population: 10.6 million.
Screens: 139 (plus around 100 open air screens in summer).
Admissions: 6.0 million.
Box Office Gross: approx. $1 million.
Average Ticket Price: $6.25-$7.25.
Domestic Feature Production: 11 films.
Top Five Domestic Films of 1995: End of an Era, Quartet in
Four Movements, Love Knot, The Dawn, The Charioteer.
Top Ten Films of 1995: Heat, Pocahontas, Braveheart,
Underground, Seven, Waterworld, Die Hard With A Vengeance,
Nine Months, The Bridges of Madison County, First Knight.
Greek audiences, discouraged by the poor quality of local TV
programming, turned to the movies, resulting in a 15% increase
in attendance during 1996. Encouraged by this new turn in the
industry, exhibitors renovated their theaters, adding air condi-
tioning, Dolby Stereo and other modern equipment. Film distributors also released over fifty first run films during the summer
months in which the number of screens in Greece doubles, as
Greece has traditionally had a thriving open-air summer cinema
business. Yet, the number of these cinemas fell from a high of
900 nationwide in the 1970's to around 100 in 1996. Open air
cinemas are a seasonal business, yet contribute notably to
Greece's annual theater grosses. After several steps taken by
the Union of Exhibitors of Open Air Cinemas, the Ministry of
Culture designated 22 open air cinemas situated in the center of
Athens as "Preserved Monuments" so as to protect them from
destruction. However, these gains are offset by new government
legislation which would force the termination of leases on certain cinemas to protect designated national "heritage sites". On
a more positive note, the Australian distributor, Village Roadshow,
will be opening a multiplex in Maroussi, a suburb of Athens. The
theater which will have 10 screens and 2600 seats, constructed
at a cost of $28.5 million, should be open by the end of 1996.
Village Roadshow plans another 12 sites with an unnamed local
partner over the next five years. Negotiations for another multiplex to be owned and operated by British based Virgin Cinemas
Ltd. are under way.

ASSOCIATIONS & ORGANIZATIONS
CINEMA & TELEVISION TECHNICIANS GUILD (ETEKT)
25 Valtetsiou St., Athens 10680. Tel: (301) 360 2379. FAX:
(301) 361 6442.
GREEK DIRECTORS GUILD
11 Tositsa St., Athens, 10683. Tel: (301) 822 3205. FAX: (301)
821 1390.
GREEK FILM & TELEVISION PRODUCERS UNION (SEPKT)
1A Egyptou Sq., Athens 10434. Tel: (301) 883 8460. FAX:
(301) 883 0410.
GREEK FILM CENTER
10 El Venizelou, Athens 10671. Tel: (301) 363 4586. FAX: (301)
361 4336.
MINISTRY OF CULTURE
Cubena Department, 17 Ermou St., Athens 10563. Tel: (301)
323 9317. FAX: (301) 322 2247.
PANHELLENIC FEDERATION OF FILM DISTRIBUTORS
96 Akadimias St., Athens 10677. Tel: (301) 801 1045.
THESSALONIKI FILM FESTIVAL
36 Sina St., Athens 10672. Tel: (301) 361 0418. FAX: (301) 362
1023. Director: Michael Demopoulos.
TENIOTHIKI TIS ELLADOS (GREEK FILM ARCHIVES) I
1 Kanari St., Athens 10671. Tel: (301) 361 2046. FAX: (301)
362 8468.

DISTRIBUTORS AND PRODUCERS
AMA FILMS
26 Tositsa St., Athens 10553. General Manager: George
Stergiakis.
HELLINIKI KINIMSTROGRAFIKI ENOSSI (ELKE)
(Distributes films of Warner Bros, Goldcrest, Carolco, Lorimar,
Globe, Rank, Thames International, etc.)
96-98 Academias St., Athens 10677. Tel: (301) 382 3801. FAX:
(301) 380 301. General Manager: George V. Michaelides.
NEA KINISSI
(Distributes films of Dino de Laurentis, Atlantis International,
Entertainment Group and European Films.)
9-13 Gravias St., Athens, 10677. Tel: (301) 3828 4545. FAX:
(301) 383 9008. General Manager: Antonis Karatzopoulos.
OVO ENTERTAINMENT
27 Themistocleous St., Athens 10677. Tel: (301) 330 4521.
FAX: (301) 330 4523.

PROOPTIKI S. A.
(Distributes films of Columbia Pictures, Orion, Touchstone,
Walt Disney, Tri Star, Cannon.)
40-42 Kileti St., Athens 10682. Tel: (301) 384 4541. FAX: (301)
381 3762. General Manager: Pantelis Metropoulos.
ROSEBUD MOTION PICTURES ENTERPRISES
(Distributes independent American, European & Int'l films.)
96 Academias St., Athens 10677. Tel: (301) 384 4293. FAX:
(301) 383 9208. General Manger: Zenos Panayotides.
SPENTZOS FILMS S. A.
(Distributes films of Twentieth Century Fox, New Line Cinema,
independent and European films.)
9-13 Gravias St., Athens 10678. Tel: (301) 382 0957. FAX:
(301) 382 1438. General Manager: George Spentzos.
UNITED INTERNATIONAL PICTURES (UIP)
(distributes films of MGM, Paramount, Universal, United
Artists.)
4 Gamveta St., Athens 10678. Tel: (301) 381 1472. FAX: (301)
3873 5396. General Manager: John Takaziadis.

EXHIBITORS
AMA FILMS
168B Mavromihali St., Athens 11472. Tel: (301) 862 7640. FAX:
(301) 646 7117.
ELKE
96-98 Akadimias St., Athens 10677. Tel: (301) 382 3801. FAX:
(301) 380 361.
APOSTOLOS FOUKIS
6 Messouguion St., Athens 11527.
K. GEORGOPOULOU S.A.
109 Kifissias St., Athens 11524.
V. HAPSIS HEIRS
14 Kifissias St., Athens 11526.
IONNIDES FILMS E.P.E.
12A Nikiforou Lytra St., Athens 11474.
STAVROS ISAAKIDES
26 Velvedous St., Athens 11364.
CHRISTOS KARAVIAS & CO.
192 Alexandras Ave., Athens 11521.
A. KARAVOKYROS/K.FRANTZIS S.A.
122 Patission St., Athens 11257.
E. KONYOULIS
152 El. Venizelou St., Calithea, Athens.
VICTOR MICHAELIDES S.A.
1 Voukourestiou St., Athens 10564.
N. PANAYOTOPOULOS S.A.
3 Patriarchou Iokem, Athens 10673.
D.P. SKOURAS FILMS
19 Stadium St., Athens 10561.
SPENTZOS FILMS
9-13 Gravias St., Athens 10678. Tel: (301) 382 0957. FAX:
(301) 382 1438.
P. TSAKALAKIS E.P.E.
1 Themistocleous St., Athens 10677.
VILLAGE ROADSHOW, GREECE
11 Mistral St., Neo Psyhiko, Athen 15451. Tel: (301) 685 6833.
FAX: (301) 685 6830.

—Rena Velissariou

HONG KONG

Population: 6.3 million.
Admissions: 14.2 million.
Movie Theatres: 161
Domestic Feature Production: 140 films.
1997 is the year that the People's Republic will assume control
over Hong Kong. While Beijing has claimed that no changes will
occur, many Hong Kong-based talents have already emigrated
to the U. S., most notably Jacky Chan, John Woo, and Quentin
Tarantino influence Ringo Lam. Golden Harvest wanted to double the number of screens they have in Hong Kong, Singapore,
Thailand, Malaysia and Taiwan, with expansion into South
Korea. American Multi Cinemas is building a theater in Hong
Kong that will open after the 1997 accord takes place. Editor's
note: from 1997 forward, Hong Kong will appear in the section
on China in the Almanacs.

ASSOCIATIONS & ORGANIZATIONS
EAST ASIA FILM AND VIDEO SECURITY
13/F, Rm B, Lockhart Centre, 301 Lockhart Rd., Wanchai. Tel:
(852) 575 7842. FAX: (852) 838 0937.
**HONG KONG AND KOWLOON CINEMA AND THEATRICAL
ENTERPRISE FREE GENERAL ASSOCIATION**
Flat A-B, 9/F, 88 Nathan Rd., Kowloon. Tel: (852) 376 3833.
FAX: (852) 721 9225.
**KOWLOON & NEW TERRITORIES MOTION PICTURE
INDUSTRY ASSOCIATION**
319 Beverley Commercial Centre, 87-105 Chatham Rd.,
Tsimshatsui, Kowloon. Tel: (852) 311 2692. FAX: (852) 311
1178.

FILM DISTRIBUTORS AND PRODUCERS

ATLAS FILM
Rm. 905-6, Winning Commercial Bldg., 46-48 Hillwood Rd.,Tsimshatsui, Kowloon. Tel: (852) 367 1057. FAX: (852) 369 0855.

CAPITAL ARTISTS
No. 1, Leighton Rd., Causeway Bay. Tel: (852) 833 9192. FAX: (852) 832 5055.

CITY ENTERTAINMENT
Flat E, 14/F, Tung Nam Bldg., 475 Hennessy Rd., Wanchai. Tel: (852) 892 0155. FAX: (852) 838 4930.

CLEVELAND FILM
Imperial Cinema, 29 Burrows St., Wanchai. Tel: (852) 572 0002. FAX: (852) 834 0723.

CONTINENTAL FILM DISTRIBUTORS
Unit 1922, Star House, 3 Salisbury Rd., Tsimshatsui, Kowloon. Tel: (852) 730 4373. FAX: (852) 730 2977.

CRYSTAL CORPORATION
10/F, Lee Kar Bldg., 4-4A Carnarvon Rd., Tsimshatsui, Kowloon. Tel: (852) 367 4077. FAX: (852) 723 3054.

D & B FILM COMPANY
5 Kent Rd., Kowloon Tong, Kowloon. Tel: (852) 338 7888. FAX: (852) 338 6721.

DELON INTERNATIONAL FILM
7B Astoria Bldg., 24-30 Ashley Rd., Tsimshatsui, Kowloon. Tel: (852) 376 1168. FAX: (852) 376 2569.

EKDO FILMS
19/F Fung Hse, 19-20 Connaught Rd., Central. Tel: (852) 523 1152. FAX: (852) 810 6670.

ERA COMMUNICATIONS
Unit 604, Taikoktsui Centre, 11-15 Kok Cheung St., Kowloon. Tel: (852) 787 3612. FAX: (852) 787 4367.

FILM CITY DISTRIBUTION
Flat A-F, 16/F, Marvel Bldg., 25-31 Kwai Fung Cres, Kwai Chung, New Territories. Tel: (852) 423 4272. FAX: (852) 420 0352.

FILM CONSORTIUM
Rm. 1302, 1 Hysan Av., Causeway Bay. Tel: (852) 5760321. FAX: (852) 895 5471.

FOX COLUMBIA TRISTAR
Rm. 1014, World Commerce Centre, 11 Canton Rd., Tsimshatsui, Kowloon. Tel: (852) 736 6277. FAX: (852) 736 3872.

GOLDEN COMMUNICATIONS
8 Hammer Hill Rd., Kowloon. Tel: (852) 726 5541. FAX: (852) 351 1683.

GOLDEN GLOBE FILM
1203 Tak Woo Hse, 17-19 D'Aguilar St., Central. Tel: (852) 576 0321.

GOLDEN HARVEST (INTERNATIONAL)
8 Hammer Hill Rd., Kowloon. Tel: (852) 352 8222. FAX: (852) 351 1683.

GOLDEN HARVEST ENTERTAINMENT CO. LTD.
8 King Tung Street, Hammer Hill Rd., Kowloon. Tel: (852) 2352 8222. FAX: (852) 2351 1683.

GOLDEN PRINCESS AMUSEMENT
6th Floor, 742-744 Nathan Rd., Kowloon. Tel: (852) 391 9988. FAX: (852) 789 1365.

HAPPY INTERNATIONAL ENTERTAINMENT
Rm. 1205, Shun Tak Centre, 200 Connaught Rd., Central. Tel: (852) 559 1051. FAX: (852) 858 2657.

WILLIAM HAY & CO.
5th Floor Rear, 234 Nathan Road. Central. Tel: (852) 368 8319. FAX: (852) 311 6727.

IMPACT FILMS PRODUCTION
22/F Horizon Plaza, 53-55 Waterloo Rd., Kowloon. Tel: (852) 332 1762. FAX: (852) 783 8225.

IN-GEAR FILM DISTRIBUTION INTERNATIONAL
14th Floor, 206-208 Prince Edward Rd., Kowloon. Tel: (852) 397 1452. FAX: (852) 380 5216.

INTERCONTINENTAL FILM DISTRIBUTORS LTD.
27/F Wyler Centre, Phase 2, 200 Tai Lin Pai Rd., Kwai Chung, New Territories. Tel: (852) 2481 6693. FAX: (852) 2481 6377.

JOY SALES FILM & VIDEO DISTRIBUTORS
2/F Hang On Mansion, 239-249 Portland St., Mongkok, Kowloon. Tel: (852) 771 6161. FAX: (852) 770 6218.

KOREAN MOTION PICTURE PROMOTION (HK)
Ste. B1, 14/F, Golden Crown Ct, 68 Nathan Rd., Tsimshatsui, Kowloon. Tel: (852) 369 2789. FAX: (852) 311 3425.

MANDARIN FILMS DISTRIBUTION
10/F, Rms. B-C, China Overseas Bldg., 139 Hennessy Rd., Wanchai. Tel: (852) 527 3691. FAX: (852) 865 0600.

MEDIA AND ENTERTAINMENT INTERNATIONAL AL
1413 Seaview Est, Block A, 2-8 Watson Rd., North Point. Tel: (852) 510 9138. FAX: (852) 510 0410.

NEWPORT ENTERTAINMENT
19/F, Southland Bldg., 47 Connaught Rd., Central. Tel: (852) 543 6973. FAX: (852) 544 9574.

PARSONS INTERNATIONAL
11J Far East Mansion, 5-6 Middle Rd., Tsimshatsui, Kowloon. Tel: (852) 721 8647. FAX: (852) 311 5383.

SAM LOON INTERNATIONAL
12/F, Vincent Commercial Centre, 21 Hillwood Rd., Tsimshatsui, Kowloon. Tel: (852) 723 6239. FAX: (852) 721 4954.

SKYNOX INTERNATIONAL
Room 3, 81F, James Lee Mansion, 33-35 Carnarvon Rd., Tsimshatsui, Kowloon. Tel: (852) 723 1336. FAX: (852) 723 0085.

SOUTHERN FILM
1902 Dominion Centre, 37-59 Queens Rd. East, Wanchai. Tel: (852) 527 7282. FAX: (852) 865 1449.

UIP INTERNATIONAL SERVICES
Ste. 1501, Dina Hse., 11 Duddell St., Central. Tel: (852) 526 6841. FAX: (852) 845 9581.

THE WALT DISNEY STUDIOS HONG KONG
15th floor, Citibank Tower, Citibank Plaza, 3 Garden Rd., Central. FAX: (852) 2536 2453.

WARNER BROS. (FAR EAST)
12/F Siberian Fur Bldg., 38-40 Haiphong R., Tsimshatsui, Kowloon. Tel: (852) 376 3963. FAX: (852) 376 1302.

HUNGARY

Population: 10.3 million.
Screens: 595.
Admissions: 14.3 million.
Box Office Gross: $20 million.
Average Ticket Price: $1.26.
Domestic Feature Production: 9
Top Domestic Films 1995: Witness Again, Red Colibri, With Kiss and Nails, The Outpost, Awakening.
Top Ten Films 1995: Die Hard with a Vengeance, Dumb and Dumber, The Specialist, The Mask, Outbreak, Junior, Casper, Waterworld, Apollo 13, Streetfighter.

Box office grosses continued to slide in 1995, with admissions down by almost 2 tickets million for the year. Domestic production also dropped to nine films from 25 in 1994. Hungarian films still account for less than 1% of the national box office. The government has cut the state budget for the Motion Picture Foundation, raising fears that domestic production will be halved in the coming years. Mafilm Studio, Hungary's former state film production studio, is being sold by the state in ongoing efforts to privatize the industry. The 12 existing independent production companies in Hungary shared a total of $7 million in funding last year from the Hungarian Motion Picture Foundation. Accordingly, producers are seeking foreign investors for co-productions, the first of which is Szamba, a joint venture with HBO International. The Corvin, Budapest's largest cinema, is due to be turned into a multiplex in the fall of 1996.

ASSOCIATIONS & ORGANIZATIONS

ASSOCIATION OF CINEMAS OF HUNGARY
Maria u 19, Szolnok H-5000. Tel. (3656) 420 612.

GUILD OF HUNGARY
Varosligeti Fasor 38, Budapest H-1068. Tel: (361) 342 4760. FAX: (361) 342 4760.

HUNGARIAN FILM INSTITUTE & ARCHIVE
Budakeszi u 51B, Budapest H-1021. Tel: (361) 176 0205. FAX: (361) 176 7106.

MOTION PICTURE FOUNDATION OF HUNGARY
Szalaiu 10, Budapest H-1054. Tel. (361) 1126417.

DISTRIBUTORS AND PRODUCERS

BUDAPEST FILM
Batori u 10, Budapest H-1054. (361) 111 6650. FAX: (361) 131 5946.

CINEMAGYAR KFT (HUNGAROFILM EX)
Batori u 10, Budapest H-1054. (361) 111 4614. FAX: (361) 153 1317.

DUNA/UIP DANUBE
Tarogato u 24, Budapest H-1021. Tel: (361) 174 7291. FAX: (361) 176 7291.

EUROFILM STUDIO
Rona u 174, Budapest H-1145. Tel: (361) 252 5069. FAX: (361) 251 3986. email: eurofilm@hungary.net

FLAMEX
Labanc u 22B, Budapest H-1021. Tel: (361) 176 1543. FAX: (361) 176 0596.

FOCUSFILM LTD.
Psareti u 122, Budapest H-1026. Tel: (361) 176 7484. FAX: (361) 176 7493.

HUNNIA FILMSTUDIO
Rona u 174, Budapest H-1145. Tel: (361) 252 3170. FAX: (361) 251 6269.

INTERCOM
Karolina ut. 65, Budapest H-1113. Tel: (361) 209 0933. FAX: (361) 209 0930.

MOKEP
Bathori u 10, Budapest H-1054. Tel: (361) 111 2097. FAX: (361) 153 1613.
UIP—DANUBE INTERNATIONAL PICTURES
Tarogato u 2-4/2nd floor, Budapest H-1021. Tel: (361) 176 7291. FAX: (361) 274 2177. Manager: Peter Balint.
EXHIBITORS
BUDAPEST FILM
Bathori u 10, Budapest H-1054,(361) 111 6650. FAX: (361) 131 5946.
HUNGARIAN FILM INSTITUTE & FILM ARCHIVE
Budakeszi u 51B, Budapest H-1021. Tel: (361) 176 0205. FAX: (361) 176 7106.

ICELAND

Population: 265,998.
Screens: 24
Admissions: 1.2 million.
Gross Box Office: $10.8 million.
Average Ticket Price: $7.05.
Domestic Feature Production: 2.
Top Ten Films of 1995: The Lion King, Dumb and Dumber, Die Hard With A Vengeance, Batman Forever, Golden Eye, Casper, French Kiss, Apollo 13, Outbreak, Waterworld.

Iceland remains the only to country to rival the U.S. in number of visits per person to the cinema. Spending on films in Iceland ($40 per person) actually exceeds that of the U.S. However, the Icelandic government does little to support the domestic film industry and over 60% of movies' budgets comes from foreign funding.

ASSOCIATIONS & ORGANIZATIONS
ASSOCIATION OF FILM DISTRIBUTORS IN ICELAND
Stjornubio, Laugaveg 94, Reykjavik 101. Tel: (3541) 551 6500. FAX: (3541) 554 4630.
ASSOCIATION OF ICELANDIC FILM DIRECTORS
Hverfisgata 46, Reykjavik 121. (3541) 562 1850. FAX: (3541) 552 5154.
ASSOCIATION OF ICELANDIC FILM PRODUCERS
Posthusstraeti 13, Reykjavik 101. (3541) 152 8188. FAX: (3541) 162 3424.
DIRECTORS GUILD OF ICELAND
Hverfisgata 46, Reykjavij 101. Tel: (3541) 551 2260. FAX: (3541) 552 5154.
ICELANDIC FILM FUND
Laugavegur 24, Reykjavik 101. (3541) 562 3580. FAX: (3541) 562 7171.
ICELANDIC FILMMAKERS ASSOCIATION
Laugavegur 24, P. O. Box 320, Reykjavik 101. (3541) 562 3225. FAX: (3541) 562 7171.
MINISTRY OF CULTURE & EDUCATION
Solvholsgotu 4, Reykjavik 105. Tel: (3541) 560 9500. FAX: (3541) 562 3068.
DISTRIBUTORS AND PRODUCERS
BERGVIK
Armula 44, Reykjavik. Tel: (3541) 588 7966. FAX: (3541) 588 0288.
HASKOLABIO UNIVERSITY CINEMA
Hagatorg, Reykjavik 107. Tel: (3541) 561 1212. FAX: (3541) 562 7135. email: cinema@centrum.is
ICELANDIC FILM COMPANY
Hverfisgata 46, Reykjavik 101. Tel: (3541) 551 2260. FAX: (3541) 552 5154.
LAUGARASBIO
Laugaras, Reykjavik 104. Tel: (3541) 563 8150. FAX: (3541) 568 0910.
MYNDFORM
Holshraun 2, Hafnarfirdi 220. (354) 565 1288. FAX: (354) 565 0188.
SAM FILM
Alfabakki 8, Reykjavik 109. Tel: (3541) 587 8900. FAX: (3541) 587 8930.
SKIFAN
Skeifan 17, Reykjavik 108. Tel: (354) 525 5000. FAX: (3541) 525 5001.
STJOERNUBIO
Laugavegi 94, Reykjavik 101. Tel: (3541) 551 6500. FAX: (3541) 554 4630.
EXHIBITORS
BORGARBIO
Akuyeri. Tel: (354) 462 3500. FAX: (354) 461 2796.
HASKOLABIO-UNIVERSITY CINEMA
Hagatorg, Reykjavik 107. Tel: (3541) 561 1212. FAX: (3541) 562 7135. email: cinema@centrum.is
LAUGARASBIO
Laugaras, Reykjavik 104. Tel: (3541) 563 8150. FAX: (3541) 568 0910.

REGNBOGINN
Hverfisgata 54, Reykjavik 101. Tel: (3541) 462 3500. FAX: (3541) 461 2796.
SAM FILM
Alfabakka 8, Reykjavik 109. Tel: (3541) 587 8900. FAX: (3541) 587 8930.
STJOERNUBIO
Laugavegi 94, Reykjavik 101. Tel: (3541) 551 6500. FAX: (3541) 554 4630.

INDIA

Population: 936 million.
Theatres: 12,942.
Admissions: 110 million per week, up from 90 million in 1994.
Box Office Gross: approx. $440 million.
Average Ticket Price: approx. 50¢.
Domestic Feature Production: 795.
Top Ten Films of 1995: Hum Aapke Hain Koun, Dilwale Dulhania Le Jayenge, Karan Arjun, Coolie No. 1, Bewafa Sanam, Raja, Bombay, Hum Se Hai Muqabla. Rangeela, Bandit Queen.

India continued to produce the largest number of films in the world with 795 feature films in 16 languages at its three major centres of production, Bombay, Madras, and Calcutta. Growing audience presence in the theatres and swelling box office receipts augur well for the Indian film industry. Two other important developments during 1995 were a growing rejection of violent themes and the diminishing superstar phenomenon at the box office. The trend seems to have shifted to moderate budget family dramas and teenage romantic love stories. Hollywood films always had a very substantial presence on Indian screens. Of late, starting with Jurassic Park, many more blockbusters such as Speed, The Mask, True Lies and Goldeneye (dubbed in Hindi) have made inroads into the Indian market, largely due to the increase of dubbing in local languages. As in other countries, the multiplex boom has come to India. Decatron, a division of the Bert-Clays exhibition group of Belgium, has joined with local partner, Group Beautiful to design and construct a number of the mega-theaters in India.

EXPORT
With the liberalization of import and export controls, no precise figures of the volume of export are available. Indian films are exported to U. K., Singapore, Gulf countries, Fiji, Indonesia, Malaysia, U. S. A., Mauritius, Canada and Kenya all of which have sizeable Indian populations.

IMPORT
The Indian government's recent trade liberalization policy, eliminating control on the import of foreign films, has opened up the market for world cinema, particularly for established organizations like MPEAA (Motion Picture Export Association of America). As there is no limit on the import of films or prints into the country, nor any restriction on the repatriation of revenue earned, more Hollywood blockbusters are available in theatres and on video at the same time as they are released around the world.

CENSORSHIP
Films can only be exhibited in India after having been certified by the Central Board of Film Certification. The Board has headquarters in Bombay and regional offices in Madras and Calcutta. All members of the Board are appointed by the government. The Board grants 'A' certification for exhibition restricted to Adults above 18 years and 'U' certification for unrestricted exhibition. The Board has 2 other categories for certificates 'UA' and 'S'—UA being the rating between Universal and Adults, and is the equivalent of American PG. The S rating is a certificate for exhibition issued to films of a professional nature, and exhibition is restricted to members of the intended profession. The Board can refuse or ask for modifications to a film before issuing a certificate.

ASSOCIATIONS & ORGANIZATIONS
CINEMATOGRAPH EXIBITOR'S ASSOCIATION OF INDIA
Flat 22/23 B, 1st floor, Vellard View, Tardeo Rd, Bombay 400034.
EASTERN INDIA MOTION PICTURE ASSOCIATION
98E Chowringhee Square, Calcutta.
FEDERATION OF FILM SOCIETIES OF INDIA
C7 Bharat Bhavan, 3 Chittaranjan Avenue, Calcutta 72.
FILM FEDERATION OF INDIA
91 Walkeshwar Rd, Bombay 400006.
INDIAN DOCUMENTARY PRODUCERS ASSOCIATION
305 Famous Cine Bldg., Mahalaxmi, Bombay 400018.
INDIAN FILM EXPORTERS ASSOCIATION
305 Famous Cine Bldg., Mahalaxmi, Bombay 400018.
INDIAN MOTION PICTURE PRODUCERS' ASSOCIATION
Dr. Ambedkar Road, Bandra (W), Bombay 400050.
THE INDIAN MOTION PICTURE DISTRIBUTOR'S ASSOCIATION
33 Vijay Chamber, Tribhuvan Rd, Bombay 400004.
SOUTH INDIA'S FILM CHAMBER OF COMMERCE
122 Mount Road, Madras 60002.

PRINCIPAL EXPORTERS

ANAND EXPORTS
730 Chandra Niwas, Annex Shop 2, 11th Road, Khar, Bombay 400052. Tel: (9122) 646 2755.

CITIZEN INTERNATIONAL
B/6 3rd floor, Everest, Tardeo Road, Bombay 400034. Tel: (9122) 495 1688.

FAIRDEAL EXPORTS LTD.
10 Kashi Kunj, 2nd Flr, Waterfield Road, Bandra, Bombay 400050. FAX: (9122) 604 2429.

NATIONAL FILM DEVELOPMENT CORP. LTD.
Nehru Centre, Dr. A. Besant Road, Worli, Bombay 400018. Tel: (9122) 495 2662.

NEPTUNE ENTERPRISES
c-8/9 Everest 4th flr, Tardeo Road, Bombay 400042. FAX: (9122) 492 0890.

TRIMURTI EXPORTS
B/11 Commerce Centre, Tardeo Road, Bombay 400034. FAX: (9122) 811 667.

RAJSHRI PRODUCTIONS LTD.-BHAVNA
1st floor, Opp Kismat Cinema, Prabhadevi, Bombay 400025. FAX: (9122) 422 9181.

PRINCIPAL IMPORTERS

ALLIED ARTS OF INDIA INC.
Metro House, M. G. Road, Bombay 400020.

COLUMBIA TRISTAR FILMS OF INDIA LTD.
Metro House, 1st floor, M. G. Road, Bombay 400020. Tel: (9122) 201 4264. FAX: (9122) 201 4321.

METRO-GOLDYN-MAYER INDIA LTD.
Metro House, M. G. Road, Bombay 400020.

MODI FILMS INTERNATIONAL
4 Lands End, 54 Byramjee Jeejibhoy Rd., Bandra Bandstand, Bombay 400025. Tel: (9122) 645 8000. FAX: (9122) 645 8282.

PARAMOUNT FILMS OF INDIA LTD.
(also representing Universal), Hague Building, Ballard Estate, P.O. Box 623, Bombay 400038. Tel: (9122) 261 3877. FAX: (9122) 261 2856. Manager: Sarabjit Singh.

TWENTIETH CENTURY FOX CORP. (INDIA) LTD.
Metro House, 3rd floor, M. G. Road, Bombay 400020. Tel: (9122) 205 4290. Calcutta: Tel: (9133) 249 5623. New Delhi: (9111) 332 0351. Madras: Tel: (9144) 852 0078. General Manager: Sunder Kimatrai.

UNITED ARTISTS CORP.
Metro House, M. G. Road, Bombay 400020.

UNIVERSAL PICTURES INDIA P LTD.
Hague Bldg, Sprott Road, Bombay 400020. Tel: (9122) 266 6146. FAX: (9122) 261 2856.

WARNER BROS (F. E.) INDIA
Eros Theatre Bldg., 42 M. Karve Road, Bombay 400020. Tel: (9122) 285 6557. FAX: (9122) 285 0984. Managing Director: Blaise J. Fernandes.
Leslie House, 19A Jawarharlal Nehru Rd., Calcutta 700087. Tel: (9133) 249 5613.
Dinroze Estate, 69 Mount Rd., Madras 600002. Tel: (9144) 852 5964.
Plaza Thatre Bldg., Connaught Circus, New Delhi 110001. Tel: (9111) 332 1544.

—B.D. Garga

INDONESIA

Population: 203 million.
Screens: 2,202.

DISTRIBUTORS

UNITED INTERNATIONAL PICTURES (UIP)
c/o PT Camila Internuse Film, Subentra Bank Building, Suite 716, Jl. Jend, Gatot Subroto Kaz 21, Jakarta 12930, Indonesia. Tel: (6221) 522 0063. FAX: (6221) 522 0064. Representative: Douglas Lee.

ISRAEL

Population: 5.1 million.

ASSOCIATIONS & ORGANIZATIONS

ISRAEL FILM CENTRE
Ministry of Industry & Trade, 30 Gershon Agron St., P. O. Box 299, Jerusalem 94190. Tel: (9722) 750 433. FAX: (9722) 245 110.

ISRAEL FILM SERVICE
Ministry of Education & Culture, P. O. Box 13240, Hakirya Romema, Jerusalem 91130. Tel: (9722) 512 248. FAX: (9722) 526 818.

DISTRIBUTORS AND PRODUCERS

ALBERT D. MATALON & CO.
(Agency for Columbia TriStar & Twentieth Century Fox), 13 Yona Hanavi St., Tel Aviv 63302. Tel: (9723) 516 2020. FAX: (9723) 516 1888. Contact: Amnon Matalon, Charlotte Matalon.

ARGO FILMS
43 Ben Yehuda St., Tel Aviv 63341. Tel: (9723) 522 8251. FAX: (9723) 524 6910.

FORUM FILM LTD.
P.O. Box 12598, Herzlia Pituah, Industrial Zone 46766. Tel: (9729) 562 111. FAX: (9729) 561 581.

NACHSHON FILMS
22 Harakeuel St., Tel Aviv 66183. Tel: (9723) 356 40015. FAX: (9723) 350 05112.

NOAH FILMS/UNITED INTERNATIONAL PICTURES (UIP)
10 Glickson St., Tel Aviv 63567. Tel: (9723) 200 221. FAX: (9723) 202 071. Representative: Jonathan Chissick.

SHAPIRA FILMS
34 Allenby Rd., P. O. Box 4842, Tel Aviv 63325.

SHOVAL-FILM PRODUCTION
32 Allenby Rd., Tel Aviv. Tel: (9723) 659 288. FAX: (9723) 659 289.

TAMUZ FILMS
5 Pinsker St., Tel Aviv. Tel: (9723) 201 512. FAX: (9723) 528 1564.

EXHIBITOR

TAMUZ FILMS
5 Pinsker St., Tel Aviv. Tel: (9723) 201 512. FAX: (9723) 528 1564.

STUDIOS

G. G. ISRAEL STUDIOS
Communications Centre, Neve Ilan, D. N. Harei, Yehuda 90850. Tel: (9722) 349 111. FAX: (9722) 349 9000.

JERUSALEM CAPITAL STUDIOS
P. O. Box 13172, 206 Jaffa Rd., Jerusalem 91131. Tel: (9722) 701 711. FAX: (9722) 381 658.

ORION FILMS
4 Shamgar St., Jerusalem 90058. Tel: (9722) 238 0221. FAX: (9722) 238 0925.

TEL AD JERUSALEM STUDIOS
20 Marcus St., P. O. Box 4111, Jerusalem Theatre Building, Jerusalem 91040. Tel: (9722) 619 988. FAX: (9722) 611 451.

ITALY

Population: 58.2 million.
Screens: 2,000.
Admissions: 97 million.
Box Office Gross: $344 million.
Average Ticket Price: $3.70.
Domestic Feature Production: 75 films.
Top ten Domestic Films of 1995: Viaggi di nozze, Vacanze di natale, La scuola, SPQR—2000e 1/2 anni fa, Al di la delle nuvole, Uomini uomini uomini, L'Uomo delle stelle, Io no spik inglish, Belle al bar, Occhiopinocchio.
Top Ten Films of 1995: Stargate, Pocohontas, Disclosure, Viaggi di nozze, The Mask, Dumb and Dumber, Apollo 13, Vacanze di natale, First Knight, Waterworld.

Italian box office revenues showed moderate gains for the 1995-96 season (which runs September to May), particularly in the first five months of 1996, with a 5.7% increase over the previous year. In the 1994-95 season, admissions had been down by 5.9%, due mainly to a lack of U. S. produced block-busters. However, American films still control 75% of ticket sales, and the success of Stargate and Pocahontas rallied the box office. Italian films Honeymoon (Viaggi di nozze) and Christmas Vacation '95 (Vacanze di natale) brought in a combined $28 million.

The new deputy prime minister of the Italian government, Walter Veltroni, will supervise the Cultural and Environmental Heritage ministry and the Department of Entertainment, both of which are concerned with film production. Veltroni immediately announced his support for tax incentives to aid the ailing Italian production industry. The Italian state producer and distributor Luce joined forces with two smaller distributors and Roman exhibitor Fabio Fefe to develop an alternative theatre circuit to ensure distribution for smaller productions. In the hope that the industry's recovery will continue distributors are offering exhibitors over 400 films for the 1996-97 exhibition season. This is a marked increase over the 295 features of the 1995-96 season.

Only two-thirds of the screens in Italy are open year-round. Eighty-eight percent of the theatres in Italy are single screen. To remedy this, UCI plans to begin building multiplexes in six major Italian cities, in spite of the difficult licensing laws that require each screen within a theater to be licensed individually. Australian Village Roadshow and U.S. based Warner Bros., as well as local exhibitors, have begun construction on multiplexes throughout the country. Progress, however, has been limited due to continued difficulty with municipal authorities and planning commissions.

ASSOCIATIONS & ORGANIZATIONS

ANICA
Viale Regina Margherita 286, Rome 00198. Tel: (396) 4423 1480. FAX: (396) 440 4128.

CINECITTA INTERNATIONAL
Via Tuscolana 1055, Rome 00173. Tel: (396) 722 2824. FAX: (396) 722 3131.

ENTE AUTONOMO GESTIONE CINEMA
Via Tuscolana 1055, Rome 00173. Tel: (396) 722 861. FAX: (396) 722 1883.

PRESIDENZA DEL CONSIGLIO DEI MINISTRI
Via Della Ferracella in Laterano 51, Rome 00184. Tel: (396) 77321. FAX: (396) 759 2602.

DISTRIBUTORS AND PRODUCERS

AB FILM DISTRIBUTORS
Via Monte Zebio 28, Rome 00195. Tel: (396) 321 9554. FAX: (396) 361 3641.

ACADEMY PICTURES
Via F. Ruspoli 8, Rome 00198. Tel: (396) 884 0424. FAX: (396) 841 7043.

ADRIAN CHIESA ENTERPRISES
Via Barnaba Oriani 24A, Rome 00197. Tel: (306) 807 0400. FAX: (306) 8068 7855.

ARTISTI ASSOCIATI INTERNAZIONALE
Via Degli Scipioni 281-283, Rome 00192. Tel: (396) 321 0367. FAX: (396) 321 7245.

BIM DISTRIBUZIONE
Via G. Antonelli 47, Rome 00196. Tel: (396) 323 1057. FAX: (396) 321 1984.

BUENA VISTA INTERNATIONAL ITALIA
Via Palestro 24, Rome 00185. Tel: (396) 445 2269. FAX: (396) 445 1202.

CDI (COMPAGNIA DISTRIBUZIONE INTERNAZIONALE)
Via Saleria 292, Rome 00199. Tel: (309) 854 8821. FAX: (396) 854 1691.

CECCHI GORI GROUP
Via Valadier 42, Rome 00193. Tel: (306) 324 721. FAX: (306) 3247 2300.

CHALLENGE FILM INTERNATIONAL
Via Lazio 9, Rome 00187. Tel: (396) 481 8117. FAX: (396) 482 4890.

CHANCE FILM
Via G. Mercalli 19, Rome 00197. Tel: (396) 808 5041. FAX: (396) 807 0506.

CIDIF
Via Vicenza 5a, Rome 00185. Tel: (396) 446 9636. FAX: (396) 446 9636.

CLEMI CINEMATOGRAFICA
Via Salaria 292, Rome 00199. Tel: (396) 854 8821. FAX: (396) 841 9749.

COLUMBIA TRISTAR FILMS ITALIA
Via Palestro N. 24, Rome 00185. Tel: (396) 494 1196. FAX: (396) 446 9936.

DARC
Via Brenta 2A, Rome 00198. Tel: (396) 854 1144. FAX: (396) 854 1987.

DELTA
Via Elenora Duse 37, Rome 00197. Tel: (396) 808 4458. FAX: (396) 807 9331.

EAGLE PICTURES
Via M. Buonarroti 5, Milan 20149. Tel: (392) 481 4169. FAX: (392) 481 3389.

EDIZIONI EDEN
Via A. Grandi 1, Mazzo Di Rho, Milan 20017. Tel: (392) 9350 9822.

ENRICO GAMBI
Via C. Sul Clitunno 20, Rome 00181. Tel: (396) 788 7746. FAX: (396) 780 6803.

EUPHON TECHNICOLOUR
Via Po 13-15, San Giuliano Milanes 20098. Tel: (392) 9828 0406.

FILMAURO
Via Della Vasca Navale 58, Rome 00146. Tel: (396) 556 0788. FAX: (396) 559 0670.

FULVIA FILM
Via Bruno Nuozzi 36, Rome 00197. Tel: (396) 808 1575. FAX: (396) 808 1510.

GRANATO PRESS
Via Marconi 47, Bologna 40122. Tel: (3951) 237 737.

GRUPPO BEMA
Via N. Martelli 3, Rome 00197. Tel: (396) 808 8551. FAX: (396) 807 5454.

GRUPPO CURTI COMMUNICAZIONE
Via Domenico Cimarosa 18, Rome 00198. Tel: (396) 854 3382. FAX: (396) 855 8105.

IMPERIAL BULLDOG PRODUCTIONS
Via B. Eustachi 12, Milan 20129. Tel: (392) 2952 2363.

INTERNATIONAL MOVIE COMPANY
Lungotevere Flaminio 66, Rome 00196. Tel: (396) 361 0344. FAX: (396) 361 2676.

ISTITUTO LUCE
Via Tuscolana 1055, Rome 00173. Tel: (396) 722 2492. FAX: (396) 722 2493.

ITALIAN INTERNATIONAL FILM
Via Gian Domenico Romagnosi 20, Rome 00196. Tel: (396) 361 1377. FAX: (396) 322 5965.

KINA
Piazza Duomo 16, Milan 20122. Tel: (392) 8646 4102. FAX: (392) 7200 1817.

LIFE INTERNATIONAL
Via Monte Zebio 43, Rome 00195. Tel: (396) 321 5972. FAX: (396) 361 0036.

LUCKY RED
Via Antonio Baiamonti 10, Rome 00195. Tel: (396) 3735 2296. FAX: (396) 3735 2310.

MARGY FILM
Via Orti 2, Milan 20122. Tel: (392) 551 7545. FAX: (392) 545 9918.

MEDUSA FILM
Via Aurelia Antica 422-424, Rome 00165. Tel: (396) 66301. FAX: (396) 663 960.

MFD
Largo A., Ponchielli 6, Rome 00198. Tel: (396) 854 0542. FAX: (396) 854 1691.

MIKADO FILM
Via Victor Pisani 12, Milan 20124. Tel: (392) 6671 1476. FAX: (392) 6671 1488.

MIMA FILMS
Largo V. Alpini 12, Milan 20145. Tel: (392) 349 2860.

MOVIETIME
Via Nicola Ricciotti 11, Rome 00195. Tel: (396) 322 6709. FAX: (396) 3600 0950.

MUSIC BOX FILM
Piazzale Belle Arti 6, Rome 00196. Tel: (396) 322 6685.

MULTIMEDIA FILM DISTRIBUTION
Via L. Ximenes 21, Florence 50125. Tel: (3955) 225 622. FAX: (3955) 233 6726.

NEMO DISTRIBUZIONE CINEMATOGRAFICA
Via Livigno 50, Rome 00188. Tel: (396) 331 851. FAX: (396) 3367 9491.

NINI GRASSIA COMMUNICATIONS
Via Velletri 49, Rome 00198. Tel: (396) 855 1745. FAX: (396) 844 3572.

NUOVE INIZIATIVE COMMERCIALI SRL
Via Flaminia 872, Rome 00191. Tel: (396) 333 9416. FAX: (396) 333 6367.

PAG FILM
Via Velletri 49, Rome 00198. Tel: (396) 855 1745. FAX: (396) 855 2705.

PEGASO INTER-COMMUNICATION
L. Gen. Gonzaga del Vodice 4, Rome 00195. Tel: (396) 360 0830. FAX: (396) 3611 13251.

PENTA DISTRIBUZIONE
Via Aurelia Antica 422, Rome 00165. Tel: (396) 663 901. FAX: (396) 663 9040.

ROYAL FILM ENTERPRISES
Via A. Caroncini 47. Rome 00197. Tel: (396) 808 3506.

SACIS
Via Teulada 66, Rome 00195. Tel: (396) 374 981. FAX: (396) 372 3492.

SILVIO BERLUSCONI COMMUNICATIONS
Corporate Headquarters: Palazzo, Michelangelo, Via Cassanese 224, Segrate , Milan 20090. Tel: (392) 21621. FAX: (392) 2162 8724.

SIRIO FILM
Viale Parioli 28 Int. 1, Rome 00197. Tel: (396) 808 2144. FAX: (396) 808 8748.

SKORPION
Via L. Caro 12-A, Rome 00193. Tel: (396) 324 2223. FAX: (396) 321 0890.

SO CINEMATOGRAFICA
Lungotevere Delle Navi 19, Rome 00196. Tel: (396) 321 5114. FAX: (396) 361 2852.

STARLIGHT
Via Bellerio 30, Milan 20161. Tel: (392) 646 6441. FAX: (392) 646 6444.

SURF FILM
Via Padre Filippini 130, Rome 00144. Tel: (396) 529 3811. FAX: (396) 529 3816

TWENTIETH CENTURY FOX
Largo Amilcare Ponchielli 6, Rome 00198. Tel: (396) 8530 1060. FAX: (396) 8530 0971. Managing Director: Osvaldo De Santis.

UNITED INTERNATIONAL PICTURES
Via Bissolati 20, Rome 00187. Tel: (396) 482 0626. FAX: (396) 482 0628. Manager: Richard Borg.

VARIETY FILMS COMMUNICATIONS
Via Nomentana 257, Rome 00161. Tel: (396) 3600 1409. FAX: (396) 3600 1022.
VISTARAMA
Via Savoia 72, Italy 00198. Tel: (396) 854 6646. FAX: (396) 8535 0050.
WARNER BROS. ITALIA
Via Varesse 16B, Rome 00185. Tel: (396) 446 3191. FAX: (396) 675 1022.
ZENITH DISTRIBUZIONE
Via Soperga 36, Milan 20127. Tel: (392) 261 3207. FAX: (392) 261 0768.

EXHIBITORS
CECCHI GORI GROUP
Via Valadier 42, Rome 00193. Tel: (396) 324 721. FAX: (396) 3247 2300.
CINEMA 5
Via Aurelia Antica 422, Rome 00165. Tel: (396) 663 901. FAX: (396) 6639 0440.
CIRCUITO GERMANI
Piazza Strozzi 2, Florence 50123. Tel: (3955) 295 051.
DAVID QUILLERI
Via Ville Patrizi 10, Rome. Tel: (396) 884 4731.
ERNESTO DI SARRO
Via Soperga 36, Milan 20127. Tel: (392) 260 3207.
ISTITUTO LUCE
Via Tuscolana 1055, Rome 00173. Tel: (396) 722 2492. FAX: (396) 722 2493.
LORENZO VENTAVOLI
Via Pomba 18, Turin 10123. Tel: (3911) 544 083.
LUIGI DE PEDYS
Via Sorpega 43, Milan 20127. Tel: (392) 284 6756.
RAFFAELE GAUDAGNO
Cinema President, Largo Augusto 1, Milan 20122. Tel: (392) 7602 1410. FAX: (392) 7602 2223.
UGO POGGI
Via Fiume 11, Florence 50123. Tel: (3955) 218 682.

JAPAN

Population: 125.5 million.
Screens: 1,734 screens.
Admissions: 130.7 million.
Average Ticket Price: $15.
Domestic Feature Production: 57.
Domestic film themes are becoming more mixed, with romances such as Shall We Dance? beating out local box office staples of animation and monster films. Japan has been the subject of a great deal of interest from foreign exhibitors in 1995-96 given the size of the population and the amount of disposable income. American Multi Cinemas, United Cinemas International and Warner International Theatres have all made inroads, building multiplexes. After the U.S., Japan leads the world in box office revenue. However, most of the 1700 screens in Japan need to be renovated and the equipment upgraded to current standards. AMC plans to build a 16-screen theater and new entertainment center in front of Tokyo Disneyland. The biggest problem that remains for foreign investors is the difficulty of acquiring sufficient real estate and overcoming complex zoning laws to build the kind and number of multiplexes that exist elsewhere. Production and exhibition giant, Shochiku Co., established Shochiku Multiplex Theatres Inc. The new conglomerate is a joint venture with eight construction and real estate companies which is expected to help Shochiku overcome Japan's prohibitive land prices and zoning laws. They have announced plans to build 100 new screens by 1998. Their first project, the Rokko Island seven screen multiplex in Kobe, will open in early 1997. The Toho Towa Company has begun a series of renovations on its existing theaters, and has constructed new theaters on a smaller scale. In spite of these large capital outlays, Japanese exhibitors are under pressure to keep ticket prices "down" to the current $12-$18 range. Accordingly, Shochiku, Toho and Toei, the three largest exhibitors in the country, have planned to expand their concession services and auxiliary facilities to generate more income.

ASSOCIATIONS & ORGANIZATIONS
HI-VISION PROMOTION ASSOCIATION
1-9-6 Sendagaya, Shibuya-ku 151, Tokyo. Tel: (813) 3746 1125. FAX: (813) 3746 1138.
HI-VISION PROMOTION CENTER
Kowa Kawasaki Nishiguchi Bldg. 4F, 66-2, Horikawa-Cho, Saiwai-ku 210, Kanagawa-Ken. Tel: (8144) 541 6331. FAX: (8144) 541 6335.

DISTRIBUTORS AND PRODUCERS
ASCII PICTURES
12 Mori Bldg SF. 1-17-3 Toranomon, Minato-ku, Tokyo 105. Tel: (813) 3581 9501. FAX: (813) 3581 9510.
BUENA VISTA INTERNATIONAL JAPAN
Roppongi DK Bldg., 7-18-23 Roppongi 106, Minato-ku. Tel: (813) 3746 5009. FAX: (813) 3746 0009.

CINE SAISON
Asako Kyobashi Bldg., 2F, 6-13 Kyobasai 1-Chome, Chuo-ku 104, Tokyo. Tel: (813) 3567 1203. FAX: (813) 3567 1295.
DAIEI
1-18-21 Shimbashi, Minato-ku 105, Tokyo. Tel: (813) 3508 2631. FAX: (813) 3508 2030.
DELA CORPORATION
Rozan Bldg. 813, 7-15-13, Roppongi, Minato-ku, 106, Tokyo. Tel: (813) 479 0591. FAX: (813) 479 0602.
EURO SPACE
24-8-601 Sakuragaoka-Cho, Shibuya-ku 150, Tokyo. Tel: (813) 3461 0212. FAX: (813) 3770 1179.
GAGA COMMUNICATIONS
East Roppongi Bldg., 3-16-35 Roppongi, Minato-ku, Tokyo 106. Tel: (813) 5410 3507. FAX: (813) 5410 3558.
MARUBENI CORPORATION
4-2, Ohtemachi 1-Chome, Chiyoda-u, Tokyo. Tel: (813) 282 4136. FAX: (813) 3282 4835.
MEDIA INTERNATIONAL CORPORATION
2-14-5 Akasaka, Minato-ku, Tokyo 107. Tel: (813) 5561 9571. FAX: (813) 5561 9550/49.
MITSUBISHI CORPORATION
3-1, Marunouchi 2-Chome, Chiyoda-ku, Tokyo 100-86. Tel: (813) 3210 7795. FAX: (813) 3210 7397.
OPTO-ELECTRONICS MEDIA DEPT.
New Select, Nakamura Bldg., 7th Floor, 5-9-13 Ginza, Chuo-ku. Tel: (813) 3573 7571. FAX: (813) 3572 0139.
SHIBATA ORGANIZATION
2-10-8 Ginza, Chuo-ku, Tokyo. Tel: (813) 3545 3411. FAX: (813) 3545 3519.
SHOCHIKU COMPANY
13-5, Tsukiji, 1-Chome, Chuo-ku 104, Tokyo. Tel: (813) 3542 5551. FAX: (813) 3545 0703.
SONY PICTURES ENTERTAINMENT, JAPAN
Hamamatsucho-TS Bldg. 5F, 8-14, Chome, Hamamatsucho Minato-ku, Tokyo 105. Tel: (813) 5476 8361. FAX: (813) 5473 8369.
TOEI COMPANY
2-17, 3-Chome, GinzaJapan, Chuo-ku 104, Tokyo. Tel: (813) 535 4641.
TOHO INTERNATIONAL (A DIVISION OF TOHO)
1-8-1, Yurakucho, Chiyoda-ku, Tokyo 100. Tel: (813) 3213 6821. FAX: (813) 3213 6825.
TOHO TOWA COMPANY
6-4, Ginza 2-Chome, Chuo-ku, Tokyo 104. Tel: (813) 3562 0109. FAX: (813) 3535 3656.
TV MAN UNION
30-13 Motoyoyogi-Cho, Shibuya-ku, Tokyo. Tel: (813) 5478 1611. FAX: (813) 5478 8141.
TWENTIETH CENTURY FOX (FAR EAST)
Fukide Bldg. 4-1-13 Toranomon, Minato-ku, Tokyo. Tel: (813) 3436 3421. FAX: (813) 3433 5322.
UNITED INTERNATIONAL PICTURES (FAR EAST)
Riccar Kaikan Bldg. 6-2-1 Ginza, Chuo-ku 104, Tokyo. Tel: (813) 3248 1771. FAX: (813) 3248 6274.
WARNER BROS. THEATRICAL DISTRIBUTION JAPAN
1-2-4 Hamamatsu-Cho, Minato-ku 105, Tokyo. Tel: (813) 5472 8000. FAX: (813) 5472 8029.
WORLD TELEVISION CORPORATION
6F 8-10 Ban Bldg., 8-10-8 Ginza, Chuo-ku, Tokyo 104. Tel: (813) 3571 8047. FAX: (813) 3572 2307.

EXHIBITORS
SHOCHIKU COMPANY
13-5, Tsukiji, 1-Chome, Chuo-ku 104, Tokyo. Tel: (813) 3542 5551. FAX: (813) 3545 0703.
TOEI COMPANY
2-17, 3-Chome, GinzaJapan, Chuo-ku 104, Tokyo. Tel: (813) 535 4641.
TOHO INTERNATIONAL (A DIVISION OF TOHO)
1-8-1, Yurakucho, Chiyoda-ku, Tokyo 100. Tel: (813) 3213 6821. FAX: (813) 3213 6825.
TOHO TOWA COMPANY
6-4, Ginza 2-Chome, Chuo-ku, Tokyo 104. Tel: (813) 3562 0109. FAX: (813) 3535 3656.

MALAYSIA

Population: 19.7 million.
Malaysia, with its rapidly expanding economy, has attracted the attention of Village Roadshow Ltd., Tanjong PLC and the Golden Harvest Group who have planned a number of multiplexes, and have already opened the eight-screen Tanjong Golden Village Bukitr Raja and the seven-screen Tanjong Golden Village Butama. Malaysian audiences have access to feaures from a number of different countries, including Hollywood fare, Malay, Indian, and Cantonese films. Malaysia has traditionally had strict censorship laws, but in 1997 the government intends to introduce film classifications that will prevent films from being cut or banned.

STATE ASSOCIATIONS

MALAYSIAN MINISTRY OF INFORMATION
Angkasapuri, 50610 Kuala Lumpur. Tel: (603) 282 5333. FAX: (603) 282 1255.

MINISTRY OF INTERNATIONAL TRADE & INDUSTRY
Block 10, Government Offices Complex, Jalan Duta 50622, Kuala Lumpur. Tel: (603) 254 0033. FAX: (603) 255 0827.

EXHIBITORS & DISTRIBUTORS
(Local addresses and telephone numbers are listed where available, otherwise please contact the corporate headquarters below)

CATHAY ORGANISATION
Cathay Organisation, 11 Dhoby Ghant #05-00, Cathay Building, Singapore 0922. Tel: 65 337 6855. FAX: (65) 339 5609.

GOLDEN COMMUNICATIONS
8 Hammer Hill Rd., Kowloon, Hong Kong. Tel: (852) 726 5541. FAX: (852) 351 1683.

GOLDEN HARVEST (INTERNATIONAL)
8 Hammer Hill Rd., Kowloon, Hong Kong. Tel: (852) 352 8222. FAX: (852) 351 1683.

TANJONG PLC
17th floor, Menara Boustead, Jln Raja Chulan, 50200 Kuala Lumpur. Tel: (603) 244 3388. FAX: (603) 244 3388.

TWENTIETH CENTURY FOX FILM
Sendirian Berhad, 22 Jalan Padang Walter Grenier off Jalan Imbi, 55100 Kuala Lumpur. Tel: (603) 242 4396. FAX: (603) 248 3129.

UNITED INTERNATIONAL PICTURES
No. 22 Jalan SS26/6, Taman Mayang Jaya, 47301 Petaling Jaya, Selangor, Malaysia. Tel: (603) 704 4899. FAX: (603) 703 7833. Manager: Nicholas Yong.

WARNER BROS.
24 Jalan Padang Walter Grenier off Jalan Imbi, 55100 Kuala Lumpur. Tel: (603) 242 3669. FAX: (603) 248 9670.

MEXICO

Population: 93.9 million.
Screens: 1,550.
Admissions: 63 million.
Domestic feature production: 13 films.
Despite a location close to Hollywood, on average only four U.S. production crews a year ventured into Mexico in the 1990's. Mexican film unions are now easier to deal with, and the Government is launching a national film commission and other steps to woo producers back. Since the fall of the peso, currency rates are favorable for foreign visitors. Activity should be increasing, but it is slow. Texas-based exhibitor Cinemark has opened four multiplexes in Mexico.

DISTRIBUTORS

COLUMBIA TRISTAR FILMS DE MEXICO
Av. Ejercito Nacional, 343-3er Piso, Col. Granada, Delegacion Miguel Hidalgo, Mexico D.F. 11520. Tel: (525) 531 1428. FAX: (525) 545 1986.

UNITED INTERNATIONAL PICTURES
Apartado Postal No. 70 bis, Mexico D.F. 06000. Tel: (525) 255 5727. FAX: (525) 255 5657.

NETHERLANDS

Population: 15.4 million.
Admissions: 17.2 million.
Number of screens: 440 (165 theatres).
Average Ticket Price: $6.70.
Gross box Office: $115 million.
Domestic Feature Production: 16 films.
Top Five Domestic Films of 1995: Flimpje, Flodder 2, Lang Leve Koningin, Antonia, Tot Ziens.
Top Ten Films of 1995: The Lion King, Goldeneye, Filmpje, Die Hard With A Vengeance, Pocahontas, Waterworld, Disclosure, Flodder 3, Dumb and Dumber, Outbreak.
Holland was home to three new multiplexes owned and operated by French media conglomerate Chargeurs SA (owner of the Pathe exhibition circuit). Pathe is now the largest exhibitor in the Netherlands, after buying the 65 screen MGM circuit. A new "co-production protocol" agreement has been signed between the American Film Marketing Association and the Dutch Association of Feature Film Producers that will grant Americans easier access to European co-production deals. The agreement will also qualify many co-productions as European films thus making them ineligible for the laws setting quotas on U.S. entertainment products. And, while U.S. films still reign in the theaters with a reported 90% market share, two native films made the top ten in 1995, grossing a combined $8 million. 1995 was a very strong year for the Dutch box office, showing a 1.2 million ticket increase in admissions, while the number of theatrical releases stayed constant at 239.

ASSOCIATIONS & ORGANIZATIONS

AMSTERDAMSE ARTS COUNCIL
Kloveniersburgwal 47, Amsterdam 1011 JX. Tel: (3120) 626 4315. FAX: (3120) 626 7584.

AMSTERDAM FUND FOR THE ARTS
Keizerstraat 223, Amsterdam 1016 DV. Tel: (3120) 624 2443. FAX: (3120) 624 6053.

ASSOCIATION FOR FILM & TELEVISION PROGRAMME MAKERS (NBF)
Jan Luykenstraat 2, Amsterdam 1071 CM. Tel: (3120) 664 6588. FAX: (3120) 664 3707.

ASSOCIATION OF DUTCH FILM THEATRES
2e der Helstraat 38, 1072 PE Amsterdam. Tel: (3120) 671 67 76. FAX: (3120) 673 08 04.

AUDIOVISUAL PLATFORM/,MEDIA DESK NETHERLANDS
Postbus 256, Sumatralaan 45, Hilversum 1200 AG. Tel: (3135) 623 8641. FAX: (3135) 621 8541.

CARTOON
E Hoogt 4, Utrecht 3512 GW. Tel: (3130) 233 1733. FAX: (3130) 233 1079.

CIRCLE OF DUTCH FILM CRITICS (KNF)
Snelliuslaasn 78, Hilversum 1222 TG. Tel: (3135) 685 6115.

COMMISSARIAAT VOOR DE MEDIA
Emmastraat 51-53, P. O. Box 1426, Hilversum 1200 BK. Tel: (3135) 672 1721. FAX: (3135) 672 1722.

DUTCH ARTS COUNCIL
RJ Schimmelpennincklaan 3, The Hague 2517 JN. Tel: (3170) 346 9619. FAX: (3170) 361 4727.

DUTCH CULTURAL BROADCASTING PROMOTION FUND
Korte Leidsedwarsstraat 12, Amsterdam 1017 RC. Tel: (3120) 623 3901. FAX: (3120) 625 7456.

DUTCH FILM & TELEVISION ACADEMY
Ite Boeremastratt 1, Amsterdam 1054. Tel: (3120) 683 0206. FAX: (3120) 612 6266.

DUTCH FILM MUSEUM
Vondelpark 3, Amsterdam 1071 AA. Tel: (3120) 589 1400. FAX: (3120) 683 3401.

DUTCH FOUNDATION FOR AUDIOVISUAL CONGRESSES (SAM)
Honongstraat 14B, P.O. Box 262, Hilversum 1200 AG. Tel: (3135) 624 5589. FAX: (3135) 623 8208.

FILM INFORMATION & DOCUMENTATION SERVICE (FID)
Postbus 805, Utrecht 3500 AV. Tel: (3130) 332 328. FAX: (3130) 334 018.

FILM MAKERS SOCIETY OF THE NETHERLANDS (GNS)
P. O. Box 581, Amsterdam 1000. Tel: (3120) 676 5088. FAX: (3120) 676 5837.

HOLLAND FILM PROMOTION
Jan Luykenstraat 2, Amsterdam 1071 CM. Tel: (3120) 664 4649. FAX: (3120) 664 9171.

NEDERLANDS FEDERATION FOR CINEMTOGRAPHY
Jan Luykenstraat 2, P. O. Box 75048, Amsterdam 1070 AA. Tel: (3120) 679 9261. FAX: (3120) 675 0398.

NEDERLANDS INSTITUTE FOR AUDIOVISUAL MEDIA
Neuyskade 94, P.O. Box 97734, The Hague 2509 GC. Tel: (3170) 356 4107. FAX: (3170) 364 7756

THE PRODUCERS WORKSHOP (RBS)
Aalbrechtskade 129, Rotterdam 3023 JE. Tel: (3110) 425 7477. FAX: (3110) 425 7193.

SOURCES
Jan Luykenstraat 92, Amsterdam 1071 CT. Tel: (3120) 672 0801. FAX: (3120) 672 0399.

STICHTING FUURLAND/FILMKRANT
Prinsengracht 770-IV, Amsterdam. Tel: (3120) 623 0121. FAX: (3120) 627 5923.

UNITED AUDIOVISUAL PRODUCTION COMPANIES (UAP)
c/o H. Wennink, Mozartlaan 27, Hilversum 1217 CM. Tel: (3135) 623 8677. FAX: (3135) 623 8674.

VEVAM
P.O. Box 581, Amsterdam 1000 AN. Tel: (3120) 676 5088. FAX: (3120) 676 5837.

DISTRIBUTORS AND PRODUCERS

ARGUS FILM
P. O. Box 18269, Amsterdam 1001 ZD. Tel: (3120) 625 4585. FAX: (3120) 626 8978. email: argusfilm@xs4all.nl

BIOSCOOP EXPLOITATIE MINERVA BV
P. O. Box 7220, Amsterdam 1007 JE. Tel: (3120) 644 6823. FAX: (3120) 644 8946.

BUENA VISTA INTERNATIONAL (NETHERLANDS)
P.O. Box 349, Badhoevedorp 1170 AH. (3120) 658 0300. FAX: (3120) 659 3349.

CINEMA EUROPE
Oranje Nassaulaan 53, P. O. Box 5242, 1007 AE Amsterdam. Tel: (3120) 676 7841. FAX: (3120) 671 4968.

CINEMA INTERNATIONAL
P.O. Box 9228, Amsterdam 1006 AE. Tel: (3120) 617 7575. FAX: (3120) 617 7434.

CINEMIEN FILM AND VIDEO DISTRIBUTORS
Entrepotdok 66, Amsterdam 1018 AD. Tel: (3120) 625 8857.
FAX: (3120) 620 9857.
CNR FILM RELEASING
Amstellandlaan 78, Weesp 1382 CH. Tel: (3129) 446 1800.
COLUMBIA TRISTAR FILMS
Van Eeghenst 70, Amsterdam 1071 GK. Tel: (3120) 673 6611.
FAX: (3120) 573 7656.
CONCORDE FILM BENELUX
Lange Voorhout 35, Den Haag 2514 EC. Tel: (3170) 3605810.
FAX: (3170) 360 4925.
THE FILM COMPANY AMSTERDAM
Entrepotdok 66, Amsterdam 1018 AD. Tel: (3120) 620 9504.
FAX: (3120) 620 9857.
HUNGRY EYE PICTURES
Duivendrechtsekade 82, Amsterdam 1096. Tel: (3120) 668
6126. FAX: (3120) 668 3452.
INTERNATIONAL ART FILM
Vodelpark 3, Amsterdam 1071 AA. Tel: (3120) 589 1418. FAX:
(3120) 683 3401.
LAVA FILM DISTRIBUTION & SALES
Korte Leidsedwarstraat 12, Amsterdam 1017 RC. Tel: (3120)
625 5442. FAX: (3120) 620 2426.
MELIOR FILMS
Steynlaan 8, Hilversum 1217 JS. Tel: (3135) 624 5542. FAX:
(3135) 623 5906.
METEOR/POLYGRAM FILM
P.O. Box 432, Hilversum 1217 JS. Tel: (3135) 626 1500. FAX:
(3135) 624 8418.
MOONLIGHT FILMS
Geerdinkhof 236, Amsterdam 1103 PZ. Tel: (3120) 695 3811.
FAX: (3120) 588 4343.
THE MOVIES ARTHOUSES & FILM DISTRIBUTION
Haarlemmerdjik 161, Amsterdam 1013 KH. Tel: (3120) 624
5790. FAX: (3120) 620 6758.
NETHERLANDS INSTITUTE FOR ANIMATION FILM
P.O. Box 9358, Tillburg 5000 HJ. Tel: (3113) 535 4555. FAX:
(3113) 535 0953.
NFM/IAF
Vondelpark 3, Amsterdam 1071 AM. Tel: (3120) 589 1418.
FAX: (3120) 683 3401.
NIS FILM DISTRIBUTION HOLLAND
Abba Paulownastraat 76, The Hague 2518 BJ. Tel: (3170) 356
4208. FAX: (3170) 356 4681.
POLYGRAM FILMED ENTERTAINMENT
P.O. Box 432, Hilversum 1200 AK. Tel: (3135) 626 1700. FAX:
(3135) 624 8418.
SHOOTING STAR FILM COMPANY
Prinsengracht 546, Amsterdam 1017 KK. Tel: (3120) 624 7272.
FAX: (3120) 626 8533.
STICHTING STEMRA
Prof. E. M. Meijerslaan 3, 1183 AV Amstelveen. Tel: (3120)
5407911. FAX: (3120) 5407496.
THREE LINES PICTURES
Laapersveld 68, Hilversum 1213 VB. Tel: (3135) 623 0555.
FAX: (3135) 623 9966.
TWENTIETH CENTURY FOX
Mozartlaan 27, Hilversum 1217 CM. Tel: (3135) 622 2111. FAX:
(3135) 623 9966.
TWIN FILM
Sarphatistraat 183, Amsterdam 1018 GG. Tel: (3120) 6228206.
FAX: (3120) 6248729.
UNITED DUTCH FILM COMPANY
Jan Luykenstraat 5-7, Amsterdam 1071 CJ. Tel: (3120) 675
7774. FAX: (3120) 675 7754.
UNITED INTERNATIONAL PICTURES
Willemsparkweg 112, Amsterdam 1071 HN. Tel: (3120) 662
2991. FAX: (3120) 662 3240. Manager: Max van Praag.
WARNER BROS.
De Boelelaan 16 3H, Amsterdam 1083 HJ. Tel: (3120) 541
1211. FAX: (3120) 644 9001.
EXHIBITORS
ASSOCIATION OF DUTCH FILM THEATRES
2E Der Helstraat 38, Amsterdam 1072 PE. Tel: (3120) 671
6776. FAX: (3120) 673 0804.
BIOSCOOP EXPLOITATIE MINERVA
P.O. Box 7220, Amsterdam 1007 IE. Tel: (3120) 644 6823.
FAX: (3120) 644 8946.
BIOSCOOPONDERNEMING A. F. WOLFF
Ondegracht 154, P.O. Box 777, Utrecht 3500 AT. Tel: (3130)
233 1312. FAX: (3130) 231 5227.
DUTCH FILM MUSEUM
Vondelpark 3, Amsterdam 1071 AA. Tel: (3120) 589 1400. FAX:
(3120) 683 3401.
JOGCHEM'S THEATRES
Veenestraat 31, Bunschoten 3751 GE. Tel: (3133) 298 4884.
FAX: (3133) 298 4908.

PATHE CINEMAS B.V.
P.O. Box 75948, Amsterdam 1070 AX. Tel: (3020) 575 1751.
FAX: (3020) 679 3316. Managing Director: Lauge Neilson.
De Lairessestraat 111-115, Amsterdam 1075 HH. Tel: (3120)
575 1751. FAX: (3120) 662 2085.
THE MOVIES ARTHOUSES & FILM DISTRIBUTION
Haarlemmerdjik 161, Amsterdam 1013 KH. Tel: (3120) 624
5790. FAX: (3120) 620 6758.
UNITED DUTCH FILM COMPANY
Jan Luykenstraat 5-7, Amsterdam 1071 CJ. Tel: (3120) 675
7774. FAX: (3120) 675 7754.
WARNER–MORGAN CREEK–CHARGEURS CINEMAS
De Boelelaan 16, Amsterdam 1083. Tel: (4620) 541 1211. FAX:
(4620) 644 9001.

NEW ZEALAND

Population: 3.4 million.
Screens: 232.
ASSOCIATIONS AND ORGANIZATIONS
CHIEF CENSOR OF FILMS
1 Fairway Dr., P.O. Box 46 009, Lower Hutt. Tel: (644)
5673241. FAX: (644) 5673450.
INDEPENDENT PRODUCERS AND DIRECTORS GUILD
P.O. Box 3969, Wellington. Tel: (644) 385 8055. FAX: (644) 385
8055.
MANU AUTE
P.O. Box 38-141, Petone, Wellington. Tel: (644) 385 9387. FAX:
(644) 384 2580.
NEW ZEALAND FEDERATION OF FILM SOCIETIES INC.
P.O. Box 9544, Te Aro, Wellington. Tel: (644) 385 0162. FAX:
(644) 801 7304.
NEW ZEALAND FILM AND VIDEO TECHNICIANS GUILD
P.O. Box 2949, Auckland. Tel: (649) 372 8917. FAX: (649) 372
8917.
NEW ZEALAND FILM ARCHIVE
Corner Cable St. and Jervois Quay, P.O. Box 9544, Wellington.
Tel: (644) 384 7647. FAX: (644) 384 9719.
NEW ZEALAND FILM COMMISSION
Floor 2, Film Centre, Corner Cable St. and Jervois Quay,
Wellington. Tel: (644) 385 9754. FAX: (644) 384 9719.
QE II ARTS COUNCIL OF NZ
Old Public Trust Bldg., P.O. Box 3806, Wellington. Tel: (644)
473 0880. FAX: (644) 471 2865.
DISTRIBUTORS AND PRODUCERS
ENDEAVOUR ENTERTAINMENT
P.O. Box 68-445, Auckland. Tel: (649) 378 1900. FAX: (649)
378 1905.
EVERARD FILMS
P.O. Box 3664, Auckland 1. Tel: (649) 302 1193. FAX: (649)
302 1192.
FIRST TRAINING
P.O. Box 17096, Auckland. Tel: (649) 579 1332. FAX: (649) 579
5113.
FOOTPRINT FILMS
P.O. Box 1852, Auckland. Tel: (649) 309 8388. FAX: (649)
373 4722.
HOYTS CORPORATION (NZ)
P.O. Box 6445, Auckland. Tel: (649) 303 2739. FAX: (649) 307
0011.
UNITED INTERNATIONAL PICTURES
P.O. Box 105263, Auckland. Tel: (649) 379 6269. FAX: (649)
379 6271.
WARNER BROS (NZ)
P.O. Box 8687, Mt. Eden, Auckland. Tel: (649) 377 5223. FAX:
(649) 309 2795.
EXHIBITORS
EVERARD FILMS
P.O. Box 3664, Auckland 1. Tel: (649) 302 1193. FAX: (649)
302 1192.
HOYTS CORPORATION (NZ)
P.O. Box 6445, Auckland. Tel: (649) 303 2739. FAX: (649) 307
0011.
WELLINGTON FILM SOCIETY
P.O. Box 1584, Wellington. Tel: (644) 384 6817. FAX: (644) 384
6248.

NORWAY

Population: 4.3 million.
Screens: 394.
Average Ticket Price: $5.62.
Box Office Gross: $73.2 million.
Domestic Feature Production: 13 films.
Top Five Domestic Films of 1995: Kirstin Lavransdatter,
Frederiksson's Fashion, Dangerous Waters, Two Green
Feathers, Shut Up and Listen!

Top Ten Films of 1995: The Lion King, Kirstin Lavransdatter, Die Hard With A Vengeance, Dumb and Dumber, The Bridges of Madison County, 101 Dalmations, While You Were Sleeping, House of Angels—The Second Summer, The River Wild, Disclosure.

Unlike most other European countries, with the notable exception of Finland, Norway is not participating in the multiplex boom. The number of multiplex screens has increased from 32 in 1990 to the current 37 with no plans for further construction. Other than a 3% drop in admissions, the only box office event of note in 1995 was the unprecedented success of a Norwegian film, Kirstin Lavransdatter, which grossed almost $4 million.

ASSOCIATIONS & ORGANIZATIONS

NORSK FILMFORBUND
Storengvn 8 B, Jar N-1342. Tel: (47) 2259 1000. FAX: (47) 2212 4865.

NORSK FILMINSTITUTT
Grev Wedelsplass 1, P. O. Box 482 Sentrum, Oslo N-0105. Tel: (47) 2242 8740. FAX: (47) 2233 2277.

NORSK FILMKLUBBFORBUND
Teatergata 3, Oslo N-0180. Tel: (47) 2211 4217. FAX: (47) 2220 7981.

NORSK FILMKRITIKERLAG
Norwegian Society of Film Critics, Radhusgata 7, N-0151 Oslo 1. Tel: (47) 2241 9409. FAX: (47) 2242 0356.

DISTRIBUTORS AND PRODUCERS

ACTION FILM
Valerenggata 47, P. O. Box 9343, Valerenga, Oslo N-0610. Tel: (47) 2267 3131. FAX: (47) 2267 3005.

ARTHAUS
Teatergaten 3, Oslo N-0180. Tel: (47) 2211 2612. FAX: (47) 2220 7981.

BV-FILM INTERNATIONAL
N-4262, Avaldnsnes. Tel: (47) 5284 3544. FAX: (47) 5284 3575.

EGMONT FILM
P. O. Box 417, Asker N-1370. Tel: (47) 6690 4121. FAX: (47) 6690 4175.

EUROPAFILM
Stortingsgt 30, Oslo N-0161. Tel: (47) 2283 4290. FAX: (47) 2283 4151, Mobile: 9202 1017.

FIDALGO
P. O. Box 2054 Posebyen, Kristiansand N-4602. Tel: (47) 3802 4004. FAX: (47) 3802 2354.

HOLLYWOOD FILM
Baneviksgt 7, Stavanger N-4014. Tel: (47) 5153 4045. FAX: (47) 5152 7398.

KIKU VISUAL PRODUCTIONS
Gange Rolvsgt 1, Oslo N-0273. Tel: (47) 2244 9650. FAX: (47) 2244 5098, Mobile: 9424 5294.

KOMMUNENES FILM-CENTRAL
Nedre Voligt 9, Oslo N-0158. Tel: (47) 2241 4325. FAX: (47) 2242 1469

NORSK FILM DISTRIBUTION
Stortingsgt 12, Oslo N-0161. Tel: (47) 2242 3600. FAX: (47) 2242 2313.

ROYAL FILM
Hedmarksgt 15, Oslo N-0658. Tel: (47) 2268 5140. FAX: (47) 2219 7393.

SF NORGE
P. O. Box 6868 St Olavs Plass, Grensen 3, Oslo N-0130. Tel: (47) 2233 4750. FAX: (47) 2242 7293.

UNITED INTERNATIONAL PICTURES
Hegdehaugsvn 27, P. O. Box 7134, Homansbyen, Oslo N-0307. Tel: (47) 2256 6115. FAX: (47) 2256 7181.

WARNER BROS (NORWAY)
Oscarsgt 55, P. O. Box 7053, Homansbyen, Oslo N-0258. Tel: (47) 2243 1800. FAX: (47) 2255 4683.

EXHIBITORS

BERGEN CINEMAS
P.O. Box 4413, Nygardstangen, Bergn N-5028. Tel: (47) 5597 9050. FAX: (47) 5597 9056.

OSLO MUNICIPAL CINEMAS
P.O. Box 1584, Vika, Oslo N-0118. Tel: (47) 2242 7154. FAX: (47) 2233 3945.

TRONDHEIM MUNICIPAL CINEMAS
Prinsensgt. 2B, Kino, Trondheim N-7013. Tel: (47) 7254 7369. FAX: (7352 2550.

PAKISTAN

Population: 131.5 million.
Screens: 650 (includes 200 touring screens)
Average Ticket Price: varies widely between $.15-$1.00.
Box Office Gross: est. Rs. 612 million.
Top Ten Domestic Films of 1995: Munda Bigra Jae, Jeeva, Jo Dar Gaya Woh Mar Gaya, Sargam, Madam Raani, Aakhiri Mujra, Jungle Ka Qanoon, Mushkil, Nange Paaon, Sarak and Khazana.

Top Ten Foreign Films of 1995: Speed, Armour of God, Wonder, Street Fighter, Barbarian Brothers, Shalon Popy Wonder, The Last of the Mohicans, Terminator 2, The Big Brawl, Crystal Hunt.

In spite of the high cost of production, high rates of cinema admission tickets, video piracy, daily telecast of feature films, dish antennas and political disturbances, the number of Pakistani films released stood at 64 as compared to 78 during 1994. Most of the Urdu (national language) films proved big box office hits and helped to change the thematic trend of terrorism to romantic and musical movies. Because of the poor response from filmgoers in the past, co-productions with neighboring countries (excluding India) was down; only one film Tilasmi Jazira (Mysterious Island), a Russian co-production, was released but was not received well at the box office. However, over 12 pictures were shot in foreign locations including Singapore, Sri Lanka, Turkey, the Phillipines, Russia and the United Kingdom. The exhibition of Indian films has been banned since the last war betwen the two countries in 1965, but current Indian films on video are smuggled into Pakistan and are available on the open market. To protect the rights of filmmakers, the government has approved amendments in the existing Copyright Act under which violators can be sentenced to jail for three years with a fine of Rs. 100,000.

Admission costs vary widely in Pakistan. The highest rate, Rs. 30 (including entertainment tax), is charged for a balcony seat in the big cities. Cinemas, showing exclusively imported films, are considering raising the cost to Rs. 40 per seat. The theaters in suburbs and villages generally charge at most half of that price because they provide lesser facilities and filmgoers cannot afford higher prices. Entertainment tax is levied by provincial governments and paid by all cinemagoers. Rates vary by province from a high of 65% to a low of 37.5%. The taxes charged on theater admissions are the highest of all entertainment venues.

Films can be imported by anyone and released upon the receipt of a certificate from the Central Board of Film Censors in Islamabad. Cinemas showing foreign films must allot 15% of their playing time to domestic product. New releases are down considerably over the past year due to a new law which dictates that for the purpose of taxation, all imported films are assessed at $15,000. As a result, over 150 films have remained in customs over the past year. Many of the cinemas which had in the past shown only foreign films are now screening Pakistani features due to the import taxes. The Pakistani film industry is one of the most heavily taxed businesses. Cinemas houses pay 27 different types of taxes. Similarly, every producer, distributor, artist and technician has to pay numerous taxes, including income tax, wealth tax and professional tax among others.

The Central Board of Film Censors has its head office in Islamabad and branches in Lahore and Karachi. The branches examine domestic films while Islamabad certifies imported pictures and films rejected by branches.

ASSOCIATION & ORGANIZATIONS

PAKISTAN FILM DISTRIBUTORS' ASSOCIATION
Geeta Bhawan, Lakshmi Chowk, Lahore. (9242) 58785.

PAKISTAN FILM EXHIBITORS' ASSOCIATION
National Auto Plaza, C Block, Marston Road, Karachi. Tel.: (9221) 776 5806.

PAKISTAN FILM PRODUCERS' ASSOCIATION
Regal Cinema Building, The Mall, Lahore. Tel.: (9242) 322 904.

PAKISTAN MOTION PICTURE INVESTORS' ASSOC.
National Auto Plaza, Marston Road, Karachi. Tel: (9221) 776 5806.

THE CENTRAL BOARD OF FILM CENSORS
Street No. 55-F, Blue Area, Islamabad.

THE NATIONAL FILM DEVELOPMENT CORPORATION LTD.
NAFDEC Complex, Blue Area, Islamabad. Tel: (9251) 821 154. FAX: (9251) 221 863.

IMPORTERS

AJRAK ENTERTAINMENT
357 Hotel Metropole, Karachi. Tel: (9221) 566 1046.

CARRY-ON FILMS
Moon Bldg., 4 Royal Parl, Lahore. Tel: (9242) 222 543.

CONTINENTAL TRADERS
Ex-rally Bros. Bldg., Talpur Rd., Karachi.

MANDVIWALA ENTERTAINMENT
Bishat Cinema Bldg., M.A. Jinnah Rd., Karachi. Tel: (9221) 721 9505. FAX: (9221) 722 7259.

PAKISTAN INTERNATIONAL CORPORATION
Lyric Cinema Bldg., Garden Rd., Karachi. Tel: (9221) 772 7273.

STARLING INTERNATIONAL
Zaibunnisa St., Saddar, Karachi. Tel: (9221) 516 280.

TEE JEES ENTERPRISES
367 Hotel Metropole, Karachi. Tel: (9221) 522 540.

ZEE RAY ENTERPRISES
209 Hotel Metropole, Karachi. Tel: (9221) 514 089. FAX: (9221) 568 0671.

EXHIBITORS
AFSHAN CINEMA
Marston Rd., Karachi.
ALFALAH CINEMA
The Mall, Lahore.
BAMBINO CINEMA
Sh. Imtiaz Husain, Garden Rd., Karachi.
CAPRI CINEMA
Choudhary Bros., M.A. Jinnah Rd., Karachi.
GODEON CINEMA
Marston Rd., Karachi.
GULISTAN CINEMA
Abbot Rd., Lahore.
Also: Murree Rd., Rawalpindi.
LYRIC CINEMA
Haroon Rashid, Garden Rd., Karachi.
JUBILEE CINEMA
Marston Rd., Karachi.
MOTI MAHAL CINEMA
Murree Rd., Rawalpindi.
NAFDEC CINEMA
Blue Area, Islamabad.
NAGHAMA CINEMA
Abbot Rd., Lahore.
NASHEMAN CINEMA
Marston Rd., Karachi.
NISHAT CINEMA
Mr. Nadeem Madviwala, M.A. Jinnah Rd., Karachi.
ODEON CINEMA
The Mall, Lahore.
Also: The Mall, Rawalpindi.
PLAZA CINEMA
Queens Rd., Lahore.
Also: The Mall, Rawalpindi.
RATTAN CINEMA
McLeod Rd., Lahore.
REGAL CINEMA
The Mall, Lahore.
SHABISTAN CINEMA
Abbot Rd., Lahore.
STAR CINEMA
Z.S. Ramzi, Garden Rd., Karachi.

— A. R. Slote

PHILIPPINES

Population: 73.2 million.
Movie Theatres: 270
The Philippines has no quotas on importation of foreign films and no government funding. In spite of this, domestic features continue to outperform films from every other country including the U.S. SM Prime Holdings is the Philippines' largest exhibitor, with 58 movie theaters.

DISTRIBUTORS & PRODUCERS
COLUMBIA PICTURES INDUSTRIES, INC.
Rooms 306-308, Philippine President Lines Bldg., 1000 United Nations Ave., Ermita, Metro Manila 1000. Tel: (632) 521 1381. FAX: (632) 521 3684. Manager: Victor R. Cabrera
MEVER FILMS, INC.
9th floor, Avenue Theatre Bldg., Rizal Ave., Manila.
TWENTIETH CENTURY FOX PHILIPPINES
9th floor, Avenue Theatre Bldg., Rizal Ave., Manila. Tel: (632) 733 8156. FAX: (632) 733 4010. Manager: Rodrigo Dulfo.
UNITED INTERNATIONAL PICTURES
Room 310, Philippine Presidential Lines Bldg., 1000 United Nations Ave., Ermita Metro Manila 1000. Tel: (632) 509304. FAX: (632) 521 6133. Manager: Tristan Leveriza.
WARNER BROS.
Room 311, Philippine Presidential Lines Bldg., 1000 United Nations Ave., Ermita Metro Manila 1000. Tel: (632) 596 991. FAX: (632) 521 2673. Manager: Lucas Pasiliao.

POLAND

Population: 38.7 million.
Average Ticket Price: $1.48.
Admissions: 22.5 million.
Gross Box Office: $40 million.
Theatres: 788.
Domestic Feature Production: 20
Top Five Domestic Films of 1995: Mlode Wilki, Faustyna, Awantura O Basie, Spis Cudzoloznic, Krolestwo Sielonej Polany.
Top Ten Films of 1995: Casper, Lion King, Pocahontas, The Mask, Dumb and Dumber, Waterworld, Forrest Gump, Stargate, Priest, Baby's Day Out.

Poland's exhibition industry continued its recovery in 1995 with 22.5 million admissions against 13.5 million in 1994. In spite of this obvious growth, the 1995 figure is over 80% lower than the 130 million of the industry's largest admission figures in the early 1970's. Of the 200 films released in Poland each year, over two-thirds are from the U.S. The Polish film industry only releases about 10-20 domestic films per year. United Cinemas International and Polish media group ITI plan to build 10 multiplexes with at least 8 screens, each at a cost of $70 million.

ASSOCIATIONS & ORGANIZATIONS
ASSOCIATION OF POLISH FILM PRODUCERS AND PRODUCTION MANAGERS
Pulawska 61, Warsaw 02595. Tel: (482) 245 5586.
ASSOCIATION OF POLISH FILMMAKERS
Krakowskie Przedmiescie, Warsaw 00071. Tel: (482) 227 6785. FAX: Tel: (482) 263 51927.
FEDERATION OF FILM TRADE GUILDS
Pulawska 61, Warsaw 02595. Tel: (482) 628 4855. FAX: (482) 245 5586.
FEDERATION OF NON-PROFESSIONAL FILM CLUBS
Pulawska 61, Warsaw 02595. Tel: (482) 245 5382.
FILM ART FOUNDATION
Krakowskie Przedmiescie 21/23, Warsaw 00071. Tel: (482) 226 1409. FAX: (482) 635 2001.
POLISH FEDERATION OF FILM SOCIETIES
Plocka 16/34, Warsaw 01138. Tel: (482) 232 1187.
POLISH FILM AND TV DIRECTOR'S GUILD
Pulawska 67, Warsaw 02595. Tel: (482) 245 5316. FAX: (482) 245 5316.
POLISH SCREENWRITERS GUILD
Al. Jerozolimskie 49m 41, Warsaw 00697. Tel: (482) 262 81158.
PRIVATE FILM PRODUCERS CLUB
Walbrzyska 14/11, Warsaw 02738. Tel: (482) 243 2861.
SOCIETY OF AUTHORS-ZAIKS
Hipoteczna 21, P. O. Box P-16, Warsaw 00092. Tel: (482) 227 7950. FAX: (482) 635 1347.

DISTRIBUTORS AND PRODUCERS
ANWA FILM INTERNATIONAL
Str. Smolensk 27/3, Krakow 31-12. Tel: (4812) 215 634.
BEST FILM
Ul. Twarda 16a, Warsaw 00105. Tel: (482) 220 1201. FAX: (482) 220 1201.
BLACK CAT
Magnoliowa 2, Lublin. Tel: (4881) 774 654. FAX: (4881) 774 654.
CASS FILM
Wolowska Str. 5, Warsaw 02675. Tel: (482) 243 1431. FAX: (482) 247 3964.
EUROKADR
Potocka Str. 14, Warsaw 01639.Tel: (482) 233 2491. FAX: (482) 233 2491.
EUROPOL
Chelmzynska 180, Warsaw 04464. Tel: (482) 611 1140. FAX: (482) 610 8717.
FILM ART FOUNDATION
Krakowskie Przedmiescie 21/23, Warsaw 00071. Tel: (482) 261 409. FAX: (482) 635 2001.
FILM DISTRIBUTION AGENCY
Trebacka 3, Warsaw 00074. Tel: (482) 635 2038. FAX: (482) 635 1543.
FILM STUDIO HELIOS
Przybyszewskiego 167, Lodz 93120. Tel: (4842) 812 196. FAX: (4842) 812 481.
GRAFFITI
Ul, SW. Gertrudy 5, Krakow 31306. Tel: (4812) 214 294. FAX: (4812) 211 402.
IMP
Ul. Hoza 66, Warsaw 00950. Tel: (482) 6287081. FAX: (482) 628 7691.
ITI CINEMA POLAND
Marszalkowska 138, Warsaw 00004. Tel: (482) 640 4447. FAX: (482) 642 5001.
Wernyhory 14, Warsaw 02727. Tel: (482) 243 3488. FAX: (482) 243 4532.
KRAKATAU
Ul, Kaminskiego 29/12, Lodz. Tel: (4842) 788 536.
NEPTUN FILM
Piwna 22, Gdansk 80831. Tel: (4858) 314 876. FAX: (4858) 313 744.
NEPTUN VIDEO CENTRE
Grzybowska Str. 6-10, Warsaw 00131. Tel: (482) 224 0395. FAX: (482) 224 5969.
ODRA FILM
Ul. Boguslawskiego 14, Wroclaw 50023. Tel: (4871) 33487. FAX: (4871) 441 088.
SILESIA-FILM
Head Office: Plebiscytowa 46, Katowice 40041. Tel: (483) 251 2284. FAX: (483) 251 2245.

STARCUT FILM-POLAND
6 Wybickiego St, Rumia 84230. Tel: (4858) 219 769.
SYRENA ENTERTAINMENT GROUP
Marsz al kowska 115, Warsaw 00102. Tel: (482) 220 9053.
FAX: (482) 227 3500.
VISION
Rydygiera 7, Warsaw 01793. Tel: (482) 239 0753. FAX: (482)
239 2575.
WARNER BROS. POLAND
Ul. Palawska 37/39, Warsaw 02508. Tel: (482) 249 5959. FAX:
(482) 249 3598.

EXHIBITORS
APOLLO-FILM STATE FILM DISTRIBUTOR
Pychowicka 7, Krakow 30960. Tel: (4812) 671 355. FAX: (4812)
671 552
FILM STUDIO HELIOS
Przybyszewskiego 167, Lodz 93120. Tel (4842) 812 196. FAX:
(4842) 812 481.
IFDF MAX
Jagiellonska Str 26, Warsaw 03719. Tel: (482) 219 0481. FAX:
(482) 218 1783.
ITI CINEMA POLAND
Marszalkowska 138, Warsaw 00004. Tel: (482) 640 4447. FAX:
(482) 642 5001.
NEPTUN FILM
Piwna 22, Gdansk 80831. Tel: (4858) 313 744. FAX: (4858) 313
744.

PORTUGAL

Population: 10.5 million.
Screens: 249.
Admissions: 12.5 million.
Box Office Gross: $18.1 million.
Average Ticket Price: $2.83.
U.S. films hold a 95% market share in Portugal. Lusomundo, the
exhibition giant, commands a 40% share of the market and has
entered into an agreement with Warner Bros. International
Theaters to exploit the expanding multiplex market. The joint
venture aims to open 15 new multiplexes over the next four
years. Cinesa, a Spanish subsidiary of UCI, will open its first
multiplex in Lisbon in 1997, followed by another six in major
cities. AMC, not to be outdone, has opened a 20-screen cinema
in Portugal. The expansion will continue in spite of the fact that
Portugal's admissions have fallen 33% since 1990, and cinema
admissions per capita are the second lowest in the EU, only
slightly ahead of Greece.

ASSOCIATIONS & ORGANIZATIONS
CINEMA, TELEVISION & VIDEO TRADE UNION
Rua D Pedro V 60, 1 Esq., Lisbon 1200. Tel: (3511) 342 2660.
FAX: (3511) 342 6943.
CINEMATICA PORTUGUESA
Rua Barata Salgueiro 39, Lisbon 1200. Tel: (3511) 354 6279.
FAX: (3511) 352 3180.
PORTUGUESE FILM INSTITUTE
Rua Sao Pedro de Alcantara 45, 1st floor, Lisbon 1250. Tel:
(3511) 345 6634. FAX: (3511) 347 2777.
SECRETARY OF STATE FOR CULTURE
Palacio Nacional da Ajuda, Lisbon 1300. Tel: (3511) 364 9867.
FAX: (3511) 364 9872.
DISTRIBUTORS AND PRODUCERS
ATALANTA FILMES
Avenida D. Carlos 1, 72 D-3, Lisbon 1200. Tel: (3511) 397
0680. FAX: (3511) 397 4723.
COLUMBIA TRISTAR & WARNER FILMES DE PORTUGAL
Av Duque De Loule 90 3 Esq., Lisbon 1000. Tel: (3511) 572
007. FAX: (3511) 315 5389.
FILMES LUSOMUNDO S.A.
Praca de Aleguia 22, Apartado 1063, Lisbon 1294. Tel: (3511)
347 4561. FAX: (3511) 346 5349.
FILMES CASTELLO LOPES
Rua de St. Amaro Estrelo 17-A, 5955. Tel: (3511) 395 5955.
FAX: (3511) 395 5924.
MEDIA
Avenida Joao Crisostomo, 38 C-1, Escr. 3, Lisbon 1050. Tel:
(3511) 353 1616. FAX: (3511) 353 1636.
UNITED INTERNATIONAL PICTURES
(see Filmes Lusomundo)
VITORIA FILME
Avenida Duquer de Loul, 75, 3 Dt, Lisbon 1000. Tel: (3511) 546
195. FAX: (3511) 546 195.

EXHIBITORS
ATALANTA FILMES
Avenida D. Carlos 1, 72 D-3, Lisbon 1200. Tel: (3511) 397
0680. FAX: (3511) 397 4723.
FILMES CASTELO LOPES
Rua de St Amaro Estrelo 17-A, 5955. FAX: (3511) 395 5924.

LUSOMUNDO
Praca da Alegria 22, Lisbon 1294. Tel: (3511) 347 4561. FAX:
(3511) 346 5349.
PAULO MARTINS
Avenida Duque de Loul, 75, 3 Dt, Lisbon 1000. Tel: (3511) 546
195. FAX: (3511) 546 195.
WARNER LUSOMUNDO—SOCIEDADE IBERICA
DE CINEMAS, LDA.
Rua Luciano Cordeiro 113, 10 Lisbon 1150. Tel: (3511) 315
0860. FAX: (3511) 355 7784.

RUSSIAN FEDERATION

Population: 149.9 million.
Screens: 1,468.
Admissions: 100 million.
Domestic Feature Production: 90 films.
Top Five Films of 1995: Beethoven 2, Leon, True Lies, Farinelli,
Un indien a Paris.
Cinema admissions have fallen by 80% in Russia since 1992.
Due to the loss of revenue, cinemas have closed by the hundreds, with some estimating that up to 40% of existing screens
close each year. Yet, in 1996, the Russian film industry experienced a wave of renewal with homegrown films becoming a big
box office draw. Audiences are tired of the usual fare—independent Hollywood 'B' movies—and have expressed a preference
for Russian films with nostalgic themes. The U.S. majors have
thus far avoided Russia, due largely to the immense piracy problems.

ASSOCIATIONS & ORGANIZATIONS
COMMITTEE OF CINEMATOGRAPHY OF THE RUSSIAN
FEDERATION (ROSKOMKINO)
7 Mal Gnezdnikovsky Ln., Moscow 103877. Tel: (7095) 229
8224. FAX: (7095) 229 4522.
CONFEDERATION OF FILMMAKERS UNIONS
Maly Kozikhinsky Per 11, Moscow 103001. Tel: (7095) 299
7020. FAX: (7095) 299 3880.
FEDERATION OF CINEMA CLUBS
Konstantin Simonov St. 5, Cor 3, Apt. 41, Moscow 125167. Tel:
(7095) 255 9105. FAX: (7095) 393 4896.
FILMMAKERS UNION OF REPUBLIC OF BELARUS
5 Karl Marx St., Minsk, Belarus 220050. Tel: (70172) 271 002.
FAX: (70172) 271 451.
KAZAKHINO
Abylai Khana St. 93/95, Alma-Ata 480091, Kazakhstan. Tel:
(7327) 269 2418.
STATE FILM CONCERN GRUZIA-FILM
Akhmedeli St. 10a, Tbilisi 308059, Georgia. Tel: (99532) 510
627. FAX: (99532) 510 010.
STATE FILM CONCERN MOLDOVA FILM
Enunesku St. 10, Kishinev 277012, Moldova. Tel: (3732) 234
405. FAX: (3732) 234 405.
ST. PETERSBURG CULTURE FUND
Nevsky Prosp. 31, St. Petersburg 191011. Tel: (7812) 311
8349. FAX: (7812) 315 1701.
DISTRIBUTORS AND PRODUCERS
ARGUS
Olypissicis Prospect 16, Moscow 129090. Tel: (7095) 288
4027. FAX: (7095) 288 9147.
ATLANT CO
Kirovogradskaya St. 9A, Moscow 113587. Tel: (7095) 312 5203.
FAX: (7095) 312 8127.
EAST WEST CREATIVE ASSOCIATES
Bldg. 4, Stankevich St., Moscow 113587. Tel: (7095) 229 7100.
FAX: (7095) 200 4429.
EKATERINBURG ART
Chebyshev St., 5th floor, Ekaterinburg 620062. Tel: (73432)
442 1120. FAX: (73432) 442 343.
GEMINI FILM
Bldg. 6, Myansnitskaya St. 40, Moscow 101000. Tel: (7095) 921
0854. FAX: (7095) 921 2394.
GORKY FILM STUDIOS
8 Einstein St., Moscow 129226. Tel: (7095) 181 0183. FAX:
(7095) 188 9871.
KINOTON
Okruzhnoy Proyezd 16, Moscow 105058. Tel: (7095) 290 3412.
FAX: (7095) 200 5612.
KREDO-ASPEK
Novy Arbat St. 11, Moscow 121019. Tel: (7095) 291 7269. FAX:
(7095) 219 6880.
MOST MEDIA
Maly Gnezdnikovsky 7, Moscow 103877. Tel: (7095) 229 1172.
FAX: (7095) 229 1274.
PARADISE LTD. AGENCY
12a Christoprudny Blvd., Suite 601, Moscow 101000. FAX:
(7095) 924 1331.
RUSSKOYE VIDEO
Malaya Nevka 4, St. Petersburg 191035. Tel: (7812) 234 4207.

SKIP CENTRE
2 Flievskaya St. 7/19, Moscow 121096. Tel: (7095) 145 2459. FAX: (7095) 145 3355.
SOVENTURE
Bolshiye Kamenshchiki 17, Lorpus 1, Moscow 109172. Tel: (7095) 912 3065. FAX: (7095) 911 0665.
SOVEXPORTFILM
14 Kalashny Pereulok St., Moscow 103009. Tel: (7095) 290 2053. FAX: (7095) 200 1256.
TRETYAKOVKA
8 Maly Tolmachevsky per, Moscow 109017. Tel: (7095) 231 0183. FAX: (7095) 231 4857.

SINGAPORE

Population: 2.8 million.
Screens: 90 screens.
Golden Harvest, the Hong Kong exhibition giant that currently co-owns three cinemas in Singapore, plans to open four new multiplexes with a total of 26 screens by the end of 1997.

ORGANIZATIONS
MINISTRY OF INFORMATION & THE ARTS
#36-00 PSA Bldg., 460 Alexandra Rd., Singapore. Tel: (65) 279 9707. FAX: (65) 279 9784.
SINGAPORE FILM SOCIETY
Robinson Rd., P. O. Box 3714, Singapore. Tel: (65) 235 2088. FAX: (65) 732 2088.
DISTRIBUTORS AND PRODUCERS
ALLSTAR FILM
Block 136, Alexandra Rd., 01-161, Singapore 0315. Tel: (65) 472 7554. FAX: (65) 474 2676.
CATHAY ASIA FILMS
11 Dhoby Ghant #05-00, Cathay Building, Singapore 0922. Tel: (65) 337 6855. FAX: (65) 339 5609.
CINEMA VISION
2 Leng Kee Rd., Singapore 0315. Tel: (65) 472 2233. FAX: (65) 475 3346.
ENG WAH FILM
400 Orchard Rd., 16-06 Orchard Towers, Singapore 0923. Tel: (65) 734 0028.
FAIRMOUNT INTERNATIONAL
200 Jalan Sultan, 08-02 Textile Centre, Singapore 0719. Tel: (65) 296 5904. FAX: (65) 293 4742.
GLOBE FILM DISTRIBUTORS
Block 1, Rochor Rd., Singapore 0718. Tel: (65) 296 6324. FAX: (65) 296 6742.
GOLDEN VILLAGE ENTERTAINMENT
11 Dhoby Ghaut, #15-04 Cathay Bldg., Singapore 0922. Tel: (65) 334 3766. FAX: (65) 334 8397. Managing Director: John Crawford.
KIM FONG FILM
05-03, Block 8, Lorong Bakur Batu, Singapore 1334. Tel: (65) 7480265. FAX: (65) 7470939.
OVERSEAS MOVIE
#04-21 People's Park Complex, Singapore 0106. Tel: (65) 535 0555. FAX: (65) 535 0783.
SHAW ORGANISATION
Shaw Centre, 1 Scotts Rd., Singapore 0922. Tel: (65) 235 2077. FAX: (65) 235 2860.
TWENTIETH CENTURY FOX FILM (EAST)
400 Orchard Rd., 17-064 Orchard Towers, Singapore 0923. Tel: (65) 723 0952. FAX: (65) 235 4957.
UNITED INTERNATIONAL PICTURES
15-04 Shaw Centre, 1 Scotts Rd., Singapore 0922. Tel: (65) 737 2484. FAX: (65) 235 3667.
WARNER BROS. SINGAPORE
04-02 Midlands House, 122 Middle Rd., Singapore 0718. Tel: (65) 337 5060. FAX: (65) 339 1709.

SOUTH AFRICA

Population: 45 million.
Number of Screens: 650.
Admission Prices: From approx. $4.00 in Johannesburg to ¢20 in rural areas.
Of 51 nations in Africa, South Africa, Egypt and Zimbabwe are the only nations that have legitimate exhibitors who pay royalties and fees to distributors. Until 1990, apartheid laws banned blacks from attending theatres in the predominately white enclaves. All exhibition to the black majority was by pirates, who occasionally showed films on bedsheets attached to trees. Recently a small chain of theatre franchises aimed at the black market, Maxi Movies, has begun operating in the townships and rural areas. Maxi Movies is controlled by Ster-Kinekor

ASSOCIATIONS & ORGANIZATIONS
AFRICAN FILM AND TELEVISION COLLECTIVE
P. O. Box 42723, Fordsbury 2033. Tel: (2711) 804 5186. FAX: (2711) 838 3034.

CINEMA THEATRE AND VIDEO UNION
P. O. Box 81338, Parkhurst 2120. Tel: (2711) 782 4273. FAX: (2711) 492 1221.
DEPARTMENT OF HOME AFFAIRS-FILM DEPARTMENT
Private Bag X114, Pretoria 0001. Tel: (2712) 314 3328.
FILM AND ALLIED WORKERS ORGANISATION
P. O. Box 16939, Doornfontein 2028. Tel: (2711) 402 4570. FAX: (2711) 402 0777.
PROFESSIONAL PHOTOGRAPHERS OF SOUTHERN AFRICA
P. O. Box 47044, Parklands, Johannesburg 2121. Tel: (2711) 880 9110. FAX: (2711) 880 1648.
SOUTH AFRICAN SOCIETY OF CINEMATOGRAPHERS
P. O. Box 17465, Sunward Park 1470. Tel: (2711) 902 2826.
SOUTH AFRICAN FILM AND TELEVISION INSTITUTE
P. O. Box 3512, Halfway House 1685. Tel: (2711) 315 0140. FAX: (2711) 315 0146.

DISTRIBUTORS AND PRODUCERS
ATLAS MOTION PICTURE CORPORATION
P. O. Box 87385, Houghton 2041. Tel: (2711) 728 4912. FAX: (2711) 728 5287.
CONCORD FILMS
P. O. Box 8112, Johannesburg 2000. Tel: (2711) 337 5581. FAX: (2711) 337 3913.
EMS
24 Napier Road, Richmond, Johannesburg. Tel: (2711) 482 4470. FAX: (2711) 482 2552.
ENTERTAINMENT WORKERS' UNION
P. O. Box 81338, Parkhurst 2120. Tel: (2711) 782 4273.
FILM FARE INTERNATIONAL
P. O. Box 24, Crawford 7770. Tel: (2721) 637 8028. FAX: (2721) 637 3138.
GENESIS RELEASING
Charter House, 3 Robertson St. Observatory Ext 2198, Johannesburg. Tel: (2711) 487 1060. FAX: (2711) 487 1040.
JAGUAR FILM DISTRIBUTORS
P. O. Box 53126, Yellowood Park 4011. Tel: (2731) 420 610.
MIMOSA FILM DISTRIBUTORS
P. O. Box 50019, Randburg 2125. Tel: (2711) 787 1075.
SAVAGE EYE FILMWORKS
6A Glade Rd., Rondebosch, Cape Town 7700. Tel: (2721) 686 3858. FAX: (2721) 244 313.
STER-KINEKOR (PTY) LIMITED
Interleisure Park, 185 Katherine St., Eastgate, Sandton. Tel: (2711) 4457 7300. FAX: (2711) 444 1003.
UNITED INTERNATIONAL PICTURES
Castrol House, 7 Junction Ave., Parktown, Johannesburg 2193. Tel: (2711) 484 4215. FAX: (2711) 484 3339.

STUDIOS
FRAMEWORK TELEVISION
P. O. Box 5200, Horizon 1730. Tel: (2711) 475 4220. FAX: (2711) 475 5333.
SONNEBLOM FILM PRODUCTIONS
P. O. Box 3940, Honeydew 2040. Tel: (2711) 794 2100. FAX: (2711) 794 2061.
SONOVISION STUDIOS
P. O. Box 783133, Sandton 2146. Tel: (2711) 783 1100. FAX: (2711) 883 3834.
TORON INTERNATIONAL
P. O. Box 89271, Lyndhurst 2106. Tel: (2711) 786 2360. FAX: (2711) 440 5132.

SOUTH KOREA

Population: 45.5 million.
DISTRIBUTORS
COLUMBIA TRISTAR FILMS OF KOREA
Songpa Bldg., 505 Shinsa-Dong, Kangnam-Gu, Seoul. Tel: (9822) 545 0101. FAX: (822) 546 0020.
DAEWOO
(Agency for New Line International), 12th floor, Daewood Foundation Bldg., 526 5 Ga Namdaemoon Ro, Jung Gu 100-095, Seoul.
TWENTIETH CENTURY FOX KOREA
Asia Cement Bldg., 8th floor, 726 Yeok Sam-dong, Kangnam-ku, Seoul. Tel: (822) 3452 5980. FAX: (822) 3452 7223.
UIP—CIC FILM & VIDEO DISTRIBUTION
Jang Choong Bldg., 2nd floor, 120-1, 1Ka, Jang Choong-Dong, Jung-ku, Seoul. Tel: (822) 276 0077. FAX: (822) 273 8208. Manager: H.K. Lee.
WALT DISNEY KOREA
4th floor, Samboo Bldg., 676 Yeok Sam-dong, Kangam-ku, Seoul. Tel: (822) 527 0400. FAX: (822) 527 0399.
WARNER BROS KOREA
M Bldg., 6th floor, 221-5 Nonhyun-dong, Kangnam-ku, Seoul. Tel: (822) 547 0181. FAX: (822) 547 8396.

SPAIN

Population: 39.4 million.
Screens: 2,042.
Admissions: 90 million.
Average Ticket Price: $3.77.
Domestic Feature Production: 56 films.
Top Five Domestic Films of 1995: Turkish Passion, Historis Del Kronen, Los Hombres Siempre Mienten, Running Out of Time, Land and Freedom.
Top Ten Films of 1995: Pulp Fiction, Die Hard With A Vengeance, Disclosure, Legends of the Fall, The Lion King, Mary Shelley's Frankenstein, Dumb and Dumber, Color of Night, Interview With A Vampire, The Shawshank Redemption.
Admissions continue to rise dramatically, hitting 90 million in 1995, one million more than 1994. Additionally, domestic fims drew an increase of 43% over 1994 at the box office. 1995 saw the contruction of 112 new screens, with another 100 expected by the beginning of 1997. The boom in admissions has encouraged foreign investment. Warner Bros. International Theaters, Prisa, and the Portuguese company Lusomundo have announced that they will jointly build 20 multiplexes across the country; UCI, French company UGC, Belgian exhibitor Kinepolis and American Multi Cinemas all begun construction on multplexes, most of them in, or around, Madrid. By 1997, over 10% of Spain's theaters will have five or more screens.
Distributor Prime Films entered the production business with the aim of moving into the Latin American and European markets.

ASSOCIATIONS & ORGANIZATIONS

ASSEMBLY OF SPANISH DIRECTORS & PRODUCERS
San Lorenzo 11, Madrid 28004. Tel: (341) 319 6844.

ASSOCIATION OF NATIONAL FILM DISTRIBUTORS & PRODUCERS
Blanca de Navarra 7, Madrid 28010. Tel: (341) 308 0120. FAX: (341) 319 0036.

CATALONIA FILM COMMISSION
Alicante 27, 3F, Barcelona 08022. Tel: (343) 417 9551. FAX: (343) 418 2205.

FEDERACION ESPANOLA DE PRODUCTORAS DE CINE PUBLICITARIO Y CORTOMETRAJE
Sanchez Pacheco 64 Entreplanta, Madrid 28002. Tel.: (341) 413 2454. FAX: 34 1 519 2019.

FEDERATION OF SPANISH FILM COMPANIES
Velazquez 10 3 deha., Madrid 28001. Tel: (341) 576 9913. FAX: (341) 576 2774.

FEDERATION OF THEATRICAL DISTRIBUTORS
Velazquez 10, 3 deha., Madrid 28001. Tel: (341) 576 0820. FAX: (341) 576 0028.

MINISTRY OF CULTURE
Plaza del Rey 1, Madrid 28071. Tel: (341) 532 0093. FAX: (341) 522 9377.

PROCINE FOUNDATION
Ayala 20-5 B, Madrid 28001. Tel.: (341) 576 6066. FAX: (341) 578 1915.

DISTRIBUTORS AND PRODUCERS

ALAS FILMS
Maestro Guerrero 4, Madrid 28015. Tel.: (341) 547 6664. FAX: (341) 542 7887.

ALTA FILMS
Martin de los Heros 12, Madrid 28008. Tel: (341) 542 2702. FAX: (341) 542 8777.

ARABA FILMS
Dr. Arce 1b, Madrid 28002. Tel: (341) 564 9498. FAX: (341) 564 5738.

BARTON FILMS S.I.
Iturribide 68, Lonja, Bolbao. Tel: (344) 433 7103. FAX: (344) 433 5086.

BRB INTERNATIONAL
Autovia Fuencarral Alcobendas, Km. 12 220 Edificio Auge 1, Madrid 28049. Tel: (341) 358 9596. FAX: (341) 358 9818.

BREPI FILMS
Corredera Baja de San Pablo, 2-30, Madrid 28004. (341) 522 3108. FAX: (341) 522 5721.

BUENA VISTA INTERNATIONAL SPAIN
Jose Bardasano Baos 9-11, Edificio Gorbea 3, Madrid 28016. Tel: (341) 383 0732. FAX: (341) 766 9241.

CINE COMPANY
Zurbano 74, Madrid 28010. Tel: (341) 442 2944. FAX: (341) 441 0098.

CINEMUSSY
Quintana No. 1, 2 B, Madrid 28029. Tel: (341) 542 0036. FAX: (341) 559 9069.

COLUMBIA TRI-STAR FILMS DE ESPANA
c/o Hernandez de Tejada 3, Madrid 28027. Tel: (341) 377 7100. FAX: (341) 377 7128.
Edificio Piovera Azul, Peonias 2, Madrid 28042. Tel: (341) 320 0744. FAX: (341) 320 6105.

DAGA FILMS
Desengano 12 Madrid 28004. Tel: (341) 522 7218.

DISTRIBUIDORA COQUILLAT
Denia 43, Valencia 46006. Tel: (346) 341 7000. FAX: (346) 380 4270.

ESICMA
Maestro Lasalle 15, 28016 Madrid. Tel: (341) 345 8708. FAX: (341) 355 7991.

FILMAX GROUP
P. San Gervasio 16-20, Barcelona 08022. Tel: (343) 453 0303. FAX: (343) 453 0608.

FILMAYER INTERNATIONAL
Arda Brugos, 8-A Planta 10-1, Madrid 28036. Tel: (341) 383 0265. FAX: (341) 383 0845.

GOLEM DISTRIBUCION
Corezonde Maria 56-9A, Madrid 28002. Tel: (341) 519 1737. FAX: (341) 416 3626.

HISPANO FOXFILM S.A.E.
Avenida de Bourgos 8-A, Planta 18, Madrid 28036. Tel: (341) 343 4640. FAX: (341) 343 4646.

IBEROAMERICANA FILMS INTERNACIONAL
Velazquez 12, 7 & 8, Madrid 28001. Tel: (341) 4314246. FAX: (341) 435 5994. Contact: Andres Vicente Gomez.

IMPALA MONTILLA
Manuel Motilla 1, Madrid 28016. Tel: (341) 350 6200. FAX: (341) 345 1948. Contact: Jose Antonio Sainz de Vicuna.

JOSE ESTEBAN ALENDA
Trujillos 7, Madrid 28013. Tel: (341) 541 1838. FAX: (341) 548 3791.

KALEKIA
Comino del Obispo 25, Mostcles, Madrid 28935. Tel: (341) 616 3710. FAX: (341) 616 3710.

LAUREN FILM
Tetuan 29-2, Madrid 28013. Tel: (341) 521 8284. FAX: (341) 522 0616.

LECAS FILM DISTRIBUCION
Galileo 82, Madrid 28015. Tel: (341) 447 4657. FAX: (341) 448 8978.

LIDER FILMS
Isla de Fuenteventura No, 21-10, San Sebastian de los Reyes, Madrid 28700. Tel: (341) 663 9000. FAX: (341) 663 9320.

MOVIERECORD
Martires de Alcala 4, Madrid 28015. Tel: (341) 559 9205. FAX: (341) 547 5985. Contact: Jesus Martin Sanz.

MULTIVIDEO
La Luna 15, Madrid 28004. Tel: (341) 522 9347. FAX: (341) 532 8695.

MUSIDORA FILMS
Calle Princesa 17, Madrid 28008. Tel: (341) 541 6869. FAX: (341) 541 5482. Contact: Javier de Garcillan.

NEPTUNO FILMS
Cardaire 36-38, Terassa, Barcelona 08221. Tel: (341) 784 1622. FAX: (341) 784 2938.

ORO FILMS
Amigo 17-Bajo, Barcelona 08021. Tel: (343) 200 4911. FAX: (343) 200 4321. Contact: Luis Lopez Val.

POLYGRAM FILM ESPANA
Manuel Montilla 1, Madrid 28016. Tel: (341) 350 6200. FAX: (341) 350 1371.

PRIME FILMS
Padre Xitre 5-7C, Madrid 28002. Tel: (341) 519 0181. FAX: (341) 413 0772.

REX FILMS
Provenza 197-199. Barcelona 08008. Tel: (343) 451 3315. FAX: (343) 453 5391.

SOGEPAQ DISTRIBUCION
Manual Montilla 1, Madrid 28016. Tel: (341) 350 6200. FAX: (341) 345 1948.

SUCESORES DES JESUS RODRIGUEZ DORESTA
Triana 68-1, Las Palmas de Gran Canaria 35002. Tel: (3428) 371 560. FAX: (3428) 371 560.

SUPER FILMS S.A.
Provenza 197/199, Barcelona 08008. Tel: (343) 451 3315. FAX: (343) 453 5391.

SURF FILMS
Zurbano 74, Madrid 28010. Tel: (341) 442 2944. FAX: (341) 0441 0098.

TRIPICTURES
Doce Octubre 28, Madrid 28009. Tel: (341) 574 9008. FAX: (341) 574 9005.

U FILMS/UNION FILMS
Maestro Guerrero 4, Madrid 28015. Tel: (341) 547 6664. FAX: (341) 542 7887.

UNITED INTERNATIONAL PICTURES
Plaza del Callao 4-6, Madrid 28013. Tel: (341) 522 7261. FAX: (341) 532 2384. Manager: Gaulberto Bana.

VHERO FILMS
Capitan Haya 58 3H, Madrid 28020. Tel: (341) 571 6490. FAX: (341) 572 0280.

VICTORY FILMS
Cuesta de Santo Domingo 11, Madrid 28013. Tel: (341) 541 8734. FAX: (341) 541 4612.
VIRGIN VISION
Gran Via 36 8, Madrid 28013. Tel: (341) 523 3870. FAX: (341) 532 0122.
WANDA FILMS
Avenida de Europa 9, Pozuelo, Madrid 28224. Tel: (341) 352 8376. FAX: (341) 345 1948.
WARNER ESPANOLA
Manual Montilla 1, Madrid 28016. Tel: (341) 350 6200. FAX: (341) 345 1948.

EXHIBITORS
ALPHAVILLE
Martin de Los Heros 14, Madrid 28008. Tel: (341) 559 3836. FAX: (341) 541 5482.
ALTA FILMS
Martin de los Heros 12, Madrid 28008. Tel: (341) 542 2702. FAX: (341) 541 8777.
AREA CATALANA D'EXHIBICIO CINEMATOGRAFICA
Mallorca 221 6 1, Barcelona 08008. Tel: (341) 323 6426. FAX: (341) 323 7223.
BAUTISTA SOLER
Abada 14, Madrid 28013. Tel: (341) 531 6107. FAX: (341) 522 2202.
CASABLANCA CINEMA
Paseo de Gracia 115, Barcelona 08008. Tel: (343) 218 4345.
CINESA
Florida Blanca 135, Barcelona 08011. Tel: (343) 423 2455. FAX: (343) 423 0622.
COLISEO ALBIA
Alameda de Urquijo 13, Bilbao 48008. Tel: (344) 423 2148. FAX: (344) 423 1001.
DIFUSARA CULTURAL CINEMATOGRAFICA
Cines Golem, Avenida de Bayona 52, Pamplona 31008. Tel: (3448) 174 141. FAX: (3448) 171 058.
DIFUSORA BURGOS
Avenida Sanjurjo 36, Cines Can Golem, Burgos 09004. Tel: (3448) 174 141. FAX: (3448) 171 058.
DIFUSORA LOGRONO
Cines Golem, Parque de San Adrian s/n, Logrono 26006. Tel: (3448) 174 141. FAX: (3448) 171 058.
EMPRESA BALANA
Provenza 266, 5, Barcelona 08008. Tel: (343) 215 9570. FAX: (343) 215 6740.
FRANCISCO HERAS
Van Dyke Cinema, Van Dyke 59-61, Salamanca 37005. Tel: (3423) 243 538.
IZARO FILMS
Raimundo Fernandez Villaverde 65, Madrid 28003. Tel: (341) 555 8041. FAX: (341) 555 8292.
LAUREN FILMS VIDEO HAGAR
Balmes 87, Barcelona 08008. Tel: (343) 451 7189. FAX: (343) 323 6155.
PALAFOX CINEMA
Luchana 15, Madrid 28010. Tel: (341) 446 1887. FAX: (341) 447 3441.
PEDRO BALANA
Provenza 266, Barcelona 08008. Tel: (343) 215 9570. FAX: (343) 215 6740.
REAL CINEMA
Plaza de Isabel II 7, Madrid 28013. Tel: (341) 547 4577. FAX: (341) 547 4650.
TABEXSA CINE
Albatros Minicines, Plaza Fray Luis Colomer 4, Valencia 46021. Tel: (346) 369 4530. FAX: (346) 360 1469.
YELMO FILMS
Jacometrezo 4 7 piso, Madrid 28013. Tel: (341) 523 1560. FAX: (341) 523 1658.

SWEDEN

Population: 8.8 million.
Screens: 1,165; 845 theaters.
Admissions: 14.9 million.
Total Box Office Gross: $130.3 million.
Average Ticket Price: $8.75.
Domestic Feature Production: 21 films.
Top Five Domestic Films of 1995: Anglagard-andra Sommaren, Vendetta, En Pa Miljonen, Jonssonligans Storsta Kupp, Lust Och Fagring Stor.
Top Ten Films of 1995: Anglagard-andra Sommaren, The Lion King, Vendetta, Forrest Gump, Die Hard With A Vengeance, Goldeneye, Leon, Pocahontas, En Pa Miljonen, 101 Dalmations. 1995 cinema admissions fell by one million from 15.9 million in 1994. SF/Svensk Filmindustri controls the lion's share of the exhibition market with over 50%, followed by Sandrew Film with 26%. Plagued by poor funding, and in spite of a number of successful films, the Swedish film industry is dependent on government subsidies. In 1995, Swedish films represented an impressive 20% of ticket sales, with early figures from 1996 showing an uptrend. In February, 1996, domestic product took in 32%, the highest number of the last several years. Swedish exhibitors continue to build multiplexes at the rate of 10 screens per year.

ASSOCIATIONS & ORGANIZATIONS
FILM-OCH VIDEOBRANCHENS SAMAR
Film and Video Joint Industry, P. O. Box 49084, Stockholm S-100 28. Tel: (468) 785 0400. FAX: (468) 653 2425.
INDEPENDENT FILMMAKERS ASSOCIATION
Tantogaten 49, Stockholm S-117 42. Tel: (468) 720 7728.
PRODUCERS CONTROL BUREAU
Box 1147, Solna S-171 23. Tel: (468) 735 9780. FAX: (468) 730 2560.
SVENSKA TEATERFORBUNDET
Hantverkargatan 4, Stockholm S-112 21. Tel: (468) 785 0330. FAX: (468) 653 9507.
SWEDISH DISTRIBUTORS ASSOCIATION
P. O. Box 49084, Stockholm S-100 28. Tel: (468) 785 0400. FAX: (468) 730 2560.
SWEDISH MEDIA EMPLOYERS' ASSOCIATION-FILM, VIDEO AND BROADCASTING
Birger Jarlsgatan 53, P. O. Box 1720, Stockholm S-111 87. Tel: (468) 762 7700. FAX: (468) 678 6933.

DISTRIBUTORS AND PRODUCERS
ATLANTIC FILM
P. O. Box 79008, Stockholm S-100 28. Tel: (468) 305 230. FAX: (468) 305 280.
BUENA VISTA INTERNATIONAL
Box 5631, Stockholm S-114 86. Tel: (468) 679 1550. FAX: (468) 678 01728. General Manager: Eric Broberg.
CAPITOL FILM DISTRIBUTION
Sodravagen 12, Kalmar S-392 33. Tel: (46480) 12215. FAX: (46480) 24085.
CINEMA SWEDEN
P.O. Box 20105, Bromma S-161 02. Tel: (468) 280 738. FAX: (268) 299 091.
COLUMBIA TRISTAR FILMS (SWEDEN)
Hornsbruksgatan 19, 1 Tr, P. O. Box 9501, Stockholm S-102 74. Tel: (468) 658 1140. FAX: (468) 841 204. General Manager: Peter Jansson.
EGMONT FILM
P.O. Box 507, Taby S-183 25. Tel: (468) 5101 0050. FAX: (468) 5101 2046.
FOLKETS BIO
P. O. Box 2068, Stockholm S-103 12. Tel: (468) 203059. FAX: (468) 204023.
FOX FILM
Box 9501, Stockholm S-102 74. Tel: (468) 658 1144. FAX: (468) 841 204.
NORDISK FILM TV DISTRIBUTION
P. O. Box 9011, Soder Malarstrand 27, Stockholm S-10271. Tel: (468) 440 9070. FAX: (468) 440 9080.
PLANBORG FILM
Granhallsvagen 23, Stocksund S-182 75. Tel: (468) 655 80 70. FAX: (468) 655 03 40.
SANDREW FILM & TEATR
P. O. Box 5612, Stockholm S-114 86. Tel: (468) 234 700. FAX: (468) 103 850.
SONET FILM
Tappvagen 24, P. O. Box 20105, Bromma S-161 02. Tel: (468) 799 7700. FAX: (468) 285 834.
SVENSK FILMINDUSTRI
Suder Malerstrand 27, Stockholm S-127 83. Tel: (468) 680 3500. FAX: (468) 710 4460.
SVENSKA FILMINSTITUTET
Filmhuset, Borgvagen 1-5, P. O. Box 27126, Stockholm S-102 52. Tel: (468) 665 1100. FAX: (468) 661 1820.
UNITED INTERNATIONAL PICTURES (SWEDEN)
P.O. Box 9502, Stockholm S-102 74. Tel: (468) 616 7400. FAX: (468) 843 870.
WARNER BROS. SWEDEN
Hornsbruksgatan 19, 4th floor, Stockholm S-117 34. Tel: (468) 658 1050. FAX: (468) 658 6482.

EXHIBITORS
FILMOVID R REISS
Ralangsvegen 6, Enskede S-120 42. Tel: (468) 910 316. FAX: (468) 910 316.
FOLKETS BIO
P. O. Box 2068, Stockholm S-103 12. Tel: (468) 402 0820. FAX: (468) 402 0827.
SANDREWS
P. O. Box 5612, Stockholm S-114 86. Tel: (468) 234 700. FAX: (468) 796 8105.
SVENSK FILMINDUSTRI
Suder Malerstrand 27, Stockholm S-127 83. Tel: (468) 680 3500. FAX: (468) 710 4460.

STUDIOS

EUROPA STUDIOS
Tappvagen 24, P. O. Box 20105, Stockholm S-16102. Tel: (468) 764 7700.

FILM HOUSE STUDIOS
P. O. Box 27 066, Stockholm S-102 51. Tel: (468) 665 1200. FAX: (468) 661 1053.

MEXFILM
P. O. Box 17607, Stockholm S-11892. Tel: (468) 642 0035. FAX: (468) 642 9850.

STUDIO 24
Sibyllegatan 24, Stockholm S-114 42. Tel: (468) 662 5700. FAX: (468) 662 9240.

SWITZERLAND

Population: 7 million.
Screens: 483.
Admissions: 16.2 million.
Box Office Gross: $146 million.
Average Ticket Price: $9.00.
Domestic Feature Production: 35 films.
Top Five Domestic Films: Adultere, Liebe Lügen, Er Nannte Sich Surava, Der Stand Der Bäume, Krauter und Krafte.
Top Ten Films of 1995: Disclosure, Nell, The Lion King, Apollo 13, Pocahontas, Forrest Gump, The Bridges of Madison County, French Kiss, While You Were Sleeping, Die Hard With A Vengeance.

Local production of features has decreased, largely due to France's decision in 1994 to withdraw funding for Swiss co-productions. Admissions continue to rise, although Switzerland has the highest ticket rates in Europe. Unlike other western European countries, Switzerland has not been caught up in the multiplex building boom. It is currently home to 35 multiplex screens with no plans to construct more.

ASSOCIATIONS AND ORGANIZATIONS

CINELIBRE
Swiss Associations of Film Societies and Non-Commercial Screening Organisations, Postfach, CH-4005 Basel. Tel: (4161) 681 3844. FAX: (4161) 691 1040.

FEDERAL OFFICE OF CULTURE
Sektion Film, Hallwylstrasse 15, CH-3003 Bern. Tel: (4131) 322 9271. FAX: (4131) 322 9273.

FEDERAL DEPARTMENT OF FOREIGN AFFAIRS
Sektion fur internationale kulturelle und UNESCO-Angelegenheiten, Schwarztorstrasse 59, CH-3003 Bern. Tel: (4131) 325 9267. FAX: (4131) 325 9358.

SUISSIMAGE
Neuengasse 23, CH-3001 Bern. Tel: (4131) 312 1106. FAX: (4131) 311 2104.

SWISS CINEMATHEQUE
Case Postale 2512, CH-1002 Lausanne. Tel: (4121) 331 0101. FAX: (4121) 320 4888.

SWISS FILM DISTRIBUTORS ASSOCIATION
Effingerstrasse 11. P.O. Box 8175. CH-3001 Bern. Tel: (4131) 381 5077. FAX: (4131) 382 0373.

SWISS FILM THEATRES ASSOCIATION
Effingerstrasse 11. P.O. Box 8175. CH-3001 Bern. Tel: (4131) 381 5077. FAX: (4131) 382 0373.

DISTRIBUTORS AND PRODUCERS

ALEXANDER FILM
Lagernstrasse 6, CH-8037 Zurich. Tel: (411) 362 8443. FAX: (411) 361 1603.

ALPHA FILMS S. A.
4 Place du Cirque, Case Postale 5311, CH-1211 Geneve 11. (4122) 328 0204. FAX: (4122) 781 0676.

BERNARD LANG AG
Dorf Strasse 14D, Freienstein, CH-8427 Zurich. Tel: (411) 865 6627. FAX: (411) 865 6629.

BUENA VISTA INTERNATIONAL (SWITZERLAND) LTD.
Am Schanzengraben 27, CH-8002 Zurich. Tel: (411) 201 6655. FAX: (411) 201 7770.

CACTUS FILM AG
Neugasse 6, Postfach 299, CH-8021 Zurich. Tel: (411) 272 8711. FAX: (411) 271 2616. Telex: 822 843 CF CH.

COLUMBUS FILM AG
Steinstrasse 21, CH-8036 Zurich. Tel: (411) 462 7377. FAX: (411) 462 0112.

CONDOR FILMS
Restelbergstrasse 107, CH-8044 Zurich. Tel: (411) 361 9612.

FAMA-FILM AG
Balthasarstrasse 11, CH-3027 Bern. Tel: (4131) 992 9280. FAX: (4131) 992 6404.

FILMCOOPERATIVE ZURICH
Fabrikstrasse 21, Postfach 172, CH-8031 Zurich. Tel: (411) 271 8800. FAX: (411) 271 8038. Contact: Wolfgang Blosche.

IMPERIAL FILMS S. A.
Avenue de la Gare 17, CH-1002 Lausanne. Tel.: (4121) 732 1830. FAX: (4121) 738 7882.

MASCOTTE-FILM AG
Dienerstrasse 16-18, CH-8026 Zurich. Tel: (411) 296 9070. FAX: (411) 296 9089.

MONOPOLE PATHE FILMS S. A.
Neugasse 6, CH-8005 Zurich. Tel: (4311) 271 1003. FAX: (411) 271 5643.

REGINA FILM S. A.
4 Rue de Rive, CH-1204 Geneve. Tel: (4122) 310 8136. FAX: (4122) 310 9476.

RIALTO FILM AG
Neugasse 6, CH-8021 Zurich. Tel: (411) 271 4200. FAX: (411) 2714203.

SPIEGEL FILM AG
Ebelstrasse 25, Postfach 179, CH-8030 Zurich. Tel: (411) 252 7406. FAX: (411) 251 1354.

STAMM-FILM AG
Lowenstrasse 20, CH-8023 Zurich. Tel: (411) 211 6615.

TWENTIETH CENTURY-FOX FILM CORPORATION
P.O. Box 1049, CH-1211 Geneva 26. Tel: (4122) 343 3315. FAX: (4122) 343 9255. Manager: Peter Danner.

UNITED INTERNATIONAL PICTURES (SCHWEIZ)
Signaustrasse 6, CH-8032 Zurich. Tel: (411) 383 8550. FAX: (411) 383 6112. Manager: Hans Ulrich Daetwyler.

WARNER BROS. (TRANSATLANTIC)
Studerweg 3, Postfach, CH-8802 Kilchberg. Tel: (411) 715 5911. FAX: (411) 715 3451. Sales: Richard Broccon.

EXHIBITORS

CINEMAX
Tel: (411) 273 2222. FAX: (411) 273 3354.

CINEMOBIL OPEN AIR CINEMA
Dorfstrasse 77, CH-8105 Regensdorf. Tel: (411) 840 5342.

CINETYP
Obergrundstrasse 101, CH-6005 Lucerne. Tel: (4141) 422 257. FAX: (4141) 422 746.

ERNO INTERNATIONAL
Niedergaslistrasse 12, CH-8157 Dielsdorf. Tel: (411) 855 5353. FAX: (411) 855 5350.

FILMCOOPERATIVE ZURICH
Fabrikstrasse 21, Postfach 172, CH-8031 Zurich. Tel: (411) 271 8800. FAX: (411) 271 8038.

KITAG KINO THEATER
Lowenstrasse 11, CH-8021 Zurich. Tel: (411) 225 2550. FAX: (411) 225 2005.

LIAG CAPITOL
Bergstrasse 42, CH-8032 Zurich. Tel: (411) 251 5228. FAX: (411) 251 4444.

METROCINE
Ch. de Rosenack 6, CH-1000 Lausanne 13. Tel: (4121) 614 3333. FAX: (4121) 614 3399.

SALAFA
Perolles 5, CH-1204 Fribourg. Tel: (4137) 221 150. FAX: (4137) 231 952.

V ESPOSITO
4 Rue de Reve, CH-1204 Geneva. Tel: (4122) 782 1417. FAX: (4122) 310 9476.

WALCH KINOBETRIEBS
Steinentorstrasse 8, CH-4051 Basel. Tel: (4161) 281 0908. FAX: (4161) 281 6564.

TAIWAN

Population: 21.5 million.
Theatres: 255.
Screens: 569.
Taiwan has lifted its restrictions on the import of mainland Chinese films, allowing up to 10 films per year to run in Taiwan. Western films continued to do well at the box office in 1994, while the local movie industry continued to lag.

ORGANIZATION

MOTION PICTURE DEVELOPMENT FOUNDATION
2 Tien-Tsin St., Taipei. 866 2 3516625. FAX: (8862) 341 6252.

DISTRIBUTORS

BUENA VISTA FILM CO. LTD.
4th floor, No. 1, Hsiang Yang Rd., Taipei. Tel: (8862) 383 6309. FAX: (8862) 382 5348.

COLUMBIA TRISTAR FILMS OF CHINA, LTD.
City Hero Plaza, 8F-A No. 59, Chung-hua Rd., Section 1, Taipei 100. Tel: (8862) 331 9456. FAX: (8862) 381 4492.

PARAMOUNT FILMS OF CHINA, INC.
(Also: MGM of China, Inc., United Artists of China, Inc, Universal Picture Corp of China, Inc.)
2nd floor, 18 Kwei Yang St., Section 2, Taipei. Tel: (8862) 331 4929. FAX: (8862) 331 1967.

TWENTIETH CENTURY FOX
City Hero Plaza, 8F-A No. 59, Chung-hwa Rd., Section 1, Taipei 100. Tel: (8862) 315 3773. FAX: (8862) 381 4492.

WARNER BROS.
P.O. Box 167, Taipei 100. Tel: (8862) 389 0159. FAX: (8862) 311 8526.

THAILAND

Population: 60.2 million.
Screens: approx. 300.
Average Ticket Price: $2.80.
Thailand's film censorhip system is under review. The Federation of the National Film Association of Thailand and other government agencies have proposed a formal rating system that would prevent films from being cut or banned. Thailand produces an average of 125 films per year. The 1995 hit, Sia Dan (Wasted Youths), was the highest grossing domestic film ever, and second for the year, just behind Die Hard With A Vengeance. Over 60 new screens opened in Bangkok in 1995-96, many of them owned and operated by Entertain Golden Village, a joint venture of Village Roadshow (Australia), Golden Harvest (Hong Kong) and Entertain Theaters Network (Thailand). As these multiplexes spring up, Dolby and THX are becoming common, forcing the owners of older theaters to renovate their facilites.

ASSOCIATIONS & ORGANIZATIONS

AMERICAN MOTION PICTURE ASSOCIATION
Rm. 602, Akane Bldg., 315 Silom Rd., Bangkok 10500. Tel: (662) 234 0240.
MOTION PICTURE EXHIBITORS ASSOC. OF THAILAND
352 Siam Theatre, Tama 1 Rd., Pathumwan, Bangkok 10500.
THAILAND FILM PROMOTION CENTRE
599 Bumrung Muang Rd., Bangkok 10100. Tel: (662) 223 4690. FAX: (662) 253 1817.
THAI MOTION PICTURES PRODUCERS ASSOCIATION
15/79 Soi Chokchairuammit, Viphavadee-Rangsit Rd., Bangkhen, Bangkok 10900. Tel: (662) 275 8833. FAX: (662) 281 8460.

DISTRIBUTORS AND PRODUCERS

APEX INTERNATIONAL CORP.
215 1 6 Rama 1 Rd., Slam Sq., Pathumwa, Bangkok 10500. Tel: (662) 251 8476. FAX: (662) 255 3131.
BSY PRODUCTIONS
17 Theves Soi, 1 Krung Kasem Rd., Bangkok 10200. Tel: (662) 281 2515. FAX: (662) 281 8460.
CINEAD GROUP
40 19 Sol Amonphannivas 4, Vipavadee Rangsit Road, Bangkok 10900. Tel: (662) 561 1965. FAX: (662) 561 1887.
CO BROTHERS ORGANISATION
117/2 Phayathai Rd., Rajthevi, Bangkok 10400. Tel: (662) 251 7163. FAX: (662) 254 7714.
FIVE STARS
31 345 Petchburi Rd., Phayathai, Bangkok 10400. Tel: (662) 215 0704.
GOLDEN TOWN FILM
69/55 Phayathai Atehn Theater Rd., Bangkok 10400. Tel: (662) 251 9168. FAX: (662) 259 3117. Jinsirivanic, Managing Director.
HOLLYWOOD FILM DISTRIBUTION
420 Petchburi Rd., Phayathai, Bangkog 10400. Tel: (662) 251 5211.
IVS FILM DISTRIBUTION
Rm. 5002, 99 Ratchaparop Tower Mansion, Soi Boom Parop, Makasan, Phayathai, Bangkok 10400. Tel: (662) 246 9301. FAX: (662) 246 5468.
MOVIELINK
40/19 Soi Amorn Pannives 4, Vipavadee-Rangsit Rd., Bangkok. Tel: (662) 561 1915.
NONTANUND ENTERTAINMENT
113/10 Suriwong Centre, Suriwong Rd., Bangkok 10500. Tel: (662) 236 7504. FAX: (662) 253 4830.
PYRAMID ENTERTAINMENT
216/1-6 Rama Rd., Siam Square, Bangkok 10500. Tel: (662) 252 7416.

SAHA MONGKOL FILM
1081/5 Phaholyothin Rd., Bangkok 10400. Tel: (662) 279 8456. FAX: (662) 271 0620.
SUPREME IMPORTEX
GPO Box 2758, Bangkok 10501. Tel: (662) 377 4382.
TWENTIETH CENTURY FOX/WARNER BROS.
Rm. 603, South East Insurance Bld., 315 Silom Road, Bangkok 10500. Tel: (662) 233 0920. FAX: (662) 236 4384.
UNITED INTERNATIONAL PICTURES (UIP)
Rm. 605 South East Insurance Bldg., 315 Silom Road, Bangkok 10500. Tel: (662) 233 4225. FAX: (662) 236 7597.

TURKEY

Population: 63.4 million.

ASSOCIATIONS & ORGANIZATIONS

ISTANBUL FOUNDATION FOR CULTURE & ARTS
Besiktas, Istanbul 80700. Tel: (90216) 259 1738. FAX: (90216) 261 8823.
SE-SAM
Istiklal Cad 122/4, Beyoglu, Istanbul. Tel: (90216) 245 4645. FAX: (90216) 245 2747.
SOCIETY OF IMPORTERS AND DISTRIBUTORS
Yesilcam Sok 7/1, Beyoglu, Istanbul. Tel: (90216) 249 0986.
SODER, THE SOCIETY OF ACTORS
Mete Cad Yani Prefabrik Binasi, Taksim, Istanbul. Tel: (90216) 252 6566.

DISTRIBUTORS AND PRODUCERS

ACAR FILM
2. Tasocagi Cad. 13, Me Cidi Yekoy, Istanbul. Tel: (90216) 266 6092.
BARLIK FILM
Ahududu Cad 32/3, Beyoglu, Istanbul 80060. Tel: (90216) 244 1542. FAX: (90216) 251 0386.
FID MOTION PICTURE IMPORTS
Yesilcam Sokak No: 29, Beyoglu, Istanbul. Tel: (90216) 249 0986.
FIYAP-MOTION PIC PRODUCERS
Alyan Sokak Erman Han 5/2, Beyoglu, Istanbul. Tel: (90216) 245 4645.
KILIC FILM
Yesilcam SK 26/2, Beyoglu, Istanbul 80070. Tel: (90216) 249 5804. FAX: (90216) 244 1612.
WARNER BROS. A.S. TURKEY
Bronz Sokak, Bronz Apt. 3/6, Macka, Istanbul 80200. Tel: (90216) 231 2569. FAX: (90216) 231 7070.
UNITED INTERNATIONAL PICTURES
Filmcilik ve Ticaret Ltd. Sti, Spor Cad. Acisu Sok. 1/7-8, Macka, Istanbul 80200. Tel: (90216) 227 8205. FAX: (90216) 227 8207.

VIETNAM

Population: 74.3 million.
Average Ticket Price: $1.00-$2.00.
Vietnam is an emerging market for the exhibition industry. A U.S.-Hong Kong partnership, ChinAmerica plans to establish a circuit of up to 150 screens in Vietnam in a joint venture with the Vietnamese government. Multiplex sites will be built in Da Nang, Hanoi, Ho Chi Minh City. Plans to renovate the 50 existing cinemas are included. Trinity Australasia Group established the first foreign industry presence in 1995 with the 150 seat New Age Cinema, a hi-tech video screening complex, that showed such favorites as Speed. TAG plans to continue building theaters throughout Vietnam in 1997.